KU-303-682

WHO'S WHO 2016

AN ANNUAL
BIOGRAPHICAL DICTIONARY

ONE HUNDRED AND SIXTY-EIGHTH
YEAR OF ISSUE

A & C BLACK

AN IMPRINT OF

B L O O M S B U R Y

LONDON • OXFORD • NEW YORK • NEW DELHI • SYDNEY

A&C Black
An Imprint of Bloomsbury Publishing Plc

50 Bedford Square
London
WC1B 3DP
UK

1385 Broadway
New York
NY 10018
USA

www.bloomsbury.com

A&C BLACK and the 'WHO'S WHO PUBLISHED ANNUALLY SINCE 1849' belt logo are trademarks of Bloomsbury Publishing Plc

British Library Cataloguing-in-Publication Data
A catalogue record for this book is available from the British Library.
ISBN: HB: 978-1-472-90470-6
Online: 978-1-472-93392-8
www.ukwhoswho.com

2 4 6 8 10 9 7 5 3 1

Printed and bound in Italy by L.E.G.O. S.p.A.

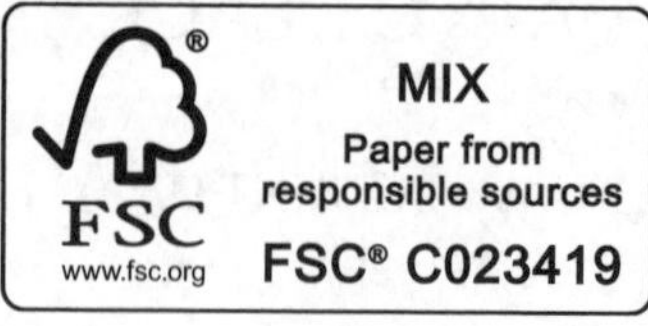

CONTENTS

HISTORICAL NOTE

The first edition of *Who's Who* was published in 1849. It consisted of an almanac followed by thirty-nine lists of ranks and appointments and the names of those holding them. As might be expected, there were lists of peers, members of the House of Commons, judges, archbishops and bishops. Additionally, however, there were the names of the Governor and board of directors of the Bank of England, of British envoys abroad, of the directors of the East India Company and of the officers (including the actuaries) of the life and fire assurance companies in London.

The range of lists was expanded over the next half century to more than two hundred and fifty, to include, amongst others, the Police Commissioners, the officers of the principal railways, the members of the London School Board and the Crown Agents – together with the editors of significant newspapers and magazines whose names, the editor noted, were "given here, not for contributors, but that the public may know who lead public opinion".

In 1897 substantial changes were made to the nature and content of the book. The major change was the addition of a section of biographies in which details were given of the lives of some five and a half thousand leading figures of the day.

Now, as then, the book aims to list people who, through their careers, affect the political, economic, scientific and artistic life of the country. *Who's Who* places its emphasis on careers whilst giving opportunity for the inclusion of family and other individual details, such as the recreations which have become a distinctive feature of the book.

An invitation to appear in *Who's Who* has, on occasion, been thought of as conferring distinction; that is the last thing it can do. It recognises distinction and influence. The attitude of the present editorial board remains that of the editor of the 1897 edition, who stated in his preface that the book seeks to recognise people whose "prominence is inherited, or depending upon office, or the result of ability which singles them out from their fellows in occupations open to every educated man or woman".

PREFACE

Who's Who is the recognised source book of information on people of influence and interest in all fields.

This, the 2016 edition, contains more than 33,000 biographies, approximately one thousand of these making their first appearance in *Who's Who*. They are of all kinds of people from all parts of the world and from all walks of life: the arts, business and finance, the church, the civil service, education, entertainment and sport, government, the law, local government, the media, medicine, professional institutions, science and the trade unions.

Each entry is in a standard form, full name and present post being followed by date of birth and family details, education, career in date order, publications, recreations and address.

The entries are carefully updated both from information supplied by biographees on their annual proofs and from many independent sources of reference. As a result, tens of thousands of amendments are made, more than half the entries requiring change. The book includes an obituary and a comprehensive list of abbreviations used in the entries.

OBITUARY

Deaths notified from mid-September 2014 to mid-September 2015

Abrahams, Ivor, RA, 6 Jan. 2015.
Abse, Dannie, CBE, 28 Sept. 2014.
Adeane, Hon. (George) Edward, CVO, 20 May 2015.
Ailsa, 8th Marquess of; Archibald Angus Charles Kennedy, 15 Jan. 2015.
Alexander, Andrew Clive, 5 July 2015.
Allan, Ian, OBE, 28 June 2015.
Alldis, Air Cdre Cecil Anderson, CBE, DFC, AFC, 5 Oct. 2014.
Allen, James Hendricuss, QC, 26 Nov. 2013.
Allen, Sir John Derek, CBE, 24 Oct. 2014.
Allen, Very Rev. John Edward, 9 Sept. 2015.
Allenby, 3rd Viscount; Michael Jaffray Hynman Allenby, 3 Oct. 2014.
Alston, John Alistair, CBE, 22 Feb. 2015.
Anderson, Rev. David, 30 Dec. 2014.
Anderson, Prof. Joan Mary, (Jan), FRS, 28 Aug. 2015.
Andrew, His Honour Herbert Henry, QC, 25 Dec. 2014.
Anson, Vice-Adm. Sir Edward Rosebery, KCB, 22 Sept. 2014.
Armstrong, Rear Adm. John Herbert Arthur James, (Louis), CBE, 31 Dec. 2014.
Armytage, Captain David George, CBE, RN, 8 Feb. 2015.
Ash, Raymond, Oct. 2012.
Aspinwall, Jack Heywood, 19 May 2015.
Aston, Margaret Evelyn, (Hon. Mrs Paul Buxton), CBE, FBA, 22 Nov. 2014.
Atkinson, Frank, CBE, 30 Dec. 2014.
Atkinson, Sir John Alexander, (Sir Alec), KCB, DFC, 7 Aug. 2015.
Atkinson, Sir Robert, DSC, RD, 25 Jan. 2015.
Atkinson, Prof. Thomas, 6 Dec. 2014.

Balderstone, Sir James Schofield, AC, 15 Oct. 2014.
Baldwin, Maj.-Gen. Peter Alan Charles, CBE, 15 Sept. 2015.
Balston, His Honour Antony Francis, 10 Dec. 2014.
Banfield, Ven. David John, 2 Oct. 2014.
Banham, Belinda Joan, CBE, 13 Oct. 2014.
Barber, Prof. James Peden, 24 July 2015.
Barbour, Very Rev. Prof. Robert Alexander Stewart, KCVO, MC, 18 Oct. 2014.
Barclay, Christopher Francis Robert, CMG, 20 March 2015.
Barker, Sir Colin, 10 June 2015.
Barnett, Baron (Life Peer); Joel Barnett, PC, 1 Nov. 2014.
Baron, Sir Thomas, CBE, 22 Dec. 2014.
Barrot, Jacques, 3 Dec. 2014.
Bartlett, (Harold) Charles, 19 Dec. 2014.
Bayley, Prof. John Oliver, CBE, FBA, 12 Jan. 2015.
Bayly, Sir Christopher Alan, FBA, 19 April 2015.
Beard, Allan Geoffrey, CB, CBE, 5 Jan. 2015.
Beattie, (George) Anthony, 31 March 2014.
Bellotti, David Frank, 10 June 2015.
Benaud, Richard, OBE, 10 April 2015.
Bennett, Seton John, CBE, 14 Sept. 2015.
Bennion, Francis Alan Roscoe, 28 Jan. 2015.
Benson, Prof. Frank Atkinson, OBE, 23 Nov. 2014.
Bentley, His Honour David Ronald, QC, 1 March 2012.
Beynon, Prof. John Herbert, FRS, 24 Aug. 2015.
Bhagwati, Jaimini, 23 Feb. 2015.
Bicester, 3rd Baron; Angus Edward Vivian Smith, 11 Dec. 2014.
Bilk, Bernard Stanley, (Acker), MBE, 2 Nov. 2014.
Bills, David James, CBE, 30 March 2014.
Birch, Prof. Anthony Harold, 13 Dec. 2014.
Birch, Dennis Arthur, CBE, 15 Dec. 2012.
Birdwood, 3rd Baron; Mark William Ogilvie Birdwood, 11 July 2015 (*ext*).
Birkett, 2nd Baron; Michael Birkett, 3 April 2015.
Black, Cilla, OBE, 2 Aug. 2015.
Black, Timothy Reuben Ladbroke, CBE, 11 Dec. 2014.
Bond, Alan, 5 June 2015.
Bonsall, Sir Arthur Wilfred, KCMG, CBE, 26 Nov. 2014.
Bosnich, Prof. Brice, FRS, 13 April 2015.
Bosworth, Prof. Clifford Edmund, FBA, 28 Feb. 2015.
Bowering, Ven. Michael Ernest, 25 April 2015.
Bowman-Shaw, Sir (George) Neville, 11 July 2015.
Bown, Jane Hope, (Mrs M. G. Moss), CBE, 21 Dec. 2014.
Bowyer, (Arthur) William, RA, 1 March 2015.
Bradbourn, Philip Charles, OBE, 19 Dec. 2014.
Bradfield, Sir John Richard Grenfell, CBE, 13 Oct. 2014.
Bradley, Prof. Donald Charlton, FRS, 20 Dec. 2014.
Bradley, Richard Alan, 25 March 2015.
Bragg, Stephen Lawrence, 15 Nov. 2014.
Brandon, (David) Stephen, QC, 15 Feb. 2015.
Brassey of Apethorpe, 3rd Baron; David Henry Brassey, OBE, 7 May 2015.
Brewis, Marion Teresa, CVO, 31 Dec. 2014.
Bridges, Rt Rev. Dewi Morris, 18 May 2015.
Bridges, Ven. Peter Sydney Godfrey, 24 Jan. 2015.
Bridle, Ronald Jarman, 2 Sept. 2015.
Brink, Prof. André Philippus, 6 Feb. 2015.
Brittan of Spennithorne, Baron (Life Peer); Leon Brittan, PC, QC, 21 Jan. 2015.
Brittenden, (Charles) Arthur, 25 April 2015.
Brock, Prof. William Ranulf, FBA, 12 Nov. 2014.
Brookes, Beata Ann, CBE, 18 Aug. 2015.
Brooks, Douglas, 6 Sept. 2014.
Brown, Rev. Canon Geoffrey Harold, 27 May 2015.
Brown, John, CMG, 24 Sept. 2014.
Brown, John Russell, 25 Aug. 2015.
Brown, Joseph Lawler, CBE, TD, 22 May 2015.
Browne, Sheila Jeanne, CB, 27 Aug. 2015.
Brownlow, Peter, 16 April 2014.
Buchan of Auchmacoy, Captain David William Sinclair, 16 July 2015.
Buchanan, Sir John Gordon St Clair, 13 July 2015.
Buckley, Martin Christopher Burton, 11 Dec. 2014.
Bull, (Oliver) Richard (Silvester), 11 Sept. 2015.
Bullock, (Edward) Anthony (Watson), 21 Feb. 2015.
Bunce, Michael John, OBE, 31 Dec. 2014.
Burgess, Gen. Sir Edward Arthur, KCB, OBE, 8 May 2015.
Burkett, Mary Elizabeth, OBE, 12 Nov. 2014.
Burrows, General Eva, AC, 20 March 2015.
Burrows, Rt Rev. Simon Hedley, 5 Aug. 2015.
Burston, Sir Samuel Gerald Wood, OBE, 14 July 2015.
Byrne, Douglas Norman *[Deceased.*

Cadbury, Sir (George) Adrian (Hayhurst), CH, 3 Sept. 2015.
Cairncross, Neil Francis, CB, 26 Feb. 2015.
Caldwell, Maj.-Gen. Frank Griffiths, OBE, MC, 22 Nov. 2014.
Calvert, Barbara Adamson, (Lady Lowry), QC, 22 July 2015.
Cameron Watt, Prof. Donald, FBA, 30 Oct. 2014.
Campbell, John Davies, CVO, CBE, MC, 30 July 2015.
Carbery, Prof. Thomas Francis, OBE, 22 Feb. 2015.
Carlile, Thomas, CBE, 29 Sept. 2014.
Carr, Sir (Albert) Raymond (Maillard), FBA, 19 April 2015.
Carter, Sir John Alexander, 7 July 2015.
Carter, Sir Philip David, CBE, 23 April 2015.
Cassidy, Most Rev. Joseph, 31 Jan. 2013.
Catherwood, Sir (Henry) Frederick (Ross), 30 Nov. 2014.
Catherwood, Herbert Sidney Elliott, CBE, 24 Aug. 2013.
Chadwick, Rev. Prof. (William) Owen, OM, KBE, FBA, 17 July 2015.
Chalmers, Ian Pender, CMG, OBE, 10 Dec. 2014.
Chamberlain, Prof. Geoffrey Victor Price, RD, 30 Oct. 2014.
Chapman, Sir Sydney Brookes, 9 Oct. 2014.
Charlton, Philip, OBE, 28 March 2015.
Chauvin, Yves, 27 Jan. 2015.
Chester, Maj.-Gen. John Shane, OBE, 10 Sept. 2015.
Chetwynd, 10th Viscount; Adam Richard John Casson Chetwynd, 20 Aug. 2015.
Chetwynd, Sir Robin John Talbot, 9th Bt, 18 May 2012.
Chilwell, Hon. Sir Muir Fitzherbert, 10 June 2014.
Chinnery, (Charles) Derek, 22 March 2015.
Chisholm, Prof. Alexander William John, 26 July 2014.
Clark, Alistair Campbell, 26 Jan. 2015.
Clark, Robert Joseph, CBE, 23 Sept. 2012.
Clark, (Thomas) Alastair, CBE, 11 Feb. 2015.
Clarke, Geoffrey, RA, 30 Oct. 2014.
Clarke, Mary, 20 March 2015.
Clatworthy, Robert, RA, 16 March 2015.
Cleall, Charles, 11 Jan. 2015.
Clegg, Prof. Edward John, 1 March 2015.
Clough, Philip Gerard, 16 Feb. 2015.
Cockburn, Sir John Elliot, 12th Bt of that Ilk, 12 June 2015.
Coe, Denis Walter, 3 March 2015.
Cohen, Prof. Robert Donald, CBE, 17 Oct. 2014.
Cole, George, OBE, 5 Aug. 2015.
Coleman, John Ennis, CB, 10 Nov. 2014.
Colyer, Peter John, 10 Dec. 2014.
Conlan, Bernard, 12 Dec. 2013.
Conquest, (George) Robert (Acworth), CMG, OBE, 3 Aug. 2015.
Cooke, Rear-Adm. David John, CB, MBE, 1 Dec. 2014.
Coombs, Derek Michael, 30 Dec. 2014.
Coombs, Douglas Stafford, 19 Sept. 2014.
Cooper, Ronald Cecil Macleod, CB, 2 Aug. 2014.
Coppock, Surgeon Rear-Adm. (D) David Arthur, CB, 1 Dec. 2014.
Corner, Frank Henry, CMG, 27 Aug. 2014.
Correa, Charles Mark, 16 June 2015.
Coultass, (George Thomas) Clive, 24 April 2015.
Couzens, Brian William, 17 April 2015.

Coward, (John) Stephen, QC, 19 Oct. 2014.
Cowderoy, Brenda, 21 July 2015.
Cowley, Prof. Roger Arthur, FRS, 27 Jan. 2015.
Cox, Graham Loudon, QC (Scot.), 27 Dec. 2014.
Cox, Philip Joseph, DSC, QC, 14 Nov. 2014.
Cranfield, Rev. Prof. Charles Ernest Burland, FBA, 27 Feb. 2015.
Crawford, Robert Gammie, CBE, 2 May 2015.
Crowe, His Honour Gerald Patrick, QC, 4 Nov. 2014.
Croxon, Raymond Patrick Austen, QC, 30 Nov. 2014.
Cubbon, Sir Brian Crossland, GCB, 20 May 2015.
Cunningham-Jardine, Ronald Charles, CVO, 25 May 2015.
Cuomo, Mario Matthew, 1 Jan. 2015.
Cutts, Adrian Clive Tylden, 16 Jan. 2015.

Dalgarno, Prof. Alexander, FRS, 9 April 2015.
Davey, Prof. William, CBE, 7 Jan. 2015.
Davies, Prof. Anna Elbina, (Anna Morpurgo Davies), Hon. DBE, FBA, 27 Sept. 2014.
Davies, Sir (Charles) Noel, 10 Feb. 2015.
Davies, Hon. Sir (David Herbert) Mervyn, MC, TD, 12 May 2015.
Davis, Christine Agnes Murison, CBE, 17 Feb. 2015.
Dawood, Nessim Joseph, 20 Nov. 2014.
Day, Sir Derek Malcolm, KCMG, 7 March 2015.
Delbridge, Richard, 23 July 2015.
Denison, His Honour (William) Neil, QC, 21 Dec. 2014.
Devon, 18th Earl of; Hugh Rupert Courtenay, 18 Aug. 2015.
Devonshire, Dowager Duchess of; Deborah Vivien Cavendish, DCVO, 24 Sept. 2014.
Dickinson, Brian Henry Baron, 11 May 2014.
Di Palma, Vera June, (Mrs Ernest Jones), OBE, 7 June 2015.
Docker, Rt Rev. (Ivor) Colin, 3 Nov. 2014.
Doctorow, Edgar Lawrence, 21 July 2015.
Dodds, Sir Ralph Jordan, 2nd Bt, 24 May 2015 (*ext*).
Donald, Air Marshal Sir John George, KBE, 6 Nov. 2014.
Dorey, Sir Graham Martyn, 25 June 2015.
Doughty, Sir William Roland, 21 March 2015.
Dow, Andrew Richard George, 24 April 2015.
Downward, Maj.-Gen. Sir Peter Aldcroft, KCVO, CB, DSO, DFC, 18 Oct. 2014.
Draycott, Simon Douglas, QC, 22 Aug. 2015.
Drinkall, John Kenneth, CMG, 30 May 2015.
Duckworth, John Clifford, 8 Jan. 2015.
Dugdale, Sir William Stratford, 2nd Bt, CBE, MC, 13 Nov. 2014.
Duthie, Prof. Sir Herbert Livingston, 24 April 2015.
Dymoke, Lt-Col John Lindley Marmion, MBE, 21 March 2015.

Eardley-Wilmot, Sir Michael John Assheton, 6th Bt, 15 Nov. 2014.
East, Kenneth Arthur, CMG, 20 June 2014.
Ebsworth, Prof. Evelyn Algernon Valentine, CBE, 16 July 2015.
Edmonds, John Christopher, CMG, CVO, 17 Aug. 2015.
Edwards, Rear Adm. (John) Phillip, CB, LVO, 12 Dec. 2014.
Edwards, Prof. Sir Samuel Frederick, (Sir Sam Edwards), FRS, 7 May 2015.
Ellingworth, Richard Henry, 31 March 2015.
Ellis, Carol Jacqueline, (Mrs Ralph Gilmore), CBE, QC, 12 July 2015.
Ellis, Richard Peter, 10 Feb. 2015.
Ellis, Dr (William) Herbert (Baxter), AFC, 4 Oct. 2014.
Elphinston of Glack, Sir John, 11th Bt, 28 May 2015.
Emerton, Rev. Prof. John Adney, FBA, 12 Sept. 2015.
Ensor, Michael de Normann, CMG, OBE, 13 Feb. 2015.
Evans, John Robert, CC, OOnt, 13 Feb. 2015.
Evans, Lloyd Thomas, AO, FRS, 23 March 2015.
Evans, Valerie Jean, CBE, 26 July 2015.
Eveleigh, Rt Hon. Sir Edward Walter, PC, ERD, 24 Sept. 2014.
Ewington, John, OBE, 15 Aug. 2015.
Eyre, Brian Leonard, CBE, FRS, 28 July 2014.

Faber, Michael Leslie Oglivie, 26 Feb. 2015.
Fairclough, Anthony John, CMG, 9 Feb. 2014.
Faith, (Irene) Sheila, 28 Sept. 2014.
Farmer, Paul Roy, 4 June 2014.
Fatt, Prof. Paul, FRS, 28 Sept. 2014.
Fearn, John Martin, CB, 18 Oct. 2014.
Fearnley, David, 23 Dec. 2014.
Fell, Robert, CB, CBE, 19 Jan. 2015.
Fendall, Prof. Neville Rex Edwards, 25 May 2014.
Fenner, Dame Peggy Edith, DBE, 15 Sept. 2014.
Fenwick, Very Rev. Jeffery Robert, 14 Sept. 2014.
Ferguson, John Alexander, 20 Dec. 2014.
Fife, 3rd Duke of; James George Alexander Bannerman Carnegie, 22 June 2015.
Fisher, Desmond Michael, 30 Dec. 2014.
Fishwick, Avril, OBE, 28 Oct. 2014.
Fitch, Rodney Arthur, CBE, 20 Oct. 2014.
Flanagan, Sir Maurice, KBE, 7 May 2015.
Foot, Michael Colin, OBE, 24 Jan. 2015.
Fowler, Dennis Houston, OBE, 20 April 2015.
France, Sir Christopher Walter, GCB, 21 Oct. 2014.
Fraser, Rt Hon. (John) Malcolm, AC, CH, PC, 20 March 2015.
Frazer, Prof. Malcolm John, CBE, 20 April 2014.
Freeman, David John, 23 Feb. 2015.
Freeman, Ernest Allan, 10 Jan. 2015.
Freeman, Rt Hon. John, MBE, PC, 20 Dec. 2014.
Frere, Prof. Sheppard Sunderland, CBE, FBA, 26 Feb. 2015.
Friend, Rev. Frederick James, 23 April 2014.
Froude, Andrew Christopher Haysom, 19 Dec. 2014.
Frutiger, Adrian, 10 Sept. 2015.
Fry, Sir Peter Derek, 12 May 2015.
Fyfe, Prof. William Sefton, CC, FRS, 11 Nov. 2013.

Gallacher, John, 17 June 2015.
Garner, Sir Anthony Stuart, 22 March 2015.
Gaskell, Sir Richard Kennedy Harvey, 17 July 2015.
Gavron, Baron (Life Peer); Robert Gavron, CBE, 7 Feb. 2015.
Gemmill, Moira Elizabeth, 9 April 2015.
Gerard, Ronald, OBE, 10 Jan. 2015.
Gibson, Madeline, 28 Oct. 2014.
Gilbert, Rt Hon. Sir Martin John, CBE, PC, 3 Feb. 2015.
Glen Haig, Dame Mary Alison, DBE, 15 Nov. 2014.
Glover, Myles Howard, 29 Sept. 2014.
Goddard, David Rodney, MBE, 30 June 2015.
Godwin, William Henry, 24 Oct. 2012.
Goff, Martyn, CBE, 25 March 2015.
Gold, Jack, 9 Aug. 2015.
Goldstein, His Honour Simon Alfred, 18 Dec. 2014.
Goodbourn, David Robin, 9 Nov. 2014.
Goodhart, Sir Philip Carter, 5 July 2015.
Goodson, Sir Mark Weston Lassam, 3rd Bt, 1 Feb. 2015.
Goodwyn, Charles Wyndham, LVO, 10 June 2015.
Goody, Sir John Rankine, (Sir Jack), FBA, 16 July 2015.
Gordon, Rt Rev. (Archibald) Ronald (McDonald), 8 Aug. 2015.
Gorman, Teresa Ellen, 28 Aug. 2015.
Goss, Wayne Keith, 10 Nov. 2014.
Graaff, Sir David de Villiers, 3rd Bt, 24 Jan. 2015.
Grabham, Sir Anthony Herbert, 22 Feb. 2015.
Grady, Terence, MBE, 27 Oct. 2014.
Graham, (Malcolm Gray) Douglas, 21 March 2015.
Graham, His Honour Martin, QC, 16 Sept. 2014.
Graham, (William) Gordon, MC, 24 April 2015.
Grant, Donald Blane, CBE, TD, 21 Sept. 2014.
Grass, Günter Wilhelm, 13 April 2015.
Gray, (Edna) Eileen (Mary), CBE, 20 May 2015.
Gray, Richard Paul, QC, 14 Oct. 2014.
Green, John Michael, CB, 25 Jan. 2015.
Greenaway, Sir John Michael Burdick, 3rd Bt, 16 March 2015.
Greenfield, Edward Harry, OBE, 1 July 2015.
Grierson, Sir Ronald Hugh, 23 Oct. 2014.
Griffiths, Baron (Life Peer); William Hugh Griffiths, MC, PC, 30 May 2015.
Griffiths, Howard Barton, 7 June 2015.
Gruffydd, Prof. (Robert) Geraint, FBA, 24 March 2015.
Guild, Ivor Reginald, CBE, 3 Jan. 2015.
Gunn, Sir Robert Norman, 29 March 2015.
Guthrie, Roy David, (Gus), AM, 12 Jan. 2013.

Hague, Prof. Sir Douglas Chalmers, CBE, 1 Feb. 2015.
Haigh, Brian Roger, 3 Aug. 2015.
Hall, Prof. Alan, FRS, 3 May 2015.
Hallett, Victor George Henry, 18 Nov. 2014.
Halnan, His Honour Patrick John, 14 Dec. 2014.
Halsey, Prof. Albert Henry, FBA, 14 Oct. 2014.
Hamilton, Martha, (Mrs R. R. Steedman), OBE, 3 March 2015.
Hampton, Bryan, 29 March 2015.
Hancock, Ronald John, 22 Feb. 2015.
Hanson, James Donald, 29 Oct. 2014.
Hanson, Neil, 16 Feb. 2015.
Harbottle, (George) Laurence, 1 May 2015.
Hare Duke, Rt Rev. Michael Geoffrey, 15 Dec. 2014.
Hargreaves, Prof. John Desmond, 14 Feb. 2015.
Harker, (Ronald) David, CBE, 2 March 2015.
Harris, Sir Henry, FRS, 31 Oct. 2014.
Harris, Joanne Olga Charlotte; Her Honour Judge Harris, 17 April 2014.
Harris, Prof. Roy, 9 Feb. 2015.
Harrison, Jessel Anidjah, 18 Dec. 2013.
Harriss, Gerald Leslie, FBA, 2 Nov. 2014.
Hawley, Henry Nicholas, (8th Bt), 10 Jan. 2015.
Haworth, His Honour Richard James, 6 July 2015.
Hayward, Sir Jack Arnold, OBE, 13 Jan. 2015.
Heath, Bernard Oliver, OBE, 11 Aug. 2014.
Heather, Stanley Frank, CBE, 28 Aug. 2015.
Hepburn, John William, 10 Dec. 2014.

Hepple, Prof. Sir Bob Alexander, FBA, 21 Aug. 2015.
Herbert-Jones, Hugh Jarrett, (Hugo), CMG, OBE, 19 Nov. 2014.
Herdman, (John) Mark (Ambrose), CBE, LVO, 5 Aug. 2015.
Herries of Terregles, Lady (14th in line); Anne Elizabeth Fitzalan-Howard, 23 Nov. 2014.
Higginbotham, Prof. James Taylor, FBA, 25 April 2014.
Higham, Norman, OBE, 2 July 2014.
Hill, Prof. Alan Geoffrey, FBA, 14 April 2015.
Hillier-Fry, (William) Norman, CMG, 11 Jan. 2015.
Ho, Eric Peter, CBE, 25 March 2015.
Hoad, Air Vice-Marshal Norman Edward, CVO, CBE, AFC, 29 Nov. 2014.
Hobday, Sir Gordon Ivan, 27 May 2015.
Hobhouse, (Mary) Hermione, MBE, 17 Oct. 2014.
Hodgson, Sir Maurice Arthur Eric, 1 Oct. 2014.
Hogwood, Christopher Jarvis Haley, CBE, 24 Sept. 2014.
Holmes, Christopher John, CBE, 2 Dec. 2014.
Holroyd, John Hepworth, CB, CVO, 29 Nov. 2014.
Holt, (James) Richard (Trist), 22 Oct. 2014.
Honeysett, Martin, 21 Jan. 2015.
Hooley, Frank Oswald, 21 Jan. 2015.
Hope, Sir Colin Frederick Newton, 31 Aug. 2015.
Hopewell, John Prince, 14 Jan. 2015.
Hord, Brian Howard, CBE, 30 Aug. 2015.
Horlock, Sir John Harold, FRS, 22 May 2015.
Hoskyns, Sir (Edwyn) Wren, 17th Bt, 19 Feb. 2015.
Hoskyns, Sir John Austin Hungerford Leigh, 20 Oct. 2014.
Houston, Maj.-Gen. David, CVO, CBE, 10 Nov. 2014.
Howard, Alan Mackenzie, CBE, 14 Feb. 2015.
Howard, Philip Nicholas Charles, 5 Oct. 2014.
Howell, Prof. John Bernard Lloyd, CBE, 1 Jan. 2015.
Huang, Rayson Lisung, Hon. CBE, 8 April 2015.
Huckstep, Prof. Ronald Lawrie, CMG, 10 April 2015.
Hughes, Catherine Eva, CMG, 10 Dec. 2014.
Hussain, Karamat, SQA, 24 Aug. 2014.

Inglis, Sir Brian Scott, AC, 24 Sept. 2014.
Ingram, Sir John Henderson, CBE, 1 April 2015.
Innes, William James Alexander, 18 July 2015.
Irby, Charles Leonard Anthony, 15 Sept. 2015.
Irvin, Albert, OBE, RA, 26 March 2015.
Isaac, Maurice Laurence Reginald, 11 Jan. 2015.

Jackson, (Walter) Patrick, CB, 7 Nov. 2014.
Jacobs, Hon. Sir Kenneth Sydney, KBE, 24 May 2015.
Jaeger, Prof. Leslie Gordon, CM, 20 Aug. 2013.
James of Holland Park, Baroness (Life Peer); Phyllis Dorothy White, (P. D. James), OBE, 27 Nov. 2014.
James, (Arthur) Walter, 5 Aug. 2015.
James, His Honour Charles Edwin Frederic, 20 Sept. 2013.
Jarman, Nicholas Francis Barnaby, QC, 17 Feb. 2015.
Jefferies, Sheelagh, CBE, 22 May 2014.
Jefferson, (John) Bryan, CB, CBE, 19 Oct. 2014.
Jenkins, Ven. David Thomas Ivor, 16 Sept. 2014.
Johnson, Richard Keith, 6 June 2015.
Jolliffe, William Orlando, 16 Feb. 2015.
Jones, (David) Alan, 19 Dec. 2014.
Jones, David Evan Alun, CBE, 16 March 2015.

Kafity, Rt Rev. Samir, 21 Aug. 2015.
Kalam, (Avul Pakir Jainulabdeen) Abdul, 27 July 2015.
Katin, Peter Roy, 19 March 2015.
Kavanagh, P. J., (Patrick Joseph Gregory Kavanagh), 26 Aug. 2015.
Keller, Prof. Rudolf Ernst, 19 Oct. 2014.
Kelly, Charles Henry, CBE, QPM, 31 Dec. 2014.
Kemp, Robert Thayer, 24 June 2014.
Kennedy, Rt Hon. Charles Peter, PC, 2 June 2015.
Kennedy, (George) Michael (Sinclair), CBE, 31 Dec. 2014.
King, (Albert) Norman, CMG, LVO, OBE, 27 June 2015.
King, Sir John Christopher, 4th Bt, 5 Dec. 2014.
Kingdon, Roger Taylor, CBE, 12 May 2015.
Kirkness, Donald James, CB, 30 Dec. 2013.
Kirner, Hon. Joan Elizabeth, AC, 1 June 2015.
Kitzinger, Sheila Helena Elizabeth, MBE, 11 April 2015.
Knights, Baron (Life Peer); Philip Douglas Knights, CBE, QPM, 11 Dec. 2014.
Knowlton, Richard James, CBE, QFSM, 19 Sept. 2014.
Knox, (Alexander) David, CMG, 29 Nov. 2014.
Knox, John, (Jack), 12 April 2015.
Knox, Sir John Leonard, 28 May 2015.
Kreisel, Prof. Georg, FRS, 1 March 2015.

Lacon, Sir Edmund Vere, 8th Bt, 17 Oct. 2014.
Lainson, Prof. Ralph, OBE, FRS, 5 May 2015.
Laird, Endell Johnston, 8 July 2015.
Lambert, Sir John Henry, KCVO, CMG, 6 July 2015.
Lane, Dr Anthony John, 11 June 2014.
Langford, Prof. Paul, FBA, 27 July 2015.
Latour-Adrien, Hon. Sir (Jean François) Maurice, 31 July 2014.
Lawrence, Sir William Fettiplace, 5th Bt, OBE, 10 Feb. 2015.
Laws, Richard Maitland, CBE, FRS, 7 Oct. 2014.
Lawson, Richard Henry, CBE, 17 Feb. 2015.
Lea, Vice-Adm. Sir John Stuart Crosbie, KBE, 20 May 2015.
Leaning, Very Rev. David, 28 July 2015.
Leaper, Prof. Robert Anthony Bernard, CBE, 22 Dec. 2014.
Ledwith, Prof. Anthony, CBE, FRS, 5 Jan. 2015.
Lee, Sir Christopher Frank Carandini, CBE, 7 June 2015.
Lee Kuan Yew, Hon. CH, Hon. GCMG, 23 March 2015.
Lee, Rt Rev. Paul Chun Hwan, Hon. CBE, 26 March 2010.
Leech, Rev. Kenneth, 12 Sept. 2015.
Le Fleming, Peter Henry John, 16 Oct. 2014.
Leicester, 7th Earl of; Edward Douglas Coke, CBE, 25 April 2015.
Lepping, Sir George Geria Dennis, GCMG, MBE, 24 Dec. 2014.
Lewers, Very Rev. Benjamin Hugh, 25 March 2015.
Lewis, (Alun) Kynric, QC, 4 June 2015.
Lewis, Prof. Gwynne, 10 Dec. 2014.
Lewis, Henry Nathan, 31 Jan. 2015.
Lewis, Julian Hart, FRS, 30 April 2014.
Lewis, Trevor Oswin, (disclaimed as 4th Baron Merthyr), CBE, 5 Aug. 2015.
Liddiard, Ronald, 6 July 2014.
Lightbody, Ian Macdonald, CMG, 10 March 2015.
Lim Fat, Sir (Maxime) Edouard (Lim Man), 2 March 2015.
Linacre, Sir (John) Gordon (Seymour), CBE, AFC, DFM, 5 Feb. 2015.
Littman, Mark, QC, 19 June 2015.
Livingston, Air Vice-Marshal Graham, 5 Oct. 2014.
Lloyd, Air Vice-Marshal Darrell Clive Arthur, CB, 18 Feb. 2015.
Lobo, Sir Rogerio Hyndman, (Sir Roger), CBE, 18 April 2015.
Ludlow, Her Honour Caroline Mary, 10 Dec. 2014.
Lund, John Walter Guerrier, CBE, FRS, 21 March 2015.
Lyddon, (William) Derek (Collier), CB, 7 Feb. 2015.
Lyon, Mary Frances, FRS, 25 Dec. 2014.

McAlister, Maj.-Gen. Ronald William Lorne, CB, OBE, 8 Sept. 2015.
McCabe, John, CBE, 13 Feb. 2015.
McCabe, Thomas, 19 April 2015.
McClelland, George Ewart, CB, 7 Jan. 2015.
McCluney, Ian, CMG, 17 July 2015.
MacCormick, Ian Somerled MacDonald, 19 Sept. 2014.
McDermid, Ven. Norman George Lloyd Roberts, 30 Sept. 2014.
McDonald, Alistair, 1 May 2014.
MacDonald, Hon. Flora Isabel, CC, PC (Can.), 26 July 2015.
Macdonald, Prof. William Weir, 30 April 2015.
Macdonald-Buchanan, John, MC, 11 Oct. 2014.
McEwan, Geraldine, 30 Jan. 2015.
McGregor, Harvey, CBE, QC, 27 June 2015.
Mackey, William Gawen, 12 May 2015.
Mackie of Benshie, Baron (Life Peer); George Yull Mackie, CBE, DSO, DFC, 17 Feb. 2015.
Mackintosh, Prof. Nicholas John, FRS, 8 Feb. 2015.
Macklin, David Drury, CBE, 29 March 2015.
McKuen, Rod, 29 Jan. 2015.
Macleod, Ian Buchanan, 2 Dec. 2013.
Macmillan, Robert Hugh, 10 May 2015.
McMullen, His Honour Jeremy John, QC, 10 Feb. 2015.
McMurray, David Bruce, 7 June 2015.
McNair, Archibald Alister Jourdan, (Archie), 2 July 2015.
Macpherson of Biallid, Sir (Ronald) Thomas (Stewart), (Tommy), CBE, MC, TD, 6 Nov. 2014.
Macready, Sir Nevil John Wilfrid, 3rd Bt, CBE, 27 Sept. 2014.
MacWilliam, Very Rev. Alexander Gordon, 24 Oct. 2014.
Mais, Francis Thomas, 22 Sept. 2014.
Makgill Crichton Maitland, Major John David, 7 May 2015.
Malcolm, Prof. Hon. David Kingsley, AC, QC, 20 Oct. 2014.
Manduca, John Alfred, 6 Nov. 2014.
Mangham, Maj.-Gen. William Desmond, CB, 23 Nov. 2014.
Manley, Brian William, CBE, 20 Dec. 2014.
Mann, Dr Felix Bernard, 2 Oct. 2014.
Manzie, Sir (Andrew) Gordon, KCB, 24 Sept. 2014.
Margesson, 2nd Viscount; Francis Vere Hampden Margesson, 11 Nov. 2014.
Markl, Prof. Hubert, 8 Jan. 2015.
Marks, Dennis Michael, 2 April 2015.
Marlborough, 11th Duke of; John George Vanderbilt Henry Spencer-Churchill, 16 Oct. 2014.
Marler, Dennis Ralph Greville, 12 Nov. 2014.
Marmion, Prof. Barrie P., AO, 12 July 2014.
Marrack, Rear-Adm. Philip Reginald, CB, 29 May 2014.
Marriott, Arthur Leslie, QC, 4 Sept. 2015.
Marsh, Rear-Adm. Geoffrey Gordon Ward, CB, OBE, 24 Oct. 2014.
Marsh, Prof. Leonard George, OBE, 3 Oct. 2014.

Marshall, Prof. Christopher John, FRS, 8 Aug. 2015.
Marshall, John Alexander, CB, 29 March 2013.
Marshall, Prof. Sir (Oshley) Roy, CBE, 2 Feb. 2015.
Martin, (Arthur) Bryan, CB, 30 Dec. 2014.
Mason of Barnsley, Baron (Life Peer); Roy Mason, PC, 20 April 2015.
Mason, Sir (Basil) John, CB, FRS, 6 Jan. 2015.
Masse, Hon. Marcel, OQ, PC (Can.), 25 Aug. 2014.
Master, (Humphrey) Simon Harcourt, 16 Jan. 2015.
Maunsell, Susan Pamela, 4 Aug. 2015.
Maxey, Peter Malcolm, CMG, 23 Oct. 2014.
May, Gordon Leslie, OBE, 24 Nov. 2013.
Mazrui, Prof. Ali A., 12 Oct. 2014.
Meade, Richard John Hannay, OBE, 8 Jan. 2015.
Medawar, His Honour Nicholas Antoine Macbeth, QC, 30 Jan. 2015.
Messer, Cholmeley Joseph, 21 July 2015.
Metcalf, Prof. Donald, AC, FRS, 15 Dec. 2014.
Metcalf, Ven. Robert Laurence, 26 Dec. 2014.
Michael, Ian Lockie, CBE, 24 Oct. 2014.
Michie, Prof. David Alan Redpath, OBE, 24 Aug. 2015.
Middleton, Donald King, CBE, 21 Jan. 2015.
Miller, Sir Hilary Duppa, (Sir Hal), 21 March 2015.
Miller, Prof. Karl Fergus Connor, 24 Sept. 2014.
Miller, Keith William, 16 Oct. 2014.
Miller, Kenneth Allan Glen, CBE, 5 April 2015.
Miller, Terence George, TD, 17 Jan. 2015.
Molony, (Sir) (Thomas) Desmond, 3rd Bt, 3 Oct. 2014.
Molyneaux of Killead, Baron (Life Peer); James Henry Molyneaux, KBE, PC, 9 March 2015.
Monier-Williams, His Honour Evelyn Faithfull, 30 June 2015.
Monk, Arthur James, 29 June 2014.
Montagu of Beaulieu, 3rd Baron; Edward John Barrington Douglas-Scott-Montagu, 31 Aug. 2015.
Morby, Grainne, 7 Aug. 2014.
Morgan, Kenneth, OBE, 5 Aug. 2015.
Morgan, Prof. Roger Pearce, 19 Feb. 2015.
Morris, Christopher, 11 March 2015.
Morris, David Elwyn, 29 April 2015.
Moser, Baron (Life Peer); Claus Adolf Moser, KCB, CBE, FBA, 4 Sept. 2015.
Mott, Sir John Harmar, 3rd Bt, 15 May 2015.
Mountevans, 3rd Baron; Edward Patrick Broke Evans, 21 Dec. 2014.
Mtesa, Love, 17 Nov. 2014.
Mustill, Baron (Life Peer); Michael John Mustill, PC, FBA, 24 April 2015.

Nambu, Prof. Yoichiro, 5 July 2015.
Neighbour, Oliver Wray, FBA, 20 Jan. 2015.
Nevin, Prof. Norman Cummings, OBE, 28 June 2014.
Newall, Sir Paul Henry, TD, 28 July 2015.
Newman, Prof. Ronald Charles, FRS, 30 July 2014.
Newton, David Alexander, 15 Jan. 2007.
Nicholson, Brian Thomas Graves, CBE, 12 Aug. 2015.
Ninis, Ven. Richard Betts, 15 Oct. 2014.
Nobbs, David Gordon, 9 Aug. 2015.
Nugee, Edward George, TD, QC, 30 Dec. 2014.
Nugee, Rachel Elizabeth, 11 Aug. 2015.
Nunan, Manus, 4 Aug. 2015.

Oates, Sir Thomas, CMG, OBE, 28 June 2015.
O'Brien, Prof. Michael, FBA, 6 May 2015.
O'Connor, Rory, CBE, 10 Aug. 2015.
O'Hara, Prof. Michael John, FRS, 24 Nov. 2014.
Oliver, Prof. Michael Francis, CBE, 7 June 2015.
Orr, Dr James Henry, 7 Oct. 2014.
O'Sullevan, Sir Peter John, CBE, 29 July 2015.
Overbury, (Henry) Colin (Barry), CBE, 23 March 2015.

Palmer, Thomas Joseph, (Joe), CBE, 15 Aug. 2015.
Parkes, John Hubert, CB, 23 Nov. 2013.
Parsons, Susie, 6 June 2015.
Pasco, Richard Edward, CBE, 12 Nov. 2014.
Pasco, Rowanne, (Mrs William FitzGerald), 14 March 2015.
Pasqua, Charles Victor, 29 June 2015.
Patten, (Hilda Elsie) Marguerite, CBE, 4 June 2015.
Peake, David Alphy Edward Raymond, 7 Sept. 2015.
Peel, Rev. Jonathan Sidney, CBE, MC, 11 Dec. 2014.
Pelly, Derek Roland, (Derk), 14 Feb. 2015.
Penfold, Maj.-Gen. Robert Bernard, CB, LVO, 22 April 2015.
Pentecost, Prof. Brian Leonard, OBE, 16 Jan. 2015.
Perham, Prof. Richard Nelson, FRS, 14 Feb. 2015.
Perl, Prof. Martin Lewis, 30 Sept. 2014.
Perry, George Henry, 1998.
Perry, Rev. Canon Michael Charles, 22 Jan. 2015.
Petre, His Honour Francis Herbert Loraine, 25 Feb. 2015.
Pettigrew, Sir Russell Hilton, 20 March 2015.
Phelps, Anthony John, CB, 9 Nov. 2014.
Phillips, (Mervyn) John, AO, 3 Nov. 2014.
Phillips, Robin, OC, 25 July 2015.
Pilkington, Air Vice-Marshal Michael John, CB, CBE, 29 Jan. 2015.
Pinder, John Humphrey Murray, OBE, 7 March 2015.
Pinkerton, Prof. John Henry McKnight, CBE, 22 Sept. 2013.
Pinsent, Sir Christopher Roy, 3rd Bt, 19 Aug. 2015.
Platt of Writtle, Baroness (Life Peer); Beryl Catherine Platt, CBE, 1 Feb. 2015.
Platt, Prof. Colin Peter Sherard, 23 July 2015.
Pöhl, Karl Otto, 9 Dec. 2014.
Porter, Andrew Brian, 3 April 2015.
Postgate, Prof. John Raymond, FRS, 22 Oct. 2014.
Potter, John Herbert, MBE, 14 Feb. 2015.
Potter, Rev. Philip Alford, 30 March 2015.
Powell, Prof. Michael James David, FRS, 19 April 2015.
Powerscourt, 10th Viscount; Mervyn Niall Wingfield, 25 July 2015.
Pratchett, Sir Terence David John, OBE, 12 March 2015.
Pratt, (Arthur) Geoffrey, CBE, 20 July 2014.
Price, Christopher, 20 Feb. 2015.
Probert, David Henry, CBE, 11 Oct. 2014.
Prosser, Rt Hon. Lord; William David Prosser, PC, 22 March 2015.
Pulleyblank, Prof. Edwin George, 13 April 2013.

Quayle, Maj.-Gen. Thomas David Graham, CB, 25 June 2015.

Rabinovitch, Prof. Benton Seymour, FRS, 2 Aug. 2014.
Rackham, Oliver, OBE, FBA, 12 Feb. 2015.
Rainer, Luise, 30 Dec. 2014.
Randolph, Denys, 27 Jan. 2015.
Ranger, Prof. Terence Osborn, FBA, 3 Jan. 2015.
Rankin, Andrew, QC, 11 Feb. 2015.
Rawley, Alan David, QC, 26 Aug. 2014.
Raychaudhuri, Prof. Tapan Kumar, 26 Nov. 2014.
Read, Air Marshal Sir Charles Frederick, KBE, CB, DFC, AFC, 17 Sept. 2014.
Read, Brig. Gregory, CBE, 7 Oct. 2014.
Read, Sir John Emms, 4 April 2015.
Reddish, Prof. Vincent Cartledge, OBE, 2 Jan. 2015.
Reeve, Sir Anthony, KCMG, KCVO, 6 Nov. 2014.
Regan, Charles Maurice, 31 March 2015.
Rendell of Babergh, Baroness (Life Peer); Ruth Barbara Rendell, CBE, 2 May 2015.
Reynolds, Barbara, 29 April 2015.
Reynolds, Sir David James, 3rd Bt, 13 Feb. 2015.
Richardson, Rt Hon. Sir Ivor Lloyd Morgan, PCNZM, PC, 29 Dec. 2014.
Richardson, Lt-Gen. Sir Robert Francis, KCB, CVO, CBE, 21 Nov. 2014.
Richardson, Maj.-Gen. Thomas Anthony, (Tony), CB, MBE, 26 March 2015.
Rickus, Gwenneth Margaret, CBE, 28 Jan. 2015.
Roads, Peter George, 2 June 2015.
Roberts, John Arthur, 2 Sept. 2013.
Roberts, Michael Guist, MBE, 14 Nov. 2014.
Roborough, 3rd Baron; Henry Massey Lopes, 8 Feb. 2015.
Rochdale, 2nd Viscount; St John Durival Kemp, 27 Feb. 2015.
Rogers, Maj.-Gen. Anthony Peter Vernon, OBE, 16 April 2015.
Ropner, (William Guy) David, 16 April 2015.
Rose, Irwin A., (Ernie), 1 June 2015.
Ross-Munro, Colin William Gordon, QC, 5 Sept. 2015.
Rossi, Marie-Louise Elizabeth, 27 Oct. 2014.
Rudden, Prof. Bernard Anthony, FBA, 4 March 2015.
Rule, Margaret Helen, CBE, 9 April 2015.
Russell, Terence Francis, 24 April 2014.

Sachs, Prof. Leo, FRS, 12 Dec. 2013.
Sacks, Oliver Wolf, CBE, 30 Aug. 2015.
Sadler, Anthony John, CBE, 1 Oct. 2014.
St Omer, Sir Dunstan Gerbert Raphael, KCMG, MBE, SLC, 5 May 2015.
Samuel, 3rd Viscount; David Herbert Samuel, OBE, 7 Oct. 2014.
Sarei, Sir Alexis Holyweek, CBE, 22 Sept. 2014.
Saward, Rev. Canon Michael John, 31 Jan. 2015.
Sawdy, Peter Bryan, 20 March 2015.
Scott, John Gavin, LVO, 12 Aug. 2015.
Scott-Joynt, Rt Rev. Michael Charles, 27 Sept. 2014.
Scrivener, Anthony Frank Bertram, QC, 27 March 2015.
Scroggs, Cedric Annesley, 11 Feb. 2015.
Seccombe, Sir (William) Vernon (Stephen), 6 Dec. 2014.
Sedgemore, Brian Charles John, 5 May 2015.
Seipp, Walter, 4 Feb. 2015.
Shackleton, Keith Hope, MBE, 17 April 2015.
Shaw, Maj.-Gen. Anthony John, CB, CBE, 27 July 2015.
Shaw, Colin Don, CBE, 18 Sept. 2014.
Shaw, Geoffrey Peter, QC, 12 Oct. 2014.
Shaw, Captain Peter Jack, CBE, RN, 10 Feb. 2015.
Shepherdson, Prof. John Cedric, FBA, 8 Jan. 2015.

Sheppard of Didgemere, Baron (Life Peer); Allen John George Sheppard, KCVO, 25 March 2015.
Sheppard, Prof. Norman, FRS, 10 April 2015.
Sherrington, Prof. David Colin, FRS, 4 Oct. 2014.
Short, Rt Rev. Kenneth Herbert, AO, 19 Oct. 2014.
Silberston, Prof. (Zangwill) Aubrey, CBE, 24 March 2015.
Simeon, Sir Richard Edmund Barrington, 8th Bt, 11 Oct. 2013.
Simmons, Peter Patrick, 28 Oct. 2014.
Singh, Prof. Ajit, 23 June 2015.
Sirs, William, 16 June 2015.
Slive, Prof. Seymour, 14 June 2014.
Small, David Purvis, CMG, MBE, 3 Sept. 2015.
Smallman, Prof. Raymond Edward, CBE, FRS, 25 Feb. 2015.
Smith, His Honour David Arthur, QC, 30 March 2015.
Smith, David John Harry, CBE, 1 Sept. 2015.
Smith, Ven. Donald John, 22 Aug. 2014.
Smith, Prof. Harry, FRS, 9 Feb. 2015.
Snaith, George Robert, 15 Oct. 2013.
Somerset, David Henry Fitzroy, 25 Oct. 2014.
Sorley Walker, Kathrine, 15 April 2015.
Southampton, 6th Baron; Charles James FitzRoy, 10 Jan. 2015.
Speirs, John Garrett, CBE, LVO, 27 Dec. 2014.
Spicer, Sir James Wilton, 21 March 2015.
Sporborg, Christopher Henry, CBE, 2 Jan. 2015.
Stallworthy, Prof. Jon Howie, FBA, 19 Nov. 2014.
Stanbridge, Ven. Leslie Cyril, 19 March 2015.
Staughton, Rt Hon. Sir Christopher Stephen Thomas Jonathan Thayer, PC, 15 Oct. 2014.
Steinberg, Gerald Neil, (Gerry), 21 Aug. 2015.
Stephenson, His Honour Jim, 29 July 2015.
Stephenson, Maj.-Gen. John Aubrey, CB, OBE, 24 May 2015.
Stephenson, Stanley, CMG, 23 Dec. 2014.
Stevens, Sir Jocelyn Edward Greville, CVO, 9 Oct. 2014.
Stevenson, Sir Simpson, 4 May 2015.
Stewart, Brian Thomas Webster, CMG, 16 Aug. 2015.
Stowe, Sir Kenneth Ronald, GCB, CVO, 29 Aug. 2015.
Strang, 2nd Baron; Colin Strang, 19 Dec. 2014 (*ext*). *[(ext).*
Sugden, John Goldthorp, 27 Dec. 2014.
Sullivan, David Douglas Hooper, QC, 9 July 2015.
Sutton, Air Marshal Sir John Matthias Dobson, KCB, 21 Nov. 2014.
Swaffield, Sir James Chesebrough, CBE, RD, 4 July 2015.
Swainson, Eric, CBE, 15 Dec. 2014.
Sykes, Rt Rev. Prof. Stephen Whitefield, 24 Sept. 2014.

Tallboys, Richard Gilbert, CMG, OBE, 2 Nov. 2013.
Tamblin, Air Cdre Pamela Joy, CB, 8 March 2015.
Tamuno, Prof. Tekena Nitonye, CON, OFR, 11 April 2015.
Taylor, Phyllis Mary Constance, 21 Oct. 2014.
Templeton, John Marks, Jr, 16 May 2015.
Théodore, Jean-François, 18 May 2015.
Thomas, Susan Kanter, 5 Sept. 2012.
Thompson, Christopher Ronald, 6 April 2015.
Thompson, James, 30 Jan. 2015.
Thomson, Prof. Andrew William John, OBE, 26 Dec. 2014.
Thorpe, Rt Hon. (John) Jeremy, PC, 4 Dec. 2014.
Tizard, Prof. Barbara, FBA, 4 Jan. 2015.
Tobias, Richard David, OBE, 8 Jan. 2015.
Todd, Sir Ian Pelham, KBE, 21 April 2015.
Tomlinson, Prof. (Alfred) Charles, CBE, 22 Aug. 2015.
Toohey, Hon. John Leslie, AC, 9 April 2015.
Topolski, Daniel, 21 Feb. 2015.
Townes, Prof. Charles Hard, 27 Jan. 2015.
Townsend, Lady Juliet Margaret, DCVO, 29 Nov. 2014.
Trainor, Roy, 11 Feb. 2015.
Treadgold, Very Rev. John David, LVO, 15 Feb. 2015.
Tremblay, Marc-Adélard, OC, GOQ, 20 March 2014.
Trewin, Ion Courtenay Gill, 8 April 2015.
Tupman, William Ivan, 29 June 2015.
Turcotte, His Eminence Cardinal Jean-Claude, 8 April 2015.
Turnbull, Jeffrey Alan, CBE, 22 Feb. 2015.
Turner, Christopher John, CBE, 30 Oct. 2014.
Turner, Wilfred, CMG, CVO, 26 June 2015.
Tyrrell, Alan Rupert, QC, 23 Oct. 2014.
Tyrrell, Anne Elizabeth, MBE, 6 Feb. 2015.
Tysoe, John Sidney, 5 Aug. 2015.

Underwood, Hon. Peter George, AC, 7 July 2014.
Urquhart, James Graham, CVO, 14 July 2015.
Utley, (Clifton) Garrick, 20 Feb. 2014.

Vaux of Harrowden, 11th Baron; Anthony William Gilbey, 16 Dec. 2014.
Venables, (Harold) David (Spenser), CB, 3 Oct. 2014.
Vickers, Jon, CC (Can.), 10 July 2015.
Voelcker, Christopher David, TD, 23 Oct. 2014.
von Weizsäcker, Richard, 31 Jan. 2015.

Wade-Gery, Sir Robert Lucian, KCMG, KCVO, 16 Feb. 2015.
Waine, Dr Colin, OBE, 4 Aug. 2014.
Wales, Daphne Beatrice, 20 March 2015.
Walker, Air Marshal Peter Brett, CB, CBE, 6 Sept. 2015.
Wallenberg, Peter, Hon. KBE, 19 Jan. 2015.
Waller, Rt Rev. John Stevens, 3 Sept. 2015.
Wallis, Jeffrey Joseph, 27 Oct. 2014.
Warburton, Dame Anne Marion, DCVO, CMG, 4 June 2015.
Ware, Cyril George, CB, 8 Oct. 2014.
Wareing, Robert Nelson, 12 Feb. 2015.
Warren, Ian Scott, 23 Feb. 2015.
Warren, Maurice Eric, 14 March 2015.
Warren, Prof. Michael Donald, 25 Jan. 2015.
Waterford, 8th Marquess of; John Hubert de la Poer Beresford, 11 Feb. 2015.
Waterstone, David George Stuart, CBE, 1 Oct. 2014.
Watson, Sir David John, 8 Feb. 2015.
Watson, Sir Duncan Amos, CBE, 21 April 2015.
Watson, Victor Hugo, CBE, 25 Feb. 2015.
Webb, Michael Alfred Healey, OBE, 25 April 2015.
Welch, Rear Adm. John Edwin Nugent, CB, 12 Sept. 2014.
Weller, Walter, 14 June 2015.
Wellington, 8th Duke of; Arthur Valerian Wellesley, KG, LVO, OBE, MC, 31 Dec. 2014.
West, Christopher John, CBE, 22 April 2015.
West, John James, 27 April 2014.
West, Martin Litchfield, OM, FBA, 13 July 2015.
Westcott, Prof. John Hugh, FRS, 14 Oct. 2014.
White, Air Vice-Marshal George Alan, CB, AFC, 8 June 2015.
White, Norman Arthur, 13 Jan. 2015.
Whitelaw, Billie, CBE, 21 Dec. 2014.
Whiting, Alan, 14 June 2015.
Whitlam, Hon. (Edward) Gough, AC, QC, 21 Oct. 2014.
Whittaker, Geoffrey Owen, OBE, 24 Feb. 2015.
Whittall, (Harold) Astley, CBE, 28 Aug. 2015.
Whittall, Michael Charlton, CMG, OBE, 9 Nov. 2014.
Wiggin, Sir Alfred William, (Sir Jerry Wiggin), TD, 12 March 2015.
Wilkinson, Prof. Tony James, FBA, 25 Dec. 2014.
Will, Ronald Kerr, 11 Sept. 2014.
Willett, Allan Robert, CMG, CVO, 18 July 2015.
Williams, Rt Hon. Alan John, PC, 21 Dec. 2014.
Williams, Rear-Adm. Charles Bernard, CB, OBE, 11 June 2015.
Williams, Very Rev. Mgr John Noctor, CBE, 11 June 2014.
Williams, Prof. Robert Joseph Paton, MBE, FRS, 21 March 2015.
Williams, Ronald William, 20 Nov. 2014.
Williamson of Horton, Baron (Life Peer); David Francis Williamson, GCMG, CB, PC, 30 Aug. 2015.
Willson, Prof. (Francis Michael) Glenn, 13 Aug. 2014.
Wilson, Prof. Henry Wallace, 7 Nov. 2014.
Wilson, William Desmond, OBE, MC, DSC, 3 Jan. 2014.
Winstone, Dame Dorothy Gertrude, DBE, CMG, 3 April 2014.
Winton, Sir Nicholas George, MBE, 1 July 2015.
Wistrich, Ernest, CBE, 7 May 2015.
Withers, Rt Hon. Reginald Greive, PC, 15 Nov. 2014.
Wolters, Gwyneth Eleanor Mary, 25 April 2015.
Wood, Robert Noel, 14 July 2015.
Wood, Rt Rev. (Stanley) Mark, 28 Sept. 2014.
Woodhead, Sir Christopher Anthony, 23 June 2015.
Worskett, Prof. Roy, 23 Aug. 2014.
Worth, Prof. Katharine Joyce, 28 Jan. 2015.
Worthington, His Honour George Noel, 19 Nov. 2014.
Wrenbury, 3rd Baron; Rev. John Burton Buckley, 27 Sept. 2014.
Wright, (Charles) Christopher, 1 Sept. 2014.
Wright, Prof. Michael Thomas, 10 Jan. 2015.
Wyatt, Arthur Hope, CMG, 4 March 2015.

Yates, Ivan Ray, CBE, 2 Aug. 2015.
Young, (David) Junor, 18 June 2015.
Young, Kenneth Middleton, CBE, 7 Feb. 2015.

Zapf, Hermann, 4 June 2015.

ABBREVIATIONS USED IN THIS BOOK

Some of the designatory letters in this list are used merely for economy of space and do not necessarily imply any professional or other qualification.

A

AA Anti-aircraft; Automobile Association; Architectural Association; Augustinians of the Assumption; Associate in Arts

AAA Amateur Athletic Association; American Accounting Association; Abdominal Aortic Aneurysm

AAAL American Academy of Arts and Letters

AA&QMG Assistant Adjutant and Quartermaster-General

AAArb Member, Association of Arbitrators (South Africa)

AAAS American Association for the Advancement of Science

AABC (Register of) Architects Accredited in Building Conservation

AAC Army Air Corps; Amateur Athletic Club

AACE Association for Adult and Continuing Education

AADB Accountancy and Actuarial Discipline Board

AAF Auxiliary Air Force (*now see* RAuxAF)

AAFCE Allied Air Forces in Central Europe

AAG Assistant Adjutant-General

AAI Associate, Chartered Auctioneers' and Estate Agents' Institute (later, after amalgamation, ARICS)

AAIL American Academy and Institute of Arts and Letters (*now see* AAAL)

AAM Association of Assistant Mistresses in Secondary Schools

AAMC Australian Army Medical Corps (*now see* RAAMC)

A&AEE Aeroplane and Armament Experimental Establishment

A&E Accident and Emergency

A&R Artists and Repertoire

A and SH Argyll and Sutherland Highlanders

AAPS Aquatic and Atmospheric Physical Sciences

AAS American Astronomical Society

AASA Associate, Australian Society of Accountants (*now see* FCPA)

AASC Australian Army Service Corps

AATSE Australian Academy of Technological Sciences and Engineering

AAUQ Associate in Accountancy, University of Queensland

AB Bachelor of Arts (US); able-bodied seaman; airborne; Alberta (postal)

ABA Amateur Boxing Association; Antiquarian Booksellers' Association; American Bar Association

ABBSI Associate Member, British Boot and Shoe Institute

ABC Australian Broadcasting Commission; American Broadcasting Companies; Amateur Boxing Club; Associate, Birmingham Conservatoire; Accredited Business Communicator

ABCC Association of British Chambers of Commerce

ABF Army Benevolent Fund

ABI Association of British Insurers

ABIA Associate, Bankers' Institute of Australasia

ABINZ Associate, Bankers' Institute of New Zealand

ABIPP Associate, British Institute of Professional Photography

ABIS Association of Burglary Insurance Surveyors

ABM Advisory Board of Ministry

ABNM American Board of Nuclear Medicine

ABP Associated British Ports

Abp Archbishop

ABPI Association of British Pharmaceutical Industry

ABPsS Associate, British Psychological Society (*now see* AFBPsS)

ABRC Advisory Board for the Research Councils

ABSA Association for Business Sponsorship of the Arts

ABSM Associate, Birmingham and Midland Institute School of Music

ABTA Association of British Travel Agents

ABTAPL Association of British Theological and Philosophical Libraries

AC Companion, Order of Australia; *Ante Christum* (before Christ)

ACA Associate, Institute of Chartered Accountants

Acad. Academy

ACARD Advisory Council for Applied Research and Development

ACAS Advisory, Conciliation and Arbitration Service; Assistant Chief of the Air Staff

ACC Association of County Councils; Anglican Consultative Council

ACCA Associate, Association of Chartered Certified Accountants (*formerly* Chartered Association of Certified Accountants)

ACCE Association of County Chief Executives

ACCEL American College of Cardiology Extended Learning

ACCM Advisory Council for the Church's Ministry (*now see* ABM)

AcDip Academic Diploma in the History of Art

AcDipEd Academic Diploma in Education

ACDP Australian Committee of Directors and Principals

ACDS Assistant Chief of Defence Staff

ACE Association of Consulting Engineers; Member, Association of Conference Executives; Allied Command Europe

ACENVO Association of Chief Executives of National Voluntary Organisations (*now see* ACEVO)

ACEO Association of Chief Education Officers

ACertCM Archbishops' Certificate in Church Music

ACEVO Association of Chief Executives of Voluntary Organisations

ACF Army Cadet Force

ACFA Army Cadet Force Association

ACFAS Association Canadienne-Française pour l'avancement des sciences

ACFHE Association of Colleges for Further and Higher Education

ACG Assistant Chaplain-General

ACGI Associate, City and Guilds of London Institute

ACGS Assistant Chief of the General Staff

ACI Airports Council International (Europe)

ACIArb Associate, Chartered Institute of Arbitrators

ACIB Associate, Chartered Institute of Bankers

ACIBS Associate, Chartered Institute of Bankers in Scotland

ACIEA Associate, Chartered Institute of Educational Assessors

ACIHort Associate, Chartered Institute of Horticulture

ACII Associate, Chartered Insurance Institute

ACIM Associate, Chartered Institute of Marketing

ACIS Associate, Institute of Chartered Secretaries and Administrators (*formerly* Chartered Institute of Secretaries)

ACLS American Council of Learned Societies

ACM Association of Computing Machinery

ACMA Associate, Chartered Institute of Management Accountants (*formerly* Institute of Cost and Management Accountants)

ACMI Associate, Chartered Management Institute

ACNS Assistant Chief of Naval Staff

ACommA Associate, Society of Commercial Accountants (*now see* ASCA)

ACORD Advisory Committee on Research and Development

ACOS Assistant Chief of Staff

ACOST Advisory Council on Science and Technology

ACP Association of Clinical Pathologists; Associate, College of Preceptors; African/Caribbean/Pacific

ACPO Association of Chief Police Officers

ACR Accredited Conservator-Restorer

ACRE Action with Rural Communities in England

ACS American Chemical Society; Additional Curates Society

acsc passed Advanced Command and Staff Course

ACSEA Allied Command South East Asia

ACSM Associate, Camborne School of Mines

AcSS Member, Academy of Learned Societies for the Social Sciences (*now see* FAcSS)

ACT Australian Capital Territory; Australian College of Theology; Associate, College of Technology; Association of Corporate Treasurers

ACTSS Association of Clerical, Technical and Supervisory Staff

ACTT Association of Cinematograph, Television and Allied Technicians

ACTU Australian Council of Trade Unions

ACU Association of Commonwealth Universities

ACWA Associate, Institute of Cost and Works Accountants (*now see* ACMA)

AD Dame of the Order of Australia; *Anno Domini* (in the year of the Lord); Air Defence

aD ausser Dienst

ADAS Agricultural Development and Advisory Service

ADASS Association of Directors of Adult Social Services

ADB Asian Development Bank; Associate of the Drama Board (Education)

ADB/F African Development Bank/Fund

ADC Aide-de-camp; Association of District Councils

ADCM Archbishop of Canterbury's Diploma in Church Music

AD Corps Army Dental Corps (*now* RADC)

ADC(P) Personal Aide-de-camp to HM The Queen

ADEME Assistant Director Electrical and Mechanical Engineering

Ad eund *Ad eundem gradum* ; and *see under* aeg

ADFManc Art and Design Fellow, Manchester

ADGMS Assistant Director-General of Medical Services

ADipC Advanced Postgraduate Diploma in Management Consulting

Adjt Adjutant

ADJAG Assistant Deputy Judge Advocate General

ADK Order of Ahli Darjah Kinabalu

ADM Advanced Diploma in Midwifery

Adm. Admiral

ADMS Assistant Director of Medical Services

ADOS Assistant Director of Ordnance Services

ADP Automatic Data Processing

ADPA Associate Diploma of Public Administration

ADS&T Assistant Director of Supplies and Transport

ADSS Association of Directors of Social Services

ADSW Association of Directors of Social Work

Adv. Advisory; Advocate

AdvDip Advanced Diploma
ADVS Assistant Director of Veterinary Services
ADWE&M Assistant Director of Works, Electrical and Mechanical
AE Air Efficiency Award
AEA Atomic Energy Authority; Air Efficiency Award (*now see* AE); American Economic Association
AEAF Allied Expeditionary Air Force
AEC Agriculture Executive Council; Army Educational Corps (*now see* RAEC); Atomic Energy Commission
AECMA Association Européenne des Constructeurs de Matériel Aérospatial
AEE Atomic Energy Establishment
AEEU Amalgamated Engineering and Electrical Union
AEF Amalgamated Union of Engineering and Foundry Workers (later AEU, then AEEU); American Expeditionary Forces; Air Experience Flight
aeg *ad eundem gradum* (to the same degree-of the admission of a graduate of one university to the same degree at another without examination)
AEI Associated Electrical Industries
AELTC All England Lawn Tennis Club
AEM Air Efficiency Medal
AER Army Emergency Reserve
AERE Atomic Energy Research Establishment (Harwell)
Æt. or **Ætat.** *Ætatis* (aged)
AEU Amalgamated Engineering Union (later AEEU)
AEWVH Association for the Education and Welfare of the Visually Handicapped
AF Admiral of the Fleet
AFAIAA Associate Fellow, American Institute of Aeronautics and Astronautics
AFASIC Association for All Speech Impaired Children
AFB Air Force Base
AFBPsS Associate Fellow, British Psychological Society
AFC Air Force Cross; Association Football Club
AFCEA Armed Forces Communications and Electronics Association
AFCENT Allied Forces in Central Europe
AFD Doctor of Fine Arts (US)
AFDS Air Fighting Development Squadron
AFGE Associate Fellow, Guild of Glass Engravers
AFHQ Allied Force Headquarters
AFI American Film Institute
AFIAP Artiste, Fédération Internationale de l'Art Photographique
AFIAS Associate Fellow, Institute of Aeronautical Sciences (US) (*now see* AFAIAA)
AFIMA Associate Fellow, Institute of Mathematics and its Applications
AFM Air Force Medal
AFNORTH Allied Forces in Northern Europe
AFOM Associate, Faculty of Occupational Medicine
AFRAeS Associate Fellow, Royal Aeronautical Society (*now see* MRAeS)
AFRC Agricultural and Food Research Council (*now see* BBSRC)
AFRSPSoc Associate Fellow, Remote Sensing and Photogrammetry Society
AFSOUTH Allied Forces in Southern Europe
AFV Armoured Fighting Vehicles
AG Attorney-General
AGAC American Guild of Authors and Composers
AGARD Advisory Group for Aerospace Research and Development
AGAvA Associate, Guild of Aviation Artists
AGC Adjutant General's Corps
AGH Australian General Hospital
AGI Alliance Graphique Internationale; Associate, Institute of Certificated Grocers
AGR Advanced Gas-cooled Reactor
AGRA Army Group Royal Artillery; Association of Genealogists and Record Agents
AGRI Animal Genetic Resources Information
AGSM Associate, Guildhall School of Music and Drama; Australian Graduate School of Management
AHA Area Health Authority; American Hospitals Association; Associate, Institute of Health Service Administrators (later AHSM)
AHA(T) Area Health Authority (Teaching)
AHI Association of Heritage Interpretation
AHQ Army Headquarters
AHRB Arts and Humanities Research Board (*now see* AHRC)
AHRC Arts and Humanities Research Council
AHSM Associate, Institute of Health Services Management
ai *ad interim*
AIA Associate, Institute of Actuaries; American Institute of Architects; Association of International Artists
AIAA American Institute of Aeronautics and Astronautics
AIACE Association Internationale des Anciens des Communautés Européennes
AIAgrE Associate, Institution of Agricultural Engineers
AIAS Associate Surveyor Member, Incorporated Association of Architects and Surveyors
AIB Associate, Institute of Bankers (*now see* ACIB)
AIBD Associate, Institute of British Decorators
AIC Agricultural Improvement Council; Associate of the Institute of Chemistry (later ARIC, MRIC; *now see* MRSC)
aic armour infantry course
AICA Associate Member, Commonwealth Institute of Accountants; Association Internationale des Critiques d'Art
AICE Associate, Institution of Civil Engineers
AIChE American Institute of Chemical Engineers
AICPA American Institute of Certified Public Accountants
AICS Associate, Institute of Chartered Shipbrokers
AID Artificial Insemination by Donor
AIDB Accountancy Investigation and Discipline Board (*now see* AADB)
AIDS Acquired Immunity Deficiency Syndrome
AIE Associate, Institute of Education
AIEE Associate, Institution of Electrical Engineers
AIF Australian Imperial Forces
AIFireE Associate, Institution of Fire Engineers
AIG Adjutant-Inspector-General
AIH Associate, Institute of Housing
AIHort Associate, Institute of Horticulture (*now see* ACIHort)
AIIA Associate, Insurance Institute of America; Associate, Indian Institute of Architects
AIIMR Associate, Institute of Investment Management and Research (later ASIP; *now see* CFA)
AIIRA Associate, International Industrial Relations Association
AIL Associate, Institute of Linguists
AILA Associate, Institute of Landscape Architects (later ALI)
AIM Associate, Institution of Metallurgists (later MIM); Australian Institute of Management; Alternative Investment Market; Advanced Institute of Management Research
AIMarE Associate, Institute of Marine Engineers
AIMBE American Institute for Medical and Biological Engineering
AIMC Associate, Institute of Management Consultants
AIME American Institute of Mechanical Engineers
AIMgt Associate, Institute of Management (*now see* ACMI)
AIMSW Associate, Institute of Medical Social Work
AInstP Associate, Institute of Physics
AIP Association of Independent Producers; American Institute of Physics
AIPR Associate, Institute of Public Relations
AIQS Associate Member, Institute of Quantity Surveyors
AIRCENT Allied Air Forces Central Europe
AIRTO Association of Independent Research and Technology Organizations
AIS Associate, Institute of Statisticians (later MIS)
AIStructE Associate, Institution of Structural Engineers
AITP Associate, Institute of Town Planners, India
AJAG Assistant Judge Advocate General
AJEX Association of Jewish Ex-Service Men and Women
AK Knight, Order of Australia; Alaska (postal)
AKC Associate, King's College London
AL Alabama (postal)
ALA Associate, Library Association (*now see* MCLIP); Association of London Authorities
Ala Alabama
ALAA Associate, Library Association of Australia
ALAI Associate, Library Association of Ireland
ALAM Associate, London Academy of Music and Dramatic Art
ALCD Associate, London College of Divinity
ALCM Associate, London College of Music
ALCM (TD) Associate, London College of Music (Teaching Diploma)
ALCS Authors Lending and Copyright Society
ALFSEA Allied Land Forces South-East Asia
ALI Argyll Light Infantry; Associate, Landscape Institute (*now see* MLI)
ALICE Autistic and Language Impaired Children's Education
ALLC Association for Literary and Linguistic Computing
ALP Australian Labor Party
ALPSP Association of Learned and Professional Society Publishers
ALS Associate, Linnean Society; Amyotrophic Lateral Sclerosis
Alta Alberta
ALVA Association of Leading Visitor Attractions
AM Albert Medal; Member, Order of Australia; Master of Arts (US); Alpes Maritimes
AMA Association of Metropolitan Authorities; Assistant Masters Association (later AMMA, *now see* ATL); Associate, Museums Association; Australian Medical Association
AMARC Associated Marine and Related Charities
Amb. Ambulance; Ambassador
AMBIM Associate Member, British Institute of Management (later AIMgt)
AMC Association of Municipal Corporations
AMCST Associate, Manchester College of Science and Technology
AMCT Associate, Manchester College of Technology
AMDEA Association of Manufacturers of Domestic Electrical Appliances
AMF Australian Military Forces
AMFL Allied Command Europe Mobile Force Land
AMICE Associate Member, Institution of Civil Engineers (*now see* MICE)
AMIChemE Associate Member, Institution of Chemical Engineers
AMIEE Associate Member, Institution of Electrical Engineers (later MIEE)

AMIERE Associate Member, Institution of Electronic and Radio Engineers
AMIMechE Associate Member, Institution of Mechanical Engineers (*now see* MIMechE)
AMInstCE Associate Member, Institution of Civil Engineers (*now see* MICE)
AmInstEE American Institute of Electrical Engineers
AMMA Assistant Masters & Mistresses Association (*now see* ATL)
AMN Ahli Mangku Negara (Malaysia)
AMP Advanced Management Program; Air Member for Personnel
AMRAeS Associate Member, Royal Aeronautical Society
AMRC Association of Medical Research Charities
AMREF African Medical and Research Foundation
AMRI Associate Member, Royal Institution
AMRS Associate, Market Research Society
AMRSH Associate Member, Royal Society of Health
AMS Assistant Military Secretary; Army Medical Services
AMSI Associate Member, Securities Institute
AMSO Air Member for Supply and Organisation
AMTRI Advanced Manufacturing Technology Research Institute
ANAF Arab Non-Arab Friendship
Anat. Anatomy; Anatomical
ANC African National Congress
Anon. Anonymously
ANU Australian National University
ANZAAS Australian and New Zealand Association for the Advancement of Science
Anzac Australian and New Zealand Army Corps
AO Officer, Order of Australia; Air Officer
AOA Air Officer in charge of Administration
AOC Air Officer Commanding
AOC-in-C Air Officer Commanding-in-Chief
AOD Army Ordnance Department
AOE Alberta Order of Excellence
AOER Army Officers Emergency Reserve
APA American Psychiatric Association
APACS Association of Payment and Clearing Systems
APD Army Pay Department
APEX Association of Professional, Executive, Clerical and Computer Staff
APHA American Public Health Association
APIS Army Photographic Intelligence Service
APM Assistant Provost Marshal
APMI Associate, Pensions Management Institute
APNI Alliance Party of Northern Ireland
APR Accredited Public Relations Practitioner
APS Aborigines Protection Society; American Physical Society
APSW Association of Psychiatric Social Workers
APT&C Administrative, Professional, Technical and Clerical
APTC Army Physical Training Corps
AQ Administration and Quartering
AQMG Assistant Quartermaster-General
AR Associated Rediffusion (Television); Arkansas (postal)
ARA Associate, Royal Academy; Armada de la República Argentina
ARACI Associate, Royal Australian Chemical Institute
ARAD Associate, Royal Academy of Dancing
ARAeS Associate, Royal Aeronautical Society
ARAgS Associate, Royal Agricultural Societies (*ie* of England, Scotland and Wales)
ARAIA Associate, Royal Australian Institute of Architects
ARAM Associate, Royal Academy of Music
ARAS Associate, Royal Astronomical Society
ARB Architects' Registration Board
ARBA Associate, Royal Society of British Artists
ARBS Associate, Royal Society of British Sculptors
ARC Architects' Registration Council (*now see* ARB); Agricultural Research Council (later AFRC); Aeronautical Research Council; Arthritis and Rheumatism Council
ARCA Associate, Royal College of Art; Associate, Royal Canadian Academy
ARCamA Associate, Royal Cambrian Academy of Art
ARCIC Anglican-Roman Catholic International Commission
ARCM Associate, Royal College of Music
ARCO Associate, Royal College of Organists
ARCO(CHM) Associate, Royal College of Organists with Diploma in Choir Training
ARCP Affiliate, Royal College of Physicians
ARCS Associate, Royal College of Science; Accreditation Review and Consulting Service (*now see* ISI)
ARCST Associate, Royal College of Science and Technology (Glasgow)
ARCUK Architects' Registration Council of the United Kingdom (*now see* ARB)
ARCVS Associate, Royal College of Veterinary Surgeons
ARE Associate, Royal Society of Painter-Printmakers (*formerly* of Painter-Etchers and Engravers); Arab Republic of Egypt; Admiralty Research Establishment
AREINZ Associate, Real Estate Institute, New Zealand
ARELS Association of Recognised English Language Schools
ARHistS Associate, Royal Historical Society
ARIAS Associate, Royal Incorporation of Architects in Scotland
ARIBA Associate, Royal Institute of British Architects (*now see* RIBA)
ARIC Associate, Royal Institute of Chemistry (later MRIC; *now see* MRSC)
ARICS Professional Associate, Royal Institution of Chartered Surveyors (*now see* MRICS)
ARINA Associate, Royal Institution of Naval Architects
ARLIS Art Libraries Association
ARLT Association for the Reform of Latin Teaching
ARMS Associate, Royal Society of Miniature Painters
ARP Air Raid Precautions
ARPS Associate, Royal Photographic Society
ARR Association of Radiation Research
ARRC Associate, Royal Red Cross; Allied (formerly Allied Command Europe) Rapid Reaction Corps
ARSA Associate, Royal Scottish Academy
ARSC Association of Recorded Sound Collections
ARSCM Associate, Royal School of Church Music
ARSM Associate, Royal School of Mines
ARTC Associate, Royal Technical College (Glasgow) (*now see* ARCST)
ARVO Association for Research in Vision and Ophthalmology
ARWA Associate, Royal West of England Academy
ARWS Associate, Royal Society of Painters in Water-Colours
AS Anglo-Saxon
ASA Associate Member, Society of Actuaries; Associate of Society of Actuaries (US); Australian Society of Accountants; Army Sailing Association; Advertising Standards Authority; Alment Aksjeselskap
ASAA Associate, Society of Incorporated Accountants and Auditors
ASAI Associate, Society of Architectural Illustrators
ASAQS Association of South African Quantity Surveyors
ASBAH Association for Spina Bifida and Hydrocephalus
ASC Administrative Staff College, Henley
ASCAP American Society of Composers, Authors and Publishers
ASCE American Society of Civil Engineers
ASCHB Association for Study of Conservation of Historic Buildings
ASCL Association of School and College Leaders
AScW Association of Scientific Workers (later ASTMS)
ASD Armament Supply Department
ASE Amalgamated Society of Engineers (later AUEW, then AEU, subsequently AEEU); Association for Science Education
ASEAN Association of South East Asian Nations
ASH Action on Smoking and Health
ASIAD Associate, Society of Industrial Artists and Designers
ASIP Associate, UK Society of Investment Professionals (*now see* CFA)
ASLE American Society of Lubrication Engineers
ASLEF Associated Society of Locomotive Engineers and Firemen
ASLIB or Aslib Association for Information Management (*formerly* Association of Special Libraries and Information Bureaux)
ASM Association of Senior Members; Australian Service Medal
ASME American Society of Mechanical Engineers; Association for the Study of Medical Education
ASO Air Staff Officer
ASSET Association of Supervisory Staffs, Executives and Technicians (later ASTMS)
Asst Assistant
ASTA Association of Short Circuit Testing Authorities
ASTC Administrative Service Training Course
ASTMS Association of Scientific, Technical and Managerial Staffs (subsequently part of MSF)
ASTS Army School of Training Support
ASVU Army Security Vetting Unit
ASWE Admiralty Surface Weapons Establishment
ATA Air Transport Auxiliary
ATAE Association of Tutors in Adult Education
ATAF Allied Tactical Air Force
ATC Air Training Corps; Art Teacher's Certificate
ATCDE Association of Teachers in Colleges and Departments of Education (*now see* NATFHE)
ATCL Associate, Trinity College of Music, London
ATD Art Teacher's Diploma
ATI Associate, Textile Institute
ATII Associate Member, Chartered Institute (*formerly* Incorporated Institute, then Institute) of Taxation
ATL Association of Teachers and Lecturers
ato Ammunition Technical Officer
ATP Association of Tennis Players
ATPL (A) or (H) Airline Transport Pilot's Licence (Aeroplanes), or (Helicopters)
ATR (BC) Art Therapist Registered (Board Certified)
ATS Auxiliary Territorial Service (later WRAC)
ATTI Association of Teachers in Technical Institutions (*now see* NATFHE)
ATV Associated Television (*formerly* Association TeleVision)
AUA American Urological Association; Association of University Administrators
AUCAS Association of University Clinical Academic Staff
AUEW Amalgamated Union of Engineering Workers (later AEU, then AEEU)
AUS Army of the United States

AUT Association of University Teachers
AVCC Australian Vice-Chancellors' Committee
AVCM Associate, Victoria College of Music
AVD Army Veterinary Department
AVMA Association for Victims of Medical Accidents
AVR Army Volunteer Reserve
AWA Anglian Water Authority
AWHCT Associate, West Ham College of Technology
AWO Association of Water Officers (*now see* IWO)
AWRE Atomic Weapons Research Establishment
aws Graduate of Air Warfare Course
AZ Arizona (postal)

B

b born; brother
BA Bachelor of Arts
BAA British Airports Authority; British Accounting Association
BAAB British Amateur Athletic Board
BAAL British Association for Applied Linguistics
BAAS British Association for the Advancement of Science
BAB British Airways Board
BAC British Aircraft Corporation
BAcc Bachelor of Accountancy
BaccPhil Baccalaureate in Philosophy
BACS British Academy of Composers & Songwriters (*now see* BASCA)
BACSA British Association for Cemeteries in South Asia
BACUP British Association of Cancer United Patients
BADA British American Drama Academy
BAe British Aerospace
BAED Bachelor of Arts in Environmental Design
B&FBS British and Foreign Bible Society
BAFO British Air Forces of Occupation
BAFTA British Academy of Film and Television Arts
BAG Business Art Galleries
BAgricAdmin Bachelor of Agricultural Administration
BAgrSc Bachelor of Agricultural Science
BAI *Baccalarius in Arte Ingeniaria* (Bachelor of Engineering)
BAIE British Association of Industrial Editors
BALPA British Air Line Pilots' Association
BAO Bachelor of Art of Obstetrics
BAOMS British Association of Oral and Maxillo-Facial Surgeons
BAOR British Army of the Rhine (*formerly* on the Rhine)
BAOS British Association of Oral Surgeons (*now see* BAOMS)
BAppSc(MT) Bachelor of Applied Science (Medical Technology)
BAPS British Association of Plastic Surgeons
BARB Broadcasters' Audience Research Board
BARC British Automobile Racing Club
BArch Bachelor of Architecture
Bart Baronet
BAS Bachelor in Agricultural Science
BASc Bachelor of Applied Science
BASCA British Academy of Songwriters, Composers and Authors
BASE British Association for Service to the Elderly
BASEEFA British Approvals Service for Electrical Equipment in Flammable Atmospheres
BASES British Association of Sport and Exercise Sciences
BASHH British Association for Sexual Health and HIV
BASIC British American Security Information Council
BASW British Association of Social Workers
Batt. Battery
BBA British Bankers' Association; Bachelor of Business Administration
BBB of C British Boxing Board of Control
BBC British Broadcasting Corporation
BBFC British Board of Film Classification
BBS Bachelor of Business Studies
BBSRC Biotechnology and Biological Sciences Research Council
BC Before Christ; British Columbia; Borough Council
BCA Bachelor of Commerce and Administration
BCC British Council of Churches (later CCBI)
BCE Bachelor of Civil Engineering; Before the Christian Era
BCh or **BChir** Bachelor of Surgery
BChD Bachelor of Dental Surgery
BCIA British Clothing Industries Association
BCL Bachelor of Civil Law
BCMF British Ceramic Manufacturers' Federation
BCMS Bible Churchmen's Missionary Society
BCOF British Commonwealth Occupation Force
BCom or **BComm** Bachelor of Commerce
BCompt Bachelor of Accounting
BComSc Bachelor of Commercial Science
BCPC British Crop Protection Council
BCS Bengal Civil Service; British Computer Society; Bachelor of Combined Studies
BCSA British Constructional Steelwork Association
BCSC British Council of Shopping Centres
BCTS Bristol Certificate in Theological Studies
BCURA British Coal Utilization Research Association
BCYC British Corinthian Yacht Club
BD Bachelor of Divinity
Bd Board
BDA British Dental Association; British Deaf Association; British Dyslexia Association
Bde Brigade
BDQ Bachelor of Divinity Qualifying
BDS Bachelor of Dental Surgery
BDSc Bachelor of Dental Science
BE Bachelor of Engineering; British Element
BEA British East Africa; British European Airways; British Epilepsy Association
BEAMA Federation of British Electrotechnical and Allied Manufacturers' Associations (*formerly* British Electrical and Allied Manufacturers' Association)
BE&A Bachelor of Engineering and Architecture (Malta)
BEARR British Emergency Aid for Russia and the Republics
BEC Business Education Council (*now see* BTEC)
BEc Bachelor of Economics
BECTU Broadcasting, Entertainment, Cinematograph and Theatre Union
BEd Bachelor of Education
Beds Bedfordshire
BEE Bachelor of Electrical Engineering
BEF British Expeditionary Force; British Equestrian Federation
BEM British Empire Medal
BEMAS British Educational Management and Administration Society
BEME Brigade Electrical and Mechanical Engineer
BEng Bachelor of Engineering
BEO Base Engineer Officer
Berks Berkshire
BERR Department for Business, Enterprise and Regulatory Reform
BES Bachelor of Environmental Studies
BESO British Executive Service Overseas
BEVA British Equine Veterinary Association
BFA Bachelor of Fine Arts
BFI British Film Institute
BFMIRA British Food Manufacturing Industries Research Association
BFPO British Forces Post Office
BFSS British Field Sports Society
BFUW British Federation of University Women (*now see* BFWG)
BFWG British Federation of Women Graduates
BGCStJ Bailiff Grand Cross, Most Venerable Order of the Hospital of St John of Jerusalem
BGS Brigadier General Staff
BHA British Hospitality Association
BHB Bachelor of Human Biology
Bhd Berhad
BHF British Heart Foundation
BHL Bachelor of Hebrew Letters
BHRA British Hydromechanics Research Association
BHRCA British Hotels, Restaurants and Caterers' Association (*now see* BHA)
BHS British Horse Society
BHSc Bachelor of Home Science
BI British Invisibles
BIBA British Insurance Brokers' Association
BIBRA British Industrial Biological Research Association
BICC British Insulated Callender's Cables
BICERA British Internal Combustion Engine Research Association (*now see* BICERI)
BICERI British Internal Combustion Engine Research Institute
BICSc British Institute of Cleaning Science
BIDA British Interior Design Association
BIEC British Invisible Exports Council (*now see* BI)
BIEE British Institute of Energy Economics
BIFA British Independent Film Awards
BIFU Banking Insurance and Finance Union
BII British Institute of Innkeeping
BIIBA British Insurance & Investment Brokers' Association (*now see* BIBA)
BIM British Institute of Management
BIR British Institute of Radiology
BIS Bank for International Settlements; British Interplanetary Society; Department for Business, Innovation and Skills
BISPA British Independent Steel Producers Association
BISRA British Iron and Steel Research Association
BITC Business in the Community
BJ Bachelor of Journalism
BJOG British Journal of Obstetrics and Gynaecology
BJP Bharatiya Janata Party
BJSM British Joint Services Mission
BJur Bachelor of Law
BKSTS British Kinematograph, Sound and Television Society
BL Bachelor of Law; British Library
BLA British Liberation Army
BLDSA British Long Distance Swimming Association

BLE Bachelor of Land Economy
BLegS Bachelor of Legal Studies
BLESMA British Limbless Ex-Servicemen's Association
BLitt Bachelor of Letters
BM British Museum; Bachelor of Medicine; Brigade Major; British Monomark
BMA British Medical Association
BMedSci Bachelor of Medical Science
BMEO British Middle East Office
BMet Bachelor of Metallurgy
BMEWS Ballistic Missile Early Warning System
BMG British Military Government
BMH British Military Hospital
BMilSc Bachelor of Military Science
BMJ British Medical Journal
BMM British Military Mission
BMR Bureau of Mineral Resources
BMRA Brigade Major Royal Artillery
BMS Bachelor of Management Studies
Bn Battalion
BNA British Nursing Association
BNAF British North Africa Force
BNC Brasenose College
BNEC British National Export Council
BNF British National Formulary
BNFL British Nuclear Fuels Ltd
BNOC British National Oil Corporation; British National Opera Company
BNP Banque Nationale de Paris; British National Party
BNSC British National Space Centre
BNSc Bachelor of Nursing Science
BOAC British Overseas Airways Corporation
BoT Board of Trade
Bot. Botany; Botanical
BOTB British Overseas Trade Board
BOU British Ornithologists' Union
Bp Bishop
BPA British Paediatric Association (later CPCH; *now see* RCPCH); Bachelor of Performing Arts
BPG Broadcasting Press Guild
BPharm Bachelor of Pharmacy
BPIF British Printing Industries Federation
BPMF British Postgraduate Medical Federation
BProc Bachelor of Procurations
BPsS British Psychological Society
BR British Rail
Br. Branch
BRA Brigadier Royal Artillery; British Rheumatism & Arthritis Association
BRB British Railways Board
BRCS British Red Cross Society
BRE Building Research Establishment
Brig. Brigadier
BRIT British Recording Industry Trust
BritIRE British Institution of Radio Engineers (*now see* IERE)
BRNC Britannia Royal Naval College
BRS British Road Services
BRTP Bachelor of Regional and Town Planning
BRurSc Bachelor of Rural Science
BS Bachelor of Surgery; Bachelor of Science; British Standard
BSA Bachelor of Scientific Agriculture; Birmingham Small Arms; Building Societies' Association
BSAP British South Africa Police
BSAS British Society of Animal Science
BSBI Botanical Society of the British Isles
BSC British Steel Corporation; Bengal Staff Corps
BSc Bachelor of Science
BScA or **BScAgr** Bachelor of Science in Agriculture
BSc(Dent) Bachelor of Science in Dentistry
BScEcon Bachelor of Science in Economics
BScEng Bachelor of Science in Engineering
BSc (Est. Man.) Bachelor of Science in Estate Management
BScN Bachelor of Science in Nursing
BScSoc Bachelor of Social Sciences
BSE Bachelor of Science in Engineering (US); Bovine Spongiform Encephalopathy
BSEE Bachelor of Science in Electrical Engineering
BSES British Schools Exploring Society
BSF British Salonica Force
BSFA British Science Fiction Association
BSFS Bachelor of Science in Foreign Service
BSI British Standards Institution
BSIA British Security Industry Association
BSJA British Show Jumping Association
BSME Bachelor of Science in Mechanical Engineering; British Society of Magazine Editors
BSN Bachelor of Science in Nursing
BSNS Bachelor of Naval Science
BSocSc Bachelor of Social Science
BSocStud Bachelor of Social Studies
BSRA British Ship Research Association
BSRIA Building Services Research and Information Association
BSS Bachelor of Science (Social Science)
BSSc Bachelor of Social Science
BST Bachelor of Sacred Theology
BSurv Bachelor of Surveying
BSW Bachelor of Social Work
BT Bachelor of Teaching; British Telecommunications
Bt Baronet; Brevet
BTA British Tourist Authority (*formerly* British Travel Association)
BTC British Transport Commission
BTCV British Trust for Conservation Volunteers
BTDB British Transport Docks Board (*now see* ABP)
BTEC Business and Technology (*formerly* Technician) Education Council
BTech Bachelor of Technology
BTh Bachelor of Theology
BTP Bachelor of Town Planning
BTS Bachelor of Theological Studies
Btss Baronetess
BUAS British Universities Association of Slavists
Bucks Buckinghamshire
BUGB Baptist Union of Great Britain
BUNAC British Universities North America Club
BUniv Bachelor of the University
BUPA British United Provident Association
BURA British Urban Regeneration Association
BV Besloten Vennootschap
BVA British Veterinary Association; British Video Association
BVC Bar Vocational Course
BVCA British Private Equity and Venture Capital Association
BVetMed Bachelor of Veterinary Medicine
BVI British Virgin Islands
BVM Blessed Virgin Mary
BVMS Bachelor of Veterinary Medicine and Surgery
BVPA British Veterinary Poultry Association
BVSc Bachelor of Veterinary Science
BWI British West Indies
BWM British War Medal

C

C Conservative; 100
c child; cousin; *circa* (about)
CA Central America; County Alderman; Chartered Accountant (Scotland and Canada); California (postal)
CAA Civil Aviation Authority
CAABU Council for the Advancement of Arab and British Understanding
CAAV (Member of) Central Association of Agricultural Valuers
CAB Citizens' Advice Bureau; Centre for Agricultural and Biosciences (*formerly* Commonwealth Agricultural Bureau)
CABE Commission for Architecture and the Built Environment
CACTM Central Advisory Council of Training for the Ministry (later ACCM; *now see* ABM)
CAER Conservative Action for Electoral Reform
CAF Charities Aid Foundation
CAFCASS Child and Family Court Advisory and Support Service
CAFOD Catholic Agency for Overseas Development
CAJ Committee on the Administration of Justice
Calif California
CAM Communications, Advertising and Marketing
Cambs Cambridgeshire
CAMC Canadian Army Medical Corps
CAMRA Campaign for Real Ale
CAMS Certificate of Advanced Musical Study
C&G City and Guilds of London Institute
Cantab *Cantabrigiensis* (of Cambridge)
Cantuar *Cantuariensis* (of Canterbury)
CAP Common Agricultural Policy
Capt. Captain
CARD Campaign against Racial Discrimination
CARDS Community Assistance for Reconstruction, Development and Stabilisation
CARE Cottage and Rural Enterprises
CARICOM Caribbean Community
CARIFTA Caribbean Free Trade Area (*now see* CARICOM)
Carms Carmarthenshire
CAS Chief of the Air Staff
CASE Council for the Advancement and Suppport of Education
CAT College of Advanced Technology; Countryside Around Towns
CATE Council for the Accreditation of Teacher Education
Cav. Cavalry
CAWU Clerical and Administrative Workers' Union (later APEX)
CB Companion, Order of the Bath; County Borough
CBC County Borough Council
CBE Commander, Order of the British Empire

CBI	Confederation of British Industry
CBII	Companion, British Institute of Innkeeping
CBIM	Companion, British Institute of Management (later CIMgt)
CBiol	Chartered Biologist
CBNS	Commander British Navy Staff
CBS	Columbia Broadcasting System
CBSI	Chartered Building Societies Institute (*now see* CIB)
CBSO	City of Birmingham Symphony Orchestra
CC	Companion, Order of Canada; City Council; County Council; Cricket Club; Cycling Club; County Court
CCAB	Consultative Committee of Accountancy Bodies
CCAHC	Central Council for Agricultural and Horticultural Co-operation
CCBE	Commission Consultative des Barreaux de la Communauté Européenne
CCBI	Council of Churches for Britain and Ireland (*now see* CTBI)
CCC	Corpus Christi College; Central Criminal Court; County Cricket Club
CCE	Chartered Civil Engineer
CCETSW	Central Council for Education and Training in Social Work
CCF	Combined Cadet Force
CCFM	Combined Cadet Forces Medal
CCG	Control Commission Germany; Clinical Commissioning Group
CCH	Cacique's Crown of Honour, Order of Service of Guyana
CChem	Chartered Chemist
CCHMS	Central Committee for Hospital Medical Services
CCIA	Commission of Churches on International Affairs
CCIPD	Companion, Chartered Institute of Personnel and Development
CCIS	Command Control Information System
CCJ	Council of Christians and Jews
CCLRC	Council for the Central Laboratory of the Research Councils
CCMI	Companion, Chartered Management Institute
CCMS	Committee on the Challenges of Modern Society
CCPR	Central Council of Physical Recreation
CCQI	Companion, Chartered Quality Institute
CCRA	Commander Corps of Royal Artillery
CCRE	Commander Corps of Royal Engineers
CCREME	Commander Corps of Royal Electrical and Mechanical Engineers
CCRSigs	Commander Corps of Royal Signals
CCS	Casualty Clearing Station; Ceylon Civil Service; Countryside Commission for Scotland
CCSU	Council of Civil Service Unions
CCTA	Commission de Coöpération Technique pour l'Afrique; Central Computer and Telecommunications Authority
CCTS	Combat Crew Training Squadron
CD	Canadian Forces Decoration; Commander, Order of Distinction (Jamaica); Civil Defence; Compact Disc
CDA	Co-operative Development Agency; Christian Democratic Alliance
CDC	Centers for Disease Control and Prevention
CDEE	Chemical Defence Experimental Establishment
CDipAF	Certified Diploma in Accounting and Finance
CDir	Chartered Director
CDISS	Centre for Defence and International Security Studies
Cdo	Commando
Cdre	Commodore
CDS	Chief of the Defence Staff
CDU	Christlich-Demokratische Union
CE	Civil Engineer
CEA	Central Electricity Authority
CEC	Commission of the European Communities
CECAM	Centre Européen de Calcul Atomique et Moléculaire
CECD	Confédération Européenne du Commerce de Détail
CECG	Consumers in European Community Group
CEDA	Committee for Economic Development of Australia
CEDEP	Centre Européen d'Education Permanente
CEDR	Centre for Effective Dispute Resolution
CEE	Communauté Economique Européenne
CEED	Centre for Economic and Environmental Development
CEF	Canadian Expeditionary Force
CeFA	Certificate for Financial Advisers
CEFAS	Centre for Environment, Fisheries and Aquaculture Science
CEFIC	Conseil Européen des Fédérations de l'Industrie Chimique
CEGB	Central Electricity Generating Board
CEH	Centre for Ecology & Hydrology
CEI	Council of Engineering Institutions
CEIR	Corporation for Economic and Industrial Research
CEM	Council of European Municipalities (*now see* CEMR); College of Emergency Medicine
CEMA	Council for the Encouragement of Music and Arts
CeMAP	Certificate in Mortgage Advice and Practice
CeMGA	Centre for the Measurement of Government Activity
CEMR	Council of European Municipalities and Regions
CEMS	Church of England Men's Society
CEN	Comité Européen de Normalisation
CENELEC	European Committee for Electrotechnical Standardization
CEng	Chartered Engineer
Cento	Central Treaty Organisation
CEnv	Chartered Environmentalist
CEO	Chief Executive Officer
CEPES	Comité européen pour le progrès économique et social
CEPS	Center for Economic Policy Studies
CEPT	Conférence Européenne des Postes et des Télécommunications
CERA	Chartered Enterprise Risk Analyst
CeRGI	Certificate of Regulated General Insurance
CERL	Central Electricity Research Laboratories
CERN	Organisation (*formerly* Centre) Européenne pour la Recherche Nucléaire
CERT	Charities Effectiveness Review Trust
CertCPE	Certificate in Clinical Pastoral Education
CertDS	Certificate in Dramatic Studies
Cert Ed	Certificate of Education
CertHE	Certificate in Higher Education
CertITP	Certificate of International Teachers' Program (Harvard)
CertTP	Certificate in Town Planning
CEST	Centre for Exploitation of Science and Technology
CET	Council for Educational Technology
CETSW	Council for Education and Training in Social Work
CF	Chaplain to the Forces; Companion, Order of Fiji; Corporate Finance; Corporate Financier
CFA	Canadian Field Artillery; Chartered Financial Analyst
CFE	Central Fighter Establishment
CFM	Cadet Forces Medal
CFPS	Certificate of Further Professional Studies
CFR	Commander, Order of the Federal Republic of Nigeria
CFS	Central Flying School; Chronic Fatigue Syndrome
CGA	Community of the Glorious Ascension; Country Gentlemen's Association
CGeog	Chartered Geographer
CGeol	Chartered Geologist
CGIA	Insignia Award of City and Guilds of London Institute (*now see* FCGI)
CGLI	City and Guilds of London Institute (*now see* C&G)
CGM	Conspicuous Gallantry Medal
CGMA	Chartered Global Management Accountant
CGRM	Commandant-General Royal Marines
CGS	Chief of the General Staff
CH	Companion of Honour
Chap.	Chaplain
ChapStJ	Chaplain, Order of St John of Jerusalem (*now see* ChStJ)
CHAR	Campaign for the Homeless and Rootless
CHB	Companion of Honour of Barbados
ChB	Bachelor of Surgery
CHC	Community Health Council
Ch.Ch.	Christ Church
CHIU	Committee for Heads of Irish Universities
ChLJ	Chaplain, Order of St Lazarus of Jerusalem
(CHM)	*see under* ARCO(CHM), FRCO(CHM)
ChM	Master of Surgery
Chm.	Chairman or Chairwoman
CHN	Community of the Holy Name
CHSC	Central Health Services Council
ChStJ	Chaplain, Most Venerable Order of the Hospital of St John of Jerusalem
CI	Imperial Order of the Crown of India; Channel Islands
CIA	Chemical Industries Association; Central Intelligence Agency
CIAD	Central Institute of Art and Design
CIAgrE	Companion, Institution of Agricultural Engineers
CIAL	Corresponding Member of the International Institute of Arts and Letters
CIArb	Chartered Institute of Arbitrators
CIB	Chartered Institute of Bankers
CIBS	Chartered Institution of Building Services (*now see* CIBSE)
CIBSE	Chartered Institution of Building Services Engineers
CIC	Chemical Institute of Canada; Community Interest Company
CICAP	Criminal Injuries Compensation Appeal Panel
CICB	Criminal Injuries Compensation Board
CICHE	Committee for International Co-operation in Higher Education
CICI	Confederation of Information Communication Industries
CID	Criminal Investigation Department
CIE	Companion, Order of the Indian Empire; Confédération Internationale des Etudiants
CIES	Companion, Institution of Engineers and Shipbuilders in Scotland
CIEx	Companion, Institute of Export
CIFE	Council (*formerly* Conference) for Independent Further Education
CIGasE	Companion, Institution of Gas Engineers (*now see* CIGEM)
CIGEM	Companion, Institution of Gas Engineers and Managers
CIGRE	Conférence Internationale des Grands Réseaux Electriques
CIGS	Chief of the Imperial General Staff (*now see* CGS)
CIHM	Companion, Institute of Healthcare Management
CIHR	Canadian Institutes of Health Research
CIIA	Canadian Institute of International Affairs
CIL	*Corpus inscriptionum latinarum*
CILT	Chartered Institute of Logistics and Transport
CIM	China Inland Mission; Chartered Institute of Marketing
CIMA	Chartered Institute of Management Accountants

CIMarE Companion, Institute of Marine Engineers
CIMEMME Companion, Institution of Mining Electrical and Mining Mechanical Engineers
CIMgt Companion, Institute of Management (*now see* CCMI)
CIMGTechE Companion, Institution of Mechanical and General Technician Engineers
CIMO Commission for Instruments and Methods of Observation
CIMR Cambridge Institute for Medical Research
C-in-C Commander-in-Chief
CINCHAN Allied Commander-in-Chief Channel
CInstLM Companion, Institute of Leadership and Management
CINOA Confédération Internationale des Négotiants en Œuvres d'Art
CIOB Chartered Institute of Building
CIPA Chartered Institute of Patent Agents
CIPD Companion, Institute of Personnel and Development (*now see* CCIPD); Chartered Institute of Personnel and Development
CIPFA Chartered Institute of Public Finance and Accountancy
CIPL Comité International Permanent des Linguistes
CIPM Companion, Institute of Personnel Management (later CIPD)
CIPR Chartered Institute of Public Relations
CIQA Companion, Institute of Quality Assurance (*now see* CCQI)
CIR Commission on Industrial Relations
CIRES Co-operative Institute for Research in Environmental Sciences
CIRIA Construction Industry Research and Information Association
CIRP Collège Internationale pour Recherche et Production
CIS Institute of Chartered Secretaries and Administrators (*formerly* Chartered Institute of Secretaries); Command Control Communications and Information Systems; Commonwealth of Independent States
CISAC Confédération Internationale des Sociétés d'Auteurs et Compositeurs; Centre for International Security and Arms Control
CISI Chartered Institute for Securities & Investment
CIT Chartered Institute of Transport; California Institute of Technology
CITB Construction Industry Training Board
CITD Certificate of Institute of Training and Development
CITP Chartered Information Technology Professional
CIV City Imperial Volunteers
CIWEM Chartered Institution of Water and Environmental Management
CJM Congregation of Jesus and Mary (Eudist Fathers)
CL Commander, Order of Leopold
cl *cum laude*
Cl. Class
CLA Country Land & Business Association (*formerly* Country Landowners' Association)
CLIC Cancer and Leukemia in Childhood
CLIP Chartered Institute of Library and Information Professionals
CLit Companion of Literature (Royal Society of Literature Award)
CLJ Commander, Order of St Lazarus of Jerusalem
CLP Constituency Labour Party
CLRAE Congress (*formerly* Conference) of Local and Regional Authorities of Europe
CLY City of London Yeomanry
CM Member, Order of Canada; Congregation of the Mission (Vincentians); Master in Surgery; Certificated Master; Canadian Militia
CMA Canadian Medical Association; Cost and Management Accountant (NZ); Competition and Markets Authority
CMarSci Chartered Marine Scientist
CMath Chartered Mathematician
CMB Central Midwives' Board
CMC Certified Management Consultant; Civil Mediation Council
CME Continuing Ministerial Education
CMet Chartered Meteorologist
CMF Commonwealth Military Forces; Central Mediterranean Force
CMG Companion, Order of St Michael and St George
CMgr Chartered Manager
CMILT Chartered Member, Chartered Institute of Logistics and Transport
CMIWSc Certified Member, Institute of Wood Science
CMJ Commander, Supreme Military Order of the Temple of Jerusalem
CMLI Chartered Member, Landscape Institute
CMLJ Commander of Merit, Order of St Lazarus of Jerusalem
CMM Commander, Order of Military Merit (Canada)
CMO Chief Medical Officer
CMP Corps of Military Police (*now see* CRMP)
CMS Church Mission (*formerly* Church Missionary) Society; Certificate in Management Studies
CMT Chaconia Medal of Trinidad
CNAA Council for National Academic Awards
CND Campaign for Nuclear Disarmament
CNI Companion, Nautical Institute
CNO Chief of Naval Operations
CNOCS Captain Naval Operational Command Systems
CNR Canadian National Railways
CNRS Centre National de la Recherche Scientifique
CNZM Companion, New Zealand Order of Merit
CO Commanding Officer; Commonwealth Office (after Aug. 1966) (*now see* FCO); Colonial Office (before Aug. 1966); Conscientious Objector; Colorado (postal); Congregation of the Oratory
Co. County; Company
Coal.L or Co.L Coalition Liberal
Coal.U or Co.U Coalition Unionist
COBSEO Confederation of British Service and Ex-Service Organisations
CODEST Committee for the Development of European Science and Technology
C of E Church of England
C of I Church of Ireland
C of S Chief of Staff; Church of Scotland
COHSE Confederation of Health Service Employees
COI Central Office of Information
CoID Council of Industrial Design (*now* Design Council)
Col Colonel
Coll. College; Collegiate
Colo Colorado
Col.-Sergt Colour-Sergeant
Com Communist
Comd Command
Comdg Commanding
Comdr Commander
Comdt Commandant
COMEC Council of the Military Education Committees of the Universities of the UK
COMET Committee for Middle East Trade
Commn Commission
Commnd Commissioned
CompICE Companion, Institution of Civil Engineers
CompIEE Companion, Institution of Electrical Engineers (later FIEE)
CompIERE Companion, Institution of Electronic and Radio Engineers
CompIGasE Companion, Institution of Gas Engineers
CompILE Companion, Institution of Lighting Engineers
CompIMechE Companion, Institution of Mechanical Engineers
CompInstE Companion, Institute of Energy
CompInstMC Companion, Institute of Measurement and Control
CompOR Companion, Operational Research Society
CompTI Companion of the Textile Institute
Comr Commissioner
Comy-Gen. Commissary-General
CON Commander, Order of the Niger
ConfEd Confederation of Education Service Managers
Conn Connecticut
Const. Constitutional
CONUL Council of National and University Librarians
Co-op. Co-operative
COPA Comité des Organisations Professionels Agricoles de la CEE
COPEC Conference of Politics, Economics and Christianity
COPUS Committee on the Public Understanding of Science
Corp. Corporation; Corporal
Corresp. Mem. Corresponding Member
COS Chief of Staff; Charity Organization Society
CoSIRA Council for Small Industries in Rural Areas
COSLA Convention of Scottish Local Authorities
COSPAR Committee on Space Research
COSSAC Chief of Staff to Supreme Allied Commander
COTC Canadian Officers' Training Corps
CP Central Provinces; Cape Province; Congregation of the Passion
CPA Commonwealth Parliamentary Association; Chartered Patent Agent; Certified Public Accountant (USA)
CPAG Child Poverty Action Group
CPAGB Credit, Photographic Alliance of Great Britain
CPAS Church Pastoral Aid Society
CPC Conservative Political Centre
CPCH College of Paediatrics and Child Health (*now see* RCPCH)
CPD Continuing Professional Development
CPE Common Professional Examination; Clinical Pastoral Education
CPEng Chartered Professional Engineer (of Institution of Engineers of Australia)
CPFA Member or Associate, Chartered Institute of Public Finance and Accountancy
CPHVA Community Practitioners & Health Visitors' Association
CPhys Chartered Physicist
CPL Chief Personnel and Logistics
CPLS Certificate of Professional Legal Studies
CPM Colonial Police Medal
CPR Canadian Pacific Railway
CPRE Campaign to Protect Rural England (*formerly* Council for the Protection of Rural England)
CPRW Campaign for the Protection of Rural Wales
CPS Crown Prosecution Service; Certificate in Pastoral Studies
CPSA Civil and Public Services Association (*now see* PCS); Church of the Province of South Africa
CPSU Communist Party of the Soviet Union
CPsychol Chartered Psychologist
CPU Commonwealth Press Union
CQ Chevalier, National Order of Quebec

CQI Chartered Quality Institute
CQP Chartered Quality Professional
CQSW Certificate of Qualification in Social Work
CR Community of the Resurrection
cr created or creation
CRA Commander, Royal Artillery
CRAC Careers Research and Advisory Centre
CRadP Chartered Radiation Protection Professional
CRAeS Companion, Royal Aeronautical Society
CRAG Clinical Resources and Audit Group
CRASC Commander, Royal Army Service Corps
CRC Cancer Research Campaign (*now see* CRUK); Community Relations Council
CRE Commander, Royal Engineers; Commission for Racial Equality; Commercial Relations and Exports; Conference of Rectors of European Universities (*formerly* Association of European Universities)
Cres. Crescent
CRMP Corps of Royal Military Police
CRNCM Companion, Royal Northern College of Music
CRO Commonwealth Relations Office (*now see* FCO)
CRSNZ Companion, Royal Society of New Zealand
CRUK Cancer Research United Kingdom
CS Civil Service; Clerk to the Signet; Companion, Order of Samoa
CSA Confederate States of America; Child Support Agency
CSAB Civil Service Appeal Board
CSB Bachelor of Christian Science
CSC Conspicuous Service Cross; Congregation of the Holy Cross
CSCA Civil Service Clerical Association (later CPSA)
CSCE Conference on Security and Co-operation in Europe
CSci Chartered Scientist
CSD Civil Service Department; Co-operative Secretaries Diploma; Chartered Society of Designers
CSDE Central Servicing Development Establishment
CSEU Confederation of Shipbuilding and Engineering Unions
CSG Companion, Order of the Star of Ghana; Company of the Servants of God
CSI Companion, Order of the Star of India; Cross, Order of Solomon Islands
CSIR Commonwealth Council for Scientific and Industrial Research (*now see* CSIRO); Council of Scientific and Industrial Research, India
CSIRO Commonwealth Scientific and Industrial Research Organization (Australia)
CSM Civil Service Medal (Fiji); Companion, Star of Merit (Federation of Saint Kitts and Nevis); Companion, Star of Melanesia (Papua New Guinea)
CSO Chief Scientific Officer; Chief Signal Officer; Chief Staff Officer; Central Statistical Office (*now see* ONS)
CSP Chartered Society of Physiotherapists; Civil Service of Pakistan
CSPQ Certificat de Spécialiste de la Province de Québec
CSS Companion, Star of Sarawak; Council for Science and Society; Certificate in Social Studies
CSSB Civil Service Selection Board
CSSD Czech Social Democratic Party
CSSp Holy Ghost Father
CSSR Congregation of the Most Holy Redeemer (Redemptorist Order)
CStat Chartered Statistician
CSTI Council of Science and Technology Institutes
CStJ Commander, Most Venerable Order of the Hospital of St John of Jerusalem
CSU Christlich-Soziale Union in Bayern
CSV Community Service Volunteers
CSW Certificate in Social Work
CT Connecticut (postal)
CTA Chaplain Territorial Army; Chartered Tax Adviser
CTBI Churches Together in Britain and Ireland
CTC Cyclists' Touring Club; Commando Training Centre; City Technology College
CText Chartered Textile Technologist
CTh Certificate in Theology
CTL Companion, Trinity Laban
CTM Certificate of Theology for Ministry
CTS Certificate in Terrorism Studies
CU Cambridge University
CUAC Cambridge University Athletic Club; Colleges and Universities of the Anglican Communion
CUAFC Cambridge University Association Football Club
CUCC Cambridge University Cricket Club
CUF Common University Fund
CUNY City University of New York
CUP Cambridge University Press
CUPGRA Cambridge University Postgraduate Research Association
CURUFC Cambridge University Rugby Union Football Club
CV Cross of Valour (Canada)
CVCP Committee of Vice-Chancellors and Principals of the Universities of the United Kingdom (*now see* UUK)
CVO Commander, Royal Victorian Order
CVS Council for Voluntary Service
CVSNA Council of Voluntary Service National Association
CWA Crime Writers Association
CWEM Chartered Water and Environmental Manager
CWGC Commonwealth War Graves Commission
CWS Co-operative Wholesale Society
CWU Communication Workers Union

D

D Duke
d died; daughter
DA Dame of St Andrew, Order of Barbados; Diploma in Anaesthesia; Diploma in Art; Doctor of Arts
DAA Diploma in Archive Administration
DAA&QMG Deputy Assistant Adjutant and Quartermaster-General
DAAD Designers and Art Directors Association
DAAG Deputy Assistant Adjutant-General
DA&QMG Deputy Adjutant and Quartermaster-General
DAC Development Assistance Committee; Diocesan Advisory Committee
DAcad Doctor of the Academy
DACG Deputy Assistant Chaplain-General
DACLAM Diplomate, American College of Laboratory Animal Medicine
DACOS Deputy Assistant Chief of Staff
DAD Deputy Assistant Director
DAdmin Doctor of Administration
DADMS Deputy Assistant Director of Medical Services
DADOS Deputy Assistant Director of Ordnance Services
DADQ Deputy Assistant Director of Quartering
DADST Deputy Assistant Director of Supplies and Transport
DAEd Diploma in Art Education
DAG Deputy Adjutant-General
DAgr Doctor of Agriculture
DAgrFor Doctor of Agriculture and Forestry
DAgrSc Doctor of Agricultural Science
DAMS Deputy Assistant Military Secretary
D&AD Design and Art Direction (*formerly* Designers and Art Directors Association)
DAppSc Doctor of Applied Science
DAQMG Deputy Assistant Quartermaster-General
DArch Doctor of Architecture
DArt Doctor of Art
DArts Doctor of Arts
DASc Doctor in Agricultural Sciences
DASS Diploma in Applied Social Studies
DATA Draughtsmen's and Allied Technicians' Association (later AUEW(TASS))
DATEC Art and Design Committee, Technician Education Council
DAvMed Diploma in Aviation Medicine, Royal College of Physicians
DBA Doctor of Business Administration
DBE Dame Commander, Order of the British Empire
DBTS Diploma in Biblical and Theological Studies
DBus Doctor of Business
DC District Council; District of Columbia
DCA Doctor of Creative Arts; Department for Constitutional Affairs
DCAe Diploma of College of Aeronautics
DCAS Deputy Chief of the Air Staff
DCB Dame Commander, Order of the Bath
DCC Diploma of Chelsea College
DCCH Diploma in Community Child Health
DCDS Deputy Chief of Defence Staff
DCE Diploma of a College of Education
DCG Deputy Chaplain-General
DCGS Deputy Chief of the General Staff
DCh Doctor of Surgery
DCH Diploma in Child Health
DChA Diploma in Charity Accounting
DCHS Dame Commander, Order of the Holy Sepulchre
DCL Doctor of Civil Law; Dr of Canon Law
DCLG Department for Communities and Local Government
DCLI Duke of Cornwall's Light Infantry
DCLJ Dame Commander, Order of St Lazarus of Jerusalem
DCM Distinguished Conduct Medal
DCMG Dame Commander, Order of St Michael and St George
DCMS Department for Culture, Media and Sport
DCnL Doctor of Canon Law
DCNZM Distinguished Companion, New Zealand Order of Merit
DCO Duke of Cambridge's Own
DCom or **DComm** Doctor of Commerce
DCP Diploma in Clinical Pathology; Diploma in Conservation of Paintings
DCS Deputy Chief of Staff; Doctor of Commercial Sciences
DCSF Department for Children, Schools and Families
DCSG Dame Commander, Order of St Gregory the Great
DCSO Deputy Chief Scientific Officer
DCT Doctor of Christian Theology
DCVO Dame Commander, Royal Victorian Order
DD Doctor of Divinity

DDAM Diploma in Disability Assessment Medicine
DDes Doctor of Design
DDGAMS Deputy Director General, Army Medical Services
DDH Diploma in Dental Health
DDL Deputy Director of Labour
DDME Deputy Director of Mechanical Engineering
DDMI Deputy Director of Military Intelligence
DDMO Deputy Director of Military Operations
DDMS Deputy Director of Medical Services
DDMT Deputy Director of Military Training
DDNI Deputy Director of Naval Intelligence
DDO Diploma in Dental Orthopaedics
DDPH Diploma in Dental Public Health
DDPR Deputy Director of Public Relations
DDPS Deputy Director of Personal Services
DDR Deutsche Demokratische Republik
DDRA Deputy Director Royal Artillery
DDra Doctor of Drama
DDS Doctor of Dental Surgery; Director of Dental Services
DDSc Doctor of Dental Science
DDSD Deputy Director Staff Duties
DDSM Defense Distinguished Service Medal
DDST Deputy Director of Supplies and Transport
DDWE&M Deputy Director of Works, Electrical and Mechanical
DE Doctor of Engineering; Delaware (postal)
DEA Department of Economic Affairs; Diplôme d'Etudes Approfondies
DEc Doctor of Economics
DECC Department of Energy and Climate Change
decd deceased
DEcon Doctor of Economics
DEconSc Doctor of Economic Science
DEd Doctor of Education
DEFRA Department for Environment, Food and Rural Affairs
Deleg. Delegate
DEME Directorate of Electrical and Mechanical Engineering
DEMS Defensively Equipped Merchant Ships
(DemU) Democratic Unionist
DenD Docteur en Droit
DEng Doctor of Engineering
DenM Docteur en Médicine
DEOVR Duke of Edinburgh's Own Volunteer Rifles
DEP Department of Employment and Productivity; European Progressive Democrats
Dep. Deputy
DERA Defence Evaluation and Research Agency
DES Department of Education and Science (later DFE); Dr in Environmental Studies
DèsL Docteur ès lettres
DèS or **DèsSc** Docteur ès sciences
DesRCA Designer of the Royal College of Art
DESS Diplôme d'Etudes Supérieures Specialisées
DESU Diplôme d'Etudes Supérieures d'Université
DETR Department of the Environment, Transport and the Regions
DFA Doctor of Fine Arts
DFAS Decorative and Fine Art Society
DFC Distinguished Flying Cross
DFE Department for Education
DFEE or **DfEE** Department for Education and Employment (later DFES)
DFES or **DfES** Department for Education and Skills
DFFP Diploma in Fertility and Family Planning
DFH Diploma of Faraday House
DFID Department for International Development
DFil Doctor en Filosofía
DFLS Day Fighter Leaders' School
DFM Distinguished Flying Medal
DFPHM Diplomate Member, Faculty of Public Health Medicine
DfT Department for Transport
DG Director General; Directorate General; Dragoon Guards
DGAA Distressed Gentlefolks Aid Association
DGAMS Director-General Army Medical Services
DGCHS Dame Grand Cross, Order of the Holy Sepulchre
DGDP Diploma in General Dental Practice, Royal College of Physicians
DGEME Director General Electrical and Mechanical Engineering
DGLP(A) Director General Logistic Policy (Army)
DGMS Director-General of Medical Services
DGMT Director-General of Military Training
DGMW Director-General of Military Works
DGNPS Director-General of Naval Personal Services
DGP Director-General of Personnel
DGPS Director-General of Personal Services
DGS Diploma in Graduate Studies
DGStJ Dame of Grace, Order of St John of Jerusalem (*now see* DStJ)
DGU Doctor of Griffith University
DH Doctor of Humanities; Doctor of Health
DHA District Health Authority
Dhc or **DHC** Doctor *honoris causa*
DHE Defence Housing Executive
DHEW Department of Health Education and Welfare (US)
DHL Doctor of Humane Letters; Doctor of Hebrew Literature
DHLitt Doctor of Humane Letters
DHM Dean Hole Medal
DHMSA Diploma in the History of Medicine (Society of Apothecaries)
DHQ District Headquarters
DHS Dame, Order of the Holy Sepulchre
DHSS Department of Health and Social Security
DHum Doctor of Humanities
DHumLit Doctor of Humane Letters
DIA Diploma in Industrial Administration
DIAS Dublin Institute of Advanced Sciences
DIB Doctor of International Business
DIC Diploma of the Imperial College
DICTA Diploma of Imperial College of Tropical Agriculture
DIFC Dubai International Financial Centre
DIG Deputy Inspector-General
DIH Diploma in Industrial Health
DIMP Darjah Indera Mahkota Pahang (Malaysia)
DIntLaw Diploma in International Law
Dio. Diocese
DipA Diploma of Arts in Theology
DipAA Diploma in Applied Art
DipABRSM Diploma, Associated Board of Royal Schools of Music
DipAD Diploma in Art and Design
DipAE Diploma in Adult Education
DipAe Diploma in Aeronautics
DipAgr Diploma in Agriculture
DipArch Diploma in Architecture
DipASE Diploma in Advanced Study of Education, College of Preceptors
DipASS Diploma in Applied Social Studies
DipBA Diploma in Business Administration
DipBS Diploma in Fine Art, Byam Shaw School
DipCAM Diploma in Communications, Advertising and Marketing of CAM Foundation
DipCAT Diploma in Cognitive Analytic Therapy
DipCC Diploma of the Central College
DipCD Diploma in Civic Design
DipCE Diploma in Civil Engineering; Diploma of a College of Education (Scotland)
DipChA Diploma in Chartered Accounting
DipCons Diploma in Conservation
DipCS Diploma in Classical Studies
DipECLAM Diplomate, European College of Laboratory Animal Medicine
DipEcon Diploma in Economics
DipECVO Diploma in Veterinary Ophthalmology, European College of Veterinary Ophthalmologists
DipEd Diploma in Education
DipEE Diploma in Electrical Engineering
DipEl Diploma in Electronics
DipESL Diploma in English as a Second Language
DipEth Diploma in Ethnology
DipEurHum Diploma in European Humanities
DipEVPC Diplomate, European Veterinary Parasitology College
DipFBOM Diploma in Farm Business Organisation and Management
DipFD Diploma in Funeral Directing
DipFE Diploma in Further Education
DipFM Diploma in Forensic Medicine; Diploma in Financial Management
DipFMS Diploma in Forensic Medicine and Science
DipFS Diploma in Financial Services
DipGSM Diploma in Music, Guildhall School of Music and Drama
DipHA Diploma in Hospital Administration
DipHE Diploma in Higher Education
DipHSM Diploma in Health Services Management
DipHIC Diploma in Hospital Infection Control
DipHum Diploma in Humanities
DipHV Diploma in Health Visiting
DipICArb Diploma in International Commercial Arbitration
DipIT Diploma in Information Technology
DipLA Diploma in Landscape Architecture
DipLaw Diploma in Law
DipLib Diploma of Librarianship
DipLLP Diploma in Law and Legal Practice
DipLP Diploma in Legal Practice
DipLS Diploma of Legal Studies
DipM Diploma in Marketing
DipMed Diploma in Medicine
DipMin Diploma in Ministry
DipN Diploma in Nursing
DipNEC Diploma of Northampton Engineering College (*now* City University)
DIPP Diploma of Interventional Pain Practice
DipPA Diploma of Practitioners in Advertising (*now see* DipCAM)
DipPE Diploma in Physical Education
DipPSA Diploma in Public Service Administration
DipPSW Diploma in Psychiatric Social Work
DipPsych Diploma in Psychology
DipRE Diploma in Religious Education

DipREM Diploma in Rural Estate Management
DipRS Diploma in Religious Studies
DipSMS Diploma in School Management Studies
DipSoc Diploma in Sociology
DipSocSc Diploma in Social Science
DipSRAA Diploma in the Study of Records and Administration of Archives
DipStat Diploma in Statistics
DipSW Diploma in Social Work
DipTA Diploma in Tropical Agriculture
DipT&CP Diploma in Town and Country Planning
DipTh Diploma in Theology
DipTMHA Diploma in Training and Further Education of Mentally Handicapped Adults
DipTP Diploma in Town Planning
DipTPT Diploma in Theory and Practice of Teaching
DipTRP Diploma in Town and Regional Planning
DipYCS Diploma in Youth and Community Studies
DIS Diploma in Industrial Studies
DistTP Distinction in Town Planning
DIur Doctor of Law
DIUS Department for Innovation, Universities and Skills
Div. Division; Divorced
Div.Test Divinity Testimonium (of Trinity College, Dublin)
DJAG Deputy Judge Advocate General
DJPD Dato Jasa Purba Di-Raja Negeri Sembilan (Malaysia)
DJStJ Dame of Justice, Order of St John of Jerusalem (*now see* DStJ)
DJur *Doctor Juris* (Doctor of Law)
DK Most Esteemed Family Order (Brunei)
DL Deputy Lieutenant; Democratie Libérale
DLAS Diploma in Laboratory Animal Science, Royal College of Veterinary Surgeons
DLaws Doctor of Laws
DLC Diploma of Loughborough College
DLES Doctor of Letters in Economic Studies
DLI Durham Light Infantry
DLIS Diploma in Library and Information Studies
DLit or **DLitt** Doctor of Literature; Doctor of Letters
DLittS Doctor of Sacred Letters
DLJ Dame of Grace, Order of St Lazarus of Jerusalem
DLO Diploma in Laryngology and Otology
DLP Diploma in Legal Practice; Democratic Labour Party
DLR Docklands Light Railway
DM Doctor of Medicine
DMA Diploma in Municipal Administration
DMan Doctor of Management
DMCC Diploma in the Medical Care of Catastrophe, Society of Apothecaries
DMD Doctor of Medical Dentistry (Australia)
DME Director of Mechanical Engineering
DMed Doctor of Medicine
DMedSci Doctor of Medical Science
DMet Doctor of Metallurgy
DMI Director of Military Intelligence
DMin Doctor of Ministry
DMiss Doctor of Missiology
DMJ Diploma in Medical Jurisprudence
DMJ(Path) Diploma in Medical Jurisprudence (Pathology)
DMLJ Dame of Merit, Order of St Lazarus of Jerusalem
DMO Director of Military Operations
DMR Diploma in Medical Radiology
DMRD Diploma in Medical Radiological Diagnosis
DMRE Diploma in Medical Radiology and Electrology
DMRT Diploma in Medical Radio-Therapy
DMS Director of Medical Services; Decoration for Meritorious Service (South Africa); Diploma in Management Studies
DMSc Doctor of Medical Science
DMT Director of Military Training
DMus Doctor of Music
DN Diploma in Nursing
DNB Dictionary of National Biography
DNE Director of Naval Equipment
DNH Department of National Heritage
DNI Director of Naval Intelligence
DNZM Dame Companion, New Zealand Order of Merit
DO Diploma in Ophthalmology
DOAE Defence Operational Analysis Establishment
DObstRCOG Diploma of Royal College of Obstetricians and Gynaecologists (*now see* DRCOG)
DOC District Officer Commanding
DocArts Doctor of Arts
DocEng Doctor of Engineering
DoE Department of the Environment
DoH Department of Health
DoI Department of Industry
DOL Doctor of Oriental Learning
Dom. *Dominus* (Lord)
DOMS Diploma in Ophthalmic Medicine and Surgery
DOR Director of Operational Requirements
DOrthRCS Diploma in Orthodontics, Royal College of Surgeons
DOS Director of Ordnance Services; Doctor of Ocular Science
DP Data Processing
DPA Diploma in Public Administration; Discharged Prisoners' Aid; Doctor of Public Administration
DPD Diploma in Public Dentistry
DPEc Doctor of Political Economy
DPed Doctor of Pedagogy
DPH Diploma in Public Health
DPh or **DPhil** Doctor of Philosophy
DPharm Doctor of Pharmacy
DPhilMed Diploma in Philosophy of Medicine
DPhysMed Diploma in Physical Medicine
DPLG Diplômé par le Gouvernement
DPM Diploma in Psychological Medicine; Diploma in Personnel Management
DPMS Dato Paduka Mahkota Selangor (Malaysia)
DPMSA Diploma in Philosophy and Ethics of Medicine, Society of Apothecaries
DPP Director of Public Prosecutions
DPR Director of Public Relations
DPS Director of Postal Services; Director of Personal Services; Doctor of Public Service; Diploma in Pastoral Studies
DPSA Diploma in Public and Social Administration
DPSE Diploma in Professional Studies in Education
DPSM Diploma in Public Sector Management
DPSN Diploma in Professional Studies in Nursing
DPsych Doctor of Psychology
DQMG Deputy Quartermaster-General
Dr Doctor
DRA Defence Research Agency (later DERA)
DRAC Director Royal Armoured Corps
DRC Diploma of Royal College of Science and Technology, Glasgow
DRCOG Diploma of Royal College of Obstetricians and Gynaecologists
DRD Diploma in Restorative Dentistry
Dr hab. Doctor of Habilitation
Dr ing Doctor of Engineering
Dr jur Doctor of Laws
DrŒcPol *Doctor Œconomiæ Politicæ* (Doctor of Political Economy)
Dr phil Doctor of Philosophy
Dr rer. nat. Doctor of Natural Science
Dr rer. pol. Doctor of Political Science
Dr rer. soc. oec. Doctor of Social and Economic Sciences
DRS Diploma in Religious Studies
Drs Doctorandus
DRSAMD Diploma of the Royal Scottish Academy of Music and Drama
DS Directing Staff; Doctor of Science
DSA Diploma in Social Administration
DSAC Defence Scientific Advisory Council
DSAO Diplomatic Service Administration Office
DSC Distinguished Service Cross
DSc Doctor of Science
DScA Docteur en sciences agricoles
DSc(Eng) Doctor of Engineering Science
DSCHE Diploma of the Scottish Council for Health Education
DSCM Diploma of the Sydney Conservatorium of Music
DScMil Doctor of Military Science
DSc (SocSci) Doctor of Science in Social Science
DSD Director Staff Duties; Diploma in Speech and Drama
DSF Director Special Forces
DSG Dame, Order of St Gregory the Great
DSIR Department of Scientific and Industrial Research (later SRC; then SERC)
DSL Doctor of Sacred Letters
DSLJ Dato Seri Laila Jasa (Brunei)
DSM Distinguished Service Medal
DSNB Dato Setia Negara Brunei
DSNS Dato Setia Negeri Sembilan (Malaysia)
DSO Companion of the Distinguished Service Order
DSocSc Doctor of Social Science
DSP Director of Selection of Personnel; Docteur en sciences politiques (Montreal)
dsp *decessit sine prole* (died without issue)
DSport Doctor of Sport
DSS Department of Social Security; Doctor of Sacred Scripture
Dss Deaconess
DSSc Doctor of Social Science
DST Director of Supplies and Transport
DStJ Dame of Grace, Most Venerable Order of the Hospital of St John of Jerusalem; Dame of Justice, Most Venerable Order of the Hospital of St John of Jerusalem
DSTL Defence Science and Technology Laboratory
DTA Diploma in Tropical Agriculture
DTech Doctor of Technology
DTH Diploma in Tropical Hygiene
DTh or **DTheol** Doctor of Theology
DThMin Doctor of Theology and Ministry
DThPT Diploma in Theory and Practice of Teaching
DTI Department of Trade and Industry
DTLR Department for Transport, Local Government and the Regions

DTM&H Diploma in Tropical Medicine and Hygiene
DU or **DUniv** Honorary Doctor of the University
Dunelm *Dunelmensis* (of Durham)
DUP Democratic Unionist Party; Docteur de l'Université de Paris
DVA Diploma of Veterinary Anaesthesia
DVH Diploma in Veterinary Hygiene
DVLA Driver and Vehicle Licensing Agency
DVLC Driver and Vehicle Licensing Centre
DVM or **DVetMed** Doctor of Veterinary Medicine
DVMS or **DVM&S** Doctor of Veterinary Medicine and Surgery
DVO Driver, Vehicle and Operator
DVOphthal Diploma in Veterinary Ophthalmology
DVR Diploma in Veterinary Radiology
DVSc Doctor of Veterinary Science
DVSM Diploma in Veterinary State Medicine
DWP Department for Work and Pensions

E

E East; Earl; England; E-mail
e eldest
EA Environment Agency
EAA Edinburgh Architectural Association
EACR European Association for Cancer Research
EADS European Aeronautics Defence and Space Company
EAF East African Forces
EAGA Energy Action Grants Agency
EAHY European Architectural Heritage Year
EAP East Africa Protectorate
EASD European Association of Securities Dealers; European Association for the Study of Diabetes
EBC English Benedictine Congregation
Ebor *Eboracensis* (of York)
EBRD European Bank for Reconstruction and Development
EBU European Broadcasting Union
EC Etoile du Courage (Canada); European Community; European Commission; Emergency Commission
ECA Economic Co-operation Administration; Economic Commission for Africa
ECAFE Economic Commission for Asia and the Far East (*now see* ESCAP)
ECB England and Wales Cricket Board
ECCTIS Education Courses and Credit Transfer Information Systems
ECE Economic Commission for Europe
ECGD Export Credits Guarantee Department
ECHR European Court of Human Rights
ECLAC United Nations Economic Commission for Latin America and the Caribbean
ECOSOC Economic and Social Committee of the United Nations
ECR European Conservatives and Reformists Group
ECSC European Coal and Steel Community
ED Efficiency Decoration; Doctor of Engineering (US); European Democrat
ed edited
EdB Bachelor of Education
EDC Economic Development Committee
EdD Doctor of Education
EDF European Development Fund
EDG European Democratic Group; Employment Department Group
Edin. Edinburgh
Edn Edition
EDP Executive Development Programme
EdS Specialist in Education
EDSAC Electronic Delay Storage Automatic Calculator
Educ Educated
Educn Education
EEA European Environment Agency
EEC European Economic Community (*now see* EC); Commission of the European Communities
EEF Engineering Employers' Federation; Egyptian Expeditionary Force
EETPU Electrical Electronic Telecommunication & Plumbing Union (later AEEU)
EETS Early English Text Society
EFCE European Federation of Chemical Engineering
EFIAP Excellence, Fédération Internationale de l'Art Photographique
EFQM European Foundation Quality Management
EFTA European Free Trade Association
EGCLJ Ecclesiastical Grand Cross Chaplain, Order of St Lazarus of Jerusalem
eh ehrenhalber (honorary)
EI East Indian; East Indies
EIA Engineering Industries Association
EIB European Investment Bank
EIEMA Electrical Installation Equipment Manufacturers' Association
E-in-C Engineer-in-Chief
EIS Educational Institute of Scotland
EISCAT European Incoherent Scatter Association
EIU Economist Intelligence Unit
ELBS English Language Book Society
ELDR European Liberal, Democrat and Reform Party
ELSE European Life Science Editors
ELT English Language Teaching
EM Edward Medal; Earl Marshal
EMBL European Molecular Biology Laboratory
EMBO European Molecular Biology Organisation
EMEA European Medicines Agency (*formerly* European Agency for the Evaluation of Medical Products); Europe, Middle East and Africa
EMI European Monetary Institute
EMP Electro Magnetic Pulse; Executive Management Program Diploma
EMS Emergency Medical Service
EMU European Monetary Union
Eng. England
EngD Doctor of Engineering
Engr Engineer
ENO English National Opera
ENSA Entertainments National Service Association
ENT Ear Nose and Throat
ENTO Employment National Training Organisation
EO Executive Officer
EOC Equal Opportunities Commission
EOPH Examined Officer of Public Health
EORTC European Organisation for Research on Treatment of Cancer
EP European Parliament
EPOS Electronic Point of Sale
EPP European People's Party
EPSA Excellence, Photographic Society of America
EPSRC Engineering and Physical Sciences Research Council
EPsS Experimental Psychology Society
er elder
ER Eastern Region (BR); East Riding
ERA Electrical Research Association
ERC Electronics Research Council
ERD Emergency Reserve Decoration (Army)
ESA European Space Agency
ESART Environmental Services Association Research Trust
ESC European Society of Cardiology
ESCAP Economic and Social Commission for Asia and the Pacific
ESCP-EAP Ecole Supérieure de Commerce de Paris-Ecole des Affaires de Paris
ESF European Science Foundation
ESL English as a Second Language
ESNS Educational Sub-Normal Serious
ESOL English for Speakers of Other Languages
ESP English for Special Purposes
ESPID European Society for Paediatric Infectious Diseases
ESRC Economic and Social Research Council; Electricity Supply Research Council
ESRO European Space Research Organization (*now see* ESA)
ESSKA European Society for Surgery of the Knee and Arthroscopy
ESTA European Science and Technology Assembly
ESU English-Speaking Union
ETA Engineering Training Authority
ETH Eidgenössische Technische Hochschule
ETS Educational and Training Services
ETS(A) Educational and Training Services (Army)
ETU Electrical Trades Union
ETUC European Trade Union Confederation
ETUCE European Trade Union Committee for Education
EU European Union
Euratom European Atomic Energy Community
EurBiol European Biologist (*now see* EurProBiol)
EurChem European Chemist
EurGeol European Geologist
Eur Ing European Engineer
EUROM European Federation for Optics and Precision Mechanics
EurProBiol European Professional Biologist
EUW European Union of Women
eV eingetragener Verein
EVPC European Veterinary Parasitology College
Ext Extinct; external

F

FA Football Association
FAA Fellow, Australian Academy of Science; Fleet Air Arm
FAAAI Fellow, American Association for Artificial Intelligence
FAAAS Fellow, American Association for the Advancement of Science
FAAHMS Fellow, Australian Academy of Health and Sciences
FAAN Fellow, American Academy of Neurology; Fellow, American Academy of Nursing
FAAO Fellow, American Academy of Optometry
FAAP Fellow, American Academy of Pediatrics
FAARM Fellow, American Academy of Reproductive Medicine

FAAV Fellow, Central Association of Agricultural Valuers
FAAVCT Fellow, American Academy of Veterinary and Comparative Toxicology
FABE Fellow, Association of Building Engineers
FAcadMed Fellow, Academy of Medical Educators
FACB Fellow, National Academy of Clinical Biochemistry, USA
FACC Fellow, American College of Cardiology
FACCA Fellow, Association of Certified and Corporate Accountants (*now see* FCCA)
FACCP Fellow, American College of Chest Physicians
FACD Fellow, American College of Dentistry
FACDS Fellow, Australian College of Dental Surgeons (*now see* FRACDS)
FACE Fellow, Australian College of Educators (*formerly* of Education)
FACerS Fellow, American Ceramic Society
FAChAM Fellow, Australasian Chapter of Addiction Medicine, Royal Australian College of Physicians
FAChPM Fellow, Australasian Chapter of Palliative Medicine, Royal Australian College of Physicians
FACHSE Fellow, Australian College of Health Service Executives
FACI Fellow, Australian Chemical Institute (*now see* FRACI)
FACM Fellow, Associaton of Computing Machinery
FACMA Fellow, Australian College of Medical Administrators (*now see* FRACMA)
FACMG Fellow, American College of Medicinal Genetics
FACOG Fellow, American College of Obstetricians and Gynæcologists
FACOM Fellow, Australian College of Occupational Medicine
FACP Fellow, American College of Physicians
FACPM Fellow, American College of Preventive Medicine
FACR Fellow, American College of Radiology
FACRM Fellow, Australian College of Rehabilitation Medicine
FACS Fellow, American College of Surgeons
FAcSS Fellow, Academy of Social Sciences
FACVSc Fellow, Australian College of Veterinary Scientists
FACVT Fellow, American College of Veterinary Toxicology (*now see* FAAVCT)
FADM Fellow, Academy of Dental Materials
FADO Fellow, Association of Dispensing Opticians
FAEM Faculty of Accident and Emergency Medicine (*now see* CEM)
FAeSI Fellow, Aeronautical Society of India
FAFMS Fellow, Academy of Forensic Medical Sciences
FAfN Fellow, Association for Nutrition
FAFPHM Fellow, Australian Faculty of Public Health Medicine
FAGS Fellow, American Geographical Society
FAHA Fellow, Australian Academy of the Humanities; Fellow, American Heart Association
FAI Fellow, Chartered Auctioneers' and Estate Agents' Institute (*now* (after amalgamation) *see* FRICS); Fédération Aéronautique Internationale
FAIA Fellow, American Institute of Architects; Fellow, Association of International Accountants
FAIAA Fellow, American Institute of Aeronautics and Astronautics
FAIAS Fellow, Australian Institute of Agricultural Science (*now see* FAIAST)
FAIAST Fellow, Australian Institute of Agricultural Science and Technology
FAIB Fellow, Australian Institute of Bankers
FAIBF Fellow, Australasian Institute of Bankers + Finance
FAIBiol Fellow, Australian Institute of Biology
FAICD Fellow, Australian Institute of Company Directors
FAIE Fellow, Australian Institute of Energy
FAIEx Fellow, Australian Institute of Export
FAIFST Fellow, Australian Institute of Food Science and Technology
FAII Fellow, Australian Insurance Institute
FAIIA Fellow, Australian Information Industry Association
FAIM Fellow, Australian Institute of Management
FAIMBE Fellow, American Institute for Medical and Biological Engineering
FAIP Fellow, Australian Institute of Physics
FAISB Fellow, Society for the Study of Artificial Intelligence and the Simulation of Behaviour
FAM Fellow, Academy of Marketing
FAMA Fellow, Australian Medical Association
FAMI Fellow, Australian Marketing Institute
FAMINZ(Arb) Fellow, Arbitrators and Mediators Institute of New Zealand
FAMM Fellow, Academy of Medicine, Malaysia
FAmNucSoc Fellow, American Nuclear Society
FAMS Fellow, Ancient Monuments Society; Fellow, Academy of Medicine, Singapore
FANA Fellow, American Neurological Association
F and GP Finance and General Purposes
FANY First Aid Nursing Yeomanry
FANZCA Fellow, Australian and New Zealand College of Anaesthetists
FANZCP Fellow, Australian and New Zealand College of Psychiatrists (*now see* FRANZCP)
FAO Food and Agriculture Organization of the United Nations
FAOrthA Fellow, Australian Orthopaedic Association
FAPA Fellow, American Psychiatric Association
FAPHA Fellow, American Public Health Association
FAPI Fellow, Association of Physicians of India
FAPM Fellow, Association for Project Management (*formerly* of Project Managers)
FAPS Fellow, American Phytopathological Society
FAPT Fellow, Association for Preservation Technology (US)
FArborA Fellow, Aboricultural Association
FARE Federation of Alcoholic Rehabilitation Establishments
FARELF Far East Land Forces
FAS Fellow, Antiquarian Society; Fellow, Nigerian Academy of Science; Funding Agency for Schools
FASA Fellow, Australian Society of Accountants (*now see* FCPA)
FASc Fellow, Indian Academy of Sciences
fasc. fascicule
FASCE Fellow, American Society of Civil Engineers
FASI Fellow, Architects' and Surveyors' Institute
FASME Fellow, American Society of Mechanical Engineers
FASPOG Fellow, Australian Society for Psychosomatic Obstetrics and Gynaecology
FASSA Fellow, Academy of the Social Sciences in Australia
FAusIMM Fellow, Australasian Institute of Mining and Metallurgy
FAustCOG Fellow, Australian College of Obstetricians and Gynæcologists (later FRACOG; *now see* FRANZCOG)
FAWT Farm Animal Welfare Trust
FBA Fellow, British Academy; Federation of British Artists
FBAHA Fellow, British Association of Hotel Accountants
FBAM Fellow, British Academy of Management
FBC Fellow, Birmingham Conservatoire
FBCartS Fellow, British Cartographic Society
FBCO Fellow, British College of Optometrists (*formerly* of Ophthalmic Opticians (Optometrists)) (*now see* FCOptom)
FBCS Fellow, British Computer Society
FBCS CITP Fellow, British Computer Society, with Chartered Professional Status
FBEC(S) Fellow, Business Education Council (Scotland)
FBEng Fellow, Association of Building Engineers
FBES Fellow, Biological Engineering Society (*now see* FIPEM)
FBHA Fellow, British Hospitality Association
FBHI Fellow, British Horological Institute
FBHS Fellow, British Horse Society
FBI Federation of British Industries (*now see* CBI); Federal Bureau of Investigation
FBIA Fellow, Bankers' Institute of Australasia
FBIAT Fellow, British Institute of Architectural Technicians
FBIBA Fellow, British Insurance Brokers' Association (*now see* FBIIBA)
FBID Fellow, British Institute of Interior Design
FBIDA Fellow, British Interior Design Association
FBIDST Fellow, British Institute of Dental and Surgical Technologists
FBII Fellow, British Institute of Innkeeping
FBIIBA Fellow, British Insurance and Investment Brokers' Association
FBIM Fellow, British Institute of Management (later FIMgt)
FBINZ Fellow, Bankers' Institute of New Zealand
FBIPM Fellow, British Institute of Payroll Management (*now see* FIPPM)
FBIPP Fellow, British Institute of Professional Photography
FBIR Fellow, British Institute of Radiology
FBIRA Fellow, British Institute of Regulatory Affairs
FBIS Fellow, British Interplanetary Society
FBKS Fellow, British Kinematograph Society (*now see* FBKSTS)
FBKSTS Fellow, British Kinematograph, Sound and Television Society
FBNA Fellow, British Naturalists' Association
FBOA Fellow, British Optical Association
FBOU Fellow, British Ornithologists' Union
FBPharmacolS Fellow, British Pharmacological Society (*now see* FBPhS)
FBPhS Fellow, British Pharmacological Society
FBPICS Fellow, British Production and Inventory Control Society
FBPsS Fellow, British Psychological Society
FBritIRE Fellow, British Institution of Radio Engineers (later FIERE)
FBS Fellow, Building Societies Institute (later FCBSI; *now see* FCIB)
FBSE Fellow, Biomaterials Science and Engineering
FBSI Fellow, Boot and Shoe Institution (*now see* FCFI)
FBSM Fellow, Birmingham School of Music (*now see* FBC)
FBTS Fellow, British Toxicology Society
FC Football Club
FCA Fellow, Institute of Chartered Accountants; Fellow, Institute of Chartered Accountants in Australia; Fellow, New Zealand Society of Accountants; Federation of Canadian Artists
FCAHS Fellow, Canadian Academy of Health Sciences
FCAI Fellow, New Zealand Institute of Cost Accountants; Fellow, Canadian Aeronautical Institute (*now see* FCASI); Fellow, College of Anaesthetists of Ireland
FCAM Fellow, CAM Foundation
FCAnaes Fellow, College of Anaesthetists (*now see* FRCA)
FCARCSI Fellow, College of Anaesthetists, Royal College of Surgeons of Ireland
FCA(SA) Fellow, College of Anaesthetists (South Africa)
FCASI Fellow, Canadian Aeronautics and Space Institute
FCBSI Fellow, Chartered Building Societies Institute (merged with Chartered Institute of Bankers; *now see* FCIB)
FCCA Fellow, Chartered Association of Certified Accountants
FCCEA Fellow, Commonwealth Council for Educational Administration

FCCP Fellow, American College of Chest Physicians
FCCS Fellow, Corporation of Secretaries (*formerly* of Certified Secretaries)
FCCT Fellow, Canadian College of Teachers
FCDSHK Fellow, College of Dental Surgeons of Hong Kong
FCEC Federation of Civil Engineering Contractors
FCEM Fellow, College of Emergency Medicine (*now see* FRCEM)
FCFI Fellow, Clothing and Footwear Institute
FCGA Fellow, Certified General Accountants of Canada
FCGC Fellow, Council of Geriatric Cardiology
FCGI Fellow, City and Guilds of London Institute
FCGP Fellow, College of General Practitioners (*now see* FRCGP)
FChS Fellow, Society of Chiropodists
FCI Fellow, Institute of Commerce
FCIA Fellow, Corporation of Insurance Agents
FCIArb Fellow, Chartered Institute of Arbitrators
FCIB Fellow, Corporation of Insurance Brokers; Fellow, Chartered Institute of Bankers
FCIBS Fellow, Chartered Institution of Building Services (*now see* FCIBSE); Fellow, Chartered Institute of Bankers in Scotland
FCIBSE Fellow, Chartered Institution of Building Services Engineers
FCIC Fellow, Chemical Institute of Canada (*formerly* Canadian Institute of Chemistry)
FCIEEM Fellow, Chartered Institute of Ecology and Environmental Management
FCIEH Fellow, Chartered Institute of Environmental Health
FCIH Fellow, Chartered Institute of Housing
FCIHort Fellow, Chartered Institute of Horticulture
FCIHT Fellow, Chartered Institution of Highways & Transportation
FCII Fellow, Chartered Insurance Institute
FCIJ Fellow, Chartered Institute of Journalists
FCIL Fellow, Chartered Institute of Linguists
FCILA Fellow, Chartered Institute of Loss Adjusters
FCILT Chartered Fellow, Chartered Institute of Logistics and Transport
FCIM Fellow, Chartered Institute of Marketing; Fellow, Institute of Corporate Managers (Australia)
FCInstCES Fellow, Chartered Institution of Civil Engineering Surveyors
FCIOB Fellow, Chartered Institute of Building
FCIPA Fellow, Chartered Institute of Patent Agents (*now see* CPA)
FCIPD Fellow, Chartered Institute of Personnel and Development
FCIPHE Fellow, Chartered Institute of Plumbing and Heating Engineering
FCIPR Fellow, Chartered Institute of Public Relations
FCIPS Fellow, Chartered Institute of Purchasing and Supply
FCIS Fellow, Institute of Chartered Secretaries and Administrators (*formerly* Chartered Institute of Secretaries)
FCISA Fellow, Chartered Institute of Secretaries and Administrators (Australia)
FCIT Fellow, Chartered Institute of Transport (*now see* FCILT)
FCIWEM Fellow, Chartered Institution of Water and Environmental Management
FCIWM Fellow, Chartered Institution of Wastes Management
FCJEI Fellow, Commonwealth Judicial Education Institute
FCLIP Fellow, Chartered Institute of Library and Information Professionals
FCM Faculty of Community Medicine
FCMA Fellow, Chartered Institute of Management Accountants (*formerly* Institute of Cost and Management Accountants); Fellow, Communications Management Association
FCMC Fellow grade, Certified Management Consultant
FCMI Fellow, Chartered Management Institute
FCMSA Fellow, College of Medicine of South Africa
FCNA Fellow, College of Nursing, Australia
FCO Foreign and Commonwealth Office
FCOG(SA) Fellow, South African College of Obstetrics and Gynæcology
FCollH Fellow, College of Handicraft
FCollP Fellow, College of Preceptors
FCollT Fellow, College of Teachers
FCommA Fellow, Society of Commercial Accountants (*now see* FSCA)
FCOphth Fellow, College of Ophthalmologists (*now see* FRCOphth)
FCOptom Fellow, College of Optometrists
FCOT Fellow, College of Teachers
FCP Fellow, College of Preceptors
FCPA Fellow, Australian Society of Certified Practising Accountants
FCPath Fellow, College of Pathologists (*now see* FRCPath)
FCPCH Fellow, College of Paediatrics and Child Health (*now see* FRCPCH)
FCPodMed Fellow, College of Podiatric Medicine
FCPS Fellow, College of Physicians and Surgeons
FCP(SoAf) Fellow, College of Physicians, South Africa
FCPSO(SoAf) Fellow, College of Physicians and Surgeons and Obstetricians, South Africa
FCPS (Pak) Fellow, College of Physicians and Surgeons of Pakistan
FCQI Fellow, Chartered Quality Institute
FCRA Fellow, College of Radiologists of Australia (*now see* FRACR)
FCS Federation of Conservative Students
FCS or **FChemSoc** Fellow, Chemical Society (now absorbed into Royal Society of Chemistry)
FCSD Fellow, Chartered Society of Designers
FCSFS Fellow, Chartered Society of Forensic Sciences
FCSHK Fellow, College of Surgeons of Hong Kong
FCSI Fellow, Chartered Institute for Securities & Investment
FCSLT Fellow, College of Speech and Language Therapists (*now see* FRCSLT)
FCSM Fellow, Cambridge School of Music
FCSP Fellow, Chartered Society of Physiotherapy
FCSSA or **FCS(SoAf)** Fellow, College of Surgeons, South Africa
FCSSL Fellow, College of Surgeons of Sri Lanka
FCST Fellow, College of Speech Therapists (later FCSLT; *now see* FRCSLT)
FCT Federal Capital Territory (*now see* ACT); Fellow, Association of Corporate Treasurers; Fellow, College of Teachers
FCTB Fellow, College of Teachers of the Blind
FCU Fighter Control Unit
FCWA Fellow, Institute of Costs and Works Accountants (*now see* FCMA)
FD Doctor of Philosophy
FDA Association of First Division Civil Servants
FdA Foundation Degree of Arts
FDF Food and Drink Federation
FDI Fédération Dentaire Internationale
FDP Freie Demokratische Partei
FDS Fellow in Dental Surgery
FDSRCPSGlas Fellow in Dental Surgery, Royal College of Physicians and Surgeons of Glasgow
FDSRCS or **FDS RCS** Fellow in Dental Surgery, Royal College of Surgeons of England
FDSRCSE Fellow in Dental Surgery, Royal College of Surgeons of Edinburgh
FE Far East; Further Education
FEA Fellow, English Association
FEAF Far East Air Force
FEANI Fédération Européenne d'Associations Nationales d'Ingénieurs
FEBS Federation of European Biochemical Societies; Fellow, European Board of Surgery
FECI Fellow, Institute of Employment Consultants
FECTS Fellow, European Association for Cardiothoracic Surgery
FEE Fédération des Expertes Comptables Européens
FEF Far East Fleet
FEFC or **FEFCE** Further Education Funding Council for England
FEFCW Further Education Funding Council for Wales
FEI Fédération Equestre Internationale; Fellow, Energy Institute
FEIDCT Fellow, Educational Institute of Design Craft and Technology
FEIS Fellow, Educational Institute of Scotland
FEMAC Fellow, European Marketing Academy
FEng Fellow, Royal Academy (*formerly* Fellowship) of Engineering (*now see* FREng)
FEPS Federation of European Physiological Societies
FERS Fellow, European Respiratory Society
FES Fellow, Entomological Society; Fellow, Ethnological Society
FESC Fellow, European Society of Cardiology
FETCS Fellow, European Board of Thoracic and Cardiovascular Surgeons
FF Fianna Fáil; Field Force
FFA Fellow, Faculty of Actuaries (in Scotland); Fellow, Institute of Financial Accountants
FFAEM Fellow, Faculty of Accident and Emergency Medicine (later FCEM)
FFARACS Fellow, Faculty of Anaesthetists, Royal Australasian College of Surgeons (*now see* FANZCA)
FFARCS Fellow, Faculty of Anaesthetists, Royal College of Surgeons of England (*now see* FRCA)
FFARCSI Fellow, Faculty of Anaesthetists, Royal College of Surgeons in Ireland (*now see* FCAI)
FFAS Fellow, Faculty of Architects and Surveyors, London (*now see* FASI)
FFA(SA) Fellow, Faculty of Anaesthetists (South Africa) (*now see* FCA(SA))
FFB Fellow, Faculty of Building
FFCM Fellow, Faculty of Community Medicine (*now see* FFPH); Fellow, Faculty of Church Music
FFCMI Fellow, Faculty of Community Medicine of Ireland
FFCS Founding Fellow, Contemporary Scotland
FFDRCSI Fellow, Faculty of Dentistry, Royal College of Surgeons in Ireland
FFFLM Fellow, Faculty of Forensic and Legal Medicine, Royal College of Physicians
FFFP Fellow, Faculty of Family Planning & Reproductive Health Care of the Royal College of Obstetricians and Gynaecologists (*now see* FFSRH)
FFGDP(UK) Fellow, Faculty of General Dental Practitioners of the Royal College of Surgeons
FFHom Fellow, Faculty of Homoeopathy
FFI Finance for Industry; Fauna & Flora International
FFICM Fellow, Faculty of Intensive Care Medicine
FFOM Fellow, Faculty of Occupational Medicine
FFOMI Fellow, Faculty of Occupational Medicine of Ireland
FFOP (RCPA) Fellow, Faculty of Oral Pathology, Royal College of Pathologists of Australasia
FFPath, RCPI Fellow, Faculty of Pathologists of the Royal College of Physicians of Ireland
FFPH Fellow, Faculty of Public Health

FFPHM Fellow, Faculty of Public Health Medicine (*now see* FFPH)
FFPHMI Fellow, Faculty of Public Health Medicine of Ireland
FFPM Fellow, Faculty of Pharmaceutical Medicine
FFPRHC Faculty of Family Planning & Reproductive Health Care, Royal College of Obstetricians and Gynaecologists
FFPS Fauna and Flora Preservation Society (*now see* FFI)
FFR Fellow, Faculty of Radiologists (*now see* FRCR)
FFRRCSI Fellow, Faculty of Radiologists of the Royal College of Surgeons in Ireland
FFSEM Fellow, Faculty of Sports and Exercise Medicine, Royal College of Physicians of Ireland and Royal College of Surgeons in Ireland
FFSRH Fellow, Faculty of Sexual and Reproductive Healthcare of the Royal College of Obstetricians and Gynaecologists
FFSSoc Fellow, Forensic Science Society (*now see* FCSFS)
FFTM(Glas) Fellow, Faculty of Travel Medicine, Royal College of Physicians and Surgeons of Glasgow
FG Fine Gael
FGA Fellow, Gemmological Association
FGCL Fellow, Goldsmiths' College, London
FGCM Fellow, Guild of Church Musicians
FGDP(UK) Fellow, Faculty of General Dental Practice of the Royal College of Surgeons of England
FGDS Fédération de la Gauche Démocratique et Socialiste
FGE Fellow, Guild of Glass Engravers
FGGE Fellow, Guild of Glass Engravers (*now see* FGE)
FGI Fellow, Institute of Certificated Grocers
FGMS Fellow, Guild of Musicians and Singers
FGS Fellow, Geological Society; Fellow, Guildhall School of Music and Drama
FGSM Fellow, Guildhall School of Music and Drama (*now see* FGS)
FGSM(MT) Fellow, Guildhall School of Music and Drama (Music Therapy)
FHA Fellow, Institute of Health Service Administrators (*formerly* Hospital Administrators) (later FHSM); Fellow, Historical Association
FHAS Fellow, Highland and Agricultural Society of Scotland
FHCIMA Fellow, Hotel Catering and International (formerly Institutional) Management Association (*now see* FIH)
FHEA Fellow, Higher Education Academy
FHKAES Fellow, Hong Kong Academy of Engineering Sciences
FHKAM Fellow, Hong Kong Academy of Medicine
FHKCCM Fellow, Hong Kong College of Community Medicine
FHKCP Fellow, Hong Kong College of Physicians
FHKCPath Fellow, Hong Kong College of Pathologists
FHKCS Fellow, Hong Kong College of Surgeons
FHKIE Fellow, Hong Kong Institution of Engineers
FHMAAAS Foreign Honorary Member, American Academy of Arts and Sciences
FHRS Fellow, Heart Rhythm Society
FHS Fellow, Heraldry Society; Forces Help Society and Lord Roberts Workshops (*now see* SSAFA)
FHSA Family Health Services Authority
FHSM Fellow, Institute of Health Services Management (later FIHM)
FIA Fellow, Institute and Faculty of Actuaries (formerly Institute of Actuaries)
FIAA Fellow, Institute of Actuaries of Australia
FIAAS Fellow, Institute of Australian Agricultural Science
FIAA&S Fellow, Incorporated Association of Architects and Surveyors
FIACM Fellow, International Association of Computational Mechanics
FIAE Fellow, Irish Academy of Engineering
FIAFoST Fellow, International Academy of Food Science and Technology
FIAgrE Fellow, Institution of Agricultural Engineers
FIAgrM Fellow, Institute of Agricultural Management
FIAL Fellow, International Institute of Arts and Letters
FIAM Fellow, International Academy of Management
FIAMBE Fellow, International Academy for Medical and Biological Engineering
FIAP Fellow, Institution of Analysts and Programmers; Fellow, Indian Academy of Paediatrics
FIArb Fellow, Institute of Arbitrators (*now see* FCIArb)
FIArbA Fellow, Institute of Arbitrators of Australia
FIAS Fellow, Institute of Aeronautical Sciences (US) (*now see* FAIAA)
FIASc Fellow, Indian Academy of Sciences
FIASSID Fellow, International Association for the Scientific Study of Intellectual Disability
FIB Fellow, Institute of Bankers (*now see* FCIB)
FIBA Fellow, Institute of Business Administration, Australia (*now see* FCIM)
FIBC Fellow, Institute of Business Consulting (*now see* FIC)
FIBI Fellow, Institute of Bankers of Ireland
FIBiol Fellow, Institute of Biology (later FSB, *now see* FRSB)
FIBiotech Fellow, Institute for Biotechnical Studies
FIBMS Fellow, Institute of Biomedical Sciences
FIBScot Fellow, Institute of Bankers in Scotland (*now see* FCIBS)
FIC Fellow, Institute of Chemistry (then FRIC; *now see* FRSC); Fellow, Imperial College, London; Fellow, Institute of Consulting
FICA Fellow, Commonwealth Institute of Accountants; Fellow, Institute of Chartered Accountants in England and Wales (*now see* FCA)
FICAI Fellow, Institute of Chartered Accountants in Ireland
FICB Fellow, Institute of Canadian Bankers
FICD Fellow, Institute of Civil Defence; Fellow, Indian College of Dentists; Fellow, International College of Dentists
FICE Fellow, Institution of Civil Engineers
FICeram Fellow, Institute of Ceramics (later FIM)
FICES Fellow, Institution of Chartered Engineering Surveyors
FICFM Fellow, Institute of Charity Fundraising Managers (*now see* FInstF)
FICFor Fellow, Institute of Chartered Foresters
FIChemE Fellow, Institution of Chemical Engineers
FICM Fellow, Institute of Credit Management
FICMA Fellow, Institute of Cost and Management Accountants
FICOG Fellow, Indian College of Obstetricians and Gynaecologists
FICorr Fellow, Institute of Corrosion
FICorrST Fellow, Institution of Corrosion Science and Technology (*now see* FICorr)
FICPD Fellow, Institute of Continuing Professional Development
FICPEM Fellow, Institute of Civil Protection and Emergency Management
FICS Fellow, Institute of Chartered Shipbrokers; Fellow, International College of Surgeons
FIDA Fellow, Institute of Directors, Australia (*now see* FAICD)
FIDDA Fellow, Interior Decorators and Designers Association (*now see* FBIDA)
FIDE Fédération Internationale des Echecs; Fellow, Institute of Design Engineers; Fédération Internationale pour le Droit Européen
FIDEM Fédération Internationale de la Médaille d'Art
FIDM Fellow, Institute of Direct Marketing
FIDPM Fellow, Institute of Data Processing Management
FIEAust Fellow, Institution of Engineers, Australia
FIED Fellow, Institution of Engineering Designers
FIEE Fellow, Institution of Electrical Engineers (*now see* FIET)
FIEEE Fellow, Institute of Electrical and Electronics Engineers (NY)
FIEEIE Fellow, Institution of Electronics and Electrical Incorporated Engineers (later FIIE)
FIEEM Fellow, Institute of Ecology and Environmental Management (*now see* FCIEEM)
FIEHK Fellow, Institution of Engineering, Hong Kong
FIEI Fellow, Institution of Engineering Inspection (later FIQA); Fellow, Institution of Engineers of Ireland
FIEIE Fellow, Institution of Electronic Incorporated Engineers (later FIEEIE)
FIEJ Fédération Internationale des Editeurs de Journaux et Publications
FIEMA Fellow, Institute of Environmental Management and Assessment
FIEnvSc Fellow, Institution of Environmental Sciences
FIERE Fellow, Institution of Electronic and Radio Engineers (later FIEE)
FIES Fellow, Illuminating Engineering Society (later FIllumES; *now see* FCIBSE); Fellow, Institution of Engineers and Shipbuilders, Scotland
FIET Fédération Internationale des Employés, Techniciens et Cadres; Fellow, Institution of Engineering and Technology
FIEx Fellow, Institute of Export
FIExpE Fellow, Institute of Explosives Engineers
FIFA Fédération Internationale de Football Association
FIFEM Fellow, International Federation of Emergency Medicine
FIFF Fellow, Institute of Freight Forwarders (*now see* FIFP)
FIFireE Fellow, Institution of Fire Engineers
FIFM Fellow, Institute of Fisheries Management
FIFor Fellow, Institute of Foresters (*now see* FICFor)
FIFP Fellow, Institute of Freight Professionals
FIFST Fellow, Institute of Food Science and Technology
FIGasE Fellow, Institution of Gas Engineers (*now see* FIGEM)
FIGCM Fellow, Incorporated Guild of Church Musicians
FIGD Fellow, Institute of Grocery Distribution
FIGEM Fellow, Institution of Gas Engineers and Managers
FIGO International Federation of Gynaecology and Obstetrics
FIH Fellow, Institute of Housing (*now see* FCIH); Fellow, Institute of the Horse; Fellow, Institute of Hospitality
FIHE Fellow, Institute of Health Education
FIHEEM Fellow, Institute of Healthcare Engineering and Estate Management
FIHM Fellow, Institute of Housing Managers (later FIH; *now see* FCIH); Fellow, Institute of Healthcare Management
FIHort Fellow, Institute of Horticulture (*now see* FCIHort)
FIHospE Fellow, Institute of Hospital Engineering
FIHT Fellow, Institution of Highways & Transportation (*now see* FCIHT)
FIHVE Fellow, Institution of Heating & Ventilating Engineers (later FCIBS and MCIBS)
FIIA Fellow, Institute of Industrial Administration (later CBIM and FBIM); Fellow, Institute of Internal Auditors
FIIB Fellow, International Institute of Biotechnology
FIIC Fellow, International Institute for Conservation of Historic and Artistic Works
FIIDA Fellow, International Interior Design Association
FIIE Fellow, Institution of Incorporated Engineers in Electronic, Electrical and Mechanical Engineering (*now see* FIET)
FIIM Fellow, Institution of Industrial Managers
FIInfSc Fellow, Institute of Information Scientists (*now see* FCLIP)

FIIP Fellow, Institute of Incorporated Photographers (*now see* FBIPP)
FIIPC Fellow, India International Photographic Council
FIIT Fellow, Institute of Indirect Taxation
FIL Fellow, Institute of Linguists (*now see* FCIL)
FILA Fellow, Institute of Landscape Architects (*now see* FLI)
FILAM Fellow, Institute of Leisure and Amenity Management
FILDM Fellow, Institute of Logistics and Distribution Management (later FILog)
FilDr Doctor of Philosophy
Fil.Hed. Filosofie Hedersdoktor
FIllumES Fellow, Illuminating Engineering Society (*now see* FCIBSE)
FILog Fellow, Institute of Logistics (later FILT)
FILT Fellow, Institute of Logistics and Transport (*now see* FCILT)
FIM Fellow, Institute of Materials (*formerly* Institution of Metallurgists, then Institute of Metals) (*now see* FIMMM)
FIMA Fellow, Institute of Mathematics and its Applications
FIMarE Fellow, Institute of Marine Engineers (*now see* FIMarEST)
FIMarEST Fellow, Institute of Marine Engineering, Science and Technology
FIMatM Fellow, Institute of Materials Management (later FILog)
FIMBRA Financial Intermediaries, Managers and Brokers Regulatory Association
FIMC Fellow, Institute of Management Consultants (*now see* FCMC)
FIMCB Fellow, International Management Centre from Buckingham
FIMCRCSE Fellow in Immediate Medical Care, Royal College of Surgeons of Edinburgh
FIMechE Fellow, Institution of Mechanical Engineers
FIMF Fellow, Institute of Materials Finishing
FIMfgE Fellow, Institution of Manufacturing Engineers (later FIEE)
FIMgt Fellow, Institute of Management (*now see* FCMI)
FIMH Fellow, Institute of Materials Handling (later FIMatM); Fellow, Institute of Military History
FIMI Fellow, Institute of the Motor Industry
FIMinE Fellow, Institution of Mining Engineers (later FIMM)
FIMIT Fellow, Institute of Musical Instrument Technology
FIMLS Fellow, Institute of Medical Laboratory Sciences (*now see* FIBMS)
FIMLT Fellow, Institute of Medical Laboratory Technology (later FIMLS)
FIMM Fellow, Institution of Mining and Metallurgy (*now see* FIMMM)
FIMMA Fellow, Institute of Metals and Materials Australasia
FIMMM Fellow, Institute of Materials, Minerals and Mining
FIMS Fellow, Institute of Mathematical Statistics
FIMT Fellow, Institute of the Motor Trade (*now see* FIMI)
FIMTA Fellow, Institute of Municipal Treasurers and Accountants (*now see* IPFA)
FIMunE Fellow, Institution of Municipal Engineers (now amalgamated with Institution of Civil Engineers)
FIN Fellow, Institute of Navigation (*now see* FRIN)
FINRA Financial Industry Regulatory Authority
FInstAM Fellow, Institute of Administrative Management
FInstArb(NZ) Fellow, Institute of Arbitrators of New Zealand
FInstBiol Fellow, Institute of Biology (later FIBiol)
FInstCES Fellow, Institution of Civil Engineering Surveyors (*now see* FCInstCES)
FInstD Fellow, Institute of Directors
FInstE Fellow, Institute of Energy (*now see* FEI)
FInstF Fellow, Institute of Fuel (later FInstE); Fellow, Institute of Fundraising
FInstFF Fellow, Institute of Freight Forwarders Ltd (later FIFF)
FInstHE Fellow, Institution of Highways Engineers (later FIHT, *now see* FCIHT)
FInstKT Fellow, Institute of Knowledge Transfer
FInstLEx Fellow, Institute of Legal Executives
FInstLM Fellow, Institute of Leadership and Management
FInstM Fellow, Institute of Meat; Fellow, Institute of Marketing (*now see* FCIM)
FInstMC Fellow, Institute of Measurement and Control
FInstMSM Fellow, Institute of Marketing and Sales Management (later FInstM; *now see* FCIM)
FInstMet Fellow, Institute of Metals (later part of Metals Society; then FIM)
FInstNDT Fellow, Institute of Non-Destructive Testing
FInstP Fellow, Institute of Physics
FInstPet Fellow, Institute of Petroleum (*now see* FEI)
FInstPkg Fellow, Institute of Packaging
FInstPS Fellow, Institute of Purchasing and Supply (*now see* FCIPS)
FInstRE Fellow, Institution of Royal Engineers
FInstSM Fellow, Institute of Sales Management (*now see* FInstSMM)
FInstSMM Fellow, Institute of Sales and Marketing Management
FInstTT Fellow, Institute of Travel & Tourism
FInstW Fellow, Institute of Welding (*now see* FWeldI)
FINucE Fellow, Institution of Nuclear Engineers (*now see* FNucI)
FIOA Fellow, Institute of Acoustics
FIOB Fellow, Institute of Building (*now see* FCIOB)
FIOH Fellow, Institute of Occupational Hygiene
FIOM Fellow, Institute of Office Management (*now see* FIAM)
FIOP Fellow, Institute of Printing (*now see* FIP3)
FIOSH Fellow, Institution of Occupational Safety and Health
FIP Fellow, Australian Institute of Petroleum
FIPA Fellow, Institute of Practitioners in Advertising; Fellow, Insolvency Practitioners Association
FIPAA Fellow, Institute of Public Administration Australia
FIPD Fellow, Institute of Personnel and Development (*now see* FCIPD)
FIPDM Fellow, Institute of Physical Distribution Management (later FILDM)
FIPEM Fellow, Institute of Physics and Engineering in Medicine
FIPENZ Fellow, Institution of Professional Engineers, New Zealand
FIPG Fellow, Institute of Professional Goldsmiths
FIPharmM Fellow, Institute of Pharmacy Management
FIPHE Fellow, Institution of Public Health Engineers (later FIWEM)
FIPlantE Fellow, Institution of Plant Engineers
FIPM Fellow, Institute of Personnel Management (later FIPD)
FIPPM Fellow, Institute of Payroll and Pensions Management
FIPR Fellow, Institute of Public Relations (*now see* FCIPR)
FIProdE Fellow, Institution of Production Engineers (later FIMfgE)
FIPSM Fellow, Institute of Physical Sciences in Medicine (*now see* FIPEM)
FIP3 Fellow, Institute of Paper, Printing and Publishing
FIQ Fellow, Institute of Quarrying
FIQA Fellow, Institute of Quality Assurance (*now see* FCQI)
FIRA Furniture Industry Research Association
FIRI Fellow, Institution of the Rubber Industry (later FPRI)
FIRM Fellow, Institute of Risk Management
FIRO Fellow, Institution of Railway Operators
FIRSE Fellow, Institute of Railway Signalling Engineers
FIRTE Fellow, Institute of Road Transport Engineers
FIS Fellow, Institute of Statisticians
FISA Fellow, Incorporated Secretaries' Association; Fédération Internationale des Sociétés d'Aviron
FISE Fellow, Institution of Sales Engineers; Fellow, Institution of Sanitary Engineers
FISITA Fédération Internationale des Sociétés d'Ingénieurs des Techniques de l'Automobile
FISM Fellow, Institute of Supervisory Managers (*now see* FInstLM); Fellow, Institute of Sports Medicine
FISOB Fellow, Incorporated Society of Organ Builders
FISPAL Fellow, Institute for Sport, Parks and Leisure
FISTC Fellow, Institute of Scientific and Technical Communicators
FISTD Fellow, Imperial Society of Teachers of Dancing
FIStructE Fellow, Institution of Structural Engineers
FITD Fellow, Institute of Training and Development (later FIPD)
FITE Fellow, Institution of Electrical and Electronics Technician Engineers
FITSA Fellow, Institute of Trading Standards Administration
FIW Fellow, Welding Institute (*now see* FWeldI)
FIWE Fellow, Institution of Water Engineers (later FIWES)
FIWEM Fellow, Institution of Water and Environmental Management (*now see* FCIWEM)
FIWES Fellow, Institution of Water Engineers and Scientists (later FIWEM)
FIWM Fellow, Institution of Works Managers (*now see* FIIM); Fellow, Institute of Wastes Management (*now see* FCIWM)
FIWO Fellow, Institute of Water Officers
FIWPC Fellow, Institute of Water Pollution Control (later FIWEM)
FIWSc Fellow, Institute of Wood Science
FIWSP Fellow, Institute of Work Study Practitioners (*now see* FMS)
FJI Fellow, Institute of Journalists (*now see* FCIJ)
FJIE Fellow, Junior Institution of Engineers (*now see* CIMGTechE)
FKC Fellow, King's College London
FKCHMS Fellow, King's College Hospital Medical School
FL Florida (postal)
FLA Fellow, Library Association (*now see* FCLIP)
Fla Florida
FLAI Fellow, Library Association of Ireland
FLAS Fellow, Chartered Land Agents' Society (*now* (after amalgamation) *see* FRICS)
FLCM Fellow, London College of Music
FLI Fellow, Landscape Institute
FLIA Fellow, Life Insurance Association
FLLA Fellow, Association of Lawyers and Legal Advisers
FLS Fellow, Linnean Society
FLSW Fellow, Learned Society of Wales
Flt Flight
FM Field-Marshal
FMA Fellow, Museums Association
FMAAT Fellow Member, Association of Accounting Technicians
FMBA Fellow, Marine Biological Association
FMedSci Fellow, Academy of Medical Sciences
FMES Fellow, Minerals Engineering Society
FMI Foundation for Manufacturing and Industry
FMinSoc Fellow, Mineralogical Society of Great Britain and Ireland
FMS Federated Malay States; Fellow, Medical Society; Fellow, Institute of Management Services
FMSA Fellow, Mineralogical Society of America
FNA Fellow, Indian National Science Academy
FNAEA Fellow, National Association of Estate Agents
FNCO Fleet Naval Constructor Officer

FNECInst Fellow, North East Coast Institution of Engineers and Shipbuilders
FNI Fellow, Nautical Institute; Fellow, National Institute of Sciences in India (*now see* FNA)
FNIA Fellow, Nigerian Institute of Architects
FNM Free National Movement
FNMCP Fellow, Nigerian Medical College of Physicians
FNMSM Fellow, North and Midlands School of Music
FNucI Fellow, Nuclear Institute
FNZIA Fellow, New Zealand Institute of Architects
FNZIAS Fellow, New Zealand Institute of Agricultural Science
FNZIC Fellow, New Zealand Institute of Chemistry
FNZIE Fellow, New Zealand Institution of Engineers (*now see* FIPENZ)
FNZIM Fellow, New Zealand Institute of Management
FNZPsS Fellow, New Zealand Psychological Society
FO Foreign Office (*now see* FCO); Field Officer; Flag Officer; Flying Officer
FODC Franciscan Order of the Divine Compassion
FOIC Flag Officer in charge
FOMA Flag Officer, Maritime Aviation
FOMI Faculty of Occupational Medicine of Ireland
FONA Flag Officer, Naval Aviation
FONAC Flag Officer, Naval Air Command
FOR Fellowship of Operational Research
For. Foreign
FOREST Freedom Organisation for the Right to Enjoy Smoking Tobacco
FOST Flag Officer Sea Training
FOX Futures and Options Exchange
FPA Family Planning Association
FPC Family Practitioner Committee (later FHSA); Financial Planning Certificate
FPH Faculty of Public Health
FPHM Faculty of Public Health Medicine (*see now* FPH)
FPhS Fellow, Philosophical Society of England
FPhysS Fellow, Physical Society
FPI Fellow, Plastics Institute (later FPRI)
FPIA Fellow, Plastics Institute of Australia; Fellow, Planning Institute of Australia
FPM Faculty of Pharmaceutical Medicine
FPMI Fellow, Pensions Management Institute
FPRI Fellow, Plastics and Rubber Institute (later FIM)
FPS Fellow, Pharmaceutical Society (*now also* FRPharmS); Fauna Preservation Society (later FFPS)
FPWI Fellow, Permanent Way Institution
FQNI Fellow, Queen's Nursing Institute
f r fuori ruole
FRA Fellow, Royal Academy
FRAC Fellow, Royal Agricultural College
FRACDS Fellow, Royal Australian College of Dental Surgeons
FRACGP Fellow, Royal Australian College of General Practitioners
FRACI Fellow, Royal Australian Chemical Institute
FRACMA Fellow, Royal Australian College of Medical Administrators
FRACO Fellow, Royal Australian College of Ophthalmologists
FRACOG Fellow, Royal Australian College of Obstetricians and Gynaecologists (*now see* FRANZCOG)
FRACP Fellow, Royal Australasian College of Physicians
FRACR Fellow, Royal Australasian College of Radiologists
FRACS Fellow, Royal Australasian College of Surgeons
FRAD Fellow, Royal Academy of Dancing
FRAeS Fellow, Royal Aeronautical Society
FRAgS Fellow, Royal Agricultural Societies (*ie* of England, Scotland and Wales)
FRAHS Fellow, Royal Australian Historical Society
FRAI Fellow, Royal Anthropological Institute of Great Britain & Ireland
FRAIA Fellow, Royal Australian Institute of Architects
FRAIB Fellow, Royal Australian Institute of Building
FRAIC Fellow, Royal Architectural Institute of Canada
FRAIPA Fellow, Royal Australian Institute of Public Administration
FRAM Fellow, Royal Academy of Music
FRAME Fund for the Replacement of Animals in Medical Experiments
FRANZCOG Fellow, Royal Australian and New Zealand College of Obstetricians and Gynaecologists
FRANZCP Fellow, Royal Australian and New Zealand College of Psychiatrists
FRANZCR Fellow, Royal Australian and New Zealand College of Radiologists
FRAPI Fellow, Royal Australian Planning Institute (*now see* FPIA)
FRAS Fellow, Royal Astronomical Society; Fellow, Royal Asiatic Society
FRASE Fellow, Royal Agricultural Society of England
FRBS Fellow, Royal Society of British Sculptors; Fellow, Royal Botanic Society
FRCA Fellow, Royal College of Art; Fellow, Royal College of Anaesthetists
FRCCO Fellow, Royal Canadian College of Organists
FRCD(Can.) Fellow, Royal College of Dentists of Canada
FRCEM Fellow, Royal College of Emergency Medicine
FRCGP Fellow, Royal College of General Practitioners
FRCM Fellow, Royal College of Music
FRCN Fellow, Royal College of Nursing
FRCO Fellow, Royal College of Organists
FRCO(CHM) Fellow, Royal College of Organists with Diploma in Choir Training
FRCOG Fellow, Royal College of Obstetricians and Gynaecologists
FRCOphth Fellow, Royal College of Ophthalmologists
FRCP Fellow, Royal College of Physicians, London
FRCPA Fellow, Royal College of Pathologists of Australasia
FRCP&S (Canada) Fellow, Royal College of Physicians and Surgeons of Canada
FRCPath Fellow, Royal College of Pathologists
FRCPC Fellow, Royal College of Physicians of Canada
FRCPCH Fellow, Royal College of Paediatrics and Child Health
FRCPE or **FRCPEd** Fellow, Royal College of Physicians, Edinburgh
FRCPGlas Fellow, Royal College of Physicians and Surgeons of Glasgow
FRCPI Fellow, Royal College of Physicians of Ireland
FRCPSGlas Hon. Fellow, Royal College of Physicians and Surgeons of Glasgow
FRCPsych Fellow, Royal College of Psychiatrists
FRCR Fellow, Royal College of Radiologists
FRCS Fellow, Royal College of Surgeons of England
FRCSCan Fellow, Royal College of Surgeons of Canada
FRCSE or **FRCSEd** Fellow, Royal College of Surgeons of Edinburgh
FRCSGlas Fellow, Royal College of Physicians and Surgeons of Glasgow
FRCSI Fellow, Royal College of Surgeons in Ireland
FRCSLT Fellow, Royal College of Speech and Language Therapists
FRCSoc Fellow, Royal Commonwealth Society
FRCS (OMFS) Fellow, Royal College of Surgeons of England (Oral and Maxillofacial Surgery)
FRCST Fellow, Royal College of Surgeons of Thailand
FRCUS Fellow, Royal College of University Surgeons (Denmark)
FRCVS Fellow, Royal College of Veterinary Surgeons
FREconS Fellow, Royal Economic Society
FREng Fellow, Royal Academy of Engineering
FRES Fellow, Royal Entomological Society of London
FRFPSG Fellow, Royal Faculty of Physicians and Surgeons, Glasgow (*now see* FRCPGlas)
FRG Federal Republic of Germany
FRGS Fellow, Royal Geographical Society
FRGSA Fellow, Royal Geographical Society of Australasia
FRHistS Fellow, Royal Historical Society
FRHS Fellow, Royal Horticultural Society (*now see* MRHS)
FRI Fellow, Royal Institution
FRIAI Fellow, Royal Institute of the Architects of Ireland
FRIAS Fellow, Royal Incorporation of Architects of Scotland; Royal Institute for the Advancement of Science
FRIBA Fellow, Royal Institute of British Architects (*and see* RIBA)
FRIC Fellow, Royal Institute of Chemistry (*now see* FRSC)
FRICS Fellow, Royal Institution of Chartered Surveyors
FRIH Fellow, Royal Institute of Horticulture (NZ)
FRIN Fellow, Royal Institute of Navigation
FRINA Fellow, Royal Institution of Naval Architects
FRIPA Fellow, Royal Institute of Public Administration (the Institute no longer has Fellows)
FRIPH Fellow, Royal Institute of Public Health (*now see* FRSPH)
FRIPHH Fellow, Royal Institute of Public Health and Hygiene (later FRIPH; *now see* FRSPH)
FRMCM Fellow, Royal Manchester College of Music
FRMedSoc Fellow, Royal Medical Society
FRMetS Fellow, Royal Meteorological Society
FRMIA Fellow, Retail Management Institute of Australia
FRMS Fellow, Royal Microscopical Society
FRNCM Fellow, Royal Northern College of Music
FRNS Fellow, Royal Numismatic Society
FRPharmS Fellow, Royal Pharmaceutical Society
FRPS Fellow, Royal Photographic Society
FRPSL Fellow, Royal Philatelic Society, London
FRS Fellow, Royal Society
FRSA Fellow, Royal Society of Arts
FRSAI Fellow, Royal Society of Antiquaries of Ireland
FRSAMD Fellow, Royal Scottish Academy of Music and Drama
FRSB Fellow, Royal Society of Biology
FRSC Fellow, Royal Society of Canada; Fellow, Royal Society of Chemistry
FRS(Can) Fellow, Royal Society of Canada (used when a person is also a Fellow of the Royal Society of Chemistry)
FRSCM Hon. Fellow, Royal School of Church Music
FRSC(UK) Fellow, Royal Society of Chemistry (used when a person is also a Fellow of the Royal Society of Canada)
FRSE Fellow, Royal Society of Edinburgh
FRSGS Fellow, Royal Scottish Geographical Society
FRSH Fellow, Royal Society for the Promotion of Health (*now see* FRSPH)
FRSL Fellow, Royal Society of Literature
FRSM Fellow, Royal Schools of Music
FRSN Fellow, Royal Society of New South Wales
FRSocMed Fellow, Royal Society of Medicine
FRSNZ Fellow, Royal Society of New Zealand
FRSPH Fellow, Royal Society for Public Health

FRSPS Fellow, Remote Sensing and Photogrammetry Society
FRSSA Fellow, Royal Scottish Society for the Arts
FRSSAf Fellow, Royal Society of South Africa
FRSTM&H Fellow, Royal Society of Tropical Medicine and Hygiene
FRSV Fellow, Royal Society of Victoria
FRTPI Fellow, Royal Town Planning Institute
FRTS Fellow, Royal Television Society
FRUSI Fellow, Royal United Services Institute
FRVA Fellow, Rating and Valuation Association (*now see* IRRV)
FRVC Fellow, Royal Veterinary College
FRWCMD Fellow, Royal Welsh College of Music and Drama
FRZSScot Fellow, Royal Zoological Society of Scotland
FS Field Security
fs Graduate, Royal Air Force Staff College
FSA Fellow, Society of Antiquaries; Financial Services Authority
FSAC Fast Stream Assessment Centre
FSACOG Fellow, South African College of Obstetricians and Gynaecologists
FSAE Fellow, Society of Automotive Engineers; Fellow, Society of Art Education
FSAI Fellow, Society of Architectural Illustrators
FSArc Fellow, Society of Architects (merged with the RIBA 1952)
FSaRS Fellow, Safety and Reliability Society
FSAScot Fellow, Society of Antiquaries of Scotland
FSASM Fellow, South Australian School of Mines
FSB Fellow, Society of Biology (*now see* FRSB)
fsc Foreign Staff College
FSCA Fellow, Society of Company and Commercial Accountants
FScotvec Fellow, Scottish Vocational Education Council
FSCRE Fellow, Scottish Council for Research in Education
FSDC Fellow, Society of Dyers and Colourists
FSE Fellow, Society of Engineers; Fellow, Society for the Environment
FSEDA Fellow, Staff and Higher Educational Development Association
FSES Fellow, Society for Educational Studies
FSG Fellow, Society of Genealogists
FSGD Fellow, Society of Garden Designers
FSGT Fellow, Society of Glass Technology
FSI Fellow, Chartered Surveyors' Institution (*now see* FRICS); Fellow, Securities Institute (later Securities & Investment Institute, *now see* FCSI)
FSIA Fellow, Securities Institute of Australia
FSIAD Fellow, Society of Industrial Artists and Designers (*now see* FCSD)
FSIP Fellow, Society of Investment Professionals
FSLCOG Fellow, Sri Lankan College of Obstetrics and Gynaecology
FSLCPaed Fellow, Sri Lanka College of Paediatricians
FSLTC Fellow, Society of Leather Technologists and Chemists
FSMA Fellow, Incorporated Sales Managers' Association (later FInstMSM, then FInstM)
FSMC Freeman of the Spectacle-Makers' Company
FSME Fellow, Society of Manufacturing Engineers
FSMPTE Fellow, Society of Motion Picture and Television Engineers (US)
FSMS Fellow, Strategic Management Society
FSNAD Fellow, Society of Numismatic Artists and Designers
FSNAME Fellow, American Society of Naval Architects and Marine Engineers
FSOE Fellow, Society of Operations Engineers
FSOGC Fellow, Society of Obstetricians and Gynaecologists of Canada
FSPI Fellow, Society of Practitioners of Insolvency
FSQA Fellow, Scottish Qualifications Authority
FSRHE Fellow, Society for Research into Higher Education
FSRP Fellow, Society for Radiological Protection
FSS Fellow, Royal Statistical Society
FSSI Fellow, Society of Scribes and Illuminators
FSTD Fellow, Society of Typographic Designers
FSVA Fellow, Incorporated Society of Valuers and Auctioneers (*now see* RICS)
FT Financial Times
FTC Flying Training Command; Full Technological Certificate, City and Guilds of London Institute
FTCD Fellow, Trinity College, Dublin
FTCL Fellow, Trinity College of Music, London
FTI Fellow, Textile Institute
FTII Fellow, Chartered Institute (*formerly* Incorporated Institute, then Institute) of Taxation
FTMA Fellow, Telecommunications Managers Association (*now see* FCMA)
FTS Fellow, Australian Academy of Technological Sciences and Engineering (*now see* FTSE); Flying Training School; Fellow, Tourism Society
FTSE Fellow, Australian Academy of Technological Sciences and Engineering
FUCEB Fellow, University of Central England in Birmingham
FUCUA Federation of University Conservative and Unionist Associations (*now see* FCS)
FUMIST Fellow, University of Manchester Institute of Science and Technology
FVCM Fellow, Victoria College of Music
FVRDE Fighting Vehicles Research and Development Establishment
FWAAS Fellow, World Academy of Arts and Sciences
FWACP Fellow, West African College of Physicians
FWAG Farming and Wildlife Advisory Group
FWCB Fellow, Worshipful Company of Blacksmiths
FWCMD Fellow, Welsh College of Music and Drama (*now see* FRWCMD)
FWeldI Fellow, Welding Institute
FWSOM Fellow, Institute of Practitioners in Work Study, Organisation and Method (*now see* FMS)
FZS Fellow, Zoological Society
FZSScot Fellow, Zoological Society of Scotland (*now see* FRZSScot)

G

GA Geologists' Association; Gaelic Athletic (Club); Georgia (postal)
Ga Georgia
GAI Guild of Architectural Ironmongers
GAICD Graduate Member, Australian Institute of Company Directors
GAP Gap Activity Projects
GAPAN Guild of Air Pilots and Air Navigators
GATT General Agreement on Tariffs and Trade (*now* World Trade Organisation)
GB Great Britain
GBA Governing Bodies Association
GBE Knight or Dame Grand Cross, Order of the British Empire
GBGSA Governing Bodies of Girls' Schools Association (*formerly* Association of Governing Bodies of Girls' Public Schools)
GBM Grand Bauhinia Medal (Hong Kong)
GBS Gold Bauhinia Star (Hong Kong)
GBSM Graduate of Birmingham and Midland Institute School of Music
GC George Cross
GCB Knight or Dame Grand Cross, Order of the Bath
GCBS General Council of British Shipping
GCC General Chiropractic Council
GCCC Gonville and Caius College, Cambridge
GCCF Grand Commander, Companion Order of Freedom (Zambia)
GCCS Government Code and Cipher School
GCFR Grand Commander, Order of the Federal Republic of Nigeria
GCH Knight Grand Cross, Hanoverian Order
GCHQ Government Communications Headquarters
GCIE Knight Grand Commander, Order of the Indian Empire
GCL Grand Chief, Order of Logohu (Papua New Guinea)
GCLJ Grand Cross, Order of St Lazarus of Jerusalem
GCLM Grand Commander, Order of the Legion of Merit of Rhodesia
GCM Gold Crown of Merit (Barbados)
GCMG Knight or Dame Grand Cross, Order of St Michael and St George
GCMJ Knight or Dame Grand Cross, Supreme Military Order of the Temple of Jerusalem
GCON Grand Cross, Order of the Niger
GCSE General Certificate of Secondary Education
GCSG Knight Grand Cross, Order of St Gregory the Great
GCSI Knight Grand Commander, Order of the Star of India
GCSJ Knight Grand Cross of Justice, Sovereign Order of St John of Jerusalem (Knights Hospitaller)
GCSK Grand Commander, Order of the Star and Key of the Indian Ocean (Mauritius)
GCSL Grand Cross, Order of St Lucia
GCStG Knight Grand Cross, Order of St George
GCStJ Bailiff or Dame Grand Cross, Most Venerable Order of the Hospital of St John of Jerusalem
GCVO Knight or Dame Grand Cross, Royal Victorian Order
gd grand-daughter
GDBA Guide Dogs for the Blind Association
GDC General Dental Council
Gdns Gardens
GDR German Democratic Republic
GDST Girls' Day School Trust
Gen. General
Ges. Gesellschaft
GFD Geophysical Fluid Dynamics
GFS Girls' Friendly Society
ggd great-grand-daughter
ggs great-grandson
GGSM Graduate in Music, Guildhall School of Music and Drama
GHQ General Headquarters
Gib. Gibraltar
GIMechE Graduate, Institution of Mechanical Engineers
GIS Geographic Information Systems
GKT Guy's, King's and St Thomas' (Medical and Dental School of King's College London)
GL Grand Lodge
GLA Greater London Authority
GLAA Greater London Arts Association (*now see* GLAB)
GLAB Greater London Arts Board
GLC Greater London Council
Glos Gloucestershire
GM George Medal; Grand Medal (Ghana); genetically modified
GMB (Union for) General, Municipal, Boilermakers

GMBATU General, Municipal, Boilermakers and Allied Trades Union (*now see* GMB)
GmbH Gesellschaft mit beschränkter Haftung
GMBPS Graduate Member, British Psychological Society
GMC General Medical Council; Guild of Memorial Craftsmen; General Management Course (Henley)
GMH Gibraltar Medallion of Honour
GMWU General and Municipal Workers' Union (later GMBATU; *now see* GMB)
GNC General Nursing Council
GNVQ General National Vocational Qualification
GNZM Knight or Dame Grand Companion, New Zealand Order of Merit
GOC General Officer Commanding
GOC-in-C General Officer Commanding-in-Chief
GOE General Ordination Examination
GOMLJ Grand Officer of Merit, Order of St Lazarus of Jerusalem
GOQ Grand Officer, National Order of Quebec
GOSK Grand Officer, Order of the Star and Key of the Indian Ocean (Mauritius)
Gov. Governor
Govt Government
GP General Practitioner; Grand Prix
Gp Group
GPDST Girls' Public Day School Trust (*now see* GDST)
GPMU Graphical, Paper and Media Union
GPO General Post Office
GR General Reconaissance
Gr. Greek
GRNCM Graduate of the Royal Northern College of Music
GRSM Graduate of the Royal Schools of Music
GS General Staff; Grammar School
g s grandson
GSA Girls' Schools Association
GSD Gibraltar Social Democrats
GSM General Service Medal; (Member of) Guildhall School of Music and Drama
GSMD Guildhall School of Music and Drama
GSO General Staff Officer
GTCL Graduate, Trinity College of Music
GTS General Theological Seminary (New York)
GWR Great Western Railway

H

HA Historical Association; Health Authority
HAA Heavy Anti-Aircraft
HAC Honourable Artillery Company
HACAS Housing Association Consultancy and Advisory Service
Hants Hampshire
HAT Housing Action Trust
HBM His (or Her) Britannic Majesty (Majesty's); Humming Bird Gold Medal (Trinidad)
hc *honoris causa* (honorary)
HCA Hospital Corporation of America
HCF Honorary Chaplain to the Forces
HCIMA Hotel, Catering and International (*formerly* Institutional) Management Association
HCO Higher Clerical Officer
HCSC Higher Command and Staff Course
HDA Hawkesbury Diploma in Agriculture (Australia); Health Development Agency
HDD Higher Dental Diploma
HDE Higher Diploma in Education
HDFA Higher Diploma in Fine Art
HDipEd Higher Diploma in Education
HE His (or Her) Excellency; His Eminence; Higher Education
HEA Health Education Authority (later HDA)
HEC Ecole des Hautes Etudes Commerciales; Higher Education Corporation
HEFCE Higher Education Funding Council for England
HEFCW Higher Education Funding Council for Wales
HEH His (or Her) Exalted Highness
Heir-pres. Heir-presumptive
HEO Higher Executive Officer
HEQC Higher Education Quality Council (*now see* QAA)
HERDA-SW Higher Education Regional Development Association - South West
HERO Higher Education Research Opportunities
Herts Hertfordshire
HFEA Human Fertilisation and Embryology Authority
HG Home Guard
HGTAC Home Grown Timber Advisory Committee
HH His (or Her) Highness; His Holiness; Member, Hesketh Hubbard Art Society
HHA Historic Houses Association
HHD Doctor of Humanities (US)
HI Hawaii (postal)
HIH His (or Her) Imperial Highness
HIlH His (or Her) Illustrious Highness
HIM His (or Her) Imperial Majesty
HIV Human Immunodeficiency Virus
HJ Hilal-e-Jurat (Pakistan)
HKIA Hong Kong Institute of Architects
HKSAR Hong Kong Special Administrative Region
HLD Doctor of Humane Letters
HLF Heritage Lottery Fund
HLI Highland Light Infantry
HM His (or Her) Majesty, or Majesty's
HMA Head Masters' Association
HMAS His (or Her) Majesty's Australian Ship
HMC Headmasters' and Headmistresses' (*formerly* Headmasters') Conference; Hospital Management Committee
HMCIC His (or Her) Majesty's Chief Inspector of Constabulary
HMCS His (or Her) Majesty's Canadian Ship
HMHS His (or Her) Majesty's Hospital Ship
HMI His (or Her) Majesty's Inspector
HMMTB His (or Her) Majesty's Motor Torpedo Boat
HMNZS His (or Her) Majesty's New Zealand Ship
HMOCS His (or Her) Majesty's Overseas Civil Service
HMP His (or Her) Majesty's Prison
HMRC His (or Her) Majesty's Revenue and Customs
HMS His (or Her) Majesty's Ship
HMSO His (or Her) Majesty's Stationery Office
HNC Higher National Certificate
HND Higher National Diploma
H of C House of Commons
H of L House of Lords
Hon. Honourable; Honorary
HPA Health Protection Agency
HPk Hilal-e-Pakistan
HPV Human Papilloma Virus
HQ Headquarters
HQA Hilali-Quaid-i-Azam (Pakistan)
HR Human Resources
HRA Horseracing Regulatory Authority
HRGI Honorary Member, The Royal Glasgow Institute of the Fine Arts
HRH His (or Her) Royal Highness
HRHA Honorary Member, Royal Hibernian Academy
HRI Honorary Member, Royal Institute of Painters in Water Colours
HROI Honorary Member, Royal Institute of Oil Painters
HRSA Honorary Member, Royal Scottish Academy
HRSW Honorary Member, Royal Scottish Water Colour Society
HRUA Hon. Member, Royal Ulster Academy
HSC Health and Safety Commission; Higher School Certificate
HSE Health and Safety Executive
HSH His (or Her) Serene Highness
HSO Higher Scientific Officer
HSS Health and Social Services
Hum. Humanity; Humanities (Classics)
Hunts Huntingdonshire
HVCA Heating and Ventilating Contractors' Association
HVCert Health Visitor's Certificate

I

I Island; Ireland
IA Indian Army; Iowa (postal)
IAA International Academy of Architecture
IAAF International Association of Athletics Federations (formerly International Amateur Athletic Federation)
IABSE International Association of Bridge and Structural Engineers
IAC Indian Armoured Corps; Institute of Amateur Cinematographers
IACP International Association of Chiefs of Police
IACR Institute of Arable Crops Research
IADB Inter American Development Bank
IADR International Association for Dental Research
IAEA International Atomic Energy Agency
IAF Indian Air Force; Indian Auxiliary Force
IAHS International Association of Hydrological Sciences
IAM Institute of Advanced Motorists; Institute of Aviation Medicine
IAMAS International Association of Meteorology and Atmospheric Sciences
IAMC Indian Army Medical Corps
IAML International Association of Music Libraries
IAO Incorporated Association of Organists
IAOC Indian Army Ordnance Corps
IAPS Independent Association of Prep Schools (*formerly* Incorporated Association of Preparatory Schools)
IAPSO International Association for the Physical Sciences of the Oceans
IARO Indian Army Reserve of Officers
IAS Indian Administrative Service; Institute for Advanced Studies; International Academy of Science
IASC International Arctic Science Committee
IASE Institute of Advanced Studies in Education
IASPEI International Association of Seismology and Physics of the Earth's Interior

IATA International Air Transport Association
IATUL International Association of Technological University Libraries
IAU International Astronomical Union
IAVCEI International Assembly of Volcanology and Chemistry of the Earth's Interior
IAWPRC International Association on Water Pollution Research and Control
ib. or ibid. *ibidem* (in the same place)
IBA Independent Broadcasting Authority; International Bar Association
IBBY International Board for Books for Young People
IBCA International Braille Chess Association
IBG Institute of British Geographers (now part of RGS)
IBRD International Bank for Reconstruction and Development (World Bank)
IBRO International Bank Research Organisation; International Brain Research Organisation
IBTE Institution of British Telecommunications Engineers
IBVM Institute of the Blessed Virgin Mary
i/c in charge; in command
ICA Institute of Contemporary Arts; Institute of Chartered Accountants in England and Wales (*now see* ICAEW)
ICAC Independent Commission Against Corruption, Hong Kong
ICAEW Institute of Chartered Accountants in England and Wales
ICAI Institute of Chartered Accountants in Ireland
ICAO International Civil Aviation Organization
ICAS Institute of Chartered Accountants of Scotland
ICBP International Council for Bird Preservation
ICC International Chamber of Commerce; International Cricket Council (*formerly* International Cricket Conference)
ICCA International Council for Commercial Arbitration
ICCROM International Centre for Conservation at Rome
ICD *Iuris Canonici Doctor* (Doctor of Canon Law); Independence Commemorative Decoration (Rhodesia)
ICD.D Institute of Corporate Directors Director (Canada)
ICE Institution of Civil Engineers
ICED International Council for Educational Development
ICEF International Federation of Chemical, Energy and General Workers' Unions
ICES International Council for the Exploration of the Sea
ICF International Federation of Chemical and General Workers' Unions (*now see* ICEF)
ICFC Industrial and Commercial Finance Corporation (later part of Investors in Industry)
ICFR International Centre for Financial Regulation
ICFTU International Confederation of Free Trade Unions
ICH International Conference on Harmonisation
ICHCA International Cargo Handling Co-ordination Association
IChemE Institution of Chemical Engineers
ICI Imperial Chemical Industries
ICJ International Commission of Jurists
ICL International Computers Ltd
ICM International Confederation of Midwives
ICMA Institute of Cost and Management Accountants (*now see* CIMA)
ICME International Commission for Mathematical Education
ICNL International Center for Not for Profit Law
ICOM International Council of Museums
ICOMOS International Council on Monuments and Sites
ICorrST Institution of Corrosion Science and Technology (*now see* ICorr)
ICPO International Criminal Police Organization (Interpol)
ICRC International Committee of the Red Cross
ICREA Institució Catalana de Recerca i Estudis Avançats
ICRF Imperial Cancer Research Fund (*now see* CRUK)
ICS Indian Civil Service
ICSA Institute of Chartered Secretaries and Administrators
ICSC International Council of Shopping Centres
ICSD International Council for Scientific Development
ICSID International Council of Societies of Industrial Design; International Centre for Settlement of Investment Disputes
ICSM Imperial College School of Medicine
ICSTIS Independent Committee for Supervision of Telephone Information Services
ICSTM Imperial College of Science, Technology and Medicine, London
ICSU International Council for Science (*formerly* International Council of Scientific Unions)
ICT International Computers and Tabulators Ltd (later ICL); Information and Communications Technology
ID Independence Decoration (Rhodesia); Idaho (postal)
IDA International Development Association
IDB Internal Drainage Board; Industrial Development Board
IDC Imperial Defence College (*now see* RCDS); Inter-Diocesan Certificate
idc completed a course at, or served for a year on the Staff of, the Imperial Defence College (*now see* rcds)
IDDA Interior Decorators and Designers Association (*now see* BIDA)
IDeA Improvement and Development Agency for Local Government
IDRC International Development Research Centre
IDS Institute of Development Studies; Industry Department for Scotland
IEA Institute of Economic Affairs
IEC International Electrotechnical Commission
IED Institution of Engineering Designers; improvised explosive device
IEE Institution of Electrical Engineers (*now see* IET)
IEEE Institute of Electrical and Electronics Engineers (NY)
IEEIE Institution of Electrical and Electronics Incorporated Engineers (later IIE)
IEETE Institution of Electrical and Electronics Technician Engineers (later IIE)
IEI Institution of Engineers of Ireland
IEIE Institution of Electronics and Electrical Incorporated Engineers (later IIE)
IEMA Institute of Environmental Management Assessment
IEME Inspectorate of Electrical and Mechanical Engineering
IEng Incorporated Engineer
IERE Institution of Electronic and Radio Engineers
IES Indian Educational Service; Institution of Engineers and Shipbuilders in Scotland; International Electron Paramagnetic Resonance Society
IET Institution of Engineering and Technology
IExpE Institute of Explosives Engineers
IFAC International Federation of Automatic Control; International Federation of Accountants
IFAD International Fund for Agricultural Development (UNO)
IFAW International Fund for Animal Welfare
IFBWW International Federation of Building Woodworkers
IFC International Finance Corporation
IFIAS International Federation of Institutes of Advanced Study
IFIP International Federation for Information Processing
IFLA International Federation of Library Associations; Institute of Family Law Arbitrators
IFMGA (Member of) International Federation of Mountain Guides Associations
IFOR Implementation Force
IFORS International Federation of Operational Research Societies
IFPI International Federation of the Phonographic Industry
IFRA World Press Research Association
IFS Irish Free State; Indian Forest Service; Institute for Fiscal Studies
IG Instructor in Gunnery
IGasE Institution of Gas Engineers
IGCSE International General Certificate of Secondary Education
IGPP Institute of Geophysics and Planetary Physics
IGS Independent Grammar School
IGU International Geographical Union; International Gas Union
IHA Institute of Health Service Administrators (later IHSM)
IHBC (Member of) Institute of Historic Building Conservation
IHM Institute of Healthcare Management
IHospE Institute of Hospital Engineering
IHSM Institute of Health Services Management (*now see* IHM)
IHVE Institution of Heating and Ventilating Engineers (later CIBS)
IIE Institution of Incorporated Engineers (*now see* IET)
IIEB Institut International d'Etudes Bancaires
IIExE Institution of Incorporated Executive Engineers
IILS International Institute for Labour Studies
IIM Institution of Industrial Managers
IInfSc Institute of Information Scientists
IIRSM International Institute of Risk and Safety Management
IIS International Institute of Sociology
IISI International Iron and Steel Institute
IISS International Institute of Strategic Studies
IIT Indian Institute of Technology
IL Illinois (postal)
ILA International Law Association
ILAC International Laboratory Accreditation Co-operation
ILAM Institute of Leisure and Amenity Management
ILEA Inner London Education Authority
Ill Illinois
ILM Institute of Leadership and Management
ILO International Labour Office; International Labour Organisation
ILP Independent Labour Party
ILR Independent Local Radio; International Labour Review
ILT Institute for Learning and Teaching in Higher Education
ILTM Member, Institute for Learning and Teaching in Higher Education (*now see* FHEA)
IM Individual Merit
IMA International Music Association; Institute of Mathematics and its Applications
IMC Instrument Meteorological Conditions
IMCB International Management Centre from Buckingham
IMCO Inter-Governmental Maritime Consultative Organization (*now see* IMO)
IME Institute of Medical Ethics
IMechE Institution of Mechanical Engineers
IMechIE Institution of Mechanical Incorporated Engineers (later IIE)
IMEDE Institut pour l'Etude des Méthodes de Direction de l'Entreprise
IMF International Monetary Fund
IMGTechE Institution of Mechanical and General Technician Engineers
IMinE Institution of Mining Engineers
IMM Institution of Mining and Metallurgy (*now see* IMMM)
IMMM Institute of Materials, Minerals and Mining

IMO International Maritime Organization
Imp. Imperial
IMRO Investment Management Regulatory Organisation
IMS Indian Medical Service; Institute of Management Services; International Military Staff
IMTA Institute of Municipal Treasurers and Accountants (*now see* CIPFA)
IMU International Mathematical Union
IMunE Institution of Municipal Engineers (now amalgamated with Institution of Civil Engineers)
IN Indian Navy; Indiana (postal)
INASFMH International Sports Association for People with Mental Handicap
Inc. Incorporated
INCA International Newspaper Colour Association
Incog. Incognito
Ind. Independent
Inf. Infantry
INFORM Information Network Focus on New Religious Movements
INFORMS Institute for Operations Research and the Management Sciences
INSA Indian National Science Academy
INSEA International Society for Education through Art
INSEAD or **Insead** Institut Européen d'Administration des Affaires
Insp. Inspector
INSS Institute of Nuclear Systems Safety
Inst. Institute
Instn Institution
InstSMM Institute of Sales and Marketing Management
INTELSAT International Telecommunications Satellite Organisation
IOC International Olympic Committee; Intergovernmental Oceanographic Commission
IOCD International Organisation for Chemical Science in Development
IoD Institute of Directors
IODE Imperial Order of the Daughters of the Empire
I of M Isle of Man
IOM Isle of Man; Indian Order of Merit
IOP Institute of Painters in Oil Colours
IOSCO International Organisation of Securities Commissions
IOSH Institution of Occupational Safety and Health
IOTA (Fellow of) Institute of Transport Administration
IoW Isle of Wight
IP Intellectual Property
IPA International Publishers' Association
IPC International Property Corporation
IPCIS International Institute for Practitioners in Credit Insurance and Surety
IPCS Institution of Professional Civil Servants
IPE International Petroleum Exchange
IPFA Member or Associate, Chartered Institute of Public Finance and Accountancy (*now see* CPFA)
IPHE Institution of Public Health Engineers (later IWEM)
IPI International Press Institute; Institute of Patentees and Inventors
IPM Institute of Personnel Management (later CIPD)
IPPA Independent Programme Producers' Association
IPPF International Planned Parenthood Federation
IPPR Institute for Public Policy Research
IPPS Institute of Physics and The Physical Society
IPR Institute of Public Relations (*now see* CIPR)
IPRA International Public Relations Association
IProdE Institution of Production Engineers (later Institution of Manufacturing Engineering)
IPS Indian Police Service; Indian Political Service; Institute of Purchasing and Supply
IPSM Institute of Public Sector Managers
IPSO Independent Press Standards Organisation
IPU Inter-Parliamentary Union
IRA Irish Republican Army
IRAD Institute for Research on Animal Diseases
IRC Industrial Reorganization Corporation; Interdisciplinary Research Centre
IRCAM Institute for Research and Co-ordination in Acoustics and Music
IRCert Industrial Relations Certificate
IREE(Aust) Institution of Radio and Electronics Engineers (Australia)
IRI Institution of the Rubber Industry (*now see* PRI)
IRO International Refugee Organization
IRPA International Radiation Protection Association
IRRV (Fellow/Member of) Institute of Revenues, Rating and Valuation
IRTE Institute of Road Transport Engineers
IS International Society of Sculptors, Painters and Gravers; Information Systems
Is Island(s)
ISAA International Spill Response Accreditation Association
ISABE International Society for Air Breathing Engines
ISAF International Sailing Federation; International Security Assistance Force
ISAKOS International Society for Arthroscopy and Knee Surgery
ISBA Incorporated Society of British Advertisers
ISC Imperial Service College, Haileybury; Indian Staff Corps; Independent Schools Council
ISCis Independent Schools Council Information Service
ISCM International Society for Contemporary Music
ISCO Independent Schools Careers Organisation
ISE Indian Service of Engineers
ISI International Statistical Institute; Independent Schools Inspectorate
ISIS Independent Schools Information Service (*see now* ISCis)
ISJC Independent Schools Joint Council (*now see* ISC)
ISM Incorporated Society of Musicians
ISMAR International Society of Magnetic Resonance
ISME International Society for Musical Education
ISMP International Senior Management Program
ISO Imperial Service Order; International Organization for Standardization
ISPRS International Society for Photogrammetry and Remote Sensing
ISSA International Social Security Association
ISTAR Intelligence, Surveillance, Target Acquisition and Reconnaissance
ISTC Iron and Steel Trades Confederation; Institute of Scientific and Technical Communicators
ISTD Imperial Society of Teachers of Dancing; Institute for the Study and Treatment of Delinquency
IStructE Institution of Structural Engineers
ISVA Incorporated Society of Valuers and Auctioneers
IT Information Technology; Indian Territory (US)
It. or **Ital.** Italian
ITA Independent Television Authority (later IBA)
ITAB Information Technology Advisory Board
ITB Industry Training Board
ITC International Trade Centre; Independent Television Commission
ITCA Independent Television Association (*formerly* Independent Television Companies Association Ltd)
ITDG Intermediate Technology Development Group
ITF International Transport Workers' Federation; International Tennis Federation
ITN Independent Television News
ITO International Trade Organization
ITSA Information Technology Services Agency
ITU International Telecommunication Union
ITUC International Trade Union Confederation
ITV Independent Television
ITVA International Television Association
IUA International Union of Architects
IUB International Union of Biochemistry (*now see* IUBMB)
IUBMB International Union of Biochemistry and Molecular Biology
IUC Inter-University Council for Higher Education Overseas (*now see* IUPC)
IUCN International Union for Conservation of Nature (*formerly* International Union for the Conservation of Nature and Natural Resources, then World Conservation Union)
IUF International Union of Food, Agricultural, Hotel, Restaurant, Catering, Tobacco and Allied Workers' Associations
IUGG International Union of Geodesy & Geophysics
IUGS International Union of Geological Sciences
IUHPS International Union of the History and Philosophy of Science
IULA International Union of Local Authorities
IUPAB International Union of Pure and Applied Biophysics
IUPAC International Union of Pure and Applied Chemistry
IUPAP International Union of Pure and Applied Physics
IUPC Inter-University and Polytechnic Council for Higher Education Overseas
IUPS International Union of Physiological Sciences
IUSSP International Union for the Scientific Study of Population
IUTAM International Union of Theoretical and Applied Mechanics
IVF In-vitro Fertilisation
IVS International Voluntary Service
IWA Inland Waterways Association
IWEM Institution of Water and Environmental Management (*now see* CIWEM)
IWES Institution of Water Engineers and Scientists (later IWEM)
IWGC Imperial War Graves Commission (*now see* CWGC)
IWM Institution of Works Managers (*now see* IIM)
IWO Institution of Water Officers
IWPC Institute of Water Pollution Control (later IWEM)
IWSA International Water Supply Association
IWSOM Institute of Practitioners in Work Study Organisation and Methods (*now see* IMS)
IWSP Institute of Work Study Practitioners (*now see* IMS)
IYRU International Yacht Racing Union (*now see* ISAF)
IZ I Zingari

J

JA Judge Advocate
JACT Joint Association of Classical Teachers
JAG Judge Advocate General
Jas James
JCB *Juris Canonici* (or *Civilis*) *Baccalaureus* (Bachelor of Canon (or Civil) Law)
JCR Junior Common Room

JCS Journal of the Chemical Society
JCD *Juris Canonici* (or *Civilis*) *Doctor* (Doctor of Canon (or Civil) Law)
JCHMT Joint Committee on Higher Medical Training, Royal Medical Colleges (*now see* JRCPTB)
JCI Junior Chamber International
JCL *Juris Canonici* (or *Civilis*) *Licentiatus* (Licentiate in Canon (or Civil) Law)
JCO Joint Consultative Organisation (of AFRC, MAFF, and Department of Agriculture and Fisheries for Scotland)
JCPTGP Joint Committee on Postgraduate Training for General Practice
JD Doctor of Jurisprudence
jd *jure dignitatis* (by virtue of status)
JDipMA Joint Diploma in Management Accounting Services
JG Junior Grade
JILA Joint Institute for Laboratory Astrophysics
JInstE Junior Institution of Engineers (*now see* IMGTechE)
JISC Joint Information Systems Committee, Higher Education Funding Council
jl(s) journal(s)
JMB Joint Matriculation Board
JMN Johan Mangku Negara (Malaysia)
JMOTS Joint Maritime Operational Training Staff
JNCC Joint Nature Conservation Committee
Jno. or **Joh.** John
JP Justice of the Peace
Jr Junior
JRCPTB Joint Royal Colleges of Physicians Training Board
jsc qualified at a Junior Staff Course, or the equivalent, 1942-46
JSCSC Joint Services Command and Staff College
jscsc completed a course at Joint Services Command and Staff College
JSD Doctor of Juristic Science
JSDC Joint Service Defence College
jsdc completed a course at Joint Service Defence College
JSLO Joint Service Liaison Officer
JSLS Joint Services Liaison Staff
JSM Johan Setia Mahkota (Malaysia); Master of the Science of Jurisprudence
JSPS Japan Society for the Promotion of Science
JSSC Joint Services Staff College
jssc completed a course at Joint Services Staff College
JSU Joint Support Unit
jt, jtly joint, jointly
JUD *Juris Utriusque Doctor* (Doctor of Both Laws (Canon and Civil))
Jun. Junior
Jun.Opt. Junior Optime
JWS or **jws** Joint Warfare Staff

K

KA Knight of St Andrew, Order of Barbados
Kans Kansas
KAR King's African Rifles
KBE Knight Commander, Order of the British Empire
KC King's Counsel
KCB Knight Commander, Order of the Bath
KCC Commander, Order of the Crown, Belgium and Congo Free State
KCGSJ Knight Commander of Magisterial Grace, Order of St John of Jerusalem (Knights Hospitaller)
KCH King's College Hospital; Knight Commander, Hanoverian Order
KCHS Knight Commander, Order of the Holy Sepulchre
KCIE Knight Commander, Order of the Indian Empire
KCJSJ Knight Commander of Justice, Sovereign Order of St John of Jerusalem (Knights Hospitaller)
KCL King's College London
KCLJ Knight Commander, Order of St Lazarus of Jerusalem
KCMG Knight Commander, Order of St Michael and St George
KCN Knight Commander, Most Distinguished Order of the Nation (Antigua and Barbuda)
KCSA Knight Commander, Military Order of the Collar of St Agatha of Paternò
KCSG Knight Commander, Order of St Gregory the Great
KCSHS or **KC*HS** Knight Commander with Star, Order of the Holy Sepulchre
KCSI Knight Commander, Order of the Star of India
KCSJ Knight Commander, Sovereign Order of St John of Jerusalem (Knights Hospitaller)
KCSS Knight Commander, Order of St Silvester
KCVO Knight Commander, Royal Victorian Order
KDG King's Dragoon Guards
KEO King Edward's Own
KFOR Kosovo Force
KG Knight, Order of the Garter
KGB Komitet Gosudarstvennoi Bezopanosti (Committee of State Security, USSR)
KGCHS Knight Grand Cross, Order of the Holy Sepulchre
KGCSS Knight Grand Cross, Order of St Silvester
KGN Knight Grand Collar, Most Distinguished Order of the Nation (Antigua and Barbuda)
KGSJ Knight of Grace, Sovereign Order of St John of Jerusalem (Knights Hospitaller)
KGStJ Knight of Grace, Order of St John of Jerusalem (*now see* KStJ)
KH Knight, Hanoverian Order
KHC Hon. Chaplain to the King
KHDS Hon. Dental Surgeon to the King
KHNS Hon. Nursing Sister to the King
KHP Hon. Physician to the King
KHS Hon. Surgeon to the King; Knight, Order of the Holy Sepulchre
K-i-H Kaisar-i-Hind
KJSJ Knight of Justice, Sovereign Order of St John of Jerusalem (Knights Hospitaller)
KJStJ Knight of Justice, Order of St John of Jerusalem (*now see* KStJ)
KLJ Knight, Order of St Lazarus of Jerusalem
KM Knight of Malta
KMJ Knight, Supreme Military Order of the Temple of Jerusalem
KMLJ Knight of Merit, Order of St Lazarus of Jerusalem
KNH Knight Companion, Most Exalted Order of National Hero (Antigua and Barbuda)
KNZM Knight Companion, New Zealand Order of Merit
KOM Companion, National Order of Merit (Malta)
KORR King's Own Royal Regiment
KOSB King's Own Scottish Borderers
KOYLI King's Own Yorkshire Light Infantry
KP Knight, Order of St Patrick
KPM King's Police Medal
KrF Kristelig Folkeparti
KRRC King's Royal Rifle Corps
KS King's Scholar; Kansas (postal)
KSC Knight of St Columba
KSG Knight, Order of St Gregory the Great
KSJ Knight, Sovereign Order of St John of Jerusalem (Knights Hospitaller)
KSLI King's Shropshire Light Infantry
KSS Knight, Order of St Silvester
KStJ Knight, Most Venerable Order of the Hospital of St John of Jerusalem
KStJ(A) Associate Knight of Justice, Most Venerable Order of the Hospital of St John of Jerusalem
KT Knight, Order of the Thistle
Kt Knight
KUOM Companion of Honour, National Order of Merit (Malta)
KY Kentucky (postal)
Ky Kentucky

L

L Liberal
LA Los Angeles; Library Association; Liverpool Academy; Louisiana (postal)
La Louisiana
LAA Light Anti-Aircraft
Lab Labour
LAC London Athletic Club; Los Angeles County
LACSAB Local Authorities Conditions of Service Advisory Board
LAMDA London Academy of Music and Dramatic Art
LAMSAC Local Authorities' Management Services and Computer Committee
LAMTPI Legal Associate Member, Town Planning Institute (*now see* LMRTPI)
Lance-Corp. Lance-Corporal
Lancs Lancashire
LAPADA London & Provincial Antique Dealers' Association
LARSP Language Assessment, Remediation and Screening Procedure
Lautro Life Assurance and Unit Trust Regulatory Organisation
LBC London Broadcasting Company; London Borough Council
LBHI Licentiate, British Horological Institute
LBIPP Licentiate, British Institute of Professional Photography
LC Cross of Leo
LCA Licensed Companies Auditor
LCAD London Certificate in Art and Design (University of London)
LCC London County Council (later GLC)
LCCI London Chamber of Commerce and Industry
LCD Lord Chancellor's Department
LCh Licentiate in Surgery
LCJ Lord Chief Justice
LCL Licentiate of Canon Law
LCM (Member of) London College of Music and Media
LCP Licentiate, College of Preceptors
LCSP London and Counties Society of Physiologists
LCST Licentiate, College of Speech Therapists
LD Liberal and Democratic; Licentiate in Divinity
LDC Limited Duration Company (US)
LDDC London Docklands Development Corporation
LDiv Licentiate in Divinity
LDP Liberal Democratic Party (Japan)
Ldr Leader
LDS Licentiate in Dental Surgery

LDV Local Defence Volunteers
LEA Local Education Authority
LEAD Leadership in Environment and Development
LEADR Lawyers Engaged in Alternative Dispute Resolution
LEDU Local Enterprise Development Unit
LEP Local Ecumenical Project
LEPRA British Leprosy Relief Association
LèsL Licencié ès lettres
LèsSc Licencié ès Sciences
LG Lady Companion, Order of the Garter
LGA Local Government Association
LGBT Lesbian, gay, bisexual and transgender
LGBTI Lesbian, gay, bisexual, transgender and intersex
LGSM Licentiate, Guildhall School of Music and Drama
LGTB Local Government Training Board
LH Light Horse
LHD *Literarum Humaniorum Doctor* (Doctor of Literature)
LHSM Licentiate, Institute of Health Services Management
LI Light Infantry; Long Island
LIBA Lloyd's Insurance Brokers' Association
Lib Dem Liberal Democrat
LIBER Ligue des Bibliothèques Européennes de Recherche
LicMed Licentiate in Medicine
Lieut Lieutenant
LIFFE London International Financial Futures and Options Exchange
LIFT Local Improvement Finance Trust
LIMA Licentiate, Institute of Mathematics and its Applications; International Licensing Industry Merchandisers' Association
Lincs Lincolnshire
LIOB Licentiate, Institute of Building
LISTD Licentiate, Imperial Society of Teachers of Dancing
Lit. Literature; Literary
LitD Doctor of Literature; Doctor of Letters
Lit.Hum. *Literae Humaniores* (Classics)
LittD Doctor of Literature; Doctor of Letters
LJ Lord Justice
LLAM Licentiate, London Academy of Music and Dramatic Art
LLB Bachelor of Laws
LLC Limited Liability Company
LLCM Licentiate, London College of Music
LLD Doctor of Laws
LLL Licentiate in Laws
LLM Master of Laws
LLP Limited Liability Partnership
LLSC Local Learning and Skills Council
LM Licentiate in Midwifery
LMBC Lady Margaret Boat Club
LMC Local Medical Committee
LMCC Licentiate, Medical Council of Canada
LMed Licentiate in Medicine
LMH Lady Margaret Hall, Oxford
LMR London Midland Region (BR)
LMS London, Midland and Scottish Railway; London Missionary Society; London Mathematical Society
LMSSA Licentiate in Medicine and Surgery, Society of Apothecaries
LMRTPI Legal Member, Royal Town Planning Institute
LNat Liberal National
LNER London and North Eastern Railway
LOB Location of Offices Bureau
LOCOG London Organising Committee of the Olympic and Paralympic Games
L of C Library of Congress; Lines of Communication
LP Limited Partnership
LPh Licentiate in Philosophy
LPO London Philharmonic Orchestra
LPTB London Passenger Transport Board (later LTE)
LRAD Licentiate, Royal Academy of Dancing
LRAM Licentiate, Royal Academy of Music
LRCP Licentiate, Royal College of Physicians, London
LRCPE Licentiate, Royal College of Physicians, Edinburgh
LRCPI Licentiate, Royal College of Physicians of Ireland
LRCPSGlas Licentiate, Royal College of Physicians and Surgeons of Glasgow
LRCS Licentiate, Royal College of Surgeons of England
LRCSE Licentiate, Royal College of Surgeons, Edinburgh
LRCSI Licentiate, Royal College of Surgeons in Ireland
LRelSc Licentiate in Religious Sciences
LRFPS(G) Licentiate, Royal Faculty of Physicians and Surgeons, Glasgow (*now see* LRCPSGlas)
LRIBA Licentiate, Royal Institute of British Architects (*now see* RIBA)
LRPS Licentiate, Royal Photographic Society
LRSM Licentiate, Royal Schools of Music
LRT London Regional Transport
LSA Licentiate, Society of Apothecaries; Licence in Agricultural Sciences
LSC Learning and Skills Council
LSE London School of Economics and Political Science
LSHTM London School of Hygiene and Tropical Medicine
LSO London Symphony Orchestra
LSS Licentiate in Sacred Scripture
Lt Lieutenant; Light
LT Lady, Order of the Thistle; London Transport (later LRT); Licentiate in Teaching
LTA Lawn Tennis Association
LTB London Transport Board (later LTE)
LTCL Licentiate of Trinity College of Music, London
Lt Col Lieutenant Colonel
LTE London Transport Executive (later LRT)
Lt Gen. Lieutenant General
LTh Licentiate in Theology
LTS London Topographical Society
LU Liberal Unionist
LUOTC London University Officers' Training Corps
LVO Lieutenant, Royal Victorian Order (*formerly* MVO (Fourth Class))
LWT London Weekend Television
LXX Septuagint

M

M Marquess; Member; Monsieur
m married
MA Master of Arts; Military Assistant; Massachusetts (postal)
MAA Manufacturers' Agents Association of Great Britain
MAAF Mediterranean Allied Air Forces
MAAT Member, Association of Accounting Technicians
MACE Member, Australian College of Education; Member, Association of Conference Executives
MACI Member, American Concrete Institute
MACM Member, Association of Computing Machines
MACS Member, American Chemical Society
MADO Member, Association of Dispensing Opticians
MAE Member, Academia Europaea
MAEE Marine Aircraft Experimental Establishment
MAF Ministry of Agriculture and Fisheries
MAFF Ministry of Agriculture, Fisheries and Food
MAHL Master of Arts in Hebrew Letters
MAI *Magister in Arte Ingeniaria* (Master of Engineering)
MAIAA Member, American Institute of Aeronautics and Astronautics
MAIBC Member, Architectural Institute of British Columbia
MAICD Member, Australian Institute of Company Directors
Maj. Gen. Major General
MALD Master of Arts in Law and Diplomacy
Man Manitoba
M&A Mergers and Acquisitions
MAO Master of Obstetric Art
MAOT Member, Association of Occupational Therapists
MAOU Member, American Ornithologists' Union
MAP Ministry of Aircraft Production
MAPM Member, Association for Project Management
MAppSc Master of Applied Science
MAPsS Member, Australian Psychological Society
MARAC Member, Australasian Register of Agricultural Consultants
MArch Master of Architecture
MARIS Multi-State Aquatic Resources Information System
Marq. Marquess
MAS Minimal Access Surgery
MASc Master of Applied Science
MASCE Member, American Society of Civil Engineers
MASME Member, American Society of Mechanical Engineers
Mass Massachusetts
MAT Master of Arts and Teaching (US)
MATh Master of Arts in Theology
Math. Mathematics; Mathematical
MAusIMM Member, Australasian Institute of Mining and Metallurgy
MB Medal of Bravery (Canada); Bachelor of Medicine; Manitoba (postal)
MBA Master of Business Administration
MBASW Member, British Association of Social Workers
MBC Metropolitan/Municipal Borough Council
MBCS Member, British Computer Society
MBE Member, Order of the British Empire
MBES Member, Biological Engineering Society
MBFR Mutual and Balanced Force Reductions (negotiations)
MBHI Member, British Horological Institute
MBIFD Member, British Institute of Funeral Directors
MBII Member, British Institute of Innkeeping
MBIID Member, British Institute of Interior Design
MBIM Member, British Institute of Management (later MIMgt)
MBKS Member, British Kinematograph Society (*now see* MBKSTS)
MBKSTS Member, British Kinematograph, Sound and Television Society
MBL Master of Business Leadership
MBOU Member, British Ornithologists' Union
MBPsS Graduate Member, British Psychological Society
MBritIRE Member, British Institution of Radio Engineers (later MIERE)
MBS Member, Building Societies Institute (*now see* MCBSI)

MBSc Master of Business Science
MC Military Cross; Missionaries of Charity
MCAM Member, CAM Foundation
MCB Master in Clinical Biochemistry; Muslim Council of Britain
MCBSI Member, Chartered Building Societies Institute
MCC Marylebone Cricket Club; Metropolitan County Council
MCCDRCS Member in Clinical Community Dentistry, Royal College of Surgeons
MCD Master of Civic Design
MCE Master of Civil Engineering
MCFP Member, College of Family Physicians (Canada)
MCGI Member, City and Guilds of London Institute
MCh or **MChir** Master in Surgery
MChD Master of Dental Surgery
MChE Master of Chemical Engineering
MChemA Master in Chemical Analysis
MChOrth Master of Orthopaedic Surgery
MCIArb Member, Chartered Institute of Arbitrators
MCIBS Member, Chartered Institution of Building Services (*now see* MCIBSE); Member, Chartered Institute of Bankers in Scotland
MCIBSE Member, Chartered Institution of Building Services Engineers
MCIEEM Member, Chartered Institute of Ecology and Environmental Management
MCIfA Member, Chartered Institute for Archaeologists
MCIH Member, Chartered Institute of Housing
MCIHort Member, Chartered Institute of Horticulture
MCIHT Member, Chartered Institution of Highways & Transportation
MCIJ Member, Chartered Institute of Journalists
MCIL Member, Chartered Institute of Linguists
MCIM Member, Chartered Institute of Marketing
MCIMarE Member, Canadian Institute of Marine Engineers
MCIOB Member, Chartered Institute of Building
MCIPD Member, Charted Institute of Personnel and Development
MCIPR Member, Chartered Institute of Public Relations
MCIPS Member, Chartered Institute of Purchasing and Supply
M.CIRP Member, International Institution for Production Engineering Research
MCIS Member, Institute of Chartered Secretaries and Administrators
MCIT Member, Chartered Institute of Transport (*now see* CMILT)
MCIWEM Member, Chartered Institution of Water and Environmental Management
MCIWM Member, Chartered Institution of Wastes Management
MCL Master in Civil Law
MCLIP Member, Chartered Institute of Library and Information Professionals
MCMI Member, Chartered Management Institute
MCollP Member, College of Preceptors
MCom Master of Commerce
MCommH Master of Community Health
MConsE Member, Association of Consulting Engineers
MConsEI Member, Association of Consulting Engineers of Ireland
MCOphth Member, College of Ophthalmologists (*now see* MRCOphth)
MCP Member of Colonial Parliament; Master of City Planning (US)
MCPA Member, College of Pathologists of Australia (*now see* MRCPA)
MCPP Member, College of Pharmacy Practice
MCPS Member, College of Physicians and Surgeons
MCS Malayan Civil Service
MCSD Member, Chartered Society of Designers
MCSEE Member, Canadian Society of Electrical Engineers
MCSI Member, Chartered Institute for Securities & Investment
MCSP Member, Chartered Society of Physiotherapy
MCST Member, College of Speech Therapists
MCT Member, Association of Corporate Treasurers
MD Doctor of Medicine; Military District; Maryland (postal)
Md Maryland
MDA Masters in Defence Administration
MDC Metropolitan District Council
MDes Master of Design
MDiv Master of Divinity
MDS Master of Dental Surgery
MDSc Master of Dental Science
ME Mining Engineer; Middle East; Master of Engineering; Maine (postal); Myalgic Encephalomyelitis
MEAF Middle East Air Force
MEC Member of Executive Council; Middle East Command
MEc Master of Economics
MECAS Middle East Centre for Arab Studies
Mech. Mechanics; Mechanical
MECI Member, Institute of Employment Consultants
Med. Medical
MEd Master of Education
MED Master of Environmental Design
MEdSt Master of Educational Studies
MEF Middle East Force
MEI Member, Energy Institute
MEIC Member, Engineering Institute of Canada
MELF Middle East Land Forces
Mencap Royal Society for Mentally Handicapped Children and Adults
MEng Master of Engineering
MEnvS Master of Environmental Studies
MEO Marine Engineering Officer
MEP Member of the European Parliament
MES Master of Environmental Studies
MESc Master of Engineering Science
MetSoc Metals Society (formed by amalgamation of Institute of Metals and Iron and Steel Institute; now merged with Institution of Metallurgists to form Institute of Metals)
MEWI Member, Expert Witness Institute
MEXE Military Engineering Experimental Establishment
MF Master of Forestry
MFA Master of Fine Arts
MFC Mastership in Food Control
MFCM Member, Faculty of Community Medicine (later MFPHM)
MFFP Member, Faculty of Family Planning, Royal College of Obstetricians and Gynaecologists
MFGB Miners' Federation of Great Britain (*now see* NUM)
MFGDP Member, Faculty of General Dental Practitioners, Royal College of Surgeons
MFH Master of Foxhounds
MFHom Member, Faculty of Homoeopathy
MFOM Member, Faculty of Occupational Medicine
MFPaed Member, Faculty of Paediatrics, Royal College of Physicians of Ireland
MFPH Member, Faculty of Public Health
MFPHM Member, Faculty of Public Health Medicine (*now see* MFPH)
MFPHMI Member, Faculty of Public Health Medicine of Ireland
MFPM Member, Faculty of Pharmaceutical Medicine
MGA Major General in charge of Administration
MGC Machine Gun Corps
MGDSRCS Member in General Dental Surgery, Royal College of Surgeons
MGGS Major General, General Staff
MGI Member, Institute of Certificated Grocers
MGO Master General of the Ordnance; Master of Gynaecology and Obstetrics
Mgr Monsignor
MHA Member of House of Assembly; Master of Health Administration
MHCIMA Member, Hotel Catering and International (*formerly* Institutional) Management Association (*now see* MIH)
MHK Member of the House of Keys
MHM Master of Health Management
MHort (RHS) Master of Horticulture, Royal Horticultural Society
MHR Member of the House of Representatives
MHRA Modern Humanities Research Association
MHRF Mental Health Research Fund
MHSM Member, Institute of Health Services Management (*now see* MIHM)
MI Military Intelligence; Michigan (postal)
MIAeE Member, Institute of Aeronautical Engineers
MIAgrE Member, Institution of Agricultural Engineers
MIAM Member, Institute of Administrative Management
MIAS Member, Institute of Aeronautical Science (US) (*now see* MAIAA); Member, Institute of Architects and Surveyors
MIBC Member, Institute of Business Counsellors; Member, Institute of Building Control
MIBF Member, Institute of British Foundrymen
MIBiol Member, Institute of Biology (later MSB, *now see* MRSB)
MIBritE Member, Institution of British Engineers
MICE Member, Institution of Civil Engineers
MICEI Member, Institution of Civil Engineers of Ireland
MICeram Member, Institute of Ceramics (later MIM)
MICFor Member, Institute of Chartered Foresters
Mich Michigan
MIChemE Member, Institution of Chemical Engineers
MICM Member, Institute of Credit Management
MICorr Member, Institute of Corrosion
MICorrST Member, Institution of Corrosion Science and Technology (*now see* MICorr)
MICS Member, Institute of Chartered Shipbrokers
MIDPM Member, Institute of Data Processing Management
MIE(Aust) Member, Institution of Engineers, Australia
MIED Member, Institution of Engineering Designers
MIEE Member, Institution of Electrical Engineers (*now see* MIET)
MIEEE Member, Institute of Electrical and Electronics Engineers (NY)
MIEEM Member, Institute of Ecology and Environmental Management (*now see* MCIEEM)
MIEI Member, Institution of Engineering Inspection
MIEMA Member, Institute of Environmental Management and Assessment
MIEMgt Member, Institute of Environmental Management (*now see* MIEMA)
MIEnvSc Member, Institution of Environmental Sciences
MIERE Member, Institution of Electronic and Radio Engineers (later MIEE)
MIES Member, Institution of Engineers and Shipbuilders, Scotland
MIET Member, Institution of Engineering and Technology (*formerly* Member, Institute of Engineers and Technicians)
MIEx Member, Institute of Export
MIExpE Member, Institute of Explosives Engineers

MIfA Member, Institute for Archaeologists (*now see* MCIfA)
MIFA Member, Institute of Field Archaeologists (later MIfA)
MIFF Member, Institute of Freight Forwarders (*now see* MIFP)
MIFireE Member, Institution of Fire Engineers
MIFM Member, Institute of Fisheries Management
MIFor Member, Institute of Foresters (*now see* MICFor)
MIFP Member, Institute of Freight Professionals
MIGasE Member, Institution of Gas Engineers (*now see* MIGEM)
MIGEM Member, Institution of Gas Engineers and Managers
MIGeol Member, Institution of Geologists
MIH Member, Institute of Housing (*now see* MCIH); Member, Institute of Hospitality
MIHM Member, Institute of Housing Managers (later MIH); Member, Institute of Healthcare Management
MIHort Member, Institute of Horticulture (*now see* MCIHort)
MIHT Member, Institution of Highways and Transportation (*now see* MCIHT)
MIHVE Member, Institution of Heating and Ventilating Engineers (later MCIBS)
MIIA Member, Institute of Industrial Administration (later FBIM)
MIIE Member, Institution of Incorporated Engineers in Electronic, Electrical and Mechanical Engineering (*now see* MIET)
MIIM Member, Institution of Industrial Managers
MIInfSc Member, Institute of Information Sciences (*now see* MCLIP)
MIL Member, Institute of Linguists (*now see* MCIL)
Mil. Military
MILGA Member, Institute of Local Government Administrators
MILocoE Member, Institution of Locomotive Engineers
MILog Member, Institute of Logistics (*now see* MILT)
MILT Member, Chartered Institute of Logistics and Transport
MIM Member, Institute of Materials (*formerly* Institution of Metallurgists, then Institute of Metals) (*now see* MIMMM)
MIMA Member, Institute of Mathematics and its Applications
MIMarE Member, Institute of Marine Engineers (*now see* MIMarEST)
MIMarEST Member, Institute of Marine Engineering, Science and Technology
MIMC Member, Institute of Management Consultants
MIMechE Member, Institution of Mechanical Engineers
MIMEMME Member, Institution of Mining Electrical & Mining Mechanical Engineers (later MIMinE)
MIMgt Member, Institute of Management (*see now* MCMI)
MIMGTechE Member, Institution of Mechanical and General Technician Engineers
MIMI Member, Institute of the Motor Industry
MIMinE Member, Institution of Mining Engineers (later MIMM)
MIMM Member, Institution of Mining and Metallurgy (*now see* MIMMM)
MIMMM Member, Institute of Materials, Minerals and Mining
MIMunE Member, Institution of Municipal Engineers (now amalgamated with Institution of Civil Engineers)
MIN Member, Institute of Navigation (*now see* MRIN)
Min. Ministry
Minn Minnesota
MInstAM Member, Institute of Administrative Management
MInstBE Member, Institution of British Engineers
MInstCE Member, Institution of Civil Engineers (*now see* FICE)
MInstD Member, Institute of Directors
MInstE Member, Institute of Energy (*now see* MEI)
MInstF Member, Institute of Fuel (later MInstE)
MInstHE Member, Institution of Highway Engineers (later MIHT, *now see* MCIHT)
MInstKT Member, Institute of Knowledge Transfer
MInstLM Member, Institute of Leadership and Management
MInstM Member, Institute of Marketing (*now see* MCIM)
MInstMC Member, Institute of Measurement and Control
MInstME Member, Institution of Mining Engineers
MInstMet Member, Institute of Metals (later part of Metals Society; then MIM)
MInstP Member, Institute of Physics
MInstPet Member, Institute of Petroleum (*now see* MEI)
MInstPkg Member, Institute of Packaging
MInstPS Member, Institute of Purchasing and Supply
MInstRA Member, Institute of Registered Architects
MInstRE Member, Institution of Royal Engineers
MInstT Member, Institute of Transport (later MCIT)
MInstTA Member, Institute of Transport Administration
MInstTM Member, Institute of Travel Managers in Industry and Commerce
MInstW Member, Institute of Welding (*now see* MWeldI)
MInstWM Member, Institute of Wastes Management (*now see* MCIWM)
MINucE Member, Institution of Nuclear Engineers (*now see* MNucI)
MIOA Member, Institute of Acoustics
MIOB Member, Institute of Building (*now see* MCIOB)
MIOM Member, Institute of Office Management (*now see* MIAM)
MIOSH Member, Institution of Occupational Safety and Health
MIPA Member, Institute of Practitioners in Advertising
MIPD Member, Institute of Personnel and Development (*now see* MCIPD)
MIPEM Member, Institute of Physics and Engineering in Medicine
MIPlantE Member, Institution of Plant Engineers
MIPM Member, Institute of Personnel Management (later MIPD)
MIPR Member, Institute of Public Relations (*now see* MCIPR)
MIProdE Member, Institution of Production Engineers (later MIEE)
MIQ Member, Institute of Quarrying
MIQA Member, Institute of Quality Assurance
MIRE Member, Institution of Radio Engineers (later MIERE)
MIREE(Aust) Member, Institution of Radio and Electronics Engineers (Australia)
MIRM Member, Institute of Risk Management
MIRO Mineral Industry Research Organisation; Member, Institution of Railway Operators
MIRPM Member, Institute of Residential Property Management
MIRT Member, Institute of Reprographic Technicians
MIRTE Member, Institute of Road Transport Engineers
MIS Member, Institute of Statisticians
MISI Member, Iron and Steel Institute (later part of Metals Society)
Miss Mississippi
MIStructE Member, Institution of Structural Engineers
MIT Massachusetts Institute of Technology
MITA Member, Industrial Transport Association
MITD Member, Institute of Training and Development (later MIPD)
MITE Member, Institution of Electrical and Electronics Technician Engineers
MITI Member, Institute of Translation & Interpreting
MITSA Member, Institute of Trading Standards Administration
MITT Member, Institute of Travel and Tourism
MIWE Member, Institution of Water Engineers (later MIWES)
MIWEM Member, Institution of Water and Environmental Management (*now see* MCIWEM)
MIWES Member, Institution of Water Engineers and Scientists (later MIWEM)
MIWM Member, Institution of Works Managers (*now see* MIIM)
MIWPC Member, Institute of Water Pollution Control (later MIWEM)
MIWSP Member, Institute of Work Study Practitioners (*now see* MMS)
MJA Medical Journalists Association
MJI Member, Institute of Journalists (*now see* MCIJ)
MJIE Member, Junior Institution of Engineers (*now see* MIGTechE)
MJS Member, Japan Society
MJur *Magister Juris* (Master of Law)
ML Licentiate in Medicine; Master of Laws
MLA Member of Legislative Assembly; Modern Language Association; Master in Landscape Architecture; Museums, Libraries and Archives Council
MLC Member of Legislative Council; Meat and Livestock Commission
MLCOM Member, London College of Osteopathic Medicine
MLI Member, Landscape Institute
MLib Master of Librarianship
MLitt Master of Letters
Mlle Mademoiselle
MLO Military Liaison Officer
MLR Modern Language Review
MLS Master of Library Science
MM Military Medal; Merchant Marine
MMA Metropolitan Museum of Art
MMan Master of Management
MMath Master of Mathematics
MMB Milk Marketing Board
MMD Movement for Multi-Party Democracy
MME Master of Mining Engineering
Mme Madame
MMechE Master of Mechanical Engineering
MMEd Master in Medical Education
MMedSci Master in Medical Science
MMet Master of Metallurgy
MMGI Member, Mining, Geological and Metallurgical Institute of India
MMin Master of Ministry
MML Masters in Medical Law
MMLJ Member of Merit, Order of St Lazarus of Jerusalem
MMM Member, Order of Military Merit (Canada)
MMRS Member, Market Research Society
MMS Member, Institute of Management Services
MMSA Master of Midwifery, Society of Apothecaries
MMus Master of Music
MN Merchant Navy; Minnesota (postal)
MNAS Member, National Academy of Sciences (US)
MND Motor Neurone Disease
MNECInst Member, North East Coast Institution of Engineers and Shipbuilders
MNI Member, Nautical Institute
MNIMH Member, National Institute of Medical Herbalists
MNSE Member, Nigerian Society of Engineers
MNucI Member, Nuclear Institute
MNZIS Member, New Zealand Institute of Surveyors
MNZPI Member, New Zealand Planning Institute
MO Medical Officer; Military Operations; Missouri (postal)
Mo Missouri
MoD Ministry of Defence
Mods Moderations (Oxford)
MOF Ministry of Food

MOH Medical Officer(s) of Health
MOI Ministry of Information
MoJ Ministry of Justice
MOM Member, Order of Merit (Malta)
MOMA Museum of Modern Art
MOMI Museum of the Moving Image
Mon Monmouthshire
Mont Montgomeryshire
MOP Ministry of Power
MOrthRCS Member in Orthodontics, Royal College of Surgeons
MoS Ministry of Supply
Most Rev. Most Reverend
MoT Ministry of Transport
MOV Member, Order of Volta (Ghana)
MP Member of Parliament
MPA Master of Public Administration; Member, Parliamentary Assembly, Northern Ireland
MPAGB Member, Photographic Alliance of Great Britain
MPBW Ministry of Public Building and Works
MPH Master of Public Health
MPhil Master of Philosophy
MPhys Master of Physics
MPIA Master of Public and International Affairs
MPMI Member, Property Management Institute
MPO Management and Personnel Office
MPodA Member, Podiatry Association
MPP Member, Provincial Parliament; Master in Public Policy (Harvard)
MPRISA Member, Public Relations Institute of South Africa
MProf Masters in Professional Studies
MPS Member, Pharmaceutical Society (*now see* MRPharmS)
MPTS Medical Practitioners Tribunal Service
MR Master of the Rolls; Municipal Reform
MRAC Member, Royal Agricultural College
MRACP Member, Royal Australasian College of Physicians
MRACS Member, Royal Australasian College of Surgeons
MRad Master of Radiology
MRAeS Member, Royal Aeronautical Society
MRAIC Member, Royal Architectural Institute of Canada
MRAS Member, Royal Asiatic Society
MRC Medical Research Council
MRCA Multi-Role Combat Aircraft
MRCGP Member, Royal College of General Practitioners
MRC-LMB Medical Research Council Laboratory of Molecular Biology
MRCOG Member, Royal College of Obstetricians and Gynaecologists
MRCOphth Member, Royal College of Ophthalmologists
MRCP Member, Royal College of Physicians, London; Member, Royal College of Physicians, United Kingdom
MRCPA Member, Royal College of Pathologists of Australia
MRCPath Member, Royal College of Pathologists
MRCPCH Member, Royal College of Paediatrics and Child Health
MRCPE Member, Royal College of Physicians, Edinburgh
MRCPGlas Member, Royal College of Physicians and Surgeons of Glasgow
MRCPI Member, Royal College of Physicians of Ireland
MRCPsych Member, Royal College of Psychiatrists
MRCS Member, Royal College of Surgeons of England
MRCSE Member, Royal College of Surgeons of Edinburgh
MRCSI Member, Royal College of Surgeons in Ireland
MRCVS Member, Royal College of Veterinary Surgeons
MRD RCS Member in Restorative Dentistry, Royal College of Surgeons
MRE Master of Religious Education
MRes Master of Research
MRHS Member, Royal Horticultural Society
MRI Magnetic Resonance Imaging; Member, Royal Institution
MRIA Member, Royal Irish Academy
MRIAI Member, Royal Institute of the Architects of Ireland
MRIC Member, Royal Institute of Chemistry (*now see* MRSC)
MRICS Member, Royal Institution of Chartered Surveyors
MRIN Member, Royal Institute of Navigation
MRINA Member, Royal Institution of Naval Architects
MRNZCGP Member, Royal New Zealand College of General Practitioners
MRPharmS Member, Royal Pharmaceutical Society
MRSB Member, Royal Society of Biology
MRSC Member, Royal Society of Chemistry
MRSH Member, Royal Society for the Promotion of Health (*now see* MRSPH)
MRSL Member, Order of the Republic of Sierra Leone
MRSocMed Member, Royal Society of Medicine
MRSPH Member, Royal Society for Public Health
MRTPI Member, Royal Town Planning Institute
MRurSc Master of Rural Science
MRUSI Member, Royal United Service Institution
MRVA Member, Rating and Valuation Association
MS Master of Surgery; Master of Science (US); Mississippi (postal); Multiple Sclerosis; Motor Ship
MS, MSS Manuscript, Manuscripts
MSA Master of Science, Agriculture (US); Mineralogical Society of America; Motor Sports Association
MSAAIE Member, Southern African Association of Industrial Editors
MSAE Member, Society of Automotive Engineeers (US)
MSAICE Member, South African Institution of Civil Engineers
MSAInstMM Member, South African Institute of Mining and Metallurgy
MS&R Merchant Shipbuilding and Repairs
MSB Member, Society of Biology (*now see* MRSB)
MSC Manpower Services Commission; Missionaries of the Sacred Heart
MSc Master of Science
MScD Master of Dental Science
MScE Master of Science in Engineering
MSci Master of Natural Sciences
MScSoc Master of Social Sciences
MScSocMed Master of Science in Social Medicine
MSD Meritorious Service Decoration (Fiji)
MSE Master of Science in Engineering (US)
MSF (Union for) Manufacturing, Science, Finance
MSFA Member, Society of Financial Advisers
MSHyg Master of Science in Hygiene
MSI Member, Securities Institute (later Securities & Investment Institute, *now see* MCSI)
MSIA Member, Society of Industrial Artists
MSIAD Member, Society of Industrial Artists and Designers (*now see* MCSD)
MSIT Member, Society of Instrument Technology (*now see* MInstMC)
MSLS Master of Science in Library Science
MSM Meritorious Service Medal; Madras Sappers and Miners; Master in Science Management
MSN Master of Science in Nursing
MSocAdmin Master of Social Administration
MSocIS Member, Société des Ingénieurs et Scientifiques de France
MSocSc Master of Social Sciences
MSocWork Master of Social Work
MSoFHT Member, Society of Food Hygiene Technology
MSP Member, Scottish Parliament; Managing Successful Programmes
MSR Member, Society of Radiographers
MSRP Member, Society for Radiological Protection
MSSc Master of Social Sciences
MSSC Marine Society & Sea Cadets
MSt Master of Studies
MSTD Member, Society of Typographic Designers
MStJ Member, Most Venerable Order of the Hospital of St John of Jerusalem
MSW Master of Social Work
MSzP Magyar Szocialista Párt
MT Mechanical Transport; Montana (postal)
Mt Mount; Mountain
MTA Music Trades Association
MTAI Member, Institute of Travel Agents
MTB Motor Torpedo Boat
MTCA Ministry of Transport and Civil Aviation
MTD Midwife Teachers' Diploma
MTech Master of Technology
MTEFL Master in the Teaching of English as a Foreign or Second Language
MTh Master of Theology
MTIA Metal Trades Industry Association
MTIRA Machine Tool Industry Research Association (*now see* AMTRI)
MTPI Member, Town Planning Institute (*now see* MRTPI)
MTS Master of Theological Studies; Ministerial Training Scheme
MUniv Honorary Master of the University
MusB Bachelor of Music
MusD Doctor of Music
MusM Master of Music
MV Merchant Vessel, Motor Vessel (naval)
MVB Bachelor of Veterinary Medicine
MVEE Military Vehicles and Engineering Establishment
MVO Member, Royal Victorian Order
MVSc Master of Veterinary Science
MW Master of Wine
MWA Mystery Writers of America
MWeldI Member, Welding Institute
MWSOM Member, Institute of Practitioners in Work Study Organisation and Methods (*now see* MMS)

N

N Nationalist; Navigating Duties; North
n nephew
NA National Academician (America)
NAACP National Association for the Advancement of Colored People
NAAFI Navy, Army and Air Force Institutes
NAAS National Agricultural Advisory Service
NAB National Advisory Body for Public Sector Higher Education
NABC National Association of Boys' Clubs (later NABC-CYP)
NABC-CYP National Association of Boys' Clubs - Clubs for Young People
NAC National Agriculture Centre
NACAB National Association of Citizens' Advice Bureaux
NACCB National Accreditation Council for Certification Bodies

NACETT National Advisory Council for Education and Training Targets
NACF National Art-Collections Fund
NACRO National Association for the Care and Resettlement of Offenders
NADFAS National Association of Decorative and Fine Arts Societies
NAE National Academy of Engineering
NAEW Nato Airborn Early Warning
NAHA National Association of Health Authorities (*now see* NAHAT)
NAHAT National Association of Health Authorities and Trusts
NAHT National Association of Head Teachers
NALGO or **Nalgo** National and Local Government Officers' Association
NAMAS National Measurement and Accreditation Service
NAMCW National Association for Maternal and Child Welfare
NAMH MIND (National Association for Mental Health)
NAMMA NATO MRCA Management Agency
NAPAG National Academies Policy Advisory Group
NARM National Association of Recording Merchandisers (US)
NAS National Academy of Sciences
NASA National Aeronautics and Space Administration (US)
NASD National Association of Securities Dealers
NASDAQ National Association of Securities Dealers Automated Quotation System
NASDIM National Association of Security Dealers and Investment Managers (later FIMBRA)
NAS/UWT National Association of Schoolmasters/Union of Women Teachers
NATCS National Air Traffic Control Services (*now see* NATS)
NATFHE National Association of Teachers in Further and Higher Education (combining ATCDE and ATTI)
NATLAS National Testing Laboratory Accreditation Scheme
NATO North Atlantic Treaty Organisation
NATS National Air Traffic Services
Nat. Sci. Natural Sciences
NATSOPA National Society of Operative Printers, Graphical and Media Personnel (*formerly* of Operative Printers and Assistants)
NAYC Youth Clubs UK (*formerly* National Association of Youth Clubs)
NB New Brunswick; Nebraska (postal)
NBA North British Academy
NBC National Book Council (later NBL); National Broadcasting Company (US)
NBL National Book League
NBPI National Board for Prices and Incomes
NC National Certificate; North Carolina
NCA National Certificate of Agriculture
NCARB National Council of Architectural Registration Boards
NCAS Natural Environment Research Council Centres for Atmospheric Science
NCB National Coal Board
NCC National Computing Centre; Nature Conservancy Council (later NCCE); National Consumer Council
NCCE Nature Conservancy Council for England (English Nature)
NCCI National Committee for Commonwealth Immigrants
NCCL National Council for Civil Liberties
NCD National Capital District, Papua New Guinea
NCDAD National Council for Diplomas in Art and Design
NCEA National Council for Educational Awards
NCET National Council for Educational Technology
NCH National Children's Homes
NCLC National Council of Labour Colleges
NCOP National Council of Provinces (South Africa)
NCOPF National Council for One Parent Families
NCRI National Cancer Research Institute
NCSE National Council for Special Education
NCSS National Council of Social Service
NCTA National Community Television Association (US)
NCTJ National Council for the Training of Journalists
NCU National Cyclists' Union
NCVCCO National Council of Voluntary Child Care Organisations
NCVO National Council for Voluntary Organisations
NCVQ National Council for Vocational Qualifications
NCYPE National Centre for Young People with Epilepsy
ND North Dakota
NDA National Diploma in Agriculture
NDC National Defence College; NATO Defence College
NDD National Diploma in Dairying; National Diploma in Design
NDEA National Defense Education Act
NDH National Diploma in Horticulture
NDIC National Defence Industries Council
NDP New Democratic Party
NDRI National Disease Research Interchange
NDTA National Defense Transportation Association (US)
NE North-east
NEAB Northern Examinations and Assessment Board
NEAC New English Art Club
NEAF Near East Air Force
NEARELF Near East Land Forces
NEB National Enterprise Board
NEC National Executive Committee
NECInst North East Coast Institution of Engineers and Shipbuilders
NEDC National Economic Development Council; North East Development Council
NEDO National Economic Development Office
NEH National Endowment for the Humanities
NEL National Engineering Laboratory
NERC Natural Environment Research Council
NESTA National Endowment for Science, Technology and the Arts
NF Newfoundland and Labrador (postal)
NFC National Freight Consortium (*formerly* Corporation, then Company)
NFCG National Federation of Consumer Groups
NFER National Foundation for Educational Research
NFHA National Federation of Housing Associations
NFMS National Federation of Music Societies
NFS National Fire Service
NFSH National Federation of Spiritual Healers
NFT National Film Theatre
NFU National Farmers' Union
NFWI National Federation of Women's Institutes
NGO Non-Governmental Organisation(s)
NGTE National Gas Turbine Establishment
NH New Hampshire
NH&MRC National Health and Medical Research Council (Australia)
NHBC National House-Building Council
NHMF National Heritage Memorial Fund
NHS National Health Service
NHSU National Health Service University
NI Northern Ireland; Native Infantry
NIAB National Institute of Agricultural Botany
NIACE National Institute of Adult Continuing Education
NIACRO Northern Ireland Association for the Care and Resettlement of Offenders
NIAE National Institute of Agricultural Engineering
NIAID National Institute of Allergy and Infectious Diseases
NICE National Institute for Health and Care Excellence (formerly National Institute of Clinical Excellence, then National Institute for Health and Clinical Excellence)
NICEC National Institute for Careers Education and Counselling
NICEIC National Inspection Council for Electrical Installation Contracting
NICG Nationalised Industries Chairmen's Group
NICRO National Institute for Crime Prevention and Re-integration of Offenders
NICS Northern Ireland Civil Service
NID Naval Intelligence Division; National Institute for the Deaf; Northern Ireland District; National Institute of Design (India)
NIESR National Institute of Economic and Social Research
NIH National Institutes of Health (US)
NIHCA Northern Ireland Hotels and Caterers Association
NIHEC Northern Ireland Higher Education Council
NIHR National Institute of Health Research
NII Nuclear Installations Inspectorate
NILP Northern Ireland Labour Party
NIMR National Institute for Medical Research
NISTRO Northern Ireland Science and Technology Regional Organisation
NISW National Institute of Social Work
NIU Northern Ireland Unionist
NJ New Jersey
NL National Liberal; No Liability; Newfoundland and Labrador
NLCS North London Collegiate School
NLF National Liberal Federation
NLYL National League of Young Liberals
NM New Mexico (postal)
NMC Nursing and Midwifery Council
NMR Nuclear Magnetic Resonance
NMRS National Monuments Record of Scotland
NMSI National Museum of Science and Industry
NNMA Nigerian National Merit Award
NNOM Nigerian National Order of Merit
NO Navigating Officer
NODA National Operatic and Dramatic Association
Northants Northamptonshire
Notts Nottinghamshire
NP Notary Public
NPA Newspaper Publishers' Association
NPFA National Playing Fields Association
NPG National Portrait Gallery
NPk Nishan-e-Pakistan
NPL National Physical Laboratory
NPQH National Professional Qualification for Headship
NRA National Rifle Association; National Recovery Administration (US); National Rivers Authority
NRAO National Radio Astronomy Observatory
NRCC National Research Council of Canada
NRD National Registered Designer
NRDC National Research Development Corporation
NRMA National Roads and Motorists' Association
NRPB National Radiological Protection Board
NRR Northern Rhodesia Regiment

NRSA National Research Service Award (US)
NS Nova Scotia; New Style in the Calendar (in Great Britain since 1752); National Society; National Service
ns Graduate of Royal Naval Staff College, Greenwich
NSA National Skating Association (*now see* NISA)
NSAIV Distinguished Order of Shaheed Ali (Maldives)
NSERC Natural Sciences and Engineering Research Council, Canada
NSF National Science Foundation (US)
NSM Non-Stipendiary Minister
NSMHC National Society for Mentally Handicapped Children (*now see* Mencap)
NSPCC National Society for Prevention of Cruelty to Children
NSQT National Society for Quality through Teamwork
NSRA National Small-bore Rifle Association
N/SSF Novice, Society of St Francis
NSW New South Wales
NT New Testament; Northern Territory (Australia); Northwest Territories (Canada); National Theatre; National Trust
NT&SA National Trust & Savings Association
NTO National Training Organisation
NTUC National Trades Union Congress
NUAAW National Union of Agricultural and Allied Workers
NUBE National Union of Bank Employees (later BIFU)
NUFLAT National Union of Footwear Leather and Allied Trades (*now see* NUKFAT)
NUGMW National Union of General and Municipal Workers (later GMBATU)
NUHKW National Union of Hosiery and Knitwear Workers (*now see* NUKFAT)
NUI National University of Ireland
NUJ National Union of Journalists
NUJMB Northern Universities Joint Matriculation Board
NUKFAT National Union of Knitwear, Footwear and Apparel Trades
NUM National Union of Mineworkers
NUMAST National Union of Marine, Aviation and Shipping Transport Officers
NUPE National Union of Public Employees
NUR National Union of Railwaymen (*now see* RMT)
NUS National Union of Students; National University of Singapore
NUT National Union of Teachers
NUTG National Union of Townswomen's Guilds
NUTGW National Union of Tailors and Garment Workers
NUTN National Union of Trained Nurses
NUU New University of Ulster
NV Nevada (postal)
NVQ National Vocational Qualification
NW North-west
NWC National Water Council
NWFP North-West Frontier Province
NWP North-Western Province
NWT North-Western Territories
NY New York
NYC New York City
NYO National Youth Orchestra
NYT National Youth Theatre
NZ New Zealand
NZEF New Zealand Expeditionary Force
NZIA New Zealand Institute of Architects
NZRSA New Zealand Retired Services Association
NZTF New Zealand Territorial Force

O

o only
OAM Medal of the Order of Australia
O&E Operations and Engineers (US)
O&M organisation and method
O&O Oriental and Occidental Steamship Co.
OAP Old Age Pensioner
OAS Organisation of American States; On Active Service
OASC Officer Aircrew Selection Centre
OAU Organisation for African Unity
OB Order of Barbados; Order of Belize
OBC Order of British Columbia
OBE Officer, Order of the British Empire
OC Officer, Order of Canada (equivalent to former award SM)
OC or **o/c** Officer Commanding
oc only child
OCC Order of the Caribbean Community
OCDS or **ocds Can** Overseas College of Defence Studies (Canada)
OCF Officiating Chaplain to the Forces
OCHA Office for the Coordination of Humanitarian Affairs
OCPA Office of the Commissioner for Public Appointments
OCS Officer Candidates School; Officer Cadet School
OCSS Oxford and Cambridge Shakespeare Society
OCTU Officer Cadet Training Unit
OCU Operational Conversion Unit
OD Officer, Order of Distinction (Jamaica); Order of Distinction (Antigua)
ODA Overseas Development Administration
ODI Overseas Development Institute
ODM Ministry of Overseas Development
ODPM Office of the Deputy Prime Minister
ODSM Order of Diplomatic Service Merit (Lesotho)
OE Order of Excellence (Guyana)
OECD Organization for Economic Co-operation and Development
OED Oxford English Dictionary
OEEC Organization for European Economic Co-operation (*now see* OECD)
OF Order of the Founder, Salvation Army
OFCOM or **Ofcom** Office of Communications
OFEMA Office Française d'Exportation de Matériel Aéronautique
OFFER Office of Electricity Regulation
Ofgem Office of Gas and Electricity Markets
OFM Order of Friars Minor (Franciscans)
OFMCap Order of Friars Minor Capuchin (Franciscans)
OFMConv Order of Friars Minor Conventual (Franciscans)
Ofqual Office of Qualifications and Examinations Regulation
OFR Order of the Federal Republic of Nigeria
OFS Orange Free State
OFSTED Office for Standards in Education
OFT Office of Fair Trading
Oftel Office of Telecommunications
Ofwat Office of Water Services
OGC Office of Government Commerce
OGS Oratory of the Good Shepherd
OH Ohio (postal)
OHMS On His (or Her) Majesty's Service
O i/c Officer in charge
OJ Order of Jamaica
OK Oklahoma (postal)
OL Officer, Order of Leopold; Order of the Leopard (Lesotho)
OLJ Officer, Order of St Lazarus of Jerusalem
OLM Officer, Legion of Merit (Rhodesia); Ordained Local Minister
OM Order of Merit; Order of Manitoba
OMCS Office of the Minister for the Civil Service
OMFIF Official Monetary and Financial Institutions Forum
OMI Oblate of Mary Immaculate
OMLJ Officer, Order of Merit, Order of St Lazarus of Jerusalem
OMM Officer, Order of Military Merit (Canada)
ON Order of the Nation (Jamaica); Ontario (postal)
OND Ordinary National Diploma
ONDA Ordinary National Diploma in Agriculture
ONS Office for National Statistics
Ont Ontario
ONZ Order of New Zealand
ONZM Officer, New Zealand Order of Merit
OON Officer, Order of the Niger
OOnt Order of Ontario
OOV Officer, Order of the Volta (Ghana)
OP *Ordinis Praedicatorum* (of the Order of Preachers (Dominican)); Observation Post
OPCON Operational Control
OPCS Office of Population Censuses and Surveys (*now see* ONS)
OPCW Organisation for the Prohibition of Chemical Weapons
OPEC Organisation of Petroleum Exporting Countries
OPEI Order of Prince Edward Island
OPM Owner President Management program
OPRA Occupational Pensions Regulatory Authority
OPS Office of Public Service
OPSS Office of Public Service and Science (later OPS)
OQ Officer, National Order of Quebec
OR Order of Rorima (Guyana); Operational Research; Oregon (postal)
ORC Orange River Colony
ORGALIME Organisme de Liaison des Industries Métalliques Européennes
ORHA/CPA Office of Reconstruction and Humanitarian Assistance/Coalition Provisional Authority
ORL Otorhinolaryngology
ORS Operational Research Society
ORSA Operations Research Society of America (*now see* INFORMS)
ORSL Order of the Republic of Sierra Leone
ORT Organization for Rehabilitation through Training
ORTF Office de la Radiodiffusion et Télévision Française
ORTT Order of the Republic of Trinidad and Tobago
o s only son
OSA Order of St Augustine (Augustinian); Ontario Society of Artists
OSB Order of St Benedict (Benedictine)
OSC Order of Simon of Cyrene
osc Graduate of Overseas Staff College
OSCE Organisation for Security and Co-operation in Europe
OSCHR Office for Strategic Co-ordination of Health Research
OSFC Franciscan (Capuchin) Order
O/Sig Ordinary Signalman
OSMTH Ordo Supremus Militaris Templi Hierosolymitani (Supreme Military Order of the Temple of Jerusalem)

OSNC Orient Steam Navigation Co.
osp *obiit sine prole* (died without issue)
OSS Office of Strategic Services
OST Office of Science and Technology
OStJ Officer, Most Venerable Order of the Hospital of St John of Jerusalem
OSUK Ophthalmological Society of the United Kingdom
OT Old Testament
OTC Officers' Training Corps
OTL Officer, Order of Toussaint L'Ouverture (Haiti)
OTS Office of the Third Sector
OTU Operational Training Unit
OTWSA Ou-Testamentiese Werkgemeenskap in Suider-Afrika
OU Oxford University; Open University
OUAC Oxford University Athletic Club
OUAFC Oxford University Association Football Club
OUBC Oxford University Boat Club
OUCC Oxford University Cricket Club
OUDS Oxford University Dramatic Society
OUP Oxford University Press; Official Unionist Party
OURC Oxford University Rifle Club
OURFC Oxford University Rugby Football Club
OURT Order of the United Republic of Tanzania
Oxon Oxfordshire; *Oxoniensis* (of Oxford)

P

PA Pakistan Army; Personal Assistant; Pennsylvania (postal)
PAA President, Australian Academy of Science
pac passed the final examination of the Advanced Class, The Military College of Science
PACE Protestant and Catholic Encounter; Property Advisers to the Civil Estate
PACTA Professional Associate, Clinical Theology Association
PALS Partnership for Active Leisure Scheme for Disabled Children
P&O Peninsular and Oriental Steamship Co.
P&OSNCo. Peninsular and Oriental Steam Navigation Co.
PAO Prince Albert's Own
PASOK Panhellenic Socialist Movement
PBFA Provincial Booksellers Fairs Association
PBS Public Broadcasting Service
PC Privy Counsellor; Police Constable; Perpetual Curate; Peace Commissioner (Ireland); Progressive Conservative (Canada)
pc *per centum* (in the hundred)
PCC Parochial Church Council; Protected Cell Company (Guernsey); Private Cell Company
PCE Postgraduate Certificate of Education
pce passed command examinations
PCEF Polytechnic and Colleges Employers' Forum
PCFC Polytechnics and Colleges Funding Council
PCG Primary Care Group
PCL Polytechnic of Central London
PCMO Principal Colonial Medical Officer
PCNZM Principal Companion, New Zealand Order of Merit
PCS Parti Chrétien-Social; Public and Commercial Services Union
PCT Primary Care Trust
PdD Doctor of Pedagogy (US)
PDG Président Directeur Général
PDipHEd Postgraduate Diploma in Health Education
PDR People's Democratic Republic
PDRA post doctoral research assistant
PDSA People's Dispensary for Sick Animals
PDTC Professional Dancer's Training Course Diploma
PDTDip Professional Dancer's Teaching Diploma
PE Procurement Executive; Prince Edward Island (postal)
PEI Prince Edward Island
PEN Poets, Playwrights, Editors, Essayists, Novelists (Club)
PEng Registered Professional Engineer (Canada); Member, Society of Professional Engineers
Penn Pennsylvania
PEP Political and Economic Planning (*now see* PSI)
PER Professional and Executive Recruitment
PES Party of European Socialists
PEST Pressure for Economic and Social Toryism
PF Procurator-Fiscal
PFA Professional Footballers' Association
pfc Graduate of RAF Flying College
PFE Program for Executives
PFI Private Finance Initiative
PGA Professional Golfers' Association
PGCA Post Graduate Certificate of Adjudication
PGCE Post Graduate Certificate of Education
PGCFHE Post Graduate Certificate in Further and Higher Education
PGCHE Post Graduate Certificate in Higher Education
PGCTh Postgraduate Certificate in Theology
PGDCCI Postgraduate Diploma in Computing for Commerce and Industry
PGDipMin Postgraduate Diploma in Ministry
PGDPT Postgraduate Diploma in Pastoral Theology
PGTC Postgraduate Teaching Certificate
PGTCSE Postgraduate Teaching Certificate in Secondary Education
PH Presidential Order of Honour (Botswana)
PHAB Physically Handicapped & Able-bodied
PhB Bachelor of Philosophy
PhC Pharmaceutical Chemist
PhD Doctor of Philosophy
PHE Public Health England
Phil. Philology; Philological; Philosophy; Philosophical
PhL Licentiate in Philosophy
PHLS Public Health Laboratory Service
PhM Master of Philosophy (USA)
PhmB Bachelor of Pharmacy
Phys. Physical
PIA Personal Investment Authority
PIARC Permanent International Association of Road Congresses
PIB Prices and Incomes Board (later NBPI)
PICAO Provisional International Civil Aviation Organization (*now* ICAO)
PICTFOR Parliamentary Internet Communications and Technology Forum
pinx. *pinxit* (he painted it)
PITCOM Parliamentary Information Technology Committee (*now see* PICTFOR)
PJG Pingat Jasa Gemilang (Singapore)
PJHQ Permanent Joint Headquarters
PJK Pingkat Jasa Kebaktian (Malaysia)
Pl. Place; Plural
PLA Port of London Authority
PLAB Professional and Linguistic Assessments Board
PLC or **plc** public limited company
Plen. Plenipotentiary
PLI President, Landscape Institute
PLP Parliamentary Labour Party; Progressive Liberal Party (Bahamas)
PLR Public Lending Right
PMA Personal Military Assistant
PMC Personnel Management Centre
PMD Program for Management Development
PMedSci President, Academy of Medical Sciences
PMETB Postgraduate Medical Education and Training Board
PMG Postmaster-General
PMN Panglima Mangku Negara (Malaysia)
PMO Principal Medical Officer; Princess Mary's Own
PMRAFNS Princess Mary's Royal Air Force Nursing Service
PMS Presidential Order of Meritorious Service (Botswana); President, Miniature Society
PNBS Panglima Negara Bintang Sarawak
PNEU Parents' National Educational Union
PNG Papua New Guinea
PNP People's National Party
PO Post Office
POB Presidential Order of Botswana
POMEF Political Office Middle East Force
Pop. Population
POST Parliamentary Office of Science and Technology
POUNC Post Office Users' National Council
POW Prisoner of War; Prince of Wales's
PP Parish Priest; Past President
pp pages
PPA Periodical Publishers Association
PPARC Particle Physics and Astronomy Research Council
PPCLI Princess Patricia's Canadian Light Infantry
PPCSD Past President, Chartered Society of Designers
PPDF Parti Populaire pour la Démocratie Française
PPE Philosophy, Politics and Economics
PPInstHE Past President, Institution of Highway Engineers
PPIStructE Past President, Institution of Structural Engineers
PPITB Printing and Publishing Industry Training Board
PPP Private Patients Plan; Psychology, Philosophy and Physiology
PPRA Past President, Royal Academy
PPRBA Past President, Royal Society of British Artists
PPRBS Past President, Royal Society of British Sculptors
PPRE Past President, Royal Society of Painter-Printmakers (*formerly* of Painter-Etchers and Engravers)
PPRIBA Past President, Royal Institute of British Architects
PPRNCM Diploma in Professional Performance, Royal Northern College of Music
PPROI Past President, Royal Institute of Oil Painters
PPRP Past President, Royal Society of Portrait Painters
PPRSA Past President, Royal Scottish Academy
PPRSW Past President, Royal Scottish Society of Painters in Water Colours
PPRTPI Past President, Royal Town Planning Institute
PPRWA Past President, Royal Watercolour Association
PPRWS Past President, Royal Society of Painters in Water Colours
PPS Parliamentary Private Secretary
PPSA Proficiency, Photographic Society of America
PPSIAD Past President, Society of Industrial Artists and Designers
PQ Province of Quebec

PQCCC Post Qualification Certificate in Child Care
PQE Professional Qualifying Examination
PR Public Relations; Parti républicain
PRA President, Royal Academy
PRASEG Associate Parliamentary Renewable and Sustainable Energy Group
PRBS President, Royal Society of British Sculptors
PRCA Public Relations Consultants Association
PRCS President, Royal College of Surgeons
PrD Doctor of Professional Practice
PRE President, Royal Society of Painter-Printmakers (*formerly* of Painter-Etchers and Engravers)
Preb. Prebendary
Prep. Preparatory
Pres. President
PRHA President, Royal Hibernian Academy
PRI President, Royal Institute of Painters in Water Colours; Plastics and Rubber Institute
PRIA President, Royal Irish Academy
PRIAS President, Royal Incorporation of Architects in Scotland
Prin. Principal
PRISA Public Relations Institute of South Africa
PRL Liberal Reform Party (Belgium)
PRO Public Relations Officer; Public Records Office
Proc. Proctor; Proceedings
Prof. Professor; Professional
PROI President, Royal Institute of Oil Painters
PRO NED Promotion of Non-Executive Directors
PRORM Pay and Records Office, Royal Marines
Pro tem. *Pro tempore* (for the time being)
ProtU Protestant Unionist Party
Prov. Provost; Provincial
Prox. *Proximo* (next)
Prox.acc. *Proxime accessit* (next in order of merit to the winner)
PRS President, Royal Society; Performing Right Society Ltd
PRSA President, Royal Scottish Academy
PRSE President, Royal Society of Edinburgh
PRSH President, Royal Society for the Promotion of Health
PRSW President, Royal Scottish Water Colour Society
PRUAA President, Royal Ulster Academy of Arts
PRWA President, Royal West of England Academy
PRWS President, Royal Society of Painters in Water Colours
PS Pastel Society; Paddle Steamer
ps passed School of Instruction (of Officers)
PSA Property Services Agency; Petty Sessions Area
psa Graduate of RAF Staff College
psc Graduate of Staff College († indicates Graduate of Senior Wing Staff College); Personal Services Company
PSD Petty Sessional Division; Social Democratic Party (Portugal); Panglima Setia Diraja
PSE Party of European Socialists
PSGB Pharmaceutical Society of Great Britain (*now see* RPSGB)
PSI Policy Studies Institute
PSIAD President, Society of Industrial Artists and Designers
PSM Panglima Setia Mahkota (Malaysia)
psm Certificate of Royal Military School of Music
PSMA President, Society of Marine Artists
PSNC Pacific Steam Navigation Co.
PSO Principal Scientific Officer; Personal Staff Officer
PSOE Partido Socialista Obrero Español
PSS Society of Priests of St Sulpice
PsyD Doctor of Psychology
PTA Passenger Transport Authority; Parent-Teacher Association
PTC Personnel and Training Command
PTE Passenger Transport Executive
Pte Private
ptsc passed Technical Staff College
Pty Proprietary
PUP People's United Party; Progressive Unionist Party
PVSM Param Vishishc Seva Medal (India)
PWD Public Works Department
PWE Political Welfare Executive
PWO Prince of Wales's Own
PWO(CEW) Principal Warfare Officer (Communications and Electronic Warfare)
PWO(U) Principal Warfare Officer (Underwater Warfare)
PWR Pressurized Water Reactor
PYBT Prince's Youth Business Trust

Q

Q Queen
QAA Quality Assurance Agency for Higher Education
QAIMNS Queen Alexandra's Imperial Military Nursing Service
QARANC Queen Alexandra's Royal Army Nursing Corps
QARNNS Queen Alexandra's Royal Naval Nursing Service
QBD Queen's Bench Division
QC Queen's Counsel; Quebec (postal)
QCA Qualifications and Curriculum Authority
QCB Queen's Commendation for Bravery
QCDA Qualifications and Curriculum Development Agency
QCVS Queen's Commendation for Valuable Service
QCVSA Queen's Commendation for Valuable Service in the Air
QDR Qualified in Dispute Resolution
QEH Queen Elizabeth Hall
QEO Queen Elizabeth's Own
QFSM Queen's Fire Service Medal for Distinguished Service
QGM Queen's Gallantry Medal
QHC Honorary Chaplain to the Queen
QHDS Honorary Dental Surgeon to the Queen
QHNS Honorary Nursing Sister to the Queen
QHP Honorary Physician to the Queen
QHS Honorary Surgeon to the Queen
Qld Queensland
Qly Quarterly
QMAAC Queen Mary's Army Auxiliary Corps
QMC Queen Mary College, London
QMG Quartermaster-General
QMIPRI Queen Mary Intellectual Property Research Institute
QMO Queen Mary's Own
QMUL Queen Mary, University of London
QMW Queen Mary and Westfield College, London (*now see* QMUL)
QO Qualified Officer
QOOH Queen's Own Oxfordshire Hussars
Q(ops) Quartering (operations)
QOY Queen's Own Yeomanry
QPM Queen's Police Medal
QPSM Queen's Public Service Medal (New Zealand)
Qr Quarter
QRIH Queen's Royal Irish Hussars
QS Quarter Sessions; Quantity Surveying
qs RAF graduates of the Military or Naval Staff College
QSM Queen's Service Medal (NZ)
QSO Queen's Service Order (NZ)
QTS Qualified Teacher Status
QUB Queen's University, Belfast
qv *quod vide* (which see)
QVRM Queen's Volunteer Reserve Medal
qwi Qualified Weapons Instructor

R

(R) Reserve
RA Royal Academician; Royal Academy; Royal (Regiment of) Artillery
RAA Regional Arts Association; Royal Australian Artillery
RAAF Royal Australian Air Force
RAAMC Royal Australian Army Medical Corps
RABI Royal Agricultural Benevolent Institution
RAC Royal Automobile Club; Royal Agricultural College; Royal Armoured Corps
RACDS Royal Australian College of Dental Surgeons
RACGP Royal Australian College of General Practitioners
RAChD Royal Army Chaplains' Department
RACI Royal Australian Chemical Institute
RACO Royal Australian College of Ophthalmologists
RACOG Royal Australian College of Obstetricians and Gynaecologists
RACP Royal Australasian College of Physicians
RACS Royal Australasian College of Surgeons; Royal Arsenal Co-operative Society
RAD Royal Academy of Dance
RADA Royal Academy of Dramatic Art
RADAR Royal Association for Disability Rights (*formerly* Royal Association for Disability and Rehabilitation)
RADC Royal Army Dental Corps
RADIUS Religious Drama Society of Great Britain
RAE Royal Australian Engineers; Royal Aerospace Establishment (*formerly* Royal Aircraft Establishment); Research Assessment Exercise
RAEC Royal Army Educational Corps
RAEng Royal Academy of Engineering
RAeS Royal Aeronautical Society
RAF Royal Air Force
RAFA Royal Air Forces Association
RAFO Reserve of Air Force Officers (*now see* RAFRO)
RAFR Royal Air Force Reserve
RAFRO Royal Air Force Reserve of Officers
RAFVR Royal Air Force Volunteer Reserve
RAI Royal Anthropological Institute of Great Britain & Ireland; Radio Audizioni Italiane
RAIA Royal Australian Institute of Architects
RAIC Royal Architectural Institute of Canada
RAM (Member of) Royal Academy of Music
RAMC Royal Army Medical Corps
RAN Royal Australian Navy
R&D Research and Development

RANR Royal Australian Naval Reserve
RANVR Royal Australian Naval Volunteer Reserve
RAOC Royal Army Ordnance Corps
RAPC Royal Army Pay Corps
RARDE Royal Armament Research and Development Establishment
RARO Regular Army Reserve of Officers
RAS Royal Astronomical Society; Royal Asiatic Society; Recruitment and Assessment Services
RASC Royal Army Service Corps (*now see* RCT)
RASE Royal Agricultural Society of England
RAU Royal Agricultural University
RAuxAF Royal Auxiliary Air Force
RAVC Royal Army Veterinary Corps
RB Rifle Brigade
RBA Member, Royal Society of British Artists
RBK&C Royal Borough of Kensington and Chelsea
RBL Royal British Legion
RBS Royal Society of British Sculptors
RBSA (Member of) Royal Birmingham Society of Artists
RBY Royal Bucks Yeomanry
RC Roman Catholic
RCA Member, Royal Canadian Academy of Arts; Royal College of Art; (Member of) Royal Cambrian Academy
RCAC Royal Canadian Armoured Corps
RCAF Royal Canadian Air Force
RCamA Member, Royal Cambrian Academy
RCAnaes Royal College of Anaesthetists
RCAS Royal Central Asian Society (*now see* RSAA)
RCCM Research Council for Complementary Medicine
RCDS Royal College of Defence Studies
rcds completed a course at, or served for a year on the Staff of, the Royal College of Defence Studies
RCGP Royal College of General Practitioners
RCHA Royal Canadian Horse Artillery
RCHME Royal Commission on Historical Monuments of England
RCM (Member of) Royal College of Music
RCN Royal Canadian Navy; Royal College of Nursing
RCNC Royal Corps of Naval Constructors
RCNR Royal Canadian Naval Reserve
RCNVR Royal Canadian Naval Volunteer Reserve
RCO Royal College of Organists
RCOG Royal College of Obstetricians and Gynaecologists
RCP Royal College of Physicians, London
RCPA Royal College of Pathologists of Australia
RCPath Royal College of Pathologists
RCPCH Royal College of Paediatrics and Child Health
RCPE or **RCPEd** Royal College of Physicians, Edinburgh
RCPI Royal College of Physicians of Ireland
RCPSG Royal College of Physicians and Surgeons of Glasgow
RCPsych Royal College of Psychiatrists
RCR Royal College of Radiologists
RCS Royal College of Surgeons of England; Royal Corps of Signals; Royal College of Science
RCSE or **RCSEd** Royal College of Surgeons of Edinburgh
RCSI Royal College of Surgeons in Ireland
RCT Royal Corps of Transport
RCVS Royal College of Veterinary Surgeons
RD Rural Dean; Royal Naval and Royal Marine Forces Reserve Decoration
Rd Road
RDA Diploma of Roseworthy Agricultural College, South Australia; Regional Development Agency
RDC Rural District Council
RDF Royal Dublin Fusiliers
RDI Royal Designer for Industry (Royal Society of Arts)
RE Royal Engineers; Fellow, Royal Society of Painter-Printmakers (*formerly* of Painter-Etchers and Engravers); Religious Education
REACH Retired Executives Action Clearing House
react Research Education and Aid for Children with potentially Terminal illness
Rear Adm. Rear Admiral
REconS Royal Economic Society
REF Research Excellence Framework
Regt Regiment
REIT Real Estate Investment Trust
REME Royal Electrical and Mechanical Engineers
REngDes Registered Engineering Designer
REOWS Royal Engineers Officers' Widows' Society
REPAC Regional Environmental Protection Advisory Committee
REPC Regional Economic Planning Council
RERO Royal Engineers Reserve of Officers
Res. Resigned; Reserve; Resident; Research
Rev. Reverend; Review
RFA Royal Field Artillery
RFC Royal Flying Corps (*now* RAF); Rugby Football Club
RFCA Reserve Forces and Cadets Association
RFD Reserve Force Decoration
RFH Royal Festival Hall
RFN Registered Fever Nurse
RFP Registered Forensic Practitioner
RFPS(G) Royal Faculty of Physicians and Surgeons, Glasgow (*now see* RCPSG)
RFR Rassemblement des Français pour la République
RFU Rugby Football Union
RGA Royal Garrison Artillery
RGI Royal Glasgow Institute of the Fine Arts
RGJ Royal Green Jackets
RGN Registered General Nurse
RGS Royal Geographical Society
RGSA Royal Geographical Society of Australasia
RHA Royal Hibernian Academy; Royal Horse Artillery; Regional Health Authority
RHASS Royal Highland and Agricultural Society of Scotland
RHB Regional Hospital Board
RHBNC Royal Holloway and Bedford New College, London
RHC Royal Holloway College, London (later RHBNC)
RHF Royal Highland Fusiliers
RHG Royal Horse Guards
RHistS Royal Historical Society
RHQ Regional Headquarters
RHR Royal Highland Regiment
RHS Royal Horticultural Society; Royal Humane Society
RHUL Royal Holloway, University of London
RHV Royal Health Visitor; Registered Health Visitor
RI (Member of) Royal Institute of Painters in Water Colours; Rhode Island
RIA Royal Irish Academy
RIAI Royal Institute of the Architects of Ireland
RIAS Royal Incorporation of Architects in Scotland
RIASC Royal Indian Army Service Corps
RIBA (Member of) Royal Institute of British Architects
RIBI Rotary International in Great Britain and Ireland
RIC Royal Irish Constabulary; Royal Institute of Chemistry (*now see* RSC)
RICS (Member of) Royal Institution of Chartered Surveyors
RIE Royal Indian Engineering (College)
RIF Royal Inniskilling Fusiliers
RIIA Royal Institute of International Affairs
RILEM Réunion internationale des laboratoires d'essais et de recherches sur les matériaux et les constructions
RIM Royal Indian Marines
RIN Royal Indian Navy
RINA Royal Institution of Naval Architects
RINVR Royal Indian Naval Volunteer Reserve
RIPA Royal Institute of Public Administration
RIPH Royal Institute of Public Health (*now see* RSPH)
RIPH&H Royal Institute of Public Health and Hygiene (later RIPH; *now see* RSPH)
RIrF Royal Irish Fusiliers
RLC Royal Logistic Corps
RLFC Rugby League Football Club
RLSS Royal Life Saving Society
RM Royal Marines; Resident Magistrate; Registered Midwife
RMA Royal Marine Artillery; Royal Military Academy Sandhurst (*now* incorporating Royal Military Academy, Woolwich)
RMB Rural Mail Base
RMC Royal Military College Sandhurst (*now see* RMA)
RMCM (Member of) Royal Manchester College of Music
RMCS Royal Military College of Science
RMedSoc Royal Medical Society, Edinburgh
RMetS Royal Meteorological Society
RMFVR Royal Marine Forces Volunteer Reserve
RMIT Royal Melbourne Institute of Technology
RMLI Royal Marine Light Infantry
RMN Registered Mental Nurse
RMO Resident Medical Officer(s)
RMP Royal Military Police
RMPA Royal Medico-Psychological Association
RMS Royal Microscopical Society; Royal Mail Steamer; Royal Society of Miniature Painters; Royal Mail Ship
RMT National Union of Rail, Maritime and Transport Workers; Registered Massage Therapist
RN Royal Navy; Royal Naval; Registered Nurse
RNAS Royal Naval Air Service
RNAY Royal Naval Aircraft Yard
RNC Royal Naval College
RNCM (Member of) Royal Northern College of Music
RNEC Royal Naval Engineering College
RNIB Royal National Institute of Blind People (*formerly* Royal National Institute for the Blind, then Royal National Institute of the Blind)
RNID Royal National Institute for Deaf People (*formerly* Royal National Institute for the Deaf)
RNLI Royal National Life-boat Institution
RNLO Royal Naval Liaison Officer
RNLTA Royal Naval Lawn Tennis Association
RNR Royal Naval Reserve
RNRU Royal Navy Rugby Union

RNS Royal Numismatic Society
RNSA Royal Naval Sailing Association
RNSC Royal Naval Staff College
RNT Registered Nurse Tutor; Royal National Theatre
RNTNEH Royal National Throat, Nose and Ear Hospital
RNUR Régie Nationale des Usines Renault
RNVR Royal Naval Volunteer Reserve
RNVSR Royal Naval Volunteer Supplementary Reserve
RNXS Royal Naval Auxiliary Service
RNZA Royal New Zealand Artillery
RNZAC Royal New Zealand Armoured Corps
RNZAF Royal New Zealand Air Force
RNZIR Royal New Zealand Infantry Regiment
RNZN Royal New Zealand Navy
RNZNVR Royal New Zealand Naval Volunteer Reserve
ROC Royal Observer Corps
ROF Royal Ordnance Factories
R of O Reserve of Officers
ROI Member, Royal Institute of Oil Painters
RoSPA Royal Society for the Prevention of Accidents
(Rot.) Rotunda Hospital, Dublin (after degree)
RP (Member of) Royal Society of Portrait Painters
RPC Royal Pioneer Corps
RPE Rocket Propulsion Establishment
RPF Rassemblement pour la France
RPMS Royal Postgraduate Medical School
RPO Royal Philharmonic Orchestra
RPP Registered Project Professional
RPR Rassemblement pour la République
RPS Royal Photographic Society
RPSGB Royal Pharmaceutical Society of Great Britain
RRC Royal Red Cross; Rapid Reaction Corps
RRE Royal Radar Establishment (later RSRE)
RRF Royal Regiment of Fusiliers
RRS Royal Research Ship
RSA Royal Scottish Academician; Royal Society of Arts; Republic of South Africa
RSAA Royal Society for Asian Affairs
RSAF Royal Small Arms Factory
RSAI Royal Society of Antiquaries of Ireland
RSAMD Royal Scottish Academy of Music and Drama
RSanI Royal Sanitary Institute (later RSH; *now see* RSPH)
RSAS Royal Surgical Aid Society
RSC Royal Society of Canada; Royal Society of Chemistry; Royal Shakespeare Company
RSCM (Member of) Royal School of Church Music
RSCN Registered Sick Children's Nurse
RSE Royal Society of Edinburgh
RSF Royal Scots Fusiliers
RSFSR Russian Soviet Federated Socialist Republic
RSGS Royal Scottish Geographical Society
RSH Royal Society for the Promotion of Health (*now see* RSPH)
RSL Royal Society of Literature; Returned Services League of Australia
RSM Royal School of Mines
RSM or RSocMed Royal Society of Medicine
RSMA (Member of) Royal Society of Marine Artists
RSME Royal School of Military Engineering
RSMHCA Royal Society for Mentally Handicapped Children and Adults (*see* Mencap)
RSNC Royal Society for Nature Conservation
RSO Rural Sub-Office; Railway Sub-Office; Resident Surgical Officer
RSPB Royal Society for Protection of Birds
RSPCA Royal Society for Prevention of Cruelty to Animals
RSPH Royal Society for Public Health
RSRE Royal Signals and Radar Establishment
RSSAf Royal Society of South Africa
RSSAILA Returned Sailors, Soldiers and Airmen's Imperial League of Australia (*now see* RSL)
RSSPCC Royal Scottish Society for Prevention of Cruelty to Children
RSTM&H Royal Society of Tropical Medicine and Hygiene
RSUA Royal Society of Ulster Architects
RSV Revised Standard Version; Respiratory Syncytial Virus
RSW Member, Royal Scottish Society of Painters in Water Colours
RTE Radio Telefis Eireann
Rt Hon. Right Honourable
RTL Radio-Télévision Luxembourg
RTO Railway Transport Officer
RTPI Royal Town Planning Institute
RTR Royal Tank Regiment
Rt Rev. Right Reverend
RTS Religious Tract Society; Royal Toxophilite Society; Royal Television Society
RTYC Royal Thames Yacht Club
RU Rugby Union
RUA Royal Ulster Academy
RUC Royal Ulster Constabulary
RUI Royal University of Ireland
RUKBA Royal United Kingdom Beneficent Association
RUR Royal Ulster Regiment
RURAL Society for the Responsible Use of Resources in Agriculture & on the Land
RUSI Royal United Services Institute for Defence and Security Studies (*formerly* Royal United Service Institution)
RVC Royal Veterinary College
RVS Royal Voluntary Service
RWA (Member of) Royal West of England Academy
RWAFF Royal West African Frontier Force
RWCMD Royal Welsh College of Music and Drama
RWF Royal Welch Fusiliers
RWS (Member of) Royal Society of Painters in Water Colours
RYA Royal Yachting Association
RYS Royal Yacht Squadron
RZSScot Royal Zoological Society of Scotland

S

(S) (in Navy) Paymaster; Scotland
S Succeeded; South; Saint
s son
SA South Australia; South Africa; Société Anonyme; Society of the Atonement
SAAF South African Air Force
SABC South African Broadcasting Corporation
SAC Scientific Advisory Committee
sac qualified at small arms technical long course
SACC South African Council of Churches
SACEUR Supreme Allied Commander Europe
SACIF sociedad anónima commercial industrial financiera
SACLANT Supreme Allied Commander Atlantic
SACRO Scottish Association for the Care and Resettlement of Offenders
SACSEA Supreme Allied Command, SE Asia
SA de CV sociedad anónima de capital variable
SADF Sudanese Auxiliary Defence Force
SADG Société des Architectes Diplômés par le Gouvernement
SAE Society of Automobile Engineers (US)
SAHFOS Sir Alister Hardy Foundation for Ocean Science
SAMC South African Medical Corps
SAN Senior Advocate of Nigeria
SARL Société à Responsabilité Limitée
Sarum Salisbury
SAS Special Air Service
Sask Saskatchewan
SASO Senior Air Staff Officer
SAT Senior Member, Association of Accounting Technicians
SATB Soprano, Alto, Tenor, Bass
SATRO Science and Technology Regional Organisation
SB Bachelor of Science (US)
SBAA Sovereign Base Areas Administration
SBAC Society of British Aerospace Companies (*formerly* Society of British Aircraft Constructors)
SBS Special Boat Service; Silver Bauhinia Star (Hong Kong)
SBStJ Serving Brother, Most Venerable Order of the Hospital of St John of Jerusalem
SC Star of Courage (Canada); Senior Counsel; South Carolina
sc student at the Staff College
SCA Society of Catholic Apostolate (Pallottine Fathers); Société en Commandité par Actions
SCAA School Curriculum and Assessment Authority
SCAO Senior Civil Affairs Officer
SCAR Scientific Committee for Antarctic Research
ScD Doctor of Science
SCDC Schools Curriculum Development Committee
SCDI Scottish Council for Development and Industry
SCF Senior Chaplain to the Forces; Save the Children Fund
Sch. School
SChStJ Senior Chaplain, Order of St John of Jerusalem
SCI Society of Chemical Industry
SCIE Social Care Institute of Excellence
SCIS Scottish Council of Independent Schools
SCL Student in Civil Law
SCLC Short Service Limited Commission
SCLI Somerset and Cornwall Light Infantry
SCM State Certified Midwife; Student Christian Movement
SCOB Supreme Counsellor of Baobab (South Africa)
SCONUL Standing Conference of National and University Libraries
SCOP Standing Conference of Principals
Scot. Scotland
ScotBIC Scottish Business in the Community
SCOTMEG Scottish Management Efficiency Group
SCOTVEC Scottish Vocational Education Council
SCRL Sociedade Cooperativa de Responsabilidade Limitada
SCVO Scottish Council for Voluntary Organisations
SD Staff Duties; South Dakota (postal)
SDA Social Democratic Alliance; Scottish Diploma in Agriculture; Scottish Development Agency

SDF Sudan Defence Force; Social Democratic Federation
SDI Strategic Defence Initiative
SDLP Social Democratic and Labour Party
SDP Social Democratic Party
SE South-east
SEAC South-East Asia Command
SEALF South-East Asia Land Forces
SEATO South-East Asia Treaty Organization
SEC Security Exchange Commission
Sec. Secretary
SED Scottish Education Department
SEE Society of Environmental Engineers
SEEDA South East England Development Agency
SEFI European Society for Engineering Education
SEN State Enrolled Nurse; Special Educational Needs
SEP Stanford Executive Program
SEPA Scottish Environmental Protection Agency
SEPM Society of Economic Palaeontologists and Mineralogists
SERC Science and Engineering Research Council
SERT Society of Electronic and Radio Technicians (later IEIE)
SESO Senior Equipment Staff Officer
SF Sinn Féin
SFA Securities and Futures Authority
SFC Scottish Further and Higher Education Funding Council
SFHEA Senior Fellow, Higher Education Academy
SFOR Stabilisation Force
SFSEDA Senior Fellow, Staff and Higher Educational Development Association
SFTA Society of Film and Television Arts (*now see* BAFTA)
SFTCD Senior Fellow, Trinity College Dublin
SG Solicitor-General
SGA Member, Society of Graphic Art
Sgt Sergeant
SHA Secondary Heads Association (*now see* ASCL); Special Health Authority
SHAC London Housing Aid Centre
SHAEF Supreme Headquarters, Allied Expeditionary Force
SHAPE Supreme Headquarters, Allied Powers, Europe
SHEFC Scottish Higher Education Funding Council (*now see* SFC)
SHHD Scottish Home and Health Department
SHND Scottish Higher National Diploma
SHO Senior House Officer
SIA Security Industry Authority
SIAD Society of Industrial Artists and Designers (*now see* CSD)
SIAM Society of Industrial and Applied Mathematics (US)
SIB Shipbuilding Industry Board; Securities and Investments Board (*now see* FSA)
SICA-FICA Foundation for International Commercial Arbitration
SICAV Société d'Investissement à Capital Variable
SICOT Société Internationale de Chirurgie Orthopédique et de Traumatologie
SID Society for International Development
SIESO Society of Industrial and Emergency Services Officers
SIMA Scientific Instrument Manufacturers' Association of Great Britain
SIME Security Intelligence Middle East
SIMG *Societas Internationalis Medicinae Generalis*
SinDrs Doctor of Chinese
SIROT Société Internationale pour Recherche en Orthopédie et Traumatologie
SIS Secret Intelligence Service
SITA Société Internationale de Télécommunications Aéronautiques
SITPRO Simpler Trade Procedures Board (*formerly* Simplification of International Trade Procedures)
SJ Society of Jesus (Jesuits)
SJAB St John Ambulance Brigade
SJD Doctor of Juristic Science
SK Saskatchewan (postal)
SL Serjeant-at-Law; Sociedad Limitada
SLA Special Libraries Association
SLAC Stanford Linear Accelerator Centre
SLC St Lucia Cross
SLD Social and Liberal Democrats
SLJ Seri Laila Jasa (Brunei)
SLP Scottish Labour Party
SLS Society of Legal Scholars
SM Medal of Service (Canada) (*now see* OC); Master of Science; Officer qualified for Submarine Duties
SMA Society of Marine Artists (*now see* RSMA)
SMB Setia Mahkota Brunei
SMCC Submarine Commanding Officers' Command Course
SME School of Military Engineering (*now see* RSME)
SMEO Squadron Marine Engineer Officer
SMHO Sovereign Military Hospitaller Order (Malta)
SMIEE Senior Member, Institute of Electrical and Electronics Engineers (New York)
SMMT Society of Motor Manufacturers and Traders Ltd
SMN Seri Maharaja Mangku Negara (Malaysia)
SMO Senior Medical Officer; Sovereign Military Order
SMP Senior Managers' Program
SMPTE Society of Motion Picture and Television Engineers (US)
SMRTB Ship and Marine Requirements Technology Board
SNAME Society of Naval Architects and Marine Engineers (US)
SNCF Société Nationale des Chemins de Fer Français
SND Sisters of Notre Dame
SNH Scottish Natural Heritage
SNP Scottish National Party
SNTS Society for New Testament Studies
SO Staff Officer; Scientific Officer; Symphony Orchestra
SOAF Sultan of Oman's Air Force
SOAS School of Oriental and African Studies
Soc. Society; Socialist (France, Belgium)
SOCA Serious and Organised Crime Agency
Soc & Lib Dem Social and Liberal Democrats (*now see* Lib Dem)
SocCE(France) Société des Ingénieurs Civils de France
Soc Dem Social Democrats
SOE Special Operations Executive; Society of Operations Engineers
SOGAT Society of Graphical and Allied Trades (*now see* GPMU)
SOLACE or **Solace** Society of Local Authority Chief Executives
SOLT Society of London Theatre
SOM Society of Occupational Medicine; Saskatchewan Order of Merit (Canada)
SOSc Society of Ordained Scientists
SOTS Society for Old Testament Study
sowc Senior Officers' War Course
SP Self-Propelled (Anti-Tank Regiment)
sp *sine prole* (without issue)
SpA Società per Azioni
SPAB Society for the Protection of Ancient Buildings
SPARKS Sport Aiding Medical Research for Children
SPCA Society for the Prevention of Cruelty to Animals
SPCK Society for Promoting Christian Knowledge
SPCM Darjah Seri Paduka Cura Si Manja Kini (Malaysia)
SPD Salisbury Plain District; Sozialdemokratische Partei Deutschlands
SPDK Seri Panglima Darjal Kinabalu
SPG Society for the Propagation of the Gospel (*now see* USPG)
SPk Sitara-e-Pakistan
SPMB Seri Paduka Makhota Brunei
SPMK Darjah Kebasaran Seri Paduka Mahkota Kelantan (Malaysia)
SPMO Senior Principal Medical Officer
SPNC Society for the Promotion of Nature Conservation (*now see* RSNC)
SPNM Society for the Promotion of New Music
SPR Society for Psychical Research
sprl société de personnes à responsabilité limitée
SPSO Senior Principal Scientific Officer
SPTL Society of Public Teachers of Law (*now see* SLS)
SPUC Society for the Protection of Unborn Children (*formerly* the Unborn Child)
Sq. Square
sq staff qualified
SQA Sitara-i-Quaid-i-Azam (Pakistan)
Sqdn or **Sqn** Squadron
SR Special Reserve; Southern Railway; Southern Region (BR)
SRA Solicitors Regulation Authority
SRC Science Research Council (later SERC); Students' Representative Council
SRCh State Registered Chiropodist
SRHE Society for Research into Higher Education
SRIS Science Reference Information Service
SRN State Registered Nurse
SRNA Shipbuilders and Repairers National Association
SRO Supplementary Reserve of Officers; Self-Regulatory Organisation
SRP State Registered Physiotherapist
SRY Sherwood Rangers Yeomanry
SS Saints; Straits Settlements; Steamship
SSA Society of Scottish Artists; Side Saddle Association
SSAC Social Security Advisory Committee
SSAFA Soldiers, Sailors, Airmen and Families Association (*formerly* Soldiers', Sailors', and Airmen's Families Association, then Soldiers, Sailors, Airmen and Families Association Forces Help)
SSBN Nuclear Submarine, Ballistic
SSC Solicitor before Supreme Court (Scotland); Sculptors Society of Canada; *Societas Sanctae Crucis* (Society of the Holy Cross); Short Service Commission
SSEB South of Scotland Electricity Board
SSEES School of Slavonic and East European Studies
SSF Society of St Francis
SSJE Society of St John the Evangelist
SSLC Short Service Limited Commission
SSM Society of the Sacred Mission; Seri Setia Mahkota (Malaysia)
SSO Senior Supply Officer; Senior Scientific Officer
SSR Soviet Socialist Republic
SSRC Social Science Research Council (*now see* ESRC)
SSSI Sites of Special Scientific Interest

SSSR Society for the Scientific Study of Religion
SSStJ Serving Sister, Most Venerable Order of the Hospital of St John of Jerusalem
St Street; Saint
STA Sail Training Association
STB *Sacrae Theologiae Baccalaureus* (Bachelor of Sacred Theology)
STC Senior Training Corps
STD *Sacrae Theologiae Doctor* (Doctor of Sacred Theology)
STEP Skills To Empower Programme
STETS Southern Theological Education and Training Scheme
STFC Science and Technology Facilities Council
STh Scholar in Theology
Stip. Stipend; Stipendiary
STL *Sacrae Theologiae Lector* (Reader or a Professor of Sacred Theology)
STM *Sacrae Theologiae Magister* (Master of Sacred Theology)
STP *Sacrae Theologiae Professor* (Professor of Divinity, old form of DD)
STSO Senior Technical Staff Officer
STV Scottish Television
SUNY State University of New York
Supp. Res. Supplementary Reserve (of Officers)
Supt Superintendent
Surg. Surgeon
Surv. Surviving
SW South-west
SWET Society of West End Theatre (*now see* SOLT)
SWIA Society of Wildlife Artists
SWO Staff Warfare Officer
SWPA South West Pacific Area
SWRB Sadler's Wells Royal Ballet

T

T Telephone; Territorial
TA Telegraphic Address; Territorial Army
TAA Territorial Army Association
TAF Tactical Air Force
T&AFA Territorial and Auxiliary Forces Association
T&AVR Territorial and Army Volunteer Reserve
TANS Territorial Army Nursing Service
TANU Tanganyika African National Union
TARO Territorial Army Reserve of Officers
TAS Torpedo and Anti Submarine Course
TASS Technical, Administrative and Supervisory Section of AUEW (now part of MSF)
TAVRA or TA&VRA Territorial Auxiliary and Volunteer Reserve Association (*now see* RFCA)
TC Order of the Trinity Cross (Trinidad and Tobago)
TCCB Test and County Cricket Board (*now see* ECB)
TCD Trinity College, Dublin (University of Dublin, Trinity College)
TCF Temporary Chaplain to the Forces
TCPA Town and Country Planning Association
TD Territorial Efficiency Decoration; Efficiency Decoration (T&AVR) (since April 1967); Teachta Dala (Member of the Dáil, Eire)
TDA Training and Development Agency for Schools
TDD Tubercular Diseases Diploma
TE Technical Engineer
TEAC Technical Educational Advisory Council
TEC Technician Education Council (later BTEC); Training and Enterprise Council
Tech(CEI) Technician
TechRICS Technical Member, Royal Institution of Chartered Surveyors
TEFL Teaching English as a Foreign Language
TEFLA Teaching English as a Foreign Language to Adults
TEM Territorial Efficiency Medal
TEMA Telecommunication Engineering and Manufacturing Association
Temp. Temperature; Temporary
TEng(CEI) Technician Engineer (*now see* IEng)
Tenn Tennessee
TEO Teaching English Overseas
TeolD Doctor of Theology
TES Times Educational Supplement
TESL Teaching English as a Second Language
TESOL Teaching English to Speakers of other Languages
Tex Texas
TF Territorial Force
TfL Transport for London
TFR Territorial Force Reserve
TFTS Tactical Fighter Training Squadron
TGEW Timber Growers England and Wales Ltd
TGO Timber Growers' Organisation (*now see* TGEW)
TGWU Transport and General Workers' Union
ThD Doctor of Theology
THED Transvaal Higher Education Diploma
THES Times Higher Education Supplement
ThL Theological Licentiate
ThM Master of Theology
ThSchol Scholar in Theology
TIMS The Institute of Management Sciences (*now see* INFORMS)
TISCA The Independent Schools Christian Alliance
TLS Times Literary Supplement
TMA Theatrical Management Association
TN Tennessee (postal)
TNC Theatres National Committee
TOPSS Training Organisation for the Personal Social Services
TPI Town Planning Institute (*now see* RTPI)
TPP Transport Planning Professional
TPsych Trainer in Psychiatry
TQ Teaching Qualification
TRA Tenants' and Residents' Association
Trans. Translation; Translated
Transf. Transferred
TrATB Treble, Alto, Tenor, Bass
TRC Thames Rowing Club
TRE Telecommunications Research Establishment (later RRE)
TRH Their Royal Highnesses
TRIC Television and Radio Industries Club
Trin. Trinity
TRL Transport Research Laboratory
TRRL Transport and Road Research Laboratory (*now see* TRL)
TS Training Ship
TSB Trustee Savings Bank
tsc passed a Territorial Army Course in Staff Duties
TSE Transmissible Spongiform Encephalopathies
TSSA Transport Salaried Staffs' Association
TSSF Tertiary, Society of St Francis
TSWA Television South West Arts
TTA Teacher Training Agency (*now see* TDA)
TUC Trades Union Congress
TUS Trade Union Side
TUSC Trade Unionist and Socialist Coalition
TUV Traditional Unionist Voice
TV Television
TVEI Technical and Vocational Education Initiative
TWA Thames Water Authority
TX Texas (postal)

U

U Unionist
u uncle
UA Unitary Authority
UACE Universities Association for Continuing Education
UAE United Arab Emirates
UAL University of the Arts London
UAR United Arab Republic
UAU Universities Athletic Union
UBC University of British Columbia
UBI Understanding British Industry
UC University College
UCAS Universities and Colleges Admissions Service
UCCA Universities Central Council on Admissions
UCCF Universities and Colleges Christian Fellowship of Evangelical Unions
UCD University College Dublin
UCE University of Central England
UCEA Universities and Colleges Employers Association
UCET Universities Council for Education of Teachers
UCH University College Hospital (London)
UCL University College London
UCLA University of California at Los Angeles
UCLES University of Cambridge Local Examinations Syndicate
UCLH University College London Hospital
UCMSM University College and Middlesex School of Medicine
UCNS Universities' Council for Non-academic Staff
UCNW University College of North Wales
UCRN University College of Rhodesia and Nyasaland
UCS University College School
UCSB University of California at Santa Barbara
UCSD University of California at San Diego
UCSF University of California at San Francisco
UCUNF Ulster Conservatives and Unionists - New Force
UCW University College of Wales; Union of Communication Workers (*now see* CWU)
UDC Urban District Council; Urban Development Corporation
UDF Union Defence Force; Union pour la démocratie française
UDM United Democratic Movement (South Africa)
UDR Ulster Defence Regiment; Union des Démocrates pour la Vème République (later RPR)
UDSR Union Démocratique et Socialiste de la Résistance
UEA University of East Anglia
UED University Education Diploma
UEFA Union of European Football Associations

UEL University of East London
UEMS Union Européenne des Médecins Spécialistes
UF United Free Church
UFAW Universities Federation for Animal Welfare
UFC Universities' Funding Council
UGC University Grants Committee (later UFC)
UHI University of the Highlands and Islands (*formerly* University of the Highlands and Islands Millennium Institute)
UIAA Union Internationale des Associations d'Alpinisme
UICC Union Internationale contre le Cancer
UIE Union Internationale des Etudiants
UISPP Union Internationale des Sciences Préhistoriques et Protohistoriques
UITP International Union of Public Transport
UJD *Utriusque Juris Doctor* (Doctor of both Laws, Doctor of Canon and Civil Law)
UK United Kingdom
UKAC United Kingdom Automation Council
UKAEA United Kingdom Atomic Energy Authority
UKCC United Kingdom Central Council for Nursing, Midwifery and Health Visiting
UKCCCR United Kingdom Co-ordinating Committee on Cancer Research
UKCICC United Kingdom Commanders-in-Chief Committees
UKCISA United Kingdom Council for International Student Affairs
UKCOSA United Kingdom Council for Overseas Student Affairs (*now see* UKCISA)
UKCP United Kingdom Council for Psychotherapy
UKERNA United Kingdom Education and Research Networking Association
UKIAS United Kingdom Immigrants' Advisory Service
UKIC United Kingdom Institute for Conservation
UKIP United Kingdom Independence Party
UKLF United Kingdom Land Forces
UKMEA United Kingdom, Middle East and Africa
UKMF(L) United Kingdom Military Forces (Land)
UKMIS United Kingdom Mission
UKOLN United Kingdom Office of Library Networking
UKOOA United Kingdom Offshore Operators Association
UKPIA United Kingdom Petroleum Industry Association Ltd
UKSC United Kingdom Support Command
UKSLS United Kingdom Services Liaison Staff
UKTI UK Trade & Investment
UKU United Kingdom Unionist
ULPS Union of Liberal and Progressive Synagogues
UMDS United Medical and Dental Schools
UMIST University of Manchester Institute of Science and Technology
UMP Union pour un Mouvement Populaire (*formerly* Union pour la Majorité Présidentielle)
UN United Nations
UNA United Nations Association
UNCAST United Nations Conference on the Applications of Science and Technology
UNCIO United Nations Conference on International Organisation
UNCITRAL United Nations Commission on International Trade Law
UNCSTD United Nations Conference on Science and Technology for Development
UNCTAD or **Unctad** United Nations Commission for Trade and Development
UNDP United Nations Development Programme
UNDRO United Nations Disaster Relief Organisation
UNECA United Nations Economic Commission for Asia
UNECE United Nations Economic Commission for Europe
UNED United Nations Environment and Development
UNEP United Nations Environment Programme
UNESCO or **Unesco** United Nations Educational, Scientific and Cultural Organisation
UNFAO United Nations Food and Agriculture Organisation
UNFICYP United Nations Force in Cyprus
UNHCR United Nations High Commissioner for Refugees
UNICE Union des Industries de la Communauté Européenne
UNICEF or **Unicef** United Nations Children's Fund (*formerly* United Nations International Children's Emergency Fund)
UNIDO United Nations Industrial Development Organisation
UNIDROIT Institut International pour l'Unification du Droit Privé
UNIFEM United Nations Development Fund for Women
UNIFIL United Nations Interim Force in Lebanon
UNIPEDE Union Internationale des Producteurs et Distributeurs d'Energie Electrique
UNISIST Universal System for Information in Science and Technology
UNITAR United Nations Institute of Training and Research
Univ. University
UNO United Nations Organization
UNODC United Nations Office on Drugs and Crime
UNRRA United Nations Relief and Rehabilitation Administration
UNRWA United Nations Relief and Works Agency
UNSCOB United Nations Special Commission on the Balkans
UP United Provinces; Uttar Pradesh; United Presbyterian
UPGC University and Polytechnic Grants Committee
UPNI Unionist Party of Northern Ireland
UPU Universal Postal Union
UPUP Ulster Popular Unionist Party
URC United Reformed Church; Urban Regeneration Company
URSI Union Radio-Scientifique Internationale
US United States
USA United States of America
USAAF United States Army Air Force
USAF United States Air Force
USAID United States Agency for International Development
USAR United States Army Reserve
USC University of Southern California
USDAW Union of Shop Distributive and Allied Workers
USM Unlisted Securities Market
USMA United States Military Academy
USMC United States Marine Corps
USN United States Navy
USNR United States Naval Reserve
USPG United Society for the Propagation of the Gospel
USPHS United States Public Health Service
USPS United States Postal Service
USS United States Ship
USSR Union of Soviet Socialist Republics
USVI United States Virgin Islands
UT Utah (postal)
UTC University Training Corps
U3A University of the Third Age
UTS University of Technology, Sydney
UU Ulster Unionist
UUK Universities UK
UUUC United Ulster Unionist Coalition
UUUP United Ulster Unionist Party
UWCC University of Wales College of Cardiff
UWCM University of Wales College of Medicine
UWE University of the West of England
UWIC University of Wales Institute, Cardiff
UWIST University of Wales Institute of Science and Technology
UWP United Workers' Party (Dominica)
UWS University of the West of Scotland
UWT Union of Women Teachers

V

V Five (Roman numerals); Version; Vicar; Viscount; Vice
v *versus* (against)
v or **vid.** *vide* (see)
VA Virginia (postal)
Va Virginia
VAD Voluntary Aid Detachment
V&A Victoria and Albert
VAT Value Added Tax
VC Victoria Cross; Voluntary Controlled
VCAS Vice Chief of the Air Staff
VCDS Vice Chief of the Defence Staff
VCGS Vice Chief of the General Staff
VCM Member, Victoria College of Music
VCNS Vice Chief of the Naval Staff
VCT Venture Capital Trust
VD Royal Naval Volunteer Reserve Officers' Decoration (*now* VRD); Volunteer Officers' Decoration; Victorian Decoration
VDC Volunteer Defence Corps
Ven. Venerable
Vet. Veterinary
VetMB Bachelor of Veterinary Medicine
VG Vicar-General
Vic Victoria
Vice Adm. Vice Admiral
VIP Very Important Person
Visc. Viscount
VLSI Very Large Scale Integration
VLV Voice of the Listener and Viewer
VM Victory Medal
VMA Fixed Wing Marine Attack
VMGO Vice Master General of the Ordnance
VMH Victoria Medal of Honour (Royal Horticultural Society)
VMI Virginia Military Institute
VMSM Voluntary Medical Services Medal
Vol. Volume; Voluntary; Volunteers
VP Vice-President
VPP Volunteer Political Party
VPRP Vice-President, Royal Society of Portrait Painters
VQMG Vice-Quartermaster-General
VR *Victoria Regina* (Queen Victoria); Volunteer Reserve
VRD Royal Naval Volunteer Reserve Officers' Decoration
VRSM Volunteer Reserves Service Medal
VSO Voluntary Service Overseas
VT Vermont (postal)
Vt Vermont
VUP Vanguard Unionist Party
VVD Volkspartij voor Vrijheiden Democratie

W

W	West; Website
WA	Western Australia; Washington (postal)
WAAF	Women's Auxiliary Air Force (later WRAF)
WACL	Women in Advertising and Communications, London
WAOS	Welsh Agricultural Organisations Society
Wash	Washington State
WCC	World Council of Churches
W/Cdr	Wing Commander
WCMD	Welsh College of Music and Drama (*now see* RWCMD)
WDA	Welsh Development Agency
WEA	Workers' Educational Association; Royal West of England Academy
WEF	World Economic Forum
WEU	Western European Union
WFEO	World Federation of Engineering Organisations
WFSW	World Federation of Scientific Workers
WFTU	World Federation of Trade Unions
WhF	Whitworth Fellow
WHO	World Health Organization
WhSch	Whitworth Scholar
WI	West Indies; Women's Institute; Wisconsin (postal)
Wilts	Wiltshire
WIPO	World Intellectual Property Organization
Wis	Wisconsin
Wits	Witwatersrand
WJEC	Welsh Joint Education Committee
WLA	Women's Land Army
WLD	Women Liberal Democrats
WLF	Women's Liberal Federation
Wm	William
WMA	World Medical Association
WMO	World Meteorological Organization
WNO	Welsh National Opera
WO	War Office; Warrant Officer
Worcs	Worcestershire
WOSB	War Office Selection Board
WR	West Riding; Western Region (BR)
WRAC	Women's Royal Army Corps
WRAF	Women's Royal Air Force
WRNS	Women's Royal Naval Service
WRVS	Women's Royal Voluntary Service (*now see* RVS)
WS	Writer to the Signet
WSAVA	World Small Animal Veterinary Association
WSET	Wine and Spirits Educational Trust
WSPA	World Society for the Protection of Animals
WSPU	Women's Social and Political Union
WTO	World Trade Organisation
WUS	World University Service
WV	West Virginia (postal)
WVS	Women's Voluntary Services (later WRVS)
WWF	World Wide Fund for Nature (*formerly* World Wildlife Fund)
WY	Wyoming (postal)

XYZ

X	Ten (Roman numerals)
XO	Executive Officer
y	youngest
YC	Young Conservative
YCNAC	Young Conservatives National Advisory Committee
Yeo.	Yeomanry
YHA	Youth Hostels Association
YMCA	Young Men's Christian Association
YOI	Young Offenders Institute
Yorks	Yorkshire
YPTES	Young People's Trust for Endangered Species
yr	younger
yrs	years
YT	Yukon Territory (postal)
YTS	Youth Training Scheme
YVFF	Young Volunteer Force Foundation
YWCA	Young Women's Christian Association
ZANU PF	Zimbabwe African National Union Patriotic Front
ZAPU	Zimbabwe African People's Union
ZIPRA	Zimbabwe People's Revolutionary Army

THE ROYAL FAMILY

Born

THE SOVEREIGN

Her Majesty Queen Elizabeth II, (Elizabeth Alexandra Mary) . . . . 21 April 1926

Succeeded her father, King George VI, 6 February 1952

Married 20 Nov. 1947, HRH The Duke of Edinburgh, *now* HRH The Prince Philip, Duke of Edinburgh, KG, KT, OM, GBE, ONZ, QSO, AK, GCL, CC, CMM (*b* 10 June 1921, *s* of HRH Prince Andrew of Greece (*d* 1944) and of HRH Princess Andrew of Greece (*d* 1969), *gg-d* of Queen Victoria; *cr* 1947, Baron Greenwich, Earl of Merioneth and Duke of Edinburgh)

Residences: Buckingham Palace, SW1A 1AA; Windsor Castle, Berkshire SL4 1NJ; Sandringham House, Norfolk PE35 6EN; Balmoral Castle, Aberdeenshire AB35 5TB.

SONS AND DAUGHTER OF HER MAJESTY

HRH The Prince of Wales, (Prince Charles Philip Arthur George), ... 14 Nov. 1948

KG, KT, GCB, OM, AK, QSO, ADC; *cr* 1958, Prince of Wales and Earl of Chester; Duke of Cornwall; Duke of Rothesay, Earl of Carrick and Baron of Renfrew; Lord of the Isles and Great Steward of Scotland

Married 1st, 29 July 1981, Lady Diana Frances Spencer (*b* 1 July 1961, *y d* of 8th Earl Spencer, LVO, she *d* 31 Aug. 1997), (marriage dissolved, 1996), and has issue –

HRH The Duke of Cambridge (Prince William Arthur Philip Louis), KG, KT, ADC;

cr 2011, Baron Carrickfergus, Earl of Strathearn and Duke of Cambridge . . . 21 June 1982

Married 29 April 2011, Catherine Elizabeth Middleton, *d* of Michael and Carole Middleton, and has issue –

HRH PRINCE GEORGE OF CAMBRIDGE, (PRINCE GEORGE ALEXANDER LOUIS). . 22 July 2013

HRH PRINCESS CHARLOTTE OF CAMBRIDGE, (PRINCESS CHARLOTTE ELIZABETH DIANA) 2 May 2015

HRH PRINCE HENRY OF WALES, (PRINCE HENRY CHARLES ALBERT DAVID), KCVO . 15 Sept. 1984

Married 2nd, 9 April 2005, Mrs Camilla Rosemary Parker Bowles (*now* HRH The Duchess of Cornwall, GCVO), *d* of late Major Bruce Shand, MC

Office: Clarence House, SW1A 1BA; *residences:* Highgrove, Doughton, Tetbury, Gloucestershire GL8 8TN; Birkhall, Ballater, Aberdeenshire.

HRH The Duke of York, (Prince Andrew Albert Christian Edward), KG, GCVO, ADC; . 19 Feb. 1960

cr 1986, Baron Killyleagh, Earl of Inverness and Duke of York

Married 23 July 1986, Sarah Margaret Ferguson, *now* Sarah, Duchess of York (*b* 15 Oct. 1959, 2nd *d* of late Major Ronald Ivor Ferguson, Life Guards), (marriage dissolved, 1996), and has issue –

HRH PRINCESS BEATRICE OF YORK, (PRINCESS BEATRICE ELIZABETH MARY) . . 8 Aug. 1988

HRH PRINCESS EUGENIE OF YORK, (PRINCESS EUGENIE VICTORIA HELENA). . . 23 March 1990

Office: Buckingham Palace, SW1A 1AA; *residence:* Royal Lodge, Windsor Great Park, Windsor, Berkshire SL4 2HW.

HRH The Earl of Wessex, (Prince Edward Antony Richard Louis), KG, GCVO, ADC; . 10 March 1964

cr 1999, Viscount Severn and Earl of Wessex

Married 19 June 1999, Sophie Helen Rhys-Jones, GCVO (*b* 20 Jan. 1965, *d* of Christopher and late Mary Rhys-Jones), and has issue –

JAMES ALEXANDER PHILIP THEO MOUNTBATTEN-WINDSOR, (VISCOUNT SEVERN, *qv*) . 17 Dec. 2007

LOUISE ALICE ELIZABETH MARY MOUNTBATTEN-WINDSOR, (LADY LOUISE WINDSOR) . 8 Nov. 2003

Office: Buckingham Palace, SW1A 1AA; *residence:* Bagshot Park, Bagshot, Surrey GU19 5PL.

HRH The Princess Royal, (Princess Anne Elizabeth Alice Louise), KG, KT, GCVO, QSO . 15 Aug. 1950

Married 1st, 14 Nov. 1973, Captain Mark Anthony Peter Phillips, *qv* (marriage dissolved, 1992), and has issue –

PETER MARK ANDREW PHILLIPS . . . . 15 Nov. 1977

Married 17 May 2008, Autumn Patricia, *d* of Brian Kelly, and has issue –

SAVANNAH ANNE KATHLEEN PHILLIPS . . . . 29 Dec. 2010

ISLA ELIZABETH PHILLIPS . . . . 29 March 2012

ZARA ANNE ELIZABETH PHILLIPS, MBE, (MRS M. J. TINDALL) . . . . . . 15 May 1981

Married 30 July 2011, Michael James Tindall, MBE, *s* of Philip and Linda Tindall, and has issue –

MIA GRACE TINDALL . . . . 17 Jan. 2014

Married 2nd, 12 Dec. 1992, Vice Admiral Sir Timothy James Hamilton Laurence, *qv*

Office: Buckingham Palace, SW1A 1AA; *residence:* Gatcombe Park, Minchinhampton, Stroud, Gloucestershire GL6 9AT.

NEPHEW AND NIECE OF HER MAJESTY

Children of HRH The Princess Margaret (Rose), (Countess of Snowdon, CI, GCVO, *b* 21 Aug. 1930, *d* 9 Feb. 2002) and 1st Earl of Snowdon, *qv*

Viscount Linley, (David Albert Charles Armstrong-Jones), *qv* . . . . 3 Nov. 1961

Married 8 Oct. 1993, Hon. Serena Alleyne Stanhope, *o d* of Earl of Harrington, *qv* and has issue –

HON. CHARLES PATRICK INIGO ARMSTRONG-JONES . . . . 1 July 1999

HON. MARGARITA ELIZABETH ALLEYNE ARMSTRONG-JONES . . . . . . 14 May 2002

Lady Sarah Chatto, (Sarah Frances Elizabeth Chatto) . . . . 1 May 1964

Married 14 July 1994, Daniel Chatto, *s* of late Thomas Chatto and Rosalind Chatto, and has issue –

SAMUEL DAVID BENEDICT CHATTO . . . . 28 July 1996

ARTHUR ROBERT NATHANIEL CHATTO . . . . 5 Feb. 1999

COUSINS OF HER MAJESTY

Child of HRH The Duke of Gloucester (Prince Henry William Frederick Albert, *b* 31 March 1900, *d* 10 June 1974) and HRH Princess Alice Christabel, Duchess of Gloucester, GCB, CI, GCVO, GBE (*b* 25 Dec. 1901, *d* 29 Oct. 2004), 3rd *d* of 7th Duke of Buccleuch

HRH The Duke of Gloucester, (Prince Richard Alexander Walter George), KG, GCVO . 26 Aug. 1944

Married 8 July 1972, Birgitte Eva van Deurs, GCVO (*b* 20 June 1946, *d* of Asger Preben Wissing Henriksen), and has issue –

ALEXANDER PATRICK GREGERS RICHARD, (EARL OF ULSTER, *qv*) . . . . . . 24 Oct. 1974

Married 22 June 2002, Dr Claire Alexandra, *d* of Mr and Mrs Robert Booth, and has issue –

XAN RICHARD ANDERS, (LORD CULLODEN, *qv*) . . . . 12 March 2007

COSIMA ROSE ALEXANDRA, (LADY COSIMA WINDSOR) . . . . . 20 May 2010

DAVINA ELIZABETH ALICE BENEDIKTE, (LADY DAVINA LEWIS) . . . . . 19 Nov. 1977

Married 31 July 2004, Gary Christie Lewis, and has issue –

TĀNE MAHUTA LEWIS . . . . 25 May 2012

SENNA KOWHAI LEWIS . . . . 22 June 2010

ROSE VICTORIA BIRGITTE LOUISE, (LADY ROSE GILMAN) . . . . . . 1 March 1980

Married 19 July 2008, George Edward Gilman, and has issue –

LYLA BEATRIX CHRISTABEL GILMAN . . . . 30 May 2010

RUFUS FREDERICK MONTAGU GILMAN . . . . 2 Nov. 2012

Residence: Kensington Palace, W8 4PU.

Children of HRH The Duke of Kent (Prince George Edward Alexander Edmund, *b* 20 Dec. 1902, *d* 25 Aug. 1942) and HRH Princess Marina, Duchess of Kent (*b* 13 Dec. 1906, *d* 27 Aug. 1968), *y d* of late Prince Nicholas of Greece

HRH The Duke of Kent, (Prince Edward George Nicholas Paul Patrick), KG, GCMG, GCVO 9 Oct. 1935

Married 8 June 1961, Katharine Lucy Mary Worsley, GCVO (*b* 22 Feb. 1933, *o d* of Sir William Worsley, 4th Bt), and has issue –

GEORGE PHILIP NICHOLAS, (EARL OF ST ANDREWS, *qv*) . . . . 26 June 1962

Married 9 Jan. 1988, Sylvana Tomaselli, and has issue –

EDWARD EDMUND MAXIMILIAN GEORGE, (BARON DOWNPATRICK, *qv*) . . . 2 Dec. 1988

MARINA-CHARLOTTE ALEXANDRA KATHARINE HELEN, (LADY MARINA-CHARLOTTE WINDSOR) 30 Sept. 1992

AMELIA SOPHIA THEODORA MARY MARGARET, (LADY AMELIA WINDSOR) . . 24 Aug. 1995

NICHOLAS CHARLES EDWARD JONATHAN, (LORD NICHOLAS WINDSOR) . . . . 25 July 1970

Married 19 Oct. 2006, Princess Paola Doimi de Lupis Frankopan Šubic Zrinski, and has issue –

ALBERT LOUIS PHILIP EDWARD WINDSOR . . . . 22 Sept. 2007

LEOPOLD ERNEST AUGUSTUS GUELPH WINDSOR . . . . 8 Sept. 2009

LOUIS ARTHUR NICHOLAS FELIX WINDSOR . . . . 27 May 2014

HELEN MARINA LUCY, (LADY HELEN TAYLOR) . . . . 28 April 1964

Married 18 July 1992, Timothy Verner Taylor, *e s* of Commander Michael Taylor, RN and Mrs Colin Walkinshaw, and has issue –

COLUMBUS GEORGE DONALD TAYLOR . . . . 6 Aug. 1994

CASSIUS EDWARD TAYLOR . . . . 26 Dec. 1996

ELOISE OLIVIA KATHARINE TAYLOR . . . . 2 March 2003

ESTELLA OLGA ELIZABETH TAYLOR . . . . 21 Dec. 2004

Office: St James's Palace, SW1A 1BQ; *residence:* Wren House, Palace Green, W8 4PY.

HRH Prince Michael of Kent, (Prince Michael George Charles Franklin), GCVO . . 4 July 1942

Married 30 June 1978, Baroness Marie-Christine Agnes Hedwig Ida von Reibnitz (*b* 15 Jan. 1945, *d* of Baron Günther Hubertus von Reibnitz), and has issue –

FREDERICK MICHAEL GEORGE DAVID LOUIS, (LORD FREDERICK WINDSOR) . . . 6 April 1979

Married 12 Sept. 2009, Sophie Lara, *d* of Barry and Cynthia Winkleman, and has issue –

MAUD ELIZABETH DAPHNE MARINA WINDSOR . . . . 15 Aug. 2013

GABRIELLA MARINA ALEXANDRA OPHELIA, (LADY GABRIELLA WINDSOR) . . . 23 April 1981

Residence: Kensington Palace, W8 4PU.

HRH Princess Alexandra (Helen Elizabeth Olga Christabel), The Hon. Lady Ogilvy, . . 25 Dec. 1936
KG, GCVO

Married 24 April 1963, Rt Hon. Sir Angus (James Bruce) Ogilvy, KCVO, PC (*b* 14 Sept. 1928, *d* 26 Dec. 2004, *s* of 12th Earl of Airlie, KT, GCVO, MC), and has issue –

JAMES ROBERT BRUCE OGILVY . . . . 29 Feb. 1964

Married 30 July 1988, Julia, *d* of Charles Frederick Melville Rawlinson, *qv*, and has issue –

ALEXANDER CHARLES OGILVY . . . . 12 Nov. 1996

FLORA ALEXANDRA OGILVY . . . . 15 Dec. 1994

MARINA VICTORIA ALEXANDRA OGILVY . . . . 31 July 1966

Married 2 Feb. 1990, Paul Julian Mowatt (marriage dissolved, 1997), and has issue –

CHRISTIAN ALEXANDER MOWATT . . . . 4 June 1993

ZENOUSKA MAY MOWATT . . . . 26 May 1990

Office: Buckingham Palace, SW1A 1AA; *residence:* Thatched House Lodge, Richmond, Surrey TW10 5HP.

EDITORS' NOTE

A proof of each entry is sent to its subject every year for personal revision. Any editorial queries concerning content and accuracy are raised with the biographee at this stage, for amendment in the next edition.

Addresses printed in *Who's Who* are those which the subjects of the entries have submitted for publication. Addresses in London, and the names of London clubs, are unaccompanied by the word 'London'.

Entries are listed alphabetically by surname; forenames follow, those which are not customarily used by the subject being placed within brackets. Where a diminutive or alternative name is preferred, this is shown in brackets after all the given names.

Inclusion in *Who's Who* has never, at any time, been a matter for payment or of obligation to purchase.

The Cat Survival Trust

The only British Charity devoted to the care, rescue and conservation of wild cats as well as the preservation of their natural habitat.

Do you want to help Save Our Planet for all life forms?

We have a solution if you want to help.

Not only do we rescue endangered cats from bankrupt zoos and illegal collections, we purchase forest and other habitats to save cats, and the original genetic stocks of foods and Medicines also found there. This helps preserve water courses for farm lands, which rely on pure water for food for all of us. This work also helps to stabilise the world's climate, thereby reducing flooding and landslides.

Your donations and legacies will help preserve this planet for future generations. Saving the last of the world's wild places is essential for our common survival and for the future survival of all species.

For more information please contact us at:

The Cat Survival Trust

The Centre, 46-52 Codicote Road,

Welwyn, Hertfordshire, AL6 9TU.

Tel: 01438 716873/716478 Fax: 717535

Email: cattrust@aol.com Charity No: 272187

Web address www.catsurvivaltrust.org

Also, search 'Cat Survival Trust' on.com www.youtube www.vimeo.com and www.flickr.com

The Trust's achievements since it's registration in 1976 are due to the combined efforts of all those volunteers past and present and an increasing team of enthusiastic sponsors and members. It is important to note that here in the UK, the charity has never had a single paid member of staff in the 37 years of operation. Our successes are all the more remarkable, when you consider that many of the wildlife, conservation and environmental groups and associations have still failed to carry out practical conservation work, including habitat purchase and management, even though many of them have millions in their bank accounts!

For every 10,000 acres of tropical or sub-tropical forest saved, an average of 5 million trees, billions of insects and hundreds of thousands of plants, mammals, primates, reptiles, fish, birds and many endangered cats are protected at the same time in a reserve that can obtain legal protection for ever. As cats are at the terminal end of the food chain, it is necessary to protect the whole ecosystem for all of us, in order to preserve these cats.

There are well over 29,000 conservation, wildlife and environmental organisations around the world. When considering donations and bequests to charities, please investigate which charities are doing the work at minimum cost, rather than those who have huge incomes just to pay for expensive headquarters and huge staff numbers sitting at desks, writing reports and doing little practical work.

Remember, leaving this planet intestate provides governments with more income for projects of little or no benefit to the environment! Unless urgent practical steps are taken to protect our common support system, planet Earth, all of man's other achievements will be wasted.

A donation or bequest to a charity like 'The Cat Survival Trust' could help save more habitats for cats and every other life form on this planet, including the most destructive life form....the human! It is possible to have part or all of a reserve named after you or your company for posterity and to inspire others to do the same.

Working for Endangered Wild Cats and our common habitats

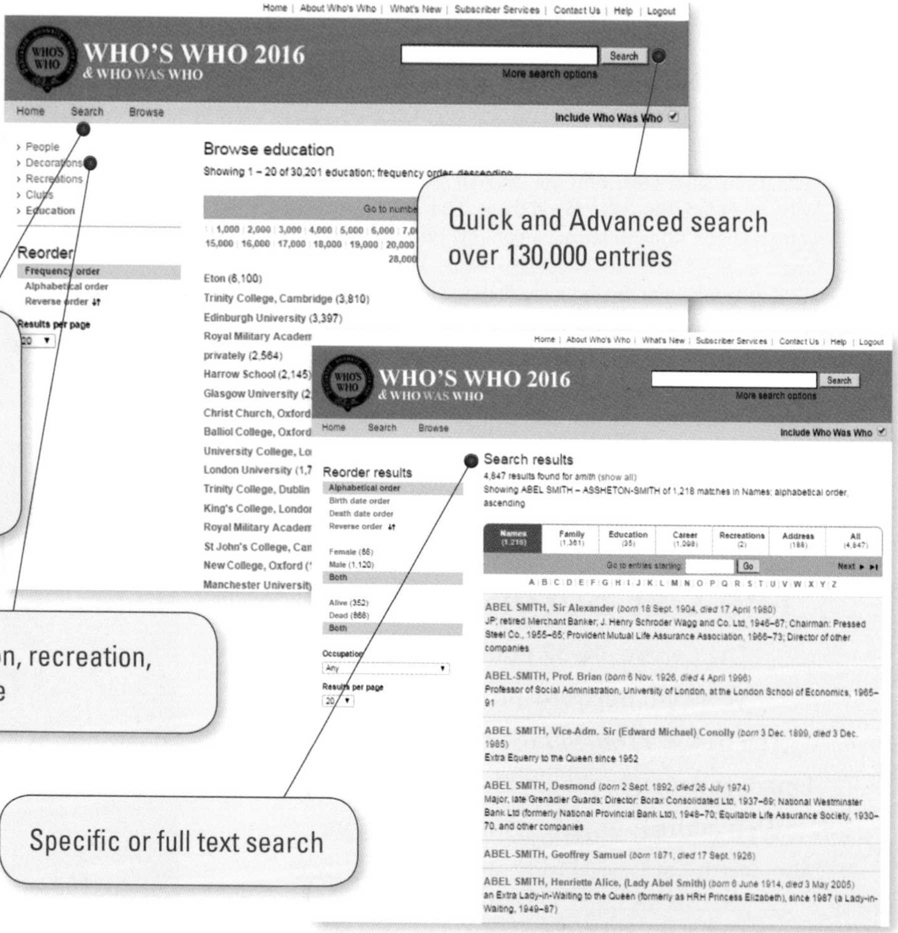

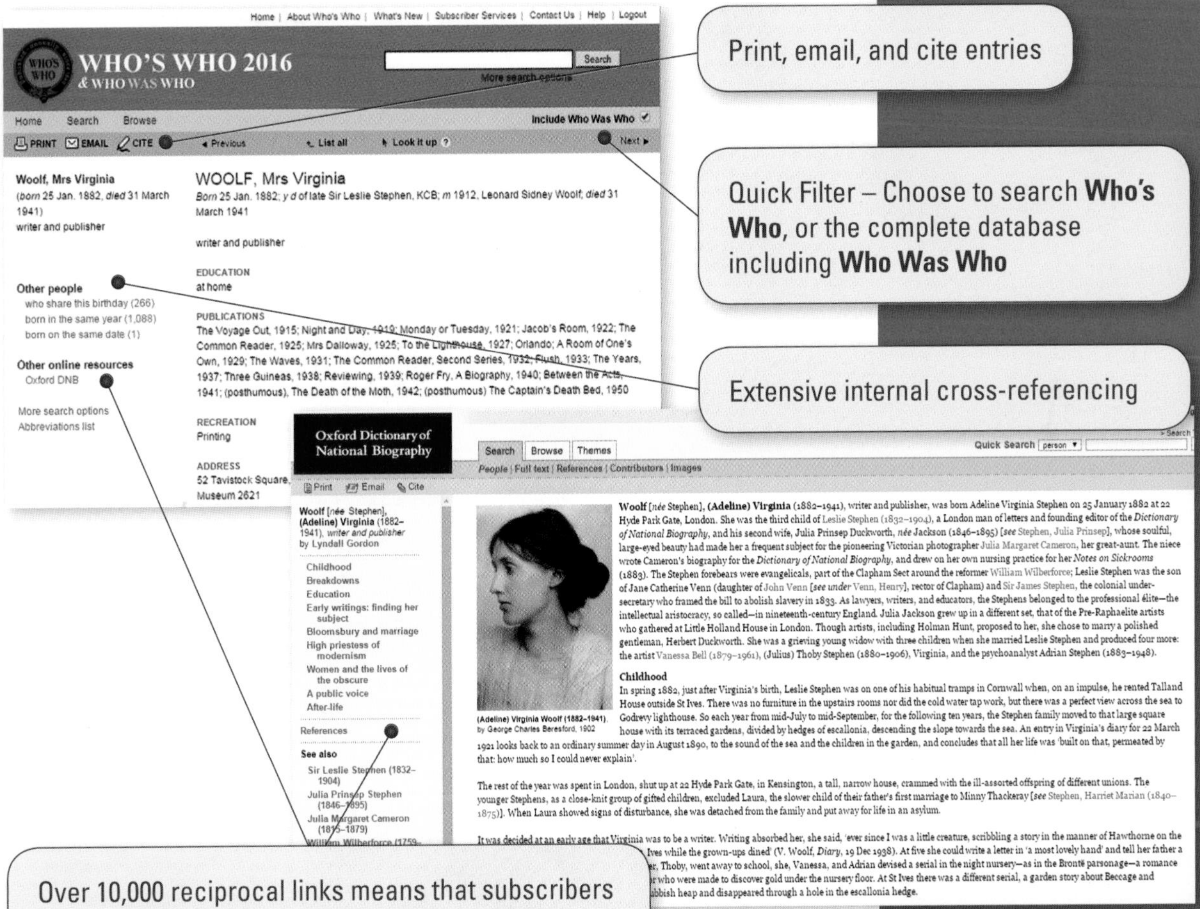

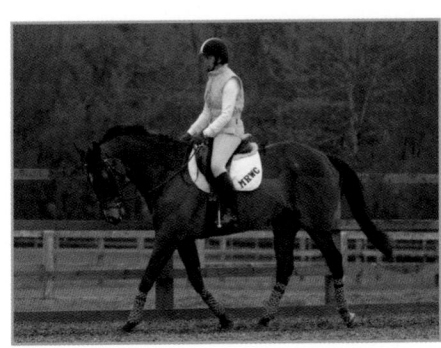

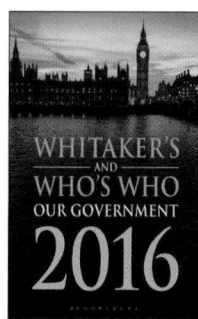

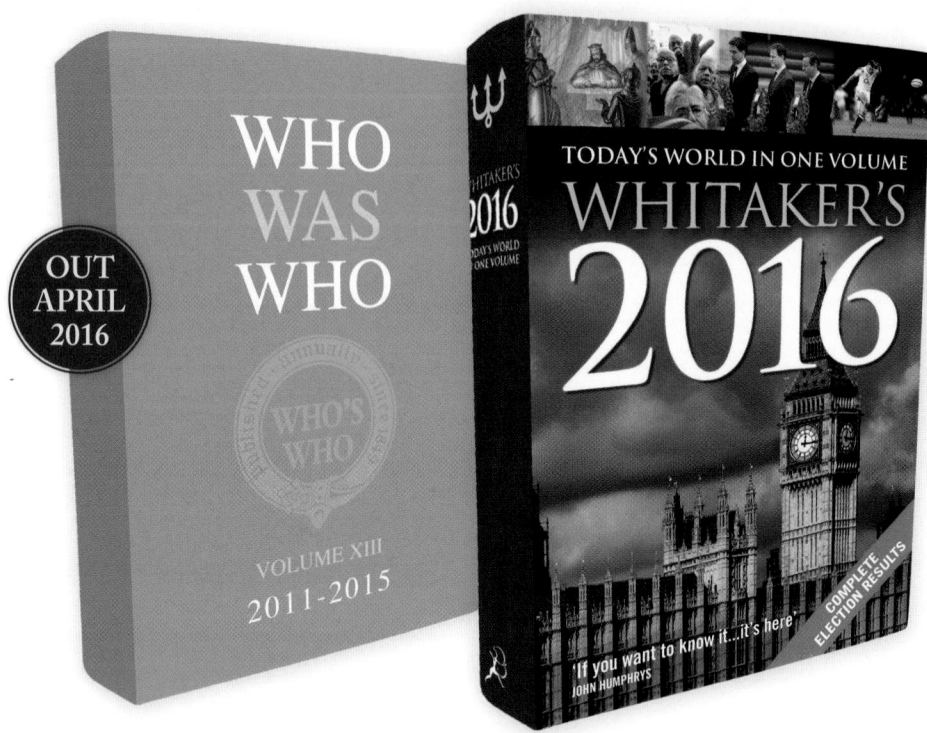

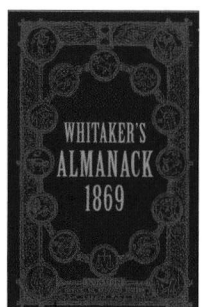

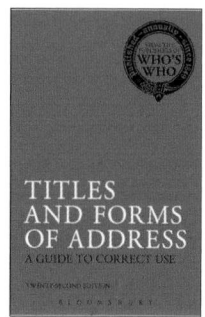

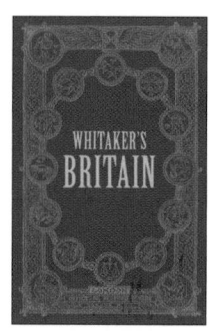

A

AARONBERG, David Jeffrey; QC 2010; a Recorder, since 2007; *b* Edgware, Middx, 16 June 1958; *s* of Sidney and Yvonne Aaronberg; *m* 1990, Linda Aaronson; two *d. Educ:* Merchant Taylors' Sch.; Poly. of Central London (BA Law). Called to the Bar, Inner Temple, 1981; in practice as barrister, specialising in criminal and regulatory law. *Recreations:* theatre, cinema, travel, ski-ing. *Address:* 15 New Bridge Street, EC4V 6AU. *T:* (020) 7842 1900. *E:* david.aaronberg@15nbs.com.

AARONOVITCH, David Morris; columnist, The Times, since 2005; *b* 8 July 1954; *s* of Dr Sam Aaronovitch and Lavender Aaronovitch; *m* 2005, Sarah Powell; three *d. Educ:* William Ellis Sch., Highgate; Manchester Univ. (BA Hons Hist.). Pres., NUS, 1980–82. Researcher and producer, Weekend World, LWT, 1982–87; BBC: Ed., On the Record, 1988–90; Hd, Political News, 1990–93; Managing Ed., Current Affairs, 1993–94; Chief Leader Writer, Independent, 1995–97; columnist: Independent, 1997–2003; Guardian and Observer, 2003–05. *Publications:* Paddling to Jerusalem, 2000; Voodoo Histories: the role of the conspiracy theory in shaping modern history, 2009. *Recreations:* running, theatre, film, watching football. *Address:* The Times, 1 London Bridge Street, SE1 9GF. *E:* David.Aaronovitch@btinternet.com.

AARONSON, Graham Raphael; QC 1982; *b* 31 Dec. 1944; *s* of late John and Dora Aaronson; *m*; two *s* one *d*; *m* 1993, Pearl Isobel Buchler; two step *s* one step *d. Educ:* City of London Sch.; Trinity Hall, Cambridge (Thomas Waraker Law Schol.; MA). Called to the Bar, Middle Temple, 1966, Bencher 1991; practised Revenue law, 1968–73 and 1978–; Founding Mem. and Partner, Joseph Hage Aaronson LLP, 2013–. Chairman: Tax Law Review Cttee, 1994–97; Revenue Bar Assoc., 1995–98; Gen. Anti-Avoidance Rule Study Gp, HM Treasury, 2010–11; Interim Gen. Anti-Abuse Rule Adv. Panel, 2012–13. Advr on tax reform to Treasury, Israel, 1986–90. Chm., Dietary Res. Foundn, 1989–93. Founder, Standford Grange residential rehabilitation centre for ex-offenders, 1974; Man. Dir, Worldwide Plastics Development, 1973–77; Dir, Bridgend Group PLC, 1973–92. *Address:* Joseph Hage Aaronson LLP, 280 High Holborn, WC1V 7EE.

AARONSON, Sir Michael John, Kt 2006; CBE 2000; Chairman, Frimley Health (Frimley Park Hospital) NHS Foundation Trust, since 2006; Director, Oxford Policy Management Ltd, since 2006; Professorial Research Fellow and Executive Director of cii - The Centre for International Intervention, University of Surrey, since 2011; *b* 8 Sept. 1947; *s* of Edward John Aaronson and late Marian Aaronson (*née* Davies); *m* 1988, Andrene Margaret Sutherland; two *s* one *d. Educ:* Merchant Taylors' Sch.; St John's Coll., Oxford (Sir Thomas White Scholar, Trevelyan Scholar; MA). Field Co-ordinator, SCF, Nigeria, 1969–71; HM Diplomatic Service, 1972–88, served Paris, Lagos, Rangoon; Save the Children Fund: Overseas Dir, 1988–95; Dir-Gen., 1995–2005. A Civil Service Comr, 2007–12. Chm. Bd, Centre for Humanitarian Dialogue (Geneva), 2001–08; Gov., Westminster Foundn for Democracy, 2001–07 (Vice-Chm., 2005–07); non-exec. Dir, Nat. Sch. of Govt Internat., 2012–15. Mem. Council, RSA, 2004–09. Vis. Fellow, Nuffield Coll., Oxford, 2004–12 (Hon. Fellow, 2012–); Hon. Vis. Prof., Univ. of Surrey, 2008–11. Freeman: City of London, 1989; Merchant Taylors' Co., 1989. DUniv Surrey, 2011. *Recreations:* sports, the performing arts. *Address:* Dingley Dell, 166 Glaziers Lane, Normandy, Guildford, Surrey GU3 2EB. *T:* (01483) 811655. *Club:* MCC.

AARTS, Prof. Sebastiaan Henri Lucas Marie, (Bas), PhD; Professor of English Linguistics, University College London, since 2003; *b* Nijmegen, The Netherlands; *s* of Florent Gérard Antoin Marie Aarts and Marie Josephine Victoria Servatia Postmes; *m* 2002, Dr Gergana Popova; two *d. Educ:* Elshof Coll., Nijmegen; Univ. of Utrecht (Drs); University Coll. London (MA; PhD 1990). University College London: Lectr, 1989–96; Sen. Lectr, 1996–99; Reader, 1999–2003. Jt Founding Editor, English Lang. and Linguistics, 1997–2004. *Publications:* Small Clauses in English: the nonverbal types, 1992; (ed with C. F. Meyer) The Verb in Contemporary English, 1995; English Syntax and Argumentation, 1997, 4th edn 2013; (jtly) Investigating Natural Language: working with the British component of the international corpus of English, 2002; (ed jtly) Fuzzy Grammar: a reader, 2004; (ed with A. McMahon) The Handbook of English Linguistics, 2006; Syntactic Gradience: the nature of grammatical indeterminacy, 2007; Oxford Modern English Grammar, 2011; (ed jtly) The Verb Phrase in English: investigating recent language change with corpora, 2013; (jtly) Oxford Dictionary of English Grammar, 2nd edn, 2014; articles in jls and books. *Address:* Department of English, University College London, Gower Street, WC1E 6BT. *T:* (020) 7679 3130. *E:* b.aarts@ucl.ac.uk.

ABAS, Madeleine Nasim; Senior Partner, Osborn Abas Hunt, since 2004; *b* Bangor, Gwynedd, 26 Aug. 1970; *d* of Dr Jan Abas and Rosemary Ann Abas; *m* 2002, Jason Harvey Osborn. *Educ:* David Hughes Sch., Anglesey; Nottingham Trent Univ. (LLB Hons Law); Nottingham Law Sch. (Postgrad. DipLP). Trainee, Asst Solicitor and Associate, Irwin Mitchell Solicitors, 1988–2000; Associate, DLA Piper, 2000–02; Partner, Cooper Kenyon Burrows, 2002–04. Mem., Inst. of Industrial Accident Investigators. Founder, and Chair, 2005–12, Health and Safety Lawyers Assoc. Mem., Editl Panel, Construction Industry Pubns Health and Safety Manual, 2011–. *Recreation:* Formula 1. *Address:* OAH Law Ltd, 3 Oxford Court, Bishopsgate, Manchester M2 3WQ. *T:* (0161) 200 8450, *Fax:* (0161) 236 6522. *E:* madeleine.abas@oahlaw.com.

ABBERLEY, Robert; self-employed consultant, since 2013; Assistant General Secretary, UNISON, 2002–13; *b* 29 Oct. 1952; *s* of late Fred Abberley and of Lillian Abberley. *Educ:* Kingsland Co. Primary Sch., Hereford; Wigmore Co. Secondary Sch., Hereford. C&G Operating Dept Practitioner. Labourer, 1969; apprentice toolmaker, Halls Engrg, Shrewsbury, 1969–70; driver, builders merchants, 1971–72; operating dept asst, Hereford Hosps, 1972–79. Trade Union officer, COHSE, 1979–93; Hd of Health, UNISON, 1993–2002. Member: Adv. Bd, TUC Partnership Inst.; TUC Gen. Council, 2005; Bd, TUC Stakeholder Pension, 2009–; Trustee: UNISON Pension Fund, 2012–; COHSE Pension Scheme, 2014–. Non-exec. Dir, UIA, 2013–. Member: NHS Task Force on Staff Involvement in decision making, 1998–99; NHS Modernisation Bd, 1999–; NHS shifting the balance of power task force, 2001; Community Cohesion Rev. Team, 2001–02; Ministerial Adv. Panel on Social Cohesion, 2002; NHSUniv. SHA, 2003–05; NHS Nat. Leadership Network, 2005–; NHS Ministerial Sounding Bd, 2006; Chair, NHS widening participation in learning steering gp, 2005–. Board Member: Care Connect Learning, until 2009; Coll. of Operating Dept Practitioners, 2007; Managers in Partnership, 2007–13; Skills for Health, 2009– (Mem., Shadow Bd, Nat. Skills Acad., 2011–13); Nat. Cohesion Forum, Inst. of Community Cohesion, 2009–; Involvement and Participation Assoc., 2010–; TUC Unionlearn, 2010–; Movement for Change, 2012– (Vice Chair, 2014–). Pres., Health and Social Services Cttee, Eur. Fedn of Trade Unions, 1983–2002. Member: IAM (Middx); TR Register. *Recreations:* classic car restoration, motorcycling, music, going to the gym, Manchester United, watching movies, reading biographies, watching Hereford United. *E:* bobabberley1@gmail.com.

ABBOTT, Anthony John, CMG 2001; OBE 1997 (MBE 1986); HM Diplomatic Service, retired; Head, Pitcairn Logistics Team, New Zealand, 2001–04; *b* Ashton-under-Lyne, 9 Sept. 1941; *s* of Walter Abbott and Mary Abbott (*née* Delaney); *m* 1962, Margaret Stuart Green; three *s* one *d. Educ:* All Souls' Sch., Salford; De La Salle Coll., Pendleton. Joined HM Diplomatic Service, 1959: Vice-Consul, Khorramshahr, 1963–65; Helsinki, 1965–68; Press Officer, FCO, 1969–72; Passport Officer, Lusaka, 1972–75; Consul, Santiago, 1976–80; UK Presidency Secretariat to EC, 1981; on secondment to BOTB, 1981–82; Consul, Lisbon, 1983–87; First Sec., Calcutta, 1987–91; EC Monitor, Croatia and Bosnia Herzogovina, 1991; Dep. Head, Trng Dept, FCO, 1992–93; Consul-Gen., Perth, 1993–97; Governor, Montserrat, 1997–2001. Pres., Como Conf., St Vincent de Paul Soc., WA, 2009–. EC Monitoring Medal, 1994. Officer, Order of Enfante Dom Henrique (Portugal), 1985. *Recreations:* travel, driving, golf, spectator (all sports). *Address:* 6 James Street, Shenton Park, WA 6008, Australia. *Club:* Royal Over-Seas League (Chm., WA Br., 2011–).

ABBOTT, Hon. Anthony John; MP (L) Warringah, New South Wales, since 1994; Prime Minister of Australia, 2013–15; Leader of the Liberal Party, Australia, 2009–15; *b* 4 Nov. 1957; *s* of Richard Abbott and Fay Abbott; *m* 1988, Margaret Aitken; three *d. Educ:* St Ignatius' Coll., Riverview; Univ. of Sydney (BEc; LLB); Queen's Coll., Oxford (Rhodes Schol. 1981; MA PPE). Journalist and feature writer, The Bulletin and The Australian; Press Sec. and Political Advr to Leader of Opposition, 1990–93; Exec. Dir, Australians for Constitutional Monarchy, 1993–94; Parly Sec. to Minister for Employment, Educn, Trng and Youth Affairs, 1996–98; Minister for Employment Services, 1998–2001, for Employment, Workplace Relns and Small Business, 2001, for Employment and Workplace Relns, 2001–03, asstg Prime Minister for Public Service, 2001–03; Leader, House of Reps, 2001–07; Minister for Health and Ageing, 2003–07; Shadow Minister for Families, Community Services, Indigenous Affairs and Voluntary Sector, then for Families, Housing, Community Services and Indigenous Affairs, 2008–09; Leader of the Opposition, 2009–13. Centenary Medal (Australia), 2003. *Publications:* The Minimal Monarch, 1995; How to Win the Constitutional War, 1997; Battlelines, 2009. *Address:* Parliament House, Canberra, ACT 2600, Australia.

ABBOTT, Diane Julie; MP (Lab) Hackney North and Stoke Newington, since 1987; *b* 27 Sept. 1953; *d* of late Reginald and Julia Abbott; *m* 1991, David Thompson (marr. diss. 1993); one *s. Educ:* Harrow County Girls' Grammar Sch.; Newnham Coll., Cambridge. Formerly: Admin. Trainee, Home Office; Race Relations Officer, NCCL; Researcher, Thames Television; Reporter, TV-am; Equality Officer, ACTT; Press and PR Officer, GLC; Principal Press Officer, Lambeth Borough Council. Joined Labour Party, 1971; Mem., NEC, 1994–97. Mem., Westminster City Council, 1982–86. Mem. resp. for equality and women's issues, Mayor of London's Cabinet, 2000–08. Shadow Minister of Public Health, 2010–13; Shadow Sec. of State for Internat. Develt, 2015–. *Address:* House of Commons, SW1A 0AA.

ABBOTT, John Martin, CBE 2000; QPM 1996; Director General, National Criminal Intelligence Service, 1997–2003; Vice President, Interpol, 1999–2002; *b* 22 March 1949; *s* of late Geoffrey Lowick Abbott and Gladys Lilian Abbott; *m* 1972, Christine Sowter; two *d. Educ:* Univ. of Sussex (BA Hons History 1982). Joined Sussex Police, 1968: served in various ranks throughout Sussex, 1968–86; Supt, seconded to Royal Hong Kong Police, 1986–88; Chief Supt, seconded to Police Staff Coll., Bramshill, 1989–91; Asst Chief Constable, 1991–94; Asst Insp. of Constabulary, 1994–96. *Recreations:* reading, history, golf, cricket.

ABBOTT, Paul; film and television writer; *b* 22 Feb. 1960; *s* of Alan Abbott and late Doreen Abbott; *m* 1993, Saskia; one *s* one *d. Educ:* Barden High Sch., Burnley. Writer: television series: Coronation Street, 1985–89; Cracker (episodes), 1993 (Best Drama Series, BAFTA award, 1995); Reckless, 1997; Touching Evil, 1997; Butterfly Collectors, 1999; Secret Life of Michael Fry, 2000; Clocking Off, 2000–03 (Best Drama Series, BAFTA award, 2001); Linda Green, 2001; State of Play, 2003; Shameless, 2004–13 (Best Drama Series, BAFTA award, 2005); Hit and Miss, 2012; No Offence, 2015; TV film, Reckless: The Movie, 1999. Exec. Prod., State of Play (film), 2009. *Recreations:* film, theatre, novels, rumours. *Address:* c/o The Agency, 24 Pottery Lane, Holland Park, W11 4LZ. *Clubs:* Ivy; Writers' Guild of Great Britain.

ABBOTT, Adm. Sir Peter (Charles), GBE 1999; KCB 1994; Vice Chief of the Defence Staff, 1997–2001; Commissioner, Commonwealth War Graves Commission, 2001–06; *b* 12 Feb. 1942; *s* of late Lieut-Col Dennis Abbott, Royal Garwhal Rifles and Delphine McConaghey; *m* 1965, Susan Phillippa Grey; three *d. Educ:* St Edward's Sch., Oxford; Queens' College, Cambridge (MA 1966). Articled Clerk, Blackburn, Robson Coates, 1963; 2nd Lieut, RMFVR 1963; Sub Lieut, RN 1964; Commanding Officer, HM Ships Chawton, 1972, Ambuscade, 1976, Ajax, 1983 (and First Frigate Sqdn); RCDS 1985; Flag Officer, Flotilla Two, 1989; ACNS, 1991–93; Dep. SACLANT, 1993–95; C-in-C Fleet, C-in-C Eastern Atlantic Area and Comdr Naval Forces N Western Europe, 1995–97. Chairman: Trustees, 2003–10, Mgt Bd, 2010–, Royal Naval Mus.; Bd of Dirs, Nat. Mus. of Royal Navy, 2008–10. King of Arms, Order of the British Empire, 2010–. Officer, US Legion of Merit, 1995.

ABBOTT, Roderick Evelyn; consultant, international trade; *b* 16 April 1938; *e s* of late Stuart Abbott, OBE; *m* 1963, Elizabeth Isobel McLean; three *d. Educ:* Rugby Sch.; Merton Coll., Oxford. Board of Trade, 1962–68 (Private Sec. to Pres. of BoT, 1965–66; seconded to DEA, 1966–68); UK Mission to UN, Geneva, 1968–71; Foreign Office, London, 1971–73; EEC, Brussels, 1973–75; EEC Delegation, Geneva, 1975–79; EEC, Brussels,

1979–82; Dir, D-G of External Relns, then External Econ. Relns, EC, Brussels, 1982–96; Ambassador and Perm. Rep. of EC to UN and WTO, Geneva, 1996–2000; Dep. Dir Gen., Trade, EC, Brussels, 2000–02; Dep. Dir-Gen., WTO, 2002–05. Sen. Trade Advr, Eur. Centre for Internat. Pol Economy, 2006–. *Recreation:* travel. *Address:* Avenue Grandchamp 98A, 1150 Brussels, Belgium.

ABBOTT-WATT, Thorhilda Mary Vivia, (Thorda); HM Diplomatic Service; Acting Head, Project Task Force, Foreign and Commonwealth Office, since 2012 (Deputy Head, 2012); *b* 11 Feb. 1955; *d* of Samuel Abbott-Watt and Elva Mary Abbott-Watt (*née* Clare Gibson); partner, Reef Talbot Hogg. *Educ:* Stonar Sch., Atworth, Wilts. Joined HM Diplomatic Service, 1974; Third Sec., FCO, 1974–79; temp. duty tours in Latin America, Middle and Far East, 1979–80; Vice Consul, Paris, 1981–84; Third Sec. (Chancery), UK Repn to EU, 1984–86; Second Secretary: FCO, 1986–88; Bonn, 1988–91; First Sec., EU Dept and Western Eur. Dept, FCO, 1991–95; Hd, Commercial Section, Kiev, 1995–98; First Sec. (Political), Belgrade, 1998–99; Hd, Visa Policy Section, Jt Entry Clearance Unit, FCO, 1999–2001; Chargé d'Affaires, Tajikistan, 2001–02; Ambassador to Armenia, 2003–06; Conflict Issues Gp, FCO, 2006; Hd, Political/Military Gp, Kabul, 2006; Afghanistan Gp, FCO, 2006–07; Migration Directorate, FCO, 2007–08; Hd of Strategy and Performance, UKTI, 2008; Ambassador to Mongolia, 2008–09 and 2011–12; Finance Directorate, FCO, 2009–10; Internat. Liaison Section, MoD, 2010. Life Mem., NACF. *Recreations:* riding, theatre, the arts, sitting in a comfortable chair with a good book. *Address:* c/o Foreign and Commonwealth Office, King Charles Street, SW1A 2AH. *E:* Thorda.Abbott-Watt@fco.gov.uk.

ABDALLA, Hossam Ibrahim, (Sam), FRCOG; Clinical Director, Lister Fertility Clinic, London, since 1988; *b* Illinois, 23 May 1952; *s* of Ibrahim Abdalla and Alia Abdalla; *m* 1975, Mediha Elsawi; one *s* one *d*. *Educ:* Orman High Sch., Cairo; University of Baghdad (MB ChB 1977). MRCOG 1983, FRCOG 2001. Infertility and IVF Specialist, Cromwell Hosp., London, 1986–87. Mem. Bd, HFEA, 2004–14. *Publications:* Fast Facts: endometriosis, 1998, 2nd edn 2003; articles in learned jls. *Address:* Lister Hospital, Lister Fertility Clinic, Chelsea Bridge Road, SW1W 8RH. *T:* (020) 7881 4035. *E:* pa@lfclinic.com.

ABDEL-HAQ, Prof. Mohammed Kayed, PhD; Founder and Chief Executive Officer, Oakstone Merchant Bank, since 2012; Chairman: Centre for Opposition Studies, since 2010; Centre for Islamic Finance, University of Bolton, since 2012; *b* Jordan, 22 April 1964; *s* of Dr Kayed Abdel-Haq and Fatima Abdel-Haq; *m* 1993, Lynn Rhymes; four *d*. *Educ:* Islamic Scientific Coll., Amman; Yarmouk Univ., Jordan (BSc; MA); Oxford Brookes Univ. and Centre for Islamic Studies, St Cross Coll., Univ. of Oxford (PhD 1993). With Aitken Hume Bank, then Arbuthnot Latham & Co., 1994–95; UK Bank of Kuwait, London, 1995–96; Vice-Pres., Private Bank, ME Reg., ABN Amro Bank, London, 1997–99; Dir and Sen. Private Banker, Saudi Arabia and Levant, Citigroup Private Bank, London, 1999–2003; Dir and Hd, ME and N Africa Div., Deutsche Bank AG, London, 2003–04; Man. Dir and Global Hd, HSBC Amanah Private Banking, 2004–07; CEO, Barwa Capital (UK) Ltd, 2007–11; Chm., Complyport Ltd (UK), 2008–12; CEO and Founder Mem., Rosette Merchant Bank LLP, 2011–12. Chm., Ministerial Adv. Gp on Extremism in Univs and Further Educn Colls, 2011. Member: Adv. Bd, Centre for Social Justice, 2011–; Council, Chatham Hse, 2011–; Adv. Bd, Centre for Contemp. Arab Music, Brunel Univ., 2012–. Pres., Disability Partnership, 2009–. Chm., Amman Arab Univ., 2008–12. Chm., Adv. Bd, Cons. ME Council, 2010–. Contested (C) Swansea W, 2005. Chm., Oxford E Cons. Assoc., 2004. Freeman, City of Oxford, 2010. MInstD 2009. *Publications:* (jtly) Islamic Banking: theory, practice and challenges, 1996. *Recreations:* swimming, squash, chess. *Address:* University of Bolton, Deane Road, Bolton BL3 5AB. *T:* 07881 506785. *E:* Mabdelhaq1@aol.com; Oakstone Merchant Bank, 53 Davies Street, W1K 5JH. *Clubs:* Carlton, Lansdowne; Royal Automobile (Amman).

ABDELA, Lesley Julia, MBE 1990; journalist and broadcaster, since 1986; Chief Executive: Project Parity, since 1996; Project Parity Partnerships for Peace, since 2005; Senior Partner: Eyecatcher Associates, since 1986; Shevolution, since 1998; specialist in post-conflict reconstruction, since 1999; *b* London, 17 Nov. 1945; *d* of late Frederick Abdela and Henrietta (*née* Hardy); *m* 1972 (marr. diss.); one *s*; partner, Tim Symonds. *Educ:* Queen Anne's Sch., Caversham; Châtelard Sch., Les Avants, Switzerland; Queen's Coll., Harley Street; Hammersmith Coll. of Art and Building; London Coll. of Printing. Advertising Exec., Royds of London, 1968–72; Derek Forsyth Design Partnership, 1972–73; researcher for Liberal Party, H of C, 1977–79; Founder, 1980, Chair, 1980–85, Trustee, 1980–95, 300 Group (for women in politics). UK Consultant, Project Liberty, Kennedy Sch. of Govt, Harvard Univ., 1992–98. OSCE Dep. Dir for Democracy, UN Interim Admin in Kosovo, 1999; Sen. Civil Soc. Expert in governance, democratisation, gender and human rights, Kosovo, Sierra Leone, Iraq, Afghanistan and Aceh (Indonesia); Sen. Gender Advr to UN OCHA Chief Coordinator Kathmandu, 2007–08. Political Editor: Cosmopolitan, 1993–96 (first Pol Ed. of a women's mag.); Radio Viva!, 1995; regular contributor to Exec. Woman mag., Mail on Sunday, Sunday Times, Guardian, Times, Independent, Glasgow Herald, etc; writer, researcher and presenter of radio and TV documentaries, incl. Women with X Appeal, 1993, Breaking Glass, 1994. Board Member: Internat. Inst. for Envmt and Develt, 1992–96; British Council, 1995–2000; Mem. Exec. Bd, Women in Mgt, 1985–88. Vice Pres., Electoral Reform Soc., 1995–. Contested (L) E Herts, 1979. Gov., Nottingham Trent Univ., 1997–2000. FRGS; FRSA; MCIJ. Hon. DLitt Nottingham Trent, 1996. Political Journalist of the Year, Women in Public Life Awards, 2009. *Publications:* Women with X Appeal, 1989; Breaking Through the Glass Ceilings, 1991; What Women Want, 1994; Do It! - Walk the Talk, 1995. *Recreations:* painting, ski-ing, scuba, reading, looking forward to true equality between women and men in politics and society. *Address:* Park Farm Oast, Bateman's Lane, Burwash, Etchingham, East Sussex TN19 7DR. *E:* lesley.abdela@shevolution.com.

ABDIN, Dr Hasan; Ambassador of Sudan to the Court of St James's, 2000–06; *b* 1 Jan. 1939; *m* 1966, Manahil A. Abu Kashwa; two *s* three *d*. *Educ:* Univ. of Khartoum (BA 1965); Univ. of Wisconsin (MA 1967; PhD 1970). Lectr in African Hist., Univ. of Khartoum, 1970–77; State Minister, Sudan, 1977–78; Mem., Nat. Assembly, 1978–80; Asst Prof. of Hist., Univ. of King Saud, Riyyadh, Saudi Arabia, 1983–88; Inst. of Asian and African Studies, Univ. of Khartoum, 1988–90; Ambassador to: Algeria, 1990–92; Iraq, 1993–97; Under Sec., Min. of Foreign Affairs, Khartoum, 1998–2000. *Publications:* Introduction to African History (in Arabic), 1974; Early Sudanese Nationalism, 1986. *Recreations:* reading, walking. *Address:* c/o Embassy of the Republic of the Sudan, 3 Cleveland Row, St James's, SW1A 1DD.

ABDULAH, Frank Owen; Deputy Secretary-General, Caribbean Community Secretariat, Guyana, 1989–93; Member, Public Service Commission of Trinidad and Tobago, since 2012; *b* 8 Nov. 1928; *m*; four *d*. *Educ:* Queen's Royal Coll., Trinidad; Oxford (MA, DipEd Oxon). Held several govt posts, 1953–62, before entering Diplomatic Service at Trinidad and Tobago's Independence, 1962; Dep. Perm. Rep. (Minister Counsellor), 1970–73, Perm. Rep. (Ambassador), 1975–83, Trinidad and Tobago Perm. Mission to UN, NY; Perm. Sec. (Acting), Ministry of External Affairs, Port of Spain, 1973–75; High Comr for Trinidad and Tobago in London with concurrent accreditations as Ambassador to Denmark, Finland, France, FRG, Norway and Sweden, 1983–85; Permanent Sec., Min. of External Affairs and Internat. Trade, Trinidad and Tobago, 1985–88. Caribbean Community Special Advr to Pres. of UN Gen. Assembly, 1993–94. Pres., UNA Trinidad and Tobago, 1987–88, 1997–2001. *Recreations:* music, sports. *Address:* 8 Nock Road, Maraval, Trinidad and Tobago.

ABDY, Sir Robert Etienne Eric, 7th Bt *cr* 1850, of Albyns, Essex; *b* 22 Feb. 1978; *o s* of Sir Valentine Robert Duff Abdy, 6th Bt and of Mathilde (*née* Coche de la Ferté); *S* father, 2012, but his name does not appear on the Official Roll of the Baronetage. *Heir:* none.

ABED, Sir Fazle Hasan, KCMG 2010; Founder and Chairman, BRAC (formerly Bangladesh Rural Advancement Committee), 1972; *b* Bengal, 27 April 1936; *m* Syeda Sarwat; one *s* one *d*. *Educ:* Dhaka Univ.; Glasgow Univ. Chartered Mgt Accountant; Sen. Exec., Shell Oil, Pakistan. Founder Mem., Global Acad. for Social Entrepreneurship; Mem., Eminent Persons Gp for Least Developed Countries, UN, 2010–. Hon. DHL Yale, 2007; Hon. LLD: Queen's, 1994; Columbia, 2008; Bath, 2010; Hon. DLitt Oxon, 2009. Magsaysay Award, 1980; Maurice Pate Award, UNICEF, 1992; Olof Palme Award, 2002; Mahbub ul Haq Award for Outstanding Contribn in Human Develt, UNDP, 2004; Gates Award for Global Health, Bill and Melinda Gates Foundn, 2004; Inaugural Clinton Global Citizen Award, 2007; Kravis Leadership Prize, 2007; David Rockefeller Bridging Leadership Award, 2008; World Innovation Summit for Educn Prize, Qatar, 2011. Order of Civil Merit (Spain), 2014. *Address:* BRAC, BRAC Centre, 75 Mohakhali, Dhaka 1212, Bangladesh.

ABED, Ringo F.; Head of Mission, Namibian Embassy in Beijing, since 2013; *b* 6 June 1956; *s* of late Benjamin Abed and Albertina Matheus; *m* 1979, Johanna; three *d* (two *s* decd). *Educ:* UN Inst. for Namibia (Dip. Mgt and Develt Studies 1981); Makerere Univ., Kampala (BA Hons Pol Sci. and Public Admin 1986). Mem., SW African People's Orgn; in exile in Zambia, then Angola, 1974–89; Dep. Dir, reception and food distribn centres for returning veterans, 1989–92; Mem., OAU Observer Mission to SA, 1992–94; Ministry of Foreign Affairs, Namibia: First Sec. (Pol) and Dep. Hd of Mission, Botswana, 1995; First Sec. (Pol), SA, 1996; Hd, Privileges and Immunities, 1999, Functions and Ceremonies, 2000, Protocol Dept, Min. of Foreign Affairs; Counsellor and Dep. Hd of Mission, Congo, 2000–03; Dir, Protocol, Office of the Prime Minister, 2003–04; Actg Chief of Protocol, Min. of Foreign Affairs, 2004–05; High Comr to the Court of St James's, 2005–06; Ambassador to Democratic Republic of the Congo and (non-resident) to Republic of Congo, 2006–13. *Recreations:* reading, music, travelling. *Address:* Namibian Embassy in Beijing, 2–9–2 Ta Yuan, Diplomatic Office Building, Beijing 100600, China.

ABEL, Prof. Edward William, CBE 1997; PhD, DSc; FRSC; Professor of Inorganic Chemistry, University of Exeter, 1972–97, now Emeritus (Head of Department of Chemistry, 1977–88; Deputy Vice-Chancellor, 1991–94); *b* 3 Dec. 1931; *s* of Sydney and Donna Abel; *m* 1960, Margaret R. Edwards; one *s* one *d*. *Educ:* Bridgend Grammar Sch.; University Coll., Cardiff (BSc 1952); Northern Polytechnic, London (PhD 1957). Served Army, 1953–55. Research Fellow, Imperial Coll., 1957–59; Lectr, later Reader, Univ. of Bristol, 1957–71. Vis. Professor: Univ. of British Columbia, 1970; Japanese Soc. for Promotion of Science, 1971; Tech. Univ. of Braunschweig, 1973; ANU, Canberra, 1990; Robert E. Welch Lectures, Texas, 1994. Royal Society of Chemistry: Mem. Council, 1977–82, 1983–87 and 1989–2002; Pres., 1996–98; Chairman: Local Affairs Bd, 1983–87; Divl Affairs Bd, 1989–92; Scientific Affairs Bd, 1992–95; Parly Cttee, 1995–2003; Laboratory of the Govt Chemist Adv. Cttee, 1998–2003; Mem., Dalton Div. Council, 1977–83, 1987–91 (Sec./Treasurer, 1977–82; Vice-Pres., 1983, 1989–91; Pres., 1987–89); Main Group Chem. Medal, 1976; Tilden Medal and Lectr, 1981; Service Medal, 2007. Perm. Sec., Internat. Confs on Organometallic Chem., 1972–89; Mem., UGC, 1986–89 (Chm., Phys. Scis Sub-Cttee, 1986–89); Nat. Advr for Chem., UFC, 1989–92; CNAA: Mem., 1991–93; Chm., Phys. Scis Cttee, 1987–91; Mem., Cttee for Academic Affairs, 1989–91. DUniv North London, 1998; Hon. DSc: Exeter, 2000; Glamorgan, 2004. *Publications:* (ed jtly) Organometallic Chemistry, vols 1–25, 1970–95; (exec. editor) Comprehensive Organometallic Chemistry, 9 vols, 1984; (exec. editor) Comprehensive Organometallic Chemistry II, 14 vols, 1995; papers to learned jls. *Address:* 1A Rosebarn Avenue, Exeter EX4 6DY. *T:* (01392) 270272. *E:* mea@rosebarn.eclipse.co.uk.

ABEL, Keith Russell; Founding Director, Abel & Cole, organic food business, since 1988; *b* London, 13 Nov. 1963; *s* of Keith Paterson Abel and Sally Anne Neame; *m* 1992, Catherine Ciapparelli; one *s* one *d*. *Educ:* Rugby Sch.; Leeds Univ. (BA Hons); City Univ. (CPE Law); Inns of Court Sch. of Law. Called to the Bar, 1992. Queen's Award for Industry (Sustainable Develt), 2005. *Publications:* Cooking Outside the Box, 2005. *Recreations:* ski-ing, tennis, shooting, sleeping on Sunday afternoons! *Address:* Abel & Cole Ltd, 16 Waterside Way, Plough Lane, Wimbledon, SW17 0HB. *T:* (01264) 387540. *E:* organics@abelandcole.co.uk.

ABEL, Roger Lee; Director, Cygnus Oil and Gas Corporation (formerly Touchstone Resources USA Inc.), 2005–07 (Chairman and Chief Executive Officer, 2005–06); *b* Nebraska, 12 Aug. 1943. *Educ:* Colorado Sch. of Mines (BSc Petroleum Engrg 1965); MIT (MSc 1979). FInstPet. Served US Army, 1966–68 (Capt.). Joined Conoco Inc., 1968: prodn engr, 1968–72; Supervising Reservoir Engr, Lake Charles, Louisiana, 1972–73; Staff Engr, N America, 1973–74; Co-ordinator for W Hemisphere Planning Dept, 1974–75; Manager, Planning and Budgets, 1975–77; Exec. Asst to Conoco's Dep. Chm., 1977–78; Sloan Fellow, MIT, 1978–79; Asst Div. Manager, Offshore Div., 1979–80; Vice Pres. and Gen. Manager of Ops for Dubai Petroleum Co., 1980–82; Manager: of Ops, UK and Europe, 1982–84; of Planning, Admin and Engrg, N American Prodn, 1984–86; General Manager: Offshore and Frontier, N American Prodn, 1986–88; Prodn Engrg and Res. Dept, 1988–90; Vice-Pres. and Gen. Manager, Prodn Engrg and Res., 1990–91; Vice Pres., Exploration Prodn-Russia, 1991–93; Chm., Conoco Exploration Prodn Europe Ltd, 1993–97; Pres. and Chief Operating Officer, Occidental Oil & Gas Corp., 1997–99; Exec. Vice Pres., Occidental Petroleum Corp., 1999–2000; Pres., Austex Production Co. LLC, 2002–05. Chm. Bd, Offshore Technol. Conf., 1994–2002; Co-Vice Chm., Mgt Cttee, E&P Forum, 1995–97; Chm., Energy Sub-Cttee, Gore-Chernomyrdin Commn, 1997–98. Dist. Mem., Soc. of Petroleum Engrs (Pres., 1992). Former Mem., Adv. Cttee, Petroleum Engrg Dept, and Trustee Develt Council, Colorado Sch. of Mines. Dist. Achievement Medal, Colorado Sch. of Mines, 1998; Bronze Star Medal, 1967 (USA). *Address:* 8045 Chalk Knoll Drive, Austin, TX 78735–1706, USA.

ABELL, Prof. Christopher, PhD; FMedSci; Professor of Biological Chemistry, since 2002, and Director of Postdoctoral Affairs, since 2013, University of Cambridge; Fellow, since 1986, and Todd-Hamied Fellow, since 1997, Christ's College, Cambridge; *b* Fulford, 11 Nov. 1957; *s* of Norman and Barbara Abell; *m* 1981, Dr Katherine Tang; one *s*. *Educ:* St John's Coll., Cambridge (BA 1st Cl. Chem. 1979; PhD Chem. 1982). SERC NATO Postdoctoral Fellow, Brown Univ., RI, 1982–83; Res. Fellow, King's Coll., Cambridge, 1983–86; Department of Chemistry, University of Cambridge: demonstrator, 1984–88; Lectr, 1988–89; Reader, 1999–2002. Co-Founder and Mem., Scientific Adv. Bd, Astex Therapeutics, then Astex Pharmaceuticals, 1999–; Co-Founder and Dir, Sphere Fluidics, 2010–; Co-Founder: Akubio, 2002; Aqdot, 2013. Iberdrola Vis. Prof., Univ. of Santiago de Compostela, Spain, 1999–2000; David P. Craig Vis. Prof., ANU, 2003; Vis. Prof., Univ. Paul Sabatier, Toulouse, 2008–09; Erskine Fellow, 2000, BIC Internat. Fellow, 2011, Univ. of Canterbury, Christchurch, NZ. FMedSci 2012. *Publications:* over 250 articles in scientific jls. *Recreation:* running. *Address:* Department of Chemistry, University of Cambridge, Lansfield Road, Cambridge CB2 1EW.

ABELL, (John) David; Chairman, Jourdan (formerly Thomas Jourdan) plc, since 1997; Director, Leicester Football Club plc, since 1999; *b* 15 Dec. 1942; *s* of Leonard Abell and Irene (*née* Anderson); *m* 1st, 1967, Anne Janette Priestley (marr. diss. 1977); three *s*; 2nd, 1981, Sandra Dawn Atkinson (marr. diss. 1986); one *s* one *d*; 3rd, 1988, Juliana, *d* of late Prof. J. L. I. Fennell, PhD, FRSL and of Marina Lopukhin. *Educ:* Univ. of Leeds (BAEcon); London School of Economics (Dip. Business Admin). Assistant to Cash and Investment Manager, Ford Motor Co., 1962–65; Asst, Treasurer's Office, AEI, 1965–67; British Leyland: Central Staffs,

1968–69; Manager, Investments and Banking, 1969–70; Chm. and Chief Exec., Prestcold Div., 1970–72; Corporate Treasurer, 1972; First Nat. Finance Corp., Nov. 1972–Aug. 1973; re-joined British Leyland as Man. Dir, Leyland Australia, 1974–75; Group Man. Dir, Leyland Special Products, 1975; Man. Dir, BL Commercial Vehicles, Chm. and Chief Exec., Leyland Vehicles Ltd, 1978–81; Chm. and Chief Exec., Suter Electrical, subseq. Suter plc, 1981–96. *Recreations:* horse racing and breeding, wine, tennis, music, Rugby, soccer. *Address:* Jourdan plc, Elm House, Elmer Street North, Grantham, Lincs NG31 6RE.

ABELL, Stephen Paul, (Stig); Managing Editor, The Sun, since 2013; *b* Nottingham, 10 April 1980; *s* of Steve Abell and Vera Abell; *m* 2008, Nadine Sanders; one *s* one *d*. *Educ:* Loughborough Grammar Sch.; Emmanuel Coll., Cambridge (BA 2001). Press Complaints Commission: Complaints Officer, 2001–04; Asst Dir, 2004–08; Dep. Dir, 2008–10; Dir, 2010–12; Partner, Pagefield Communications, 2012–13. Fiction Reviewer: TLS, 2001–12; Spectator, 2003–12; Telegraph, 2005–13. Contributor, Sky News, 2012–. Presenter, Sunday Morning Breakfast, LBC, 2014–. *Recreations:* reading, writing, pogonotrophy. *E:* stigabell@gmail.com.

ABELSON, Michael Andrew; a District Judge (Magistrates' Courts), Merseyside, since 2001; a Recorder, since 2000; *b* 22 March 1952; *s* of Harvey Abelson and Eva Abelson (*née* Newman); *m* 1994, Angela Bernadette Therese Walsh, BEd, DipEFL, *d* of Joseph Walsh and Frances Walsh (*née* Begley); one *s*. *Educ:* Leyton County High Sch.; University Coll., London (LLB Hons 1975). Called to the Bar, Middle Temple, 1976; in practice at the Bar, Northern, and Wales and Chester Circuits, 1977–98; Asst Recorder, 1997–2000; acting Stipendiary Magistrate: S Yorks, 1993–98; Gtr Manchester, 1995–98; Stipendiary Magistrate, later a Dist Judge (Magistrates' Courts), Gtr Manchester, 1998–2001. *Recreations:* travel, ski-ing, tennis, badminton. *Address:* Liverpool City Magistrates' Court, Dale Street, Liverpool L2 2JQ. *T:* (0151) 243 5596.

ABENSUR, Eric; Group Chief Executive Officer, Venda Ltd, since 2008 (Deputy Managing Director, 2007–08); *b* 7 Jan. 1964. *Educ:* Univ. Paris IX Dauphine (DESS Finance d'Entreprise). Sen. Manager, Ernst & Young, Paris and Los Angeles, 1989–98; Finance Dir, Pay-TV Div., France Telecom, 1998–2001; Chief Finance Officer, 2001–02, CEO, 2002–06, Freeserve, then Wanadoo UK, plc; Vice Pres., Orange Home UK plc, 2006–07. *Recreations:* cinema, history of 20th century, golf, squash. *Address:* Venda Ltd, 101 St Martin's Lane, WC2N 4AZ. *T:* (020) 7070 7227, *Fax:* (020) 7070 7111. *E:* eabensur@venda.com.

ABERCONWAY, 4th Baron *cr* 1911, of Bodnant; **Henry Charles McLaren;** Bt 1902; *b* 26 May 1948; *s* of 3rd Baron Aberconway and his 1st wife, Deirdre Knewstub; *S* father, 2003; *m* 1st, 1981, Sally (marr. diss. 1993), *yr d* of Captain C. N. Lentaigne, RN; one *s* one *d*; 2nd, 2005, Brigitte E. Hasler (*d* 2007). *Educ:* Eton; Sussex Univ. (BA). *Heir: s* Hon. Charles Stephen McLaren, *b* 27 Dec. 1984. *Address:* 10 Rose Farm Cottages, Shotley, Ipswich, Suffolk IP9 1PH.

ABERCORN, 5th Duke of, *cr* 1868; **James Hamilton,** KG 1999; Lord of Paisley, 1587; Lord of Abercorn, 1603; Earl of Abercorn and Lord of Hamilton, Mountcastle and Kilpatrick, 1606; Baron of Strabane, 1617; Viscount of Strabane, 1701; Viscount Hamilton, 1786; Marquess of Abercorn, 1790; Marquess of Hamilton, 1868; Bt 1660; Chancellor, Order of the Garter, since 2012; Lord Lieutenant of Co. Tyrone, 1987–2009; Lord Steward of HM Household, 2001–09; company director; *b* 4 July 1934; *er s* of 4th Duke of Abercorn, and Lady Mary Kathleen Crichton (Dowager Duchess of Abercorn, GCVO) (*d* 1990); *S* father, 1979; *m* 1966, Anastasia Alexandra (OBE 2008), *e d* of late Lt-Col Harold Phillips, Checkendon Court, Reading; two *s* one *d*. *Educ:* Eton Coll.; Royal Agricultural Coll., Cirencester, Glos. Joined HM Army, Oct. 1952; Lieut, Grenadier Guards. MP (UU) Fermanagh and South Tyrone, 1964–70. Dir, Northern Bank Ltd, 1970–97. Chm., Laganside Develt Corp., 1989–96 (Laganside Ltd, 1986–89); Dir, NI Industrial Develt Bd, 1982–87. Member: Council of Europe, 1968–70; European Economic and Social Cttee, 1973–78. President: Royal UK Beneficent Assoc., 1979–2013; Building Socs Assoc., 1986–92; Patron, Royal Ulster Agricl Soc., 1990–96. Trustee, Winston Churchill Meml Trust, 1991–2001. Col, Irish Guards, 2000–08. High Sheriff of Co. Tyrone, 1970. Hon. Mem., RICS, 1995. Hon. LLB QUB, 1997. *Recreations:* shooting, ski-ing. *Heir: s* Marquess of Hamilton, *qv*. *Address:* Barons Court, Omagh, Northern Ireland BT78 4EZ. *T:* (028) 8166 1470. *E:* duke.baronscourt@btinternet.com. *Club:* Brooks's.

ABERCROMBIE, Ian Ralph; QC (Scot.) 1994; Sheriff Principal of South Strathclyde, Dumfries and Galloway, since 2015; *b* 7 July 1955; *s* of late Ralph Abercrombie and Jean Abercrombie (*née* Lithgow). *Educ:* Edinburgh Univ. (LLB Hons 1978). Called to the Bar: Scotland, 1981; Lincoln's Inn, 1992. Sheriff of Grampian, Highland and Islands at Inverness, 2009–13, of Tayside Central and Fife at Dunfermline, 2013–15. *Address:* Sheriff Principal's Chambers, Sheriff Court House, Graham Street, Airdrie ML6 6EE. *T:* (01236) 439170.

ABERDARE, 5th Baron *cr* 1873, of Duffryn, co. Glamorgan; **Alastair John Lyndhurst Bruce;** DL; *b* 2 May 1947; *s* of 4th Baron Aberdare, KBE, PC and Lady Aberdare (*née* (Maud Helen) Sarah Dashwood); *S* father, 2005; *m* 1971, Elizabeth Mary Culbert Foulkes; one *s* one *d*. *Educ:* Eton; Christ Church, Oxford (MA Hons Lit.Hum.). IBM, 1969–91; Partner, Bruce Naughton Wade, 1991–99; Dir, ProbusBNW Ltd (corporate reputation consultants), 1999–2009; Dir, WALTZ Programmes Ltd, 2009–13. Trustee: Nat. Botanic Gdn of Wales, 1994–2006; St John Cymru Wales, 2008–; Berlioz Soc., 2008–; Nat. Liby of Wales, 2012–. Vice President: Fountain Soc., 2008–11; Public Monuments and Sculpture Assoc., 2011–. Elected Mem., H of L, July 2009. FRGS 1997; FRSA. Hon. Fellow, Cardiff Univ., 2008. DL Dyfed, 2009. *Publications:* (trans. and ed.) Hector Berlioz: the musical madhouse, 2003; (contrib.) Berlioz: scenes from the life and work, 2008. *Recreations:* music (esp. Berlioz), Wales, family, crosswords. *Heir: s* Hon. Hector Morys Napier Bruce, *b* 25 July 1974. *Address:* 16 Beverley Road, SW13 0LX. *Club:* MCC.

ABERDEEN, Bishop of, (RC), since 2011; **Rt Rev. Hugh Gilbert,** OSB; *b* Emsworth, Hants, 15 March 1952; *s* of Robert Gilbert and Philippa Gilbert (*née* Fordyce Jones). *Educ:* St Paul's Sch., London; King's Coll. London (BA Hons History). Entered Benedictine community of Pluscarden, 1974; ordained deacon, 1981, priest, 1982; Abbot, Pluscarden Abbey, Moray, 1992–2011. *Publications:* Unfolding the Mystery: monastic conferences on the liturgical year, 2007; Living the Mystery: monastic markers on the Christian way, 2008. *Recreations:* arts, walking. *Address:* Bishop's House, 3 Queen's Cross, Aberdeen AB15 4XU. *T:* (01224) 319154, *Fax:* (01224) 325570.

ABERDEEN, (St Andrew's Cathedral), Provost of; *see* Poobalan, Very Rev. Dr I. M.

ABERDEEN AND ORKNEY, Bishop of, since 2007; **Rt Rev. Robert Arthur Gillies;** *b* 21 Oct. 1951; *s* of Duncan and Vera Gillies; *m* 1976, Katherine Elizabeth Greening Tucker; three *s* (and one *s* decd). *Educ:* Univ. of Edinburgh (BD Hons 1978); Univ. of St Andrews (PhD 1991). Medical Lab. Technician, 1968–72; ordained deacon, 1977, priest, 1978; Curate, Christ Church, Falkirk, 1977–80; Curate, Christ Church, Edinburgh and Chaplain, Napier Coll., 1980–84; Chaplain, Univ. of Dundee, 1984–90; Rector, St Andrews Episcopal Church, St Andrews, 1991–2007; Synod Clerk, 2005–07, Dean, 2007, Dio. of St Andrews, Dunkeld and Dunblane. Hon. Lectr in Philosophy, Univ. of Dundee, 1985–94. *Publications:* A Way for Healing, 1995; Informing Faith, 1996; Healing Broader and Deeper, 1998; New Language of Faith, 2001; Where Earth and Heaven Meet, 2005; Sounds Before the Cross, 2007; Three Days in Holy Week, 2014. *Recreations:* climbing Scotland's mountains, travelling England's canals, watching ice hockey. *Address:* Diocesan Office, St Clement's House, Mastrick Drive, Aberdeen AB16 6UF. *T:* (01224) 662247. *E:* bishop@aberdeen.anglican.org.

ABERDEEN AND ORKNEY, Dean of; *see* Nimmo, Very Rev. Dr A. E.

ABERDEEN AND TEMAIR, 7th Marquess of, *cr* 1915; **Alexander George Gordon;** DL; landowner and property developer; Bt (NS) 1642; Earl of Aberdeen, Viscount Formartine, Lord Haddo, Methlic, Tarves, and Kellie, 1682 (Scot.); Viscount Gordon 1814, Earl of Haddo 1915 (UK); *b* 31 March 1955; *s* of 6th Marquess of Aberdeen and Temair and Anne, *d* of Lt-Col Gerald Barry, MC; *S* father, 2002; *m* 1981, Joanna Clodagh Houldsworth; three *s* one *d*. *Educ:* Cothill House, Abingdon; Harrow School; Polytechnic of Central London (DipBE). ARICS 1979–95. With Gardiner and Theobald, Chartered Quantity Surveyors, 1976–82; Speyhawk plc, Property Developers, 1982–86; London & Edinburgh Trust plc, Property Developers, 1986–94; Managing Director: Letinvest, 1989–94; Kellie Estates Ltd, 1995–2008; Gordon Land Ltd, 2000–; Braiklay Estates Ltd, 2007–; non-executive Director: Mobile Cardiovascular Science plc, 1992–99; Gordon Enterprise Trust, 1998–2002. DL Aberdeenshire, 1998. *Recreations:* golf, music, theatre. *Heir: s* Earl of Haddo, *qv*. *Address:* House of Formartine, Methlick, Ellon, Aberdeenshire AB41 7EQ. *T:* (01651) 851664. *Clubs:* MCC; New (Edinburgh); Royal Aberdeen Golf; Meldrum House Golf.

ABERDOUR, Lord; John Stewart Sholto Douglas; *b* 17 Jan. 1952; *s* and *heir* of 22nd Earl of Morton, *qv*; *m* 1985, Amanda, *yr d* of David Mitchell, Kirkcudbright; one *s* two *d*. *Educ:* Dunrobin Castle School. Studied Agriculture, Aberdeen Univ. Partner, Dalmahoy Farms, Kirknewton. Pres., Convention of Baronage of Scotland. *Heir: s* Master of Aberdour, *qv*. *Address:* Haggs Farm, Kirknewton, Midlothian EH27 8EE.

ABERDOUR, Master of; Hon. John David Sholto Douglas; *b* 28 May 1986; *s* and *heir* of Lord Aberdour, *qv*. *Educ:* Merchiston Castle Sch., Edinburgh; RAC, Cirencester (BSc Hons Agric. (Land Mgt) 2008).

ABERGAVENNY, 6th Marquess of, *cr* 1876; **Christopher George Charles Nevill;** Baron Abergavenny 1450; Earl of Abergavenny and Viscount Nevill 1784; Earl of Lewes 1876; DL; landowner; *b* 23 April 1955; *yr s* of Lord Rupert Charles Montacute Nevill, CVO, *yr s* of 4th Marquess of Abergavenny and of Lady Anne Camilla Eveline Wallop, *d* of 9th Earl of Portsmouth; *S* uncle, 2000; *m* 1985, Venetia Jane, *er d* of late Frederick Gerard Maynard; one *d* (one *s* decd). *Educ:* Harrow. Dir, Nevill Estate Co. Ltd, 1985–. Mem. (C), Wealden DC, 1999. Chm., St John Ambulance, Kent, 2004–10. President: Royal Tunbridge Wells Civic Soc., 2008–; Friends of Tunbridge Wells Mus. and Art Gall., 2008–; S of England Agricl Soc., 2009–10. Patron: Sussex Housing Care, 2007–; Rotherfield St Martin, 2007–; Spa Valley Rly, 2008–; Pepenbury Residential Care Home, 2008–; Searchlight, 2009–12. Trustee, Royal British Legion Industries, 2010–. DL E Sussex, 2011. *Heir:* (to Earldom and Barony of Abergavenny and Viscountcy of Nevill only) *kinsman* David Michael Ralph Nevill [*b* 20 June 1941; *m* 1972, Katherine Mary, *d* of Rossmore Derrick Westenra; one *s* two *d*]. *Address:* Eridge Park, Eridge Green, Tunbridge Wells, Kent TN3 9JT. *T:* (01892) 752808. *Club:* White's.

ABERNETHY, Rt Hon. Lord; John Alastair Cameron; PC 2005; a Senator of the College of Justice in Scotland, 1992–2007; *b* 1 Feb. 1938; *s* of William Philip Legerwood Cameron and Kathleen Milthorpe (*née* Parker); *m* 1968, Elspeth Mary Dunlop Miller; three *s*. *Educ:* Clergy Sch., Khartoum; St Mary's Sch., Melrose; Trinity Coll., Glenalmond; Pembroke Coll., Oxford (MA 1961; Hon. Fellow, 1993). Nat. Service, 1956–58 (2nd Lieut, RASC). Called to the Bar, Inner Temple, 1963; admitted Mem., Faculty of Advocates, 1966, Vice-Dean, 1983–92; QC (Scotland) 1979. Advocate-Depute, 1972–75; Standing Jun. Counsel; to Dept of Energy, 1976–79; to Scottish Develt Dept, 1978–79. Legal Chm., Pensions Appeal Tribunals for Scotland, 1979–92 (Pres., 1985–92). Dir, Faculty Services Ltd, 1979–89 (Chm., 1983–89). International Bar Association: Chm., Judges' Forum, 1994–98 (Vice-Chm., 1993–94); Mem. Council, Section on Legal Practice, 1998–2002; Mem. Council, Human Rights Inst., 1998–2000, 2002–05. Mem., Internat. Legal Assistance Consortium, 2002–. Comr, NI (Remission of Sentences) Act 1995, 2008–. Justice of Appeal, Botswana, 2009–; Judge of Interim Ind. Constitutional Dispute Resolution Ct, Kenya, 2010. Pres., Scottish Medico-Legal Soc., 1996–2000. Mem. Exec. Cttee, Soc. for Welfare and Teaching of the Blind (Edinburgh and SE Scotland), 1979–92. Trustee: Arthur Smith Meml Trust, 1975–2001 (Chm., 1990–2001); Faculty of Advocates 1985 Charitable Trust, 1985–; Southern Africa Litigation Centre, 2008–15. Gov., St Mary's Sch. (Melrose) Ltd, 1998–2012 (Dep. Chm., 2004–12). *Publications:* Medical Negligence: an introduction, 1983; (contrib.) Reproductive Medicine and the Law, 1990. *Recreations:* travel, nature conservation, Africana. *Address:* 4 Garscube Terrace, Edinburgh EH12 6BQ. *T:* (0131) 337 3460, *Fax:* (0131) 240 6711. *Club:* New (Edinburgh).

ABERNETHY, Rt Rev. Alan Francis; *see* Connor, Bishop of.

ABINERI, Claudia; *see* Rosencrantz, C. E.

ABINGDON, Earl of; *see* Lindsey and Abingdon, Earl of.

ABINGER, 9th Baron *cr* 1835; **James Harry Scarlett;** Director General, A-Music, since 2005; *b* 28 May 1959; *er s* of 8th Baron Abinger and Isla Carolyn, *o d* of Vice-Adm. J. W. Rivett-Carnac, CB, CBE, DSC; *S* father, 2002; *m* 1995, Tracy Lee, *d* of N. Cloutier, Ottawa; one *s* one *d* (adopted twins). *Educ:* Eton; Univ. of Aberdeen (BSc 1982); Magdalene Coll., Cambridge (MPhil 1994). FRGS, FLS. *Recreations:* diving for treasure, playing the cello. *Heir: b* Hon. Peter Richard Scarlett [*b* 21 March 1961; *m* 1992, Sharon Elizabeth Turl; one *s* one *d*].

ABLE, Graham George; Deputy Chairman, Alpha Plus Group, since 2014 (Chief Executive Officer, 2009–14); Master, Dulwich College, 1997–2009; *b* 28 July 1947; *s* of George Jasper Able and Irene Helen Able (*née* Gaff); *m* 1969, Mary Susan Munro; one *s* one *d*. *Educ:* Worksop Coll.; Trinity Coll., Cambridge (MA Nat. Scis 1968, PGCE 1969); MA Social Scis Dunelm 1983. Teacher, Sutton Valence Sch., 1969–83 (Boarding Housemaster, 1976–83); Second Master, Barnard Castle Sch., 1983–88; Headmaster, Hampton Sch., 1988–96. Co-Chm., HMC and GSA Educn and Academic Policy Cttee, 1998–2001; Chairman: HMC, 2003; Exporting Educn (UK), 2012–. Member: Council and Court, ICSTM, 1999–2006; Council, Roedean Sch., 2000–09. Pres., Internat. Boys' Schs' Coalition, 2006–09; Sen. Vice-Pres. (Acad.), Dulwich Coll. Mgt Internat., 2009–. Governor: Beeston Hall Sch., 2012–; Gresham's Sch., 2013–. Fellow, Dulwich Coll., 2009. Mem., Bd of Trustees, Cricket Foundn, 2009–14. FRSA 1994. MInstD 1995. *Publications:* (jtly) Head to Head, 1992; (jtly) Head to HoD, 1998; (jtly) Education: A Great British Export?, 2012. *Recreations:* cricket, golf, sailing, contract bridge. *Address:* The Old Smithy, High Street, Wighton, Norfolk NR23 1AL. *Clubs:* MCC, East India (Hon. Mem.).

ABNEY-HASTINGS, family name of **Earl of Loudoun**.

ABOUSEIF, Doris B.; *see* Behrens-Abouseif.

ABOYNE, Earl of; Alistair Granville Gordon; *b* 26 July 1973; *s* and *heir* of Marquess of Huntly, *qv*; *m* 2004, Sophia, *d* of Michael Cunningham; one *s* three *d*. *Educ:* Harrow. *Heir: s* Lord Strathavon, *qv*. *Address:* c/o Aboyne Castle, Aberdeenshire AB34 5JP.

ABRAHAM, Ann; UK Parliamentary Ombudsman and Health Service Ombudsman for England, 2002–12; *b* 25 Aug. 1952; *d* of John Kenneth and Kathleen Mary Marsden; *m* 2011, Geoffrey Leonard Mitchell. *Educ:* Bedford Coll., Univ. of London (BA Hons German);

Postgrad. DMS. MCIH. Housing Manager, Local Govt, 1975–80; Ops Manager, Regional Dir and Ops Dir, Housing Corp., 1980–90; Chief Exec., NACAB, 1991–97; Legal Services Ombudsman for England and Wales, 1997–2002; Health Service Comr for Wales, 2002–03; Welsh Admin Ombudsman, 2002–04. Non-executive Director: Benefits Agency, 1997–2001; Health Educn England, 2012–14. Mem., Cttee on Standards in Public Life, 2000–02; ex officio Member: Commn for Local Admin in England, 2002–11; Administrative Justice and Tribunals Council (formerly Council on Tribunals), 2002–11 (Mem., Scottish Cttee, 2002–11, Welsh Cttee, 2008–11). Mem. Validation Cttee, Ombudsman Assoc. (formerly British and Irish Ombudsman Assoc.), 2006–11, 2012– (Mem. 2001–06, Chair, 2004–06, Exec. Cttee). Trustee, Picker Inst. Europe, 2013–. Chair, Dorset Healthcare Univ. NHS Foundn Trust, 2014– (non-exec. Dir, 2013–14). Hon LLD Winchester, 2012. *Recreations:* family, friends, walking, gardening. *E:* ann.abraham@btinternet.com.

ABRAHAM, David; Chief Executive, Channel Four, since 2010; *b* Lincs, 7 Aug. 1963; *s* of Esmond and Jeanette Abraham; one *s* one *d*. *Educ:* Ingatestone Sch.; Magdalen Coll., Oxford (BA Modern Hist. 1984). Account Manager, Benton & Bowles, 1984–87; Account Manager, 1987–88, Account Dir, 1989–90, CDP; Account Dir, 1990–93, Dep. Man. Dir, 1993–95, Chiat Day; Founder and Chief Operating Officer, St Luke's, 1995–2000; Gen. Manager, Discovery Networks UK, 2001–04; Pres., TLC, USA, 2005–07; Chief Exec., UKTV, 2007–10. Mem. Bd, Creative Skillset, 2008–. Member: BAFTA; RTS. *Address:* Channel Four Television, 124 Horseferry Road, SW1P 2TX. *T:* (020) 7396 4444.

ABRAHAM, Eric Antony; film, theatre and television producer; *b* Cape Town, S Africa, 3 March 1954; *s* of George Abraham; *m* 1st, 1978, Katarina Krausova (marr. diss. 2002); one *s* one *d*; 2nd, 2003, Sigrid Maria Elisabet Rausing, *qv*. *Educ:* Univ. of Cape Town (BA Comparative African Govt and Law 1976). Organiser, Amnesty Internat. first global campaign against torture and Conf. for Abolition of Torture, Paris, 1973–74; human rights worker and foreign corresp., S Africa, 1974–76; banned and house-arrested by apartheid govt, 1976; adopted as Amnesty Prisoner of Conscience; escaped and granted political asylum in UK, 1977. Producer, Panorama, BBC TV, 1977–82; Exec. Producer, Primetime TV, 1983–86; Founder, Portobello Pictures, 1987; productions include: *films:* Danny, the Champion of the World, 1989; A Murder of Quality, 1991; Kolya, 1996; IDA, 2013; *television:* Dalziel & Pascoe, 1997–99; Mojo, 1997; *theatre:* Embers, Duke of York's, 2006; South African version of Mozart's Magic Flute, Young Vic, transf. Duke of York's, 2008; Exec. Producer and Founder, Fugard Th., Cape Town, 2010–. Member: BAFTA, 1990–; Acad. of Motion Picture Arts and Scis, 1997–; Czech Film Acad., 1997–; Eur. Film Acad., 1998–. *Recreations:* cinema, theatre, ski-ing, walking. *Address:* Portobello Pictures, 12 Addison Avenue, W11 4QR. *Clubs:* Chelsea Arts, Soho House, Groucho.

ABRAHAM, Maj. Gen. Kevin David, CB 2014; Director General Army Reform, Army Headquarters, 2012–14; *b* Magherafelt, 11 Feb. 1960; *s* of David Abraham and Mary Patricia Abraham (*née* Nesbitt); *m* 1996, Julia Caroline Williams; two step *s*. *Educ:* Dr Challoner's Grammar Sch.; Univ. of St Andrews (MA 1983); King's Coll. London (MA 2000). Jun. officer posts in Germany and UK, 1983–2000; psc 1992; psc JSCSC 1999; CO, 1st Regt RHA, 2000–02; ACOS Plans, HQ ARRC, 2002–04; hcsc 2003; Comdr, 1st UK Armd Div., RA, 2004–05; rcds 2006; ACOS J7, PJHQ, 2006–08; Director: Jt Capability, MoD, 2008–10; Force Develt, Army HQ, 2010–12. Mem., Regtl Council, HAC, 2013–. Hon. Col, Tayforth Univ. OTC, 2013–. *Recreations:* village cricket, ski-ing, sailing, Rugby, birding. *Club:* Naval and Military.

ABRAHAM, Neville Victor, CBE 2001; Chairman: Liberty Wines Ltd, since 2003; Metabolic Services Ltd, since 2013; Groupe Chez Gérard plc, 1994–2003 (Joint Founder, 1986; Chief Executive, 1994–99); *b* 22 Jan. 1937; *s* of late Solomon Abraham and of Sarah (*née* Raphael); *m* 2005, Nicola Leach. *Educ:* Brighton Coll.; London Sch. of Econs (BSc Hons). Marketing Asst, Young & Rubicam, 1961–63; Sen. Principal, DTI, 1963–71; Corporate Policy Advr, Harold Whitehead & Partners, 1971–74; Founder, Les Amis du Vin, 1974 (Man. Dir, 1974–86); Chm., Amis du Vin Gp, 1980–84; Dir, Kennedy Brookes plc, 1984–86. Non-exec. Dir, Draft House Hldgs Ltd, 2009–. Vis. Lectr, several business schools, 1972–81. Chairman: Exec. Cttee, Covent Garden Fest., 1993–99; London String Quartet Foundn, 2000–06. Gov., Brighton Coll., 2006–. *Publications:* Big Business and Government: the new disorder, 1974. *Recreations:* music, opera, walking, good food and wine, cricket. *Clubs:* Royal Automobile, Home House, MCC.

ABRAHAM, Sigrid Maria Elisabeth; *see* Rausing, S. M. E.

ABRAHAM-WILLIAMS, Rev. Gethin; ecumenist; Tutor, Department of History, Archaeology and Religion (formerly School of Religion and Theological Studies), Cardiff University, since 2009; *s* of late Lt Col Emlyn Abraham-Williams, TD, DL, and of Anne Elizabeth Abraham-Williams; *m* 1977, Denise Frances Harding; one *s* one *d*. *Educ:* Ysgol yr Urdd, Aberystwyth; Ardwyn Grammar Sch., Aberystwyth; UC of Wales, Aberystwyth; Regent's Park Coll., Oxford (BA Hons Theol. 1964; MA 1967; Chm., Oxford Theol Colls' Union, 1963). Ordained 1965; Asst Minister, Queen's Road Baptist Ch (with Lenton's Lane, Hawkesbury), Coventry, 1964–68; Minister: Chester Rd Baptist Ch, Sutton Coldfield, 1968–73; Sutton Baptist Ch, Surrey, 1973–80; Ecumenical Officer and Exec. Sec., Milton Keynes Christian Council, 1981–90; Bp of Oxford's Ecumenical Officer, Milton Keynes, 1981–90; Gen. Sec., ENFYS: Covenanted Churches in Wales, with Provincial Officer for Ecumenism, Ch in Wales, 1990–98; Gen. Sec., CYTÛN: Churches Together in Wales, 1998–2006. Ed., Baptist Ministers' Fellowship Jl, 1998–2002. Baptist Union of GB: Member: Council, 1971–73 and 1993–95; Wkg Gp on LEPs, 1982–90; Worship and Doctrine Cttee, 1993–95. Mem., 1981–90, Moderator, 1988–90, Consultative Cttee for LEPs in England; British Council of Churches: Mem., Bd for Ecumenical Affairs, 1987–90; Observer: Nat. (RC) Conf. of Priests, 1983 and 1984; English ARC, 1988–90; Delegated Rep., WCC, 1991–2006; Mem., Steering Cttee, CCBI, 1992–96, 1998–; Mem., Free Church Fed. Council, 1991–96; Mem. Council, CYTÛN, 1995–98; Mem., Ecumenical Adv. Gp, ACC, 1997; Chm., Commn of Covenanted Churches in Wales, 2010–13. Co-Chair, Cardiff Branch, Council of Christians and Jews, 2012–. Member: Warwicks Probationary and After Care Service, 1970–73; Ind. Monitoring Bd, HM Prison and Young Offenders Instn Parc, Bridgend, 2009–14. Mem., Marjory Fry and St Leonard's Trust Housing Cttee, 1970–73; Westlake Pastoral Lectr, Regent's Pk Coll., Oxford, 1973. Religions and Beliefs Consultant, Univ. of Glamorgan Chaplaincy, 2007–08. Mem., Order of St Luke, 1961; CStJ and Sub Prelate 2010 (ChStJ, Priory for Wales, 2002). Radio presenter, BBC World Service, Radio 4, Radio Wales, etc. Cross of St Augustine, 2006. *Publications:* (ed) Christian Baptism and Church Membership, Vol. II, 1994; (ed jtly) Letters to Friends, 1996; (ed) Towards the Making of an Ecumenical Bishop in Wales, 1997; (ed) Women, Church and Society in Wales, 2004; (ed) No, please, I don't want to die!, 2006; Spirituality or Religion? Do we have to choose?, 2008; Seeing the Good in Unfamiliar Spiritualities, 2011; Why the Gospel of Thomas Matters, 2015; contrib. to Birmingham Post, Expository Times, Epworth Rev., Baptist Times, Cristion, etc. *Recreations:* radio, travel, theatre, books, eating out. *Address:* 13 Millbrook Road, Dinas Powys, Vale of Glamorgan CF64 4BZ. *T:* (029) 2051 5884. *E:* gethin@theaws.com. *W:* www.twitter.com/DownTimeRev.

ABRAHAMS, David; *see* Abrahams, I. D.

ABRAHAMS, Deborah Angela Elspeth; MP (Lab) Oldham East and Saddleworth, since Jan. 2011; *b* Sheffield, 1960; *m* John Abrahams; two *d*. *Educ:* Univ. of Salford; Univ. of Liverpool. FFPH 2012. Hd, Healthy Cities for Knowsley, 1992–2000; Sen. Res. Fellow, Univ. of Liverpool, full time, 2000–02, pt time, 2002–06; Chm., Rochdale PCT, 2002–06; Dir, Internat. Health Impact Assessment Consortium, Univ. of Liverpool, 2006–10. Mem. Bd, Bury and Rochdale HA, 1998–2002. Contested (Lab) Colne Valley, 2010. Mem., Work and Pensions Select Cttee, 2011–. *Address:* House of Commons, SW1A 0AA.

ABRAHAMS, Prof. (Ian) David, PhD; Beyer Professor of Applied Mathematics, University of Manchester, since 1998; *b* Manchester, 15 Jan. 1958; *s* of late Harry Abrahams and of Leila Abrahams; *m* 2004, Penelope Lawrence Warwick; one *d* and two step *s*. *Educ:* Imperial Coll. London (BSc Eng. Hons 1979; PhD Applied Maths 1982; DIC 1982). Temp. Lectr, Dept of Maths, Univ. of Manchester, 1982–83; Lectr, Sch. of Maths, Univ. of Newcastle upon Tyne, 1983–90; Reader, 1990–93, Prof., 1994–98, Dept of Maths, Keele Univ.; Hd, Applied Maths, Sch. of Maths, Univ. of Manchester, 1998–2007. Nuffield Foundn Sci. Res. Fellow, 1990–91; Royal Soc. Leverhulme Trust Sen. Res. Fellow, 2002–03. Member: Council: IMA, 1998– (Pres., 2008–09); Eur. Mechanics Soc., 2000–06; LMS, 2002–06; Bd, Internat. Council for Industrial and Applied Maths, 2003–. *Publications:* contrib. scientific papers on propagation, refraction and diffraction of waves in solids, fluids and electromagnetics. *Recreations:* distance running, motorcycling, fiddling with ALL things mechanical and electrical, watching (almost) all sports. *Address:* School of Mathematics, University of Manchester, Oxford Road, Manchester M13 9PL. *T:* (0161) 275 5901, *Fax:* (0161) 275 5819.

ABRAHAMS, Michael David, CBE 1994 (MBE 1988); DL; Chairman, Ferrexpo plc, since 2007; *b* 23 Nov. 1937; *s* of Alexander Abrahams and Anne Abrahams (*née* Sokoloff); *m* 1968, Amanda Atha; one *s* two *d*. *Educ:* Shrewsbury; Worcester Coll., Oxford. Nat. Service, RM (commnd). Man. Dir, AW (Securities) Ltd, 1968–73; Chairman: Champion Associated Weavers Ltd, 1974–80; Associated Weavers Europe NV, 1974–83; Weavercraft Carpets Ltd, 1980–85; Dep. Chm., John Crowther PLC, 1985–88; Director: Prudential Corp. plc, 1984–2000 (Dep. Chm., 1991–2000); John Waddington plc, 1984–2000; Cavaghan & Gray plc, 1987–98 (Chm., 1992–98); Drummond Gp plc, 1989–2001. Chairman: Prudential Staff Pension Scheme, 1991–; Minorplanet Systems plc, 1997–2004; Kingston Communications plc, 1999–2009; imJack plc (formerly Amteus plc), 2006–11. Chm., The London Clinic, 1996–2012. Pres., British Carpet Mfrs Assoc., 1979–80. Dep. Chm. Council, Prince of Wales's Inst. of Architecture, 1991–96; Dir, Rank Foundn, 1992–2007; Regl Chm., NT for Yorks, 1996–2003; Chm., Ripon City Partnership, 2005–09. Jt Chm., Yorks Children's Hosp. Fund (Co-founder), 1989–2011; Trustee, Hackfall Trust, 1987–. Pres., Yorks Agricl Soc., 2007–08. Master, Woolmen's Co., 1996–97. High Sheriff, 1993–94, DL, 1994, N Yorks. Hon. Freeman, City of Ripon, 2002. *Recreations:* art, architecture. *Address:* Newfield, Mickley, Ripon, N Yorks HG4 3JH. *T:* (01765) 635426. *Clubs:* Garrick, Pratt's.

ABRAHAMSEN, Egil; Comdr, Order of St Olav, 1987 (Kt Comdr 1979); Chairman, Norwegian Telecommunications, 1980–95; *b* 7 Feb. 1923; *s* of Anker Christian Abrahamsen and Aagot (*née* Kjølberg); *m* 1950, Randi Wiborg; one *s* two *d*. *Educ:* Technical Univ. of Norway (Naval Architect, 1949); Durham Univ., King's Coll., Newcastle upon Tyne (post-grad. studies and res.); Univ. of Calif, Berkeley (post-grad. studies). Sales Engr, Maschinen-Fabrik Augsburg-Nürnberg, and Karlstads Mekaniska Verkstad AB, Sweden, 1949–50; projects and planning, A/S Rosenberg Mekaniske Verksted, Stavanger, 1951–52; Det Norske Veritas, 1952–85: Surveyor, 1952; Sen. Surveyor, 1954 (resp. for building up Res. Dept); Principal Surveyor, 1957; Dep. Pres., 1966; Vice Pres., 1966; Pres., 1967. Chairman: Norsk Hydro, 1985–92; OPAK, 1985–99; Royal Caribbean Cruise-Line, 1987–88; Kosmos, 1988–99; IKO Group, 1988–; Eikland, 1990–99; IM Skaugen ASA, 1990–99. Editor, European Shipbuilding, 1952–60. Fellow, Nat. Acad. of Engrg, USA, 1978; Member: Norwegian Acad. of Technical Scis, 1968 (Hon. Mem., 2008); Royal Swedish Acad. of Engrg Scis, 1979; Hon. Mem., Soc. of Naval Architects and Marine Engrs, USA, 1987. DTech *hc* Royal Inst. of Technol., Sweden, 1977. Owes Hon. Prize, for contribn to res. and educn, 1971. Grand Officer, Order of Infante Dom Henrique (Portugal), 1977; Comdr, Order of the Lion (Finland), 1982; Kt, Nat. Order of Merit (France), 1982. *Address:* Borgenveien 50, 0373 Oslo, Norway.

ABRAM, Henry Charles, VRD 1958 (bar 1968); Chairman: Henry Abram Ltd, since 1955; Henry Abram & Sons, 1989–2012; Vice Lord-Lieutenant of Renfrewshire, 1995–2002; *b* 3 March 1924; *s* of Henry Kerr Abram and Madge Ballantyne, Glasgow; *m* 1950, Marie Kathleen Janet Paterson, *d* of Andrew Paterson, Glasgow; four *s*. *Educ:* Kelvinside Acad. Joined family shipping firm, Henry Abram Ltd, 1941; Dir, 1948–; Man. Dir, 1953. Joined RNVR, 1942; served in HMSs Ganges, Porcupine (torpedoed) and Meadowsweet; Lieut, 1946; Lieut-Comdr, 1954; Comdr, 1963; assumed comd and commnd HMS Dalriada, RNR Trng Estabt, Greenock, 1965; retd 1972. Dir, Glasgow Aged Seamen Relief Fund, 1974–2002; Pres., Glasgow Shipowners' and Shipbrokers' Benevolent Assoc., 1976–77; Hon. Vice-Pres., Clyde Maritime Trust, 1990; Mem., Scottish Council, King George's Fund for Sailors, 1988–2001. Deacon Convenor, Trades House of Glasgow, 1978–79; Chm., Trades Hall of Glasgow Trust, 1987–2004; Dir, Merchants House of Glasgow, 1988–2005. Dir, Glasgow Sch. of Art, 1977– (Vice-Chm., 1985; Chm., 1989–92). MRIN 1957; FRSA 1987. DL Strathclyde, 1987. OStJ 1978. *Recreations:* sailing, shooting, stalking, golf, gardening. *Address:* Enterkin, Kilmacolm, Renfrewshire PA13 4NR. *T:* (01505) 872018. *Clubs:* Caledonian, Royal Thames Yacht; Kilmacolm Golf, Prestwick Golf.

ABRAM, Rev. Paul Robert Carrington, MVO 2007; a Deputy Priest in Ordinary to the Queen, 1996–2007; Chaplain of the Chapel Royal of St Peter ad Vincula, Tower of London, 1996–2007; *b* 21 July 1936; *s* of Norman and Madge Alice Abram; *m* 1961, Joanna Rose (*née* Headley); four *d*. *Educ:* The English Sch., Cairo; King Alfred Sch., Plon; Hymers Coll., Hull; Keble Coll., Oxford (BA 1962; MA 1965); Chichester Theol Coll. Ordained deacon, 1962, priest, 1963; Asst Curate, Redcar, 1962–65; Chaplain to the Forces, 1965–89; Vicar of Salcombe and Chaplain, Missions to Seamen, 1989–96; Chaplain for the Pool of London, Mission to Seafarers (formerly Missions to Seamen), 1996–2007. Chaplain: HMS President, 1996–2007; Solicitors' Co., 1996–2007; Builders' Merchants' Co., 1996–2007 (Life Liveryman, 2007); Aldermanic Sheriff, 1999–2000; Security Professionals, 2001–07; NEAC, 2001–07; Lord Mayor of London, 2003–04. FRGS 1960. Medal, Order of St Melitus, 2007. *Recreations:* sailing, pre-nineteenth century maps, travel, people. *Address:* Paddock End, Kimpton, Andover, Hants SP11 8PG. *Club:* Special Forces.

ABRAMS, Dominic; *see* Abrams, W. D. J.

ABRAMS, Dr Michael Ellis, CB 1992; FRCP, FFPH; public health consultant, since 1992; Chairman, Whittington Hospital NHS Trust, 1998–2003; Deputy Chief Medical Officer, Department of Health (formerly of Health and Social Security), 1985–92; *b* 17 Sept. 1932; *s* of late Sam Philip and Ruhamah Emmie Abrams; *m* 1962, Rosalind J. Beckman; four *c*. *Educ:* King Edward's Sch., Birmingham; Univ. of Birmingham (BSc 1st Cl. Anat. and Physiol. 1953; MB ChB Distinction in Medicine 1956). FRCP 1972; MFCM (Founder Mem.) 1972, FFCM 1983. Ho. Officer posts in United Birmingham Hosps, 1957–58; Univ. Research Fellow, Dept of Exp. Pathology, Univ. of Birmingham, and Medical Registrar, Queen Elizabeth Hosp., Birmingham, 1959; Medical Registrar and MRC Clinical Res. Fellow, Queen Elizabeth Hosp., Birmingham, 1959–62; MRC Clin. Res. Fellow, Dept of Medicine, Guy's Hosp., London, 1962–63; Rockefeller Travelling Fellow, Cardiovascular Res. Inst., Univ. of California Med. Centre, San Francisco, 1963–64; Lectr/Sen. Lectr and Hon. Cons. Phys., Guy's Hosp., 1964–75; Chief Med. Adviser, Guy's Hosp./Essex Gen. Practice Computing Unit, 1968–73; Dir, Inter-Deptl Laboratory, Guy's Hosp., 1971–75; DHSS: SMO, 1975–78; PMO, 1978–79; SPMO, 1979–85. Vice-Chm., Haringey Healthcare NHS Trust, 1993–98; Chm., N Thames Reg., Metropolitan Housing Trust, 1999–2004 (Vice-Chm., 1998–99). Mem. Bd, Dalco Homes Ltd, 1997–98. UK Deleg., Council of Europe Steering Cttee on

Bioethics, 1990–97; Mem., WHO Council on Earth Summit Action Prog. for Health and Envmt, 1993–. Hon. Cons. Phys. Emeritus, Guy's Hosp. and Hon. Lectr in Medicine, Guy's Hosp. Med. Sch.; Examr in Human Communication, London Univ., 1972–84. Pres., Section of Measurement in Medicine, RSM, 1981–83; Chm., Computer Cttee, RCP, 1981–89. Gov., Moselle Sch., 2000–04. Hon. Officer, Muswell Hill Synagogue, 1974–95. Chm. Editl Bd, Health Trends, 1988–99. *Publications:* (ed) Medical Computing Progress and Problems, 1970; (ed) Spectrum 71, 1971; (ed) The Computer in the Doctor's Office, 1980; articles on medical manpower planning, biomedical computing, pulmonary surfactant and glucose tolerance in diabetes. *Recreations:* reading, gardening, beachcombing. *Address:* 97 Wood Vale, N10 3DL.

ABRAMS, Prof. (William) Dominic (Joshua), PhD; FBA 2013; FAcSS; Professor of Social Psychology, since 1993 and Director, Centre for the Study of Group Processes, since 1995, University of Kent; *b* Cambridge, 11 April 1958; *s* of late Prof. Philip Abrams and of Prof. Sonia Jackson (*née* Edelman); *m* 1989, Prof. Diane Margaret Houston; one *s* two *d*. *Educ:* Impington Village Coll.; Brooksbank Comp. Sch.; Greenhead Coll.; Univ. of Manchester (BA Hons Psychol.) London Sch. of Econs and Pol Sci. (MSc Social Psychol.); Univ. of Kent (PhD Social Psychol. 1984). CPsychol 1989. Lectr in Social Psychol., Univ. of Bristol, 1983–85; Lectr in Social Cognition, Dundee Univ., 1985–89; Lectr, 1989–91, Sen. Lectr, 1991–92, Reader, 1992–93, in Social Psychol., Univ. of Kent. Member: res. bds, ESRC, 2008–13; HEFCE Res. Evaluation Framework Panel 4, 2013–14. British Psychological Society: Sec./Treas., Social Psychol. Section, 1985–89; Chm., Res. Bd and Mem., Bd of Trustees, 2003–06; Fellow, 2011. Mem. Council and Chm., Learned Socs, Acad. of Social Scis, 2000–06, 2009–14; Sec., Eur. Assoc. of Social Psychol., 2002–05; Pres., Soc. for Psychol Study of Social Issues, 2012–14 (Fellow, 1999). Trustee, Anne Frank Trust, 2013–15. Editor, Group Processes and Intergroup Relations, 1997–. Fellow: Soc. of Experimental Social Psychol., 2006; Soc. for Personality and Social Psychol., 2009. FAcSS (AcSS 2004). *Publications:* with M. A. Hogg: Social Identifications: a social psychology of intergroup relations and group processes, 1988; (ed) Social Identity Theory: constructive and critical advances, 1990; (ed) Group Motivation: social psychological perspectives, 1993; Social Identifications: a social psychology of intergroup relations and group processes, 1995; (ed) Social Identity and Social Cognition, 1999; Intergroup Relations, 2001; (ed jtly) The Social Psychology of Exclusion and Inclusion, 2005; (ed jtly) Multidisciplinary Handbook of Social Exclusion Research, 2007; over 200 papers on prejudice, social cohesion and social gps in jls. *Recreations:* folk, blues and jazz guitar and violin. *Address:* Centre for the Study of Group Processes, University of Kent, Canterbury CT2 7NP. *E:* D.Abrams@kent.ac.uk.

ABRAMSKY, Dame Jennifer (Gita), DBE 2009 (CBE 2001); Chair: National Heritage Memorial Fund and Heritage Lottery Fund, 2008–14; Board of Trustees, University of London, 2008–14; Royal Academy of Music, since 2014; *b* 7 Oct. 1946; *d* of late Prof. Chimen Abramsky and Miriam (*née* Nirenstein); *m* 1976, Alasdair Donald MacDuff Liddell, CBE (*d* 2012); one *s* one *d*. *Educ:* Holland Park Sch.; Univ. of East Anglia (BA Hons English) (Dep. Chm., New Univs Fest., 1968). BBC: joined as Prog. Operations Asst, 1969; Producer, World at One, 1973; Jt Producer and Compiler of Special Prog. on 'Nixon', 1974; Editor: PM Prog., 1978–81; Radio Four Budget Prog., 1979–86; World at One, 1981–86; Today, 1986–87; News and Current Affairs, BBC Radio, 1987–93; set up Radio 4 News FM for duration of Gulf War, 1991; Controller, BBC Radio Five Live, 1993–96; Dir, Continuous News Services, BBC, incl. Radio 5 Live, BBC World, 24 Hour UK TV News, Ceefax and Multimedia News, 1996–98; Dir, BBC Radio, 1999–2000; Dir, BBC Radio and Music, subseq. Audio and Music, 2000–08. Member: ESRC, 1992–96; Editl Bd, British Journalism Rev., 1993–98. Director: Hampstead Th., 2003– (Chm., 2005–12); Birmingham Royal Ballet, 2011–. A Governor, BFI, 2000–06; Vice Chm., Digital Radio Devlt Bureau, 2002–08. News Internat. Vis. Prof. of Broadcast Media, Oxford Univ., 2001–02. Gov., Royal Ballet, 2008– (Chair, Bd of Govs, 2012–); Trustee: Central Sch. of Ballet, 2007–13; Shakespeare Schs Fest., 2008–; English Touring Th., 2015–. Fellow, Radio Acad., 1998. Hon. Fellow, Central Sch. of Speech and Drama, 2009. Hon. RAM 2002. Hon. MA Salford, 1997; Hon. LittD UAE, 2003; Hon. DLitt: Westminster, 2005; Kent, 2012. Woman of Distinction, Jewish Care, 1990; Sony Radio Acad. Award, 1995. *Recreations:* theatre, music, dance.

ABRAMSKY, Prof. Samson, PhD; FRS 2004; FRSE; Christopher Strachey Professor of Computing, University of Oxford, since 2000; Fellow, Wolfson College, Oxford, since 2000; *b* 12 March 1953; *s* of Moshe and Chaya-Sarah Abramsky; *m* 1976, Rosalind Susan Herman; two *s*. *Educ:* King's Coll., Cambridge (BA 1975; MA Philosophy 1979; Dip. Computer Sci.); Queen Mary Coll., London (PhD Computer Sci. 1988). FRSE 2000. Programmer, GEC Computers Ltd, 1976–78; Lectr, Dept of Computer Sci. and Stats, QMC, 1980–83; Lectr, 1983–88, Reader, 1988–90, Prof., 1990–95, Dept of Computing, Imperial Coll., London; Prof. of Theoretical Computer Sci., Univ. of Edinburgh, 1996–2000. MAE 1993. *Publications:* (ed jtly) Handbook of Logic in Computer Science, 5 vols, 1992–2000; contrib. numerous articles to computer sci. jls and confs. *Recreations:* reading, music, walking. *Address:* Computing Laboratory, Wolfson Building, Parks Road, Oxford OX1 3QD. *T:* (01865) 283558; Wolfson College, Linton Road, Oxford OX2 6UD.

ABRIKOSOV, Alexei Alexeyevich, DS; Distinguished Scientist, Argonne National Laboratory, since 1991; *b* Moscow, 25 June 1928; *s* of Alexei Ivanovich Abrikosov and Fanny Davidovna (Vulf) Abrikosov; *m* 1977, Svetlana Yuriyevna Bun-kova; two *s* one *d*. *Educ:* Univ. of Moscow (MS 1948); Inst. of Physical Problems, Moscow (DS Physics and Maths 1955). Postgrad. res. associate, then sen. res. worker, Inst. of Physical Problems, USSR Acad. of Scis, 1948–65; Asst Prof., 1951–66, Full Prof., 1966–68, Univ. of Moscow; Hd of Dept, L. D. Landau Inst. of Theoretical Physics, 1965–88; Professor: Gorky Univ., 1971–72; Moscow Physical Engrg Inst., 1974–75; Hd Chair of Theoretical Physics, Moscow Inst. of Steel and Alloys, 1976–92; Dir, Inst. of High Pressure Physics, Moscow, 1988–91. Member: Russian (formerly USSR) Acad. of Scis, 1987; NAS, 2000. Fellow, Amer. Physics Soc., 1992. Foreign Hon. Mem., AAAS, 1991; Foreign Mem., Royal Soc., 2001; Hon. Mem., Hungarian Acad. of Scis, 2007. Hon. DS: Lausanne, 1975; Bordeaux, 2003; Loughborough, 2004; Tsukuba, 2005; Hong Kong, 2005; Orléans, 2006. Lenin Prize, Govt of USSR, 1966; Fritz London Award, 1972; State Prize, USSR, 1982; Landau Prize, Acad. of Scis, USSR, 1989; Internat. John Barden Award, 1991; (jtly) Nobel Prize for Physics, 2003. *Publications:* Quantum Field Theory Methods in Statistical Physics, 1962; Introduction to the Theory of Normal Metals, 1972; Fundamentals of the Theory of Metals, 1987; contrib. articles to professional jls. *Address:* Argonne National Laboratory, 9700 South Cass Avenue, Argonne, IL 60439–4803, USA. *T:* (630) 2525482.

ABTS, Tomma; artist; Professor of Painting, Kunstakademie, Düsseldorf, since 2010; *b* Kiel, 26 Dec. 1967; *d* of Hermann Abts and Imke Tammena. *Educ:* Hochschule der Künste, Berlin (Dip. 1993, MA 1995). Trustee, Tate, 2011–15. *Solo exhibitions* include: greengrassi, London, 1999, 2002, 2005, 2011; Galerie Giti Nourbakhsch, Berlin, 2001, 2004, 2009; Wrong Gall., NY, 2003; Galerie Daniel Buchholz, Cologne, 2003, 2006; Douglas Hyde Gall., Dublin, Kunsthalle Basel, 2005; Kunsthalle Kiel, 2006; David Zwirner, NY, New Mus. of Contemporary Art, NY, travelling to Hammer Mus., LA, 2008; Kunsthalle Düsseldorf, 2011; Galerie Daniel Buchholz, Berlin, 2013; David Zwirner, NY, 2014; Aspen Art Mus., 2014; *group exhibitions* include: Egofugal, 7th Internat. Istanbul Biennial, 2001; deutschemalereizweitausenddrei, Frankfurter Kunstverein, 2003; 54th Carnegie Internat., Carnegie Mus. of Art, Pittsburgh, 2004; British Art Show 6, Gateshead, Manchester, Nottingham and Bristol, 2005; Of Mice and Men, 4th Berlin Biennale, Shanghai Biennale - Hyper Design, 2006; Turner Prize: a retrospective 1986–2007, London, transf. Mori Art Mus., Tokyo, 2007; Art Sheffield 08, 2008. Stipendium for London, DAAD, 1995; Paul Hamlyn Foundn Award, 2004; Turner Prize, 2006. *Publications:* exhibition catalogues.

ABULAFIA, Prof. David Samuel Harvard, PhD, LittD; FBA 2010; FRHistS, FSA; Professor of Mediterranean History, History Faculty, University of Cambridge, since 2000; Fellow, since 1974, and Papathomas Professorial Fellow, since 2014, Gonville and Caius College, Cambridge; *b* Twickenham, 12 Dec. 1949; *s* of Leon and Rachel Abulafia; *m* 1979, Anna Sapir; two *d*. *Educ:* St Paul's Sch.; King's Coll., Cambridge (BA 1971; MA); PhD 1975, LittD 1994, Cantab. FRHistS 1981. FSA 2010. Rome Schol., British Sch. at Rome, 1972–74; Cambridge University: Asst Lectr, 1978–83; Lectr, 1983–91; Reader, 1991–2000; Chm., History Faculty, 2003–05; Tutor for Grad. Students, Gonville and Caius Coll., 1984–91. Dorfler Meml Lectr, Leo Baeck Coll., 1992; Guest Lectr, project on Objective Cultural Resources, Tokyo Univ., 2000; Crayenborgh Lectr, Leiden Univ., 2002. Project co-ordinator, EU Culture 2000, 2000–03. Mem., Rev. Cttee, Ben Gurion Univ. of the Negev, 1999–2000. Member, Council: Mediterranean Studies Assoc., 1998–2003; Cambridge Univ., 2008–12. Chm., Historians for Britain, 2015–. Gov., Perse Sch., 2002–10. Gen. Ed., Jl of Medieval Hist., 1989–95. MAE 2002. British Acad. Medal, 2013. Commendatore dell'Ordine della Stella della Solidarietà Italiana (Italy), 2003; Mediterranean Award (Malta), 2014. *Publications:* The Two Italies, 1977 (trans. Italian 1991); Italy, Sicily and the Mediterranean, 1987; Frederick II, 1988, 3rd edn 2002 (trans. Italian 1990, German 1991); Spain and 1492, 1992; (ed jtly) Church and City, 1992; Commerce and Conquest in the Mediterranean, 1993; A Mediterranean Emporium, 1994 (trans. Spanish 1996); (ed) The French Descent into Renaissance Italy, 1995 (trans. Italian 2005); The Western Mediterranean Kingdoms, 1997 (trans. Italian 1999); (ed jtly) En las costas del Mediterráneo occidental, 1997; (ed) New Cambridge Medieval History, vol. 5, 1999; Mediterranean Encounters, 2000; (ed jtly) Medieval Frontiers, 2002; (ed) The Mediterranean in History, 2003 (trans. Spanish and German, 2003, French and Greek, 2004, Turkish, 2005); (ed) Italy in the Central Middle Ages, 2004; The Discovery of Mankind, 2008 (trans. Spanish 2009, Italian 2010); (with M. Naro) Il Duomo di Monreale, 2009 (trans. French 2013); The Great Sea (Mountbatten Maritime Award for Literary Excellence, Maritime Foundn), 2011 (trans. Dutch, 2011, Greek, Turkish, 2012, Spanish, German, Italian, Korean, 2013, Romanian, Portuguese (Brazil), 2014). *Recreation:* travel in reality and in imagination. *Address:* Gonville and Caius College, Cambridge CB2 1TA. *T:* (01223) 332473. *Club:* Athenæum.

ABUSSEITOV, Kairat; Ambassador of the Republic of Kazakhstan to the Court of St James's, 2008–14; *b* Almaty, 20 Oct. 1955; *s* of Khuat Abusseitov and Maira Abusseitova; *m* Rosa Aidarova; one *s*. *Educ:* Kazakh State Univ. (degree 1979); Moscow State Univ. (PhD 1984). Sen. Lectr, Dep. of Dean, Kazakh State Univ., Almaty, 1985–89; Sen. Lectr, World Pols and Internat. Relns, Almaty High Party Sch., 1989–91; Hd, Foreign Policy and Nat. Security Prog. of Presidential Center for Strategic Studies, 1991–93; Ministry of Foreign Affairs: Hd, Internat. Security and Arms Control Section, 1993–94; Hd, Internat. Security and Arms Control Dept, 1994–96; Counsellor, Embassy of Kazakhstan to USA, 1996–98; Dir, Multilateral Cooperation Dept, and Ambassador-at-Large, Min. of Foreign Affairs, 1998–99; Dep. Minister of Foreign Affairs, 1999–2002; First Dep. Minister of Foreign Affairs, 2002–04; Ambassador to Switzerland, 2004–08. Kurmet Order, 2002. *Publications:* more than 40 scientific articles on internat. security, arms control and disarmament issues. *Recreations:* jazz music, tennis. *Address:* c/o Embassy of the Republic of Kazakhstan, 125 Pall Mall, SW1Y 5EA. *Club:* Institute of Directors.

ACHER, Sir Gerald, Kt 2012; CBE 1999; LVO 2002; Deputy Chairman, Camelot UK Lotteries Ltd (formerly Camelot Group plc), since 2002 (non-executive Director, since 2002; Interim Chairman, 2004); *b* 30 April 1945; *s* of late David Acher and Andrée Diana Acher (*née* Laredo); *m* 1970, Joyce Kathleen White; two *s*. *Educ:* King's Coll. Sch., Wimbledon. Articled clerk, Bird Potter & Co., 1961–66; Peat, Marwick, Mitchell & Co., subseq. KPMG: Asst Manager, 1967–73; Manager, 1973–75; Sen. Manager, 1975–80; Partner, 1980–2001; Mem., UK Bd, 1987–2001; Hd, Corporate Finance, 1990–93; UK Hd of Audit and Accounting, 1993–98; Sen. Partner, London Office, 1998–2001; Chairman: Worldwide Audit and Accounting Cttee, 1995–98; UK Client Service Bd, 1998–2001; Sen. Advr, 2002–10. Non-executive Director: BPB Industries plc, 2002–05; Imperial Coll. Healthcare NHS Trust, 2012– (Dep. Chm., 2015). Member: Adv. Cttee on Business and the Envmt, 1999–2004; DTI Foresight Panel on Crime and Business, 2001–02. Dep. Chm., London First, 2000–05; Dir, London First Centre, 1998–2001; Chm., London Mayoral Commn investigating feasibility of an internat. convention centre in London, 2004–06. Institute of Chartered Accountants in England and Wales: Mem., 1967–; Mem. Council, 1995–2001; Chm., Audit and Assce Faculty, 1995–2001. Trustee, KPMG Foundn, 2005–. MCSI (MSI 1992). Hon. Treas., Queen's Golden Jubilee Weekend Trust, 2001–02. Chairman: Heart of the City, 2005–12; London Climate Change Partnership, 2005–12; Cobham Conservation and Heritage Trust, 2005–; Cobham Community Bus CIC; Chm. and Trustee, Brooklands Mus. Trust, 2015. Pres., Young Epilepsy, 2011–; Gov., 1990–, and Vice Chm., 1995–, Motability; Trustee, Motability Tenth Anniversary Trust, 1991–. Trustee, Aston Martin Heritage Trust, 2001–07; Chm., Awards for Young Musicians, 1998–2004. Royal Society of Arts: Fellow, 1998; Treas., 1999; Trustee, 2000–09; Chm., 2006–09; Mem. Council, 2000–04. Liveryman, Chartered Accountants' Co. (Mem., Ct of Assistants; Master, 2003–04). Chm. Govs, Milbourne Lodge Jun. Sch., 1986–2007. *Recreations:* classic and vintage car rallying, restoring old houses, mountain walking, opera, classical music, travel, gardening. *Club:* Travellers.

ACHESON, family name of **Earl of Gosford**.

ACHESON, Peter Newton; DL; Vice Lord-Lieutenant of County Tyrone, 2009–13; Solicitor and Senior Partner, Ronald Rosser & Co., 1974–98; *b* Belfast, 21 April 1938; *s* of David A. Acheson and Kathleen F. Acheson (*née* Newton); *m* 1962, Hilary J. McMaster (*d* 2010); one *s* three *d*. *Educ:* Elm Park Sch., Armagh; Merchiston Castle Sch., Edinburgh; Brasenose Coll., Oxford (BA Modern Hist. 1960). Dir, David Acheson Ltd, linen manufacturers, 1960–70. Admitted solicitor, 1973. Pres., Solicitors Disciplinary Tribunal (NI), 1996–98. Chm. Govs, Charles Sheils Charity, 1975–. DL Co. Tyrone, 1997. *Recreations:* boating, lawnmowing and weeding. *Address:* Castlecaulfield House, Castlecaulfield, Dungannon, Co. Tyrone, Northern Ireland BT70 3NY. *T:* (028) 8776 1223. *E:* pnacheson@yahoo.com. *Clubs:* Armagh; Kildare St and University (Dublin).

See also Sir D. R. J. B. Finlay, Bt.

ACHONRY, Bishop of, (RC), since 2008; **Most Rev. Brendan Kelly;** *b* Loughrea, Co. Galway, 20 May 1946; *s* of Seán Kelly and Annie Kelly (*née* Monahan). *Educ:* Craughwell Nat. Sch.; St Mary's Coll., Galway; St Patrick's Coll., Maynooth (BA 1967; BD 1970); University Coll., Galway (DipEd 1973). Ordained priest, 1971; Teacher, Coláiste Éinde, Galway, 1972–80; Teacher, 1980–86, Principal, 1986–95, Our Lady's Coll., Gort, Co. Galway; Parish Priest: Lisdoonvarna, Co. Clare, 1996–2003; Spiddal, Co. Galway, 2003–08. *Address:* Bishop's House, Ballaghaderreen, Co. Roscommon, Ireland. *T:* (94) 9860021. *E:* bishop@achonrydiocese.org.

ACKERMAN, Roy, CBE 2004 (OBE 1991); Chairman, Tadema Studios, since 1980; Founder, executive producer and presenter, Coolcucumber.tv, since 2010; *b* 22 Feb. 1944; *m* Sally Simpson; one *s* three *d*. Trained as apprentice chef; restaurateur and owner, Quincy's Bistro, Oxford, 1975–79; Dep. Chm. and Devlt Dir, Kennedy Brooks plc, 1979–88; Chairman: 190 Queensgate plc, 1989–94; Restaurant Partnership plc, 1989–99; Simpsons of Cornhill plc, 1994–97; Parallel Hotel Outsourcing Co., 2002–08. Chairman: Hotel and

Catering Trng Bd/Hospitality Trng Foundn, 1988–99; Catering Review Bd, Millennium Dome, 1999–2001. Chm., then Pres., Restaurant Assoc., 1985–95, now Hon. Vice-Pres. Pres., Acad. of Food and Wine Service, 2008 (Hon. Fellow); Chm. and Vice Chancellor, Wine Guild of UK, 2012–; Chm., Bd of Govs, Royal Acad. (formerly Acad.) of Culinary Arts (Hon. Mem.). Hon. Pres., Henley Fest. of Music and the Arts, 1983 (former Chm.). Presenter, TV series: The Chef's Apprentice; Chef for a Night; Best of British; Cookery Clinic; Cafés of Europe; presenter and producer, coolcucumber.tv. FRSA. Hon. FCGI; Hon. Fellow: Hotel Catering Inst.; Acad. Culinaire Française; British Hospitality Assoc.; Acad. of Culinary Arts. Hon. DBA De Montfort; Hon. Dr Thames Valley. Personnalité de l'année distinction internat., Paris, 1991. *Publications:* Ackerman Guide, 1987; Roy Ackerman's Recipe Collection, 1988; The Chef's Apprentice, 1992; The Ackerman Martell Guide to Europe, annually, 1992–96; The Chef's Compendium, 1993; The Ackerman Charles Heidsieck Guide, annually, 1993–96; Café Crème Guide to Cafés of Europe, annually, 1998–2003. *Recreations:* Chelsea Arts Club/Garrick Members Table, Mornington Crescent (non league). *Address:* Tadema Studios, 7 Dilke Street, SW3 4JE. *E:* tadema.studios@btconnect.com. *Clubs:* Garrick, Chelsea Arts.

ACKLAND, Joss, (Sidney Edmond Jocelyn), CBE 2001; actor; *b* 29 Feb. 1928; *s* of Norman Ackland and Ruth Izod; *m* 1951, Rosemary Jean Kirkcaldy (*d* 2002); one *s* five *d* (and one *s* decd). *Educ:* Dame Alice Owen's Sch.; Central Sch. of Speech Training and Dramatic Art. Has worked in theatre, 1945–; repertory includes Stratford-upon-Avon, Arts Th., Buxton, Croydon, Embassy, Coventry, Oxford, Chesterfield, Windsor, Pitlochry; tea planter, Central Africa, 1954–55; disc jockey, Cape Town, 1955–57; Mem., Old Vic Theatre Co., 1958–61: parts include Toby Belch, in Twelfth Night, Caliban, in The Tempest, Pistol, in Henry IV, Lord Froth, in The Double Dealer, Aegisthus, in The Oresteia, Falstaff, in Henry IV Pt I and the Merry Wives of Windsor; Associate Dir, Mermaid Theatre, 1961–63: dir, The Plough and the Stars; parts include title rôle, Galileo, Bluntschli, in Arms and the Man, Scrofulovsky, in The Bedbug, Kirilov, in The Possessed. *West End theatre* rôles include: title rôle, The Professor, 1966; Gus, in Hotel in Amsterdam, 1968–69; Come As You Are, 1969–70; Brassbound, in Captain Brassbound's Conversion, 1971; Sam, in The Collaborators, 1973; Mitch, in A Streetcar Named Desire, 1974; Stewart, in A Pack of Lies, 1984; Clarence Darrow, in Never the Sinner, 1990; Weller Martin, in The Gin Game, 1999; King George V, in The King's Speech, 2002; *West End musicals:* Justice Squeezum, in Lock up your Daughters, 1962; title rôle, Jorrocks, 1967; Frederik, in a Little Night Music, 1975–76; Juan Perón, in Evita, 1978; Captain Hook and Mr Darling, in Peter Pan—the musical, 1985–86; *other musical rôles:* Honoré Lachailles, in Gigi; The King, in The King and I; *National Theatre:* Eustace Perry State, in The Madras House, 1977; Romain Gary, in Jean Seberg (musical), 1983; *Barbican Theatre:* Falstaff, in Henry IV pts I and II (opening prodn), 1982; Captain Hook and Mr Darling, in Peter Pan, 1982; *Chichester Theatre:* Gaev, in The Cherry Orchard, 1981; Ill, in The Visit, 1995; John Tarleton in Misalliance, 1997; Captain Shotover, in Heartbreak House, 2000; *tours:* Petruchio, in The Taming of the Shrew, 1977; Sir, in The Dresser, 1981; title rôle, King Lear, gala play reading, Old Vic and St James Theatres, 2013. *Films* include: Seven Days to Noon, 1949; Crescendo, 1969; The House that Dripped Blood, Villain, 1970; The Happiness Cage, England Made Me, 1971; The Little Prince, The Black Windmill, S-P-Y-S, The Three Musketeers, 1973; Great Expectations, One of our Dinosaurs is Missing, 1974; Operation Daybreak, Royal Flash, 1975; The Silver Bears, 1976; The End of Civilisation as we know it, The Greek Tycoon, Who is Killing the Great Chefs of Europe, 1977; Saint Jack, The Apple, Rough Cut, 1978; Lady Jane, 1984; A Zed and Two Noughts, 1985; Don Masino, in The Sicilian, 1987; Sir Jock Broughton, in White Mischief, The Colonel, in To Kill a Priest, 1988; Lethal Weapon II, The Hunt for Red October, The Palermo Connection, 1989; The Object of Beauty, The Sheltering Desert, 1991; The Bridge, Nowhere to Run, Pin for the Butterfly, The Mighty Ducks, 1992; Occhio Pinocchio (Italy), 1993; Miracle on 34th Street, Mad Dogs and Englishmen, A Kid in King Arthur's Court, Citizen X, 1994; Daisies in December, 'Til the End of Time, Mighty Ducks 3, Surviving Picasso, Deadly Voyage, Giorgino (France), 1995; Firelight, Swept from the Sea, 1996; Son of Sandokan, Game of Mirrors, Milk, 1999; Mumbo Jumbo, 2000; K-19: The Widowmaker, No Good Deed, I'll Be There, 2002; A Different Loyalty, Asylum, 2003; These Foolish Things, 2004; Tolstoy, in Moscow Zero, 2005; Flawless, How About You, 2007. Numerous TV plays and serials, incl. title rôle in Kipling, Alan Holly in First and Last, C. S. Lewis in Shadowlands, Barrett in The Barretts of Wimpole Street, Archie in Voices in the Garden, Terence Fielding in A Murder of Quality, Isaac in The Bible, Onassis in A Woman Named Jackie, Goering in The Man who lived at the Ritz, Heat of the Sun, Henry VII in Henry VIII, title rôle in Icon, 2004; Sir Winston Churchill in Above and Beyond, 2005; John Narbutowiz in Kingdom, Ridcully in The Hogfather, 2006; Pinocchio, 2008. *Radio* includes: title rôle in Macbeth; Falstaff in Henry IV, parts 1 and 2; Victor Hugo in Les Misérables; The Dog in Investigations of a Dog; God in The Little World of Don Camillo; 1966 And All That; Flashman in Flashman at the Charge; Big Daddy in Cat on a Hot Tin Roof; Socrates in The Life and Death of Socrates. Ambassador, MND Assoc.; Member: Drug Helpline; Amnesty Internat. *Publications:* I Must Be in There Somewhere (autobiog.), 1989; (with Rosemary Ackland) My Better Half and Me, 2009. *Recreations:* writing, painting, thirty-two grandchildren, fourteen great-grandchildren.

ACKNER, Hon. Claudia Madeleine, (Hon. Mrs Hughes); Her Honour Judge Ackner; a Circuit Judge, since 2007; *b* 13 Dec. 1954; *d* of Baron Ackner, PC and Joan May Evans; *m* 1978, Iain Hughes, *qv*; one *s* one *d* (and one *s* decd). *Educ:* Roedean Sch.; Girton Coll., Cambridge (BA 1976; MA). Called to the Bar, Middle Temple, 1977, Bencher, 2009; District Judge, 2000–07; Recorder, 2002–07. *Recreations:* theatre, opera. *Address:* c/o Courts of Justice, Winston Churchill Avenue, Portsmouth, Hants PO1 2EB.

ACKROYD, Keith, CBE 1994; FRPharmS; Chairman, Silentnight Holdings plc, 1995–2002 (Director, 1993–2002); *b* 6 July 1934; *s* of Edward Ackroyd and Ethel (*née* Bate); *m* 1958, Ellen Gwenda Thomas; one *s* one *d* (and one *s* decd). *Educ:* Heath Grammar Sch.; Bradford Sch. of Pharmacy; London Business Sch. FRPharmS 1981. Boots The Chemists Ltd: Apprentice Pharmacist, 1952; Dir, 1975–94; Midlands Area Dir, 1976–77; Man. Dir, 1983–89; Pres., Boots Drug Stores (Canada) Ltd, 1977–79; Boots Company plc: Dir, 1979–94; Man. Dir, Retail Div., 1984–94; Chairman: Halfords Ltd, 1989–94; A. G. Stanley, 1989–94; Do It All Ltd, 1992–94; Director: Carefirst (formerly Takare) plc, 1994–98 (Dep. Chm., 1996–98); Navara (formerly Nottingham Gp) plc, 1994–2001; Cowie plc, 1994–96; Victoria plc, 1998–2008. Chairman: Company Chemists Assoc., 1983–89; British Retailers Assoc., 1988–92; British Retail Consortium, 1992–94; Regl Chm., Trent RHA, later NHS Exec., Trent, 1994–97; Mem., NHS Policy Bd, 1994–97. Member: Passport Agency Bd, 1991–2000; Nat. Bd for Crime Prevention, 1993–95. CCMI (CIMgt 1981); FInstD 1979. Liveryman, Soc. of Apothecaries, 1990–. *Recreations:* drinking wine, country sport. *Address:* Millfield, Bradmore, Nottingham NG11 6PF. *T:* (0115) 921 6052.

ACKROYD, Norman, CBE 2007; RA 1991 (ARA 1988); RE 1985; artist (painter and etcher); *b* 26 March 1938; *s* of late Albert Ackroyd, master butcher, and Clara Briggs, weaver; *m* 1st, 1963, Sylvia Buckland (marr. diss. 1975); two *d*; 2nd, 1978, Penelope Hughes-Stanton; one *s* one *d*. *Educ:* Cockburn High Sch., Leeds; Leeds Coll. of Art; Royal Coll. of Art (ARCA 1964; Sen. FRCA 2000). Teaches occasionally at RA, Slade, RCA and in N America; Tutor in Etching, Central Sch. of Arts, London, 1965–93; Prof. of Etching, London Inst., 1992. Over 50 one-man exhibns, 1970–, mainly in UK and USA; work in public collections includes: Tate Gall.; BM; V&A; Arts Council; British Council; Mus. of Modern Art, NY; Nat. Galls of Scotland, Norway, Canada, S Africa; Albertina, Vienna; Rijksmus. and Stedelijk, Amsterdam; Musée d'Art Histoire, Geneva; Nat. Gall. of Art, Washington. Mural commissions include: Albany, Glasgow, 1975; Haringey Cultural Centre, 1985; Lloyds Bank Technol. Centre, London, 1990; British Airways, 1991; Freshfields, London, 1992; Tetrapak, London, 1993; British Embassy, Moscow, 2000; Lazards Bank, London, 2003; Sainsbury Lab. for the Study of Plant Develt, Univ. of Cambridge, 2010. TV work includes: Artists in Print (etching), 1981; A Prospect of Rivers, 1988; Painting with Acid, 2000. Awards: Bradford Internat. Biennale, 1972, 1982; Royal Soc. of Etchers and Engravers, 1984, 1985; Bronze Medal, Frechen, Germany, 1986. *Publications:* A Cumberland Journey, 1981; Travels with Copper and Zinc, 1983; (with Douglas Dunn) The Pictish Coast, 1988; St Kilda: the furthest land, 1989; Windrush, 1990; A Song for Ireland, 1999; Aran Islands, 2001; Skellig to Skibbereen, 2002; High Islands, 2003; Brancaster Roads, 2004; The Furthest Lands, 2005; From Cuillin to Kintyre, 2006; Shannon, 2007; Malin, 2008; Random Journeys, 2009; St Kilda Revisited, 2010; Beyond Cape Wrath, 2011; Shetland, 2012; Donegal Bay, 2013; numerous collections of etchings from travels in the British Isles, occasionally with poets. *Recreations:* cricket, archæology. *Address:* Royal Academy of Arts, Piccadilly, W1J 0BD. *T:* (020) 7378 6001. *Clubs:* Chelsea Arts, Arts.

ACKROYD, Peter, CBE 2003; writer; Chief Book Reviewer, The Times, 1986–2010; *b* 5 Oct. 1949; *s* of Graham Ackroyd and Audrey Whiteside. *Educ:* St Benedict's Sch., Ealing; Clare Coll., Cambridge (MA; Hon. Fellow, 2006); Yale Univ. (Mellon Fellow). Literary Editor, 1973–77, Jt Managing Editor, 1978–82, The Spectator. Writer and presenter, TV series: Dickens, 2003; Peter Ackroyd's London, 2004; The Romantics, 2006; Peter Ackroyd's Thames, 2008; Peter Ackroyd's Venice, 2009. Freeman, City of London, 2006. FRSL 1984. Hon. Fellow, Amer. Acad. of Arts and Scis, 2006; Hon. FRIBA 2009. Hon. DLitt: Exeter, 1992; London Guildhall, 1999; City, 2000; London, 2001; Brunel, 2006. *Publications: poetry:* London Lickpenny, 1973; Country Life, 1978; The Diversions of Purley, 1987; *novels:* The Great Fire of London, 1982; The Last Testament of Oscar Wilde, 1983 (Somerset Maugham Award, 1984); Hawksmoor, 1985 (Whitbread Award; Guardian Fiction Prize); Chatterton, 1987; First Light, 1989; English Music, 1992; The House of Doctor Dee, 1993; Dan Leno and the Limehouse Golem, 1994; Milton in America, 1996; The Plato Papers, 1999; The Clerkenwell Tales, 2003; The Lambs of London, 2004; The Fall of Troy, 2006; The Casebook of Victor Frankenstein, 2008; Three Brothers, 2013; *non-fiction:* Notes for a New Culture, 1976; Dressing Up, 1979; Ezra Pound and his World, 1980; T. S. Eliot, 1984 (Whitbread Award; Heinemann Award); Dickens, 1990; Introduction to Dickens, 1991; Blake, 1995; The Life of Thomas More, 1998; London: the biography, 2000; The Collection, 2001; Albion, 2002; Dickens: public life and private passion, 2002; Chaucer, 2004; Turner, 2005; Shakespeare: the biography, 2005; Newton, 2006; Thames: sacred river, 2007; Poe: a life cut short, 2008; Venice: pure city, 2009; The English Ghost: spectres through time, 2010; London Under, 2011; The History of England, vol. 1, Foundation, 2011, vol. 2, Tudors, 2012, vol. 3, Civil War, 2014; Wilkie Collins, 2012; Charles Chaplin, 2014; Hitchcock, 2015; *translation:* The Canterbury Tales, 2009; The Death of King Arthur, 2010. *Address:* c/o Anthony Sheil Associates Ltd, 43 Doughty Street, WC1N 2LF. *T:* (020) 7405 9351.

ACKROYD, Sir Timothy Robert Whyte, 3rd Bt *cr* 1956, of Dewsbury, West Riding of Yorkshire; actor; *b* 7 Oct. 1958; *er s* of Sir John Robert Whyte Ackroyd, 2nd Bt and Jennifer Eileen McLeod (*d* 1997), *d* of H. G. S. Bishop; *S* father, 1995. *Educ:* Bradfield; LAMDA. *Theatre* includes: Agamemnon, 1976; On Approval, 1979; Much Ado About Nothing, 1980; Macbeth, Old Vic Co., 1980; Man and Superman, 1982; A Sleep of Prisoners, 1983; Pygmalion, 1984; Another Country, 1986; No Sex Please - We're British, 1987; Black Coffee, 1988; Jeffrey Bernard is Unwell, 1989, 1999 (televised); Journey's End, 1993; Bad Soldier Smith, 1995; Saki, 1997; The Rivals, Iphigenia at Aulis, 2000; A Step Out of Time, 2000; A Village Wooing, 2002; Red Lanterns, 2002; Falstaff, in Henry IV, Part I, 2003; Les Parents Terribles, 2004; Hogarth: the compassionate satirist, 2005–07; narrator, Gogol with Jurowski, 2009; narrator, An Oxford Elegy, 2010; The Fuse, 2011; *television:* Jack Be Nimble, 1979; Luther, 1983; Man and Superman, 1985; Pied Piper, 1989; A Royal Scandal, 1996; The New Professionals, 1998; *films:* Creator, 1984; Bullseye, 1990; Tembo Kali, 1992; *radio* includes: Fugitive Pieces, 1999; Life Story, 2004; Beau Geste, 2009. Director: Martingale Productions, 1985–86; Archview Films, 1991–95; Ackroyd Pullan, 1995–98; Zuma Productions, 2000–; Messiah Pictures, 2001; Ackroyd & Company, 2004–. Hon. Mem., Theatre of Comedy, 1984. Chm., Ackroyd Trust; Hon. Vice-Pres., Tusk Trust; Trustee, Marjorie and Dorothy Whyte Meml Fund; Patron, London & Internat. Sch. of Acting. Freeman and Liveryman, Carpenters' Co., 1982. *Publications:* Ackroyd's Ark, 2004, vol. II, 2010; Tripe (poetry), 2009. *Recreations:* Rugby, cricket, literature, Sumo wrestling. *Heir: b* Andrew John Armitage Ackroyd, *b* 17 Sept. 1961. *Clubs:* Garrick, MCC; Lazarusians.

ACLAND, family name of **Baroness Valentine**.

ACLAND, Sir Antony (Arthur), KG 2001; GCMG 1986 (KCMG 1982; CMG 1976); GCVO 1991 (KCVO 1976); HM Diplomatic Service, retired; Provost of Eton, 1991–2000; *b* 12 March 1930; *s* of late Brig. P. B. E. Acland, OBE, MC, TD and Bridget Susan (*née* Barnett); *m* 1956, Clare Anne Verdon (*d* 1984); two *s* one *d*; *m* 1987, Jennifer McGougan (*née* Dyke). *Educ:* Eton; Christ Church, Oxford (MA 1956). Joined Diplomatic Service, 1953; ME Centre for Arab Studies, 1954; Dubai, 1955; Kuwait, 1956; FO, 1958–62; Asst Private Sec. to Sec. of State, 1959–62; UK Mission to UN, 1962–66; Head of Chancery, UK Mission, Geneva, 1966–68; FCO, 1968, Hd of Arabian Dept, 1970–72; Principal Private Sec. to Foreign and Commonwealth Sec., 1972–75; Ambassador to Luxembourg, 1975–77, to Spain, 1977–79; Deputy Under-Sec. of State, FCO, 1980–82, Perm. Under-Sec. of State, FCO, and Head of Diplomatic Service, 1982–86; Ambassador to Washington, 1986–91. Director: Shell Transport and Trading, 1991–2000; Booker plc, 1992–99. Chairman: Council, Ditchley Foundn, 1991–96; Tidy Britain Gp, 1992–96 (Pres., 1996–2002). Trustee: Nat. Portrait Gall., 1991–98; Esmée Fairbairn Foundn, 1991–2005. Chancellor, Order of St Michael and St George, 1994–2005. Pres., Exmoor Soc., 2007–. Hon. DCL: Exeter, 1988; William and Mary Coll., USA, 1990; Reading, 1992. *Address:* Staddon Farm, near Winsford, Minehead, Som TA24 7HY. *T:* (01643) 831489. *Club:* Brooks's.

ACLAND, Lt-Col Sir (Christopher) Guy (Dyke), 6th Bt *cr* 1890; LVO 1999 (MVO 1990); an Extra Equerry to the Queen, since 1999; Vice Lord-Lieutenant, Isle of Wight, since 2006; *b* 24 March 1946; *s* of Major Sir Antony Guy Acland, 5th Bt, and Margaret Joan, *e d* of late Major Nelson Rooke; *S* father, 1983; *m* 1971, Christine Mary Carden, *y d* of late Dr John Waring, Totland Bay, Isle of Wight; two *s*. *Educ:* Allhallows School; RMA Sandhurst. Commissioned RA, 1966; served BAOR (26 Field Regt), 1967–70; UK and Hong Kong (3 RHA), 1970–73; BAOR and UK (22 AD Regt), 1974–77; Staff Coll., Camberley, 1978 (psc); served on Staff of HQ Eastern District, 1979–80; commanded Q (Sanna's Post) Bty in BAOR (5 Regt), 1981–83; SO2, Army Staff Duties Directorate, MoD, 1983–85; 2 i/c 1 RHA BAOR, 1986–88; Equerry to HRH The Duke of Edinburgh, 1988–90; SO1, Management Services Orgn 3, MoD, 1990–92; CO, Southampton Univ. OTC, 1992–94; retired 1994. Dep. Master of the Household and Equerry to the Queen, 1994–99. Administrator, HSA Charitable Trust, 2000–06. DL Isle of Wight, 2002. *Recreations:* sailing, gardening. *Heir: s* Alexander John Dyke Acland [*b* 29 May 1973; *m* 2007, Susannah Katharine Janet, *d* of Charles James Bell; two *d*]. *Clubs:* Royal Solent Yacht, Royal Artillery Yacht.

ACLAND, Sir Dominic (Dyke), 17th Bt *cr* 1644, of Columb John, Devon; Managing Director, Embercombe, since 2014; *b* 19 Nov. 1962; *er s* of Sir John Dyke Acland, 16th Bt and of Virginia, *yr d* of Roland Forge; *S* father, 2009, but his name does not appear on the Official Roll of the Baronetage; *m* 1990, Sarah Anne, 3rd *d* of Ven. Kenneth Unwin, *qv*; two

s two *d* (of whom one *s* one *d* are twins). *Educ:* Edinburgh Univ. (MA). Dir, Torbay Coast and Countryside Trust, 1999–2013. *Heir: s* Patrick Acland, *b* 18 Nov. 1993.
See also P. D. Acland.

ACLAND, Lt-Col Sir Guy; *see* Acland, Lt-Col Sir C. G. D.

ACLAND, Piers Dyke; QC 2010; barrister; *b* Nairobi, 2 Feb. 1965; *yr s* of Sir John Dyke Acland, 16th Bt and Virginia Acland; *m* 1993, Lucinda Raiman; one *s* two *d. Educ:* University Coll. London (BSc Biochem. 1987); Imperial Cancer Research Fund, Univ. of London (PhD 1991). Called to the Bar, Lincoln's Inn, 1993; in practice as barrister, specialising in intellectual property, 1993–. *Address:* 11 South Square, Gray's Inn, WC1R 5EY. *E:* pacland@11southsquare.com.
See also Sir D. D. Acland, Bt.

ACLAND-HOOD-GASS, Dame Elizabeth Periam; *see* Gass, Dame E. P. A. H.

ACOSTA QUESADA, Carlos Yunior, (Carlos Acosta), CBE 2014; ballet dancer; Principal Guest Artist, Royal Ballet, since 2003; *b* Havana, Cuba, 1973; partner, Charlotte Holland; one *d.* Trained with Nat. Ballet Sch. of Cuba; guest performer with cos incl. Compagnia Teatro Nuovo, Turin, 1989–91; Principal, English Nat. Ballet, 1991–92; with Nat. Ballet of Cuba, 1992–93 and 1994; Principal, Houston Ballet, 1993–98; with Royal Ballet, 1998–; Guest Principal Artist with ballet companies including: American Ballet Th., 2002 (and Principal Dancer, 2003); Paris Opera, 2008; Australian Ballet, 2008. Performances include: English National Ballet: Polovtsian Dances from Prince Igor, 1991; The Nutcracker, Cinderella, 1992; National Ballet of Cuba: Giselle, Don Quixote, Swan Lake, 1994; Houston Ballet: The Nutcracker, Swan Lake, La Bayadère, Don Quixote, 1993; Royal Ballet: In the middle somewhat elevated, 1998; Raymonda, Swan Lake, My Brother, My Sisters, Rhapsody, Le Corsaire, The Nutcracker, Coppelia, Shadowplay, 2000; Don Quixote, 2001; Apollo, 2002; Manon, 2003; Mayerling, Giselle, 2004; La Fille mal gardée, 2005; Romeo and Juliet, 2006; Spartacus with Bolshoi Ballet, 2007; writer and choreographer, Tocororo, 2003; choreographer: Premieres, 2010; Guys and Dolls, 2014. Hon. DLitt London Metropolitan, 2006. Gold Medal, Prix de Lausanne, 1990; Grand Prix, Concours Internat. de Danse de Paris, 1990; Vignale Danza Prize, Italy, 1990; Frédéric Chopin Prize, Polish Artistic Corp., 1990; Best Male Dancer, Nat. Dance Awards, 2004; Outstanding Achievement in Dance, Laurence Olivier Awards, 2007. *Publications:* No Way Home: a Cuban dancer's story (autobiog.), 2007; Pig's Foot (novel), 2013. *Address:* c/o Carlos Acosta Management, Aviation House, 1–7 Sussex Road, Haywards Heath, W Sussex RH16 4DZ; Royal Opera House, Covent Garden, WC2E 9DD.

ACRES, Paul, QPM 1997; Chief Constable of Hertfordshire, 2000–04; Chairman, Sefton NHS Primary Care Trust, 2006; *b* 15 April 1948; *s* of Albert George Acres and Kathleen Acres (*née* Jones); *m* 1971, Jean Parsons; three *s. Educ:* City of Bath Boys' Sch. Liverpool and Bootle Constabulary, 1968–74; joined Merseyside Police, 1974: Asst Chief Constable, 1992–94; rcds, 1994; Dep. Chief Constable, 1995–2000. Police Long Service and Good Conduct Medal, 1991. *Recreations:* walking, motor cycling, golf, cycling. *Club:* West Lancashire Golf.

ACTON, 5th Baron *cr* 1869, of Aldenham, Salop; **John Charles Ferdinand Harold Lyon-Dalberg-Acton;** Bt 1644; *b* 19 Aug. 1966; *o s* of 4th Baron Acton and Hilary Juliet Sarah (*née* Cookson); *S* father, 2010; *m* 1998, Lucinda, *d* of Brig. James Percival, OBE. *Educ:* Winchester; Balliol Coll., Oxford. *Heir: uncle* Rev. Canon the Hon. John Charles Lyon-Dalberg-Acton, *b* 26 Jan. 1943.

ACTON, Prof. Edward David Joseph Lyon-Dalberg-, PhD; Vice-Chancellor, University of East Anglia, 2009–14; *b* Harare; *s* of 3rd Baron Acton, CMG, MBE, TD and Hon. Daphne, *o d* of 4th Baron Rayleigh, FRS; *m* 1972, Stella, *d* of Henry Conroy; two *d. Educ:* St George's Coll., Harare; Univ. of York (BA Hons Hist.); St Edmund's Coll., Cambridge (PhD Hist. 1976). Bank of England, 1975–76; Lectr, Univ. of Liverpool, 1976–88; Sen Lectr, Univ. of Manchester, 1988–91; University of East Anglia: Prof. of Modern Eur. Hist., 1991–; Pro-Vice-Chancellor, 2003–09. *Publications:* Alexander Herzen and the role of the intellectual revolutionary, 1979; Russia: the present and the past, 1986; Rethinking the Russian Revolution, 1990; Russia: the Tsarist and Soviet legacy, 1995; (ed jtly) Critical Companion to the Russian Revolution, 1914–1921, 1997; Nazism and Stalinism: a suitable case for comparison?, 1998; (ed jtly) La transición a la política de masas, 2001; The Soviet Union: a documentary history, vol. I, 1917–1940, 2005, vol. II, 1939–1991, 2007. *Recreations:* bridge, racing. *Address:* 365 Unthank Road, Norwich NR4 7QG. *Club:* Athenæum.
See also Baron Acton.

ACTON DAVIS, Jonathan James; QC 1996; a Recorder, since 2000; a Deputy High Court Judge, since 2008; *b* 15 Jan. 1953; *s* of Michael James and Elizabeth Acton Davis; *m* 1987, Lindsay Alice Boswell, *qv*; one *s. Educ:* Harrow Sch.; Poly. of Central London (LLB London). Called to the Bar, Inner Temple, 1977 (Bencher, 1995, Master of the House, 1999–2005); an Asst Recorder, 1997–2000. General Council of the Bar: Mem., 1993–98; Chm., Professional Conduct and Complaints Cttee, 2001–02 (Vice-Chm., 1999–2000); Mem., Legal Services Consultative Panel, 2004–09. *Recreations:* cricket, walking, South West France. *Address:* 1 Atkin Building, Gray's Inn, WC1R 5AT. *T:* (020) 7404 0102. *E:* clerks@atkinchambers.law.co.uk. *Clubs:* Garrick, Beefsteak, MCC, Chelsea Arts.

ACTON DAVIS, Lindsay Alice; *see* Boswell, L. A.

ACTON SMITH, Michael, OBE 2014; Chief Executive Officer and Founder, Mind Candy, since 2004; *b* London, 3 Sept. 1974; *s* of Charles and Colette Smith. *Educ:* Danesfield Primary Sch.; Sir William Borlase Grammar Sch.; Birmingham Univ. (BSc Geog.). Co-founder and Chm., Firebox.com, 1998–; Co-founder: Second Chance Tuesday, 2006; Calm.com, 2012. Inventor, Shot Glass Chess Set, 1998; creator of games: Perplex City, 2005; Moshi Monsters, 2008. *Publications:* Calm, 2015. *Recreations:* games, memes, monsters, poker, puzzles, parties and prime numbers. *Address:* Mind Candy, Floor 4, 15 Bonhill Street, EC2A 4DN. *T:* (020) 7501 1901. *E:* michael@mindcandy.com. *Clubs:* Soho House, Adam Street, Paramount.

ACWORTH, Ven. Richard Foote; Archdeacon of Wells, 1993–2003; *b* 19 Oct. 1936; *s* of late Rev. Oswald Roney Acworth and Jean Margaret Acworth; *m* 1966, Margaret Caroline Marie Jennings; two *s* one *d. Educ:* St John's Sch., Leatherhead; Sidney Sussex Coll., Cambridge (BA Hist. and Theol. 1962; MA 1965); Cuddesdon Theol Coll. Nat. service, RNVR, 1956–58. Ordained deacon, 1963, priest, 1964; Assistant Curate: St Etheldreda's, Fulham, 1963; All Saints and Martyrs, Langley, Mancs, 1964–66; St Mary's, Bridgwater, 1966–69; Vicar, Yatton, 1969–81; Priest-in-charge, St John's and St Mary's, Taunton, 1981–85; Vicar of St Mary Magdalene, Taunton, 1985–93. Trustee, Rethink Mental Illness, 2014–. *Recreations:* walking, gardening, DIY, ornithology. *Address:* Corvedale Cottage, Croscombe, Wells, Som BA5 3QJ. *T:* (01749) 342242.
See also Brig. R. W. Acworth.

ACWORTH, Brig. Robert William, CBE 1986; Registrar of St Paul's Cathedral, 1991–2001; *b* 11 Dec. 1938; *s* of late Rev. Oswald Roney Acworth and Jean Margaret (*née* Coupland); *m* 1967, Elizabeth Mary, *e d* of late J. N. S. Ridgers; two *s* one *d. Educ:* St John's Sch., Leatherhead; RMA, Sandhurst. Commnd, Queen's Royal Regt, 1958; served in Germany, Holland, Norway, Gibraltar, Aden, Oman, Hong Kong, UK and NI; sc 1970; staff and regtl duty, 1971–81; Comdr, 10 UDR, 1981–83 (despatches 1983); Asst COS, HQ NI, 1983–85; Coll. Comdr, RMA, Sandhurst, 1985–87; Asst COS (Intelligence), HQ AFCENT, 1987–90; Dep. Comdr and COS, SE Dist, 1990–91, retd. Deputy Colonel: Queen's Regt, 1986–92; Princess of Wales's Royal Regt, 1992–94. Pres., Queen's Royal Surrey Regt Assoc., 1995–2005. *Recreations:* gardening, shooting, fishing, golf. *Address:* The Close, Netton, Salisbury, Wilts SP4 6AP. *T:* (01722) 782539. *Club:* Army and Navy.
See also Ven. R. F. Acworth.

ADAIR, Brian Campbell, TD 1979; NP 1975; Senior Partner, 1973–2005, Consultant, 2005–08, Adairs, Solicitors, Dumbarton; President, Law Society of Scotland, 1992–93; *b* 28 Aug. 1945; *s* of Alan William Adair and Helen Mary Scott or Adair; *m* 1969, Elaine Jean Morrison; one *s* two *d. Educ:* Milngavie Primary Sch.; High Sch., Glasgow; Glasgow Univ. (LLB 1967). Commnd TA 1965, 1st Bn Glasgow Highlanders; served Glasgow & Strathclyde Univs OTC, 1967–73, 2nd Bn Lowland Volunteers, 1973–79; retired rank Major. Apprentice Solicitor, McGrigor Donald, Glasgow, 1967–70; Solicitor, Dumbarton CC, 1970–73; constituted own firm, 1973. Temp. Sheriff, 1995–99; part-time Sheriff, 2000–. Mem., Scottish Legal Aid Bd, 1998–2002. Mem. Council, Law Soc. of Scotland, 1980–94 (Vice Pres., 1991–92). Elder, St Paul's Church, Milngavie. Chm. of Govs, High Sch. of Glasgow, 2006– (Gov., 1992–). *Recreations:* holidaying in Arran, entertaining, golf. *Address:* 21 James Watt Road, Milngavie, Glasgow G62 7JX. *T:* (0141) 956 3070. *Clubs:* Milngavie Golf (Captain, Centenary Year, 1995), Whiting Bay Golf.

ADAIR, John Eric, PhD; author and teacher of leadership; *b* Luton, 18 May 1934; *s* of Robin and Dorothy Adair; *m* 1977, Thea Talbot; two *s* one *d. Educ:* St Paul's Sch.; Hull Nautical Coll. (qualified Arctic trawler deckhand 1955); Trinity Hall, Cambridge (BA 1959); Univ. of London (PhD 1966); Jesus Coll., Oxford (BLitt 1971). FRHistS 1966. National Service: 2nd Lt Scots Guards and Adjutant 9 Regt Arab Legion, 1953–55. Arctic trawler deckhand, 1955. Sen. Lectr, RMA Sandhurst, 1961–67; Hon. Dir of Studies, St George's House, Windsor Castle, 1968; Asst Dir and Hd, Leadership Dept, 1969–71, Associate Dir, 1972–75, Industrial Soc.; Prof. of Leadership Studies, Univ. of Surrey, 1979–84. Vis. Prof., Univ. of Exeter, 1990–2000; Hon. Prof. of Leadership, China Exec. Leadership Acad., Pudong, 2006–; Chair, Strategic Leadership Studies, UN System Staff Coll., 2009–. Pres., John Hampden Soc., 1992–. Fellow, Windsor Leadership Trust, 2001–. *Publications:* Hastings to Culloden: battles of Britain (with Peter Young), 1964, 4th edn 2009; Training for Leadership, 1968; Training for Decisions, 1969; Roundhead General: the life of Sir William Waller, 1969, 2nd edn 1997; Cheriton 1644: the campaign and the battle, 1973; Training for Communication, 1973; Action Centred Leadership, 1973; Management and Morality: the problems and opportunities of social capitalism, 1974; A Life of John Hampden The Patriot 1594–1643, 1976; The Becoming Church, 1976; The Pilgrims' Way: shrines and saints in Britain and Ireland, 1978; The Royal Palaces of Britain, 1981; Founding Fathers: the Puritans in England and America, 1982, 2nd edn 1998; By the Sword Divided: eyewitness accounts of the English Civil War, 1983, 2nd edn 1998; Effective Leadership, 1983, 2nd edn 2009; Effective Decision-Making, 1985, 2nd edn 2009; Effective Teambuilding, 1986, 2nd edn 2009; How to Manage Your Time, 1987, 3rd edn as Effective Time Management, 2009; No Bosses But Leaders, 1987, 3rd edn 2003; Developing Leaders, 1988; Great Leaders, 1989, 2nd edn as Inspiring Leadership, 2002; Understanding Motivation, 1990, 2nd edn as Leadership and Motivation, 2006; The Challenge of Innovation, 1990, 2nd edn as Leadership for Innovation, 1990; The Art of Creative Thinking, 1990, 2nd edn 2007; Effective Innovation, 1994, 2nd edn 2009; Effective Motivation, 1996, 2nd edn 2009; Leadership Skills, 1996, 2nd edn as Develop Your Leadership Skills, 2007; Effective Communication, 1997, 2nd edn 2009; Decision Making and Problem Solving, 1997, 2nd edn as Decision Making and Problem Solving Strategies; How to Find Your Vocation, 2000; The Leadership of Jesus, 2001; Effective Strategic Leadership, 2002, 2nd edn 2010; The Inspirational Leader, 2003; How to Grow Leaders, 2005; Effective Leadership Development, 2006; The Leadership of Muhammad, 2010; Lexicon of Leadership, 2011; John Adair's 100 Greatest Ideas (series), 2011; Confucius on Leadership, 2013. *Recreations:* English countryside, sketching, reading. *Address:* Westbury Manor, Compton, Guildford GU3 1EE. *T:* (01483) 810241. *E:* ja@johnadair.co.uk.

ADAM, Prof. Andreas Ntinou, CBE 2012; FRCR, FRCP, FRCS, FMedSci; Professor of Interventional Radiology, Guy's, King's and St Thomas' School of Medicine (formerly United Medical and Dental Schools of Guy's and St Thomas' Hospital and King's College Medical School), since 1992; President, Royal College of Radiologists, 2007–10; Dean, Medical School, University of Cyprus, since 2012; *b* 4 May 1951; *s* of Constantinos Adam and Hera Adam (*née* Spanou); *m* 1977, Dr Jane Williams; two *d. Educ:* Middlesex Hosp. Med. Sch. (MB BS Hons 1977). MRCP 1979, FRCP 1994; FRCR 1985; FRCS 1998. Hse physician, Middx Hosp., 1977–78; hse surgeon, Kettering Gen. Hosp., 1978; Senior House Officer: Hammersmith Hosp., 1978–79; Middx Hosp., 1979; National Hosp., 1979–80; Registrar: Whittington Hosp., 1980–81; UCH, 1981; Hammersmith Hosp., 1981–83; Senior Registrar: Hammersmith and Hillingdon Hosps, 1983–84; Hammersmith Hosp., 1984–86; Sen. Lectr, 1987–91, Reader, 1991–92, RPMS; Hon. Consultant Radiologist, Guy's and St Thomas' NHS Foundn Trust, 1992–. Jt Ed.-in-Chief, Jl Interventional Radiol., 1992–95; Ed.-in-Chief, Cardiovascular and Interventional Radiol., 1995–2003; Asst Ed., Jl Hepato-Pancreato-Biliary Assoc., 1998–2001; mem., editl bds of numerous jls. Advr to EU on digital imaging, 1991–92; Consultant in Radiol. to WHO, 1999; Specialist Advr on Interventional Radiol., NICE, 2000–; Mem., Adv. Gp on Ionising Radiation, Subgp on High Dose Radiation Effects and Tissue Injury, HPA, 2005–. Rep. of Eur. Assoc. of Radiol., Eur. Agency for Evaluation of Medicinal Products, 2000–04. Lectures include: Alan Goldin Oration, Royal Australasian Coll. of Radiologists, 1993; John Wickham, Internat. Soc. Minimally Invasive Therapy, 1998; Hounsfield, BIR, 2006; Haughton, RCSI, 2007; Holmes, New England Roentgen Ray Soc., 2008. President: Soc. for Minimal Invasive Therapy, 1996–97; British Soc. Interventional Radiologists, 1997–99; BIR, 1998–99; Internat. Soc. Hepatobiliary Radiol., 1998–99; Cardiovascular and Interventional Radiol Soc. of Europe, 2005–07; Eur. Congress of Radiol., 2006; Soc. of Gastrointestinal Intervention, 2007–09; Eur. Soc. Radiol., 2007–08. Fellow: Soc. of Cardiovascular and Interventional Radiol., USA, 1993; Eur. Soc. Gastrointestinal and Abdominal Radiol., 1998; FBIR 2007; FMedSci 2009; Academician, Russian Acad. Med. Scis, 2005. Hon. FRANZCR 2007; Hon. Fellow: Faculty of Radiologists, RCSI, 2007; Greek Soc. Interventional Radiol., 2007; Hong Kong Coll. of Radiologists, 2010; American Coll. of Radiol., 2011. Hon. PhD Crete, 2012. Medal, Russian Acad. Med. Scis, 2004; Gold Medal, British Soc. Interventional Radiologists, 2005; President's Medal, RCR, 2006; Gold Medal, Cardiovascular and Interventional Radiol Soc. Europe, 2007; Gold Medal, Soc. of Interventional Radiol., USA, 2009; Gold Medal, Eur. Soc. of Radiol., 2010. *Publications:* Clinical Gastroenterology: interventional radiology of the abdomen, 1993; Practical Interventional Radiology of the Hepatobiliary System and Gastrointestinal Tract, 1994; Interventional Radiology: a practical guide, 1995; A Textbook of Metallic Stents, 1996; Interventional Radiology: a multimedia virtual textbook, 1997; Practical Management of Oesophageal Disease, 2000; Diagnostic Radiology, 4th edn 2001, 5th edn 2008; Interventional Radiology in Cancer, 2003; Interventional Radiological Treatment of Liver Tumours, 2008; Interventional Oncology, 2012; contrib. numerous scientific papers on aspects of interventional radiol., esp. focusing on use of metallic stents in various organs. *Recreation:* reading history. *Address:* Department of Radiology, 1st Floor Lambeth Wing, St Thomas' Hospital, SE1 7EH. *T:* (020) 7188 5550, *Fax:* (020) 7188 5454. *E:* andy.adam@kcl.ac.uk. *Club:* Athenæum.

ADAM, George; Lord Provost and Lord-Lieutenant of Aberdeen, since 2012; *b* Montrose, 26 Jan. 1957; *s* of late George Smith Adam and of Helen Adam (*née* Aitken). *Educ:* Brechin High Sch.; Duncan of Jordanstone Coll. of Art, Dundee. Graphic Designer, 1979–83, Event Producer and Co-Dir, 1983–90, Format Communications, Aberdeen; Owner, The

Presentation Business, Aberdeen, 1990–2012. *Recreations:* gardening, visual arts, music, cinema and theatre. *Address:* City of Aberdeen, Town House, Aberdeen AB10 1LP. *T:* (01224) 522637, *Fax:* (01224) 523747. *E:* lordprovost@aberdeencity.gov.uk.

ADAM, Gordon Johnston, PhD; Member (Lab) North East Region, England, European Parliament, Feb. 2000–2004; *b* 28 March 1934; *s* of John Craig Adam and Deborah Armstrong Johnston; *m* 1973, Sarah Jane Seely; one *s*. *Educ:* Leeds Univ. (BSc Hons, PhD). CEng, MIMMM; FEI. NCB, 1959–79. Mem., Whitley Bay Bor. Council, 1971–74; Mem. 1973–80, and Dep. Leader 1975–80, North Tyneside Metrop. Bor. Council (Chm., 1973–74; Mayor, 1974–75). Mem., Whitley Bay Playhouse Theatre Trust, 1975–2007 (Chm., 1975–80). MEP (Lab) Northumbria, 1979–99; contested (Lab) NE Region, 1999; Vice-Chm., Energy, Res. and Technol. Cttee, EP, 1984–99; Chm., Jt Parly Cttee, EU-Lithuania, 2000–04. Chairman: Northumbria Energy Advice Centre, 1994–; Northern Energy Initiative, 1996–2000; NE Reg. Energy Forum, 2004–06; Member: Northern Econ. Planning Council, 1974–79; Northern Arts Gen. Council, 1975–78; Northern Sinfonia Management Cttee, 1978–80; Bd, Northern Stage Co., 1989–2001; Bd, S Tyneside & Newcastle Groundwork Trust, 2004–10; NE Energy Leadership Council, 2011–. Sen. Advr, Energy Policy Consulting, 2006–08. Contested (Lab): Tynemouth, 1966; Berwick-upon-Tweed, Nov. 1973 (by-election), Feb. 1974 and 1992. *Recreation:* gardening. *Address:* The Old Farm House, East House Farm, Killingworth Village, Newcastle upon Tyne NE12 6BQ. *T:* (0191) 216 0154.

ADAM, Ian Clark; Chairman, Britannia Building Society, 2004–08 (Director, 1998–2008); *b* 2 Sept. 1943; *s* of George Adam and Natalie Jane Gibson Adam; *m* 1967, Betty Anne Crosbie; one *s* one *d*. *Educ:* Harris Acad., Dundee. CA 1967. Partner, 1976, Sen. Partner, Scotland, 1985–95, Price Waterhouse; Finance Dir, Christian Salvesen plc, 1995–98. Mem., SHEFC, 2003–05, SFC, 2005–11. Chm., St Columba's Hospice, 2011– (Gov., 2010–11). Gov., St Leonards Sch., St Andrews, 2010–. *Recreations:* gardening, golf, reading. *Address:* Gowanfield, 2 Cammo Road, Edinburgh EH4 8EB. *T:* (0131) 339 6401. *E:* iancadam@talktalk.net. *Clubs:* Royal and Ancient Golf (St Andrews); Royal Burgess Golfing Society (Edinburgh); Kilspindie Golf.

ADAM, Sir Kenneth (Klaus Hugo), Kt 2003; OBE 1995; RDI 2009; freelance film production designer; *b* 5 Feb. 1921; *s* of Fritz Adam and Lilli Adam (*née* Saalfeld); *m* 1952, Maria-Letizia Moauro. *Educ:* Collège Français, Berlin; St Paul's Sch., London; Bartlett Sch. of Architecture, London (Ext.). Film art dir/prodn designer, 1947–; collaborated on approx. 70 films, including: seven early Bond films; Chitty Chitty Bang Bang, 1967; Sleuth, 1972; Pennies from Heaven, 1981; Addams Family Values, 1993. Exhibitions of designs: Meisterwerke der Film Architektur, touring, Germany and Austria, 1994; Serpentine Gall., 1999–2000; Ken Adam Visionäre Film Welten, Frankfurt, 2002, Berlin, 2002–03; Moonraker, Strangelove and Other Celluloid Dreams: the visionary art of Ken Adam, Hollywood, 2003. Dr *hc* RCA, 1995; Hon. DArts Greenwich, 2000. Academy Awards for Production Design: Barry Lyndon, 1975; The Madness of King George, 1995; BAFTA Awards: Dr Strangelove, 1964; The Ipcress File, 1965; Lifetime Achievement Award, Hollywood Art Directors, 2002. *Relevant publications:* Moonraker, Strangelove and Other Celluloid Dreams: the visionary art of Ken Adam, by David Sylvester, 1999; Ken Adam and the Art of Production Design, by Sir Christopher Frayling, 2005. *Publications:* (with Sir Christopher Frayling) Ken Adam Designs the Movies: James Bond and beyond, 2008. *Recreation:* swimming. *Address:* 34 Montpelier Street, SW7 1HD. *T:* (020) 7589 9372, *Fax:* (020) 7584 7090. *Club:* Royal Automobile.

ADAM, Robert, RIBA; Director, ADAM Architecture (formerly Robert Adam Architects), since 1995; *b* 10 April 1948; *s* of Dr Robert Wilson Adam and Margaret Adam; *m* 1970, Sarah Jane Chalcraft; one *s* one *d*. *Educ:* Canford Sch., Dorset; Regent Street Poly. (DipArch 1973). RIBA 1977. Partner, 1977–, Dir, 1987–, Evan Roberts & Partners, subseq. Winchester Design (Architects) Ltd, later Robert Adam Architects, then ADAM Architecture. Principal buildings include: Sackler Liby, Oxford; Solar House, Wakeham; Dogmersfield Park, Odiham; Millennium Pavilion, Preston Candover, Hants; 198–202 Piccadilly; new country houses in Hants, Dorset and Wilts; New district, Leith masterplans; William Wake House, Northampton. Trustee, 1989–98, Chm., Faculty of Fine Arts, 1993–97, British Sch. at Rome; Chm., Popular Housing Gp, 1995–2003; Mem. Council, RIBA, 1999, 2002 (Hon. Sec., 2000–03); Design Advr, CABE, 1999–2003; Founder and Chair, Coll. of Chapters, Internat. Network for Traditional Building, Architecture and Urbanism, 2000–12 (Chair, UK Chapter, 2009–); Academician, Acad. of Urbanism, 2006–; Mem., Design Review Panel, London CABE, 2012–. Hon. FRIAS 2014. *Publications:* Classical Architecture: a complete handbook, 1990; (contrib.) Building Classical, 1993; (contrib.) Companion to Contemporary Architectural Thought, 1993; Buildings by Design, 1994; (ed jtly and contrib.) Tradition Today, 2008; The 7 Sins of Architects, 2010; (contrib.) Urban Identity, Learning from Place 2, 2011; The Globalisation of Modern Architecture, 2012; (contrib.) Architecture and Globalisation in the Persian Gulf Region, 2013; (contrib.) The Architectural Capriccio, 2014; *relevant publication:* Robert Adam: the search for a modern classicism, by Richard John, 2010; papers in Architectl Review, Architects Jl, RIBA Jl, Architectl Design, Context 79, City Jl (USA), Archis (Holland). *Recreations:* ceramics, politics, economics. *Address:* Old Hyde House, 75 Hyde Street, Winchester, Hants SO23 7DW. *T:* (01962) 843843. *Clubs:* Athenæum, Home House.

ADAM, Sheila Anne, MD; FRCP, FFPH, FRCGP; Interim Director of Public Health, NHS London (Strategic Health Authority for London), 2006–07; *b* 24 Nov. 1949. *Educ:* Nottingham High Sch. for Girls; Edinburgh Univ. (MB ChB 1972; MD 1983); DCH 1974. MRCP 1976, FRCP 1993; MFPHM 1981, FFPHM 1986; FRCGP 2002. Public Health Registrar, 1975–77, Sen. Registrar and MRC Trng Fellow in Public Health, 1977–81, Oxford RHA; Public Health Consultant, Brent HA, 1981–83; Public Health Consultant, 1983–89, Dir of Public Health, 1989–95, NW Thames RHA; NHS Executive, Department of Health: Hd of Mental Health and NHS Community Care, 1995–97; Dep. Dir of Health Services, 1997–99; Dir of Health Services, 1999–2001; Dep. CMO, 1999–2002, and Dir of Policy, 2001–02, DoH; Dir of Public Health, NE London Strategic HA, 2002–06. QHP 1996–99.

ADAM, Rev. Sir Stephen Timothy Beilby F.; *see* Forbes Adam.

ADAM, Thomas Noble; QC 2008; *b* London, 6 Jan. 1965; *s* of Bruce and Sheila Adam; *m* 1991, Helen Gooch; three *s*. *Educ:* Norwich Sch.; Trinity Coll., Cambridge (BA 1987). Solicitor, Macfarlanes, 1988–91; called to the Bar, Inner Temple, 1991; in practice at the Bar, specialising in commercial law, 1991–. *Publications:* (with C. Hollander) Documentary Evidence, 7th edn, 2000; (contrib.) Professional Negligence and Liability Encyclopedia. *Recreations:* family time, fishing, shooting, Munro-walking, light verse, wine and whisky, boxing. *Address:* c/o Brick Court Chambers, 7–8 Essex Street, WC2R 3LD. *Club:* Hawks.

ADAMI, Edward F.; *see* Fenech-Adami.

ADAMISHIN, Dr Anatoly; Consultant, Sistema Joint-Stock Financial Corporation, Russia, since 2003 (Vice President, International Affairs, 1998); *b* 11 Oct. 1934; *s* of Leonid Adamishin and Vera Gusovskaya; *m* 2000, Svetlana Kharlamova; one *d* by previous marriage. *Educ:* Lomonosov Moscow State Univ.; Diplomatic Acad. of USSR (Dr in Historic Sci. 1979). Joined USSR Diplomatic Service, 1957; First European Dept, Min. of Foreign Affairs, 1957–59; served embassy in Italy, 1959–65; First European Dept, 1965–71; Foreign Policy Planning Dept, 1971–73; Head, Gen. Internat. Issues Dept, 1973–78; Head, First European Dept and Mem., Min. of Foreign Affairs Collegium, 1978–86; Dep. Minister for Foreign Affairs, 1986–90; also Head, USSR Commn for UNESCO Affairs, 1987–90; Ambassador to Italy, 1990–92; First Dep. Minister for Foreign Affairs of Russia, 1992–94; Ambassador to UK, 1994–97; Minister for relations with CIS, Min. of Foreign Affairs, 1997–98. Sen. Fellow, US Inst. of Peace, Washington, 2005–06. *Publications:* Tramonto e rinascita di una grande potenza, 1995; The White Sun of Angola, 2001; (with R. Schifter) Human Rights, Perestroika, and the End of the Cold War, 2009. *Recreation:* lawn tennis. *Address:* (office) 13 Mokhovaya Street, 125009 Moscow, Russia.

ADAMKUS, Valdas; President, Republic of Lithuania, 1998–2003 and 2004–09; *b* Kaunas, 3 Nov. 1926; *s* of Ignas Adamkavičius and Genovaite Bacevičiūte; *m* 1951, Alma Adamkiene. *Educ:* Munich Univ.; Illinois Inst. of Technology, Chicago. Qualified civil engr, 1960; Chicago Car Plant, 1949–50; Draftsman, Meissner Consulting Engrs, 1950–59; owner and operator, summer resort, Sodus, Michigan, 1960–69; Dir, Envmt Res. Centre, US Envmt Protection Agency, 1969–71; Dep. Adminr, 1971–81, Adminr, 1981–97, Reg. 5 (Great Lakes), US Envmt Protection Agency. Mem., US Delegn in Co-operation with USSR under bilateral envmtl agreement, 1972–91; Chm., US Delegn, Internat. Jt Commn for Great Lakes (US-Canada), 1980–97. Vice Chm., 1958–65, Chm., 1967–97, Santara-Sviesa Cultural-political Fedn; Vice-Chm., Exec. Cttee, American-Lithuanian Community; Mem., American-Lithuanian Council. Hon. Dr: Vilnius, 1989; Indiana St Joseph Coll., 1991; Northwestern, 1994; Kaunas Technology Univ., 1998. *Publications:* Lithuania: the name of my destiny, 1997. *Recreations:* sport activities (golf, swimming), classical music.

ADAMS, family name of **Baroness Adams of Craigielea**.

ADAMS OF CRAIGIELEA, Baroness *cr* 2005 (Life Peer), of Craigielea in Renfrewshire; **(Katherine Patricia) Irene Adams;** JP; *b* 27 Dec. 1947; *m* 1968, Allen S. Adams (*d* 1990), MP Paisley North; one *s* two *d*. *Educ:* Stanley Green High Sch., Paisley. Councillor, Paisley Town, 1970; Member: Renfrew DC, 1974–78; Strathclyde Regl Council, 1979–84. MP (Lab) Paisley North, Nov. 1990–2005. *Address:* House of Lords, SW1A 0PW.

ADAMS, Dr Aileen Kirkpatrick, CBE 1988; FRCS; FRCA; Emerita Consultant Anaesthetist, Addenbrooke's Hospital, Cambridge, since 1983; *b* 5 Sept. 1923; *d* of F. Joseph Adams and M. Agnes Adams (*née* Munro). *Educ:* Farringtons School, Chislehurst; Sheffield Univ. MB ChB Sheffield, 1945; MA Cantab 1977; FFARCS 1954; FFA(SA) 1987; FRCS 1988; FDSRCS 1989. Fellow in anaesthesia, Harvard Univ. and Mass. Gen. Hosp., Boston, 1955–57; Consultant Anaesthetist, Addenbrooke's Hosp., Cambridge, 1960–83; Associate Lectr, Univ. of Cambridge, 1977–85; Dean, Faculty of Anaesthetists, RCS, 1985–88. Sen. Lectr, Lagos Univ. Med. Sch., Nigeria, 1963–64. Mem., Cambridge Health Authy, 1978–82. Royal College of Surgeons of England: Mem. Council, 1982–88; Hunterian Prof., 1993; Trustee, Hunterian Collection, 1996–2012; Royal Society of Medicine: Hon. Treas., 1995–99; Hon. Mem., Anaesthesia Section, 1998– (Pres., 1985–86); Pres., History of Medicine Section, 1994–95; Vice-Pres., Comparative Medicine Section, 2003–04. Hon. Mem., History of Anaesthesia Soc., 1994– (Pres., 1990–92); Pres., British Soc. for the History of Medicine, 2003–05. Hon. Archivist, Royal Coll. of Anaesthetists, 1989–98. Former Examr, Cambridge Univ. and FFARCS. Hon. Mem., Assoc. of Anaesthetists, GB and Ire. Lectures: Monckton Copeman, Soc. of Apothecaries, 2002; Arthur Thompson, Univ. of Birmingham, 2004. Mem., Editl Bd, Anaesthesia, 1972–85. *Publications:* book chapters and papers in med. jls on anaesthetic and related topics, and on history of medicine. *Recreations:* choral singing, outdoor activities, including walking, ski-ing, history of medicine and music. *Address:* 12 Redwood Lodge, Grange Road, Cambridge CB3 9AR. *T:* (01223) 356460.

ADAMS, Alan Edgar; Director, A. A. Leadership Ltd, since 2007; Deputy Chief Executive for Families, London Borough of Waltham Forest, since 2012; *b* 1 June 1954; *s* of Anthony Adams and Olive Adams; one *d*. *Educ:* Nottingham Univ. (BA (Sociol.) 1976; MA (Social Work), Cert. Social Work 1978); Paddington Coll. of Further Educn, London (Further Educn Teachers' Cert.); Hendon Business Sch., Middlesex Poly. (MBA 1991). Dir, Housing and Social Services, Wokingham UA, 1997–2002; Exec. Dir for Adults and Community Care, Surrey CC, 2002–06; Interim Director: Havering LBC, 2007; Newham LBC, 2008–09. *Recreations:* family, watching sport, flying light aircraft, drums, writing, optimism. *Address:* 9 Edgcumbe Park Drive, Crowthorne, Berks RG45 6HB. *T:* (01344) 773955. *E:* alan32b@hotmail.co.uk.

ADAMS, Alastair Christian, RP; portrait painter, since 1995; President, Royal Society of Portrait Painters, 2008–14; *b* Kingston upon Thames, 24 Dec. 1969; *s* of Gordon and Carolyn Adams; *m* 1997, Amy Wilkinson; one *s* one *d*. *Educ:* Formby High Sch.; Hugh Baird Coll., Bootle (Foundn Course 1989); Leicester Poly. (BA Hons Illustration 1992). RP 2002. Commissions include: Rear-Adm. Nicholas Wilkinson, Sir Ian Blair, Tony Blair, Dame Sandra Burslem, Sir Colin Campbell, Sir William Dale, Rt Hon. Lord Hope of Craighead, Sir John Jennings, Sir Rob Margetts, Rt Hon. Lord Nolan, Capt. John Powell, Rt Hon. Lord Scarman, Rt Hon. Lord Woolf, David Swensen. Prog. Coordinator, Sch. of the Arts, Loughborough Univ., 2006–13. Treas., RP, 2006–08. Trustee, Fedn of British Artists, 2008–14. *Publications:* contribs to Internat. Jl Humanities, Internat. Jl Arts in Society. *Recreations:* family, painting, travel, music, charity work. *T:* 07808 585366. *E:* alastair.adams@virgin.net.

ADAMS, Prof. Alfred Rodney, FRS 1996; Professor of Physics, 1987–2003, Distinguished Professor of Physics, 2003–08, University of Surrey, now Emeritus; *b* 11 Nov. 1939; *s* of Alfred Walter Adams and Lucy Elizabeth Adams; *m* 1966, Helga Fehringer; two *d*. *Educ:* Rayleigh Technical Sch.; Westcliff High Sch.; Univ. of Leicester (BSc, PhD, DSc). FInstP 1982; FIET 1997, Hon. FIET 2012; FIEEE 2001, Life FIEEE 2011. Research Fellow: Univ. of Leicester, 1964; Univ. of Karlsruhe, 1965; Lectr, 1967, Reader, 1984, Univ. of Surrey. Royal Soc./Japanese Soc. for Promotion of Science Fellow, 1980, Hitachi Prof., 1992, Tokyo Inst. Tech; CNRS Vis. Researcher, Univ. of Montpellier, 1993. Duddell Medal and Prize, Inst. of Physics, 1995; Rank Prize for Optoelectronics, 2014. *Publications:* (ed with Y. Suematsu) Semiconductor Lasers and Photonic Integrated Circuits, 1994; numerous papers in jls on physics and on quantum electronics. *Recreations:* walking, travel, sailing. *Address:* Advanced Technology Institute, Faculty of Engineering and Physical Sciences, University of Surrey, Guildford, Surrey GU2 7XH. *T:* (01483) 689310.

ADAMS, Prof. Anthony Peter, FRCA, FANZCA; Professor of Anaesthetics in the University of London, 1979–2001, now Emeritus, and Joint Vice-Chairman, Division of Surgery and Anaesthesia, 1998–2001, at Guy's, King's and St Thomas' Medical and Dental School of King's College, London; *b* 17 Oct. 1936; *s* of late H. W. J. Adams and W. L. Adams; *m* 1973, Veronica Rosemary John; three *s* one *d*. *Educ:* Epsom College; London Univ. MB BS 1960, PhD 1970; DA 1962; MRCS 1960, LRCP 1960, FRCA (FFARCS 1964); FANZCA (FFARACS 1987). Wellcome Res. Fellow, RPMS, 1964–66; Consultant Anaesthetist and Clinical Lectr, Nuffield Dept of Anaesthetics, Univ. of Oxford, 1968–79; Guy's Hosp. Med. Sch., subseq. UMDS of Guy's and St Thomas' Hospitals, 1979–98: Chm., Div. of Anaesthetics, 1984–89, 1996–97; Vice-Chm., Div. of Surgery and Anaesthesia, 1997–98; Mem., Council of Govs, 1997–98. Civilian Consultant in Anaesthesia to Army, 1988–2001, Consultant Emeritus, 2001–. Member: Standing Cttee, Bd of Studies in Surgery, London Univ., 1979–92; Academic Bd of Medicine, London Univ., 1980–83; Jt Cttee for Higher Trng of Anaesthetists, 1985–90; Specialist Adv. Cttee on Accident and Emergency Medicine, Jt Cttee for Higher Trng in Medicine, 1986–90; Exec. Cttee, Fedn of Assocs of Clin. Profs, 1979–87; Exec. Cttee, Anaesthetic Res. Soc., 1983–94 (Chm., 1991–94; Hon. Mem., 2002–); Council, Assoc. of Anaesthetists of GB and Ireland, 1984–89 (Chm., Safety

Cttee, 1987–89); Council, Royal Coll. of Anaesthetists, 1989–97; Chm., Assoc. of Profs of Anaesthesia, 1984–88; Senator, Eur. Acad. of Anaesthesiology, 1985–95, 2000–03 (Mem. Exec. Cttee, 1997–2003). Regional Educnl Adviser (SE Thames RHA) to Faculty of Anaesthetists of RCS, 1980–87; Examiner: FFARCS, 1974–86; DVA, 1986–93; DA and DM, Univ. of WI, 1986–88, 1995, 1997, 1998; MSc, Univ. of Wales Coll. of Medicine, 1988–93; PhD: Univ. of London, 1989, 1997, 1999, 2001, 2004; Univ. of Manchester, 1993; Univ. of Liverpool, 1995; NUI, Galway, 2000; MB ChB Chinese Univ. of Hong Kong, 1990; Professional and Linguistic Assessment Bd Pt 2, GMC, UK, 2001–06; Mem. of Faculty, Key Skills in Surgery Courses, RCSE, 2006–10. Mem., Bd of Govs, Sutton High Sch. for Girls, 1988–95 (Chm., 1991–95). President: Sutton & Dist Med. Soc., 2006–08; Cheam Br., Arthritis Research UK (formerly Arthritis and Rheumatism Council), 2011–14. Hon. Life Mem., Assoc. Dental Anaesthetists, 2006. Asst Editor, Anaesthesia, 1976–82; Associate Editor: Survey of Anesthesiology, 1984–2001; European Jl of Anaesthesiology, 1987–94; Jl of Anesthesia (Japan), 1995–2002; Mem. Editl Bd, British Jl of Anaesthesia, 1984–97; Chm. Editl Bd, 1997–2000, Editor-in-Chief, 2000–03, European Jl of Anaesthesiology. *Publications:* Principles and Practice of Blood-Gas Analysis, 1979, 2nd edn 1982; Intensive Care, 1984 (trans. Spanish 1987, Greek 1990); (ed jtly) Recent Advances in Anaesthesia and Analgesia, vol. 15, 1985, vol. 16, 1989, vol. 17, 1992, vol. 18, 1994, vol. 19, 1995, vol. 20, 1998, vol. 21, 2000, vol. 22, 2003; (ed jtly) Emergency Anaesthesia, 1986 and 1988, Japanese edn 1998; (ed jtly) Anaesthesia, Analgesia and Intensive Care, 1991; contribs to medical jls. *Recreations:* badger watching, English castles, history, tennis, croquet, cinema, theatre, ballet. *Clubs:* Royal Automobile, Royal Society of Medicine; Halifax House (Oxford).

ADAMS, Rev. David; *see* Adams, Rev. J. D. A.

ADAMS, Prof. David, PhD; Ian Mactaggart Professor of Property and Urban Studies, University of Glasgow, since 2004; *b* Menston, 10 Sept. 1954; *s* of Richard Adams and Sylvia Adams; *m* 1989, Judith Banks; one *s* one *d*. *Educ:* Emmanuel Coll., Cambridge (BA Hons Land Economy 1976; PhD 1997); Univ. of Liverpool (MCD 1978). MRTPI 1981, FRTPI 2001; MRICS 1999, FRICS 2012. Planning Asst, Leeds CC, 1978–83; Res. Asst, Univ. of Reading, 1983–84; Lectr in Urban Planning and Develt, Univ. of Manchester, 1984–93; University of Aberdeen: Sen. Lectr, 1993–95, Reader, 1995–97, in Land Economy; Prof. of Land Economy, 1997–2004. Dep. Chair, Architecture, Planning and Built Envmt Sub-Panel, REF 2014. FRSA 1998; FAcSS (AcSS 2013). *Publications:* Urban Planning and the Development Process, 1994; (jtly) Land for Industrial Development, 1994; (with C. Watkins) Greenfields, Brownfields and Housing Development, 2002; (ed jtly) Planning, Public Policy and Property Markets, 2005; (ed jtly) Urban Design in the Real Estate Development Process, 2011; (with S. Tiesdell) Shaping Places: urban planning, design and development, 2013. *Recreations:* walking, reading, classical music. *Address:* Urban Studies, School of Social and Political Sciences, University of Glasgow, 25 Bute Gardens, Glasgow G12 8RD. *T:* (0141) 330 6280, *Fax:* (0141) 330 6032. *E:* david.adams@glasgow.ac.uk.

ADAMS, David H.; *see* Hempleman-Adams.

ADAMS, Prof. David Harvey, MD; FRCP, FMedSci; Professor of Hepatology, since 1997, Dean of Medicine, since 2013 and Pro-Vice Chancellor and Head, College of Medical and Dental Sciences, since 2015, University of Birmingham; Consultant Physician, Queen Elizabeth Hospital, Birmingham, since 1993; *b* Nottingham, 26 Feb. 1958; *s* of Stewart Adams and late Mary Adams (*née* Harvey); *m* 1984, Rosalind Hicks; two *s* one *d*. *Educ:* Univ. of Birmingham (MB ChB 1981; MD 1990). MRCP 1984, FRCP 1996. University of Birmingham: Lectr, Dept of Medicine, 1985–87; MRC Res. Fellow, 1987–90; MRC Travelling Fellow and Vis. Associate, Fogarty Exchange Prog., Experimental Immunol. Br., Nat. Cancer Inst., NIH, Bethesda, Md, 1991–93; Dir, Birmingham NIHR Biomed. Unit for Liver Disease, 2008–; Dir, Translational Res. MRC Centre for Immune Regulation, 2009–, Hd, Sch. of Immunity and Infection, 2011–13, Univ. of Birmingham. Mem., Clin. Trng and Career Develt Panel, MRC, 2009–. Chm., Wkg Gp on Mentoring, 2009–, Mem. Council, 2011–, Acad. of Med. Scis; Chm., Academic Cttee, British Soc. of Gastroenterol., 2011–. Mem. Council, Eur. Soc. for Organ Transplantation, 2004–08; Mem., Scientific Cttee and Gov. Bd, 2004–07, Founder Mem., Ethics Cttee, 2011–, Eur. Assoc. for Study of the Liver. Associate Editor: Liver, 1997–2002; Gut, 1998–2004; Clinical Sci., 1998–2010; Transplant Internat., 2006–10; Liver Transplantation, 2009–; Amer. Jl of Physiol., 2009–; Jl of Hepatol., 2009–. *Publications:* over 200 articles in scientific jls on immunol. and liver disease. *Recreations:* walking, fishing, reading, music. *Address:* Centre for Liver Research, School of Immunity and Infection, University of Birmingham Medical School, Birmingham B15 2TT. *T:* (0121) 415 8700. *E:* d.h.adams@bham.ac.uk.

ADAMS, David Robert Hutchinson, (Robin); Librarian and College Archivist, Trinity College Dublin, 2002–12; *b* 9 June 1951; *s* of Cecil David and Ann Gilmore Adams; *m* 1984, Linda Jean Carter (*d* 2011); one *s* one *d*. *Educ:* Royal Belfast Academical Instn; Univ. of Ulster (BA); Queen's Univ. of Belfast (Dip. Liby Studies); Univ. of Dublin (MA). Asst Librarian, QUB, 1975–78; Asst Under-Librarian, Cambridge Univ., 1978–86; Principal Asst Librarian, Glasgow Univ., 1986–90; Dep. Librarian, TCD, 1991–2002. Member: Bd, Nat. Preservation Office, 2002–09; An Chomhairle Leabharlanna (Liby Council), 2002–12; Consortium of Nat. and Univ. Libraries, 2002–12; Legal Deposit Adv. Panel, 2005–09; Bd, NI Publications Resource, 2006– (Chm., 2013–); Council, Liby Assoc. of Ireland, 2012–; BL Adv. Council, 2013–. Dir, Res. Libraries UK (formerly Consortium of Univ. Res. Libraries), 2002–12; Chm., Newsplan Ireland, 2008–12. Dir, Iris Document Delivery Services Ltd, 2002–12. Trustee, Worth Liby, 2002–12. *Publications:* contrib. articles to professional jls. *Recreations:* fishing, theatre, walking, permaculture and organic gardening, choral singing, distance running. *Address:* 44 York Road, Dun Laoghaire, Co. Dublin, Ireland. *E:* radams@tcd.ie.

ADAMS, Dr Derek Westwood, FRPharmS; Director, Pharmaceutical Compliance Europe, Merck Sharpe and Dohme, 1996–99; *b* Leeds, 13 April 1941; *s* of Ernest Wilfred Adams and Hilda Adams (*née* Wightman); *m* 1972, Kathryn Robinson. *Educ:* Archbp Holgate's Grammar Sch., York; Roundhay Sch., Leeds; Univ. of Manchester (BSc Pharmacy); Wolfson Coll., Cambridge (MA Hist.); Univ. of Hertfordshire (PhD 2010). Qualified Person status under provisions of Directive EEC 75/319, 1982. FRPharmS 1989. Merck Sharpe and Dohme: formulation pharmacist, Pharmaceutical R&D Dept, 1966–78; Manufg Manager, 1978–79; Prodn Manager, 1979–84; Distribn Services Manager, 1984–87; Gp Quality Control Manager, 1987–92; Director: Quality Ops, GB and Ireland, 1992–94; Ext. Quality Ops, 1994–96. Assessor of applicants for Qualified Persons under provisions of Directive EEC 75/319, RPharmS, 1980–99. RPharmS Nominee, Pharmacy Practices Cttee, FPC, 1983–88; Mem., Antibiotics Sub-Cttee, British Pharmacopoeia Commn, 1988–99. Society of Apothecaries: Sen. Warden, 2015–Aug. 2016; Master, Aug. 2016–. Diocesan Gov., Tewin Cowper C of E Primary Sch., 2011–. Mem., Rotary Club of Amwell (Pres., 1995–96); Gov., Rotary Internat. Dist 1260 (Beds, Bucks and Herts), 2000–01. *Recreations:* cycling, walking, music, reading. *Club:* Oxford and Cambridge.

ADAMS, Sir Geoffrey (Doyne), KCMG 2008 (CMG 2003); HM Diplomatic Service; Ambassador to the Netherlands, since 2013; *b* 11 June 1957; *s* of late Sir Philip George Doyne Adams, KCMG, and Hon. (Mary) Elizabeth, *e d* of Baron Trevethin and Oaksey (3rd and 1st Baron respectively); *m* 1999, Mary Emma Baxter; two *s* one *d*. *Educ:* Eton; Magdalen Coll., Oxford (BA). Joined HM Diplomatic Service, 1979; Third, later Second, Sec., Jedda, 1982–85; Ecole Nat. d'Admin, Paris, 1985–87; Private Sec. to Perm. Under-Sec. of State, FCO, 1987–91; First Sec., Pretoria and Cape Town, 1991–94; European Secretariat, Cabinet Office, 1995–98; Counsellor and Dep. Hd of Mission, Cairo, 1998–2001; Consul-Gen., Jerusalem, 2001–03; Principal Private Sec. to Sec. of State for Foreign and Commonwealth Affairs, 2003–05; Ambassador to Iran, 2006–09; Dir Gen. (Political), FCO, 2009–12. *Address:* c/o Foreign and Commonwealth Office, King Charles Street, SW1A 2AH.

ADAMS, Gerard, (Gerry); Member of the Dáil (TD) (SF) Louth, since 2011; President, Sinn Féin, since 1983 (Vice-President, 1978–83); *b* 6 Oct. 1948; *s* of late Gerard Adams and Annie (*née* Hannaway); *m* 1971, Colette McArdle; one *s*. *Educ:* St Mary's Christian Brothers' Sch., Belfast. Interned for suspected terrorist activity, 1971, 1973; subseq. imprisoned; released, 1976. Mem., NI Assembly, 1982; MP (SF) Belfast W, 1983–92; contested (SF) same seat, 1992; MP (SF) Belfast W, 1997–Jan. 2011; Mem. (SF) Belfast W, NI Assembly, 1998–Dec. 2010. Thorr Award, Switzerland, 1995. Blog, www.leargas/blogspot.com. *Publications:* Falls Memories (autobiog.), 1982; Politics of Irish Freedom, 1986; Pathway to Peace, 1988; Cage Eleven (autobiog.), 1990; The Street and Other Stories, 1992; Selected Writings, 1994; Before the Dawn (autobiog.), 1996; An Irish Voice: the quest for peace, 1997; An Irish Journal, 2001; Hope and History (memoirs), 2003; The New Ireland: a vision for the future, 2005; An Irish Eye, 2007. *Address:* Houses of the Oireachtas, Leinster House, Kildare Street, Dublin 2, Ireland.

ADAMS, Sir James; *see* Adams, Sir W. J.

ADAMS, James Noel, CBE 2015; DPhil; FBA 1992; FAHA; Senior Research Fellow, All Souls College, Oxford, 1998–2010; *b* 24 Sept. 1943. *Educ:* North Sydney Boys' High Sch.; Univ. of Sydney (BA); Brasenose Coll., Oxford (MA; DPhil); MA Cantab. Teaching Fellow, Dept of Latin, Univ. of Sydney, 1965–66; Commonwealth Schol., Brasenose Coll., Oxford, 1967–70; Rouse Res. Fellow in Classics, Christ's Coll., Cambridge, 1970–72; University of Manchester: Lectr and Sen. Lectr in Greek and Latin, 1972–82; Reader in Latin, 1982–93; Prof. of Latin, 1993–95; Prof. of Latin, Univ. of Reading, 1995–97. Vis. Sen. Res. Fellow, St John's Coll., Oxford, 1994–95; Professorial Res. Fellow, Univ. of Manchester, 2013–14. FAHA 2002. Kenyon Medal, British Acad., 2009. *Publications:* The Text and Language of a Vulgar Latin Chronicle (Anonymus Valesianus), 1976; The Vulgar Latin of the Letters of Claudius Terentianus, 1977; The Latin Sexual Vocabulary, 1982; Wackernagel's Law and the Placement of the Copula *Esse* in Classical Latin, 1994; Pelagonius and Latin Veterinary Terminology in the Roman Empire, 1995; Bilingualism and the Latin Language, 2003; The Regional Diversification of Latin 200 BC–AD 600, 2007; Social Variation and the Latin Language, 2013; articles in learned jls. *Recreation:* cricket. *Address:* All Souls College, Oxford OX1 4AL.

ADAMS, Jennifer, LVO 1993; OBE 2008; Director of Open Spaces, City of London Corporation (formerly Corporation of London), 2001–08; *b* 1 Feb. 1948; *d* of Arthur Roy Thomas Crisp and Joyce Muriel Crisp (*née* Davey); *m* 1968, Terence William Adams (*d* 2011). *Educ:* City of London School for Girls. Final Diploma, Inst. of Leisure and Amenity (FILAM DipPRA); FCIHort. Various positions in Parks Dept, London Borough of Wandsworth, 1971–83; Manager, Inner Parks, 1983–90; Acting Bailiff, Royal Parks, 1990–92; Hd of Inner Parks and Commerce, Royal Parks, 1992–2001. Pres., Inst. of Horticulture, 1996–98. Vice Chm. and Treas., Royal Parks Guild, 2006–. Liveryman, Gardeners' Co., 1985. Associate of Honour, RHS, 1999. *Recreations:* walking, gardening, nature conservation.

ADAMS, John; composer; *b* 15 Feb. 1947. *Educ:* Harvard Univ. (scholar). Teacher, San Francisco Conservatory of Music, 1972–82; Music Advr, 1978–82, Composer-in-Residence, 1982–85, San Francisco Symphony; Creative Chair, LA Philharmonic, 2006–. *Compositions include: opera:* Nixon in China, 1987; The Death of Klinghoffer, 1990; I Was Looking at the Ceiling and Then I Saw the Sky, 1995; El Niño, 2000; Doctor Atomic, 2005; A Flowering Tree, 2007; The Gospel According to the Other Mary, 2013; *orchestral works:* Shaker Loops, 1978; Common Tones in Simple Time, 1979; Harmonium, 1980–81; Grand Pianola Music, 1981–82; Harmonielehre, 1984–85; The Chairman Dances, 1985; Short Ride in a Fast Machine, 1986; Tromba Lontana, 1986; Fearful Symmetries, 1988; The Wound-Dresser, 1988–89; Eros Piano, 1989; El Dorado, 1991; Violin Concerto, 1993 (Grawemeyer Award for Music Composition, 1995); Gnarly Buttons, 1996; Century Rolls, piano concerto, 1998; Guide to Strange Places, 2002; My Father Knew Charles Ives, 2003; The Dharma at Big Sur, 2004; City Noir, 2010; Absolute Jest, string quartet and orch., 2012; Saxophone Concerto, 2013; Scheherezade.2, 2015; *chorus and orchestra:* On the Transmigration of Souls, 2002 (Pulitzer Prize, 2003); *chamber and ensemble works:* Christian Zeal and Activity, 1973; China Gates, 1977; Phrygian Gates, 1977; Chamber Symphony, 1992; John's Book of Alleged Dances, 1994; Road Movies, 1995; Son of Chamber Symphony, 2007; String Quartet, 2008; numerous recordings. *Publications:* Hallelujah Junction: composing an American life (memoir), 2008. *Address:* c/o Boosey & Hawkes Music Publishers Ltd, Aldwych House, 71–91 Aldwych, WC2B 4HN.

ADAMS, Rev. (John) David (Andrew); Headmaster, Weydon School, 1982–98; Chaplain to the Queen, 1994–2007; Secondary School consultant, 1998–2010; *b* 27 Nov. 1937; *s* of John McCullough McConnell Adams and Sylvia Pansy (*née* Pinner); *m* 1970, Maria Carmen de Azpiazu-Cruz; one *s* one *d*. *Educ:* Trinity Coll., Dublin (BA 1960; Div. Test. 1961; MA 1964; BD 1965); Univ. of Reading (MEd 1974). Curate, St Stephen's, Belfast, 1962–65; part-time teaching and vol. chaplaincy in Europe, 1965–67; Hd, Religious Educn, Tower Ramparts, Ipswich, 1967–70; Counsellor, later Sen. Teacher, Robert Haining Sch., Surrey, 1970–74; Headmaster, St Paul's, Addlestone, 1974–82. Non-stipendiary Curate, 1976–2007, Hon. Priest, 2007–, St Thomas-on-the-Bourne, Farnham. Bishop's Assessor, Dio. of Guildford, 2005–. *Recreations:* gardening, household chores, birding; the life of George Morley, Bishop of Winchester, 1597–1684. *Address:* Brookside Farm, Oast House Crescent, Farnham, Surrey GU9 0NP. *T:* (01252) 726888.

ADAMS, His Honour John Douglas Richard; a Circuit Judge, 1998–2002; *b* 19 March 1940; *o s* of late Gordon Arthur Richard Adams and Marjorie Ethel Adams (*née* Ongley); *m* 1966, Anne Easton Todd, *o d* of late Robert Easton Todd and Mary Ann Margaret Todd; two *d*. *Educ:* Watford Grammar School; Durham Univ. (LLB 1963). Called to Bar, Lincoln's Inn, 1967; Bencher, Inner Temple, 1997. Lecturer: Newcastle Univ., 1963–71; University College London, 1971–78; also practised at Revenue Bar until 1978; Special Comr of Income Tax, 1978–82; Registrar of Civil Appeals, 1982–98; a Recorder, 1992–98. Hon. Lecturer, St Edmund Hall, Oxford, 1978–2008; Vis. Lectr, Oxford Univ., 1995–2008. Mem. Bd of Trustees, Hospice of St Francis, Berkhamsted, 2004–11. *Publications:* (with J. Whalley) The International Taxation of Multinational Enterprises, 1977; (contrib.) Atkin's Court Forms, 1984, 1992; (ed jtly) Supreme Court Practice, 1985, 1991, 1993, 1995, 1997, 1999; (ed jtly) Chitty and Jacob's Queen's Bench Forms, 21st edn, 1986; (ed jtly) Sweet & Maxwell's County Court Litigation, 1993; (ed jtly) Emergency Remedies in the Family Courts, 3rd edn, 1997; (ed jtly) Jordan's Civil Court Service, 2002; (ed jtly) Halsbury's Laws of England, 4th edn, vol. 10. *Recreations:* music, walking, dining. *E:* johndradams@btinternet.com.

ADAMS, (John) Giles Selby C.; *see* Coode-Adams.

ADAMS, His Honour (John) Roderick (Seton); a Circuit Judge, 1990–2003; *b* 29 Feb. 1936; *s* of George Adams and Winifred (*née* Wilson); *m* 1965, Pamela Bridget, *e d* of Rev. D. E. Rice, MC; three *s*. *Educ:* Whitgift Sch.; Trinity Coll., Cambridge. BA, 1959, MA 1963. Commnd, Seaforth Highlanders, 1955–56; Parachute Regt, TA, 1959–66. Legal Adviser in industry, 1960–66. Called to the Bar, Inner Temple, 1962; began practice at the Bar, 1967; Dep. Circuit Judge, 1978–80; a Recorder, 1980–90. *Recreations:* hill-walking, fishing, growing

old roses, microlight flying. *Address:* 8 Melville Road, Eskbank, Midlothian EH22 3BY. *T:* (0131) 654 9274; Melness House, Sutherland IV27 4YR. *T:* (01847) 601255.
See also R. G. S. Adams.

ADAMS, Lewis Drummond, OBE 1999; General Secretary, Associated Society of Locomotive Engineers and Firemen, 1994–99; *b* London, 16 Aug. 1939; *s* of Lewis John Adams and Margaret (*née* Drummond); *m* 1958, Jean Marion Bass; one *s* one *d*. *Educ:* Impington Coll., Cambridge; NCLC; Tavistock Inst., London. British Railways: engine cleaner, 1954–55; engine fireman and driver asst, 1955–67; engine driver, 1967–80. Associated Society of Locomotive Engineers and Firemen: Sec., London Dist Council No 1, 1970–80; Executive Committee: Mem., 1981–90; Vice-Pres., 1985–90; Asst Gen. Sec., 1990–93. British Railways: Mem., later Chm., Pension Fund, 1982–93; Member: Wages Grade Pension Fund, 1982–93; Superannuation Fund, 1982–93. Dir, Millennium Drivers Ltd, 1998–. Bd Mem., SRA, 1999–2004. Member: TUC Pension Cttee, 1987–90; Railway Industries Adv. Cttee, 1985–90; British Transport Police Authy, 2004– (Mem. Mgt Cttee, Superannuation Pension Fund, 2006–). *Recreations:* travel, gardening.

ADAMS, Rev. Prof. Marilyn McCord, PhD, DD; Regius Professor of Divinity, University of Oxford, 2004–09; Canon Residentiary of Christ Church, Oxford, 2004–09; Recurrent Visiting Professor of Philosophy, Rutgers University, since 2013; *b* 12 Oct. 1943; *d* of William Clark McCord and Wilmah Brown McCord; *m* 1966, Prof. Robert Merrihew Adams, *qv*. *Educ:* Univ. of Illinois (AB); Cornell Univ. (PhD 1967); Princeton Theol Seminary (ThM 1984, 1985); Univ. of Oxford (DD 2008). University of California, Los Angeles: Associate Prof. of Philosophy, 1972–78; Prof., 1978–93; Chair of Philosophy, 1985–87; Prof. of Histl Theology, 1993–2003, Horace Tracy Pitkin Prof. of Histl Theology, 1998–2003, Yale Univ. Divinity Sch. Dist. Res. Prof. of Philosophy, Univ. of N Carolina at Chapel Hill, 2009–13. Hon. Prof., Australian Catholic Univ., 2012–. Ordained deacon and priest, Episcopal Church, USA, 1987; served in parishes in LA, Calif, New Haven, Conn, Chapel Hill, NC and Trenton, NJ. Hon. DD Berkeley Divinity Sch., Yale, 2011. *Publications:* (with Norman Kretzmann) Ockham's Treatise on Predestination, God's Foreknowledge, and Future Contingents, 1969, 2nd edn 1983; (trans.) Paul of Venice, On the Truth and Falsity of Propositions and On the Significatum of a Proposition, 1977; William Ockham, 2 vols, 1987; (ed with Robert Merrihew Adams) The Problem of Evil, 1990; Horrendous Evils and the Goodness of God, 1999; Wrestling for Blessing, 2005; Christ and Horrors: the coherence of Christology, 2006; Opening to God: childlike prayers for adults, 2008; Some Later Medieval Theories of the Eucharist, 2010; articles in learned jls.

ADAMS, Air Vice-Marshal Michael Keith, CB 1986; AFC 1970; FRAeS; *b* 23 Jan. 1934; *s* of late William Frederick Adams and Jean Mary Adams; *m* 1966, Susan (*née* Trudgian); two *s* one *d*. *Educ:* Bedford Sch.; City of London Sch. FRAeS 1978. Joined RAF, 1952; qualified Pilot, 1954; Flying Instr, 1960; Test Pilot, 1963 (QCVSA 1967); Staff Coll., Toronto, 1969; CO Empire Test Pilots' Sch., 1975; Dir of Operational Requirements, 1978–81; RCDS, 1982; AOC Training Units, 1983; ACAS (Op. Requirements), MoD, 1984; ACDS (Op. Requirements) Air, MoD, 1985–86; Sen. Directing Staff (Air), RCDS, 1987–88; retd. Dir, Thomson-CSF (UK) Ltd, 1988–94; Dir, International Aerospace, 1989–96 (Chm., 1996). Vice-Pres., RAeS, 1992–95. Chm. Govs, Duke of Kent Sch., Cranleigh, Surrey, 1997–2003. *Recreations:* walking, silversmithing.

ADAMS, Nigel; MP (C) Selby and Ainsty, since 2010; *b* Goole, E Yorks, 30 Nov. 1966; *s* of Derek Adams and late Isabella Adams; *m* 1992, Claire Robson; one *s* three *d*. *Educ:* Selby Grammar Sch.; Selby High Sch. Sales and mktg roles in advertising and telecommunications industry, 1985–93; Founder and Man. Dir, Advanced Digital Telecom Ltd, 1993–99; Dir, JWE Telecom plc, 1999–2000; non-exec. Chm., Pareto Law plc, 2001–02; Director: Ebor Events Ltd, 2003–05; Yorks Tourist Bd, 2005–06; NGC Networks Ltd, 2006–; NGC Network Services Ltd, 2007–. Hon. Sec., All Party Parly Cricket Gp, 2010–. *Recreations:* cricket, playing and watching (Member: Yorks CCC; Carlton Club CC; Hovingham CC; Sec., Lords and Commons CC). *Address:* House of Commons, SW1A 0AA. *E:* nigel.adams.mp@parliament.uk; 17 High Street, Tadcaster, N Yorks LS24 9AP. *Club:* Carlton.

ADAMS, Paul Nicholas; Chief Executive, British American Tobacco plc, 2004–11; *b* 12 March 1953; *s* of Peter Adams and Joan Adams (*née* Smith); *m* 1978, Gail Edwina McCann; one *s* two *d*. *Educ:* Culford Sch.; Ealing Coll., London (BA Hons 1977). Mktg Dir, Beecham Products Internat., 1983–86; Vice Pres. Mktg Europe, Pepsi-Cola Internat., 1986–91; British American Tobacco plc: Regl Dir, Asia Pacific, 1991–98, Europe, 1999–2001; Dep. Man. Dir, 2001; Man. Dir, 2002–03. Non-exec. Dir, Allied Domecq plc, 2003–05. *Recreations:* reading, country pursuits, theatre. *Address:* c/o British American Tobacco plc, Globe House, 4 Temple Place, WC2R 2PG.

ADAMS, Piers Dermot Meredith; musician; professional virtuoso recorder player, since 1985; *b* 21 Dec. 1963; *s* of late John Adams and of Susan Adams; one *d*. *Educ:* Reading Blue Coat Sch.; Univ. of Bristol (BSc Physics 1984); Guildhall Sch. of Music & Drama (Cert. Perf. in Early Music 1985). Winner (jtly), Moeck Recorder Competition, 1985; début recital, Wigmore Hall, London, 1985; performed, 1986–, in all Eur. countries, most US states, Canada, Mexico, Cuba, Russia, China, Japan, Singapore, Thailand and Australia; soloist: in all South Bank concert halls, London; with many orchs incl. BBC Symphony, Philharmonia, Acad. of Ancient Music and Singapore Symphony; commnd over 25 works by mod. composers, 1986–; Founder and Dir, Red Priest (cult baroque ensemble), 1997–; Co-Founder, Red Priest Recordings, 2009–; performed private concerts for the Prince of Wales and the Duke of Edinburgh, 2001, 2002; frequent radio broadcasts; many TV appearances. Ten CD recordings (début CD, 1988). *Address:* c/o Maureen Phillips, Upbeat Classical Management, 170 Thirlmere Gardens, Northwood HA6 2RU. *T:* (01923) 836220. *E:* admin@upbeatclassical.co.uk.

ADAMS, Richard Clive; Chairman, Crosswater Solutions Ltd, 2000–14; *b* 22 June 1945; *s* of William Henry Adams and Alberta Sarah Adams (*née* Steed); *m* 1971, Elizabeth Anne Coleman; two *s*. *Educ:* Cotham Grammar Sch., Bristol; Exeter Univ. (BA). Post Office: Asst Postal Controller, 1966–78; Dir of Studies, PO Mgt Coll., 1978–82; Head Postmaster, Northampton, 1982–85; Asst Dir, Corporate Planning, 1985–92; Gp Planning Dir, 1992–97; Sec., 1997–99. Chm., Postal and Logistics Consulting Worldwide Ltd, 2003–06. Mem. Council, CBI, 1998–99. Sec., Postal Heritage Trust, 2004–15. *Recreations:* applied arts, railways, wine. *Address:* 48 Overton Drive, Wanstead, E11 2NJ. *T:* (020) 8989 0021.

ADAMS, Richard George; author; *b* 10 May 1920; *s* of Evelyn George Beadon Adams, FRCS, and Lilian Rosa Adams (*née* Button); *m* 1949, Barbara Elizabeth Acland; two *d*. *Educ:* Bradfield Coll., Berks; Worcester Coll., Oxford (MA, Mod. Hist.). Entered Home Civil Service, 1948; retd as Asst Sec., DoE, 1974. Writer-in-residence: Univ. of Florida, 1975; Hollins Univ., Virginia, 1976. Pres., RSPCA, 1980–82. Carnegie Medal, 1972; Guardian Award for Children's Literature, 1972. FRSL 1975. *Publications:* Watership Down, 1972 (numerous subseq. edns in various languages; filmed 1978); Shardik, 1974; (with Max Hooper) Nature through the Seasons, 1975; The Tyger Voyage, 1976; The Ship's Cat, 1977; The Plague Dogs, 1977 (filmed 1982); (with Max Hooper) Nature Day and Night, 1978; The Girl in a Swing, 1980 (filmed 1988); The Iron Wolf, 1980; (with Ronald Lockley) Voyage through the Antarctic, 1982; Maia, 1984; The Bureaucats, 1985; A Nature Diary, 1985; (ed and contrib.) Occasional Poets (anthology), 1986; The Legend of Te Tuna, 1986; Traveller, 1988; The Day Gone By (autobiog.), 1990; Tales from Watership Down, 1996; The Outlandish Knight, 2000; Daniel, 2006; (contrib.) Gentle Footprints: a collection of animal stories, 2010. *Recreations:* folk-song, chess, fly-fishing.

ADAMS, Robert George Seton; His Honour Judge Adams; a Circuit Judge, since 2014; *b* London, 5 Jan. 1966; *s* of His Honour (John) Roderick (Seton) Adams, *qv*; *m* 1994, Theresa Campbell; two *s* one *d*. *Educ:* Dulwich Coll.; Trinity Coll., Cambridge (BA 1987; MA 1991). Commnd Queen's Own Highlanders, 1987–92. Called to the Bar, Inner Temple, 1993; a Recorder, 2008–14. *Recreations:* running, swimming, walking, fly-fishing. *Address:* Durham Crown Court, Old Elvet, Durham DH1 3HW. *T:* (0191) 386 6714; Newcastle upon Tyne Crown Court, Quayside, Newcastle upon Tyne NE1 2LA. *T:* (0191) 201 2000. *E:* HHJ.Adams@judiciary.gsi.gov.uk. *Clubs:* Old Alleynian; Northern Counties (Newcastle upon Tyne).

ADAMS, Prof. Robert Merrihew, PhD; FBA 2006; Visiting Professor of Philosophy, Rutgers University, since 2013; *b* 8 Sept. 1937; *s* of Rev. Arthur Merrihew Adams and Margaret Baker Adams; *m* 1966, Marilyn McCord (*see* Rev. Prof. M. McC. Adams). *Educ:* Princeton Univ. (AB 1959); Mansfield Coll., Oxford (BA 1961, MA 1965); Princeton Theological Seminary (BD 1962); Cornell Univ. (MA 1967; PhD 1969). Pastor, Montauk Community Ch (Presbyterian), Montauk, NY, 1962–65; Lectr, 1968, Asst Prof., 1969–72, Univ. of Michigan, Ann Arbor; University of California, Los Angeles: Assoc. Prof., 1972–76; Prof., 1976–93; Chm., Philos. Dept, 1975–79; Yale University: Prof., 1993–2003; Clark Prof. of Philos., 1995–2003, Emeritus, 2004–; Chm., Philos. Dept, 1993–2001. Vis. Prof. of Philos., Univ. of Oxford, 2004–09; Sen. Res. Fellow, Mansfield Coll., Oxford, 2004–11. Dist. Res. Prof. of Philos., Univ. of N Carolina at Chapel Hill, 2009–13. Wilde Lectr in Natural Religion, Univ. of Oxford, 1989; Gifford Lectr, Univ. of St Andrews, 1999. Fellow, Amer. Acad. of Arts and Scis, 1991. *Publications:* The Virtue of Faith and Other Essays in Philosophical Theology, 1987; (ed with Marilyn McCord Adams) The Problem of Evil, 1990; Leibniz: determinist, theist, idealist, 1994; Finite and Infinite Goods: a framework for ethics, 1999; A Theory of Virtue, 2006; jl articles on topics in ethics, metaphysics, philos. of religion and hist. of mod. philos. *Recreations:* travel, museum visits, birdwatching.

ADAMS, Robin; *see* Adams, D. R. H.

ADAMS, Roderick; *see* Adams, His Honour J. R. S.

ADAMS, Sheenagh; Keeper of the Registers of Scotland, since 2009; *b* Dundee, 31 Aug. 1957; *d* of James McIntosh Adams and Isabella Bruce Adams (*née* Ross); *m* 1997, Peter William Craig; two *d*. *Educ:* Harris Acad., Dundee; St Andrews Univ. (MA Hons Medieval Hist.); Glasgow Univ. (Dip. Housing Studies). Welfare Rights Officer, Strathclyde Regl Council, 1979–82; Tenant Participation Officer, Clydebank DC, 1982–83; Develt Manager, Tenant Participation Adv. Service, 1983–85; Principal Mgt Officer, Falkirk DC, 1985–90; various hd of branch posts, Scottish Office, 1990–99; Hd, Voluntary Issues Unit, Scottish Govt, 1999–2002; Dir of Policy, Historic Scotland, 2002–06; Man. Dir, Registers of Scotland, 2006–09. *Recreations:* reading, theatre, Spain. *Address:* Registers of Scotland, Meadowbank House, 153 London Road, Edinburgh EH8 7AU. *T:* (0131) 659 6111, *Fax:* (0131) 459 1221. *E:* sheenagh.adams@ros.gov.uk.

ADAMS, Suzanne; *see* Cory, S.

ADAMS, Terence David, CMG 1997; Managing Director, Monument Oil and Gas, 1998–2000; *b* 22 Feb. 1938; *s* of F. E. Adams and E. S. Adams; *m* 1990, Caroline Mary (*née* Hartley); two *s* four *d* by previous marriage. *Educ:* UCW, Aberystwyth (BSc Hons; PhD 1963; Fellow, 2002); Univ. of Dundee (LLM 2004). International service in petroleum industry with Shell and BP, 1959–98; served in N America, Europe, ME and SE Asia. Pres., Azerbaijan Internat. Operating Co., Baku, 1994–98. Sen. Associate, Cambridge Energy Associates, Cambridge, Mass, 2001–. British Oil Advr, Coalition Provisional Authy, Iraq, 2003–04. Mem. Council, RSAA, 1999–2002. Fellow, East-West Inst., NY, 1999–2002. Medal of Honour, Republic of Azerbaijan, 1998; Hon. Citizen, Republic of Georgia, 1999. *Publications:* numerous scientific articles on micropalaeontology, geomorphology, world energy predictions and geopolitics of the Caspian, Central Asia and the Middle East. *Recreations:* archaeology, palaeontology, music, literature. *Address:* 2 Pearsons Road, Holt, Norfolk NR25 6EJ. *T:* (01263) 711443. *Club:* Tanglin (Singapore).

ADAMS, William David B.; *see* Butler-Adams.

ADAMS, Sir (William) James, KCMG 1991 (CMG 1976); HM Diplomatic Service, retired; *b* 30 April 1932; *s* of late William Adams and late Norah (*née* Walker); *m* 1961, Donatella, *d* of late Andrea Pais-Tarsilia; two *s* one *d*. *Educ:* Wolverhampton Grammar Sch.; Shrewsbury Sch.; Queen's Coll., Oxford. 2nd Lieut RA, MELF, 1950–51. Foreign Office, 1954; MECAS, 1955; 3rd Sec., Bahrain, 1956; Asst Political Agent, Trucial States, 1957; FO, 1958; 2nd Sec., 1959; Manila, 1960; 1st Sec. and Private Sec. to Minister of State, FO, 1963; 1st Sec. (Information), Paris, 1965–69; FCO, 1969; Counsellor, 1971; Head of European Integration Dept (2), FCO, 1971–72; seconded to Economic Commn for Africa, Addis Ababa, 1972–73; Counsellor (Developing Countries), UK Permanent Representation to EEC, 1973–77; Head of Chancery and Counsellor (Economic), Rome, 1977–80; Asst Under-Sec. of State (Public Depts, then Energy), FCO, 1980–84; Ambassador and Consul-Gen. to Tunisia, 1984–87; Ambassador to Egypt, 1987–92. Consultant, Control Risks Group, 1992–2001. Chm., Egyptian-British Chamber of Commerce, 1992–99. Mem., RC Cttee for Other Faiths, 1995–2002. Chairman: Egyptian Growth Investment Co. Ltd, 1997–2012; Coral Growth Investments Ltd Funds, 2011–. Order of the Star of Honour (Hon.), Ethiopia, 1965; Order of the Two Niles (Hon.), Sudan, 1965. *Address:* 20 Park Close, Ilchester Place, W14 8ND. *Club:* Reform.

ADAMS, Prof. William Mark, PhD; Moran Professor of Conservation and Development, University of Cambridge, since 2006; Fellow, Downing College, Cambridge, since 1984; *b* 4 July 1955; *s* of Jimmie and Margaret Adams; *m* 1983, Dr Francine Hughes; one *s* one *d*. *Educ:* Downing Coll., Cambridge (BA 1976; PhD 1984); University Coll. London (MSc). Asst Lectr, 1984–89, Lectr, 1989–99, Reader, 1999–2004, and Prof. of Conservation and Develt, 2005–06, Dept of Geog., Univ. of Cambridge. *Publications:* Nature's Place, 1986; Green Development, 1990, 3rd edn 2009; Wasting the Rain, 1992; Future Nature, 1995; (with M. Mortimore) Working the Sahel, 1999; (with M. Mulligan) Decolonising Nature, 2003; Against Extinction, 2004. *Recreations:* poetry, mountains, cycling. *Address:* Downing College, Cambridge CB2 1DQ.

ADAMS-CAIRNS, (Andrew) Ruaraidh; Head of Litigation Support, Savills, since 1995; *b* 12 Oct. 1953; *s* of late Alastair Adams-Cairns and Fiona Lauder (*née* Paton of Grandhome); *m* 1983, Susan Ann Foll; two *s*. *Educ:* Gordonstoun Sch.; Reading Univ. (BSc Est. Man.); RMA Sandhurst. FRICS; MCIArb. Commissioned Queen's Own Highlanders, 1971; Platoon Comdr, Germany, UK, Belize, Gibraltar; Royal Guard, Balmoral (Capt.); Intell. Officer, NI, 1978–79. Joined Savills, 1980; Partner in charge, Salisbury office, 1985–87; Dir, Mixed Develt, 1987–91; Man. Dir, Savills Propriedades, Portugal, 1989–96; Dir, Savills (UK) Ltd (formerly Land and Property), 1987–; Dir and Hd, Residential Valuations, 1998–2004; Hd of Training and Talent Develt, 2004–11. FRGS. *Publications:* The Somme Battlefield: a pocket guide to places and people with maps, 2014; occasional contribs to Estates Gazette, Family Law and Liability Today. *Recreations:* field sports, carpentry, tennis, Somme Battlefield. *Address:* Savills, 33 Margaret Street, W1G 0JD. *T:* (020) 7499 8644. *Club:* Army and Navy.

ADAMSON, Clare Anne; Member (SNP) Scotland Central, Scottish Parliament, since 2011; *b* Motherwell, 1 Aug. 1967; *d* of George Pickering and Eileen Pickering; *m* 2002, John Adamson; one *s*, and three step *c*. *Educ:* Glasgow Caledonian Univ. (BSc Computer Information Systems). MBCS. Mem. (SNP), N Lanarkshire Council, 2007–. Parly Liaison Officer to Cabinet Sec. for Culture and External Affairs, Scottish Govt, 2011–. Vice Chm., Home Safety Cttee, Scottish Accident Prevention Council; Mem., Organising Cttee, Lanarkshire 2011 Internat. Children's Games. *Address:* Scottish Parliament, Edinburgh EH99 1SP. *T:* (0131) 348 6377.

ADAMSON, Clive Peter; Director, Supervision, and Executive Director of Board, Financial Conduct Authority, 2013–15; *b* Bath, 17 March 1956; *s* of David Adamson and Cynthia Adamson; *m* 1988, Barbara Elizabeth; two *s* one *d*. *Educ:* Trinity Hall, Cambridge (BA 1977). Asst Manager, Citibank, London, 1977–81; Sen. Vice Pres., and Hd, UK and N Europe Reg., Bank of America, London, 1981–97; Sen. Advr, 1997–2008, Dir, Supervision (formerly Major Retail Gps) Div., 2008–13, FSA. Non-executive Director: Prudential UK, 2015–; JP Morgan, 2015–. Gov., St Paul's Cathedral Sch., 2005–. *Recreations:* sailing, ski-ing, reading.

ADAMSON, Hamish Christopher, OBE 1996; Director (International), The Law Society, 1987–95; *b* 17 Sept. 1935; *s* of John Adamson, Perth, Scotland, and Denise Adamson (*née* Colman-Sadd). *Educ:* Stonyhurst Coll.; Lincoln Coll., Oxford (Schol.; MA Hons Jurisprudence). Solicitor (Hons). Law Society: Asst Sec., then Sen. Asst Sec. (Law Reform), 1966–81; Sec., Law Reform and Internat. Relations, 1981–87. Sec., UK Delegn, Council of the Bars and Law Socs of EC, 1981–95; Exec. Sec., Commonwealth Lawyers' Assoc., 1983–95. Chm., Trustee Cttee, Commonwealth Human Rights Initiative, 1993–95; Mem. Bd Trustees, Acad. of European Law, 1995–2003. Dir, Franco-British Lawyers' Soc., 1991–2009. *Publications:* The Solicitors Act 1974, 1975; Free Movement of Lawyers, 1992, 2nd edn 1998. *Recreations:* plants, books, travel. *Address:* 133 Hartington Road, SW8 2EY.

ADAMSON, Ian; *see* Adamson, S. I. G.

ADAMSON, Martin Gardiner, CA; Chairman, Associated British Foods, 2002–09 (non-executive Director, 1999–2009); *b* Shanghai, 14 Sept. 1939; *s* of Alan S. Adamson and Janet J. Adamson (*née* Gardiner); *m* 1964, Kathleen Jane Darby; two *s* one *d*. *Educ:* St Mary's Sch., Melrose; Sedbergh Sch. CA (with Dist.) 1962. Trained with Graham, Smart & Annan, Edinburgh, 1957–62; joined Thomson McLintock & Co., London, 1963: Partner, 1967; Staff Partner, i/c audit practice, 1970–83; Man. Partner, London Office, 1983–86, until merger with Peat Marwick Mitchell to form KPMG; mgt roles with KPMG, 1986–96, including: Partner i/c risk mgt; Mem. Bd. *Recreations:* gardening, golf, reading, theatre. *Clubs:* Caledonian, MCC; Royal Cinque Ports Golf; Wildernesse Golf (Sevenoaks); Tantallon Golf (N Berwick).

ADAMSON, Nicolas Clark, CVO 2008 (LVO 2002); OBE 1982; Private Secretary to the Duke and Duchess of Kent, 1993–2011; an Extra Equerry to the Duke of Kent, since 2011; *s* of Joseph Clark Adamson and Prudence Mary (*née* Paine); *m* 1971, Hilary Jane Edwards; two *d*. *Educ:* St Edward's Sch., Oxford; RAF Coll., Cranwell. Commnd RAF, 1959; served various fighter Sqdns, UK and ME, 1960–65; Flt Lieut 1962; Flying Instructor, 1965–67; ADC to Chief of Defence Staff, MoD, 1967–69; transferred to FCO, 1969 as First Sec.; served: Brussels (EC), 1972–75; Islamabad, 1979–82; Paris, 1985–90; Counsellor, FCO, 1990–92; attached CBI, 1992–93; retd from FCO, 1993. *Club:* Athenæum.

ADAMSON, (Samuel) Ian (Gamble), OBE 1998; medical practitioner; Member (UU), Belfast City Council, 1989–2011 (Lord Mayor of Belfast, 1996–97); *b* 28 June 1944; *s* of John Gamble Sloan Adamson and Jane (*née* Kerr); *m* 1998, Kerry Christian Carson. *Educ:* Bangor GS; Queen's Univ., Belfast (MB, BCh; BAO 1969). DCH RCSI 1974; DCH RCPSG 1974; MFCH 1988; FRSPH (FRIPHH 1998). Registrar in Paediatrics: Royal Belfast Hosp. for Sick Children, 1975–76; Ulster Hosp., Dundonald, 1976–77; specialist in community child health and travel medicine, N and W Belfast HSS Trust (formerly Community Unit of Mgt), 1981–2004. Mem. (UU) Belfast East, NI Assembly, 1998–2003. Chm., Farset Youth and Community Develt, 1988–90. Exec. Bd Mem., Assoc. of Port Health Authies, 2005–11 (Chairman: Border Inspection Post Cttee, 2005–06; Imported Food Cttee, 2006–11). First Pres., Ullans Acad., 1992–; Founder Rector, 1994, Chm., 1994–2004, Mem., Implementation Gp, 2005–, Ulster-Scots Acad.; Mem., Ulster-Scots Agency, 2003–; Chm., Grand Unionist Centenary Cttee, 2010–11; Founder Chairman: Somme Assoc., 1989–2015; Ulster-Scots Lang. Soc., 1992–2002 (Vice-Pres., 2002–); Founder Member: Cultural Traditions Gp, NI CRC, 1988; Ultach Trust, 1990; Pres., Belfast Civic Trust, 2001–; Convenor Gen., Posse Comitatus, 2011–. Historical Advr to Rev. Dr Ian R. K. Paisley, MP, now Rev. and Rt Hon. Lord Bannside, 2007–14; First Hon. Historian, UU Party, 2009–14. Librarian, OStJ Commandery of Ards, NI, 2014–. Patron, Dalaradia, 2014–. High Sheriff, Belfast, 2011. SBStJ 1998. Fluent in ten langs, incl. Lakota; holds Wisdom-Keeper status among Lakota (Sioux) nation. *Publications:* The Cruthin, 1974, 6th edn 2014; Bangor: light of the world, 1979, 3rd edn 2015; The Battle of Moira, 1980; The Identity of Ulster, 1982, 4th edn 1995; The Ulster People, 1991; 1690, William and the Boyne, 1995; Dalaradia: kingdom of the Cruthin, 1998; Stormont: the house on the hill, 2008; Bombs on Belfast: the Blitz 1941, 2011; The Old Testament in Scots, 2014. *Recreations:* oil painting, theatre, travel. *Address:* Marino Villa, 5 Marino Park, Holywood, Co. Down, N Ireland BT18 0AN. *T:* (028) 9042 1005. *Clubs:* Ulster Reform (Belfast); Clandeboye Golf.

ADCOCK, Christopher John; Chief Financial Officer, since 2003, and Member of Council, since 2007, Duchy of Lancaster; *b* Berlin, 7 Aug. 1962; *s* of late Col Alfred John Adcock, OBE and of Eileen Joan Adcock (*née* Linton); *m* 1990, Joanna Sarah Mackinder; one *s* one *d*. *Educ:* Wellington Coll., Berks; Exeter Coll., Oxford (BA 1984). ACA 1988. With Ernst & Whinney, 1984–89. *Recreations:* golf, running, tennis, ski-ing. *Address:* Duchy of Lancaster Office, 1 Lancaster Place, WC2E 7ED. *T:* (020) 7269 1700. *Club:* East Berkshire Golf.

ADCOCK, Fleur, CNZM 2008; OBE 1996; FRSL; poet; *b* 10 Feb. 1934; *d* of Cyril John Adcock and Irene Adcock (*née* Robinson); *m* 1952, Alistair Teariki Campbell (marr. diss. 1958); two *s*. *Educ:* numerous schs in England and NZ; Victoria Univ., Wellington, NZ (MA 1st cl. Hons (Classics) 1956). Worked in libraries, NZ, 1959–62; settled in England, 1963; asst librarian, FCO, 1963–79. Arts Council Writing Fellow, Charlotte Mason Coll. of Educn, Ambleside, 1977–78; Northern Arts Fellow in Lit., Univs of Newcastle upon Tyne and Durham, 1979–81; Eastern Arts Fellow, UEA, 1984. FRSL 1984. Awards include: Cholmondeley, Soc. of Authors, 1976; NZ Nat. Book Award, 1984; Queen's Gold Medal for Poetry, 2006. *Publications:* The Eye of the Hurricane, 1964; Tigers, 1967; High Tide in the Garden, 1971; The Scenic Route, 1974; The Inner Harbour, 1979; (ed) The Oxford Book of Contemporary NZ Poetry, 1982; Selected Poems, 1983; (trans.) The Virgin and the Nightingale: medieval Latin poems, 1983; The Incident Book, 1986; (ed) The Faber Book of 20th Century Women's Poetry, 1987; (trans.) Orient Express: poems by Grete Tartler, 1989; Time Zones, 1991; (trans.) Letters from Darkness: poems by Daniela Crasnaru, 1991; (ed and trans.) Hugh Primas and the Archpoet, 1994; (ed jtly) The Oxford Book of Creatures, 1995; Looking Back, 1997; Poems 1960–2000, 2000; Dragon Talk, 2010; Glass Wings, 2013. *Recreation:* genealogy. *Address:* 14 Lincoln Road, N2 9DL. *T:* (020) 8444 7881.

ADDERLEY, family name of **Baron Norton**.

ADDERLEY, Mark David; Director of Human Resources, Heriot-Watt University, since 2011; *b* 15 Jan. 1965; *s* of David Adderley and Gill Adderley (now Boden); *m* 1989, Miranda Jones; four *d*. *Educ:* King Edward's Sch., Birmingham; Emmanuel Coll., Cambridge (BA 1987; MEng 1988); London Business Sch. (MBA 1999). Analyst, then Sen. Analyst, Associate, then Sen. Associate, Gemini Consulting, 1988–94; Head of Ops, then Sen. Manager Group Integration, Royal Bank of Scotland, 1994–2002; Dir, Scottish Water, 2002–07; Chief Exec., Nat. Trust for Scotland, 2007–08; Dir, Adderley Associates Ltd, 2008–11; Exec. Dir, People and Orgnl Develt, NHS Ayrshire and Arran, 2009–11. Director: Quality Scotland, 2003–07; Scottish Bible Soc., 2012–; Social Investment Scotland, 2013–; Scottish Squash and Rocketball Ltd, 2013–. FCIPD 2011; CDir 2011; FInstD 2012. *Recreations:* family, outdoor activity, sport, keeping track of five girls. *Address:* 18 Murrayfield Gardens, Edinburgh EH12 6DF.

ADDINGTON, family name of **Viscount Sidmouth**.

ADDINGTON, 6th Baron *cr* 1887; **Dominic Bryce Hubbard;** *b* 24 Aug. 1963; *s* of 5th Baron Addington and of Alexandra Patricia, *yr d* of late Norman Ford Millar; *S* father, 1982; *m* 1999, (Elizabeth) Ann Morris; one *d*. *Educ:* Aberdeen Univ. (MA Hons). Lib Dem spokesman on disability and on sport, H of L; elected Mem., H of L, 1999. Vice President: British Dyslexia Assoc.; Adult Dyslexia Orgn; UK Sport Assoc. for People with Learning Disability; Lonsdale Sporting Club; Lakenham Hewett RFC. *Recreation:* Rugby football. *Heir:* *b* Hon. Michael Walter Leslie Hubbard [*b* 6 July 1965; *m* 1999, Emmanuella Ononye]. *Address:* House of Lords, SW1A 0PW.

ADDIS, Richard James; Editor-in-Chief, Europe, Newsweek, since 2014; Founder and Editor-in-Chief, since 2010, and Chairman, since 2014, The Day; *b* 23 Aug. 1956; *s* of Richard Thomas Addis and Jane Addis; *m* 1983, Eunice Minogue (marr. diss. 2000); one *s* two *d*; partner, Helen Slater; two *s*. *Educ:* West Downs Prep. Sch.; Rugby; Downing Coll., Cambridge (MA). Evening Standard, 1985–89; Dep. Editor, Sunday Telegraph, 1989–91; Exec. Editor, Daily Mail, 1991–95; Editor, The Express, 1995–98; Consultant Editor, Mail on Sunday, 1998–99; Editor, The Globe and Mail, Toronto, 1999–2002; Asst Editor, Financial Times, 2002–06; Founder and Man. Partner, Shakeup Media, 2006–10; Man. Dir, The Day, 2010–14. *Recreations:* tennis, flute, cycling, skipping, herb-surfing, dendron-leaping, portacenare. *Clubs:* Boodle's, Garrick, Academy.

ADDISON, family name of **Viscount Addison**.

ADDISON, 4th Viscount *cr* 1945, of Stallingborough; **William Matthew Wand Addison;** Baron Addison 1937; consultant, environmental impact assessment, 2002–09; *b* 13 June 1945; *s* of 3rd Viscount Addison and Kathleen Amy, *d* of Rt Rev. and Rt Hon. J. W. C. Wand, PC, KCVO; *S* father, 1992; *m* 1st, 1970, Joanna Mary (marr. diss. 1990), *e d* of late J. I. C. Dickinson; one *s* two *d*; 2nd, 1991, Lesley Ann, *d* of George Colin Mawer. *Educ:* Westminster; King's Sch., Bruton; Essex Inst. of Agriculture. Chm., DCL Telecommunications, 1997–99; Dir, Commensus, 1999–2002. Mem., Cttee on Jt Statutory Instruments, 1993–99. Vice President: Council for Nat. Parks, 1994–; British Trust for Conservation Volunteers, 1996–2006. Pres., Motor Activities Trng Council, 1996–2009. *Heir:* *s* Hon. Paul Wand Addison, *b* 18 March 1973.

ADDISON, Lynda Helen, OBE 2007; freelance consultant, 2011–14; Director, Malcolm Baker Consulting Ltd, since 2014; Managing Director, Addison & Associates, 1996–2011; *b* Manchester, 2 Dec. 1945; *d* of Cyril Shepley and Kathleen Shepley; *m* 1973, Alan Addison (marr. diss. 1998); one *s* one *d*; *m* 2014, Malcolm Baker. *Educ:* Gainsborough High Sch. for Girls; Portsmouth Poly. (BSc Geog. 1967); Central London Poly. (DipTP 1972). Asst Bor. Planner, Southwark LBC, 1978–83; Controller, Planning, Harrow LBC, 1983–87; Dir, Planning, 1987–91, Dir, Planning and Transport, 1991–95, Hounslow LBC. Historic England (formerly English Heritage): Comr, 2008–; Chm., London Adv. Cttee, 2011–. Dir, Paddington Business Improvement District, 2005–13. Trustee: TCPA, 2004–; Living Streets, 2009–; Mem. Council, Nat. Infrastructure Planning Assoc., 2011–; Chm., Sustainable Transport Panel, Chartered Instn of Highways and Transportation, 2012–. Vis. Prof., Univ. of Westminster, 2008–. Academician, Acad. of Urbanism, 2009. FRSA 1992; FCIHT 2012. *Publications:* best practice guidance and research reports for DfT and DCLG; various articles in professional jls. *Recreations:* family, theatre, opera, walking, ski-ing, sailing. *E:* lynda@lynda-addison.co.uk. *T:* (020) 7087 4123.

ADDISON, Mark Eric, CB 2005; Director General, Department for Environment, Food and Rural Affairs, 2001–06; *b* 22 Jan. 1951; *s* of Sydney Robert James Addison and Prudence Margaret Addison (*née* Russell); *m* 1987, Lucinda Clare Booth. *Educ:* Marlborough Coll.; St John's Coll., Cambridge (BA, MA); City Univ. (MBA); Imperial Coll. (DIC, PhD). Department of Employment, 1978–95: Private Sec. to Parly Under-Sec. of State, 1982; Private Sec. to Prime Minister (Home Affairs, then Parly Affairs), 1985–88; Regl Dir for London, Training Agency, 1988–91; Dir, Finance and Resource Management, 1991–94; DoE, 1995–97; Dir, Safety Policy, HSE, 1994–97; Dir, Better Regulation Unit, OPS, 1997–98; Chief Exec., Crown Prosecution Service, 1998–2001. A Civil Service Comr, 2007–12; Public Appts Assessor, 2012–. Mem., Adv. Cttee on Business Appts, 2012–. Chm., Nursing and Midwifery Council, 2012–14. Non-executive Director: Salix Finance Ltd, 2006–11; National Archives, 2007–12. Mem., Council, Which?, 2010–. *Recreations:* classic motorbikes, gardening, photography. *E:* mark@addisonbooth.com.

ADDISON, His Honour Michael Francis; a Circuit Judge, 1987–2014; *b* 14 Sept. 1942; *s* of late Joseph Addison and Wendy Blyth Addison; *m* 1979, Rosemary Hardy (*d* 1994); one *s*; *m* 1998, Lucy Carter; one *s* one *d*. *Educ:* Eton; Trinity College, Cambridge (BA). Called to the Bar, Inner Temple, 1965. *Recreation:* gardening.

ADDYMAN, Peter Vincent, CBE 2000; FSA; Director, York Archaeological Trust, 1972–2002; *b* 12 July 1939; *y s* of Erik Thomas Waterhouse Addyman and Evelyn Mary (*née* Fisher); *m* 1965, Shelton (*née* Oliver), Atlanta, Ga; one *s* one *d*. *Educ:* Sedbergh Sch.; Peterhouse, Cambridge (MA). MCIfA (MIFA 1982); FSA 1967. Asst Lectr in Archaeology, 1962–64, Lectr, 1964–67, QUB; Lectr in Archaeol., Univ. of Southampton, 1967–72. Hon. Fellow, Univ. of York, 1972; Hon. Reader, Univ. of Bradford, 1974–81. Directed excavations: Maxey, 1960; Lydford, 1964–67; Ludgershall Castle, 1964–72; Chalton, 1970–72. Vice-President: Council for British Archaeol., 1981–85 (Pres., 1992–95); Royal Archaeol. Inst., 1979–83; Chairman: Standing Conf. of Archaeol Unit Managers, 1975–78; Inst. of Field Archaeologists, 1983–85; Standing Conf. on Portable Antiquities, 1995–2005; Standing Conf. on London Archaeology, 2005–07; Yorks Dales Landscape Res. Trust, 2006–; Malton Museum Foundn, 2012–; York Civic Trust, 2012–; Member: RCHME, 1997–99; Ancient Monuments Adv. Cttee, 1998–2001, Places of Worship Panel, 2001–04, English Heritage. Chm., Cultural Resource Management Ltd, 1989–95 (Dir, 1979–95); Academic Director, Heritage Projects Ltd, 1984–2007; Dir, Continuum Gp Ltd, 2007–; Jt Instigator, Jorvik Viking Centre, York. President: Yorks Archaeol Soc., 1999–2005; Yorks Philosophical Soc., 1999–2013. Trustee, Nat. Coal Mining Mus., 1995–2002. Gov., Co. of Merchant Adventurers of York, 2006–07. Hon. Freeman, City of York, 2008. Honorary Professor: Univ. of Bradford, 1998; Univ. of York, 1998. Hon. DSc Bradford, 1984; DUniv York, 1985. Comdr, Royal Norwegian Order of Merit, 2004. *Publications:* (gen. editor) The Archaeology of York, vols 1–20, 1976–2002; (ed with V. E. Black) Archaeological Papers from York, 1984; papers in archaeol jls. *Recreations:* gardening, watercolours, travel. *Address:* 15 St Mary's, York YO30 7DD. *T:* (01904) 624311. *Club:* Athenæum.

ADEAGBO, Dr Ade; Chairman, Non-executive Directors Network, since 2009, and Treasurer, since 2010, NHS Alliance; *b* Nigeria, 9 Nov. 1960; *s* of Joseph and Christiana Adeagbo; *m* 1992, Ibironke Bawala; one *s* three *d*. *Educ:* Ogun State Univ., Nigeria (BA

Philosophy); Thames Valley Univ. (MBA 1998); Bournemouth Univ. (DBA 2008). Admin Manager, London Bor. of Southwark, 1992–96; Retail Manager, Shell UK, 1996–2001; Res., Systems and Admin Manager, Help the Aged, 2001–03; Chief Exec., Age Concern Bexley, 2003–07; Ops Dir, Mission Care, 2007–08; Dir, Organisational Develt, and Interim CEO, National Voices, 2008–09; Interim CEO, African Health Policy Network, 2009–11; Interim Dir, African Diaspora Youth Network in Europe, 2011–12. Chair, Community Alliance, 2009–11. Non-exec. Dir and Chm., Audit Cttee, NHS Greenwich, 2001–11. Dir, Nest Exchange, 2010–. Chm., EU Community Health Orgns, Netherlands, 2010–. Fellow and Mem., Coll. of Medicine, 2010–. *Address:* 28 Birkdale Road, Abbey Wood, SE2 9HX. *T:* (020) 8311 2207. *E:* dr.adeagbo@gmail.com.

ADEBAYO, Oludiran Oludele Abimbola, (Diran), FRSL; writer, novelist, academic; *b* London, 30 Aug. 1968; *s* of Dr Solomon Layi Adebayo and Phebean Olufunke Adebayo (*née* Agbe). *Educ:* Malvern Coll., Worcs (Major Schol.); Wadham Coll., Oxford (BA Hons Law 1989; MA). Reporter, then Chief News Reporter, The Voice, 1989–91; Reporter/Researcher, BBC TV, 1991–93; Sen. Researcher, LWT, 1994–95; Lectr (pt-time) in English and Creative Writing, Lancaster Univ., 2009–12. Fellow, Santa Maddalena Foundn, 2002; Internat. Writing Fellow, Southampton Univ., 2006–07; Royal Literary Fund Fellow, London Coll. of Fashion, 2012–14. Dir, Book Trust, 2000–04; Trustee, Nat. Council, Arts Council of England, 2004–10. FRSL 2006. *Publications:* Some Kind of Black, 1996; My Once Upon A Time, 2000; (ed jtly) New Writing, 2003. *Recreations:* music, sports, cricket history, general knowledge.

ADEBOWALE, Baron *cr* 2001 (Life Peer), of Thornes in the County of West Yorkshire; **Victor Olufemi Adebowale,** CBE 2000; Chief Executive Officer, Turning Point, since 2001; *b* 21 July 1962; *s* of Ezekiel Adebowale and Grace Adebowale. *Educ:* Thornes House Sch., Wakefield; Poly. of E London; City Univ. (MA Adv. Organisational Consulting 2008); Tavistock Inst., London (Dip. Adv. Organisational Consulting 2008). London Borough of Newham: Private Sector Repairs Administrator and Estate Officer, 1983–84; Sen. Estate Manager, 1984–86; Perm. Property Manager, Patchwork Community Housing Assoc., 1986–88; Regl Dir, Ujima Housing Assoc., 1988–90; Dir, Alcohol Recovery Project, 1990–95; Chief Exec., Centrepoint, 1995–2001. Dir, Leadership in Mind Ltd, 2006–; non-executive Director: Three Sixty Action Ltd, 2011–; Mem. Bd, THP Innovate, 2012–. Member: Nat. Council, NFHA, 1991; Adv. Gp, New Deal Task Force, 1997–; Nat. Employment Panel, 2000–; Mental Health Task Force; UK Commn for Employment and Skills, 2009–; Adv. Council on Misuse of Drugs; Locality; NHS Commng Bd. Mem. Council, Inst. for Fiscal Studies. Chair, Collaborate CIC, London South Bank Univ., 2012–; Member, Board: English Touring Theatre; Urban Development. Director: Leadership in Mind, 2005–; 360; THP. Fellow, Sunningdale Inst. Mem. Bd Trustees, New Economics Foundn, 2006–07. Patron, British Nursing Council on Alcohol. Chancellor, Lincoln Univ., 2008– (Hon. Vis. Prof., 2007–). DUniv UCE, 2001; Hon. Dr UEL. *Recreations:* poetry writing, kite flying, music, playing the saxophone. *Address:* Turning Point, Standon House, 21 Mansell Street, E1 8AA. *T:* (020) 7481 7600.

See also M. Adebowale.

ADEBOWALE, Maria; Director, Living Space Project, since 2013; *b* 1968; *d* of Ezekiel Adebowale and Grace Olurin Adebowale; *m* 2002, Christoph Schwarte; one *s* one *d*. *Educ:* Lancaster Univ. (BA Hons Orgn Studies and Business Law); Huddersfield Poly. (Postgrad. Dip. Law); SOAS, London Univ. (LLM Public Internat. Law). Prog. Asst, Climate Change and Trade, Foundn for Internat. Envmtl Law and Develt, 1994–98; Public Law Tutor, SOAS, 1996–97; Director: Envmtl Law Foundn, 1998–2001; Capacity Global, 2001–13; Shared Assets, 2012. Mem., UK Sustainable Develt Commn, 2000–03 (Chair, World Summit for Sustainable Develt Wkg Gp, 2002); Comr, English Heritage, 2003–11; London Leader, London Sustainable Develt Commn, 2011–. Mem., Adv. Gp, Artist Project Earth, 2011–. Chair, Waterwise, 2005–09. Trustee: Allavida, 2006–09; Conservation Volunteers, 2013–; Matron, Women's Envmtl Network, 2006–; Patron, UK Envmtl Law Assoc., 2011–. Clore Social Leadership Fellow (Envmt), 2013–. FRSA 2001. *Publications:* contribs to acad. and non-acad. pubns on urban place making and green spaces, envmtl justice, and inclusive participation. *Recreations:* arguing about politics with my husband, collecting and reading knackered old Penguin paperback books, watching my daughter and son play. *Address:* Living Space Project, The Hub Kings Cross, 34b York Way, N1 9AB. *T:* (020) 8938 3210. *E:* hello@livingspaceproject.com.

See also Baron Adebowale.

ADEKUNLE, Rev. Elizabeth; Chaplain, St John's College, Cambridge, until April 2016; Archdeacon of Hackney (with title Ven.), from April 2016; *b* N London. *Educ:* Birmingham Univ. (BTh); Sch. of Oriental and African Studies, Univ. of London (MA African Christianity and Develt); Ridley Hall, Cambridge (MA Pastoral Care and Counselling). Curate, later Priest-in-charge, St Luke's Church, Homerton, 2007–11. Chaplain: St Mellitus Theol Coll., London; Homerton Hosp., Hackney. Mem., Archbishops' Task Gp on Evangelism. *Address:* (until April 2016) St John's College, Cambridge CB2 1TP.

ADELAIDE, Archbishop of, since 2005; **Most Rev. Jeffrey William Driver,** PhD; Metropolitan of South Australia, since 2005; *b* 6 Oct. 1951; *s* of Ernest Leslie Driver and Joyce Mary Driver; *m* 1978, Lindy Mary Muffet; one *s* one *d*. *Educ:* Aust. Coll. of Theol. (ThL 1977, ThSchol 1983); Sydney Coll. of Divinity (MTh 1991); Charles Sturt Univ. (PhD 2008). Newspaper journalist, 1970–74. Ordained deacon, 1977, priest, 1978; Asst Curate, dio. Bathurst, 1977–80; Rector: Mid-Richmond, 1980–84; Jamison, ACT, 1984–89; Archdeacon, Young, NSW, 1989–95; Exec. Dir, St Mark's Nat. Theol Centre, 1995–97; Head, Sch. of Theol., Charles Sturt Univ., 1996–97; Diocesan Archdeacon, Canberra, and Rector of Manuka, 1997–2001; Bishop of Gippsland, 2001–05. *Publications:* A Polity of Persuasion: gift and grief of Anglicanism, 2014; various articles and reviews in St Mark's Review. *Recreations:* fly-fishing, gardening. *Address:* Bishop's Court, 45 Palmer Place, North Adelaide, SA 5006, Australia.

ADELAIDE, Archbishop of, (RC), since 2001; **Most Rev. Philip Edward Wilson,** DD; *b* 2 Oct. 1950; *s* of John and Joan Wilson. *Educ:* St Joseph's Coll., Hunters Hill, NSW; St Columba's Coll., Springwood; St Patrick's Coll., Manly; Catholic Inst. of Sydney (BTh 1974); JCL 1992, DD 1996, Catholic Univ. of America, Washington. Ordained priest, 1975; Asst Priest, E Maitland, 1975–77; studied RE, NY, 1977–78; Maitland Diocese: Dir of RE, 1978–80; Bishop's Sec. and Master of Ceremonies, 1980–83; Parish Priest, 1983–87; VG, Diocesan Management and Admin, 1987–90; Dir of Tribunal, 1993–94; Bp of Wollongong, 1996–2000; Coadjutor Archbp of Adelaide, 2000–01. Australian Catholic Bishops' Conference: Pres., 2006–12; Vice Pres., 2012–; Chm., Justice, Ecol. and Develt Commn, 2012–; Mem., Canon Law Commn, 2012–. Co-Chm., Nat. Professional Standards Cttee, 2003–. Chairman: Catholic Earthcare Australia, 2012–; Caritas Australia, 2012–. Hon. DLitt Newcastle, 2003. Prelate of Honour, 1995. *Address:* 39 Wakefield Street, Adelaide, SA 5000, Australia. *T:* (8) 82108108, *Fax:* (8) 82232307.

ADER, Peter Charles; His Honour Judge Ader; a Circuit Judge, since 1999; *b* 14 May 1950; *s* of late Max Ader and Inge Ader (*née* Nord); *m* 1979, Margaret Taylor (marr. diss. 2005); one *s* two *d*. *Educ:* Highgate Sch.; Southampton Univ. (LLB). Called to the Bar, Middle Temple, 1973; a Recorder, 1995–99. *Recreations:* squash, tennis, golf, ski-ing, travel. *Address:* 3 Temple Gardens, Temple, EC4Y 9AU. *T:* (020) 7353 3102.

ADERIN-POCOCK, Dr Margaret Ebunoluwa, MBE 2009; Managing Director, Science Innovation Ltd, since 2004; *b* London, 9 March 1968; *d* of Justus Adebayo Aderin and Caroline Philips; *m* 2002, Dr Martin Pocock; one *d*. *Educ:* La Sainte Union Convent Sch.; Imperial Coll. London (BSc Phys; PhD Mech. Engrg 1994). System Scientist, 1996–97, Project Manager, 1997–99, DERA; Project and Engrg Manager, UCL, 1999–2004; Sen. Project Manager, Surrey Satellite Technol. Ltd, 2004–06; Sen. Res. Fellow, UCL, 2006–; Optical Instrumentation Manager UK, Astrium Ltd, 2006–10. Television and radio presenter, incl. BBC TV: Do We Really Need the Moon?, 2011; In Orbit: How Satellites Rule Our Lives, 2012; CBeebies Stargazing, 2014; The Sky at Night (series), 2014–. *Recreations:* star gazing, travel, cinema, cooking, art, photography. *E:* m.aderin@science-innovation.com.

ADÈS, Prof. (Josephine) Dawn, CBE 2013 (OBE 2002); FBA 1996; Professor of Art History and Theory, University of Essex, since 1989; *b* 6 May 1943; *d* of A. E. Tylden-Pattenson, CSI; *m* 1966, Timothy Raymond Adès; three *s*. *Educ:* St Hilda's Coll., Oxford (BA 1965); MA London 1968. Essex University: Lectr, 1971–85; Sen. Lectr, 1985–88; Reader, 1988–89; Head of Dept of Art History and Theory, 1989–92. Prof. of History of Art, Royal Acad., 2009–; Slade Prof. of the History of Art, Oxford Univ., 2010. Trustee: Tate Gall., 1995–2005; Nat. Gall., 1998–2005; Elephant Trust, 2000–; Henry Moore Foundn, 2003–13. *Publications:* Dada and Surrealism Reviewed, 1978; Salvador Dali, 1982, 2nd edn 1995; (jtly) The Twentieth Century Poster: design of the avant garde, 1984; (jtly) Francis Bacon, 1985; Photomontage, 1986; Art in Latin America: the modern era 1820–1980, 1989; Andre Masson, 1994; Figures and Likenesses: the paintings of Siron Franco, 1995; Surrealist Art: the Bergman Collection in the Art Institute of Chicago, 1997; (jtly) Marcel Duchamp, 1999; Salvador Dali's Optical Illusions, 2000; Dali: centenary retrospective, 2004; (jtly) Undercover Surrealism: Georges Bataille and Documents, 2006; (jtly) Close-Up, 2008; The Colour of My Dreams: the Surrealist revolution in art, 2011; Selected Writings, 2015. *Address:* Department of Art History and Theory, Essex University, Wivenhoe Park, Colchester, Essex CO4 3SQ.

See also T. J. E. Adès.

ADÈS, Thomas Joseph Edmund; composer, pianist and conductor; *b* 1 March 1971; *s* of Timothy Adès and Prof. Dawn Adès, *qv*. *Educ:* University Coll. Sch.; Guildhall Sch. of Music and Drama; King's Coll., Cambridge (MA); St John's Coll., Cambridge (MPhil; Hon. Fellow, 2013). Composer in Association, Hallé Orch., 1993–95; Lectr, Univ. of Manchester, 1993–94; Fellow Commoner in Creative Arts, Trinity Coll., Cambridge, 1995–97; Benjamin Britten Prof. of Music, RAM, 1997–2000; Musical Dir, Birmingham Contemporary Music Gp, 1998–2000; Artistic Dir, Aldeburgh Fest., 1999–2008. *Principal compositions:* Five Eliot Landscapes, 1990; Chamber Symphony, 1990; Catch, 1991; Darknesse Visible, 1992; Still Sorrowing, 1993; Life Story, 1993; Living Toys, 1993; … but all shall be well, 1993; Sonata da Caccia, 1993; Arcadiana (for string quartet), 1994; Powder Her Face (Chamber opera), 1995; Traced Overhead, 1996; These Premises are Alarmed, 1996; Asyla, 1997 (Grawemeyer Award for Music Composition, 2000); Concerto Conciso, 1997–98; America (A Prophecy), 1999; Piano Quintet, 2000; Brahms, 2001; The Tempest (opera), 2003; Violin Concerto, 2005; Tevót, 2007; Dances from Powder Her Face, 2007; In Seven Days, 2008; Concert Paraphrase on Powder Her Face, 2009; Lieux retrouvés, 2009; Three Mazurkas, 2010; Polaris, 2010; The Four Quarters, 2010; Totentanz (song-cycle), 2013. Works performed at numerous festivals incl. Musica Nova, Helsinki, 1999; Salzburg Easter Fest., 2004; Présences, Radio France, 2007; Traced Overhead, Barbican, 2007; Tonsattarfestival, Stockholm, 2009; Composer in Focus, Melbourne, 2010; Aspects of Adès, LA, 2011; Portrait at Gulbenkian, Lisbon, 2012. *Address:* c/o Faber Music, Bloomsbury House, 74–77 Great Russell Street, WC1B 3DA. *T:* (020) 7908 5310, *Fax:* (020) 7908 5339. *Club:* Black's.

ADEY, John Fuller; company director; Chief Executive, National Blood Authority, 1993–98; *b* 12 May 1941; *s* of Frank Douglas Adey and Doreen Adey (*née* Fuller); *m* 1965, Marianne Alyce Banning; two *s* two *d*. *Educ:* Glyn GS, Epsom; St Edmund Hall, Oxford (MA); Harvard Univ. (MBA). CEng 1970; MIMechE 1970; MIEE 1976. Graduate Trainee, AEI Ltd, 1963–65; Design Engineer: Montreal Engrg, 1965–67; Nat. Steel & Shipbuilding, San Diego, 1967–70; various positions, Raychem Ltd, 1972–83; Chief Exec., Chemicals and Plastics, Courtaulds, 1983–86; Man. Dir, Baxter Healthcare, 1986–93. Director: API, 1987–97; Seton Healthcare Gp, 1996–98; non-executive Chairman: Adams Healthcare, 1999–2000; Medical Engineering Investments, 2003–05; non-executive Director: Swindon and Marlborough NHS Trust, 2002–06; New Horizons Ltd, 2005–08. Chm., Aldbourne Nursing Home, 2000–. A Gen. Comr of Income Tax, 1985–2009. Trustee, Royal Merchant Navy Sch. Foundn, 1999– (Chm., 2002–); Gov., John O'Gaunt Sch., Hungerford, 2000 (Chm. Govs, 2001–12). Treas., St Michael's Ch, Aldbourne, 2006–14. *Recreations:* tennis, tinkering with old cars, village life. *Address:* The Old Malt House, Aldbourne, Marlborough, Wilts SN8 2DW.

ADIE, Kathryn, (Kate), OBE 1993; DL; author and freelance broadcaster; Presenter, From Our Own Correspondent, BBC Radio 4, since 1998; *b* 19 Sept. 1945; *d* of Babe Dunnet (*née* Issitt), and adopted *d* of late John Wilfrid Adie and Maud Adie (*née* Fambely). *Educ:* Sunderland Church High Sch.; Newcastle Univ. (BA Hons Scandinavian Studies). FJI 1990. Technician and Producer, BBC Radio, 1969–76; Reporter, BBC TV South, 1977–78; Reporter, TV News, 1979–81, Correspondent, 1982; Chief News Correspondent, BBC TV, 1989–2003. Trustee: Imperial War Mus., 1998–2007; Services Sound and Vision Corp., 2004–11. Mem., First World War Centenary Adv. Gp, 2014–. Hon. Prof., Broadcasting and Journalism, Univ. of Sunderland, 1995. Freeman, City of London, 1995; Liveryman, Glaziers' Co., 1996. DL Dorset, 2013. Hon. Freeman, Borough of Sunderland, 1989. Hon. Fellow: Royal Holloway, London Univ., 1996; Univ. of Central Lancs, 2002; Cardiff Univ., 2004; York St John UC, 2006. Hon. MA: Bath, 1987; Newcastle upon Tyne, 1990; MUniv Open, 1996; Hon. DLitt: City, 1989; Loughborough, 1991; Sunderland, 1993; Robert Gordon, 1996; Nottingham, 1998; Nottingham Trent, 1998; Plymouth, 2013; Queen Margaret, 2014; DUniv: Anglia Polytechnic Univ., 1999; Oxford Brookes, 2002; Hon. DLaws: St Andrews, 2010; Bristol, 2012. RTS News Award, 1981 and 1987, Judges' Award, 1989; Monte Carlo Internat. TV News Award, 1981 and 1990; BAFTA Richard Dimbleby Award, 1989. *Publications:* The Kindness of Strangers (memoirs), 2002; Corsets to Camouflage: women and war, 2003; Nobody's Child: the lives of abandoned children, 2005; Into Danger, 2008; Fighting on the Home Front: the legacy of women in World War One, 2013. *Address:* c/o PO Box 317, Brentford TW8 8WX. *E:* louisegreenberg@msn.com.

ADIE, Rt Rev. Michael Edgar, CBE 1994; Bishop of Guildford, 1983–94; *b* 22 Nov. 1929; *s* of Walter Granville Adie and Kate Emily Adie (*née* Parrish); *m* 1957, Anne Devonald Roynon; one *s* three *d*. *Educ:* Westminster School; St John's Coll., Oxford (MA). Assistant Curate, St Luke, Pallion, Sunderland, 1954–57; Resident Chaplain to the Archbishop of Canterbury, 1957–60; Vicar of St Mark, Sheffield, 1960–69; Rural Dean of Hallam, 1966–69; Rector of Louth, 1969–76; Vicar of Morton with Hacconby, 1976–83; Archdeacon of Lincoln, 1977–83. Chm., Gen. Synod Bd of Education and of National Soc., 1989–94. DUniv Surrey, 1995. *Publications:* Held Together: an exploration of coherence, 1997. *Recreations:* gardening, walking. *Address:* 4 Lochnager Way, Ballater, Aberdeenshire AB35 5PB.

ADIE, Susan Myraid; *see* Sinclair, S. M.

ADJAYE, David, OBE 2007; Founder, and Principal Architect, Adjaye Associates, since 2000; *b* 22 Sept. 1966; *s* of Affram Adjaye and Cecilia Affram-Adjaye. *Educ:* South Bank Univ. (BA Hons Arch. 1990; RIBA Pt 1); Royal Coll. of Art, London (MA Arch. 1993; Sen. Fellow 2007). RIBA 1998. *Building projects* include: Nobel Peace Center, Oslo, 2005; Idea Store

Whitechapel, London, 2005 (Inclusive Design Award, RIBA, 2006); Bernie Grant Centre, Stephen Lawrence Centre and Rivington Place, London, 2007 (London Award, RIBA, 2008); Mus. of Contemporary Art, Denver, 2007 (Internat. Award, RIBA, 2008); Moscow Sch. of Mgt, Skolkovo, 2010. Advr, Thames Gateway Design Panel, 2004. Mem. Bd, Greenwich Dance Agency, 2004–; Trustee: Architectl Educn Trust; South London Gall., 2003–; V&A Mus., 2008–10. Hon. Dr Arts UEL, 2007. W. E. B. Du Bois Medal, Harvard Univ., 2014. *Publications:* (ed Peter Allison) David Adjaye Houses: recycling, reconfiguring, rebuilding, 2005; (ed Peter Allison) David Adjaye: making public buildings, 2006; contribs to jls incl. Frame, Domus, RIBA Jl, Architects Jl, Archithese, Architectural Record, A+U, El Croquis. *Address:* Adjaye Associates, Edison House, 223–231 Old Marylebone Road, NW1 5QT. *E:* info@adjaye.com. *Club:* Shoreditch House.

ADKIN, Jonathan William; QC 2013; *b* Leicester, 2 March 1973; *s* of David and Prudence Adkin; *m* 2010, Ruth. *Educ:* Loughborough Grammar Sch.; Balliol Coll., Oxford (MA). Called to the Bar, Gray's Inn, 1997; in practice as barrister, 1997–. *Recreations:* riding, walking. *Address:* Serle Court, 6 New Square, Lincoln's Inn, WC2A 3QS. *T:* (020) 7242 6105, *Fax:* (020) 7405 4004.

ADKINS, Richard David; QC 1995; *b* 21 Oct. 1954; *s* of late Walter David Adkins and Patricia (*née* Chimes); *m* 1977, Jane Margaret, *d* of late Derek and of Ella Sparrow; two *s* one *d*. *Educ:* Leamington Coll. for Boys; Hertford Coll., Oxford (MA). Admitted as solicitor, 1978; called to the Bar, Middle Temple, 1982. Cttee Mem., Chancery Bar Assoc., 1991–93. *Publications:* Encyclopaedia of Forms and Precedents, Vol. 3: Arrangements with Creditors, 1985; Company Receivers: a new status?, 1988; contrib. Gore Browne on Companies, 50th edn, 1992–2008. *Recreation:* opera. *Address:* 3–4 South Square, Gray's Inn, WC1R 5HP. *T:* (020) 7696 9900.

ADLER, Prof. Jeremy David, PhD; Professor of German, 1994–2003, Visiting Professor, 2003–05, Emeritus Professor and Senior Research Fellow, Department of German, since 2005, King's College London; *b* 1 Oct. 1947; *s* of H. G. and Bettina Adler; *m* 1983, Eva Mikulašová. *Educ:* St Marylebone GS; Queen Mary Coll., Univ. of London (BA 1st cl. Hons 1969); Westfield Coll., Univ. of London (PhD 1977). Lectr in German, Westfield Coll., 1970–89; Queen Mary and Westfield College, London: Reader, 1989–91; Prof. of German, 1991–94; Founding Chm., Centre for Modern European Studies, 1990–94. Mem., Council, 1997–99, Senate, 2000–01, London Univ. Mem. Council, Poetry Soc., 1973–77; Jt Hon. Sec., English Goethe Soc., 1987–2004; Member: Bielefeld Colloquium für Neue Poesie, 1979–2002; Council, Goethe Ges., Weimar, 1995–2003; Res. Cttee, Freies Deutsches Hochstift, 2003–; Editl Bd, Central Europe, 2003–; Res. Gp on Prague and Dublin Lit., Osaka, 2006–. Chm., M. L. v. Motesiczky Trust, 1997–2006. Schol., Herzog August Bibliothek, Wolfenbüttel, 1979; Fellow, Inst. of Advanced Study, Berlin, 1985–86, 2012. Corresp. Mem., German Acad. of Lang. and Lit., 2005. Goethe Prize, English Goethe Soc., 1977. *Publications:* (ed with J. J. White) August Stramm: Kritische Essays und unveröffentlichtes Quellenmaterial aus dem Nachlass des Dichters, 1979; (ed) Allegorie und Eros: Texte von und über Albert Paris Gütersloh, 1986; Eine fast magische Anziehungskraft: Goethes Wahlverwandtschaften und die Chemie seiner Zeit, 1987; (with Ulrich Ernst) Text als Figur: Visuelle Poesie von der Antike bis zur Moderne, 1987, 3rd edn 1990; (ed) August Stramm: Die Dichtungen, Sämtliche Gedichte, Dramen, Prosa, 1990; (ed) August Stramm: Alles ist Gedicht: Briefe, Gedichte, Bilder, Dokumente, 1990; (ed) Friedrich Hölderlin: Poems and Fragments, 1998; (ed) H. G. Adler: Der Wahrheit verpflichtet, 1998; (ed) E. T. A. Hoffmann: The Life and Opinions of the Tomcat Murr, 1999; (ed) H. G. Adler: Eine Reise, 1999; (ed jtly) F. B. Steiner: Selected Writings, 2 vols, 1999; (ed jtly) Goethe at 250, 2000; (ed) F. B. Steiner: Am Stürzenden Pfad, Gesammelte Gedichte, 2000; Franz Kafka, 2001; (ed jtly) Models of Wholeness, 2002; (ed jtly) From Prague poet to Oxford anthropologist: Franz Buermann Steiner celebrated, 2003; (ed) H. G. Adler: Die Dichtung der Prager Schule, 2003; (ed) H. G. Adler: Theresienstadt 1941–1945, 2005; (ed) E. Canetti: Aufzeichnungen für Marie-Louise, 2005; (ed jtly) Marie-Louise von Motesiczky 1906–1996: the paintings, 2006; (ed jtly) H. G. Adler: über Franz Baermann Steiner, 2006; (ed jtly) F. B. Steiner: Zivilization und Gefahr, 2008; (ed jtly) Friedrich Hölderlin: essays and letters, 2009; (with Gesa Dane) Literatur und Anthropologie: H. G. Adler, Elias Canetti und Franz Baermann Steiner in London, 2014; The Magus of Portobello Road (novel), 2015; *poetry:* Alphabox, 1973; Alphabet Music, 1974; Fragments Towards the City, 1977; Even in April, Ferrara and Liberty, 1978; A Short History of London, 1979; The Wedding and Other Marriages, 1980; Triplets, 1980; Homage to Theocritus, 1985; Notes from the Correspondence, 1983; The Electric Alphabet, 1986, 3rd edn 2001; To Cythera!, 1993; At the Edge of the World, 1994; Big Skies and Little Stones, 1997; pamphlets; articles in learned jls, daily press, New York Times, TLS, London Rev. of Books. *Recreations:* mountaineering, painting and drawing, music. *Address:* Department of German, King's College London, WC2R 2LS. *T:* (020) 7848 2124.

ADLER, Prof. Michael William, CBE 1999; MD; FRCP, FFPH; Professor of Genito Urinary Medicine and Consultant Physician, University College London (formerly Middlesex Hospital) Medical School, 1979–2004, now Emeritus Professor; *b* 12 June 1939; *s* of late Gerhard and of Hella Adler; *m* 1st, 1966, Susan Jean (marr. diss. 1978); 2nd, 1979, Karen Hope Dunnell (*see* Dame K. H. Dunnell) (marr. diss. 1994); two *d*; 3rd, 1994, Margaret Jay (*see* Baroness Jay of Paddington). *Educ:* Bryanston Sch.; Middlesex Hosp. Med. Sch. MB BS 1965, MD 1977; MRCP 1970, FRCP 1984; FFPH (MFCM 1977, FFCM 1983). House Officer and Registrar in Medicine, Middlesex, Central Middlesex and Whittington Hosps, 1965–69; Lectr, St Thomas' Hosp. Med. Sch., 1970–75; Sen. Lectr, Middlesex Hosp. Med. Sch., 1975–79. Consultant Physician: Middlesex Hosp., 1979–; Camden and Islington Community Health Services NHS Trust, 1992– (non-exec. Dir, 1992–94); non-exec. Dir, Health Develt Agency, 1999–2003. Advr in Venereology, WHO, 1983–2010; Department of Health (formerly DHSS): Mem., Expert Adv. Gp on AIDS, 1984–92; Mem., Sub-Gps on Monitoring and Surveillance, 1987–88 and Health Care Workers, 1987–92; Mem., AIDS Action Gp, 1991–92; Mem., Stocktake Gp, 1997–99; Chief Scientist's Advr, Res. Liaison Gp (Child Health), 1985–90; Mem., and Chm. Steering Gp, Develt of Sexual Health and HIV Strategy, 1999–2001; Mem., Ind. Adv. Gp on Sexual Health, 2000–. Medical Research Council: Member: Res. Adv. Gp on Epidemiol Studies of Sexually Transmitted Diseases, 1975–80; Working Party to co-ordinate Lab. Studies on the Gonococcus, 1979–83; Working Party on AIDS, 1981–87; Sub-Cttee on Therapeutic Studies, 1985–87; Cttee on Epidemiol Studies on AIDS, 1985–94; Cttee on Clinical Studies of Prototype Vaccines against AIDS, 1987–89; RCS Cttee on HIV infection/AIDS, 1991–96. Member: Med. Adv. Cttee, Brook Adv. Centres, 1984–94; Working Gp on AIDS, European Commn, 1985–; AIDS Working Party, BMA, 1986–92; Exec. Cttee, Internat. Union Against Sexually Transmitted Infections (formerly Against the Venereal Diseases and Treponematoses), 1986–; DFID (formerly ODA) Health and Population Adv. Cttee on R&D, 1995–99; Steering Cttee, Assoc. of NHS Providers of AIDS Care and Treatment, 1996–2003; Exec. Cttee, Assoc. of Genito Urinary Medicine, 1997–99. Mem., Specialist Adv. Cttee on Genito Urinary Medicine, Jt Cttee of Higher Med. Trng, 1981–86 (Sec., 1981–82; Chm., 1983–86). Royal College of Physicians: Member: Cttee on Genito Urinary Medicine, 1984–91 (Sec., 1984–87; Chm., 1987–91); Working Gp on AIDS, FCM (now FPH), 1985–; Lumleian Lectr, 1996; Member Council: Med. Soc. for the Study of Venereal Diseases, 1999–2002 (Pres., 1997–99); RIPH&H, 1993–94; RCP, 1999–2002. Dir, Terrence Higgins Trust, 1982–88; Mem. Governing Council, Internat. AIDS Soc., 1993–98; Trustee, 1987–2000, Chm., 1991–2000, Nat. AIDS Trust (Chm., Grants and Gen. Purposes Cttee, 1988–91); Member, Board: Care UK, 2007–; LEPRA, 2007–; Adviser: AIDS Crisis Trust, 1986–98; Parly All Party Cttee on AIDS, 1987–. Mem. Bd, Rose Th., Kingston, 2009–11. Patron, Albany Soc., 1987–91. Evian Health Award, 1990. Member, Editorial Panel: Sexually Transmitted Infections; Current Opinion on Infectious Diseases; Enfermedades de Transmission Sexual; Venereology; also Ed., AIDS, 1986–94; Consultant Editor, AIDS Letter, RSM, 1987–89. *Publications:* ABC of Sexually Transmitted Diseases, 1984, 5th edn 2004; (ed) ABC of AIDS, 1987, 6th edn 2012; (ed) Diseases in the Homosexual Male, 1988; (jtly) Sexual Health and Care Guidelines for Prevention and Treatment, 1998; articles on sexually transmitted diseases and AIDS in med. jls. *Recreations:* yoga, walking, theatre.

ADLER, Rachel Vivienne; *see* Karp, R. V.

ADNAMS, Jonathan Patrick Adair, OBE 2009; Chairman, Adnams plc, since 2006; *b* Halesworth, 25 Nov. 1956; *s* of John Adnams and Patricia Adnams. *Educ:* Framlingham Coll. Adnams: Brewery Engr, 1973–88; Pubs and Property Dir, 1988–97; Man. Dir, 1997–2006. Helmsman, Southwold RNLI, 1973–2001. *Recreations:* sailing, bluegrass banjo, Lithuanian language. *Address:* Adnams, Sole Bay Brewery, East Green, Southwold, Suffolk IP18 6JW. *T:* (01802) 727200, *Fax:* (01802) 727201. *E:* jonathan.adnams@adnams.co.uk.

ADONIS, family name of **Baron Adonis**.

ADONIS, Baron *cr* 2005 (Life Peer), of Camden Town in the London Borough of Camden; **Andrew Adonis;** PC 2009; Director, Institute for Government, 2010–12; *b* 22 Feb. 1963; *m* 1994, Kathryn Davies; one *s* one *d*. *Educ:* Kingham Hill Sch., Oxon; Keble Coll., Oxford; Christ Church, Oxford (DPhil 1988). Mem., HQ Secretariat, British Gas Corp., 1984–85; Nuffield College, University of Oxford: Res. student, 1985–86; Fellow in Politics, 1988–91; Financial Times: Public Policy corresp., 1991–93; Industry corresp., 1993–94; Public Policy Editor, 1994–96; political columnist and contributing editor, The Observer, 1996–98; Mem., Prime Minister's Policy Unit, 1998–2001; Head of Policy, 2001–03, Sen. Advr on Educn and Public Services, 2003–05, Prime Minister's Office. Parly Under-Sec. of State, DFES, later DCSF, 2005–08; Minister of State, DfT, 2008–09; Sec. of State for Transport, 2009–10. Non-exec. Dir, HS2 Ltd, 2015–. Mem., Oxford City Council, 1987–91. Chm., Commn on East Thames Crossings, 2014. Chm. Trustees, IPPR, 2012–. *Publications:* Parliament Today, 1990; Making Aristocracy Work: the peerage and the political system in Britain 1884–1914, 1993; (with T. Hames) A Conservative Revolution?: the Thatcher-Reagan decade in perspective, 1994; (with D. Butler and T. Travers) Failure in British Government: the politics of the poll tax, 1994; (with S. Pollard) A Class Act: the myth of Britain's classless society, 1997; (ed with Keith Thomas) Roy Jenkins: a retrospective, 2004; Five Days in May, 2013. *Address:* House of Lords, SW1A 0PW. *T:* (020) 7219 5904.

ADRIANO, Dino, FCCA, FCIM; Director, 1990–2000, Group Chief Executive, 1998–2000, J. Sainsbury plc (Joint Group Chief Executive, 1997–98); Chairman and Chief Executive, Sainsbury's Supermarkets Ltd, 1997–2000; *b* 24 April 1943; *s* of Dante Adriano and Yole Adriano; *m* 1966, Susan Rivett; two *d*. *Educ:* Highgate Coll.; Strand Grammar Sch. ACCA 1965, FCCA 1980. Articled clerk, George W. Spencer & Co., Chartered Accountants, 1959–64; joined J. Sainsbury plc, 1964: trainee, Accounting Dept, 1964–65; Financial Accounts Dept, 1965–73; Br. Financial Control Manager, 1973–80; Gen. Manager, Homebase, 1981–86; Area Dir, Sainsbury's Central and Western Area, 1986–89; Homebase: Man. Dir, 1989–95; Chm., 1991–96; Shaw's Supermarkets Inc.: Dep. Chm., 1994; Chm., 1994–96; Dir, Giant Food Inc., 1994–96; J. Sainsbury plc: Asst Man. Dir, 1995–96; Dep. Chief Exec., 1996–97. Dir, Laura Ashley plc, 1996–98. Oxfam: Trustee, 1990–96, 1998–2004; Advr on Retail Matters, 1996–98, 2004–06; Vice-Chm., 2001–04; Trustee: WRVS, 2001–07; Sainsbury Archive, 2007–; Sainsbury Veterans Welfare Scheme, 2008–. Chm. Bd Govs, Thames Valley Univ., 2004–09. FCIM 2011. DUniv Thames Valley, 2009. *Recreations:* opera, music, soccer, culinary arts. *E:* dino_adriano@tiscali.co.uk.

ADSETTS, Sir (William) Norman, Kt 1999; OBE 1988; President, Sheffield Theatres Trust, since 2006 (Chairman, 1996–2006); *b* 6 April 1931; *s* of Ernest Norman Adsetts and Hilda Rachel Adsetts (*née* Wheeler); *m* 1956, Eve Stefanuti; one *s* one *d*. *Educ:* King Edward VII Sch., Sheffield; Queen's Coll., Oxford (BA 1955; MA). Commissioned RAF, 1950–52; Marketing Manager, Fibreglass Ltd, 1955–66; Sheffield Insulating Co.: Dir, 1966–89; Man. Dir, 1970–85; Chm., 1985–89; Chm., 1989–96, Pres., 1996–, Sheffield Insulations Gp, subseq. SIG plc. Dir, 1988–91, Dep. Chm., 1991–97, Sheffield Develt Corp.; Chairman: Kelham Riverside Develt Agency, 1998–2002; Sheffield Supertram Trust, 1993–98; Sheffield Partnerships, 1988–93; Sheffield First for Investment, 1999–2002. Chairman: Assoc. for Conservation of Energy, 1985–90, 1993–95; Yorkshire Humberside CBI, 1989–91; Pres., Sheffield Chamber of Commerce, 1988–89. Mem., Arts Council England, 2002–05 (Chm., Yorks Arts Regl Council, 2002–05). Chairman: Autism Plus, 2007–12; Adsetts Partnership, 2009–; Trustee, Research Autism, 2006– (Chm., 2006–14). Chairman of Governors: Sheffield Hallam Univ., 1993–99; Mount St Mary's Coll., 1999–2009 (Pres., 2010–). Patron of local charities. *Recreations:* writing family history, two autistic grandchildren, reading. *Address:* Danes Balk, 8 Rotherham Road, Eckington, Sheffield S21 4FH. *T:* (01246) 431008.

ADSHEAD, Fiona Jane, FRCP, FFPH; Senior Sustainability and Health Advisor, PricewaterhouseCoopers; *b* 31 July 1962; *d* of late Lt Comdr and Mrs J. R. Adshead. *Educ:* University Coll. London (BSc 1983; MB BS 1986; MSc 1994). MRCP 1989, FRCP 2005; MFPHM 1999, FFPH 2003. Sen. hse officer posts, Nat. Hosp. for Nervous Diseases, Royal Marsden Hosp., Brompton Hosp. and RPMS, 1987–89; Med. Registrar, St George's Hosp., 1989–90; Clinical Res. Fellow, Inst. of Cancer Res. and Royal Marsden Hosp., 1990–92; Registrar, then Sen. Registrar, Croydon HA, 1993–96; Clinical Lectr, St George's Hosp. Med. Sch., 1996–2000; Consultant in Public Health Medicine, Camden and Islington HA, 2000–02; Dir of Public Health, Camden PCT, 2002–04; Dep. Chief Med. Officer, DoH, 2004–08; Dir, Chronic Diseases and Health Promotion, WHO, 2009. *Publications:* contrib. numerous articles to scientific jls. *Recreations:* art, travel, gardening, film, theatre.

ADYE, Sir John (Anthony), KCMG 1993; Director, Government Communications Headquarters, 1989–96; *b* 24 Oct. 1939; *s* of Arthur Francis Capel Adye and Hilda Marjorie Adye (*née* Elkes); *m* 1961, Anne Barbara, *d* of Dr John Aeschlimann, Montclair, NJ; two *s* one *d*. *Educ:* Leighton Park Sch.; Lincoln Coll., Oxford (MA). Joined GCHQ, 1962; Principal, 1968; British Embassy, Washington, 1973–75; Nat. Defence Coll., Latimer, 1975–76; Asst Sec., 1977–83; Under Sec., 1983–89; Dep. Sec., 1989–92; 2nd Perm. Sec., 1992–96. Chairman: Country Houses Assoc., 1999–2002; CPRE Glos, 2005–11; Identity Assurance Systems Ltd, 2010–. Dir, Nat. Biometric Security Project, Washington, 2003–. Gov., Dean Close Sch., Cheltenham. *Address:* c/o Campaign to Protect Rural England, Community House, Gloucester GL1 2LZ. *Club:* Naval and Military.

AEPPLI, Prof. Gabriel, PhD; FRS 2010; Quain Professor of Physics and Hon. Professor of Medicine, University College London, since 2002; Head, Department of Synchrotron Radiation and Nanotechnology, Paul Scherrer Institute, Switzerland, since 2014; Professor of Physics, ETH Zurich and École Polytechnique Fédérale de Lausanne, since 2014; *b* Zurich, 25 Nov. 1956; *s* of late Alfred Aeppli and of Dorothea Aeppli; *m* 2005, Yeong-Ah Soh; one *d*. *Educ:* Massachusetts Inst. of Technol. (BSc Electrical Engrg and Maths 1978; MSc Electrical Engrg; PhD Electrical Engrg 1983). Res. asst, MIT, 1978–82; Mem., Tech. Staff, 1982–93, Dist. Mem., Tech. Staff, 1993–96, AT&T Bell Labs, Murray Hill, NJ; Sen. Res. Scientist, Nippon Electric Co. Res. Inst. Inc., Princeton, NJ, 1996–2002; Dir, London Centre for Nanotechnol., UCL, 2002–14. Resident, Bellagio Study and Conf. Center, Rockefeller Foundn, 2007. Lectures: Mildner, Dept of Electronic and Electrical Engrg, UCL, 2002; Liddiard Meml, Inst. Materials, Minerals and Mining, London, 2006; James A. Morrison, McMaster Univ., Ontario, 2008; J. C. Bose Meml, Saha Inst. of Nuclear Physics, Kolkata,

2009. Fellow: Japan Soc. for Promotion of Sci., 1996; Amer. Physical Soc., 1997; Riso Nat. Lab., Denmark, 2002. Mem., Physical Soc. Club, London, 2003. Wolfson Res. Merit Award, Royal Soc., 2002; (jtly) Neel Medal/Magnetism Prize, IUPAP, 2003; Majumdar Meml Award, Indian Assoc. for Cultivation of Sci., 2005; (jtly) Oliver Buckley Prize, APS, 2005; Mott Medal, Inst. of Physics, 2008. *Publications:* contribs to jls incl. Nature, Science, Proceedings of NAS, Physics Rev. Letters, Nature Materials, Nanomedicine and Jl Applied Physics. *Address:* London Centre for Nanotechnology, 17–19 Gordon Street, WC1H 0AH. *T:* (020) 7679 0055, *Fax:* (020) 7679 0595. *E:* lcn-administrator@ucl.ac.uk.

AFFLECK, Prof. Ian Keith, PhD; FRS 2010; FRSC; Killam University Professor, University of British Columbia, since 2003; *b* Vancouver, BC, 2 July 1952; *s* of William Burchill Affleck and Evelyn Mary Colenso Affleck (*née* Carter); *m* 1977, Glenda Ruth Harman; one *s* one *d*. *Educ:* Trent Univ., Ont (BSc 1975); Harvard Univ. (AM Physics 1976; PhD Physics 1979). Jun. Fellow, Harvard Soc. of Fellows, 1979–81; Asst Prof., Princeton Univ., 1981–87; Prof., Univ. of BC, 1987–; on leave as Prof., Boston Univ., 2001–03. Fellow: Canadian Inst. for Advanced Res., 1987–2001 and 2008–; Inst. for Theoretical Physics, UCSB, 1999–2000. FRSC 1991; Fellow: APS, 2003; Japanese Soc. for Promotion of Sci., 2004. Hon. LLD Trent, 1998. Steacie Prize, NRCC, 1988; Herzberg Medal, Canadian Assoc. Physicists, 1990; Rutherford Medal in Physics, RSC, 1991; Lars Onsager Prize, APS, 2012. *Publications:* contribs to scientific jls, incl. Nuclear Physics, Physics Letters, Physics Rev. Letters, Physics Rev. D and B, Jl of Physics A, Jl of Statistical Mechanics. *Recreations:* bicycling, swimming, hiking, wind-surfing, ski-ing. *Address:* Department of Physics and Astronomy, University of British Columbia, Vancouver, BC V6T 1Z1, Canada. *T:* (604) 8222137, *Fax:* (604) 8225324. *E:* iaffleck@phas.ubc.ca.

AFRIYIE, Adam; MP (C) Windsor, since 2005; *b* 4 Aug. 1965. *Educ:* Addey and Stanhope Sch., New Cross; Imperial Coll., London (BSc 1987). Man. Dir, then non-exec. Chm., Connect Support Services, 1993–; Exec. Chm., DeHavilland Inf. Services, 1998–2005; non-exec. Chm., Axonn Media Ltd (formerly Adfero), 2005–. Shadow Minister for Sci. and Innovation, 2007–10. Chairman: Parly Space Cttee, 2010–; Parly Office of Sci. and Technol., 2010–; Members' Expenses Cttee, 2011–15. Mem. Bd, Policy Exchange, 2003–05. Gov., Mus. of London, 1999–2005. *Address:* (office) 87 St Leonards Road, Windsor SL4 3BZ; House of Commons, SW1A 0AA.

AFSHAR, Baroness *cr* 2007 (Life Peer), of Heslington in the County of North Yorkshire; **Haleh Afshar,** OBE 2005; PhD; FAcSS; Professor of Politics and Women's Studies, University of York, 1999–2011, now Emeritus; *b* 1944; *d* of Hassan Afshar and Pouran Afshar (*née* Khabir); *m* 1974, Maurice Dodson; one *s* one *d*. *Educ:* Ecole Jean d'Arc, Tehran; St Martin's Sch., Solihull; Davis's Coll., Brighton; Univ. of York (BA Hons Soc. Scis 1967); Univ. of Strasbourg (Diplôme de Droit Comparé Communauté Européen 1972); PhD Land Economy Cantab 1974. Sen. Res. Officer, Ministry of Co-operatives and Rural Develt, Rural Res. Centre, Tehran; Econ. and Envmt Corresp. and Feature Writer, Kayhan International, English lang. daily newspaper, Tehran, 1971–74; Lectr in Develt, Univ. of Bradford, 1976–85; University of York: Dep. Dir and Lectr in Health Econs, Inst. for Res. in Social Scis, 1985–87; Dept of Politics and Centre for Women's Studies, 1987–. Founder and Co-Chm., 2002–09, Pres., 2009–, Muslim Women's Network; Chm. and Facilitator, Listening to Women exercise, conducted by Muslim Women's Network and Women's Nat. Commn, 2005–06. Advr to various pts of Govt on public policy on Muslim women and Islamic law; speaker on various media on Muslim community. Member: Wkg Gp on Ethics and Pharmacogenetics, Nuffield Council on Bioethics, 2002–04; UK Drug Policy Commn, 2006–; Educn Honours Cttee, 2007–; Women's Nat. Commn, 2008–10. FAcSS (AcSS 2009). Launched Democracy Series, Hansard Soc., with Democracy and Islam (pamphlet), 2006. Mem. editl bds of 10 learned jls. *Publications:* Islam and the Post-revolutionary State in Iran (as Homa Omid), 1994; Islam and Feminisms, 1998; edited: Iran: a revolution in turmoil, 1985; Women, Work and Ideology in the Third World, 1985; Women, State and Ideology, 1987; (jtly) Women, Poverty and Ideology, 1989; Women, Development and Survival in the Third World, 1991; (jtly) Women and Adjustment Policies in the Third World, 1992; Women in the Middle East, 1993; (jtly) The Dynamics of Race and Gender, 1994; Women and Politics in the Third World, 1996; (jtly) Empowering Women for Development, 1997; Women and Empowerment: illustrations from the Third World, 1998; (jtly) Women and Globalization and Fragmentation in the Developing World, 1999; (jtly) Development, Women, and War, 2004; (jtly) Women in Later Life, 2008; Women and Fluid Identities, 2012. *Recreations:* music, opera, ballet, movies, books, cooking, entertaining, Paris, the Pennines. *Address:* House of Lords, SW1A 0PW; Department of Politics, University of York, York YO10 5DD.

AGA KHAN (IV), His Highness Prince Karim, granted title His Highness by the Queen, 1957, granted title His Royal Highness by the Shah of Iran, 1959; KBE 2004; *b* Genthod, Geneva, 13 Dec. 1936; *s* of late Prince Aly Salomon Khan and Princess Joan Aly Khan, later Viscountess Camrose (*née* Joan Barbara Yarde-Buller, *e d* of 3rd Baron Churston, MVO, OBE); became Aga Khan, spiritual leader and hereditary Imam of Ismaili Muslims all over the world on the death of his grandfather, Sir Sultan Mahomed Shah, Aga Khan III, GCSI, GCIE, GCVO, 11 July 1957; *m* 1969, Sarah Frances Croker-Poole (marr. diss. 1995); two *s* one *d*; *m* 1998, Princess Gabriele zu Leiningen (Begum Inaara Aga Khan) (marr. diss. 2014); one *s*, and one step *d*. *Educ:* Le Rosey, Switzerland; Harvard University (BA Hons 1959). Founder and Chairman: Aga Khan Foundn, Geneva, 1967 (also branches/affiliates in Afghanistan, Bangladesh, Canada, India, Kenya, Kyrgyzstan, Mozambique, Pakistan, Portugal, Syria, Tajikistan, Tanzania, Uganda, UK and US); Aga Khan Award for Architecture, 1977–; Inst. of Ismaili Studies, 1977–; Aga Khan Fund for Econ. Develt, Geneva, 1984–; Aga Khan Trust for Culture, Geneva, 1988; Aga Khan Agency for Microfinance, 2005. Founder and Chancellor: Aga Khan Univ., Pakistan, 1983; Univ. of Central Asia, 2001. Leading owner and breeder of race horses in France, Ireland and UK; won: Derby, 1981 (Shergar), 1986 (Shahrastani), 1988 (Kahyasi), 2000 (Sinndar); Irish Derby, 1981 (Shergar), 1986 (Shahrastani), 1988 (Kahyasi), 2000 (Sinndar), 2003 (Alamshar); King George VI and Queen Elizabeth Diamond Stakes, 2003 (Alamshar), 2005 (Azamour); St James's Palace Stakes, 2004 (Azamour); Prix de L'Arc de Triomphe, 1982 (Akiyda), 2000 (Sinndar), 2003 (Dalakhani), 2008 (Zarkava); Prix du Jockey Club, 1960 (Charlottesville), 1979 (Top Ville), 1984 (Darshaan), 1985 (Mouktar), 1987 (Natroun), 2003 (Dalakhani); Prix de Diane, 1993 (Shemaka), 1997 (Vereva), 1998 (Zainta), 1999 (Daryaba), 2008 (Zarkava). Hon. Citizen of Canada, 2010. Hon. FRIBA 1991; Hon. Mem., AIA, 1992. Associate Foreign Mem., Académie des Beaux Arts, France, 2008. Doctor of Laws (*hc*): McGill, 1983; McMaster, 1987; Wales, 1993; Brown, 1996; Toronto, 2004; Ireland, 2006; Hon. DLitt London, 1989; DHLitt (*hc*) Amer. Univ. Beirut, 2005; Hon. Dr: Evora, 2005; Ottawa, 2012; Hon. DHumLit Amer. Univ., Cairo, 2006; Hon. DD Cambridge, 2008. Thomas Jefferson Meml Foundn Medal in Architecture, 1984; Amer. Inst. of Architects' Inst. Honor, 1984; Médaille d'argent, Académie d'Architecture, Paris 1991; Vincent Scully Prize, USA, 2005; Die Quadriga, Germany, 2005; Carnegie Medal of Philanthropy, Scotland, 2005; Grand Patron and Grand Donor of Culture, France, 2009; Medal, UCSF, 2011; J. C. Nichols Prize for Visionaries in Urban Develt, Urban Land Inst., 2011. Grand Croix: Order of Prince Henry the Navigator, Portugal, 1960; Ordem Militar de Cristo, Portugal, 2005; Order of Merit, Portugal, 1998; Cavaliere, Gran Croce, Ordine al Merito della Repubblica Italiana, 1977; Grand Cordon, Ouissam-al Arch, Morocco, 1986; Cavaliere del Lavoro, Italy, 1988; Commandeur, Légion d'Honneur, France, 1990; Gran Cruz, Orden del Mérito Civil, Spain, 1991; Order of Bahrain (1st cl.), 2003; Hon. CC, 2004; Comdr, Order of Arts and Letters (France), 2010. *Address:* Aiglemont, 60270 Gouvieux, France. *Clubs:* Royal Yacht Squadron; Yacht Club Costa Smeralda (Founder Pres.) (Sardinia).

AGAR, family name of **Earl of Normanton**.

AGARWAL, Prof. Girish Saran, PhD; FRS 2008; Noble Foundation Chair and Regents' Professor, Department of Physics, Oklahoma State University, since 2004; *b* Bareilly, Uttar Pradesh, 7 July 1946; *s* of late Keladevi and Bhagwat Saran; *m* 1970, Sneh (*d* 2006); two *d*. *Educ:* Banaras Hindu Univ., India (MSc 1966); Univ. of Rochester, USA (PhD 1969). Res. Associate, 1969–71, and Asst Prof., 1970–71, Dept of Physics and Astronomy, Univ. of Rochester, NY; Asst Prof., Inst. für Theoretische Physik, Univ. of Stuttgart, 1971–73; Prof. and Hd, Dept of Physics, Inst. of Sci., Bombay, 1975–77; University of Hyderabad: Prof., Sch. of Physics, 1977–95; Dean, Sch. of Physics, 1977–80; Dir and Dist. Scientist, Physical Res. Lab., Ahmedabad, 1995–2006. Albert Einstein Centenary Res. Prof., Indian Nat. Sci. Acad., 2001–05; Hon. Prof., Jawaharlal Nehru Centre for Advanced Scientific Res., Jakkur, Bangalore, 1995–2000; Visiting Professor: Univ. of Ulm, Germany; Univ. of Essen, Germany; Max-Planck-Inst. für Quantenoptik, Garching; Technische Univ., Vienna; Vis. Fellow, 1973–75, J. R. D. Tata Vis. Prof., 2011–13, Tata Inst. of Fundamental Res., Mumbai; Vis. Fellow, Jt Inst. for Lab. Astrophysics, Univ. of Colo, Boulder, 1981–82; SERC Sen. Vis. Fellow, UMIST, 1985–86. Dr *hc* Liege, 2007; Hon. Dr Hyderabad, 2011. Fellow: Amer. Physical Soc., 1981; Indian Acad. of Scis, 1981; Indian Nat. Sci. Acad., 1985; Optical Soc. of America, 1988; Third World Acad. of Scis, 1997. Eastman Kodak Prize, Univ. of Rochester, 1969; Shanti Swaroop Bhatnagar Award in Physical Scis, Govt of India, 1982; Max-Born Award, Optical Soc. of America, 1988; Einstein Medal, Optical and Quantum Electronics Soc., USA, 1994; G. D. Birla Prize for Scientific Res., K. K. Birla Foundn, 1994; Third World Acad. of Scis Prize in Physics, 1994; R. D. Birla Prize, Indian Physics Assoc., 1997; Humboldt Res. Award, Germany, 1997; Eminent Faculty Award, Oklahoma State Univ., 2012. *Publications:* Quantum Optics, 2013; monographs; papers on stochastic processes and quantum optics; contrib. res. articles to jls of Amer. Physical Soc., Inst. of Physics, Optical Soc. of America. *Recreations:* reading magazines and newspapers, watching comedy and movies with message. *Address:* Department of Physics, Oklahoma State University, Stillwater, OK 74078, USA. *T:* (405) 7443862, *Fax:* (405) 7446811. *E:* girish.agarwal@okstate.edu.

AGASSI, André; tennis player; *b* Las Vegas, 29 April 1970; *s* of Emmanuel (Mike) and Betty Agassi; *m* 1997, Brooke Shields (marr. diss.); *m* 2001, Stefanie Graf, *qv*; one *s* one *d*. Trained at Nick Bollettieri Tennis Acad., Fla. Professional tennis player, 1986–2006; winner: (inaugural) ATP World Championship, Frankfurt, 1991; Wimbledon, 1992; US Open, 1994, 1999; Australian Open, 1995, 2000, 2001, 2003; French Open, 1999 (one of only five players ever to win all four men's grand-slam titles); Gold Medallist, Olympic Games, 1996. Founder, André Agassi Charitable Foundn, 1996. *Publications:* Open: an autobiography, 2009. *Address:* c/o IMG, 1360 East 9th Street, Suite 100, Cleveland, OH 44114, USA.

AGG, Stephen James, FCILT; Chief Executive, Chartered Institute of Logistics and Transport, since 2006; *b* 25 Sept. 1952; *s* of Douglas and Ivy Agg; *m* 2007, Maggie; one *s* one *d* by a previous marriage. Lowfield Distribn, 1981–86; Jacob's Bakery, 1986–96; Distribn Dir, Danone UK, 1996–99; Logistics Dir, Danone Waters UK, 1999–2002; Man. Dir, Business Services, Freight Transport Assoc., 2002–06. Director: Eur. Logistics Assoc., 2011–; PTRC Educn and Res. Services; Mem., Adv. Bd, Cranfield Centre for Logistics and Supply Mgt. FCILT 2006. *Recreations:* classic cars, walking, rural life, English Setters. *Address:* Chartered Institute of Logistics and Transport, Earlstrees Court, Earlstrees Road, Corby, Northants NN17 4AX. *T:* (01536) 740109. *E:* steve.agg@ciltuk.org.uk.

AGGARWAL, Prof. Varinder Kumar, PhD; FRS 2012; Professor of Synthetic Chemistry, University of Bristol, since 2000; *b* Kalianpur, N India, 1961. *Educ:* Pembroke Coll., Cambridge (BA 1st Cl. Hons Natural Scis 1983; PhD 1987). Harkness Fellow, 1986–88; Postdoctoral Res. Fellow, Columbia Univ., NY, 1986–88; Lectr in Chem., Bath Univ., 1988–91; Lectr in Chem., 1991–95, Reader, 1995–97, Prof. of Chem., 1997–2000, Sheffield Univ. Hickinbottom Fellow, RSC, 1997; Nuffield Foundn Fellow, 1997–98. Pfizer Academic Award, 1996, 1998; Glaxo Wellcome Academic Award, 1996; Zeneca Academic Award, 1996; Corday Morgan Prize and Medal, 1999, Green Chem. Award, 2003, RSC. *Address:* School of Chemistry, University of Bristol, Cantock's Close, Bristol BS8 1TS.

AGGLETON, Prof. John Patrick, DPhil; FRS 2012; Professor of Cognitive Neuroscience, Cardiff University, since 1994; *b* Cardiff, 14 June 1955; *s* of Patrick and Judy Aggleton; *m* 1978, Jane; two *s*. *Educ:* Trinity Sch., Croydon; Clare Coll., Cambridge (BA Natural Scis 1976); Jesus Coll., Oxford (DPhil 1980). Lectr, Durham Univ., 1983–94. FMedSci 2002; FLSW 2011. *Recreations:* bird watching, fell running, cycling. *Address:* c/o School of Psychology, Cardiff University, Tower Building, 70 Park Place, Cardiff CF10 3AT. *T:* (029) 2087 4563, *Fax:* (029) 2087 4858. *E:* aggleton@cf.ac.uk. *Club:* Mynyddwyr de Cymru.

AGGLETON, Prof. Peter Jeremy, PhD; CPsychol, FBPsS; FAcSS; Professor of Education and Health, Centre for Social Research in Health (formerly National Centre in HIV Social Research), since 2012, and Scientia Professor, since 2015, UNSW Australia (formerly University of New South Wales); *b* 16 Oct. 1952; *s* of David Charles and Pauline Betty Aggleton; partner, Preecha Anurakpongpee. *Educ:* Worcester Coll., Oxford (BA 1974); Aberdeen Univ. (MEd 1977); PhD London 1984. CPsychol 1989; FBPsS 1996; FRSPH (FRIPHH 2001); FAcSS (AcSS 2004). Lecturer: Psychol. and Sociol., Worthing Coll. of Technol., 1975–76; Teacher Educn, City of Bath Tech. Coll., 1977–84; Sen. Lectr, Sociol., Bath Coll. of Higher Educn, 1984–85; Sen. Lectr, 1985–89, Hd, 1989–90, Educn Policy Studies, Bristol Poly.; Dir, Health and Educn Res. Unit, Goldsmiths' Coll., Univ. of London, 1991–92; Chief, Social and Behavioural Studies and Support Unit, Global Prog. on AIDS, WHO, Geneva, 1992–94; Prof., 1994–2009, and Dir, 1996–2006, Thomas Coram Res. Unit, Inst. of Educn, Univ. of London; Prof. of Educn, Health and Social Care, and Hd, Sch. of Educn and Social Work, Univ. of Sussex, 2009–11. Visiting Professor: Univ. of NSW, 2003–12; Univ. of Oslo, 2006–; Inst. of Educn, Univ. of London, 2012–. Editor: Culture, Health and Sexuality, 1999–; Sex Education, 2011–; Health Educn Jl, 2013–. *Publications:* (with H. A. Chalmers) Nursing Models and the Nursing Process, 1986; Deviance, 1987; Health, 1990; Health Promotion and Young People, 1996; (with H. A. Chalmers) Nursing Models and Nursing Practice, 2000; (ed jtly) Young People and Mental Health, 2000; (ed jtly) Sex, Drugs and Young People, 2006; contribs to learned jls incl. Science, Lancet, AIDS Care, AIDS Educn and Prevention, Health Educn Res. *Recreations:* walking, writing, travel, learning foreign languages. *Address:* Centre for Social Research in Health, UNSW Australia, Sydney, NSW 2052, Australia. *T:* (2) 93856776, *Fax:* (2) 93856455. *E:* csrh@unsw.edu.au.

AGIUS, Prof. Dionisius A., PhD; FBA 2011; Al Qasimi Professor of Arabic Studies and Islamic Material Culture, University of Exeter, since 2007; *b* Mosta, Malta, 21 Dec. 1945; *s* of Pietro Agius and Giovanna Agius (*née* Griscti Soler); *m* 1987, Anne Phillips; one *d*, and one step *s* one step *d*. *Educ:* Univ. St Joseph, Beirut (Diplôme d'Etudes Arabes 1967); Pontificio Istituto di Studi Arabi, Rome (Diploma di Studi Arabi *cum laude* 1974); Univ. of Toronto (MA 1977; PhD 1984). Teacher Assistant, in Classical and Modern Arabic, 1977–84, in Field Methods, 1979–81, Univ. of Toronto; Teacher, Arabic as Second Lang., Kuwait Univ., 1984–85; Burnham Lectr in Arabic, Defence Sch. of Langs, 1986–87; University of Leeds: Teaching Fellow, 1987–89, Lectr, 1989–94, Sen. Lectr, 1994–98, in Arabic; Reader in Arabic and Medieval Mediterranean, 1998–2003; Prof. of Arabic and Islamic Material Culture, 2003–07. FRSA 2013. *Publications:* Arabic Literary Works as a Source of Documentation for Technical Terms of the Material Culture, 1984; Siculo Arabic, 1996; In the Wake of the Dhow: the Arabian Gulf and Oman, 2002, 2nd edn 2009; Seafaring in the Arabian Gulf and Oman: people of the dhow, 2005; Classic Ships of Islam: from Mesopotamia to the Indian

Ocean, 2008; (ed) Georgio Scala and the Moorish Slaves: the Inquisition Malta 1598, 2013. *Recreations:* walking, reading, travel. *Address:* Institute of Arab and Islamic Studies, University of Exeter, Exeter EX4 4ND. *T:* (01395) 445538. *E:* d.a.agius@exeter.ac.uk.

AGIUS, Kate Juliette de R.; *see* Rothschild Agius.

AGIUS, Marcus Ambrose Paul; Chairman, PA Consulting Group, since 2014; *b* 22 July 1946; *s* of late Lt-Col Alfred Victor Louis Benedict Agius, MC, TD and Ena Eleanora Alberta Agius (*née* Hueffer); *m* 1971, Kate Juliette de Rothschild (*see* K. J. de Rothschild Agius); two *d*. *Educ:* Trinity Hall, Cambridge (MA); Harvard Business Sch. (MBA). With Vickers plc, 1968–70; joined Lazard Brothers & Co. Ltd, subseq. Lazard London, 1972; Chm., 2001–06; a Dep. Chm., Lazard LLC, 2002–06; Chm., Barclays PLC, 2007–12. Non-executive Director: Exbury Gardens Ltd, 1977–; BAA plc, 1995–2006 (Dep. Chm., 1998–2002; Chm., 2002–06); Sen. Ind. Dir, BBC, 2006–12. Chm., BBA, 2010–12. British Business Ambassador, 2010–12. Member: Adv. Council, TheCityUK, 2010–12; Exec. Cttee, IIEB, 2010–12; Takeover Panel, 2010–12. Chm., Bd of Trustees, Royal Botanic Gdns, Kew, 2009– (Chm., Foundn and Friends, 2004–; Trustee, 2006–09). *Recreations:* gardening, shooting, ski-ing, fine art, sailing. *Address:* PA Consulting Group, 123 Buckingham Palace Road, SW1W 9SR. *Clubs:* White's; Swinley Forest Golf; Beaulieu River Sailing.

AGLIONBY, Dr Julia Catherine Weir, FRGS; Executive Director, Foundation for Common Land, since 2012; *b* London, 4 Oct. 1969; *d* of late Francis John Aglionby and of Susan Victoria Mary Aglionby; *m* 2000, Charles Alexander Forbes Weir; one *s* one *d*. *Educ:* St Paul's Girls' Sch.; Somerville Coll., Oxford (MA); University Coll. London (MSc); Newcastle Univ. (PhD 2014). MRICS. ODA, 1993–96; Land Agent, H&H Bone Ltd, 1997–2013. Director: Nat. Centre for the Uplands, 2013; Swan's Farm, CLC, 2015–. Mem. Bd, Natural England, 2014–. *Publications:* contribs on common land and natural park mgt. *Recreations:* wild swimming, Racing Demon expeditions. *Address:* Wallacefield, Armathwaite, Carlisle CA4 9SR. *T:* 07702 100111. *E:* julia.aglionby@wallacefield.org.

AGNELLO, Raquel, (Mrs Michel Hanns); QC 2009; *b* London, 29 July 1963; *d* of Jose Agnello de Vaz Carreiro and Maria Eduarda Tavares Botelho Machado de Vaz Carreiro; *m* 2000, Michel Hanns; one *s* one *d*. *Educ:* Norra Reals Gymnasium, Stockholm; Univ. of Sussex (BA Hons Law with French); Univ. of Strasbourg (Dip. d'Etudes Juridiques Françaises). MCIArb 1989. Called to the Bar, Inner Temple, 1986, Bencher, 2011; Dep. Registrar in Bankruptcy, 2001–. *Recreations:* ski-ing, listening to music (opera and classical). *Address:* Erskine Chambers, 33 Chancery Lane, WC2A 1EN. *T:* (020) 7242 5532, *Fax:* (020) 7831 0125. *E:* ragnello@erskinechambers.com.

AGNEW, Christine; QC 2015; *b* Northern Ireland; *d* of Robert and Amy Agnew; *m* 1997, Caspar Hilary Gordon Glyn, *qv*; two *s* one *d*. *Educ:* Methodist Coll., Belfast; Univ. of W of England (LLB). Called to the Bar, Inner Temple, 1992. *Recreations:* theatre, eating out, ski-ing, home, friends and family, Chelsea Football and Ireland Rugby supporter, touchline Mum. *Address:* 2 Bedford Row, WC1R 4BU. *T:* (020) 7440 8888. *E:* cagnew@2bedfordrow.co.uk.

AGNEW of Lochnaw, Sir Crispin Hamlyn, 11th Bt *cr* 1629; QC (Scot.) 1995; Rothesay Herald of Arms, since 1986; Chief of the Name and Arms of Agnew; *b* 13 May 1944; *s* of (Sir) Fulque Melville Gerald Noel Agnew of Lochnaw, 10th Bt and Swanzie, *d* of late Major Esmé Nourse Erskine, CMG, MC; *S* father, 1975; *m* 1980, Susan (careers adviser, formerly journalist, broadcaster, Advertising Exec.), *yr d* of late J. W. Strang Steel, Logie, Kirriemuir, Angus; one *s* three *d*. *Educ:* Uppingham; RMA, Sandhurst. Major (retd 1981), late RHF. Admitted to Faculty of Advocates, 1982. A Dep. Upper Tribunal Judge (formerly Dep. Social Security and Child Support Comr), 2000–; Part-time Chm., Pension Appeal Tribunal, 2002–12. Slains Pursuivant of Arms to Lord High Constable of Scotland, 1978–81; Unicorn Pursuivant of Arms, 1981–86. Trustee, John Muir Trust, 1989–2005. Leader: Army Expedn to E Greenland, 1968; Jt Services Expedn to Chilean Patagonia, 1972–73; Army Expedn to Api, NW Nepal, 1980; Member: RN Expedn to E Greenland, 1966; Jt Services to Elephant Island (Antarctica), 1970–71; Army Nuptse Expedn, 1975; Jt British and Royal Nepalese Army Everest Expedn, 1976 (reached the South Col). Mem. Council, 2008–10, Mem. Bd, 2010–12, Scottish Youth Hostels Assoc. Patron, UK Envmtl Law Assoc., 2010– (Convenor, Scottish Cttee, 2010–12). *Publications:* (jtly) Allan and Chapman, Licensing (Scotland) Act 1976, 2nd edn 1989, 5th edn 2002; (jtly) Connell on the Agricultural Holdings Acts, 7th edn 1996; Agricultural Law in Scotland, 1996; Land Obligations, 1999; Crofting Law, 2000; (contrib.) The Law of Trees, Forests and Hedgerows, 2nd edn, 2011; articles in newspapers and magazines, and in legal and heraldic jls. *Recreations:* mountaineering, sailing (Yacht Pippa's Song), heraldry, mountain biking. *Heir: s* Mark Douglas Noel Agnew of Lochnaw, yr, *b* 24 April 1991. *Address:* 6 Palmerston Road, Edinburgh EH9 1TN.

AGNEW, Fraser; *see* Agnew, W. A. F.

AGNEW, Sir George (Anthony), 7th Bt *cr* 1895, of Great Stanhope Street, London; joint owner, Rougham Estate, Suffolk, since 1994; *b* Rougham, 18 Aug. 1953; *yr s* of Major Sir (George) Keith Agnew, 5th Bt, TD and Anne Merete Louise Schaffalitzky de Muckadell; *S* brother, 2011; civil partnership 2007, Adrian Paul White. *Educ:* Gresham's Sch., Holt; Univ. of East Anglia (BA Hons). Director: Blackthorpe Barn Arts, 1993–; Summer Music at Blackthorpe Barn, 1993–2011. Chm. Trustees, Rougham Estate Trust, 2014–. *Recreations:* gardening, classical music, cooking, travel. *Heir: cousin* John Stuart Agnew [*b* 30 Aug. 1949; *m* 1982, Diana Margaret Zoë Baker; three *s*]. *Address:* Estate Office, Rougham, Bury St Edmunds, Suffolk IP30 9LZ. *T:* (01359) 270091, *Fax:* (01359) 271555. *E:* george@roughamestate.com.

AGNEW, (John) Stuart; Member (UK Ind) Eastern, European Parliament, since 2009; *b* Oulton, Norwich, 30 Aug. 1949; *s* of Stephen William Agnew and Elizabeth Agnew (*née* Close); *m* 1982, Diana Margaret Zoe Baker; three *s*. *Educ:* Gordonstoun Sch.; Royal Agricultural Coll. (NDA 1971; McClennan Silver Medal 1971). MRAC 1971. Teacher, Church Mission Sch., Srinaga, Kashmir, 1968; farm pupil, Maj. C. Maude, 1968–69; Farm Manager, Narford Farm, 1971–74; Soil and Water Conservation Officer, Min. of Agric., Rhodesia, 1975–76; Rhodesian Army, 1976; Farm Manager, C. W. Cave, 1976–77 and 1978–81, Rogate Farms Ltd, 1977–83; farmer, free-range eggs, sheep and arable crops, 1983–. Chm., Norfolk Co., NFU, 1997; Norfolk Deleg., NFU Council, 2000–09; Local Dir, NFU Mutual Insce Soc., 2001–09. *Recreations:* country sports, cricket, snooker. *Address:* Paxfield Farm, Helhoughton, Fakenham, Norfolk NR21 7HJ. *T:* (01485) 528917, 07850 269424. *E:* eastern@ukip.org. *Club:* Farmers.

AGNEW, Jonathan Geoffrey William; Chairman: The Cayenne Trust, since 2006; Fleet Mortgages Ltd, since 2014; *b* 30 July 1941; *er s* of Sir Geoffrey Agnew and Hon. Doreen Maud, *y d* of 1st Baron Jessel, CB, CMG; *m* 1st, 1966, Hon. Joanna Campbell (marr. diss. 1985); one *s* two *d*; 2nd, 1990, Marie-Claire Dreesmann; one *s* one *d*. *Educ:* Eton College; Trinity College, Cambridge (MA). The Economist, 1964–65; World Bank, 1965–67; Hill Samuel & Co., 1967–73, Dir, 1971–73; Morgan Stanley & Co., 1973–82, Man. Dir, 1977–82; J. G. W. Agnew & Co., 1983–86; Kleinwort Benson Gp, 1987–93, Gp Chief Exec., 1989–93; Chairman: Limit, 1993–2000; Gerrard Gp, 1998–2000; Nationwide Bldg Soc., 2002–07 (Dep. Chm., 1999–2002; non-exec. Dir, 1997–2007); Beazley (formerly Beazley Gp), 2003–12 (non-exec. Dir, 2002–12); LMS Capital (formerly Leo Capital), 2006–10; Ashmore Global Opportunities, 2007–13; non-executive Director: Thos Agnew & Sons Ltd, 1969–2007; Thos Agnew and Sons Hldgs Ltd, 2007–13; Sen. Ind. Dir, Rightmove plc, 2007–15. Mem. Council, Lloyd's, 1995–99. *Address:* Flat E, 51 Eaton Square, SW1W 9BE. *Clubs:* White's; Automobile (Paris).

AGNEW, Jonathan Philip; cricket correspondent, BBC, since 1991; *b* 4 April 1960; *s* of Philip Agnew and Margaret Agnew; *m* 1996, Emma Norris; two *d* by former marriage. *Educ:* Uppingham Sch. Professional cricketer: début, Leics CCC, 1978; played for England, 1984–85; retd from first class cricket, 1990; cricket corresp., Today, 1990–91. Sports Reporter of Year, Sony, 1992. *Publications:* 8 Days a Week, 1988; (ed) Cricket Year (annually), 1989–2010; Over to You, Aggers (autobiog.), 1997; (with Peter Baxter) Inside the Box, 2009; (with Bill Frindall) Ask Bearders, 2009; Thanks, Johnners, 2010; Aggers' Ashes, 2011; Cricket: a modern anthology, 2013. *Address:* c/o Jane Morgan Management, Argentum, 2 Queen Caroline Street, W6 9DX. *T:* (020) 3178 8071.

AGNEW, Sir Rudolph (Ion Joseph), Kt 2002; Chairman, Stena International BV, 1990–2007; Director, 2004–09, Consultant, 2009–11, Petropavlovsk (formerly Peter Hambro Mining) PLC; *b* 12 March 1934; *s* of Rudolph John Agnew and Pamela Geraldine (*née* Campbell); *m* 1980, Whitney Warren. *Educ:* Downside School. Commissioned officer, 8th King's Royal Irish Hussars, 1953–57. Joined Consolidated Gold Fields, 1957; Dep. Chm., 1978–82; Gp Chief Exec., 1978–89; Chm., 1983–89; Mem., Cttee of Man. Dirs, 1986–89. Chairman: TVS Entertainment, 1990–93; Federated Aggregates PLC, 1991–95; Global Stone Corp. (Canada), 1993–94; Bona Shipholding Ltd, Bermuda, 1993–98; LASMO PLC, 1994–2000; Redland plc, 1995–97; Star Mining Corp., 1995–98; Wentworth Wooden Jigsaw Co., 2011–; non-executive Director: Internat. Tool and Supply (formerly New London) PLC, 1985–96; Standard Chartered PLC, 1988–97; Newmont Mining Corp., USA, 1989–98; Newmont Gold Co., USA, 1989–98; Stena (UK) Ltd, 1990–99; Director: Gold Fields of South Africa Ltd, 1978–89; Renison Goldfields Consolidated, 1978–90; Anglo American Corp. of South Africa, 1980–88; Hanson PLC, 1989–91. Vice President: Nat. Assoc. of Boys' Clubs; Game Conservancy (Fellow); Hawk Trust; Chm., World Conservation Monitoring Centre, 1989–2006 (Hon. Pres., 2013); Fellow, WWF (UK), 2006 (Trustee, 1983–89). CCMI (FBIM 1980); FRSA. *Recreations:* shooting, racing. *Clubs:* White's, Cavalry and Guards.

AGNEW, Stanley Clarke, CB 1985; FREng; FICE; Chief Engineer, Scottish Development Department, 1976–87, retired; *b* 18 May 1926; *s* of Christopher Gerald Agnew and Margaret Eleanor Agnew (*née* Clarke); *m* 1950, Isbell Evelyn Parker (*née* Davidson) (*d* 2012); two *d*. *Educ:* Royal Belfast Academical Instn; Queen's Univ., Belfast (BSc Civil Eng., 1947). FIWEM. Service with contractors, consulting engineers and local authorities, 1947–62; Eng. Inspector, Scottish Develt Dept, 1962–68, Dep. Chief Engr, 1968–75. FREng (FEng 1985). *Recreations:* golf, photography, motoring, gardening. *Club:* Murrayfield Golf (Edinburgh).

AGNEW, Steven; Member (Green) North Down, Northern Ireland Assembly, since 2011; *b* Dundonald, Belfast, 12 Oct. 1979; *s* of H. Bell and step *s* of R. Bell; partner, D. Hanna; one *s* one *d*. *Educ:* Brooklands Primary Sch., Dundonald, Belfast; Grosvenor Grammar Sch., Belfast; Queen's Univ., Belfast (BA Hons Philosophy). Porter, HSE NI, 2002; Homeless Support Worker: First Housing Aid and Support Services, 2003–04; Simon Community, 2004–07; Res. Officer to Brian Wilson, MLA, 2007–11. Contested (Green) N Down, 2015. *Recreations:* music, film, football, acting (appeared in I Wanted to Talk to You Last Night and Endless Life, directed by Michael MacBroom). *Address:* Northern Ireland Assembly, Parliament Buildings, Stormont, Belfast BT4 3XX. *T:* (028) 9052 1790. *E:* steven.agnew@mla.niassembly.gov.uk; (office) 76 Abbey Street, Bangor BT20 4JB. *T:* (028) 9145 9110.

AGNEW, Stuart; *see* Agnew, J. S.

AGNEW, Sir Theodore (Thomas More), Kt 2015; DL; philanthropist; *b* UK, 17 Jan. 1961; *s* of Stephen and Elizabeth Agnew; *m* 1993, Clare; one *s* one *d*. *Educ:* Rugby Sch. Non-executive Board Member: DfE, 2010–15 (Chm., Acads Bd, 2013–15); MoJ, 2015–. Founder and Chm., Inspiration Trust, 2012–; Trustee, New Schs Network, 2009–12. DL Norfolk, 2012. *Recreation:* European military history. *Clubs:* Boodle's, Cavalry and Guards.

AGNEW, (William Alexander) Fraser, MBE 2015; Cultural Co-ordinator, Newtownabbey Borough Council, 1981; *b* 16 Aug. 1942; *s* of late James Agnew and Maureen Barbara Agnew (*née* Fraser); *m* 1972, Lila McCausland; one *s*. *Educ:* Ballyclare High Sch.; Univ. of Ulster at Jordanstown; Belfast Tech. Coll.; Coll. of Business Studies. MCIOB (MIOB 1968). Architectural draughtsman and company dir, until 1990; part-time sports journalist; presenter, history programmes on community radio; lecturer. Mem., NI Assembly, 1982–86; Mem. (UU) Belfast North, NI Assembly, 1998–2003. Mem. (UU, 1980–90 and 2011–, Ind., 1990–2011) Newtownabbey BC (Chairman: Corporate Services Cttee, 1993–94, 1995–96; Culture and Tourism Cttee, 1995–); Mayor, Newtownabbey, 1990–91, 2013–14. Formerly Chm., Ulster Tourist Develt Assoc. Chm., Ulster Young Unionist Council, 1970. Associate Mem., Inst. of Engrg Technol., 1969. Freeman, Newtownabbey, 2007. *Publications:* numerous pamphlets on aspects of Ireland's history. *Recreations:* soccer coaching for children (qualified coach), 5-a-side football, golf. *Address:* 1 Knockview Crescent, Newtownabbey BT36 6UD. *T:* (028) 9050 6147; (office) Mossley Mill, Newtonabbey, Co. Antrim BT36 5QA.

AGNEW-SOMERVILLE, Sir (James) Lockett (Charles), 3rd Bt *cr* 1957, of Clendry, Co. Wigtown; plumbing and heating engineer; *b* Dublin, 26 May 1970; *o s* of Sir Quentin Agnew-Somerville, 2nd Bt and of Hon. April Drummond, *y d* of 15th Baron Strange; *S* father, 2010. *Educ:* Headfort, Co. Meath; Milton Abbey. NVQ Level 3 Plumbing and Heating; Gas Safe. *Publications:* (as Lockett Somerville) The London Eye (poetry). *Recreations:* tents, dogs, music. *Heir:* none. *Address:* 6 Albion Terrace, Ramsey, Isle of Man IM8 2LW.

AGRAN, Linda Valerie; Executive Producer, Sky Arts Theatre Live!, 2009; *b* 9 May 1947; *d* of Albert and Gertrude Agran; *m* 1991, Alexander Gordon Scott. *Educ:* Queen Elizabeth's Girls' Grammar Sch., Barnet. William Morris Agency, Columbia Pictures, Paramount Pictures, Warner Bros, 1973–76; Head of Development, 1976, Director, 1982, Euston Films; Writer in Residence, Aust. Film & TV Sch.; Dep. Controller of Drama and Arts, LWT, 1986; Chief Exec., Paravision (UK) Ltd, 1989; completed management buyout to form Agran Barton TV, 1993, Jt Chief Exec., 1993–2000; Founder, Linda Agran Clothes Storage, 2004. FRSA. *Television* (as producer or executive producer): series include: Minder; Widows; Paradise Postponed; London's Burning; Hercule Poirot; Moving Story. *Recreations:* cooking good food, drinking fine wines, horse racing, reading, all in the company of close friends.

AGRE, Prof. Peter Courtland, MD; Director, Malaria Research Institute, Johns Hopkins Bloomberg School of Public Health, since 2008; *b* 30 Jan. 1949; *s* of late Courtland Leverne Agre and of Ellen Violet Agre (*née* Swedberg); *m* 1975, Mary Macgill; one *s* three *d* (and one *d* decd). *Educ:* Theodore Roosevelt High Sch., Minneapolis; Augsburg Coll., Minneapolis (BA 1970); Johns Hopkins Univ. (MD 1974). Fellow, 1978–80, Asst Prof. of Medicine, 1980–81, Univ. of N Carolina; Sen. Clin. Res. Scientist, Wellcome Labs, Research Triangle Park, NC, 1980–81; Johns Hopkins University: Res. Associate, 1981–83, Asst Prof., 1984–88, Associate Prof., 1988–93, Sch. of Medicine; Prof. of Biol Chemistry and of Medicine, 1993–2005; Vice-Chancellor for Sci. and Technol., Duke Univ. Med. Center, 2005–07. (Jtly) Nobel Prize for Chemistry, 2003. *Publications:* articles in learned jls. *Address:* Malaria Research Institute, Johns Hopkins Bloomberg School of Public Health, Room E5132, 615 North Wolfe Street, Baltimore, MD 21205, USA.

AGUIRRE, Marcelino O.; *see* Oreja Aguirre.

ÁGÚSTSSON, Helgi, Hon. GCVO 1990; Icelandic Grand Order of the Falcon, 1990 (Order of the Falcon, 1979); Headmaster, Diplomatic School, Ministry of Foreign Affairs, Iceland, 2010–11; *b* 16 Oct. 1941; *s* of Ágúst Pétursson and Helga Jóhannesdóttir; *m* 1963, Hervör Jónasdóttir; three *s* one *d*. *Educ:* Univ. of Iceland (Law degree 1970); Icelandic Sch. of Travel and Tourism (dip. tour guide, 2010). Joined Foreign Ministry, 1970; served London, 1973–77; Counsellor, 1977; Dir, Defence Div., Foreign Min., 1979 and Chm., US-Icelandic Defence Council; Minister-Counsellor, 1980; served Washington, 1983–87; Dep. Perm. Under-Sec., Foreign Min., 1987, in rank of Ambassador; Ambassador to UK, 1989–94, and to Ireland, Holland and Nigeria, 1990–94; Perm. Under-Sec., Min. for Foreign Affairs, Iceland, 1995–99; Ambassador: to Denmark, also accredited to Lithuania, Turkey, Israel and Romania, 1999–2002; to USA, also accredited to Argentina, Brazil, Chile, El Salvador, Guatemala, Mexico and Uruguay, 2002–06; Special Assignments, Min. of Foreign Affairs, 2007–08; Chief of Protocol, Min. of Foreign Affairs, Iceland, 2008; Advr, 2008–09. Chm. Bd, Save the Children, Iceland, 2009–12. Former Pres., Icelandic Basketball Fedn. Decorations from Finland, Denmark, Sweden, Norway, Italy, Spain, Netherlands. *Recreations:* theatre, music, reading, salmon fishing.

AGUTTER, Jennifer Ann, OBE 2012; actress; *b* 20 Dec. 1952; *d* of Derek and Catherine Agutter; *m* 1990, Johan Tham; one *s*. *Educ:* Elmhurst Ballet School, Camberley. *Films:* East of Sudan, 1964; Ballerina, 1964; Gates of Paradise, 1967; Star, 1968; Walkabout, I Start Counting, The Railway Children, 1969 (Royal Variety Club Most Promising Artist, 1971); Logan's Run, 1975; The Eagle Has Landed, Equus (BAFTA Best Supporting Actress, 1977), The Man In The Iron Mask, 1976; Dominique, Clayton and Catherine, 1977; The Riddle of the Sands, Sweet William, 1978; The Survivor, 1980; An American Werewolf in London, 1981; Secret Places, 1983; Dark Tower, 1987; King of the Wind, 1989; Child's Play 2, 1991; Freddie as Fro7, 1992; Blue Juice, 1995; The Parole Officer, 2001; Number One, Longing, Number Two, Regret, 2004; Heroes and Villains, 2006; Irina Palm, 2008; Glorious 39, 2009; Outside Bet, 2012; Avengers Assemble, 2012; Captain America: The Winter Soldier, 2014; *stage:* School for Scandal, 1972; Rooted, Arms and the Man, The Ride Across Lake Constance, 1973; National Theatre: The Tempest, Spring Awakening, 1974; Hedda, Betrayal, 1980; Peter Pan, 1997; Royal Shakespeare Co.: Arden of Faversham, Lear, King Lear, The Body, 1982–83; Breaking the Silence, 1985; Shrew, The Unified Field, LA, 1987; Breaking the Code, NY, 1987; Love's Labour's Lost, Barbican, 1995; Mothers and Daughters, Chichester, 1996; Equus, Gielgud, 2007; *television includes:* Long After Summer, 1967; The Wild Duck, The Cherry Orchard, The Snow Goose (Emmy Best Supporting Actress), 1971; A War of Children, 1972; School Play, 1979; Amy, 1980; Love's Labour's Lost, This Office Life, 1984; Silas Marner, 1985; Murder She Wrote, 1986; The Equaliser, Magnum, 1988; Dear John, 1989; Not a Penny More, Not a Penny Less, Tecx, 1990; The Good Guys, Puss in Boots, 1991; The Buccaneers, 1995; And the Beat Goes On, 1996; Bramwell, A Respectable Trade, 1998; The Railway Children, 2000; Spooks, 2002, 2003; The Alan Clark Diaries, 2004; The Invisibles, 2008; Monday Monday, 2009; Call the Midwife, 2012–. Hon. DLitt Bradford, 2004. *Publications:* Snap, 1983. *Address:* c/o The Artists Partnership, 101 Finsbury Pavement, EC2A 1RS. *T:* (020) 7439 1456.

AGUTTER, Richard Devenish; corporate finance adviser, since 1976; Senior Adviser, KPMG, 1998–2005; *b* 17 Sept. 1941; *s* of late Anthony Tom Devenish Agutter and Joan Hildegare Sabina (*née* Machen); *m* 1968, Lesley Anne Ballard; three *s*. *Educ:* Marlborough Coll. CA 1964. With W. T. Walton, 1960–64; joined Peat Marwick Mitchell, subsequently KPMG, 1964: Partner, 1977–98; Chm., KPMG Internat. Corporate Finance, 1990–96. City of London: Alderman, Ward of Castle Baynard, 1995–2005; Sheriff, 2000–01. Liveryman: Goldsmiths' Co., 1979– (Mem., Ct of Assts, 1999–; Prime Warden, 2013–14); Co. of Marketors, 1999–; Hon. Liveryman, Co. of Tax Advisers, 2005 (Mem., Ct of Assts, 2005–; Master, 2008–09); Master, Guild of Freemen, 2004. Hon. Fellow, Birkbeck, Univ. of London, 2011. *Recreations:* wine, gardening, sailing. *Address:* Leabridge Farmhouse, West Burton, near Pulborough, West Sussex RH20 1HD. *T:* (01798) 839169.

AHEARNE, Stephen James, FCA; Chief Financial Officer, 1990–96, and Managing Director, 1992–96, British Petroleum Company PLC; *b* 7 Sept. 1939; *s* of James Joseph Ahearne and Phyllis Eva (*née* Grigsby); *m* 1965, Janet Elizabeth Edwards; two *s*. Qualified as Chartered Accountant, 1962; joined British Petroleum, 1964: Man. Dir, BP Denmark, 1978–81; Exec. Dir, BP Chems, 1981–86; Gp Controller, 1986–88; Gp Planner, 1988–90. Mem., Restrictive Practices Court, 1993–99. Gov., Felsted Sch., 1996–. *Recreations:* tennis, gardening, walking, reading, learning languages.

AHERN, Bertie; Member of the Dáil (TD) (FF), 1977–2011; Taoiseach (Prime Minister of Ireland), 1997–2008; President, Fianna Fáil, 1994–2008; *b* 12 Sept. 1951; *s* of Cornelius and Julia Ahern; *m* 1975 (separated); two *d*. *Educ:* Rathmines Coll. of Commerce; University Coll., Dublin. Accountant. Asst Chief Whip, 1980–81; spokesman on youth affairs, 1981; Govt Chief Whip and Minister of State at Depts of Taoiseach and Defence, 1982; Minister for Labour, 1987–91; Minister for Finance, 1991–94; Leader of the Opposition, 1994–97. Lord Mayor of Dublin, 1986–87. Member, Board of Governors, 1991–94: IMF; World Bank; EIB (Chm., 1991–92). Grand Cross, Order of Merit with Star and Sash (Germany), 1991. *Recreations:* sports, reading. *Address:* Drumcondra Business Centre, 120 Upper Drumcondra Road, Drumcondra, Dublin 9, Ireland.

AHERN, Dermot; Member of the Dáil (TD) (FF) for Louth, 1987–2011; Minister for Justice, Equality and Law Reform, Republic of Ireland, 2008–11; *b* 2 Feb. 1955; *s* of Jerry Ahern; *m* 1980, Maeve Coleman; two *d*. *Educ:* St Mary's Coll. Secondary Sch., Dundalk; University Coll., Dublin (BCL); Law Soc. of Ireland. Mem. (FF) Louth CC, 1979–91. Asst Govt Whip, 1988–91; Minister of State, Dept of Defence and Dept of Taoiseach, and Govt Chief Whip, 1991–92; Minister: for Social, Community and Family Affairs, 1997–2002; for Communications, Marine and Natural Resources, 2002–04; for Foreign Affairs, 2004–08. Mem., British-Irish Parly Body, 1991–97 (Co-Chm., 1993–95). *Recreations:* windsurfing, skiing, golf. *Address:* Blackrock, Dundalk, Co. Louth, Ireland.

AHERNE, Gerald Paul; Chairman, Cenkos Securities plc, since 2012; Managing Partner, Javelin Capital Partners LLP, since 2003; *b* London, 15 Jan. 1946; *s* of John Aherne and Eileen Aherne (*née* Peters); *m* 1st, 1971, Mary Wright (marr. diss. 1987); one *s* one *d*; 2nd, 1995, Robina Handley (marr. diss. 2006); two *d*. *Educ:* St Joseph's Acad., Blackheath; Univ. of Surrey (BSc Maths). AIA 1980. Actuarial and investment mgt rôles in UK and Europe, Equity & Law, 1968–86; Investment Dir, Schroder Investment Mgt, 1986–2002; Founding Dir, PRI Gp plc, 2002–03; Founding Partner and Chief Exec., Javelin Capital LLP, 2009–11; Chm., Electric & General Investment Fund (formerly Trust plc), 2012– (non-exec. Dir, 2003–11); non-executive Director: Henderson Global Investors Ltd, 2004–12; Majedie Investments plc, 2006–09, 2011–; Hadleigh plc, 2007–11; Mecom Gp plc, 2009–12; TSM Agencies Ltd, 2010–12; Omnis Investments Ltd, 2012–; Iveagh Ltd, 2012–; Linear Investments, 2013–. *Recreations:* film, fishing, travel, politics, gardening. *Address:* Cenkos Securities plc, 6, 7, 8 Tokenhouse Yard, EC2R 7AS. *T:* (020) 7397 8910. *E:* gaherne@cenkos.com. *Club:* City of London.

AHMAD, family name of **Baron Ahmad of Wimbledon**.

AHMAD OF WIMBLEDON, Baron *cr* 2011 (Life Peer), of Wimbledon in the London Borough of Merton; **Tariq Mahmood Ahmad;** Parliamentary Under-Secretary of State, Home Office and Department for Transport, since 2015; *b* London, 3 April 1968; *s* of Chaudhry Mansoor Ahmad, BT and Amtul Matin Ahmad (*née* Mir); *m* 2011, Siddiquea Masud; two *s* one *d*. *Educ:* Rutlish Sch.; London South Bank Univ. (BA Hons Business 1990); City Univ. (ACIB 1996). Mgt roles in corporate banking and Hd Office, NatWest Gp, 1991–2000; Vice Pres., and Dir, Marketing, Alliance Berstein, 2000–03; Dir, Strategy and Marketing, Sucden Financial Ltd, 2004–12. Mem. (C) Merton LBC, 2002–12 (Mem. Cabinet for Envmt, 2006–08, for Community Safety and Policing, 2008–09). A Lord in Waiting (Govt Whip), 2012–14; Parly Under-Sec. of State, DCLG, 2014–15. Contested (C) Croydon N, 2005. Vice Chm., Conservative Party, 2008–10. MInstD. *Recreations:* charity work, various sports, charity runs. *Address:* House of Lords, SW1A 0PW. *E:* ahmadt@parliament.uk.

AHMAD, Asif Anwar; HM Diplomatic Service; Ambassador to the Philippines, since 2013; *b* London, 21 Jan. 1956; *s* of late Salahuddin Ahmad and of Bandana Ahmad; *m* 1994, Zubeda Khamboo; three *s* one *d*. *Educ:* Community High Sch., Tehran; Carlisle Tech. Coll.; Durham Univ. (BA Hons Econs 1977); INSEAD (Internat. Exec. Prog. 1991). Nat. Westminster Bank, later NatWest, 1977–96, Sen. Manager, internat., domestic and private banking; business advr, Business Link London, 1996–99; joined FCO, 1999; Dep. Hd, Resource Budgeting Dept, 1999–2000; Hd, Commonwealth Co-ordination Dept, 2001–04; Hd, Communication and Inf. Centre, Prime Minister's Office, 2003–04; Dir, Asia, UK Trade and Investment, 2004–08; Hd, SE Asia and Pacific Dept, FCO, 2008–10; Ambassador to Thailand, 2010–12. *Recreations:* passionate Liverpool FC fan, cricket, theatre, music, travel. *Address:* c/o Foreign and Commonwealth Office, King Charles Street, SW1A 2AH. *E:* asif.ahmad@fco.gov.uk.

AHMAD, Khurshid; Chairman: Institute of Policy Studies, Islamabad, Pakistan, since 1979; Board of Trustees, Islamic Foundation, Leicester, since 1985; Member, Senate of Pakistan, 1985–97, and 2003–12; *b* 23 March 1932; three *s* three *d*. *Educ:* Karachi Univ. (LLB; MA Economics; MA Islamic Studies). Dir-Gen., Islamic Foundn, Leicester, 1973–78; Federal Minister for Planning and Develt and Dep. Chm., Planning Commn, Govt of Pakistan, 1978–79. Chm., Internat. Inst. of Islamic Econs, Islamic Univ., Islamabad, 1983–87. Hon. PhD: Educn, Nat. Univ. of Malaya; Internat. Islamic Univ., Kuala Lumpur; Hon. DLitt Loughborough, 2003. Islamic Develt Bank Laureate for dist. contribn to Islamic econs, 1988; King Faisal, Internat. Prize for service to Islam, 1990. *Publications:* Essays on Pakistan Economy (Karachi), 1958; An Analysis of Munir Report (Lahore), 1958; (ed) Studies in the Family Law of Islam (Karachi), 1960; (ed) The Quran: an Introduction (Karachi), 1966; The Prophet of Islam (Karachi), 1967; Principles of Islamic Education (Lahore), 1970; Fanaticism, Intolerance and Islam (Lahore), 1970; Islam and the West (Lahore), 1972; The Religion of Islam (Lahore), 1973; (ed) Islam: its meaning and message (London, Islamic Council of Europe), 1976; Development Strategy for the Sixth Plan (Islamabad), 1983; Islamic Approach to Development: some policy implications (Islamabad), 1994; Islamic Resurgence: challenges, directions and future perspectives, ed I. M. Abu-Rabi, 1995; The Crisis of the Political System in Pakistan and the Jamaat-e-Islami, 1996; *for Islamic Foundation, Leicester:* Islam: Basic Principles and Characteristics, 1974; Family Life in Islam, 1974; Islamic Perspectives: Studies in honour of Maulana Mawdudi, 1979; The Quran: Basic Teachings, 1979; Studies in Islamic Economics, 1980; contrib. The Third World's Dilemma of Development, Non-Aligned Third World Annual, (USA) 1970. *Recreations:* travelling, reading. *Address:* Islamic Foundation, Markfield Conference Centre, Ratby Lane, Markfield, Leics LE67 9SY. *T:* (01530) 244944; Institute of Policy Studies, House 1, Street 8, F-6/3, Islamabad 44000, Pakistan. *T:* (51) 8438391. *E:* khurshid@ips.net.pk.

AHMAD, Mushtaq, OBE 2007; JP; Lord-Lieutenant of Lanarkshire, since 2010; *b* Chhinah, India, 12 Nov. 1942; *s* of Choudary Inayat Ali Ahmadi and Khurshaid Begum; three *s* two *d* by Ann-Marie Razia Anne. *Educ:* Punjab Univ. (BA 1962); Univ. of Glasgow (MA 1969; Dip. Adult Educn 1993); Jordanhill Coll. of Educn, Glasgow (PGCE 1971). Migrated to Pakistan, 1947, moved to UK, 1963; worked in British industry, 1963–66; teacher: of modern studies, Earnock High Sch., Hamilton, 1972–74; of English, Daneford High Sch., London, 1974–77; Specialist Organiser of Adult Basic Educn, Lanarks, 1977–97. Chm.-Consultant (pt-time), Lifeskills Central, 2007–; Chm., Hamilton Dist, CAB, 2008–. Mem., Hamilton DC, then South Lanarks Council, 1988–2007, Provost, South Lanarks Council, 2003–07. Founder Pres., 2003–08, Vice Pres., 2008–, Scottish Provost's Assoc. JP Hamilton, 1988 (Chm., Justice's Cttee, 1988–2003). Mem., Amnesty Internat. *Recreations:* charity work to help alleviate the difficulties experienced by the disadvantaged, reading, current affairs. *Address:* 79 Rosevale Crescent, Hamilton, Lanarks ML3 8NX. *T:* and *Fax:* (01698) 429993, *T:* 07768 093979. *E:* mushtaq.ahmad@blueyonder.co.uk.

AHMADI, Hon. Aziz Mushabber; Chief Justice of India, 1994–97; *b* 25 March 1932; *s* of M. I. Ahmadi and Shirin I. Ahmadi; *m* 1960, Amena A. Muchhala; one *s* one *d*. *Educ:* Ahmedabad and Surat (LLB). Called to the Bar, Ahmedabad, 1954; Judge, City Civil and Sessions Court, Ahmedabad, 1964–74; Sec., Legal Dept, Govt of Gujarat, 1974–76; Judge, High Court of Gujarat, 1976–88; Judge, Supreme Court of India, 1988–94. Pres., Supreme Court Legal Aid Cttee, 1989; Exec. Chm., Cttee for Implementing Legal Aid Schemes in India, 1994. Chairman: Adv. Bd, Conservation of Foreign Exchange and Prevention of Smuggling Activities Act, 1974; Adv. Bd, Prevention of Black Marketing, Maintenance of Supplies of Essential Commodities Act, 1982–83; Gujarat Third Pay Commn, 1982–85. Member: UN Commn of Inquiry, East Timor, 1999; Internat. Bar Assoc. Mission to Zimbabwe, 2001. Chancellor, Aligarh Muslim Univ., 2003–06. Hon. Bencher, Middle Temple, 1996. Hon. LLD: Kurukshetra, 1994; Maharishi Dayanand, 1995; Kanpur, 1995; Sardar Patel, 1996; Cochin, 1997; Leicester, 1998. *Recreations:* reading, music. *Address:* C-3 Kant Enclave, near Dr Karni Singh Shooting Ranges, Anangpur, Haryana 121003, India. *T:* (129) 2511291, (129) 2511293, *Fax:* (129) 2511285, (11) 26966389. *E:* amahmadi@bol.net.in. *Clubs:* Delhi Gymkhana, India International Centre (New Delhi).

AHMED, Baron *cr* 1998 (Life Peer), of Rotherham in the co. of South Yorkshire; **Nazir Ahmed;** business development manager; *b* 24 April 1957; *s* of Haji Sain Mohammed and Rashim Bibi; *m* 1974, Sakina Bibi; two *s* one *d*. *Educ:* Thomas Rotherham Coll.; Sheffield Hallam Univ. Business development manager: mini-markets, 1979–82; fish and chip shops, 1979–2003; petrol station, 1982–84; marble mining, Azad, Kashmir, 1985–87; business park and property develt, 1990–. Advisor to Nestlé, 2003–06. Mem. (Lab) Rotherham MBC, 1990–2000. Founder, British Muslim Councillors Forum; founder Chm., Muslims for Labour. Chm., S Yorks Lab. Party, 1993–98. Chairman: All-Pty Parly Libya Gp, 1999–2001; All-Pty Parly Gp on Kashmir, 2010; All-Pty Parly Interfaith Inter-religious Gp; All-Pty Parly Financial Exploitation Gp; founder and Chm., All-Pty Parly Entrepreneurship Gp; founder, All-Pty Parly Enterprise Gp, 2009–13. Founder and Co-Chm., Govt's Forced Marriage Wkg Gp, 1999–; Chm., Preventing Extremism Together Working Gp on Imams trng and role of mosques, 2005. Mem., Channel 4 Hate Commn (on hate crime), 1999–. Mem. Council, BHF, 2007–. Pres., S Yorks Victim Support. Led first Hajj delegn on behalf of British govt, 2000; leader, British Muslim Peace and Reconciliation Initiative, 2009–. Advr to many internat. orgns on dialogue, tolerance and co-operation. Chancellor, British Inst. of Technol. and E-commerce, 2009–13. JP Rotherham, 1992. *Recreation:* volleyball. *Address:* 152 East Bawtry Road, Rotherham S60 4LG. *T:* (01709) 730140; House of Lords, SW1A 0PW.

AHMED, Aaqil; Head of Religion and Ethics, BBC, since 2009; *b* Wigan, 5 June 1969; *s* of Maqbool Ahmed and Farhat Ahmed; *m* 1996, Saima Javed; one *s* two *d*. *Educ:* Univ. of Westminster (BA Hons Photography, Film and Video); London Business Sch. (Accelerated Develt Prog. 2010). BBC: Researcher, 1992–94, Asst Producer, 1994–95, Producer, 1995–96, Network TV; Producer, Network News and Current Affairs, 1997–2000; Exec. Producer, Religion and Ethics, 2000–03; Hd, Religion and Multicultural Progs, Channel 4, 2003–09. Chair: Mosaic Media Network, 2008–11; Cultural Diversity Network North, 2009–13; Mem. Bd, Mosaic, 2009–; Pres., BBC Black and Asian Workers Forum, 2014–. Trustee: Runnymede Trust, 2008–11; Rugby League Foundn, 2014–; Patron, Curriculum for Cohesion, 2013–. Prof. of Media, Middlesex Univ., 2013– (Vis. Prof. of Media, 2011–13). Hon. Dr: Lancaster, 2012; Bolton, 2012. *Publications:* (contrib.) The Future of Public Service Broadcasting, 2008. *Recreations:* keen cyclist and regular five-a-side football player, coach and manager of under 15s football team, supporter of Bolton Wanderers, keen gardener and cook, learning the Arabic language in between reliving my youth on my Vespa scooter. *Address:* BBC, Dock House, MediaCityUK, Salford M50 2LH. *E:* Aaqil.ahmed@bbc.co.uk.

AHMED, Prof. Haroon, ScD; FREng; Professor of Microelectronics, University of Cambridge, 1992–2003, now Emeritus; Fellow, 1967–2007, now Honorary Fellow, Master, 2000–06, Corpus Christi College, Cambridge (Warden of Leckhampton, 1993–98); *b* 2 March 1936; *s* of Mohammad Nizam Ahmed and Bilquis Jehan Ahmed; *m* 1969, Evelyn Anne Travers Goodrich; one *s* two *d*. *Educ:* St Patrick's Sch., Karachi; Imperial College London; King's College, Cambridge (PhD 1963); ScD Cantab 1996. GEC and Hirst Research Centre, 1958–59; Turner and Newall Res. Fellow, 1962–63; University of Cambridge: Univ. Demonstrator, Engineering Dept, 1963–66; Lectr, Engineering Dept, 1966–84; Reader in Microelectronics, 1984–92. Vis. Prof., Computer Lab., 2010–, Engrg Dept, 2015–, Univ. of Cambridge. Non-exec. Dir, Addenbrooke's NHS Trust, 2001–04. Pres., Cambridge Philosophical Soc., 2004–06. Syndic, CUP, 1996–2002. Higher Educn Advr, Govt of Pakistan, 2006–08. Trustee: Noon Educnl Foundn, 2001–; Edith Evelyn Wali Mohammad Trust, 2009–. Mem., Develt Bd, Imperial Coll. London, 2006–10. FREng (FEng 1990). *Publications:* (with A. H. W. Beck) Introduction to Physical Electronics, 1968; (with P. J. Spreadbury) Electronics for Engineers, 1973, 2nd edn 1984; Cambridge Computing, 2013; (with P. N. Denbigh) Cambridge Depicted, 2013. *Recreation:* golf. *Address:* Corpus Christi College, Cambridge CB2 1RH.

AHMED, Kamal; Business Editor, BBC, since 2014; *b* London, 8 Nov. 1967; *s* of Abubaker Ismail Ahmed and Elaine Ahmed (*née* Sturman); *m* 2011, Elizabeth Day; one *s* one *d* from a previous marriage. *Educ:* Drayton Manor High Sch.; Univ. of Leeds (BA Hons Politics); City University (Dip. Newspaper Journalism). Reporter, Lennox Herald, 1990–92; Chief Reporter, Scotland on Sunday, 1992–95; Royal Corresp., 1995–97, Media Editor, 1997–2000, The Guardian; Political Editor, 2000–04, Hd, News, 2004–07, The Observer; Dir, Communications, Equality and Human Rights Commn, 2007–09; Business Editor, Sunday Telegraph, 2009–14. *Recreation:* gardening (badly). *Address:* BBC News, Broadcasting House, Portland Place, W1A 1AA.

AHMED, Masood; Director, Middle East and Central Asia, International Monetary Fund, since 2008; *b* 13 Jan. 1953; *s* of late Aziz Ahmed and Phool Aziz Ahmed; *m* 1979, Priscilla Macleod; one *d*. *Educ:* St Joseph's Sch., Dhaka; Karachi Grammar Sch., Karachi; LSE (BSc Econ. 1974, MSc Econ. with dist. 1975). Res. Asst, then Lectr, LSE, 1975–78; joined World Bank, 1979: Economist, then Dep. Div. Chief, Energy Dept, 1980–86; Div. Chief, N Africa Country Dept, 1987–91; Div. Chief, Internat. Debt and Finance, 1991–93; Dir, Internat. Econs Dept, 1993–97; Vice Pres., Poverty Reduction and Econ. Mgt, 1997–2000; Dep. Dir, Policy Develt and Review, IMF, 2000–03; Dir Gen., Policy and Internat., DFID, 2003–06; Dir, External Relns, IMF, 2006–08. *Recreations:* Urdu poetry, biographies, walking. *Address:* Middle East and Central Asia Department, International Monetary Fund, Washington, DC 20431, USA. *E:* mahmed@imf.org. *Club:* Reform.

AHMED, Samira; freelance journalist and broadcaster, BBC Radio and TV, since 2011; *b* 15 June 1968; *d* of Athar Ahmad and Lalita Ahmed (*née* Chatterjee); *m* 1996, Brian Michael Millar; one *s* one *d*. *Educ:* Wimbledon High Sch.; St Edmund Hall, Oxford (BA Hons English 1989); City Univ., London (Postgrad. Dip. Newspaper Journalism 1990). BBC: news trainee, 1990–92; network radio news reporter, 1992; Presenter, World Service TV, 1993; Reporter, Newsnight, 1993–94; News Corresp., 1994–97; LA Corresp., 1996–97; Presenter: Deutsche Welle TV, Berlin, 1998; BBC News 24/BBC World, 1998–99; (and writer) Islam Unveiled, documentary series, Channel 4, 2004; Presenter/Corresp., Channel 4 News, 2000–11. Vis. Prof. of Journalism, Kingston Univ., 2011–. Broadcaster of the Year, Stonewall, 2009. *Recreations:* reading, cinema, theatre, Berlin, collecting Amar Chitra Katha comics, swimming. *Address:* c/o Knight Ayton Management, 35 Great James Street, WC1N 3HB. *W:* www.samiraahmed.co.uk.

AHMED-SHEIKH, Tasmina, OBE 2014; MP (SNP) Ochil and South Perthshire, since 2015; *b* Chelsea; *m* Zulfikar Sheikh; two *s* two *d*. *Educ:* Univ. of Edinburgh (MA 1991); Strathclyde Univ. (LLB 1995; Postgrad. DipLaw 1996). NP; WS 2009. Mem., Faculty of Procurators, 1996; admitted as solicitor, 1997; Partner, 2005–10, Equity Partner, 2010–15, Hamilton Burns, WS. Columnist, The National. City of Glasgow College: Chm., Internat. and Commercial Develt Cttee, 2011–; Mem. Bd, Remuneration and Nominations Cttee, 2011–. Mem., Adv. Bd, Yes Scotland Campaign, Yes Scotland Ltd, 2012–14. Scottish National Party: Mem. Bd, Finance and Audit Cttee, 2012–; Nat. Women's and Equalities Officer, 2012–. Founder and Chair, Scottish Asian Women's Assoc., 2012–. *Address:* House of Commons, SW1A 0AA.

AHO, Esko Tapani; Senior Fellow, Mossavar-Rahmani Center for Business and Government, Harvard University, 2012–14; Prime Minister of Finland, 1991–95; *b* Veteli, 20 May 1954; *s* of Kauko Kaleva Aho and Laura Kyllikki Aho (*née* Harjupatana); *m* 1980, Kirsti Hannele Söderkultalahti; three *s* one *d*. *Educ:* Univ. of Helsinki (Master of Pol Scis). Political Sec. to Minister for Foreign Affairs, Finland, 1979–80; MP (Centre Party), Helsinki, 1983–2003; Chm., Finnish Parlt, April 1991; Member: Traffic Commn, 1983–86; Finances Commn, 1987–90. Member: CSCE Cttee, 1984–90; Finnish Delegn, Nordic Council, 1983–89; Finnish Delegn, Council of Europe, 1989–91. Chairman: League, Centre Party Youth, 1974–80; Finnish Centre Party, 1990–2002. Vice-Chm., Liberal Internat., 1994–2002; Chm., Finnish Ski Assoc., 1996–2000; Vice-Chm., Finnish Olympic Cttee, 1997–2000. Elector, Presidential Elections, 1978, 1982 and 1998. Member, Advisory Board: Outokumpu Oy (Metal Ind.), 1985–91; OKO (Bank), 1991; SOK (Diversified Co-op.), 1990–91. Lectr, Harvard Univ., 2001–02; Chm., Verbatum Oy, corporate consulting co., 2002–04; Pres., Finnish Nat. Fund for Res. and Develt (Sitra), 2004–08; Exec. Vice Pres., Corporate Relns and Responsibility, Nokia Corp., 2008–12 (Mem., Nokia Leadership Team, 2009–12; Consultative Partner, 2012–); Member: Bd, Fortum Corp., 2006–; Bd of Dirs, Russian Venture Co., 2007–10; Bd of Dirs, Terveystalo Gp, 2012–. Vice-Chm. Bd, Technol. Industries of Finland, 2009–; Mem., Bd of Dirs, Technol. Acad. of Finland, 2009–; Mem., Sci. and Technol. in Soc. Forum. Member: Club of Madrid; InterAction Council. Mem., World Council, and Vice Chm., Finland, ICC, 2009–. Grand Cross, Order of White Rose (Finland), 1992; Cavaliere di Gran Croce, Order of Merit (Italy), 1993. *Recreations:* literature, golf.

AHRENDS, Peter; Founding Partner, 1961, Director, 1961–2009, and Consultant, 2009–12, Ahrends, Burton & Koralek, Architects; *b* 30 April 1933; *s* of Steffen Bruno Ahrends and Margarete Marie Sophie Visino; *m* 1954, Elizabeth Robertson (*d* 2007); two *d*. *Educ:* King Edward VII Sch., Johannesburg; Architectural Assoc. Sch. of Architecture (Dipl., Hons). RIBA 1959. Steffen Ahrends & Partners, Johannesburg, 1957–58; Denys Lasdun & Partners, 1959–60; Julian Keable & Partners; major projects, 1961–, include: *public buildings:* Hampton Site, Nat. Gall. Extn, 1982–85 (comp. winning entry); St Mary's Hosp., Newport, IoW (nucleus low energy hosp.), 1990; White Cliffs Heritage Centre, Dover, 1991; Techniquest Science Centre, 1995 (RIBA Arch. Award); Dublin Dental Hosp., 1994–; Sculpture Court, Whitworth Art Gall., Manchester, 1995 (RIBA Arch. Award); Waterford Visitor Centre, 1998; N Tipperary Council civic offices, Nenagh, 2000–; Offaly Council offices, Tullamore, 2002 (RIBA Award, 2003); Galway Council office extension, library and HQ, 2002; *educational buildings:* New Liby, TCD, 1961 (internat. comp.); Templeton Coll., Oxford, phased completion over 25 years from 1969; residential bldg, Keble Coll., Oxford, 1976 (RIBA Arch. Award, 1978); Arts Faculty Bldg, TCD, 1979; Loughborough Univ. Business Sch., 1997; IT bldg and catering bldg, Inst. of Technology, Tralee, 1998; tourism and leisure bldg, Waterford Inst. of Technology, 1999; first phase bldgs, Inst. of Technology, Blanchardstown, 1999; *residential buildings:* Nebenzahl House, Jerusalem, 1972; Whitmore Court Housing, 1975 (RIBA Good Design in Housing Award, 1977); housing, Newcastle West, Limerick, 2004; *commercial/industrial buildings:* warehouse, showroom and offices, Habitat, 1974 (Structural Steel Design Award, FT Industrial Arch. Award, 1976); factory, Cummins Engines (Struct. Steel Design Award, 1980); Sainsbury supermarket, Canterbury, 1984 (Struct. Steel Design Award, 1985); W. H. Smith offices, Swindon, 1985; British Embassy, Moscow, 1988–99; John Lewis dept store, Kingston-upon-Thames, 1990; office develt for Stanhope Trafalgar, 1990–; office building, Tel Aviv, 1998; *sports buildings:* Carrickmines Croquet and Lawn Tennis Club, Dublin, 1998; *transport:* Docklands Light Railway Beckton Extension stations, 1987–93; *development plans:* MBA Sch., Templeton Coll., Univ. of Oxford, 1992; Falmer Develt Plan, Univ. of Brighton, 1992; Cardiff Inner Harbour, 1993; Inst. of Technology, Tralee, 1998; Waterford Inst. of Technology, 1998; City Block, Dublin, 2000; Dublin Corp. NEIC Civic Centre, Dublin, 2000; TCD Dublin Docklands Innovation Centre, 2001; Inst. of Technol., Blanchardstown, 2002; Arts Faculty Extension Bldg, TCD, 2002; Bexhill Town Centre Develt Plan, 2004; *competition wins:* Campus Develt Plan, Univ. of Grenoble, 1990–93; Designs on Democracy, Stockport, 2003. Chair: UK Architects Against Apartheid, 1988–93; Newham Design Review Panel, 2007–13 (Design Advr, Newham Strategic Develt Cttee, 2010–13); Member: Design Council, 1988–93; Council, AA, 1965–67. Vis. Prof. of Architecture, Kingston Poly., 1983–84; Bartlett Prof. of Arch., Bartlett Sch. of Arch. and Planning, UCL, 1986–89; part-time teaching posts and workshops at AA Sch. of Arch., Canterbury Sch. of Art, Edinburgh Univ., Winter Sch. Edinburgh, Plymouth Poly., Kingston Poly., and Plymouth Sch. of Art; vis. critic and/or ext. examr at Kumasi Univ., AA Sch. of Arch., Nova Scotia Tech. Univ., Strathclyde Univ. Exhibitions of drawings and works: RIBA Heinz Gall., 1980; RIAI, 1981; Douglas Hyde Gall., Dublin, 1981; Braunschweig Tech. Univ., Tech. Univ. of Hanover, Museum of Finnish Arch., 1982; Univ. of Oulu, Alvar Aalto Museum, Finland, 1982; AA HQ, Oslo, 1983. *Publications:* (contrib.) Ahrends Burton & Koralek, Architects (monograph), 1991; *relevant publications:* Collaborations: the work of ABK, ed by Kenneth Powell, 2002; Ahrends, Burton and Koralek, 2012, by Kenneth Powell; papers and articles in RIBA Jl and other prof. jls. *Recreations:* architecture, France. *Address:* 16 Rochester Road, NW1 9JH. *E:* pahrends@gmail.com.

AHTISAARI, Martti Oiva Kalevi; President, Republic of Finland, 1994–2000; Founder and Chairman of Board, Crisis Management Initiative, since 2000; *b* 23 June 1937; *s* of Oiva and Tyyne Ahtisaari; *m* 1968, Eeva Irmeli Hyvärinen; one *s*. Finnish diplomat; joined Ministry for Foreign Affairs, 1965; Ambassador to Tanzania, 1973–76; Under-Sec. of State, Internat. Develt Co-operation, 1984–86; Under-Sec. Gen., Admin and Mgt, 1987–91; Sec. of State for Foreign Affairs, 1991–94; UN envoy; UN Comr for Namibia, 1977–81; head, operation monitoring Namibia's transition to independence, 1989–90; senior envoy in Yugoslavia, 1992–93; EU Special envoy in Kosovo, 1999; Mem., observer gp on Austrian govt human rights record, 2000; co-inspector, IRA arms dumps, 2000; Chm., panel on security and safety of UN personnel in Iraq, 2003; special envoy of UN Secretary-General: for the Horn of Africa, 2003–06; for future status process for Kosovo, 2005–08. Chairman: Balkan Children and Youth Foundn, 2000–; Governing Council, Interpeace, 2000–09, now Chm. Emeritus and Special Advr; Ind. Commn on Turkey, 2004–; Co-Chair, Eur. Council on Foreign Relns, 2007–. Dir-at-Large, ImagineNations Gp, 2008–. Member: Internat. Sen. Adv. Bd, W Asia N Africa Regl Forum, 2008–; The Elders, 2009–; Bd of Trustees, Silatech. Mem., Prize Cttee, Mo Ibrahim Foundn, 2007–. Chm. Supervisory Bd, Finnish Nat. Opera, 2004–. Holds numerous honorary doctorates. Hon. AO 2002. Nobel Peace Prize, 2008. *Address:* (office) Eteläranta 12, 2nd Floor, 00130 Helsinki, Finland.

AIKEN, Philip Stanley, AM 2013; Chairman: Aveva Group plc, since 2012; Balfour Beatty, since 2015; *b* Sydney, Australia, 9 Jan. 1949; *s* of Stanley Ernest Aiken and Aileen Winifred Aiken; *m* 1976, Frances Barbara McCluskey; three *s*. *Educ:* Univ. of Sydney (BE Chem. Engrg 1970); Harvard Business Sch. (AMP 1989). BOC: Prodn Engr, 1970–72; Gas Supply Manager, 1972–78; Deptl Manager, 1978–82; Gen. Manager, W Australia, 1983–85, Medishield, 1985–87; Chief Exec., Gases, 1987–89; Man. Dir, CIG and Regl Dir, S Pacific, 1989–93; Man. Dir, Gases Europe, 1993–95; Man. Dir, BTR Nylex, 1995–97 and Exec. Dir, BTR, 1996–97; Pres. and CEO, 1997–2004, Gp Pres., Energy, 2004–06, BHP Petroleum Billiton Pty Ltd. Senior Independent Director: Kazakhmys, 2006–13; Essar Energy plc, 2010–14; non-executive Director: National Grid plc, 2008–15; Newcrest Mining Ltd, 2013–. *Recreations:* golf, ski-ing, Rugby, football, cricket. *Address:* 12/36 Sloane Court West, SW3 4TB. *T:* (020) 7730 4167. *E:* philipaiken1@gmail.com. *Clubs:* Wentworth; Melbourne; Royal Sydney Yacht Squadron.

AIKENS, Rt Hon. Sir Richard (John Pearson), Kt 1999; PC 2008; **Rt Hon. Lord Justice Aikens;** a Lord Justice of Appeal, since 2008; *b* 28 Aug. 1948; *s* of late Basil Aikens and Jean Eleanor Aikens; *m* 1979, Penelope Anne Hartley Rockley (*née* Baker); two *s* two step *d*. *Educ:* Norwich Sch.; St John's Coll., Cambridge (BA 1970, MA; Hon. Fellow, 2005). Called to Bar, Middle Temple, 1973 (Harmsworth scholar, 1974; Bencher, 1994); in practice, 1974–99; a Junior Counsel to the Crown, Common Law, 1981–86; QC 1986; a Recorder, 1993–99; a Judge of the High Court of Justice, QBD, 1999–2008; Presiding Judge, SE Circuit, 2001–04; Judge in charge of Commercial Ct, 2005–06. Mem., Supreme Court Rules Cttee, 1984–88. Dir, Bar Mutual Indemnity Fund Ltd, 1988–2000 (Chm., 1998–99). Dir, ENO, 1995–2004. Chm., Temple Music Foundn, 2002–. Governor, Sedbergh Sch., 1988–97. *Publications:* (contributing editor) Bullen and Leake and Jacob, Precedents of Pleading, 13th edn 1990; (jtly) Bills of Lading, 2006; (contrib.) Reforming Marine and Commercial Insurance Law, 2008; (contrib.) Tom Bingham and the Transformation of the Law: a liber amicorum, 2009; (ed jtly) Law and Society: who shall be master?, 2011. *Recreations:* music, cycling, wine, le pays basque. *Address:* Royal Courts of Justice, Strand, WC2A 2LL. *Clubs:* Groucho; Leander.

AIKIN, Olga Lindholm, (Mrs J. M. Driver), CBE 1997; Partner, Aikin Driver Partnership, since 1988; Visiting Lecturer, London Business School, since 1985; Council Member, Advisory Conciliation and Arbitration Service, 1982–95; *b* 10 Sept. 1934; *d* of Sidney Richard Daly and Lilian May Daly (*née* Lindholm); *m* 1st, 1959, Ronald Sidney Aikin (marr. diss. 1979); one *d*; 2nd, 1982, John Michael Driver; one step *d*. *Educ:* London School of Economics (LLB); King's Coll., London. Called to Bar, Gray's Inn, 1956. Assistant Lecturer, King's Coll., London, 1956–59; Lecturer, London School of Economics, 1959–70; London Business School: Sloan Fellowship Programme, 1970–71; Vis. Lectr, 1971–79; Lectr in Law, 1979–85. Dir, Gen. Law Div., Lion Internat. (Keiser Enterprises Inc.), 1985–90; Chm. Bd of Mgt, Nat. Conciliation Service of Qualitas Furnishing Standards Ltd, 1992–94. *Publications:* (with Judith Reid) Employment, Welfare and Safety at Work, 1971; (with Sonia Pearson) Legal Problems of Employment Contracts, 1990; (ed) IPM Law and Employment series (Discipline; Industrial Tribunals; Redundancy), 1992; articles in Personnel Management. *Recreation:* collecting cookery books and pressed glass. *Address:* 22 St Luke's Road, W11 1DP. *T:* (office) (020) 7727 9791.

See also Hon. F. L. Daly.

AILESBURY, 8th Marquess of, *cr* 1821; **Michael Sydney Cedric Brudenell-Bruce;** Bt 1611; Baron Brudenell 1628; Earl of Cardigan 1661; Baron Bruce 1746; Earl of Ailesbury 1776; Earl Bruce 1821; Viscount Savernake 1821; 30th Hereditary Warden of Savernake Forest; *b* 31 March 1926; *e s* of 7th Marquess of Ailesbury and Joan (*d* 1937), *d* of Stephen Salter, Ryde, Isle of Wight; *S* father, 1974; *m* 1st, 1952, Edwina Sylvia de Winton (from whom he obtained a divorce, 1961), *yr d* of Lt-Col Sir (Ernest) Edward de Winton Wills, 4th Bt; one *s* two *d*; 2nd, 1963, Juliet Adrienne (marr. diss. 1974), *d* of late Hilary Lethbridge Kingsford and Mrs Latham Hobrow, Marlborough; two *d*; 3rd, 1974, Mrs Caroline Elizabeth Romilly (marr. diss. 1990), *d* of late Commander O. F. M. Wethered, RN, DL, JP. *Educ:* Eton. Lt RHG, 1946. *Heir: s* Earl of Cardigan, *qv*. *Address:* 4 Abdale Road, W12 7ET.

AILION, Philipa Ann, (Pippa); Director, Pippa Ailion Casting, since 1997; *b* London, 20 Sept. 1947; *d* of Philip and Pamela Mary Ailion; one *s* by Roger Sell; *m* 2008, Paul Hale. *Educ:* Hove Co. Grammar Sch. for Girls; Bulmershe Coll. of Educn, Reading (Teachers' Cert. and Dip. 1968). Hd of Drama, Dick Sheppard Sch., London, 1968–71; actor, Greenwich Th. and Northcott Th., Exeter, 1971–73; asst to Neil Simon, playwright, NYC, 1974; Asst to Hd of Wardrobe (pt-time), Th. Dept, Dartington Coll. of Arts, Devon, 1975–81; Asst Dir and Co. Manager, Children of a Lesser God, Mermaid, then Albery, Dublin, Australia, SA, 1981–84; Resident Dir and Co. Manager, West End, incl. West Side Story, Her Majesty's Th. and Opera House Manchester, When We Are Married, Whitehall Th., Italian Straw Hat, Shaftesbury Th., A Month of Sundays, Duchess Th., 1984–87; Resident Associate Dir and Casting Dir, Old Vic Th., 1987–91; freelance casting dir, 1991–94; Hd, BA Acting, Central Sch. of Speech and Drama, 1994–97. Mem., Bd of Trustees, Regent's Park Open Air Th., 2012–. Mem., BAFTA. Hon. Companion, Liverpool Inst. Performing Arts, 2009. *Recreations:* theatre, gardening, travel, swimming, film. *Address:* Pippa Ailion Casting, Unit 67B Eurolink Business Centre, SW2 1BZ. *T:* (020) 7738 7556. *E:* pippa@lineone.net.

AILSA, 9th Marquess of, *cr* 1831; **David Thomas Kennedy;** Baron Kennedy 1452; Earl of Cassillis 1509; Baron Ailsa (UK) 1806; *b* Ayrshire, 3 July 1958; *yr s* of 7th Marquess of Ailsa, OBE and Mary Kennedy (*née* Burn); *S* brother, 2015; *m* 1991, Anne Kelly; one *s* one *d*. *Educ:* Strathallan Sch.; Berks Coll. of Agriculture. *Heir: s* Lord Archibald David Kennedy, Earl of Cassillis, *b* 7 Sept. 1995. *Address:* Morriston, Culzean, Maybole, Ayrshire KA19 8LB. *Clubs:* New (Edinburgh); Glasgow Art.

AINA, Benjamin Adejuwon Olufemi; QC 2009; barrister; *b* London, 14 Feb. 1964; *s* of Johnson Olusola Aina and Elizabeth Taiwo Awolesi; *m* 2002, Mwanida Elizabeth Sakala; three *s* four *d* (and one *s* decd). *Educ:* Woolverstone Hall, Ipswich; Chelmer Inst. of Higher Educn (LLB Hons 1985); University Coll. London (LLM 1986). Called to the Bar, Lincoln's Inn, 1987. Admitted Attorney at Law, Cayman Is, 2010. Standing Counsel to Revenue and Customs Prosecution Office, 2008–; QC List, Serious Fraud Office, 2009–. *Publications:* Holborn Law Tutors Company Law Manual, rev. edn 1989. *Recreations:* running, travelling. *Address:* Thomas Bingham Chambers, 33 Bedford Row, WC1R 4JH. *T:* (020) 7242 6476, *Fax:* (020) 7831 6065. *E:* baqc@tbchambers.co.uk.

AINGER, Nicholas Richard, (Nick); *b* Sheffield, 24 Oct. 1949; *m* 1976, Sally Robinson; one *d*. *Educ:* Netherthorpe Grammar Sch., Staveley. Rigger, Marine and Port Services Ltd, Pembroke Dock, 1977–92. Mem. (Lab) Dyfed CC, 1981–93. Branch Sec., TGWU, 1978–92. MP (Lab) Pembroke, 1992–97, Carmarthen W and Pembrokeshire S, 1997–2010; contested (Lab) same seat, 2010. PPS to Sec. of State for Wales, 1997–2001; a Lord Comr, HM Treasury (Govt Whip), 2001–05; Parly Under-Sec. of State, Wales Office, 2005–07. *E:* nick.ainger@live.co.uk.

AINGER, Stephen David; Chief Executive, Partnerships For Renewables, since 2007; *b* 27 Nov. 1951; *s* of Peter Jackson Ainger and Aileen (*née* Simpson); *m* 1992, Nicola Jane Corbett; one *s* one *d*. *Educ:* Towcester Grammar Sch.; Bath Univ. (BSc 1st cl. Hons (Physics) 1974). Exploration and Prodn posts with British Petroleum Co. Plc, London, Colombia, Brazil, Spain, Venezuela and Kuwait, 1974–99; Strategy and Business Develt Dir, Transco Plc, BG Gp, 1999–2000; Dir, Business Develt, Lattice Gp Plc, 2000–02; Chief Exec., Charities Aid Foundn, 2002–06. Trustee, Artsadmin, 2003–14. Non-exec. Dir, Royal Free Hampstead NHS Trust, 2011–. *Recreations:* classic cars, architectural heritage. *Address:* (office) 12 Melcombe Place, NW1 6JJ. *T:* (020) 7170 7077. *E:* stephen.ainger@pfr.co.uk. *Club:* Reform.

AINLEY, (David) Geoffrey, CEng, FIMechE; FRAeS; AGAvA; Deputy Director (Projects and Research), Military Vehicles and Engineering Establishment, Chertsey, 1978–84; *b* 5 July 1924; *s* of Cyril Edward and Constance Ainley; *m* 1st, 1948, Dorothy Emily (*née* Roberts); one *s* one *d*; 2nd, 1959, Diana Margery Hill (*née* Sayles); one *d*; 3rd, 1988, Joyce Dinah (*née* Jessett). *Educ:* Brentwood Sch., Essex; Queen Mary Coll., London Univ. (BSc, 1st Cl. Hons). Engine Dept, RAE, Farnborough, 1943–44; Power Jets (R&D) Ltd, 1944–46; National Gas Turbine Estabt, Pyestock, 1946–66; idc 1967; Dir of Engine Develt, MoD (Procurement Exec.), 1968–78. George Stephenson Research Prize, IMechE, 1953. *Publications:* contrib. books and learned jls on gas turbine technology. *Recreations:* painting, sketching, golf. *Address:* 20 Hampton Close, Church Crookham, Fleet, Hants GU52 8LB.

AINLEY, Prof. Janet Mary, PhD; Professor of Education, University of Leicester, since 2006 (Director, School of Education, 2007–14); *b* London, 13 March 1952; *d* of (James) Henry and Joyce Ainley; *m* 2001, Ronnie Goldstein; one *d* and two step *s* one step *d*. *Educ:* Sydenham High Sch.; Univ. of York (BA Hons Phil.); St Luke's Coll., Exeter (PGCE); Univ. of Warwick (MEd; PhD 1996). Primary sch. teacher, Solihull LEA, 1974–81; University of Warwick: Res. Asst, 1981–83; Lectr, 1983–98; Sen. Lectr, 1998–2002; Reader, 2002–06; Dep. Dir, 1999–2004, Dir of Teacher Educn, 2004–06, Warwick Inst. of Educn. Vice-Pres., Internat. Gp for Psychol. of Maths Educn, 1999–2000; Treas., Eur. Soc. for Res. in Maths Educn, 2007–13; Chair, British Soc. for Res. in Learning of Maths, 2008–11. *Publications:* (with R. Goldstein) Making Logo Work, 1988; Enriching Primary Mathematics with IT, 1996; contrib. For the Learning of Maths, Educnl Studies in Maths, Internat. Jl Computers for Math. Learning, British Educnl Res. Jl. *Recreations:* gardening, cooking, reading, family history. *Address:* School of Education, University of Leicester, 21 University Road, Leicester LE1 7RF. *T:* (0116) 252 3690, *Fax:* (0116) 252 3653. *E:* janet.ainley@le.ac.uk.

AINLEY, Nicholas John; His Honour Judge Ainley; a Circuit Judge, since 2003; Vice President, Immigration Appeal Tribunal, 2003–05; *b* 18 March 1952; *s* of late Edgar Ainley and of Jean Olga Ainley (*née* Simister); *m* 1980, Susan Elizabeth Waugh; two *s* one *d*. *Educ:* Sevenoaks Sch. Called to the Bar, Lincoln's Inn, 1973; Supplementary Panel Counsel to the Crown (Common Law), 1995–2001; Asst Recorder, 1996–2000; a Recorder, 2000–03. *Publications:* (jtly) Disclosure and Confidentiality, 1996. *Recreations:* family, travel, books. *Address:* c/o The Law Courts, Altyre Road, Croydon CR9 5AB. *Clubs:* Sussex Yacht (Shoreham); Royal de Panne Sand Yacht (Belgium); Hove Deep Sea Anglers.

AINLEY, Vivien Lesley; Headmistress, South Hampstead High School, 2001–04; *b* 29 March 1950; *d* of late Herbert John Matthews and Win Matthews; *m* 1975, Eric Michael Ainley (marr. diss. 2015); two *d*. *Educ:* Univ. of Durham (BA Econs 1971); Hughes Hall, Cambridge (PGCE with distinction 1979); Univ. of Maryland (MA Secondary Educn (Maths) 1982); Royal Holloway, Univ. of London (Postgrad. Dip. Psychol. with distinction 2008; MSc Human Neurosci. with distinction 2010; PhD 2015). CSIR, Pretoria, South Africa, 1972–73; Bank of England, 1973–77; UCNW, Bangor, 1976–77; CEGB, 1977–78; Teacher of Econs and Stats, 1985–91, Hd of Sixth Form, 1991–94, Haberdashers' Aske's Sch. for Girls; Sen. Mistress, Oundle Sch., 1994–96; Surmistress, St Paul's Girls' Sch., 1996–2001. Researcher, Lab. of Action and Body, RHUL, 2015–. *Recreations:* theatre, travel, gardening, voluntary work in mental health. *Address:* 52 Sterndale Road, W14 0HU.

AINSCOUGH, Jill Patricia; Chief Operating Officer, 2007–14 and Board Member, 2010–14, Ofcom; *b* Leicester, 28 Dec. 1957; *d* of Philip and Jean Needham; three *d*. *Educ:* Univ. of Sheffield (BA Hons); Univ. of Warwick (MBA). ACIS 1988, FCIS 2012. Sen. Financial Analyst, Granada Gp, 1990–92; Business Planner, Cambridge Cable Gp, 1994–95; Financial Planning and Analysis Manager, Barclaycard, 1995–97; Head, Marketing Develt, NTL; Man. Dir, Easynet, 2001–06. Non-exec. Dir, BMJ. Mem. Bd, Sport England, 2007–13. Gov., Univ. of Northampton.

AINSCOW, Prof. Melvin, (Mel), CBE 2012; PhD; Professor of Education, University of Manchester, since 1995; *b* Manchester, 25 May 1943; *s* of Richard and Sarah Ainscow; one *s* one *d*. *Educ:* Ducie High Sch., Manchester; Univ. of Birmingham (MEd); Univ. of E Anglia (PhD 1995). Teacher, 1964–74; Headteacher, Castle Sch., Walsall, 1974–79; School Inspector, 1979–85; Lectr, Univ. of Cambridge, 1985–95. Chief Adviser, Greater Manchester Challenge, 2007–11. FRSA 2012. *Publications:* Understanding the Development of Inclusive Schools, 1999; Improving Schools, Developing Inclusion, 2006; Developing Equitable Education Systems, 2012. *Recreations:* music, reading, sport. *Address:* 31 Appleby Lodge, Manchester M14 6HQ. *T:* (0161) 275 3503. *E:* Mel_Ainscow@yahoo.co.uk.

AINSCOW, Robert Morrison, CB 1989; Deputy Secretary, Overseas Development Administration, Foreign and Commonwealth Office, 1986–96; *b* 3 June 1936; *s* of Robert M. Ainscow and Hilda Ainscow (*née* Cleminson); *m* 1965, Faye Bider; one *s* one *d*. *Educ:* Salford Grammar School; Liverpool Univ. (BA Econ Hons). Statistician: Govt of Rhodesia and Nyasaland, 1957–61; UN Secretariat, New York, 1961–65 and 1966–68; Dept of Economic Affairs, London, 1965–66. Ministry of Overseas Development: Economic Adviser, 1968–70; Senior Economic Adviser, 1971–76; Head, South Asia Dept, 1976–79; Under Secretary and Principal Finance Officer, FCO (ODA), 1979–86. Chm., OECD (DAC) Working Party on Financial Aspects of Develt Assistance, 1982–86; Member: World Bank/IMF Develt Cttee Task Force on Concessional Flows, 1983–85, on Multilateral Develt Banks, 1994–96; Asian Develt Bank Inspection Panel, 1996–2002. Consultant to UN, World Bank, OECD, DFID, Ireland Aid, and Overseas Develt Council, Washington, 1996–. Mem. Bd Trustees, BRCS, 2000–06. *T:* (020) 7435 2218. *E:* robain@hotmail.co.uk.

AINSLEY, John Mark; tenor; *b* 9 July 1963; *s* of John Alwyn Ainsley and Dorothy Sylvia (*née* Anderson). *Educ:* Royal Grammar Sch., Worcester; Magdalen Coll., Oxford. Début in Stravinsky's Mass, RFH, 1984; subsequent débuts: USA, in NY and Boston, 1990; with Berlin Philharmonic Orch., 1992; Glyndebourne Fest., in Così fan Tutte, 1992; Aix-en-Provence, in Don Giovanni, 1993; San Francisco, in Don Giovanni, 1995; appears regularly with ENO, Royal Opera, and leading orchestras incl. LPO, LSO, Scottish Chamber Orch. and Orchestre de Paris. Has made numerous recordings. Grammy Award for best opera recording, 1995. *Recreation:* chocolate. *Address:* Askonas Holt Ltd, Lincoln House, 300 High Holborn, WC1V 7JH. *T:* (020) 7400 1700.

AINSLIE, Sir Charles Benedict, (Sir Ben), Kt 2013; CBE 2009 (OBE 2005; MBE 2001); professional yachtsman; Principal, Ben Ainslie Racing, since 2014; *b* 5 Feb. 1977; *s* of Michael Roderick and Susan Linda Ainslie; *m* 2014, Georgie Thompson. *Educ:* Truro Sch.; Peter Symonds Coll., Winchester. Laser Cl. World Champion, 1998 and 1999; Silver Medal, Laser Cl. Sailing, Atlanta Olympics, 1998; Gold Medal, Laser Cl. Sailing, Sydney Olympics, 2000; Finn Cl. World Champion, 2002, 2003, 2004, 2005, 2008 and 2012; Gold Medal, Finn Cl. Sailing, Athens Olympics, 2004, Beijing Olympics, 2008, London Olympics, 2012; ISAF World Match Racing Champion, 2010. Crew, Oracle Team USA, America's Cup winners, San Francisco, 2013. ISAF World Sailor of the Year, 1998, 2002, 2008 and 2012. Hon. MSc UC Chichester, 2001; Hon. LLD Exeter, 2005; Hon. DSport Southampton Solent, 2007. *Publications:* The Laser Campaign Manual, 2002; Close to the Wind, 2009. *Recreations:* motor racing, cycling, flying. *Address:* Carne Vean, Manaccan, Helston, Cornwall TR12 6HD. *Clubs:* Royal Thames Yacht (Hon. Mem.), Royal Cornwall Yacht (Hon. Mem.), Stokes Bay Sailing (Gosport) (Hon. Mem.), Restronguet Sailing (Falmouth) (Hon. Mem.), Royal Lymington Yacht (Hon. Mem.), Royal Southern Yacht (Hon. Mem.), Royal Corinthian Yacht (Hon. Mem.), Royal Yacht Squadron (Hon. Mem.), Royal Ocean Racing Club (Hon. Mem.).

AINSWORTH, Sir Anthony (Thomas Hugh), 5th Bt *cr* 1916, of Ardanaiseig, co. Argyll; Director, Richard Glynn Consultants, since 2000; *b* 30 March 1962; *er s* of Sir David Ainsworth, 4th Bt and Sarah Mary, *d* of Lt-Col H. C. Walford; *S* father, 1999; *m* 2003, Anong Pradith; one *d*. *Educ:* Harrow. Lt, Royal Hussars (PWO), 1982–85. *Heir: b* Charles David Ainsworth, *b* 24 Aug. 1966. *Address:* 12th Floor, 208 Wireless Road, Lumpini, Bangkok 10330, Thailand. *E:* anthony@rglynn.th.com.

AINSWORTH, James Bernard; restaurant consultant; Editor, Good Food Guide, 1994–2002 (Consultant Editor, 2003); *b* 1 Feb. 1944; *s* of Henry Bernard Ainsworth and Margaret Ainsworth (*née* Fletcher); *m* 2002, Valerie (*née* McCully); two step *d*. *Educ:* Duke St Primary Sch.; Chorley Grammar Sch.; Liverpool Univ. (BA Psychol.). Lectr in Psychol. and Educn, Chorley Coll. of Educn, 1970–78; Proprietor, Vineyard Restaurant, Northampton, 1979–84; drinks columnist, Punch, 1984–92; freelance wine writer and restaurant reviewer, 1984–. *Publications:* Mitchell Beazley Red Wine Guide, 1990; Mitchell Beazley White Wine Guide, 1990. *Recreation:* eating home produce including suckling pig and super-fresh eggs. *Address:* Bicton Pool House, Bicton, Kingsland, Leominster, Herefordshire HR6 9PR.

AINSWORTH, Rev. Janina Helen Margaret; Chief Education Officer, Church of England, 2007–14; General Secretary, National Society, 2007–14; House for Duty Team Vicar, Turton Moorland Team Ministry, Manchester, since 2014; *b* 23 Dec. 1950; *d* of Paul and Isobel Brych; *m* 1974, Michael Ronald Ainsworth; two *s* two *d*. *Educ:* Nottingham High Sch. for Girls; Homerton Coll., Cambridge (Cert Ed 1972); Newnham Coll., Cambridge (BEd 1973); Lancaster Univ. (MA Religious Studies 1974); Ripon Coll., Cuddesdon. RE Teacher: Manor Sch., Arbury, 1974–75; Greaves Sch., Lancaster, 1975–78; pt-time Lectr and Warden, St Martin's Coll., Lancaster, 1978–82; Manchester Diocesan Board of Education: Children's Work Advr, 1986–91; RE and Schs Advr, 1991–98; Diocesan Dir of Educn, 1998–2007. Ordained deacon, 2005, priest, 2006; non-stipendiary Curate, E Farnworth and Kearsley, 2005–07; Asst Priest, St George-in-the-East with St Paul, London, 2012–14. FRSA. *Publications:* (with Alan Brown) Moral Education, 1994; Clergy and Church Schools, 1995. *Recreations:* singing church music, cinema, crime novels.

AINSWORTH, (Mervyn) John, OBE 2008; FCIS; Chief Executive and Secretary, Institute of Chartered Secretaries and Administrators, 1990–2007; *b* 28 Jan. 1947; *s* of late Gordon John Ainsworth and Eileen Ainsworth; *m* 1973, Marta Christina Marmolak; two *s* one *d*. *Educ:* Stanfields Technical High Sch., Stoke-on-Trent; Goldsmiths' Coll., Univ. of London (CertEd; DipEd). Asst Clerk to Govs and Bursar, Dulwich Coll., 1969–74; Principal Assistant, Sec. and Solicitors' Dept, CEGB, 1974–77; Secretarial Asst, BTDB, 1977–78; Sec., 1978–83, Sec. and Dir of Finance, 1983–84, BPIF; Sec. General, Inst. of Administrative Management, 1984–90. Director: ICSA Publishing, 1990–2007; ICSA Consultants, 1992–2007; ICSA Software, 1993–2007; Inst. of Business Administration, 1992–2007. Special Advr, Assets Reunited (UK) LLP, 2008–10. Member: Bd, Nat. Examining Bd for Supervisory Management, 1984–99; Academic Bd, Greenwich Coll., 1984–97; Court, Cranfield Univ. (formerly Inst. of Technology), 1990–2010; Council for Admin (formerly Admin Lead Body),

1991–2007; Open and Distance Learning Quality Council (formerly Council for Certification of Correspondence Colls), 1994– (Chm., 1998–); City & Guilds Quality Standards Cttee, 1999–2005; Commonwealth Assoc. for Corporate Governance, 2000–07. Gov., Rokeby Sch., 2010– (Vice-Chair, 2014). Sec., Shepway Econ. Regeneration Partnership, 2010–14. Liveryman, Worshipful Co. of Chartered Secs and Administrators, 1992– (Mem. Ct of Assts, 2006–12); Mem., Livery Cos Financial Service Gp, 2008–14. Hon. Fellow, Canadian Inst. of Certified Administrative Managers, 1987; Hon. MCGI 2006. Hon. DBA Bournemouth, 1997; DUniv Anglia Ruskin, 2006. *Publications:* articles on management education and administrative systems. *Recreations:* golf, motoring, travel. *Address:* 2 Aspen House, West Terrace, Folkestone, Kent CT20 1TH.

AINSWORTH, Peter Michael; *b* 16 Nov. 1956; *s* of late Lt-Comdr Michael Lionel Yeoward Ainsworth, RN and Patricia Mary Ainsworth (*née* Bedford, later Beeny); *m* 1981, Claire Alison Burnett; one *s* two *d*. *Educ:* Ludgrove, Wokingham; Bradfield Coll.; Lincoln Coll., Oxford (MA Eng. Lit. and Lang.). Res. Asst to Sir J. Stewart-Clark, MEP, 1979–81; Investment Analyst, Laing & Cruickshank, 1981–85; Sen. Investment Analyst, S. G. Warburg Securities, 1985–87; Asst Dir, 1987–89, Dir, 1989–92, S. G. Warburg Securities Corporate Finance. Mem., Wandsworth Borough Council, 1986–94 (Chm., Cons. Group, 1990–92). MP (C) E Surrey, 1992–2010. PPS to Chief Sec. to HM Treasury, 1994–95, to Sec. of State for Nat. Heritage, 1996; an Asst Govt Whip, 1996–97; Opposition Dep. Chief Whip, 1997–98; Shadow Secretary of State: for Culture, Media and Sport, 1998–2001; for Envmt, Food and Rural Affairs, 2001–02, 2005–09. Member, Select Committee: on Envmt, 1993–94; on Public Affairs, 1996; on Envmtl Audit, 2003–05 (Chm., 2003–05); on Culture, Media and Sport. Sec., All-Party Conservation Gp, 1994–97; Chm., All-Party Parly Gp for the Envmt; Chm., All-Party Parly Gp for Sustainable Aviation; Treas., All-Party Parly Climate Change Gp. Mem., Speaker's Adv. Cttee on Works of Art. Mem. Council, Bow Group, 1984–86. Chairman: Cons. Arts and Creative Industries Network, 2009–10; Cons. Environment Network, 2010–12. Chm., UK Big Lottery Fund, 2011–; Mem. Bd, Envmt Agency, 2012–. Founder Partner, Robertsbridge Gp, 2010–. Member: Bd, Plantlife, 2003– (Chm., 2010–); CPRE; Friends of the Earth; Surrey Wildlife Trust. Chm., Elgar Foundn, 2005–13 (Trustee, 2013–); Vice-Pres., Arthur Bliss Soc. Trustee, Surrey CPRE, 2010–11. Hon. Fellow: CIWM, 2010; Soc. for the Envmt, 2013. Presenter, Discord, Music and Dissent, radio, 2000. FRSA 1998. *Recreations:* family, music, doggerel. *Clubs:* MCC, Garrick.

AINSWORTH, Rt Hon. Robert (William); PC 2005; *b* 19 June 1952; *s* of late Stanley Ewart Ainsworth and Monica Pearl Ainsworth (later Mrs D. J. Scullion); *m* 1974, Gloria Jean Sandall; two *d*. *Educ:* Foxford Comprehensive School. Sheet metal worker and fitter, Jaguar, 1971–91 (Shop Steward, MSF, 1974–91; Sec., Joint Stewards, 1980–91). City Councillor, Coventry, 1984–93 (Dep. Leader, 1988–91; Chm., Finance, 1989–92). MP (Lab) Coventry NE, 1992–2015. An Opposition Whip, 1995–97; a Lord Comr of HM Treasury (Govt Whip), 1997–2001; Parly Under-Sec. of State, DETR, 2001, Home Office, 2001–03; Treasurer of HM Household (Dep. Chief Whip), 2003–07; Minister of State, MoD, 2007–09; Sec. of State for Defence, 2009–10; Shadow Sec. of State for Defence, 2010. Member: Select Cttee on environmental affairs, 1993–95; Foreign Affairs Select Cttee, 2010–15. Vice-Chm., W Midlands Gp of Labour MPs, 1995–97. *Recreations:* walking, reading, chess. *Clubs:* Bell Green Working Men's (Coventry); Broad Street Old Boy's RFC (Coventry).

AINSWORTH, Prof. Roger William, DPhil; FRAeS; Master, St Catherine's College, Oxford, since 2002; Professor of Engineering Science, since 1998, and Pro Vice-Chancellor, since 2003, University of Oxford; *b* 17 Nov. 1951; *s* of Harold Ainsworth and Mary Ainsworth (*née* Reynolds); *m* 1978, Sarah Pilkington; one *s* two *d*. *Educ:* Lancaster Royal Grammar Sch.; Jesus Coll., Oxford (BA 1st Cl. 1973; DPhil 1976; Hon. Fellow, 2002). FRAeS 2004. Research Section Leader: Aero Engines Div., Rolls-Royce Ltd, 1976–77; Engrg Scis Div., AERE Harwell, 1977–85; University of Oxford: Fellow and Tutor in Engrg, St Catherine's Coll., 1985–2002; Univ. Lectr in Fluid Mechanics, 1985–96; Reader in Engrg Sci., 1996–98; Sen. Proctor, 1998–99; Chairman: Faculty Bd of Mgt Studies, 1999–2001; Bd of Continuing Educn, 2004–08; Mem., Council, 2002–05; Delegate, 1998–2009, Mem., Finance Cttee, 2001–09, OUP; Chm., Visitors of Botanic Garden, 2002–14. Vice-Chm. and Mem. Bd, Oxford Inst. for Energy Studies, 2002–14 (Chm., 2014–). Vis. Prof., EPFL Lausanne, 1998–2000. Recorder, Engrg Section, BAAS, 1988–92. Trustee: Oxford Preservation Trust, 1989–95 (Chm., 2009–); Emmott Foundn, 2003–; Oxford Sch. of Drama, 2005–12; Chm., Voltaire Foundn, 2015–. Governor: Abingdon Sch., 1997–2010; Dragon Sch., Oxford, 2004– (Chm., 2015–). Royal Society Esso Energy Award, 1996. Knight, Order of Dannebrog (Denmark), 2006. *Publications:* various contribs related to turbomachinery in sci. jls. *Recreations:* Baroque music, technical pursuits and digital image making. *Address:* The Master's Lodgings, St Catherine's College, Oxford OX1 3UJ. *T:* (01865) 271762. *Club:* Oxford and Cambridge.

AIRD, Fiona Violet, (Lady Aird), CVO 2001 (LVO 1980); Extra Lady-in-Waiting to HRH Princess Margaret, Countess of Snowdon, 1963–2002; *b* 24 Sept. 1934; *d* of late Lt Col Ririd Myddelton, LVO, and of Lady Margaret Myddelton; *m* 1963, Capt. Sir Alastair Sturgis Aird, GCVO (*d* 2009); two *d*. *Educ:* Westonbirt Sch.; in France. Lady-in-Waiting to HRH Princess Margaret, 1960–63. Mem. Council, UCL, 1987–97 (Hon. Fellow, 2003). Chm., Middx Hosp. League of Friends, 1987–2002; Vice-Pres., England, Attend (formerly Nat. Assoc. of Hosp. and Community Friends), 2000–; Chm., Florence Nightingale Aid in Sickness Trust, 1994–. *Recreations:* reading, fishing. *Address:* The Paddock, Lovells Court, Marnhull, Sturminster Newton, Dorset DT10 1JJ.

AIRD, Sir (George) John, 4th Bt *cr* 1901; Chairman, Matcon plc, 1980–2013; Chairman and Managing Director, Sir John Aird & Co. Ltd, 1969–96; *b* 30 Jan. 1940; *e s* of Sir John Renton Aird, 3rd Bt, MVO, MC, and Lady Priscilla Aird, *yr d* of 2nd Earl of Ancaster; *S* father, 1973; *m* 1st, 1968, Margaret (*d* 2010), *yr d* of Sir John Muir, 3rd Bt; one *s* two *d*; 2nd, 2011, Xiao Fen, *d* of Jin Fen Wang, Beijing. *Educ:* Eton; Oxford Univ.; Harvard Business Sch. MICE. Trainee, Sir Alexander Gibb & Partners, 1961–65; Manager, John Laing & Son Ltd, 1967–69. Dir, Healthcare Development Services Ltd, 1994–2006. *Recreations:* ski-ing, tennis, hunting. *Heir: s* James John Aird [*b* 12 June 1978; *m* 2007, Dr Tara Clare Harrop, *d* of Dr Brian Harrop, Nairobi]. *Address:* Two Leys, Evenlode, Moreton-in-Marsh, Glos GL56 0NT. *T:* (01608) 650607. *E:* johnaird@aol.com.

See also Baroness Willoughby de Eresby.

AIREY, David Lawrence; Managing Director, Bunge & Co. Ltd, 1987–90, retired; *b* 28 April 1935; *s* of Samuel Airey and Helena Florence Lever; *m* 1961, Joan Mary Stewart; three *d*. *Educ:* Oldershaw Grammar Sch., Wallasey. J. Bibby & Sons Ltd: Management trainee, various sales/commercial management positions, 1952–74; Chief Exec., Edible Oils Div., 1974–78; Man. Dir, J. Bibby Edible Oils Ltd, 1979–86; Dep. Man. Dir, Bunge & Co. Ltd, 1986. Chm., Seed Crushers & Oil Processors Assoc., 1980–82. Trustee, Wiltshire and Swindon Community Foundn, 1996–2002. JP Liverpool, 1980–86. *Recreations:* Rugby Union football (Birkenhead Park FC, 1955–66, Cheshire, 1958–65, North West Counties, 1964, Barbarians, 1965), cooking, gardening. *Address:* Darnley, Church Road, Woodborough, Pewsey, Wilts SN9 5PH. *T:* (01672) 851647. *Club:* Birkenhead Park FC.

AIREY, Dawn Elizabeth; Chief Executive, Getty Images Inc., since 2015; *b* Preston, Lancs, 15 Nov. 1960; civil partnership 2007, Jacqueline Lawrence; two *d*. *Educ:* Kelly College; Girton College, Cambridge (MA Hons). Central TV: management trainee, 1985–86; Channel 4 Liaison Officer, 1987; Associate Producer, 1988; Controller, later Dir, Programme Planning, Central Broadcasting, 1988–93; Controller of Network Children's and Daytime Progs, ITV Network Centre, 1993–94; Controller of Arts and Entertainment, Channel 4, 1994–96; Dir of Progs, 1996–2000, Chief Exec., 2000–02, Channel 5; Man. Dir, Sky Networks, 2003–07, Man. Dir, Channels and Services, 2006–07, BSkyB; Man. Dir, Global Content, ITV, 2007–08; Chm. and Chief Exec., Five, 2008–10; Man. Dir, 2010–11, Pres., 2011–13, CLT-UFA UK Television, RTL Gp; Sen. Vice-Pres. for EMEA, Yahoo!, 2013–15. Non-executive Director: easyJet, 2004–08; Thomas Cook, 2010–. Member: Film Council, 1999–2002; Bd, Internat. Acad. of Television Arts and Scis, 2003–08; British Liby Bd, 2007–13. Patron, Birmingham Film and TV Festival, 1996–; Gov., Banff Fest., 1999–2008; Chm., Edinburgh Internat. Television Fest., 2000; Exec. Chm., Guardian Edin. Internat. Television Fest., 2002–06. Chairman: Grierson Trust, 2010–13; NYT, 2011–. Patron, Skillset, 2002–08. Trustee, Media Trust, 2004–11. FRSA 1996; FRTS 1999 (Vice-Pres., 2002–). *Recreations:* tennis, fine wines, cinema, TV, theatre, collecting antique maps.

AIREY, Janet Claire; *see* Bazley, J. C.

AIRLIE, 13th Earl of, *cr* 1639 (*de facto* 11th Earl, 13th but for the Attainder); **David George Coke Patrick Ogilvy,** KT 1985; GCVO 1984; PC 1984; Royal Victorian Chain, 1997; JP; Baron Ogilvy of Airlie, 1491; Captain late Scots Guards; Lord Chamberlain of HM Household, 1984–97; Lord-Lieutenant of Angus, 1989–2001; a Permanent Lord-in-Waiting to the Queen, since 1997; Chancellor, Order of the Thistle, since 2007; *b* 17 May 1926; *e s* of 12th Earl of Airlie, KT, GCVO, MC, and Lady Alexandra Marie Bridget Coke (*d* 1984), *d* of 3rd Earl of Leicester, GCVO; *S* father, 1968; *m* 1952, Virginia Fortune Ryan (*see* Countess of Airlie); three *s* three *d*. *Educ:* Eton. Lieutenant Scots Guards, 1944; serving 2nd Battalion Germany, 1945; Captain, ADC to High Comr and C-in-C Austria, 1947–48; Malaya, 1948–49; resigned commission, 1950. Ensign, 1975–85, Lieutenant, 1985–2000, Pres., 2000, Captain-Gen. and Gold Stick, 2004–12, Queen's Body Guard for Scotland, Royal Company of Archers. Chancellor, Royal Victorian Order, 1984–97. Chairman: Schroders plc, 1977–84; Gen. Accident Fire & Life Assurance Corp., 1987–97 (Dir, 1962–97; Dep. Chm., 1975–87); Director: J. Henry Schroder Wagg & Co. Ltd, 1961–84 (Chm., 1973–77); Scottish & Newcastle Breweries plc, 1969–83; The Royal Bank of Scotland Gp, 1983–93; Baring Stratton Investment Trust (formerly Stratton Investment Trust), 1986–97. Chm., Historic Royal Palaces Trust, 1998–2002; Dep. Chm., Royal Collection Trust, 1992–97; Pres., NT for Scotland, 1997–2002; Trustee, Prince's Foundn for Built Envmt, 2003–06. Treasurer, Scout Assoc., 1962–86; Hon. Pres., Scottish Council of Scout Assoc., 1988–2001. Gov., Nuffield Nursing Homes Trust, 1985–89; Chancellor, Univ. of Abertay Dundee, 1994–2009. DL Angus, 1964; JP Angus, 1990. Hon. LLD Dundee, 1990. *Heir: s* Lord Ogilvy, *qv*. *Address:* Airlie House, Cortachy, Kirriemuir, Angus DD8 4QJ; 36 Sloane Court West, SW3 4TB. *T:* (020) 7823 6246.

See also Hon. J. D. D. Ogilvy, Sir H. Wake.

AIRLIE, Countess of; Virginia Fortune Ogilvy, DCVO 1995 (CVO 1983); Lady of the Bedchamber to the Queen, since 1973; *b* 9 Feb. 1933; *d* of John Barry Ryan, Newport, RI, USA; *m* 1952, Lord Ogilvy (now Earl of Airlie, *qv*); three *s* three *d*. *Educ:* Brearley School, New York City. Founder Governor, Cobham School, Kent, 1958. Mem., Industrial Design Panel, British Rail, 1974–94; Comr, Royal Fine Arts Commn, 1975–88. Trustee: Tate Gallery, 1983–95 (Chm. Friends of Tate Gallery, 1978–83); Amer. Mus. in Britain, 1985–89 (Chm., 2001); Nat. Gallery, 1989–95; Nat. Galls of Scotland, 1995 (Chm., 1997–2000). Pres., Angus Br., BRCS, 1988. *Address:* Cortachy Castle, Kirriemuir, Angus DD8 4LX; 36 Sloane Court West, SW3 4TB.

AIRS, Prof. Malcolm Russell, DPhil; FSA, FRHistS; Fellow, Kellogg College (formerly Rewley House), Oxford, 1991–2008, now Emeritus (Director, Centre for the Historic Environment, 2008–12); Professor of Conservation and the Historic Environment, University of Oxford, 2002–06; *b* 7 March 1941; *s* of George William Laurence Airs and Gwendoline Elizabeth Airs (*née* Little); partner, 1971, Megan Parry; one *s*. *Educ:* Bushey Grammar Sch.; Oriel Coll., Oxford (BA Hons Modern Hist. 1963, MA, DPhil 1970). FSA 1980; IHBC 1998; FRHistS 2003. Historian, Historic Bldgs Div., GLC, 1966–73; Architectural Ed., Survey of London, 1973–74; Conservation Officer, S Oxfordshire DC, 1974–91; Lectr, 1991–96, Reader, 1996–2002, in Conservation and Historic Envmt, Univ. of Oxford; Vice-Pres., Kellogg Coll., Oxford, 2006–08. Member: Historic Bldgs and Areas Adv. Cttee, 1988–2003, Adv. Cttee, 2012–, English Heritage; Historic Buildings and Land Panel, Heritage Lottery Fund, 2004–05; Architectural Panel, 2004–, Council, 2012–14, NT; Comr, RCHM, 1993–99. Chm., 1998–2001, Pres., 2001–03, Inst. of Historic Building Conservation; Pres., Soc. of Architectl Historians of GB, 2008–13. Trustee: Oxford Preservation Trust, 1993–; Standing Conf. on Trng of Architects in Conservation, 1996–2004; Landmark Trust, 2007–. Pres., Oxford Architectl and Histl Soc., 2001–05; Vice-Pres., Assoc. of Small Historic Towns and Villages, 2006–. *Publications:* The Making of the English Country House 1500–1640, 1975; The Buildings of Britain: Tudor and Jacobean, 1982; The Tudor and Jacobean Country House, 1995; numerous articles on architectural hist. and historic conservation. *Recreations:* visiting buildings, cultivating my allotment, following the lost cause of Oxford United. *Address:* 39 High Street, Dorchester on Thames, Wallingford OX10 7HN. *Club:* Oxford United Supporters.

AIRY, Maj.-Gen. Sir Christopher (John), KCVO 1989; CBE 1984; General Officer Commanding London District and Major General Commanding Household Division, 1986; an Extra Equerry to the Prince of Wales, since 1991; *b* 8 March 1934; *m* 1959, Judith Stephenson; one *s* two *d*. *Educ:* Marlborough Coll.; RMA Sandhurst. 2nd Lieut, Grenadier Guards, 1954; Scots Guards, 1974. PMA to Sec. of State for War, 1960; sc 1966; DAAG, Regtl Adjt, 1967; Bde Major, 4th Guards Armoured Bde, 1971; ndc 1973; CO, 1st Bn Scots Guards, 1974; Mil. Asst (GSO1) to Master Gen. of the Ordnance, 1976; Comdr 5th Field Force, 1979; rcds 1981; ACOS, HQ UKLF, 1982–83; Sen. Army Mem., RCDS, 1984–85; retd 1989. Private Sec. and Treas. to TRH The Prince and Princess of Wales, 1990–91. Chm., C. N. Unwin Ltd, 2006–09 (non-exec. Dir, 2003–06). Chairman: Not Forgotten Assoc., 1992–2001; Nat. Assoc. of Air Ambulance Services, 1999–2002; Comr, Royal Hosp., Chelsea, 1990–96; Mem., Prince of Wales's Council, 1990–91. Vice-Pres., Brainwave, 2000–. Trustee: Hedley Foundn, 1994–2002; The Voices Foundn, 2003–13. Patron, Soc. of Mary and Martha, 1998–. *Recreations:* gardening, smallholding with herd of alpacas, music, art, churches. *Address:* c/o Headquarters Scots Guards, Wellington Barracks, Birdcage Walk, SW1E 6HQ.

AITCHISON, Prof. Cara Carmichael, PhD; FAcSS; Vice-Chancellor and Chief Executive, University of St Mark & St John, Plymouth, since 2013; *b* Falkirk, 5 Feb. 1965; *d* of James Aitchison and Norma Nicol. *Educ:* High Sch. of Stirling; Univ. of Edinburgh (MA Hons Geog. 1987); Moray House Coll. of Educn (Postgrad. Dip. Recreation and Leisure Practice 1988); Thames Poly. (CertEd Further and Higher Educn 1990); Middlesex Univ. (MA Gender and Society 1993); Univ. of Bristol (PhD Soc. Sci. 1999). Lectr, Croydon Coll., 1988–89; Polytechnic, then University of North London: Lectr, 1989–90; Sen. Lectr, 1990–93; Prin. Lectr, 1993–97; Cheltenham and Gloucester College of Higher Educn, then University of Gloucestershire: Sen. Res. Fellow, 1997–99; Reader, 1999–2003; Hd, Leisure and Sport Res. Unit, 2001–03; Prof. in Human Geog., UWE Bristol (formerly UWE), 2003–08; University of Bedfordshire: Dean, Faculty of Educn and Sport, 2008–10; Prof. in Leisure and Tourism Studies, 2008–10; University of Edinburgh: Hd, Moray House Sch. of Educn, 2010–13; Prof. in Social and Envmtl Justice, 2010–13. FAcSS (AcSS 2003). *Publications:* (jtly) Leisure and Tourism Landscapes: social and cultural geographies, 2000; Gender and Leisure: social and cultural perspectives, 2003; (ed jtly) Geographies of Muslim Identities: diaspora, gender and belonging, 2007; (ed) Sport and Gender Identities:

masculinities, femininities and sexualities, 2007; articles in jls on educn, geog., sociol., gender, disability, leisure, sport, tourism and rural studies. *Recreations:* travel, camping, active outdoor recreation including swimming and kayaking, contemporary landscape art, music. *Address:* Vice-Chancellor's Office, University of St Mark & St John, Derriford Road, Plymouth PL6 8BH. *T:* (01752) 636872. *E:* caitchison@marjon.ac.uk.

AITCHISON, Sir Charles (Walter de Lancey), 4th Bt *cr* 1938; *b* 27 May 1951; *er s* of Sir Stephen Charles de Lancey Aitchison, 3rd Bt, and (Elizabeth) Anne (Milburn), *er d* of late Lt-Col Edward Reed, Ghyllheugh, Longhorsley, Northumberland; *S* father, 1958; *m* 1984, Susan (marr. diss. 2009), *yr d* of late Edward Ellis; one *s* one *d*. Lieut, 15/19th The King's Royal Hussars, 1974; RARO, 1974–78. *Recreation:* fishing. *Heir: s* Rory Edward de Lancey Aitchison, *b* 7 March 1986.

AITCHISON, Prof. Jean Margaret; Rupert Murdoch Professor of Language and Communication, University of Oxford, 1993–2003; Fellow, Worcester College, Oxford, 1993–2003, now Emeritus; *b* 3 July 1938; *d* of late John Frederick and Joan Eileen Aitchison; *m* 2000, John Robert Ayto. *Educ:* Wimbledon High Sch.; Girton Coll., Cambridge (BA 1st Cl. Hons Classics 1960; MA 1964); Radcliffe Coll., Harvard (AM Linguistics 1961). University of London: Asst Lectr in Ancient Greek, Bedford Coll., 1960–65; Lectr, 1965–82, Sen. Lectr, 1982–92, Reader, 1992, in Linguistics, LSE. Reith Lectr, BBC, 1996. *Publications:* Linguistics, 1972, 7th edn (as Aitchison's Linguistics) 2010; The Articulate Mammal: an introduction to psycholinguistics, 1976, 5th edn 2008; Language Change: progress or decay?, 1981, 4th edn 2013; Words in the Mind: an introduction to the mental lexicon, 1987, 5th edn 2012; The Seeds of Speech: language origin and evolution, 1996, extended edn 2000; The Language Web: the power and problem of words (Reith lectures), 1997; A Glossary of Language and Mind, 2003; (ed with Diana Lewis) New Media Language, 2003; The Word Weavers: newshounds and wordsmiths, 2007; Linguistics Made Easy, 2012. *Recreations:* gardening, reading. *Address:* 45 Malvern Road, E8 3LP. *T:* (020) 7249 3734. *E:* jean.aitchison@worc.ox.ac.uk.

AITCHISON, June Rosemary, (Mrs T. J. Aitchison); *see* Whitfield, J. R.

AITCHISON, Thomas Nisbet, CBE 2005; Chief Executive, City of Edinburgh Council, 1995–2010; *b* 24 Feb. 1951; *s* of Thomas Aitchison and Mary (*née* Millar); *m* 1973, Kathleen Sadler; one *s* two *d*. *Educ:* Univ. of Glasgow (MA 1st Class Hons); Heriot-Watt Univ. (MSc). Lothian Regional Council: various posts, 1975–91; Depute Chief Exec., 1991–94; Chief Exec., 1994–95. Regl Returning Officer for Scotland Region, European elecns, 1999, 2004 and 2009. Chm., SOLACE Scotland, 2001–03. Mem. Court, Napier Univ., 1997–2002. Sec., Edinburgh Internat. Fest. Soc., 1996–2010. *Recreations:* hill-walking, football, music, fine wines and malt whiskies.

AITHRIE, Viscount; Charles Adrian Bristow William Hope; *b* 25 July 2001; *s* and *heir* of Earl of Hopetoun, *qv*. A Page of Honour to the Queen, 2013–15.

AITKEN, family name of **Baron Beaverbrook**.

AITKEN, Anne Elizabeth, (Mrs Charles Collinson); District Judge, Principal Registry, Family Division, since 2008; *b* Dewsbury, W Yorks, 14 Oct. 1952; *d* of late William Allen Crowther and of Mary Eileen Crowther; *m* 1st, 1979, Robert Aitken (marr. diss.); 2nd, 1990, Charles Collinson; one *d*. *Educ:* St Margaret Clitherow Grammar Sch., Bradford; Univ. of Warwick (BA Hons 1974); College of Law. Admitted solicitor, 1982; solicitor in private practice, 1982–92; Partner, Aitken Associates, Islington, 1992–2008; Dep. District Judge, 2000–08. *Address:* Principal Registry of the Family Division, First Avenue House, 42–49 High Holborn, WC1V 6NP.

AITKEN, Cairns; *see* Aitken, R. C. B.

AITKEN, Gill; General Counsel and Solicitor, HM Revenue and Customs, since 2014; *b* 23 March 1960; *d* of Bill and Pamela Parker; *m* 1998, Robert Aitken; one *s*, and two step *s*. *Educ:* St Hugh's Coll., Oxford (BA Hons Philosophy and Theol. 1982). Admitted solicitor, 1988; solicitor in private practice, 1988–93; lawyer in Govt Legal Service, 1993–; Department for Environment, Food and Rural Affairs: Dir, Legal Services, 2004–07; Director General: Law and Human Resources (formerly Legal Gp), 2007–09; Law and Corporate Services, 2009–10. *Recreations:* family, cycling, art history, theatre, conversation and ideas.

AITKEN, Gillon Reid; literary agent; Chairman, Aitken Alexander Associates (formerly Gillon Aitken, then Aitken, Stone & Wylie, subsequently Aitken & Stone, latterly Gillon Aitken Associates) Ltd, since 1977; *b* 29 March 1938; *s* of James Aitken and Margaret Joane Aitken (*née* Simpson); *m* 1982, Cari Margareta Bengtsson (marr. diss. 2000; she *d* 2011); (one *d* decd). *Educ:* Charterhouse Sch.; privately. Private schoolmaster, Surbiton, 1955–56; National Service, 1956–58: Somerset LI; Intelligence Corps; Jt Services Sch. for Linguists (Russian course); Royal Signal Corps, Berlin. Stuart's Advertising Agency Ltd, 1958–59; Editor: Chapman & Hall Ltd, 1959–66; Hodder & Stoughton Ltd, 1966–67; Dir, Anthony Sheil Associates Ltd, 1967–71; Man. Dir, Hamish Hamilton Ltd, 1971–74; Vice-Pres., Wallace, Aitken & Sheil, Inc. (NY), 1974–77; Chairman: Christy & Moore Ltd, 1977–; Hughes Massie Ltd, 1985–. *Publications:* translations from Russian: The Captain's Daughter & Other Stories by Alexander Sergeyevitch Pushkin, 1962; The Complete Prose Tales of Pushkin, 1966; One Day in the Life of Ivan Denisovich by Alexander Solzhenitsyn, 1970. *Recreations:* crossword puzzles, ping-pong. *Address:* c/o Aitken Alexander Associates Ltd, 291 Gray's Inn Road, WC1X 8EB. *T:* (020) 7373 8672; The Garden Flat, 4 The Boltons, SW10 9TB. *T:* (020) 7373 7438.

AITKEN, Ian Levack; columnist, Tribune, since 1998; *b* 19 Sept. 1927; *s* of George Aitken and Agnes Levack Aitken; *m* 1956, Dr Catherine Hay Mackie (*d* 2006), *y d* of late Maitland Mackie, OBE; two *d*. *Educ:* King Alfred Sch., Hampstead; Regent Street Polytechnic; Lincoln Coll., Oxford (BA PPE; MA); LSE. Served Fleet Air Arm, 1945–48. HM Inspector of Factories, 1951; Res. Officer, CSEU, 1952; Industrial Reporter, Tribune, 1953–54; Industrial Reporter, subseq. Foreign Correspondent and Political Correspondent, Daily Express, 1954–64; political staff, The Guardian, 1964–92 (Political Editor, 1975–90; political columnist, 1990–92; columnist, 1992; contributor, 1992–); columnist and contributing editor, New Statesman, 1993–96. Gerald Barry Award for journalism, 1984. *Publications:* (with Mark Garnett) Splendid! Splendid!: the authorised biography of William Whitelaw, 2002. *Recreation:* music. *Address:* 8 Fitzwarren House, 12 Hornsey Lane, N6 5LX. *T:* (020) 7272 2314. *Club:* Garrick.

AITKEN, Jonathan William Patrick; *b* 30 Aug. 1942; *s* of Sir William Traven Aitken, KBE and Hon. Penelope Loader Maffey, MBE, JP; *m* 1st, 1979, Lolicia Olivera (marr. diss. 1998), *d* of Mr and Mrs O. Azucki, Zürich; one *s* twin *d*; one *d* by Soraya Khashoggi; 2nd, 2003, Hon. Elizabeth Harris, *d* of 1st Baron Ogmore, TD, PC. *Educ:* Eton Coll.; Christ Church, Oxford (MA Hons Law); HMPs Belmarsh and Standford Hill; Wycliffe Hall, Oxford (CTh Dist.). Private Sec. to Selwyn Lloyd, 1964–66; Foreign Corresp., London Evening Standard, 1966–71; Man. Dir, Slater Walker (Middle East) Ltd, 1973–75; Dep. Chm., Aitken Hume Internat. PLC, 1990–92 (Co-founder, 1981; Chm., 1981–90); Dir, TV-am PLC, 1981–88. Contested (C) Meriden, 1966; MP (C) Thanet East, Feb. 1974–83, Thanet South, 1983–97; contested (C) Thanet South, 1997. Minister of State for Defence Procurement, MoD, 1992–94; PC, 1994–97; Chief Sec. to HM Treasury, 1994–95. Mem., Select Cttee on Employment, 1979–82. Dir, Prison Fellowship Internat., 2003–; Exec. Dir, Trinity Forum Europe, 2006–; Chm., Prison Reform Gp, Centre for Social Justice, 2007– (Fellow, 2014); Advr to World Bank on offender rehabilitation projects, 2010–. Trustee: Caring for Ex-Offenders, 2003–; Saïd Foundn, 2007–; NACRO, 2011–. Pres., Christian Solidarity Worldwide, 2006–; Vice Pres., New Bridge Soc., 2007–. *Publications:* A Short Walk on the Campus, 1966; The Young Meteors, 1967; Land of Fortune: A Study of Australia, 1969; Officially Secret, 1970; Richard Nixon: a life, 1993; Pride and Perjury, 2000; Psalms for People under Pressure, 2004; Prayers for People under Pressure, 2004; Porridge and Passion, 2005; Charles W. Colson: a life redeemed, 2005; Heroes and Contemporaries, 2006; John Newton: from disgrace to amazing grace, 2007; Nazarbayev and the Making of Kazakhstan, 2009; Margaret Thatcher: power and personality, 2013; Meaningful Mentoring, 2014; articles in Spectator, Sunday Telegraph, Sunday Times, Guardian, American Spectator, Sydney Morning Herald, Washington Post, Independent, Daily Mail, Mail on Sunday, etc. *Address:* 83 Barkston Gardens, SW5 0EU. *T:* (office) (020) 7373 5800. *E:* jonathanaitken@jwpaitken.co.uk.

See also M. P. K. Aitken.

AITKEN, Maria Penelope Katharine; actress; Director, Dramatis Personae Co.; *b* 12 Sept. 1945; *d* of Sir William Traven Aitken, KBE and Hon. Penelope Loader Maffey, MBE, JP; *m* 1st, 1968, Mark Durden-Smith (marr. diss.); 2nd, 1972, (Arthur) Nigel Davenport (marr. diss.; he *d* 2013); one *s*; 3rd, 1991, Patrick McGrath, *qv*. *Educ:* Riddlesworth Hall, Norfolk; Sherborne Girls' Sch.; St Anne's Coll., Oxford. Associate Prof., Yale Sch. of Drama, 1990; Faculty Member: Juilliard Sch., NY, 1991–97; Drama Dept, NY Univ., 1995–96. *Stage includes:* first professional appearance, Belgrade Th., Coventry, 1967; rep., Th. Royal, Northampton, 1970–71; Travesties, RSC, 1974; A Little Night Music, Adelphi, 1975; Blithe Spirit, NT, 1976; Bedroom Farce, NT, 1977; Private Lives, Duchess, 1980; Design for Living, Queen's, 1982; Sister Mary Ignatius (also dir.), Ambassadors, 1983; Happy Family (dir.), Duke of York's, 1983; Private Lives (also dir.), 1984; After the Ball (dir.), Old Vic, 1985; The Rivals (dir.), Court, Chicago, 1985; Waste, RSC, 1985; The Women, Old Vic, 1986; The Vortex, Garrick, 1989; Other People's Money, Lyric, 1990; The Mystery of Irma Vep (dir.), Ambassadors, 1990; As You Like It (dir.), Regent's Park Open Air Th., 1992; Hay Fever, Albery, 1992; The Picture of Dorian Gray, Lyric, Hammersmith, 1994; Sylvia, Lyric, 1997; Easy Virtue (dir.), Chichester, 1999; Humble Boy, Gielgud, 2002; Man and Boy (dir.), Duchess, 2005; The 39 Steps (dir.), Criterion, 2006; Sherlock's Last Case (dir.), Watermill Th., Newbury, 2013; *films:* A Fish Called Wanda, 1988; Fierce Creatures, 1997; Jinnah, 1998; Asylum, 2005; producer, director and actor for TV and radio. *Publications:* A Girdle Round the Earth, 1986; Style: acting in high comedy, 1996.

See also J. W. P. Aitken, J. A. Davenport.

AITKEN, Prof. Martin Jim, FRS 1983; FSA, FRAS, FInstP; Professor of Archaeometry, 1985–89, and Deputy Director, Research Laboratory for Archaeology, 1957–89, Oxford University; Fellow of Linacre College, Oxford, 1965–89; *b* 11 March 1922; *s* of Percy Aitken and Ethel Brittain; *m* Joan Killick; one *s* four *d*. *Educ:* Stamford Sch., Lincs; Wadham Coll. and Clarendon Lab., Oxford Univ. (MA, DPhil). Served War, RAF Radar Officer, 1942–46 (Burma Star, 1945). Mem., Former Physical Soc., 1951–; MRI, 1972–89. Editor, Archaeometry, 1958–89. *Publications:* Physics and Archaeology, 1961, 2nd edn 1974; Thermoluminescence Dating, 1985; Science-based dating in Archaeology, 1990; Introduction to Optical Dating, 1998. *Recreation:* walking. *Address:* Le Garret, 63930 Augerolles, France.

AITKEN, Oonagh Melrose; Chief Executive, Volunteering Matters (formerly Community Service Volunteers), since 2014 (Director, Social Action, Volunteering, Fundraising and Policy, 2012–14); *b* 11 March 1956. *Educ:* Paisley Grammar Sch.; Glasgow University (MA Hons, MEd); Open Univ. (MA Art Hist. 2008). Teacher of modern languages, Linwood High Sch., Braidfield High Sch., and Garrion Acad., Wishaw (also Asst Head Teacher), 1982–90; Strathclyde Regional Council: Educn Officer, 1990–93; Brussels Officer, 1993–95; Actg Asst Chief Exec., 1995–96; Hd, Social Policy, Glasgow CC, 1996; Corporate Manager (Social Strategy), Fife Council, 1996–99; Chief Exec., COSLA, 1999–2001; Improvement and Development Agency: Regl Associate Dir, 2001–02, Regl Associate, 2002–03, South East; Acting Dir, Strategy, Inf. and Develt, 2003–04; Consultant, 2004–05; sessional lectr, project manager and researcher, McGill Sch. of Social Work, Montreal, 2006–09; Nat. Advr, Children, Young People and Families, Improvement and Develt Agency, subseq. Local Govt Improvement and Develt, 2009–12. *Recreations:* literature, cinema, current affairs. *Address:* Volunteering Matters, The Levy Centre, 18–24 Lower Clapton Road, E5 0PD.

AITKEN, Prof. (Robert) Cairns (Brown), CBE 1998; MD; FRCPE, FRCPsych; Chairman, Royal Infirmary of Edinburgh NHS Trust, 1993–97; *b* 20 Dec. 1933; *s* of late John Goold Aitken and Margaret Johnstone (*née* Brown); *m* 1959, Audrey May Lunn; one *s* one *d* (and one *d* decd). *Educ:* Cargilfield Sch., Edinburgh; Sedbergh Sch., Yorks; Univ. of Glasgow (MB, ChB 1957; MD 1965). FRCPE 1971; FRCPsych 1974. Univ. of Glasgow-McGill Univ. Exchange Schol., Montreal, 1958–59; RAF Inst. of Aviation Medicine, 1960–62; Registrar in Medicine, Orpington Hosp., Kent, 1962–64; Registrar, then Sen. Registrar, Maudsley Hosp., 1964–66; University of Edinburgh: Lectr and Sen. Lectr, Dept of Psychiatry, 1966–74; Prof. of Rehabilitation Studies and Hon. Consultant Physician, 1974–94; Dir, Disability Mgt Res. Gp, Assoc. of British Insurers, 1980–94; Dean, Faculty of Medicine, 1990–91; Vice-Principal (Planning and Budgeting), 1991–94. Visiting Professor: Univ. of Pennsylvania, 1971; Saragossa Univ., 1976; Monash Univ., 1982; Univ. of Malaya, 1993. Ed., Jl of Psychosomatic Res., 1979–86. Dir, Lothian Health Bd, 1991–93. Member: Council, RCPsych, 1972–74; Scottish Council on Disability, 1975–84; Council, Professions Supplementary to Medicine, 1983–90; Scottish Cttee for Hosp. Med. Services, 1985–87; GMC, 1991–96; Human Genetics Adv. Commn, 1996–99; Pres., Internat. Coll. of Psychosomatic Medicine, 1985–87. For. Associate Mem., Inst. of Medicine, Amer. Acad. of Sci., 1995. Hon. Fellow: Napier Poly. of Edinburgh, 1990; Internat. Coll. of Psychosomatic Medicine, 1994. Hon. DSc CNAA, 1992. Officers' Cross, Order of Merit (Poland), 1994. *Publications:* on stress in aircrew, measurement of mood and assessment and management of disability. *Recreations:* people, places and pleasures of Edinburgh, Scotland and beyond. *Address:* 11 Succoth Place, Edinburgh EH12 6BJ. *T:* (0131) 337 1550. *Club:* New (Edinburgh).

AITKEN, William Mackie; JP; DL; Member (C) Glasgow, Scottish Parliament, 1999–2011; *b* 15 April 1947; *s* of William Aitken and Nell Aitken. *Educ:* Allan Glen's Sch., Glasgow; Glasgow Coll. of Technol. ACII 1971. Underwriter and sales exec., insurance industry, 1965–98. Glasgow City Council: Mem. (C), 1976–99; Convenor, Licensing Cttee, 1977–80; Leader of Opposition, 1980–84 and 1992–96; Bailie of City, 1980–84, 1988–92 and 1996–99. Scottish Parliament: Dep. Opposition spokesman on justice, 2001–03; Vice Convenor, Justice 2 Cttee, 2000–03; Cons. Chief Whip and Parly Business Mgr, 2003–07; Shadow Sec. for Justice, 2007–11; Convener, Justice Cttee, 2007–11. JP 1985, DL 1992, Glasgow. *Publications:* contrib. articles to newspapers. *Recreations:* reading, walking, foreign travel, wining and dining with friends.

AITKIN, Prof. Donald Alexander, AO 1998; PhD; Chairman: Cultural Facilities Corporation, 2002–11; National Capital Authority, 2008–11; Chief Executive Officer, Agrecon Pty Ltd, 2002–03 (Chairman, 1992–2002); *b* 4 Aug. 1937; *e s* of late Alexander George Aitkin and Edna Irene (*née* Taylor); *m* 1st, 1958, Janice Wood (marr. diss. 1977); one *s* three *d*; 2nd, 1977, Susan Elderton (marr. diss. 1991); one *s*; 3rd, 1991, Beverley Benger. *Educ:* Univ. of New England (MA 1961); ANU (PhD 1964). Postdoctoral Travelling Fellow, Nuffield Coll., Oxford, 1964–65; Australian National University: Res. Fellow in Pol Sci., 1965–68; Sen. Res. Fellow, 1968–71; Prof. of Politics (Foundn Prof.), Macquarie Univ.,

1971–80; Institute of Advanced Studies, Australian National University: Prof. of Pol Sci., 1980–88; Chm. Bd, 1986–88; Vice-Chancellor, 1991–2002, Pres., 1997–2002, Prof. Emeritus, 2003–, Univ. of Canberra. Chairman: Aust. Res. Grants Cttee, 1986–87; Aust. Res. Council, 1988–90; ACT Schs Legislation Review, 1999–2000; Dep. Chm., ACT Sci. and Technol. Council, 1999–; Member: Aust. Sci. and Technol. Council, 1986–92; Tourism Ministerial Adv. Council, 2006–08. Vice-Pres., Australian Vice-Chancellors' Cttee, 1994–95. Chairman: Aust. Maths Trust, 1995–2004; Nat. Olympiad Council, 1996–2004; NRMA/ ACT Road Safety Trust, 2001–. Mem. Bd, Canberra Theatre Trust, 1993–97; Pres., Pro Musica Inc., 2002–09; Chm., Canberra Internat. Music Fest., 2009–12; Dir, Artsound FM, 2004–06. FASSA 1975; FACE 1995; Hon. Fellow, Royal Aust. Planning Inst., 2001. DUniv Canberra, 2002; Hon. DLitt New England, 2004. *Publications:* The Colonel, 1969; The Country Party in New South Wales, 1972; Stability and Change in Australian Politics, 1977, 2nd edn 1982; The Second Chair (novel), 1977; (with B. Jinks) Australian Political Institutions, 1980 (trans. Japanese, 1985), 10th edn 2012; (ed) The Life of Politics, 1984; (ed) Surveys of Australian Political Science, 1985; What Was It All For? The Reshaping of Australia, 2005; Edna and Alec: a memoir, 2006. *Recreations:* walking, music, cooking. *Address:* 80 Banks Street, Yarralumla, ACT 2600, Australia.

AITMAN, David Charles; Global Managing Partner, Freshfields Bruckhaus Deringer LLP, since 2014. *Educ:* Clifton Coll.; Univ. of Sheffield (BA). Admitted as solicitor, 1982; Partner, Denton Wilde Sapte, 1988–2001; Freshfields Bruckhaus Deringer LLP: Partner, 2001–; Deptl Man. Partner, 2003–06; Global Practice Leader, 2006–10. *Publications:* contributor: Butterworth's Encyclopaedia of Competition Law, 1991; Practical Intellectual Property; Yearbook of Media Law; Bellamy & Child's European Community Law of Competition. *Recreations:* tennis, windsurfing, music (performing and concert going). *Address:* Freshfields Bruckhaus Deringer LLP, 65 Fleet Street, EC4Y 1HS. *T:* (020) 7832 7240. *E:* david.aitman@ freshfields.com.

AITMAN, Prof. Timothy John, DPhil; FRCP; FRSB; FMedSci; Professor of Molecular Pathology and Genetics, and Director, Centre for Genomic and Experimental Medicine, University of Edinburgh, since 2014; *b* Northwood, 9 June 1958; *s* of Gabriel and Irene Aitman; *m* 1989, Megan Rowley; one *s* one *d. Educ:* Birmingham Med. Sch. (BSc Physiol. 1979; MB ChB 1982); King's Coll. London (MSc Gen. Biochem. 1988); Wolfson Coll., Oxford (DPhil 1992). MRCP 1985, FRCP 2000; FRSB (FSB 2012). Clinical Res. Fellow and Hon. Sen. Registrar, Nuffield Dept of Surgery and Radcliffe Infirmary, Univ. of Oxford, 1989–92; Sen. Registrar, St Bartholomew's Hosp., 1993; Gp Hd and Section Chair, Physiol Genomics and Medicine Gp, MRC Clin. Scis Centre, Hammersmith Hosp., 1993–2014; Hon. Consultant Physician, Hammersmith Hosps NHS Trust, 1994–2014; Prof. of Clin. and Molecular Genetics, Faculty of Medicine, Imperial Coll. London, 2001–14. Specialist Advr for H of L Genomic Medicine Report, 2009. FMedSci 2001. *Address:* Centre for Genomic and Experimental Medicine, Room N2.13, Institute of Genetics and Molecular Medicine, University of Edinburgh, Western General Hospital, Crewe Road South, Edinburgh EH4 2XU. *T:* (0131) 651 2081. *E:* tim.aitman@ed.ac.uk.

AITTCHISEN, Sir Lance Walter; *see* Aitchison, Sir C. W. de L.

AJEGBO, Sir Keith Onyema, Kt 2007; OBE 1994; education consultant; Headteacher, Deptford Green School, 1986–2006; *b* 31 Oct. 1946; *s* of late Michael Ajegbo and Dorothy Ajegbo; *m* 1991, Deborah Caroline Fry; one *s* one *d. Educ:* Greenacres Primary Sch., Eltham; Eltham Coll.; Downing Coll., Cambridge (BA Eng. Lit. 1969); Univ. of Nottingham (PGCE 1970); Birkbeck, Univ. of London (MA Culture, Diaspora, Ethnicity 2014). Dep. Hd, Elliott Sch., Putney, 1981–86. Education consultant for: DFES, subseq. DCSF, later DFE, 2006–10, researched and wrote report for Sec. of State for Educn (Curriculum Review: Diversity and Citizenship, 2007); London Bor. of Newham, 2004–10; UBS Investment Bank, 2006–07; Leadership Develt Advr, Future Leaders, 2006–; Chm., 14–19 Diploma in Humanities Steering Gp, DFE (formerly DCSF), 2008–10; Mem., Speaker's Adv. Cttee on Public Engagement, 2010–. Governor: Nat. Coll. of Sch. Leadership, 2001–03; Goldsmiths, London, 2003–07; Bridge Acad., Hackney, 2007–. Trustee: Citizenship Foundn, 2007–11; Stephen Lawrence Trust, 2007– (Vice Chair, 2011). Hon. Fellow, Goldsmiths, London, 1997. Hon. DEd De Montfort, 2002; Hon. DLit(Ed) London, 2011. *Publications:* Black Lives, White Worlds, 1982; numerous articles for educn jls. *Recreations:* playing tennis (Capt., Cambridge Univ., 1969, Prentice Cup tour, 1968; Kent county team, 1966–82, county colours), reading novels, extensive library of pop music. *Club:* All England Lawn Tennis (Wimbledon).

AJIBOLA, Prince Bola Adesumbo, Hon. KBE 1989; CFR; SAN 1986; High Commissioner for Nigeria in the United Kingdom, 1999–2002; Leader of Nigerian Delegation, Cameroon-Nigeria Mixed Commission, since 2002; Founder, Bola Ajibola & Co., 1963; *b* 22 March 1934; *s* of Oba A. S. Ajibola and Adikatu Ashakun Ajibola; *m* 1961, Olu Olugbemi; three *s* two *d. Educ:* Owu Baptist Day Sch., Abeokuta, Nigeria; Baptist Boys' High Sch., Abeokuta. Called to the Bar, Lincoln's Inn, London, 1962. Principal Partner, Bola Ajobola & Co., Nigeria, 1967–85 (specialising in commercial law and internat. arbitration); Hon. Attorney-Gen. and Minister of Justice, Nigeria, 1985–91; Judge: Internat. Court of Justice, The Hague, 1991–94; World Bank Admin. Tribunal, 1994; Constitutional Court, Fedn of Bosnia and Herzegovina, 1995; delegate to numerous internat. confs. President: Nigerian Bar Assoc., 1984–85 (Chm., Human Rights Cttee, 1980–84); Pan African Council, London Court of Internat. Arbitration, 1994; Pres. and Founder, African Concern, 1995–; Chairman: Gen. Council of the Bar, Nigeria, 1985–91; Body of Sen. Advocates of Nigeria, 1985–91; Adv. Cttee of Prerogative of Mercy, Nigeria, 1989–91; Task Force for Revision of Laws, Nigeria, 1990; Member: Privileges Cttee, Nigerian Bar, 1985–91; Nigerian Police Council, 1989–91; Internat. Bar Assoc.; Internat. Chamber of Commerce; World Arbitration Inst.; Perm. Court of Arbitration, The Hague (also Mem., Bd of Trustees); Governing Bd, Internat. Maritime Law Inst., IMO; Internat. Law Commn, UN, 1986–91; Internat. Court of Arbitration, ICC (Vice Chm., Commn; arbitrator, numerous internat. cases); Internat. Maritime Arbitration Commn; Governing Body, African Soc. of Internat. and Comparative Law. Fellow, Nigerian Inst. of Advanced Legal Studies; FCIArb. Editor: All Nigeria Law Reports, 1961–90; Nigeria's Treaties in Force, 1970–90; Ed.-in-Chief, Justice; Gen. Editor, Federal Min. of Justice Law Review Series. *Publications:* Law Development and Administration in Nigeria, 1987; Towards a Better Administration of Justice System in Nigeria, 1988; Narcotics, Law and Policy in Nigeria, 1989; Compensation and Remedies for Victims of Crime, 1989; Banking Frauds and Other Financial Malpractices in Nigeria, 1989; Unification and Reform of Criminal Laws and Procedure Codes of Nigeria, 1990; Women and Children under Nigerian Law, 1990; Customary Law in Nigeria, 1991; Democracy and the Law; Dispute Resolution by International Court of Justice; papers and articles in learned jls. *Address:* Bola Ajibola & Co., PO Box 6624, Marina, Lagos, Nigeria. *Clubs:* Abeokuta (Abeokuta); Metropolitan (Lagos); Yoruba Tennis.

AKAM, Prof. Michael Edwin, DPhil; FRS 2000; FRES, FLS; Professor of Zoology (1866), and Head, Department of Zoology, University of Cambridge, since 2010; Fellow, Darwin College, Cambridge, since 2006; *b* 19 June 1952; *s* of William Edwin Akam and Evelyn Warriner Akam (*née* Thorne); *m* 1979, Margaret Madeleine Bray; two *s. Educ:* King's Coll., Cambridge (BA Nat. Scis 1974); Magdalen Coll., Oxford (DPhil Genetics 1978). FRES 1985; FLS 1999. Australian Sci. Schol., Royal Instn, 1970. Coll. Lectr in Zoology, Magdalen Coll., Oxford, 1978; Res. Fellow, King's Coll., Cambridge, 1978–86; MRC Fellow, Lab. of Molecular Biology, Cambridge, 1978–79; Fellow, Dept of Biochemistry, Stanford Univ., 1979–81 (Damon-Runyan/Walter Winchell Fellow, 1979); Cambridge University: MRC Sen. Fellow, Dept of Genetics, 1982–90; Wellcome Principal Fellow, and Founding Mem., Wellcome/CRC Inst., 1990–97; Prof. of Zoology, 1997–2010; Dir, Univ. Mus. of Zoology, 1997–2010. Chm., British Soc. for Developmental Biology, 1989–94 (Waddington Medal, 2005). Mem., EMBO, 1987. FAAAS 2006. Kowalevsky Medal, St Petersburg Soc. of Naturalists, 2007; Linnean Medal for Zool., Linnean Soc., 2009; Frink Medal, ZSL, 2013. *Publications:* (ed jtly) The Evolution of Developmental Mechanisms, 1994; res. papers and reviews in jls, Proc. Royal Soc., etc. *Recreation:* the living world. *Address:* Department of Zoology, University of Cambridge, Downing Street, Cambridge CB2 3EJ. *T:* (01223) 336601.

AKENHEAD, Hon. Sir Robert, Kt 2008; **Hon. Mr Justice Akenhead;** a Judge of the High Court of Justice, Queen's Bench Division, since 2007; Judge in charge, Technology and Construction Court, 2010–13; *b* 15 Sept. 1949; *s* of late Edmund and Angela Akenhead; *m* 1972, Elizabeth Anne Jackson; one *s* three *d. Educ:* Rugby School; Exeter Univ. (LLB). Called to the Bar, Inner Temple, 1972, Bencher, 1997; in practice as barrister, 1973–2007; QC 1989; Head of Chambers, 2001–06; Asst Recorder, 1991–94; Recorder, 1994–2007. Examiner, Dio. of Canterbury, 1991–2007. Ed., Building Law Reports, 1999–. *Publications:* Site Investigation and the Law, 1984; Technology and Construction Court Practice and Procedure, 2006. *Recreations:* theatre, cricket, ski-ing, golf. *Address:* Royal Courts of Justice, Strand, WC2A 2LL.

AKER, Tim Mark; Member (UK Ind) Eastern Region, European Parliament, since 2014; *b* Orsett, Essex, 23 May 1985. *Educ:* Havering Sixth Form Coll.; Univ. of Nottingham. Public affairs, TaxPayers' Alliance and Get Britain Out; Hd, Policy Unit, UKIP, 2013–15. Mem. (UK Ind) Thurrock Council, 2014–. Contested (UK Ind) Thurrock, 2015. *Address:* European Parliament, 60 Rue Wiertz, 1047 Brussels, Belgium; (office) 64a Orsett Road, Grays Thurrock, Essex RM17 5EB.

AKERLOF, Prof. George Arthur, PhD; Professor of Economics, University of California at Berkeley, since 1980; Cassel Professor of Economics, London School of Economics and Political Science, 1978–81; *b* 17 June 1940; *s* of Gosta C. Akerlof and Rosalie C. Akerlof; *m* 1978, Janet Yellen; one *s. Educ:* Yale Univ. (BA 1962); MIT (PhD 1966). Fellowships: Woodrow Wilson, 1962–63; National Science Co-op., 1963–66; Fulbright, 1967–68; Guggenheim, 1973–74. Univ. of Calif, Berkeley: Asst Prof. of Econs, 1966–70; Associate Prof., 1970–77; Prof., 1977–78. Vis. Prof., Indian Statistical Inst., New Delhi, 1967–68. Sen. Economist, Council of Econ. Advisors, USA, 1973–74; Vis. Economist, Bd of Governors of Fed. Reserve System, USA, 1977–78. (Jtly) Nobel Prize for Economics, 2001. *Publications:* contrib. American Econ. Rev., Econ. Jl, Qly Jl Econs, Jl Polit. Econ., Rev. of Econ. Studies, Internat. Econ. Rev., Jl Econ. Theory, Indian Econ. Rev., and Rev. of Econs and Stats. *Address:* Department of Economics, University of California, Berkeley, CA 94720–3880, USA. *Club:* Piggy (Center Harbor, NH, USA).

AKERS-DOUGLAS, family name of **Viscount Chilston**.

AKERS-JONES, Sir David, KBE 1985; CMG 1978; GBM 2002; Chief Secretary, Hong Kong, 1985–86; Acting Governor, Hong Kong, Dec. 1986–April 1987; *b* 14 April 1927; *s* of Walter George and Dorothy Jones; *m* 1951, Jane Spickernell (MBE 1988) (*d* 2002); one *d* (one *s* decd). *Educ:* Worthing High Sch.; Brasenose Coll., Oxford (MA; Hon. Fellow, 2005). British India Steam Navigation Co., 1945–49. Malayan Civil Service (studied Hokkien and Malay), 1954–57; Hong Kong Civil Service, 1957–86; Government Secretary: for New Territories, 1973–81; for City and New Territories, 1981–83; for Dist Admin, 1983–85; Advr to Gov., April–Sept. 1987. Chm., Hong Kong Housing Authy, 1988–93; Advr to China on Hong Kong Affairs. Chm., Operation Smile China Medical Mission, 1992–. Pres., Business and Professionals Fedn, 2005–. Hon. Pres., Outward Bound Trust, Hong Kong, 1996– (Pres., 1986–95); Vice-Patron, Hong Kong Football Assoc. Hon. Member: RICS, 1991; HKIA, 2006. Hon. DCL Kent, 1987; Hon. LLD Chinese Univ. of Hong Kong, 1988; Hon. DSSc City Univ. of Hong Kong, 1993. *Recreations:* painting, music. *Address:* Flat C, 33rd Floor, Tower 1, Sorrento, 1 Austin Road West, West Kowloon, Hong Kong. *Clubs:* Royal Over-Seas League; Hong Kong, Dynasty, China, Gold Coast and Country (Hong Kong).

AKHTAR, Prof. Muhammad, FRS 1980; Professor of Biochemistry, University of Southampton, 1973–98, now Emeritus; Distinguished National Professor, School of Biological Sciences, University of the Punjab, Lahore, since 2004; *b* 23 Feb. 1933; *m* 1963, Monika E. Schurmann; two *s. Educ:* Punjab Univ., Pakistan (MSc 1st class 1954); Imperial College, London (PhD, DIC 1959). Research Scientist, Inst. for Medicine and Chemistry, Cambridge, Mass, USA, 1959–63; University of Southampton: Lecturer in Biochemistry, 1963–66; Senior Lectr, 1966–68; Reader, 1968–73; Hd of Dept of Biochemistry, 1978–93; Chm., Sch. of Biochem. and Physiol. Scis, 1983–87; Dir, SERC Centre for Molecular Recognition, 1990–94. Chm., Inst. of Biomolecular Scis, 1989–90. Member: Chemical Soc. of GB; American Chemical Soc.; Biochemical Soc. of GB; Council, Royal Soc., 1983–85; Founding Fellow, Third World Acad. of Sciences, 1983 (Mem. Council and Treas., 1993–98; Vice-Pres., 1998–2004; Medal, 1996). Fellow, UCL, 2010. Hon. DSc Karachi, 2002. Flintoff Medal, RSC, 1993. Sitara-I-Imtiaz (Pakistan), 1981. *Publications:* numerous works on: enzyme mechanisms; synthesis and biosynthesis of steroids and porphyrins; biochemistry of vision; synthesis of anti-microbial compounds. *Address:* Centre for Biological Sciences, University of Southampton, Southampton SO17 1BJ. *T:* (home) (023) 8076 7718.

AKIHITO, HM the Emperor of Japan; Collar, Supreme Order of Chrysanthemum, 1989; KG 1998; *b* Tokyo, 23 Dec. 1933; *e s* of Emperor Hirohito (Showa) and Empress Nagako (Kojun); *S* father, 1989; *m* 1959, Michiko Shoda; two *s* one *d. Educ:* Gakushuin Primary, Jun. and Sen. High Schs; Dept of Politics, Faculty of Politics and Econs, Gakushuin Univ. Official Investiture as Crown Prince of Japan, 1952. Res. Associate, Australian Mus.; Mem., Ichthyological Soc. of Japan; For. Member: Linnean Soc. of London; Zool Soc. of London, 1992. King Charles II Medal, Royal Soc., 1998. *Publications:* (contrib. jtly) Fishes of the Japanese Archipelago, 1984; (jtly) The Fresh Water Fishes of Japan, 1987; 30 papers on gobies. *Recreation:* tennis. *Heir: er s* Crown Prince Naruhito [*b* Tokyo, 23 Feb. 1960; *m* 1993, Masako Owada; one *d*]. *Address:* Imperial Palace, 1–1 Chiyoda, Chiyoda-ku, Tokyo 100–8111, Japan. *T:* (3) 32131111.

AKINKUGBE, Prof. Oladipo Olujimi, NNOM 1997; CON 1979; CFR 2004; Officier de l'Ordre National de la République de Côte d'Ivoire, 1981; MD, DPhil; FRCP, FWACP, FAS; Professor of Medicine, University of Ibadan, Nigeria, 1968–95, now Emeritus; *b* 17 July 1933; *s* of late Chief David Akinbobola and Chief (Mrs) Grace Akinkugbe; *m* 1965, Dr Folasade Modupeore Dina, *d* of late Chief I. O. Dina, CFR, OBE; two *s. Educ:* Univs of Ibadan (Fellow, 1998), London (MD), Liverpool (DTM&H) and Oxford (DPhil). FRCP 1968 (Hon. FRCP 2012); FWACP 1975; FAS 1980. House Surg., London Hosp., 1958; House Phys., King's Coll. Hosp., London, 1959; Commonwealth Res. Fellow, Balliol Coll. and Regius Dept of Medicine, Oxford, 1962–64; Head of Dept of Medicine, 1972, Dean of Medicine, 1970–74, and Chm., Cttee of Deans, 1972–74, Univ. of Ibadan; Vice-Chancellor: Univ. of Ilorin, 1977–78 (Principal, 1975–77); Ahmadu Bello Univ., Zaria, 1978–79. Rockefeller Vis. Fellow, US Renal Centres, 1966; Vis. Fellow in Medicine, Univs of Manchester, Cambridge and London, 1969; Visiting Professor of Medicine: Harvard Univ., 1974–75; Univ. of Oxford (and Vis. Fellow, Balliol Coll.), 1981–82; Univ. of Cape Town, 1996. Adviser on Postgrad. Med. Educn to Fed. Govt of Nigeria, 1972–75; Chairman: Nat. Implementation Commn on Rev. of Higher Educn in Nigeria, 1992; Presidential Project on Revamping Teaching Hosps, 2003–07; Member: Univ. Grants Commn, Uganda Govt; OAU Scientific Panels on Health Manpower Develt; Council, Internat. Soc. of Hypertension, 1982–90; Bd of Trustees, African Assoc. of Nephrology, 1986–94; Bd of Trustees, Nigerian

Educare Trust, 1997–; internat. socs of hypertension, cardiology, and nephrology; Med. Res. Soc. of GB; Scientific Adv. Panel, Ciba Foundn, 1970–98; WHO Expert Adv. Panels on Cardiovascular Diseases, 1973–78, on Health Manpower, 1979–, on Health Sci. and Technol., 2003–; WHO Adv. Council on Health Res., 1990–95; Sec. to WHO 1984 Technical Discussions. Pro-Chancellor, and Chm. of Council, Univ. of Port-Harcourt, Nigeria, 1986–90; Chairman: Bd of Mgt, UCH, Ibadan, 2000–; Bd of Trustees, Ajayi Crowther Univ., Oyo, 2004–; Bd of Trustees, Bells Univ. of Technol., Ota, 2011–; Member: Governing Council and Bd of Trustees, Obafemi Awolowo Foundn, 1992; Governing Council, Nigeria Heart (formerly Heartcare) Foundn, 1994– (Chm., Bd of Trustees, 2000–); Exec. Council, World Innovation Foundn, 1998–; Bd of Trustees, Heritage Resources Conservation, 1999–; Bd, World Heart Fedn, 2004–; Chairman: Governing Council, Ajumogobia Science Foundn, 1997–; Bd of Trustees and Governing Council, Nigeria Soc. for Inf., Arts and Culture, 2002. President: Nigerian Assoc. of Nephrology, 1987–90; Nigerian Hypertension Soc., 1994; African Heart Network, 2001. Member, Editorial Bd: Jl of Hypertension, 1984–90; Jl of Human Hypertension, 1988–; Kidney International, 1990–98; Blood Pressure, 1991–; News in Physiological Scis, 1992–98. Hon. Fellow, Balliol Coll., Oxford, 2009. Hon. DSc: Ilorin, 1982; Fed. Univ. of Technol., Akure, 1992; Port Harcourt, 1997; Ogun State, 1998; Ibadan, 2006; Obafemi Awolowo, Ile-Ife, 2009; Bells Univ. of Technol., Ota, 2010. Searle Dist. Res. Award, 1989; Boehringer Ingelheim Award, Internat. Soc. of Hypertension, 2004; Hallmarks of Labour Award, 2004; Life Achievement Award: Nigerian Acad. of Sci., 2004; Nat. Univs Commn, 2006. Traditional title, Atobase of Ife, 1991; Babalofin of Ijebu-Igbo, 1994; Adengbua of Ondo, 1995; Ikolaba Balogun Basegun of Ibadan, 1997; Aare Basegun of Ibadan, 2008. *Publications:* High Blood Pressure in the African, 1972; (ed) Priorities in National Health Planning, 1974; (ed) Cardiovascular Disease in Africa, 1976; (ed) Nigeria and Education: the challenges ahead, 1994; (ed jtly) Nigeria's Health in the 90s, 1996; (ed) Non-Communicable Diseases in Nigeria: final report of a national survey, 1997; (ed jtly) A Compendium of Clinical Medicine, 1999; (ed jtly) Clinical Medicine in the Tropics Series, 1987–; Footprints and Footnotes: an autobiography, 2010; papers on hypertension and renal disease in African, Eur. and Amer. med. jls, and papers on med. and higher educn. *Recreations:* music, gardening, clocks, birdwatching, golf. *Address:* c/o Department of Medicine, University of Ibadan, Ibadan, Nigeria; The Little Summit, Olubadan Aleshinloye Way, Iyaganku, Ibadan, Nigeria. *T:* 8036063327. *E:* akinihc@yahoo.com. *Clubs:* Dining (Ibadan); Oxford and Cambridge (Nigeria).

AKINOLA, Most Rev. Peter Jasper, CON 2003; Metropolitan, Archbishop and Primate of Nigeria, 2000–10; *b* 27 Jan. 1944; *m* 1969, Susan A. Akinola; three *s* three *d*. *Educ:* Diocesan Trng Centre, Wusasa; Theol Coll. of Northern Nigeria (Higher Dip. in Theol.); Virginia Theol Seminary, USA (MTS 1981). Catechist, Nguru, Nigeria, 1972; ordained deacon, 1978, priest, 1979; Vicar, St James, Suleija, Abuja, 1978–83; Canon (Missioner), Abuja, 1983–88; Bishop of Abuja, 1989–2010; Archbishop, Province Three, Nigeria, 1998–2000. Chairman: Global South, 2002; Conf. of Anglican Provinces in Africa, 2003–; Global Anglicans Future Conf. Primates' Council.

AKKER, John Richard, MBE 2012; Visiting Professor, Human Rights Centre, University of Essex, since 2012; Executive Secretary, Council for Assisting Refugee Academics, 1999–2012; *b* 6 May 1943; *s* of Alec Louis Morris Akker and Ruby (*née* Bryant); *m* 1st, 1967, Jean-Anne Roxburgh (marr. diss. 1990); two *d*; 2nd, 2007, Elaine Hill. *Educ:* SW Essex Tech. Coll.; Ruskin Coll., Oxford (L. C. White Schol.; Dip. Econ./Pol.); Univ. of York (BA Hons 1969); Cranfield Inst. of Technol. Mgt Sch. Clerical Officer, Ministry of Works, 1959–64; Asst Nat. Officer, 1969–71, Dep. Nat. Local Govt Officer, 1972–73, NALGO; Association of University Teachers: Asst Gen. Sec., 1973–77; Dep. Gen. Sec., 1978–94; Gen. Sec., NATFHE, 1994–97. Advr to EC, 1985–88. Exec. Dir, Network for Educn and Academic Rights, 2001–12. Visiting Lecturer: CIT, 1970–74; Univ. of Wisconsin, 1977–78; Vis. Prof., London South Bank Univ., 2005–12. Winston Churchill Fellowship, USA, 1976. Trustee: Refugee Council, 2000–09; Immigration Adv. Service, 2002–09; Student Action for Refugees, 2012– (Chm., 2012–). Arbitrator, ACAS, 2012–. Freeman, Guild of Educators, 2009–. *Recreations:* motor sport, sailing, football. *Address:* Human Rights Centre, University of Essex, Wivenhoe Park, Colchester CO4 3SQ. *E:* jakker@essex.ac.uk. *Clubs:* National Liberal; Colchester United FC Supporters.

ALABASTER, Rear Adm. Martin Brian, CBE 2011; CEng, FIET; Managing Director, Martin Alabaster Associates Ltd, since 2012; *b* 10 Aug. 1958; *s* of late Instructor Comdr Alan James Alabaster, RN and of Eileen Muriel (*née* Willshee); *m* 1981, Moira Bain; one *s* one *d*. *Educ:* Dulwich Coll.; Queens' Coll., Cambridge (BA Engrg Tripos 1980); Southampton Univ. (MSc Electronics 1985). CEng 2007; FIET 2007. HMS Bristol, 1982–84; Seawolf Project, MoD, 1985–89; RN Staff Course, Greenwich, 1989; BRNC Dartmouth, 1990–91; HMS London, 1992–93; Fleet Support, MoD, 1993–96; Project Horizon, 1996–98; Operational Requirements, MoD, 1998–2000; rcds 2001; Hd, Project Mgt, MoD, 2002–05; Sen. Engr, Fleet HQ, 2005–07. Cdre, BRNC Dartmouth, 2007–08; FO Scotland, Northern England and NI and FO Reserves, 2008–11. FInstLM 2007. Hon. DTech Plymouth, 2008. *Recreations:* running, sailing, bird-watching (Chm., RN Birdwatching Soc., 2006–), photography.

ALAGIAH, George Maxwell, OBE 2008; presenter: BBC TV News at Six (formerly BBC TV 6 o'clock News), since 2003; GMT with George Alagiah, since 2010; *b* 22 Nov. 1955; *s* of Donald and Therese Alagiah; *m* 1984, Frances Robathan; two *s*. *Educ:* St John's Coll., Southsea; Van Mildert Coll., Durham Univ. South Magazine, 1982–89; BBC Foreign Affairs Correspondent, 1989–99, Africa Correspondent, 1994–99; News Presenter and journalist, BBC, 1999–2002. Monte Carlo TV Fest. Award; BAFTA commendation; awards as Journalist of the Year from: Amnesty Internat., 1994; BPG, 1994; James Cameron Meml Trust, 1995; Bayeux Award for War Reporting, 1996. *Publications:* A Passage to Africa, 2001; (jtly) The Day That Shook the World, 2001; A Home from Home, 2006. *Recreations:* sport, tennis, music, hiking. *Address:* BBC News Centre, Broadcasting House, Portland Place, W1A 1AA.

ALAGNA, Roberto; Chevalier de la Légion d'honneur, 2008; French tenor; *b* 7 June 1963; *m* 1st, Florence (*d* 1994); one *d*; 2nd, 1996, Angela Gheorghiu, *qv*; one *d* by Aleksandra Kurzak. Worked as accountant, electrician and cabaret singer; studied under Rafael Ruiz; Pavarotti Internat. Voice Competition Prize, 1988. Débuts: Alfredo in La Traviata, Glyndebourne Touring Opera, 1988; Royal Opera, Covent Garden, 1992; La Scala, Milan, 1994; Théâtre du Châtelet, Paris, 1996; Metropolitan Opera, NY, 1996. Rôles include: Roméo in Roméo et Juliette (Laurence Olivier Award, Covent Garden, 1995); title rôle in Don Carlos; Rodolpho in La Bohème; Nemorino in L'elisir d'amore; Edgard in Lucia di Lammermoor; Cavaradossi in Tosca; Radamès in Aida; title rôle in Gounod's Faust. Film, Tosca, 2002. Numerous recordings. Officier des Arts et des Lettres (France), 2002 (Chevalier, 1996); Ordre Nat. du Mérite (France), 2003. *Publications:* Je ne suis pas le fruit du hasard (autobiog.), 2007.

ALAMBRITIS, Stephen; Leader of the Council, Merton London Borough Council, since 2010 (Member (Lab), since 2003; Leader, Labour Group, since 2007); *b* Larnaca, Cyprus, 22 Feb. 1957; *s* of late Andreas Alambritis, Cyprus and Christina Alambritis (*née* Skardashi); *m* 1987, Athanasia Georgiou; one *s* one *d*. *Educ:* Elliott Sch., Putney; Birmingham Poly. (BA Hons Govt); London Sch. of Econs (MSc); City Poly. (MA Business Law). Researcher, Assoc. of Ind. Businesses, 1984–88; Hd of Public Affairs, Fedn of Small Businesses, 1988–2010 (Mem., 2011–). Owner of small unincorporated property business, 2009–. Member: Better Regulation Task Force, Cabinet Office, 1998–2001; Rural Affairs Task Force, DEFRA, 2001–02; Consumer Adv. Panel, DCA, then MoJ, 2005–10. Member: Disability Rights Commn, 2004–07; Equality and Human Rights Commn, 2009–12. Trustee, Enterprise Insight UK, later Enterprise UK, 2009–10. Member, Board: London Pensions Fund Authy, 2010–; South London Business Ltd, 2010–12; Sutton, Croydon and Merton Credit Union Ltd, 2011–12; Smart Energy Gp (formerly Smart Meter Central Delivery Body), 2013–. Chair, South London Partnership, 2012–. Consultant, Adam Smith Internat., 2012–. Member: Labour Party Small Business Task Force, 2011–; Labour Party Skills Task Force, 2012–; EU Cttee of the Regions, 2015–. Member: NUJ, 1985–2010; Unite (formerly Amicus), 1999–2010; GMB, 2009–; CWU, 2009–10; London Councils, 2010–. Mem., CAMRA, 1995. FCIPR 2008 (MIPR 1990). *Recreation:* FA referee grade 1. *Address:* 10 Woodland Way, Morden, Surrey SM4 4DS. *T:* (020) 8543 6003, 07958 139498. *E:* stephen.alambritis@btinternet.com. *W:* www.twitter.com/cllr_alambritis; The Leader's Office, Merton London Borough Council, Civic Centre, London Road, Morden, Surrey SM4 5DX. *T:* (020) 8545 3424. *E:* stephen.alambritis@merton.gov.uk.

ALANBROOKE, 3rd Viscount *cr* 1946; **Alan Victor Harold Brooke;** Baron Alanbrooke, 1945; *b* 24 Nov. 1932; *s* of 1st Viscount Alanbrooke, KG, GCB, OM, GCVO, DSO, and Benita Blanche (*d* 1968), *d* of Sir Harold Pelly, 4th Bt; *S* half-brother, 1972. *Educ:* Harrow; Bristol Univ. (BEd Hons 1976). Qualified teacher, 1975. Served Army, 1952–72; Captain RA, retired. *Heir:* none.

ALAZREG, Abdullahi Hamad Ali; Under-Secretary, Ministry of Foreign Affairs, Sudan, since 2014; *b* El Gadaref, Sudan, 1 Jan. 1955; *s* of Hamad Ali Alazreg and Nafeesa Albashir Ahmad; *m* 2010, Sumaya Omer Hussain Abdelrahman; one *s* three *d*. *Educ:* Omdurman Univ., Sudan (BA Econs); Lincoln Univ., USA (MA Sociol.); NY Poly. (Dip. Energy Resources and Technol.). Min. of Energy and Mining, Sudan, 1980–88; Islamic African Relief Agency, Sudan, 1989–90; diplomat serving in Saudi Arabia, Kenya, USA, UN Office, Geneva, China, 1990–2004; Ambassador to Bulgaria, 2004–08; Dir, Res. and Studies Dept, Arab Affairs Dept and Dir Gen., Bilateral Relns Directorate, Min. of Foreign Affairs, 2008–10; Ambassador to UK, 2010–14. *Publications:* contrib. magazines in Sudan and Bulgaria. *Recreations:* reading, writing poetry. *Address:* Ministry of Foreign Affairs, University Street, Khartoum, Sudan. *E:* abalazreg@yahoo.com.

ALBANESE, Thomas; Chairman, Vedanta Resources Holdings Ltd, since 2013; Chief Executive, Vedanta Resources plc, since 2014; *b* 9 Sept. 1957; *s* of Paul Albanese and Rosemarie Albanese (*née* Helm); *m* 1979, Mary Delane; two *d* (and one *d* decd). *Educ:* Univ. of Alaska (BS Mining Econs (*cum laude*) 1979; MS Mining Engrg 1981). Chief Operating Officer, Nerco Minerals Co., 1982–93; Rio Tinto plc, 1993–2013: Gen. Manager, Greeks Creek Mine, Alaska, 1993–95; Gp Exploration Exec., London, 1995–97; Vice Pres. Engrg and Gen. Manager Smelting and Refining, Kennecott Utah Copper, Salt Lake City, 1997–2000; Man. Dir, North Ltd, Australia, 2000–01; Chief Executive: Industrial Minerals Div., 2001–04; Copper, and Hd of Exploration, 2004–06; Dir, Gp Resources, 2006–07; CEO, Rio Tinto plc, 2007–13. *Recreations:* walking, swimming, canal boats. *Address:* Woodpeckers, Pachesham Park, Oxshott, Surrey KT22 0DJ.

ALBARN, Damon; musician, singer and songwriter; *b* 23 March 1968; partner, Suzi Winstanley; one *d*. *Educ:* Stanway Sch., Colchester. Lead singer, Blur, 1989–; co-creator, Gorillaz, 1998–; *albums:* with Blur: Leisure, 1991; Modern Life is Rubbish, 1993; Parklife, 1994 (BRIT Award, 1995); The Great Escape, 1995; Blur, 1997; 13, 1999; Think Tank, 2003; The Magic Whip, 2015; with Gorillaz: Gorillaz, 2001; Demon Days, 2005; Plastic Beach, 2010; The Fall, 2011; other projects: Mali Music, 2002; The Good, The Bad & The Queen, 2007; Monkey: Journey to the West, 2008; Kinshasa One Two, 2011; Rocket Juice & The Moon, 2012; Dr Dee, 2012; solo: Everyday Robots, 2014. Composer of musical, wonder.land, 2015. BRIT Award for best group (jtly), 1995, for outstanding contribution to music (jtly), 2012. *Address:* c/o Eleven Management, Suite B, Park House, 206–208 Latimer Road, W10 6QY.

ALBEE, Edward; American dramatist; *b* 12 March 1928. Has directed prodns of own plays, 1961–, mainly at English Th., Vienna, and Alley Th., Houston. *Publications: plays:* The Zoo Story, 1958; The Death of Bessie Smith, 1959; The Sandbox, 1959; Fam and Yam, 1959; The American Dream, 1960; Who's Afraid of Virginia Woolf?, 1962; (adapted from Carson McCullers' novella) The Ballad of the Sad Café, 1963; Tiny Alice, 1964; (adapted from the novel by James Purdy) Malcolm, 1965; A Delicate Balance, 1966 (Pulitzer Prize, 1967); (adapted from the play by Giles Cooper) Everything in the Garden, 1967; Box and Quotations from Chairman Mao Tse-Tung, 1968; All Over, 1971; Seascape, 1974 (Pulitzer Prize, 1975); Listening, 1975; Counting the Ways, 1976; The Lady from Dubuque, 1978; Lolita (adapted from V. Nabokov), 1979; The Man Who Had Three Arms, 1981; Finding the Sun, 1982; Marriage Play, 1986; Three Tall Women, 1991 (Pulitzer Prize, 1994); The Lorca Play, 1992; Fragments, 1993; The Play About the Baby, 1997; The Goat, or Who is Sylvia?, 2000; Occupant, 2001; Peter and Jerry, 2004 (retitled At Home at the Zoo); Me, Myself and I, 2007. *Address:* (office) 14 Harrison Street, New York, NY 10013, USA.

ALBEMARLE, 10th Earl of, *cr* 1696; **Rufus Arnold Alexis Keppel;** Baron Ashford, 1696; Viscount Bury, 1696; *b* 16 July 1965; *s* of Derek William Charles Keppel, Viscount Bury (*d* 1968), and Marina, *yr d* of late Count Serge Orloff-Davidoff; *S* grandfather, 1979; *m* 2001, Sally Claire Tadayon, *d* of Dr Jamal Tadion; one *s*. *Educ:* Central Sch. of Art (BA (Hons) Industrial Design, 1990). *Heir:* *s* Viscount Bury, *qv*. *Address:* Hurst Barns Farm, East Chiltington, Lewes, Sussex BN7 3QU.

ALBERTI, Sir (Kurt) George (Matthew Mayer), Kt 2000; DPhil; FRCP, FRCPE, FRCPath; Senior Research Investigator, Imperial College, London, since 2002; Professor of Medicine, University of Newcastle upon Tyne, 1985–2002 (Dean of Medicine, 1995–97); President, Royal College of Physicians, 1997–2002; *b* 27 Sept. 1937; *s* of late William Peter Matthew Alberti and Edith Elizabeth Alberti; *m* 1st, 1964; three *s*; *m* 2nd, 1998, Prof. Stephanie Anne Amiel, *qv*. *Educ:* Balliol Coll., Oxford (MA; DPhil 1964; BM, BCh 1965; Hon. Fellow 1999). FRCP 1978; FRCPath 1985; FRCPE 1988. Res. Fellow, Harvard Univ., Boston, USA, 1966–69; Res. Officer, Dept of Medicine, Oxford Univ., 1969–73; Prof. of Chemical Pathology and Human Metabolism, 1973–78, Prof. of Clinical Biochemistry and Metabolic Medicine, 1978–85, Univ. of Southampton; Prof. of Medicine, ICSTM, 2000–02. Vis. Prof. of Diabetes and Metabolism, KCL, 2013–. Mem., WHO Expert Adv. Panel on Diabetes, 1979–. Nat. Clin. Dir for Emergency Access, DoH, 2002–09; Clin. Advr, NHS London, 2009–10. Pres., Internat. Diabetes Fedn, 2000–03 (Vice-Pres., 1988–94); Vice-Chm., British Diabetic Assoc., 1996–99; Chm., Diabetes UK, 2009–12 (Vice Pres., 2000–09). Chm., King's College Hosp. NHS Foundn Trust, 2011–15 (non-exec. Dir, 2010–). Founder FMedSci 1998 (Mem. Council, 1998–2002). Hon. FRCPGlas 1999; Hon. FRCPI 1999. Hon. Member: Hungarian Diabetes Assoc., 1986; Argentinian Diabetes Assoc., 1991. Hon. MD: Aarhus, 1998; Athens, 2002; Hon. DM Southampton, 1999; Hon. DSc: Warwick, Cranfield, 2005. *Publications:* edited more than 30 medical books, including: Diabetes Annual, Vols 1–6; Internat. Textbook of Diabetes Mellitus, 1992, 2nd edn 1997; author of more than 1100 pubns in learned jls. *Recreations:* hill walking, jogging, crime fiction, opera.

ALBERTI, Stephanie Anne, (Lady Alberti); *see* Amiel, S. A.

ALBERY, Ian Bronson; theatre producer, manager and consultant, West End, London; Theatre Design Consultant, Nimax Theatres Ltd, since 2007; *b* 21 Sept. 1936; *s* of Sir Donald Albery and Rubina Albery (*née* McGilchrist); *m* Barbara Yu Ling Lee (*d* 1997); two *s*; one *d* by Jenny Beavan; *m* 2003, Judy Monahan. *Educ:* Stowe; Lycée de Briançon, France. Joined

New Theatre, Oxford as Box Office trainee, 1952, Dep. Box Office Manager, 1955, Asst Stage Manager, 1956, 1st Electrical Dayman, 1957; Jt Dep. Stage Manager for H. M. Tennent, 1958. Stage, Production or Technical Manager for over 100 West End productions, 1958–70; Chief Electrician, American Ballet Th., Eur. and USSR tour, first cultural exchange between the West and USSR, 1960; Technical Dir, London Festival Ballet, 1964–68; Producer or Co-Producer for over 50 West End prodns, 1978–; Managing Director: Wyndham Theatres, Piccadilly Theatre, Donmar Productions, Omega Stage (Donmar Warehouse Th.), 1978–87; Theatre of Comedy, 1987–90; Dep. Chm., English Nat. Ballet, 1984–90; Dir, Ticketmaster (UK) Ltd, 1985–92; Chief Exec. and Producer, Sadler's Wells, Peacock and Lilian Baylis Theatres, 1994–2002; Theatre Consultant for rebuilding of Sadler's Wells Th., 1995–99; Chief Exec., Guildford Sch. of Acting Conservatoire, 2002–04. Consultant, Japan Satellite Broadcasting, 1991–92. Member: Bd of Mgt, British Th. Assoc., 1968–79; Drama Panel, Arts Council of GB, 1974–76; Drama and Dance Adv. Panel, British Council, 1978–88. Vice-Chm., Assoc. of British Th. Technicians, 1974–78 (Hon. Mem., 2007; Fellow, 2013). Trustee, Theatres Trust, 1977–96. Pres., 1977–79, Vice-Pres., 1979–80, Soc. of West End Th., later Soc. of London Th. (Hon. Mem., 2003–); Hon. Treas., Soc. of Th. Consultants, 1990–96 (Founder Mem., 1964–); Hon. Vice Pres., Sadler's Wells Foundn, 2009–. *Address:* 1090 Chemin de la Rochette, 26450 Roynac, France. *T:* (4) 75901221. *E:* ian@albery.com.

ALBERY, Tim; theatre and opera director; *b* 20 May 1952. *Theatre* productions include: War Crimes, ICA, 1981; Secret Gardens, Amsterdam and ICA, 1983; Venice Preserv'd, Almeida, 1983; Hedda Gabler, Almeida, 1984; The Princess of Cleves, ICA, 1985; Mary Stuart, Greenwich, 1988; As You Like It, Old Vic, 1989; Berenice, NT, 1990; Wallenstein, RSC, 1993; Macbeth, RSC, 1996; Attempts on her Life, Royal Court, 1997; Nathan the Wise, Toronto, 2005; *opera* productions include: for English National Opera: Billy Budd, 1988; Beatrice and Benedict, 1990; Peter Grimes, 1991; Lohengrin, 1993; From the House of the Dead, 1997; La Bohème, 2000; War and Peace, 2001; Boris Godunov, 2008; for Opera North: The Midsummer Marriage, 1985; The Trojans, 1986; La finta giardiniera, 1989; Don Giovanni, 1991; Don Carlos, 1992; Luisa Miller, 1995; Così fan Tutte, 1997, 2004; Katya Kabanova, 1999; Idomeneo, 2003; King Croesus, Madama Butterfly, 2007; Macbeth, 2008; Giulio Cesare, 2012; Otello, 2013; Poppea, 2014; for Royal Opera: Chérubin, 1994; Der Fliegende Hollander, 2009; Tannhäuser, 2010; for Welsh National Opera: The Trojans, 1987; La finta giardiniera, 1994; Nabucco, 1995; for Scottish Opera: The Midsummer Marriage, 1988; The Trojans, 1990; Fidelio, 1994, 2005; The Ring Cycle, 2000–03; Don Giovanni, 2006; for Australian Opera: The Marriage of Figaro, 1992; for Netherlands Opera: Benvenuto Cellini, 1991; La Wally, 1993; Beatrice and Benedict, 2001; for Santa Fé Opera: Beatrice and Benedict, 1998; The Magic Flute, 2006; Arabella, 2012; for Batignano Fest., Italy, The Turn of the Screw, 1983; for Bregenz Fest., Austria, La Wally, 1990; for Bayerische Staatsoper, Munich: Peter Grimes, 1991; Simon Boccanegra, 1995; Ariadne auf Naxos, 1996; for Metropolitan Opera, NY: A Midsummer Night's Dream, 1996; The Merry Widow, 2000; for Canadian Opera: Rodelinda, 2005; Götterdämmerung, 2006; War and Peace, 2008; Aida, 2010; for Glimmerglass Fest., Così fan Tutti, 2005; for Boston Lyric Opera, The Lighthouse, 2012; for Luminato Festival, Toronto: The Children's Crusade, 2009; Prima Donna, 2010; for Aldeburgh Fest., Peter Grimes, 2013; for Dallas Opera, The Aspern Papers, 2013; for Soundstreams, Toronto, Airline Icarus, 2014; *musicals* include: Passion, Minnesota Opera, 2004; One Touch of Venus, Opera North, 2004.

ALBON, Sarah; Chief Executive Officer and Inspector General, Insolvency Service, since 2015. Principal Private Sec. to Lord Chancellor, 2001–03; Dep. Dir, Finance, DCA, 2004; Dep. Dir, Criminal Legal Aid Strategy, 2005–09, Dir, Civil Family and Legal Aid Policy, 2009–11, MoJ; Dir, Strategy and Change, HM Courts and Tribunal Service, 2011–15. *Address:* Insolvency Service, 4 Abbey Orchard Street, SW1P 2HT. *T:* (020) 7291 6713. *E:* sarah.albon@insolvency.gsi.gov.uk. *W:* www.twitter.com/insolvencyCEO.

ALBRIGHT, Madeleine Korbel, PhD; Secretary of State, United States of America, 1997–2001; Chairman, Albright Stonebridge Group, since 2009 (founder and Principal, Albright Group LLC, 2001–09); *b* 15 May 1937; *m* Joseph Albright (marr. diss.); three *d. Educ:* Wellesley Coll. (BA Hons Pol Sci. 1959); Sch. of Advanced Internat. Studies, Johns Hopkins Univ.; Columbia Univ. (BA 1968; PhD 1976). Chief Legislative Asst to Senator Edmund Muskie, 1976–78; Staff Mem., Nat. Security Council and Mem., White House Staff, 1978–81; Sen. Fellow in Soviet and E European Affairs, Center for Strategic and Internat. Studies; Fellow, Woodrow Wilson Internat. Center for Scholars, 1981–82; Res. Prof. of Internat. Affairs and Dir, Women in Foreign Service Program, Georgetown Univ. Sch. of Foreign Service, 1982–92; Pres., Center for Nat. Policy, 1989–92 (Mem., Bd of Dirs); US Perm. Rep. to UN, 1993–96; Mem., Nat. Security Council, USA, 1993–2001. Member: Bd of Dirs, Atlantic Council of US; US Nat. Commn, UNESCO. Chm., Nat. Democratic Inst. for Internat. Affairs, 2001–. Presidential Medal of Freedom (USA), 2012. *Publications:* Poland: the role of the press in political change, 1983; Madam Secretary (autobiog.), 2003; The Mighty and the Almighty: reflections on America, God, and world affairs, 2006; Memo to the President: how we can restore America's reputation and leadership, 2008; Read My Pins: stories from a diplomat's jewel box, 2009; articles in professional jls and chapters in books.

ALBROW, Susan Jane; *see* Owen, S. J.

ALBU, Sir George, 3rd Bt *cr* (UK) 1912, of Grosvenor Place, City of Westminster, and Johannesburg, Province of Transvaal, South Africa; farmer; *b* 5 June 1944; *o s* of Major Sir George Werner Albu, 2nd Bt, and Kathleen Betty (*d* 1956), *d* of Edward Charles Dicey, Parktown, Johannesburg; *S* father, 1963; *m* 1969, Joan Valerie Millar (*d* 2015), London; two *d. Recreation:* horse racing. *Heir:* none. *Address:* Glen Hamish Farm, PO Box 62, Richmond, Natal, 3780, South Africa. *T:* (33) 2122587. *Clubs:* Victoria Country (Pietermaritzburg); Durban Country; Richmond (Natal) Country (Richmond).

ALCOCK, Michael Reginald; Literary Agent, Johnson & Alcock Ltd, since 2003; *b* Hammersmith, London, 11 Feb. 1948; *s* of Rex Alcock and Venetia Alcock; *m* 1993, Nadia Manuelli; one *s* one *d. Educ:* Rugby Sch.; Univ. of Bristol (BA Classics 1970). N Eur. Rep., OUP, 1970–72; Editor, Tom Stacey Ltd, 1972–73; Editl Dir, Macmillan London, 1974–86; Publishing Dir, Aurum Press, 1986–90; Book Publisher, Newspaper Publishing plc, 1991; Publishing Dir, Boxtree, 1991–97; Literary Agent, Michael Alcock Mgt, 1997–2003. *Recreations:* music (especially opera, flamenco, blues), reading, classical antiquity, feasting. *Address:* 27 Manchester Street, W1U 4DJ. *E:* michael@johnsonandalcock.co.uk. *Club:* Garrick.

ALCOCK, Air Chief Marshal Sir (Robert James) Michael, GCB 1996 (CB 1989); KBE 1992; FREng; Royal Air Force, retired; aerospace consultant, since 1997; Director, Cygnae Ltd, 1997–2013; Chairman, AMSS Ltd, 2003–13; *b* 11 July 1936; *s* of late William George and Doris Alcock; *m* 1965, Pauline Mary Oades; two *d. Educ:* Victoria College, Jersey; Royal Aircraft Establishment. FIMechE; FRAeS. Commissioned, Engineer Branch, RAF, 1959; RAF Tech. Coll., Henlow, 1961; Goose Bay, Labrador, 1964; Units in Bomber Comd, 1959–69; RAF Staff Coll., Bracknell, 1970; PSO to DG Eng (RAF), 1971–73; OC Eng. Wing, RAF Coningsby, 1973–75; OC No 23 Maintenance Unit, RAF Aldergrove, 1975–77; Group Captain (Plans), HQ RAF Support Command, 1977–79; MoD, 1979–81; Dep. Comdt, RAF Staff Coll., Bracknell, 1981–84; RCDS, 1984; Dir Gen. of Communications, Inf. Systems and Orgn (RAF), 1985–88; AO Engrg, HQ Strike Comd, 1988–91; Chief Engr (RAF), 1991–96; Chief of Logistic Support, RAF, 1991–93; Air Mem. for Supply and Orgn, MoD, 1993–94; Air Member for Logistics and AOC-in-C, Logistics Comd, 1994–96. Trustee, RAF Benevolent Fund, 1996–2002. Chm., Bd of Mgt, Princess Marina Hse, 1996–2002. Pres., British Model Flyers' Assoc., 2000–; Mem., RAF Sailing Assoc. Governor, Victoria Coll., Jersey, 1995–2004. FREng (FEng 1995). Hon. DSc Cranfield, 1994. *Recreations:* golf, model aircraft, sailing. *Address:* c/o National Westminster Bank, PO Box 61, 2 Alexandra Road, Farnborough, Hants GU14 6YR. *Clubs:* Royal Air Force; Berkshire Golf, St Enodoc Golf.

ALDENHAM, 6th Baron *cr* 1896, of Aldenham, Co. Hertford, **AND HUNSDON OF HUNSDON,** 4th Baron *cr* 1923, of Briggens, Co. Hertford; **Vicary Tyser Gibbs;** *b* 9 June 1948; *s* of 5th Baron Aldenham and of Mary Elizabeth, *o d* of late Walter Parkyns Tyser; *S* father, 1986; *m* 1980, Josephine Nicola, *er d* of John Richmond Fell, Lower Bourne, Farnham, Surrey; three *s* one *d. Educ:* Eton; Oriel College, Oxford; RAC, Cirencester. Capel-Cure Myers Ltd, 1975–79; Dir, 1986–, Chm., 2012–, Montclare Shipping Co.; Man. Partner, Aldenham Aviation, 2004–. Chairman: Herts CLA, 1995–98; Watling Chase Community Forest, 1997–99. Freeman, City of London, 1979; Liveryman, Merchant Taylors' Co., 1979. *Heir: s* Hon. Humphrey William Fell Gibbs, *b* 31 Jan. 1989. *Address:* c/o Aldenham Estate Office, Elstree Aerodrome, Hogg Lane, Elstree, Herts WD6 3AR.

ALDER, Debbie, (Mrs M. A. T. Johnstone); Human Resources Director General, Department for Work and Pensions, since 2014; *b* Bexley, Kent, 1 March 1966; *m* Mark Alexander Talbot Johnstone; two step *d. Educ:* Haberdashers' Aske's Hatcham Girls' Sch.; Univ. of Bristol (BSc Hons Psychol. and Zool. 1988). FCIPD. Hd, HR, W London, Marks and Spencer plc, 1988–2000; Hd, Internal HR Consultancy, Ford Motor Co. (Europe), 2000–04; Associate Consultant, Aspiren; Dir, Change 2 Perform; Human Resources Director: DWP, 2009–10; DEFRA, 2011–13; MoJ, 2013–14. *Recreations:* solo and choral singing, travel, movies, dog walking. *Address:* Department for Work and Pensions, Level 7, Caxton House, 6–12 Tothill Street, SW1H 9NA. *T:* (020) 7340 4193. *E:* debbie.alder@dwp.gsi.gov.uk.

ALDER, Lucette, (Mrs Alan Alder); *see* Aldous, L.

ALDER, Michael; Controller, English Regional Television, British Broadcasting Corporation, 1977–86, retired; *b* 3 Nov. 1928; *s* of late Thomas Alder and Winifred Miller; *m* 1955, Freda, *d* of late John and Doris Hall; two *d. Educ:* Ranelagh Sch., Bracknell, Berks; Rutherford Coll., Newcastle-upon-Tyne. Newcastle Evening Chronicle, 1947–59; BBC North-East: Chief News Asst, Newcastle; Area News Editor, Newcastle; Representative, NE England, 1959–69; Head of Regional Television Development, BBC, 1969–77. Mem., Exec. Cttee, Relate (formerly Nat. Marriage Guidance Council), 1987–94 (Chm., S Warwicks, 1987–89; Chm., Appeals Cttee, 1988–94). Chm., Tanworth Educnl Foundn, 2004–08 (Vice Chm., 1994–2004). Mem., Incorporated Co. of Butchers, 1948. Freeman, City of Newcastle upon Tyne. *Recreations:* gardening, fishing, walking, country pursuits. *Address:* 1 Lune Close, Kirkby Lonsdale, Carnforth, Lancs LA6 2DA.

ALDER, Prof. Roger William, DPhil, DSc; FRS 2006; FRSC; Professor of Organic Chemistry, University of Bristol, 1996–2002, now Professor Emeritus and Senior Research Fellow; *b* 26 April 1937; *s* of William John Alder and Mona Amelia Alder (*née* Nevitt); *m* 1961, Judy Anne Sweet; one *s* two *d. Educ:* Rendcomb Coll., Cirencester; Pembroke Coll., Oxford (MA, DPhil); DSc Bristol. FRSC 1980. Lectr in Organic Chem., 1966–81, Reader, 1981–96, Univ. of Bristol. *Publications:* (jtly) Mechanism in Organic Chemistry, 1971; contrib. numerous papers on aspects of organic chem. *Address:* School of Chemistry, University of Bristol, Cantock's Close, Bristol BS8 1TS. *T:* (0117) 928 7657, *Fax:* (0117) 929 8611. *E:* rog.alder@bris.ac.uk.

ALDERDICE, family name of **Baron Alderdice**.

ALDERDICE, Baron *cr* 1996 (Life Peer), of Knock, in the City of Belfast; **John Thomas Alderdice,** FRCPsych; consultant psychiatrist in psychotherapy, Belfast Health and Social Services Trust (formerly Eastern Health and Social Services Board, then South and East Belfast Health and Social Services Trust), 1988–2010; Convenor, Liberal Democrat Parliamentary Party, House of Lords, 2010–14; *b* 28 March 1955; *s* of late Rev. David Alderdice and Helena Alderdice (*née* Shields); *m* 1977, Dr Joan Margaret Alderdice (*née* Hill), former consultant pathologist; two *s* one *d. Educ:* Ballymena Acad.; Queen's Univ., Belfast (MB, BCh, BAO 1978). MRCPsych 1983; FRCPsych 1997; Jun. House Officer, Lagan Valley Hosp., 1978–79; Sen. House Officer, Belfast City Hosp., 1979–80; Registrar: Holywell and Whiteabbey Hosps, 1980–81; Shaftesbury Square Hosp., 1981–82; Lissue and Belfast City Hosps, 1982–83; Sen. Tutor and Sen. Registrar, Belfast City Hosp. and Queen's Univ., Belfast, 1983–87. Exec. Med. Dir, S and E Belfast HSS Trust, 1993–97. Hon. Lectr/Sen. Lectr, QUB, 1991–99; Hon. Prof., Univ. of San Marcos, Peru, 1999; Vis. Prof., Dept of Psychiatry and Neurobehavioral Scis, Univ. of Virginia, USA, 2006–10; Sen. Res. Fellow, 2012–, Dir, Centre for Resolution of Intractable Conflict, 2013–, Harris Manchester Coll., Oxford; Res. Associate, Centre for Internat. Studies, Oxford, 2014–. Chm., Centre for Democracy and Peace Bldg, Belfast, 2014–. Dir, NI Inst. of Human Relns, 1991–94. Contested (Alliance): Belfast E, 1987, 1992; NI, European Parly Election, 1989. Alliance Party of Northern Ireland: Mem., Exec. Cttee, 1984–98; Chm., Policy Cttee, 1985–87; Vice-Chm., March–Oct. 1987; Leader, 1987–98; Leader: delegn at Inter-Party and Inter-Governmental Talks on the future of NI, 1991–98; delegn at Forum for Peace and Reconciliation, Dublin Castle, 1994–96; Mem., NI Forum, 1996–98; Speaker, NI Assembly, 1998–2004 (Mem. for Belfast East). European Liberal, Democrat and Reform Party (formerly Fedn of European Liberal, Democratic and Reform Parties): Mem., Exec. Cttee, 1987–2003; Treas., 1995–99; Vice-Pres., 1999–2003; Pres., Liberal International, 2005–09 (Mem. Bureau, 1996–2014; Vice Pres., 1992–99; Dep. Pres., 2000–05). Member: Ind. Monitoring Commn, 2004–11; Commonwealth Commn on Respect and Understanding, 2006–07; Cttee on Standards in Public Life, 2010–. Mem. (Vic. Area), Belfast City Council, 1989–97. Pres., ARTIS (Europe) Ltd, 2009–. Trustee, Ulster Museum, 1993–97. Hon. FRCPI 1997; Hon. FRCPsych 2001; Hon Mem., Peruvian Psychiatric Assoc., 2000; Hon. Affiliate, British Psychoanalytical Soc., 2001. Hon. DLitt UEL, 2008; Hon. LLD Robert Gordon, Aberdeen, 2009; DUniv Open 2014. Silver Medal, Congress of Peru, 1999; Medal of Honour, Coll. of Medicine, Peru, 1999; Erice Prize, World Fedn of Scientists, 2005; Extraordinarily Meritorious Service to Psychoanalysis Award, Internat. Psychoanalytical Assoc., 2005; Prize for Freedom, Liberal Internat., 2015. Kt Comdr, Royal Order of Francis I, 2002. *Publications:* professional articles on psychology of fundamentalism, radicalisation, terrorism, violent political conflict and its resolution and rule of law; political articles. *Recreations:* reading, music, gastronomy, travel. *Address:* House of Lords, SW1A 0PW. *T:* (020) 7219 5050, (Belfast) (028) 9079 3097. *E:* john.alderdice@hmc.ox.ac.uk, alderdicej@parliament.uk. *Clubs:* National Liberal (Trustee, 2010–; Chm. Trustees, 2011–14); Ulster Reform (Belfast).
See also D. K. Alderdice.

ALDERDICE, David King, OBE 1999; Consultant Dermatologist, Ulster Hospital, since 2010; Lord Mayor of Belfast, 1998–99; *b* 2 June 1966; *s* of Rev. David and Helena Alderdice; *m* 1989, Fiona Alison Johnston; one *s* two *d. Educ:* Queen's Univ., Belfast (MB BCh BAO 1989); Manchester Coll., Oxford (BA PPE 1994; MA 1998). MRCPI 1996, FRCPI 2008. Jun., subseq. Sen., House Officer, Royal Victoria Hosp., Belfast, 1989–92; Specialist Registrar in Dermatology, Royal Victoria Hosp., Belfast and Belfast City Hosp., 1997–2002; Clin. Res. Fellow, Ulster Hosp., Dundonald, 1997–98; Consultant Dermatologist, Causeway Hosp., Coleraine, 2002–10. Contested (Alliance), N Antrim, Forum, 1996, parly elecns, 1997. Member (Alliance): Belfast CC, 1997–2005; N Down BC, 2005–10. Chair, Youth Lyric, 2002–12. *Publications:* articles in dermatology, genitourinary and psychol learned jls.

Recreations: squash racquets, hill walking. *Address:* c/o Ulster Hospital, Newtownwards Road, Dundonald, Belfast BT16 1RH.

See also Baron Alderdice.

ALDERMAN, Richard John; Director, Serious Fraud Office, 2008–12; *b* 5 Aug. 1952; *s* of John Edward Alderman and Patricia Eileen Alderman; *m* 1981, Joyce Sheelagh, *d* of late Herrick Edwin and Joyce Hilda Wickens; one *d. Educ:* Woking Grammar Sch.; University College London (LLB). Called to the Bar, Gray's Inn, 1974; joined Solicitor's Office, Inland Revenue, 1975; seconded to Legal Secretariat to the Law Officers, 1991–93; Principal Asst Solicitor, 1996–2003, Dir, Special Compliance Office, 2003–05, Bd of Inland Revenue; Dir, Special Civil Investigations, HMRC, 2005–08. Member: Adv. Council, Sch. of Ethics and Law, UCL, 2011–; Anti-Corruption Council, WEF, 2011–13. *Recreations:* family life, country walking.

ALDERSLADE, Prof. Richard, FRCP, FFPH; Special Professor of Health Policy, Nottingham University, since 1993; Adjunct Associate Professor of Public Health Administration, Robert F. Wagner Graduate School of Public Service, New York University, since 2008; *b* 11 Aug. 1947; *s* of Herbert Raymond Alderslade and Edna F. Alderslade; *m* 1st, 1974, Elizabeth Rose (marr. diss. 1999); two *s* one *d* (and one *d* decd); 2nd, 1999, Angela Hendriksen (marr. diss. 2010); one step *d. Educ:* Chichester High Sch. for Boys; Christ Church, Oxford (BM BCh; MA); St George's Hosp. FFPH (FFPHM 1987); FRCP 1993. GP, 1974–76; Registrar in Community Medicine, 1976–78, Lectr, 1978–79; MO and SMO, DHSS, 1979–85; Specialist in Community Medicine, 1985–88 and Community Unit Gen. Manager, 1986–88, Hull HA; Regl Dir of Public Health and Regl MO, Trent RHA, 1988–94; Prof. of Community Care, Univ. of Sheffield, 1994–95; Regl Advr, Humanitarian Assistance, WHO Regl Office for Europe, Copenhagen, 1995–2001; Chief Officer, High Level Gp for Romanian Children and Advr to Prime Minister of Romania, 2001–02; Sen. External Relns Officer, WHO Office, UN, NY, 2002–06; Chief Exec., Children's High Level Gp, 2006–10; Sen. Health Policy Advr, WHO Regl Office for Europe, 2010–12. Teaching Fellow in Public Health, St George's Hosp. Med. Sch., 2013–. *Publications:* articles on public health, BMJ and other jls. *Recreations:* walking, railways, photography. *Address:* 112A Osborne Street, Hull HU1 2PN.

ALDERSON, Brian Wouldhave; freelance editor and writer; Children's Books Consultant, The Times, since 1995 (Children's Books Editor, 1967–95); *b* 19 Sept. 1930; *s* of John William Alderson and Helen Marjory Alderson; *m* 1953, Valerie Christine (*née* Wells) (*d* 2005); three *s* (and two *s* decd). *Educ:* Ackworth Sch.; University College of the South-West, Exeter (BA Hons). Work in the book trade, 1952–63; Tutor-librarian, East Herts Coll. of Further Educn, 1963–65; Sen. Lectr, (on Children's Literature and on the Book Trade), Polytechnic of N London, 1965–83. Visiting Professor: Univ. of Southern Mississippi, 1985; UCLA, 1986. Lectr, London Rare Books Sch., 2008–. Founder and first Chm., Children's Books Hist. Soc., 1969–78 and 1995–2001. Pres., Beatrix Potter Soc., 1995–. Exhibition organiser: (with descriptive notes): Early English Children's Books, BM, 1968; Looking at Picture Books, NBL, 1973; Grimm Tales in England, British Library, 1985–86; Randolph Caldecott and the Art of the English Picture Book, British Library, 1986–87; Be Merry and Wise: the early development of English children's books, Pierpont Morgan Library, NY, 1990–91; Childhood Re-Collected, Christ Church, Oxford, 1994; This Book Belongs To Me, Nat. Liby of Scotland, Edinburgh, 2002. DUniv Surrey, 2002. Eleanor Farjeon Award, 1968. *Publications:* Sing a Song for Sixpence, 1986; (with Iona and Robert Opie) Treasures of Childhood, 1989; The Arabian Nights, 1992; Ezra Jack Keats: artist and picture book maker, vol. 1, 1994, vol. 2, 2002; Edward Ardizzone: a bibliographic commentary, 2003; (with Felix de Marez Oyens) Be Merry and Wise: origins of children's book publishing in England 1650–1800, 2006; (with Andrea Immel) Tommy Thumb's Pretty Song-Book: a commentary, 2013; (with Lorraine Johnson) The Ladybird Story, 2014; *translations:* Hürlimann: Three Centuries of Children's Books in Europe, 1967; Picture-book World, 1968; Grimm, Popular Folk Tales, 1978; Andersen, The Swan's Stories, 1997; Andersen, Fairy Tales, 2013; *edited:* The Juvenile Library, 1966–74; The Colour Fairy Books, by Andrew Lang, 1975–82; Lear, A Book of Bosh, 1975; Children's Books in England, by F. J. Harvey Darton, 1982; Hans Christian Andersen and his Eventyr in England, 1982. *Recreations:* bibliography, dale-walking. *Address:* 28–30 Victoria Road, Richmond, North Yorks DL10 4AS. *T:* (01748) 823648.

ALDERSON, Daphne Elizabeth, (Mrs J. K. A. Alderson); *see* Wickham, D. E.

ALDERSON, (George) Lawrence (Hastings), CBE 2004; FRAgS; Chairman: Countrywide Livestock Ltd, since 1974; PigBioDiv (Europe), since 2008; Trustee and Founder Chairman, Rare Breeds International, since 1991; *b* 24 June 1939; *s* of late John Henry Alderson and Mary Hilda Alderson (*née* Hastings), Teesdale; *m* 2nd, 1971, Jacqueline Mary (marr. diss. 1983), *y d* of John Pasfield, OBE; one *s* one *d*; 4th, 1994, Marie Bridgette (marr. diss. 2014), *e d* of John Lynch. *Educ:* Barnard Castle Sch.; Selwyn Coll., Cambridge (BA 1962, MA; boxing blue). Farmer, 1968–92: created new breed, British Milksheep; Chm., Westwater Farm Partners, 1974–81. Consultant: on internat. genetic resources, 1974–; EEC studies of endangered breeds, 1992–93. Dir, Traditional Breeds Meat Mktg Co., 1998–2000. Chm., Preserving Cttee, DEFRA Nat. Steering Cttee, 2003–06. Consultant: Internat. Evaluation Cttee, Danish Farm Animal Genetic Resources, 2001–02; Indian Horse Breeds, 2013–. Rare Breeds Survival Trust: Tech. Consultant, 1973–90; Dir, 1990–2000; Chm., 2003–07; Internat. Ambassador, 2010–13; Chm., Traditional Livestock Foundn, 1994–2003; Dir, Kelmcott Rare Breeds Foundn, USA, 1995–2003. Member: Council, Grazing Advice Partnership, 1997–2009; Council, Eur. Livestock Assoc. (formerly Eur. Livestock Alliance), 2001–; Mgt Bd, PigBioDiv (Eur.), 2002–; Mgt Bd, Semen Archive, 2003–08; Co-Chm., Mgt Bd, Ovine Semen Archive, 2010–13. President: White Park Cattle Soc., 1988–; Red Poll Cattle Soc., 2001–02 (Mem. Council, 2001–04). Chm., Combined Flock Book, 1974–81, 2007–08; Mem., Editl Adv. Bd, AGRI (FAO), 2003–. FRAgS 2012. Hon. Fellow, Rare Breeds Internat., 2011. *Publications:* The Chance to Survive, 1978, 3rd edn 1994; Rare Breeds, 1984, 4th edn 2001; Genetic Conservation of Domestic Livestock, Vol. I 1990, Vol. II 1992; Saving the Breeds, 1994; Coloured Sheep, 1994; A Breed of Distinction, 1997; The Adaptation of Rare Breeds of British Livestock to Different Environments, 1998; Conservation Genetics of Endangered Horse Breeds, 2005; A Pennine Dynasty (novel), 2009. *Recreations:* sport, writing, genealogy, travel, breeding White Park cattle. *E:* ecnewal@gmail.com. *Club:* Farmers.

ALDERSON, Joanne Hazel; District Judge (Magistrates' Courts) (formerly Stipendiary Magistrate), Derbyshire, 1997–2014; *b* 18 March 1954; *d* of Colin and Joan Fleetwood; *m* 1983, Richard Alderson; two *s. Educ:* Wolverhampton Girls' High Sch.; Liverpool Univ. (LLB Hons); College of Law. Called to the Bar, Middle Temple, 1978. Legal Advr, W Midlands Prosecuting Solicitors' Dept, 1977–78; Court Clerk/Principal Asst, Wolverhampton Magistrates' Court, 1978–85; Deputy Clerk: to Warley Justices, 1985–86; to Wolverhampton Justices, 1986–97; Dep. Chief Exec., Wolverhampton Magistrates' Courts Cttee, 1995–97. *Recreations:* travel, bridge, swimming, reading.

ALDERSON, Lawrence; *see* Alderson, G. L. H.

ALDERSON, Margaret Hanne, (Maggie); journalist and novelist; *b* 31 July 1959; *d* of Douglas Arthur Alderson and Margaret Dura Alderson (*née* Mackay); *m* 1st, 1991, Geoffrey Francis Laurence (marr. diss. 1996); 2nd, 2002, Radenko Popovic; one *d. Educ:* Alleyne's Sch., Stone, Staffs; Univ. of St Andrews (MA Hons History of Art). Features Editor: Look Now, 1983; Honey, 1984; Commng Editor, You, 1985; Metropolitan Features Editor, Evening Standard, 1986; Editor: ES Magazine, 1988; Elle, 1989–92; Dep. Editor, Cleo magazine, 1993–94; Editor, Mode, 1994–95; sen. writer, Sydney Morning Herald, 1996–2001. Editor of the Year, Colour Supplements, British Soc. of Magazine Eds, 1989. *Publications:* Shoe Money, 1998; Pants On Fire, 2000; Handbag Heaven, 2001; (ed jtly) Big Night Out, 2002; Mad About the Boy, 2002; Handbags and Gladrags, 2004; (ed jtly) Ladies Night, 2005; Cents and Sensibility, 2006; How to Break Your Own Heart, 2008; (ed jtly) In Bed With, 2009; Shall We Dance?, 2010; Style Notes, 2011; Evangeline, the Wish Keeper's Helper, 2011; Everything Changes But You, 2012; Secret Keeping For Beginners, 2015. *Address:* Bentinck House, Hastings, East Sussex. *W:* www.maggiealdersonstylenotes.wordpress.com. *Club:* Groucho.

ALDERSON, Martha, (Matti); international advisor on regulatory policy and strategy; Managing Director, FireHorses Ltd, since 2000; *b* 20 Dec. 1951; *d* of Edward Connelly and Helen Connelly (*née* Peacock); *m* 1970, Alan Alderson. *Educ:* Bearsden Acad., Dunbartonshire; Open Univ. (BA Hons 1994). Legal Exec., Scotland, 1970–72; Advertising Agency Poster Bureau, 1972–74; Advertising Standards Authority: Executive, 1975–80; Manager, 1980–89; Dep. Dir Gen., 1989–90; Dir Gen., 1990–2000. Vice Chm., European Advertising Standards Alliance, Brussels, 1991–2000. Member: Food Adv. Cttee, MAFF, 1997–2002; Better Regulation Task Force, 1998–2004; Doctors' and Dentists' Remuneration Review Body, 1998–2001; Press Complaints Commn, 2002–10; Bd, PhonepayPlus, 2008–14; IMCB, 2008–14; Cttee, BSI, 2008–11; Chm., Direct Mkting Commn (formerly Authy), 2007–10; Removals Ombudsman, 2008–11. Patron, Westminster Media Forum, 2001–. Mem., IAM 2008. FCAM 1993; FRSA 1993; CCMI 2010. *Publications:* Report on Children, Advertising and Regulation in Europe, 2001; Alcohol Regulation in the Asia Pacific Region, 2006; columnist and contrib. numerous advertising and mktg textbooks, and jls in UK and EU. *Recreations:* design, cars, reading, studying. *Address:* Raglan House, Windsor Road, Gerrards Cross, Bucks SL9 7ND. *Club:* Royal Over-Seas League.

ALDERTON, Clive, LVO 2013; HM Diplomatic Service; Principal Private Secretary to the Prince of Wales and the Duchess of Cornwall, since 2015; *b* 9 May 1967; *m* 1990, Catriona Canning; one *s* one *d.* Joined FCO, 1986; Vice-Consul, Poland, 1988–90; Third Sec., UK Repn to EU, Brussels, 1990–93; Desk Officer, Far Eastern Dept, FCO, 1993–96; Hd, Indo-China Section, SE Asia Dept, FCO, 1996–98; Hd of Chancery and Dep. Hd of Mission, Singapore, 1998–2003; Consul-Gen., Lille, 2004–06; Dep. Private Sec., 2006–08, Private Sec. 2009–12, to the Prince of Wales and the Duchess of Cornwall; Ambassador to Morocco and concurrently (non-resident) Ambassador to Mauritania, 2012–15. *Address:* Clarence House, SW1A 1BA.

ALDERTON, John; actor (stage, films, television); *b* Gainsborough, Lincs, 27 Nov. 1940; *s* of Gordon John Alderton and Ivy Handley; *m* 1st, 1964, Jill Browne (marr. diss. 1970; she *d* 1991); 2nd, Pauline Collins, *qv*; two *s* one *d. Educ:* Kingston High Sch., Hull. *Stage:* 1st appearance (Rep.) Theatre Royal, York, in Badger's Green, 1961; cont. Rep.; 1st London appearance, Spring and Port Wine, Mermaid (later Apollo), 1965; Dutch Uncle, RSC, Aldwych, 1969; The Night I Chased the Women with an Eel, Comedy, 1969; Punch and Judy Stories, Howff, 1973; Judies, Comedy, 1974; The Birthday Party, Shaw, 1975; Confusions (4 parts), Apollo, 1976; Rattle of a Simple Man, Savoy, 1980; Special Occasions, Ambassadors, 1983; The Maintenance Man, Comedy, 1986; Waiting for Godot, NT, 1987; What the Butler Saw, RNT, 1995; Honeymoon Suite, Royal Court, 2004; *films:* (1962–): incl. Duffy, Hannibal Brooks, Zardoz, It Shouldn't Happen to a Vet, Please Sir, Calendar Girls; *television:* series: Please Sir, No Honestly, My Wife Next Door, P. G. Wodehouse, Thomas and Sarah, Father's Day, Forever Green, Little Dorrit and various plays. *Address:* c/o Curtis Brown, Haymarket House, 28–29 Haymarket, SW1Y 4SP.

ALDHOUSE-GREEN, Prof. Miranda Jane, PhD; FSA, FLSW; Professor of Archaeology, Cardiff University, 2006–13, now Emeritus; *b* 24 July 1947; *d* of Eric Aldhouse and Eunice Henriques; *m* 1970, Stephen Green (now Aldhouse-Green); one *d. Educ:* Cardiff Univ. (BA Hons Archaeol. 1969); Lady Margaret Hall, Oxford (MLitt 1974); Open Univ. (PhD 1981). FSA 1979. Pt-time Classical Studies Tutor, OU in Wales, 1982–94; Lectr, Cardiff Univ., 1990–94; University of Wales College, Newport, subseq. University of Wales, Newport: Sen. Lectr, 1994–97; Reader, 1997–98; Head, SCARAB Res. Centre, 1996–2006; Prof. of Archaeology, 1998–2006. Prof. John Mulvaney Lecture, ANU, 2011. Mem., Ancient Monuments Bd for Wales, 2001–10. Pres., Prehistoric Soc., 2005 (Vice-Pres., 2002). FLSW 2011. Hon. Fellow, Centre for Advanced Welsh and Celtic Studies, Univ. of Wales, Aberystwyth, 1990–2001. *Publications:* The Gods of the Celts, 1986; Symbol and Image in Celtic Religious Art, 1989; The Sun Gods of Ancient Europe, 1991; Animals in Celtic Life and Myth, 1992; Dictionary of Celtic Myth and Legend, 1992; Celtic Goddesses, 1995; (ed) The Celtic World, 1995; Celtic Art, 1996; The World of the Druids, 1997; Dying for the Gods, 2001; An Archaeology of Images, 2004; (with S. Aldhouse-Green) The Quest for the Shaman in European Antiquity, 2005; Boudica Britannia, 2006; Caesar's Druids: archaeology of an ancient priesthood, 2010; The Celtic Myths; a guide to the ancient gods and legends, 2015; about 80 articles in learned archaeol. jls. *Recreations:* choral singing, wine, travel, early and baroque music, swimming, Burmese cats, walking. *Address:* Department of Archaeology, School of History, Archaeology and Religion, Cardiff University, John Percival Building, Colum Drive, Cardiff CF10 3EU. *T:* (029) 2087 5651. *E:* Aldhouse-GreenMJ@cardiff.ac.uk.

ALDINGTON, 2nd Baron *cr* 1962; **Charles Harold Stuart Low;** Chairman, 2002–09, Senior Adviser, 2009–12, Deutsche Bank London; Chairman, Intramuros Ltd, since 2009; *b* 22 June 1948; *s* of 1st Baron Aldington, KCMG, CBE, DSO, TD, PC and Araminta Bowman, *d* of Sir Harold MacMichael, GCMG, DSO; *S* father, 2000; *m* 1989, Dr Regine, *d* of Erwin von Csongrady-Schopf and Liselotte (*née* Horstmann); one *s* twin *d. Educ:* Winchester Coll.; New Coll., Oxford (BA Hons); INSEAD; Baden-Badener Unternehmergespräche. Citibank NA (NY), Hong Kong and Dusseldorf, 1971–77; Head of Ship Finance, then Head of UK Corporate Lending, then Dir, Continental Europe, Grindlays Bank, 1978–86; Deutsche Bank AG: Dir, Duisburg Br., 1986–87; Man. Dir, London, 1988–96; Man. Dir, Investment Banking, 1996–2002. Chm., Stramongate Ltd, 2007–11. Chairman: Eur. Vocational Coll., 1991–96; CENTEC, subseq. FOCUS Central London, Central London TEC, 1995–99; Member: Council, British-German Chamber of Commerce and Industry, 1995–2008; Chairman's Cttee, LIBA, 2003–09; Chairman's Cttee, BBA, 2003–09. Member: Oxford Univ. Ct of Benefactors, 1990–2012; Business Adv. Council, Saïd Business Sch., 2001–11; Chm., New Coll. 2019 Cttee, New Coll., Oxford, 2009–. Dep. Chm., Royal Acad. Trust, 2003–12 (Trustee, 2012–); Trustee: English Internat., 1979–86; Whitechapel Art Gall. Foundn, 1991–96; Inst. for Philanthropy, 2008–14. Vice Pres., Nat. Churches Trust, 2008–. Gov., Ditchley Foundn, 2006– (Chm., Finance and Gen. Purposes Cttee, 2013–). *Heir: s* Hon. Philip Toby Augustus Low, *b* 1 Sept. 1990. *Address:* Knoll Farm, Aldington, Ashford TN21 7BY. *Clubs:* Brooks's; Hong Kong.

See also Hon. Dame P. J. S. Roberts.

ALDISS, Brian Wilson, OBE 2005; writer; critic; *b* 18 Aug. 1925; *s* of Stanley and Elizabeth May Aldiss; *m* 1965, Margaret Manson (*d* 1997); one *s* one *d*; and one *s* one *d* by previous *m. Educ:* Framlingham Coll.; West Buckland School. FRSL 1994. Royal Signals, 1943–47; book-selling, 1947–56; writer, 1956–; Literary Editor, Oxford Mail, 1958–69. Pres., British Science Fiction Assoc., 1960–64. Editor, SF Horizons, 1964–. Chairman, Oxford Branch Conservation Soc., 1968–69; Vice Pres., The Stapledon Soc., 1975–; Jt Pres., European SF Cttees, 1976–79; Society of Authors: Mem., Cttee of Management, 1976–78, Chm., 1978; Chm., Cultural Exchanges Cttee, 1979–; Member: Arts Council Literature Panel, 1978–80; Internat. PEN, 1983–; Pres., World SF, 1982–84; Vice-President: H. G. Wells Soc., 1983–; Soc. for Anglo-Chinese Understanding, 1987–91. Mem. Council, Council for Posterity,

1990–. Vice Pres., West Buckland Sch., 1996–. Two art exhibns of isolées, Jam Factory, Oxford, 2010. Hon. DLitt: Reading, 2001; Liverpool, 2008. Observer Book Award for Science Fiction, 1956; Ditmar Award for Best Contemporary Writer of Science Fiction, 1969; first James Blish Award, for SF criticism, 1977; Pilgrim Award, 1978; first Award for Distinguished Scholarship, Internat. Assoc. for the Fantastic in the Arts, Houston, 1986; Prix Utopie, France, 1999; Grand Master of Science Fiction, Science Fiction Writers of America, 2000; Prix Européen, Grand Prix de l'Imaginaire, 2006; Outstanding Literary Contribn Award, SFX Mag., 2012. *Publications: science-fiction:* Space, Time and Nathaniel, 1957; Non-Stop, 1958 (Prix Jules Verne, 1977); Canopy of Time, 1959; The Male Response, 1961; Hothouse, 1962 (Hugo Award, 1961); Best Fantasy Stories, 1962; The Airs of Earth, 1963; The Dark Light Years, 1964; Introducing SF, 1964; Greybeard, 1964; Best SF Stories of Brian W. Aldiss, 1965; Earthworks, 1965; The Saliva Tree, 1966 (Nebula Award, 1965); An Age, 1967; Report on Probability A, 1968; Farewell, Fantastic Venus!, 1968; Intangibles Inc. and other Stories, 1969; A Brian Aldiss Omnibus, 1969; Barefoot in the Head, 1969; The Moment of Eclipse, 1971 (BSFA Award, 1972); Brian Aldiss Omnibus II, 1971; Frankenstein Unbound, 1973 (filmed, 1990); The Eighty-Minute Hour, 1974; (ed) Space Opera, 1974; (ed) Space Odysseys: an Anthology of Way-Back-When Futures, 1975; (ed) Hell's Cartographers, 1975; (ed) Evil Earths, 1975; Science Fiction Art: the fantasies of SF, 1975 (Ferrara Silver Comet, 1977); (ed with H. Harrison) Decade: the 1940s, 1976; (ed with H. Harrison) Decade: the 1950s, 1976; The Malacia Tapestry, 1976; (ed) Galactic Empires, vols 1 and 2, 1976; (ed with H. Harrison) The Year's Best Science Fiction No 9, 1976; Last Orders, 1977; (ed with H. Harrison) Decade: the 1960s, 1977; Enemies of the System, 1978; (ed) Perilous Planets, 1978; New Arrivals, Old Encounters, 1979; Moreau's Other Island, 1980; Helliconia Spring, 1982 (BSFA Award, John W. Campbell Meml Award); Helliconia Summer, 1983; Helliconia Winter, 1985; Helliconia Trilogy (boxed set of Helliconia Spring, Helliconia Summer, and Helliconia Winter), 1985; Cracken at Critical, 1987; Best SF Stories of Brian W. Aldiss, 1988; Science Fiction Blues, 1988; A Romance of the Equator, 1989; Dracula Unbound, 1991; A Tupolev Too Far, 1993; (with Roger Penrose) White Mars or, The Mind Set Free, 1999; Cultural Breaks, 2005; Sanity and the Lady, 2005; *fiction:* The Brightfount Diaries, 1955; The Hand-Reared Boy, 1970; A Soldier Erect, 1971; Brothers of the Head, 1977; A Rude Awakening, 1978; Life in the West, 1980; Foreign Bodies, 1981; Seasons in Flight, 1984; The Horatio Stubbs Saga, 1985; Ruins, 1987; Forgotten Life, 1988; Remembrance Day, 1993; Somewhere East of Life, 1994; The Secret of This Book, 1995; The Squire Quartet, 1998; Supertoys Last All Summer Long, 2001; Super-State, 2002; The Cretan Teat, 2002; Affairs at Hampden Ferrers, 2004; Jocasta, 2005; Harm, 2007; Walcot, 2009; The Invention of Happiness, 2013; Comfort Zone, 2014; *non-fiction:* Cities and Stones: A Traveller's Jugoslavia, 1966; The Shape of Further Things, 1970; Billion Year Spree: a history of science fiction, 1973 (Special BSFA Award, 1974; Eurocon Merit Award, 1976); This World and Nearer Ones, 1979; The Pale Shadow of Science, 1985; …And the Lurid Glare of the Comet, 1986; (with David Wingrove) Trillion Year Spree, 1986 (Hugo Award, 1987); Bury My Heart at W. H. Smith's, 1990; The Detached Retina, 1995; The Twinkling of an Eye (autobiog.), 1998; When the Feast is Finished, 1999; Art after Apogee, 2000; Researches and Churches in Serbia, 2002; *verse:* Home Life with Cats, 1992; At the Caligula Hotel, 1995; Songs from the Steppes of Central Asia, 1996; The Dark Sun Rises, 2002; Oedipus on Mars, 2004; The Prehistory of Mind, 2008; Mortal Morning, 2011; An Exile on Planet Earth, 2012; Finches of Mars, 2013. *Recreations:* fame, obscurity, trances. *Address:* Hambleden, 39 St Andrews Road, Old Headington, Oxford OX3 9DL. *Clubs:* Groucho; Writers in Oxford.

ALDOUS, Charles; QC 1985; *b* 3 June 1943; *s* of Guy Travers Aldous, QC and Elizabeth Angela Aldous (*née* Paul); *m* 1969, Hermione Sara de Courcy-Ireland; one *s* two *d* (and one *d* decd). *Educ:* Harrow; University College London (LLB). Called to the Bar, Inner Temple, 1967 (Bencher, 1994), Lincoln's Inn *ad eund*, 1967 (Bencher, 1993). *Address:* Ravensfield Farm, Bures Hamlet, Suffolk CO8 5DP.

See also Rt Hon. Sir W. Aldous.

ALDOUS, Prof. David John, PhD; FRS 1994; Professor of Statistics, University of California, Berkeley, since 1986; *b* 13 July 1952; *s* of Kenneth George Aldous and Joyce Minnie Aldous (*née* Finch); *m* 1986, Katy Edwards; one *s*. *Educ:* St John's Coll., Cambridge (BA 1973; PhD 1977). Res. Fellow, St John's Coll., Cambridge, 1977–79; Asst Prof., 1979–82, Associate Prof., 1982–86, Univ. of Calif, Berkeley. *Publications:* Probability Approximations via the Poisson Clumping Heuristic, 1989. *Recreations:* volley-ball, science fiction. *Address:* Department of Statistics, University of California, 367 Evans Hall #3860, Berkeley, CA 94720–3860, USA. *T:* (510) 6422781.

ALDOUS, Grahame Linley; QC 2008; a Recorder, since 2000; *b* London, 8 June 1956; *s* of Howard Aldous and Jocelyn Murray Aldous; partner, Vanessa Knapp, OBE; three *s*. *Educ:* Univ. of Exeter (LLB Hons 1978). Called to the Bar, Inner Temple, 1979, Bencher, 2009; in practice at the Bar, specialising in clinical and professional negligence and personal injury; Hd of Chambers, 9 Gough Square, 2008–13. Fellow, Assoc. of Personal Injury Lawyers, 2007. Contributing Ed., Kemp & Kemp Personal Injury Law Practice and Procedure, 2000–. *Publications:* Housing Law for the Elderly, 1982; Applications for Judicial Review, 1985, 2nd edn 1993; Work Accidents at Sea, 2008; Clinical Negligence Claims, 2008, 2nd edn 2011; APIL Guide to Catastrophic Injury Claims, 2010. *Recreations:* ocean racing, naval history. *Address:* 9 Gough Square, EC4A 3DG. *T:* (020) 7832 0500, *Fax:* (020) 7353 1344. *E:* galdous@9goughsquare.co.uk. *Club:* Royal Ocean Racing.

ALDOUS, Hugh (Graham Cazalet), FCA; Partner, Grant Thornton UK LLP (formerly Robson Rhodes, then RSM Robson Rhodes LLP), 1976–2008; Member, Competition Commission (formerly Monopolies and Mergers Commission), 1998–2001; *b* 1 June 1944; *s* of Maj. Hugh Francis Travers Aldous and Emily Aldous; *m* 1967, Christabel Marshall. *Educ:* Leeds Univ. (BCom). ACA 1970, FCA 1976. Robson Rhodes, later RSM Robson Rhodes, then Grant Thornton, 1967–2008: on secondment to Depts of Transport and the Envmt, 1976–79; Man. Partner, 1987–97; DTI Inspector: House of Fraser Hldgs plc, 1987–88; TransTec plc, 2000–03. Chairman: RSM Internat., 1997–2000; Eastern European (formerly First Russian Frontiers) Trust plc, 2000–09 (Dir, 1995–2011); Protocol Associates NV, 2000–02; Craegmoor Ltd, 2001–05; Smart Educn Ltd, 2005–14; Capita Sinclair Henderson Ltd, 2007–; Melorio plc, 2009–10 (Dir, 2007–10); SPL Guernsey ICC Ltd, 2010–; Director: Freightliner Ltd, 1979–84; Sealink UK Ltd, 1981–84; British Waterways Bd, 1983–86; CILNTEC Ltd, 1991–96; FOCUS Ltd, 1996–98; Elderstreet VCT plc (formerly Gartmore Venture Capital Trust plc, then Millennium Venture Capital Trust), 1996–; Asian Total Return Investment Co. plc (formerly Henderson TR Pacific Investment Trust plc, then Henderson Asian Growth Trust plc), 2003–14; Innospec Inc., 2005–; Polar Capital Holdings plc, 2007–. *Publications:* Guide to Government Incentives to Industry, 1979; Study of Businesses Financed under the Small Business Loan Guarantee Scheme, 1984; (with H. Brooke) Report into the affairs of House of Fraser Holdings plc, 1988; Review of the UK Financial and Professional Services Industry, 1992; (with R. Kaye) Report into the affairs of TransTec plc, 2003; Performance Fees: a question of purpose, 2008. *Recreations:* music, walking. *Club:* Royal Automobile.

ALDOUS, Lucette; Senior Lecturer in Classical Ballet, Edith Cowan University, since 1994; Head of Classical Dance, Dance Department, Western Australian Academy of Performing Arts, 1984–99, now Senior Lecturer; Senior Adjudicator, National Eisteddfods, since 1979; *b* 26 Sept. 1938; *d* of Charles Fellows Aldous and Marie (*née* Rutherford); *m* 1972, Alan Alder; one *d*. *Educ:* Toronto Public Sch., NSW; Brisbane Public Sch., Qld; Randwick Girls' High Sch., NSW. Awarded Frances Scully Meml Schol. (Aust.) to study at Royal Ballet Sch., London, 1955; joined Ballet Rambert, 1957, Ballerina, 1958–63; Ballerina with: London Fest. Ballet, 1963–66; Royal Ballet, 1966–71; Prima Ballerina, The Australian Ballet, 1971; Master Teacher, Australian Ballet Sch., 1979; Guest Teacher: Australian Ballet, 1988–; Royal NZ Ballet Co., 1988–; West Australian Ballet Co., 1988–. Rep. Australia, 1st Internat. Ballet Competition, Jackson, Miss, USA, 1979; Guest, Kirov Ballet and Ballet School, Leningrad, 1975–76. Guest appearances: Giselle, with John Gilpin, NY, 1968; Lisbon, 1969; with Rudolf Nureyev, in Don Quixote: Aust., 1970, NY, Hamburg and Marseilles, 1971; Carmen, Johannesburg, 1970; The Sleeping Beauty: E Berlin, 1970, Teheran, 1970, 1975; partnered Edward Villela at Expo '74, Spokane, USA. *Television:* title rôle, La Sylphide, with Fleming Flindt, BBC, 1960. *Films:* as Kitri, in Don Quixote, with Rudolf Nureyev and Robert Helpmann, Aust., 1972; The Turning Point, 1977. Mem., Australia Council for the Arts, 1996–98. Patron, Australian Cecchetti Soc., 1991–. Hon. DLitt Edith Cowan, 1999. DStJ 2008. *Recreations:* music, reading, gardening, breeding Burmese cats. *Address:* c/o Dance Department, Western Australian Academy of Performing Arts, 2 Bradford Street, Mount Lawley, Perth, WA 6050, Australia.

ALDOUS, Peter; MP (C) Waveney, since 2010; *b* Ipswich, 26 Aug. 1961. *Educ:* Harrow Sch.; Reading Univ. (BSc Land Mgt 1982). Chartered Surveyor, in private practice, Norwich and Ipswich, 1983–2010. Member (C): Waveney DC, 1999–2002; Suffolk CC, 2001–05 (Dep. Leader, Cons. Gp, 2002–05). *Recreations:* cricket, squash, football, horse racing. *Address:* House of Commons, SW1A 0AA. *E:* peter.aldous.mp@parliament.uk.

ALDOUS, Rt Hon. Sir William, Kt 1988; PC 1995; a Lord Justice of Appeal, 1995–2003; Justice of Appeal, Gibraltar, 2005–15; *b* 17 March 1936; *s* of Guy Travers Aldous, QC; *m* 1960, Gillian Frances Henson; one *s* two *d*. *Educ:* Harrow; Trinity Coll., Cambridge (MA). Barrister, Inner Temple, 1960, Bencher, 1985; Jun. Counsel, DTI, 1972–76; QC 1976; appointed to exercise appellate jurisdiction of BoT under Trade Marks Act, 1981–88; a Judge of the High Court, Chancery Div., 1988–95. Chm., Performing Rights Tribunal, 1986–88. Chm., British Eventing, 2005–06. *Address:* Layham Lodge, Lower Layham, Ipswich, Suffolk IP7 5RW.

See also C. Aldous.

ALDRED, Brian Gordon; Chief Executive, Lancashire Police Authority, 2003–07; *b* 27 April 1951; *s* of late James Bernard Aldred and of Jean Margaret Layton Aldred; *m* 1973, Miriam Constance Shaw; one *s* one *d*. *Educ:* Queen Elizabeth's Grammar Sch., Blackburn; Jesus Coll., Oxford (BA Modern Hist.; MA); Liverpool Poly. CIPFA. Cheshire CC, 1972–82; Dep. Dir of Finance, Bolton MBC, 1982–85; Lancashire County Council: Dep. County Treas., 1985–92; County Treas., 1992–2000; Dir of Resources, 2000–02. *Recreations:* cycling, fell-walking, archaeology.

ALDRED, Margaret; *see* Aldred, P. M.

ALDRED, Micheala Ann, PhD; Assistant Staff, Genomic Medicine Institute, Cleveland Clinic, and Assistant Professor, Department of Genetics, Case Western Reserve University School of Medicine, Cleveland, Ohio, since 2006; *b* 16 Oct. 1966; *d* of Spencer and Barbara Aldred; *m* 1991, Keith Niven Mitchell. *Educ:* University Coll. London (BSc Hons); Open Univ. (PhD 1993); DipRCPath 1998. Postdoctoral Research Associate: MRC Human Genetics Unit, Edinburgh, 1991–94; Univ. of Cambridge, 1994–96; University of Leicester: Lectr in Med. Molecular Genetics, 1996–2001; Res. Fellow, 2001–04; Sen. Lectr in Med. Molecular Genetics, 2004–06. Mem., Human Genetics Adv. Commn, 1997–99. Trustee, Retinoblastoma Soc., 1992–2001. *Publications:* papers in jls on human genetics. *Recreations:* charity work, photography, hiking.

ALDRED, (Patricia) Margaret, CB 2009; CBE 1991; Secretary, Iraq Inquiry (on secondment from Cabinet Office), since 2009. Joined Civil Service as grad. trainee, 1975; posts at MoD incl. Principal Private Sec., 1994–97; Asst Under-Sec. of State, Service Personnel, 1997–98, and Dir Gen., Mgt and Orgn, 1998–2000; Dir, Public Services, HM Treasury, 2001; Dir Gen., Resources and Performance, Home Office, 2001–04; Dep. Hd, Defence and Overseas Secretariat, Cabinet Office, 2004–09. *Address:* Iraq Inquiry, 35 Great Smith Street, SW1P 3BG.

ALDRIDGE, (Harold Edward) James; author; *b* 10 July 1918; *s* of William Thomas Aldridge and Edith Quayle Aldridge; *m* 1942, Dina Mitchnik; two *s*. With Herald and Sun, Melbourne, 1937–38; Daily Sketch, and Sunday Dispatch, London, 1939; subsequently Australian Newspaper Service and North American Newspaper Alliance (war correspondent), Finland, Norway, Middle East, Greece, USSR, until 1945; also correspondent for Time and Life, Teheran, 1944. Rhys Meml Award, 1945; Lenin Peace Prize, 1972. *Play:* The 49th State, Lyric, Hammersmith, 1947. *Publications:* Signed With Their Honour, 1942; The Sea Eagle, 1944; Of Many Men, 1946; The Diplomat, 1950; The Hunter, 1951; Heroes of the Empty View, 1954; Underwater Hunting for Inexperienced Englishmen, 1955; I Wish He Would Not Die, 1958; Gold and Sand (short stories), 1960; The Last Exile, 1961; A Captive in the Land, 1962; The Statesman's Game, 1966; My Brother Tom, 1966; The Flying 19, 1966; (with Paul Strand) Living Egypt, 1969; Cairo: Biography of a City, 1970; A Sporting Proposition, 1973; The Marvellous Mongolian, 1974; Mockery in Arms, 1974; The Untouchable Juli, 1975; One Last Glimpse, 1977 (adapted as stage play, Prague Vinohrady Th., 1981); Goodbye Un-America, 1979; The Broken Saddle, 1983; The True Story of Lilli Stubek, 1984 (Australian Children's Book of the Year, 1985); The True Story of Spit MacPhee, 1986 (Guardian Children's Fiction Prize; NSW Premier's Literary Award, 1986); The True Story of Lola MacKellar, 1993; The Girl from the Sea, 2003. *Recreations:* trout fishing, etc. *Address:* c/o Curtis Brown, 28/29 Haymarket, SW1Y 4SP.

ALDRIDGE, Dr John Frederick Lewis, OBE 1990, FRCP, FRCPEd, FFOM; consultant in occupational medicine, 1987–97; Civil Consultant in Occupational Medicine to the Royal Navy, 1983–92, Emeritus Consultant, since 1992; *b* 28 Dec. 1926; *s* of Dr Frederick James Aldridge and Kathleen Marietta Micaela (*née* White); *m* 1955, Barbara Sheila Bolland (*d* 2014); three *s* one *d*. *Educ:* Gresham's Sch.; St Thomas's Hosp. Med. Sch. (MB, BS 1951). DIH 1963; FRCPEd 1980; FFOM 1981; FRCP 1984. Served RAMC, 1953–60 (retd, Major). Indust. MO, Reed Paper Gp, 1960–63; CMO, IBM United Kingdom Ltd, 1963–87; part-time Hon. Clin. Asst, Dept of Psychol Medicine, UCH, 1970–76. Faculty of Occupational Medicine, Royal Coll. of Physicians: Vice-Dean, 1984–86; Dean, 1986–88; Chm., Ethics Cttee, 1991–96; Royal Soc. of Medicine: Fellow, 1964–2002; Hon. Sec., 1970–72 and Vice-Pres., 1974–77, Occupl Medicine Section; Soc. of Occupational Medicine: Mem., 1960–; Hon. Meetings Sec., 1969–71. Member: Specialist Adv. Cttee on Occupl Medicine, Jt Cttee of Higher Med. Trng, 1970–74; Nat. Occupl Health and Safety Cttee, RoSPA, 1979–81; Standing Med. Adv. Cttee, DHSS, 1986–88; Defence Med. Emergency Steering Cttee, 1986–88; Indust. Soc. Med. Adv. Cttee, 1986–89 (Chm., 1987–89); CEGB Med. Adv. Cttee, 1988–89. Mem., Council and Cttee of Management, Shipwrecked Mariners' Royal Benevolent Soc., 1987–96; Dir, Shipwrecked Mariners' Trading Ltd, 1999–2001. Chm., W Sussex Assoc. for the Disabled, 1995–97 (Mem. Council and Mgt Cttee, 1991–2006; Vice-Pres., 1997–2012); Vice Chm., Chichester DFAS, 2000–04 (Librarian, 1999–2003); Trustee, Southampton and Wessex Med. Sch. Trust, 1978–82. Liveryman, Worshipful Soc. of Apothecaries, 1984–. *Publications:* papers on occupnl med. topics and occupnl mental health. *Recreations:* art in general, geriatric golf, my family. *Address:* 2 Summersdale Road, Chichester, W Sussex PO19 6PL. *T:* (01243) 784705. *Clubs:* Lansdowne; Vintage Sports Car.

ALDRIDGE, Sir Rodney (Malcolm), Kt 2012; OBE 1994; Founder and Chairman, Capita Group, 1984–2006; Chair, Aldridge Foundation, since 2006. Qualif. accountant, CIPFA 1970. With CIPFA, 1974, latterly as Tech. Dir; work in local govt, E Sussex CC, Brighton BC, Crawley DC and W Sussex CC. Non-exec. Dir, Xafinity. Chair, Dance Champions Gp, DoH, 2009–. Member Board: NESTA Lab.; Equiniti; Centre for Public Sector Partnerships, Univ. of Birmingham. Chm., Public Services Strategy Bd, CBI, 2003–06. Chairman: V, 2006–; Acorn Care and Educn; The Lowry, Salford, 2007–. Mem., Prince of Wales Charities Council; Patron, Prince's Trust. Freeman, City of London, 1996; Mem. Court, Information Technologists' Co. *Address:* Aldridge Foundation, First Floor, Swan Gardens, 10 Piccadilly, W1J 0DD.

ALDRIDGE, Stephen Charles, CB 2007; Director, Analysis and Innovation, Department for Communities and Local Government, since 2009; *b* 30 April 1957; *s* of Dennis and Pamela Aldridge; *m* 1995, Katie Iakovleva; one *d. Educ:* City Univ., London (BSc Econ 1978); University Coll. London (MSc Econ 1982). Public Services Econs Div., HM Treasury, 1991–93; Housing and Urban Econs, DoE, subseq. DETR, 1993–98; Cabinet Office: Chief Economist, Perf. and Innovation Unit, 1998–2002; Dep. Dir, 2002–04, Dir, 2004–09, Strategy Unit. *Address:* Department for Communities and Local Government, 2 Marsham Street, SW1P 4DF. *T:* 0303 444 3339.

ALDRIN, Dr Buzz; President, Starcraft Enterprises International (research and development of space technology, manned flight to Mars), since 1988; *b* Montclair, NJ, USA, 20 Jan. 1930; *s* of late Col Edwin E. Aldrin, USAF retd, Brielle, NJ, and Marion Aldrin (*née* Moon); named Edwin Eugene, changed legally to Buzz, 1979; *m* 1988, Lois Driggs-Cannon; two *s* one *d* of former marriage. *Educ:* Montclair High Sch., Montclair, NJ (grad.); US Mil. Academy, West Point, NY (BSc); Mass Inst. of Technology (DSc in Astronautics). Received wings (USAF), 1952. Served in Korea (66 combat missions) with 51st Fighter Interceptor Wing. Aerial Gunnery Instr, Nellis Air Force Base, Nevada; attended Sqdn Officers Sch., Air Univ., Maxwell Air Force Base, Alabama; Aide to Dean of Faculty, USAF Academy; Flt Comdr with 36th Tactical Fighter Wing, Bitburg, Germany. Subseq. assigned to Gemini Target Office of Air Force Space Systems Div., Los Angeles, Calif; later transf. to USAF Field Office, Manned Spacecraft Center. One of 3rd group of astronauts named by NASA, Oct. 1963; served as back up pilot, Gemini 9 Mission and prime pilot, Gemini 12 Mission (launched into space, with James Lovell, 11 Nov. 1966), 4 day 59 revolution flight which brought Gemini Program to successful close; he established a new record for extravehicular activity and obtained first pictures taken from space of an eclipse of the sun; also made a rendezvous with the previously launched Agena; later assigned to 2nd manned Apollo flight, as back-up command module pilot; Lunar Module Pilot, Apollo 11 rocket flight to the Moon; first lunar landing with Neil Armstrong, July 1969; left NASA to return to USAF as Commandant, Aerospace Res. Pilots Sch., Edwards Air Force Base, Calif, 1971; retired USAF 1972. Mem., Soc. of Experimental Test Pilots; FAIAA; Tau Beta Pi, Sigma Xi. Further honours include Presidential Medal of Freedom, 1969; Air Force DSM with Oak Leaf Cluster; Legion of Merit; Air Force DFC with Oak Leaf Cluster; Air Medal with 2 Oak Leaf Clusters; and NASA DSM, Exceptional Service Medal, and Group Achievement Award. Various hon. memberships and hon. doctorates. *Publications:* Return to Earth (autobiography), 1973; Men From Earth: the Apollo Project, 1989; (jtly) Encounter with Tiber (science fiction), 1996; The Return (science fiction), 2000; Reaching for the Moon (for children), 2005; (with K. Abraham) Magnificent Desolation: the long journey home from the Moon, 2009; Look to the Stars (for children), 2009. *Recreations:* athletics, scuba diving, ski-ing, golf, etc. *Address:* 10380 Wilshire Boulevard #703, Los Angeles, CA 90024, USA.

ALEKSANDER, Prof. Igor, PhD; FREng; Professor of Neural Systems Engineering, and Head of Department of Electrical Engineering, Imperial College of Science, Technology and Medicine, University of London, 1988–2002, now Emeritus, and Senior Research Investigator, since 2002; *b* 26 Jan. 1937. *Educ:* Marist Brothers' Coll., S Africa; Univ. of the Witwatersrand (BSc Eng); Univ. of London (PhD). Section Head of STC, Footscray, 1958–61; Lectr, Queen Mary Coll., Univ. of London, 1961–65; Reader in Electronics, Univ. of Kent, 1965–74; Prof. of Electronics and Head of Electrical Engrg Dept, Brunel Univ., 1974–84; Prof. of Information Technology Management, Computing Dept, Imperial Coll., 1984–88. FREng (FEng 1989); FCGI 1994. *Publications:* An Introduction to Logic Circuit Theory, 1971; Automata Theory: an engineering approach, 1976; The Human Machine, 1978; Reinventing Man, 1983 (USA 1984); Designing Intelligent Systems, 1984; Thinking Machines, 1987; An Introduction to Neural Computing, 1990; Neurons and Symbols: the stuff that mind is made of, 1993; Impossible Minds: my neurons, my consciousness, 1996, rev. edn 2015; How to Build a Mind, 2000; The World in My Mind, 2005; Aristotle's Laptop, 2012; *c* 120 papers on computing and human modelling. *Recreations:* tennis, ski-ing, music, architecture. *Address:* Imperial College of Science, Technology and Medicine, Exhibition Road, SW7 2AZ. *T:* (020) 7594 6176.

ALEKSIC, Jocelyn; *see* Pook, J.

ALESSI, Charles, (Charles Sammut Alessi); Co-Chairman, National Association of Primary Care, since 2014 (Chairman, 2012–14); Senior Adviser, NHS Clinical Commissioners, since 2014 (Chairman, 2012–14); Senior Advisor, since 2012, Lead for Dementia, since 2014, and Lead for Wellness, since 2014, Public Health England; *b* Mgarr, Malta, 1 May 1954; *s* of William and Mary Sammut Alessi; *m* 2008, Dr Anu Jain. *Educ:* St Aloysius Coll., Malta; St George's Hosp. Med. Sch., Univ. of London (LRCP 1980). MRCS 1980. Kingston Hospital: Hse Officer, 1980–81; Anaesthetic SHO, 1981–82; Registrar, 1983–84; in practice as GP, SW London, 1984–2013; Dir, Medicine and Clin. Governance, SSAFA/Guy's and St Thomas's Care LLP, British Armed Forces, Germany, 2008–11; Med. Dir, Kingston PCT, subseq. CCG, 2009–11. Vice Chm., Kingston and Richmond HA, 2002–. Adjunct Res. Prof. of Health Innovation, Richard Ivey Sch. of Business, 2012–, Adjunct Res. Prof. of Clin. Neuroscis, Schulich Sch. of Medicine, 2013–, Univ. of Western Ont; Vis. Prof., Psychol. and Lang. Scis, Clinical Educnl and Health Psychol., UCL, 2014–. *Recreation:* opera. *Address:* National Association of Primary Care, Lettsom House, 11 Chandos Street, Cavendish Square, W1G 9DP. *T:* (020) 7636 7228. *E:* charles@napc.co.uk. *Club:* Royal Society of Medicine.

ALESSI, Prof. Dario Renato, PhD; FMedSci; FRS 2008; FRSE; Principal Investigator, since 1997, and Director, since 2012, MRC Protein Phosphorylation and Ubiquitylation Unit, University of Dundee (Deputy Director, 2006–12); *b* Dec. 1967. *Educ:* Univ. of Birmingham (BSc 1st Cl. Hons Biochem. with Biotech. 1988; PhD 1991). Postdoctoral res., MRC Protein Phosphorylation Unit, Univ. of Dundee, 1991–96. Hon. Reader, 2001, Hon. Prof. of Signal Transduction, 2003, Univ. of Dundee. R. D. Lawrence Lectr, Diabetes UK, 2004; Francis Crick Prize Lectr, Royal Soc., 2006. Mem., EMBO, 2005. FRSE 2002; FMedSci 2012. Colworth Medal, British Biochem. Soc., 1999; Eppendorf Young Eur. Investigator, 2000; Morgagni Young Investigator Prize, Servier Labs, 2002; Pfizer Acad. Award for Europe, 2002; Makdougall Brisbane Prize, RSE, 2002; Philip Leverhulme Prize, Leverhulme Trust, 2002; FEBS Anniv. Prize, 2003; Jun. Chamber Internat. Young Persons of Year Award, 2005; Gold Medal, EMBO, 2005. *Address:* MRC Protein Phosphorylation and Ubiquitylation Unit, Sir James Black Centre, University of Dundee, Dundee DD1 5EH. *T:* (01382) 385602, *Fax:* (01382) 223778. *E:* d.r.alessi@dundee.ac.uk.

ALEX; *see* Peattie, C. W. D. and Taylor, R. P.

ALEXANDER, family name of **Earl Alexander of Tunis** and **Earl of Caledon**.

ALEXANDER, Viscount; Frederick James Alexander; *b* 15 Oct. 1990; *s* and *heir* of Earl of Caledon, *qv. Educ:* Stowe.

ALEXANDER OF TUNIS, 2nd Earl *cr* 1952; **Shane William Desmond Alexander;** Viscount, 1946; Baron Rideau, 1952; Lieutenant Irish Guards, retired, 1958; Director: International Hospitals Group and associated companies, since 1981; Pathfinder Financial Corporation, Toronto, since 1980; *b* 30 June 1935; *er s* of 1st Earl Alexander of Tunis, KG, PC, GCB, OM, GCMG, CSI, DSO, MC, and Lady Margaret Diana Bingham (Countess Alexander of Tunis), GBE, DStJ, DL (*d* 1977), *yr d* of 5th Earl of Lucan, PC, GCVO, KBE, CB; *S* father, 1969; *m* 1981, Hon. Davina Woodhouse (LVO 1991; Lady-in-Waiting to Princess Margaret, 1975–2002), *y d* of 4th Baron Terrington; two *d. Educ:* Ashbury Coll., Ottawa, Canada; Harrow. A Lord in Waiting (Govt Whip), 1974. Dir, Marketform Ltd, 1996–2009. Trustee, 1987–, and Chm., 1989–, Canada Meml Foundn; Pres., British-American-Canadian Associates, 1989–94. Patron, British-Tunisian Soc., 1979–99. Freeman, City of London, 1964; Liveryman, Mercers Company. Freedom, City of New Orleans, 1993. Order of Republic of Tunisia, 1995. *Heir: b* Hon. Brian James Alexander, *qv. Address:* 28 Clonmel Road, SW6 5BJ. *T:* (020) 7736 2604. *Clubs:* MCC; Quis Separabit; Stoke Park Golf and Country.

See also Viscount Somerton.

ALEXANDER, Prof. Alan, OBE 2010; FRSE; General Secretary, Royal Society of Edinburgh, since 2013; Chairman, Waterwise, since 2010; Professor of Local and Public Management, University of Strathclyde, 1993–2000, now Emeritus (Professor of Management in Local Government, 1987–93); *b* 13 Dec. 1943; *s* of Alexander Alexander and Rose (*née* Rein); *m* 1964, Morag MacInnes (*see* M. Alexander); one *s* one *d. Educ:* Possil Secondary Sch., Glasgow; Albert Secondary Sch., Glasgow; Univ. of Glasgow (MA 1965). Lectr/Asst Prof. of Political Sci., Lakehead Univ., Ontario, 1966–71; Lectr in Politics, Univ. of Reading, 1971–87; Dir, Scottish Local Authorities Management Centre, 1987–93, and Hd, Dept of Human Resource Mgt, 1993–96, Univ. of Strathclyde. Scholar-in-Residence, Rockefeller Foundn, Villa Serbelloni, Bellagio, Italy, Feb.–March 1984; Fulbright Vis. Prof. of Politics, Randolph-Macon Woman's Coll., Virginia, 1986; Vis. Prof., Univ. of Edinburgh Mgt Sch., 2006–. Member: Board, Housing Corp., 1977–80; Council, Quarriers', 1995–2000; Ind. Commn on Relations between Local Govt and the Scottish Parlt, 1998–99; Accounts Commn for Scotland, 2002–08; ESRC, 2003–09. Chairman: Glasgow Regeneration Fund, 1998–2001; W of Scotland Water Authy, 1999–2002; Scottish Water, 2002–06; Distance Lab Ltd, 2006–10; Postwatch Scotland, 2007–08; Res. Councils UK/Univs UK Rev. of Full Economic Costing of Univ. Res., 2008–09; Data Access Cttee and Mem., Scientific Adv. Cttee, Understanding Soc., ESRC, 2010–15. Pres., Instn of Water Officers, 2005–06; Mem. Exec. Cttee, Advanced Inst. of Mgt Res., 2003–08. Member: Reading BC, 1972–74; Berks CC, 1973–77. Member: Standing Res. Cttee on Local and Central Govt Relns, Joseph Rowntree Foundn, 1988–92; Adv. Bd, Edinburgh Univ. Mgt Sch., 2004–07. Conducted independent inquiry into relations between Western Isles Islands Council and Bank of Credit and Commerce Internat., 1991. Contested (Lab) Henley, Feb. 1974. Pres., Raglan Housing Assoc., 1987–2014 (Chm., 1975–87); Trustee: WaterAid, 2001–06; David Hume Inst., 2012–; Mem., Scottish Council, Outward Bound, 2011–14 (Chm., 2012–14). Mem. Council, RSE, 2012– (Vice Chm., Digital Scotland Spreading the Benefits (formerly Digital Scotland: Reaping the Social Benefits) Inquiry, 2012–). FRSE 2003. *Publications:* Local Government in Britain since Reorganisation, 1982 (Italian edn, revised, 1984); The Politics of Local Government in the United Kingdom, 1982; Borough Government and Politics: Reading 1835–1985, 1985; Managing the Fragmented Authority, 1994; articles in Local Govt Studies, Public Admin, Brit. Jl Pol Sci. and others. *Recreations:* walking, theatre, opera, cinema, avoiding gardening. *Address:* Royal Society of Edinburgh, 22–26 George Street, Edinburgh EH2 2PQ.

ALEXANDER, Anthony George Laurence; Deputy Chairman, Imperial Tobacco Group, 1996–2008; *b* 4 April 1938; *s* of George and Margaret Alexander; *m* 1962, Frances, *d* of Cyril Burdett; one *s* two *d. Educ:* St Edward's School, Oxford. FCA. Hanson plc: Dir, 1976–96; UK Chief Operating Officer, 1986–96. *Recreations:* tennis, golf. *Address:* Crafnant, Gregories Farm Lane, Beaconsfield, Bucks HP9 1HJ. *T:* (01494) 672882.

ALEXANDER, Bill, (William Alexander Paterson); Artistic Director, Birmingham Repertory Theatre, 1993–2000; Hon. Associate Director, Royal Shakespeare Company, since 1991 (Associate Director, 1984–91); *b* 23 Feb. 1948; *s* of Bill and Rosemary Paterson; *m* 1977, Juliet Harmer; two *d. Educ:* St Lawrence Coll., Ramsgate; Keele Univ. (BA Hons English/Politics). Seasons with The Other Company, Bristol Old Vic, Royal Court, 1972–78; Asst Dir, 1978–80, Resident Dir, 1980–84, RSC. Laurence Olivier award, Best Director, 1986. *Productions directed: Bristol Old Vic:* The Ride Across Lake Constance; Twelfth Night; Old Times; Butley; How the Other Half Loves; Merchant of Venice, 2015; *Royal Court:* Sex and Kinship in a Savage Society, 1976; Amy and the Price of Cotton, 1977; Class Enemy, 1978; Sugar and Spice, 1979; *Royal Shakespeare Company:* Factory Birds, 1977; Shout Across the River, The Hang of the Gaol, Captain Swing, 1978; Men's Beano, 1979; Bastard Angel, Henry IV tour, 1980; Accrington Pals, 1981; Money, Clay, Molière, 1982; Tartuffe, Volpone, 1983; Richard III, Today, The Merry Wives of Windsor, 1984; Crimes in Hot Countries, Downchild (co-dir), 1985; Country Dancing, A Midsummer Night's Dream, 1986; Cymbeline, Twelfth Night, The Merchant of Venice, 1987; The Duchess of Malfi, Cymbeline, 1989; Much Ado About Nothing, The Taming of the Shrew (dir, regional tour), 1990; The Bright and Bold Design, 1991; The Taming of the Shrew, The School of Night, 1992; Titus Andronicus, 2003; King Lear, 2004, transf. Albery, 2005; *Birmingham:* Othello, Volpone, Old Times, 1993; The Snowman, 1993, 1997, transf. Peacock Th., London, annually, 1997–; Awake and Sing, The Tempest, 1994; The Servant, Macbeth, The Way of the World, 1995; Divine Right, The Alchemist, 1996; The Merchant of Venice, 1997; Frozen, Hamlet, 1998; The Four Alice Bakers, Jumpers, Nativity, 1999; Quarantine, Twelfth Night, 2000; *National Theatre:* Mappa Mundi, Frozen, 2002; *other productions* include: Entertaining Mr Sloane, Nottingham Playhouse, 1977; The Gingerbread Lady, Ipswich, 1977; The Last of the Knuckle Men, Edin. Fest. Fringe, 1977; Julius Caesar, Newcastle upon Tyne, 1979; One White Day, Soho Poly, 1976; Mates, Leicester Square, 1976; Betrayal, 1980; Anna Christie, 1981, Cameri Th., Tel Aviv; Talk of the Devil, Watford Palace, 1986; Romeo and Juliet, Victory Theatre, NY, 1990; Troilus and Cressida, 1992, Henry IV, 2004, Shakespeare Theatre, Washington; The Importance of Being Earnest, Th. Royal, Northampton, 2002; Enemy of the People, Th. Clywd, 2002; The School of Night, Mark Taper Forum, LA, 2008; Glamour, Nottingham Playhouse, 2009; Bette and Joan, Arts Th., 2011; Twelfth Night, 2012, Summerfolk, Measure for Measure, 2013, LAMDA; Othello, Northwest Classical Th. Co., Portland, Oregon, 2012; Merchant of Venice, LAMDA, 2015; The Sea, adaption for Radio 4, 2015. *Recreation:* tennis. *Address:* Rose Cottage, Tunley, Glos GL7 6LP.

ALEXANDER, Hon. Brian (James), CMG 2000; Managing Director, Mustique Co., 1980–2008, now Chairman Emeritus; *b* 31 July 1939; *s* of 1st Earl Alexander of Tunis, KG, GCB, OM, GCMG, CSI, DSO, MC, PC, and Lady Margaret Diana Bingham, GBE, DStJ, DL (*d* 1977), *yr d* of 5th Earl of Lucan, GCVO, KBE, CB, PC; *heir-presumptive* to brother, Earl Alexander of Tunis, *qv*; *m* 1999, Johanna Williamson Miller. *Educ:* Ashbury Coll., Ottawa; Harrow Sch.; Grenoble Univ. Served Irish Guards, 1958–61. Mgt trainee, Bowater Corp., 1961–62; Advertising Films Div., then Central Marketing Dept, subseq. Marketing Exec., Hotels Div., Rank Orgn, 1962–68; Manager, Previews Internat., 1968–71; self-employed,

1971–80; Mustique Co., 1980–2008. Resort Consultant, 2008–. *Recreations:* windsurfing, tennis, golf, reading. *Address:* Sapphire House, Mustique, St Vincent, W Indies. *E:* brian@mustique.vc; PO Box 349, Kingstown, St Vincent, W Indies. *Club:* White's.

ALEXANDER of Ballochmyle, Sir Claud Hagart-, 4th Bt *cr* 1886, of Ballochmyle; *b* 5 Nov. 1963; *s* of Sir Claud Hagart-Alexander of Ballochmyle, 3rd Bt and Hilda Etain Acheson; *S* father, 2006; *m* 1994, Elaine Susan, *d* of Vincent Park, Winnipeg; one *s*. *Educ:* Trinity Coll., Glenalmond; Glasgow Univ. (BSc). *Heir: s* Claud Miles Hagart-Alexander, *b* 28 Sept. 1998.

ALEXANDER, Rt Hon. Sir Daniel (Grian), Kt 2015; PC 2010; *b* 15 May 1972; *s* of Dion Ralph Alexander and Jane Alexander; *m* 2005, Rebecca Louise Hoar; two *d*. *Educ:* St Anne's Coll., Oxford (BA Hons Philos., Politics and Econs). Researcher, Campaign for Freedom of Information, 1991; Press Officer, Scottish Lib Dems, 1993–96; Press Officer, 1996–97, Hd of Communications, 1997–2003, European Movt, subseq. Britain in Europe; Hd of Communications, Cairngorms Nat. Park, 2004–05. MP (Lib Dem) Inverness, Nairn, Badenoch and Strathspey, 2005–15; contested (Lib Dem) same seat, 2015. Lib Dem spokesman on disability, 2005–07; Lib Dem Shadow Sec. of State for Work and Pensions, 2007–08; COS to Rt Hon. Nicholas Clegg, 2007–10; Sec. of State for Scotland, 2010; Chief Sec. to the Treasury, 2010–15. Chairman: All Party Gp on Media Literacy, 2006–08; Manifesto Gp, 2007–10; Vice-Chm., All Party Gp on Citizens Advice, 2006–10. Trustee, Joseph Rowntree Reform Trust, 2007–. *Publications:* Why Vote Liberal Democrat?, 2010. *Recreations:* hill-walking, fishing, cricket.

ALEXANDER, Maj.-Gen. David Crichton, CB 1976; Commandant, Scottish Police College, 1979–87, retired; *b* 28 Nov. 1926; *s* of James Alexander and Margaret (*née* Craig); *m* 1st, 1957, Diana Joyce (Jane) (*née* Fisher) (*d* 1995); one *s* two *d* and one step *s*; 2nd, 1996, Elizabeth Patricia (*née* Herrington). *Educ:* Edinburgh Academy. Joined RM, 1944; East Indies Fleet; 45 Commando, Malaya, Malta, Canal Zone, 1951–54; Parade Adjt, Lympstone, 1954–57; Equerry and Acting Treasurer to Duke of Edinburgh, 1957–60; psc 1960; Directing Staff, Staff Coll., Camberley, 1962–65; 45 Commando (2IC), Aden, 1965–66; Staff of Chief of Defence Staff, incl. service with Sec. of State, 1966–69; CO 40 Commando, Singapore, 1969–70; Col GS to CGRM, 1970–73; ADC to the Queen, 1973–75; RCDS 1974; Comdr, Training Gp RM, 1975–77. Dir-Gen., English-Speaking Union, 1977–79. Governor, Corps of Commissionaires, 1978–97 (Pres., 1994–97); Member: Civil Service Final Selection Bd, 1978–88; MoD Police Review Cttee, 1985; Transport Users' Consultative Cttee for Scotland, 1989–93. Dir, Edinburgh Acad., 1980–89 (Chm., 1985–89). Pres., SSAFA, Fife, 1990–94. Freeman, City of London; Liveryman, Painter Stainers' Co., 1978. *Recreation:* gardening. *Address:* Baldinnie, Park Place, Elie, Fife KY9 1DH. *T:* (01333) 330882. *Club:* Army and Navy.

ALEXANDER, Sir Douglas, 3rd Bt *cr* 1921; with Cowen & Co.; *b* 9 Sept. 1936; *s* of Lt-Comdr Archibald Gillespie Alexander (*d* 1978) (2nd *s* of 1st Bt), and of Margery Isabel, *d* of Arthur Brown Griffith; *S* uncle, 1983; *m* 1st, 1958, Marylon, *d* of Leonidas Collins Scatterday; two *s*; 2nd, Deborah J. Marcus. *Educ:* Rice Univ., Houston, Texas (MA 1961); PhD 1967 (Univ. of N Carolina). Formerly Assoc. Prof. and Chairman, French, State Univ. of New York at Albany. *Heir: s* Douglas Gillespie Alexander [*b* 24 July 1962; *m* 1993, Marsha Sue, *d* of Robert Fink]. *Address:* 2866 Polo Island Drive, Wellington, FL 33414–7218, USA.

ALEXANDER, Rt Hon. Douglas (Garven); PC 2005; *b* 26 Oct. 1967; *s* of Rev. Douglas N. Alexander and Dr Joyce O. Alexander; *m* 2000, Jacqueline Christian; one *s* one *d*. *Educ:* Univ. of Edinburgh (MA 1st cl. Hons 1990; LLB (Dist.) 1993; DipLP 1994); Univ. of Pennsylvania. Admitted Solicitor, 1995; Brodies WS, 1994–96; Digby Brown, 1996–97. MP (Lab) Paisley S, Nov., 1997–2005, Paisley S and Renfrewshire S, 2005–15; contested (Lab) same seat, 2015. Minister of State: (Minister for E-Commerce and Competitiveness), DTI, 2001–02; Cabinet Office, 2002–03; Minister for the Cabinet Office and Chancellor of the Duchy of Lancaster, 2003–04; Minister of State: FCO and DTI, 2004–05; for Europe, 2005–06; Sec. of State for Transport, and for Scotland, 2006–07, for Internat. Develt, 2007–10; Shadow Sec. of State for Internat. Develt, 2010, for Work and Pensions, 2010–11, for Foreign and Commonwealth Affairs, 2011–15. *Recreation:* fishing on the Isle of Mull.
See also W. C. Alexander.

ALEXANDER, Fiona Jane, (Mrs Stanko Ilic); Director of Communications, University Hospital Birmingham NHS Foundation Trust, since 2006; *b* 18 July 1967; *d* of David Charles Alexander and Susan Margaret Heywood (*née* Lewis); *m* 2004, Stanko Ilic; one *d*. *Educ:* S Glamorgan Inst. of Higher Educn, Cardiff (NCTJ); DipM; ACIM. Asst Ed., MATCH mag., 1989–96; Editor: Leics Herald Post, 1996–97; Sunday Mercury, 1997–2000; Editor-in-Chief, Midland Independent Mags, 2000–02; Business Develt Dir, Trinity Mirror Midlands, 2002–03; Ed., Birmingham Post, 2003–06. *Recreations:* football clubs Arsenal and Birmingham City, fine food and wine. *Address:* University Hospital Birmingham NHS Foundation Trust, Queen Elizabeth Medical Centre, Edgbaston, Birmingham B15 2TH. *T:* (0121) 371 4325. *E:* fiona.alexander@uhb.nhs.uk.

ALEXANDER, Heidi; MP (Lab) Lewisham East, since 2010; *b* Swindon, 17 April 1975; *d* of Malcolm and Elaine Alexander; *m* 2011, Martin Ballantyne. *Educ:* Churchfields Secondary Sch., Swindon; Durham Univ. (BA Geog. 1996; MA Eur. Urban and Regl Change 1999). Researcher to Joan Ruddock, MP, 1999–2005; Campaign Manager, Clothes Aid, 2006. Dir and Chair, Gtr London Enterprise, 2007–09; Dir, Lewisham Schs for the Future Local Educn Partnership, 2007–09. Mem. (Lab) Lewisham LBC, 2004–10 (Dep. Mayor, 2006–10; Cabinet Mem. for Regeneration, 2006–10). Shadow Health Sec., 2015–. *Address:* House of Commons, SW1A 0AA.

ALEXANDER, Dame Helen (Anne), DBE 2011 (CBE 2004); Chairman: Incisive Media, since 2009; Port of London Authority, since 2010; UBM, since 2012; President, Confederation of British Industry, 2009–11 (Vice-President, 2008–09); *b* 10 Feb. 1957; *d* of late Bernard Alexander and Tania Alexander (*née* Benckendorff); *m* 1985, Tim Suter; two *s* one *d*. *Educ:* Hertford Coll., Oxford (MA 1978; Hon. Fellow, 2002); INSEAD, France (MBA 1984). Gerald Duckworth, 1978–79; Faber & Faber, 1979–83; Economist Gp, 1985–2008, Chief Exec., 1997–2008. Non-executive Director: Northern Foods plc, 1994–2002; British Telecom plc, 1998–2002; Centrica plc, 2003–11; Rolls-Royce Gp plc, 2007–; Huawei Technologies (UK), 2015–. Sen. Advr, Bain Capital, 2008–; Dep. Chm., esure Gp Hldgs. Trustee, Tate, 2003–11. Chancellor, Univ. of Southampton, 2011–. Chair, Business Adv. Council, Saïd Business Sch., Univ. of Oxford. Gov., St Paul's Girls' Sch., 2003–.

ALEXANDER, His Honour Ian Douglas Gavin; QC 1989; a Circuit Judge, 2002–11; *b* 10 April 1941; *s* of late Dr A. D. P. Alexander, MB ChB, and of Mrs D. Alexander; *m* 1969, Rosemary Kirkbride Richards; one *s* one *d*. *Educ:* Tonbridge; University College London (LLB). Called to Bar, Lincoln's Inn, 1964, Bencher, 1998; a Recorder, Midland and Oxford Circuit, 1982–2002. A Pres., Mental Health Review Tribunal, 2000–11. Freemason; Grand Registrar of Craft and Chapter, United Grand Lodge of England, 2001–07. *Recreations:* horses, sailing, gardening, ski-ing, Church of England. *Address:* The Folly, Fifield, Chipping Norton, Oxon OX7 6HW. *Club:* Naval and Military.

ALEXANDER, Jonathan James Graham, DPhil; FBA 1985; FSA 1981; Sherman Fairchild Professor of Fine Arts, Institute of Fine Arts, New York, 2002–11, now Emeritus (Professor of Fine Arts, 1988–2011); *b* 20 Aug. 1935; *s* of Arthur Ronald Brown and Frederica Emma Graham (who *m* 2nd, Boyd Alexander); *m* 1st, 1974, Mary Davey (marr. diss. 1995); one *s*; 2nd, 1996, Serita Winthrop (marr. diss. 2001). *Educ:* Magdalen Coll., Oxford (BA, MA, DPhil). Assistant, Dept of Western MSS, Bodleian Library, Oxford, 1963–71; Lecturer, 1971–73, Reader, 1973–87, History of Art Dept, Manchester Univ. Lyell Reader in Bibliography, Univ. of Oxford, 1982–83; Sen. Kress Fellow, Center for Adv. Study in Visual Arts, Nat. Gall. of Art, Washington DC, 1984–85; Sandars Reader in Bibliography, Cambridge Univ., 1984–85. Vis. Prof., UCL, 1991–93; John Simon Guggenheim Meml Fellow, 1995–96; Rio Tinto Distinguished Vis. Fellow, La Trobe Univ., Melbourne, 1997; Vis. Fellow, All Souls Coll., Oxford, 1998; J. Clawson Mills Art Hist. Fellowship, Met. Mus. of Art, NY, 2002; Samuel H. Kress Prof., Center for Advanced Study in the Visual Arts, Nat. Gall. of Art, Washington DC, 2004–05; J. Paul Getty Mus. Guest Scholar, 2006. Panizzi Lectures, BL, 2007–08. Fellow, Medieval Acad. of America, 1999. Hon. Fellow, Pierpont Morgan Liby, NY, 1995. *Publications:* (with Otto Pächt) Illuminated Manuscripts in the Bodleian Library, Oxford, 3 vols, 1966, 1970, 1973; (with A. C. de la Mare) Italian Illuminated Manuscripts in the Library of Major J. R. Abbey, 1969; Norman Illumination at Mont St Michel *c* 966–1100, 1970; The Master of Mary of Burgundy, A Book of Hours, 1970; Italian Renaissance Illuminations, 1977; Insular Manuscripts 6th–9th Century, 1978; The Decorated Letter, 1978; (with E. Temple) Illuminated Manuscripts in Oxford College Libraries, 1986; (ed with Paul Binski) Age of Chivalry: Art in Plantagenet England 1200–1400, 1987; Medieval Illuminators and Their Methods of Work, 1993; (ed) The Painted Page: Italian Renaissance book illumination 1450–1550, 1994; The Towneley Lectionary illuminated for Cardinal Alessandro Farnese by Giulio Clovio, 1997; Studies in Italian Manuscript Illumination, 2002; articles in Burlington Magazine, Arte Veneta, Pantheon, etc. *Recreation:* music. *Address:* Institute of Fine Arts, 1 East 78th Street, New York, NY 10075–0178, USA.

ALEXANDER, Lesley-Anne, CBE 2012; Chief Executive, Royal National Institute of Blind People (formerly Royal National Institute of the Blind), since 2004; *b* 20 Sept. 1959; *d* of N. J. Davies and D. E. Davies; *m*; one *s*; *m* 1995, Colin James Reith. *Educ:* Thames Valley Univ. (MSc Ops Mgt). Housing Department: Ealing LBC, 1980–92; Enfield LBC, 1992–98; Dir of Ops, Peabody Trust, 1998–2003. Chairman: British Judo Assoc., 1997–2001; ACEVO, 2009–15. *Address:* Royal National Institute of Blind People, 105 Judd Street, WC1H 9NE. *T:* (020) 7391 2200, *Fax:* (020) 7383 0508. *E:* lesley-anne.alexander@rnib.org.uk.

ALEXANDER, McNeill; *see* Alexander, R. McN.

ALEXANDER, Michael Richard, CEng, FIET; FIGEM; FIChemE; CSci; Chief Executive, British Energy plc, 2003–05; Senior Independent Director, Seplat Petroleum Development Company plc, since 2013; *b* 17 Nov. 1947; *s* of Humphrey and Pauline Alexander; *m* (marr. diss. 2011); two *s*. *Educ:* King George Grammar Sch., Southport; Univ. of Manchester Inst. of Sci. and Technol. (BSc 1st Cl. Hons Chem. Engrg; MSc Control Engrg). CEng 1975; MIChemE 1975, FIChemE 2004; FIGEM (FIGasE 1995); FIET (FIEE 2001); CSci 2004. Dir, CIS, Eastern Europe, British Gas Exploration and Production Ltd, 1991–93; Managing Director: Public Gas Supply, British Gas plc, 1993–96; British Gas Trading Ltd, 1996–2001; Exec. Dir, 1996–2003, Chief Operating Officer, 2002–03, Centrica plc. Chairman: Goldfish Bank Ltd, 2002–03; TGE Marine AG, 2008–10; Dep. Chm. and Sen. Ind. Dir, Russian Platinum, 2011–13; non-executive Director: Associated British Foods plc, 2002–07; Costain plc, 2007–13; Board Adviser: Marwyn Investment Mgt LLP, 2006–09; Landis+Gyr Gp, 2007–; EGS Energy Ltd, 2010–. Ind. Dir, UK Payments Council, 2007–14. Chm., Assoc. of Train Operating Cos, 2008–09. *Recreations:* Rugby, walking, family. *Address:* c/o Seplat Petroleum Development Company plc, 4th Floor, 50 Pall Mall, SW1Y 5JH.

ALEXANDER, Michael Stuart; Chief Reporter, The Courier, Fife, since 2012; *b* St Andrews, 17 Jan. 1973; *s* of Robert and Lorraine Alexander; *m* 2006, Lindsey Quinn; one *s* one *d*. *Educ:* Madras Coll., St Andrews; Univ. of Dundee (MA Hons Geog. 1995). Cinema projectionist (pt-time), St Andrews, 1990–95; The Courier, Dundee: reporter, 1995–2005; features writer, 2005–06; News Ed., 2007–12. *Recreations:* mountain biking, hill walking, cinema, family, community events. *Address:* The Courier, 14 Hunter Street, Kirkcaldy, Fife KY1 1ED. *T:* (01592) 260385. *E:* malexander@thecourier.co.uk. *Club:* St Andrews Golf.

ALEXANDER, Morag, OBE 2001; Member and Scotland Commissioner, Equality and Human Rights Commission, 2007–10; Convener, Scottish Social Services Council, 2001–07; *b* 10 Oct. 1943; *d* of Coll MacInnes and Sarah MacInnes (*née* Carberry); *m* 1964, Prof. Alan Alexander, *qv*; one *s* one *d*. *Educ:* Our Lady of Lourdes Sch., Glasgow; Glasgow Univ.; Lakehead Univ., Ont. (BA Hons). Res. Asst, ASTMS, 1971–73; editor and researcher, RIPA, 1973–82; freelance journalist and consultant, 1982–90; Founding Dir, TRAINING 2000 (Scotland) Ltd, Scottish Alliance for Women's Trng, 1990–92; Dir, EOC, Scotland, 1992–2001. Board Member: Children in Scotland, 1995–2000 (Chm., Early Years Adv. Gp, 1995–2002); Scottish Commn for Regulation of Care, 2001–07; Chairman: Fair Play Scotland, 2001–06; TOPSS UK Alliance, 2002–05. Member: Bd, Partnership for a Parliament, 1997; Scottish Senate, the Windsor Meetings, 1997–2000; Women's Adv. Gp to Scottish Exec. (formerly Scottish Office), 1997–2000; Expert Panel on Procedures and Standing Orders, Scottish Parlt, 1997–98; Bd, Turning Point Scotland, 1998–2006; Bd, Skills for Health, 2003–05; Skills for Care and Develt, 2005–07; Bd and Trustee, ELCAP, 2010– (Vice Chm., 2012–). Mem., Gen. Optical Council, 2009–. Mem., Cttee of Inquiry into Student Finance, 1999–2000. Member: Governing Body, Queen Margaret UC, 2001–07; Court, Queen Margaret Univ., Edinburgh, 2007–08. Founding Ed., Women in Europe, 1985–89; UK corresp., Women of Europe, 1987–92. *Recreations:* reading, walking, theatre, opera, spending time with family.

ALEXANDER, Pamela Elizabeth, OBE 2012; Chair, Covent Garden Market Authority, since 2013; *b* 17 April 1954; *d* of late Reginald William Purchase Alexander and Marion Elizabeth Alexander (*née* Ross); *m* 1994, Dr Roger Booker; three step *s* one step *d*. *Educ:* Lady Eleanor Holles Sch.; Newnham Coll., Cambridge (BA Hons Geog.; MA). CGeog 2005. Department of the Environment, 1975–94: Asst Private Sec. to Minister for Housing, 1978–81; seconded to UK Rep., EC, Brussels, 1981–82; Hd, Publicity, 1987–90; Hd, Finance, Deptl Services, 1990–92; Hd, Housing Assocs Div., 1992–94; Dep. Chief Exec. (Ops), Housing Corp., 1995–97; Chief Exec., Historic Buildings and Monuments Commn (English Heritage), 1997–2001; Leader, Agency Policy Rev., Cabinet Office, 2001–02; Chief Exec., SEEDA, 2004–11. Non-executive Director: Housing Finance Corp., 2002–11; Quintain E&D plc, 2003; Crest Nicholson Hldgs plc (formerly Ltd), 2011–. Chair: Thanet Regeneration Bd, 2011–14; Design Council Cabe, 2014– (non-exec. Dir, 2011–; Built Envmt Expert, 2012–); non-exec. Dir, Acad. of Urbanism, 2010–. Member: London Mayor's Design Adv. Gp, 2012–; Watts Gall. Limnerslease Appeal Cttee, 2012–14. Governor, Peabody Trust, 2000–09 (Chm., 2004–09); Trustee: Brighton Dome and Festival Ltd, 2006–; Design Council, 2011–. Advr, Joseph Rowntree Foundn Res. Cttee, 1997–2004. Associate, New Economics Foundn, 2002–06. FRSA 1998; FRGS 1999. Academician, Acad. of Urbanism, 2006. *Recreations:* choral singing, tennis, walking, talking. *E:* pamalexander@bookeralexander.com.

ALEXANDER, Lt-Col Sir Patrick Desmond William C.; *see* Cable-Alexander.

ALEXANDER, Prof. Paul, PhD; Professor of Radio Astronomy, University of Cambridge, since 2010; Fellow, Jesus College, Cambridge, since 1989; *b* Brighton, 20 Dec. 1960; *s* of Reginald and Iris Alexander; partner, Prof. Lynn Faith Gladden, *qv*. *Educ:* Brighton, Hove and Sussex Grammar Sch. and Sixth Form Coll.; Trinity Coll., Cambridge (BA 1982; PhD 1986). Res. Fellow, Sidney Sussex Coll., Cambridge, 1985–89; Lectr, 1989–2008, Reader, 2008–10, Univ. of Cambridge. UK Sci. Dir, Square Kilometre Array Orgn, 2011–. *Publications:* contribs on astrophysics and data analysis. *Recreations:* gardening, cooking, wine. *Address:* Cavendish Laboratory, JJ Thomson Avenue, Cambridge CB3 0HE. *T:* (01223) 337477. *E:* p.alexander@mrao.cam.ac.uk.

ALEXANDER, Maj.-Gen. Paul Donald, CB 1989; MBE 1968; Policy Director (Army), Ministry of Defence, 1989–94; *b* 30 Nov. 1934; *s* of Donald Alexander and Alice Louisa Alexander (*née* Dunn); *m* 1958, Christine Winifred Marjorie Coakley; three *s. Educ:* Dudley Grammar Sch.; RMA Sandhurst; Staff Coll., Camberley; NDC; RCDS. Enlisted 1953; commissioned Royal Signals, 1955; served Hong Kong, E Africa, Germany; Comd 1st Div. Signal Regt, 1974–76; MoD, 1977–79; Comdr, Corps Royal Signals, 1st (Br) Corps, 1979–81; Dep. Mil. Sec. (B), 1982–85; Signal Officer in Chief (Army), 1985–89, retired. Col Comdt, RCS, 1989–95; Hon. Col, 35th Signal Regt, 1991–96. Chm., Royal Signals Assoc., 1990–95; Mem., E Anglian TA&VRA, 1991–2001 (County Chm., 1996–2000). Vice Pres., Lady Grover's Hosp. Fund, 2005– (Chm., 1998–2005). *Recreation:* gardening. *Clubs:* Army and Navy; Royal Signals Yacht (Adm., 1989–93).

ALEXANDER, Prof. Philip Stephen, DPhil; FBA 2005; Professor of Post-Biblical Jewish Literature, Manchester University, 1995–2011, now Emeritus; Co-Director, Manchester University Centre for Jewish Studies, 1995–2011; *b* 10 March 1947; *s* of Robert and Priscilla Alexander; *m* 1973, Loveday Constance Anne Earl (Rev. Canon Prof. L. Alexander); one *s* one *d. Educ:* Pembroke Coll., Oxford (Hon. Mods Greek and Latin Lit. 1967; BA Oriental Studies 1969; DPhil Oriental Studies 1974; MA 1992). University of Manchester: Nathan Laski Lectr in Post-Biblical Jewish Studies, Dept of Near Eastern Studies, 1972–86; Sen. Lectr in Jewish Studies, 1986–91; Prof. of Post-Biblical Jewish Lit., Dept of Middle Eastern Studies, 1991–92; University of Oxford: Speaker's Lectr (pt-time), 1985–88; Pres., Oxford Centre for Hebrew and Jewish Studies, 1992–95; Hebrew Centre Lectr, Oriental Faculty, 1992–95; Fellow, St Cross Coll., 1992–95. *Publications:* Textual Sources for the Study of Judaism, 1984; (with G. Vermes) Serekh ha-Yahad and Two Related Texts, 1998; The Targum of Canticles: translated with a critical introduction, apparatus and notes, 2003; Companions to the Dead Sea Scrolls: the Mystical Texts, 2005; contrib. to major ref. works in field of Jewish studies; contribs to Jl Jewish Studies, Jl Semitic Studies. *Recreations:* hill-walking, swimming, Rembrandt, Bach, Shakespeare. *Address:* c/o Centre for Jewish Studies, Religions and Theology, School of Arts, Histories and Cultures, Faculty of Humanities, University of Manchester, Manchester M13 9PL. *T:* (0161) 275 3977, *Fax:* (0161) 275 3151. *E:* philip.s.alexander@man.ac.uk.

ALEXANDER, Sir Richard, 3rd Bt *cr* 1945, of Sundridge Park, co. Kent; *b* London, 1 Sept. 1947; *o s* of Sir Charles Gundry Alexander, 2nd Bt, and of Mary Neale, *oc* of Stanley Richardson; S father, 2009; *m* 1971, Lesley Jane Jordan (marr. diss. 2002); two *s. Educ:* Bishop's Stortford Coll. MCIPR (MIPR 1980). Manager, Burntisland Shipbuilding, 1966–68; Shipbroker, Cory Mann George, 1968–70; Ship Manager, Houlder Brothers, 1970–79; PR Officer, Furness Gp, 1979–90; PR consultant, 1990–2012. Dir, Bentley Drivers Club Ltd, 1997–2014; Editor, The BDC Review, 1997–2014. Chm., Detling Village Hall, 1999–. Freeman, City of London; Liveryman, Merchant Taylors' Co. *Recreations:* vintage motoring, clay pigeon shooting, barebow archery. *Heir: s* Edward Samuel Alexander [*b* 1 Oct. 1974; *m* 2005, Michelle, *d* of Nicholas Goodhew, Sittingbourne; two *d*]. *Address:* 1 Northdowns View, Harrietsham, Maidstone, Kent ME17 1AQ. *T:* 07976 413091.

ALEXANDER, Prof. (Robert) McNeill, CBE 2000; FRS 1987; FRSB; Professor of Zoology, University of Leeds, 1969–99; *b* 7 July 1934; *s* of Robert Priestley Alexander and Janet McNeill; *m* 1961, Ann Elizabeth Coulton; one *s* one *d. Educ:* Tonbridge School; Trinity Hall, Cambridge (MA, PhD); DSc Wales. Asst Lectr in Zoology, University Coll. of North Wales, 1958, Lectr 1961, Sen. Lectr 1968; Head, Dept of Pure and Applied Zoology, Univ. of Leeds, 1969–78 and 1983–87. Visiting Professor: Harvard, 1973; Duke, 1975; Nairobi, 1976, 1977, 1978; Basle, 1986; St Francis Xavier Univ. (NS), 1990; Univ. of Calif, Davis, 1992. Mem., Biological Scis Cttee, SRC, 1974–77. Sec., Zool Soc. of London, 1992–99 (Mem. Council, 1988–91); Vice Pres., 1990–91); President: Soc. for Experimental Biology, 1995–97 (Vice Pres., 1993–95); Internat. Soc. for Vertebrate Morphology, 1997–2001. Ed., Royal Soc. Proc. B, 1998–2004. Hon. FZS 2002. Hon. Mem., Soc. for Integrative and Comparative Biol. (formerly Amer. Soc. of Zoologists), 1986; Member: Academia Europaea, 1996; European Acad. of Scis, 2004; Foreign Hon. Mem., Amer. Acad. of Arts and Scis, 2001. Hon. DSc Aberdeen, 2002; Hon. Dr Wageningen, 2003. Scientific Medal, Zoological Soc., 1969; Linnean Medal, Linnean Soc., 1979; Muybridge Medal, Internat. Soc. for Biomechanics, 1991; Borelli Award, Amer. Soc. for Biomechanics, 2003. *Publications:* Functional Design in Fishes, 1967, 3rd edn 1974; Animal Mechanics, 1968, 2nd edn 1983; Size and Shape, 1971; The Chordates, 1975, 2nd edn 1981; Biomechanics, 1975; The Invertebrates, 1979; Locomotion of Animals, 1982; Optima for Animals, 1982, 2nd edn 1996; Elastic Mechanisms in Animal Movement, 1988; Dynamics of Dinosaurs and other Extinct Giants, 1989; Animals, 1990; The Human Machine, 1992; Exploring Biomechanics, 1992; Bones, 1994; Energy for Animal Life, 1999; Principles of Animal Locomotion, 2003; Human Bones, 2005; papers on mechanics of human and animal movement. *Recreations:* history of natural history, history of tableware. *Address:* 14 Moor Park Mount, Leeds LS6 4BU. *T:* (0113) 275 9218.

ALEXANDER, Prof. Robin John, PhD, LittD; FBA 2011; Chairman, Cambridge Primary Review Trust, since 2012 (Director, Cambridge Primary Review, 2006–12); Hon. Professor of Education, University of York, since 2013; Fellow of Wolfson College, Cambridge, 2004–09, now Emeritus; Professor of Education, University of Warwick, 1995–2001, now Emeritus; *b* 10 Nov. 1941; *s* of Donald Alexander and Isabel Alexander (*née* Manton); *m* 1st, 1964, Elizabeth Walbank (marr. diss. 1986); one *s* one *d*; 2nd, 2001, Karen Lennox Mills. *Educ:* Downing Coll., Cambridge (BA 1964; MA 1968; PhD 1985; LittD 2006); Durham Univ. (PGCE 1966); London Univ. (AcDipEd 1970); Univ. of Manchester (MEd 1975). Teacher, schs and colls, 1964–77; University of Leeds: Lectr, Sen. Lectr, then Reader in Educn, 1977–90; Prof. of Educn, 1990–95; Leverhulme Res. Fellow, 1994–95; Leverhulme Emeritus Fellow, 2002–04. Dir, Dialogos UK Ltd, 2004–. Vis. Fellow, Hughes Hall, Cambridge, 2001–02; Sir Edward Youde Vis. Prof., Hong Kong Inst. of Educn, 2005–06; C. K. Koh Prof., Nat. Inst. of Educn, Singapore, 2010; Miegunyah Dist. Vis. Fellow, Univ. of Melbourne, 2010. Internat. educational consultant to DFID, EC, Ofsted, UGC of HK Govt, Knowledge and Human Develt Authy, Dubai. Member: Cttees, CNAA, 1975–84; Council, CATE, 1989–94; DES Inquiry into Curriculum Orgn and Classroom Practice in Primary Schs, 1991–92; BFI/TES Commn on Teaching of English, 1992–93; Bd and Cttees, QCA, 1997–2002; Teach First Global Strategy Adv. Gp, 2011; Internat. Steering Cttee, Van Leer Jerusalem Inst., 2012–13; Strategic Bd, Expert Subject Adv. Gp, DFE, 2013–; Chm., Assoc. for Study of Primary Educn, 1987–89; Pres., British Assoc. for Internat. and Comparative Educn, 2008–09; Vice-Pres., Early Educn, 2014–. Advr, Artis Educn, 2013–. Trustee, Prince's Foundn for Children and the Arts, 2015–. Gov., Bath Spa Univ., 2013–. FRSA 2006; FAcSS (AcSS 2011). Hon. FCollT 2009. Hon. DEd Manchester Metropolitan, 2010; DUniv Bishop Grosseteste, 2010. Award for Services to Educn, Assoc. of Managers in Educn, 2010; Fred and Anne Jarvis Award, NUT, 2011. *Publications:* (jtly) The Self-Evaluating Institution, 1982; Primary Teaching, 1984; (jtly) Change in Teacher Education, 1984; (jtly) Changing Primary Practice, 1989; Policy and Practice in Primary Education, 1992, 2nd edn 1997; Versions of Primary Education, 1995; (jtly) Learning from Comparing, vol 1, Classrooms, Contexts and Outcomes, 1999, vol. 2, Policy, Professionals and Development, 2000; Culture and Pedagogy, 2001 (Outstanding Book Award, Amer. Educnl Res. Assoc., 2002; First Prize, Soc. for Educn Studies Book Awards, 2002); Towards Dialogic Teaching, 2004, 4th edn 2008; Essays on Pedagogy, 2008; Education for All: the quality imperative and the problem of pedagogy, 2008; (jtly) Children, their World, their Education: final report of the Cambridge Primary Review, 2010 (1st Prize, Soc. for Educn Studies Book Awards, 2011); (jtly) The Cambridge Primary Review Research Surveys, 2010. *Recreations:* the arts, travel. *Address:* Wolfson College, Cambridge CB3 9BB. *E:* rja40@cam.ac.uk.

ALEXANDER, Roger Michael; non-executive Group Chairman, Walker Books Ltd, since 2010 (non-executive Director, 1999–2009); *b* Edinburgh, 29 June 1942; *s* of Hyman and Anna Alexander; *m* 1966, Monica Anne Freedman; two *d. Educ:* Dulwich Coll.; Coll. of Law. Admitted as solicitor, 1965; Lewis Silkin LLP: articled to Hon. John E. Silkin, 1960–65; Partner, 1965–2010; Head: Corporate Dept, 1986–89; Mktg Services Law Gp, 1986–99; Lead Partner, 1989–99; Sen. Partner, 1999–2005; Chm., 2005–10. Non-executive Director: EDS Financial Services Div., 1995–96; The Communications Agency Ltd, 2010–13; Advr to Bd, Strategy & Investment Partners LLP, 2010–. Non-executive Director: London String Quartet Foundn, 2001–07; Royal Central Sch. of Speech and Drama (formerly Central Sch. of Speech and Drama), 2005–14; Mem., Strategy Develt Cttee, Dulwich Coll., 2013–. Non-exec. Dir, and Hon. Solicitor, London Marriage Guidance Council, 1983–89. *Recreations:* literature, theatre, photography, cricket, gardening, bridge, family, reading to my grandchildren, travel, opera. *Address:* 24 Lyndhurst Road, NW3 5NX. *E:* roger.m.alexander@btinternet.com.

ALEXANDER, Rosemary Anne, (Mrs G. L. S. Dobry); Founder and Principal, English Gardening School, since 1983; *b* 15 Dec. 1937; *d* of late Charles Sleigh and Violet Allison (*née* Petrie); *m* 1st, 1956, Walter Ronald Alexander, CBE (marr. diss. 1975; he *d* 2006); two *s* two *d*; 2nd, 1982, His Honour George Leon Severyn Dobry, *qv. Educ:* Beacon Sch., Bridge of Allan, Stirlingshire. ACIHort (AIHort 1994). Trained as landscape architect; with Brian Clouston & Partners, Glasgow and London, 1973–79, then in private practice as garden designer. Expert witness, historic gardens, 2011–12. Internat. lectr, Kiev, 2012, NZ and Australia, 2013. Show Gardens Judge, RHS, 2011–15; Judge, Imperial Russian Flower and Garden Show, St Petersburg, 2014. FSGD 1981. Veitch Meml Medal, RHS, 2011. *Publications:* (with Tony Aldous) Landscape By Design, 1979; The English Gardening School, 1987; A Handbook for Garden Designers, 1994; Terraced, Town and Village Gardens, 1999; Garden Design, 2000; Caring for Your Garden, 2001; The Essential Garden Design Workbook, 2004, 2nd edn 2009; The Garden Maker's Manual, 2005; The Essential Garden Maintenance Workbook, 2006; Dear Christo, 2010. *Recreations:* opera, travel to remote places, horse racing, walking. *Address:* Sandhill Farm House, Rogate, Petersfield, Hants GU31 5HU. *T:* (01730) 818373; English Gardening School, Chelsea Physic Garden, 66 Royal Hospital Road, SW3 4HS. *T:* (020) 7352 4347; Whitelands House, Cheltenham Terrace, SW3 4RA.

ALEXANDER, Steven; Chief Executive, Pre-School Learning Alliance, 2004–10; *b* 23 Oct. 1954; *s* of late Louisa and James Alexander; two *s. Educ:* Blue Coat C of E Sch.; Coventry Univ. (CQSW; CSS; DMS; MBA); Putteridge Bury Business Sch. (PhD 1994). Operational Services Manager, Coventry Social Services, 1976–92; Asst Gen. Manager, S Birmingham Community NHS Trust, 1992–95; Dir of Ops, Sense, 1995–2001; CEO, British Dyslexia Assoc., 2001–04. Associate Consultant, Nat. Develt Team, 1992–94. Dir, Children's Workforce Develt Council, 2005–. Mem., Disability Employment Adv. Cttee, DWP, 2003–. Treas., Eur. Dyslexia Assoc. FRSA. *Recreations:* classic cars, antiques, supporting Coventry FC, music, horses. *Address:* Potfords Dam Farm, Coventry Road, Cawston, Rugby CV23 9JP. *T:* (020) 7697 2519.

ALEXANDER, Wendy Cowan; Associate Dean, London Business School, since 2012; *b* 27 June 1963; *d* of Rev. Douglas N. Alexander and Dr Joyce O. Alexander; *m* 2003, Prof. Brian Ashcroft; one *s* one *d* (twins). *Educ:* Park Mains Sch., Erskine; Pearson Coll., Canada; Glasgow Univ. (MA Hons); Warwick Univ. (MA Econ); INSEAD, France (MBA). Research Officer, Lab. Party, 1988–92; with Booz & Co., 1994–97; Advr to Sec. of State for Scotland, 1997–98. Mem. (Lab) Paisley N, Scottish Parlt, 1999–2011. Scottish Executive, subseq. Scottish Government: Minister for Communities, 1999–2000; Minister for Enterprise and Lifelong Learning, 2000–02, and for Transport, 2001–02; Convenor: Finance Cttee, 2006–07; Scotland Bill Cttee, 2010–11; Lab Shadow Cabinet Sec. for Finance and Sustainable Growth, 2007. Leader, Scottish Labour Party, 2007–08. Vis. Prof., Univ. of Strathclyde Business Sch., 2003–12. FRSA 2011. DUniv Strathclyde, 2007; DUniv UWS, 2012.

See also Rt Hon. D. G. Alexander.

ALEXANDER, William John, CBE 2005; FREng, FIMechE; Chairman: Invesco Perpetual Income and Growth Investment Trust, since 2006; Beyond Analysis Ltd, since 2008; *b* 15 Feb. 1947; *s* of late John Fryer Alexander and of Kathleen Mary (*née* Berry); *m* 1968, Dorothy Full; one *s* one *d.* FIMechE 1987; FREng (FEng 1996). British Coal: trng scheme, 1970; Chief Engr, Scottish Reg., 1982–86; Chief Mechanical Engr, 1986–87; Hd of Engrg, 1987–89; Thames Water Utilities: Engrg Dir, 1989–91; Technical Dir, 1991–92; Man. Dir, 1992–96; Dir, 1994–2005, Gp Man. Dir, 1996–97, Chief Executive, 1997–2005, Thames Water plc, later RWE Thames Water plc. Non-exec. Dir, RMC, 2001–05; Chairman: Henley Festival Ltd, 2003–11; Xansa plc, 2004–07; Clearview Traffic Ltd, 2006–09. Mem. Bd, CBI, 2005–09. Freeman, City of London, 1994; Liveryman, Engineers' Co., 1997–. Hon. FIMMM (Hon. FIMinE 1990); Hon. FCIWEM 2002. Hon. DSc: Cranfield, 2003; Reading, 2003. *Recreations:* classic cars, travel, golf. *Address:* Invesco Perpetual Income and Growth plc, 30 Finsbury Square, EC2A 1AG. *Club:* Phyllis Court (Henley).

ALEXANDER-SINCLAIR of Freswick, James Boyd; garden designer, writer, lecturer and broadcaster; *b* Münster, Germany, 30 July 1959; *s* of Maj.-Gen. David Boyd Alexander-Sinclair of Freswick, CB; *m* 1987, Celestria Fenwick; two *s* one *d. Educ:* Eton Coll. Estabd Terra Firma Landscapes, 1984–; gardens designed and built throughout UK and parts of Europe; freelance garden journalist, 2000–; columnist, Gardeners' World mag., 2007–. Co-presenter, Chelsea Flower Show coverage, BBC, 2008–. Gardens Judge, 2008–, Mem. Council, 2011–, RHS. Blog of Year, Garden Media Guild, 2008, 2009, 2013. *Recreations:* gardening, cinema, drainage. *Address:* Green Rise, Ledwell, Oxon OX7 7AN. *E:* james@jamesalexandersinclair.com.

AL FAYED, Mohamed; Chairman: Harrods Holdings Ltd, 1994–2010; Harrods Ltd, 1985–2010; Fulham Football Club, 1997–2013; Chairman and Owner, Ritz Hotel, Paris, since 1979; *b* Egypt, Jan. 1933; *m*; two *s* two *d* (and one *s* decd). *Educ:* Alexandria Univ. Hon. Mem., Emmanuel Coll., Cambridge, 1995. Officier, Légion d'Honneur, 1993 (Chevalier, 1985); La Grande Médaille de la Ville de Paris, 1985; Plaque de Paris, 1989; Commendatore, Order of Merit (Italy), 1990.

ALFEROV, Prof. Zhores Ivanovich, DSc; Professor of Optoelectronics, since 1973, and Dean, Faculty of Physical Science and Technical Engineering, since 1988, St Petersburg State Polytechnical University (formerly V. I. Ulyanov Electrotechnical Institute, Leningrad); Rector, St Petersburg Academic University Center for Research and Education, since 2009; *b* Belorussia, USSR, 15 March 1930; *s* of Ivan Karpovich and Anna Vladimirovna; *m* 1967, Tamara Darskaya; two *c. Educ:* V. I. Ulyanov Electrotechnical Inst., Leningrad (DSc 1970). Jun. Researcher, 1953–64, Sen. Researcher, 1964–67, Head of Lab., 1967–87, Dir, 1987–2003, A. F. Ioffe Physico-Technical Inst., Leningrad, later St Petersburg. Chm., St Petersburg Scientific Centre, 1989–. Mem., State Duma, 1995–. USSR, subseq. Russian, Academy of Science: Corresp. Mem., 1972, Mem., 1979; Vice-Pres., 1989–. (Jtly) Nobel Prize for Physics, 2000. *Publications:* four books; articles in jls on semiconductor technology. *Address:* St Petersburg Academic University, Nanotechnology Research Education Centre RAS, 8/3 Khlopina str., St Petersburg 194021, Russia.

ALFÖLDY, Tádé; Chairman, since 1997, and Chief Executive Officer, since 2005, ATI Depo Zrt; Chairman: Preventiv Security Rt, since 2000; ATI Sziget Industrial Park Kft, since 2005; Managing Director, Gundel Kft, since 2010; *b* 6 Aug. 1946; *s* of László Alföldy and Erzsébet (*née* Újvári); *m* 1968, Orsolya Baraczka; two *d*. *Educ:* Karl Marx Univ. of Economics, Budapest. Hungarian Shipping Agency, 1968–70; Hungarian Youth Union, 1970–74; Sec.-Gen., Internat. Cttee, Children's and Adolescents' Movements, 1974–79; joined Ministry of Foreign Affairs, Hungary, 1979; Arab Desk Officer, 1979–80; 2nd, later 1st, Sec., Kuwait, 1980–85; British Desk Officer, 1985–89; Dir, N Atlantic Dept, 1989–90; Dep. State Sec., 1990–91; Ambassador: to Greece, 1991–94; to the UK, 1994–97. Jt Chm., Investor Holding Rt, 1997–2005; Sen. Exec. Officer, Investor/Interag Gp, 1997–. Vice Pres., 1997–2002, Mem. Bd of Auditors, 2002–, Hungarian Atlantic Council, Budapest. Mem., Foreign Policy Assoc., Budapest, 1991–. *Recreations:* family, tennis, gardening. *Address:* Interag Zrt, Budapest 1051, Szent István tér 11, Hungary.

ALFORD, Richard Harding, CMG 2003; OBE 1988; Secretary, Charles Wallace India Trust, since 2004; British Council Director, Italy, 1996–2003; *b* 28 Dec. 1943; *s* of Jack Harding Alford and Sylvia Alford; *m* 1968, Penelope Jane Wort; one *s* two *d*. *Educ:* Dulwich Coll.; Keble Coll., Oxford (MA; Diploma in History and Philosophy of Science). Asst Cultural Attaché, British Embassy, Prague, 1969–72; posts in ME Dept, Policy Res. Dept, and Educnl Contracts Dept, British Council, 1972–77; Project Planning Centre, Bradford Univ., 1977; Inst. of Educn, London Univ., 1978; British Council: Asst Rep., New Delhi, 1978–81; Dir, E Europe and N Asia Dept, 1982–85; Rep., Poland, 1985–89; Dir of Personnel, 1989–93; Regl Dir, Central Europe, 1993–96. Chm., Adv. Panel, British Centre for Literary Translation, 2009–11. Governor: Centre for Internat. Briefing, Farnham Castle, 1992–96; British Inst., Florence, 1996–2003; Atlantic Coll., 2005–14 (Mem., Adv. Council, 2014–). *Recreations:* tennis, theatre. *Address:* c/o British Council, 10 Spring Gardens, SW1A 2BN. *Club:* Friends of Dulwich College Sports.

ALFORD, Stuart Robert; QC 2014; Head of Division (Fraud), Serious Fraud Office, since 2013; *b* Westminster, 20 May 1967; *s* of Philip Alford and Heather Alford (*née* Porter); *m* 1995, Sylvia Philippa Theresa de Bertodano, *qv*; two *s* two *d*. *Educ:* Kenilworth Sch.; Univ. of Reading (BSc Hons Geog. 1989); Univ. of Westminster (DipLaw 1991); Inns of Court Sch. of Law. Called to the Bar, Middle Temple, 1992; in practice as barrister, 1992–2001 and 2003–12; UN Prosecutor (E Timor), 2001–03; Legal Advr, Iraq High Tribunal, 2005–06; Special Advocate of Attorney Gen., 2009–; Case Controller, Serious Fraud Office, 2012–13. Chm., War Crimes Cttee, Internat. Bar Assoc., 2008–13. Chm. Govs, St Mary's Catholic Primary Sch., Aston-le-Walls, Northants, 2010–. *Publications:* (contrib.) Oxford Companion to International Criminal Justice, 2009; contribs to Internat. Criminal Law Rev. *Recreations:* flying (Private Pilot's Licence Australia and Europe), scuba diving, opera (Mem., Glyndebourne Fest. Soc.), collecting fossilised wood. *Address:* Serious Fraud Office, 2–4 Cockspur Street, SW1Y 5BS. *T:* (020) 7239 7272. *E:* Stuart.Alford@sfo.gsi.gov.uk. *W:* www.stuartalford.net.

ALFORD, Sylvia Philippa Theresa; *see* de Bertodano, S. P. T.

ALHAJI, Alhaji Abubakar, Hon. KBE 1989; Economic Adviser to Nigerian States of Sokoto, Kebbi and Zamfara, since 1999; High Commissioner for Nigeria in the United Kingdom, 1992–97; *b* 22 Nov. 1938; *m* Hajiya Amina Abubakar; three *s* three *d*. *Educ:* Univ. of Reading (BA Hons Political Economy); IMF Inst. course in public finance, 1974; Hague Inst. for Social Scis (course on industrialisation, 1970). Permanent Secretary, Ministries of: Trade, 1975–78; Industries, 1978–79; Finance, 1979–84; Nat. Planning, 1984–88; Hon. Minister, Ministries of: Budget and Planning, 1988–90; Finance and Economic Develt, 1990–92. Chm., Group 24 Cttee, 1991–92. Vice-Pres., Commonwealth Soc. for the Deaf. Sardauna of Sokoto, 1991. Hon. DSc Sokoto Univ., 1991. *Recreations:* horse riding, walking, reading. *Address:* c/o Government House, Sokoto State, Nigeria.

AL HINAI, Shaikh Abdulaziz Abdullah Zahir; Ambassador of Oman to the Court of St James's, since 2009; *b* Bahla Al Ghafat, 20 Jan. 1961. *Educ:* Univ. of Jordan (Bachelor Pol Sci. 1983). Joined Min. of Foreign Affairs, Oman, 1983; Second Sec., 1983–88; Chargé d'Affaires *ad interim*, London, 1988–90; Ambassador: to Netherlands, 1990–94; to Russian Fedn, 1994–2000; to Egypt, and Perm. Rep. to Arab League, 2000–09. *Address:* Embassy of Oman, 167 Queen's Gate, SW7 5HE. *T:* (020) 7589 3233, *Fax:* (020) 7589 2505. *E:* London2@mofa.gov.om.

ALI, Ebrahim Mahomed; Solicitor, Reynolds Porter Chamberlain LLP, 2013–14; *b* 9 April 1951; *s* of Mahomed and Katija Ali; *m* 1981, Susan Linda Kirkby; two *s* one *d*. *Educ:* Morgan High Sch., Harare; Univ. of Zimbabwe (LLB); UCL (LLM); Columbia Univ., NY (LLM). Called to the Bar, Middle Temple, 1978; admitted as legal practitioner, Zimbabwe, 1982; Attorney Gen.'s Chambers, Zimbabwe, 1982–83; Kantor & Immerman, Zimbabwe, 1983–84; admitted solicitor, England and Wales, 1989; Solicitor, Inland Revenue: Principal Legal Officer, 1989–94; on secondment to Competition Br., Legal Dept, OFT, 1994–97; Asst Solicitor (special appeals, internat., EC, oil), 1997–2002; on secondment to Legal Dept, Ofgem, 2002–03; Principal Assistant Solicitor (Taxes), Bd of Inland Revenue, subseq. HMRC, 2003–06; Consultant, Freshfields Bruckhaus Deringer, 2006–08; with PricewaterhouseCoopers Legal, 2008–09. *Recreations:* relaxing, sport.

ALI, Rt Rev. Dr Michael N.; *see* Nazir-Ali.

ALI, Monica; writer; *b* Dhaka, 20 Oct. 1967; *m* 2002, Simon Torrance; one *s* one *d*. *Educ:* Bolton Sch.; Wadham Coll., Oxford (BA Hons PPE). Mktg Manager, Verso, 1992–94; Account Dir, Newell & Sorrell (Interbrand), 1995–97; Gp Account Dir, Lambie-Nairn, 1997–98; freelance copy-writer, 1999–2001. *Publications:* Brick Lane, 2003; Alentejo Blue, 2006; In the Kitchen, 2009; Untold Story, 2011. *Recreations:* eating, cooking, yoga, riding, having baths. *Address:* c/o Curtis Brown, Haymarket House, 28–29 Haymarket, SW1Y 4SP.

ALI, Muhammad; former professional heavyweight boxer; *b* Cassius Marcellus Clay, Louisville, Ky, 17 Jan. 1942; *s* of Cassius Marcellus Clay, Sr and Odessa L. Clay (*née* Grady); changed name on conversion to Islam, 1964; *m* 1st, 1964, Sonji Roi (marr. diss. 1966); 2nd, 1967, Belinda Kalilah Boyd (marr. diss. 1977); one *s* three *d* (incl. twin *d*); 3rd, 1977, Veronica Porche (marr. diss. 1986); four *d*; 4th, 1986, Yolanda Williams; one *s*. *Educ:* Central High Sch., Louisville. Amateur boxer, 1954–60; Gold Medal, Light Heavyweight Boxing, Olympic Games, Rome, 1960; turned professional, 1960: 61 bouts; 37 knockouts; won 19 by decision; World Heavyweight Champion, 1964, 1974, 1978. Special Envoy of US Pres. to Africa, 1980, to Iraq, 1990; Messenger of Peace, UN, 2000. *Films:* The Greatest, 1977; Freedom Road, 1979. Lifetime Achievement Award, Amnesty Internat. US Presidential Medal of Freedom, 2005. *Publications:* (with Richard Durham) The Greatest: my own story, 1975; (with T. Hauser) Healing, 1996; (with Hana Ali) More than a Hero, 2000; (with Hana Ali) The Soul of a Butterfly, 2004. *Address:* PO Box 160, Berrien Springs, MI 49103, USA.

ALI, Rushanara; MP (Lab) Bethnal Green and Bow, since 2010; *b* Bangladesh, 14 March 1975. *Educ:* Mulberry Sch. for Girls; Tower Hamlets Coll.; St John's Coll., Oxford (BA PPE). Res. asst to Lord Young of Dartington on estabt of Tower Hamlets Summer Univ., 1995; helped to develop Language Line; Parly Asst to Oona King, MP, 1997–99; FCO, 2000–01; Communities Directorate, Home Office, 2002–05; Associate Dir, Young Foundn, 2005–10. Res. Fellow, IPPR, 1999–2002. Shadow Minister: for Internat. Develt, 2010–14; for Educn, 2013–14. Mem., Treasury Select Cttee, 2014–15. Chair, UpRising Leadership Prog. *Address:* House of Commons, SW1A 0AA.

ALI, Tariq; writer; *b* 21 Oct. 1943; *s* of Tahira Hyat and Mazhar Ali Khan; partner, Susan Watkins; one *s* two *d*. *Educ:* Government Coll., Lahore (BA Hons); Exeter Coll., Oxford (PPE). Editor: The Black Dwarf, 1968–70; The Red Mole, 1970–73; Mem., Editorial Bd, New Left Review, 1982– (Chm., 1999–); Series Producer, Channel Four TV: Bandung File, 1984–89; Rear Window, 1990–94; Editorial Dir, 2001–05, Chm., 2005–, Verso Books. *Publications: non-fiction:* Pakistan: military rule or people's power, 1970; 1968 and After: inside the Revolution, 1978; Can Pakistan Survive?, 1982; Who's Afraid of Margaret Thatcher?, 1984; The Nehrus and the Gandhis: an Indian dynasty, 1985, 4th edn 2005; Streetfighting Years: an autobiography of the sixties, 1987, 2nd edn 2005; Revolution from Above: where is the Soviet Union going?, 1988; The Clash of Fundamentalisms, 2002; Bush in Babylon, 2003; Speaking of Empire and Resistance (interviews with David Barsamian), 2005; Rough Music: Blair/bombs/Baghdad/London/terror, 2005; Pirates of the Caribbean: axis of hope, 2006; The Duel: Pakistan on the flight path of American power, 2008; The Idea of Communism, 2009; The Protocols of the Elders of Sodom and other essays, 2009; The Obama Syndrome, 2010; On History: Tariq Ali and Oliver Stone in conversation, 2011; The Extreme Centre, 2015; *fiction:* Redemption, 1990; Shadows of the Pomegranate Tree, 1992; The Book of Saladin, 1998; Fear of Mirrors, 1998; The Stone Woman, 2000; A Sultan in Palermo, 2005; Night of the Golden Butterfly, 2010; *plays:* Spinoza, 1993; Necklaces, 1994; The Illustrious Corpse, 2003; Zahra, 2007; (with Thorvald Steen) Desert Storms, 2010; The New Adventures of Don Quixote, 2013; with Howard Brenton: Iranian Nights, 1989; Moscow Gold, 1990; Ugly Rumours, 1998. *Recreations:* swimming, cinema, cricket, theatre. *Address:* 6 Meard Street, W1F 0EG. *T:* (020) 7437 3546, *Fax:* (020) 7734 0059. *E:* tariq.ali3@btinternet.com. *W:* www.tariqali.org. *Clubs:* Groucho; Bolivarian Circle (Caracas); Société Stendhal (Paris).

ALI, Sayyid Zafar Gilani; QC 2012; *b* London, 22 Feb. 1965; *s* of Mohsin and Jamila Ali; *m* 2004, Melissa Tollman; two *d*. *Educ:* Sutton Valence Sch., Kent; Pakistan Mil. Acad.; Warwick Univ. (BA Hons 1990); City Univ. (DipLaw 1992); Inns of Court Sch. of Law. Called to the Bar, Middle Temple, 1994; in practice as barrister, specialising in criminal defence, 1994–. *Recreations:* boxing, family, study of Shia Islam. *Address:* 25 Frenchay Road, Oxford OX2 6TG; 5 Sheffield Terrace, W8 7NG. *Club:* Cavalry and Guards.

ALIBHAI-BROWN, Yasmin; journalist and author; weekly columnist, The Independent, since 1998; Professor (part-time) of Journalism, Middlesex University, since 2013; *b* 10 Dec. 1949; *d* of Kassim Damji and Jena Ramji; *m* (marr. diss.); one *s*; *m* 1990, Colin Brown; one *d*. *Educ:* Makerere Univ., Uganda (BA Hons 1972); MPhil Oxon 1975. Arrived in UK from Uganda, 1972; journalist; contributions to: Guardian; Observer; NY Times; Time mag.; Newsweek; Daily Mail; radio and TV broadcaster. Res. Fellow, IPPR, 1996–2001. Advr to instns on race matters. Pres., Inst. Family Therapy. One-woman show, commnd and dir by RSC, 2005–06, UK and Indian tour, 2007. Visiting Professor in Journalism: Cardiff Univ., 2008; Univ. of Lincoln, 2008; UWE, 2008. Winston Churchill Meml Trust Fellow, 2011. DUniv: Open, 1999; Oxford Brookes, 2004; Hon. Dr Liverpool John Moore's, 2003; DLitt York St John, 2008. Asia Award for achievement in writing, BBC, 1999; Special Award for outstanding contrib. to journalism, CRE, 2000; Media Personality of Year Award, 2000, Award for Journalism, 2004, Ethnic Minority Media Award; Windrush Outstanding Merit Award, 2000; GG2 Leadership and Diversity Award for Media Personality of Year, 2001; George Orwell Prize for political journalism, 2002; Columnist of the Year, Asian Voice Political and Public Life Awards, 2011. *Publications:* No Place Like Home, 1995; After Multiculturalism, 2000; Who Do We Think We Are?, 2001; Mixed Feelings, 2001; Some of My Best Friends Are, 2004; The Settler's Story: a memoir of love, migration and food, 2009; Exotic England, 2013. *Recreations:* theatre, reading, volunteering to assist children in need. *Address:* The Independent, Northcliffe House, 2 Derry Street, W8 5HF. *E:* y.alibhai-brown@independent.co.uk.

AL JABER, Mohamed Bin Issa; Founder and Chairman, MBI Group; *b* Jeddah, 17 Jan. 1959; *m*; one *s* two *d*. Founder and Chairman: Jadawel Internat. Construction and Develt, 1982–; JJW Hotels and Resorts, 1989–; AJWA Gp for Agro and Food Industries, 1992–. UNESCO Special Envoy, 2004–; UN spokesperson for global forums on reinventing govt, 2007–. Founder, MBI Trust at SOAS, 2000; Founder and Chairman: MBI Foundn, 2002–; MBI Al Jaber Foundn (also br. in France); Vice-Chm., Internat. Adv. Bd, 2002–, Mem., Adv. Bd, London Middle East Inst., 2002–, SOAS, Univ. of London. Hon. Fellow: SOAS, Univ. of London, 2002; Corpus Christi Coll., Oxford, 2009; UCL, 2012. Senator, Modul Univ., 2013–. Hon. DLitt Westminster, 2004; Hon. DSc City, 2004. Gold Medal: Arab League Educnl, Cultural and Scientific Orgn, 2007; UNESCO, 2007; City of Vienna, 2009; Islamic Educnl, Cultural and Scientific Orgn, 2012. Medaille d'Or du Tourisme (France), 2005. *Publications:* Yes, the Arabs Can Too, Arabic edn 2009, English edn 2013, French edn 2014, German edn 2015. *Recreations:* poetry, history, reading. *Address:* MBI Group, 78 Wigmore Street, W1U 2SJ. *T:* (020) 7935 5859, *Fax:* (020) 7535 1569.

ALKER, Doug; Chair, since 1980, and Managing Director, since 2001, East Lancashire Deaf Society; Chief Executive, Royal National Institute for Deaf People, 1995–97; *b* 23 Nov. 1940. *Educ:* London Univ. (BSc 1967); Birmingham Univ. (MBA 1993). Analytical Chemist, Pilkington Bros, 1959–64; Exptl Officer, ICI, 1964–85; Researcher, BBC, 1985–87; Royal National Institute for Deaf People: Principal Regl Officer, 1987; Dir, Community Services, 1987–90; Dir, Quality and Res., 1990–94. Member: Nat. Disability Council, 1995–2000; Exec. Cttee, RADAR, 1997–2000; Chair: Fedn of Deaf People, 1997–2001 (Pres., 2001–); BDA, 2002–. Chair, Kings Court (Blackburn) Ltd, 2000–. Ind. Assessor for DETR, 1999–. Hon. Fellow, Univ. of Central Lancashire, 1995. *Address:* Playing Field Cottage, Darwen, Lancs BB3 3PN.

ALKER, Rt Rev. Mgr (John) Stephen, MBE 1997; Pastor and Parish Priest, St Leonhard's International English-speaking Roman Catholic Parish, Frankfurt am Main and St Mary's, Lieberbach, Germany, since 2010; *b* 1 July 1953; *s* of John Alker and Alice Alker (*née* Ashurst). *Educ:* St Joseph's Coll., Upholland, Wigan; St Cuthbert's Coll., Ushaw, Durham; Pontifical N American Coll., Rome (Inst. of Continuing Theol Educn Course, 2009). Ordained priest, Liverpool Archdio., 1978; Assistant Priest: St Joseph's, Leigh, 1978–80; Metropolitan Cath., Liverpool, 1980–83; Chaplain, TA, 1981, Regular Army, 1983–2009, served Germany, NI, Australia, Cyprus, Bosnia, UK; first RC Asst Chaplain Gen., RAChD, 2003–09; Principal RC Chaplain and Vicar Gen. to the Army, 2006–09; Asst Chaplain Gen., HQ Land Comd, later HQ Land Forces, 2006–09. QHC, 2007–09. Prelate of Honour, 2006. KCHS 2010 (KHS 2002). *Recreations:* ornithology, country walks, classical music, ecclesiastical heraldry. *Address:* c/o St Leonhard's International English Speaking Parish, Vilbeler Str. 36, 60313 Frankfurt am Main, Germany. *T:* (69) 283177.

AL KHALIFA, Shaikh Abdul Aziz bin Mubarak; International Media Advisor, Information Affairs Authority, Bahrain; *b* 10 Oct. 1962; *m* 1988, Shaikha Lamees Daij Al Khalifa. *Educ:* Wellington Sch., Som; Newbury Coll. (HND); Amer. Univ. Sch. of Internat. Service, Washington (BA); Inst. for Social and Economic Policy in Middle East, Harvard. Prime Minister's Court, Bahrain: Researcher on Political and Economic Affairs, 1987–90; Asst Dir of Information, 1990–94; acting Dir of Admin and Public Relations, 1994–96; Ambassador for Bahrain to UK, Denmark, Ireland, Holland, Norway and Sweden, 1996–2001; Asst Under Sec. for Policy Co-ordination, 2001, Asst Under Sec. for Co-ordination and Follow-up, 2002, Ministry of Foreign Affairs, Bahrain. *Address:* Information Affairs Authority, PO Box 253, Isa Town, Bahrain.

AL KHALIFA, Shaikh Khalifa bin Abdullah; Secretary General, Supreme Defence Council, Bahrain, and National Security Adviser to the King of Bahrain, since 2011; *b* 4 March 1965; *m* 1989, Shaikha Mayar bint Khalifa Al Khalifa; three *s* one *d*. *Educ:* West Rifaa Sch. for Boys; Huston Tillotson Univ., Texas (BBA); South West Texas State Univ. (MBA). Ministry of Information, Bahrain: Tourism Sector, 1989–96; set up and expanded Foreign Media Affairs, 1996–2002; Asst Under Sec. for Foreign Media Affairs, 2002–06; Chief Exec., Bahrain Radio and TV Corp., 2006–07; Ambassador of Bahrain to the Court of St James's, 2007–08; Hd, Nat. Security Agency, Bahrain, 2008–11. Chm. of regl, nat. and internat. seminars and confs in media field. Shaikh Isa bin Salman Al Khalifa Medal 4th class. *Recreation:* reading about politics and social affairs.

AL-KHALIFA, Shaikh Khalifa bin Ali bin Rashid; Ambassador of Bahrain to the Court of St James's, 2008–11; *b* 1957; *m*; one *s* three *d*. *Educ:* Royal Mil. Coll. of Sci., Shrivenham (BSc Hons Aeronautical Engrg 1979); Southampton Univ. (MSc Aeronautical Engrg 1981); RAF Cranwell (Initial Officers Trng Course with dist. 1982). Joined Bahrain Defence Force, 1976; operational and staff posts, then Dep. Comdr, Bahraini Amiri Air Force, 1982–94 (Air Comd and Staff Course, Maxwell AFB, Ala); Defence Attaché, Washington, 1994–2001; Brig. 2001; Ambassador to USA and Canada, 2001–04; Hd, Nat. Security Agency, Bahrain, 2005–08. Trustee, Bahrain Centre for Strategic, Internat. and Energy Studies, 2011–. *Address:* c/o Embassy of Bahrain, 30 Belgrave Square, SW1X 8QB. *T:* (020) 7201 9170, *Fax:* (020) 7201 9183. *Clubs:* Mark's, Mosimann's, Harry's Bar.

AL-KHALILI, Prof. Jameel S., (Jim), OBE 2008; PhD; FInstP; scientist, author and broadcaster; Professor of Physics and Professor of Public Engagement in Science, University of Surrey, since 2005; *b* Baghdad, 20 Sept. 1962; *s* of Sadik and Jean Al-Khalili; *m* 1986, Julie Frampton; one *s* one *d*. *Educ:* Univ. of Surrey (BSc Hons Physics 1986; PhD 1989). FInstP 2000. Res. Fellow, UCL, 1989–91; University of Surrey: Res. Fellow, 1991–92; Lectr in Physics, 1992–94; Advanced Res. Fellow, 1994–99; Sen. Lectr, 2000–05. Adjunct Prof., Michigan State Univ., 1999–2000. Sen. Advr on Sci. and Technol. to British Council, 2007–. British Association for Advancement of Science, later British Science Association: Trustee, 2006–; Vice Pres., 2008–; Hon. Fellow, 2007; Pres., British Humanist Assoc., 2013–. Presenter: *television* documentaries: The Riddle of Einstein's Brain, 2004; Atom, 2007; Lost Horizons: The Big Bang, 2008; Science and Islam, 2009; The Secret Life of Chaos, 2010; Chemistry: A Volatile History, 2010; Everything and Nothing, 2011; Shock and Awe: The Story of Electricity, 2011; Horizon: Is Nuclear Power Safe, 2012; Horizon: The Search for the Higgs, 2012; Order and Disorder, 2012; Light and Dark, 2013; The Secrets of Quantum Physics, 2014; *radio:* The Secret Scientists, 2009; The Life Scientific, 2011–. Hon. DSc Royal Holloway, 2013. Michael Faraday Medal for Sci. Communication, Royal Soc., 2007; Kelvin Medal for Public Awareness of Physics, Inst. of Physics, 2011. *Publications:* Black Holes, Wormholes and Time Machines, 1999; Nucleus: a trip into the heart of matter, 2001; Quantum: a guide for the perplexed, 2004; (ed) Lecture Notes in Physics: Nuclear Physics with Exotic Beams, vol I 2004, vol II 2006, vol III 2008; Pathfinders: the golden age of Arabic science, 2010; Paradox: the nine greatest enigmas in science, 2012; (with J. McFadden) Life on the Edge: the coming of the age of quantum biology, 2014; contrib. res. papers in jls, newspaper and mag. articles. *Recreations:* reading non-fiction (particularly history and philosophy), hiking, running, cycling, oil painting, playing guitar, following Leeds United FC. *Address:* Department of Physics, University of Surrey, Guildford, Surrey GU2 7XH. *T:* (01483) 686808, *Fax:* (01483) 686781. *E:* j.al-khalili@surrey.ac.uk.

ALKIN, Lawrence Michael; Chairman, Metro Inns Ltd; *b* 16 June 1939; *s* of Henry and Phyllis Alkin. *Educ:* Mill Hill Sch.; University Coll. London (LLM). Sen. Partner, Alkin Colombotti and Partners, 1965–72; Managing Director: Filross Securities, 1972–; Holmes Place Ltd, 1979–96; Jt CEO, Holmes Place PLC, 1997–2000. *Recreations:* fishing (badly), cooking (moderately), dining out (well). *Address:* Flat 101, Block E, Montevetro Building, 100 Battersea Church Road, SW11 3YL.

ALLABY, (John) Michael; author, since 1973; *b* 18 Sept. 1933; *s* of Albert Theodore Allaby and Jessica May Allaby (*née* King); *m* 1957, Ailsa Marthe McGregor; one *s* one *d*. *Educ:* George Dixon Grammar Sch., Birmingham; Birmingham Sch. of Speech Training and Dramatic Art. Left sch. at 15, 1948; clerk, 1949; police cadet, Birmingham City Police, 1950–51; pilot, RAF, 1952–54; actor, 1955–64; Editorial Asst, Soil Assoc., 1964–72; Managing Editor, The Ecologist, 1972–73. *Publications:* The Eco-Activists, 1971; Who Will Eat?, 1972; (with Floyd Allen) Robots Behind the Plow, 1974; Ecology, 1975; (jtly) The Survival Handbook, 1975; Inventing Tomorrow, 1976; World Food Resources: actual and potential, 1977; (with Colin Tudge) Home Farm, 1977; (ed) A Dictionary of the Environment, 1977, 4th edn 1994; Making and Managing a Smallholding, 1979, 2nd edn 1986; Animals that Hunt, 1979; Wildlife of North America, 1979; (with Peter Bunyard) The Politics of Self-Sufficiency, 1980; A Year in the Life of a Field, 1981; (with Peter Crawford) The Curious Cat, 1982; Animal Artisans, 1982; (with James Lovelock) The Great Extinction, 1983; The Food Chain, 1984; (with James Lovelock) The Greening of Mars, 1984; (ed) The Oxford Dictionary of Natural History, 1985; Your Child and the Computer, 1985; (with Jane Burton) Nine Lives, 1985; 2040: our world in the future, 1985; (with Jane Burton) A Dog's Life, 1986; The Woodland Trust Book of British Woodlands, 1986; Ecology Facts, 1986, 2nd edn as Green Facts, 1989; The Ordnance Survey Outdoor Handbook, 1987; (with Jane Burton) A Pony's Tale, 1987; Conservation at Home, 1988; (ed) Thinking Green: an anthology of essential ecological writing, 1989; Guide to Gaia, 1989; Into Harmony with the Planet, 1990; Living in the Greenhouse, 1990; (ed with Ailsa Allaby) The Concise Oxford Dictionary of Earth Sciences, 1991, (ed) 4th edn as Oxford Dictionary of Geology and Earth Sciences, 2013; (ed) The Concise Oxford Dictionary of Zoology, 1991, 3rd edn as Oxford Dictionary of Zoology, 2009; (ed) The Concise Oxford Dictionary of Botany, 1992, 3rd edn as Oxford Dictionary of Plant Sciences, 2012; Elements: water, 1992; Elements: air, 1992; Elements: earth, 1993; Elements: fire, 1993; (with Neil Curtis) Planet Earth: a visual factfinder, 1993; (ed) The Concise Oxford Dictionary of Ecology, 1994, 5th edn as Oxford Dictionary of Ecology, 2015; How the Weather Works, 1995; Facing the Future, 1995; Basics of Environmental Science, 1996, 2nd edn 2000; (with Michael Kent) Collins Pocket Reference Biology, 1996; How it Works: the environment, 1996; Ecosystem: temperate forests, 1999, 2nd edn 2007; Biomes of the World, 9 vols, 1999; DK Guide to Weather, 2000; Plants and Plant Life, 5 vols of 10-vol. series: Plant Ecology, Plants Used By People, Conifers, Flowering Plants - The Monocotyledons, Flowering Plants - The Dicotyledons, 2001; Ecosystem: deserts, 2001, 2nd edn 2007; Megabites: tornadoes and other dramatic weather systems, 2001; (with Derek Gjertsen) Makers of Science, 5 vols, 2001; Encyclopedia of Weather and Climate, 2 vols, 2002, 2nd edn 2007; How it Works: the world's weather, 2002; The Facts on File Weather and Climate Handbook, 2002; (ed with Chris Park) Oxford Dictionary of Environment and Conservation, 2nd edn 2013; Gardener's Dictionary of Science, 2015; Gardener's Guide to Weather and Climate, 2015; *series:* Dangerous Weather: Hurricanes, 1997, 2nd edn 2003, Tornadoes, 1997, 2nd edn 2003, Blizzards, 1997, 2nd edn 2003, Droughts, 1998, 2nd edn 2003, A Chronology of Weather, 1998, 2nd edn 2003, Floods, 1998, 2nd edn 2003, A Change in the Weather, 2003, Fog, Smog, and Poisoned Rain, 2003; Biomes of the Earth: Deserts, 2005, Grasslands, 2005, Temperate Forests, 2005, Tropical Forests, 2005; Countries of the World: India, 2005; Discovering the Earth: Earth Sciences, 2009, Atmosphere, 2009, Oceans, 2009, Ecology, 2009, Animals, 2010, Plants, 2010, Exploration, 2010. *Recreations:* gardening, reading, watching movies. *Address:* Braehead Cottage, Tighnabruaich, Argyll PA21 2ED. *T:* and *Fax:* (01700) 811332. *E:* m.allaby@btinternet.com. *W:* www.michaelallaby.com.

ALLAIN, Prof. Jean-Pierre Charles, MD, PhD; FRCPath, FMedSci; Professor of Transfusion Medicine, University of Cambridge, 1991–2011, now Emeritus; *b* 26 Jan. 1942; *s* of Jacques Louis Allain and Marthe Charlotte (*née* Petitjean); *m* 1st, 1962, DucDung Nguyen (marr. diss.); two *s* two *d*; 2nd, 1978, Helen Lee. *Educ:* Univ. of Paris (MD 1967; PhD 1986; MSc 1995). FRCPath 1992. Asst Prof. of Haematol., Univ. of Paris, 1967–70; Dir, French Red Cross Haemophilia Centre, 1970–77; Head, Coagulation Res. Lab., Nat. Blood Transfusion Centre, Paris, 1977–81; Head, Dept of R&D Plasma Protein Derivatives, Nat. Blood Transfusion Centre, Paris, 1981–86; Dir of Med. Res., Diagnostic Div., Abbott Labs, Chicago, 1986–91; Dir, E Anglian Blood Transfusion Centre, 1991–94. FMedSci 2000. *Publications:* over 300 articles in Nature, N Engl. Jl Med., Lancet, Jl of Clin. Invest., BMJ, Blood, PLoS Medicine, Hepatology, Jl Hepatol., Jl of Infectious Diseases, Transfusion. *Recreations:* tennis, ceramics.

ALLAIN CHAPMAN, Ven. Dr Justine Penelope Heathcote; Archdeacon of Boston, since 2013; *b* Durham, 30 June 1967; *d* of Albert and Eileen Chapman; *m* 1990, Thomas Allain; one *s* three *d*. *Educ:* King's Coll. London (BA Hons 1988; AKC 1988; PGCE 1989; DThMin 2012); Lincoln Theol Coll. (MDiv Nottingham Univ. 1993). Hd of Religious Studies, S Hampstead High Sch., 1989–91; ordained deacon, 1993, priest, 1994; Curate, Christ Church and St Paul, Forest Hill, 1993–96; Vicar, St Paul, Clapham, 1996–2004; Dir of Mission and Pastoral Studies, 2004–13, Vice-Principal, 2007–13, SE Inst. for Theol Educn. *Publications:* Resilient Pastors: the role of adversity in healing and growth, 2012. *Recreations:* family, Norfolk, detective fiction, yoga, music. *Address:* Archdeacon's House, Castle Hill, Welbourn, Lincoln LN5 0NF. *T:* (01400) 273335. *E:* archdeacon.boston@lincoln.anglican.org.

ALLAM, Peter John; Architect Principal in private practice of Peter Allam, Chartered Architect, Dollar and Edinburgh, 1964–68, 1971–78 and 1981–2008; *b* 17 June 1927; *er s* of late Leslie Francis Allam and Annette Farquharson (*née* Lawson); *m* 1961, Pamela Mackie Haynes; two *d*. *Educ:* Royal High Sch., Edinburgh; Glasgow Sch. of Architecture. War service, 1944–48, Far East; commnd in Seaforth Highlanders, 1946. Architectural trng, 1948–53. Bahrain Petroleum Co., Engrg Div., 1954–55; Asst in private architectural practices, 1956–64; Partner in private practice of Haswell-Smith & Partners, Edinburgh, 1978–79; Director, Saltire Soc., 1968–70; Dir of Sales, Smith & Wellstood Ltd, Manufg ironfounders, 1979–81. ARIBA 1964; FRIAS 1985 (Associate, 1964). VMSM 1999. *Recreations:* trying to keep up with all my grandchildren and their modern technology, also some drawing and painting. *Address:* 15 St Thomas' Place, Stirling FK7 9LX. *T:* 07803 205620.

ALLAM, Roger William; actor; *b* 26 Oct. 1953; *s* of Rev. William Sydney Allam and Kathleen Allam (*née* Service); partner, Rebecca Saire; two *s*. *Educ:* Christ's Hosp.; Univ. of Manchester (BA). With Royal Shakespeare Co., 1981–, Associate Artist, 1990–: rôles include: Mercutio in Romeo and Juliet, Oberon in Midsummer Night's Dream, 1984; Javert in Les Misérables, transf. Palace Th., 1985; Brutus in Julius Caesar, Duke Vincentio in Measure for Measure, Toby Belch in Twelfth Night, 1987; Benedick in Much Ado About Nothing, 1990; title rôle in Macbeth, 1996; National Theatre, 1999–: rôles include: Graves in Money (Olivier Award for Best Supporting Actor, 2000), Ulysses in Troilus and Cressida (Clarence Derwent Award), Bassov in Summerfolk, 1999; Hitler in Albert Speer, Lophakin in The Cherry Orchard, 2000; Willy Brandt in Democracy, 2003, transf. Wyndham's, 2004; Reinhardt in Afterlife, 2008; West End includes: City of Angels, Prince of Wales, 1993; Arcadia, Haymarket, 1994; Importance of Being Earnest, Old Vic, 1995; Art, Wyndham's, 1997; Privates on Parade, Donmar, 2001 (Olivier Award for Best Actor, 2002); Aladdin, Old Vic, 2004, 2005; Boeing-Boeing, Comedy, 2007; La Cage aux Folles, Playhouse, 2009; Henry IV Parts I and II, Shakespeare's Globe, 2010 (Olivier Award for Best Actor, 2011); The Tempest, Shakespeare's Globe, 2013; other performances include: Blackbird, Edinburgh Fest., 2005, transf. Albery, 2006; Pravda, Chichester Festival Th., 2006; God of Carnage, Th. Royal Bath, 2009; Uncle Vanya, Chichester Festival Th., 2012; Seminar, Hampstead Th., 2014; *films* include: A Cock & Bull Story, 2005; V for Vendetta, The Wind That Shakes the Barley, The Queen, 2006; Speed Racer, 2008; Tamara Drewe, 2010 (Peter Sellers Award for Comedy, Evening Standard British Film Awards, 2011); The Iron Lady, The Angel's Share, 2011; The Book Thief, 2014; Mr Holmes, A Royal Night Out, 2015; *television* includes: The Thick of It (series), 2007–12; Endeavour, 2012, 2013, 2014; Parades End (series), 2012. *Publications:* contrib. chapters to Players of Shakespeare, vol. II and vol. III. *Recreations:* playing and listening to music, cooking. *Address:* c/o Claire Maroussas, Independent Talent Group Ltd, 40 Whitfield Street, W1T 2RH. *T:* (020) 7636 6565, *Fax:* (020) 7323 9867. *Club:* 2 Brydges.

ALLAN; *see* Havelock-Allan.

ALLAN, family name of **Baron Allan of Hallam**.

ALLAN OF HALLAM, Baron *cr* 2010 (Life Peer), of Ecclesall in the County of South Yorkshire; **Richard Beecroft Allan;** Director of European Public Policy, Facebook, since 2009; *b* 11 Feb. 1966; *s* of John and Elizabeth Allan; *m* 1991, Louise Maria Netley (marr. diss. 2001); one *d*. *Educ:* Pembroke Coll., Cambridge (BA Hons Archaeology and Anthropology); Bristol Poly. (MSc IT). Archaeologist, 1988–90; NHS Computer Manager, 1991–97. MP (Lib Dem) Sheffield, Hallam, 1997–2005. Hd of Govt Relns, UK and Ireland, Cisco Systems, 2005–09. Chm., Power of Inf. Task Force, 2008–. *Recreation:* visiting sites of historical interest and natural beauty. *E:* richard@richardallan.org.uk.

ALLAN, Dr Alasdair James; Member (SNP) Na h-Eileanan an Iar, Scottish Parliament, since 2011 (Western Isles, 2007–11); Minister for Learning, Science and Scotland's Languages (formerly Learning and Skills), since 2011; *b* Edinburgh, 6 May 1971; *s* of John H. Allan and Christine M. Allan. *Educ:* Selkirk High Sch.; Glasgow Univ. (MA Scottish Lang. and Lit.); Aberdeen Univ. (PhD Scots Lang. 1998). Sen. Vice Pres., Students' Rep. Council, Glasgow Univ., 1991–92. Teaching asst, English Dept, Aberdeen Univ., 1995–97; researcher, SNP HQ, 1998–99; Parliamentary Assistant: to Michael Russell, MSP, 1999–2002; to Alex Salmond, MP, 2002–04; Policy and Parly Affairs Manager, Carers Scotland, 2004–05; Sen. Media Relns Officer, Ch of Scotland, 2005–06; Parly Asst to Angus MacNeil, MP, 2006–07. Nat. Sec., SNP, 2003–06. Vice-Pres., Scots Lang. Soc., 1996–99. *Publications:* Talking Independence, 2001. *Recreations:* campaigning for independence, cutting peat, singing in local Gaelic choir (Mem., Back Gaelic Choir, Isle of Lewis), learning Norwegian. *Address:* (office) 31 Bayhead, Stornoway, Isle of Lewis HS1 2DU. *T:* (01851) 702272, *Fax:* (01851) 701767. *E:* alasdair.allan.msp@scottish.parliament.uk. *W:* www.alasdairallan.net.

ALLAN, Sir Alexander (Claud Stuart), (Sir Alex), KCB 2012; Independent Adviser to Prime Minister on Ministers' Interests, since 2011; *b* 9 Feb. 1951; *s* of Lord Allan of Kilmahew, DSO, OBE and of Maureen (*née* Stuart Clark); *m* 1st, 1978, Katie Christine Clemson (*d* 2007); 2nd, 2012, Sarah Stacey. *Educ:* Harrow Sch.; Clare College, Cambridge; University College London (MSc). HM Customs and Excise, 1973–76; HM Treasury, 1976–92; secondments in Australia, 1983–84; Principal Private Sec. to Chancellor of the Exchequer, 1986–89; Under Sec. (Internat. Finance), 1989–90; Under Sec. (Gen. Expenditure Policy), 1990–92; Principal Private Sec. to PM, 1992–97; High Comr, Australia, 1997–99; UK Govt e-envoy, 1999–2000; Perm. Sec., DCA, subseq. MoJ, 2004–07; Chm., Jt Intelligence Cttee and Hd of Intelligence Assessment, Cabinet Office, 2007–11. Mem., QC Selection Panel, 2013–. Mem., Premier's Science Council, WA, 2001–04. Mem., Senate, Univ. of WA, 2002–04. Mem., Royal S Beach Cycling Assoc., WA, 1983–. Trustee, Treloar Trust, 2010–. *Recreations:* Grateful Dead music, sailing, computers. *E:* alex@whitegum.com. *Club:* Royal Ocean Racing.

ALLAN, (Christopher) David; QC 1995; a Recorder, since 1993; a Deputy High Court Judge, since 2007; *b* 5 April 1952; *s* of Herbert Roy Allan and Joan (*née* Womersly); *m* 1977, Lynne Margaret Hosking; one *s* three *d*. *Educ:* Teignmouth Grammar Sch.; Manchester Univ. (LLB). Called to the Bar, Gray's Inn, 1974; Mem., Northern Circuit, 1975–. *Recreations:* tennis, theatre, walking. *Address:* 12 Byrom Street, Manchester M3 4PP. *T:* (0161) 829 2100.

ALLAN, Christopher John; HM Diplomatic Service; Ambassador to Uzbekistan, since 2015; *b* Edinburgh, 18 Dec. 1975; *s* of John Richard Allan and Margaret Anne Allan; *m* 2004, Alice Mary Edith; two *d*. *Educ:* George Watson's Coll., Edinburgh; Pembroke Coll., Cambridge (BA Natural Scis and Social and Pol Scis 1996); London Sch. of Econs and Pol Sci. (MSc Envmt and Develt). Joined FCO, 2000; First Sec., Energy and Envmt, Tokyo, 2003–06; Hd, Nuclear and Missile Defence Team, FCO, 2007–08; Dep. Hd, 2009, Hd, 2009–10, S Asia Gp, FCO; Dep. Hd of Mission, Addis Ababa, 2011–14. *Recreations:* mountain walking, cycling, bridge, music. *Address:* c/o Foreign and Commonwealth Office, King Charles Street, SW1A 2AH.

ALLAN, Prof. Cliff Charles; Vice-Chancellor, Birmingham City University, since 2012; *b* Tynemouth, 20 Feb. 1959; *s* of James and Irene Allan; *m* 1988, Alison Francis; one *s* one *d*. *Educ:* Allerton Grange High Sch., Leeds; Coventry Poly. (BA Hons Modern Studies 1981); Univ. of Birmingham (MA W African Studies 1982); Univ. of Bristol (MA Res. and Professional Studies in Educn 2007). Hd, Regl Activities (S), ActionAid, 1985–89; Sen. Prog. Officer, PCFC, 1989–93; Mgt Consultant, JM Consulting, 1993; Principal Policy Officer, 1993–96, Hd, Teaching and Learning, 1996–2000, HEFCE; Dir, Learning and Teaching Support Network, 2000–04; Dep. CEO, Higher Educn Acad., 2004–07; Deputy Vice-Chancellor: Teesside Univ., 2007–09; Sheffield Hallam Univ., 2010–12. FRSA. *Recreations:* swimming, cycling, walking, cinema, Leeds United. *Address:* Vice-Chancellor's Office, Birmingham City University, City North Campus, Perry Barr, Birmingham B42 2SU. *T:* (0121) 331 5555. *E:* cliff.allan@bcu.ac.uk.

ALLAN, David; *see* Allan, C. D.

ALLAN, Diana Rosemary, (Mrs R. B. Allan); *see* Cotton, D. R.

ALLAN, Douglas; *see* Allan, J. D.

ALLAN, Douglas George; freelance wildlife and documentary cameraman, since 1984; Director, Tartan Dragon Ltd, since 2002; *b* Dunfermline, 17 July 1951; *s* of Morris and Betty Allan; *m* 1st, 1985, Elisabeth Smith (marr. diss. 2000); one *s*; 2nd, 2000, Sue Flood (marr. diss. 2011). *Educ:* Dunfermline High Sch.; Univ. of Stirling (BSc Hons Biol. 1973). Pearl diver, 1974; res. diver, 1974; dive instructor, 1975; diver, scientist, 1976–84, Base Comdr, 1983, British Antarctic Survey. Live tour, In the Company of Giants, 2014. Fellow, NY Explorer's Soc., 2007; Hon. FRPS 2012; Hon. FRSGS 2015; Hon. Fellow, Falmouth Univ., 2014. DUniv Stirling, 2007; Hon. DA Edinburgh Napier, 2009; Hon. DSc St Andrews, 2010. Cherry Kearton Photographic Award, RGS, 1993; BAFTA Awards for Cinematography: Life in the Freezer, 1993; Wildlife Special, 1997; The Blue Planet, 2002; Human Planet, 2011; Emmy Awards for Cinematography, 1994, 1995, 2002, 2007, 2010, 2012, 2014. Fuchs Medal, British Antarctic Survey, 1982; Polar Medal, 1983, and Bar, 2012. *Publications:* Freeze Frame: a wildlife cameraman's adventures on ice, 2012. *Recreations:* travelling slowly, reading, meeting and talking with unknown people. *Address:* 13 Rockleaze Court, Rockleaze Avenue, Bristol BS9 1NN. *T:* 07876 032608; c/o Jo Sarsby Management, 58 St Johns Road, Clifton, Bristol BS8 2HG. *T:* (0117) 927 9423. *E:* jo@josarsby.com. *W:* www.dougallan.com, www.twitter.com/dougallancamera.

ALLAN, Gary James Graham; QC (Scot.) 2007; *b* Aberdeen, 21 Jan. 1958; *s* of Stanley Gibson Allan and Margaret Harrison Allan (*née* Graham); *m* 1986, Margaret Muriel Glass; one *s* one *d*. *Educ:* Aberdeen Grammar Sch.; Univ. of Aberdeen (LLB Hons). Apprentice solicitor, McGrigor Donald and Co., Glasgow, 1980–82; Hughes Dowdall, Glasgow: Solicitor, 1982–86; Partner, 1986–93; admitted Faculty of Advocates, 1994; in practice at Scottish Bar; Senior Advocate Depute (Crown Counsel), 2007–11. Appeal Chm., Judicial Panel, Scottish FA, 2011–. *Recreations:* watching sport, music, reading, food and drink with friends, the pursuit of opportunities to do absolutely nothing. *Address:* Advocates Library, Parliament House, Edinburgh EH1 1RF. *T:* (0131) 226 5071. *E:* gary.allan@advocates.org.uk.

ALLAN, George Alexander, MA; Headmaster, Robert Gordon's College, Aberdeen, 1978–96; *b* 3 Feb. 1936; *s* of William Allan and Janet Peters (*née* Watt); *m* 1962, Anne Violet Veevers; two *s*. *Educ:* Daniel Stewart's Coll., Edinburgh; Edinburgh Univ. (MA 1st Cl. Hons Classics; Bruce of Grangehill Scholar, 1957). Classics Master, Glasgow Acad., 1958–60; Daniel Stewart's College: Classics Master, 1960–63; Head of Classics, 1963–73; Housemaster, 1966–73; Schoolmaster Fellow, Corpus Christi Coll., Cambridge, 1972; Dep. Headmaster, Robert Gordon's Coll., 1973–77. Headmasters' Conference: Sec., 1980–86, Chm., 1988, 1989, Scottish Div.; Mem. Cttee, 1982, 1983; Mem., ISIS Scotland Cttee, 1984–93; Council Mem., Scottish Council of Ind. Schs, 1988–96, 1997–2002. Dir, Edinburgh Acad., 1996–2003; Governor: Welbeck Coll., 1980–89; Longridge Towers Sch., 2004–08. Mem., Scottish Adv. Cttee, ICRF, 1996–97. *Recreations:* gardening, music. *Address:* Maxwiel, 5 Abbey View, Kelso TD5 8HX. *T:* (01573) 225128.
See also T. E. D. Allan.

ALLAN, James Nicholas, CMG 1989; CBE 1976; HM Diplomatic Service, retired; *b* 22 May 1932; *s* of late Morris Edward Allan and Joan Bach; *m* 1961, Helena Susara Crouse (*d* 2001); one *s* one *d*. *Educ:* Gresham's Sch.; London Sch. of Economics (BSc (Econ)). HM Forces, 1950–53. Asst Principal, CRO, 1956–58; Third, later Second Sec., Cape Town/Pretoria, 1958–59; Private Sec. to Parly Under-Sec., 1959–61; First Secretary: Freetown, 1961–64; Nicosia, 1964; CRO, later FCO, 1964–68; Head of Chancery, Peking, 1969–71; Luxembourg, 1971–73; Counsellor, seconded to Northern Ireland Office, Belfast, 1973–75; Counsellor, FCO, 1976; Head of Overseas Inf. Dept, FCO, 1978–81 (Governor's Staff, Salisbury, Dec. 1979–March 1980); High Comr in Mauritius, 1981–85, concurrently Ambassador (non-resident) to the Comoros, 1984–85; Ambassador to Mozambique, 1986–89; Sen. Directing Staff, RCDS, 1989–92. Mem., Commonwealth Observer Gp, S African elecns, 1994. *Address:* 7 The Orchard, SE3 0QS. *Club:* Athenæum.
See also Baron Bach.

ALLAN, Prof. James Wilson, DPhil; Professor of Eastern Art, University of Oxford, 1996–2012, now Emeritus; Fellow of St Cross College, Oxford, 1990–2005, now Emeritus; *b* 5 May 1945; *s* of John Bellerby Allan and Evelyn Mary Allan; *m* 1970, Jennifer Robin Hawksworth; two *s* two *d*. *Educ:* Marlborough Coll.; St Edmund Hall, Oxford (MA 1966; DPhil 1976). Ashmolean Museum: Asst Keeper, 1966–88, Sen. Asst Keeper, 1988–91, Keeper, 1991–2005, Eastern Art Dept; Dir, Ashmolean Inter-Faith Exhibitions Service, 2005–06. *Publications:* Medieval Middle Eastern Pottery, 1971; Persian Metal Technology 700–1300 AD, 1978; Islamic Metalwork: the Nuhad Es-Said Collection, 1982; Nishapur: metalwork of the early Islamic period, 1982; Metalwork of the Islamic World: the Aron Collection, 1986; (ed) Creswell: A Short Account of Early Muslim Architecture, 1989; (with B. Gilmour) Persian Steel: the Tanavoli Collection, 2000; The Art and Architecture of Twelver Shi'ism: Iraq, Iran and the Indian Sub-Continent, 2012. *Recreations:* music, ornithology, walking, travel.

ALLAN, (John) Douglas, OBE 2006; Sheriff of Lothian and Borders at Edinburgh, 2000–08; *b* 2 Oct. 1941; *s* of late Robert Taylor Allan and Christina Helen Blythe Reid or Allan; *m* 1966, Helen Elizabeth Jean Aiton or Allan; one *s* one *d*. *Educ:* George Watson's Coll.; Edinburgh Univ. (BL); Napier Coll., Edinburgh (DMS). Solicitor and Notary Public. Solicitor, 1963–67; Depute Procurator Fiscal, 1967–71; Sen. Legal Asst, Crown Office, 1971–76; Asst Procurator Fiscal, Glasgow, 1976–77; Sen. Asst Procurator Fiscal, Glasgow, 1978–79; Asst Solicitor, Crown Office, 1979–83; Regl Procurator Fiscal for Lothian and Borders and Procurator Fiscal for Edinburgh, 1983–88; Sheriff of South Strathclyde, Dumfries and Galloway at Lanark, 1988–2000. Bd Mem., Scottish Children's Reporter Admin, 1995–2003 (Dep. Chm., 2002–03); Mem., Judicial Appts Bd for Scotland, 2002–08. Chm., Judicial Commn, Gen. Assembly of C of S, 1998–2003 (Mem., 2009–). Pres., Sheriffs' Assoc., 2000–02 (Vice Pres., 1997–2000; Sec., 1991–97); Regl Vice-Pres., Commonwealth Magistrates' and Judges' Assoc., 2003–09 (Mem., Council, 2000–03, 2009–). Chm., Exec. Cttee, Scottish Council, 2009–13, Vice-Pres., SE Scotland Reg., 2014–, Scout Assoc. *Recreations:* youth work, church work, walking. *Address:* Minard, 80 Greenbank Crescent, Edinburgh EH10 5SW. *T:* (0131) 447 2593. *E:* jdouglasallan@lumison.co.uk.

ALLAN, John Murray, CBE 2005; Chairman: Care UK, since 2010; Barratt Developments, since 2014; Tesco plc, since 2015; *b* 20 Aug. 1948; *s* of Archibald John and Anna Allan; *m* 1st, 1970, Ewa Gaczol (marr. diss. 1998); two *d*; 2nd, 1999, Carole Thomas. *Educ:* Edinburgh Univ. (BSc Hons Mathematical Sci.). Brand Manager, Lever Bros, 1970–73; Mkting Manager, Bristol Myers, 1973–77; Fine Fare: Mkting Dir, 1977–83; Dir, 1980; Mkting and Buying Dir, 1983–84; Dir and Gen. Manager, 1984–85; BET: Divl Chm., 1985–87; Dir, 1987–94; Chief Exec., Ocean Gp, later Exel plc, 1994–2005; Chief Exec., DHL Logistics, 2006–07; Chief Financial Officer, Deutsche Post World Net, 2007–09 (Mem., Mgt Bd, 2006–09). Chm., CBI Transport Policy Cttee, 1998–2001; Mem., CBI President's Cttee, 2001–. Chm., Dixons Retail (formerly DSG internat.) plc, 2009–14; Co-Dep. Chm. and Sen. Ind. Dir, Dixons Carphone plc, 2014–15; Chm., Worldpay, 2011–15; non-executive Director: Wolseley plc, 1999–2004; PHS plc, 2001–05; 3i, 2009–11; Royal Mail Gp, 2013–15. Chm., Freight Forwarders Europe, 2006–07 (Vice Chm., 2002–06). Chm., Mkting Soc. of GB, 1983–84. Mem., Internat. Adv. Cttee, Singapore Economic Develt Bd, 2002–07. Trustee, Univ. of Edinburgh Develt Trusts, 1991–2000; Mem., Univ. of Edinburgh Campaign Bd, 2000–. FInstD 1986 (Mem. Council, 1991–99); CCMI (CIMgt 1995). FRSA 1995. *Recreations:* reading, conversation, history. *Address:* Tesco plc, New Tesco House, Delamare Road, Cheshunt, Herts EN8 9SL.

ALLAN, Keith Rennie; HM Diplomatic Service; Consul General, St Petersburg, since 2013; *b* 25 Aug. 1968; *m* 1996, Marja Harriette Medendorp; one *s* two *d*. *Educ:* Bannerman High Sch., Glasgow. MoD 1986–88; entered FCO, 1988; Botswana, 1990–93; worldwide floater duties, 1993–95; Counter Terrorism Policy Dept, FCO, 1996–97; Dep. Hd of Mission, Uzbekistan, 1997–2000; Hd, Central NW Eur. Dept, FCO, 2000–02; Consul, Kabul, 2002; Dep. Dir, Africa and ME, UK Trade and Investment, 2002–03; Dep. High Comr, Trinidad and Tobago, 2003–06; Consul Gen., Miami, 2006–09; Ambassador to Turkmenistan, 2010–13. *Address:* c/o Foreign and Commonwealth Office, King Charles Street, SW1A 2AH.

ALLAN, Lucy; MP (C) Telford, since 2015; *b* Cheltenham, 2 Oct. 1964; *m* Robin; one *s*. *Educ:* Durham Univ. (BA Hons Anthropol. 1986); Kingston Univ. (LLM Employment Law 2006). CA 1992. Insolvency Manager, Price Waterhouse, 1987–94; Mercury Asset Mgt plc, 1994–95; De La Rue plc, 1995–97; Hd, Investment Trusts, Gartmore Investment, 1997–2001; Dir, Investment Trust Team, UBS Warburg, 2001–02; Hd, Investment Trusts, First State Investment, 2002–04; freelance employment law advr, Workplacelaw Ltd, 2004–. Mem. (C) Wandsworth LBC, 2006–12. *Address:* House of Commons, SW1A 0AA.

ALLAN, Timothy Edward Douglas; Chief Executive, Unicorn Property Group, since 2006; *b* Edinburgh, 5 June 1966; *s* of George Alexander Allan, *qv*; *m* 1994, Kim Cowan; two *d*. *Educ:* Robert Gordon's Coll., Aberdeen; Univ. of St Andrews (MA Hist. 1988); Royal Mil. Acad. Sandhurst. Officer, RTR, British Army, 1988–98; Equerry to the Duke of York, 1996–98; Vice Pres., Citigroup Private Bank, 1998–2003; Dir, UBS Wealth Mgt, 2003–06. Non-exec. Dir, Motor Fuel Gp, 2011–. Pres., Dundee and Angus Chamber of Commerce, 2014–. Dir, 2003–09, Chm., 2006–09, Young Enterprise Scotland; Mem. Cttee, Big Lottery Fund, Scotland, 2007–14; Vice Chm., V&A Mus. of Design Campaign, 2011–. FRSA 2010. Queen's Award for Enterprise Promotion, 2010. *Recreations:* field sports, theatre, wine, our farm, holding horses and ponies under instructions from my family. *Address:* Unicorn Property Group, DundeeOne, 5 West Victoria Dock Road, Dundee DD1 3JT. *T:* (01382) 224555. *E:* tallan@unicornpropertygroup.com. *Clubs:* Cavalry and Guards; Kate Kennedy (St Andrews).

ALLAN, Timothy Neil; Managing Director, Portland, since 2001. *Educ:* Royal Grammar Sch., Guildford; Godalming Sixth Form Coll.; Pembroke Coll., Cambridge (BA 1992); INSEAD (MBA). Researcher to Tony Blair, MP, 1992–94; producer, A Week in Politics, 1994; Press Officer to Rt Hon. Tony Blair, MP, Leader of the Opposition, 1994–97; Dep. Press Sec., 10 Downing St, 1997–98; Dir, Corporate Communications, BSkyB plc, 1998–2000. *Recreations:* golf, ski-ing. *Address:* Portland, 1 Red Lion Court, EC4A 3EB. *T:* (020) 7842 0110. *E:* Tim.Allan@portland-communications.com. *Clubs:* Oxford & Cambridge, Soho House.

ALLAN, William Roderick Buchanan; formerly Arts Consultant to United Technologies Corporation, working with Tate Gallery, National Portrait Gallery and National Maritime Museum; *b* 11 Sept. 1945; *s* of James Buchanan Allan and Mildred Pattenden; *m* 1973, Gillian Gail Colgan (*d* 2004); two *s*. *Educ:* Stowe; Trinity Coll., Cambridge (MA Hons History, 1970). Joined staff of The Connoisseur, 1972, Editor 1976–80; Editorial Consultant to Omnific, 1980–83. Author of seven radio plays with nineteenth century historical themes. *Publications:* contrib. to several books dealing with British history; contrib. to History Today, The Connoisseur, and Antique Collector. *Recreations:* military history, cooking. *Address:* 52 Jamieson House, Edgar Road, Hounslow, Middlesex TW4 5QH.

ALLARD, Christian; Member (SNP) Scotland North East, Scottish Parliament, since May 2013; *b* Dijon, France, 31 March 1964; *s* of Maurice and Solange Allard; *m* Jacqueline Kerrigan (*d* 2000); three *d*. *Educ:* Lycée Montchapet, Dijon. With STEF-TFE (seafood haulage), 1982–93, Scottish Develt Manager, 1987–93; Seafood Export Manager, Charles & Caie (seafood export), 1994–2013. *Recreations:* campaigning for an independent Scotland, family, swimming. *Address:* Scottish Parliament, Edinburgh EH99 1SP. *T:* (0131) 348 5764. *E:* christian.allard.msp@scottish.parliament.uk.

ALLARDYCE, Samuel; Manager, West Ham United Football Club, 2011–15; *b* Dudley, 19 Oct. 1954; *s* of Robert Allardyce and Mary Agnes Maxwell Allardyce; *m* 1974, Lynne Ward; one *s* one *d*. *Educ:* Wren's Nest Comp. Sch., Dudley; St Helen's Coll. UEFA Pro Licence 2005. Football player for: Bolton Wanderers, 1973–80; Sunderland, 1980–81; Millwall, 1981–83; Tampa Bay Rowdies, 1983; Coventry City, 1983–84; Huddersfield Town, 1984–85; Bolton Wanderers, 1985–86; Preston North End, 1986–89; West Bromwich Albion, 1989–91; player and Manager, Limerick, 1991–92; Coach and Asst Manager, then Manager, Preston North End, 1992; Manager: Blackpool, 1994–96; Notts County, 1997–99; Bolton Wanderers, 1999–2007; Newcastle United, 2007–08; Blackburn Rovers, 2008–10. Mem. Cttee, League Managers Assoc., 1997–. Patron, Prince's Trust, 2004–. Hon. Dr Bolton, 2010. *Recreations:* golf, tennis, food and wine.

ALLAS, Tera; independent strategic and economic adviser, since 2014; *b* Finland, 1968; *m* 1992, Petri Allas; one *s* one *d*. *Educ:* Helsinki Univ. of Technol. (MSc Technol./Industrial Econs); INSEAD (MBA). Consultant, McKinsey & Co., Inc., 1992–2004; Chief Energy Economist, DTI, then BERR, later DECC, 2004–09; Dir, Transport Analysis and Econs, and Chief Economist, DfT, 2009–10; Dir Gen., Strategy, Analysis and Better Regulation (formerly Economics, Strategy and Better Regulation), and Dep. Hd, Govt Economic Service, 2011–13, Dir Gen., Strategic Advise, 2013–14, BIS. Mem., States of Jersey Fiscal Policy Panel, 2014–. Mem., Sci., Technol. and Innovation Adv. Bd, OECD, 2014–. Observer, non-exec. Bd, Green Investment Bank, 2015–; Mem., Governing Bd, Innovate UK, 2015–. Gov., NIESR, 2014–.

ALLASON, Rupert William Simon; European Editor, World Intelligence Review (formerly Intelligence Quarterly), since 1985; *b* 8 Nov. 1951; *s* of Lt-Col James Harry Allason, OBE and Nuala Elveen Allason; *m* 1st, 1979, Nicole Jane (marr. diss. 1996), *y d* of late M. L. Van Moppes; one *s* one *d*; 2nd, 2012, Nicola Loud. *Educ:* Downside; Grenoble Univ.; London Univ. (external). Special Constable, 1975–82. BBC TV, 1978–82. Contested (C): Kettering, 1979; Battersea, 1983. MP (C) Torbay, 1987–97; contested (C) same seat, 1997. *Publications:* The Branch: A History of the Metropolitan Police Special Branch 1883–1983, 1983; *as Nigel West:* non-fiction: Spy! (with Richard Deacon), 1980; MI5: British Security Service Operations 1909–45, 1981; A Matter of Trust: MI5 1945–72, 1982; MI6: British Secret Intelligence Service Operations 1909–45, 1983; Unreliable Witnesses: espionage myths of World War II, 1984; Garbo (with Juan Pujol), 1985; GCHQ: The Secret Wireless War, 1986; Molehunt, 1987; The Friends: Britain's post-war secret intelligence operations, 1988; Games of Intelligence, 1989; Seven Spies Who Changed the World, 1991; Secret War, 1992; The Illegals, 1993; (ed) Faber Book of Espionage, 1993; (ed) Faber Book of Treachery, 1995; The Secret War for the Falklands, 1997; Counterfeit Spies, 1998; (with Oleg Tsarev) The Crown Jewels: the British secrets at the heart of the KGB archives, 1998; (ed) British Security Co-ordination: the secret history of British Intelligence in the Americas 1940–1945, 1998; Venona: the greatest secret of the Cold War, 1999; The Third Secret, 2000; Mortal Crimes, 2004; (ed) The Guy Liddell Diaries, 2005; Mask, 2005; Historical Dictionary of British Intelligence, 2005; At Her Majesty's Secret Service, 2006; Historical Dictionary of International Intelligence, 2006; Historical Dictionary of Cold War Counterintelligence, 2007; Historical Dictionary of World War II Intelligence, 2008; (with Oleg Tsarev) TRIPLEX, 2009; Historical Dictionary of Naval Intelligence, 2010; (with Madoc Roberts) Snow: the double life of a WW II spy, 2011; Historical Dictionary of Signals Intelligence, 2012; (with I. C. Smith) Historical Dictionary of Chinese Intelligence, 2012; Historical Dictionary of World War I Intelligence, 2014; MI5 and the Great War, 2014; Double Cross in Cairo, 2015; fiction: The Blue List, 1989; Cuban Bluff, 1990; Murder in the Commons, 1992; Murder in the Lords, 1994. *Recreations:* sailing, ski-ing. *Clubs:* White's, Special Forces.

ALLCOCK, Anthony, MBE 1998; Chief Executive, Bowls England, since 2008; *b* Thurmaston, Leics, 11 June 1955; *s* of Ernest Stacey Allcock and Joan Winifred Allcock. *Educ:* Norwich City Coll. Teacher, Millfield Day Centre, Hinckley; Head Teacher; company and managing director. Bowls player: world outdoor champion, 1980, 1984, 1988; world outdoor singles champion, 1992, 1996; world indoor singles champion, 1986, 1987, 2002; world indoor pairs champion, 1986, 1987, 2002, 2003; England Bowls Captain, 1998–2002. Performance Dir, Bowls England, 1998–2002; Chief Exec., English Bowling Assoc., 2003–08. *Publications:* Improve Your Bowls, 1987; Step by Step Guide to Bowls, 1988; End to End, 1989; Bowl to Win, 1994. *Recreation:* dog show exhibitor and international judge. *Address:* Bowls England, Riverside House, Milverton Hill, Royal Leamington Spa, Warwickshire CV32 5HZ. *E:* tony@bowlsengland.com. *Clubs:* Kennel; Cheltenham Bowling, Falcon (Painswick) Bowling.

ALLCOCK, Stephen James; QC 1993; *b* 29 Jan. 1952; *s* of James Allcock and Pamela Eve Allcock. *Educ:* Bristol Grammar Sch.; Jesus Coll., Cambridge (BA). Called to the Bar, Gray's Inn, 1975; private practice, 1977–99; with PricewaterhouseCoopers, 2001–04. *Recreations:* motor cars, business, stock market, piano.

ALLDEN, Alison; Chief Executive, Higher Education Statistics Agency, 2009–15; *b* 3 April 1954; *d* of late Michael Allden and Jean Allden (*née* Reynolds); *m* 1989, David McCutcheon (*d* 2004); one *s* one *d*. *Educ:* Sch. of St Helen and St Katharine, Abingdon; Univ. of Bristol (BA Hons 1976); London Sch. of Econs (MSc Dist. 1988). MCIfA (MIFA 1985); MBCS 1988, FBCS 2007; MCLIP 1992. Archaeologist, DoE, 1977–82; Co. Archaeologist, Glos CC, 1982–85; Researcher: BM, 1985–89; Nat. Maritime Mus., 1989–91; Hd, IT, CCETSW, 1991–94; Computer Services Manager, Goldsmiths' Coll., Univ. of London, 1994–98; Dir, IT Services, Univ. of Warwick, 1998–2003; Dep. Registrar, Librarian and Dir of Inf. Services, Univ. of Bristol, 2003–09. Member: Res. Resources Bd, ESRC, 2002–05; JISC Bd, HEFC, 2005–12 (Mem., 1998–2011, Chm., 2005–11, JISC sub-cttees); Educn and Trng Forum, BCS, 2007–10. Mem., Bd of Govs, Northumbria Univ., 2011–. Mem., Glos Co. History Trust, 2012–. Trustee and Governor: Sch. of St Helen and St Katharine, Abingdon, 2002–; Badminton Sch., Bristol, 2009–. FRSA 2010. *Publications:* contrib. articles on archaeol., computing and mus. mgt to books and jls. *Recreations:* family, archaeology and culture, life-long learning.

ALLEN OF KENSINGTON, Baron *cr* 2013 (Life Peer), of Kensington in the Royal Borough of Kensington and Chelsea; **Charles Lamb Allen,** Kt 2012; CBE 2003; FCMA; Chairman: Global Radio Group, since 2007; 2 Sisters Food Group, since 2011; ISS A/S, since 2013; Senior Advisor, Goldman Sachs Equity Partners, since 2008; *b* 4 Jan. 1957. *Educ:* Bell Coll., Hamilton. FCMA 1989. Accountant, British Steel, 1974–79; Dep. Audit Manager, Gallaghers plc, 1979–82; Dir, Management Services, Grandmet Internat. Services Ltd, 1982–85; Gp Man. Dir, Compass Vending, Grandmet Innovations Ltd, 1986–87; Man. Dir, Compass Gp Ltd, 1988–91; Chief Exec., Leisure Div., Granada Gp, 1991–92; Chief Exec., 1992–96, Chm., 1996–2006, Granada TV; Chief Exec., 1994–96, Chm., 1996–2006, LWT; Chief Exec., Granada Gp, 1996–2000; Exec. Chm., Granada Media, subseq. Granada plc, 2000–04; Chief Exec., ITV plc, 2004–06; Chief Advr to Home Office, 2006–08. Chairman: Granada Leisure and Services, 1993–2000; Boxclever, 1994–2000; Tyne Tees TV, 1997–2006; Yorkshire TV, 1997–2006; Anglia TV, 2000–06; Meridian TV, 2000–06; ITV Digital, 2001–02; non-exec. Chm., 2009–10, Exec. Chm., 2010, Advr, 2010–, EMI Music; Dep. Chm., 1994–96, Chm., 1996–2000, GMTV; non-executive Director: Tesco plc, 1999–2010; Endemol, 2008–14; Virgin Media, 2008–13; Get AS, 2009–14. Dep. Chm., BITC, 1997–2007. Vice-Pres., RTS, 1996–2010. Chairman: British Commonwealth Games, 2000–02; Manchester 2002 Ltd, 2000–02; Vice-Chm., London 2012 Olympic Bid, 2004–05; Dir, London Organising Cttee of the Olympic Games, 2005–13. Chm., Creative Industries Adv. Gp, 1999–2002; Mem., Talent and Enterprise Taskforce Adv. Gp, 2006–. Chairman: Join In Trust Ltd, 2012–; British Red Cross, 2013–14. Mem., Internat. Acad. of Television Arts and Scis, 1996. FRSA. Hon. DBA Manchester Metropolitan, 1999; Hon. DLitt Salford, 2002; Hon. DEcon Southampton Solent, 2006. *Recreations:* visual and performing arts, international travel.

ALLEN, Anthony John, CBE 1994; Chief Executive, and Clerk to Lieutenancy, Royal County of Berkshire, 1986–93; public sector consultant, 1996–2010; *b* 7 Oct. 1939; *s* of late Raymond Houghton Allen and Elsie Zillah Allen; *m* 1st, 1964, Suzanne Myfanwy Davies; two *s*; 2nd, 1987, Helen Leah Graney; two *s*. *Educ:* Battersea Grammar Sch.; Univ. of Exeter (LLB 1961). Admitted Solicitor, 1964. Asst Solicitor: Hendon Bor. Council, 1964–65; Barnet Bor. Council, 1965; Watford Bor. Council, 1966–68; Asst Town Clerk, Coventry CBC, 1968–71; Asst Chief Exec., Lewisham Bor. Council, 1971–72; Solicitor to the Council and Dep. Town Clerk, Southwark Bor. Council, 1972–76; Chief Exec., Hammersmith and Fulham Bor. Council, 1976–86; Chief Exec., NHBC, 1994–96. Lay Inspector of Constabulary, 1997–2001. Non-exec. Dir, BSI, 1992–95. Vice Pres. and Founder Dir, London Youth Games Ltd, 1979–2013 (Vice Chm., 2006–13). Chm., Working Party on Social and Psychol Aspects of Major Disasters (report published, 1990). CCMI (CIMgt 1992). Trustee, W Berks CAB, 2003–09 (Chm., 2005–09). Gov., Newbury Coll., 1997– (Chm., 2003–11); Mem., Govs' Council, Assoc. of Colleges, 2008–13 (non-exec. Dir, 2006–08); non-exec. Dir, AoC Create (formerly Mgt Services), 2008–. *Recreations:* golf, travel. *Address:* Appledown, School Lane, Frilsham, Thatcham, Berks RG18 9XB. *T:* (01635) 201445.

ALLEN, Benedict Colin; author, adventurer; *b* 1 March 1960; *s* of late Colin Allen and Virginia Stafford; *m* 2007, Lenka Flidrova; one *s* one *d*. *Educ:* Bradfield Coll.; Univ. of E Anglia (BSc Hons). Television programmes: Raiders of the Lost Lake, 1995; Great Railway Journeys: Mombasa to the Mts of the Moon, 1996; The Skeleton Coast, 1997; Edge of Blue Heaven, 1998; The Bones of Col Fawcett, 1998; Last of the Medicine Men, 2000; Icedogs, 2002; Adventure for Boys: the Lost Worlds of Rider Haggard, 2006; Traveller's Century, 2008; Unbreakable, 2008; Expedition Africa, 2009. Mem. Council and Trustee, RGS, 2010–13. Patron: Save the Rhino Trust; Envmtl Justice Foundn; Tony Trust. *Publications:* Mad White Giant, 1985; Into the Crocodile Nest, 1987; Hunting the Gugu, 1989; The Proving Grounds, 1991; Through Jaguar Eyes, 1994; (jtly) More Great Railway Journeys, 1996; The Skeleton Coast, 1997; Edge of Blue Heaven, 1998; Last of the Medicine Men, 2000; Faber Book of Exploration, 2002; Into the Abyss, 2006. *Recreations:* writing diary, maintaining fitness, reading biographies at home. *E:* info@benedictallen.com.

ALLEN, Brian, PhD; FSA; Chairman, Hazlitt Group, since 2012; *b* 3 Oct. 1952; *s* of Herbert and Mary Allen; *m* 1978, Katina Michael; two *s*. *Educ:* Univ. of East Anglia (BA 1974); Courtauld Inst. of Art, Univ. of London (MA 1975; PhD 1984). Research Asst, Witt Library, Courtauld Inst. of Art, 1975–76; Paul Mellon Centre for Studies in British Art: Asst Dir and Librarian, 1977–85, Dep. Dir of Studies, 1985–92; Dir of Studies, 1993–2012. Adjunct Prof. of History of Art, Yale Univ., 1993–2012; Vis. Prof. of History of Art, Birkbeck Coll., Univ. of London, 1999–2004. Hon. Sec. and Editor, 1977–85, Chm., 1996–2003, Walpole Soc.; Pres., Johnson Club, 1993–97. Member: Paintings and Sculpture Cttee, Victorian Soc., 1981–84; Bd of Studies in History of Art, Univ. of London, 1986–93; Adv. Cttee, Yale Center for British Art, 1993–2012; Bd, Assoc. of Research Insts in Art History, 1993–2003; Council, Attingham Trust for Study of Country Houses and Collections, 1995–2005; Scientific Cttee, Birth of Modernity exhibn, Fondazione Roma, Rome, 2001–14; Adv. Council, Sotheby's Inst. of Art, 2002–; Adv. Cttee, Getty Res. Inst. Provenance Index, 2002–04; Council, Tate Britain, 2003–08; Internat. Adv. Bd, Ben Uri Gall., London Jewish Mus. of Art, 2003–; Adv. Council, NACF, 2004–12 (Mem. Exec. Cttee, 1998–2004; Chm., 2003–04); Appeal Cttee, Holburne Mus. of Art, Bath, 2005–12 (Trustee, 2000–03; Vice-Chm., Trustees, 2011–); Adv. Cttee, Chantrey Proj., Ashmolean Mus., Oxford, 2006–09; Kettle's Yard Appeal Gp, Univ. of Cambridge, 2009–12; Steering Cttee, Walpole Collection and Houghton Hall exhibn, 2011–13; Nat. Steering Gp, Wright of Derby Campaign, 2011–; Appeals Cttee, Limnerslease Proj., Watts Gall., 2011–; Acceptance in Lieu Panel, Arts Council England, 2012–; Adv. Panel, Nat. Heritage Meml Fund, 2012–; Exhibns and Prog. Cttee, Nat. Horse Racing Mus., Newmarket Heritage Centre, 2014–; Vetting Cttee, Eur. Fine Art Fair Maastricht, 2014–; Res. Adv. Council, NPG, 2014–. Lectures: Opening, Newport Symposium, Newport Histl Soc., USA, 1998; Meml, Christie's/Nat. Art Collections Fund, 2003; Spring, Scottish Nat. Art Collections Fund, 2004; 1st Paul Mellon, World Monuments Fund, 2004; 1st Lunar Soc., 2004. Trustee and Gov., Dr Johnson's House Trust, 1998–2012; Trustee: Foundling Mus., 1998–2007 (Vice Pres., 2010–); The Buildings Book Trust, 2002–11; Strawberry Hill Collections Trust, 2011–; Hermitage Foundn UK, 2011– (Chm., 2012–); NPG, 2012–; British Sporting Art Trust, 2012–; Gov., Gainsborough's House Trust, 2000–05; Member Committee: Friends of Strawberry Hill, 2000–03; American Friends of the Strawberry Hill Trust, 2007–; Co. Sec., UK Friends, Yale Charitable Corp., 2003–12; Mem. Council, Academia Rossica, 2004–. Chm., Judging Panel, Sunday Times/Singer and Friedlander Watercolour Competition, subseq. RWS and Sunday Times Watercolour Competition, 1997–2009; Judge, Garrick/Milne Prize, 2000. Chm., Works of Art Cttee, Garrick Club, 2005–13. Chm., Modern Art Press, 2007–12. Mem., Editorial Adv. Panel, Apollo, 1990–2010; Associate Editor, Oxford DNB, 1997–2004; Member: Panel of Specialist Advrs, Architectural Heritage, 1998–2012; Internat. Adv. Bd, British Art Jl, 1999–2012; Adv. Bd, Visual Culture in Britain, 2000–10; Internat. Adv. Bd, Courtauld Inst. of Art Res. Forum, 2004–10; Editl Bd, English Heritage Histl Rev., 2006–; Advr to Editl Bd, Art and Architecture of Ireland, 2010–12. FSA 2000. Hon. DLitt: Southampton Inst. (Nottingham Trent Univ.), 1999; Birmingham, 2006. *Publications:* Francis Hayman, 1987; (ed.) Towards a Modern Art World, 1995; (ed with L. Dukelskaya) British Art Treasures from Russian Imperial Collections in The Hermitage, 1996; The Paul Mellon Centre for Studies in British Art: a history 1970–2010, 2011; numerous articles in Apollo, Burlington Mag., Jl RSA, etc. *Recreations:* watching association football, opera. *Address:* 7 Frances Road, Windsor, Berks SL4 3AE. *Club:* Garrick.

ALLEN, David Charles Keith, AO 1990; Chairman, Florey Neuroscience Institutes, 2007–12; *b* 3 April 1936; *s* of G. Keith Allen and Dorothy M. Allen; *m* 1st, 1964, Angela Mary Evatt (*d* 2001); two *s* one *d*; 2nd, 2002, Jocelyn Claire Searby. *Educ:* Oundle Sch.; Corpus Christi Coll., Cambridge (MA); Imperial Coll., London (MSc, DIC). Nat. Service, RE, Malaya, 1954–56. Joined Shell International, 1961: geophysicist, in Holland, NZ, Turkey and Nigeria, 1961–71; Chief Geophysicist, Shell Expro, London, 1971–74; Area Geologist, Shell Internat. Petroleum, The Hague, 1974–75; Western Division, Shell BP, Nigeria: Ops Manager, 1975–77; Divl Manager, 1977–79; Chm., NW Shelf LNG Project, 1980–95; Woodside Petroleum Ltd: Exec. Dir, 1980–82; Man. Dir, 1982–96; Chm., CSIRO, 1996–2001. Chm., National Australia Bank Ltd, 2001–04 (Dir, 1992–2004); Director: Metals Manufacturers Ltd, 1990–92; Amcor Ltd, 1996–2005; AGL, 1996–2008; Air Liquide (Aust.), 1997–2008 (Chm., 2005–08). Pres., Aust. Mines and Metals Assoc., 1989–91; Chm., Cambridge Australia Trust, 1996–2002; Director: Aust. Confedn of Commerce and Industry, 1989–91; Earthwatch Australia, 1994–2005. Hon. LLD: Monash, 1994; Melbourne, 2013. Reg Spriggs Gold Medal, 1996, Lewis G. Weeks Gold Medal, 2001, Australian Petroleum Prodn and Exploration Assoc. Centenary Medal (Australia), 2003. *Recreations:* golf, travel, fishing, music. *Clubs:* MCC; Grannies Cricket (UK); Australian, Melbourne (Melbourne).

ALLEN, David James, OBE 2012; Chair, Higher Education Funding Council for Wales, since 2014 (Board Member, since 2008); *b* Cardiff, 11 Feb. 1952; *s* of Aubrey and Joyce Allen; *m* 2008, Elaine Cotter; three *s* two *d*. *Educ:* Barry Comprehensive Sch.; University Coll. of Swansea (BA English 1973); University Coll., Cardiff (MEd 1986). Travel, casual and temp. work, 1973–74; Housing Asst, Vale of Glamorgan BC, 1974–76; Admin. Asst, Univ. of Wales Registry, 1976–80; Asst Registrar, Univ. of Wales Coll. of Medicine, 1980–86; Dep. Dir, Admin. Services, Univ. of Southampton, 1986–91; Sec., Jt Planning and Resources Cttee, Univ. of Wales, 1991–94; Registrar, Univ. of Nottingham, 1994–98; Registrar and Sec., Univ. of Birmingham, 1998–2003; Registrar and Dep. Chief Exec., Univ. of Exeter, 2003–13; Principal Consultant, Perrett Laver Exec. Recruitment, 2013–14. Chair: Assoc. of Univ. Administrators, 1998–2000; Assoc. of Heads of Univ. Admin, 2003–06; Member, Board: Leadership Foundn for Higher Educn, 2005–11; Heart of SW Local Enterprise Partnership, 2011–13. Non-exec. Dir, S Devon Healthcare NHS Foundn Trust, 2011– (Vice-Chair, 2014–). Gov., Exeter Coll., 2014–. Hon. LLD Exeter, 2013. *Recreations:* supporting Exeter Chiefs Rugby team, boating, gardening, walking. *Address:* Higher Education Funding Council for Wales, Linden Court, The Orchards, Ilex Court, Llanishen, Cardiff CF14 5DZ. *T:* (029) 2068 2280. *E:* david.allen@hefcw.ac.uk. *Club:* Lansdowne.

ALLEN, David Kenneth; a Judge of the Upper Tribunal (Immigration and Asylum Chamber) (formerly a Vice-President, Immigration Appeal Tribunal, later a Senior Immigration Judge, Asylum and Immigration Tribunal), since 2000; Legal Member, Special Immigration Appeals

Commission, since 2002; *b* 23 Feb. 1950; *yr s* of late Philip Hernaman Allen and of Dorothy Allen (*née* Modral); *m* 1974, Joan Rosalind, *d* of late Rev. E. N. O. Gray and V. Gray; two *s* one *d*. *Educ:* Loughborough Grammar Sch.; Merton Coll., Oxford (BA Hons Juris; MA); McGill Univ., Montreal (LLM). Called to the Bar, Middle Temple, 1975; Lectr in Law, Inns of Court Sch. of Law, 1974–76; Department of Law, University of Leicester: Lectr, 1976–88; Sen. Lectr, 1988–99; Hd of Dept, 1993–96; Hon. Vis. Fellow, 1999–; in practice, Midland and Oxford Circuit, 1990–99. Immigration Adjudicator, 1989–2000 (pt-time, 1989–99). Vis. Prof., Dalhousie Univ., Halifax, NS, 1982–83. *Publications:* (jtly) Accident Compensation after Pearson, 1979; (jtly) Civil Liability for Defective Premises, 1982; (jtly) Fire, Safety and the Law, 1983, 2nd edn 1990; Misrepresentation, 1988; (jtly) Damages in Tort, 2000; essays; contrib. articles and notes in various jls. *Recreations:* golf, music. *Address:* Upper Tribunal (Immigration and Asylum Chamber), Field House, 15–25 Bream's Buildings, EC4A 1DZ.

See also P. R. H. Allen.

ALLEN, David Paul; Director, Finance (formerly Finance and Shared Services), Department for Business, Innovation and Skills, since 2010; *b* Bracknell, 1 Jan. 1979; *s* of John Allen and Linda Allen; *m* 2007, Nadia Mortali; two *s*. *Educ:* Trinity Catholic High Sch. CIMA 2004. Joined NHS, 1999; Deputy Director of Finance: DWP, 2007–08; DFE, 2008–10. *Recreation:* hill walking. *Address:* Department for Business, Innovation and Skills, 1 Victoria Street, SW1H 0ET. *T:* (020) 7215 5889. *E:* David.p.allen@bis.gsi.gov.uk.

ALLEN, Elizabeth Martin, (Mrs T. Bennett), CBE 2014; MA; Headteacher, Newstead Wood School for Girls, 2001–13; *b* 5 March 1946; *d* of Alfred (David) Trory and Alvena Trory (*née* Fisk); *m* 1st, 1967, Trevor Winston Allen (marr. diss. 1985); two *d*; 2nd, 1999, Terence Bennett; three step *s*. *Educ:* Whitelands Coll. of Educn (Cert Ed Divinity); Birkbeck Coll., Univ. of London (BA Hons English); Inst. of Educn, Univ. of London (MA Curriculum Studies). Hd of Religious Studies, Wallington High Sch. for Girls, 1969–73; 2nd i/c English Dept, St Bede's Ecumenical Sch., Redhill, 1981–84; Hd of English, Court Lodge Sch., Horley, 1984–88; Dep. Headteacher, Carshalton High Sch. for Girls, 1988–93; Headteacher, Altwood C of E Sch., Maidenhead, 1993–2001. FRSA 2000. *Recreations:* literature, the theatre, the garden, adding to the porcelain collection, the children and grandchildren.

ALLEN, Fergus Hamilton, CB 1969; ScD, MA, MAI; FRSL; First Civil Service Commissioner, Civil Service Department, 1974–81; *b* 3 Sept. 1921; *s* of late Charles Winckworth Allen and Marjorie Helen, *d* of F. J. S. Budge; *m* 1947, Margaret Joan, *d* of Prof. M. J. Gorman; two *d*. *Educ:* Newtown Sch., Waterford; Trinity Coll., Dublin. ScD 1966. Asst Engineer, Sir Cyril Kirkpatrick and Partners, 1943–48; Port of London Authority, 1949–52; Asst Director, Hydraulics Research Station, DSIR, 1952–58; Dir of Hydraulics Research, DSIR, 1958–65; Chief Scientific Officer, Cabinet Office, 1965–69; Civil Service Comr, 1969–74; Scientific and Technological Advr, CSD, 1969–72. Consultant, Boyden Internat. Ltd, 1982–86. Instn Civil Engrs: Mem., 1947–57; Fellow, 1957–86; Telford Gold Medal, 1958; Mem. Council, 1962–67, 1968–71. FRSL 2000. *Publications: poems:* The Brown Parrots of Providencia, 1993; Who Goes There?, 1996; Mrs Power Looks Over the Bay, 1999; Gas Light & Coke, 2006; Before Troy, 2010; New & Selected Poems, 2013; papers in technical journals. *Address:* Dundrum, Wantage Road, Streatley, Berks RG8 9LB. *T:* (01491) 873234. *Club:* Athenæum.

See also M. F. Allen.

ALLEN, Prof. Sir Geoffrey, Kt 1979; PhD; FRS 1976; FREng; FRSC; FInstP; Executive Adviser, Kobe Steel Ltd, 1990–2000; Head of Research, Unilever PLC, 1981–90 (Director, Unilever PLC and NV, 1982–90); *b* 29 Oct. 1928; *s* of John James and Marjorie Allen; *m* 1973, Valerie Frances Duckworth; one *d*. *Educ:* Clay Cross Tupton Hall Grammar Sch.; Univ. of Leeds (BSc, PhD). FInstP 1972; FPRI 1974; FRSC 1984; Hon. FIMMM 2002 (FIM 1991); FREng (FEng 1993). Postdoctoral Fellow, Nat. Res. Council, Canada, 1952–54; Lectr, Univ. of Manchester, 1955–65, Prof. of Chemical Physics, 1965–75; Prof. of Polymer Science, 1975–76, Prof. of Chemical Technology, 1976–81, Imperial Coll. of Science and Technology (Fellow, 1986); Vis. Fellow, Robinson Coll., Cambridge, 1980–. Non-exec. Dir, Courtaulds, 1987–93. Member: Science Research Council, 1976, Chm., 1977–81; Royal Commn on Envmtl Pollution, 1991–99; Nat. Consumer Council, 1993–96; Council, Foundn for Sci. and Technol., 1995–2000; President: SCI, 1989–91; PRI, 1990–92; Inst. of Materials, 1994–95. A Vice-Pres., Royal Soc., 1991–93. Chancellor, UEA, 1994–2003. Fellow, St Catherine's Coll., Oxford, 1992. Hon. FUMIST 1993. Hon. FIChemE 1988; Hon. FCGI 1990; Hon. FIM 2002. Hon. MSc Manchester; DUniv Open, 1981; Hon. DSc: Durham, East Anglia, 1984; Bath, Bradford, Loughborough, 1985; Essex, Keele, Leeds, 1986; Cranfield, 1988; Surrey, 1989; Sheffield, 1993; London Metropolitan, 1998. Monbu Daijin Sho, Min. of Sci. and Educn, Japan, 2000. *Publications:* papers on chemical physics of polymers in Trans Faraday Soc., Polymer. *Recreations:* opera, walking, talking. *Address:* Flat 6.12, St Johns Building, 79 Marsham Street, SW1P 4SB.

ALLEN, Graham Leslie; consultant to local authorities on arts, museum and cultural services; *b* 27 May 1949; *s* of William Leslie Allen and Doris Allen (*née* Fraser). *Educ:* Ladywood Comprehensive Sch., Birmingham. Joined Birmingham City Council, 1973; Assistant Director: Museums Services, 1990–94; Mgt Services, 1994–95; acting Head of Museums Services, 1995; Asst Dir (Museums and Arts), 1995–2001; Sen. Asst Dir (Museums and Heritage Projects), 2001–04. Associate: 4ps Consultancy; Invigour Consultancy. Trustee and Director: Thinktank, Birmingham Mus. of Sci. and Industry, 2004–12; Birmingham Mus Trust, 2011–; Trustee: Birmingham Mus Develt Bd, 2010–12; Birmingham Mus Trust, 2011–; Millennium Point Birmingham, 2014–. Chm., Selly Park Residents' Assoc., 2007–10. *Recreations:* the arts, museums, hill walking, gardening, environmental issues. *Address:* 61 Sir Johns Road, Selly Park, Birmingham B29 7EP. *T:* (0121) 472 7953.

ALLEN, Graham William; MP (Lab) Nottingham North, since 1987; *b* 11 Jan. 1953; *s* of William and Edna Allen. *Educ:* Robert Shaw Primary Sch.; Forest Fields Grammar Sch.; City of London Polytechnic; Leeds Univ. Warehouseman, Nottingham, 1971–72; Labour Party Res. Officer, 1978–83; Local Govt Officer, GLC, 1983–84; Trades Union National Co-ordinator, Political Fund Ballots Campaign, 1984–86; Regional Res. and Educn Officer, GMBATU, 1986–87. Opposition front bench spokesman on social security, 1991–92, on democracy and the constitution, 1992–94, on the media, 1994, on transport, 1995, on environment, 1996–97; a Lord Comr of HM Treasury (Govt Whip), 1997–98; Vice Chamberlain of HM Household, 1998–2001. Member: Public Accounts Cttee, 1988–91; Procedure Cttee, 1989–91; 1990 Financial Bill Cttee. Chm., PLP Treasury Cttee, 1990–91. Chm., One Nottingham, 2005–10. *Publications:* Reinventing Democracy, 1995; The Last Prime Minister: being honest about the UK Presidency, 2002; (jtly) Early Intervention: good parents, great kids, better citizens, 2009. *Recreations:* cricket, golf, painting, cooking. *Address:* House of Commons, SW1A 0AA. *T:* (020) 7219 4343. *Clubs:* Strelley Social, Beechdale Community Centre, Bulwell Community Centre, Basford Hall Miners Welfare (Nottingham).

ALLEN, Heidi Suzanne; MP (C) South Cambridgeshire, since 2015; *b* Notton, Yorks; *m* Phil Allen. *Educ:* University Coll. London (BSc Hons Astrophysics 1996); London Business Sch. (Exxon Develt prog.); BPP London (DipLaw 2007). *Address:* House of Commons, SW1A 0AA.

ALLEN, Dame Ingrid (Victoria), (Dame Ingrid Barnes Thompson), DBE 2001 (CBE 1993); DL; MD, DSc, FRCPath, FMedSci; MRIA; Director of Research and Development, Health and Personal Social Services, Northern Ireland, 1997–2001; Professor of Neuropathology, Queen's University of Belfast, 1979–97, now Emerita; *b* 30 July 1932; *d* of Rev. Robert Allen, MA, PhD, DD and Doris V. Allen (*née* Shaw); *m* 1st, 1972, Alan Watson Barnes, MA, ARIBA, Past Pres., RSUA (*d* 1987); 2nd, 1996, Prof. John Thompson (*d* 2010). *Educ:* Ashleigh House, Cheltenham Ladies' College; QUB. House Officer, Royal Victoria Hosp., Belfast, 1957–58; Musgrave Res. Fellow, Tutor in Path., Calvert Res. Fellow, QUB, 1958–64; Sen. Registrar, RVH, 1964–65; Sen. Lectr and Consultant in Neuropathol., QUB/RVH, 1966–78; Reader and Consultant, 1978–79; Head, NI Regional Neuropathol. Service, RVH, Belfast, 1979–97. Vis. Prof., Univ. of Ulster, 1988. Mem., MRC, 1989–92 (Chm., Neuroscis Bd, 1989–92); President: British Neuropathological Soc., 1993–95; Irish Neurological Assoc., 1993–; Vice-President: Internat. Soc. of Neuropathol., 1988–92; RCPath, 1993–96 (Mem. Council and Coll. Cttees, 1990–97). MRIA 1993 (Fellow, 1993). Founder FMedSci 1998. DL Belfast 1989. Mem. editl bds of various scientific jls. *Publications:* (contrib.) Greenfield's Neuropathology, 1984; (contrib.) McAlpine's Multiple Sclerosis, 1990; contribs to jls on neuropathology, demyelinating diseases, neurovirology and neuro-oncology. *Recreations:* doing research on molecular virology and demyelinating diseases, church activities, reading, playing the piano (badly), idling on an island in Donegal. *Address:* 95 Malone Road, Belfast BT9 6SP. *T:* (028) 9066 6662.

ALLEN, Janet Rosemary; Headmistress of Benenden School, Kent, 1976–85; *b* 11 April 1936; *d* of John Algernon Allen and Edna Mary Allen (*née* Orton). *Educ:* Cheltenham Ladies' Coll.; University Coll., Leicester; Hughes Hall, Cambridge. BA London 1958; CertEd Cambridge 1959. Asst Mistress, Howell's Sch., Denbigh, North Wales, 1959: Head of History Dept, 1961; in charge of First Year Sixth Form, 1968; Housemistress, 1968 and 1973–75. Acting Headmistress: Sch. of St Mary and St Anne, Abbots Bromley, Sept.–Dec. 1988; Selwyn Sch., Gloucester, 1989–90. Member: E-SU Scholarship Selection Panel, 1977–85; South East ISIS Cttee, 1978–84; Boarding Schs Assoc. Cttee, 1980–83; GSA Educnl sub-cttee, 1983–85; Gloucester Diocesan Bd of Educn, 1992–97; Mem., Winchcombe Ministry Leadership Team, 1997–2010. Vice-Pres., Women's Career Foundn (formerly Girls of the Realm Guild), 1981–90. Governor: St Catherine's Sch., Bramley, 1986–91; The King's Sch., Worcester, 1996–2008. *Recreations:* music, theatre, pottery, helping to preserve national heritage. *Address:* Bourne Rise, Queen's Square, Winchcombe, Cheltenham, Glos GL54 5LR.

ALLEN, Prof. John Anthony, PhD, DSc; FRSB; FRSE; Professor of Marine Biology, University of London, and Director, University Marine Biological Station, Millport, Isle of Cumbrae, 1976–91, now Professor Emeritus; Hon. Research Fellow, University Marine Biological Station, 1991–2013; *b* 27 May 1926; *s* of George Leonard John Allen and Dorothy Mary Allen; *m* 1st, 1952, Marion Ferguson Crow (marr. diss. 1983); one *s* one *d*; 2nd, 1983, Margaret Porteous Aitken; one adopted step *s*. *Educ:* High Pavement Sch., Nottingham; London Univ. (PhD, DSc). FRSB (FIBiol 1969); FRSE 1968 (Mem. Council, 1970–73). Served in Sherwood Foresters, 1945–46, and RAMC, 1946–48. Asst Lectr, Univ. of Glasgow, 1951–54; John Murray Student, Royal Soc., 1952–54; Lectr/Sen. Lectr in Zool., then Reader in Marine Biol., Univ. of Newcastle upon Tyne, 1954–76. Post Doctoral Fellow and Guest Investigator, Woods Hole Oceanographic Instn, USA, 1965–2005; Vis. Prof., Univ. of Washington, 1968, 1970, 1971; Royal Soc. Vis. Prof., Univ. of West Indies, 1976. Member: NERC, 1977–83 (Chm., Univ. Affairs Cttee, 1978–83); Council, Scottish Marine Biol Assoc., 1977–83; Council, Marine Biol Assoc. UK, 1981–83, 1990–93; Life Sciences Bd, CNAA, 1981–84; Nature Conservancy Council, 1982–90 (Chm., Adv. Cttee Sci., 1984–90); British Nat. Cttee for Oceanic Res., 1988–90. Pres., Malacological Soc. of London, 1982–84. *Publications:* many papers on decapod crustacea and molluscs, and deep sea benthos, in learned jls. *Recreations:* travel, appreciation of gardens, pub-lunching. *Address:* Drialstone, Millport, Isle of Cumbrae, Scotland KA28 0EP. *T:* (01475) 530479.

ALLEN, Prof. John Robert Lawrence, DSc; FRS 1979; Research Professor, Postgraduate Research Institute for Sedimentology, University of Reading, 1993–2001 (Director, 1988–93), Professor Emeritus and Visiting Professor, Department of Archaeology, since 2001; *b* 25 Oct. 1932; *s* of George Eustace Allen and Alice Josephine (*née* Formby); *m* 1959, Jean Mary (*née* Wood); four *s* one *d*. *Educ:* St Philip's Grammar Sch., Birmingham; Univ. of Sheffield (BSc; DSc 1972). Academic career in University of Reading, 1959–, Prof. of Geology, then of Sedimentology, 1972. Mem., NERC, 1992–94. FGS 1955; FSA 1991. Assoc. Mem., Royal Belgian Acad. of Scis, 1991. Hon. LLD Sheffield, 1994; Hon. DSc Reading, 2010. Lyell Medal, Geol Soc., 1980; David Linton Award, British Geomorphological Research Group, 1983; Twenhofel Medal, Soc. of Economic Paleontologists and Mineralogists, 1987; G. K. Warren Prize, Nat. Acad. of Scis, USA, 1990; Sorby Medal, Internat. Assoc. of Sedimentologists, 1994; Penrose Medal, Geol Soc. of Amer., 1996. *Publications:* Current Ripples, 1968; Physical Processes of Sedimentation, 1970; Sedimentary Structures, 1982; Principles of Physical Sedimentology, 1985; numerous contribs to professional jls; several archaeol books on bldgs, monuments and bldg materials. *Recreations:* cooking, music, opera, pottery. *Address:* 17c Whiteknights Road, Reading RG6 7BY. *T:* (0118) 926 4621.

ALLEN, Jonathan Guy; HM Diplomatic Service; Director, National Security, Foreign and Commonwealth Office, since 2015; *b* Nottingham, 5 March 1974; *s* of late Jeremy Allen and of Maggie Allen; *m* 2010, Elizabeth Sleeman; one *s* one *d*. *Educ:* Nottingham High Sch.; St Catharine's Coll., Cambridge (BA 1996; MPhil 1997). Joined FCO, 1997; Second Sec. (Press/Pol), Cyprus, 1999–2002; Hd, Cyprus Section, FCO, 2002–03; Spokesman, UK Perm. Repn to the EU, Brussels, 2003–06; Asst Dir, Internat. Directorate, Home Office, 2006–07; Hd, Res., Inf. and Communications Unit, Office for Security and Counter-Terrorism, 2007–09; Hd, Africa Dept (E Africa, Great Lakes and Strategy), FCO, 2009–11; Ambassador to Bulgaria, 2012–15. *Recreations:* reading, theatre, walking, flying, travelling, Nottingham Forest, Strollers Cricket Club, Yacht Fund, eating and drinking well. *Address:* c/o Foreign and Commonwealth Office, King Charles Street, SW1A 2AH.

ALLEN, Joyce; *see* Moseley, J.

ALLEN, Katherine, (Kate); Director, Amnesty International UK, since 2000; *b* 25 Jan. 1955; *d* of William Allen and Patricia Allen (*née* Middleton). *Educ:* Brasenose Coll., Oxford (BA Hons PPE; Hon. Fellow, 2006). Policy Officer, GLC, 1977–79; Scientific Officer, SSRC, 1979–80; Policy Officer, Haringey LBC, 1980–81; Sen. Policy Officer (Social Services), ACC, 1981–87; Dep. Chief Exec., Refugee Council, 1987–99.

ALLEN, Kay, OBE 2011; consultant on social action; Director, Diverse Advice Ltd consultancy, since 2003; Founding Director: Trading for Good, since 2011; Really Useful Stuff, since 2012; *b* 31 Jan. 1964; *d* of Frank Garside Allen and Gladys Allen. *Educ:* Oldham Coll.; Huddersfield Univ. (BA Hons Business Studies 1989). CIPD 1991, MCIPD 1994. Personnel Manager, Shorrock Security, 1986–90; Dir of Human Resources, Royal Philharmonic Orch., 1990–95; Head of Diversity, B&Q, 1995–2000; Consultant, Grass Roots Gp, 2000–02; Head of Diversity, BSkyB, 2002–07; Gp Hd of Social Policy and Inclusion, 2007–10, Special Advr on Social Action, 2010–11, Royal Mail Gp. Commissioner: Disability Rights Commn, 2000–03; Commn for Equality and Human Rights, 2007–09. Mem., Prime Minister's Council on Social Action, 2007–09; non-exec. Dir, Pension, Disability and Carers Bd, DWP, 2010–11. Dir, Every Business Commits, Prime Minister's Office, 2011–13. Mem. Bd of Advrs, Helen Hamlyn Centre, 2004–. Mem., Editl Bd, Equal Opportunities Rev., 2003–. Chm., Tollard Royal Parish Council, 2014–. FRSA 2011. Lord Dahrendorf Award for Responsible Capitalism, First Mag., 2014. *Publications:* (jtly) Equality and Diversity, 2001; Corporates are from Mars, Charities are from Venus, 2012. *Recreations:*

passionate about Arabian horses (owner of two Arabian stallions), country pursuits. *Address:* Salisbury, Wilts. *T:* (01725) 553099. *E:* kay.allen@diverseadvice.com. *Club:* Royal Over-Seas League.

ALLEN, Kenton Paul Benbow; Chief Executive, Big Talk Productions, since 2008; *b* Birmingham, 16 June 1965; *s* of Benbow Robert Sydney Allen and Pauline Allen; *m* 1999, Imogen Edwards-Jones; two *s* one *d*. *Educ:* Grange Comprehensive Sch., Stourbridge; King Edward's Sixth Form, Stourbridge. Producer: BBC Radio 4, 1990–94; BBC Radio 1, 1994–98; The Royle Family, 1998–2000; Creative Dir, Shine, 2000–02; Hd of Comedy, BBC, 2002–08. Producer, Six Shooter, 2005 (Academy Award for Best Short Film, 2006). *Recreations:* sailing, looking at boats, sitting on a hill in Ibiza, gazing into space, child taming. *Address:* Big Talk Productions, 26 Nassau Street, W1W 7AQ; Finca 15, St Joan, Ibiza. *E:* kenton@bigtalkproductions.com. *Clubs:* Royal Automobile, Groucho, Soho House.

ALLEN, Sir Mark (John Spurgeon), Kt 2005; CMG 2002; HM Diplomatic Service, retired; Special Adviser to BP Group, since 2004; *b* 3 July 1950; *s* of Peter Muir Spurgeon Allen and Heather Anne Allen (*née* Roney); *m* 1976, Margaret Mary Watson; one *s* one *d*. *Educ:* Dragon Sch.; Downside; Exeter Coll., Oxford (MA). Entered FCO, 1973; MECAS, 1974; Third Secretary: Abu Dhabi, 1975–77; FCO, 1977–78; Second, later First, Sec., Cairo, 1978–81; First Secretary: Belgrade, 1982–86; FCO, 1986–90; Counsellor: Amman, 1990–94; FCO, 1994–2004. Senior Adviser: Monitor Gp, 2006–11; Palantir Technologies, Palo Alto, 2006–; Mem., Adv. Bd, Millennium Finance Corp., Private Equity Energy Fund, 2008–10. Sen. Associate Mem., St Antony's Coll., Oxford, 2004–10 (Hon. Fellow, 2010). Member: Adv. Council, London ME Inst., 2005–09; IDEAS Centre, LSE, 2008–14. Trustee, St John and St Elizabeth Hosp., 2008–. KCSG 2009. Hon. Medal, Pres. of Republic of Bulgaria, 2011. *Publications:* Falconry in Arabia, 1980; (with Ruth Burrows) Letters on Prayer, 1999; First Holy Communion, 2002; Arabs, 2006; (ed) Sacred Script: Muhaqqaq in Islamic calligraphy, 2010. *Recreations:* falconry, Islamic calligraphy (traditional qualification (ijaza) in Arabic calligraphy (Muhaqqaq) from Nassar Mansour and Hasan Çelebi, 2010). *E:* mjsa@btinternet.com. *Clubs:* Travellers, Beefsteak, Grillions; Leander.

ALLEN, Mary Fitzgerald; executive coach and mentor; *d* of Dr Fergus Hamilton Allen, *qv* and Joan Allen; *m* 1st, 1980, Robin George Woodhead, *qv* (marr. diss. 1990); 2nd, 1991, Nigel Pantling (marr. diss. 2004). *Educ:* School of St Helen and St Katharine; New Hall, Cambridge; UEA (MA Creative Writing 2002). Actress, West End and repertory, 1973–76; Agent, London Management, 1977–78; Arts, Sponsorship Manager, Mobil Oil Co., 1978–81; Assoc. for Business Sponsorship of the Arts, 1982–83; arts management consultant, 1983–90; Dir, Watermans Arts Centre, 1990–92; Dir, Cheek by Jowl Theatre Co., 1989–92; Dep. Sec.-Gen., Arts Council of GB, 1992–94; Sec.-Gen., Arts Council of England, 1994–97; Chief Exec., Royal Opera House, Covent Garden, 1997–98. Mem., Brighton and Hove Arts and Creative Industries Commn, 2013–. Dir, City of London Fest., 2003–06; Chairman: High Tide Fest., 2008–12; Wonderful Beast, 2009–11; New Writing South, 2013–; Director: Zap Art, 2013–; Brighton Fringe, 2014–. Public Art Develt Trust: Trustee, 1983–92; Chm., 1987–92. Chm., Breast Cancer Campaign, 2002–06. *Publications:* Sponsoring the Arts: new business strategies for the 1990s, 1990; A House Divided, 1998. *Recreations:* opera, theatre, collecting contemporary art, gardening, playing the spoons, astronomy, poetry.

ALLEN, Michael David Prior, FRICS; FCIArb; QC 2008; a Recorder, since 2005; *b* Liverpool, 24 March 1963; *s* of late Terence Roy Allen and of Margaret Prior Allen; *m* 1995, Lorraine Brown; one *s* one *d*. *Educ:* BSc Building Econs; LLB; LLM; MA. ARICS 1987, FRICS 1992; FCIArb 2006. Called to the Bar, Gray's Inn, 1990; in practice at the Bar, 1990–. *Publications:* Company Law and the Human Rights Act, 2000. *Recreations:* playing and teaching squash, ski-ing, cheering the children on in their sports. *Address:* 7 King's Bench Walk, Temple, EC4Y 7DS. *T:* (020) 7583 0404, *Fax:* (020) 7583 0950. *E:* dallen@7kbw.co.uk.

ALLEN, Prof. Myles Robert, DPhil; FInstP; Professor of Geosystem Science, School of Geography and the Environment and Department of Physics, University of Oxford, since 2011; *b* Farnham, 11 Aug. 1965; *s* of Hubert Allen and Phoebe Allen; *m* 1994, Prof. Irene Mary Tracey; two *s* one *d*. *Educ:* British Sch. in the Netherlands; St John's Coll., Oxford (MA Phys and Philos. 1987; DPhil 1992). Tech. Manager, Bellerive Foundn, 1987–89; Consultant, UN Envmt Prog., 1989; Research Fellow, Rutherford Appleton Lab., 1993–94 and 1996–2001; Nat. Oceanic and Atmospheric Admin Postdoctoral Res. Fellow, MIT, 1994–95; Univ. Lectr, Dept of Phys, Univ. of Oxford, 2001–11. FInstP 2010. Appleton Medal, Inst. of Phys, 2010. *Publications:* contrib. and review ed. of chapters in Intergovtl Panel on Climate Change reports. *Recreations:* being a father, husband, son. *Address:* School of Geography and the Environment, University of Oxford, South Parks Road, Oxford OX1 3QY. *T:* (01865) 275848. *E:* myles.allen@ouce.ox.ac.uk.

ALLEN, Sir Patrick (Linton), ON 2009; GCMG 2009; CD 2006; PhD; Governor-General of Jamaica, since 2009; *b* Fruitful Vale, Portland, Jamaica, 7 Feb. 1951; *s* of Ferdinand Linton Allen and Christiana Eugenia Allen; *m* 1975, Patricia Denise; two *s* one *d*. *Educ:* Moneague Coll. (DipEd); Andrews Univ. (BA Hist. and Religion 1985; MA Systematic Theol. 1986; PhD Educnl Admin and Supervision 1998). Teacher, Water Valley All-age Sch., 1972–76; Principal: Robin's Bay All-age Sch., 1976–79; Hillside Primary Sch., 1979–81; Port Maria High Sch., 1981–83; Dir, Educn and Communication, Central Jamaica Conf. (Reg.), 1986–89 (Pres., 1998–2000); Dir, Educn and Family Life, WI Union Conf. of Seventh Day Adventists, 1990–93 (Pres., 2000–09); Asst Registrar, Andrews Univ., 1996–98. Chairman: Northern Caribbean Univ., 2000–09; Andrews Meml Hosp., 2000–09; Adventist Develt and Relief Agency, 2000–09; Book and Nutrition Centre, 2004–08. Dir, Educn and Communication, 1986–89, Pres., 1998–2000, Central Jamaica Conf. (Reg.); Dir, Educn and Family Life, 1990–93, Pres., 2000, WI Union Conf. of Seventh Day Adventists. Vice-Chm., Bible Soc. of WI, 2006–09. Hon. Dr Public Service N Caribbean Univ., 2009; Hon. DLaws Andrews, 2010; Hon. Dr Oakwood, 2010. KStJ 2013. *Recreations:* avid sports fan, enjoys badminton, track and field, basketball and cricket. *Address:* Office of the Governor-General, King's House, Kingston 6, Jamaica, West Indies. *T:* 9276424, ext. 2030, *Fax:* 9786025. *E:* kingshouse@kingshouse.gov.jm. *Clubs:* Kiwanis (Kingston, Jamaica), Rotary, Lions.

ALLEN, Paul Gardner; Chairman, Vulcan Inc., since 1983; *b* 21 Jan. 1953; *s* of late Kenneth Allen and of Faye Allen. *Educ:* Lakeside High Sch., Seattle; Washington State Univ. Programmer, Honeywell, Boston; Co-founder, Micro-Soft, later Microsoft Corp., 1975: Exec. Vice-Pres. of Res. and Product Develt, 1975–83; Dir, 1983–2000; Sen. Strategy Advr, 2000–. Founder: Asymetrix Corp., 1985; Vulcan Ventures, 1986; Starwave Corp., 1992; Interval Res., 1992; Paul Allen Group, 1994. Chairman: Portland Trailblazers, 1988–; Ticketmaster Hldgs Gp, 1993–; Seattle Seahawks, 1997–. *Publications:* Idea Man, 2011. *Address:* Vulcan Inc., 505 5th Avenue S, Suite 900, Seattle, WA 98104–3821, USA.

ALLEN, Hon. Sir Peter (Austin Philip Jermyn), Kt 1987; High Court Judge, Lesotho, 1987–89; *b* 20 Oct. 1929; *yr s* of late Donovan Jermyn Allen and Edith Jane Bates. *Educ:* Headlands School, Swindon; LLB London. Army service, 1947–55, Lieut RA, 1952–55. HM Overseas Police Service, Asst Supt Uganda Police, 1955–62; ADC to Governor of Uganda, 1957; called to the Bar, Gray's Inn, 1964; Lectr, 1962–64, Principal, 1964–70, Uganda Law School; Judicial Adviser, Buganda Kingdom, 1964; Advocate, High Court of Uganda, 1965; Chief Magistrate, Uganda, 1970–73; Judge, Uganda High Court, 1973–85; Chief Justice (Head of Uganda Judiciary, Chm., Judicial Service Commn), 1985–86. Member: Uganda Law Reform Commn, 1964–68; Foundn Cttee, Uganda YMCA, 1959; Dir, Mbarara Branch, YMCA, 1970–73; Chairman: Presidential Commn of Inquiry into Kampala City Council, 1971; Judicial Review of Caribbean Dependent Territories (Allen Report for FCO), 1990; Commn of Inquiry into Grand Cayman New Hospital Contracts, 1993; Mem., Uganda Law Soc., 1964–70. Uganda Independence Medal, 1962. *Publications:* An Introduction to the Law of Uganda (co-author), 1968; Days of Judgment, 1987; Interesting Times—Uganda Diaries 1955–1986, 2000; Inspector Beadle's Progress (fiction), 2007. *Address:* PO Box 38, Savannah, Grand Cayman KY1-1501, Cayman Islands, British West Indies.

ALLEN, Peter William, FCA; Managing Partner, 1984–90, Deputy Chairman, 1990–94, Coopers & Lybrand; *b* 22 July 1938; *s* of late Alfred William Allen, Sittingbourne, Kent, and Myra Nora (*née* Rogers); *m* 1965, Patricia Mary, *d* of late Joseph Frederick Dunk, FCA, Sheffield; three *d*. *Educ:* Borden Grammar Sch.; Cambridge Univ. (MA). Served RAF, 1957–59. Joined Coopers & Lybrand, 1963; qualified CA, 1966; Partner, 1973; Chm., Internat. Personnel Cttee, 1975–78; Partner in Charge, London Office, 1983; Member: UK Bd, 1984–94; Internat. Exec. Cttee, 1988–90, 1992–94. Non-executive Director: Charter, 1994–2001; Schroder Ventures, 1994–; Bd Mem., Post Office, 1995–98. Mem. and Hon. Treas., Governing Bd, Lister Inst. of Preventive Medicine, 1998–2005; Bd Mem., BRCS, 1999–2000. CCMI (CIMgt 1993). Freeman, City of London, 1988; Liveryman, Co. of Glaziers and Painters of Glass, 1989–2003. *Recreations:* golf, painting. *Address:* Fordham House, Abbotsbrook, Bourne End, Bucks SL8 5QS. *Club:* Reform.

ALLEN, (Philip) Richard (Hernaman), CB 2006; independent management and change consultant; author and composer; *b* 26 Jan. 1949; *s* of late Philip Hernaman Allen and Dorothy Allen (*née* Modral); *m* 1970, Vanessa (*née* Lampard); two *d*. *Educ:* Loughborough Grammar Sch.; Merton Coll., Oxford (BA (Hons) Mod. History). Asst Principal, HM Customs and Excise, 1970; Assistant Private Secretary: to Paymaster Gen., 1973; to Chancellor of the Duchy of Lancaster, 1974; HM Customs and Excise: Principal, 1975; Asst Sec., 1984; Comr of Customs and Excise, 1990; Director: Internal Taxes, 1990; Orgn, 1991; Dir, Policy, DSS, 1994; HM Customs and Excise: Comr, 1997–2001; Director: Ops (Compliance), 1997–98; Personnel and Finance, 1998–2000; Human Resources, 2000–01; Prin. Estabs Officer and Dir Reorgn Project, 2001; Dir, Corporate Services, DEFRA, 2001–05. FRSA. *Publications:* The Waterguard, 2012; The Summer of Love, 2013; Through Fire, 2014; Bankers' Draught, 2014. *Recreations:* music, badminton, running, writing.

See also D. K. Allen.

ALLEN, Richard Ian Gordon; consultant on public finance issues, International Monetary Fund, since 2010 (Deputy Division Chief, Fiscal Affairs Department, 2005–09); Senior Research Associate, Overseas Development Institute, since 2011; *b* 13 Dec. 1944; *s* of Reginald Arthur Hill Allen and Edith Alice Allen (*née* Manger). *Educ:* Edinburgh Academy; Edinburgh Univ. (MA); York Univ. (BPhil). Consultant, UN Economic Commn for Europe, Geneva, 1970; Research Officer, NIESR, 1971–75; Economic Adviser: Dept of Energy, 1975–78; HM Treasury, 1978–81; Senior Economic Adviser, later Asst Sec., HM Treasury, 1981–85; Counsellor (Economic), Washington, 1985–87; Press Sec. to Chancellor of the Exchequer, 1987–88; Under Sec., HM Treasury, 1988–95; Financial Advr, Govt of Bahrain, 1995–96; Sen. Counsellor, SIGMA prog., OECD, Paris, 1996–2001; Sen. Advr on Governance, Asian Develt Bank, 2001; World Bank: Dir, Public Expenditure and Financial Accountability Prog., 2001–03; Lead Economist for Public Sector Issues, ME and N Africa Reg., 2003–05. Mem., Bd of Dirs, European Investment Bank, 1988–90. *Publications:* (with Daniel Tommasi) Managing Public Expenditure: a reference book for transition countries, 2001; (with Salvatore Schiavo-Campo and Thomas Columkill Garrity) Assessing and Reforming Public Financial Management, 2004; (with Richard Hemming and Barry Potter) International Handbook of Public Financial Management, 2013. *Recreations:* collecting art, music, golf. *Club:* Royal Wimbledon Golf.

ALLEN, Prof. Robert Carson, PhD; FRSCan; FBA 2003; Professor of Economic History, University of Oxford, 2002; Fellow, Nuffield College, Oxford, 2001, now Emeritus; *b* 10 Jan. 1947; *s* of Richard Carson Allen and Barbara Tudbury Allen; *m* 1990, Dianne Frank; one *s*. *Educ:* Carleton Coll. (BA 1969); Harvard Univ. (MA 1972; PhD 1975). FRSCan 1994. Asst Prof., Hamilton Coll., 1973–75; University of British Columbia: Asst Prof., 1975–80; Associate Prof., 1980–85; Prof., 1985–2000; Reader in Recent Social and Econ. Hist., Oxford Univ., 2001–02. Vis. Prof., Harvard Univ., 1993–94, 1999–2000. *Publications:* (with G. Rosenbluth) Restraining the Economy: social credit economic policies for BC in the Eighties, 1986; (with G. Rosenbluth) False Promises: the failure of conservative economics, 1992; Enclosure and the Yeoman: agrarian change and English economic development 1450–1850, 1992; Farm to Factory: a reinterpretation of the Soviet industrial revolution, 2003; The British Industrial Revolution in Global Perspective, 2009; Global Economic History: a very short introduction, 2011. *Recreations:* mountaineering, carpentry, gardening. *Address:* Nuffield College, New Road, Oxford OX1 1NF. *T:* (01865) 278589, *Fax:* (01865) 278621. *E:* bob.allen@nuffield.ox.ac.uk.

ALLEN, Robert Geoffrey Bruère, (Robin); QC 1995; a Recorder, since 2000; *b* 13 Feb. 1951; *s* of Rev. Canon R. E. T. Allen and Isabel (*née* Otter-Barry); *m* 1977, Elizabeth Gay Moon; two *s*. *Educ:* Rugby; University Coll., Oxford (BA PPE 1972). Called to the Bar, Middle Temple, 1974 (Bencher, 2004), NI, 2009; in practice, specialising in discrimination, employment and public law, and human rights, 1976–; an Asst Recorder, 1997–2000; Hd of Chambers, 2002– (Jt Head, 2002–05). Co-organiser and first Treas., Free Representation Unit, 1973. Employment Law Advr to Legal Action Gp, 1978–80; Legal Advr to Local Govt Gp, Inst. Public Relns, 1988–90; expert advr to EC on law affecting most disadvantaged, 1993. Founder Mem. Cttee, Employment Law Bar Assoc., 1994–99 (Chm., 1997–99); Chairman: Bar in the Community, 2000–02; Bar Pro Bono Unit, 2000–02; Mem., Bar Council, 1999–2001 and 2013– (Chm., Equality and Diversity Cttee, 2013–, Social Mobility Cttee, 2015–); Chm., Bar Conf. Organising Bd, 2002. Mem., Home Office Human Rights Task Force, 1999–2001. Special Advr to Disability Rights Commn, 2002–07; Consultant: Age Concern and Age Europe, 2004–09; Age UK, 2012–14. Trustee, London Bombing Relief Charitable Fund, 2005–08; Patron, Andrea Adams Trust, 2008–09. Mem., Eur. Social Platform Virtual Network of Legal Experts, 2009–. Sec., Lambeth Central CLP, 1977. Chm., London Youth Adv. Centre, 1984–90. Chairman: Bd of Govs, Eleanor Palmer Primary Sch., 1988–91; Brandon Centre for Psychotherapy, 1991–93. Chambers and Partners Employment Law Silk Award, 2008, 2012. *Publications:* How to Prepare a Case for an Industrial Tribunal, 1987; (ed and contrib.) Home Office/Bar Council Study Guide to the Human Rights Act, 2000, rev. edn for Dept of Constitutional Affairs/Bar Council, 2004; Employment Law and Human Rights, 2002, 2nd edn 2007; Family Rights at Work, 2012; contributed to: The Legal Framework and Social Consequences of Free Movement of Persons in the European Union, 1998; Women, Work and Inequality: the challenge of equal pay in a de-regulated labour market, 1999; Anti-Discrimination: the way forward, 1999; Race Discrimination: developing and using a new legal framework, 2000; Bullen and Leake and Jacob's Precedents of Pleadings, 2000; The Legal Regulation of the Employment Relationship, 2001; Equality Law in an Enlarged Europe, 2007; Blackstone's Guide to the Equality Act, 2010, 2nd edn 2012. *Recreations:* family life, fireworks, fishing, growing chrysanthemums, singing. *Address:* Cloisters, 1 Pump Court, Temple, EC4Y 7AA. *T:* (020) 7827 4000, *Fax:* (020) 7827 4100. *Club:* Vincent's (Oxford).

ALLEN, Shane; Controller, Comedy Commissioning, BBC, since 2013; *b* Carrickfergus, 24 Nov. 1972; *s* of Joe Allen and Carole Allen; partner, Catherine Lovesey; two *s*. *Educ:* Belfast Royal Acad.; Univ. of Edinburgh (MA Hons Social Hist. 1996). Producer and writer, 11 O'Clock Show and Brass Eye, Talkback TV, 1998–2001; writer, Shooting Stars, BBC, 2002; Dir, Ali G in da USAiii, Talkback TV, 2003; Commng Editor, Comedy, Channel 4, 2004–09;

Hd of Comedy, Channel 4, 2009–12. Mem., BAFTA, 2005–. *Recreations:* snooker, table tennis, American literature, print collecting, snail genocide. *Address:* 3 West Drive, Brighton BN2 0GD.

ALLEN, Sir Thomas, Kt 1999; CBE 1989; singer; *b* 10 Sept. 1944; *s* of Thomas Boaz Allen and Florence Allen; *m* 1st, 1968, Margaret Holley (marr. diss. 1986); one *s*; 2nd, 1988, Jeannie Gordon Lascelles. *Educ:* Robert Richardson Grammar Sch., Ryhope; Royal College of Music. ARCM; FRCM 1988. Welsh Nat. Opera, 1969–72; Principal Baritone, Royal Opera, Covent Garden, 1972–78; appearances include: Glyndebourne Fest. Opera; English Opera Group; Paris Opera; Florence; Teatro Colon, Buenos Aires; Met. Opera, NY; Hamburg; La Scala, Milan; BBC TV (The Gondoliers, The Marriage of Figaro); all major orchestras and various concert engagements abroad. Major rôles include: Figaro in Barber of Seville; Figaro and the Count in Marriage of Figaro; Papageno in The Magic Flute; Billy Budd; Marcello in La Bohème; Belcore in l'Elisir d'Amore; Sid in Albert Herring; Tarquinius in Rape of Lucretia; Guglielmo, and Don Alfonso, in Così fan Tutte; Demetrius in A Midsummer Night's Dream; Valentin in Faust; Dr Falke, and Eisenstein, in Die Fledermaus; King Arthur; The Count in Voice of Ariadne; Silvio in Pagliacci; Pelléas in Pelléas and Mélisande; Germont in La Traviata; Don Giovanni; Mandryka in Arabella; Malatesta in Don Pasquale; title rôle in Il ritorno d'Ulisse; Beckmesser in Die Meistersinger; Prosdocimo in The Turk in Italy; Music Master in Ariadne auf Naxos; title rôle in Sweeney Todd, and many others. Director: Albert Herring, RCM, 2002; Il Barbiere di Siviglia, Th. Royal, Glasgow, 2007; Don Giovanni, Sage, Gateshead, 2007; Marriage of Figaro, Scottish Opera, 2010; The Magic Flute, Th. Royal, Glasgow, 2012; prod., Così fan Tutte, Sage, Gateshead. Hambro Vis. Prof. of Opera, Oxford Univ., 2000–01. Kammersänger, Bayerische Staatsoper, 2003. Chancellor, Durham Univ., 2012–. Patron, Samling Foundn. Hon. RAM 1988. Hon. MA Newcastle, 1984; Hon. DMus Durham, 1988. Queen's Medal for Music, 2013. *Publications:* Foreign Parts: a singer's journal, 1993. *Recreations:* gardening, golf, sailing, painting, ornithology. *Address:* c/o Askonas Holt Ltd, Lincoln House, 300 High Holborn, WC1V 7JH.

ALLEN, Thomas Michael Chard; QC 2015; *b* Beaconsfield, Bucks, 21 Feb. 1968; *s* of Michael and Susan Allen; *m* 1998, Natalie Baylis; two *s* one *d*. *Educ:* King's Sch., Bruton, Som; Durham Univ.; Inns of Court Sch. of Law. Called to the Bar, Middle Temple, 1994. Wilmer Oscar Moore/Screen Internat. Screenplay Award, 2000. *Recreations:* daydreaming, Radio 3 world music programmes, travel. *Address:* 5 Paper Buildings, Temple, EC4Y 7HB. *T:* (020) 7583 6117, *Fax:* (020) 7353 0075. *E:* clerks@5pb.co.uk.

ALLEN, Twink; *see* Allen, W. R.

ALLEN, William Anthony; economic consultant, since 2004; Visiting Senior Fellow, Faculty of Finance, Cass Business School, since 2004; *b* 13 May 1949; *s* of Derek William Allen and Margaret Winifred Allen (*née* Jones); *m* 1972, Rosemary Margaret Eminson; one *s* two *d*. *Educ:* King's College Sch., Wimbledon; Balliol College, Oxford (BA); LSE (MScEcon). Joined Bank of England, 1972; Economic Intell. Dept, 1972–77; Gold and Foreign Exchange Office, 1977–78; seconded to Bank for Internat. Settlements, Basle, 1978–80; Bank of England: Asst Adviser, Economics Div. (working on monetary policy), 1980–82; Manager, Gilt-Edged Div., 1982–86; Hd of Money Market Operations Div., 1986–90; Hd of Foreign Exchange Div., 1990–94; Dep. Dir, 1994–2003; Dir for Europe, 2002–04; Econ. Advr, Brevan Howard Asset Mgt LLP, 2004–07; Chief Economist, Denholm Hall Gp, 2007–10. Specialist Adviser: Treasury Cttee, H of C, 2010–; Parly Commn on Banking Standards, 2012–13. Pt-time Advr, Nat. Bank of Poland, 1990–2001. *Publications:* International Liquidity and the Financial Crisis, 2013; Monetary Policy and Financial Repression in Britain, 1951–59, 2014; articles in economics jls. *Recreations:* gardening, jazz. *E:* bill@allen-economics.com.

ALLEN, Hon. Sir William (Clifford), KCMG 2000; JP; Minister of Finance and Planning, Bahamas, 1995–2002; *b* 15 March 1937; *m* 1960, Aloma Munnings; three *s* one *d*. *Educ:* St Augustine's Coll., Nassau; Rhodes Sch., NYC; NY Univ. (BSc Accounting); CUNY (MBA). Internal auditor, Stone and Webster Securities Corp., NY, 1965–68; budget supervisor, J. C. Penny Co., NY, 1968–70; Res. Manager, Bahamas Monetary Authy, 1970–74; Dep. Gov., 1974–80, Gov., 1980–87, Central Bank of Bahamas; Pres., Matrix Investment Ltd, 1987–92. Mem., Bahamas Senate, 1992–94; MP (Free Nat. Movt) Montagu, Bahamas, Nov. 1994–2002; Minister of State, Ministry of Finance and Planning, 1992–93; Minister of Planning and Public Service, 1993–95. *Address:* Old Fort Bay, POB CB10993, Nassau, Bahamas.

ALLEN, Sir William (Guilford), Kt 1981; Chairman, family group of companies; *b* 22 April 1932; *s* of Sir William Guilford Allen, CBE, and Mona Maree Allen; *m* 1959, Elaine Therese Doyle; two *s* one *d*. *Educ:* Downlands Coll., Toowoomba, Qld. In grazing industry, Merino sheep; Principal, Historic Malvern Hills Registered Merino Stud; stud Santa Gertrudis cattle breeder. Commercial broadcasting industry. Chm., Qld Transport and Technology Centre, 1984; Director: Qantas, 1981; Suncorp Insurance and Building Soc., 1985–89; Power Brewing Co., 1989. Former Mem. Bd, Care Australia. Mem., Longreach Base Hosp. Bd, 1960–83. Treas., 1981, Trustee, 1989–, Nat. Party, Qld. Councillor, Longreach Shire, 1958. Fellow, Hon. Co. of Air Pilots (formerly GAPAN). *Recreation:* aviation. *Clubs:* Brisbane, Tattersalls, Australian, Longreach, Queensland Turf, Brisbane Amateur Turf (Brisbane); Australian, Royal Sydney Golf (Sydney).

ALLEN, Maj.-Gen. William Maurice, CB 1983; FCIT, FIMI, FILDM; MInstPet; Senior Military Consultant to Mondial Defence Systems (formerly Mondial & Co.), 1985–95; Regional Vice President and Senior Defence Adviser, Fortis Aviation Group, 1995–99; *b* 29 May 1931; *s* of William James Allen and Elizabeth Jane Henrietta Allen; *m* 1st, 1955, Patricia Mary (*née* Fletcher) (*d* 1998); one *d* decd; 2nd, 1998, Elizabeth (*née* Irving). *Educ:* Dunstable Sch. FCIT 1972; FIMI 1982; FILDM (FIPDM 1982); FCMI (FBIM 1983); MInstPet 1982. Commnd RASC, 1950; RCT, 1965; regtl and staff appts, Korea, Cyprus, Germany and UK; Student, Staff Coll., Camberley, 1961; Instructor, Staff Coll., Camberley and RMCS Shrivenham, 1968–70; Student, RCDS, 1976; Asst Comdt, RMA Sandhurst, 1979–81; Dir Gen. of Transport and Movements (Army), 1981–83. Dir of Educn and Trng, Burroughs Machines Ltd, 1983–85. Jt Man. Dir, Marina Moraira Yacht Brokers, 1989–92; Man. Dir, Fortis Internat. Ltd, 1991–92; Director: Govt Projects, Unisys Corp. (formerly Systems Develt Corp.), Heidelberg, 1985–86; Fortis Aviation Gp, Spain, 1988–89; European Management Information, 1989–92. Member, Council: IAM, 1982–85; NDTA, 1983–90. Chm., Milton Keynes Information Technol. Trng Centre, 1983–85. Associate, St George's House. Freeman, City of London, 1981; Hon. Liveryman, Worshipful Co. of Carmen, 1981. *Recreations:* economics, trout fishing, gardening, vigneron et oleiculteur de Languedoc. *Address:* c/o Royal Bank of Scotland, Holts Farnborough Branch, Lawrie House, 31–37 Victoria Road, Farnborough, Hants GU14 7NR.

ALLEN, Prof. William Richard, (Twink), CBE 2002; PhD, ScD; FRCVS; Jim Joel Professor of Equine Reproduction, Department of Veterinary Medicine (formerly Clinical Veterinary Medicine), University of Cambridge, 1995–2007, now Professor Emeritus; Fellow, Robinson College, Cambridge, 1995–2007, now Emeritus; Director, Thoroughbred Breeders' Association Equine Fertility Unit, Newmarket, 1989–2007; Scientific Director, Paul Mellon Laboratory of Equine Reproduction, since 2008; *b* 29 Aug. 1940; *s* of Francis Cecil Allen and Rose St Ledger Allen (*née* Sinclair); *m* 1965, Diana Margaret Emms; one *s* two *d*. *Educ:* Auckland Grammar Sch.; Univ. of Auckland; Univ. of Sydney (BVSc 1965); Univ. of Cambridge (PhD in Equine Reproductive Physiology 1970); Royal Coll. of Veterinary Surgeons (Dip. Equine Stud Medicine 1986). FIBiol 2002–09; FRCVS 2004. In vet. practice, Kaitaia, NZ, 1965; res. student, Dept of Clinical Vet. Medicine, Univ. of Cambridge, 1966–70; Post Doctoral Scientist, AFRC Unit of Reproductive Physiol. and Biochem., Cambridge, 1970–72; Prin. Vet. Res. Officer, Thoroughbred Breeders' Assoc. Equine Fertility Unit, Animal Res. Stn, Cambridge, 1972–89. *Publications:* (ed) Equine Reproduction, vols I–V, 1975–91; contrib. Proc. Internat. Symposia on Equine Reproduction; numerous papers in scientific jls and reference books. *Recreations:* fox hunting, horse racing, wildlife conservation. *Address:* Paul Mellon Laboratory of Equine Reproduction, Brunswick, 18 Woodditton Road, Newmarket, Suffolk CB8 9BJ. *T:* (01638) 666930. *E:* pml777@virginmedia.com.

See also L. Dettori.

ALLEN, Woody, (Allen Stewart Konigsberg); writer, actor, director; *b* Brooklyn, 1 Dec. 1935; *s* of late Martin and of Nettie Konigsberg; *m* 1966, Louise Lasser (marr. diss.); one *s* by Mia Farrow, *qv*; *m* 1997, Soon-Yi Previn. TV script writer, 1953–64, and appeared as a comedian in nightclubs and on TV shows. Sylvania Award, 1957. *Plays:* (writer) Don't Drink the Water, 1966; (writer and actor) Play It Again Sam, 1969 (filmed 1972); The Floating Light Bulb, 1990; (writer and dir) A Second Hand Memory, 2005. *Films:* (writer and actor) What's New Pussycat?, 1965; (actor): Casino Royale, 1967; Scenes from a Mall, 1991; Fading Gigolo, 2014; (writer, actor and director): What's Up Tiger Lily?, 1966; Take the Money and Run, 1969; Bananas, 1971; Everything You Always Wanted to Know About Sex But Were Afraid to Ask, 1972; Sleeper, 1973; Love and Death, 1975; The Front, 1976; Annie Hall (Academy Award), 1977; Manhattan, 1979; Stardust Memories, 1980; A Midsummer Night's Sex Comedy, 1982; Zelig, 1983; Broadway Danny Rose, 1984; Hannah and her Sisters (Academy Award), 1986; New York Stories, 1989; Shadows and Fog, 1992; Husbands and Wives, 1992; Manhattan Murder Mystery, 1994; Mighty Aphrodite, 1995; Everyone Says I Love You, 1996; Deconstructing Harry, 1997; Small Time Crooks, 2000; The Curse of the Jade Scorpion, 2002; Hollywood Ending, 2002; Anything Else, 2003; Whatever Works, 2010; To Rome with Love, 2012; (writer and director): Interiors, 1978; The Purple Rose of Cairo, 1985; Radio Days, 1987; September, 1988; Another Woman, 1989; Crimes and Misdemeanours, 1989; Alice, 1990; Bullets over Broadway, 1995 (writer, stage version, 2014); Celebrity, 1999; Sweet and Lowdown, 1999; Melinda and Melinda, 2005; Match Point, 2007; Cassandra's Dream, 2008; Vicky Cristina Barcelona, 2009; You Will Meet a Tall Dark Stranger, 2011; Midnight in Paris, 2011 (Academy Award for Best Original Screenplay. 2012); Blue Jasmine, 2013; Magic in the Moonlight, 2014; Irrational Man, 2015. *Publications:* Getting Even, 1971; Without Feathers, 1975; Side Effects, 1981; Three One-Act Plays, 2004; Mere Anarchy (short stories), 2007; The Insanity Defense, 2007; contribs to New Yorker, etc.

ALLEN-JONES, Charles Martin; Senior Partner, Linklaters (formerly Linklaters & Paines), 1996–2001; Joint Chairman, Linklaters & Alliance, 1998–2001; *b* 7 Aug. 1939; *s* of late Air Vice-Marshal John Ernest Allen-Jones, CBE, and Margaret Allen-Jones (*née* Rix); *m* 1966, Caroline Beale; one *s* two *d*. *Educ:* Clifton Coll., Bristol. Admitted Solicitor, 1963. Articled Clerk: to the Clerk to the Justices, Uxbridge Magistrates Court, 1958–60; Vizard Oldham Crowder & Cash, London, 1960–63; Solicitor, Supreme Court, London, 1963; Linklaters & Paines, subseq. Linklaters: Solicitor, 1964; Partner, 1968–2001; Head, Hong Kong office, 1976–81; Head, Corporate Dept, 1985–91. Director: Caledonia Investments plc, 2001–; Hongkong Land Holdings Ltd, 2001–; Jardine Strategic Hldgs Ltd, 2008–. Mem., Financial Reporting Council, 2001–07 (Member: Corporate Governance Cttee, 2004–07; Financial Reporting Review Panel, 2006–11). Trustee: BM, 2000–04; Asia House, 2001–09 (Chm., 2005–06). Member: Barbican Adv. Council, 1997–2005; Council, RCA, 2004– (Vice Chm., 2007–); Internat. Adv. Council, SOAS, 2007–10. Mem., Cttee, Hong Kong Assoc., 2002–. Consultant Ed., CUP Law Practitioner Series, 2003–09. *Recreations:* keeping in touch, Asia, travel, tennis, golf. *Address:* 6 Kensington Place, W8 7PT. *Clubs:* Brooks's; Hong Kong (Hong Kong).

ALLENBY, family name of **Viscount Allenby**.

ALLENBY, 4th Viscount *cr* 1919; **Henry Jaffray Hynman Allenby;** *b* 29 July 1968; *o s* of 3rd Viscount Allenby and of Sara Margaret Allenby (*née* Wiggin); *S* father, 2014; *m* 1996, Louise Victoria, *yr d* of Michael Green; two *s*.

ALLENBY, Katherine Fiona, MBE 2007; athlete; Games Teacher, Paragon School, Bath, since 2009; Fencing Manager of Modern Pentathlon, London 2012 Olympic Games, 2011–12; *b* London, 16 March 1974; *d* of William James and Gillian Mary Allenby; *m* 2005, Ian David Pocock; two *d*. *Educ:* St Joseph's Sch., Launceston; Kelly Coll., Tavistock; Brighton Univ. (BSc Hons Sport Sci.); QTS 2005. Modern Pentathlon athlete, 1993–2004: Individual bronze medal, 1994, silver medal, 1995, World Jun. Modern Pentathlon Championships; Eur. Champion, 1997; Eur. Team Champion, 1999, 2000, 2001, 2002, 2003; World Cup Champion, 1998, 2004; World Team Champion, 2000, 2001, 2003, 2004; Bronze Medal, Sydney Olympics, 2000; Individual bronze medal, 2003, silver medal, 2004, World Modern Pentathlon Championships; National Fencing Champion, 2005. Trainee teacher of Physical Educn, Wellington Sch., Som, 2004–05; PE teacher and Hd of Modern Pentathlon, Whitgift Sch., Croydon, 2005–09. Dir of Fencing in Modern Pentathlon for 2011 Eur. Modern Pentathlon Championships and 2011 World Cup trial and Olympic Test event, 2010–11. Motivational/public speaker, 2000–. Chm., British Athletes' Commn, 2003–07; Member: Athletes' Cttee, British Olympic Assoc., 1997–2003, 2010–12; Nat. Olympic Cttee, 2000–09; Athlete Steering Gp advising Exec. Bd of London 2012 Olympics, 2003–05. Member: Athletes' Cttee, Union Internat. de Pentathlon Moderne, 2004–08; Tetrathlon Nat. Cttee, Pony Club, 2009–13. Founder Mem. and Vice Chm., Modern Pentathlon Club, Bath, 2009–11. Jim Fox Award for Excellence in Modern Pentathlon, Pentathlon GB, 2004. *Recreations:* foreign languages, cooking, especially with chocolate, reading paperback bestsellers, global exploration. *Address:* c/o British Olympic Association, 60 Charlotte Street, W1T 2NU. *E:* ktlnb@hotmail.com.

ALLENDALE, 4th Viscount *cr* 1911; **Wentworth Peter Ismay Beaumont;** Baron 1906; *b* 13 Nov. 1948; *e s* of 3rd Viscount Allendale and of Hon. Sarah, 2nd *d* of 1st Baron Ismay, KG, GCB, CH, DSO, PC; *S* father, 2002; *m* 1975, Theresa Mary Magdalene (*née* More O'Ferrall); one *s* three *d*. *Educ:* Harrow. Landowner. *Recreations:* shooting, ski-ing, horseracing. *Heir: s* Hon. Wentworth Ambrose Ismay Beaumont [*b* 11 June 1979; *m* 2011, Vanessa, *d* of Peter Webb; two *s*]. *Address:* Bywell Estate Office, Stocksfield, Northumberland NE43 7AQ. *T:* (01661) 843296, *Fax:* (01661) 842838. *Clubs:* Jockey, White's; Northern Counties, Recorders (Newcastle upon Tyne).

ALLENDE, Isabel; writer; *b* 2 Aug. 1942; *d* of Tomás Allende Pesce and Francisca Llona Barros; *m* 1st, 1962, Miguel Frías (marr. diss. 1987); one *s* (one *d* decd); 2nd, 1988, William C. Gordon. *Educ:* Ursulinas (German nuns), Chile; Dunalastaid Amer. Sch., La Paz; British Lebanese Trng Coll., Lebanon; La Maisonette, Chile. Journalist: Chile, 1964–74 (Paula (women's mag.), Mampato (children's mag.), TV programmes, film documentaries); El Nacional, Venezuela, 1975–84; Lecturer in Literature: Montclair Coll., USA; Univ. of Calif at Berkeley, 1988; Univ. of Virginia, 1988. Member: Academía de la Lengua, Chile, 1989; Academía de Artes y Ciencias, Puerto Rico, 1995. Hon. Prof. of Literature, Univ. of Chile, 1991. Lecture tours, N America and Europe. Work has been translated into more than 27 languages and has received numerous literary awards. Hon. DLitt: SUNY, 1991; Bates Coll., USA, 1994; Dominican Coll., USA, 1994; Columbia Coll., USA, 1996; Hon. DHL Florida Atlantic, 1996. Condecoración Gabriela Mistral (Chile), 1994; Chevalier, Ordre des Arts et des Lettres (France), 1994. *Plays:* El Embajador, 1971; La Balada del Medio Pelo, 1973; Los Siete Espejos, 1974. *Publications: novels:* La Casa de los Espíritus (The House of Spirits), 1982 (filmed; adapted for stage); De Amor y de Sombra (Of Love and Shadows), 1984 (filmed); Eva

Luna, 1985 (adapted for stage); El Plan Infinito (The Infinite Plan), 1991; Paula, 1994 (adapted for stage); Hija de la Fortuna (Daughter of Fortune), 1999; Retrato en Sepia (Portrait in Sepia), 2000; La Ciudad de las Bestias (City of the Beasts), 2002; El reino del Dragón de Oro (Kingdom of the Golden Dragon), 2003; El Bosque de los Pigmeos (Forest of the Pygmies), 2005; Zorro, 2005; Inés del Alma Mía (Inés of My Soul), 2006; La Isla Bajo el Mar (The Island Beneath the Sea), 2010; El Cuaderno de Maya (Maya's Notebook), 2011; Ripper, 2014; *short stories:* La Gorda de Porcelana, 1983; Cuentos de Eva Luna (Stories of Eva Luna), 1989 (adapted for theatre, opera, and ballet); Afrodita (Aphrodite), 1997; *memoirs:* Mi país inventado (My Invented Country), 2003; The Sum of Our Days, 2008; articles in jls in N America and Europe. *Address:* 116 Caledonia Street, Sausalito, CA 94965, USA.

ALLEYNE, Sir George (Allanmore Ogarren), Kt 1990; OCC 2001; MD, FRCP; Director, Pan American Health Organization, 1995–2003 (Assistant Director, 1990–95), now Director Emeritus; Special Envoy of the UN Secretary-General for HIV/AIDS in the Caribbean, 2003–10; *b* 7 Oct. 1932; *s* of Clinton O. Alleyne and Eileen A. Alleyne (*née* Gaskin); *m* 1958, Sylvan Ionie (*née* Chen); two *s* one *d. Educ:* Harrison College, Barbados; University College of the West Indies (MB BS London 1977, MD). Completed training as physician in Barbados and UCH, London, 1958–62; Sen. Med. Registrar, UCH, Jamaica, 1962–63; Res. Fellow, Sen. Res. Fellow, MRC Tropical Metabolism Res. Unit, 1963–72; Prof. of Medicine, Univ. of W Indies, 1972–81 (Chm., Dept of Medicine, 1976–81); Pan American Health Organization: Head of Res. Unit, 1981–83; Dir of Health Programs Develt, 1983–90. Mem., Lancet Commn on Investing in Health; Chm., Bd of Dirs, Centre for Disease Dynamics, Econs and Policy, Washington. Chancellor, Univ. of W Indies, 2003–. Sir Arthur Sims Travelling Prof., 1977. Hon. FACP. Hon. DSc Univ. of W Indies, 1989. Jamaica Assoc. of Scientists Award, 1979. Jamaica Centenary Medal, 1980. *Publications:* contribs to learned jls on medicine, renal physiology and biochemistry, health and develt issues. *Recreations:* reading, gardening. *Address:* Pan American Health Organization, 525 23rd Street NW, Washington, DC 20037, USA. *T:* (202) 9743057.

ALLEYNE, Rev. Sir John (Olpherts Campbell), 5th Bt *cr* 1769; Rector of Weeke, Diocese of Winchester, 1975–93; *b* 18 Jan. 1928; *s* of Captain Sir John Meynell Alleyne, 4th Bt, DSO, DSC, RN, and Alice Violet (*d* 1985), *d* of late James Campbell; *S* father, 1983; *m* 1968, Honor, *d* of late William Albert Irwin, Belfast; one *s* one *d. Educ:* Eton; Jesus Coll., Cambridge (BA 1950, MA 1955). Deacon 1955, priest 1956; Curate, Southampton, 1955–58; Chaplain: Coventry Cathedral, 1958–62; Clare Coll., Cambridge, 1962–66; to Bishop of Bristol, 1966–68; Toc H Area Sec., SW England, 1968–71; Vicar of Speke, 1971–73, Rector, 1973–75. *Heir: s* Richard Meynell Alleyne, *b* 23 June 1972. *Address:* 2 Ash Grove, Guildford, Surrey GU2 8UT.

ALLEYNE, Selwyn Eugene, CBE 1986; Hong Kong Commissioner in London, 1987–89, retired; *b* 4 Dec. 1930; *s* of Gilbert Sydney Alleyne and Dorothy Alleyne; *m* 1956, Ellie Lynn Wong, MBE. *Educ:* Queen's Royal Coll., Trinidad; Jesus Coll., Oxford (MA). Joined Hong Kong Govt, 1956; Dep. Dir of Urban Services, 1974; Dep. Sec. for Civil Service, 1979; Dir of Social Welfare, and MLC, 1980; Dep. Financial Sec., 1983–87. *Recreations:* tennis, chess, collecting Chinese ceramics. *Clubs:* Civil Service; Hong Kong Jockey.

ALLI, Baron *cr* 1998 (Life Peer), of Norbury in the London Borough of Croydon; **Waheed Alli;** Chairman, Chorion Ltd, 2003–11; *b* 16 Nov. 1964. *Educ:* Norbury Manor Sch. Formed televised production co., 24 Hour Productions, later Planet 24 Productions Ltd, with partner Charlie Parsons, Jt Man. Dir, 1992–99; Man. Dir, Carlton Productions, 1998–2000; Dir, Carlton Television, 1998–2000. Director: Shine Entertainment Ltd, 2000; Silvergate Media Ltd, 2011– (Chm.); Castaway Television; Chm., ASOS, 2001–12. Chancellor, De Montfort Univ., 2006–. Pres., NYT. Trustee, Elton John Aids Foundn. *Address:* House of Lords, SW1A 0PW.

ALLIANCE, Baron *cr* 2004 (Life Peer), of Manchester in the County of Greater Manchester; **David Alliance,** Kt 1989; CBE 1984; Chairman, N. Brown Group plc, 1968–2012; *b* 2 June 1932; *s* of Eliahoo and Sarahi Alliance. *Educ:* Iran. First acquisition, Thomas Hoghton (Oswaldtwistle), 1956; acquired Spirella, 1968, then Vantona Ltd, 1975, to form Vantona Group, 1975; acquired Carrington Viyella to form Vantona Viyella, 1983, Nottingham Manufacturing, 1985, Coats Patons to form Coats Viyella, 1986; Gp Chief Exec., 1975–90, Chm., 1989–99; Chm., Tootal Gp, 1991–99. Gov., Tel Aviv Univ., 1989–. CCMI (CBIM 1985); CompTI 1984. FRSA 1988. Hon. Fellow: UMIST 1988; Shenkar Coll. of Textile Tech. and Fashion, Israel, 1990. Hon. FCGI 1991. Hon. LLD: Victoria Univ. of Manchester, 1989; Liverpool, 1996; Hon. DSc Heriot-Watt, 1991; Hon. DPhil Tel Aviv, 2009. *Publications:* A Bazaar Life (autobiog.), 2015. *Address:* House of Lords, SW1A 0PW.

ALLIES, Edgar Robin, (Bob); Partner, Allies and Morrison, architects, since 1983; *b* 5 Sept. 1953; *s* of Edgar Martyn Allies, MBE, DFC and Lily Maud Allies; *m* 1991, Jill Anne Franklin; one *s* one *d. Educ:* Reading Sch.; Univ. of Edinburgh (MA Hons 1976; DipArch 1977). Rome Schol. in Architecture, 1981–82; Lectr, Univ. of Cambridge, 1984–88; George Simpson Vis. Prof., Univ. of Edinburgh, 1995; Vis. Prof., Univ. of Bath, 1996–99; Kea Dist. Vis. Prof., Univ. of Maryland, 1999. Mem., Faculty of Fine Arts, Brit. Sch. at Rome, 1997–2002. Mem. Council, AA, 2004–07. Chair, South+East Reg. Design Rev. Panel, 2013–. With G. Morrison, founded Allies and Morrison, 1983; *completed projects* include: Clove Bldg, London, 1990 (RIBA Award 1991); Pierhead, Liverpool, 1995; Sarum Hall Sch., London, 1995 (RIBA Award 1996); Nunnery Sq., Sheffield, 1995 (RIBA Award 1996); British Embassy, Dublin, 1995 (RIBA Award 1997); Rosalind Franklin Bldg, Newnham Coll., Cambridge, 1995 (RIBA Award 1996); Abbey Mills Pumping Station, Stratford (RIBA Award), 1997; Rutherford Inf. Services Bldg, Goldsmiths Coll., London, 1997 (RIBA Award 1998); Extension to Horniman Mus., 2002 (RIBA Award 2004); One Piccadilly Gdns, Manchester, 2003 (RIBA Award 2004); 85 Southwark Street, 2003 (RIBA London Bldg of the Year, 2004; Corporate Workplace Bldg Nat. Winner, British Council for Offices Awards, 2004); BBC Media Village, White City, 2004 (RIBA Award 2005); Fitzwilliam Coll. Gatehouse and Auditorium, 2004 (RIBA Award 2005); Girton Coll. Library, Cambridge, 2005 (RIBA Award 2006); British Council, Lagos, 2005 (RIBA Internat. Awards); Farnborough Business Park, 2006 (RIBA Award 2007); Royal Festival Hall, 2007 (RIBA Design for London Space Award, 2007; RIBA Award 2008); The Planetarium at Royal Observatory, Greenwich, 2007 (RIBA Award 2008); Paradise Street, Liverpool One, 2009 (RIBA Award 2009); Charles Street Car Park, Sheffield, 2009 (RIBA Award 2009); One Vine Street, The Quadrant, Regent Street, 2009 (RIBA Award 2009); Highbury Square, London, 2009 (RIBA Award 2010); Bankside 123, London, 2009 (RIBA Award 2010); Mint Hotel, Leeds (RIBA Award 2011); Royal Albert Meml Mus., 2013 (RIBA Award 2013); Simon Smith Bldg, Brighton Coll., 2013 (RIBA Award 2013); Masterplan London 2012 Stratford (RIBA Nat. Award 2013); Rambert London, 2014 (RIBA Award 2014); Ash Court, Girton Coll., 2014 (RIBA Award 2014); *exhibitions* include: New British Architecture, Japan, 1994; Allies and Morrison Retrospective, USA Schools of Architecture, 1996–98, Helsinki, Delft, Strasbourg, 1999. Edinburgh Architectural Assoc. Medal for Architecture, 1977; Allies and Morrison winner of Architectural Practice of the Year, Bldg Awards, 2004; Architect of the Year Award, Building Design Awards, 2007. *Publications:* Model Futures, 1983; Allies and Morrison, 1996; Cultivating the City: London before and after 2012, 2010; Allies and Morrison 1, 2011; The Fabric of Place, 2014. *Recreation:* contemporary music. *Address:* Allies and Morrison, 85 Southwark Street, SE1 0HX. *T:* (020) 7921 0100; 12 Well Road, NW3 1LH. *T:* (020) 7443 9309.

ALLIN, George, RCNC; Director General Ship Refitting, Ministry of Defence, 1989–93, retired; *b* 21 June 1933; *s* of late Henry Richard Allin and Mary Elizabeth Allin (*née* Wyatt); *m* 1st, 1956, Barbara May Short (marr. diss.); two *s*; 2nd, 1977, Janice Annette Richardson-Sandell. *Educ:* Devonport High Sch.; Devonport Dockyard Tech. Coll.; RNEC Manadon; RNC Greenwich. WhSch, BSc. Asst Elect. Engineer, 1957–59; HMS Belfast, 1959; Admiralty, Bath, 1959–62; Elect. Engineer, MoD (Navy), Bath, 1963–68; HM Dockyard, Devonport: Line Manager, 1968–70; Project Manager Frigates, 1970–71; Supt Elect. Engineer, Dep. Personnel Manager, 1971–74; Industrial Relations Manager, 1975; Org. and Develt Div., Dockyard HQ, Bath, 1975–79; rcds 1979; HM Dockyard, Rosyth: Project Manager, SSBN Refit, 1980–81; Production Dir, 1981–83; Dockyard HQ, Bath: Management Systems and Audit Div., 1984–85; Principal Dir, Policy and Plans, 1985–86; Principal Dir, Ship Refitting, MoD (Navy), Bath, 1986–87; Dir, Aldermaston Projects, Brown & Root (on secondment), 1987–89. *Recreations:* chess, music, bowls, snooker, philately.

ALLINSON, Sir (Walter) Leonard, KCVO 1979 (MVO 1961); CMG 1976; HM Diplomatic Service, retired; *b* 1 May 1926; *o s* of Walter Allinson and Alice Frances Cassidy; *m* 1951, Margaret Patricia Watts; three *d* (of whom two are twins). *Educ:* Friern Barnet Grammar Sch.; Merton Coll., Oxford (First class in History, 1947; MA). Asst Principal, Ministry of Fuel and Power (Petroleum Div.), 1947–48; Asst Principal, later Principal, Min. of Education, 1948–58 (Asst Private Sec. to Minister, 1953–54); transf. CRO, 1958; First Sec. in Lahore and Karachi, 1960–62, Madras and New Delhi, 1963–66; Counsellor and Head of Political Affairs Dept, March 1968; Dep. Head, later Head, of Permanent Under Secretary's Dept, FCO, 1968–70; Counsellor and Head of Chancery, subsequently Deputy High Comr, Nairobi, 1970–73; RCDS, 1974; Diplomatic Service Inspectorate, 1975; Dep. High Comr and Minister, New Delhi, 1975–77; High Comr, Lusaka, 1978–80; Asst Under-Sec. of State (Africa), 1980–82; High Comr in Kenya and Ambassador to UN Environment Programme, 1982–86. Vice Pres., Royal African Soc., 1982–99; Mem. Council, East Africa Inst., 1986–92; Hon. Vice Chm., Kenya Soc., 1989–; Chm., Finance Cttee, Cornwall Red Cross, 1996–98. Gov., Wendron Voluntary Primary Sch., 1990–2003. *Address:* Tregarthen, Wendron, Helston, Cornwall TR13 0PY.

See also N. Syfret.

ALLIOT-MARIE, Dr Michèle Yvette Marie-Thérèse; Minister of Foreign and European Affairs, France, 2010–11; *b* 10 Sept. 1946; *d* of Bernard Marie and Renée Leyko. *Educ:* Lycée Folie St-James, Neuilly-sur-Seine; Paris Sorbonne Univ. (BA Private Law, Pol Scis and Hist. of Law; Cert. Law and Econs in African Countries; MA Ethnol.; PhD Law and Politics). Sen. Lectr, Paris Sorbonne Univ., 1984–. Jun. Minister i/c teaching affairs, 1986–88; Mem. (RPR) EP, 1989–94; Minister: of Youth and Sports, 1993–95; of Defence, 2002–07; of the Interior, 2007–09; of Justice, 2009–10. Deputy for Pyrénées-Atlantiques: (RPR), 1986, 1988, 1993, 1995, 1997; (UMP), 2002, 2007. Member: Municipal Council: Ciboure, 1983–88; Biarritz, 1989–91; and First Vice-Pres., Gen. Council, Pyrénées-Atlantiques, 1994–2001. Mayor, St-Jean-de-Luz, 1995–2002. Rassemblement pour la République: various posts including: Mem., Central Cttee, 1984–, Exec. Cttee, 1985–; Dep. Gen. Sec. i/c foreign affairs, 1990–93; Mem., Party Exec., 1991–; National Secretary: i/c social affairs, 1998–99; i/c elections, 1999; Party Chm., 1999–2002. Decorations include: Commandeur: Mérite de l'Educn Nat. and Croix de Comdr, Ordre Nat. (Ivory Coast); Ordre de la République (Egypt); Palmes magistrales 1st Cl. (Peru); Ordre de Stara Planina (Bulgaria); Grand Officier, Ordre Nat. du Lion (Senegal). *Publications:* La Décision Politique: attention! une République peut en cacher une autre, 1983; La Grande Peur des Classes Moyennes, 1996; Les Boursiers Étrangers en France: errements et potentialités, 1997; La République des Irresponsables, 1999; Le Chêne qu'on relève, 2005; La tentation totalitaire de la Gauche, 2014.

ALLIOTT, Sir John (Downes), Kt 1986; Judge of the High Court of Justice, Queen's Bench Division, 1986–2001; *b* 9 Jan. 1932; *er s* of late Alexander Clifford Alliott and Ena Kathleen Alliott (*née* Downes); *m* 1957, Patsy Jennifer, *d* of late Gordon Beckles Willson; two *s* one *d. Educ:* Charterhouse; Peterhouse, Cambridge (Schol., BA). Coldstream Guards, 1950–51; Peterhouse, 1951–54; called to Bar, Inner Temple, 1955, Bencher 1980; QC 1973. Dep. Chm., E Sussex QS, 1970–71; Recorder, 1972–86; Leader, 1983–86, Presiding Judge, 1989–92, SE Circuit. Member: Home Office Adv. Bd on Restricted Patients, 1983–86; Parole Bd, 1994–98 (Vice Chm., 1996–98). *Recreations:* rural pursuits, France and Italy, military history. *Address:* Park Stile, Love Hill Lane, Langley, Slough SL3 6DE.

ALLISON, Brian George; Senior non-executive Director, Goodwood Estate Company Ltd, since 2007; *b* 4 April 1933; *s* of late Donald Brian Allison and Edith Maud Allison (*née* Humphries); *m* 1st, 1958, Glennis Mary Taylor (*d* 1993); one *s* one *d*; 2nd, 1996, Joanne Valerie Norman (*d* 2010); 3rd, 2012, Alisa Ann Topham. *Educ:* Hele's Sch., Exeter; University Coll. London (BSc Econ). FCIM 1981. Flying Officer, RAF, 1955–58. Economist Statistician, Shell-Mex & BP, 1958; Marketing Res. Manager, Spicers, 1958–64; Business Intelligence Services, subseq. The BIS Group: Dir, 1964–91; Gen. Manager, 1964–69; Man. Dir and Dep. Chm., 1969–74; Chm. and Man. Dir, 1974–81; Chm. and Chief Exec., 1981–85; Exec. Chm., 1985–87. Director: NYNEX Inf. Solutions Gp, 1987–90; NYNEX Network Systems Co. (Brussels) SA, 1991–93; non-executive Director: English China Clays plc, subseq. ECC Gp, 1984–92; Brammer plc, 1988–97; Electra Corporate Ventures Ltd, 1989–96; Microgen Holdings plc, 1992–98; Unitech plc, 1993–96; Flexible Management Systems Ltd, 1998–2001; Mem., London Bd, Halifax Building Soc., 1991–95; Chm., Holt Lloyd Gp, 1995–97; Chm. and non-exec. Dir, Amtico Holdings Ltd, 1996–2006; Chm. and non-exec. Dir, Smith Gp Holdings, later Detica Gp plc, 1997–2001; Operating Partner, Electra Partners Europe Ltd, later Cognetas LLP, 2001–09. Mem., ESRC, 1986–90. University of Surrey: Vis. Prof., 1976–92, 1994–2009, 2010–; Chm., Industrial Adv. Panel, Sch. of Mechanical and Materials Engrg, 1998–2001. Distinguished Scholar, QUB, 1989. *Recreations:* tennis, travel, motoring, restoring historic properties. *Clubs:* Reform; Goodwood Road Racing, Bentley Drivers, Rolls-Royce Enthusiasts.

ALLISON, David William; QC 2014; *b* England, 25 June 1975; *s* of Graham and Susan Allison; *m* Fiona Crookall; one *s* one *d. Educ:* Norwich Sch.; Downing Coll., Cambridge (BA 1st Cl. 1997). Called to the Bar, Middle Temple, 1998. *Publications:* contribs to legal textbooks. *Recreations:* tennis, ski-ing, riding, wine. *Address:* South Square Chambers, 3–4 South Square, Gray's Inn, WC1R 5HP. *T:* (020) 7696 9900. *E:* davidallison@southsquare.com.

ALLISON, Air Vice-Marshal Dennis, CB 1987; Chief Executive, North Western Regional Health Authority, 1990–94 (General Manager, 1986–90); *b* 15 Oct. 1932; *m* 1964, Rachel Anne, *d* of Air Vice-Marshal J. G. Franks, CB, CBE; one *s* four *d. Educ:* RAF Halton; RAF Coll., Cranwell; Manchester Univ. (MA 1994). Commnd, 1954; No 87 Sqdn, 1955–58; cfs 1958; Flying Instructor and Coll. Adjt, RAF Coll., 1958–61; CO, RAF Sharjah, 1961–62; Indian Jt Services Staff Coll., 1965; HQ 224 Gp, 1965–68; MoD Central Staffs, 1968–70; ndc, 1973; MoD Central Staffs, 1973–74; CO, RAF Coningsby, 1974–76; Canadian Nat. Defence Coll., 1977; MoD Central Staffs, 1978–79; Comdt, Central Flying Sch., 1979–83; Dir of Training (Flying), MoD, 1983–84; Dir of Management and Support of Intelligence, MoD, 1985–86; retired 1987. Chm., Family Health Service Computer Unit, 1992–94; Member: NHS Trng Authority, 1988–91; Standing Cttee on Postgrad. Medical Educn, 1988–93; Steering Cttee on Pharmacist Postgrad. Educn, 1991–94; Adv. Bd, NHS Estates, 1991–95; Nat. Blood Authority, 1993–2001 (Vice Chm., 1994–2001). Gov., Salford Coll. of Technology, 1987–89. QCVSA 1959. *Address:* 5 Castlegate, Castle Bytham, Grantham, Lincs NG33 4RU. *T:* (01780) 410372. *Club:* Royal Air Force (Hon. Life Mem., 2004).

ALLISON, Gillian Margaret Clarkson; a District Judge (Magistrates' Courts), since 2005; *b* 23 Dec. 1960; *d* of Murray Penman Clarkson and Margaret Gladys Clarkson; *m* 1985, Glen Stuart Allison; two *s*. *Educ:* Merchant Taylors' Sch. for Girls; Surrey Univ.; Central London Poly. (Dip. Law, ext.); Inns of Court Sch. of Law. Called to the Bar, Gray's Inn, 1990; Bench Legal Manager, HM Courts Service, and Dep. Dist Judge, 2003–05. *Recreations:* family, friends, sport, theatre. *Address:* Highbury Corner Magistrates' Court, 51 Holloway Road, N7 8JA.

ALLISON, John, PhD; Editor, Opera, since 2000; Music Critic, Sunday Telegraph, since 2005; *b* 20 May 1965; *s* of David Allison and Adele Myrtle Allison (*née* Kirby); *m* 1991, Nicole Galgut; one *s*. *Educ:* Rondebosch Boys' High Sch., Cape Town; Univ. of Cape Town (BMus 1986, PhD 1989); ARCO. Asst Organist, St George's Cathedral, Cape Town, 1985–89; Music Master, Culford Sch., 1990–91; Asst Ed., 1991–97, Co-ed., 1998–99, Opera mag.; Music Critic, The Times, 1995–2005. Ed., Glyndebourne Fest. prog., 1999–. *Publications:* Edward Elgar: sacred music, 1994; The Pocket Companion to Opera, 1994; (contrib.) New Grove Dictionary of Music and Musicians, 2nd edn 2001; (contrib.) Words on Music: essays in honour of Andrew Porter on the occasion of his 75th birthday, 2004. *Recreations:* travel, art. *Address:* Opera Magazine, 36 Black Lion Lane, W6 9BE. *T:* (020) 8563 8893. *E:* john@opera.co.uk.

ALLISON, Air Chief Marshal Sir John (Shakespeare), KCB 1995; CBE 1986 (MBE 1971); Member, Criminal Injuries Compensation Tribunal (formerly Appeals Panel), 2000–13; *b* 24 March 1943; *o s* of Walter Allison and Mollie Emmie Allison (*née* Poole); *m* 1966, Gillian Patricia Middleton; two *s* three *d*. *Educ:* Royal Grammar Sch., Guildford; RAF College, Cranwell; psc, rcds. Commissioned 1964; flying and staff appts include: 5 Sqn; 226 OCU; 310 TFTS (USAF), Arizona; OC 228 OCU; Station Comdr, RAF Wildenrath; Sec., Chiefs of Staff Cttee; Dir, Air Force Plans and Programmes, 1987–89; ACDS Operational Requirements (Air), MoD, 1989–91; AOC No 11 Gp, 1991–94; COS and Dep. C-in-C, Strike Command, 1994–96; Air Member for Logistics and AOC-in-C, Logistics Comd, 1996–97; AOC-in-C, Strike Comd, 1997–99; Air ADC to Queen, 1997–99. Gentleman Usher to Sword of State, 2005–13. Dir of Strategy, 2001–02, Ops Dir, 2002–04, Jaguar Racing Ltd; Project Director: Filton Site Develt, Rolls-Royce plc, 2005–07; Griffon Hoverwork Ltd, 2009–10. Non-exec. Dir, Oxford Health NHS Foundn Trust, 2015–. Dir and Trustee, Shuttleworth Trust, 1999–2013. President: Europe Air Sports, 2004–09; Light Aircraft Assoc. (formerly Popular Flying Assoc.), 2006–. FRAeS 1995–2013. *Recreation:* private flying. *Address:* c/o National Westminster Bank, 24 Broadgate, Coventry CV1 1ZZ. *Club:* Royal Air Force.

ALLISON, Julia, PhD; General Secretary, 1994–97, Vice President, since 1997, Royal College of Midwives; *b* 26 Sept. 1939; *d* of Alfred Arthur Richley and Amelia (*née* Douglas); *m* 1960, Barrie Allison; one *s* one *d*. *Educ:* Lilley and Stone Foundn for Girls, Newark, Notts; Univ. of Nottingham (MA); Wolverhampton Poly. (CertEd (Dist.)); Univ. of Manchester (PhD English and American Studies 2013). RM; ADM; MTD. Clerical officer, Civil Service, 1956–62; liby officer, Nottingham City Libraries, 1963–66; resident in Australia, 1966–68; liby officer, Nottingham City Libraries, 1968–79; direct entry pupil midwife, 1970–72; dist midwife, Nottingham Local Authy, 1972–76; midwifery sister, night duty, Nottingham AHA, 1976–77; registered foster mother, Nottingham Social Services, 1977–79; community midwife, Nottingham HA, 1979–86; midwife teacher, Kingsmill Hosp., 1986–89; Associate Researcher and Sen. Midwife Advr, Univ. of Nottingham, 1989–91; Head of Midwifery Educn, Norfolk Coll. of Nursing and Midwifery, 1991–94. Hon. Associate Prof., Univ. of Nottingham. Norwich Diocesan Pres., Mother's Union, 2001–06; Lay Canon, Norwich Cathedral, 2002–08, now Lay Canon Emeritus. Hon. DSc Nottingham, 2013. *Publications:* Delivered at Home, 1996; The Organisation of Midwifery Care, 1998; (ed) First World War Diary of Robert Douglas, 2002; A Lifetime of Happiness, 2007; The Oldest Oriental Carpet Emporium, 2007; Maternal Mortality in Six East Anglian Parishes, 1539–1619, 2015. *Recreations:* painting, writing. *Address:* Victory Cottage, 6 Jermyns Road, Reydon, Southwold, Suffolk IP18 6QB.

ALLISON, Prof. Robert John, PhD; Vice-Chancellor and President, Loughborough University, since 2012; *b* Bristol, 4 Feb. 1961; *s* of Gordon Allison and Elizabeth Ann Allison (*née* Oman). *Educ:* Northallerton Grammar Sch.; Hull Univ. (BA Geog.); King's Coll. London (PhD Geog. 1986). CGeog RGS (with IBG) 2002. Addison Wheeler Res. Fellow, Durham Univ., 1986–89; Lectr in Engrg Sedimentology, UCL, 1989–93; Durham University: Lectr in Geog., 1993–95; Reader in Geog., 1995–99; Prof. of Geog., 1999–2006; Chm., Bd of Studies in Geog. (Head of Dept), 2000–03; Dean, Faculty of Social Scis and Health, 2003–06; Sussex University: Prof. of Geog. and Pro-Vice-Chancellor for Res., 2006–12; Dep. Vice-Chancellor, 2010–11. Tutor, EPSRC Graduate Schs Trng Prog., 1996–2005; Prog. Dir, ESRC/NERC Graduate Sch., 1999; Scientist: Oman Wahiba Sands Res. Proj., RGS (with IBG), 1988; Kimberly Res. Proj., RGS (with IBG), 1988; Geomorphology Prog. Dir, 1992–94, Mem. Steering Cttee, 1998–2001, Jordan Badia Res. and Develt Prog., RGS (with IBG). Chm., British Geomorphol Res. Gp, 2006–07 (Jun. Vice-Chm., 2004–05; Vice-Chm., 2005–06). Gen. Sec., Internat. Assoc. of Geomorphologists, 1993–97; Hon. Sec., RGS (with IBG), 1998–2001. Director and Chairman: Sussex Innovation Centre Ltd, 2006–12; Sussex IP Ltd, 2006–12; Chm., West Sussex Envmt and Climate Change Bd, 2010–12. Convener, keynote speaker and plenary lectr at internat. confs and symposia. Jan De Ploey Prize, Katholieke Universiteit Leuven, 1993; Charles Lyell Award, BAAS, 1995; Cuthbert Peek Award, RGS (with IBG), 1997. *Publications:* (ed) Landslides of the Dorset Coast, 1990; (ed) The Coastal Landforms of West Dorset, 1992; (ed jtly) Landscape Sensitivity, 1993; Australia: country fact file, 1999; (ed jtly) Applied Geomorphology: theory and practice, 2002; (ed jtly) Sediment Cascades: an integrated approach, 2010; over 100 articles in jls and other pubns. *Recreations:* mountain biking when not falling off, reading a good book preferably on the beach, exploring remote places. *Address:* Vice-Chancellor's Office, Loughborough University, Leics LE11 3TU. *T:* (01509) 222001. *E:* r.j.allison@lboro.ac.uk.

ALLISON, Roderick Stuart, CB 1996; Joint Chairman and Head of UK Delegation, Channel Tunnel Safety Authority, 1997–2003; Member, Inter-Governmental Commission, 1997–2003; *b* 28 Nov. 1936; *s* of Stuart Frew Allison and Poppy (*née* Hodges); *m* 1968, Anne Sergeant; one *s* one *d*. *Educ:* Manchester Grammar Sch.; Balliol Coll., Oxford. Entered Ministry of Labour, 1959; Private Sec. to Perm. Sec., 1963–64; Principal, 1964; Civil Service Dept, 1969–71; Asst Sec., 1971, Under Sec., 1977, Dept of Employment; Health and Safety Executive, 1989–96: Dir, Safety Policy Div., 1992–94; Chief Exec., Offshore Safety Div., 1994–96; Mem., 1995–96. *Recreations:* reading, swimming, music, grandchildren. *Address:* c/o Channel Tunnel Safety Authority, 1 Kemble Street, WC2B 4AN.

ALLISON, Ronald William Paul, CVO 1978; journalist, author, broadcaster; television consultant; *b* 26 Jan. 1932; *o s* of Percy Allison and Dorothy (*née* Doyle); *m* 1st, 1956, Maureen Angela Macdonald (*d* 1992); two *d*; 2nd, 1993, Jennifer Loy Weider; one *s*. *Educ:* Weymouth Grammar Sch.; Taunton's Sch., Southampton. Reporter, Hampshire Chronicle, 1952–57; Reporter, BBC, 1957–67; freelance broadcaster, 1968–69; special correspondent, BBC, 1969–73; Press Sec. to Queen, 1973–78; regular presenter and commentator, Thames TV, 1978–90; Controller of Sport and Outside Broadcasts, 1980–85, Dir of Corporate Affairs, 1986–89, Thames TV; Chm. and Man. Dir, Grand Slam Sports, 1992–96; Dir, Corporate Affairs, BAFTA, 1993–98. Dir, Corporate Affairs, API Gp, 1996–98. Consultant on Royal Family to ITN, 1991–. Editor, BAFTA News, 1993–99. *Publications:* Look Back in Wonder, 1968; The Queen, 1973; Charles, Prince of our Time, 1978; The Country Life Book of Britain in the Seventies, 1980; (ed with Sarah Riddell) The Royal Encyclopedia, 1991; The Queen: 50 years—a celebration, 2001. *Recreations:* photography, watching football. *Clubs:* Lord's Taverners; Old Tauntonians (Southampton).

ALLISS, Peter; golfer; television commentator; golf course architect; writer; *b* 28 Feb. 1931; *s* of Percy Alliss and Dorothy Alliss (*née* Rust); *m* 1st, 1953, Joan; one *s* one *d*; 2nd, 1969, Jacqueline Anne; two *s* one *d* (and one *d* decd). *Educ:* Queen Elizabeth's Grammar Sch., Wimborne; Crosby House, Bournemouth. Nat. Service, RAF Regt, 1949–51. Professional golfer, 1946; played in 8 Ryder Cup matches and 10 Canada Cup (now World Cup) matches; winner of 21 major events; open championships of Spain, Portugal, Italy, Brazil. Past Pres., Ladies' PGA and British Green Keepers' Assoc.; twice Captain, British PGA. Hon. Member, Golf Clubs: Royal & Ancient, 2004; Royal Cinque Ports; Professional Golfers' Assoc.; Combe Hill; Moor Allerton; Beaconsfield; Trevose; Parkstone; Ferndown; Stoke Poges; W Cornwall; Peel; Muirfield Village; Wentworth; Guildford; Rosses Point; Lahinch; Broadstone; Chestfield; Auchterarder; Hindhead; Royal Porthcawl; Kemper Lakes; Helsby; Loch Lomond; Churston; President: Old Thorns; Remedy Oak. Hon. LLD St Andrews, 2005; Hon. DLitt: Humberside, 1993; Bournemouth, 2002. *Publications:* Easier Golf (with Paul Trevillion), 1969; Bedside Golf, 1980; Shell Book of Golf, 1981; The Duke, 1983; Play Golf with Peter Alliss, 1983; The Who's Who of Golf, 1983; (with Michael Hobbs) The Open, 1984; Golfer's Logbook, 1984; Lasting the Course, 1984; More Bedside Golf, 1984; Peter Alliss' Most Memorable Golf, 1986; Peter Alliss' Supreme Champions of Golf, 1986; (ed) Winning Golf, 1986; Yet More Bedside Golf, 1986; Play Better Golf with Peter Alliss, 1989; (with Michael Hobbs) Peter Alliss' Best 100 Golfers, 1989; (with Bob Ferrier) The Best of Golf, 1989; The Lazy Golfers' Guide, 1995; Peter Alliss' Golf Heroes, 2002; Alliss's 19th Hole, 2005; Golf: the cure for a grumpy old man, 2008; *autobiography:* Alliss through the Looking Glass, 1964; Peter Alliss: an autobiography, 1981; My Life, 2004. *Recreation:* talking and taking wine with chums. *Address:* Bucklands, Hindhead, Surrey GU26 6HY. *Clubs:* Lansdowne, Crockfords, Ritz Casino.

ALLISTER, Rt Rev. Donald Spargo; *see* Peterborough, Bishop of.

ALLISTER, James Hugh; QC (NI) 2001; Member (TUV) North Antrim, Northern Ireland Assembly, since 2011; Leader, Traditional Unionist Voice, since 2007; *b* 2 April 1953; *s* of Robert Allister and Mary Jane Allister (*née* McCrory); *m* 1978, Ruth McCullagh; two *s* one *d*. *Educ:* Regent House Grammar Sch., Newtownards; Queen's Univ., Belfast. Called to the NI Bar, 1976. Mem. (DemU) N Antrim, NI Assembly, 1982–86. Mem. for NI, European Parlt, 2004–09 (DemU, 2004–07, Traditional Unionist, 2007–09). Contested (TUV) North Antrim, 2010. *Address:* Northern Ireland Assembly, Parliament Buildings, Stormont, Belfast BT4 3XX.

ALLMENDINGER, Prof. Philip Michael, PhD; Professor of Land Economy, since 2008, Head, School of Humanities and Social Sciences, since 2015, University of Cambridge; Fellow of Clare College, Cambridge; *b* North Ferriby, 20 Jan. 1968; *s* of Michael Antoon Allmendinger and Janet Mary Allmendinger; *m* 2002, Claudia Wilma Alföldi; three *d*. *Educ:* BSc Hons, MA, PhD, Dip. Law. MRTPI; MRICS. Reader in Land Economy, Univ. of Aberdeen, 1998–2004; Prof. of Planning, Univ. of Reading, 2004–08; Hd, Dept of Land Econ. and Dep. Hd, Sch. of Humanities and Social Scis, Univ. of Cambridge, 2012–15. *Publications:* Planning and Thatcherism, 1997; Planning in Postmodern Times, 2001; Planning Theory, 2002, 2nd edn 2009; New Labour New Planning, 2011. *Recreations:* ski-ing, reading. *Address:* Department of Land Economy, 19 Silver Street, Cambridge CB3 9EP. *E:* pma32@cam.ac.uk.

ALLNUTT, Denis Edwin; former Director of Analytical Services, Department for Education and Employment; *b* 17 May 1946; *m* 1968, Patricia Livermore; one *s* one *d*. *Educ:* Hampton Sch., Middlesex; Univ. of Birmingham (BSc 1967). Statistician, Min. of Housing and Local Govt, DoE and Dept of Transport, 1967–82; Chief Statistician: Dept of Employment, 1982–88; DoE, 1988–90; Hd, subseq. Dir, Analytical Services, DES, then DFE, later DFEE, 1990–2000.

ALLNUTT, (Ian) Peter, OBE; MA; *b* 26 April 1917; *s* of Col E. B. Allnutt, CBE, MC, and Joan C. Gainsford; *m* 1st, 1946, Doreen Louise Lenagan (*d* 1995); four *d*; 2nd, 1997, Doreen Laven. *Educ:* Imperial Service Coll., Windsor; Sidney Sussex Coll., Cambridge. HM Colonial Service, 1939–46, Nigeria, with break, 1940–45, for service in World War II, Nigeria Regt, RWAFF (despatches). Service with the British Council in Peru, E Africa, Colombia, Argentina, Malta, London and Mexico, 1946–77. OBE 1976; Insignia of Aztec Eagle, 1975. *Recreations:* rowing, swimming, pre-Columbian America, the Hispanic world.

ALLOTT, Nicholas David, OBE 2014; Managing Director, Cameron Mackintosh Ltd, since 2000; *b* 25 March 1954; *s* of late Brig. David Allott and of Shirley Allott; *m* 1989, Anneka Rice (separated 1993); two *s*; partner, Christa D'Souza; two *s*. *Educ:* Geelong Grammar Sch., Australia; Copthorne Sch., Sussex; Charterhouse, Surrey; Exeter Univ. Exec. Dir, Royal Th., Northampton, 1977–81; Cameron Mackintosh Ltd: Prodn Adminr, 1981–86; Exec. Producer, 1986–2000. UK Trade Ambassador, 2014–. Chm., Soho Th., 2005–. Member: London Cultural Strategy Gp, 2013–; Selection Cttee for UK City of Culture, 2013–. Trustee: Foundn for Sport and the Arts, 1996–2014; Oxford Sch. of Drama, 2000–; Roundhouse Trust, 2005–; Member: Bd, Cultural Olympiad, 2010–13; Theatres Trust, 2011–. British Business Ambassador, 2014–. *Recreations:* shooting, sailing, keeping the peace. *Address:* 101 Gunterstone Road, W14 9BT. *T:* (020) 7602 0412, *Fax:* (020) 7610 4346. *E:* nick@camack.co.uk. *Clubs:* Garrick, Soho House, Century, Ivy.

ALLOTT, Prof. Philip James, LLD; FBA 2004; Professor of International Public Law, University of Cambridge, 2000–04, now Professor Emeritus; Fellow, Trinity College, Cambridge, since 1973; *b* Sheffield, 29 May 1937; *s* of Reginald William Allott and Dorothy Allott (*née* Dobson). *Educ:* Downside Sch.; Trinity Coll., Cambridge (MA, LLM; LLD 1998). Called to the Bar, Gray's Inn, 1960; HM Diplomatic Service, 1960–73: Asst Legal Advr, then Legal Counsellor, 1965, FCO; Legal Advr, BMG, Berlin, 1965–68; Legal Counsellor, UK Perm. Repn to EC, Brussels, 1972–73; Law Faculty, University of Cambridge: Mem., 1976–; Lectr, 1980–97; Reader, 1997–2000. Bertha Wilson Dist. Vis. Prof., Dalhousie Univ. Law Sch., 1992; Ganshof van der Meersch Chair, Univ. Libre de Bruxelles, 1996; Faculty Mem., Hauser Global Law Sch. Prog., NY Univ. Law Sch., 1995–. Alternate Rep., UK Delegn to UN Law of the Sea Conf., 1976–80. Internat. Envmtl Law Award, Center for Internat. Envmtl Law, 2014. *Publications:* Eunomia: new order for a new world, 1990, 2nd edn 2001; The Health of Nations: society and law beyond the state, 2002; Towards the International Rule of Law, 2005; Invisible Power: a philosophical adventure story, 2005; Invisible Power 2: a metaphysical adventure story, 2008; Trinity Minds 1317–1945: an intellectual account of Trinity College, Cambridge, 2015. *Recreations:* high culture, the fine arts, conversation, gardening. *Address:* Trinity College, Cambridge CB2 1TQ. *E:* pja1001@cam.ac.uk. *Club:* Oxford and Cambridge.

See also R. M. Allott.

ALLOTT, Robin Michael; Under-Secretary, Departments of Industry and Trade, 1978–80; *b* 9 May 1926; *s* of late Reginald William Allott and Dorothy (*née* Dobson). *Educ:* The Oratory Sch., Caversham; New Coll., Oxford; Sheffield Univ. Asst Principal, BoT, 1948; UK Delegn to OECD, Paris, 1952; Private Sec. to Sec. for Overseas Trade, 1953; Principal, Office for Scotland, Glasgow, 1954; UK Delegn to UN Conf. on Trade and Develt, Geneva, 1964; Asst Sec., BoT, 1965; Counsellor, UK Delegn to EEC, Brussels, 1971; sabbatical year, New Coll., Oxford, 1974–75; Dept of Industry (motor industry), 1975; Under-Sec., Dept of Trade, 1976.

Member: European Sociobiol Soc., 1992; NY Acad. of Scis, 1995; AAAS, 1996. Herder/Jan Wind Prize Essay, 2015. *Publications:* The Physical Foundation of Language, 1973; The Motor Theory of Language Origin, 1989; (ed) Studies in Language Origins 3, 1994; (ed jtly) Dorothy Dobson's Commonplace Book, 2000; The Natural Origin of Language, 2000; The Great Mosaic Eye, 2001, 2nd edn as The Great Mosaic Eye: embodied language, evolution and society, 2012; The Child and the World, 2005; contrib. Jl of Social and Evolutionary Systems; contrib. collections on lang. and origin of semiosis, sound symbolism, syntax, etc. *Recreations:* studying the evolutionary relation of language, perception and action and language acquisition. *Address:* 5 Fitzgerald Park, Seaford, East Sussex BN25 1AX. *T:* (01323) 492300.

See also P. J. Allott.

ALLPRESS, Dr Stephen Alan, FREng; FIET; Chief Technology Officer for Modern Software Development, since 2011, and Senior Vice President, since 2014, Nvidia, (Vice President, 2011–14); *b* Billericay, Essex, 24 July 1968; *s* of Alan and Valerie Kathleen Allpress; *m* 2005, Sarah Bryn; two *d. Educ:* Univ. of Bristol (BEng Hons 1990; PhD 1994). FIET 2000; FREng 2013. Mem., tech. staff, 1994–98, Tech. Manager, 1998–2000, Bell Labs, USA; Principal Scientist, Broadcom, NJ, 2000–01; Chief Res. Fellow, Toshiba Res. Labs, Bristol, 2001–02; Co-Founder, Mem. Bd, Chief Tech. Officer and Vice Pres., Icera Inc., 2002–11. *Recreations:* family, running, cycling, squash.

ALLSHIRE, Prof. Robin Campbell, PhD; FRS 2011; Professor of Chromosome Biology, and Wellcome Trust Principal Research Fellow, Wellcome Trust Centre for Cell Biology, University of Edinburgh. *Educ:* Trinity College, Dublin; Univ. of Edinburgh (PhD). Postdoctoral researcher, MRC Human Genetics Unit, Univ. of Edinburgh; Vis. Scientist, Cold Spring Harbor Labs; established own res. gp, MRC Human Genetics Unit, 1990, subseq. moved to Wellcome Trust Centre for Cell Biol., 2002, Univ. of Edinburgh. Mem. EMBO, 1988. FRSE 2002. Genetics Soc. Medal, 2013. *Publications:* articles in jls. *Address:* Wellcome Trust Centre for Cell Biology, University of Edinburgh, Michael Swann Building, King's Buildings, Mayfield Road, Edinburgh EH9 3JR.

ALLSOP, Malcolm Vincent; Director, Town House Films Ltd, since 2009; *b* 9 Sept. 1950; *s* of Bernard and Irene Allsop; *m* 1975, Elaine Jessica Cox; one *s. Educ:* Highbury Grammar Sch., London. Reporter: Ormskirk Advertiser, Lancs, 1967–68; W Lancs Press Agency, 1968–70; and Producer, BBC Radio Merseyside, 1970–71; BBC TV Manchester, 1971–72; Anglia TV, Norwich, 1973; BBC TV East, Norwich, 1974–77; Anglia Television: Political Ed., 1978–84; Sen. Producer, Current Affairs, 1984–89; Controller, Current Affairs and Religion, 1990–94; Dep. Dir of Progs, 1994–96; Controller of Progs and Prodn, 1996–97; Dir of Progs and Prodn, 1998–2000; Controller of Factual Entertainment, Formats and Daytime, LWT/United Prodns, 2001–02; Dir, Anglia TV, until 2002; Controller, Format Sales and Acquisitions, Granada Media, 2002–03; Creative Dir, TéVé Media Gp, 2004; CEO, TéVé Partners, 2004; Man. Dir, Town House TV Prodns Ltd, 2004–09. Mem., Cringleford Parish Council, 2014–. *Publications:* (jtly) Painting Light in Oil, 2011. *Recreations:* painting, bird-watching, Victorian criminology, lawn bowling, metal detecting, archaeology, history. *Address:* Town House Films Ltd, PO Box 3482, Norwich NR7 7PP.

ALLSOP, Prof. Richard Edward, OBE 1997; PhD, DSc; FREng, FICE; Professor of Transport Studies, University College London, 1976–2005, now Professor Emeritus; *b* 2 May 1940; *s* of Edward James Allsop and Grace Ada Allsop (*née* Tacey); *m* 1990, Frances Elizabeth Killick. *Educ:* Bemrose Sch., Derby; Queens' Coll., Cambridge (MA Maths); University Coll. London (PhD Maths, DSc Engrg). CEng, FICE, 1990; FREng 1996; FCILT (FCIT 1981); FCIHT (FIHT 1983); TPP 2009. Scientific Officer, Road Res. Lab., 1964–66; Res. Fellow, 1967–69, Lectr in Transport Studies, 1970–72, UCL; Dir, Transport Ops Res. Gp, Univ. of Newcastle upon Tyne, 1973–76; Dean of Engrg, UCL, 1983–85. Visiting Professor: Univ. of Karlsruhe, 1977; Univ. of Natural Resources and Applied Life Scis, Vienna, 2002; Newcastle Univ., 2006–; Adjunct Prof., Qld Univ. of Technol., 2006–; Hon. Professor: Tech. Univ. of Cracow, 2000–; Moscow Automobile and Roads Inst. (State Tech. Univ.), 2001–; Vis. Fellow, Univ. of Osaka, 1981; Vis. Erskine Fellow, Univ. of Canterbury Christchurch, 1997; Vis. Choi Kin Chung Fellow, Univ. of Hong Kong, 2012. Ext. Res. Advr, Dept for Transport, 1993–; Dir, Parly Adv. Council for Transport Safety, 1995–2015. Mem., Road Traffic Law Rev., 1985–88. Visitor to Traffic Gp, Transport & Road Res. Lab., 1987–92. Bd Mem., Eur. Transport Safety Council, 2005–. Member: Northumberland and Newcastle Soc., 1973–; Chiltern Soc., 1977–. Highways and Transportation Award, Instn of Highways and Transportation, 1997; Prince Michael Internat. Road Safety Award, 2011. *Publications:* (with D. Zumkeller) Kleines Fachwörterbuch Verkehrswesen, 2003; (ed jtly) Transportation and Traffic Theory 2007, 2007; numerous papers in learned jls, edited proceedings. *Recreations:* photography, theatre, walking. *Address:* Centre for Transport Studies, University College London, Gower Street, WC1E 6BT. *E:* r.e.allsop@ucl.ac.uk.

ALLSOPP, family name of **Baron Hindlip**.

ALLSOPP, Ven. Christine; Archdeacon of Northampton, 2005–13, now Archdeacon Emeritus; *b* 19 Jan. 1947; *d* of John Rupert Goddard and Phyllis May Goddard; *m* 1970, Dr Dennis Allsopp; two *s* one *d. Educ:* St Albans Grammar Sch. for Girls; Univ. of Aston (BSc (Chem.) 1968); Salisbury and Wells Theol Coll. Res. Chemist, 1968–70, Inf. Officer, 1970–72, Albright and Wilson; freelance scientific ed. and abstractor, 1977–86. Ordained deacon, 1989, priest, 1994; Asst Curate, Caversham and Mapledurham, 1989–94; Team Vicar, Bracknell, 1994–98; Team Rector, Bourne Valley, 1998–2005. RD, Alderbury, 1999–2005; Canon and Preb., Salisbury Cathedral, 2002–05; Hon. Canon, Peterborough Cathedral, 2005–13. Dep. to Archdeacon of Berks for church building matters, 2014–. Mem., Gen. Synod of C of E, 2005–13. Mem., Oxford DAC, 2014–. Trustee, Sons & Friends of the Clergy, 2012–. *Recreations:* walking, swimming, Asian cooking. *Address:* Mellor Cottage, Sunnybank, 2 Walker's Lane, Lambourn, Berks RG17 8YE. *T:* 07801 096345. *E:* venchrisallsopp@gmail.com.

ALLSOPP, Christopher John, CBE 2004; Director, Oxford Institute for Energy Studies, 2006–13; Fellow of New College, 1967–2008, now Emeritus, and Senior Research Fellow, Department of Economics, 2006, now Emeritus, Oxford University; *b* 6 April 1941; twin *s* of late (Harold) Bruce Allsopp, FSA; *m* 1967, Marian Elizabeth Pearce. *Educ:* Balliol Coll., Oxford (MA 1967); Nuffield Coll., Oxford (BPhil Econs 1967). Econ. Asst, HM Treasury, 1966–67; Oxford University: Tutor in Econs, New Coll., 1967–2008; Lectr in Econs, 1968–97 (on leave to OECD, Paris, 1973–74); Reader in Econ. Policy, 1997–2006. Bank of England: Advr, 1980–83; Mem., Ct of Dirs, 1997–2000; Mem., Monetary Policy Cttee, 2000–03. Leader, ind. Review of Statistics for Economic Policymaking, 2003. Ed., Oxford Review of Econ. Policy, 1985–.

ALLTHORPE-GUYTON, Marjorie; Secretary General, Association Internationale des Critiques d'Art, since 2015 (President, UK section, since 2009; Chair, Congress Commission, 2012–14); *b* 29 July 1948; *d* of Maurice Jack Allthorpe-Guyton and Edith Florence (*née* Clark); *m* 1st, 1970, Brian Collison (marr. diss. 1977); 2nd, 1989, John Mullis (marr. diss. 2000); one *s* one *d*; 3rd, 2000, Paul Dale. *Educ:* Univ. of East Anglia (BA Hons Fine Art); Courtauld Inst. AMA 1974. Asst Keeper, Norwich Castle Mus., 1969–79; Researcher, Norwich Sch. of Art, 1980–82; Selector, British Art Show, Arts Council, 1982–84; Associate Ed., 1988–91, Ed., 1990–92, Artscribe; Dir of Visual Arts, Arts Council of England, later Arts Council England, 1993–2006. External Assessor, Fine Art degrees, 1988–95, Mem. Council, 1997–2005, Goldsmiths' Coll., London Univ.; External Assessor: Fine Art, Oxford Brookes Univ., 1998–2000; Art Theory, City Univ., 2003–07; Ext. Examr, Painting, Slade Sch. of Art, UCL, 2010–14; Panel Mem., Art and Design RAE, HEFC, 2008. Trustee: Kenneth Armitage Foundn, 2011–; City and Guilds of London Art Sch., 2011–. FRSA 1994; FRCA 1999; RIBA 2003. Hon. Dr Anglia Ruskin Univ., 2005. Previews writer, Royal Acad. Mag. *Publications:* A Happy Eye: history of Norwich Sch. of Art 1845–1982, 1982; (jtly) Ian McKeever (monograph), 2009; catalogues: Henry Bright, 1973; John Sell Cotman, 1975; John Thirtle, 1977; Norwich Castle Museum, 1979; many essays and articles on contemporary art. *Recreations:* film, cooking, sailing, growing pomegranates. *Address:* 1 Thornhill Road, N1 1HX. *Clubs:* Chelsea Arts, Blacks, Two Brydges.

ALLUM, Sarah Elizabeth Royle, (Mrs R. G. Allum); *see* Walker, S. E. R.

ALLWEIS, Martin Peter; His Honour Judge Allweis; a Circuit Judge, since 1994; Designated Family Judge for Greater Manchester, 1996–2005; *b* 22 Dec. 1947; *s* of late Jack Allweis and Iris Allweis (*née* Mosco); *m* 1984, Tracy Ruth, *d* of late Hyam Barr and of Bernice Barr; one *s* one *d. Educ:* Manchester Grammar Sch.; Sidney Sussex Coll., Cambridge (BA Hons 1969). Called to the Bar, Inner Temple, 1970; in practice on Northern Circuit, 1971–94; a Recorder, 1990–94. *Recreations:* family interests, football (Manchester City FC), squash. *Address:* c/o Manchester County Court, Manchester Civil Justice Centre, 1 Bridge Street, Manchester M60 9DJ.

ALLWOOD; *see* Muirhead-Allwood.

ALMOND, David John; novelist, short story writer and playwright for children and adults; Professor of Creative Writing, Bath Spa University, since 2012; *b* 15 May 1951; *s* of James Arthur Almond and Catherine Almond (*née* Barber); partner, Sara Jane Palmer; one *d. Educ:* St John's, Felling; St Aidan's, Sunderland; St Joseph's Hebburn; Univ. of E Anglia (BA Hons Eng. and American Lit.); Univ. of Newcastle upon Tyne (PGCE). Postman; teacher (primary, adults and special needs), Tyneside, 1976–98. Vis Prof. of Creative Writing, Nottingham Trent Univ., 2007–12; Dist. Writing Fellow, Newcastle Univ., 2013–. Commune mem., 1982–83. Ed., Panurge (fiction mag.), 1987–93. Artistic Dir, Bath Fest. of Children's Lit., 2013, 2014. Freeman, City of Gateshead, 2011. Hon. DLitt: Sunderland, 2001; Leicester, 2005; Newcastle, 2011. Hans Christian Andersen Award, 2010; Eleanor Farjeon Award, 2013. *Plays:* Wild Girl, Wild Boy, nat. tours, 2001, 2002; My Dad's a Birdman, Young Vic, 2003, 2010; *libretto:* Skellig, 2008, UK tour, 2009–10, Broadway, 2011; Angelo: an opera for Sunderland, 2015. *Publications:* Sleepless Nights, 1985; A Kind of Heaven, 1997; Counting Stars (short stories), 2000; Noah and the Fludd (play), 2010; Nesting (short stories), 2013; Half a Creature from the Sea (short stories), 2014; Harry Miller's Run, 2015; *for children:* Skellig, 1998 (Library Assoc. Carnegie Medal, Whitbread Children's Book of the Year; Silver Pencil (Holland), 2000) (adapted for radio, and staged, Young Vic, 2003; adapted as opera, The Sage, Gateshead, 2008, and as film, 2009); Kit's Wilderness, 1999 (Smarties Silver Award, 1999; Silver Kiss (Holland), Michael L. Printz Award (USA), 2001; adapted for TV); Heaven Eyes, 2000 (adapted for radio, and staged, 2004); Secret Heart, 2001 (adapted for stage); Wild Girl, Wild Boy (play), 2002; The Fire-Eaters, 2003 (Smarties Gold Award, Whitbread Children's Book of the Year, 2003; Boston Globe-Horn Book Award (USA), 2004); Kate, the Cat and the Moon (illus. Stephen Lambert), 2004; Clay, 2005 (adapted for TV, 2008); My Dad's a Birdman, 2007; The Savage, 2008 (Le Prix Sorcières, 2011); Jackdaw Summer, 2008; Slog's Dad, 2010; The Boy who Climbed into the Moon, 2010; My Name is Mina, 2010; The Boy who Swam with Piranhas, 2012; Mouse Bird Snake Wolf, 2013; A Song for Ella Grey, 2014; Klaus Vogel and the Bad Lads, 2014; *for children and adults:* The True Tale of the Monster Billy Dean, 2011; The Tightrope Walkers, 2014; books trans. into more than 30 langs. *Recreation:* walking (Yorkshire Dales, Northumbrian beaches). *Address:* c/o Catherine Clarke, Felicity Bryan, 2a North Parade Avenue, Oxford OX2 6LX, W6 0HJ.

ALMOND, George Haylock, CBE 2001 (MBE 1993); DL; international fire consultant, since 2002; Commander, St John Ambulance for Greater Manchester, 2002–07; *b* 19 Jan. 1944; *s* of late Arthur Ernest Almond and of Mrs Constance Violet Almond; *m* 1968, Elizabeth Allcock; one *s* one *d. Educ:* Portsmouth Tech. High Sch.; Eastleigh Tech. Coll. Fireman, then Leading Fireman, and Sub-Officer, Hants Fire Service, 1962–70; Cheshire Fire Brigade: Station Officer, 1970–72; Asst Divl Officer, 1972–75; Divl Officer, Grade III, 1975–77; Divl Officer, Grade I, 1977–82; Divl Comdr, 1978–82; Greater Manchester County Fire Service: Asst County Fire Officer, 1982–90; Dep. County Fire Officer, 1990–95; County Fire Officer and Chief Exec., 1995–2002. Chm., Fire Services Nat. Benevolent Fund, 2000; Vice Chm., Emmaus Bolton, 1998–; Vice Chm., 1998–2012, Chm., 2012–, Emmaus North West Partnership. Life Patron, Fire Fighters Charity, 2010. Vice Chm., Broughton Hse for ex-service men and women, 2013–. Mem., Rotary Club, Manchester, 1996–2014 (Pres., 2002–03). FIFireE 1988 (Internat. Pres., 1996–97); FRSPH (FRSH 1989–2013); FCIPD (FIPD 1991). Freeman, City of London, 1999. DL 1999, High Sheriff 2012–13, Greater Manchester. Hon. Fellow, Bolton Inst., 2000. Hon. MSc Salford, 2004; Hon. DEng Bolton, 2010. OStJ 2004 (SBStJ 2001). Fire Bde Long Service and Good Conduct Medal, 1982; Queen's Jubilee Medal, 2002. *Publications:* Accidents, Injuries and Illnesses to Firemen in Great Britain, 1972; (contrib.) Fire Service Drill Book, 1985; IFE Preliminary Certificate Students Handbook, 1994; Elementary Fire Engineering Handbook, 2004; contrib. papers to technical jls. *Recreations:* music, reading, walking. *Address:* 4 Stonehouse, Chapeltown Road, Bromley Cross, Bolton, Lancs BL7 9NB.

ALMOND, Prof. Jeffrey William, PhD; FMedSci; Vice President, Discovery Research (formerly Global Research) and External Research and Development, Sanofi Pasteur, 1999–2014; *b* 28 June 1951; *s* of Stanley Peter Almond and Joyce Mary Almond (*née* Fountain); *m* 1976, Karen Elizabeth Batley, BSc, PhD; two *s* one *d. Educ:* Univ. of Leeds (BSc); Downing Coll., Cambridge (PhD 1978). Lectr in Virology, Univ. of Leicester, 1979–85; Fellow, Lister Inst. of Preventive Medicine, 1985; University of Reading: Prof. of Microbiol., 1985–99; Hd, Sch. of Animal and Microbial Scis, 1991–95; Vis. Prof., 1999–. Vis. Prof. of Microbiol., Univ. of Oxford, 2013–. Mem., Spongiform Encephalopathies Adv. Cttee, UK Govt, 1995–99. Chm., Virology Div., Internat. Union of Microbiol Socs, 1996–99. Mem. Council, MRC, 2008–14. Fellow, Amer. Acad. of Microbiol., 1996; FMedSci 2006 (Mem. Council, 2008–11). Ivanosky Medal for Virology, Russian Acad. Med. Scis, 1999. *Publications:* over 160 scientific papers, book chapters and rev. articles in jls. *Recreations:* Alpine sports, jardinage, golf, fitness, jogging. *T:* (France) 6033 60851.

ALMOND, Thomas Clive, OBE 1989; HM Diplomatic Service, retired; Consul-General, Bordeaux, 1992–98; *b* 30 Nov. 1939; *s* of late Thomas and Eveline Almond; *m* 1965, Auriol Gala Elizabeth Annette Hendry (*d* 2014). *Educ:* Bristol Grammar Sch.; London Univ. Entered HM Diplomatic Service, 1967; Accra, 1968; Paris, 1971; FCO, 1975; Brussels, 1978; Jakarta, 1980; Brazzaville, 1983; Ambassador to People's Republic of the Congo, 1987–88; Asst Marshal of the Diplomatic Corps and Asst Head of Protocol Dept, 1988–92. *Recreations:* travelling, golf.

AL-MULLA, Shwan Mohammad, CBE 2011; President, Iraqi Consultants and Construction Bureau, since 2003; *b* Baghdad, 20 Oct. 1960; *s* of Mohammad and Neimat Al-Mulla; *m* 1981, Suzan; three *s* two *d. Educ:* Richmond Coll., London (BA(Econ)). Pres. and CEO, Sheermans Ltd, 1993–2004; Co-Founder and Pres., Empire Hldgs, 2006–09. Mem., Adv. Bd, Amar Internat. Charitable Foundn, 2012–. *Recreations:* art, car racing, boating. *Address:* Iraqi Consultants and Construction Bureau Centre, Queen Rania Al Abdullah Street, opposite Arena Hotel, Amman, Jordan. *E:* info@iccb.com.

ALMUNIA AMANN, Joaquín; Member, 2004–14, and a Vice-President, 2010–14, European Commission; *b* 17 June 1948; *m*; two *c. Educ:* Univ. of Deusto, Bilbao. Economist, Council Bureau, Spanish Chambers of Commerce, Brussels, 1972–75; Chief Economist,

Unión Gen. de Trabajo, 1976–79. MP (PSOE), Spain, 1979–2004; Minister: of Employment and Social Security, 1982–86; of Public Admin, 1986–91. Parly Leader, 1994–97, Sec. Gen., 1997–2000, PSOE. *Publications:* Memorias Políticas, 2001.

ALMUTAIWEE, Abdulrahman Ghanem, Hon. CVO 2013; Ambassador of the United Arab Emirates to the Court of St James's, since 2009; *b* Dubai, 1 July 1953; *m*; six *s* two *d*. *Educ:* Cairo Univ. (BSc Econs 1979); Dip. Banking and Financial Studies, Bankers Trust Co., NY, 1983. Nat. Bank of Abu Dhabi, Dubai, 1980–83; Dir-Gen., Dubai Chamber of Commerce and Industry, 1983–2006. Chm., Al Fordous PSCo., 2008–; Vice-Chm., Emirates Glass Co., 2007–; Mem. Bd, Emirates Petroleum Corp., 1990–2006. Board Member: Trade Agencies Cttee, Min. of Econ. and Trade, Dubai, 1990–2003; Higher Cttee, Econ. and Trade Exec. Office, Dubai, 2005–06; Government of Dubai: Board Member: Higher Cttee, Dubai Shopping Fest., 1997–2006; Higher Cttee, Dubai Quality Award, 1998–2006; Vice-Chm., Exec. Council, Central Grievance Cttee, 2008–. Member: Bd, Jebel Ali Free Zone, 1985–2000; Dubai Commerce and Tourism Promotion Bd, 1989–95. Mem. Bd, UAE Nat. Cttee for Internat. Chamber of Commerce, 2003–06. Chm., Mohammed bin Rashid Al Maktoum Business Award Cttee, 2004–06. Member, Board of Governors: Dubai UC, 1983–2006; Dubai Ethics Resource Centre, 2003–06. Mem. Bd, UAE Red Crescent, 2007–. Officer, Order of Civil Merit (Spain), 1999. *Recreations:* reading, swimming, jogging. *Address:* United Arab Emirates Embassy, 30 Prince's Gate, SW7 1PT. *T:* (020) 7590 7212, *Fax:* (020) 7581 9616.

ALPASS, John; Head of Fraud Strategy, Department for Work and Pensions (formerly Head of Fraud Intelligence, Department of Social Security), 2000–05. Security Service, 1973–95; Intelligence Co-ordinator, Cabinet Office, 1996–99. Mem., Security Vetting Appeals Panel, 2009–15. Chm., Fees Adv. Commn, Gen. Synod, 2012–; Member: Guildford Diocesan Adv. Cttee, 2003– (Chm., 2011–); Bishop's Council, Dio. of Guildford, 2007–.

ALPE, Pauline; *see* Wallace, P.

ALPERS, Prof. Michael Philip, AO 2005; CSM 2008; FRS 2008; FAA; John Curtin Distinguished Professor of International Health, Curtin University, since 2005. *Educ:* Gonville and Caius Coll., Cambridge (BA 1957); Univ. of Adelaide (BSc, MB BS). FAA 2012. Kuru Res. Officer, Dept of Public Health, PNG, 1961–63; Vis. Scientist, NIH, 1964–67; Res. Fellow, Dept of Microbiol., Univ. of Western Australia, 1968–76; Dir, Inst. of Med. Res., PNG, 1977–2000; Adjunct Prof., Centre for Internat. Health, Curtin Univ. of Technol., 2001–04. Mem., Aust. TSE Adv. Cttee, 2001–12. Fellow: Australasian Coll. of Tropical Medicine, 1992; Qld Inst. of Med. Res., 1992; Faculty of Public Health Medicine, RACP, 2001; PNG Inst. of Med. Res., 2005. Fellow, World Acad. of Scis (Associate Fellow, Third World Acad. of Scis, 1991). Hon. Internat. Fellow (formerly Hon. Mem.), Amer. Soc. of Tropical Medicine and Hygiene, 1993; Hon. Life Mem., Australasian Soc. for Infectious Diseases, 1999; Life Member: Med. Soc. of PNG, 2002; Australasian Epidemiol Assoc., 2011. DUniv Adelaide, 2012. Medal, Collège de France, 1984; Macdonald Medal, RSTM&H, 1990; Lifetime Achievement Award, Monash Univ., 2008. *Address:* Room 108, Shenton Park Campus, Curtin University, GPO Box U1987, Perth, WA 6845, Australia; 3 Watkins Street, Fremantle, WA 6160, Australia.

ALPHANDÉRY, Edmond Gérard; President, Centre for European Policy Studies, Brussels, since 2014; non-voting Director, Crédit Agricole Corporate and Investment Bank (formerly Calyon), since 2002; Director: ENGIE (formerly Suez, then GDF Suez), since 2003; Néovacs, since 2011; Senior Adviser, Nomura France, since 2012; *b* 2 Sept. 1943; *m* 1972, Laurence Rivain; one *s*. *Educ:* Frédéric Mistral Lycée, Avignon; Inst. of Political Studies, Paris; Univs of Chicago and California at Berkeley. Asst Lectr, Univ. of Paris, IX, 1968–69; Lectr, Univ. of Aix-en-Provence, 1970–71; Sen. Lectr, and Dean, Faculty of Econ. Sci., Univ. of Nantes, 1971–74; Prof., Univ. of Angers, 1973; Associate Prof., Univ. of Pittsburgh, 1975; Prof. of Political Economy, Univ. of Paris II, 1974–92. Deputy (UDF-CDS) for Maine-et-Loire, French Nat. Assembly, 1978–93 (Mem., Finance Cttee, 1979–93); Minister of the Economy, France, 1993–95; Mem., Maine-et-Loire General Council, 1976–2008 (Vice-Pres., 1991–94, Pres., 1994–95); Mayor of Longué-Jumelles, 1977–2008. Vice-Pres., Centre des Démocrates Sociaux; numerous positions with economic and monetary bodies, incl. Chm., Adv. Cttee, Omnès Capital, 2013–; Mem., Governance Cttee, Caisse des Dépôts et Consignations, 2003– (Mem., Supervisory Bd, 1988–93); Member: Consultative Cttee, Banque de France, 1998–; Adv. Cttee, A. T. Kearney, France, 2013–. Chairman: Bd of Dirs, CNP Insurance SA, 1992–93; Electricité de France, 1995–98; Caisse Nationale de Prévoyance, subseq. CNP Assurances, 1998–2012; Dir, Icade, 2004–12. Founder and Chm., Euro (50) Gp, 1999–. Chm., Centre des Professions financières, 2003–14. Mem., Trilateral Commn, 1996–2014 (Hon. Mem., 2014). *Publications:* Les Politiques de stabilisation (with G. Delsupehe), 1974; Cours d'analyse macroéconomique, 1976; Analyse monétaire approfondie, 1978; 1986: le piège, 1985; La Rupture: le liberalisme à l'épreuve des faits (with A. Fourçans), 1987; La Réforme obligée: sous le soleil de l'euro, 2000.

ALPS, Tess; Chair, Thinkbox, since 2013 (Founding Chief Executive Officer, 2006–13); *b* Retford, Notts, 1953; *m* 1976, Tim Alps; one *s*. *Educ:* Durham Univ. (BA Hons Eng. Lang. and Lit.); Mountview Theatre Sch. (Postgrad. Dip. Drama). Sales, ITV, incl. ATV, TSW and YTV, 1977–92; Dir, PHD, 1993–2003; Chm., PHD Gp UK, 2003–06. Member, Advisory Panel: ASA; BBC Magazines. Trustee, Nat. Advertising Benevolent Soc. Former Pres., WACL. Member: Mktg Gp of GB; BAFTA. FRTS; Fellow, Marketing Soc. Outstanding Achievement Award, Women in Film and TV, 2007; Media Leader of Decade, 2013. *Recreations:* classical music, theatre, literature, gardening, lots of TV of course. *Address:* Thinkbox, Manning House, 22 Carlisle Place, SW1P 1JA. *T:* (020) 7630 2320. *E:* tess.alps@thinkbox.tv.

ALPTUNA, Akin, PhD; Ambassador of Turkey to the Court of St James's, 2003–07; *b* 23 May 1942; *s* of Huseyin Kamil Alptuna and Cahide Alptuna; *m* 1967, Esin Arman; two *s*. *Educ:* Ankara Univ. (BA; PhD in Internat. Relns). Joined Min. of Foreign Affairs, Turkey, 1967; Second, then First Sec., Copenhagen, 1972–75; First Sec., Nicosia, 1975–77; Hd of Section, Internat. Econ. Agreements Dept and Mem. of Cabinet for Minister of Foreign Affairs, 1977–79; Counsellor, Perm. Delegn of Turkey to EC, Brussels, 1979–81; Consul, Düsseldorf, 1981–83; Hd, Dept for Internat. Econ. Orgns, 1983–85; Dep. Hd of Mission, Turkish Perm. Delegn to UN, 1985–89; Dep. Dir Gen., Multilateral Political Affairs, 1989–93; Dir Gen., EU Dept, 1993–95; Ambassador: Helsinki, 1995–97; Perm. Repn of Turkey to OECD, 1997–2000; Dep. Under-Sec. for EU and W Europe, 1999–2003. Lectr, TOBB Univ. of Econs and Technol. *Clubs:* Athenæum, Travellers, Cavalry and Guards.

AL SAUD, HRH Prince Mohammed Nawaf; Ambassador of the Kingdom of Saudi Arabia to the Court of St James's and to Ireland, since 2005; *b* 22 May 1953; *s* of HRH Prince Nawaf bin Abdulaziz and HH Princess Sharifa; *m* 1979, HH Princess Fadwa Khalid Abdullah; two *s* three *d*. *Educ:* Capital Institute High Sch., Riyadh; Sch. of Foreign Service, Georgetown Univ., Washington; John F. Kennedy Sch. of Govt, Harvard Univ. Diplomat; joined Royal Commn for Jubail and Yanbu, Saudi Arabia, 1981; joined Min. of Foreign Affairs, 1984, Minister's Cabinet; promoted to Inspector Gen.; Ambassador of Saudi Arabia to Italy and Malta, 1995; promoted to rank of Minister, 2005. Formerly: Dean, Arab Ambassadors in Italy; Chm., Islamic and Cultural Centre, Rome. Pres., Harvard Alumni Assoc., Saudi Arabia. *Recreations:* football, tennis. *Address:* Royal Embassy of Saudi Arabia, 30 Charles Street, W1J 5DZ. *T:* (020) 7917 3000, *Fax:* (020) 7917 3001. *Clubs:* Brooks's, Travellers.

AL-SHAIKH-ALI, Dr Anas, CBE 2009; Academic Advisor, International Institute of Islamic Thought, since 1991; *b* Mosul, 29 Sept. 1942; *s* of Saddiq and Khadija Al-Shaikh-Ali; *m* 1972, Dr Maryam Mahmood; one *s* one *d*. *Educ:* Al-Hikma Univ., Baghdad (BA English Lit. 1969); American Univ. of Beirut (MA English Lit. 1972); Univ. of Manchester (PhD American Studies 1983). Lectr, and Cultural and PR Dir, Univ. of Mosul, Iraq, 1973–79; Res. Fellow, Manchester Univ., 1983–85; Res. Fellow, St David's UC, Wales, 1985–86; personal res. work, 1986–91. Chair, Assoc. of Muslim Social Scientists, UK, 1999–. Mem., Mgt Bd, Islamic Centre, Cambridge Univ., 2008–. Vice-Pres., Inst. of Epistemological Res., 2010–. *Publications:* (contrib.) Citizenship, Security and Democracy: Muslim engagement with the West, 2009; (contrib.) Islamophobia: the challenge of pluralism in the 21st century, 2011; (contrib.) Genocidal Nightmares: narratives of insecurity and the logic of mass atrocities, 2014. *Recreations:* reading, gardening, walking. *E:* iiit@iiituk.com.

ALSOP, Marin; conductor; Music Director: Baltimore Symphony Orchestra, since 2007; São Paulo Symphony Orchestra, since 2013 (Chief Conductor, 2012–13); Artist in Residence, Southbank Centre, since 2011; *b* 16 Oct. 1956; *d* of K. LaMar Alsop and Ruth (*née* Condell). *Educ:* Juilliard Sch. (BM 1977, MM 1978). Music Director: Long Island Philharmonic Orch., 1989–96; Eugene SO, Oregon, 1989–96; Cabrillo Fest., 1992–; Colorado SO, 1993–2003 (Music Dir Laureate, 2003–); Principal Conductor, Bournemouth SO, 2002–08 (Conductor Emeritus, 2008–); Principal Guest Conductor: City of London Sinfonia, 2000–03; Royal Scottish Nat. Orch., 2000–03. Regular guest conductor: Philadelphia Orch.; Cleveland Orch., Los Angeles Philharmonic; NY Philharmonic; LSO; LPO. Conductor, Last Night of the Proms, 2013, 2015. MacArthur Foundn Fellow, 2005. Fellow, Amer. Acad. of Arts and Scis, 2008. Hon. RAM, 2011; Hon. Mem., Royal Philharmonic Soc., 2014. Grammy Award, 2010. *Recreations:* running, swimming, antique collecting, reading. *Address:* c/o Intermusica Artists' Management Ltd, Crystal Wharf, 36 Graham Street, N1 8GJ. *T:* (020) 7608 9900.

ALSOP, William Allen, OBE 1999; RA 2000; Director, ALL Design, since 2011; *b* 12 Dec. 1947; *s* of Francis John Alsop and Brenda Hight; *m* 1972, Sheila E. Bean; two *s* one *d*. *Educ:* Architectural Association (DipAA 1973). ARB 1978; RIBA 1978. Maxwell Fry, 1971; Cedric Price, 1973–77; Rodrick Ham, 1977–79; Principal, Alsop & Stormer, then Alsop, later SMC Alsop Architects, 1979–2009, then Consultant; Principal, RMJM, 2009–11. Professor of Architecture: Technical Univ., Vienna, 1996–; Univ. for Creative Arts, Canterbury, 2013–; Tutor in Sculpture, Central St Martin's Coll. of Art and Design, 1973 (Hon. Prof., 1997). Principal buildings: Hamburg Ferry Terminal; Cardiff Visitor Centre (RIBA Nat. Award, 1991); Cardiff Barrage; N Greenwich Underground station; Tottenham Hale Interchange station; Nat. Mus., Nuremberg; Govt HQ, Marseilles (RIBA Nat. Award, 1997); Peckham Library (RIBA Stirling Prize, 2000); Ontario Coll. of Art and Design, Toronto, 2004; Sch. of Medicine and Dentistry, QMW, 2004; Fawood Children's Centre; Blizard Building; Palestra; other projects include: Blackfriars, London, 2000; Calypso, Rotterdam, 2006; Clarke Quay, Singapore, 2006; Chips, Manchester, 2009; Raffles City, Beijing, 2009; Michael Faraday Community Sch., London, 2010; RiversideOne, Middlesbrough, 2011. Hamburgische Architektenkammer, 1992; Chm., Architectl Foundn, 2000–07; Member: Design Council, 1994–98; Russian Architectl Inst., 1995; Russian Acad. of Art, 1995; Urban Renaissance Panel, Yorkshire Forward, 2001–03; Internat. Design Cttee, Thames Gateway, 2004–; Kensington and Chelsea Architectl Adv. Bd, 2009–. SADG 1973; FRSA 1981. Hon. Fellow: Royal Soc. of British Sculptors, 1996; Sheffield Hallam Univ., 2002; Univ. Coll. Northampton, 2005; QMW, 2006. Hon. LLD Leicester, 1996; Hon. Dr (Design) Nottingham Trent, 2001; DUniv Sheffield Hallam, 2001; Hon. Dr: Ontario Coll. of Art and Design, Toronto, 2004; UEA, 2007; Ryerson Univ., Toronto, 2010. *Publications:* City of Objects, 1992; William Alsop Buildings and Projects, 1992; William Alsop Architect, Four Projects, 1993; Will Alsop and Jan Störmer, Architects, 1993; Le Grand Bleu-Marseille, 1994; Will Alsop, Book 1, 2001, Book 2, 2002. *Recreations:* fishing, writing. *Address:* ALL Design, 33 Parkgate Road, SW11 4NP.

ALSTON, David Ian; Arts Director, Arts Council of Wales, since 2005; *b* 26 June 1952; *s* of Cyril Alston and Dorothy Alston; *m* 1975, Christine Bodin (marr. diss. 1987); two *d*; partner, Lesley Webster; one *s* one *d*. *Educ:* Corpus Christi Coll., Oxford (Open Exhibn, MA; Postgrad. Dip. in History of Art (Dist.)). Asst Curator of Pictures, Christ Church, Oxford, 1978–82; Asst Keeper of Art (Ruskin Collection), Sheffield, 1982; Dep. Dir of Arts, Sheffield MDC, 1982–93; Sen. Principal Keeper, Sheffield Arts and Museums, 1993–94; Keeper of Art, Nat. Museums and Galls of Wales, 1994–98; Galls Dir, 1998–2002, Acting Chief Exec., 2001–02, The Lowry. Co-Founder Ed., Oxford Art Jl, 1978. *Publications:* Under the Cover of Darkness: Night Prints, 1986; Piranesi's Prisons: a perspective, 1987; Graham Sutherland: nature into art, 2004; Into Painting: Brendan Stuart Burns, 2007; sundry exhibn texts and articles. *Recreations:* listening, looking, cooking, talking, drinking, walking, playing, loving, musing and other 'ings. *Address:* Arts Council of Wales, Bute Place, Cardiff CF10 5AL. *E:* david.alston@artscouncilofwales.org.uk.

ALSTON, Richard John William, CBE 2001; choreographer; Artistic Director, The Place, and Richard Alston Dance Company, since 1994; *b* 30 Oct. 1948; *s* of late Gordon Walter Alston and Margot Alston (*née* Whitworth). *Educ:* Eton; Croydon Coll. of Art. Choreographed for London Contemporary Dance Theatre, 1970–72; founded Strider, 1972; worked in USA, 1975–77; Resident Choreographer, 1980–86, Artistic Dir, 1986–92, Ballet Rambert, subseq. Rambert Dance Co. Principal Ballets: Nowhere Slowly; Tiger Balm; Blue Schubert Fragments; Soft Verges; Rainbow Bandit; Doublework; Soda Lake; for Ballet Rambert: Rainbow Ripples, 1980; The Rite of Spring, 1981; Apollo Distraught, 1982; Dangerous Liaisons, 1985; Zansa, 1986; Dutiful Ducks, 1986; Pulcinella, 1987; Strong Language, 1987; Hymnos, 1988; Roughcut, 1990; Cat's Eye, 1992. Created: The Kingdom of Pagodas, for Royal Danish Ballet, 1982; Midsummer, for Royal Ballet, 1983; Le Marteau Sans Maitre, for Compagnie Chopinot, 1992; Delicious Arbour, for Shobana Jeyasingh Dance Co., 1993; Movements from Petrushka, Lachrymae, Rumours Visions, for Aldeburgh Festival, 1994; Sheer Bravado, for Ballet Theatre Munich, 2006; Walk Through A Storm, for Ballet Black, 2008; Carmen, for Scottish Ballet, 2009, for Miami City Ballet, 2015; All Alight for Phoenix Dance Th., 2013; for Richard Alston Dance Co.: Shadow Realm, Something in the City, 1994; Stardust, 1995; Orpheus Singing and Dreaming, Beyond Measure, Okho, 1996; Brisk Singing, Light Flooding into Darkened Rooms, 1997; Red Run, Waltzes in Disorder, Sophisticated Curiosities, 1998; Slow Airs Almost All, A Sudden Exit, 1999; The Signal of a Shake, Tremor, 2000; Fever, Strange Company, Water Music, 2001; Touch and Go, Stampede, 2002; Overdrive, 2003; Shimmer, Gypsy Mixture, 2004; Such Longing, 2005; Volumina, 2005; The Devil in the Detail, Proverb, 2006; Fingerprint, Nigredo, 2007; Shuffle it Right, Blow Over, The Men in My Life, 2008; Alert, Serene Beneath, 2009; Out of the Strong, 2010; Unfinished Business, 2011; A Ceremony of Carols, Isthmus, Darknesse Visible, 2012; Buzzing Round the Hunisuccle, Phaedra, Hölderlin Fragments, 2013; Rejoice in the Lamb, 2014; Nomadic, 2015. Chm., Youth Dance England, 2009–. DUniv Surrey, 1993. Chevalier, Ordre des Arts et des Lettres (France), 1995; Ninette de Valois Award for Outstanding Achievement, Nat. Dance Critics Circle, 2009. *Recreations:* music, reading. *Address:* The Place, 17 Duke's Road, WC1H 9PY.

ALSTON, Hon. Richard Kenneth Robert, AO 2015; High Commissioner for Australia in the United Kingdom, 2005–08; *b* 19 Dec. 1941; s of late Robert Bruce Alston and of Sheila Gertrude Alston; *m* 1973, Margaret Mary, (Megs), Kennedy; one *s* one *d*. *Educ:* Xavier Coll., Melbourne; Univ. of Melbourne (BA, LLB; BCom); Monash Univ. (LLM; MBA). Government of Australia: Senator (Lib) for Victoria, 1986–2004; Shadow Minister: for Communications, 1989–90 and 1993–96; for Social Security, Child Care and Retirement

Incomes, 1990–92; for Superannuation and Child Care, 1992–93; for the Arts, 1994–96; Dep. Leader of the Opposition in Senate, 1993–96; Dep. Leader of Govt in Senate, 1996–2003; Minister for Communications, IT and the Arts, 1996–2003. Chm., Senate Select Cttees, 1991–96; Mem., Senate Standing Cttees on Finance and Public Admin, 1987–90, and Legal and Const. Affairs, 1989–90. Chm., Broadcasting Services Australia Ltd, 2004–05; Dir, Hansen Technologies Ltd, 2004–05. Chm., TFS Ltd, 2011–12; non-exec. Dir, Chime plc, 2008–13; Mem. Internat. Bd, CQS LLP, 2008–. Adjunct Prof. of Information Technol., Bond Univ., 2004–. Federal Pres., Liberal Party, 2014–. Centenary Medal (Australia), 2003. *Recreations:* Aboriginal art, modern literature, oriental rugs, walking, pumping iron.

ALSTON, Robert John, CMG 1987; QSO 2004; HM Diplomatic Service, retired; High Commissioner to New Zealand, Governor (non-resident) of Pitcairn, Henderson, Ducie and Oeno Islands, and High Commissioner (non-resident) to Western Samoa, 1994–98; *b* 10 Feb. 1938; *s* of late Arthur William Alston and of Rita Alston; *m* 1969, Patricia Claire Essex; one *s* one *d*. *Educ:* Ardingly Coll.; New Coll., Oxford (MA Mod. Hist.). Third Sec., Kabul, 1963; Eastern Dept, FO, 1966; Head of Computer Study Team, FCO, 1969; First Sec. (Econ.), Paris, 1971; First Sec. and Head of Chancery, Tehran, 1974; Asst Head, Energy Science and Space Dept, FCO, 1977; Head, Joint Nuclear Unit, FCO, 1978; Political Counsellor, UK Delegn to NATO, 1981; Head, Defence Dept, FCO, 1984; Ambassador to Oman, 1986–90; seconded to NI Office, 1990–92; Asst Under-Sec. of State (Public Depts), FCO, 1992–94. Chm., Link Foundn for UK-NZ Relations, 1999–2004; Advr, Internat. Trade & Investment Missions Ltd, 1999–2002; Trustees Rep., Commonwealth Inst., 2002–. Chm., Anglo-Omani Soc., 2014–. Dir, Romney Resource Centre, 1999–2006. Consultant on Anglican Communion affairs to Archbishop of Canterbury, 1999–2002. Trustee, Antarctic Heritage Trust, 1998–2008; Dir, Antarctic Heritage Ltd, 2008–12; Member: Cttee, Romney Marsh Historic Churches Trust, 2003–10; Cttee, The Pilgrims, 2010– (Chm., Membership Cttee, 2010–). Chairman of Governors: Ardingly Coll., 2005–10; Marsh Acad., New Romney, 2007–13. Mem. Ct, World Traders' Co., 2003–13 (Master, 2007–08). DL Kent, 2004. *Publications:* (with Stuart Laing) Unshook Till the End of Time: a history of relations between Britain and Oman, 2012. *Recreations:* gardening, travel, music. *Address:* 97 Coast Drive, Lydd on Sea, Romney Marsh, Kent TN29 9NW. *T:* (01797) 321686.

ALSTON-ROBERTS-WEST, Lt-Col George Arthur; *see* West, Lt-Col G. A. A.-R.-.

ALT, Deborah; *see* Gribbon, D.

AL TAJIR, Sayed Mohamed Mahdi; Patron, Al Tajir World of Islam Trust, since 1977; *m*; five *s* one *d*. *Educ:* Bahrain Govt Sch.; Preston Grammar Sch. Director: Port and Customs, Dubai, 1955–63; HH the Ruler's Affairs and Petroleum Affairs Dept, Dubai, 1963–72; Ambassador of UAE: to UK, 1972–91; to France, 1972–91. Vice Chm., World of Islam Fest. Trust, 1974–77. *Address:* c/o Al Tajir World of Islam Trust, 11 Elvaston Place, SW7 5QG.

ALTANGEREL, Bulgaa; Ambassador of Mongolia to United States of America, and (non-resident) to Israel and Mexico, since 2013; *b* Khovd Province, Mongolia, 25 Oct. 1955; *s* of Puntsag Bulgaa and Dansran Nansalmaa; *m* 1980, Erdenee Chuluuntsetseg; three *d*. *Educ:* Secondary Sch., Khovd Province, Mongolia; Moscow Inst. of Internat. Relns (Master in Internat. Law 1979); Moscow Inst. Political Scis (Master in Pol Scis 1990); Columbia Univ., USA (Special Trng for Internat. Law and Internat. Public Affairs 1992); Kiev Nat. Taras Shevchenko Univ., Ukraine (PhD Internat. Law 2003); Harvard Kennedy Sch. (Sen. Exec. Prog. 2013); Asia-Pacific Center for Security Studies, Hawaii (Sen. Exec. course, 2014). Attaché, Min. of Foreign Affairs, Mongolia, 1979–81; Attaché, later Third Sec., Embassy of Mongolia in Afghanistan, 1981–85; Third, later Second Sec., Min. of Foreign Affairs, 1985–88; State Great Hural-SGH (Parliament of Mongolia): Advr on Foreign Policy, 1991; Dir, Foreign Relns Dept, SGH Secretariat, 1991–97; Ambassador to Turkey and Ambassador (non-resident) to Bulgaria, Lebanon, Romania and Uzbekistan, 1997–2003; Dir Gen. for Legal and Consular Affairs, Min. of Foreign Affairs, 2003–08; Ambassador to UK and Ambassador (non-resident) to RSA, Ireland and Iceland, 2008–13. Mem., Inter-Govtl Commn on inspection of state boundaries between Mongolia and USSR, 1985–88. Responsible Sec., Mongolian Inter-Parly Gp, 1990–97. Chair, Internat. Law Dept, Mongolian Nat. Univ., 1993–97; Professor: Law and Security Acad., Russian Fedn, 2006; Mongolian Nat. Inst., 2008. Hon. Prof., Law Sch., Nat. Univ. of Mongolia, 2011. Mem., Bd of Dirs, Trust Fund for Victims, Internat. Criminal Court, 2007–12. *Address:* Embassy of Mongolia, 2833 M Street NW, Washington, DC 20007, USA. *T:* (202) 3337117, ext. 119, (202) 4316344, *Fax:* (202) 2989227. *E:* ambassador@mongolianembassy.us.

ALTARAS, Jonathan; Chairman and Managing Director, Jonathan Altaras Associates, 1990–2006; *b* 5 Aug. 1948; *s* of Leonard and Joy Altaras. *Educ:* Cheadle Hulme Sch.; Manchester Univ. (MA). Trustee, V&A Mus., 2003–06. Chm., Mus. of Performance, 2003–; Mem. Bd, Drama Centre, 1990–. *Recreation:* eating. *Club:* Garrick.

ALTHAM, John Robert Carr; His Honour Judge Altham; a Circuit Judge, since 2011; *b* Morecambe, 30 March 1966; *s* of John Altham and Linda Altham; *m* 1992, Fiona Aubrey; one *s* two *d*. *Educ:* Lancaster Royal Grammar Sch.; University Coll. London (BA Hons Classics); Univ. of Birmingham (Common Professional Exam.). Called to the Bar, Gray's Inn, 1993; Junior, Northern Circuit, 1996–97; Recorder, 2008–11. *Recreations:* family, hiking, running, piano. *Address:* Preston Crown Court, Openshaw Place, Ringway, Preston, Lancs PR1 2LL.

ALTHORP, Viscount; Louis Frederick John Spencer; *b* 14 March 1994; *o s* and *heir* of Earl Spencer, *qv*. *Educ:* Western Province Prep. Sch., Cape Town; Reddam House Sch., Cape Town; Bishops, Dio. Coll., Cape Town; Edinburgh Univ. *Address:* Althorp, Northampton NN7 4HG.

ALTMAN, Brian; QC 2008; a Recorder, since 2003; *b* 16 Aug. 1957; *s* of late Stanley Altman and of Pauline Altman; *m* 1996, Charlotte Parkin; one *s* one *d* and one *s* one *d* from previous *m*. *Educ:* Chingford Sen. High Sch.; King's Coll. London (LLB); Univ. of Amsterdam (Dip. Eur. Int.). Called to the Bar, Middle Temple, 1981, Bencher, 2010; Central Criminal Court: Jun. Treasury Counsel, 1997–2002; Sen. Treasury Counsel, 2002–10; First Sen. Treasury Counsel, and Chm., Bar Mess, 2010–13. *Recreations:* weight and fitness training, music, scuba diving. *Address:* (chambers) 2 Bedford Row, WC1R 4BU. *T:* (020) 7440 8888, *Fax:* (020) 7242 1738. *E:* baltman@2bedfordrow.co.uk.

ALTMAN, Prof. Douglas Graham, CStat, CSci; FMedSci; Director, Cancer Research UK Medical Statistics Group, Oxford (formerly Head, Imperial Cancer Research Fund Medical Statistics Laboratory, London), since 1988; Founding Director, Centre for Statistics in Medicine, since 1995, and Professor of Statistics in Medicine, since 1998, University of Oxford; Co-Director, Oxford Clinical Trials Research Unit, since 2005; *b* London, 12 July 1948; *s* of Jack and Decima Altman; *m* 2009, Susan Wilkinson; one *s* one *d*. *Educ:* Bath Univ. (BSc Stats 1970); Univ. of London (DSc Med. Stats 1997). CStat 1993; CSci 2009. Lectr, St Thomas's Hosp. Med. Sch., London, 1970–76; Med. Statistician, MRC, 1976–88. FMedSci 2011. *Publications:* Practical Statistics for Medical Research, 1991; contrib. articles to jls on methods and applications of med. stats, and guidelines for reporting research. *Recreations:* music (especially if little-known), cycling. *Address:* Centre for Statistics in Medicine, University of Oxford, Botnar Research Centre, Windmill Road, Oxford OX3 7LD.

ALTMAN, John; His Honour Judge Altman; a Circuit Judge, since 1991; Senior Circuit Judge and Designated Family Judge for London, since 2007; *b* 21 June 1944; *s* of Lionel and Vita Altman; *m* 1968, Elizabeth Brown; two *d*. *Educ:* Bootham Sch., York; Univ. of Bristol (LLB); Council of Legal Education. Called to the Bar, Middle Temple, 1967; part-time Chm., Industrial Tribunals, 1983; Asst Recorder, 1985; Chm., Industrial Tribunals, 1986; a Recorder, 1989; Designated Family Judge: for Milton Keynes, 2003–07; for Oxford, 2005–07. Chm., W Yorks Family Mediation Service, 1997–2002. *Publications:* contribs to Law Guardian. *Recreations:* reading, photography, music, theatre. *Address:* c/o Central Family Court, 42–49 High Holborn, WC1 6NP.

ALTMANN, Baroness *cr* 2015 (Life Peer), of Tottenham in the London Borough of Haringey; **Rosalind Miriam Altmann,** CBE 2014; PhD; Minister of State (Minister for Pensions), Department for Work and Pensions, since 2015; *b* 8 April 1956; *d* of Leo and Renate Altmann; *m* 1982, Paul Richer; one *s* two *d*. *Educ:* University Coll. London (BSc Econ 1st Cl. Hons); Harvard Univ. (Kennedy Schol.); London Sch. of Econs (PhD 1981). Investment Mgt Cert. Fund Manager, Prudential Assce, London, 1981–84; Hd, Internat. Equities, Chase Manhattan Bank, 1984–89; Director: Rothschild Asset Mgt, 1989–91; Natwest Investment Mgt, 1991–93; ind. policy advr on pensions, investment, savings and retirement, 1993–2015; Dir-Gen., Saga Gp, 2010–13. Consultant to HM Treasury on Pension Fund Investment, 2000; Mem., Lord Chancellor's Strategic Investment Bd, 2004–; Policy Advr to Number 10 Policy Unit on pensions, investments and savings, 2000–05. Non-exec. Mem., Court Funds Office, 2004–15; Mem. Bd, IPSO, 2014–15. Gov., 1989–, and non-exec. Dir, 2004–, LSE. Life Gov., Nightingale House for the Elderly, 1985. MCSI (MSI 1992); MInstD 2000. Hon. DLitt Westminster, 2009. *Publications:* articles in newspapers, jls and industry magazines, incl. Financial Times, The Times, Pensions Week, Financial Advr, Money Mktg, Pensions World, Wall St Jl, Professional Investor, Global Finance, Instnl Investor. *Recreations:* charity fund-raising, swimming, walking, table tennis. *E:* altmannr@parliament.uk.

ALTON, family name of **Baron Alton of Liverpool**.

ALTON OF LIVERPOOL, Baron *cr* 1997 (Life Peer), of Mossley Hill, in the Co. of Merseyside; **David Patrick Paul Alton;** Chairman, Banner Ethical Investment Fund, 1999–2011; Chairman and Director, Merseyside Special Investment Fund, 2001–06; Professor of Citizenship, 1997, and Director, since 1997, Roscoe Foundation for Citizenship, Liverpool John Moores University; *b* 15 March 1951; *s* of Frederick and Bridget Alton; *m* 1988, Dilys Elizabeth, *yr d* of Rev. Philip Bell; three *s* one *d*. *Educ:* Edmund Campion Sch., Hornchurch; Christ's College of Education, Liverpool; St Andrews Univ. Elected to Liverpool City Council as Britain's youngest City Councillor, 1972; CC, 1972–80; Deputy Leader of the Council and Housing Chairman, 1978; Vice-Pres., AMA, later LGA, 1979–. MP Liverpool, Edge Hill (by-election), March 1979–83, Liverpool, Mossley Hill, 1983–97 (L, 1979–88, Lib Dem, 1988–97). Liberal Party spokesman on: the environment and race relations, 1979–81; home affairs, 1981–82; NI, 1987–88 (Alliance spokesman on NI, 1987); Chief Whip, Liberal Party, 1985–87; Member: Select Cttee on the Environment, 1981–85; H of C Privileges Cttee, 1994–97; cross-bencher, 1997. All-Party Groups: Treasurer: Pro-Life, 1993–2004; Landmines, 1996–2000; Friends of CAFOD; Chairman: Street Children, 1992–97; British-N Korea, 2003–; Vice Chairman: Tibet Gp, 2005–; Blood Cord and Adult Stem Cells, 2009–; Foreign Affairs, 2010–; Freedom of Religion and Belief; Sec., Sudan Gp, 2005–. Chm., Liberal Candidates Cttee, 1985. Nat. Pres., Nat. League of Young Liberals, 1979. Co-founder, Movement for Christian Democracy in Britain, 1990. Vis. Fellow, St Andrews Univ., 1996. Former Chm., Council for Educn in Commonwealth. Nat. Vice-Pres., Life; former Pres., Liverpool Br., NSPCC; Vice-President: Liverpool YMCA; Crisis; Past Chairman: Forget-me-not Appeal (Royal Liverpool Hosp.); Merseyside CVS. Vice-Pres., Assoc. of Councillors. Patron: Jubilee Campaign for the release of prisoners of conscience, 1986–; Nat. Assoc. Child Contact Centres, 1997–; Karen Aid; Merseyside Kidney Res.; Jospice; Liverpool Sch. of Tropical Medicine; G. K. Chesterton Inst.; Motec Life; Asylum Link Merseyside; Internat. Young Leaders Network. Mem., Catholic Writers' Guild; Trustee: Catholic Central Liby, 1998–2004; Partners In Hope, 1999–2006; Metta Educn Trust, 2002–06. Columnist, The Universe, 1989–2013. Kt Comdr, Constantinian Order of St George, 2003; KCSG 2008. *Publications:* What Kind of Country?, 1987; Whose Choice Anyway?, 1988; Faith in Britain, 1991; Signs of Contradiction, 1996; Life After Death, 1997; Citizen Virtues, 1999; Citizen 21, 2001; Pilgrim Ways, 2001; Passion and Pain, 2003; Euthanasia: getting to the heart of the matter, 2005; Abortion: getting to the heart of the matter, 2005; Building Bridges: is there hope for North Korea?, 2013. *Recreations:* gardening, reading, walking. *Address:* House of Lords, SW1A 0PW. *E:* altond@parliament.uk. *W:* www.davidalton.net.

ALTON, Roger; Executive Editor, The Times, 2010–15; *b* 20 Dec. 1947; *s* of late Reginald Ernest Alton, MC and Jeannine Beatrice Alton (*née* Gentis); divorced; one *d*. *Educ:* Clifton Coll.; Exeter Coll., Oxford. Liverpool Post, 1969–74; The Guardian, 1974–98; Editor: The Observer, 1998–2007; The Independent, 2008–10. Editor of the Year: What the Papers Say Awards, 2000; GQ Men of the Year Awards, 2005. *Recreations:* sports, films, ski-ing, climbing. *Clubs:* Climbers', Soho House, Groucho; Ski Club of GB.

ALTRINCHAM, 3rd Baron *cr* 1945, of Tormarton, co. Gloucester; **Anthony Ulick David Dundas Grigg;** *b* 12 Jan. 1934; *yr s* of 1st Baron Altrincham, KCMG, KCVO, DSO, MC, PC and Hon. Joan Dickson-Poynder; *S* brother, 2001; *m* 1965, Eliane, *d* of Marquis de Miramon; two *s* one *d*. *Educ:* Eton; New Coll., Oxford. *Heir: s* Hon. (Edward) Sebastian Grigg [*b* 18 Dec. 1965; *m* 1993, Rachel Sophia Kelly; three *s* two *d* (of whom one *s* one *d* are twins)]. *Address:* La Musclera, Tamariu 17212, Palafrugell, Girona, Spain.

ALTY, John Henry Myers, CB 2010; Chief Executive, Intellectual Property Office, since 2010; Acting Director General, Knowledge and Innovation, Department for Business, Innovation and Skills, 2012–13; *b* Liverpool, 2 Dec. 1956; *s* of Henry and Heather Alty; *m* 1981, Jane Cocks; three *s* one *d*. *Educ:* Liverpool Coll.; Worcester Coll., Oxford (BA Classics). Department of Industry, subseq. Department of Trade and Industry, later Department for Business, Enterprise and Regulatory Reform, then Department for Business, Innovation and Skills: various trng posts, 1978–81; Private Sec. to Minister of State, 1981–83; Grade 7, 1984–91, incl. period in Eur. Secretariat, Cabinet Office and as Prin. Private Sec. to Chancellor of Duchy of Lancaster; Competition Policy, 1992–94; Insce Regulation, 1994–95; Prin. Private Sec. to Sec. of State for Trade and Industry, 1995–98; Director: Europe, 1998–2002; Business Relations, 2002–05; Dir Gen., Fair Mkts Gp, 2005–10. *Publications:* contrib. Jl Hellenic Studies. *Recreation:* Liverpool Football Club. *Address:* UK Intellectual Property Office, Concept House, Cardiff Road, Newport, Gwent NP10 8QQ. *E:* john.alty@ipo.gov.uk.

ALVAREZ, Al(fred); poet and author; *b* London, 1929; *s* of late Bertie Alvarez and Katie Alvarez (*née* Levy); *m* 1st, 1956, Ursula Barr (marr. diss. 1961); one *s*; 2nd, 1966, Anne Adams; one *s* one *d*. *Educ:* Oundle Sch.; Corpus Christi Coll., Oxford (BA 1952, MA 1956; Hon. Fellow, 2001). Research Schol., CCC, Oxon, and Research Schol. of Goldsmiths' Company, 1952–53, 1954–55. Procter Visiting Fellowship, Princeton, 1953–54; Vis. Fellow of Rockefeller Foundn, USA, 1955–56, 1958; gave Christian Gauss Seminars in Criticism, Princeton, and was Lectr in Creative Writing, 1957–58; D. H. Lawrence Fellowship, New Mexico Univ., 1958; Poetry Critic and Editor, The Observer, 1956–66. Visiting Professor: Brandeis Univ., 1960; New York State Univ., Buffalo, 1966. Adv. Ed., Penguin Modern European Poets in Translation, 1966–78. Hon. DLitt East London, 1998. Vachel Lindsay Prize for Poetry (from Poetry, Chicago), 1961; Benson Medal for Literature, RSL, 2010, 2012. *Publications:* The Shaping Spirit (US title, Stewards of Excellence), 1958; The School of Donne, 1961; The New Poetry (ed and introd), 1962; Under Pressure, 1965; Beyond All This Fiddle, 1968; Lost (poems), 1968; Penguin Modern Poets, No 18, 1970; Apparition (poems, with paintings by Charles Blackman), 1971; The Savage God, 1971; Beckett, 1973; Hers (novel), 1974; Hunt (novel), 1978; Autumn to Autumn and Selected Poems 1953–76, 1978; Life After Marriage, 1982; The Biggest Game in Town, 1983; Offshore, 1986; Feeding the Rat, 1988; Rain Forest (with paintings by Charles Blackman), 1988; Day of Atonement (novel), 1991; The Faber Book of Modern European Poetry (ed and introd.), 1992; Night, 1995; Where Did It All Go Right? (autobiog.), 1999; Poker: bets, bluffs and bad beats, 2001; New and Selected Poems, 2002; The Writer's Voice, 2005; Risky Business, 2007; Pondlife: a swimmer's journal, 2013. *Recreations:* music, poker, cold water swimming. *Address:* c/o Aitken Alexander Associates, 291 Gray's Inn Road, WC1X 8EB. *Clubs:* Climbers', Alpine; Highgate Lifebuoys.

ALVEY, John, CB 1980; FREng; Chairman, SIRA Ltd, 1987–94; *b* 19 June 1925; *s* of George C. V. Alvey and Hilda E. Alvey (*née* Pellatt); *m* 1955, Celia Edmed Marson; three *s*. *Educ:* Reed's Sch.; London Univ.; BSc (Eng), DipNEC. FIET. London Stock Exchange, to 1943. Royal Navy, 1943–46; Royal Naval Scientific Service, 1950; Head of Weapons Projects, Admiralty Surface Weapons Estabt, 1968–72; Dir-Gen. Electronics Radar, PE, MoD, 1972–73; Dir-Gen., Airborne Electronic Systems, PE, MoD, 1974–75; Dir, Admiralty Surface Weapons Estabt, 1976–77; Dep. Controller, R&D Estabts and Res. C, and Chief Scientist (RAF), MoD, 1977–80; Senior Dir, Technology, 1980–83, Man. Dir, Develt and Procurement, and Engr-in-Chief, 1983–86, British Telecom. Dir (non-exec.), LSI Logic Ltd, 1986–91. Member Council: Fellowship of Engrg, 1985–92 (Vice-Pres., 1989–92); Foundn for Sci. and Technology, 1986–90; City Univ., 1985–93. Fellow, Queen Mary and Westfield Coll. (formerly QMC), London, 1988. FREng (FEng 1984). FRSA 1983. Hon. DSc City, 1984; Hon. DTech CNAA, 1991. *Recreations:* reading, Rugby, ski-ing, theatre going. *Address:* 9 Western Parade, Emsworth, Hants PO10 7HS.

ALVINGHAM, 2nd Baron *cr* 1929, of Woodfold; **Maj.-Gen. Robert Guy Eardley Yerburgh,** CBE 1978 (OBE 1972); DL; *b* 16 Dec. 1926; *s* of 1st Baron and Dorothea Gertrude (*d* 1927), *d* of late J. Eardley Yerburgh; *S* father, 1955; *m* 1952, Beryl Elliott, *d* of late W. D. Williams; one *s* one *d*. *Educ:* Eton. Commissioned 1946, Coldstream Guards; served UK, Palestine, Tripolitania, BAOR, Farelf, British Guiana; Head of Staff, CDS, 1972–75; Dep. Dir, Army Staff Duties, 1975–78; Dir of Army Quartering, 1978–81, retired. Patron, Royal British Legion, Oxfordshire, 1994–2009; Co-Patron, Henley and District Agricultural Assoc., 2008–. DL Oxfordshire, 1996. *Heir: s* Captain Hon. Robert Richard Guy Yerburgh, 17th/21st Lancers, retired [*b* 10 Dec. 1956; *m* 1st, 1981, Vanessa, *yr d* of Captain Duncan Kirk (marr. diss. 1993); two *s*; 2nd, 1994, Karen, *er d* of Antony Baldwin; one *s* one *d*].

ALWARD, Peter Andrew Ulrich; Intendant and Managing Director, Salzburg Easter Festival, 2010–15; President, EMI Classics, 2002–05; *b* 20 Nov. 1950; *s* of late Herbert Andrew Alward and Marion Evelyne (*née* Schreiber). *Educ:* Mowden Prep. Sch., Hove; Bryanston; Guildhall Sch. of Music and Drama. Simrock Music Publishers, London, 1968–70; with EMI, 1970–2005: EMI Records UK, London, 1970–74; Eur. Co-ordinator, EMI Classical Div., Munich, 1975–83; Exec. Producer, with Herbert von Karajan, for all EMI recordings, 1976–89; Artists and Repertoire, UK: Manager, 1983–84; Internat. Dir, 1985–88; Vice-Pres., 1989–97; Sen. Vice-Pres., 1998–2001. Trustee: Royal Opera House Enterprises Ltd, 2007–; Bd, Opera Rara, 2007–11. Artistic Consultant, 2006–09, Mem., Eur. Adv. Bd, 2009–10, Cleveland Orch.; Hon. Artistic Consultant, West-Eastern Divan Orch., 2007–09; Consultant, BR Klassik, 2008–. Member: Adv. Bd, Royal Opera House, Covent Garden, 1998–99; Artistic Cttee, Herbert von Karajan Stiftung, 2003–10; Kuratorium, Internationale Stiftung Mozarteum, Salzburg, 2008–13; Jury Mem., Salzburg Fest. and Nestlé Young Conductor's Award, 2010–; Chm., ARD Piano Competition, 2011; Vice-Chm., Santander Internat. Piano Competition, 2012. Mem., Bd of Trustees, Young Concert Artists Trust, 1999–2004; Trustee, Masterclass Media Foundn, 2006–14. Mem., Editl Adv. Bd, BBC Music, 2006–15. *Recreations:* all classical music sectors, exhibitions of painting and sculpture, theatre, books, collecting stage designs and costume designs, cooking, travelling. *Address:* 24 Midway, Walton-on-Thames, Surrey KT12 3HZ. *T:* (01932) 248985; Reiteralpestrasse 19, 83395 Freilassing, Germany. *T:* (8654) 3558. *Club:* Arts.

AMAN, Dato' Sri Anifah; Minister of Foreign Affairs, Malaysia, since 2009; *b* Keningau, Sabah, Malaysia, 16 Nov. 1953; *m* Siti Rubiah Abdul Samad; three *s*. *Educ:* Sabah Coll., Kota Kinabalu, Sabah, Malaysia; Univ. of Buckingham (BA Philosophy, Econs and Law 1979). Deputy Minister: of Primary Industries, 1999–2004; of Plantation Industries and Commodities, 2004–08. JP 1996. Ahli Setia Darjah Kinabalu, 1994; Panglima Gemilang Darjah Kinabalu, 1998; Darjah Indera Mahkota Pahang, 2004; Darjah Sri Sultan Ahmad Shah Pahang, 2009. *Recreations:* football, golf. *Address:* Ministry of Foreign Affairs, No 1, Jalan Wisma Putra, Precinct 2, 62602 Putrajaya, Malaysia.

AMANN, Prof. Ronald, PhD; Professor of Comparative Politics (formerly of Soviet Politics), University of Birmingham, 1986–2003, now Emeritus; *b* 21 Aug. 1943; *s* of George James Amann and Elizabeth Clementson Amann (*née* Towell); *m* 1965, Susan Frances Peters; two *s* one *d*. *Educ:* Heaton Grammar Sch., Newcastle upon Tyne; Univ. of Birmingham (MSocSc, PhD). Consultant, OECD, and Res. Associate, 1965–68; University of Birmingham: Asst Lectr, then Lectr and Sen. Lectr, 1968–83; Dir, Centre for Russian and E European Studies, 1983–89; Dean, Faculty of Commerce and Soc. Sci., 1989–91; Pro-Vice-Chancellor, 1991–94; Chief Exec. and Dep. Chm., ESRC, 1994–99; Dir-Gen., Centre for Mgt and Policy Studies, Cabinet Office, 1999–2002. Vis. Fellow, Osteuropa Inst., Munich, 1975. Special Advr, H of C Select Cttee on Sci. and Technol., 1976. Member: Technology Foresight Steering Cttee, 1995–2000; COPUS, 1996–99; Adv. Bd, Centre for Analysis of Risk and Regulation, LSE, 2000–; Chm. Adv. Bd, Centre for Res. on Innovation and Competitiveness, Univ. of Manchester, 2001–. Ind. Mem., W Midlands Police Authy, 2007–12. Mem. Council, SSEES, London Univ., 1986–89. Founding AcSS, 1999. FRSA. *Publications:* jointly: Science Policy in the USSR, 1969; The Technological Level of Soviet Industry, 1977; Industrial Innovation in the Soviet Union, 1982; Technical Progress and Soviet Economic Development, 1986. *Recreations:* modern jazz, walking. *Address:* 26 Spring Road, Edgbaston, Birmingham B15 2HA. *T:* (0121) 440 6186.

AMANO, Yukiya; Director General, International Atomic Energy Agency, since 2009; *b* 1947; married. *Educ:* Faculty of Law, Tokyo Univ.; Univ. of Besançon; Univ. of Nice. Entered Min. of Foreign Affairs, Japan, 1972; Director: for Res. Coordination and Sen. Res. Fellow, Japan Inst. of Internat. Affairs, Tokyo, 1988–90; OECD Pubns and Information Center, Tokyo, 1990–93; Lectr in Internat. Politics, Yamanashi Univ., Japan, 1991–92; Dir, Nuclear Sci. Div., 1993, Nuclear Energy Div., 1993–94, Min. of Foreign Affairs; Counsellor, Delegn to Conf. on Disarmament, Geneva, 1994–97; Consul Gen., Marseilles, 1997–99; Dep. Dir-Gen. for Arms Control and Scientific Affairs, Min. of Foreign Affairs, 1999–2000; Chm., G7 Nuclear Safety Gp, 2000; Lectr in Internat. Politics, Sophia Univ., Japan, 2000–01; Govtl Expert on Missiles to UN Panel, 2001, on Disarmament and Non-Proliferation Educn to UN Gp, 2001; Ambassador and Dir-Gen. for Disarmament, Non-Proliferation and Sci. Dept, Min. of Foreign Affairs, 2002–05; Perm. Rep. and Ambassador to Internat. Orgns in Vienna, 2005–09; Gov., IAEA, 2005–09 (Chm. Govs, 2005–06). Chm., First Session of Prep. Cttee for 2010 Non-Proliferation Treaty Rev. Conf., 2007. Fellow, Weatherhead Center for Internat. Affairs, Harvard Univ., 2001; Vis. Schol., Monterey Inst. of Internat. Studies, USA, 2001–02. *Publications:* Sea Dumping of Liquid Radioactive Waste by Russia, 1994; (contrib.) Proliferation et Non-Proliferation Nucléaire, 1995; (contrib.) Future Restraints on Arms Proliferation, 1996; contrib. Non-Proliferation Rev. *Address:* International Atomic Energy Agency, Vienna International Centre, Wagramer Strasse 5, PO Box 100, 1400 Vienna, Austria.

AMARATUNGA, Prof. Gehan Anil Joseph, PhD; CEng, FREng, FIET; 1966 Professor of Engineering (Electrical), University of Cambridge, since 1998; Fellow, Churchill College, Cambridge, 1987–95 and since 1998; *b* 6 April 1956; *s* of Carl Hermen Joseph Amaratunga and Mallika Swarna; *m* 1981, Praveen Dharshini Hitchcock; one *s* two *d*. *Educ:* Royal Coll., Colombo; Pelham Meml High Sch., NY; University Coll. Cardiff (BSc Hons); Wolfson Coll., Cambridge (PhD 1983). CEng, FREng 2004; FIET (FIEE 2004). University of Southampton: Res. Fellow in Microelectronics, 1983; Lectr in Electronics, 1984–86; Vis. Prof., Dept of Electronics and Computer Sci., 1998–; Lectr in Electrical Engrg, Univ. of Cambridge, 1987–95; Prof. of Electrical Engrg, Univ. of Liverpool, 1995–98. Nanyang Prof., 2010–12, Tan Chin Tuan Centennial Prof., 2012–14, Nangyang Vis. Prof., 2014–, Nanyang Technol Univ., Singapore. Founder, Chief Scientific and Technol. Officer, Cambridge Semiconductor Ltd, 2000–15; Founder and Chief Scientific Officer, Camutronics, 2012–; Chm. and Dir, Wind Technologies Ltd, 2006–; Founder and Director: Enecsys Ltd, 2004–; Nanoinstruments Ltd, 2005; Chief of Res. and Innovation, Sri Lanka Inst. of Nanotechnol., 2011–. Royal Acad. Engrg Vis. Researcher, Stanford Univ., Calif, 1989. FRSA 2009. Silver Medal, Royal Acad. of Engrg, 2007. *Publications:* contrib. IEEE Trans, Physical Rev., Nature. *Recreations:* jazz, opera, cricket, classic cars, avant garde cinema. *Address:* Electrical Engineering Division, Engineering Department, Cambridge University, Cambridge CB3 0FA. *T:* (01223) 748320. *E:* gaja1@cam.ac.uk.

AMBACHE, Jeremy Noel; Trustee: Age UK (Wandsworth) (formerly Wandsworth Age Concern), since 2008; Wandsworth LINK, 2009–12 (Chairman, 2009); *b* 16 Dec. 1946; *s* of Nachman and Stella Ambache; *m* 1973, Ann Campbell; two *d*. *Educ:* Bedales Sch.; Sussex Univ. (BA); York Univ. (MPhil); Kingston Univ. (MA). Social worker, Birmingham Social Services, 1971–73; Team Manager, Hammersmith Social Services, 1974–80; Co-ordinator for Community Homes, Brent Social Services, 1981–84; Area Manager, Croydon Social Services, 1984–90; Divl Dir, Berks Social Services, 1990–91; Asst Dir, Bedfordshire Social Services, 1991–93; Dir of Social Services, Knowsley, 1993–2000; Dir of Social Services and Housing, Bromley, 2000–02; mgt consultant in health and social care, 2002–05. Member, Board: Wandsworth PCT, 2011–12; Wandsworth CCG, 2012–14. Mem. (Lab) Wandsworth BC, 2014–. Pol advr and campaigner, Liberal Democrats, 2004–10. Contested (Lib Dem) Putney, 2005. Sec., and Vice Chair (Campaigns), Putney Constituency, Lab. Party, 2011–14. *Recreations:* tennis, yoga, travel, walking. *Address:* 17 Hazlewell Road, Putney, SW15 6LT. *T:* (020) 8785 9650. *Club:* Putney Lawn Tennis.

AMBLER, John Doss; Vice-President, 1980–96, Vice-President, Human Resources, 1989–96, Texaco Inc.; *b* 24 July 1934; *m*; one *s* one *d*. *Educ:* Virginia Polytechnic Inst. and State Univ. (BSc Business Admin). Texaco Inc., USA: various assignments, Marketing Dept, Alexandra, Va, 1956–65; Dist Sales Manager, Harrisburg, Pa, 1965–67; Asst Divl Manager, Norfolk, Va, 1967–68; Staff Asst to Gen. Manager Marketing US, New York, 1968; various assignments, Chicago and New York, 1969–72; Gen. Manager, Texaco Olie Maatschappij BV, Rotterdam, 1972–75; Man. Dir, Texaco Oil AB, Stockholm, 1975–77; Asst to Pres., 1977, Asst to Chm. of the Bd, 1980, Texaco Inc.; Pres., Texaco Europe, New York, 1981–82; Chm. and Chief Exec. Officer, Texaco Ltd, 1982–89. *Recreations:* hunting, fishing, tennis, photography.

AMBROSE, Euan James; His Honour Judge Ambrose; a Circuit Judge, since 2009; *b* 23 Nov. 1967. *Educ:* Magdalene Coll., Cambridge (BA 1989). Called to the Bar, Middle Temple, 1992; Treasury Counsel, 2000–09; Recorder, 2005–09. *Address:* Bristol Crown Court, Small Street, Bristol BS1 1DA.

AMED, Imran; Founder and Chief Executive Officer, The Business of Fashion, since 2007; *b* Calgary, Canada, 20 April 1975; *s* of Miles Ahmed and Hamida Ahmed. *Educ:* McGill Univ. (BCom 1997); Harvard Business Sch. (MBA 2002). Associate, Braxton Associates, 1997–2000; Engagement Manager, McKinsey & Co., 2002–06. Contrib. Editor, GQ, 2014–. *Publications:* (jtly) Pattern: 100 fashion designers, 10 curators, 2013. *Address:* The Business of Fashion, 2 Kingly Court, W1B 5PW. *E:* editor@businessoffashion.com.

AMENT, Sharon Ann; Director, Museum of London, since 2012; *b* London, 29 Sept. 1962; *d* of Horace Cecil Ament and Pauline Ament (*née* Anderson); *m* 2006, Nicholas Lane. *Educ:* Sterrix Lane Comprehensive Sch., Litherland, Liverpool; Univ. of Leeds (BA Hons Hist. of Art). PR Manager, Merseyside Council for Voluntary Service, 1985–86; Hd of Mktg, Martin Mere Wildfowl Centre, 1986–89; Nat. Mktg Manager, Wildfowl and Wetlands Trust, 1989–92; Hd of Mktg, Zool Soc. London, 1992–2000; Dir, Public Engagement, Natural Hist. Mus., 2000–12. Vice Pres., Eur. Network for Sci. Centres and Mus, 2009–12. Chair, Exhibn Rd Culture Gp, 2008–12. Mem., Internat. Bd, ArtSci. Mus., Singapore, 2012–. Fellow: Salzburg Seminar, 2011; Noyce Leadership Inst., 2011. *Recreations:* cycling (keen), wine, walking, culture, birdwatching, wild places, knitting. *Address:* Museum of London, 150 London Wall, EC2Y 5HN. *T:* (020) 7814 5700. *E:* Director@museumoflondon.org.uk.

AMERY, Colin Robert; architectural writer, critic and historian; Director, World Monuments Fund in Britain, 1999–2008 (Trustee, 1992–98); *b* 29 May 1944; *yr s* of late Kenneth George Amery and Florence Ellen Amery (*née* Young). *Educ:* King's College London; Univ. of Sussex (BA Hons). Editor and Inf. Officer, TCPA, 1968–70; Asst Editor and Features Editor, Architectural Review, 1970–79; Architecture Corresp., Financial Times, 1979–99. Advr for Sainsbury Wing, Nat. Gall., 1985–91; Arch. consultant to J. Sainsbury plc, 1985–2002. Vis. Fellow, Jesus Coll., Cambridge, 1989. Member: Arts Panel, Arts Council, 1984–86; Exec. Cttee, Georgian Gp, 1985–93; Adv. Cttee, Geffrye Mus., 1985–87; Architecture Panel, NT, 1986–; London Adv. Cttee, English Heritage, 1987–90; Building Cttee, Nat. Gallery, 1988–92; British Council, Visual Art Adv. Cttee, 1989–93; Chm., Fabric Adv. Cttee, St Edmundsbury Cathedral, 2001–14. Dir, Sir John Soane Soc., 1987–2002; Dir of Develt, Prince of Wales's Inst. of Architecture, 1993–96; President: Lutyens Trust, 1999– (Chm., 1984–93); St Marylebone Soc., 2008–14; Chairman: Organising Cttee, Lutyens Exhibn, 1981–82; Duchy of Cornwall Commercial Property Develt Cttee, 1990–98; Perspectives on Architecture Ltd, 1994–98; Fabric Adv. Cttee, St George's Chapel, Windsor Castle, 2012–14. Trustee: Spitalfields Trust, 1977–85; Save Britain's Heritage, 1980–; Brooking Collection, 1985–94; Nat. Museums and Galls on Merseyside, 1988–97; Architectural Heritage Fund, 1998–2011; Heather Trust for the Arts; War Memorials Trust, 2004–14; Advr, Auckland Castle Trust, 2013–14. Governor: Museum of London, 1992–99; Compton Verney, 2000–09. Hon. FRIBA 1998. *Publications:* Period Houses and Their Details, 1974; (jtly) The Rape of Britain, 1975; Three Centuries of Architectural Craftsmanship, 1977; (jtly) The Victorian Buildings of London 1837–1887, 1980; (compiled jtly) Lutyens 1869–1944, 1981; (contrib.) Architecture of the British Empire, 1986; Wren's London, 1988; A Celebration of Art and Architecture: the National Gallery Sainsbury Wing, 1991; Bracken House, 1992; Architecture, Industry and Innovation: the early work of Nicholas Grimshaw & Partners, 1995; Vanishing Histories, 2001; (jtly) The Lost World of Pompeii, 2002; (jtly) St Petersburg, 2006; (with Kerry Downes) St George's Bloomsbury, 2008; I. M. Pei Oare Pavilion, 2010; Windmill Hill Waddesdon, Architecture, Archives and Art, 2011; articles in professional jls. *Address:* 72 Valiant House, Vicarage Crescent, SW11 3LX. *Clubs:* Pratt's, Arts.

AMESS, Sir David (Anthony Andrew), Kt 2015; MP (C) Southend West, since 1997 (Basildon, 1983–97); *b* Plaistow, 26 March 1952; *s* of late James Henry Valentine Amess and of Maud Ethel Martin; *m* 1983, Julia Monica Margaret Arnold; one *s* four *d*. *Educ:* St Bonaventure's Grammar Sch.; Bournemouth Coll. of Technol. (BScEcon Hons 2.2, special subject Govt). Teacher, St John the Baptist Jun. Mixed Sch., Bethnal Green, 1970–71; Jun.

Underwriter, Leslie & Godwin Agencies, 1974–76; Sen. Manager, Accountancy Personnel, 1976–79; Senior Consultant: Executemps Co. Agency, 1979–81; AA Recruitment Co., 1981–87; Chairman and Chief Executive: Accountancy Solutions, 1987–90; Accountancy Gp, 1990–96. Mem., Redbridge Council, 1982–86 (Vice Chm., Housing Cttee, 1982–85). Contested (C) Newham NW, 1979. Parliamentary Private Secretary: to Parly Under-Secs of State (Health), DHSS, 1987–88; to Minister of State and Parly Under-Sec. of State, Dept of Transport, 1988–90; to Minister of State, DoE, 1990–92; to Chief Sec. to the Treasury, 1992–94; to Sec. of State for Employment, 1994–95; to Sec. of State for Defence, 1995–97. Member: Broadcasting Select Cttee, 1994–97; Health Select Cttee, 1998–2007; Chairman's Panel, 2001–. All-Party Groups: Chairman: Solvent Abuse, 2000; Fire Safety and Rescue, 2001–; Rheumatoid Arthritis, 2002; Hepatology, 2004–; Holy See, 2006; FRAME, 2006; Maldives, 2009–; Democracy in Bahrain, 2013; Maternity, 2013–; Jt Chm., Scouts, 1997; Vice-Chairman: Guides, 2000; Hungary, 2003–; Obesity, 2003; Deep Vein Thrombosis Awareness, 2003–; Asthma, 2003; Funerals and Bereavement, 2005–; Bermuda, 2005–; Warm Homes, 2005; Thrombosis, 2006–; Lions Club Internat., 2006; Mauritius, 2010–; MS, 2010–; Sec., Eye Health and Visual Impairment, 2003; Treasurer: ME (Myalgic Encephalomyelitis), 2001; N Korea, 2004–; Zoos and Aquariums, 2010–; Cardiac Risk in the Young, 2011–. Chm., Cons. Back Bench Health Cttee, 1999–; Member: Backbench Business Cttee, 2012–15; Admin Cttee, 2015–. Mem. Exec., 1922 Cttee, 2004–12. Vice Pres., Nat. Lotteries Council, 1998. Chm. Trustees, Industry and Parlt Trust, 2014–. Dir, Parly Broadcasting Unit Ltd, 1997–99. Chm., 1912 Club, 1996–; Vice Chm., Assoc. of Cons. Clubs, 1997–. Hon. Sec., Cons. Friends of Israel, 1998–. Fellow, Industry and Parliament Trust, 1994 (Chm., Fellowship Cttee, 2007–). *Publications:* The Road to Basildon, 1993; Basildon Experience: Conservatives fight back, 1994; Against All Odds, 2012; Party of Opportunity, 2014, 2nd edn 2015; contrib. magazines and pamphlets. *Recreations:* gardening, music, sport, animals, theatre, travel. *Address:* c/o House of Commons, SW1A 0AA.

AMET, Hon. Sir Arnold (Karibone), Kt 1993; CBE 1987; MP (Nat. Alliance) Madang, Papua New Guinea, 2007–12; Attorney General, Papua New Guinea, 2010–11; *b* 30 Oct. 1952; *m* 1972, Miaru (*d* 2009); three *s* two *d. Educ:* Univ. of PNG (LLB 1975); Legal Trng Inst., PNG. Joined Public Solicitor's Office, PNG, 1976; qualified as barrister and solicitor, 1977; Legal Officer and Sec., Nat. Airline Commn, 1979–80; Dep. Public Solicitor, 1980–81; Public Solicitor, 1981–83; Judge of National Trial Court and Supreme Court of Appeal, 1983–93; Chief Justice, Papua New Guinea, 1993–2003; Governor, Madang, 2007. Hon. LLD PNG, 1993. *Recreations:* Christian Ministry, watching Rugby and cricket.

AMEY, Julian Nigel Robert; Chief Executive, Institute of Healthcare Engineering and Estate Management, since 2012; *b* 19 June 1949; *s* of Robert Amey and Diana Amey (*née* Coles); *m* 1972, Ann Victoria Brenchley; three *d. Educ:* Wellingborough Sch.; Magdalene Coll., Cambridge (BA 1971, MA 1973). Longman Group: Exec. Trainee, 1971; Manager: Spain, 1972–76; Brazil, 1977–79; Latin America, 1979–83; Regional Manager, Asia Pacific Region, 1983–85; Dir, Internat. Sales and Mktg, 1985–89; Exec. Dir, BBC English, World Service, 1989–94; apptd to DTI, to assist in internat. promotion of British educn and media interest, 1994–96; Dir Gen., Canning House, 1996–2001; Chief Executive: CIBSE, 2001–06; Trinity Coll. London, 2006–09 (Gov., 2003–06); ISTD, 2009–11. Chm., Anglo-Chilean Soc., 2002–06. Gov., Bath Spa Univ. (formerly Univ. Coll.), 1996–2013. Chm., Ambassadors Circle, Bath Spa Univ., 2013–. Mem., Samuel Pepys Club, 2010– (Mem. Cttee, 2011; Chm., 2013–). FRSA 2009. *Publications:* Spanish Business Dictionary, 1979; Portuguese Business Dictionary, 1981. *Recreations:* cricket, tennis, ornithology, travel. *Clubs:* English-Speaking Union, Rumford; Hawks (Cambridge).

AMHERST OF HACKNEY, 5th Baron *cr* 1892; **Hugh William Amherst Cecil;** maritime lawyer; *b* 17 July 1968; *s* of 4th Baron Amherst of Hackney and of Elisabeth, *d* of Hugh Humphrey Merriman, DSO, MC, TD; *S* father, 2009; *m* 1996, Nicola Jane, *d* of Major Timothy Michels; one *s* two *d. Educ:* Eton; Bristol Univ. (BSc Hons Psychology). Admitted solicitor, 1994. *Recreation:* sailing. *Heir: s* Hon. Jack William Amherst Cecil, *b* 13 July 2001. *Club:* Royal Yacht Squadron.

AMIEL, Prof. Stephanie Anne, (Lady Alberti), MD; FRCP; R. D. Lawrence Professor of Diabetic Medicine, King's College London, since 1995; *b* Farnborough, Kent, 17 Oct. 1954; *d* of Gerald Joseph Amiel and Trudie Amiel; *m* 1998, Sir (Kurt) George (Matthew Mayer) Alberti, *qv*; three step *s. Educ:* Baston Sch. for Girls, Kent; Guy's Hosp. Sch. of Medicine, Univ. of London (BSc 1975; MB BS 1978; MD 1988). FRCP 1993. Res. Fellow, Yale Univ., 1983–86; Res. Fellow and Hon. Sen. Registrar, St Bartholomew's Hosp., London, 1986–89; Sen. Lectr and Hon. Consultant, Guy's Hosp., London, 1989–95. *Publications:* contrib. papers on diabetes, hypoglycaemia in diabetes and central control of metabolism. *Recreations:* fell-walking, painting, opera. *Address:* Diabetes Research Offices, King's College London School of Medicine, Denmark Hill Campus, Weston Education Centre, 10 Cutcombe Road, SE5 9RJ. *T:* (020) 7878 5639. *E:* stephanie.amiel@kcl.ac.uk. *Club:* Royal Society of Medicine.

AMIN, Prof. Ash, CBE 2014; PhD; FBA 2007; Professor of Geography, University of Cambridge, since 2011; *b* 31 Oct. 1955; *s* of late Harish and Vilas Amin; *m* 1989, Lynne Marie Brown; one *s* two *d. Educ:* Reading Univ. (BA Hons Italian Studies 1979; PhD Geog. 1986). Newcastle University: Res. Associate, Centre for Urban and Regl Develt Studies, 1982–89; Lectr, then Sen. Lectr, Geog., 1989–94; Prof. of Geog., 1994–95; University of Durham: Prof. of Geography, 1995–2011; Exec. Dir, Inst. of Advanced Study, 2005–11. Visiting Professor: Naples, 1989; Rotterdam, 1995; Copenhagen, 1995; International Fellow: Naples, 1987; Uppsala, 1999 and 2011. FAcSS (AcSS 2000). Corresp. Life Mem., Società Geografica Italiana, 1999. Edward Heath Award, RGS/IBG, 1998. *Publications:* (ed jtly) Technological Change, Industrial Restructuring and Regional Development, 1986; (ed jtly) Towards a New Europe?, 1991; (ed) Post-Fordism: a reader, 1994; (ed with N. Thrift) Globalisation, Institutions and Regional Development, 1994; (ed jtly) Behind the Myth of European Union, 1995; (ed with J. Hausner) Beyond Market and Hierarchy, 1997; (with D. Massey and N. Thrift) Cities for the Many not the Few, 2002 (trans. Italian); (with N. Thrift) Cities: reimagining the urban, 2002; (with A. Cameron and R. Hudson) Placing the Social Economy, 2002; (with D. Massey and N. Thrift) Decentering the Nation: a radical approach to regional inequality, 2003; (jtly) Organisational Learning: the role of communities, 2003; (ed jtly) The Blackwell Cultural Economy Reader, 2004; (with P. Cohendet) Architectures of Knowledge: firms, capabilities and communities, 2004; (ed jtly) Community, Economic Creativity and Organisation, 2008; (ed jtly) Thinking About Almost Everything, 2009; (ed) The Social Economy: international perspectives, 2009; Land of Strangers, 2012; (with N. Thrift) Arts of the Political: new openings for the Left, 2013. *Recreations:* music, walking, tennis. *Address:* Department of Geography, University of Cambridge, Downing Place, Cambridge CB2 3EN. *T:* (01223) 768418.

AMIS, Prof. Andrew Arthur, PhD, DSc(Eng); FREng; CEng, FIMechE; Professor of Orthopaedic Biomechanics, and Head, Medical Engineering Research Group, Imperial College London, since 2000; *b* London, 10 Oct. 1951; *s* of Peter Amis and Hilda Amis; *m* 1974, Teresa; one *s* one *d. Educ:* Univ. of Leeds (BSc Mech. Engrg 1973; PhD Biomechanics 1978); Univ. of London (DSc(Eng) 1999). FIMechE 1988; CEng 1988; FREng 2014. Imperial College London: Lectr, 1979–89, Sen. Lectr, 1989–94, in Mech. Engrg; Reader in Orthopaedic Biomechanics, 1994–2000. FRSA 1995. *Publications:* approx. 300 articles in orthopaedic surgery res. *Recreations:* sailing, travel, theatre, wine, underwater photography. *Address:* Mechanical Engineering Department, Imperial College London, SW7 2AZ. *T:* (020) 7594 7062. *E:* a.amis@imperial.ac.uk.

AMIS, Martin Louis; author; Professor of Creative Writing, Manchester University, 2007–11; special writer for The Observer, since 1980; *b* 25 Aug. 1949; *s* of Sir Kingsley Amis, CBE, and Hilary Bardwell; *m* 1984, Antonia Phillips (marr. diss. 1996); two *s*; *m* 1998, Isabel Fonseca; two *d. Educ:* various schools; Exeter Coll., Oxford (BA Hons 1st cl. in English). Fiction and Poetry Editor, TLS, 1974; Literary Editor, New Statesman, 1977–79. *Publications:* The Rachel Papers, 1973 (Somerset Maugham Award, 1974); Dead Babies, 1975; Success, 1978; Other People: a mystery story, 1981; Money, 1984; The Moronic Inferno and Other Visits to America, 1986; Einstein's Monsters (short stories), 1987; London Fields, 1989; Time's Arrow, 1991; Visiting Mrs Nabokov and Other Excursions, 1993; The Information, 1995; Night Train, 1997; Heavy Water and Other Stories, 1998; Experience (memoir), 2000 (James Tait Black Meml Prize); The War Against Cliché: essays and reviews 1971–2000, 2001; Koba the Dread, 2002; Yellow Dog, 2003; House of Meetings, 2006; The Second Plane: September 11, 2001–2007, 2008; The Pregnant Widow, 2010; Lionel Asbo: state of England, 2012; The Zone of Interest, 2014. *Recreations:* tennis, chess, snooker. *Address:* c/o Wylie Agency (UK), 17 Bedford Square, WC1B 3JA. *E:* mail@wylieagency.co.uk. *Club:* Oxford and Cambridge.

AMLOT, Roy Douglas; QC 1989; barrister; *b* 22 Sept. 1942; *s* of Douglas Lloyd Amlot and Ruby Luise Amlot; *m* 1969, Susan Margaret (*née* McDowell); two *s. Educ:* Dulwich Coll. Called to the Bar, Lincoln's Inn, 1963 (Bencher, 1986; Treas., 2007). Second Prosecuting Counsel to the Inland Revenue, Central Criminal Court and London Crown Courts, 1974; First Prosecuting Counsel to the Crown, Inner London Crown Court, 1975; Jun. Prosecuting Counsel to the Crown, Central Criminal Court, 1977, Sen. Prosecuting Counsel, 1981; First Sen. Prosecuting Counsel, 1987–89. Chairman: Criminal Bar Assoc., 1997; Bar Council, 2001; Mem., QC Appts Cttee, 2006–09. *Publications:* (ed) 11th edn, Phipson on Evidence. *Recreations:* ski-ing, cycling, windsurfing, music. *Address:* Treasury Office, Lincoln's Inn, WC2A 3TL.

AMMON, Dr (Niels) Peter (Georg), Cross, Order of Merit (Federal Republic of Germany), 1999; Ambassador of Germany to the Court of St James's, since 2014; *b* Frankfurt am Main, Germany, 23 Feb. 1952; *s* of Georg Ammon and Rita Ammon (*née* Nielsen); *m* 1979, Marliese Heimann; two *d. Educ:* Augustinergymnasium, Friedberg; Clausthal Univ. of Technol. (Dip. Maths); Freie Univ. Berlin (PhD Econs 1978); German Govt Diplomatic Sch., Bonn. Entered German Federal Foreign Office, 1978; Second Sec. and COS to Ambassador, London, 1980–82; First Sec. (Press, Cultural and Develt), Dakar, 1982–85; Econ. Dept, Bonn, 1985–89; Press Attaché, New Delhi, 1989–91; Policy Planning Office, Bonn, 1991–96; Hd, Policy Planning Staff of German Federal President, 1996–99; Minister (Econs), Washington, 1999–2001; Dir-Gen. for Econ. Affairs, Bonn, 2001–07; Ambassador to France, 2007–08; State Sec., Berlin, 2008–11; Ambassador to USA, 2011–14. *Address:* Embassy of Federal Republic of Germany, 23 Belgrave Square, SW1X 8PZ. *T:* (020) 7824 1301, *Fax:* (020) 7824 1315. *E:* amboffice@german-embassy.org.uk.

AMORIM, Celso; Minister of Defence, Brazil, since 2011; *b* 3 June 1942; *s* of Vicente Matheus Amorim and Beatriz Nunes Amorim; *m* 1966, Ana Maria Carvalho; three *s* one *d. Educ:* Brazilian Diplomatic Acad., Rio Branco Inst.; Diplomatic Acad. of Vienna (Postgrad. Dip. Internat. Relns 1967). Postgrad. work in Pol Sci./Internat. Relns, LSE, 1968–71. Chm., Brazilian Film Corp., 1979–82; Dep. Hd of Mission, Brazilian Embassy, Netherlands, 1982–85; Asst Sec., Min. of Sci. and Technol., 1985–88; Dir for Cultural Affairs, 1989, Dir for Econ. Affairs, 1990–91, Min. of Foreign Relns; Perm. Rep. to UN, GATT and Conf. on Disarmament, Geneva, 1991–93; Minister of Foreign Affairs, 1993–94; Perm. Rep. to UN, NY, 1995–99; Perm. Rep. to UN and WTO, Geneva, 1999–2000; Ambassador to UK, 2001–02; Minister of Foreign Affairs, 2003–10. Chairman: UN Security Council, 1999; Conf. on Disarmament, 2000; Gov. Body, ILO, 2000–01; Convention on Tobacco Control, 2000–01; WTO Council for Trade in Services, 2001. US Foreign Policy Assoc. Medal, 1999. Nat. and foreign decorations, incl. many Grand Crosses. *Publications:* articles in Brazilian and foreign pubns in fields of political theory, internat. relations, cultural policy, sci. and technological development. *Recreations:* reading, travelling, art, film. *Address:* Ministry of Defence, Esplanada dos Ministérios, Bloco Q, 70049-900, Brasilia DF, Brazil.

AMORY; *see* Heathcoat Amory and Heathcoat-Amory.

AMOS, Baroness *cr* 1997 (Life Peer), of Brondesbury in the London Borough of Brent; **Valerie Ann Amos;** PC 2003; Director, School of Oriental and African Studies, University of London, since 2015; *b* 13 March 1954; *d* of E. Michael Amos and Eunice Amos. *Educ:* Univ. of Warwick (BA Sociol.); Univ. of Birmingham (MA Cultural Studies); Univ. of E Anglia (doctoral research). With London Boroughs: Lambeth, 1981–82; Camden, 1983–85; Hackney, 1985–89 (Head of Trng; Head of Management Services); Management Consultant, 1984–89; Chief Exec., Equal Opportunities Commn, 1989–94; Dir, Amos Fraser Bernard, 1995–98. A Baroness in Waiting (Govt Whip), 1998–2001; Parly Under-Sec. of State, FCO, 2001–03; Sec. of State for Internat. Develt, 2003; Leader of H of L, 2003–07. High Comr to Australia, 2009–10; Under Sec. Gen. for Humanitarian Affairs and Emergency Relief Coordinator, UN, 2010–15. Mem., Fulbright Commn, 2009–. Chairman: Bd of Govs, RCN Inst., 1994–98; Afiya Trust (formerly Black Heath Foundn), 1995–98; Royal African Soc., 2008–10. Member: Adv. Cttee, Centre for Educnl Develt Appraisal and Res., Univ. of Warwick, 1991–98; Gen. Council, King's Fund, 1992–98; Council, Inst. of Employment Studies, 1993–98; Adv. Bd, Global Health Gp, UCSF, 2008–10; Trustee, IPPR, 1994–98. External Examiner: (MA Equal Opportunities), Univ. of Northumbria, at Newcastle (formerly Newcastle Poly.), 1989–93; Liverpool Univ., 1992–97. Fellow, Centre for Corporate Reputation, Saïd Business Sch., Oxford Univ., 2008–. Dir, UCL Hosps NHS Trust, 1995–98; Fellow, UCL Hosps, 2000–. Dir, Hampstead Theatre, 1992–98; Dep. Chm., Runnymede Trust, 1990–98; Trustee: VSO, 1997–98; Project Hope, 1997–98; NPG, 2003–07. Hon. LLD: Warwick, 2000; Staffordshire, 2000; Manchester, 2001; Bradford, 2006; Leicester, 2007; Birmingham, 2008; E Anglia, 2009; Stirling, 2010; Nottingham, 2012; Durham, 2013. *Publications:* various articles on race and gender issues. *Address:* School of Oriental and African Studies, Thornaugh Street, WC1H 0XG. *T:* (020) 7898 4014.

AMOS, Alan Thomas; investigator with Local Government Ombudsman, since 1993; Complaints Manager, Camden and Islington Health Authority, 2002–05; *b* 10 Nov. 1952; *s* of William Edmond Amos and Cynthia Florence Kathleen Amos. *Educ:* St Albans Sch.; St John's Coll., Oxford (MA(PPE) Hons); London Univ. Inst. of Educn (PGCE 1976). Pres., Oxford Univ. Cons. Assoc., 1974–75. Dir of Studies, Hd of Sixth Form, Hd of Econs and Politics Dept, Dame Alice Owen's Sch., Potters Bar, 1976–84; Hd of Agric. and Environment Sect., Cons. Res. Dept, 1984–86; Asst Prin., College of Further Educn, 1986–87. PA to Sec. of State for the Envmt, 1993. Councillor, 1978–90, Dep. Leader, and Chm. Educn Cttee, 1983–87, Enfield Bor. Council; Chm., London Boroughs Assoc. Educn Cttee, 1986–87; Member (Lab): Tower Hamlets LBC, 1998–2006 (Chm., Overview and Scrutiny Cttee, 2002–06); Worcester CC, 2008–; Worcestershire CC, 2009– (Dep. Leader, Lab Gp, 2009–; Dep. Leader of Opposition, 2013–; Mayor, City of Worcester, 2014–15). Contested (C): Tottenham, GLC, 1981; Walthamstow, 1983; MP (C) Hexham, 1987–92; contested (Lab) Hitchin and Harpenden, 2001. Mem., Agriculture Select Cttee, 1989–92; Chairman: Cons. backbench Forestry Cttee, 1987–92; Parly ASH Gp, 1991–92; Secretary: Cons. backbench Transport Cttee, 1988–92 (Vice Chm., 1991–92); Cons. backbench Educn Cttee, 1989–92; British-Bulgarian All Party Gp, 1991–92; Chm., Northern Gp of Cons. MPs, 1991–92. Joined Labour party, 1994; Mem. Exec. Cttee, Poplar and Canning Town Lab Party, 1996– (Treas., 1997–); Chm., Millwall Lab Party, 2000–; Vice Chm., Worcestershire Co. Lab Party, 2009–. Sec., Nat. Agricl and Countryside Forum, 1984–86. Lay Chm., NHS Ind. Review Panel,

1998–; Mem., Candidates Panel for appt to NHS Authorities, 1999–. A Vice-Pres., Gtr London YCs, 1981. Member: ESU, 1982–; ASH, 1987– (Mem. Council, 1991–); SPUC, 1987–. Hon. US Citizen, 1991. *Recreations:* travel, badminton, USA politics, bibliophilia.

AMOS, Brad; *see* Amos, W. B.

AMOS, Timothy Robert, (Tim); QC 2008; a Recorder, since 2009; *b* 13 Jan. 1964; *s* of Edward and Jean Miriam Amos; *m* 1995, Elke Mund, Cologne. *Educ:* King's Sch., Canterbury; Oriel Coll., Oxford (BA Hist. 1985); Poly. of Central London. Called to the Bar, Lincoln's Inn, 1987; in practice at the Bar, specialising in family law, esp. big money family finance cases, those with a foreign or internat. element and particularly Anglo-German cases. Standing Counsel to Queen's Proctor, 2001–08. *Recreation:* music and wine (separately and together). *Address:* Queen Elizabeth Building, Temple, EC4Y 9BS.

AMOS, William Bradshaw, (Brad), PhD; FRS 2007; biologist and optical designer; Research Staff Member, since 1981, and Emeritus Group Leader, since 2010, MRC Laboratory of Molecular Biology, Cambridge; Visiting Research Scientist, since 2010, and Visiting Professor, since 2012, Strathclyde Institute of Pharmacology and Biomedical Sciences; *b* 21 Nov. 1945; *s* of James and Edna Amos; *m* 1969, Linda Ann Richardson; two *s*. *Educ:* King Edward VII Sch., Sheffield; Queen Elizabeth's Hosp., Bristol; Queen's Coll., Oxford (MA Natural Scis 1966); Pembroke Coll., Cambridge (PhD 1970). University of Cambridge: Res. Fellow, King's Coll., 1970–74; Univ. Demonstrator and Balfour Student, Dept of Zoology, 1978–81. Chief Design Consultant, Bio-Rad Microsciences Ltd, 1986–2002; Co-Founder and Dir, Mesolens Ltd, 2009–. Principal Organiser, MRC Course in Advanced Optical Microscopy (annual), Plymouth, 2003–. Leeuwenhoek Lect., Royal Soc., 2012. Hon. FRPS 2002. Mullard Award, Royal Soc., 1994; Rank Prize for Optoelectronics, 1995; Ernst Abbe Award, NY Microscopical Soc., 2005. *Publications:* Molecules of the Cytoskeleton (with L. A. Amos), 1991; numerous articles in learned sci. jls; five patents in field of laser scanning microscopy. *Recreations:* aquatic microscopy, gemstone faceting, amateur dramatics, metalwork. *Address:* MRC Laboratory of Molecular Biology, Francis Crick Avenue, Cambridge CB2 0QH. *T:* (01223) 411640, *Fax:* (01223) 213556. *E:* ba@mrc-lmb.cam.ac.uk. *W:* http://homepage.ntlworld.com/w.amos2.

AMPLEFORTH, Abbot of; *see* Madden, Rt Rev. C.

AMPTHILL, 5th Baron *cr* 1881; **David Whitney Erskine Russell;** *b* London, 27 May 1947; *s* of 4th Baron Ampthill, CBE, PC and Susan Mary Sheila (*d* 2001), *d* of Hon. Charles John Frederic Winn; *S* father, 2011; *m* 1st, 1980, April McKenzie Arbon (marr. diss. 1998); two *d*; 2nd, 2002, Christia, *d* of Harold Noregaard Ipsen and *widow* of Prince Rostislav Romanoff. *Educ:* Stowe Sch. Member (C): Mid Sussex DC, 1999–2003; Rother DC, 2007– (Chm., 2011–12). *Heir: b* Hon. Anthony John Mark Russell [*b* 10 May 1952; *m* 1st, 1985, Christine O'Dell; one *s*; 2nd, 1999, Mrs Catherine Agnès Lefebvre (*née* Veinstein)]. *Address:* Mountsfield, Rye Hill, E Sussex TN31 7NH. *Club:* White's.

AMRAN, Mohammed; *b* 20 Nov. 1975; *s* of Mohammed Ramzan and Rakhmat Jan; *m* 1999, Saima Tabassum; two *s* one *d*. *Educ:* Huddersfield Tech. Coll. (BTEC Nat. Public Services 1995); Bradford and Ilkley Community Coll. (DipHE 1998). Youth work, Grange Interlink Community Centre, Bradford, 1994–96; Play Scheme Leader, Manningham Sport Centre, 1994–97, and Girlington Action Gp, 1996, Bradford; Co-ordinator, Youth for Understanding UK, 1996–97; Recruitment Officer, Prince's Trust Volunteers, 1997–98; remand worker, Youth Offending Team, 1998–99; Outreach Manager, Prince's Trust, 1999–2002; Fundraiser, Yorks Air Ambulance Service Charity, 2002–04; Lay Advisor: Developing Policy Excellence, Central Police Trng Develt Authy, 2005–07; Nat. Police Improvement Agency, 2007–09; Community Cohesion Manager, Greenhead High Sch., 2004–06. Mem., CRE, 1998–2002. Chm., Courts Bd, DCA, subseq. MoJ, 2004–; Member: Home Office Adv. Panel on Futurebuilders, 2005–08; England Cttee, Big Lottery Fund, 2007–. Mem. Panel, EC Cities Anti-Racism Project, 1996–97. Volunteer Trainer, Nat. Police Trng Sch., 1996–97. Member: Policy Action Team, DCMS, 1999–2000; IPPR (Criminal Justice Reform), 2000–02; Advr, Steering Gp, Holocaust Meml Day, Home Office, 2000–01; Home Sec.'s Rep., Selection Panel, Police Authy, 2008–. Mem., Duke of York's Community Initiative, Bradford, 2001–03; Mem., Police Liaison Cttee, Bradford and Dist Minority Ethnic Communities, 1998–; Dir, Bradford Youth Develt Partnership, 2000–. Eur. Rep., Prince's Trust Action, 1996–99. Mem. Court, Univ. of Leeds, 2002–. FRSA 2002. DUniv Bradford, 2002. Awards include: Imran Foundn Special Award in Recognition of Promotion of Asian Community, 2001; Gold Standard Winner, Arts and Community, Windrush Achievement Awards, 2001; Community and Campaigning Volunteer of Year, Whitbread Volunteers Action Awards, 2001; Beacon Prize (Community Builder), 2004. *Address:* 8 Highfield Drive, Heaton, Bradford, Yorks BD9 6HN.

AMWELL, 3rd Baron *cr* 1947, of Islington; **Keith Norman Montague;** former consulting civil engineer, engineering geologist and company director; *b* 1 April 1943; *o s* of 2nd Baron Amwell and of Kathleen Elizabeth Montague (*née* Fountain); *S* father, 1990; *m* 1970, Mary, *d* of Frank Palfreyman; two *s*. *Educ:* Ealing Grammar Sch. for Boys; Nottingham Univ. (BSc Civil Engrg 1964); CEng 1972; FICE 1992; CGeol 1992; FGS 1971. Consulting civil engineer, 1965–96. Dir, Construction Industry Res. and Inf. Assoc., 1996–2005; independent consultant, 2005–10. *Publications:* papers to international construction confs. *Recreations:* gardening, walking, photography, badminton. *Heir: s* Hon. Ian Keith Montague [*b* 20 Sept. 1973; *m* 2001, Amanda, *d* of George Sweetland; one *s* one *d*].

AMY, Dennis Oldrieve, CMG 1992; OBE 1984; HM Diplomatic Service, retired; Ambassador to the Democratic Republic of Madagascar, 1990–92, and Ambassador (non-resident) to Federal Islamic Republic of the Comoros, 1991–92; *b* 21 Oct. 1932; *s* of late George Arthur Amy and Isabella Thompson (*née* Crosby); *m* 1956, Helen Rosamunde (*d* 2005), *d* of late Wilfred Leslie Clemens and Nellie (*née* Brownless); one *s* one *d*. *Educ:* Southall Grammar Sch. Served RM, 1951–53. Entered HM Foreign, later HM Diplomatic Service, 1949; FO, 1949–51 and 1953–58; Athens, 1958–61; Second Sec. and Vice Consul, Moscow, 1961–63; FO, 1963–65; DSAO, 1965; Second Sec. and Passport Officer, Canberra, 1966–70; First Sec., Ibadan, 1971–74; seconded to Dept of Trade, 1974–75; FCO, 1976–78; First Sec. (Commercial), Santiago, 1978–83 (Chargé d'Affaires, 1979); FCO, 1983–86 (Counsellor, 1985–86); Consul Gen., Bordeaux, 1986–89. *Recreations:* church, walking, badminton, gardening.

AMY, Ronald John, OBE 1998; FFA; Chairman, Review Body on Doctors' and Dentists' Remuneration, 2007–13; *b* 17 June 1950; *s* of Ernest and Grace Amy; *m* 1st, 1975, Evelyn Morrison (marr. diss.); two *d*; 2nd, 1997, Patricia Groves. *Educ:* Glasgow Univ. (BSc Hons Pure Maths). FFA 1977. London Actuary, Scottish Mutual Assce Soc., 1978–80; UK Pensions Manager, Philips Electronics, 1980–84; Gp Pensions Dir, Metal Box Plc, 1984–86; Dir, New Business Develt, BZW Investment Mgt, 1986–87; Gp Pensions Dir, 1987–88, Gp Compensation and Benefits Dir, 1988–96, Grand Metropolitan PLC; Chm. and Chief Exec., Alexander Clay, 1996–97; Chief Exec., 1998–2005, Chm., 1998–2007, Aon Consulting. Non-exec. Dir, Aon Ltd, 2007–11. Chairman: Jersey Public Employees Contributory Retirement Scheme, 1990–2014; DHL Master Trust, 2000–; Jersey Teachers' Superannuation Fund, 2007–14; Chairman of Trustees: Allied Domecq Pension Fund, 2004–13; Santander UK Retirement Plan, 2008–; Alliance & Leicester Pension Scheme, 2009–12; Scottish Mutual Assurance plc Staff Pension Scheme, 2011–12; Scottish Provident Instn Staff Pension Fund, 2011–12. Member: Occupational Pensions Bd, 1989–97; Bd, OPRA, 1996–2003. Chm., Nat. Assoc. of Pension Funds, 1993–95. *Recreation:* golf. *Clubs:* Royal Automobile, Caledonian; Cruden Bay Golf (Captain, 2015–), Royal Aberdeen Golf.

AMYOT, Léopold Henri, CVO 1990; Secretary to Governor General of Canada and Secretary General of Order of Canada and of Order of Military Merit, 1985–90; Herald Chancellor of Canada, 1988–90; *b* 25 Aug. 1930; *s* of S. Eugène Amyot and Juliette Gagnon; *m* 1958, (Marie Jeanne) Andrée Jobin; one *s* two *d*. *Educ:* Laval Univ., Québec (BLSc, BScSoc); Ottawa Univ. (BA); Geneva Univ. (course on Internat. Instns). Joined External Affairs, 1957; Second Secretary: Canberra, 1960; New Delhi, 1961; Counsellor, Paris, 1968; Amb. to Lebanon (with accredn to Syria, Jordan, Iraq), 1974; Dep. Sec. Gen., Agence de Co-opération culturelle et technique, Paris, 1976; Chief of Protocol, Ext. Affairs, Ottawa, 1980; Exec. Dir, Task Force, on Pope's Visit to Canada, 1983; Amb. to Morocco, 1983. Chm., Official Residences Collections (formerly Official Residences Arts) Adv. Cttee, 1985–. Member: Professional Assoc. of For. Service Officers, Ottawa, 1957–; Inst. canadien des Affaires internat., Québec, 1985–90. Prix d'honneur (Sect. de Québec), Inst. canadien des Affaires internat., 1985. *Recreations:* tennis, golf, swimming, contemporary art collector.

ANAND, Anjum, (Mrs Adarsh Sethia); author, television presenter; Founder and Creative Director, The Spice Tailor, since 2010; *b* London, 25 Aug. 1971; *d* of Prem and Santosh Anand; *m* 2003, Adarsh Sethia; one *s* one *d*. *Educ:* Queen's Coll., London; European Business Sch., London (BA Eur. Business Admin). Cookery writer, 2003–; presenter of TV series, Indian Food Made Easy, 2007, 2008. *Publications:* Indian Every Day, 2003; Indian Food Made Easy, 2007; Anjum's New Indian, 2008; Eat Right for your Body Type, 2010; I Love Curry, 2010; Anjum's Indian Vegetarian Feast, 2012; Quick and Easy Indian, 2014. *Recreations:* travelling, contemporary Indian art, theatre, ski-ing, yoga, friends and family. *Address:* The Spice Tailor, 37 Warren Street, W1T 6AD. *T:* (0151) 245 0178, *Fax:* (0151) 244 5401. *E:* anjum.anand@thespicetailor.com.

ANANDALINGAM, Prof. Gnanalingam, (Anand), PhD; Dean, Imperial Business School, Imperial College London, since 2013; *b* Cambridge, UK, 27 Oct. 1953; *s* of Dr S. Gnanalingam and Pushpa Gnanalingam; *m* 1987, Dr Deepa Ollapally; one *s* one *d*. *Educ:* Trinity Coll., Cambridge (BA 1975); Harvard Univ. (PhD 1981). Prof., Wharton Sch. and Systems Engrg, Univ. of Pennsylvania, 1987–2001; Chair and Prof., Dept of Decision and Inf. Technol., 2001–07, Dean, 2007–13, Robert H. Smith Sch. of Business, Univ. of Maryland. MInstD. *Publications:* Beware the Winner's Curse, 2004; Telecommunications Planning, 2006. *Recreations:* tennis, jazz, cinema, walking, biking. *Address:* Imperial Business School, Imperial College London, Exhibition Road, SW7 2AZ. *T:* (020) 7594 9100. *E:* anand@imperial.ac.uk. *Club:* Bangalore (Bangalore).

ANANIA, Giorgio, PhD; Co-Founder and Vice President, Executive Board, Phototonics 21, since 2006; Co-Founder, Chief Executive Officer and Chairman, Aledia (formerly HelioDel), since 2012; *b* 18 Oct. 1958; *s* of Spartaco and Fanny Anania; *m* 1979, Regine Boucher (*d* 2012); two *d*. *Educ:* Princeton Univ. (MA, PhD); Magdalen Coll., Oxford (BA). Sen. Associate, Booz-Allen & Hamilton, New York, 1982–87; Strategic Marketing Manager, and Gen. Manager Miniplex Product, Raychem Corp., California, 1987–91; Principal, OCC Strategy Consultants, Paris, 1991–93; Vice Pres., Sales, Mktg and Business Develt, Flamel Technologies, Lyon, 1993–98; Sen. Vice Pres., Sales and Mktg, 1998–2000, Pres., 2000–07, CEO, 2001–07, Bookham Technology plc; Chm., Cube Optics AG, 2007–14. Advr on Acquisitions, Trilantic Capital Partners, 2009–11. *Recreations:* flying private planes, guitar, most water sports, reading (non-fiction). *T:* (France) 626694007. *E:* giorgio.anania@gmail.com.

ANASTASIADES, Nicos; President of Cyprus, since 2013; *b* Limassol, Cyprus, 1945; *m* Andri Moustakoudi; two *d*. *Educ:* Univ. of Athens (Law); Univ. of London (postgrad. studies in Maritime Law). In practice as lawyer, 1972–. MHR (Democratic Rally), 1981–2013 (Vice-Pres., House of Reps, 1996–2001); Chairman: Cttee of Foreign Affairs; Cttee on Educnl Affairs; Inter-Parly Cttee on Foreign Affairs, until 2006. Mem., Nat. Council, 1995–2013. Hd, Cyprus delegn to IPU. Pres., Democratic Rally Party, 1997–2012 (Hon. Pres., 2013). *Address:* Presidential Palace, 1400 Nicosia, Cyprus.

ANAWOMAH, Margo Ciara Essi B.; *see* Boye-Anawomah.

ANCONA, Ronni; *see* Ancona, V. J.

ANCONA, Rear Adm. Simon James; Assistant Chief of Defence Staff (Military Strategy), since 2013; *b* Emsworth, Hants, 7 Jan. 1963; *s* of Derek Thomas and Jane Ancona; *m* 1996, Lisa Maree Daniel; one *s* one *d*. *Educ:* Daniel Stewart's and Melville Coll., Edinburgh; King's Coll. London (MA Strategic Studies and Internat. Affairs). Flying and sea appts, 1982–96; CO, HM Ships Birmingham, Newcastle and Starling (Hong Kong), 1996–2000; MA to Minister of State for Armed Forces, 2001–03; CO, HMS Cumberland, 2005–06; Hd, Iraq Commitment and Global Maritime Commitments, MoD, 2006–09; Comdr, UK Carrier Strike Gp and Dep. Comdr, UK Maritime Force, 2009–11; Comdr, ME, UK Maritime Component, 2011–13. Mem. Council, RUSI, 2005–. QCVS 2014. *Address:* c/o Naval Secretary, Navy Command Headquarters, Mail Point 3.1, Leach Building, Whale Island, Portsmouth PO2 8BY.

See also V. J. Ancona.

ANCONA, Veronica Jane, (Ronni); actress, comedienne and author; *b* 4 July 1968; *d* of Derek Thomas Ancona and Jane Ancona; *m* 2004, Dr Gerard Hall; two *d* (one *s* decd). *Educ:* Marr Coll., Troon; St Martins and Central Sch. of Art and Design (BA Hons); Inst. of Educn, Univ. of London (PGCE). Art, Design and Technol. Teacher, Holloway Boys Sch., Islington, 1993–95; worked extensively in radio, theatre, TV and film, 1995–; *theatre* includes: Miss Conceptions, Edinburgh Fest., 1996; Singin' in the Rain, Sadler's Wells, 2004; The Hypochondriac, 2005, Little Revolution, 2014, Almeida; *television* includes: The Big Impression (with Alistair McGowan), 1999–2005 (Variety Club Comedy Award (jtly), 2002); Gideon's Daughter, 2005; Ronni Ancona & Co, 2007; Hope Springs, 2009; Skins, 2009–10; Last Tango in Halifax, 2012, 2013; various appearances in Bremner, Bird and Fortune; regular panellist on QI, 2006–; *films* include: The Calcium Kid, 2004; Stella Street—The Movie, 2004; A Cock and Bull Story, 2006; Penelope, 2006. Ambassador for: Prince's Foundn for Children and the Arts, 2008–; Prince's Trust, 2010–; Sightsavers, 2011–. Mem., BAFTA. Best Actress, British Comedy Awards, 2003. *Publications:* A Matter of Life and Death, 2009. *Recreations:* cinema, walking, family, painting, running. *Address:* c/o ARG, 4A Exmoor Street, W10 6BD. *Club:* Soho House.

See also Rear Adm. S. J. Ancona.

ANCRAM, Rt Hon. Michael; *see* Lothian, Marquess of.

ANDERSEN, Thomas Thune; Chairman, Lloyd's Register Group Ltd, since 2010; *b* Gentofte, Denmark, 4 March 1955; *s* of William Thune Andersen and Mette Munck; *m* 1981, Eva Lillan Hansen; one *s* one *d*. *Educ:* Rungsted Gymnasium; Copenhagen Business Sch. (Higher Dip. Foreign Trade 1979); Columbia Univ. (Sen. Mgt Course 1988); Harvard Univ. (Sen. Mgt Prog. 1992). Served Danish Navy, 1972–73. A. P. Møller Maersk: Personal Asst to Chm. and CEO, 1979–81; various roles, Hong Kong and China, 1981–88; Country Manager, Maersk Line Jakarta, Indonesia, 1989–91; Man. Dir, Maersk Taiwan Gp of Cos, Taiwan, 1992–94; CEO and Man. Dir, Maersk Co., UK, 1994–2000; Pres. and CEO, Maersk Contractors, Denmark, 2000–01; Pres. and CEO, Maersk Inc., USA, 2001–04; CEO, Maersk Oil Denmark, 2004–09. Director: Scottish and Southern Energy, 2008–14; Petrofac Ltd,

2009– (Sen. Ind. Dir, 2014–); Chairman: DeepOcean Gp Hldg BV, 2011–; Dong Energy A/S, 2014–; Vice Chm., VKR Hldg, 2010–; Mem. Bd, Blue Water Energy LLP, 2011–. Vice Chm., British Chamber of Commerce, 2009–. Fellow, Churchill Coll., Cambridge, 2001. Freeman, City of London, 2000; Liveryman, Shipwrights' Co., 2001. *Recreations:* golf, hunting. *Address:* Lloyd's Register Group Ltd, 71 Fenchurch Street, EC3M 4BS. *T:* (020) 7423 2228. *E:* thomas.andersen@lr.org. *Clubs:* Travellers, Special Forces.

ANDERSON, family name of **Viscount Waverley** and **Baron Anderson of Swansea**.

ANDERSON OF SWANSEA, Baron *cr* 2005 (Life Peer), of Swansea in the county of West Glamorgan; **Donald Anderson;** PC 2001; DL; barrister-at-law; *b* 17 June 1939; *s* of David Robert Anderson and Eva (*née* Mathias); *m* 1963, Dr Dorothy Trotman, BSc, PhD; three *s*. *Educ:* Swansea Grammar Sch.; University Coll. of Swansea (Hon. Fellow, 1985). 1st cl. hons Modern History and Politics, Swansea, 1960. Barrister; called to Bar, Inner Temple, 1969. Member of HM Foreign Service, 1960–64: Foreign Office, 1960–63; 3rd Sec., British Embassy, Budapest, 1963–64; lectured in Dept of Political Theory and Govt, University Coll., Swansea, 1964–66. Councillor, Kensington and Chelsea, 1971–75. MP (Lab): Monmouth, 1966–70; Swansea E, Oct. 1974–2005. Mem. Estimates Cttee, 1966–69; Vice-Chm., Welsh Labour Group, 1969–70, Chm., 1977–78; PPS to Minister of Defence (Administration), 1969–70; PPS to Attorney General, 1974–79; opposition front-bench spokesman on foreign affairs, 1983–92, on defence, 1993–94; Shadow Solicitor General, 1994–95. Member: Select Cttee on Welsh Affairs, 1980–83 (Chm., 1981–83); Select Cttee on Home Affairs, 1992–93; Speaker's Panel of Chairmen, 1995–99; Chm., Foreign Affairs Cttee, 1997–2005. Chairman: Parly Lab. Party Environment Gp, 1974–79; Welsh Lab. Gp, 1977–78. Former: Chm., British-French, -S African and -Norwegian Parly Gps; Vice Chm., British-German, -Spanish, -Netherlands, -Hungarian, Parly Gps; Mem. Exec., IPU, 1983–2001, 2005 (Vice-Chm. Exec., 1985–88; Treas., 1988–90, 1992); Chm., UK Br., CPA, 1997–2001 (Vice-Chm., 1986–97, 2010–11; Treas., 1990–93). Sen. Vice-Pres., Assoc. of European Parliamentarians for Africa (Southern), 1984–97; Member: North Atlantic Assembly, subseq. NATO Parly Assembly, 1992–2005 (Ldr, UK Delegn, 1997–98; Chm., Socialist Gp, 1997–2001); UK Delegn to OSCE, 1997–2001; UK Delegn, Parly Assembly Council of Europe, 2008– (Vice-Chm., 2012–14, Chm., 2014–, Middle East Cttee). Mem., H of L Sub-Cttee C, 2006–10, EU Cttee, 2006–10, Sub-Cttee E, 2011–. Pres., Gower Soc., 1976–78. Chairman: Parly Christian Fellowship, 1990–93; Nat. Prayer Breakfast, 1989; President: Boys' Brigade of Wales, 1992–94; Swansea Male Choir; Mem. Bd, Mercy Ships, 2005–12; Hon. Mem., Morriston Rotary Club, 2000; Hon. Vice Pres., Swansea Business Club, 2006. Vis. Parly Fellow, St Antony's Coll., Oxford, 1999–2000. DL W Glam, 2006. Freeman: City of London, 2005; City and County of Swansea, 2000. Hon. Fellow, Swansea Inst. of Higher Educn, 2005. Commander's Cross, Order of Merit (FRG), 1986; Foreign Minister's Medal (Republic of Slovakia), 2004; Chevalier, Légion d'Honneur (France), 2005; Officer's Cross, Order of Merit (Hungary), 2007. *Recreations:* church work, walking and talking. *Address:* House of Lords, SW1A 0PW.

ANDERSON, Ailsa Jane, LVO 2009; Director of Communications, Lambeth Palace, since 2013; *b* Pembury, Kent, 20 April 1969; *d* of Roderick and Patricia McIntyre; *m* 2000, Rear Adm. Mark Anderson, CB; one *s* one *d*. *Educ:* John Warner Sch., Herts; Univ. of Essex (BA English Lit.). Journalist, London and Essex Guardian Newspapers, 1989–92; Sen. Press Officer and Press Sec. to Minister of State to Armed Forces, 1993–99; Chief Press Officer, Cabinet Office, 1999–2001; Royal Household: Asst Press Sec., 2001–06; Dep. Press Sec. to the Queen and Hd of News, 2007–10; Communications and Press Sec. to the Queen, 2010–13. MIPR 2007. *Recreations:* riding, cinema and theatre, walking my black labrador. *Address:* Lambeth Palace, SE1 7JU. *T:* (020) 7898 1224, 07990 574916. *E:* ailsa.anderson@lambethpalace.org.uk.

ANDERSON, Alexander Beveridge, CBE 2015 (OBE 2010); DL; FREng, FIChemE; Chairman, Tees Valley Local Enterprise Partnership, since 2010; *b* Methil, Fife, 16 April 1944; *s* of John Weir Anderson and Elizabeth Warrender Anderson; *m* 1970, May Wemyss (*d* 2001); three *s*. *Educ:* Buckhaven High Sch.; Heriot-Watt Univ. (BSc). FIChemE 1982. ICI: Gen. Manager, Teesside Ops, 1989–94; Dir, Engrg, 1994–96; Ops Dir, Tioxide Gp, 1994–97; Dir, ICI Pakistan, 1997–2000; Sen. Vice Pres., Technol., 1997–2000. Chm., Ensus UK, 2006–11; Dir, Eutech Engrg Solutions, 1997–2001. Chairman: Teesside Trng Enterprise, 1989–94; Teesside Tomorrow Ltd, 1990–94; Director: Teesside Develt Corp., 1989–2005; Teesside Trng and Enterprise Council, 1989–2004; Centre for Process Innovation, 2004–. Chm., S Durham NHS Health Trust, 2002–04. Chm., Univ. of Teesside, 2004–14. Gov., Durham Sch., 2002–12. FREng 1997. DL Durham, 1991. *Recreations:* jazz, golf, gardening, travel. *Address:* Carperby Lodge, 39 Abbey Road, Darlington, Co. Durham DL3 8LR. *E:* sandy_anderson.t21@btinternet.com.

ANDERSON, Maj.-Gen. Alistair Andrew Gibson, CB 1980; *b* 26 Feb. 1927; *s* of Lt-Col John Gibson Anderson and Margaret Alice (*née* Scott); *m* 1953, Dr Margaret Grace Smith (*d* 2013); one *s* two *d*. *Educ:* George Watson's Boys' Coll., Edinburgh; University Coll. of SW of England, Exeter (Short Univ. Course, 1944); Staff Coll., Camberley; Jt Services Staff Coll., Latimer. Enlisted 1944; commnd Royal Corps of Signals, 1946; comd 18 Signal Regt, 1967–69; Defence Ops Centre, 1969–72; staff of Signal Officer-in-Chief, 1972–74; Comdt, Sch. of Signals, 1974–76; Signal Officer-in-Chief (Army), 1977–80, retired; Dir, Communications and Electronics Security Gp, GCHQ, 1980–85. Col Comdt, Royal Corps of Signals, 1980–86; Chm., Royal Signals Assoc., 1982–87. *Recreations:* walking, gardening as far as limited ability will allow.

ANDERSON, Dr Alun Mark; writer and publisher; Senior Consultant, New Scientist, since 2005 (Editor 1992–99; Editor-in-Chief and Publishing Director, 1999–2005); *b* 27 May 1948; *s* of Peter Marchmont Anderson and Jane Watkin Anderson (*née* James). *Educ:* Univ. of Sussex (BSc 1968); Univ. of Edinburgh (PhD 1972). IBM Res. Fellow, 1972–74, Jun. Res. Fellow, Wolfson Coll., 1972–76, Oxford; Royal Soc. Res. Fellow, Kyoto Univ., 1977–79; Nature: News and Views Ed., 1980–83; Tokyo Bureau Chief, 1984–86; Washington Ed., 1986–90; Internat. Ed., Science, 1991–92. Dir, IPC Magazines Ltd, 1997–98; Dir and Co-owner, Xconomy, 2007–. Member: Royal Soc. COPUS, 1997–2000; Royal Soc. Faraday Prize Cttee, 1999–2004; British Council Sci., Engrg and Envmt Adv. Cttee, 2001–07. Member Council: Univ. of Sussex, 1998–2001; Royal Instn, 2005–10; Soc. for Experimental Biol., 2007–. Trustee, St Andrews Prize, 1999–. Mem., Editl Adv. Bd, Oxford Today, 2010–. Editor of the Year (Special Interest Magazines), BSME, 1993, 1995, 1997; Editors' Editor of the Year, BSME, 1997. *Publications:* Science and Technology in Japan, 1984, 2nd edn 1991; After the Ice: life, death and politics in the New Arctic, 2009; (contrib.) The Fast-Changing Arctic: rethinking Arctic security for a warmer world, 2013. *Recreations:* mountain walking, travel. *Address:* New Scientist, 110 High Holborn, WC1V 6EU. *T:* (020) 7611 1200. *E:* alun.anderson@gmail.com.

ANDERSON, Prof. Anne Harper, OBE 2002; PhD; FRSE; Vice Principal, and Head, College of Social Sciences, University of Glasgow, since 2010; *b* Glasgow, 19 Feb. 1954; *d* of James and Jean Thomson; *m* 1975, Ian Anderson; one *s* one *d*. *Educ:* Hutchesons' Girls' Grammar Sch., Glasgow; Univ. of Glasgow (MA Hons Psychol. 1976; PhD 1982). Res. Fellow, Univ. of Edinburgh, 1979–86; University of Glasgow: Lectr, 1986–97; Prof. of Psychol., 1997–2006; Dep. Dean, Faculty of Law, Business and Social Sci., 2005–06; Vice Principal, and Hd, Coll. of Art, Sci. and Engrg, Univ. of Dundee, 2006–10. Director: ESRC Cognitive Engrg Prog., 1995–2000; ESRC/EPSRC/DTI People at the Centre of Communication and Inf. Technols Prog., 2000–06; Mem., EPSRC, 2008–15. FRSE 2015. *Publications:* (jtly) Teaching Talk, 1983; (with Tony Lynch) Listening, 1988; papers in learned jls incl. Jl of Memory and Lang., Lang. and Cognitive Processes, Computers in Human Behavior. *Recreations:* travel to nice places, good food, good fiction, relaxing with the family. *Address:* College of Social Sciences, University of Glasgow, Florentine House, Glasgow G12 8QF. *T:* (0141) 330 6076, *Fax:* (0141) 330 7491. *E:* anne.anderson@glasgow.ac.uk.

ANDERSON, Anthony John; QC 1982; a Recorder, 1995–99; *b* 12 Sept. 1938; *s* of late A. Fraser Anderson and Margaret Anderson; *m* 1970, Fenja Ragnhild Gunn. *Educ:* Harrow; Magdalen Coll., Oxford. MA. 2nd Lieut, The Gordon Highlanders, 1957–59. Called to the Bar, Inner Temple, 1964, Bencher, 1992; retired from practice, 2001. Chm. of Tribunals, SFA (formerly The Securities Assoc.), 1988–2001. *Recreations:* golf, fishing, gardening, choral singing. *Address:* Mariners, Mariners Lane, Bradfield, Berkshire RG7 6HU. *Clubs:* Garrick, MCC.

ANDERSON, Mrs Beverly Jean; educator; former journalist and broadcaster; *b* 9 Dec. 1940; *d* of Arthur Benjamin Phillpotts and Sylvia Phillpotts; *m* 1st, 1968, Angus Walker, *qv* (marr. diss. 1976); 2nd, 1976, Andrew Anderson (marr. diss. 1986); one *s*. *Educ:* Wellesley Coll., Mass (BA History, and Politics 1962); London Univ. (PGCE 1967). Jamaican Foreign Service, Kingston and Washington, 1963–66; primary sch. teacher, London, 1968–71, Oxfordshire primary schs, 1971–81; Headteacher, Berwood First Sch., Oxford, 1981–83; Sen. Lectr in Educn, Oxford Poly., 1985–89; Lectr in Educn, Warwick Univ., and educn consultant, 1989–93; Chief Exec., Book Trust, 1993–94; Head, Village Sch., Pacific Palisades, Calif, 1995–99; Middle School Principal: Trinity Sch., NY, 1999–2004; Rye Country Day Sch., Rye, NY, 2004–06. Dir, Railtrack, 1993–94. Chairman: Equal Opportunities Wkg Gp, NAB, 1987–88; CNAA Steering Cttee on Access Courses to HE Framework, 1988–89; Member: Nat. Curriculum Council, 1989–91; Council, ABSA, 1989–95; Arts Council, 1990–94; Governor: BFI, 1985–93; Oxford Stage Co. Bd, 1986–96; S Bank Bd, 1989–94. Mem., Nuffield Council on Bioethics, 1991–94; Chm. Council, Charter '88, 1989–93. Columnist, TES, 1989–93. Television includes: Presenter: Black on Black, 1982–83; Nothing but the Best; Sixty Minutes; After Dark, 1989–90; Behind the Headlines, 1990–91. FRSA 1991. Hon. Fellow, Leeds Metropolitan Univ., 1991. Hon. LLM Teesside, 1993. *Publications:* Learning with Logo: a teacher's guide, 1985; numerous articles on education, social issues and media education. *Recreations:* plays, paintings, poems, movies, dancing.

ANDERSON, Brian David Outram, AO 1993; PhD; FRS 1989; Distinguished Professor, Australian National University, since 2002 (Professor of Systems Engineering, 1981–2002); Distinguished Researcher, National ICT Australia, since 2006 (Chief Executive Officer and President, 2002–03; Chief Scientist, 2003–06); *b* 15 Jan. 1941; *s* of late David Outram Anderson and Nancy Anderson; *m* 1968, Dianne, *d* of M. Allen; three *d*. *Educ:* Sydney Univ.; Stanford Univ. (PhD 1966); California Univ. Res. Asst, Stanford Electronics Labs, 1964; Lectr in Electrical Engrg, Stanford Univ., 1965; Asst Prof. and Staff Consultant, Vidar Corp., Mount View, Calif., 1966; Hd of Dept, 1967–75, Prof., 1967–81, Dept of Electrical Engrg, Univ. of Newcastle; Dir, Res. Sch. of Information Scis and Engrg, ANU, 1994–2002. Mem., Scientific Adv. Bd, Rio Tinto (formerly CRA) Ltd, 1982–98; Director: Telectronics Hldgs Ltd, 1986–88; Nucleus Ltd, 1988–95; Cochlear Ltd, 1995–2005; Crasys Ltd, 1996–98; Anutech Pty Ltd, 1997–2000. Member: Aust. Res. Grants Cttee, 1972–77; Aust. Science and Technology Council, 1977–82; UNESCO Nat. Commn, 1982–83; Aust. Industrial Res. and Develt Incentives Bd, 1984–86; Prime Minister's Sci. and Engrg Council, 1989–93; Prime Minister's Sci., Engrg and Innovation Council, 1998–2002; Aust. Res. Council, 2000–01; Aust. Res. Council Bd, 2001–03; Nat. Res. Priorities Standing Cttee, 2005–07; DEST e-Res. Co-ordinating Cttee, 2005–06. Member, Advisory Board: Inst. for Telecoms Res., 2004–07; Centre for Complex Dynamic Systems and Control, Univ. of Newcastle, NSW, 2004–; Centre for Applied Philos. and Public Ethics, 2005–. Pres., Australian Acad. of Sci., 1998–2002. FAA; FTS; FIEEE; Hon. FIE(Aust). For. Assoc., US NAE, 2002. Dr *hc*: Louvain, 1991; Swiss Federal Inst. of Technol., 1993; Hon. DEng: Sydney, 1995; Melbourne, 1997; Newcastle, NSW, 2005; Hon. DSc NSW, 2001. Order of the Rising Sun, Gold Rays with Neck Ribbon (Japan), 2007. *Publications* include: Linear Optimal Control, 1971; Network Analysis and Synthesis, 1975; Optimal Filtering, 1980; Optimal Control, 1990. *Address:* Research School of Engineering, Australian National University, Canberra, ACT 0200, Australia.

ANDERSON, Campbell McCheyne; Managing Director, North Ltd, 1994–98; *b* 17 Sept. 1941; *s* of Allen Taylor Anderson and Ethel Catherine Rundle; *m* 1965, Sandra Maclean Harper; two *s* one *d*. *Educ:* The Armidale Sch., NSW, Aust.; Univ. of Sydney (BEcon). AASA. Trainee and General Administration, Boral Ltd, Australia, 1962–69; Gen. Manager/Man. Dir, Reef Oil NL, Australia, 1969–71; Asst Chief Representative, Burmah Oil Australia Ltd, 1972; Corporate Development, Burmah Oil Incorporated, New York, 1973; Corporate Development, 1974; Finance Director and Group Planning, Burmah Oil Trading Ltd, UK, 1975; Special Projects Dir, 1976, Shipping Dir, 1978, Industrial Dir, 1979, Man. Dir, 1982–84, Burmah Oil Co.; Man. Dir, 1985–93, Chief Exec. Officer, 1986–93, Renison Goldfields Consolidated. Director: Consolidated Gold Fields, 1985–89; Ampolex Ltd, 1991–97 (Chm., 1991–96); Macquarie Direct Investments Ltd, 1999–2006; Aviva Australia Hldgs (formerly CGNU Australia), 1999–2009; IBJ Australia Bank, 2000–02; Reconciliation Australia Ltd, 2001–07; Clough Ltd, 2003–08; ThoroughVisioN Ltd, 2004–11. Dir, Aust. Mines and Metals Assoc., 1985–93 (Pres., 1988–89); Councillor: Aust. Mining Industry Council, 1985–98 (Pres., 1991–93); Business Council of Aust., 1986–2000 (Pres., 1999–2000); Sentient Gp, 2001–; Chairman: Energy Resources Aust. Ltd, 1994–98; Southern Pacific Petroleum NL, 2001–08; Landcare Aust. Ltd, 2012–. Pres., Australia-Japan Soc., Victoria, 1995–98. *Recreations:* golf, swimming, horse-racing. *Address:* 77 Drumalbyn Road, Bellevue Hill, NSW 2023, Australia. *Clubs:* Australian (Sydney); Royal Sydney Golf; Australian Turf (formerly Jockey); Elanora Country (NSW).

ANDERSON, (Clarence) Eugene; business consultant; Chairman and Chief Executive, Ferranti International plc, 1990–94; *b* 31 Aug. 1938; *s* of Clarence Leslie Anderson and Wilda Faye Anderson; *m* 1977, Daniela Leopolda Proche; one *d*, and one *s* two *d* from a previous marriage. *Educ:* Univ. of Texas (BSc Chem. Engrg, 1961); Harvard Univ. (MBA 1963). Process Engr, New Orleans, 1961, Ops Analyst, Houston, 1963–66, Tenneco Oil Co.; Man. Dir, Globe Petroleum Sales Ltd, Lincs, 1966–69; Dir, Supply and Transportation, Houston, 1969–72, Dir, Operational Planning, Houston, 1972, Tenneco Oil Co.; Vice Pres., Tenneco International Co., Houston, 1973; Exec. Dir, Albright & Wilson Ltd, London, 1973–75; Vice Pres., Corporate Develt, Tenneco Inc., Houston, 1975–78; Dep. Man. Dir, Ops, Albright & Wilson Ltd, London, 1979–81; Pres., Celanese International Co., and Vice Pres., Celanese Corp., New York, 1981–85; Chief Exec., Johnson Matthey PLC, London, 1985–89. Pres., Eugene and Daniela Scholarship Foundn, 1990–. *Publications:* (jtly) report on microencapsulation. *Recreations:* music, literature, theatre, sailing, various sports.

ANDERSON, Clive Stuart; barrister; television and radio presenter and writer; *b* 10 Dec. 1952; *s* of Gordon Menzies Randall Anderson and late Doris Elizabeth Anderson; *m* 1981, Jane Hughes, (Prof. Jane Anderson); one *s* two *d*. *Educ:* Harrow County Sch. for Boys; Selwyn Coll., Cambridge (MA). Called to the Bar, Middle Temple, 1976. *Radio:* Host, Cabaret Upstairs, 1986–88; Chm., Whose Line is it Anyway?, 1988; Presenter: Devil's Advocate, 1991–92; Unreliable Evidence, 1998–; The Real…, 2002–; Clive Anderson's Chat Room, 2004–; *television:* Whose Line is it Anyway?, 1988–98; Clive Anderson Talks Back, 1989–95; Notes & Queries, 1993; Our Man In, 1995, 1996; Clive Anderson All Talk, 1996–99; If I Ruled the World, 1998–99; Clive Anderson Now, 2001–; various other progs. Pres., Woodland Trust, 2003–. Patron: Afghan Connection; Save the Rhino International.

Publications: (jtly) Great Railway Journeys, 1994; (with Ian Brown) Patent Nonsense, 1994; Our Man In, 1995; Our Man in Heaven & Hell, 1996. *Recreations:* history, comedy, football. *Address:* Curtis Brown, Haymarket House, 28–29 Haymarket, SW1Y 4SP. *T:* (020) 7393 4400; 6 King's Bench Walk, Temple, EC4Y 7DR. *T:* (020) 7583 0410.

ANDERSON, David; Chairman: Reclaim Fund, 2010–14; Vice Chairman, NFU Mutual Insurance Society, 2012–14 (non-executive Director, 2010–14); *b* 23 Oct. 1955; *s* of Donald and Gweneth Anderson; *m* 1980, Fiona Ellen Hamilton; one *s* one *d*. *Educ:* Cheadle Hulme Sch.; St Edmund Hall, Oxford (MA PPE). Graduate trainee, Aveling Barford Ltd, construction equipment manufr, 1977–80; Dun and Bradstreet, 1980–83; PA Mgt Consultants, 1983–87; Dep. Gen. Manager (Mkting), 1987–90, Dir, 1990–2003, Chief Exec., 1996–2003, Yorkshire Building Soc.; Chief Executive: Jobcentre Plus, DWP, 2003–05; Co-operative Financial Services Ltd, 2005–09. Non-exec. Dir, John Lewis Partnership, 2011–14. *Recreations:* golf, sailing.

ANDERSON, David; MP (Lab) Blaydon, since 2005; *b* 2 Dec. 1953; *s* of Cyril and Janet Anderson; *m* 1973, Elizabeth Eva Jago. *Educ:* Doncaster and Durham Tech. Colls; Durham Univ. (DipSocSc); Moscow Higher Trade Union Sch. Colliery mechanic, 1969–89; care worker, 1989–2005. PPS to Minister of State, DIUS, 2007–08, FCO, 2008–09, MoD, 2009–10; an Opposition Whip, 2010–11. Chm., All-Party Parly Gp on Third World Solidarity, on Muscular Dystrophy, on Coalfield Communities, on Industrial Heritage; Sec., All-Party Parly Gp on Kurdistan. Trade Union Lay Official: NUM, 1978–89; UNISON, 1989–2005; Pres., UNISON, 2003–04; Mem., TUC Gen. Council, 2000–05. *Recreations:* walking, travel, music, caravanning. *Address:* House of Commons, SW1A 0AA. *T:* (020) 7219 4348. *E:* andersonda@parliament.uk.

ANDERSON, David Heywood, CMG 1982; Judge of the International Tribunal for the Law of the Sea, 1996–2005 (Judge *ad hoc* in Arctic Sunrise case, 2013); *b* 14 Sept. 1937; *s* of late Harry Anderson; *m* 1961, Jennifer Ratcliffe; one *s* one *d*. *Educ:* King James' Grammar Sch., Almondbury; LLB (Leeds); LLM (London). Called to Bar, Gray's Inn, 1963. HM Diplomatic Service, 1960–96: Asst Legal Adviser, FCO 1960–69; Legal Adviser, British Embassy, Bonn, 1969–72; Legal Counsellor, FCO, 1972–79; Legal Adviser, UK Mission to UN, NY, 1979–82; Legal Counsellor, 1982–87, Dep. Legal Advr, 1987–89, Second Legal Advr, 1989–96, FCO. Mem., Greenwich Forum, 1996–2014. *Publications:* Modern Law of the Sea - Selected Essays, 2008; (contrib.) International Maritime Boundaries, 1993–; contribs to British Yearbook of Internat. Law and learned jls. *Recreation:* gardening.

ANDERSON, David James Charles, OBE 1999; Director General, Amgueddfa Cymru-National Museum Wales, since 2010; *b* Belfast, 22 Aug. 1952; *s* of Trevor and Sylvia Anderson; *m* 1977, Josephine Harrison; one *s* two *d*. *Educ:* Lawrence Sheriff Sch., Rugby; Lewes Comprehensive Sch.; Edinburgh Univ. (MA Hist. 1976); Univ. of Sussex (PGCE 1977). History teacher, Oathall Comprehensive Sch., Haywards Heath, 1977–79; Educn Officer, Royal Pavilion, Art Gall. and Museums, Brighton, 1979–85; Hd of Educn, Nat. Maritime Mus., 1985–89; Hd of Educn, 1990–2001, Dir of Learning and Interpretation, 2001–10, V&A Mus. Pres., Museums Assoc., 2013–15. *Publications:* The Spanish Armada, 1988; (jtly) The Mutiny on the Bounty, 1989; A Common Wealth: museums and learning in the United Kingdom, 1997, 2nd edn as A Common Wealth: museums in the learning age, 1999. *Recreations:* family, Celtic literature and music, opera, visual arts, Irish Rugby, film. *Address:* Amgueddfa Cymru-National Museum Wales, Cathays Park, Cardiff CF10 3NP. *T:* (029) 2039 7951. *E:* david.anderson@museumwales.ac.uk.

ANDERSON, Prof. David McBeath, PhD; Professor of African History and Politics, University of Warwick, since 2013; *b* Wick, 12 May 1957; *s* of William Anderson and Isobel Anderson; *m* 1983, Angela Parrott; two *s* two *d*. *Educ:* Kingswood Sch., Northants; Sussex Univ. (BA 1st Cl. Hons); Trinity Coll., Cambridge (PhD Hist. 1982). Res. Associate, Hist. Dept, Univ. of Nairobi, 1980–81; Sen. Rouse-Ball Scholar (Postdoctoral), Trinity Coll., Cambridge, 1982–83; Res. Fellow in Hist., New Hall, Cambridge, 1983–84; Lectr in Imperial and Commonwealth Hist., Birkbeck Coll., Univ. of London, 1984–91; Leverhulme Trust Res. Fellow, 1990–91; Sen. Lectr in Hist., SOAS, 1991–2002, Dir, Centre of African Studies, 1998–2002, Univ. of London; University of Oxford: Res. Fellow, St Antony's Coll., Oxford, 2002–05; Lectr in African Politics, 2005–06; Prof. of African Politics, 2006–12; Dir, African Studies Centre, 2006–09; Fellow, St Cross Coll., Oxford, 2005–12. Actg Dir, British Inst. in Eastern Africa, Nairobi, 2009–10. Evans-Pritchard Vis. Lectr, All Souls Coll., Oxford, 2002. *Publications:* (ed) Conservation in Africa: people, policies and practice, 1987; (ed) The Ecology of Survival: case studies from Northeast African history, 1988; (ed) Policing the Empire: government, authority and control, 1830–1940, 1991; (ed) Policing and Decolonisation: nationalism, politics and the police, 1917–1965, 1992; (ed) Revealing Prophets: prophecy and history in Eastern Africa, 1998; Maasai: people of cattle, 1998; (ed) Africa's Urban Past, 1999; Eroding the Commons: politics of ecology in Baringo, Kenya, 1890–1963, 2002; Supporting Ownership: Swedish development cooperation with Kenya, Tanzania and Uganda, 2 vols, 2002; (ed) The Poor Are Not Us: poverty and pastoralism in Eastern Africa, 2002; Histories of the Hanged: Britain's dirty war in Kenya and the end of empire, 2005; The Khat Controversy - Stimulating the Debate on Drugs, 2007; (ed) Routledge Handbook of African Politics, 2013; (ed) Politics and Violence in Eastern Africa: struggles of emerging states, 2015. *Recreations:* football, ski-ing, reading good history. *Address:* Department of History, University of Warwick, Humanities Building, University Road, Coventry CV4 7AL. *T:* (024) 7615 0991. *E:* d.m.anderson@warwick.ac.uk.

ANDERSON, David Munro; Chairman, Anderson Quantrend (formerly Allingham Anderson Roll Ross) Ltd, since 1990; *b* 15 Dec. 1937; *s* of Alexander Anderson and Jessica Anderson (*née* Vincent-Innes); *m* 1st, 1965, Veronica Jane (*née* Stevens) (marr. diss.); two *s* one *d*; 2nd, 1989, Ruth Lewis-Bowen. *Educ:* Morrison's Academy, Perthshire; Strathallan, Perthshire. Commissioned Black Watch; served W Africa; tea production with James Finlay & Co., India, 1959–62; London Chamber of Commerce and Industry, 1962–63; joined E. D. & F. Man Ltd, 1963; formed Anderson Man Ltd, 1981; formed E. D. & F. Man International Ltd, 1985, Chm., 1986–90; Man. Dir, Commodity Analysis Ltd, 1968; numerous directorships. Chairman, formation cttees: Internat. Petroleum Exchange; Baltic Internat. Freight Futures Exchange (jtly); former Vice-Chm., London Commodity Exchange; Dir, SIB, 1986–87. MCSI (MSI 1992). *Recreations:* ski-ing, shooting. *Address:* The Old Gardens, Kersey, Suffolk IP7 6ED. *Club:* Caledonian.

ANDERSON, David William Kinloch; QC 1999; Independent Reviewer of Terrorism Legislation, since 2011; Judge of Courts of Appeal of Guernsey and Jersey, since 2015; *b* 5 July 1961; *s* of Sir (William) Eric (Kinloch) Anderson, *qv* and Poppy (*née* Mason); *m* 1989, Margaret Beeton; two *d*. *Educ:* Eton Coll. (King's Schol.); New Coll., Oxford (Open Schol.; MA Ancient and Modern Hist. 1982); Downing Coll., Cambridge (BA Law 1984); Inns of Court Sch. of Law. Called to the Bar, Middle Temple, 1985, Bencher, 2007; Lawyer from Abroad, Covington & Burling, Washington, 1985–86; Stagiaire, Cabinet of Lord Cockfield, European Commn, 1987–88; in practice as barrister, Brick Court Chambers, 1988–; a Recorder, 2004–13. Vis. Lectr in European Law, 1989–95, Vis. Res. Fellow, 1995–99, Vis. Prof., 1999–, KCL. Ind. Expert monitoring freedom of expression and inf., Council of Europe, 2000–03. Mem. Exec. Cttee, Lord Slynn of Hadley European Law Foundn, 2002–09. Member: Governing Body, British Assoc. for Central and Eastern Europe, 2002–08; Adv. Bd, SSEES, 2007–10. Trustee, British Inst. of Internat. and Comparative Law, 2005–09. Mem., RIIA, 2012–. *Publications:* References to the European Court, 1995, 2nd edn 2002; various articles in legal jls. *Recreations:* kayaking, off-road cycling, mountains, history. *Address:* Brick Court Chambers, 7–8 Essex Street, WC2R 3LD. *T:* (020) 7379 3550. *Clubs:* Alpine, Athenæum.

ANDERSON, Prof. Declan John; Professor of Oral Biology, University of Bristol, 1966–85, now Professor Emeritus; Founder, The Oral and Dental Research Trust, 1989 (Director, 1989–92); *b* 20 June 1920; *s* of Arthur John Anderson and Katherine Mary Coffey; *m* 1947, Vivian Joy Dunkerton; four *s* three *d*. *Educ:* Christ's Hospital; Guy's Hospital Medical School, Univ. of London. BDS (London) 1942; LDSRCS 1943, BSc 1946, MSc 1947, PhD 1955. Prof. of Physiology, Univ. of Oregon, USA, 1957–58; Prof. of Physiology in Relation to Dentistry, Univ. of London, 1963–66. *Publications:* Physiology for Dental Students, 1952; (with R. Buxton) How to Dissect and Understand Medical Terms, 1992; Introducing Silver, 2000; (with J. Flowerday) Introducing Silversmithing, 2002; scientific papers in professional jls. *Recreations:* silversmithing, forging, music.

ANDERSON, Dr Digby Carter; Director, Social Affairs Unit, 1980–2004; *b* 25 May 1944; *s* of late Donald Anderson and Elizabeth Nance Ethel Anderson; *m* 1965, Judith Harris. *Educ:* St Lawrence Coll.; Univ. of Reading (BA Hons); Brunel Univ. (MPhil, PhD). Lectr, then Sen. Lectr, Luton Coll. of Higher Educn, 1965–77; Tutor, Brunel Univ. Youth Work Trng Unit, 1974–78; Res. Fellow, Univ. of Nottingham, 1977–80; Associate Lectr, Brunel Univ., 1977–78. Mem., ESRC, 1989–93. Mem., Health Studies Cttee, CNAA, 1987–92. Columnist: The Times, 1984–88; Sunday Telegraph, 1988–89; Sunday Times, 1989–90; Spectator, 1984–2000; National Review, 1991–2000. Ordained deacon 1985, priest 1986; asst priest, St Saviour's, Luton, 1986–. Mem., Mont Pelerin Soc. *Publications:* (ed) Health Education in Practice, 1979; Evaluation by Classroom Experience, 1979; Evaluating Curriculum Proposals, 1980; (ed) The Ignorance of Social Intervention, 1980; Breaking the Spell of the Welfare State, 1981; (ed) The Kindness that Kills, 1984; (ed) A Diet of Reason, 1986; The Spectator Book of Imperative Cooking, 1987; (ed) Full Circle, 1988; (ed) Health, Lifestyle and Environment, 1992; (ed) The Loss of Virtue: moral confusion and social disorder in Britain and America, 1993; (ed) This Will Hurt: the restoration of civic order in America and Britain, 1995; (ed) Gentility Recalled: mere manners and the making of social order, 1996; (ed jtly) Faking It: the sentimentalisation of modern society, 1998; (compiler) The Dictionary of Dangerous Wars, 2000; Losing Friends, 2001; All Oiks Now, 2004; The English at Table, 2006; contrib. Sociology, Jl Curriculum Studies, Econ. Affairs, Social Policy Rev. *Recreations:* non-Germanic music, the seaside, dinner. *Address:* 17 Hardwick Place, Woburn Sands, Bucks MK17 8QQ. *T:* (01908) 584526.

ANDERSON, Prof. Donald Thomas, AO 1986; PhD, DSc; FRS 1977; Challis Professor of Biology, University of Sydney, 1984–91, Professor Emeritus, since 1992 (Professor of Biology, 1972–84); *b* 29 Dec. 1931; *s* of Thomas and Flora Anderson; *m* 1960, Joanne Trevathan (*née* Claridge). *Educ:* King's Coll., London Univ. DSc London, 1966; DSc Sydney, 1983. Lectr in Zoology, Sydney Univ., 1958–61; Sen. Lectr, 1962–66; Reader in Biology, 1967–71. Clarke Medal, Royal Soc. of NSW, 1979; Alexander Kowalevsky Medal, St Petersburg Soc. Naturalists, 2001. *Publications:* Embryology and Phylogeny of Annelids and Arthropods, 1973; Barnacles: structure, function, development and evolution, 1993; Atlas of Invertebrate Anatomy, 1996; Invertebrate Zoology, 1998, 2nd edn 2001; papers in zool. jls. *Recreations:* gardening, photography. *Address:* 5 Angophora Close, Wamberal, NSW 2260, Australia. *T:* (2) 43847218.

ANDERSON, Edmund John Seward; Chairman, Yorkshire Building Society, 2007–15 (Director, 2003–15); *b* Singapore, 22 Dec. 1950; *s* of late Dick Anderson and of Irene Anderson (*née* Seward); *m* 1982, Heather Medcalf (*see* H. Anderson); two *s* two *d*. *Educ:* Beaumont Coll.; Stonyhurst Coll.; Leeds Poly. (BSc Econs). CPFA 1973. Various local govt appts, 1973–87; Dep. Man. Dir, E Midlands Airport, 1987–90; Exec. Dir, Leeds CC, 1990–97; Man. Dir, Leeds Bradford Internat. Airport, 1997–2007. Non-executive Director: Kelda Gp plc, 2005–08; Marketing Leeds Ltd, 2005–09. Chm., Airport Operators Assoc., 2008– (Hon. Chm., 2001–02). Leeds, York and North Yorkshire (formerly Leeds) Chamber of Commerce: non-exec. Dir, 1998–2010; Pres., 2000–02; Chm., 2005–10. Chm., Mid Yorks Hosps NHS Trust, 2009–12. Non-executive Director: Opera North, 2014–; Tablet Publishing Co., 2015–. Leeds Trinity University (formerly Leeds Trinity and All Saints College, then Leeds Trinity University College): Mem., Bd of Govs, 2001–13; Chm., 2007–13; Pro-Chancellor, 2014–; Mem. Council, Univ. of Leeds, 2007–. Trustee: St Gemma's Hospice, 1999–2011; Leeds Internat. Pianoforte Competition, 2004–14. High Sheriff, W Yorks, 2015–March 2016. KSG 2011. *Recreations:* watching sport, music, walking in the Yorkshire Dales. *Clubs:* Royal Over-Seas League; Collingham and Linton Cricket; Scarcroft Golf.

ANDERSON, Sir Eric; *see* Anderson, Sir W. E. K.

ANDERSON, Eugene; *see* Anderson, C. E.

ANDERSON, Gillian Leigh; actress; *b* Chicago, 9 Aug. 1968; *d* of Edward Homer Anderson, III, and Rosemary Alyce Anderson; two *s* one *d*. *Educ:* Goodman Theater Sch., De Paul Univ. (BA). *Theatre* includes: A Streetcar Named Desire, Young Vic, 2014 (Best Actress, Evening Standard Theatre Awards, 2014); *television* includes: The X Files, 1993–2002 (Screen Actors Guild Award, 1996, 1997; Emmy Award, Golden Globe Award for Best Actress in a Drama Series, 1997); Bleak House, 2005; Any Human Heart, 2010; Great Expectations, 2011; The Fall, 2013, 2014; Hannibal, 2013, 2014; War and Peace, 2015; *films* include: The X Files, 1998; House of Mirth, 2000 (Best Actress, BIFA Awards); The Last King of Scotland, 2006; The X Files: I Want to Believe, 2008; How to Lose Friends and Alienate People, 2008; Johnny English Reborn, 2011; Shadow Dancer, 2012; Mr Morgan's Last Love, 2014; Robot Overlords, 2014. *Publications:* (jtly) A Vision of Fire, 2014. *Address:* c/o Jane Epstein, Independent Talent Group Ltd, 40 Whitfield Street, W1T 2RH. *T:* (020) 7636 6565.

ANDERSON, Rt Rev. Gregory David; *see* Northern Territory (Australia), Bishop of the.

ANDERSON, Prof. Harry Laurence, PhD; FRS 2013; FRSC; Professor of Chemistry, University of Oxford, since 2004; *b* Kingston upon Thames, 12 Jan. 1964; *s* of late Douglas Alexander Anderson and of Elinor Anderson; *m* 1992, Sally Nicholson; two *d*. *Educ:* Haslemere Prep. Sch.; Brecon High Sch.; Hereford Cathedral Sch.; Rugby Sch.; Christ Ch, Oxford (BA 1st Cl. Chem. 1987); Trinity Hall, Cambridge (PhD Chem. 1991). FRSC 2003. Res. Fellow, Magdalene Coll., Cambridge, 1990–93; Postdoctoral Res. Fellow, ETH, Zurich, 1993–94; Lectr in Organic Chem., Univ. of Oxford, 1994–2004. *Publications:* contribs to scientific jls. *Recreation:* playing with fire. *Address:* Department of Chemistry, University of Oxford, Chemistry Research Laboratory, Mansfield Road, Oxford OX1 3TA. *T:* (01865) 275704. *E:* harry.anderson@chem.ox.ac.uk.

ANDERSON, Heather; Her Honour Judge Heather Anderson; a Circuit Judge, since 2013; *b* Withernsea, 20 Nov. 1954; *d* of Edward Harry Medcalf and late Marjorie Medcalf; *m* 1982, Edmund John Seward Anderson, *qv*; two *s* two *d*. *Educ:* Withernsea High Sch.; Univ. of Warwick (BA Hons). Admitted as solicitor, 1978; in practice as solicitor, 1978–2000; called to the Bar, Inner Temple, 2000; in practice as barrister, 2000–01; a Dep. Dist Judge, 1998–2001; a Dist Judge, 2001–13; a Recorder, 2005–13. Chm., Child Support Appeal Tribunal, 1993–99. *Recreations:* walking, music, eating with family and friends, Rugby League, travel. *Address:* Leeds Combined Court Centre, The Courthouse, 1 Oxford Row, Leeds, W Yorks LS1 3BG. *T:* (0113) 306 2800. *Clubs:* Royal Over-Seas League; Collingham and Linton Cricket.

ANDERSON, Sir Iain; *see* Anderson, Sir J. I. W.

ANDERSON, James Frazer Gillan, CBE 1979; JP; DL; Member, Scottish Development Agency, 1986–89; *b* 25 March 1929; *m* 1956, May Harley; one *s* one *d. Educ:* Maddiston Primary Sch.; Graeme High Sch., Falkirk. Member: Stirling CC, 1958–75 (Convener, 1971–75); Central Regional Council, Scotland, 1974–96 (Convener, 1974–86). Mem., Health and Safety Commission, 1974–80. DUniv Stirling, 1987. *Recreations:* gardening, walking.

ANDERSON, Sir (James) Iain (Walker), Kt 2008; CBE 2000; PhD; Director, Unilever PLC and NV, 1988–98; *b* Glasgow, 30 June 1938; *s* of John and Alice Anderson; *m* 1963, Katie McCrone; two *s. Educ:* King's Park Sch., Glasgow; Univ. of Glasgow (BSc Hons, PhD 1962). Res. Manager, Unilever, 1965–76; Chairman: Marine Harvest Ltd, 1976–79; Food Industries Ltd, 1979–80; PPF Ltd, 1980–82; Ops Dir, Unilever Chemicals Div., 1982–85; Chm., Batchelors Foods Ltd, 1985–88. Director: British Telecom plc, 1995–2001; BT Scotland, 1997–2004 (Chm., 1999–2004); Scottish and Newcastle plc, 1998–2006. Chairman: Intense Photonics Ltd, 2000–06; Schs Enterprise Scotland Ltd, 2000–06. Special Advr to Prime Minister on Millennium Compliance (Y2K), 1998–2000; conducted ind. inquiry into Lessons to be Learned from 2001 outbreak of foot and mouth disease in UK, 2001–02; conducted ind. rev. of Govt's handling of foot and mouth outbreak in England in 2007, 2007–08. Gov., NIESR, 1992–98. Trustee: British Occupational Health Res. Foundn, 1996–98; Scottish Sci. Trust, 1997–2002; Leverhulme Trust, 1999–. FRSE 2010. Hon. DEng Glasgow, 2012. *Recreations:* food and wine, finding better restaurants, garden plants, travel, photography, thinking about things. *Address:* Burnbank, Acharn, by Aberfeldy, Perthshire PH15 2HU. *Club:* New (Edinburgh).

ANDERSON, Janet; Associate Consultant, Pandic (Political and Industrial Connections) Ltd, since 2012; Director, Pearson-Anderson Communications Ltd, since 2015; *b* Newcastle upon Tyne, 6 Dec. 1949; *d* of late Thomas Anderson and Ethel Pearson; *m* (marr. diss.); two *s* one *d. Educ:* Kingswood Grammar Sch.; Kingsfield Comprehensive Sch.; Polytechnic of Central London; Univ. of Nantes (Dip. Bi-lingual Business Studies in French and German). Asst to Rt Hon. Barbara Castle, 1974–81, to Jack Straw, MP, 1981–87; Campaign Officer, PLP, 1988–89; Regl Organiser, Shopping Hours Reform Council, 1991–92. Contested (Lab) Rossendale and Darwen, 1987. MP (Lab) Rossendale and Darwen, 1992–2010; contested (Lab) same seat, 2010. PPS to Dep. Leader of Labour Party, 1992–93; an Opposition Whip, 1995–97; Vice Chamberlain of HM Household, 1997–98; Parly Under-Sec. of State, DCMS, 1998–2001. Mem., H of C Commn, 1993–94; Member, Select Committee: on Home Affairs, 1994–95 (Home Affairs Campaigns Co-ordinator, 1994–95); on Culture, Media and Sport, 2002–10. Secretary: All-Party Footwear Gp, 1992–97; All-Party Tourism Gp, 2002–10; Chairman: All-Party Intellectual Property Gp, 2005–10; All-Party Writers Gp, 2008–10; All-Party Performers Alliance Gp, 2008–10; Mem., Chairmen's Panel, 2004–10. Sec., Tribune Gp of Lab MPs, 1993–97. Vis. Fellow, St Antony's Coll., Oxford, 1993–94. Mem. and Consultant, Authors' Licensing and Collecting Soc., 2010–. *Recreations:* gardening, reading, cooking, playing with my grandchildren.

ANDERSON, Jennifer Elizabeth; HM Diplomatic Service; Head, Counter-Terrorism Department, Foreign and Commonwealth Office, since 2014; *m* 1997, Stephen Ashworth; one *s* one *d. Educ:* Australian Nat. Univ. (BA Hons, LLB Hons). ME and Africa analyst, Australian Office of Nat. Assessments, Canberra, 1993–95; Advr, Internat. Div., Australian Dept of Prime Minister and Cabinet, 1995; Harkness Fellow, Inst. of War and Peace Studies, Columbia Univ., NY, 1995–96; Res. Associate, IISS, 1996–97; entered FCO, 1997; Head: Visegrad Sect., Central Eur. Dept, FCO, 1997–99; Bosnia and Croatia Sect., Eastern Adriatic Dept, FCO, 1999–2000; Resident Clerk, FCO, 2000–01; First Sec. (Pol/Mil.), UK Perm. Representation to EU, Brussels, 2001–03; Dep. Hd, Security Policy Gp, FCO, 2003–05; Business Change Manager and Hd, Business Engagement Gp, Inf. and Technol. Directorate, FCO, 2006–09; High Comr to Botswana, 2010–13; Dep. Hd of Mission, Jakarta, 2013. *Address:* c/o Foreign and Commonwealth Office, King Charles Street, SW1A 2AH.

ANDERSON, Jeremy David Bruce, CBE 2005; Chairman, Global Financial Services, KPMG LLP, since 2010; *b* Penang, 8 June 1958; *s* of Bruce Anderson and Sheila Anderson; *m* 1985, Rachel Priscilla Naish; two *s* one *d. Educ:* Mill Sch., Potterne; Dauntsey's Sch.; University Coll. London (BSc (Econ) 1980). IT develt, Triad Computing Systems, 1980–85; Mgt Consulting - Financial Services, KPMG, 1985–98; Dep. CEO, 1998–2001, CEO, 2001–02, KPMG Consulting UK; Mem. Bd, KPMG UK LLP, 1998–2002; Mem. Mgt Bd, Atos Origin SA, 2002–04; KPMG: UK Financial Services Leader, 2004–06; Eur. Financial Services Leader, 2006–08; Eur. Hd of Mkts, 2008–10; Mem. Bd, KPMG Europe LLP, 2008–11. Member: Nat. Employment Panel, 2002–08 (Chm., 2006–08); Ethnic Minority Employment Task Force, 2006–08; UK Commn for Employment and Skills, 2008–. Mem., Bretton Woods Cttee, 2014–. Trustee, Kingham Hill Trust, 2014–. Chm. Council, Oakhill Theol Coll., 2015–. Churchwarden, St Helen's, Bishopsgate. *Recreations:* walking, ski-ing, travel, wine, family. *Address:* KPMG LLP, 15 Canada Square, E14 5GL. *T:* (020) 7311 5800. *Club:* National.

ANDERSON, Prof. John, FRCP; FRCPGlas; FRCOG; Postgraduate Dean and Director, Postgraduate Institute for Medicine and Dentistry, and Professor of Medical Education, University of Newcastle upon Tyne, 1985–98, now Professor Emeritus; *b* 2 Feb. 1936; *s* of John and Norah Anderson, Newcastle upon Tyne; *m* Mary Bynon, Whitley Bay; one *s* one *d. Educ:* Royal Grammar Sch., Newcastle upon Tyne; Med. Sch., King's Coll., Univ. of Durham (MB, BS 2nd Cl. Hons). FRCP 1973 (MRCP 1961); FRCOG (*ad eundem*) 1983; FRCPGlas 1992. Med. Registrar, Royal Victoria Inf., Newcastle upon Tyne, 1962–64; Res. Fellow, Univ. of Virginia, Charlottesville, 1965–66; University of Newcastle upon Tyne: First Asst in Medicine 1967–68; Sen. Lectr in Medicine 1968–85; Academic Sub-Dean, Med. Sch., 1975–85. Hon. Cons. Phys., Royal Victoria Infirmary, 1968–2009. Mem. Council, RCP, 1974–77; Member: Assoc. of Phys of GB and Ire., 1976–; Exec. Cttee, ASME, 1979–2013 (Hon. Treas., 1980–88; Gen. Sec., 1990–92; Chm. Council, 1992–95; Vice-Pres., 1996–2013); GMC, 1980–2001; GDC, 1986–99. Vice-Pres., Durham and Newcastle Med. Graduates Assoc., 2013–. *Publications:* The Multiple Choice Question in Medicine, 1976, 2nd edn 1982; numerous chapters in books, and papers in sci. jls on medicine, diabetes and med. educn. *Recreations:* listening to music, walking, watching cricket, computing, reading, thinking. *Address:* 6 Wilson Gardens, Newcastle upon Tyne NE3 4JA. *T:* (0191) 285 4745. *Club:* Durham CC.

ANDERSON, John Adrian; His Honour Judge Anderson; a Circuit Judge, since 2009; *b* Manchester, 11 Jan. 1950; *s* of Robert and Stella Anderson; *m* 1995, Helen Gordon. *Educ:* Trent Coll., Long Eaton, Notts. Commercial apprenticeship, Rolls Royce Aero Engine Div., 1967–71; commnd RN as pilot, Fleet Air Arm, 1972–88 (South Atlantic Medal, Falklands War, 1982); Commercial and Airline Transport Pilot's Licences (Fixed and Rotary Wing), 1988. Called to the Bar, Middle Temple, 1989; in practice at the Bar, specialising in crime and serious fraud, 1990–2009. Standing Counsel to Revenue and Customs Prosecutions Office, 2005–09. *Recreations:* boating, walking, DIY, Cornwall, getting beaten at Wii tennis by nieces. *Address:* Harrow Crown Court, Hailsham Drive, Harrow HA1 4TU. *Club:* Torpoint Mosquito Sailing.

ANDERSON, Sir John (Anthony), KBE 1994; FCA, FAIBF, FNZIM; Chief Executive and Director: South Pacific Merchant Finance Ltd, 1979–2005; National Bank of New Zealand Ltd, 1990–2005; ANZ National Bank Ltd, 2003–05; Chairman: Television New Zealand Ltd, 2006–12; NPT Ltd, since 2011; *b* 2 Aug. 1945; *s* of Donald Ian Mogine Anderson and Elizabeth Grace Anderson (*née* Plummer); *m* 1970, Carol Margaret Tuck; two *s* one *d. Educ:* Christ's Coll.; Victoria Univ. of Wellington. ACA 1967, FCA 1991; FNZIM 1993. With Deloitte Ross Tohmatsu, Wellington, 1962–69; Guest & Bell, Melbourne, 1969–72. Chairman: Petroleum Corp. of NZ, 1986–88; NZ Venture Investment Fund, 2007–13; PGG Wrightson, 2010–13; Director: NZ Steel, 1986–87; Lloyds Merchant Bank (London), 1986–92; Lloyds Bank NZA, 1989–96; Commonwealth Bank of Australia, 2007–; non-executive Director: NZIER, 2011–; Steel and Tube Hldgs, 2011– (Chm., 2011–); Dep. Chm., Turners and Growers Ltd, 2012–. Chairman: Adv. Bd, NZ Debt Mgt Office, 1989–2001; Prime Minister's NZ Employment Taskforce, 1994. Chairman: NZ Merchant Banks Assoc., 1982–89; NZ Bankers' Assoc., 1991–92 and 1999–2000; Pres., NZ Bankers' Inst., 1990. Bd Dir, ICC, 1996–2008; Chairman: NZ Cricket Bd, 1995–2008; NZ Sports Foundn, 1999–2002. Chm., Capital & Coast District Health Bd, 2007–10; Comr, Hawkes Bay District Health Bd, 2008–10. Sen. Fellow, Financial Services Inst. of Australasia. FInstD; FCSAP; Fellow, Inst. of Financial Professionals NZ, 2002. DCom Wellington, 2012. First Blake Medal, Sir Peter Blake Trust, 2005; Halberg Trust Award, 2010; CFO Lifetime Achievement Award, Fairfax Media, 2013; Inducted NZ Business Hall of Fame, 2013. NZ Commemoration Medal, 1990. *Recreations:* cricket, bridge. *Address:* 3 Bayview Terrace, Oriental Bay, Wellington, New Zealand. *T:* (4) 4990162. *Club:* Wellington (NZ).

ANDERSON, Hon. John (Duncan), AO 2011; Chairman, Eastern Star Gas, 2007–11; Director, Crawford Fund, since 2006; *b* 14 Nov. 1956; *s* of Duncan Anderson and Beryl Anderson (*née* Mann); *m* 1987, Julia Gillian Robertson; one *s* three *d. Educ:* Univ. of Sydney (MA). Farmer and grazier. MP (Nat.) Gwydir, NSW, 1989–2007; Minister for: Primary Industries and Energy, 1996–98; Transport and Regl Services, 1998–2005; Dep. Prime Minister, 1999–2005. Dep. Leader, 1993–99, Leader, 1999–2005, Nat. Party of Australia. *Club:* Australian (Sydney).

ANDERSON, John Ferguson; Chief Executive, Glasgow City Council, 1995–98; *b* 13 Dec. 1947; *s* of Charles and Isabella Anderson; *m* 1970, Sandra McFarlane; one *s* one *d. Educ:* Edinburgh Univ. (LLB Hons 1969). Legal Assistant, then Solicitor, later Asst Chief Solicitor, Glasgow Corp., 1969–75; Strathclyde Regional Council: Prin. Solicitor, 1975–78; Asst Dir of Admin, 1978–80; Sen. Exec. Officer, 1980–86; Prin. Exec. Officer, 1986–90; Dep. Chief Exec., 1990–95. *Recreations:* golf, watching football, transportation issues, church. *Address:* Balwearie, 41 Scott Brae, Kippen FK8 3DL.

ANDERSON, John Graeme, CBE 1989; CEng, FInstE; Deputy Chairman, Northern Engineering Industries plc, 1986–89; Director, Team General Partner, 1993–2002; *b* 3 June 1927; *s* of John Anderson and Ella (*née* Pusey); *m* 1953, Nancy Clarice Taylor Johnson; one *s* twin *d. Educ:* Merchant Taylors' Sch., Sandy Lodge; London Univ. (BScEng Hons). MIMechE. Served RN, Fleet Air Arm, 1945–48. International Combustion Ltd: graduate apprentice, 1952; Dir, 1968; Dep. Chief Exec., 1969; Man. Dir, 1974; Northern Engineering Industries: Man. Dir, NEI-Internat. Combustion Ltd, 1977; Managing Director: Mechanical Gp, 1980; Power Gp, 1982; Internat. and Projects Gp, 1984; Chm., NEI Pacific, 1984–88. Chm., Internat. Combustion-HUD Hong Kong, 1978–82; Dir, British Nuclear Associates, 1985–88; Alternate Dir, Nat. Nuclear Corp., 1986–88; Director: Tyne and Wear Develt Corp., 1987–93; The Newcastle Initiative, 1988–90. Mem., Duke of Kent's BOTB mission to Turkey, 1984. Chairman: Solid Waste Assoc., 1972–74; Watertube Boilermakers' Assoc., 1976–80; Member: Process Plant Assoc., 1968–87; Process Plant, EDC, 1972–76; Heavy Electrical, EDC, 1976–80. Gov., Derby Coll. of Technology, 1969–74. Chm., Upstage, 1977–79. *Recreations:* shooting, painting, music, fell walking. *Address:* Trinity Barns, Corbridge, Northumberland NE45 5HP. *T:* (01434) 633228.

ANDERSON, John Huxley Fordyce, OBE 2010; FCIOB; property and development consultant, since 2009; Consultant, Deerbrook Group, since 2011; *b* 13 Jan. 1945; *s* of Alexander Robert Fordyce Anderson and Agnes Joan (*née* Huxley); *m* 1973, Tucker Lee Etherington; one *s* one *d. Educ:* Fan Court Sch.; Milton Abbey Sch.; Brixton Sch. of Building; Harvard Business Sch. (post-grad. PMD 1983). FCIOB 1988. Joined Higgs & Hill as indentured student, 1962; Project Planner on projects such as BBC TV Centre, RMA Sandhurst, 1966–69; Contract Manager, Sales and Marketing Manager then Dep. Man. Dir, Costains, Vale do Lobo, Portugal, 1969–74; with Town & City Properties in Holland, 1975–76; Develt Project Manager, Town & City Develts in London, 1976–83; Man. Dir, Town & City, then P&O, Develts, 1984–92; Director: Chelsea Harbour, 1984–92; P&O Property Hldgs, 1985–99; Managing Director: Bovis Construction Ltd, 1993–2000; Bovis Europe, 1996–2000; Jt Man. Dir, Bovis Construction Gp, 1997–2000 (Dir, 1988–2000). Man. Dir, PSA Building Mgt (on secondment to Govt), 1991–93. Non-exec. Dir, Maxxiom, 1997–2000. Director: British Council for Offices, 1996–2003; Land Securities Properties, 2000–03; Chelsfield plc, 2003–05; of Develt, Parkview (Battersea Power Station), 2006–07; Buckingham Develts Ltd, 2007–08; of Projects and Develts, Tellesma LLP, 2008–09; Construction Adviser: Sammy Ofer Wing Develt, Nat. Maritime Mus., 2009–; Cutty Sark Conservation Project, 2009–; Chief Advr of Major Projects and Infrastructures, Olympic Park Legacy Co., 2010–11. Chairman: Export Gp for Construction Industries, 1999–2001; Special Purpose Vehicle St Martin in the Fields Develts Ltd, 2006–11. Hon. Property Consultant, Queen Elizabeth Foundn for the Disabled, 2001–. Chm., Lighthouse Club, 2005–08. Mem., Hambledon Parish Council, 1984– (Chm., 2004–). Dir, Hambledon Village Shop, 2007–. *Recreations:* parish council, golf, ski-ing, gardening, Rugby, opera, theatre, ballet, eating and drinking with friends. *Club:* Royal Automobile.

ANDERSON, Prof. John Kinloch, FSA; Professor of Classical Archaeology, University of California, Berkeley, 1958–93, now Emeritus; *b* 3 Jan. 1924; *s* of late Sir James Anderson, KCIE, and Lady Anderson; *m* 1954, Esperance (*d* 2000), *d* of late Guy Batham, Dunedin, NZ; one *s* two *d. Educ:* Trinity Coll., Glenalmond; Christ Church, Oxford (MA). Served War, in Black Watch (RHR) and Intelligence Corps, 1942–46 (final rank, Lieut). Student, British Sch. at Athens, 1949–52; Lecturer in Classics, Univ. of Otago, NZ, 1953–58. FSA 1976. Award for Distinction in Teaching, Phi Beta Kappa (N Calif. Chapter), 1988. *Publications:* Greek Vases in the Otago Museum, 1955; Ancient Greek Horsemanship, 1961; Military Theory and Practice in the Age of Xenophon, 1970; Xenophon, 1974; Hunting in the Ancient World, 1985; articles and reviews in Annual of British Sch. at Athens; Jl of Hellenic Studies, etc. *Recreation:* gardening. *Address:* 1020 Middlefield Road, Berkeley, CA 94708, USA. *T:* (510) 8415335.

ANDERSON, John M., PhD; FBA 1991; Professor of English Language, University of Edinburgh, 1988–2001, now Emeritus. *Educ:* Edinburgh Univ. (MA, PhD). Lectr until 1975, Reader, 1975–88, Edinburgh Univ. *Publications:* The Grammar of Case: towards a localistic theory, 1971; An Essay Concerning Aspect, 1973; (ed with C. Jones) Historical Linguistics, 2 vols, 1974; (with R. Lass) Old English Phonology, 1975; On Case Grammar, 1977; (with C. Jones) Phonological Structure and the History of English, 1977; (with C. J. Ewen) Principles of Dependency Phonology, 1987; Linguistic Representation: structural analogy and stratification, 1992; Notional Theory of Syntactic Categories, 1997; Modern Grammars of Case, 2006; The Grammar of Names, 2007; The Substance of Language (3 vols), 2011. *Address:* PO Box 348, Methoni Messinias 24006, Greece. *E:* frohn@otenet.gr.

ANDERSON, Dame Josephine; *see* Barstow, Dame J. C.

ANDERSON, Julian Anthony; Director General, Country Landowners' Association, 1990–2000; *b* 12 June 1938; *s* of Sir Kenneth Anderson, KBE, CB. *Educ:* King Alfred Sch.; Wadham Coll., Oxford (MA). Entered MAFF as Asst Principal, 1961; Asst Private Sec. to Minister of Agriculture, 1964–66; Principal, 1966; seconded to FCO, 1970–73; Asst Sec.,

1973, Under Sec., 1982–90, MAFF; seconded as Minister (Food and Agriculture), UK Perm. Rep. to EEC, 1982–85. *Recreations:* music, sport, travel, photography, gardening, DIY. *Clubs:* Oxford and Cambridge, Civil Service.

ANDERSON, Julian David; composer; *b* 6 April 1967. *Educ:* Royal Coll. of Music (BMus London 1st cl.); Gonville and Caius Coll., Cambridge, 1990–91; King's Coll., Cambridge, 1992–94 (MPhil Composition). Prof. of Music, Harvard Univ., 2004–07; Prof. of Composition and Composer-in-Residence, Guildhall Sch., 2007–. Composer-in-Association, CBSO, 2001–05; Daniel R. Lewis Young Composer Fellow, Cleveland Orch., 2005–07; Composer-in-Residence: London Philharmonic Orch., 2010–; Wigmore Hall, 2013–. Works performed by numerous ensembles and orchestras in Europe, Japan, E Asia and USA, incl. Cleveland Orch., Boston SO, Deutsche SO, Orch. de Paris, NY Philharmonic Orch., Tokyo Metropolitan SO, Malaysian Philharmonic Orch., Seoul Philharmonic Orch., London Sinfonietta, Tokyo Sinfonietta, Schoenberg, Nash and Asko Ensembles. Broadcast talks on music on BBC Radio, French, German, Swiss, Finnish and American radios. *Compositions* include: Symphony, 2003; Book of Hours, 2004; The Comedy of Change, 2009; Fantasias, 2009; The Discovery of Heaven, 2012; Violin Concerto, 2015; commissions from: London Sinfonietta, 1994 (Khorovod) and 2000 (Alhambra Fantasy); BBC Proms, 1998 (The Stations of the Sun), 2006 (Heaven is Shy of Earth) and 2013 (Harmony); Cheltenham Festival, 1997 (The Crazed Moon); ENO, 2014 (Thebans). Young Composer Prize, 1990, Award, 2006, Royal Philharmonic Soc.; South Bank Show Award, 2002; BASCA Award, 2004, 2007, 2011 (two awards); South Bank Sky Arts Award, 2013. *Publications:* articles on music in Musical Times, Tempo, The Independent, Guardian, The Times, FT. *Recreations:* films, reading, poetry, swimming. *Address:* c/o Faber Music, Bloomsbury House, 74–77 Great Russell Street, WC1B 3DA.

ANDERSON, Kenneth Walter; Senior Advisor, Greenhill and Co. International LLP, since 2014; *b* 22 Feb. 1960; *s* of late Walter Anderson and of Barbara Anderson; *m* 1983, Pamela Davison; three *s*. *Educ:* American Community Sch., London; Texas A&M Univ. Director: of Strategic Investment, MG Technologies AG, Germany, 2000–01; of Healthcare, Amey plc, 2001–02; Department of Health: Dir, Contract Procurement Prog., 2002–03; Commercial Dir Gen., 2003–06; Man. Dir, 2006–11, a Vice Chm., 2011–14, UBS Investment Bank. Advr to Texas A&M Genetics Res. Prog., 2012–. Dir, West One Restaurants Ltd, 2013–. Non-exec. Dir, Real Asset Energy Fund, 2012–. Adjunct Prof. of Finance, Imperial Business Coll. (formerly Tanaka Business Sch., Imperial Coll. London), 2005–. *Recreations:* ski-ing, reading, fishing. *Address:* Greenhill and Co. International LLP, Landsdowne House, 57 Berkeley Square, W1J 6ER. *T:* (020) 7198 7412. *E:* ken.anderson@greenhill.com.

ANDERSON, Lesley Jane, (Mrs C. Crawford); QC 2006; a Recorder, since 2006; a Deputy High Court Judge, Chancery Division, since 2008; *b* 6 April 1963; *d* of Ian Anderson and late Rosemary Campbell Anderson; *m* 1996, Colin Crawford; one step *s* one step *d*. *Educ:* King Edward VI Camp Hill Sch. for Girls, Birmingham; Univ. of Manchester (LLB Hons 1984). CEDR Accredited Mediator, 2000. Lectr in Law, Univ. of Manchester, 1984–89; called to the Bar, Middle Temple, 1989; Trng Manager, Norton Rose M5 Gp of Legal Practices, 1989–91; barrister, 40 King St Chambers, subseq. Kings Chambers, Manchester, 1991–, and Hardwicke Chambers, 2011–. *Publications:* articles in legal and professional jls. *Recreations:* food, wine, theatre, cinema, modern jazz. *Address:* Kings Chambers, 36 Young Street, Manchester M3 3FT. *T:* (0161) 819 8261, *Fax:* (0161) 835 2139. *E:* anderson.lesley@ntlworld.com.

ANDERSON, Lucy; Member (Lab) London Region, European Parliament, since 2014. Policy and legal expert, TUC, 1997–2006; Business Manager, GLA; Sen. Manager, NUT. Mem. (Lab) Camden LBC, 2002–06. *Address:* European Parliament, 60 Rue Wiertz, 1047 Brussels, Belgium; (office) 20 Hanson Street, W1W 6UF.

ANDERSON, Prof. Malcolm Grove; Professor of Physical Geography, 1989–2012, Professorial Research Fellow, Department of Civil Engineering, since 2012, University of Bristol; *b* 27 June 1949; *s* of Wilfred Roy Anderson and Frances Betty Anderson; *m* 1972, Elizabeth Ann Roger; one *d*. *Educ:* Univ. of Nottingham (BSc); Univ. of Cambridge (PhD); Univ. of Bristol (DSc). FICE 1996. Research Fellow, Sidney Sussex Coll., Cambridge, 1972; University of Bristol: Lectr, 1973; Reader, 1985; Head, Dept of Geography, 1990–96, 2002–05; Dir, Inst. for Advanced Studies, 1997–2000 (Vice-Provost, 2000–02); Pro-Vice-Chancellor, 2005–09. Res. Hydrologist, US Corps of Engrs, 1981–82; Sen. Res. Geotechnical Engr, Hong Kong Govt, 1982–83; Nuffield Foundn, Sen. Science Fellowship, 1988–89; Quater Centenary Vis. Fellowship, Emmanuel Coll., Cambridge, 1989. Vis. Prof. of Hydrology, Univ. of Oxford, 2010–13. Technical Advr, Poverty Reduction Fund, 2004–09, Chm., Management of Slope Stability in Communities (MoSSaiC) Cttee, 2004–11, Govt of St Lucia, WI; Mem., Sustainable Develt Gp, Latin America and Caribbean, World Bank, 2009–. Natural Environment Research Council: Mem., AAPS Cttee, 1990–93; Chm., Land-Ocean Interaction Study Steering Cttee, 1998–2001; Member: Council, 2002–07; Audit Cttee, 2003–07; Mem., Science Grants Panel, Nuffield Foundn, 1992–2007; Mem., Technology Opportunities Panel, EPSRC, 2009–11; Scholarship Assessor, ACU, 1993–97. Mem., Bristol Cathedral Council, 2002–09. Editor-in-Chief, Hydrological Processes, 1986–2014. Life Fellow, Indian Assoc. of Hydrologists, 1995. Gill Meml Award, RGS, 1986; Trevithick Premium Award, ICE, 1996, 2007. *Publications:* edited jointly: Hydrological Forecasting, 1985; Slope Stability: geotechnical engineering and geomorphology, 1987; Modelling Geomorphological Systems, 1988; Process Studies in Hillslope Hydrology, 1990; Floodplain Processes, 1996; Advances in Hillslope Processes, 1996; Model Validation: perspectives in hydrological science, 2001; Encyclopaedia of Hydrological Sciences, 2005; Landslides: hazard and risk, 2005; (authored jtly) Community-based Landslide Risk Reduction: managing disasters in small steps, 2013; numerous res. pubns in hydrological scis and geotechnics. *Recreations:* Anse la Voutte Bay, West Indies. *Address:* Department of Civil Engineering, University of Bristol, Bristol BS8 1TR. *T:* (0117) 331 5731.

ANDERSON, Mark Roger; QC 2010; a Recorder, since 2003; a Deputy High Court Judge, Chancery Division, since 2013; *b* Birmingham, 1960; *s* of Roger John Anderson and Ethel Ann Anderson (*née* Beale); *m* 1986, Katharine Elizabeth Anne Dillon; one *s* one *d*. *Educ:* King Edward's Sch., Birmingham; Exeter Coll., Oxford (MA). Called to the Bar, Middle Temple, 1983; in practice as barrister, specialising in commercial dispute resolution and professional negligence. Chm., Midland Chancery and Commercial Bar Assoc., 2010–. *E:* markandkateanderson@googlemail.com.

ANDERSON, Martina; Member (SF) Northern Ireland, European Parliament, since June 2012; *b* Derry, NI, 16 April 1962. *Educ:* St Cecilia's Coll. BA 1st Cl. Hons Social Scis 1996. Spent 13 years in prisons in England and Ireland; released under terms of Good Friday Agreement, 1998. Political researcher, 1999–2002; All Ireland Coordinator, 2002–06, Dir, Unionist Engagement, 2006–07, SF. Mem. (SF) Foyle, NI Assembly, 2007–June 2012; Jun. Minister, Office of First Minister and Dep. First Ministers, 2011–12. Mem., NI Policing Bd, 2007–11. Mem., All Party Gp on Internat. Develt, 2007–09, on Disability, 2008–11, NI Assembly. Mem., Cttee on Envmt, Public Health and Food Safety, 2012–, Cttee on Regl Develt, 2012–, Eur. Parlt. *Address:* European Parliament, Rue Wiertz, 1047 Brussels, Belgium.

ANDERSON, Prof. Michael, OBE 1999; FRSE; FBA 1989; Professor of Economic History, University of Edinburgh, 1979–2007, now Emeritus; *b* 21 Feb. 1942; *s* of Douglas Henry and Rose Lillian Anderson; *m* 1st, 1966, Rosemary Elizabeth Kitching (marr. diss.); one *s* one *d*; 2nd, 2007, Elspeth Catriona MacArthur. *Educ:* Kingston Grammar Sch.; Queens' Coll., Cambridge (BA 1964; MA 1968; PhD 1969). FRSE 1990. University of Edinburgh: Department of Sociology: Asst Lectr, 1967; Lectr, 1969; Reader, 1975; Department of Economic and Social History, 1979; Dean, Faculty of Social Scis, 1985–89; Vice-Principal, 1989–93, 1997–2000; Acting Principal, April–Aug. 1994; Sen. Vice-Principal, 2000–07. Member: Economic and Social History Cttee, SSRC, 1974–78; Computing Cttee, SSRC, 1980–82; Scot. Records Adv. Council, 1984–93; ESRC, 1990–94 (Member: Res. Resources and Methods Cttee, 1982–84; Society and Politics Res. Develt Gp, 1989–92; Chm., Res. Resources Bd, 1992–94); History of Medicine Cttee, Wellcome Trust, 1988–92; BL Bd, 1994–2003 (Dep. Chm., 2000–03); Council, British Acad., 1995–98; Res. Information Network Adv. Bd, 2005–11; HEFCE Res. and Innovation Cttee, 2006–09; Adv. Cttee, Nat. Statistics Centre for Demography, 2006–12; Scottish Census Steering Cttee, 2009–11; Population Theme Adv. Bd, ONS, 2012–. Chm., Res. Support Libraries Programme, 1998–2003. Curator, RSE, 1997–99. Chm., Bd of Trustees, Nat. Library of Scotland, 2000–12 (Trustee, 1998–2012). Hon. FFA 2007. Dr *hc* Edinburgh, 2007; Hon. LittD Leicester, 2014. *Publications:* Family Structure in Nineteenth Century Lancashire, 1971; (ed) Sociology of the Family, 1972; Approaches to the History of the Western Family 1500–1914, 1981; The 1851 Census: a national sample of the enumerators returns, 1987; Population Change in Northwestern Europe 1750–1850, 1988; (ed) Social and Political Economy of the Household, 1995; (ed) British Population History, 1996; numerous papers on family sociology, population and family history. *Recreations:* natural history, gardening, study of ancient civilizations.

ANDERSON, Michael James; Senior Vice President, External Affairs, Government Relations and Security, Kosmos Energy, since 2015; *b* 3 April 1961; *s* of James and Beryl Anderson; *m* 1987, Julie Dickens; two *s* one *d*. *Educ:* Newcastle Royal Grammar Sch.; Hymers Coll., Hull; Trinity Coll., Cambridge (BA Hons Law 1983). Law Lectr, Univ. of Ill, Urbana-Champaign, 1983–84; Foreign and Commonwealth Office, 1984–2003: Moscow, 1988–89; UK Delegn to Conf. on Disarmament, Geneva, 1992–97; Private Secretary: to Sir David Spedding, 1997–99; to Sir Richard Dearlove, 1999–2000; UK Mission to UN, NY, 2000–03; Prin. Private Sec. to the Lord Chancellor and Sec. of State for Constitutional Affairs, 2003–06; Dir of Strategy and Communication, DCA, 2006–07; Dir Gen., Climate Change Gp, DEFRA, later DECC, 2007–09; on secondment to Nat. Grid, 2009; Dir Gen., Strategy, Finance, Perf. and Evidence Gp, later Green Economy and Corp. Services, DEFRA, 2009–11; Dir Gen., Internat. and Immigration Policy Gp (formerly Strategy, Immigration and Internat. Gp), Home Office, 2011–15. *Recreations:* doing, thinking, family, sports.

ANDERSON, Michael Roy, CB 2014; Chief Executive Officer, Children's Investment Fund Foundation, since 2013; *b* Bellingham, WA, USA, 9 April 1962; *s* of Jerry McCush Anderson and Maria Schmitt Anderson; *m* 2002, Sian Harris; one *s*. *Educ:* Univ. of Washington (Marshall Schol.; BA Pol Sci. *summa cum laude*; President's Medal); St John's Coll., Oxford (Rhodes Schol.; MLitt Social Anthropol. 1988); Sch. of Oriental and African Studies, Univ. of London (LLM 1988). Consultant in internat. law and litigation, 1988–2002; Lectr in Law, SOAS, Univ. of London, 1988–96; Dir of Studies, British Inst. of Internat. and Comparative Law, 1996–2001; Co-founder and Chief Operating Officer, Bazian Ltd, 2000–02; Department for International Development: Team Leader for Justice, 2002–03, for Fragile States, 2003–05; Head, ME, 2005–08, India, 2008–10; Dir Gen., Policy and Global Issues, then Policy and Global Progs, 2010–13; Prime Minister's Special Envoy for UN Develt Goals, 2012–13. Vis. Fellow in Law, LSE, 1996–. *Publications:* books include: Human Rights Approaches to Environmental Protection, 1996; The International Law Commission and the Future of International Law, 1998; International Environmental Law in National Courts, 2001; Constitutional Human Rights in the Commonwealth, 2002; Seafarers' Rights, 2005. *Recreations:* hiking, theatre. *Address:* Children's Investment Fund Foundation, 7 Clifford Street, W1S 2FT. *E:* manderson@ciff.org.

ANDERSON, Paul James; journalist and author; Lecturer in Journalism, University of Essex, since 2014; *b* 3 Oct. 1959; *s* of James George Anderson and Marjorie Rosemary Anderson (*née* Thorpe). *Educ:* Ipswich Sch.; Balliol Coll., Oxford (BA Hons PPE 1981); London College of Printing. Dep. Ed., European Nuclear Disarmament Jl, 1984–87; Reviews Ed., 1986–91, Editor, 1991–93, Tribune; Dep. Ed., New Statesman, 1993–96; News Ed., Red Pepper, 1997–99; Dep. Ed., New Times, 1999–2000; Lecturer in Journalism: City Univ., 2000–12; Brunel Univ., 2012–14; Univ. Campus Suffolk, 2012–14. Dir, People's Europe 98, 1998. *Publications:* (ed jtly) Mad Dogs: The US Raid on Libya, 1986; (with Nyta Mann) Safety First: the making of New Labour, 1997; (ed) Orwell in Tribune: 'As I Please' and other writings, 2006; (with K. Davey) Moscow Gold?: the Soviet Union and the British Left, 2014. *Address:* 119 Woodbridge Road, Ipswich IP4 2NJ.

ANDERSON, Prof. Philip Warren; Joseph Henry Professor of Physics, Princeton University, New Jersey, 1975–96, now Emeritus; *b* 13 Dec. 1923; *s* of Prof. H. W. Anderson and Mrs Elsie O. Anderson; *m* 1947, Joyce Gothwaite; one *d*. *Educ:* Harvard Univ. BS 1943; MA 1947; PhD 1949, Harvard. Naval Res. Lab., Washington, DC, 1943–45 (Chief Petty Officer, USN). Mem., Technical Staff, 1949–76, Dir, 1976–84, Bell Telephone Labs. Fulbright Lectr, Tokyo Univ., 1953–54; Overseas Fellow, Churchill Coll., Cambridge, 1961–62; Vis. Prof. of Theoretical Physics, Univ. of Cambridge, 1967–75, and Fellow of Jesus College, Cambridge, 1969–75, Hon. Fellow, 1978–; Cherwell-Simon Meml Lectureship, 1979–80, George Eastman Prof., 1993–94, Oxford Univ. Member: Amer. Acad. of Arts and Sciences, 1966; Nat. Acad. of Sciences, US, 1967; Amer. Philosophical Soc., 1991; Foreign Member: Royal Society, London, 1980; Japan Acad., 1988; Indian Nat. Acad. of Scis, 1990; Russian Nat. Acad. of Sci., 1994; Foreign Associate: Accademia Lincei, Rome, 1985; Indian Acad. of Sci., 1996. Hon. FInstP, 1986. Hon. DSc: Illinois, 1978; Rutgers, 1991; Ecole Normale Supérieure, Paris, 1995; Gustavus Adolphus Coll., Minn, 1995; Sheffield, 1996; Tsinghua, Beijing, 2008; Hon. PhD Tokyo, 2002. O. E. Buckley Prize, Amer. Phys. Soc., 1964; Dannie Heinemann Prize, Akad. Wiss. Göttingen, 1975; (jtly) Nobel Prize for Physics, 1977; Guthrie Medal, Inst. of Physics, 1978; Centennial Medal, Harvard, 1996; John Bardeen Prize, 1997; Prange Prize and Lectr, Univ. of Maryland, 2009. Nat. Medal of Science, US, 1984. *Publications:* Concepts in Solids, 1963; Basic Notions of Condensed Matter Physics, 1984; A Career in Theoretical Physics, 1994, 2nd edn 2004; The Theory of Superconductivity in the High Tc Cuprates, 1996; More and Different, 2011; numerous articles in scholarly jls. *Recreations:* go (Japanese game), rank sho-dan, rank 3-Dan (honorary). *Address:* 2439 Windrows Drive, Princeton, NJ 08540, USA.

ANDERSON, Ray Thomas, OAM 2005; Chairman, Educang Pty Ltd, 2006–08; Board Member, Epic Employment Service Inc., 2000–13; *b* 23 Nov. 1936; *s* of late Thomas James Anderson and Daisy Eva D'Arcy-Irvine (*née* Woodhouse); *m* 1962, Margaret, *d* of Ronald George Geach; one *s* three *d*. *Educ:* State Commercial High Sch., Brisbane; Univ. of Queensland (BCom Hons); Macquarie Univ. (BLegS). Public servant, Brisbane, 1956–60; RAAF Psychologist, Brisbane, 1961–62; Trainee Trade Comr, Canberra, 1963; First Sec. and Asst Trade Comr, Australian High Commn, Singapore, 1964–67; Trade Commissioner: Johannesburg, 1968; Cape Town, 1969–70; Counsellor (Commercial) and Sen. Trade Comr, Aust. High Commn, New Delhi, 1971–73; Regl Dir, DTI, Brisbane, 1974–76; Counsellor (Commercial) and Trade Comr (Mktg), Aust. Embassy, Tokyo, 1977–80; Asst Sec., Dept of Trade, 1980–82; First Asst Sec., Depts of Foreign Affairs and Trade, Trade, Immigration and Ethnic Affairs, 1982–87; Manager, Nat. Ops, AUSTRADE, 1987–89; Minister (Marketing) and Sen. Trade Comr, London and Minister (Commercial), The Hague, 1990–91; Agent-Gen. for Qld in London, 1991–95; Exec. Dir, 1996, Asst Dir-Gen. 1997, Dept of Econ. Develt and Trade, Qld; Gen. Manager, Evans Deakin Industries, 1997–99; Exec. Dir,

Anglicare, 1999–2005. Admitted Barrister, Supreme Court, NSW and High Court of Australia, and Barrister and Solicitor, Supreme Court, ACT, 1989. Dir, EAC Ltd, 2000–05. Mem., Diocesan Council, Dio. of Brisbane, 1999–2005. Freeman, City of London, 1991. Flying Officer, RAAF Reserve. Hon. FAIEx. KGSJ 2007. Centenary Medal, Australia, 2003; Nat. Service Medal, Australia, 2006; Australian Defence Medal, 2007. *Recreations:* tennis, reading, travel, theatre. *Address:* Box 464, PO Tugun, Qld 4224, Australia. *Clubs:* Singapore Town; United Services, Queensland (Brisbane).

ANDERSON, Robert Edward; QC 2006; barrister; *b* 12 Nov. 1963; *s* of Edward and Ivy Anderson; one *s. Educ:* Oundle Sch.; Pembroke Coll., Cambridge (BA Hons Law 1985). Called to the Bar, Gray's Inn and Middle Temple, 1986; in practice, specialising in commercial, sports and media law, 1986–. *Recreations:* literature, baroque music, cricket, the Turf. *Address:* Blackstone Chambers, Temple, EC4Y 9BW. *T:* (020) 7583 1770, *Fax:* (020) 7822 7350. *E:* robertanderson@blackstonechambers.com. *Club:* Home House.

ANDERSON, Robert Geoffrey William; Fellow, Clare Hall, Cambridge, since 2006 (Vice-President, 2009–13); *b* 2 May 1944; *er s* of late Herbert Patrick Anderson and of Kathleen Diana Anderson (*née* Burns); *m* 1st, 1973, Margaret Elizabeth Callis Lea (marr. diss. 2003); two *s*; 2nd, 2005, Jane Virginia Portal. *Educ:* Woodhouse Sch., London; St John's Coll., Oxford (Casberd exhibitioner; BSc, MA, DPhil; Hon. Fellow, 2000). FSA 1986; FRSE 1990. Assistant Keeper: Royal Scottish Museum, 1970–75; Science Museum, 1975–78; Dep. Keeper, Wellcome Museum of History of Medicine, and Sec., Adv. Council, Science Museum, 1978–80; Keeper, Dept of Chemistry, Science Mus., 1980–84; Director: Royal Scottish Mus., 1984–85; Nat. Museums of Scotland, 1985–92; British Mus., 1992–2002; Fellow, IAS, Princeton, 2002–03; By Fellow, Churchill Coll., Cambridge, 2003–04; Vis. Fellow, CCC, Cambridge, 2004–05. Sec., Royal Scottish Soc. of Arts, 1973–75; Member Council: Soc. for History of Alchemy and Chemistry, 1978– (Chm., 2007–); Gp for Scientific, Technological and Medical Collections, 1979–83; British Soc. History of Science, 1981–84 (Pres., 1988–90); Scottish Museums, 1984–91; Museums Assoc., 1988–92; Mem., British Nat. Cttee for Hist. of Science, 1985–89; Pres., Scientific Instrument Commn, IUHPS, 1982–97; Visitor, Mus. of the Hist. of Sci., Oxford, 2002–14; Mem., Bd of Dirs, Chemical Heritage Foundn, Philadelphia, 2006– (Vice-Chm., 2012–). Mem., Internat. Acad. of Hist. of Sci., 2002. Member Editorial Board: Annals of Science, 1981–; Annali di Storia della Scienza, 1986–. Trustee, Boerhaave Mus., Leiden, 1994–99. Hon. FSAScot 1991. Hon. DSc: Edinburgh, 1995; Durham, 1998. Dexter Prize, Amer. Chemical Soc., 1986. Comdr, Ordre des Arts et des Lettres (France), 2002. *Publications:* The Mariner's Astrolabe, 1972; Edinburgh and Medicine, 1976; (ed) The Early Years of the Edinburgh Medical School, 1976; The Playfair Collection and the Teaching of Chemistry at the University of Edinburgh, 1978; (contrib.) The History of Technology, Vol. VI, ed T. I. Williams, 1978; Science in India, 1982; (ed) Science, Medicine and Dissent: Joseph Priestley (1733–1804), 1987; Scientific Instrument Makers Trade Catalogues, 1990; (ed) A New Museum for Scotland, 1990; (with G. Fyffe) Joseph Black: a Bibliography, 1992; (ed) Making Instruments Count, 1993; The Great Court at the British Museum, 2000; (ed) Chymica Acta, 2007; The Correspondence of Joseph Black, 2012. *Recreation:* books. *Address:* 15 King Street, King's Lynn, Norfolk PE30 1ET. *T:* (01533) 691567. *Club:* Athenæum.

ANDERSON, Prof. Robert Henry; Joseph Levy Professor of Paediatric Cardiac Morphology, Institute of Child Health, University College London, 1999–2007 (at National Heart and Lung Institute, Imperial College School of Medicine, 1979–99), University of London, now Emeritus (Professorial Fellow, 2007–08); Professor of Pediatrics, Medical University of South Carolina, since 2008; *b* 4 April 1942; *s* of Henry Anderson and Doris Amy Anderson (*née* Callear); *m* 1966, Christine (*née* Ibbotson); one *s* one *d. Educ:* Wellington Grammar Sch., Shropshire; Manchester Univ. BSc (Hons); MD; FRCPath. House Officer, Professorial Surgical Unit, 1966, Medical Unit, 1967, Manchester Royal Infirmary; Asst Lectr in Anatomy, 1967–69, Lectr, 1969–73, Manchester Univ.; MRC Travelling Fellow, Dept of Cardiology, Univ. of Amsterdam, 1973–74; Cardiothoracic Institute, now National Heart and Lung Institute, University of London: British Heart Foundn Sen. Res. Fellow and Sen. Lectr in Paediatrics, 1974–77; Joseph Levy Reader, 1977–79, Joseph Levy Prof., 1979–2007, Paediatric Cardiac Morphology. Hon. Consultant: Royal Brompton & Harefield NHS Trust, 1974–99; Gt Ormond St Hosp., 1999–2007. Hon. Prof. of Surgery, Univ. of N Carolina, USA, 1984–; Visiting Professor: Univ. of Pittsburgh, Pa, 1985–; Liverpool Univ., 1989–; St George's Hosp. Med. Sch., 2000–; Paediatrics, Baylor Coll. of Med., Houston, Texas, 2012–; Vis. Professorial Fellow, Inst. of Med. Genetics, Univ. of Newcastle, 2008–; Emeritus Vis. Prof., Univ. of Manchester, 2009–. Excerpta Medica Travel Award, 1977; British Heart Foundn Prize for Cardiovascular Research, 1984. Associate Editor, Internat. Jl of Cardiology, 1985–91; Ed.-in-Chief, Cardiology in the Young, 1997–2007 (Exec. Ed., 1992–97). *Publications:* (ed jtly) Paediatric Cardiology, 1977, vol. 3, 1981, vol. 5, 1983, vol. 6, 1986; (with A. E. Becker) Cardiac Anatomy, 1980; (with E. A. Shinebourne) Current Paediatric Cardiology, 1980; (with A. E. Becker) Pathology of Congenital Heart Disease, 1981; (with M. J. Davies and A. E. Becker) Pathology of the Conduction Tissues, 1983; (jtly) Morphology of Congenital Heart Disease, 1983; (with A. E. Becker) Cardiac Pathology, 1984; (with G. A. H. Miller and M. L. Rigby) The Diagnosis of Congenital Heart Disease, 1985; (with B. R. Wilcox) Surgical Anatomy of the Heart, 1985, 3rd edn 2004; (jtly) Paediatric Cardiology, 2 vols, 1987, 2nd edn 2002; (with P. J. Oldershaw and J. R. Dawson) Clinician's Illustrated Dictionary of Cardiology, 1988; (jtly) Atlas of the Heart, 1988; (jtly) Transoesophageal Echocardiography in Clinical Practice, 1991; (with A. E. Becker) The Heart Structure in Health and Disease, 1992; over 250 invited chapters in published books and over 800 papers in jls. *Recreations:* golf, music, wine. *Address:* 60 Earlsfield Road, SW18 3DN. *T:* (020) 8870 4368. *Clubs:* Saintsbury, Roehampton; Walton Heath Golf.

ANDERSON, Rodney Brian; Director of Marine and Fisheries, Department for Environment, Food and Rural Affairs, 2006–08; *b* 12 July 1948; *s* of Guy and Phyllis Anderson; *m* 1974, Mavis Barker; two *d.* ACIS 1972. Local Govt career, 1964–89; various posts, DoE, subseq. DETR, then DEFRA, 1989–2008; Hd, Water Supply and Regulation, 2000–04; Director: Water, 2004; Fisheries, 2004–06. Member, Board: Greenwich Forum, 2007–; Marine Mgt Orgn, 2010–13; Adviser: North Sea Marine Cluster, 2008–; (internat.), Marine Planning Consultants, 2012–. Advr, Agric., Fisheries, Envmt and Energy Sub-Cttee, EU Cttee, H of L, 2014–15. Dir, IRIS Consulting Ltd, 2008–. Trustee, Travel Foundn, 2009–. *Recreations:* spending time with my grandchildren and family, reading, walking, travelling, angling. *E:* rb.anderson@btinternet.com.

ANDERSON, Rolande Jane Rita; Director General, Office for Civil Society, Cabinet Office, 2009–10; Lay Member, Bar Standards Board, since 2012 (Chairman, Equalities and Diversity Committee, since 2012); *d* of late Arthur Ingham Anderson and of Rolande Marie Anderson. *Educ:* Lycée Français de Londres; Newnham Coll., Cambridge (BA Hons Mod. and Mediaeval Langs, MA Mod. Langs). Fast Stream Admin Trainee, Depts of Industry and of Prices and Consumer Protection, 1976–79; HEO, Dept of Trade, 1979–83; Principal and Hd of Section, DTI, 1983–89; Grade 7, Eur. Secretariat, Cabinet Office, 1989–91; Hd (Asst Sec.), Policy and Planning, Insolvency Service Exec. Agency, 1991–92; Dir, Aerospace and Defence Industries Policy, 1992–96, Regl Eur. Funds, 1996–99, Competition Policy, 1999–2002, DTI; Chief Exec., Radiocommunications Agency, 2002–03; Dep. Dir Gen., Innovation Gp, DTI, 2003–05; Regl Dir, Govt Office for the SE, 2006–08; Dir-Gen. for Transformation and Corporate Services, 2008, for Corporate Ops, 2008–09, ONS. Mem., panel of assessors for Fast Stream recruitment, CSSB, 1988–91; DTI Member, Steering Board: Patent Office, 2004–05; Nat. Weights and Measures Lab., 2004–05. Non-exec. Dir, Genesis Housing Assoc., 2005–14 (Chm., Remuneration and Diversity Cttees, 2007–14; Sen. Ind. Dir, 2012–14). Selector and Mentor, Minority Ethnic Talent Assoc., 2010–11. Newnham College, Cambridge: Associate Fellow, 2004–07; Pres. of Associates, 2009–11, now Hon. Associate; Mem., Campaign Bd, 2012–. Trustee and Mem. Council, Community Service Volunteers, 2012– (Chm., HR, Remuneration and Pensions Cttee, 2014–); Trustee, Brightside Trust, 2011–. Life FRSA. *Club:* Athenæum.

ANDERSON, Prof. Ross John, PhD; FRS 2009; FREng; FIMA, FIET, FInstP; Professor of Security Engineering, University of Cambridge, since 2003; computer security consultant, since 1984; *b* 1956; *s* of William and Anne Anderson; *m* Shireen; one *d. Educ:* High Sch. of Glasgow; Trinity Coll., Cambridge (BA 1978; MA 1982; PhD 1995). FIMA 1993; FIET (FIEE 2000); FREng 2009; FInstP 2009. University of Cambridge: Lectr, 1995–2000, Reader, 2000–03; Mem. Council, 2003–10 and 2015–. Ed., Computer and Communications Security Reviews, 1992–99. Chm., Foundn for Information Policy Research, 1998–. *Publications:* Fast Software Encryption, 1993; Security in Clinical Information Systems, 1996; Information Hiding, 1996; Personal Medical Information: security, engineering and ethics, 1997; Security Engineering: a guide to building dependable distributed systems, 2001, 2nd edn 2008. *Recreation:* music. *Address:* Computer Laboratory, University of Cambridge, J. J. Thomson Avenue, Cambridge CB3 0FD. *T:* (01223) 334733. *E:* info@ross-anderson.com.

ANDERSON, Prof. Sir Roy (Malcolm), Kt 2006; FRS 1986; FMedSci; Professor of Infectious Disease Epidemiology, Imperial College London, since 2000 (Head of Department, 2000–04; Rector, 2008–09); Chief Scientific Adviser, Ministry of Defence, 2004–08; *b* 12 April 1947; *s* of James Anderson and Betty Watson-Weatherburn; *m* 1st, 1975, Dr Mary Joan Anderson (marr. diss. 1989); 2nd, 1990, Dr Claire Baron (marr. diss. 2013); 3rd, 2014, Janet Louise Meyrick. *Educ:* Duncombe Sch., Bengeo; Richard Hale Sch., Hertford; Imperial Coll., London (BSc, ARCS, PhD, DIC). CBiol, FRSB. IBM Research Fellow, Univ. of Oxford, 1971–73; Lectr, King's Coll., London, 1973–77; Lectr, 1977–80, Reader, 1980–82, Prof., 1982–93, Head of Dept of Biology, 1984–93, Imperial Coll., London Univ.; University of Oxford: Linacre Prof. of Zoology, 1993–2000, and Hd, Zoology Dept, 1993–98; Dir, Wellcome Trust Centre for Epidemiology of Infectious Diseases, 1994–2000; Fellow, Merton Coll., Oxford, 1993–2000. Vis. Prof., McGill Univ., 1982–; Alexander Langmuir Vis. Prof., Harvard, 1990–; Genentech Vis. Prof., Univ. of Washington, 1998; James McLaughlin Vis. Prof., Univ. of Texas, 1999. Nuffield Medal Lect., RSocMed, 2002. Member: NERC, 1988–91 (Chm., Services and Facilities Cttee, 1989–90); ACOST, 1989–93 (Chm., Standing Cttee on Envmt, 1990–93); Spongiform Encephalopathy Adv. Cttee, 1998–2003; EPSRC, 2004–08; Chm., Sci. Adv. Council, DEFRA, 2004–; Mem., Govt's China Task Force, 2009–12. Chm., Oxford Biologica Ltd (formerly IBHSC Ltd), 1999–2001; non-executive Director: GlaxoSmithKline, 2007–; Imperial Coll. Healthcare NHS Trust, 2008–09; Mem. Internat. Adv. Bd, Hakluyt and Co. Ltd; Chm., Baccalaureate Adv. Panel, Pearson plc, 2012–. Member, Scientific Advisory Board: IMS, 1997–99; deCode, 1998–2002; Bill & Melinda Gates Foundn Initiative on Grand Challenges in Global Health, 2003–11; Singapore Nat. Res. Foundn, 2009–13; Member: Bio-Internat. Adv. Panel, Malaysia, 2009–; Adv. Bd, Partnership for Child Develt, 2012–; Chairman: Adv. Bd, Schistosomiasis Control Initiative, 2000–; Sci. Adv. Bd, Neglected Tropical Diseases prog., WHO, 2008–12; Dir, London Centre for Neglected Tropical Disease Res., 2012–. Member, Council: Zoological Soc., 1988–90; Royal Soc., 1989–91; RSTM&H, 1989–92; RPMS, 1994–97; Mem. Ct, LSHTM, 1993–2003. Governor: Wellcome Trust Ltd, 1992–2000 (Trustee, Wellcome Trust, 1991–92; Chairman: Infection and Immunity Grant Panel, 1990–92; Population Studies Panel); Inst. for Government, 2008–13. Trustee, Natural Hist. Mus., 2008–. Mem. Internat. Adv. Cttee, Nat. Sci. and Technol. Develt Agency, Thailand, 2009–; Chm., Internat. Adv. Panel Sci., PTT Public Co. Ltd, Thailand. Foreign Associate Member: Inst. of Medicine, NAS, USA, 2000; French Acad. of Scis, 2010. Founder FMedSci 1998. Hon. FIA 2000; Hon. FRCPath 2000; Hon. FSS 2002; Hon. FRAgS 2002. Hon. Fellow, Linacre Coll., Oxford, 1993. Hon. DSc: East Anglia, 1997; Stirling, 1998; Aberdeen, 2008. Zoological Soc. Scientific Medal, 1982; Huxley Meml Medal, Imperial Coll., London, 1983; Wright Meml Medal, British Soc. of Parasitology, 1986; David Starr Jordan Medal, Univs of Stanford, Cornell and Indiana, 1986; Chalmers Medal, RSTM&H, 1988; Weldon Medal, Oxford Univ., 1989; John Hill Grundy Medal, Royal Army Med. Coll., 1990; Frink Medal, Zoological Soc. of London, 1993; Joseph Smadel Medal, Infectious Diseases Soc. of Amer., 1994; Distinguished Statistical Ecologist Award, 1998; Dist. Parasitologists Award, Amer. Soc. of Parasitology, 1999. *Publications:* (ed) Population Dynamics of Infectious Disease Agents: theory and applications, 1982; (ed jtly) Population Biology of Infectious Diseases, 1982; (with R. M. May) Infectious Diseases of Humans: dynamics and control, 1991. *Recreations:* wildlife photography, croquet, natural history. *Address:* Department of Infectious Disease Epidemiology, Faculty of Medicine, Imperial College London, St Mary's Campus, Norfolk Place, Paddington, W2 1PG. *Club:* Athenæum.

ANDERSON, Roy William; District Judge (Magistrates' Courts) (formerly Stipendiary Magistrate), West Yorkshire, 1999–2015; *b* 10 Feb. 1950; *s* of William Patterson Bruce Anderson and Thirza Elizabeth Anderson (*née* Wakeham); *m* 1974, Pauline Mary Rylands; two *s. Educ:* King Edward VI Sch., Stratford-upon-Avon; University Coll. London (LLB). Articled clerk, City of Swansea, 1972–74; Prosecuting Solicitor, W Midlands CC, 1974–80; Solicitor, Jacobs Bird & Co., Birmingham, 1980–84; Sole Principal, Roy Anderson Solicitor, Birmingham, 1984–99. *Recreations:* reading, theatre, tennis, golf. *Clubs:* Silsden Golf; Ilkley Wharfedale Rotary.

ANDERSON, Sarah Lilian, CBE 2000; Member, Equality and Human Rights Commission, 2011; a Public Appointments Assessor, since 2012; *b* London, 19 June 1956; *d* of Derek and Joan Anderson; *m* 1989, Terrence Ivor Collis; one *s* one *d. Educ:* Queen's Coll., London; Westminster Coll. (HND Hotel and Catering Admin). Personnel and Trng Manager, Compass Gp, 1977–86; owner and Chief Exec., Mayday Gp, 1986–2006; Chair, Teddies Nurseries Ltd, 1991–95. Dir, Simple Solutions Ltd, 1994–; non-executive Director: Job Centre Plus, 2003–11; Albatross Gp Hldgs Ltd, 2009–; Action for Employment; Chair, Call Britannia, 2009–12. Member: Women and Work Commn, 2004–09; Commn for Employment and Skills, 2007–09; Leader, Ind. Rev. on Regulatory Guidance (Anderson Rev.), 2008–09. Member: Better Regulation Task Force, 1997–2002; Small Business Council, 2000–04; Council, ACAS, 2004–11. Chair, Small and Medium-sized Enterprises Council, CBI, 2000–04. Dir, Central London Samaritans, 2005–08. *Recreations:* eating out, Samaritans, fostering. *Address:* 45 Sussex Street, SW1V 4RJ. *T:* (020) 7821 5530, 07836 274968. *E:* sarah@anderson2.demon.co.uk.

ANDERSON, Air Marshal Sir Timothy (Michael), KCB 2013 (CB 2009); DSO 1999; independent consultant, since 2013; *b* 2 Feb. 1957; *s* of George Anderson and Beatrice Anderson; *m* 1979, Ursula Henderson; two *d. Educ:* Belfast Royal Acad.; King's Coll. London (MA 1994). Ops Flight Comdr No 1 Sqn, RAAF, 1988–90; Mil. Asst to DCDS (Systems), 1996–98; OC No 14 Sqdn, RAF, 1999–2000; CO RAF Bruggen, 2000–01; Dir, Equipment Capability (Deep Target Attack), MoD, 2003–05; Comdt, RAF Air Warfare Centre, 2005–07; ACAS, 2007–10; Dir Gen., Mil. Aviation Authy, 2010–13. Non-exec. Dir, Flybe Gp plc, 2014–. President: NI Wing Air Training Corps, 2008–; No 14 Sqdn Assoc., 2009–; RAF Rugby Union, 2009–13. Hon. Air Cdre, No 622 Sqdn, RAuxAF, 2013–. Vice Patron, Royal Internat. Air Tattoo, 2013–. FRAeS 2002. *Recreations:* cycling, military history, golf, Asian cooking, motor sport. *Club:* Royal Air Force.

ANDERSON, Victor Frederick; Visiting Professor, Global Sustainability Institute, Anglia Ruskin University, since 2013; *b* 7 Feb. 1952; *s* of Tom and Iris Anderson; *m* 1987, Joan Rawlinson; one *s*. *Educ:* Whitgift Sch.; Brasenose Coll., Oxford (BA). Lectr, 1980–88, at Paddington Coll. of FE, 1982–88; Researcher: New Econs Foundn, 1987–92; Plaid Cymru Gp of MPs, 1992–2000 and 2004–05; Higher Economic Analyst, Sustainable Develt Commn, 2006–09; One Planet Economy Leader, 2009–12, economist, 2011–13, WWF-UK. Mem. (Green), London Assembly, GLA, 2000–03. Mem. Bd, London Develt Agency, 2000–04. Envmt Advr to Mayor of London, 2001–04; Mem., London Sustainable Develt Commn, 2002–04. Develt Manager, Green Econs Inst., 2005. Dir, Planetary Boundaries Initiative, 2014–. Mem., Mgt Cttee, Compass, 2011–14. Mem. Editl Bd, Internat. Jl of Green Economics, 2006–. *Publications:* Alternative Economic Indicators, 1991, reissued 2013; Energy Efficiency Policies, 1993; Greens and the New Politics, 2001. *Recreations:* dancing, visiting museums. *Address:* 12 Glynwood Court, Dartmouth Road, Forest Hill, SE23 3HU.

ANDERSON, Sir (William) Eric (Kinloch), KT 2002; MA, MLitt, DLitt, FRSE; Provost of Eton College, 2000–09; *b* 27 May 1936; *er s* of late W. J. Kinloch Anderson and Margaret (*née* Harper), Edinburgh; *m* 1960, Poppy, *d* of late W. M. Mason, Skipton; one *s* one *d*. *Educ:* George Watson's Coll.; Univ. of St Andrews (MA); Balliol Coll., Oxford (MLitt; Hon. Fellow, 1989). Asst Master: Fettes Coll., 1960–64; Gordonstoun, 1964–66; Asst Master, Fettes Coll., and Housemaster, Arniston House, 1967–70; Headmaster: Abingdon Sch., 1970–75; Shrewsbury Sch., 1975–80; Eton Coll., 1980–94; Rector, Lincoln Coll., Oxford, 1994–2000 (Hon. Fellow, 2000). Chairman: King George VI and Queen Elizabeth Foundn of St Catharine's, Cumberland Lodge, 1997–2009; Nat. Heritage Meml Fund, 1998–2001 (Trustee, 1996–2001). President: Edinburgh Sir Walter Scott Club, 1981; Johnson Soc., 1992; Mem., DCMS Adv. Panel for Public Appointments, 1997–2004. Trustee: Said (formerly Karim Rida Said) Foundn, 1994–98, 2004–09; Wordsworth Trust, 1996–97; Royal Collection, 2000–06; Shakespeare Birthplace Trust, 2001–; Farmington Trust, 2005–; Manifold Trust, 2008–15; Abbotsford Trust, 2012–15. Mem. Visiting Cttee, Harvard Meml Church, 2001–07. Council Mem., Royal Holloway, London Univ. (formerly RHBNC), 1990–95; Gov., Shrewsbury Sch., 1994–2000; Visitor, Harris Manchester Coll., Oxford Univ., 2001–. Chm. of Judges, Whitbread Book Awards, 2000. FRSE 1985. Hon. DLitt: St Andrews, 1981; Hull, 1994; Siena, 1999; Birmingham, 2010; Aberdeen, 2013. *Publications:* The Written Word, 1964; (ed) The Journal of Sir Walter Scott, 1972, rev. edn 1998; (ed) The Percy Letters, vol IX, 1988; The Sayings of Sir Walter Scott, 1995; (with Adam Nicolson) About Eton, 2010; Sir Walter's Wit and Wisdom, 2013; Sir Walter's Verse, 2013; articles and reviews. *Recreations:* theatre, golf, fishing. *Address:* The Homestead, Kingham, Oxon OX7 6YA.

See also D. W. K. Anderson.

ANDERSSON, Hilary Harper; correspondent, Panorama, BBC, since 2006; *b* 23 Sept. 1967; *d* of Alfred McRae Andersson and Zosha Mary Andersson; two *s*. *Educ:* Cheltenham Ladies' Coll.; Univ. of Edinburgh (MA Hons Politics). Joined BBC, 1991: producer, World Service, 1992–94; sen. broadcast journalist, 1994–96; Lagos Corresp., 1996–99; Jerusalem Corresp., 1999–2001; Africa Corresp., 2001–05; special reports for Panorama: Secrets of the Camps, 2005; The New Killing Fields, 2005; Climate of Fear, 2006; Is America Ready for a Black President?, 2008; What Next Mr President?, 2009; Licence to Torture, 2009; Zimbabwe's Blood Diamonds, 2011; Poor America, 2012; The Brothers who Bombed Boston, 2013; America's Gun Addiction, 2013; Bedlam Behind Bars, 2014; Bagram Airbase, BBC Radio 4, 2010 (Radio Prize, Amnesty Internat. Media Awards). *Publications:* Mozambique: a war against the people, 1992. *Recreations:* ski-ing, windsurfing, writing. *Address:* c/o BBC News Centre, Broadcasting House, Portland Place, W1A 1AA. *E:* Hilary.Andersson.01@bbc.co.uk.

ANDERTON, Prof. Brian Henry, PhD; FMedSci; Director, MRC Centre for Neurodegeneration Research, 2005–08, and Professor of Neuroscience, Institute of Psychiatry, 1989–2008, at King's College London; *b* 25 Dec. 1945; *s* of Henry Anderton and Mary Anderton (*née* Ashcroft); *m* 1969, Thérèse L. F. Loviny; one *s*. *Educ:* Alsop High Sch. for Boys, Liverpool; University College London (BSc 1967; PhD 1970). MRC Biophysics Unit, KCL, 1970–72; Lectr in Biochem., Poly. of Central London, 1972–77; Lectr in Biochem. and Immunology, Chelsea Coll., Univ. of London, 1977–79; St George's Hospital Medical School, University of London: Lectr in Immunology, 1979–81; Sen. Lectr in Immunology, 1981–86; Reader in Molecular Pathology, 1986–88. FMedSci 2007. *Publications:* contribs to sci. jls on nervous system and molecular pathology of Alzheimer's disease and other neurodegenerative diseases. *Recreations:* hill walking, cycling, general reading, theatre, cinema, listening to music, drawing, painting. *Address:* 19 Speldhurst Road, W4 1BX.

ANDERTON, Sir (Cyril) James, Kt 1991; CBE 1982; QPM 1977; DL; Chief Constable, Greater Manchester Police Force, 1976–91 (Deputy Chief Constable, 1975); *b* 24 May 1932; *o s* of late James Anderton and Lucy Anderton (*née* Occleshaw); *m* 1955, Joan Baron; one *d*. *Educ:* St Matthew's Church Sch., Highfield; Wigan Grammar Sch. Certif. Criminology, Manchester Univ., 1960; Sen. Comd Course, Police Coll., 1967. Corps of Royal Mil. Police, 1950–53; Constable to Chief Inspector, Manchester City Police, 1953–67; Chief Supt, Cheshire Constab., 1967–68; Asst Chief Constable, Leicester and Rutland Constab., 1968–72; Asst to HM Chief Inspector of Constab. for England and Wales, Home Office, London, 1972–75; Dep. Chief Constable, Leics Constabulary, 1975. Mem., ACPO, 1968–91 (Pres., 1986–87). FCO lect. tour, FE and SE Asia, 1973. UK Govt deleg., UN Congress on Prevention of Crime, Budapest, 1974. British Institute of Management: Pres., Manchester Br., 1984–93; Chm., 1986–90, Mem., 1985–90, NW Regl Bd; Cert. of Merit, 1990. President: Manchester NSPCC Jun. League, 1979–93; Christian Police Assoc., 1979–81; Manchester and Dist RSPCA, 1984–2000 (Vice-Pres., 1981–84); Wigan and Dist RSPCA, 1999–2000 (Patron, 1986–99); Wythenshawe Hosp. League of Friends, 1991–2004; Altrincham Town Centre Partnership, 1994–2003; Disabled Living, Manchester, 1995–2005 (Patron, 1991–; Hon. Life Mem., 2006); Bolton Outward Bound Assoc., 1995–2002 (Vice-Pres., 1991–95); NW Reg., YMCA, 1996–2002; Manchester YMCA, 2000–02 (Vice-Pres., 1976–2000); Greater Manchester Fedn of Clubs for Young People (formerly Boys' Clubs), 2001–05 (Vice-Pres., 1984–2001; Patron, 2005–). Member: Manchester Adv. Bd, Salvation Army, 1977–2001 (Chm., 1993–2001; Hon. Life Mem., Salvation Army Adv. Bd, 2000); Salvation Army Territorial Adv. Bd, 1996–2001; Exec. Cttee, Manchester NSPCC, 1979–93; Bd, Henshaws Soc. for the Blind, 1991–95; Royal Soc. of St George, 1992–; CCJ, 1992–; Friends of Israel Assoc., 1992–; Broughton Catholic Charitable Soc., 1996–; Nat. Adv. Gp, YMCA, 1997–2002 (Chm., Prisons Steering Gp, 1994–2002). Comdr, St John Amb., Greater Manchester, 1989–96 (County Dir, 1976–89); Vice-President: Manchester and District RLSS, 1976–2000; Adelphi Lads' Club, Salford, 1979–2006; Sharp Street Ragged Sch., Manchester, 1982–2002; Manchester Schools Football Assoc., 1976–91; Greater Manchester East Scout Council, 1977–91; Wigan Hospice, 1990–; Greater Manchester West Scout Council, 1992–; Manchester and Dist NSPCC, 1994–. Boys' Brigade: Pres., Leics Bn, 1972–76; Hon. Nat. Vice-Pres., 1983–. Patron: NW Counties Schs ABA, 1980–91; NW Campaign for Kidney Donors, 1983–91; NW Eye Res. Trust, 1982–91; Internat. Spinal Res. Trust (Greater Manchester Cttee), 1983–91; Stockport Lourdes Gp HCPT (formerly ACROSS), 1993–2009; Trafford Multiple Sclerosis Soc., 1994–2004; Mottram and Hattersley ABC, 1994–2003; Rhodes Foundn Scholarship Trust, 1996–; Lancashire and Cheshire (formerly Gtr Manchester) Lupus Gp, 1996–2005; Gtr Manchester Youth Field Gun Assoc., 1996–2003 (Pres., 1992–96); Police Boxing Assoc. of England, 1997–2003; Manchester Stedfast Assoc., 1999–. British College of Accordionists: Chm., Governing Council, 1972–77; Vice-Pres., 1977–84; Pres., 1984–91; Patron, 1991–2002. Trustee, Manchester Olympic Bid Cttee, 1985–93; Chm. of Trustees, S Manchester Accident Rescue Team, 1996–2001; Chm., Manchester Concerts Cttee, Sargent Cancer Care for Children, 1992–2003. Hon. FBCA 1976; Hon. RNCM 1984. Member: Catholic Union of GB; NT; Wigan Little Theatre; Royal Exchange Th., Manchester; Corps of Royal Mil. Police Assoc. Mancunian of The Year, 1980. DL Greater Manchester, 1989. Freeman, City of London, 1990. KStJ 1989 (OStJ 1978; CStJ 1982; Mem., Chapter-Gen., 1993–99). KMLJ 1998; KHS 1999. Cross Pro Ecclesia et Pontifice, 1982. Chevalier de la Confrérie des Chevaliers du Tastevin, 1985. *Recreations:* opera, theatre, walking; Rugby League supporter. *Address:* 9 The Avenue, Sale, Cheshire M33 4PB.

ANDERTON, Hon. James Patrick, (Jim); MP Wigram, New Zealand, 1996–2011 (MP Sydenham, 1984–96) (Lab 1984–89, NewLab, then Alliance, 1989–2002, Progressive, 2002–11); *b* 21 Jan. 1938; *m* 1st, Joan Caulfield (marr. diss.); three *s* two *d*; 2nd, Carole Dianne. *Educ:* Seddon Meml Technical Coll.; Auckland Teachers' Trng Coll. Formerly: teacher; Child Welfare Officer, Educn Dept, Wanganui; Export Manager, UEB Textiles, 1969–70; Man. Dir, Anderton Hldgs, 1971–84. Member: Manukau CC, 1965–68; Auckland CC, 1974–80; Auckland Regl Authy, 1977–80. Dep. Prime Minister of NZ, 1999–2002; Minister: for Econ. Develt, and for Industry and Regl Develt, 1999–2005; of Forests, 2004–08; of Agriculture, of Fisheries and for Biosecurity, 2005–08. Labour Party, 1963–89: Pres., 1979–84; Mem., Policy Council, 1979–89; Leader, NewLabour Party, 1989–2002; Jt Founder, 1991, Leader, 1992–2001, Alliance; Leader, Progressive Party, 2002–11. Co-Chm., Gtr Christchurch Bldgs Trust, 2012–; Chm., AMI Stadium, Christchurch, 2012–. Dir of Habitat, Humanity Bd, Christchurch, 2012–. Organiser, Catholic Youth Movt, 1960–65; Sec., Catholic Diocesan Office, Auckland, 1967–69.

ANDERTON, Stephen Hugh Garth; garden journalist and author; *b* Skipton, 3 Feb. 1955; *s* of William and Winifred Anderton; *m* 1976, Judith Symonds; three *d*. *Educ:* Ermysted's Grammar Sch., Skipton; Univ. of Birmingham (BA Drama and Classics 1976). Gardener and Hd Gardener for private estates incl. Cadogan Estate, Abbots Ripton Hall, Great Comp, Belsay Hall and Brodsworth Hall, 1976–85; English Heritage: Horticultural Officer, 1985–95; Nat. Gardens Manager, 1995–96; garden writer, The Times, 1993–; contrib. consumer mags, garden tour leader, lectr and horticultural consultant; TV presenter, Britain's Best Back Gardens, 2004, 2005. Cttee work for Garden Media Guild, Plant Heritage, RHS, Professional Gardener's Guild, Garden Hist. Soc. Founder, Thinkingardens Gp, 2005. Patron, Professional Gardener's Guild, 2008. Garden Media Guild Awards, 1995, 1996, 2000, 2003. *Publications:* Stephen Anderton's Garden Answers, 1998; Rejuvenating a Garden, 1998; Urban Sanctuaries: creating peaceful havens for the city gardener, 2006; Discovering Welsh Gardens, 2009; Christopher Lloyd: his life at Great Dixter, 2010. *Recreations:* gardening, writing music and lyrics, opera. *Address:* c/o Greene and Heaton, 37 Goldhawk Road, W12 8QQ. *E:* stephenanderton95@btinternet.com; Abergavenny, Mon.

ANDO, Tadao, Hon. RA 2002; architect; Director, Tadao Ando Architect and Associates, since 1969; *b* 13 Sept. 1941; *s* of Mitsugu Kitayama and Asako Kitayama; adopted by grandparents Hikoichi Ando and Kikue Ando; *m* 1970, Yumiko Kato. *Educ:* self-educated in architecture. Visiting Professor: Yale Univ., 1987; Columbia Univ., 1988; Harvard, 1990. *Works include:* Row House, Sumiyoshi (Azuma House), 1975; Rokko Housing I and II, 1978–89; Kidosaki House, 1982; Church of The Light, Osaka, 1987; Japanese Pavilion, Expo '92, Seville, 1989. *Exhibitions include:* Mus. of Modern Art, NY, 1991; Centre Georges Pompidou, Paris, 1993; Basilica Palladiana, Vicenza, 1994; RA, 1998. Hon. FAIA 1991; Hon. FRIBA 1993. Chevalier, Ordre des Arts et des Lettres (France), 1995. Alvar Aalto Medal, Finnish Assoc. Architects, 1986; Gold Medal of Architecture, French Acad. Architecture, 1989; Arnold W. Brunner Meml Prize, AAIL, 1991; Carlsberg Architectural Prize, 1992; Pritzker Architecture Prize, 1995; Royal Gold Medal, RIBA, 1997; Gold Medal, AIA, 2002. *Publications:* Tadao Ando Monographies, 1982; Tadao Ando: buildings, projects, writings, 1984; Tadao Ando Complete Works, 1995; (with Richard Pare) The Colours of Light, 1996. *Address:* 5–23 Toyosaki 2–chome, Kita-ku, Osaka 531–0072, Japan. *T:* (6) 63751148.

ANDOR, László; Member, European Commission, 2010–14; *b* Zalaegerszeg, Hungary, 3 June 1966; *m* Varsányi; one *s* one *d*. *Educ:* High Sch., Zalaegerszeg; Univ. of Budapest; Univ. of Manchester (MA Develtl Econs 1993). Res. Fellow, Econ. and Social Res. Inst. of Trade Unions, Hungary, 1989–91; Hd, Coll. for Advanced Studies in Social Theory, Budapest Univ. of Econ. Scis and Public Admin, 1993–97; Vis. Prof., Rutgers Univ., 1997–98; Advisor: Budgetary and Finance Cttee, Hungarian Nat. Assembly, 1998–99; World Bank on Structural Adjustment Participatory Rev. Initiative, 1999–2001; Sen. Researcher, Inst. for Political Scis, Hungary, 2002–05; Sen. Advr to Prime Minister's Office, Hungary, 2003–05; Mem., Bd of Dirs, EBRD, 2005–. Associate Prof., Econs Dept, Corvinus Univ. of Budapest and King Sigismund Coll., 2000– (on unpaid leave). *Publications:* Amerikai politika a XX században, 1998; Pénz beszél, 1998; (jtly) Market Failure: a guide to the East European economic miracle, 1998; (jtly) Roosevelt - Churchill, 1999; Hungary on the Road to the European Union: transition in Blue Westport, 2000; (jtly) Tiz év után…, 2000; Amerika évszázada, 2002; Nemzetek és pénzügyek, 2003; (jtly) Paneltöl az óceánig, 2003; Irak: háborúra ítélve, 2004; (ed) Közgazdaság, 2005; (ed) Világgazdaság, 2006; (ed) Magyar gazdaság, 2008; Összehasonlító gazdaságtan, 2008; (ed) Az adóparadicsomtól a zöldmozgalomig, 2008. *Recreations:* listening to music, playing soccer.

ANDOVER, Viscount; Alexander Charles Michael Winston Robsahm Howard; Managing Director, guntrader.co.uk Ltd, since 1997; *b* 17 Sept. 1974; *s* and *heir* of 21st Earl of Suffolk and Berkshire, *qv*; *m* 2011, Victoria, *d* of James Hamilton; one *d*. *Educ:* Eton Coll.; Bristol Univ. *E:* andover@charltonpark.com.

ANDRE, Carl; sculptor; *b* 16 Sept. 1935; *s* of George Hans Andre and Margaret Andre (*née* Johnson). First exhibn, 1964; represented in collections in: Tate Gall.; Mus. of Modern Art, NYC; Guggenheim Mus., NYC; La Jolla Mus. Contemporary Art; Mönchengladbach Mus., Germany; Kunstmuseum Basel, Switzerland; Stedelijk Mus., Amsterdam; Musée Nationale d'Art Moderne, Paris; Nat. Gall. of Canada, Ottawa; Seattle Art Mus.; Musèo de Arte Moderno, Bogotá; *solo exhibitions:* Tibor de Nagy Gall., NY, 1965; Konrad Fischer Gall., Düsseldorf, 1967, 2006; Guggenheim Mus., 1970; Univ. Art Mus., Berkeley, Calif, 1979; Paula Cooper Gall., NY, 1983; (retrospective) Whitechapel Art Gall., 2000; Sadie Coles HQ, London, 2001; Ace Gall., LA, 2002; Galerie Tschudi, Switzerland, 2003; Galerie Arnaud Lefebvre, Paris, 2004; Kunsthalle Basel, Switzerland, 2005; Andrea Rosen Gall., NY, 2007; Yvon Lambert, Paris, 2008; Turner Contemporary, Margate, 2013. *Address:* c/o Konrad Fischer Galerie, Platanenstrasse 7, 40233 Düsseldorf, Germany; c/o Paula Cooper, 534 W 21 St, New York, NY 10011, USA.

ANDREAE, Sophie Clodagh Mary, (Mrs D. E. Blain), FSA; Trustee, Historic Royal Palaces, 2009–14; *b* 10 Nov. 1954; *d* of Herman Kleinwort (Sonny) Andreae and Clodagh Mary (*née* Alleyn); *m* 1984, Douglas Ellis Blain; three *s* one *d*. *Educ:* St Mary's, Ascot; Newnham Coll., Cambridge. FSA 2012. SAVE Britain's Heritage: Sec., 1976–84; Chm., 1984–88; Head, London Div., English Heritage (Historic Bldgs and Monuments Commn for England), 1988–93. Member: Royal Fine Art Commn, 1996–99; CABE, 1999–2004 (Chm., CABE Educn Foundn, 2002–06); English Heritage/CABE Urban Panel, 2004–07; Places of Worship Forum, English Heritage, 2005–; Council, Nat. Trust, 2006–15. Trustee: Heritage of London Trust, 1985–2003; Greenwich Foundn, 2007–15. Member: London DAC, 1988–2001; St Paul's Cathedral Fabric Adv. Cttee, 1991–2011; Exec. Cttee, 1993–2011, Council, 2011–, Georgian Gp, 1993–2013; Council, London Historic Parks and Gardens

Trust, 1993–2002. Vice Chm., Patrimony Cttee, RC Bishops' Conf., 2002–. Dir, Action for Mkt Towns, 1998–2003. High Sheriff, Powys, 2002–03. Chm., Friends of St Andrew's Church, Presteigne, Powys, 1998–; Trustee, Judge's Lodging Mus., Presteigne, Powys, 2007–. DSG 2011. *Publications:* (contrib.) Preserving the Past: the rise of heritage in modern Britain, 1996; ed and contrib. to numerous SAVE Britain's Heritage reports. *Address:* 23 Brompton Square, SW3 2AD.

ANDREAE-JONES, William Pearce; QC 1984; a Recorder of the Crown Court, since 1982; *b* 21 July 1942. *Educ:* Canford Sch.; Corpus Christi Coll., Cambridge (MA Hons). Called to the Bar, Inner Temple, 1965. Legal Mem., Mental Health Review Tribunal, 2002–12. *Address:* Citadel Chambers, 190 Corporation Street, Birmingham B4 6QD; King's Bench Chambers, Wellington House, 175 Holdenhurst Road, Bournemouth, Dorset BH8 8DQ.

ANDREASEN, Marta; Member for South East Region, European Parliament, 2009–14 (UK Ind, 2009–13, C, 2013–14); *b* 26 Nov. 1954; *d* of Svend Andreasen and Maria Elena Salaverri; *m* 1979, Octavio Otaño; one *s* one *d*. *Educ:* Catholic Univ., Argentina (CPA); Babson Coll., Boston (Postgrad. Exec. Educn). Economist, Educn Ministry, Spain; Auditor, Price Waterhouse, 1977–82; Regl Finance Dir, cos incl. Lotus Develt, Rockwell Automation, 1983–98; Hd of Accounting, OECD, 1998; Chief Accounting Officer, European Commn, 2002. Contested (C) SE Reg., EP, 2014. *Publications:* Brussels Laid Bare, 2009. *Recreations:* sailing, trekking, swimming, water ski-ing, reading.

ANDRES, Dame Clare; *see* Tickell, Dame O. C.

ANDRESEN GUIMARÃES, Fernando; Ambassador of Portugal to the Court of St James's, 2003–06; *b* 13 Nov. 1941; *s* of Fernando João Andresen Guimarães and Maria Carlota da Rocha Vasconcelos Meireles de Lacerda Andresen Guimarães; *m* 1984, Graça Trocado; two *s* from a previous marriage. *Educ:* Univ. of Lisbon (Econs degree). Joined Portuguese Diplomatic Service, 1969; Sec., Malawi, 1970–73; First Sec., London, 1973–76; Min. of Foreign Affairs, 1976–77; NATO Defence Coll., Rome, 1977–78; Counsellor, UN, NY, 1978–82; Consul Gen., Angola, 1982–86; Ambassador to: Iraq, 1986–88; Algeria, 1988–91; Dir Gen., Aid to Develt, 1991–92; Pres., Interministerial Commn on Macau and Portuguese-Chinese Jt Liaison Gp, 1992–95; Ambassador to USA, 1995–99; Perm. Rep. to NATO, 1999–2003. Decorations include: Grand Cross, Order of Christ (Portugal); Grand Cross, Order Infante D. Henrique (Portugal); Naval Cross, 1st cl. (Portugal). *Recreations:* reading, golf, opera (as spectator).

ANDREW, Prof. Christopher Maurice, PhD; FRHistS; Professor of Modern and Contemporary History, 1993–2008, Director of Research, Department of History, 2008–11, University of Cambridge; Fellow, Corpus Christi College, Cambridge, since 1967; *b* 23 July 1941; *s* of Maurice Viccars Andrew and Freda Mary (*née* Sandall); *m* 1962, Jennifer Ann Alicia Garratt; one *s* two *d*. *Educ:* Norwich Sch.; Corpus Christi Coll., Cambridge (MA, PhD). FRHistS 1976. Res. Fellow, Gonville and Caius Coll., Cambridge, 1965–67; Dir of Studies in History, 1967–81 and 1988–, Sen. Tutor, 1981–87, Corpus Christi Coll., Cambridge; Univ. Lectr in History, 1972–89, Reader in Mod. and Contemp. Hist., 1989–93, Univ. of Cambridge. Ext. Examr in History, NUI, 1977–84. Specialist Adviser, H of C Select Cttee on Educn, Science and the Arts, 1982–83. Chm., British Intelligence Study Gp, 1999–. Official historian, MI5, 2002–. Visiting Professor: Univ. of Toronto, 1991; Harvard Univ., 1992. Visiting Fellow: ANU, 1987; Wilson Center, Washington, 1987. TV Presenter: The Fatal Attraction of Adolf Hitler, 1989; Hess: an edge of conspiracy, 1990; The Cambridge Moles, 1990; All the King's Jews, 1990; A Cold War, 1991; BBC Radio Presenter (series): Tampering with the Past, 1990; What if?, 1990–94; Hindsight, 1993–95. Editor: The Historical Journal, 1976–85; Intelligence and National Security, 1986–. *Publications:* Théophile Delcasse and the making of the Entente Cordiale, 1968; The First World War: causes and consequences, 1970 (vol. 19 of Hamlyn History of the World); (with A. S. Kanya-Forstner) France Overseas: the First World War and the climax of French imperial expansion, 1981; (ed with Prof. D. Dilks) The Missing Dimension: governments and intelligence communities in the Twentieth Century, 1984; Secret Service: the making of the British Intelligence Community, 1985; Codebreaking and Signals Intelligence, 1986; (ed with Jeremy Noakes) Intelligence and International Relations 1900–1945, 1987; (with Oleg Gordievsky) KGB: the inside story of its foreign operations from Lenin to Gorbachev, 1990; (with Oleg Gordievsky) Instructions from The Centre: top secret files on KGB foreign operations, 1991; (with Oleg Gordievsky) More Instructions from The Centre, 1992; For The President's Eyes Only: secret intelligence and the American presidency from Washington to Bush, 1995; (with Vasili Mitrokhin) The Mitrokhin Archive: the KGB in Europe and the West, 1999, vol. II: the KGB and the world, 2005; The Defence of the Realm: the authorized history of MI5, 2009; broadcasts and articles on mod. history, Association football, secret intelligence, internat. relations. *Address:* 67 Grantchester Meadows, Cambridge CB3 9JL. *T:* (01223) 353773.

ANDREW, Christopher Robert, (Rob), MBE 1995; Professional Rugby Director, Rugby Football Union, since 2011 (Elite Rugby Director, 2006–11; Operations Director, 2011); *b* 18 Feb. 1963; *m* 1989, Sara (marr. diss. 2014); three *d*. *Educ:* Barnard Castle; St John's Coll., Cambridge (BA 1985; MA 1989; Rugby blue, cricket blue). MRICS (ARICS 1988). Chartered surveyor with Debenham, Tewson & Chinnocks, until 1995; Develt Dir, Newcastle RFC, then Dir of Rugby, Newcastle Falcons, 1995–2006. Played for: Nottingham RFC, 1984–87; Wasps FC, 1987–91, 1992–96; Toulouse RFC, 1991–92; Barbarians RFC, and Newcastle RFC, 1996–99; England, 1985–97 (71 caps); World Cup team 1987, 1991, 1995; Grand Slam side, 1991, 1992, 1995; British Lions tour, Australia, 1989, NZ 1993. *Publications:* A Game and a Half, 1994. *Address:* c/o Rugby Football Union, Rugby House, 200 Whitton Road, Twickenham TW2 7BA.

ANDREW, Prof. Colin; Professor of Manufacturing Engineering, 1986–94, and Chairman of Council, School of Technology, 1993–94, Cambridge University; Fellow, Christ's College, Cambridge, 1986–94; *b* 22 May 1934; *s* of Arnold Roy and Kathleen Andrew; *m* 1952, Ruth E. Probert; two *s* two *d*. *Educ:* Bristol Grammar Sch.; Christ's Coll., Cambridge Univ. MA; PhD. Res. Engr, Rolls-Royce, 1955–58; research, Cambridge, 1958–60; Develt Engr, James Archdale & Co., 1960–61; Bristol University: Lectr, 1961–68; Reader, 1968–71; Prof. of Applied Mechanics, 1971–82; Hon. Prof., 1982–86. Managing Director: Flamgard Ltd, 1982–85; Bristol Technical Develts Ltd, 1985–94. Chairman: Engrg Processes Cttee, SERC, 1981–83; Production Cttee, SERC, 1983–84; Main Engrg Panel, and Mech., Aeronautical and Manufacturing Panel, UFC Res. Assessment Exercise, 1992; Mech., Aeronautical and Manufacturing Panel, HEFCE Res. Assessment Exercise, 1996; Member: Technology Sub-Cttee, UGC, 1986–89; Engrg Council, 1990–94 (Chm., Bd of Engrs Registration, 1992–94). *Publications:* (jtly) Creep Feed Grinding, 1985; papers in scientific jls. *Address:* Hybank, Itton, Chepstow NP16 6BZ.

ANDREW, Hon. (John) Neil, AO 2008; arbitrator and mediator, since 2006; Speaker, House of Representatives, Australia, 1998–2004; *b* 7 June 1944; *s* of Jack Clover Andrew and Elsie Mavis Andrew; *m* 1971, Carolyn Ann Ayles; two *s* one *d*. *Educ:* Waikerie High Sch.; Urrbrae Agricl Coll.; Australian Nuffield Schol. in Agric., UK, 1975; Univ. of Adelaide. Horticulture (fruit and vineyards), 1964–83. MP (L) Wakefield, SA, 1983–2004; Dep. Opposition Whip, 1985–89, 1990–93; Chief Govt Whip, House of Reps, 1997–98. Chm., Murray Darling Basin Authy, 2015–. Chm., AATSE, 2005–11, now Hon. Mem. *Recreations:* horticulture, camping, reading, aviation. *Address:* c/o Box 495, Walkerville, SA 5081, Australia.

ANDREW, Rob; *see* Andrew, C. R.

ANDREW, Sir Robert (John), KCB 1986 (CB 1979); civil servant, retired; *b* 25 Oct. 1928; *s* of late Robert Young Andrew and Elsie (*née* Heritage); *m* 1963, Elizabeth Bayley (OBE 2000); two *s*. *Educ:* King's College Sch., Wimbledon; Merton Coll., Oxford (MA; Hon. Fellow 2005). Intelligence Corps, 1947–49. Joined Civil Service, 1952: Asst Principal, War Office, Principal, 1957; Min. of Defence, 1963; Asst Sec., 1965; Defence Counsellor, UK Delegn to NATO, 1967–70; Private Sec. to Sec. of State for Defence, 1971–73; Under-Sec., CSD, 1973–75; Asst Under-Sec. of State, MoD, 1975–76; Dep. Under-Sec. of State, Home Office, 1976–83; Perm. Under-Sec. of State, NI Office, 1984–88; Cabinet Office, Review of Govt Legal Services, 1988. Dir, Esmée Fairbairn Charitable Trust, 1989–94. Conservator of Wimbledon and Putney Commons, 1973–2009. Governor, King's College Sch., 1975–2000 (Chm., 1990–2000; Hon. Fellow 2003). Mem. Council, Royal Holloway, Univ. of London (formerly RHBNC), 1989–99 (Chm., 1992–99; Hon. Fellow, 2000). Trustee, BBC Children in Need Appeal, 1993–99. FRSA 1992–2013. *Recreations:* reading, current affairs, grandchildren. *Address:* 8 High Cedar Drive, Wimbledon, SW20 0NU. *Club:* Oxford and Cambridge.

ANDREW, Her Honour Sandra Christine; a Circuit Judge, 1999–2004; Designated Family Judge, Canterbury Combined Court, 2000–04; a Deputy Circuit Judge, 2004–11; *b* 5 Nov. 1941; *d* of Albert Hugh Dudley Tyas and Anne Florence (*née* Preston); *m* 1963, John Andrew (*d* 2001); two *s*. *Educ:* various prep. schools; E Grinstead Co. Grammar Sch. Admitted Solicitor, 1964; in private practice, 1964–83; Registrar, SE Circuit, Bromley Co. Court, 1983, transf. to Maidstone, 1990; Trng Registrar, then Dist Judge, 1986–99; Care Dist Judge, 1991–99. Member: President's Ancillary Relief Adv. Gp (formerly Lord Chancellor's Adv. Cttee on Ancillary Relief), 1993–2004; Family Proceedings Rules Cttee, 1993–97; Litigant Inf. Sub-Cttee, Civil Justice Council, 1998–2001; Tutor team for Dep. Dist Judges, Judicial Studies Bd, 1998–2001. Chm., SE Circuit Assoc. Dist Judges, 1992–95; SE Circuit (S) Rep., Nat. Cttee, Assoc. Dist Judges, 1996–99 (Co-opted Mem., Family Sub-Cttee, 1993–96). *Recreations:* music, bridge, travel, reading. *Address:* c/o The Law Courts, Chaucer Road, Canterbury, Kent CT1 1ZA.

ANDREW, Stuart James; MP (C) Pudsey, since 2010; *b* Bangor, N Wales, 25 Nov. 1971; *s* of James Edward and Maureen Catherine Andrew; partner, 2001, Robin Rogers. *Educ:* Ysgol David Hughes, Menai Bridge. Fundraiser: BHF, 1994–98; Hope House Children's Hospice, 1998–2000; Hd of Fundraising, E Lancs Hospice, 2000–03. Mem. (C) Leeds CC, 2003–. PPS to Minister for Cabinet Office and Paymaster Gen., 2012–. Treas., All Party Parly Gp on Hospice and Palliative Care, 2010–. *Recreations:* walking Yorkshire Dales, attending gym, socialising. *Address:* House of Commons, SW1A 0AA. *T:* (020) 7219 7130. *E:* stuart.andrew.mp@parliament.uk.

ANDREWS, Baroness *cr* 2000 (Life Peer), of Southover in the co. of East Sussex; **Elizabeth Kay Andrews,** OBE 1998; DPhil; Chair, English Heritage, 2009–13; *b* 16 May 1943; *d* of Clifford and Louisa Andrews; *m* 1970, Prof. Roy MacLeod (marr. diss. 1992); one *s*. *Educ:* Univ. of Wales (BA 1964); Univ. of Sussex (MA 1970; DPhil 1975). Res. Fellow, Science Policy Res. Unit, Univ. of Sussex, 1968–70; Res. Clerk, then Sen. Res. Clerk, H of C, 1970–85; Special Advr, Rt Hon. Neil Kinnock, MP, Leader of the Opposition, 1985–92; Dir, Education Extra (nat. charity for out-of-sch. learning), 1992–2002. A Baroness in Waiting (Govt Whip), 2002–05; Parly Under-Sec. of State, ODPM, later DCLG, 2005–09. Hon. DLaws Sussex, 2012. *Publications:* (with J. B. Poole) The Government of Science, 1972; (with John Jacobs) Punishing the Poor, 1990; Good Practice & Policy for After School, 1997; Extra Learning, 2001; articles in history, science policy and social policy jls. *Recreations:* music, museums, walking, friends. *Address:* House of Lords, SW1A 0PW.

ANDREWS, Ann; *see* Beynon, A.

ANDREWS, Anthony Peter Hamilton; Chairman: Countryside Learning Scotland (formerly Scottish Country Alliance Educational Trust), since 2003; South Esk Catchment Management Partnership, since 2004; Chief Executive (formerly Executive Director), Atlantic Salmon Trust, since 2008; *b* 23 Dec. 1946; *s* of late Col Peter Edward Clinton Andrews and Jean Margaret Hamilton (*née* Cooke); *m* 1973, Alison Margaret Dudley Morgan; two *d* (one *s* decd). *Educ:* King's Sch., Worcester; Univ. of St Andrews (MA); UCNW, Bangor (Dip. TEFL). Served RM, 1964–71. Land agent, 1975–76; with British Council, 1976–2002: Kano, Nigeria, 1976–78; Belgrade, 1979–81; Muscat, Oman, 1981–85; Recife, Brazil, 1985–89; Director: Scotland, 1989–95; Russia and Central Asia, 1996–2000; Germany, 2000–02; Chief Exec., Scottish Countryside Alliance, 2002–08. *Recreations:* angling, river management, sailing, the arts. *Address:* Milton of Finavon House, by Forfar, Angus DD8 3PY. *T:* (01307) 850275; (office) King James VI Building, Friarton Road, Perth PH2 8DG. *T:* (01738) 472032. *Clubs:* Flyfishers'; New (Edinburgh).

ANDREWS, Rev. Canon Christopher Paul; Rector of Grantham, 1996–2013; Priest-in-charge, Grantham Manthorpe St John, 2010–13; Chaplain to the Queen, since 2009; *b* Leicester, 29 April 1947; *s* of Stephen James Andrews and Patricia Margaret Andrews (*née* Eyre); *m* 1975, Christine Helen Hawkins; one *s* one *d*. *Educ:* Brighton Grammar Sch., Melbourne; Bishop Wordsworth's Sch., Salisbury; Fitzwilliam Coll., Cambridge (BA 1970; MA 1973); Westcott House, Cambridge. Ordained deacon, 1972, priest, 1973; Assistant Curate: St John the Baptist, Croydon, 1972–75; All Saints', Gosforth, Newcastle upon Tyne, 1975–78; Team Vicar, Kingston Park, Newcastle upon Tyne, 1978–87; Rural Dean, Newcastle Central, 1982–87; Vicar of Alnwick, 1987–96. Canon and Preb., Lincoln Cathedral, 2004–13. Mem. Cttee, Egypt Diocesan Assoc. Volunteer, Embrace the Middle East. *Recreations:* walking, gardening, reading, music and singing, drawing and watercolour painting, Arabic and Islamic faith and culture of Islam. *Address:* 74 Daisy Avenue, Bury St Edmunds, Suffolk IP32 7PH. *T:* (01284) 723785.

ANDREWS, David; Member of the Dáil (TD) (FF) for Dún Laoghaire, 1965–2002; Minister for Foreign Affairs, Republic of Ireland, 1997–2000; *b* 15 March 1935; *s* of Christopher Andrews and Mary Coyle; *m* Annette Cusack; two *s* three *d*. *Educ:* Coláiste Mhuire, Christian Brothers' Sch.; Cistercian College, Roscrea; University College Dublin (BCL). Called to the Bar, King's Inns, 1962; Senior Counsel. Parly Sec. to Taoiseach, and Govt Chief Whip, 1970–73; opposition frontbench spokesman on justice and social welfare, 1973–77; Minister of State: Dept of Foreign Affairs, 1977–79; Dept of Justice, 1978–79; Minister: for Foreign Affairs, 1992–93; for Defence and the Marine, 1993–94; opposition spokesman on tourism and trade, 1995–97; Minister for Defence, 1997. Member: Cttee on the Constitution, 1967; New Ireland Forum, 1983–84. Mem., British-Irish Interparly Body, 1990–92. Hon. FRCPI 2010. Chevalier, Légion d'Honneur, 2006. *Recreations:* fly fishing, walking, theatre.

ANDREWS, Prof. David John, PhD; FREng, FIMechE; FRINA; Professor of Engineering Design, Department of Mechanical Engineering, University College London, since 2000; *b* 9 Aug. 1947; *m* 1970, Philippa Vanette Whitehurst; one *s* one *d*. *Educ:* Stationers' Co. Sch.; University Coll. London (BSc Eng 1970; MSc 1971; PhD 1984). FRINA 1987; FREng 2000; FIMechE 2002. RCNC Cadetship, 1965; Constructor Lieut, RCNC, 1971; Ministry of Defence: professional design on in-service and new build submarines, Submarine Design Section, Ship Dept, Bath, 1972–75; Constructor Grade, working on Invincible carrier design and subseq. Forward Design Gp, 1975–80; Lectr in Naval Architecture, UCL, 1980–84; Ministry of Defence: Hd, Trident Submarine Hull Design Section, Bath, 1984–86; Hd, Amphibious Gp (Chief Constructor), Replacement Amphibious Shipping Prog., 1986–90; Hd, Concept Design Div., Future Projects (Naval), Whitehall, 1990–93; Prof. of Naval

Architecture, UCL, 1993–98; Dir, Frigates and Mine Countermeasures, Defence Procurement Agency, then Integrated Project Team Leader, Future Surface Combatant, MoD, Bristol, 1998–2000. Royal Institution of Naval Architects: Chm., Membership Cttee, 1993–2000; Chm., Future Directions Cttee, 2000–; Vice Pres., 2005–; Mem. Council, Exec. Cttee and Bd of Trustees, 2005–; Vice Chm., Council, 2010–12. Mem., Panel 28, 2008 RAE. FRSA 1996. Dep. Ed., Internat. Jl of Maritime Engrg, 2008–. *Publications:* Synthesis in Ship Design (thesis), 1984; (contrib.) Finite Element Methods Applied to Thin Walled Structures, 1987; (contrib.) Technology and Naval Combat in the Twentieth Century and Beyond, 2001; (contrib.) Ship Design and Construction, 2004; (contrib) The Royal Institution of Naval Architects, 1860–2010, 2010; (contrib.) Dreadnought to Daring, 2013; contrib. numerous papers on ship design published by RINA, Royal Soc., etc, and in conf. proc. *Recreations:* painting and sketching, reading, cinema and theatre going, re-exploring London with my wife. *Address:* Department of Mechanical Engineering, University College London, Torrington Place, WC1E 7JE. *T:* (020) 7679 3874. *E:* d_andrews@meng.ucl.ac.uk.

ANDREWS, David Roger Griffith, CBE 1981; Chairman, Gwion Ltd, 1986–95; *b* 27 March 1933; *s* of C. H. R. Andrews and G. M. Andrews; *m* 1963, Dorothy Ann Campbell; two *s* one *d*. *Educ:* Abingdon Sch.; Pembroke Coll., Oxford (MA). FCMA. Pirelli-General, 1956–59; Ford Motor Company, 1960–69: Controller: Product Engrg, 1965–66; Transmission and Chassis Div., 1967; European Sales Ops, 1967–69; Asst Controller, Ford of Europe, 1969; BLMC: Controller, 1970; Finance Dir, Austin Morris, 1971–72; Man. Dir, Power and Transmission Div., 1973–75; British Leyland Ltd: Man. Dir, Leyland International, 1975–77; Exec. Vice Chm., BL Ltd, 1977–82; Chm., Leyland Gp and Land Rover Gp, 1981–82; Chm. and Chief Exec., Land Rover-Leyland, 1982–86. Director: Clarges Pharmaceutical Trustees Ltd, 1983–91; Glaxo Trustees Ltd, 1983–91; Ex-Cell-O Ltd, 1987–88; Foundn for Sci. and Technology, 1990–95 (Mem. Council, 1990–95, and Hon. Treas., 1990–95; Foundn Medal, 1996). Member: CBI Council, 1981–86; Exec. Cttee, SMMT, 1981–86; Open Univ. Visiting Cttee, 1982–85. FRSA. *Recreation:* reading.

ANDREWS, Sir Derek (Henry), KCB 1991 (CB 1984); CBE 1970; Permanent Secretary, Ministry of Agriculture, Fisheries and Food, 1987–93, retired; Chairman, Residuary Milk Marketing Board, 1994–2002; *b* 17 Feb. 1933; *s* of late Henry Andrews and Emma Jane Andrews; *m* 1st, 1956, Catharine May (*née* Childe) (*d* 1982); two *s* one *d*; 2nd, 1991, Alison Margaret Blackburn, OBE, *d* of Sir William Nield, GCMG, KCB. *Educ:* LSE (BA (Hons) 1955). Ministry of Agriculture, Fisheries and Food: Asst Principal, 1957; Asst Private Sec. to Minister of Agriculture, Fisheries and Food, 1960–61; Principal, 1961; Asst Sec., 1968; Private Sec. to Prime Minister, 1966–70; Harvard Univ., USA, 1970–71; Under-Sec., 1973; Dep. Sec., 1981. FRGS. *Clubs:* Reform; Aldeburgh Yacht.

ANDREWS, Finola Mary Lucy; *see* O'Farrell, F. M. L.

ANDREWS, Hon. Dame Geraldine (Mary), DBE 2013; **Hon. Mrs Justice Andrews;** a Judge of the High Court of Justice, Queen's Bench Division, since 2013; *b* 19 April 1959; *d* of Walter and Mary Andrews. *Educ:* King's Coll. London (LLB 1st Cl. Hons 1980, LLM 1982; AKC; Dip.). Called to the Bar, Gray's Inn, 1981, Bencher, 2004; barrister, 1983–2013, specialising in commercial law, esp. banking; called to Irish Bar, 1993; QC 2001; a Recorder, 2001–13; a Dep. High Ct Judge, 2006–13. *Publications:* (with S. Gee) Mareva Injunctions, 1988; (with R. Millett) The Law of Guarantees, 1992, 7th edn 2015. *Recreations:* keen violinist, theatre, music, sport, reading, learning modern languages. *Address:* Royal Courts of Justice, Strand, WC2A 2LL. *T:* (020) 7947 7303.

ANDREWS, Gillian Margaret, FSA; President, Society of Antiquaries of London, since 2014; *b* Manchester, 19 April 1953; *d* of Harold Victor Walker and Margaret Esther Walker; *m* 1978, Richard Duncan Andrews; two *d*. *Educ:* Kendal High Sch. for Girls; Univ. of Bristol (BA Archaeol., Ancient Hist. and Latin); Hughes Hall, Cambridge (PGCE). MCIfA (MIfA 1982); FSA 2002. Finds Officer, Central Excavation Unit, DoE, 1976–84; Archaeol and cultural heritage consultant, 1984–2015. *Recreations:* Lake District mountains, South Coast beach hut. *Address:* 4 Beechworth Road, Havant, Hants PO9 1AX. *E:* gill.andrews@virgin.net.

ANDREWS, Sir Ian (Charles Franklin), Kt 2007; CBE 1992; TD 1989; senior consultant to organisations in public and third sectors and academia; Chairman, Serious Organised Crime Agency, 2009–13; *b* 26 Nov. 1953; *s* of Peter Harry Andrews and Nancy Gwladys Andrews (*née* Franklin); *m* 1985, Moira Fraser McEwan; two *s* one *d*. *Educ:* Solihull Sch.; Univ. of Bristol (BSc Social Sci.). Joined Ministry of Defence, 1975: Private Sec. to 2nd Perm. Under Sec. of State, 1979–81; short service volunteer commn, RRF, 1981–82; Principal, 1982; NATO Defence Coll., 1984–85; Asst Private Sec. to Sec. of State for Defence, 1986–88; Head: Defence Lands, 1988–90; Resources and Prog. (Army), 1990–93; Civil Sec., British Forces Germany/BAOR, 1993–95; Man. Dir (Facilities), DERA, 1995–97; Chief Exec., Defence Estates Agency, 1998–2002; Second Perm. Under-Sec. of State, MoD, 2002–08. Non-exec. Dir, Health and Social Care Inf. Centre, 2013–. Conservator, Wimbledon and Putney Commons, 2009–; Trustee, Chatham Historic Dockyard, 2010–. Served TA in rank of Major, 1972–93. FRGS 1996. *Recreations:* travel, ski-ing.

ANDREWS, Prof. John Albert, CBE 2000; Pro Chancellor, University of South Wales (formerly University of Glamorgan), since 2005 (Member, Board of Governors, since 2002; Vice Chairman, 2005–08; Chairman, 2008–13); *b* 29 Jan. 1935; *s* of late Arthur George Andrews and Hilda May Andrews (*née* Banwell); *m* 1960, Elizabeth Ann Mary Wilkes; two *d*. *Educ:* Newport High Sch.; Wadham Coll., Oxford (MA, BCL). Called to the Bar, Gray's Inn, 1960, Bencher, 1991. Asst Lectr, Univ. of Manchester, 1957–58; Lectr in English Law, Univ. of Birmingham, 1958–67; University College of Wales, Aberystwyth: Prof. of Law, 1967–92; Hon. Prof., 1992–2000; Emeritus Prof., 2000–; Head of Dept of Law, 1970–92; Vice-Principal, 1985–88. Chief Exec., FEFCW and HEFCW, 1992–2000; Chm., Gen. Teaching Council for Wales, 2000–04. Visiting Professor: Thessaloniki, 1974, 1990; Cracow, 1978; Maryland, 1983. Former chm. or mem., numerous educnl, police and adv. bodies; Member: Police Trng Council, 1987–2002 (Academic Advr, 1997–2002); Lord Chancellor's Adv. Cttee on Legal Educn, 1987–90; Welsh Econ. Council, 1994–96; Criminal Injuries Compensation Appeals Panel, 2000–06; Police Skills and Standards Orgn, 2001–04; Police Accreditation and Licensing Bd, 2002–06; Justice Sector Skills Council, Policing Cttee, 2004–06; Actuarial Profession Disciplinary Panel, 2004–13; Practice Assce Cttee, CIPFA, 2007–14; Chairman: Council of Validating Universities, 1987–90 (Vice Chm., 1982–87); Police Promotions Exams Bd, 1987–2002; Agricl Wages Bd, 1999–2003. Member Council: Cardiff Univ., 2000–08; Univ. of Wales Coll. of Medicine, 2000–04; Member, Court of Governors: Univ. of Wales, 1969–92, 2001–04; Nat. Liby of Wales, 1979–92; Member, Board of Governors: Penglais Sch., 1974–80; Llanishen High Sch., 2005– (Chm., 2010–14); Mem., Bd of Dirs, Royal Welsh Coll. of Music and Drama, 2006–14. Hon. Fellow: Univ. of Wales Coll., Newport, 2000; Cardiff Univ., 2008. Trustee: SLS (formerly SPTL), 1990–2004 (Pres., SPTL, 1988–89); Hamlyn Trust, 1969–2000; AHRB, 2001–05. Mem., Welsh Cttee, Action for Children (formerly NCH), 2004–10. FRSA 1992; FLSW 2014. JP N Ceredigion, 1975–91. Editor, Legal Studies, 1981–93. *Publications:* (ed) Welsh Studies in Public Law, 1970; (ed) Human Rights in Criminal Procedure, 1982; (with L. G. Henshaw) The Welsh Language in the Courts, 1984; (with W. D. Hines) Keyguide to the International Protection of Human Rights, 1987; (with D. M. Hirst) Criminal Evidence, 1987, 3rd edn 1997; Criminal Evidence: statutes and materials, 1990; contribs to legal and educnl books and jls. *Recreations:* walking, theatre, food, opera. *Address:* The Croft, 110 Mill Road, Lisvane, Cardiff CF14 0UG. *T:* (029) 2075 3980; c/o Office of the Vice-Chancellor, University of South Wales, Pontypridd CF37 1DL. *T:* (01443) 482001. *Clubs:* Brynamlwg (Aberystwyth); Cardiff and County.

ANDREWS, Rev. John Robert; General Secretary, Professional Association of Teachers, 1992–97 (Assistant General Secretary, 1982–91); Local Minister, Parish of Farewell, Diocese of Lichfield, 2004–10; *b* 15 June 1942; *s* of late John Henry Andrews, ERD, MA, FCCA, and Marjorie Andrews (*née* Kirkman); *m* 1966, Minna D. L. Stevenson; two *d*. *Educ:* Nottingham High Sch.; Nottingham Coll. of Educn (CertEd 1963). ACP 1973; FCollP 1982; DipSMS 1982. Teacher in primary and secondary schs, 1963–72; Headteacher, Birmingham LEA, 1972–81; Professional Association of Teachers: Mem. Council, 1972–81; Chairman: Educn Cttee, 1975–77; Pay and Conditions Cttee, 1977–81. Mem., Council, Managerial and Professional Staffs, later Managerial and Professional Staffs Assoc., 1988–2000 (Pres., 1990–92; Chm., 1997–2000). Mem., Econ. and Social Cttee, EU, 1994–98. Chm., Ind. Unions Trng Council, 1989–96; Vice-Pres., European Confedn of Ind. Trade Unions, 1992–94; Bd Mem., 1994–2002, Treas., 1996–2002, Confédération Européenne des Cadres; Bd Mem. and Treas., Eur. Managers Inst., 2000–02; Chartered Management Institute: Chm., 2001–04, Pres., 2004–08, Derby Br.; Mem., Chartered Manager Assessment Panel, 2002–08. Mem., Schs Orgn Cttee for Staffordshire, 1999–2010. Dir, GTC (England & Wales) Trust, 1992–99. Member: Lichfield Deanery Synod, 1970–2004; Lichfield Diocesan Synod, 1979–2003; Exec. Cttee, Lichfield Diocesan Bd of Finance, 1987–2003; Lichfield Diocesan Bd of Educn, 1998–2010 (Chm. Cttee for Mgt and Finance of Dio. Schs, 1998–2010; Mem. Exec. Cttee, 2001–10); Bishop's Council, 1999–2003; Reader, Lichfield Diocese (Gentleshaw and Farewell), 1967–2004. Ordained deacon, 2004, priest, 2005. Mem., Parish Council, Longdon, Staffs, 1973–2011 (Chm., 1991–93, 2003–06). Governor, Gentleshaw Sch., 1993–97, 1999–2010 (Chm. Govs, 1996–97, 2006–10, Vice-Chm., 2004–06). FCMI (FIMgt 1992; MBIM 1982); FRSA 1992. *Publications:* (contrib.) Butterworth's Law of Education, 1997; contribs to various jls on multi-cultural educn, general educnl issues and educn law. *Recreation:* listening to music. *Address:* Footherley Hall, Shenstone, nr Lichfield, Staffs WS14 0HG. *T:* (01543) 480253.

ANDREWS, Dame Julie (Elizabeth), DBE 2000; actress; *b* 1 Oct. 1935; *m* 1st, Anthony J. Walton (marr. diss. 1968); one *d*; 2nd, 1969, Blake Edwards (*d* 2010); one step *s* one step *d*, and two adopted *d*. *Educ:* Woodbrook Girls' Sch., Beckenham and private governess. Appeared in The Boy Friend, NY, 1954; My Fair Lady: New York, 1956, London, 1958; Camelot, New York, 1960; Victor/Victoria, New York, 1995; directorial début, The Boy Friend, Bay Street Th., NY, 2003; The Gift of Music, 0_2 Arena, 2010. *Films:* (Walt Disney) Mary Poppins, 1963 (Academy Award, 1964); Americanisation of Emily, 1964; Sound of Music, 1964; Hawaii, 1965; Torn Curtain, 1966; Thoroughly Modern Millie, 1966; Star, 1967; Darling Lili, 1970; The Tamarind Seed, 1973; "10", 1980; Little Miss Marker, 1980; S.O.B., 1981; Victor/Victoria, 1982; The Man Who Loved Women, 1983; Duet for One, 1987; That's Life, 1987; Relative Values, 2000; The Princess Diaries, 2001; The Princess Diaries II, 2004; Shrek II, 2004; Shrek III, 2007; Enchanted, 2007; The Tooth Fairy, 2010; *television:* Cinderella, 1957; Julie & Carol at Carnegie Hall, 1961; An Evening with Julie Andrews and Harry Belafonte, 1969; Julie & Carol at Lincoln Center, 1971; The Julie Andrews Hour, 1972–73 (7 Emmy Awards); Julie & Dick at Covent Garden, 1973–74; Julie & Jackie—How Sweet it is, 1973–74; Julie & Perry & The Muppets, 1973–74; My Favourite Things, 1975; The Puzzle Children, 1976; ABC's Silver Anniversary Celebration, 1978; Julie Andrews… One Step into Spring, 1978; The Sound of Christmas (Emmy Award), 1987; Julie & Carol Together Again, 1989; Great Performances Live in Concert, 1990; Our Sons, 1991; The Julie Show, 1992; One Special Night, 1999; On Golden Pond, 2001; Eloise at the Plaza, 2003; Eloise at Christmastime, 2003. *Publications:* (as Julie Andrews Edwards) Mandy, 1972; Last of the Really Great Whangdoodles, 1973; Little Bo, 1999; Little Bo in France, 2002; (with Emma Walton Hamilton): Dumpy the Dump Truck, 2000; Dumpy at School, 2000; Dumpy Saves Christmas, 2001; Dumpy and His Pals; Dumpy's Friends on the Farm; Dumpy and the Big Storm, 2002; Dumpy and the Firefighters, 2003; Dumpy's Apple Shop, 2004; Dumpy's Happy Holiday, 2005; Dumpy's Valentine, 2008; Dumpy's Extra-Busy Day, 2008; Simeon's Gift, 2003; Dragon, 2004; The Great American Mousical, 2006; Thanks to You: wisdom from mother and child, 2007; Julie Andrews' Collection of Poems, Songs and Lullabies, 2010; The Very Fairy Princess, 2010; (as Julie Andrews) Home: a memoir of my early years, 2008. *Recreations:* gardening, boating, writing.

ANDREWS, Hon. Kevin James; MHR (L) Menzies, Victoria, since 1991; *b* Sale, Vic, Australia, 9 Nov. 1955; *s* of Roy Gebhardt Andrews and Sheila Andrews; *m* 1979, Margaret; three *s* two *d*. *Educ:* Rosedale Primary Sch.; St Patrick's Coll., Sale; Univ. of Melbourne (BA, LLB); Monash Univ. (LLM). Res. solicitor, 1980–81, Co-ordinator, Contg Legal Educn, 1981–83, Law Inst. of Vic; Associate to Hon. Sir James Gobbo, Supreme Court of Vic, 1983–85; in practice as barrister, 1985–91. Minister: of Ageing, 2001–03; for Employment and Workplace Relns, 2003–07; for Immigration and Citizenship, 2007; for Social Services, 2013–14; for Defence, 2014–15. *Publications:* Maybe 'I do': modern marriage and the pursuit of happiness, 2012. *Recreations:* cycling, horse racing. *Address:* Parliament House, Canberra, ACT 2600, Australia. *T:* (02) 62777800.

ANDREWS, Leighton Russell; Member (Lab) Rhondda, National Assembly for Wales, since 2003; *b* 11 Aug. 1957; *s* of Len and Peggy Andrews; *m* 1996, Ann Beynon, *qv*; one step *s* one step *d*. *Educ:* University Coll. of N Wales, Bangor (BA Hons English and Hist.); Univ. of Sussex (MA Hist.). Vice-Pres., NUS, 1980–81; Parly Officer, Age Concern, 1982–84; Campaign Dir, Internat. Year of Shelter, 1984–87; Dir, then Man. Dir, Sallingbury Casey, subseq. Rowland Sallingbury Casey, 1988–93; Hd, Public Affairs, BBC, 1993–96; Chm., Political Context, 1996–99; Dir, then Man. Dir, Westminster Strategy, 1999–2001; Man. Dir, Smart Co., 2001–02; Lectr, Sch. of Journalism, Cardiff Univ., 2002–03. Vis. Prof., Univ. of Westminster, 1997–; Hon. Prof., Cardiff Univ., 2004–. Welsh Government: Dep. Minister for Social Justice and Public Service Delivery, 2007, for Regeneration, 2007–09; Minister for Children, Educn and Lifelong Learning, then for Educn and Skills, 2009–13; Minister for Public Services, 2014–. *Publications:* Wales Says Yes, 1999; Ministering to Education, 2014; contrib. various articles and chapters. *Recreations:* watching Cardiff City FC, winding up nationalists, music, cinema, theatre, reading literature, history and political biography. *Address:* National Assembly for Wales, Cardiff Bay, Cardiff CF99 1NA. *T:* 0300 200 7119. *E:* leighton.andrews@assembly.wales.

ANDREWS, Mark Björnsen; Partner (formerly Deputy Chairman), SNR Denton UK LLP (formerly Denton Wilde Sapte), solicitors, 2000–11; Consultant, Dentons UKMEA LLP (formerly SNR Denton UK), 2011–13; *b* 12 July 1952; *s* of Harry Field Andrews and Ruth Margaret Andrews (*née* Legge). *Educ:* Reading Grammar Sch.; Hertford Coll., Oxford (BA Jurisp.). Articled Clerk, Clarks, solicitors, Reading, 1974–76; Wilde Sapte, subseq. Denton Wilde Sapte: Asst Solicitor, 1976–79; Partner, 1979–2000; Head of Insolvency Gp, 1989–2000; Sen. Partner, 1996–2000; Head, Restructuring and Insolvency Gp, 2000–10. Non-exec. Dir, Healthcare Locums plc, 2011–13; Sen. Ind. Dir, Zolfo Cooper LLP, 2013–; Dir, AI Scheme Ltd, 2014–. Chairman of Trustees: Pimlico Opera, 1991–2015; Grange Park Opera Endowment Fund, 2005–14; Trustee: Dulwich Picture Gall., 2012–; The Crescent, 2013–. *Recreations:* music, art, history, ornithology, walking. *E:* m.bjornsen@hotmail.com.

ANDREWS, Nigel John; Film Critic, Financial Times, since 1973; *b* 3 April 1947; *s* of Francis Yardley Andrews and Marguerite Joan Andrews. *Educ:* Lancing Coll., Sussex; Jesus Coll., Cambridge (MA English). Contributor and reviewer, Sight and Sound and Monthly Film Bulletin, 1969–73; Asst Ed., Cinema One books and Sight and Sound mag., 1972–73; regular broadcaster, BBC Radio; writer and presenter, Kaleidoscope, Radio 4, and other arts programmes, 1975–. Mem., BFI, 1971–. Critic of Year, British Press Awards, 1985, 2002. FRSA 2002. *Publications:* (contrib.) The Book of the Cinema, 1979; Horror Films, 1985; True Myths: the life and times of Arnold Schwarzenegger, 1995; Travolta: the life, 1998; Jaws, 1999. *Address:* c/o Curtis Brown, Haymarket House, 28–29 Haymarket, SW1Y 4SP.

ANDREWS, Peter John; QC 1991; a Recorder of the Crown Court, 1990–2012; a Deputy High Court Judge, Queen's Bench Division, 1998–2012; *b* 14 Nov. 1946; *s* of Reginald and Dora Andrews; *m* 1976, Ann Chavasse; two *d. Educ:* Bishop Vesey's Grammar Sch.; Bristol Univ. (Undergraduate Scholar; LLB); Christ's Coll., Cambridge (DCrim). Called to the Bar, Lincoln's Inn (Hardwicke Scholar), 1970, Bencher, 1999; barrister specialising in catastrophic personal injury and clinical negligence litigation; Junior, Midland and Oxford Circuit, 1973–74; Asst Recorder, 1986–90. Chm., Fountain Court Chambers (Birmingham) Ltd, 1994–2004; Head of Chambers, 199 Strand, 1997–2000. Mem., Professional Conduct Cttee, GMC, 2001–12; Legal Mem., Mental Health Rev. Tribunals, 2007–. Contributing Ed. and Mem., Editl Bd, The Quantum of Damages, 2004–12. *Publications:* Catastrophic Injuries: a guide to compensation, 1997; (contrib.) Personal Injury Handbook, 1997, 3rd edn 2005; (contrib.) Kemp and Kemp, The Quantum of Damages, 1998–; (contrib.) Guide to Catastrophic Injury Claims, 2010.

ANDREWS, Robert Graham M.; *see* Marshall-Andrews.

ANDREWS, Rt Rev. Rodney Osborne; Bishop of Saskatoon, 2004–10; *b* 11 Nov. 1940; *s* of George William Andrews and Mary Isabel (*née* Smith); *m* 1990, Jacqueline Plante; one *s* one *d. Educ:* Univ. of Saskatchewan (BA 1963); Coll. of Emmanuel and St Chad, Saskatoon (BTh 1965; MDiv 1981). Ordained deacon, 1964, priest, 1965; parish work and native ministry, Dio. Calgary, 1965–84; parish work and military chaplaincy, Dio. Montreal, 1984–87; parish work, Dio. Ottawa, 1988–91; Exec. Archdeacon, Dio. Algoma, 1991–2000; Rector of St Alban's, Richmond, and Univ. Chaplain: UBC, Dio. New Westminster, BC, 2000–03; Royal Canadian Mounted Police, 2011–. Columnist, Country Guide, Canada's nat. farm mag., 1994–. Holds airline transport pilot's licence, Canada. Hon. DD Coll. of Emmanuel and St Chad, Saskatoon, 2009. Medal commemorating 100th anniv. of treaty betw. southern Alberta native tribes and Queen Victoria, 1977; Saskatchewan Centennial Medal, 2006. *Recreations:* flying, curling, camping. *Address:* 310 Kutz Court, Saskatoon, SK S7N 4S4, Canada.

ANDREWS, Maj. Gen. Stephen Michael, CBE 2001 (MBE 1992); CEng, FIET; thought leader enabling people and organisations to succeed, since 2012; Executive Director, Hamad Medical Corporation, Qatar, since 2012; *b* Plymouth, 8 Jan. 1957; *s* of Gordon James Andrews and Monica Marion Andrews (*née* Mansfield); *m* 1988, Kim Victoria White; two *s* one *d. Educ:* Ravensbourne Sch.; Welbeck Coll.; RMA, Sandhurst; Pembroke Coll., Cambridge (MA 1981). CEng 1993; MIET (MIEE 1993), FIET 2009. Joined Army, 1975; commnd REME, 1976; served UK and BAOR, 1976–88; Staff Coll., Camberley, 1989; DCOS 22 Armd Bde, 1990–91; OC 3 Field Workshop, 1992–94; jsdc 1994; Mem. Directing Staff, RMCS, 1995–96; CO, 3 Bn REME, 1996–98; Col Army Discipline Policy, 1999–2001; rcds 2002; Director: Personal Services (Army), 2003–06; Personnel Strategy, MoD, 2006–09; Dir, Strategy and Change, Defence Medical Services, 2009–12. Col Comdt, REME, 2010–. Trustee, ABF, 2007–12. Patron, Defence Medical Welfare Service, 2012–. FRSA. *Recreations:* Wessex landscapes, running for pleasure, radio drama, crime fiction, Jane Austen. *Address:* c/o Corps Secretary, Regimental Headquarters Royal Electrical and Mechanical Engineers, MoD Lyneham, Lyneham, Chippenham SN15 9HB. *E:* stephenmandrews@btinternet.com.

ANDREWS, Stuart Morrison; Head Master of Clifton College, 1975–90; *b* 23 June 1932; *s* of William Hannaford Andrews and Eileen Elizabeth Andrews; *m* 1962, Marie Elizabeth van Wyk; two *s. Educ:* Newton Abbot Grammar Sch.; St Dunstan's Coll.; Sidney Sussex Coll., Cambridge (MA). Nat. service with Parachute Bde, 1952–53. Sen. History Master and Librarian, St Dunstan's Coll., 1956–60; Chief History Master and Librarian, Repton Sch., 1961–67; Head Master, Norwich Sch., 1967–75. Chm., Direct-grant Sub-cttee, HMC, 1974–75; Dep. Chm., Assisted Places Cttee, 1982–91; Nat. Rep., HMC, 1987–89; HMC Lead Inspector of Schs, 1994–96. Trustee, Glastonbury Abbey Develt Trust, 1992–96; Chm. Trustees and Managers, Wells & Mendip Mus., 1999–2004 (Hon. Librarian, 2004–). Chm., Emmott Foundn, 1999–2006. Editor, Conference, 1972–82. *Publications:* Eighteenth-century Europe, 1965; Enlightened Despotism, 1967; Methodism and Society, 1970; Rediscovery of America, 1998; British Periodical Press and the French Revolution, 2000; Unitarian Radicalism: political rhetoric 1770–1814, 2003; Irish Rebellion: Protestant polemic 1798–1900, 2006; Robert Southey: history, politics, religion, 2011; articles in various historical and literary jls. *Recreations:* walking, writing. *Address:* 34 St Thomas Street, Wells, Somerset BA5 2UX.

ANDREWS, William Denys Cathcart, CBE 1980; WS; Partner, Shepherd & Wedderburn, WS, Edinburgh, 1962–91; *b* 3 June 1931; *s* of Eugene Andrews and Agnes Armstrong; *m* 1955, May O'Beirne; two *s* two *d. Educ:* Girvan High Sch.; Worksop Coll.; Edinburgh Univ. (BL). Served RASC, 1950–52. Law Society of Scotland: Mem. Council, 1972–81; Vice Pres., 1977–78; Pres., 1978–79. Examr in Conveyancing, Edinburgh Univ., 1974–77. Pt-time Mem., Lands Tribunal for Scotland, 1980–91. Fiscal to Soc. of Writers to HM Signet, 1987–91. *Recreation:* gardening. *Address:* Auchairne, Ballantrae, South Ayrshire KA26 0NX. *T:* (01465) 831344.

ANDRIESSEN, Prof. Frans, (Franciscus H. J. J.), Kt, Order of Dutch Lion; Grand Cross, Order of Orange-Nassau; LLD; Member, 1981–92, Vice-President, 1985–92, the European Commission (responsible for Competition, Agriculture and Fisheries and Trade and External Relations); *b* Utrecht, 2 April 1929; *m*; four *c. Educ:* Univ. of Utrecht (LLD). Served at Catholic Housing Institute, latterly as Director, 1954–72. Member: Provincial States of Utrecht, 1958–67; Lower House of the States-General (Netherlands Parliament), initially as specialist in housing matters, 1967–77; Chairman, KVP party in Lower House, 1971–77; Minister of Finance, Netherlands, 1977–80; Member, Upper House of States-General (Senate), 1980. Prof. of European Integration, Rijksuniversiteit, Utrecht, 1989–99, now Emeritus. Grand Cross: Order of Leopold II (Belgium); Order of Isabel the Catholic (Spain); Order of Merit (Austria); Order of the Falcon (Iceland); Order of the Finnish Lion (Finland). *Address:* H. Vaesgaarde 1, 1950 Kraainem, Belgium.

ANELAY OF ST JOHNS, Baroness *cr* 1996 (Life Peer), of St Johns in the county of Surrey; **Joyce Anne Anelay,** DBE 1995 (OBE 1990); PC 2009; JP; Minister of State, Foreign and Commonwealth Office, since 2014; Prime Minister's Special Representative on Preventing Sexual Violence in Conflict, since 2015; *b* 17 July 1947; *d* of late Stanley Charles Clarke and of Annette Marjorie Clarke; *m* 1970, Richard Alfred Anelay, *qv*. *Educ:* Merryhills Primary Sch., Enfield; Enfield Co. Sch.; Bristol Univ. (BA Hons Hist.); London Univ. Inst. of Educn (Cert Ed); Brunel Univ. (MA Public and Social Admin). Teacher, St David's Sch., Ashford, Middx, 1969–74; Voluntary Advr, Woking CAB, 1976–85 (Chm., 1988–93; Pres., 1996–). Member: Social Security Appeal Tribunal, 1983–96; Social Security Adv. Cttee for GB and NI, 1989–96. Opposition spokesman on agriculture, 1997–98, on culture, media and sport, 1998–2002, on Home Affairs, 2002–07; an Opposition Whip, 1997–98, Opposition Chief Whip, 2007–10, H of L; Captain of the Honourable Corps of Gentlemen at Arms (Govt Chief Whip in H of L), 2010–14. Mem., Procedure Cttee, 1997–2000, 2007–. Conservative Women's Committee: Chm., SE Area, 1987–90; Vice-Chm., SE Area Exec. Cttee, 1990–93; Chm., Nat. Cttee, 1993–96; Member: Nat. Union of Cons. Party, 1987–97 (Vice-Pres., 1996–97); Women's Nat. Commission, 1990–93. Trustee: UNICEF UK, 2004–07; Just a Drop, 2004–06. JP NW Surrey, 1985–97. Chm. Govs, Hermitage First and Middle Schs, 1981–88. FRSA 1991. Hon. DSocSc Brunel, 1997. *Recreations:* golf, reading. *Address:* House of Lords, SW1A 0PW. *Club:* Woking Golf.

ANELAY, Richard Alfred; QC 1993; a Recorder, since 1992; a Deputy High Court Judge, Family Division, since 1995; *b* 26 March 1946; *s* of late Maurice Alfred Anelay and Bertha Anelay; *m* 1970, Joyce Anne Clarke (*see* Baroness Anelay of St Johns). *Educ:* Dodmire Primary Sch., Darlington; Queen Elizabeth Grammar Sch., Darlington; Bristol Univ. (BA Classics and Philosophy); Council of Legal Educn. Called to the Bar, Middle Temple, 1970, Bencher, 2003; Asst Recorder, 1987. Hd of Chambers, 2006–13. Acting Deemster, 2007–09, Deemster, 2009–, I of M. Dir, Bar Mutual Indemnity Fund, 2005–13. Consulting Ed., Encyclopedia of Financial Provision in Family Matters, 1998–2014. Fellow, Internat. Acad. of Matrimonial Lawyers, 2008–. *Recreation:* golf. *Address:* 1 King's Bench Walk, Temple, EC4Y 7DB. *T:* (020) 7936 1500. *Club:* Woking Golf.

ANFOM, Emmanuel E.; *see* Evans-Anfom.

ANGEL, Anthony Lionel; Senior Partner, DLA Piper International, and Global Co-Chairman, DLA Piper, since 2011; *b* 3 Dec. 1952; *s* of William and Frances Angel; *m* 1975, Ruth Hartog; two *s. Educ:* Haberdashers' Aske's Sch., Elstree; Queens' Coll., Cambridge (MA). Admitted Solicitor, 1978. Linklaters: Articled Clerk, 1976; Partner, 1984–2008; Hd of Tax, 1994–98; Man. Partner, 1998–2007; Exec. Man. Dir and Hd of Europe, Middle East and Africa, Standard & Poor's, 2008–10; Chief Exec., Vantage Diagnostics Ltd, 2010–11. Vis. Prof., Cass Business Sch., 2011. Hon. DSc City, 2009. *Recreations:* golf, ski-ing, tennis, theatre. *Address:* DLA Piper UK LLP, 3 Noble Street, EC2V 7EE. *T:* (020) 7153 7500.

ANGEL, Gerald Bernard Nathaniel Aylmer; Senior District Judge, Family Division of the High Court, 1991–2004 (Registrar, 1980–90; District Judge, 1991); *b* 4 Nov. 1937; *s* of late Bernard Francis and Ethel Angel; *m* 1968, Lesley Susan Kemp; three *s* one *d* (and one *s* decd). *Educ:* St Mary's Sch., Nairobi; Inns of Court Sch. of Law. Served Kenya Regt, 1956–57. Called to Bar, Inner Temple, 1959, Bencher 1992; Advocate, Kenya, 1960–62; practice at Bar, 1962–80. Member: Judicial Studies Bd, 1989–90 (Mem., Civil and Family Cttee, 1985–90); Supreme Ct Procedure Cttee, 1990–95; Matrimonial Causes Rule Cttee, 1991; Family Proceedings Rule Cttee, 1991–2003. *Publications:* (ed) Industrial Tribunals Reports, 1966–78; (contrib.) Atkin's Court Forms (Adv. Editor), 1988–2003. *Recreations:* reading, walking. *Address:* Garden House, 12 Aylsham Road, North Walsham, Norfolk NR28 0BH. *T:* (01692) 402401.

ANGEL, Heather, FRPS, FBIPP; professional wildlife photographer, author and lecturer; *b* 21 July 1941; *d* of Stanley Paul Le Rougetel and Hazel Marie Le Rougetel (*née* Sherwood); *m* 1964, Martin Vivian Angel; one *s. Educ:* 14 schools in England and NZ; Bristol Univ. (BSc Hons (Zoology) 1962; MSc 1965). FRPS 1972; FBIPP 1974. Solo exhibitions: The Natural History of Britain and Ireland, Sci. Mus., 1981; Nature in Focus, Natural Hist. Mus., 1987; The Art of Wildlife Photography, Gloucester, 1989; Natural Visions, UK tour, 2000–04, Cairo, 2002, Kuala Lumpur, 2002, Beijing, 2003; Wild Kew, Royal Botanic Gdns, Kew, 2010; Haslemere Mus., 2012. Television: demonstrating photographic techniques, Me and My Camera I, 1981; Me and My Camera II, 1983; Gardener's World, 1983; Nature, 1984; Nocon on Photography, 1988. Led British Photographic Delegn to China, 1985. Photos used worldwide in books, magazines, on TV, advertising, etc, 1972–. Hon. (formerly Special Prof.), Dept of Life Sci., Nottingham Univ., 1994–. Hon. FRPS 1986 (Pres., 1984–86). Hon. DSc Bath, 1986. Hood Medal, RPS, 1975; Médaille de Salverte, Soc. Française de Photographie, 1984; Louis Schmidt Award, Biocommunications Assoc., 1998. *Publications:* Nature Photography: its art and techniques, 1972; All Colour Book of Ocean Life, 1975; Photographing Nature: Trees, 1975, Insects, 1975, Seashore, 1975, Flowers, 1975, Fungi, 1975; Seashore Life on Rocky Shores, 1975; Seashore Life on Sandy Beaches, 1975; Seashells of the Seashore, 1976; Wild Animals in the Garden, 1976; Life in the Oceans, 1977; Life in our Estuaries, 1977; Life in our Rivers, 1977; British Wild Orchids, 1977; The Countryside of the New Forest, 1977; The Countryside of South Wales, 1977; Seaweeds of the Seashore, 1977; Seashells of the Seashore, Book 1, 1978, Book 2, 1978; The Countryside of Devon, 1980; The Guinness Book of Seashore Life, 1981; The Natural History of Britain and Ireland, 1981; The Family Water Naturalist, 1982; The Book of Nature Photography, 1982; The Book of Close-up Photography, 1983; Heather Angel's Countryside, 1983; A Camera in the Garden, 1984; Close-up Photography, 1986; Kodak Calendar, The Thames, 1987; A View from a Window, 1988; Nature in Focus, 1988; Landscape Photography, 1989; Animal Photography, 1991; Kew: a world of plants, 1993; Photographing the Natural World, 1994; Outdoor Photography: 101 tips and hints, 1997; How to Photograph Flowers, 1998; Pandas, 1998; How to Photograph Water, 1999; Natural Visions, 2000; Giant Pandas, 2006; Puffins, 2007; Green China, 2008; Snow Monkeys, 2009; Living Dinosaurs, 2009; Heather Angel's Wild Kew, 2009; Exploring Natural China, 2010; Digital Outdoor Photography: 101 top tips, 2012; *for children:* Your Book of Fishes, 1972; The World of an Estuary, 1975; Fact Finder—Seashore, 1976; The World of a Stream, 1976; Fungi, 1979; Lichens, 1980; Mosses and Ferns, 1980. *Recreations:* exploring wilderness areas and photographing unusual aspects of animal behaviour, reading and writing haiku at airports and in planes. *W:* www.heatherangel.co.uk.

ANGEL, Prof. (James) Roger (Prior), FRS 1990; Regents' Professor of Astronomy, since 1990, Regents' Professor of Optical Sciences, and Director, Steward Observatory Mirror Laboratory, since 1985, University of Arizona; *b* 7 Feb. 1941; *s* of James Lee Angel and Joan Angel; *m* 1965, Ellinor M. Goonan; one *s* one *d. Educ:* St Peter's Coll., Oxford (Hon. Schol.; BA 1963; Hon. Fellow, 1993); Calif Inst. of Technology (MS 1966); DPhil Oxon 1967. Post Doctoral Assistant, then Asst Prof., later Associate Prof. of Physics, Columbia Univ., 1967–72; Alfred P. Sloan Res. Fellow, 1970–74; Associate Prof. and Prof. of Astronomy, Arizona Univ., 1973–90. Dir, Center for Astronomical Adaptative Optics, 1996–2011. Vice-Pres., Amer. Astronomical Soc., 1987–90 (Pierce Prize, 1976); Fellow, Amer. Acad. of Arts and Scis, 1990. MacArthur Fellow, John D. and Catherine T. MacArthur Foundn, 1996–2001. MNAS 2000. Kavli Prize in Astrophysics, 2010. *Publications:* numerous papers on white dwarf stars, quasars, the search for extra-solar planetary systems, astronomical mirrors, telescopes and their instruments, adaptive optics, geoengrg and current research in photovoltaic solar energy. *Recreation:* grandchildren. *Address:* Steward Observatory, University of Arizona, Tucson, AZ 85721–0065, USA. *T:* (520) 6216541.

ANGELINI, Prof. Gianni Davide, MD; FRCSGlas, FMedSci; British Heart Foundation Professor of Cardiac Surgery, Bristol Heart Institute, University of Bristol, since 1992; Director, Biomedical Research Unit for Cardiovascular Medicine, National Institute of Health Research, Bristol, since 2008; Professor of Cardiothoracic Surgery, Imperial College London, since 2010; *b* Murlo, Siena, 29 Jan. 1953; *s* of Marzio and Erina Angelini; *m* 1985, Rosalind Gwendolin John; three *s. Educ:* Istituto T Sarrochi, Siena (Dip. Mech. Engrg 1972); Univ. of Siena (MD 1979; Fellow in Thoracic Surgery 1984); Univ. of Wales Coll. of Medicine, Cardiff (MCh 1986). FRCSGlas 1986. Senior House Officer: Cardiothoracic Surgery, Llandough Hosp., Cardiff, 1981; Gen. Surgery, University Hosp. of Wales, Cardiff, 1981–82; Casualty/Accident, Royal Gwent Hosp., Newport, 1982–83; Registrar in Cardiothoracic Surgery, 1983–86, Sen. Registrar, 1986–88, University Hosp. of Wales, Cardiff; Sen. Registrar, Cardiothoracic Surgery, Thoraxcenter, Erasmus Univ., Rotterdam, 1988–89; Lectr and BHF Intermediate Res. Fellow in Cardiothoracic Surgery, University Hosp. of Wales, April–Oct. 1989; Sen. Lectr and Consultant in Cardiothoracic Surgery, Univ. of Sheffield, 1989–92. Sen. Investigator, NIHR, 2009–. FETCS 1998; FMedSci 2011. Cavaliere, Order of Merit (Italy) 2003. *Publications:* (jtly) Arterial Conduits in Myocardial

Revascularisation, 1995; contribs to jls incl. Lancet, Nature, Circulation, BMJ, Jl of Thoracic and Cardiovascular Surgery, Jl of the American Coll. of Cardiol. *Recreations:* running, tennis. *Address:* Bristol Heart Institute, Bristol Royal Infirmary, Bristol BS2 8HW. *T:* (0117) 928 3145; Hammersmith Hospital, Du Cane Road, W12 0HS. *E:* g.d.angelini@imperial.ac.uk.

ANGEST, Sir Henry, Kt 2015; Chairman and Chief Executive Officer, and Principal Shareholder, Arbuthnot Banking Group plc, since 1985; Chairman: Secure Trust Bank plc, since 1982; Arbuthnot Latham & Co. Ltd, since 1994; *b* Winterthur, Switzerland, 6 July 1940; *m* Dorothy Block; one *s* one *d*. *Educ:* Univ. of Basel, Switzerland (LLL). Nat. Service, Switzerland (1st Lieut (Intelligence and Mil. Court)) (pt-time), 1959–79. International Executive: Dow Chem. Co. and Dow Banking Corp., Zurich, Miami, Sao Paulo, Hong Kong, 1967–85. Chm., Banking Cttee, London Investment Banking Assoc., 1997–2009. Mem., Council and Bd, IoD, 1999–2004. Nat. Treas. and Banker, Cons. Party, 2000–. Patron: Royal Botanic Gdn, Edinburgh, 2001–; Royal Botanic Gdns, Kew, 2011–. Founder Fellow, RHS 2011. Hon. Fellow, Univ. of Highlands and Is, 2007. Master, Internat. Bankers' Co., 2008–09. *Recreations:* dendrology, farming, science, cosmology, politics. *Address:* Arbuthnot Banking Group plc, Arbuthnot House, 7 Wilson Street, EC2M 2SN. *T:* (020) 7012 2420. *E:* henryangest@arbuthnot.co.uk. *Clubs:* White's, 5 Hertford St, Mosimann's, Carlton.

ANGIOLINI, Rt Hon. Dame Elish (Frances), DBE 2011; PC 2006; Principal, St Hugh's College, Oxford, since 2012; *b* 24 June 1960; *d* of James McPhilomy and Mary McPhilomy (*née* Magill); *m* 1985, Domenico Angiolini; two *s*. *Educ:* Notre Dame Sch., Glasgow; Univ. of Strathclyde (LLB Hons; DipLP). Admitted solicitor, 1985; admitted Mem., Faculty of Advocates, 2008; Depute Procurator Fiscal, Airdrie; Mgt Services Gp, Crown Office; Sen. Depute Procurator Fiscal, Asst Procurator Fiscal 1995–97, Glasgow; with Crown Office, 1997–2000; Regl Procurator Fiscal, Grampian, Highlands and Is, 2000–01; QC (Scot.) 2001; Solicitor Gen. for Scotland, 2001–06; Lord Advocate, Scottish Exec., later Scottish Govt, 2006–11. Practising Mem., Terra Firma Chambers, 2011–. Vis. Prof., Univ. of Strathclyde, 2011–; Hon. Prof., Univ. of Aberdeen, 2011–. *Recreations:* travel, walking, picking wild mushrooms, cinema, eating out. *Address:* Terra Firma Chambers, Parliament House, Edinburgh EH1 1RF; St Hugh's College, St Margaret's Road, Oxford OX2 6LE.

ANGLE, Martin David, FCA; Chairman, National Exhibition Centre Group, since 2006; *b* London, 8 April 1950; *s* of Robert William Angle and Mary Angle; *m* 1977, Lindsey Blake (separated); two *s* one *d*. *Educ:* St Dunstan's Coll., London; Univ. of Warwick (BSc Hons). FCA 1975; MCSI 1992. Articled Clerk, Peat, Marwick, Mitchell & Co., London, 1972–76; Asst to Chief Exec., UAE Currency Bd, 1976–77; Dir, S G Warburg & Co. Ltd, 1978–88; Man. Dir, Morgan Stanley, 1988–92; Gp Dir, Kleinwort Benson, 1992–96; Gp Finance Dir, TI Gp plc, 1997–2000; Operational Man. Dir, Terra Firma Capital Partners, 2001–06. Non-executive Director: Savills plc, 2007–; OAO Severstal, 2007–15; Pennon Gp plc, 2008–; Shuaa Capital psc, 2009–. Vice Chm., Trustee and Treas., FIA Foundn, 2010–. Member: Governing Council, Univ. of Warwick, 2001–07; Adv. Bd, Warwick Business Sch., 2001–11. FRSA. *Recreations:* music and opera, mountain walking, historic motor racing, modern history, boating. *Address:* NEC Group, Birmingham B40 1NT. *T:* (0121) 767 3891. *E:* martindangle@aol.co.uk. *Club:* Royal Automobile.

ANGLESEY, 8th Marquess of, *cr* 1815; **Charles Alexander Vaughan Paget;** Baron Paget of Beaudesert 1549; Earl of Uxbridge 1784; Bt 1730; *b* 13 Nov. 1950; *s* of 7th Marquess of Anglesey and of Dowager Marchioness of Anglesey, *qv*; *S* father, 2013; *m* 1986, Georganne Elizabeth Elliott (marr. diss. 2011), *d* of Col John Alfred Downes, MBE, MC; one *s* one *d*. *Educ:* Dragon School, Oxford; Eton; Exeter Coll., Oxford; Sussex Univ. (MA, DPhil). *Heir:* *s* Earl of Uxbridge, *qv*. *Address:* Plâs-Newydd, Llanfairpwll, Gwynedd LL61 6DZ.

ANGLESEY, Dowager Marchioness of; (Elizabeth) Shirley Vaughan Paget, DBE 1983 (CBE 1977); LVO 1993; Member of Board, British Council, 1985–95 (Chairman, Drama and Dance Advisory Committee, 1981–91); Vice-Chairman, Museums and Galleries Commission, 1989–96 (Member, 1981–96); *b* 4 Dec. 1924; *d* of late Charles Morgan and Hilda Vaughan (both novelists); *m* 1948, 7th Marquess of Anglesey (*d* 2013); two *s* three *d*. *Educ:* Francis Holland Sch., London; St James', West Malvern; Kent Place Sch., USA. Personal Secretary to Gladwyn Jebb, FO, until marriage. Chm., Broadcasting Complaints Commn, 1987–91. Dep. Chm., Prince of Wales Cttee, 1970–80. Member: Civic Trust for Wales, 1967–76; Arts Council, 1972–81 (Chm., Welsh Arts Council, 1975–81); Royal Commn on Environmental Pollution, 1973–79; IBA, 1976–82; Radioactive Waste Management Adv. Cttee, 1981–92; Vice-Chm., Govt Working Party on Methods of Sewage Disposal, 1969–70. Chm., NFWI, 1966–69. A Vice-Pres., C&G, 1998– (Hon. FCGI 2003). Mem., Theatres Trust, 1992–95. Trustee, Pilgrim Trust, 1982–2001. Hon. Fellow, UCNW, Bangor, 1990. Hon. LLD Wales, 1977. *Address:* Plâs-Newydd, Llanfairpwll, Gwynedd LL61 6DZ. *T:* (01248) 714330.

See also R. H. V. C. Morgan.

ANGLIN, Prof. Douglas (George); Professor of Political Science, Carleton University, Ottawa, Canada, 1958–89, Adjunct Research Professor, 1989–93, Professor Emeritus, since 1993; *b* Toronto, Canada, 16 Dec. 1923; *s* of George Chambers Anglin, MD, and Ruth Cecilia Cale, MD; *m* 1948, Mary Elizabeth Watson; two *d*. *Educ:* Toronto Univ.; Corpus Christi and Nuffield Colls, Oxford Univ. BA Toronto; MA, DPhil Oxon. Lieut, RCNVR, 1943–45. Asst (later Associate) Prof. of Political Sci. and Internat. Relations, Univ. of Manitoba, Winnipeg, 1951–58; Associate Prof. (later Prof.), Carleton Univ., 1958–89. Vice-Chancellor, Univ. of Zambia, Lusaka, Zambia, 1965–69; Associate Research Fellow, Nigerian Inst. of Social and Economic Research, Univ. of Ibadan, Ibadan, Nigeria, 1962–63; Research Associate, Center of Internat. Studies, Princeton Univ., 1969–70. Canadian Association of African Studies: Pres., 1973–74; Distinguished Africanist Schol., 1989. Consultant, Educn for Democracy Prog., South African Council of Churches, Johannesburg, 1992–94. Hon. DLitt Zambia, 2011. *Publications:* The St Pierre and Miquelon Affaire of 1941: a study in diplomacy in the North Atlantic quadrangle, 1966, repr. 1999; Zambia's Foreign Policy: studies in diplomacy and dependence, 1979; Zambian Crisis Behaviour: confronting Rhodesia's unilateral declaration of independence 1965–1966, 1994; Confronting Rwandan Genocide: the military options, 2002; edited jointly: Africa: Problems and Prospects 1961; Conflict and Change in Southern Africa, 1978; Canada, Scandinavia and Southern Africa, 1978; articles on Internat. and African affairs in a variety of learned jls. *Address:* 302–43 Aylmer Avenue, Ottawa, Ontario K1S 5R4, Canada.

ANGLO, Margaret Mary, (Mrs Sydney Anglo); *see* McGowan, M. M.

ANGLO, Prof. Sydney, PhD; FBA 2005; Professor of the History of Ideas, 1981–86, Research Professor, 1986–99, now Professor Emeritus, University of Wales Swansea (formerly University College of Swansea); *b* 1 March 1934; *s* of Harry Anglo and Ray (*née* Pelter); *m* 1964, Margaret Mary McGowan, *qv*. *Educ:* Pinner Co. Grammar Sch.; London Sch. of Economics (BA 1955; PhD 1959). Sen. Res. Fellow, Univ. of Reading, 1958–61; Lectr in the Hist. of Ideas, 1961–69, Sen. Lectr, 1969–75, Reader, 1975–81, UC of Swansea. Sen. Fellow, Warburg Inst., 1970–71. Mem., Adv. Cttee, Ref. Div., BL, 1975–84. Sec., 1967–70, Chm., 1986–89, Soc. for Renaissance Studies. FSA 1965. Founding FLSW 2010. Lectr, Conférences Léopold Delisle, Bibliothèque nationale de France, 2010. Numerous contribs to BBC Radio; features include: The Leonardo Cylinders, 1989; The Big Fight Fiasco of 1467, 1992; Piping the Blues, 1992; The Great Snooker Final, 1994; Great Spy, Lousy Tapdancer, 1996; Cheese, 1997. Arms and Armour Soc. Medal, 2002. *Publications:* The Great Tournament Roll of Westminster, 1968; Spectacle, Pageantry and Early Tudor Policy, 1969, 2nd edn 1997; Machiavelli, a Dissection, 1969; La tryumphante Entrée de Charles Prince des Espagnes, 1974; (ed) The Damned Art: essays in the literature of witchcraft, 1977; (ed) Chivalry in the Renaissance, 1990; Images of Tudor Kingship, 1992; The Martial Arts of Renaissance Europe, 2000; Machiavelli - the First Century: studies in enthusiasm, hostility and irrelevance, 2005; L'escrime, la danse et l'art de la guerre: le livre et la représentation du mouvement, 2011; numerous contribs to learned jls, periodicals and collaborative vols. *Recreations:* telephone conversation with friends, listening to and reading about pianists past and present. *Address:* 59 Green Ridge, Brighton BN1 5LU. *Club:* East India.

ANGUS, Robert James Campbell; Social Security and Child Support Commissioner, 1995–2007; *b* 7 Feb. 1935; *s* of James Angus and Jessie Macrae Angus; *m* 1968, Jean Anne, *d* of Andrew and Jessie Martin. *Educ:* Shawlands Acad.; Univ. of Glasgow (BL 1957). Nat. service, RA, 1958–60. Admitted solicitor, Scotland, 1960; in private practice, 1960–71; Legal Asst, Office of Solicitor to Sec. of State for Scotland, 1972–74, Sen. Legal Asst, 1974; on secondment as Administrator, SHHD, 1974–78; Solicitor's Office, 1978–82; Inquiry Reporter, Scottish Office, 1982–84; Chairman: Social Security, Medical and Vaccine Damage Appeal Tribunals, 1984–95; Child Support Appeal Tribunals, 1992–95. *Recreations:* history, music, history and mechanics of pianos, rough gardening. *Address:* Hunter Gap, Keenley, Allendale, Northumberland NE47 9NT. *Club:* Royal Scots (Edinburgh).

ANGUS, Tracey Anne; QC 2012; *b* Amersham, 10 Jan. 1967; *d* of Athol James Angus and Roberta Anne Angus (*née* Scott); *m* 1997, John Simon Jones; one *s* one *d*. *Educ:* St George's Sch., Edinburgh; Rugby Sch.; Edinburgh Univ. (MA Hons English Lit.); City Univ. (DipLaw). Called to the Bar, Inner Temple, 1991. *Publications:* Inheritance Act Claims, 2007; (ed) Heywood & Massey Court of Protection Practice. *Address:* 5 Stone Buildings, Lincoln's Inn, WC2A 3XT. *T:* (020) 7242 6201.

ANHOLT, Trudy Frances Charlene; *see* Mackay, T. F. C.

ANKERSON, Dr Dudley Charles, CMG 2013; HM Diplomatic Service, retired; Managing Director, Latin Insight Consulting, since 2006; *b* Hereford, 4 Sept. 1948; *s* of Richard and Norah Ankerson; *m* 1973, Silvia Galicia Morales; one *s* one *d*. *Educ:* Hereford Cathedral Sch.; Sidney Sussex Coll., Cambridge (BA 1971; MA 1975; PhD 1982). Entered FCO, 1976; Second Sec., Buenos Aires, 1978–81; Falkland Is Dept, FCO, 1982–85; First Sec., Mexico City, 1985–88; Soviet and Eastern Europe Dept, FCO, 1988–93; Counsellor: Madrid, 1993–97; Budapest, 1998–2001; Permanent Under-Sec.'s Dept, FCO, 2001–06. Vis. Lectr, Univ. of San Luis Potosí, Mexico, 2008; Vis. Fellow, Latin American Centre, Cambridge Univ., 2009. Consultant: BP, Latin America, 2006–; British cos in Latin America, incl. Anglo-American, HSBC, Smiths Gp, G3, BG Gp, 2006–; Special Adviser: on Latin America to FCO, 2006–; to Mexican Govt, 2008–; to Govt of Colombia, 2011–. Participant in N American Tri-Lateral Commn, 2013. Mil. Medal, 1st Cl. (Hungary), 2000. *Publications:* Agrarian Warlord: Saturnino Cedillo and the Mexican Revolution in San Luis Potosí, 1984; La Memoria Viva del General Saturnino Cedillo, 2010; Caudillo Agrarista, 2011. *Recreations:* history (especially of Latin America), classical studies, family, travel, cinema, theatre, sport. *Address:* c/o Latin Insight Consulting, 11 Quernmore Road, Bromley, Kent BR1 4EH. *T:* (020) 8290 0386. *E:* Ankergal@aol.com. *Clubs:* Athenæum, MCC; Penguins Internat. Rugby Football.

ANNALY, 6th Baron *cr* 1863; **Luke Richard White;** a Lord in Waiting (Government Whip), 1994; *b* 29 June 1954; *o s* of 5th Baron Annaly and Lady Marye Isabel Pepys (*d* 1958), *d* of 7th Earl of Cottenham; *S* father, 1990; *m* 1983, Caroline Nina (marr. diss.), *yr d* of Col Robert Garnett, MBE; one *s* three *d*. *Educ:* Eton; RMA Sandhurst. Commnd Royal Hussars, 1974–78, RARO, 1978–86. Freeman, Haberdashers' Co., 1997. *Heir:* *s* Hon. Luke Henry White, *b* 20 Sept. 1990.

ANNAN, Kofi Atta, Hon. GCMG 2007; President, Kofi Annan Foundation, since 2007; Secretary-General, United Nations, 1997–2006; *b* 1938; *m*; one *s* two *d*. *Educ:* Univ. of Sci. and Technol., Kumasi, Ghana; Macalester Coll., St Paul, Minnesota, USA; Institut des Hautes Etudes Internationales, Geneva, Switzerland; MIT (Alfred P. Sloan Fellow, 1971–72). Various posts in UN, Addis Ababa and NY, and WHO, Geneva, 1962–71; Admin. Officer, UN, Geneva, 1972–74; Chief Civilian Personnel Officer, UNEF, Cairo, 1974; Man. Dir, Ghana Tourist Develt Co., 1974–76; Dep. Chief of Staff Services, 1976–80, Dep. Dir, Div. of Admin and Hd, Personnel Service, 1980–83, UNHCR, Geneva; UN, New York: Dir of Admin Mgt Services, then of Budget, 1984–87; Asst Sec.-Gen., Human Resources Mgt, 1987–90; Controller, Programme Planning, Budget and Finance, 1990–92; Under Sec.-Gen., 1993–95, Dept of Peace Keeping Ops; UN Special Envoy to former Yugoslavia, 1995–96. Pres., Global Humanitarian Forum, 2007–10. Vis. Prof., Lee Kuan Yew Sch. of Public Policy, Nat. Univ. of Singapore, 2010–. Chancellor, Univ. of Ghana, 2008–. Hon. DCL Oxford, 2001. Nobel Peace Prize, 2001. *Publications:* (with Elie Wiesel) Confronting Anti-Semitism (essays), 2006; Interventions: a life in war and peace, 2012. *Address:* Kofi Annan Foundation, PO Box 157, 1211 Geneva 20, Switzerland.

ANNANDALE AND HARTFELL, 11th Earl of, *cr* 1662 (S) with precedence to 1643; **Patrick Andrew Wentworth Hope Johnstone of Annandale and of that Ilk;** Earl of the territorial earldom of Annandale and Hartfell, and of the Lordship of Johnstone; Hereditary Steward of the Stewartry of Annandale; Hereditary Keeper of the Castle of Lochmaben; Chief of the Name and Arms of Johnstone; landowner; Vice-Lord Lieutenant, Dumfries and Galloway Region, districts of Nithsdale, Annandale and Eskdale, since 1992; *b* 19 April 1941; *s* of Major Percy Wentworth Hope Johnstone of Annandale and of that Ilk, TD (*d* 1983) (*de jure* 10th Earl) and Margaret Jane (*d* 1998), *d* of Herbert William Francis Hunter-Arundell; claim to earldom admitted by Committee for Privileges, House of Lords, 1985; *m* 1969, Susan Josephine, *d* of late Col Walter John Macdonald Ross, CB, OBE, MC, TD, Netherhall, Castle Douglas; one *s* one *d*. *Educ:* Stowe School; RAC, Cirencester. Member: Dumfries CC, 1970–75; Dumfries and Galloway Regional Council, 1974–86; Scottish Valuation Advisory Council, 1983–85. Director: Bowring Members Agency, 1985–88; Murray Lawrence Members Agency, 1988–92; Solway River Purification Bd, 1970–86; Raehills Farms Ltd, 1997–; Skairfield Ltd, 1998–; Maclay Gp plc, 2001–15; Dir and Trustee, River Annan Trust, 2010–; Chm., River Annan District Fishery Bd, 1988–2012. Chm., Royal Jubilee and Prince's Trusts for Dumfries and Galloway, 1984–88. Underwriting Member of Lloyds, 1976–2004. DL Nithsdale and Annandale and Eskdale, 1987. *Recreations:* golf, shooting. *Heir:* *s* Lord Johnstone, *qv*. *Address:* Annandale Estates Office, St Ann's, Lockerbie, Dumfriesshire DG11 1HQ. *Club:* Puffin's (Edinburgh).

ANNAS, Rt Rev. Geoffrey Peter; *see* Stafford, Bishop Suffragan of.

ANNESLEY, family name of **Earl Annesley** and **Viscount Valentia**.

ANNESLEY, 12th Earl *cr* 1789 (Ire.), of Castelwellan, co. Down; **Michael Robert Annesley;** Baron Annesley 1758; Viscount Glerawly 1766; *b* Egham, Surrey, 4 Dec. 1933; 3rd *s* of 9th Earl Annesley and Nora, *y d* of Walter Harrison; *S* brother, 2011; *m* 1956, Audrey Mary Goodwright (*d* 2013); two *s* one *d*. *Educ:* Sir Henry Strode's Sch., Egham; No 1 Sch. of Tech. Training, RAF Halton. RAF, 1949–73: aircraft engineer and aircrew, then Warrant Officer, retd. Flight simulator engineer and sen. installation mgr, 1976–91. *Recreation:* classic motorcycle racing. *Heir:* *er s* Viscount Glerawly, *qv*.

ANNESLEY, (Arthur) Noël (Grove); Hon. Chairman, Christie's UK (formerly Christie's International UK Ltd), since 2004; *b* 28 Dec. 1941; *s* of late E. P. Grove Annesley, OBE and Ruth, *d* of A. Norman Rushforth; *m* 1968, Caroline Lumley; two *s*. *Educ:* Harrow Sch.

(entrance schol.); Worcester Coll., Oxford (Open Schol. in classics; MA). Joined Christie Manson & Woods Ltd, fine art auctioneers, 1964; founded Dept of Prints, Drawings and Watercolours; auctioneer, 1967–; holds world records for Michelangelo and Leonardo da Vinci drawings and for British watercolours (J. M. W. Turner); authority on Old Master Drawings; discoveries incl. drawings by Michelangelo, Sebastiano del Piombo, Raphael and Rubens; Dep. Chm., 1985–91; Dir, Christie's Internat. plc, 1989–98 (Dep. Chm., 1992–98); Dep. Chm., Christie's Fine Art Ltd, 1998–2000; Chairman: Christie's Fine Art Specialist Gp, 2000–03; Christie's Educn, 2000–11. Mem. Adv. Panel, Nat. Heritage Meml Fund, 2006–12. Mem. Council, American Mus. in Britain, 1988–; Trustee: Villiers David Foundn, 1996–2009; Dulwich Picture Gall., 1999–2010 (Vice Chm., 2006–10); Yehudi Menuhin Sch., 2000– (Chm., Appeal Cttee to raise funds for concert hall, 2000–05); Michael Marks Charitable Trust, 2007–. *Publications:* contribs to specialist books and jls. *Recreations:* music (especially chamber), exploring classical sites, gardening. *Address:* c/o Christie's, 8 King Street, St James's, SW1Y 6QT. *T:* (020) 7389 2241. *Clubs:* Brooks's, Garrick, MCC.

ANNESLEY, Sir Hugh (Norman), Kt 1992; QPM 1986; Chief Constable, Royal Ulster Constabulary, 1989–96; *b* 22 June 1939; *s* of late William Henry Annesley and of Agnes Annesley (*née* Redmond); *m* 1970, Elizabeth Ann (*née* MacPherson); one *s* one *d*. *Educ:* St Andrew's Prep. Sch., Dublin; Avoca Sch. for Boys, Blackrock. Joined Metropolitan Police, 1958; Chief Supt, 1974; Police Staff College: Special Course, 1963; Intermed. Comd Course, 1971; Sen. Comd Course, 1975; Asst Chief Constable, Personnel and Ops, Sussex Police, 1976; RCDS 1980; Metropolitan Police, Deputy Assistant Commissioner: Central and NW London, 1981; Personnel, 1983; Dir, Force Re-organisation Team, 1984; Assistant Commissioner: Personnel and Training, 1985; Specialist Ops, 1987. Graduate: Nat. Exec. Inst., FBI, 1986; Mem. Exec. Cttee, Interpol (British Rep.), 1987–90, and 1993–94. Bd of Govs, Burgess Hill Sch. for Girls, 1997 (Chm. Govs, 2000–05). *Recreations:* hockey, sailing. *Address:* Brooklyn, 65 Knock Road, Belfast BT5 6LE.

ANNESLEY, Noël; *see* Annesley, A. N. G.

ANNETTS, Deborah Claire; Chief Executive, Incorporated Society of Musicians, since 2008; *b* 7 Oct. 1960; *d* of Robert John Annetts and Patricia Margaret Annetts; *m* 2008, Simon Thomsett. *Educ:* St Albans Girls' Grammar Sch.; St Hilda's Coll., Oxford (BA PPE 1983). Admitted solicitor, 1989; Hd, Employment Law, 1994–99, Partner, 1998–99, Stephens Innocent, solicitors; Partner and Hd, Employment Law, Tarlo Lyons, Solicitors, 1999–2000; Asst Dir, Public Concern at Work, 2000–01; Chief Executive: Voluntary Euthanasia Soc., subseq. Dignity in Dying, 2001–07; YWCA, 2007. Board Member: London Museums Agency, 2001–03; Medic Alert, 2003–07 (Vice Chair, 2005–07); Law Soc. Charity, 2003–09; Fair Trials International, 2008– (Chair, 2014–); Nat. Music Council, 2009–12; Music Educn Council, 2009– (Chm., 2010–13); NYO, 2011–13; Educnl Resource Agency, 2011– (Interim Chair, 2012–13; Chair, 2013–). *Recreations:* music, theatre, film, social history, tennis, yoga. *Address:* Incorporated Society of Musicians, 4/5 Inverness Mews, W2 3JQ.

ANNING, Raymon Harry, CBE 1982; QPM 1975; Commissioner of Police, The Royal Hong Kong Police Force, 1985–90; *b* 22 July 1930; *s* of Frederick Charles Anning and Doris Mabel Anning (*née* Wakefield); *m* 1949, Beryl Joan Boxall; one *s* (and one *d* decd). *Educ:* Richmond and East Sheen Grammar School. Army (East Surrey Regt and Royal Military Police), 1948–50. Metropolitan Police, 1952–79: Constable to Chief Supt, Divisions and Headquarters, 1952–69; Officer i/c Anguilla Police Unit, W Indies, 1969; Chief Supt i/c Discipline Office, New Scotland Yard, 1970–72; Commander i/c A 10 (Complaints Investigation) Branch, NSY, 1972–75; seconded to Hong Kong Govt, 1974; Dep. Asst Commissioner C (CID) Dept, 1975–78; Inspector of Metropolitan Police (Dep. Asst Comr), 1979; HM Inspector of Constabulary for England and Wales, 1979–83; Dep. Comr of Police, Hong Kong, 1983–85. Graduate of Nat. Exec. Inst., FBI Academy, Quantico, Virginia, USA, 1979. *Recreation:* walking. *Clubs:* Royal Automobile; Hong Kong Golf.

ANNIS, Francesca; actress; *b* 1945. *Theatre:* Royal Shakespeare Company: Romeo and Juliet, 1976; Troilus and Cressida, 1976; Luciana in Comedy of Errors, 1976; Natalya in A Month in the Country, NT, 1981; Masha in Three Sisters, Albery, 1987; Melitta in Mrs Klein, NT, 1988; Rosmersholm, Young Vic, 1992; Lady Windermere's Fan, Albery, 1994; Hamlet, Hackney Empire, 1995; Ghosts, Comedy, 2001; The Vortex, Donmar Warehouse, 2002; Blood, Royal Court, 2003; Henry IV, Donmar Warehouse, 2004; The Shoreditch Madonna, Soho Th., Epitaph for George Dillon, Comedy, 2005; Time and the Conways, NT, 2009; Company, Sheffield Crucible, 2011; Versailles, Donmar Warehouse, 2014. *Films* include: Penny Gold, 1972; Macbeth, 1973; Krull, 1983; Dune, 1984; The Golden River; Under the Cherry Moon; The Debt Collector, 1999; The Libertine, 2004; Revolver, 2005. *Television:* A Pin to see the Peepshow, 1973; Madame Bovary, 1975; Stronger than the Sun, 1977; The Ragazza, 1978; Lillie (series), 1978; Partners in Crime (series), 1983; Inside Story (series), 1986; Parnell and the Englishwoman, Absolute Hell, 1991; The Gravy Train Goes East (series), 1991; Between the Lines (series), 1993; Reckless (series), 1997; Deadly Summer, 1997; Wives and Daughters, Milk, 1999; Deceit, 2000; Jericho, 2005; Cranford, 2007, 2009; The Little House, 2010; Loving Miss Hatto, 2012; Home Fires (series), 2015. *Address:* c/o Independent Talent Group Ltd, 40 Whitfield Street, W1T 2RH.

ANSBRO, David Anthony; Chairman, SFL Ltd, 2006–10; *b* 3 April 1945; *s* of late David T. Ansbro and Kathleen Mary Ansbro (*née* Mallett); *m* 1967, Veronica Mary (*née* Auton); two *d*. *Educ:* Xaverian Coll., Manchester; Leeds Univ. (LLB Hons). Articled to Town Clerk, Leeds, 1966–69; admitted Solicitor, 1969; Solicitor, Leeds City Council, 1969–73; Asst Dir of Admin, 1973–77, Dep. Dir of Admin, 1977–81, W Yorks County Council; Town Clerk and Chief Exec., York City Council, 1981–85; Chief Exec., Kirklees Council, 1985–87; Rees & Co., Solicitors, Huddersfield, 1987–88; Chief Exec., Leeds City Council, 1988–91; Partner, Hepworth & Chadwick, then Eversheds, 1991–2003, Managing Partner, 2000–03; Managing Partner, Eversheds, Leeds and Manchester, 1995–2000. Consultant, Grant Thornton, 2003–08. Mem., Local Govt Commn for England, 1992–95. Dir, Leeds TEC, 1990–99; Chm., Leeds Renaissance Partnership, 2005–10. Pro-Chancellor, Leeds Univ., 2000–07. Chm., Airton Parish Meeting, 2011–. Trustee: Henry Moore Foundn, 2003–10; Nat. Centre for Early Music, 2003–09. Hon. LLD Leeds, 2007. Papal Medal Pro Ecclesia et Pontifice, 1982; KSG 2008. *Recreations:* family, friends, golf, watching Manchester City, visiting Thorpeness and Singapore. *Address:* The Green, Airton, Skipton, N Yorks BD23 4AH. *T:* (01729) 830451. *Clubs:* Honley Cricket; Skipton Golf; Wharfedale Rugby Union Football.

ANSELL, Anthony Ronald Louis; His Honour Judge Ansell; a Circuit Judge, since 1995; a Deputy High Court Judge, Family Division, since 2009; *b* 9 Sept. 1946; *s* of Samuel Ansell and Joan Ansell; *m* 1970, Karen Kaye; one *s* one *d*. *Educ:* Dulwich Coll.; University Coll. London (LLB). Called to the Bar, Gray's Inn, 1968; in practice at the Bar, 1968–80; admitted Solicitor, 1980; in practice as solicitor, 1980–95; Asst Recorder, 1987–91; Recorder, 1991–95; a Judge of Employment Appeal Tribunal, 2002–10. Mem., Sentencing Adv. Panel, 2005–10. Vice-Pres., United Synagogue, 1992–97. *Publications:* (jtly) A Time for Change: the Kalms review of United Synagogue, 1992. *Recreations:* walking, opera, Chelsea Football Club. *Address:* c/o Central Family Court, First Avenue House, 42–49 High Holborn, WC1V 6NP. *T:* (020) 7421 8594.

ANSELL, Caroline Julie Porte; MP (C) Eastbourne, since 2015; *b* 1971; *m* 1997, Nicholas Ansell; three *s*. *Educ:* Royal Holloway Coll., Univ. of London (BA French); MEd 2001. NPQH. Teacher; Schs Inspector. Mem. (C) Eastbourne BC, 2012–15. *Address:* House of Commons, SW1A 0AA.

ANSELL, Maj.-Gen. Nicholas George Picton, CB 1992; OBE 1980; JP, DL; Clerk of the Course, Exeter Racecourse, 1995–2002; Director, Devon and Exeter Steeplechases Ltd, 2003–07; *b* 17 Aug. 1937; *s* of Col Sir Michael Ansell, CBE, DSO and Victoria Jacintha Fleetwood Fuller; *m* 1961, Vivien, *e d* of Col Anthony Taylor, DSO, MC; two *s* one *d*. *Educ:* Wellington Coll.; Magdalene Coll., Cambridge (MA). Commnd into 5th Royal Inniskilling Dragoon Guards, 1956; served BAOR, Libya, Cyprus; sc Camberley, 1970; Bde Major RAC HQ 1 (BR) Corps, 1971–72; Instructor Staff Coll., 1976–77; CO 5th Royal Inniskilling Dragoon Guards, 1977–80; Col GS Staff Coll., 1980–81; comd 20 Armd Bde, 1982–83; RCDS, 1984; Dep. Chief of Staff HQ BAOR, 1985–86; Dir, RAC, 1987–89; Sen. DS, Army, RCDS, 1990–92. JP N Devon, 1994; DL Devon, 1996; High Sheriff, Devon, 2002–03. *Recreations:* fishing, bird watching. *Address:* The Potting Shed, Pillhead, Bideford, Devon EX39 4NF.

ANSELL, Rachel Louise; QC 2014; *b* Amersham, Bucks, 14 June 1973; *d* of Michael and Laraine Ansell. *Educ:* St Clement Danes Sch., Chorleywood; Downing Coll., Cambridge (BA 1st Cl. Law 1994). Called to the Bar, Middle Temple, 1995. *Recreations:* avid Rugby fan supporting Wales and Saracens (season ticket holder) and cricket enthusiast supporting England cricket team and Middlesex County Cricket Club; working out at the gym, going to the ballet and opera. *Address:* 4 Pump Court, Temple, EC4Y 7AN. *T:* (020) 7842 5555, *Fax:* (020) 7583 2036. *E:* ransell@4pumpcourt.com.

ANSIP, Andrus; Member and a Vice-President, European Commission, since 2014; Prime Minister of Estonia, 2005–14; *b* Tartu, Estonia, 1 Oct. 1956; *m*; three *d*. *Educ:* Tartu Univ. (Dip. Chem. 1979); York Univ., Toronto (Business Mgt 1992). Hd, Tartu Regl Office, Jt Venture Estkompexim, 1989–93; Mem., Bd of Dirs, Rahvapank (People's Bank), 1993–95; Chairman, Management Board: Radio Tartu Ltd, 1994–98; Fondijuhtide AS (Fundmanager Ltd), 1995–96; Livonia Privatization IF, 1995–96; Bankruptcy Trustee, Tartu Commercial Bank, 1995–98; Mayor of Jartu, 1998–2004; Minister of Econ. Affairs and Communications, Estonia, 2004–05. Mem., Estonia Reform Party. Order of White Star, 3rd Cl. (Estonia), 2005; Officer, Nat. Order of Merit (Malta), 2001. *Address:* European Commission, Rue de la Loi 200, 1049 Brussels, Belgium.

ANSON, family name of **Earl of Lichfield**.

ANSON, Viscount; (Thomas) Ossian (Patrick Wolfe) Anson; *b* 20 May 2011; *s* and *heir* of Earl of Lichfield, *qv*.

ANSON, Charles Vernon, CVO 1996 (LVO 1983); DL; Vice Chairman, Cubitt Consulting PR, since 2002; Associate Director, Siren Communications, since 2003; *b* 11 March 1944; *s* of Philip Vernon Anson and Stella Anson; *m* 1st, 1976, Clarissa Rosamund Denton (marr. diss. 2005); one *s* one *d*; 2nd, 2009, Juliet Nicolson, *qv*. *Educ:* Lancing College; Jesus College, Cambridge (BA History). Joined Diplomatic Service, 1966; Third, later Second Sec. (Commercial), Washington, 1968–71; FCO, 1971–74; Asst Private Sec. to Minister of State, 1974–76; Second Sec. (Commercial), Tehran, 1976–79; seconded to Press Office, 10 Downing St, 1979–81; First Sec. (Inf.), Washington, 1981–85; FCO, 1985–87; Dir of Public Relations, Kleinwort Benson, 1987–90; Press Sec. to the Queen, 1990–97; Gp Corporate Relns Dir, Grand Metropolitan, later Diageo plc, 1997–98; Hd of Communications, EBU, 1998–2000; Dir of Corporate Commns, Hilton Gp, 2000–01; Communications Advr, The Queen's Golden Jubilee Weekend Trust, 2001–02. Mem., Press Complaints Commn, 2012–14. Mem., Regl Adv. Bd for London and SE, Nat. Trust, 2013–. Trustee: Elizabeth Finn Trust, 2002–08; Brogdale Horticultural Trust, 2002–08. Chm., S Downs Jt Cttee, 2009–11. DL E Sussex, 2011. *Address:* Winton House, Winton Street, Alfriston, E Sussex BN26 5UH. *T:* (01323) 871769. *Club:* Hurlingham.

ANSON, Dame Elizabeth (Audrey), (Lady Anson), DBE 1995; JP, DL; Chairman, Independent Appeals Authority for School Examinations, 1990–99; Independent Monitor to Parliament on Entry Clearance Refusals, 1994–2000; *b* 9 Jan. 1931; *d* of late Rear-Adm. Sir Philip Clarke, KBE, CB, DSO, and Audrey (*née* White); *m* 1955, Rear-Adm. Sir Peter Anson, Bt, *qv*; two *s* two *d*. *Educ:* Weirfield Sch., Taunton; Royal Naval Sch., Haslemere; King's Coll., London (LLB). Called to Bar, Inner Temple, 1953; joined Western Circuit, 1953; practice at Bar, 1952–56; part-time Adjudicator, 1979–87, an Adjudicator, 1987–91, Immigration Appeals. Councillor, Waverley Bor. Council, 1974–95, Mayor, 1987–88. Association of District Councils of England and Wales: Mem., 1983–95; Vice-Chm., 1989–91; Chm., 1991–93; Dep. Chm., and Chm. Exec. Cttee, 1993–95; Chm., Housing and Environmental Health Cttee, 1987–89. Dep. Chm., Local Govt Management Bd, 1991–93; Member: Local Govt Audit Commn, 1987–90; Cons. Nat. Local Govt Adv. Cttee, 1991–95; Nat. Union Exec. Cttee, 1992–95; Local and Central Govt Relations Res. Cttee, Joseph Rowntree Meml Trust, 1992–96; EU Cttee of the Regions, 1993–98; Packaging Standards Council, 1992–96. Chm., Eagle Radio (formerly Surrey and NE Hampshire Radio Ltd, then County Sound Radio Network Ltd), 1994–2006. Chm., Nat. Mobility Scheme, 1987–88. Mem. Council and Chm. W Surrey Br., IoD, 2002–05; Chair of Judges, Surrey Business Awards, 2005–07. Vice President: Inst. of Envmtl Health Officers, 1989–2001; Assoc. of Drainage Authorities, 1995–2010. Vice Pres., SW Surrey Conservative Assoc., 2006– (Pres., 2003–06). Mem. Schs Forum, Hants CC, 2005–10. Gov., Rowledge C of E Primary Sch., 1981–2013 (Chm., 1995–2003). President: Farnham Venison Dinner, 2012– (Chm., 2005–10); Farnham and Alton Talking Newspapers, 2012–. FRSA 1992. JP 1977, DL 1984, Surrey. *Recreations:* travel, needlecraft, swimming. *Address:* Rosefield, Rowledge, Farnham, Surrey GU10 4AT. *T:* (01252) 792724.

ANSON, Sir John, KCB 1990 (CB 1981); Second Permanent Secretary (Public Expenditure), HM Treasury, 1987–90; *b* 3 Aug. 1930; *yr s* of Sir Edward Anson, 6th Bt, and Alison (*née* Pollock) (*d* 1997); *m* 1957, Myrica Fergie-Woods; one *s* two *d* (and one *s* decd). *Educ:* Winchester; Magdalene Coll., Cambridge (MA; Smith's Prize). Served in HM Treasury, 1954–68; Financial Counsellor, British Embassy, Paris, 1968–71; Asst Sec., 1971–72, Under-Sec., 1972–74, Cabinet Office; Under-Sec., 1974–77, Dep. Sec., 1977–87, HM Treasury; Economic Minister, British Embassy, Washington, and UK Exec. Dir, IMF and World Bank, 1980–83. Chairman: Public Finance Foundn, 1991–94; Retirement Income Inquiry, 1994–96. Hon. Treas., Council of Churches for Britain and Ireland, 1990–92; Chair, House of Laity, Southwark Diocesan Synod, 1996–97.

See also Sir Peter Anson, Bt.

ANSON, Rear-Adm. Sir Peter, 7th Bt, *cr* 1831; CB 1974; DL; Chairman, IGG Component Technology Ltd, 1992–97; *b* 31 July 1924; *er s* of Sir Edward R. Anson, 6th Bt, and Alison (*d* 1997), *o d* of late Hugh Pollock; *S* father 1951; *m* 1955, Elizabeth Audrey Clarke (*see* Dame Elizabeth Anson); two *s* two *d*. *Educ:* RNC, Dartmouth. Joined RN 1938; Lieut 1944. Served War of 1939–45, HMS Prince of Wales, HMS Exeter. Lieut-Comdr, 1952; Comdr 1956. Commanding Officer, HMS Alert, 1957–58; Staff of RN Tactical Sch., Woolwich, 1959–61; Commanding Officer, HMS Broadsword, 1961–62; Captain, 1963; Director Weapons, Radio (Naval), 1965–66 (Dep. Director, 1963–65); CO HMS Naiad and Captain (D) Londonderry Squadron, 1966–68; Captain, HM Signal School, 1968–70; Commodore, Commander Naval Forces Gulf, 1970–72; ACDS (Signals), 1972–74, retired 1975. Marconi Space and Defence Systems, later Marconi Space Systems: Divl Manager, Satellites, 1977–84; Man. Dir, 1984–85; Chm., 1985–91. Chm., UK Industrial Space Cttee, 1980–82. FIERE 1972. High Sheriff, Surrey, 1993. DL Surrey, 1993. *Heir:* *s* Philip Roland Anson, *b* 4 Oct. 1957. *Address:* Rosefield, Rowledge, Farnham, Surrey GU10 4AT. *T:* and *Fax:* (01252) 792724.

See also Sir John Anson.

ANSTEE, Eric Edward, FCA, FFA; Chairman of Council, Institute of Financial Accountants, since 2007; *b* 1 Jan. 1951; *s* of Reginald Thomas Anstee and Margaret Doris Anstee (*née* Hampshire); *m* 1982, Suzanne Joy Piller; one *s* three *d*. *Educ:* St Albans Sch. FCA 1974. Ernst and Young: London and Singapore, 1974–83; on secondment as Commercial Accountancy Advr to HM Treasury, 1983–86; Partner, London, 1986–93; Gp Finance Dir, Eastern Electricity plc, 1993–95; Advr to Lord Hanson, Hanson plc, 1995–96; Group Finance Director: Energy Gp plc, 1996–98; Old Mutual plc, 1998–2000; Chief Executive: Old Mutual Financial Services plc, 2000–01; Old Mutual Asset Management Inc., 2000–01; non-exec. Chm., Mansell plc, 2001–03; Chief Exec., ICAEW, 2003–06; Chief Exec., City of London Gp, 2009–13. Non-executive Director: Severn Trent plc, 1999–2003; Insight Investment Funds Mgt Ltd, 2006–; Insight Investment Mgt (Global) Ltd, 2006–; Financial Reporting Council, 2007–11; Paypoint plc, 2008–; Sun Life Financial of Canada (UK) Ltd, 2011–. Chm., Eastern Reg. Industrial Develt Bd, DTI, 1993–99. Mem., Takeover Panel Appeals Bd, 2006–. FFA 2007. *Recreations:* tennis, golf, gardening. *Address:* 30 Cannon Street, EC4M 6XH. *E:* eric@ansteeassociates.com. *Club:* Athenæum.

ANSTEE, Dame Margaret (Joan), DCMG 1994; lecturer, writer and consultant on UN issues and peacekeeping training; Adviser to: President and Government of Bolivia (*ad honorem*), 1993–97 and 2002–05; Under-Secretary-General of the United Nations, 1987–93; *b* 25 June 1926; *d* of Edward Curtis Anstee and Anne Adaliza (*née* Mills). *Educ:* Chelmsford County High Sch. for Girls; Newnham Coll., Cambridge (MA; 1st cl. Hons, Mod. and Med. Langs Tripos; Hon. Fellow, 1991); BSc(Econ) London. Lectr in Spanish, QUB, 1947–48; Third Sec., FO, 1948–52; Admin. Officer, UN Technical Assistance Bd, Manila, Philippines, 1952–54; Spanish Supervisor, Cambridge Univ., 1955–56; UN Technical Assistance Board: O i/c Bogotá, Colombia, 1956–57; Resident Rep., Uruguay, 1957–59; Resident Rep., UN Tech. Assistance Bd, Dir of Special Fund Progs, and Dir of UN Inf. Centre, Bolivia, 1960–65; Resident Rep., UNDP, Ethiopia, and UNDP Liaison Officer with UN Econ. Commn for Africa, 1965–67; Sen. Econ. Adviser, Prime Minister's Office, UK, 1967–68; Sen. Asst to Comr i/c Study of Capacity of UN Develt System, 1968–69; Resident Rep., UNDP, Morocco, 1969–72; Resident Rep., UNDP, Chile, and UNDP Liaison Officer with UN Econ. Commn for Latin America, 1972–74; Dep. to UN Under Sec.-Gen. i/c UN Relief Operation to Bangladesh, and Dep. Co-ordinator of UN Emergency Assistance to Zambia, June–Dec. 1973; United Nations Development Programme, New York: Dep. Asst Adminr, and Dep. Reg Dir for Latin America, 1974–76; Dir, Adminr's Unit for Special Assignments, Feb.–July 1976; Asst Dep. Adminr, July–Dec. 1976; Asst Adminr and Dir, Bureau for Prog. Policy and Evaluation, 1977–78; Asst Sec.-Gen. of UN (Dept of Technical Co-operation for Develt), NY, 1978–87; Dir-Gen., UN Office, Vienna, and Head, Centre for Social Develt and Humanitarian Affairs, 1987–92. Special Representative of Secretary-General: for Bolivia, 1982–92; for co-ordination of internat. assistance to Mexico following the earthquake, 1985–87; for UN Conf. for adoption of convention against illicit traffic in narcotic drugs and psychotropic substances, 1988; for Peru, 1991–92; Special Rep. of Sec.-Gen. for Angola, and Head, UN Angola Verification Mission (UNAVEM II), 1992–93; Sec.-Gen.'s Personal rep., to co-ordinate UN efforts, Kuwait (burning oil wells and envmtl impact of Gulf war in whole reg.), 1991–92. Chm., Adv. Gp on review of World Food Council, UN, 1985–86; Special Co-ordinator of UN Sec.-Gen. to ensure implementation of Gen. Assembly resolution on financial and admin. reform of UN, 1986–87; Co-ordinator for all UN Drug-Control-Related Activities, 1987–90; UN Co-ordinator of Internat. Co-operation for Chernobyl, 1991–92; Chm., Expert Adv. Gp to Lessons Learned Unit, UN Dept of Peacekeeping Ops, 1996–2001. Sec.-Gen., 8th UN Congress on Prevention of Crime and Treatment of Offenders, 1990. Vice Pres., UN Assoc. of UK, 2002–. Hon. Life Vice Pres., British Assoc. of Former UN Civil Servants, 2010–. Member: Bd of Trustees, HelpAge Internat., 1993–96; Council of Advisers, Yale Univ. UN Studies, 1996–; Adv. Council, Oxford Res. Gp, 1997–; Adv. Bd, British-Angola Forum, 1998–2010; Internat. Adv. Council, UN Intellectual Hist. Project, 1999–2010; President Jimmy Carter's Internat. Council on Conflict Resolution, 2001–; Editorial Bd, Global Governance, 2004–; Strategic Adv. Bd, Durham Global Security Inst., 2011–. DU Essex, 1994; Hon. LLD: Westminster, 1996; Cambridge, 2004; Hon. DSc (Econ) London, 1998. Reves Peace Prize, Coll. of William and Mary, Williamsburg, USA, 1993; Sir Brian Urquhart Award for distinguished service to UN, UNA-UK, 2011. Comdr, Order of Ouissam Alaouite, Morocco, 1972; Dama Gran Cruz, Condor of the Andes, Bolivia, 1986; Grosse Goldene Ehrenzeichen am Bande, Austria, 1992; Gran Caballero, Orden de Bernardo O'Higgins, Chile, 2006. *Publications:* The Administration of International Development Aid, USA 1969; Gate of the Sun: a prospect of Bolivia, 1970 (USA 1971); (ed with R. K. A. Gardiner and C. Patterson) Africa and the World (Haile Selassie Prize Trust Symposium), 1970; Orphan of the Cold War; the inside story of the collapse of the Angolan peace process 1992–93, 1996 (USA 1996; Portugal, 1997); Never Learn to Type: a woman at the United Nations, 2003; The House on the Sacred Lake and other Bolivian Dreams - and Nightmares, 2009; JB - An Unlikely Spanish Don: the life and times of Professor John Brande Trend, 2013; numerous articles and chapters in books on UN reform, peacekeeping, economic and social development. *Recreations:* writing, gardening, hill-walking (preferably in the Andes), bird-watching, swimming. *Address:* The Walled Garden, Knill, near Presteigne, Powys LD8 2PR. *T:* (01544) 267411. *Club:* Oxford and Cambridge.

ANSTEE, Nicholas John, FCA; Senior Director, S J Berwin LLP, since 2007; Lord Mayor of London, 2009–10; *b* 27 May 1958; *s* of Wing Comdr Peter John Anstee and Ann Tudor Anstee (*née* Price); *m* 1983, Claire Mary Carson Cooper; three *d*. *Educ:* Stamford Sch. ICAEW 1982; FCA 1987. Dearden Farrow, 1984–86; Binder Hamlyn, 1987–94; Partner, Andersen, 1994. Director: London Marathon, 2004–; Barts and The London Charity, 2008–. Common Councilman, City of London, 1987–96; Alderman, Aldersgate Ward, 1996–; Sheriff, City of London, 2003–04; Liveryman: Butchers' Co., 1996– (Master, 2014–15); Plaisterers' Co., 2005–. Mem., Adv. Council, LSO, 2010–. Trustee, Cricket Foundn, 2010–. Governor: City of London Sch. for Girls, 1993–2003; Christ's Hosp., 1996–; King Edward Sch., 1996–. KStJ 2010. *Recreations:* marathon running, cricket, tennis. *Address:* 8 Wallside, Monkwell Square, Barbican, EC2Y 8BH. *T:* (020) 7588 6851. *E:* nick.anstee@btinternet.com. *Clubs:* Aldersgate Ward, MCC.

ANSTRUTHER, Sir Sebastian Paten Campbell, 9th Bt *cr* 1694 (NS), of Balcaskie, and 14th Bt *cr* 1700 (NS) of Anstruther; *b* 13 Sept. 1962; *s* of Sir Ian Fife Campbell Anstruther of that Ilk, 8th, 13th and 10th Bt and Susan Margaret Walker (*née* Paten); *S* to father's NS Baronetcies, 2007; *m* 1992, Pornpan Pinitwong, Thailand; one *s* one *d*. *Heir: s* Maximilian Sengtawan Pinitwong Anstruther, *b* 27 Jan. 1995. *Address:* The Barlavington Estate Office, Dye House Lane, Duncton Mill, Petworth, W Sussex GU28 0LF.

ANSTRUTHER-GOUGH-CALTHORPE, Sir Euan (Hamilton), 3rd Bt *cr* 1929; Director, Calthorpe Holdings Ltd, since 2000; *b* 22 June 1966; *s* of Niall Hamilton Anstruther-Gough-Calthorpe (*d* 1970) and of Martha Rodman (who *m* 2nd, 1975, Sir Charles C. Nicholson, Bt, *qv*), *d* of Stuart Warren Don; *S* grandfather, 1985; *m* 2002, Anna Joan Wright; two *s* two *d*. *Educ:* Hawtreys, Savernake Forest; Harrow School; Royal Agricultural Coll., Cirencester (Dip. in Estate Mgt). Pres., Birmingham Botanical Gdns, 1985–99. Director: STG Hldgs plc, 1999–2004; Estate Insce Gp, 1999–2003; Enterprise Heritage Capital Ltd, 2000–06; HTTP Technol. Inc., 2000–03; Richmond & Hampshire Ltd, 2001–; Beck & Call Delivery Ltd, 2001–04; Quantum Land Ltd, 2005–11; Capstone Foster Care Ltd, 2007–. DUniv Birmingham, 2008. *Heir: s* Barnaby Charles Anstruther-Gough-Calthorpe, *b* 28 Oct. 2005. *Clubs:* Brooks's; Edgbaston Priory (Pres., 1985–).

ANTELME, Alexander John; QC 2014; *b* London, 2 Oct. 1968; *s* of Leopold Antelme and Patricia Antelme (*née* Kane); *m* 1992, Rachel Alexa McMullen; one *s* two *d*. *Educ:* St Bede's, Bishton Hall, Staffs; Douai Sch., Berks; Exeter Coll., Oxford (Open Schol.; MA Hons); City Univ., London (DipLaw). Called to the Bar, Gray's Inn, 1993; in practice as barrister, 1994–. *Address:* Crown Office Chambers, 2 Crown Office Row, Temple, EC4Y 7HJ. *T:* (020) 7797 8100.

ANTHONY, Rear Adm. Derek James, MBE 1983; Clerk to the Shipwrights' Company, 2003–08; *b* 2 Nov. 1947; *s* of late James Kenwood Anthony and Nora Evelyn Anthony (*née* Honnor); *m* 1970, Denyse Irene Hopper Wright; two *d*. *Educ:* New Beacon Prep. Sch., Sevenoaks; Eastbourne Coll.; BRNC, Dartmouth. Joined Royal Navy, 1966: sea-going appts, HM Ships Opossum, Revenge, Andrew, Oxley, Oberon, Sovereign, 1970–80; CO, HMS Onslaught, 1981–82; Exchange Service, USN, 1982–84; jsdc, 1985; CO, HMS Warspite, 1986–88; CO, Submarine Comd Course, 1988–90; Head, RN Seaman Officers Policy, MoD, 1990–91; CO, HMS Cumberland, 1991–93; Dir, Naval Service Conditions, 1993–96; hcsc, Camberley, 1996; Dep. Flag Officer Submarines, 1996–97; Naval Attaché, Asst Defence Attaché, Washington, and UK Nat. Liaison Rep. to SACLANT, 1997–2000; FO Scotland, Northern England and NI, 2000–03. Chairman: Assoc. of RN Officers, 2004–13; RN Officers' Charity, 2004–13. Trustee and Dir, Medway Kingfisher Trust, 2010–. Liveryman, Shipwrights' Co., 2009–. Mem., Incorp. of Wrights of Glasgow, 2002–. *Recreations:* golf, music, clarinet, history, family, fly fishing. *Address:* Bocton House, Faversham Road, Boughton Lees, Ashford, Kent TN25 4HS. *Clubs:* Royal Navy of 1765 and 1785, Victory Services.

ANTHONY, Rt Hon. Douglas; *see* Anthony, Rt Hon. J. D.

ANTHONY, Evelyn Bridget Patricia, (Mrs Michael Ward-Thomas); DL; author; *b* 3 July 1928; *d* of Henry Christian Stephens, inventor of the Dome Trainer in World War II, and Elizabeth (*née* Sharkey); *ggd* of Henry Stephens of Cholderton, Wilts, inventor of Stephens Ink; *m* 1955, Michael Ward-Thomas (*d* 2004); four *s* one *d* (and one *d* decd). *Educ:* Convent of Sacred Heart, Roehampton. Freeman, City of London, 1987; Liveryman, Needlemakers' Co., 1987. High Sheriff, Essex, 1994–95, DL Essex, 1995. *Publications:* Imperial Highness, 1953; Curse Not the King, 1954; Far Fly the Eagles, 1955; Anne Boleyn, 1956 (US Literary Guild Award); Victoria, 1957 (US Literary Guild Award); Elizabeth, 1959; Charles the King, 1961; Clandara, 1963; The Heiress, 1964; Valentina, 1965; The Rendezvous, 1967; Anne of Austria, 1968; The Legend, 1969; The Assassin, 1970; The Tamarind Seed, 1971; The Poellenberg Inheritance, 1972; The Occupying Power, 1973 (Yorkshire Post Fiction Prize); The Malaspiga Exit, 1974; The Persian Ransom, 1975; The Silver Falcon, 1977; The Return, 1978; The Grave of Truth, 1979; The Defector, 1980; The Avenue of the Dead, 1981; Albatross, 1982; The Company of Saints, 1983; Voices on the Wind, 1985; No Enemy But Time, 1987; The House of Vandekar, 1988; The Scarlet Thread, 1989; The Relic, 1991; The Doll's House, 1992; Exposure, 1993; Bloodstones, 1994; The Legacy, 1997. *Recreations:* racing (National Hunt), gardening, going to sale rooms (Christie's or Sotheby's).

ANTHONY, Graham George, CEng; Director, Industry and Regions, Engineering Council, 1983–90; *b* 25 Oct. 1931; *s* of George Alfred and Dorothy Anthony; *m* 1957, Thelma Jane Firmstone; two *s* one *d*. *Educ:* Fletton Grammar Sch.; King's College London (BSc Eng). Projects Manager, ICI Fibres, 1956; Works Engineer, ICI India, 1964; Chief Engineer, Ilford Ltd, 1968; Gen. Manager, Bonded Structures, 1975; Commercial Dir, Ciba-Geigy (UK) Ltd, 1979. FRSA. *Recreations:* offshore sailing, woodworking, lecturing as a maritime historian. *Address:* 11 North Terrace, Cambridge CB5 8DJ. *T:* (01223) 360553.

ANTHONY, Guy; *see* Anthony, M. G.

ANTHONY, Rt Hon. (John) Douglas, AC 2003; CH 1982; PC 1971; company director and farmer; *b* 31 Dec. 1929; *s* of late H. L. Anthony; *m* 1957, Margot Macdonald Budd; two *s* one *d*. *Educ:* Murwillumbah Primary and High Schs, The King's Sch., Parramatta; Queensland Agricultural Coll. (QDA). MP, Country Party, later National Party, Richmond, NSW, 1957–84, (Mem., Exec. Council, 1963–72, 1975–83). Minister for Interior, 1964–67; Minister for Primary Industry, 1967–71; Dep. Prime Minister and Minister for Trade and Industry, 1971–72; Minister for Overseas Trade, Minerals and Energy, Nov.–Dec. 1975; Dep. Prime Minister and Minister for Trade and Resources, 1975–83. Dep. Leader, Aust. Country Party, 1966–71; Leader, Nat. Country Party, later Nat. Party, 1971–84. Chairman: Pan Australian Mining Ltd, then Mt Leyshon Gold Mines, 1986–92; Resource Finance Corp., 1986–2003; Commonwealth Regl Telecommunications Infrastructure Fund, then Networking Nation, 1997–2002; Director: John Swires & Sons Pty Ltd (Australia), 1987–2007; Clyde Agriculture Ltd, 1988–2008; Normandy Mining Ltd, 1992–2000. Chm. Governing Council, Old Parlt House, 1998–2008. Hon. Fellow, AATSE, 1990. Hon. LLD Victoria Univ. of Wellington, NZ, 1983; DUniv: Sydney, 1997; Southern Cross, 2014. Council Gold Medal, Qld Agricl Coll., 1985. Canberra Medal, 1989; NZ Commemorative Medal, 1990. *Recreations:* golf, tennis, fishing, swimming. *Address:* PO Box 71, Murwillumbah, NSW 2484, Australia. *Clubs:* Australian, Royal Sydney Golf (Sydney); Queensland (Brisbane).

ANTHONY, Louise Frances; *see* Chunn, L. F.

ANTHONY, (Michael) Guy; His Honour Judge Anthony; a Circuit Judge, since 1998; *b* 5 March 1950; *s* of Kenneth Anthony and June Anthony (*née* Gallifent); *m* 1974, Jane Farrer; one *s*. *Educ:* St Paul's Sch.; Magdalen Coll., Oxford (BA 1971; MA). Called to the Bar, Middle Temple, 1972; in practice at the Bar, 1972–98; an Asst Recorder, 1989–93; a Recorder, 1993–98; SE Circuit. Mem., Mental Health Review Tribunal, 2002–14. *Recreations:* travel, reading, spending time with family, Rugby and other sports. *Address:* Lewes Combined Crown and County Court Centre, The Law Courts, High Street, Lewes, E Sussex BN7 1YB. *T:* (01273) 480400. *Club:* Army and Navy.

ANTHONY, Robert Brown; QC (Scot.) 2002; Sheriff of Glasgow and Strathkelvin, 2007–10; *b* Bathgate, 1 June 1962; *s* of Michael Anthony and Elizabeth Campbell Anthony (*née* Brown); *m* 1987, Shona Catherine Struthers; one *s* two *d*. *Educ:* Univ. of Aberdeen (LLB 1983). Admitted solicitor, 1984; admitted to Faculty of Advocates, 1988; Advocate Depute, 2001–02; Sen. Advocate Depute, 2002–04; pt-time Sheriff, 2005–07; in practice at Scottish Bar, 2010–13. Part-time Chairman: Judicial Panel, Scottish FA, 2011–; Anti-Discriminatory Disciplinary Panel, FA. Mem., Scottish Criminal Cases Review Commn, 2007.

ANTHONY, Ronald Desmond; consultant in safety and engineering, since 1986; Chief Inspector of Nuclear Installations, Health and Safety Executive, 1981–85; *b* 21 Nov. 1925; *s* of William Arthur Anthony and Olive Frances Anthony (*née* Buck); *m* 1948, Betty Margaret Croft; four *d*. *Educ:* Chislehurst and Sidcup Grammar School; City and Guilds Coll., Imperial Coll. of Science and Technology (BSc, ACGI). CEng, FIMechE, MRAeS. Vickers Armstrongs (Supermarine), 1950; Nuclear Power Plant Co., 1957; Inspectorate of Nuclear Installations, 1960; Deputy Chief Inspector, 1973; Dir, Safety Policy Div., 1977, Hazardous Installations Gp, 1981–82, Health and Safety Exec. *Publications:* papers in technical journals. *Recreation:* golf. *Address:* 30 The Landway, Kemsing, Sevenoaks, Kent TN15 6TG. *T:* (01732) 490141.

ANTHONY, Vivian Stanley; educational consultant; Reporting Inspector of Independent Schools, 1994–2010; Secretary, Headmasters' and Headmistresses' (formerly Headmasters') Conference, 1990–2000; *b* 5 May 1938; *s* of Captain and Mrs A. S. Anthony; *m* 1969, Rosamund Anne MacDermot Byrn; one *s* one *d*. *Educ:* Cardiff High Sch.; LSE (1st Div. 2nd

Cl. Hons BSc Econ); Fitzwilliam Coll., Cambridge (DipEd); Merton Coll., Oxford (schoolmaster student). Asst Master, Leeds Grammar Sch., 1960–64; Asst Master and Housemaster, Tonbridge Sch., 1964–69; Lectr in Educn, Univ. of Leeds, 1969–71; Dep. Headmaster, The King's Sch., Macclesfield, 1971–76; Headmaster, Colfe's Sch., London, 1976–90. Asst Examr, Econ. Hist., London Univ., 1964–71; Asst Examr, Econs, Oxford and Cambridge Bd, 1970–76, Chief Examr (Awarder), Econs, 1976–92; Ext. Examr, Educn, Univs of Manchester, 1972–75, Birmingham, 1975–78, and Lancaster, 1977–79. Mem., DFEE Wkg Gp on Sch. Security, 1996–2000. Chm., Econs Assoc., 1974–77; Member: Schools Council Social Science Cttee, 1976–83; London Univ. Schs Examinations Cttee, 1981–85; Secondary Examinations Council Economics Panel, 1984–89; CBI/Schools Panel, 1984–88. Sabbatical tour, US indep. schools, 1983. Chm., London Area, 1988–89, Mem. Council, 1989–2000, SHA; Headmasters' Conference: elected, 1980; Chm., Academic Policy Cttee, 1988–90 (Mem., 1983–2000); Mem., Professional Develt Cttee, 1985–2004, Teacher Shortage Wkg Party, 1987–88, Assisted Places Cttee, 1987–89; Chm., Records of Achievement Wkg Party, 1987–90; Trng Co-ordinator, 2000–04; Hon. Associate, 2000. Member: Exec. Cttee, Nat. Professional Qualification for Headship (E Midlands), 1996–99; Exec., Boarding Schs Assoc., 2000–04. Mem., Admiralty Interview Bd, 1980–2004. Comr, Inland Revenue, 1989–90. Mem. Court, Univ. of Kent, 1985–90; Governor: Stamford Sch., 1992–2009 (Chm. of Educn, 1996–2009); King's Sch., Macclesfield, 1993–96; Bromsgrove Sch., 1995–2010 (Chm. of Educn, 2001–10; Pres., 2010–; Mem., Hd Selection team, 2013); Uppingham Sch., 1996–2006; British Sch. in Colombo, 1999–2007; Hosp. of St John and St Anne Oakham, 2007– (Chm., 2010–); Bromsgrove Internat. Sch. in Thailand, 2009–13. Mem., Uppingham PCC, 2009–12; Chairman: Allexton Parish Meeting, 2005–14; Three Villages Conservation Trust, 2005–. Member: Uppingham Local Hist. Study Gp, 2005– (Chm., 2014–); Rutland Decorative and Fine Arts Soc., 2005–. Volunteer, Churches Conservation Trust (Allexton), 2003–. Founder Chm., 2006–09, Pres., 2009–, Uppingham White Hart Dining Club. Hon. Freeman, Leathersellers' Co., 1990. Hon. FCP 1991. Hon. DEd De Montfort, 1999. *Publications:* Monopoly, 1968, 3rd edn 1976; Overseas Trade, 1969, 4th edn 1981; Banks and Markets, 1970, 3rd edn 1979; Objective Tests in A Level Economics, 1971, 2nd edn 1974; Objective Tests in Introductory Economics, 1975, 3rd edn 1983; History of Rugby Football at Colfe's, 1980; US Independent Schools, 1984; 150 Years of Cricket at Colfe's, 1986; (ed) Head to Head, 1993; (ed) Manual of Guidance, 1995; (ed) Head to HoD, 1998; (ed) Head to House, 2000; Allexton Church Guide, 2007; The Survival of a Village: the history of Allexton, 2009; Good Wit and Capacity: the history of Colfe's School 1972–2002, 2012; *contributor:* The Teaching of Economics in Secondary Schools, 1970; Curriculum Development in Secondary Schools, 1973; Control of the Economy, 1974; Comparative Economics in Teaching Economics, 1984; The Search for Standards, 1992; Access and Affordability, 1994; Uppingham in Peacetime, 2007; The History of Uppingham to 1800, 2015; articles in Economics, Leicestershire & Rutland Life. *Recreations:* choral singing (Chm., 1998–2004, Pres., 2007–, Leics Chorale; Chm., Youth Find A Voice, 2005–), Rugby football (Leicester FC), local and family history, travelling. *Address:* Bridge House, Allexton, Leics LE15 9AB. *T:* (01572) 717400. *Clubs:* East India, Devonshire, Sports and Public Schools, Old Colfeians' Association; Uppingham Probus (Mem., 2000–; Sec., 2008–09; Pres., 2011–12; Speaker Sec., 2012–).

ANTONIADES, Reno Michael; Managing Partner, Lee & Thompson LLP, since 2012; *b* London, 27 July 1966; *s* of Michael and Joy Antoniades; *m* 1997, Julieanne Cunningham; one *s* one *d*. *Educ:* Alleyn's Sch., Dulwich; Leicester Univ. (LLB Hons 1987). Trainee solicitor, then Solicitor, Herbert Smith, 1989–93; Solicitor: Olswang, 1993–94; Lee & Thompson LLP, 1994–. Mem., Edward Alleyn Club. *Recreations:* cinema, football, family. *Address:* 34 Herondale Avenue, SW18 3JL. *T:* 07872 118422. *E:* renoantoniades@leeandthompson.com. *Club:* Soho House.

ANTONIAZZI, Manon Bonner, LVO 2012 (MVO 1998); PhD; Chief Executive Officer, Tourism and Marketing, Welsh Government, since 2012; *b* Cardiff, 15 April 1965; *d* of (John) Emyr Jenkins, *qv*; *m* 1991, Jeremy Huw Williams (marr. diss. 2009); one *d*; *m* 2014, John Lawrence Antoniazzi. *Educ:* Llanhari Welsh Comp. Sch.; St John's Coll., Cambridge (BA 1986; PhD 1990). Hd, Press and Public Relns, S4C, 1991–93; Asst Private Sec. to the Prince of Wales, 1994–98; Dir, Communications Services, Nat. Assembly for Wales, 1999–2000; Sec. and Hd of Public Affairs, BBC Wales, 2000–03; Hd, Public Policy, BBC Nations and Regions, 2003–04; Private Sec. for Wales to the Prince of Wales and the Duchess of Cornwall, 2004–12. Associate, CMi, 2011–12. Mem., Tourism Panel, Welsh Govt, 2011–12. Trustee, Wales: Prince's Trust, 2001–04; Nat. Heritage Meml Fund and Heritage Lottery Fund, 2012–15. Gov., RSC, 2001–04; Non-exec. Dir, London Philharmonic Orch., 2012–. *Recreations:* music (as a harpist), walking, old languages and buildings. *Address:* Department for Enterprise, Science and Transport, QED Centre, Main Avenue, Treforest, Rhondda Cynon Taf CF37 5YR. *E:* manon@manonbonner.com. *Club:* Royal Automobile.

See also F. L. Hague.

ANTONIW, Michael; Member (Lab) Pontypridd, National Assembly for Wales, since 2011; *b* 2 Sept. 1954; *s* of Mychajlo Antoniw and Agnes Rigmor Antoniw (*née* Sørensen); *m* 1983, Elaine Baynton; one adopted *s* two adopted *d*. *Educ:* Presentation Coll., Reading; University Coll., Cardiff (LLB Hons). Thompsons Solicitors, 1980–2011, Partner, 1987–2011. Fellow, Assoc. of Personal Injury Lawyers, 2006–. Vis. Fellow, Univ. of S Wales. *Recreations:* football, playing the mandolin. *Address:* National Assembly for Wales, Cardiff Bay, Cardiff CF99 1NA. *Club:* Llantrisant Working Men's.

ANTRIM, 14th Earl of, *cr* 1620; **Alexander Randal Mark McDonnell;** Viscount Dunluce; Keeper of Conservation, 1975–95, and Director (formerly Head) of Collection Services, 1990–95, Tate Gallery; *b* 3 Feb. 1935; *er s* of 13th Earl of Antrim, KBE, and Angela Christina (*d* 1984), *d* of Sir Mark Sykes, 6th Bt; *S* father, 1977 (but continued to be known as Viscount Dunluce until 1995); *m* 1963, Sarah Elizabeth Anne (marr. diss. 1974), 2nd *d* of St John Harmsworth; one *s* two *d*; *m* 1977, Elizabeth, *d* of late Michael Moses Sacher; one *d*. *Educ:* Downside; Christ Church, Oxford; Ruskin Sch. of Art. Restorer: the Ulster Museum, 1969–71; Tate Gall., 1965–75. Dir, Ulster Television, 1982–2000; Chm., Northern Salmon Co. Ltd, 2000–08 (Dir, 2000–14). Mem., Exec. Cttee, City and Guilds Art School, 1983–2009. FRSA 1984. Prime Warden, Fishmongers' Co., 1995–96. *Recreations:* painting, vintage cars. *Heir:* *s* Viscount Dunluce, *qv*. *Address:* Deerpark Cottage, Castle Lane, Glenarm, Ballymena, Co. Antrim BT44 0BQ. *Club:* Beefsteak.

ANTROBUS, Sir Edward (Philip), 8th Bt *cr* 1815, of Antrobus, Cheshire; *b* 28 Sept. 1938; *er s* of Sir Philip Coutts Antrobus, 7th Bt and his 1st wife, Dorothy Margaret Mary (*d* 1973), *d* of Rev. W. G. Davis; *S* father, 1995; *m* 1st, 1966, Janet Sarah Elizabeth (*d* 1990), *d* of Philip Sceales, Johannesburg; one *s* one *d* (and one *d* decd); 2nd, 1996, Rozanne Penelope, *d* of Neville Simpson. *Educ:* Witwatersrand Univ. (BSc Mining Engrg); Magdalene Coll., Cambridge (MA). *Heir:* *s* Francis Edward Sceales Antrobus, BSc Eng Cape Town, *b* 24 Oct. 1972. *Address:* 54A 3rd Avenue, Parktown North, 2193 Johannesburg, South Africa.

ANWYL, Her Honour Shirley Anne; QC 1979; a Circuit Judge, 1995–2008; Resident Judge, Woolwich Crown Court, 1999–2007; *b* 10 Dec. 1940; *d* of James Ritchie and Helen Sutherland Ritchie; *m* 1969, Robin Hamilton Corson Anwyl; two *s*. *Educ:* St Mary's Diocesan Sch. for Girls, Pretoria; Rhodes Univ., S Africa (BA, LLB). Called to the South African Bar, 1963; called to the Bar, Inner Temple, 1966, Bencher, 1985. A Recorder, 1981–95. Member: Senate of Inns of Court and Bar, 1978–81; Gen. Council of the Bar, 1987; Criminal Injuries Compensation Bd, 1980–95; Mental Health Review Tribunal, 1983–99. Chm., Barristers' Benevolent Assoc., 1989–95. FRSA 1989. Freeman, City of London, 1994; Liveryman, Fruiterers' Co., 1996. *Recreations:* theatre, music, reading. *Address:* 30/31 The Cedars, St George's Park, Ditchling Common, Burgess Hill, E Sussex RH15 0GR. *Club:* Guild of Freemen of City of London.

ANYAOKU, Eleazar Chukwuemeka, (Emeka), CFR 2003; CON 1982; Hon. GCVO 2000; Ndichie Chief Adazie of Obosi; Ugwumba of Idemili; Secretary-General of the Commonwealth, 1990–2000; *b* 18 Jan. 1933; *e s* of late Emmanuel Chukwuemeka Anyaoku, Ononukpo of Okpuno Ire, Obosi, Nigeria, and Cecilia Adiba (*née* Ogbogu); *m* 1962, Ebunola Olubunmi, *yr d* of late barrister Olusola Akanbi Solanke, of Abeokuta, Nigeria; three *s* one *d*. *Educ:* Merchants of Light Sch., Oba; Univ. of Ibadan (Schol.), Nigeria; courses in England and France. Exec. Asst, Commonwealth Develt Corp., in London and Lagos, 1959–62. Joined Nigerian Diplomatic Service, 1962; Mem. Nigerian Permanent Mission to the UN, New York, 1963–66; seconded to Commonwealth Secretariat as Asst Dir, 1966–71, and Dir, 1971–75, Internat. Affairs Div.; Asst Sec.-Gen., 1975–77, Dep. Sec.-Gen. (Political), 1977–83 and 1984–90, of the Commonwealth. Minister of External Affairs, Nigeria, Nov.–Dec. 1983. Chm., Presidential Adv. Council on Internat. Relns, Nigeria, 2001–. Served as Secretary: Review Cttee on Commonwealth inter-governmental organisations, June–Aug., 1966; Commonwealth Observer Team for Gibraltar Referendum, Aug.–Sept., 1967; Anguilla Commn, WI, Jan.–Sept. 1970; Leader, Commonwealth Mission for Mozambique, 1975; Commonwealth Observer, Zimbabwe Talks, Geneva, 1976; accompanied Commonwealth Eminent Persons Gp, SA, 1986. Pres., Royal Commonwealth Society, London, 2000–08 (Vice-Pres., 1975–2000); Mem. Council, Overseas Develt Inst., 1979–90. Trustee, BM, 2005–. Mem., Governing Council: SCF, 1984–90; IISS, London, 1987; Mem., Governing Bd, South Centre, Geneva, 2002–10; Hon. Mem., Club of Rome, 1992–. Internat. Pres., WWF, 2001–09. FRSA 1984. Hon. Fellow, Inst. of Educn, Univ. of London, 1994. Hon. DLitt: Ibadan, 1990; Buckingham, 1994; Bradford, 1995; Rhodes, 2002; Lagos, 2010; Internat. Univ. of Geneva, 2010; Hon. DPhil Ahmadu Bello, 1991; Hon. LLD: Nigeria, 1991; Aberdeen, Reading, 1992; Bristol, Oxford Brookes, 1993; Leeds, South Bank, 1994; New Brunswick, North London, 1995; Liverpool, London, 1997; Nottingham. Livingstone Medal, RSGS, 1996. Freeman, City of London, 1998. Trinity Cross, Trinidad and Tobago, 1999; Grand Officer, Nat. Order of Valour, Cameroon, 1999; Comdr, Most Courteous Order of Lesotho, 1999; Order of Welwitchia (1st Class), Namibia, 2000; highest nat. civilian honour, Madagascar, 2005; Supreme Companion of O. R. Tambo (Gold), S Africa, 2008. *Publications:* The Missing Headlines, 1997; The Inside Story of the Modern Commonwealth, 2004; essays in various pubns. *Recreations:* tennis, swimming, reading. *Address:* 36 Lugard Avenue, PO Box 56236, Ikoyi, Lagos, Nigeria. *Clubs:* Travellers; Metropolitan (Lagos).

AOTEAROA, Archbishop of, since 2006; **Most Rev. William Brown Turei;** Co-Primate of Aotearoa, New Zealand and Polynesia, since 2006; *b* 12 Dec. 1924; *s* of Honehiki and Heneriata Waititi; adopted by Nehe and Hariata Turei; *m* 1957, Mary Jane King; one *s* two *d*. *Educ:* Te Aute Coll. Secondary; St John's Theol Coll., Auckland (LTh). Ordained priest, 1950; served in parishes: Tauranga, Whangara, Te Puke, Whakatane, Manutuke, Christchurch and Waipatu, 1949–82; Archdeacon of Tairawhiti, 1982–92; Bishop of Tairawhiti, 1992–2008; Bishop of Aotearoa, 2005–08. *Recreation:* of late a couch participant (did play Rugby, tennis, cricket and golf). *Address:* PO Box 568, Gisborne 4040, New Zealand. *E:* browntmihi@xtra.co.nz.

AOTEAROA, NEW ZEALAND AND POLYNESIA, Archbishop and Co-Primate of; *see* Aotearoa, Archbishop of.

APLIN, Paul Stephen, OBE 2009; Tax Partner, A C Mole & Sons, since 1992; *b* Taunton, 11 June 1957; *s* of James Aplin and Marjorie Aplin (*née* Townsley); *m* 1991, Sharon Binns. *Educ:* Cambridge Coll. of Arts and Technol. (BSc Jt Hons Biol. and Chem. 1978). ACA 1985, FCA 1996; CTA 1989, CTA (Fellow) 2010. A C Mole & Sons, 1980–. Mem. Council, ICAEW, 2007– (Chm. Tax Faculty, 2007–09 (Chm., Tech. Cttee, 2010–); Mem., Tech. Strategy Bd, 2007–09). Mem., Tech. Cttee, Chartered Inst. of Taxation, 2010–. Mem., Admin. Burdens Adv. Bd, 2008–, Powers Oversight Forum, 2009–13, HMRC. Mem., Editl Bd, Tax Jl, 2012–. Lectr and broadcaster on tax issues. Freeman, Tax Advisers' Co., 2009. Tax Personality of Year, Taxation Awards, 2007; External Engagement Award, HMRC, 2012; Outstanding Industry Contribution Award, British Accountancy Awards, 2013. *Publications:* contrib. Tax Jl, Taxation, TAXLine, Economia and other tax and accountancy jls. *Recreations:* photography (LRPS 1999), hillwalking and mountaineering, ballroom dancing, reading, theatre, early music, endeavouring (generally unsuccessfully) to stay one intellectual step ahead of my border collie. *Address:* A C Mole & Sons, Stafford House, Blackbrook Park Avenue, Taunton, Somerset TA1 2PX. *T:* (01823) 624450. *E:* paulaplin@acmole.co.uk.

APPIGNANESI, Dr Lisa, OBE 2013; FRSL; writer, since 1990; *b* Poland, 4 Jan. 1946; *d* of Aron Borenstein and Hena Borenstein; *m* 2013, Prof. John Forrester; one *d*; one *s* by a previous marriage. *Educ:* McGill Univ., Montreal (BA 1966; MA 1967); Univ. of Sussex (PhD 1970). Lecturer: Univ. of Essex, 1971–73; New England Coll., 1974–81; Institute of Contemporary Arts: Dir, Talks, 1981–86; Dep. Dir, 1986–90; Mem. Bd, 2001–05. Dep. Pres., 2003–07, Pres., 2008–11, English PEN. Chm., Freud Mus., 2006–14. Vis. Prof., KCL, 2012–. FRSL 2015. Chevalier, Ordre des Arts et des Lettres (France), 1987. *Publications: non-fiction:* Dialogue of the Generations, 1974; Femininity and the Creative Imagination: James, Proust and Musil, 1974; Cabaret: the first hundred years, 1976, 2nd edn 1986 (trans. several langs); (ed with Steven Rose), Science and Beyond, 1986; Simone de Beauvoir, 1988, 2nd edn 2005 (trans. several langs); (ed) Postmodernism, 1989; (ed) Ideas from France, 1989; (ed with Hilary Lawson) Dismantling Truth, 1989; (ed with Sara Maitland) The Rushdie File, 1989; (with John Forrester) Freud's Women, 1992, 3rd edn 2004 (trans. German, Spanish and other langs); Losing the Dead, 1999, 2nd edn 2014; (ed) Free Expression is No Offence, 2005; Mad, Bad and Sad: a history of women and the mind doctors since 1800, 2008 (BMA Award for Public Understanding of Sci., 2009); All About Love: anatomy of an unruly emotion, 2011; (ed jtly) Fifty Shades of Feminism, 2013; Trials of Passion: crimes in the name of love and madness, 2014; *fiction:* Memory and Desire, 1991; Dreams of Innocence, 1994; A Good Woman, 1996; The Things We Do for Love, 1997; The Dead of Winter, 1999; Sanctuary, 2000; Paris Requiem, 2002, 2nd edn 2014; The Memory Man, 2004 (Holocaust Literature Award, 2005); Sacred Ends, 2014; *translations* include: (with John Berger) Bielski, Oranges for the Son of Alexander Levy, 2000; Latifa, My Forbidden Face: a memoir of an Afghan girl, 2002; (with John Berger) Bielski, The Year is 42, 2003 (Scott Moncrieff Prize for French Trans., 2005); articles in Guardian, Observer, Independent, Telegraph. *Recreation:* friends. *Address:* c/o Matias Lopez-Portillo, Aitken Alexander Associates, 291 Gray's Inn Road, WC1X 8EB.

APPLEBY, Bernadette Joan; *see* Kenny, B. J.

APPLEBY, His Honour Brian John; QC 1971; a Circuit Judge, 1988–2003, a Deputy Circuit Judge, since 2003; *b* 25 Feb. 1930; *s* of Ernest Joel and Gertrude Appleby; *m* 1st, 1958, Rosa Helena (*née* Flitterman) (*d* 1996); one *s* one *d*; 2nd, 1998, Lynda Jane Eaton (*d* 2014). *Educ:* Uppingham; St John's Coll., Cambridge (BA). Called to Bar, Middle Temple, 1953; Bencher, 1980. Dep. Chm., Notts QS, 1970–71; a Recorder, 1972–88. Mem., Nottingham City Council, 1955–58 and 1960–63. District Referee, Nottinghamshire Wages Conciliation Board, NCB, 1980–88. President, Court of Appeal: St Helena, 1998–2007; Falkland Is, 2002–07; Indian Ocean Territory, 2002–07. *Recreations:* watching good football (preferably Nottingham Forest: Mem. Club Cttee, 1965–82, Life Mem., 1982; Vice-Chm., 1972–75,

Chm., 1975–78); swimming, reading and enjoying, when possible, company of wife and children. *Address:* The Briars, Old Melton Road, Normanton on the Wolds, Nottingham NG12 5NN.

APPLEBY, Douglas Edward Surtees; farmer; retired Managing Director, The Boots Co. Ltd; *b* 17 May 1929; *s* of Robert Edward Appleby, MSc and Muriel (*née* Surtees); one *s* one *d. Educ:* Durham Johnston Sch.; Univ. of London (BSc); Univ. of Nottingham (BSc). Chartered Accountant, 1957. Commissioned, RAF, Cranwell, 1950–54. Moore, Stephens & Co., Chartered Accountants, London, 1954–57; Distillers Co. Ltd, 1957–58; Corn Products Co., New York, 1959–63; Wilkinson Sword Ltd, 1964–68; The Boots Co. Ltd, 1968–81 (Finance Dir, 1968–72, Man. Dir, 1973–81). Regional Dir, Nat. Westminster Bank, 1979–88; Chairman: John H. Mason Ltd, 1982–96; Meadow Farm Produce plc, 1984–86; Sims Food Gp plc, 1987–89. Member Council: Inst. Chartered Accountants, 1971–75; Loughborough Univ., 1973–75; CBI, 1977–81. *Address:* c/o Bank of Scotland, The Mound, Edinburgh EH1 1YZ.

APPLEBY, Elizabeth; *see* Appleby, L. E.

APPLEBY, Dame Hazel Gillian; *see* Genn, Dame H. G.

APPLEBY, Prof. (James) Louis (John), CBE 2006; MD; FRCPE, FRCPsych, FRCP; Professor of Psychiatry, University of Manchester, since 1996; *b* 27 Feb. 1955; *s* of late James Appleby and of Doris May Appleby; *m* 1992, Juliet Haselden; two *s* two *d. Educ:* Bathgate Acad.; Univ. of Edinburgh (BSc Hons; MB ChB; MD 1995). MRCP 1983, FRCPE 1995; MRCPsych 1986, FRCPsych 1997; FRCP 2008. Sen. Lectr, Univ. of Manchester, 1991–96. Nat. Dir for Mental Health, DoH, 2000–10; Nat. Clinical Dir for Health and Criminal Justice, DoH, 2010–14. Dir, Nat. Confidential Inquiry into suicide and homicide by people with mental illness, 1996–; Chm., Nat. Suicide Prevention Strategy Adv. Gp, 2002–. Non-exec. Dir, Care Quality Commn, 2013–. Hon. FRCPsych 2011. *Publications:* A Medical Tour Through the Whole Island of Great Britain, 1994, 2nd edn 1995; contrib. numerous res. pubns on suicide, homicide and parental mental illness. *Recreations:* trying to impress my kids, cleaning my clarinet, keeping lists. *Address:* Centre for Mental Health and Safety, University Place, University of Manchester, Oxford Road, Manchester M13 9PL.

APPLEBY, John Laurence; Chief Economist, King's Fund, since 1998; *b* 26 April 1958; *s* of Will Appleby and Margaret Sheila Appleby; partner, Claire Helen Melamed; three *s* one *d. Educ:* Univ. of Essex (BA Hons Econs 1979); Univ. of York (MSc Health Econs 1981). Economist in NHS, Birmingham and London, 1981–88; Manager of Res., NAHAT, 1988–93; Senior Lecturer in Health Economics: Univ. of Birmingham, 1993–95; Univ. of East Anglia, 1995–98. Hon. Vis. Prof., Dept of Econs, City Univ., London, 2002–. *Publications:* Financing Health Care in the 1990s, 1992; (jtly) The Reorganised NHS, 5th edn 1995, 6th edn 1998; numerous book chapters and peer-reviewed papers. *Recreations:* when not painting, reading, iPodding or DIYing, slumped in front of TV with a bottle of wine. *Address:* King's Fund, 11–13 Cavendish Square, W1G 0AN. *T:* (020) 7307 2400, *Fax:* (020) 7307 2807.

APPLEBY, His Honour John Montague; a Circuit Judge, Northern Circuit, 2003–15; *b* 8 Nov. 1945; *s* of Montague Eric Appleby and Carmen Irene Appleby; *m* 1970, Barbara Joan Plumb; one *s. Educ:* Dauntsey's; Univ. of Nottingham (LLB Hons). Admitted solicitor, 1970; Asst Solicitor, Leicester, 1970–72; joined Truman & Appleby, later Truman Close Kendall & Appleby, 1972: Partner, 1974–88; Man. Partner, 1988–98; merged to form Nelsons, 1999: Mem., Mgt Bd, 1999–2000; Partner, 1999–2003; Asst Recorder, 1993–99; Recorder, 1999–2003. Mem. Council, Law Soc., 1984–99; Pres., Notts Law Soc., 1997. Pres., Notts Hockey Assoc., 1994–96. *Publications:* (contrib.) Professional Management of a Solicitor's Practice, 1980. *Recreations:* golf, travel, wine, theatre. *Clubs:* Nottingham Hockey (Vice-Pres.), Bacchanalians Hockey (Midlands); Nottingham Cricket (Vice-Pres.); Hale Golf.

APPLEBY, (Lesley) Elizabeth, (Mrs Michael Kenneth Collins); QC 1979; barrister-at-law; a Deputy High Court Judge, since 1985; a Recorder, since 1989; *b* 12 Aug. 1942; *o d* of late Arthur Leslie Appleby and Dorothy Evelyn Appleby (*née* Edwards); *m* 1978, Michael Kenneth Collins, OBE, BSc, MICE (*d* 2008); one *s* one *d. Educ:* Dominican Convent, Brewood, Staffs; Wolverhampton Girls' High Sch.; Manchester Univ. (LLB Hons). Called to Bar, Gray's Inn, 1965 (Richardson Schol.); *ad eundem* Lincoln's Inn, 1975, Bencher, 1986, Treas., 2009–10; in practice at Chancery Bar, 1966–; inspector of five cos, Dept of Trade, 1983; Chm., Inquiry into Lambeth BC, 1993. Mem., Senate of Inns of Court and Bar, 1977–80, 1981–82. Chm., Ethics and Integrity Cttee, Cons. Party, 1998–. *Recreations:* walking, gardening. *Address:* 4/5 Gray's Inn Square, Gray's Inn, WC1R 5AH. *T:* (020) 7404 5252.

APPLEBY, Lindsay C.; *see* Croisdale-Appleby, L.

APPLEBY, Louis; *see* Appleby, J. L. J.

APPLEBY, Malcolm Arthur, MBE 2014; engraver designer, mentor and teacher; *b* 6 Jan. 1946; *s* of James William and Marjory Appleby; *m* 2000, Philippa Swann; one *d. Educ:* Hawes Down County Secondary Modern School for Boys; Beckenham Sch. of Art; Ravensbourne Coll. of Art and Design; Central Sch. of Arts and Crafts; Sir John Cass Sch. of Art; Royal Coll. of Art. Set up trade, 1968; bought Crathes station, 1970; moved workshop to Perthshire, 1996; developed fresh approaches to engraving on silver, forging after engraving; created first pure gold and pure silver pieces to bear Scottish hallmark, 1999; works designed and executed include: engraving on Prince of Wales coronet; model of moon (subseq. gift to first moon astronauts); steel and gold cylinder box for Goldsmiths' Co.; steel, gold, ivory and silver chess set, 1977; 500th anniv. silver for London Assay Office; King George VI Diamond Stakes trophy, 1978; seal for the Board of Trustees, V & A; silver condiment set for 10 Downing Street, commnd by Silver Trust; major silver commn for Royal Mus. of Scotland; silver table centre for new Scottish Parlt; gold Royal Medal for RSE, 2000; sporting guns (product designer, Holland & Holland, gunmakers, 1991–97), 'Loving Cups' for 35th anniv. of George Heriot's Sch., Edinburgh, silver bowls, jewels, prints; Banchory Bangle award for Children First charity, annually, 1976–; Diamond Jubilee Jewel; Prime Ministers' catch phrases silver beaker series, 2011–; medal for FIDEM XXXII Art Medal Congress, 2012; Candlesticks for St Giles' Cath., Edinburgh, 2013. Goldsmiths' Craftsmanship and Design Awards: Gold Awards, Trafalgar Medal, 2007, Peacock Bangle, 2008; Silver Award, Raven Beaker, 2009; Gold, Silver and Special Awards for engraving, 2011; Gold and Special Council Award, 2012. Work in collections: Aberdeen Art Gallery; Royal Scottish Museum; Scottish Craft Collection; East Midlands Arts; Fitzwilliam Mus., Cambridge; BM; Goldsmiths' Co.; V&A; Crafts Council; Contemporary Arts Soc.; Tower of London Royal Armouries; Nat. Mus. of Finland; Åland Maritime Mus.; S Australia Maritime Mus.; Perth Art Gall. and Mus.; Ashmolean Mus. Exhibitions: one-man retrospective, Aberdeen Art Gall., 1998; (contrib.) Creation, Goldsmiths' Hall, 2004; (jt retrospective) Precious Statements, Goldsmiths' Hall, 2006; The Cutting Edge, Royal Mus. of Scotland, Mus. of Modern Art Glasgow, Aberdeen Art Gall. and Mus., 2007; Raising the Bar, Dovecot, Edinburgh, Ruthin Craft Centre, Wales, Middlesbrough Inst. of Modern Art, 2008; Contemporary Silver for Bishopsland, V&A, 2009, Dovecot, Edinburgh, 2010; Maker, Scottish Gall., Edinburgh, 2012; Silver, the Aberdeen Story, Aberdeen Art Gall., 2012; Passing it On, Scottish Gall., 2014. Fellow, Bishopsland Educnl Trust. Founder, British Art Postage Stamp Soc., 1986; Mem., British Art Medal Soc., 1987–; Founding Mem., British Hand Engravers Assoc.; estab. Malcolm Appleby Hand Engraving Award, British Silver Week, 2010. Chm., Crathes Drumoak Community Council, 1981. Life Member: NT for Scotland, 1971; SPAB, 1989; British Dragon Fly Soc., 2001; Orkney Boat Mus.; Cluny Gardens; Highland Perthshire Community Land Trust; McLaren Soc. Member: Silver Soc.; Butterfly Conservation Soc.; John Muir Trust; Bumble Bee Conservation Trust. Sponsor, Friends of Birks Cinema, Aberfeldy restoration project. Hon. Mem., Grandtully and Strathtay Br., Women's Rural Inst., 1997. Liveryman, Goldsmiths' Co. Hon. DLitt Heriot-Watt, 2000. Lifetime Achievement Award, Hand Engravers Assoc., 2015. *Recreations:* work, walking, garden design, drinking herbal tea with friends, acting in pantomime, conservation matters, tree planting with Philippa Swann, playing pom pom ping pong with daughter May, inventor of celebrity frisbee quoits. *Address:* Aultbeag, Grandtully, by Aberfeldy, Perthshire PH15 2QU. *T:* (01887) 840484.

APPLEBY, Dom Raphael, OSB; *b* 18 July 1931; *s* of Harold Thompson Appleby and Margaret Morgan. *Educ:* Downside; Christ's Coll., Cambridge (MA). Downside novitiate, 1951; Housemaster at Downside, 1962–75, Head Master, 1975–80; Nat. Chaplain, Catholic Students' Council, 1974–94; Parish Priest, St Joseph's, Great Malvern, 1996–2003; Mem., Sch. Chaplaincy Team, Downside, 2003–10. Nat. Co-ordinator for RC Chaplains in Higher Educn, 1980–87; Diocesan Youth Chaplain, Clifton Dio., 1983–89. *Publications:* Dear Church, What's the Point?, 1984; Glimpses of God, 1993. *Recreations:* books, music. *Address:* Downside Abbey, Bath BA3 4RH.

APPLEBY, Rt Rev. Richard Franklin; Bishop of the Northern Region and an Assistant Bishop, Diocese of Brisbane, 1999–2006; *b* 17 Nov. 1940; *s* of Julian Paul Leonard Appleby and Lilian Margaret Appleby (*née* Pragnell); *m* 1966, Elizabeth Clark; two *d. Educ:* Eltham High Sch.; Univ. of Melbourne (BSc); St John's Coll., Morpeth (ThL (Hons)). Curate of Glenroy, 1967–68; Curate of N Balwyn and Chaplain to Apprentices and Probation Hostels, 1969–70; Chaplain to Christchurch Grammar Sch., 1970–71; Warden of Wollaston Coll. and Chaplain to the Archbishop of Perth, 1972–75; Rector of Belmont, 1975–80; Dean of Bathurst and Examining Chaplain to the Bishop of Bathurst, 1980–83; Auxiliary Bishop of Newcastle, 1983–92; Bishop of the Northern Territory (Australia), 1992–99. President: NSW Ecumenical Council, 1987–89; Qld Churches Together, 2004–05; Nat. Council of Churches in Australia, 2006–09. *Recreations:* gardening, walking, listening to music. *Address:* PO Box 112, Waratah, NSW 2298, Australia. *T:* (2) 49674628. *E:* rfappleby@gmail.com.

APPLEGARTH, Adam John; Chief Executive, Northern Rock plc, 2001–07; *b* 3 Aug. 1962; *s* of late John Speed Applegarth and of Mary Applegarth; *m* 1984, Patricia Catherine Killeen; two *s. Educ:* Sedbergh Sch.; Grey Coll., Durham Univ. (BA). Gen. Manager, 1993–96, Exec. Dir, 1996–97, Northern Rock Building Soc.; Exec. Dir, Northern Rock plc, 1997–2007; Dir, Northern Rock (Guernsey) Ltd, 1996–2001; non-exec. Dir, Persimmon, 2006–07. Senior Adviser: Apollo Mgt, 2009–13; to private equity, 2014–. Trustee, Internat. Centre for Life Trust, 1997–2001. Gov., RGS, Newcastle, 2002–. *Recreation:* cricket. *Club:* Ashbrooke Sporting.

APPLEGATE, Ven. John, PhD; Principal, All Saints Centre for Mission and Ministry (formerly Course Principal, Southern North-West Training Partnership), since 2008; Archdeacon of Bolton, 2002–08, now Emeritus; *b* 1956. *Educ:* Bristol Univ. (BSc 1975); Trinity Coll., Bristol (DipHE; PhD). Ordained deacon, 1984, priest, 1985; Curate: Collyhurst, Dio. of Manchester, 1984–87; St John, Broughton and St James, Higher Broughton, and St Clement with St Matthias, Lower Broughton, 1987–92; St John, Broughton and St James with St Clement, and St Matthias, Broughton, 1992–94; Rector, St John, Broughton, 1994–96; Team Rector, Broughton, 1996–2002. Area Dean, Salford, 1996–2002. Pt-time Lectr and Hon. Res. Fellow, Univ. of Manchester, 2001–.

APPLEGATE, Lt Gen. Richard Arthur David, CB 2010; OBE 1996; Managing Director, Eagle Strategic Consulting Ltd, since 2010; Head of Strategy and New Business, Elbit Systems (UK), since 2011; *b* 20 March 1955; *s* of late Arthur Applegate and Elsie Applegate; *m* 1979, Rachael Bridgeman; two *d. Educ:* Chislehurst and Sidcup Grammar Sch.; Manchester Univ. (BA Hons Politics and Mod. Hist.); Staff Coll., Camberley (psc† 1987); Joint Staff Coll., Bracknell (hcsc(j) 1998); Boeing Exec. Leadership Prog. 2009; IoD 2009. Service in Bosnia, Kosovo, NI, Belize, Hong Kong, Kenya, Germany, Belgium and UK; Mil. Asst/Speechwriter to SACEUR, 1992–94; Comdr UN and European Rapid Reaction Bde Artillery Gps, Mount Igman/Sarajevo, 1995; CO 19th Regt RA (Highland Gunners), 1994–96; Col Force Develt, 1996–98; CRA 3rd (UK) Div., 1998–2000; Director: Indirect Battlefield Engagement; Deep Target Attack, 2000–03; Capability Manager (Battlespace Manoeuvre), MoD, 2003–06, and Master Gen. of the Ordnance, 2006; Chief of Materiel (Land), Defence Equipment and Support Orgn, 2007–09; Quartermaster Gen., 2007–09; Defence Career Partner, 2009–10. Col Comdt, RA, 2006–11 (Chm., RA Fundraising, 2009–). Director: Design Blue, 2011–; UAV Tactical Systems Ltd, 2011–; Ferranti Technologies Ltd, 2012–; Remitia Ltd. Patron, Heropreneurs, 2012–. CCMI 2010; FCGI 2011. City and Guilds Inst. Award, 1986; Légionnaire 1st cl. d'Honneur, Légion Étrangère, 1996; Officer, Legion of Merit (USA), 2007. *Publications:* numerous articles in RUSI Jl, Defense Analysis and in-house jls; winner, Thales essay competition, 2002. *Recreations:* walking, coarse gardening, military history, game shooting.

APPLETON, His Honour John Fortnam; a Circuit Judge, 1992–2011; Designated Civil Judge, Lancashire and Cumbria (formerly Preston) Group of Courts, 1998–2011; *b* 8 April 1946; *s* of late George Fortnam Appleton, OBE, TD, JP, DL and Patricia Margaret Appleton; *m* 1983, Maureen Sellers; one *s. Educ:* Harrow; Bristol Univ. (LLB Hons). Called to the Bar, Middle Temple, 1969; Asst Recorder, 1981–85; a Recorder of the Crown Court, 1985–92. *Recreations:* family, country pursuits. *Address:* Park Cottage, Deer Park Lane, Hornby, Lancaster LA2 8LF. *E:* jfappleton@btinternet.com.

APPLETON, Margaret Mary, MBE 2012; Chief Executive, Royal Air Force Museum, since 2015; *b* Lytham, Lancs, 1965; *d* of Thomas Appleton and Veronica Ball; partner, 1986, *m* 2005, Anthony Nicolson; two *s. Educ:* Lark Hill House Sch., Preston; Cardinal Newman Coll., Preston; Univ. of Liverpool (BA Hons Med. and Mod. Hist. 1988); Univ. of Birmingham (MSocSc Heritage Mgt 1991). AMA. Asst Registrar, Royal Armouries, 1990; Asst Curator, then Curator/Cultural Services Manager, Stevenage BC, 1991–2002; Dir, Museums, Luton BC, 2003–08; Chief Exec., Luton Culture, 2008–15. Mem., E of England Cttee, HLF. Vice Pres., Mus Assoc.; Co-Chair, Women Leaders in Mus Network. *Recreations:* book group, cycling, museums, theatre. *Address:* Royal Air Force Museum, Grahame Park Way, NW9 5LL. *T:* (020) 8358 4823. *E:* maggie.appleton@rafmuseum.org.

APPLEYARD, James; *see* Appleyard, W. J.

APPLEYARD, Joan Ena, (Lady Appleyard); DL; Headmistress, St Swithun's School, Winchester, 1986–94; *b* 15 Aug. 1946; *d* of William Jefferson and Ruth Ena Leake; *m* 1994, Sir Leonard Appleyard, *qv. Educ:* Univ. of Newcastle (BA Hons History); Westminster Coll., Oxford (Dip Ed). Asst Mistress, 1968–70, Head of History, 1970–73, Scarborough Girls' High Sch.; Head of Humanities, Graham Sch., Scarborough, 1973–75; Dep. Head, 1975–79, Headmistress, 1979–86, Hunmanby Hall Sch., Filey. President: GSA, 1992–93; Soc. for Promoting the Training of Women, 2007–. Dep. Chm., ESU, 1999–2005. Chm., Hants Historic Churches Trust, 2008–. DL Hants, 2010. *Recreations:* drama, opera, reading, cooking.

APPLEYARD, Sir Leonard (Vincent), KCMG 1994 (CMG 1986); Pro Chancellor, Bournemouth University, 2004–12; Senior Fellow and Visiting Professor, Southampton University, since 2009; *b* 2 Sept. 1938; *s* of Thomas William Appleyard; *m* 1st, 1964, Elizabeth Margaret West (marr. diss. 1994); two *d*; 2nd, 1994, Joan Ena Jefferson (*see* J. E. Appleyard).

Educ: Read School, Drax, W Yorks; Queens' Coll., Cambridge (MA). Foreign Office, 1962; Third Secretary, Hong Kong, 1964; Second Secretary, Peking, 1966; Second, later First, Secretary, Foreign Office, 1969; First Secretary, Delhi, 1971, Moscow, 1975; HM Treasury, 1978; Financial Counsellor, Paris, 1979–82; Head of Economic Relations Dept, FCO, 1982–84; Principal Private Sec. to Sec. of State for Foreign and Commonwealth Affairs, 1984–86; Ambassador to Hungary, 1986–89; Dep. Sec., Cabinet Office, 1989–91 (on secondment); Political Dir and Dep. Under-Sec. of State, FCO, 1991–94; Ambassador to People's Republic of China, 1994–97. Vice-Chm., Barclays Capital, 1998–2003. Chairman: Farnham Castle Conf. Centre, 2003–07; Hants Archives Trust, 2011–12. Chm., Council, Winchester Cathedral, 2007–12. *Recreations:* music, shooting.

APPLEYARD, Sir Raymond (Kenelm), KBE 1986; PhD; Director-General for Information Market and Innovation, Commission of the European Communities, 1981–86; *b* 5 Oct. 1922; *s* of late Maj.-Gen. K. C. Appleyard, CBE, TD, DL, and Monica Mary Louis; *m* 1947, Joan Greenwood (*d* 2015); one *s* two *d. Educ:* Rugby; Cambridge. BA 1943, MA 1948, PhD 1950. Instructor, Yale Univ., 1949–51; Fellow, Rockefeller Foundn, California Inst. of Technology, 1951–53; Research Officer, Atomic Energy of Canada Ltd, 1953–56; Sec., UN Scientific Cttee on effects of atomic radiation, 1956–61; Dir, Biology Services, Commn of European Atomic Energy Community, 1961–73; Dir-Gen. for Scientific and Tech. Information and Information Management, EEC Commn, 1973–80. Exec. Sec., European Molecular Biology Organisation, 1965–73; Sec., European Molecular Biology Conf., 1969–73; President: Inst. of Information Scientists, 1981–82; Inst. of Translation and Interpreting, 1989–94. Hon. Dr.med Ulm, 1977. *Publications:* contribs to: Nature, Jl Gen. Microbiol., Genetics, Jl of Radiol Protection. *Recreation:* bridge.

APPLEYARD, Dr (William) James, FRCP; Dean of Clinical Sciences, Kigesi International School of Medicine, Uganda, 2000–04; Consultant Paediatrician, 1971–98, Hon. Consultant Paediatrician, 1998–99, and Clinical Director, Paediatric Directorate, 1992–98, Kent and Canterbury Hospitals NHS Trust (formerly Canterbury and Thanet Health District); *b* 25 Oct. 1935; *s* of late E. R. Appleyard and Maud Oliver Collingwood (*née* Marshall); *m* 1964, Elizabeth Anne Ward; one *s* two *d. Educ:* Canford Sch.; Exeter College, Oxford (BM BCh, MA); Guy's Hosp. Med. Sch., Univ. of London. DObstRCOG; FRCP 1978; FRCPCH 1998. Junior paediat. posts, Guy's and Gt Ormond St; Resident in Pediat., Univ. of Louisville, 1964–65; Dyers' Co. Res. Registrar, St Thomas' Hosp., 1968–69. British Medical Association: Treas., 1996–2002; Member: Jt Consultants Cttee, 1976–95; Consultants Cttee, 1971–2002 (Dep. Chm., 1979–83); Dep. Chm., 1989–91, Chm., 1992–95, Rep. Body. Treasurer, BPA, 1983–88; Mem., GMC, 1984–2003 (Mem., Educn Cttee, 1993–96); Member Council: RCP, 1988–91 (Member: Standing Cttee, 1970–72; Res. Cttee, 1971–74; Paed. Cttee, 1987–91; Examng Bd, 1992–98); World Med. Assoc., 1995–2005 (Chm., Med. Ethics Cttee, 1996–99; Pres., 2003–04; immed. Past Pres., 2005); Chm. Ethics Cttee and a Site Visitor, 2006–, Vice Pres., 2012–, Internat. Assoc. of Med. Colls (Hon. Sec. to Bd of Trustees, 2007–12); Pres., Internat. Coll. of Person Centered Medicine, 2013–15. Member: Health Service Inf. Steering Gp, Korner Cttee, 1985; DoH Inf. Adv. Gp, 1986–90; Nat. Specialist Commissioning Adv. Gp, DoH, 1995–96; London Univ. Nominee, Kent AHA, 1974–78. Mem. Bd, Urbani Internat., Geneva, 2004–. Hon. Tutor in Paed., Guy's Hosp.; Hon. Lectr in Paed., St Thomas' Hosp.; Dean of Clin. Studies, (UK), St George's Univ. Sch. of Medicine, Grenada, 1995–97 (Associate Prof., 1985–90; Prof. of Paediatrics, 1991–95; Chm., Senate, 1991–93). Hon. Treas., Kent Postgrad. Med. Centre, Canterbury, 1998–2000. Patron, Dyspraxia Trust, 1988–. Trustee, St John's Hosp., Canterbury, 2007– (Chm., 2012). Liveryman, Apothecaries' Soc., 1983. Hon. FRCPCH 2002. Hon. DM Kent at Canterbury, 1999; Hon. DHL St George's, Grenada, 2000. Alumnus Award for Paed. Res., Univ. of Louisville, 1965. Member, Editorial Board: Jl Chinese Med. Assoc., 2003–13; Internat. Jl of Person Centered Medicine, 2011–. *Publications:* contribs to med. jls. *Recreations:* croquet, photography, erstwhile allotment digger. *Address:* Thimble Hall, Blean Common, Blean, Kent CT2 9JJ. *T:* (01227) 781771. *Club:* Athenæum.

ApSIMON, Prof. Helen Mary, CBE 2013; PhD; Professor of Air Pollution Studies, Imperial College London, since 2001; *b* Ashby-de-la-Zouche, 28 April 1942; *d* of Dr Geoffrey and Margery Hollingsworth; *m* 1967, Dr Hugh Ellis Gardiner ApSimon (*d* 1998). *Educ:* Northampton High Sch.; Somerville Coll., Oxford (MA Maths 1963); St Andrews Univ. (PhD Astrophysics 1967). Res., W S Atkins, 1972–74; Imperial College London: pt-time PDRA, 1974–86; Res. Fellow, 1986–91; Reader in Air Pollution Studies, 1991–2000; Churchill Travelling Fellowship on air pollution in Eastern Europe, 1988; work for UK govt on air pollution, 1991–. Mem., task forces under UNECE Convention on Long-Range Transboundary Air Pollution, 1991–. Founder Mem. and Pres., Eur. Assoc. for Sci. of Air Pollution, 1994–2000; Founder Mem. and Chair, Air Pollution Res. in London res. network, 2000–10. Mem., expert gps, incl. Air Quality Expert Gp, 2003–12, Air Quality Modelling Steering Gp, 2013–, DEFRA; Mem., Expert Panel, Airports Commn, 2013–. *Recreations:* keeping a horse, dressage competing and judging, walking, gardening, reading, volunteer in A&E at Frimley Park Hospital. *Address:* Centre for Environmental Policy, Imperial College London, Exhibition Road, SW7 2AZ. *T:* (020) 7594 9292. *E:* h.apsimon@imperial.ac.uk.

APSLEY, Lord; Benjamin George Henry Bathurst; Captain, 40 Commando Royal Marines; *b* 6 March 1990; *s* and *heir* of Earl Bathurst, *qv.*

APSLEY, Dr Norman, OBE 2012; FREng; FInstP; FIAE; Chief Executive, Northern Ireland Science Park Foundation Ltd, since 2000; *b* Larne, Co. Antrim, 9 Dec. 1950; *s* of Robert and Edith Muriel Apsley; *m* 2009, Jacqui McCarroll; one *s* one *d. Educ:* Larne Grammar Sch.; Ulster Univ. (BSc Physics 1st Cl.); Peterhouse, Cambridge (MA 1976); Jesus Coll., Cambridge (PhD 1977). FInstP 1996; FREng 2011. Res. Fellow, Jesus Coll., Cambridge, 1976–79; Sen. Res. Scientist, 1979–83, Principal Res. Scientist, 1983–90, Royal Signals & Radar Estabt Malvern; Superintendent, Optical and Display Sci., 1990–92, Business Develt Manager, 1992–96, DRA; Dir, Electronics Sector, DERA, 1996–2000. Vis. Prof., Ulster Univ., 2000–. Vice Pres. (Business and Innovation), Inst. of Physics, 2008–. FIAE 2011. *Publications:* contribs to learned jls. *Recreations:* photography, walking, camping, music. *Address:* Northern Ireland Science Park, The Innovation Centre, Queen's Road, Belfast BT3 9DT. *T:* (028) 9073 7800, *Fax:* (028) 9073 7801. *E:* n.apsley@nisp.co.uk.

APTED, Michael David, CMG 2008; director and producer of television and films; *b* 10 Feb. 1941; *m* (marr. diss.); two *s*; *m* Jo; one *s. Educ:* Downing Coll., Cambridge (BA 1963). With Granada TV, 1963–70: researcher, 1963; dir, episodes of Coronation Street; investigative reporter, World in Action, incl. research, 1964, on 7 Up, which became first of series (director: Seven Plus Seven, 1970; 21 Up, 1977; 28 Up, 1985; 35 Up, 1991; 42 Up, 1998; 49 Up, 2005; 56 Up, 2012; 21 Up New Generation, 2014). Director: *television:* series: Big Breadwinner Hog, 1969; The Lovers, 1970; Folly Foot (for children), 1972; My Life and Times, 1991; plays and films: Slattery's Mounted Foot, 1970; The Mosedale Horseshoe, 1971; The Reporters, 1972; Kisses at Fifty, 1972; Another Sunday and Sweet FA, 1972; The Collection, 1975; Stronger than the Sun, 1977; P'tang Yang Kipperbang, 1982; The Long Way Home, 1989; Always Outnumbered, 1998; Nathan Dixon, 1999; *films include:* Triple Echo, 1973; Stardust, 1975; The Squeeze, 1977; Agatha, 1979; Coal Miner's Daughter, 1980; Continental Divide, 1981; Gorky Park, 1983; Firstborn, 1984; Bring on the Night, 1985; Critical Condition, 1987; Gorillas in the Mist, 1988; Class Action, 1991; Incident at Oglala, 1992; Thunderheart, 1992; Blink, 1994; Moving the Mountain, 1994; Nell, 1995; Extreme Measures, 1997; (also prod) Inspirations (documentary), 1997; The World is Not Enough, 1999; Me and Isaac Newton, 1999; Enigma, 2001; Enough, 2002; Amazing Grace, 2007; The Chronicles of Narnia: the Voyage of the Dawn Treader, 2010; *executive producer:* The River Rat, 1984; Dracula, 1992. Prod., TV series, Rome, 2006. *Publications:* 7 Up, 1999. *Address:* c/o United Agents, 12–26 Lexington Street, W1F 0LE.

APTHORP, John Dorrington, CBE 2014 (OBE 1999); Chairman, Majestic Wine Warehouses (formerly Wizard Wine), 1989–2005; *b* 25 April 1935; *s* of late Eric and Mildred Apthorp; *m* 1959, Jane Frances Arnold; three *s* one *d. Educ:* Aldenham School. Sub-Lieut RNVR, 1953–55. Family business, Appypak, 1956–68; started Bejam Group, 1968, Exec. Chm., 1968–87, non-exec. Chm., 1987–88. Mem., Tay River Bd, 2002–09. Councillor, London Bor. of Barnet, 1968–74. Liveryman: Butchers' Co., 1974–; Vintners' Co., 1999–. Gov., London Acad., 2004–. FCMI (FBIM 1977); FInstD 1978; FIGD 1981. Hon. DArts Herts, 2014. Guardian Young Business Man of Year, 1974. Commandeur d'Honneur pour Commanderie du Bontemps de Medoc et des Graves, 1977. Freedom, Bor. of Barnet, 2009. *Recreations:* shooting, wine. *Address:* The Field House Farm, 29 Newlands Avenue, Radlett, Herts WD7 8EJ. *T:* (01923) 855201. *Club:* Radlett Tennis and Squash.

ARAD, Prof. Ron, RDI 2002; RA 2013; architect and designer; Professor of Product Design, Royal College of Art, 1998–2009; *b* 24 April 1951; *s* of Grisha and Itai Arad; *m* 1975, Dr Alma Erlich; two *d. Educ:* Jerusalem Acad. of Art; Architectural Assoc. (dip. 1979). Professor: of Product Design, Hochschule für Angewandte Kunst, Vienna, 1994–97; of Furniture Design, RCA, 1997. Retrospective exhibn, Restless, Barbican, 2010. Guest Ed., Internat. Design Yearbook, 1994. Designer of Year, Salon du Meuble, Paris, 1994; Barcelona Primavera Internat. Award for Design, 2001; Gio Ponti Internat. Design Award, Denver, 2001; Oribe Art and Design Award, Japan, 2001; Architektur und Wohnen Designer of the Year Award, 2004; FX Mag. Designer of the Year Award, 2005; Visionary Award, Mus. of Arts & Design, NY, 2006; Laureate, Contemporary Art Prize, French Friends of Tel Aviv Mus. of Art, 2007; London Design Medal, 2011. *Recreations:* tennis, ping-pong. *Address:* 62 Chalk Farm Road, NW1 8AN. *T:* (020) 7284 4963. *W:* www.ronarad.com.

ARAGONA, Giancarlo, Hon. KCVO 2005; Ambassador of Italy to the Court of St James's, 2004–09; Chairman: Mediterranean Institute of Hematology, since 2010; Sogin SpA, since 2010; *b* 14 Nov. 1942; *s* of late Giovanni Aragona and of Bianca Maria Aragona (*née* Vinci); *m* 1968, Sandra Pauline Jackson; two *d. Educ:* Messina Univ., Italy (degree in Internat. Law). Entered Italian Diplomatic Service, 1969: served in Vienna, Freiburg im Breisgau and Lagos, 1969–80; Foreign Ministry, Rome, 1980–84; First Counsellor (Political), London, 1984–87; First Counsellor, then Minister-Counsellor and Dep. Perm. Rep., Delegn to NATO, 1987–92; Diplomatic Advr to Defence Minister, Rome, 1992–95; Dir of Cabinet of Foreign Minister, 1995–96; Sec. Gen., OSCE, 1996–99; Ambassador to Russian Fedn, 1999–2001; Dir Gen., Political Affairs and Human Rights, Min. of Foreign Affairs, 2001–04. Cavaliere di Gran Croce dell'Ordine al Merito della Repubblica Italiana, 2007. *Address:* Largo dell'Olgiata 15, 00123 Roma, Italy.

ARAM, Zeev, OBE 2014; FCSD; Chairman, Aram Designs Ltd and Aram Store, since 2002; *b* 5 Oct. 1931; *s* of Aaron and Palma Ungar; *m* 1958, Elizabeth Bunzl; one *s* three *d. Educ:* Central Sch. of Arts and Design (NDD). Worked in architects practices of Ernő Goldfinger, RIBA, Sir Basil Spence & Partners and Andrew Renton Associates, 1960–63; estabd own design practice, Zeev Aram and Associates, 1963; founded Aram Designs, 1964; opened furniture and design showroom in Chelsea, 1964, 2nd showroom in Hampstead, 1991; design and furniture showrooms, Aram Store, Drury Lane, opened 2002. Estabd Grad. Show of Young Designers, 1987. FCSD 1973; FRSA 1982. Hon. FRIBA 2006; Hon. FRCA 1992; Hon. Fellow, Univ. of the Arts, London, 2004. Arts Bicentenary Medal, RSA, 1996. *Recreations:* walking, music, sailing. *Address:* c/o Aram Designs Ltd, 110 Drury Lane, Covent Garden, WC2B 5SG. *T:* (020) 7240 3933, *Fax:* (020) 240 3697. *E:* admin@aram.co.uk. *Club:* Chelsea Arts.

ARBER, Prof. Sara Lynne, PhD; FBA 2008; FAcSS; Professor of Sociology, since 1994, and Co-Director, Centre for Research on Ageing and Gender, since 2000, University of Surrey; *b* Essex, 19 March 1949; *d* of late George Arber and Katie Arber; *m* 1979, Geoff Herrington (*d* 2005); one *s* two *d. Educ:* London Sch. of Econs (BSc 1st Cl. Sociol. 1972); Bedford Coll., Univ. of London (MSc Med. Sociol. 1973); Univ. of Surrey (PhD 1991). University of Surrey: Lectr, 1974–86; Sen. Lectr, 1986–94; Head: Dept of Sociol., 1996–2002; Sch. of Human Scis, 2001–04. Member: SW Surrey Community Health Council, 1976–81; SW Surrey District HA, 1981–89; Social Affairs Bd, 1984–87, Res. Grants Bd, 2008–10, Grants Assessment Panel, 2010–12, ESRC; Statistics Users Council, 1999–2006. British Sociological Association: Treas., 1988–90; Pres., 1999–2001; Vice Pres., 2002–; Vice Pres., Eur. Sociol Assoc., 2005–07; Pres., Res. Cttee 11 on Ageing, Internat. Sociol Assoc., 2006–10. FAcSS (AcSS 2000). Fellow, Gerontol Soc. of America, 2012; FRSA 2012. Chm., Edtl Bd, Sociology, 1992–95. Outstanding Achievement Award, British Soc. of Gerontology, 2011. *Publications:* Gender and Later Life, 1991; (ed) Women and Working Lives, 1991; (ed) Ageing, Independence and the Life Course, 1993; (ed) Connecting Gender and Ageing, 1995; (ed) The Myth of Generational Conflict, 2000; (ed) Gender and Ageing, 2003; (ed) Contemporary Grandparenting, 2012; over 300 articles on health inequalities, gender, ageing and sociology of sleep. *Recreations:* travel, walking, swimming, ruins in exotic places. *Address:* Department of Sociology, University of Surrey, Guildford, Surrey GU2 7XH. *T:* (01483) 686973, *Fax:* (01483) 689551. *E:* S.Arber@surrey.ac.uk.

ARBER, Prof. Werner; Professor of Molecular Microbiology, Basle University, 1971–96; President, Pontifical Academy of Sciences, since 2011. President, International Council of Scientific Unions, 1996–99. Discovered restriction enzymes at Geneva in 1960s; Nobel Prize in Physiology or Medicine (jointly), 1978. *Address:* Department of Microbiology, Biozentrum der Universität Basel, 50–70 Klingelbergstrasse, 4056 Basel, Switzerland.

ARBIB, Sir Martyn, Kt 2003; DL; Founder and Chairman, Perpetual plc, 1973–2000; *b* 27 June 1939; *s* of late Richard Arbib and Denise Arbib; *m* 1969, Anne Hermione Parton; two *s* two *d. Educ:* Felsted Sch. FCA 1962. Trained with Spicer & Pegler, 1956–62; qualified Chartered Accountant, 1962; Kelsey Industries PLC, 1966–72 (non-exec. Dir, 1975–2000). Dir, Perpetual Income & Growth Investment Trust, 1996–. Trustee: Arbib Foundn, 1987–; Langley Acad. Trust, 2006–; Dir, 1991–, Dep. Chm., 1994–2001, Chm., 2001–12, River and Rowing Mus. Foundn, Henley on Thames; Dir, 1992, Jt Chm., 1994–2003, Henley Fest. of Music and the Arts. DL Oxon, 2001. *Recreations:* golf, dry fly fishing, flat racehorse owner and breeder. *Address:* 61 Grosvenor Street, W1K 3JE. *Clubs:* Alfred's; Huntercombe Golf, Queenwood Golf, Royal Westmorland Golf.

ARBOUR, Anthony Francis; JP; Member (C) South West, London Assembly, Greater London Authority, since 2000; *b* 30 Aug. 1945; *s* of late Charles Foster Arbour and of Magdalen Arbour; *m* 1970, Caroline Anne Cooper; three *s* one *d. Educ:* St Andrew's Sch., Ham Common; Surbiton Co. Grammar Sch.; Kingston Coll. of Technol. (BSc Econ); City Univ. Business Sch. (MBA). Admitted to the Bar, Gray's Inn, 1967. Sen. Lectr, Kingston Univ. Business Sch., 1967–2000 (Vis. Hon. Fellow, 2000–08). Mem., Employment Tribunals, London Central (formerly Industrial Tribunals, London North), 1993–2012. Member (C): Richmond upon Thames BC, 1968– (Chm., Planning Cttee, 1974–80; Leader, Cons. Gp, 1996–2002; Leader of Council, 2002–06); Surbiton, GLC, 1983–86. London Assembly, GLA: Chm., Planning Cttee, 2000–02; Cons. spokesman on planning and standards, 2004–; Chm., Planning and Spatial Develt Cttee, 2005–08. Vice-Chm., Kingston and Richmond FHSA, 1990–96; Member: Metropolitan Police Authy, 2000–08, 2010–12; London Fire and Emergency Planning Authy, 2008–. JP Richmond upon Thames, 1974. Chm., Hampton Wick United Charity, 1972–. Governor: Kingston Poly., 1988–90; Tiffin

Sch., 1988–92; St Mary's Univ. Coll., 2010–. *Recreations:* book collecting, watching TV soap operas, car booting, eBaying. *Address:* 3 Holmesdale Road, Teddington, Middx TW11 9LJ; Greater London Authority, City Hall, Queen's Walk, SE1 2AA.

ARBUCKLE, Andrew, FRAgS; Member (Lib Dem) Scotland Mid and Fife, Scottish Parliament, Jan. 2005–2007; *b* 12 April 1944; *s* of John and Lydia Arbuckle; *m* Margaret Elizabeth Arbuckle (marr. diss. 1985); two *d. Educ:* Bell Baxter High Sch., Cupar; Elmwood Coll., Cupar (NDA). Farmer, E Fife; Agricl Ed., Dundee Courier & Advertiser, 1986–2005. Lib Dem spokesman on finance, Scottish Parlt, 2005–07. Member (Lib Dem): Fife Regl Council, 1986–95; Fife Council, 1995–2012. Mem., Tay Bridge Bd, 1996–2012. Pres., Fife NFU, 1989–91. Mem. Ct, St Andrews Univ., 1990–95. Chm., Fife Athletic Club, 1980–81. FRAgS 2000. *Recreations:* sport, reading, music. *Address:* Fliskmillan Cottage, Newburgh, Cupar, Fife KY14 6HN.

ARBUTHNOT, family name of **Baron Arbuthnot of Edrom**.

ARBUTHNOT OF EDROM, Baron *cr* 2015 (Life Peer), of Edrom in the County of Berwick; **James Norwich Arbuthnot;** PC 1998; barrister; *b* 4 Aug. 1952; 2nd *s* of Sir John Arbuthnot, 1st Bt, MBE, TD and of Margaret Jean, *yr d* of late Alexander G. Duff; *m* 1984, Emma Louise Broadbent (*see* E. L. Arbuthnot); one *s* three *d. Educ:* Wellesley House, Broadstairs; Eton Coll. (Captain of School); Trinity Coll., Cambridge (MA). Called to the Bar, 1975; practising barrister, 1977–92 and 2002–03. Councillor, Royal Bor. of Kensington and Chelsea, 1978–87. Contested (C) Cynon Valley, 1983, May 1984. MP (C) Wanstead and Woodford, 1987–97, NE Hampshire, 1997–2015. An Asst Govt Whip, 1992–94; Parly Under-Sec. of State, DSS, 1994–95; Minister of State for Defence Procurement, MoD, 1995–97; Opposition Chief Whip, 1997–2001; Shadow Sec. of State for Trade, 2003–05. Chm., Defence Select Cttee, 2005–14. Non-exec. Dir, Gusbourne Estates plc, 2015–. Mem., Adv. Bd, Thales UK, 2015–. Pres., Cynon Valley Cons. Assoc., 1983–92. *Recreations:* playing guitar, ski-ing.

See also Sir W. R. Arbuthnot, Bt.

ARBUTHNOT, Emma Louise; a District Judge (Magistrates' Courts), since 2005; a Recorder, since 2002; Deputy Chief Magistrate of England and Wales and Deputy Senior District Judge (Magistrates' Courts), since 2012; *b* 9 Jan. 1959; *d* of (John) Michael Broadbent, *qv*; *m* 1984, Rt Hon. James Norwich Arbuthnot (*see* Baron Arbuthnot of Edrom); one *s* three *d. Educ:* Lycée Français de Londres; Queen Mary Coll., Univ. of London (BA); City Univ. (Dip. Law); Coll. of Legal Educn. Called to the Bar, Inner Temple, 1986, Bencher, 2007; Tenant, 6 King's Bench Walk, 1988–2005; a Dep. Dist Judge, 2000–05. Member: Cttee, Criminal Bar Assoc., 1996–2002; Bar Council, 1998–2005 (Mem., Professional Conduct and Complaints Cttee, 1998–2005; Vice-Chm., Public Affairs Cttee, 2003–05). Chm., 1987–2008, Vice Chm., 2008–, Earls Court Youth Club; Dir, Feathers' Clubs Assoc., 1999–. Judge: Asian Women of Achievement Awards, 2004–13; Women of the Future Awards, 2006–08. *Recreations:* city cycling, su doku, weeding, reading. *Address:* c/o Westminster Magistrates' Court, 181 Marylebone Road, NW1 5BR.

ARBUTHNOT, Sir Keith Robert Charles, 8th Bt *cr* 1823, of Edinburgh; *b* 23 Sept. 1951; *s* of Sir Hugh Fitz-Gerald Arbuthnot, 7th Bt and Elizabeth Kathleen (*d* 1972), *d* of late Sqdn-Ldr G. G. A. Williams; *S* father, 1983; *m* 1st, 1982, Anne (marr. diss. 2001), *yr d* of late Brig. Peter Moore; two *s* one *d*; 2nd, 2003, Alison Jane, *d* of John Warner and Ann Casson. *Educ:* Wellington; Univ. of Edinburgh. BSc (Soc. Sci.). *Heir: s* Robert Hugh Peter Arbuthnot, *b* 2 March 1986. *Address:* Ivy House, High Street, Edgmond, Newport, Shropshire TF10 8JY.

ARBUTHNOT, Sir William (Reierson), 2nd Bt *cr* 1964, of Kittybrewster, Aberdeen; *b* 2 Sept. 1950; *s* of Sir John Sinclair-Wemyss Arbuthnot, 1st Bt, MBE, TD, sometime MP (C) Dover Div. of Kent, and of (Margaret) Jean, *yr d* of late Alexander Gordon Duff; *S* father, 1992; one *d*; *m* 2010, Louise Alexandra Mary Barry; two *s* (twins). *Educ:* Eton; Coll. of Law, London. Arbuthnot Latham Holdings, 1970–76; Joynson-Hicks & Co., solicitors, 1978–81. Dir, Assoc. of Lloyd's Members, 1997–2005. Dep. Chm., High Premium Gp, 1994–2010. Liveryman, Grocers' Co., 1981. *Recreations:* genealogy; webmaster, Arbuthnott Family Assoc. and Kittybrewster.com. *Heir: s* Henry William Arbuthnot, *b* 21 March 2011. *Address:* 37 Cathcart Road, SW10 9JG. *T:* (020) 7795 0707. *E:* wra@kittybrewster.com.

ARBUTHNOTT, family name of **Viscount of Arbuthnott**.

ARBUTHNOTT, 17th Viscount of, *cr* 1641; **John Keith Oxley Arbuthnott,** DL; *b* 18 July 1950; *o s* of 16th Viscount of Arbuthnott, KT, CBE, DSC and Mary Elizabeth Darley Oxley (*d* 2010); *S* father, 2012; *m* 1974, Jillian Mary, *er d* of late Captain Colin Farquharson of Whitehouse; one *s* two *d. Educ:* Fettes College; Aberdeen Univ. Mem., Grampian Health Bd, 1993–97; Vice-Convenor, Scottish Landowners' Fedn, 2003–05; Chm., Scottish Rural Property and Business Assoc., 2005–08. DL Kincardineshire, 2000. *Heir: s* Master of Arbuthnott, *qv*. *Address:* Kilternan, Arbuthnott, Laurencekirk, Kincardineshire AB30 1NA. *T:* (01561) 320417.

ARBUTHNOTT, Master of; Hon. Christopher Keith Arbuthnott; *b* 20 July 1977; *o s* and *heir* of 17th Viscount of Arbuthnott, *qv*; *m* 2003, Emily Jane Agg-Manning; one *s* two *d*.

ARBUTHNOTT, Hugh James, CMG 1984; HM Diplomatic Service, retired; *b* 27 Dec. 1936; *m*; two *s* (and one *s* decd). *Educ:* Ampleforth Coll., Yorks; New Coll., Oxford. Nat. Service, Black Watch, 1955–57. Joined Foreign (subseq. Diplomatic) Service, 1960; 3rd Sec., Tehran, 1962–64; 2nd, later 1st Sec., FO, 1964–66; Private Sec., Minister of State for Foreign Affairs, 1966–68; Lagos, 1968–71; 1st Sec. (Head of Chancery), Tehran, 1971–74; Asst, later Head of European Integration Dept (External), FCO, 1974–77; Counsellor (Agric. and Econ.), Paris, 1978–80; Head of Chancery, Paris, 1980–83; Under Sec., Internat. Div., ODA, 1983–85; Ambassador to Romania, 1986–89, to Portugal, 1989–93, to Denmark, 1993–96. Chm., Martin Currie Eur. Investment Trust, 1997–2004. Chm., Charities Evaluation Services, 1997–2003. Chm., Iran Soc., 2006–08. Trustee, Children at Risk Foundn (UK), 1997–2007. *Publications:* Common Man's Guide to the Common Market (ed with G. Edwards), 1979, 2nd edn (co-author with G. Edwards), 1989; (jtly) British Missions around the Gulf 1575–2005, 2008.

ARBUTHNOTT, Sir John (Peebles), Kt 1998; PhD, ScD; FRCPath, FMedSci; FRSE; FRSB; President, Royal Society of Edinburgh, 2011–14; Chairman, Greater Glasgow and Clyde (formerly Greater Glasgow) NHS Board, 2002–07; *b* 8 April 1939; *s* of James Anderson Arbuthnott and Jean (*née* Kelly); *m* 1962, Elinor Rutherford Smillie; one *s* two *d. Educ:* Univ. of Glasgow (BSc 1960; PhD 1964); Trinity Coll., Dublin (ScD 1984; Hon. FTCD 1992). FRSB (FIBiol 1988); FRSE 1993; FIIB 1993; FRCPath 1995. University of Glasgow: Lectr, Dept of Bacteriology, 1963–67; Alan Johnston, Lawrence and Moseley Res. Fellow of Royal Soc., 1968–72; Sen. Lectr, Dept of Microbiol., 1972–73; Sen. Lectr, Dept of Bacteriol., 1973–75; Professor of Microbiology: TCD, 1976–88 (Bursar, 1983–86); Univ. of Nottingham, 1988–91; Prin. and Vice Chancellor, Strathclyde Univ., 1991–2000. Vis. Lectr, Dept of Microbiol., New York Univ. Med. Centre, 1966–67. Sec. and Treas., Carnegie Trust for Univs of Scotland, 2000–04. Chair, External Adv. Bd, Wolfson Inst. for Health & Wellbeing, Univ. of Durham, 2000–08 (Mem., Internat. Adv. Bd, 2012–). Chair, Med. and Scientific Bd, Lamellar Biomedical Ltd, 2011–. Bd Mem., Food Standards Agency and Chm., Scottish Food Adv. Cttee, 2000–02; Member: Bd, PHLS, 1991–97; Bd, Glasgow Development Agency, 1995–2000; Bd, British Council Educn Counselling Service, 1995–96; Cttee, DTI Multimedia Industry Adv. Gp, 1995–97; Nat. Cttee of Inquiry into Higher Educn, 1996–97; Chm., Commn on Boundary Changes and Voting Systems, 2004–05 (report, 2006). Chm., Jt Inf. Systems Cttee, HEFC, 1994–98; Convenor, Cttee of Scottish Higher Educn Principals, 1994–96. Pres., Scottish Assoc. of Marine Sci., 2004–10. Treas., Soc. for Gen. Microbiol., 1987–92. Chairman: Nat. Review of allocation of health resources in Scotland, 1998–2000 (report, 2000); Standing Cttee on resource allocation to health services in Scotland, 2001–03; Clyde Valley Review, 2008; Chair: Expert Gp on Integrated and Social Care in Scotland, 2010–11; Adv. Bd, Fiscal Affairs Scotland, 2014–. Foundn Trustee, Africa Oxford Cancer Foundn, 2007–13; Trustee, Lloyds TSB Foundn for Scotland, 2009–. Hon. Sec., UK Bioscis Fedn, 2002–06. Founder FMedSci 1998. Hon. FRCPSGlas 1997. MRIA 1985. Hon. Fellow, Internat. Med. Univ., Kuala Lumpur; Hon. Principal Fellow, Dept of Clinical Pharmacol., Univ. of Oxford, 2008. Hon. DSc: Łódź, 1995; Univ. Teknologi, Malaysia, 1997; Glasgow, 1999; Durham, 2007; Edinburgh Napier, 2013; Open, 2014; Hon. LLD: QUB, 1996; Aberdeen, 1998; Hon. DEd Queen Margaret's UC, 2000. *Publications:* edited: (jtly) Isoelectric Focusing, 1975; (jtly) The Determinants of Bacterial and Viral Pathogenicity, 1983; (jtly) Foodborne Illness: a Lancet review, 1991; more than 100 in prestigious scientific learned jls and books. *Recreations:* golf, birdwatching. *Address:* 9 Curlinghall, Broomfield Crescent, Largs KA30 8LB. *Club:* New (Edinburgh) (Hon. Mem.).

ARBUTHNOTT, Robert, CBE 1991; Minister (Cultural Affairs), India, British Council, 1988–93; *b* 28 Sept. 1936; *s* of late Archibald Arbuthnott, MBE, ED, and Barbara Joan (*née* Worters); *m* 1962, Sophie Robina (*née* Axford); one *s* two *d. Educ:* Sedbergh Sch. (scholar); Emmanuel Coll., Cambridge (exhibnr; BA Mod Langs, MA). Nat. service, 1955–57 (2nd Lieut The Black Watch RHR). British Council, 1960–94: Karachi, 1960–62; Lahore, 1962–64; London, 1964–67; Representative, Nepal, 1967–72; London Inst. of Education, 1972–73; Representative, Malaysia, 1973–76; Director, Educational Contracts Dept, 1976–77; Controller, Personnel and Staff Recruitment Div., 1978–81; Representative, Germany, 1981–85; RCDS, 1986; Controller, America, Pacific and S Asia Div., 1987. Member: Adv. Panel, Nehru Centre, 1998–2002; Council, Royal Soc. for Asian Affairs, 2006–09. Member: Mgt Cttee, St Anthony's Cheshire Home, Wolverhampton, 1995–2000; English Haydn Fest. Cttee, Bridgnorth, 1995–2000; Internat. Cttee, Leonard Cheshire Foundn, 1997–2003. FRAS 1995 (Mem. Council, 1996–2000). *Recreations:* music-making, the arts, historic buildings. *Club:* Oxford and Cambridge.

ARCAYA, Ignacio; international and political consultant; Ambassador of Venezuela to the United States of America, 2001–02; *b* Caracas, 3 June 1939; *s* of Ignacio Luis Arcaya and Antonieta (*née* Smith); *m* 1966, Lydia Vincenti; one *s* one *d. Educ:* Central Univ. of Venezuela (Internat. Affairs, 1964; Law, 1968). Third Sec., Perm. Mission of Venezuela to UN, Geneva, 1966–68; Second Sec., Min. for Foreign Affairs, 1968–69; First Sec., Mission to OAS, Washington, 1969–72; Counsellor, Inst. of Foreign Trade, Min. for Foreign Affairs, 1972–75; Minister Counsellor of Econ. Affairs, Paris, 1975–78; Ambassador to Australia and non-resident Ambassador to NZ, Fiji and Philippines, 1978–84; Sec. Gen., Assoc. of Iron Ore Exporting Countries, Geneva, 1984–88; Ambassador-at-large, Min. for Foreign Affairs, 1988; Ambassador: to Chile, 1988–92; to UK, 1992–95 and (non-resident) to Ireland, 1994–95; to Argentina, 1995–98; Perm. Rep. to UN, 1998–99 and 2000–01; Minister of Govt and Justice, 1999–2000; acting Pres. of Venezuela, Oct. 1999. Venezuelan orders: Order of Liberator, 1992; Orden Francisco de Miranda, 1995; Orden Andrés Bello, 1995; Orden al Merito en el Trabajo, 1998; Orden J. C. Falcón, 1999; numerous foreign orders. *Recreation:* golf. *Address:* Residencia Castellalta Torre A Apt. 4-A, Avenida Mohedano, La Castellana, Caracas 1060, Venezuela. *T:* (212) 2636263. *E:* ia@arcaya.com. *Clubs:* Caracas Country; Royal Berkshire Polo; Royal & Ancient Golf (St Andrews); Chantilly Polo (Paris).

ARCHARD, Prof. David William, PhD; Professor of Philosophy, Queen's University Belfast, since 2012; *b* Reading, 19 Jan. 1951; *s* of John Frederick Archard and Peggy Muriel Archard (*née* Pratt); *m* 2015, Marie Bernarde Lynn. *Educ:* Wyggeston Boys' Sch., Leicester; Corpus Christi Coll., Oxford (Open Scholar; BA PPE 1972); London Sch. of Econs and Political Sci. (PhD 1976). Lectr, then Sen. Lectr, Ulster Poly., subseq. Univ. of Ulster, Jordanstown, 1976–85; Reader in Moral Philos., Univ. of St Andrews, 1985–2003; Prof. of Philosophy and Public Policy, Univ. of Lancaster, 2003–12. *Publications:* Marxism and Existentialism: the political philosophy of Jean-Paul Sartre and Maurice Merleau-Ponty, 1980; Consciousness and the Unconscious, 1984; (ed) Philosophy and Pluralism, 1996; Sexual Consent, 1998; (jtly) The Moral and Political Status of Children, 2002; Children, Family and the State, 2003; Children: rights and childhood, 2004; The Family: a liberal defence, 2010; (ed jtly) Procreation and Parenthood: the ethics of bearing and rearing children, 2010; (ed jtly) Reading Onora O'Neill, 2013. *Recreations:* walking, offbeat travel, food and drink, growing spuds. *Address:* School of Politics, International Studies and Philosophy, Queen's University Belfast, University Road, Belfast BT7 1NN. *T:* (028) 9097 5028. *E:* d.archard@qub.ac.uk.

ARCHDALE, Sir Nicholas (Edward), 4th Bt *cr* 1928, of Riversdale, co. Fermanagh; *b* 2 Dec. 1965; *o s* of Sir Edward Folmer Archdale, 3rd Bt and of Elizabeth Ann Stewart Archdale (*née* Lukis); *S* father, 2009 but his name does not appear on the Official Roll of the Baronetage. *Heir: cousin* Mervyn Talbot Archdale [*b* 30 Oct. 1924; *m* 1951, Aureole Helen Whelan (*d* 1998); one *s* one *d*].

ARCHER, family name of **Baron Archer of Weston-super-Mare**.

ARCHER OF WESTON-SUPER-MARE, Baron *cr* 1992 (Life Peer), of Mark in the County of Somerset; **Jeffrey Howard Archer;** author; *b* 15 April 1940; *s* of late William Archer and Lola Archer (*née* Cook); *m* 1966, Mary Weeden (*see* Dame M. D. Archer); two *s*. *Educ:* by my wife since leaving Wellington Sch., Somerset; Brasenose Coll., Oxford. Athletics Blues, 1963–65, Gymnastics Blue, 1963, Pres. OUAC 1965; ran for Great Britain (never fast enough); Oxford 100 yards record (9.6 sec.), 1966. Mem. GLC for Havering, 1966–70; MP (C) Louth, Dec. 1969–Sept. 1974. Dep. Chm., Cons. Party, 1985–86. Former Pres., Somerset AAA; Pres., World Snooker Assoc. (formerly World Professional Billiards & Snooker Assoc.), 1997–99. Co-ordinator, Simple Truth Campaign, 1991. *Plays:* Beyond Reasonable Doubt, Queen's, 1987; Exclusive, Strand, 1990; The Accused (and acted), Haymarket Theatre Royal, 2000. *Publications:* Not a Penny More, Not a Penny Less, 1975 (televised, 1990); Shall We Tell the President?, 1977; Kane and Abel, 1979, rev. 30th anniv. edn 2009 (televised, 1986); A Quiver Full of Arrows (short stories), 1980; The Prodigal Daughter, 1982; First Among Equals, 1984 (televised, 1986); A Matter of Honour, 1986; A Twist in the Tale (short stories), 1988; As the Crow Flies, 1991; Honour Among Thieves, 1993; Twelve Red Herrings (short stories), 1994; The Fourth Estate, 1996; The Collected Short Stories, 1997; The Eleventh Commandment, 1998; To Cut a Long Story Short (short stories), 2000; A Prison Diary, vol. I, Hell, 2002, vol. II, Purgatory, 2003, vol. III, Heaven, 2004; Sons of Fortune, 2003; False Impression (also screenplay), 2006; Cat O'Nine Tales (short stories), 2006; (with Francis J. Moloney) The Gospel according to Judas, 2007; A Prisoner of Birth, 2008; Paths of Glory (also screenplay), 2009; And Thereby Hangs a Tale (short stories), 2010; Only Time Will Tell, 2011; The Sins of the Father, 2012; Best Kept Secret, 2013; Be Careful What You Wish For, 2014; Mightier Than The Sword, 2015. *Recreations:* charity auctioneer, theatre, watching Somerset try to win the County Championship. *Address:* 93 Albert Embankment, SE1 7TY. *W:* www.jeffreyarcher.com.

ARCHER OF WESTON-SUPER-MARE, Lady; *see* Archer, Dame M. D.

ARCHER, Anthony William; Partner, JWA Governance Services LLP, since 2012; Managing Partner, Bridgewater Leadership Advisory (formerly Bridgewater Associates), since 2010; *b* 17 Jan. 1953; *s* of late George William Frederic Archer and Mary Archer (*née* Deeming); *m* 1979, Louise Marion Rhodes; one *s* two *d. Educ:* St Edward's Sch., Oxford; Univ. of Birmingham (LLB Hons 1975). ACA 1979. Asst Manager, Tax, Price Waterhouse

& Co., 1975–80; Asst Manager, Corporate Finance, S. G. Warburg & Co. Ltd, 1980–83; various posts in London and NY, County NatWest Ltd, 1983–88 (Dir, 1988); Man. Dir, MacLennan & Partners, 1988–92; Principal, TASA Ltd, 1992–95; Partner, Ray & Berndtson, later Odgers Berndtson, 1995–2010. Mem., Crown Nominations Commn, 2005–07. Chm., Council for Discipleship and Ministry, Dio. of St Albans, 2014–. Mem., Gen. Synod of C of E, 1993–2010. Member, Council: Oak Hill Coll., 1995–2000; Wycliffe Hall, Oxford, 2000–11. Freeman, City of London, 2001; Liveryman, Wheelwrights' Co., 2001–. *Recreations:* gardening, narrow boating, grandparenting. *Address:* Barn Cottage, Little Gaddesden, Berkhamsted, Herts HP4 1PH. *T:* (01442) 842397. *E:* anthony.archer@jwagovernance.com.

ARCHER, Gilbert Baird; Vice Lord-Lieutenant for Tweeddale, since 2008; Chairman, Tods of Orkney Ltd (oatcake and biscuit manufacturers), since 1970; *b* Edinburgh, 24 Aug. 1942; *s* of late John Mark Archer, CBE and Marjorie Carmichael (*née* Baird); *m* 1967, Irené, *er d* of late Rev. Dr John C. M. Conn and Jess (*née* Stewart); two *d*. *Educ:* Melville Coll. Chairman: John Dickson & Son Ltd, 1985–97; Borders 1996 Ltd, 1996–98; Dir, EPS Moulders Ltd, 1985–88. Dir, Scottish Council Develt and Industry, 1993–96. Chm., Leith Chamber of Commerce, 1986–88; Pres., Edinburgh Chamber of Commerce, 1990–92; Chm., Assoc. of Scottish Chambers of Commerce, 1993–96; Dep. Pres., British Chambers of Commerce, 1995–96. Chm., Edinburgh Common Purpose, 1991–94. Dir, Scottish Council of Ind. Schs, 1988–91; Mem. Council, Governing Bodies Assoc. of Ind. Schs, 1988–91. Chm., St Columba's Hospice, 1998–2004 (now Vice Pres.). Vice Convener, George Watson's Coll., 1978–80; Governor: Fettes Coll., 1986–90; Napier Univ., 1991–97. Master: Co. of Merchants of the City of Edinburgh, 1997–99; Gunmakers' Co., 2006–07. Moderator, High Constables of Port of Leith, 1990–91. DL Tweeddale, 1994. *Recreations:* previously flying, now country pursuits. *Address:* 10 Broughton Place Lane, Edinburgh EH1 3RS. *T:* (0131) 556 4518. *Clubs:* Army and Navy; New (Edinburgh).

ARCHER, Graham Robertson, CMG 1997; HM Diplomatic Service, retired; High Commissioner to Malta, 1995–99; *b* 4 July 1939; *s* of late Henry Robertson Archer and Winifred Archer; *m* 1963, Pauline Cowan; two *d*. *Educ:* Judd School, Tonbridge. Joined Commonwealth Relations Office, 1962; British High Commission, New Delhi, 1964; Vice Consul, Kuwait, 1966; CRO (later FCO), 1967; Second Secretary (Commercial), Washington, 1970; First Secretary: FCO, 1972; Wellington, NZ, 1975; FCO, 1979; Counsellor: Pretoria, 1982; The Hague, 1986; FCO, 1990. Chm., Commonwealth Soc. for the Deaf, 2001–03; Dep. Chm., Adv. Bd, London and SE Reg. (formerly Cttee, SE and London Reg.), NT, 1999–2012. KStJ 1999. *Club:* Royal Over-Seas League (Mem., Council and Exec. Cttee).

ARCHER, Malcolm David, FRCO; Director of Chapel Music, Winchester College, since 2007; *b* 29 April 1952; *s* of Gordon Austin Archer and Joan Eddleston Archer; *m* 1994, Alison Jane Robinson; one *s* one *d*. *Educ:* King Edward VII Sch., Lytham; Royal Coll. of Music (ARCM 1971); Jesus Coll., Cambridge (Organ Schol.; MA, CertEd). FRCO 1974. Asst Dir of Music, Magdalen Coll. Sch., Oxford, 1976–78; Asst Organist, Norwich Cathedral, 1978–83; Organist and Master of the Choristers, Bristol Cathedral, 1983–90; freelance organist, conductor and composer, 1990–96; music staff, 1990–96, Head of Chapel Music, 1994–96, Clifton Coll.; Organist and Master of the Choristers, Wells Cathedral, 1996–2004; Organist and Dir of Music, St Paul's Cathedral, 2004–07. Founder and Musical Dir, City of Bristol Choir, 1991–2000; Conductor, Wells Cathedral Oratorio Soc., 1996–2004. Hon. FNMSM, 2002; Hon. FGCM, 2005; Hon. FRSCM 2009. *Publications:* A Year of Praise, 1991; (ed jtly) Carols Old and New, 1991; After the Last Verse, 1995; (ed jtly) Advent for Choirs, 1999; (ed jtly) Epiphany to All Saints for Choirs, 2004; over 200 compositions; major works include: Love Unknown, 1992; Requiem, 1993; The Coming of the Kingdom, 1999; Three Psalms of David, 2000; Veni Creator Spiritus, 2004; The Garden of Love, 2004; Nowell! Nowell!, 2010; George and the Dragon, 2014. *Recreations:* watercolour painting, cooking, classic cars, antique clocks. *Address:* Winchester College, College Street, Winchester SO23 9NA.

ARCHER, Dame Mary (Doreen), DBE 2012; PhD; Chair: Science Museum Group, since 2015 (Trustee, Science Museum, 1990–2000); Imperial College Health Partners Expert Advisory Board, since 2013; External Advisory Board, Centre for Personalised Medicine, St Anne's College, Oxford, since 2013; *b* 22 Dec. 1944; *d* of late Harold Norman Weeden and Doreen Weeden (*née* Cox); *m* 1966, Jeffrey Howard Archer (*see* Baron Archer of Weston-super-Mare); two *s*. *Educ:* Cheltenham Ladies' College; St Anne's Coll., Oxford (Nuffield Schol.; MA 1972); Imperial Coll., London Univ. (PhD 1968); MA Cantab 1976. FRSC 1987. Junior Res. Fellow, St Hilda's Coll., Oxford, 1968–71; temp. Lectr in Chemistry, Somerville Coll., Oxford, 1971–72; Res. Fellow, Royal Instn of GB, 1972–76 (Dewar Fellow, 1975–76); Lector in Chemistry, Trinity Coll., Cambridge, 1976–86; Fellow and Coll. Lectr in Chem., Newnham Coll., Cambridge, 1976–86 (Bye-Fellow, 1987–2002). Sen. Academic Fellow, De Montfort Univ. (formerly Leicester Polytechnic), 1990–; Vis. Prof., Dept of Biochem., 1991–99, Centre for Energy Policy and Technol., 2000–03, Imperial Coll., London; Visitor, Univ. of Hertfordshire, 1993–2005. Chm., Cambridge Univ. Hosps NHS Foundn Trust (formerly Addenbrooke's NHS Trust), 2002–12 (Dir, 1992–2012; Vice-Chm., 1999–2002). Member: Renewable Energy Adv. Gp, Dept of Energy/DTI, 1991–92; Energy Adv. Panel, DTI, 1992–98; COPUS, 1995–2000; Energy Policy Adv. Gp, Royal Soc., 1998–2004. Chm., E of England Stem Cell Network Steering Gp, 2004–08. Convenor (formerly Chm.), UK Univ. Hosps Chairs' Gp, 2008–12. Trustee: UK Stem Cell Foundn, 2005–; CRAC, 2007–12; icould, 2012–. Mem. Council, Cheltenham Ladies' Coll., 1991–2000. Mem. Bd of Dirs, Internat. Solar Energy Soc., 1975–81 (Sec., UK Section, 1973–76); Manager, 1982–84, Mem. Council, 1984–85 and 1997–2002, Royal Instn; Chm., Nat. Energy Foundn, 1990–2000 (Pres., 2000–); Pres., Solar Energy Soc., 2001–. Director: Anglia Television Gp, 1987–95; Mid Anglia Radio, 1988–94; Q103 (formerly Cambridge & Newmarket FM Radio), 1988–97. Mem. Council of Lloyd's, 1989–92. Pres., Guild of Church Musicians, 1989–; non-exec. Dir, Britten Sinfonia, 1998–. Hon. DSc Hertfordshire, 1994. Melchett Medal, Inst. of Energy, 2002; Eva Philbin Award, Inst. of Chem. of Ireland, 2007. *Publications:* Rupert Brooke and the Old Vicarage, Grantchester, 1989; (ed jtly) Clean Electricity from Photovoltaics, 2001, 2nd edn 2014; (ed jtly) Molecular to Global Photosynthesis, 2004; (ed jtly) Transformation and Change: the 1702 Chair of Chemistry at Cambridge, 2004; (ed jtly) Solar Photon Conversion in Nanostructured and Photoelectrochemical Systems, 2008; The Story of The Old Vicarage, Grantchester, 2012; contribs to chem. jls. *Recreations:* reading, writing, singing. *Address:* The Old Vicarage, Grantchester, Cambridge CB3 9ND. *T:* (01223) 840213.

ARCHER, Nicholas Stewart, MVO 2001; HM Diplomatic Service; Managing Director, Policy and Network Development, UK Trade and Investment, since 2014; *b* 24 Dec. 1960; *s* of Thomas Stewart Archer and Marjorie Anne Archer (*née* Mackenzie); *m* 1999, Erica Margaret Power; two *s*. *Educ:* Denstone Coll.; Univ. of Durham (BA 1982). With Sotheby's, 1983; entered FCO, 1983: Third, later Second Sec., Amman, 1986–89; FCO, 1989–92; Private Sec. to Minister of State, FCO, 1992–94; First Sec., Oslo, 1995–97; Asst Private Sec. to the Prince of Wales, 1997–2000; Head: NE Asia and Pacific Dept, FCO, 2001–02; Near East and N Africa Dept, FCO, 2002–05; High Comr, Malta, 2006–08; Ambassador to Denmark, 2008–12; Dir, Strategic Trade, UK Trade and Investment, 2012–14. Trustee, St Catherine Foundn, 1997–2000. *Address:* UK Trade and Investment, 1 Victoria Street, SW1H 0ET.

ARCHER, Thomas; Controller, Factual Production, BBC, 2008–12; *b* Tunbridge Wells, 7 Jan. 1953; *s* of Michael and Carol Carr-Archer; two *d*. *Educ:* Tonbridge Sch.; Univ. of Bristol (BA; PhD African Hist. 1982). Freelance investigative journalist, 1982–95; Head: of Factual Progs, HTV, 1995–96; of Factual Progs, United News and Media, 1997–2000; of Factual, Granada West, 2000–02; of Progs, BBC TV, Bristol, 2002–04; Comr, Features and Documentaries, BBC, 2004–08. Vis. Prof., UWE, 2013–.

ARCHER, Timothy John; Consultant, Reed Smith LLP (formerly Richards Butler, then Reed Smith Richards Butler), since 2001 (Partner, 1973–2001; Senior Partner, 1991–2000); *b* 9 Feb. 1943; *s* of Jack Valentine Archer and Phyllis Emma Archer (*née* Cotton); *m* 1972, Gillian Karen Davies; one *s* one *d*. *Educ:* Sutton Valence Sch.; Merton Coll., Oxford (MA); Coll. of Law. Alfred Syrett Prizeman, Law Soc., 1966; admitted Solicitor, 1969. Richards Butler, Solicitors, subseq. Reed Smith Richards Butler, later Reed Smith LLP, 1965–. Associate, Byrne Dean Associates Ltd, 2003–. Part-time Chm., Employment Tribunals, 2002–06. Director: Royal Philharmonic Orch., 1993–95; Philharmonia Orch. Trust, 1997–2010; Harefield Res. Foundn, 2002–03; NSO Trust Ltd, 2010–. Mem., Management Cttee, Univ. of Exeter Centre for Legal Practice, 1993–96. *Publications:* (contrib.) International Handbook on Contracts of Employment, 1988, 2nd edn 1991; with Prof. G. S. Morris: Trade Unions, Employers and the Law, 1991; Collective Labour Law, 2000. *Recreations:* sport, travel, music, art. *Club:* City of London.

ARCHER, William Ernest; Chairman, Focus DIY Ltd (formerly Focus DIY, later Focus Do It All, then Focus Wickes Group), 1992–2007 (Chief Executive Officer, 1992–2002); *b* 6 May 1944; *s* of Joseph and Elizabeth Archer; *m* 1963, Shirley Patricia Clarke; one *s* two *d*. *Educ:* Wellington Sch. for Boys. Sales Manager Nat. Accounts, Crown Dec. Prod., Reed Internat. Ltd, 1968–83; Man. Dir, Signpost/Ashfield Paints, 1983–87; (with business partner) acquired retailer Choice DIY Ltd, 1987; Man. Dir, Choice DIY Ltd, subseq. Focus DIY, 1987–92. MInstD; MCIM. *Recreations:* golf, swimming, walking, reading, football, tennis. *Address:* Withington Hall Offices, Holmes Chapel Road, Lower Withington, Cheshire SK11 9DS. *E:* vicki@bandscharters.com. *Clubs:* Pleasington Golf; La Manga.

ARCULUS, Sir David; *see* Arculus, Sir T. D. G.

ARCULUS, Sir Ronald, KCMG 1979 (CMG 1968); KCVO 1980; HM Diplomatic Service, retired; *b* 11 Feb. 1923; *s* of late Cecil Arculus, MC and Ethel L. Arculus; *m* 1953, Sheila Mary Faux (*d* 2015); one *s* one *d*. *Educ:* Solihull; Exeter Coll., Oxford (MA; Hon. Fellow, 1989). 4th Queen's Own Hussars (later Queen's Royal Hussars), 1942–45 (Captain). Joined HM Diplomatic Service, 1947; FO, 1947; San Francisco, 1948; La Paz, 1950; FO, 1951; Ankara, 1953; FO, 1957; Washington, 1961; Counsellor, 1965; New York, 1965–68; IDC, 1969; Head of Science and Technology Dept, FCO, 1970–72; Minister (Economic), Paris, 1973–77; Ambassador and Permt Leader, UK Delegn to UN Conf. on Law of the Sea, 1977–79; Ambassador to Italy, 1979–83. Dir, 1983–91, Trustee, 1986–93, Consultant, 1992–95, Glaxo Hldgs. Special Advr to Govt on Channel Tunnel trains, 1987–88. Consultant: Trusthouse Forte, 1983–86; London and Continental Bankers Ltd, 1985–90. Dir of Appeals, King's Med. Res. Trust, 1984–88. Pres., Kensington Soc., 2001–11 (Chm., 1999–2001). Governor, British Institute, Florence, 1983–94. FCMI (FBIM 1984). Freeman, City of London, 1981. Kt Grand Cross, Order of Merit, Italy, 1980. *Recreations:* travel, music, fine arts, antiques. *Address:* 20 Kensington Court Gardens, W8 5QF. *Clubs:* Hurlingham; Cowdray Park Polo.

ARCULUS, Sir (Thomas) David (Guy), Kt 2005; Chairman: O_2 plc (formerly mmO_2), 2004–06; Aldermore Bank plc, 2010–13; *b* 2 June 1946; *s* of Thomas Guy Arculus and Mary (*née* Barton); *m* 1973, Anne Murdoch Sleeman; two *s* one *d*. *Educ:* Bromsgrove Sch.; Oriel Coll., Oxford (MA 1968); London Graduate Sch. of Business Studies (MSc 1972). VSO, 1964–65. BBC Producer, 1968–70; EMAP plc: Publisher, 1972–84; Dep. Man. Dir, 1984–89; Gp Man. Dir, 1989–97; Chief Operating Officer, United News and Media plc, 1997–98; Chairman: ipc Gp, 1998–2001; Severn Trent plc, 1998–2004; Earls Court and Olympia Ltd, 2002–04; Shortlist Media, 2007–14; Boat Internat., 2007–10; LIEC, 2008–12 (non-exec. Dir, LIEC Hldgs, 2008–12); Numis Corp., 2009–14. Non-executive Director: Norcros, 1993–96; Barclays plc, 1997–2006; Guiton Gp, 2000–02; Telefónica (formerly Telefónica O_2) Europe plc, 2006–12; Telefónica SA, 2006–12; Pearson plc, 2006–. Chm., Better Regulation Task Force, Cabinet Office, 2002–05. Mem., President's Cttee, 2003–, Dep. Pres., 2005–06, CBI. Chairman: PPA, 1988–90; NCC, 1993–96. Deleg., Finance Cttee, OUP, 2000–06; Chm., Investment Cttee, Oriel Coll., Oxford, 2000–04. A Comr, Public Works Loan Bd, 2001–02. Trustee, Industry and Parliament Trust, 2006–11 (Fellow, 1994). Freeman, City of London, 1989. DUniv Central England, 2003. Marcus Morris Award, PPA, 1993. *Recreations:* cricket, hill walking, reading. *E:* david.arculus@integral2.com. *Clubs:* Oxford and Cambridge, Groucho, Thirty, MCC.

ARDAGH, Philip; *see* Roxbee Cox, P. A.

ARDAGH AND CLONMACNOISE, Bishop of, (RC), since 2013; **Most Rev. Francis Duffy;** *b* Templeport, Co. Cavan, 21 April 1958; *s* of late Frank Duffy and of Mary Catherine Duffy (*née* Dolan). *Educ:* Munlough Nat. Sch., Bawnboy; St Patrick's Coll., Co. Cavan; St Patrick's Coll., Maynooth. Ordained priest, 1982; Teacher of history, religion and Irish, St Patrick's Coll., Co. Cavan; Principal, Fatima and Felim's Secondary Sch., Ballinamore, Co. Leitrim, 1996–2008; Diocesan Sec. and Chancellor, Dio. of Kilmore, 2009; Resident Priest, Parish of Laragh, Co. Cavan, 2009–13. *Address:* Diocesan Office, Ballinalee Road, Longford, Co. Longford, Ireland.

ARDEE, Lord; Anthony Jacques Brabazon; *b* 30 Jan. 1977; *o s* of Earl of Meath, *qv*; *m* 2004, Fionnuala, *d* of Joseph Aston; one *s* one *d*. *Educ:* Harrow Sch. *Heir: s* Hon. Aldus Jack Brabazon, *b* 21 April 2010.

ARDEN, Andrew Paul Russel; QC 1991; *b* 20 April 1948; *m* 1991, Joanne Leahy; one *d*. *Educ:* Stowe; University College Sch.; University Coll. London (LLB). MCIH 2002. Called to the Bar, Gray's Inn, 1974; Dir, Small Heath Community Law Centre, Birmingham, 1976–78. Local government inquiries/reviews: for GLC, 1982–83; for Bristol CC, 1985; for Hackney LBC, 1985–87, 1993–94; for Camden LBC, 1992. Founder, Arden Chambers, 1993. Vis. Prof. of Law, Faculty of Develt and Soc., Sheffield Hallam Univ., 2001–07. General Editor: Encyclopaedia of Housing Law, 1978–; Housing Law Reports, 1981–; Jl of Housing Law, 1997–; Consultant Ed., Local Government Law Reports, 2000–01 (Gen. Ed., 1999–2000). *Publications:* Manual of Housing Law, 1978, 9th edn (with Andrew Dymond), 2012; Housing Act 1980 (annotations), 1980; (with Prof. M. Partington) Quiet Enjoyment, 1980, 6th edn (with D. Carter and A. Dymond) 2002; (with Prof. M. Partington) Housing Law, 1983, 2nd edn (also with C. Hunter), 1994; (with Prof. J. T. Farrand) Rent Acts & Regulations, amended and annotated, 1981; (with C. Cross) Housing & Building Control Act 1984 (annotations), 1984; Private Tenants Handbook, 1985, 2nd edn 1989; Public Tenants Handbook, 1985, 2nd edn 1989; (with S. McGrath) Landlord & Tenant Act 1985 (annotations), 1986; Housing Act 1985 (annotations), 1986; (with J. Ramage) Housing Associations Act 1985 (annotations), 1986; Homeless Persons Handbook, 1986, 2nd edn 1988; (with C. Hunter) Housing Act 1988 (annotations), 1989; (with Sir Robert Megarry) Assured Tenancies, Vol. 3, The Rent Acts, 11th edn 1989; (with C. Hunter) Local Government & Housing Act 1989 (annotations), 1990; (with C. Hunter) Local Government Finance Law, 1994; (with C. Hunter) Housing Act 1996 (annotations), 1996; (with C. Hunter) Housing Grants, Construction and Renewal Act 1996 (annotations), 1996; Homeless Persons Act, 1982, 9th edn (with E. Orme and T. Vanhegan) 2012; (jtly) Local Government

Constitutional and Administrative Law, 1999, 2nd edn 2008; *fiction:* The Motive Not The Deed, 1974; No Certain Roof, 1985; The Object Man, 1986; The Programme, 2001; four thrillers under pseudonym Bernard Bannerman, 1990–91. *Recreations:* Southern Comfort, Hill Street Blues, Camel cigarettes. *Address:* Arden Chambers, 20 Bloomsbury Square, WC1A 2NS. *T:* (020) 7242 4244, *Fax:* (020) 7242 3224. *E:* Andrew.Arden@Ardenchambers.com.

ARDEN, Annabel Kate, (Mrs Stephen Jeffreys); freelance theatre and opera director; Co-Founder, Complicité (formerly Théâtre de Complicité), since 1983; *b* London, 11 Nov. 1959; *d* of Prof. Geoffrey Bernard Arden and Sheila Barbara Arden (*née* Gordon); *m* 1999, Stephen Jeffreys; two *s*. *Educ:* St Paul's Girls' Sch.; Newnham Coll., Cambridge (BA Hons English Lit. 1981). For Complicité: *as performer:* Put It on Your Head, 1983; Foodstuff, 1986; Anything for a Quiet Life, 1987 (adapted for TV, 1989); The Street of Crocodiles, world tour, 1992–93 and revival, 1998–99; *as director:* productions include: Please, Please, Please, 1986; The Lamentations of Thel, 1989; (with S. McBurney) The Visit, 1989, revival, 1991; (with A. Castledine) The Winter's Tale, 1992; (with A. Castledine) India Song, 1993; Lionboy, 2013; for Opera North: The Magic Flute, 1993, 1997; The Return of Ulysses, 1995–97; La Traviata, 2001, 2002, 2003, 2004; The Cunning Little Vixen, 2001; La Traviata, Sadler's Wells, 1999; Picasso's Women, RNT, 1999; The Rake's Progress, ENO, 2001; Gianni Schicchi, The Miserley Knight, Glyndebourne, 2004; L'Elisir d'Amore, Glyndebourne on Tour, 2007, Houston, 2009, revival at Glyndebourne, 2011; Little Red Riding Hood, Almeida, 2005; The Art of War, Sydney Th. Co., 2007; Heldenplatz, Arcola, 2010; concert. perf., The Soldier's Tale, Chicago SO, 2012; La Bohème, WNO, 2012; The Commission/Café Kafka, Linbury Studio Th., 2014; has created many concert stagings incl. (with Sir John Eliot Gardiner) Leonore, 1996 and (with V. Jurowski) Faust, 2012–14. Has conducted internat. workshops. Union of Eur. Women of Achievement Award, 2003. *Publications:* (contrib.) Actor Training, 2010. *Recreations:* family, gardening, singing. *E:* annabelarden@me.com.

ARDEN, Rt Hon. Dame Mary (Howarth), DBE 1993; PC 2000; **Rt Hon. Lady Justice Arden;** a Lady Justice of Appeal, since 2000; Head, International Judicial Relations for England and Wales, since 2005; *d* of late Lt-Col E. C. Arden, LLB, TD and M. M. Arden (*née* Smith); *m* 1973, Jonathan Hugh Mance (*see* Baron Mance); one *s* two *d*. *Educ:* Huyton College; Girton College, Cambridge (MA, LLM; Hon. Fellow, 1995); Harvard Law School (LLM). Called to the Bar, Gray's Inn, 1971 (Arden and Birkenhead Scholarships, 1971); admitted *ad eundem* to Lincoln's Inn, 1973 (Bencher, 1993); QC 1986; Attorney Gen., Duchy of Lancaster, 1991–93; a Judge of the High Ct of Justice, Chancery Div., 1993–2000; UK *ad hoc* Judge, Eur. Ct of Human Rights, 2000. Chm., Law Commn, 1996–99. Bar Mem., Law Society's Standing Cttee on Company Law, 1976–2007; Member: Financial Law Panel, 1993–2000; Steering Gp, Company Law Review Project, 1998–2001; Chairman: Wking Party of Judges' Council on Constitutional Reform, 2004–06; Papers Cttee, Commonwealth Law Conf., 2005. DTI Inspector, Rotaprint PLC, 1988–91. Mem. Council, Statute Law Soc., 2001–07. Member: Exec. Cttee, 2004–05, Advr to Bd of Trustees, 2005–, British Inst. of Internat. and Comparative Law; Ext. Adv. Bd, Faculty of Modern History, Univ. of Oxford, 2000–06; Amer. Law Inst., 2003–; Adv. Bd, Centre of European Law, KCL, 2008–; Permanent Ct of Arbitration, 2011–; Visitor, Royal Holloway, Univ. of London, 2008–; Dist. Judicial Visitor, UCL, 2008–. Acad. Trustee, Kennedy Meml Trust, 1995–2005. Pres., Assoc. of Women Barristers, 1994–98. Chair, CAB, Royal Cts of Justice, 1994–97; Patron, Free Repn Unit, 2007–. Hon. Fellow, Liverpool John Moores Univ., 2006. DUniv Essex, 1997; Hon. LLD: Liverpool, 1998; Warwick, 1999; RHBNC, 1999; Nottingham, 2002; UCL, 2011. Editor, Chancery Guide, 1995, 1999. *Publications:* Negligence and the Public Accountant (contrib.), 1972; Legal Editor, Current Accounting Law and Practice, by Robert Willott, 1976; (with George Eccles) Tolley's Companies Act 1980, 1980; Legal Consultant Editor: Tolley's Companies Act 1981, 1981; Tolley's Accounting Problems of the Companies Acts, 1984; Accounting Provisions of the Companies Act 1985, 1985; Coopers & Lybrand Deloitte Manual of Accounting, vols 1 and 2, 1990, 1995; Jt Gen. Editor and Contributor, Buckley on the Companies Acts, 14th edn: Special Bulletin, 1990, 15th edn 2000 (updated biannually); (contrib.) Accounting and the Law, 1992; (contrib.) Perspectives on Company Law, 1995; (contrib.) Law, Society and Economy, 1997; Human Rights and European Law: building new legal orders, 2015; articles in legal jls. *Recreations:* travel, reading, theatre. *Address:* Royal Courts of Justice, Strand, WC2A 2LL.

ARDEN, Peter Leonard; QC 2006; *b* 5 April 1960; *s* of Surgeon Captain Leonard Arden and Ann Arden; *m* 1999, Zia Kurban Bhaloo, *qv*; one *d*. *Educ:* University Coll. London (LLB); Queens' Coll., Cambridge (LLB 1982). Called to the Bar, Gray's Inn, 1983.

ARDEN, Sian S.; *see* Sutherland-Arden.

ARDEN, Zia; *see* Bhaloo, Z. K.

ARFIELD, John Alan; University Librarian, University of Western Australia, 1996–2010; *b* 15 March 1949; *s* of Donald Sidney Arfield and Barbara Winifred Arfield (*née* Alderton); *m* 1st, 1970, Paula May Perrin (marr. diss. 1998); one *s* two *d*; 2nd, 2004, Susan June Henshall. *Educ:* Kingston Grammar Sch.; Jesus Coll., Cambridge (BA 1971; MA 1975); Univ. of Sheffield (MA 1973). Cambridge University Library: Asst Liby Officer, 1973–78; Asst Under-Librarian, 1978–79; Under-Librarian, 1979–81; Sub-Librarian (Tech. Services), UC, Cardiff, 1981–88; Dep. Librarian, Reading Univ., 1988–92; University Librarian, Loughborough Univ., 1992–96. *Publications:* articles in librarianship. *Recreations:* cricket, theatre, music, gardening.

ARFON-JONES, Elisabeth, (Mrs B. Watkins); DL; Senior Tribunals Liaison Judge (Wales), since 2011; a Vice President, Upper Tribunal (Immigration and Asylum Chamber) (formerly Deputy President, Asylum and Immigration Tribunal), 2005–14; a Public Appointments Assessor, since 2012; *b* 2 July 1950; *d* of late Arfon Arfon-Jones and Margaret Arfon-Jones (*née* Price); *m* 1982, Brian Watkins, *qv*; one *d*. *Educ:* University Coll. London (LLB 1971). Called to the Bar, Gray's Inn, 1972 (William Shaw Schol.; Fellow, 2008; Bencher, 2010); in practice at the Bar, 1973–77; Sen. Prosecuting Solicitor, Cheshire, 1977–80; Crown Counsel, Bermuda, 1980–81; Registrar, Supreme Court, Bermuda, 1981–83; an Immigration Adjudicator, 1997–2005; Dep. Chief Immigration Adjudicator, 2001–04; Chief Immigration Adjudicator, 2004–05. A Civil Service Comr, 2007–12. A Lay Chm., NHS Complaints Rev. Panels in Wales, 1995–2006. US Liby of Congress Rep. (pt-time), Islamabad, 1984–86; Chm., Internat. Cttee, BC Red Cross, Vancouver, 1986–90; Founding Chm., Swaziland Hospice at Home, 1990–93. Mem. Bd, Community Fund (formerly National Lottery Charities Bd), 1998–2004 (Chm., Wales Cttee, 2000–02). Member: Ministerial Adv. Gp on Community Volunteering, 1999–2004; Multi-Centre Res. Ethics Cttee for Wales, 2001–03. Lay Mem., Lord Chancellor's Adv. Cttee for Appointment of JPs in Gwent, 2000–09. Hon. Sec., Assoc. of Women Barristers, 1999–2001. Member, Council: Barnardo's, 2001–08 (Chm., Wales Cttee, 2007–08); Canada-Royal Commonwealth Ex-Services League, 2013–. Mem., Livery Co. of Wales (formerly Welsh Livery Guild), 2009–. Trustee, Lord Edmund-Davies Legal Educn Trust, 2013–. DL Gwent, 2006. *Recreations:* 'laughter and the love of friends' (worldwide), theatre, ski-ing. *Address:* c/o Coutts & Co., 440 Strand, WC2R 0QS. *E:* libby.watkins@gmail.com. *Clubs:* Athenæum, Royal Over-Seas League.

ARGAR, Edward John Comport; MP (C) Charnwood, since 2015; *b* Ashford, Kent, 9 Dec. 1977; *s* of Edward Henry Argar and Patricia Joan Argar. *Educ:* Harvey Grammar Sch., Folkestone; Oriel Coll., Oxford (BA; MSt). Political Advr to Shadow Foreign Sec., 2001–05; Mgt Consultant, Hedra plc, then Mouchel, 2005–11; Hd, Public Affairs, UK and Europe, Serco Gp plc, 2011–14. Non-exec. Mem. Bd, NHS Westminster PCT, 2008–10. Trustee, Groundwork London, 2010–15. Mem., Westminster CC, 2006–15. *Recreations:* reading, ski-ing, tennis, cricket, gardening. *Address:* House of Commons, SW1A 0AA. *T:* (020) 7219 8140. *E:* edward.argar.mp@parliament.uk. *Club:* Travellers.

ARGENT, Malcolm, CBE 1985; Deputy Chairman, Civil Aviation Authority, 1995–98; *b* 14 Aug. 1935; *s* of Leonard James and Winifred Hilda Argent; *m* 1st, 1961, Mary Patricia Addis Stimson (marr. diss. 1983); one *s* one *d*; 2nd, 1986, Thelma Hazel Eddleston. *Educ:* Palmer's Sch., Grays, Essex. General Post Office, London Telecommunications Region: Exec. Officer, 1953–62; Higher Exec. Officer, 1962–66; Principal, PO Headquarters, 1966–70; Private Sec., Man. Dir, Telecommunications, 1970–74; Personnel Controller, External Telecommun. Exec., 1974–75; Dir, Chairman's Office, PO Central Headquarters, 1975–77; Dir, Eastern Telecommun. Region, 1977; Secretary: of the Post Office, 1978–81; British Telecommunications Corp., 1981–94; British Telecommunications plc, 1984–94 (Dir, 1989–98); Chm., NATS, 1996–98. Trustee, British Telecommunications Staff Superannuation Fund, 1981–94. Director: McCaw Cellular Communications Inc., 1989–94; Westminster Health Care plc, 1992–99; Clerical, Medical & Gen. Assce Soc., 1994–2001; Clerical Medical Investment Gp, 1997–2001; Chm., Envision Licensing Ltd, 1999. Member: Council, CBI, 1994–95; Cttee, Essex Magistrates' Courts, 2000–04. Freeman, City of London, 1987. CCMI (CIMgt 1992; CBIM 1991; FBIM 1980). Hon. DSc Aston, 2004. *Recreation:* golf. *Address:* 64 Tor Bryan, Ingatestone, Essex CM4 9HN.

ARGENTA, Nancy Maureen; soprano; *b* Nelson, Canada, 17 Jan. 1957; *d* of Hugh and Agnes Herbison; adopted Argenta as professional name. *Educ:* Vancouver Community Coll.; Univ. of Western Ontario (Artist Dip. in Performance). Début, Hippolyte and Aricie, Fest. d'Aix en Provence, 1983; has performed in Australia, Europe, Japan, N America, S America, with major orchestras and companies, including Boston SO, Leipzig Gewandhaus Orch., Montreal SO, LPO and Philharmonia Orch.; also tours as a recitalist. Has made over 50 recordings. *Recreations:* walking, gardening, cycling, woodwork. *Address:* c/o Askonas Holt Ltd, Lincoln House, 300 High Holborn, WC1V 7JH. *T:* (020) 7400 1700.

ARGENTINA, Bishop of, since 2002; **Most Rev. Gregory James Venables;** *b* 6 Dec. 1949; *s* of Rev. Dudley James Venables and May Norah Venables (*née* Saddington); *m* 1970, Sylvia Margaret Norton; one *s* two *d*. *Educ:* Chatham House; Kingston Univ.; Christchurch Coll., Canterbury. Computer Systems Officer, Sterling Winthrop, 1971–72; English master, Holy Cross Sch., Broadstairs, 1974–77; Headmaster, St Andrews Coll., Asunción, Paraguay, 1978–89; ordained deacon, March 1984, priest, Nov. 1984; Asst Curate, St Helen's and St Giles, Rainham with St Mary's, Wennington, dio. of Chelmsford, 1990–93; Asst Bishop, dio. of Peru and Bolivia, 1993–95; Bishop of Bolivia, and Vice-Primate, Province of the Southern Cone of America, 1995–2000; Coadjutor Bishop of Argentina, 2000–02; Presiding Bishop (Primate) of the Province of the Southern Cone of America, 2001–10. *Publications:* Look to the Scars, 1973. *Recreations:* reading, music, walking. *Address:* 25 de Mayo 282, 1001 Buenos Aires, Argentina. *T:* (11) 43424618, *Fax:* (11) 43310234. *E:* diocesisanglibue@fibertel.com.ar.

ARGERICH, Martha; pianist; *b* Buenos Aires, 5 June 1941; *m* 1st, 1963, Robert Chen (marr. diss.); one *d*; 2nd, 1969, Charles Dutoit, conductor (marr. diss.); one *d*. Studied with Vincenzo Scaramuzza, Madeleine Lipatti, Nikita Magaloff, Friedrich Gulda, Arturo Benedetti Michelangeli, Stefan Askenase. Début in Buenos Aires, 1949, in London, 1964; soloist with leading orchestras. Gen. Dir, Argerich's Meeting Point, Beppu, 1996–; Founder, Martha Argerich Project, 2002; Co-Founder, Alink-Argerich Foundn. Numerous recordings. First Prize: Ferruccio Busoni Internat. Competition, Bolzano, Italy, 1957; Internat. Music Competition, Geneva, 1957; Internat. Chopin Competition, Warsaw, 1965. *Address:* c/o Jacques Thelen Agence Artistique, 15 avenue Montaigne, 75008 Paris, France.

ARGUS, Donald Robert, AC 2010 (AO 1998); Chairman, BHP Billiton (formerly BHP Ltd), 1999–2010 (Director, 1996–2010); *b* 1 Aug. 1938; *s* of Dudley Francis and Evelyn Argus; *m* 1961, Patricia Anne Hutson; three *d*. *Educ:* C of E GS, Brisbane; RMIT; Harvard Univ. FAIB; FCPA; FAICD. National Australia Bank: General Manager: Credit Bureau, 1984–87; Gp Strategic Devel t, 1987–89; Chief Operating Officer, 1989–90; Man. Dir and Chief Exec., 1990–99. Chm. and Dir, Brambles Ltd (formerly Brambles Industries), 1999–2008; Director: Southcorp Ltd, 1999–2003; Australian Foundn Investment Co., 1999–; Member: Allianz Internat. Adv. Bd, 2000–09; Internat. Adv. Bd, NYSE, 2005–09; Global Adv. Council, Bank of America Merrill Lynch, 2013–. Hon. LLD Monash; DUniv Griffith. *Recreations:* golf, reading, hockey. *Address:* PO Box 252, Caulfield East, Melbourne, Vic 3145, Australia. *T:* (3) 96592726, *Fax:* (3) 90171313. *Clubs:* Australian, Melbourne (Melbourne); Kingston Heath Golf; Queensland Cricketers (Brisbane).

ARGYLL, 13th Duke of, *cr* 1701 (Scotland), 1892 (UK); **Torquhil Ian Campbell;** Marquess of Lorne and Kintyre; Earl of Campbell and Cowal; Viscount Lochow and Glenyla; Baron Inveraray, Mull, Morvern and Tiry, 1701; Baron Campbell, 1445; Earl of Argyll, 1457; Baron Lorne, 1470; Baron Kintyre, 1633 (Scotland); Baron Sundridge, 1766; Baron Hamilton of Hameldon, 1776; Bt 1627; 37th Baron and 47th Knight of Lochow; Celtic title, Mac Cailein Mor, Chief of Clan Campbell; Hereditary Master of the Royal Household, Scotland; Hereditary High Sheriff of the County of Argyll; Admiral of the Western Coast and Isles; Keeper of the Great Seal of Scotland and of the Castles of Dunstaffnage, Dunoon, and Carrick and Tarbert; *b* 29 May 1968; *s* of 12th Duke of Argyll, and Iona Mary, *d* of Capt. Sir Ivar Colquhoun, 8th Bt; *S* father, 2001; *m* 2002, Eleanor Mary, *d* of Peter H. G. Cadbury; two *s* one *d*. *Educ:* Craigflower; Cargilfield; Glenalmond Coll.; Royal Agricultural Coll., Cirencester. A Page of Honour to the Queen, 1981–83. Pres., Scottish Chapter, World Elephant Polo Assoc., 2006–. Patron, Keeper of the Quaich, 2006–. Liveryman, Distillers' Co., 2006–. *Heir: s* Marquess of Lorne, *qv*. *Address:* Inveraray Castle, Inveraray, Argyll PA32 8XF.

ARGYLL AND THE ISLES, Bishop of, since 2011; **Rt Rev. Kevin Pearson;** *b* 27 Aug. 1954; s of Edward and Nancy Pearson; *m* 1992, Dr Elspeth Atkinson. *Educ:* Leeds Univ. (BA 1975); Edinburgh Univ. (BD 1979); Edinburgh Theol Coll. Ordained deacon, 1979, priest, 1980; Curate, St Mary, Horden, 1979–81; Chaplain, Leeds Univ., 1981–87; Rector, St Salvador, Edinburgh, 1987–93; Chaplain, Napier Poly., subseq. Napier Univ., 1988–94; Diocesan Dir of Ordinands, Dio. Edinburgh, 1990–95; Provincial Dir of Ordinands, Scottish Episcopal Church, 1991–2011; Associate Rector, Old St Paul, Edinburgh, 1993–94; Priest-in-charge, Linlithgow, 1994–95; Rector, St Michael and All Saints, Edinburgh, 1995–2011; Dean, Dio. of Edinburgh, 2004–10. Hon. Canon, St Mary's Cathedral, Edinburgh, 2003–04. *Recreations:* Italy, the Victorian novel, food and drink. *Address:* Bishop's House, Ganavan Sands, Oban PA34 5TB. *T:* (01631) 562617. *E:* bishop@argyll.anglican.org; St Moluag's Diocesan Centre, Croft Avenue, Oban PA34 5JJ. *T:* (01631) 570870.

ARGYLL AND THE ISLES, Bishop of, (RC); *no new appointment at time of going to press.*

ARGYLL AND THE ISLES, Dean of; *see* Swift, Very Rev. A. C.

ARGYLL AND THE ISLES, Provost in; *see* McNelly, Very Rev. N.

ARGYRIS, Nicholas John; Director, Communications Services: policy and regulatory framework (formerly Telecommunications Trans European Networks and Services and Postal Services), European Commission, 1993–2001; *b* 22 March 1943; *s* of late Costas Argyris, (Costas Hadjiargyris), and Eileen Argyris (*née* Pollard); *m* 1st, 1966, Carol Bartlett (marr. diss. 1991); one *s* two *d*; 2nd, 1992, Danielle Canneel. *Educ:* St Paul's Sch.; Clare Coll., Cambridge (BA Hons Econs 1965; Cert. Ed. 1966). Schoolmaster, 1966–68; with Govt Econ. Service, in

Depts of Econ. Affairs, Technol. and Trade and Ind., 1969–73; joined European Commission, 1973: worked in Directorate General for: Competition, 1973–84 (State Aids); Develt, 1985–86 (Trade and Private Investment Issues); Competition, 1987–91 (Head of Div., Transport and Tourist Industries); Dir for internal market, DG for Energy, 1991–93. Former Mem., England junior chess team (London junior champion, 1960). *Publications:* articles on air transport, energy and telecommunications policy. *Recreations:* reading, walking, music, gardening, chess problems, cinema.

ARIAS SÁNCHEZ, Oscar, PhD; President of Costa Rica, 1986–90 and 2006–10; President, Arias Foundation for Peace, 1990–2010; *b* 13 Sept. 1940; *m* Margarita; one *s* one *d*. *Educ:* Univ. of Costa Rica; Univ. of Essex. Prof., Sch. of Political Sciences, Univ. of Costa Rica, 1969–72; Minister of Nat. Planning and Economic Policy, 1972–77; Gen. Sec., 1979–86, Liberación Nacional Party; Congressman, 1978–82. Formulated Central American Peace Agreement, 1986–87. Member: Stockholm Internat. Peace Res. Inst.; Carter Center; Inst. for Internat. Studies, Stanford Univ.; ILD Rockefeller Foundn; Internat. Centre for Human Rights and Democratic Develt; Inter Press Service; Bd of Dirs, WWF. Hon. PhD: Harvard, 1988; Essex, 1988; Dartmouth, 1992. Nobel Peace Prize, 1987; Martin Luther King Peace Prize, Martin Luther King Foundn, 1987; Prince of Asturias Prize, 1988; Nat. Audubon Soc. Prize, 1988; Liberty Medal, Univ. of Pennsylvania, 1991. *Publications:* Pressure Groups in Costa Rica, 1970; Who Governs in Costa Rica?, 1976; Latin American Democracy, Independence and Society, 1977; Roads for Costa Rica's Development, 1977; New Ways for Costa Rican Development, 1980. *Address:* c/o Arias Foundation/Center for Peace, PO Box 8–6410–1000, San José, Costa Rica. *T:* 2552955, *Fax:* 2552244.

ARIE, Prof. Thomas Harry David, CBE 1995; FRCPsych, FRCP, FFPH; Foundation Professor of Health Care of the Elderly, University of Nottingham, 1977–95, now Professor Emeritus, and Hon. Consultant Psychiatrist, Nottingham Health Authority, 1977–95; *b* 9 Aug. 1933; *s* of late Dr O. M. Arie and Hedy Arie; *m* 1963, Eleanor, FRCP, *yr d* of Sir Robert Aitken, FRCP, FRACP; two *d* one *s*. *Educ:* Reading Sch.; Balliol Coll., Oxford (Open Exhibnr in Classics; 1st cl. Hons, Classical Mods); MA, BM 1960; DPM. Training, Radcliffe Infirmary, Oxford, and Maudsley and London Hosps; Consultant Psychiatrist, Goodmayes Hosp., 1969–77; Sen. Lectr in Social Medicine, London Hosp. Med. Coll.; Hon. Sen. Lectr in Psychiatry, UCH Med. Sch. Royal College of Psychiatrists: Mem. Council, 1975–79, 1981–86, 1991–97; Vice-Pres., 1984–86; Chm., Specialist Section on Psychiatry of Old Age, 1981–86; Jt Cttee on Higher Psychiatric Training, 1978–84; Hon. FRCPsych 2001; Royal College of Physicians: Geriatrics Cttee, 1984–90; Examining Bd for Dip. in Geriatric Medicine, 1983–92. Member: Central Council for Educn and Trng in Social Work, 1975–81; Standing Med. Adv. Cttee, DHSS, 1980–84; Cttee on Review of Medicines, 1981–90; Res. Adv. Council, Nat. Inst. for Social Work, 1982–90; Med. Adv. Cttee to Registrar General, 1990–93; Council, AgeCare, Royal Surgical Aid Soc., 1995– (Vice-Chm., 1998–2007; Vice-Pres., 2008–). Fotheringham Lectr, Univ. of Toronto, 1979; Vis. Prof., NZ Geriatrics Soc., 1980; Dozor Vis. Prof., Univ. of the Negev, Israel, 1988; Fröhlich Vis. Prof., UCLA, 1991; Vis. Prof., Keele Univ., 1997. Chm., Geriatric Psych. Section, World Psych. Assoc., 1989–93. Governor, Centre for Policy on Ageing, 1992–98. Founders' Medal, British Geriatrics Soc., 2005; Lifetime Award, Internat. Psychogeriatric Assoc., 1999; Lifetime Award, Old Age Faculty, RCPsych, 2012. *Publications:* (ed) Health Care of the Elderly, 1981; (ed) Recent Advances in Psychogeriatrics, Vol. 1 1985, Vol. 2 1992; articles in med. jls and chapters in other people's books. *Address:* Cromwell House, West Church Street, Kenninghall, Norfolk NR16 2EN.

ARIS, Aung San Suu Kyi, (Mrs M. V. Aris); *see* Aung San Suu Kyi.

ARKELL, John Hardy, MA; Headmaster, Gresham's School, Holt, 1991–2002; *b* 10 July 1939; *s* of Hardy Arkell and Vivienne (*née* Le Sueur); *m* 1963, Jean Harding, JP; two *s* one *d*. *Educ:* Stowe Sch.; Selwyn Coll., Cambridge (BA Hons English Tripos; MA). National Service, HM Submarines, 1958–60 (Sub Lieut). Asst Master, Abingdon Sch., 1963–64; Head of VI form English, Framlingham Coll., 1964–70; Fettes College, 1970–83: Head of English Dept, 1971–73, 1976–78; Founder Headmaster, Fettes Jun. Sch., 1973–79; Housemaster, Glencorse House, 1979–83; Headmaster, Wrekin Coll., 1983–91. Chm., ISIS, Central England, 1989–91; Sec., HMC Midland Div., 1990–91; HMC Rep., ISC (formerly ISJC) Special Needs Cttee, 1991–2002. Governor: Oakham Sch., 2001–; Beeston Hall Prep. Sch., 2003–11. Lay Reader, Benefice of Weybourne, 2006–. Mem., Fishmongers' Co., 2002–. *Recreations:* tennis, sailing, motor cars, drama. *Address:* Church Farm House, Lower Bodham, Holt, Norfolk NR25 6PS. *T:* (01263) 715582.

ARKLESS, Richard Lambert Thomas; MP (SNP) Dumfries and Galloway, since 2015; *b* Stranraer, 1975; *m* Anne; two *c*. *Educ:* Glasgow Caledonian Univ. (BA Hons Financial Services); Strathclyde Univ. (LLB); Glasgow Grad. Sch. of Law (DipLP). Solicitor trainee, Edinburgh incl. secondment to RBS; solicitor, specialising in consumer litigation, Cheshire, until 2013; set up small online business, 2013. *Address:* House of Commons, SW1A 0AA.

ARKLEY, Alistair Grant, CBE 2006; DL; Chairman, New Century Enterprises (formerly New Century Inns) Ltd, since 1999; *b* 13 May 1947; *s* of Alexander Arkley and Victoria Margaret Arkley (*née* Grant); *m* 1972, Kathleen Ann Raeburn; three *s*. *Educ:* Aberdeen Acad.; Aberdeen Univ. (BSc Engrg). Engrg Officer, R&D, ICI, 1971–72; various posts, selling and mktg, Procter & Gamble, 1972–79; Sales and Mktg Dir, Scottish Breweries, Scottish & Newcastle plc, 1979–85; Man. Dir, J. W. Cameron & Co. Ltd, 1985–91; Chief Exec., Century Inns plc, 1991–99. Chairman: Chameleon Pub. Co., 1999–; Steelite Internat. plc, 2006–; Hospitality Data Insights, 2012–; Dir, S. A. Brains & Co. Ltd, 2014. Dir, UK (formerly British) Business Angels Assoc., 2008–. Hon. ML, Teesside Univ., 2000. DL Co. Durham, 2007. *Recreations:* countryside, gardening, football (spectating). *Address:* New Century Enterprises Ltd, Belasis Business Centre, Coxwold Way, Billingham, Tees Valley TS23 4EA. *T:* (office) (01642) 343415, *Fax:* (01642) 345729. *E:* a.arkley@new-century.co.uk. *Clubs:* Royal Automobile; Northern Counties (Newcastle upon Tyne).

ARKWRIGHT, Paul Thomas; HM Diplomatic Service; High Commissioner to Nigeria, since 2015; *b* Bolton, 2 March 1962; *s* of Thomas Arkwright and Muriel Arkwright (*née* Hague); *m* 1997, Patricia Holland; one *s* one *d*. *Educ:* Ampleforth Coll.; Trinity Coll., Cambridge (BA Hons English 1983). Entered FCO, 1987; Second Sec. (Political), BMG Berlin (later Berlin Office), 1988–91; Hd, Conventional Arms Section, Non-proliferation and Defence Dept, FCO, 1991–93; First Sec. (Political), UK Mission to UN, 1993–97; on secondment to Min. of Foreign Affairs, France, 1997–98; First Sec. (Political), Paris, 1998–2001; Political Counsellor, UK Delegn to NATO, 2001–05; Hd, Counter-proliferation Dept, FCO, 2006–09; Ambassador to the Netherlands, 2009–13; Dir, Multilateral Policy, FCO, 2013–15. *Recreations:* cycling, swimming, watching football. *Address:* c/o Foreign and Commonwealth Office, King Charles Street, SW1A 2AH. *Club:* London Supporters of Bolton Wanderers Football.

ARLINGTON, Baroness (11th in line), *cr* 1664; **Jennifer Jane Forwood;** *b* 7 May 1939; *er d* of Maj.-Gen. Sir John Nelson, KCVO, CB, DSO, OBE, MC, and Lady Jane Nelson; *S* in 1999 to Barony of uncle, 9th Duke of Grafton, which had fallen into abeyance in 1936; *m* 1964, Rodney Forwood (*d* 1999); two *s*. *Educ:* Downham. *Recreations:* horse racing, bridge, gardening. *Heir:* *s* Hon. Patrick John Dudley Forwood [*b* 23 April 1967; *m* 2001, Alexandra, *yr d* of late Anthony Psychopulos and of Mrs Neil Maconochie].

ARLOW, Ruth Marian; barrister; Chancellor, Diocese of Norwich, since 2012 (Deputy Chancellor, 2008–12); *b* Bristol, 31 Jan. 1975; *d* of James Terence Arlow and Lynne Margaret Arlow (*née* Martinson); *m* 1997, Jonathan Chambers; three *d*. *Educ:* St Edmund Hall, Oxford (BA 1996); Cardiff Univ. (LLM Canon Law 2003). Called to the Bar, Inner Temple, 1997; Mem., Pump Court Chambers, 1997–. Deputy Chancellor: Dio. of Chichester, 2006–; Dio. of Oxford, 2014–. Lectr and Dir of Teaching, Postgraduate Dip. in Legal Practise, Monash Univ., 2003–06; Vis. Lectr, Bristol Law Sch., 2007–. Gov., Berrow C of E Primary Sch., Som, 2009–. Casenotes Ed., Ecclesiastical Law Jl, 2001–. *Recreations:* family, reading, walking. *Address:* Norwich Diocesan Registry, Kingfisher House, 1 Gilders Way, Norwich NR3 1UB. *T:* (01603) 756501, *Fax:* (01603) 756554.

ARMAGH, Archbishop of, and Primate of All Ireland, since 2012; **Most Rev. Richard Lionel Clarke,** PhD; *b* 25 June 1949; *s* of Dudley Hall Clarke and Norah Constance (*née* Quine); *m* 1975, Linda Margaret Thompson (*d* 2009); one *s* one *d*. *Educ:* Trinity Coll., Dublin (MA 1979; PhD 1990); King's Coll., London (BD 1975). Ordained deacon, 1975, priest, 1976; Assistant Curate: Holywood, Down, 1975–77; St Bartholomew with Christ Church, Leeson Park, Dublin, 1977–79; Dean of Residence, Trinity Coll., Dublin, 1979–84; Rector, Bandon Union of Parishes, Dio. of Cork, 1984–93; Dean of Cork and Incumbent of St Fin Barre's Union of Parishes, Cork, 1993–96; Bishop of Meath and Kildare, 1996–2012. *Publications:* And Is It True?, 2000; A Whisper of God, 2006. *Recreation:* music. *Address:* Church House, 46 Abbey Street, Armagh BT61 7DZ. *T:* (028) 3752 7144.

ARMAGH, Archbishop of, (RC), and Primate of All Ireland, since 2014; **Most Rev. Eamon Martin;** *b* Derry, 30 Oct. 1961; *s* of John James Martin and Catherine Martin (*née* Crossan). *Educ:* St Columb's Coll., Derry; St Patrick's Coll., Maynooth (BSc Math. Scis; BD Theol.); Queen's Univ. Belfast; St Edmund's Coll., Cambridge (MPhil). Ordained priest, 1987; Asst Priest, St Eugene's Cathedral, Derry, 1987–89; Teacher, 1990–98, Pres., 1999–2008, St Columb's Coll., Derry; Sec. Gen., Irish Episcopal Conf., 2008–10; Vicar Gen., 2010–11, Diocesan Administrator, 2011–13, Diocese of Derry; Coadjutor Archbishop of Armagh, (RC), 2013–14. Chaplain to HH The Pope, 2010–13. *Address:* Ara Coeli, Cathedral Road, Armagh BT61 7QY. *T:* (028) 3752 2045, *Fax:* (028) 3752 6182. *E:* admin@aracoeli.com.

ARMAGH, Dean of; *see* Dunstan, Very Rev. G. J. O.

ARMANI, Giorgio; Italian fashion designer; *b* 11 July 1934; *s* of late Ugo Armani and of Maria Raimondi. *Educ:* Univ. of Milan. Mil. Service, 1957. La Rinascente, Milan, 1957–64; Designer and Product Developer, Nino Cerruti, 1964–70; freelance designer, 1970–; founded Giorgio Armani SpA, 1975 and created own-label ready-to-wear clothing; has since introduced other Armani lines, incl. accessories, fragrances and eyewear. Dr *hc* RCA, 1991. Numerous fashion awards. Gran Cavaliere dell'ordine al merito della Repubblica Italiana, 1987 (Commendatore, 1985; Grand'Ufficiale, 1986). *Publications:* Giorgio Armani (autobiog.), 2015. *Address:* Giorgio Armani SpA, Via Borgonuovo 11, 20121 Milan, Italy. *T:* (02) 723181; Giorgio Armani Corporation, 114 Fifth Avenue, New York, NY 10011, USA.

ARME, Prof. Christopher, PhD, DSc; CBiol, FRSB; Professor of Zoology, University of Keele, 1979–2007, now Emeritus; *b* 10 Aug. 1939; *s* of Cyril Boddington and Monica Henrietta Arme; *m* 1962; three *s*. *Educ:* Heanor Grammar Sch.; Univ. of Leeds (BSc 1961; PhD 1964); Univ. of Keele (DSc 1985). FRSB (FIBiol 1980); CBiol 1980. SRC/NATO Res. Fellow, Univ. of Leeds, 1964–66; Res. Associate, Rice Univ., Texas, 1966–68; Lectr, later Reader, QUB, 1968–76; Head of Biology Gp, N Staffs Polytechnic, 1976–79; Head, Dept of Biol Scis, 1981–88, Dean of Natural Scis, 1998–2001, Univ. of Keele; Dir of Terrestrial and Freshwater Scis, NERC, 1993–95 (on leave of absence from Keele Univ.). British Society for Parasitology: Hon. Gen. Sec., 1980–83; Silver Jubilee Lectr, 1987; Vice Pres., 1988–90; Pres., 1990–92; Hon. Mem., 1992. Chm., Heads of Zool. Depts of Univs Gp, 1981–82; Institute of Biology: Hon. Treas. and Chm., Finance Cttee, 1986–93; Chm., Staffing Cttee, 1993–99; Treas., Eur. Fedn of Parasitologists, 1992–2000. Mem., Biol Scis Cttee, and Chm., Animal Scis and Psychol. Sub-Cttee, SERC, 1989–92; Chairman: Steering Cttee, NERC special topic prog. on wildlife diseases, 1992–93; Policy Adv. Cttee, Envmtl Res. Prog., DFID (formerly ODA), 1995–99; Molecular Genetics in Ecology Initiative, Aberdeen Univ./Inst. of Terrestrial Ecology, Banchory, 1995–99; Mem., Adv. Cttee, Centre for Ecology and Hydrology, NERC, 1998–2002. Mem. Bd of Govs, Harper Adams Agricl Coll., 1996–2002. Hon. Member: Czechoslovakian Parasitological Soc., 1989; All-Russia Soc. of Helminthologists, 1992; Bulgarian Soc. for Parasitology, 1995. Jt Editor, Parasitology, 1987–2006; Ed.-in-Chief, Parasites and Vectors, 2008–. Hon. DSc Slovak Acad. of Scis, 1995. K. I. Skryabin Medal, All-Russian Soc. of Helminthologists, 1994; Hovorka Medal, Slovak Acad. of Scis, 1995; Charter Award Medal, Inst. of Biology, 1995. *Publications:* (ed jtly) Biology of the Eucestoda, Vols I and II, 1983; (ed) Molecular Transfer across Parasite Membranes, 1988; (ed jtly) Toxic Reactions of the Liver, 1992; contribs to parasitological jls. *Address:* School of Life Sciences, University of Keele, Keele, Staffs ST5 5BG. *T:* (01782) 733028.

ARMES, Rt Rev. John Andrew; *see* Edinburgh, Bishop of.

ARMFIELD, Diana Maxwell, (Mrs Bernard Dunstan), RA 1991 (ARA 1989); RWS 1983 (ARWS 1977); RWA; RCA; painter, since 1965; *b* 11 June 1920; *d* of Joseph Harold Armfield and Gertrude Mary Uttley; *m* 1949, Bernard Dunstan, *qv*; two *s* (and one *s* decd). *Educ:* Bedales; Bournemouth Art Sch.; Slade Sch.; Central School of Arts and Crafts. MCSD. Textile/wallpaper designer, 1949–65; work in Fest. of Britain, 1951, and Permanent Collection, V&A Mus. One woman exhibitions: Browse & Darby (London), regularly, 1979–, 90th Birthday show, 2010; RCA Conwy, and Cardiff, 2001; other exhibitions include: regular contribs RA Summer Exhibn, 1966–; Friends' Room, RA, also Cardiff and Llanbedrog, 1995; Bala, 1996; Wassenaar, Holland, 1998; Nat. Mus. of Cardiff, 1998; Bedales Art & Design Centenary Exhibn, 1999; Kentucky, USA, 2005; Arts Club, London, 2006; Curwen & New Acad. Gall. 50th Anniv. Show, 2008; Director's Choice, Curwen & New Academy Gall., 2009; Pure Gold: 50 Years of the FBA, Mall Gall., 2011; Featured Artist, RWS Spring Exhibn, 2011; RA Now Exhibn, 2012; exhibn with Bernard Dunstan, Belle Shenkman Room, RA, 2015. Artist in Residence: Perth, WA, 1985; Jackson, Wyoming, 1989. Work in Permanent Collections: Govt picture collection, RWA; Yale Center for British Art; Nat. Trust; Contemporary Art Soc. for Wales; Lancaster City Mus.; Faringdon Trust; RWS Queen's birthday collection, 1996; Royal Acad. Queen's Diamond Jubilee Collection, 2012; Commissions: Reuters, Nat. Trust, 1989; Prince of Wales, 1989; Royal Acad. diploma collection. RWA 1975, now Hon. Retired RWA; RCA 1991, now Hon. Retired RCA; Hon. Mem., Pastel Soc., 1988; Hon. NEAC 2000. *Publications:* (jtly) Painting in Oils, 1982; (jtly) Drawing, 1982; *relevant publication:* The Art of Diana Armfield, by Julian Halsby, 1995. *Recreations:* music, gardening, travel. *Address:* 10 High Park Road, Kew, Richmond, Surrey TW9 4BH; Llwynhir, Parc, Bala, Gwynedd, North Wales LL23 7YU. *Club:* Arts.

ARMFIELD, James Christopher, CBE 2010 (OBE 2000); Technical Consultant, Football Association and Professional Footballers' Association, since 1994; Sports Commentator, BBC, since 1980; *b* Denton, Gtr Manchester, 21 Sept. 1935; *s* of Christopher Armfield and Doris Armfield; *m* 1958, Anne Ashurst; two *s*. *Educ:* Arnold Sch., Blackpool. Professional footballer, Blackpool FC, 1954–71; England Internat., 1959–66, World Cup, 1962, 1966; Manager: Bolton Wanderers FC, 1971–75; Leeds Utd FC, 1975–79; journalist and broadcaster, 1980–. Chm., Lancs Partnership Against Crime; President: Trinity Hospice of the Fylde; Age UK (formerly Age Concern), Blackpool; Patron, Lancs Outward Bound Assoc. Lay Canon and

Mem. Council, Blackburn Cathedral Treas., St Peter's PCC, Blackpool. High Sheriff Lancs, 2005–06. Freeman of Blackpool, 2003. *Publications:* Fighting Back, 1963; Right Back to the Beginning, 2004. *Recreations:* music (church organist), gardening, walking, crosswords. *Address:* 41 Stonyhill Avenue, Blackpool FY4 1PR. *T:* (01253) 401663. *E:* jarmfield@thepfa.co.uk. *Club:* St Annes Old Links Golf.

ARMIDALE, Bishop of, since 2012; **Rt Rev. Richard Alexander Lewers;** *b* Sydney, 18 March 1958; *s* of Basil Richard Lewers and Lois Lewers; *m* 1981, Janene; three *c. Educ:* Sydney Missionary and Bible Coll. (Dip.); Moore Coll. (DipA; BTh). Curate, Liverpool, NSW, 1988–92; Asst Minister, later Rector, Wanniassa, ACT, 1992–2002; Evangelism Ministries, 2002–05; Engadine Anglican Church, 2005–12. Dep. Chair, Evangelical Fellowship Anglican Church; Mem., Gospel Coalition (Australia). *Recreations:* fishing, golf, family. *Address:* PO Box 198, Armidale Diocesan Office, NSW 2350, Australia. *T:* (2) 67724491. *E:* bishop@armidaleanglicandiocese.com. *Club:* Armidale Golf.

ARMITAGE, Edward, CB 1974; Comptroller-General, Patent Office and Industrial Property and Copyright Department, Department of Trade (formerly Trade and Industry), 1969–77; *b* 16 July 1917; *s* of Harry and Florence Armitage; *m* 1st, 1940, Marjorie Pope (*d* 1997); one *s* two *d*; 2nd, 1999, Marjorie Malby. *Educ:* Huddersfield Coll.; St Catharine's Coll., Cambridge. Patent Office, BoT: Asst Examr 1939; Examr 1944; Sen. Examr 1949; Principal Examr 1960; Suptg Examr 1962; Asst Comptroller 1966. Governor, Centre d'Etudes Internationales de la Propriété Industrielle, Strasbourg, 1975–85; Mem. Council, Common Law Inst. of Intellectual Property, 1981–97; Pres., Internat. Assoc. for Protection of Industrial Property, 1983–86. *Recreations:* bowls, bridge, gardening. *Address:* Richmond House, Plud Street, Wedmore, Somerset BS28 4BE. *T:* (01934) 712756.

See also P. Armitage.

ARMITAGE, His Honour (Ernest) Keith; QC 1994; a Circuit Judge, 2001–15; *b* 15 May 1949; *s* of Selwyn and Marjorie Armitage; *m* 1972, Anita Sharples; one *s* one *d. Educ:* Trent Coll., Notts; Univ. of Liverpool (LLB Hons). Called to the Bar, Middle Temple, 1970; in practice, Northern Circuit, 1971–2001; a Recorder, 1989–2001. *Recreations:* travel, gliding (soaring).

ARMITAGE, John Vernon, PhD; Principal, 1975–97, and Hon. Senior Fellow in Mathematical Sciences, since 1997, College of St Hild and St Bede, Durham; *b* 21 May 1932; *s* of Horace Armitage and Evelyn (*née* Hauton); *m* 1963, Sarah Catherine Clay; two *s. Educ:* Rothwell Grammar Sch., Yorks; UCL (BSc, PhD); Cuddesdon Coll., Oxford. Asst Master: Pontefract High Sch., 1956–58; Shrewsbury Sch., 1958–59; Lectr in Maths, Univ. of Durham, 1959–67; Sen. Lectr in Maths, King's Coll., London, 1967–70; Prof. of Mathematical Educn, Univ. of Nottingham, 1970–75; Special Prof., Nottingham Univ., 1976–79. Chm., Math. Instruction Sub-Cttee, Brit. Nat. Cttee for Maths, Royal Soc., 1975–78. *Publications:* (with H. B. Griffiths) A Companion to Advanced Mathematics, 1969; (with W. F. Eberlein) Elliptic Functions, 2006; papers on theory of numbers in various jls. *Recreations:* railways, cricket and most games inexpertly. *Address:* 7 Potters Close, Potters Bank, Durham DH1 3UB.

ARMITAGE, Prof. Judith Patricia, PhD; FRS 2013; Professor of Biochemistry, University of Oxford, since 1996; Fellow, Merton College, Oxford, since 1996; *b* Shelley, Yorks, 21 Feb. 1951; *d* of George Arthur Armitage and Eleanor Armitage (*née* Emmott); *m* 1975, John Gordon R. Jefferys; two *d. Educ:* Selby Girls' High Sch.; University Coll. London (BSc Hons 1972; PhD 1976). Lister Inst. Res. Fellow, 1982–85; Lectr, Univ. of Oxford, 1985–96. *Publications:* contrib. papers to scientific jls. *Recreations:* theatre, travel, art, good food and wine, reading history. *Address:* Department of Biochemistry, University of Oxford, South Parks Road, Oxford OX1 3QU. *T:* (01865) 613293. *E:* judith.armitage@bioch.ox.ac.uk.

ARMITAGE, Keith; *see* Armitage, E. K.

ARMITAGE, Air Chief Marshal Sir Michael (John), KCB 1983; CBE 1975; Commandant, Royal College of Defence Studies, 1988–89; *b* 25 Aug. 1930; *m* 1st, 1955 (marr. diss. 1969); three *s*; 2nd, 1970, Gretl Renate Steinig. *Educ:* Newport Secondary Grammar Sch., IW; Halton Apprentice; RAF Coll., Cranwell. psc 1965, jssc 1970, rcds 1975. Commnd 1953; flying and staff appts, incl. 28 Sqn, Hong Kong, and No 4 and No 1 Flying Trng Schools; Personal Staff Officer to Comdr 2ATAF, 1966; OC 17 Sqdn, 1967–70; Directing Staff, JSSC and NDC, 1971–72; Stn Comdr, RAF Luqa, Malta, 1972–74; Dir Forward Policy, Ministry of Defence (Air Force Dept), 1976–78; Dep. Comdr, RAF Germany, 1978–80; Senior RAF Mem., RCDS, 1980–81; Dir of Service Intelligence, 1982; Dep. Chief of Defence Staff (Intelligence), 1983–84; Chief of Defence Intelligence and Dep. Chm., Jt Intelligence Cttee, 1985–86; Air Mem. for Supply and Orgn, Air Force Dept, MoD, 1986–87. Mem. Council, RUSI, 1986. Trustee: RAF Mus., 1986–87; Headley Ct, 1986–87; Chm., Mus. of E Asian Art, Bath, 1996–2000. Freeman, City of London, 1996. *Publications:* (jtly) Air Power in the Nuclear Age, 1982; Unmanned Aircraft, 1988; The Royal Air Force: an illustrated history, 1993, 3rd edn 1999; (ed) Great Air Battles of the Royal Air Force, 1996; contrib. prof. jls. *Recreations:* military history, shooting, reading, writing. *Address:* c/o Lloyds, Cox & King's Branch, 7 Pall Mall, SW1Y 5NA. *Club:* Royal Air Force.

ARMITAGE, Prof. Peter, CBE 1984; Professor of Applied Statistics (formerly of Biomathematics), 1976–90, now Emeritus, and Fellow, St Peter's College, University of Oxford, 1976–90, now Emeritus Fellow; *b* 15 June 1924; *s* of Harry and Florence Armitage, Huddersfield; *m* 1st, 1947, Phyllis Enid Perry (*d* 2001), London; one *s* two *d*; 2nd, 2003, Cecil Dione Rowlatt, Abingdon. *Educ:* Huddersfield Coll.; Trinity Coll., Cambridge (Wrangler, 1947; MA 1952); PhD London, 1951. Ministry of Supply, 1943–45; National Physical Laboratory, 1945–46; Mem. Statistical Research Unit of Med. Research Council, London Sch. of Hygiene and Trop. Med., 1947–61; Prof. of Medical Statistics, Univ. of London, 1961–76. President: Biometric Soc., 1972–73 (Hon. Life Mem., 1998); Royal Statistical Soc., 1982–84 (Hon. Sec., 1958–64); Internat. Soc. for Clinical Biostatistics, 1990–91; Mem., International Statistical Institute, 1961. Hon. FFPM 1991. Hon. DSc De Montfort, 1998. (Jtly) J. Allyn Taylor Prize, John P. Robarts Res. Inst., London, Ont, 1987; Guy Medals in bronze, silver and gold, Royal Statistical Soc., 1962, 1978, 1990. Editor, Biometrics, 1980–84. *Publications:* Sequential Medical Trials, 1960, 2nd edn 1975; Statistical Methods in Medical Research, 1971, 4th edn (jtly), 2001; (ed with H. A. David) Advances in Biometry, 1996; (ed with T. Colton) Encyclopedia of Biostatistics, 1998, 2nd edn 2005; papers in statistical and medical journals. *Recreations:* music, genealogy. *Address:* 2 Reading Road, Wallingford, Oxon OX10 9DP. *T:* (01491) 835840.

See also E. Armitage.

ARMITAGE, Simon Robert, CBE 2010; poet, novelist, playwright, song-lyricist, screen-writer and broadcaster; Professor of Poetry: University of Sheffield, since 2011; University of Oxford, since 2015; *b* 26 May 1963. Writer of song-lyrics for film, Feltham Sings, 2002 (BAFTA and Ivor Novello Awards, 2004). *Publications: poetry:* Zoom!, 1989; Xanadu, 1992; Kid, 1992; Book of Matches, 1993; (with G. Maxwell) Moon Country, 1995; The Dead Sea Poems, 1996; CloudCuckooLand, 1997; Killing Time, 1999; Selected Poems, 2001; The Universal Home Doctor, 2002; Travelling Songs, 2002; Tyrannosaurus Rex Versus the Corduroy Kid, 2006; The Not Dead, 2008; Seeing Stars, 2010; Black Roses: the killing of Sophie Lancaster, 2012; *prose:* All Points North, 1998; Walking Home: travels with a troubadour on the Pennine Way, 2012; Walking Away: further travels with a troubadour on the South West Coast Path, 2015; *plays:* Mister Heracles, 2000; Jerusalem, 2005; Gig, 2008; *novels:* Little Green Man, 2001; The White Stuff, 2004; *dramatisation:* The Odyssey, 2005; *libretto:* The Assassin Tree, 2006; *translations:* Sir Gawain and the Green Knight, 2007; The Death of King Arthur, 2012. *Address:* c/o DGA, 55 Monmouth Street, WC2H 9DG.

ARMITSTEAD, Claire Louise, (Mrs J. C. Yandell); Books Editor, Guardian News and Media, since 2011 (Literary Editor, The Guardian, 1999–2011); *b* 2 Dec. 1958; *d* of Charles Henry Wilfrid Armitstead and Gillian Louise Armitstead (*née* Bartley); *m* 1983, John Christopher Yandell; one *s* one *d. Educ:* Zaria Children's Sch., Nigeria; Bedales Sch.; St Hilda's Coll., Oxford (BA). Reporter, S Wales Argus, 1980–84; sub-ed. and Theatre Critic, Hampstead and Highgate Express, 1984–88; Theatre Critic, Financial Times, 1988–92; Theatre Critic, 1992–95, Arts Ed., 1995–99, The Guardian. Trustee, English PEN, 2013–. *Recreations:* reading, writing, gardening, trying to play the piano. *Address:* The Guardian, Kings Place, 90 York Way, N1 9AG.

ARMITT, Sir John (Alexander), Kt 2012; CBE 1996; FREng, FICE, FCGI; Chairman: City and Guilds, since 2012; National Express, since 2013 (non-executive Director, since 2013); *b* 2 Feb. 1946; *s* of Alexander Walter Armitt and Lily Irene (*née* Dunce); *m* 1969, Mavis Dorothy Sage (marr. diss.); one *s* one *d. Educ:* Portsmouth Northern Grammar Sch.; Portsmouth Coll. of Technology. FREng (FEng 1993); FICE 1989. John Laing Construction, 1966–93; Jt Man. Dir, 1988–93; Chairman: J. Laing Internat., 1988–93; Laing Civil Engrg, 1988–93; Chief Executive: Union Railways, 1993–97; Costain Gp, 1997–2001; Railtrack plc, 2001–02; Network Rail, 2002–07. Chairman:: EPSRC, 2007–12; Olympic Delivery Authy, 2007–14. Non-exec. Dir, Berkeley Gp, 2007– (Dep. Chm., 2012–). Member, Advisory Board: Siemens UK, 2009–12; PricewaterhouseCoopers, 2010–12. Council Member: ICE, 1989–92 (Chm., Mgt Bd, 1989–92; Pres., 2015–Nov. 2016); FCEC, 1986–93 (Chm., European Affairs Cttee, 1989–92). Pres., Export Gp for Constructional Inds, 1992–93; Member: Overseas Project Bd, DTI, 1992–93; Export Guarantees Adv. Council, 2001–04; Commn for Integrated Transport, 2004–07; Bd, TfL, 2012–. Mem. Bd, Major Projects Assoc., 1994–2004. FCGI 2010. *Recreations:* sailing, fishing, golf, theatre, music. *E:* john_armitt@hotmail.com.

ARMOND, Ralph Peter; Director General, Zoological Society of London, since 2004; *b* 30 May 1957; *s* of John Walter Armond and Helene Maria Armond; *m* 1984, Jane Caroline Everitt; one *s* one *d. Educ:* King's Coll. Sch., Wimbledon; Emmanuel Coll., Cambridge (BA Geog. 1978). Retail Mktg, Boots Co. Plc, 1978–84; Mktg Manager, Dixons Stores Gp, 1984–88; Tussauds Group Ltd, 1988–2004: Mktg Manager, Chessington World of Adventures, 1988–91; Gen. Manager, Warwick Castle, 1991–95; Divl Dir, Alton Towers Resort, 1995–2004. Outstanding Personal Contribn to Tourism award, Heart of England Tourist Bd, 2003. *Recreations:* mountain biking, jogging, learning to play the saxophone. *Address:* Zoological Society of London, Regent's Park, NW1 4RY. *T:* (020) 7449 6207.

ARMOUR, Prof. Sir James, Kt 1995; CBE 1989; FRSE; FMedSci; Vice-Principal, 1990–95, and Professor of Veterinary Parasitology, 1976–95, now Emeritus, University of Glasgow; Chairman, Glasgow Dental Hospital and School NHS Trust, 1995–98; *b* 17 Sept. 1929; *s* of James Angus Armour and Margaret Brown Roy; *m* 1st, 1953, Irene Morris (*d* 1988); two *s* two *d*; 2nd, 1992, Christine Strickland. *Educ:* Marr Coll., Troon; Univ. of Glasgow (PhD 1967; BVMS 2010). MRCVS 1952 (Hon. FRCVS 1995); FRSE 1991. Colonial Service, Nigeria: Vet. Officer, 1953–57; Vet. Parasitologist, 1957–60; Parasitologist, Cooper Technical Bureau, Berkhamsted, 1960–63; University of Glasgow: Research Fellow, 1963–67; Lectr, 1967–70; Sen. Lectr, 1970–73; Reader, 1973–76; Dean, Vet. Faculty, 1986–91. Chairman: Vet. Products Cttee, Medicines Commn, 1987–96; Governing Body, Inst. of Animal Health, Compton, 1991–97; Member: Adv. Bd, Inst. of Aquaculture, Univ. of Stirling, 1997–2003; Bd, Hannah Res. Inst., Ayr, 1999–2011; RSE Inquiry into Foot and Mouth Disease in Scotland, 2001–03; Chm., HEFCE RAE Panels for Agriculture, Food Sci. and Vet. Sci., 1999–2001. Chairman: Moredun Foundn for Animal Health and Welfare, 2000–04; St Andrews Clinics for Children in Africa, 1996–2010; Vice Chm., Hannah Trust, 2012–; Trustee, Scottish Sci. Trust, 1999–2001. Vice-Pres., RSE, 1998–2000. Founder FMedSci 1998. Hon. FIBiol 2001. Dr *hc* Utrecht, 1981; DVM&S Edinburgh, 1995; DU: Glasgow, 2001; Stirling, 2005. John Henry Steel Medal, RCVS, 1979; Bledisloe Award, Royal Agricl Soc., 1990; Wooldridge Medal, BVA, 1990; World Assoc. for Advancement of Vet. Parasitol./Pfizer Award, 1993; Chiron Medal, BVA, 1997; Bicentenary Medal, RSE, 2002. *Publications:* (with Urquhart and Duncan) Veterinary Parasitology, 1988; numerous contribs to vet. and parasitology jls. *Recreations:* golf (British Boys Golf Champion, Hoylake, 1947), watching soccer and Rugby. *Address:* 4b Towans Court, Prestwick KA9 2AY. *Clubs:* Royal Troon Golf (Captain, 1990–92; Hon. Pres., 2007–10); Atlanta Athletic (USA).

ARMOUR, Prof. John Hamish; Hogan Lovells (formerly Lovells) Professor of Law and Finance, Oxford University, since 2007; Fellow, Oriel College, Oxford, since 2007; *b* Nottingham, 24 Dec. 1971; *s* of Edward and Suzanne Armour; *m* 2007, Rebecca Ann Williams; two *d. Educ:* Pembroke Coll., Oxford (BA 1994; BCL 1995); Yale Law Sch. (LLM 1996). University of Nottingham: Lectr in Law, 1996–2000; Norton Rose Lectr in Corporate and Financial Law, 2000–01; University of Cambridge: Res. Fellow, Centre for Business Res., 1999–2000; Sen. Res. Fellow, 2001–02; Lectr in Law, 2002–05; Sen. Lectr in Law, 2005–07. *Publications:* (ed) Vulnerable Transactions in Corporate Insolvency, 2003; (ed) After Enron: modernising corporate and securities law in Europe and the US, 2006; The Anatomy of Corporate Law, 2nd edn 2009; (ed) Rationality in Company Law, 2009; contrib. to academic jls. *Recreations:* cycling, hill-walking. *Address:* Faculty of Law, University of Oxford, St Cross Building, St Cross Road, Oxford OX1 3UL. *T:* (01865) 281616. *E:* john.armour@law.ox.ac.uk.

ARMOUR, Nicholas Hilary Stuart; HM Diplomatic Service, retired; business consultant, since 2013; Director and Chief Executive, International Chambers of Commerce UK, 2012–13; *b* 12 June 1951; *s* of late Brig. William Stanley Gibson Armour and of Penelope Jean Armour; *m* 1982, Georgina Elizabeth Fortescue (*d* 2003); two *d. Educ:* Ampleforth Coll.; Exeter Univ. (BA). FCO, 1974; MECAS: Lebanon, Beaconsfield, Jordan, 1975; Beirut, 1977; FCO, 1980; Head of Chancery, Athens, 1984; Asst Head of Dept, FCO, 1989; Counsellor, Muscat, 1991; on loan to DTI, 1994–97; Consul-Gen., Dubai and the Northern Emirates, 1997–99; on loan to Royal Mail ViaCode, 2000; Head, North America Dept, FCO, 2000–03; Sen. DS (Civil), RCDS, 2003–05 (on secondment); Consul-Gen., Toronto, and Dir, UK Trade and Investment, Canada, 2005–09; Dir, Internat. Gp, UK Trade and Investment, 2009–12. Mem., Madrigal Soc., 1995–. *Recreations:* music, singing, sailing, ski-ing.

ARMSON, (Frederick) Simon (Arden); mental health professional, since 2004; *b* 11 Sept. 1948; *s* of late Frank Gerald Arden Armson and Margaret Fenella Armson (*née* Newton); *m* 1975, Marion Albinia (*née* Hamilton-Russell); one *s* two *d. Educ:* Denstone Coll.; MSc (Mental Health Studies) Guy's Hosp. Med. Sch., London, 1996; Dip. Clin. Psychotherapy, CAT, 2002; Dip. Neuro-linguistic programming, Internat. Neuro-linguistic Programming Trainers' Assoc., 2007; registered UKCP, 2005. Various administrative and managerial posts, NHS, 1970–84; Asst Gen. Sec. 1984–89, Gen. Sec. 1989, Chief Exec., 1990–2004, The Samaritans. Dir, The Samaritans Enterprises Ltd, 1996–2004. Clinical Psychotherapist, 2004–; Develt Coach, 2004–. Chair: BBC Radio Helpline Adv. Gp, 1995–98; Telephone Helplines Gp, 1992–96; Develt Adv. Cttee, Cancer Bacup Service, 1998–2001. UK Rep., 1996–2005, Chm., Nat. Delegs, 2001–03, Mem. Exec. Cttee, 2001–03, Internat. Assoc. for Suicide Prevention; Member: Suicide Prevention Sub-Gp, DoH Wider Health Wkg Gp, 1995–97; RCN Men's Health Forum, 1995–97; Steering Cttee for Structure Review of British Red Cross, 1995; Adv. Cttee, Inst. of Volunteer Research, 1996–2002; Wkg Gp, Rev. of BACUP

Cancer Counselling Service, 1997; Cttee, ICSTIS, 2001–07; Ind. Adv. Panel to Ministerial Council on Deaths in Custody, 2009–14; Lay Mem., Mental Health Rev. Tribunal, later Specialist Mem., First-tier Tribunal (Mental Health), 2006–. Mental Health Act Comr, 2002–08 and 2009–12 (Mem. Bd, 2004–09; Chm., Mental Health Act Commn, 2008–09); Ind. Mem., Mkt Res. Disciplinary Authy, 2009–; Mental Health Act Manager, W London Mental Health NHS Trust, 2012–. Trustee: Yoxall Town Lands Charity, 1974–; Yoxall United Charities, 1982–; ChildLine, 1999–2006; Broadcasting Support Services, 2003–09; Mental Health Media Trust, 2004–09; National Nightline, 2005–06; Maytree Respite Centre, 2005–14 (Chm., 2009–14; Patron, 2015–); CLIC Sargent, 2006–09; Partnership for Children, 2009– (Vice Chm., 2012–15). Hon. Mem., Telephone Helplines Assoc., 1999. Chairman of Judges: Guardian Jerwood Award, 1995–99; Guardian Charity Award, 2000–03; Mem. Cttee, Ringel Award, 2001–03. CCMI (CIMgt 1995; Pres., Mid Thames Br., 2006–). FRSA 1993. *Publications:* (contrib.) International Handbook of Suicide and Attempted Suicide, 2000; (contrib.) Every Family in the Land, 2004; (contrib.) Prevention and Treatment of Suicidal Behaviour, 2005. *Recreations:* music, cycling (cross country), walking, sailing, mental health and emotional wellbeing; grand paternal activities. *Address:* Broad Oak, Old Honey Lane, Hurley, Maidenhead, Berkshire SL6 5LW. *T:* (01628) 824322, 07788 186339. *E:* armson@btinternet.com. *Club:* Reform.

ARMSON, Rev. Canon John Moss, PhD; Canon Residentiary, Rochester Cathedral, 1989–2001, now Canon Emeritus; *b* 21 Dec. 1939; *s* of Arthur Eric Armson and Edith Isobel Moss. *Educ:* Wyggeston Sch.; Selwyn Coll., Cambridge (MA); St Andrews Univ. (PhD); College of the Resurrection, Mirfield. Curate, St John, Notting Hill, 1966; Chaplain and Fellow, Downing Coll., Cambridge, 1969; Chaplain, 1973–77, Vice-Principal, 1977–82, Westcott House, Cambridge; Principal, Edinburgh Theol Coll., 1982–89. Mem., Hengrave Ecumenical Community, 2001–03. *Recreations:* music, theatre, gardening, landscaping. *Address:* Stuart Court, High Street, Kibworth, Leics LE8 0LR. *T:* (01162) 793341.

ARMSON, Simon; *see* Armson, F. S. A.

ARMSTRONG, family name of **Baron Armstrong of Ilminster**.

ARMSTRONG OF HILL TOP, Baroness *cr* 2010 (Life Peer), of Crook in the County of Durham; **Hilary Jane Armstrong;** PC 1999; DL; *b* 30 Nov. 1945; *d* of Rt Hon. Ernest Armstrong, PC and of Hannah P. Lamb; *m* 1992, Dr Paul Corrigan. *Educ:* Monkwearmouth Comp. Sch., Sunderland; West Ham Coll. of Technology (BSc Sociology); Univ. of Birmingham (Dip. in Social Work). VSO, Murray Girls' High Sch., Kenya, 1967–69; Social Worker, Newcastle City Social Services Dept, 1970–73; Community Worker, Southwick Neighbourhood Action Project, Sunderland, 1973–75; Lectr, Community and Youth Work, Sunderland Polytechnic, 1975–86. MP (Lab) NW Durham, 1987–2010. Frontbench spokesperson on education, 1988–92 (under-fives, primary, and special educn), on Treasury affairs, 1994–95; PPS to Leader of the Opposition, 1992–94; Minister of State, DETR, 1997–2001; Parly Sec. to HM Treasury (Govt Chief Whip), 2001–06; Chancellor of the Duchy of Lancaster and Minister for the Cabinet Office, 2006–07. DL Durham, 2010. *Recreations:* reading, theatre, football. *Address:* House of Lords, SW1A 0PW.

ARMSTRONG OF ILMINSTER, Baron *cr* 1988 (Life Peer), of Ashill in the county of Somerset; **Robert Temple Armstrong,** GCB 1983 (KCB 1978; CB 1974); CVO 1975; Secretary of the Cabinet, 1979–87, and Head of the Home Civil Service, 1983–87 (Joint Head, 1981–83), retired; director of companies; *b* 30 March 1927; *o s* of Sir Thomas (Henry Wait) Armstrong, DMus, FRCM; *m* 1st, 1953, Serena Mary Benedicta (marr. diss. 1985; she *d* 1994), *er d* of Sir Roger Chance, 3rd Bt, MC; two *d*; 2nd, 1985, (Mary) Patricia, *d* of late C. C. Carlow. *Educ:* Dragon Sch., Oxford; Eton; Christ Church, Oxford (Hon. Student 1985). Asst Principal, Treasury, 1950–55; Private Secretary to: Rt Hon. Reginald Maudling, MP (when Economic Sec. to Treasury), 1953–54; Rt Hon. R. A. Butler, CH, MP (when Chancellor of the Exchequer), 1954–55; Principal, Treasury, 1955–57; Sec., Radcliffe Cttee on Working of Monetary System, 1957–59; returned to Treasury as Principal, 1959–64; Sec., Armitage Cttee on Pay of Postmen, 1964; Asst Sec., Cabinet Office, 1964–66; Sec. of Kindersley Review Body on Doctors' and Dentists' Remuneration and of Franks Cttee on Pay of Higher Civil Service, 1964–66; Asst Sec., Treasury, 1967–68; Jt Prin. Private Sec. to Rt Hon. Roy Jenkins, MP (Chancellor of the Exchequer), 1968; Under Secretary (Home Finance), Treasury, 1968–70; Principal Private Sec. to Prime Minister, 1970–75; Dep. Sec., 1973; Dep. Under-Sec. of State, Home Office, 1975–77, Permt Under Sec. of State, 1977–79. Director: BAT Industries, 1988–97; Inchcape, 1988–95; Bristol and West plc (formerly Bristol and West Building Soc.), 1988–97 (Chm., 1993–97); N. M. Rothschild & Sons, 1988–97; RTZ Corporation, 1988–97; Shell Transport & Trading Co., 1988–97; Lucas Industries, 1989–92; Biotechnology Investments Ltd, subseq. 3i Bioscience Investment Trust, 1989–2002 (Chm., 1989–2001); Carlton Television, 1991–95; IAMGold Ltd, 1996–2003; Bank of Ireland, 1997–2001; Chm., Forensic Investigative Associates, 1997–2003; Mem., Supervisory Bd, Robeco Gp, 1988–97. Chancellor, Univ. of Hull, 1994–2006. Chairman: Bd of Trustees, V & A Museum, 1988–98; Hestercombe Gardens Trust, 1996–2005; Bd of Govs, RNCM, 2000–05; Sir Edward Heath Charitable Foundn, 2005–13; Trustee: Ralph Vaughan Williams Trust, 1956–; Leeds Castle Foundn, 1988–2007 (Chm., 2001–07); Derek Hill Foundn, 2000–; Wells Cathedral Sch. Foundn, 2007–12; Dir, RAM, 1975–98 (Hon. Fellow 1985); Member: Council of Management, Royal Philharmonic Soc., 1975–2002; Rhodes Trust, 1975–97; Bd of Dirs, Royal Opera House, Covent Garden, 1988–93 (Sec., 1968–88); Royal Acad. of Music Foundn, 1988–2000. Fellow of Eton Coll., 1979–94. Hon. Bencher, Inner Temple, 1986. *Recreation:* music. *Address:* House of Lords, SW1A 0PW. *Clubs:* Brooks's, Garrick.

ARMSTRONG, Hon. Lord; Iain Gillies Armstrong; a Senator of the College of Justice in Scotland, since 2013; *b* 26 May 1956; *s* of John Gillies Armstrong and June Bell Armstrong (*née* Black); *m* 1977, Deirdre Elizabeth Mary Mackenzie; one *s* one *d*. *Educ:* Inverness Royal Acad.; Glasgow Univ. Called to Scottish Bar, 1986; QC (Scot.) 2000; Clerk of Faculty of Advocates, 1995–99 (Vice Dean, 2008–13); Standing Jun. Counsel in Scotland, DSS, 1998–2000; Crown Counsel, 2000–03. Member: Jt Standing Cttee on Legal Educn in Scotland, 1995–99; Adv. Panel, Sch. of Law, Univ. of Glasgow, 2009–; Judicial Appts Bd for Scotland, 2010–12. Gov., Fettes Coll., 2000–11. *Address:* Court of Session, Parliament House, Parliament Square, Edinburgh EH1 1RQ. *T:* (0131) 225 2595. *Club:* New (Edinburgh).

ARMSTRONG, Alan Gordon; Senior Lecturer in Economics, University of Bristol, 1977–97; *b* 11 Feb. 1937; *s* of late Joseph Gordon Armstrong and Evelyn Armstrong (*née* Aird); *m* 1963, Margaret Louise Harwood; one *s* one *d*. *Educ:* Bede Grammar Sch., Sunderland; Queens' Coll., Cambridge (MA). Economist, Reed Paper Gp, 1960–62; Res. Officer, Dept of Applied Econs, Univ. of Cambridge, 1962–69; Fellow, Selwyn Coll., Cambridge, 1967–69; Lectr in Econs, Univ. of Bristol, 1970–77. Part-time Mem., Monopolies and Mergers Commn, 1989–95; Consultant on Economic Statistics to: UN Statistical Office, OECD, EEC, ONS, DTI, NEDO, various times, 1970–2001; Member: EC Adv. Cttee on Econ. and Social Statistics, 1992–97; UK Central Statistical Office (formerly Central Statistical Office Users') Adv. Cttee, 1992–96. *Publications:* Input-Output Tables and Analysis, 1973; Structural Change in UK, 1974; Review of DTI Statistics, 1989; res. papers and jl articles on input-output, nat. accounts and the motor industry. *Recreations:* gardening (by necessity), family history, cricket, church affairs. *Address:* 70 Causeway View, Nailsea, Bristol BS48 2XL. *T:* (01275) 853197.

ARMSTRONG, Alexander Henry Fenwick; television presenter, comedian and actor, since 1996; *b* Rothbury, Northumberland, 2 March 1970; *s* of Angus and Virginia Armstrong; *m* 2004, Hannah Snow; four *s*. *Educ:* Durham Sch.; Trinity Coll., Cambridge (Choral Schol.; BA 1992). *Television* includes: Beast, 2000–01; (with Ben Miller) The Armstrong and Miller Show, 2000–01 and 2007–10; Life Begins, 2004–06; The Trial of Tony Blair, 2007; Mutual Friends, 2008; Dr Who, 2008, 2011; Pointless, 2009–; SJA: Alien Files, 2010; Reggie Perrin, 2010; The Sarah Jane Adventures, 2011; Love Life, 2012; The Twelve Drinks of Christmas, 2013; Rome's Invisible City, 2015. Dir, Toff Media, 2006–. Pres., Newcastle Literary and Philosophical Soc., 2011–. Mem. Cttee, St Paul's Knightsbridge Foundn, 2006–. *Publications:* (with R. Osman) The Very Pointless Quiz Book, 2014. *Recreations:* wine, fishing, friends, singing. *Address:* The Old Vicarage, Minster Lovell, Oxon OX29 0RR. *E:* xander.armstrong@mac.com. *Clubs:* Brooks's, Groucho, Aspinalls.

ARMSTRONG, Very Rev. Christopher John; Dean of Blackburn, since 2001; *b* 18 Dec. 1947; *s* of John Armstrong and Susan Elizabeth Armstrong; *m* 1976, Geraldine Anne Clementsen; two *s* one *d*. *Educ:* Dunstable Grammar Sch.; Bede Coll., Univ. of Durham (Cert Ed 1969); Kelham Theol Coll.; Univ. of Nottingham (BTh 1975). Ordained deacon, 1975, priest, 1976; Asst Curate, All Saints, Maidstone, 1975–79; Chaplain, Coll. of St Hild and St Bede, Univ. of Durham, 1979–85; Domestic Chaplain to Archbp of York and Diocesan Dir of Ordinands, Dio. York, 1985–91; Vicar, St Martin, Scarborough, 1991–2001, Chm., Lancs Fairness Commn, 2014–15. *Recreations:* sport, mountaineering, gardening, theatre and cinema, travel. *Address:* The Deanery, Preston New Road, Blackburn, Lancs BB2 6PS. *T:* (01254) 52502.

ARMSTRONG, Lt-Col Sir Christopher (John Edmund Stuart), 7th Bt *cr* 1841, of Gallen Priory, King's County; MBE 1979; *b* 15 Jan. 1940; *s* of Sir Andrew Clarence Francis Armstrong, 6th Bt, CMG and Laurel May (*née* Stuart; *d* 1988); *S* father, 1997; *m* 1972, Georgina Elizabeth Carey, *d* of Lt-Col W. G. Lewis; three *s* one *d*. *Educ:* Ampleforth; RMA, Sandhurst. Lt-Col, RCT. *Heir:* *s* Charles Andrew Armstrong, *b* 21 Feb. 1973.

ARMSTRONG, Prof. (Christopher) Mark, DPhil; FBA 2007; Professor of Economics, University of Oxford, since 2011; Fellow, All Souls College, Oxford, since 2011; *b* 26 Dec. 1964; *s* of John Armstrong and Jane Armstrong; *m* 1999, Carli Coetzee; one *s* one *d*. *Educ:* Bedales Sch., Petersfield; Queens' Coll., Cambridge (BA Hons Math. 1987); St John's Coll., Oxford (DPhil Econs 1992). Lectr in Econs, Univ. of Cambridge, 1992–94; Eric Roll Prof. of Econ. Policy, Univ. of Southampton, 1994–97; Fellow in Econs, Nuffield Coll., Oxford, 1997–2003; Prof. of Econs, UCL, 2003–11. Editor: Rev. of Econ. Studies, 1999–2003; Rand Jl of Econs, 2005–. *Publications:* (with S. Cowan and J. Vickers) Regulatory Reform: economic analysis and UK experience, 1994; articles in academic jls on industrial economics, competition policy and consumer behaviour. *Recreations:* playing the piano, dragging my children Harriet and Joseph around old buildings. *Address:* Department of Economics, University of Oxford, Manor Road, Oxford OX1 3UL.

ARMSTRONG, Colin Robert, CMG 2012; OBE 1995; Founder, and Executive President, since 1976, Agripac SA (Manager, 1972–76); *b* Manchester, 9 Sept. 1945; *s* of Gerald Armstrong and Margaret Armstrong (*née* Wilson); *m* 1974, Cecilia Alexandra Luna; one *s* two *d*. *Educ:* Rossall Sch.; Harper Adams Agricl Coll. (NDA); Essex Inst. of Agric. (Dip. Mgt). ICI Plant Protection Div., Malaysia, Mexico and Ecuador, 1968–76. Hon. Consul, Guayaquil, 1982–. Designer, Forbidden Corner, Coverdale, N Yorks (visitor attraction, opened 1994). *Publications:* Behind the Forbidden Corner, 1999. *Recreations:* reading, opera, walking, riding and cattle ranching in Ecuador. *Address:* Agripac SA, PO Box 09 01 8598, Guayaquil, Ecuador. *E:* carmstrong@agripac.com.ec. *Club:* Union (Guayaquil).

ARMSTRONG, Dean Paul; QC 2014; *b* Halstead, Kent; *s* of Paul Armstrong and Merle Armstrong; one *s*. *Educ:* Sevenoaks Sch.; Fitzwilliam Coll., Cambridge (BA 1983; MA 1986). Called to the Bar, Gray's Inn, 1985; in practice as barrister, specialising in serious crime and fraud. Regular commentator on Sky News and BBC TV and Radio. *Recreations:* follower of Chelsea Football Club and Kent County Cricket Club, music. *Address:* 2 Bedford Row, WC1R 4BU. *T:* (020) 7440 8888, *Fax:* (020) 7242 1378. *E:* darmstrong@2bedfordrow.co.uk. *Club:* Arts.

ARMSTRONG, Douglas; *see* Armstrong, R. D.

ARMSTRONG, Dr Ernest McAlpine, CB 2005; FRCSE, FRCPE, FRCPGlas, FRCGP, FFPH; Chief Medical Officer, Scottish Executive Department of Health, 2000–05; Chairman, Alcohol Focus Scotland, since 2011; *b* 3 June 1945; *s* of Ernest Armstrong and Mary Brownlie McLean Armstrong (*née* McAlpine); *m* 1970, Dr Katherine Mary Dickson Young; two *s*. *Educ:* Hamilton Acad.; Glasgow Univ. (BSc (Hons) 1968; MB ChB (Hons) 1970). MRCP 1975; FRCGP 1987; FRCPGlas 1988; FRCPE 1996; FFPH (FFPHM 2001); FRCSE 2001. Lectr in Pathology, Glasgow Univ., 1971–74; Trainee Assistant, Douglas, 1974–75; Principal in gen. practice, Argyll, 1975–93; Sec., BMA, 1993–2000. Chm., Oban Hospice Ltd, 2007–13. Hon. Col, 205 (S) Field Hosp. (V), 2005–12. Hon. LLD Aberdeen, 2008. *Publications:* articles on ultrastructure, clinical immunology and med. politics. *Recreations:* church music, opera, sailing, travelling. *Address:* 29/1 Inverleith Place, Edinburgh EH3 5QD.

ARMSTRONG, Frank William, FREng; FIMechE; FRAeS; independent technical consultant, since 1991; *b* 26 March 1931; *s* of Frank Armstrong and Millicent L. Armstrong; *m* 1957, Diane T. Varley; three *d*. *Educ:* Stretford Grammar Sch.; Royal Technical Coll., Salford; Queen Mary Coll., Univ. of London (BSc Eng; MSc Eng 1956). FIMechE 1981; FRAeS 1981; FREng (FEng 1991). Massey-Harris Ltd, 1947–51; De Havilland Engine Co., 1956–58; Admiralty Engineering Lab., 1958–59; NGTE, 1959–78; Engine Div., MoD (PE), 1978–81; Dep. Dir, R&D, NGTE, 1981–83; Royal Aircraft, later Royal Aerospace, Establishment: Head of Propulsion Dept, 1983–87; Dep. Dir (Aircraft), 1987–88; Dep. Dir (Aerospace Vehicles), 1988–90; Dir (Aerospace Vehicles), 1990–91. *Publications:* contribs on aeronautics research, gas turbines and aircraft propulsion to learned jls. *Recreations:* mountaineering, music, aviation history. *Address:* 6 Corringway, Church Crookham, Fleet, Hants GU52 6AN. *T:* (01252) 616526.

ARMSTRONG, Prof. Fraser Andrew, PhD; FRS 2008; Professor of Chemistry, University of Oxford; Fellow of St John's College, Oxford, since 1993. *Educ:* Univ. of Leeds (BSc; PhD 1978); Univ. of Oxford (MA). Royal Soc. Univ. Res. Fellow, Univ. of Oxford, 1983–89; Chemistry Faculty, Univ. of Calif, Irvine, 1989–93; Lectr, then Reader, Dept of Chem., Univ. of Oxford, 1993. European Medal for Biol Inorganic Chem., 1998; Award for Inorganic Biochem., 2000, Medal for Interdisciplinary Chem., 2006, RSC; Carbon Trust Innovation Award, 2003; Max Planck Award for Frontiers in Biol Chem., 2004. *Publications:* Bioinorganic Chemistry, 1990; (jtly) Inorganic Chemistry, 4th edn 2006, 5th edn as Shriver & Atkins' Inorganic Chemistry, 2009; (jtly) Energy… beyond oil, 2007; articles in learned jls. *Address:* Department of Chemistry, University of Oxford, South Parks Road, Oxford OX1 3QR.

ARMSTRONG, Iain Gillies; *see* Armstrong, Hon. Lord.

ARMSTRONG, Prof. Isobel Mair, PhD; FBA 2003; Professor of English, Birkbeck College, University of London, 1989–2002, now Professor Emeritus, and Hon. Fellow, 2002; *b* 25 March 1937; *d* of Richard Aneurin Jones and Marjorie Jackson; *m* 1961, John Michael Armstrong; two *s* one *d*. *Educ:* Friends' Sch., Saffron Walden; Univ. of Leicester (BA 1959; PhD 1963). Asst Lectr and Lectr in English, UCL, 1963–70; Lectr and Sen. Lectr in English, Univ. of Leicester, 1971–79; Prof. of English, Univ. of Southampton, 1979–89. Vis. Prof.,

Princeton Univ., 1983–84; Frank and Eleanor Griffiths Chair, Bread Loaf Sch. of English, 1990, Robert Frost Chair, 2002, Middlebury Coll.; Vis. Prof., Harvard Univ., 1995–96, 1999, 2004, 2008; Sen. Res. Fellow, Inst. of English Studies, 2002; John Hinkley Vis. Prof., Johns Hopkins Univ., 2005, 2013. Warton Lect. on English Poetry, British Acad., 2011. For. Mem., Amer. Acad. of Arts and Scis, 2014. Hon. DLitt Leicester, 2005. Jt Editor, Women: a cultural review, 1990–; Gen. Editor, Writers and their Work, British Council, 1992–2006. *Publications:* Victorian Scrutinies: reviews of poetry 1830–70, 1972; Language as Living Form in Nineteenth Century Poetry, 1982; Jane Austen: Mansfield Park, 1988; Victorian Poetry, 1993; Jane Austen: Sense and Sensibility, 1994; Nineteenth Century Women Poets, 1996; (ed with Virginia Blain) Women's Poetry in the Enlightenment, 1999; (ed with Virginia Blain) Women's Poetry, Late Romantic to Late Victorian, 1999; The Radical Aesthetic, 2000; Victorian Glassworlds: glass culture and the imagination, 1830–1880, 2008 (John Russell Lowell Prize, MLA, 2009). *Recreation:* drawing in pen and ink. *Address:* Department of English and Humanities, Birkbeck College, Malet Street, WC1E 7HX. *T:* (020) 7631 6078.

ARMSTRONG, Dr Jennifer Louise, FFPH; Medical Director, NHS Greater Glasgow and Clyde, since 2012; *b* Glasgow, 19 Nov. 1965; *d* of James Armstrong and Irene Armstrong; *m* 1993, Prof. Martin McIntyre; two *s* one *d*. *Educ:* Laurel Bank Sch., Glasgow; Langside Coll., Glasgow; Univ. of Glasgow (MB ChB 1988; MPH 1995); Caledonian Univ. (Dip. Mgt 1999). MRCPGlas 1993; MFPH 1998, FFPH 2007. Trng in clin. posts, 1988–94; specialty trng in public health, West of Scotland, 1994–2000; Gen. Manager, N Glasgow Trust, 2000–04; Dir, Acute Services Rev., 2001–02; Consultant in Public Health Medicine, Nat. Services Div., NHS Nat. Services Scotland, 2004–07; SMO, Health Dept, Scottish Govt, 2007–12. *Recreations:* running 10K, script writing, cycling. *Address:* NHS Greater Glasgow and Clyde, J B Russell House, Gartnavel, 1055 Great Western Road, Glasgow G12 0XH. *T:* (0141) 201 4407. *E:* Jennifer.Armstrong2@ggc.scot.nhs.uk.

ARMSTRONG, Karen Andersen, OBE 2015; writer, since 1982; *b* 14 Nov. 1944; *d* of John Oliver Seymour Armstrong and Eileen Hastings Armstrong (*née* McHale). *Educ:* Convent of Holy Child Jesus, Edgbaston; St Anne's Coll., Oxford (MA; MLitt). Mem., Soc. of the Holy Child Jesus, 1962–69. Tutorial Res. Fellow, Bedford Coll., Univ. of London, 1973–76; Hd of English, James Allen's Girls' Sch., Dulwich, 1976–82. Trustee, British Mus., 2008–. Hon. DLitt: Georgetown; Exeter; Aston; St Andrews; Hon. DD Kingston, Ont. TED Prize, 2008; Franklin D. Roosevelt Four Freedoms Medal, 2008; Leopold Lucas Meml Prize, Tubingen Univ., 2009; Internat. Hon. Knowledge Award (Sweden), 2011; Jack P. Blaney Award for Dialogue, Simon Fraser Univ., 2012; Al-Rodhan Prize, British Acad., 2013. *Publications:* Through the Narrow Gate, 1981; Beginning the World, 1983; The First Christian, 1984; Tongues of Fire, 1985; The Gospel According to Woman, 1986; Holy War: the Crusades and their impact on today's world, 1988; Muhammad: a biography of the Prophet, 1991; A History of God, 1993; In the Beginning, 1996; Jerusalem, One City, Three Faiths, 1996; The Battle for God: a history of Fundamentalism, 2000; Islam: a short history, 2000; Buddha, 2001; The Spiral Staircase: a memoir, 2004; A Short History of Myth, 2005; The Great Transformation: the world at the time of Buddha, Socrates, Confucius and Jeremiah, 2006; Muhammad: a prophet for our time, 2006; The Bible: a biography, 2007; The Case for God: what religion really means, 2009; Twelve Steps to a Compassionate Life, 2011; Fields of Blood: religion and the history of violence, 2014. *Recreations:* literature, music, theatre. *Address:* c/o Felicity Bryan, 2A North Parade, Banbury Road, Oxford OX2 6LX. *T:* (01865) 513816, *Fax:* (01865) 310055.

ARMSTRONG, Lance; professional cyclist, retired 2005, returned to racing, 2009–11; *b* Plano, Texas, 18 Sept. 1971; *s* of Linda Armstrong (*née* Walling); *m* 1998, Kristin Richard (marr. diss. 2003); one *s* twin *d*; one *s* one *d* by Anna Hansen. Nat. Amateur Champion, USA, 1991; Member: US Olympic Team, 1992, 1996, 2000 (Bronze Medal, subseq. disqualified); Motorola Team, 1993–96; Cofidis Team, 1996–97; US Postal Service, subseq. Discovery Channel, Pro Cycling Team, 1998–2005; Team Astana, 2009; RadioShack, 2009–11. Winner, numerous races, including: World Cycling Championships, Oslo, 1993; Tour DuPont, 1995, 1996; Tour de Luxembourg, 1998; Tour de France, 1999, 2000, 2001, 2002, 2003, 2004, 2005 (1st person to win 7 consecutive races, but subseq. stripped of titles); Grand Prix du Midi Libre, 2002. Founder and Chm., Lance Armstrong Foundn for Cancer, later Livestrong Foundn, 1996–2012. *Publications:* It's Not About the Bike: my journey back to life, 2000; (jtly) The Lance Armstrong Performance Program, 2001; (with S. Jenkins) Every Second Counts, 2003. *Address:* c/o Capital Sports & Entertainment, 300 West 6th Street, Suite 2150, Austin, TX 78701, USA; c/o Livestrong Foundation, 2201 E Sixth Street, Austin, TX 78702, USA.

ARMSTRONG, Lisa, (Mrs P. Hadaway); Fashion Director, The Daily Telegraph, since 2011; Contributing Editor, Vogue, since 1999; *b* 12 Oct. 1961; *d* of Royston Myers and Rosalind Armstrong, and step *d* of Clement Armstrong; *m* 1988, Paul Hadaway; two *d*. *Educ:* Dorchester Grammar Sch. for Girls; Bristol Univ. (BA Hons English Lit.); City Univ. (Postgrad. Dip. Journalism). Asst Ed., Fitness Mag., 1985–86; Insight Ed., Elle, 1986–88; Dep. Features Ed., Vogue, 1988–91; Fashion Ed., The Independent and Independent on Sunday, 1991–93; Fashion Features Dir, Vogue, 1993–98; Fashion Ed., The Times, 1998–2011. Trustee, Style for Soldiers. Fashion Writer of the Year, British Fashion Council, 2001. Hon. Dr London Univ. of Arts 2011. *Publications:* Front Row, 1998; Dead Stylish, 2001; Bad Manors, 2003; Deja View, 2004. *Recreations:* reading, riding, needlepoint, finding places to put finished needlepoint. *Address:* Daily Telegraph, 111 Buckingham Palace Road, SW1W 0DT.

ARMSTRONG, Lucy Victoria Winwood; Chief Executive, The Alchemists Ltd, since 2003; *b* Manchester, 13 July 1968; *d* of late David Winwood Armstrong and of Jennifer Susan Armstrong. *Educ:* Aylesbury High Sch.; St Hilda's Coll., Oxford (BA Hons PPE 1989); Open Univ. (MBA 1999; MSc Forensic Psychol. and Criminol. 2010). Investment Controller, 3i plc, 1989–96; Business Develt Manager, Courtaulds Textiles plc, 1996–98; Consultant, Tyzack & Partners, 1998–2003. Non-executive Chairman: Hotspur, 2008–; Capital for Enterprise Ltd, 2012–13. Mem., Adv. Bd, IP Gp plc, 2010–12, 2014–. Actg Chair, Northumbria Univ., 2010–12. Non-exec. Chm., Small and Medium Enterprises Council, CBI, 2004–13. Chair: Professional Standards Council, Asset Based Finance Assoc., 2013–; Enterprise Res. Centre, 2014–; Tyneside Cinema, 2015–. Trustee and Vice-Chm., NCFE, 2008–; Chair, TDI, 2008–; Trustee, Northern Sinfonia Trust, 2011–13. FRSA. *Recreations:* church bell ringing, chain-sawing, diving. *Address:* The Alchemists Ltd, Vertu House, Kingsway North, Gateshead NE11 0JH. *T:* (0191) 491 2391. *E:* lucy.armstrong@the-alchemists.com. *Club:* Northern Counties (Newcastle upon Tyne).

ARMSTRONG, Mark; *see* Armstrong, C. M.

ARMSTRONG, Sir Patrick (John), Kt 2002; CBE 1989; JP; Chairman, Police Authority of Northern Ireland, 1996–2001; *b* 16 Sept. 1927; *s* of Andrew and Hannah Armstrong; *m* 1949, Agnes Carson; two *s* two *d*. *Educ:* Ruskin Coll., Oxford (DipEcon and Pol Sci.); Queen's Univ., Belfast (BA, Dip. Social Studies); Univ. of Newcastle upon Tyne (Dip. Applied Social Studies). Factory worker, 1947–57; Dep. Co. Welfare Officer, 1966–71, Chief Welfare Officer, 1971–73, Co. Antrim; Dep. Chief Inspector of Social Services for NI, 1973–83, Chief Inspector of Social Services, 1983–89. Vice-Chm., Police Authy for NI, 1994–96. JP 1994. *Recreations:* walking, cycling, reading. *Address:* 13 North Parade, Belfast BT7 2GF. *T:* (028) 9064 3616. *Club:* Ulster Reform (Belfast).

ARMSTRONG, Prof. Peter; Professor of Diagnostic Radiology, St Bartholomew's Hospital, 1989–2005; President, Royal College of Radiologists, 1998–2001; *b* 31 Aug. 1940; *s* of Alexander Armstrong and Ada Armstrong (*née* Lapidas); *m* 1967, Carole J. Gray; one *s* one *d* (and one *s* decd). *Educ:* Marylebone Grammar Sch.; Middlesex Hosp. Med. Sch. (MB BS 1963). Jun. hosp. posts, Middlesex Hosp. and Guy's Hosp., 1963–70; Consultant Radiologist, KCH, 1970–77; Prof. of Radiology and Dir, Diagnostic Radiology Dept, Univ. of Virginia, 1977–89. Ed., Clinical Radiology, 1990–94. Warden for Clinical Radiology, RCR, 1994–98. *Publications:* (with M. Wastie) Diagnostic Imaging, 1981, 6th edn 2009; (jtly) Imaging Diseases of the Chest, 1990, 4th edn 2005; contrib. numerous articles on radiological topics to med. jls and books. *Recreations:* reading, theatre, opera. *Address:* 8 Westrow, SW15 6RH. *Club:* Shadows Radiology.

ARMSTRONG, Peter John Bowden; His Honour Judge Armstrong; a Circuit Judge, since 2000; *b* 19 Dec. 1951; *s* of late William David Armstrong, MBE and Kathleen Mary Armstrong; *m* 1976, Joanna Cox; two *d*. *Educ:* Durham Johnston Grammar Technical Sch.; Trinity Coll., Cambridge (MA). Called to the Bar, Middle Temple, 1974; in practice at the Bar, Middlesbrough, 1976–2000; Asst Recorder, 1990–94; a Recorder, 1994–2000; North Eastern Circuit. *Recreations:* golf, cricket, Rugby, music. *Address:* c/o Teesside Court Centre, Russell Street, Middlesbrough TS1 2AE. *Clubs:* Eaglescliffe Golf (Stockton-on-Tees); Durham CC.

ARMSTRONG, Sir Richard, Kt 2004; CBE 1993; FRSE; conductor; Music Director, Scottish Opera, 1993–2005; *b* 7 Jan. 1943. *Educ:* Wyggeston School, Leicester; Corpus Christi College, Cambridge (Hon. Fellow, 1994). Music staff, Royal Opera House, Covent Garden, 1966–68; Welsh National Opera: head of music staff, 1968–73; Musical Director, 1973–86; Principal Guest Conductor, Frankfurt Opera, 1987–90. FRSE 2002. Hon. DMus: De Montfort, 1992; Glasgow, 2001; Aberdeen, 2002; St Andrews, 2004. Janáček Medal, 1978. *Recreations:* walking, food. *Address:* c/o Ingpen & Williams, 7 St George's Court, 131 Putney Bridge Road, SW15 2PA.

ARMSTRONG, (Robert) Douglas; QC (Scot.) 2005; *m* Sally Grossart; two *d*. *Educ:* Melville Coll., later Daniel Stewart's and Melville Coll.; Aberdeen Univ. (LLB Hons 1986; DipLP 1987). Admitted Faculty of Advocates, 1990; called to the Bar, Inner Temple, 1999; in practice as barrister, 1999–, specialising in planning, envmt and admin. and constitutional law; Vice Chm., Terra Firma Chambers, 2008–12. *Address:* Terra Firma Chambers, Advocates' Library, Parliament House, Edinburgh EH1 1RF. *Clubs:* Lansdowne; New (Edinburgh); Hon. Company of Edinburgh Golfers (Muirfield).

ARMSTRONG, Sheila Ann; soprano; *b* 13 Aug. 1942; *m* 1980, Prof. David Edward Cooper, *qv* (marr. diss. 1998). *Educ:* Hirst Park Girls' Sch., Ashington, Northumberland; Royal Academy of Music, London. Debut Sadler's Wells, 1965, Glyndebourne, 1966, Covent Garden, 1973. Sang all over Europe, Far East, N and S America; has made many recordings. Pres., Kathleen Ferrier Soc., 1996–2012 (former Trustee, Kathleen Ferrier Awards). K. Ferrier and Mozart Prize, 1965; Hon. RAM 1970, FRAM 1973. Hon. MA Newcastle, 1979; Hon. DMus Durham, 1991. *Recreations:* interior design and decoration, collecting antique keys, gardening, flower arranging, sewing.

ARMSTRONG-JONES, family name of **Earl of Snowdon**.

ARMYTAGE, John McDonald G.; *see* Green-Armytage.

ARMYTAGE, Sir (John) Martin, 9th Bt *cr* 1738, of Kirklees, Yorkshire; *b* 26 Feb. 1933; *s* of Sir John Lionel Armytage, 8th Bt, and of Evelyn Mary Jessamine, *d* of Edward Herbert Fox, Adbury Park, Newbury; *S* father, 1983. *Educ:* Eton; Worcester Coll., Oxford. *Heir: cousin* Hugh Anthony Armytage [*b* 6 Aug. 1955; *m* 1999, Rachel, *yr d* of Michael Wesson; one *s* one *d*]. *Address:* 5 St James's Place, Cheltenham, Glos GL50 2EG. *T:* (01242) 525869.

ARNAULT, Bernard Jean Etienne, Hon. KBE 2012; President, since 1984, and Chairman, Christian Dior; President, since 1989, and Chairman, since 1992, Louis Vuitton Moët Hennessy; *b* Roubaix, 5 March 1949; *s* of Jean Arnault and Marie-Jo (*née* Savinel); *m* 1991, Hélène Mercier; three *s*; one *s* one *d* by former marriage. *Educ:* Ecole Polytechnique, Paris. Qualified as engineer, 1971. President: Ferret Savinel, 1978–84; Financière Agache SA, 1984–89. Man of the Year, NY, 1991. Officier, 2001, Commandeur, 2007, Légion d'Honneur; Commandeur, Ordre des Arts et des Lettres, 2002. *Recreations:* music, piano, tennis. *Address:* Louis Vuitton Moët Hennessy, 22 avenue Montaigne, 75008 Paris, France. *T:* (1) 44132222.

ARNELL, Prof. Nigel William, PhD; FRGS; Professor of Climate Systems Science, and Director, Walker Institute for Climate System Research, University of Reading, since 2007; *b* Newport, IoW, 10 Dec. 1959; *s* of Roy and Audrey Arnell; *m* 1993, Hilary Kathryn Stevens (*née* Burn); one *d*, and one step *s* one step *d*. *Educ:* W Kidlington Primary Sch.; Gosford Hill Secondary Sch.; Univ. of Southampton (BSc Hons Geog.; PhD Geog. 1985). FRGS 2003. Hydrologist, Inst. of Hydrol., 1984–94; University of Southampton: Reader in Geog., 1995–99; Prof. of Geog., 1999–2007; Hd, Sch. of Geog., 2003–07. Vis. Prof., NUI, Maynooth, 2007–. *Publications:* Global Warming, River Flows and Water Resources, 1996; Hydrology and Global Environmental Change, 2002; lead author, 2nd, 3rd, 4th and 5th Assessment Reports of InterGovtl Panel on Climate Change, 1995, 2001, 2007, 2013; contrib. jls incl. Climatic Change, Jl Hydrol., Jl Geophysical Res., Nature Climate Change, Global Envmtl Change. *Recreations:* walking in the country, especially the remoter parts of the British Isles, gardening, badminton, old maps, 10k runs. *Address:* Walker Institute for Climate System Research, University of Reading, Earley Gate, Reading RG6 6BB. *E:* n.w.arnell@reading.ac.uk.

ARNEY, Claudia Isobel; non-executive Director and Chair of Remuneration Committee, Halfords plc, since 2011; Senior Independent Director, Telecity plc, since 2013; *b* 25 Jan. 1971; *d* of Hon. Martin Jay, *qv*; *m* 2000, John Arney; one *s* two *d*. *Educ:* Hertford Coll., Oxford (BA English Lit.); INSEAD (MBA). Business Analyst, McKinsey and Co., 1992–94; Strategy and Develt Exec., Pearson plc, 1994–97; Product Develt Manager, FT, 1997–99; Man. Dir, thestreet.co.uk, 1999–2000; Exec. Dir, Goldman Sachs, 2000–06; Dir, Enterprise and Growth Unit, HM Treasury, 2006–08; Gp Man. Dir, Digital, Emap, 2008–10. Non-executive Director: Partnerships UK, 2006–10; Transport for London, 2009–12; Which?, 2011–15; Huawei, 2011–14. Mem., Adv. Bd, Shareholder Exec., 2008–. Chair, Public Data Gp, 2013–.

ARNISON, Maj.-Gen. Peter Maurice, AC 2001 (AO 1992); CVO 2002; company director; Governor of Queensland, Australia, 1997–2003; Chancellor, Queensland University of Technology, 2004–12; *b* 21 Oct. 1940; *s* of Frank and Norma Arnison; *m* 1964, Barbara Ruth Smith; one *s* one *d*. *Educ:* Lismore High Sch.; Royal Mil. Coll., Duntroon; Army Staff Coll., Queenscliff; Univ. of Queensland (BEc 1976); Securities Inst. of Australia (Grad. Dip. in Applied Finance and Investment 1993). CO 5th 7th Bn Royal Aust. Regt, 1981–82; COS HQ 1st Div., Brisbane, 1983–84; Comdt Land Warfare Centre, Canungra, Qld, 1985–86; Comdr 3rd Bde, Townsville, Qld, 1987–88; jssc, Canberra; rcds 1989; Dir-Gen. Jt Ops and Plans, HQ Aust. Defence Force, Canberra, 1990; Comdr 1st Div., Brisbane, Qld, 1991–94; Land Comdr Australia, Sydney, 1994–96. Exec. Dir, Allied Rubber Products (Qld), 1996–97; Mem. Bd, Energex Ltd, 2004–. Chairman: Centre for Military and Veterans' Health, 2004–10; Australian Bravery Decorations Council, 2009–10. DUniv: Griffith, 1998; Qld Univ. of Technology, 1999; Southern Cross, 2009. Hon. DLit Southern Qld, 2001; Hon. LLD Qld, 2002. KStJ 1997. *Publications:* Australia's Security Arrangements in the South West Pacific, 1989. *Recreations:* golf, watching Rugby and cricket, theatre, opera, ballet, reading, computing. *Address:* 86 Yabba Street, Ascot, Qld 4007, Australia. *Clubs:* Queensland, Brisbane, United Service (Brisbane); Royal Queensland Golf.

ARNOLD, Anne Mary; a District Judge (Magistrates' Courts), Hampshire, since 2006; a Recorder, since 2005; *b* 16 March 1958; *d* of late Lt Comdr Stanley Hugh Childs Plant, RNR, RD, and of Enid Edith Plant (*née* Morgan); *m* 1987, Peter Roderick Arnold. *Educ:* Talbot Heath, Bournemouth; Dorset Inst. Higher Educn and Université de Caen (BA Hons); Univ. of Birmingham (MBA Public Service); Homerton Coll., Cambridge (AdvDip Professional Trng and Develt). Called to the Bar, Inner Temple, 1981; Dorset Magistrates' Courts, 1979–99: Legal Advr, 1980–82; Principal Legal Advr, 1982–92; Dep. Justices' Trng Officer, 1991–94; Bench Legal Advr, 1992–94; Dir of Legal Services, 1994–99; Jt Staff Trng Officer, 1995–99; Associate Inspector, HM Magistrates' Courts Inspectorate, 1998; Actg Provincial Stipendiary Magistrate, E and W Sussex Commn Areas, 1997–99; a Provincial Stipendiary Magistrate, then District Judge (Magistrates' Cts), E Sussex, 1999–2006. Adjudicator, Prison Rule 53(A)2 and Young Offender Instn Rule 58(A)2, 2002–. Mem., Sentencing Council for England and Wales, 2010–14. *Publications:* (contrib.) Atkin's Court Forms, vol. 5, 2nd edn (2012 issue), 2012, vol. 25, 2002, vol. 5(i), 2nd edn, 2004, vol. 19(1A) and 19(1B), 2005, vol. 25(1), 2007. *Recreations:* running and cycling (for softies), messing about in boats, travel. *Address:* The Law Courts, Winston Churchill Avenue, Portsmouth, Hants PO1 2DQ. *T:* (023) 9281 9421. *Club:* Bar Yacht.

ARNOLD, Dr Bruce, OBE 2003; writer; *b* 6 Sept. 1936; *s* of George Croft Arnold and Margaret Shaw; *m* 1959, Ysabel Mavis Cleave; one *s* one *d* (and one *s* decd). *Educ:* Kingham Hill Sch., Oxon; Trinity Coll., Dublin (MA); National Univ. of Ireland (DLitt 2000). Political commentator and arts journalist: Irish Times, 1961–67; Sunday Independent, 1967–70; Irish Independent, 1972–2014: Literary Ed., 1986–2001; Chief Critic, 1986–2014. *Publications:* A Concise History of Irish Art, 1969, rev. edn 1998; Coppinger quartet: A Singer at the Wedding, 1978; The Song of the Nightingale, 1980; The Muted Swan, 1981; Running to Paradise, 1983; Orpen: mirror to an age, 1981; What Kind of Country, 1984; Margaret Thatcher: a study in power, 1984; An Art Atlas of Britain and Ireland, 1991; The Scandal of Ulysses, 1991, rev. edn 2004; Mainie Jellett and the Modern Movement in Ireland, 1991 (Amer. Conf. for Irish Studies Prize); Haughey: his life and unlucky deeds, 1993, rev. edn 2007; Jack Yeats, 1998; Jonathan Swift: an illustrated life, 1999; Jack Lynch: hero in crisis, 2001; The Spire and other essays in Irish culture, 2003; He That Is Down Need Fear No Fall, 2008; The Fight for Democracy: the Libertas voice in Europe, 2009; The Irish Gulag: how the Irish state betrayed its innocent children, 2009; Derek Hill, 2010; (with Jason O'Toole) The End of the Party: how Fianna Fail lost its grip on power, 2011. *Recreations:* camellias, snowdrops, singing madrigals. *E:* arnoldbruce@mac.com. *Club:* Athenæum.

ARNOLD, Prof. Dana Rebecca, PhD; FSA; Professor of Architectural History, Middlesex University, since 2012; *b* 22 June 1961; *d* of late Edward Cyril Arnold and of Josephine Arnold; *m* 1989, Dr Kenneth Haynes (marr. diss. 2007). *Educ:* Westfield Coll., London (BA 1983); Bartlett Sch. of Architecture, UCL (MSc 1984; PhD 1997). Sen. Lectr, Dept of Fine Art, Univ. of Leeds, 1994–99; Prof. of Architectural History, 1999–2012, Hd of Res., Sch. of Humanities, 2003–12, Univ. of Southampton. Research Fellow: Yale Univ., 1997 and 2005; Getty Res. Inst., Calif, 2002; Univ. of Cambridge, 2003, 2013. Hon. Prof., Faculty of Architecture, Middle East Tech. Univ., Ankara, 2010–; Guest Prof., Internat. Res. Centre for Chinese Cultural Heritage Conservation, Tianjin Univ., 2011–. Member: AHRC (formerly AHRB), 2004–; Adv. Panel, AHRC/EPSRC Sci. and Heritage Res. Prog., 2008–14. FRSA 2000; FSA 2006; FRHistS 2007. Ed., Art History jl, 1997–2002; General Editor: New Interventions in Art History (book series), 2002–; Blackwell Companions to Art History, 2004–; Jt Ed., special issue of Synergies jl, London and Paris: capitals of the nineteenth century, 2009. *Publications:* (ed) Belov'd by Ev'ry Muse: Richard Boyle, 3rd Earl of Burlington and 4th Earl of Cork (1694–1753), 1994; (ed) Squandrous and Lavish Profusion: George IV, his image and patronage of the arts, 1995; (ed) The Georgian Villa, 1995, 2nd edn 1998; (ed) The Georgian Country House, 1998, 2nd edn 2003; (ed) The Metropolis and its Image, 1999; Re-presenting the Metropolis: architecture, urban experience and social life in London 1800–1840, 2000; Reading Architectural History, 2002; (ed jtly) Tracing Architecture, 2003; (ed jtly) Art and Thought, 2003; Art History: a very short introduction, 2004; (ed) Cultural Identities and the Aesthetics of Britishness, 2004; (ed jtly) Architecture as Experience, 2004; Rural Urbanism: London landscapes in the early nineteenth century, 2006; (ed jtly) Re-thinking Architectural Historiography, 2006; (ed jtly) Biographies and Space, 2007; (ed) Art History: contemporary perspectives on method, 2010; (ed jtly) A Companion to British Art 1600 to the Present, 2013; The Spaces of the Hospital: spatiality and urban change in London 1680–1820, 2013; An Introduction to Art, 2014; (ed) Interdisciplinary Encounters: hidden and visible explorations of the work of Adrian Rifkin, 2014; A Short Book about Art, 2015; (ed jtly) Londres et Paris s'observent, 2015. *Address:* School of Art and Design, Middlesex University, The Burroughs, NW4 4BT. *E:* darnold@talk21.com.

ARNOLD, David George; film composer, songwriter and record producer; *b* 23 Jan. 1962; *s* of George and Rita Arnold; one *s* twin *d*. Composer: for *films* including: The Young Americans, 1993; Stargate, 1994; Last of the Dogmen, 1995; Independence Day (Grammy Award for Best Film Score), 1996; Tomorrow Never Dies, A Life Less Ordinary, 1997; Godzilla, 1998; The World is not Enough, 1999 (Ivor Novello Award for Best Film Score, 2003); Shaft, 2000; Zoolander, Baby Boy, 2001; Enough, Changing Lanes, Die Another Day, 2002; 2 Fast 2 Furious, 2003; Stepford Wives, 2004; Stoned, Four Brothers, 2005; Casino Royale, Venus, Amazing Grace, 2006; Hot Fuzz, 2007; How to Lose Friends and Alienate People, Quantum of Solace, 2008; Narnia: The Voyage of the Dawn Treader, 2010; Made in Dagenham, 2010; Paul, 2011; for *television* including: The Visitor (series), 1997; Randall & Hopkirk Deceased (series), 2000; Little Britain (series), 2003 (RTS Award for Best Music, 2005); Sherlock, 2010 (Emmy Award, 2014); Made In Dagenham - The Musical, Adelphi, 2014. Music Dir, London 2012 Olympics Closing and Paralympics Closing Ceremonies, 2012. Composer and producer of numerous recordings. Fellow, British Acad. of Composers & Songwriters, 2005. *Recreations:* watching cooking on TV, wandering round streets in a daze, Twitterer @davidgarnold. *Address:* Air Studios, Lyndhurst Road, NW3 4DJ. *T:* (020) 7794 0660, *Fax:* (020) 7794 8518. *E:* davidgarnold@gmail.com.

ARNOLD, Prof. David John, DPhil; FBA 2004; Professor of Asian and Global History, University of Warwick, 2006–11, now Emeritus; *b* 1 Oct. 1946; *s* of Mansel John and May Arnold; *m* 1988, Juliet Elizabeth Miller. *Educ:* Univ. of Exeter (BA Hons (Hist.) 1968); Univ. of Sussex (DPhil 1973). Lectr in History, Univ. of Dar es Salaam, 1972–75; Res. Fellow, Flinders Univ., Australia, 1975–77; Res. Fellow, SOAS, 1977–78; Lectr in History, Univ. of Lancaster, 1979–88; Prof. of S Asian Hist., 1988–2006, Hd, Dept of Hist., 1992–96, Pro-Dir for Res., 1999–2002, SOAS. Dist. Vis. Prof., Dept of Hist., Univ. of Chicago, 2008; Vis. Prof., ETH, Zurich, 2013. *Publications:* The Age of Discovery 1400–1600, 1983, 2nd edn 2002; Famine: social crisis and historical change, 1988; Colonizing the Body: state medicine and epidemic disease in nineteenth-century India, 1993; The Problem of Nature: environment, culture and European expansion, 1996; Science, Technology and Medicine in Colonial India, 2000; Gandhi, 2001; The Tropics and the Travelling Gaze: India, landscape and science 1800–1856, 2005; Everyday Technology: machines and the making of India's modernity, 2013. *Recreations:* travel, gardening. *Address:* 12 Eyot Green, Chiswick, W4 2PT. *E:* d.arnold@warwick.ac.uk.

ARNOLD, Rev. Duane Wade-Hampton, PhD; Principal, St Chad's College, University of Durham, 1994–97; *b* 5 Aug. 1953; *s* of Wade H. Arnold and Louise Elizabeth (*née* Hensley); *m* 1980, Janet Lee Drew. *Educ:* Univ. of State of New York (BA 1979); Concordia Theological Seminary (MA 1981); St Chad's Coll., Durham (PhD 1989); STh (Lambeth Dip. in Theol.), 1984. Minister, First Church, Detroit, Michigan, 1985–87; Precentor, St Paul's Cathedral, Detroit, 1987; Chaplain, Wayne State Univ., Detroit, 1988–91; Curate, St Thomas Church, Fifth Ave, NY, 1991–93. Tutor, St Chad's Coll., Durham, 1983–85; Adjunct Lecturer: in Religious Studies, Univ. of Detroit, 1985–88; in Church History, Ashland Seminary, Ohio, 1987–91. Producer, CD, Martyrs Prayers, 2012. Fellow, Coll. of Preachers, Washington Nat. Cathedral, 1991. ChStJ 1990. Governor's Award, Michigan, 1988. *Publications:* A Lutheran Reader, 1982; The Way, the Truth and the Life, 1982; Francis, A Call to Conversion, 1990; Prayers of the Martyrs, 1991; The Early Episcopal Career of Athanasius of Alexandria, 1991; Praying with John Donne and George Herbert, 1992; *De Doctrina Christiana*, Classic of Western Civilization, 1995; with R. Hudson: Beyond Belief: what the Martyrs said to God, 2002; Más allá de la Fe, 2004; Fiés até o Fim, 2008; contribs to learned jls. *Recreation:* shooting. *Club:* Columbia (Indianapolis).

ARNOLD, Glynis, (Mrs Elliott Arnold); *see* Johns, G.

ARNOLD, Jacques Arnold; DL; consultant on Latin America; *b* London, 27 Aug. 1947; *s* of late Samuel Arnold and Eugenie (*née* Patentini); *m* 1976, Patricia Anne, *er d* of late Dennis Maunder, Windsor; one *s* two *d*. *Educ:* schools in Brazil and by correspondence; London School of Economics (BSc (Econ) 1972). Asst Gp Rep., Midland Bank, São Paulo, 1976–78; Regl Dir, Thomas Cook Gp, 1978–84; Asst Trade Finance Dir, Midland Bank, 1984–85; Dir, American Express Europe Ltd, 1985–87; Adviser for Latin America: GEC plc, 1998–2000; BAE Systems, 2000–04; FIRST Mag., 2006–; has travelled to over 90 countries on business. County Councillor for Oundle, Northants, 1981–85. Contested (C) Coventry SE, 1983. MP (C) Gravesham, 1987–97; contested (C) same seat, 1997, 2001. PPS to Minister of State: for Envmt and Countryside, 1992–93; Home Office, 1993–95. Member: Educn, Arts and Sci. Select Cttee, 1989–92; Treasury and CS Select Cttee, 1997; Sec., Cons. Backbench Cttee on Foreign and Commonwealth Affairs, 1990–92, 1995–97; Vice-Chm., 1995–96, Chm., 1996–97, Cons. Backbench Cttee on Constitutional Affairs. Secretary: British-Latin-American Parly Gp, 1987–97; Scout Assoc. Parly Gp, 1987–97; Chairman: British Brazilian Parly Gp, 1992–97; British Portuguese Parly Gp, 1995–97. Chm., LSE Cons. Soc., 1971–72; Treasurer, Nat. Assoc. of Cons. Graduates, 1974–76; Chairman: Hyde Park Tories, 1975–76; Tonbridge and Malling Cons. Assoc., 2012–; Vice-Chairman: Croydon NE Cons. Assoc., 1974–76; Corby Cons. Assoc., 1983–85. Chm., Kent County Scout Council, 1998–2000. Trustee, Environment Foundn, 1989–2003. DL Kent, 2013. Grand Official, Order of Southern Cross (Brazil), 1993. *Publications:* Democracy for Europe, 1977; (ed) Royal Houses of Europe (series), 1998–2015; (ed) History of Britain's Parliamentary Constituencies (annually), 2009–15; A Senate of Interests: a proposal for reform of the House of Lords, 2013. *Recreations:* family life, travel, genealogy. *Address:* Fairlawn, 243 London Road, West Malling, Kent ME19 5AD. *T:* and *Fax:* (01732) 848388. *Club:* Carlton.

ARNOLD, Jennette, OBE 2009; Member (Lab), London Assembly, Greater London Authority, since July 2000 (London, 2000–04, North East, since 2004) (Chairman, 2008–09 and 2011–13; Deputy Chairman, 2009–11). Formerly: nurse; health visitor; Regl Dir, RCN. Mem. (Lab) Islington BC, 1994–2002 (Dep. Mayor, 1999–2000). Chair: Cultural Strategy Gp for London, 2000–04; London Health Commn, 2004–; Vice-Chair, London Cultural Commn, 2005–. Member: Metropolitan Police Authy, 2000–12; Mayor of London's Adv. Cabinet, 2000–; UK Delegn to EU Cttee of the Regions, 2002–. Mem. Bd, Arts Council England - London, 2002–06. *Address:* Greater London Authority, City Hall, Queen's Walk, SE1 2AA.

ARNOLD, Prof. John André, FCA; Director, Manchester Business School, and KPMG Professor of Accounting and Financial Management, University of Manchester, 1994–2006; *b* 30 April 1944; *s* of André Eugene Arnold and May Arnold (*née* Vickers); *m* 1997, Sylvia Bailey; two *d*. *Educ:* London Sch. of Econs (MSc 1969). FCA 1967. Teaching Fellow, LSE, 1967–69; Lectr in Accounting, Univ. of Kent, 1969–71; Lectr, 1971–75, Sen. Lectr, 1975–77, Prof. of Accounting, 1977–94, Univ. of Manchester. Vis. Prof., Grad. Sch. of Business, Univ. of Washington, 1981–82. Chm., pro.manchester, 2007–08; non-exec. Dir, PZ Cussons plc, 2007–. Pres., Manchester Soc. of Chartered Accountants, 1991–92. CCMI 1995. Chm., Feelgood Theatre Prodns, 2008–. *Publications:* Pricing and Output Decisions, 1973; Accounting for Management Decisions, 1983, 3rd edn 1996; Financial Accounting, 1985, 2nd edn 1994; contrib. numerous articles to learned jls. *Recreations:* tennis, golf, watching Stockport County FC. *Address:* 3 Green Meadows, Marple, Stockport, Cheshire SK6 6QF. *T:* (0161) 449 9432. *E:* john.arnold@mbs.ac.uk. *Club:* Marple Golf.

ARNOLD, Very Rev. John Robert, OBE 2002; Dean of Durham, 1989–2002, now Emeritus; *b* 1 Nov. 1933; *s* of John Stanley and Ivy Arnold; *m* 1963, Livia Anneliese Franke; one *s* two *d*. *Educ:* Christ's Hospital; Sidney Sussex Coll., Cambridge (MA); Westcott House Theol College. Curate of Holy Trinity, Millhouses, Sheffield, 1960–63; Sir Henry Stephenson Fellow, Univ. of Sheffield, 1962–63; Chaplain and Lectr, Univ. of Southampton, 1963–72; Secretary, Board for Mission and Unity, General Synod of the Church of England, 1972–78; Dean of Rochester, 1978–89. Pt-time Lectr, Univ. of Durham, 1992–2002. Hon. Canon of Winchester Cathedral, 1974–78; Mem., General Synod, 1980–2002. Mem., European Ecumenical Commn for Church and Society, 1986–98; Pres., Conference of European Churches, 1986–2001 (Vice-Chm., 1986–92; Chm., 1993–97). Pres., Anglican-Lutheran Soc., 1999–; Vice Pres., Faith in Europe, 2005–. Patron, ChildAid to Russia and the Republics, 1978–; Trustee, St Ethelburga's Centre for Peace and Reconciliation, 2003–13. Hon. Fellow, St Chad's Coll., Univ. of Durham, 2002. DD Lambeth, 1999; Hon. DD Dunelm, 2002. Order of Saint Vladimir (Russian Orthodox Church), 1977. Officers' Cross, Order of Merit (Germany), 1991. *Publications:* (trans.) Eucharistic Liturgy of Taizé, 1962; (contrib.) Hewitt, Strategist for the Spirit, 1985; Rochester Cathedral, 1987; (contrib.) Cathedrals Now, 1996; (contrib.) Preaching from Cathedrals, 1998; Life Conquers Death, 2007; contribs to Theology, Crucible, St Luke's Journal of Theology, Ecclesiology. *Recreations:* music, European languages and literature. *Address:* 26 Hawks Lane, Canterbury CT1 2NU.

ARNOLD, Rt Rev. John Stanley Kenneth; Auxiliary Bishop of Westminster, (RC), since 2006; Titular Bishop of Lindisfarne, since 2006; *b* 12 June 1953; *s* of late Stanley Kenneth Arnold and Mary Arnold (*née* Murray). *Educ:* Ratcliffe Coll., Leics; Trinity Coll., Oxford (MA Juris.); Council of Legal Educn, London; Gregorian Univ., Rome (DCL 1985). Called to the Bar, Middle Temple, 1976, Bencher, 2010; ordained priest, 1983; Chaplain, 1985–89, Sub-Adminr, 1989–93, Westminster Cathedral; Parish Priest, Our Lady of Mt Carmel and St George, Enfield, 1993–2001; Westminster Diocese: VG and Chancellor, 2001–06; Moderator of the Curia, 2005– (Chancellor, 2005–10). *Publications:* Quality of Mercy: a fresh look at the Sacrament of Reconciliation, 1993. *Address:* Archbishop's House, Ambrosden Avenue, SW1P 1QJ. *T:* (020) 7931 6062. *E:* johnarnold@rcdow.org.uk.

ARNOLD, Rt Rev. Keith Appleby; Hon. Assistant Bishop, Diocese of Oxford, since 1996; *b* 1 Oct. 1926; *s* of Dr Frederick Arnold, Hale, Cheshire, and Alice Mary Appleby Arnold (*née* Holt); *m* 1955, Deborah Noreen Glenwright; one *s* one *d*. *Educ:* Winchester; Trinity Coll., Cambridge (MA); Westcott House, Cambridge. Served as Lieut, Coldstream Guards, 1944–48. Curate: Haltwhistle, Northumberland, 1952–55; St John's, Princes St, Edinburgh, 1955–61; Chaplain, TA, 1956–61; Rector of St John's, Edinburgh, 1961–69; Vicar of Kirkby Lonsdale, Cumbria, 1969–73; Team Rector of Hemel Hempstead, 1973–80; Bishop Suffragan of Warwick, 1980–90; Hon. Assistant Bishop: dio. Newcastle, 1991–96; dio. Oxford, 1997–2009. Vice-Pres., Abbeyfield Soc., 1981–91; Chairman: Housing Assocs

Charitable Trust, 1980–86; Rural Housing Trust, 1987–2008. Pres., S Warwicks Marriage Guidance Council, subseq. Relate, 1980–90. *Recreations:* 19th century history, gardening. *Address:* 9 Dinglederry, Olney, Bucks MK46 5ES. *T:* (01234) 713044.

ARNOLD, Hon. Rev. Lynn Maurice Ferguson, AO 2004; Priest Assistant, St Peter's Cathedral, Adelaide, since 2014; Chief Executive Officer, Anglicare SA, 2008–12; *b* 27 Jan. 1949; *s* of Maurice and Jean Arnold; *m* 1978, Elaine Palmer; two *s* three *d. Educ:* Adelaide Boys' High Sch.; Univ. of Adelaide (BA, BEd; PhD 2003). Dip. en la Alta Dirección de Empresas, ESADE, 1996. Teacher, Salisbury N High Sch., 1971–74; Adv. Teacher, Health Educn Project Team, 1975–76; Personal Assistant to MHR, 1977–79; MHA (ALP) Salisbury, 1979–87; MP (ALP) Ramsay, 1987–93, Taylor, 1993–94; Minister of: Education, 1982–85; Technology, 1982–87; Children's Services, 1985; Employment and Further Educn, and State Develt, 1985–89; Industry, Trade & Technol., also Agriculture, Fisheries, and Ethnic Affairs, 1989–92; Economic Develt, and Multicultural and Ethnic Affairs, 1992–93; Premier of S Australia, 1992–93; Leader of the Opposition and Shadow Minister of Econ. Develt and of Multicultural and Ethnic Affairs, 1993–94; Vis. Scholar, Univ. of Oviedo, Spain, 1994–95; student, Escuela Superior de Administración y Dirección de Empresas, Barcelona, 1995–96; CEO, World Vision Australia, 1997–2003; Regl Vice-Pres. (Asia/Pacific), World Vision Internat., 2003–08. Chair, Board: Ahava Holdings Pty Ltd, 2009–; Ahava Energy Pty Ltd, 2009–. Sec. and Pres., Campaign for Peace in Vietnam, 1970–73. Mem. Council, Univ. of Adelaide, 1979–82; Mem. Bd, ICFAI Australia, 2008–. Ordained deacon, 2013, priest, 2014. Mem. Council, Anglicare Australia Council, 2008–; Pres., SA Br., CMS, 2009–; Mem., Gen. Synod, Anglican Ch of Australia, 2010–. Reconciliation Ambassador for SA, 2010–. Trustee, Cttee for the Economic Develt of Australia, 1997–2003, 2008–; Chair, Bd of Trustees, Don Dunstan Foundn, 2009–. Mem., Australian Inst. of Co. Dirs, 1997–. *Publications:* Nigeria-Biafra Conflict, 1968; (jtly) Hoa Binh Third Force in Vietnam, 1970; (jtly) You and Me, 1975; (jtly) All Together, 1976. *Recreations:* sociolinguistics, history. *Address:* St Peter's Cathedral, St Peter's Cathedral Close, 27 King William Road, North Adelaide, SA 5006, Australia.

ARNOLD, Mark Graham; QC 2013; *b* Colwyn Bay, 1965; *s* of Alan Arnold and Carole Arnold (*née* McCann); *m* 1991, Halldis Gribbin; two *s* one *d. Educ:* Rydal Sch.; Norwich Sch.; Downing Coll., Cambridge (BA 1987; MA 1990). Called to the Bar, Middle Temple, 1988; in practice as barrister, specialising in company, insolvency and restructuring, 1989–. *Publications:* (contrib.) Company Directors: duties, liabilities and remedies, 2009, 2nd edn 2013; (contrib.) Cross Border Insolvency, 3rd edn 2012, 4th edn 2015. *Recreations:* music, wine, playing the piano. *Address:* South Square, 3–4 South Square, Gray's Inn, WC1R 5HP. *T:* (020) 7696 9900. *E:* markarnold@southsquare.com.

ARNOLD, Dr Richard Bentham; Executive Vice-President, International Federation of Pharmaceutical Manufacturers' Associations, 1984–97; *b* 29 Aug. 1932; *s* of George Benjamin and Alice Arnold; *m* 1956, Margaret Evelyn Racey; one *s* one *d. Educ:* Stamford Sch.; King Edward VII Sch., King's Lynn; Nottingham Univ. BSc, PhD. Joined May & Baker Ltd, 1959; Commercial Manager, Pharmaceuticals Div., 1974–76; Dir Designate, 1976, Dir, 1977–83, Assoc. of British Pharmaceutical Industry. *Recreations:* gardening, internet browsing, nature watching.

ARNOLD, Hon. Sir Richard David, Kt 2008; **Hon. Mr Justice Arnold;** a Judge of the High Court of Justice, Chancery Division, since 2008; Judge in charge, Patents Court, since 2013; *b* 23 June 1961; *s* of late Francis Arnold and of Ann Arnold (*née* Churchill); *m* 1990, Mary Elford; two *d. Educ:* Highgate Sch.; Magdalen Coll., Oxford (BA Nat. Sci. 1983, MA 1986); Univ. of Westminster (Dip. Law 1984). Called to the Bar, Middle Temple, 1985, Bencher, 2008. QC 2000; Dep. High Court Judge, 2004–08. Chm. Cttee, Code of Practice for Promotion of Animal Medicines, Nat. Office of Animal Health, 2002–08. Apptd to hear Trade Mark appeals, 2003–08; Mem., Panel of Chairmen, Competition Appeal Tribunal, 2008–. Ed., Entertainment and Media Law Reports, 1993–2004. *Publications:* Performers' Rights, 1990, 4th edn 2008; (jtly) Computer Software: legal protection in the UK, 2nd edn 1992; (ed) Halsbury's Laws—Trade Marks, 4th edn reissue, 5th edn. *Recreations:* music, cinema, theatre, opera, exhibitions, cooking, walking in Suffolk. *Address:* Rolls Building, Fetter Lane, EC4A 1NL. *Club:* MCC.

ARNOLD, Sir Thomas (Richard), Kt 1990; theatre producer; publisher; consultant in Middle East affairs; *b* 25 Jan. 1947; *s* of late Thomas Charles Arnold, OBE and Helen Breen; *m* 1984, Elizabeth Jane (marr. diss. 1993), *widow* of Robin Smithers; one *d. Educ:* Bedales Sch.; Le Rosey, Geneva; Pembroke Coll., Oxford (MA). Contested (C): Manchester Cheetham, 1970; Hazel Grove, Feb. 1974. MP (C) Hazel Grove, Oct. 1974–1997. PPS to Sec. of State for NI, 1979–81, to Lord Privy Seal, FCO, 1981–82; Chm., Treasury and CS Select Cttee, 1994–97 (Mem., 1992–94). Vice-Chm., Conservative Party, 1983–92. *Address:* No 1 Manchester Square, W1U 3AB.

ARNOLD, Wallace; *see* Brown, C. E. M.

ARNOLD, William; Director, Corporate Services, Supreme Court of the United Kingdom, since 2009; *b* 13 May 1953; *s* of Rev. William and Mrs Ruth Arnold; *m* 1992, Elizabeth Anne McLellan; twin *s. Educ:* Bury Grammar Sch.; King's Coll., Cambridge (MA Classics). Joined Lord Chancellor's Department, 1974: Asst Private Sec. to Lord Chancellor, 1977–79; Principal, 1979; Head of Legal Services Div., 1987; Hd of Remuneration and Competition Div., 1988; Hd, Courts and Legal Services Bill Div., 1989; Dir of Corporate Services and Principal Estabt and Finance Officer, PRO, 1991–92; on loan to Dept of PM and Cabinet, Canberra, Australia, 1993–94; Hd, Family Policy Div., LCD, 1994–99; Hd of Govt Offices and Regl Policy, then Regl Policy and Regeneration, Div. 1, DETR, 1999–2001; Dir, Regl Develt Agency Policy, Finance and Sponsorship, DTI, 2001–03; Hd, Criminal Justice System Confidence Unit, Home Office, 2003; Sec. to the Judicial Appointments Comrs, 2004–06; Interim Chief Exec., Family Justice Council, 2006; Hd, Court Broadcasting Unit, Min. of Justice, 2006–07; Chief Exec., Law Commn, 2008–09. Reader: St Margaret's Church, Putney, 1989–2008; Mortlake with East Sheen, 2008–. FRSA 2000. *Recreations:* ski-ing, swimming, long-distance trekking, opera, ballet. *Address:* Supreme Court of the United Kingdom, Parliament Square, SW1P 3BD. *E:* william.arnold@supremecourt.uk.

ARNOT, Prof. Madeleine Mary, (Lady Young), PhD; Professor of Sociology of Education, University of Cambridge, since 2004; Fellow, Jesus College, Cambridge, since 1990; *b* 9 Jan. 1950; *d* of Eric Maxwell-Arnot and Marie Madeleine (*née* Rzewuska); *m* 1st, 1973, Neil MacDonald (marr. diss. 1980); 2nd, 1982, R. Allan Drummond (*d* 1994); one *s* one *d*; 3rd, 1998, Sir Robin Urquhart Young, *qv. Educ:* More House Convent, London; Univ. of Edinburgh (MA 1st Cl. Hons 1972); Univ. of London Inst. of Educn; PhD Open 1989; MA Cantab 1998. Lectr, Open Univ., 1975–88; Lectr, 1988–2000, Reader, 2000–04, Cambridge Univ.; Leverhulme Trust Res. Fellow, 1996–97; Dir of Studies in Educn, Jesus Coll., Cambridge, 1990–. Noted Schol., Univ. of BC, 1993; George A. Miller Vis. Prof., Univ. of Illinois, Champagne Urbana, 2000; Visiting Professor: Univ. of Porto, 2001–; Aristotle Univ. of Thessaloniki, 2003–; Univ. of Stockholm, 2005. Member: Wkg Gp on Citizenship and Initial Teacher Educn, 2000, DfEE; Gender Policy Gp, QCA, 1998–99; Consultative Gp, EOC, 1999–2002; Steering Gp Global Monitoring Report, UNESCO, 2003; Gender expert for Council of Europe Jt Cttee on Human Rights and Educn, 1999. FRSA 1996; FAcSS (AcSS 2004). FilDr *hc* Uppsala, 2008. *Publications:* (jtly) Educational Reforms and Gender Equality in Schools, 1996; (jtly) Recent Research on Gender and Educational Performance, 1998; (jtly) Closing the Gender Gap: post-war education and social change, 1999; Reproducing Gender?: essays on educational theory and feminist politics, 2002; (jtly) Consultation in the Classroom, 2004; Educating the Gendered Citizen, 2009; (jtly) Education, Asylum and the 'Non-Citizen' Child, 2010; (jtly) School Approaches to the Education of EAL Students, 2014; (jtly) Girls' Education and Gender Equality 2014; *anthologies:* as M. M. MacDonald: (ed jtly) Schooling and Capitalism, 1977; Education and the State, Vol. 1: Schooling and the National Interest, 1981, Vol. 2: Politics, Patriarchy and Practice, 1981; as M. Arnot: (ed) Race and Gender: equal opportunities policies in education, 1985; (ed) The Sociology of Disability and Inclusive Education: a tribute to Len Barton, 2012; edited jointly: Gender and the Politics of Schooling, 1987; Gender Under Scrutiny: new inquiries in education, 1987; Voicing Concerns: sociological perspectives on contemporary education reforms, 1992; Feminism and Social Justice in Education, 1993; Challenging Democracy?: international perspectives on gender, education and citizenship, 2000; Gender Education and Equality in a Global Context, 2008; Youth Citizenship and the Politics of Belonging, 2013. *Address:* Jesus College, Cambridge CB5 8BL. *T:* (01223) 339339, *Fax:* (01223) 339313.

ARNOTT, Sir Alexander John Maxwell, 6th Bt *cr* 1896, of Woodlands, Shandon, Co. Cork; *b* 18 Sept. 1975; *s* of Sir John Robert Alexander Arnott, 5th Bt, and of Ann Margaret, *d* of late T. A. Farrelly, Kilcar, Co. Cavan; *S* father, 1981. *Heir: b* Andrew John Eric Arnott, *b* 20 June 1978.

ARNOTT, Very Rev. (Andrew) David (Keltie); Moderator of the General Assembly of the Church of Scotland, 2011–12; *b* Dunfermline, Fife, 22 July 1945; *s* of Robert Scott Gibb Arnott and Christian Keltie Arnott (*née* Taylor); *m* 1972, Rosemary Jane Batchelor; two *s* one *d. Educ:* George Watson's Coll., Edinburgh; Univ. of St Andrew (MA); Univ. of Edinburgh (BD). Ordained, 1971; Minister: Gorebridge, Midlothian, 1971–77; Netherlee, Glasgow, 1977–96; Hope Park, St Andrews linked with Strathkinness, 1996–2010. *Recreations:* golf, photography. *Address:* 53 Whitehaugh Park, Peebles EH45 9DB. *T:* (01721) 725979.

ARNOTT, (Ann) Rosemary, OBE 2001; Country Director, Burma, Voluntary Service Overseas, since 2014; *b* Hull, 30 Jan. 1961; *d* of Prof. W(illiam) Geoffrey Arnott, FBA and Vera Arnott (*née* Hodson); *m* 1993, Abdu Mozayen (*d* 2013); twin *s. Educ:* Leeds Girls' High Sch.; Trinity Coll., Cambridge (BA Mod. Langs 1984); Univ. of Muenster; Inst. of Educn, Univ. of London (PGCE TESOL 1987); Univ. of Manchester (MA Econ Develt Studies (Dist.) 2000). Teacher of English: Hubei Teachers Coll., Wuhan, China, 1984–85; Lhasa Educn Office, Lhasa, Tibet, 1985–86; British Council, 1987–2014: Assistant Director: Romania, 1988–89; Ethiopia, 1989–93; Ghana, 1993–95; Consultant, gender and social develt, Manchester, 1996–98; Country Dir, Ethiopia, 1999–2003; Regl Dir, Southern Africa, 2003–08; Dir, Turkey and Black Sea, 2008–11; Dir, Bangladesh, 2011–14. *Recreations:* literature, travel, cultural relations. *Address:* 65 Little Normans, Longlevens, Gloucester GL2 0EH.

ARNOTT, Deborah; Chief Executive (formerly Director), Action on Smoking and Health, since 2003; *b* 23 June 1955; *d* of Michael MacMillan Arnott and Felicity Arnott (*née* Hugh-Jones); *m* 1996, Jon Davies; two *s. Educ:* Brunel Univ. (BSc Hons Govt, Politics and Mod. Hist. 1977); Cranfield (MBA 1981). Grad. trainee and Industrial Relns Officer, Triumph Cars, 1977–80; business consultant, planning, research and systems, 1981–82; journalist, Management Today, 1982–83; LWT Factual Programmes: researcher, 1984–86; producer director, 1986–93; series producer and prog. editor, 1993–98; Hd, Consumer Educn, Financial Services Authy, 1998–2002. Equality Officer and Shop Steward, ACTT, later BECTU, at LWT, 1983–93; Mem., Nat. Exec. and Standing Orders Cttees, ACTT, 1984–86. Chair, Mgt Cttee, and Special Advr to Bd, Personal Finance Educn Gp, 1998–2002; Mem., Govt Task Force on Tackling Over-indebtedness, 2000–02. Member: Eur. Bd, Framework Convention Alliance, 2003–12; Tobacco Adv. Gp, RCP, 2003–; Bd, IMPRESS, 2015. Numerous policy submissions to govt depts, incl. HM Treasury and DoH, and to EC and WHO. Mem. Cttee, Kingsway workplace nursery, 1983–94; Governor: Walnut Tree Walk Primary Sch., 1995–2001; Pimlico Comprehensive, Westminster, 2002–06. Hon. Associate Prof., Univ. of Nottingham, 2011–. Hon. FRCP 2012. Alwyn Smith prize for most outstanding contrib. to public health, FPH, 2007. *Publications:* letters, articles and editls in sci. jls incl. The Lancet and BMJ's Tobacco Control; articles in The Guardian and other newspapers and pubns. *Recreation:* the usual. *Address:* Action on Smoking and Health, New House, 67–68 Hatton Garden, EC1N 8JY. *T:* (020) 7404 0242. *E:* deborah.arnott@ash.org.uk.

See also J. J. Arnott.

ARNOTT, Edward Ian W.; *see* Walker-Arnott.

ARNOTT, John Jacob, (Jake); novelist; *b* 11 March 1961; *s* of Michael MacMillan Arnott and Felicity Arnott (*née* Hugh-Jones); one *s. Educ:* Aylesbury Grammar Sch. Labourer, lab technician, theatrical agent's asst, artist's life model, actor, sign lang. interpreter, 1978–91; care worker, Leeds Social Services, 1991–98. *Publications:* The Long Firm, 1999; He Kills Coppers, 2001; truecrime, 2003; Johnny Come Home, 2006; The Devil's Paintbrush, 2009; The House of Rumour, 2012. *Recreations:* t'ai chi chuan, swimming, wandering. *Address:* c/o Curtis Brown Group Ltd, Haymarket House, 28–29 Haymarket, SW1Y 4SP. *T:* (020) 7393 4409.

See also D. Arnott.

ARNOTT, Jonathan; Member (UK Ind) North East Region, European Parliament, since 2014; *b* Sheffield, 12 Jan. 1981; *m. Educ:* Sheffield Univ. (MMath Hons). Former teacher. Gen. Sec., UKIP, 2008–14. *Address:* European Parliament, 60 Rue Wiertz, 1047 Brussels, Belgium; (office) 41 Elwick Road, Hartlepool TS26 9AE.

ARNOTT, Rosemary; *see* Arnott, A. R.

ARON, Michael Douglas; HM Diplomatic Service; Ambassador to Sudan, since 2015; *b* 22 March 1959; *s* of late Maurice Aron and of Sheila Aron (*née* Torrens); *m* 1986, Rachel Ann Golding Barker (*see* R. A. G. Aron) (separated); two *s* two *d. Educ:* Exeter Sch.; Leeds Univ. (BA Hons Arabic and French); Poly. of Central London. English lang. teacher, Sudan, 1981–83; joined FCO, 1984: Conf. Support Officer, UK Mission to UN, NY, 1985; on secondment to EC, 1986; Second, later First Sec., FCO, 1986–88; First Secretary: (Commercial and Econ.), Brasilia, 1988–91; FCO, 1991–93; UK Mission to UN, 1993–96; Dep. Hd, ME Dept, FCO, 1996–97; Head: Comprehensive Spending Review Unit, FCO, 1997–98; Mgt Consultancy Services, FCO, 1998–99; Counsellor and Dep. Hd of Mission, Amman, Jordan, 1999–2002; Political Counsellor, UK Repn to EU, Brussels, 2002–06; EU Dir and Hd, Scottish Govt (formerly Exec.) EU Office, Brussels (on secondment), 2006–08; Ambassador to Kuwait, 2008–09; Hd of Middle East Gp, FCO, 2010–11; Ambassador to Iraq, 2011–12; Acting Hd of Mission, Libya, 2012; Ambassador to Libya, 2013–15. *Recreations:* football, Arsenal, tennis, walking, France. *Address:* c/o Foreign and Commonwealth Office, King Charles Street, SW1A 2AH.

ARON, Rachel Ann Golding, PhD; HM Diplomatic Service, retired; executive coach and consultant, since 2010; *b* 18 July 1951; *d* of Guy Barker and Ailsa Barker (*née* Gladdish); *m* 1986, Michael Douglas Aron, *qv* (separated); two *s* two *d. Educ:* Ashford Sch. for Girls; Westfield Coll., Univ. of London (BA Hons Hist. 1973); Inst. of Educn, Univ. of London (PGCE 1974); Darwin Coll., Cambridge (PhD 1978). Res. Asst to Sir Frederick Catherwood, MEP, 1979–84; joined FCO, 1984; First Sec. and Cyprus Desk Officer, 1984–86; Privileges and Immunities Desk Officer, 1987–88; Hd of Chancery, Brasilia, 1988–91; Asst Hd, Eastern Dept, 1991–93; First Sec. (Pol), UK Mission to UN, NY, 1993–96; FCO Chair, CSSB, 1997–99; remote project work for HR Directorate in Amman and Brussels, 2000–03; Ambassador to Belgium, 2007–10. Chair, Parents' Assoc., 2003–05, Bd of Govs, 2005–07,

Trustee, British Sch. of Brussels, 2010–. Chair, Stanmore Community Assoc., 2011–; Vice Chair, Winchester Dist CAB, 2012–. *Publications:* Conscience, Government and War, 1978. *Recreations:* walking, gardening. *Address:* 76 Romsey Road, Winchester, Hants SO22 5PH. *E:* rachel.aron12@gmail.com.

ARONSOHN, Lotte Therese; *see* Newman, L. T.

ARONSON, Hazel Josephine; *see* Cosgrove, Rt Hon. Lady.

ARORA, Rev. Arun; Director of Communications, Church of England, since 2012; *b* Birmingham, 10 Oct. 1971; *s* of Gucharan and Sodarhan Arora; *m* 2006, Joanne Logan; one *d. Educ:* King Edward VI Five Ways Sch., Birmingham; Univ. of Birmingham (LLB 1993); Univ. of Durham (BA 2006). Admitted solicitor, 1998; with Thompsons Solicitors, 1996–2000; Diocesan Communications Officer, Dio. of Birmingham, 2000–07; Dir of Communications for Archbishop of York, 2006–09; ordained deacon, 2007, priest, 2008; Curate, St Marks, Harrogate, 2007–10; Team Leader, Wolverhampton Pioneer Ministries, 2010–12. *Publications:* (with A. Francis) The Rule of Lawyers, 1998. *Address:* Church House, Great Smith Street, SW1P 3AZ. *T:* (020) 7898 1000. *E:* arun.arora@churchofengland.org. *Club:* Aston Villa Football.

ARORA, Simon; Chief Executive, B&M Retail Ltd, since 2005; *b* UK, 1969; *s* of Surjit and Rani Arora; *m* 1995, Shalni; two *d. Educ:* Manchester Grammar Sch.; Fitzwilliam Coll., Cambridge (BA 1991). McKinsey & Co., 1992–94; 3i plc, 1994–95; Barclays Bank plc, 1995–96; Orient Sourcing Services Ltd, 1996–2003. Mem., Young Presidents' Orgn, 2002–. *Recreations:* travel, art, fine dining. *Address:* B&M Retail Ltd, The Vault, Dakota Drive, Estuary Commerce Park, Speke, Liverpool L24 8RJ. *Clubs:* Arts, 5 Hertford Street.

ARRAN, 9th Earl of, *cr* 1762, of the Arran Islands, Co. Galway; **Arthur Desmond Colquhoun Gore;** Bt 1662; Viscount Sudley, Baron Saunders, 1758; Baron Sudley (UK), 1884; *b* 14 July 1938; *er s* of 8th Earl of Arran and Fiona Bryde, *er d* of Sir Iain Colquhoun of Luss, 7th Bt, KT, DSO; *S* father, 1983; *m* 1974, Eleanor, (MBE 2008), *er d* of Bernard van Cutsem and Lady Margaret Fortescue; two *d. Educ:* Eton; Balliol College, Oxford. 2nd Lieutenant, 1st Bn Grenadier Guards (National Service). Asst Manager, Daily Mail, 1972–73; Man. Dir, Clark Nelson, 1973–74; Asst Gen. Manager, Daily and Sunday Express, June–Nov. 1974. Dir, Waterstone & Co. Ltd, 1984–87. A Lord in Waiting (Govt Whip), 1987–89; Parliamentary Under-Secretary of State: for the Armed Forces, MoD, 1989–92; NI Office, 1992–94; Parly Under-Sec. of State, DoE, 1994; Captain of the Yeomen of the Guard (Dep. Govt Chief Whip), 1994–95; elected Mem., H of L, 1999. Director: HMV, 1995–98; Bonham's, 1997–2000; Weather World, 2005–. Chm., Waste Mgt Industry NTO, 2000–. Pres., Children's Country Holidays Fund. Trustee, Chelsea Physic Garden, 1994–2014. *Recreations:* tennis, shooting, gardening, croquet. *Address:* c/o House of Lords, SW1A 0PW. *Clubs:* White's, Pratt's, Turf, Beefsteak.

ARRAN, Graham Kent; His Honour Judge Arran; a Circuit Judge, since 2007; Resident Judge, Harrow Crown Court, since 2013; *b* Manchester, 13 April 1947; *s* of Carl and Dorothy Arran; *m* 1st, 1973, Carol Quellmalz (*d* 1986); one *s* two *d*; 2nd, 1992, Susan Duncan. *Educ:* N Manchester Grammar Sch.; London Sch. of Econs and Pol Sci. (LLB). Called to the Bar, Lincoln's Inn, 1969; in practice at the Bar, London, specialising in criminal law, 1969–2007; Asst Recorder, 1990–94; Recorder, 1994–2007. Chm., Lord Chancellor's Adv. Cttee on JPs for London West, 2012–. *Recreations:* being a grandfather, the occasional holiday. *Address:* Harrow Crown Court, Hailsham Drive, Harrow HA1 4TU. *T:* (020) 8424 2294.

ARRAND, Ven. Geoffrey William; Archdeacon of Suffolk, 1994–2009, now Archdeacon Emeritus; *b* 24 July 1944; *s* of Thomas Staniforth Arrand and Alice Ada Arrand; *m* 1st, 1968, Mary Marshall (marr. diss.); one *s* two *d*; 2nd, 2005, Margaret Elizabeth Frost. *Educ:* King's Coll., London (BD 1966, AKC). Ordained deacon, 1967, priest, 1968; Assistant Curate: Washington, dio. of Durham, 1967–70; S Ormsby Gp, 1970–73; Team Vicar, Great Grimsby, 1973–79; Team Rector, Halesworth, 1979–85; Dean of Bocking and Rector of Hadleigh with Layham and Shelley, 1985–94; RD of Hadleigh, 1986–94. Hon. Canon, St Edmundsbury Cathedral, 1991–. Mem., Gen. Synod, 2005–09. OStJ 1994 (County Chaplain, Suffolk, 1995–2009). *Recreations:* golf, bowls. *Address:* 8 Elm Close, Saxilby, Lincoln LN1 2QH. *T:* (01522) 826967. *E:* garrand@virginmedia.com. *Club:* Lincoln Golf.

ARROW, Kenneth Joseph; Professor of Economics and Operations Research, Stanford University, 1979–91, Professor Emeritus, 1991; *b* 23 Aug. 1921; *s* of Harry I. and Lillian Arrow; *m* 1947, Selma Schweitzer; two *s. Educ:* City College (BS in Social Science 1940); Columbia Univ. (MA 1941, PhD 1951). Captain, US AAF, 1942–46. Research Associate, Cowles Commn for Research in Economics, Univ. of Chicago, 1947–49; Actg Asst Prof., Associate Prof. and Prof. of Economics, Statistics and Operations Research, Stanford Univ., 1949–68; Prof. of Econs, later University Prof., Harvard Univ., 1968–79. Staff Mem., US Council of Economic Advisers, 1962. Consultant, The Rand Corp., 1948–. Fellow, Churchill Coll., Cambridge, 1963–64, 1970, 1973, 1986 (Hon. Fellow, 1992); Vis. Fellow, All Souls Coll., Oxford, 1996. President: Internat. Economic Assoc., 1983–86; Internat. Soc. for Inventory Res., 1984–90; Member: Inst. of Management Sciences (Pres., 1963); Nat. Acad. of Sciences; Amer. Inst. of Medicine; Amer. Philosoph. Soc.; Pontifical Acad. of Social Scis; Fellow: Econometric Soc. (Pres., 1956); Amer. Acad. of Arts and Sciences (Vice Pres., 1979–80, 1991–94); Amer. Assoc. for Advancement of Science (Chm., Section K, 1982); Amer. Statistical Assoc.; Amer. Financial Assoc.; Dist. Fellow: Amer. Econ. Assoc. (Pres., 1972); Western Econ. Assoc. (Pres., 1980–81); Corresp. Fellow, British Acad., 1976; Foreign Mem., Royal Soc., 2006; Foreign Hon. Mem., Finnish Acad. of Sciences. Hon. LLD: Chicago, 1967; City Univ. of NY, 1972; Univ. of Pennsylvania, 1976; Washington Univ., St Louis, Missouri, 1989; Ben-Gurion Univ., 1989; Hon. Dr Soc. and Econ. Sciences, Vienna, 1971; Hon. ScD Columbia, 1973; Hon. DSocSci Yale, 1974; Hon. Dr: Paris, 1974; Hebrew Univ. of Jerusalem, 1975; Helsinki, 1976; Aix-Marseille III, 1985; Sacro Cuore, Milan, 1994; Uppsala, 1995; Buenos Aires, 1999; Cyprus, 2000; Tel Aviv, 2001; Hitotsubashi, 2004; Waseda, 2009; Hon. LittD Cambridge, 1985. John Bates Clark Medal, American Economic Assoc., 1957; Nobel Meml Prize in Economic Science, 1972; von Neumann Prize, Inst. of Management Scis and Ops Res. Soc. of America, 1986; US Nat. Medal of Science, 2004; (jtly) Benjamin E. Lippincott Award, Amer. Pol Sci. Assoc., 2009. Order of the Rising Sun (2nd class), Japan, 1984. *Publications:* Social Choice and Individual Values, 1951, 2nd edn 1963; (with S. Karlin and H. Scarf) Studies in the Mathematical Theory of Inventory and Production, 1958; (with M. Hoffenberg) A Time Series Analysis of Interindustry Demands, 1959; (with L. Hurwicz and H. Uzawa) Studies in Linear and Nonlinear Programming, 1959; Aspects of the Theory of Risk Bearing, 1965; (with M. Kurz) Public Investment, the Rate of Return, and Optimal Fiscal Policy, 1971; Essays in the Theory of Risk-Bearing, 1971; (with F. Hahn) General Competitive Analysis, 1972; The Limits of Organization, 1974; (with L. Hurwicz) Studies in Resource Allocation Processes, 1977; Collected Papers, Vols 1–6, 1984–86; (with H. Raynaud) Social Choice and Multicriterion Decision-Making, 1986; 270 articles in jls and collective vols. *Address:* Department of Economics, Stanford University, Stanford, CA 94305–6072, USA.

ARROWSMITH, Amanda Jane Elizabeth; Chair, Eastern Region Committee, Heritage Lottery Fund, 2001–04; *b* 28 Dec. 1947; *d* of late Michael St George Arrowsmith and Elizabeth Arrowsmith (*née* Bartlett). *Educ:* Lady Margaret Hall, Oxford (MA); MBA Open Univ. Archive trng, Bodleian Liby, Oxford, 1971–72; asst, sen. asst and dep. archivist posts, Northumberland and Suffolk CCs, 1972–79; Co. Archivist, Berks, 1979–82, Suffolk, 1982–87; Dep. Dir of Arts and Libraries, 1987–90, Dir of Libraries and Heritage, 1990–2001, Suffolk. Comr, RCHME, 1994–98; Mem., Hist. Bldgs and Monuments Commn (Eng. Heritage), 1998–2001. Member: Adv. Council on Public Records, 1995–2000; Eastern Reg. Cttee, SE Museums Service, 1999–2003; Exec. Cttee, Friends of Nat. Libraries, 1993–96 and 1999–2003; Reviewing Cttee on Export of Works of Art, 2002–06 (Chm., Manuscripts and Documents Wkg Gp, 2002–06); Pres., 1996–99, Vice-Pres., 2002–, Soc. of Archivists. Dir, Victim Support Suffolk, 2002–03 (Chm., Magistrates' Courts Witness Support Service Cttee, 2002–03). Mem. Bd, Living East, 1999–2002. Hon. Ed., Chapels Soc., 2004–07. *Publications:* contrib. articles to Archives, Jl Soc. Archivists, New Liby World. *Address:* 30 Underhill, Stowmarket, Suffolk IP14 1QY.

ARROWSMITH, Pat; peace activist and socialist; on staff of Amnesty International, 1971–94, retired; *b* 2 March 1930; *d* of late George Ernest Arrowsmith and late Margaret Vera (*née* Kingham); *m* Mr Gardner, 11 Aug. 1979, separated 11 Aug. 1979; lesbian partnership with Wendy Butlin, 1962–76. *Educ:* Farringtons; Stover Sch.; Cheltenham Ladies' Coll.; Newnham Coll., Cambridge (BA history); Univ. of Ohio; Liverpool Univ. (Cert. in Social Science). Has held many jobs, incl.: Community Organizer in Chicago, 1952–53; Cinema Usher, 1953–54; Social Caseworker, Liverpool Family Service Unit, 1954; Child Care Officer, 1955 and 1964; Nursing Asst, Deva Psychiatric Hosp., 1956–57; Reporter for Peace News, 1965; Gardener for Camden BC, 1966–68; Researcher for Soc. of Friends Race Relations Cttee, 1969–71; Case Worker for NCCL, 1971; and on farms, as waiter in cafes, in a factory, as a toy demonstrator, as a 'temp' in numerous offices, as asst in children's home, as newspaper deliverer and sales agent, as cleaner, as bartender, and in a holiday camp. Organizer for Direct Action Cttee against Nuclear War, Cttee of 100 and Campaign for Nuclear Disarmament, 1958–68; gaoled 11 times as political prisoner, 1958–85 (adopted twice as Prisoner of Conscience by Amnesty International); awarded: Holloway Prison Green Band, 1964; Girl Crusaders knighthood, 1940; Americans Removing Injustice, Suppression and Exploitation peace prize, 1991; Unsung Woman award, Haringey Council, 2001. Contested: Fulham, 1966 (Radical Alliance) and 1970 (Hammersmith Stop the SE Asia War Cttee), on peace issues; Cardiff South East (Independent Socialist), 1979. Member: War Resisters' Internat.; Campaign for Nuclear Disarmament (Vice-Pres., 2008–). *Publications:* Jericho (novel), 1965; Somewhere Like This (novel), 1970; To Asia in Peace, 1972; The Colour of Six Schools, 1972; Breakout (poems and drawings from prison), 1975; On the Brink (anti-war poems with pictures), 1981; The Prisoner (novel), 1982; Thin Ice (anti-nuclear poems), 1984; Nine Lives (poems and pictures), 1990; I Should Have Been a Hornby Train (fiction-cum-memoir), 1995; Many are Called (novel), 1998; Drawing to Extinction (poems and pictures), 2000; Going On (poems), 2005; Dark Light (poems and pictures), 2009. *Recreations:* water colour painting (has held and contrib. exhibns), swimming, writing poetry. *Address:* 132c Middle Lane, N8 7JP. *T:* (020) 8340 2661.

ARROYO, Gloria M.; *see* Macapagal-Arroyo.

ARSCOTT, John Robert Dare, FRAeS; Director, Airspace Policy, Civil Aviation Authority, 1999–2009; *b* 19 April 1947; *s* of Richard Arscott and Janet Arscott (*née* Knibbs); *m* 1971, Kyrle Margaret Bradley; one *d* and one *s* decd. *Educ:* Lindisfarne Coll. RAF, 1966; jsdc 1984; awc 1987; posts in NATS and Mil. Air Traffic Ops, 1990–95; AOC Mil. Air Traffic Ops, 1996–99; retired in rank of Air Vice-Marshal, 2001. Dep. Chm., 2007–09, Chm., 2009–11, Eurocontrol Performance Rev. Commn. FRAeS 2001. *Recreations:* aviation, railways, walking, DIY, grandfathering. *Address:* Lilac Cottage, Kemble Wick, Cirencester, Glos GL7 6EQ. *Club:* Royal Air Force.

ARSHAD, Rowena, (Mrs M. Q. Parnell), OBE 2001; Director, Centre for Education for Racial Equality in Scotland, since 1994, Senior Lecturer, since 1997, and Head, Moray House School of Education, since 2013, University of Edinburgh; *b* 27 April 1960; *d* of Zainal Arshad bin Zainal Abidin and Teoh Phaik Choo; *m* 1985, Malcolm Quarrie Parnell; one *s* one *d. Educ:* Methodist Girls' Sch., Penang, W Malaysia; St Francis' Coll., Letchworth; Bulmershe Coll. of Higher Educn (Cert. in Youth and Community Work 1985); Moray House, Heriot-Watt Univ. (MEd 1995); Univ. of Edinburgh (DEd). Scottish Educn and Action for Develt, 1985–88; Multicultural Educn Centre, Edinburgh, 1988–91; Lectr, Moray House Inst. of Educn, Edinburgh, 1991–97; Hd, Inst. for Educn, Community and Soc., Univ. of Edinburgh, 2010–13. Member: SHEFC, then SFC, 1999–2008; Independent Inquiry into Student Finance, 1999; Working Party on Guidelines in Sex Educn in Scottish Schs, 2000; Equal Opportunities Commn, 2001–07; Scotland Cttee, Equality and Human Rights Commn; Convenor Educn Sub Gp, Race Equality Adv. Forum, Scottish Exec., 1999–2001. Board Member: Telford Coll., Edinburgh, 2001–03; Inspectorate of Educn, 2001–05; Member: Governance Adv. Team, British Council, 2002–08; Inst. of Contemporary Scotland, 2002–. *Recreations:* reading political literature on Scotland, equity, justice, travelling (particularly to favourite city Toronto), cooking for family and friends, playing with border collie Perry. *Address:* St John's Land, Moray House School of Education, University of Edinburgh, Holyrood Road, Edinburgh EH8 8AQ. *T:* (0131) 651 6371, *Fax:* (0131) 651 6511. *E:* Rowena.Arshad@ed.ac.uk.

ARTER, Anthony Lewis; Pensions Ombudsman and Pension Protection Fund Ombudsman, since 2015; *b* Harrow, 9 Jan. 1947; *s* of Jack and Louise Arter; *m* Catherine; one *s* one *d. Educ:* Wandsworth Comprehensive Sch.; Jesus Coll., Cambridge (BA 1988); Coll. of Law. Detective Superintendent, Metropolitan Police, 1990–92; admitted as solicitor, 1995; Eversheds LLP: Partner, 2001–14; Hd, Pensions Gp, 2005–13; London Sen. Partner, 2009–14. London Ambassador for Employee Volunteering, BITC, 2009. Police Long Service and Good Conduct Medal, 1991. *Recreations:* sailing, cycling, walking. *Address:* Pensions Ombudsman, 11 Belgrave Road, SW1V 1RB. *E:* anthony.arter@pensions-ombudsman.org.uk. *Clubs:* Reform; Royal Fowey Yacht.

ARTHANAYAKE, Nihal; BBC Radio 1 Disc Jockey, since 2002; *b* 1 June 1971; *s* of Tilak Arthanayake and Rohini Arthanayake; *m* 2005, Eesha; one *s* one *d. Educ:* St Mary's Coll., Strawberry Hill (BA Hons). Television presenter: The Drop, 2001; Saturday Show Extra; Whitey Blighty (documentary), 2003; Desi DNA, 2004–07; Where's Your F***ing Manners (documentary), 2004; God is a DJ for Heaven and Earth Show, 2007; jt programmer, with Radio 1, London Flavas stage, 2004–; promoter and creator, Bombay Bronx clubnight. Member, Board: British Council, 2006–12; Metal Arts Think Tank, 2007–. Cultural Ambassador, London 2012 Olympics, 2004–12; Ambassador, Football Aid Charity, 2007. *Recreations:* walking my Staffordshire Bull Terrier, Luna, swimming, going to see the mighty Tottenham Hotspur, listening to music, DJing, looking at my My Space page, messageboards. *E:* dj.nihal@bbc.co.uk.

ARTHUIS, Jean Raymond Francis Marcel; Member for Mayenne, Senate, France; *b* 7 Oct. 1944; *m* 1971, Brigitte Lafont; one *s* one *d. Educ:* Ecole Supérieure de Commerce, Nantes; Institut d'Etudes Politiques, Paris. Sen. consultant in internat. auditing office; Founder of a soc. for accounting expertise and auditors. Senator, Mayenne, 1983–86, 1988–95 and 1997– (President: Gpe de l'Union Centriste, 1998–2002; Finance Commn, 2002–); Pres., Gen. Council of Mayenne, 1992– (Rapporteur général of budget to Senate, 1992–95). Secretary of State: Ministry of Social Affairs and Employment, 1986–87; for competition and consumption, Ministry of Economy, Finance and Privatization, 1987–88; Minister of: Economic Development and Planning, May–Aug. 1995; the Economy, Finance and Planning, Aug.–Nov. 1995; the Economy and of Finance, 1995–97. Mayor, Château-Gontier, Mayenne, 1971–2001. *Publications:* (with H. Haenel) Justice Sinistrée: démocratie en danger, 1991; Les Délocalisations et l'emploi, 1993; Dans les coulisses de Bercy, 1998; Mondialisation: la France à contre emploi, 2007; SOS Finances publiques: osons les vraies réformes, 2011; (with Michel Sapin) La France peut s'en sortir, 2012. *Recreation:* horse-riding. *Address:* Sénat, 15 rue de Vaugirard, 75006 Paris, France; 8 rue René Homo, 53200 Château-Gontier, France.

ARTHUR, family name of **Baron Glenarthur**.

ARTHUR, Adrian; Editor, The Courier, Dundee, 1993–2002; *b* 28 Sept. 1937; *s* of Alastair and Jean Arthur, Kirkcaldy; *m* 1962, Patricia Mill; one *s* two *d*. *Educ:* Harris Academy, Dundee; Univ. of St Andrews (BL). Sub-Editor, People's Journal, 1954–56; Nat. Service, RAF, 1956–58; editorial staff, The Courier, Dundee, 1958–2002 (Dep. Editor, 1978–93). Hon. Fellow, Univ. of Abertay, Dundee, 2003. *Recreations:* golf, reading, travel, Rotary. *Address:* 33 Seaforth Crescent, West Ferry, Dundee DD5 1QD. *T:* (01382) 776842. *Club:* Dalhousie Golf (Carnoustie).

ARTHUR, Sir Benjamin Nathan, 7th Bt *cr* 1841, of Upper Canada; *b* 27 March 1979; *o s* of Sir Stephen John Arthur, 6th Bt, and of Carolyn Margaret, *d* of Burney Lawrence Diamond, Cairns, Qld; *S* father, 2010, but his name does not yet appear on the Official Roll of the Baronetage. *Heir: (presumptive) kinsman* Sir Gavyn Farr Arthur, *qv*.

ARTHUR, Sir Gavyn (Farr), Kt 2004; **His Honour Judge Sir Gavyn Arthur;** a Circuit Judge, since 2007; a Deputy High Court Judge, since 2008; Lord Mayor of London, 2002–03; *b* 13 Sept. 1951; *s* of late Maj. the Hon. Leonard Arthur, sometime Chm., Natal Provincial Assembly, and Raina Arthur (*née* Farr); *heir presumptive (kinsman)* to Sir Benjamin Nathan Arthur, 7th Bt, *qv*. *Educ:* Harrow Sch.; Christ Church, Oxford (MA Jurisprudence). Called to the Bar, Middle Temple, 1975 (Bencher, 2001); in practice as barrister, 1977–2007; Recorder, 2002–07. Mem. Cttee, Western Circuit, 1985–88. Common Councilman, Ward of Farringdon Without, 1988–91; Alderman, Cripplegate Ward, 1991–2007; Sheriff, City of London, 1998–99; HM Lieut, City of London, 2002–; Chief Magistrate, City of London, 2002–03; Admiral, Port of London, 2002–03. Freeman, City of London, 1979 (Master, Guild of Freemen of City of London, 2009–10); Liveryman: Gardeners' Co., 1990– (Master, 2007–08); Wax-Chandlers' Co., 1996– (Mem., Ct of Assts; Master, 2012); Mem., Guild of Public Relations Practitioners, 2000– (Mem., Ct of Assts; Master, 2010); Hon. Liveryman, Lightmongers' Co., 2008–. Chm., Arab Financial Forum, 2004–. Vice-President: British Red Cross, 1993–; Inst. of Export, 1999–. Member: Anglo-Austrian Soc.; British Assoc. for Cemeteries in SE Asia; British Lebanese Soc.; British Tunisia Soc.; British Ukrainian Law Assoc.; City of London Sheriffs Soc. (Patron); Cttee, Save the Children; Council, Imperial Soc. of Knights Bachelor, 2005– (Registrar, 2012–); Gov., 2004–07, Vice-Adm. of the Northern Waters, 2004–, Hon. the Irish Soc. Trustee: Sir John Soane Mus., 1996–2004; Cripplegate Foundn; Lord Kitchener Nat. Meml Fund; St Paul's Cathedral. Patron: Royal Soc. of St George; Three Faiths Forum; Vice-Patron, Treloar Coll. Appeal. Chancellor, City Univ., 2002–03; Vice-Patron, London Metropolitan Univ. Governor: Christ's Hosp., 1991–2007; King Edward's Sch., Witley, 1991–2007; City of London Sch. for Girls, 1991–2007; City of London Freemen's Sch., 1994–2007. Hon. DCL City, 2002. KStJ 2002. Order of Honour (Georgia), 2003; Kt Grand Cross, Royal Order of Francis I, 2011 (Kt Comdr, 2006); Comdr, Order of the Crown (Romania), 2012; Kt, Order of Vila Viçosa (Portugal), 2014; Kt Comdr, Order of the Eagle (Georgia), 2014. *Recreations:* travel, Alpine walking. *Address:* c/o Brooks's, St James's Street, SW1A 1LE. *Clubs:* Brooks's; Bedford (Eastern Cape).

ARTHUR, Hugh Anthony Victor, OBE 2010; High Commissioner for Barbados in the United Kingdom, 2008–13; *b* Bridgetown, Barbados, 1945; *s* of Beresford Arthur and Louise Arthur; *m* 1972, Rose Anne Burnham (marr. diss. 2000); one *s* one *d*. *Educ:* Modern High Sch., Bridgetown; Trent Univ., Ont (BA Hons Sociol. and Econs 1969); Univ. of Surrey (MSc Tourism 1977). Barbados Tourist Board: Travel Develt Officer, Toronto, 1971–74; Exec. Officer, Bridgetown, 1974–76; Lectr in Tourism, Univ. of West Indies, Nassau, 1979–80; Barbados Tourist Board, subseq. Barbados Board of Tourism, then Barbados Tourism Authority: Mktg Manager, 1980–85; Dep. Dir of Tourism, 1985–91; Dir, Mktg and Sales, N America, 1991–92; CEO, 1992–95; Tourism Develt Planner, Grenada Tourism Master Plan Proj., Govt of Grenada/Orgn of Amer. States, 1995–97; Lectr/Coordinator, Hospitality and Mgt Degree Prog., Univ. of West Indies, Cave Hill, 1998–2008. *Recreations:* reading, walking, guitar. *Address:* 9 Roehampton Gate, Roehampton, SW15 5JR. *T:* (020) 7299 7150, *Fax:* (020) 7323 6872.

ARTHUR, Prof. James Greig, FRS 1992; FRSC 1981; University Professor, since 1987, and Professor of Mathematics, since 1979, University of Toronto; *b* 18 May 1944; *s* of John Greig Arthur and Katherine Mary Patricia Scott; *m* 1972, Dorothy Pendleton Helm; two *s*. *Educ:* Upper Canada Coll.; Univ. of Toronto (BSc, MSc); Yale Univ. (PhD). Instructor, Princeton Univ., 1970–72; Asst Prof., Yale Univ., 1972–76; Prof., Duke Univ., 1976–79. Sloan Fellowship, 1976; E. W. R. Steacie Meml Fellowship, 1982. Synge Award, RSC, 1987. *Publications:* Simple Algebras, Base Change and the Advanced Theory of the Trace Formula (with Laurent Clozel), 1989. *Recreations:* tennis, golf. *Address:* 23 Woodlawn Avenue W, Toronto, ON M4V 1G6, Canada. *T:* (416) 9640975.

ARTHUR, Lt-Gen. Sir (John) Norman (Stewart), KCB 1985; CVO 2007; Lord-Lieutenant, Stewartry of Kirkcudbright (Dumfries and Galloway Region), 1996–2006; General Officer Commanding Scotland and Governor of Edinburgh Castle, 1985–88, retired; *b* 6 March 1931; *s* of Col Evelyn Stewart Arthur, DL, and Mrs E. S. Arthur (*née* Burnett-Stuart); *m* 1st, 1960, Theresa Mary Hopkinson (*d* 2011); one *s* one *d* (and one *s* decd); 2nd, 2012, Jillian Constance Andrews. *Educ:* Eton Coll.; RMA, Sandhurst. rcds, jssc, psc. Commnd Royal Scots Greys, 1951; commanded: Royal Scots Dragoon Guards, 1972–74 (despatches, 1974); 7th Armoured Bde, 1976–77; Brig., Gen. Staff, Intelligence, MoD, 1978–80; GOC 3rd Armoured Div., 1980–82; Dir of Personal Services (Army), MoD, 1983–85. Col Comdt, Military Provost Staff Corps, 1985–88; Col, The Royal Scots Dragoon Gds (Carabiniers and Greys), 1984–92; Hon. Col, 205 (Scottish) Gen. Hosp., RAMC(V), 1988–93, The Scottish Yeomanry, 1993–97. Chm., Cavalry Colonels, 1987–92. Officer, Royal Co. of Archers, Queen's Body Guard for Scotland. Chairman: Scotland, Army Benevolent Fund, 1988–2000; Leonard Cheshire Services, SW Scotland, 1994–2000; President: Combined Cavalry Old Comrades Assoc., 1995–2000; Lowland RFCA, 2001–06; Vice Pres., Edinburgh and Borders, Riding for the Disabled Assoc., 1988–94; Dir, Edinburgh Mil. Tattoo Co., 1988–91; Pres., Scottish Conservation Projects, 1989–94; Mem., Automobile Assoc. Cttee, 1990–98. Humanitarian aid work to Balkans, 1992–2013. Mem., British Olympic Team, Equestrian Three-Day Event, 1960. DL Stewartry, 1989; JP 1996. *Recreations:* field and country sports and pursuits, horsemanship, military history. *Address:* Newbarns, Dalbeattie, Kirkcudbrightshire DG5 4PY. *T:* (01556) 630227.

ARTHUR, Sir Michael (Anthony), KCMG 2004 (CMG 1992); HM Diplomatic Service, retired; President, Boeing UK, since 2014; consultant, since 2010; *b* 28 Aug. 1950; *s* of late John Richard Arthur and of Mary Deirdre (*née* Chaundy); *m* 1974, Plaxy Gillian Beatrice (*née* Corke); two *s* two *d*. *Educ:* Watford GS; Rugby; Balliol Coll., Oxford. Entered HM Diplomatic Service, 1972; UK Mission to UN, NY, 1972; FCO, 1973; 3rd, later 2nd Sec., UK Perm. Representation to Eur. Communities, 1974–76; 2nd Sec., Kinshasa, 1976–78; FCO, 1978–83; Private Secretary: to Lord Privy Seal, 1981; to Minister of State, FCO, 1982; 1st Sec., Bonn, 1984–88; Hd, EC Dept (Internal), FCO, 1988–93; Sen. Associate Mem., St Antony's Coll., Oxford, 1993; Counsellor and Hd of Chancery, Paris, 1993–97; Dir (Resources) and Chief Inspector, FCO, 1997–99; Minister and Dep. Hd of Mission, Washington, 1999–2000; Econ. Dir, then Dir-Gen., EU and Econ., FCO, 2001–03; High Comr, India, 2003–07; Ambassador to Germany, 2007–10. UK Chm., Koenigswinter, 2010. Non-exec. Dir, Diligentia plc, 2012–. Member: FCO Locarno Gp, 2011–; Sen. European Experts Gp, European Movement, 2013–; Member, Advisory Board: Kings India Inst., 2011–; Global Economic Symposium, 2011–; Humboldt Univ. GB Centre, 2011–15. Associate Mem., BUPA. Trustee: Orbis, 2011–; Nehru Trust. Regular speaker on India, Germany and Europe. Freeman, City of Oxford, 1970. *Recreations:* music, travel, books.

ARTHUR, Prof. Michael James Paul, DM; FRCP, FMedSci; Provost and President, University College London, since 2013; *b* 3 Aug. 1954; *s* of Reginald Alfred John Arthur and Patricia Margaret Arthur; *m* 1979, Elizabeth Susan McCaughey; one *s* two *d*. *Educ:* Burnt Mill Comprehensive Sch., Harlow; Sch. of Medicine, Univ. of Southampton (BM 1977; DM 1986). FRCP 1993. Med. Registrar, Wessex Reg., 1980–82; University of Southampton: Lectr in Medicine, 1982–89; Sen. Lectr, 1989–92; Prof. of Medicine, 1992–2004; Hd, Sch. of Medicine, 1998–2001; Dir of Res., Sch. of Medicine, 2001–02; Dean, Faculty of Medicine, Health and Life Scis, 2003–04; Vice-Chancellor, Univ. of Leeds, 2004–13. Fogarty Internat. Travelling Fellow, Liver Center Lab., Univ. of Calif, San Francisco, 1986–88; Fulbright Dist. Scholar, Mount Sinai Sch. of Medicine, NY, 2002. Mem., Adv. Gp on Hepatitis, 1998–2004, Chm., Adv. Gp on Nat. Specialist Services, 2010–13, DoH. Member: Molecular and Cell Panel, Wellcome Trust, 1998–2002 and 2003–04 (Vice-Chm., 2000; Chm., 2003–04); Council, MRC, 2008–14. US/UK Fulbright Comr, 2008–. Pres., British Assoc. for Study of the Liver, 2001–03. Chair, Nat. Student Survey Steering Gp, 2006–08; Mem. Bd, QCA, later QCDA, 2007–10. Board Member: Yorkshire Forward, 2007–11; Opera North, 2007–; Nat. Sci. Learning Centre, 2006–. Chair: Worldwide Univs Network, 2007–09; Russell Gp of Univs, 2009–12. FMedSci 1998; FRSA 2006. Hon. Fellow, Assoc. of Physicians of GB and Ireland, 2006. Hon. DLitt Southampton, 2010. Res. Prize, Amer. Liver Foundn, 1987; Linacre Medal, RCP, 1994. *Publications:* (ed jtly) Wright's Liver and Biliary Disease, 3rd edn 1992; numerous contribs to biomed. jls relating to liver disease and the pathogenesis of liver fibrosis. *Recreation:* sailing and yacht racing in the Solent. *Address:* Provost's Office, University College London, Gower Street, WC1E 6BT. *T:* (020) 7679 7234. *Club:* Royal Southern Yacht (Hamble).

ARTHUR, Lt-Gen. Sir Norman; *see* Arthur, Lt-Gen. Sir J. N. S.

ARTHUR, Rt Hon. Owen Seymour; PC 1995; MP (Lab) Barbados, since 1984; Leader of the Opposition, 2010–13; *b* 17 Oct. 1949; *m* 1st, 1978, Beverley Jeanne Batchelor (marr. diss.); 2nd, 2006, Julie Ann Price. *Educ:* Harrison Coll., Barbados; Univ. of West Indies at Cave Hill (BA) and at Mona (MSc). Research Asst, UWI, Jamaica, 1973; Asst Economic Planner, then Chief Econ. Planner, Nat. Planning Agency, Jamaica, 1974–79; Dir of Econs, Jamaica Bauxite Inst., 1979–81; Chief Project Analyst, Min. of Finance, Barbados, 1981–83; Lectr, Dept of Management, UWI, Cave Hill, 1986, Res. Fellow, 1993. Mem., Barbados Senate, 1983–84; Parly Sec., Min. of Finance, 1985–86; Chm., Barbados Labour Party, 1993–96, 1998–99; Leader of Opposition, 1993–94; Prime Minister of Barbados, 1994–2008; Minister of Finance and Econ. Affairs, Defence and Security and Civil Service, 1994–2008. *Publications:* The Commercialisation of Technology in Jamaica, 1979; Energy and Mineral Resource Development in the Jamaica Bauxite Industry, 1981; The IMF and Economic Stabilisation Policies in Barbados, 1984. *Recreations:* cooking, gardening.

ARTHUR, Richard Andrew; Chairman, Camden and Islington NHS Foundation Trust, 2009–13; *b* 24 March 1944; *s* of late Cyril Stuart Arthur and Cicely Arthur; *m* 1st, 1968, Diana Thompson (marr. diss.); one *s* one *d*; 2nd, 1986, Akiko Shindo; one step *s*. *Educ:* King's Sch., Canterbury; Christ's Coll., Cambridge (MA Econs); London Business Sch. (MSc Business). Commonwealth Development Finance Co.: Regl Dir, SE Asia, 1976–80; Chief Exec., Australia, 1981–82; Hd of Ops, 1982–86; Exec. Dir, Scimitar Develt Capital, 1986–93. Mem., Audit Commn, 1995–2003; Bd Mem., Housing Corp., 2000–04 (Chm., Regulation and Supervisory Cttee, 2001–04); Chm., CSA, 2006–08. Chm., Public Private Partnerships Prog., 1998–2000; Vice-Chm., Central London Partnership, 1998–2000. Dir, Accord plc, 2000–07. Chm., Renaissance Bedford, 2005–11. London Borough of Camden: Mem. (Lab), 1971–76 and 1990–2002; Chm. of Staff, 1975–76; Chm., Social Services, 1991–93; Leader, 1993–2000. Vice-Chm., Assoc. of London Govt, 2000–02. Mem. Ct, Middlesex Univ., 1996–2000. *Recreations:* swimming, gardening, reading, travel. *Address:* 11d Highgate West Hill, N6 6JR. *T:* (020) 8341 9148. *Club:* Singapore Cricket.

ARTHUR, Sandra Joy; Midwife Lecturer, School of Nursing and Midwifery Studies, Cardiff University, since 1998; *b* 16 April 1957; *d* of William Chapman and Evelyn Joy Chapman; *m* 1981, Stephen Laurence Arthur; two *s*. *Educ:* Queen Elizabeth Hosp., Birmingham (SRN 1979); Good Hope Hosp., Sutton Coldfield (SCM 1980); Cardiff Univ. (PGCE; LLM Legal Aspects in Med. Practice). Midwife, S Glamorgan, Cardiff and Vale NHS Trust, 1980. Hon. Supervisor of Midwives, 1996–. Mem. Council, Royal Coll. of Midwives, 1993–98; President: Assoc. of Supervisors of Midwives, 2002–; NMC, 2006–07. *Recreations:* tennis, sailing, gardening. *Address:* Cardiff School of Nursing and Midwifery Studies, Ty Dewi Sant, Heath Park Campus, Cardiff CF14 4XN. *E:* Arthursj@cf.ac.uk. *Clubs:* Penarth Yacht, Penarth Lawn Tennis.

ARTHURS, Prof. Harry William, OC 1989; OOnt 1995; FRSC 1982; University Professor, Osgoode Hall Law School, York University, Canada, 1995–2005, now Emeritus (Professor of Law, 1968–95); *b* 9 May 1935; *s* of Leon and Ellen Arthurs; *m* 1974, Penelope Geraldine Ann Milnes; two *s*. *Educ:* Univ. of Toronto (BA, LLB); Harvard Univ. (LLM). Barrister and Solicitor, 1961. York University: Asst Prof. 1961, Associate Prof. 1964, Associate Dean 1967, Dean 1972–77, Osgoode Hall Law Sch.; Pres., 1985–92, Pres. Emeritus, 1992–. Mem., Economic Council of Can., 1978–82; Bencher, Law Soc. of Upper Can., 1979–84; Chm., Consultative Gp on Res. and Educn in Law, 1981–84; Arbitrator, Mediator in Labour Disputes, 1962–84; Chair, Council of Ontario Univs, 1987–89; a Dir, Internat. Centre for Human Rights and Democratic Develt, 1999–2002; Commissioner: Rev. of Federal Labour Standards, 2004–06; Rev. of Ontario Pensions Legislation, 2006–08; Chm., Ind. Funding Review, Workplace Safety and Insurance Bd, 2010–12. Visiting Professor: Univ. of Toronto, 1965; McGill, 1967; Visiting Scholar: Clare Hall, Cambridge, 1971; Inst. for Socio-Legal Res., Oxford, 1977–78; Vis. Research Prof., UCL, 1984, 2003. Killam Laureate, 2002. Corresp. FBA 2003. Hon. LLD: Sherbrooke, 1986; Brock, 1986; Law Soc. of Upper Can., 1987; McGill, 1995; Montreal, 2002; Toronto, 2002; York, 2008; Simon Fraser, 2012; Hon. DLitt Lethbridge, 1991; Hon. DCL Windsor, 2004. (jtly with J. Stiglitz) Decent Work Res. Prize, ILO, 2008. *Publications:* Law and Learning, 1983; (jtly) Industrial Relations and Labour Law in Canada, 1979, 3rd edn 1988; Without the Law, 1985; (ed jtly) Rethinking Workplace Regulation: beyond the standard contract of employment, 2013. *Address:* Osgoode Hall Law School, York University, 4700 Keele Street, Toronto, Ontario M3J 1P3, Canada. *T:* (416) 7365407.

ARTHURSON, Paul Andrew; QC (Scot.) 2005; Sheriff of Lothian and Borders at Edinburgh, since 2011; Temporary Judge, Court of Session and High Court of Justiciary, since 2013; *b* 16 Dec. 1964; *s* of Dr Iain Hayden Arthurson and Margaret Arthurson; *m* 1997, Dr Sharon Elizabeth McAuslane; two *d*. *Educ:* Daniel Stewart's and Melville Coll., Edinburgh; Univ. of Edinburgh (LLB Hons 1986); Worcester Coll., Oxford (Dip Law 1990). Advocate, 1991–2005; Temp. Sheriff, 1999; Pt-time Sheriff, 2003–05; All Scotland Floating Sheriff, 2005–11. Chm., Mental Health Tribunals (restricted patients), 2008–09; Legal Mem., Parole Bd for Scotland, 2008–11. *Recreations:* family life, hill-walking in Scotland, choral singing.

ARTIS, Prof. Michael John, FBA 1988; Director, Manchester Regional Economics Centre, Institute for Political and Economic Governance, and Professor of Economics, Manchester University, 2005–08, now Emeritus; Welsh Assembly Visiting Research Professor, Swansea

University, 2008–10, now Emeritus; *b* 29 June 1938; *s* of Cyril John and Violet Emily Artis; *m* 1st, 1961, Lilian Gregson (marr. diss. 1982); two *d*; 2nd, 1983, Shirley Knight. *Educ:* Baines Grammar Sch., Poulton-le-Fylde, Lancs; Magdalen Coll., Oxford. BA Hons (PPE) Oxon. Assistant Research Officer, Oxford Univ., 1959; Lectr in Economics, Adelaide Univ., 1964; Lectr and Sen. Lectr in Economics, Flinders Univ., 1966; Research Officer and Review Editor, Nat. Inst. of Economic and Social Research, London, 1967; Prof. of Applied Economics, Swansea Univ. Coll., 1972; Prof. of Econs, Manchester Univ., 1975–99 (on leave of absence, 1995–99); Prof. of Econs, 1995–2003, Professorial Fellow, 2004–05, now Emeritus, European Univ. Inst., Florence; Sen. Houblon-Norman/George Fellow, Bank of England, 2004. *Publications:* Foundations of British Monetary Policy, 1964; (with M. K. Lewis) Monetary Control in the United Kingdom, 1981; Macroeconomics, 1984; (with S. Ostry) International Economic Policy Co-ordination, 1986; (with M. K. Lewis) Money in Britain, 1991; (ed jtly) The Central and Eastern European Countries and the European Union, 2006; contribs on economics, economic policy to books and learned jls. *Recreation:* eating out. *Address:* 76 Bexton Road, Knutsford, Cheshire WA16 0DX.

ARTON, Simon Nicholas B.; *see* Bourne-Arton.

ARULKUMARAN, Prof. Sabaratnam, Kt 2009; PhD; FRCS, FRCOG; Professor and Head of Obstetrics and Gynaecology, St George's, University of London (formerly St George's Hospital Medical School), 2001–13, now Emeritus; President, British Medical Association, 2013–14; *b* Jaffna, Ceylon, 17 Jan. 1948; *s* of Kathiravelu Sabaratnam and Gnanambikai Sabaratnam; *m* 1975, Gayatri Muttuthamby; two *s* one *d*. *Educ:* Univ. of Ceylon (MB BS Hons 1972); Univ. of Singapore (PhD 1992). FRCS 1979; FRCOG 1993. Hon. Sen. Lectr, Inst. of Obstetrics and Gynaecol., Queen Charlotte's Hosp., London, 1988–89. National University of Singapore: Associate Prof., 1990–92, Prof., 1992–97, of Obstetrics and Gynaecol.; Dep. Hd, 1992–94, Hd, 1994–97, of Obstetrics and Gynaecol.; Prof. of Obstetrics and Gynaecol., Univ. of Nottingham, 1997–2001. Vice Pres., 2005–07, Pres., 2007–10, RCOG. Treas. and Sec. Gen., Internat. Fedn of Obstetrics and Gynaecol., 1997–2006. Ed.-in-Chief, Best Practice in Clin. Res. in Obstetrics and Gynaecol., 1998–. *Publications:* (ed jtly) Fetal Monitoring in Practice, 1992, 3rd edn 2008; (ed jtly) Management of Labour, 1996, 2nd edn 2005; Emergencies in Obstetrics and Gynaecology, 2006; (ed jtly) Munro Kerr's Operative Obstetrics, 11th edn 2007; (ed jtly) Oxford Handbook of Obstetrics and Gynaecology, 2nd edn 2008; Best Practice in Labour and Delivery, 2009; (ed jtly) Obstetrics and Gynaecology for Postgraduates, vols 1 and 2, 3rd edn 2009; contrib. chapters in books and peer-reviewed indexed articles. *Recreations:* reading, philosophy, walking, listening to classical music. *Address:* Division of Obstetrics and Gynaecology, St George's, University of London, Cranmer Terrace, SW17 0RE. *T:* (020) 8725 5956, *Fax:* (020) 8725 5958. *E:* sarulkum@sgul.ac.uk.

ARUNDEL AND BRIGHTON, Bishop of, (RC), since 2015; **Rt Rev. (Charles Phillip) Richard Moth;** *b* Chingola, Zambia, 8 July 1958; *s* of Charles Ernest Moth and Barbara Yvonne Moth (*née* Hambly). *Educ:* Judd Sch., Tonbridge; St John's Seminary, Wonersh; St Paul Univ., Ottawa (MA; JCL 1987). Ordained priest, 1982; Assistant Priest: Clapham Park, 1982–85; Lewisham, 1987–92; Private Sec. to Archbishop of Southwark, 1992–2001; Vocations Dir, 1992–2001; Vicar Gen. and Chancellor, RC Archdio. of Southwark, 2001–09; RC Bishop of the Forces, 2009–15. Liaison Bishop for Catholic Scouting, 2010–, for Prisons, 2013–. Pres., Southwark Metropolitan Appeal Tribunal, 1994–2002; Catholic Bishops' Conference: Mem., Dept of Christian Responsibility and Citizenship, 2009–; Chair, Mental Health Reference Gp, 2009–. Chair of Govs, St Mary's UC, later St Mary's Univ., Twickenham, 2011–. Mem., Canon Law Soc. of GB and Ireland, 1985. Freeman: City of London, 2013; Skinners' Co., 2013. KC*HS 2009. *Recreations:* horse riding, walking, music. *Address:* High Oaks, Old Brighton Road North, Pease Pottage, W Sussex RH11 9AJ. *Club:* Naval and Military.

ARUNDEL AND SURREY, Earl of; Henry Miles Fitzalan-Howard; *b* 3 Dec. 1987; *s* and *heir* of Duke of Norfolk, *qv*. *Educ:* Radley College; Bristol Univ. Formula BMW UK Rookie Champion, 2006.

ARUNDELL; *see* Monckton-Arundell, family name of Viscount Galway.

ARUNDELL, family name of **Baron Talbot of Malahide**.

ARVILL, Robert; *see* Boote, R. E.

ASANTE, Kwaku Baprui, GM 1976; OOV 2008 (MOV 1978); High Commissioner for Ghana in London, 1991–93; *b* 26 March 1924; *s* of Kweku Asante and Odorso Amoo; *m* 1958, Matilda Dzagbele Anteson; three *s* two *d*. *Educ:* Achimota Coll.; Durham Univ. (BSc); Final Exam., Inst. Statisticians (AIS), London. Sen. Maths Master, Achimota, 1954–56; joined Ghana Foreign Service, 1956; Hd, African Dept of Foreign Ministry, 1957–60; 2nd Sec., London, 1957–58; Chargé d'Affaires, Tel Aviv, 1958–60; Principal Sec., African Affairs Secretariat, Office of Pres., 1960–66; Head of Admin, OAU, 1966–67; Ambassador to Switzerland and Austria and Permanent Delegate to UN Office, Geneva, 1967–72; Principal Sec., Min. of Foreign Affairs, 1972; Sen. Principal Sec., Ministries of Trade and Tourism, 1973–76; Ambassador to Belgium, Luxembourg and EEC, 1976–79; Sec.-Gen., Social Democratic Front, 1979–81; Sec. (Minister) for Trade and Tourism, 1982; Private Consultant, 1982–88; Sec. (Minister) for Educn, 1988–91. Chairman: Unimax Macmillan, 2001–09; La Community Bank, 2006–14. Pres., Gadangme Council, 1998–2012. Columnist, Daily Graphic. Hon. LLD Ghana, 1999; Hon. DLit Univ. of Develt Studies, Tamale, 2004. *Publications:* Foreign Policy Making in Ghana, 1997; Voice From Afar: a Ghanaian experience, 2003; articles in Ghanaian and foreign newspapers and jls. *Recreations:* music, cricket. *Address:* Asanteson, Palm Wine Junction, La, PO Box CT 4075, Accra, Ghana. *T:* (302) 774344.

ASANTE-MENSAH, Evelyn Justina, OBE 2006; Chairman, NHS Manchester (formerly Manchester Primary Care Trust), 2006–13 (Chairman: Central Manchester Primary Care Trust, 2000–06; Manchester Locality Assurance, 2011–13); *b* 11 Oct. 1965; *d* of late Kwaku Asante-Mensah and of Beatrice Gyamfi (*née* Amoo-Mensah); step *d* of Alfred Gyamfi; partner, Yoni Ejo; one *s* three *d*. *Educ:* Nicholls Ardwick High Sch., Manchester; Manchester Metropolitan Univ. (MA 2001). Joined Black Health Agency, 1992; Chief Exec., Black Health Agency, 1999–2005; Strategic Advr on Community Cohesion and Diversity, Govt Office for NW, 2006–07; Head of Equality and Econ. Inclusion, NW Develt Agency, 2007–10. Non-executive Director: Manchester HA, 1998–2000; NHS Greater Manchester, 2010–. Dir, EAM Solutions Ltd, 2011–. Chairman: Race for Health, 2002–08; Appt Commn, Black and Minority Ethnic Adv. Gp, 2004–07; Brook, 2007–09; Member: Equal Opportunities Commn, 2005–07; Community, Voluntary and Local Services Hons Cttee, Cabinet Office, 2011–; Bd, Partners of Prisoners, 2011–; EHRC, 2013–. Gov., St Mary's C of E Primary Sch., Moss Side, 2012–. Hon. DLitt Manchester Metropolitan, 2003. *Recreations:* reading, gardening, cooking, spending time with family. *E:* evelynasante-mensha@hotmail.co.uk, evelyn@eamsolutions.co.uk.

ASBIL, Rt Rev. Walter Gordon; Bishop of Niagara, 1991–97; *b* 3 Oct. 1932; *m* 1957, Mavis Asbil; three *s* one *d*. *Educ:* Concordia Univ., Montreal (BA); McGill Univ. (BD, STM). Ordained deacon, 1957, priest, 1957; Rector: Aylwin River Desert, 1957–60; Montreal South Shore, 1960–65; St Stephen's, Montreal, 1965–67; St George, St Anne de Bellevue, 1967–70; St George, St Catharine's, 1970–86; Rector and Dean, Christ Church Cathedral, Ottawa, 1986–90; Co-adjutor Bishop of Niagara, 1990–91. Hon. DD Montreal Dio. Theol Coll., 1991. *Address:* 1107, 3 Towering Heights Boulevard, St Catharines, ON L2T 4A4, Canada.

ASBRIDGE, Sir Jonathan (Elliott), Kt 2006; Programme Director, Reconfiguration of Health Services, North East Sector, Greater Manchester, 2008–12; *b* 16 Feb. 1959; *s* of late Roy Derek Asbridge and Doris Enid Asbridge; *m* 1986, Helen Catherine Lewis-Smith; two *s* two *d*. *Educ:* Nightingale Sch., St Thomas' Hosp., London (SRN 1980); UC Swansea (DipN 1987). Dir, Clinical Care Services, Addenbrooke's Hosp., 1989–92; Executive Nurse Director: Llandough Hosp., Cardiff, 1992–94; Oxford Radcliffe Hosp., 1994–97; Chief Nurse, Barts and the London NHS Trust, 1997–2003; Nat. Clinical Dir, Emergency Care, DoH, 2003–06; Dir of Nursing and Clinical Services, 2007–08, Ops Dir, 2008–12, Clinicenta Ltd. Pres., NMC, 2001–06. Mem., Council for Health Regulatory Excellence, 2002–06 (Vice Chm., 2004–05). Chm., Eur. Health Wkg Gp, Conseil Européen des Professions Libérales, 2004–; Mem., Internat. Council of Nurses Observatory of Licensure and Regulation, 2004–. Council Mem., Florence Nightingale Foundn, 2002–06; Life Vice Pres., Nightingale Fellowship, 2005–. Hon. DSc City, 2004. *Recreations:* tennis, walking, biographies, aviation.

ASCHERSON, (Charles) Neal; journalist and author; *b* 5 Oct. 1932; *s* of late Stephen Romer Ascherson and Evelyn Mabel Ascherson; *m* 1st, 1958, Corinna Adam (marr. diss. 1982; she *d* 2012); two *d*; 2nd, 1984, Isabel Hilton; one *s* one *d*. *Educ:* Eton College; King's College, Cambridge (MA; Hon. Fellow, 1993). Served RM, 1950–52. Reporter and leader writer, Manchester Guardian, 1956–58; Commonwealth corresp., Scotsman, 1959–60; The Observer: reporter, 1960–63; Central Europe corresp., 1963–68; Eastern Europe corresp., 1968–75; foreign writer, 1979–85; columnist, 1985–90; Associate Editor, 1985–89; columnist, The Independent on Sunday, 1990–98. Scottish politics corresp., Scotsman, 1975–79. Asst Lectr, 1998–2009, Hon. Prof., 2008–, Inst. of Archaeology, UCL; Hon. Fellow: UCL, 2010; UHI, 2010. Hon. FSAScot 2011. Hon. DLitt: Strathclyde, 1988; Bradford, 2006; Aberdeen, 2010; Goldsmiths, Univ. of London, 2014; Hon. DSc (SocSci) Edinburgh, 1990; DUniv: Open, 1991; Paisley, 2003; Hon. LLD St Andrews, 1999. Reporter of the Year 1982, Journalist of the Year 1987, Granada Awards; James Cameron Award, 1989; David Watt Meml Prize, 1991; (jtly) George Orwell Award, Political Qly, 1993; Saltire Award for Literature, 1995. Golden Insignia, Order of Merit (Poland), 1992; Bene Merito Insignia (Poland), 2011. *Publications:* The King Incorporated, 1963; The Polish August, 1981; The Struggles for Poland, 1987; Games with Shadows, 1988; Black Sea, 1995; Stone Voices, 2002. *Address:* 27 Corsica Street, N5 1JT. *Club:* Ognisko Polskie (Polish Hearth Club).

ASFARI, Ayman; Group Chief Executive, Petrofac plc, since 2002; *b* 8 July 1958; *s* of Dr Adeeb Asfari and Lamia Haroun; *m* 1983, Sawsan El-Himani; four *s*. *Educ:* Villanova Univ. (BSc Civil Engrg 1979); Univ. of Pennsylvania (MSc Civil and Urban Engrg 1980). Resident Engr, Conser Consulting Gp, 1980–81; Man. Dir, Desert Line Projects (DLP), Muscat, Oman, 1982–91; Man. Dir, Petrofac UK Ltd, Chm. and Chief Exec., Petrofac Internat. Ltd, and Dir in all other Petrofac cos, 1991–2002. *Recreations:* tennis, golf, ski-ing, boating. *Address:* Petrofac plc, 4th Floor, 117 Jermyn Street, SW1Y 6HH. *T:* (020) 7811 4900. *Club:* Royal Automobile.

ASGHAR, Mohammad; Member (C) South Wales East, National Assembly for Wales, since 2009 (Plaid Cymru, 2007–09); *b* Peshawar, 30 Sept. 1945; *s* of M. Aslam Khan and Zubaida Aslam; *m* 1983, Firdaus; one *d*. *Educ:* Peshawar Univ. (BA 1968). Certified Public Accountant. Asst to Principal, R. J. Minty, chartered accountants, 1972–83; Principal, MA Associates, accountants, 1983–. Shadow Minister for Equalities and Sport, Nat. Assembly for Wales, 2011. Member: Assoc. of Accounting Technicians, 1975–; Inst. of Financial Accountants, 2001–. *Recreations:* holder of Private Pilot's Licence, keen sportsman, cricket, athletics, badminton. *Address:* National Assembly for Wales, Cardiff Bay, Cardiff CF99 1NA. *T:* 0300 200 7239. *E:* mohammad.asghar@assembly.wales.

ASH, Brian Maxwell; QC 1990; *b* 31 Jan. 1941; *s* of late Carl Ash and of Irene Ash (*née* Atkinson); *m* 1971, Barbara Anne Maxwell, creator and founding editor of BBC TV Question Time; two *s* one *d*. *Educ:* Mercers' Sch.; City of London Sch.; New Coll., Oxford (Open Exhibnr; BA). BBC TV Current Affairs Producer, Reporter and Programme Presenter, 1967–73; called to the Bar, Gray's Inn, 1975. Chm. of Panel, Examination in Public of First Alteration to Devon Structure Plan, 1986; Sec., Local Govt, Planning and Envmtl Bar Assoc., 1990–92. *Recreations:* golf, sailing, ski-ing, music. *Address:* Thirty Nine Essex Street Chambers, 39 Essex Street, WC2R 3AT. *T:* (020) 7832 1111. *Clubs:* Royal Mid-Surrey Golf; Royal Norwich Golf.

ASH, Daniel Victor, FRCP, FRCR; Consultant in Clinical Oncology, Cookridge Hospital, Leeds, 1979–2007; President, Royal College of Radiologists, 2001–04 (Dean, Faculty of Clinical Oncology, 1998–2000); *b* 18 Oct. 1943; *s* of Vivien and Isidore Ash; *m* 1969, Deirdre Meikle; one *s* one *d*. *Educ:* Royal London Hosp. Medical Coll. (MB BS). FRCR 1976; FRCP 1992. Lectr in Medicine, Makerere Univ., Kampala, 1971–72; Registrar in Radiotherapy, Churchill Hosp., Oxford, 1973–76; Lectr in Radiotherapy, Royal Marsden Hosp., London, 1976–79. President: British Oncology Assoc., 1994–97; European Brachytherapy Gp, 1995–98. *Publications:* (jtly) Practical Radiotherapy Planning, 1985, 3rd edn 2000; (jtly) Effective Treatment of Prostate Cancer, 2002; clinical res. papers on radiation sensitisers, photodynamic therapy and brachytherapy. *Recreations:* music (classical and jazz), walking, ceramics. *Address:* 10 Oakwood Park, Leeds LS8 2PJ.

ASH, Prof. Sir Eric (Albert), Kt 1990; CBE 1983; FRS 1977; FREng; Emeritus Professor of Electrical Engineering, University College London, since 1993; *b* 31 Jan. 1928; *s* of Walter and Dorothea Ash; *m* 1954, Clare (*née* Babb); five *d*. *Educ:* University College Sch.; Imperial Coll. of Science and Technology. BSc(Eng), PhD, DSc; FCGI, DIC. FREng (FEng 1978); FIET; FIEEE; FInstP. Research Fellow: Stanford Univ., Calif, 1952–54; QMC, 1954–55; Res. Engr, Standard Telecommunication Laboratories Ltd, 1955–63; Sen. Lectr, 1963–65, Reader, 1965–67, Prof., 1967–85, Pender Prof. and Head of Dept, 1980–85, Dept of Electronic and Electrical Engrg, UCL (Hon. Fellow, 1985); Rector, Imperial Coll., London Univ., 1985–93 (Hon. Fellow, 1995). Dir (non-exec.), BT (formerly British Telecom), 1987–93; Chairman: Hydroventuri Ltd, 2001–03; Ocean Power Technologies, Inc., 2003–08. Pres., IEE, 1987–88 (Vice-Pres., 1980–83; Dep. Pres., 1984–86); Treas. and Vice-Pres., Royal Soc., 1997–2002; Mem., Exec. Bd, Fellowship of Engrg, 1981–84. Chm., BBC Science Advisory Cttee, 1987–90. Trustee: Science Mus., 1987–91; Wolfson Foundn, 1988–. Sec., Royal Instn, 1984–88 (Vice Pres., 1980–82; Manager, 1980–84; Vice Pres. and Chm. of Council, 1995–99). Foreign Member: NAE, US, 2001; Russian Acad. of Sci., 2003. Marconi International Fellowship, 1984. Dr *hc* Aston, 1987; Leicester, 1987; Institut National Polytechnique de Grenoble, 1987; Edinburgh, 1988; Polytechnic Univ., NY, 1988; Westminster, 1992; Sussex, 1993; Glasgow, 1994; Chinese Univ. of Hong Kong, 1994; City Univ. of Hong Kong, 1998; Surrey, 2001; Nanyang Technol Univ., Singapore, 2002. Faraday Medal, IEE, 1980; Royal Medal, Royal Soc., 1986. National Order of Merit (France), 1990. *Publications:* patents; papers on topics in physical electronics in various engrg and physics jls. *Recreations:* music, swimming. *Address:* 11 Ripplevale Grove, N1 1HS.

ASH, Dame Margaret; *see* Barbour, Dame M.

ASH, Timothy John G.; *see* Garton Ash.

ASHBERG, Judith; *see* Piatkus, J.

ASHBOURNE, 4th Baron *cr* 1885; **Edward Barry Greynville Gibson;** Lieutenant-Commander RN, retired; *b* 28 Jan. 1933; *s* of 3rd Baron Ashbourne, CB, DSO, and Reta Frances Manning (*d* 1996), *e d* of E. M. Hazeland, Hong Kong; *S* father, 1983; *m* 1967, Yvonne Georgina, *d* of Mrs Flora Ham, of Malin, County Donegal; three *s*. *Educ:* Rugby. RN, 1951–72; Kitcat and Aitken, stockbrokers, 1972–73, 1976–79; Vickers, da Costa & Co. Ltd, stockbrokers, 1973–76; Save & Prosper Gp, 1979–81; GT Management, 1981–88; MoD, 1989–93. Pres., Christian Broadcasting Council, 1998–. Pres., Hampshire Autistic Soc. *Heir: s* Hon. Edward Charles d'Olier Gibson [*b* 31 Dec. 1967; *m* 2001, Tanya Louise (marr. diss. 2013), *d* of Bryan Beckett, OBE; two *s* one *d*]. *Address:* Colebrook Barn, East Harting Farm, Petersfield, Hants GU31 5LU.

ASHBOURNE, (Kenneth) John (Turner); artist (primarily sculpture and photography); public and private sector chief executive and company chairman, now retired; *b* 16 July 1938; *s* of Ernest John Ashbourne and Phyllis Turner Ashbourne; *m* 1959, Valerie Anne Sado; one *s* one *d*. *Educ:* St Dunstan's Coll.; London Sch. of Econs (BSc Econs 1959). Teacher, then lectr, 1959–68; Mgt Develt Officer, BAC, 1968–71; Hd, Corporate Planning, London Borough of Lewisham, 1971–74; Asst Chief Exec., Suffolk CC, 1974–77; Chief Exec., Royal Borough of Kingston-upon-Thames, 1977–80; Dep. Man. Dir, Express Newspaper Gp, 1980–83; Sen. Consultant, Hay-MSL, 1983–85; Chief Executive: Cambridge HA, 1985–91; Addenbrooke's Hosp., then Addenbrooke's NHS Trust, 1991–98; E Anglian Ambulance NHS Trust, 1999. Chairman: Chapter Ltd, 1999–2012; Enterprise Cradle Ltd, 2001–12. Sen. Mem., Hughes Hall, 1992–2000, and Affiliate Lectr, Clinical Sch., 1994–2000, Univ. of Cambridge. Chm., UK Univ. Hosps Forum, 1998–2000. Founder and Hon. Dir, Shelby Transplant Trust, 1994–2000. Gov., Anglia Poly. Univ., 1996–2000. Mem. Nat. Council, British Falconers' Club, 1977–88; Mem., 1980–86, Vice-Chm., 1983–86, Hawk Bd, DoE. Mem., Ontario Soc. of Artists. *Recreations:* music, birds of prey. *Address:* 248400 5th Side Road, Mono, ON L9W 6L2, Canada.

ASHBROOK, 11th Viscount *cr* 1751 (Ire.); **Michael Llowarch Warburton Flower;** JP; DL; Baron Castle Durrow 1733; landowner; Vice Lord-Lieutenant, Cheshire, 1990–2010; *b* 9 Dec. 1935; *s* of 10th Viscount Ashbrook and Elizabeth, *er d* of Capt. John Egerton-Warburton and Hon. Mrs Waters; *S* father, 1995; *m* 1971, Zoë Mary Engleheart; two *s* one *d*. *Educ:* Eton; Worcester Coll., Oxford (MA Mod. Hist.). 2nd Lieut, Grenadier Guards, 1955. Solicitor, 1963; Partner, Farrer & Co., Solicitors, 1966–76; Partner, then Consultant, Pannone & Partners (formerly March Pearson & Skelton), 1985–96. Chm., Taxation Sub-Cttee, 1984–86, Pres., Cheshire Branch, 1990–99, CLA. Hon. DBA Chester, 2012. DL 1982, JP 1983, Cheshire. *Recreations:* gardening, the countryside, shooting. *Heir: s* Hon. Rowland Francis Warburton Flower [*b* 16 Jan. 1975; *m* 2004, Annika Jane, *d* of Julian Beavan; one *s* two *d*]. *Address:* The Old Parsonage, Arley Green, Northwich, Cheshire CW9 6LZ. *T:* (01565) 777277. *Club:* Brooks's.

See also Sir C. J. Hoare, Bt.

ASHBROOK, Kate Jessie; General Secretary, Open Spaces Society, since 1984; *b* 1 Feb. 1955; *d* of John Ashbrook and Margaret Balfour; lives with Christopher Myles Hall, *qv*. *Educ:* Benenden Sch., Kent; Exeter Univ. (BSc). Mem., Exec. Cttee, Open Spaces Soc., 1978–84; Campaign for National Parks (formerly Council for National Parks): Mem., Exec. Cttee, later Trustee, 1983–; Vice-Chm., 1998–2003; Chm., 2003–09; Ramblers' Association: Trustee, 1982–2012; Vice-Chm., 1993–95; Chm., Exec. Cttee, later Bd of Trustees, 1995–98, 2006–09; Pres., 2012–; Chm., Access Cttee, 1997–2009; Footpath Sec., Bucks and W Middx, 1986–; Member: Common Land Forum, 1984–86; Countryside Agency, 1999–2006; Nat. Parks Review Adv. Panel, DEFRA, 2002; Common Land Stakeholder Wkg Gp, DEFRA, 2002–03; Natural England Rights of Way Stakeholder Gp, 2008–; Adv. Mem., Thames Basin Heaths Special Protection Area Jt Strategic Partnership Bd, 2007–. Chm., Central Rights of Way Cttee, 1991–98; Sec., Countryside Link, 1989–92; Pres., Dartmoor Preservation Assoc., 1995–2011 (Hon. Sec., 1981–84; Trustee, 2011–). Mem., Inst. of Public Rights of Way and Access Mgt (formerly Inst. of Public Rights of Way Officers), 1999–. Patron, Walkers are Welcome Towns Network, 2008–. Chm., Turville Sch. Trust, 1994–95. Editor, Open Space, 1984–. *Publications:* (contrib.) The Walks of South-East England, 1975; (contrib.) Severnside: a guide to family walks, 1976; Saving Open Spaces, 2015; pamphlets; contribs to Oxford DNB, The Countryman and various jls. *Recreations:* pedantry, finding illegally blocked footpaths, learning British birdsong. *Address:* Telfer's Cottage, Turville, Henley-on-Thames RG9 6QL. *T:* (01491) 638396, (office) (01491) 573535.

ASHBURNER, Prof. Michael, PhD, ScD; FRS 1990; Professor of Biology, University of Cambridge, 1991–2009, Professor Emeritus, 2010 (Director of Research, 2009–11); Fellow, Churchill College, Cambridge, since 1980; *b* 23 May 1942; *s* of Geoffrey Staton Ashburner and Diane Ashburner (*née* Leff); *m* 1963, Francesca Ryan, *d* of Desmond Francis Ryan and Isabel Ryan; one *s* two *d*. *Educ:* Royal Grammar Sch., High Wycombe; Churchill Coll., Cambridge (BA 1964, PhD 1968, ScD 1978). FRES 1975. University of Cambridge: Asst in Research, 1966–68; Univ. Demonstrator, 1968–73; Univ. Lectr, 1973–80; Reader in Developmental Genetics, 1980–91. Gordon Ross Res. Fellow, Calif Inst. of Technology, 1968–69; Visiting Professor: Univ. of California Sch. of Medicine, San Francisco, 1977–78; Univ. of Crete, 1985; Univ. of Pavia, Italy, 1990–96; Miller Vis. Prof., Univ. of California at Berkeley, 1986. Lectures: Goldschmidt, Hebrew Univ., Jerusalem, 1985; Osborne, Edinburgh Univ., 1991; Dacre, Peterhouse, Cambridge, 1992. Res. Co-ordinator, EMBL, 1994–98; Jt Hd, EMBL-European Bioinformatics Inst., 1998–2001. Member: EMBO, 1977, Council, 1988–91; Governing Council, Internat. Centre for Insect Physiology and Ecology, Nairobi, 1991–96; Council, Royal Soc., 2001–03. Pres., Genetical Soc., 1997–2000. Mem., Academia Europaea, 1989; Fellow, Japan Soc. for Promotion of Sci., 1992. Hon. Foreign Mem., Amer. Acad. of Arts and Scis, 1993; Hon. FRES 2012. Hon. Dr Biol Crete, 2002; Hon. DSc Edinburgh, 2003. *Publications:* (ed) The Genetics and Biology of Drosophila, 1976–86, 12 vols; (ed) Insect Cytogenetics, 1980; (ed) Heat Shock: from bacteria to man, 1982; Drosophila: a laboratory handbook, 1989, (jtly) 2nd edn 2005; Won for All: how the Drosophila genome was sequenced, 2006; contribs to scientific jls. *Recreations:* walking, watching birds. *Address:* 26 Commercial End, Swaffham Bulbeck, Cambs CB25 0NE. *T:* (01223) 812451.

ASHBURNHAM, Sir James Fleetwood, 13th Bt *cr* 1661, of Broomham, Sussex; *b* 17 Dec. 1979; *s* of John Anchitel Fleetwood Ashburnham (*d* 1981) and of Corinne Ashburnham (*née* O'Brien, now Merricks); *S* grandfather, 1999; *m* 2011, Yasmin, *er d* of Jurgen Effertz; one *s*. *Educ:* Sherborne; King's Coll., London. *Heir: s* Levent John Ashburnham, *b* 12 April 2013.

ASHBURTON, 7th Baron *cr* 1835; **John Francis Harcourt Baring,** KG 1994; KCVO 1990 (CVO 1980); Kt 1983; DL; Chairman: Barings plc, 1985–89 (non-executive Director, 1989–94); Baring Brothers & Co. Ltd, 1974–89 (a Managing Director, 1955–74); BP Co. plc, 1992–95 (Director, 1982–95); *b* 2 Nov. 1928; *er s* of 6th Baron Ashburton, KG, KCVO, DL and Hon. Doris Mary Thérèse Harcourt (*d* 1981), *e d* of 1st Viscount Harcourt; *S* father, 1991; *m* 1st, 1955, Susan Mary Renwick (marr. diss. 1984), *e d* of 1st Baron Renwick, KBE, and Mrs John Ormiston; two *s* two *d*; 2nd, 1987, Mrs Sarah Crewe, *d* of late J. G. Spencer Churchill. *Educ:* Eton (Fellow, 1982–97); Trinity Coll., Oxford (MA; Hon. Fellow 1989). Dep. Chm., Royal Insurance Co. Ltd, 1975–82 (Dir, 1964–82); Chairman: Outwich Investment Trust Ltd, 1968–86; Baring Stratton Investment Trust, 1986–97; Director: Trafford Park Estates Ltd, 1964–77; Dunlop Holdings Ltd, 1981–84; Jaguar, 1989–91; Mem. Court, Bank of England, 1983–91. Receiver-Gen., 1974–90, Lord Warden of the Stannaries, 1990–94, Duchy of Cornwall. Vice-Pres., British Bankers' Assoc., 1977–81; Pres., Overseas Bankers' Club, 1977–78. Chm., Accepting Houses Cttee, 1977–81; Chm., Cttee on Finance for Industry, NEDC, 1980–86. Member: British Transport Docks Bd, 1966–71; President's Cttee, CBI, 1976–79; Trustee and Hon. Treas., Police Foundn, 1989–2001; Member: Council, Baring Foundn, 1971–98 (Chm., 1987–98); Exec. Cttee, NACF, 1989–99. Trustee: Rhodes Trust, 1970–99 (Chm., 1987–99); Southampton Univ. Develt Trust, 1986–96 (Chm., 1989–96); Nat. Gall., 1981–87; Winchester Cathedral Trust, 1989– (Chm., 1993–2006). High Steward, Winchester Cathedral, 1991–2013. DL Hants, 1994. Hon. Fellow, Hertford Coll., Oxford, 1976. DUniv Southampton, 2007. *Heir: s* Hon. Mark Francis Robert Baring [*b* 17 Aug. 1958; *m* 1983, Miranda Caroline (marr. diss. 2014), *d* of Captain Charles St John Graham Moncrieff; two *s* two *d*]. *Address:* Lake House, Northington, Alresford, Hants SO24 9TG; 52 Carthew Road, W6 0DX. *Clubs:* Pratt's, Flyfishers', Beefsteak.

ASHBY, David Glynn; barrister; *b* 14 May 1940; *s* of Robert M. Ashby and Isobel A. Davidson; *m* 1965, Silvana Morena (marr. diss. 1998); one *d*. *Educ:* Royal Grammar Sch., High Wycombe; Bristol Univ. (LLB Hons). Called to the Bar, Gray's Inn, 1963; formerly in practice on SE Circuit. Member: Hammersmith Bor. Council, 1968–71; for W Woolwich, GLC, 1977–81; ILEA, 1977–81. MP (C) NW Leics, 1983–97. *Recreations:* gardening, sailing (Transatlantic 2003–04, Mediterranean 2005–06), music. *Address:* 7B Westleigh Avenue, SW15 6RF.

ASHBY, Prof. Deborah, OBE 2009; PhD; FMedSci; Professor of Medical Statistics and Clinical Trials, Imperial College London, since 2008; NIHR Senior Investigator, since 2010; *b* London, 21 Aug. 1959; *d* of George Herbert Davis and Jean Davis (*née* Martin); *m* 1982, Michael Owen Ashby (marr. diss. 2014); one *s* one *d*. *Educ:* Southend High Sch. for Girls; Univ. of Exeter (BSc Maths 1980); London Sch. of Hygiene and Tropical Medicine (MSc Med. Stats 1981); Royal Free Hosp. Sch. of Medicine (PhD 1984). CStat 1994. Res. Fellow, Royal Free Hosp. Sch. of Medicine, 1983–86; Lectr, 1987–92, Sen. Lectr, 1992–95, Reader, 1995–97, in Medical Statistics, Univ. of Liverpool; Prof. of Med. Stats, QMUL, 1997–2008. Member: Cttee on Safety of Medicines, 1999–2005; Commn on Human Medicines, 2005–14. Royal Statistical Society: Mem. Council, 1992–97; Vice Pres., 1993–95; Hon. Sec., 1998–2004. FMedSci 2012. *Publications:* (with S. Eldridge) Statistical Concepts, 2000. *Recreations:* seeing family and friends, walking and cycling in cities and countryside, genealogy, visiting art galleries. *Address:* Imperial Clinical Trials Unit, School of Public Health, Imperial College London, Norfolk Place, W2 1PG. *T:* (020) 7594 8704. *E:* deborah.ashby@imperial.ac.uk.

ASHBY, Francis Dalton, OBE 1975; Director, National Counties Building Society, 1980–90; retired; *b* 20 Jan. 1920; *s* of late John Frederick Ashby and late Jessie Ashby; *m* 1948, Mollie Isabel Mitchell (*d* 1999); one *s* one *d* (and one *d* decd). *Educ:* Watford Grammar Sch. Diploma in Govt Admin. War Service, Royal Signals, 1940–46: POW, Far East, 1942–45. National Debt Office: Exec. Officer, 1938; Asst Comptroller and Estabt Officer, 1966–76; Comptroller-General, 1976–80. *Recreations:* listening to music, retirement village activities, brain games. *Address:* 21 Badgers Walk, Chorleywood, Herts WD3 5GA.

ASHBY, Rt Rev. Godfrey William Ernest Candler; an Honorary Assistant Bishop, Diocese of Exeter, since 2012; *b* 6 Nov. 1930; *s* of late William Candler Ashby and Vera Fane Ashby (*née* Hickey); *m* 1957, Sally Hawtree; four *s* two *d*. *Educ:* King's School, Chester; King's Coll., London (BD, AKC, PhD). Deacon 1955, priest 1956; Assistant Curate: St Peter, St Helier, Morden, 1955–57; Clydesdale Mission, 1958; Priest-in-charge, St Mark's Mission, 1958–60; Subwarden, St Paul's Coll., Grahamstown, 1960–65; Priest-in-charge, St Philip's, Grahamstown, 1962–63; Rector of Alice and Lectr, Federal Theological Seminary, 1966–68; Sen. Lecturer, Old Testament and Hebrew, Rhodes Univ., Grahamstown, 1969–75; Assoc. Professor, 1974–75; Overseas Visiting Scholar, St John's Coll., Cambridge, 1975; Dean and Archdeacon, Cathedral of St Michael and St George, Grahamstown, 1976–80; Bishop of St John's (Transkei and S Africa), 1980–84; Prof. of Divinity, Univ. of Witwatersrand, Johannesburg, 1985–88; Asst Bp of Leicester, 1988–95; Priest-in-Charge, Newtown Linford, 1992–95; Hon. Assistant Bishop: George, S Africa, 1995–2008; Portsmouth, 2008–12. Hon. Canon, Leicester Cathedral, 1994. *Publications:* Theodoret of Cyrrhus as Exegete of the Old Testament, 1970; Sacrifice, 1988; Exodus (commentary), 1998; articles in theological jls. *Recreations:* ornithology, French literature. *Address:* 3 Gracey Court, Broadclyst, Devon EX5 3GA.

ASHBY, Prof. Michael Farries, CBE 1997; FRS 1979; FREng; Royal Society Research Professor, Department of Engineering, University of Cambridge, since 1989 (Professor of Engineering Materials, 1973–89); *b* 20 Nov. 1935; *s* of Baron Ashby, FRS; *m* 1962, Maureen Stewart; two *s* one *d*. *Educ:* Campbell Coll., Belfast; Queens' Coll., Cambridge (BA, MA, PhD). Post-doctoral work, Cambridge, 1960–62; Asst, Univ. of Göttingen, 1962–65; Asst Prof., Harvard Univ., 1965–69; Prof. of Metallurgy, Harvard Univ., 1969–73. Mem., Akad. der Wissenschaften zu Göttingen, 1980–. FREng (FEng 1993). Hon. MA Harvard, 1969. Editor: Acta Metallurgica, 1974–96; Progress in Materials Science, 1995–. *Publications:* Deformation Mechanism Maps, 1982; Engineering Materials, pt 1 1986, pt 2 1996; Materials Selection in Design, 1992, 3rd edn 2004; Cellular Solids, 1997; Materials and Design, 2002; Materials: engineering, properties, science, design, 2007; Materials and the Environment, 2009; Materials: engineering, science, processing and design, 2014; Materials and Sustainable Development, 2015. *Recreations:* music, design. *Address:* 51 Maids Causeway, Cambridge CB5 8DE. *T:* (01223) 301333.

ASHCOMBE, 5th Baron *cr* 1892; **Mark Edward Cubitt;** *b* 29 Feb. 1964; *s* of Mark Robin Cubitt and Juliet Perpetua Cubitt (*née* Woodall); *S* cousin 2013; *m* 1992, Melissa Mary, *o d* of Maj. Charles Hay; two *s*. *Heir: s* Hon. Richard Robin Alexander Cubitt, *b* 14 June 1995.

ASHCROFT, Baron *cr* 2000 (Life Peer), of Chichester in the County of West Sussex; **Michael Anthony Ashcroft,** KCMG 2000; PC 2012; international businessman and entrepreneur; *b* 4 March 1946; *s* of Frederic Parker Ashcroft and Mary Lavinia Long; *m* 1st, 1972, Wendy Mahoney (marr. diss. 1984); two *s* one *d*; 2nd, 1986, Susi Anstey. *Educ:* King Edward VI Grammar Sch., Norwich; Royal Grammar Sch., High Wycombe; Mid-Essex Tech. Coll., Chelmsford. Varied business interests in public and private cos in UK, USA and Caribbean. Chairman: Hawley Group, later ADT Ltd, 1977–97; BB Hldgs, later BCB Hldgs, 1987–2010; Dir, Tyco Internat., 1984–2002. Ambassador from Belize to the UN, 1998–2000. Party Treas., Conservative Party, 1998–2001; a Dep. Chm., Conservative and Unionist Party, 2005–10; Treas., Internat. Democratic Union, 2007–. Mem., H of L, 2000–15. Sen. Ind. Advr on Sovereign Base Areas, Cyprus, 2011; Govt Special Rep. for Veterans' Transition, 2012– (report, Veterans' Transition Review, 2014). Founder and Chm., Crimestoppers Trust, 1988–. Chm., Ashcroft Technology Acad. (formerly ADT Coll.), 1991–; Chancellor, Anglia Ruskin Univ., 2001–. Pres. and Trustee, W India Cttee, 2011–; Trustee: Cleveland Clinic, 2004–; Imperial War Mus. and Foundn, 2010–. Vice Patron, Intelligence Corps Mus., 2009–. *Publications:* Smell the Coffee: a wake up call to the Conservative Party, 2005; Dirty Politics, Dirty Times, 2005; Victoria Cross Heroes, 2006; Special Forces Heroes, 2008; George Cross Heroes, 2010; Minority Verdict: the Conservative Party, the voters and the 2010 election, 2010; Heroes of the Skies, 2012; Special Ops Heroes, 2014. *Recreations:* researching the Victoria Cross, entertaining friends, trying something new, messing about in boats. *W:* www.lordashcroft.com.

ASHCROFT, Andrew Richard; HM Diplomatic Service, retired; Chief Executive, Ambassador Communications, since 2008; Joint Director: Astro Inc./Koolskools Ethical School Clothing, since 2009; FAIR4DR, since 2011; *b* 28 May 1961; *s* of Ivor John Ashcroft and Amy Joan Ashcroft; *m* 1st, 2001, Dr Amanda Sives (marr. diss. 2006); 2nd, 2012, Anna

Zofia Danielewicz. *Educ:* Worle Sch., Weston-super-Mare; Millfield Sch. Entered FCO, 1980; Finance Dept, then S Asian Dept, FCO, 1980–82; 3rd Sec. (Commercial), Muscat, 1982–86; 3rd, later 2nd Sec. (Chancery), Tel Aviv, 1987–91; Asst Private Sec. to Minister of State (ME, Near East, N Africa and Former Soviet Union and Central Eastern Europe), FCO, 1991–95; 1st Sec. (Commercial), Harare, 1996–99; Hd, Caribbean Section, FCO, 1999–2001; Ambassador, Dominican Republic and Haiti, 2002–06; FCO, London, 2006–07. Mem. Bd, New Forest Business Partnership, 2010–. *Recreations:* music (trumpet, piano and singing), cricket, golf, tennis. *Address:* 103 The Meadows, Lyndhurst, Hants SO43 7EJ. *T:* (023) 8028 3723, 07757 978898. *Club:* Royal Harare Golf.

ASHCROFT, Emma Georgina Annalies; *see* Fielding, E. G. A.

ASHCROFT, Dame Frances Mary, DBE 2015; PhD, ScD; FRS 1999; Professor of Physiology, University of Oxford, 1996–2001 and since 2011 (Royal Society GlaxoSmithKline Research Professor, 2001–11); Fellow, Trinity College, Oxford, since 1992; *b* 15 Feb. 1952; *d* of John and Kathleen Ashcroft. *Educ:* Talbot Heath Sch., Bournemouth; Girton Coll., Cambridge (BA 1974; MA 1978; PhD 1979; ScD 1996). MRC Trng Fellow, Physiol., Leicester Univ., 1978–82; Oxford University: Demonstrator in Physiol., 1982–85; EPA Cephalosporin Jun. Res. Fellow, Linacre Coll., 1983–85; Royal Soc. 1983 Univ. Res. Fellow, Physiol., 1985–90; Lecturer in Physiology: Christ Church, 1986–87; Trinity Coll., 1988–89; Univ. Lectr in Physiol., 1990–96; Tutorial Fellow in Medicine, St Hilda's Coll., 1990–91. Grass Foundn Fellow, 1978; Muscular Dystrophy Assoc. Fellow, Physiol., UCLA, 1981–82. G. L. Brown Prize Lectr, 1997; Peter Curran Lectr, Yale Univ., 1999; Charitable Infirmary Lectr, RCSI, 2003; Linacre Lect., Cambridge Univ., 2006; Kroc Lect., Uppsala Univ., 2008; Rodney Porter Lect., Oxford Univ., 2008; Mendel Lect., Brno, 2009; Croonian Lect., Royal Soc., 2013. FMedSci 1999. DUniv Open, 2003; Hon. DSc: Leicester, 2007; Radboud, 2013. Frank Smart Prize, Cambridge Univ., 1974; Andrew Cudworth Meml Prize, 1990; G. B. Morgagni Young Investigator Award, 1991; Charter Award, Inst. of Biology, 2004; Walter Cannon Award, Amer. Physiol. Soc., 2007; Albert Renold Prize, Eur. Assoc. for the Study of Diabetes, 2007; Feldberg Foundn Prize, 2010; Eur. Laureate, L'Oréal/UNESCO Women in Sci. Award, 2010; Lewis Thomas Prize for Writing about Science, Rockefeller Univ., 2013. *Publications:* (with S. J. H. Ashcroft) Insulin-Molecular Biology to Pathology, 1992; Ion Channels and Disease, 1999; Life at the Extremes: the science of survival, 2000; The Spark of Life, 2012; res. papers in Nature, Jl Physiology, etc. *Recreations:* reading, writing, walking, sailing. *Address:* Department of Physiology, Anatomy and Genetics, Parks Road, Oxford OX1 3PT.

ASHCROFT, Jane Rachel, CBE 2014; Chief Executive, Anchor Trust, since 2010; *b* Liverpool, 17 June 1966; *d* of Alan Geoffrey and June Rachel Williams; *m* 1990, Andrew Jonathan Ashcroft. *Educ:* Univ. of Stirling (BA Hons Modern Hist. 1988). Grad. trainee, 1988–89, Co. Secretarial Asst, 1989–91, Personnel Officer, 1991–93, Midlands Electricity plc; HR Mgr, 1993–95, Co. Sec., 1995–97, Bromford Housing Gp; Personnel Dir (Care First), BUPA, 1997–99; Hd of HR, then Man. Dir, Care Services, Anchor Trust, 1999–2010. Non-executive Director: Stroud and Swindon Building Soc., 2007–10; Dignity plc, 2012–. Care England (formerly English Community Care Assoc.), 2009–. MCIPD 1995. FCIS 2006. *Recreations:* reading, historical biography, running, theatre, ballet. *Address:* Anchor Trust, The Heals Building, 22–24 Torrington Place, WC1E 7HJ. *T:* (020) 7759 7200, *Fax:* (020) 7759 7201. *E:* jane.ashcroft@anchor.org.uk.

ASHCROFT, Hon. John David, JD; Attorney General of the United States of America, 2001–04; Founder and Chairman, Ashcroft Group, LLC, since 2005; *b* Chicago, 9 May 1942; *m* Janet Elise; two *s* one *d*. *Educ:* Yale Univ.; Univ. of Chicago (JD 1967). Admitted: Missouri State Bar; US Supreme Court Bar. In private practice, Springfield, Mo, 1967–73; Associate Prof., SW Missouri State Univ., Springfield, 1967–72; State Auditor, 1973–75, Asst Attorney Gen., 1975–77, Attorney Gen., 1977–84, Gov., 1985–93, Missouri; Attorney, Suelthaus and Kaplan, 1993–94; US Senator Missouri, 1995–2001. *Publications:* (with Janet E. Ashcroft) College Law for Business; (with Janet E. Ashcroft) It's the Law, 1979; Lessons From a Father to his Son, 1998.

ASHCROFT, John Kevin, CBE 1990; Chief Executive, pro.manchester, since 2009; *b* 24 Dec. 1948; *s* of Cumania Manion and late John Ashcroft; *m* 1972, Jennifer Ann (*née* King); two *s* one *d*. *Educ:* Upholland Grammar School; LSE (BSc Econ Hons); PhD Manchester Metropolitan Univ., 1996. Marketing Trainee, Tube Investments, 1970; Brand Manager, Crown Wallcoverings Internat. Div., 1974; Marketing Dir, Crown Wallcoverings French Subsidiary, 1976; Man. Dir, Coloroll, 1978–82, Dep. Chm. and Chief Exec., 1982–86, Chm., 1986–90; Chief Exec., Crabtree Consultancy Gp Ltd, 1990–2007. Dir, Marketing Manchester, 2010–; Mem., Gtr Manchester Business Leadership Council, 2010–. Vis. Prof., Business Sch., Manchester Metropolitan Univ., 2010–; Executive in Residence, Manchester Business Sch., 2012. Young Business Man of the Year, The Guardian, 1987. *Recreations:* fine arts, opera, sports, wine.

ASHCROFT, Prof. Margaret, PhD; FRSB; Professor of Hypoxia Signalling and Cell Biology, University of Cambridge, since 2014; *b* Stirling, Scotland, 22 Jan. 1969; *d* of James Galbraith and Ann Armour Galbraith (*née* Miller); *m* 1991, Neville Richard Ashcroft; one *s*. *Educ:* Univ. of Bristol (BSc Hons Pharmacol. 1991; PhD Molecular/Cellular Biol. 1995). FRSB (FSB 2010). Postdoctoral Researcher, Eukaryotic Signal Transduction Section, 1995–97, Sen. Postdoctoral Researcher, Molecular Carcinogenesis Section, 1997–2000, Nat. Cancer Inst., Frederick Cancer Res. and Develt Center, Frederick, Md; Team Leader, Inst. of Cancer Res., 2000–07 (Hon. Team Leader, 2007–08); Reader in Cancer Biol., Imperial Coll. London, 2007–08; University College London: Reader in Cancer Biol., 2008–12; Hd, Centre for Cell Signalling and Molecular Genetics, 2008–14; Prof. of Molecular Cell Biol., 2012–14 (Hon. Prof. of Molecular Cell Biol., 2014–). Principal Investigator affiliated with: KCL/UCL Comprehensive Imaging Cancer Centre, 2009–14; CRUK and UCL Cancers Centre, UCL Cancer Inst., 2010–14. Postdoctoral Fellow, Human Frontier Scientific Prog., 1997–2000. Young Investigator Award: Nat. Cancer Inst., Frederick Cancer Res. and Develt Center, 1997, 1998, 1999; EACR, 2005. *Publications:* (contrib.) Tumor Suppressor Genes in Human Cancer, 2000; articles in learned jls. *Recreations:* martial arts, running (cross country and marathon), golf. *Address:* Department of Medicine, University of Cambridge, Clifford Allbutt Building, Cambridge Biomedical Campus, Hills Road, Cambridge CB2 0AH. *E:* m.ashcroft@medschl.cam.ac.uk.

ASHCROFT, Ven. Mark David; Archdeacon of Manchester, since 2009; *b* Rugby, 3 Sept. 1954; *s* of David Ashcroft and Joan Ashcroft; *m* 1977, Sally; three *s*. *Educ:* Ridley Hall, Cambridge; Fitzwilliam Coll., Cambridge (BA 1981); Worcester Coll., Oxford (MA 1982). Manager, Cairngorm Restaurant, Edinburgh, 1978–79; ordained deacon, 1982, priest, 1983; Curate, St Margaret, Burnage, 1982–85; Tutor, subseq. Principal, St Paul's Theol Coll., Kapsabet, Kenya, 1986–95; Rector, Christ Church, Harpurhey, 1996–2009; Area Dean, N Manchester, 2000–06. Hon. Canon, Manchester Cathedral, 2004–09. *Recreations:* RSPB (Mem.), photography, sport. *Address:* 14 Moorgate Avenue, Withington, Manchester M20 1HE. *E:* ArchdeaconManchester@manchester.anglican.org.

ASHCROFT, Noel Graham, AM 2012; JP; company director, leadership training and change management consultant; Company Executive, Griffin Group, Australia, since 2008; Agent General for Western Australia in London, 2005–08; *b* 2 May 1944; *s* of Arthur Joseph Ashcroft and late Eileen May Ashcroft; *m* 1st, 1968, Penelope Anthea Edwards (marr. diss. 2000); four *d*; 2nd, 2003, Susan Mary Feeney (*née* Zanco); two step *s*. *Educ:* St Francis Xavier Coll., Bunbury; St Ildephonsus Coll., New Norcia; Australian National Univ. (BSc Forestry 1967); Linacre Coll., Oxford (MSc 1974). Divl Forest Officer, 1968–80, Regl Forest Manager, 1980–83, Forests Dept, WA; Project Manager, Govt of WA Functional Review Cttee, 1983–86; Associate Dir, Barrack House Gp Pty, Ltd, 1986–89; Government of Western Australia: Dir, Dept of Resources Develt, 1989–2001; Exec. Dir, Office of Major Projects, 2001–03; Dep. Dir Gen., Dept of Industry and Resources, 2003–05. Member, Board: Australian Coal Research Ltd, 2010–; Geraldton Port Authy, 2012–; Dep. Chm., Mid West Ports Authy, WA, 2012–. Member: Oxford Soc. (WA), 2001–; Britain-Australia Soc., 2005–; Cook Soc., 2005–. JP WA, 2005–. Mem., Guild of Freemen of City of London, 2006–10. *Recreations:* building, furniture restoration, golf, fishing, sightseeing and touring, spiritual reading. *Address:* PO Box 955, Mount Lawley, WA 6929, Australia. *Club:* Western Australian (Perth).

ASHCROFT, Philip Giles; Solicitor, British Telecommunications, 1981–87; *b* 15 Nov. 1926; *s* of Edmund Samuel Ashcroft and Constance Ruth Ashcroft (*née* Giles); *m* 1st, 1968, Kathleen Margaret Senior (marr. diss. 1983); one *s*; 2nd, 1985, Valerie May Smith, *d* of late E. T. G. Smith. *Educ:* Royal Grammar Sch., Newcastle upon Tyne; Durham Univ. Admitted solicitor, 1951. Joined Treasury Solicitor's Dept, 1955; Asst Legal Adviser, Land Commn, 1967; Asst Treasury Solicitor, 1971; Under-Sec. (Legal), DTI, 1973; Legal Adviser, Dept of Energy, 1974–80; Dep. Solicitor to the Post Office, 1980–81. Legal Consultant, Registry of Friendly Socs and Building Socs Commn, 1988–96. *Recreations:* reading, listening to music.

ASHCROFT, Wendy Cowan, (Mrs B. Ashcroft); *see* Alexander, W. C.

ASHCROFT, Zoë Jane; Co-Founder, Capital Partner and Head, Corporate and Finance Group, Winston & Strawn London LLP, since 2003; *b* 6 Oct. 1965; *d* of Peter Ashcroft and Christine Zillah (*née* Hawley); *m* 2014, Piers Alexander Adamson. *Educ:* Clifton Prep. Sch., York; York Coll. for Girls; St Peter's Sch., York; Univ. of Bristol (LLB 1986); Guildford Coll. of Law. Lawyer, Turner Kenneth Brown, London and Hong Kong, 1987–94; Morgan, Lewis & Bockius: Associate, 1994–98; Partner, 1998–2003; Hd, UK Corporate/Business and Finance Gp, 2000–03. Dir, Sponsors for Educnl Opportunity, 2003–; Trustee, Climate Gp, 2006–. *Recreations:* travel, art, comedy, horse racing. *Address:* Winston & Strawn London LLP, CityPoint, One Ropemaker Street, EC2Y 9AW. *E:* zashcroft@winston.com. *Clubs:* Home House, Morton's.

ASHDOWN, family name of **Baron Ashdown of Norton-sub-Hamdon**.

ASHDOWN OF NORTON-SUB-HAMDON, Baron *cr* 2001 (Life Peer), of Norton-sub-Hamdon in the County of Somerset; **Jeremy John Durham Ashdown, (Paddy),** GCMG 2006; CH 2015; KBE 2000; PC 1989; High Representative of the International Community and EU Special Representative in Bosnia and Herzegovina, 2002–06; *b* 27 Feb. 1941; *s* of late John W. R. D. Ashdown and Lois A. Ashdown; *m* 1962, Jane (*née* Courtenay); one *s* one *d*. *Educ:* Bedford Sch. Served RM, 1959–71: 41 and 42 Commando; commanded 2 Special Boat Section; Captain RM; HM Diplomatic Service, 1st Sec., UK Mission to UN, Geneva, 1971–76; Commercial Manager's Dept, Westlands Gp, 1976–78; Sen. Manager, Morlands Ltd, 1978–81; employed by Dorset CC, 1982–83. Contested (L) Yeovil, 1979; MP Yeovil, 1983–2001 (L 1983–88, Lib Dem 1988–2001); Leader, Liberal Democrats, 1988–99. L spokesman for Trade and Industry, 1983–86; Lib/SDP Alliance spokesman on education and science, 1987; Lib Dem spokesman on NI, 1988–97. Pres., UNICEF (UK), 2009–. *Publications:* Citizen's Britain, 1989; Beyond Westminster, 1994; Making Change our Ally, 1994; The Ashdown Diaries, vol. 1, 2000, vol. 2, 2001; Swords and Ploughshares: bringing peace to the 21st century, 2007; A Fortunate Life (autobiog.), 2009; A Brilliant Little Operation: the cockleshell heroes and the most courageous raid of WW2, 2012; The Cruel Victory: the French Resistance and the battle for the Vercors 1944, 2014. *Recreations:* walking, gardening, wine making. *Address:* House of Lords, SW1A 0PW. *Club:* National Liberal.

ASHE, Ven. (Francis) John; Archdeacon of Lynn, and Warden of Readers, Diocese of Norwich, since 2009; *b* London, 11 Feb. 1953; *s* of Francis Patrick Bellesme and Marion Islay Ashe; *m* 1979, Shelagh Lesley Prouse; three *d*. *Educ:* Christ's Hospital, Horsham; Univ. of Sheffield (BMet 1974); Ridley Hall, Cambridge (CTh 1979). Metallurgist, Hadfield's Steel, Sheffield, 1974–75; Dir, Witley Enterprises, 1976–77; ordained deacon, 1979, priest, 1980; Curate, Parish of St Giles and St George, Ashtead, 1979–82; Priest-in-charge, St Faith's, Plumstead, SA, 1982–87; Rector, Wisley with Pyrford, Guildford, 1987–93; Vicar, Godalming, 1993–2001; Rural Dean of Godalming, 1996–2002; Team Rector, Godalming, 2001–09. Hon. Canon, Guildford Cathedral, 2003–09. Chaplain (pt-time), Rowley Bristow Hosp., Pyrford, 1987–91; Hon. Chaplain, Dunkirk Veterans, Pyrford Br., 1987–93. Mem., Gen. Synod, 2004–09. *Recreations:* woodturning/carpentry, gardening, running, photography. *Address:* Holly Tree House, Whitwell Road, Sparham, Norwich NR9 5PN. *T:* (01362) 688032. *E:* archdeacon.lynn@dioceseofnorwich.org.

ASHE, (Thomas) Michael; QC 1994; QC (NI) 1998; SC (Ire.) 2000; a Recorder, since 2000; *b* 10 March 1949; *s* of John Ashe and Nancy (*née* O'Connor); *m* 1977, Helen Morag Nicholson (marr. diss. 2007). *Educ:* Finchley Catholic Grammar Sch. Called to the Bar, Middle Temple, 1971, Bencher, 1998; called to Irish Bar, 1975, Northern Irish Bar, 1993. Estate Duty Office, CS, 1967–70; merchant banking, 1971–76; practice at the Bar, 1978–. Dep. Public Prosecutor, Min. of Finance, Singapore, 1988–90; an Asst Recorder, 1998–2000. Editor, Company Lawyer, 1983–2007. Hon. General Counsel to Brit. Inst. of Securities Laws, 1980–; Hon. Consultant to Commercial Crime Unit, Commonwealth Secretariat, 1980–84. Mem. Bd, Centre for Internat. Documentation on Organised and Economic Crime, Cambridge, 1990–; Guest Lectr, Fac. of Laws, Univ. of Cambridge, 1990–95. Diocese of Brentwood: Auditor and Notary, 1997–; Defender of the Bond, 2006–; Mem., Safeguarding Commn, Dio. of Westminster, 2012–. *Publications:* (jtly) Insider Trading, 1990, 2nd edn 1994; (jtly) Insider Dealing (Ireland), 1992; (jtly) Insider Crime, 1994; (jtly) Money Laundering, 2000, 2nd edn 2007; (jtly) Anti-Money Laundering Risks, Compliance and Governance, 2013; contrib. Money, 1980, and (jtly) Injunctions, 1991, in Halsbury's Laws of England, 4th edn; articles in legal periodicals. *Recreations:* walking, railways, Gregorian Chant, classical music, Irish traditional music. *Address:* 9 Stone Buildings, Lincoln's Inn, WC2A 3NN. *T:* (020) 7404 5055.

ASHENDEN, Rev. Canon Dr Gavin Roy Pelham; Vicar, St Martin de Gouray, Jersey, since 2012; Chaplain to the Queen, since 2008; *b* London, 3 June 1954; *s* of Michael Roy Edward Ashenden and Carol Ashenden (*née* Simpson, now Salmon); *m* 1996, Helen Mary Lowe; one *s* two *d*. *Educ:* Univ. of Bristol (LLB 1976); Oak Hill Theol Coll. (BA 1980); Heythrop Coll., Univ. of London (MTh 1989); Univ. of Sussex (DPhil 1998). Ordained deacon, 1980, priest, 1981; Curate, St James, Bermondsey, 1980–82; Vicar, St Antony's, Hamsey Green, Sanderstead, 1982–89; University of Sussex: Univ. Chaplain, 1989–2012; Sen. Lectr, Dept of English, 1989–2012. Canon, later Bursalis Canon, Chichester Cathedral, 2005–. Presenter: on faith and ethics, BBC Radio, BBC Sussex, BBC Surrey, 2008–11; Faith in England, BBC podcast, 2009–. Dir, Aid to Russian Christians, 1982–92; Patron, Child Aid to Russia, 2005–. Mem. Council, Keston Coll., 1982–92 (Vice Chm., 1990–92). *Publications:* Charles Williams: alchemy and integration, 2007; (contrib.) Charles Williams and His Contemporaries, 2009; (contrib.) Persona and Paradox: issues of identity in C. S. Lewis, 2012; contrib. to jls incl. Church Times, Anglo American Literary Jl, Seven, Third Way. *Recreations:* singing opera and oratorio, sailing off the Normandy Coast and walking expeditions from my water mill on the Cotentin Peninsula, discussing metaphysics with the sceptical and inquisitive. *Address:* The Vicarage, Le Grande Route de Faldouet, St Martin, Jersey JE3 6UA. *E:* Gavin@ashenden.org. *Club:* Sussex Yacht (Shoreham-by-Sea).

ASHER, Bernard Harry; Director and Vice-Chairman, Legal & General Group plc, 1998–2004; Chairman, Liontrust Asset Management plc, 2004–10; *b* 9 March 1936; *s* of Samuel Asher and Rebecca (*née* Fisher); *m* 1961, Batia Sislin; one *s* two *d*. *Educ:* LSE (BSc). S. Japhet & Co., 1957–59; English Electric Co., 1960–67; ITT Inc., 1967–74 and 1978–80; on secondment to NEDO, 1975–78; Hong Kong Bank, 1980–92; Chairman: HSBC Investment Bank Ltd, 1992–98; James Capel & Co., 1991–98; Samuel Montagu, 1993–98; Lonrho Africa, 1998–2004. Non-executive Director: Rémy Cointreau SA, 1992–95; The China Fund Inc., 1995–99; Randgold Resources Ltd, 1997–2008; Morgan Sindall plc, 1998–2009; China Shoto, 2005–; Hansard Global Investments, 2005–12; Medicapital Bank, 2005–. Investment Advr, RCP, 1998–. Trustee, The Health Foundn (formerly Healthcare Med. Trust, then PPP Foundn), 1998–. Vice Chm. Governors, LSE, 1998–2004. *Recreations:* opera, walking. *Clubs:* Reform; Hong Kong, Hong Kong Jockey.

ASHER, Jane; actress, writer and businesswoman; *b* 5 April 1946; *d* of late Richard A. J. Asher, MD, FRCP and Margaret Asher (*née* Eliot); *m* Gerald Scarfe, *qv*; two *s* one *d*. *Educ:* North Bridge House; Miss Lambert's PNEU. *Stage:* Will You Walk a Little Faster, Duke of York's, 1960; Wendy in Peter Pan, Scala, 1961; Bristol Old Vic, 1965; Romeo and Juliet and Measure for Measure, NY, 1967; Look Back in Anger, Royal Court, 1969; The Philanthropist, Mayfair and NY, 1970; Treats, Royal Court, 1975; National Theatre, 1976; Whose Life is it Anyway?, Mermaid and Savoy, 1978; Before the Party, Queen's, 1978; Blithe Spirit, Vaudeville, 1986; Henceforward, Vaudeville, 1988; The School for Scandal, NT, 1990; Making it Better, Criterion, 1992; The Shallow End, Royal Court, 1997; Things We Do For Love, Gielgud, 1998; House, and Garden, RNT, 2000; What the Butler Saw, tour, 2001; Festen, Almeida, transf. Lyric, 2004; The World's Biggest Diamond, Royal Court, 2005; Bedroom Farce, Rose Th., Kingston, 2009; Snow White and the Seven Dwarfs, Richmond Th., 2009; The Reluctant Debutante, tour, 2011; Farewell to the Theatre, The Importance of Being Earnest, Rose Th., Kingston, 2011; Charley's Aunt, Menier Chocolate Factory, 2012; Pride & Prejudice, Regent's Park, 2013; Moon Tiger, tour, 2014; The Gathered Leaves, Park Th., 2015; *films include:* Mandy, 1951; Greengage Summer, 1961; Alfie, 1966; Deep End, 1970; Henry VIII and his Six Wives, 1970; Runners, 1984; Dream Child, 1985; Paris by Night, 1988; The Maidens' Conspiracy, 2005; Death at a Funeral, 2007; I Give It a Year, 2013; *television includes:* Brideshead Revisited, 1981; The Mistress, 1986; Wish Me Luck, 1987–89; Eats for Treats, 1990; Tonight at 8.30, Murder Most Horrid, 1991; Closing Numbers, 1993; The Choir, 1995; Good Living, 1997, 1998; Crossroads, 2003; Miss Marple, 2004; New Tricks, 2005; A For Andromeda, 2006; Holby City, 2007, 2008, 2009, 2010; The Palace (series), 2008; Maestro, 2008; The Old Guys, 2009, 2010; Poirot, 2009; Dancing on the Edge, 2012; Eve, 2015; Stella, 2015; numerous plays for radio; Radio Actress of the Year Award, 1986. Member: BBC Gen. Adv. Council, 1991–; BAFTA, 1985; Forum, 1993–. President: Nat. Autistic Soc., 1997– (Vice Pres., 1990–97); Arthritis Care, 2003–; Parkinson's UK (formerly Parkinson's Disease Soc.), 2007–; Vice-President: Nat. Deaf Children's Soc., 2003–08; Autistica, 2010–; Trustee: Child Accident Prevention Trust, 1992–96; Ford Martin Trust for Cancer in Children, 1993–95; WWF, 1994–98; Children in Need, 1995–99. Governor, Molecule Theatre. Started business, Jane Asher Party Cakes, London, 1990; designer and consultant for Sainsbury's cakes, 1992–99; Consultant, Debenhams, 1999–2004. Columnist: Today newspaper, 1994–95; The Express, 1998–2001. FRSA 1989. Hon. LLD Bristol, 2001. *Publications:* Jane Asher's Party Cakes, 1982; Jane Asher's Fancy Dress, 1983; Silent Nights for You and Your Baby, 1984; Jane Asher's Quick Party Cakes, 1986; Moppy is Happy, 1987; Moppy is Angry, 1987; Easy Entertaining, 1987; Keep Your Baby Safe, 1988; Children's Parties, 1988; Calendar of Cakes, 1989; Eats for Treats, 1990; Jane Asher's Book of Cake Decorating Ideas, 1993; Round the World Cookbook, 1994; Time to Play, 1995; The Longing, 1996; 101 Things I wish I'd known before…, 1996; The Best of Good Living, 1998; The Question, 1998; Good Living at Christmas, 1998; Tricks of the Trade, 1999; Losing It, 2002; Cakes For Fun, 2005; Moppy is Calm, 2005; Moppy is Sad, 2005; Beautiful Baking, 2007; journalism for newspapers and magazines. *Recreations:* reading, The Times crossword. *Address:* c/o United Agents, 12–26 Lexington Street, W1F 0LE. *T:* (020) 3214 0800.

ASHFOLD, Prof. Michael Norman Royston, PhD; FRS 2009; Professor of Physical Chemistry, University of Bristol, since 1992; *b* Bridgwater, Som, 19 June 1954; *s* of Kenneth Norman George and Gwendoline May Ashfold; *m* 1977, Julie Carolyn Favell; two *s*. *Educ:* Weston-super-Mare Grammar Sch. for Boys; Birmingham Univ. (BSc Hons Chem.; PhD Phys. Chem. 1978). Guy Newton Jun. Res. Fellow, Jesus Coll., Oxford, 1978–81; School of Chemistry, University of Bristol: Lectr in Chem. Physics, 1981–90; Reader in Chem. Physics, 1990–92. Vis. Fellow, Jt Inst. for Lab. Astrophysics, Univ. of Colo, 1990; EPSRC Sen. Res. Fellow, 1997–2002; Royal Soc. Leverhulme Trust Sen. Res. Fellow, 2011–12. Royal Society of Chemistry: Pres., Faraday Div., 2009–12; Chair, Sci., Educn and Industry Bd, 2012–. *Publications:* contribs to physical chem./chem. physics jls describing res. in broad areas of gas-phase and gas-surface chemistry. *Recreations:* family, walking, half-marathons, watching many other sports. *Address:* School of Chemistry, University of Bristol, Bristol BS8 1TS. *T:* (0117) 928 8312, *Fax:* (0117) 925 0612. *E:* mike.ashfold@bris.ac.uk.

ASHFORD, Archdeacon of; *see* Down, Ven. P. R.

ASHKEN, Kenneth Richard, CB 1996; JP; Director (Policy), Crown Prosecution Service, 1990–95; *b* 13 June 1945; *s* of Karol and Dulcinea Ashken; *m* 1st, 1969, Linda Salemink (marr. diss.); two *s* one *d*; partner, 1986, *m* 2nd, 1996, Patricia Almond (*d* 1996); one *d*; partner, Linda Demaris Wood. *Educ:* Whitgift Sch., Croydon; London Univ. (LLB Hons); Cambridge Inst. of Criminology (DipCrim). Admitted solicitor, 1972. Office of Director of Public Prosecutions, 1972; Asst Dir of Public Prosecutions, 1984; Hd of Policy and Inf. Div., 1986, Dir, Policy and Communications Gp (Grade 3), 1990, Crown Prosecution Service. UK Govt consultant to S African Ministry of Justice, 1998–99. Lay Chm., ind. review panels, NHS, 1998–2001; non-exec. Dir, Bromley Primary Care NHS Trust, 2001–04. Member: Cttee, SE London Probation Service, 1997–2001; London Area Bd, Nat. Probation Service, 2001–07. Mem., Funding Panel, Victim Support, 1997–2008 (Vice-Chair, 2006–08); Chair: S London Youth Panel, 2012; S London Trng and Devel t Cttee, 2014. FRSA 1990. JP SE London, 2000. *Recreations:* travel, opera, wine and other decadent retirement activities, working an allotment. *Club:* Royal Automobile.

ASHKENAZY, Vladimir; concert pianist; conductor; Music Director, European Union Youth Orchestra, since 2000; *b* Gorky, Russia, 6 July 1937; *m* 1961, Thorunn Johannsdottir, *d* of Johann Tryggvason, Iceland; two *s* three *d*. *Educ:* Central Musical Sch., Moscow; Conservatoire, Moscow. Studied under Sumbatyan; Lev Oborin class, 1955: grad 1960. Internat. Chopin Comp., Warsaw, at age of 17 (gained 2nd prize); won Queen Elisabeth Internat. Piano Comp., Brussels, at age of 18 (gold medal). Joint winner (with John Ogdon) of Tchaikovsky Piano Comp., Moscow, 1962. London debut with London Symph. Orch. under George Hurst, and subseq., solo recital, Festival Hall, 1963. Music Dir, RPO, 1987–94; Chief Conductor, Berlin Radio SO, subseq. Deutsches Symphonie-Orchester Berlin, 1989–99; Music Dir and Chief Conductor, Czech Philharmonic Orchestra, 1998–2003; Music Dir, NHK SO, Tokyo, 2004–07; Principal Guest Conductor, Orch. della Svizzera Italiana, Lugano, 2012–; Prin. Conductor and Artistic Advr, Sydney SO, 2009–13. Has played in many countries. Makes recordings (Grammy Awards, 1973, 1978, 1981, 1985, 1987; 1999, 2009). Hon. RAM 1972. Icelandic Order of the Falcon, 1971. *Publications:* (with Jasper Parrott) Beyond Frontiers, 1985. *Address:* Pilatusstrasse 13, 6045 Meggen, Switzerland.

ASHLEY, Cedric, CBE 1984; PhD; CEng, FIMechE; automotive engineering and e-learning consultant; Chairman: Cedric Ashley and Associates, since 1989; Euromotor Autotrain LLP, since 2006; Kings Gate Management Company (Cambridge) Ltd, since 2008; Director, AlphaPillars Ltd, since 2012; *b* 11 Nov. 1936; *s* of Ronald Ashley and Gladys Fincher; *m* 1st, 1960, Pamela Jane Turner (decd); one *s*; 2nd, 1965, (Marjorie) Vivien Gooch (marr. diss. 1991); one *s* one *d*; 3rd, 1991, Auriol Mary Keogh. *Educ:* King Edward's Sch., Birmingham; Mech. Engrg Dept, Univ. of Birmingham (BSc 1958, PhD 1964). CEng 1972; FIMechE 1978. Rolls-Royce Ltd, Derby, 1955–60; Univ. of Birmingham, 1960–73: ICI Res. Fellow, 1963; Lectr, 1966; Internat. Technical Dir, Bostrom Div., Universal Oil Products Ltd, 1973–77; Dir, Motor Industry Res. Assoc., 1977–87; Man. Dir, Lotus Engineering, 1987; Chief Exec., BICERI, 1989–91. Dir, Euromotor, Univ. of Birmingham, 1992–2006. Chairman: SEE, 1970–72; RAC Tech. Cttee, 1980–87; Member: SMMT Technical Bds, 1977–87; Board, Assoc. Ind. Contract Res. Orgns, 1977–86 (Pres., 1982–84); Automobile Div., IMechE, 1978–93 (Chm., 1990–91); Court, Cranfield Inst. of Technol., 1977–87; Engine and Vehicles Cttee, DTI, 1980–88; Three-Dimensional Design Bd, CNAA, 1981–87. Trustee, Sir Henry Royce Meml Foundn, 2006–13, 2014–. Liveryman, Carmen's Co., 1987. FRSA 1983. Cementation Muffelite Award, SEE, 1968; Design Council Award, 1974. TA, 1959–68. *Publications:* (contrib.) Infrasound and Low Frequency Vibration, ed Tempest, 1976; over 40 papers on various automotive and ICT topics incl. engine technol., vehicle ride, effect of vibration and shock on man and buildings, and e-learning, in learned jls. *Recreations:* travel, reading, classic cars. *Address:* (office) Euromotor Autotrain LLP, 58 Jacoby Place, Priory Road, Birmingham B5 7UW. *T:* (0121) 472 2082. *E:* c.ashley@autotrain.org.

ASHLEY, Jacqueline; President, Lucy Cavendish College, Cambridge, since 2015; *b* 10 Sept. 1954; *d* of Baron Ashley of Stoke, CH, PC; *m* 1987, Andrew William Stevenson Marr, *qv*; one *s* two *d*. *Educ:* Rosebery Grammar Sch., Epsom; St Anne's Coll., Oxford (MA PPE). Producer and Newsreader, Newsnight, BBC TV, 1980–83; Producer and Reporter, TV-am, 1983–84; Politics Producer, Channel 4 News, 1984–87; Editor, Their Lordships' House, Channel 4, 1987–88; Presenter, The Parliament Programme, Channel 4, 1988–89; Political Corresp., ITN, 1989–98; Presenter, People and Politics, BBC World Service, 1998–2000; Political Editor, New Statesman, 2000–02; columnist, The Guardian, 2002–15. Presenter, The Week in Westminster, BBC Radio 4, 1999–2015. *Recreations:* reading, swimming. *Address:* Lucy Cavendish College, Lady Margaret Road, Cambridge CB3 0BU.

ASHLEY, Michael St John, FCA; non-executive Director, since 2013, and Chairman, Audit Committee, since 2014, Barclays plc; *b* Redhill, Surrey, 19 Sept. 1954; *s* of John Gordon Ashley and Alice Ellen Ashley; *m* 1977, Janet Perry; four *s*. *Educ:* Dulwich Coll.; Trinity Coll., Cambridge (BA Maths 1976). ACA 1979, FCA 2002. Peat, Marwick, Mitchell & Co., later KPMG: Trainee Acct, 1976–78; Sen. Acct, 1978–79; Supervising Sen. Acct, 1979–81; Asst Manager, 1981–82; Consultant, 1982–84; Manager, 1984–85; Sen. Manager, 1985–89; Partner, 1989–95; Chief Financial Officer, NatWest Mkts, 1995–97; Partner, KPMG LLP, 1997–2013; Hd, Quality and Risk Mgt, KPMG Europe LLP, 2007–13. Chairman: Audit and Risk Cttee, Asset Protection Agency, 2009–12; Govt Internal Audit Agency, 2014–; Member: Audit and Risk Cttee, HM Treasury, 2009–15; Charity Commn, 2014– (Chm., Audit and Risk Cttee, 2014–). Member: Accounting Standards Bd, 2004–10; Ethics Standards Cttee, ICAEW, 2006–; Steering Gp, Financial Reporting Lab, 2011–. Mem., Tech. Expert Gp, Eur. Financial Reporting Adv. Gp, 2005– (Vice Chm., 2010–). Gov., Dulwich Coll. Prep. Sch. Trust, 2013–. *Recreations:* genealogy, dinghy sailing, fine wine. *Address:* Barclays plc, Level 31, One Churchill Place, E14 5HP. *Club:* Athenæum.

ASHLEY, Neil; Founder Chairman, Amey plc, 1989–2001; *b* 14 Nov. 1936; *s* of late Bernard Stephenson Ashley and of Nora Ashley (*née* Dixon); *m* 1st, 1961, Jane Evelyn Victoria (*d* 1995), *d* of late Granville Canty and of Vera Canty; two *s*; 2nd, 2002, Dr Shirley Anne, *d* of late Col George Frederick Preston Bradbrooke and Lillian (*née* Sibley). *Educ:* Barton-on-Humber Grammar Sch.; Battersea Poly.; Ashridge Mgt Coll. Man. Dir, ARC Construction Ltd, 1971–79; Dir, Balfour Beatty Construction Ltd, 1979–84; Man. Dir, Balfour Beatty Internat. Ltd, 1984–88; Jt Man. Dir, Balfour Beatty plc, 1985–89; Chairman: Balfour Beatty Projects Ltd, 1985–88; Balfour Beatty Canada Ltd, 1986–89; Balfour Beatty Malaysia SND BYD, 1986–88; Balfour Beatty Inc., 1987–89; Heery Internat. Inc. USA, 1987–89; Amey Construction Ltd, 1989–98; Amey Facilities Mgt Ltd, 1990–98; Amey Homes Ltd, 1991–98; Amey Building Ltd, 1992–98; Amey Railways Ltd, 1996–98. Chairman: Energy Power Resources, 1997–2003; Heritage Property Gp, 1997–2009; Courtenay Develts, 1998–2004; BPO Gp, 1999–2004; Oxford Radcliffe Hospitals NHS Trust, 2000–03; Vectra Gp, 2003–07; BPOSS Ltd, 2005–09. Non-executive Director: Volvere plc, 2002–11; Clarsen Goff Mgt Ltd, 2008–12. Mem., Nat. Council, 1994–2000, Chm., Southern Regl Council, 1995–97, CBI. Mem. Bd, British Road Fedn, 1993–98. Mem. Court, Oxford Brookes Univ., 2005– (Ind. Gov., 1997–2005; Chm., Audit Cttee, 1999–2005); Member: Med. Scis Bd, Oxford Univ., 2000–03; Inst. of Cancer Res., 2004 (Dep. Chm., Develt Bd, 2004–). Vice Pres. and Mem. Council, Lighthouse Club (Construction Ind. Charity), 1991– (Chm., 1998–2001); Chairman: Oxford Radcliffe Charities and Radcliffe Med. Foundn, 2000–03; Oxford Cancer Campaign, 2008–10; Oxford Univ. Hosps Trust (formerly Oxford Radcliffe Hosps Charitable Funds) Cancer Benefactors' Bd, 2010–. Chm. Trustees, Occtopus, 2004–; Trustee, Ashley (formerly Jane Ashley) Charitable Trust, 1995–; Patron: Dorchester Abbey Appeal, 1998–2006; Mulberry Bush Sch. (for care and educn of troubled children), 1998–; Vice-Patron, Purley Park Trust, 2003–07. FRSA 1993. Freeman, City of London, 1979; Liveryman, and Mem. Ct, Paviors' Co., 1979–. DUniv Oxford Brookes, 2006; Hon. Bachelor Surrey, 2011. *Publications:* contrib. numerous technical and commercial papers to jls and presentations on wide range of business topics. *Recreations:* boating, shooting, dogs, pyrotechnics. *Address:* Burcot Grange, Burcot, Oxon OX14 3DJ. *T:* (01865) 407106, *Fax:* (01865) 409969; 52 Upper Montagu Street, W1H 1SJ. *T:* and *Fax:* (020) 7569 8595. *E:* neil@bpogroup.com. *Clubs:* Leander (Henley); Middlesex CC; Clifton Hampton Cricket; Henley Rugby.

ASHLEY-COOPER, family name of **Earl of Shaftesbury**.

ASHLEY-MILLER, Dr Michael, CBE 1995; DPH; FFPH; FRCPE; FRCP; Secretary, Nuffield Provincial Hospitals Trust, London, 1986–95; *b* 1 Dec. 1930; *s* of Cyril and Marjorie Ashley-Miller; *m* 1958, Yvonne Townend; three *d*. *Educ:* Charterhouse; Oxford Univ.; King's Coll. Hosp.; London Sch. of Hygiene and Tropical Med. MA Oxon; BM BCh; DObstRCOG. FFPH (FFCM 1977); FRCPE 1985; FRCP 1990. Ho. Surg., Ho. Phys., King's Coll. Hosp., 1956–57; SMO, Dulwich Hosp., 1957; MO/SMO, RAF, 1958–61; SMO, IoW CC, 1961–64; MO/SMO, MRC (HQ Staff), 1964–74; PMO, SPMO, Scottish Home and Health Dept, 1974–86. Mem. Council, RSocMed, 1998–2002 (Pres., Gen. Practice Sect., 1994–95). Mem. Council, Stroke Assoc., 1997–2006. Hon. MRCP 1986; Hon. FRCGP 1994. FRSocMed 1996. *Publications:* (contrib.) Textbook of Public Health, Vol. III, 1985; (ed jtly) Screening for Risk of Coronary Heart Disease, 1987. *Recreations:* theatre, reading, visiting cathedrals. *Club:* Royal Society of Medicine.

ASHLEY-SMITH, Jonathan, PhD; FMA, FRSC, FIIC; consultant in collections risk; Secretary General, International Institute for Conservation, 2003–06; *b* 25 Aug. 1946; *s* of Ewart Trist and Marian Tanfield Ashley-Smith; *m* 1967, Diane Louise (*née* Wagland); one *s* one *d*. *Educ:* Sutton Valence Public Sch.; Bristol Univ. (BSc (Hons), PhD). FMA 1988. Post-doctoral research, Cambridge Univ., 1970–72; Victoria and Albert Museum, 1973–2004: Hd of Conservation, 1977–2002; Sen. Res. Fellow (Conservation Studies), 2002–04. Leverhulme Fellow, 1995; Sen. Mem., Wolfson Coll., Cambridge, 1995. Gp leader, EU Climate for Culture project on effects of climate change on cultural heritage, 2009–14. Member: UKIC,

1974– (Accredited Mem., 1999; Mem., Exec Cttee, 1978–; Vice-Chm., 1980; Chm., 1983–84); Crafts Council, 1980–83 (Mem., Conservation Cttee, 1978–83); Council for Care of Churches Conservation Cttee, 1978–85; Board of Governors, London Coll. of Furniture, 1983–85. Vis. Prof., RCA, 1999. Trustee, Leather Conservation Centre, 2009–13. FRSC 1987; FIIC 1985; Hon. FRCA 1992; FRSA 2000. Scientific Editor, Science for Conservators (Crafts Council series), 1983–84. Plowden Medal, Royal Patentholders Assoc., 2000. *Publications:* Risk Assessment for Object Conservation, 1999; articles in learned jls on organometallic chemistry, conservation risk, spectroscopy and scientific examination of art objects. *Recreations:* loud music, strong cider. *E:* jonathan.ashley.smith.1994@wolfsonemail.com.

ASHMORE, Admiral of the Fleet Sir Edward Beckwith, GCB 1974 (KCB 1971; CB 1966); DSC 1942; *b* 11 Dec. 1919; *er s* of late Vice-Admiral L. H. Ashmore, CB, DSO and late Tamara Vasilevna Schutt, St Petersburg; *m* 1942, Elizabeth Mary Doveton Sturdee (*d* 2014), *d* of late Rear-Admiral Sir Lionel Sturdee, 2nd Bt, CBE; one *s* one *d* (and one *d* decd). *Educ:* RNC, Dartmouth. Served HMS Birmingham, Jupiter, Middleton, 1938–42; qualified in Signals, 1943; Staff of C-in-C Home Fleet, Flag Lieut, 4th Cruiser Sqdn, 1944–45; qualified Interpreter in Russian, 1946; Asst Naval Attaché, Moscow, 1946–47; Squadron Communications Officer, 3rd Aircraft Carrier Squadron, 1950; Commander 1950; comd HMS Alert, 1952–53; Captain 1955; Chief Signal Officer, AFNORTH, 1956; Captain (F) 6th Frigate Sqdn, and CO HMS Blackpool, 1958; Director of Plans, Admiralty and Min. of Defence, 1960–62; Commander British Forces Caribbean Area, 1963–64; Rear-Adm., 1965; Asst Chief of the Defence Staff, Signals, 1965–67; Flag Officer, Second-in-Command, Far East Fleet, 1967–68; Vice-Adm. 1968; Vice-Chief, Naval Staff, 1969–71; Adm. 1970; C-in-C Western Fleet, Sept.–Oct. 1971; C-in-C, Fleet, 1971–74; Chief of Naval Staff and First Sea Lord, 1974–77; First and Principal Naval Aide-de-Camp to the Queen, 1974–77; CDS, Feb.–Aug. 1977. Dir, Racal Electronics plc, 1978–97. Gov., Suttons Hosp. in Charterhouse, 1976–2000. Queen's Diamond Jubilee Medal, 2012; Arctic Star, 2013; Ushakov Medal, 2014. *Publications:* The Battle and the Breeze: the naval reminiscences of Admiral of the Fleet Sir Edward Ashmore, 1997. *Recreations:* usual.

See also Sir John Sykes, Bt.

ASHMORE, Gillian Margaret; Recording Clerk, Society of Friends (Quakers), 2007–10; *b* 14 Oct. 1949; *d* of John Oxenham and Joan Oxenham; *m* 1971, Frederick Scott Ashmore; three *s* one *d*. *Educ:* Walthamstow Hall, Sevenoaks; Winchester Co. High Sch. for Girls; Newnham Coll., Cambridge (BA Hons Hist.). Depts of the Envmt and Tspt, 1971–86; seconded to Housing Corp., 1974; Dep. Dir, Enterprise and Deregulation Unit, Dept of Employment, 1986–87, then DTI, 1987–89; Head, Central Finance Div., Dept of Transport, 1990–92; Dir, Privatisation Studies, BRB, 1992–94; Regl Dir, Govt Office for SE, 1994–98; Principal, Mulberry Consulting, 1999–2007. Chief Exec., EOC, 2001–02. Chair: Kingston Victim Support, 1998–2001; Refugee Housing Assoc., 1999–2006; Exec. Dir, Fostering Network, 2003; Trustee: Metropolitan Housing Trust, then Metropolitan Housing Partnership, 1999–2006; Victim Support London, 1999–2001; Quaker Social Action, 2011–; Joseph Rowntree Foundn, 2011– (Chair, Audit Cttee, 2008–11). Gov., Richmond Adult and Community Coll., 2000–06. Associate, Newnham Coll., Cambridge, 1998–2009. FRSA 1995. *Recreations:* novels, history, talking, learning about science, walking, Religious Society of Friends (Quakers). *Address:* 47 Lower Teddington Road, Hampton Wick, Kingston, Surrey KT1 4HQ.

ASHMORE, Prof. Jonathan Felix, PhD; FRS 1996; FMedSci; Bernard Katz Professor of Biophysics, University College London, since 1996; *b* 16 April 1948; *s* of late Eric Peter Ashmore, theatre director, and Rosalie Sylvia Crutchley, actress; *m* 1974, Sonia Elizabeth Newby; one *s* one *d*. *Educ:* Westminster; Univ. of Sussex (BSc 1st cl. Mathematical Physics); Imperial Coll., London (PhD); University College London (MSc Physiology). Vis. Scientist, Internat. Centre for Theoretical Physics, Trieste, Italy, 1971–72; Nuffield Biological Scholar, 1972–74; Res. Asst, Dept of Biophysics, UCL, 1974–77; Fulbright Scholar, and Vis. Physiologist, Ophthalmology Dept, Univ. of California, San Francisco, 1977–80; Lectr, Univ. of Sussex, 1980–83; Lectr, 1983–88, Reader in Physiology, 1988–93, Prof. of Biophysics, 1993–96, Univ. of Bristol; Dir, UCL Ear Inst., 2004. Chaire Blaise Pascal, Institut Pasteur, Paris, 2007–09. G. L. Brown Lectr, Physiol Soc., 1992. Chief Scientific Advr, Defeating Deafness, subseq. Deafness Res. UK, 2002–07. Pres., Physiol Soc., 2012–14 (Vice Pres., 2010–12). Acted in film, A Kid for Two Farthings, 1955. FMedSci 2001. *Publications:* contribs to learned jls on cellular basis of hearing. *Recreation:* travel. *Address:* Department of Neuroscience, Physiology and Pharmacology, University College London, Gower Street, WC1E 6BT. *T:* (020) 7679 2141, *Fax:* (020) 7813 0530. *E:* j.ashmore@ucl.ac.uk.

ASHRAWI, Hanan; Media Director and spokesperson, Arab League, since 2001; Member, Palestinian Legislative Council, since 1996; *b* 1946; *m* Emile Ashrawi; two *d*. *Educ:* American Univ., Beirut; Univ. of Virginia. Prof. of English Literature, Chm. of English Dept, and Dean of Arts, Birzeit Univ., West Bank, 1973–90; Dir Gen., Human Rights Instn, Jerusalem. Joined Fatah, PLO; official spokesperson, Palestinian Delegn, 1991–93; Mem., and former Head, Palestinian Independent Commn for Palestinian Republic; Minister of Higher Educn, Palestinian Legislative Council, 1996–98; Mem. Exec. Cttee, Palestine Liberation Orgn, 2009–. *Publications:* A Passion for Peace, 1994; This Side of Peace, 1995. *Address:* c/o Palestinian Legislative Council, Jerusalem, West Bank, via Israel.

ASHTIANY, Saphieh, (Mrs P. L. Davies); Principal, Ashtiany Associates, since 2010; Special Counsel, Nabarro LLP, 2010–14; *b* Teheran, 2 Aug. 1949; *d* of Ali Asghar Nouredin Ashtiany and Amir Banou Faily; *m* 1973, Prof. Paul Lyndon Davies, *qv*; two *d*. *Educ:* Huntington Hse Sch.; Univ. of Warwick (BA Hons Philosophy and Politics); Univ. of Birmingham (MSocSc Pt 1 Internat. Relns). Refugee counsellor, UNHCR/UKIAS, 1976–79; volunteer, CAB, 1980–84; admitted as solicitor, 1986; Cole & Cole Solicitors, subseq. Morgan Cole: trainee and solicitor, 1984–89; Partner and Hd, Employment Dept, 1989–2000; Partner and Hd, Employment and Discrimination Gp, Nabarro Nathanson, subseq. Nabarro LLP, 2001–10. Vis. Professorial Fellow, QMUL, 2012–. Commissioner: EOC, 2000–07; LSE Commn of Inquiry into women, power and inequality. Non-exec. Dir, 1993–2003, Vice-Chair, 1996–2001, Actg Chair, 2001–03, Oxon Ambulance NHS Trust. Non-exec. Dir, Channel 4 Corp., 2003–09. Vice Chair, CAF, 2012– (non-exec. Dir, 2009–). Trustee: Oxford Philomusica, 2010– (Chair, Adv. Council); Equal Rights Trust (Chair, 2014–); Dir, Oxford Playhouse, 2011–; Mem., Adv. Bd, WNO, 2013–. *Publications:* (contrib.) Tottles Encyclopaedia on Employment Law, 1996–; contribs to Solicitors' Jl. *Recreations:* music, theatre, walking, cricket. *Address:* 21 Warnborough Road, Oxford OX2 6JA. *T:* (01865) 310232, 07585 771373. *E:* saphieh@ashtianyassociates.com.

ASHTON, family name of **Baron Ashton of Hyde**.

ASHTON OF HYDE, 4th Baron *cr* 1911; **Thomas Henry Ashton;** a Lord in Waiting (Government Whip), since 2014; *b* 18 July 1958; *s* of 3rd Baron Ashton of Hyde and Pauline Trewlove Ashton (*née* Brackenbury); *S* father, 2008; *m* 1987, Emma Louise, *d* of C. N. G. Allinson and Mrs J. R. W. Palmer; four *d*. *Educ:* Eton; Trinity Coll., Oxford (MA). Late Lt Royal Hussars (PWO), Royal Wessex Yeo. Vice Pres., Guy Carpenter & Co., Inc., 1990–92; Director: C. T. Bowring Reinsurance Ltd, 1992–93; D. P. Mann Ltd, 1996–99; Chief Executive Officer: Faraday Underwriting Ltd, 2005–13 (Dir, 1999–2013); Faraday Reinsurance Co. Ltd, 2005–13 (Dir, 2002–13). Member: Council of Lloyd's, 2010–13; Adv. Council, Century Capital LLP, Boston, 2006–14. Elected Mem., H of L, 2011. Mem., RCDS, 2013–14. Jt Master, Heythrop Hunt, 2007–09. *Heir: b* Hon. John, (Jack), Edward Ashton, *b* 30 Jan. 1966. *Address:* Broadwell Hill, Moreton-in-Marsh, Glos GL56 0UD. *Club:* Boodle's.

ASHTON OF UPHOLLAND, Baroness *cr* 1999 (Life Peer), of St Albans in the county of Hertfordshire; **Catherine Margaret Ashton,** GCMG 2015; PC 2006; High Representative of the European Union for Foreign Affairs and Security Policy, 2009–14, and a Vice-President, European Commission, 2010–14 (Member, 2008–14); *b* 20 March 1956; *d* of late Harold and Clare Margaret Ashton; *m* 1988, Peter Jon Kellner, *qv*; one *s* one *d*. *Educ:* Upholland Grammar Sch.; Bedford Coll., Univ. of London (BSc 1977). Admin. Sec., CND, 1977–79; Business Manager, The Coverdale Orgn, 1979–81; Dir of Public Affairs, BITC, 1983–89; freelance policy advr, 1989–99; on secondment from London First to Home Office, 1998–2001. Chm., E and N Herts, subseq. Herts, HA, 1998–2001. Parliamentary Under-Secretary of State: DFES, 2001–04; DCA, subseq. MoJ, 2004–07; Leader of the H of L, 2007–08. Vice Pres., Nat. Council for One-Parent Families. Trustee, Verulamium Mus. Chm. Governors, Spencer Jun. Sch., 1995–2001. *Recreations:* theatre, family. *Address:* House of Lords, SW1A 0PW.

ASHTON, Rt Rev. Cyril Guy; Bishop Suffragan of Doncaster, 2000–11; an Honorary Assistant Bishop in the Diocese of Liverpool and in the Diocese of Blackburn, since 2011, and in the Diocese of Carlisle, since 2015; *b* 6 April 1942; *s* of William Joseph Ashton and Margaret Anne Ashton (*née* Todd); *m* 1965, Muriel Ramshaw; three *s* one *d*. *Educ:* Oak Hill Theol Coll.; Lancaster Univ. (MA 1986). Ordained deacon, 1967, priest, 1968; Curate, St Thomas', Blackpool, 1967–70; Vocations Sec., CPAS, 1970–74; Vicar, St Thomas', Lancaster, 1974–91; Dir of Training, Dio. Blackburn, 1991–2000. Hon. Canon, Blackburn Cathedral, 1991–2000. *Publications:* Church on the Threshold, 1988, 2nd edn 1991; Threshold God, 1992; (with Jack Nicholls) A Faith Worth Sharing?: a Church Worth Joining?, 1995. *Recreations:* poetry, writing, music. *Address:* Charis, 17c Quernmore Road, Lancaster LA1 3EB.

ASHTON, John, CBE 2012; independent speaker and writer on contemporary questions, including climate politics, since 2012; Founder, E3G, 2004 (Chief Executive, 2004–06; Director, 2004–14); *b* 7 Nov. 1956; *s* of Prof. John Ashton and Prof. Heather Ashton; *m* 1983, Kao Fengning, (Judy); one *s*. *Educ:* Royal Grammar Sch., Newcastle upon Tyne; St John's Coll., Cambridge (MA). Radio Astronomy Gp, New Cavendish Lab., Cambridge, 1977–78; FCO 1978; Science Officer, Peking, 1981–84; Head, China Section, FCO, 1984–86; Cabinet Office, 1986–88; Rome, 1988–93; Dep. Political Advr to Governor, Hong Kong, 1993–97; Vis. Fellow, Green Coll., Oxford, 1997–98; Hd of Envmt, Sci. and Energy, then Envmt Policy, Dept, FCO, 1998–2002; Dir for Strategic Partnerships, LEAD Internat., 2002–04. Foreign Sec.'s Special Rep. for Climate Change, FCO, 2006–12. Vis. Prof., 2006–13, Dist. Policy Fellow, Grantham Inst. for Climate Change, 2013–14, Imperial Coll. London; Vis. Prof., Grantham Res. Inst., LSE, 2013–. Trustee: Tipping Point, 2012–; UK Youth Climate Coalition, 2012–. FRSA; Mem., ICA. *Recreations:* cricket, nature. *Address:* c/o E3G, 47 Great Guildford Street, SE1 0ES. *Clubs:* MCC; Kew Cricket; Kowloon Cricket.

ASHTON, Prof. John Richard, CBE 2000; Professor of Public Health Policy and Strategy, University of Liverpool, since 1993; President: Faculty of Public Health, Royal Colleges of Physicians, since 2013; Epidemiology and Public Health Section, Royal Society of Medicine, since 2014; Honorary Professor, Faculty of Public Health and Policy, London School of Hygiene and Tropical Medicine, since 2014; *b* Liverpool, 27 May 1947; *s* of Edward Ashton and Irene Ashton (*née* Pettit); *m* 1st, 1968, Pamela Scott (marr. diss. 2001); three *s*; 2nd, 2004, Catherine Benedicte, (Maggi), Morris; one *s*, and two step *s*. *Educ:* Quarry Bank High Sch., Liverpool; Univ. of Newcastle upon Tyne (MB BS 1970); London Sch. of Hygiene and Trop Medicine (MSc Soc. Med. 1978). FFPHM 1986; FRCPsych 1993; FFSRH (MFFP 1993), FRCPE 2003; FRCP 2004; FRSocMed 2004. House physician and surgeon, Newcastle Univ. Hosps, 1970–71; Registrar in Psychiatry and Family Practitioner, Newcastle, 1971–75; Lectr in Primary Care, Southampton Univ., 1975–76; Sen. Lectr in Preventive Medicine, LSHTM, 1980–82; Sen. Lectr in Public Health, Univ. of Liverpool, 1983–93; Regional Director of Public Health and Regional Medical Officer: Mersey, 1993–94; Govt Office for NW (formerly NW RHA, then NW Region, NHS Exec., DoH), 1994–2006; Dir of Public Health and County Medical Officer, NHS Cumbria (formerly Cumbria PCT) and Cumbria CC, 2007–13. Visiting Professor: Valencia Inst. Public Health, 1988; Liverpool John Moores Univ., 1998; Med. Sch., Univ. of Manchester, 2001–; Univ. of Central Lancs, 2004–; Univ. of Cumbria, 2008–; Professorial Fellow, Liverpool Sch. of Trop. Medicine, 1994; Fellow, Liverpool John Moores Univ., 2003. Advr on Urban Health, Health Policy, Public Health Educn and Violence, WHO; Neighbourhood Renewal Advr to UK govt, 2006–09. Mem., Liverpool Med. Instn, 1990–. Member: John Snow Soc.; Duncan Soc., 1998– (Life Pres., 2011); Chm., Woolton Soc., 2001–03. Trustee and Chm., UK Public Health Assoc., 2009–11; Trustee: Carlisle Youth Zone, 2010–13; Mus and Galls Liverpool, 2011–15; Kendal Arts Internat., 2012–13. FRSA 2012. Ed., Jl of Epidemiology and Community Health, 1997–2008. *Publications:* Everyday Psychiatry, 1980; The New Public Health, 1988; Esmedune 2000, 1988; Healthy Cities, 1992; (ed) The Epidemiological Imagination, 1994; The Pool of Life, 1997; contrib. articles on medical, public health and social issues. *Recreations:* Liverpool FC, fell walking, cycling, keeping chickens, contributing to regenerating Liverpool, outdoor education. *Address:* Ginny Hall, Dent, Cumbria LA10 5TD. *T:* (01539) 625281. *Club:* Athenæum (Liverpool).

ASHTON, Joseph William, OBE 2007; journalist; *b* 9 Oct. 1933; *s* of Arthur and Nellie Ashton, Sheffield; *m* 1957, Margaret Patricia Lee; one *d*. *Educ:* High Storrs Grammar Sch.; Rotherham Technical Coll. Engineering Apprentice, 1949–54; RAF National Service, 1954–56; Cost Control Design Engineer, 1956–68; Sheffield City Councillor, 1962–69. MP (Lab) Bassetlaw Div. of Notts, Nov. 1968–2001. PPS to Sec. of State for Energy, formerly Sec. of State for Industry, 1975–76; an Asst Govt Whip, 1976–77; Opposition Spokesman on Energy, 1979–81. Member, Select Committee: on Trade and Industry, 1987–92; on Home Affairs, 1989–92; on Nat. Heritage, 1992–97; on Modernising the House, 1997–98; Chm., Parly All-Party Football Cttee, 1992–2001. Dir, Sheffield Wednesday, 1990–99. Founder and Chm., Assoc. of Former Members of Parliament, 2001–11. Columnist for: Sheffield Star, 1970–75, 1979–80, 1990–91; Labour Weekly, 1971–82; Daily Star, 1979–87; Sunday People, 1987–88; Plus magazine, 1988–89. Columnist of the Year, What the Papers Say, Granada TV, 1984. *Publications:* Grass Roots, 1977; A Majority of One (stage play), 1981; Red Rose Blues (memoirs), 2000; Joe Blow, 2014. *Recreations:* football, reading, do-it-yourself, motoring, travel, films, theatre. *Address:* 16 Ranmoor Park Road, Sheffield S10 3GX. *T:* (0114) 230 7175.

ASHTON, Robin James; Chairman, Leeds Building Society, since 2013 (non-executive Director, since 2011); non-executive Director, Shawbrook Bank Ltd, since 2011; *b* 19 Jan. 1958; *s* of late Frederick James Ashton and of Florence Mary Ashton; *m* 1st, 1985, Elizabeth Miles (marr. diss. 2002); one *s* one *d*; 2nd, 2004, Jasna Mozetič; one *s*. *Educ:* Bradford Grammar Sch.; Durham Univ. (BA Hons Econs and Law). ACA. Coopers & Lybrand, 1979–83; Finance Dir, Provident Insurance plc, 1983–85; Finance Dir and Dep. Man. Dir, H. T. Greenwood Ltd, 1986–88; Man. Dir, Provident Investments Ltd, 1989; Provident Financial plc: Gp Treas., 1989–93; Finance Dir, 1993–99; Dep. Chief Exec., 1999–2001; Chief Exec., 2001–06; Chief Exec., London Scottish Bank plc, 2007–09; non-exec. Chm., Apple Holdco Ltd, 2010–11; non-executive Director: Albermarle & Bond Hldgs plc, 2012–13; Non-Standard Finance plc, 2014–. *Address:* 105 Albion Street, Leeds LS1 5AS.

ASHTON, Prof. Rosemary Doreen, OBE 1999; FRSL; FBA 2000; Quain Professor of English Language and Literature, University College London, 2002–12, now Emeritus; *b* 11 April 1947; *d* of late David Thomson and Doreen Sidley Thomson (*née* Rose); *m* 1971, Gerard Ashton (*d* 1999); two *s* one *d*. *Educ:* Univ. of Aberdeen (MA Hons English and German 1969); Newnham Coll., Cambridge (PhD 1974). Temp. Lectr, English Dept, Univ. of Birmingham, 1973–74; Lectr, 1974–86, Reader, 1986–91, Prof., 1991–2002, English Dept, UCL. Sen. Res. Fellow, Sch. of Advanced Study, Univ. of London, 2012–. FRSL 1999; Founding Fellow, English Assoc., 1999. FRSA 2002. Hon. Fellow, UCL, 2013. *Publications:* The German Idea: four English writers and the reception of German thought 1800–1860, 1980; Little Germany: exile and asylum in Victorian England, 1986; The Mill on the Floss: a natural history, 1990; G. H. Lewes: a life, 1991; The Life of Samuel Taylor Coleridge: a critical biography, 1996; George Eliot: a life, 1996; Thomas and Jane Carlyle: portrait of a marriage, 2002; 142 Strand: a radical address in Victorian London, 2006; Victorian Bloomsbury, 2012. *Recreations:* gardening, table tennis, listening to music.

ASHTON, Ruth Mary, (Mrs E. F. Henschel), OBE 1991; RN, RM, MTD; non-executive Director and Vice-Chairman, Bromley Primary Care NHS Trust, 2001–07; *b* 27 March 1939; *d* of Leigh Perry Ashton and Marion Lucy Ashton (*née* Tryon); *m* 1984, E. Fred Henschel. *Educ:* Kenya High Sch. for Girls; Clarendon Sch. (lately Abergele); London Hosp. and Queen Mother's Hosp., Glasgow; High Coombe Midwife Teachers' Training College (RN 1964; RM 1967; MTD 1970). Staff Midwife and Midwifery Sister, Queen Mother's Hosp., Glasgow, 1967–69; Nursing Officer and Midwifery Tutor, King's College Hosp., 1971–75; Tutor, 1975–79, Professional Officer, 1979, Gen. Sec., 1980–94, Royal College of Midwives. Non-executive Director: Optimum Health Services NHS Trust, 1994–99; Community Health S London NHS Trust, 1999–2000. Chm., Workforce Develt Confedn, NHS SE London, 2002–06. Temp. Advr on Midwifery, WHO, 1995. Treas., Internat. Confedn of Midwives, 1997–2002. Temp. Prof. March of Dimes, Los Angeles, 1982. Lay Mem., London Deanery Sch. of Gen. Practice Bd, 2007–11. ACIArb 1995. OStJ 1988. *Publications:* midwifery related articles. *Recreations:* gardening, travel, photography. *Address:* c/o National Westminster Bank, PO Box 192, 116 Fenchurch Street, EC3M 5AN. *T:* (home) (020) 8851 7403. *E:* ruhens@tiscali.co.uk.

ASHTON, William Michael Allingham, OBE 2010 (MBE 1978); Founding Musical Director, National Youth Jazz Orchestra of Great Britain, 1968–2010, now Life President; *b* Blackpool, 6 Dec. 1936; *s* of Eric Sandiford Ashton and Zilla Dorothea (*née* Miles); *m* 1966, Kay Carol Watkins; two *s* one *d*. *Educ:* Rossall Sch., Fleetwood; St Peter's Coll., Oxford (MA Hons Mod. Langs; DipEd 1962). Nat. Service, RAF, 1955–57. Professional musician, 1962–63; teacher of French in London schs, 1963–73. Founded London Schs Jazz Orch., 1965; became Nat. Youth Jazz Orch., 1968. Editor, News from NYJO, 1988–. Appeared in Royal Variety Perf., 1978; visits to America, Russia, Australasia, France, Poland, Portugal, Germany, Bulgaria, Turkey, Malta, Spain, Italy, etc.; appearances at festivals, film premières, etc. Numerous recordings. Has written over 60 recorded songs, incl. Wait and See, Much Too Much, It's Over, Accident Prone, Thought I'd Ask, Let's Settle Down, Why Don't They Write Songs Like This Any More?, Don't Go to Her. Member: Arts Sub-cttee, Internat. Year of the Child, 1979; Cttee, Assoc. British Jazz Musicians, 1988–. Fellow, City of Leeds Coll. of Music, 1995. BP ABSA Award, 1991; Music Retailers Assoc. Annual Awards for Excellence, 1984, 1990; NYJO voted Best British Big Band, British Jazz Awards, 1993, 1995, 1998, 2002; BBC R2 Award for services to British jazz, 1995; Silver Medal for Jazz, Musicians' Co., 1996; Special Award, All Party Jazz Appreciation Gp, 2007. *Recreations:* song writing, snorkelling, reading. *Address:* 11 Victor Road, Harrow, Middx HA2 6PT. *T:* (020) 8863 2717. *E:* bill.ashton@virgin.net.

ASHTOWN, 8th Baron *cr* 1800 (Ire.); **Roderick Nigel Godolphin Trench;** *b* 17 Nov. 1944; *o s* of 7th Baron Ashtown, KCMG and Marcelle Clotterbooke Patijn; *S* father, 2010; *m* 1st, 1967, Janet (*d* 1971), *d* of Harold Hamilton-Faulkner; one *s*; 2nd, 1973, Susan Barbara Wright, *d* of Lewis Frank Day, FRCS, DLO; one *d*. *Educ:* Eton; Stanford Univ., USA. Mem. Cttee, Irish Peers Assoc., 2006–. *Recreations:* reading, family history. *Heir:* *s* Hon. Timothy Roderick Hamilton Trench [*b* 29 Feb. 1968; partner; one *d*]. *Address:* Plonk Barn, Lullington Road, Lullington, Polegate, E Sussex BN26 5QU. *E:* roderickashtown@gmail.com.

ASHURST, Deborah Ann; *see* Sherwin, D. A.

ASHURST, (Kenneth William) Stewart; DL; Chief Executive and Clerk, Essex County Council, 1995–2005; Partner, Odgers Ray & Berndtson, 2006–07; *b* 19 May 1945; *s* of late Kenneth Latham Ashurst, OBE and Helen Ferguson Ashurst (*née* Rae); *m* 1984, Catherine Mary Sample; two *s* one *d*. *Educ:* Royal Grammar Sch., Newcastle upon Tyne; King Edward VI Grammar Sch., Lichfield; Exeter Coll., Oxford Univ. (MA); Guildford Coll. of Law; Birmingham Univ. (MSocSc). Trainee solicitor, Leicester and Newcastle upon Tyne CBCs, 1967–68; Assistant Solicitor: Newcastle upon Tyne, 1968–71; Cumberland CC, 1972–73; Asst Co. Clerk, Cumbria CC, 1973–79; Dep. Co. Sec., 1979–81, Co. Solicitor and Dep. Co. Clerk, 1981–85, Suffolk CC; Dep. Chief Exec. and Clerk, Essex CC, 1985–94. Clerk to: Essex Police Authy, 1995–2002; Essex Fire Authy, 1998–2004; Essex Lieutenancy, 1995–2004; River Crouch Harbour Authy, 1995–2004; Secretary: Lord Chancellor's Adv. Cttee in Essex, 1995–2004; Stansted Airport Consultative Cttee, 1995–2004 (Chm., 2007–); Mem., Essex TEC Bd, 1995–2001. Director: Disability Essex, 2005–07; Children's Legal Centre, Essex Univ., 2006–07. Nat. Chm., ACCE, 2003–04. Law Society: Council Mem., 1989–97; Chm., Local Govt Gp, 1986–87. Mem. Council, Industrial Soc., 1997–2001. Chairman: Trustees, Aldeburgh Mus., 2008–13; Alde and Ore Assoc., 2010–12. Dir, Year of Opera and Musical Theatre, 1996–97. DL Essex, 2004. FCMI (FIMgt 1982); FRSA 1998. *Recreations:* wine and dining, art, music, loafing. *Address:* 3 The Cygnets, Saxmundham Road, Aldeburgh, Suffolk IP15 5PD.

ASHURST, Stephen John; His Honour Judge Ashurst; a Circuit Judge, since 2004; *b* 19 April 1957; *s* of John Anthony Ashurst and Doris Ashurst; *m* 1981, Deborah Ann Sherwin, *qv*; one *s* one *d*. *Educ:* South Hunsley Sch., E Yorks; Univ. of Newcastle upon Tyne (LLB). Called to the Bar, Inner Temple, 1979; in practice as barrister, Leeds and Middlesbrough, 1979–2004; an Asst Recorder, 1994–98, Recorder, 1998–2004; Resident Judge, York Crown Court, 2007–15. Judicial Mem., N Yorks Probation Bd, 2006–10. Hon. Pres., N Yorks Magistrates' Assoc., 2011–. Mem. Council, 2010–, Mem., Ethics Cttee, 2011–, Univ. of York. Hon. Recorder, City of York, 2008. *Recreations:* music, cycling, walking. *Address:* Teesside Combined Court Centre, Russell Street, Middlesbrough TS1 2AE.

ASHWIN, Mary Christine; *see* Vitoria, M. C.

ASHWORTH, Prof. Alan, PhD; FRS 2008; President, Helen Diller Family Comprehensive Cancer Center, Professor of Medicine, Division of Hematology/Oncology, E. Dixon Heise Distinguished Professor in Oncology, and Senior Vice President for Cancer Services, University of California, San Francisco, since 2015; *b* 26 Aug. 1960; *s* of Arthur and Dorothy Ashworth; *m* 2011, Dr Amanda McGuigan. *Educ:* Thornleigh Salesian Coll., Bolton; Imperial Coll. London (BSc Hons 1981); UCL (PhD 1984). Institute of Cancer Research, University of London: Gp Leader, 1988–2014; Prof. of Molecular Biology, 1997–2014; Chm., Section of Gene Function, 1997–99; Dir, Breakthrough Breast Cancer Res. Centre, 1999–2011; Chief Exec., 2011–14. Mem., EMBO, 1999. FMedSci 2002. *Publications:* contribs to scientific jls. *Recreations:* cinema, theatre, reading, writing. *Address:* Helen Diller Family Comprehensive Cancer Center, University of California, San Francisco, 1450 3rd Street, San Francisco, CA 94158, USA.

ASHWORTH, Prof. Andrew John, CBE 2009; PhD, DCL; FBA 1993; Vinerian Professor of English Law, University of Oxford, 1997–2013, now Emeritus; Fellow of All Souls College, Oxford, 1997–2013, now Emeritus; *b* 11 Oct. 1947; *s* of late Clifford Ashworth and Amy Ashworth (*née* Ogden); *m* 1st, 1971, Gillian Frisby (marr. diss. 2002); two *d*; 2nd, 2006, Veronica Bagnall. *Educ:* London Sch. of Economics (LLB 1968); New Coll., Oxford (BCL 1970; DCL 1993); Manchester Univ. (PhD 1973). Lectr, then Sen. Lectr, in Law, Manchester Univ., 1970–78; Fellow and Tutor in Law, Worcester Coll., Oxford, 1978–88; Edmund-Davies Prof. of Criminal Law and Criminal Justice, KCL, 1988–97. Mem., Sentencing Adv. Panel, 1999–2010 (Chm., 2007–10). Editor, Criminal Law Rev., 1975–99. Hon. QC 1997. Hon. LLD De Montfort, 1998; Hon. DJur Uppsala, 2003. *Publications:* Sentencing and Penal Policy, 1983; Principles of Criminal Law, 1991, 7th edn (with Jeremy Horder) 2013; Sentencing and Criminal Justice, 1992, 6th edn 2015; The Criminal Process, 1994, 4th edn (with Mike Redmayne) 2010; (with Ben Emmerson) Human Rights and Criminal Justice, 2001, 3rd edn 2012; Human Rights, Serious Crime and Criminal Procedure, 2002; Positive Obligations in Criminal Law, 2013; (with Lucia Zedner) Preventive Justice, 2014. *Recreations:* bridge, travel. *Address:* All Souls College, Oxford OX1 4AL.

ASHWORTH, Anne Mary Catherine; Assistant Editor (Property), The Times, since 2006; *b* 13 June 1954; *d* of Peter Ashworth and Joan Ashworth (*née* Kay); *m* 1985, Tom Maddocks; one *s*. *Educ:* Ursuline Convent High Sch., Wimbledon; King's Coll. London (BA Hons French and German). Reporter: Sunday Express, 1982–86; Today, 1986; Daily Mail, 1986–87; Personal Finance Editor: Mail on Sunday, 1987–94; The Times, 1994–2006. Property Columnist of the Year, Property Press Awards, 2014. *Recreations:* art, architecture, cinema. *Address:* The Times, News Building, 1 London Bridge Street, SE1 9GF. *T:* (020) 7782 5083. *E:* anne.ashworth@thetimes.co.uk.

ASHWORTH, Auriol, (Lady Ashworth); *see* Stevens, A.

ASHWORTH, Prof. Graham William, CBE 1980; DL; Visiting Professor: of Environmental Policy, University of Salford, 2004–12; International Baptist Theological Seminary, Prague, 2003–12; *b* 14 July 1935; *s* of Frederick William Ashworth and Ivy Alice Ashworth; *m* 1960, Gwyneth Mai Morgan-Jones; three *d*. *Educ:* Devonport High Sch., Plymouth; Univ. of Liverpool (Master of Civic Design, BArch). RIBA, PPRTPI, FRSA, FIEnvSc, FCMI. LCC (Hook New Town Project), 1959–61; consultancy with Graeme Shankland, 1961–64; architect to Civic Trust, 1964–65; Dir, Civic Trust for North-West, 1965–73 (Chm., Exec. Cttee, 1973–87); Prof. of Urban Envmtl Studies, Univ. of Salford, 1973–87; Director: Univ. of Salford Environmental Inst., 1978–87; CAMPUS (Campaign to Promote Univ. of Salford), 1981–87; Dir Gen., Keep Britain Tidy, then Tidy Britain, Gp, 1987–2000. Chairman: Going for Green, 1994–2000; World of Glass, 2000–09; Envmtl Campaigns, 2000–03. Member: Skeffington Cttee on Public Participation in Planning, 1969; North-West Adv. Council of BBC, 1970–75 (Chm.); NW Economic Planning Council (and Sub-gp Chm.), 1968–79; Countryside Commn, 1974–77; Merseyside Urban Develt Corp., 1981–92; (non-exec.) North Western Electricity Bd, 1985–88; Chairman: Ravenhead Renaissance, 1988–2002; Rural Recovery Trust, 2002–04. Governor, Northern Baptist Coll., 1966–82; President: RTPI, 1973–74; Foundn for Envmtl Educn, 1988–2004 (Pres., 1996–2004); Vice-Pres., Chartered Inst. of Envmtl Health, 2000–. Chm., Instn of Environmental Sciences, 1980–82. Member: Council, St George's House, Windsor, 1982–88; Council, Baptist Union, 1983– (Pres., 2000–01). Trustee: Manchester Mus. of Science and Industry, 1988–90; Tatton Trust, 2002–. Chm., Samlesbury and Cuerdale Parish Council, 2007–. Editor, Internat. Jl of Environmental Educn, 1981–2001. DL Lancs, 1991. *Publications:* An Encyclopædia of Planning, 1973; Britain in Bloom, 1991; The Role of Local Government in Environmental Protection, 1992. *Recreations:* gardening, painting, church and social work. *Address:* Spring House, Preston New Road, Samlesbury, Preston PR5 0UP. *E:* ashworth260@btinternet.com.

ASHWORTH, Ian Edward; Planning Inspector, Department of the Environment, 1987–95; *b* 3 March 1930; *s* of late William Holt and Cicely Ashworth, Rochdale; *m* Pauline, *er d* of late Maurice James Heddle, MBE, JP, and Gladys Heddle, Westcliff-on-Sea; two *s* one *d*. *Educ:* Manchester Grammar Sch.; The Queen's Coll., Oxford (BCL, MA). Admitted Solicitor, 1956; FGA 1983. Asst Solicitor, Rochdale, 1956–58; Dep. Town Clerk, Dep. Clerk of Peace, Canterbury, 1958–63; Town Clerk, Clerk of Peace, Deal, 1963–66; Town Clerk, Rugby, 1966–70; Circuit Administrator, Western Circuit, Lord Chancellor's Dept (Under Sec.), 1970–87. *Recreations:* music, gemmology, gardening. *Address:* Westdale Edge, Beer Road, Seaton, Devon EX12 2PT. *T:* (01297) 21212. *Club:* Oxford and Cambridge.

ASHWORTH, Jennifer Elizabeth; *see* Anderson, J. E.

ASHWORTH, Sir John (Michael), Kt 2008; DSc; Chairman, Barts and the London NHS Trust, 2003–07; *b* 27 Nov. 1938; *s* of late Jack Ashworth and late Constance Mary Ousman; *m* 1st, 1963, Ann Knight (*d* 1985); one *s* three *d*; 2nd, 1988, Auriol Stevens, *qv*. *Educ:* West Buckland Sch., N Devon; Exeter Coll., Oxford (MA, DSc; Hon. Fellow, 1983); Leicester Univ. (PhD). FRSB (FIBiol 1974). Dept of Biochemistry, Univ. of Leicester: Res. Demonstr, 1961–63; Lectr, 1963–71; Reader, 1971–73; Prof. of Biology, Univ. of Essex, 1974–79 (on secondment to Cabinet Office, 1976–79); Under-Sec., Cabinet Office, 1979–81 and Chief Scientist, Central Policy Review Staff, 1976–81; Vice-Chancellor, Univ. of Salford, 1981–90; Dir, LSE, 1990–96; Chm., British Liby Bd, 1996–2001. Harkness Fellow of Commonwealth Fund, NY, at Brandeis Univ. and Univ. of Calif, 1965–67. NEDO: Chm., Information Technology EDC, 1983–86; Mem., Electronics EDC, 1983–86. Chairman: Nat. Accreditation Council for Certification Bodies, BSI, 1984–88; NCC, 1983–92. Director: Granada TV, 1987–89; Granada Group, 1990–2002; J. Sainsbury, 1993–97; London First, 1993–98. Non-exec. Dir, Colchester Hosp. Univ. Foundn Trust, 2010–14. Fellow, Inst. of Cancer Res., 2007 (Mem. Council, 2000–07). Pres., Council for Assisting Refugee Academics, 2002–06. Colworth Medal, Biochem. Soc., 1972. *Publications:* Cell Differentiation, 1972; (with J. Dee) The Slime Moulds, 1976; over 100 pubns in prof. jls on biochem., genet., cell biol. and educnl topics. *Recreation:* sailing. *Address:* Garden House, Wivenhoe, Essex CO7 9BD. *Clubs:* Royal Overseas League; Wivenhoe Sailing.

ASHWORTH, Jonathan Michael Graham; MP (Lab) Leicester South, since May 2011; *b* Salford, 14 Oct. 1978; *m* 2010, Emilie Oldknow; one *d*. *Educ:* Philips High Sch.; Bury Coll.; Durham Univ. (BA Hons Politics and Philosophy). Pol Res. Officer, 2001, Econs and Welfare Policy Officer, 2002–03, Labour Party; Special Advr, HM Treasury, 2003–07; Dep. Political Sec. to Prime Minister, 2007–10; Political Sec. to Acting Leader, Labour Party, 2010; Hd, Labour Party Relns for Rt Hon. Edward Miliband, MP, 2010–11. Shadow Cabinet Office Minister, 2013–15; Shadow Minister without Portfolio, 2015–. *Address:* House of Commons, SW1A 0AA.

ASHWORTH, Lance Dominic Piers; QC 2006; a Recorder of the Crown Court, since 2005 and of the County Court, since 2007; *b* 13 June 1964; *s* of Piers Ashworth, QC and of Iolene Jennifer Scholes (*née* Foxley); *m* 1989, Sally Elizabeth Downs (marr. diss. 2015); two *s* one *d*. *Educ:* Oundle Sch.; Pembroke Coll., Cambridge (BA 1986, MA 1990). Called to the Bar, Middle Temple, 1987; specialises in commercial and insolvency law. Chm., Midlands Legal Support Trust, 2008–11. Founder Trustee, Medical Res. Foundn, Coventry and Warwicks, 2004–; Trustee, Access to Justice Foundn, 2014–. Mem., W Midlands Cttee, 2010–12, Middlesex Cttee, 2012–, Lord's Taverners. *Publications:* (contrib.) Mithani: Directors' Disqualification, nos 8 to 27, 1995–2007. *Recreations:* tennis, golf, cricket (Earlswood CC). *Address:* Serle Court, 6 New Square, Lincoln's Inn, WC2A 3QS. *T:* (020) 7242 6105. *E:* lashworth@serlecourt.co.uk.

ASHWORTH, Patrick; HM Diplomatic Service, retired; High Commissioner to Belize, 2009–13 (Acting High Commissioner, 2008–09); *b* Maryport, Cumberland, 2 Nov. 1950; *s* of late Tom Ashworth and of Mary Josephine Ashworth (*née* Mulgrew); *m* 1973, Pauline Mary Harrison; one *s* one *d*. *Educ:* St Patrick's RC Sch., Maryport; Cockermouth Grammar Sch. Joined HM Diplomatic Service, 1968; Dar es Salaam, 1971–75; Castries, 1975–78; Attaché, Moscow, 1978–80; Security Dept, FCO, 1980–81; Diplomatic Service Trade Union Side Sec., FCO, 1981–83; Consular Officer, Valletta, 1983–87; Vice Consul Commercial, Sao Paulo, 1987–92; Second Sec., UN Conf. on Envmt and Develt Co-ordinator, Brasilia/Rio de Janeiro, 1992; Hd, Council of Europe Section, W Eur. Dept, FCO, 1992–95; Press Officer, The Hague, 1995–2000; Dep. Consul Gen., Sao Paulo and Dep. Dir of Trade for Brazil, 2000–05; Hd of Liaison, Whitehall Liaison Dept, FCO, 2005–08. *Recreations:* walking, running, sport, music, reading, photography. *Club:* Civil Service.

ASHWORTH, Peter Anthony Frank; Director, Leeds Permanent Building Society, 1971–92 (President, 1978); *b* 24 Aug. 1935; *s* of Peter Ormerod and Dorothy Christine Ashworth; *m* 1964, Elisabeth Crompton; one *s* one *d*. *Educ:* Leeds Grammar School. Articled to Hollis & Webb, Chartered Surveyors, Leeds (later Weatherall, Green & Smith, now Sanderson Weatherall), 1953–56; Partner, 1961–80. *Recreations:* golf, gardening. *Address:* 4 Bridge Paddock, Collingham, Wetherby LS22 5BN. *T:* (01937) 572953. *Club:* Alwoodley Golf (Leeds).

ASHWORTH, Richard James; Member (C) South East Region, European Parliament, since 2004; *b* 17 Sept. 1947; *s* of late Maurice Ashworth and Eileen Ashworth; *m* 1972, Sally Poulton; three *d*. *Educ:* King's Sch., Canterbury; Seale-Hayne Coll., Devon (DipAgr; Dip. in Farm Mgt; NDA). Farmer, 1970–2001. Chairman: United Milk Plc, 1996–2002; NFU Corporate, 2000–02. Contested (C) Devon North, 1997. European Parliament: Member: Budget Cttee, 2005–; Climate Change Cttee, 2005–09; Agriculture Cttee, 2009–; Chief Whip, 2006–09; Dep. Leader, 2009–11, Leader, 2012–, British Cons. MEPs. *Recreations:* sport, music, theatre, country pursuits. *Address:* Pollard House, Church Road, Lingfield, Surrey RH7 6AH. *E:* rashworth@europarl.eu.int. *Club:* Farmers.

ASHWORTH, Thomas Leslie, MSc; Head Master, Ermysted's Grammar School, Skipton, 1998–2008; *b* 17 Sept. 1949; *s* of late William Leslie Ashworth and Katharine Elizabeth Ashworth; *m* 1979, Roslyn Williams; two *d*. *Educ:* Birkenhead Inst.; Queen Mary Coll., London (BSc Hons Maths 1971); Univ. of Liverpool (MSc Maths 1973). Maths teacher, Birkenhead Sch., 1973–83; Sen. Teacher and Hd of Maths, Ripon GS, 1983–88; Dep. Head Master, Reading Sch., 1988–98. Trustee, Skipton Mechanics Inst., 2005– (Vice Chm., 2012–). *Recreations:* Rugby (RFU panel referee, 1988–2000; Member: Yorks Referees' Soc., 1983–88, 2008–; London Soc. of Rugby Referees, 1989–99), golf, Rotary (Skipton Craven, 2009–, Treas., 2011–), philately, ICT, travel. *Address:* 22 Cross Bank, Skipton, N Yorks BD23 6AH. *E:* tla179@aol.com. *Clubs:* Birkenhead Park Football; Skipton Golf.

ASIF, (Mohammed) Jalil (Akhter); QC 2010; a Recorder, since 2004; *b* London, 25 March 1965; *s* of Mohammed Asif and Carola Mary Asif (*née* Paine); *m* 1994, (Katharine) Clare Harding Price; one *s* two *d*. *Educ:* Twyford High Sch., London; St Paul's Sch., London; Peterhouse, Cambridge (BA 1987). Called to the Bar, Lincoln's Inn, 1988, Bencher, 2011; in practice as a barrister, 1988–. Mem. Bd and Trustee, Royal and Derngate Theatres, Northampton, 2010–. *Publications:* (ed jtly) Professional Negligence Liability Reports, 1996–; contributing editor: Jackson & Powell's Professional Liability Precedents, 2000; APIL Clinical Negligence, 2008, 2nd edn 2014; The Law and Regulation of Medicines, 2008. *Recreations:* scuba diving, ski-ing, cinema, music. *Address:* Kobre & Kim LLP, Tower 42, 25 Old Broad Street, EC2N 1HQ. *T:* (020) 3301 5700, *Fax:* (020) 3301 5720. *E:* jalil.asif@kobrekim.com.

ASIM, Dr Mohamed; Minister/Chargé d'affaires, Belgium and Maldives Mission to European Union, 2013–14; *b* 1960; *m* Mariyam Ali Manik; one *s* one *d*. *Educ:* American Univ. of Beirut (BA Public Admin); California State Univ., Sacramento (MA Internat. Relns); Australian National Univ. (PhD Pol Sci. and Internat. Relns 1999). Government of the Maldives: admin. officer, Min. of Educn, 1982–83; President's Office, 1983–96; Dir Gen., Employment Affairs, 1996–99; Dir Gen., Public Service Div., President's Office, 1999–2004; High Comr, Sri Lanka and concurrently to Bangladesh and Pakistan, 2004–07; High Comr, UK, 2007–08; Addnl Sec., Min. of Foreign Affairs, Maldives, 2009. *Publications:* contrib. articles on public admin and public sector reform in the Maldives to Labour and Mgt in Develt Jl and Public Admin and Develt Jl.

ASKARI, Hasan; Chairman, New India Investment Trust plc, since 2014 (Director, since 2012); non-executive Director, Sun Life of Canada (UK) Ltd, since 2011; *s* of late Syed Mohammad and Kishwar Jahan Askari; *m* 1976, Nasreen Hassam Ismail; one *s* one *d*. *Educ:* University Coll., Oxford (MA 1975). S. G. Warburg & Co. Ltd, London, 1975–80; Chase Manhattan Bank: Dir, Hong Kong, 1981–85; Man. Dir, Tokyo, 1985–89; Man. Dir, Barclays de Zoete Wedd Ltd, Tokyo, 1989–92, London, 1992–99; Dir, 1999–2003, Chief Exec., 2003–07, Old Mutual Financial Services plc. Chm., Aqua Resources Fund Ltd, 2008–; Sen. Advr, Kotak Mahindra Bank Gp, India, 2008–. Dir, Gt Ormond St Hosp. for Children NHS Trust, 1999–2007. Chm., Turquoise Mountain Foundn, 2007–08. Trustee, BM, 1999–2007. Mem., RSAA, 1979; FRAS 1979. *Recreations:* cricket, South Asian art, walking (preferably in solitude). *Address:* 22 Ovington Square, SW3 1LR. *E:* hasan.askari@btinternet.com. *Clubs:* Oriental, Walbrook; American (Tokyo).

ASKE, Sir Robert John Bingham, 3rd Bt *cr* 1922; *b* 12 March 1941; *s* of late Robert Edward Aske (*yr s* of Sir Robert Aske, 1st Bt) and of Joan, *o d* of late Capt. Eric Bingham Ackerley; *S* uncle, 2001. *Educ:* King's Sch., Canterbury. *Heir:* none. *Address:* 5 Bicton Place, Heavitree, Exeter EX1 2PF.

ASKEW, Sir Bryan, Kt 1989; Personnel Director, Samuel Smith Old Brewery (Tadcaster), 1982–95; Chairman, Yorkshire Regional Health Authority, 1983–94; *b* 18 Aug. 1930; *s* of John Pinkney Askew and Matilda Askew; *m* 1955, Millicent Rose Holder; two *d*. *Educ:* Wellfield Grammar Sch., Wingate, Co. Durham; Fitzwilliam Coll., Cambridge (MA Hons History). ICI Ltd, 1952–59; Consett Iron Co. Ltd (later part of British Steel Corporation), 1959–71; own consultancy, 1971–74; Samuel Smith Old Brewery (Tadcaster), 1974–95. Chm., Advanced Digital Telecom Ltd, 1997–99. Member, Consett UDC, 1967–71; contested (C) General Elections: Penistone, 1964 and 1966; York, 1970. Mem., Duke of Edinburgh's Third Commonwealth Study Conf., Australia, 1968. Mem., Working Gp on Young People and Alcohol, Home Office Standing Conf. on Crime Prevention, 1987. Chm., British Polio Fellowship, 2004–08. Mem. Court, 1985–2006, Mem. Council, 1988–2000, Univ. of Leeds. Chm., Burgage Holders of Alnmouth Common, 2003–13. FRSA 1986 (Chm., Yorks Region, 1997–99); FRSocMed 1988. Hon. LLD Hull, 1992. *Recreations:* listening to music, reading, writing to The Times. *Address:* 27 Golf Links Avenue, Tadcaster LS24 9HF. *T:* (01937) 833216.

ASKEW, Christopher Richard Thompson; Chief Executive, Breakthrough Breast Cancer, since 2010; *b* Amersham, 1965; *s* of Canon Richard George Askew and Margaret Askew; *m* 2002, Liza Juliet; one *s* one *d*. *Educ:* Monkton Combe Sch., Bath; Brasenose Coll., Oxford (BA Hons Classics). Dir, GMT Shipping and Chartering Ltd, 1994–97; Asst Dir, External Affairs, NCH, 2001–03; Director of Fundraising: Crisis, 2003–06; Breakthrough Breast Cancer, 2006–10. *Recreations:* cycling, sailing, family. *Address:* Breakthrough Breast Cancer, Weston House, 246 High Holborn, WC1V 7EX. *T:* (020) 7025 2453. *E:* chrisa@breakthrough.org.uk.

ASKEW, Clinton Graham; Chairman, Smaller Business Practitioner Panel, Financial Conduct Authority, since 2015; Founder and Director, Citywide Financial Partners Ltd, since 2004; *b* Cardiff, 31 May 1958; *s* of Douglas Askew and Muriel Askew; *m* 1991, Dr Leslie Becker; two *s* two *d*. *Educ:* Univ. of West of England (BA Hons Business Studies). Mem., Smaller Business Practitioner Panel, FCA (formerly FSA), 2009–. Mem., RYA. *Recreations:* Scout group leader, rock climbing, sailing, cycling. *Address:* Citywide Financial Partners Ltd, Fetcham Park House, Lower Road, Fetcham, Surrey KT22 9HD. *T:* (01372) 371137. *E:* clinton.askew@citywidefinancial.co.uk.

ASLET, Clive William; Editor-at-Large, Country Life, since 2006 (Deputy Editor, 1989–92; Editor, 1993–2006); Editor in Chief, Country Life Books, 1994–2006; Co-founder, Remember WW1, since 2013; *b* 15 Feb. 1955; *s* of Kenneth and Monica Aslet; *m* 1980, Naomi Roth; three *s*. *Educ:* King's College Sch., Wimbledon; Peterhouse, Cambridge. Joined Country Life, 1977, Architectural Editor, 1984–88; Ed. in Chief, New Eden, 1999–. Dir, Country and Leisure Media Ltd, 1999–. Founding Hon. Sec., Thirties Soc., 1979–87. Gov., St Peter's Eaton Sq. C of E Sch., 1999–2006. FRSA. *Publications:* The Last Country Houses, 1982; (with Alan Powers) The National Trust Book of the English House, 1985; Quinlan Terry, the Revival of Architecture, 1986; The American Country House, 1990; Countryblast, 1991; (introd.) The American Houses of Robert A. M. Stern, 1991; Anyone for England? a search for British identity, 1997; (with Derry Moore) The House of Lords, 1998; The Story of Greenwich, 1999; Greenwich Millennium, 2000; A Horse in the Country: a diary of a year in the heart of England, 2001; The Landmarks of Britain, 2005; The English House: the story of a nation at home, 2008; Villages of Britain, 2010; The Edwardian Country House, 2012; War Memorial: the story of one village's sacrifice from 1914 to 2003, 2012; Exuberant Catalogue of Dreams, 2013; The Birdcage, 2014. *Recreations:* pleasures of the table, wool gathering. *Address:* c/o Country Life, 9th floor, Blue Fin Building, 110 Southwark Street, SE1 0SU. *W:* www.cliveaslet.com. *Club:* Garrick.

ASLETT, Anne; Executive Director, Elton John Aids Foundation, since 2009; *b* Sydney, Australia, 5 Aug. 1964; *d* of Derek Anthony Ewen Maclaren and Pamela Anne Maclaren; *m* 1993, William David Aslett; one *s* one *d*. *Educ:* Francis Holland Girls Sch., London; OISE, Paris (Dip. Business French 1993). Editl asst, House & Garden, 1983–85; prodn asst, Strategy Prodns, 1985–86; Prodn Manager, Park Prodns Ltd, 1986–88; photographic assignment, Middle East, 1988; Publications Manager, Profile Systems Ltd, News Media Information, 1989–92; freelance journalist and documentary/film researcher (pt-time), BBC and Channel 4, 1994–97; Prog. Officer (pt-time), 1997–2001, Internat. Develt Dir, 2001–09, Elton John Aids Foundn. Chm., Eur. Funders Gp, 2010–. Mem., Internat. Grants Cttee, Comic Relief, 2004–. *Recreations:* reading, family, badminton, art, travel. *Address:* Elton John Aids Foundation, 1 Blythe Road, W14 0HG. *T:* (020) 7603 9996, *Fax:* (020) 7348 4848. *E:* anne.aslett@ejaf.com.

ASPEL, Michael Terence, OBE 1993; broadcaster and writer; *b* 12 Jan. 1933; *s* of late Edward and of Violet Aspel; *m* 1st, 1957, Dian; one *s* (and one *s* decd); 2nd, 1962, Ann; twin *s* and *d*; 3rd, 1977, Elizabeth; two *s*. *Educ:* Emanuel School. Tea boy, publishers, 1949–51. Nat. Service, KRRC and Para Regt, TA, 1951–53. Radio actor, 1954–57; television announcer, 1957–60, newsreader, 1960–68; freelance broadcaster, radio and TV, 1968–; presenter: Aspel and Company, 1984–93; This is Your Life, 1988–2003; Antiques Roadshow, 2000–08; A Hundred Years of Us, 2011; occasional stage appearances. Vice-Pres., BLISS (Baby Life Support Systems), 1981–; Patron: Plan International, 1986–; Evacuees Reunion Assoc., 2005–. Member: Equity, 1955–; Lord's Taverners; RYA. Hon. Fellow, Cardiff Univ., 2002. Mem., RTS Hall of Fame, 1996. Hon. Freeman, Elmbridge, 2008. *Publications:* Polly Wants a Zebra (autobiog.), 1974; Hang On! (for children), 1982; (with Richard Hearsey) Child's Play, 1985; regular contribs to magazines. *Recreations:* water sports, theatre, cinema, eating, travel. *Address:* c/o Shepherd Management, 4th Floor, 45 Maddox Street, W1S 2PE.

ASPINALL, Beverley Ann; Managing Director, Bond Street Development Group, New West End Company, since 2013; *b* Dunstable, 4 Dec. 1958; *d* of late D. Thomas and of Mrs R. J. Browning; *m* 2002, David Aspinall; one *s* one *d*. *Educ:* Redbourne Community Coll., Ampthill; Univ. of York (BA Hons). Managing Director: John Lewis, Peterborough, 1996–98; Peter Jones, 1998–2005; Fortnum & Mason plc, 2005–12. Dir, Aspinalls Gp, 2012–; non exec. Dir, W. & G. Foyle Ltd, 2014–. Dir, V&A Enterprises, 2007–. Dir, Develt Bd, Univ. of York, 2007–. Gov., King's Sch., Ely, 2008–11. *Recreations:* classical music, gardening.

ASPINALL, John Michael; QC 1995; a Recorder, 1990–98; *b* 19 Feb. 1948; *s* of Kenneth James Aspinall and Joan Mary Aspinall; *m* 1980, Frances Helen Parks. *Educ:* Kampala Kindergarten; Wigan and Dist Mining and Tech. Coll.; Liverpool Univ. (LLB Hons). Called to the Bar, Inner Temple, 1971; Asst Recorder, 1985–90. RAC Motor Sports Council: Mem., 1990, Chm., 1994, Judicial Cttee; Mem., 1994. Winner, Observer Mace Nat. Debating Comp., 1971. *Recreations:* motor sports, being with my wife and friends at the Drax Arms. *Address:* Church Court Chambers, 2nd Floor, Goldsmith Buildings, Temple, EC4Y 7BL. *Club:* Savile.

ASPINALL, John Michael, CEng, FICE; Director of Major Projects, Ministry of Justice, 2012–13; Member, International Tennis Federation, playing on Seniors Tennis Tour, since 2013; *b* Leeds, 3 July 1959; *s* of Ronald and Margaret Aspinall; *m* 1983, Jill Hutton; one *s* two *d*. *Educ:* Allerton Grange High Sch., Leeds; Bradford Univ. (BEng Hons Civil and Structural Engrg). CEng 1986; MCIHT (MIHT 1991); FICE 2008. Grad. Civil Engr, S Yorks CC, 1982–86; Sen. Section Engr, W Yorks Highways Engrg and Tech. Services, 1986–91; Associate, Smithers Purslow, Cons. Engrs, 1991–93; Project Manager, Highways Agency, 1993–98; Policy Advr, World Bank, Washington, 1998–99 (on secondment); Gp Leader, Highways Agency, 1999–2002; Divl Manager, Rail Directorate, DfT, 2002–04; Regl Dir for SE, Highways Agency, 2004–08; Ministry of Justice: Dir of Estate Capacity, Nat. Offender Mgt Service, 2008–09; Strategic Estates Dir, 2009–11; Dir, Transforming Justice Portfolio and Estates, 2011–12. *Recreations:* cricket, reading, pottering about. *Address:* 92 Kennylands Road, Sonning Common, Oxon RG4 9JX. *T:* (0118) 9242567. *E:* aspinall562@btinternet.com.

ASPINALL, Margaret Mary, CBE 2015; Chairman, Hillsborough Family Support Group, since 1999; *b* Liverpool, 25 Sept. 1946; *d* of James and Margaret McCormick; *m* 1970, James Aspinall; two *s* two *d* (and one *s* decd). *Educ:* St Augustine's Secondary Modern RC High Sch. Voluntary work for Hillsborough Family Support Gp, 1989– (Mem. Cttee; Vice Chm.). Voluntary work for Liverpool Capital of Culture, 2008. *Address:* Hillsborough Family Support Group, Anfield Sports Community Centre, Lower Breck Road, Anfield, Liverpool L6 0AG. *T:* (0151) 263 8138. *E:* info@HFSG.co.uk.

ASPINALL, Most Rev. Phillip John; *see* Brisbane, Archbishop of.

ASPINALL, Wilfred; European Union policy and strategy adviser; Director, Aspinall & Associates, since 1988; Hon. Chairman (formerly Director) and Strategy Adviser, Forum in the European Parliament for Construction and Energy Users (formerly European Parliament Forum for Construction, then Forum in the European Parliament for Construction, Energy, Finance and Sustainability, then Forum in the European Parliament for Construction and Sustainable Energy), since 20022; *b* 14 Sept. 1942; *s* of late Charles Aspinall and Elizabeth Aspinall; *m* 1973, Judith Mary (*d* 2005), *d* of late Leonard James Pimlott and Kathleen Mary Pimlott; one *d*. *Educ:* Poynton Secondary Modern; Stockport Coll. for Further Educn. Staff, National Provincial Bank Ltd, 1960–69; Asst Gen. Sec., National Westminster Staff Assoc., 1969–75; Dep. Sec. (part-time), Council of Bank Staff Assocs, 1969–75; Mem., Banking Staff Council, 1970–77; Gen. Sec., Confedn of Bank Staff Assocs, 1975–79; Exec. Dir, Fedn of

Managerial, Professional and Gen. Assocs, 1978–94. Advr, Eversheds Financial Services Forum, 1998–2009. Mem., European Economic and Social Cttee, 1986–98. Dir, The Strategy Centre, Brussels, 2004–14. Vice-Pres., Confédération Internat. des Cadres, 1979–94. Member: N Herts DHA, 1981–86; NW Thames RHA, 1986–88; Hammersmith and Queen Charlotte's SHA, 1981–90; Professions Allied to Medicine, Whitley Management Negotiating Cttee, 1983–87. *Recreations:* motoring, travel - particularly to places of historical interest, social affairs and political history. *Address:* The Coach House, Shillington Road, Pirton, Hitchin, Herts SG5 3QJ. *T:* 07872 953922, (Belgium) 475952225. *E:* wa@wilfredaspinall.eu, wilfredaspinall@me.com.

ASPLIN, Hon. Dame Sarah (Jane), (Hon. Dame Sarah Sherwin), DBE 2012; **Hon. Mrs Justice Asplin;** a Judge of the High Court of Justice, Chancery Division, since 2012; *b* 16 Sept. 1959; *d* of Raymond Asplin and Florence Grace Asplin; *m* 1986, Nicholas Adrian Sherwin; two *d. Educ:* Southampton Coll. for Girls; Fitzwilliam Coll., Cambridge (MA; Hon. Fellow, 2013); St Edmund Hall, Oxford (BCL). Called to the Bar, Gray's Inn, 1984, Bencher, 2006; in practice as barrister, specialising in Chancery and pensions law and life assurance, 1985–2012; QC 2002; Dep. High Court Judge, Chancery Div. Head of Chambers, 3 Stone Bldgs, 2009–12. Member: Chancery Bar Assoc., 1985–2012; Assoc. Pension Lawyers, 1990–2012 (Mem., Litigation Sub-Cttee, 2000–09; Hon. Mem., 2014); Fees Collection Cttee and Implementation Cttee, Bar Council. *Recreations:* playing the violin, classical music. *Address:* Royal Courts of Justice, Rolls Building, 7 Rolls Buildings, Fetter Lane, EC4 1NL.

ASPRAY, Rodney George, FCA; Managing Director, Worthbase Ltd, 1990–2000; *b* 1934. Secretary, Manchester and Salford Cooperative Society, 1965–69; Chief Exec. Officer, Norwest Co-op. Soc., 1969–91. Director: Co-operative Bank, 1980–89 (Chm., 1986–89); Co-operative Wholesale Soc. Ltd, 1980–89; Mersey Docks & Harbour Co., 1987–94; Piccadilly Radio Plc, 1989–90. Mem., Monopolies and Mergers Commn, 1975–81. FCA 1960.

ASQUITH, family name of **Earl of Oxford and Asquith**.

ASQUITH, Viscount; Mark Julian Asquith; *b* 13 May 1979; *o s* and heir of Earl of Oxford and Asquith, *qv*; *m* 2008, Helen, *d* of Christopher Norman Russell Prentice, *qv*. *Educ:* Ampleforth; St Andrews Univ. (MA 2001). Investment manager, Somerset Capital Management LLP.

ASQUITH, Hon. Sir Dominic (Anthony Gerard), KCMG 2012 (CMG 2004); HM Diplomatic Service, retired; Ambassador to Libya, 2011–12; *b* 7 Feb. 1957; *y s* of 2nd Earl of Oxford and Asquith, KCMG; *m* 1988, Louise Cotton; two *s* two *d*. Joined HM Diplomatic Service, 1983; FCO, 1983–86; Second Sec., Damascus, 1986–87; First Secretary: Muscat, 1987–89; FCO, 1989–92; Washington, 1992–96; Minister and Dep. Hd of Mission, Argentina, 1997–2001; Dep. Hd of Mission and Consul Gen., Saudi Arabia, 2001–04; Dep. Special Rep. and Dep. Head of Mission, Iraq, 2004; Dir, Iraq Directorate, FCO, 2004–06; Ambassador to: Iraq, 2006–07; Egypt, 2007–11. Sen. Advr, Dentons US LLP, 2013–; Senior Director: Macro Advisory Partners, 2014–; Strategic Advr, Gp DF Internat., 2014–. Chm., Libyan British Business Council, 2014–. *Address:* 22 Cyril Mansions, Prince of Wales Drive, SW11 4HP.

See also Earl of Oxford and Asquith.

ASSAMBA, Aloun N.; *see* Ndombet-Assamba, A.

ASSHETON, family name of **Baron Clitheroe**.

ASSIRATI, Robert, CBE 2012; Major Projects Director, Office of Government Commerce, HM Treasury, 2007–11 (Executive Director, 2001–07); Vice President, BCS - The Chartered Institute for IT, 2008–13; *b* 27 May 1947; *s* of late Frederick Louis Assirati and Mary Violet Assirati (*née* Dillon); *m* 1968, Lynne Elizabeth Yeend; one *s* one *d*. *Educ:* Stationers' Company's Sch., London; Hertford Coll., Oxford (MA PPE). MCIPS 1997; CITP 2007. Nat. Coal Bd, 1968; Data Processing Manager, Eli Lilly & Co., 1972; Management Services Manager, British Carpets, 1976; Company Dir, C Squared, 1984; Commercial Dir, Inland Revenue IT Office, 1986; Chief Exec., CCTA, 1996–2001. Freeman, City of London; Liveryman, Co. of Information Technologists, 2003. FBCS. Hon. FAPM 1997. *Recreations:* bridge, tennis, travel, theatre. *Address:* The Alders, Capel, Tonbridge, Kent TN12 6SU. *T:* (01892) 836609.

ASTAIRE, Jarvis Joseph, OBE 2004; Chairman: GRA (formerly Greyhound Racing Association), 1993–2005; First Artist Corporation plc, 2006–09; *b* 6 Oct. 1923; *s* of late Max and Esther Astaire; *m* 1st, 1948, Phyllis Oppenheim (*d* 1974); one *s* one *d*; 2nd, 1981, Nadine Hyman (*d* 1986). *Educ:* Kilburn Grammar Sch., London. Dir, Lewis & Burrows Ltd, 1957–60; Managing Director: Mappin & Webb Ltd, 1958–60; Hurst Park Syndicate, 1962–71; Dep. Chm., Wembley Stadium, 1984–99; Director: Perthpoint Investments Ltd, 1959–70; Associated Suburban Properties Ltd, 1963–81; Anglo-Continental Investment & Finance Co. Ltd, 1964–75; William Hill Org., 1971–82; First Artists Prodns Inc. (USA), 1976–79; Wembley PLC (formerly GRA Gp), 1987–99; Revlon Group Ltd, 1991–98. Mem. Bd, British Greyhound Racing, 1991–2004. Introduced into UK showing of sporting events on large screen in cinemas, 1964. Pres., Royal Free Hosp. and Med. Sch. Appeal Trust, 1991–97 (Chm., 1974); Hon. Treas., 1976–, and Vice Pres., 1982–, Fedn of London Youth Clubs (formerly London Fedn of Boys' Clubs); Chm., Police Dependants' Trust Appeal, 1999–; Trustee: Nightingale House Home for Aged Jews, 1984–; Bowles Outdoor Centre, 1985–; Royal Free Cancer Res. Trust, 2001–. Chm., Associated City Properties, 1981–2001. Chief Barker (Pres.), Variety Club of GB, 1983; Pres., Variety Clubs Internat. (Worldwide), 1991–93. Mem. Adv. Council, LSO, 1996–2004. Freeman, City of London, 1983. *Recreations:* playing tennis, watching cricket and football. *Clubs:* East India, MCC, Queen's; Friars (USA).

ASTBURY, Prof. Alan, PhD; FRS 1993; FRS(Can) 1988; R. M. Pearce Professor of Physics, University of Victoria, British Columbia, 1983–2000, now Emeritus; Director, TRIUMF Laboratory, Vancouver, 1994–2001; *b* 27 Nov. 1934; *s* of Harold Astbury and Jane Astbury (*née* Horton); *m* 1964, Kathleen Ann Stratmeyer; two *d*. *Educ:* Nantwich and Acton Grammar Sch.; Univ. of Liverpool (BSc, PhD). Leverhulme Research Fellow, Univ. of Liverpool, 1959–61; Res. Associate, Lawrence Radiation Lab., Berkeley, Calif., 1961–63; Res. Physicist, Rutherford Appleton Lab., UK, 1963–83. Vis. Scientist, CERN, Geneva, 1970–74 and 1980–83. Pres., IUPAP, 2005–08. Hon. DSc: Liverpool, 2003; Victoria, BC, 2003; Simon Fraser, BC, 2006. Rutherford Medal, Inst. Physics, 1986; Gold Medal, Canadian Assoc. of Physics, 2002. *Publications:* numerous in learned jls. *Recreations:* jazz, playing piano. *Address:* Department of Physics and Astronomy, University of Victoria, PO Box 3055, Station Commercial Service Centre, Victoria, BC V8W 3P6, Canada. *T:* (250) 7217725; 1383 St Patrick Street, Victoria, BC V8S 4Y5, Canada.

ASTBURY, Nicholas John, FRCS, FRCOphth, FRCP; Clinical Senior Lecturer (part-time), International Centre for Eye Health, London School of Hygiene and Tropical Medicine, since 2014 (Consultant Adviser, 2006–14); *b* 21 Feb. 1949; *s* of late Dr John Schonberg Astbury and of Dr Noel Hope Astbury (*née* Gunn); *m* 1970, Susan Patricia Whall; two *s* two *d*. *Educ:* Rugby Sch.; Guy's Hosp. Med. Sch. (MB BS 1972). LRCP 1972; MRCS 1972, FRCS 1977; DO 1974; FRCOphth 1989; FRCP 2005. Sen. Registrar, KCH and Moorfields Eye Hosp., 1981–83; Consultant Ophthalmic Surgeon (part-time), W Norwich Hosp., later Norfolk and Norwich Univ. Hosp. NHS Trust, 1983–2013. Vice-Chm., Impact Foundn, 2004–; Chairman: Duke-Elder Foundn, 2004–; VISION 2020 UK, 2008–; Regional Co-Chm. for Europe, Internat. Agency for the Prevention of Blindness, 2009–. Med. Advr, St John of Jerusalem Eye Hosp., 2009–. Pres., Royal Coll. of Ophthalmologists, 2003–06. Hon. FCOptom. *Recreations:* walking, cycling, sailing, horology, photography, making automata. *Address:* Rectory Farmhouse, The Street, Shotesham, Norwich NR15 1YL. *T:* (01508) 550377. *E:* nick.astbury@virgin.net.

ASTBURY, Nicholas Paul; HM Diplomatic Service; Deputy Consul General and Deputy Head of Mission, New York, since 2012; *b* 13 Aug. 1971; *s* of Nigel Astbury and Yvonne Susan Astbury (*née* Harburn). *Educ:* Hills Rd Sixth Form Coll., Cambridge; University Coll. London (BA Internat. Historical Studies; MA Legal and Political Theory); Open Univ. (MBA). Entered FCO, 1994; Second Secretary: Colombo, 1995–99; FCO, 1999–2001; Private Sec. to Parly Under-Sec. of State, 2001–02; Deputy Head: UKvisas, 2002–04; Drugs Team, Kabul, 2005; Ambassador to Eritrea, 2006–08; Hd of Sudan Unit, FCO, 2009–11. FRSA 2014. *Recreations:* photography, diving, numismatics, beer. *Address:* c/o Foreign and Commonwealth Office, King Charles Street, SW1A 2AH. *Club:* Bentham Boat.

ASTILL, Prof. Grenville George, PhD; FSA; Professor of Archaeology, University of Reading, since 1999; *b* Coventry, 15 June 1950; *s* of George and Hazel Astill. *Educ:* Warwick Sch., Warwick; Univ. of Birmingham (BA Hons Hist.; PhD 1978). FSA 1987. Tutorial Fellow, Sch. of Hist., Univ. of Birmingham, 1974–75; Dir, Berks Archaeol Unit, 1975–78; University of Reading: Lectr in Eur. Medieval Archaeol., 1978–95; British Acad. Reader, 1990–92; Reader in Archaeol., 1995–99. *Publications:* Historic Towns in Berkshire, 1978; (ed with A. Grant) The Countryside of Medieval England, 1988; A Medieval Industrial Complex and its Landscape: the metalworking watermills and workshops of Bordesley Abbey, 1993; (with W. Davies) The East Brittany Survey: fieldwork and field data, 1994; (with W. Davies) A Breton Landscape, 1997; (ed with J. Langdon) Medieval Farming and Technology: the impact of agricultural change in Northwest Europe, 1997; (with W. Davies) Un Paysage Breton, 2001; over 70 chapters and articles on Eur. and British urbanisation, rural soc., medieval industry and technol change, medieval religion, particularly monasticism. *Recreations:* early and contemporary music, vegetable gardening, cooking, walking to find monuments. *Address:* Department of Archaeology, University of Reading, Whiteknights, PO Box 218, Reading RG6 6AA. *T:* (0118) 378 7363. *E:* g.g.astill@reading.ac.uk.

ASTILL, Hon. Sir Michael (John), Kt 1996; a Judge of the High Court of Justice, Queen's Bench Division, 1996–2004; *b* 31 Jan. 1938; *s* of Cyril Norman Astill and Winifred Astill; *m* 1968, Jean Elizabeth, *d* of Dr J. C. H. Mackenzie; three *s* one *d*. *Educ:* Blackfriars School, Laxton, Northants. Admitted solicitor, 1962; called to the Bar, Middle Temple, 1972, Bencher, 1996; a Recorder, 1980–84; a Circuit Judge, 1984–96; a Pres., Mental Health Tribunals, 1986–96; Presiding Judge, Midland and Oxford Circuit, 1999–2002. Mem., Judicial Studies Bd, 1995–99 (Chm., Magisterial Cttee, 1995–99). *Recreations:* music, reading, sport. *Address:* c/o Royal Courts of Justice, Strand, WC2A 2LL.

ASTLEY, family name of **Baron Hastings**.

ASTLEY, Neil Philip; Editor and Managing Director, Bloodaxe Books Ltd, since 1978; *b* 12 May 1953; *s* of Philip Thomas Astley and late Margaret Ivy Astley (*née* Solman). *Educ:* Price's Sch., Fareham; Alliance Française, Paris; Univ. of Newcastle upon Tyne (BA 1st Cl. Hons). Journalist, England and Australia, 1972–74. Hon. DLitt Newcastle upon Tyne, 1996. Eric Gregory Award, Soc. of Authors, 1982. *Publications:* (ed) Ten North-East Poets, 1980; The Speechless Act, 1984; (ed) Bossy Parrot, 1987; Darwin Survivor (Recommendation, Poetry Book Soc.), 1988; (ed) Poetry with an Edge, 1988, 2nd edn 1993; (ed) Tony Harrison (critical anthology), 1991; Biting My Tongue, 1995; (ed) New Blood, 1999; The End of My Tether (novel), 2002; (ed) Staying Alive: real poems for unreal times, 2002; (ed) Pleased to See Me, 2002; (ed) Do Not Go Gentle, 2003; (ed) Being Alive: the sequel to Staying Alive, 2004; The Sheep Who Changed the World (novel), 2005; (ed) Passionfood: 100 love poems, 2005; (ed) Bloodaxe Poetry Introductions: vol. 1, 2006, vol. 2, 2006, vol. 3, 2007; (ed jtly) Soul Food: nourishing poems for starved minds, 2007; (ed) Earth Shattering: ecopoems, 2007; (ed jtly) In Person: 30 poets filmed by Pamela Robertson-Pearce, 2008; (ed) Being Human, 2011; (ed) Ten Poems About Sheep, 2012; (ed) Essential Poems from the Staying Alive Trilogy, 2012; (ed jtly) The World Record, 2012; (ed) The Hundred Years' War: modern war poems, 2014. *Recreations:* reading, film, enjoying countryside, folklore, sheep. *Address:* Bloodaxe Books Ltd, Eastburn, South Park, Hexham, Northumberland NE46 1BS. *T:* (01434) 611581.

ASTLEY, Philip Sinton, CVO 1999 (LVO 1979); HM Diplomatic Service, retired; Ambassador to Denmark, 1999–2003; *b* 18 Aug. 1943; *s* of Bernard Astley and Barbara Astley (*née* Sinton); *m* 1966, Susanne Poulsen; two *d*. *Educ:* St Albans Sch.; Magdalene Coll., Cambridge (BA 1965). Asst Representative, British Council, Madras, 1966–70; British Council, London, 1970–73; First Sec., FCO, 1973–76, Copenhagen, 1976–79; First Sec. and Head of Chancery, East Berlin, 1980–82; First Sec., FCO, 1982–84; Counsellor and Head of Management Review Staff, FCO, 1984–86; Econ. Counsellor and Consul Gen., Islamabad, 1986–90; Dep. Head of Mission, Copenhagen, 1990–94; Counsellor, and Hd of Human Rights Policy Dept, FCO, 1994–96; Asst Under-Sec. of State, FCO, and HM Vice-Marshal of the Diplomatic Corps, 1996–99. Freeman, City of London, 1999. Grand Cross, Order of Dannebrog (Denmark), 2000. *Recreations:* oriental ceramics and textiles, vernacular furniture, gardening, cooking. *Address:* Lark Hill, Egerton, Ashford, Kent TN27 9BG.

ASTLEY, Rita Ann; *see* Clifton, R. A.

ASTLING, (Alistair) Vivian, OBE 2005; DL; Chairman, National Forest Co., 1999–2005; *b* 6 Sept. 1943; *s* of late Alec William Astling, MBE and Barbara Grace Astling; *m* 1967, Hazel Ruth Clarke. *Educ:* Glyn Grammar Sch., Epsom; Sheffield Univ. (LLB 1965; LLM 1967); Birmingham Univ. (MSocSci 1973). West Bromwich County Borough Council: articled clerk, 1967; Asst Solicitor, 1971; Asst Town Clerk, 1973; Walsall Metropolitan Borough Council: Corporate Planner, 1974; Chief Exec. and Town Clerk, 1982–88; Chief Exec., Dudley MBC, 1988–99. Clerk to W Midlands Police Authy, 1988–99; Sec. to Shareholders' Forum, 1988–97, Chm., Consultative Cttee, 2002–12, Birmingham Internat. Airport. Member Board: Midlands Arts Centre, 1999–2013; Artsites, 2002–06; Dudley Coll. Corp., 2003–11 (Chm., 2004–11). Mem., Birmingham Art Circle, 2009–. RBSA 2012 (Hon. Sec., 2011–). Trustee, Heart of the Nat. Forest Foundn, 2005–10. DL W Midlands, 2008. Hon. MBA Wolverhampton, 1999. *Recreations:* sculpture, theatre, music, planting trees. *Address:* 16 Knighton Drive, Sutton Coldfield, W Midlands B74 4QP.

ASTON, Bishop Suffragan of, since 2015; **Rt Rev. Anne Elizabeth Hollinghurst;** *b* 4 March 1964; *d* of William and Audrey Bailey; *m* 1984, Rev. Steve Hollinghurst. *Educ:* Trinity Coll., Bristol (BA 1996); Hughes Hall, Cambridge (MSt 2010). Youth worker, Sussex, then Nottingham; ordained deacon, 1996, priest, 1997; Curate, St Saviours in the Meadows, Nottingham, 1996–99; Chaplain, Derby Univ. and Derby Cathedral, 1999–2005; Bishop's Domestic Chaplain and Canon Res., Manchester Cathedral, 2005–10; Vicar, St Peter's, St Albans, 2010–15. *Address:* Diocesan Office, 1 Colmore Row, Birmingham B3 2BJ.

ASTON, Archdeacon of; *see* Heathfield, Ven. S. D.

ASTOR, family name of **Viscount Astor** and **Baron Astor of Hever**.

ASTOR, 4th Viscount *cr* 1917, of Hever Castle; **William Waldorf Astor;** Baron 1916; *b* 27 Dec. 1951; *s* of 3rd Viscount Astor; *S* father, 1966; *m* 1976, Annabel Lucy Veronica Sheffield (*see* Viscountess Astor); two *s* one *d*. *Educ:* Eton Coll. A Lord in Waiting (Govt Whip), 1990–93. Parliamentary Under-Secretary of State: DSS, 1993–94; Dept of Nat. Heritage,

1994–95; an Opposition spokesman, H of L, 1996–2009; elected Mem., H of L, 1999; Director: Networkers Internat. plc, 1996–; Silvergate Media Ltd, 2012–. Trustee, Sir Stanley Spencer Gall., Cookham, 1975–. *Heir:* *s* Hon. William Waldorf Astor [*b* 18 Jan. 1979; *m* 2009 Lohralee Stutz; one *s* one *d*]. *Address:* Ginge Manor, Wantage, Oxon OX12 8QT. *Club:* White's.

ASTOR, Viscountess; **Annabel Lucy Veronica Astor;** Founder and Chief Executive Officer, Oka Direct Ltd, 1999–2014 (Director, since 1999); *b* London, 14 Aug. 1948; *d* of late Timothy Angus Jones and Pandora Jones (*née* Clifford); *m* 1st, 1969, Sir Reginald Adrian Berkeley Sheffield, Bt, *qv* (marr. diss. 1975); two *d*; 2nd, 1976, Viscount Astor, *qv*; two *s* one *d*. *Educ:* Hatherop Castle Sch.; Lycée Français de Londres. Owner, Annabel Jones Ltd, jewellery, 1969–99. *Address:* Ginge Manor, Wantage, Oxon OX12 8QT. *E:* aastor@okadirect.com.

See also Rt Hon. D. W. D. Cameron.

ASTOR OF HEVER, 3rd Baron *cr* 1956, of Hever Castle; **John Jacob Astor;** PC 2015; DL; *b* 16 June 1946; *s* of 2nd Baron Astor of Hever and Lady Irene Haig, *d* of Field Marshal 1st Earl Haig, KT, GCB, OM, GCVO, KCIE; *S* father, 1984; *m* 1st, 1970, Fiona Diana Lennox Harvey (marr. diss. 1990), *d* of Captain Roger Harvey; three *d*; 2nd, 1990, Hon. Elizabeth, *d* of 2nd Viscount Mackintosh of Halifax, OBE, BEM; one *s* one *d*. *Educ:* Eton College. Lieut Life Guards, 1966–70, Malaysia, Hong Kong, Ulster. Director: Terres Blanches Services Sarl, 1975–77; Valberg Plaza Sarl, 1977–82; Managing Director: Honon et Cie, 1982–; Astor France Sarl, 1989–. An Opposition Whip, H of L, 1998–2010; elected Mem., H of L, 1999. Shadow Defence Minister, 2003–10; a Lord in Waiting (Govt Whip), 2010–11; Parly Under-Sec. of State, MoD, 2010–15. Vice-Chm., All Party Parly Gp for the Army; Secretary: Anglo-Swiss Parly Assoc., 1992–2010; All Party Motor Gp, 1998–2010; All Party Gp on Autism, 2000–10; All Party Gp on Shooting and Conservation, 2002–10; Jt Treas., British-S African Parly Assoc., 1994. Trustee: Astor Foundn; Astor of Hever Trust; Pres., RoSPA, 1996–99. Gov., Cobham Hall Sch., 1993–96. DL Kent, 1996. Chm., Council of St John, Kent, 1987–97; KStJ 1998. *Heir:* *s* Hon. Charles Gavin John Astor, *b* 10 Nov. 1990. *Address:* Frenchstreet House, Westerham, Kent TN16 1PW. *Club:* White's.

ASTOR, David Waldorf, CBE 1994; DL; farmer, since 1973; *b* 9 Aug. 1943; *s* of late Michael Langhorne Astor and Barbara Mary (*née* McNeill); *m* 1968, Clare Pamela St John; two *s* two *d*. *Educ:* Eton Coll.; Harvard Univ. Short service commn in Royal Scots Greys, 1962–65. United Newspapers, 1970–72; Housing Corp., 1972–75; Head of Develt, National Th., 1978–79; Director: Jupiter Tarbutt Merlin, 1985–91; Priory Investments Ltd, 1990–2007. Chairman: CPRE, 1983–93; Southern Arts Bd, 1998–2002. Chairman: Action for Prisoners' Families, 2003–09; Turn2Us, 2007–09. Trustee: Glyndebourne Arts Trust, 1995–2005; Elizabeth Finn Care (formerly Elizabeth Finn Trust), 2004–11; Oxford Community Foundn, 2010–. Patron: Mulberry Bush Sch., 1998–; Wychwood Project, 2010–; Oxfordshire Family Mediation, 2010–. Contested (SDP/Alliance) Plymouth Drake, 1987. FRSA. DL Oxon, 2007. *Recreations:* books, sport. *Address:* Bruern Grange, Milton under Wychwood, Oxford OX7 6HA. *T:* (01993) 830413. *Clubs:* Brooks's, Beefsteak, Academy, MCC.

ASTWOOD, Hon. Sir James (Rufus), KBE 1994; Kt 1982; JP; President, Court of Appeal: Bermuda, 1994–2003; Turks and Caicos Islands, 1997–2002; *b* 4 Oct. 1923; *s* of late James Rufus Astwood, Sr, and Mabel Winifred Astwood; *m* 1952, Gloria Preston Norton; one *s* two *d*. *Educ:* Berkeley Inst., Bermuda; Univ. of Toronto, Canada. Called to the Bar, Gray's Inn, London, Feb. 1956, Hon. Bencher, 1985; admitted to practice at Jamaican Bar, Oct. 1956; joined Jamaican Legal Service, 1957; Dep. Clerk of Courts, 1957–58; Clerk of Courts, Jamaica, 1958–63; Stipendiary Magistrate and Judge of Grand Court, Cayman Islands (on secondment from Jamaica), 1958–59; Resident Magistrate, Jamaica, 1963–74; Puisne Judge, Jamaica, during 1971 and 1973; retd from Jamaican Legal Service, 1974; Sen. Magistrate, Bermuda, 1974–76; Solicitor General, 1976–77; Acting Attorney General, during 1976 and 1977; Acting Dep. Governor for a period in 1977; Chief Justice, 1977–93, Justice of Appeal, 1993–94, Bermuda. Has served on several cttees, tribunals and bds of enquiry, in both Bermuda and Jamaica. *Recreations:* golf, cricket, photography, reading, bridge, travel. *Address:* The Pebble, 7 Astwood Walk, Warwick WK08, Bermuda; PO Box HM 1674, Hamilton HMGX, Bermuda. *Club:* Bermuda Senior Golfers Society (Bermuda).

ATALLA, Ashraf Albert; Managing Director, Roughcut Television Ltd, since 2007; *b* Cairo, 18 June 1972; *s* of Albert and Adele Atalla. *Educ:* Lord Mayor Treloar Coll.; Bath Univ. (BSc Business Admin 1994). Stockbroker, Panmure Gordon, 1995–97; Researcher, BBC, 1997–2001; Producer, The Office, BBC TV, 2001–04; Hd of Comedy, Talkback Thames, 2004–07. Exec. Producer, TV series incl. The IT Crowd, 2006–07, Clone, 2008, Trinity, 2009, Trollied, 2011–12. Columnist, Guardian, 2006–08. *Publications:* contribs to newspapers. *Recreations:* audio books, sitting in the sun, Indian food, watching any football that happens to be on. *Address:* PBJ Management, 22 Rathbone Street, W1T 1LG. *Clubs:* Groucho, Soho House, Ivy.

ATCHERLEY, Sir Harold Winter, Kt 1977; Chairman: Suffolk and North Essex Branch, European Movement, 1995–98 (President, 1998–2002); Aldeburgh Foundation, 1989–94 (Deputy Chairman, 1988–89); Toynbee Hall, 1985–90 (Member, Management Committee, 1979–90); *b* 30 Aug. 1918; *s* of L. W. Atcherley and Maude Lester (*née* Nash); *m* 1st, 1946, Anita Helen (*née* Leslie) (marr. diss. 1990); one *s* two *d*; 2nd, 1990, Mrs Elke Jessett (*d* 2004), *d* of late Dr Carl Langbehn; 3rd, 2005, Mrs Sarah, (Sally), Mordant. *Educ:* Gresham's Sch.; Heidelberg and Geneva Univs. Joined Royal Dutch Shell Gp, 1937. Served War: Queen's Westminster Rifles, 1939; commissioned Intelligence Corps, 1940; served 18th Inf. Div., Singapore; POW, 1942–45. Rejoined Royal Dutch Shell Gp, 1946: served Egypt, Lebanon, Syria, Argentina, Brazil, 1946–59. Personnel Co-ordinator, Royal Dutch Shell Group, 1964–70, retd. Recruitment Advisor to Ministry of Defence, 1970–71. Chm., Tyzack & Partners, 1979–85; Dir, British Home Stores Ltd, 1973–87. Chairman: Armed Forces Pay Review Body, 1971–82; Police Negotiating Bd, 1983–86 (Dep. Chm., 1982); Member: Top Salaries Review Body, 1971–87; Nat. Staff Cttee for Nurses and Midwives, 1973–77; Cttee of Inquiry into Pay and Related Conditions of Service of Nurses, 1974; Cttee of Inquiry into Remuneration of Members of Local Authorities, 1977. Vice-Chm., Suffolk Wildlife Trust, 1987–90; Mem. Management Cttee, Suffolk Rural Housing Assoc., 1984–87. Empress Leopoldina Medal (Brazil), 1958. *Publications:* Prisoner of Japan, 2012. *Recreations:* music, good food and wine with family and friends. *Address:* 27 Sussex Square, W2 2SL.

ATHA, Bernard Peter, CBE 2007 (OBE 1991); Principal Lecturer in Business Studies, Huddersfield Technical College, 1973–90; Lord Mayor, City of Leeds, 2000–01; *b* 27 Aug. 1928; *s* of Horace Michael Atha and Mary Quinlan; unmarried. *Educ:* Leeds Modern Sch.; Leeds Univ. (LLB Hons). Barrister-at-law, Gray's Inn. Commn, RAF, 1950–52. Variety artist on stage; Mem. Equity; films and TV plays. Elected Leeds City Council, 1957–2014 (Hon. Alderman, 2014); Chm., Leeds Leisure Services Cttee, 1988–99; former Chairman: Watch Cttee; Social Services Cttee; Educn Cttee. Vice-Chm., W Leeds HA, 1988–90. Contested (Lab): Penrith and the Border, 1959; Pudsey, 1964. Pres., Leeds Co-op. Soc., 1976–96; Chairman: Leeds Playhouse, 1974–2007; Northern Ballet Theatre, 1995–2010. Member: Arts Council, 1979–82; Ministerial Working Party on Sport and Recreation, 1974, on Sport for the Disabled, 1989; EU (formerly EC) Sport for Disabled Cttee, 1992–99 (Vice-Chm., 1997–99); Internat. Paralympic Cttee, 1993–98; Sports Lottery Bd, 1995–2003; Vice-Chm., Sports Council, 1976–80; Chairman: Yorks and Humberside Reg. Sports Council, 1966–76; Nat. Water Sports Centre, 1978–84; UK Sports Assoc. for People with Learning Disability (formerly UK Sports Assoc. for People with Mental Handicap), 1980– (Pres., INASFMH 1993–2007); British Paralympics Assoc., 1989. Vice-Chm., St James' Univ. Hosp. NHS Trust, 1993–98 (Dir, 1990–98); Chm., United Leeds Teaching Hosps NHS Trust, subseq. United Leeds Hosps Charitable Foundn, 2009–14 (Mem., 2000–14; Vice Chm., 2001–09); Chairman: Disability Sports Develt Trust (formerly British Paralympic Trust), 1990–; English Fedn Disability Sport, 1999–2009. Chairman: Yorks Dance Centre Trust, 1987–2007; Red Ladder Theatre Co., 1987–2014; Craft Centre and Design Gall., Leeds, 1988–; Liz Dawn Cancer Appeal; Yorkshire Youth Ballet (formerly Yorkshire Youth Dance), 2006–08. Pres., British and Internat. Fedn of Festivals, 2002–14, now Emeritus. Mem., Lord Renton Foundn, 1991–; Trustee, London Marathon Charitable Foundn, 2007–11. Governor, Sports Aid Foundn. FRSA. Hon. Fellow, Leeds Coll. of Music, 2002. British Gas/Arts Council Award, 1993. *Recreations:* sport, the arts, travel. *Address:* 25 Moseley Wood Croft, Leeds, West Yorks LS16 7JJ. *T:* (0113) 267 2485. *E:* bernard.atha@outlook.com.

ATHA, Air Vice-Marshal Stuart David, CB 2015; DSO 2003; Chief of Staff (Operations), Permanent Joint Headquarters, since 2014; *b* Irvine, 30 April 1962; *s* of Wright Atha and Myra Atha; *m* 1989, Caroline Dick; one *s* four *d*. *Educ:* Kilmarnock Acad.; Univ. of Glasgow (BSc 1984); King's Coll. London (MA 2000). Joined RAF, 1984; Hawk flying instructor, 1986–90; Harrier pilot, 1 (Fighter) Sqdn, IV (Army Cooperation) Sqdn and Air Warfare Centre, 1990–2000; OC 3 (Fighter) Sqdn, 2000–03; PSO to CAS, 2003–05; Station Comdr, RAF Coningsby, 2006–08; AOC No 83 Expeditionary Air Gp, 2009–10; Hd, Jt Capability, MoD, 2010–11; AOC No 1 Gp, RAF, 2011–14. *Recreations:* high handicap piano player and golfer, children's taxi driver. *Club:* Royal Air Force.

ATHANASOU, Prof. Nicholas Anthony, PhD, MD; FRCPath; Professor of Musculoskeletal Pathology, University of Oxford, since 2002; Fellow of Wadham College, Oxford, since 2002; *b* Perth, Australia, 26 April 1953; *s* of Anthony Athanasou and Angelina Athanasou (*née* Pappas); *m* 1985, Linda Hulls. *Educ:* Sydney High Sch.; Univ. of Sydney (MB BS 1978; MD 1998); St Bartholomew's Hosp. Medical Coll., Univ. of London (PhD 1985). MRCP 1981; FRCPath 1986. Arthritis Res. Campaign Fellow in Osteoarticular Pathology, Univ. of Oxford, 1988–91; Consultant Pathologist, Nuffield Orthopaedic Centre, Oxford, 1991–; Reader, Univ. of Oxford, 1997–2002. Res. Line Leader, EuroBoNeT, 2006–11. Committee Member: Nat. Cancer Intelligence Network, 2008–; Nat. Cancer Res. Network (sarcoma), 2011–14; Nat. Cancer Peer Rev. (sarcoma), 2012–14. *Publications:* Hybrids: stories of Greek Australia, 1995; The Greek Liar (novel), 2002; Atlas of Bone, Joint and Soft Tissue Pathology, 1999; Pathological Basis of Orthopaedic and Rheumatic Disease, 2001; The Person of the Man (novel), 2012. *Recreations:* walking, music, theatre, sports, travel. *Address:* Department of Pathology, Nuffield Orthopaedic Centre, Oxford OX3 7LD. *T:* (01865) 738136, *Fax:* (01865) 738140. *E:* nick.athanasou@ndorms.ox.ac.uk.

ATHERTON, Alan Royle, CB 1990; Director, The Argyll Consultancies PLC, 1991–9[illegible] (Deputy Chairman, 1992–94; Chairman, 1994–99); *b* 25 April 1931; *s* of Harold Atherton and Hilda (*née* Royle); *m* 1959, Valerie Kemp (marr. diss. 1996); three *s* one *d*. *Educ:* Cowley Sch., St Helens; Sheffield Univ. (BSc (Hons Chem.)). ICI Ltd, 1955–58; Department of Scientific and Industrial Research: SSO, 1959–64; Private Sec. to Permanent Sec., 1960–64; PSO, Road Res. Lab., 1964–65; Principal, Min. of Housing and Local Govt, 1965–70; Asst Sec., Ordnance Survey, 1970–74; Under-Sec., 1975–87, Dep. Sec., 1987–91, DoE. Chm., Local Govt Staff Commn (Eng.), 1993–98. Vice Chm., CS Med. Assoc., then CS Healthcare, 1987–98. Chm., Queen Elizabeth II Conf. Centre Bd, 1990–93; Dir, Internat. Centre for Facilities, Canada, 1993–2001; Member: Letchworth Garden City Corp., 1991–94; Historic Royal Palaces Agency Adv. Gp, 1991–98. *Recreations:* walking, gardening, ballet, Rugby, bonsai. *Club:* Athenæum.

ATHERTON, Candice Kathleen, (Candy); freelance journalist, since 1980; political consultant, since 2005; Managing Director, Atherton Associates, since 2007; *b* 21 Sept. 1955; *d* of late Denis G. W. Atherton and of Pamela A. M. Osborne; *m* 2002, Broderick Ross. *Educ:* Poly. of N London (BA Hons Applied Social Studies). Journalist, Portsmouth News, 1974; West Sussex Probation Service, 1975–76; Founder, Women's Aid Refuge, 1977; Co-Founder, Everywoman Magazine, 1984; freelance journalist, 1980–. Member: (Lab), Islington LBC, 1986–92 (Mayor, 1989–90); Islington HA, 1986–90. Contested (Lab), Chesham and Amersham, 1992. MP (Lab) Falmouth and Camborne, 1997–2005; contested (Lab) same seat 2005. Member: Select Committee: on Educn and Employment, 1997–2001; on Envmt, Food and Rural Affairs, 2002–05. Chair: All-Party (formerly Associate) Parly Water Gp, 1997–2005; Rural Housing Adv. Gp, 2007–11. Treas., Parly Waterways Gp, 1999–2005; Sec., All-Party Parly Objective 1 Areas Gp, 2000–05. Member, Board: Housing Corp., 2005–08; Homes and Communities Agency, 2008–11. Chair: Cornwall Labour Party, 2011–13; Truro and Falmouth Labour Party, 2010–. Mem. (Lab and Co-op), Falmouth Town Council, 2013– (Chair, Finance and Gen. Purposes Cttee, 2013–); Vice Chair, Health and Adult Care, Cornwall Council, 2013–. Freeman, City of London, 1989. *Recreations:* bird-watching, canal boats, keeping chickens, archaeology. *Address:* Osprey, Swanpool, Falmouth TR11 5BD.

ATHERTON, David, OBE 1999; Founder and Artistic Director, Mainly Mozart Festival, Southern California and Northern Mexico, 1988–2013; Conductor Laureate, Hong Kong Philharmonic Orchestra, 2000–09 (Music Director and Principal Conductor, 1989–2000); *b* 3 Jan. 1944; *s* of Robert and Lavinia Atherton; *m* 1970, Ann Gianetta Drake (marr. diss. 2012); one *s* two *d*; *m* 2012, Eleanor Ann Roth. *Educ:* Cambridge Univ. (MA). LRAM, LTCL. Music Dir, London Sinfonietta, 1967–73 and 1989–91 (Co-Founder, 1967); Repetiteur, Royal Opera House, Covent Garden, 1967–68; Resident Conductor, Royal Opera House, 1968–80; Principal Conductor and Artistic Advr, 1980–83, Principal Guest Conductor, 1983–86, Royal Liverpool Philharmonic Orch.; Music Dir and Principal Conductor, San Diego Symphony Orch., 1980–87; Artistic Director and Conductor: London Schubert/Webern Fest., 1978–79; Stravinsky Fest., 1979–82; Ravel/Varèse Fest., 1983–84; Principal Guest Conductor: BBC SO, 1985–89; BBC Nat. Orch. of Wales, 1994–97. Co-Founder, Pres. and Artistic Dir, Global Music Network, 1998–2002. Became youngest conductor in history of Henry Wood Promenade Concerts at Royal Albert Hall, and also at Royal Opera House, 1968; Royal Festival Hall debut, 1969; from 1968 performances in Europe, Middle East, Far East, Australasia, N and S America. Adapted and arranged Pandora by Roberto Gerhard for Royal Ballet, 1975. Conductor of the Year Award (Composers' Guild of GB), 1971; Edison Award, 1973; Grand Prix du Disque award, 1977; Koussevitzky Award, 1981; Internat. Record Critics Award, 1982; Prix Caecilia, 1982. *Publications:* (ed) The Complete Instrumental and Chamber Music of Arnold Schoenberg and Roberto Gerhard, 1973; (ed) Pandora and Don Quixote Suites by Roberto Gerhard, 1973; contrib., The Musical Companion, 1978, The New Grove Dictionary, 1981. *Recreations:* travel, computers, theatre. *Address:* Askonas Holt Ltd, Lincoln House, 300 High Holborn, WC1V 7JH. *T:* (020) 7400 1700, *Fax:* (020) 7400 1799.

ATHERTON, James Bernard; Secretary-General, British Bankers' Association, 1982–85; *b* 3 Dec. 1927; *s* of late James Atherton and Edith (*née* Atkinson); *m* 1953, Eileen Margaret Birch; two *s*. *Educ:* Alsop High Sch., Liverpool. Served RAF, 1946–48; Martins Bank, 1943–46 and 1948–69 (Asst Chief Accountant, 1966–69); Barclays Bank, 1969–82 (Chief Clearing Manager, 1969–73, Asst Gen. Manager, 1973–78, Divl Gen. Manager, 1978–82). *Recreations:* opera, gardening. *Address:* c/o Barclays Bank, 10 The Square, Petersfield, Hants GU32 3HW.

ATHERTON, Jason; chef; Chief Executive Officer, Jason Atherton Restaurants, since 2010; *b* Worksop, Notts, 6 Sept. 1971; *s* of Vic and Sandra Atherton; *m* 2004, Irha; two *d*. *Educ:* Earl of Scarborough High Sch.; Boston Coll. of Further Educn. Commis chef, La Tante Claire; chef de partie: Chez Nico; The Restaurant; L'Auberge de l'Ill, France; sous chef, Coast; hd chef, Mash and Air; chef de partie, El Bulli, Spain; hd chef, Frith St Restaurant; Exec. Chef, Maze Restaurants, 2001–10, incl. Verre, Dubai, 2001–05, Maze London, Maze Grill and Maze Prague; Chef: Pollen St Social Restaurant, 2011– (Michelin Star, 2012); Little Social, 2013; Social Eating House, 2013 (Michelin Star, 2013); City Social, 2014; Chef/owner, restaurants in China, Hong Kong and Singapore. Presenter, TV series, My Kitchen Rules, 2014. Chef of Year, Catey Awards, 2012. *Publications:* Maze: the cookbook, 2008; Gourmet Food for a Fiver, 2010. *Recreations:* golf, keeping fit, running. *Address:* 7B Balham Grove, SW12 8AZ. *E:* jason@pollenstreetsocial.com.

ATHERTON, Brig. Maurice Alan, CBE 1981; JP; Vice Lord-Lieutenant, Kent, 2000–02; *b* 9 Oct. 1926; *s* of late Rev. Harold Atherton and Beatrice Atherton (*née* Shaw); *m* 1954, Guendolene Mary Upton; one *s* one *d*. *Educ:* St John's Sch., Leatherhead; Staff Coll., Camberley (psc). Commnd E Yorks Regt, 1946 (served in Egypt, Sudan, Malaya, Austria, Germany, UK); MA to Comdr British Forces, Hong Kong, 1959–62; coll. chief instructor, RMA Sandhurst, 1964–67; CO 1 Green Howards, 1967–69; GSO 1, NI, 1969–71; defence advr, Ghana, 1971–73; Comdr, Dover Shorncliffe Garrison and Dep. Constable, Dover Castle, 1976–81. Co. Pres., Kent, RBL, 1982–91; Chm., Kent Cttee, Army Benevolent Fund, 1984–96. Gov., Christ Church UC, Canterbury, 1985–99 (Chm. Govs, 1993–99); Comr, Duke of York's Royal Mil. Sch., 1992–2003. JP 1982–91, High Sheriff 1983–84, DL 1984, Kent. Hon. DCL Kent, 1996. *Recreations:* gardening, shooting. *Address:* Digges Place, Barham, Canterbury, Kent CT4 6PJ. *T:* (01227) 831420. *Club:* Lansdowne.

ATHERTON, Michael Andrew, OBE 1997; sports commentator and broadcaster; *b* 23 March 1968; *s* of Alan and Wendy Atherton; two *s*. *Educ:* Manchester Grammar Sch.; Downing Coll., Cambridge (BA Hons History; MA). 1st class début, Cambridge *v* Essex, 1987; played for Lancashire CCC, 1987–2001; Captain: Young England, Sri Lanka 1987, Australia 1988; Cambridge Univ., 1988–89; Combined Universities, 1989; Mem., England Test team, 115 matches, 1989–2001; captained 54 Test matches, 1993–98 and 2001; scored 16 Test centuries. Mem., Editl Board, Wisden Cricket Monthly, 1993–2003; columnist: Sunday Telegraph, 2001–07; The Times, 2008–. Cricket commentator: Channel 4, 2001–05; BSkyB, 2006–. *Publications:* Opening Up: my autobiography, 2002; Gambling: a story of triumph and disaster, 2007. *Recreations:* golf, reading, writing. *Address:* c/o Jon Holmes Media Ltd, 3 Wine Office Court, EC4A 3BY. *Club:* Groucho.

ATHERTON, Air Vice-Marshal Paul Ashley, OBE 2005; Director Operations, Military Aviation Authority, since 2012; *b* W Hartlepool, 10 Feb. 1964; *s* of Wilfred and Melva Atherton; *m* 1987, Jane Mary Richards; two *d*. *Educ:* Peterlee Grammar Tech. Sch.; RAF Coll., Cranwell. VIP and trng pilot, Sqdn Exec., No 10 Sqdn, 1985–95; sc 1996; Directorate of Jt Warfare, MoD, 1997–99; OC No 216 Sqdn, 1999–2002; Future Strategic Tanker Aircraft Project Team, Defence Procurement Agency, 2002–04; Comdr, Basrah Air Stn, Iraq, 2004–05; OC, RAF Lyneham, 2006–07; rcds, 2008; ACOS Strategy, Policy and Plans, 2008–10, AO Ops, 2010–12, HQ Air Comd. Chm., Combined Services Cricket Assoc., 2012–; President: RAF Cricket Assoc., 2008–; 216 Sqdn Assoc., 2009–. Freeman, Fuellers' Co., 2002. *Recreations:* growing vegetables from seed, reading, the countryside, watching football, Rugby Union and cricket (sadly no longer playing!). *Address:* Military Aviation Authority, MoD Abbey Wood, Bristol BS34 8QW. *T:* 0306 798 4178, 07557 053677. *E:* maa-op-d@mod.uk. *Clubs:* Royal Air Force Innominate; Adastrian Cricket (Pres., 2007–).

ATHERTON, Rev. Mgr Richard, OBE 1989; Chaplain to the Archbishop of Liverpool, 1996–2002; *b* 15 Feb. 1928; *s* of Richard Atherton and Winifred Mary Atherton (*née* Hurst). *Educ:* St Francis Xavier's Coll., Liverpool; Upholland Coll., Wigan; Dip. Criminology, London Univ., 1979; BA Hons Maryvale Inst., Birmingham, 1995; MA Durham, 1997. Ordained priest, 1954; Curate: St Cecilia's, Tuebrook, Liverpool, 1954–60; St Philip Neri's, Liverpool, 1960–65; Prison Chaplain: Walton, Liverpool, 1965–75; Appleton Thorne, Warrington, 1975–77; Principal RC Prison Chaplain, 1977–89; Parish Priest, St Joseph's, Leigh, Lancs, 1989–91; Pres., Ushaw Coll., 1991–96. *Publications:* Summons to Serve, 1987; New Light on the Psalms, 1993; Praying the Prayer of the Church, 1998; Praying the Sunday Psalms, Year A, 2001, Year B, 2003, Year C, 2004; Let's Meet the Prophets, 2008. *Recreations:* walking, reading. *Address:* 27 Seabank Road, Southport PR9 0EJ. *T:* (01704) 631071.

ATHERTON, His Honour Robert Kenneth; a Circuit Judge, 2000–15; *b* 22 June 1947; *s* of late John and Evelyn Atherton; civil partnership 2006, Michael Montgomery. *Educ:* Boteler Grammar Sch., Warrington; Univ. of Liverpool (LLB Hons). Called to the Bar, Gray's Inn, 1970; in practice at the Bar, 1971–2000; Asst Recorder, 1994–99; a Recorder, 1999–2000. Legal Mem., Mental Health Review Tribunal, 1989–2000 (Mem., Restricted Panel, 2001–). Asst Comr, Parly Boundary Commn, 1993–95. Mem., Council of HM Circuit Judges, 2006–14 (Chm., Criminal Sub-cttee, 2011–14). Mem., Lincoln's Inn, 2008, Bencher, 2012. *Recreations:* travel, music, gardening.

ATHERTON, Stephen Nicholas; QC 2006; barrister; *b* 6 May 1966; *s* of James Alan Atherton and late Ann Margaret Atherton; *m* 1992, Lucy-Jane Coppock; one *d*. *Educ:* West Park Sch.; Univ. of Lancaster (LLB Hons); Magdalene Coll., Cambridge (LLM 1988). Called to the Bar, Middle Temple, 1989, and Gray's Inn. Barrister specialising in domestic and internat. corporate insolvency and restructuring, and civil aspects of domestic and internat. commercial fraud. *Publications:* various legal texts and articles. *Recreations:* Rugby Union, Rugby League, cricket, films, food, family, collecting ancient Chinese ceramics and British watercolours and drawings. *Address:* 20 Essex Street, WC2R 3AL. *T:* (020) 7842 1200. *E:* satherton@20essexst.com; Old Isleworth, Middlesex; Hinton St George, Somerset. *Club:* Hinton St George Cricket.

ATHOLL, 12th Duke of, *cr* 1703; **Bruce George Ronald Murray;** Lord Murray of Tullibardine 1604; Earl of Tullibardine 1606; Earl of Atholl 1629; Marquess of Atholl, Viscount of Balquhidder, Lord Murray, Balvenie and Gask, 1676; Marquess of Tullibardine, Earl of Strathtay and Strathardle, Viscount Glenalmond and Glenlyon, 1703 - all in the peerage of Scotland; *b* 6 April 1960; *er s* of 11th Duke of Atholl and of Margaret Yvonne Murray (*née* Leach); *S* father, 2012; *m* 1st, 1984, Lynne Elizabeth (marr. diss. 2003), *e d* of Nicholas Andrew; two *s* one *d*; *m* 2nd, 2009, Charmaine Myrna, *d* of Dirk Du Toit. Lieut, Transvaal Scottish, 1983; Col, Atholl Highlanders, 2012. *Heir: s* Marquess of Tullibardine, *qv*. *Address:* PO Box 1522, Louis Trichardt, 0920, South Africa.

ATIYAH, Sir Michael (Francis), OM 1992; Kt 1983; FRS 1962; FRSE 1985; President, Royal Society of Edinburgh, 2005–08; Master of Trinity College, Cambridge, 1990–97, Fellow since 1997; Director, Isaac Newton Institute for Mathematical Sciences, Cambridge, 1990–96; *b* 22 April 1929; *e s* of late Edward Atiyah and Jean Levens; *m* 1955, Lily Brown; two *s* (and one *s* decd). *Educ:* Victoria Coll., Egypt; Manchester Grammar Sch.; Trinity Coll., Cambridge (BA 1952; PhD 1955). Research Fellow, Trinity Coll., Camb., 1954–58, Hon. Fellow, 1976–97; First Smith's Prize, 1954; Commonwealth Fund Fellow, 1955–56; Mem. Inst. for Advanced Study, Princeton, 1955–56, 1959–60, 1967–68, 1987; Asst Lectr in Mathematics, 1957–58, Lectr 1958–61, Univ. of Cambridge; Fellow, Pembroke Coll., Cambridge, 1958–61 (Hon. Fellow, 1983); Reader in Mathematics, Univ. of Oxford, and Professorial Fellow of St Catherine's Coll., Oxford, 1961–63 (Hon. Fellow, 1992); Savilian Prof. of Geometry, and Fellow of New College, Oxford, 1963–69 (Hon. Fellow 1999); Prof. of Mathematics, Inst. for Advanced Study, Princeton, NJ, 1969–72; Royal Soc. Res. Prof., Mathematical Inst., Oxford, and Professorial Fellow, St Catherine's Coll., Oxford, 1973–90. Hon. Prof., Univ. of Edinburgh, 1997–. Visiting Lecturer, Harvard, 1962–63 and 1964–65. Member: Exec. Cttee, Internat. Mathematical Union, 1966–74; SERC, 1984–89; ACOST, 1991–93; President: London Mathematical Soc., 1975–77; Mathematical Assoc., 1981–82; Royal Soc., 1990–95; Chm., European Mathematical Council, 1978–90. Pres., Pugwash, 1997–2002. Chancellor, Univ. of Leicester, 1995–2005. Freeman, City of London, 1996. Fellow, Univ. of Wales Swansea, 1999. Founder FMedSci 1998 (Hon. FMedSci 2001). Hon. FREng (Hon. FEng 1993); Hon. FFA 1999. Foreign Member: Amer. Acad. of Arts and Scis; Swedish Royal Acad.; Leopoldina Acad.; Nat. Acad. of Scis, USA; Acad. des Sciences, France; Royal Irish Acad.; Czechoslovak Union of Mathematicians and Physicists; Amer. Philos. Soc.; Indian Nat. Science Acad.; Australian Acad. of Scis; Ukrainian Acad. of Scis; Russian Acad. of Scis; Georgian Acad. of Scis; Venezuelan Acad. of Scis; Accad. Nazionale dei Lincei, Rome; Moscow Mathematical Soc.; Royal Norwegian Acad. of Sci. and Letters, 2001; Spanish Royal Acad. of Sci., 2002; Norwegian Acad. of Sci. and Letters, 2009; Hon. Mem., Royal Spanish Mathematical Soc., 2011. Hon. Prof., Chinese Acad. of Scis; Hon. Fellow, Darwin Coll., Cambridge, 1992; Hon. Dist. Fellow, Leicester Univ., 2007. Hon. DSc: Bonn, 1968; Warwick, 1969; Durham, 1979; St Andrew's, 1981; Dublin, Chicago, 1983; Edinburgh, 1984; Essex, London, 1985; Sussex, 1986; Ghent, 1987; Reading, Helsinki, 1990; Leicester, 1991; Salamanca, Rutgers, 1992; Wales, Montreal, Waterloo, 1993; Lebanese Univ., Birmingham, Keele, Queen's (Ontario), 1994; UMIST, Chinese Univ. of Hong Kong, 1996; Brown, 1997; Oxford, Prague, 1998; Heriot-Watt, 1999; Mexico, 2001; York, 2005; Harvard, 2006; Hong Kong Univ. of Sci. and Technol., 2012; Hon. ScD Cantab, 1984; DUniv Open, 1995; Hon. PhD Scuola Normale, Pisa, 2007; Dr *hc* Poly. Univ. of Catalonia, 2008; Hon. DHumLit American Univ. of Beirut, 2004. Fields Medal, Internat. Congress of Mathematicians, Moscow, 1966; Royal Medal, Royal Soc., 1968; De Morgan Medal, London Mathematical Soc., 1980; Antonio Feltrinelli Prize for mathematical sciences, Accademia Nazionale dei Lincei, Rome, 1981; King Faisal Foundn Internat. Prize for Science, Saudi Arabia, 1987; Copley Medal, Royal Soc., 1988; Gunning Victoria Jubilee Prize, RSE, 1990; Nehru Meml Medal, INSA, 1993; Franklin Medal, Amer. Phil. Soc., 1993; Royal Medal, RSE, 2003; (jtly) Abel Prize, Norwegian Acad. of Sci. and Letters, 2004; President's Medal, Inst. of Physics, 2008; Grande Médaille, French Acad. of Scis, 2011. Commander, Order of Cedars (Lebanon), 1994; Mem. (1st Class), Order of Andrés Bello (Venezuela), 1997; Mem. (1st class), Golden Order of Merit (Lebanon), 2004; Grand Cross of Order of Scientific Merit (Brazil), 2010; Grand Officier, Légion d'Honneur (France), 2011. *Publications:* Collected Works, 5 vols, 1988, vol. 6, 2004, vol. 7, 2015; The Geometry and Physics of Knots, 1990; papers in mathematical journals. *Recreation:* gardening. *Address:* 3/8 West Grange Gardens, Edinburgh EH9 2RA.

See also P. S. Atiyah.

ATIYAH, Prof. Patrick Selim, DCL; QC 1989; FBA 1978; Professor of English Law, and Fellow of St John's College, Oxford University, 1977–88, Hon. Fellow, 1988; *b* 5 March 1931; *s* of Edward Atiyah and D. J. C. Levens; *m* 1951, Christine Best; three *s* (and one *s* decd). *Educ:* Woking County Grammar Sch. for Boys; Magdalen Coll., Oxford (MA 1957, DCL 1974). Called to the Bar, Inner Temple, 1956. Asst Lectr, LSE, 1954–55; Lectr, Univ. of Khartoum, 1955–59; Legal Asst, BoT, 1961–64; Fellow, New Coll., Oxford, 1964–69; Professor of Law: ANU, 1970–73; Warwick Univ., 1973–77; Visiting Professor: Univ. of Texas, 1979; Harvard Law Sch., 1982–83; Duke Univ., 1985. Lectures: Lionel Cohen, Hebrew Univ., Jerusalem, 1980; Oliver Wendell Holmes, Harvard Law Sch., 1981; Cecil Wright Meml, Univ. of Toronto, 1983; Viscount Bennett, Univ. of New Brunswick, 1984; Chorley, LSE, 1985; Hamlyn, Leeds Univ., 1987. Hon. LLD Warwick, 1989. General Editor, Oxford Jl of Legal Studies, 1981–86. *Publications:* The Sale of Goods, 1957, 8th edn 1990, 10th edn (ed John Adams), 2000; Introduction to the Law of Contract, 1961, 6th edn (ed Stephen Smith), 2007; Vicarious Liability, 1967; Accidents, Compensation and the Law, 1970, 6th edn (ed Peter Cane), 1999; The Rise and Fall of Freedom of Contract, 1979; Promises, Morals and Law, 1981 (Swiney Prize, RSA/RSP, 1984); Law and Modern Society, 1983, 2nd edn 1995; Essays on Contract, 1987; Pragmatism and Theory in English Law, 1987; (with R. S. Summers) Form and Substance in Anglo-American Law, 1987; The Damages Lottery, 1997; articles in legal jls. *Recreations:* gardening, cooking. *Address:* 65 Seaview Road, Hayling Island, Hants PO11 9PD. *T:* (023) 9246 2474.

See also Sir M. F. Atiyah.

ATKIN, Becky; *see* Parker, B.

ATKIN, Gavin Mark; journalist and editor, Wellards, since 2012; *b* 2 Jan. 1956; *s* of Alistair Brian and Sunya Mary Atkin; one *s* one *d*; *m* 2009, Julie Arnott. *Educ:* Univ. of Newcastle upon Tyne (BSc Gen. Scis). Man. Editor, 1994–2000, Ed., 2000–06, The Practitioner; Clin. Ed., Chemist & Druggist, 2006–10; Ed. and Publisher, intheboatshed.net, 2006–. *Publications:* Ultrasimple Boatbuilding, 2007. *Recreations:* enjoying, performing and teaching traditional music; playing Jeffries duet concertina; sailing, boat building and design; weblogging about boats at intheboatshed.net.

ATKIN, Timothy John; freelance wine writer and photographer; *b* Dartford, 26 Aug. 1961; *s* of Ronald George Atkin and late Brenda Irene Atkin; *m* 2009, Sue Wixley. *Educ:* Durham Univ. (BA Hons French); London Sch. of Econs (MSc Eur. Studies). With Haymarket Publishing, 1985–89; wine correspondent: Guardian, 1989–93; Observer, 1993–2010. Mem., Inst. of Masters of Wine, 2001–. Chevalier du Tastevin, 2000; Master of Wine, 2001; Caballero del Vino, 2007. *Publications:* Chardonnay, 1991; Vins de Pays d'Oc, 1992; (with A. Rose) Grapevine, annually, 1993–97. *Recreations:* golf, piano, reading, cinema, guitar, collecting black and white photography. *Address:* c/o PFD, Drury House, 34–43 Russell Street, WC2B 5HA. *T:* (020) 7344 1000. *Clubs:* Groucho, Blacks; Royal Wimbledon Golf.

ATKINS, Andrew Windham; Executive Director, Friends of the Earth (England, Wales and Northern Ireland), 2008–15; *b* Eastleigh, Hants, 9 Oct. 1960; *s* of Rev. Roger Atkins and Diana Atkins (*née* Gilbard); *m* 1985, Sarah Witts; one *s* two *d*. *Educ:* University Coll. London (BA Hons Geog. 1982); Inst. of Latin American Studies, Univ. of London (MA Latin American Studies 1983). Nat. Coordinator, 1985, Gen. Sec., 1986–88, Chile Cttee for Human Rights; Partnership Scheme Coordinator, CAFOD, 1988–90; Latin America Desk Officer, Catholic Inst. for Internat. Relns, 1990–97; Tearfund: Public Policy Advr, 1997–98; Public Policy Team Leader, 1998–2000; Advocacy (Policy and Campaigns) Dir, 2000–08. Board Member: Make Poverty Hist. Campaign, 2004–06; Micah Challenge Campaign, 2004–08. FRSA. *Recreations:* landscape painting, cycling, world literature, theatre.

ATKINS, Charlotte; *b* 24 Sept. 1950; *d* of Ronald and Jessie Atkins; *m* 1990, Gus Brain; one *d*. *Educ:* Colchester County High Sch.; LSE (BSc(Econ)); MA London Univ. Asst Community Relations Officer, Luton CRC, 1974–76; Res. Officer, then Hd of Res., UCATT, 1976–80; Res. and Political Officer, AUEW (TASS), 1980–83; Press Officer, 1983–92, Parly Officer, 1992–97, COHSE, then UNISON. Contested (Lab) Eastbourne, Oct. 1990. MP (Lab) Staffordshire Moorlands, 1997–2010; contested (Lab) same seat, 2010. PPS to Minister of State for Trade, DTI and FCO, 2001–02; an Asst Govt Whip, 2002–05; Parly Under-Sec. of State, DfT, 2004–05. Member: Select Cttee on Educn and Employment, 1997–2001; Cttee of Selection, 1997–2000; Select Cttee on Health, 2005–10. Mem., PLP Parly Cttee, 1997–2000. Member (Lab): Staffordshire Moorlands DC, 2012–; Staffordshire CC, 2013– (Shadow Cabinet Mem. for Health and Social Care). Chm., Central Shires Canal and River Trust Waterways Partnership, 2012–; Mem., Staffs and Stoke on Trent Fire and Rescue Authy, 2013–14.

ATKINS, Charlotte Elizabeth Mary; *see* Voake, C. E. M.

ATKINS, Dame Eileen, DBE 2001 (CBE 1990); actress and writer; *b* 16 June 1934; *d* of Arthur Thomas Atkins and late Annie Ellen (*née* Elkins); *m* Bill Shepherd. *Educ:* Latymer Grammar Sch., Edmonton; Guildhall Sch. of Music and Drama. *Stage appearances include:* Twelfth Night, Richard III, The Tempest, Old Vic, 1962; The Killing of Sister George (Best Actress, Standard Awards), Bristol Old Vic, transf. Duke of York's, 1965; The Cocktail Party, Wyndham's, transf. Haymarket, 1968; Vivat! Vivat Regina! (Variety Award), Piccadilly, 1970; Suzanne Andler, Aldwych, 1973; As You Like It, Stratford, 1973; St Joan, Old Vic, 1977; Passion Play, Aldwych, 1981; Medea, Young Vic, 1986; The Winter's Tale, and Cymbeline (Olivier Award), Mountain Language, NT, 1988; A Room of One's Own, Hampstead, 1989; Exclusive, Strand, 1989; Prin, NY, 1990; The Night of the Iguana, NT, 1992; Vita and Virginia, Ambassadors, 1993, NY, 1994; Indiscretions, NY, 1995; John Gabriel Borkman, NT, 1996; A Delicate Balance, Haymarket (Best Actress, Evening Standard Awards), 1997; The Unexpected Man, RSC, transf. Duchess (Best Actress, Olivier Awards), 1998; Honour, NT, 2003; The Retreat from Moscow, NY, 2003; The Birthday Party, Duchess, 2005; Doubt, NY, 2006; There Came a Gypsy Riding, Almeida, 2007; The Sea, Haymarket, 2008; The Female of the Species, Vaudeville, 2008; All That Fall, Jermyn Street Th., transf. Arts, 2012 (Best Actress, Offie Awards); (one-woman show) Ellen Terry with Eileen Atkins, Sam Wanamaker Playhouse, 2014; The Witch of Edmonton, Stratford, 2014; *films include:* Equus, 1974; The Dresser, 1984; Let Him Have It, 1990; Wolf, 1994; Women Talking Dirty, 2001; Gosford Park, 2002; What a Girl Wants, 2003; Vanity Fair, 2005; Evening, 2007; Wild Target, 2008; Last Chance Harvey, 2009; Robin Hood, 2009; Beautiful Creatures, 2013; Magic in the Moonlight, 2014; Suite Française, 2015; *TV appearances include:* The Duchess of Malfi; Sons and Lovers; Smiley's People; Nelly's Version; The Burston Rebellion; Breaking Up; The Vision; Mrs Pankhurst in In My Defence (series), 1990; A Room of One's Own, 1990; The Lost Language of Cranes, 1993; The Maitlands, 1993; Cold Comfort Farm, 1995 (film, 1997); Talking Heads 2, 1998; Madame Bovary, 2000; Bertie and Elizabeth, 2002; Love Again, 2003; Waking the Dead, Cranford, 2007 (Best Actress, BAFTA, 2008; Best Supporting Actress, Emmy Awards, 2008); Upstairs Downstairs, 2010; Doc Martin, 2011, 2013, 2015; The Scapegoat, 2012. Co-created television series: Upstairs Downstairs; The House of Eliott; *screenplay:* Mrs Dalloway (Best Screenplay, Evening Standard British Film Awards), 1998. Hon. DLitt Oxford, 2010. *Address:* c/o Paul Lyon Maris, Independent Talent Group Ltd, 40 Whitfield Street, W1T 2RH.

ATKINS, Prof. Madeleine Julia, CBE 2012; DL; PhD; Chief Executive, Higher Education Funding Council for England, since 2014; *b* 2 July 1952; *d* of Harold and Juliana Dunkerley; *m* 1975, John Michael Atkins; two *s*. *Educ:* Girton Coll., Cambridge (BA Hons 1974); Lady Margaret Hall, Oxford (PGCE); Nottingham Univ. (PhD 1982). Teacher, Hinchingbrooke Comprehensive Sch., 1975–79; post-doctoral res., Nottingham Univ., 1982–83; University of Newcastle upon Tyne: Lectr, 1984–88; Sen. Lectr, 1988–2004; Head, Dept of Educn, 1991–96; Dean, Faculty of Educn, 1996–98; Pro-Vice-Chancellor, 1998–2004; Vice-Chancellor, Coventry Univ., 2004–14. Mem. Bd, HEFCE, 2009–14. Trustee, NESTA Operating Co., 2012–. DL W Midlands, 2013. *Publications:* (with G. A. Brown) Effective Teaching in Higher Education, 1988; contrib. numerous articles on mgt in higher educn and on use of multimedia applications in learning to jls. *Recreations:* theatre, walking. *Address:* Higher Education Funding Council for England, Northavon House, Coldharbour Lane, Bristol. *T:* (020) 7400 4100, *Fax:* (020) 7400 4145. *E:* m.atkins@hefce.ac.uk.

ATKINS, Rev. Dr Martyn David; Superintendent Minister and Team Leader, Methodist Central Hall, Westminster, since 2015; *b* 16 June 1955; *s* of Raymond and Marion Atkins; *m* 1980, Helen Claire Robinson; three *s*. *Educ:* Victoria Univ. of Manchester (BA; PhD 1990). Ordained Methodist Minister, 1981; Leeds (S) Methodist circuit, 1981–86; Shipley and Bingley Methodist circuit, 1986–91; Chaplain, Edgehill Coll., Bideford, Devon, 1991–96; Postgrad. Tutor, 1996–2004, Principal, 2004–08, Cliff Coll., Sheffield; Gen. Sec., Methodist Ch of GB, and Sec., Methodist Conf., 2008–15. Chm. Bd, Fresh Expressions, 2014–. Pres., Methodist Conference, 2007–08. Hon. Ecumenical Canon, Sheffield Cathedral, 2010–15. *Publications:* Preaching in a Cultural Context, 2001; Sermon on the Mount, 2002; Resourcing Renewal, 2007; Discipleship and the people called Methodists, 2010. *Recreations:* supporting Leeds United Football Club, book collecting, reading. *Address:* Methodist Central Hall, Storeys Gate, Westminster, SW1H 9NH. *T:* (020) 7654 3809.

ATKINS, Rt Rev. Peter Geoffrey; Bishop of Waiapu, 1983–90; Dean, Theological College of St John the Evangelist, Auckland, 1991–96; *b* 29 April 1936; *s* of late Lt-Col Owen Ivan Atkins and Mrs Mary Atkins; *m* 1968, Rosemary Elizabeth (*née* Allen); one *d*. *Educ:* Merchant Taylors' School, Crosby, Liverpool; Sidney Sussex Coll., Cambridge; St John's Coll., Auckland, NZ. MA (Cantab), BD (Otago), LTh (NZ). Ordained deacon, 1962, priest, 1963; Curate, Karori Parish, Wellington, 1962–66; Priest-Tutor, St Peter's Theological Coll., Siota, Solomon Is, 1966–67; Curate, Dannevirke Parish, dio. Waiapu, 1968–70; Vicar of Waipukurau Parish, 1970–73; Diocesan Sec. and Registrar, Diocese of Waiapu, 1973–79; Canon of St John's Cathedral, Napier, 1974–79; Vicar of Havelock North, 1979–83; Archdeacon of Hawkes Bay, 1979–83; Vicar-Gen., Diocese of Waiapu, 1980–83; Commissary to Archbishop of NZ, 1983; Lectr in Liturgy and Evangelism, Univ. of Auckland and Melbourne Coll. of Divinity, 1991–97. Permission to Officiate as bishop and priest, Dio. of Auckland, 2013–. Hon. Sen. Res. Fellow, Univ. of Birmingham, 1996. Contributor, Reviews in Religion and Theology, 1997–2006; Mem., Editl Bd, Rural Theology, 2006–13. *Publications:* Good News in Evangelism, 1992; (contrib.) Counselling Issues and South Pacific Communities, 1997; Worship 2000, 1999; Soul Time, 2000; (jtly) Personality Type and Scripture: exploring Luke's gospel, 2000, exploring Matthew's gospel, 2001, exploring Mark's gospel, 2002; Soul Care, 2001; Ascension Now, 2001; (jtly) Family Prayers, 2003; Memory and Liturgy, 2004; (jtly) Cool Prayers, 2004; (jtly) Prayer Kids, 2008; (contrib.) Journeying into Prayer: people and pathways, 2012. *Recreations:* writing, gardening, music, University of the Third Age. *Address:* 9A Paunui Street, St Helier's Bay, Auckland 1071, New Zealand. *T:* (9) 5754775. *E:* peter.rosemary@xtra.co.nz.

ATKINS, Prof. Peter William, PhD; FRSC; Professor of Chemistry, University of Oxford, 1998–2007; Fellow and Tutor, Lincoln College, Oxford, 1965–2007, now Supernumerary Fellow (Acting Rector, 2007); author; *b* 10 Aug. 1940; *s* of William Henry Atkins and Ellen Louise Atkins; *m* 1st, 1964, Judith Ann Kearton (marr. diss. 1983); one *d*; 2nd, 1991, Susan Adele Greenfield (*see* Baroness Greenfield) (marr. diss. 2005); 3rd, 2008, Patricia-Jean Nobes. *Educ:* Dr Challoner's Sch., Amersham; Univ. of Leicester (BSc 1961; PhD 1964); MA Oxon 1965. FRSC 2002. Harkness Fellow, UCLA, 1964–65; Lectr, Univ. of Oxford, 1965–2007. Vis. Prof. in China, Japan, France, NZ and Israel. Nyholm Lectr, 1999; Hon. Prof., Mendeleyev Univ., Moscow, 2006. Chairman: Davy-Faraday Lab. Cttee, 1999–2005; Educn Strategy Develt Cttee, 2000, Cttee on Chemistry Educn, 2002–05, IUPAC. Mem. Council, Royal Instn, 1999–2005; Mem. Ct, Leicester Univ., 2000–13. Foreign Mem., Acad. of Sci., Bologna, 2007. Hon. Associate: Rationalist Assoc., 1993; Nat. Secular Soc., 2000; Dist. Supporter, Humanist Assoc., 2010. Hon. DSc: Utrecht, 1992; Leicester, 2002; Kazan State Technol Univ., 2009. Meldola Medal, RSC, 1969. *Publications:* The Structure of Inorganic Radicals, 1967; Tables for Group Theory, 1970; Molecular Quantum Mechanics, 1970, 5th edn 2011; Physical Chemistry, 1978, 10th edn 2014; Solutions Manual for Physical Chemistry, 1978, 8th edn 2006; Quanta: a handbook of concepts, 1974, 2nd edn 1991; Principles of Physical Chemistry, 1981; The Creation, 1981; Quantization, 1981; Solutions Manual for Molecular Quantum Mechanics, 1983, 2nd edn 1997; The Second Law, 1984; Molecules, 1987, 2nd edn as Atkins' Molecules, 2003; General Chemistry, 1987, 2nd edn 1992; Chemistry: principles and applications, 1988; Inorganic Chemistry, 1990, 5th edn 2010; Atoms, Electrons and Change, 1991; The Elements of Physical Chemistry, 1992, 6th edn 2013; Creation Revisited, 1992; The Periodic Kingdom, 1995; Concepts of Physical Chemistry, 1995; Chemistry: molecules, matter, and change, 1997, 4th edn 1999; Chemical Principles, 1999, 6th edn 2013; Galileo's Finger: the ten great ideas of science, 2003; Physical Chemistry for Life Sciences, 2006, 2nd edn 2011; Four Laws that Drive the Universe, 2007; Quanta, Matter and Change, 2009, 2nd edn as Physical Chemistry: quanta, matter and change, 2014; A Very Short Introduction to: The Laws of Thermodynamics, 2010; On Being, 2011; Reactions: the private life of atoms, 2011; What is Chemistry?, 2013; Physical Chemistry: a very short introduction, 2014. *Recreation:* working. *Address:* Lincoln College, Oxford OX1 3DR. *Club:* Athenæum.

ATKINS, Richard Paul; QC 2011; a Recorder, since 2005; *b* Coventry, 31 May 1966; *s* of late Michael Richard Atkins and of Margaret Atkins; *m* 1998, Nicola Mary Rutherford-Jones; one *s* one *d*. *Educ:* King Henry VIII Sch., Coventry; St Catherine's Coll., Oxford (BA Hons Juris. 1988; MA). Called to the Bar, Gray's Inn, 1989, Bencher, 2014; in practice as a barrister: 1 Fountain Court Chambers, Birmingham, 1991–2002; St Philips Chambers, Birmingham, 2002– (Head: Criminal Gp, 2011–14; Regulatory Gp, 2014–); Leader, Midland Circuit, 2014–. Tutor Judge, Judicial Coll., 2012–; a Chm., Disciplinary Tribunal, Financial Reporting Council, 2013–. Mem., Gen. Council of the Bar, 2003– (Chairman: Member Services Bd, 2010–; Bar Conf. Organising Bd, 2014; Mem., Gen. Mgt Cttee, 2011–). Mem. Council, Birmingham Law Soc., 2013–. Gov., Coventry Sch. Foundn (King Henry VIII and Bablake Schs), 1999–2014 (Chm., 2011–14). *Recreations:* family, wine, humour, member of Coventry School of Music Old Boys' Band. *Address:* St Philips Chambers, 55 Temple Row, Birmingham B2 5LS. *T:* (0121) 246 7000, *Fax:* (0121) 246 7001. *E:* rpatkins@st-philips.com.

ATKINS, Rt Hon. Sir Robert (James), Kt 1997; PC 1995; Member (C) North West Region, England, European Parliament, 1999–2014; *b* 5 Feb. 1946; *s* of late Reginald Alfred and of Winifred Margaret Atkins; *m* 1969, Dulcie Mary (*née* Chaplin); one *s* one *d*. *Educ:* Highgate School. Councillor, London Borough of Haringey, 1968–77; Vice-Chm., Greater London Young Conservatives, 1969–70, 1971–72. Contested (C) Luton West, Feb. 1974 and Oct. 1974 general elections. MP (C) Preston North, 1979–83, South Ribble, 1983–97; contested (C) South Ribble, 1997. PPS to Minister of State, DoI, then DTI, 1982–84, to Minister without Portfolio, 1984–85, to Sec. of State for Employment, 1985–87; Parly Under Sec. of State, DTI, 1987–89, Dept of Transport, 1989–90, DoE (Minister for Sport), 1990, DES (Minister for Sport), 1990–92; Minister of State, NI Office, 1992–94; Minister of State for the Environment and the Countryside, DoE, 1994–95. Vice-Chm., Cons. Aviation Cttee, 1979–82; Jt Sec., Cons. Defence Cttee, 1979–82. Chm., NW Cons. MPs, 1996–97; Dep. Leader, British Cons. MEPs, 2004–07; Chief Whip (C), Eur. Parlt, 2008–10. President: Cons. Trade Unionists, 1984–87; Wyre & Preston N Cons. Assoc., 2007–; Preston Cons. Assoc., 2013–; Lancs Assoc. of Local Councils, 2014–. Member: Victorian Soc.; Sherlock Holmes Soc. of London; English Heritage; Historic Churches Preservation Trust; Nat. Trust. Chm., Lancs CCC Develt Assoc., 2002–12. Freeman, City of London, 1989. *Publications:* (contrib.) Changing Gear, 1981. *Recreations:* cricket, ecclesiology, wine, Holmesiana. *Address:* Manor House, Lancaster Road, Garstang, Lancs PR3 1JA. *Clubs:* Carlton, MCC, Lord's Taverners; Middlesex County Cricket, Lords and Commons Cricket, Lancashire County Cricket (Vice-Pres., 2005–), Garstang Cricket (Pres., 2007–), Preston Grasshoppers Rugby Football (Vice-Pres., 1990–), Garstang Rugby Union Football (Vice-Pres., 2007–).

See also V. M. Atkins.

ATKINS, Ronald Henry; *b* Barry, Glam, 13 June 1916; *s* of Frank and Elizabeth Atkins; *m* 1st (marr. diss. 1979); three *s* two *d*; 2nd, 2012, Elizabeth Alison Wildgoose. *Educ:* Barry County Sch.; London Univ. (BA Hons). Teacher, 1949–66 (latterly Head, Eng. Dept, Halstead Sec. Sch.); Lectr, Accrington Coll. of Further Educn, 1970–74. Member: Braintree RDC, 1952–61; (Lab) Preston Dist Council, 1974–76, 1980–2010. Contested (Lab) Lowestoft, 1964; MP (Lab) Preston North, 1966–70 and Feb. 1974–1979. *Recreations:* jazz, dancing, walking, local and national politics, connoisseur of good coffee. *Address:* 38 James Street, Preston, Lancs PR1 4JU. *T:* (01772) 251910.

ATKINS, Rosemary Jean, (Rosie), FLS; Curator, Chelsea Physic Garden, 2002–10; Member, Management Council, Royal Horticultural Society, 2010–15; *b* 9 Oct. 1947; *m* 1973, Eric James Brown; one *s* one *d*. *Educ:* St Michael's Sch. for Girls, Limpsfield; Ravensbourne Sch. of Art. Sunday Times, 1968–82; freelance journalist and gardening writer, 1982–; Jt Producer, In the Air, BBC Radio 4, 1983; gardening corresp., Today, 1985–92; launch Editor, Gardens Illustrated Mag., 1993–2002. Royal Horticultural Society: a Judge, 2004–; Mem., Nominations, Appts and Governance Cttee, 2006–13; Chm., Awards Cttee, 2010–14; Chm., Awards Wkg Party, 2014–. Member: Garden Panel, English Heritage, 2011–; Council, Metropolitan Public Gardens Assoc., 2012–. Chm., London Gardens Network, 2009–12. Trustee: Thrive, 1998–2003; Gardening for Disabled Trust, 1998–2011; Gt Dixter Charitable Trust, 2008–. FLS 2004. Editor's Editor Award, BSME, 1996. *Publications:* (jtly) The Sunday Times Book of the Countryside, 1978; (contrib.) Making a Garden: the history of the National Garden Scheme, 2001; (ed) Gardens Illustrated Plant Profiles, 2003; Roses, 2004. *Recreations:* gardening, lecturing, painting, travel. *E:* rosie19@ymail.com. *Club:* Chelsea Arts.

ATKINS, Dr Susan Ruth Elizabeth, CB 2014; Service Complaints Commissioner for the Armed Forces, 2007–15; *b* 4 March 1952; *d* of late Victor Charles Rodney Prickett and of Marian Sarah Gertrude Prickett; *m* 1977, Stephen Thomas Atkins; one *s* one *d*. *Educ:* Manchester High Sch. for Girls; Univ. of Birmingham (LLB Hons); Univ. of Calif, Berkeley (Master of Criminol.); Univ. of Southampton (PhD 1986). Admitted solicitor, 1977. Articled clerk, GLC, 1974–77; Lectr in Law, Univ. of Southampton, 1977–89; Principal, Home Office, 1989–93; Dep. Chief Exec., EOC, 1993–95; Home Office: Head: of Extradition, 1995–96; of Personnel Policy, 1996–99; of Probation, 1999–2000; Dir, Women and Equality Unit, Cabinet Office, 2000–02; Chief Exec., Ind. Police Complaints Commn, 2003–06; Interim Chief Exec., Appts Commn, 2007. Vis. Fellow, 1989–95, Vis. Prof., 1995–2001, Univ. of Southampton. Non-exec. Bd Mem., HMP Manchester, 1994–95; Bd Mem., QAA, 2004–10; non-exec. Dir, Leadership Foundn for Higher Educn, 2007–13. Member, Advisory Board: Geneva Centre for Democratic Control of Armed Forces, 2015–; Mem., Ind. Adv. Bd, RMA Sandhurst, 2015–. *Publications:* (with B. Hoggett) Women and the Law, 1984; contribs to legal jls, mainly on sex discrimination and European law. *Recreations:* reading, travel, tapestry.

ATKINS, Victoria Mary; MP (C) Louth and Horncastle, since 2015; *d* of Rt Hon. Sir Robert (James) Atkins, *qv*; *m* Paul; one *s*. *Educ:* Univ. of Cambridge (Law). Called to the Bar, 1998; in practice as barrister, specialising in serious organised crime, 1998–. *Address:* House of Commons, SW1A 0AA.

ATKINSON, Sir Anthony Barnes, (Sir Tony), Kt 2000; FBA 1984; Professor of Economics, University of Oxford, 2007–09, now Emeritus; Honorary Fellow, Nuffield College, Oxford, since 2009 (Warden, 1994–2005; Senior Research Fellow, 2005–09); Centennial Professor of Economics, London School of Economics, since 2010; *b* 4 Sept. 1944; *s* of Norman Joseph Atkinson and Esther Muriel Atkinson; *m* 1965, Judith Mary (*née* Mandeville); two *s* one *d*. *Educ:* Cranbrook Sch.; Churchill Coll., Cambridge (MA; Hon. Fellow 2015). Fellow, St John's Coll., Cambridge, 1967–71; Prof. of Econs, Univ. of Essex, 1971–76; Prof. and Hd of Dept of Political Economy, UCL, 1976–79; Prof. of Econs, LSE, 1980–92; Prof. of Political Economy, and Fellow, Churchill Coll., Cambridge, 1992–94. Vis.

Prof., MIT, 1973; Chaire Blaise Pascal, Paris Sch. of Econs, 2005–07; F. W. Taussig Res. Prof., Harvard Univ., 2009–10. Member: Royal Commn on Distribution of Income and Wealth, 1978–79; Retail Prices Index Adv. Cttee, 1984–90; Pension Law Review Cttee, 1992–93; Social Justice Commn, 1992–94; Conseil d'Analyse Economique, France, 1997–2001; European Statistics Governance Adv. Bd, 2009–12. Editor, Jl of Public Economics, 1972–97. President: European Econ. Assoc., 1989 (Vice-Pres., 1986–88); Internat. Econ. Assoc., 1989–92; Luxembourg Income Study, 2012–; Vice-Pres., British Acad., 1988–90. Fellow, Econometric Soc., 1975 (Vice-Pres., 1986–87, Pres., 1988). Hon. Mem., Amer. Econ. Assoc., 1985. Fellow, Centre for Econ. Studies, Munich, 1995. Hon. Fellow, LSE, 2005. Hon. Dr rer. pol. Univ. of Frankfurt, 1987; Hon. Dr en Sci. Econ., Univ. of Lausanne, 1988; Hon. Dr: Univ. of Liège, 1989; Athens Univ. of Econs, 1991; Stirling, 1992; Edinburgh, 1994; Essex, Bologna, and Ecole Normale Supérieure, Paris, 1995; South Bank and Univ. Catholique, Louvain, 1996; Nottingham, 2000; London Metropolitan, 2002; Gent, Antwerp, and European Univ. Inst., Florence, 2004; Molise, 2006; Univ. de la Méditerranée, Marseilles, 2010. Scientific Prize, Union des Assurances de Paris, 1986; Frank E. Seidman Dist. Award in Pol Econ., Rhodes Coll., Tenn, 1995; A.SK Social Sci. Award, WZB, Berlin, 2007; Jerzy Neyman Medal, Polish Statistical Soc., 2012. Chevalier, Légion d'Honneur (France), 2001. *Publications:* Poverty in Britain and the Reform of Social Security, 1969; Unequal Shares, 1972; The Tax Credit Scheme, 1973; Economics of Inequality, 1975; (with A. J. Harrison) Distribution of Personal Wealth in Britain, 1978; (with J. E. Stiglitz) Lectures on Public Economics, 1980; Social Justice and Public Policy, 1982; (jtly) Parents and Children, 1983; (with J. Micklewright) Unemployment Benefits and Unemployment Duration, 1985; Poverty and Social Security, 1989; (with J. Micklewright) Economic Transformation in Eastern Europe and the Distribution of Income, 1992; Public Economics in Action, 1995; Incomes and the Welfare State, 1996; The Economic Consequences of Rolling Back the Welfare State, 1999; (jtly) Social Indicators, 2002; (jtly) The EU and Social Inclusion, 2006; The Changing Distribution of Earnings in OECD Countries, 2008; Public Economics in an Age of Austerity, 2014; Inequality: what can be done?, 2015; articles in Rev. of Econ. Studies, Econ. Jl, Jl of Public Econs, Jl of Econ. Theory. *Address:* Nuffield College, Oxford OX1 1NF.

ATKINSON, Prof. Bernard, OBE 2001; FREng, FIChemE; Director-General, BRF International (formerly Director, Brewing Research Foundation), 1981–96; *b* 17 March 1936; *s* of late Thomas Atkinson and of Elizabeth Ann (*née* Wilcox); *m* 1957, Kathleen Mary Richardson; two *s*. *Educ:* Farnworth Grammar Sch.; Univ. of Birmingham (BSc); Univ. of Manchester Inst. of Science and Technology; PhD Univ. of Manchester. FREng (FEng 1980). Post-Doctoral Fellow and Asst Prof., Rice Univ., Houston, Texas, 1960–63; Lectr, Sen. Lectr in Chem. Engrg, and latterly Reader in Biochem. Engrg, University Coll. of Swansea, 1963–74 (Hon. Fellow, 1991); Prof. and Head of Dept of Chem. Engrg, UMIST, 1974–81; Visiting Professor: UMIST, 1981–86; Swansea, 1986–96; Heriot-Watt, 1991–96. European Brewery Convention: Mem., Management Cttee and Council, 1990–97; Vice Pres., 1991–97. Mem., BBSRC, 1996–2001. Gov., Queen Victoria Hosp. NHS Foundn Trust, 2004–11 (Vice-Chm., 2009–11; Gov. Rep., Bd of Dirs, 2007–10). Editor, Biochemical Engineering Journal, 1983–93. Senior Moulton Medal, IChemE, 1976; Gairn EEC Medal, Soc. of Engrs, 1985; Presidential Award, Master Brewers' Assoc. of the Americas, 1988; Donald Medal, IChemE, 1996. *Publications:* Biochemical Reactors, 1974, trans. Japanese, Russian, Spanish; (with P. F. Cooper) Biological Fluidised Bed Treatment of Water and Waste Water, 1981; (with F. Mavituna) Biochemical Engineering and Biotechnology Handbook, 1982, 2nd edn 1991; (ed) Research and Innovation in the 1990s: the chemical engineering challenge, 1986; (with C. Webb and G. M. Black) Process Engineering Aspects of Immobilised Cell Systems, 1986; numerous contribs to chemical engrg and biochemical engrg jls. *Recreations:* cycling, sailing, walking. *Address:* Little Mieders, Borers Arms Road, Copthorne, Crawley, West Sussex RH10 3LJ. *T:* (01342) 713181. *Club:* Square Rigger (Gosport) (Sec., 2007–12).

ATKINSON, Prof. Bruce Wilson, PhD; Professor of Geography, Queen Mary and Westfield College (formerly at Queen Mary College), University of London, 1983–2004, now Emeritus; *b* 28 Sept. 1941; *s* of J. and S. A. Atkinson. *Educ:* University Coll., London (BSc, PhD). CGeog 2002. Queen Mary, subseq. Queen Mary and Westfield College, University of London: Lectr, 1964–78; Reader, 1978–83; Hd, Dept of Geog., 1985–89; Dean of Social Scis, 1991–94; Mem., Senate and Acad. Council, Univ. of London, 1991–94. Natural Environment Research Council: Mem., 1982–85, Chm., 1988–91, Aquatic & Atmospheric Phys. Sci. Cttee; Mem., Atmos. Sci., Marine Sci., Terrestrial and Freshwater Sci. and Higher Educn Affairs Cttees, 1988–91. Mem., RAE (Envmtl Sci.) 2001. Member: Meteorol and Atmos. Phys. Sub-cttee, Nat. Cttee on Geodesy and Geophysics, 1988–90; Scientific Adv. Cttee, Meteorol Office, 1996–2004. Mem. Council and cttees, and Editor, Weather, RMetS, 1972–79; Chm., Pubns Cttee, 1992–98, Mem. Council, 1993–95, RGS-IBG (formerly RGS); Mem., Assoc. Brit. Climatologists, 1970– (Chm., 1976–78). Ed., Progress in Physical Geography, 1977–2008. Hugh Robert Mill Medal, RMetS, 1974; Back Award, RGS, 1981. *Publications:* Weather Business, 1968; (ed) Dynamical Meteorology, 1981; Meso-scale Atmospheric Circulations, 1981; Weather: Review of UK Statistical Sources, 1985; (ed jtly) Encyclopædic Dictionary of Physical Geography, 1986; (with A. Gadd) Weather: a modern guide to forecasting, 1986; articles in geographical, geophys. and meteorol jls. *Recreations:* walking, music. *Clubs:* Athenæum, Geographical.

ATKINSON, Carol Lesley, (Mrs C. A. Kinch); Her Honour Judge Atkinson; a Circuit Judge, since 2007; Designated Family Judge, East London, since 2014; *b* N Yorks, 29 Sept. 1962; *d* of George Atkinson and Maureen Atkinson (*née* Heslop); *m* 1994, Christopher Anthony Kinch, *qv*; one *s* two *d*. *Educ:* Cleveland Girls Grammar Sch.; Rye Hills Sch., Redcar; Sir William Turner's Sixth Form Coll.; Lancaster Univ. (LLB Hons); Inns of Court Sch. of Law. Called to the Bar, Gray's Inn, 1985 (Karmel Schol. 1986); Recorder, 2001–07. Mem., Bar Council, 1997–2007. Sec., Family Law Bar Assoc., 2004–07. *Recreations:* my children, running, swimming, music, Middlesbrough FC; Black Belt, 1st Dan, Karate, playing alto sax. *Address:* East London Family Court, 11 Westferry Circus, E14 4HD.

ATKINSON, Rt Rev. David John; Bishop Suffragan of Thetford, 2001–09; an Hon. Assistant Bishop, Diocese of Southwark, since 2009; *b* 5 Sept. 1943; *s* of Thomas John Collins and Adèle Mary Atkinson; *m* 1969, Suzan Elizabeth; one *s* one *d*. *Educ:* King's Coll., London (BSc, PhD, AKC); Bristol Univ. (MLitt); Oxford Univ. (MA). Teacher of Chemistry, Maidstone Tech. High Sch. for Boys, 1968–69. Ordained deacon, 1972, priest, 1973; Assistant Curate: St Peter Halliwell, Bolton, 1972–74; Harborne Heath, Birmingham, 1974–77; Librarian, Latimer House, Oxford, 1977–80; Chaplain, 1980–93, Fellow, 1984–93, Corpus Christi Coll., Oxford; Canon Chancellor and Missioner, Southwark Cathedral, 1993–96; Archdeacon of Lewisham, 1996–2001. Co-Founder, Oxford Christian Inst. for Counselling, 1985. Mem., SOSc, 1987. *Publications:* To Have and To Hold, 1979; The Bible Speaks Today (series): Ruth, 1983; Genesis 1–11, 1990; Job, 1991; Proverbs, 1996; Peace in Our Time?, 1985; Pastoral Ethics, 1989, 2nd edn 1994; (jtly) Counselling in Context, 1994, 2nd edn 1998; (ed jtly) New Dictionary of Christian Ethics and Pastoral Theology, 1995; Jesus, Lamb of God, 1996; God So Loved the World, 1999; Renewing the Face of the Earth: a theological and pastoral response to climate change, 2008; The Church's Healing Ministry, 2011; articles and reviews in jls. *Recreations:* music, walking, photography. *Address:* 6 Bynes Road, South Croydon CR2 0PR. *T:* (020) 8406 0895. *E:* davidatkinson43@virginmedia.com.

ATKINSON, David Rowland; Regional Chairman, British Gas East Midlands, 1987–92; *b* 18 June 1930; *s* of late Rowland Hodgson Atkinson and Nora Marian (*née* Coleman); *m* 1956, Marian Eileen Sales; one *d*. *Educ:* Wrekin College. FCA, CCMI, CompIGasE. National Coal Board: NW Div., 1955; E Midlands Div., 1961; Chief Accountant, W Midlands Gas, 1969; Dir of Finance, E Midlands Gas, 1977; Dep. Chm., SE Gas, 1983; Dir of Finance, British Gas, 1985. *Recreations:* Rugby, gardening, ciné photography. *Address:* 28 Browning Court, Bourne, Lincs PE10 9FA.

ATKINSON, Sir Frederick John, (Sir Fred), KCB 1979 (CB 1971); Hon. Fellow of Jesus College, Oxford, since 1979; *b* 7 Dec. 1919; *s* of George Edward Atkinson and of late Elizabeth Sabina Cooper; *m* 1947, Margaret Grace Gibson; two *d*. *Educ:* Dulwich Coll.; Jesus Coll., Oxford. Lectr, Jesus and Trinity Colls, Oxford, 1947–49; Economic Section, Cabinet Office, 1949–51; British Embassy, Washington, 1952–54; HM Treasury, 1955–62; Economic Adviser, Foreign Office, 1962–63; HM Treasury, 1963–69 (Dep. Dir, Economic Section, Treasury, 1965–69); Controller, Economics and Statistics, Min. of Technology, 1970; Chief Econ. Adviser, DTI, 1970–73; an Asst Sec.-Gen., OECD, Paris, 1973–75; Dep. Sec. and Chief Econ. Advr, Dept of Energy, 1975–77; Chief Econ. Advr, HM Treasury, and Head of Govt Econ. Service, 1977–79. *Publications:* (with S. Hall) Oil and the British Economy, 1983. *Recreation:* reading. *Address:* 26 Lee Terrace, Blackheath, SE3 9TZ. *T:* (020) 8852 1040; Tickner Cottage, Aldington, Kent TN25 7EG. *T:* (01233) 720514.

ATKINSON, Brig. Geoffrey Arthur; chartered engineer, retired; *b* 17 March 1931; *s* of Arthur Vivian Atkinson and Flora Muriel Atkinson (*née* Lucas); *m* 1952, Joyce Eileen Pavey; one *s* one *d*. *Educ:* Berkhamsted Sch.; Royal Military College of Science (BScEng); Manchester Business Sch. CEng, FIMechE. Commnd REME, 1950; Regtl and technical employment, UK, Malaya, BAOR, 1950–60; EME, Queen's Own Hussars, 1960; Instr, RMA Sandhurst, 1962; Technical Staff trng, RMCS, 1963; BEME 20 Armd Bde, 1965; Weapons Staff, Army Sch. of Transport, 1967; CO 7 Armd Workshop, 1970; GSO I (W) DGFVE, 1972; ADEME 1/3 HQ DEME, 1975; Mil. Dir of Studies, Weapons and Vehicles, RMCS, 1977; CCREME HQ 1 BR Corps, BAOR, 1978; Dir of Equipment Engrg, HQ DGEME, 1981; Comdr HQ REME TA, 1983, retired 1984. Hon. Col REME Specialist Units TA, 1986–89. Dep. Sec., 1984–89, Exec. Sec. 1990–93, Fellowship of Engineering, later Royal Acad. of Engrg. Member: Council, Parly and Scientific Cttee, 1991–93; Cttee, Parly Gp for Engrg Develt, 1991–93. Freeman, City of London, 1990; Liveryman, Co. of Engineers, 1991–2003.

ATKINSON, Harry Hindmarsh, PhD; consultant; Under Secretary, Director (Special Responsibilities), Science and Engineering Research Council, 1988–92; *b* 5 Aug. 1929; *s* of late Harry Temple Atkinson and Constance Hindmarsh Atkinson (*née* Shields); *m* 1958, Anne Judith Barrett; two *s* one *d*. *Educ:* Nelson Coll., Nelson, NZ; Canterbury University Coll., NZ (BSc, sen. schol.; MSc (1st cl. Hons)), 1948–52. Asst Lectr, Physics, CUC, 1952–53; Research Asst, Cornell Univ., USA, 1954–55; Corpus Christi Coll. and Cavendish Laboratory, Cambridge Univ., 1955–58 (PhD); Sen. Research Fellow, AERE, Harwell, 1958–61; Head, General Physics Group, Rutherford Laboratory, 1961–69; Staff Chief Scientific Adviser, Cabinet Office, 1969–72; Dep. Chief Scientific Officer and Head of Astronomy, Space and Radio Division, SRC, 1972–78; Dir (Astronomy, Space and Radio, and Nuclear Physics), SRC later SERC, 1979–83; Dir Science, SERC, 1983–88. Chm. Council, ESA, 1984–87 (Vice-Chm., 1981–84, UK Deleg., 1974–87); UK Member: EISCAT Council, 1976–86; Bd, Anglo-Aust. Telescope, 1979–88; Cttee, S African Astronomical Observatory, 1979–83; Council, European Synchrotron Radiation Facility, 1986–88; Chairman: Cttee on Netherlands/UK Astronomy Collaboration, 1981–88; Steering Cttee, Inst. Laue-Langevin, Grenoble, 1984 and 1987 (UK deleg., 1983–88); UK Govt Task Force on Potentially Hazardous Near-Earth Objects, 2000; Mem., Working Gp on Near Earth Objects, ESF, 2001. Assessor, UGC, 1987–89; Member: NI Cttee, UFC, 1989–93; Working Gp on Internat. Collaboration (Cabinet Office), ACOST, 1989; Co-ordinator, UK, Australia, NZ sci. collaboration, 1989–94. Chief Scientist, Loss Prevention Council, 1990–98. Consultant: UGC of HK Govt, 1993–95; Oxford Univ. Commn on future of the Univ., 1995–96. Trustee, Trans-Antarctic Assoc., 1993–. Minor planet named 5972 Harryatkinson by IAU, 2006. *Publications:* papers on various branches of physics, science and higher education policy, international comparisons. *Address:* Bampton, Oxon. *Club:* Athenæum.

ATKINSON, Prof. Helen Valerie, CBE 2014; PhD; CEng, FREng, FIMMM, FIMechE; Professor of Materials Processing, since 2002, Head, Mechanics of Materials Group, 2004–14, and Head, Department of Engineering, since 2012, University of Leicester; *b* Portadown, NI, 29 April 1960; *d* of Arthur and Sheila Bavister; *m* 1984, Rt Rev. Richard William Bryant Atkinson, *qv*; one *s* two *d*. *Educ:* South Park High Sch., Lincoln; Girton Coll., Cambridge (BA 1981); Imperial Coll. of Sci. and Technol., Univ. of London (PhD 1986; DIC 1986). MIM 1985, FIMMM 1998; CEng 1986; FIMechE 2004; FREng 2007. SO, 1981–83, HSO, 1983–87, SSO, 1987, Materials Develt Div., UKAEA, Harwell; Sen. Lectr in Materials, Sheffield City Poly., 1987–89; Lectr, 1989–96, Sen. Lectr, 1996–2000, Reader, 2000–02, in Materials, Univ. of Sheffield. Vis. Prof., Ecole d'Arts et Métiers, ParisTech, Centre Paris, 2010–11. Member: UK Foresight Panel on Materials, 1994–99; Action Gp on Sensors, Office of Sci. and Technol., 1996–97; British Transport Police Cttee, 1998–2003; Chem. and Materials Task Force, UK Foresight Crime Prevention Panel, 1999–2001; Lord Chancellor's Adv. Cttee for Appt of Magistrates in Rotherham, 2000–02; Implementation Gp for Govt's Strategy on Women in Sci., Engrg and Technol., DTI, 2004–07. Member: Bd of Dirs, Eur. Soc. of Material Forming, 2007–12; Educn and Trng Panel, EngineeringUK (formerly Engrg and Technol. Bd), 2008–12; Royal Academy of Engineering: Mem., Standing Cttee on Educn and Trng, 2008–11 (Chair, 2012–); Trustee, 2011–; Vice Pres., 2012–14. Jt Chm., Engrg Professors' Council/Engrg and Technol. Bd Cttee on costs of teaching engrg degrees, 2007–08. Member, Council: Inst. of Metals, 1989–91; Inst. of Materials, 1992–96. Mem. Cttee, Engrg Professors' Council, 2004–. Member: Oxford Diocesan Bd of Social Responsibility, 1986–87; Sheffield Diocesan Bd of Social Responsibility, 1990–91. Pres., Engrg Professors' Council, 2011–13. Member, Editorial Board: Jl Fatigue and Fracture of Engrg Materials and Structures, 1996–2002; Internat. Jl Microstructure and Material Properties, 2004–. Dr hc Liège, 2010. Plowden Prize, British Nuclear Energy Soc., 1985; (jtly) Williams Prize, IMMM, 2002; Woman of Outstanding Achievement, UK Resource Centre for Women in Sci., Engrg and Technol., 2010. *Publications:* (with B. A. Rickinson) Hot Isostatic Processing, 1991; (ed) Modelling of Semi-Solid Processing, 2008; (ed) Thixoforming Steel, 2010; contrib. papers on metallurgy and materials sci. *Recreations:* gardening, singing, walking. *Address:* Department of Engineering, University of Leicester, University Road, Leicester LE1 7RH. *T:* (0116) 252 2569.

ATKINSON, Janice Ann; Member for South East Region, European Parliament (UK Ind, 2014–15, Ind, since 2015); *b* London, 31 Aug. 1962; *m* 1st, Steve Small (marr. diss.); two *s*; 2nd, Simon; two step *c*. Owner, media and mktg agency; Global PR Dir, Byronwilde Ltd, 2012–. Jt Founder, WomenOn.org. Contested (C) Batley and Spen, 2010. *Address:* European Parliament, 60 Rue Wiertz, 1047 Brussels, Belgium.

ATKINSON, Kenneth Neil, FCIPD; Managing Director, Travel Training Co. Ltd, 1995 (Director, then Chief Executive, ABTA National Training Board, 1989–94); *b* 4 April 1931; *s* of William Atkinson and Alice Reid. *Educ:* Kingussie High Sch., Inverness-shire; BA Hons Open Univ. 2001. ARCM 1961; FCIPD (FIPM 1986). Various appts, Min. of Labour and Dept of Employment, 1948–67; Dep. Chief Conciliation Officer, Dept of Employment, 1968–72; Dir, Industry Trng Bd Relations, MSC, 1973–78; Manpower Services Dir, Scotland, 1979–82; Dir of Youth Training, Training Agency (formerly Manpower Services/

Training Commn), 1983–89. Chm., Prince's Trust Community Venture, 1989–92; Mem. Bd, Prince's Trust Volunteers, 1993–94. Mem., Council, CGLI, 1991–98. Mem., London Philharmonic Choir, 1990–2010; Musical Dir, Ruislip Operatic Soc., 1994–2008. FRSA 2003. *Recreation:* choral and solo singing. *Address:* 14/7 St Margaret's Place, Edinburgh EH9 1AY. *T:* (0131) 447 5975; 4 Morford Close, Ruislip, Middlesex HA4 8SW. *T:* and *Fax:* (020) 8866 2581. *Club:* Royal Automobile.

ATKINSON, Kent; *see* Atkinson, M. K.

ATKINSON, Dr Margaret Elizabeth; Children's Commissioner for England, 2010–15; *b* Barnsley, S Yorks, 16 Sept. 1956; *d* of Colin Cragg and Kathleen Cragg; *m* 1999, Andrew Atkinson; one step *s* one step *d.* *Educ:* Pope Pius X RC Comp. Sch., Wath-on-Dearne; Mexborough VI Form Coll.; Newnham Coll., Cambridge (BA Hons Hist. 1978); Sheffield Univ. (PGCE 1979); Keele Univ. (EdD 2008). Teacher of English and Drama, Hungerhill Comp. Sch., Doncaster, 1979–87; Hd of English, Birkdale Comp. Sch., Dewsbury, 1987–89; W and N Yorks Co-ordinator, Lang. in the Nat. Curriculum Proj., 1989–91; Educn Adviser and Inspector: Birmingham, 1991–92; Kirklees, 1992–98; Asst Dir of Educn, Warrington, 1998–99, seconded as Dep. Dir of Educn to Liverpool CC, 1999; County Manager, Cheshire LEA, 1999–2003; Gp Dir Learning and Culture and Dir of Educn, later Gp Dir Learning and Children and Dir of Children's Services, Gateshead Council, 2003–10. Member: Children and Young People's Health Outcomes Forum, 2011–14; DoH Children and Young People's Mental Health and Well-Being Taskforce, 2014–15. Chm., Bd of Dirs, A New Direction, 2015–. Hon. Prof., Keele Univ., 2013–. Leading Thinker, Nat. Educn Trust, 2012–. Pres., Assoc. of Dirs of Children's Services, 2008–09. Mem. Court, Bishop Grosseteste Univ., Lincoln, 2013–. FRSA; FIAM; Fellow, ILM; Mem., Internat. Fedn of Professional Aromatherapists. Mem., Northumberland Pipers' Soc. Hon. DCL: Northumbria, 2010; Keele, 2015. Pres.'s Medal, RCPsych, 2014. *Recreations:* playing Northumbrian small pipes, gardening, piano, singing, travel, arts (watching, making, celebrating), family, DIY, aromatherapy (qualified aromatherapist, 1997), church affairs, walking, good food, wine and company, birdwatching, range of hand crafts. *E:* maggie.e.atkinson@gmail.com. *Club:* Civil Service.

ATKINSON, (Michael) Kent; Group Finance Director, Lloyds TSB Group plc, 1994–2002 (non-executive Director, 2002–03); *b* 19 May 1945; *s* of late Carl Kent Atkinson and Edith Atkinson (*née* Gilbert); *m* 1970, Eufemia Alexandra Alarcón; two *s.* *Educ:* Blundell's Sch. Entered Bank of London & South America Ltd, 1964: sen. appts, Bank of London/Lloyds Bank Internat. Ltd in Colombia, Ecuador, Panama, Bahrain, Dubai, Paraguay and Argentina, 1967–86; Gen. Manager, Argentina, Chile, Peru, Bolivia, Paraguay and Uruguay, 1987–89; Lloyds Bank plc: Regl Exec. Dir, 1989–94; Gen. Manager, Retail Ops, 1994. Non-executive Director: Coca-Cola HBC SA (formerly Coca-Cola Beverages), 1998–2013; telent plc (formerly Marconi Corp.), 2002–07; Cookson Gp plc, 2003–05; Standard Life plc (formerly Standard Life Assurance Co.), 2005–11; Gemalto (formerly Axalto) NV, 2005–13; Millicom Internat. SA, 2007–10; Northern Rock plc, 2008–09; Northern Rock (Asset Mgt) plc, 2010–; Bradford & Bingley plc, 2010–; UK Asset Resolution Ltd, 2010–; BILT Paper plc, 2011; Bank of Ireland Gp, 2012–; Chairman: Standard Life Bank Ltd, 2007; Link Plus Corp., 2006–08. *Recreations:* tennis, golf, Rugby, soccer, opera, personal computers. *Clubs:* Effingham Golf, Horsley Sports.

ATKINSON, Michael William, CMG 1985; MBE 1970; HM Diplomatic Service, retired; *b* 11 April 1932; *m* 1963, Veronica Bobrovsky; two *s* one *d.* *Educ:* Purley County Grammar School; Queen's College, Oxford (BA Hons). Served FO, Vientiane, Buenos Aires, British Honduras, Madrid; FCO 1975; NATO Defence Coll., 1976; Counsellor, Budapest, 1977–80, Peking, 1980–82; Hd of Consular Dept, FCO, 1982–85; Ambassador: to Ecuador, 1985–89; to Romania, 1989–92; Personnel Assessor, FCO, 1992–98.

ATKINSON, Nigel John Bewley; Lord-Lieutenant of Hampshire, since 2014 (Vice Lord-Lieutenant, 2007–14); Chairman: Centurion Safety Products Ltd, since 2009; Flowrite Services Ltd, since 2012; *b* London, 25 Dec. 1953; *s* of John Bewley Atkinson, MBE and Jean Margaret Atkinson; *m* 1987, Christine Pamela Oliver; one *d* and one step *s* one step *d.* *Educ:* Haileybury Coll.; RMA Sandhurst. Served RGJ, Captain and Adjt, 1973–79. Courage Ltd: District Manager, 1979–83; Retail Services Manager, 1983–85; Regl Gen. Manager, 1985–87; Sales Dir, 1987–90; Chief Exec., George Gale & Co. Ltd, 1990–2006. Non-executive Chairman: S E Hants Enterprise Agencies, 1992–2003; Ocean Radio Gp, 2001–07. Non-executive Director: Fuller, Smith & Turner plc, 2006–12; Wadworth & Co. Ltd, 2012–. Chm., St John Ambulance, Hants, 2001–09; Vice-Pres., Duke of Edinburgh Award, Hants, 1998–2014. Trustee, HMS Warrior 1860, 2001–. Hon. Col, Hants & IoW ACF, 2009–. Patron: King Edward VI Sch., Southampton, 2014–; Hants Constabulary Volunteer Police Cadets, 2014–. Liveryman, Brewers' Co. (Master, 2010–11). DL Hants, 1999. CStJ 2007. *Recreations:* tennis, ski-ing. *Address:* c/o Hampshire Lieutenancy Office, Serle's House, Gar Street, Winchester, Hants SO23 8GQ. *Clubs:* Lansdowne, Royal Green Jackets; Royal Naval and Royal Albert Yacht (Southsea), Royal Southampton Yacht.

ATKINSON, Very Rev. Peter Gordon; Dean of Worcester, since 2007; *b* 26 Aug. 1952; *m* 1983, Lynne Wilcock; two *s* one *d.* *Educ:* St John's Coll., Oxford (BA 1974; MA 1978); Westcott House, Cambridge. Ordained: deacon, 1979; priest, 1980; Asst Curate, Clapham Old Town Team Ministry, 1979–83; Priest-in-charge, St Mary, Tatsfield, 1983–90; Rector, Holy Trinity, Bath, 1990–91; Principal, Chichester Theol Coll., 1991–94; Rector, Lavant, 1994–97; Bursalis Preb., 1991–97, Canon Residentiary and Chancellor, 1997–2007, Chichester Cathedral; Dio. Warden of Readers, Chichester, 2001–03. Mem., Gen. Synod of C of E, 2000–05. Vice-Chm., 2002–07, Chm., 2007–, Cathedral Libraries and Archives Assoc.; Mem., Cathedrals Fabric Commn for England, 2001–05. Master, St Oswald's Hosp., Worcester, 2007–. FRSA 2006. Hon. DLitt Worcester, 2014. *Publications:* (contrib.) Stepping Stones: joint essays on Anglican Catholic and Evangelical Unity, ed C. Baxter, 1987; Friendship and the Body of Christ, 2005; The Lion Encyclopedia of the Bible, 2009. *Recreations:* English literature, European history, living in Normandy. *Address:* The Deanery, 10 College Green, Worcester WR1 2LH. *T:* (01905) 732909, 732939.

ATKINSON, Peter Landreth; *b* 19 Jan. 1943; *s* of Major Douglas Wilson Atkinson, RTR (*d* Burma, 1945) and of Amy Landreth; *m* 1976, Brione, *d* of late Comdr Arthur Darley, RN and Elspeth Darley; two *d.* *Educ:* Cheltenham Coll. Journalist, 1961–87 (formerly News Editor, Evening Standard); Dep. Dir, British Field Sports Soc., 1987–92. Councillor: London Borough of Wandsworth, 1978–82; Suffolk County Council, 1989–92. MP (C) Hexham, 1992–2010. PPS to Chm. of Cons. Pty, 1994–95, 1997–98, to Sec. of State for Transport, 1996–97; an Opposition Whip, 1999–2002, 2003–05. Member: Select Cttee on Scottish Affairs, 1992–2002; Speaker's Panel of Chairmen, 1997–99, 2005–10; Procedure Cttee, 2003–05. *Recreations:* shooting, racing, gardening. *Clubs:* Carlton; Northern Counties (Newcastle).

ATKINSON, Reay; *see* Atkinson, W. R.

ATKINSON, Rt Rev. Richard William Bryant; *see* Bedford, Bishop Suffragan of.

ATKINSON, Rowan Sebastian, CBE 2013; actor and writer; *b* 6 Jan. 1955; *s* of late Eric Atkinson and Ella May Atkinson; *m* 1990, Sunetra Sastry; one *s* one *d.* *Educ:* Durham Cathedral Choristers' Sch.; St Bees Sch.; Newcastle Univ.; Oxford Univ. (BSc, MSc). *Stage:* Beyond a Joke, Hampstead, 1978; Oxford Univ. Revues at Edinburgh Festival Fringe; youngest person to have a one-man show in the West End of London, 1981; The Nerd, 1984; The New Revue, 1986; The Sneeze, 1988; Oliver!, Th. Royal, 2009; Quartermaine's Terms, Wyndham's Th., 2013; *television:* Not the Nine O'clock News, 1979–82; The Black Adder, 1983; Blackadder II, 1985; Blackadder the Third, 1987; Blackadder goes Forth, 1989; Mr Bean, 1990–94; The Thin Blue Line, 1995; *films:* The Tall Guy, The Appointment of Dennis Jennings, 1989; The Witches, 1990; Hot Shots—Part Deux, 1993; Four Weddings and a Funeral, The Lion King, 1994; Bean—The Ultimate Disaster Movie, 1997; Maybe Baby, 2000; Rat Race, Scooby Doo, 2002; Johnny English, Love Actually, 2003; Keeping Mum, 2005; Mr Bean's Holiday, 2007; Johnny English Reborn, 2011. *Recreations:* motor cars, motor sport. *Address:* c/o PBJ Management Ltd, 22 Rathbone Street, W1T 1LG. *T:* (020) 7287 1112. *E:* general@pbjmgt.co.uk.

ATKINSON, Dr Susan, (Sue), CBE 2002; FFPH; Visiting Professor, Department of Epidemiology and Public Health, University College London, since 2002; Chairman, Public Health Action Support Team; *b* 10 Aug. 1946; *d* of Fredrick Booth Atkinson and Jay Atkinson (*née* Carruthers); *m*; one *d.* *Educ:* Merchant Taylors' Sch. for Girls; UCNW (BSc Zoology); New Hall, Cambridge (MA 1976; MB BChir 1975); Middlesex Hosp. Med. Sch. DCH 1977; FFPH (FFPHM 1989). Res. Associate in animal behaviour/zool., Univ. of Cambridge, 1969–70; Registrar and SHO posts, Paediatrics, Bristol Children's Hosp. and Addenbrooke's Hosp., 1976–78; Registrar in Public Health Medicine, Avon Area HA, 1979–80; Res. Fellow, NH and MRC Perinatal Epidemiology Unit, Univ. of WA, 1980–81; GP, Bristol, 1981–82; Sen. Registrar in Public Health Medicine, Bristol and Weston HA, 1982–84; Public Health Consultant, Bristol HA, 1985–87; Dir, Public Health, and Chief Exec., SE London HA, 1987–93; Regional Director of Public Health: Wessex, then Wessex and SW RHA, 1993–94; S Thames RHA, then S Thames Regl Office, NHS Exec., 1994–99; Regl Dir of Public Health, 1999–2006, Med. Dir, 1999–2003, London, DoH; Health Advr to Mayor of London and GLA, 2000–06. Special Advr to Health Select Cttee, 1991–92. Interim Dir, Public Health Tri-borough, London, 2013–14. Chm., Greater London Alcohol and Drug Alliance, 2007–08; Mem. Bd, Food Standards Agency, 2008–13; Co-Chair, Climate and Health Council, 2009–. Non-exec. Dir, UCL Hosps NHS Foundn Trust, 2007–13. Joan H. Tisch Dist. Fellow in Public Health, Hunter Coll., NY, 2012. Mem., London Sports Bd, 2003–08; Mem. Bd and Ct, LSHTM, 2001–. FRSA. *Publications:* articles and chapters on spastic diplegia, vision screening, public health in UK and health impact assessment. *Recreations:* cinema, art, music, furniture restoration. *E:* sueatkinsonph@gmail.com. *T:* 07884 473280.

ATKINSON, (William) Reay, CB 1985; FBCS; Under Secretary, 1978–86, and Regional Director, North Eastern Region, 1981–86, Department of Industry; *b* 15 March 1926; *s* of William Edwin Atkinson and Lena Marion (*née* Haselhurst); *m*; one *s* two *d*; *m* 1983, Rita Katherine (*née* Bunn). *Educ:* Gosforth Grammar Sch., Newcastle upon Tyne; King's Coll. Durham Univ.; Worcester Coll., Oxford. Served RNVR, 1943–46. Entered Civil Service as Inspector of Taxes, 1950; Principal, 1958, Asst Sec., 1965; Secretaries Office, Inland Revenue, 1958–61 and 1962–69; Asst Sec., Royal Commn on the Press, 1961–62; Civil Service Dept, 1969; Under Sec., and Dir, Central Computer Agency, CSD, 1973–78. Chm., Northern Development Co. Ltd, 1986–90; Director: English Estates Corp., 1986–94; Northern Rock Building Soc., 1987–96; Belasis Hall Technol. Park, 1989–98; Maryport Develt Co. Ltd, 1989–95. Chm., Northern Rock Foundn, 1997–2000. Chm. of Governors, Univ. of Northumbria at Newcastle (formerly Newcastle-upon-Tyne Polytechnic), 1989–96 (Hon. Fellow, 1987). Hon. Fellow, Univ. of Newcastle upon Tyne, 2005. Hon. DCL Northumbria at Newcastle, 1998. *Recreations:* gentle walking, reading, music. *Address:* 1 Greencroft Avenue, Corbridge, Northumberland NE45 5DW. *T:* (01434) 632351.

ATKINSON, Sir William (Samuel), Kt 2008; Executive Headteacher, Phoenix Canberra Schools Federation, 2010–13 (Headteacher, Phoenix High School, Hammersmith and Fulham, 1995–2010); *b* St Ann, Jamaica, 9 April 1950; *s* of late William Benjamin Atkinson and Sara Jane Atkinson; *m* 1974, Jacqueline Ann Burley; three *s* one *d.* *Educ:* King's Coll. London (MA 1981). Teacher, Portsmouth Modern Boys' Sch., 1971–72; Asst Hd of Year, Islington Green Sch., 1973–74; Hd of Year, Holloway Boys' Sch., 1974–81; Deputy Head, Henry Thornton Sch., 1981–83; White Hart Lane Sch., Haringey, 1983–86; Headteacher, Copland Community Sch., Brent, 1986–87; Cranford Community Sch., 1987–95. Member: Special Measures Action Recovery Team, 1997, Standards Task Force, 1997–2001, DfEE; Justice Task Force, 1999, London Youth Crime Reduction Task Force, 2003–04, Home Office; London Black and Minority Ethnic Communities Cracking Crime Partnership Bd, until 2006; Adv. Panel on Children's Viewing, BBFC, until 2010; a Comr, Family Commn. Designated Nat. Leader, Nat. Coll. for Leadership of Schs and Children's Services, 2010. Nat. Judge, 2002–09, Dep. Chm., Nat. Judging Panel, 2006, Teaching Awards; Chm., London Teaching Awards Panel, 2003. Member: Fulham Sch. Commn, 2007; Haringey Educn Commn, 2012; Chm., Hammersmith and Fulham Youth Task Force, 2007. Dir, Lyric Th. Hammersmith, 2010–. Mem. Bd, RSC, 2012– (Gov., 2011–12). Trustee: Inst. for Citizenship, 2001–06; Shaftesbury Homes and Arethusa, 2001–06; Research Autism. Mem. Council, Industrial Soc. FRSA (Mem., Council, 2004–). Media roles and appearances incl. contribs to wide range of TV and radio progs; role of headteacher in The Unteachables (documentary series), 2005. Hon. Dr North London, 2002. *Recreations:* Rugby, theatre, family.

ATTALI, Jacques; Member, Conseil d'Etat, France, 1981–90 and since 1993; Président: Attali et Associés, since 1994; PlaNet Finance, since 1999; *b* 1 Nov. 1943. *Educ:* Ecole Polytechnique; Inst. d'Etudes Politiques, Paris; Ecole des Mines; Ecole Nat. d'Admin. Dr d'Etat en Sci. Econ. Conseil d'Etat: Auditeur, 1970; Maître des Requêtes, 1977; Conseiller, 1989; Special Advr to President of French Republic, 1981–91; Founding Pres., EBRD, 1991–93; Pres., Commn for Liberation of French Econ. Growth, 2007–08. *Publications:* Analyse économique de la vie politique, 1972; Modèles Politiques, 1973; (with Marc Guillaume) L'Anti-Economique, 1974; La Parole et l'outil, 1975; Bruits, 1976; La nouvelle Economie Française, 1977; L'Ordre Cannibale, 1979; Les Trois Mondes, 1981; Histoire du Temps, 1982; La figure de Fraser, 1984; Un homme d'influence, 1985; Au propre et au figuré, 1988; Lignes d'Horizon, 1990; 1492, 1991; Verbatim, 1993; Europe(s), 1994; L'Economie de l'Apocalypse, 1995; Verbatim II, 1995; Verbatim III, 1996; Chemins de Sagesse: traité du labyrinthe, 1996; Mémoire de Sabliers, 1997; Dictionnaire du XXIe siècle, 1998; Fraternités, 1999; Blaise Pascal, 2000; Economic History of the Jewish People, 2002; L'homme nomade, 2003; La Voie humaine, 2004; La confrérie des éveillés, 2004; Karl Marx ou l'esprit du monde, 2005; C'était François Mitterrand, 2005; Une brève histoire de l'avenir, 2006; Devenir soi, 2014; *fiction:* La vie éternelle, 1989; Le premier Jour après moi, 1990; Il viendra, 1994; Manuel, l'Enfant Rêve (for children), 1994; Au-delà de nulle part, 1997; La femme du menteur, 1999; *play:* Les portes du Ciel, 1999. *Address:* 27 rue Vernet, 75008 Paris, France.

ATTALIDES, Michalis A.; Rector, since 2007, and Jean Monnet Professor, since 2011, University of Nicosia (formerly Intercollege) (Dean, School of Humanities, Social Sciences and Law, 2003–06); *b* 15 Nov. 1941; *s* of Antonis Attalides and Katina Loizou; *m* 1991, Alexandra Alexandrou; one *s* one *d* from previous marriages. *Educ:* London Sch. of Econs (BSc Econ); Princeton Univ. (PhD 1975). Lectr in Sociology, Univ. of Leicester, 1966–68; sociologist, Cyprus Town and Country Planning Project, 1968–70; Counterpart of UNESCO Expert, Social Research Centre, Cyprus, 1971 and 1973–74; mil. service, 1972; Guest Lectr, Otto Suhr Inst., Free Univ. of Berlin, 1974–75; journalist, 1975–76; Internat. Relns Service, House of Representatives of Cyprus, 1977–89 (Dir, 1979–89); Dir, Pol Affairs Div. B (Cyprus Question) (with rank of Ambassador), Min. of Foreign Affairs, 1989–91; Ambassador to France, also accredited to Morocco, Portugal and Spain, 1991–95; Perm. Delegate to EU, also accredited to Belgium and Luxembourg, 1995–98; High Comr in

London, 1998–2000; Perm. Sec., Min. of Foreign Affairs, Cyprus, 2000–01; Rep. of Govt of Cyprus, Eur. Convention, 2002–03. *Publications:* Social Change and Urbanization in Cyprus: a study of Nicosia, 1971; Cyprus: nationalism and international politics, 1980; Cyprus: State, Society and International Environment (in Greek), 2009. *Address:* University of Nicosia, 46 Makedonitissas Avenue, PO Box 24005, 1700 Nicosia, Cyprus. *E:* attalides.m@unic.ac.cy.

ATTALLAH, Naim Ibrahim; Book Publisher and Proprietor: Quartet Books, since 1976; The Women's Press, since 1977; Robin Clark, since 1980; *b* 1 May 1931; *s* of Ibrahim and Genevieve Attallah; *m* 1957, Maria Attallah (*née* Nykolyn); one *s*. *Educ:* Battersea Polytechnic. Foreign Exchange Dealer, 1957; Financial Consultant, 1966; Dir of cos, 1969–; Financial Dir and Jt Man. Dir, Asprey of Bond Street, 1979–92; Gp Chief Exec., Asprey PLC, 1992–96; Managing Director: Mappin & Webb, 1990–95; Watches of Switzerland, 1990–95; Exec. Dir, Garrard, 1990–95; Magazine Proprietor: The Literary Review, 1981–2001; The Wire, 1984–2000; The Oldie, 1991–2001. Proprietor, Academy Club, 1989–96. Launched Parfums Namara, Avant l'Amour and Après l'Amour, 1985, Naïdor, 1987, l'Amour de Namara, 1990; launched Namara Fine Art, 1997. *Theatre:* co-presenter, Happy End, Lyric, 1975; presented and produced, The Beastly Beatitudes of Balthazar B, Duke of York's, 1981; co-prod, Trafford Tanzi, Mermaid, 1982; *films:* co-prod (with David Frost), The Slipper and the Rose, 1974–75; exec. producer, Brimstone and Treacle, 1982; also prod and presented TV docs. MUniv Surrey, 1993. *Publications:* Women, 1987; Singular Encounters, 1990; Of a Certain Age, 1992; More of a Certain Age, 1993; Speaking for the Oldie, 1995; A Timeless Passion (novel), 1995; Asking Questions, 1996; Tara & Claire (novel), 1996; A Woman a Week, 1998; In Conversation with Naim Attallah, 1998; Insights, 1999; Dialogues, 2000; The Old Ladies of Nazareth, 2004; The Boy in England, 2005; In Touch With His Roots, 2006; Fulfilment & Betrayal, 2007; contrib. Literary Review, Oldie, and most nat. newspapers. *Recreations:* classical music, opera, theatre, cinema, photography. *Address:* 25 Shepherd Market, W1J 7PP. *T:* (020) 7499 2901, *Fax:* (020) 7499 2914. *E:* nattallah@aol.com. *W:* http://quartetbooks.wordpress.com.

ATTANASIO, Prof. Orazio Pietro, PhD; FBA 2004; Professor of Economics, University College London, since 1995; *b* 31 Oct. 1959. *Educ:* Univ. of Bologna; London Sch. of Econs and Pol Sci. (MSc 1984; PhD 1988). Asst Prof. of Econs, 1988–94, Fellow, Hoover Instn, 1993–94, Stanford Univ.; Associate Prof. of Econs, Univ. of Bologna, 1993–95; Res. Fellow, Inst. for Fiscal Studies, 1995–; Dir, Centre for the Evaluation of Develt Policies, UCL and Inst. for Fiscal Studies, 2002–. Man. Ed., Quantitative Economics, 2009–. *Publications:* contrib. learned jls. *Address:* Department of Economics, University College London, Gower Street, WC1E 6BT; Institute for Fiscal Studies, 7 Ridgmount Street, WC1E 7AE.

ATTENBOROUGH, Sir David (Frederick), OM 2005; CH 1996; Kt 1985; CVO 1991; CBE 1974; FRS 1983; FLS; FSA; broadcaster and naturalist; *b* 8 May 1926; *s* of late Frederick Levi Attenborough; *m* 1950, Jane Elizabeth Ebsworth Oriel (*d* 1997); one *s* one *d*. *Educ:* Wyggeston Grammar Sch. for Boys, Leicester; Clare Coll., Cambridge (Hon. Fellow, 1980). Served in Royal Navy, 1947–49. Editorial Asst in an educational publishing house, 1949–52; joined BBC Television Service as trainee producer, 1952; undertook zoological and ethnographic filming expeditions to: Sierra Leone, 1954; British Guiana, 1955; Indonesia, 1956; New Guinea, 1957; Paraguay and Argentina, 1958; South West Pacific, 1959; Madagascar, 1960; Northern Territory of Australia, 1962; the Zambesi, 1964; Bali, 1969; Central New Guinea, 1971; Celebes, Borneo, Peru and Colombia, 1973; Mali, British Columbia, Iran, Solomon Islands, 1974; Nigeria, 1975; Controller, BBC2, BBC Television Service, 1965–68; Dir of Programmes, Television, and Mem., Bd of Management, BBC, 1969–72. Writer and presenter, BBC series: Tribal Eye, 1976; Wildlife on One, 1977–2004; Life on Earth, 1979; The Living Planet, 1984; The First Eden, 1987; Lost Worlds, Vanished Lives, 1989; The Trials of Life, 1990; Life in the Freezer, 1993; The Private Life of Plants, 1995; The Life of Birds, 1998; State of the Planet, 2000; The Life of Mammals, 2002; Life in the Undergrowth, 2005; Life in Cold Blood, 2008; Darwin and the Tree of Life, 2009; Life Stories, Radio 4, 2009; David Attenborough's First Life, 2010; Flying Monsters 3D, 2010; Frozen Planet, 2011; Kingdom of Plants 3D, 2011; Madagascar, 2011; 60 Years in the Wild, 2012; Galapagos 3D, 2012; Attenborough's Ark, 2012; Africa, 2013; David Attenborough's Natural Curiosities, 2013–14; Tweet of the Day, Radio 4, 2013; David Attenborough's Rise of Animals: triumph of the vertebrates, 2013; Life Story, 2014; Natural World, 2015. Huw Wheldon Meml Lecture, RTS, 1987. President: BAAS, 1990–91; RSNC, 1991–96; Mem., Nature Conservancy Council, 1973–82. Trustee: WWF UK, 1965–69, 1972–82, 1984–90; WWF Internat., 1979–86; British Museum, 1980–2001; Science Museum, 1984–87; Royal Botanic Gardens, Kew, 1986–92 (Kew Award, 1996). Corresp. Mem., Amer. Mus. Nat. Hist., 1985. Fellow, BAFTA 1980; FRSE 2006; FLS 2007 (Hon. FLS 1998); FSA 2008. Hon. Fellow: Manchester Polytechnic, 1976; UMIST, 1980; Hon. FRCP 1991; Hon. FIBiol 2000. Special Award, SFTA, 1961; Silver Medal, Zool Soc. of London, 1966; Silver Medal, RTS, 1966; Desmond Davis Award, SFTA, 1970; Cherry Kearton Medal, RGS, 1972; Kalinga Prize, UNESCO, 1981; Washburn Award, Boston Mus. of Sci., 1983; Hopper Day Medal, Acad. of Natural Scis, Philadelphia, 1983; Founder's Gold Medal, RGS, 1985; Internat. Emmy Award, 1985; Encyclopaedia Britannica Award, 1987; Livingstone Medal, RSGS, 1990; Franklin Medal, RSA, 1990; Gold Medal, RTS, 1991; Golden Kamera Award, Berlin, 1993; Edinburgh Medal, Edinburgh Sci. Fest., 1998; Internat. Cosmos Prize, Osaka, 2000; Michael Faraday Prize, Royal Soc., 2003; Raffles Medal, Zool Soc. of London, 2004; Caird Medal, Nat. Maritime Mus., 2004; Bicentennial Medal, Smithsonian Instn, 2004; Petersen Medal, Harvard, 2004; Descartes Prize, EC, 2004; Prince of Asturias Award, 2009. Hon. DLitt: Leicester, 1970; City, 1972; London, 1980; Birmingham, 1982; Hon. DSc: Liverpool, 1974; Heriot-Watt, 1978; Sussex, 1979; Bath, 1981; Ulster, Durham, 1982; Keele, 1986; Oxford, 1988; Plymouth, 1992; Bradford, 1998; Nottingham, 1999; UWE, Iceland, Guelph, 2003; UEA, 2005; Uppsala, 2007; St Andrews, 2011; Hon. LLD: Bristol, 1977; Glasgow, 1980; DUniv: Open Univ., 1980; Essex, 1987; Antwerp, 1993; Hon. ScD Cambridge, 1984; Hon. DVetMed Edinburgh, 1994. Hon. Freeman, City of Leicester, 1990. Comdr of Golden Ark (Netherlands), 1983. *Publications:* Zoo Quest to Guiana, 1956; Zoo Quest for a Dragon, 1957; Zoo Quest in Paraguay, 1959; Quest in Paradise, 1960; Zoo Quest to Madagascar, 1961; Quest under Capricorn, 1963; The Tribal Eye, 1976; Life on Earth, 1979; The Living Planet, 1984; The First Eden, 1987; The Trials of Life, 1990; The Private Life of Plants, 1994; The Life of Birds, 1998; Life on Air (memoirs), 2002, 2nd edn 2009; The Life of Mammals, 2002; Life in the Undergrowth, 2005; Life in Cold Blood, 2008; Life Stories, 2009; New Life Stories, 2011; (with Errol Fuller) Drawn from Paradise, 2012. *Recreations:* music, tribal art, natural history. *Address:* 5 Park Road, Richmond, Surrey TW10 6NS.

ATTENBOROUGH, (Hon.) Michael John, CBE 2013; freelance theatre director; *b* 13 Feb. 1950; *s* of Baron Attenborough, CBE; *m* 1st, 1971, Jane Seymour (*née* Joyce Frankenberg) (marr. diss. 1976); 2nd, 1984, Karen Lewis; two *s*. *Educ:* Westminster Sch.; Sussex Univ. (BA Hons English). Associate Director: Mercury Theatre, Colchester, 1972–74; Leeds Playhouse, 1974–79; Young Vic Theatre, 1979–80; Artistic Director: Palace Theatre, Watford, 1980–84; Hampstead Theatre, 1984–89; Turnstyle Gp, 1989–90; Exec. Producer and Resident Dir, 1990–95, Principal Associate Dir, 1995–2002, RSC; Artistic Dir, Almeida Theatre, 2002–13. Hon. Prof. of English, Univ. of Sussex, 2011–. Hon. DLitt: Sussex, 2005; Leicester, 2009. Excellence in the Theatre Award, Internat. Theatre Inst., 2012. *Recreations:* music, football, reading, being with my family. *Address:* c/o Rose Cobbe, United Agents, 12–16 Lexington Street, W1F 0LE.

ATTENBOROUGH, Peter John; Director of Educational and Community Care Projects, 1994–2004, Administrator, Leadership and Fellowship Schemes, 2004–06, The Rank Foundation; Headmaster of Charterhouse, 1982–93; *b* 4 April 1938; *m* 1967, Alexandra Deidre Campbell Page; one *s* one *d*. *Educ:* Christ's Hospital; Peterhouse, Cambridge. BA Classics 1960, MA 1964. Asst Master, Uppingham Sch., 1960–75 (Housemaster, Senior Classics Master); Asst Master, Starehe Boys' Centre, Nairobi, 1966–67; Headmaster, Sedbergh Sch., 1975–81. Chairman: Common Entrance Cttee of Independent Schs, 1983–88; Schools Arabic Project, 1986–87; Mem., HMC Cttee, 1986–90. Almoner, Christ's Hosp., 1987–2001; Governor: Ashdown House, 1983–93; Haslemere Prep. Sch., 1986–93; St Edmund's Sch., 1986–94; Brambletye Sch., 1989–99; Caldicott Sch., 1990–93; Haberdashers' Monmouth Schs, 1996–2007; Trustee, Uppingham Sch., 1993–2002. Trustee: Inner City Young People's Project, 1989–98; Starehe Endowment Fund (UK), 1995–2008. Freeman, City of London, 1965; Liveryman, Skinners' Co., 1978. *Address:* Rawmarsh Cottage, Linton, near Ross-on-Wye, Herefords HR9 7RX.

ATTERBURY, Paul Rowley; self-employed writer, lecturer, broadcaster, curator and antiques expert, since 1981; *b* London, 8 April 1945; *s* of Rowley Streatfeild Atterbury and Audrey Atterbury; *m* 1st, 1974, Avril Thompson (marr. diss. 1987); two *d*; 2nd, 2002, Chrissie Bursey; two step *d*. *Educ:* Westminster Sch.; London Sch. of Printing (Co. Cert. Typography 1967); Univ. of E Anglia (BA Hons 1972). Prodn Manager, Sotheby Pubns, 1973–76; historical advr, Royal Doulton, 1976–80; Ed., Connoisseur mag., 1980–81; exhibn curator, V&A Mus., 1976, 1979, 1994, 2001; lectr, UK and internationally, 1970–. Mem., team of experts, Antiques Roadshow, 1990–. Judge, Nat. Heritage Rlwy Awards, 2010–. Hon. DLitt Keele, 2005. *Publications:* Nicholson's Guide to the Thames, 1969; (with A. Darwin) Nicholson's Guides to the Waterways, 5 vols, 1970–74; (with J. Moran) Henry George: printer and publisher in Westerham, Kent, 1830–1946, 1972; (ed) Antiques: an encyclopedia of the decorative arts, 1979; English Pottery and Porcelain: historical survey, 1980; History of Porcelain, 1982; English Rivers and Canals, 1984; A Golden Adventure: the first 50 years of Ultramar, 1985; Moorcroft Pottery: guide to the pottery of William and Walter Moorcroft, 1897–1986, 1987, 4th edn as Moorcroft: a guide to Moorcroft Pottery, 1897–1993, 2008; See Britain by Train, 1989; (ed) The Interior Design Year Book 1989; The Parian Phenomenon: survey of Victorian Parian porcelain statuary and busts, 1989; Art Deco Patterns, 1990; South East England by Train, 1991; (with J. Henson) Ruskin Pottery: pottery of Edward Richard Taylor and William Howson Taylor, 1993; The Great Antiques Treasure Hunt, 1993, 2nd edn 1997; (ed with Lars Tharp) The Little, Brown Illustrated Encyclopedia of Antiques, 1994, 2nd edn 1998; End of the Line: exploration of Britain's threatened rural railways, 1994; (with Lars Tharp) The Bullfinch Illustrated Encyclopedia of Antiques, 1994; Exploring Britain's Canals, 1995; (with L. Hayward) Poole Pottery: Carter and Co. and their successors, 1873–1995, 1995, rev. edn as Poole Pottery: Carter and Company and their successors, 1873–2011, 2011; A. W. N. Pugin: master of Gothic revival, 1996; (with I. Burgum) Country Railways, 1996; (with T. Forrest) The Bullfinch Anatomy of Antique Furniture, 1996; (with T. Forrest) Know Your Antiques, 1996; Walking Britain's Rivers and Canals, 1997, 2nd edn 1999; (with A. Haines) Thames: from source to the sea, 1998; (with M. Batkin) The Dictionary of Minton, 1999; (jtly) Twentieth-Century Ceramics, 2000, 2nd edn 2005; (with S. F. Cooper) Victorians at Home and Abroad, 2001; Miller's 20th Century Ceramics Antiques Checklist, 2003; Branch Line Britain, 2004; (with J. Benjamin) The Jewellery and Silver of H. G. Murphy: arts and crafts to art deco, 2005; (jtly) The Antiques Roadshow, 2005; Along Country Lines: exploring the rural railways of yesterday, 2005; Tickets Please!: a nostalgic journey through railway station life, 2006; (with H. Kay) The Wedding: 150 years of down-the-aisle style, 2006; Along Lost Lines, 2007; On Holiday: the way we were, 2008; All Change: visiting the byways of Britain's railway network, 2009; (with A. Hart-Davis) Discovering Britain's Lost Railways, 2009; Life Along the Line: a nostalgic celebration of railways and railway people, 2010; An A-Z of Railways: a nostalgic celebration of British railway heritage, 2010; Along Main Lines: the great trains, stations and routes of Britain's railways, 2011; Paul Atterbury's Lost Railway Journeys: rediscover Britain's forgotten railway routes, 2011; Paul Atterbury's Railway Collection, 2012; Paul Atterbury's Wonder Book of Trains, 2012; Mapping Lost Branch Lines: a nostalgic look at Britain's branch lines in old maps and photographs, 2013; Paul Atterbury's Favourite Railway Journeys, 2013; The First World War in 100 Family Treasures, 2014. *Recreations:* going to Australia, visiting antique fairs, walking the Somme, exploring lost railways. *Address:* 27 Admiral's Quarter, Barrack Road, Weymouth, Dorset DT4 8BD. *T:* (01305) 774089. *E:* paul@pcpress.co.uk.

ATTEWELL, Brian; HM Diplomatic Service, retired; *b* 29 May 1937; *s* of late William John Geldard Attewell and Marie Evelyn Attewell; *m* 1st, 1963, Mary Gillian Tandy (*d* 2000); two *s* one *d*; 2nd, 2002, Angelika Pathak. *Educ:* Dulwich Coll.; London School of Economics and Political Science (BScEcon 1961); Birkbeck Coll., London (Dip. Hist. of Art, 2006). BoT, 1956–58, 1961–66; Private Sec. to Parly Sec., 1964–66; transf. to Diplomatic Service, 1966: Washington, 1967–70; Buenos Aires, 1970–73; FCO, 1974–78; Canberra, 1978–80; FCO, 1980–83; Dubai, 1984–87; Brussels, 1988–92; High Comr, Bahamas, 1992–96. *Recreations:* golf, walking, listening to music (classical and jazz), watercolours, following fortunes of Charlton Athletic. *Club:* Wimbledon Park Golf.

ATTFIELD, Prof. (John) Paul, DPhil; FRS 2014; FRSC; FRSE; Professor of Materials Science at Extreme Conditions, University of Edinburgh, since 2003; *b* Birmingham, 27 July 1962; *s* of David George Attfield and Janet Attfield (*née* White); *m* 1987, Diane Louise Gallagher (marr. diss. 2014); two *s* one *d*. *Educ:* Durham Johnston Sch., Durham; Magdalen Coll., Oxford (BA Hons Chem. 1984; DPhil Chem. 1987). FRSC 2005. Jun. Res. Fellow, Christ Church, Oxford, 1987–91; Lectr in Chem., 1991–2000, Reader in Materials Chem., 2000–03, Univ. of Cambridge; Fellow, Jesus Coll., Cambridge, 1991–2003. FRSE 2006. *Recreations:* walking, travel, visiting galleries and museums. *Address:* Centre for Science at Extreme Conditions, King's Buildings, University of Edinburgh, Mayfield Road, Edinburgh EH9 3JZ; School of Chemistry, King's Buildings, University of Edinburgh, West Mains Road, Edinburgh EH9 3JJ. *T:* (0131) 651 7229, *Fax:* (0131) 651 7049. *E:* j.p.attfield@ed.ac.uk.

ATTLEE, family name of **Earl Attlee**.

ATTLEE, 3rd Earl *cr* 1955; **John Richard Attlee,** TD; Viscount Prestwood, 1955; *b* 3 Oct. 1956; *s* of 2nd Earl Attlee and Anne Barbara, *er d* of late James Henderson, CBE; *S* father, 1991; *m* 2008, Teresa Ahern. *Educ:* Stowe. Engrg and automotive industries until 1993; British Direct Aid: Bosnia, 1993–94; Rwanda, 1995. TA officer, Maj. REME (V), Op. Lodestar, 1997–98, OC 150 Recovery Company, 1998–2000; Op. TELIC, 2003. Opposition Whip, H of L, 1997–99; opposition spokesman, in H of L, for transport, 1997 and 1999–2001, for NI, 1997 and 1998–99, for energy, 1998, and for defence, 1998–2001, for transport and defence, 2002–03, for trade and industry, 2003–05; for maritime and shipping, 2007–10; govt spokesman in H of L, for Transport, Home Office, and NI, 2010–, for Wales, 2012–, and for Scotland, 2013–; a Lord in Waiting (Govt Whip), 2010–13. Elected Mem., H of L, 1999. *Address:* House of Lords, SW1A 0PW. *T:* (020) 7219 6071. *E:* attleej@parliament.uk.

ATTLEE, Air Vice-Marshal Donald Laurence, CB 1978; LVO 1964; DL; fruit farmer, 1977–95, retired; *b* 2 Sept. 1922; *s* of Major Laurence Attlee; *m* 1952, Jane Hamilton Young; one *s* two *d*. *Educ:* Haileybury. Pilot trng in Canada, 1942–44; Flying Instructor, 1944–48; Staff, Trng Comd, 1949–52; 12 Sqdn, 1952–54; Air Ministry, Air Staff, 1954–55; RAF Staff Coll., 1956; 59 Sqdn, 1957–59; CO, The Queen's Flight (W/Cdr), 1960–63; HQ, RAF Germany, 1964–67; CO, RAF Brize Norton, 1968–69; IDC, 1970; MoD Policy Staff, 1971–72; Dir of RAF Recruiting, 1973–74; Air Cdre, Intell., 1974–75; AOA Trng Comd,

1975–77, retired. Chm., Mid-Devon Business Club, 1985–87; Mem. Bd, Mid-Devon Enterprise Agency, 1983–93. Mem., Mid-Devon DC, 1982–2003 (Vice-Chm., 1987–89; Chm., 1989–91; Leader, 2002–03; Hon. Alderman, 2003). DL Devon, 1991. *Recreations:* genealogy, gardening. *Address:* Wintergold, 31 Longmead, Hemyock, Devon EX15 3SG. *T:* (01823) 680317. *Club:* Royal Air Force.

ATTRIDGE, Prof. Derek, PhD; FBA 2007; Professor of English and Related Literature, University of York, since 1998 (Head, Department of English and Related Literature, 2004–07); *b* 6 May 1945; *s* of Henry Lester Attridge and Marjorie Julia Attridge (*née* Lloyd); *m* 1st, 1969, Anna Mary Ridehalgh (marr. diss. 1976); 2nd, 1986, Suzanne Hall; two *d. Educ:* Scottsville Govt Sch., S Africa; Maritzburg Coll., S Africa; Univ. of Natal (BA Hons English 1966); Clare Coll., Cambridge (BA English 1968; PhD 1972). Res. Lectr, Christ Church, Oxford, 1971–73; Lectr, then Sen. Lectr in English, Univ. of Southampton, 1973–84; Prof. of English Studies, 1984–88, Hd of Dept, 1985–86, Univ. of Strathclyde; Prof. of English, 1988–98, Dir of Grad. Studies, 1994–98, Rutgers Univ.; Leverhulme Res. Prof., Univ. of York, 1998–2003. Visiting Professor: Univ. of Illinois, 1979; Univ. of Orléans, 1990; Vis. Prof., 1984, 1987, Dist. Vis. Prof., 1998–2006, Rutgers Univ.; Vis. Scholar, New Hall, Cambridge, 1993–97; S. W. Brooks Fellow, Univ. of Qld, 2007; Vis. Fellow, All Souls Coll., Oxford, 2012; Fellow: Stellenbosch Inst. for Advanced Studies, 2013; Bogliasco Foundn, 2014; Birkelund Sen. Fellow, Nat. Humanities Center, USA, 2015. Mem., Scottish Adv. Bd, British Council, 1985–88. Mem., Bd of Trustees, Internat. James Joyce Foundn, 1986–96, 2007–12. Member, Editorial Board: Derrida Today; Interventions; James Joyce Qly, Joyce Studies Annual; Jl of Narrative Theory; Language and Literature; Modern Fiction Studies, etc. *Publications:* Well-weighed Syllables: Elizabethan verse in classical metres, 1974; The Rhythms of English Poetry, 1982; (ed with D. Ferrer) Post-structuralist Joyce: essays from the French, 1984; (ed jtly) Post-structuralism and the Question of History, 1987; (ed jtly) The Linguistics of Writing: arguments between language and literature, 1987; Peculiar Language: literature as difference from the Renaissance to James Joyce, 1988, 2nd edn 2004; (ed) The Cambridge Companion to James Joyce, 1990, 2nd edn 2004; (ed) Jacques Derrida: acts of literature, 1992; Poetic Rhythm: an introduction, 1995; (ed with R. Jolly) Writing South Africa: literature, apartheid, and democracy 1970–1995, 1998; Joyce Effects: on language, theory, and history, 2000; (ed with M. Howes) Semicolonial Joyce, 2000; (with T. Carper) Meter and Meaning: an introduction to rhythm in poetry, 2003; The Singularity of Literature, 2004; J. M. Coetzee and the Ethics of Reading: literature in the event, 2004; (ed) James Joyce's Ulysses: a casebook, 2004; How to Read Joyce, 2007; Reading and Responsibility: deconstruction's traces, 2010; (ed with J. Elliott) Theory after 'Theory', 2011; (ed with D. Attwell) The Cambridge History of South African Literature, 2012; Moving Words: forms of English poetry, 2013; The Work of Literature, 2015; (with Henry Staten) The Craft of Poetry: dialogues on minimal interpretation, 2015; articles in Essays in Criticism, Jl of Postcolonial Writing, MLN, Modernism/Modernity, New Literary History, Novel, Paragraph, PMLA, Poetics Today, South Atlantic Quarterly, etc. *Address:* Department of English and Related Literature, University of York, Heslington, York YO10 5DD. *T:* (01904) 323361, *Fax:* (01904) 323372.

ATTRIDGE, Elizabeth Ann Johnston, (Mrs John Attridge); Senior Clerk/Adviser, European Legislation Committee, House of Commons, 1994–98; *b* 26 Jan. 1934; *d* of late Rev. John Worthington Johnston, MA, CF, and Mary Isabel Giraud (*née* McFadden); *m* 1956, John Attridge (*d* 2013); one *s. Educ:* Richmond Lodge Sch., Belfast; St Andrews Univ., Fife. Assistant Principal, Min. of Education, NI, 1955, reappointed on marriage (marriage bar), MAFF, London, 1956; assisted on Agriculture Acts, 1957 and 1958; Head Plant Health Br., 1963–66, Finance, 1966–69, External Relations (GATT) Br., 1969–72; Assistant Secretary: Animal Health I, 1972–75; Marketing Policy and Potatoes, 1975–78; Tropical Foods Div., 1978–83; Under Secretary: European Community Group, 1983–85; Emergencies, Food Quality and Pest Control, 1985–89; Animal Health Gp, 1989–91; Agricl Inputs, Plant Protection and Emergencies Gp, 1991–94. Chairman, International Coffee Council, 1982–83. *Recreations:* collecting fabric, opera. *Address:* Croxley East, Cobbetts Hill, Weybridge, Surrey KT13 0UA.

ATTWELL, Prof. David Ian, PhD; FMedSci; FRS 2001; Jodrell Professor of Physiology, University College London, since 1995; *b* 18 Feb. 1953; *s* of Arthur Attwell and Vera Eileen Attwell (*née* Slade); *m* 1988, Ulrike Schmidt; one *s. Educ:* Magdalen Coll., Oxford (BA 1st Cl. Physics 1974; BA 2nd Cl. Physiological Scis 1975; PhD Physiol. 1979). Fellow, Magdalen Coll., Oxford, 1977–79 and 1980–81; University College London: Lectr in Physiol., 1981–88; Reader, 1988–91; Prof. of Physiol., 1991–95. SRC Postdoctoral Fellow, Berkeley, Calif, 1979–80; Henry Head Fellow, Royal Soc., 1984–89. FMedSci 2000. *Publications:* contribs to learned jls on neuroscience. *Recreation:* travel. *Address:* Department of Physiology, University College London, Gower Street, WC1E 6BT. *T:* (020) 7679 7342.

ATTWOOD, Alex; Member (SDLP) Belfast West, Northern Ireland Assembly, since 1998; *b* Belfast, 26 April 1959; *s* of Benjamin and Claire Attwood. *Educ:* St Malachy's Coll.; Queen's Univ. Belfast (LLB). Solicitor, Belfast. Mem. (SDLP), Belfast CC, 1985–2005 (Leader, SDLP Gp). Minister for Social Develt, 2010–11, of the Envmt, 2011–13, NI. Mem., NI Policing Bd, 2001–07, 2009–10. Contested (SDLP) Belfast W, 2015. *Address:* Northern Ireland Assembly, Parliament Buildings, Stormont, Belfast BT4 3XX.

ATTWOOD, Brian Christopher; Channel Manager, LinkedIn Employability, Open University, since 2014; *b* New Brighton, Cheshire, 29 Feb. 1960; *s* of Raymond Attwood and Eileen Attwood (*née* Power); *m* 2002, Lisa Frances Martland; one *s* one *d. Educ:* St Joseph's RC Primary Sch., South Oxhey; Watford Boys' Grammar Sch.; Univ. of Stirling (BA Hons Social Anthropol.); Centre for Journalism, Cardiff (Dip.). The Stage: Chief Reporter, 1989–92; Dep. Ed., 1992–94; Ed., The Stage Newspaper, 1994–2014; Editl Dir, The Stage Media Co. Ltd, 2011–14. *Recreations:* history (especially Irish), fine art, autism issues. *Address:* Open University, Walton Hall, Milton Keynes MK7 6AA.

ATTWOOD, Jonathan F.; *see* Freeman-Attwood.

ATTWOOD, Philip; Keeper of Coins and Medals, British Museum, since 2010; *b* Sheffield, 23 March 1954; *s* of Frank Eric Attwood and Doreen Hilda Attwood; partner, Anthony J. Daniels. *Educ:* Cambridgeshire High Sch. for Boys, Cambridge; Univ. of Birmingham (BA Hons). British Museum: mus. asst, 1978–87; Curator: of Medals, 1987–90; of Modern Coins, 1990–2002; of Medals, 2002–10. Ed., The Medal, 1990–. Hon. Curator of Medals, Cutlers' Co., 1996–. President: British Art Medal Soc., 2008–; FIDEM, 2012–. *Publications:* Artistic Circles: the medal in Britain 1880–1918, 1992; British Art Medals 1982–2002, 2002; Italian Medals, *c.* 1530–1600, in British Public Collections, 2003; Badges, 2004; (with Felicity Powell) Medals of Dishonour, 2009; Hard at Work: the diary of Leonard Wyon 1853–1867, 2014. *Recreations:* architectural history, local history, transport, swimming. *Address:* Department of Coins and Medals, British Museum, WC1B 3DG. *E:* pattwood@thebritishmuseum.ac.uk.

ATTWOOD, Thomas Jaymril; management and marketing consultant; Chairman, Cargill, Attwood and Thomas Ltd, Management Consultancy Group, 1965–97; Associate Professor of Strategic Management, International Management Centres, 1997–2004; *b* 30 March 1931; *s* of George Frederick Attwood and Avril Sandys (*née* Cargill, NZ); *m* 1963, Lynette O. E. Lewis; one *s* one *d. Educ:* Haileybury and Imperial Service Coll.; RMA Sandhurst; Harvard Grad. Sch. of Business Admin; INSEAD, Fontainebleau. Pres., Internat. Consultants' Foundn, 1978–81. Conducted seminars for UN Secretariat, European Commn and World Council of Churches, 1970–80; presented papers to Eur. Top Management Symposium, Davos, Internat. Training Conf. and to World Public Relations Conf. Mem. Exec. Cttee, Brit. Management Training Export Council, 1978–85; Chm., Post Office Users National Council, 1982–83. Mem. Court, Worshipful Company of Marketors, 1985–93 (Liveryman, 1980). FInstD. Mem., Richmond upon Thames Borough Council, 1969–71. *Publications:* (jtly) Bow Group pubn on United Nations, 1961; contrib. to reference books, incl. Systems Thinking, Innovation in Global Consultation, Handbook of Management Development, and Helping Across Cultures; articles on marketing, management and business topics. *Recreations:* travel, music, chess, City of London, cricket. *Address:* 28 Tabor Court, Cheam SM3 8RT. *T:* (020) 8643 3292. *E:* tom.attwood@btinternet.com. *Clubs:* Lord's Taverners, Directors.

ATTWOOLL, David John; Director, Attwooll Associates Ltd, since 2002; *b* 22 April 1949; *s* of Derek Attwooll and Dorothy Attwooll (*née* Hunt); *m* 1979, Trish Cowan; two *s* one *d. Educ:* Lancing Coll.; Pembroke Coll., Cambridge (BA 1970; MA). Editorial Dir, Reference and Gen., OUP, 1985–89; Random House: Man. Dir, Paperback Div., 1989–90; Man. Dir, Reference Div., 1990–92; Man. Dir, Helicon Publishing, 1992–2002. Chm., Liverpool Univ. Press, 2004–; non-executive Director: Oxfordshire Artweeks, 2003–09 (Chm., 2006–09); Oxford Inspires, 2004–11; Oxford Contemporary Music, 2011–; Associate Publisher, Oxford Internat. Centre for Publishing Studies, Oxford Brookes Univ., 1995–. FRSA. *Publications:* poetry: Surfacing, 2013; Ground Work, 2014; The Sound Ladder, 2015. *Recreations:* music (particularly jazz), travel, cricket, reading. *Address:* Attwooll Associates Ltd, 90 Divinity Road, Oxford OX4 1LN. *T:* (01865) 422230. *E:* david@attwoollassociates.com. *Club:* Southfield Cricket.

ATTWOOLL, Elspeth Mary-Ann Muncy; Member (Lib Dem) Scotland, European Parliament, 1999–2009; *b* 1 Feb. 1943; *d* of Hugh Robert Rhind Attwooll and Joan Attwooll (*née* Fidler); *m* 1990, Donald Gordon Henry. *Educ:* Tiffin Girls' Sch., Kingston upon Thames; St Andrews Univ.; Queen's Coll., Dundee (LLB, MA Hons Politics and Philosophy). University of Glasgow: Asst Lectr, Lectr, Sen. Lectr in Jurisp., 1966–98; ILO, Geneva, 1968–69. *Publications:* The Tapestry of the Law, 1997; articles and essays on legal philosophy. *Recreations:* reading, particularly detective fiction.

ATWELL, Very Rev. James Edgar; Dean of Winchester, 2006–June 2016; *b* 3 June 1946; *s* of Joseph Norman Edgar Atwell and Sybil Marion Atwell (*née* Burnett); *m* 1976, Lorna Goodwin; one *s* two *d. Educ:* Dauntsey's Sch.; Exeter Coll., Oxford (MA, BD); Harvard Univ. (ThM). Ordained deacon, 1970, priest, 1971; Assistant Curate: St John the Evangelist, E Dulwich, 1970–74; Great St Mary's, Cambridge, 1974–77; Chaplain, Jesus Coll., Cambridge, 1977–81; Vicar of Towcester, 1981–95; RD, Towcester, 1983–91; Provost, subseq. Dean, of St Edmundsbury, 1995–2006. Hon. Prof., Univ. of Winchester, 2011–16. Member: Cathedral Fabric Commn for England, 2006–16; Cttee to Visit, Harvard Meml Ch, USA, 2006–12. Pres., New Forest and Hants County Show, 2015–May 2016. Order of St Edmund, Dio. St Edmund and Ipswich, 2011. *Publications:* Sources of the Old Testament, 2004; (contrib.) Dreaming Spires?, 2005; contrib. to Jl Theol Studies. *Recreations:* countryside, walking, driving a Land Rover, travel, fairground organs, theology. *Address:* (until June 2016) The Deanery, The Close, Winchester, Hants SO23 9LS. *T:* (01962) 857205, *Fax:* (01962) 857264.

ATWELL, Rt Rev. Robert Ronald; *see* Exeter, Bishop of.

ATWOOD, Barry Thomas; public and European Community law consultant, since 1995; Principal Assistant Solicitor (Under Secretary), Ministry of Agriculture, Fisheries and Food, 1989–95; *b* 25 Feb. 1940; *s* of Percival Atwood and Vera Fanny Atwood (*née* Stoneham); *m* 1965, Jennifer Ann Burgess; two *s. Educ:* Bristol Grammar Sch.; Bristol Univ. (LLB); University College London. Solicitor. Articled John Robinson and Jarvis, Isle of Wight, 1961; Solicitor with Robert Smith & Co., Bristol, 1965; Legal Dept, Ministry of Agriculture, Fisheries and Food: conveyancing, 1966; food legislation, 1970; Common Agricultural Policy, 1977; i/c European Court litigation, 1982; Agricultural Commodities and Food Safety Bill, 1986; Legal Gp B (domestic and EC litigation and commercial work), 1989–92; Legal Gp A (legislation and adv. work), 1992–95. *Publications:* (contrib.) Law of the European Communities, 1999; Butterworth's Food Law, 2nd edn 2000, 3rd edn as Food Law (with K. Thompson and C. Willett) 2009. *Recreations:* family, music, walking, France, Italy.

ATWOOD, Margaret, CC (Can.) 1981; FRSC 1987; writer; *b* Ottawa, 18 Nov. 1939; *m* Graeme Gibson; one *d. Educ:* Univ. of Toronto (BA 1961); Radcliffe Coll., Cambridge, Mass (AM 1962); Harvard Univ., Cambridge, Mass. Lectr in English, Univ. of BC, Vancouver, 1964–65; Instructor in English: Sir George Williams Univ., Montreal, 1967–68; Univ. of Alberta, 1969–70; Asst Prof. of English, York Univ., Toronto, 1971–72; Writer-in-Residence: Univ. of Toronto, 1972–73; Macquarie Univ., Australia, 1987; Hon. Chair, Univ. of Alabama, Tuscaloosa, 1985; Berg Prof., New York Univ., 1986. Holds hon. degrees from univs and colls; recipient of awards, medals and prizes for writing. TV scripts: The Servant Girl, 1974; Snowbird, 1981; (with Peter Pearson) Heaven on Earth, 1986; radio script, The Trumpets of Summer, 1964. *Publications: poetry:* The Circle Game, 1966; The Animals in That Country, 1969; The Journals of Susanna Moodie, 1970 (illus. edn, 1997); Procedures for Underground, 1970; Power Politics, 1971; You Are Happy, 1974; Selected Poems, 1976; Two-Headed Poems, 1978; True Stories, 1981; Notes Towards a Poem that Can Never be Written, 1981; (ed) The New Oxford Book of Canadian Verse in English, 1982; Snake Poems, 1983; Interlunar, 1984; Selected Poems II: poems selected and new 1976–1986, 1986; Selected Poems 1966–1984, 1990; Margaret Atwood Poems 1965–1975, 1991; Poems 1976–1986, 1992; Morning in the Burned House, 1995; The Door, 2007; also poetry in art and small press edns; *fiction:* The Edible Woman, 1969; Surfacing, 1972; Lady Oracle, 1976; Dancing Girls (short stories), 1977; Up in the Tree (for children), 1978; Anna's Pet (for children), 1980; Life Before Man, 1979; Bodily Harm, 1981; Encounters with the Element Man, 1982; Murder in the Dark (short stories), 1983; Bluebeard's Egg (short stories), 1983; Unearthing Suite, 1983; The Handmaid's Tale, 1985 (Governor General's Award, 1986; filmed 1990); (ed with Robert Weaver) The Oxford Book of Canadian Short Stories in English, 1986, new edn as The New Oxford Book of Canadian Short Stories in English, 1995; Cat's Eye, 1989; (ed with Shannon Ravenel) The Best American Short Stories, 1989; For the Birds (for children), 1990; Wilderness Tips (short stories), 1991; Good Bones (short stories), 1992; The Robber Bride, 1993; Princess Prunella and the Purple Peanut (for children), 1995; Alias Grace (Giller Prize, Giller Foundn, Canada; Canadian Booksellers Assoc. Author of the Year; Nat. Arts Club Medal of Honor for Literature), 1996; The Blind Assassin (Booker Prize), 2000; Oryx and Crake, 2003; Rude Ramsay and the Roaring Radishes (for children), 2003; Bashful Bob and Doleful Dorinda (for children), 2004; The Penelopiad, 2005; The Tent (short stories), 2006; Moral Disorder (short stories), 2006; The Penelopiad: the play, 2007; The Year of the Flood, 2009; Wandering Wenda and the Widow Wallop (for children), 2011; MaddAddam, 2013; Stone Mattress (short stories), 2014; The Heart Goes Last, 2015; *opera:* Pauline, York Theatre, Vancouver, 2014; *non-fiction:* Survival: a thematic guide to Canadian literature, 1972; Days of the Rebels 1815–1840, 1977; Second Words: selected critical prose, 1982; Strange Things: the malevolent North in Canadian literature, 1995; Negotiating with the Dead: a writer on writing, 2002; Moving Targets: writing with intent 1982–2004, 2004; Curious Pursuits: occasional writing, 2005; Payback: debt and the shadow side of wealth, 2008; In Other Worlds: SF and the human imagination, 2011. *Address:* c/o McClelland & Stewart, 1 Toronto Street, #300, Toronto, ON M5C 2V6, Canada.

AUBREY, David John; QC 1996; Head of Advocacy, Public Defender Service, since 2014; *b* 6 Jan. 1950; *s* of Raymond John Morgan Aubrey and Dorothy Mary (*née* Griffiths); *m* 1980, Julia Catherine Drew; one *d. Educ:* Cathays High Sch., Cardiff; University Coll., Cardiff (LLB Hons); Inns of Court Sch. of Law. Called to the Bar, Middle Temple, 1976, Bencher, 2002;

a Recorder, 1998–2014; Hd of Chambers, Temple Chambers, Cardiff and Newport, 2001–11; Hd of Temple Court Chambers, Cardiff, 2012–14. Treas., Wales and Chester Circuit, 2000–03. Legal Pres., Mental Health Review Tribunal, 1998–. Member: Criminal Bar Assoc., 1988–; Bar Council, 1998–. Pres., Boys' Brigade in Wales, 2004– (Vice Pres., 2002–04). *Recreations:* gardening, music, cricket, collecting Boys' Brigade memorabilia, genealogy. *E:* david.aubrey1@virgin.net.

AUBREY-FLETCHER, family name of **Baroness Braye**.

AUBREY-FLETCHER, Sir Henry (Egerton), 8th Bt *cr* 1782, of Clea Hall, Cumberland; farmer and company director; Lord-Lieutenant of Buckinghamshire, since 2006 (Vice Lord-Lieutenant, 1997–2006); *b* 27 Nov. 1945; *s* of Sir John Henry Lancelot Aubrey-Fletcher, 7th Bt and Diana Mary Fynvola (*d* 1996), *o c* of Lt-Col Arthur Egerton; *S* father, 1992; *m* 1976, Sara Roberta, *d* of late Major Robert Gilliam Buchanan and Mrs Margaret Ogden-White; three *s*. *Educ:* Eton. Chm., Chilton House Nursing Home, 1987–. Chm., Fox FM ILR, 2000 (Dir, 1989–2006). Dep. Chm., NT, 2003–06; Member: Landscape Adv. Cttee, Dept of Transport, 1990–94. Pres., CLA, 2007–09. Chairman: Berks, Bucks and Oxon Wildlife (formerly Naturalist) Trust, 1995–2001; Cothill Educnl Trust, 2010–; Trustee, Chequers Trust, 1997–. High Sheriff, Bucks, 1995–96. KStJ 2014. *Recreations:* IT, media and rural affairs. *Heir: s* John Robert Aubrey-Fletcher, *b* 20 June 1977. *Address:* Estate Office, Chilton, Aylesbury, Bucks HP18 9LR. *T:* (01844) 265201.

AUCKLAND (Dio. Durham), **Archdeacon of;** *see* Barker, Ven. N. J. W.

AUCKLAND, 10th Baron *cr* 1789 (Ire.), 1793 (GB); **Robert Ian Burnard Eden;** *b* 25 July 1962; *s* of 9th Baron Auckland and Dorothy Margaret, *d* of H. J. Manser; *S* father, 1997; *m* 1986, Geraldine Caroll; one *d*. *Educ:* Blundell's Sch., Tiverton; Dublin City Univ. (BBS). *Heir: cousin* Henry Vane Eden [*b* 11 March 1958; *m* 1988, Alice Claire Needham; one *s* two *d* (and one *s* decd)].

AUCKLAND (NZ), Bishop of, since 2010; **Rt Rev. Ross Bay;** *b* Auckland, NZ, 22 Jan. 1965; *s* of Max and Valerie Bay; *m* 1987, Jacqueline Hedge. *Educ:* Australian Coll. of Theol. (BTh); Univ. of London (Postgrad. Dip. Pastoral Theol.). Ordained deacon, 1989, priest 1989; Vicar: of Ellerslie, Auckland, 1994–2001; of Remuera, Auckland, 2001–07; Archdeacon of Auckland, 2006–07; Dean of Auckland, 2007–10; Vicar-Gen., Dio. of Auckland, 2007–10. *Recreation:* squash. *Address:* PO Box 37242, Parnell, Auckland, New Zealand. *T:* (office) (9) 3027202. *E:* bishop@auckanglican.org.nz.

AUCKLAND (NZ), Bishop of, (RC), since 1994; **Most Rev. Patrick James Dunn;** *b* London, 5 Feb. 1950; *s* of Hugh Patrick Dunn and June Mary (*née* Grevatt). *Educ:* Sacred Heart Coll., Auckland; Canterbury Univ. (BA); Otago Univ. (BTh); Melbourne Coll. of Divinity, Australia (MTheol 1989). Ordained priest, 1976; Catholic Maori Mission, Auckland, 1976–77; Assistant Priest: Mangere E, 1978–79; Takapuna, 1980–84; Co-Pastor, Pakuranga, 1985; Dir, First Year Formation House, Dio. of Auckland, 1986–87; Parish Priest, Northcote, 1990–92; Pastoral Asst to RC Bp of Auckland, and VG, 1993–94. *Publications:* Priesthood, 1990. *Address:* Pompallier Diocesan Centre, Private Bag 47904, Ponsonby, Auckland 1144, New Zealand. *T:* (9) 3603002.

AUCKLAND, Mary Josephine, OBE 2002; independent consultant and trainer; *b* 22 Nov. 1950; *d* of Reginald George Auckland and Annie Auckland (*née* Sullivan); *m* 2003, Terence John Beck. *Educ:* Poly. of N London (LA Professional Exams 1971); University Coll. London (BSc Hons Anthropol. 1977); London Sch. of Econs (MSc Industrial Relns and Personnel Mgt 1986). MCLIP (ALA 1973). Res. Asst, Sch. of Librarianship and Inf. Studies, Poly. of N London, 1971–72; Res. Librarian, Liby and Learning Resources Service, City of London Poly., 1972–74; Asst Librarian, 1979–88, Sub-Librarian, 1988–89, British Liby of Pol and Econ. Sci., LSE; Dep. Librarian and Hd, User Services, Univ. of Southampton Liby, 1990–92; Librarian, SOAS, Univ. of London, 1992–98; Dir of Liby and Learning Resources, London Inst., subseq. Univ. of the Arts London, 1998–2005. Conf. Dir, Computers in Libraries Internat., 1993–95. Member: Cttee for Inf. Envmt (formerly for Electronic Inf.), Jt Inf. Systems Cttee, 1996–2003 (Chair, Content Wkg Gp, 1999–2000); UK Office for Liby Networking Mgt Cttee, 1999–2001; UKOLN Strategic Adv. Gp, 2002–03; British Council Knowledge and Inf. Adv. Cttee, 2002–; Artifact Exec. Bd, 2002–05; ARLIS Nat. Co-ordinating Cttee, 2004–05. Mem., Higher Educn/British Liby Task Force, 2000–01. Mem. Council, LA, 1991–99 (Chm. Council, 1997–99; Chm., Acad. and Res. Libraries Cttee, 1993–95). Acad. Gov., Ct of Govs, SOAS, 1996–98; Acad. Bd Gov., Ct of Govs, London Inst. (later Univ. of the Arts London), 1999–2005. Mem. Trustees, CLIP Benevolent Fund, 2004–. Hon. FCLIP 2002. Cawthorne Prize, LA, 1970. *Publications:* contrib. various articles, chapters, etc, in professional pubns, and conf. papers. *Recreations:* good company, travel.

AUDLAND, Sir Christopher (John), KCMG 1987 (CMG 1973); HM Diplomatic Service and Commission of the European Communities, retired; *b* 7 July 1926; *s* of late Brig. Edward Gordon Audland, CB, CBE, MC, and Violet Mary, *d* of late Herbert Shepherd-Cross, MP; *m* 1955, Maura Daphne Sullivan; two *s* one *d*. *Educ:* Twyford Sch.; Winchester Coll. RA, 1944–48 (Temp. Capt.). Entered Foreign (subseq. Diplomatic) Service, 1948; served in: Berlin and Bonn; British Representation to Council of Europe, Strasbourg; Washington; UK Delegn to negotiations for British Membership of European Communities, Brussels, 1961–63; Co-ordinator and Ed.-in-Chief, FCO report on negotiations for UK entry into EC, 1963; Buenos Aires, 1963–67; Head of Science and Technology Dept, FCO, 1968–70; Counsellor (Head of Chancery), Bonn, 1970–73; seconded to Commn of Eur. Communities, 1973: Dep. Sec.-Gen., 1973–81; Dir-Gen. for Energy, 1981–86. British Negotiator, Allied/FRG Bonn Conventions, 1950–52; Head, UK Delegn to 1st UN Conf. on Seabed and Ocean Floor, 1968; Dep. Head, UK Delegn to Four-Power Negotiations on Berlin, 1970–72. Hon. Fellow, Faculty of Law, and Vis. Lectr on European Instns, Edinburgh Univ., 1986–90. Vice President: Europa Nostra, 1988–91; Internat. Castles Inst., 1988–90 (Pres., 1990–91); Europa Nostra united with Internat. Castles Inst., 1991–96 (Exec. Pres., 1992; Hon. Pres., 1997–). Member: NW Regl Cttee, National Trust, 1987–95; European Strategy Bd, ICL, 1988–96; Lake District Nat. Park Authority, 1989–95; Pro-Chancellor, Lancaster Univ., 1990–97 (Mem., Council, 1988–97; Hon. Fellow, 2007). Trustee: Peter Kirk Meml Fund, 1989–96; Ruskin Foundn, 1994–2001; European Opera Centre, 1996–2002. DL Cumbria, 1996–2006. *Publications:* (contrib.) Berlin: von Brennpunkt der Teilung zur Brücke der Einheit, 1990; Right Place, Right Time (autobiog.), 2004; Jenny: the life and times of a Victorian Lady, 2008; contrib. Jl Soc. of Archivists. *Address:* The Old House, Ackenthwaite, Milnthorpe, Cumbria LA7 7DH. *T:* (015395) 62202. *E:* cja_ack@btinternet.com. *Club:* Oxford and Cambridge.

See also W. G. Audland.

AUDLAND, William Grant; QC 2015; *b* Buenos Aires, 27 Aug. 1966; *s* of Sir Christopher (John) Audland, *qv*; *m* 1994, Antonella Bonetti; one *s* one *d*. *Educ:* Winchester Coll.; Queen's Coll., Oxford (BA Hons Mod. Langs); City Univ., London (DipLaw). Called to the Bar, Gray's Inn, 1992 (Scarman Scholar); in practice as a barrister, 1993–; Accredited Mediator, 2011–. *Publications:* (contrib.) Personal Injury Schedules: calculating damages, 2001, 3rd edn 2010. *Recreations:* ascent and descent of mountains on foot, ski(n)s or by bicycle; hockey, diving, Italy, theatre, opera. *Address:* 12 King's Bench Walk, Temple, EC4Y 7EL. *T:* (020) 7583 0811. *E:* audland@12kbw.co.uk.

AUDLEY, Barony *cr* 1312–13; in abeyance. *Co-heiresses:* Hon. Patricia Ann Mackinnon [*b* 10 Aug. 1946; *m* 1969, Carey Leigh Mackinnon; one *s* one *d*]; Hon. Jennifer Michelle Carrington [*b* 23 May 1948; *m* 1978, Michael William Carrington; two *s* one *d*]; Hon. Amanda Elizabeth Souter [*b* 5 May 1958; one *d*].

AUDLEY, Prof. Robert John, PhD; FBPsS; Professor of Psychology, University College London, 1965–94, now Professor Emeritus; *b* 15 Dec. 1928; *s* of Walter Audley and Agnes Lilian (*née* Baker); *m* 1st, 1952, Patricia Mary Bannister (marr. diss. 1977); one *s* (and one *s* decd); 2nd, 1990, Vera Elyashiv Bickerdike. *Educ:* Battersea Grammar Sch.; University Coll. London (BSc 1st Cl. Hons Psychology, 1952; PhD 1955). Fulbright Scholar and Res. Asst, Washington State Univ., 1952; University College London: Res. Worker, MRC Gp for Exptl Investigation of Behaviour, 1955–57; Lectr in Psychology, 1957–64; Reader in Psychology, 1964; Head, Psychology Dept, 1979–93; Dean, Faculty of Science, 1985–88; Vice-Provost, 1988–94; Fellow, 1989. Vis. Prof., Columbia Univ., NY, 1962; Vis. Miller Prof., Univ. of Calif, Berkeley, 1971; Vis Fellow, Inst. for Advanced Study, Princeton, 1970. Member: UGC Social Studies Sub-Cttee, 1975–82; UGC Equipment Sub-Cttee, 1982–89; Computer Bd for Univs and Res. Councils, 1986–90; MRC/RN Personnel Res. Cttee, 1984 (Chm., Psychology Sub-Cttee, 1984–95); Chm., Jt Wkg Gp, ESRC/HEFC Jt Inf. Systems Cttee, 1990–99 (Mem., New Technology Sub-Cttee, Jt Inf. Systems Cttee, 1993–95). President: British Psychological Soc., 1969–70; Exptl Psychology Soc., 1975–76. Editor, British Jl of Math. and Stat. Psychology, 1965–70. *Publications:* papers on choice, judgement, medical mishaps. *Recreations:* crosswords, cooking, the arts. *Address:* 22 Keats Grove, NW3 2RS. *T:* (020) 7435 6655.

AUDLEY-CHARLES, Prof. Michael Geoffrey, PhD; Yates-Goldsmid Professor of Geology, 1982–93, now Emeritus Professor, and Head of the Department of Geological Sciences, 1982–92, University College London; *b* 10 Jan. 1935; *s* of Laurence Geoffrey Audley-Charles and Elsie Ada (*née* Ustonson); *m* 1965, Brenda Amy Cordeiro; one *s* one *d*. *Educ:* Royal Wanstead Sch.; Chelsea Polytechnic (BSc); Imperial Coll., London (PhD). Geologist with mining and petroleum cos, Canada and Australia, 1957–62; Imperial Coll. of Science and Technology, London: research in geology, 1962–67; Lectr in Geol., 1967–73; Reader in Geol., 1973–77; Prof. of Geol. and Head of Dept of Geol Sciences, Queen Mary Coll., London, 1977–82. Hon. Fellow, UCL, 1996. *Publications:* geological papers dealing with stratigraphy of British Triassic, regional geol. of Indonesia and Crete, evolution of Gondwanaland, and deep orogenic trough tectonic processes, in learned jls. *Recreation:* gardening. *Address:* La Serre, 46800 St Pantaléon, France. *T:* 565318067.

AUERBACH, Frank Helmuth; painter; *b* 29 April 1931; *s* of Max Auerbach, lawyer, and Charlotte Norah Auerbach; *m* 1958, Julia Wolstenholme; one *s*. *Educ:* privately; St Martin's Sch. of Art; Royal Coll. of Art. *One-man exhibitions:* Beaux Arts Gallery, 1956, 1959, 1961, 1962, 1963; Marlborough Fine Art, 1965, 1967, 1971, 1974, 1983, 1987, 1990, 1997, 2004, 2009, 2012, 2015; Marlborough Gall., New York, 1969, 1982, 1994, 1998, 2006; Villiers, Sydney, Australia, 1972; Bergamini, Milan, 1973; Univ. of Essex, 1973; Mun. Gall. of Modern Art, Dublin, 1975; Marlborough, Zurich, 1976; Anthony D'Offay, London, 1978; Arts Council Retrospective, Hayward Gall., Fruit Market Gall., Edinburgh, 1978; Jacobson, NY, 1979; Anne Berthoud, London, 1983; Venice Biennale, British Pavilion, 1986 (Golden Lion Prize); Kunstverein, Hamburg; Museum Folkwang, Essen; Centro de Arte Reina Sofia, Madrid, 1986–87; Rijksmuseum Vincent van Gogh, Amsterdam, 1989; Yale Center for British Art, New Haven, 1991; Nat. Gall., 1995; Campbell-Thiebaud Gall., San Francisco, 1995; Rex Irwin, Woollahra, 1996, 2000; Charlottenborg, Copenhagen, 2000; RA 2001; Marlborough, Madrid, 2002; (with Lucian Freud) V&A Mus., 2006; Fitzwilliam Mus., Cambridge; Abbot Hall Art Gall., Kendal, 2007–08; Courtauld Gall., London, 2009; Offer Waterman, London, 2012; Kunstmus., Bonn, 2015; Tate Britain, London, 2015–16. *Mixed exhibitions:* Carnegie International, Pittsburgh, 1958, 1961; Dunn International, Fredericton, 1963; Gulbenkian International, Tate Gallery, 1964; Peter Stuyvesant Foundn Collection, London, 1967; The Human Clay, Hayward Gall., 1976; European Painting in the Seventies, Los Angeles County Mus. and tour, 1976; Annual Exhibn, part I, Hayward Gall., 1977; Westkunst, Cologne, 1981; New Spirit in Painting, RA, 1981; Internat. Survey, MoMA, NY, 1984; The Hard Won Image, Tate Gall., 1984; The British Show, Art Gall. of WA, Perth, and tour, 1985; British Art in the Twentieth Century, RA, 1987; Current Affairs, Mus. of Modern Art, Oxford, and tour, 1987; A School of London, Kunstnernes Hus, Oslo, and tour, 1987–88; Pursuit of the Real, Manchester City Art Gall., 1990; British Figurative Painting of the Twentieth Century, Israel Mus., Jerusalem, 1992–93; From London, Scottish Nat. Gall. of Modern Art, Edinburgh, and tour, 1995–96; School of London, Fondation Dina Vierny, Musée Maillol, Paris, and tour, 1998–99; La Mirada Fuerte: Pintura Figurativa de Londres, Museo de Arte Moderno and Museo de Monterrey, Mexico, 2000; Raw Truth: Auerbach-Rembrandt, Ordovas, London and Rijkmuseum, Amsterdam, 2013; Bare Life, LWL-Mus. für Kunst und Kultur, Münster, 2014–15. *Public collections:* Arts Council; Brit. Council; Brit. Museum; Tate Gallery, London; Courtauld Gall.; Metropolitan Museum, NY; Mus. of Modern Art, NY; National Gallery of Victoria, Melbourne; Nat. Galls of Australia, W Australia and NSW; County Museum of LA, Calif; Cleveland Mus., Ohio; Art Inst., Chicago; Univ. of Cincinnati; St Louis Art Mus.; Yale Center for British Art, New Haven; Tamayo Mus., Mexico; Aberdeen, Bedford, Bolton, Cambridge, Edinburgh, Hartlepool, Huddersfield, Hull, Leeds, Leicester, Manchester, Nottingham, Oldham, Rochdale, Sheffield, Southampton, Belfast, Birmingham, Bristol, Cardiff, Glasgow, Newcastle, Wakefield, Walsall Galls; Contemporary Art Soc., etc. *Address:* c/o Marlborough Fine Art, 6 Albemarle Street, W1S 4BY.

AUGAR, Philip John; author; *b* Northampton, 18 June 1951; *s* of John and Helen Augar; *m* 1978; one *s* one *d*. *Educ:* Cambridgeshire High Sch.; Clare Coll., Cambridge (BA 1973; PhD 1979; PGCE 1974). Investment analyst, Wood Mackenzie, 1978–87; Bursar and Fellow, St Catharine's Coll., Cambridge, 1987–89; Sen. Man. Dir, NatWest Mkts, 1989–95; Gp Man. Dir, Securities, Schroders plc, 1995–2000. Non-executive Director: Fuller Smith & Turner plc, 1999–2002; TSB, 2014–. Chm., UK Border Agency, 2012–13; non-executive Director: DFE, 2004–10; Home Office, 2010–14. Member: Public Interest Cttee, KPMG, 2013–; Adv. Bd, New City Agenda, 2014–. Visiting Fellow: Cranfield Sch. of Mgt, 2001–09; Inst. of Historical Res., 2010–. *Publications:* The Death of Gentlemanly Capitalism, 2001; (with Joy Palmer) The Rise of the Player Manager, 2003; The Greed Merchants, 2005; (with Robin Cane) Skiing Better, 2006; Chasing Alpha, 2009, new edn as Reckless: the rise and fall of the City, 2010. *Recreations:* Leeds United, tennis, ski-ing, rock music. *W:* www.philipaugar.com.

AUGIER, Sir Fitzroy (Richard), Kt 1996; OJ 2014; Professor of History, University of the West Indies, 1989–95, now Professor Emeritus; *b* 17 Dec. 1924; *s* of Frank John Augier and Lucie Lastique; *m* 1959, Leila Yvette Gibbs; two *s* one *d*. *Educ:* St Mary's Coll., Castries; Univ. of St Andrews (MA 1949; PhD 1954); London Univ. Inst. of Educn (DipEd 1950); Inst. Commonwealth Studies. Served RAF, 1942–46. Pres., West Indian Students' Union, 1952–54; University of the West Indies: Jun. Res. Fellow, 1954; Lectr, Dept of Hist., 1955–65; Sen. Lectr, 1965–89; Dean, Faculty of Arts and Gen. Studies, 1967–72; Pro Vice Chancellor, 1972–90. Rockefeller Fellow, Inst. of Historical Res., London Univ., 1962. Chairman: Drafting Cttee, UNESCO Gen. Hist. of Caribbean, 1981–2014; Caribbean Exams Council, 1986–96; Teachers' Service Commn, Jamaica, 2008. Mem., Univ. Council of Jamaica, 2012–. Fellow, Inst. of Jamaica, 2003. Medal, Internat. Council on Archives, 1980; Musgrave Medal (Gold), Council, Inst. of Jamaica, 1996; Five Continents Medal, UNESCO, 2009. Chevalier, Ordre des Arts et des Lettres (France), 1989. *Publications:* (jtly) The Making of the West Indies, 1960; (jtly) Sources of West Indian History: documents with commentary,

1962; contrib. to Caribbean Qly, New World Qly, Jl Caribbean Hist. *Recreation:* gardening. *Address:* Department of History, University of the West Indies, Mona, Kingston 7, Jamaica, West Indies. *T:* 9271922. *E:* history@uwimona.edu.jm; 70 Donhead Close, Kingston 6, Jamaica, West Indies. *T:* 9275385.

AUGUST, Dame Kathryn (Mary), DBE 2014; education researcher, writer and consultant, since 2013; *b* Blackpool, 1 July 1952; *d* of James and Ann Daly; *m* 1977, Richard August; two *s*. *Educ:* Convent of Holy Child Jesus, Blackpool; Manchester Poly. (BA; PGCE; MA). North Manchester High School for Girls: Teacher of History, 1975–80; Project Leader, Alternative Curriculum, 1980–83; Dep. Headteacher, 1983–85; Headteacher, 1988–93; Headteacher, Priestall Sch., Stockport, 1993–97; Dir of Educn, Trafford MBC, 1997–99; Sen. Educn Advr, DFES, 1999–2002; Dir of Educn, Stockport MBC, 2002–03; Principal, Manchester Acad., 2003–10; Dep. Chief Exec., then Actg Chief Exec., United Learning Trust, 2010–12; Exec. Dir of Educn, The Educn Fellowship, 2012–13. *Recreations:* reading, travel, theatre. *Address:* 18 Mersey Road, Stockport SK4 3DG. *T:* 07803 525644. *E:* kathryn.august@gmail.com.

AUKIN, David; Director, David Aukin Productions Ltd, since 2003; Chief Executive Officer, Daybreak Pictures Ltd, since 2006; *b* 12 Feb. 1942; *s* of late Charles and Regina Aukin; *m* 1969, Nancy Meckler, theatre director; two *s*. *Educ:* St Paul's Sch., London; St Edmund Hall, Oxford (BA). Admitted Solicitor, 1965. Literary Advr, Traverse Theatre Club, 1970–73; Administrator, Oxford Playhouse Co., 1974–75; Administrator, 1975–79, Dir, 1979–84, Hampstead Theatre; Dir, Leicester Haymarket Theatre, 1984–86; Exec. Dir, NT, 1986–90; Hd of Drama, 1990–97, Hd of Film, 1997–98, Channel 4 Television; Jt Chief Exec., HAL Films, 1998–2000; Dir, Act Prodns Ltd, 2001–04; Hd of Drama, Mentorn, 2003–06. Chm., Artichoke Prodns Ltd, 2005–14. Chm., Soho Theatre and Writers' Centre, 1994–2005; Dir, Soho Theatre Ltd, 1995–. Gov., London Film Sch., 2008–. *Recreation:* golf. *Address:* Daybreak Pictures Ltd, 77 Fulham Palace Road, W6 8JA. *Clubs:* Century, Royal Automobile.

AULD, Alasdair Alpin, FMA; Director, Glasgow Museums and Art Galleries, 1979–88, retired; *b* 16 Nov. 1930; *s* of Herbert Bruce Auld and Janetta Isabel MacAlpine; *m* 1959, Mary Hendry Paul; one *s* one *d*. *Educ:* Shawlands Acad., Glasgow; Glasgow Sch. of Art (DA). FMA 1971. Glasgow Museums and Art Galleries: Asst Curator, 1956–72; Keeper of Fine Art, 1972–76; Depute Dir, 1976–79. Pres., Scottish Fedn of Museums and Art Galls, 1981–84. Hon. Curator, RCPSG, 1991–. Hon. FRCPSGlas 2001. *Publications:* catalogues; articles on museum subjects. *Recreations:* golf, travel, painting. *Address:* 3 Dalziel Drive, Pollokshields, Glasgow G41 4JA. *T:* (0141) 427 1720.

AULD, Very Rev. Jeremy Rodger; Provost, St Paul's Cathedral, Dundee, since 2010; *b* Perth, 5 Nov. 1966; *s* of late Derek William Auld and of Jennifer Anne Auld (*née* Rodger); *m* 2000, Christine Marie Arjun; two *s*. *Educ:* Perth Acad.; Univ. of Edinburgh (LLB 1987; DipLP; BD 2004); Theol Inst. of Scottish Episcopal Church (Cert. Theol. 2004). Admitted solicitor, Scotland, 1988; Solicitor, Tods Murray, Edinburgh, 1992–97; admitted to the Bar, Fiji, 1997; Principal Legal Officer, Govt of Fiji, 1997–99; Solicitor, MacRoberts, Edinburgh, 1999–2002; ordained deacon, 2004, priest, 2005; Asst Curate, St Peter's, Edinburgh, 2004–06; Rector, St James the Great, Dollar, 2006–10. Convenor, Provincial Cttee on Canons, 2008–13, Mem., Organisational Rev. Cttee, 2012–, Scottish Episcopal Church; Mem., Gen. Synod, 2011–; Trustee, Scottish Churches Architectural Heritage Trust, 2010–12. Chm., Bd of Dirs, Ark Nursery, Dundee, 2010–. *Publications:* contribs to Expository Times. *Recreations:* travel, music, architecture, theatre, amateur dramatics. *Address:* Castlehill House, 1 High Street, Dundee DD1 1TD. *E:* provost@saintpaulscathedral.net.

AULD, Rt Hon. Sir Robin (Ernest), Kt 1988; PC 1995; a Lord Justice of Appeal, 1995–2007; Vice-Chairman, Judicial Appointments Commission, 2006–07; a Justice of the Court of Appeal, Bermuda, since 2008; *b* 19 July 1937; *s* of late Ernest Auld and Adelaide Mackie; *m* 1st, 1963 (marr. diss. 2005); one *s* one *d*; 2nd, 2014, Prof. Catherine Alison Geissler. *Educ:* Brooklands Coll.; King's Coll. London (LLB 1st cl. Hons 1958; PhD 1963; FKC 1987). Called to Bar, Gray's Inn, 1959 (first in order of merit, Bar finals; Macaskie Schol., Lord Justice Holker Sen. Schol.), Bencher, 1984; in practice at English Bar, 1960–87; admitted to Bar: State of NY, USA, 1984; NSW, Australia, 1986. QC 1975; a Recorder, 1977–87; a Judge of the High Court of Justice, QBD, 1987–95; Presiding Judge, Western Circuit, 1991–94; Sen. Presiding Judge for England and Wales, 1995–98. Sen. Res. Scholar, Yale Law Sch., 2001; Vis. Prof., KCL, 2007–10; Arthur Goodhart Prof. in Legal Sci., Cambridge Univ., 2009–10; Vis. Fellow, Selwyn and Wolfson Colls, Cambridge, 2009–10. Legal Assessor, GMC and GDC, 1982–87. Mem., Judicial Studies Bd, 1989–91. Mem., Commn of Inquiry into Casino Gambling in the Bahamas, 1967; Chm., William Tyndale Schools' Inquiry, 1975–76; Dept of Trade Inspector, Ashbourne Investments Ltd, 1975–79; Counsel to Inquiry into Brixton Disorders, 1981; Chm., Home Office Cttee of Inquiry into Sunday Trading, 1983–84; Counsel to UK, Australian Royal Commn of Inquiry into British nuclear tests in Australia, 1984–85; conducted Criminal Courts Review, 1999–2001; Chm., Inquiry into Governmental Corruption, Turks and Caicos Islands, 2008–09; Pres., Court of Appeal, Solomon Islands, 2009–12; Mem., Tribunal of Inquiry into alleged misconduct in office of Prime Minister of PNG, 2011. Mem., Oxford Univ. Appeal Ct, 2009–. Trustee, Slynn Foundn, 2014–. Master, Woolmen's Co., 1984–85. Hon. LLD Hertfordshire, 2002. *Address:* Lamb Chambers, Lamb Building, Temple, EC4Y 7AS. *T:* (020) 7797 8301. *Clubs:* Athenæum; Yale (New York).

AUMANN, Prof. Robert John, PhD; Professor of Mathematics, 1968–2000, now Emeritus, and Member, Center for the Study of Rationality, since 1991, Hebrew University of Jerusalem; *b* Frankfurt am Main, 8 June 1930; *s* of Siegmund Aumann and Miriam Aumann (*née* Landau); *m* 1st, 1955, Esther Schlesinger (*d* 1998); four *c* (and one *s* decd); 2nd, 2005, Batya Cohn (*née* Schlesinger). *Educ:* Yeshiva High Sch., NY; City Coll. of New York (BS 1950); Mass Inst. of Technol. (SM 1952; PhD 1955). Mathematics Department, Hebrew University of Jerusalem: Instructor, 1956–58; Lectr, 1958–61; Sen. Lectr, 1961–64; Associate Prof. 1964–68. Foreign Hon. Mem., Amer. Acad. of Arts and Scis, 1974; Mem., Nat. Acad. of Scis, USA, 1985; Mem., Israel Acad. of Scis and Humanities, 1989; Corresp. FBA 1995; Corresp. Mem., Royal Acad. of Financial Sci. and Econs, Spain, 2011. Hon. dr: Bonn, 1988; Univ. Catholique de Louvain, 1989; Chicago, 1992; City Univ. of NY; Bar Ilan, 2006. Harvey Prize in Sci. and Technol., Technion-Israel Inst. of Technol., 1983; Israel Prize in Econs, 1994; Lanchester Prize in Operations Res., 1995, von Neumann Theory Prize in Operations Res., 2005, INFORMS; Erwin Plein Nemmers Prize in Econs, Northwestern Univ., USA, 1998; EMET Prize in Econs, Israel, 2002; (jtly) Nobel Prize in Econs, 2005. *Publications:* (with L. S. Shapley) Values of Non-Atomic Games, 1974; (with Y. Tauman and S. Zamir) Game Theory (2 vols), 1981; (ed jtly) Handbook of Game Theory with Economic Applications, vol. 1, 1992, vol. 2, 1994, vol. 3, 2002; (with M. Maschler) Repeated Games with Incomplete Information, 1995; Collected Papers (2 vols), 2000; articles in learned jls. *Address:* Center for the Study of Rationality, Hebrew University of Jerusalem, 91904 Jerusalem, Israel.

AUNG SAN SUU KYI; MP for Kawhmu, Burma, since 2012; Co-Founder and General Secretary, National League for Democracy, Burma, since 1988; Burmese prisoner of conscience, 1989–95; *b* Rangoon, 19 June 1945; *d* of U Aung San (assassinated, 19 July 1947) and late Daw Khin Kyi; *m* 1972, Michael Vaillancourt Aris (*d* 1999); two *s*. *Educ:* St Francis Convent, Rangoon; Methodist English High Sch., Rangoon; Lady Shri Ram Coll., Delhi Univ.; St Hugh's Coll., Oxford (BA PPE 1967; MA; Hon. Fellow, 1990). Asst Sec., Adv. Cttee on Admin. and Budgetary Questions, UN Secretariat, NY, 1969–71; Res. Officer, Min. of Foreign Affairs, Bhutan, 1972. Vis. Schol., Centre for SE Asian Studies, Kyoto Univ., Japan, 1985–86. Fellow, Indian Inst. of Advanced Studies, Simla, 1987. Hon. Mem., Worl Commn on Culture and Develt, Unesco, 1992–95; Mem., Acad. Universelle des Cultures Paris, 1993. Hon. Pres., LSE Students' Union, 1992; Hon. Life Mem., Univ. of Londo Union, 1992. Hon. doctorates: Thammasat Univ., Bangkok, 1992; Toronto Univ., 1993 Oxford Univ., 1993; Vrije Univ., Brussels, 1994; Queen's Univ., Kingston, 1995. Thoro Rafto Award for Human Rights, Norway, 1990; Nobel Peace Prize, 1991; Sakharov Prize fo Freedom of Thought, European Parlt, 1991; Annual Award, Internat. Human Rights Law Group, USA, 1992; Simón Bolívar Prize, Unesco, 1992; Prix Littéraire des Droits d l'Homme, Paris, 1992; Rose Prize, Internat. Forum of Danish Lab. Movement, 1993; Victo Jara Internat. Human Rights Award, Center for Human Rights and Constitutional Law, LA 1993; Bremen Solidarity Prize, 1993; Liberal Internat. Prize for Freedom, 1995; Jawaharla Nehru Award for Internat. Understanding, 1995; Freedom Award of Internat. Rescue Cttee 1995; Congressional Gold Medal, USA, 2012. *Publications:* (ed with Michael Aris) Tibeta Studies in Honour of Hugh Richardson, 1980; Aung San, 1984, 2nd edn as Aung San o Burma: a biographical portrait by his daughter, 1990; (contrib.) Burma and Japan: basic studie on their cultural and social structure, 1987; Burma and India: some aspects of intellectual lif under colonialism, 1990; Freedom from Fear and Other Writings, 1991, 2nd edn 1995 Towards a True Refuge (Joyce Pearce Meml Lect.), 1993; numerous speeches. *Address:* 54–(University Avenue, Rangoon, Burma.

AUST, Anthony Ivall, CMG 1995; international law consultant, writer and teacher; *b* March 1942; *s* of Ivall George Aust and Jessie Anne Salmon; *m* 1st, 1969, Jacquelin Antoinette Thérèse Paris (marr. diss. 1987); two *d*; 2nd, 1988, Dr Kirsten Kaarre Jensen. *Educ* London Sch. of Econs and Pol Science (LLB 1963, LLM 1967). Admitted Solicitor, 1967. Ass Legal Advr, FCO (formerly CO), 1967–76; Legal Advr, British Mil. Govt, Berlin, 1976–79 Asst Legal Advr, FCO, 1979–84; Legal Counsellor, FCO, 1984–88 and 1991–2000 Counsellor (Legal Advr) UK Mission to UN, NY, 1988–91; retired as Dep. Legal Advr, FCO 2002. Visiting Professor: SOAS, 1994–2007; UCL, 2002–04; LSE, 2003–08; Notre Dame London Centre, 2005–10. *Publications:* Modern Treaty Law and Practice, 2000, Chinese edi 2005, 3rd edn 2013; Handbook of International Law, 2005, 2nd edn 2010; articles i international law jls and chapters in edited books. *Recreations:* architecture, cinema, gardening parlour games. *Address:* 5 Coulter Road, W6 0BJ. *E:* aiaust@aol.com.

AUSTEN, Patrick George; Operating Partner, Nova Capital Management Ltd, since 2003 *b* 22 Sept. 1943; *m* 1968, Margaret; three *s* one *d*. *Educ:* Bristol Coll. of Commerce; Leiceste Sch. of Textiles; Leicester Poly.; Centre d'Etudes Industrielles, Geneva. ICI Fibres, 1961–83 commercial apprentice, British Nylon Spinners (later ICI Fibres), 1961–65; mgt trainee 1965–67; Trade Sales Manager, 1967–70; Fibres Manager, Republic of Ireland, 1970–73 Business Area Manager, 1974–79; Commercial Manager, Textile Fibres, 1979–83; BTR 1983–93; Managing Director: Pretty Polly, 1983–85; Pretty Polly and Dunlopillo, 1985–87 Chief Exec., Liberty plc, 1993–96. *Recreations:* golf, motor-racing. *Address:* Nova Capita Management Ltd, 1st Floor, Cayzer House, 30 Buckingham Gate, SW1E 6NN.

AUSTEN, Richard Bertram G.; *see* Godwin-Austen.

AUSTEN, Richard James, MBE 1996; HM Diplomatic Service, retired; Africa Directorate Foreign and Commonwealth Office, 2012–13; *b* 25 May 1955; *s* of late Capt. George Alber Austen, MN and Joyce Margaret Austen. *Educ:* Steyning Grammar Sch.; Univ. of Bristol (BA Hons (Theol.) 1977). Grad. trainee, Midland Bank, 1977–81; joined FCO, 1981; Des Officer, Consular Dept, 1981–82, ME Dept, 1982–83, FCO; Attaché, Dar Es Salaam 1983–87; 3rd Sec., Ottawa, 1987–90; Desk Officer, Protocol Dept, FCO, 1990–93; Dep High Comr, Banjul, 1993–96; Desk Officer, Perm. Under-Sec.'s Dept, FCO, 1996–97; Dep Hd, Conference Dept, FCO, 1997–98; Hd of Section, Latin America and Caribbean Dept FCO, 1998–2001; Dep. High Comr, Port Louis, 2001–03; Ambassador: to Mongolia 2004–06; to Panama, 2006–11; Hd, Pol Ext. Section, Moscow, 2011; Chargé d'Affaires, Mali 2012. *Recreations:* walking, cycling, religion, travelling, family history. *Address:* 8 Tunsta Court, Hatherley Road, Richmond, Surrey TW9 3LJ.

AUSTEN-SMITH, Air Marshal Sir Roy (David), KBE 1979; CB 1975; CVO 1994; DFC 1953; retired; a Gentleman Usher to HM the Queen, 1982–94, an Extra Gentleman Usher since 1994; *b* 28 June 1924; *m* 1951, Ann (*née* Alderson); two *s*. *Educ:* Hurstpierpoint College Pilot trng, Canada, 1943–44; No 41 Sqn (2 TAF), 1945; No 33 Sqdn, Malaya, 1950–53; Sq Comdr, RAF Coll., Cranwell, 1953–56; OC No 73 Sqdn, Cyprus, 1956–59; Air Min. 1960–63; OC No 57 Sqdn, 1964–66; HQ 2 ATAF, 1966–68; CO, RAF Wattisham 1968–70; MoD, 1970–72; AOC and Comdt, RAF Coll., Cranwell, 1972–75; SASO Nea East Air Force, 1975–76; Comdr British Forces, Cyprus, AOC Air HQ Cyprus an Administrator, Sovereign Base Areas, Cyprus, 1976–78; Hd of British Defence Staff Washington, and Defence Attaché, 1978–81. *Recreation:* golf. *Address:* c/o Nationa Westminster Bank, Swanley, Kent BR8 7WL. *Club:* Royal Air Force.

AUSTIN, Sir Anthony Leonard, 6th Bt *cr* 1894, of Red Hill, Castleford, West Riding; *b* 3 Sept. 1930; *yr s* of Sir William Ronald Austin, 4th Bt (*d* 1989) and his 1st wife, Dorothy Mary (*d* 1957), *d* of L. A. Bidwell, FRCS; *S* brother, 1995; *m* 1st, 1956, Mary Annette (marr. diss 1966), *d* of Richard Kelly; two *s* (one *d* decd); 2nd, 1967, Aileen Morrison Hall, *d* of William Hall Stewart; one *d*. *Educ:* Downside. *Heir:* *s* Peter John Austin [*b* 29 July 1958; *m* 1988, Jan Clare Dracup (marr. diss. 2012)]. *Address:* Stanbury Manor, Morwenstow, Bude, Cornwal EX23 9JQ.

AUSTIN, Brian Patrick; HM Diplomatic Service, retired; *b* 18 March 1938; *s* of Edwar William Austin and Winifred Alice Austin (*née* Villiger); *m* 1st, 1968, Gusti Lina (*d* 2002); on *s* one *d*; 2nd, 2007, Dr Mary Laurie-Pile. *Educ:* St Olave's Grammar Sch.; Clare Coll. Cambridge. National Service, 1956–58. Joined CRO, 1961; Central African Office, 1962 Lagos, 1963; The Hague, 1966; First Sec., FCO, 1969; Montreal, 1973; FCO, 1978; Dep High Comr, Kaduna, 1981–84; Counsellor: FCO, 1984–88; Stockholm, 1989–93; Consul Gen., Vancouver, 1993–98. *Recreation:* birdwatching. *Address:* Clinton, Nightingale Avenue West Horsley, Surrey KT24 6PB.

AUSTIN, David Charles Henshaw, OBE 2007; VMH 2002; farmer, since 1943; Chairman David Austin Roses Ltd, since 1970; *b* 16 Feb. 1926; *s* of Charles Frederick Austin and Liliar Austin; *m* 1956, Patricia Josephine Braithwaite (*d* 2007); two *s* one *d*. *Educ:* Shrewsbury Sch Non-professional rose breeder, 1946–70; nurseryman and professional rose breeder developing new race, English Roses, 1970–. Hon. MSc East London, 1997. Veitch Mem Medal, RHS, 1994; Queen Mary Commemoration Medal, 1994, Dean Hole Medal, 2000 Royal Nat. Rose Soc.; Landscape Gardening Award, Franco-British Soc., 1995. *Publications* The Heritage of the Rose, 1988; Old Roses and English Roses, 1992; Shrub Roses an Climbing Roses, 1993; David Austin's English Roses, 1993 (Gardening Book of Year Award Garden Writers' Guild, 1994); The English Roses, 2005, 2nd edn 2011; The Rose, 2009; Th Breathing Earth (poetry), 2014. *Recreations:* reading and writing poetry, current affairs gardens, the countryside. *Address:* (office) David Austin Roses Ltd, Bowling Green Lane Albrighton, Wolverhampton, W Midlands WV7 3HB. *T:* (01902) 376300; Bowling Greer House, Bowling Green Lane, Albrighton, Wolverhampton, W Midlands WV7 3HB.

AUSTIN, Gary Ronald; Deputy Chairman, East Midlands Ambulance Service NHS Trust 2009–14 (non-executive Director, 2006–14); *b* 28 May 1956; *s* of late Ronald Austin and o Doris Austin (*née* Pearce); *m* 1980, Susan Ann Horridge; one *s* one *d*. *Educ:* Univ. o Nottingham (BSc Hons (Geog.) 1978); City Univ. Business Sch. (MBA 1984). Bank clerk Nat. Westminster Bank, 1974–75; Econ. Planning Asst, N. Lichfield & Partners, 1978–79

Manpower Planner, City Area, 1980–84, City Dist, 1984–86, British Telecom plc; Dep. Regl Personnel Dir, SW Regl HA, 1986–92; Chief Exec., Blood Services SW, 1992–94; Exec. Dir, Nat. Blood Service, 1994–99; Chief Exec., Driving Standards Agency, 2000–06; Man. Dir, a^{2}om academy, 2006–08, Chief Exec., a^{2}om International, 2008–09. Non-exec. Dir, Intellectual Property Office, 2009–. Lay Mem., Employment Tribunals Service, 2010–. Trustee, Lincs and Notts Air Ambulance Charitable Trust, 2013–. London Olympic Games Maker team leader, 2012. CCMI 2003. *Recreations:* Bath Rugby, family, walking. *Address:* No 2 The Furlongs, Main Street, Bleasby, Notts NG14 7GH. *E:* tartan2clan@btinternet.com.

AUSTIN, Ven. George Bernard; Archdeacon of York, 1988–99, now Emeritus; broadcaster, writer; *b* 16 July 1931; *s* of Oswald Hulton Austin and Evelyn Austin; *m* 1962, Roberta Anise Thompson; one *s*. *Educ:* St David's Coll., Lampeter (BA); Chichester Theol Coll. Deacon 1955, priest 1956; Assistant Curate: St Peter's, Chorley, 1955–57; St Clement's, Notting Dale, 1957–59; Asst Chaplain, Univ. of London, 1960; Asst Curate, Dunstable Priory, 1961–64; Vicar: St Mary the Virgin, Eaton Bray, 1964–70; St Peter, Bushey Heath, 1970–88. Hon. Canon, St Albans, 1978–88; Canon, York, 1988–99, now Emeritus. Proctor in Convocation, 1970–95; a Church Comr, 1978–95. *Publications:* Life of our Lord, 1960; WCC Programme to Combat Racism, 1979; (contrib.) When will ye be Wise?, 1983; (contrib.) Building in Love, 1990; Journey to Faith, 1992; Affairs of State, 1995; (contrib.) Quo Vaditis, 1996; But This I Know, 1996; contrib. to national press. *Recreations:* cooking, theatre. *Address:* 1 Priory Court, 169 Sparrows Herne, Bushey Heath, Herts WD23 1EF. *T:* (020) 8420 4116. *E:* george.austin@virgin.net.

AUSTIN, Ian; MP (Lab) Dudley North, since 2005; *b* 6 March 1965; *s* of Alfred and Margaret Austin; *m* 1993, Catherine Miles; two *s* one *d*. *Educ:* Dudley Sch.; Univ. of Essex (BA Hons Govt). Communications Manager, Focus Housing, 1989–94; Press Officer, Labour Party, 1995–98; Dep. Dir of Communications, Scottish Labour Party, 1998–99; political advr to Chancellor of Exchequer, 1999–2005. Mem. (Lab) Dudley MBC, 1991–95. PPS to Prime Minister, 2007–08; an Asst Govt Whip, 2008–09; Minister for the W Midlands, 2008–10; Parly Under-Sec. of State, DCLG, 2009–10. *Recreations:* reading, watching football, cycling. *Address:* House of Commons, SW1A 0AA. *T:* (020) 7219 8012, *Fax:* (020) 7219 4408; Turner House, 157/185 Wrens Nest Road, Dudley DY1 3RU. *T:* (01384) 342503/4, *Fax:* (01384) 342523.

AUSTIN, Hon. Jacob, (Jack), CM 2014; OBC 2010; PC (Canada) 1981; QC (British Columbia) 1970; Member of the Senate, 1975–2007, and Minister and Leader of the Government in the Senate, 2003–06, Canadian Parliament; Senior Advisor, International, Stern Partners Inc., since 2007; *b* 2 March 1932; *s* of Morris Austin and Clara Edith (*née* Chetner); *m* (marr. diss.); three *d*; *m* 1978, Natalie Veiner Freeman. *Educ:* Univ. of British Columbia (BA, LLB); Harvard Univ. (LLM). Barrister and Solicitor, BC and Yukon Territory. Asst Prof. of Law, Univ. of Brit. Columbia, 1955–58; practising lawyer, Vancouver, BC, 1958–63; Exec. Asst to Minister of Northern Affairs and Nat. Resources, 1963–65; contested (Liberal) Vancouver-Kingsway, Can. Federal Election, 1965; practising lawyer, Vancouver, BC, 1966–70; Dep. Minister, Dept of Energy, Mines and Resources, Ottawa, 1970–74; Principal Sec. to Prime Minister, Ottawa, May 1974–Aug. 1975; Minister of State for Aboriginal and Northern Affairs, 1981–82; Minister of State for Social Develt, responsible for Canada Develt Investment Corp., and Minister for Expo '86, 1982–84; Chm., Ministerial Sub-Cttee on Broadcasting and Cultural Affairs, 1982–84. Pres., Internat. Div., Bank of British Columbia, 1985–86; Associate Counsel: Swinton & Co., 1986–92; Boughton Peterson & Co., 1992–2002; Chm. Board and Dir, Elite Insurance Management Ltd, 1986–90. Pres., Canada China Business Council, 1993–2001. Hon. Prof. and Sen. Fellow, Inst. of Asian Res., Univ. of BC, 2007–. Hon. DSocSc Univ. East Asia, 1987; Hon. LLD BC, 2011. Queen's Diamond Jubilee Medal, 2012. *Publications:* articles on law and public affairs in Canadian Bar Rev., Amer. Soc. of Internat. Law and other publns. *Recreations:* sailing, golf, reading, theatre. *Address:* Stern Partners Inc., Suite 2900, 650 West Georgia Street, Vancouver, BC V6B 4N8, Canada. *Clubs:* Vancouver, Shaughnessy Golf and Country (Vancouver, BC).

AUSTIN, John Eric; *b* 21 Aug. 1944; *s* of late Stanley George Austin and Ellen Elizabeth (*née* Day); adopted surname Austin-Walker, 1965, reverted to Austin, 1997; *m* 1965, Linda Margaret Walker (marr. diss. 1998); two *s* one *d*; *m* 2014, Sylvia Kelcher. *Educ:* Glyn Grammar Sch., Epsom; Goldsmiths' Coll., Univ. of London (Cert. Community and Youth Work 1972); Sch. for Advanced Urban Studies, Univ. of Bristol (MSc Policy Studies 1990). Hosp. lab. technician, 1961–63; Labour Party organiser, 1963–70; social worker/community worker, Bexley, 1972–74; Race Equality Officer (Dir, Bexley Council for Racial Equality), 1974–92. London Borough of Greenwich Council: Mem., 1970–94; Vice-Chm., 1971–74, Chm., 1974–78, Social Services; Dep. Leader, 1981–82; Leader, 1982–87; Mayor of Greenwich, 1987–88 and 1988–89. Vice-Chairman: ALA, 1983–87 (Envmt Spokesperson, 1989–92); London Strategic Policy Unit, 1986–88; Chairman: London Ecology Unit, 1990–92; London Emergency Planning Inf. Centre, 1990–92. Chairman: British Youth Council, 1969–71; Assoc. CHCs for England and Wales, 1986–88. Contested (Lab) Woolwich, 1987. MP (Lab) Woolwich, 1992–97, Erith and Thamesmead, 1997–2010. Mem., Select Cttee on Health, 1994–2005. Jt Chm., All Party Osteoporosis Gp, 1996–2010; Treasurer: Parly Human Rights Gp, 1997–98; Parly Gibraltar Gp, 1997–98; Secretary: British/Czech and Slovak Parly Gp, 1997–2010; British/Hungary Parly Gp, 1997–2010; Chairman: British/Slovenia Parly Gp, 1997–2010; British/Albania Parly Gp, 1997–2010; All Party UK Overseas Territories Parly Gp, 1998–2010; All Party Trinidad and Tobago Gp, 2005–10; Vice-Chm., British Falkland Is Gp, 1997–2006; Member: British Irish Parly Assembly, 2006–10; Jt Cttee on Human Rights, 2008–09. Vice Chm., London Gp of Labour MPs, 1992–97; Chm., Socialist Campaign Gp of Labour MPs, 1992–98. Deleg., Parly Assembly, Council of Europe and WEU, 2004–10 (Vice-Chm., Sub-Cttee on Human Trafficking); Vice-Chm., UK br., CPA, 2004–05 (Mem., 1997–2010, Chm., 2009–10, Exec. Cttee); Mem., Internat. Exec., IPU, 2004–07 (Mem. Exec. Cttee, British Gp, 1997–2010 (Chm., 2002–05); Pres., 12+ (Geopolitical Gp), 2006–10). Mem., Exec. Cttee, Assoc. of Former MPs, 2010–; Chm., Assoc. of Former MPs Parly Outreach Trust, 2015– (Sec., 2014–15). Hon. Chm., British Caribbean Assoc., 1997–2009. Mem. Bd, CAABU, 2001– (Co-Chair, 2001–11). Chm., George Croydon Marks Soc. (formerly Baron Marks Commemoration Cttee), 2011–. Trustee: London Marathon Charitable Trust, 1997–; Greenwich Community Coll. Trust, 2006–14; Crossness Engines Trust, 2007– (Chm., 2013–); Conway Sch. Trust, 2008–; Patron: Palestine Solidarity Campaign, 2007–; Archway Project, Thamesmead, 2008–; Dist. Supporter, British Humanist Assoc. *Recreations:* cooking, gardening, reminiscing about past marathons run, travel. *E:* johnaustin1944@gmail.com, john.austin@crossness.org.uk.

AUSTIN, Mark; Presenter, ITV Evening News, since 2003 (ITV News at 10.30pm, 2006–08, ITV News at Ten, 2008–15); *b* 1 Nov. 1958; *m* 1991; one *s* two *d*. *Educ:* Bournemouth Sch.; Highbury Coll., Portsmouth. Reporter, Bournemouth Evening Echo, 1976–80; newsroom writer, 1980–82, news reporter, 1982–85, sports reporter, 1985–86, BBC; joined ITV News as sports correspondent, 1986; Asia correspondent, 1990–93, 1996–98; Africa correspondent, 1993–96; Sen. Correspondent, 1998–2002. Presenter, TV series, Survivor, 2001. Best TV News Presenter, RTS, 2014, 2015. *Address:* Independent Television News Ltd, 200 Gray's Inn Road, WC1X 8XZ.

AUSTIN, Neil; lighting designer; *b* London, 22 June 1972; *s* of Anthony Charles Austin and Patricia Anne Austin (*née* Daly). *Educ:* St Paul's Sch., London; Guildhall Sch. of Music and Drama (Fellow 2008). Lighting designer for plays, musicals, opera and dance. *Productions include:* West End: Japes, Haymarket, 2000; A Life in the Theatre, Apollo, 2005; Dealer's Choice, Trafalgar, 2007; No Man's Land, Duke of York, 2008; The Prisoner of 2nd Avenue, Vaudeville, 2010; The Children's Hour, Comedy, Death and the Maiden, Pinter, Betty Blue Eyes, Novello, 2011; South Downs, The Browning Version, Pinter, The Sunshine Boys, Savoy, 2012, transf. LA, 2013; The Hothouse, Trafalgar, Henry V, Noël Coward, 2013; Shakespeare in Love, Noël Coward, Assassins, Menier Chocolate Factory, 2014; Bend it Like Beckham, Phoenix, Photograph 51, Noël Coward, 2015; National Theatre: A Prayer for Owen Meany, 2002; Henry IV Pts 1 and 2, 2005; The Man of Mode, Philistines, The Emperor Jones, The Seafarer, transf. NY, 2007; Her Naked Skin, Oedipus, 2008; England People Very Nice, The Observer, 2009; London Assurance, The White Guard (Olivier Award for Best Lighting Design, 2011), Women Beware Women, Welcome to Thebes, 2010; The Cherry Orchard, 2011; She Stoops to Conquer, The Doctor's Dilemma, 2012; Port, Liolà, 2013; The Silver Tassie, Great Britain, 2014; Dara, Rules for Living, Three Days in the Country, 2015; Donmar Warehouse: Caligula, After Miss Julie, 2003; The Wild Duck, 2005; Frost Nixon, 2006, transf. NY, 2007; Don Juan in Soho, 2006; John Gabriel Borkman, Parade, 2007; Piaf, Twelfth Night, 2008; Madame de Sade, Hamlet, transf. NY, A Streetcar Named Desire, Life is a Dream, 2009; Red, 2009, transf. NY, 2010 (Tony Award for Best Lighting Design of a Play, Drama Desk Award for Outstanding Lighting Design, 2010); The Prince of Homborg, Passion, King Lear, 2010; The 25th Annual Putnam County Spelling Bee, 2011; Julius Caesar, 2012, transf. NY, 2013; The Weir, 2013, transf. West End, 2014; The Night Alive, 2013, transf. NY, 2013; Henry IV, 2014; Royal Ballet: The Soldier's Tale, 2004; Rhapsody, 2005; As One, 2010; 24 Preludes, 2013; English National Ballet: The Sleeping Beauty, 2012; Le Corsaire, 2013; New York: Evita, 2012; Cat on a Hot Tin Roof, 2013; Macbeth, 2014. *Address:* c/o Rose Cobbe, United Agents, 12–26 Lexington Street, W1F 0LE. *W:* www.neilaustin.com.

AUSTIN, Sir Roger (Mark), KCB 1992; AFC 1973; aviation and defence consultant, 1998–2009; *b* 9 March 1940; *s* of Mark and Sylvia Joan Austin. *Educ:* King Alfred's Grammar Sch., Wantage. Commissioned in RAF, 1957; flying appts as Qualified Flying Instructor and with Nos 20 and 54 Sqns, 1960–68; commanded No 54 Sqn, 1969; flying appt with No 4 Sqn, 1970–72; Staff Coll., Camberley, 1973; commanded 233 OCU, 1974–77; PSO to AOC-in-C Strike Command, 1977–80; commanded RAF Chivenor, 1980–82; ADC to the Queen, 1980–82; Staff of HQ Strike Command, 1982–84; Dir of Op. Requirements, 1984–85; RCDS, 1986; AO i/c Central Tactics and Trials Orgn, 1987; DG Aircraft 1, MoD (PE), 1987–89; AOC and Comdt, RAF Coll., Cranwell, 1989–92; DCDS (Systems), MoD, 1992–94; Controller Aircraft, MoD, 1994–96; Dep. Chief of Defence Procurement (Ops), MoD (PE), 1995–96; Air Marshal, retd 1997. FO RAFVR (T), 1997–2009. President: RBL, 1997–2000; Victory Services Assoc., 2002–09 (Chm., 1997–2001); SE and E Area, RAFA, 2014–; Trustee, RAF Benevolent Fund, 2000–09. *Recreations:* military history, transport systems, photography. *Address:* 10 Cleveland Grove, Newbury, Berks RG14 1XF. *Club:* Royal Air Force.

AUSTIN-SMITH, Michael Gerard; QC 1990; a Recorder, 1986–2014; *b* 4 Sept. 1944; *s* of late Cyril John Austin-Smith and Joyce Austin-Smith; *m* 1971, Stephanie Maddocks; one *s* one *d*. *Educ:* Hampton Grammar Sch.; Exeter Univ. (LLB Hons). Called to the Bar, Inner Temple, 1969, Bencher, 2002. DTI Inspector, 1988–89 and 1989–90. *Clubs:* Royal Corinthian Yacht, Island Sailing, Cowes Corinthian, Baat (Cowes).

AUSTIN-WALKER, John Eric; *see* Austin, J. E.

AUSTINS, Lynne Teresa; *see* Matthews, L. T.

AUSTRALIA, Primate of; *see* Melbourne, Archbishop of.

AUSTWICK, Dawn Jacquelyn, OBE 2000; Chief Executive, Big Lottery Fund, since 2013; *b* Sheffield, 11 Dec. 1960; *d* of Prof. Kenneth Austwick, *qv*; *m* 1990, Henry Stewart; one *s* two *d*. *Educ:* Bath High Sch.; Westfield Coll., London (BA Combined Hons English and Drama); London Business Sch. (MBA). Projects Coordinator, Assoc. for Business Sponsorship of the Arts, 1983–85; Business Develt Manager, Half Moon Th., 1985–86; Principal Consultant, KPMG Mgt Consulting, 1986–94; Proj. Dir, Tate Modern, 1995–2000; Dep. Dir, BM, 2002–05; Chief Exec., Esmée Fairbairn Foundn, 2005–13. Dep. Chm., Women's Liby, 2000–05. Dir, Big Society Capital, 2011–13. Mem., Audit Cttee, AHRC, 2007–10. Trustee: Woodland Trust, 2001–09; Historic Royal Palaces, 2006–. CCMI; FRSA. Hon. DBA London Metropolitan, 2006. *Recreations:* theatre, gardening, Arsenal Football Club, yoga. *Address:* Big Lottery Fund, 1 Plough Place, EC4A 1DE. *Club:* Bath.

AUSTWICK, Prof. Kenneth; JP; Professor of Education, Bath University, 1966–91, now Emeritus; *b* 26 May 1927; *s* of Harry and Beatrice Austwick; *m* 1956, Gillian Griffin; one *s* one *d*. *Educ:* Morecambe Grammar Sch.; Sheffield Univ. BSc Maths, DipEd, MSc, PhD Sheffield. Schoolmaster, Bromsgrove, Frome and Nottingham, 1950–59; Lectr/Sen. Lectr, Sheffield Univ., 1959–65; Dep. Dir, Inst. of Educn, Reading Univ., 1965–66; Pro-Vice-Chancellor, Bath Univ., 1972–75. Vis. Lecturer: Univ. of BC, 1963; Univ. of Michigan, 1963; Univ. of Wits., 1967. Consultant, OECD, 1965; Adviser, Home Office, 1967–81; Chm., Nat. Savings SW Regional Educn, 1975–78. JP Bath 1970. FRSA. *Publications:* Logarithms, 1962; Equations and Graphs, 1963; (ed) Teaching Machines and Programming, 1964; (ed) Aspects of Educational Technology, 1972; Maths at Work, 1985; Mathematics Connections, 1985; Level by Level Mathematics, 1991; (ed) Working Science, 1991; (ed) Working English, 1991; articles and contribs on maths teaching and educnl technology. *Recreations:* painting, gardening, bridge. *Address:* The Coach House, Combe Hay, Bath BA2 7EG. *T:* (01225) 282726.

See also D. J. Austwick.

AUTON, Sylvia Jean, OBE 2014; Chairman, 2009–13, and Chief Executive, 2003–08 and 2011–13, IPC Media Ltd (Director, 1998–2013); *b* 8 June 1949; *m* 1978, William Auton; two *s*. *Educ:* Southampton Univ. (BSc Jt Hons). Publishing Dir, New Scientist, 1990–98; Man. Dir, IPC Country & Leisure Media, 1998–2003; Exec. Vice Pres., Time Inc., 2007–10. Trustee, 1998–2013, Chm., 2000–13, IPC Media Pension Trustee Ltd; Dir, PPA Ltd, 2003–13. *Recreations:* walking, travel.

AUTY, Michael Roy; QC 2013; *b* Nottingham, 30 July 1963; *s* of late Roy Mercer Auty and Phyllis Mary Auty; *m* 2007, Helen Catherine Asher-Hibbett; four *s*. *Educ:* Nottingham Bluecoat C of E Grammar Sch.; Nottingham Trent Univ. (BA Hons Law 1984); Chester Coll. of Law. Admitted as solicitor, 1987; Asst Solicitor, 1987–88, Partner, 1988–90, Messrs Fidler and Pepper; called to the Bar, Inner Temple, 1990; barrister in ind. practice, specialising in criminal law (homicide, major drugs ops and serious sexual offences), 1990–. *Recreations:* rock music, playing the guitar, food (American, Asian and Indian), motorcycling, films, relaxing with friends and family. *Address:* No 1 High Pavement Chambers, 1 High Pavement, Nottingham NG1 1HF. *T:* (0115) 941 8218, *Fax:* (0115) 941 8240. *E:* MichaelAutyqc@1highpavement.co.uk.

AVEBURY, 4th Baron *cr* 1900; **Eric Reginald Lubbock;** Bt 1806; *b* 29 Sept. 1928; *s* of Hon. Maurice Fox Pitt Lubbock (6th *s* of 1st Baron) (*d* 1957), and Hon. Mary Katherine Adelaide Stanley (*d* 1981), *d* of 5th Baron Stanley of Alderley; *S* cousin, 1971; *m* 1953, Kina Maria (marr. diss. 1983) (*see* Kina, Lady Avebury); two *s* one *d*; 2nd, 1985, Lindsay Stewart; one *s*. *Educ:* Upper Canada Coll.; Harrow Sch.; Balliol Coll., Oxford (BA Engineering; boxing blue; Hon. Fellow, 2004). MIMechE, CEng; FBCS. Welsh Guards (Gdsman, 2nd Lieut), 1949–51; Rolls Royce Ltd, 1951–56; Grad. Apprentice; Export Sales Dept; Tech. Assistant to Foundry Manager. Management Consultant: Production Engineering Ltd, 1953–60; Charterhouse

Group Ltd, 1960. MP (L) Orpington, 1962–70; Liberal Whip in House of Commons, 1963–70; elected Mem., H of L, 1999. Dir, C. L. Projects Ltd, 1966–; Consultant, Morgan-Grampian Ltd, 1970–84. President: Data Processing Management Assoc., 1972–75; Fluoridation Soc., 1972–84; Conservation Soc., 1973–83. Member: Council, Inst. of Race Relations, 1972–74; Royal Commn on Standards of Conduct in Public Life, 1974–76; Chm., British Parly Human Rights Gp, 1976–97 (Vice Pres., 1997–). Member: Information Cttee, H of L, 2001–05; Select Cttee on the EU, H of L, 2002–. Co-Chair, Chittagong Hill Tracts Commn, 2008–. Vice Pres., London Bach Soc., 1998– (Pres., 1984–98); Pres., Steinitz Bach Players, 1984–95. Patron: Buddhist Prison Chaplaincy, 1992–; Traveller Movement, 2014–. *Recreations:* listening to music, reading. *Heir: s* Hon. Lyulph Ambrose Jonathan Lubbock [*b* 15 June 1954; *m* 1977, Susan (*née* MacDonald); one *s* one *d*]. *Address:* House of Lords, SW1A 0PW; 26 Flodden Road, SE5 9LH.

AVEBURY, Kina, Lady; Kina-Maria Lubbock; consultant on health and social policy; *b* 2 Sept. 1934; *d* of late Count Joseph O'Kelly de Gallagh and Mrs M. Bruce; *m* 1953, 4th Baron Avebury, *qv* (marr. diss. 1983); two *s* one *d*. *Educ:* Convent of the Sacred Heart, Tunbridge Wells; Goldsmiths' College (BScSoc Hons) and LSE, Univ. of London. Lectr, Royal Coll. of Nursing, 1970–74; campaign organizer, European Movement, 1975; Asst Dir, Nat. Assoc. for Mental Health, 1976–82; Sociologist, Dept of Psychiatry, London Hosp. Med. Coll., 1983–85; Mental Health Planner, Tower Hamlets Social Services, 1986–94. Chairman: Nat. Marriage Guidance Council, 1975–82; Family Service Units, 1984–87; Avebury Working Party, 1982–84 (produced Code of Practice for Residential Care for DHSS); Working Party for A Better Home Life, 1996, Working Party on Nat. Required Standards for Long Term Care, 1998–99, Centre for Policy on Ageing; Mem., Central Council for Educn and Trng in Social Work, 1986–90. JP Kent, 1974–79. Trustee: Neighbours in Poplar; George Green Almshouse Trust. *Publications:* Volunteers in Mental Health, 1985; (with R. Williams) A Place in Mind, 1995; (jtly) The Substance of Young Needs, 1996; articles on mental health and related social policy. *Recreations:* painting, cooking, gardening, music.

AVERY, Brian Stuart, FDSRCS; FRCSE; Consultant Oral and Maxillofacial Surgeon, James Cook University Hospital, Middlesbrough, 1983–2009; Dean, Faculty of Dental Surgery, Royal College of Surgeons of England, 2004–08; *b* 15 Feb. 1947; *s* of Stuart and Edna Avery; *m* 1972, Fiona Gibson; two *s* two *d*. *Educ:* Fox Primary Sch., Notting Hill Gate; Abingdon Sch.; Guy's Hosp. Med. Sch., Univ. of London (BDS Hons 1970; MB BS 1974). LDSRCS 1970, FDSRCS 1976; LRCP 1974; MRCS 1974, Hon. FRCS 2005; FRCSE 1985; FRACDS 2008; FDSRCPSGlas 2009. House officer posts, Guy's Hosp., 1974–75; Registrar in Oral and Maxillofacial Surgery: Eastman Dental Hosp., 1975; Queen Mary Hosp., Roehampton and Westminster Hosp., 1976–78; Sen. Registrar in Oral and Maxillofacial Surgery, Canniesburn Hosp., Glasgow, 1978–83. Hon. Prof. of Oral and Maxillofacial Surgery, Univ. of Teesside, 2002–09. Consultant to the Army, 1995–2009. Pres., BAOMS, 2005. Member: Council, RCS, 2003–09; Acad. of Med. Royal Colls, 2004–09. Hon. Fellow: Indian Assoc. Oral and Maxillofacial Surgery, 1992; Amer. Assoc. Oral and Maxillofacial Surgery, 2005. Downs Surgical Prize, BAOMS, 2008; Colyer Gold Medal, Faculty of Dental Surgery, RCS, 2009. *Publications:* with G. Dimitroulis: Maxillofacial Injuries: a synopsis of basic principles, diagnosis and management, 1994; Oral Cancer: a synopsis of pathology and management, 1998; contrib. book chapters and articles related to oral and maxillofacial surgery. *Recreations:* reading, dining, travelling, keeping children's cars on the road, cursing inefficiency of the National Health Service. *Address:* Mordon House, Mordon, Sedgefield, Stockton-on-Tees TS21 2EY. *T:* (01740) 620634, *Fax:* (01740) 623702. *E:* averyb@live.co.uk.

AVERY, Gillian Elise, (Mrs A. O. J. Cockshut); writer; *b* 1926; *d* of late Norman and Grace Avery; *m* 1952, A. O. J. Cockshut; one *d*. *Educ:* Dunottar Sch., Reigate. Chm., Children's Books History Soc., 1987–90; Mem., American Antiquarian Soc., 1988. *Publications: children's fiction:* The Warden's Niece, 1957; Trespassers at Charlcote, 1958; James without Thomas, 1959; The Elephant War, 1960; To Tame a Sister, 1961; The Greatest Gresham, 1962; The Peacock House, 1963; The Italian Spring, 1964; The Call of the Valley, 1966; A Likely Lad, 1971 (Guardian Award, 1972); Huck and her Time Machine, 1977; *adult fiction:* The Lost Railway, 1980; Onlookers, 1983; *non-fiction:* 19th Century Children: heroes and heroines in English children's stories (with Angela Bull), 1965; Victorian People in Life and Literature, 1970; The Echoing Green: memories of Regency and Victorian youth, 1974; Childhood's Pattern, 1975; Children and Their Books: a celebration of the work of Iona and Peter Opie (ed with Julia Briggs), 1989; The Best Type of Girl: a history of girls' independent schools, 1991; Behold the Child: a history of American children and their books 1622–1922, 1994; (ed with Kimberley Reynolds) Representations of Childhood Death, 2000; Cheltenham Ladies: a history of Cheltenham Ladies' College 1853–2003, 2003; ed, Gollancz revivals of early children's books, 1967–70, and anthologies of stories and extracts from early children's books. *Address:* 32 Charlbury Road, Oxford OX2 6UU.

AVERY, Graham John Lloyd, CMG 2012; Senior Member, St Antony's College, Oxford, since 2005; Senior Adviser, European Policy Centre, Brussels, since 2006; Hon. Director General, European Commission, since 2006; *b* 29 Oct. 1943; *s* of Rev. Edward Avery and Alice Avery; *m* 1st, 1967, Susan Steele (marr. diss.); two *s*; 2nd, 2002, Annalisa Cecchi; one *s*. *Educ:* Kingswood Sch., Bath; Balliol Coll., Oxford (MA). Joined MAFF, 1965; Principal responsible for negotiations for British entry to European Communities, 1969–72; PPS to Ministers, Fred Peart, John Silkin, 1976; Commission of the European Communities, subseq. European Commission, Brussels: Member of Cabinets: of President, Roy Jenkins, 1977–80; of Vice-Pres. for External Relns, Christopher Soames, 1973–76; of Comrs for Agric., Finn Gundelach 1981, Poul Dalsager 1981, Frans Andriessen 1985–86; served: in Directorate Gen. for Agric. as Hd of Div. for Econ. Affairs and Gen. Problems, 1981–84, as Dir for Rural Develt, 1987–90; in Directorate Gen. for External Relations as Dir for relns with USA, Canada, Australia and NZ, 1990–92, as Dir for relns with Austria, Switzerland, Iceland, Norway, Sweden and Finland, 1992–93, in Task Force for Enlargement as Dir, 1993–94; in Directorate Gen. for External Political Relations, as Head of Policy Planning, 1995, as Chief Advr for Enlargement, 1996–98; Inspector Gen., 1998–2000; Chief Advr, Directorate Gen. for Enlargement, 2000–03; Chief Advr, subseq. Dir for Strategy, Co-ordination and Analysis, Directorate Gen. for External Relations, 2003–06. Sec. Gen., Trans European Policy Studies Assoc., 2006–08. Vis. Prof., Coll. of Europe, 2003–05. Fellow: Center for Internat. Affairs, Harvard Univ., 1986–87; Eur. Univ. Inst., Florence, 2002, 2009, 2010; Canterbury Univ., NZ, 2006. *Publications:* (with Fraser Cameron): The Enlargement of the European Union, 1998; chapter on Enlargement Negotiations in The Future of Europe: enlargement and integration, 2004; chapter on EU Expansion and Wider Europe in The European Union: how does it work?, 2nd edn 2008, 3rd edn 2011; articles in Internat. Affairs, World Today, Prospect, Jl of Eur. Public Policy, Internat. Spectator, Studia Diplomatica, Hungarian Qly, Internat. Jl Study of Christian Ch, Jl of Agricl Econs, etc. *Address:* 65 Southmoor Road, Oxford OX2 6RE.

AVERY, James Royle, (Roy); Headmaster, Bristol Grammar School, 1975–86; *b* 7 Dec. 1925; *s* of Charles James Avery and Dorothy May Avery; *m* 1954, Marjorie Louise (*née* Smith); one *s* one *d*. *Educ:* Queen Elizabeth's Hosp., Bristol; Magdalen Coll., Oxford; Bristol Univ. MA Oxon, CertifEd Bristol. Asst History Master, Bristol Grammar Sch., 1951–59; Sen. History Master, Haberdashers' Aske's Sch. at Hampstead, then Elstree, 1960–65; Head Master, Harrow County Boys' Sch., 1965–75. Mem. Council, Bristol Univ., 1982–95. Hon. MLitt Bristol, 1996. *Publications:* The Story of Aldenham House, 1961; The Elstree Murder, 1962; The History of Queen Elizabeth's Hospital 1590–1990, 1990; The Sky's the Limit: the story of Bristol philanthropist John James, 1906–1996, 2001; contrib. Dictionary of World History, 1973; articles, reviews in educnl jls. *Recreations:* reading, walking, sport, music, the ecumenical movement, international studies. *Address:* 6 Willow Pool, Cote Lane, Bristol BS9 3FD. *T:* (0117) 962 3423.

AVERY, John Ernest, CB 1997; Deputy Parliamentary Commissioner for Administration, 1990–2000; *b* 18 April 1940; *s* of Ernest Charles Avery and Pauline Margaret Avery; *m* 1966, Anna Meddings; two *d*. *Educ:* Plymouth Coll.; Leeds Univ. (BSc). Called to the Bar, Gray's Inn, 1972. Patent Examiner, Bd of Trade, 1964–72; Office of Fair Trading, 1972–76; Dept of Industry, later DTI, 1976–89; Dir of Investigations, Office of Parly Comr for Admin (Ombudsman), 1989–90. *Recreations:* squash, theatre.

AVERY, Mark Ian, PhD; freelance writer on environmental issues; *b* Bristol, 29 March 1958; *s* of Charles Avery and Megan Avery; *m* 1985, Rosemary Cockerill; one *s* one *d*. *Educ:* Downing Coll., Cambridge (BA 1979); Aberdeen Univ. (PhD 1983). NERC Res. Fellow, Univ. of Oxford, 1984–85; Res. Biologist, 1986–88, Sen. Res. Biologist, 1988–92, Hd of Conservation Sci., 1992–98, Dir, Conservation, 1998–2011, RSPB. *Publications:* Birds and Forestry (with R. Leslie), 1989; Blogging for Nature, 2011; Fighting for Birds, 2012; A Message from Martha, 2014; (with K. Betton) Behind the Binoculars, 2015; Inglorious, 2015. *Recreations:* National Hunt racing, opera, nature. *Address:* 9 Lawson Street, Raunds, Wellingborough, Northants NN9 6NG. *Club:* Reform.

AVERY, Roy; *see* Avery, J. R.

AVERY JONES, Dr John Francis, CBE 1987; a Judge of the Upper Tribunal (Tax and Chancery Chamber) and of the Tax Chamber of the First-tier Tribunal, 2009–11 (a Special Commissioner of Income Tax, 2002–09 (Deputy, 1991–2001); Chairman, VAT and Duties Tribunals, 2002–09 (part-time, 1991–2001)); *b* 5 April 1940; *s* of Sir Francis Avery Jones, CBE, FRCP; *m* 1994, Catherine Susan Bobbett. *Educ:* Rugby Sch.; Trinity Coll., Cambridge (MA, LLM, PhD 1993). Solicitor, 1966; Partner in Bircham & Co., 1970; Sen. Partner, Speechly Bircham, 1985–2001. Member: Meade Cttee, 1975–77; Keith Cttee, 1980–84. Pres., Inst. of Taxation, 1980–82 (Hon. FTII 2002); Chm., Law Soc.'s Revenue Law Cttee, 1983–87; Member Council: Law Soc., 1986–90; Inst. for Fiscal Studies, 1988–2011; Exec. Cttee, Internat. Fiscal Assoc., 1988–94 (1st Vice-Pres., 1993–94; Chm., British Br., 1989–91); Mem., Bd of Trustees, Internat. Bureau of Fiscal Documentation, 1989–2011 (Chm., 1991–2002). Vis. Prof. of Taxation, LSE, 1988–2009; Atax Cliffbrook Vis. Schol., Univ. of NSW, 1995. David R. Tillinghast Lectr on Internat. Taxation, New York Univ., 1997. Mem., Steering Cttee, Tax Law Rewrite, 1996–; Mem., Tax Law Review Cttee, 1997–2011 (Chm., 1997–2005). Member, Board of Governors: Voluntary Hosp. of St Bartholomew, 1984–2011; LSE, 1995–2010 (Chm., Audit Cttee, 1996–2003); Chm., Addington Soc., 1985–87. Master: Co. of Barbers, 1985–86; City of London Solicitors' Co., 1997–98. Consulting Editor: Encyclopedia of VAT, 1989–93 (Gen. Ed., 1972–89); British Tax Review, 1997– (Jt Ed., 1974–97); Mem. Editl Bd, Simon's Taxes, 1977–2001. Frans Banninck Cocq Medal, City of Amsterdam, 2002; Chartered Inst. of Taxation Council Award, 2012; Lifetime Achievement, Taxation Awards, 2014. *Publications:* (ed) Tax Havens and Measures Against Tax Avoidance and Evasion in the EEC, 1974; numerous articles on tax. *Recreations:* music, particularly opera. *Address:* Camilla, Frogham, Fordingbridge, Hants SP6 2HN. *T:* (01425) 653721. *Club:* Athenæum.

AVES, Jonathan James; HM Diplomatic Service; Joint Ambassador to Armenia, 2012–14; *m* Katherine Jane Leach, *qv*; three *c*. Joined FCO, 1996; Res. Analyst, S Caucasus and Central Asia, FCO, 1996–2000; First Sec. (Pol), Moscow, 2000–04; Hd, Pol and Human Rights Section, Iraq Policy Unit, FCO, 2004–05; Hd, Pol Section, Tokyo, 2006–11; Hd, UN Team, Human Rights and Democracy Dept, FCO, 2011. *Address:* c/o Foreign and Commonwealth Office, King Charles Street, SW1A 2AH.

AVES, Katherine Jane; *see* Leach, K. J.

AVIS, Rev. Dr Paul David Loup; Chaplain to the Queen, since 2008; Canon Theologian of Exeter Cathedral, 2008–13; *b* 21 July 1947; *s* of late Peter George Hobden Avis and Diana Joan (*née* Loup); *m* 1970, Susan Janet Haywood; three *s*. *Educ:* London Bible Coll. (BD Hons London Univ. (ext.) 1970; PhD 1976); Westcott House, Cambridge. Deacon 1975, priest 1976; Curate, South Molton, dio. Exeter, 1975–80; Vicar, Stoke Canon, Poltimore with Huxham, Rewe with Netherexe, 1980–98; Gen. Sec., C of E Council for Christian Unity, 1998–2011. Preb. of Exeter Cathedral, 1993–2008; Sub Dean of Exeter Cathedral, 1997–2008. Theol Consultant to Anglican Communion Office, 2011–12. Hon. Dir, Centre for Study of Christian Church, 1997–, Hon. Vis. Prof., 2009–, Univ. of Exeter. Jt Ed., Internat. Jl for Study of the Christian Church, 2001–03; Convening Ed., 2004–11, Ed.-in-Chief, 2011–, Ecclesiology. *Publications:* The Church in the Theology of the Reformers, 1982; Ecumenical Theology, 1986; The Methods of Modern Theology, 1986; Foundations of Modern Historical Thought, 1986; Gore: Construction and Conflict, 1988; (ed and contrib.) The Threshold of Theology, 1988; Eros and the Sacred, 1989; Anglicanism and the Christian Church, 1989, 2nd edn 2002; Authority, Leadership and Conflict in the Church, 1992; (ed and contrib.) The Resurrection of Jesus Christ, 1993; (ed and contrib.) Divine Revelation, 1997; Faith in the Fires of Criticism, 1997; God and the Creative Imagination, 1999; The Anglican Understanding of the Church, 2000, 2nd edn 2013; Church, State and Establishment, 2001; (ed and contrib.) The Christian Church: an introduction to the major traditions, 2002; A Church Drawing Near, 2003; (ed and contrib.) Public Faith?, 2003; (ed and contrib.) Seeking the Truth of Change in the Church, 2003; (ed and contrib.) Paths to Unity, 2004; A Ministry Shaped by Mission, 2005; Beyond the Reformation?: authority, primacy and unity in the conciliar tradition, 2006; The Identity of Anglicanism: essentials of Anglican ecclesiology, 2008; Reshaping Ecumenical Theology: the Church made whole?, 2010; (ed and contrib.) The Journey of Christian Initiation: theological and pastoral perspectives, 2011; In Search of Authority: Anglican theological method from the Reformation to the Enlightenment, 2014; Becoming a Bishop: theological handbook of episcopal ministry, 2015. *Recreations:* walking, literature, writing theology, logging trees. *Address:* Lea Hill, Membury, Axminster, Devon EX13 7AQ. *T:* (01404) 881881. *E:* reception@leahill.co.uk.

AVISON, Dr Gerald; Co-Founder, 1988, and Chairman, since 2007, TTP Group plc (Chief Executive, 1988–2007); *b* 23 Nov. 1940; *s* of Fred and Edith Avison; *m* 1971, Jean Margaret Mizen; one *s* one *d*. *Educ:* Manchester Grammar Sch.; Univ. of Bristol (BSc; PhD 1967). Engr, Guided Weapons Div., 1968–71, Manager, Electron Beam Welding Dept, 1971–73, BAC; PA Technology: Sen. Engr, 1973–75; Consultant, 1975–78, Sen. Consultant, 1978–85; Man. Dir, Cambridge Lab., 1985–87; Chm., TTP Communications plc, 2000–06. Director: TTP Venture Managers Ltd, 1999–; Cambridge Network, 2002–08. Trustee, Hirsch Trust for Camlab Employees, 2001–. *Recreations:* travel, family, curiosity. *Address:* 59 Victoria Park, Cambridge CB4 3EJ. *T:* (01223) 354553, *Fax:* (01763) 261582. *E:* ga@ttpgroup.com.

AVISS, Prof. Derek William, OBE 2013; 'cellist; freelance consultant, since 2012; Executive Director, Trinity Laban Conservatoire of Music and Dance, 2010–12 (Joint Principal, 2006–10), Emeritus Professor of Higher Education, 2013; *b* 21 Aug. 1948; *s* of Arthur William Archibald and Joan Gladys Aviss; *m* 1994, Jennifer Jane Smith; one *s* from previous marriage. *Educ:* Trinity Coll. of Music (LTCL 1970; Hon. FTCL 1986). FLCM 1979. Free-lance professional 'cellist, performing with Ariosti Piano Trio, Cantilena Ensemble, 1970–83. Trinity College of Music: Prof. of 'Cello, Jun. Dept, 1976–90, Prof. of 'Cello and Chamber Music, Sen. Dept, 1979–; Sen. Lectr in 'Cello and Chamber Music, 1986–90; Head: String

Dept, 1990–94; Performance Studies, 1992–94; Dep. Principal, 1994–2005; Principal, 2005–10. Hon. Vis. Prof., City Univ., 2010–. FRSA 2000. *Recreations:* granddaughters Rowan and Ilona, motor cars, cricket, literature, music, theatre, travel. *Address:* The Clock House, The Dower Court, Somerford Keynes, Glos GL7 6DN. *T:* (01285) 861974. *E:* derek.aviss@gmail.com.

AX, Emanuel; concert pianist, since 1974; *b* 8 June 1949; *m* Yoko Nazaki; one *s* one *d*. *Educ:* Juilliard Sch. (studied with Mieczylaw Munz); Columbia Univ. Regular solo appearances with symphony orchs, incl. NY Philharmonic, National Symphony, Philadelphia Orch., Boston SO, Chicago SO, Cleveland Orch., Berlin Philharmonic, LPO, etc.; recitals at Carnegie Hall, Concertgebouw, Amsterdam, Barbican Centre, Théâtre des Champs Elysées, etc.; has played duo recitals with cellist Yo-Yo Ma annually since 1976; performed world premières of piano concertos by: Joseph Schwantner, 1988; Ezra Laderman, 1992; John Adams, 1997; Christopher Rouse, 1999; Bright Sheng, 2000, 2003; Krzysztof Penderecki, 2002; Melinda Wagner, 2003. Numerous recordings; Grammy Awards, 1985–86, 1992–95. First Prize, Arthur Rubinstein Internat. Piano Competition, 1974; Michael's Award, Young Concert Artists, 1975; Avery Fisher Prize, 1979. *Address:* c/o Opus 3, 470 Park Avenue South, 9th Floor North, New York, NY 10016, USA. *T:* (212) 5847500.

AXEL, Prof. Richard, MD; Professor of Biochemistry and Molecular Biophysics, Columbia University, since 1999; *b* 2 July 1946; two *s*. *Educ:* Columbia Univ. (AB 1967); Johns Hopkins Univ. (MD 1970). Res. Associate, NIH, 1972–74; Columbia University: Asst Prof., Inst. of Cancer Res., 1974–78; Prof. of Pathol. and Biochem., 1978; Investigator, Howard Hughes Medical Inst., 1984–. Foreign Mem. Royal Soc., 2014. (Jtly) Nobel Prize in Physiology or Medicine, 2004. *Address:* Axel Laboratory, Howard Hughes Medical Institute, Columbia University, Room 1014, 701 West 168th Street, New York, NY 10032, USA.

AXFORD, David Norman, PhD; CMet, CEng, FIET; international consultant meteorologist; Adviser to Earthwatch Europe, Oxford, 1996–2000; *b* 14 June 1934; *s* of Norman Axford and Joy Alicia Axford (*née* Williams); *m* 1st, 1962, Elizabeth Anne (*née* Stiles) (marr. diss. 1980); one *s* two *d*; 2nd, 1980, Diana Rosemary Joan (*née* Bufton); three step *s* one step *d*. *Educ:* Merchant Taylors' School, Sandy Lodge; Plymouth Coll.; St John's Coll., Cambridge (Baylis Open Scholarship in Maths; BA 1956, MA 1960, PhD (Met.) 1972); MSc (Electronics) Southampton 1963; Advanced Dip., 2004, Dip., 2006 (English Local Hist.), Oxford Univ. FIET (FIEE, CEng 1982). Entered Met. Office, 1958; Flying Officer, RAF, 1958–60; Meteorological Office: Forecasting and Research, 1960–68; Met. Research Flight, and Radiosondes, 1968–76; Operational Instrumentation, 1976–80; Telecommunications, 1980–82; Dep. Dir, Observational Services, 1982–84; Dir of Services, 1984–89; Dep. Sec.-Gen., WMO, 1989–95; Special Exec. Advr to Sec.-Gen., WMO, 1995. Chm., Cttee on Operational World Weather Watch Systems Evaluation, N Atlantic (CONA), 1985–89. Pres., N Atlantic Observing Stations (NAOS) Bd, 1983–86; Vice Pres., RMetS, 1989–91 (Mem. Council and Hon. Gen. Sec., 1983–88; Mem., 1998–2004, Chm., 1999–2004, Accreditation Bd); European Meteorological Society: Chm., Accreditation Cttee, 2001–06; Vice Pres. and Treas., 2002–05. British Association of Former UN Civil Service: Mem., Exec. Cttee, 1996–; Vice Chm., 1998–99; Chm., 1999–2004, 2009–10; Vice-Pres., 2004–. Clerk/Correspondent of Trustees, Stanford-in-the-Vale Public Purposes Charity, 2002– (Chm., 2000–02); Chm., Stanford-in-the-Vale Local and Dist History Soc., 2004–13 (Hon. Mem., 2013–); Mem. and Trustee, Stanford-in-the-Vale Village Hall Mgt Cttee, 2010–. Trustee: Thames Valley Hospice, 1996–98; Friends of the Ridgeway, 2008–15. L. G. Groves 2nd Meml Prize for Met., 1970. *Publications:* (contrib.) History of the Meteorological Office, 2012; papers in learned jls on met. and aspects of met. instrumentation in GB and USA; articles on local history. *Recreations:* home and garden, music, travel, good food, family history research, local English history, twelve grandchildren, one great grandson, creating a family web-site. *Address:* Honey End, 14 Ock Meadow, Stanford-in-the-Vale, Oxon SN7 8LN. *T:* (01367) 718480.

AXON, Prof. Anthony Thomas Roger, MD; FRCP; Consultant Physician and Gastroenterologist, Leeds General Infirmary, 1975–2006, now Emeritus Consultant Gastroenterologist; Hon. Professor of Gastroenterology, University of Leeds, since 1995; *b* 21 Nov. 1941; *s* of Robert and Ruth Axon; *m* 1965, Jill Coleman; two *s* one *d*. *Educ:* Woodhouse Grove Sch., W Yorks; St Bartholomew's Hosp. Med. Coll., London (MB BS Hons, Dist. in Medicine, MD 1973). FRCP 1980. Hse Physician and Resident in Pathology, St Bartholomew's Hosp., 1965–68; Registrar, 1968–70, Sen. Registrar, 1971–75, St Thomas' Hosp., London. Mem. Council, RCP, 1992–94. Vice-Pres. Endoscopy, British Soc. Gastroenterol., 1989–91; President: N of England Gastroenterol. Soc., 1999–2000; British Soc. of Gastroenterol., 2000–01; Eur. Soc. of Gastrointestinal Endoscopy, 2000–02; World Orgn of Gastrointestinal Endoscopy, 2005–09; United European Gastroenterology Fedn, 2006–07; Mem., Educn Cttee, World Orgn of Gastroenterology, 1999–2004. *Publications:* contrib. numerous original papers on wide variety of gastrointestinal subjects, specifically inflammatory bowel disease, intestinal permeability, endoscopic retrograde cholangio-pancreatography, safety in endoscopy, Helicobacter pylori, cancer surveillance, aetiology of gastric cancer, to peer review jls and other pubns. *Recreations:* travel, gardening. *Address:* Nidd Park House, Nidd, N Yorks HG3 3BN. *T:* (01423) 779099.

AXWORTHY, Hon. Lloyd; PC (Can.) 1980; OC 2003; OM 2001; PhD; President and Vice-Chancellor, University of Winnipeg, since 2004; *b* 21 Dec. 1939; *s* of Norman Joseph and Gwen Anne Axworthy; *m* 1984, Denise Ommanney; two *s* one *d*. *Educ:* Univ. of Winnipeg (BA 1961); Princeton Univ. (MA 1963; PhD 1972). Asst Prof. of Pol Sci., 1969–79, and Dir, Inst. of Urban Studies, 1970–79, Univ. of Winnipeg. MLA(L) Manitoba, 1973–79; MP (L): Winnipeg-Fort Garry, 1979–88; Winnipeg S Centre, 1988–2001; Minister of State for Status of Women, Canada, 1980–81; Minister of Employment and Immigration, 1980–83; Minister of Transportation, 1983–84; Opposition spokesman on internat. trade, 1984–88; Liberal spokesman on external affairs, 1988–93; Minister of Human Resources Develt, and of Western Econ. Diversification, 1993–96; Minister for Foreign Affairs, 1996–2001; Dir, Liu Inst. for Global Issues, Univ. of BC, 2001–04 (Sen. Associate, 2004–). Mem., Commn for the Legal Empowerment of the Poor, UN Develt Prog., 2006–08; Head, OAS Electoral Observation Mission to Peru, 2006; Comr, Dialogue and Commn on Artic Climate Change, Aspen Inst., 2008–. *Publications:* Navigating a New World: Canada's global future, 2003. *Recreation:* golf. *Address:* President's Office, University of Winnipeg, 515 Portage Avenue, Winnipeg, MB R3B 2E9, Canada.

AXWORTHY, Dr Michael George Andrew, FRAS; Senior Lecturer, since 2012, and Director, Centre for Persian and Iranian Studies, since 2008, University of Exeter; *b* Woking, 26 Sept. 1962; *s* of Ifor and Monica Axworthy; *m* 1996, Sally Hinds; one *s* three *d*. *Educ:* King's Sch., Chester; Peterhouse, Cambridge (BA Hons Hist. 1985; MA 2002; PhD 2012). Entered FCO, 1986; Third Sec., Valletta, 1988–91; Second Secretary: FCO, 1991–93; Bonn, 1993–98; First Sec. and Hd, Iran Section, ME Dept, FCO, 1998–2000. University of Exeter: Hon. Fellow, Inst. of Arab and Islamic Studies, 2006; Lectr, 2007–12. FRAS 2007; FRSA. *Publications:* The Sword of Persia, 2006; Empire of the Mind: a history of Iran, 2007 (trans. Italian, Spanish, Dutch, Czech, German, Finnish); Revolutionary Iran, 2013. *Recreations:* reading, music, hill walking, painting, oriental rugs, old books, planting and cutting down trees, tending the Rayburn, Radio 4. *Address:* Institute of Arab and Islamic Studies, University of Exeter, Stocker Road, Exeter EX4 4ND. *T:* (01392) 724090. *E:* m.g.a.axworthy@exeter.ac.uk.

AYAZ, Sir Iftikhar Ahmad, KBE 2015 (OBE 1998); PhD; Hon. Consul of Tuvalu in the United Kingdom, since 1995; *b* 3 Jan. 1933. *Educ:* secondary educn in Tanzania; BEd Hons; DipEd; MA Applied Linguistics, UK; PhD Educn and Trng for Human Develt, USA, 1993. Planning and Programming, Teacher Educn and Curriculum Develt, Govt of Tanzania Educn Admin, 1960–76; Commonwealth Fellow, Commonwealth Inst., London, 1976–77; Sen. Lectr and Sen. Curriculum Advr, Univ. of Dar-Es-Salaam, Tanzania, 1979–81; Admin Officer, Centre on Integrated Rural Develt for Africa, UNFAO, 1981–85; Field Expert in Educn, Commonwealth Fund for Tech. Co-operation, 1985–90; Consultant: on Educn for Human Develt, UNO, 1990–93; on Educn for All, 1993–95. Associate Dir, Universal Consultants, UK; Advr, Minority Gp Rights, UN Human Rights Cttee, Geneva. Sec., E Africa Commonwealth Soc. for Prevention of Disablement. Chairman: Grass Roots Diplomat; Human Rights Cttee Internat.; Royal Soc. for Prevention of Cruelty to Animals, Tanzania. Founder and Sec. Gen., Tanzania Commonwealth Soc. Vice President: Pacific Peace Forum; NRIs Welfare Soc. of India. Member: Commonwealth Partnership for Tech. Mgt; World Council for Poverty Alleviation. Member: Pacific Is Assoc.; Commonwealth Assoc.; Dep. Gov., ABI Res. Assoc. Ambassador, Universal Peace Fedn. Award for Internat. Consultation on Skill-based Educn, OAD, 1979. *Publications:* contrib. papers on educn in small states, climate change and sustainable envmts, educn theory, philosophy and sociol., linguistics, literature and curriculum develt, human develt, culture in educn, peace educn, and universal and fundamental human rights. *Address:* Tuvalu House, 230 Worple Road, SW20 8RH. *T:* and *Fax:* (020) 8879 0985. *E:* TuvaluConsulate@netscape.net.

AYCKBOURN, Sir Alan, Kt 1997; CBE 1987; playwright and director; Artistic Director, Stephen Joseph Theatre, Scarborough, 1972–2009; *b* 12 April 1939; *s* of Horace Ayckbourn and Irene Maude (*née* Worley); *m* 1st, 1959, Christine Helen (*née* Roland); two *s*; 2nd, 1997, Heather Stoney. *Educ:* Haileybury. Worked in repertory as Stage Manager/Actor at Edinburgh, Worthing, Leatherhead, Oxford, and with late Stephen Joseph's Theatre-in-the-Round Co., at Scarborough. Founder Mem., Victoria Theatre, Stoke-on-Trent, 1962. BBC Radio Drama Producer, Leeds, 1964–70; Co. Dir, NT, 1986–87. Vis. Prof. of Contemporary Theatre, and Fellow, St Catherine's Coll., Oxford, 1991–92. Has written numerous full-length plays almost all premiered in Scarborough. London productions: Mr Whatnot, Arts, 1964; Relatively Speaking, Duke of York's, 1967, Greenwich, 1986 (televised, 1969, 1989); How the Other Half Loves, Lyric, 1970, Duke of York's, 1988; Time and Time Again, Comedy, 1972 (televised, 1976); Absurd Person Singular, Criterion, 1973 (Evening Standard Drama Award, Best Comedy, 1973) (televised, 1985); The Norman Conquests (Trilogy), Globe, 1974 (Evening Standard Drama Award, Best Play; Variety Club of GB Award; Plays and Players Award) (televised, 1977); Jeeves (musical, with Andrew Lloyd Webber), Her Majesty's, 1975, reworked as By Jeeves, Duke of York's, transf. Lyric, 1996, NY, 2001 (filmed, 2001); Absent Friends, Garrick, 1975 (televised, 1985); Confusions, Apollo, 1976; Bedroom Farce (dir), Nat. Theatre, 1977 (televised, 1980); Just Between Ourselves, Queen's, 1977 (Evening Standard Drama Award, Best Play) (televised, 1978); Ten Times Table (dir), Globe, 1978; Joking Apart (dir), Globe, 1979 (Shared Plays and Players Award); Sisterly Feelings (dir), Nat. Theatre, 1980; Taking Steps, Lyric, 1980; Suburban Strains (musical with Paul Todd) (dir), Round House, 1981; Season's Greetings (dir), Apollo, 1982 (televised, 1986); Way Upstream (dir), Nat. Theatre, 1982 (televised, 1988); Making Tracks (musical with Paul Todd) (dir), Greenwich, 1983; Intimate Exchanges (dir), Ambassadors, 1983 (filmed, 1993); A Chorus of Disapproval (dir), Nat. Theatre, 1985 (Evening Standard Drama Award, Best Comedy; Olivier Award, Best Comedy; DRAMA Award, Best Comedy, 1985), transf. Lyric, 1986 (filmed, 1989); Woman in Mind (dir), Vaudeville, 1986; A Small Family Business (dir), Nat. Theatre, 1987 (Evening Standard Drama Award, Best Play); Henceforward... (dir), Vaudeville, 1988 (Evening Standard Drama Award, Best Comedy, 1989); Man of the Moment (dir), Globe, 1990 (Evening Standard Drama Award, Best Comedy, 1990); The Revengers' Comedies (dir), Strand, 1991; Time of My Life (dir), Vaudeville, 1993; Wildest Dreams (dir), RSC, 1993; Communicating Doors (dir), Gielgud, 1995, transf. Savoy, 1996 (Writers' Guild of GB Award, Best West End Play, 1996); Things We Do For Love (dir), Gielgud, 1998 (Lloyds Pvte Banking Playwright of the Year); adapt. Ostrovsky's The Forest, RNT, 1999; Comic Potential (dir), Lyric, 1999; House & Garden (dir), RNT, 2000; Damsels in Distress (trilogy: GamePlan; FlatSpin; RolePlay), (dir), Duchess, 2002; Haunting Julia, Riverside Studios, 2011; Snake in the Grass, Print Room, 2011; Drowning on Dry Land, Jermyn St Th., 2011; Private Fears in Public Places, Orange Tree, 2011 (filmed, 2007); Neighbourhood Watch, Tricycle, 2012; Scarborough: Family Circles, 1970; It Could Be Any One Of Us, 1983; Body Language, 1990; Dreams from a Summer House (play with music by John Pattison), 1992; A Word from our Sponsor (musical with John Pattison), 1995; Sugar Daddies, 2003; Improbable Fiction, 2005; If I Were You, 2006; Life and Beth, 2008; Awaking Beauty (musical with Denis King), 2008; My Wonderful Day, 2009; Life of Riley, 2010 (filmed, 2014); Dear Uncle (adapt. Chekhov's Uncle Vanya), 2011; Surprises, 2012; Arrivals & Departures, 2013; Farcicals, 2013; Roundelay, 2014; Hero's Welcome, 2015; other plays directed: Tons of Money, Nat. Theatre, 1986; A View from the Bridge, Nat. Theatre, transf. Aldwych, 1987; 'Tis Pity she's a Whore, Nat. Theatre, 1988; Two Weeks with the Queen, Nat. Theatre, 1994; Conversations with my Father, Old Vic, 1995; The Safari Party, Scarborough, 2002, Hampstead, 2003. *Plays for children and young people include:* Callisto 5, 1990; This Is Where We Came In, 1990; My Very Own Story, 1991; Invisible Friends (dir), Nat. Theatre, 1991; Mr A's Amazing Maze Plays, Nat. Theatre, 1993; The Musical Jigsaw Play, 1994; The Champion of Paribanou, 1996; The Boy Who Fell Into A Book, 1998, Lyric, 2012 (jtly reworked as musical, 2014); Callisto #7, 1999; Whenever (musical with Denis King), 2000; The Jollies, 2002; Orvin—Champion of Champions (musical with Denis King), 2003; My Sister Sadie, 2003; Miss Yesterday, 2004. Hon. DLitt: Hull, 1981; Keele, 1987; Leeds, 1987; York, 1992; Bradford, 1994; Univ. of Wales Coll. of Cardiff, 1995; Manchester, 2003; York St John, 2011; DUniv Open, 1998. Sunday Times Award for Literary Achievement, 2000; Special Olivier Award, 2009; Critics' Circle Award for Services to the Arts, 2010; Tony Lifetime Achievement Award, 2010. *Publications:* The Crafty Art of Playmaking, 2002; the majority of his plays have been published and are currently in print. *Recreations:* music, cricket, films. *Address:* c/o Casarotto Ramsay & Associates Ltd, Waverley House, 7–12 Noel Street, W1F 8GQ. *T:* (020) 7287 4450. *W:* www.alanayckbourn.net.

AYERS, John Gilbert; Keeper, Far Eastern Department, Victoria and Albert Museum, 1970–82; *b* 27 July 1922; *s* of H. W. Ayers, CB, CBE; *m* 1957, Bridget Elspeth Jacqualine Fanshawe; one *s* two *d*. *Educ:* St Paul's Sch.; St Edmund Hall, Oxford. Served in RAF, 1941–46 (Sgt). Asst Keeper, Dept of Ceramics, Victoria and Albert Museum, 1950, Dep. Keeper 1963. Pres., Oriental Ceramic Soc., 1984–87. *Publications:* The Seligman Collection of Oriental Art, II, 1964; The Baur Collection: Chinese Ceramics, I–IV, 1968–74, Japanese Ceramics, 1982; (with R. J. Charleston) The James A. de Rothschild Collection: Meissen and Oriental Porcelain, 1971; Oriental Ceramics, The World's Great Collections: Victoria and Albert Museum, 1975; (with J. Rawson) Chinese Jade throughout the Ages, exhibn catalogue, 1975; (with D. Howard) China for the West, 2 vols, 1978; (with D. Howard) Masterpieces of Chinese Export Porcelain, 1980; Oriental Art in the Victoria and Albert Museum, 1983; (ed) Chinese Ceramics in the Topkapi Saray Museum, Istanbul, 3 vols, 1986; (with O. Impey and J. V. G. Mallet) Porcelain for Palaces: the fashion for Japan in Europe 1650–1750, 1990; Chinese Ceramic Tea Vessels: the K. S. Lo Collection, Hong Kong, 1991; A Jade Menagerie: creatures real and imaginary from the Worrell Collection, 1993; Chinese Ceramics in the Baur Collection, Geneva, 2 vols, 1999; Blanc de Chine: divine images in porcelain, exhibn catalogue, China Inst., NY, 2002; The Chinese Porcelain Collection of Marie Vergottis, Lausanne, 2004. *Address:* 3 Bedford Gardens, W8 7ED. *T:* (020) 7229 5168.

AYERS, Prof. Michael Richard, PhD; FBA 2001; Professor of Philosophy, University of Oxford, 1996–2002; Fellow of Wadham College, Oxford, 1965–2002, now Emeritus; *b* 27 June 1935; *s* of Dick Ayers and Sybil Kerr Ayers (*née* Rutherglen); *m* 1962, Delia Mary Bell; one *s* one *d*. *Educ:* Battersea Grammar Sch.; St John's Coll., Cambridge (BA 1959; MA, PhD 1965). Jun. Res. Fellow, St John's Coll., Cambridge, 1962–65; Tutor in Philosophy, Wadham Coll., Oxford, 1965; CUF Lectr in Philosophy, 1965–94, Reader in Philosophy, 1994–2002, Univ. of Oxford. Vis. Lectr, 1964–65, Vis. Prof., 1979, 2007, Univ. of Calif, Berkeley; Vis. Prof., Univ. of Oregon, 1970–71; Vis. Fellow, Res. Sch. of Social Scis, ANU, 1993; Ida Beam Dist. Vis. Prof., Univ. of Iowa, 1995. MAE 2006. *Publications:* The Refutation of Determinism, 1968; (with J. Ree and A. Westoby) Philosophy and its Past, 1978; Locke: vol. 1, Epistemology, vol. 2, Ontology, 1991; Locke: ideas and things, 1997; (ed with D. Garber) The Cambridge History of Seventeenth Century Philosophy, 2 vols, 1998; (ed) Rationalism, Platonism and God, 2007; contrib. to jls, collections and works of reference. *Recreations:* walking, gardening, natural history. *Address:* Wadham College, Oxford OX1 3PN.

AYKROYD, Sir Henry (Robert George), 5th Bt *cr* 1920, of Lightcliffe, Yorks; *b* Leeds, 4 April 1954; *o s* of Sir Michael David Aykroyd, 4th Bt and of Oenene Gillian Diana (*née* Cowling); *S* father, 2010; *m* 1975, Lucy Merlin Houghton Brown (marr. diss. 2007); two *s* three *d* (of whom two *d* are twins). *Educ:* Charterhouse; Edinburgh Univ. (MA). Farmer. *Heir: s* George Jack Aykroyd [*b* 8 Jan. 1977; *m* 1999, Jodie Askew (marr. diss. 2012); two *s* one *d*]. *Address:* Balgove House, St Andrews KY16 9SF. *T:* 07836 757845. *E:* henryaykroyd@msn.com.

AYKROYD, Sir James (Alexander Frederic), 3rd Bt *cr* 1929, of Birstwith Hall, Hampsthwaite, co. York; *b* 6 Sept. 1943; *s* of Bertram Aykroyd (*d* 1983), *y s* of Sir Frederic Alfred Aykroyd, 1st Bt, and his 1st wife, Margot (later Dame Margot Smith, DBE), *d* of Leonard Graham Brown; *S* uncle, 1993; *m* 1973, Jennifer Marshall; two *d*. *Educ:* Eton Coll.; Univ. of Aix en Provence; Univ. of Madrid. Sen. Export Dir, James Buchanan & Co. Ltd, 1965–83; Export Man. Dir, Martini & Rossi SpA, 1983–87; Chm., Speyside Distillers Co. Ltd, 2001–12. *Recreation:* active sports esp. tennis and golf. *Heir: half b* Toby Nigel Bertram Aykroyd [*b* 13 Nov. 1955; *m* 2005, Rona Louise Birnie; one *s*]. *Address:* Birstwith Hall, near Harrogate, Yorks HG3 2JW. *T:* (01423) 770250. *Club:* Alwoodley Golf.

AYLARD, Richard John, CVO 1994; External Affairs and Sustainability Director, Thames Water, since 2010; Extra Equerry to the Prince of Wales, since 1996; *b* 10 April 1952; *s* of John and Joy Aylard; *m* 1st, 1977, Sally Williams (marr. diss. 1984); 2nd, 1984, Suzanne Walker (marr. diss. 1998); two *d*; 3rd, 1998, Jennifer Jones; one *s* one *d*. *Educ:* Queen Elizabeth's Grammar Sch., Barnet; Reading Univ. (BSc Hons Applied Zoology with Maths). Joined RN as university cadet, 1972; served HM Ships Shavington, Ark Royal, Fox, 1974–77; Staff of Flag Officer Submarines, 1977–79; Flag Lieut to Dep. SACLANT, Norfolk, USA, 1979–81; Capt.'s Sec., HMS Invincible, 1981–83; Supply Officer, HMS Brazen, 1984–85; Equerry to the Princess of Wales, 1985–88; Comdr RN, 1987; Asst Private Sec. and Comptroller to the Prince and Princess of Wales, 1988–91; RN retd, 1989; Private Sec. and Treas. to the Prince of Wales, 1991–96; consultant on envmtl issues and public affairs, 1996–2002; Thames Water: Corporate Social Responsibility Dir, 2002–04; Ext. Affairs and Envmt Dir, 2004–08; Dir, 2008–10. *Recreations:* sailing, fishing, gardening, ski-ing.

AYLEN, Walter Stafford; QC 1983; a Deputy High Court Judge, 1993–2005; *b* St Helena, 21 May 1937; *s* of late Rt Rev. Charles Arthur William Aylen and Elisabeth Margaret Anna (*née* Hills); *m* 1967, Peggy Elizabeth Lainé Woodford; three *d*. *Educ:* Summer Fields Sch.; Winchester Coll. (schol.); New Coll., Oxford (schol., sen. schol.; BCL; MA). Northants County Cricket Club 2nd XI, 1955. Commnd 2nd Lieut KRRC, 1956–57. Called to the Bar, Middle Temple, 1962 (Bencher 1991); Head of Chambers, Hardwicke Bldg, 1991–2000; Mem., ADR Chambers, 2000–08. Asst Recorder, 1982; Recorder, 1985–2003. Mem., Internat. Panel, Alternative Dispute Resolution Gp, 2001–08. Mem., Bar Council, 1994–96 (Chm., Bar Services and IT Cttee, 1994; Vice-Chm., Finance Cttee, 1995–96). MCIArb 1999–2009. FRSA 1989–2009. *Recreations:* reading novels (especially his wife's), theatre, music. *Address:* 24 Fairmount Road, SW2 2BL.

AYLESFORD, 12th Earl of, *cr* 1714; **Charles Heneage Finch-Knightley;** Baron Guernsey, 1703; Vice Lord-Lieutenant for West Midlands, 1990–2015; *b* 27 March 1947; *s* of 11th Earl of Aylesford and Margaret Rosemary Tyer; *S* father, 2008; *m* 1971, Penelope Anstice, *y d* of Kenneth A. G. Crawley; one *s* four *d* (incl. twin *d*). *Educ:* Oundle; Trinity Coll., Cambridge. DL West Midlands, 1986. *Recreations:* shooting, fishing, Real tennis, cricket. *Heir: s* Lord Guernsey, *qv*. *Address:* Packington Hall, Meriden, Coventry CV7 7HF. *T:* (01676) 522274.

AYLETT, Crispin David William; QC 2008; *b* 13 Aug. 1961; *s* of late David Leonard Nankivell Aylett and Freda Emily Aylett (*née* Montague, then Whitehead); *m* 1989, Louise Sheppard; two *s* two *d*. *Educ:* Dulwich Coll.; Bristol Univ. (BA Hons 1983); City Univ., London (Dip Law 1984). Called to the Bar, Inner Temple, 1985 (Scarman Schol.), Bencher, 2014. Jun. Treasury Counsel, 2001–06, Sen. Treasury Counsel, 2006–13, Central Criminal Court. Tribunal Mem., disciplinary panel, Lloyd's of London, 2013–. Sec., Cakemaker's Dozen, 1985–2002. *Recreations:* theatre, satire, cricket. *Address:* QEB Hollis Whiteman, 1–2 Laurence Pountney Hill, EC4R 0EU. *T:* (020) 7933 8855.

AYLING, John Vernon, OBE 2007; Executive Chairman, John Ayling and Associates, since 1978; *b* Fulmer, Bucks, 18 April 1944; *s* of Stanley Harradine Ayling and Phyllis Evelyn Ayling; *m* 1982, Marilyn, (Lyn), Whinray; one *d*. *Educ:* East Grinstead Grammar Sch.; Univ. of Exeter (BA Hons Geog.). Media Manager, Garland-Compton, 1968–71; Media Dir, Kirkwood Co., 1971–78. *Recreations:* cricket, golf, travel, music, watching all sports. *Address:* John Ayling and Associates, 27 Soho Square, W1D 3QR. *T:* (020) 7439 6070, *Fax:* (020) 7437 8473. *E:* jaa@jaa-media.co.uk. *Clubs:* Lord's Taverners (Chm., 2002–03, 2010–12), MCC, Solus (Pres., 2007); Oxted Hockey; Tandridge and Wisley Golf; SWIGS Golf.

AYLING, Robert John; Chief Executive, British Airways, 1996–2000; *b* 3 Aug. 1946; *m* 1972, Julia Crallan; two *s* one *d*. *Educ:* King's Coll. Sch., Wimbledon. Admitted solicitor, 1968; joined Elborne, Mitchell & Co., Solicitors, 1969, Partner, 1971; Department of Trade, later of Trade and Industry: Legal Advr, 1974 (work on UK accession to EEC, 1974–77); Asst Solicitor and Head, Aviation Law Br., 1979 (legislation to privatise British Airways Bd); UK deleg., UN Commn for Internat. Trade Law, 1979–83; Under Sec. (Legal), 1983; British Airways: Legal Dir, 1985; Company Sec., 1987; Human Resources Dir, 1988; Marketing and Ops Dir, 1991; Gp Man. Dir, 1993. Chairman: New Millennium Experience Co., 1997–2000; Holidaybreak plc, 2003–09; Sanctuary Group plc, 2006–07. Non-executive Director: Royal & Sun Alliance, 1994–2004; Dyson Ltd, 2001–12 (Vice-Chm., 2005–10; Chm., 2010–12); Glas Cymru (Welsh Water), 2008– (Chm., 2010–). Ind. Chm., HM Courts and Tribunals Service, 2011–. Gov., King's Coll. Sch., 1996–2006. Hon. LLD Brunel, 1996. Hon. FRIBA. *Recreations:* hillwalking, sailing. *Clubs:* Brooks's; Royal Thames Yacht.

AYLING, Tracy Jane, (Mrs C. A. Hutton); QC 2006; *b* 27 April 1960; *d* of Rex John Ayling and Doreen Ayling (*née* Matthews); *m* 2004, Charles Adrian Hutton. *Educ:* Horndean Comprehensive Sch.; Durham Univ. (BA Hons 1982). Called to the Bar, Inner Temple, 1983, Bencher, 2010. *Recreations:* cuisine, travel, shoes. *Address:* 2 Bedford Row, WC1R 4BU. *T:* (020) 7440 8888, *Fax:* (020) 7242 1738.

AYLMER, family name of **Baron Aylmer**.

AYLMER, 14th Baron *cr* 1718; **(Anthony) Julian Aylmer;** Bt 1662; Partner, Reynold Porter Chamberlain LLP, 1982–2009; *b* 10 Dec. 1951; *o s* of 13th Baron Aylmer and Countes Maddalena Sofia, *d* of late Count Arbeno Attems; *S* father, 2006; *m* 1990, Belinda Rosemary e *d* of Major Peter Henry Parker; one *s* one *d*. *Educ:* Westminster; Trinity Hall, Cambridg (MA). Admitted solicitor, 1976. Chm., Irish Peers Assoc., 2011–. *Recreations:* history genealogy, architecture. *Heir: s* Hon. Michael Henry Aylmer, *b* 21 March 1991. *Address:* 1 Edgarley Terrace, SW6 6QF. *Clubs:* Brooks's, Pratt's.

AYLMER, Sir Richard John, 16th Bt *cr* 1622, of Donadea, Co. Kildare; writer; *b* 23 Apr 1937; *s* of Sir Fenton Gerald Aylmer, 15th Bt and Rosalind Boultbee (*d* 1991), *d* of J. Perciv Bell; *S* father, 1987; *m* 1962, Lise, *d* of Paul Demers; one *s* one *d*. *Educ:* Lower Canada Coll. Montreal; Western Ontario, London, Canada; Harvard Univ., Cambridge, Mass, USA. *Hei s* Fenton Paul Aylmer [*b* 31 Oct. 1965; *m* 1989, Pina Mastromonaco; two *s*]. *Address:* 446 Francis Peninsula Road, Madeira Park, BC V0N 2H1, Canada. *T:* (604) 8832130. *E* dickaylmer@gmail.com.

AYLWARD, Adrian John Francis; Headmaster, Leweston School (formerly St Antony' Leweston School), since 2006; *b* 12 Nov. 1957; *s* of John James and Cynthia Aylward; *m* 1990 Caroline Cramer; one *s* two *d*. *Educ:* Worth Sch., Sussex; Exeter Coll., Oxford (BA); King' Coll. London (PGCE). Formerly investment banker; Royal Sovereign Group (Chief Exec. 1986–91); Dir, EMESS plc, 1990–91; Housemaster and Head of Religious Studies, Downsid Sch., 1992–96; Headmaster, Stonyhurst Coll., 1996–2006. Mem., Irish Assoc. Knight o Malta. *Recreations:* fishing, philosophy, sport, travel. *Address:* Leweston School, Sherborne Dorset DT9 6EN. *T:* (01963) 210691, *Fax:* (01963) 210786. *Club:* Brooks's.

AYLWARD, (George) William, MD; FRCS, FRCOphth; Consultant Ophthalmi Surgeon, Moorfields Eye Hospital, since 1994 (Medical Director, 2002–10); Director OpenEyes Project, 2010–14; *b* 23 Dec. 1957; *s* of James Ernest Aylward and Martha Harvey Aylward; *m* 1983, Catherine Joy Otty; one *s* one *d*. *Educ:* Malvern Coll.; Corpus Christi Coll. Cambridge (MB BChir); Addenbrooke's Hosp. (Cambridge Univ. Med. Sch. (MD 1990)) FRCS 1987; FRCOphth 1989. SHO, Western Eye Hosp., London, 1985–86; Lectr, Sydney Univ., 1987–89; Sen. Registrar, 1989–92, Fellow in Vitreoretinal Surgery, 1992–93 Moorfields Eye Hosp. Fellow in Med. Retina, Bascom Palmer Eye Inst., Miami, 1993–94 President: Eur. Soc. of Retina Specialists, 2009–11 (Vice Pres., 2007–09); British and Eir Vitreoretinal Soc., 2012–14. Mem., Eur. Acad. of Ophthalmology, 2008. Vice Pres., Clu Jules Gonin, Lausanne, 2011–; Mem., Ophthalmic Club, 1999–. *Publications:* contrib. chapter to books, including: Ophthalmology, 1997; Clinical Retina, 2002; Ryan's Retina, 2005, 3r edn 2012; over 110 articles in peer-reviewed ophthalmic jls. *Recreations:* sailing, cooking *Address:* Moorfields Eye Hospital, City Road, EC1V 2PD; 8 Upper Wimpole Street, W1C 6LH. *T:* (020) 7935 1565, *Fax:* (020) 7224 1752. *E:* bill.aylward@moorfields.nhs.uk.

AYLWARD, Sir Mansel, Kt 2010; CB 2002; FRCP, FFPM, FFOM; Professor o Psychosocial and Disability Research and Director, Centre for Psychosocial and Disability Research, since 2004, Professor of Public Health Education, School of Medicine, since 2012 and Specialist Adviser to the Vice Chancellor on International Engagement, since 2013 Cardiff University; Chair, Public Health Wales NHS Trust, since 2009; *b* 29 Nov. 1942; *s* o John Aylward and Cora Doreen Aylward (*née* Evans); *m* 1963, Angela Bridget Besley; one one *d*. *Educ:* Cyfarthfa Castle Grammar Sch., Merthyr Tydfil; London Hosp. Med. Coll. Univ. of London (BSc 1964; MB BS Hons 1967); FFPM 1991; DDAM RCP 2001; FFOM 2003; FRCP 2003. MRC Clin. Res. Fellow in Exptl Surgery, London Hosp., 1968–70; Lect in Surgery, London Hosp. Med. Coll., 1969; GP, Merthyr Tydfil, 1970–73; Clin. Assistant in Dermatol. and Minor Surgery, St Tydfil's Hosp., 1970–76; Res. Physician, Singleton Hosp. Swansea and Merthyr and Cynon Valleys, 1973–76; Chm. and Man. Dir, Simbec Researc Ltd, 1974–84; Dir of Clin. Res., Berk Pharmaceuticals, 1974–76; Dir, Women's Healt Concern, London, 1976–86; Pres., Simbec Research (USA) Inc., 1980–84; Dir of Clin. Res. Lyonnaise Industrielle Pharmaceutique, France, 1982–84; Regl MO, DHSS, Cardiff 1985–88; SMO, DSS, London, 1988–90; Sec. to Attendance Allowance Bd, London, 1991 PMO and Dir of Med. Policy, R&D, Benefits Agency, London, 1991–95; CMO and Chie Scientist, DSS, subseq. DWP, 1995–2005. Hon. Prof., Sch. of Psychol., Cardiff Univ. an UWCM, 2001–04. Chief Med. Advr, War Pensions, later Veterans, Agency, MoD, 2001–05 Civilian Med. Advr in Disability Medicine to Army, 2004–. Expert Agrée Medicine Interne France, 1982. Visiting Professor: Harvard Univ., 2004–; Leuven Univ., 2006–; Karolinsk Univ., 2008–; First Ko Awatea Stevenson Chair and Vis. Prof., Univ. of Auckland, 2012– Lectures include: Thakrah, SOM, 2006; Edward Jones, Cardiff Univ., 2006; Tudor Hart Cardiff Univ., 2007; Dynamics of Disability Keynote, FLA, USA, 2008; Easter, RSM, 2009 Brackenridge Meml, Assurance Med. Soc. UK, 2011; Eumass, Padua Univ., 2013 Australasian Mil. Medicine Assoc., 2014. Chm., Standards Cttee, Merthyr Tydfil CB, 2002– Chair: Wales Centre for Health, Welsh Assembly Govt, 2004–09; Health Commn Wale Rev., 2007–08; All Wales Public Mental Health Network, 2007–; Academic Forum, Faculty of Occupational Medicine, 2007–; Royal Mail Attendance Acad., 2007–11; Bevan Commn 2008–; Wales Occupational Health Review, 2008–09; All Wales Occupational Health Review, 2009–; Expert Panel Rev. of Growing Up in NZ Longitudinal Study, 2012 Member: Health Honours Cttee UK, 2005–12; Industrial Injuries Adv. Cttee, 2005–14 Director: Elision Gp Ltd UK, 2005–07; Arkaga Health & Technology Ltd, 2008–09. Autho of Reviews: Child Protection and Safeguarding in NHS Wales, 2009; Supporting People Programme (Wales), 2010; Health Improvement Prog. (Wales), 2011. Vice Pres., Soc. o Occupational Therapists, 2012–. Pres., Dowlais Male Voice Choir, 2013–; Patron: Vocationa Rehabilitation Assoc. (UK), 2005–; Wellbeing Wales Lles Cymru, 2011–. FRSocMed 198 (Academic Dean (Wales), 2001–; Hon. Treas. and Dir, 2005–07); Fellow, Soc. o Occupational Medicine, 2006–. Hon. FFPH 2008. Hon. Mem., Soc. of Occupational Medicine, Ireland, 2004. Hon. DSc S Wales, 2013. Freeman, Merthyr Tydfil CB, 2013 *Publications:* Management of the Menopause and Post-Menopausal Years, 1975; The Disability Handbook, 1991, 2nd edn 1998; Back Pain: an international review, 2002; (contrib. Malingering and Illness Deception, 2003; Scientific Concepts and Basis of Incapacity Benefits, 2005; The Power of Belief, 2006; (contrib.) Fitness for Work, 2nd edn, 1997 to 4th edn, 2012; Models of Disability, 2010; contribs on public health, disability assessment, rehabilitation, and social security issues to learned jls. *Recreations:* military history, travel, theatre, reading, grandchildren. *Address:* Public Health Wales, 14 Cathedral Road, Cardiff CF11 9LJ; (home) Cefn Cottage, Cefn Coed-y-Cymer, Merthyr Tydfil CF48 2PH. *Club:* Athenæum.

AYLWARD, William; *see* Aylward, G. W.

AYNSLEY-GREEN, Sir Albert, Kt 2006; DPhil; FRCP, FRCPE, FRCPCH, FMedSci; Founder and Director, Aynsley-Green Consulting, since 2010; Children's Commissioner for England, 2005–10; Nuffield Professor of Child Health, Institute of Child Health, University College London, 1993–2005, now Emeritus; President, British Medical Association, 2015–June 2016; *b* 30 May 1943; *m* 1967, Rosemary Anne Boucher; two *d*. *Educ:* Glyn Grammar Sch., Epsom; Guy's Hosp. Med. Sch., Univ. of London (MB BS); Oriel Coll., Oxford (MA, DPhil; Hon. Fellow, 2007). MRCS 1967; FRCP 1982; FRCPE 1987; FRCPCH 1997 (Hon. FRCPCH 2008). House Officer posts at Guy's Hosp., London, St Luke's Hosp., Guildford, Radcliffe Infirmary, Oxford and RPMS, Hammersmith Hosp., London, 1967–70; Radcliffe Infirmary, Oxford: Wellcome Res. Fellow, 1970–72; Clinical Lectr in Internal Medicine, 1972–73; Sen. House Officer and Registrar posts in Paediatrics, Radcliffe Infirmary and John Radcliffe Hosp., Oxford, 1973–74; European Sci. Exchange Fellow, Royal Soc. and Swiss Nat. Res. Council, Univ. Children's Hosp., Zurich, 1974–75; University of Oxford: Clinical Lectr in Paediatrics, 1975–78; Univ. Lectr, 1978–83; Fellow,

Green Coll., 1980–83; Hon. Consultant Paediatrician, Oxford AHA, 1978–83; University of Newcastle upon Tyne: James Spence Prof. of Child Health and Hd of Dept, 1984–93; Hd, Sch. of Clinical Med. Scis, 1991–93; Hon. Consultant Paediatrician: Royal Victoria Infirmary, Newcastle upon Tyne, 1984–93; Gt Ormond St Hosp. and UCL, 1993–2005; Vice-Dean for Clin. Res., Inst. of Child Health, Univ. of London, at UCL, 1999–2003; Dir, Clinical R&D, Gt Ormond St Hosp. for Children, 1993–2003; NHS Nat. Clin. Dir for Children and Chm., NHS Nat. Children's Taskforce, DoH, 2001–05. Non-exec. Mem., Bd of Govs, Hosp. for Sick Children, Gt Ormond St, 1990–93; Exec. Mem., Trust Bd, Gt Ormond St Hosp. for Children NHS Trust, 1993–2003; non-exec. Dir, Salisbury Foundn NHS Trust, 2007–08. Chm., Adv. Gp on NHS Priorities for R&D in Mother and Child Health, DoH, 1994–95; Mem., Central R&D Cttee, DoH, 1999–2002. Hon. Mem. Council, NSPCC, 2006–; Pres., Contact a Family, 2007–; Patron: Childhood Bereavement Network, 2010–; Coram Life Educn, 2014–; Mosaic Bereavement Care, 2014–. Visiting Professor: Univ. of Ulm, FRG, 1986; Harvard Univ., 1987; Columbus Children's Hosp., Ohio State Univ., 1991; Vis. Paediatrician in Residence, Royal Children's Hosp., Univ. of Qld, 1989; Vis. Lectr, Children's Hosp., Camperdown, Sydney, 1992; Queen Elizabeth the Queen Mother Fellow, Nuffield Trust, 2004–05. Numerous lectures in Europe, USA and Australia including: Lockyer, RCP, 1988; Assoc. of Paediatric Anaesthetists of GB and Ire. (and Medal), 1990; Niilo Hallman, Univs of Helsinki and Tampere, Finland (and Medal), 1991; Killam, Killam Trusts, Canada, 2009. External Examiner in Paediatrics: Univ. of Malaya, 1990; Chinese Univ. of Hong Kong, 1994–98; Univ. of Kuwait, 1996. European Society for Paediatric Endocrinology: Sec., 1982–87; Pres., 1994–95; Pres., Assoc. of Clin. Profs of Paediatrics, 1999–2002. Hon. Lay Canon, Salisbury Cathedral, 2009–14, now Lay Canon Emeritus; Chair, Diocesan Bd of Educn, 2010–13. Founder FMedSci, 1998; Millennium Fellow, Paediatric Soc. NZ, 2000; FRSA 2010; Hon. FFPH 2007; Hon. Fellow, UNICEF UK, 2010. Hon. Member: Hungarian Paediatric Assoc., 1988 (Silver Medal, 2004); S African Paediatric Assoc., 1998; Finnish Paediatric Soc., 2006. Dr *hc* Pécs, 1998; Hon. DCL Northumbria, 2005; Hon. MD Liverpool, 2006; DUniv: Northampton, 2007; York, 2008; Hon. DEd Nottingham Trent, 2011. Andrea Prader Prize and Medal, 1991, (jtly) Henning Andersen Prize, 1999, European Soc. for Paediatric Endocrinology; Juvenile Justice Award, Internat. Juvenile Justice Observatory, 2010; James Spence Medal, RCPCH, 2013. *Publications:* papers and articles on children in society, child health and childhood, and scientifically on endocrinology and metabolism in infancy. *Recreations:* family, walking, music, photography. *E:* al@aynsley-green.com. *Club:* Athenæum.

AYOADE, Richard Ellef; comedian, actor, writer and director; *b* London, 23 May 1977; *s* of Layide and Dagny Ayoade; *m* Lydia; one *d*. *Educ:* St Joseph's Coll., Ipswich; St Catharine's Coll., Cambridge (BA Law 1998). Pres., Footlights, Cambridge Univ., 1997–98. Actor in TV series including: The Mighty Boosh, 2003–07; Garth Marenghi's Dark Place, 2004; The IT Crowd, 2006–11; Presenter, TV series: Gadget Man, 2013–; Travel Man, 2015– Director and writer of screenplay: Submarine, 2011; The Double, 2014; Dir, music videos for bands incl. Arctic Monkeys, Kasabian. *Publications:* (jtly) The Mighty Book of Boosh, 2008. *Address:* c/o PBJ Management, 22 Rathbone Street, W1T 1LG. *T:* (020) 7287 1112.

AYONG, Most Rev. James Simon; Primate of the Anglican Church of Papua New Guinea, 1996–2009; Bishop of Aipo Rongo, 1995–2009; *b* 3 Sept. 1944; *s* of Julius and Margaret Ayong; *m* 1967, Gawali Susuwa (*d* 2003); one *d*, and one adopted *s*. *Educ:* Martyrs' Sch.; Newton Theol Coll. (DipTh); Martin Luther Seminary (BTh). Govt Administrative Officer, 1964–71; Church Purchasing Officer and Radio Operator, 1976–79. Ordained deacon, 1982, priest, 1984; Asst Priest, Resurrection parish, Popondetta, 1985–86; Lectr, 1987–88, Principal, 1989–93, Newton Theol Coll.; locum at Burgess Hill, Sussex, UK, and student at Chichester Theol Coll., 1993–94; Parish Priest, Gerehu, Port Moresby, 1994–95. *Recreations:* reading, watching Rugby football. *Address:* Kumbun Village, PO Box 806, Kimbe, West New Britain, Papua New Guinea.

AYOUB, Fouad; Ambassador of the Hashemite Kingdom of Jordan to Canada, 2002–05; *b* 15 Aug. 1944; *m* 1974, Marie Vernazza; two *s* one *d*. *Educ:* California State Univ., San Francisco (BA; MA philosophy 1974). Press Secretary to King Hussein, 1977–91; Mem., Jordanian Delegn to Madrid Peace Conf., 1991; Ambassador of Jordan to UK, 1991–99, and (non-resident) to Iceland and Ireland, 1992–99; Ambassador of Jordan to Switzerland, 1999–2001. Fellow, Centre for Internat. Affairs, Harvard, 1983–84. Order of El Istiqlal (Jordan), 1991; numerous foreign orders. *Recreation:* reading.

AYRAULT, Jean-Marc Joseph Marcel; Prime Minister of France, 2012–14; *b* Maulévrier, France, 25 Jan. 1950; *s* of Joseph Ayrault and Georgette Ayrault (*née* Uzenot); *m* 1971, Brigitte Terrien; two *d*. *Educ:* Nantes Univ. (German degree; Teaching Cert.). German lang. teacher, Rezé, 1973–76, Saint-Herblain, 1976–86. Mem., Gen. Council, Loire-Atlantique, 1976–82; Mayor: Saint-Herblain, 1977–89; Nantes, 1989–2012; Chm., Dist of City of Nantes, 1992–2001; Pres., Nantes Métropole Urban Community, 2001–12. National Assembly: Mem. (Soc.) Loire-Atlantique, 1986–88, 3rd Dist, Loire-Atlantique, 1988–2012; Leader, Socialist Gp, 1997–2012. Mem., Steering Cttee, 1977–, Exec. Bd, 1979–, Socialist Party, France.

AYRE, Andrew; HM Diplomatic Service; High Commissioner to Guyana, and non-resident Ambassador to Suriname, 2011–15; *b* Bishop Auckland, 1966; *s* of Brian Ayre and Barbara Ayre; *m* 1990, Bettina Moosberger; one *s*. *Educ:* Douglas Ewart High Sch., Newton Stewart; King James I Comp. Sch., Bishop Auckland. Joined FCO, 1986; Accountant, Warsaw, 1988–89; Asst Mgt Officer, Rio de Janeiro, 1990–91; Travel Policy Officer, FCO, 1991–94; Entry Clearance Officer and Vice Consul, Nicosia, 1994–97; Entry Clearance Manager, Geneva, 1997; Second Secretary: Political, Tel Aviv, 1998–2001; EU, Vienna, 2001–06; Head: Arabian Peninsula Team, FCO, 2006–08; EU Budget and European Councils Team, FCO, 2009–11. *Recreations:* motorcycling, travelling, mountaineering, photography. *Address:* c/o Foreign and Commonwealth Office, King Charles Street, SW1A 2AH. *E:* andrew.ayre@fco.gov.uk, andrewayre@hotmail.co.uk.

AYRES, Andrew John William; QC 2015; *b* Bradford on Avon, 18 March 1971; *s* of Lt Col Brian William Ayres, MBE and late Margaret Elizabeth Ayres (*née* Moore); *m* 2000, Claire Alison Kavanaugh; two *s* one *d*. *Educ:* Eton Coll. (Oppidan Schol.); University Coll., Oxford (MA 1995); City Univ. (Dip. Law). Called to the Bar, Gray's Inn, 1996; in practice as barrister, specialising in commercial and chancery law, 1996–. Mem., Bar Council, 1999–2001. Asst Treas., S Eastern Circuit Bar Mess, 2003–06. Sec., Bar Boat Club, 1998–2003. *Recreations:* theatre, music, film, country pursuits. *Address:* Maitland Chambers, 7 Stone Buildings, Lincoln's Inn, WC2A 3SZ. *T:* (020) 7406 1200. *E:* aayres@maitlandchambers.com. *Club:* Ivy.

AYRES, Gillian, CBE 2011 (OBE 1986); RA; painter, artist; *b* 3 Feb. 1930; *d* of Stephen and Florence Ayres; *m* Henry Mundy (marr. diss.); two *s*. *Educ:* St Paul's Girls' Sch.; Camberwell Sch. of Art. Student, 1946–50; taught, 1959–81 (incl. Sen. Lectr, St Martin's Sch. of Art, and Head of Painting, Winchester Sch. of Art, 1978–81). ARA 1982, RA 1991–97 (resigned), rejoined 2000. One-woman Exhibitions include: Gallery One, 1956; Redfern Gall., 1958; Moulton Gall., 1960 and 1962; Kasmin Gall., 1965, 1966 and 1969; William Darby Gall., 1976; Women's Internat. Centre, New York, 1976; Knoedler Gall., 1979, 1982, 1987; Mus. of Mod. Art, Oxford, 1981; Alan Cristea Gall., 2007, 2015; retrospective exhibitions: Serpentine Gall., 1983; RA Sackler Gall., Yale British Art Center, and Iowa Mus., 1997; also exhibited: Redfern Gall., 1957; 1st Paris Biennale, 1959; Hayward Gall., 1971; Silver Jubilee Exhibn, RA, 1977; Knoedler Gall., NY, 1985; Tate Gall., 1995. Works in public collections: Tate Gall.; Mus. of Mod. Art, NY; Olinda Mus., Brazil; Gulbenkian Foundn, Lisbon; V&A Mus.; British Council. Hon. DLit London, 1994. Prize winner: Tokyo Biennale, 1963; John Moores Prize, 1982; Indian Triennale, Gold Medal, 1991. *Address:* c/o Alan Cristea Gallery, 31 Cork Street, W1S 3NU.

AYRES, Ian Leslie; Chief Officer, NHS West Kent Clinical Commissioning Group, since 2012; *b* 14 Nov. 1954; *s* of Dennis Albert Walter Ayres and Patience Ayres; *m* 1980, Catherine Tucker; two *s* one *d*. *Educ:* Univ. of Surrey (BSc Hons Psychol. and Philosophy); Univ. of Warwick (MBA). Pres., Univ. of Surrey Students' Union, 1976–77. BP Oil UK: Asst Manpower Planner, 1977–80; Business Controller, 1980–84; Sales Manager, 1984–88; Project Manager, Business Process Re-engrg, 1990–94; Project Manager, Queen Mary's Christian Care Foundn, 1994–95; National Health Service: Chief Executive Officer: SW London Total Purchasing Project, 1995–99; Nelson PCG, 1999–2000; Nelson and W Merton PCT, 2000–02; Sutton and Merton PCT, 2002–06; Hillingdon PCT, 2006; Mgt Consultant and Dir, Downsview Ltd, 2007; Associate Dir, BUPA Health Dialog, 2008–09; Dir, Strategy and Innovation, 2009–12, Dir, Commissioning Develt, 2012, NHS Norfolk. *Recreations:* church going, ski-ing, reading. *Address:* 3 Cornwall Road, Cheam, Surrey SM2 6DR. *T:* (020) 8296 8645. *E:* IanLAyres@aol.com.

AYRES, Pamela, (Mrs D. Russell), MBE 2004; writer, broadcaster and entertainer; *b* 14 March 1947; *d* of Stanley William Ayres and Phyllis Evelyn Loder; *m* 1982, Dudley Russell; two *s*. *Educ:* Stanford-in-the-Vale Village Primary Sch., Berks; Faringdon Secondary Modern Sch., Berks. Served WRAF, 1965–69. Writer and performer: *television:* début on Opportunity Knocks, 1975; The World of Pam Ayres (series), 1977; TV specials in UK, Hong Kong and Canada, 1978–79; *radio:* Pam Ayres Radio Show (series), 1995; presenter: Pam Ayres on Sunday, 1996–99; Pam Ayres' Open Road, 2000–01; Ayres on the Air (series), 2004, 2006, 2009, 2012, 2014; appeared in Royal Variety Show, Palladium, 1977; annual UK concert tours; regular concert tours in Australia and NZ; also perf. in Canada, France, Ireland, Hong Kong and Kenya. *Publications:* Some of Me Poetry, 1976; Some More of Me Poetry, 1976; Thoughts of a Late-Night Knitter, 1978; All Pam's Poems, 1978; The Ballad of Bill Spinks' Bedstead and Other Poems, 1981; Dear Mum, 1985; Pam Ayres: The Works, 1992, new edn as The Works: the classic collection, 2010; With These Hands, 1997; Surgically Enhanced, 2006; The Necessary Aptitude (autobiog.), 2011; You Made Me Late Again!, 2013; *for children:* Bertha and the Racing Pigeon, 1979; Guess Who?, 1987; Guess What?, 1987; When Dad Fills In The Garden Pond, 1988; When Dad Cuts Down The Chestnut Tree, 1988; Piggo and the Nosebag, 1990; Piggo has a Train Ride, 1990; Piggo and the Fork-lift Truck, 1991; The Bear Who Was Left Behind, 1991; Jack Crater, 1992; Guess Why?, 1994; Guess Where?, 1994; The Nubbler, 1997 (trans. Japanese 1999). *Recreations:* gardening, bee-keeping, drawing, wildlife. *Address:* PO Box 64, Cirencester, Glos GL7 5YD. *T:* (01285) 644622. *W:* www.pamayres.com.

AYRIS, Dr Paul; Director of UCL Library Services, University College London, since 1997; *b* 27 April 1957; *s* of Walter Roy Ayris and Irene Ayris (*née* Ball). *Educ:* Selwyn Coll., Cambridge (BA, MA); Gonville and Caius Coll., Cambridge (PhD 1984); Univ. of Sheffield (MA). Sir Henry Stephenson Fellow, Univ. of Sheffield, 1982–84; Cambridge University Library: Asst Librarian, Scientific Periodicals Liby, 1985–89; Automation Div., 1989–96; Hd, IT Services, 1994–96; Dep. Librarian, UCL, Jan.–Sept. 1997. Exec. Ed., Reformation & Renaissance Rev., 1999–2006. *Publications:* (ed with D. Selwyn) Thomas Cranmer, Churchman and Scholar, 1993, 2nd edn 1999. *Recreations:* ecclesiastical architecture, visiting foreign cities, classical music, sailing. *Address:* UCL Library Services, UCL, Gower Street, WC1E 6BT. *T:* (020) 7679 7834. *E:* p.ayris@ucl.ac.uk.

AYRTON, Norman Walter; international theatre and opera director; Dean, British American Drama Academy, London, 1986–96; *b* London, 25 Sept. 1924. Served War of 1939–45, RNVR. Trained as an actor at Old Vic Theatre School under Michael Saint Denis, 1947–48; joined Old Vic Company, 1948; repertory experience at Farnham and Oxford, 1949–50; on staff of Old Vic Sch., 1949–52; rejoined Old Vic Company for 1951 Festival Season; opened own teaching studio, 1952; began dramatic coaching for Royal Opera House, Covent Garden, 1953; apptd Asst Principal of London Academy of Music and Dramatic Art, 1954; taught at Shakespeare Festival, Stratford, Ont, and Royal Shakespeare Theatre, Stratford-upon-Avon, 1959–62; apptd GHQ Drama Adviser to Girl Guide Movement, 1960–74; Principal, LAMDA, 1966–72; Dean, World Shakespeare Study Centre, Bankside, 1972; Nat. Inst. of Dramatic Art, Sydney, 1973–76; Faculty, Juilliard Sch., NY, 1974–85; Dir of Opera, Royal Acad. of Music, 1986–90. *Director:* Artaxerxes, for Handel Opera Soc., Camden Festival, 1963; La Traviata, Covent Garden, 1963; Manon, Covent Garden, 1964; Sutherland-Williamson Grand Opera Season, in Australia, 1965; Twelfth Night at Dallas Theatre Center, Texas, 1967; The Way of the World, NY, 1976; Lakmé, Sydney Opera House, 1976; Der Rosenkavalier, Sydney Opera House, 1983; *Guest Director:* Australian Council for Arts, Sydney and Brisbane, 1973; Loeb Drama Center, Harvard (and teacher), 1974, 1976, 1978; Melbourne Theatre Co., 1974–; Vancouver Opera Assoc., 1975–83; Sydney Opera House, 1976–81, 1983; Williamstown Festival, USA, 1977; Hartford Stage Co. and Amer. Stage Fest., 1978–; Missouri Rep. Theatre, 1980–81; Nat. Opera Studio, London, 1980–81; Spoleto Fest., USA, 1984; Sarah Lawrence Coll., NY, 1993, 1997, 2001; Utah Shakespeare Fest., 1994; BADA Midsummer Conservatory, Oxford, 2006–13; *Resident Stage Director:* Amer. Opera Center, NY, 1981–85; Vassar Coll., NY, 1990–2001; Cornell Univ., 1995, 1998; Florida State Univ., 1997–; Asolo Theatre, Sarasota, 2002. Hon. RAM 1989; Hon. Fellow, LAMDA, 2008. *Recreations:* reading, music, gardens, travel. *Address:* 40A Birchington Road, NW6 4LJ.

AZA, Alberto; Head of the Royal Household, Spain, 2002–11; *b* 22 May 1937; *s* of Alberto Aza and Marcela Arias; *m* 1963, María Eulalia Custodio Martí; two *s* four *d*. *Educ:* Univ. de Oviedo; Law Faculty of Madrid (Law Degree); BA, BSc. Joined Diplomatic Service, 1965; served Libreville, Algiers, Rome, Madrid; Dir, Cabinet of the Spanish Prime Minister, 1977–83; Chief Dir, OAS, Latin-America Dept, Min. of Foreign Affairs, 1983; Minister Counsellor, Lisbon, 1983–85; Ambassador: to OAS, Washington, 1985–89; to Belize (resident in Washington), 1985–89; to Mexico, 1990–92; to UK, 1992–99; Dir, Office of Diplomatic Inf., 1999–2002; Sec. Gen., Royal Household, Spain, 2002. Permanent Dir, Consejo de Estado, 2012–. Hon. DLitt Portsmouth, 1997. Gran Cruz del Mérito Civil (Spain), 1979; Gran Cruz del Mérito Naval (Spain), 1996. *Recreations:* fishing, golf, walking. *Address:* Consejo de Estado, C/ Mayor 79, 28013 Madrid, Spain. *Clubs:* Puerta de Hierro, Nuevo (Madrid).

AZAPAGIC, Prof. Adisa, PhD; FREng, FIChemE, FRSC; Professor of Sustainable Chemical Engineering, University of Manchester, since 2006; *b* Tuzla, Bosnia and Herzegovina, 10 April 1961; *d* of Bahrija Azapagic and Iza Balic; *m* 1992, Dr Slobodan Perdan. *Educ:* Gymnasium, Tuzla; Univ. of Tuzla (Dip. Ing. 1984; MSc 1987); Univ. of Surrey (PhD 1997). CEng 2000; CSci 2000; FIChemE 2000; FRSC 2000; FREng 2013. Teaching and Res. Asst, Univ. of Tuzla, 1985–92; British Council Fellow, Univ. of Leeds, 1992–93; University of Surrey: Res. Asst, 1993–97; Lectr, 1996–2000; Reader, 2000–04; Prof., 2004–06; Dir of Res., Sch. of Chem. Engrg and Analytical Sci., Univ. of Manchester, 2006–09. Dir, Industrial Ecology Solutions Ltd, 2001–07. Deutscher Akademischer Austausch Dienst Sen. Scholar, 2001; Vis. Scientist, German Aerospace Agency, 2002; RAEng Industrial Secondment, WBB Minerals, 2002; RAEng Schol., 2002, Leverhulme Trust Vis. Schol., 2002, Univ. of Sydney; UNESCO/ICSU/Third World Acad. of Sci. Vis. Prof., ITAM, Mexico City, 2003; Erskine Fellow, Univ. of Canterbury, Christchurch, 2006; Vis. Prof., Technical Univ. of Dresden, 2013. Member: Strategic Adv. Cttee for Energy, UK Res.

Councils, 2005–10; UK Commonwealth Scholarships Adv. Panel, 2009–; UK REF panel for Aeronaut., Mech., Chem. and Manufg Engrg, 2011–14; Manufg Commn, 2014–. Member: Internat. Adv. Panel, Helmholtz Assoc., 2009–; Nat. Scientific Qualification Cttee for Commodity Sci., Italy, 2012–; Chm., Sustainability Section, Eur. Fedn of Chem. Engrg, 2013–. Fellow, Japanese Soc. for Promotion of Sci., 2012. Editor-in-Chief: (Envmt), Process Safety and Envmtl Protection, 2013–; Sustainable Prodn and Consumption, 2014–. Hon. FSE 2012. FRSA. Hon. Dr Envmtl Engrg Technical Univ., Iaşi, 2014. *Publications:* Polymers, the Environment and Sustainable Development, 2003 (trans. Chinese, 2005); Sustainable Development in Practice: case studies for engineers and scientists, 2004, 2nd edn 2011; papers on life cycle assessment, industrial sustainability and policy. *Recreations:* hiking, cross-country ski-ing, writing, leading even when I don't know where I'm going (and trying to find my way afterwards). *Address:* University of Manchester, The Mill, Sackville Street, Manchester M13 9PL. *T:* (0161) 306 4363. *E:* adisa.azapagic@manchester.ac.uk.

AZIZ, Mohammed Abdul; Director, Centre for Policy and Public Education, Woolf Institute, Cambridge, since 2012; *b* 28 Feb. 1971; *s* of Moinul Islam and Sundora Khatun; *m* 1998, Duaa Izzidien; two *s* one *d. Educ:* UCL (LLB Hons (Law), LLM (Jurisprudence and Human Rights Law)). Called to the Bar, Gray's Inn, 1997. London Borough of Tower Hamlets: Policy Officer, 1997–2000; Lawyer, 1998–99; Chief Executive Officer: Forum Against Islamophobia and Racism, 2000–02; British Muslim Res. Centre, 2002–04. Dir, FaithWise Ltd, 2003–11. Mem., Treasury Counsel Rev. Team, 2005; Advr on Religion and Belief Equality, DTI, 2004–07; Sen. Advr on Race, Religion and Community Cohesion, DCLG, 2007–11. Vis. Fellow, Univ. of Cambridge, 2011–12; Res. Associate, Centre of Islamic Studies, Univ. of Cambridge, 2012–; Associate Mem., St Edmund's Coll., Cambridge, 2013–; Nohoudh Scholar, Sch. of Law, SOAS, 2012–. Member: CRE, 2003–07; EOC, 2005–07; TUC Commn on Vulnerable Employment, 2006–08; Commission for Equality and Human Rights: Member: Govt Task Force, 2003–04; Govt Steering Gp, 2004–06; Equalities Reference Gp, 2005–07. Member: Mgt Cttee, UK Race & Europe Network, 2003–; Bd, European Network Against Racism, 2004–10 (Chm., 2007–10); Council, Liberty, 2004–08. Mem., Honours Cttees for State and Community, Voluntary and Local Service, 2005–10. Founder Mem., Equality and Diversity Forum, 2002– (Trustee, 2010–; Vice Chm., 2011–). Trustee: E London Mosque and London Muslim Centre, 1992–2013; Book Foundn, 2000–. *Recreations:* swimming, gardening, travelling. *T:* (01322) 408220. *E:* maziz@faithwise.co.uk, maa74@cam.ac.uk.

AZIZ, Shaukat; Member for Attock, National Assembly, Pakistan, 2004–07; Prime Minister of Pakistan, 2004–07, and Minister of Finance, 1999–2007; *b* 6 March 1949; *m*; three *c. Educ:* Gordon Coll., Rawalpindi (BSc 1967); Univ. of Karachi (MBA 1969). With Citibank, 1969–99, posts included: Hd of Corporate and Investment Banking for Asia Pacific Reg., then for Central and Eastern Europe; ME and Africa Corporate Planning Officer, Citicorp; Man. Dir, Saudi American Bank; Global Hd, Private Banking, Citigroup; Vice-Pres., 1992. Senator, Pakistan, 2002. Ind. non-exec. Dir, Millennium & Copthorne Hotels plc, 2009–; former Mem., Internat. Adv. Bd, Blackstone Gp.

AZIZ, Suhail Ibne; international management consultant, since 1981; Chairman and Managing Director, Brettonwood Partnership Ltd, since 1990; *b* Bangladesh (then India), 3 Oct. 1937; permanently resident in England, since 1966; *s* of Azizur Rahman and Lutfunnessa Khatoon; *m* 1960, Elizabeth Ann Pyne, Dartmouth, Devon; two *d. Educ:* Govt High Sec. Sch., Sylhet; Murarichand Coll., Dacca Univ., Sylhet (Intermed. in Science, 1954); Jt Services Pre-Cadet Trng Sch., Quetta; Cadet Trng Sch., PNS Himalaya, Karachi; BRNC, Dartmouth (Actg Sub-Lieut 1958); (mature student) Kingston upon Thames Polytechnic and Trent Polytech., Nottingham (Dipl. in Mgt Studies, 1970); (ext. student) London Univ. (BScEcon Hons 1972); (internal student) Birkbeck Coll., London Univ., (MScEcon 1976); Michigan Business Sch., USA (mgt courses, 1992). FCMI (FIMgt 1981); FIMC 1991; CMC 1994. Sub-Lieut and Lieut, Pakistan Navy Destroyers/Mine Sweeper (Exec. Br.), 1954–61. Personnel and indust. relations: Unilever (Pakistan); Royal Air Force; Commn on Indust. Relations, London; Ford Motor Co. (GB); Mars Ltd, 1963–78; Dir of Gen. Services Div., CRE, 1978–81; Dep. Dir of Econ. Develt, London Borough of Lewisham, 1984–89; Management Consultant, Fullemploy Consultancy Ltd, 1989–90; Mem. Exec. Sub-Cttee, and Bd Mem., Tower Hamlets, Education Business Partnership, 1993–2009. Mem., London Electricity Consumer Cttee, 1991–95. Chairman: Lambeth Healthcare NHS Trust, 1998–99; S London Community Health NHS Trust, 1999–2000; London Probation Bd, Nat. Probation Service, 2001–07. Leading Mem., Bangladesh Movement in UK, 1971. Member: Exec., Standing Conf. of Asian Orgs in UK, 1972–90; N Metropol. Conciliation Cttee, Race Relations Bd, 1971–74; Exec., Post Conf. Constituent Cttee, Black People in Britain - the Way Forward, 1975–76; Adv. Cttee to Gulbenkian Foundn on Area Resource Centre and Community Support Forum, 1976–81; Exec., Nottingham and Dist Community Relations Council, 1975–78; Dept of Employment Race Relations Employment Adv. Gp, 1977–78; BBC Asian programme Adv. Cttee, 1977–81; Industrial Tribunals, 1977–95; Exec., Nat. Org. of African, Asian and Caribbean Peoples, 1976–77; Home Sec.'s Standing Adv. Council on Race Relations, 1976–78; Steering Cttee, Asian Support Forum, 1984–86; Steering Cttee, Develt Policy Forum, DFID, 1998–2000; Jt Consultative Cttee with Ethnic Minorities, Merton BC, 1985–87; Plunkett Foundn for Co-operative Studies, 1985–97; "One World", 1986–90; Adv. Gp, City of London Polytechnic Ethnic Minority Business Develt Unit, 1987–94; Res. Adv. Bd, QMW, London Univ., 1988–99; (co-opted), Exec. Cttee, Tower Hamlets Assoc. for Racial Equality, 1988–91 (Mem., Action Tower Hamlets, 1987); Bangladeshis in Britain - a Response Forum, 1987–89; Tower Hamlets Consortium, 1994–97; Exec. Mem. and Trustee, Docklands Forum, 1991–99; Chairman: Jalalabad Overseas Orgn in UK, 1983–; London Boroughs Bangladesh Assoc., 1984–; Founder Chm., East London Bangladeshi Enterprise Agency, 1985–. CRE Bursary to study Minority Business Develt initiatives in USA, 1986. Mem., Labour Econ. Finance Taxation Assoc., 1973–80; Institute of Management Consultants: Chm., Third World Specialist Gp, 1984–92; Mem. Council, 1995–. Jt Trustee, United Action-Bangladesh Relief Fund, 1971–90; Trustee: Brixton Neighbourhood Assoc., 1979–82; Trust for Educn and Develt, 1992–2004; Community Develt Foundn, 1999–2008; pact (Prison Advice & Care Trust), 2007–13; Advr and Trustee, SE London Community Foundn, 1996–2010. Comr, Commonwealth Scholarship Commn, 1996–2002. Governor: London Guildhall Univ., 1995–2003; Lambeth Coll., 1999–2011. Deeply interested in community and race relations and believes profoundly that future health of Brit. society depends on achieving good race relations. *Recreations:* travelling, seeing places of historical interest, meeting people, reading (e.g. political economy). *Club:* Royal Air Force.

AZNAR LÓPEZ, José María; Prime Minister of Spain, 1996–2004; Distinguished Scholar in the Practice of Global Leadership, Georgetown University, USA, 2004–11; *b* Madrid, 1953; *m* 1977, Ana Botella; two *s* one *d. Educ:* Univ. Complutense, Madrid (LLB). Tax Inspector, 1976. Mem., Cortes, 1982–2004; Chief Exec., Castile-León Reg.; Premier, Castilla y León Autonomous Reg., 1987. Joined Alianza Popular, later Partido Popular, 1978: Dep. Sec. Gen., 1982; Pres., 1990–2004; Vice-Pres., European Popular Party, 1993. Dir, News Corp., 2006–. Pres., Fundación para el Análisis y los Estudios Sociales, Madrid. *Publications:* Libertad y solidaridad, 1991; España: la segunda transición, 1994; La España en que yo creo, 1995; Ocho años de Gobierno, 2004; Retratos y Perfiles: de Fraga a Bush, 2005. *Recreations:* reading, sports, music.

B

BABINGTON, Roger Vincent, FREng; FRINA; Director General Ships and Chief Executive, Ships Support Agency, Ministry of Defence, 1996–97; *b* 6 April 1943; *s* of late George Cyril Babington and Rita Mary Babington (*née* Simpkins); *m* 1967, Susan Wendy Eaton; two *s* two *d*. *Educ:* King Edward's Sch., Bath; Univ. of Birmingham (BSc); University Coll. London (MSc). RCNC. Asst Constructor, MoD, 1965–73; Constructor, MoD, Bath, 1973–76; Naval Constructor Overseer, MoD, Barrow-in-Furness, 1976–81; HM Dockyard, Rosyth: Constructor, 1981–82; Chief Constructor, 1982–86; Dir of Progs and Planning, 1986–87; Ministry of Defence, Bath: Dir, Surface Ships D, 1987–89; Dir, SSN20, 1989–91; Dir, Submarines, 1991–93; Dir-Gen., Ship Refitting, 1993; Dir-Gen., Fleet Support (Ships), 1993–95; Dir-Gen. Ships, 1995–96; Managing Director: BMT Marine Procurement Ltd, 1998–99; BMT Defence Services Ltd, 1999–2001. FREng (FEng 1995). *Recreations:* badminton, golf, house, garden and vehicle maintenance, watching sport, listening. *Address:* Shoscombe Lodge, Shoscombe, Bath BA2 8LU. *T:* and *Fax:* (01761) 432436.

BABINGTON-BROWNE, Gillian Brenda, (Mrs K. J. Wilson); a District Judge (Magistrates' Courts) (formerly Metropolitan Stipendiary Magistrate), 1991–2008; *b* 20 May 1949; *d* of Derek Keith Babington-Browne and Olive Maude (*née* Seymour); *m* 1983, Kenneth John Wilson. *Educ:* Rochester Girls' Grammar Sch.; Coll. of Law, London. Admitted Solicitor, 1973; Asst Solicitor with Arnold, Tuff & Grimwade, Rochester, 1973–74; Assistant with Ronald A. Prior, 1974, with Edward Lewis Possart, London, 1974–78; own practice, 1978–89; freelance advocate and consultant, 1989–91. Hon. Mem., London Criminal Courts Solicitors' Assoc. (Pres., 1990–91; Associate Mem., 1991–). *Publications:* contribs to legal jls. *Recreations:* gardening, interior design/decorating, reading.

BACH, family name of **Baron Bach**.

BACH, Baron *cr* 1998 (Life Peer), of Lutterworth in the co. of Leicestershire; **William Stephen Goulden Bach;** *b* 25 Dec. 1946; *s* of late Stephen Craine Goulden Bach, CBE and Joan Bach; *m* 1984, Caroline Jones, *er d* of Eric and Cynthia Smeaton; one *d*, and one *s* one *d* from former marriage. *Educ:* Westminster Sch.; New Coll., Oxford (BA). Called to the Bar, Middle Temple, 1972; Midland and Oxford Circuit; Hd of Chambers. Member (Lab): Leicester City Council, 1976–87; Harborough DC, 1995–99; Mayor, Lutterworth, 1993–94. Labour Party: Treas., Leics W Const., 1974–87; Chm., Harborough Dist, 1989–95; Chm., Northants and Blaby Euro. Const., 1992–99. Member: Lab Party Econ. Commn, 1998–99; Lab Party Nat. Policy Forum, 1998–99. Government spokesman: Home Office, DfEE, LCD, 1999–2000; FCO, BIS (formerly BERR), MoJ, 2007–10; a Lord in Waiting (Govt Whip), 1999–2000, 2007–09; Parly Sec., LCD, 2000–01; Parliamentary Under-Secretary of State: MoD, 2001–05; DEFRA, 2005–06; MoJ, 2008–10; an Opposition spokesman for Justice, 2010–12, for Foreign Affairs, 2013–; Shadow Attorney Gen., 2014–. Contested (Lab): Gainsborough, 1979; Sherwood, 1983 and 1987. Mem. Court, Leicester Univ., 1980–99. Trustee, LawWorks. Patron, Coventry Law Centre. *Recreations:* playing and watching football and cricket, Leicester City FC supporter, music, reading hard-boiled American crime fiction. *Address:* House of Lords, SW1A 0PW.

See also J. N. Allan.

BACHE, Andrew Philip Foley, CMG 1992; HM Diplomatic Service, retired; Ambassador to Denmark, 1996–99; *b* 29 Dec. 1939; *s* of late Robert Philip Sidney Bache, OBE and Jessie Bache; *m* 1963, Shân Headley; two *s* one *d*. *Educ:* Shrewsbury Sch.; Emmanuel Coll., Cambridge (MA). Joined HM Diplomatic Service, 1963; 3rd Sec., Nicosia, 1964–66; Treasury Centre for Admin. Studies, 1966; 2nd Sec., Sofia, 1966–68; FCO, 1968–71; 1st Sec., Lagos, 1971–74; FCO, 1974–78; 1st Sec. (Commercial), Vienna, 1978–81; Counsellor and Head of Chancery, Tokyo, 1981–85; Counsellor and Dep. Hd of Mission, Ankara, 1985–87; Hd of Personnel Services Dept, FCO, 1988–90; on secondment as Diplomatic Service Chm. to CSSB, 1990–91; Ambassador, Romania, 1992–96. Chief Exec., Westminster Foundn for Democracy, 2001–02. Chm., Hospices of Hope (formerly Hospices of Hope Romania Trust), 2000–12. Conseiller, Chief Pleas, Sark, 2010–14. JP West London, 2001–09. Dr *hc*: Technical Univ., Cluj, 1994; Sibiu Univ., 1995. *Recreations:* diverse, including travel, history, ornithology, fine arts, tennis, cricket, Real tennis. *Clubs:* Oxford and Cambridge, MCC.

BACHER, Dr Aron, (Ali); Chairman, Right to Care, since 2008; *b* 24 May 1942; *s* of Rose and Koppel Bacher; *m* 1965, Shira Ruth Teeger; one *s* two *d*. *Educ:* Yeoville Boys' Primary Sch.; King Edward VII High Sch.; Witwatersrand Univ. (MB BCh). Junior appts, Baragwanath and Natalspruit Hosps, 1968–69; private practice, Rosebank, Johannesburg, 1970–79. Managing Director: Delta Distributors, 1979–81; Transvaal Cricket Council, 1981–86; South African Cricket Union, 1986–91; United Cricket Bd of S Africa, 1991–2000; Executive Director: 2003 ICC Cricket World Cup, 2001–03; Wits Foundn, 2003–06. Chairman: Stella Vista, 2007–09; Seniors' Finance, 2007–10. International Cricket Council: Mem. Exec. Bd, 1997–2000; Chm., Internat. Develt Cttee, 1996–2000. Cricket début for Transvaal, 1959–60; captained S Africa, 1970; played 12 Test matches, made 120 1st cl. appearances, 7,894 runs, 18 centuries, 110 catches, one stumping; retired, 1974; Transvaal and Nat. Selectors' Panels, 1976–83; Dir, S African Cricket Develt Club, 1986. Chm., Alexander Forbes Community Trust, 2012–. Numerous awards include: Jack Cheetham Meml, 1990, for doing the most to normalise sport in S Africa; Laureate Award for Social Architecture, Da Vinci Inst., 2013. *Recreation:* jogging. *Address:* PO Box 55041, Northlands 2116, South Africa. *T:* (home) (11) 7831263.

BACK, Kenneth John Campbell, AO 1984; MSc, PhD; higher education consultant; *b* 13 Aug. 1925; *s* of J. L. Back; *m* 1950, Patricia, *d* of R. O. Cummings; two *d*. *Educ:* Sydney High Sch.; Sydney Univ. (MSc); Univ. of Queensland (PhD). Res. Bacteriologist, Davis Gelatine (Aust.) Pty Ltd, 1947–49; Queensland University: Lectr in Bacteriology, 1950–56; Sen. Lectr in Microbiology, 1957–61; Actg Prof. of Microbiology, 1962; Warden, University Coll. of Townsville, Queensland, 1963–70; Vice-Chancellor, James Cook Univ. of N Queensland, 1970–85, Prof. Emeritus, 1986–; Exec. Dir, Internat. Develt Program of Australian Univs and Colls Ltd, 1986–90. Vis. Fellow, ANU, 1996–2000. Chm., Standing Cttee, Australian Univs Internat. Develt Prog. (formerly Australian-Asian Univs Co-operation Scheme), 1977–85. Hon. DSc: Queensland, 1982; James Cook, 1995; DUniv: South Pacific, 1992; Nat. Univ. of Samoa, 1998. *Publications:* papers on microbiological metabolism, international education. *Recreations:* bridge, croquet. *Address:* 205/36 Bunker Road, Victoria Point, Qld 4165, Australia.

BACK, Philippa Lucy F.; *see* Foster Back.

BACKHOUSE, Sir Alfred (James Stott), 5th Bt *cr* 1901; *b* 7 April 2002; *s* of Sir Jonathan Roger Backhouse, 4th Bt and of Sarah Ann, *o d* of J. A. Stott; S father, 2007.

BACKHOUSE, David, FRBS, RWA; sculptor; *b* 5 May 1941; *s* of late Joseph and Jessie Backhouse; *m* 1975, Sarah Barber; one *s* two *d*. *Educ:* Lord Weymouth Sch.; W of England Coll. of Art. RWA 1978; FRBS 1983. Numerous one-man exhibns, London and NY; public sculptures include: Meml to Merchant Seamen, Bristol, 2001; Animals in War Meml, London, 2004; sculptures in public and private collections internationally. *Recreation:* habitat improvement. *Address:* Silenus, 8 Bishop Ken Close, Wells, Som BA5 3ND. *E:* db@backhousesculptures.com.

BACKHOUSE, David Miles; Chairman: South Farm Products Ltd, since 1964; Leo Consult Ltd, since 1986; *b* 30 Jan. 1939; *s* of late Jonathan Backhouse and Alice Joan (*née* Woodroffe); *m* 1969, Sophia Ann (*née* Townsend); one *s* one *d*. *Educ:* Summer Fields, Oxford; Eton Coll. Commenced career in banking with Schroders PLC, 1966; Chief Exec. Officer, Dunbar Gp, 1973–84; Chm., Henderson Admin Gp, 1990–92; Chm., Johnson Fry Hldgs, 1995–2000. Non-executive Director: Hambro Life Assce, 1982–84; TSB Group, 1985–92; Witan Investment Company, 1985–92; Royal Agricl Coll., 1987–2005. *Recreations:* tennis, riding. *Address:* South Farm House, Hatherop, Glos GL7 3PN. *T:* (01285) 712225.

BACKHOUSE, Roger Bainbridge; QC 1984; *b* 8 March 1938; *s* of late Leslie Bainbridge Backhouse and of Jean Backhouse; *m* 1962, Elizabeth Constance, *d* of Comdr J. A. Lowe, DSO, DSC; two *s* one *d*. *Educ:* Liverpool Coll.; Trinity Hall, Cambridge (History Tripos parts I & II). Nat. Service, RAF, 1956–58 (Pilot Officer). Worked in family business, 1961–62; Schoolmaster, 1962–64; called to the Bar, Middle Temple, 1965. *Recreations:* opera, military history, travel. *Address:* 14 Parchment Street, Winchester, Hants SO23 8AZ. *T:* (01962) 863053. *Clubs:* Royal Air Force; Hockley Golf.

BACKHOUSE, Prof. Roger Edward, PhD; FBA 2014; Professor of the History and Philosophy of Economics, University of Birmingham, since 1996; *b* 19 Jan. 1951; *s* of Edward Backhouse and Mary Backhouse (*née* Pillow); *m* 1980, Merida Jane Lee (*d* 1989); one *s* one *d*; *m* 2004, Ann Elizabeth Barnfield. *Educ:* Friends' Sch., Saffron Walden; Univ. of Bristol (BSc Econs and Econ. Hist. 1972); Univ. of Birmingham (PhD Econs 1977). Temp. Lectr in Econs, UCL, 1975–77; Lectr in Econs, Univ. of Keele, 1977–79; University of Birmingham: Lectr in Econs, 1980–89; Sen. Lectr, 1989–92; Reader, 1992–96. British Acad. Res. Reader, 1998–2000; Ludwig Lachman Res. Fellow, LSE, 2006–07; Leverhulme Trust Maj. Res. Fellow, 2011–14. Vis. Lectr, UCL, 1977–79; Vis. Lectr, then Vis. Prof., Univ. of Buckingham, 1992–2006; Vis. Prof., Univ. of Oporto, 1999–; Prof. of Hist. and Philosophy of Econs (pt-time), Erasmus Univ., Rotterdam, 2009–. *Publications:* Macroeconomics and the British Economy, 1983; A History of Modern Economic Analysis, 1985 (Spanish edn, 1988; Italian edn, 1990); Economists and the Economy, 1988, 2nd edn 1994 (Japanese edn); Applied UK Macroeconomics, 1991; (ed jtly) Economics and Language, 1993; Interpreting Macroeconomics: explorations in the history of macroeconomic thought, 1995; Truth and Progress in Economic Knowledge, 1997; (ed jtly) Economics and Methodology: crossing boundaries, 1997; Explorations in Economic Methodology: from Lakatos to empirical philosophy of science, 1998; (ed) Keynes: contemporary responses to the general theory, 1999; (ed with J. Creedy) From Classical Economics to the Theory of the Firm: essays in honour of D. P. O'Brien, 1999; (ed with R. Middleton) Exemplary Economists, 2 vols, 2000; (ed with A. Salanti) Macroeconomics and the Real World, 2 vols, 2000; (ed with J. Biddle) Toward a History of Applied Economics, 2000; The Ordinary Business of Life: a history of economics from ancient times to the Twenty-First Century, 2002; The Penguin History of Economics, 2002; (ed with B. W. Bateman) The Cambridge Companion to Keynes, 2006; (ed with T. Nishizawa) No Wealth but Life: welfare economics and the welfare state in Britain, 1800–1945, 2010; (ed with P. Fontaine) The History of the Social Sciences since 1945, 2010; (ed with P. Fontaine) The Unsocial Social Science? Economics and Neighbouring Disciplines since 1945, 2010; (with B. W. Bateman) Keynes: capitalist revolutionary, 2011; (with M. Boianovsky) Transforming Modern Macroeconomics: the search for disequilibrium microfoundations, 1956–2003, 2013; (ed with P. Fontaine) A Historiography of Modern Social Science, 2014. *Address:* Department of Economics, University of Birmingham, Edgbaston, Birmingham B15 2TT. *E:* R.E.Backhouse@bham.ac.uk.

BACKLER, Dr Gary George; strategy and management consultant; owner, Backler Consulting Ltd, since 2011; Visiting Research Fellow, Institute for Transport Studies, University of Leeds, since 2011; *b* 19 July 1955; *s* of Robert and Barbara Backler; *m* 1990, Elizabeth Ann Edes; two *d*. *Educ:* Merton Coll., Oxford (MA Modern Hist.); Univ. of BC (MSc Commerce & Business Admin); Leeds Univ. (PhD Econ. Studies 1987). Traffic mgt trainee, British Rail, 1976–78; res. asst, Centre for Transportation Studies, Vancouver, 1978–81; Sen. Associate, Booz, Allen & Hamilton, 1985–90; Supervising Consultant, Price Waterhouse, 1990–94; Asst Dir, Office of Passenger Rail Franchising, 1994–98; Dir, Franchise Mgt, Shadow Strategic Rail Authy, 1998–2000; Exec. Dir, Regl Networks, 2000–02, Franchise Dir, N & W, 2002–05, Strategic Rail Authy; Dir, Rail Service Delivery, DfT, 2005–10. Trustee, 2011–, Planning Dir, 2013–, Friends of River Crane Envmt. *Publications:* contribs to logistics jls. *Recreations:* gym, Brentford FC, various charities. *E:* ggbackler@hotmail.co.uk.

BACKUS, Rear Adm. Alexander Kirkwood, CB 2003; OBE 1989; Chief of Staff (Warfare) and Rear Admiral Surface Ships, 2002–03; *b* 1 April 1948; *s* of late Jake Kirkwood Backus and Jean Backus (*née* Stobie); *m* 1971, Margaret Joan Pocock; two *s* one *d*. *Educ:* Sevenoaks Sch., Kent; BRNC, Dartmouth. Joined RN, 1966; served HM Ships Fiskerton, Intrepid, Eastbourne, Cavalier, Bacchante, Blake, Arrow, Cleopatra, and Torquay, 1967–84; CO, Arethusa, 1984; JSDC Greenwich, 1986; Comdr Sea Training, 1988; Capt. 6th Frigate

Sqn, HMS Hermione, 1990; Comdr British Forces Falkland Islands, 1995–96; ACOS (Policy) to C-in-C Fleet, 1996–99; Flag Officer Sea Trng, 1999–2001; Flag Officer Surface Flotilla, 2001–02. Hon. Pres., Devon Rural Skills Trust, 2014 (Chm., 2002–12). Silver Jubilee Medal, 1977; Golden Jubilee Medal, 2002. *Recreations:* ornithology, photography. *Clubs:* Royal Naval (Argyll); Western Isles Yacht.

BACON, Gareth Andrew; Member (C) London Assembly, Greater London Authority, since 2008; *b* Hong Kong, 7 April 1972; *s* of Robert and Helen Bacon; *m* 2004, Cheryl Cooley; one *d.* *Educ:* Univ. of Kent, Canterbury (BA Hons Pols and Govt 1996; MA Eur. Pols 1997). Mem. (C), Bexley LBC, 1998– (Dep. Mayor, 2001–02; Cabinet Mem. for Envmt, 2006–14, for Finance and Corp. Services, 2014–15). Contested (C) Greenwich and Lewisham, GLA, 2004. Cons. spokesman on envmt, 2008–10, on budget, 2010–, GLA; Mem., London Fire and Emergency Planning Authy, 2010– (Chm., 2015–). Hd, public sector div., Randstad Financial & Professional (formerly Martin Ward Anderson), 2004–12. *Recreations:* former Rugby player, current squash player, season ticket holder at Manchester United Football Club. *Address:* Greater London Authority, City Hall, The Queen's Walk, SE1 2AA. *T:* (020) 7983 5784. *E:* gareth.bacon@london.gov.uk.

BACON, Jennifer Helen, CB 1995; Director-General, Health and Safety Executive, 1995–2000; *b* 16 April 1945; *d* of Dr Lionel James Bacon and Joyce Bacon (*née* Chapman). *Educ:* Bedales Sch., Petersfield; New Hall, Cambridge (BA Hons 1st cl.; Hon. Fellow, 1997). Joined Civil Service as Asst Principal, Min. of Labour, 1967; Private Sec. to Minister of State for Employment, 1971–72; Principal, 1972–78, worked on health and safety and industrial relations legislation; Principal Private Sec. to Sec. of State for Employment, 1977–78; Asst Sec., Controller of Trng Services, MSC, 1978–80; sabbatical, travelling in Latin America, 1980–81; Asst Sec., Machinery of Govt Div., CSD, later MPO, 1981–82; Under Sec., Dir of Adult (formerly Occupational) Trng, MSC, 1982–86; Under Sec., School Curriculum and Exams, DES, 1986–89; Department of Employment: Prin. Finance Officer (Grade 3), 1989–91; Dir of Resources and Strategy (Grade 2), 1991–92; Dep. Dir-Gen. (Policy), HSE, 1992–95; Head, Animal, Health and Envmt Directorate, MAFF, then DEFRA, 2000–01. Mem., External Review Gp, Water UK, 2004–09. Mem., Adv. Cttee on Degree Awarding Powers, QAA, 1998–2004. Mem. Bd, Sheffield Develt Corp., 1992–95. Vis. Fellow, Nuffield Coll., Oxford, 1989–97. Gov., Bedales Sch., 2002–05. Hon. DSc Aston, 2000. *Recreations:* classical music especially opera, travelling, walking.

BACON, John William, CB 2006; FCCA; Chairman, Community Health Partnerships Ltd, since 2011; *b* 1 Nov. 1950; *s* of late William Bacon and Joy Bacon; *m* 1975, Margaret Clapson; one *d.* *Educ:* Cambridgeshire High Sch.; Univ. of Kent (BA). FCCA 1975. UKAEA, 1972–83: Chief Finance Officer, Culham Lab., 1979–82; Head of Finance, Harwell Lab., 1983; NHS, 1983–94; Department of Health: Dir of Finance and Performance, London Reg., 1995–2000; Dir, Health and Social Care, London, 2000–03; Dir of Service Delivery, 2003–05. Healthcare Consultant, Health Works, 2006–09; Associate Consultant, Grant Thornton Internat., 2007–09; Associate, KPMG Global Health Practice, 2011–. Chm., Sussex Partnership NHS Foundn Trust, 2008–15. Sec., London Old Tablers Soc., 2007–09. *Address:* 3 Ventnor Villas, Hove BN3 3DD.

BACON, Kelyn Meher; *see* Bacon Darwin, K. M.

BACON, Maureen Anne; QC 2009; **Her Honour Judge Bacon;** a Circuit Judge, since 2015; *b* London, 8 Jan. 1954; *d* of Stanley Clarke Bacon and Violet Bacon. *Educ:* George Farmer Sch., Holbeach, Lincs; De Montfort Univ. (BA Hons Law 1983); Inns of Court Sch. of Law 1984. NHS Adminr, 1971–80; called to the Bar, Gray's Inn, 1984; a Recorder, 2001–15; a Judge, Mental Health Tribunal (Restricted Patients Panel), 2012–. *Recreations:* jazz, cinema, cooking, travel, the pursuit of all things stylish. *Address:* Norwich Crown Court, The Law Courts, Bishopsgate, Norwich NR3 1UR.

BACON, Sir Nicholas (Hickman Ponsonby), 14th Bt of Redgrave, *cr* 1611, and 15th Bt of Mildenhall, *cr* 1627; OBE 2010; Premier Baronet of England; DL; Lord Warden of the Stannaries and Keeper of the Privy Seal, Duchy of Cornwall, since 2006; *b* 17 May 1953; *s* of Sir Edmund Castell Bacon, 13th and 14th Bt, KG, KBE, TD and Priscilla Dora, *d* of Col Sir Charles Edward Ponsonby, 1st Bt, TD; *S* father, 1982; *m* 1981, Susan, *d* of Raymond Dinnis, Edenbridge, Kent; four *s.* *Educ:* Eton; Dundee Univ. (MA). Barrister-at-law, Gray's Inn. A Page of Honour to the Queen, 1966–69. Pres., RHS, 2013–. DL Norfolk, 1998. *Heir:* *s* Henry Hickman Bacon, *b* 23 April 1984. *Address:* Raveningham Hall, Norfolk NR14 6NS. *Club:* Pratt's.

BACON, Dame Patricia (Anne), DBE 2011; Principal and Chief Executive, St Helens College, 2002–11 (Deputy Principal, 1990–2002); *b* London, 16 Jan. 1951; *d* of Reginald and Florence Bacon; *m* 1989, Anthony Paul Davison. *Educ:* Leicester Univ. (BA Hons English 1973); Wolverhampton Poly. (Cert Ed 1982); Univ. of S Bank (MBA Educn 1995). Exec. Officer, DHSS, 1969–70; grad. manager, Lewis's Dept Store, 1973–76; Retail Manager, Josiah Wedgwood, 1976–78; Lectr, Stoke Coll., 1978–81; Lectr, then Sen. Lectr, Warwickshire Coll., 1981–87; Associate Vice Principal, Wellingborough Coll., 1987–90. Association of Colleges: Pres., 2009–10; Chm., Beacon Awards Steering Gp, 2012–; Trustee, 2012–. Chm. Govs, Sutton Acad., 2008–11. Non-exec. Dir, Mid-Cheshire Hosps and Foundn Trust, 2012– (Dep. Chair, 2014). Hon. DEd Edgehill, 2011; Hon. DLitt Chester, 2014. *Recreations:* travel, golf, theatre, music.

BACON, Peter James; HM Diplomatic Service, retired; Consul-General, Houston, 1995–2001; *b* 17 Sept. 1941; *s* of Alfred J. Bacon and Mildred (*née* Randall); *m* 1963, Valerie Ann Colby; one *s* one *d.* *Educ:* Huish's Grammar Sch., Taunton. GPO, 1958–63; joined HM Diplomatic Service, 1963; CRO, 1963–64; Nicosia, 1964–66; Kota Kinabalu, 1967–70; Brussels, 1970–71; Beirut, 1971–75; Asst Private Sec. to Minister of State, FCO, 1975–78; Suva, 1978–80; First Sec. (Energy), Washington, 1980–84; Hd, Parly Relns Dept, FCO, 1984–88; Consul (Commercial), Johannesburg, 1988–92; Counsellor (Commercial and Develt), Jakarta, 1992–95. *Recreations:* golf, travel. *Address:* The Pines, Blagdon Hill, Taunton, Somerset TA3 7SL.

BACON, Richard Michael; MP (C) South Norfolk, since 2001; *b* 3 Dec. 1962; s of Michael Edward Bacon and Sheila Margaret Bacon (*née* Taylor, now Campbell); *m* 2006, Victoria Louise Panton; two *s.* *Educ:* King's Sch., Worcester; LSE (BSc 1st cl. Hons 1986); Goethe Inst., Berlin. Investment banker, Barclays de Zoete Wedd Ltd, 1986–89; financial journalist, principally with Euromoney Publications, 1993–94; Dep. Dir, Mgt Consultancies Assoc., 1994–96; Associate Partner, Brunswick Public Relations, 1996–99; Founder, English Word Factory, 1999–. Member: Public Accounts Cttee, H of C, 2001–; European Scrutiny Cttee, 2003–07; Public Accounts Commn, 2005–. Chm., Hammersmith Cons. Assoc., 1995–96. Co-founder, Cons. Party Geneva project, 2000. Contested (C) Vauxhall, 1997. *Publications:* (with Christopher Hope) Conundrum, 2013. *Recreation:* playing the bongos. *Address:* House of Commons, SW1A 0AA. *T:* (constituency office) (01379) 643728. *Club:* Ronnie Scott's.

BACON DARWIN, Kelyn Meher, (Kelyn Bacon); QC 2014; *b* Bombay, 29 Oct. 1973; *d* of Martin and Barbara Bacon; *m* 2003, Peter Darwin; one *s* one *d.* *Educ:* Merton Coll., Oxford (MA Law with Law Studies in Europe 1996); Univ. of Konstanz, Germany; European Univ. Inst., Florence (LLB Eur. Law 1997); Inns of Court Sch. of Law. Called to the Bar, Inner Temple, 1998; in practice as barrister, specialising in EU and competition law, 1998–. *Publications:* European Community Law of State Aid, 2009, 2nd edn as European Union Law of State Aid, 2013. *Recreations:* walking, cycling, singing, playing cello. *Address:* Brick Court Chambers, 7–8 Essex Street, WC2R 3LD. *T:* (020) 7379 3550.

BADAWI, Zeinab; broadcaster and journalist, BBC, since 1998; *d* of Mohammed-Khair Badawi and Asia Malik; *m*; two *s* two *d.* *Educ:* St Hilda's Coll., Oxford (BA Politics Philosophy, Econs); Sch. of Oriental and African Studies, London Univ. (MA Middle East Hist.). Broadcast journalist: Yorkshire TV, 1982–86; BBC Manchester, 1986–87; New Reporter and Presenter, Channel 4 News, ITN, 1988–98. Dir, Kush Communications Ltd Chm., Article 19 (Internat. Centre Against Censorship), 1998–2002; Vice-Pres., UNA 1998–; Council Member: ODI, 1990–; Bd, Inst. of Contemporary History, 2001–; Board Member: British Council, 2004–09; NPG, 2004–12. Chm., Africa Medical Partnership Fund 2004–. Chm., Royal African Soc., 2014–. Trustee: Africa Centre, 2001–03; BBC World Service Trust, 2002–09. Hon DLitt SOAS, Univ. of London, 2011. *Recreations:* family cooking, ancient history, travel. *Address:* BBC New Broadcasting House, Portland Place W1A 1AA.

BADCOCK, Maj.-Gen. John Michael Watson, CB 1976; MBE 1959; DL; Chairman, S W. Mount & Sons, 1982–86; *b* 10 Nov. 1922; *s* of late R. D. Badcock, MC, JP and Mrs J. D Badcock; *m* 1948, Gillian Pauline (*née* Attfield) (*d* 2007); one *s* two *d.* *Educ:* Sherborne Sch. Worcester Coll., Oxford. Enlisted in ranks (Army), 1941; commnd Royal Corps of Signals 1942; war service UK and BAOR; Ceylon, 1945–47; served in UK, Persian Gulf, BAOR and Cyprus; Comdr 2 Inf. Bde and Dep. Constable of Dover Castle, 1968–71; Dep. Mil. Sec. 1971–72; Dir of Manning (Army), 1972–74; Defence Advr and Head of British Defence Liaison Staff, Canberra, 1974–77; retired. psc, jssc, idc. Col Comdt, Royal Signals, 1974–80 and 1982–90; Master of Signals, 1982–90; Hon. Col, 31 (London) Signal Regt (Volunteers) 1978–83. Chm., SE TA&VRA, 1979–85. Chief Appeals Officer, CRC, 1978–82. Founder 1981, now Pres., E Kent Br., Royal Signals Assoc., 2011–. DL Kent, 1980. *Recreations* watching Rugby football, cricket, hockey, most field sports less horsemanship. *Address:* c/o RHQ Royal Signals, Blandford Camp, Blandford, Dorset DT11 8RH. *T:* (01258) 482076.

BADDELEY, Prof. Alan David, CBE 1999; PhD; FRS 1993; FBA 2008; Professor of Psychology, University of York, since 2003; *b* 23 March 1934; *s* of Donald and Nellie Baddeley; *m* 1964, Hilary Ann White; three *s.* *Educ:* University Coll., London (BA; Fellow 1998); Princeton Univ. (MA). PhD Cantab, 1962. Walker Fellow, Princeton Univ., 1956–57 Scientist, MRC Applied Psychology Unit, Cambridge, 1958–67; Lectr then Reader, Sussex Univ., 1969–72; Prof. of Psychology, Stirling Univ., 1972–74; Dir, Applied Psychology Unit MRC, Cambridge, 1974–95; Sen. Res. Fellow, Churchill Coll., Cambridge, 1988–95; Hon Prof. of Cognitive Psychology, Cambridge Univ., 1991–95; Prof. of Psychology, Univ. of Bristol, 1995–2003. Vis. Fellow, Univ. of California, San Diego, 1970–71; Visiting Professor Harvard Univ., 1984; Univ. of Queensland, 1990; Univ. of Texas, Austin, 1991; Fellow Center for Advanced Study in Behavioral Scis, Stanford, 2001–02. President: Experimental Psychology Soc., 1984–86; European Soc. for Cognitive Psychology, 1986–90. Founder FMedSci 1998. Hon. FBPsS 1995. Mem., Academia Europaea, 1989; Hon. For. Mem. Amer. Acad. of Arts and Scis, 1996. Hon. DPhil Umeå, Sweden, 1991; DUniv: Stirling, 1996 Essex, 1999; Plymouth, 2000; Dr *hc* Edinburgh, 2005. Aristotle Prize, 2001; Dist. Scientific Contrib. Award, Amer. Psychol Assoc., 2001; Lifetime Achievement Award, BPsS, 2013 *Publications:* The Psychology of Memory, 1976; Your Memory: a user's guide, 1982; Working Memory, 1986; Human Memory: theory and practice, 1990; Essentials of Human Memory 1999; Working Memory, Thought and Action, 2007; Memory, 2009. *Recreations:* walking reading, travel. *Address:* Department of Psychology, University of York, Heslington, York YO10 5DD. *T:* (01904) 322882.

BADDELEY, Sir John (Wolsey Beresford), 4th Bt *cr* 1922; *b* 27 Jan. 1938; *s* of Sir John Beresford Baddeley, 3rd Bt, and Nancy Winifred (*d* 1994), *d* of late Thomas Wolsey; *S* father 1979; *m* 1st, 1962, Sara Rosalind Crofts (marr. diss. 1992); three *d*; 2nd, 1998, Mrs Carol Quinlan (*née* Greenham). *Educ:* Bradfield College, Berks. FCA. Qualified as Chartered Accountant, 1961. *Recreations:* inland waterways, gardening. *Heir:* *kinsman* Paul Allan Baddeley [*b* 15 Aug. 1948; *m* 1977, Lesley Springett; two *s*]. *Address:* Brooklands Farm, Swanwick Shore Road, Sarisbury Green, Southampton SO31 7EF. *T:* (01489) 880863.

BADDELEY, Jonathan Andrew; fine art auctioneer, broadcaster and author; Managing Director, Bonhams, since 2010; *b* Woking, Surrey, 15 May 1952; *s* of Denis and Verney Baddeley; *m* 2007, Josephine Olley; two *s.* *Educ:* St Edmund's Sch., Canterbury; Univ. of Manchester; London Business Sch. Hd of Collectors' Dept, Sotheby's, 1972–75; Jeremy Cooper Ltd, 1975–81; Sotheby's, 1981–2001: Sen. Dir, 1990–2001; Gp Hd, Collectors' Div. 1990–2001; Hd of sothebys.com UK, Europe and Australasia, 2000–01; Man. Dir, Windsor Hse Antiques, 2001–03; Bonhams, 2003–. Guest Curator, Mariner's Mus., Newport News USA, 1995. Expert, Antiques Roadshow, BBC TV, 1990–. *Publications:* The Birkenhead Della Robbia Pottery, 1893–1906, 1980; Nautical Antiques and Collectables, 1993, 3rd edn 2001. *Recreations:* London markets, performing arts, travel, family, scuba diving. *Address* Bonhams, Montpelier Street, Knightsbridge, SW7 1HH. *T:* (020) 7393 3872, *Fax:* (020) 7393 3873.

BADDELEY, Ven. Martin James; Archdeacon of Reigate, 1996–2000; *b* 10 Nov. 1936; *s* of Walter Hubert and Mary Katharine Baddeley; *m* 1962, Judith Clare Hill (*d* 2005); two *s* one *d.* *Educ:* Keble Coll., Oxford (BA 1960; MA 1964); Lincoln Theol Coll. Ordained deacon, 1962, priest, 1963; Asst Curate, St Matthew, Stretford, 1962–64; staff, Lincoln Theol Coll., 1965–69; Chaplain, 1969–74, Fellow, 1972–74, Fitzwilliam Coll., Cambridge Chaplain, New Hall, Cambridge, 1969–74; Canon Residentiary, Rochester Cathedral 1974–80; Principal, Southwark Ordination Course, 1980–94; Jt Principal, SE Inst. for Theol Educn, 1994–96. *Recreations:* walking, reading. *Address:* 2 Glendower, Fossil Bank, Upper Colwall, Malvern, Worcs WR13 6PJ.

BADDELEY, Stephen John; Director of Sport, University of Bath, since 2010; *b* 28 March 1961; *s* of William Baddeley and Barbara Isobel Baddeley (*née* Dufty); *m* 1984, Deirdre Ilene Sharman (marr. diss. 1997); one *s* one *d*; partner, Kirsten Irene Gwerder; one *s* one *d.* *Educ* Chelsea Coll., Univ. of London (BSc 1982); Open Univ. (BA 1990). Professional badminton player, 1982–90; Dir of Coaching and Develt, Scottish Badminton Union, 1990–92; (pt-time) Manager, British Badminton Olympic Team, 1990–92; Head Coach, Nat. Badminton Centre, Lausanne, and Asst Nat. Coach for Switzerland, 1992–96; Dir of Elite Play, 1996–97, Performance Dir, 1997–99, Chief Exec., 1998–2004, Badminton Assoc. of England Ltd; Dir Nat. Sport, Sport England, 2004–08 (Interim Chief Exec., 2006–07); Physical Activity Consultant, NHS Northants, 2008–10. Trustee: Bath Recreation Ground Trust, 2013– SkillsActive, 2015–. Mem., Gov. Bd, Royal High Sch., Bath, 2015–. *Publications:* Badminton in Action, 1988; Go and Play Badminton, 1992. *Recreations:* jogging, tennis. *Address* Department of Sports Development and Recreation, University of Bath, Claverton Down, Bath BA2 7AY.

BADEN-POWELL, family name of **Baron Baden-Powell**.

BADEN-POWELL, 3rd Baron *cr* 1929, of Gilwell; **Robert Crause Baden-Powell;** Bt 1922; Vice-President, Scout Association, since 1982; *b* 15 Oct. 1936; *s* of 2nd Baron and Carine Crause Baden-Powell (*née* Boardman) (*d* 1993); *S* father, 1962; *m* 1963, Patience Hélène Mary Batty (CBE 1986; *d* 2010). *Educ:* Bryanston (Blandford). Money broker, 1964–84; Director: City Share Trust, 1964–70; Bolton Bldg Soc., 1974–88; Managing Director: Fieldguard Ltd, 1984–; Highline Estates Ltd, 1986–95. Chief Scouts Comr, 1965–82; Pres., West Yorks Scout Council, 1972–88; Mem., 1965–, Mem. Cttee, 1972–78,

Council, Scout Assoc. Mem. Council, British Quarter Horse Assoc., 1984–90 (Chm., 1990); Chm., Quarter Horse Racing UK, 1985–88. Vice Pres., Camping and Caravanning Club, 2002– (Pres., 1992–2002); Pres., Surrey Youth Focus, 2011–. *Recreations:* horses, the arts. *Heir:* *b* Hon. David Michael Baden-Powell [*b* 11 Dec. 1940; *m* 1966, Joan Phillips, *d* of H. W. Berryman, Melbourne, Australia; three *s*]. *Address:* Weston Farmhouse, The Street, Albury, Surrey GU5 9AY. *T:* (01483) 205087.

BADENOCH, David Fraser, DM; FRCS; Hon. Consultant Urological Surgeon, St Bartholomew's and Royal London Hospitals, since 2000 (Consultant, 1988–2000); Urological Surgeon, King Edward VII Hospital for Officers, since 1996; *b* 7 Feb. 1949; 3rd *s* of late Alec Badenoch, MD, ChM, FRCS and Dr Jean Badenoch; *m* 1981, Michele Patricia Howard; two *s* two *d*. *Educ:* Marlborough Coll.; Lincoln Coll., Oxford (Rugby blue 1971; BA Animal Physiology 1970; BM BCh 1975; MA 1975; DM 1988; MCh 1988); Med. Coll., St Bartholomew's Hosp. FRCS 1979. House Surgeon, Registrar and Lectr in Surgery, St Bartholomew's Hosp., London, 1976–82; Sen. Registrar in Urology, London Hosp., 1982–87; Sen. Lectr in Urology, London Hosp. Med. Coll., London Univ., 1988–99. Surg. Lt Comdr, RNR, 1978–91. Hon. Surg., Royal Scottish Corp., 1993–2006. Vis. Prof. of Urology, Mayo Clinic, 2001. Member: British Assoc. of Urological Surgeons; Amer. Urological Assoc.; European Urological Assoc.; Société Internationale d'Urologie; British Fertility Soc.; RSocMed (Hon. Sec., 1997–99, Hon. Treas., 2000–05, Pres., 2008–09, Section of Urology); Pres., Chelsea Clin. Soc., 2011–12 (Hon. Sec., 2000–08). Trustee: King Edward VII Hosp., 2009–; London Consultants' Assoc., 2010–. Fellow, Eur. Bd of Urology, 1995. Creevy Meml Lect., Minnesota Soc. of Urology, 2001. Trustee, Orchid Cancer Charity, 2006–. Surgitek Prize, British Assoc. of Urological Surgeons, 1987; Grand Prix, European Urological Assoc., 1988. *Publications:* Aids to Urology, 1987; contribs to textbooks and jls in urology and infertility. *Recreations:* reading, piano, Rugby, opera, company of good friends. *Address:* 101 Harley Street, W1G 6AH. *T:* (020) 7935 3881. *Clubs:* Garrick, Lansdowne; Vincent's (Oxford).

BADENOCH, (Ian) James (Forster); QC 1989; a Recorder, 1987–2012; a Deputy High Court Judge, since 1994; a President, Mental Health Review Tribunal, since 2000; *b* 24 July 1945; *s* of Sir John Badenoch and of Anne, *d* of Prof. Lancelot Forster; *m* 1979, Marie-Thérèse Victoria Cabourn-Smith; two *s* one *d*. *Educ:* Dragon Sch., Oxford; Rugby Sch.; Magdalen Coll., Oxford (Open Scholar, Demyship; MA). Called to the Bar, Lincoln's Inn, 1968 (Hardwicke Scholar; Bencher, 2000); Mem., Inner Temple; admitted (*ad eundem*) Hong Kong Bar, 1999. Accredited Mediator, 2003–. Chm., Expert Witness Inst., 2004–13. Member: Medico-Legal Soc.; Harveian Soc. FRSocMed 2005. *Publications:* (contrib.) Medical Negligence, 1990, 4th edn 2008; Urology and the Law, 2007. *Recreations:* fossil hunting, travel, wildlife photography, the study of herons. *Address:* 1 Crown Office Row, Temple, EC4Y 7HH. *T:* (020) 7797 7500.

BADER, Dr Alfred, Hon. CBE 1998; President, Alfred Bader Fine Arts, since 1961; *b* Vienna, 28 April 1924; *s* of Alfred and Elisabeth Bader; *m* 1st, 1952, Helen Daniels (marr. diss.); two *s*; 2nd, 1982, Isabel Overton. *Educ:* Queen's Univ., Kingston, Ont. (BSc 1945, BA 1946, MSc 1947); Harvard Univ. (MA 1949, PhD 1950). Res. chemist, 1950–53, Gp Leader, 1953–54, Pittsburgh Plate Glass Co.; Aldrich Chemical Co.: Chief Chemist, 1954–55; Pres., 1955–81; Chm., 1981–91; Pres., 1975–80, Chm., 1980–91, Sigma-Aldrich Corp. (Chm. Emeritus, 1991–92). Guest Curator, Milwaukee Art Mus., 1976 and 1989. FRSA 1989. Honorary Fellow: RSC, 1990; UCL, 2006. Numerous hon. degrees, including: DSc: Wisconsin, Milwaukee, 1980; Purdue, 1984; Wisconsin-Madison, 1984; Northwestern, 1990; Edinburgh, 1998; Glasgow, 1999; Masaryk, 2000; Simon Fraser, 2005; Ottawa, 2006; LLD Queen's, Kingston, 1986; DUniv Sussex, 1989. Awards include: J. E. Purkyne Medal, Czech Acad. Scis, 1994; Charles Lathrop Parsons Award, 1995, Distinguished Contributors Award, 1998, ACS; Gold Medal, Amer. Inst. Chemists, 1997; Pittcon Heritage Award, Chemical Heritage Foundn, 2009. *Publications:* Adventures of a Chemist Collector, 1995; Chemistry and Art: more adventures of a chemist collector, 2008. *Address:* 2961 N Shepard Avenue, Milwaukee, WI 53211, USA. *T:* (414) 9625169.

BADER, David John; Director, Social Justice and Regeneration, Welsh Assembly Government, 2003–05; *b* 26 July 1945; *s* of Erling David Bader and Sybil Mary Bader (*née* Lewis); *m* 1969, Hilary Mary Organ; one *s* one *d*. *Educ:* Newport High Sch. for Boys. FCIH 1975. Dir, Housing and Architectural Services, Newport CBC, 1972–89; Dep. Chief Exec., Housing for Wales (Tai Cymru), 1989–98; Dir, Housing, Welsh Assembly Govt, 1998–2003. Mem., Ind. Remuneration Panel for Wales, 2008–. Director: Somer Housing Gp Ltd, 2005–10; Newport Housing Trust Ltd, 2008–; Arloes Ltd, 2011–. Trustee: Wales Community Fire Safety Trust, 2003–05; Somer Community Housing Trust, 2005–11 (Chm., 2005). *Recreations:* golf, classic car restoration, bidding on eBay, gardening, cinema, reading. *Address:* 20 Groves Road, Newport NP20 3SP. *Club:* Newport Golf.

BADGE, Sir Peter (Gilmour Noto), Kt 1998; Chief Metropolitan Stipendiary Magistrate, 1992–97; a District Judge (Magistrates' Courts) (formerly Stipendiary Magistrate, Devon), 1997–2002; *b* 20 Nov. 1931; *s* of late Ernest Desmond Badge, LDS and Marie Benson Badge (*née* Clough); *m* 1956, Mary Rose Noble; four *d*. *Educ:* Univ. of Liverpool (LLB). National Service, 1956–58: RNVR, lower deck and commnd; UK, ME and FE; RNR, 1958–62. Solicitor, 1956; Mem., Solicitor's Dept, New Scotland Yard, 1958–61; Asst Solicitor and later Partner, 1961–75, Kidd, Rapinet, Badge & Co.; Notary Public; Metropolitan Stipendiary Magistrate, 1975–97; a Recorder, 1980–92, 1997–99; a Chm., Inner London Juvenile Panel, 1979–97; Pres., Mental Health Review Tribunals, 1997–2003. Member: Lord Chancellor's Adv. Cttee for Inner London, 1983–97; Magisterial Cttee, Judicial Studies Bd, 1985–90; Chm., Legal Cttee, Magistrates' Assoc., 1990–93. Mem., Basket Makers' Assoc., 1987–2002; Pres., Coracle Soc., 1997– (Chm., 1985–97); Chm., Binney Meml Awards Cttee, 1992–97. Mem. Bd of Green Cloth, Verge of the Palaces of St James's, Whitehall etc, 1992–2003. Liveryman, Co. of Basket Makers, 1995–2001. Contested (L) Windsor and Maidenhead, 1964. *Publications:* Coracles of the World, 2009; articles on coracles.

BADGE, Robin Howard L.; *see* Lovell-Badge.

BADGER, Prof. Anthony John, PhD; Master of Clare College, Cambridge, 2003–14; Paul Mellon Professor of American History, Cambridge University, 1992–2014; *b* 6 March 1947; *s* of Kenneth Badger and Iris G. (*née* Summerill); *m* 1979, Ruth Catherine Davis; two *s*. *Educ:* Cotham Grammar Sch.; Sidney Sussex Coll., Cambridge (BA, MA; Hon. Fellow, 2003); Hull Univ. (PhD). Department of History, Newcastle University: Lectr, 1971–81; Sen. Lectr, 1981–91; Prof., 1991; Fellow, Sidney Sussex Coll., Cambridge, 1992–2003. Ind. Reviewer for migration of FCO Colonial Admin files, 2011–. Chm., Kennedy Meml Trust, 2009–. Hon. DLitt Hull, 1999; Hon. DHumLit North Carolina State, 2013. *Publications:* Prosperity Road: the New Deal, North Carolina and tobacco, 1980; North Carolina and the New Deal, 1981; The New Deal: the Depression years, 1989; (ed jtly) The Making of Martin Luther King and the Civil Rights Movement, 1996; (ed jtly) Southern Landscapes, 1996; Race and War: Lyndon Johnson and William Fulbright, 2000; (ed jtly) Contesting Democracy: substance and structure in American political history 1775–2000, 2001; New Deal/New South, 2007; FDR: the first hundred days, 2008. *Recreations:* walking, supporting Bristol Rovers.

BADHAM, Prof. Paul Brian Leslie; Professor of Theology and Religious Studies, University of Wales, Lampeter, 1991–2010, now Emeritus Professor, University of Wales Trinity St David; *b* 26 Sept. 1942; *s* of Rev. Leslie Badham, QHC and Effie (*née* Garrett); *m* 1969, Dr Linda Frances Elson; one *s*. *Educ:* Reading Sch.; Jesus Coll., Oxford (BA 1965; MA 1969); Jesus Coll., Cambridge (BA 1968; MA 1972); Westcott House, Cambridge; Univ. of Birmingham (PhD 1973). Divinity Master, Churcher's Coll., Petersfield, 1965–66; ordained deacon, 1968, priest, 1969; Curate: Edgbaston, 1968–69; Rubery, 1969–73; St David's University College, Lampeter, then University of Wales, Lampeter: Lectr, 1973–83; Sen. Lectr, 1983–88; Reader, 1988–91; Chm. of Church History, 1982–86; Chm. of Religion and Ethics, 1987–91; Dean, Faculty of Theology, 1991–97; Hd, Dept of Theology and Religious Studies, 1991–99; Hd, Sch. of Anthropology, Classics, Philosophy, Theology and Religious Studies, 1999–2002. Chm., Subject Panel for Theology and Religious Studies, Univ. of Wales, 1998–2003; Sec., Assoc. of Univ. Depts of Theology and Religious Studies, 1990–94. Sen. Res. Fellow, Ian Ramsey Centre, Oxford, 2004–07. Member: Res. Panel for Philosophy, Law and Religious Studies, AHRB, 1999–2003; Benchmarking Panel for Theology and Religious Studies, QAA, 1999–2000 (Subject Reviewer, 2000–02). Dir, Alister Hardy Religious Experience Res. Centre, 2002–10 (Trustee, 1997–2002); Hon. Sec., Alister Hardy Trust, 2010–13. Vice-Pres., Modern Church (formerly Modern Churchpeople's Union), 2001– (Mem. Council, 1974–95). Patron, Dignity in Dying, 2006–. FRSocMed 2007. Ed., Modern Believing, 2006–11. *Publications:* Christian Beliefs about Life after Death, 1976; (with Linda Badham) Immortality or Extinction?, 1982; (ed jtly) Death and Immortality in the Religions of the World, 1987; (ed jtly) Perspectives on Death and Dying, 1987; (ed) Religion, State and Society in Modern Britain, 1989; (ed) A John Hick Reader, 1990; (ed) Ethics on the Frontiers of Human Existence, 1992; The Christian Understanding of God and Christ in Relation to True Pure-Land Buddhism, 1994; (ed jtly) Facing Death, 1996; The Contemporary Challenge of Modernist Theology, 1998; (with Xinzhong Yao) Religious Experience in Contemporary China, 2007; Is there a Christian Case for Assisted Dying?, 2009; A Christianity that Can be Believed, 2009; (ed) Verdict on Jesus, 2010; Making Sense of Death and Immortality, 2013; (ed) Assisted Dying: for and against, 2015; contribs to jls. *Address:* 4 Coed y Bryn, Aberaeron, Ceredigion SA46 0DW. *T:* 07968 626902. *E:* pblbadham@hotmail.com.

BAER, Sir Jack (Mervyn Frank), Kt 1997; independent fine art consultant, since 2001; *b* 29 Aug. 1924; *yr s* of late Frank and Alix Baer; *m* 1st, 1952, Jean St Clair (marr. diss. 1969; she *d* 1973), *oc* of late L. F. St Clair and Evelyn Synnott; one *d*; 2nd, 1970, Diana Downes Baillieu, *yr d* of late Aubrey Clare Robinson and Mollie Panter-Downes; two step *d*. *Educ:* Bryanston; Slade Sch. of Fine Art, University Coll., London. Served RAF (Combined Ops), 1942–46. Proprietor, Hazlitt Gallery, 1948 until merger with Gooden & Fox, 1973; Man. Dir, 1973–92, Chm., 1992–94, Consultant, 1994–2001, Hazlitt, Gooden & Fox. Chm., Fine Arts and Antiques Export Adv. Cttee to Dept of Trade, 1971–73 (Vice-Chm., 1969–71). Member: Reviewing Cttee on Export of Works of Art, 1992–2001; Museums and Galls Commn, 1993–98 (Chm., Acceptance in Lieu of Tax Panel, 1993–2000). Pres., Fine Art Provident Institution, 1972–75. Chm., Soc. of London Art Dealers, 1977–80 (Vice Chm., 1974–77). Trustee: Burlington Magazine Foundn, 1991–2003; Nat. Mus and Galls on Merseyside Develt Trust, 1998–2008; Campaign for Museums, 1998–2008. *Publications:* over 70 exhibition catalogues of works of art; articles in various jls. *Recreation:* drawing. *Address:* 9 Phillimore Terrace, W8 6BJ. *T:* (020) 7937 6899. *Club:* Brooks's.

BAGCHI, Andrew Kumar; QC 2015; *b* Wakefield, W Yorks, 10 Dec. 1965; *s* of Dr Saral Bagchi and Angela Bagchi; *m* 2001, Carol Ann Teague; one *s*. *Educ:* Queen Elizabeth Grammar Sch., Wakefield; King's Coll. London (LLB Law). Called to the Bar, Middle Temple, 1989; in practice as a barrister, specialising in family law and court of protection. *Publications:* (contrib.) DIY Divorce and Separation: the expert guide to representing yourself, 2014. *Recreations:* cricket, golf, electronica, LUFC. *Address:* One Garden Court, Temple, EC4Y 9BJ. *E:* bagchi@1gc.com.

BAGGE, Sir (John) Jeremy (Picton), 7th Bt *cr* 1867, of Stradsett Hall, Norfolk; DL; *b* 21 June 1945; *s* of Sir John Bagge, 6th Bt, ED, DL and Elizabeth Helena (*d* 1996), *d* of late Daniel James Davies, CBE; *S* father, 1990; *m* 1979, Sarah Margaret Phipps, *d* of late Maj. James Shelley Phipps Armstrong; two *s* one *d*. *Educ:* Eton. FCA 1968. Hon. Alderman, King's Lynn, 1995. DL Norfolk, 1996; High Sheriff, Norfolk, 2003–04. Pres., Royal Norfolk Show, 2010. *Heir:* *s* Alfred James John Bagge [*b* 1 July 1980; *m* 2009, Charlotte, *e d* of Stanley Stride; one *d*]. *Address:* Stradsett Hall, King's Lynn, Norfolk PE33 9HA.

BAGGINI, Dr Julian Guiseppe; freelance writer, since 2000; *b* 1968. *Educ:* Harvey Grammar Sch.; Univ. of Reading (BA Hons Philosophy); University Coll. London (PhD Philosophy 1996). Co-Founder and Ed., The Philosophers' Mag., 1997–2010. *Publications:* Philosophy: key texts, 2002, 2nd edn (with G. Southwell), 2012; Philosophy: key themes, 2002, 2nd edn (with G. Southwell), 2012; (with P. S. Fosl) The Philosopher's Toolkit, 2002, 2nd edn 2010; Making Sense: philosophy behind the headlines, 2002; Atheism: a very short introduction, 2003; (ed with J. Stangroom) What Philosophers Think, 2003; (ed with J. Stangroom) Great Thinkers A-Z, 2004; What's It All About: philosophy and the meaning of life, 2004; The Pig That Wants to be Eaten, 2005; (with J. Stangroom) Do You Think What You Think You Think, 2006; Welcome to Everytown: a journey into the English mind, 2007; (with P. S. Fosl) The Ethics Toolkit, 2007; (ed with J. Stangroom) What More Philosophers Think, 2007; Complaint, 2008; The Duck That Won the Lottery, 2008 (pbk edn as Do They Think You're Stupid, 2010): Should You Judge This Book By Its Cover, 2009; (jtly) 30-Second Philosophies, 2010; The Ego Trick, 2011; (with N. Choksi) Really Really Big Questions About Faith, 2011; (with A. Macaro) The Shrink and the Sage: a guide to modern dilemmas, 2012; The Big Questions: Ethics, 2012; Philosophy: all that matters, 2012; The Virtues of the Table: how to eat and think, 2014. *Address:* c/o David Higham Associates, 7th Floor, Waverley House, 7–12 Noel Street, W1F 8GQ. *E:* julian@julianbaggini.com.

BAGLIN, Richard John; Chairman, Greenwich Healthcare NHS Trust, 1995–2000 (Director, 1993–2000); *b* 30 Oct. 1942; *s* of F. W. and C. C. Baglin; *m* 1964, Anne Christine; one *d*. *Educ:* Preston Manor County Grammar Sch.; St John's Coll., Cambridge (MA). Various posts with Abbey National BS, later Abbey National plc, 1964–93: Gen. Man., 1981–88; Dir, various subsidiaries, 1987–93; Man. Dir, New Businesses, 1988–92. Mem., SE London Probation Service Cttee, 1993–95. Gov., Greenwich Univ., 2001–10. Chm., Greenwich Soc., 2010–. DUniv Greenwich, 2011. *Recreations:* theatre, the arts. *Address:* 2 Feathers Place, Greenwich, SE10 9NE. *T:* (020) 8858 9895.

BAGNALL, Air Chief Marshal Sir Anthony (John Crowther), GBE 2003 (OBE 1982); KCB 1998 (CB 1994); Vice-Chief of Defence Staff, 2001–05; *b* 8 June 1945; *s* of Maurice Arthur Bagnall and Marjorie (*née* Crowther); *m* 1970, Pamela Diane Wilson; one *s* two *d*. *Educ:* Stretford Grammar Sch. RAF Coll., Cranwell, 1964; Flight Comdr, 5 Sqn, 1975; Advanced Staff College, 1978; Sqn Comdr, 43 Sqn, 1983, 23 Sqn, 1985; Dir, Air Staff Briefing and Co-ordination, 1985; Station Comdr, RAF Leuchars, 1987; RCDS 1990; Dir, Air Force Staff Duties, 1991; ACAS, 1992; AOC No 11 Gp, 1994; Dep. C-in-C, AFCENT, 1996–98; Air Mem. for Personnel, and AOC-in-C, Personnel and Trng Comd, 1998–2000; C-in-C Strike Comd, 2000–01; Air ADC to the Queen, 2000–01. Mem. Ct, St Andrews Univ., 2005–13. *Recreations:* golf, bridge, fell walking. *Address:* c/o Lloyds, 53 King Street, Manchester M60 2ES. *Club:* Royal Air Force.

BAGNALL, Kenneth Reginald; QC 1973; QC (Hong Kong) 1983; Chairman, The New Law Publishing Co. plc, 1993; Editor-in-Chief, New Property Cases, 1986; *b* 26 Nov. 1927; *s* of Reginald and Elizabeth Bagnall; *m* 1st, 1955, Margaret Edith Wall; one *s* one *d*; 2nd, 1963, Rosemary Hearn; one *s* one *d*. *Educ:* King Edward VI Sch., Birmingham; Univ. of Birmingham (LLB Hons). Yardley Scholar. Served Royal Air Force; Pilot Officer, 1947, Flt Lt, 1948. Called to the Bar, Gray's Inn, 1950; a Dep. Judge of Crown Court, 1975–83. Co-founder, 1980, Chm., 1980–82, and Life Gov., 1983, Anglo-American Real Property Inst.

Mem., Crafts Council, 1982–85; Co-founder, Bagnall Gall., Crafts Council, 1982. Founder: The New Law Fax Reporting Service, 1992; Internat. Legal Index Online, 2006; Founder and Designer, New Law Online, 1995; Co-founder and Consultant, Law Alert Ltd, 1999. Mem., Inst. of Dirs. Freeman, City and Corp. of London, 1972; Freeman and Liveryman, Barber-Surgeons' Co., 1972. *Publications:* Guide to Business Tenancies, 1956; Atkins Court Forms and Precedents (Town Planning), 1973; (with K. Lewison) Development Land Tax, 1978; Judicial Review, 1985. *Recreations:* yachting, motoring, travel. *Address:* Flat 16, Eversley Court, St Anne's Road, Eastbourne BN21 2BS. *Clubs:* 1900, United and Cecil.

BAGNALL, Peter Hill, CBE 1999; DL; Chairman, Oxford Radcliffe Hospitals NHS Trust, 1993–2000; *b* 8 Oct. 1931; *s* of Reginald Stuart Bagnall and Mary Adelaide (*née* Hill); *m* 1st, 1955, Edith Ann Wood (marr. diss. 1979); one *s* one *d* (and one *s* decd); 2nd, 1979, Diana Elizabeth Rayner. *Educ:* Newcastle-under-Lyme Sch.; St Catharine's Coll., Cambridge (MA). Nat. Service and TA Commns, N Staffs Regt. Dir, W. H. Smith & Son Ltd, 1968–88; Dir and Man. Dir, W. H. Smith PLC, 1974–88, retd; Chm., Book Club Associates, 1972–88; Director: Book Tokens Ltd, 1975–2000; W. H. Smith Pension Trustees Ltd, 1979–2002; TSB/Trustcard, 1986–89; The Book Trust, 1986–93 (Chm., 1989–91); Longman/Ladybird Books, 1987–90; British Museum Co., 1988–2000; Blackwell Ltd, Oxford, 1989–96. Dir, Oxon HA, 1989–93. Trustee, Radcliffe Med. Foundn, 1993–2003; Chm., Oxford Radcliffe Hosps Charitable Funds, 2003–. Mem., Vis. Cttee, Open Univ., 1988–92; Chm. Govs and Pro-Chancellor, Oxford Brookes Univ., 1993–98 (Gov., 1988–98). Mem. Council, St Luke's Hospital, Oxford, 2003–14. DL Oxfordshire, 1995. Hon. LLD Oxford Brookes, 1998. *Recreations:* book collecting, theatre, travel. *Address:* Orchard House, Buckland, Faringdon, Oxon SN7 8QW. *Club:* Sloane.

BAGOT, family name of **Baron Bagot**.

BAGOT, 10th Baron *cr* 1780, of Bagot's Bromley, co. Stafford; **Charles Hugh Shaun Bagot;** Bt 1627; *b* 23 Feb. 1944; *s* of 9th Baron Bagot and of Muriel Patricia (*née* Moore-Boyle); *S* father, 2001; *m* 1986, Mrs Sally A. Stone, *d* of D. G. Blunden; one *d*. *Heir: kinsman* Richard Charles Villiers Bagot, *b* 26 April 1941. *Address:* 16 Barclay Road, SW6 1EH.

BAGRI, family name of **Baron Bagri**.

BAGRI, Baron *cr* 1997 (Life Peer), of Regent's Park in the City of Westminster; **Raj Kumar Bagri,** CBE 1995; Founder, and Chairman, since 1970, Metdist Ltd; *b* 24 Aug. 1930; *m* 1954, Usha Maheshwary; one *s* one *d*. Chairman: Metdist group of cos, 1981–; Bagri Foundation, 1990–. Hon. Pres., London Metal Exchange, 2003–06 (Dir, 1983; Vice Chm., 1990; Chm., 1993–2002). Mem., Governing Body, SOAS, 1997–2007. Chm. Trustees, Rajiv Gandhi (UK) Foundn, 1997–. Mem., H of L, 1997–2010. Hon. Fellow, London Business Sch., 2004. Hon. DSc: City, 1999; Nottingham, 2000. *Address:* Metdist Enterprises Ltd, 80 Cannon Street, EC4N 6EJ.

See also Hon. A. Bagri.

BAGRI, Hon. Apurv; President and Chief Executive Officer (formerly Managing Director), Metdist Group, since 1980; *b* 11 Nov. 1959; *s* of Baron Bagri, *qv*; *m* 1982, Alka Rakyan; two *d*. *Educ:* University Coll. Sch., London; Cass Business Sch., London (BSc Business Admin 1980); Wharton Univ. (AMP 1993). Dir, Bagri Foundn, 1990–. Mem., Crown Estate Paving Commn, 1996–; non-exec. Dir and Mem. Bd, Royal Parks, 2003– (non-exec. Chm., 2008–). Mem. Bd, Dubai FSA, 2004–. Mem. Bd, Internat. Wrought Copper Council, 2000– (Chm., 2002–04). Mem. Bd, HEFCE, 2014–. Vis. Prof., Cass Business Sch., London, 2004–. Member: Governing Council, City Univ., 2002–12 (Dep. Pro-Chancellor and Acting Chm. of Council, 2009; Pro-Chancellor and Chm. of Council, 2009–12; Hon. Rector, 2012–); Bd of Govs, London Business Sch., 2003– (Dep. Chm., 2006–14; Chm., 2014–); Corp., University Coll. Sch., 1992–. Trustee: The Indus Entrepreneurs (UK) Ltd (TiE-UK), 2000– (Founding Pres.); TiE Inc., 2002– (Chm., 2005–08); Asia House, 2000–; Royal Parks Foundn, 2003–12. Mem., Adv. Bd, UK India Business Council (formerly Indo-British Partnership), 2009–11 (Mem. Bd, 2004–09). Hon. Fellow, London Business Sch., 2013. Hon. DSc City, 2006. *Recreations:* watching cricket, travel, reading. *Address:* Metdist Enterprises Ltd, 80 Cannon Street, EC4N 6EJ. *T:* (020) 7280 0000, *Fax:* (020) 7606 6650. *E:* rbarnett@metdist.com. *Club:* MCC.

BAGSHAW, (Charles) Kerry, CMG 1998; OBE 1992; Director, Arial Associates, since 2006; *b* 5 Oct. 1943; *s* of Harry Bagshaw and Frances Bagshaw (*née* Mackay); *m* 1st, 1965, Janet Bond (marr. diss.); one *d*; 2nd, 1970, Pamela Georgina Slater; two *d*. *Educ:* White Fathers. Joined RM, 1961; commnd 1965; RM Commandos (43, 40 and 45), 1963–68; SBS, 1969–74. HM Diplomatic Service, 1974–98: First Secretary: Gaborone, 1977–79; FCO, 1979–82; UK Mission to UN, Geneva, 1982–86; FCO, 1986–87; Moscow, 1988–91; Counsellor, FCO, 1992–98. De Beers: Gen. Manager, Gp Security, 2000–03; Gp Manager, Internat. Industry Analysis, 2003–05; Consultant, Internat. Security, 2005–10. *Recreations:* people, travel, literature, wine and food, the countryside (winter and summer). *Address:* Bishopdale, Leyburn, N Yorks.

BAGSHAW, Prof. Michael, FFOM; FRAeS; Professor of Aviation Medicine, King's College London, 2005–08, now Emeritus; Associate Director, Jarvis Bagshaw Ltd, since 2012; *b* 9 July 1946; *s* of Robert and Alice Bagshaw; *m* 1970, Penelope Isaac; two *d*. *Educ:* Welsh Nat. Sch. of Medicine, Cardiff (MB BCh 1973); MRCS, LRCP 1973; DAvMed 1980; MFOM 1982, FFOM 2003; DFFP 1995; FRAeS 1995. Airline Transport Pilot's Licence; CAA Flying Examr. Clerical Asst, Architect's Dept, Swansea BC, 1966; Technical Photographer, Univ. of Swansea, 1967; medical student, Cardiff, 1967–70; RAF, 1970–86: Med. Br., 1970–75; Fast Jet Pilot (Hunter, Jaguar), 1975–78; Flying Instr, RAF Coll., Cranwell, 1978–80; Sen. Med. Officer Pilot, RAF Inst. of Aviation Medicine, 1980–86; Locum Consultant in Neuro-Otology, St George's Hosp., London, 1987; Principal, General Practice, Crowthorne, 1987–90; Estabt MO, DERA, Farnborough, 1990–92; Sen. Aviation Physician, 1992–97, Hd of Med. Services, 1997–2004, British Airways. Hon. civilian consultant advr in aviation medicine to the Army, 2003–; Aeromedical Advr, Airbus, 2005–. Vis. Prof., Cranfield Univ., 2005–. Pres., Aerospace Med. Assoc., 2005–06. Lectures: Guest Technology, Royal Society, 1996; Armstrong, Aerospace Med. Assoc., 2014. Liveryman, Hon. Co. of Air Pilots (formerly GAPAN), 1992– (Award of Merit, 1997). Clarkson Trophy, RAF, 1978; Buchanan Barbour Award, RAeS, 1984; Louis H. Bauer Founders Award, Aerospace Med. Assoc., 2008; Allard Medal, Internat. Acad. of Aviation and Space Medicine, 2009; Boothby-Edwards Award, Aerospace Med. Assoc., 2011. *Publications:* Human Performance and Limitations in Aviation, 1991; (contrib.) Principles and Practice of Travel Medicine, 2001; (contrib.) Oxford Textbook of Medicine, 2002; (contrib.) Ernsting's Aviation Medicine, 2007; (contrib.) Fundamentals of Aerospace Medicine, 2008; (contrib.) Occupational and Environmental Lung Diseases, 2010; papers and articles on aviation medicine. *Recreations:* violinist; bass singer, Royal Meml Chapel, Sandhurst; general aviation (flying instructor and examiner). *Address:* 3 Bramley Grove, Crowthorne, Berks RG45 6EB. *T:* (01344) 775647. *Club:* Royal Air Force.

BAGSHAWE, Prof. Kenneth Dawson, CBE 1990; MD; FRCP, FRCOG; FRCR; FRS 1989; Professor of Medical Oncology in the University of London at Imperial College School of Medicine (formerly Charing Cross Hospital Medical School, later Charing Cross and Westminster Medical School), 1974–90, now Emeritus; Hon. Consultant Physician, Charing Cross Hospital, since 1990 (Consultant Physician, 1961–90); *b* 17 Aug. 1925; *s* of Harry Bagshawe and Gladys (*née* Dawson); *m* 1st, 1946, Ann Kelly (marr. diss. 1976; she *d* 2000); one *s* one *d*; 2nd, 1977, Sylvia Dorothy Lawler (*née* Corben) (*d* 1996); 3rd, 1998, Surinder Kanta Sharma. *Educ:* Harrow County Sch.; London Sch. of Econs and Pol Science; St Mary's Hosp. Med. Sch. (MB, BS 1952; MD 1964). FRCP 1969; FRCR 1983; FRCOG *ad eundem* 1978. Served RN, 1942–46. Fellow, Johns Hopkins Univ., Baltimore, USA, 1955–56; Sen Registrar, St Mary's Hosp., 1956–60. Visiting Professor: Down State Univ., NY, 1977; Univ of Hong Kong, 1982, 1994. Chm., DHSS Wkg Gp on Acute Cancer Services, 1980–84; Cancer Research Campaign: Chm., Scientific Cttee, 1983–88; Chm., Exec. Cttee, 1988–90; Vice Chm. Bd, 1988–2002. Chm., Aepact Ltd, 1996–2000. Hon. FRSocMed 1993. Hon DSc Bradford, 1990. Galen Medal, London Soc. of Apothecaries, 1993. *Publications:* Choriocarcinoma, 1969; Medical Oncology, 1975; 300 papers on cancer chemotherapy, tumour markers, drug targeting and antibody-directed enzyme prodrug therapy, etc. *Recreations:* (passive) music, art; (active) walking, travel, conservation. *Address:* 115 George Street, W1H 7HF. *T:* (020) 7262 8479. *Club:* Athenæum.

BAGSHAWE, Louise; *see* Mensch, L.

BAGULEY, Adrian Duncan; Director, Helicopters, Defence Equipment and Support, Ministry of Defence, 2011–15; *b* Thurso, Caithness, 29 Sept. 1964; *s* of Geoffrey and Barbara Baguley; *m* 1998, Rachel Bould; one *s*. *Educ:* Culcheth High Sch.; Imperial Coll. London (BEng 1987). CEng 1991; MIMechE 1991. Ministry of Defence: Engrg Trainee, 1987–88; Project Manager, DERA, 1988–90; Operational Analyst, Defence Operational Analysis Gp, Rheindhalen, 1990–92; Middle East Desk Officer, Overseas Secretariat, 1992–94; Avionics Lead, Eurofighter Directorate, 1994–97; Section Leader, Avionics, NATO Eurofighter and Tornado Mgt Agency, Munich, 1997–99; Private Sec. to Chief Scientific Advr, MoD, 1999–2002; Counsellor, Defence Sci. and Technol., British Embassy, Washington, DC, 2002–05; Hd, Helicopters 2, Defence Equipment and Support, MoD, 2005–11. *Recreations:* golf, photography. *Address:* Defence Equipment and Support, Walnut 2a, # 1219, MoD Abbey Wood, Bristol BS34 8JH. *T:* (0117) 913 5000. *E:* Adrian.Baguley583@mod.uk.

BAGWELL, Air Marshal Gregory Jack, CB 2012; CBE 2007; Deputy Commander Operations, Headquarters Air Command, since 2013; *b* Dartford, Kent, 6 Oct. 1961; *s* of Jack Bagwell and Maureen Bagwell; *m* 1989, Scarlett van Gelder; three *s* one *d*. *Educ:* Tonbridge Sch.; Univ. of Madras (MSc Defence and Politics). Royal Air Force: pilot, 1982–; OC IX (B) Sqdn, 1999–2004; Station Comdr, RAF Marham, 2004–07; Plans Dir, Perm. Jt HQ Northwood, 2007–09; AOC No 1 Gp, 2009–11; COS Jt Warfare Develt, 2011–13. *Recreations:* cricket, golf.

BAHL, Kamlesh, (Mrs N. Lakhani), CBE 1997; Chief Executive, Lotus Resolutions Ltd, since 2009; Vice-President, Law Society, 1999–2000; *b* 28 May 1956; *d* of Swinder Nath Bahl and Leela Wati Bahl; *m* 1986, Dr Nitin Lakhani. *Educ:* Univ. of Birmingham (LLB 1977). Admitted Solicitor, 1980. GLC, 1978–81; BSC, 1981–84; Texaco Ltd, 1984–87; Data Logic Ltd: Legal and Commercial Manager, 1987–89; Company Sec. and Manager, Legal Services, 1989–93. Chm., EOC, 1993–98. Mem., Barnet HA, 1989–90; non-exec. Dir, Parkside HA, 1990–93. Law Society: Chm., Commerce and Industry Gp, 1988–89; Mem. Council, 1990–2000 and 2003. Member: Justice Sub-Cttee on Judiciary, 1991–92; Ethnic Minorities Adv. Cttee and Tribunals Cttee (Cttees of Lord Chancellor's Judicial Studies Bd), 1991–94; Council and Standing Cttee on HAs, NAHAT, 1993–94; Council, Justice, 1993–94. Ind. Mem., Diplomatic Service Appeal Bd, FCO, 1993–99. Bd Mem., London Transport, 1999–2003. EC Rep., EC Consultative Commn on Racism and Xenophobia, 1994–97; Vice Pres., Eur. Adv. Cttee on Equal Opportunities, 1998. Mem. Council, Scout Assoc., 1996–99. Mem. Council, Open Univ., 1999; Gov., Univ. of Westminster, 1997–2003. Foundn Gov., Krishna-Avanti Primary Sch., 2008. FRSA. Hon. Fellow, Liverpool John Moores Univ., 1998. Hon. MA North London, 1997; Hon. LLD: De Montfort, 1998; Birmingham, 1999; Hon. DCL Northumbria, 1999. *Publications:* (ed) Managing Legal Practice in Business, 1989. *Recreations:* swimming, dancing, travelling, theatre.

BAILES, Alyson Judith Kirtley, CMG 2001; Adjunct Professor, Faculty of Political Science, University of Iceland, since 2009 (Visiting Professor, 2007–09); Visiting Professor, College of Europe, Bruges, since 2010; *b* 6 April 1949; *d* of John-Lloyd Bailes and Barbara (*née* Martin). *Educ:* Belvedere Sch., Liverpool; Somerville Coll., Oxford (MA Modern Hist.). HM Diplomatic Service, 1969–2002: Budapest, 1970–74; UK Delegn to NATO, 1974–76; FCO, 1976–78; Asst to EC 'Cttee of Wise Men' (which reported on ways of improving functioning of EC instns), 1979; on loan to MoD, 1979–81; Bonn, 1981–84; Dep. Head of Planning Staff, FCO, 1984–86; Counsellor, Peking, 1987–89; on attachment to RIIA, 1990; Consul-Gen. and Dep. Head of Mission, Oslo, 1990–93; Head of Security Policy Dept, FCO, 1994–96; Vice-Pres., Inst. of East West Studies, NY, 1996–97 (on special leave); Political Dir, WEU, Brussels, 1997–2000; Ambassador to Finland, 2000–02. Dir, Stockholm Internat. Peace Res. Inst., 2002–07. Comdr, Royal Order of the Polar Star (Sweden), 2008. *Recreations:* music, nature, travel. *Address:* Faculty of Political Science, University of Iceland, Gimli, 101 Reykjavik, Iceland.

BAILES, Christopher Peter; horticulturist; Curator, Chelsea Physic Garden, 2011–14; *b* London, 3 April 1951; *s* of Charles Robert and Irene Francis Bailes; *m* 2003, Sue Lee; three *s* one *d*. *Educ:* Brockley Co. Grammar Sch.; Merrist Wood Coll. (Nat. Cert. Hort. 1976); Royal Botanic Gdns, Kew (Dip. Hort. Hons 1979). Supervisor, Tropical Section, Royal Botanic Gdns, Kew, 1979–85; Manager, Eric Young Orchid Foundn, 1985–88; Curator: RHS Garden, Rosemoor, 1988–2010; RHS Regl Gardens, 1995–2001. Ed., Orchid Rev., 1985–89. Mem., Orchid Cttee, 2011–, Gardens Cttee, 2015–, RHS. Pres., Plant Heritage Devon Gp, 2008–. FCIHort (FIHort 2000). Gold Veitch Meml Medal, RHS, 2011. *Publications:* Orchids… and how to grow them, 1987; (with P. J. Cribb) Hardy Orchids, 1989; (with P. J. Cribb) Orchids: a guide to cultivation, 1993; Hollies for Gardeners, 2007; contrib. articles and papers on orchids and gen. horticulture to jls incl. The Garden, Orchid Rev., Curtis' Botanical Mag. *Address:* 21 Highfield, Northam, Bideford, Devon EX39 1BB.

BAILEY, family name of **Baron Glanusk**.

BAILEY, Adrian Edward; MP (Lab and Co-op) West Bromwich West, since Nov. 2000; *b* 11 Dec. 1945; *s* of Edward Arthur Bailey and Sylvia Alice Bailey; *m* 1989, Jill Patricia Millard (*née* Hunscott); one step *s*. *Educ:* Cheltenham Grammar Sch.; Univ. of Exeter (BA Hons Econ. Hist.); Loughborough Coll. of Librarianship (Post Grad. DipLib). Librarian, Cheshire CC, 1971–82; Pol Organiser, Co-op Party, 1982–2000. Mem. (Lab), Sandwell MBC, 1991–2000 (Dep. Leader, 1997–2000). Contested (Lab): S Worcs, 1970; Nantwich, Feb. and Oct. 1974; Wirral, March 1976; Cheshire W, EP, 1979. *Recreations:* supporting Cheltenham Town FC, cricket, dog walking. *Address:* House of Commons, SW1A 0AA; 181 Oakham Road, Tividale, Oldbury, W Midlands B69 1PZ.

BAILEY, Sir Alan (Marshall), KCB 1986 (CB 1982); Permanent Secretary, Department of Transport, 1986–91; *b* 26 June 1931; *s* of John Marshall Bailey and Muriel May Bailey; *m* 1st, 1959, Stella Mary Scott (marr. diss. 1981); three *s*; 2nd, 1981, Shirley Jane Barrett. *Educ:* Bedford Sch.; St John's and Merton Colls, Oxford (MA, BPhil; Hon. Fellow, St John's Coll., 1991). Harmsworth Senior Scholarship, 1954; Harkness Commonwealth Fellowship, USA, 1963–64. Principal Private Sec. to Chancellor of the Exchequer, 1971–73; Under-Sec., HM Treasury, 1973–78, Dep. Sec., 1978–83 (Central Policy Review Staff, Cabinet Office, 1981–82), 2nd Perm. Sec., 1983–85. Board Mem., London Transport, 1991–2000. Hon. Treas., Hist. of Parliament Trust, 1994–2011. *Address:* 56 Greenfell Mansions, Glaisher Street, SE8 3EU.

BAILEY, Prof. Allen Jackson, FRSC; Professor of Biochemistry, University of Bristol, 1980–96, now Emeritus; *b* 31 Jan. 1931; *s* of late Horace Jackson Bailey and Mabel Bailey (*née* Young); *m* 1956, Beryl Lee; twin *s* two *d. Educ:* Eccles Grammar Sch.; BSc London (Chem.) 1954; MSc (Physics) 1958, PhD (Chem.) 1960, Birmingham; MA 1967, ScD 1973, Cambridge. FIFST. Shell Chemicals, 1954–57; Low Temp. Res. Station, Univ. of Cambridge, 1960–67; Harkness Fellow, Commonwealth Fund, Biol. Dept, CIT, 1963–65; joined AFRC Meat Res. Inst., Bristol, 1967: SPSO (Special Merit), 1972; Head of Biochem. Dept, 1977–79; Director (DCSO), 1979–85; Hd of Lab., AFRC Inst. of Food Res., Bristol, 1985–90; Hd of Collagen Res. Gp, Bristol Univ., 1991–2001. Visiting Professor: São Paulo Univ., 1991; UCL, 2004–10. Scott Robertson Meml Lectr, QUB, 1986; Proctor Meml Lectr, Leeds, 1991. Hon. Fellow, British Connective Tissue Soc.; Hon. FRCP 2003. Senior Medal Food Science, RSC, 1987; Internat. Lectureship Award, Amer. Meat Sci. Assoc., 1989. Mem. Editl Bds, sci. jls. *Publications:* Recent Advances in Meat Science, 1985; Collagen as a Food, 1987; Connective Tissue in Meat and Meat Products, 1989; Elastomeric Proteins, 2003; sci. papers in learned jls. *Recreations:* travel, photography, painting. *Address:* 14A Well Close, Winscombe, N Somerset BS25 1HG. *T:* (01934) 843447.

BAILEY, Sir Brian (Harry), Kt 1983; OBE 1976; JP; DL; Chairman, Television South West Ltd, 1980–93; Director: Channel Four Television, 1985–91 (Deputy Chairman, 1989–91); Oracle Teletext Ltd, 1983–93; *b* 25 March 1923; *s* of Harry Bailey and Lilian (*née* Pulfer); *m* 1948, Nina Olive Sylvia (*née* Saunders) (*d* 2011); one *d* (and one *d* decd). *Educ:* Lowestoft Grammar Sch. RAF, 1941–45. SW Dist Organisation Officer, NALGO, 1951–82; South Western Reg. Sec., TUC, 1968–81. Chairman: South Western RHA, 1975–82; Health Educn Council, 1983–87; Health Educn Authority, 1987–89; Member: Somerset CC, 1966–84; SW Econ. Planning Council, 1969–79; Central Health Services Council, 1978–80; MRC, 1978–86; Adv. Cttee on Severn Barrage, Dept of Energy, 1978–81; Business Educn Council, 1980–84; NHS Management Inquiry Team, 1983–84. Chm. Council, Ind. Television Assoc., 1991; Vice-Chm., BBC Radio Bristol Adv. Council, 1971–78; Member: BBC West Reg. Adv. Council, 1973–78; Council, ITCA, 1982–86; South and West Adv. Bd, Legal and General Assurance Soc. Ltd, 1985–87. Director: Independent Television Publications Ltd, 1985–90; Bournemouth Orchs (formerly Western Orchestral Soc. Ltd), 1982–96 (Vice Pres., 1996–). SW Regl Pres., MENCAP, 1984–90; Nat. Pres., Hosp. Caterers Assoc., 1987–2004; Pres., European Assoc. of Commercial Television, 1991–92. Trustee, EEC Chamber Orchestra, 1987–97. Gen. Governor, British Nutrition Foundn, 1987–91. Chm. of Govs, Dartington Coll. of Arts, 1992–2003. JP Somerset, 1964 (Chm., Taunton Deane Magistrates Bench, 1987–92); DL Somerset, 1988. Hon. LLD Plymouth, 2003. *Recreations:* football, cricket, golf and tennis (watching), music. *Address:* Runnerstones, 32 Stonegallows, Taunton, Somerset TA1 5JP. *T:* (01823) 461265.

BAILEY, Christopher, MBE 2009; Chief Creative Officer, since 2009, and Chief Executive, since 2014, Burberry Ltd (Creative Director, 2001–09); *b* Yorks, 1971. *Educ:* Univ. of Westminster (BA 1990); Royal Coll. of Art (MA 1994; Hon. Fellow 2003). Womenswear Designer, Donna Karan, 1994–96; Sen. Designer, Womenswear, Gucci, Milan, 1996–2001. Co-Founder, Burberry Foundn, 2008–. Hon. DLitt Westminster, 2006; Hon. DSc Huddersfield, 2007. Designer of the Year, 2005 and 2009, Menswear Designer of the Year, 2007, 2008 and 2013, British Fashion Awards; Internat. Award, Council of Fashion Designers of America, 2010. *Address:* Burberry Ltd, Horseferry House, Horseferry Road, SW1P 2AW.

BAILEY, Colin Frederick, QPM 1993; Chief Constable, Nottinghamshire Constabulary, 1995–2000; *b* 17 Oct. 1943; *s* of late Fred Bailey and Mary (*née* Sivill); *m* 1st, 1966, Christine Lound (*d* 2009); one *s* one *d*; 2nd, 2012, Glenys Hayers. *Educ:* Queen Elizabeth's GS, Horncastle, Lincs; Univ. of Sheffield (LLB Hons). Lincolnshire Constab., 1960–86; Asst Chief Constable (Crime Ops), W Yorks Police, 1986–90; Dep. Chief Constable, Nottinghamshire Constab., 1990–95. Chairman: ACPO Race and Community Relns Sub Cttee, 1995–2000; ACPO Crime Prevention Sub Cttee, 1997–2000. Pres., Nottingham Br., RLSS, 1995–2000; Chm., E Midlands RLSS, 1998–2000. Chm., Police History Soc., 1998–2001. Pres., Carlton Male Voice Choir, 2005–. Vice Pres., Notts Br., Royal Soc. of St George, 2014–. *Recreations:* antique porcelain, wildlife, gardening, wine, foreign travel, Nottingham Forest FC. *Address:* Lauderdale, Boat Lane, Hoveringham, Notts NG14 7JP. *T:* (0115) 966 4100.

BAILEY, Prof. Colin Gareth, PhD; CEng, FREng; FICE, FIStructE; Deputy President and Deputy Vice-Chancellor, University of Manchester, since 2014; *b* Hillingdon, 1967; *s* of Norman and Iris Bailey; *m* 1999, Fiona Maclagan; two *s* one *d. Educ:* Abbotsfield Comprehensive Sch.; Slough Coll. (ONC); Richmond upon Thames Coll. (HNC); Univ. of Sheffield (BEng 1992; PhD 1995). CEng 2003; MIFireE 2004; FICE 2006; FIStructE 2011; FREng 2012. Trainee, technician/draughtsman, Design Dept, Lovell Construction Services Ltd, 1984–86; technician/draughtsman, Cameron Taylor Partners, Consulting Civil and Structural Engrs, 1986–88; Design Engr, Clarke Nicholls and Marcel, Consulting Civil and Structural Engrs, 1988–89; res. asst, Univ. of Sheffield, 1994–96; Sen. Engr, Steel Construction Inst., 1996–98; Principal Engr, BRE, 1998–2002; Prof. of Structural Engrg, 2002–07, Hd, Sch. of Mech., Aerospace and Civil Engrg, 2007–09, Vice-Pres., and Dean, Faculty of Engrg and Physical Scis, 2009–14, Univ. of Manchester. Non-executive Director: Northern Consortium, 2010–; Univ. of Manchester 13 Ltd, 2011–; Univ. of Manchester Innovation Centre Ltd, 2011–. Mem., Standing Cttee on Structural Safety, 2009–. Mem., Adv. Bd, Manchester Mus. of Sci. and Industry, 2012–. Trustee, Find a Better Way charity, 2011–. Associate Ed., Fire Safety Jl, 2010–; Member, Editorial Board: Jl Steel Construction Res., 2008–11; Jl Structural Fire Engrg, 2010–. *Publications:* Design of Steel Framed Buildings without Applied Fire Protection, 1999; Fire Safe Design: a new approach to multi-storey-steel-framed buildings, 2000, 2nd edn 2006; New Fire Design Method for Steel Frames with Composite Floor Slabs, 2003; Guide to Evaluating Design Wind Loads to BS6399-2, 2003; Designers' Guide to EN1991-1-2, EN1992-1-2, EN1993-1-2 and EN1994-1-2, 2007; contribs to BRE Digest and Steel BRE Digest. *Recreations:* football, walking, family, DIY. *Address:* 12 Carlton Road, Hale, Altrincham, Cheshire WA15 8RJ. *T:* (0161) 306 9111. *E:* colin.bailey@manchester.ac.uk.

BAILEY, David, CBE 2001; FCSD; photographer, film maker; *b* 2 Jan. 1938; *s* of William Bailey and Agnes (*née* Green); *m* 1st, 1960, Rosemary Bramble; 2nd, 1967, Catherine Deneuve, *qv* (marr. diss.); 3rd, 1975, Marie Helvin (marr. diss. 1985); 4th, 1986, Catherine Dyer; two *s* one *d. Educ:* self taught. FRPS 1972 (Hon. FRPS 1999); FSIAD 1975. Photographer for Vogue, 1959–; dir of television commercials, 1966–, of documentaries, 1968–; director and producer: Who Dealt? (TV film), 1992; Models Close-Up (TV documentary), 1998; dir, The Intruder (film), 1999. Exhibitions: Nat. Portrait Gall., 1971; one-man retrospective, V&A, 1983; Internat. Centre of Photograph, NY, 1984; Photographs from the Sudan, ICA and tour, 1985; Bailey Now!, Nat. Centre of Photography, Bath, 1989; Hamilton's Gall., annually, 1995–; Camerawork, Berlin, 1997; Carla Sozzani Gall., Milan, 1997; Galerie Claire Fontaine, Luxembourg, 1997; A Gallery for Fine Photography, New Orleans; painting exhibn, Well Hung Gall., 1997; Barbican, 1999; Nat. Mus. of Photography, Film & TV, 1999; Modern a Museet, Stockholm, 2000; Helsinki City Art Mus., 2000; Bonham's, 2010; David Bailey: New Sculpture and Photography, Pangolin, 2010; David Bailey's East End, Compressor House, 2012; Bailey's Stardust, NPG, 2014. FRSA. Hon. FCGI. Hon. DLitt Bradford, 1999. D&AD President's Award, for outstanding contrib. to creativity, 1998; awards for commercials including Clios, D&AD Gold Award, Cannes Golden Lion and Emmy. RPS Centenary Medal, 2005. *Publications:* Box of Pinups, 1964; Goodbye Baby and Amen, 1969; Warhol, 1974; Beady Minces, 1974; Papua New Guinea, 1975; Mixed Moments, 1976; Trouble and Strife, 1980; David Bailey's London NW1, 1982; Black and White Memories, 1983; Nudes 1981–84, 1984; Imagine, 1985; If We Shadows, 1992; The Lady is a Tramp, 1995 (TV film, 1995); Rock & Roll Heroes, 1997; Models Close-Up, 1998; Archive One, 1957–69, 1999; Chasing Rainbows, 2001; (with Kate Kray) The Art of Violence, 2003; Archive Two: locations, 2003; Bailey's Democracy, 2005; Havana, 2006; NY JS DB 62, 2007; Pictures That Mark Can Do, 2007; Is that so Kid, 2008; 8 Minutes: Hirst and Bailey, 2009; Eye, 2009; Flowers, Skulls, Contacts, 2010; Bailey Exposed, 2013; Bailey's Stardust, 2014; Bailey's East End, 2014; Tears and Tears, 2015; *relevant publication:* (with Jackie Higgins) David Bailey: Look, 2010. *Recreations:* aviculture, photography, travelling, painting.

BAILEY, Ven. David Charles; Archdeacon of Bolton, since 2008; *b* Shipley, W Yorks, 5 Dec. 1952; *s* of (George) Eric Bailey and Florence Violet, (Billie), Bailey; *m* 1978, Kathryn Ann Middleton; two *s* one *d. Educ:* Bradford Grammar Sch.; Lincoln Coll., Oxford (MSc 1977; MA 1978); St John's Coll., Nottingham (BA 1979). Ordained deacon, 1980, priest, 1981; Assistant Curate: St John's, Worksop, 1980–83; Edgware, 1983–87; Incumbent, S Cave and Ellerker with Broomfleet, York, 1987–97; Rural Dean, Howden, 1991–97; Incumbent, Beverley Minster, and Priest-in-charge, Routh, 1997–2008. Canon and Preb., York Minster, 1998–2008. *Recreations:* watching cricket, football (Leeds Utd), photography, music esp. jazz. *Address:* 14 Springside Road, Walmersley, Bury, Lancs BL9 5JE. *T:* (0161) 761 6117. *E:* archdeaconbolton@manchester.anglican.org.

BAILEY, David John; QC 2006; *b* 6 March 1965; *s* of John Hardy Bailey and Joyce Marion de Havilland; *m* 1993, Catherine Crick; two *s* and one step *s. Educ:* Oundle Sch.; Mansfield Coll., Oxford (Eldon Schol.; BA 1st Cl. Hons); Univ. of Calif, Los Angeles (LLM). Called to the Bar, Gray's Inn, 1989; specialising in commercial law. Chm. and Dir, English Sinfonia, 2003–. Trustee, Menat Trust, 2003–. Mem., Old Oundelian Club. *Publications:* (contrib.) Insurance Disputes, 1999, 3rd edn 2011. *Recreations:* shooting, ski-ing, music, theatre. *Address:* 7 King's Bench Walk, Temple, EC4Y 7DS. *T:* (020) 7583 0404, *Fax:* (020) 7583 0950. *E:* dbailey@7kbw.co.uk. *Clubs:* Royal Automobile, MCC.

BAILEY, Dennis, RDI 1980; ARCA; graphic designer and illustrator; Partner, Bailey and Kenny, since 1988; *b* 20 Jan. 1931; *s* of Leonard Charles Bailey and Ethel Louise Funnell; *m* 1985, Nicola Anne Roberts; one *s* one *d. Educ:* West Sussex Sch. of Art, Worthing; Royal College of Art. Asst Editor, Graphis magazine, Zürich, 1956; free-lance design practice, London, 1957–87; Paris, 1961–64; Art Dir, Town magazine, London, 1964–66; Lectr in graphic design, Chelsea Sch. of Art, 1970–81, Middlesex Polytechnic, 1985–89. *Clients and work include:* Economist Newspaper: covers and typographic advisor; Economist Publications: The World in 1987–2013; Architectural Assoc.: art dir of journal AA Files; Arts Council of GB: design of exhibn catalogues and posters for Dada and Surrealism Reviewed, 1978, Picasso's Picassos, 1981, Renoir, 1985, Torres-Garcia, 1985, Le Corbusier, 1987, Art in Latin America, 1989, Dali: the early years, 1994; Royal Academy: catalogue and graphics for Pompeii AD 79, 1977, graphics for The Genius of Venice, 1984, Inigo Jones, 1989, Frans Hals, 1990, Egon Schiele, 1990, Mantegna, 1992; RSA: housestyle, 1989; A. d'Offay Gallery: catalogues, 1990–91; design of business print for Cons. Gold Fields, London Merchant Securities and N. M. Rothschild & Sons. Design of BMJ, 1997; illustrations for The Economist, Esquire, Harpers Bazaar (USA), Illustrated London News, Listener, Nova, Observer, Olympia (Paris), Town; book jackets for Jonathan Cape and Penguin Books; illustrated book, Read to Write, 1954. Books designed: Bonnard, 1995; Francis Bacon's Studio, 2005; Performing Architecture, 2006; Hard Rain, 2007; Sir John Soane's Museum, London, 2009. *Address:* Cunningham Place, NW8 8JU.

BAILEY, Edward Henry; His Honour Judge Bailey; a Circuit Judge, Central London Civil Justice Centre, since 2000; *b* 24 May 1949; *s* of Geoffrey Henry Bailey and Ninette Bailey; *m* 1983, Claire Dorothy Ann From; two *d. Educ:* King's Sch., Canterbury; Gonville and Caius Coll., Cambridge (MA, LLB). Called to the Bar, Middle Temple, 1970; Lectr, Inns of Court Sch. of Law, 1970–72; in practice as barrister, 1972–2000. Mem., Judicial Wing, Insol-Europe, 2008–. *Publications:* Personal Insolvency: law and practice, 1987, 4th edn 2008; Corporate Insolvency: law and practice, 1992, 4th edn 2014; Law of Voluntary Arrangements, 2003, 2nd edn 2007; (contrib.) Halsbury's Laws of England, 4th edn 1989. *Recreations:* music, gardening.

BAILEY, Glenda Adrianne, OBE 2008; Editor-in-Chief, Harper's Bazaar, since 2001; *b* 16 Nov. 1958; *d* of John Ernest Bailey and Constance Groome. *Educ:* Noel Baker Sch., Derby; Kingston Poly. (BA Fashion Design; Hon. MA). Editor: Honey Magazine, 1986; Folio Magazine, 1987; Marie Claire (UK edn), 1988–96; Editor-in-Chief, Marie Claire (US edn), 1996–2001. Women's Magazine Editor of the Year, 1989, 1992, Editor's Editor of the Year, 1992, BSME; Amnesty Internat. Award, 1997; Mediaweek Editor of the Year Award. Hon. PrD Derby, 2001. *Address:* (office) 300 West 57th Street, New York, NY 10019, USA.

BAILEY, Jack Arthur; Secretary, MCC, 1974–87; Secretary, International Cricket Conference, 1974–87; *b* 22 June 1930; *s* of Horace Arthur and Elsie Winifred Bailey; *m* 1st, 1957, Julianne Mary Squier (marr. diss.); one *s* two *d*; 2nd, 1991, Vivian Mary Robins. *Educ:* Christ's Hospital; University Coll., Oxford (BA). Asst Master, Bedford Sch., 1958–60; Reed Paper Group, 1960–67; Rugby Football Correspondent, Sunday Telegraph, 1962–74; Asst Sec., MCC, 1967–74. Regular contributor to The Times, 1987–. Mem., Cricket Writers' Club. *Publications:* Conflicts in Cricket, 1989; Trevor Bailey: a life in cricket, 1993. *Recreations:* cricket (played for Essex and for Oxford Univ.), golf. *Address:* Wickets, Dippenhall Street, Crondall, Farnham, Surrey GU10 5NX. *T:* (01252) 851870. *Clubs:* MCC; Harlequins Cricket (Pres., 1988–2014), XL (Pres., 1997–99); Vincent's (Oxford).

BAILEY, Dame Jessica Lois; *see* Corner, Dame J. L.

BAILEY, John; *see* Bailey, W. J. J.

BAILEY, Sir John Bilsland, KCB 1987 (CB 1982); Chief Adjudicator, 1989–2000, and Director, 1998–2002, Independent Committee for Supervision of Standards of Telephone Information Services; Chairman, Disciplinary Tribunal of Personal Investment Authority, 1994–2001; *b* 5 Nov. 1928; *o s* of late Walter Bailey and Ethel Edith Bailey, FRAM (who *m* 2nd, Sir Thomas George Spencer); *m* 1952, Marion Rosemary (*née* Carroll); two *s* one *d. Educ:* Eltham Coll.; University Coll., London (LLB). Solicitor of Supreme Court. Under-Sec. (Legal), Dept of HM Procurator General and Treasury Solicitor, 1973–77; Legal Dir, Office of Fair Trading, 1977–79; Dep. Treasury Solicitor, 1979–84; HM Procurator Gen. and Treasury Solicitor, 1984–88. Pres., Disciplinary Cttee, 1994, Public Interest Dir, 1993–94, LAUTRO; Dir, PIA, 1994–97. Gov., Anglo-European Coll. of Chiropractic, 1990–94. Chm., Westminster Soc., 1994–2000. *Recreation:* historical perambulations.

BAILEY, Sir John Richard, 4th Bt *cr* 1919, of Cradock, Province of Cape of Good Hope, Union of South Africa; *b* 11 June 1947; *s* of Sir Derrick Thomas Louis Bailey, 3rd Bt, DFC and Katharine Nancy Stormonth Darling; *S* father, 2009; *m* 1977, Philippa Jane, *o d* of John Sherwin Mervyn Pearson Gregory; two *s* one *d. Educ:* Winchester; Christ's Coll., Cambridge (BA 1969). *Heir: s* James Edward Bailey, *b* 7 Sept. 1983.

BAILEY, Maj. Gen. Jonathan Bernard Appleton, CB 2005; MBE 1980; PhD; Director, Boeing Defence UK, 2007–13; *b* 12 April 1951; *m* 1976, Deborah Smith; two *s* one *d. Educ:* Charterhouse; Univ. of Sussex (BA 1972); Univ. of Cranfield (PhD 2004). Commnd RA 1972; served NI; comd Assembly Place "ROMEO" (ZIPRA guerillas), Rhodesia, 1979–80; OC troops, MV Baltic Ferry, sailing to S Atlantic, then Ops Officer, 4th Field Regt RA, Falklands War, 1982; psc 1983; HCSC 1994; Chief Fire Co-ordination, ARRC, 1997–99; Chief Jt Implementation Commn, HQ Kosovo Force, and Chief Liaison Officer, Yugoslav

Gen. Staff and Kosovo Liberation Army, 1999; Dir, RA, 2000–01; Dir Gen. Develt and Doctrine, MoD, 2002–05. Dir, Centre for Defence and Internat. Security Studies, 2005–06; defence analyst and consultant, 2005–07. Consultant, Leverhulme prog. on Changing Character of War, Oxford Univ., 2005–. Col Comdt, RA, 2003–08. QCVS 1999. *Publications:* Field Artillery and Firepower, 1989; Great Power Strategy in Asia 1905–2005, 2007; contributor: British Fighting Methods in the Great War, 1996; The Emerging Strategic Environment, 1999; The Dynamics of Military Revolution 1300–2050, 2001; The Past as Prologue, 2006; Contemporary Operations: reflections on and of Empire, 2007; (ed jtly) British Generals in Blair's Wars, 2013; contrib. professional jls.

BAILEY, Mark David, PhD; High Master, St Paul's School, since 2011; *b* 21 Nov. 1960; *s* of Ronald Bailey and Maureen Bailey (*née* Oates); *m* 1989, Julie Margaret Noy; one *s* one *d*. *Educ:* Univ. of Durham (BA Econ. Hist. 1982); Corpus Christi Coll., Cambridge (PhD History 1986; Rugby blue, 1982–85). Fellow, Gonville and Caius Coll., Cambridge, 1986–96; Lectr in Local History, Bd of Continuing Educn, Univ. of Cambridge, 1991–96; Fellow, Corpus Christi Coll., Cambridge, 1996–99; Headmaster, Leeds Grammar Sch., later The Grammar Sch. at Leeds, 1999–2010; Prof. of Late Medieval History, 2010–11, Vis. Prof., 2011–, UEA. Vis. Fellow, All Souls Coll., Oxford, 2010. Mem. Council, RFU, 1994–98. Played Rugby Union for England, 1984–90 (7 caps); Captain, Suffolk CCC, 1988–90. Mem. Council, Sir Winston Churchill Meml Trust, 2007–. FRHistS 1999. T. S. Ashton Award, British Econ. Hist. Soc., 1988, 1994. *Publications:* A Marginal Economy?: East Anglian Breckland in the later Middle Ages, 1989; (ed) The Bailiffs' Minute Book of Dunwich 1404–1430, 1992; (with J. Hatcher) Modelling the Middle Ages: the history and theory of England's Economic Development, 2001; The English Manor *c* 1200–*c* 1500, 2002; Medieval Suffolk: an economic and social history 1200–1500, 2007; (with S. H. Rigby) Town and Countryside in Medieval England, 2012; The Decline of Serfdom in Late Medieval England, 2014; various articles in learned jls and contribs to collections of essays on medieval England. *Recreations:* local history, walking, sport, food, music. *Address:* St Paul's School, Lonsdale Road, Barnes, SW13 9JT. *Clubs:* East India (Hon. Mem.); Hawks (Cambridge).

BAILEY, Michael John; Chairman and Chief Executive, Trusthouse Services Group, since 2008; *b* 14 Oct. 1948; *s* of Sidney William Bailey and Joyce Mary Bailey; *m* 1st (marr. diss.); two *d*; 2nd, 2007, Michelle. *Educ:* Westminster Coll., London. Gardner Merchant: various posts, from Food Service Manager to Exec. Dir, UK South, 1964–85; Pres., US subsidiary, 1985–91; Man. Dir, UK contract feeding business, 1991–92; Exec. Vice Pres., Nutrition Mgt Food Services Co., 1992; Compass Group plc: Gp Develt Dir, 1993–94; Chief Exec., N America Div., 1994–99; Gp Chief Exec., 1999–2006. Non-exec. Dir, Allmanhall Ltd, 2007–. FHCIMA 1995. *Recreations:* music, watching sports, cooking. *Address:* Trusthouse Services Group, 2201 Water Ridge Parkway, Suite 320, Charlotte, NC 28217, USA.

BAILEY, Norman Stanley, CBE 1977; operatic and concert baritone; *b* Birmingham, 23 March 1933; *s* of late Stanley and Agnes Bailey; *m* 1st, 1957, Doreen Simpson (marr. diss. 1983); two *s* one *d*; 2nd, 1985, Kristine Ciesinski. *Educ:* Rhodes Univ., S Africa; Vienna State Academy. BMus; Performer's and Teacher's Licentiate in Singing; Diplomas, opera, lieder, oratorio. Principal baritone, Sadler's Wells Opera, 1967–71; regular engagements at world's major opera houses and festivals, including: La Scala, Milan (first British Wanderer in Siegfried, 1976); Royal Opera House, Covent Garden; Bayreuth Wagner Festival (first British Hans Sachs in Meistersinger, 1969); Vienna State Opera; Metropolitan Opera, NY; Chicago Opera; Paris Opera; Edinburgh Festival; Hamburg State Opera; Munich State Opera; Opera North; Glyndebourne Fest. BBC Television performances in Falstaff, La Traviata, The Flying Dutchman, Macbeth. Recordings include The Ring (Goodall); Meistersinger and Der Fliegende Holländer (Solti); Walküre (Klemperer), among others. Hon. RAM 1981; Hon. DMus Rhodes, 1986. *Recreations:* Mem., Baha'i world community; chess, notaphily, golf, microcomputing, indoor rowing (Mem. 16 million meter club; Winner, N American Rowing Challenge, 2004). *Address:* PO Box 655, Victor, ID 83455, USA.

BAILEY, Patrick Edward Robert; Director, Dan-Air Associated Services, 1985–92; *b* 16 Feb. 1925; *s* of late Edward Bailey and Mary Elizabeth Bailey; *m* 1947, Rowena Evelyn Nichols (*d* 1995); two *s* three *d*. *Educ:* Clapham Coll.; St Joseph's Coll., Mark Cross; LSE BSc(Econ). MIPM; FCILT (FCIT 1971) (Mem. Council, 1982–85 and 1987–89). RAPC and RAEC (Captain), 1943–48; Labour Management, Min. of Supply and Army Department: ROF Glascoed, 1951–54; RAE Farnborough, 1954–58; RSAF Enfield, 1958–59; ROF Radway Green, 1959–61; ROFs Woolwich, 1961–66. British Airports Authority: Dep. Personnel Dir, 1966; Personnel Dir, 1970; Airport Services Dir, 1974; Dir, Gatwick and Stansted Airports, 1977–85. Chm. Trustees, British Airports Authority Superannuation Scheme, 1975–86. Mem., Air Transport and Travel Industry Trng Bd, 1971–76; Mem. Bd, Internat. Civil Airports Assoc., 1974–77. Mem., Mid-Sussex DC, 1986–99 (Chm., 1991–93). *Address:* 17 Lucastes Lane, Haywards Heath, W Sussex RH16 1LE.

BAILEY, Paul, (christened **Peter Harry**); freelance writer, since 1967; radio broadcaster; *b* 16 Feb. 1937; *s* of Arthur Oswald Bailey and Helen Maud Burgess. *Educ:* Sir Walter St John's Sch., London; Central School of Speech and Drama. Actor, 1956–64: appeared in first productions of Ann Jellicoe's The Sport of My Mad Mother, 1958, and John Osborne's and Anthony Creighton's Epitaph for George Dillon, 1958. Literary Fellow at Univ. of Newcastle and Univ. of Durham, 1972–74; Bicentennial Fellowship, 1976; Visiting Lectr in English Literature, North Dakota State Univ., 1977–79; Sen. Res. Fellow, Kingston Univ., 2010–. Theatre critic, The Oldie, 2010–. Frequent radio broadcaster, mainly on Radio 3; has written and presented programmes on Karen Blixen, Henry Green, I. B. Singer and Primo Levi, among others. FRSL, 1982–84 and 1990. E. M. Forster Award, 1974; George Orwell Meml Prize, 1978, for broadcast essay The Limitations of Despair. *Publications:* At the Jerusalem, 1967 (Somerset Maugham Award, 1968; Arts Council Prize, 1968); Trespasses, 1970; A Distant Likeness, 1973; Peter Smart's Confessions, 1977; Old Soldiers, 1980; An English Madam, 1982; Gabriel's Lament, 1986; An Immaculate Mistake: scenes from childhood and beyond (autobiog.), 1990; Sugar Cane, 1993; (ed) The Oxford Book of London, 1995; (ed) First Love, 1997; Kitty and Virgil, 1998; (ed) The Stately Homo: a celebration of the life of Quentin Crisp, 2000; Three Queer Lives (Fred Barnes, Naomi Jacob and Arthur Marshall), 2001; Uncle Rudolf (novel), 2002; A Dog's Life (memoir), 2003; Chapman's Odyssey, 2011; The Prince's Boy, 2014; contribs to Independent, TLS, Daily Telegraph, Guardian. *Recreations:* wandering in Eastern Europe, visiting churches, chamber music, watching tennis. *Address:* 79 Davisville Road, W12 9SH. *T:* (020) 8749 2279, 07854 414917.

BAILEY, Reginald William, CBE 2013; Chief Executive, Mothers' Union, 1999–2015; *b* London, 9 July 1950; *s* of Reginald Arthur Bailey and Katherine Eleanor Bailey (*née* Perryment); *m* 1973, Alison Ferguson; one *s* one *d* (and one *d* decd). *Educ:* Stationers' Co. Sch.; Poly. of South Bank. MIBiol 1973. Graduate trainee, J Sainsbury, 1970–73; Marketing Manager, Spillers Foods, 1973–78; Managing Director: Swift & Co., 1978–82; Carnation Petfoods plc, 1982–84; Prestige Gp plc, 1984–86; Scientific Investment Corp., 1986–89; Del Monte Foods Internat. plc, 1989–94; Chief Exec., Danish Bacon Co. plc, 1994–99. Advr to Coalition Govt on Families and Children, 2010–. Chm. Trustees, Traidcraft Foundn, 2003–12. Reader, C of E, 1991–; Hon. Canon, St Albans Abbey and Cathedral Ch, 2014. *Publications:* Letting Children be Children: a review of the commercialisation and sexualisation of children, 2011. *E:* regbailey@aol.com.

BAILEY, Sarah Joanne; *see* Storey, Dame S. J.

BAILEY, Dame Susan (Mary), DBE 2014 (OBE 2002); FRCPsych; Chair, Children and Young People's Mental Health Coalition, since 2014; Senior National Lead for Mental Health, Health Education England; President, Royal College of Psychiatrists, 2011–14; *b* Manchester, 29 Aug. 1950; *d* of Frank and Edith Mary Bailey; two *d*. *Educ:* Hulme Grammar Sch. for Girls; Watford Grammar Sch. for Girls; Univ. of Manchester (MB ChB 1973). MRCPsych 1976, FRCPsych 1996. Consultant Child and Adolescent Psychiatrist, Bolton, Salford and Trafford Mental Health Trust, subseq. Gtr Manchester W Mental Health NHS Foundn Trust, 1983; Hon. Prof. of Child Mental Health, Univ. of Central Lancs, 2004. Chair, Acad. of Royal Med. Colls, 2015– (Vice Chair, 2012–14). Section Chair, Eur. Assoc. of Child and Adolescent Psychiatry, 2005–14. Trustee: Centre for Mental Health; MAC-UK. Hon. Fellow, Coll. of Psychiatrists (SA). *Recreations:* with children and grandchildren, walking, visual arts, music. *Address:* FACTs Team, Adult & Youth Specialised Services Directorate, Adolescent Forensic Service, Greater Manchester West Mental Health NHS Foundation Trust, Bury New Road, Prestwich, Manchester M25 3BL. *T:* (0161) 772 3601. *E:* Sue.Bailey@gmw.nhs.uk.

BAILEY, Sylvia, (Sly); Chief Executive, Trinity Mirror plc, 2003–12; *b* 24 Jan. 1962; *d* of Thomas Lewis Grice and Sylvia Grice (*née* Bantick); *m* 1998, Peter Bailey. *Educ:* St Saviour's and St Olave's Grammar Sch. for Girls. IPC Magazines, 1989–2002: Ad Sales Dir, 1990–97; Bd Dir, 1994–2002; Man. Dir, TX, 1997–99; Chief Exec., IPC Media, 1999–2002; non-executive Director: Littlewoods plc, 2002; EMI, 2004–07 (Sen. Ind. Dir, and Chm., Remuneration Cttee, 2007); Ladbrokes plc, 2009– (Mem., Remuneration Cttee, 2009–); Greencore Gp, 2013–. Mem., Press Assoc. Bd, 2003–12 (Chm., Remuneration Cttee, 2009–12). Pres., NewstrAid, 2003–. Gov., English Nat. Ballet Sch. Ltd, 2009–. Hon. MA East London, 2004. Marcus Morris Award, PPA, 2002. *Recreation:* family.

BAILEY, (William) John (Joseph); journalist; *b* 11 June 1940; *s* of Ernest Robert Bailey and Josephine Smith; *m* 1963, Maureen Anne, *d* of James Gibbs Neenan and Marjorie Dorema Wrigglesworth; five *s* three *d*. *Educ:* St Joseph's, Stanford-le-Hope, Essex; Campion Hall, Jamaica; St George's Coll., Kingston, Jamaica; St Chad's Coll., Wolverhampton. Reporter: Southend Standard, Essex, and Essex and Thurrock Gazette, 1960–63; Northern Daily Mail, 1963–64; Chief Reporter, Billingham and Stockton Express, 1964–72; Sub-Editor, Mail, Hartlepool, 1972–75; Features Editor, Echo, Sunderland, 1975–97; Editor, Northern Cross, 1981–2008; Media Officer, Sunderland City Council, 1998–2005. Mem., Press Council, 1974–80 (Member: Complaints Cttee, 1974–76; Cttee for Evidence to Royal Commission on Press, 1975–76; Gen. Purposes Cttee, 1976–77; Secretariat Cttee, 1976–80). National Union of Journalists: Mem., Nat. Exec. Council, 1966–82; Pres., 1973–74; Gen. Treasurer, 1975–82; Mem. of Honour, 1999. Sec., Hartlepool People Ltd, 1983–2002. Member: NE Br., Catholic Writers' Guild of St Francis de Sales, 2003–; Tyneside Circle, Newman Assoc. Mem., Friends of Nat. Glass Centre, Sunderland. Mem., Hartlepool Local Exchange Trading System. Trustee, Journalists' Copyright Trust, 1996–. Provincial Journalist of the Year (jtly with Carol Roberton), British Press Awards, 1977 (commended, 1979); Special award Northern Cross, 1984–85, 1989, 1992, 1996, 1997, personal award, 2000, Tom Cordner North East Press Awards. *Address:* 225 Park Road, Hartlepool TS26 9NG. *Clubs:* Tyneside Irish Centre (Newcastle upon Tyne); Island Social (Seaham); Lindisfarne Social (Wallsend).

BAILHACHE, Sir Philip (Martin), Kt 1996; a Judge of the Court of Appeal, Jersey, 1994–2011, and Guernsey, 1996–2011; Senator, States of Jersey, since 2011; Minister for External Relations, since 2013; *b* 28 Feb. 1946; *s* of late Jurat Lester Vivian Bailhache (Lieut-Bailiff of Jersey, 1980–82) and Nanette Ross (*née* Ferguson); *m* 1st, 1967 (marr. diss. 1982); two *s* two *d*; 2nd, 1984, Linda (*née* Le Vavasseur dit Durell); one *s* one *d*. *Educ:* Charterhouse; Pembroke Coll., Oxford (Hon. Fellow, 1995). Called to the Bar, Middle Temple, 1968, Hon. Bencher, 2003; called to the Jersey Bar, 1969; QC (Jersey) 1989. In private practice as Advocate, Jersey, 1969–74; States of Jersey Dep. for Grouville, 1972–74; Solicitor-Gen., Jersey, 1975–85; Attorney Gen. for Jersey, 1986–93; Dep. Bailiff of Jersey, 1994–95, Bailiff, 1995–2009; Comr, Royal Court of Jersey, 2009–11. Asst Chief Minister, States of Jersey, 2011–13. Chm., Governing Body, Inst. of Law, Jersey, 2008–. Chm., Jersey Arts Council, 1987–89. Exec. Vice-Pres., Commonwealth Magistrates' and Judges' Assoc., 2009–11. Editor, Jersey and Guernsey Law Review (formerly Jersey Law Review), 1997–. *Recreations:* books, wine, gardening, the arts. *Address:* L'Anquetinerie, Grouville, Jersey, Channel Islands JE3 9UX. *T:* (01534) 852533. *Clubs:* Reform; United (Jersey).

See also W. J. Bailhache, V. M. Bird.

BAILHACHE, William James; QC 2000; Bailiff of Jersey, since 2015 (Deputy Bailiff, 2009–15); *b* 24 June 1953; *s* of late Jurat Lester Vivian Bailhache, sometime Lieut Bailiff of Jersey, and Nanette Ross Bailhache (*née* Ferguson); *m* 1975, Jennifer Laura Nudds; one *s* one *d*. *Educ:* Charterhouse; Merton Coll., Oxford (MA). Called to the Bar, Middle Temple, 1975; Advocate, Royal Court of Jersey, 1976; Partner, Bailhache & Bailhache, 1977–94, Bailhache Labesse, 1994–99; HM Attorney Gen. for Jersey, 2000–09. Chm., Barclays Bank Finance Co. (Jersey) Ltd, 1996–99 (Dir, 1982–99); Dir, Jersey Gas Co. Ltd, 1992–94. *Recreations:* golf, cricket, reading, opera. *Address:* Seymour House, La Rocque, Jersey JE3 9BB. *T:* (01534) 854708. *Clubs:* Vincent's (Oxford); Royal Jersey Golf (Captain, 1995–96).

See also Sir P. M. Bailhache, V. M. Bird.

BAILIE, Robert Ernest, (Roy), OBE 1995; Chairman, W. & G. Baird (Holdings) Ltd, since 1982; *b* 2 June 1943; s of Robert and Rosetta Bailie; *m* 1971, Paddy Clark; two *s* one *d*. *Educ:* Belfast High Sch.; Queen's Univ., Belfast; Harvard Sch. of Business (grad. 1985). MSO Ltd, 1958–65; joined W. & G. Baird, 1965, Man. Dir, 1972, led mgt buy-out, 1977; Director: W. & G. Baird Ltd, 1977–; Graphic Plates Ltd, 1977–; MSO Ltd, 1984–2013; Blackstaff Press Ltd, 1995–; Corporate Document Services Ltd, 2000–; Court, Bank of Ireland, 1999–2006 (Mem., NI Adv. Bd, 1994–98); Bank of Ireland UK Financial Services PLC, 2006–08; non-executive Director: UTV, 1997–2013; Bank of England, 1998–2003. Pres., BPIF, 1999–2001 (Mem., Exec. Bd of Mgt, 1978–80, Chm., 1980–84, NW Reg.; Vice-Pres., 1997–99). Member: NI Council for Higher Educn, 1985–90; IDB for NI, 1990–95; Adv. Council on Alcohol and Drug Educn, 1990–99; Chairman: CBI (NI), 1992–94; NI Tourist Bd, 1996–2002; Opera Company NI, 2009–; Nat. Trust NI, 2010–. *Recreations:* sailing, golf, walking. *Address:* The Look Out, 49 Main Street, Castlerock, Coleraine, Co. Derry, Northern Ireland BT51 4RA. *T:* (028) 9334 0383.

BAILIE, Rt Hon. Robin John; PC (NI) 1971; Solicitor of the Supreme Court of Judicature, Northern Ireland, since 1961; *b* 6 March 1937; *m* 1961, Margaret F. (*née* Boggs); one *s* three *d*. *Educ:* Rainey Endowed Sch., Magherafelt, Co. Londonderry; Queen's Univ., Belfast (LLB). MP (NI) for Newtonabbey, 1969–72; Minister of Commerce, Govt of NI, 1971–72. *Recreations:* wine drinking, ski-ing, squash, golf, tennis. *Address:* Calle Gamo 7, Los Monteros, Marbella 29603, Spain. *T:* (95) 2775568.

BAILIE, Roy; *see* Bailie, R. E.

BAILIN, Alexander; QC 2010; barrister; a Recorder, since 2012; a Deputy High Court Judge, since 2013; *b* Brighton, 23 Jan. 1969; *s* of Prof. David Bailin and Dr Anjali Bailin; *m* 2001, Emma Saunders; one *s* one *d*. *Educ:* Dorothy Stringer High Sch., Brighton; Brighton, Hove and Sussex Sixth Form Coll.; Emmanuel Coll., Cambridge (BA Hons 1991; MA); Univ. of Sussex (CPE 1994). Derivatives trader, 1991–93; called to the Bar, Lincoln's Inn, 1995; in practice as barrister, specialising in criminal, public and human rights law; Matrix Chambers, 2003–. *Publications: contributions to:* Criminal Justice and Human Rights, 2007; Fraud: criminal law and procedure, 2012; Blackstone's Criminal Practice, 2012; articles in nat. press and legal jls. *Recreations:* scuba diving, West African music, theatre, ski-ing, tennis. *Address:* Matrix Chambers, Griffin Building, Gray's Inn, WC1R 5LN. *T:* (020) 7404 3447. *E:* alexbailin@matrixlaw.co.uk.

BAILLIE, family name of **Baron Burton**.

BAILLIE, Sir Adrian (Louis), 8th Bt *cr* 1823, of Polkemmet, Linlithgowshire; *b* 26 March 1973; *o s* of Sir Gawaine George Hope Baillie, 7th Bt and of (Lucile) Margot Baillie; *S* father, 2003; *m* 2006, Amber Rose Laine; one *s* one *d*. *Educ:* Eton Coll.; Manchester Univ. (BA); City Univ. (Dip. Law); Inns of Court Sch. of Law; London Business Sch. (MBA). Called to the Bar, Middle Temple, 1999. Company Director. *Heir: s* Sebastian Gawaine Baillie, *b* 18 April 2011. *Address:* Freechase, Warninglid, Haywards Heath, West Sussex RH17 5SZ.

BAILLIE, Alexander; 'cellist; *b* 1956; *m* Christel; one *s* two *d*. *Educ:* Royal Coll. of Music; Hochschule für Musik, Vienna; studied with Jacqueline du Pré. Soloist with LSO, BBC SO, CBSO and orchestras worldwide; premières of works include Colin Matthew's Cello Concerto, 1984, Penderecki's 2nd Cello Concerto, and concerti by H. K. Gruber and Andrew MacDonald; recitals include Bach's Cello Suites (unaccompanied), Wigmore Hall, 1997; also appears with chamber music ensembles; Member: Villiers Piano Quartet; Heveningham Hall Piano Trio; Alia Musica, Berlin; formerly Mem., The Fires of London. Vis. Prof., Royal Coll. of Music; Prof. of Cello, Bremen Hochschule; Prof. of Cello and Chamber Music, GSMD, 2009–.

BAILLIE, Andrew Bruce; QC 2001; a Recorder, since 1989; *b* 17 May 1948; *s* of Edward Oswald Baillie and Molly Eva (Renée) Baillie (*née* Andrews); *m* 1976, Mary Lou Meech Palmer (*d* 1988); one *s* two *d*. *Educ:* King's Coll. Sch., Wimbledon; Univ. de Besançon; Univ. of Kent at Canterbury (BA Social Scis 1969). Called to the Bar, Inner Temple, 1970. *Recreations:* played Rugby for Univ. of Kent, E Kent and London Scottish; now cooking and visiting Spain. *Address:* 9 Gough Square, EC4A 3DG. *T:* (020) 7832 0500. *E:* abaillie@9goughsquare.co.uk.

BAILLIE, Jacqueline, (Jackie); Member (Lab) Dumbarton, Scottish Parliament, since 1999; *b* Hong Kong, 15 Jan. 1964; *d* of Frank and Sophie Barnes; *m* 1982, Stephen, *s* of James and Margaret Baillie; one *d*. *Educ:* Glasgow Univ. (MSc). Resource Centre Manager, Strathkelvin DC, 1990–96; Community Economic Develt Manager, E Dumbartonshire Council, 1996–99. Scottish Parliament: Dep. Minister for Communities, 1999–2000; Minister for Social Justice, 2000–01; Shadow Cabinet Secretary for Health and Wellbeing, 2008–13, for Social Justice, Equalities and Welfare, 2013–. Chair, Scottish Labour Party, 1997–98 (Mem., Exec. Cttee, 1990–99). *Address:* Scottish Parliament, Edinburgh EH99 1SP.

BAILLIE, Prof. John, CA; Chairman, Accounts Commission for Scotland, 2007–13 (Member, 2003–13); Visiting Professor of Accountancy, University of Edinburgh, since 2013; *m* 1972, Annette; one *s* one *d*. *Educ:* Whitehill Sch. CA 1967 (Gold Medal and Distinction in final exams). Partner: Thomson McLintock & Co., later Peat Marwick McLintock, then KPMG, 1978–93; Scott-Moncrieff, 1993–2001. Johnstone-Smith Prof. of Accountancy, Univ. of Glasgow, 1983–88. Visiting Professor of Accountancy: Heriot-Watt Univ., 1989–2004; Univ. of Glasgow, 1996–2013. Member: Reporting Panel, Competition Commn, 2002–11; Ind. Local Govt Finance Review Cttee, 2004–07; Audit Scotland, 2004–13 (Chm., 2007–10). Convenor, Res. Cttee, 1995–99, and Mem. various technical and professional affairs cttees, Inst. of Chartered Accountants of Scotland; Mem., CIPFA, 2008. FRSA 1996. Hon. MA Glasgow, 1983. *Publications:* Systems of Profit Measurement, 1985; Consolidated Accounts and the Seventh Directive, 1985; technical and professional papers; contribs to Accountants' Magazine and other professional jls. *Recreations:* keeping fit, reading, music, golf. *Club:* Kilmacolm Golf (Captain, 2002).

BAILLIE-HAMILTON, family name of **Earl of Haddington**.

BAILLIEU, family name of **Baron Baillieu**.

BAILLIEU, 3rd Baron *cr* 1953, of Sefton, Australia and Parkwood, Surrey; **James William Latham Baillieu;** Director, Anthony Baillieu and Associates (Hong Kong) Ltd, since 1992; Managing Director, Bank NIKoil, since 2000; *b* 16 Nov. 1950; *s* of 2nd Baron Baillieu and Anne Bayliss, *d* of Leslie William Page, Southport, Queensland; *S* father, 1973; *m* 1st, 1974, Cornelia Masters Ladd (marr. diss. 1985), *d* of William Ladd; one *s*; 2nd, 1986, Clare Stephenson (marr. diss. 1995), *d* of Peter Stephenson; 3rd, 2004, Olga Vladimirovna; one *s*. *Educ:* Radley College; Monash Univ., Melbourne (BEc 1977). Short Service Commission, Coldstream Guards, 1970–73. Banque Nationale de Paris, 1978–80; Asst Dir, Rothschild Australia Ltd, 1980–88; Dir, Manufacturers Hanover Australia Ltd, 1988–90; Dir, Standard Chartered Asia Ltd, 1990–92; Asst Dir, Credit Lyonnais Asia Ltd, 1992–94; Asst Dir, Nomura International (Hong Kong) Ltd, 1995; Gen. Dir, Regent European Securities, 1995–96; Dir, CentreInvest Gp, Moscow, 1996–99. *Heir: s* Hon. Robert Latham Baillieu, *b* 2 Feb. 1979. *Clubs:* Boodle's; Hong Kong (Hong Kong); Australian (Melbourne).

BAILLIEU, Christopher Latham, MBE 1977; Chairman, sports coach UK, since 2010; *b* 12 Dec. 1949; *s* of late Hon. Edward Baillieu and Betty Anne Baillieu (*née* Taylor); *m* 1984, Jane Elizabeth Bowie; two *s* one *d*. *Educ:* Jesus Coll., Cambridge (BA 1972). Called to the Bar, Lincoln's Inn, 1976. Rowed in winning crew, Oxford v Cambridge Boat Race, 1970–73. Represented Great Britain in rowing, 1973–83; winner: Silver Medal, double sculls, Olympic Games, 1976; Gold Medal, World Championships, 1977; competed Olympic Games, 1980. Chairman: British Swimming, 2001–08; The Olympians, 2004–12; Wandsworth Active, 2009–; SportsAid, 2012–; Vice Chm., Torch Trophy Trust, 2002–. Steward, Henley Royal Regatta, 1985– (Trustee, Henley Stewards' Trust, 1992–). *Recreations:* exploring old buildings, hills, valleys and waterways. *Address:* 11 Woodthorpe Road, Putney, SW15 6UQ. *Clubs:* Hurlingham; Hawks (Cambridge); Leander.

BAILLIEU, Colin Clive; Director, Renata Baillieu Art Tours; Member, Monopolies and Mergers Commission, 1984–93; *b* 2 July 1930; *s* of Ian Baillieu and Joanna Baillieu (*née* Brinton); *m* 1st, 1955, Diana Robinson (marr. diss. 1968); two *d*; 2nd, 1968, Renata Richter; two *s*. *Educ:* Dragon Sch.; Eton. Commissioned Coldstream Guards, 1949. Local newspaper, Evening Standard, 1951–52; British Metal Corp., 1952–58; British Aluminium, 1958–60; Monsanto Fibres, 1960–66; Arthur Sanderson, 1966–68; Ultrasonic Machines, 1968–76. Chm., Gresham Underwriting Agencies, 1990–92. Mem., Council of Lloyd's, 1983–88. Lecturer: European Business Sch., London, 1995–2008; London Coll. of Printing, 1998–2005. Contested (C) Rossendale, Lancs, 1964 and 1966. Dir, Orchestra of St John's, Smith Square, 1999–2000. Dist Comr, Cowdray Pony Club, 1998–2001. *Publications:* The Lion and the Lamb, 1996. *Recreations:* ski-ing, 17th Century history, trees. *Address:* 17 North Pallant, Chichester, W Sussex PO19 1TQ. *T:* (01243) 778675. *Clubs:* Travellers, Beefsteak, Shikar, MCC.

BAILLIEU, Hon. Edward Norman, (Hon. Ted); MLA (L) Hawthorn, Victoria, Australia, since 1999; Premier of Victoria, and Minister of the Arts, 2010–13; Leader, Parliamentary Liberal Party (Victorian Division), 2006–13; *b* Melbourne, 31 July 1953; *s* of Darren Baillieu and Diana Margaret Baillieu (*née* Knox); *m* Robyn Mary Jubb; one *s* two *d*. *Educ:* Melbourne Grammar Sch.; Univ. of Melbourne (BArch); Royal Melbourne Inst. of Technol. (Cert. Business Studies). FRAIA. Formerly Partner, Mayne & Baillieu, Architects, Melbourne. Formerly Dir, Knight Frank Hldgs. Shadow Minister: for Tertiary Educn and Trng, 1999–2001; for Gaming, 2000–02; for Planning, 2001–06; for the Arts, 2006–10. Chm., Vic Govt Anzac Centenary Cttee, 2013–. Member: Bd, Tourism Vic, 1998–99; Melbourne Convention and Exhibn Trust, 1998–99. Dir, Australian Children's TV Foundn, 1997–99. Mem., Vic Bd of Mgt, Assoc. of Consulting Architects, 1985–99. Mem., Patron's Council, Epilepsy Foundn Vic; Patron: Hawthorn Community Chest, Melbourne; Mental Health Foundn. Ashoka Award, Aust.-India Business Council, 2013. *Recreations:* golf, basketball, swimming. *Address:* 325 Camberwell Road, Camberwell, Vic 3124, Australia. *E:* ted.baillieu@parliament.vic.gov.au.

BAIN, Andrew David, OBE 1997; FRSE 1980; Visiting Professor of Political Economy, University of Glasgow, 1991–98; *b* 21 March 1936; *s* of Hugh Bain and Kathleen (*née* Eadie); *m* 1st, 1960, Anneliese Minna Frieda Kroggel (marr. diss. 1988); three *s*; 2nd, 1989, Eleanor Riches. *Educ:* Glasgow Academy; Christ's Coll., Cambridge; PhD Cantab 1963. Junior Res. Officer, Dept of Applied Econs, Cambridge Univ., 1958–60; Res. Fellow, Christ's Coll., Cambridge, 1960; Instructor, Cowles Foundn, Yale Univ., 1960–61; Lectr, Cambridge, 1961–66; Fellow, Corpus Christi Coll., Cambridge, 1962; on secondment to Bank of England, 1965–67; Prof. of Econs, 1967–70, Esmee Fairbairn Prof. of Econs of Finance and Investment, 1970–77, Univ. of Stirling; Walton Prof. of Monetary and Financial Econs, Univ. of Strathclyde, 1977–84; Gp Econ. Advr, Midland Bank, 1984–90. Member: Cttee to Review the Functioning of Financial Institutions, 1977–80; (part-time) Monopolies and Mergers Commn, 1981–82; TEC Nat. Council, 1994–97; (part-time) Appeal Panel, Competition Commn, 2000–03; Competition Appeal Tribunal, 2003–11. Bd Mem., Scottish Enterprise, 1991–98. *Publications:* The Growth of Television Ownership in the United Kingdom (monograph), 1964; The Control of the Money Supply, 1970; Company Financing in the UK, 1975; The Economics of the Financial System, 1981, 2nd edn 1992; articles on demand analysis, monetary policy and other subjects.

See also Colin D. Bain.

BAIN, Christopher Derek; Director, Catholic Agency for Overseas Development, since 2003; *b* 27 Nov. 1953; *s* of Derek Bain and Mary Bain (*née* Hill). *Educ:* Leicester Univ. (BA); Middlesex Univ. (MBA); Open Univ. (MSc Develt Mgt). VSO develt worker, Fiji, 1975–77; VSO Field Officer, S Pacific, 1977–79; Dir, Churches' Housing Trust, Fiji, 1979–82; London Area Coordinator, Christian Aid, 1982–89; Oxfam: Sen. Campaigns Advr, 1989–93; Hd of Campaigns, 1993–96; Hd of Progs, VSO, 1996–2003. Hon. Dir, Disaster Emergency Cttee, 2003–; Chm., British Overseas Aid Gp, 2005–08; Mem. Exec. Cttee, Caritas Europa, 2010–. Pres., Co-opération Internat. pour le Développement et la Solidarité (CIDSE), 2011–. *Recreations:* long distance pilgrimages, ale and malt whiskey appreciation, friends. *Address:* 4 Penton Place, SE17 3JT. *T:* (020) 7735 7500. *E:* cdb@cafod.org.uk.

BAIN, Prof. Colin David, PhD; Professor of Chemistry, since 2005, and Dean and Deputy Pro-Vice Chancellor (Research), since 2015, Durham University; *b* 2 Jan. 1963; *s* of Andrew David Bain, *qv*; *m* 1992, Emma Victoria Claudia Kauffmann (marr. diss. 2012); one *s* two *d*. *Educ:* Dollar Acad.; Corpus Christi Coll., Cambridge (BA 1983); Harvard Univ. (PhD 1989). Mr & Mrs John Jaffe Res. Fellow, Univ. of Cambridge, and Fellow, Christ's Coll., Cambridge, 1988–91; Univ. Lectr, Univ. of Oxford, 1991–2005; Fellow, Magdalen Coll., Oxford, 1991–2005, Emeritus, 2005–; Dir, Inst. of Advanced Study, Durham Univ., 2008–12. Director: Magdalen Develt Co. Ltd, 1998–2005; GTE for Oxfordshire Ltd, 1999–2004; Member, Scientific Advisory Board: Oxford Capital Partners, 2005–; Max Planck Institute for Colloid and Interface Research, 2007–14; Res. Complex, Harwell, 2011–. Mem., Faraday Council, RSC, 2006–08; Trustee, RSC Pension Fund, 2009–. *Publications:* approx. 160 book chapters and articles in learned jls. *Recreations:* hill-walking, cycling, sailing. *Address:* Department of Chemistry, Durham University, South Road, Durham DH1 3LE. *T:* (0191) 334 2138, *Fax:* (0191) 334 2051. *E:* c.d.bain@dur.ac.uk.

BAIN, Douglas John; Industrial Adviser to the Secretary of State for Scotland, 1983–85; *b* 9 July 1924; *s* of Alexander Gillan Bain and Fanny Heaford; *m* 1946, Jean Wallace Fairbairn (*d* 2012); three *d*. *Educ:* Mosspark Elementary Sch.; Pollokshields Secondary School; Royal Technical Coll., Glasgow (DRTC). ATI. Royal Tech. Coll., 1941–43 and 1948–51. Trained and flew as pilot, RAF, 1943–48. J. & P. Coats Ltd, 1951–83: graduate trainee, 1951–55; overseas management, 1955–60; Hd, Office Management, 1960–68; Director, 1968–83; seconded to Scottish Office (Scottish Econ. Planning Dept) as Under Sec., 1979–82. *Recreations:* golf, walking, cycling, reading, internet, TV, six grandchildren and three great grandchildren. *Address:* Unit 4 Viewbank Gardens, 26–46 Rutherford Road, Viewbank, Melbourne, Vic 3084, Australia.

BAIN, Prof. Sir George (Sayers), Kt 2001; DPhil; President and Vice-Chancellor, Queen's University Belfast, 1998–2004, now Professor Emeritus; *b* 24 Feb. 1939; *s* of George Alexander Bain and Margaret Ioleen Bamford; *m* 1st, 1962, Carol Lynn Ogden White (marr. diss. 1987); one *s* one *d*; 2nd, 1988, Frances Gwynneth Rigby (*née* Vickers). *Educ:* Univ. of Manitoba (BA Hons 1961, MA 1964); Oxford Univ. (DPhil 1968). Lectr in Econs, Univ. of Manitoba, 1962–63; Res. Fellow, Nuffield Coll., Oxford, 1966–69; Frank Thomas Prof. of Indust. Relations, UMIST, 1969–70; University of Warwick: Dep. Dir, 1970–74, Dir, 1974–81, SSRC Industrial Relations Res. Unit; Pressed Steel Fisher Prof. of Industrial Relations, 1979–89; Chm., Sch. of Industrial and Business Studies, 1983–89; Principal, London Business Sch., 1989–97. Sec., British Univs Indust. Relations Assoc., 1971–74. Member: Mech. Engrg Econ. Develt Cttee, NEDO, 1974–76; Cttee of Inquiry on Indust. Democracy, Dept of Trade (Chm., Lord Bullock), 1975–76; Council: ESRC, 1986–91; Nat. Forum for Management Educn and Develt, 1987–90; Chm. Council, Univ. Management Schs, 1987–90. Member: Bd of Trustees, 1990–96, and Exec. Vice-Pres., 1991–95, European Foundn for Management Develt; Internat. Affairs Cttee, 1990–92, Bd of Dirs, 1992–94, Amer. Assembly of Collegiate Schs of Business; Council, Foundn for Mgt Educn, 1991–95; Council, IMgt (formerly BIM), 1991–93; Senior Salaries Review Body, 1993–96; Internat. Council, Amer. Mgt Assoc., 1993–95; Foundn for Canadian Studies in UK, 1993–2001, 2004–06; Exec. Cttee, Co-operation Ireland GB, 1994–97 (Dep. Chm., 1996–97); Bd of Dirs, Grad. Mgt Admission Council, 1996–97; Bd of Co-operation Ireland, 1998–2004; Educn Honours Cttee, 2005–10; Trustee: Navan at Armagh, 1999–2003; Scotch-Irish Trust, 1999–2007; Council for Advancement and Support of Educn, (CASE), 2004–08; CASE Europe, 2004–07; McClay Foundn, 2008–. Chairman: Food Sector Wkg Gp, NEDO, 1991–92; Commn on Public Policy and British Business, 1995–97; Low Pay Commn, 1997–2002, 2008–09; NI Meml Fund, 1998–2002; Conf. of Univ. Rectors in Ireland, 2000–01; Work and Parents Task Force, DTI, 2001; Pensions Policy Inst., 2002–04; Ind. Review of Fire Service, ODPM, 2002; ACU, 2002–03; NI Legal Services Review Gp, 2005–06; Advr on Royal Mail to Sec. of State for Trade and Industry, 2005–06; NI Ind. Strategic Review of Educn, 2006; NI Rev. of Policy on Location of Public Sector Jobs, 2007–08; Commn on Future of Nat. Minimum Wage and Low Pay Commn, Resolution Foundn, 2013–14. Pres., Involvement and Participation Assoc., 2002–06. Director: Blackwell Publishers Ltd (formerly Basil Blackwell Ltd), 1990–97; The Economist Gp, 1992–2001; Canada Life Gp (UK) Ltd, 1994–2014; Canada Life Assce Co., 1996–2003; Electra Private Equity (formerly Electra Investment Trust PLC), 1998–2008; Bombardier Aerospace Shorts Brothers Plc, 1998–2007; NI Sci. Park Foundn, 1999–2004; NI Adv. Bd, Bank of Ireland, 2000–02; Canada Life Capital Corp., 2003–14; Iain More Associates, 2004–07; Entertainment One, 2007–10; Great-West Lifeco Inc., 2009–14. Consultant: Royal Commn on Trade Unions and Employers' Assocs (Donovan Commn), 1966–67; NBPI, 1967–69; Canadian Task Force on Labour Relns, 1968; Dept of Employment; Manitoba and Canada Depts of Labour; arbitrator and mediator in indust. disputes. Vice-Chm., Bd and Chm., Develt Trust, Lyric Theatre, Belfast, 2006–11; Chairman: Bd, Ulster Orch. Soc., 2011–; Keeper's Council, Armagh Public Liby, 2014–. Patron, Somme Assoc., 2004–12. FRSA 1987; CCMI (CIMgt 1991); Companion, Assoc. Business Schs, 2007; Fellow: British Acad. of Mgt, 1994; London Business Sch., 1999. FAcSS (AcSS 2000). Hon. Fellow, Nuffield Coll., Oxford, 2002. Hon. DBA De Montfort, 1994; Hon. LLD: NUI, 1998; Guelph, UC of Cape Breton, 1999;

Manitoba, Warwick, 2003; Queen's, Canada, 2004; QUB, 2005; Hon. DLitt: Ulster, 2002; New Brunswick, 2003; Hon. DSc Cranfield, 2005. Chief Exec. Leadership Award, CASE, 2003; Canadian High Comr's Award, 2003; Lifetime Achievement Award, British Acad. of Mgt, 2014. *Publications:* Trade Union Growth and Recognition, 1967; The Growth of White-Collar Unionism, 1970; (jtly) The Reform of Collective Bargaining at Plant and Company Level, 1971; (jtly) Social Stratification and Trade Unionism, 1973; (jtly) Union Growth and the Business Cycle, 1976; (jtly) A Bibliography of British Industrial Relations, 1979; (jtly) Profiles of Union Growth, 1980; (ed) Industrial Relations in Britain, 1983; (jtly) A Bibliography of British Industrial Relations 1971–1979, 1985; contrib. prof. and learned jls. *Recreations:* reading, genealogy, piano playing, Western riding, ice skating. *Address:* Vice-Chancellor's Office, Queen's University Belfast, University Road, Belfast BT7 1NN. *Clubs:* Reform; Ulster Reform (Belfast).

BAIN, Iain Andrew; Editor, Nairnshire Telegraph, since 1987; *b* 25 Feb. 1949; *s* of late Alastair I. R. Bain and Jean R. Forrest; *m* 1974, Maureen Beattie; three *d*. *Educ:* Nairn Acad.; Univ. of Aberdeen (MA). Research, Univ. of Durham, 1971–74; Sub-editor, 1974, Asst Editor, 1980, Editor, 1981–87, The Geographical Magazine. Chm. Trustees, Nairn Mus. Ltd, 1998–; Pres., Nairn Lit. Inst., 2002–05. *Publications:* Mountains and People, 1982; Water on the Land, 1983; Mountains and Earth Movements, 1984; various articles. *Recreations:* reading, walking, photography. *Address:* Rosebank, Leopold Street, Nairn IV12 4BE. *Club:* Nairn Golf.

BAIN, Janet; *see* Rossant, J.

BAIN, John; *see* Bain, K. J.

BAIN, Ven. (John) Stuart; Archdeacon of Sunderland, since 2002; Priest-in-charge: Parish of Hedworth, since 2003 (Assistant Priest, 2002–03); St George's, East Boldon, since 2008; St Nicholas, Boldon, since 2010; *b* 12 Oct. 1955; *s* of John and Doris Bain; *m* 1978, Angela Forster; two *s* one *d*. *Educ:* Van Mildert Coll., Univ. of Durham (BA Theol. 1977); Westcott House, Cambridge. Ordained deacon, 1980, priest, 1981; Assistant Curate: Holy Trinity, Washington, 1980–84; St Nicholas, Dunston, 1984–86; Vicar, Shiney Row and Herrington, 1986–92; Priest-in-charge: Whitworth and Spennymoor, 1992–97; Merrington, 1994–97; Vicar, Spennymoor, Whitworth and Merrington, 1997–2002. Area Dean, Auckland, 1996–2002; Hon. Canon, 1998–2002, (supernumerary) Non-Residentiary Canon, 2002–, Durham Cathedral. Chairman: DFW Adoption (formerly Durham Family Welfare), 1999–; Lord Crewe's Charity, 2006–. *Recreations:* music (very eclectic tastes), landscape photography, cooking, enjoying good wines, surfing the net, enjoying mountains. *Address:* St Nicholas' Vicarage, Hedworth Lane, Boldon Colliery NE35 9JA. *T:* (0191) 536 2300, *Fax:* (0191) 519 3369. *E:* archdeacon.of.sunderland@durham.anglican.org.

BAIN, (Kenneth) John, OBE 2000; MA; Headmaster, The Purcell School, 1983–99; *b* 8 July 1939; *s* of Allan John and Hetty Bain; *m* 1962, Cynthia Mary Spain; one *s* one *d*. *Educ:* Bancroft's School; St Peter's College, Oxford (MA). Assistant Master, Stanbridge Earls School, 1962–70; Assistant Master and Housemaster, Cranleigh School, 1970–83. Gov., Arts Educnl Sch., Tring, 1999–2002. Dir, Endymion Ensemble, 1999–2003. Churchwarden, St Candida and Holy Cross, Whitchurch Canonicorum, 2008–11; Trustee, Friends of St Candida, 2014–. Hon. RCM 1999. *Publications:* occasional articles in educational jls. *Recreations:* Spanish language and culture, music, golf, walking, rough gardening. *Address:* Candida House, Whitchurch Canonicorum, Bridport, Dorset DT6 6RQ. *T:* (01297) 489629.

BAIN, Ven. Stuart; *see* Bain, Ven. J. S.

BAIN, William Thomas; *b* Glasgow, 29 Nov. 1972; *s* of Bill and Catherine Bain. *Educ:* St Roch's Secondary Sch., Glasgow; Univ. of Strathclyde (LLB Hons, DipLP, LLM). Sessional Lectr and Tutor, Univ. of Strathclyde Law Sch., 1996–2004; Sen. Lectr in Public Law, London South Bank Univ., 2004–09. MP (Lab) Glasgow NE, Nov. 2009–2015; contested (Lab) same seat, 2015. PPS to Minister of State, DfT, 2010; Shadow Minister for Transport, 2010, for Envmt, Food and Rural Affairs, 2010–11, for Scotland, 2011–13. Mem., Business, Innovation and Skills Select Cttee, 2013–15. Chair, All Party Gp on Sudan and S Sudan, 2012–15. *Publications:* (contrib.) Devolution to Scotland: the legal aspects, 1997; (contrib.) What Next for Labour?: ideas for a new generation, 2011. *Recreations:* films, modern music, walking, reading.

BAINBRIDGE, Cyril, FCIJ; author and journalist; *b* 15 Nov. 1928; *o s* of late Arthur Herman and Edith Bainbridge; *m* 1953, Barbara Hannah (*née* Crook); one *s* two *d*. *Educ:* privately (Negus Coll., Bradford). Served Army, staff of CGS, WO, 1947–49. Entered journalism as Reporter, Bingley Guardian, 1944–45; Telegraph and Argus, and Yorkshire Observer, Bradford, 1945–54; Press Assoc., 1954–63; joined The Times, 1963: Asst News Editor, 1967; Dep. News Editor, 1967–69; Regional News Editor, 1969–77; Managing News Editor, 1977–82; Asst Managing Editor, 1982–86; Editorial Data Manager, Times Newspapers, 1986–88. Vice-Pres., 1977–78, Pres., 1978–79, Fellow, 1986, Chartered Inst. of Journalists; Member: Press Council, 1980–90; Nat. Council for Trng of Journalists, 1983–86. *Publications:* Taught With Care: a Century of Church Schooling, 1974; The Brontës and their Country, 1978, 3rd edn 1993; Brass Triumphant, 1980; North Yorkshire and North Humberside, 1984, 2nd edn 1989; (ed) One Hundred Years of Journalism, 1984; Pavilions on the Sea, 1986; (jtly) The News of the World Story, 1993; contrib. to various magazines. *Recreations:* reading, brass bands, water colour painting. *Address:* 6 Lea Road, Hemingford Grey, Huntingdon, Cambs PE28 9ED.

BAINBRIDGE, Prof. Janet Mary, OBE 2000; PhD; Chief Executive, Agricultural Technology Organisation, UK Trade and Investment, since 2013; *b* 14 April 1947; *d* of Henry George Munn and Vera Doreen Munn; *m* 1st, 1970, Geoffrey Stathers Tuffnell (marr. diss. 1985); 2nd, 1987, Dr George Bainbridge (marr. diss. 2011); one *s* one *d*. *Educ:* Gravesend Girls' Grammar Sch.; Univ. of Newcastle upon Tyne (BSc Hons); Univ. of Leeds (PGCE); Univ. of Durham (PhD 1986). Microbiol. Res., Head Office, J. Sainsbury Ltd, 1968–70; NHS, 1970–71; secondary teaching, 1971–72; lectr, further educn, 1972–80; Teesside Polytechnic, then University: Lectr, then Sen. Lectr, 1980–85; Prin. Lectr, 1985–92; Divl Leader, 1992–98; Prof., 1996–2007, now Emeritus; Dir, Sch. of Sci. and Technol., 1998–2002; Tutor Counsellor, Sci. Foundn Degree, 1989–99, and Tutor, genetics, 1990–92, Open Univ. Chief Exec., European Process Industries Competitiveness Centre, 2001–04. Sen. Specialist Advr (Govt and Europe), One Northeast, 2004–07. Global Res. and Develt Specialist, UKTI, 2007–13. Mem., EPSRC, 2000–; Dep. Chm., Gen. Adv. Cttee on Sci., Food Standards Agency, 2010–; Chair: Govt Adv. Cttee on novel foods and processes, 1997–2003; Scientific Adv. Cttee on Genetic Manipulation (Contained Use), 2004–; Mem. Council, British Potato Council, 2003–07 (Chair, R&D Cttee, 2003–07); mem., other expert cttees and foresight panels. Trustee, Sense About Science, 2002–. MSOFHT 1994; MILT 2000; FRSA 1998. *Publications:* numerous contribs to learned jls; expert papers for parly cttees, enquiries, etc. *Recreations:* family, gardening, travel.

BAINBRIDGE, Prof. Simon; freelance composer, conductor and lecturer; Professor, University of London, since 2001, and Senior Professor of Composition, since 2007, Royal Academy of Music (Senior Lecturer, 1999–2001; Head of Composition, 2001–07); *b* 30 Aug. 1952; *s* of John Bainbridge and Nan Knowles; *m* 1997, Lynda Richardson; one *d*. *Educ:* Central Tutorial Sch. for Young Musicians; Highgate Sch.; Royal Coll. of Music. Freelance composer, 1973–; Margaret Lee Crofts Fellowship (studying with Gunther Schuller), Berkshire Music Center, Tanglewood, USA, 1973; Leonard Bernstein Fellowship, 1974; Forman Fellow in Composition, Edinburgh Univ., 1976–78; US-UK Bicentennial Fellowship, 1978–79; Music Dir, Royal Nat. Theatre, 1980–82; Composer in residence, Southern Arts, 1982–86; Professor of Composition: RCM, 1989–99; GSMD, 1991–99; Composer in residence, Univ. of Wales Coll. of Cardiff, 1993–94. Hon. RAM 2002. Gemini Prize in Composition, Musicians' Co., 1988. *Compositions include:* Viola Concerto, 1978; Fantasia for Double Orchestra, 1984; Ad ora Incerta: four orchestral songs from Primo Levi, 1994 (Grawemeyer Award for Music Composition, Univ. of Louisville, 1997); Landscape and Memory, 1995; Four Primo Levi settings, 1996; (for chorus and ensemble) Chant, 1999; (for orchestra) Diptych, 2007; Music Space Reflection, 2007; (for chamber orchestra) Concerti Grossi, 2010. *Recreations:* films, reading, cooking, swimming, walking. *Address:* c/o Novello & Co. (Music Sales Ltd), 14–15 Berners Street, W1T 3LJ.

BAINES, (John) Christopher; independent environmental consultant; Director, Chris Baines Associates Ltd, since 2011; *b* Sheffield, S Yorks, 4 May 1947; *s* of Stuart and Winifred Baines; partner, 1988, Nerys Jones. *Educ:* Ecclesfield Grammar Sch.; Wye Coll., Univ. of London (BSc Hons Horticulture); City of Birmingham Poly. (Postgrad. Dip. Landscape Architecture). FRSB (FIBiol 2009). Landscape architect, Blakedown Landscapes Ltd, 1969–74; Sen. Lectr in Landscape Design and Mgt, City of Birmingham Poly., 1974–88; Partner, Landscape Design Gp, 1974–79; Dir, Baines Environmental Ltd, 1979–2011. Presenter, TV progs incl. The Wild Side of Town, The ARK, Pebble Mill at One, Countryfile, Saturday Starship, The Big E, That's Gardening, throughout 1980s. Hon. Prof., UCE, 1986. Member: Rural Affairs Adv. Bd, 1998–2001, Breathing Places Adv. Bd, 2006–, BBC; Adv. Gp, CABE Space, 2004–10; Urban Regeneration Panel, City of Bath, 2004–; Expert Panel, Heritage Lottery Fund, 2005–11; Ind. Envmtl Rev. Panel, Stratford City and 2012 Olympic Village, 2007–; CABE Design Rev. Panel for Ecotowns, 2009–11; independent adviser to: National Grid plc; Royal Palaces; Thames Water plc; Alliance for Religions and Conservation; Lendlease. Nat. Vice Pres., Royal Soc. of Wildlife Trusts (formerly of Nature Conservation), 1987– (Chm., Strategic Develt Fund, 2011–). Chm., Wyre Forest Landscape Partnership, 2013–. Hon. President: Assoc. for Envmt-Conscious Bldg, 1994–; Wildside Centre, Wolverhampton, 1997–; Urban Wildlife Partnership, 2000–12; Thames Estuary Partnership, 2001–; Essex Wildlife Trust, 2004–; Hon. Vice Pres., Wildlife Trust for Birmingham and the Black Country, 1990–. Trustee, Nat. Heritage Meml Fund, 1998–2004. Patron: Bankside Open Spaces Trust, 1999–; Landscape Design Trust, 2001–10. Hon. FRSA 2009. Hon. FCIWEM 2000. Hon. Dr Envmtl Mgt Sheffield Hallam, 1998. Medal of Honour, RSPB, 2004; Peter Scott Meml Award, British Naturalists' Assoc., 2013. *Publications:* How to Make a Wildlife Garden, 1985, 2nd edn 2000; The Wild Side of Town, 1987 (Nat. Conservation Book Prize, Royal Soc. of Wildlife Trusts, 1987); A Guide to Habitat Creation, 1988, 2nd edn 1992; *for children:* The Old Boot, The Nest, The Flower, The Picnic, 1996, 2nd edn 2002. *Recreations:* cooking, gardening, walking, nature conservation, watercolour painting, ski-ing. *Address:* 28 Parkdale West, Wolverhampton WV1 4TE. *T:* (01902) 424820. *E:* chris.baines@blueyonder.co.uk.

BAINES, Prof. John Robert, FBA 2011; Professor of Egyptology, University of Oxford, 1976–2013, Research Associate, since 2013; Fellow of Queen's College, Oxford, 1976–2013, now Emeritus; *b* 17 March 1946; *o s* of late Edward Russell Baines and Dora Margaret Jean (*née* O'Brien); *m* 1971, Jennifer Christine Ann, *e d* of S. T. Smith; one *s* one *d*. *Educ:* Winchester Coll.; New Coll., Linacre Coll., Worcester Coll., Oxford (BA 1967, MA, DPhil 1976). Lectr in Egyptology, Univ. of Durham, 1970–75; Laycock Student, Worcester Coll., Oxford, 1973–75. Visiting Professor: Univ. of Arizona, 1982, 1988; Univ. of Michigan, 1989; Ecole Pratique des Hautes Etudes, Paris, 1994, 2003, 2012; Harvard Univ., 1995–96, 1999–2000; Univ. of Basel, 2003, 2011; Dist. Vis. Prof., Amer. Univ., Cairo, 1999; Freehling Prof., Univ. of Michigan, 2002–03; Mem., Inst. for Advanced Study, Princeton, NJ, 2009–10; Old Dominion Fellow, Princeton Univ., 2014. Fellow, Humboldt-Stiftung, 1982, 1989, 1996. Vice Pres., British Acad., 2014–. Corresp. Mem., German Archaeol Inst., 1999; Mem., Amer. Philosophical Soc., 2011. *Publications:* (trans. and ed) H. Schäfer, Principles of Egyptian Art, 1974, rev. edn 1986; (with J. Malek) Atlas of Ancient Egypt, 1980 (trans. 11 langs), 2nd edn as Cultural Atlas of Ancient Egypt, 2000; (trans. and ed) E. Hornung, Conceptions of God in Ancient Egypt, 1982; Fecundity Figures, 1985; (ed jtly) Pyramid Studies and Other Essays presented to I. E. S. Edwards, 1988; (jtly) Religion in Ancient Egypt (ed B. E. Shafer), 1991; (ed) Stone Vessels, Pottery and Sealings from the Tomb of Tut'ankhamūn, 1993; (ed jtly) Civilizations of the Ancient Near East, 4 vols, 1995; (contrib.) Ancient Egyptian Kingship, 1995; Die Bedeutung des Reisens im alten Ägypten, 2004; Visual and Written Culture in Ancient Egypt, 2007; (ed jtly) The Disappearance of Writing Systems, 2008; High Culture and Experience in Ancient Egypt, 2013; articles in collections and in Acta Orientalia, American Anthropologist, Art History, Encyclopaedia Britannica, Jl Egypt. Archaeol., Man, Orientalia, Studien altägypt. Kultur, etc. *Address:* Oriental Institute, Pusey Lane, Oxford OX1 2LE.

See also P. J. Baines.

BAINES, Rt Rev. Nicholas; *see* Leeds, Bishop of.

BAINES, Priscilla Jean, CB 2004; Librarian, House of Commons, 2000–04; *b* 5 Oct. 1942; *d* of late Edward Russell Baines and (Dora Margaret) Jean Baines (*née* O'Brien). *Educ:* Tonbridge Girls' Grammar Sch.; Somerville Coll., Oxford (BA Agric. 1963; MA 1967); Linacre Coll., Oxford (BLitt 1969). Adminr, Chelsea Coll., Univ. of London, 1965–68; House of Commons: Library Clerk, 1968–77; Head: Economic Affairs Section, 1977–88; Science and Envmt Section, 1988–91; Parly Div., 1991–93; Dep. Librarian and Dir of Human Resources, 1993–99. Associate, Hist. of Parlt, 2005–. *Publications:* (contrib.) New Select Committees, 1985, (contrib.) Westminster and Europe, 1996, 2004, and other pubns of Study of Parlt Gp; Colonel Josiah Wedgwood's Questionnaire: Members of Parliament, 1885–1918, 2012. *Recreations:* food, travel, opera. *Address:* 11 Ravensdon Street, SE11 4AQ.

See also J. R. Baines.

BAINS, Lawrence Arthur, CBE 1983; DL; formerly Director: Bains Brothers Ltd; Crowland Leasings Ltd; Bains Finance Management Ltd; *b* 11 May 1920; *s* of late Arthur Bains and Mabel (*née* Payn); *m* 1954, Margaret, *d* of late Sir William and Lady Grimshaw; two *s* one *d*. *Educ:* Stationers' Company's School. Served War, 1939–46: Middlesex Yeomanry, 1939; N Africa, 1940; POW, 1942, escaped Italy, 1943. Hornsey Borough Council: Mem., 1949–65; Dep. Leader, 1958–64; Mayor, 1964–65; Council, London Borough of Haringey: Mem., 1964–74; Finance Chm., 1968–71; Greater London Council: Chm., 1977–78; Mem. for Hornsey/Haringey, 1967–81; Chm., South Area Planning Bd, 1970–73; Dep. Leader, Housing Policy Cttee, 1979–81; Chm., GLC/Tower Hamlets Jt Housing Management Cttee, 1979–81; Mem., Lee Valley Regional Park Authority, 1968–81 (Chm., 1980–81); Chm., Haringey DHA, 1982–93. Chm., N London Coll. of Health Studies, 1991–95. Trustee, Help the Homeless, 1979–2012. Liveryman, Basketmakers' Co., 1978– (Mem., Ct of Assts, 1995–). DL Greater London, 1978 (Rep. DL for Borough of Barnet, 1983–95). *Recreation:* being a grandfather. *Address:* Flat 14, Southgate Beaumont, 15 Cannon Hill, Old Southgate, N14 7DJ. *T:* (020) 8886 4679.

BAINSFAIR, Paul Jeffrey, FIPA; Director General, Institute of Practitioners in Advertising, since 2011; *b* London, 5 Jan. 1953; *s* of Leslie John and Doris May Bainsfair; *m* 1989, Sophie Giulietta Ray; two *s* one *d*. *Educ:* Watford Coll. Advertising (DipCAM). Account Exec., 1977–87, Man. Dir and Jt CEO, 1987–91, Saatchi & Saatchi; Co-Founder and Co-Chm., Bainsfair Sharkey Trott, 1991–99; Chm., 1999–2004, Pres., Europe, 2004–09, TBWA;

Chm., IRIS Worldwide, 2009–11. Mem., Mktg Gp of GB. *Recreations:* golf, shooting, art, Queens Park Rangers. *Address:* Institute of Practitioners in Advertising, 44 Belgrave Square, SW1X 8QS. *T:* (020) 7235 7020. *E:* Paul@ipa.co.uk. *Clubs:* Soho House; High Post Golf.

BAIRD, Sir Andrew; *see* Baird, Sir J. A. G.

BAIRD, Anthony; *see* Baird, E. A. B.

BAIRD, Sir Charles William Stuart, 6th Bt *cr* 1809, of Newbyth, Haddingtonshire; *b* 8 June 1939; *s* of Robert William Stuart Baird and Maxine Christine, *oc* of Rupert Darrell, NY; *S* uncle, 2000; *m* 1965, Joanna Jane, *e d* of late Brig. A. Darley Bridge; three *d*. *Educ:* Switzerland. *Heir: kinsman* Andrew James Baird [*b* 23 Oct. 1970; *m* 2005, Katherine Louise Graham-Campbell; one *s* one *d*]. *Address:* 12 Falstaff Street, Sunnybank Hills, Brisbane, Qld 4109, Australia.

BAIRD, Prof. David Tennent, CBE 2000; FRCP, FRCOG, FMedSci; FRSE; Medical Research Council Clinical Research Professor of Reproductive Endocrinology, 1985–2000, now Emeritus, and Senior Professorial Research Fellow, MRC Centre for Reproductive Health and Obstetrics and Gynaecology, since 2000, University of Edinburgh; *b* 13 March 1935; *s* of Sir Dugald Baird, MD, FRCOG and Lady (May) Baird (*née* Tennent), CBE; *m* 1st, 1965, Frances Diana Lichtveld (marr. diss. 1995); two *s*; 2nd, 2000, Anna Frances Glasier. *Educ:* Aberdeen Grammar Sch.; Aberdeen Univ.; Trinity Coll., Cambridge (BA 1st cl.); Edinburgh Univ. (MB ChB (Dist.); DSc). Junior med. posts, Royal Infirmary, Edinburgh, 1959–65; MRC Travelling Research Fellow, Worcester Foundn of Experimental Biology, USA, 1965–68; Lectr, later Sen. Lectr, Dept of Obstetrics, Univ. of Edinburgh, 1968–72; Dep. Dir, MRC Unit of Reproductive Biology, Edinburgh, 1972–77; Prof. of Obst. and Gyn., Univ. of Edinburgh, 1977–85. Consultant Gynaecologist, Royal Infirmary, Edinburgh, 1970–2000. Dir, Contraceptive Develt Network, 1995–2007. Mem., WHO Task Force on Infertility, 1976–82; Mem. and Chm., WHO Task Force on Postovulatory Methods, 1989–95. Leading developer of methods of med. abortion, contraception, ovulation induction. FRSE 1990. Founder FMedSci 1998. Hon. FRANZCOG 1997; Hon. FFPRHC 2008; Hon. FCMSA 2009. Hon. MD Nottingham, 2002. *Publications:* Contraceptives of the Future (with R. V. Short), 1976; Mechanism of Menstrual Bleeding, 1985; (jtly) Modern Methods of Inducing Abortion, 1995; contrib. 100 chapters in books and over 400 papers in med. and sci. jls on reproductive endocrinology, abortion and contraception. *Recreations:* ski mountaineering, golf. *Address:* 24 Moray Place, Edinburgh EH3 6DA. *T:* (0131) 225 3962.

BAIRD, (Eric) Anthony (Bamber); Director, Institute for Complementary Medicine, 1980–2002; *b* 11 Dec. 1920; *s* of Oswald Baird and Marion Bamber; *m* 1st, 1952, Margareta Toss (marr. diss. 1957); 2nd, 1959, Inger Bohman (marr. diss. 1977); two *d*. *Educ:* LSE (BScEcon). Served RA, 1941–46. Swedish Broadcasting Corp., 1950–65; Public Relations Ltd, 1965–72; Civil Service, 1973–78; Inst. for Complementary Medicine, 1979–2002. Chm., British Council of Complementary Medicine, 1997–2002. FRSA 1992; FRSocMed 1999. *Publications:* Notes on Canada, 1962; (jtly) The Charm of Sweden, 1962; Lindfield and Other Poems, 2010; More Lindfield and Other Poems, 2011; Still More Lindfield and Other Poems, 2012. *Recreations:* writing children's stories, gardening. *Address:* 24 Backwoods Lane, Lindfield, Haywards Heath, West Sussex RH16 2ED. *T:* (01444) 482018. *Club:* Reform.

BAIRD, Gareth Thomas Gilroy; DL; FRAgS; farmer, since 1979; Scottish Commissioner, Crown Estate, since 2010; *b* Kelso, 11 May 1957; *s* of Roger and Margaret Baird; *m* 1985, Kirsty Stobbs; one *s* two *d*. *Educ:* St Mary's Prep. Sch.; Merchiston Castle Sch.; Edinburgh Sch. of Agric. (HND). Chm., Scottish Enterprise, S of Scotland Regl Adv. Bd, 2008–. Chairman: Scott Country Potato Growers, 1995–; Pentlands Sci. Park, 2014–; Vice Chm., Grainco Ltd, 2005–; Director: Scotland Food and Drink, 2007–; Scottish Borders Produce, 2009–. Dir, RHASS, 1995–2011. Chairman: Border Union Agricl Soc., 2000–01; Scottish Agricl Orgn Soc., 2000–03 and 2006–09. Chm., St Mary's Sch., Melrose, 2005–; Dep. Chm., Merchiston Castle Sch., 2014–; Mem. Council, St George's Sch. for Girls, 2003–. FRAgS 2005. Mem., Hon. Co. of Edinburgh Golfers. DL Roxburghshire, Ettrick and Lauderdale, 2008. *Recreations:* playing golf, watching Rugby, spoofing. *Address:* Manorhill, Kelso, Roxburghshire TD5 7PA. *T:* (01573) 460237. *E:* gareth@baird.gbtbroadband.co.uk.

BAIRD, Guy Martin, FCA; Senior Adviser, European Investment Bank, Brussels, 2001–06; *b* 3 Jan. 1948; *s* of late Thomas Herbert Mertens Baird and Kathleen Florence Baird (*née* Mapley, later Ballard); *m* 1969, Juliet Hope Mears (marr. diss. 1984); two *d*. *Educ:* Wellington College. ACA 1970, FCA 1975. Bland Fielden & Co., 1966–69; Cooper Brothers & Co., subseq. Coopers & Lybrand, 1970–72; Manager, Fidital, Coopers & Lybrand SpA, Rome, 1972–74; Vice Pres. Finance, Italicor Inc., Atlanta and Milan, 1975–77; Manager, Andrew Moore & Co., 1978–79; European Investment Bank: Sen. Loan Officer, Luxembourg, 1980–83; Head of London Office, 1983–2001. *Recreations:* sailing, Wagner. *Club:* East India.

BAIRD, Sir (James) Andrew (Gardiner), 11th Bt *cr* 1695 (NS), of Saughton Hall, Edinburgh; *b* 2 May 1946; *s* of Sir James Baird, 10th Bt, MC and Mabel Ann, (Gay), *d* of A. Gill; *S* father, 1997, but his name does not appear on the Official Roll of the Baronetage; *m* 1984, Jean Margaret (marr. diss. 1988), *yr d* of Brig. Sir Ian Jardine, 4th Bt, OBE, MC; one *s*. *Educ:* Eton. *Heir: s* Alexander William Gardiner Baird, *b* 28 May 1986.

BAIRD, James Hewson; Chief Executive and Company Secretary, British Veterinary Association, 1987–2002; *b* 28 March 1944; *s* of James Baird, MBE, MRCVS and Ann Sarah Baird (*née* Hewson); *m* 1969, Clare Rosalind (*née* Langstaff); three *d*. *Educ:* Austin Friars; Creighton, Carlisle; Newcastle upon Tyne Univ. (BSc Hons Agric). Hydrologist, Essex River Authy, 1968–75; Policy Officer, Nat. Water Council, 1975–80. Institution of Civil Engineers: Asst Dir, 1980–81; Dir of Admin, 1981–86; Mem., Infrastructure Planning Gp, 1982–86; Dir, Assoc. of Municipal Engineers, 1984–86; Dir, External Affairs, Fedn of Civil Engineering Contractors, 1986–87. *Recreations:* Rugby, gardening, farming, countryside. *Address:* Hollyhock Cottage, Fen Street, Nayland, Suffolk CO6 4HT.

BAIRD, Air Marshal Sir John (Alexander), KBE 1999; DL; Surgeon General to the Armed Forces, 1997–2000; *b* 25 July 1937; *s* of late Dr David Alexander Baird, CBE and Isobel T. Baird; *m* 1963, Mary Clews. *Educ:* Merchiston Castle Sch.; Edinburgh Univ. (MB ChB). FFOM; FRCPE 1998; FRCSE 1999; DAvMed; FRAeS. Western Gen. Hosp., Edinburgh, 1961–62; MO Sarawak, 1962–63; commnd RAF, 1963; RAF Stations, UK and Singapore, 1963–80; exchange post, USA, 1970–73; HQ Strike Comd, 1980–83; MoD, 1983–86; OC Princess of Wales RAF Hosp., Ely, 1987–88; PMO, RAF Germany, 1988–91; PMO, HQ RAF Strike Comd, 1991–94; Dir Gen., RAF Med. Services, 1994–97. QHP 1991–2000. Mem., Internat. Acad. of Aviation and Space Medicine, 1993. FRSocMed 1983; Fellow: Aerospace Med. Assoc., 1992; Assoc. of Med. Secs, 2001. DL Cambs, 1998. CStJ 1997. *Publications:* contribs to med. jls on aviation medicine subjects. *Recreations:* ornithology, wildlife conservation, cricket, music. *Address:* Braeburn, Barway, Ely, Cambs CB7 5UB. *Club:* Royal Air Force.

BAIRD, Joyce Elizabeth Leslie, OBE 1991; Joint General Secretary, Assistant Masters and Mistresses Association, 1978–90; *b* 8 Dec. 1929; *d* of Dr J. C. H. Baird and Mrs J. E. Baird. *Educ:* The Abbey School, Reading; Newnham College, Cambridge (MA); secretarial training. FEIS 1987. Sec. to Ernő Goldfinger, architect, 1952; Secretary to Sir Austin Robinson and editorial assistant, Royal Economic Soc., 1952–60; Senior Geography Mistress, Hertfordshire and Essex High School, Bishop's Stortford, 1961–77 (Dep. Head, 1973–75). President: Assoc. of Assistant Mistresses, 1976–77; Internat. Fedn of Secondary Teachers, 1981–85; Vice Pres., NFER, 1991–2010. Mem., Cambridge City Council, 1992–96. Bd Mem., Granta Housing Soc., 1992–2006. Trustee, Cambridge Preservation Soc., 1998–2008. Gov., Alleyn's Sch., Dulwich, 1993–2003. *Recreations:* opera, thinking about gardening, travel. *Address:* 14 Gretton Court, High Street, Girton, Cambridge CB3 0QN. *T:* (01223) 277666.

BAIRD, Kenneth William; Project Director/Managing Director, European Opera Centre, since 1994; *b* 14 July 1950; *s* of William and Christine Baird. *Educ:* Uppingham School; St Andrews Univ. (MA); Royal College of Music; Royal Sch. of Church Music. LRAM, ARCM. English National Opera, 1974–82; Gen. Manager, Aldeburgh Foundn, 1982–88; Music Dir, Arts Council, 1988–94. Sec., New Opera Co., 1981–82. Member: NW Arts Bd, 1998–2002; Arts Council NW, 2002–04; Bd, Huddersfield Contemporary Music Fest., 1997–2004; Birmingham Contemp. Music Gp, 2000–. Adv. Dir, Sonic Arts Network (Chm., 2003–08); Dir, Bittern Press, 2011–. Chairman: Snape Historical Trust, 1986–2001; British Arts Fests Assoc., 1988. Trustee: R. A. Vestey Meml Trust, 1991–2004; Carter Preston Trust, 2015–. Mem., Nat. Adv. Council, Milapfest, 2014–. *Address:* c/o European Opera Centre, Liverpool Hope University, 1 Haigh Street, Liverpool L3 8QB. *Club:* Chelsea Arts.

BAIRD, Nicholas Graham Faraday, CMG 2010; CVO 2008; HM Diplomatic Service, retired; Group Corporate Affairs Director, Centrica plc, since 2014; *b* 15 May 1962; *s* of Colin and Elizabeth Baird; *m* 1985, Caroline Jane Ivett; one *s* two *d*. *Educ:* Dulwich Coll.; Emmanuel Coll., Cambridge (MA English Lit.). Joined FCO, 1983; Third Sec., Kuwait, 1986–89; First Sec., UK Repn to EU, Brussels, 1989–93; Private Sec. to Parly Under-Sec. of State, FCO, 1993–95; Hd, Amsterdam Intergovtl Conf. Unit, FCO, 1995–97; Counsellor and Dep. Hd of Mission, Muscat, 1997–98; Counsellor, UK Repn to EU, Brussels, 1998–2002; Hd, EU Dept (Internal), FCO, 2002–03; Sen. Dir, Internat., Immigration and Nationality Directorate, 2003–04, Policy, Immigration and Nationality Directorate, 2004–06, Home Office (on secondment); Ambassador to Turkey, 2006–09; Dir-Gen., Europe and Globalisation, 2009–11; Chief Exec., UK Trade and Investment, 2011–13. Ind. Dir, Nord Anglia Inc., 2015–. Mem., Cole Commn advising Labour Party on exports, 2014–. Mem. Adv. Council, Sheffield Univ. Sch. of Mgt, 2014–. *Recreations:* reading, theatre, running, travel. *Address:* Centrica plc, Millstream, Maidenhead Road, Windsor, Berks SL4 5GD.

BAIRD, Vice-Adm. Sir Thomas (Henry Eustace), KCB 1980; DL; *b* Canterbury, Kent, 17 May 1924; *s* of Geoffrey Henry and Helen Jane Baird; *m* 1953, Angela Florence Ann Paul (*d* 2009), Symington, Ayrshire; one *s* one *d*. *Educ:* RNC, Dartmouth. Served HM Ships: Trinidad, in support of convoys to Russia, 1941, Midshipman; Bermuda, Russian convoys and landings in N Africa, and Orwell, Russian convoys and Atlantic escort force, 1942; Howe, E Indies, 1943, Sub-Lt; Rapid, E Indies, 1944 until VJ Day, Lieut; St James, Home Fleet, 1946; Ganges, Ratings' New Entry Trng, 1948; Plucky, Exec. Officer, mine clearance in Mediterranean, 1950; Lt Comdr 1952; Veryan Bay, Exec. Officer, W Indies and Falkland Is., 1953; O-in-C, Petty Officers' Leadership Sch., Malta, 1954; Exec. Officer, HMS Whirlwind, Home Fleet and Med., for Suez Op., 1956; Comd, HMS Acute, Dartmouth Trng Sqdn, 1958; Comdr 1959; Comd, HMS Ulysses, Home Fleet, 1960; Staff, C-in-C, Home Fleet, Northwood, 1961; Exec. Officer, Jt Anti-Sub. Sch., Londonderry, 1963; EO, HMS Bulwark, Far East, 1965; Ch. Staff Officer to Cdre, Naval Drafting, 1966; Captain 1967; Dep. Dir, Naval Equipment, Adm., Bath, 1967; Captain: Mine Countermeasures; Fishery Protection and HMS Lochinvar (comd), 1969; Comd, HMS Glamorgan, Far East, W Indies, S Amer., Med., and UK Waters, 1971; Captain of the Fleet, 1973; Rear Adm. 1976; Chief of Staff to C-in-C Naval Home Comd, 1976–77; Dir Gen., Naval Personal Services, 1978–79; Vice-Adm. 1979; Flag Officer Scotland and NI, 1979–82. Chm. Exec. Cttee, Erskine Hosp., 1986–95. DL Ayrshire and Arran, 1982. *Recreations:* cricket, golf, shooting, fishing. *Address:* Craigrethill, Symington, Ayrshire KA1 5QN. *Club:* Prestwick Golf (Prestwick).

BAIRD, Vera; QC 2000; Police and Crime Commissioner (Lab) for Northumbria, since 2012; *d* of Jack Thomas and Alice (*née* Marsland); *m* 1st, 1972, David John Taylor-Gooby (marr. diss. 1978); 2nd, 1978, Robert Brian Baird (*d* 1979); two step *s*. *Educ:* Newcastle Polytechnic (LLB Hons 1972); Open Univ. (BA 1982); London Guildhall Univ. (MA 2000). Called to the Bar, Gray's Inn, 1975, Bencher, 2004. MP (Lab) Redcar, 2001–10; contested (Lab) same seat, 2010. Parly Under-Sec. of State, DCA, then MoJ, 2006–07; Solicitor Gen., 2007–10. Vis. Law Fellow, St Hilda's Coll., Oxford, 1999. Chair, Bd of Dirs and Trustee, Centre for Criminal Appeals. Hon. DCL Northumbria, 2014. *Publications:* Rape in Court, 1998; Defending Battered Women Who Kill, 2000.

BAIRD, William; Under Secretary, Scottish Home and Health Department, 1978–87; *b* 13 Oct. 1927; *s* of Peter and Christina Baird, Airdrie; *m* 1954, Anne Templeton Macfarlane (*d* 2009); two *d*. *Educ:* Airdrie Academy; Glasgow Univ. Entered Scottish Home Dept, 1952; Private Sec. to Perm. Under-Sec. of State, Scottish Office, 1957; Principal, Scottish Educn Dept, 1958–63; Private Sec. to Minister of State and successive Secs of State for Scotland, 1963–65; Asst Sec., Scottish Educn Dept, 1965–66; Dept of Agriculture and Fisheries for Scotland, 1966–71; Scottish Office Finance Div., 1971–73; Registrar General for Scotland, 1973–78. *Address:* 8 Strathearn Road, North Berwick EH39 5BZ. *T:* (01620) 893190.

BAIRSTO, Air Vice-Marshal Nigel Alexander, CB 2007; MBE 1991; CEng, FIMechE, FRAeS; FCMI; Director, Bair Solutions Ltd, since 2013; *b* 27 Aug. 1953; *s* of Air Marshal Sir Peter Edward Bairsto, *qv*; *m* 1976, Alison Margaret Philippe; one *s* one *d*. *Educ:* King's Sch., Ely; Portsmouth Poly. (BSc 1975); RAF Coll., Cranwell; Cranfield Inst. of Technol. (MSc 1986); Cranfield Univ. (MDA 1999). CEng 1989; FIMechE 1997; FRAeS 2000. Commnd RAF Eng. Officer, 1971; RAF Leuchars, 1978–80; RAF Cottesmore, 1980–82; MoD, London, 1982–87; Sen. Engr Officer 14 Sqn, RAF Bruggen, 1987–91; RAF Staff Coll., Bracknell, 1991; Wing Comdr, Tornado, Strike Command, 1992–93; OC Eng & Supply, RAF Leeming, 1993–95; Gp Capt., Logistics, Strike Command, 1996–98; Station Comdr, Sealand, and Electronics Dir, DARA, 1998–2000; rcds 2000; ACOS Ops (Force Protection), Strike Command, and Comdt Gen., RAF Regt, 2001–03; Defence Logistics Organisation, Ministry of Defence: Tornado Integrated Project Team Leader, 2003–05; 1 Gp Cluster Leader, 2005; Dir Gen. Defence Logistics Transformation, 2005–07. Associate Partner, IBM Global Business Services, 2007–09; Vice Pres., 2009–11, Sen. Vice Pres., 2011–13, Selex Galileo. Chm., Central Council, RAFA, 2010– (Northern Area Pres., 2007–10). Hon. Air Cdre, 2624 (Co. of Oxford) Regt Sqdn, RAuxAF, 2013–. FCMI 1997. *Recreations:* golf, shooting, ski-ing, private flying, gardening, sailing, scuba diving. *Address:* Swayfield, Lincs. *T:* (01476) 550097. *E:* bears178@aol.com. *Clubs:* Royal Air Force; Air Squadron; Royal and Ancient Golf; Luffenham Heath Golf; West Rheine Golf.

BAIRSTO, Air Marshal Sir Peter (Edward), KBE 1981 (CBE 1973); CB 1980; AFC 1957; DL; *b* 3 Aug. 1926; *s* of late Arthur Bairsto and Beatrice (*née* Lewis); *m* 1st, 1947, Kathleen (*née* Clarbour) (*d* 2008); two *s* one *d*; 2nd, 2010, Mrs Pamela Braid (*née* Gibson). *Educ:* Rhyl Grammar Sch. Pilot, FAA, 1944–46; 1946–62: FO RAF Regt, Palestine, Aden Protectorate; Flying Instr; Fighter Pilot, Fighter Comd and Near East; Flight Comdr, 43 Sqdn, and Leader, RAF Aerobatic Team; Sqdn Comdr, 66 Sqdn; RAF Staff Coll.; Wing Comdr, Flying, Nicosia, 1963–64; Op. Requirements, MoD, 1965–67; JSSC Latimer, 1967; Instr, RAF Staff Coll., 1968–70; Stn Comdr, RAF Honington, 1971–73; Dir, Op. Requirements, MoD, 1974–77; AOC Training Units, Support Command, 1977–79; Comdr, Northern Maritime Air Region, 1979–81; Dep. C-in-C, Strike Command, 1981–84. Vice-Chm. (Air), Highland TAVRA, 1984–90. Hon. Col, Northern Gp Field Sqns RE (Airfield Damage Repair) (Vol.), 1989–92. Mem., Scottish Sports Council, 1985–90. HM Comr, Queen Victoria Sch., Dunblane, 1984–93; Chm. Management Bd, RAF Benevolent Fund Home, Alastrean House, Tarland, 1984–94. Mem., St Andrews Links Trust, 1989–95 (Chm., 1993–95). Queen's Commendation for Valuable Services in the Air, 1955 and 1960. CCMI. DL Fife, 1992.

Recreations: golf, fishing, shooting, gardening. *Address:* Singell, 89A Hepburn Gardens, St Andrews, Fife KY16 9LT. *T:* (01334) 475505. *Clubs:* Royal Air Force; Royal and Ancient Golf.

See also Air Vice-Marshal N. A. Bairsto.

BAIRSTOW, John; Founder, 1968, Chairman, 1972–93, Queens Moat Houses PLC (formerly Queens Modern Hotels Ltd); *b* 25 Aug. 1930; *m*; four *d. Educ:* City of London Sch. FSVA. Founded Bairstow, Eves and Son, Valuers and Estate Agents, 1953. *Relevant publication:* Corporate Hijack? The John Bairstow Story, by Brian Lynch, 2005. *Recreation:* salmon fishing.

BAISTER, Stephen, PhD; Chief Bankruptcy Registrar of the High Court, Royal Courts of Justice, since 2004 (Bankruptcy Registrar, 1996–2004); *b* 15 Feb. 1952; *s* of John Norman Baister and Bridget Baister. *Educ:* Merton Coll., Oxford (BA Mod. Langs 1974); Birkbeck Coll., London (MA German 1978); University Coll. London (PhD Law 1992). Admitted solicitor, 1981; solicitor in private practice, 1981–96. Trustee, Condor Trust for Educn, 2005–. Hon. Mem., Insolvency Lawyers' Assoc., 1997–. Hon. FICM 2011 (Hon. Pres., 2011). *Publications:* with Chris Patrick: Guide to East Germany, 1990; Latvia: the Bradt travel guide, 1999, 5th edn 2007; Riga: the Bradt city guide, 2005; William Le Queux: master of mystery, 2007; *contributions to:* Atkin's Court Forms; Butterworth's Encyclopaedia of Forms and Precedents; Civil Procedure; Muir Hunter on Personal Insolvency. *Address:* Bankruptcy Chambers, Rolls Building, Fetter Lane, EC4A 1NL.

BAJWA, Ali Naseem; QC 2011; *b* Lancs, 25 Aug. 1970; *s* of Naseem Bajwa and Yasmeen Bajwa; *m* 2000, Shine Khan; one *s* one *d. Educ:* Langley Grammar Sch.; London Sch. of Econs and Pol Sci. (LLB Hons); Inns of Court Sch. of Law (BVC). Called to the Bar, Gray's Inn, 1993, Bencher, 2015; in practice as a barrister specialising in criminal law, 1993–, 25 Bedford Row, 2000–11, Garden Court Chambers, 2011–. Pegasus Scholar, Crown Law Office, NZ, 1996. *Recreations:* cricket, tennis, ski-ing, international film. *Address:* Garden Court Chambers, 57–60 Lincoln's Inn Fields, WC2A 3LJ. *T:* (020) 7993 7600, *Fax:* (020) 7993 7700. *E:* alib@gclaw.co.uk.

BAKAYA, Mohit; Commissioning Editor, current affairs, politics, ideas, science and religion, BBC Radio 4, since 2007; *b* London, 12 Nov. 1964; *s* of Madan Bakaya and Uma Bakaya; *m* 2013, Victoria Shepherd; one *s* one *d* by a previous marriage. *Educ:* Pimlico Sch.; Keble Coll., Oxford (BA Hons PPE). Trainee Producer, BBC Radio, 1993–95; Producer, Kaleidoscope, 1995–98, Sen. Producer, Front Row, 1998–2001, BBC Radio 4; Editor, Night Waves, BBC Radio 3, 2001–07. Trustee: Nat. Prison Radio Assoc., 2013–; Tamasha Theatre Co., 2014–. *Recreations:* wine, football, PJ Harvey, Bruce Springsteen, Bob Dylan, trying to cook the perfect risotto. *E:* mohit.bakaya@bbc.co.uk.

BAKER, family name of **Baron Baker of Dorking**.

BAKER OF DORKING, Baron *cr* 1997 (Life Peer), of Iford in the Co. of East Sussex; **Kenneth Wilfred Baker,** CH 1992; PC 1984; Chairman, Graphite Resources plc, 2007–12; *b* 3 Nov. 1934; *s* of late W. M. Baker, OBE and of Mrs Baker (*née* Harries); *m* 1963, Mary Elizabeth Gray-Muir; one *s* two *d. Educ:* St Paul's Sch.; Magdalen Coll., Oxford. Nat. Service, 1953–55: Lieut in Gunners, N Africa; Artillery Instructor to Libyan Army. Oxford, 1955–58 (Sec. of Union). Served Twickenham Borough Council, 1960–62. Contested (C): Poplar, 1964; Acton, 1966. MP (C): Acton, March 1968–1970; St Marylebone, Oct. 1970–1983; Mole Valley, 1983–97; Parly Sec., CSD, 1972–74; PPS to Leader of Opposition, 1974–75; Minister of State and Minister for Information Technology, DTI, 1981–84; Minister for Local Govt, DoE, 1984–85; Sec. of State for the Environment, 1985–86; Sec. of State for Educn and Sci., 1986–89; Chancellor of the Duchy of Lancaster, 1989–90; Chm., Conservative Party, 1989–90; Sec. of State for Home Dept, 1990–92. Mem., Public Accounts Cttee, 1969–70; Chm., H of L Inf. Cttee, 2002–06; Mem., House Cttee, H of L, 2007–12. Mem. Exec., 1922 Cttee, 1975–81. Chm., Teather & Greenwood plc, 2004–07. Chm., Hansard Soc., 1978–81. Sec. Gen., UN Conf. of Parliamentarians on World Population and Development, 1978. Pres., Royal London Soc. for the Blind, 1999–2010; Vice Chm., Cartoon Art Trust, 2003–; Trustee, Booker Prize Foundn, 2005–; Chm. of Trustees, Baker Dearing Educnl Trust, 2008–; Chm., Edge Foundn, 2010–. *Publications:* (ed) I Have No Gun But I Can Spit, 1980; (ed) London Lines, 1982; (ed) The Faber Book of English History in Verse, 1988; (ed) Unauthorized Versions: poems and their parodies, 1990; (ed) The Faber Book of Conservatism, 1993; The Turbulent Years: my life in politics, 1993; The Prime Ministers: an irreverent political history in cartoons, 1995; (ed) The Faber Book of War Poetry, 1996; The Kings and Queens: an irreverent cartoon history of the British monarchy, 1996; (ed) A Children's English History in Verse, 2000; (ed) The Faber Book of Landscape Poetry, 2000; George IV: a life in caricature, 2005; George III: a life in caricature, 2007; (ed) Poems by G. K. Chesterton, 2007; George Washington's War in caricature and print, 2009; (jtly) 14–18 A New Vision for Secondary Education, 2013. *Recreation:* collecting books and political caricatures. *Address:* House of Lords, Westminster, SW1A 0PW. *Clubs:* Athenæum, Garrick, Old Pauline (Pres., 2007–09).

BAKER, Prof. Alan, FRS 1973; Professor of Pure Mathematics, University of Cambridge, 1974–2006, now Professor Emeritus; Fellow of Trinity College, Cambridge, since 1964; *b* 19 Aug. 1939; *oc* of Barnet and Bessie Baker. *Educ:* Stratford Grammar Sch.; University Coll. London (Hon. Fellow 1979); Trinity Coll., Cambridge. BSc (London); MA, PhD (Cantab). Mem., Dept of Mathematics, UCL, 1964–65; Research Fellow, 1964–68, and Dir of Studies in Mathematics, 1968–74, Trinity Coll., Cambridge; Mem., Dept of Pure Maths and Math. Statistics, Univ. of Cambridge, 1966–2006; Reader in Theory of Numbers, 1972–74. Visiting Professor: Univs of Michigan and Colorado, 1969; Stanford Univ., 1974; Royal Soc. Kan Tong Po Prof., Univ. of Hong Kong, 1988; ETH, Zürich, 1989; Mem., Inst. for Advanced Study, Princeton, 1970; Mathematical Scis Res. Inst., Berkeley, 1993; First Turán Lectr, J. Bolyai Math. Soc. Hungary, 1978. MAE 1998. Foreign Fellow: Indian Nat. Sci. Acad., 1980; Nat. Acad. of Scis, India, 1993; Hon. Mem., Hungarian Acad. of Scis, 2001. Hon. Dr Univ. Louis Pasteur, Strasbourg, 1998. Fields Medal, Internat. Congress of Mathematicians, Nice, 1970; Adams Prize of Univ. of Cambridge, 1971–72. *Publications:* Transcendental Number Theory, 1975; (ed jtly) Transcendence Theory: advances and applications, 1977; A Concise Introduction to the Theory of Numbers, 1984; (ed) New Advances in Transcendence Theory, 1988; (with G. Wüstholz) Logarithmic Forms and Diophantine Geometry, 2007; A Comprehensive Course in Number Theory, 2012; papers in various mathematical jls. *Recreation:* travel. *Address:* Centre for Mathematical Sciences, Wilberforce Road, Cambridge CB3 0WB; Trinity College, Cambridge CB2 1TQ. *T:* (01223) 338400.

BAKER, Dr Alan Reginald Harold, FBA 2010; Fellow, Emmanuel College, Cambridge, since 1970; *b* Canterbury, 20 Oct. 1938; *s* of Reginald Andrew Baker and Edith Georgina Baker (*née* Hackman); *m* 1960, Sandra Walker Teale; two *s. Educ:* Kent Coll., Canterbury; University Coll. London (BA 1960; PhD 1963); DLit London 1999. Asst Lectr in Geog., 1963–64, Lectr in Geog., 1964–66, UCL; University of Cambridge: Lectr in Geog., 1966–99, pt-time, 1999–2001; Hd, Dept of Geog., 1989–94; Tutor, 1973–76, Sen. Tutor, 1976–86, Vice-Master, 1990–94, Emmanuel Coll., Cambridge. Editor: Jl Histl Geog., 1987–96; Cambridge Studies in Histl Geog., 1980–2005. Mem. (Lib Dem) Cambridge CC, 2002–10 (Chair, Planning Cttee, 2003–10). Hon. Mem., Soc. de Géographie de Paris, 2003. Gill Meml Medal, 1974, Founder's Medal, 2009, RGS. Chevalier, Ordre des Palmes Académiques (France), 1997. *Publications:* (ed jtly) Geographical Interpretations of Historical Sources, 1970; (ed) Progress in Historical Geography, 1972; (ed jtly) Studies of Field Systems in the British Isles, 1973; (ed jtly) Period and Place: research methods in historical geography, 1982; (ed jtly) Explorations in Historical Geography, 1984; (ed jtly) Ideology and Landscape in Historical Perspective, 1992; Fraternity Among the French Peasantry: sociability and voluntary associations in the Loire Valley, 1815–1914, 1999; Geography and History: bridging the divide, 2003; (ed jtly) Geographies of England: the North-South divide, imagined and material, 2004; contrib. articles to learned jls. *Recreations:* walking, appreciating the landscapes, wines and foods of France, reading political biographies and autobiographies, theatre going, visiting art galleries, trying to follow my wife's instructions in our garden. *Address:* Emmanuel College, Cambridge CB2 3AP. *T:* (01223) 334200. *E:* arb1000@cam.ac.uk.

BAKER, Alistair James; Founder and Chief Executive Officer, Cogent Healthcare Systems (formerly Cogent Business Group), 2008–14; *b* 26 July 1962; one *s* three *d. Educ:* BSc Hons Computing and Informatics; Postgrad. DipM. Joined IBM, 1984; various rôles, IBM, Hewlett Packard, Morse Computers, 1984–96; joined Microsoft, 1996; Country Manager, Scotland, 1996–98; Gp Dir, Microsoft Services Orgn, 1998–2002; Gen. Manager, Small and Mid-Mkt Solutions and Partners, 2002–04; Man. Dir, Microsoft Ltd, 2004–06; Vice Pres., Microsoft EMEA, 2004–06. FCIM. *Recreations:* cycling, snow-boarding, guitar.

BAKER, Andrew John, MA; educational consultant, since 2012; Headmaster, Westcliff High School for Boys, 1990–2012; *b* Bolton, 13 Nov. 1946; *s* of late John and Lilian Baker; *m* 1971, Lynda Ann Revell; one *s. Educ:* Farnworth Grammar Sch.; Univ. of Sheffield (BA 1969; MA 1973). Teacher of Hist., Boteler Grammar Sch., Warrington, 1969–74; Hulme Grammar School, Oldham: Sen. Hist. Master, 1974–81; Dir, Sixth Form Studies, 1981–87; Dep. Headmaster, 1987–90. Lectr to educationalists and businessmen on contemp. educnl issues, 1987–. Chairman: SE Essex Secondary Heads' Assoc., 1995–98; Southend-on-Sea Secondary Heads' Assoc., 2001–05 and 2009–12. Mem., Southend Educn Forum, 2004–12; Sch. Improvement Partner, 2007–10. *Publications:* Examining British Politics, 1979; Education, Society and the Pursuit of Values: a headmaster's reflections, 2015. *Recreations:* reading, contemporary affairs, conversation, music, theatre, cricket, walking. *Address:* 48 Burges Road, Thorpe Bay, Essex SS1 3AX. *E:* ajbaker48@hotmail.co.uk.

BAKER, Andrew William; QC 2006; a Recorder, since 2012; *b* 21 Dec. 1965; *s* of Gordon Baker and Ann Baker (now Williamson); *m* 1986, Philippa Jane Ghaut; four *s. Educ:* Lenzie Acad., Strathclyde; Merton Coll., Oxford (BA Maths 1986; MA 1990); City Univ. (PGDipLaw 1987). Called to the Bar, Lincoln's Inn, 1988 (Hardwicke, Wolfson and Kennedy Scholar); Tutor, law of internat. trade, 1988–89; in practice at the Bar, 1989–. CEDR Accredited Mediator, 2008; Reg. Practitioner, Dubai Internat. Financial Centre Courts, 2011–. Mem., Admiralty and Commercial Court Users' Cttee, 2009–. Supporting Mem., London Maritime Arbitrators Assoc., 2004–. Member: Panel of Arbitrators, Singapore Internat. Arbitration Centre, 2010–12; Singapore Maritime Arbitrators Assoc., 2010–; Kuala Lumpur Regl Centre for Arbitration, 2010–. Gov., Busbridge C of E (Aided) Jun. Sch., 2005–13 (Chm., 2011–13). Series Editor, Lloyd's Shipping Law Library, 2009–. *Publications:* (jtly) Time Charters, 6th edn 2008, 7th edn 2014. *Recreations:* time with Philippa and the Fabulous Baker Boys, golf, football (playing and coaching), Lotus and McLaren cars, playing trumpet, music, films. *Address:* 20 Essex Street, WC2R 3AL. *T:* (020) 7842 1200, *Fax:* (020) 7842 1270. *E:* abaker@20essexst.com.

BAKER, Ann Maureen, (Mrs D. R. Baker); *see* Jenner, A. M.

BAKER, Anthony Thomas; aviation consultant; Director, International Aviation Negotiations, Department for Transport, retired 2004; *b* 1944; *s* of Charles Arthur Baker and Ivy Louvain Baker; *m* 1969, Alicia Veronica Roberts; two *s* one *d. Educ:* Chatham House Grammar Sch., Ramsgate; Lincoln Coll., Oxford (BA Hons Modern History). Ministry of Transport: Asst Principal, 1965–70; Principal, 1970–75; Principal, HM Treasury, 1975–78; Asst Sec., 1978–88, and 1991–96, MOT; Dir, Internat. Aviation Negotiations, DoE, then DETR, subseq. DTLR, later DfT, 1996–2004. Dir, County NatWest Ltd, 1988–91. Co-Chair, 2008–14, Chair, 2014–, Harington Scheme. Freeman, City of London. *Recreations:* theatre, opera, history, literature. *Address:* 68 Talbot Road, N6 4RA.

BAKER, Sir Bryan (William), Kt 1997; Chairman, West Midlands Region, NHS Executive, Department of Health, 1996–97 (Chairman, West Midlands Regional Health Authority, 1993–96); *b* 12 Dec. 1932; *m* 1954, Christine Margaret (*née* Hole); one *d.* Joined Tarmac, 1952; Gp Man. Dir, Tarmac plc, 1983–92. Non-executive Director: Volvo Truck & Bus Ltd, 1992; Birse Group PLC, 1993; Pemberstone PLC, 1995; Benson Gp PLC, 1996; formerly non-exec. Dir, Polypipe PLC; Chm., Bruntcliffe Aggregates PLC, 1996–97. Formerly Chairman: W Midlands Industrial Develt Agency; W Midlands Industrial Develt Bd.

BAKER, Air Vice-Marshal Christopher Paul, CB 1991; Chairman, Taylor Curnow Ltd, since 1994; *b* 14 June 1938; *er s* of late Paul Hocking Baker, FCA and Kathleen Minnie Florence Baker; *m* 1st, 1961, Heather Ann Laity (decd), *d* of late Cecil Henry Laity and Eleanor Hocking Laity; three *s*; 2nd, 1981, Francesca R. Aghabi, *er d* of late George Khalil Aghabi and Elizabeth Maria Regina Aghabi; two *s. Educ:* Bickley Hall, Kent; Tonbridge School. Commnd RAF, 1958; served 1958–61: RAF Khormaksar (Air Movements), Aden; Supply Sqdn, RAF Coll., Cranwell; RAF Labuan, N Borneo; No 389 Maintenance Unit, RAF Seletar, Singapore; MoD Harrogate; student, RAF Staff Coll., Bracknell; OC Supply Sqdn, RAF Linton-on-Ouse; SHAPE, Two ATAF; ndc; Directing Staff, RAF Staff Coll., Bracknell; HQ RAF Support Comd; Dep. Dir, RAF Supply Systems, MoD; Comd Supply Movements Officer, HQ Strike Comd, RAF High Wycombe, 1982–84; RCDS, 1985; Dir, Supply Systems, MoD, 1986–87; Dir, Supply Policy and Logistics Plans, MoD, 1988–89; Dir Gen. of Support Management, RAF, 1989–93. Gen. Manager, Defence Sector Business Gp, TNT Express (UK) Ltd, 1993–94. Freeman, City of London; Liveryman, Bakers' Co. *Publications:* papers on the crisis of authority, oil potential of the Arctic Basin, and German reunification. *Recreations:* Rugby, rowing, ski-ing, modern history.

BAKER, Claire Josephine, PhD; Member (Lab) Scotland Mid and Fife, Scottish Parliament, since 2007; *b* Dunfermline, 4 March 1971; *d* of James Brennan and Margaret Brennan (*née* Edgar); *m* 2004, Richard James Baker, *qv*; one *d. Educ:* Edinburgh Univ. (MA Hons English Lang. and Lit.); Glasgow Univ. (PhD English Lit. 1997). Labour researcher, Scottish Parlt, 1999–2002; Amicus researcher, 2002–04; Res. and Information Manager, RCN Scotland, 2004–05; Policy Manager, SCVO, 2005–07. *Publications:* Critical Guide to the Poetry of Sylvia Plath, 1998. *Address:* Wing B, Carlyle House, Carlyle Road, Kirkcaldy, Fife KY1 1DB. *T:* (01592) 568678, *Fax:* (01592) 566401. *E:* claire.baker.msp@scottish.parliament.uk.

BAKER, David Brian, OBE 2001; FSA; consultant, historic environment conservation, since 1997; *b* 20 Jan. 1941; *s* of Henry and Maie Baker; *m* 1963, Evelyn Amos; one *s. Educ:* Hertford Coll., Oxford (BA Hons Mod. Hist. 1963); Inst. of Educn, London (PGCE 1964). FSA 1972; MCIfA (MIFA 1982); IHBC 1998. Asst Hist. Master, Bedford Sch., 1964–68; Lectr in Hist., Portsmouth Poly., 1968–71; Conservation and Archaeol. Officer, Beds County Planning Dept, 1972–97. Member: various adv. cttees, English Heritage, 1990–2011; Council, NT, 1998–2006; Vice-Pres., Council for British Archaeol., 1999–2008. Chm., Adv. Bd for Redundant Churches, C of E, 2005–08 (Mem., 2001–08); Member: St Albans DAC, 1973–; Rochester Fabric Adv. Cttee, 2007–; Cathedrals Fabric Cttee for England, 2012–. Chm., Cowdray Heritage Trust, 2009–13 (Trustee, 1998–13). *Publications:* Living with the Past, 1983; numerous papers in conservation and archaeol jls. *Recreations:* photography, music, gardening. *Address:* 3 Oldway, Bletsoe, Bedford MK44 1QG. *T:* (01234) 781179. *E:* dbb@suttons.org.uk.

BAKER, Derek Alexander; Permanent Secretary, Department for Employment and Learning, Northern Ireland, since 2013; *b* 3 Nov. 1957; *s* of Alexander James Baker and Sarah

Beatrice Baker; *m* 1989, Barbara Anne Haggan; one *s* two *d*. *Educ:* Queen's Univ., Belfast (BA Hons French and German). Joined NICS, 1980; Dept for Econ. Develt, 1980–84, and 1987–93; Harland & Wolff Shipbuilders (on secondment), 1985–87; Asst Sec., Dept of Health and Social Services, 1993–2002; Dep. Sec., Dept for Social Develt, 2002–06; Dir, Corporate HR (formerly Central Personnel Gp), Dept of Finance and Personnel, 2006–12; Dep. Sec., Dept of Educn, 2013. *Address:* Department for Employment and Learning, Adelaide House, 39/49 Adelaide Street, Belfast BT2 8FD.

BAKER, Dick; *see* Baker, F. E.

BAKER, Prof. Edward James, MD; FRCP, FRCPCH; Deputy Chief Inspector of Hospitals England, since 2014; *b* 2 May 1956; *s* of late Christopher Baker and Dr Hazel Baker; *m* 1982, Patricia Hudswell; two *d*. *Educ:* Trinity Coll., Cambridge (MB BChir 1979; MA; MD 1987); St Thomas's Hosp. Med. Sch. FRCP 1994; FRCPCH 1997. Hon. Consultant Paediatric Cardiologist, Guy's Hosp., 1987–2010; Sen. Lectr, 1987–2010, Prof. of Paediatric Cardiol., 2010, KCL; Medical Director: Guy's and St Thomas' Hosp. NHS Trust, subseq. Guy's and St Thomas' NHS Foundn Trust, 2003–10; Oxford Radcliffe NHS Trust, subseq. Oxford Univ. Hosps NHS Trust, 2010–14. Editor-in-Chief, Cardiology in the Young, 2007–13. *Publications:* (ed jtly) Paediatric Cardiology, 1986, 3rd edn 2010. *Address:* Care Quality Commission, Finsbury Tower, 103–105 Bunhill Road, EC1Y 8TG. *T:* (020) 7448 9084.

BAKER, Elizabeth Margaret; Headmistress, Wimbledon High School, 1992–95, retired; *b* 13 Sept. 1945; *d* of Walter and Betty Gale; *m*; one *d*. *Educ:* University College of Wales, Swansea (BA, DipEd). Lectr, Derby Coll. of Further Educn, 1968–71; Classics Teacher: West Monmouth Sch., 1971–74; Cheltenham Bournside, 1974–81; Cheltenham Ladies' Coll., 1981–88; Headmistress, Ellerslie, Malvern, 1988–92. *Recreations:* wine, letter-writing, keeping the classics alive.

BAKER, Francis Eustace, (Dick), CBE 1984 (OBE 1979); business interests in property and the automotive industry; Partner, Crossroads Motors, since 1988; *b* 19 April 1933; *s* of Stephen and Jessica Wilhelmina Baker; *m* 1957, Constance Anne Shilling; two *s* two *d*. *Educ:* Borden Grammar Sch.; New Coll., Oxford (MA). Nat. Service, RNVR, 1955–57 (Sub Lieut; minesweeper navigating officer). Admin. Officer, HMOCS, 1957; Solomon Islands: Dist. Officer, W Solomons, 1958; Co-operatives Develt Officer, 1960; Secretariat Officer and Clerk to Legislative Council, 1961–63; farming in UK, 1963–67; Admin. Officer, British Service Condominium of New Hebrides, 1967–79 (Chief Co-operatives Officer, 1968–73; District Agent, Northern District, 1973–78; Political and Lands Sec., British Residency Secretariat, 1978–79); Chief Sec. to Falkland Is Govt and Deputy to Gov. and High Comr, British Antarctic Territory, 1979–84; Gov. and C-in-C, St Helena and Dependencies of Ascension and Tristan Da Cunha, 1984–88. Queen's Silver Jubilee Medal, 1977. *Recreations:* swimming, reading, travelling, interesting motor cars. *Address:* Fairway, Bannister Hill, Borden, Sittingbourne, Kent ME9 8HT. *T:* (01795) 423301.

BAKER, Francis Raymond, OBE 1997; HM Diplomatic Service; Ambassador to Iraq, since 2014; *b* 27 Jan. 1961; *s* of late Raymond Albert Baker and Pamela Annis Baker; *m* 1983, Maria Pilar Fernandez; one *s* one *d*. *Educ:* Dartford Grammar Sch. Entered FCO, 1981: Third Sec., Panama City, 1983–86; Third, later Second Sec., Buenos Aires, 1986–91; Second Sec., FCO, 1991–93; First Secretary: Ankara, 1993–96; on secondment to US State Dept, Washington, 1996–98; FCO, 1998; Private Sec. to Minister of State, FCO, 1998–2000; Head, Africa Dept (Equatorial), FCO, 2000–03; Counsellor (Pol/Mil.), 2003–04, Counsellor (Foreign and Security Policy), 2004–07, Washington; Dir (Iraq), FCO, 2007–10; Ambassador to Kuwait, 2010–14. *Recreations:* cricket, watching football (Charlton Athletic FC), American football, golf, rock music, sailing, road biking, travelling. *Address:* BFPO 5422, HA4 6EP.

BAKER, Gerard Thomas; Editor-in-Chief, Dow Jones and Co., since 2013; Managing Editor, Wall Street Journal, since 2013; *b* Barnehurst, Kent, 24 Jan. 1962; *s* of Frederick Samuel Baker and Della Maria Baker (*née* O'Flynn); *m* 1993, Sally Hinton; five *d*. *Educ:* St Mary's Grammar Sch., Sidcup; Corpus Christi Coll., Oxford (MA 1st Cl. Hons PPE 1983). Analyst, Bank of England, 1984–86; economist, Lloyds Bank, 1986; researcher, Weekend World, LWT, 1987–88; British Broadcasting Corporation: producer, News and Current Affairs, 1988–89; New York producer, 1989–90; producer, Panorama, 1990–93; economics corresp., 1993–94; Financial Times: Tokyo corresp., 1994–96; Washington corresp., 1996–98; Washington Bureau Chief, 1998–2002; Associate Ed. and Chief US Commentator, 2002–04; US Ed., The Times, 2004–09; Dep. Ed.-in-Chief, Dow Jones and Wall St Jl, 2009–13. *Recreations:* travel, reading, running, co-managing five daughters. *Address:* Dow Jones and Co., 1211 Avenue of the Americas, New York, NY 10036, USA. *T:* (212) 4163070. *E:* gerard.baker@wsj.com.

BAKER, Gordon Meldrum; HM Diplomatic Service, retired; Temporary Senior Clerk, Committee Office, House of Lords, 2002–06; Clerk, Sub-Committee G (Social Policy and Consumer Affairs), European Union Select Cttee, 2004–06; *b* 4 July 1941; *o s* of Walter John Ralph Gordon Baker and Kathleen Margaret Henrietta Dawe Baker (*née* Meldrum); *m* 1978, Sheila Mary Megson (*d* 2011). *Educ:* St Andrew's Sch., Bawdrip, near Bridgwater. MSc Bradford 1976. Lord Chancellor's Dept, 1959–66; transf. to HM Diplomatic Service, 1966; Commonwealth Office, 1966–68; FO (later FCO), 1968–69; Lagos, 1969–72; First Sec., FCO, 1973–75 (Resident Clerk, 1974–75); sabbatical at Postgrad. Sch. of Studies in Industrial Technol., Univ. of Bradford, 1975–76; FCO, 1976–78 (Res. Clerk, 1976–78); First Sec. (Chancery/Information), subseq. First Sec., Head of Chancery and Consul, Brasilia, 1978–81; Asst Head, Mexico and Central America Dept, FCO, 1982–84; Counsellor, 1984; on secondment to British Aerospace, 1984–86; Counsellor, Head of Chancery then Dep. Hd of Mission, and Consul-General, Santiago, 1986–89, Chargé d'Affaires, 1986, 1987 and 1989; RCDS, 1990–91; Head of W Indian and Atlantic Dept, FCO, 1991–94; High Commissioner: Belize, 1995–98; Barbados and Eastern Caribbean States, 1998–2001; Inquiry Sec., Competition Commn, 2002. Associate Fellow and Chm., Caribbean Study Gp, RIIA, 2001–07; Mem. Adv. Panel, Centre for Positive Ageing, Univ. of Greenwich, 2013–. Mem., Local Socs Consultative Gp on Greenwich Park Olympics, 2010–12. Mem., Exec. Cttee, Anglo-Chilean Soc., 2002–06. Trustee: Friends of Georgian Soc. of Jamaica, 2003–05, 2008– (Chm., 2012–15); Blackheath Historic Bldgs Trust, 2009–13. Patron, Age Activity Centre, Wandsworth, 2001–09. Mem., Exec. Cttee, Westcombe Soc. (local community assoc.), 2002–13 (Chm., 2007–12); Trustee: Ramphal Centre, 2007–11; Carers Support (Bexley and Greenwich), 2011–12. *Publications:* (ed) No Island is an Island: the impact of globalization on the Commonwealth Caribbean, 2007. *Recreations:* walking, watching birds, browsing, enjoying the arts and the company of women and small animals, collecting clocks. *Address:* 78 Foyle Road, Blackheath, SE3 7RH. *T:* (020) 8858 3675.

BAKER, Ian Michael; a District Judge (Magistrates' Courts) (formerly Metropolitan Stipendiary Magistrate), 1990–2012; a Recorder, since 2002; *b* 8 May 1947; *s* of late David Ernest Baker and Phyllis Hinds; *m* 1st, 1976, Sue Joel (marr. diss. 1985); one *s*; 2nd, 1991, Jill Sack (*d* 2001); 3rd, 2005, Jane Hinde. *Educ:* Cynffig Grammar Sch., Mid Glam; St Catharine's Coll., Cambridge (MA). Travelled, New England, Latin America and Asia, 1969–71. Articled, then Asst Solicitor to John Clitheroe, Kingsley Napley, 1972–76; Partner, Heninghem, Ambler & Gildener, York, 1976–79; Assistant Solicitor: Claude, Hornby & Cox, 1979; Seifert Sedley, 1980–83; Clinton Davis, 1984–87; Partner, T. V. Edwards, 1987–90. Mem., Equal Treatment Adv. Cttee, Judicial Studies Bd, 2002–08. Trustee, Nat. Council for Welfare of Prisoners Abroad, 1986–99 (Chm., 1993–99). *Recreations:* travel, saxophone, theatre, music, art, gardening, bird watching, golf.

BAKER, James Addison, III; Senior Partner, Baker Botts LLP (formerly Baker & Botts), since 1993; Founder, 1993, and Hon. Chairman, James A. Baker III Institute for Public Policy, Rice University; *b* 28 April 1930; *s* of late James A. Baker, Jr and Bonner Means Baker; *m* 1973, Susan Garrett; eight *c*. *Educ:* Princeton Univ. (BA); Univ. of Texas at Austin (law degree). Served US Marine Corps, 1952–54. Practised law, firm of Andrews, Kurth, Campbell and Jones, Houston, Texas, 1957–75, 1977–81. Under Sec. of Commerce, US Govt, 1975; National Chairman: President Ford's re-elecn campaign, 1976; George Bush for President Cttee, 1979–80; Dep. Dir, Reagan-Bush Transition and Sen. Advr to 1980 Reagan-Bush Cttee, 1980–Jan. 1981; Chief of Staff to US President, 1981–85; Sec. of US Treasury, 1985–88; Sec. of State, USA, 1989–92; COS and Sen. Counsellor to Pres. of USA, 1992–93. Personal Envoy of UN Sec. Gen. for Western Sahara, 1997–2004; Co-Chm., Iraq Study Gp, US, 2006. Numerous hon. degrees. US Presidential Medal of Freedom, 1992. *Publications:* The Politics of Diplomacy, 1995; Work Hard, Study… And Keep Out of Politics! (memoir), 2006. *Recreations:* hunting, fishing, tennis, golf. *Address:* Baker Botts LLP, 1 Shell Plaza, 910 Louisiana, Houston, TX 77002–4995, USA; James A. Baker III Institute for Public Policy, 6100 Main Street, Rice University, Baker Hall, Suite 120, Houston, TX 77005, USA. *Clubs:* numerous social, civic and fraternal.

BAKER, Dame Janet (Abbott), CH 1994; DBE 1976 (CBE 1970); professional singer; *b* 21 Aug. 1933; *d* of Robert Abbott Baker and May (*née* Pollard); *m* 1957, James Keith Shelley. *Educ:* The College for Girls, York; Wintringham, Grimsby. Chancellor, Univ. of York, 1991–2004. Trustee, Foundn for Sport and the Arts, 1991–2012. Daily Mail Kathleen Ferrier Award, 1956; Queen's Prize, Royal College of Music, 1959; Shakespeare Prize, Hamburg, 1971; Copenhagen Sonning Prize, 1979; Lifetime Achievement Award, Gramophone, 2011. Hon. DMus: Birmingham, 1968; Leicester, 1974; London, 1974; Hull, 1975; Oxon, 1975; Leeds, 1980; Lancaster, 1983; York, 1984; Hon. MusD Cantab, 1984; Hon. LLD Aberdeen, 1980; Hon. DLitt Bradford, 1983. Hon. Fellow: St Anne's Coll., Oxford, 1975; Downing Coll., Cambridge, 1985. FRSA 1979. Gold Medal, Royal Philharmonic Soc., 1990. Comdr, Order of Arts and Letters (France), 1995. *Publications:* Full Circle (autobiog.), 1982. *Recreations:* reading, walking.

BAKER, Hon. Sir Jeremy (Russell); Kt 2013; **Hon. Mr Justice Jeremy Baker;** a Judge of the High Court of Justice, Queen's Bench Division, since 2013; *b* 9 Feb. 1958. Called to the Bar, Middle Temple, 1979, Bencher, 2013; QC 1999; Recorder, 2000–10; a Circuit Judge, 2010–13. *Address:* Royal Courts of Justice, Strand, WC2A 2LL.

BAKER, His Honour John Arnold; DL; a Circuit Judge, 1973–98; *b* Calcutta, 5 Nov. 1925; *s* of late William Sydney Baker, MC and Hilda Dora Baker (*née* Swiss); *m* 1954, Edith Muriel Joy Heward; two *d*. *Educ:* Plymouth Coll.; Wellington Sch., Somerset; Wadham Coll., Oxford (MA, BCL). Served RNVR, 1943–44. Treas., Oxford Union, 1948. Admitted Solicitor, 1951; called to Bar, Gray's Inn, 1960. A Recorder, 1972–73. Chm., Nat. League of Young Liberals, 1952–53; contested (L): Richmond, 1959 and 1964; Dorking, 1970; Vice-Pres., Liberal Party, 1968–69; Chm., Liberal Party Exec., 1969–70. Pres., Medico-Legal Soc., 1986–88. Trustee, 2002–06, Patron, 2006–, The Apex Trust. DL Surrey, 1986. *Publications:* Ballot Box to Jury Box (memoir), 2005. *Recreations:* music, watching sport. *Address:* c/o The Crown Court, 6–8 Penrhyn Road, Kingston upon Thames, Surrey KT1 2BB. *T:* (020) 8240 2500. *Clubs:* National Liberal, MCC; Nothing (Richmond).

BAKER, Prof. Sir John Hamilton, Kt 2003; LLD; FBA 1984; Downing Professor of the Laws of England, Cambridge University, 1998–2011, now Emeritus; Fellow, St Catharine's College, Cambridge, 1971–2011, Emeritus, 2011–12, now Honorary Fellow (President, 2004–07); *b* 10 April 1944; *s* of Kenneth Lee Vincent Baker, QPM and Marjorie (*née* Bagshaw); *m* 1st, 1968, Veronica Margaret (marr. diss. 1997), *d* of Rev. W. S. Lloyd; two *d*; 2nd, 2002, Fiona Rosalind Holdsworth (*née* Cantlay) (*d* 2005); 3rd, 2010, Prof. Elisabeth Maria Cornelia van Houts, *widow* of Thomas Erle Faber. *Educ:* King Edward VI Grammar School, Chelmsford; UCL (LLB 1965 (Andrews Medal), PhD 1968; Fellow 1990); MA Cantab 1971, LLD 1984, Yorke Prize, 1975. FRHistS 1980. Called to the Bar, Inner Temple, 1966 (Hon. Bencher 1988), *aeg* Gray's Inn, 1978 (Hon. Bencher 2013). Asst Lectr, Faculty of Laws, UCL, 1965–67, Lectr, 1967–71; Cambridge University: Librarian, Squire Law Library, 1971–73; Univ. Lectr in Law, 1973–83; Reader in English Legal History, 1983–88; Prof. of English Legal Hist., 1988–98; Junior Proctor, 1980–81; Chm., Faculty of Law, 1990–92. Visiting Professor: European Univ. Inst., Florence, 1979; Yale Law Sch., 1987; NY Univ. Sch. of Law, 1988–2010; Vis. Lectr, Harvard Law Sch., 1982; Mellon Senior Res. Fellow, H. E. Huntington Liby, San Marino, Calif., 1983; Ford Special Lectr, Oxford Univ., 1984; Vis. Fellow, All Souls Coll., Oxford, 1995. Corresp. Fellow, Amer. Soc. Legal History, 1993; Hon. Fellow, Soc. for Advanced Legal Studies, 1997; Hon. Foreign Mem., Amer. Acad. of Arts and Scis, 2001. Literary Dir, Selden Soc., 1981–2011 (Jt Dir, 1981–90). Hon. QC 1996. Hon. LLD Chicago, 1992. Ames Prize, Harvard, 1985; Gold Medal, Irish Soc. for Legal Hist., 2008. *Publications:* An Introduction to English Legal History, 1971, 4th edn 2002; English Legal Manuscripts, vol. I, 1975, vol. II, 1978; The Reports of Sir John Spelman, 1977–78; (ed) Legal Records and the Historian, 1978; Manual of Law French, 1979, 2nd edn 1990; The Order of Serjeants at Law, 1984; English Legal Manuscripts in the USA, vol. I 1985, vol. II 1991; The Legal Profession and the Common Law, 1986; (with S. F. C. Milsom) Sources of English Legal History, 1986, 2nd edn 2010; The Notebook of Sir John Port, 1986; (ed) Judicial Records, Law Reports and the Growth of Case Law, 1989; Readings and Moots in the Inns of Court, vol. II, 1990; Cases from the lost notebooks of Sir James Dyer, 1994; Catalogue of English Legal MSS in Cambridge University Library, 1996; Spelman's Reading on Quo Warranto, 1997; Monuments of Endlesse Labours, 1998; The Reports of John Caryll, 1999; The Common Law Tradition, 2000; The Law's Two Bodies, 2001; Readers and Readings at the Inns of Court, 2001; Oxford History of the Laws of England, vol. 6, 2003; An Inner Temple Miscellany, 2004; (with A. Taussig) Catalogue of the Legal Manuscripts of Anthony Taussig, 2007; The Reports of William Dalison, 2008; The English Legal Manuscripts of Sir Thomas Phillipps, 2009; The Men of Court, 2011; Collected Papers on English Legal History, 2013; articles in legal and hist. jls. *Address:* St Catharine's College, Cambridge CB2 1RL.

BAKER, Sir John (William), Kt 2007; CBE 2000; Vice Chairman, Chelsea and Westminster Hospital NHS Foundation Trust, since 2011; *b* 5 Dec. 1937; *s* of Reginald and Wilhelmina Baker; *m* 1st, 1962, Pauline (*née* Moore); one *s*; 2nd, 1975, Gillian (*née* Bullen). *Educ:* Harrow Weald County Grammar Sch.; Oriel Coll., Oxford. Served Army, 1959–61. MoT, 1961–70; DoE, 1970–74; Dep. Chief Exec., Housing Corp., 1974–78; Sec., 1979–80, Bd Mem., 1980–89, Corporate Man. Dir, 1986–89, CEGB; Chief Exec., 1990–95, Chm., 1995–97, National Power; Dir, 1995–2003, Dep. Chm., 2002–03, Royal and Sun Alliance Insurance Gp; Chm., Medeva PLC, 1996–2000; Dep. Chm., Celltech Gp, 2000–03. Chairman: Globeleq, 2003–07; The Maersk Co., 2003–10; Renewable Energy Hldgs plc, 2005–13; Momenta Hldgs, 2006–07; Bladon Jets Hldgs Ltd, 2014–; Mem. Business Adv. Council, A. P. Moller Gp, 1996–2008. Chm., Sen. Salaries Rev. Body, 2002–08. Chairman: ENO, 1996–2001; Associated Bd, Royal Schs of Music, 2000–06. Chairman: Exec. Assembly, World Energy Council, 1995–98; Groundwork Foundn, 1996–2001. Chairman: Governing Body, Holland Park Sch., 2003–13; Friends of Yehudi Menuhin Sch., 2013–. *Recreations:* tennis, golf, bridge, music, theatre.

See also Rt Rev. J. M. R. Baker.

BAKER, Hon. Sir Jonathan Leslie, Kt 2009; **Hon. Mr Justice Baker;** a Judge of the High Court, Family Division, since 2009; *b* 6 Aug. 1955; *s* of late Leslie Baker and Isobel Baker; *m* 1980, Helen Sharrock, DL; one *s* one *d*. *Educ:* St Albans Sch.; St John's Coll., Cambridge

(MA). Called to the Bar, Middle Temple, 1978, Bencher, 2009; barrister, specialising in Family Law, 1979–2009; Recorder, 2000–09; QC 2001; Dep. High Ct Judge, 2003–09; Hd, Harcourt Chambers, 2004–09; Family Division Liaison Judge, Western Circuit, 2011–. Mem. Cttee, Family Law Bar Assoc., 2005–09. Chm., Relate, Oxon, 1999–2008. Gov., Magdalen College Sch., Oxford, 2005–14. Ed.-in-Chief, Court of Protection Law Reports, 2011–. *Publications:* (jtly) Contact: the new deal, 2006; (jtly) The Public Law Outline: the court companion, 2008. *Recreations:* music, history, family life. *Address:* Royal Courts of Justice, Strand, WC2A 2LL.

BAKER, Rt Rev. Jonathan Mark Richard; *see* Fulham, Bishop Suffragan of.

BAKER, Mark Alexander Wyndham, CBE 1998; Chairman, Magnox Electric plc, 1996–98; *b* 19 June 1940; *s* of late Lt-Comdr Alexander Arthur Wyndham Baker, RN and Renée Gavrelle Stenson (*née* Macnaghten); *m* 1964, Meriel, *yr d* of late Capt. Hugh Chetwynd-Talbot, MBE and Cynthia Chetwynd-Talbot; one *s* one *d. Educ:* Prince Edward Sch., Salisbury, S Rhodesia; University Coll. of Rhodesia & Nyasaland (Beit Schol.; BA London); Christ Church, Oxford (Rhodes Schol.; MA). United Kingdom Atomic Energy Authority, 1964–89: Sec., 1976–78, Gen. Sec., 1978–81, AERE, Harwell; Dir of Personnel and Admin, Northern Div., 1981–84; Authority Personnel Officer, 1984–86; Authority Sec., 1986–89; Exec. Dir, Corporate Affairs and Personnel, Nuclear Electric plc, 1989–96. Chm., Electricity Pensions Ltd, 1996–2006; non-exec. Dir, Pension Protection Fund, 2004–09. Deputy Chairman: Police Negotiating Bd, 2000–04; Police Adv. Bd, 2001–04. Mem., Sen. Salaries Review Body, 2004–09. Mem., Adv. Cttee, Envmtl Change Inst., Oxford Univ., 1999–2004. Mem. Bd of Trustees, Save the Children, 1998–2004. Pres., Inst. of Energy, 1998–99. *Recreations:* gardening, golf, walking, poetry, words. *Address:* The Old School, Fyfield, Abingdon OX13 5LR. *T:* (01865) 390724. *E:* MarkWBaker@aol.com. *Club:* Antrobus Dining (Cheshire).

BAKER, Martin John; Master of Music, Westminster Cathedral, since 2000; recitalist; *b* 26 July 1967. *Educ:* Royal Northern Coll. of Music Jun. Sch.; Chetham's Sch. of Music; Downing Coll., Cambridge (Organ Scholar; BA 1988). Organ Scholar, Westminster Cathedral, 1988–90; Assistant Organist: St Paul's Cathedral, 1990–91; Westminster Abbey, 1992–2000. Recitals include improvisations. *Address:* Westminster Cathedral, 42 Francis Street, SW1P 1QW.

BAKER, Martyn Murray, OBE 2009; Director of Economic Development (formerly of Economic Development and Education), City of London Corporation, 1999–2008; *b* 10 March 1944; *s* of late Norman and Constance Baker; *m* 1970, Rosemary Caroline Holdich. *Educ:* Dulwich Coll.; Pembroke Coll., Oxford (MA). Asst Principal, Min. of Aviation, 1965–67; Private Sec. to Ministers, Min. of Technology, Min. of Aviation Supply, and DTI, 1968–71; Principal, 1971; Principal Private Sec. to Sec. of State for Trade, 1977–78; Counsellor, Civil Aviation and Shipping, Washington, 1978–82; Department of Trade and Industry: Asst Sec., Air Div., 1982–85; Projects and Export Policy Div., 1985–86; Under Sec., 1986; Regl Dir, NW, 1986–88; Dir, Enterprise and Deregulation Unit, 1988–90; Head of Overseas Trade Div., 1990–93; Head of Exports to Asia, Africa and Australasia Div., 1993–96; Hd of Chemicals and Biotechnology Directorate, 1996–99, and Hd of Consumer Goods, Business and Postal Services Directorate, 1997–99. Member: Export Guarantees Advisory Council, 1985–86; Cttee for ME Trade, 1990–96; Council, China Britain Trade Gp, 1993–96; Asia Pacific Adv. Gp, 1993–96; BBSRC, 1996–99. Leader, Manchester-Salford City Action Team, 1986–88; Chm., City Fringe Partnership Exec. Team, 1999–2005. Mem. Council, Chelsea Soc., 2007–. FRSA 1988–2012.

BAKER, Mary Geraldine, MBE 1995; President: European Parkinson's Disease Association, 1992–2006; European Federation of Neurological Associations, 2002–11; European Brain Council, 2010–14 (Vice President, 2002–10); *b* 27 Oct. 1936; *d* of George and Emily Wheeler; *m* 1960, Robert William John Baker; three *s. Educ:* Bromley High Sch.; Leeds Univ. (BA); Inst. of Almoners. AIMSW. Almoner, St Thomas' Hosp., 1959–61; housewife and mother, 1961–75; Social Worker, 1975–82; Principal Med. Social Worker, Frimley Park Hosp., 1982–83; Parkinson's Disease Society of UK: National Welfare Dir, 1984–91, 1992; Acting Chief Exec., 1991–92; Dir of Welfare Develt, 1994; Nat. and Internat. Develt Consultant, 1995–99; Chief Exec., 1999–2001. Mem., Adv. Gp on Rehabilitation, DoH, 1992–94; Chm., WHO Cttee of NGOs concerned with neurol disorders, 1998–2002. World Federation of Neurology: Mem., Med. Educn Res. Gp, 1998–; Mem., PR and WHO Liaison Cttee, 2002–; Mem., Code of Practice, 2001–, Council, 2007–, ABPI; Dir at Large, World Stroke Assoc., 2004–; Patient Representative Mem., Mgt Bd, EMEA, 2005–; Mem., Scientific Cttee, Innovative Medicines Initiative Jt Undertaking, 2008–. British Medical Journal: Patient Ed., 2004– (Mem., Editl Bd, 2000–); Chm., Patient Adv. Gp, 2005–. Hon. FCSLT 1991. Paul Harris Fellow, Rotary Foundn, 1997. DUniv Surrey, 2003; Hon. DSc Aston, 2013. Outstanding Contrib. to British Neurosci. and for Public Service, British Neurosci. Assoc., 2009. *Publications:* Speech Therapy in Practice, 1988; (with B. McCall) Care of the Elderly, 1990; (with P. Smith) The Role of the Social Worker in the Management of Parkinson's Disease, 1991; (jtly) The Wall between neurology and psychiatry, 2002; Practical Neurology: destigmatizing stigma in people with neurological problems, 2003; contribs to learned jls incl. BMJ. *Recreations:* music, theatre, reading, bridge, caravanning. *Address:* Kailua, Maybourne Rise, Mayford, Woking, Surrey GU22 0SH. *T:* (01483) 763626. *Club:* Soroptimists'.

BAKER, Dr Maureen, CBE 2004; FRCGP; Chair of Council, Royal College of General Practitioners, since 2013; *b* Motherwell, 20 Sept. 1958; *d* of William Murphy and Helen Murphy; *m* 1984, Peter Baker; two *d. Educ:* Holy Cross High Sch., Hamilton; Univ. of Dundee Med. Sch. (MB ChB 1981). DCH 1985; DRCOG 1985; DM 2003. FRCGP 1994. GP, 1985–, Nettletham Med. Centre, Lincoln, 2006–. Dir, Primary Care, Nat. Patient Safety Agency, 2002–07; Clin. Dir for Patient Safety, Health and Social Care Information Centre, 2007–. Hon. Sec., RCGP, 1999–2009. *Publications:* contrib. jls and books. *Recreations:* cinema, reading fiction, theme parks. *Address:* Royal College of General Practitioners, 30 Euston Square, NW1 2FB. *T:* (020) 3188 7412. *E:* chair@rcgp.org.uk.

BAKER, Maureen Anne; *see* Bacon, M. A.

BAKER, His Honour Michael Findlay; QC 1990; DL; a Circuit Judge, 1995–2012; *b* 26 May 1943; *s* of Rt Hon. Sir George Baker, PC, OBE; *m* 1973, Sarah Hartley Overton; two *d. Educ:* Haileybury; Brasenose Coll., Oxford. Called to the Bar, Inner Temple, 1966; a Recorder, 1991–95; Resident Judge, St Albans Crown Court, 2000–10. Sec., Nat. Reference Tribunals for Coal-mining Industry, 1973–95. Chairman: Herts Criminal Justice Strategy (Liaison) Cttee, 1998–2003; Vale House Stabilisation Services, 2003–11; Mem., Herts Probation Bd (formerly Cttee), 1998–2010. Gov., Univ. of Hertfordshire, 2008–14. DL Herts, 2008. *Recreations:* mountain climbing and walking, gardening. *Address:* Oakford, Standon, Ware, Herts SG11 1LT. *Clubs:* Alpine, Climbers'; Thames Hare and Hounds.
See also Rt Hon. Sir T. S. G. Baker.

BAKER, Prof. Michael John, TD 1971; Professor of Marketing, Strathclyde University, 1971–99, now Emeritus; Chairman, Westburn Publishers Ltd, since 1984; *b* 5 Nov. 1935; *s* of John Overend Baker and Constance Dorothy (*née* Smith); *m* 1959, Sheila (*née* Bell); one *s* two *d. Educ:* Worksop Coll.; Gosforth and Harvey Grammar Schs; Durham Univ. (BA); London Univ. (BScEcon); Harvard Univ. (CertITP, DBA); DipM. FRSE 1995; FCIM 1971; FCAM 1983; FScotvec 1988; FSQA 1997. 2nd Lieut, RA, 1956–57. Salesman, Richard Thomas & Baldwins (Sales) Ltd, 1958–64; Asst Lectr, Medway Coll. of Technology, 1964–66; Lectr, Hull Coll. of Technology, 1966–68; Foundn for Management Educn Fellow, 1968–71, Res. Associate, 1969–71, Harvard Business Sch.; Dean, Strathclyde Bus. Sch., 1978–84; Dep. Principal, 1984–91, Sen. Advr to Principal, 1991–94, Strathclyde Univ. Mem., Vice Chm. and Chm., Scottish Bus. Educn Council, 1973–85; Pres., Acad. of Marketing (formerly Marketing Educn Gp), 1986–2005 (Chm., 1973–86); Member: Food and Drink, EDC, 1976–78; SSRC Management and Industrial Relns Cttee, 1976–80; Nat. Councillor, Inst. of Marketing, 1977, Vice Chm. 1984–86, Chm. 1987; Trustee, CIM, 2008–14. Member: Scottish Hosps Endowment Res. Trust, 1983–96; Chief Scientist's Cttee, SHHD, 1985–96; Bus. and Management Sub-Cttee, UGC, 1985–89. Chairman: Scottish Marketing Projects Ltd, 1986–2005; IBEX Ltd, 1991–2005; Director: Stoddard Sekers International (formerly Stoddard Hldgs) PLC, 1983–97; Scottish Transport Gp, 1986–90; ARIS plc, 1990–94; Reid Gp, 1989–91; SGBS Ltd, 1990–97; STAMP Ltd, 1992–96. Dir, Scottish Med. Res. Fund, 1992–96. Visiting Professor: Univ. of Surrey, 1995–; Nottingham Trent Univ., 1999–2001; Hon. Prof., Univ. of Wales, Aberystwyth, 1999–2011; Adjunct Prof., Monash Univ., 2000–08; Special Prof., Nottingham Univ., 2001–07. Governor, Lomond Sch., 1984–96. Dean, Senate, CIM, 1994–2002. Founding Editor: Jl of Marketing Management, 1985; Jl of Customer Behaviour, 2002; Social Business, 2011. FRSA 1986. Hon. FCIM 1989; Hon. FAM 1997; Hon. FEMAC 2004. Hon. LLD Portsmouth, 2000; DUniv Surrey, 2003. *Publications:* Marketing, 1971, 7th edn 2006; Marketing New Industrial Products, 1975; (with R. McTavish) Product Policy, 1976; (ed) Marketing in Adversity, 1976; (ed) Marketing Theory and Practice, 1976, 3rd edn 1995; (ed) Industrial Innovation, 1979; Market Development, 1983; (ed) Dictionary of Marketing, 1984, 3rd edn 1998; Marketing Strategy and Management, 1985, 5th edn 2014; (with S. T. Parkinson) Organisational Buying Behaviour, 1986; (ed) The Marketing Book, 1987, 6th edn 2008; (with D. Ughanwa) The Role of Design in International Competitiveness, 1989; (with S. Hart) Marketing and Competitive Success, 1989; Research for Marketing, 1991; (ed) Perspectives on Marketing Management, vol. 1, 1991, vol. 2, 1992, vol. 3, 1993, vol. 4, 1994; Companion Encyclopedia of Marketing, 1995; The Marketing Manual, 1998; (with S. Hart) Product Strategy and Management, 1998, 2nd edn 2007; (ed) The Encyclopedia of Marketing, 1999; (ed) Marketing Theory, 2000, 2nd edn (with M. Saren) 2010; (ed) Marketing: critical perspectives, 5 vols, 2001; Business and Management Research, 2003, 3rd edn (with Anne Foy) 2010. *Recreations:* foreign travel, building bridges and mending fences. *Address:* Westburn, Helensburgh G84 9NH. *T:* (01436) 674686. *Club:* Royal Over-Seas League.

BAKER, His Honour Michael John David; a Circuit Judge, 1988–99; *b* 17 April 1934; *s* of late Ernest Bowden Baker and Dulcie Baker; *m* 1958, Edna Harriet Lane; one *s* one *d. Educ:* Trinity Sch. of John Whitgift; Bristol Univ. (LLB Hons). Admitted solicitor, 1957. Flying Officer, RAF, 1957–60. Joined firm of Glanvilles, Solicitors, Portsmouth, 1960; Partner, 1963–88; a Recorder, 1980–88. Coroner, S Hampshire, 1973–88 (Asst Dep. Coroner, 1971; Dep. Coroner, 1972). Pres., Southern Coroners Soc., 1975–76; Mem. Council, Coroners Soc. of England and Wales, 1979–88 (Jun. Vice-Pres., 1987–88). Mem., Council of Mgt, Music at Boxgrove, 1997–2010; Chm., Friends of Boxgrove Priory, 2004–08; Hon. Patron, Chichester Festival Th., 2002–; Dir (formerly Mem. Cttee), Friends of Arundel Castle CC, 2003–; Mem., Chichester Singers, 2008–. Churchwarden, St Margaret's Ch, Eartham, 2004–12. Trustee, Leonard Hawkins Trust, 2004–12. *Recreations:* walking, swimming, watching cricket, the theatre, music (particularly choral singing), photography. *Address:* c/o Glanvilles, Solicitors, Langstone Gate, Solent Road, Havant, Hants PO9 1TR. *T:* (023) 9249 2300. *Clubs:* Law Society; Keats (Chichester); Emsworth Sailing.

BAKER, Nicola Karina Christina; *see* Horlick, N. K. C.

BAKER, Nigel Marcus, OBE 2010; MVO 2003; HM Diplomatic Service; Ambassador to the Holy See, since 2011; *b* 9 Sept. 1966; *s* of late Clive Baker and Mary (*née* Appleyard, later Berg); *m* 1997, Alexandra Čechova; one *s. Educ:* Dulwich Coll.; Gonville and Caius Coll., Cambridge (BA Hons 1st cl. Hist. 1988; MA 1992). Researcher, Cons. Res. Dept, 1989; Third Sec., FCO, 1989; Third, later Second Sec., Prague, 1992–93; Dep. Hd of Mission, Bratislava, 1993–95; First Sec., FCO, 1998; Hd of Eur. Defence Section, Security Policy Dept, FCO, 1998–2000; Asst Private Sec. to Prince of Wales, 2000–03; Dep. Hd of Mission, Havana, 2003–06; Ambassador to Bolivia, 2007–11. Writer and histl researcher, Verona, 1996–97. Trustee, St Catherine's Foundn, 2000–03; Mem. Cttee, Friends of Royal Opera House, 2000–03. *Publications:* (ed) Britain and the Holy See: a celebration of 1982 and the wider relationship, 2013; articles in British and Eur. pubns on Byron, Palmerston, Italian history, European security and defence. *Recreations:* history in all its forms, good food and drink, mountains, civilisation, escaping. *Address:* British Embassy to the Holy See, Via XX Settembre 80a, Roma 00187, Italy. *E:* baker.sn@gmail.com. *Clubs:* Travellers; Crystal Palace Football.

BAKER, Nigel Robert James; QC 1988; a Recorder, since 1985; a Deputy High Court Judge, Queen's Bench Division, since 1994; *b* 21 Dec. 1942; *s* of late Herbert James Baker and Amy Beatrice Baker; *m* 1973, Stephanie Joy Stephenson; one *s. Educ:* Norwich Sch.; Univ. of Southampton (BA Law 1st cl.); Queens' Coll., Cambridge (LLM). Lectr in Law, Univ. of Leicester, 1968–70; called to the Bar, Middle Temple, 1969, Bencher, 1997; practised in London and on Midland Circuit, 1970–2007. Mem., Bar Council, 1985. *Recreations:* football (supporting Barnet FC), fell walking, gardening. *Address:* 7 Bedford Row, WC1R 4BS. *T:* (020) 7242 3555.

BAKER, Rt Hon. Norman (John); PC 2014; *b* 26 July 1957. *Educ:* Royal Holloway Coll., London Univ. (BA Hons). Our Price Records, 1978–83; teacher, 1985–97. Member: Lewes DC, 1987–99 (Leader of Council, 1991–97); E Sussex CC, 1989–97. Contested (Lib Dem) Lewes, 1992. MP (Lib Dem) Lewes, 1997–2015; contested (Lib Dem) same seat, 2015. Parly Under-Sec. of State, DfT, 2010–13; Minister of State, Home Office, 2013–14.

BAKER, His Honour Peter Maxwell; QC 1974; a Circuit Judge, 1983–2000; *b* 26 March 1930; *s* of late Harold Baker and of Rose Baker; *m* 1st, 1954, Jacqueline Mary Marshall (*d* 1986); three *d*; 2nd, 1988, Sandra Elizabeth Hughes. *Educ:* King Edward VII Sch., Sheffield; Exeter Coll., Oxford (MA). Called to Bar, Gray's Inn, 1956 (Holker Senior Exhibitioner); Junior, NE Circuit, 1960; a Recorder of the Crown Court, 1972–83. *Recreations:* fishing, shooting, yachting, music, watching others garden. *Address:* c/o North-Eastern Regional Director, 18th Floor, West Riding House, Albion Street, Leeds LS1 5AA.

BAKER, Prof. Philip Newton, DM; FRCOG, FRCSCan, FMedSci; Professor of Maternal and Fetal Health, Liggins Institute, and Director, Gravida (National Centre for Growth and Development), University of Auckland, since 2012; *b* Leicester, 31 March 1962; *s* of John and Jennifer Baker; *m* 1987, Nicola MacGregor (marr. diss. 2011); one *s* two *d. Educ:* Oakham Sch., Rutland; Nottingham Univ. Med. Sch. (BMedSci; BM BS 1985; DM 1991). FRCOG 2003. Wellbeing/Amer. Coll. of Obstetricians and Gynaecologists Travelling Res. Fellow, Magee-Women's Res. Inst., Pittsburgh, 1994–95; Sen. Lectr and Hon. Consultant, Obstetrics and Gynaecol., 1996–98, Prof. of Obstetrics and Gynaecol., 1998–2001, Univ. of Nottingham; Prof. of Maternal and Fetal Health, Univ. of Manchester and Hon. Consultant Obstetrician, St Mary's Hosp., 2001–09; Dir, Manchester NIHR Biomedical Res. Centre, 2008–09; Hd of Res., Central Manchester Foundn NHS Trust, 2008–09; University of Alberta: Dean, Faculty of Medicine and Dentistry, 2009–11; Adjunct Prof., Dept of Physiol., Heritage Medical Res. Centre, 2011; Hon. Consultant Obstetrician, Royal Alexandra Hosp., Edmonton, Alberta, 2009–11. Non-exec. Dir, NHS Direct Trust, 2007–09. Dist. Nat. Prof., Chongqing Medical Univ., 2013–. FMedSci 2008. *Publications:* (jtly) Obstetrics and Gynaecology: cases, questions and commentaries, 1997; (ed jtly) The Pathogenesis and

Management of Intrauterine Growth Restriction, 2000; (ed) Best Practice of Labour Ward Management, 2000; A Problem-based Obstetrics and Gynaecology Textbook for Undergraduates, 2003; (ed) MRCOG: an evidence-based textbook, 2004, 2nd edn 2010; (ed) The Aetiology and Management of Pre-eclampsia, 2004; (ed) Obstetrics by Ten Teachers, 17th edn 2005, 18th edn 2010; (ed) The Placenta and Neurodisability, 2005; (ed) Midwifery by Ten Teachers, 2006; (ed) Multiple Pregnancy, 2006; (ed) Cardiac Disease and Pregnancy, 2006; (ed) Teenage Pregnancy, 2007; (ed) Obesity and Reproduction, 2007; (ed) Renal Disease and Pregnancy, 2008; contrib. articles and papers. *Recreations:* Leicester City FC, cricket (ECB coach), vintage cars, grandfather clocks.

BAKER, Philip Woolf, OBE 1997; QC 2002; *b* 14 July 1955; *s* of Lionel Baker and Frances Baker (*née* Roth); *m* 1992, Bing-Sum Lau; two *s* one *d. Educ:* Haberdashers' Aske's Sch., Elstree; Emmanuel Coll., Cambridge (MA); Balliol Coll., Oxford (BCL); University Coll., London (LLM); SOAS, London (PhD 1985); London Business Sch. (MBA). Called to the Bar, Gray's Inn, 1979, Bencher, 2009; Lectr in Law, SOAS, London Univ., 1979–87; in practice as barrister, 1987–. Vis. Prof., Queen Mary Coll., Univ. of London, 1997–2008; Vis. Fellow, 2005–08, Sen. Vis. Fellow, 2008–, Inst. of Advanced Legal Studies, Univ. of London. *Publications:* Double Taxation Conventions and International Tax Law, 1991, 3rd edn 2001; contrib. articles on internat. tax law, Chinese law, Islamic law and human rights. *Recreations:* sinology, my family. *Address:* Field Court Tax Chambers, 3 Field Court, Gray's Inn, WC1R 5EP. *T:* (020) 3693 3700. *E:* pb@fieldtax.com. *Club:* Athenæum.

BAKER, Piers Howard Burton, PhD; HM Diplomatic Service, retired; Clerk, Tin Plate Workers' alias Wire Workers' Company, since 2012; *b* 23 July 1956; *s* of late Dr Donald Burton Baker and Marjorie Winifred Baker; *m* 1979, Maria Eugenia Vilaincour; three *s. Educ:* King's Sch., Canterbury; Corpus Christi Coll., Cambridge (MA 1981, PhD 1983). Joined HM Diplomatic Service, FCO, 1983; First Sec., Brussels, 1985–88; FCO, 1988–93; First Sec., UK Repn, Brussels, 1993–96; FCO, 1996–2001; Dep. Hd of Mission, Consul-Gen. and Dir, Trade Promotion, then Trade and Investment, Vienna, 2001–06. Dir, Internat. Office, Imperial Coll. London, 2007–09; Asst Dir, Engineering Professors' Council, 2009–12. *Publications:* Shahr-i Zohak and the History of the Bamiyan Valley, Afghanistan, 1991. *Recreations:* music, walking, historical research.

BAKER, Prof. Raymond, CBE 2002; PhD; FRS 1994; Chief Executive, Biotechnology and Biological Sciences Research Council, 1996–2001; *b* 1 Nov. 1936; *s* of Alfred Baker and May (*née* Golds); *m* 1960, Marian Slater; one *s* two *d. Educ:* Ilkeston Grammar Sch.; Leicester Univ. (BSc, PhD). Postdoctoral Fellow, UCLA, 1962–64; University of Southampton: Lectr in Organic Chem., 1964–72; Sen. Lectr, 1972–74; Reader, 1974–77; Prof., 1977–84; Dir, Wolfson Unit of Chemical Entomology, 1976–84; Dir 1984–89, Exec. Dir, 1989–96, of Medicinal Chem., Merck Sharp & Dohme Res. Labs. *Publications:* Mechanism in Organic Chemistry, 1971; contrib. numerous articles to Jl Chemical Soc., Jl Medicinal Chem., and other scientific jls. *Recreations:* golf, gardening. *Address:* Angeston Court, Uley, Dursley, Glos GL11 5AL. *T:* (01453) 861017.

BAKER, Richard Andrew; Chairman: Whitbread plc, since 2014 (non-executive Director, since 2009); DFS Furniture Co. Ltd, since 2010; Operating Partner, Advent International, since 2009; *b* 6 Aug. 1962; *s* of John and Mary Baker; *m* Suzanne; two *d. Educ:* Bishop Vesey's Grammar Sch., Sutton Coldfield; Downing Coll., Cambridge (BA 1984). Nat. Account Manager, Brand Mktg and Hd of Sales, UK Multiples, Mars Confectionery, 1986–95; Gp Mktg Dir, then Chief Operating Officer, ASDA, 1995–2003; CEO, Alliance Boots (formerly Boots Gp) plc, 2003–07. Chairman: Virgin Active Ltd, 2008–14; Global Adv. Council, Aimia (formerly Groupe Aeroplan), 2009–. Non-exec. Dir and Mem. Bd, LTA, 2010–. Mem., Adv. Bd, Cambridge Judge Business Sch. *Recreations:* keen sportsman playing competitive hockey, tennis and golf. *Clubs:* Royal Automobile; Hawks (Cambridge).

BAKER, Richard Douglas James, OBE 1976; RD 1979; broadcaster and author; Member, Broadcasting Standards Council, 1988–93; *b* Willesden, London, 15 June 1925; *s* of Albert and Jane Isobel Baker; *m* 1961, Margaret Celia Martin; two *s. Educ:* Kilburn Grammar Sch.; Peterhouse, Cambridge (MA). Served War, Royal Navy, 1943–46. Actor, 1948; Teacher, 1949; Third Programme Announcer, 1950–53; BBC TV Newsreader, 1954–82; Commentator for State Occasion Outside Broadcasts, 1967–70; TV Introductions to Promenade Concerts, 1960–95; Panellist on BBC2's Face the Music, 1966–79; Presenter, Omnibus, BBC TV, 1983; on Radio 4: presenter of Start the Week with Richard Baker, 1970–87; These You Have Loved, 1972–77; Baker's Dozen, 1978–87; Rollercoaster, 1984; Music in Mind, 1987–88; Richard Baker Compares Notes, 1987–95; The Musical Directors, 1998; on Radio 3: Mainly for Pleasure, 1986–92; In Tune, 1992–95; Rush Hour concerts, 1994–95; Sound Stories, 1998–99; on Radio 2: presenter of Melodies for You, 1986–95 and 1999–2003; Friday Night is Music Night, 1998–2005; Your 100 Best Tunes, 2003–07; on Classic FM: presenter, Classic Countdown, 1996; Evening Concerts, 1997–98; Baker's Choice, 1998–99. Host, P&O's Music Festival at Sea, 1985–2010. Columnist, Now! Magazine, 1979–80. Mem., Council, Friends of Covent Garden, 1975–2009; Trustee, D'Oyly Carte Opera Co., 1985–98; Governor, NYO of GB, 1985–2001. TV Newscaster of the Year (Radio Industries Club), 1972, 1974, 1979; BBC Radio Personality of the Year (Variety Club of GB), 1984; Sony Gold Award for Lifetime Achievement in Radio, 1996. Hon. FLCM 1974; Hon. RCM 1988. Hon. LLD: Strathclyde, 1979; Aberdeen, 1983. *Publications:* Here is the News (broadcasts), 1966; The Terror of Tobermory, 1972; The Magic of Music, 1975; Dry Ginger, 1977; Richard Baker's Music Guide, 1979; Mozart, 1982, rev. edn 1991; London, a theme with variations, 1989; Richard Baker's Companion to Music, 1993; Schubert: an illustrated biography, 1997; (ed) Music of the Sea, 2005. *Address:* 34 Brook View, Richmond Village, Letcombe Regis OX12 9RG.

BAKER, Richard Hugh; HM Diplomatic Service, retired; *b* 22 Oct. 1935; *s* of late Hugh Cuthbert Baker and (Muriel) Lovenda Baker (*née* Owens); *m* 1963, Patricia Marianne Haigh Thomas; one *s* three *d. Educ:* Marlborough Coll.; New Coll., Oxford. Army (2nd Lieut RA), 1954–56. Plebiscite Officer, UN Plebiscite, S Cameroons, 1960–61; joined Diplomatic Service, 1962; 3rd, later 2nd, then 1st Sec., Addis Ababa, 1963–66; Foreign Office, 1967; Private Sec. to Permanent Under-Sec. of State, Foreign Office (later FCO), 1967–70; 1st Sec. and Head of Chancery, Warsaw, 1970–72; FCO, 1973–76; RCDS 1977; Econ. and Financial Counsellor, and Dep. Head, UK Perm. Delegn to OECD, Paris, 1978–82; Dep. High Comr, Ottawa, 1982–86; Asst Under-Sec. of State, and Civilian Mem., Sen. Directing Staff, RCDS, 1986–89. *Recreations:* music, painting, literature, pottery, printmaking, writing, architecture, engineering. *Address:* 1 The Thatched Cottages, Water Lane, Radwinter, Saffron Walden CB10 2TX. *T:* (01799) 599355.

BAKER, Richard James; Member (Lab) Scotland North East, Scottish Parliament, since 2003; *b* 29 May 1974; *s* of Rev. Canon James Baker, MBE and Rev. Anne Baker; *m* 2004, Claire Josephine Brennan (*see* C. J. Baker); one *d. Educ:* Aberdeen Univ. (MA English Lit.). Pres., NUS Scotland, 1998–2000; Scottish Press Officer, Help the Aged, 2000–02. Contested (Lab Co-op) Aberdeen N, 2015. *Recreations:* choral singing, football, cinema, reading. *Address:* Scottish Parliament, Edinburgh EH99 1SP. *T:* (constituency office) (01224) 641171, *Fax:* (01224) 645450. *E:* richard.baker.msp@scottish.parliament.uk.

BAKER, Sir Robert George Humphrey S.; *see* Sherston-Baker.

BAKER, Dr Robin William, CMG 2005; Vice-Chancellor, Canterbury Christ Church University, 2010–12; Visiting Professor of Old Testament and Ancient Near East Studies, University of Winchester, since 2015; Visiting Scholar, Sarum College, since 2015; *b* 4 Oct. 1953; *s* of late William John David Baker and Brenda Olive Baker (*née* Hodges); *m* 1974, Miriam Joy Turpin (marr. diss. 1997); two *s. Educ:* Bishop Wordsworth's Sch., Salisbury; Sch. of Slavonic and East European Studies, Univ. of London (BA 1976); Univ. of East Anglia (PhD 1984). MoD, 1976–80; res. student, 1980–84; British Council: S Africa, 1984–89; Head of Recruitment, 1989; Hungary, 1990–93; Thessaloniki, Greece, 1994–96; Russia, 1996–99; Director: W and S Europe, 1999; Europe, 1999–2002; Dep. Dir-Gen., 2002–05; Pro-Vice-Chancellor, Univ. of Kent, 2005–07; Vice-Chancellor, Univ. of Chichester, 2007–10. Sen. Vis. Fellow, Inst. for Balkan Studies, Thessaloniki, 1995–; Vis. Fellow, SSEES, 1995–97, 1999. Member: Council for Assisting Refugee Academics, 2003–13; Council, Univ. of Kent, 2003–05; Internat. Policy Cttee, Royal Soc., 2003–05; Jamestown 2007 British Cttee, 2006–07. Member, Advisory Council: Inst. of Romance Studies, Univ. of London, 1999–2002; SSEES, 2000–09; W Sussex Econ. Skills and Enterprise Bd, 2008–10. Trustee and Director: Chichester Festival Th., 2007–10; Canterbury Fest., 2010–12; Creative Foundn, 2010–12; Trustee, Finnish Inst. UK and Ireland, 2009–. Fellow, UCL, 2005. FRSA 1998. *Publications:* The Development of the Komi Case System: a dialectological investigation, 1985; papers on history and languages of E Europe. *Recreations:* jazz, opera, walking on Mount Olympus. *Club:* Travellers.

BAKER, Roger, QPM 2008; HM Inspector of Constabulary, 2009–14; *b* 15 Nov. 1958; *s* of William Ernest Baker and Norah Margaret Baker; *m* 1999, Patricia Anne O'Callaghan; two *d* (and one *d* decd). *Educ:* Shirebrook Comp. Sch., Mansfield; Univ. of Derby (MBA 1998); Univ. of Manchester (MA Organisational Mgt 2000). Derbyshire Constabulary, 1977–2001, Chief Supt, 1999; Asst Chief Constable, Staffs Police, 2001–03; Dep. Chief Constable, N Yorks Police, 2003–05; Chief Constable, Essex Police, 2005–09. *Recreations:* equestrian pursuits, golf, walking the dogs.

BAKER, Samantha Jayne, (Sam); novelist, editor, writer and brand consultant; *b* 7 July 1966; *d* of Cliff Baker and Di (*née* Riglar); *m* 1993, Jon Courtenay Grimwood; one step *s. Educ:* Winton Sch.; Cricklade Coll.; Birmingham Univ. (BSocSc Pol Sci.). Chat mag., 1988–92; writer, Take a Break, 1992–93; Features Ed., then Dep. Ed., New Woman, 1993–96; Editor: Just Seventeen, 1996–97; Minx, 1997–98; Company, 1998–2003; Cosmopolitan, 2004–06; Ed.-in-Chief, Red, 2006–13. *Publications:* Fashion Victim, 2005; This Year's Model, 2008; The Stepmothers Support Group, 2009; To My Best Friends, 2011. *Clubs:* Black's, Shoreditch House.

BAKER, Rt Hon. Sir Scott; *see* Baker, Rt Hon. Sir T. S. G.

BAKER, Ven. Simon Nicholas Hartland; Rector, United Benefice of St Michael and St Mary with St John at Wall, since 2013; Archdeacon of Lichfield, since 2013; *b* 1957; *m* Diana. *Educ:* King's Coll. London (BD 1978); Queen's Coll., Birmingham. Ordained deacon, 1981, priest, 1982; Asst Curate, St Paul, Tupsley, 1981–85; Vicar, Shinfield, 1985–98; Principal, Berks Christian Trng Scheme, 1993–98; Lay Trng Officer, 1998–2002; Dir of Discipleship and Ministry, and Warden of Readers, Dio. of Winchester, 2002–13. Hon. Canon, Winchester Cath., 2008–13, now Canon Emeritus. *Address:* c/o Diocese of Lichfield, St Mary's House, The Close, Lichfield WS13 7LD.

BAKER, Steven John; MP (C) Wycombe, since 2010; *b* St Austell, 6 June 1971; *s* of Michael Baker and Diane Vivienne Baker (*née* Brimble); *m* 1996, Julia Elizabeth Perks. *Educ:* Poltair Comp. Sch., St Austell; St Austell Sixth Form Coll.; Univ. of Southampton (BEng Aerospace Systems Engrg 1992); St Cross Coll., Oxford (MSc Computation (Computer Sci.) 2000). CEng 1999. Engr Officer (Aerosystems), RAF, 1989–99; Hd, Consulting and Product Manager, DecisionSoft Ltd, Oxford, 2000–01; Chief Technol. Officer, BASDA Ltd, Great Missenden, 2002–07; Dir, Product Develt, CoreFiling Ltd, Oxford, 2005–06; Chief Architect, Global Financing and Asset Servicing Platforms, Lehman Brothers, 2006–08. Principal, Ambriel Consulting Ltd, 2001–10. Associate Consultant, Centre for Social Justice, 2008–10; Corporate Affairs Dir, 2009–10, Trustee, 2010–, Cobden Centre. Dir, Thermal Engineering Ltd, 2013. Trustee, GB Job Clubs, 2010–13. FRSA 2012. *Recreations:* skydiving, sailing, ski-ing, motorcycling, driving. *Address:* (office) 150A West Wycombe Road, High Wycombe HP12 3AE. *T:* (01494) 448408. *Club:* Royal Air Force.

BAKER, Stuart William; His Honour Judge Stuart Baker; a Circuit Judge, since 1998; *b* 1 June 1952; *s* of Henry Baker and Elizabeth Baker (*née* Hooker); *m* 1975, Christine Elizabeth Bennett; (one *s* decd). *Educ:* Univ. of Newcastle upon Tyne (LLB Hons 1973). Called to the Bar, Inner Temple, 1974; in practice at the Bar, 1975–98; Asst Recorder, 1991–94; a Recorder, 1994–98; Northern Circuit; Dep. Judge, High Court of Justice, 2001–. Mem., Legal Aid Area Appeal Cttee, 1991–98; Legal Mem., Mental Health Review Tribunal, 1996–98. *Recreations:* fell walking, golf, woodturning, playing viola. *Address:* Preston Combined Court Centre, Openshaw Place, Ringway, Preston PR1 2LL.

BAKER, Rt Hon. Sir (Thomas) Scott (Gillespie), Kt 1988; PC 2002; a Lord Justice of Appeal, 2002–10; a Surveillance Commissioner, since 2010; President, Court of Appeal, Bermuda, since 2015 (Member, since 2011); *b* 10 Dec. 1937; *s* of late Rt Hon. Sir George Baker, PC, OBE and Jessie McCall Baker; *m* 1973, (Margaret) Joy Strange; two *s* one *d. Educ:* Haileybury; Brasenose Coll., Oxford (Hon. Fellow 2003). Called to the Bar, Middle Temple, 1961 (Astbury Schol.), Bencher 1985, Treasurer 2004; a Recorder, 1976–88; QC 1978; a Judge of the High Court, Family Div., 1988–92, QBD, 1993–2002; Family Div. Liaison Judge (Wales and Chester Circuit), 1990–92; Presiding Judge, Wales and Chester Circuit, 1991–95; Lead Judge, Administrative Ct, 2000–02. Member: Senate, Inns of Court, 1977–84; Bar Council, 1988. Chm., Panel apptd by Sec. of State for Home Office to review UK's extradition arrangements, 2010–11; Member: Govt Cttee of Inquiry into Human Fertilisation (Warnock Cttee), 1982–84; Parole Bd, 1999–2002 (Vice-Chm., 2000–02); Ind. Parly Standards Authy, 2010–13. Asst Dep. Coroner for Inquest into the deaths of Diana, Princess of Wales and Dodi Al Fayed, 2007–08. Mem., Chorleywood UDC, 1965–68. Dep. Chm., Cricket Council Appeals Cttee, 1986–88. Hon. Mem., Coroners' Soc., 2008–. Gov., Caldicott Sch., 1991–2005 (Chm., 1996–2003). *Recreations:* golf, fishing, shooting. *Address:* c/o Royal Courts of Justice, Strand, WC2A 2LL. *Clubs:* MCC; Denham Golf (Captain, 1992, Chm., 1995–2001).

See also M. F. Baker.

BAKER, William John Clovis M.; *see* Meath Baker.

BAKER-BATES, Merrick Stuart, CMG 1996; HM Diplomatic Service, retired; Historical Records Adviser, Foreign and Commonwealth Office, since 2000; *b* 22 July 1939; *s* of late E. T. Baker-Bates, MD, FRCP, and of Norah Stuart (*née* Kirkham); *m* 1963, Chrystal Jacqueline Goodacre; one *s* one *d. Educ:* Shrewsbury Sch.; Hertford Coll., Oxford (MA); College of Europe, Bruges. Journalist, Brussels, 1962–63; entered HM Diplomatic Service, 1963; 3rd, later 2nd Sec., Tokyo, 1963–68; 1st Secretary: FCO, 1968–73; (Inf.), Washington, 1973–76; (Commercial), Tokyo, 1976–79; Counsellor (Commercial), Tokyo, 1979–82. Dir, Cornes & Co., Tokyo, 1982–85; Representative Dir, Gestetner Ltd (Japan), 1982–85; Dep. High Comr and Counsellor (Commercial/Econ.), Kuala Lumpur, 1986–89; Hd of S Atlantic and Antarctic Dept, FCO, and Comr, British Antarctic Territory, 1989–92; Consul-Gen., Los Angeles, 1992–97. Youth Offending Team mentor, Leicester Probation, 2002–07. Mem., Mgt Cttee, British-Malaysia Soc., 2004–08. Comdr, 1998–2005, Pres., 2005–12, St John Ambulance (Northants). Shakespeare's Globe Trust: Mem., Develt Council, 1998–2003;

Chm., Internat. Cttee, 1999–2005; Bd Mem., 2001–05; Mem., Adv. Council, 2005–. Trustee, Oxford Univ. Soc., 2001–08. CStJ 2010 (OStJ 2000). *Recreations:* photography, golf, hill-walking, talking. *E:* merrick@bakerbates.com. *Club:* Tokyo (Tokyo).

See also R. P. Baker-Bates.

BAKER-BATES, Rodney Pennington; Chairman, Willis Ltd, since 2010; *b* 25 April 1944; *s* of Eric Tom Baker-Bates and Norah Stuart (*née* Kirkham); *m* 1972, Gail Elizabeth Roberts; one *s*. *Educ:* Shrewsbury Sch.; Hertford Coll., Oxford (MA History). FICA 1975; AIMC 1975; FCIB 1991. Glyn Mills & Co., 1966–68; Arthur Andersen & Co., 1968–77; Chase Manhattan Bank, 1977–84; Midland Bank, 1984–92; Dir of Finance and IT, BBC, 1993–98; Man. Dir, Corporate Pensions Business, Prudential Corp., 1998–99; Chief Exec., Gp Pensions, 1999–2000, Prudential Financial Services, 2000–01, Consultant, 2001–02, Prudential plc. Director: Dexia Municipal Bank, 1997–2000; Aspen Group, 1997–99; Lloyds Register of Shipping, 1998–2007; Prudential Assce Co. Ltd, 2000–01; Bedlam Asset Mgt plc, 2003–13; Chairman: Change Partnership Ltd, 1998–2001; Hydra Associates, 1999–2001; CoralEurobet plc, 1999–2002; Burns e-Commerce Solutions, 2002–04; Stobart Gp plc (formerly Westbury Property Fund), 2002–13; EG Consulting Ltd, 2003–13; First Assist Gp Ltd, 2003–09; The Music Solution Ltd, 2004–08; Cabot Financial Hldgs Gp, 2004–06; Helphire Gp plc, 2005–08; G's Mktg Gp Ltd, 2006–; Britannia Bldg Soc., 2008–09 (Mem. Bd, 2007–09); Assura Gp plc, 2008–10; Ridgeons Gp, 2012–; Deputy Chairman: Co-operative Bank, 2009–12; Co-operative Insurance Gp Ltd, 2009–12; Co-operative Life Fund, 2009–12; Co-operative Financial Services, 2009–12; non-executive Director: C. Hoare & Co., 2001–10 (Chm., Exec. Man. Partners, 2001–06); AtlasFram Gp Ltd, 2008– (Vice Chm., 2010–). Dir, City of London Fest., 2001–04; Gov., RSC, 2003–08. Governor, Bedales Sch., 1993–2002. Trustee: Royal Nat. Pension Fund for Nurses, 2001–; Burdett Trust for Nursing, 2001–09; Dolphin Square Trust, 2001–13; Mem. Audit Cttee, Wellcome Trust, 2005–07; Chm., Outset Foundn, 2014. *Recreations:* gardening, performing arts, country pursuits. *Address:* c/o Mrs Stacy Willis, Willis Ltd, The Willis Building, 51 Lime Street, EC3M 7DQ. *T:* (020) 3124 6323. *Club:* Farmers.

See also M. S. Baker-Bates.

BAKER WILBRAHAM, Sir Richard, 8th Bt *cr* 1776; DL; Director, J. Henry Schroder Wagg & Co. Ltd, 1969–89; Chairman, Bibby Line Group, 1992–97 (Deputy Chairman, 1989–92); *b* 5 Feb. 1934; *s* of Sir Randle Baker Wilbraham, 7th Bt, and Betty Ann, CBE (*d* 1975), *d* of W. Matt Torrens; *S* father, 1980; *m* 1962, Anne Christine Peto, *d* of late Charles Peto Bennett, OBE; one *s* three *d*. *Educ:* Harrow. Welsh Guards, 1952–54. J. Henry Schroder Wagg & Co. Ltd, 1954–89. Director: Westpool Investment Trust, 1974–92; Brixton Estate, 1985–2001 (Dep. Chm., 1994–2001); The Really Useful Group plc, 1985–90; Charles Barker Group, 1986–89; Grosvenor Estates Hldgs, 1989–99 (Dep. Chm., 1989–99); Severn Trent, 1989–94; Majedie Investments, 1989–2001; Christie Hosp. NHS Trust, 1990–96. Mem., Gen. Council, King Edward's Hosp. Fund for London, 1986–98. Gov., Nuffield Hosps, 1990–2001. A Church Comr, 1994–2001. Trustee, Grosvenor Estate, 1981–99. Governor: Harrow Sch., 1982–92; The King's Sch., Macclesfield, 1986–2006; Manchester Metropolitan Univ., 1998–2001. Upper Bailiff, Weavers' Co., 1994–95. High Sheriff, Cheshire, 1991–92; DL Cheshire, 1992. *Recreation:* field sports. *Heir: s* Randle Baker Wilbraham [*b* 28 May 1963; *m* 1997, Amanda, *e d* of Robert Glossop; one *s* two *d*]. *Address:* Rode Hall, Scholar Green, Cheshire ST7 3QP. *T:* (01270) 882961. *Club:* Brooks's.

BAKEWELL, family name of **Baroness Bakewell**.

BAKEWELL, Baroness *cr* 2011 (Life Peer), of Stockport in the County of Greater Manchester; **Joan Dawson Bakewell,** DBE 2008 (CBE 1999); broadcaster and writer; *b* 16 April; *d* of John Rowlands and Rose Bland; *m* 1st, 1955, Michael Bakewell (marr. diss. 1972); one *s* one *d*; 2nd, 1975, Jack Emery (marr. diss. 2001). *Educ:* Stockport High Sch. for Girls; Newnham Coll., Cambridge (MA History and Econs). Associate, 1980–91, Associate Fellow, 1984–87, Newnham Coll., Cambridge. TV critic, The Times, 1978–81; columnist: Sunday Times, 1988–90; Guardian, 2003–05; Independent, 2006–08; The Times, 2008–09; Daily Telegraph, 2012–. Gov., BFI, 1994–2003 (Dep. Chm., 1997–99; Chm., 1999–2003); Mem. Bd, RNT, 1996–2003. Chm., Nat. Campaign for the Arts, 2004–10. Chair, Shared Experience Theatre Co., 2007–12. Pres., Soc. of Arts Publicists, 1984–90. Mem. Council, Aldeburgh Foundn, 1985–99. Hon. Prof., Dept of Film and Media, Univ. of Stirling, 2006–. Hon. FRCA 1994; Hon. Fellow, RHBNC, 1997. Hon. DLitt: Queen Margaret UC, Edinburgh, 2005; Chester, 2007; Univ. of Arts, London, 2008; Staffordshire, 2009; Lancaster, 2010; Open, 2010; Essex, 2011; RHUL; Hon. DCL Newcastle, 2011. *Television:* BBC Television includes: Meeting Point, 1964; The Second Sex, 1964; Late Night Line Up, 1965–72; The Youthful Eye, 1968; Moviemakers at the National Film Theatre, 1971; Film 72, and Film 73, 1972–73; For the Sake of Appearance, Where is Your God?, Who Cares?, and The Affirmative Way (series), 1973; Holiday '74, '75, '76, '77 and '78 (series); What's it all About? (2 series) and Time Running Out (series), 1974; The Shakespeare Business, The Brontë Business, and Generation to Generation (series), 1976; My Day with the Children, 1977; Panorama, 2011–12; Arts UK: OK?, 1980; Arts Correspondent, 1981–87; The Heart of the Matter, 1988–2000; Travels with Pevsner: Derbyshire, 1998; My Generation (series), 2000; Taboo (series), 2001; ITV includes: Sunday Break, 1962; Home at 4.30, 1964; (writer and producer) Thank You, Ron (documentary), 1974; Fairest Fortune and Edinburgh Festival Report, 1974; Reports Action (4 series), 1976–78; Portrait Artist of the Year (series), Sky Arts, 2013, 2014. *Radio:* Away from it All, 1978–79; PM, 1979–81; Artist of the Week, 1998–2000; Midsummer Sins, 2004; Chm., The Brains Trust, 1998–2001; Belief, 2001–13; Inside the Ethics Cttee, 2010–; Joan Bakewell's Lovers, 2013; BBC Radio 4 plays: There and Back; Parish Magazine: 3 editions; Brought to Book, 2005. *Theatre:* Brontës: The Private Faces, Edinburgh Fest., 1979. *Publications:* (with Nicholas Garnham) The New Priesthood: British television today, 1970; (with John Drummond) A Fine and Private Place, 1977; The Complete Traveller, 1977; The Heart of Heart of the Matter, 1996; The Centre of the Bed (autobiog.), 2003; Belief, 2005; The View from Here, 2006; All the Nice Girls (novel), 2009; She's Leaving Home (novel), 2011. *Recreations:* theatre, travel, cinema. *Address:* Knight Ayton Management, 35 Great James Street, WC1N 3HB. *T:* (020) 7831 4400.

BAKEWELL OF HARDINGTON MANDEVILLE, Baroness *cr* 2013 (Life Peer), of Hardington Mandeville in the County of Somerset; **Catherine Mary Bakewell,** MBE 1999. Member (Lib Dem): Somerset CC, 1993–2013 (Leader, 2001–07); South Somerset DC, 2009–. *Address:* House of Lords, SW1A 0PW.

BAKHURST, Kevin Alexander; Deputy Director-General, since 2014, and Managing Director, News and Current Affairs, and Member, Executive Board, since 2012, RTÉ; *b* 10 Dec. 1965; *s* of Christopher and Elizabeth Bakhurst; *m* 1990, Barbara King; two *s* one *d*. *Educ:* Haberdashers' Aske's Sch. for Boys, Elstree; St John's Coll., Cambridge (BA Modern Langs 1988). Audit Asst, Price Waterhouse, 1988–89; BBC: researcher and asst producer, Business Breakfast, 1989–90; Producer, Nine O'Clock News, 1990–94; Europe Producer, Brussels, 1994–95; Asst Ed., News, 1996–2001; News Ed., BBC Millennium Eve prog., 2000; Evenings Ed., News 24, 2001–03; Ed., Ten O'Clock News, BBC TV, 2003–06 (BAFTA Award for News Coverage, 2004, 2005); Controller, BBC News Channel, BBC News at One O'Clock, 2006–12; Ed., Olympics Decision 2012 prog., 2005; Dep. Hd, BBC Newsroom, 2010–12. JP St Albans, 2000–06. *Recreations:* travel, speaking French, film and cinema, watching Chelsea, reading and political autobiography, history. *Address:* RTÉ, Donnybrook, Dublin 4, Ireland. *E:* kevin.bakhurst@rte.ie.

BALASUBRAMANIAN, Prof. Shankar, PhD; FRS 2012; FMedSci; Herchel Smith Professor of Medicinal Chemistry, University of Cambridge, since 2008; Fellow, Trinity College, Cambridge, since 1994; Senior Group Leader, CRUK Cambridge Research Institute, since 2010; *b* Madras, 30 Sept. 1966; *s* of Venkataraman Balasubramanian and Padma Balasubramanian; *m* 1999, Veena Krishnan; one *s* one *d*. *Educ:* Fitzwilliam Coll., Cambridge (BA Natural Sci 1988); PhD Cantab 1991. SERC/NATO Res. Fellow, Pennsylvania State Univ., 1991–93; University of Cambridge: Royal Soc. Res. Fellow, 1994–98; Lectr, 1998–2003; Reader in Chem. Biol., 2003–07; Prof. of Chem. Biol., 2007–08. Founder, 1998, and Dir, 1998–2004, Solexa Ltd UK; Founder, 2012, and Dir, 2012–, Cambridge Epigenetix Ltd. FMedSci 2011. *Recreations:* running, cycling, football, music, family. *Address:* Department of Chemistry, University of Cambridge, Lensfield Road, Cambridge CB2 1EW. *T:* (01223) 336347. *E:* sb10031@cam.ac.uk.

BALÁZS, Prof. Péter; Professor of International Relations and European Studies, since 2005, and Director, Center for EU Enlargement Studies, Central European University, Budapest; *b* 5 Dec. 1941; *s* of Sándor Balázs and Klára Pecz. *Educ:* Budapest Sch. of Econs (Dip. in Econs 1963; Dr habil 2000); Hungarian Acad. of Scis (Dr 2003). Economist, Elektroimpex Hungarian Foreign Trading Co., 1963–68; Desk Officer, then Dir, Min. of Foreign Trade, 1969–82; Counsellor i/c EC, Hungarian Embassy, Brussels, 1982–87; Prime Minister's Office, 1987–88; Dir Gen. for multilateral relns, Min. of Internat. Econ. Relns, 1988–92; Perm. State Sec., Min. of Industry and Trade, 1992–93; Ambassador of Hungary: to Denmark, 1994–96; to Germany, 1997–2000; Prof., Budapest Univ. of Econs and Public Admin, 2000–02; State Sec. for Integration and Ext. Econ. Relns, Min. of Foreign Affairs, 2002–03; Ambassador, Perm. Repn to EU, 2003–04; Mem., European Commn, 2004; Minister for Foreign Affairs, Hungary, 2009–10. *Publications:* Az Európai Unió külkapcsolatai és Magyarország, 1996; (contrib.) Enlarging the European Union, 1997; (contrib.) Öszinte Könyv az Európai Unióról, 1999; (contrib.) Az Európai Unió politikái, 2000; (contrib.) Európai Közjog és politika, 2000; (contrib.) Unser Europa-Gemeinsam stärker: die kooperation der Klein- und Mittelstaaten im EU-Konvent, 2004. *Recreations:* classical music, horse riding.

BALBUS, Prof. Steven Andrew, PhD; Savilian Professor of Astronomy, since 2012 and Head of Astrophysics, since 2014, University of Oxford; Fellow, New College, Oxford, since 2012; *b* Philadelphia, 23 Nov. 1953; *s* of Theodore G. Balbus and Rita S. Balbus (*née* Frucht); *m* 2002, Caroline Terquem; three *s* one *d*. *Educ:* Massachusetts Inst. of Technol. (BSc Maths and Physics); Univ. of Calif, Berkeley (PhD Physics 1981). Research Associate: MIT, 1981–83; Princeton Univ., 1983–85; Asst Prof., 1985–91, Associate Prof., 1991–97, Prof., 1997–2004, of Astronomy, Univ. of Virginia; Prof. des Universités, Physics Dept, École Normale Supérieure de Paris, 2004–12. Chaire d'Excellence, 2004; Shaw Prize in Astronomy, 2013. *Publications:* contribs to Astrophysical Jl, Monthly Notices of RAS. *Recreations:* reading, music, cycling, cooking. *Address:* Physics Department, University of Oxford, Denys Wilkinson Building, Keble Road, Oxford OX1 3RH. *T:* (01865) 273639, *Fax:* (01865) 273390. *E:* Steven.Balbus@astro.ox.ac.uk.

BALCHIN, family name of **Baron Lingfield**.

BALCOMBE, David Julian; QC 2002; a Recorder, since 2000; *b* 4 Feb. 1958; *s* of Rt Hon. Sir (Alfred) John Balcombe and Jacqueline Rosemary, (Lady Balcombe); *m* 1992, Sally Jane Spence; two *s*. *Educ:* Winchester Coll.; Univ. of Kent at Canterbury (BA). Called to the Bar, Lincoln's Inn, 1980. *Address:* 1 Crown Office Row, Temple, EC4Y 7HH. *T:* (020) 7797 7500.

BALDING, Clare Victoria, OBE 2013; freelance sports presenter and author; *b* 29 Jan. 1971; *d* of Ian Balding, LVO, and Lady Emma Balding, *sister* of Earl of Huntingdon, *qv*. *Educ:* Downe House; Newnham Coll., Cambridge (BA 2nd Cl. Hons English; Pres., Cambridge Union, 1992). Racing reporter, BBC Radio 5 Live, 1993–94; sports presenter, BBC Radio, 1994–; presenter: BBC horse-racing coverage, incl. Royal Ascot; Badminton, Derby and Grand National; BBC Grandstand and Sunday Grandstand, 2000–07; Sydney Olympics and Paralympics, 2000; Salt Lake City Winter Olympics, 2002; Athens Olympics and Paralympics, 2004; Crufts, 2005–; Commonwealth Games, Melbourne, 2006; Beijing Olympics and Paralympics, 2008; Vancouver Winter Olympics, 2010; Saturday Live and Woman's Hour, BBC Radio 4, 2008–09; Britain by Bike (BBC TV series), 2010; Countryfile, Britain's Hidden Heritage, 2011; London Olympics, BBC, 2012; London Paralympics, Channel 4, 2012; The Clare Balding Show, 2013–; horse-racing coverage, Channel 4, 2013–; Britain's Brightest, 2013; Sochi Winter Olympics, 2014; Operation Wild, 2014; Sports Personality of the Year, 2014; Wimbledon 2day, BBC, 2015. Sports columnist: Evening Standard, 1997–2003; Observer, 2004–07. Presenter, BBC Radio 4: Ramblings, 1998–; Sport and the British, 2012; Good Morning Sunday, BBC Radio 2, 2013. Sports Presenter of the Year, 2004, Presenter of the Year, 2013, RTS; BAFTA Special Award, 2013. *Publications:* My Animals and Other Family (Autobiog. of the Year, Nat. Book Awards), 2012; Walking Home: my family and other rambles, 2014. *Recreations:* riding, tennis, ski-ing, theatre, cinema, travel. *Address:* c/o James Grant Media Ltd, 94 Strand on the Green, Chiswick, W4 3NN.

BALDOCK, Anne Elizabeth; Partner, Allen & Overy LLP, 1990–2012; consultant and lecturer on project finance and infrastructure, since 2012; *b* Kent, 1959; *d* of Alec John Baldock and Violet Margery Baldock; *m* 1990, Graham David Vinter; two *s* one *d*. *Educ:* Wombwell Hall Sch. for Girls; London Sch. of Econs and Pol Sci. (LLB). Admitted as solicitor, 1982; Lawyer, Allen & Overy LLP, 1982–90. Non-executive Director: Hydrogen plc, 2012–; Thames Tideway Tunnel Ltd, 2014–; Low Carbon Contracts Co. Ltd, 2014–; Electricity Settlements Co. Ltd, 2014–. Mem., Nuclear Liabilities Financial Assce Bd, 2009–. Trustee, CRUK, 2011–. *Publications:* contrib. articles to jls incl. Project Finance Internat. *Recreations:* riding, running. *E:* abaldock@hotmail.com. *Club:* Royal Automobile.

BALDOCK, Brian Ford, CBE 1997; Chairman, Mencap, 1998–2011; independent coach, since 2010; *b* 10 June 1934; *s* of Ernest A. and Florence F. Baldock; *m* 1st, 1956, Mary Lillian Bartolo (marr. diss. 1966); two *s*; 2nd, 1968, Carole Anthea Mason; one *s*. *Educ:* Clapham Coll., London. Army Officer, 1952–55. Procter & Gamble, 1956–61; Ted Bates Inc., 1961–63; Rank Orgn, 1963–66; Smith & Nephew, 1966–75; Revlon Inc., 1975–78; Imperial Group, 1978–86; Guinness PLC: Dir, 1986–96; Gp Man. Dir, 1989–96; Dep. Chm., 1992–96. Chairman: Portman Group, 1989–96; Wellington Investments Ltd, 1997–2002; Dalgety, later Sygen Internat., 1998–2005 (Dir, 1992–2005); Marks & Spencer plc, 1999–2000 (non-exec. Dir, 1996–2004); First Artist Corp., 2001–03; Dir, Cornhill Insurance, 1996–2002. Trustee, RTR Foundn, 2002–. Freeman, City of London, 1989. CInstM 1991 (FInstM 1976); Fellow, Marketing Soc., 1988. FRSA 1987. Hon. DA E London, 2008. *Recreations:* theatre (opera), cricket, travel. *E:* brian.baldock@pobox.co.uk. *Clubs:* Garrick, MCC, Lord's Taverners (Mem. Council; Chm., 1992–95).

BALDOCK, (Richard) Stephen; High Master, St Paul's School, 1992–2004; *b* 19 Nov. 1944; *s* of John Allan Baldock and Marjorie Procter Baldock; *m* 1969, Dr Janet Elizabeth Cottrell; one *s* three *d*. *Educ:* St Paul's Sch.; King's Coll., Cambridge (John Stewart of Rannoch schol. in Greek and Latin 1964; BA 1967 Part I Classics, Part II Theology, MA 1970). St Paul's School: Asst Master, 1970–77; Housemaster, School House, 1977–84; Surmaster, 1984–92. Council Mem. and Educnl Advr, Overseas Missionary Fellowship, 1989–2010. Trustee, South Square Trust, 2007–. Governor: Monkton Combe Sch., Bath, 2003–15; Gordonstoun Sch., 2006–; Visitor, Collingham coll., SW London, 2004–.

Recreations: family, computers, sport. *Address:* c/o Old Pauline Club, St Paul's School, Lonsdale Road, Barnes, SW13 9JT. *Club:* MCC.

See also S. R. Baldock.

BALDOCK, Sarah Ruth, FRCO; Music Teacher, Cheltenham Ladies' College, since 2014; *b* Wembley, 5 April 1975; *d* of (Richard) Stephen Baldock, *qv*. *Educ:* St Paul's Girls' Sch., London; Pembroke Coll., Cambridge (BA 1996). FRCO 1997. Organist-in-Residence, Tonbridge Sch., 1996–98; Asst Organist and Dir of Girls' Choir, 1998–2002, Asst Dir of Music, 2002–08, Winchester Cathedral; Organist and Master of the Choristers, Chichester Cathedral, 2008–14. *Recreations:* cooking and eating, gardening. *Address:* Cheltenham Ladies' College, Bayshill Road, Cheltenham, Glos GL50 3EP.

BALDOCK, Stephen; *see* Baldock, R. S.

BALDRY, Rt Hon. Sir Antony Brian, (Rt Hon. Sir Tony), Kt 2012; PC 2013; *b* 10 July 1950; *e s* of Peter Edward Baldry and Oina (*née* Paterson); *m* 1st, 1979, Catherine Elizabeth (marr. diss. 1996), 2nd *d* of Captain James Weir, RN and Elizabeth Weir; one *s* one *d*; 2nd, 2001, Pippa Isbell, *e d* of Lt Col Penny Payne and Betty Payne. *Educ:* Leighton Park Sch., Reading; Univ. of Sussex (MA, LLB). Called to the Bar, Lincoln's Inn, 1975; barrister; Hd of Chambers, 1 Essex Court, 2007–. Director: New Opportunity Press, 1975–90; Newpoint Publishing Gp, 1983–90; Transense Technologies plc, 1998–2008; Gatenet plc, 2015–; Chairman: Woburn Energy (formerly Black Rock Oil & Gas) plc, 2005–; Westminster Oil Ltd, 2007–12; Mastermailer plc, 2008–10; Curve Capital Ltd, 2008–10; Partner Capital Ltd, 2008–10; Kazakhstan Kagazy plc, 2013–. Contested (C) Thurrock, 1979. MP (C) Banbury, 1983–2015. PPS to Minister of State for Foreign and Commonwealth Affairs, 1986–87, to Lord Privy Seal and Leader of the House, 1987–89, to Sec. of State for Energy, 1989–90; Parliamentary Under-Secretary of State: Dept of Energy, 1990; DoE, 1990–94; FCO, 1994–95; Minister of State, MAFF, 1995–97. Mem., Parly Select Cttee on Employment, 1983–86; on Trade and Industry, 1997–2001; on Standards and Privileges, 2001; on Internat. Develt, 2001–05 (Chm., 2001–05). Second Church Estates Comr, 2010–15; Mem., Gen. Synod, 2010–15. Chm., Church Bldgs Council, 2015–. Lay Canon, Christ Ch Cath., Oxford, 2015–. Joined Sussex Yeomanry, 1971; TA Officer, resigned 1990; Hon. Col, RLC (TA), 1997–2001. Robert Schuman Silver Medal, Stiftung FVS Hamburg, 1978. *Recreations:* walking in the country, reading historical biography, gardening, cricket. *Clubs:* Carlton, Garrick, Brass Monkey.

BALDRY, Lorraine, OBE 2012; Chairman: Inventa Partners, since 2002; London & Continental Railways Ltd, since 2011; Schroder Real Estate Investment Trust, since 2014; *b* 22 May 1949; *m* 1973, Don Baldry. Prudential Corp. plc, 1990–98; Man. Dir, Regus plc, 1999–2000; Sen. Advr, Investment Banking Div., Morgan Stanley, 2000–02; Chief Exec., Chesterton plc, 2002–03; Chm., London Thames Gateway Develt Corp., 2004–08. Chairman: Central London Partnership, 1998–2008; Tri-Air Develts Ltd, 2009– (Dir, 2006–09); non-executive Direcctor: DTZ Gp plc, 2010–11; Thames Water Utilities Ltd, 2014–; Sen. Ind. Dir, Circle Hldgs plc, 2011–. Mem. Bd, Olympic Delivery Authy, 2006–14 (Chm., Planning, 2006–12). Gov., Univ. of Arts, London, 2008–. *Address:* Inventa Partners Ltd, Golden Cross House, 8 Duncannon Street, Strand, WC2N 4JF. *E:* lorraine.baldry@inventapartners.com.

BALDRY, Rupert Patrick Craig; QC 2010; *b* Guildford, 30 March 1962; *s* of Brian and Patricia Baldry. *Educ:* Marlborough Coll.; Bedford Coll., Univ. of London (BA Hons); City Univ. (Dip. Law). Called to the Bar, Middle Temple, 1987; Jun. Counsel to the Crown, 1999–2005. *Recreations:* fly-fishing, Shakespeare, astronomy. *Address:* Pump Court Tax Chambers, 16 Bedford Row, WC1R 4EF. *T:* (020) 7414 8080, *Fax:* (020) 7414 8099. *E:* rbaldry@pumptax.com. *Club:* Travellers.

BALDRY, Tony; *see* Baldry, Rt Hon. Sir A. B.

BALDWIN, family name of **Earl Baldwin of Bewdley**.

BALDWIN OF BEWDLEY, 4th Earl *cr* 1937; **Edward Alfred Alexander Baldwin;** Viscount Corvedale, 1937; *b* 3 Jan. 1938; *o s* of 3rd Earl Baldwin of Bewdley and Joan Elspeth, *y d* of late C. Alexander Tomes, New York, USA; *S* father, 1976; *m* 1st, 1970, Sarah MacMurray (*d* 2001), *er d* of late Evan Maitland James; three *s*; 2nd, 2015, Lydia Segrave, widow of Dr I. M. D. Little. *Educ:* Eton; Trinity Coll., Cambridge (MA, PGCE). Chm., British Acupuncture Accreditation Bd, 1990–98. Joint Chairman: Parly Gp for Alternative and Complementary Medicine, 1992–2002; All Party Parly Gp Against Fluoridation, 2005–10; Sec., Associate Parly Food and Health Forum; elected Mem., H of L, 1999; Mem., H of L Select Cttee inquiry into complementary and alternative medicine, 2000. *Publications:* (ed jtly) Baldwin Papers: a Conservative statesman 1908–47, 2004. *Heir: s* Viscount Corvedale, *qv*. *Address:* 2 Scholar Place, Cumnor Hill, Oxford OX2 9RD. *Club:* MCC.

BALDWIN, Alan Charles; a District Judge (Magistrates' Courts) (formerly Metropolitan Stipendiary Magistrate), 1990–2013; *b* 14 April 1948; *s* of Frederick Baldwin and Millicent Baldwin (*née* McCarthy); *m* 1974, Denise Maureen Jagger; two *s*. Admitted Solicitor, 1976.

BALDWIN, (Anna) Lisbet (Kristina); *see* Rausing, A. L. K.

BALDWIN, Brian Paul; HM Diplomatic Service, retired; British High Commissioner, Solomon Islands, 2001–04; *b* 7 Dec. 1944; *s* of late Dennis and Violet Baldwin; *m* 1966, Elizabeth Mary Evans, MBE; three *s* one *d*. *Educ:* St Albans Grammar Sch. Joined Diplomatic Service, 1967; Vice Consul (Commercial), Johannesburg, 1970–72; Third Sec., Belgrade, 1973–75; Vice Consul (Political), Johannesburg, 1979–83; First Sec., Muscat, 1988–93; Dep. High Comr, Port Moresby, 1993–97; Administrator, Tristan Da Cunha, 1998–2001. *Recreations:* athletics, golf, tennis, photography. *Address:* PO Box 470, Noordhoek 7979, South Africa.

BALDWIN, David Arthur, CBE 1990; CEng, FIET; Director Emeritus, Hewlett-Packard Ltd, since 1996 (Chairman, 1988–96); *b* 1 Sept. 1936; *s* of late Isaac Arthur Baldwin and Edith Mary Baldwin (*née* Collins); *m* 1961, (Jacqueline) Anne Westcott; one *s* one *d*. *Educ:* Twickenham Technical Coll.; Wimbledon Technical Coll. (qualified electronic engineer). CEng; FIET (FIEE 1989). R&D Engineer, EMI, 1954–63; Sales Engineer, Solartron, 1963–65; Hewlett-Packard: Sales Engineer and Sales Manager, 1965–73; European Marketing Manager, 1973–78; Man. Dir, Hewlett-Packard Ltd, 1978–88. Man. Dir, Hewlett-Packard Eur. Multi-Country Region, 1990; Pres., Hewlett-Packard Belgium, 1991; Chm., Hewlett-Packard Spain, 1991; Dir, Hewlett-Packard Finland, Sweden, Denmark, Netherlands and Austria, 1991–96. Mem., BOTB, 1994–98 (Chm., European Trade Cttee, 1994–98); Chm., Thames Action and Res. Gp for Educn and Trng Ltd, 1996–. Mem. Council, RSA, 1994–. Member, Court: Cranfield Univ. (formerly Inst. of Technol.), 1987–; Brunel Univ., 1988–. CCMI; FInstD; FInstM. Freeman City of London, 1988; Liveryman, Inf. Technologists' Co., 1994. DUniv Strathclyde, 1990. *Recreations:* golf, ski-ing, photography, painting, sailing. *Address:* c/o Hewlett-Packard Ltd, Cain Road, Bracknell, Berks RG12 1HN. *T:* (01344) 360000.

BALDWIN, Prof. Graham, PhD; Vice Chancellor, Southampton Solent University, since 2014; *b* Carshalton, 28 July 1963; *s* of Brian Ernest Jones and Ruth Jones (*née* Pearson), and step *s* of Ralph Duncan Baldwin; *m* 1990, Sarah Moxon; two *s* one *d*. *Educ:* Madeley Sch. of Physical Educn (BA Hons Sport and Recreation Studies 1984); Univ. of Wales (PGCE 1985); Loughborough Univ. (MSc Sports Sci. 1991); Univ. of Wales, Bangor (PhD 2002). Teacher of Physical Educn, Coopers Sch., Chislehurst, 1985–87; Lectr, Stoke on Trent Coll., 1987–91; Liverpool Hope University College: Lectr, 1991–95; Dep. Hd, Sport Recreation and Physical Educn Dept, 1995–97; Hd, Dept of Sport and Health, 1997–2001; University of Central Lancashire: Hd, Dept of Tourism and Leisure Mgt, 2001–03; Dir for Cumbria, 2004–06; Dean, Academic Develt, 2006–07; Nat. Skills Res. Dir, Nuclear Decommng Authy (on secondment), 2007–08; University of Central Lancashire: Pro-Vice Chancellor, 2008–09; Dep. Vice Chancellor, 2010–13; Dep. Pres., 2013–14. Hon. Prof., Hebei Univ., 2014–. Dir, Business South, 2015–. *Recreations:* family, cycling, walking, watching sport, beer, wine, coffee. *Address:* Vice Chancellor's Office, Southampton Solent University, East Park Terrace, Southampton, Hants SO14 0YN. *T:* (023) 8201 3216, *Fax:* (023) 8023 7627. *E:* graham.baldwin@solent.ac.uk.

BALDWIN, Harriett Mary Morison; MP (C) West Worcestershire, since 2010; Economic Secretary, HM Treasury, since 2015; *b* Watford, 2 May 1960; *d* of Anthony Francis Eggleston, *qv*; *m* 2004, James Stanley Baldwin; two step *d*; one *s* by a previous marriage. *Educ:* Friends' Sch., Saffron Walden; Marlborough Coll.; Lady Margaret Hall, Oxford (BA French and Russian 1982); McGill Univ. (MBA 1985). J. P. Morgan, 1986–2008, Man. Dir, 1998–2008; Vice Chm., Social Investment Business, 2008–12. PPS to Minister for Employment, 2012–14; an Asst Govt Whip, 2014; a Lord Comr of HM Treasury (Govt Whip), 2014–15. Contested (C) Stockton N, 2005. *Recreations:* family, walking, swimming, travel. *Address:* House of Commons, SW1A 0AA. *T:* (020) 7219 7187. *E:* harriett.baldwin.mp@parliament.uk. *Club:* Carlton.

BALDWIN, Sir Jack (Edward), Kt 1997; PhD; FRS 1978; Waynflete Professor of Chemistry and Fellow of Magdalen College, University of Oxford, 1978–2006, now Professor Emeritus and Hon. Fellow; *b* 8 Aug. 1938; *s* of Frederick Charles Baldwin and Olive Frances Headland; *m* 1977, Christine Louise, *d* of William B. Franchi. *Educ:* Lewes County Grammar Sch.; Imperial Coll., London Univ. (BSc, DIC, PhD). ARCS. Asst Lectr in Chem., Imperial Coll., 1963, Lectr, 1966; Asst Prof. of Chem., Pa State Univ., 1967, Associate Prof., 1969; Alfred P. Sloan Fellow, 1969–70, Associate Prof. of Chem., 1970, Prof., 1972, MIT; Daniell Prof. of Chem., King's Coll., London, 1972; Prof. of Chem., MIT, 1972–78. Dir, Oxford Centre for Molecular Sciences, 1988–98. Mem., BBSRC, 1994–97. Lectures: Tilden, RSC, 1979; Simonsen, RSC, 1982. Corresp. Mem., Academia Scientiarum Gottingensis, Göttingen, 1988; For. Mem., Amer. Acad. of Arts and Scis, 1993. Hon. DSc: Warwick, 1988, Strathclyde, 1989. Corday Morgan Medal and Prize, Chem. Soc., 1975; Medal and Prize for Synthetic Organic Chemistry, RSC, 1980; Paul Karrer Medal and Prize, Zürich Univ., 1984; Medal and Prize for Natural Product Chemistry, RSC, 1984; Hugo Müller Medal, RSC, 1987; Max Tischler Award, Harvard Univ., 1987; Dr Paul Jansen Prize for Creativity in Organic Synthesis, Belgium, 1988; Davy Medal, 1994, Leverhulme Medal, 1999, Royal Soc.; Nakanishi Prize, Chem. Soc. of Japan, 2002; Paracelsus Prize, Swiss Chem. Soc., 2006. *Publications:* res. pubns in Jl of Amer. Chem. Soc., Jl of Chem. Soc., Tetrahedron. *Address:* Broom, Hinksey Hill, Oxford OX1 5BH.

BALDWIN, John Paul; QC 1991; barrister; a Recorder, since 2004; a Deputy High Court Judge, since 2008; *b* 15 Aug. 1947; *s* of late Frank Baldwin and Marjorie Baldwin (*née* Jay); *m* 1981, Julie Campbell; two *d*. *Educ:* Nelson Grammar Sch.; Univ. of Leeds (BSc 1st Cl. Hons 1968); St John's Coll., Oxford (DPhil 1972). Res. Fellow, Univ. of Oxford, 1972–75; called to the Bar, Gray's Inn, 1977, Bencher, 2000. Judge: Chancery Div., Patents Court, 2006–; Intellectual Property Enterprise Court (formerly Patents County Court), 2006–. *Publications:* numerous scientific pubns, 1969–75. *Recreations:* tennis, gardening. *Address:* 8 New Square, Lincoln's Inn, WC2A 3QP. *T:* (020) 7405 4321. *Clubs:* Queen's, Campden Hill.

BALDWIN, Mark Phillip, OBE 2015; founder and choreographer, Mark Baldwin Dance Co., since 1992; Artistic Director, Rambert Dance Company, since 2002; *b* 16 Jan. 1954; *s* of late Ronald William Baldwin and Rose Theresa Evans. *Educ:* St Kentigerns Coll., NZ; Pakuranga Coll., NZ; Suva Grammar Sch., Fiji; Elam Sch. of Fine Arts, Univ. of Auckland. Founder Dancer, Limbs Dance Co., NZ, New Zealand Ballet, Australian Dance Theatre, Rambert Dance Co., 1979–92; choreographer-in-residence, Sadler's Wells, 1993; resident artist, The Place, 1995–96; choreographer-in-residence, Scottish Ballet, 1996. Works choreographed for Rambert Dance Co. include: Island to Island, 1991; Gone, 1992; Spirit, 1994; Banter Banter, 1994; Constant Speed, 2005; Eternal Light, 2008; The Comedy of Change, 2009; Seven for a Secret, never to be told, 2011; What Wild Ecstasy, 2012; The Strange Charm of Mother Nature, 2014; Dark Arteries, 2015; for Scottish Ballet: Haydn Pieces, 1995; Ae Fond Kiss, 1996; More Poulenc, 1996; for Staatsoper, Berlin: Labyrinth, 1997; The Demon, 1998; The Man with a Moustache (for City Ballet of London), 1998; Towards Poetry (for Royal Ballet), 1999; Pointe Blank (for TV), 1999; Ihi FrENZY (for Royal NZ Ballet), 2001; Frankenstein (for BBC4), 2003; The Wedding (for Royal NZ Ballet), 2006; M is for Man (for Dansgroep Amsterdam), 2009; The Rite of Spring (for Rambert Sch.), 2013; Not a Cloud in the Sky (for Staatstheater, Saarbrücken), 2014; Inala, Edinburgh Playhouse, then touring, 2014. *Address:* Rambert, 99 Upper Ground, SE1 9PP.

BALDWIN, Nicholas Peter, CEng, CDir, FIMechE, FIET; Chairman, Office for Nuclear Regulation, since 2011; *b* 17 Dec. 1952; *s* of Desmond Stanley Frederick Baldwin and Beatrix Marie Baldwin (*née* Walker); *m* 2002, Adrienne Ann Plunkett; one *s* one *d*. *Educ:* City Univ. (BSc Mechanical Engrg); Birkbeck Coll., Univ. of London (MSc Econs). CEng 1979; FIMechE 1996; FIET (FIEE 2002); CDir 2007. Metropolitan Water Bd, 1971–74; Thames Water Authy, 1974–80; CEGB, 1980–89, Sen. Energy Analyst, 1986–89; PowerGen plc, 1989–2002: Econ. Studies Manager, 1989–90; Business Planning Manager, 1990–92; Head of Strategic Planning, 1992–94; Director: Strategy, 1994–95; Generation, 1995–96; Man. Dir, UK Electricity Prodn, 1996–98; Exec. Dir, UK Ops, 1998–2001; Chief Exec., 2001–02. Non-executive Director: Energy Gp Advisory Bd, DTI, 2002–06; Forensic Sci. Service, 2004–; Nuclear Decommng Authy, 2004–11 (Chm., 2007–08); Scottish and Southern Energy, 2006–11; Sanctuary Housing, 2008–09 (Chm., 2009–). Chm., Public Weather Service Customer Gp, 2007–13. Mem., HSE, 2011–. Vice Chm., Worcs Local Area Partnership, 2014–. Chm., Ambitious About Autism (formerly TreeHouse Trust), 2008–14; Trustee, Land Trust, 2010–11. FRSA 1998. *Publications:* articles in Energy Policy and Energy Economics. *Recreations:* long distance walking, photography, cinema, music, reading, family activities. *Club:* Worcester County Cricket.

BALDWIN, Air Vice-Marshal Nigel Bruce, CB 1996; CBE 1992; Chairman, RAF Historical Society, since 1997; *b* 20 Sept. 1941; *s* of Peter William Baldwin and Doris Baldwin; *m* 1963, Jennifer; one *d* (and one *d* decd). *Educ:* Peter Symonds' Sch., Winchester; RAF Coll., Cranwell. Pilot, Vulcans, 9/35 Sqns, 1963–68; ADC to AOC 11 Gp, 1968–70; Sqn Ldr, Vulcans, 35 Sqn, Cyprus, 1970–73; Staff Coll., Bracknell, 1974; HQ Strike Command, 1975–76; OC 50 Sqn, Vulcans, 1977–79; US Air War Coll. and Faculty, US Air Command and Staff Coll., 1979–82; Gp Captain and Station Comdr, Wyton, 1983–85; Internat. Fellow, Nat. Defense Univ., Washington, 1986; Asst Dir of Defence Policy, MoD, 1986–88; Air Cdre Plans, HQ Strike Command, 1989–92; ACDS (Overseas), 1993–96. Pres., RAF Vol. Band Assoc., 1996–; Vice-President: 50/61 Sqn Assoc., 1996–; Ex-Services Mental Welfare Soc., 2007– (Chm., 1997–2007). *Recreations:* hill walking, Schubert, Nelson. *Club:* Royal Air Force.

BALDWIN, Prof. Thomas Raymond, PhD; Professor of Philosophy, University of York, since 1995; *b* 10 April 1947; *s* of Raymond Baldwin and Penelope Baldwin (*née* Barlow); *m* 1973, Anna Barber; two *d*. *Educ:* Trinity Coll., Cambridge (BA (Moral Scis) 1968); PhD (Philos.) 1971). Lectr in Philos., Makerere Univ., Kampala, 1971–72; Jun. Res. Fellow, Churchill Coll., Cambridge, 1973–74; Lecturer: Univ. of York, 1974–84; Philos. Faculty,

Cambridge Univ., 1984–95; Fellow, Clare Coll., Cambridge, 1984–95. Ed., Mind, 2005–15. Member: Nuffield Council on Bioethics, 2000–06; HFEA, 2001–05 (Dep. Chm., 2002–05); Expert Adv. Cttee on Obesity, DoH, 2008–11; Human Genetics Commn, 2009–12. *Publications:* G. E. Moore, 1990; Contemporary Philosophy, 2001; Cambridge History of Philosophy, 2003. *Recreations:* walking, visiting gardens. *Address:* Department of Philosophy, University of York, York YO10 5DD. *T:* (01904) 433252. *E:* thomas.baldwin@york.ac.uk.

BALFE, family name of **Baron Balfe**.

BALFE, Baron *cr* 2013 (Life Peer), of Dulwich in the London Borough of Southwark; **Richard Andrew Balfe;** President, European Parliament Members Pension Fund, since 2004; Member, Actuarial and Technical Committee, Organisation Européenne pour la Recherche Nucléaire (CERN) Pension Fund, since 2011 (Director, 2009–14); *b* 14 May 1944; *s* of Dr Richard J. Balfe and Mrs Dorothy L. Balfe (*née* de Cann); *m* 1986, Susan Jane Honeyford; one *s* one *d*, and one *s* by a previous marriage. *Educ:* Brook Secondary Sch., Sheffield; LSE (BSc Hons 1971). Fellow Royal Statistical Soc., 1972. HM Diplomatic Service, 1965–70; Res. Officer, Finer Cttee on One Parent Families, 1970–73; Political Sec., RACS, 1973–79; Dir, RACS and associated cos, 1978–85. European Parliament: Mem. (Lab 1979–2001, C 2002–04) London S Inner, 1979–99, London Reg., 1999–2004; Quaestor, 1994–2004; Member: Foreign Affairs Cttee, 1981–99; Security Cttee, 1989–99; Econ. and Monetary Cttee, 1999–2004; Petitions Cttee, 2001–04. Mem., Eur. Econ. and Social Cttee, 2012–13. Parly Candidate (Lab), Paddington South, 1970; contested (Lab) Southwark and Bermondsey, 1992. Mem., GLC for Southwark/Dulwich, 1973–77; Chairman: Thamesmead New Town Cttee, 1973–75; GLC Housing Cttee, 1975–77. Member: Exec. Cttee, Fabian Soc., 1981–82; London Labour Party Exec., 1973–95 (Chair, Policy Cttee, 1983–85); Chair, Political Cttee, Royal Arsenal Co-op (CWS), 1984–95. Cons. Party Envoy to Trades Union and Co-op movements, 2008–12, 2014–. Trustee, Pension Scheme, Royal Statistical Soc., 2012–13. Mem., Ct of Governors, LSE, 1973–91. Chm., Anglia Community Leisure, 2008–13. *Recreations:* collecting books and pamphlets on political and social history topics, opera, Wagner, walking. *Address:* House of Lords, SW1A 0PW. *E:* richard.balfe@balfes.com. *Club:* Reform (Chm., Finance Cttee, 2013–14; Member: Gen. Cttee, 2011–; Liby Cttee, 2015–).

BALFOUR, family name of **Earl of Balfour** and **Barons Kinross** and **Riverdale**.

BALFOUR, 5th Earl of, *cr* 1922; **Roderick Francis Arthur Balfour;** Viscount Traprain 1922; *b* 9 Dec. 1948; *s* of Eustace Arthur Goschen Balfour and Anne (*née* Yule); *S* cousin, 2003; *m* 1971, Lady Tessa Mary Isabel Fitzalan-Howard, *e d* of 17th Duke of Norfolk, KG, GCVO, CB, CBE, MC; four *d*. *Educ:* Eton; London Business Sch. Mem., London Stock Exchange, 1975–81; Dir, Union Discount Co. of London plc, 1983–90; Dir, Rothschild Trust Corp. Ltd, 1990–2005; Founder and Dir, Virtus Trust Gp, 2005–. Non-executive Director: Bateman Engrg NV, 2005–09; Nikanor plc, 2006–08; Dir, CTTC Archway (China), 2008–. Mem., Adv. Bd, Gateway Commodity Fund, Basel, 2009–. Member: City of London Cttee and Soc. of Trust and Estate Practitioners, 1996–; Internat. Tax Planning Assoc., 2010–. Liveryman, Clothworkers' Co., 1986. *Heir: b* Hon. Charles George Yule Balfour [*b* 23 April 1951; *m* 1st, 1978, Audrey Margaret Hoare; 2nd, 1987, Svea Maria Cecily Lucrezia von Goëss; one *s* one *d*]. *E:* EofBPrivate@aol.com. *Clubs:* White's, I Zingari, Eton Ramblers, Old Etonian Lawn Tennis and Racquets; Brook (New York).

BALFOUR OF BURLEIGH, Lord *cr* 1607 (*de facto* 8th Lord, 12th but for the Attainder); **Robert Bruce,** CEng, FIET; FRSE; Chancellor, Stirling University, 1988–98; Vice Lord-Lieutenant, Clackmannan, 1995–2001; *b* 6 Jan. 1927; *e s* of 11th Lord Balfour of Burleigh and Dorothy (*d* 1976), *d* of late R. H. Done; *S* father, 1967; *m* 1st, 1971, Mrs Jennifer Brittain-Catlin (marr. diss. 1993), *d* of late E. S. Manasseh; two *d*; 2nd, 1993, Janet Morgan (*see* Lady Balfour of Burleigh). *Educ:* Westminster Sch. Served Home Guard, 1944–45 as Private, 2nd Herefordshire Bn; RN, 1945–48, as Ldg Radio Electrician's Mate. Joined English Electric Co. Ltd, 1951; DFH; graduate apprentice, 1951–52; Asst Foreman, Heavy Electrical Plant Dept, Stafford Works, 1952–54; Asst Superintendent, Heavy Electrical Plant Dept, Netherton Works, Liverpool, 1954–57; Manager, English Electric Co. of India (Pvte) Ltd, Madras, 1957–60; Dir and Gen. Manager, English Electric Co. India Ltd, 1960–64; Dep. Gen. Manager, English Electric Co. Ltd, Netherton, Liverpool, 1964–65, Gen. Manager 1965–66; Dir and Gen. Manager, D. Napier & Son Ltd, 1966–68; Dep. Gov., Bank of Scotland, 1977–91 (Dir, 1968–91). Chairman: Viking Oil, 1971–80; NWS Bank (formerly North West Securities), 1978–91; Capella Nova, 1988–2009; Canongate Press, 1991–93; United Artists Communications (Scotland), 1993–96; Director: Scottish Investment Trust, 1971–97; Tarmac, 1981–90; William Lawson Distillers Ltd, 1984–97; Television Educnl Network, 1990–96; UAPT Infolink, 1991–94; Member: British Railways (Scottish) Board, 1982–93; Forestry Commn, 1971–74. Chm., Fedn of Scottish Bank Employers, 1977–86. Chairman: Scottish Arts Council, 1971–80; NBL Scotland, 1981–85; Turing Inst., 1983–91; Scottish Cttee, ABSA, 1990–94 (Mem. Council, 1976–94); Dir, Edinburgh Book Fest., 1981–97 (Chm., 1981–87). Pres., Friends of Vellore, 1973–. Vice-President: RNID, 1987–2004; Bletchley Park Trust, 2009– (Trustee, 2000–09); Treasurer: Royal Scottish Corp., 1967–2004; RSE, 1989–94; Trustee, John Muir Trust, 1989–96; Dir, Eur. Brandenburg Ensemble, 2007–. Hon. FRIAS, 1982. DUniv Stirling, 1988; Hon. DLitt Robert Gordon, 1995. Chevalier, Ordre Grand-Ducal de la Couronne de Chêne (Luxembourg), 2014. *Recreations:* music, climbing, woodwork, open air ice-skating. *Heir: d* Hon. Victoria Bruce-Winkler [*b* 7 May 1973; *m* 2002, Michail Winkler; two *d*]. *Address:* Brucefield, Clackmannanshire FK10 3QF.

See also G. J. D. Bruce.

BALFOUR OF BURLEIGH, Lady; Janet Bruce, CBE 2008; writer and company director; *b* 5 Dec. 1945; *e d* of Frank Morgan and Shiela Sadler; *m* 1993, Lord Balfour of Burleigh, *qv*. *Educ:* Newbury Co. Girls Grammar Sch.; St Hugh's Coll., Oxford. MA, DPhil Oxon, MA Sussex. FSAScot 1992; FRSE 1999. Kennedy Meml Scholar, Harvard Univ., 1968–69; Student, Nuffield Coll., Oxford, 1969–71; Res. Fellow, Wolfson Coll., Oxford and Res. Officer, Univ. of Essex, 1971–72; Res. Fellow, Nuffield Coll., Oxford, 1972–74; Lectr in Politics, Exeter Coll., Oxford, 1974–76; Dir of Studies, St Hugh's Coll., Oxford, 1975–76 and Lectr in Politics, 1976–78; Mem., Central Policy Rev. Staff, Cabinet Office, 1978–81. Mem. Bd, British Council, 1989–99. Vis. Fellow, All Souls Coll., Oxford, 1983. Dir, Satellite Television PLC, 1981–83; Special Advr to Dir-Gen., BBC, 1983–86; Advr to Bd, Granada Gp, 1986–89; Mem., London Adv. Bd, Nat. and Provincial Bldg Soc., 1988–89; Chairman: Cable & Wireless Flexible Resource Ltd, 1993–97; Nuclear Liabilities Fund (formerly Nuclear Generation Decommissioning Co.), 2003–14 (Dir, 1996–2003); Nuclear Liabilities Financing Assurance Bd, 2008–; Espirito Ltd, 2011–; non-executive Director: Cable & Wireless, 1988–2004; W. H. Smith, 1989–95; Midlands Electricity, 1990–96; Pitney Bowes, 1991–93; Scottish American Investment Trust, 1991–2008; Scottish Med. Res. Fund, 1993–96; Scottish Life, 1995–2001; Scottish Oriental Smaller Cos Investment Trust, 1995–; NMT Gp, 1997–2004; BPB, 2000–05; Stagecoach Gp, 2001–10; Murray Internat. Investment Trust, 2003–; Albion Enterprise (formerly Close Enterprise) VCT, 2006–; NDA Archives Ltd, 2014–. Vice-Pres., Videotext Industries Assoc., 1985–91; Dir, Hulton Deutsch Collection, 1988–90. Member: Lord Chancellor's Adv. Council on Public Records, 1982–86; Scottish Museums Council Develt Resource, 1988–96; Adv. Council, Inst. for Advanced Studies in the Humanities, Univ. of Edinburgh, 1988–96; Ancient Monuments Bd for Scotland, 1990–97; Book Trust (Scotland), 1992–99; Scottish Econ. Council, 1993–96; Chairman: Scotland's Book Campaign, 1994–96; Readiscovery Touring Ltd, 1996–99. Trustee: Amer. Sch. in London, 1985–88; Fairground Heritage Trust, 1987–90; Cyclotron Trust, 1988–90; Scottish Hosp. Endowments Res. Trust, 1992–96; Carnegie Trust for Univs of Scotland, 1994–; Nuclear Trust, 1996–2014; Scottish Science Trust, 1997–99; Nat. Library of Scotland, 2002–11; Trusthouse Charitable Foundn, 2006–; Royal Anniversary Trust, 2010–; Chairman: Dorothy Burns Charitable Trust, 1992–2002; Scottish Cultural Resources Access Network Ltd, 1996–2004; Scottish Mus. of Year Awards, 1999–2004; Patron, Porthcurno Submarine Telegraph Mus., 2004–; Vice-Patron, Intelligence Corps Mus., 2014–. Mem., Editorial Bd, Political Quarterly, 1980–90. Mem., Amer. Philosophical Soc., 2012. Hon. LLD Strathclyde, 1999; Hon. DLitt Napier, 1999. Chevalier, Ordre Grand-Ducal de la Couronne de Chêne (Luxembourg), 2014. *Publications:* (as Janet Morgan): The House of Lords and the Labour Government 1964–70, 1975; Reinforcing Parliament, 1976; (ed) The Diaries of a Cabinet Minister 1964–70 by Richard Crossman, 3 vols 1975, 1976, 1977; (ed) Backbench Diaries 1951–63 by Richard Crossman, 1980; (ed with Richard Hoggart) The Future of Broadcasting, 1982; Agatha Christie: a biography, 1984; Edwina Mountbatten: a life of her own, 1991; The Secrets of rue St Roch, 2004. *Recreations:* music of Handel, sea-bathing, ice-skating out of doors, pruning. *Address:* Brucefield, Clackmannanshire FK10 3QF. *T:* (01259) 730228.

BALFOUR, Alexander William; Chief Digital Officer, Haymon Boxing Management, since 2014; *b* 26 Feb. 1971; *s* of late Peter Edward Gerald Balfour, CBE and of Diana Rosemary Balfour; *m* 2000, Samantha, (Sam), Walker; one *s* one *d*. *Educ:* St John's Coll., Cambridge (BA 1993). Reporter, Euromoney mag., 1994–95; freelance journalist, 1995–97; Editor, GE '97, 1997; Content Dir, UK Citizens Online Democracy, 1998; Producer, The Guardian, 1998–99; Dir, Business Develt, 2000–01, Chm., 2001–06, CricInfo Ltd; Hd of New Media, LOCOG, 2006–12; Chief Digital Officer, Engine Gp, 2013. Non-executive Director: Pensions Adv. Service, 2010–14; DTracks Ltd, 2011–. Comr, Historic England (formerly English Heritage), 2014–. *Recreations:* riding fixed gear bicycles, being bullied by my children, swimming in the sea, reading, watching cricket, DJing, surfing the Interweb. *Address:* c/o DBS, Camburgh House, 27 New Dover Road, Canterbury, Kent CT1 3DN. *Clubs:* Lansdowne, MCC; London Dynamo, Rye Wheelers.

BALFOUR, (Elizabeth) Jean, CBE 1981; FRSE 1980; FRSA; FICFor; JP; Chairman, Countryside Commission for Scotland, 1972–82; *b* 4 Nov. 1927; 2nd *d* of late Maj.-Gen. Sir James Syme Drew, KBE, CB, DSO, MC, and late Victoria Maxwell of Munches; *m* 1950, John Charles Balfour, OBE, MC (*d* 2009); three *s*. *Educ:* Edinburgh Univ. (BSc). Partner/Owner, Balbirnie Home Farms; Director: A. & J. Bowen & Co. Ltd; Loch Duart Ltd, 1999–2008 (Chm., 1999–2006); Mem. Bd, Scottish Quality Salmon, 2005–06. Pres., Royal Scottish Forestry Soc., 1969–71; Mem., Fife CC, 1958–70; Chm., Fife County and City and Royal Burgh of Dunfermline Joint Probation Cttee, 1967–69; Governor, East of Scotland Coll. of Agriculture, 1958–88, Vice Pres. 1982–88; Dir, Scottish Agricl Colls, 1987–88, Dir, Council, 1974–87; Member: Scottish Agric. Develt Council, 1972–77; Verney Working Party on Natural Resources, 1971–72; Nature Conservancy Council, 1973–80; Oil Develt Council, 1973–78; Scottish Economic Council, 1978–83; Forth River Purification Bd, 1992–96; Council, Scottish Landowners Fedn, 1996–99 (Chm., Forestry Cttee, 1997–99); Chairman: Regional Adv. Cttee, East (Scotland) Forestry Commn, 1976–85; Regional Adv. Cttee, Mid (Scotland) Forestry Commn, 1987–2000; Food and Farming Adv. Cttee, Scottish Cons. and Unionist Assoc., 1985–88; Crarae Gardens Charitable Trust, 1986–93; W Sutherland Fisheries Trust, 1996–99; Hon. Vice Pres., Scottish Wildlife Trust (Vice-Chm., 1968–72; Founder Council Mem.). Deputy Chairman: Seafish Industry Authority, 1987–90; Cttee on Women in Science, Engrg and Technol., OST, Cabinet Office, 1993–94. Member: Cttee of Enquiry on handling of geographical information, 1985–87; RSE Foot and Mouth Enquiry, 2001–02. Trustee: Buckland Foundn, 1989–94; Royal Botanic Gdns, Edinburgh, 1992–98. Mem. Council, RSE, 1983–86; Mem. Council and Chm., Policy and Legislation Cttee, Inst. of Chartered Foresters, 1986–88; Council Mem. and Chm., Mid Scotland Timber Growers' Assoc., 2000–02. Hon. Vice-Pres., Scottish YHA, 1983–. Mem. Court, St Andrews Univ., 1983–87 (Chm. Ct Cttee, Estates and Buildings, 1983–87); Gov., Duncan of Jordanstone Coll. of Art, 1992–96. JP Fife, 1963. FRSA 1981; FRZSScot 1983; FRSB (FIBiol 1988); FRSGS 1997. Hon. DSc St Andrews, 1977; DUniv Stirling, 1991. Forestry Medal, Inst. of Chartered Foresters, 1996; Forestry Award, Confedn of Forest Industries, 2015. Order of the Falcon (Iceland), 1994. Report to Government, A New Look at the Northern Ireland Countryside, 1984–85. *Recreations:* hill walking, fishing, painting, exploring arctic vegetation, shooting. *Address:* Kirkforthar House, Markinch, Fife KY7 6LS. *T:* (01592) 752233; Scourie, by Lairg, Sutherland IV27 4TH. *Clubs:* Farmers; New (Edinburgh).

See also R. W. Balfour.

BALFOUR, Maj. Gen. James Melville John, CBE 2001 (OBE 1992); DL; Director General, Winston Churchill Memorial Trust, 2007–15; *b* 6 May 1951; *s* of late Comdr Colin James Balfour, RN; *m* 1981, Carolyn Laing; one *s* two *d*. *Educ:* Eton Coll.; Mons Officer Cadet Sch.; Army Staff Coll. Commnd into 3rd Bn RGJ, 1970; ADC to CGS, 1977; Defence Services Staff Coll., India, 1983; Major, Mil. Ops, MoD, 1984–85; Co. Comdr, 3rd Bn RGJ, 1986–88; JSDC, Greenwich, 1988; Directing Staff, Army Staff Coll., Camberley, 1988–90; CO, 3rd Bn, RGJ, 1990–92; MA to QMG, 1993; HCSC 1994; Col, Mil. Ops, MoD, 1994–95; Comdr, 3rd Inf. Bde, 1996–97; RCDS 1998; COS, HQ NI, 1999–2001; Comdr, British Forces, Bosnia, 2001; Dir, Infantry, MoD, 2002–04; Co-ordinator, Kosovo Protection Corps, 2005–06; Pres., Gen. Court Martial, 2006–07. Chm., Youth Clubs Hants and IoW, 2007–09; Hants County Chairman: Game and Wildlife Conservancy Trust, 2008–11; ABF, 2008–15 (Vice Pres., 2015–); Pres., Hants CLA, 2015–. DL, 2009, High Sheriff, 2014–15, Hants. *Recreations:* field sports, gardening.

BALFOUR, Jean; *see* Balfour, E. J.

BALFOUR, Michael William, OBE 2008; FCA; Founder, The Hideaways Club Ltd, since 2006; Chairman, Pure Jatomi Fitness Ltd (formerly Pure Health and Fitness Sp. z o.o.), since 2010; *b* 3 May 1949; *s* of Alexander and Winifred Balfour; *m* 1978, Margaret; one *s* one *d*. Gen. Manager, Lucas (Latina America) Inc., 1978–81; Man. Dir, Bytex Ltd, 1982–85; Dir, Mannai Investment Co., 1985–92; Fitness First Holdings Ltd: Founder, CEO, 1992–2004; Dep. Chm., 2005–06; Chm., 2006–09. Director: Fitness Industry Assoc., 2003–; Skills Active, 2005–. Hon. DBA Bournemouth, 2004. *Recreations:* sailing, golf. *T:* (office) (01202) 331932.

BALFOUR, Neil Roxburgh; Chairman: Mermaid Holdings Ltd, since 1991; Mermaid Properties Sp. z o.o., since 2005; *b* 12 Aug. 1944; *s* of Archibald Roxburgh Balfour and Lilian Helen Cooper; *m* 1st, 1969, HRH Princess Elizabeth of Yugoslavia; one *s*; 2nd, 1978, Serena Mary Spencer-Churchill Russell; two *s* one *d*. *Educ:* Ampleforth Coll., Yorks; University Coll., Oxford Univ. (BA History). Called to the Bar, Middle Temple, 1969. Baring Brothers & Co., 1968–74; European Banking Co. Ltd, 1974–83 (Exec. Dir, 1980–83). Chm., York Trust Group plc, 1986–91; Pres., and CEO, Mostostal Warszawa SA, 2000–02. Mem. (C) N Yorks, European Parlt, 1979–84. *Publications:* Paul of Yugoslavia (biography), 1980. *Recreations:* bridge, golf, tennis, shooting, fishing. *Address:* Alma Grove, Combe, near Witney, Oxon OX29 8NA. *Clubs:* Turf, Pratt's, White's; Royal St George's (Sandwich), Sunningdale; Arcangues (Biarritz).

BALFOUR, Robert William, FRICS; Managing Partner, Balbirnie Home Farms, since 1991; Lord-Lieutenant of Fife, since 2014; *b* Edinburgh, 25 March 1952; *s* of late John Charles Balfour, OBE, MC and of (Elizabeth) Jean Balfour, *qv*; *m* 1975, Jessica McCrindle; three *s* (and one *s* decd). *Educ:* Eton Coll.; Univ. of Edinburgh (BSc Hons). FRICS 1990. Mgt trainee, Ocean Gp, 1974–78; Surveyor, Bell-Ingram, Perth, 1978–88; Bidwells, Chartered Surveyors, Perth, 1988–94 (Associate Partner, 1991–94). Chm., Kettle Growers Ltd, 2006–11. Dir, Paths for All Partnership, 2005–13. Mem., W Area Bd, Scottish Natural Heritage, 2003–07.

Convener, Scottish Landowners Fedn, 1999–2002. Chm., RICS Rural Practice Div. (Scotland), 1990–91. Chm., Assoc. of Deer Mgt Gps, 2005–11. Dir, Fife Coast and Countryside Trust, 2003–15 (Chm., 2007–15). Gen. Trustee, Church of Scotland, 2012–. Mem., Bd of Mgt, Elmwood Coll., 2000–08. Mem., Royal Co. of Archers (Queen's Body Guard for Scotland), 1992–. DL Fife, 1994. Elder, Markinch Parish Ch, 1982–. *Address:* Pitillock Farm, Freuchie, Fife KY15 7JQ. *T:* (01337) 857437, 07774 833620. *E:* robertwbalfour@gmail.com. *Clubs:* Farmers; Royal and Ancient Golf.

BALKWILL, Prof. Frances Rosemary, OBE 2008; FMedSci; Professor of Cancer Biology and Centre Lead, Centre for Cancer and Inflammation (formerly Centre for Translational Oncology), Barts Cancer Institute (formerly Cancer Research UK Translational Oncology Laboratory, then Institute of Cancer), Barts and The London School of Medicine and Dentistry, Queen Mary University of London (formerly Barts and The London, Queen Mary's Medical School), since 2000; *b* 18 March 1952; *d* of late Elson Howard Lucas Leach and Rosemary Emily Leach; *m* 1973, Lewis Balkwill (marr. diss. 1987); one *s* one *d*. *Educ:* Surbiton High Sch.; Bristol Univ. (BSc); Univ. of London (PhD). Prin. Scientist and Lab. Hd, ICRF, 1979–2000; Dir, Centre of the Cell (sci. centre for children), Barts and The London Sch. of Medicine and Dentistry (formerly Barts and the London, Queen Mary's Med. Sch.), 2002–. Non-Parly Bd Mem., POST, 2000–. Chairman: Public Engagement Strategy Cttee, Wellcome Trust, 2008–11; Understanding Animal Res., 2010–; Mem., Scientific Adv. Cttee, Breakthrough Breast Cancer, 2012–15. Series Ed., Making Sense of Science, 1995–99. FMedSci 2006. Award for Communication in the Life Scis, EMBO, 2004; Michael Faraday Prize, Royal Soc., 2005. *Publications:* Cytokines in Cancer Therapy, 1989; (ed) Cytokines: a practical approach, 1991, 3rd edn 2000; (ed jtly) Interleukin 2, 1992; (ed) Frontiers in Molecular Biology: the cytokine network, 2000; *books for children* (designed and illustrated by Mic Rolph): Cells are Us, 1990; Cell Wars, 1990; DNA is Here to Stay, 1992; Amazing Schemes within your Genes, 1993; The Egg and Sperm Race, 1994; Microbes, Bugs, and Wonder Drugs, 1995; Enjoy Your Cells (series), 2001–02; Staying Alive: fighting HIV/AIDS, 2002; SuperCells, 2003; You, Me and HIV, 2004; approx. 240 pubns in scientific jls. *Recreations:* writing, travel, bird watching, piano. *Address:* Centre for Cancer and Inflammation, Barts Cancer Institute, Barts and The London School of Medicine and Dentistry, Charterhouse Square, EC1M 6BQ. *T:* (020) 7882 3587, *Fax:* (020) 7882 3885.

BALL, Alison; QC 1995; a Recorder, since 1998; *b* 12 Jan. 1948; *d* of Winifred Alice Ball and Hilary Noble Ball; *m* 1980, Richard; two *d*. *Educ:* Bedales Sch.; King's Coll., London (LLB Hons). Called to the Bar, Middle Temple, 1972, Bencher, 2002; founded Specialist Family Law Chambers, 1989, Joint Head, 1989–2010. *Recreation:* my family and other animals. *Address:* 1 Garden Court, Temple, EC4Y 9BJ. *T:* (020) 7797 7900.

BALL, Anthony George, (Tony), MBE 1986; FCIM; FIMI; FCGI; Founder, 1983, and Chairman, 1983–2006, Tony Ball Associates (TBA) plc; *b* 14 Nov. 1934; *s* of Harry Ball and Mary Irene Ball, Bridgwater; *m* 1st, 1957, Ruth Parry Davies (marr. diss. 1997); two *s* one *d*; 2nd, 2000, Ms Jan Kennedy. *Educ:* Grammar Sch., Bridgwater. Indentured engineering apprentice, Austin Motor Co., 1951–55; responsible for launch of Mini, 1959; UK Car and Commercial Vehicle Sales Manager, 1961–66, Austin Motor Co.; Sales and Marketing Exec., British Motor Corp., 1966–67; Chm. and Man. Dir, Barlow Rand UK Motor Gp, 1967–78; Managing Director: Barlow Rand Ford, S Africa, 1971–73; Barlow Rand European Operations, 1973–78; returned to British Leyland as Man. Dir, Overseas Trading Operations, 1978; Dep. Man. Dir, Austin Morris Ltd, 1979; Chm. and Man. Dir, British Leyland Europe & Overseas, 1979–82; Director, 1979–82: BL Cars Ltd (World Sales Chief, 1979–82; responsible for launch of the Austin Metro in 1980); Austin Morris Ltd; Rover Triumph Ltd; Jaguar Rover Triumph Inc. (USA); Dir, Jaguar Cars Ltd, 1979–82; Chief Exec., Henlys plc, 1981–83. Dep. Chm., Lumley Insce Gp, 1983–95; Director: Jetmaster UK, 1989–97; Theatrical Agents Billy Marsh Associates Ltd, 1993–; Royal Carlton Hotel, Blackpool, 1998–2007. Dir, producer and stager of 'Industrial Theatre' Motivational confs, sponsorship, marketing, promotions, special events and new product launches, 1983–2014. Responsible for: staging new product launches for British Leyland, Austin, Rover, MG, Jaguar, General Motors, Vauxhall, Proton, Mercedes-Benz, Daihatsu, LDV, Land Rover, Bedford trucks, Optare buses, Pioneer-UK, Fiat and Gillette; production and staging of opening ceremony of Rugby World Cup, Twickenham, 1991; DoH European drug abuse prevention campaign, 1992. Apptd Marketing Adviser: to Minister of Agric. and 'Food from Britain', 1979–83; to Sec. of State for Energy, 1984–87; to Sec. of State for Wales, 1988–91; to SMMT for producing and promoting: British Internat. Motor Show, 1992–96; Scottish Motor Show, 1997–2001; to FA for producing opening and closing ceremonies of European Football Championships, Wembley, 1996, FA Cup Finals, 1996–2000 and promotional and presentation work for England World Cup Bid, 2006; to RFU for 125th Anniversary celebrations, 1996, for 5 Nations Championship activities, Twickenham, 1997–2006; to RFU Français for prodn of opening ceremony at Stade de France, Paris, 1998; to Welsh RU for producing opening and closing ceremonies, Rugby World Cup, Millennium Stadium, Cardiff Arms Park, 1999; to ECB for producing opening ceremony, Cricket World Cup, Lord's, 1999; responsible for: promoting London Zoo relaunch, 1993; creating and producing Lloyds Bank's Playwright of the Year Award, annually 1994–2003. President: Austin Ex-Apprentices Assoc., 2006–14; Fellowship of Motor Industry, 2011–14 (Chm., 2009–11). Lectr, public and after dinner speaker; guest after dinner speaker, P&O Cruises, 2008–; TV and radio broadcasts on motivation, marketing, public speaking and industrial subjects; producer, The Birth of Rugby (TV); panellist, Any Questions (TV and radio). Mason Meml Lecture, Birmingham Univ., 1983. Governor, N Worcs Coll., 1984–91. Patron, Wordsworth Trust, 2004–14. Freeman of City of London, 1980; Liveryman: Worshipful Co. of Coach Makers and Coach Harness Makers, 1980; Worshipful Co. of Carmen, 1982. Fellowship of Inst. of Marketing awarded 1981, for services to Brit. Motor Industry; FCGI 1999; Hon. Mem. CGLI, 1982, for services to technical and vocational educn; Prince Philip Medal, CGLI, 1984, for outstanding lifetime contribution to British marketing. Benedictine Award, Business After-Dinner Speaker of the Year, 1992, 1993. *Publications:* (contrib.) Metro: the book of the car, 1981; (contrib.) Tales out of School: misdeeds of the famous, 1983; A Marketing Study of the Welsh Craft Industry (Welsh Office report, 1988); (contrib.) Making Better Business Presentations, 1988; (contrib.) Men and Motors of 'The Austin', 2000; contribs to numerous industrial, management, marketing and public speaking books and jls. *Recreations:* theatre, British military history, sharing good humour. *Address:* Roe Lodge, Sowerby Row, Penrith, Cumbria CA4 0QH. *Club:* Lord's Taverners.

See also M. A. Ball.

BALL, Sir Christopher (John Elinger), Kt 1988; MA; Chancellor, University of Derby, 1995–2003; *b* 22 April 1935; *er s* of late Laurence Elinger Ball, OBE, and Christine Florence Mary Ball (*née* Howe); *m* 1958, Wendy Ruth Colyer, *d* of late Cecil Frederick Colyer and Ruth Colyer (*née* Reddaway); three *s* three *d*. *Educ:* St George's School, Harpenden; Merton College, Oxford (Harmsworth Scholar 1959; Hon. Fellow, 1987); 1st Cl. English Language and Literature, 1959; Dipl. in Comparative Philology, 1962; MA Oxon, 1963. 2nd Lieut, Parachute Regt, 1955–56. Lectr in English Language, Merton Coll., Oxford, 1960–61; Lectr in Comparative Linguistics, Sch. of Oriental and African Studies (Univ. of London), 1961–64; Fellow and Tutor in English Language, Lincoln Coll., Oxford, 1964–79 (Bursar, 1972–79; Hon. Fellow, 1981); Warden, Keble College, Oxford, 1980–88 (Hon. Fellow, 1989). Founding Fellow, Kellogg Forum for Continuing Educn, Univ. of Oxford, 1988–89; Vis. Prof. in Higher Educn, Leeds Poly., 1989–91; Fellow in Continuing Educn, 1989–92, Dir of Learning, 1992–97, RSA. Sec., Linguistics Assoc. of GB, 1964–67; Pres., Oxford Assoc. of University Teachers, 1968–71; Publications Sec., Philological Soc., 1969–75; Chairman: Oxford Univ. English Bd, 1977–79; Bd of NAB, 1982–88; Higher Educn Inf. Services Trust, 1987–90; Member: General Bd of the Faculties, 1979–82; Hebdomadal Council, 1985–89; CNAA, 1982–88 (Chm., English Studies Bd, 1973–80, Linguistics Bd, 1977–82); BTEC, 1984–89 (Chm., Quality Assurance & Control Cttee, 1989–90); IT Skills Shortages Cttee (Butcher Cttee), 1984–85; CBI IT Skills Agency, 1985–88; CBI Task Force, 1988–89. Chairman: NICEC, 1989–93; Pegasus, 1989–92; Strategic Educn Fora for Kent, 1992–97, Oxfordshire, 1992–97, and Gtr Peterborough, 1992–95; Educn Policy Cttee, RSA Exams Bd, 1993–96; Patron: Campaign for Learning, RSA, 1998– (Chm., 1996–98); Research Autism, 2007–15; Vice-Pres., Autistica, 2009–15. Vice-Chm., Jigsaw Gp, 1998–2004; founding Chm., The Talent Foundn, 1999–2004 (Patron, 2004–); Chairman: Global Univ. Alliance, 2000–04; WAVE Trust, 2004–07; Down Syndrome Educn Internat., 2010–15. Member: Council and Exec., Templeton Coll., Oxford, 1981–92; Centre for Medieval and Renaissance Studies, Oxford, 1987–90; Brathay Hall Trust, 1988–91 (Chm, 1990–91; Fellow, 2003–); Manchester Polytechnic, 1989–91 (Hon. Fellow, 1988). President: ACFHE, 1990–92; SEAL, 2000–05. Gov., St George's Sch., Harpenden, 1985–89; Trustee, Langley Hall Primary Acad., 2011–. Jt Founding Editor (with late Angus Cameron), Toronto Dictionary of Old English, 1970; Member Editorial Board: Oxford Rev. of Education, 1984–96; Science and Public Affairs, 1989–94. FRSA 1987. Hon. Fellow: Univ. of Westminster (formerly Poly. of Central London), 1991; Auckland Inst. of Technol., NZ, 1992; Glendower Univ. (formerly NE Wales Inst., Wrexham), 1996; Oxford Brookes Univ., 2007; Millennium Fellow, Auckland Univ. of Technol., NZ, 2000. Hon. DLitt CNAA, 1989; DUniv: N London, 1993; Open, 2002; Derby, 2003; Hon. DEd Greenwich, 1994. *Publications:* Fitness for Purpose, 1985; Aim Higher, 1989; (ed jtly) Higher Education in the 1990s, 1989; More Means Different, 1990; Learning Pays, 1991; Sharks and Splashes, 1991; Profitable Learning, 1992; Start Right, 1994; *poetry* (as John Elinger): Still Life, 2008; Operatic Interludes, 2008; That Sweet City, 2013; That Mighty Heart, 2014; pamphlets and various contributions to philological, linguistic, poetic and educational jls. *Address:* 45 Richmond Road, Oxford OX1 2JJ. *T:* and *Fax:* (01865) 310800.

BALL, Colin George; Director, Commonwealth Foundation, 2000–04 (Deputy Director, 1998–99); *b* 22 July 1943; *s* of George Heyward Ball and Bessie Margaret Ball (*née* Henry); *m* 1st, 1968, Maureen Sheelagh Bryan (marr. diss. 1996); one *s* one *d*; 2nd, 1998, Susan Helen Armstrong. *Educ:* Sevenoaks Sch.; Univ. of Keele (BA (Hons)). Teaching, Malaysia, Ghana, Nigeria, UK, 1961–62, 1966–70; Dir Schs Adv. Service, CSV, 1970–72; Asst Principal, Birstall Community Coll., 1973–74; Principal, Home Office and MSC, 1975–79; Founder, Chm. and CEO, Centre for Employment Initiatives, 1980–88; freelance researcher, consultant and writer, 1988–97. Chm., Commonwealth Assoc. for Local Action and Econ. Devel., 1990–96. *Publications:* Education for a Change, 1973; Community Service and the Young Unemployed, 1977; Fit for Work?, 1979; Whose Business is Business, 1980; Locally Based Responses to Long-term Unemployment, 1988; Towards an Enterprising Culture, 1989; Non-governmental Organisations: guidelines for good policy and practice, 1995; Dupuytren's Contracture, 2010; It's the Community, Stupid!, 2011. *Recreations:* music, reading, writing, Italy. *Address:* 1/41 Griffith Street, New Farm, Qld 4005, Australia.

BALL, David Christopher James; Director, Human Resources, Defence Equipment and Support, Ministry of Defence, since 2010; *b* Cardiff, 20 June 1959; *s* of late Peter Alec James Ball and Anne Stephen Ball; *m* 1998, Felicity Jane Unwin; two *s* one *d*. *Educ:* Winchester Coll.; Merton Coll., Oxford (BPhil Philos. 1983; MA Lit.Hum.). Chartered FCIPD 2012. Ministry of Defence, 1983–: Asst Private Sec. to Sec. of State, 1986–88; Legal Secretariat, 1988–90; on loan to Cabinet Office, 1990–92; Army Resources and Plans, 1992–95, Hd of Finance and Secretariat, Land Systems, 1995–98, Gp Leader, Central Finance and Planning Gp, 1998–2001, Defence Procurement Agency; Chief Exec., Pay and Personnel Agency, subseq. People, Pay and Pensions Agency, 2001–09. *Recreations:* family, singing in chamber choir, gardening. *Address:* Defence Equipment and Support, Ministry of Defence, Abbey Wood, Bristol BS34 8JH. *E:* david.ball248@mod.uk.

BALL, Gillian, OBE 2012; Director of Finance, University of Birmingham, 1995–2014; *b* Birmingham, 10 Nov. 1959; *d* of late John Henry Allcutt and Winifred Allcutt; *m* 1997, Michael Ball. *Educ:* Erdington Girls' Grammar Sch., Birmingham. ACCA 1983, FCCA 1988. Trainee Accountant, 1980–82, Internal Auditor, 1982–83, West Midlands CC; Accountant for Higher and Further Educn, Coventry CC, 1983–85; University of Birmingham: Systems Accountant, 1985–87; Principal Accountant, 1987–89; Dep. Dir, Finance, 1989–95; Actg Registrar and Sec., 2007–08. Mem. Bd, UM Assoc. Ltd and UM Services Ltd, 1999–2007 (Dep. Chm., 2003–07); Sec., British Univs Finance Dirs Gp, 2002–05. Mem. Council, 2001–10, Pres., 2007–08, ACCA. Ind. Mem., Audit Cttee, ESRC, 2004–06; Mem., STFC, 2009– (Mem., 2009–, Chm., 2015–, Audit Cttee; Chm., 2010–15, Mem., 2015–, Remuneration Cttee); Mem., Audit Cttee, Manufacturing Technol. Centre, 2012–14; Chm., Audit and Assurance Supervisory Bd, UK Res. Councils. Gov., King Edward VI Foundn, Birmingham, 2003– (Chm., Audit Cttee, 2009–; Bailiff, 2014–15). *Recreations:* racketball, golf, ski-ing, cooking. *E:* g.ball@bham.ac.uk.

BALL, Dr Harold William; Keeper of Palæontology, British Museum (Natural History), 1966–86; *b* 11 July 1926; *s* of Harold Ball and Florence (*née* Harris); *m* 1955, Patricia Mary (*née* Silvester); two *s* two *d*. *Educ:* Yardley Gram. Sch.; Birmingham Univ. BSc 1947, PhD 1949, Birmingham. Geologist, Nyasaland Geological Survey, 1949–51; Asst Lectr in Geology, King's Coll., London, 1951–54; Dept of Palæontology, British Museum (Nat. Hist.), 1954–86: Dep. Keeper, 1965; Keeper, 1966. Adrian Vis. Fellow, Univ. of Leicester, 1972–77. Sec., 1968–72, Vice-Pres., 1972–73, 1984–86, Geological Soc. of London; Pres., 1981–84, Vice-Pres., 1984–86, Soc. for the History of Natural History. Wollaston Fund, Geological Soc. of London, 1965. *Publications:* papers on the stratigraphy of the Old Red Sandstone and on the palæontology of the Antarctic in several scientific jls. *Recreations:* music, gardening. *Address:* Wilderbrook, Dormans Park, East Grinstead, West Sussex RH19 2LT. *T:* (01342) 870426.

BALL, Sir James; *see* Ball, Sir R. J.

BALL, Sir John (Macleod), Kt 2006; DPhil; FRS 1989; FRSE; FIMA; Sedleian Professor of Natural Philosophy, since 1996, and Director, Oxford Centre for Nonlinear PDE, since 2007, University of Oxford; Fellow, Queen's College, Oxford, since 1996; *b* 19 May 1948; *s* of Ernest Frederick Ball and Dorothy Forbes Ball; *m* 1st, 1973, Mary Judith Hodges (marr. diss. 1977); 2nd, 1992, Sedhar Chozam; two *s* one *d*. *Educ:* Mill Hill Sch.; St John's Coll., Cambridge (BA Maths, 1969; Hon. Fellow, 2005); Univ. of Sussex (DPhil 1972). FRSE 1980; FIMA 2003. SRC Postdoctoral Res. Fellow, Dept of Maths, Heriot-Watt Univ., and Lefschetz Center for Dynamical Systems, Brown Univ., USA, 1972–74; Lectr in Maths, 1974–78, Reader in Maths, 1978–82, SERC Sen. Fellow, 1980–85, Prof. of Applied Analysis, 1982–96, Heriot-Watt Univ. Visiting Professor: Dept of Maths, Univ. of Calif, Berkeley, 1979–80; Laboratoire d'Analyse Numérique, Université Pierre et Marie Curie, Paris, 1987–88, 1994; Inst. for Advanced Study, Princeton, 1993–94, 2002–03; Univ. Montpellier II, 2003; Hon. Prof., Heriot-Watt Univ., 1998–. Member Council: EPSRC, 1994–99; Edinburgh Mathematical Soc., 1972 (Pres., 1989–90); London Math. Soc., 1982 (Pres., 1996–98 and 2009); Amer. Math. Soc., 1987–; Soc. for Nat. Phil., 1978–; Pres., IMU, 2003–06. Member: Programme Cttee, Internat. Centre for Mathematical Scis, Edinburgh, 1991– (Mem. Exec. Cttee, 1991–96, Chm., 1991–93); Bd of Govs, Weizmann Inst., 1998–; Exec. Bd, ICSU, 2011–; Comité d'orientation stratégique, Sorbonne Univs, 2012–. Delegate, OUP, 1998–2008. Member, Conseil Scientifique: CNRS, 2010–14; EDF, 2010–14. John von Neumann Lect., Soc. for Industrial and Applied Maths, 2012. Associé Etranger, Acad. des

Sciences, Paris, 2000; Foreign Member: Instituto Lombardo, 2005; Norwegian Acad. of Sci. and Letters, 2007; MAE, 2008; Hon. Mem., Edinburgh Math. Soc., 2008; Fellow, Amer. Math. Soc., 2012. Hon. DSc: Ecole Polytechnique Fédérale, Lausanne, 1992; Heriot-Watt, 1998; Sussex, 2000; Montpellier II, 2003; Edinburgh, 2004; Pierre et Marie Curie, Paris, 2010. Whittaker Prize, Edinburgh Math. Soc., 1981; Jun. Whitehead Prize, 1982, Naylor Prize, 1994, London Math. Soc.; Keith Prize, RSE, 1990; Theodore von Karman Prize, SIAM, 1999; David Crighton Medal, LMS/IMA, 2003; Royal Medal, RSE, 2006; Sylvester Medal, 2009, Wolfson Res. Merit Award, 2010, Royal Soc. Mem. Editorial Boards of various math. and scientific jls and book series. *Publications:* articles in math. and scientific jls. *Recreations:* travel, music, chess. *Address:* Mathematical Institute, University of Oxford, Andrew Wiles Building, Radcliffe Observatory Quarter, Woodstock Road, Oxford OX2 6GG. *T:* (01865) 615110.

BALL, Prof. Keith Martin, PhD; FRS 2013; FRSE; Professor, University of Warwick, since 2012; *b* New York, 26 Dec. 1960; *s* of Michael John and Margaret Ball; *m* 1995, Dr Sachiko Kusukawa. *Educ:* Berkhamsted Sch.; Trinity Coll., Cambridge (BA 1982; PhD 1987). Prof., Texas A&M Univ., 1987–2006; University College London: Lectr, 1990–92; Reader, 1992–96; Prof., 1996–2007; Astor Prof. of Maths, 2007–11; Scientific Dir, Internat. Centre for Math. Scis, Edinburgh, 2010–14. Chair, Eur. Res. Centres on Maths, 2013–14. FRSE 2013. *Publications:* Strange Curves, Counting Rabbits and Other Mathematical Explorations, 2003; contrib. res. articles to math. jls. *Address:* Institute of Mathematics, University of Warwick, Coventry CV4 7AL. *T:* (024) 7652 3736. *E:* K.M.Ball@warwick.ac.uk.

BALL, Michael Ashley, OBE 2015; actor and singer; *b* 27 June 1962; *s* of Anthony George Ball, *qv*; partner, Cathy McGowan. *Educ:* Plymouth Coll.; Farnham Sixth Form Coll.; Guildford Sch. of Acting (Dip. Acting). *Theatre* includes: first professional rôle as Judas/John the Baptist, Godspell, 1984; first starring rôle, Frederick, The Pirates of Penzance, Manchester Opera House, 1985; West End début: created rôle of Marius, Les Misérables, Barbican and Palace, 1985; other major rôles include: Raoul, Phantom of the Opera, Her Majesty's, 1987; created rôle of Alex, Aspects of Love, Prince of Wales, 1989, NY 1990; Giorgio, Passion, Queen's, 1996; Alone Together, Divas Season, Donmar Warehouse, 2001; Caractacus Potts, Chitty Chitty Bang Bang, Palladium, 2002–03; Count Fosco, Woman in White, Palace, 2005; Kismet, ENO, 2007; Hairspray, Shaftesbury, 2007 (Laurence Olivier Award, 2008); Sweeney Todd, Chichester, 2011 (Olivier Award for Best Actor in a Musical, 2013), Adelphi, 2012; Mack & Mabel, Chichester Festival Th., 2015; *film:* England My England, 1996; *television* includes: GB rep., Eurovision Song Contest, 1992; two series of Michael Ball, 1993, 1994; That Day We Sang, 2014; Royal Variety Performances; numerous nat. and internat. concert tours; has made numerous recordings. Patron and Co-Founder, charity, Res. into Ovarian Cancer (ROC). Most Promising Artiste Award, 1989, Best Recording Artiste, 1998, Variety Club of GB; Most Popular Musical Actor, Theatregoers Club of GB, 1999. *Recreations:* collecting graphic novels and single malt whiskeys, country walking, music, theatre. *Address:* c/o Live Nation (Music) UK Ltd, Regent Arcade House, 19–25 Argyll Street, W1F 7TS.

BALL, Rt Rev. Michael Thomas; Bishop of Truro, 1990–97; *b* 14 Feb. 1932; *s* of Thomas James Ball and Kathleen Obena Bradley Ball. *Educ:* Lancing Coll., Sussex; Queens' Coll., Cambridge (BA 1955; MA 1959). Schoolmastering, 1955–76; Co-Founder, Community of the Glorious Ascension, 1960; Prior at Stroud Priory, 1963–76; Curate, Whitehall, Stroud, Glos, 1971–76; Priest-in-charge of Stanmer with Falmer, and Senior Anglican Chaplain to Higher Education in Brighton, including Sussex Univ., 1976–80; Bishop Suffragan of Jarrow, 1980–90. Mem., H of L, 1996–97. Advr to Tyne Tees Television, 1983–89. Mem. Council, St Luke's Hosp. for the Clergy, 1994–2006. *Publications:* So There We Are, 1997; Foolish Risks of God, 2002. *Recreations:* music, housework. *Address:* The Coach House, The Manor, Aller, Langport, Somerset TA10 0RA.

See also Rt Rev. P. J. Ball.

BALL, Rt Rev. Peter John, CGA; Bishop of Gloucester, 1992–93; *b* 14 Feb. 1932; *s* of Thomas James and Kathleen Obena Bradley Ball. *Educ:* Lancing; Queens' Coll., Cambridge; Wells Theological College. MA (Nat. Sci.). Ordained, 1956; Curate of Rottingdean, 1956–58; Co-founder and Brother of Monastic Community of the Glorious Ascension, 1960 (Prior, 1960–77); Suffragan Bishop of Lewes, 1977–92; Prebendary, Chichester Cathedral, 1978, Canon Emeritus, 2000. Fellow of Woodard Corporation, 1962–71; Member: Archbishops' Council of Evangelism, 1965–68; Midlands Religious Broadcasting Council of the BBC, 1967–69; Admin. Council, Royal Jubilee Trusts, 1986–88. Archbishop of Canterbury's Adviser to HMC, 1985–90. Governor: Wellington Coll., 1985–93; Radley Coll., 1986–93; Lancing Coll., 1972–82, 1990–. Freeman, Bor. of Eastbourne, 1992. DUniv Sussex, 1992. *Recreation:* squash (Cambridge Blue, 1953) and music. *Address:* The Coach House, The Manor, Aller, Langport, Somerset TA10 0RA.

See also Rt Rev. M. T. Ball.

BALL, Rev. Canon Peter William; Canon Emeritus, St Paul's Cathedral, since 1990 (Residentiary Canon, 1984–90); Public Preacher, diocese of Salisbury, since 1990; *b* 17 Jan. 1930; *s* of Leonard Wevell Ball and Dorothy Mary Ball; *m* 1956, Angela Jane Dunlop (*d* 2004); one *s* two *d*. *Educ:* Aldenham School; Worcester Coll., Oxford (MA); Cuddesdon Coll., Oxford. Asst Curate, All Saints, Poplar, 1955; Vicar, The Ascension, Wembley, 1961; Rector, St Nicholas, Shepperton, 1968; Area Dean of Spelthorne, 1972–83; Prebendary of St Paul's Cathedral, 1976. Dir, Post Ordination Trng and Continuing Ministerial Educn, Kensington Episcopal Area, 1984–87. Chaplain: Rediffusion Television, 1961–68; Thames Television, 1970–93. First Dir, Brent Samaritans, 1965–68; Dep. Dir, NW Surrey Samaritans, 1973–79. Mem., European Conf. on the Catechumenate, 1975– (Chm., 1983). Member: Spiritual Directors Internat., 1992–; Spiritual Directors Europe, 2000–. *Publications:* Journey into Faith, 1984; Adult Believing, 1988; Adult Way to Faith, 1992; Journey into Truth, 1996; Anglican Spiritual Direction, 1998; (with Ven. Malcolm Grundy) Faith on the Way, 2000; Introducing Spiritual Direction, 2003. *Recreations:* gardening, walking, music. *Address:* Whittonedge, Whittonditch Road, Ramsbury, Marlborough, Wilts SN8 2PX.

BALL, Sir Richard Bentley, 5th Bt *cr* 1911, of Merrion Square, Dublin and Killybegs, Donegal; *b* 29 Jan. 1953; *o s* of Sir Charles Ball, 4th Bt and Alison Mary (*née* Bentley); *S* father, 2002; *m* 1991, Beverley Ann, *d* of late Bertram Joffre Wright (marr. diss. 2015); one *d*. *Educ:* Sherborne; Leicester Univ. ACA. *Heir: cousin* Christopher Nigel Morton Ball [*b* 3 Nov. 1951; *m* 1974, Melanie Fenner; one *s* one *d*].

BALL, Prof. Sir (Robert) James, Kt 1984; MA, PhD; Professor of Economics, 1965–97, now Emeritus, Principal, 1972–84, London Business School; Chairman, Legal and General Group Plc, 1980–94 (Director, 1978–94); *b* 15 July 1933; *s* of Arnold James Hector Ball; *m* 1st, 1954, Patricia Mary Hart Davies (marr. diss. 1970); two *d* (and one *s* two *d* decd); 2nd, 1970, Lindsay Jackson (*née* Wonnacott); one step *s*. *Educ:* St Marylebone Grammar Sch.; The Queen's College, Oxford (Styring Schol.; George Webb Medley Junior Schol. (Univ. Prizeman), 1956; BA 1957 (First cl. Hons PPE), MA 1960; Hon. Fellow, 2010); Univ. of Pennsylvania (PhD 1973). RAF 1952–54 (Pilot-Officer, Navigator). Research Officer, Oxford University Inst. of Statistics, 1957–58; IBM Fellow, Univ. of Pennsylvania, 1958–60; Lectr, Manchester Univ., 1960, Sen. Lectr, 1963–65; London Business School: Governor, 1969–84; Dep. Principal, 1971–72; Fellow, 1998. Chm., Royal Bank of Canada Holdings (UK) Ltd, 1995–98; Director: Ogilvy and Mather Ltd, 1969–71; Economic Models Ltd, 1971–72; Barclays Bank Trust Co., 1973–86; Tube Investments, 1974–84; IBM UK Hldgs Ltd, 1979–95; LASMO plc, 1988–94; Royal Bank of Canada, 1990–98; IBM UK Pensions Trust Ltd, 1994–2004; Part-time Mem., NFC, 1973–77. Economic Advr, Touche Ross & Co., 1984–95; Mem., Adv. Bd, IBM UK Ltd, 1995–98. Member: Cttee to Review National Savings (Page Cttee), 1971–73; Economics Cttee of SSRC, 1971–74; Cttee on Social Forecasting, SSRC, 1971–72; Cttee of Enquiry into Electricity Supply Industry (Plowden Cttee), 1974–75; Chm., Treasury Cttee on Policy Optimisation, 1976–78. Marshall Aid Commemoration Comr, 1987–94. Governor, NIESR, 1973–. Vice-Pres., Chartered Inst. of Marketing, 1991–94; Member Council: REconS, 1973–79; BIM, 1974–82 (Chm., Economic and Social Affairs Cttee, 1979–82); British-N American Cttee, 1985–98. Pres., Sect. F, BAAS, 1990–91. Vice-Pres., CAM Foundn, 1983–92; Trustee: Foulkes Foundn, 1984–2006; Civic Trust, 1986–91; The Economist, 1987–99; Re Action Trust, 1991–93. Fellow, Econometric Soc., 1973; CCMI (CBIM 1974); FIAM 1985. Freeman, City of London, 1987. Hon. DSc Aston, 1987; Hon. DSocSc Manchester, 1988. *Publications:* An Econometric Model of the United Kingdom, 1961; Inflation and the Theory of Money, 1964; (ed) Inflation, 1969; (ed) The International Linkage of National Economic Models, 1972; Money and Employment, 1982; (with M. Albert) Toward European Economic Recovery in the 1980s (report to European Parliament), 1984; (ed) The Economics of Wealth Creation, 1992; The British Economy at the Crossroads, 1998; articles in professional jls. *Recreations:* gardening, chess. *Address:* London Business School, Sussex Place, Regent's Park, NW1 4SA. *T:* (020) 7262 5050. *Club:* Royal Automobile.

BALL, Simon Coryndon L.; *see* Luxmoore-Ball.

BALL, Simon Peter, FCA; Deputy Chairman, Cable & Wireless Communications plc, since 2010; *b* 2 May 1960; *s* of Peter Terence Ball and Maureen Eleanor Ball (*née* Bishop); *m* 1992, Sandra Marie Cameron; two *d*. *Educ:* Chislehurst and Sidcup Grammar Sch.; UCL (BSc (Econ)). ACA 1985; MCSI (MSI 2001); FCA 2009. Price Waterhouse & Co., 1981–85; Kleinwort Benson Group plc, 1985–98: Finance Dir, Kleinwort Benson Securities Ltd, 1990–93; Finance Dir, Kleinwort Benson Ltd, 1994–95; Chief Operating Officer, 1995–98; Robert Fleming Holdings Ltd, 1998–2000: Gp Finance Dir, 1998–2000; Chm., Robert Fleming Inc., 1999–2000; Exec. Dir, Intelligent Energy Ltd, 2001–02; Dir Gen., Finance, DCA, 2003–05; Gp Finance Dir, 3i Gp plc, 2005–08. Chm., Anchura Gp Ltd, 2014–; non-executive Director: Leica Geosystems AG, Switzerland, 2001–05; Cable & Wireless, 2006–10; Tribal Gp plc, 2010–14; Allied Irish Bank Gp, 2011–. Mem. Bd, Commonwealth Games England, 2013–. FRSA 2003. *Recreations:* golf, cinema, theatre, cooking. *Clubs:* Roehampton; Royal Mid Surrey Golf.

BALL, Prof. Stephen John, DPhil; FBA 2006; Karl Mannheim Professor of Sociology of Education, since 2001, and Associate Director, Centre for Critical Education Policy Studies, since 2005, Institute of Education, University College London (formerly Institute of Education, University of London); *b* 21 Jan. 1950; *s* of John and Betty Flora Joan Ball; *m* 1975, Trinidad Fructuoso-Gallego. *Educ:* Univ. of Essex (BA Hons Sociol. 1972); Univ. of Sussex (MA Sociol Studies 1975; DPhil Sociol. 1978). Lectr in Educn, Univ. of Sussex, 1975–85; King's College, London: Tutor in Urban Educn, 1985–89; Reader in Sociol. of Educn, 1990–91; Prof. of Educn, 1991–2001. FAcSS (AcSS 2000). Hon. Dr Turku, 2003; Hon. DLitt Leicester, 2014. *Publications:* Beachside Comprehensive, 1981; The Micropolitics of the School, 1987; Politics and Policy-making in Education, 1990; Education Reform, 1994; Class Strategies in the Education Market, 2003; Education Policy and Social Class: selected works, 2006; Education Plc, 2007; The Education Debate, 2008, 2nd edn 2013; Global Education Inc., 2012; Foucault, Power and Education, 2012. *Recreations:* film, novels, walking, horse-riding. *Address:* Centre for Critical Education Policy Studies, UCL Institute of Education, 20 Bedford Way, WC1H 0AL. *T:* (020) 7612 6973. *E:* s.ball@ioe.ac.uk.

BALLADUR, Edouard; Grand Officier, Légion d'Honneur; Grand Croix de l'Ordre National du Mérite; Member, Conseil d'Etat, France, since 1984; Prime Minister of France, 1993–95; *b* 2 May 1929; *s* of Pierre Balladur and Emilie Latour; *m* 1957, Marie-Josèphe Delacour; four *s*. *Educ:* Lycée Thiers, Marseilles; Faculté de Droit, Aix-en-Provence; Inst. d'études Politiques; Ecole Nat. d'Admin. Jun. Auditeur, 1957, Maître des Requêtes, 1963, Conseil d'Etat; Adviser to Dir-Gen., ORTF, 1962–63 (Mem. Admin Council, 1967–68); Tech. Adviser, Office of Prime Minister Pompidou, 1963–68; Pres., French Co. for routier tunnel under Mont Blanc, 1968–80; Mem., Admin Council, Nat. Forestry Office, 1968–73; Asst Sec. Gen., later Sec. Gen., French President's Office, 1969–74; Chm. and Chief Exec., Générale de Service Informatique, 1977–86; Chm. and Chief Exec., Co. européenne d'accumulateurs, 1980–86; Deputy (RPR, later UMP) for Paris, French Nat. Assembly, 1986–2007 (re-elected 1988, 1993, 1995, 1997 and 2002); Minister for Economy, Finance and Privatization, 1986–88; Mem., Paris City Council, 1989–. President: Comité de réflexion et de proposition sur la modernisation et le rééquilibrage des instns de la Ve République, 2007; Comité pour la réforme des collectivités locales, 2009. Numerous medals and awards, incl. Jacques Rueff Prize, NY, 1986; Euromoney Prize, IMF, 1987; Gold Medal for patronage, French Acad., 1988; Louise Michel Prize, 1993. *Publications:* L'Arbre de mai, 1979; Je crois en l'homme plus qu'en l'Etat, 1987; (jtly) Passion et longueur de temps, 1989; Douze lettres aux Français trop tranquilles, 1990; Des modes et des convictions, 1992; Le dictionnaire de la réforme, 1992; Deux ans à Matignon, 1995; Caractère de la France, 1997; Avenir de la différence, 1999; Renaissance de la droite, pour une alternance décomplexée, 2000; Les aventuriers de l'histoire, 2001; Jeanne d'Arc et la France, 2003; La fin de l'illusion jacobine, 2005; Machiavel en démocratie, 2006; l'Europe autrement, 2006; Laissons de Gaulle en paix!, 2006; Pour une Union occidentale entre l'Europe et les Etats-Unis, 2007; Une Ve République plus démocratique, 2008; Il est temps de décider, 2009; Le pouvoir ne se partage pas, 2009 (Aujourd'hui Prize, François Guizot Prize, 2010).

BALLANCE, Chris(topher); playwright; Development Manager (formerly Development Officer), Moffat CAN, since 2009; *b* 7 July 1952; *s* of Howard and Gwyneth Ballance; *m* 2005, Alis Taylor; two *s*. *Educ:* Alderman Newton's Sch., Leicester; Reigate Grammar Sch.; St Andrews Univ. Work in anti-nuclear power and public transport campaigns; Co-founder, First of May Radical Bookshop, Edinburgh, 1977; self-employed writer for theatre and radio, 1990–; jt-owner, secondhand bookshop, Wigtown, 2000–. MSP (Green) Scotland S, 2003–07. Member: Scottish Soc. of Playwrights, 1992–; Writers Guild of GB, 1995–. Mem., Equity, 1994–. *Recreations:* film, theatre, hill-walking, swimming.

BALLANTINE, (David) Grant, FFA; Directing Actuary, Government Actuary's Department, 1991–2004; *b* 24 March 1941; *s* of James Williamson Ballantine and Robertha (*née* Fairley); *m* 1969, Marjorie Campbell Brown; one *s* one *d*. *Educ:* Daniel Stewart's Coll.; Edinburgh Univ. (BSc 1st Cl.). Scottish Widows' Fund, 1963–68; Asst Vice-Pres., Amer. Insce Gp (Far East), 1968–73; Government Actuary's Department, 1973–2004: Actuary, 1973–82; Chief Actuary, 1983–90. Mem. Council, Faculty of Actuaries, 1991–94. *Publications:* articles in trade and professional jls.

BALLANTYNE, Fiona Catherine, OBE 2014; Chair, Love Music Productions Ltd, since 2009; *b* Bristol, 9 July 1950; *d* of James Douglas and Marjorie Mackay; *m* 1973, (Andrew) Neil Ballantyne. *Educ:* Univ. of Edinburgh (MA). FCIM 2004. Scottish Development Agency: Hd, Small Business Services, 1984–88; Dir, Tayside and Fife, 1988–90; Principal, Ballantyne Mackay Consultants, 1990–2012. Chm., Essentia Gp, 1997–2001; Director: 4-consulting Ltd, 2001–12; RIO Ltd, 2014–; Member, Board: Edinburgh Print Studios Ltd, 2004–08; Music at the Brewhouse Ltd, 2009–. Vice Chm., BBC Broadcasting Council for Scotland, 1991–96; Member: Bd, Edinburgh Healthcare Trust, 1994–96; Consumer Panel, OFCOM, 2004–12; Bd, Office of the Scottish Charity Regulator, 2008–; Water Customer Forum for Scotland, 2013–; Chm., Museums Galls Scotland, 2007–12. Chm., Edinburgh Br., IoD, 2002–06. Vice

Chairman: Duncan of Jordanstone Coll. of Art, 1988–94; Queen Margaret University, 2002–05. *Recreations:* walking, gardening, reading, photography. *E:* fiona@balmac.co.uk.

BALLANTYNE, Sir Frederick (Nathaniel), GCMG 2002; Governor General, St Vincent and the Grenadines, since 2002; *b* 5 July 1936; *s* of Samuel and Olive Ballantyne; *m* 1996, Sally Ann; eight *c* (and one *c* decd). *Educ:* Syracuse Univ., NY (MD); Bd Certified Internal Medicine Cardiology. Med. Dir, Kingstown Gen. Hosp., 1970–83; CMO, St Vincent and Grenadines, 1983–88. *Recreations:* sailing, tennis, bridge. *Address:* Government House, Montrose, St Vincent and the Grenadines, West Indies. *T:* 4561401, *Fax:* 4579710. *E:* govthouse@vincysurf.com.

BALLARAT, Bishop of, since 2011; **Rt Rev. Garry John Weatherill;** *b* 3 Oct. 1956; *s* of Trevor Donald and Lorna Beryl Weatherill. *Educ:* Univ. of Adelaide (BA Hons 1978; DipEd 1979); St Barnabas' Theol Coll.; Flinders Univ. of SA (BTh 1991). Asst Master, Pulteney Grammar Sch., Adelaide, 1980–81; ordained deacon 1986, priest 1987; Asst Curate, St Jude's Ch, Brighton, 1986–88; Asst Priest, St Peter's Cathedral, Adelaide, 1988–90; Rector, Semaphore, 1990–97 and Area Dean, Western Suburbs of Adelaide, 1995–97; Ministry Develt Officer, 1997–2000, Archdeacon, 1999–2000, Willochra; Bishop of Willochra, 2001–11. Mem., Standing Cttee, Gen. Synod, 2007–14; Chairman: Liturgy Commn of Anglican Church of Aust., 2013–; Adv. Council for Anglican Religious Life in Aust., 2013–; Anglican Bd of Mission, Australia, 2015–. Warden, Community of the Holy Name, 2013–; Episcopal Visitor, Southern Province, Soc. of the Sacred Mission, 2014–; Episcopal Consultant, Oratory of Good Shepherd, 2015–. Chm., Australia Council of the Mission to Seafarers, 2006–12. Bp Protector, Third Order, Soc. of St Francis, 2014–. *Recreations:* contemporary fiction, poetry, drama, garden, godchildren. *Address:* The Diocesan Centre, PO Box 89, Ballarat, Vic 3353, Australia. *E:* bishop@ballaratanglican.org.au.

BALLARD, Ven. Andrew Edgar; Archdeacon of Manchester, 2005–09; *b* 14 Jan. 1944; *s* of Arthur Henry and Phyllis Marian Ballard; *m* 1970, Marian Caroline Conolly; one *s* two *d*. *Educ:* Rossall Sch.; St John's Coll., Durham Univ. (BA Hons Theol. 1966); Westcott House, Cambridge. Ordained deacon 1968, priest 1969; Asst Curate, St Mary, Bryanston Sq., and Asst Chaplain, Middlesex Hosp., London, 1968–72; Sen. Asst Curate, St Mary, Portsea, 1972–76; Vicar: St James, Haslingden with St Stephen, Haslingden Grane, 1976–82; St Paul, Walkden, 1982–93; Team Rector, St Paul, Walkden with St John the Baptist, Little Hulton, 1993–98; Area Dean, Farnworth, 1990–98; Priest in charge, 1998–2000, Team Rector, 2000, Rochdale Team Ministry; Archdeacon of Rochdale, 2000–05. Permission to officiate, dio. of Lincoln, 2010–. Hon. Canon, Manchester Cathedral, 1998–2000. *Recreations:* church music, playing the organ. *Address:* 30 Swift Drive, Scawby Brook, Brigg, N Lincs DN20 9FL.

BALLARD, Jacqueline Margaret, (Jackie); Chief Executive, Alcohol Concern, since 2014; *b* 4 Jan. 1953; *d* of late Alexander Mackenzie and Daisy Mackenzie (*née* Macdonald); *m* 1975, Derek Ballard (marr. diss. 1989); one *d*. *Educ:* Monmouth Sch. for Girls; London Sch. of Economics (BSc Social Psychology). Social Worker, Waltham Forest, 1974–76; Further Educn Lectr, Yeovil Coll., 1982–90. Member: (L then Lib Dem) S Somerset DC, 1987–91 (Leader, 1990–91); (Lib Dem) Somerset CC, 1993–97 (Dep. Leader, 1993–95); Council Support Officer, Assoc. of Lib Dem Councillors, 1993–97. MP (Lib Dem) Taunton, 1997–2001. Contested (Lib Dem) Taunton, 2001. Dir Gen., RSPCA, 2002–07; Chief Executive: RNID, later Action on Hearing Loss, 2007–12; Womankind Worldwide, 2012–13; Associate Dir, BB Gp, 2013–14. Member: Youth Justice Bd, 2003–05; Ind. Parly Standards Authy, 2009–13. *Address:* Alcohol Concern, 25 Corsham Street, N1 6DR.

BALLARD, John Frederick, CB 2001; non-executive Director, Lewisham and Greenwich NHS Trust, since 2013 (Senior Independent Director, since 2014); *b* 8 Aug. 1943; *s* of Frederick and Margaret Ballard; *m* 1st, 1975, Ann Helm (marr. diss. 1999); one *s* two *d*; 2nd, 2000, Helena (*née* Rose). *Educ:* Roundhay Grammar Sch., Leeds; Ifield Grammar Sch., W Sussex; Southampton Univ. (BA); Exeter Univ. (CertEd). Academic Registrar's Dept, Univ. of Surrey, 1965–69; Asst Principal, MoT, 1969; Principal, DoE, 1972; Treasury, 1976; Asst Sec. 1978, Sec., Top Salaries Review Body and Police Negotiating Bd; DoE, 1979; Prin. Private Sec. to Sec. of State for the Environment, 1983–85; Under Sec., DoE and Dept of Transport, and Regl Dir, Yorks and Humberside Region, 1986; Dir, Housing Assocs and the Private Sector, DoE, 1990–92; Dir, Maxwell Pensions Unit, DSS, 1992–93 (on secondment); Dir, Town and Country Planning, DoE, 1993–97; Dir Finance, and Principal Finance Officer, DoE, subseq. DETR, 1997–2001; Dir, Water and Land, DETR, subseq. DEFRA, 2001–03. Dir, British Water, 2004–06; non-exec. Dir, NI Water, 2007–10. Mem. Steering Bd, Marine Fisheries Agency, 2005–10. Non-executive Director: Queen Elizabeth Hosp. NHS Trust, 2008–09; S London Healthcare NHS Trust, 2009–13 (Dep. Chm., 2010–12; Actg Chm., 2011–13). Trustee, Maxwell Pensioners Trust, 1993–97; Associate Special Trustee, 1992–99, Special Trustee, 1999–2010, Gt Ormond St Hosp. for Sick Children Charity (Chm., 2006–08). Gov., Brooklands Sch., Blackheath, 2005–09. *Recreations:* trekking, tennis, singing, reading. *Address:* 81 Humber Road, Blackheath, SE3 7LR.

BALLARD, Mark; Assistant Director, Barnardo's Scotland, since 2009; *b* 27 June 1971; *s* of Roger and Cathy Ballard; *m* 2002, Heather Stacey; two *s*. *Educ:* Edinburgh Univ. (MA Hons (Econ. and Social Hist.) 1994). Various positions, European Youth Forest Action, Edinburgh and Amsterdam, 1994–98; Ed., Reforesting Scotland Jl, 1998–2001; estd and ran EMBE Environmental Communications, consultancy co., 2002–03. Scottish Green Party: spokesperson on internat. develt, 1999–2000; Convener, Nat. Council, 2000–02; Nat. Sec., 2002–03. Mem. (Green) Lothians, Scottish Parlt, 2003–07. Communications Manager, SCVO, 2008–09. Rector, Edinburgh Univ., 2006–09. *Recreations:* cycling, Indian cookery. *Address:* Barnardo's Scotland, 235 Corstorphine Road, Edinburgh EH12 7AR.

BALLARD, Ven. Peter James; Chief Executive, DBE Services, since 2010; Archdeacon of Lancaster, 2006–10; *b* 10 March 1955; *m* 1978, Helen Lees; two *d*. *Educ:* Grammar Sch. for Boys, Chadderton; St Hild and St Bede's Coll., Durham (BEd 1978); DipTheol London (ext.) 1985; Sarum and Wells Theol Coll. Various posts with TEC, then BTEC, 1978–85; ordained deacon, 1987, priest, 1988; Asst Curate, Grantham, 1987–91; Vicar, Christ Ch, Lancaster, 1991–98; RD Lancaster, 1995–98; Canon Residentiary, Blackburn Cathedral, 1998–2006; Diocesan Dir of Educn, dio. of Blackburn, 1998–2010. Mem., Gen. Synod of C of E, 2000–10. Consulting Ed., Internat. Jl of Comparative Religious Educn and Values, 2001–. Non-exec. Dir, Lancashire Care NHS Foundn Trust (formerly Lancashire NHS Trust), 2009– (Sen. Ind. Dir, 2012–; Dep. Chm., 2013–). Hon. Treas., Nat. Soc., 2011. Gov., St Martin's Coll. of Higher Educn, 1999–2007 (Actg Chm., 2005); Chm. and Pro Chancellor, Univ. of Cumbria, 2007–10 (Vice Chm., 2006–07). FRSA 2009. *Publications:* (with Brian Boughton) Construction Mathematics, vols I and II, 1983; (contrib.) Mission Shaped Youth, 2007. *Recreations:* bad golf, electronic gardening, watching most sports, spending time with the family. *Address:* Chapel House, Chapel Lane, Ellel, Lancaster LA2 0PW. *T:* (01524) 752466, 07970 923141. *E:* peter.j.ballard@btinternet.com.

BALLARD, Dr Robert Duane; oceanographer and marine explorer; Founder and President, Ocean Exploration Center (formerly Institute for Exploration), Mystic Aquarium, since 1995; *b* 30 June 1942; *s* of Chester P. Ballard and Harriett N. Ballard; *m* 1991, Barbara Earle; two *s* one *d*. *Educ:* Univ. of California, Santa Barbara (BS 1965); Univ. of Hawaii; Univ. of Southern California; Univ. of Rhode Island (PhD 1974). 2nd Lieut, US Army Intelligence, 1965–67; USN, 1967–70, served Vietnam War; Comdr, USNR, 1987–2001. Woods Hole Oceanographic Institution: Res. Associate, 1969–74; Asst Scientist, 1974–76; Associate Scientist, 1976–83; Founder, Deep Submergence Lab., and Sen. Scientist, Dept of Applied Ocean Physics and Engrg, 1983–99; Dir, Center for Marine Exploration, 1989–95; Scientist Emeritus, 1997–. Founder, Jason Project (use of remotely operated vehicles for deep-sea exploration), 1989; Founder, 1989, and Chm. of Bd, 1990–95, Jason Foundn for Educn. Expeditions include: exploration of Mid-ocean Ridge, 1974, of Galapagos Rift, 1977; discovery of polymetallic sulphides, 1979; Titanic, 1985; German battleship Bismarck, 1989; warships from lost fleet of Guadalcanal, 1992; Lusitania, 1994; Roman ships off coast of Tunisia, 1997; USS Yorktown, 1998; Black Sea, 2000. Presenter, Nat. Geographic Explorer TV prog., 1989–91; award-winning films for television incl. Secrets of the Titanic, 1985, and Last Voyage of the Lusitania, 1994. Many scientific, academic and multi-media awards and honours. *Publications:* Photographic Atlas of the Mid-Atlantic Ridge Rift Valley, 1977; (jtly) The Discovery of the Titanic, 1987 (trans. 10 langs); The Discovery of the Bismarck, 1990 (trans. 8 langs); Bright Shark (novel), 1992 (trans. 6 langs); The Lost Ships of Guadalcanal, 1993 (trans. 5 langs); (jtly) Exploring the Lusitania, 1995 (trans. 2 langs); Explorations (autobiog.), 1995 (trans. 2 langs); Lost Liners, 1997 (trans. 5 langs); History of Deep Submergence Science and Technology, 1998; At the Water's Edge: coastal images of America, 1998; Return to Midway, 1999; The Eternal Darkness: a personal history of deep-sea exploration, 2000; *for children:* Exploring the Titanic, 1988 (trans. 7 langs); The Lost Wreck of the Isis, 1990 (trans. 5 langs); Exploring the Bismarck, 1991 (trans. 2 langs); Explorer, 1992; Ghost Liners, 1998; contrib. many learned jls. *Address:* Ocean Exploration Center, Mystic Aquarium, 55 Coogan Blvd, Mystic, CT 06355, USA.

BALLARD, Ronald Alfred; Head of Technical Services of the Central Computers and Telecommunications Agency, HM Treasury (formerly Civil Service Department), 1980–85; consultant, 1985–95; voluntary work, Help the Aged, 1989–2007; *b* 17 Feb. 1925; *s* of Joseph William and Ivy Amy Ballard; *m* 1948, Eileen Margaret Edwards; one *d*. *Educ:* Univ. of Birmingham (BSc (Hons) Physics). National Service, RN, 1945–47. Admiralty Surface Weapons Establishment, Portsmouth: Scientific Officer, then Sen. Scientific Officer, Research and Development Seaborne Radar Systems, 1948–55; Application of Computers to Naval Comd and Control Systems, 1955–69; PSO, 1960, responsibilities for Action Data Automation (ADA), on HMS Eagle and destroyers; SPSO, to Head Computer Systems and Techniques in Civil Service Dept (Central Computers Agency in 1972), 1969; Head of Central Computers Facility, 1972–76; DCSO, to Head Technical Services Div. of Central Computers Agency, 1977; CSO(B), 1980–85. Treasurer: Sutton Assoc. for the Blind, 1985–98; Carshalton Assoc. for the Elderly, 2000–04; Asst Treas., League of Friends, Queen Mary's Hosp., Carshalton, 1986–95.

BALLENTYNE, Donald Francis, CMG 1985; HM Diplomatic Service, retired; Consul-General, Los Angeles, 1985–89; *b* 5 May 1929; *s* of late Henry Q. Ballentyne and Frances R. MacLaren; *m* 1950, Elizabeth Heywood, *d* of late Leslie A. Heywood; one *s* one *d*. *Educ:* Haberdashers' Aske's Hatcham Sch. FO, 1950–53; Berne and Ankara, 1953–56; Consul: Munich, 1957; Stanleyville, 1961; Cape Town, 1962; First Secretary: Luxembourg, 1965–69, Havana, 1969–72; FCO, 1972–74; Counsellor (Commercial), The Hague, 1974–78, Bonn, 1978–81; Counsellor, E Berlin, 1982–84. *Address:* Orford, Suffolk.

BALLMER, Steve; Owner, Los Angeles Clippers, since 2014; *b* March 1956; *m* Connie; three *c*. *Educ:* Harvard Univ. (BA); Stanford Univ. Graduate Sch. of Business. Asst Product Manager, Procter & Gamble Co.; joined Microsoft Corp., 1980; Vice-Pres., Marketing; Sen. Vice-Pres., Systems Software; Exec. Vice-Pres., Sales and Support, until 1998; Pres., 1998–2000; CEO, 2000–14. Dir, Accenture, 2001–06.

BALLS, Alastair Gordon, CB 1995; DL; Chairman, The International Centre for Life, since 2007 (Chief Executive, 1998–2007); *b* 18 March 1944; *s* of late Dr Ernest George Balls and Elspeth Russell Balls; *m* 1978, Beryl May Nichol; one *s* one *d*. *Educ:* Hamilton Acad.; Univ. of St Andrews (MA); Univ. of Manchester (MA). Economist: Treasury, Govt of Tanzania, 1966–68; Min. of Transport, UK, 1969–74; Sec., Adv. Cttee on Channel Tunnel, 1974–75; Sen. Econ. Adviser, HM Treasury, 1976–79; Asst Sec., Dept of Environment, 1979–83; Regl Dir, Depts of Environment and Transport (Northern Region), 1984–87; Chief Exec., Tyne and Wear Develt Corp., 1987–98. Chairman: Newcastle Gateshead Initiative, 2004–07; Northern Rock Foundn, 2006–. Non-executive Director: Northumbrian Water Ltd, 2002–11; N Star Venture Capital, 2004–10. Mem. Bd, HEFCE, 2006–12. Mem., ITC, 1998–2003. Chm., Alzheimer's Soc., 2007–13. Vice-Chm., Council, Univ. of Newcastle upon Tyne, 1994–2000. DL Tyne and Wear, 2009. *Recreations:* sailing, fishing, maintaining rusty old cars. *Address:* The International Centre for Life Trust, Times Square, Newcastle upon Tyne NE1 4EP.

BALLS, Rt Hon. Edward (Michael); PC 2007; Senior Fellow, Mossavar-Rahmani Center for Business and Government, Harvard Kennedy School, Harvard University, 2015–June 2016; *b* 25 Feb. 1967; *s* of Prof. Michael Balls and Carolyn Janet Balls; *m* 1998, Rt Hon. Yvette Cooper, *qv*; one *s* two *d*. *Educ:* Bawburgh Co. Primary Sch.; Crossdale Drive Primary Sch., Keyworth; Nottingham High Sch.; Keble Coll., Oxford (Keble Coll. Scholar; BA 1st Cl. Hons PPE; Hon. Fellow); John F. Kennedy Sch. of Govt, Harvard Univ. (Kennedy Scholar; MPA). Teaching Fellow, Dept of Econs, Harvard Univ., and Nat. Bureau of Econ. Res., 1989–90; econs leader writer and columnist, Financial Times, 1990–94; Econ. Advr to Shadow Chancellor, 1994–97; Sec., Labour Party Econ. Policy Commn, 1994–97; Econ. Advr to Chancellor of the Exchequer, HM Treasury, 1997–99; Chief Econ. Advr, HM Treasury, 1999–2004. Chm., Cttee of Deputies, IMF, 2002–04. Sen. Res. Fellow, Smith Inst., 2004–05. MP (Lab and Co-op) Normanton, 2005–10, Morley and Outwood, 2010–15; contested (Lab and Co-op) same seat, 2015. Econ. Sec. to HM Treasury, 2006–07; Sec. of State for Children, Schs and Families, 2007–10; Shadow Sec. of State for Educn, 2010, for Home Dept, 2010–11; Shadow Chancellor of the Exchequer, 2011–15. Chm., Fabian Soc., 2007. Co-Chair, Commn on Inclusive Prosperity, Center for Amer. Progress, 2013–15 (Report, 2015). Hon. LLD Nottingham, 2003. Spectator Parliamentarian of the Year Award, 2010; Opposition Politician of the Year, Political Studies Assoc., 2011. *Publications:* (Principal Ed.) World Bank Development Report, 1995; (ed with Gus O'Donnell) Reforming Britain's Economic and Financial Policy, 2002; (ed with Joe Grice and Gus O'Donnell) Microeconomic Reform in Britain, 2004; contribs to learned jls, incl. Scottish Jl Pol Economy, World Economics, and to reports published by Fabian Soc. and Social Justice Commn. *Recreations:* learning the piano, running marathons, playing football with daughters Ellie and Maddy and son Joel. *Address:* (until June 2016) Harvard Kennedy School, 79 John F. Kennedy Street, Cambridge, MA 02138, USA. *E:* ed@edballs.com.

BALLS, Rt Hon. Yvette; *see* Cooper, Rt Hon. Y.

BALMER, Colin Victor, CB 2001; Managing Director, Cabinet Office, 2003–06; *b* 22 Aug. 1946; *s* of Peter Lionel Balmer and Adelaide Currie Balmer; *m* 1978, Frances Mary Montrésor (marr. diss. 2006); two *s* one *d*; *m* 2006, Lesley Ann Pasricha. *Educ:* Liverpool Inst. High Sch. War Office, 1963, later Ministry of Defence: Asst Private Sec. to Minister of State, 1972; Private Sec. to Parly Under-Sec. of State (RAF), 1973; Civil Advr to GOC N Ireland, 1973; Cabinet Office, 1977; Private Sec. to Minister of State (Defence Procurement), 1980; UK Delegn to NATO, 1982; MoD 1984; Minister (Defence Materiel), Washington, 1990; Ministry of Defence: Asst Under-Sec. of State, 1992–96; Dep. Under-Sec. of State (Resources, Programmes and Finance), 1996–98; Finance Dir, 1998–2003. Non-executive Director: QinetiQ Gp plc, 2006–14; Royal Mint, 2007–13. *Recreations:* golf, gardening, bridge, rock and roll music, playing guitar (badly) and ukulele. *E:* colinvbalmer@btinternet.com.

BALMER, Derek Rigby, RWA 1970; painter and photographer; President, Royal West of England Academy, 2001–10; *b* 28 Dec. 1934; *s* of Geoffrey Johnstone Balmer and Barbara

Winifred Balmer (*née* Rigby); *m* 1962, Elizabeth Mary Rose Hawkins; one *s* one *d*. *Educ:* Waterloo House Sch.; Sefton Park Sch.; West of England Coll. of Art. *One-man exhibitions* include: Fimbarrus Gall., Bath, 1960; Arnolfini Gall., Bristol, 1966, 1968; City Art Gall., Bristol, 1975; Sharples Gall., RWA, 1980; Anthony Hepworth Fine Art, Bath, 1992, 1994, 2005, London, 1994, 2000; Gisela van Beers, London, 1992; Montpelier Sandelson, London, 1995; Smelik and Stokking Galls, Holland, 1996, 1998, 2000, 2001; New Gall., RWA, 2003; Campden Gall., Chipping Campden, 2005, 2008, 2011; Catto Gall., London, 2010, 2012, 2014, 2016; Cube Gall., London, 2013; Bath Contemporary, Bath, 2015; *retrospective exhibition:* President's Eye: 1950–2007, RWA Galls, 2007; *group exhibitions* include: Arnolfini Gall., Bristol, 1963, 1964, 1983; Arts Council Touring Exhibn, 1967; Leicester Galls, London, 1968, 1969, 1970; Victoria Art Gall., Bath, 1970; New Art Centre, London, 1982; Louise Hallet Gall., London, 1985; London Contemp. Art Fair, annually 1990–; Campden Gall., Chipping Campden, 2004; RA Summer Show, 2005–10; Browse & Darby Gall., London, 2010; Hilton Fine Art, Bath, 2014. Chm., RWA, 1997–2000. Pro-Chancellor, UWE, 2003–10. Hon. DArts UWE, 2001. Hon. RA 2003. *Publications:* (monograph) Derek Balmer: a singular vision, 2012. *Recreations:* art history, reading, cricket, walking Newfoundland dogs and Leonberger dog. *Address:* Mulberry House, 12 Avon Grove, Sneyd Park, Bristol BS9 1PJ. *T:* (0117) 968 2953; c/o Catto Gallery, Heath Street, Hampstead, NW3 1DP. *T:* (020) 7435 6660. *Club:* Chelsea Arts.

BALMFORD, Prof. Andrew Paul, PhD; FRS 2011; Professor of Conservation Science, University of Cambridge, since 2007; Fellow, Clare College, Cambridge, since 2008; *b* Birmingham, 8 March 1963; *s* of John Edwin Balmford and Marie Diana Ruth Balmford; *m* 1989, Sarah Blakeman; two *s*. *Educ:* King Edward's Sch., Birmingham; Clare Coll., Cambridge (BA 1985; PhD 1990). Research Fellow: Girton Coll., Cambridge, 1991–92; Inst. of Zool., London, 1993–95; Lectr in Zool., Dept of Animal and Plant Scis, Univ. of Sheffield, 1995–98; University of Cambridge: Univ. Lectr, 1998–2001; Sen. Lectr, 2001–04; Reader in Conservation Sci., 2004–07. Pola Pasvolsky Prof. of Conservation Biol., Univ. of Cape Town, 2004–05. Marsh Award for Conservation Biol., Zool Soc. of London, 2000. *Publications:* Conservation in a Changing World (ed jtly), 1998; Wild Hope: on the frontlines of conservation success, 2012; contribs to learned jls. *Recreations:* enjoying wild nature, especially with my family. *Address:* Department of Zoology, Downing Street, Cambridge CB2 3EJ. *T:* (01223) 336600.

BALMFORTH, Dr David John, CEng, FICE; Executive Technical Director, MWH, 2007–15; President, Institution of Civil Engineers, 2014–15 (Vice President, 2009–14); *b* Grappenhall, Cheshire, 3 Feb. 1947; *s* of Philip and Ella Balmforth; *m* 1968, Gillian Waller; three *s* one *d*. *Educ:* Botelier Grammar Sch., Warrington; Hampton Grammar Sch., Middx; Bristol Univ. (BSc 1st Cl. Hons Civil Engrg 1968); Sheffield Univ. (PhD Civil Engrg 1976). CEng 1983; FCIWEM 1987; FICE 1999. Lectr, 1970–72, Sen. Lectr, 1972–87, Sheffield Poly.; Principal Lectr, 1988, Dean, Faculty of the Envmt, 1988–89, Sheffield City Poly.; Dir, Sch. of Construction, Sheffield Hallam Univ., 1989–99; Sen. Principal Engr, MWH, 1999–2007. Vis. Prof., Imperial Coll. London, 2003–. Ed., Jl Flood Risk Mgt, 2007–13. Pres., Engrg Section, British Sci. Acad., 1998–99. Non-exec. Dir, Construction Industry Res. and Information Assoc., 1999–2010. *Publications:* contribs to technical jls and conf. procs on flood risk mgt. *Recreation:* canal boating. *Address:* Institution of Civil Engineers, One Great George Street, SW1P 3AA. *T:* (020) 7665 2002, *Fax:* (020) 7222 0267. *E:* david.balmforth@ice.org.uk.

BALNIEL, Lord; Anthony Robert Lindsay; DL; Partner, James Hambro and Partners, since 2010; *b* 24 Nov. 1958; *s* and *heir* of Earl of Crawford and Balcarres, *qv*; *m* 1989, Nicola A., *y d* of Antony Bicket; two *s* two *d*. *Educ:* Eton Coll.; Univ. of Edinburgh. Dir, 1987–2009, CEO, 2004–07, J. O. Hambro Investment Mgt. DL Fife, 2013. *Heir: s* Master of Lindsay, *qv*. *Address:* Balcarres, Colinsburgh, Leven, Fife KY9 1HN. *Clubs:* New (Edinburgh); XII.

BALOGUN-LYNCH, Christopher Charles, FRCSE, FRCOG; Consultant Obstetrician and Gynaecological Surgeon, Milton Keynes General Hospital, 1984–2010, now Emeritus; *b* 1 Oct. 1947; *s* of late Prof. Prince E. Balogun-Lynch and Jane A. Balogun-Lynch; *m* 1986, Julia Caroline Klinner; one *s* three *d*. *Educ:* Christ Church, Oxford (MA); St Bartholomew's Hosp., London (MB BS 1974). FRCSE 1979; FRCOG 1991; MCIArb 1999; QDR 1994. Surgeon in private practice, Harley St, 1984–. Royal Coll. Tutor and Trainer in Minimal Access Surgery, 1995–2010; Internat. Lectr and Simulation Trainer in post-partum haemorrhage, 2008–. Hon. Vis. Gynaecological Cancer Surgeon, Northampton Gen. Hosp., 2001. Introduced carbon dioxide laser, YAG laser and keyhole surgery techniques to Milton Keynes Hosp., 1985–2003; innovator of new technology and obstetric and gynaecological surgical techniques incl. the control of post-partum haemorrhage now in worldwide application. Vis. Prof., Cranfield Univ., 2006–; has lectured in Sydney, Cape Town, USA, Italy and various centres in UK, 1988–. Obstetrics and gynaecol. undergrad. Trainer and Examiner, Oxford Univ., 2007–. Publications Referee: British Jl Obstetrics and Gynaecol.; Eur. Jl Obstetrics and Gynaecol.; Internat. Jl Obstetrics and Gynaecol.; American Jl Obstetrics and Gynaecol. Mem., WHO Commn for Women's Health Improvement, 2010–; Hon. Comr, WHO Women's Health Prog., 2011–. Founder and Chair, Myrtle Peach Trust for Gynaecological Cancer Prevention and Res., 1985–. Liveryman, Soc. of Apothecaries, 1983–. MAE 1992; FLLA 1997. Fellow, Royal Soc. of St George, 2002. DUniv Open, 1997. Serono Labs (UK) Award for Assisted Conception, 1987. Grand Commanding Officer, Republic of Sierra Leone, 2007. *Publications:* (jtly) The Surgical Management of Post Partum Haemorrhage, 2005; (ed jtly) A Textbook of Postpartum Hemorrhage, 2006; (ed jtly) A Textbook of Preconceptional Medicine and Management, 2012; numerous contribs to medical, surgical, scientific, clinical, endoscopic surgery, medico-legal and educational papers in leading jls. *Recreations:* Rugby, cricket, occasional golf, family outings. *Address:* Linford Court, Church Lane, Little Linford, Bucks MK19 7EB. *T:* and *Fax:* (01908) 615717. *Clubs:* Athenæum, Royal Automobile.

BALSDON, Paula; *see* Hodges, P.

BALSHAW, Maria Jane, CBE 2015; DPhil; Director: Whitworth Art Gallery, University of Manchester, since 2006; Manchester City Galleries, since 2011; *b* 24 Jan. 1970; *d* of Walter and Colette Balshaw; one *s* one *d*; *m* Nicholas Merriman. *Educ:* Univ. of Liverpool (BA Hons Eng. and Cultural Studies 1991); Univ. of Sussex (MA Critical Theory 1992; DPhil African American Visual Culture and Lit. 1997). Lectr in Cultural Studies, UC Northampton, 1993–97; Res. Fellow in American Urban Culture, Univ. of Birmingham, 1997–2002; Dir, Creative Partnerships Birmingham, 2002–05; Dir of External Relns and Develt, Arts Council England, W Midlands, 2005–06. Mem. Bd, Arts Council England, 2014–. Clore Leadership Fellow, 2004–05. *Publications:* Urban Space and Representation (ed with Liam Kennedy), 1999; Looking for Harlem: African American urban culture, 2000; (ed jtly) City Sites: multimedia essays on Chicago and New York, 2000. *Recreations:* dancing (especially in kitchen with my kids), gardening, travelling anywhere, visiting art galleries, cooking, eating out. *Address:* The Whitworth Art Gallery, University of Manchester, Oxford Road, Manchester M15 6ER. *T:* (0161) 275 5740. *E:* maria.balshaw@manchester.ac.uk.

BALSOM, Alison Louise; classical trumpet soloist, since 2001; Professor of Trumpet, Guildhall School of Music and Drama, since 2006; music educator, campaigner, producer, arranger and presenter; *b* 7 Oct. 1978; *d* of William and Zena Balsom. *Educ:* Tannery Drift Primary Sch.; Greneway Middle Sch.; Meridian Sch., Royston; Hills Rd Sixth Form Coll., Cambridge; Guildhall Sch. of Music and Drama (BMus Hons 2001; FGS 2012); Paris Conservatoire. Has appeared as soloist with many of world's major orchestras incl. Last Night of the Proms, 2009. Young Concert Artists Trust Artist, 2001–04; BBC New Generation Artist, 2004–06. Commnd, produced and appeared in Gabriel, Shakespeare's Globe, 2013. Patron: Cherubim Music Trust, 2010–; Mayor's Fund for Young Musicians, 2011–; OHMI Trust, 2012–; Brass for Africa, 2013–. Pres., Deal Fest., 2014. Hon. DA Anglia Ruskin, 2009. Brass Winner, BBC Young Musician of Year, 1998; Gramophone Award, Classic FM Listeners' Choice, 2006; Young British Classical Performer, 2006, Female Artist of the Year, 2009, 2011, Classical Brit Awards; Echo Klassik Award, Deutsche Phono-Akademie, 2007, 2010, 2012; Artist of the Year, Gramophone Awards, 2013; Silver Clef Award, Nordoff Robbins, 2013. *Recreations:* sailing, construction and design, furniture restoration. *Address:* c/o Alison Balsom Enquiries, 32 Newmarket Road, Royston, Herts SG8 7EL.

BALSTON, Michael Edward; Senior Director, Balston Agius Ltd (formerly Balston & Company Ltd), since 1983; *b* London, 11 June 1944; *s* of Comdr Edward Francis Balston, DSO, RN and Diana Beatrice Louise Balston (*née* Ferrers); *m* 1978, Meriel Frances Stirling-Aird; two *s* one *d*. *Educ:* Downside Sch.; BRNC Dartmouth; Christ's Coll., Cambridge (BA 1968; DipArch 1972); Thames Poly. (DipLA). RIBA 1972; CMLI 1979. Landscape Architect and Planner, Robert Matthew Johnson-Marshall and Partners, 1972–77; Partner, Lennox-Boyd and Balston, 1978–83. Mem., Panel, Europa Nostra UK Awards, 1999–2003. Royal Horticultural Society: Gardens Judge, 1993–2012; Mem. Council, 2003–12; Vice Pres., 2013–. *Publications:* The Well-Furnished Garden, 1986; Ten Landscapes, 2001. *Recreations:* gardening, arts. *Address:* Balston Agius Ltd, Manor Farm Lane, Patney, Devizes, Wilts SN10 3RB. *T:* (01380) 848181, *Fax:* (01380) 848189. *E:* mb@balstonagius.co.uk.

BALTIMORE, David, PhD; Robert Andrews Millikan Professor of Biology, California Institute of Technology, since 2006 (President, 1997–2006, now Emeritus); *b* New York, 7 March 1938; *s* of Richard and Gertrude Baltimore; *m* 1968, Alice Huang; one *d*. *Educ:* Swarthmore Coll. (BA 1960); Rockefeller Univ. (PhD 1964). Postdoctoral Fellow, MIT, 1963–64; Albert Einstein Coll. of Med., NY, 1964–65; Research Associate, Salk Inst., La Jolla, Calif, 1965–68; Massachusetts Institute of Technology: Associate Prof., 1968–72; Amer. Cancer Soc. Prof. of Microbiol., 1973–83; Prof. of Biology, 1972–90; Dir, Whitehead Inst., 1982–90; Prof., 1990–94, Pres., 1990–91, Rockefeller Univ.; Ivan R. Cottrell Prof. of Molecular Biol. and Immunol., MIT, 1994–97. FAAAS 1980 (Pres., 2007–08; Chm., 2008–09). Chm., AIDS Vaccine Adv. Cttee, NIH, 1996–2002. Member: Nat. Acad. of Scis, 1974; Amer. Acad. of Arts and Scis, 1974; Pontifical Acad. of Scis, 1978; Foreign Mem., Royal Soc., 1987. Eli Lilly Award in Microbiology and Immunology, 1971; US Steel Foundn Award in Molecular Biology, 1974; (jtly) Nobel Prize for Physiology or Medicine, 1975; US Nat. Medal of Science, 1999; Warren Alpert Foundn Prize, 2000; AMA Scientific Achievement Award, 2002. *Address:* California Institute of Technology, 147–75, 1200 E California Boulevard, Pasadena, CA 91125, USA.

BAMBERG, Harold Rolf, CBE 1968; FRAeS; Chairman: Glos Air Ltd, 1985–2010; Via Nova Properties Ltd, 1985–2011; Bamberg Farms Ltd, since 1996; *b* 17 Nov. 1923; *m* 1957 (marr. diss. 1990); one *s* two *d*, and one *s* one *d* of a former marriage. *Educ:* Hampstead. Former Chm., British Independent Air Transport Assoc.; Life Vice Pres., British Business and Gen. Aviation (formerly GAMTA) (Chm., 1978–80); former Director: Cunard Steamship Co.; BOAC Cunard, etc; Founder: British Eagle International Airlines, 1948; Lunn Poly Ltd, 1956. Mem., NFU. FRAeS 1993. Kt, Order of Merit, Italian Republic, 1960. *Recreations:* horses, agriculture. *Address:* 18 Cheniston Court, Ridgemount Road, Ascot, Berks SL5 9SF. *T:* (01344) 625950, *Fax:* (01344) 872285. *E:* h.bamberg489@btinternet.com. *Club:* Guards' Polo (Life Mem.).

BAMERT, Matthias; conductor; Principal Conductor and Artistic Advisor, Malaysian Philharmonic Orchestra, 2005–08; Chief Conductor, West Australian Symphony Orchestra, 2004–06; *b* Switzerland, 5 July 1942; *m* 1969, Susan Exline; one *s* one *d*. Asst conductor to Leopold Stokowski, 1970–71; Resident Conductor, Cleveland Orch., USA, 1971–78; Music Director: Swiss Radio Orch., Basel, 1977–83; London Mozart Players, 1993–2000. Principal Guest Conductor: Scottish Nat. Orch., 1985–90; NZ SO, 2000–02; Associate Guest Conductor, RPO, 2001–. Director: Musica Nova fest., Glasgow, 1985–90; Lucerne Fest., 1992–98. Has worked with orchestras incl. LPO, BBC Philharmonic, BBC SO, CBSO, Orchestre de Paris, Rotterdam Philharmonic, Cleveland Orchestra, Pittsburgh Symphony, Houston Symphony, Montreal Symphony, and appears regularly at Promenade concerts; tours each season in Europe, N America, Australia, NZ, Hong Kong and Japan, and has made over 60 recordings. *Address:* MusicVine, 2576 Broadway, #239, New York, NY 10025, USA.

BAMFORD, family name of **Baron Bamford**.

BAMFORD, Baron *cr* 2013 (Life Peer), of Daylesford in the County of Gloucestershire and of Wootton in the County of Staffordshire; **Anthony Paul Bamford,** Kt 1990; DL; Chairman, J. C. Bamford Group, since 1975; *b* 23 Oct. 1945; *s* of late Joseph Cyril Bamford, CBE; *m* 1974, Carole Gray Whitt (OBE 2006); two *s* one *d*. *Educ:* Ampleforth Coll.; Grenoble Univ. FIAgrE 2003. Joined JCB, 1964. Dir, Tarmac, 1987–95. Member: Design Council, 1987–89; President's Cttee, CBI, 1986–88. Pres., Staffs Agricl Soc., 1987–88. Pres., Burton on Trent Cons. Assoc., 1987–90. High Sheriff, Staffs, 1985–86. DL Staffs, 1989. Hon. FCGI 1993; Hon. FCSD 1994; Hon. FIED 2008; Hon. FREng 2014. Hon. MEng Birmingham, 1987; DUniv Keele, 1988; Hon. DSc: Cranfield, 1994; Harper Adams Univ. Coll., 2010; Hon. DTech: Staffordshire, 1998; Loughborough, 2002; Hon. DBA Robert Gordon, 1996. Young Exporter of the Year, 1972; Young Businessman of the Year, 1979; Top Exporter of the Year, 1995; Entrepreneurial Award, British Amer. Business Inc., 2003; Hall of Fame, Assoc. of Equipment Manufacturers, USA, 2008. Chevalier, l'Ordre National du Mérite (France), 1989; Commendatore al merito della Repubblica Italiana, 1995. *Recreations:* farming, gardening. *Address:* c/o J. C. Bamford Excavators Ltd, Rocester, Uttoxeter, Staffs ST14 5JP. *Clubs:* White's, British Racing Drivers'.

BAMFORD, Louis Neville Jules; Legal Executive with Margetts & Ritchie, Solicitors, Birmingham, since 1960; *b* 2 July 1932; *s* of Neville Barnes Bamford and Elise Marie Bamford; unmarried. *Educ:* local schools in Birmingham. Member (Lab): Birmingham CC, 1971–74; W Midlands CC, 1974–86 (Chm., 1981–82); Birmingham CC, 1986–2002 (Chm., Gen. Purposes Cttee; Chief Whip, Lab Gp; Hon. Alderman, 2002). *Recreations:* sport, music. *Address:* Apartment 25, Tudor Lodge, 331–335 Warwick Road, Solihull B92 7AA; (office) Coleridge Chambers, 177 Corporation Street, Birmingham B4 6RL.

BAMPFYLDE, family name of **Baron Poltimore**.

BANATVALA, Prof. Jehangir Edalji, (Prof. Jangu Edal Banatvala), CBE 1999; MD; FRCP, FRCPath, FMedSci; Professor of Clinical Virology, Guy's, King's College and St Thomas' Hospitals Medical and Dental School, 1975–99, now Emeritus; Hon. Consultant Virologist, Guy's and St Thomas' Hospital Trust, 1975–99; *b* 7 Jan. 1934; *s* of Dr Edal Banatvala and Ratti Banatvala (*née* Shroff); *m* 1959, Roshan (*née* Mugaseth); three *s* (one *d* decd). *Educ:* Forest Sch., London; Gonville and Caius Coll., Cambridge (MA, MB BChir 1958; MD (Whitby Medal) 1964); London Hosp. Med. Coll. DPH London 1961 (Dist.); DCH 1961; MRCPath 1965, FRCPath 1977; MRCP 1986, FRCP 1995. Polio Fund Res. Fellow, Univ. of Cambridge, 1961–64; Fulbright Schol. and Amer. Thoracic Soc. Fellow, Yale Univ., 1964–65; Sen. Lectr, 1965–71, Reader, 1971–75, St Thomas' Hosp. Med. Sch., then UMDS of Guy's and St Thomas' Hosp.; Chm., St Thomas' Hosp. Mgt Team and Med. Adv. Cttee, 1983–84. Royal College of Pathologists: Registrar, 1985–87; Vice Pres., 1987–90; Mem. Council, 1993–96; Member: Council, Med. Defence Union, 1987–2004; Jt Cttee on Vaccination and Immunisation, DoH, 1986–95; PHLS Bd, 1995–2001; Chm., Adv.

Gp on Hepatitis, DoH, 1990–98; Mem., European Soc. of Clin. Virology, 1997–; Pres., European Assoc. Against Virus Disease, 1981–83. Hon. Cons. Microbiologist to the Army, 1992–97. Dir, Clinical Pathology Accreditation (UK) Ltd, 1997–2002. Chm., Res. Cttee, CFS Foundn, 2008–; Trustee, Hepatitis B Foundn UK, 2008–. Vis. Prof., Univ. of Auckland Med. Sch., 1983. Examiner, Univs of London, Cambridge, Colombo, West Indies and Riyadh. Mem. Senate, London Univ., 1987–94; Governor: Forest Sch., E17, 1993–2014; Mill Hill Sch., 2001–14. Founder FMedSci 1998. Freeman, City of London, 1987; Liveryman, Co. of Apothecaries, 1986. *Publications:* (ed) Current Problems in Clinical Virology, 1971; (ed jtly) Principles and Practice of Clinical Virology, 1987, 6th edn 2009; (ed) Viral Infections of the Heart, 1993; papers in gen. and specialised med. jls on intrauterine and perinatal infections, blood-borne virus infections, viral vaccines, etc. *Recreations:* watching sports in which one no longer performs (rowing, cricket), playing tennis, music, good company in good restaurants. *Address:* Little Acre, Church End, Henham, Bishop's Stortford, Herts CM22 6AN. *T:* (01279) 850386. *Clubs:* Athenæum, MCC; Leander (Henley-on-Thames); Hawks (Hon. Mem.) (Cambridge).

BANBURY, family name of **Baron Banbury of Southam.**

BANBURY OF SOUTHAM, 3rd Baron *cr* 1924, of Southam; **Charles William Banbury;** Bt 1902; *b* 29 July 1953; *s* of 2nd Baron Banbury of Southam and of Hilda Ruth, *d* of late A. H. R. Carr; *S* father, 1981; *m* 1st, 1984, Lucinda Trehearne (marr. diss. 1986); 2nd, 1989, Inger Marianne Norton; three *d*. *Educ:* Eton College. *Heir:* none. *Address:* The Mill, Fossebridge, Glos GL54 3JN.

BANCROFT, Anna Louise; Her Honour Judge Bancroft; a Circuit Judge, since 2013; *b* Blackburn, 15 March 1961; *d* of Russell and Valerie Bancroft; *m* 1988, Stuart Henry MacDonald Denney, *qv*; one *s*. *Educ:* Casterton Sch., Cumbria; St Anne's Coll., Oxford (MA); Univ. of Westminster (Grad. DipLaw). Called to the Bar, Inner Temple, 1985; in practice as barrister, Deans Court Chambers, Manchester, 1985–2013; a Recorder, 2002–13. Governor: Casterton Sch., 2007–13; Sedbergh Sch., 2013–. *Recreation:* choral singing. *Address:* Liverpool Civil and Family Court, 35 Vernon Street, Liverpool, Merseyside L2 2BX.

BAND, Adm. Sir Jonathon, GCB 2008 (KCB 2002); DL; non-executive Director: Carnival Corporation and Carnival plc, since 2010; Lockheed Martin UK, since 2010; *b* 2 Feb. 1950; *s* of Victor and Muriel Band; *m* 1979, Sarah Asbury; two *d*. *Educ:* Brambletye Sch.; Haileybury Coll.; Exeter Univ. (BA 1972). Served: HMS Soberton, 1979–81; Fleet HQ, 1981–83; HMS Phoebe, 1983–85; MoD, 1986–89; HMS Norfolk and Ninth Frigate Sqn, 1989–91; MoD, 1991–95; HMS Illustrious, 1995–97; ACNS, MoD, 1997–99; Team Leader, Defence Trng and Educn Study, MoD, 2000–01; Dep. C-in-C Fleet, 2001–02; C-in-C Fleet, 2002–05; Comdr Allied Naval Forces N, 2002–04; Comdr Allied Maritime Component Comd Northwood, 2004–06; Chief of Naval Staff and First Sea Lord, 2006–09; First and Principal Naval ADC to the Queen, 2006–09. Chairman: Nat. Mus. of RN, 2010–; White Ensign Assoc., 2013–. Younger Brother, Trinity House, 1998–. Liveryman, Shipwrights' Co., 2006–. DL Hants, 2009. *Recreations:* family dominated, including boating, tennis. *Clubs:* Naval, Buck's; Royal Naval and Royal Albert Yacht (Portsmouth).

BAND, Thomas Mollison, FSAScot; Chairman, Perthshire Housing Association, 2003–09 (Director, since 1994); *b* 28 March 1934; *s* of late Robert Boyce Band and Elizabeth Band; *m* 1959, Jean McKenzie Brien (*d* 2011); one *s* two *d*. *Educ:* Perth Academy. National Service, RAF, 1952–54. Joined Civil Service, 1954; Principal, BoT, 1969; Sen. Principal, Dept of Industry, 1973; Scottish Econ. Planning Dept, 1975, Asst Sec., 1976; Scottish Development Dept, 1978; Scottish Office, Finance, 1981; Dir, Historic Bldgs and Monuments, Scottish Develt Dept, 1984–87; Chief Exec., Scottish Tourist Bd, 1987–94. Chairman: Made in Scotland Ltd, 1994–95; Anderson Enterprises Ltd, 1994–98; Edinburgh Europa Ltd, 1994–98; Perth Repertory Th. Ltd, 1995–2002. Dir, Edinburgh Telford Coll., 1989–98. Chm., Industrial Cttee, Napier Univ. (formerly Napier Poly. of Edinburgh), 1989–95. Gov., Queen Margaret UC, Edinburgh, 1995–2002. President: Perthshire Soc. of Natural Sci., 2004–07; Scots Lang. Soc., 2004–08; Eur. Bureau of Lesser Used Langs (UK), 2005–08. FRSA 1993. *Recreations:* ski-ing, gardening. *Address:* Heathfield, Pitcairngreen, Perthshire PH1 3LS. *T:* (01738) 583403.

BANDA, Prof. Enric, DSc; President, Euroscience, 2006–12; *b* 21 June 1948; *s* of Emilio and Maria Banda; *m* 1st, 1973 (marr. diss. 1982); 2nd, 1983, Gemma Lienas, writer. *Educ:* Univ. of Barcelona (BSc Physics 1974; DSc Physics 1979). Researcher, ETH-Zürich, 1980–83; Head, Geophysical Survey, Catalan Govt, 1983–87; Res. Prof., Consejo Superior de Investigaciones Científicas, 1987; Head, Inst. of Earth Sciences, Barcelona, 1988–91; Sec. Gen., Nat. Plan R&D, Spain, 1994; Sec. of State for Universities and Research, Spain, 1995–96; Sec. Gen., ESF, 1998–2003. Dir, Catalan Res. and Innovation Foundn, 2004; Dir of Sci., Res. and Envmt, La Caixa Foundn, 2009–11. Chevalier de la Légion d'Honneur (France), 1997. *Publications:* more than 150 scientific papers.

BANERJEE, Urmila, (Millie), CBE 2002; Chairman and Member, British Transport Police Authority, since 2008; Chairman, Working Links, since 2011; *b* Calcutta, 30 June 1946; *d* of late Shankar Ray-Chaudhuri and of Maya Ray-Chaudhuri; *m* 1st, 1970, Pradip Banerjee (marr. diss. 1985); 2nd, 1991, Christopher Anthony Seymour (*d* 2014). *Educ:* University Coll. London (BSc Zool.); Poly. of N London (DMS); Massachusetts Inst. of Technol. (Sen. Exec. Prog.). Post Office Telecommunications: Operational Manager, Internat. Telephones, 1970–76; Tutor, Telecoms Mgt Coll., 1976–79; Exec. Asst to MD Telecoms, 1979–84; British Telecommunications: Dep. Gen. Manager, London SW, 1984–88; Dist Gen. Manager, London Networks, 1988–90; Director: Personnel, Worldwide Networks, 1990–92; Integrated Systems, 1992–95; Pricing, 1995; Vice Pres., Prog. Mgt, 1995–97, Exec. Vice Pres., Ops, 1997–2000, ICO Global Communications. Non-exec. Dir, Channel 4 TV, 2000–02. Mem. Bd, Ofcom, 2003–11; Chairman: Postwatch, 2005–08; Postal Services Commn, 2011; non-executive Director: Prison Service Agency, 1990–95; Focus Central London, 1997–2000; Cabinet Office Bd, 1999–2005; Sector Skills Develt Agency, 2001–04; Strategic Rail Authy, 2002–05; E London and City Primary Care Cluster (formerly Newham PCT), 2009–12; Member: Nurses and Allied Professions Pay Rev. Bd, 1999–2002; Judicial Appts Commn, 2001–05; Bd, Barts Health, 2012–13; Bd, E London Foundn Trust, 2014–. Gov., S Bank Univ., 1993–98; Mem. Adv. Bd, Tanaka Imperial Business Sch., 2003–07. Trustee, 2001–07, and Chm., 2005–07, Carnegie Trust UK; Gov., Peabody Trust, 2008–11; Chm., Nominet Trust, 2011–14. High Sheriff, Greater London, 2012–13. *Recreations:* cooking, France. *Address:* 14 Marlborough Street, SW3 3PS. *T:* (020) 7581 1399, *Fax:* (020) 7581 5155. *E:* millie.banerjee@btinternet.com.

BANFIELD, John Martin, FEI; Deputy Chairman and non-executive Director, Surrey and Borders NHS Trust, 2002–11; *b* 15 Nov. 1947; *s* of late Jack Banfield and Peggy Winifred Banfield (*née* Parker); *m* 1978, Mary Gerrey Morton; one *s* one *d*. *Educ:* Haberdashers' Aske's; St John's Coll., Cambridge (MA Geography). FEI (FInstPet 1996). Joined Mobil Oil Co., 1969; Man. Dir, Mobil Cyprus, 1986–87; Director: Mobil Benelux, 1988–89; Mobil Oil Co., 1990–91; Pres., Mobil Benelux, 1992; Dir, Mobil Germany, 1993; Chm., Mobil Oil Co., 1994–96; Dir, Mobil Europe, 1996–2001. Vice-Pres., Inst. of Petroleum, 1996–99; Pres., Oil Industries Club, 1997–98. Mem., Standing Cttee, Dio. of Cyprus and the Gulf, 2007–; Hon. Lay Canon, St Christopher's Cathedral, Bahrain, 2011–. Chm. of Govs, Box Hill Sch., 2009–. *Recreations:* music, sailing, travel. *Address:* Garden Corner, Mickleham, Surrey. *Club:* MCC.

BANGAY, Deborah Joanna Janet; QC 2006; *b* 29 Nov. 1957; *d* of Joe and Janet Bangay; *m* (marr. diss. 2001); two *s* (twins). *Educ:* Cranwell Primary Sch.; Sleaford High Sch.; Wycombe High Sch.; Univ. of Exeter (LLB Hons 1979); Council of Legal Educn. Called to the Bar, Gray's Inn, 1981; in practice, specialising in family law. *Recreations:* swimming, football, fly fishing, theatre, ballet. *Address:* 1 Hare Court, Temple, EC4Y 7BE. *T:* (020) 7797 7070, *Fax:* (020) 7797 7435. *E:* bangay@1hc.com. *Club:* Soho House.

BANGEMANN, Dr Martin; a Member, European Commission (formerly Commission of the European Community), 1989–99 (a Vice-President, 1989–93); *b* 15 Nov. 1934; *s* of Martin Bangemann and Lotte Telge; *m* 1962, Renate Bauer; three *s* two *d*. *Educ:* Univ. of Tübingen; Univ. of Munich (DJur). Lawyer, 1964–. Mem., Bundestag, 1972–80 and 1986–89; Mem., European Parliament, 1973–84; Minister of Econs, FRG, 1984–88. Freie Demokratische Partei: Mem., 1963–; Chm., 1985–88. Fed. Cross of Merit with star (Germany); Bavarian Order of Merit.

BANGOR, 8th Viscount *cr* 1781 (Ire.); **William Maxwell David Ward;** Baron 1770 (Ire.); antiquarian bookseller; *b* 9 Aug. 1948; *s* of 7th Viscount Bangor and his 3rd wife, Leila Mary Heaton (*d* 1959); *S* father, 1993; *m* 1976, Sarah Mary Malet Bradford, *qv*. *Educ:* University Coll., London. *Recreations:* history, music, antiquity, Bolton Wanderers. *Heir: presumptive: b* Hon. (Edward) Nicholas Ward [*b* 16 Jan. 1953; *m* 1985, Rachel Mary, *d* of Hon. Hugh Waldorf Astor; two *d*]. *Address:* 31 Britannia Road, SW6 2HJ. *Club:* Chelsea Arts.

BANGOR, Viscountess; *see* Bradford, S. M. M. W.

BANGOR, Bishop of, since 2008; **Rt Rev. Andrew Thomas Griffith John;** *b* 1964; *m* Caroline; one *s* three *d*. *Educ:* Ysgol Penglais, Aberystwyth; Univ. of Wales (LLB 1986); Univ. of Nottingham (BA Theology 1988); St John's Coll., Nottingham (Dip. in Pastoral Studies 1989). Ordained deacon, 1989, priest, 1990; Asst Curate, St Mary's, Cardigan with Mwnt and Y Ferwg, 1989–91; Asst Curate, 1991–92, Team Vicar/Minister, 1992–99, St Michael's, Aberystwyth; Vicar: St David, Henfynyw with Aberaeron and Llanddewi Aberarth, 1999–2006; St Patrick, Pencarreg and Llanycrwys, 2006–08; Archdeacon of Cardigan, 2006–08. *Address:* Ty'r Esgob, Upper Garth Road, Bangor LL57 2SS. *T:* (01248) 362895. *E:* bishop.bangor@churchinwales.org.uk.

BANGOR, Dean of; *no new appointment at time of going to press.*

BANHAM, Sir John (Michael Middlecott), Kt 1992; DL; Chairman: Future Homes Commission, 2011–13; Innoveas International Ltd, since 2014; *b* 22 Aug. 1940; *s* of late Terence Middlecott Banham, FRCS and Belinda Joan Banham, CBE; *m* 1965, Frances Barbara Molyneux Favell; one *s* two *d*. *Educ:* Charterhouse; Queens' Coll., Cambridge (Foundn Schol.; BA 1st cl. in Natural Scis, 1962; Hon. Fellow, 1989). Asst Principal, HM Foreign Service, 1962–64; Dir of Marketing, Wallcoverings Div., Reed International, 1965–69; McKinsey & Co. Inc.: Associate, 1969–75; Principal, 1975–80; Dir, 1980–83. Controller, Audit Commn, 1983–87; Dir-Gen., CBI, 1987–92; Chm., Local Govt Commn for England, 1992–95. Chm., Retail and Consumer Affairs Foresight Panel, 1997–2001. Chairman: John Labatt (Europe), subseq. Labatt Breweries of Europe, 1992–95; Westcountry Television, 1992–95; Tarmac, 1994–2000 (Dir, 1992–2000); Kingfisher, 1996–2001; ECI Ventures, 1992–2005; Whitbread, 2000–05 (Dir, 1999–2005); Geest, 2002–05; Cyclacel Ltd, 2002–06; Spacelabs Healthcare Inc., 2005–08; Johnson Matthey plc, 2006–11; Director: National Westminster Bank, 1992–98; National Power, 1992–98; Merchants Trust, 1992–2005; Cyclacel Pharmaceuticals Inc., 2006–; Sen. Ind. Dir, Invesco Inc. (formerly Amvescap plc), 1999–2014. Mem., BOTB, 1989–92; Dir and Mem. Bd, Business in the Community, 1989–92. Member Council: PSI, 1986–92; Forum for Management Educn and Develt, 1988–93; BESO, 1991–92. Member: Council of Management, PDSA, 1982–93; Governing Body, London Business Sch., 1987–92; Managing Trustee, Nuffield Foundn, 1988–97; Hon. Treas., Cancer Res. Campaign, 1991–2002. DL Cornwall, 1999. Hon. LLD Bath, 1987; Hon. DSc: Loughborough, 1989; Exeter, 1993; Strathclyde, 1995. *Publications:* Future of the British Car Industry, 1975; Realizing the Promise of a National Health Service, 1977; The Anatomy of Change: blueprint for a new era, 1994; numerous reports for Audit Commn on education, housing, social services and local government finance, 1984–87, and for CBI on UK economy, skills, transport, the infrastructure, urban regeneration and manufacturing. *Recreations:* walking, ground clearing, gardening. *Address:* Penberth, St Buryan, Penzance, Cornwall TR19 6HJ. *Fax:* (01736) 810722. *Club:* Travellers.

BANISTER, Prof. David John, PhD; Professor of Transport Studies, and Director, Transport Studies Unit, University of Oxford, and Fellow of St Anne's College, Oxford, since 2006; *b* 10 July 1950; *s* of late Stephen Michael Alvin Banister and of Rachel Joan Banister; *m* 1985, Elizabeth Dawn Bucknell; three *d*. *Educ:* Royal Grammar Sch., Guildford; Nottingham Univ. (BA 1st Cl. Hons Geog.); Leeds Univ. (PhD Transport Studies 1976). CMILT (MCIT 1976; MILT 1999). Lectr in Geog., Univ. of Reading, 1975–78; University College London: Lectr in Transport Policy, 1979–88; Sen. Lectr, 1988–90; Reader in Transport Planning, 1990–95; Prof. of Transport Planning, 1995–2006; Acting Dir, Envmtl Change Inst., Oxford Univ., 2009–10. Vis. VSB Prof., Tinbergen Inst., Amsterdam, 1994–97; Vis. Prof., Univ. of Bodenkultur, Vienna, 2007. Jt Ed., Built Envmt, 1992–; Ed., Transport Reviews, 2001–; Mem., editl bds of several jls. Non-exec. Dir, Taylor and Francis Gp PLC, 1990–2004. Dir, Res. Prog. on Transport and Envmt, ESRC, 1992–96; Chair, BIVEC-GIBET, 2012–13. Member: Adv. Gps on Future Integrated Transport, Inland Surface Transport, Cities and Sustainability, EPSRC, 1994–2004; Team for Town and Country Planning, RAE 2001 and 2008, HEFCE. Chm., Econ. Commn for Europe's Task Force on Urban Transport Patterns and Land Use Planning, UN, 2000–02. FRSA 1988. Trustee: Ferguson Charitable Trust, 1979–; Civic Trust, 2005–09 (Chm., Policy Cttee, 2006–09). Editor, Spon series on Transport, Development and Sustainability, 1999–2006. *Publications:* Transport Mobility and Deprivation in Inter-Urban Areas, 1980; (jtly) Transport and Public Policy Planning, 1981; Rural Transport and Planning, 1985; (jtly) Urban Transport and Planning, 1989; (jtly) Transport in a Free Market Economy, 1991; (jtly) Transport in Unified Europe: policies and challenges, 1993; (jtly) Transport, the Environment and Sustainable Development, 1993; Transport Planning, 1994, 2nd edn 2002; Transport and Urban Development, 1995; (jtly) European Transport and Communications Networks: policy evolution and change, 1995; (jtly) Telematics and Transport Behaviour, 1996; Transport Policy and the Environment, 1998; (jtly) Environment, Land Use and Urban Policy, 1999; (jtly) European Transport Policy and Sustainable Mobility, 2000; (jtly) Encouraging Transport Alternatives: good practice in reducing travel, 2000; (jtly) Transport Investment and Economic Development, 2000; Unsustainable Transport, 2005; (jtly) Land Use and Transport: European perspectives on integrated policies, 2007; (jtly) Integrated Transport: from policy to practice, 2010; (jtly) The Transport System and Transport Policy, 2012; (jtly) Moving Towards Low Carbon Mobility, 2013; (jtly) Transport, Climate Change and the City, 2014; (jtly) Transport and Development, 2015; contrib. books and internat. jls. *Recreations:* gardening, farming, walking, good company and conversation. *Address:* Transport Studies Unit, Oxford University Centre for the Environment, South Parks Road, Oxford OX1 3QY. *T:* (01865) 285066.

BANKES-JONES, William Michael Roger; Artistic Director, Tête à Tête, since 1998; *b* London, 23 Aug. 1963; *s* of Roger Myddleton Bankes-Jones and Patricia Mary Russell Bankes-Jones. *Educ:* Marlborough Coll., Wilts; Univ. of St Andrews (MA Hons Logic and Metaphysics and Moral Philosophy 1986). ITV Regl Th. Young Directors' Scheme, 1989–91: Associate Dir, Thorndike Th., Leatherhead, 1989; Associate Dir, Redgrave Th., Farnham, 1989–91; Staff Dir, ENO, 1991–97; productions for Tête à Tête include: Shorts, 1999–2001; Six-Pack, 2002; Push!, 2006; Odysseus Unwound, 2006; Salad Days, 2009–13; Britten's Canticles in Westminster Abbey for Tête à Tête and Streetwise Opera, 2002; A Nitro at the Opera for Royal Opera and BBC TV, 2003; directed and translated: Fledermaus, English

Touring Opera, 2003; Hansel and Gretel, Scottish Opera, 2012. Founder and Artistic Dir, Tête à Tête: the Opera Fest., 2007–. Chm., Opera and Music Th. Forum, 2002–. *Recreations:* surfing, cycling, campaigning, swimming against the tide. *Address:* c/o Performing Arts, 6 Windmill Street, W1T 2JB. *T:* (020) 7255 1362. *E:* info@performingarts.co.uk. *Club:* London Surf.

BANKS, (Arthur) David; journalist and broadcaster; Columnist, The Journal, Newcastle, since 2006; Contributing Editor, Press Gazette, since 2006; *b* 13 Feb. 1948; *s* of Arthur Banks and Helen (*née* Renton); *m* 1975, Gemma Newton; one *s* one *d*. *Educ:* Boteler Grammar Sch., Warrington. Asst Man. Editor, NY Post, 1979–81; Night Editor, then Asst Editor, The Sun, 1981–86; Dep. Man. Editor, NY Daily News, 1986–87; Dep. Editor, The Australian, 1987–89; Editor: Daily Telegraph Mirror (Sydney), 1989–92; Daily Mirror, 1992–94; Editl Dir, Mirror Gp Newspapers, 1994–97; Consultant Ed., Sunday Mirror, 1997–98; Dir of Information, Mirror Gp, 1998–99. Presenter, Breakfast Show, Talk Radio, 1999–2000. *Recreations:* journalism, celebrating my second life. *Address:* Ross Cottage, 4 Crookham, Cornhill-on-Tweed, Northumberland TD12 4SY. *T:* 07931 501252. *E:* david_banks@hotmail.com.

BANKS, Caroline; non-executive Director, Financial Ombudsman Service, 2004–08; Director, Consumer Regulation Enforcement Division, Office of Fair Trading, 1998–2003; *b* 24 April 1950; *d* of Geoffrey Banks and Pamela Dane Banks. *Educ:* Kitwe Girls' High Sch., Zambia; Middlesex Poly. (BA Hons). Office of Fair Trading: various posts, 1975–82; Head, Consumer Credit Licensing Bureau, 1982–88; Principal Estabt and Finance Officer, 1988–97. Member: Billing and Direct Selling Codes Panel, Energy Retail Assoc., 2003–14; CSAB, 2004–12. Trustee, Homestart Westminster, 2014–. *Recreations:* gardening, family history. *Address:* 40 Meadowcroft Road, Palmers Green, N13 4EA.

BANKS, Charles Augustus, III; Partner, Clayton, Dubilier & Rice Inc., 2006–10; *b* Greensboro, N Carolina, 20 Dec. 1940; *s* of late Charles Augustus Banks, Jr and Madge McMillan Banks; *m* 1962, Marie Ann Sullivan; two *s* one *d*. *Educ:* Brown Univ. (BA 1962); Young Exec. Inst. of Professional Mgt, Univ. of N Carolina; Wharton Sch., Univ. of Pennsylvania (AMP 1989). Ensign/Lt, USNR (Active), 1962–64. Plant manager, Minerals Recovery Corp., 1964–65; mortgage banker, Cameron-Brown Co., 1965–67; Ferguson Enterprises Inc.: Peebles Supply Div., 1967–69; Outside Sales, Lenz Supply Div., 1969–70; Vice-Pres. and Gen. Manager, Alexandria, Va, 1970–77; Pres. and Gen. Manager, Herndon, Va, 1977–81; Dir, 1977; Regl Manager, 1981–87; Sen. Exec. Vice-Pres., 1987–89; Pres. and Chief Ops Officer, 1989–93; Pres. and CEO, 1993–2001; Chm., 2001–06; Dir, Wolseley plc (parent co. of Ferguson Enterprises), 1992–2006, Chief Exec., 2001–06. Chm., US Foodservice Inc., 2007; non-exec. Dir, Bunzl PLC, 2002–11.

BANKS, Christopher Nigel, CBE 2003; Chairman: Public Chairs' Forum, since 2009; Quality Assurance Agency for Higher Education, since 2014; Founder, Big Thoughts, since 2001; *b* 1 Sept. 1959; *s* of James Nigel Alexander and Pamela Ethel Banks; *m* 1982, Karen Jane Dauber; one *s* two *d*. *Educ:* Bristol Cathedral Sch.; Birmingham Univ. (BA Combined Hons Latin and French); Aston Univ. (MBA). Client Services, A. C. Nielsen, 1983–85; Marketing Manager, Mars Inc., 1985–89; Marketing Dir, H. P. Bulmer, 1989–92; Man. Dir, URM Agencies, part of Allied Domecq, 1992–95; CEO, Justerini & Brooks, part of Grand Metropolitan, 1996–97; Man. Dir, Coca-Cola GB, 1997–2001. Mem., Women and Work Commn, 2004–07. Chairman: London Employer Coalition, 1999–2004; Directgov, 2009–10; Mem., Nat. Council, and Chm., Young People's Learning Cttee, 2000–04, Chm., 2004–10, LSC; Dep. Chm., Nat. Employment Panel, 2001–08. Dep. Pro Chancellor, Univ. of Birmingham, 2009–14. Pres., British Soft Drinks Assoc., 2003–05. Gov., University of Birmingham Sch. *Address:* Public Chairs' Forum, Institute for Government, 2 Carlton Gardens, SW1Y 5AA.

BANKS, David; *see* Banks, A. D.

BANKS, Elizabeth Christina; DL; President, Royal Horticultural Society, 2010–13, now Emeritus; *b* Rockingham Castle, 30 Sept. 1941; *d* of Leslie Swain Saunders and Elizabeth Saunders; *m* 1963, (William) Lawrence Banks; two *s*. *Educ:* Fritham House Sch.; New York Botanical Gardens; Greenwich Univ. (Dip. Landscape Architecture 1981). CMLI 1982. Associate, Land Use Consultants, 1981–86; Chm. and Man. Dir, Elizabeth Banks Associates, 1986–2006. Chairman: Gardens Cttee, Historic Houses Assoc., 1989–93; Queenswood Coronation Fund, 1999–2010; Trustee: Gateway Gardens Trust, 2006–09; Member: Arboreta Adv. Cttee, Westonbirt Arboretum and Bedgebury Pinetum, 2004–; Council, RHS, 2007–13. Mem., Kington Town Council, 2001– (Mayor, 2006–10). Liveryman, Gardeners' Co., 2011. DL Herefordshire, 2008. FCIHort (FIHort 2011). Hon. DDes Greenwich, 2011; Hon. DSc Worcester, 2011. *Publications:* Creating Period Gardens, 1991; articles in Country Life and other mags. *Recreations:* gardening, fishing, travelling, walking. *Address:* Ridgebourne, Kington, Herefordshire HR5 3EG. *T:* (01544) 230218. *E:* banks@hergest.co.uk. *Club:* Boodle's.

BANKS, Frank David, DPhil; FCA; Chairman, H. Berkeley (Holdings) Ltd, 1984–90; *b* 11 April 1933; *s* of Samuel and Elizabeth Banks; *m* 1st, 1955, Catherine Jacob; one *s* two *d*; 2nd, 1967, Sonia Gay Coleman; one *d*. *Educ:* Liverpool Collegiate Sch.; Carnegie Mellon Univ. (PFE); Open Univ. (BA 1988); Univ. of Sussex (MA 1992; DPhil 2003). British Oxygen Co. Ltd, 1957–58; Imperial Chemical Industries Ltd, 1959–62; English Electric Co. Ltd, 1963–68; Finance Dir, Platt International Ltd, 1969–71; Industrial Advr, DTI, 1972–73; Constructors John Brown Ltd, 1974–80; Man. Dir, Agribusiness Div., Tate & Lyle Ltd, 1981–83. *Recreations:* music, history. *Address:* 14a Luton Road, Wilstead, Bedford, Beds MK45 3HD.

BANKS, Mrs Gillian Theresa, CB 1990; *b* 7 Feb. 1933; *d* of Percy and Enid Brimblecombe; *m* 1960, John Anthony Gorst Banks (marr. diss. 1993); one *s* two *d*. *Educ:* Walthamstow Hall Sch., Sevenoaks; Lady Margaret Hall, Oxford (BA). Asst Principal, Colonial Office, 1955; Principal, Treasury, 1966; Department of Health and Social Security: Asst Sec., 1972; Under Sec. 1981; Dir, Health Authy Finance, 1985; Dir, OPCS and Registrar Gen. for Eng. and Wales, 1986; Dir, Carnegie Inquiry into the Third Age, 1990; led Functions, Manpower and Sen. Management Review of Wider DoH, 1994; Dir, Retirement Income Inquiry, 1994; Mem., Camden and Islington HA, 1995; non-exec. Dir, Royal Free Hampstead NHS Trust, 1997–2004. Policy Consultant, Age Concern, England, 1996; Hon. Treas., Age Concern Camden, 1997–2002. Lay Mem., Council, RPSGB, 1996–2001. *Recreation:* hill walking. *Address:* Flat 3, Andrew Court, 2 Wedderburn Road, NW3 5QE. *T:* (020) 7435 4973.

BANKS, Gordon Raymond; *b* 14 June 1955; *s* of William Banks and Patricia Marion Banks (*née* Macknight); *m* 1981, Lynda Nicol; one *s* one *d*. *Educ:* Univ. of Stirling (BA Hons Hist. and Politics); Glasgow Coll. of Building and Printing (Construction Technician). Chief Buyer: Barratt (Edinburgh) Ltd, 1975–84; Barratt (Falkirk) Ltd, 1984–86; Man. Dir, Cartmore Bldg Supply Co. Ltd, 1986–. Parly Officer for Dr Richard Simpson, MP, 1999–2003; researcher for Martin O'Neill, MP, 2003–05. Mem., Nat. Policy Forum, and Quality of Life Policy Forum, Lab. Party, 2002–05. MP (Lab) Ochil and S Perthshire, 2005–15; contested (Lab) same seat, 2015. PPS to Minister for Pension Reform, DWP, 2006–07, to Sec. of State for Culture, Media and Sport, 2007–08, to Sec. of State for Work and Pensions, 2008–10; Shadow Business Minister, 2010–11; Shadow Scotland Office Minister, 2012–15. *Recreations:* music (song-writing), motor sport, football.

BANKS, Jeremy, (Banx); pocket cartoonist, Financial Times, since 1989; Cartoon Editor, The Reaper, since 2015; *b* London, 10 May 1959; *s* of Peter William Banks and Sheila Lascelles Banks (*née* Fleming); *m* 1998, Elaine Pennicott; four *d*. *Educ:* Lycée français de Londres; Hounslow Bor. Coll.; Maidstone Coll. of Art. Freelance cartoonist, 1980–, for: Private Eye; Punch; London Evening Standard; Daily Express; Mail on Sunday; New Statesman; She; Men Only; Mayfair; Penthouse; Oink!; Toxic. Float designer, Nice Carnival, 2002–09. Pocket Cartoonist of Year, Cartoon Art Trust, 2008, 2012. *Publications:* Cubes, 1982; The Many Deaths of Norman Spittal, 1997; Big Fat Sleepy Cat, 2001; The Dewsburys, 2006; Frankenthing, 2014. *Recreations:* family, art, reading, watching DVD box sets, swimming. *E:* banxcartoons@gmail.com.

BANKS, John, FREng, FIET; Chairman, Adacom 3270 Communications Ltd, 1986–90; *b* 2 Dec. 1920; *s* of John Banks and Jane Dewhurst; *m* 1943, Nancy Olive Yates; two *s*. *Educ:* Univ. of Liverpool (BEng Hons; MEng). FREng (FEng 1983); FIET (FIEE 1959). Chief Engr, Power Cables Div., BICC, 1956–67; Divl Dir and Gen. Man., Supertension Cables Div., BICC, 1968–74; Exec. Dir, 1975–78, Chm., 1978–84, BICC Research and Engineering Ltd; Exec. Dir, BICC, 1979–84. Vis. Prof., Liverpool Univ., 1987. Pres., IEE, 1982–83. *Recreations:* golf, swimming, music and the arts. *Club:* Seaford Golf.

BANKS, Lynne Reid; writer; *b* 1929; *d* of Dr James Reid-Banks and Muriel (Pat) (*née* Marsh); *m* 1965, Chaim Stephenson, sculptor; three *s*. *Educ:* schooling mainly in Canada; RADA. Actress, 1949–54; reporter for ITN, 1955–62; English teacher in kibbutz in Western Galilee, Israel, 1963–71; full-time writer, 1971–; writing includes plays for stage, television and radio. J. M. Barrie Award, Action for Children's Arts, 2013. *Publications: plays:* It Never Rains, 1954; All in a Row, 1956; The Killer Dies Twice, 1956; Already, It's Tomorrow, 1962; (for children) Travels of Yoshi and the Tea-Kettle, 1993; *fiction:* The L-Shaped Room, 1960 (trans. 10 langs; filmed 1962); An End to Running, 1962 (trans. 2 langs); Children at the Gate, 1968; The Backward Shadow, 1970; Two is Lonely, 1974; Defy the Wilderness, 1981; The Warning Bell, 1984; Casualties, 1986; Fair Exchange, 1998; *biographical fiction:* Dark Quartet: the story of the Brontes, 1976 (Yorks Arts Lit. Award, 1977); Path to the Silent Country: Charlotte Bronte's years of fame, 1977; *history:* Letters to my Israeli Sons, 1979; Torn Country, 1982; *for young adults:* One More River, 1973; Sarah and After, 1975; My Darling Villain, 1977 (trans. 3 langs); The Writing on the Wall, 1981; Melusine, 1988 (trans. 3 langs); Broken Bridge, 1994 (trans. 2 langs); *for children:* The Adventures of King Midas, 1976 (trans. 4 langs); The Farthest-Away Mountain, 1977; I, Houdini, 1978 (trans. 4 langs); The Indian in the Cupboard, 1980 (trans. 24 langs) (Pacific NW Choice Award, 1984; Calif. Young Readers Medal, 1985; Va Children's Choice, 1988; Mass. Children's Choice, 1988; Rebecca Caudill Award, Ill, 1989; Arizona Children's Choice, 1989; filmed, 1995); Maura's Angel, 1984 (trans. 2 langs); The Fairy Rebel, 1985 (trans. 3 langs); Return of the Indian, 1986 (trans. 5 langs); The Secret of the Indian, 1989 (trans. 4 langs); The Magic Hare, 1992; Mystery of the Cupboard, 1993 (trans. 3 langs); Harry the Poisonous Centipede, 1996; Angela and Diabola, 1997 (trans. 2 langs); The Key to the Indian, 1999; Moses in Egypt, 1998 (trans. 3 langs); Alice-by-Accident, 2000; Harry the Poisonous Centipede's Big Adventure, 2000; The Dungeon, 2002; Stealing Stacey, 2004; Tiger, Tiger, 2004; Harry the Poisonous Centipede Goes to Sea, 2005; Bad Cat, Good Cat, 2011; The Wrong-Coloured Dragon, 2012; Uprooted: a Canadian war-story, 2014; short stories; articles in The Times, The Guardian, Sunday Telegraph, Observer, TES, TLS, Independent on Sunday, Sunday Times, Spectator, Saga Magazine, and in overseas periodicals. *Recreations:* theatre, gardening, visiting schools overseas and at home. *Address:* c/o Abner Stein, 10 Roland Gardens, SW7 3PH. *W:* www.lynnereidbanks.com.

BANKS, Matthew Richard William; *see* Gordon Banks, M. R. W.

BANKS, Rt Rev. Norman; *see* Richborough, Bishop Suffragan of.

BANKS, Richard Lee; Chief Executive Officer: Bradford & Bingley plc, since 2010 (Managing Director, 2009–10); UK Asset Resolution Ltd, since 2010; Northern Rock (Asset Management) plc, since 2010; *b* 15 June 1951; *s* of Richard Cyril Banks and Mary Banks; *m* 1978, Elaine Helena Kret; two *s*. *Educ:* Stockport Secondary Technical High Sch.; Manchester Poly. (BA Hons Business Studies). Joined Midland Bank, 1974, various mgt posts, 1978–87; Girobank: Gen. Manager, 1987–91; Sen. Gen. Manager, 1991–94; Dir, Corporate Banking, 1994–96; Man. Dir, 1996–2000; Alliance & Leicester plc: Dir, 1998–2008; Distribution Ops Dir, 2000–02; Man. Dir, Wholesale Banking, 2002–08. *Recreations:* reading, cottage renovation. *Address:* Bradford & Bingley plc, PO Box 88, Croft Road, Crossflatts, Bingley BD16 2UA.

BANKS, Robert George; *b* 18 Jan. 1937; *s* of late George Walmsley Banks, MBE, and Olive Beryl Banks (*née* Tyler); *m* 1967, Diana Margaret Payne Crawfurd (marr. diss. 2004); four *s* one *d* (of whom one *s* one *d* are twins). *Educ:* Haileybury. Lt-Comdr RNR. Jt Founder Dir, Antocks Lairn Ltd, 1963–67. Mem., Alcohol Educn and Res. Council, 1982–88. Mem., Paddington BC, 1959–65. MP (C) Harrogate, Feb. 1974–97. PPS to Minister of State and to Under-Sec. of State, FCO, 1979–82. Member: Select Cttee on Foreign Affairs (and its Overseas Develt Sub-Cttee), 1982; Select Cttee on Trade and Industry, 1994–97; Jt Sec., Cons. Defence Cttee, 1976–79; Chairman: British-Sudan All Party Parly Gp, 1984–97; All-Party Tourism Gp, 1992–97 (Sec., 1973–79; Vice-Chm., 1979–92); Vice-Chm., Yorks Cons. Mems' Cttee, 1983–97. Member: Council of Europe, 1977–81; WEU, 1977–81; N Atlantic Assembly, 1981–95. Introd Licensing (Alcohol Educn and Res.) Act, 1981; sponsored Licensing (Restaurants Meals) Act, 1987. Reports: for Mil. Cttee of WEU, Report on Nuclear, Biol. and Chem. Protection, adopted by WEU Assembly April 1980; North Atlantic Assembly document, The Technology of Military Space Systems, 1982. *Publications:* (jtly) Britain's Home Defence Gamble (pamphlet), 1979; New Jobs from Pleasure, report on tourism, 1985; Tories for Tourism, 1995. *Recreations:* travel, architecture, contemporary art. *Address:* Brett House, 305 Munster Road, SW6 6BJ.

BANKS, Prof. William McKerrell, PhD; FREng, FIMechE; FRSE; Professor of Advanced Materials, University of Strathclyde, Glasgow, 1991–2008, now Emeritus; President, Institution of Mechanical Engineers, 2008–09; *b* Dreghorn, Ayrshire, 28 March 1943; *s* of William and Jeanie Banks; *m* 1966, Martha Ruthven (*née* Hair); three *s*. *Educ:* Univ. of Strathclyde (BSc 1st Cl. Hons Mech. Engrg 1965; MSc 1966; PhD 1977). FIMechE 1987; FIMMM 1993; FREng 2001. Sen. Res. Engr, G & J Weir Ltd, 1966–70; University of Strathclyde: Lectr, Sen. Lectr, then Reader, 1970–91; Dir, External Relns and Dir of Res., Dept of Mech. Engrg, 1990–2004. Director: Centre for Advanced Structural Materials, 1995–2008; Scottish Polymer Technol. Network, 1997–2006; Dir of Res. and Trng, Faraday Plastics Partnership, 2002–06; Pres., Engrg Professors' Council, 2001–03 (Mem. Cttee, 1999–2013); Assessor, DTI Technol. Prog., 2001–06; Member: DSAC, 1997–2002 (Mem., Wkg Party on Rev. of use of polymer composite materials in platforms, 1997–99); EPSRC Peer Rev. Coll., 2000–13; Exec. Cttee, Campaign for Sci. and Engrg, 2002–11; Fellowship Sectional Cttee for Engrg, RSE, 2003–07; Engrg Council, 2006–08; Engrg Technol. Bd, 2008–09; Educn and Skills Panel, Engrg UK, 2009–; Qualifications Design Team for Technol Studies and Engrg, Scottish Qualifications Authy, 2010–14. Mem. and Lead Assessor for Mech. Engrg Res. and Secondments Cttee, 2007–11, Professorial Mentor, 2012–, Royal Acad. of Engrg. External Advr, Materials Prog., QinetiQ, 2002–06. Chm., Professional Engineering Publishing, 2004–06. Mem. Council, Inst. of Materials, 1997–2001; Chairman: Trustee Bd and Council, IMechE, 2008–09 (Chm., Awards Cttee, Trustee Bd, 2010–11); Resolution Panel, BCS, 2011–. Pres., Engrg and Technol. Assoc. (Scotland), 2010–11. FRSE 2003. Lectures internat. incl. China, Russia, Malaysia, Singapore, Australia. Ed. in Chief, IMechE Procs Jl of Materials: Design and Applications, 2000–14; served on several editl panels. James Clayton Res. Prize, 1977, 2011, Donald Julien Groen Prize, 1994, 2001, 150th

Anniv. Gold Medal Award, 1998, IMechE; James Alfred Ewing Medal, Royal Soc. and ICE, 2007. *Publications:* co-edited: Advances in Turbine Materials: design and manufacturing, 1997; Advanced Materials for 21st Century Turbines and Power Plant, 2000; Pressure Equipment Technology: theory and practice, 2003; Engineering Issues in Turbine Machinery, Power Plant and Renewables, 2003; What God hath Joined: an answer to contemporary issues in marriage, 2005; Power Generation in an Era of Climate Change, 2007; over 200 papers and chapters in books. *Recreations:* involved extensively in Bible teaching, enjoy gardening, reading, family and travelling. *Address:* 19 Dunure Drive, Hamilton ML3 9EY. *T:* (01698) 823730, *Fax:* (01698) 823730. *E:* bill.banks@strath.ac.uk.

BANN, Prof. Stephen, CBE 2004; PhD; FBA 1998; FSA; Professor of History of Art, 2000–08, now Emeritus, and Senior Research Fellow, since 2008, University of Bristol; *b* 1 Aug. 1942; *s* of Harry Bann, OBE and Edna Bann (*née* Pailin). *Educ:* Winchester Coll. (schol.); King's Coll., Cambridge (schol.; BA Hist. 1963; MA; PhD 1967). FSA 2009. State Res. Studentship, 1963–66, in Paris, 1964–65; University of Kent: Lectr, 1967–75, Sen. Lectr, 1975–80, in History; Reader in Modern Cultural Studies, 1980–88; Prof. of Modern Cultural Studies, 1988–2000; Sen. Fellow, 2003–08, Beatrix Farrand Distinguished Fellow, 2009, Dumbarton Oaks Res. Liby, Washington; Sen. Mellon Fellow, Canadian Centre for Architecture, Montreal, 2003; Leverhulme Emeritus Fellow, 2009–10. Visiting Professor: Rennes Univ., 1994; Johns Hopkins Univ., 1996–98; Bologna Univ., 1998; Warburg Foundn, Hamburg, 2002; Inst Nat. d'Histoire de l'Art, Paris, 2003; Edmond J. Safra Prof., Center for Advanced Studies in the Visual Arts, Washington, 2005; Pilkington Vis. Prof., Univ. of Manchester, 2010; Sen. Vis. Scholar, Yale Center for British Art, 2012–14; Hon. Prof., Univ. of Kent, 2011–14. Getty Lectures, Univ. of Southern Calif, 2004. Member: Art Panel, Arts Council of GB, 1975–78; Humanities Res. Bd, British Acad., 1997–98; Chm. Res. Cttee, AHRB, 1998–2000; Res. Awards Adv. Cttee, Leverhulme Trust, 1998–2005. Pres., Comité Internat. d'Histoire de l'Art, 2000–04. Mem. Council, Friends of Canterbury Cathedral, 1990–2000. Trustee, Little Sparta Trust, 1994–2013. Dep. Ed., then Ed., 20th Century Studies, 1969–76; Adv. Ed., Reaktion Books, 1985–. MAE 2014. R. H. Gapper Prize for French Studies, Soc. for French Studies, 2002. *Publications:* Experimental Painting, 1970; (ed) The Tradition of Constructivism, 1974; The Clothing of Clio, 1984; The True Vine: on visual representation and the Western tradition, 1989; The Inventions of History, 1990; Under the Sign: John Bargrave as collector, traveler and witness, 1994; The Sculpture of Stephen Cox, 1995; Romanticism and the Rise of History, 1995; Paul Delaroche: history painted, 1997; Parallel Lines: printmakers, painters and photographers in nineteenth-century France, 2001; Jannis Kounellis, 2003; (ed) The Reception of Walter Pater in Europe, 2004; Ways Around Modernism, 2007; (ed) The Coral Mind: Adrian Stokes' engagement with architecture, art history, criticism and psychoanalysis, 2007; (with L. Whiteley) Painting History: Delaroche and Lady Jane Grey, 2010; (ed) Art and the Early Photographic Album, 2011; (ed) Interlacing Words and Things: bridging the nature-culture opposition in gardens and landscape, 2012; Distinguished Images: prints in the visual economy of nineteenth-century France, 2013; (ed) Midway: letters from Ian Hamilton Finlay to Stephen Bann 1964–69, 2014; Bernard Lassus, the Landscape Approach, 2014. *Recreations:* travel, collecting. *Address:* 2 New Street, St Dunstan's, Canterbury, Kent CT2 8AU. *T:* (01227) 761135; Department of History of Art, University of Bristol, Bristol BS8 1TB. *Club:* Savile.

BANNATYNE, Hon. Lord; Iain Alexander Scott Peebles; a Senator of the College of Justice in Scotland, since 2008. *Educ:* Strathclyde Univ. Admitted to Faculty of Advocates, 1979; Temp. Sheriff, 1991; Advocate Depute, 1992–95; QC (Scot.) 1993; Sheriff of Glasgow and Strathkelvin, 1995–99; Commercial Sheriff, 1999; Temp. Judge, Court of Session and High Court of Justiciary, 2003–08. *Address:* Court of Session, Parliament House, Edinburgh EH1 1RQ.

BANNATYNE, (Walker) Duncan, OBE 2004; Chairman: Bannatyne Fitness Ltd, since 1996; Bannatyne Hotels Ltd, since 1996; Bannatyne Casinos Ltd, since 2003; Bannatyne Housing Ltd, since 2005; *b* 2 Feb. 1949; one *s* five *d.* RN, 1964–68. Started own business, Duncan's Super Ices; established: Quality Care Homes, 1986, sold 1996; Just Learning, 1996, sold 2002. Has appeared in BBC TV series, Dragons' Den, 2005–14. Funded Bannatyne Hospices for Children with HIV and Aids, Romania and Colombia; Founder, Bannatyne Charitable Trust, 2008. *Publications:* Anyone Can Do It: my story, 2006; Wake Up and Change Your Life, 2008; How to be Smart with Your Money, 2009; How to be Smart with Your Time, 2010; 43 Mistakes Businesses Make and How to Avoid Them, 2011; 37 Questions Everyone in Business Needs to Answer, 2012. *Address:* Bannatyne Fitness Ltd, Power House, Haughton Road, Darlington, Co. Durham DL1 1ST. *T:* (01325) 382565, *Fax:* (01325) 355588.

BANNENBERG, Jennifer Bridget; *see* Tanfield, J. B.

BANNER, Rev. Prof. Michael Charles, DPhil; Dean of Chapel, Director of Studies, and Fellow, Trinity College, Cambridge, since 2006; *b* 19 April 1961; *s* of Maurice Banner and Maureen (*née* Ince); *m* 1st, 1983, Elizabeth Jane Wheare (marr. diss. 2001); two *d*; 2nd, 2007, Sally-Ann Gannon; one *d. Educ:* Bromsgrove Sch.; Balliol Coll., Oxford (BA Philos. and Theol. 1st cl. 1983; MA 1985; DPhil 1986). Ordained deacon 1986, priest 1987. Bampton Res. Fellow, St Peter's Coll., Oxford, 1985–88; Dean, Chaplain, Fellow and Dir of Studies in Philosophy and Theol., 1988–94, Tutor 1989–94, Peterhouse, Cambridge; F. D. Maurice Prof. of Moral and Social Theology, KCL, 1994–2004; Prof. of Public Policy and Ethics in the Life Scis, Univ. of Edinburgh, 2004–06; Dir, ESRC Genomics Policy and Res. Forum, 2004–06. Vis. Res. Fellow, Merton Coll., Oxford, 1993; Peden Sen. Fellow, Rice Univ., 2012. Chairman: HM Govt Cttee of Enquiry on Ethics of Emerging Technologies in Breeding of Farm Animals, 1993–95; Home Office Animal Procedures Cttee, 1998–2006; CJD Incidents Panel, DoH, 2000–04; Shell Panel on Animal Testing, 2002–09. Member: Royal Commn on Envmtl Pollution, 1996–2002; Agric. and Envmt Biotech. Commn, 2000–03; Human Tissue Authy, 2005–14; Cttee of Reference, F&C Asset Mgt, 2007–14; Working Gp on animals containing human material, Acad. of Med. Scis, 2010–11; Scientific Adv. Cttee on Medical Implications of Less Lethal Weapons, MoD, 2012–; Adv. Stewardship Cttee, Friends Life, 2014–; Nuffield Council on Bioethics, 2015–. Asst Curate, Balsham, W Wratting, Weston Colville and W Wickham, 2000–04. Member: C of E Bd for Social Responsibility, 1995–2001; C of E Doctrine Commn, 1996–99. Trustee, Scott Holland Fund, 1996–99. Baron de Lancey Lectr, Cambridge Univ., 1998; Bampton Lectr, Oxford Univ., 2013. Consultant Editor, Studies in Christian Ethics, 1996–2007; Corresp. Editor, Jl of Ethical Theory and Moral Practice, 1997–2004; Mem. Editl Bd, Internat. Jl of Systematic Theology, 1998–2004. *Publications:* The Justification of Science and the Rationality of Religious Belief, 1990; The Practice of Abortion: a critique, 1999; Christian Ethics and Contemporary Moral Problems, 1999; The Doctrine of God and Theological Ethics, 2006; Christian Ethics: a brief history, 2009; Ethics of Everyday Life, 2014; various articles in learned jls. *Recreations:* galleries, mountain biking, cross country ski-ing, horse riding, rowing. *Address:* Trinity College, Cambridge CB2 1TQ. *Club:* National.

BANNERMAN, Bernard; *see* Arden, A. P. R.

BANNERMAN, David C.; *see* Campbell Bannerman.

BANNERMAN, Sir David (Gordon), 15th Bt *cr* 1682 (NS), of Elsick, Kincardineshire; OBE 1977; Ministry of Defence, 1963–97; *b* 18 Aug. 1935; *s* of Lt-Col Sir Donald Arthur Gordon Bannerman, 13th Bt and Barbara Charlotte, *d* of late Lt-Col Alexander Cameron, OBE, IMS; *S* brother, Sir Alexander Patrick Bannerman, 14th Bt, 1989; *m* 1960, Mary Prudence, *d* of Rev. Philip Frank Ardagh-Walter; four *d. Educ:* Gordonstoun; New Coll., Oxford (MA); University Coll. London (MSc 1999). 2nd Lieut Queen's Own Cameron Highlanders, 1954–56. HMOCS (Tanzania), 1960–63. Chm., Gordonstoun Assoc., 1997–2000. *Recreations:* painting, ornithology, architecture. *Address:* Old Hall Cottage, Woodley's Yard, Southwold, Suffolk IP18 6HP.

See also M. A. O'Neill.

BANNISTER, Clive Christopher Roger; Group Chief Executive, Phoenix Group plc, since 2011; *b* London, 28 Oct. 1958; *s* of Sir Roger Gilbert Bannister, *qv*; *m* 1992, Marjorie Barfuss; three *s. Educ:* Exeter Coll., Oxford (BA PPE 2000; MA 2005). Banker, First Nat. Bank of Boston, 1981–85; Partner, Booz Allen and Hamilton, 1985–94; Gp Man. Dir, HSBC, 1994–2010. Chm., Mus. of London, 2013–. *Recreations:* woodwork, military history, running, cycling. *Address:* Phoenix Group plc, Juxon House, 100 St Paul's Churchyard, EC4M 8BU. *T:* (020) 3735 0900, *Fax:* (020) 7489 4860. *E:* clive.bannister@thephoenixgroup.com. *Club:* Athenæum.

BANNISTER, (Richard) Matthew; broadcaster and journalist; presenter: Last Word, Radio 4, since 2006; Outlook, BBC World Service, since 2008; *b* 16 March 1957; *s* of late Richard Neville Bannister and of Olga Margaret Bannister; *m* 1st, 1984, Amanda Gerrard Walker (*d* 1988); one *d*; 2nd, 1989, Shelagh Margaret Macleod (*d* 2005); one *s*; 3rd, 2007, Katherine Jane Hood (marr. diss. 2013). *Educ:* King Edward VII Sch., Sheffield; Nottingham Univ. (LLB Hons). Presenter, BBC Radio Nottingham, 1978–81; Reporter/Presenter: Capital Radio, 1981–83; Newsbeat, Radio 1, 1983–85; Dep. Head, 1985–87, Head, 1987–88, News and Talks, Capital Radio; BBC, 1988–2000: Man. Ed., Gtr London Radio, 1988–91; Project Co-ordinator: Charter Renewal, 1991–93; Prog. Strategy Review, 1993; Controller, BBC Radio 1, 1993–98; Dir, BBC Radio, 1996–98; Chief Exec., BBC Prodn, 1999–2000; Dir of Mkting and Communications, BBC, 2000; presenter, BBC Radio 5 Live, 2002–06; Chairman: Trust the DJ, 2001–02; Wire Free Prodns Ltd, 2012–. Mem. Bd, Chichester Fest. Theatre, 1999–2003. Fellow, Radio Acad., 1998. Hon. DLitt Nottingham, 2011. *Recreations:* rock music, theatre, collecting P. G. Wodehouse first editions. *Address:* c/o Knight Ayton Management, 35 Great James Street, WC1N 3HB. *T:* (020) 7831 4400. *E:* info@knightayton.co.uk.

BANNISTER, Sir Roger (Gilbert), Kt 1975; CBE 1955; DM (Oxon); FRCP; Master of Pembroke College, Oxford, 1985–93; Hon. Consultant Physician, National Hospital for Neurology and Neurosurgery, Queen Square, WC1 (formerly Consultant Physician, National Hospital for Nervous Diseases; non-executive Director, 1992–96); Hon. Consultant Neurologist: St Mary's Hospital and Western Ophthalmic Hospital, W2 (formerly Consultant Neurologist); Oxford Regional and District Health Authorities, 1985–95; *b* 23 March 1929; *s* of late Ralph and of Alice Bannister, Harrow; *m* 1955, Moyra Elver, *d* of late Per Jacobsson, Chairman IMF; two *s* two *d. Educ:* City of Bath Boys' Sch.; University Coll. Sch., London; Exeter and Merton Colls, Oxford; St Mary's Hospital Medical Sch., London. Amelia Jackson Studentship, Exeter Coll., Oxford, 1947; BA (hons) Physiology, Junior Demonstrator in Physiology, Harmsworth Senior Scholar, Merton Coll., Oxford, 1950; Open and State Schol., St Mary's Hosp., 1951; MSc Thesis in Physiology, 1952; MRCS, LRCP, 1954; BM, BCh Oxford, 1954; DM Oxford, 1963. William Hyde Award for research relating physical education to medicine; MRCP 1957. President: OU Athletics Club; Exeter Coll. Jun. Common Room. Junior Medical Specialist, RAMC, 1958; Radcliffe Travelling Fellowship from Oxford Univ., at Harvard, USA, 1962–63. Correspondent, Sunday Times, 1955–62. Chm., Hon. Consultants, King Edward VII Convalescent Home for Officers, Osborne, 1979–87. Chm., Medical Cttee, St Mary's Hosp., 1983–85; Deleg., Imperial Coll., representing St Mary's Hosp. Med. Sch., 1988–92; Trustee, St Mary's Hosp. Med. Sch. Develt Trust, 1994–98 (Chm. Trustees, 1998–2006). Inaugural Annual Sir Roger Bannister Lecture, Eur. Autonomic Soc., 2004. President: National Fitness Panel, NABC, 1956–59; Alzheimer's Disease Soc., 1982–84; Sports Medicine Sect., RSM, 1994–95; Gen. Sect., BAAS, 1995; Founder and Chm., Clinical Autonomic Res. Soc., 1982–84. Mem. Council, King George's Jubilee Trust, 1961–67; Pres., Sussex Assoc. of Youth Clubs, 1972–79; Chm., Res. Cttee, Adv. Sports Council, 1965–71; Mem., Min. of Health Adv. Cttee on Drug Dependence, 1967–70; Chm., Sports Council, 1971–74; Pres., Internat. Council for Sport and Physical Recreation, 1976–83. Mem., Management Cttee, 1979–84, Council, 1984–, King Edward's Hosp. Fund for London; Trustee: King George VI and Queen Elizabeth Foundn of St Catharine's, Cumberland Lodge, Windsor, 1985–2005; Leeds Castle, 1989–2006; Henry and Proctor Amer. Fellowships, 1987–99; Winston Churchill Fellowships, 1988–2006; Med. Commn on Accident Prevention, 1994–99; Mem. of Commn, Marshall Fellowships, 1986–94; Steering Cttee, Fulbright Fellowships, 1996–97. Patron, British Assoc. of Sport and Medicine, 1996–2007. Pres., Bath Inst. of Biomedical Engrg, 1998–2004; Governor: Atlantic Coll., 1985–93; Abingdon Sch., 1985–93; Sherborne Sch., 1989–93. Winner Oxford *v* Cambridge Mile, 1947–50; Pres. OUAC, 1948; Capt. Oxford & Cambridge Combined American Team, 1949; Finalist, Olympic Games, Helsinki, 1952; British Mile Champion, 1951, 1953, 1954; World Record for One Mile, 1954 (3 mins 59.4 secs); British Empire Mile winner and record, 1954; European 1500 metres title and record, 1954. Hon. Freeman: City of Oxford, 2004; London Bor. of Harrow, 2004. Hon. FUMIST 1972; Hon. Fellow: Exeter Coll., Oxford, 1979; Merton Coll., Oxford, 1986; Pembroke Coll., Oxford, 1994; Harris Manchester Coll., Oxford, 2007; Brunel Univ., 2008; Hon. FIC 1999. Hon. FRCSE 2002; Hon. FRSocMed 2010. Hon. LLD Liverpool, 1972; Hon. DLitt Sheffield, 1978; hon. doctorates: Jyvaskyla, Finland, 1982; Bath, Grinnell, USA, 1984; Rochester, NY, 1985; Pavia, Italy, 1986; Williams Coll., USA, 1987; Victoria Univ., Canada, 1987; Wales, Cardiff, 1994; Loughborough, 1996; UEA, 1997; Cranfield, 2002; Manchester Combined Univs, 2002; QMUL, 2010; Oxford Brookes, 2014; Buckingham, 2015. Hans-Heinrich Siegbert Prize, 1977; First Lifetime Achievement Award, Amer. Acad. Neurol., 2005. Chm. Editorial Bd, Clinical Autonomic Res., 1991–97; Mem., Editorial Bd, Jl of the Autonomic Nervous System, 1980–95; Associate Editor, Jl Neurol Sci., 1985–95. *Publications:* First Four Minutes, 1955, 50th Anniversary edn 2004; (ed) Brain's Clinical Neurology, 3rd edn 1969 to 6th edn 1985, 7th edn 1992 (as Brain and Bannister's Clinical Neurology); (ed) Autonomic Failure: a textbook of clinical disorders of the autonomic nervous system, 1982, 2nd edn 1988, (ed with C. J. Mathias) 3rd edn 1992 to 5th edn 2013; Roger Bannister, Twin Tracks (autobiog.), 2014; papers on neurological subjects, disorders of the autonomic nervous system, physiology of exercise and heat illness. *Address:* 21 Bardwell Road, Oxford OX2 6SU. *T:* (01865) 511413. *Clubs:* Athenæum; Vincent's (Oxford) (Pres., 1949).

See also C. C. R. Bannister.

BANNON, Michael Joseph, FRCPI, FRCPCH; Postgraduate Dean, Department of Postgraduate Medical and Dental Education, Oxford, since 2003; *b* 2 May 1954; *s* of Christopher Bannon and Ann (*née* Kelly); *m* 1988, Prof. Yvonne Helen Carter, CBE (*d* 2009); one *s. Educ:* Trinity Coll., Dublin (MB BCh, BAO 1978; MA 1992; DCH 1979); MA Oxon; Univ. of Keele (MSc). FRCPI 1993; FRCPCH 1993. Consultant Paediatrician: City Gen. Hosp., N Staffs, 1990–92; Warwick Hosp., 1992–96; Northwick Park Hosp., 1996–2003. Sen. Lectr, Warwick Univ., 1992–96. *Publications:* Protecting Children from Abuse and Neglect in Primary Care, 2003; contrib. papers on child protection and med. educn. *Recreation:* Irish folk music. *Address:* Department of Postgraduate Medical and Dental Education, The Triangle, Roosevelt Drive, Headington, Oxford OX3 3XP. *T:* (01865) 740605.

BANO, (Ernest) Andrew (Louis); an Upper Tribunal Judge (formerly a Social Security and Child Support Commissioner), 2000–13; *b* 7 May 1944; *s* of late Imre Bano and Susanne Bano; *m* 1985, Elizabeth Anne Sheehy; three *s* one *d. Educ:* Cardinal Vaughan Meml Sch.;

Inns of Court Sch. of Law. Trng Consultant, 1966–69; Trng Develt Officer, BEA, 1969–72; called to the Bar, Gray's Inn, 1973; in practice at Common Law Bar, 1973–88; Head of Chambers, 1986–88; Chm. (part-time), Industrial Tribunals, 1984–88; Chm., Employment Tribunals, 1988–2000; Dep. Social Security Comr, 1996–2000; Legal Chm. (part-time), Pensions Appeal Tribunals, 2001–05; Pres., War Pensions and Armed Forces Compensation Chamber, First-tier Tribunal, 2009–12. *Recreations:* opera, amateur radio, woodwork. *Club:* Athenæum.

BANTING, Ven. (Kenneth) Mervyn (Lancelot Hadfield); Archdeacon of the Isle of Wight, 1996–2003, now Archdeacon Emeritus; *b* 8 Sept. 1937; *s* of late Rev. Canon H. M. J. Banting and P. M. Banting; *m* 1970, Linda (*née* Gick); four *d*. *Educ:* Pembroke Coll., Cambridge (MA 1965); Cuddesdon Coll., Oxford; Univ. of Wales (MA 2007). Ordained deacon, 1965, priest, 1966; Chaplain, Winchester Coll., 1965–70; Asst Curate, St Francis, Leigh Park, Portsmouth, 1970–73; Team Vicar, Highfield, Hemel Hempstead, 1973–79; Vicar, Goldington, Bedford, 1979–88; Priest-in-charge, Renhold, 1980–82; RD, Bedford, 1984–87; Vicar, St Cuthbert's, Portsmouth, 1988–96; RD, Portsmouth, 1994–96. *Recreations:* sailing, horology. *Address:* Furzend, 38A Bosham Hoe, W Sussex PO18 8ET. *T:* (01243) 572340. *E:* furzend@merlinbanting.plus.com.

BANTON, Prof. Michael Parker, CMG 2001; JP; PhD, DSc; Professor of Sociology, 1965–92, now Emeritus, and Pro-Vice-Chancellor, 1985–88, University of Bristol; *b* 8 Sept. 1926; *s* of Francis Clive Banton and Kathleen Blanche (*née* Parkes); *m* 1952, Rut Marianne (*née* Jacobson), Luleå; one *s* two *d* (and one *s* decd). *Educ:* King Edward's Sch., Birmingham; London Sch. of Economics. BSc Econ. 1950; PhD 1954; DSc 1964. Served RN, 1944–47 (Sub-Lieut, RNVR). Asst, then Lecturer, then Reader, in Social Anthropology, University of Edinburgh, 1950–65. Dir, SSRC Res. Unit on Ethnic Relations, 1970–78. Visiting Professor: MIT, 1962–63; Wayne State Univ., Detroit, 1971; Univ. of Delaware, 1976; ANU, 1981; Duke Univ., 1982; National Univ. of Malaysia, 2010. Editor, Sociology, 1966–69. President: Section N, 1969–70 and Section H, 1985–86, BAAS; Royal Anthropological Inst., 1987–89; Mem., Vetenskapssocieteten, Lund, Sweden, 1972; Member: Royal Commn on Criminal Procedure, 1978–80; Royal Commn on Bermuda, 1978; UK National Commn for UNESCO, 1963–66 and 1980–85; UN Cttee for the Elimination of Racial Discrimination, 1986–2001 (Chm., 1996–98); Ethnic Minorities Adv. Cttee, Judicial Studies Bd, 1993–96; SW Regl Hosp. Board, 1966–70. JP Bristol, 1966. FRSA 1981. FilDr *hc* Stockholm, 2000. *Publications:* The Coloured Quarter, 1955; West African City, 1957; White and Coloured, 1959; The Policeman in the Community, 1964; Roles, 1965; Race Relations, 1967; Racial Minorities, 1972; Police-Community Relations, 1973; (with J. Harwood) The Race Concept, 1975; The Idea of Race, 1977; Racial and Ethnic Competition, 1983; Promoting Racial Harmony, 1985; Investigating Robbery, 1985; Racial Theories, 1987, 2nd edn 1998; Racial Consciousness, 1988; Discrimination, 1994; International Action Against Racial Discrimination, 1996; Ethnic and Racial Consciousness, 1997; The International Politics of Race, 2002. *Address:* Fairways, Luxted Road, Downe, Orpington BR6 7JT. *T:* (01959) 576828. *E:* michael@banton.demon.co.uk.

BANVILLE, John; writer; *b* Wexford, 8 Dec. 1945; *s* of Martin and Agnes Banville; two *s* with Janet Dunham Banville; two *d* with Patricia Quinn. *Educ:* Christian Brothers' Schs; St Peter's Coll., Wexford, Ireland. Journalist, 1970–99; Literary Ed., Irish Times, 1988–99. *Theatre:* The Broken Jug, Abbey Th., Dublin, 1994; God's Gift, Dublin Th. Fest. and tour, 2000; The Book of Evidence, Kilkenny Th. Fest., 2002 and Gate Th., Dublin, 2003; *television:* screenplay: Reflections, 1984; play: Seachange, 1994; *radio* includes: Stardust, series of monologues, 2004; plays: Kepler, 2004; Todtnauberg, 2005; Bowen and Betjeman, 2014; *film screenplays:* The Last September, 2000; (jtly) Albert Nobbs, 2012; The Sea, 2014. *Publications:* Long Lankin (short stories), 1970; *novels:* Nightspawn, 1971; Birchwood, 1974; Doctor Copernicus (James Tait Black Meml Prize), 1976; Kepler (Guardian Fiction Prize), 1980; The Newton Letter, 1982 (filmed for TV as Reflections, 1984); Mefisto, 1986; The Book of Evidence, 1989 (Guinness Peat Aviation Award, Premio Ennio Flaiano, Italy, 1991); Ghosts, 1993; Athena, 1995; The Untouchable, 1997; Eclipse, 2000; Shroud, 2002; The Sea (Man Booker Prize), 2005 (filmed 2014); The Infinities, 2009; Ancient Light, 2012; The Blue Guitar, 2015; *non-fiction:* Prague Pictures: portraits of a city, 2003; *adaptations* of dramas by Heinrich von Kleist: The Broken Jug, 1994; God's Gift, 2000; Love in the Wars, 2005; as Benjamin Black: Christine Falls, 2006; The Silver Swan, 2007; The Lemur, 2008; Elegy for April, 2010; A Death in Summer, 2011; Vengeance, 2012; The Black-Eyed Blonde, 2014. *Recreation:* work. *Address:* c/o Ed Victor Ltd, 6 Bayley Street, Bedford Square, WC1B 3HE. *T:* (020) 7304 4100, *Fax:* (020) 7304 4111. *Clubs:* Kildare Street and University, St Stephen's Green (Dublin).

BANX; *see* Banks, Jeremy.

BAPTISTA, João P. A.; President, Nordics, Southern Europe and South America, and Member, Executive Committee, CGI, since 2012; *b* Lisbon, Portugal, 1958; *s* of Milton Baptista and Maria Baptista; *m* 1997, Elizabeth P. A. Allen; two *s* one *d*. *Educ:* Stanford Graduate Sch. of Business (MBA 1985); Swiss Federal Inst. of Technology, Lausanne (Dip. Mechanical Engrg and Energy). Man. Dir, Bd Mem., Hd of Technol., Information, Communication and Entertainment Worldwide, Mercer Management Consulting, 1985–2005; Global Leader of Technol., Information, Communication and Entertainment, Marsh & McLennan Cos, Inc., 2004–05; Lead Partner, UK Telecommunication Team, Booz Allen Hamilton, 2005–06; Chm. and CEO of Internat. Investments, Mem. of Exec. Cttee and Dir, Main Bd, Portugal Telecom SGPS, 2006–08; CEO, N and Central Europe, Iberia and Latam, Chm., Utilities and Telecommunications Practices and Special Businesses, and Mem., Exec. Cttee, Logica plc, 2008–12. Vice-Chm., Vivo, Brazil, 2006–08; CEO, Africatel Hldgs, 2006–08. Trustee, V&A Mus., 2011– (Chm., Audit Cttee, 2011–; Mem., Finance Cttee, 2011–). FRSA. *Publications:* (jtly) Grow to be Great, 1995, 2nd edn 2010. *Recreations:* painting, modern art, cinema, travelling, ski-ing, sailing.

BAPTISTA DA SILVA, Dr Carlos Boaventura; Secretary, Board of Trustees, Calouste Gulbenkian Foundation, 1974–2005; Executive Director, Grémio Literário Committee, Lisbon, since 2001; *b* 13 Feb. 1935; *s* of Fernando Baptista da Silva and Virginia Boaventura Baptista da Silva; *m* 1961, Emilia de Almeida Nadal; two *s* one *d*. *Educ:* Univ. of Lisbon (Lic. in Law). Lawyer, 1968–. Mem., Portuguese Mint Consulting Cttee. Mem., Gen. Cttee, Oliveira Martins Foundn, Lisbon, 1980–. Pres., 2000–07, Counsellor, 2007–12, FIDEM (Hon. Mem., 2012); Vice-Pres., Gen. Assembly, Nat. Soc. of Fine Arts, Lisbon, until 2013. Comdr, Order of Public Instruction (Portugal), 1968. *Publications:* several texts on medal art. *Recreations:* collector of medals and modern art, music, reading. *Address:* Rua dos Navegantes 53–5° DT°, 1200–730 Lisbon, Portugal. *T:* 213974242, 916000276, *Fax:* 213974242. *E:* cbsilva935@gmail.com.

BAR-HILLEL, Mira; Property and Planning Correspondent, Evening Standard, since 1986; *b* 30 Sept. 1946; *d* of late Prof. Yehoshua Bar-Hillel and Shulamit (*née* Aschkenazy); partner, 2014, Peter Fermoy. *Educ:* Hebrew Gymnasia, Jerusalem; Hebrew Univ., Jerusalem (BA Soviet Studies 1972). Military Service, Israel Defence Forces, 1963–65. News reporter: Voice of Israel, 1965–72; Building mag., 1973–82 (News Editor, 1978–82); freelance writer on property and also architecture and planning, 1982–; writes regularly for The Oldie, London Mag., Property Week. LBC Radio Property Expert, 1993–94. Commentator on Israel/Palestine, Independent Voices and other media, 2008–. Internat. Bldg Press Award, 1979, 1980, 1983, 1988, 1994, 1995, 1996; RICS Award, 1985; Incorporated Soc. Valuers and Auctioneers Award, 1986, 1996; Laing Homes Award, 1989, 1991, 1993; Lifetime Achievement Award, LSL Property Press Awards, 2013. *Recreations:* cats, fighting Modernism, meeting interesting people, countering Zionist propaganda. *Address:* Evening Standard, Northcliffe House, 2 Derry Street, High Street, Kensington, W8 5EE. *T:* 07711 495158. *E:* mira.barhillel@standard.co.uk. *W:* www.twitter.com/mirabarhillel.

BARAGWANATH, Hon. Sir (William) David, KNZM 2011; QC (NZ) 1983; President, Special Tribunal for Lebanon, The Hague, 2011–15 (Judge, Appeals Chamber, since 2009); *b* Balclutha, NZ, 3 Aug. 1940; *s* of Very Rev. Owen Thomas Baragwanath and Eileen Georgia Baragwanath; *m*; four *c*. *Educ:* Auckland Grammar Sch.; Univ. of Auckland (LLB 1964); Balliol Coll., Oxford (Rhodes Scholar 1964; BCL 1966). Called to the Bar, NZ, 1964; Partner, Meredith Connell & Co., Auckland, 1966–77; Judge, High Court, 1995; Judge, Court of Appeal of NZ, 2008–10. Pres., NZ Law Commn, 1996–2001; Chm., Rules Cttee, Court of NZ, 2004–08. Presiding Judge, Court of Appeal, Samoa, 2006–12; NZ Mem., Perm. Court of Arbitration, The Hague, 2007–13. Sen. Academic Visitor, Wolfson Coll., Cambridge, 2010; Dist. Judicial Visitor, Univ. of Hong Kong, 2010; Dist. Vis. Fellow, QMUL, 2011; HUGO Fellow-in-Residence, Netherlands Inst. of Advanced Studies, 2011. Hon. Prof., Univ. of Waikato. Overseas Bencher, Inner Temple, 2010. Fulbright travel award to Univ. of Virginia, 1983. *Publications:* articles in legal jls. *Recreations:* ski-ing, walking, reading. *Address:* Special Tribunal for Lebanon, PO Box 115, 2260 Leidschendam, Netherlands. *Club:* Northern (Auckland).

BARAK, Jeff(rey); Corporate Editor, Amdocs, since 2009; *b* 26 April 1961; *s* of Malcolm and Estelle Black; *m* 1989, Yemima Rabin; two *s* one *d*. *Educ:* Leeds Grammar Sch.; Univ. of Newcastle upon Tyne (BA Hons English Lit.). Formerly ME analyst for assorted media; Ed.-in-Chief, Jerusalem Post, 1996–2002; Dep. Ed., 2002–05, Man. Ed., 2005–06, Jewish Chronicle; Ed.-in-Chief, Ynetnews.com, 2007; Sen. Ed., Ha'aretz (English-language edn), 2007–08. *Recreation:* watching televised sport. *Address:* PO Box 85285, Mevasseret Zion 90805, Israel. *T:* 526453637.

BARAŃSKI, Prof. Zygmunt Guido; Serena Professor of Italian, University of Cambridge, 2002–11, now Emeritus; Fellow, Murray Edwards College (formerly New Hall), Cambridge, 2002–11; Notre Dame Professor of Dante and Italian Studies, University of Notre Dame, since 2011; *b* 13 April 1951; *s* of Henryk Barański and Sonia Mariotti; *m* 1979, Margaret Ellen Watt; one *s* one *d*. *Educ:* St Bede's Coll., Manchester; Hull Univ. (BA 1973). Lectr in Italian, Univ. of Aberdeen, 1976–79; University of Reading: Lectr, 1979–89, Sen. Lectr, 1989–92, in Italian Studies; Prof. of Italian Studies, 1992–2002. Visiting Professor: McGill Univ., 1988, 1997; Univ. of Virginia, Charlottesville, 1991; Univ. of Connecticut, 1993; Yale Univ., 1995; Univ. of Notre Dame, 1996, 1998, 2004, 2007, 2010; Univ. of Bari, 2001; Univ. of California, Berkeley, 2002; Univ. of Reading, 2002–; UCLA, 2008; Univ. of Leeds, 2011–14. Pres., Internat. Dante Seminar, 2003–08. Commendatore, Ordine della Stella della Solidarietà (Italy), 2005. *Publications:* (ed) *Libri poetarum in quattuor species dividuntur*: essays on Dante and genre, 1995; *Luce nuova, sole nuovo*: saggi sul rinnovamento culturale in Dante, 1996; Pasolini Old and New, 1999; Dante e i segni, 2000; *Chiosar con altro testo*: leggere Dante nel trecento, 2001; Petrarch and Dante: anti-Dantism, metaphysics, tradition, 2009; Dante in Context, 2015; contribs to learned jls. *Recreations:* following Manchester United, cycling, music. *Address:* Department of Romance Languages and Literatures, University of Notre Dame, Notre Dame, IN 46556, USA. *T:* (574) 6316886, *Fax:* (574) 6313493. *E:* baranski.1@nd.edu, zgb20@cam.ac.uk.

BARBARITO, Mgr Luigi, Hon. GCVO 1996; DD, JCD; Titular Archbishop of Fiorentino; Apostolic Nuncio (formerly Pro-Nuncio) to the Court of St James's, 1986–97; *b* Atripalda, Avellino, Italy, 19 April 1922; *s* of Vincenzo Barbarito and Alfonsina Armerini. *Educ:* Pontifical Seminary, Benevento, Italy; Gregorian Univ., Rome (JCD); Papal Diplomatic Academy, Rome (Diploma). Priest, 1944; served Diocese of Avellino, 1944–52; entered Diplomatic Service of Holy See, 1953; Sec., Apostolic Delegn, Australia, 1953–59; Secretariat of State of Vatican (Council for Public Affairs of the Church), 1959–67; Counsellor, Apostolic Nunciature, Paris, 1967–69; Archbishop and Papal Nuncio to Haiti and Delegate to the Antilles, 1969–75; Pro-Nuncio to Senegal, Bourkina Fasso, Niger, Mali, Mauritania, Cape Verde Is and Guinea Bissau, 1975–78; Apostolic Pro-Nuncio to Australia, 1978–86. Mem., Mexican Acad. of Internat. Law. Grand Cross, National Order of Haiti, 1975; Grand Cross, Order of the Lion (Senegal), 1978; Knight Commander, Order of Merit (Italy), 1966, (Portugal), 1967; Knight Grand Cross of Grace, Sacred Military Constantinian Order of St George, 2013. *Recreations:* music, walking. *Address:* c/o Suore Francescane, Casa San Giuseppe, via Grottone 28, 83030 Pietradefusi, AV, Italy. *T:* (0825) 462636.

BARBER OF TEWKESBURY, Baron *cr* 1992 (Life Peer), of Gotherington in the County of Gloucestershire; **Derek Coates Barber,** Kt 1984; Chairman: Booker Countryside Advisory Board, 1990–96; Countryside Commission, 1981–91; *s* of Thomas Smith-Barber and Elsie Coates; 1st marr. diss. 1981; *m* 2nd, 1983, Rosemary Jennifer Brougham, *o d* of late Lt-Comdr Randolph Brougham Pearson, RN, and Hilary Diana Mackinlay Pearson (*née* Bennett). *Educ:* Royal Agricl Coll., Cirencester (MRAC; Gold Medal, Practical Agriculture; FRAC 1999). Served War: invalided, Armed Forces, 1942. Farmed in Glos Cotswolds; Mem., Cheltenham Rural District Council, 1948–52; Dist Adv. Officer, National Agricl Adv. Service, MAFF, 1946–57; County Agricl Advisor, Glos, 1957–72; Environment Consultant to Humberts, Chartered Surveyors, 1972–93; MAFF Assessor: Pilkington Cttee on Agric. Educ., 1966; Agric. and Hort. Trng Bd, 1968. Member: H of L Sub-Cttee D (Food and Agric.), 1992–96; H of L Select Cttee on Sustainable Develt, 1994–95. Chairman: BBC's Central Agricl Adv. Cttee, 1974–80 (*ex officio* Mem., BBC's Gen. Adv. Council, 1972–80); New National Forest Adv. Bd, 1991–95. Royal Soc. for Protection of Birds: Mem., 1970–75, Chm., 1976–81, Council; Chm., Educn Cttee, 1972–75; Vice-Pres., 1982; Pres., 1990–91. President: RASE, 1991–92; Rare Breeds Survival Trust, 1991–95, 1997–99 (Mem. Council, 1987–99); Hawk and Owl Trust, 1992–96; British Pig Assoc., 1995–96 (Vice-Pres., 1997–99); Glos Naturalists' Soc., 1981–; Vice-Pres., Ornithol Soc. of Mid-East, 1987–97; Mem. Council, British Trust for Ornithology, 1987–90; Founder Mem., 1969, Farming and Wildlife Adv. Gp of landowning, farming and wildlife conservation bodies; Member: Ordnance Survey Adv. Bd, 1982–85; Bd, RURAL Council, 1983–94; Bd, CEED, 1984–98; Centre for Agricl Strategy, 1985–91; Arable Res. Insts Assoc., 1991–95; Long Ashton Res. Stn Cttee, 1991–95. Dep. Chm., Bd, Groundwork Foundn, 1985–91; Patron, Woodland Trust, 1991–. FRAgS 1992; FIAgrM 1992. Hon. FRASE 1986. Hon. DSc Bradford, 1986. First Recipient, Summers Trophy for services to agric. in practice or science, 1955; Bledisloe Gold Medal for distinguished service to UK agriculture, 1967; RSPB Gold Medal for services to bird protection, 1982; Massey-Ferguson Award for services to agric., 1989; RASE Gold Medal, for distinguished service to UK agric., 1991. Silver Jubilee Medal, 1977. Editor, Humberts Commentary, 1973–88; columnist, Power Farming, 1973–91; Spec. Correspondent, Waitaki NZR Times, 1982–88. *Publications:* (with Keith Dexter) Farming for Profits, 1961, 2nd edn 1967; (with J. G. S. and Frances Donaldson) Farming in Britain Today, 1969, 2nd edn 1972; (ed) Farming with Wildlife, 1971; A History of Humberts, 1980; contrib. farming and wildlife conservation jls. *Recreations:* birds, wildlife conservation, farming. *Address:* House of Lords, SW1A 0PW.

BARBER, Sir Brendan (Paul), Kt 2013; General Secretary, Trades Union Congress, 2003–12; Chairman, Advisory Conciliation and Arbitration Service, since 2014 (Council Member, 1995–2004); *b* 3 April 1951; *s* of John and Agnes Barber; *m* 1981, Mary Rose Gray; two *d*. *Educ:* St Mary's Coll., Crosby; City Univ., London (BSc Hons; Pres. Students Union, 1973–74). Volunteer teacher, VSO, Ghana, 1969–70; Researcher, ceramics, glass and mineral products, ITB, 1974–75; Trades Union Congress: Asst, Orgn Dept, 1975–79; Hd, Press and

Information Dept, 1979–87; Hd, Orgn Dept, 1987–93; Dep. Gen. Sec., 1993–2003. Member: Council, Sport England, 1999–2002; Court, Bank of England, 2003–12; UK Commn on Employment and Skills, 2008–12; Bd, TfL, 2013–; Banking Standards Bd, 2015–. Visiting Fellow: Saïd Business Sch., Oxford, 2012–; Nuffield Coll., Oxford, 2013–. Member: Council, City Univ., 2013–; Bd of Trustees, Mountview Acad. of the Theatre Arts, 2014–. *Recreations:* golf, football, theatre, cinema. *Club:* Muswell Hill Golf.

BARBER, Chris; *see* Barber, D. C.

BARBER, Sir David; *see* Barber, Sir T. D.

BARBER, (Donald) Chris(topher), OBE 1991; band leader, The Chris Barber Band; *b* 17 April 1930; *s* of Henrietta Mary Evelyn Barber, MA Cantab and Donald Barber, CBE, BA Cantab; *m*; one *s* one *d*; *m* Kate; one step *d*. *Educ:* King Alfred School; St Paul's School. Formed first amateur band, 1949; present band commenced on professional basis, 1954; plays trombone, baritone horn, double bass and trumpet. Hon. Citizen, New Orleans. Numerous recordings, including over 150 LPs and 100 CDs, with records in the hit parade of over 40 countries world wide. Hon. DMus Durham, 2006. *Recreations:* collecting jazz and blues records, snooker, motor racing. *Address:* c/o Belmont, Wycombe Road, Studley Green, High Wycombe, Bucks HP14 3XB. *T:* and *Fax:* (01494) 484488. *E:* sitedc@aol.com.

BARBER, Edward Simon Dominic, OBE 2013; RDI 2007; Founding Director and Co-owner: BarberOsgerby, since 1996; Universal Design Studio, since 2001; Map Project Office Ltd, since 2011; *b* Shrewsbury, 6 April 1969; *s* of Simon Barber and Penelope Barber (*née* Baldock). *Educ:* Leeds Poly. (BA Hons Interior Design); Royal Coll. of Art (MA Arch. and Interior Design). Prof., University Coll. Falmouth. *Commissions* include: design for Torch for London 2012 Olympic Games, 2011; design for £2 coin to commemorate 150 years of London Underground. Co-Curator of exhibitions including: In the Making, Design Mus., London, 2014; Precision and Poetry in Motion, V&A Mus., 2014. FRSA 2005. Jerwood Applied Arts Prize (jtly), Jerwood Foundn, 2004. *Address:* BarberOsgerby, 37–42 Charlotte Road, EC2A 3PG. *T:* (020) 7033 3884, *Fax:* (020) 7033 3882. *E:* mail@barberosgerby.com.

BARBER, Frank; Senior Partner, Morgan, Fentiman & Barber, 1993–97; Deputy Chairman of Lloyd's, 1983, 1984; *b* 5 July 1923; *s* of Sidney Barber and Florence (*née* Seath); *m* 1st, 1945, Gertrude Kathleen Carson (decd); one *s* one *d* (and one *s* decd); 2nd, 1994, Elizabeth Joan Charvet (*d* 2011). *Educ:* West Norwood Central School. RAFVR, 1942–46. Entered Lloyd's, 1939; Underwriter, Lloyd's syndicate, Frank Barber & others, 1962–81; Member: Cttee of Lloyd's, 1977–80, 1982–85 and 1987; Council of Lloyd's, 1983–85 and 1987; Chm., Finance Cttee, Lloyd's, 1984; Dep. Chm., Lloyd's Underwriters' Non-Marine Assoc., 1971, Chm., 1972; Dep. Chm., British Insurers' European Cttee, 1983. Partner: Morgan, Fentiman & Barber, 1968–97; G. S. Christensen & Partners, 1985–2000; Chairman: A. E. Grant (Underwriting Agencies) Ltd, 1991–96; Frank Barber Underwriting Ltd, 2000–13. *Recreations:* music, walking, sailing. *Address:* Lime Cottage, Horseshoe Lane, Ipthorpe, Hants SP11 0BY.

BARBER, Prof. James, PhD; FRS 2005; FRSC; Ernst Chain Professor of Biochemistry, since 1989, and Senior Research Investigator, since 2013, Imperial College London (formerly Imperial College of Science, Technology and Medicine) (Head of Department of Biochemistry, 1989–99); *b* 16 July 1940; *s* of Stanley William George Barber and Sophia Helen Barber; *m* 1965, Marilyn Jane Emily Tyrrell; one *s* one *d*. *Educ:* Portsmouth Southern Grammar Sch.; Univ. of Wales (BSc Hons Chem.); Univ. of East Anglia (MSc, PhD Biophy.). FRSC 1983. Unilever Biochem. Soc. European Fellow, Univ. of Leiden, 1967–68; Imperial College: Lectr, Dept of Botany, 1968–74; Reader in Plant Physiology, 1974–79, Prof., 1979–89; Dean, Royal Coll. of Science, 1989–91. Miller Prof., Univ. of Calif at Berkeley, 1989–90, 2001; Burroughs Wellcome Fund Prof., Univ. of Calif, 2000. Lectures: Brookhaven Sci. Associates Dist., 2005; Drummond, Queen Mary, London, 2005; G8 Univ., Torino, 2009; Sir Ernst Chain Distinguished, Imperial Coll. London, 2011. Lee Kuan Yew Dist. Visitor, Singapore, 2008. Selby Fellow, Australian Acad. of Scis, 1996; Foreign Mem., Swedish Royal Acad. of Scis, 2003. Mem., Academia Europaea, 1989. Hon. Dr Univ. of Stockholm, 1992; Hon. DSc UEA, 2010. Flintoff Medal, RSC, 2002; Italgas Prize for Energy and Envmt, Academia Europaea, 2005; Novartis Medal and Prize, Biochem. Soc., 2006; Wheland Medal and Prize, Univ. of Chicago, 2007; Arnon Lect. and Prize, UC Berkeley, 2008; Interdisciplinary Medal and Prize, RSC, 2013. *Publications:* The Intact Chloroplast, 1976; Primary Processes in Photosynthesis, 1977; Photosynthesis in Relation to Model Systems, 1979; Electron Transport and Photophosphorylation, 1982; Chloroplast Biogenesis, 1984; Photosynthetic Mechanisms and the Environment, 1986; The Light Reactions, 1987; The Photosystems: structure, function and molecular biology, 1992; Molecular Processes of Photosynthesis, 1994; Molecular to Global Photosynthesis, 2004; articles and reviews. *Recreations:* running, sailing, gardening. *Address:* Sir Ernst Chain-Wolfson Building, Department of Life Sciences, Imperial College London, SW7 2AZ. *T:* (020) 7594 5266. *E:* j.barber@imperial.ac.uk.

BARBER, Prof. Karin Judith, CBE 2012; PhD; FBA 2003; Professor of African Cultural Anthropology, Department of African Studies and Anthropology, University of Birmingham, since 1999; *b* 2 July 1949; *d* of Charles and Barbara Barber; partner, Dr Paulo Fernando de Moraes Farias. *Educ:* Lawnswood High Sch., Leeds; Girton Coll., Cambridge (BA English 1st cl., MA); UCL (Dip. in Soc. Anthropol.); Univ. of Ife (PhD). Lectr, Dept of African Langs and Lits, Univ. of Ife, 1977–84; Centre of West African Studies, University of Birmingham: Lectr, 1985–93; Sen. Lectr, 1993–97; Reader, 1997–99; Dir, 1998–2001. Vis. Preceptor, Inst. for Adv. Study and Res. in African Humanities, 1993–94, Melville J. Herskovits Vis. Chair in African Studies, 1999, Northwestern Univ., Illinois. *Publications:* Yorùbá Dùn ún So: a beginners' course in Yorùbá, 1984, 2nd edn 1990; (ed with P. F. de Moraes Farias) Discourse and its Disguises: the interpretation of African oral texts, 1989; (ed with P. F. de Moraes Farias) Self-assertion and Brokerage: early cultural nationalism in West Africa, 1990; I Could Speak Until Tomorrow: Oríkì, women and the past in a Yorùbá town (Amaury Talbot Prize, RAI), 1991; (with Bayo Ogundijo) Yorùbá Popular Theatre: three plays by the Oyin Adejobi Company, 1994; (jtly) West African Popular Theatre, 1997; (ed) Readings in African Popular Culture, 1997; (with Akin Oyetade) Yorùbá Wuyì, 1999; The Generation of Plays: Yorùbá popular life in theater (Herskovits Award, African Studies Assoc., USA), 2000; (ed) Africa's Hidden Histories: everyday literacy and making the self, 2006; The Anthropology of Texts, Persons and Publics, 2007; Print Culture and the First Yoruba Novel (Paul Hair Prize, African Studies Assoc., USA), 2012. *Recreations:* theatre, music. *Address:* Department of African Studies and Anthropology, University of Birmingham, Edgbaston, Birmingham B15 2TT. *T:* (0121) 414 5125, *Fax:* (0121) 414 3228. *E:* k.j.barber@bham.ac.uk.

BARBER, Lionel; Editor, Financial Times, since 2005; *b* 18 Jan. 1955; *s* of Frank Douglas Barber and Joan Elizabeth Barber (*née* Nolan); *m* 1986, Victoria Greenwood; one *s* one *d*. *Educ:* Dulwich Coll.; St Edmund Hall, Oxford (BA Jt Hons German and Modern Hist.). Reporter, Scotsman, 1978–81; business reporter, Sunday Times, 1981–85; Financial Times: UK company news reporter, 1985–86; Washington Corresp., 1986–92; Brussels Bureau Chief, 1992–98; News Ed., 1998–2000; European Ed., 2000–02; US Managing Ed., 2002–05. Trustee, Tate, 2011–. *Publications:* (jtly) The Delorean Tapes, 1984; (jtly) The Price of Truth: the story of Reuter's millions, 1985; (jtly) Not with Honour, 1986. *Recreations:* cycling, tennis, working out, reading American history, watching Rugby. *Address:* Financial Times, Number One, Southwark Bridge, SE1 9HL. *T:* (020) 7873 4222.

BARBER, Prof. Sir Michael (Bayldon), Kt 2005; Chief Education Advisor, Pearson plc, since 2011; Special Representative on Education in Pakistan, Department for International Development, since 2011; *b* 24 Nov. 1955; *s* of Christopher and Anne Barber; *m* 1982, Karen Alderman; three *d*. *Educ:* Bootham Sch., York; Queen's Coll., Oxford (BA Hons 1977); Georg-August Univ., Göttingen; Westminster Coll., Oxford (PGCE 1979); Inst. of Educn, London Univ. (MA 1991). History Teacher: Watford, 1979–83; Zimbabwe, 1983–85; Policy and Res. Officer, 1985–89, Education Officer, 1989–93, NUT; Professor of Education: Keele Univ., 1993–95; Inst. of Educn, London Univ., 1995–97; Dir, Standards and Effectiveness Unit, and Chief Advr to Sec. of State on Sch. Standards, DFEE, 1997–2001; Chief Advr to Prime Minister on Delivery, and Hd, Prime Minister's Delivery Unit, 2001–05; Expert Partner, Global Public Sector Practice, later Head of Global Educn Practice, McKinsey & Co., 2005–11. Visiting Professor: Univ. of London, 2001–; Moscow Higher Sch. of Economics, 2009–. Mem. (Lab), Hackney LBC, 1986–90 (Chair, Educn Cttee, 1988–89). Contested (Lab) Henley-on-Thames, 1987. FRSA 1993. Hon. EdD Wolverhampton, 2003; Hon. DLaws Exeter, 2009; Hon. DLitt Wales, 2014. *Publications:* Education and the Teacher Unions, 1992; The Making of 1944 Education Act, 1994; The National Curriculum: a study in policy, 1996; The Learning Game: arguments for an education revolution, 1996, revd edn 1997; Instruction to Deliver: Tony Blair, reform of public services and achievement of targets, 2007, 2nd edn as Instruction to Deliver: the battle to reform Britain's public services, 2008; (with Mona Mourshed) How the World's Best Performing Education Systems Come Out on Top, 2007; Deliverology 101: a field guide for education leaders, 2011; How to Run a Government so that Citizens Benefit and Taxpayers don't go Crazy, 2015. *Recreations:* mountain walking, Liverpool Football Club, cycling, reading history books. *Address:* N Devon. *T:* (020) 7010 2347.

BARBER, Nicholas Charles Faithorn, CBE 2004; Chairman, Bolero International Ltd, since 1998; *b* 7 Sept. 1940; *s* of Bertram Harold and Nancy Lorraine Barber; *m* 1966, Sheena Macrae Graham; two *s* one *d*. *Educ:* Ludgrove Sch.; Shrewsbury Sch.; Wadham Coll., Oxford (MA; Hon. Fellow 2007); Columbia Univ., New York, 1969–71 (MBA). Lectr, Marlboro Coll., Vermont, USA, 1963–64; joined Ocean Steam Ship, subseq. Ocean Transport and Trading, later Ocean Group, 1964; Dir, 1980–94; Chief Exec., 1986–94. Divl Dir, NEB, 1977–79. Chairman: IEC Gp plc, 1996–99; Orion Publishing Gp, 1997–98; Kappa IT Ventures, 1998–2007; Director: Overseas Containers Ltd, 1984–86; Costain Gp, 1990–93; Royal Insurance Hldgs plc, 1991–96 (Dep. Chm., 1994–96); Royal & Sun Alliance Insurance Gp plc, 1996–2003; Barings plc, 1994–95; Bank of Ireland UK Financial Services plc (formerly Bristol & West Bldg Soc., then Bristol and West plc), 1994–2003 (Dep. Chm., 2001–03); Albright & Wilson plc, 1995–99; Fidelity Japanese Values PLC, 2000–12; The Maersk Co., 2004–08. Mem., NW Industrial Develt Bd, 1982–85; Gov., NIESR, 1991– (Mem., Exec. Cttee, 2001–). Mem. Bd, Liverpool Playhouse, 1982–87; Mem., Adv. Cttee, Tate Gall., Liverpool, 1988–92; Trustee: Nat. Museums and Galls on Merseyside, 1986–94; Shrewsbury Sch. Foundn, 1990–2006; British Mus., 1993–2003; Country Houses Foundn, 2004–; Chairman: British Mus. Friends (formerly British Mus. Soc.), 1992–2003; British Mus. Co. Ltd, 1996–2003; Ashmolean Mus., 2003–10. Governor: Shrewsbury Sch., 1983–2003 (Dep. Chm., 1997–2003); London Business Sch., 1993–2001; Vice-Pres., Liverpool Sch. of Tropical Medicine, 1988–2014, now Vice-Pres. Emeritus; Chm., Huron Univ. USA in London Ltd, 1998–2007; Member Council: Liverpool Univ., 1985–88; Industrial Soc., 1993–99; Mem., Adv. Council, Asia House, 1996–; Dir, Hult Internat. Business Sch., Boston, 2008–; Fellow, Ashridge Business Sch., 2015–. Chm., Classics for All, 2013–. FRSA 1994. Hon. DHL Marlboro Coll., Vermont, 2005. Distinguished Friend, Oxford Univ., 2010; Fellow, Ashmolean Mus., 2011. *Recreations:* history, museums, woodland gardening, mountain walking, cricket. *Address:* 6 Lytton Court, 14 Barter Street, WC1A 2AH. *Clubs:* Brooks's, MCC; Denham Golf.

BARBER, Pamela Gay, (Mrs Paul Barker); DL; Headteacher, Lancaster Girls' Grammar School, 1987–2007; *b* 8 May 1947; *d* of Harold and Muriel Nunwick; *m* Paul Barker. *Educ:* N Western Poly., London (BA Hons Geog.); Leeds Univ. (PGCE). Class teacher, then Hd of Geog. and Hd of Sixth Form, Belle Vue Girls' Sch., Bradford, 1969–80; Deputy Head: Crossley and Porter Sch., Halifax, 1980–85; Crossley Heath Sch., Halifax, 1985–86. Boarding Headteacher, Admiralty Interview Bd, 1992–2005. Non-exec. Dir, Lancaster HA, 1990–93. Mem. Bd, Bay Radio, 1999–2003. Mem. Council, Lancaster Univ., 1989–95. Mem., Adv. Cttee, Arkwright Trust, 1998–2007; Trustee, Community Foundn for Lancs, 2008–. Constable, Lancaster Castle, 2013–. DL Lancs, 2007. Hon. Fellow, Lancaster Univ., 2011. *Recreations:* foreign travel, horse riding, donkey keeping, gardening, fell-walking.

BARBER, Rt Rev. Paul Everard; Bishop Suffragan of Brixworth, 1989–2001; an Hon. Assistant Bishop, Diocese of Bath and Wells, since 2001; *b* 16 Sept. 1935; *s* of Cecil Arthur and Mollie Barber; *m* 1959, Patricia Jayne Walford; two *s* two *d* (and one *s* decd). *Educ:* Sherborne School; St John's Coll., Cambridge (BA 1958, MA 1966); Wells Theological College. Deacon 1960, priest 1961, dio. Guildford; Curate of St Francis, Westborough, 1960–66; Vicar: Camberley with Yorktown, 1966–73; St Thomas-on-the-Bourne, Farnham, 1973–80; Rural Dean of Farnham, 1974–79; Archdeacon of Surrey, 1980–89; Hon. Canon: of Guildford, 1980–89; of Peterborough, 1997–2001. General Synod, 1979–85; Member, Council of College of Preachers, 1969–98. Archbp of Canterbury's Advr to HMC, 1993–2001. Gov., Millfield Sch., 2002–08. *Recreations:* sport, theatre, cinema, walking. *Address:* 41 Somerton Road, Street, Somerset BA16 0DR. *T:* (01458) 442916.

BARBER, Stephen James; social services consultant; Chief Children's Officer, and Director of Social Services, London Borough of Barnet, 1999–2000; *b* 15 Nov. 1946; *s* of John Barber and Jenny Barber (*née* Roshan Mirza); *m* 1972, Mary Margaret Hoffman; three *d*. *Educ:* Hall Sch., Hampstead; Uppingham Sch., Rutland; Trinity Coll., Cambridge (BA, MA); Brunel Univ. (MA, CQSW). Res. student, 1970–73; nursing asst, Cassell Hosp., 1973–74; social worker, 1974–79, Team Leader, 1979–85, Principal Officer, 1985–88, RBK&C; Asst Dir (Children and Families), London Borough of Ealing, 1988–93; Controller of Community Services, London Borough of Barnet, 1993–99. Safeguarding Adviser (formerly Child Protection Adviser), Dio. of Oxford, 2003–; Chair, Local Safeguarding Children Bds, W Berks, Reading and Wokingham, 2009–14. Chm., Springboard Family Project, 2004–09. Trustee: British Assoc. (formerly Agencies) for Adoption and Fostering, 1999–2000; Parents and Children Together, 2004–09; Hampshire and Thames Valley Circles of Support and Accountability, 2008–09. Treas., Charles Williams Soc., 2001–. *Publications:* contrib. reviews and articles to TES, Community Care, Adoption and Fostering, etc. *Recreations:* playing the piano, collecting books and CDs, visiting cathedral cities. *Address:* c/o Diocesan Church House, North Hinksey, Oxford OX2 0NB.

BARBER, Sir (Thomas) David, 3rd Bt *cr* 1960, of Greasley, Nottingham; self-employed philatelist; *b* 18 Nov. 1937; *o s* of Col Sir William Francis Barber, 2nd Bt and his 1st wife, Diana Constance Barber (*née* Lloyd) (*d* 1984); *S* father, 1995; *m* 1st, 1971, Amanda Mary Healing (*née* Rabone) (marr. diss. 1976); one *s*; 2nd, 1978 Jeannine Mary Boyle (*née* Gurney); one *s* one *d*. *Educ:* Eton; Trinity Coll., Cambridge (MA). 2nd Lieut, RA, 1958–61. *Heir: s* Thomas Edward Barber [*b* 14 March 1973; *m* 2004, Davina Alice, *o d* of Anthony Duckworth-Chad, OBE; one *s* three *d* (of whom two *d* are twins)]. *Address:* Wicket House, Rivar Road, Shalbourne, Marlborough, Wilts SN8 3PU. *Club:* Free Foresters.

BARBER, His Honour Trevor Wing; a Circuit Judge, 1992–2014; *b* 10 June 1943; *s* of Robert and Margaret Barber; *m* 1967, Judith Penelope Downey; one *s* one *d*. *Educ:* Worksop Coll.; Newcastle Univ. (LLB). Called to the Bar, Inner Temple, 1967; practice in Sheffield,

1967–92. *Recreations:* gardening, golf, reading. *Address:* Juniper Lodge, Hillfoot Road, Totley, Sheffield S17 3AX.

BARBER, Prof. William Joseph, Hon. OBE 1981; Professor of Economics, Wesleyan University, Middletown, Conn, USA, 1965–93; *b* 13 Jan. 1925; *s* of Ward Barber; *m* 1955, Sheila Mary Marr; three *s*. *Educ:* Harvard Univ. (AB); Balliol Coll., Oxford (BA 1st Cl. Hons, 1951, MA 1955); DPhil (Nuffield Coll.) 1958. Served War, US Army, 1943–46. Lectr in Econs, Balliol Coll., Oxford, 1956; Wesleyan University: Dept of Economics, 1957–93; Asst Prof., 1957–61; Associate Prof., 1961–65; Prof., 1965–93; Andrews Prof., 1972–93; Andrews Prof. Emeritus, 1994–; Acting Pres., Aug.–Oct. 1988. Research Associate: Oxford Univ. Inst. of Economics and Statistics, 1962–63; Twentieth Century Fund, South Asian Study, 1961–62. Amer. Sec., Rhodes Scholarship Trust, 1970–80. Pres., Hist. of Econs Soc., 1989–90 (Distinguished Fellow, 2002). Hon. DLitt Wesleyan, 2005. *Publications:* The Economy of British Central Africa, 1961; A History of Economic Thought, 1967; contributor to Asian Drama: an inquiry into the poverty of nations (with Gunnar Myrdal and others), 1968; British Economic Thought and India 1600–1858, 1975; (jtly) Exhortation and Controls: the search for a wage-price policy, 1975; Energy Policy in Perspective, 1981; From New Era to New Deal: Herbert Hoover, the economists, and American economic policy 1921–1933, 1985; (ed, and jt author) Breaking the Academic Mould: economists and American higher learning in the nineteenth century, 1988; (ed) Perspectives on the History of Economic Thought, vols V and VI, 1991; Designs within Disorder: Franklin D. Roosevelt, the economists, and the shaping of American economic policy 1933–1945, 1996; (ed) Works of Irving Fisher, 14 vols, 1997; (ed) Early American Economic Thought series, 6 vols, 2004; Gunnar Myrdal: an intellectual biography, 2007; contribs to professional jls. *Address:* 52 Missionary Road, Apartment 215, Cromwell, CT 06416, USA. *T:* (860) 6321514.

BARBIERI, Margaret Elizabeth, (Mrs M. E. Barbieri-Webb); freelance ballet teacher and coach, since 1990; Assistant Director, Sarasota Ballet Company, Florida, since 2012; *b* 2 March 1947; *d* of Ettore Barbieri and Lea Barbieri; *m* 1982, Iain Webb, Artistic Dir, Sarasota Ballet Co.; one *s*. *Educ:* Convent High Sch., Durban, S Africa. Trained with Iris Manning and Brownie Sutton, S Africa; Royal Ballet Sen. Sch., 1963; joined Royal Ballet, 1965; Principal, 1970; Sen. Principal, SWRB, 1974–89. Dir, Classical Graduate Course, London Studio Centre, 1990–2012; Artistic Dir, Images of Dance, 1990–2012; guest teacher, Royal Ballet Sch., 1990–94. Roles: Gypsy Girl, Two Pigeons, 1966; 1st Giselle, Covent Garden, 1968; 1st Sleeping Beauty, Leeds, 1969; 1st Swan Lake, Frankfurt, 1977, Covent Garden, 1983; 1st Romeo and Juliet, Covent Garden, 1979; 1st Sleeping Beauty, Covent Garden, 1985. Other roles with Royal Ballet: La Fille mal Gardée, Two Pigeons, The Dream, Façade, Wedding Bouquet, Rendezvous (Ashton); Lady and the Fool, Card Game, Pineapple Poll (Cranko); The Invitation, Solitaire, (Summer) The Four Seasons (MacMillan); Checkmate, The Rake's Progress (de Valois); Grosse Fugue, Tilt (van Manen); Lilac Garden (Tudor); Fête Etrange (Howard); Grand Tour (Layton); Summer Garden (Hynd); Game Piano (Thorpe), 1978; Cinderella (Killar), 1978; Cinderella (Rodrigues), 1979; Papillon, The Taming of the Shrew, 1980; Coppélia, Les Sylphides, Raymonda Act III, Spectre de la Rose; La Vivandière, 1982; Petrushka, 1984. Roles created: Knight Errant (Tudor), 1968; From Waking Sleep (Drew), 1970; Ante-Room (Cauley), 1971; Oscar Wilde (Layton), 1972; Sacred Circles and The Sword (Drew), 1973; The Entertainers (Killar), 1974; Charlotte Brontë (Hynd), 1974; Summertide (Wright), 1977; Metamorphosis (Bintley), 1984; Flowers of the Forest (Bintley), 1985; The Wand of Youth (Corder), 1985. Recreated: Pavlova's Dragonfly Solo, 1977; The Dying Swan, produced by Dame Alicia Markova after Fokine, 1985. Guest artist, 1990–92, guest teacher, 1991–92, Birmingham Royal Ballet. Staged for Images of Dance: Les Sylphides, Façade, 1991; Rake's Progress, 1992; Pineapple Poll, La Bayadère, 1993; Raymonda, 1994; Swan Lake, 1995; Paquita, 1996; staged: Façade and Raymonda Act 3 for K Ballet Co., Japan, 2003; Façade for Oregon Ballet Th. Co., Portland, 2004; The Two Pigeons for K Ballet Co., Japan and State Ballet of Georgia, Tbilisi, 2006; staged for Sarasota Ballet, 2007–: Two Pigeons, Façade, Rendezvous, Les Patineurs, Birthday Offering, Valses Nobles et Sentimentales, La Fille mal Gardée, The Rake's Progress, Checkmate, The American and There Where She Loves (Wheeldon), Pineapple Poll, Grand Tour, Giselle, Les Sylphides, Boutique (Bourne), Scottish Dances (Bintley). Travelled with Royal Ballet to Australia, Canada, China, Egypt, Far East, France, Germany, Greece, Holland, Israel, Italy, Japan, New Zealand, Portugal, Spain, Switzerland, Yugoslavia, India and North and South America; guest appearances, USA, Germany, S Africa, France, Norway, Czechoslovakia. TV Appearances in: Spectre de la Rose; Grosse Fugue; Giselle; Coppelia; Checkmate; Metamorphosis; Markova master classes. Gov., Royal Ballet, 1994–2000. Ashton Associate, Frederick Ashton Foundn, 2013–. (Jtly) Luminaire Award, Fine Arts Soc. of Sarasota, 2014. *Recreations:* music (classical), theatre, gardening.

BARBIZET, Patricia Marie Marguerite; Commandeur: de l'ordre national du Mérite, 2010; de la Légion d'honneur, 2015; Chief Executive Officer, Artémis, since 1992; Chief Executive Officer and Chairman, Christie's International, since 2014; *b* Paris, 17 April 1955; *d* of late Philippe Dussart and of Monique Dussart (*née* Cartier); *m* 1979, Jean Barbizet; one *d*. *Educ:* ESCP Europe (Master's degree 1976). Internat. Treas., Renault Véhicules Industriels, 1979–82; Chief Financial Officer, Renault Crédit Internat., 1982–89; Groupe Pinault: Chief Financial Officer, 1989; Dep. CEO, Pinault-CFAO, 1990–92; CEO, Financière Pinault, 1992; Vice-Chm., Kering (formerly PPR), 2005–. Member Board: Total, 2008–; PSA Peugeot-Citroën, 2013–. Pres., Assoc. des Amis de la Philharmonie de Paris. *Recreations:* classical music, opera, theatre, literature. *Address:* Artémis, 12 rue François 1er, 75008 Paris, France. *T:* (1) 44112019. *E:* pbarbizet@groupeartemis.com.

BARBOSA, Rubens Antonio, Hon. GCVO 1997 (Hon. LVO 1969); President and Chief Executive Officer, Rubens Barbosa & Associates, since 2004; Senior Director, Albright Stonebridge Group, since 2005; board member of several industrial companies; *b* 13 June 1938; *s* of José Orlando Barbosa and Lice Farina Barbosa; *m* 1969, Maria Ignez Correa da Costa Barbosa; one *s* one *d*. *Educ:* Univ. of São Paulo, Brazil (BA Law); Foreign Service Acad., Brazil (BA Diplomacy); LSE (MA Latin Amer. Politics); other degrees in economics, finance and politics. Exec. Sec., Brazilian Trade Commn with socialist countries of Eastern Europe, 1976–84; Head of Staff, Min. of External Relations, 1985–86; Under-Sec. Gen., Multilateral and Special Pol Affairs, 1986; COS, Min. of Foreign Relations, 1986–87; Sec., Internat. Affairs, Min. of Economy, 1987–88; Ambassador and Perm. Rep. to Latin-Amer. Integration Assoc., 1988–91; Pres., Commn of Reps, 1991–92; Under-Sec. Gen., Trade, Regl Integration, Econ. Affairs and Foreign Trade, Min. of External Relations, and Co-ordinator for Mercosur, Brazil, 1991–93; Vice-Pres., Perm. Commn on Foreign Trade, 1992–93; Ambassador: to UK, 1994–99; to USA, 1999–2004. Pres., Assoc. of Coffee Producing Countries, 1993–99. Grand Cross, Order of Rio Branco (Brazil); French Legion of Honour; orders from Argentina and Mexico; honours from Germany, Belgium, Italy, Iran, Portugal. Publisher and Ed., Interesse Nacional, qly jl on pol, econ. and social issues, 2008–. *Publications:* America Latina em Perspectiva: a integração regional da retórica à realidade, 1991; The Mercosur Codes, 2000; Mercosur and Regional Integration, 2010; The Dissent in Washington, 2011 (Washington Dissensus, 2014); National Interest and Vision of the Future, 2012; articles in newspapers and learned jls. *Recreations:* tennis, classical music. *Address:* (office) Avenida Brigadeiro Faria Lima 2413, Sobreloja, Conjunto B, 01452–000 São Paulo, Brazil.

BARBOUR, James Jack, OBE 1992; FRCPE; Chief Executive, Lothian NHS Board, 2001–12; *b* 16 Jan. 1953; *s* of late Thomas Jack Barbour and Flora Jean Barbour (*née* Murray); one *s* two *d*; *m* Julie Barnes. *Educ:* Madras Coll., St Andrews; Univ. of Strathclyde (BA Jt Hons Politics, Sociol., Econs). MHSM 1983, CIHM 2010; FRCPE 2008. Grad. Mgt Trainee, NHS in Scotland, 1977–79; Administrator, Gtr Glasgow Health Bd, 1979–83; EEC Exchange scholarship in Germany, 1981; Unit Administration, Gt Ormond St Gp of Hosps, 1983–86; General Manager: Royal Manchester Children's Hosp., 1986–87; Aberdeen Royal Infirmary, 1987–92; Chief Executive: Aberdeen Royal Hosps NHS Trust, 1992–94; Central Manchester Healthcare NHS Trust, 1994–98; Sheffield HA, 1998–2001. Alumnus, London Business Sch. Develt Prog., 1989. Hon. Professor: Queen Margaret Univ. (formerly Queen Margaret UC) 2002–14; Univ. of Strathclyde, 2012. Burgess, City of Aberdeen, 1992. *Recreations:* travel keeping fit.

BARBOUR, Dame Margaret, DBE 2002 (CBE 1991); DL; Chairman, J. Barbour & Sons Ltd, since 1972 (Director, 1969–72); *b* 1 Feb. 1940; *d* of David and Mary Ann Davies; *m* 1st, 1964, John Malcolm Barbour (*d* 1968); one *d*; 2nd, 1991, David William Ash. *Educ:* Middlesborough High Sch.; Battersea Poly. (DipEd). Teacher: Elliot Sch., Putney, 1961–64; Church High Sch., Newcastle upon Tyne, 1964–66. DL Tyne and Wear, 1992. Hon. DBA Sunderland, 1994; Hon. DCL Newcastle, 1998. *Recreations:* swimming, bridge. *Address:* J. Barbour & Sons Ltd, Simonside, South Shields, Tyne and Wear NE34 9PD. *T:* (0191) 455 4444, *Fax:* (0191) 427 4259.

BARBOUR, Muriel Janet; *see* Gray, M. J.

BARCA, Manuel David; QC 2011; *b* Kensington, 14 Aug. 1962; *o s* of Emilio Barca and Sara Lazaro de Barca. *Educ:* Wimbledon Coll.; Churchill Coll., Cambridge (MA Law Tripos). Called to the Bar, Lincoln's Inn, 1986; in practice as a barrister, specialising in media and information law, One Brick Court, 1987–. *Recreations:* theatre, music, cinema, art history, Spain. *Address:* 1 Brick Court, Temple, EC4Y 9BY. *T:* (020) 7353 8845, *Fax:* (020) 7583 9144. *E:* clerks@onebrickcourt.com.

BARCLAY, Prof. (Alan) Neil, DPhil; E. P. Abraham Professor of Chemical Pathology, 2011–15, and Titular Professor of Molecular Immunology, 1998–2015, now Professor Emeritus, University of Oxford; Fellow of Lincoln College, Oxford, since 2011; *b* 12 March 1950; *s* of late Frank Rodney Barclay and Betty Cowie Barclay (*née* Watson); *m* 1975, Ella Geraldine Quinn; two *s* one *d*. *Educ:* Hardye's Sch., Dorchester; Oriel Coll., Oxford (DPhil Biochem. 1976). Res. Fellow, Inst. of Neurobiology, Univ. of Göteborg, Sweden, 1976–78; Scientific Staff: MRC, Sir William Dunn Sch. of Pathol., Univ. of Oxford, 1978–2011; MRC Cellular Immunol. Unit, Oxford, 1978–99. Academic Advr, Oxford Univ. Bioinformatics Centre, 1990–2000. Chairman: Everest Biotech Ltd, 1999–; Absolute Antibody Ltd, 2012–. Chm., 2009–14, Treas., 2014–, CIU Trust; Chm., EPA Cephalosporin Trust Fund, 2012–. Hon. Mem., Scandinavian Soc. of Immunology, 1993. *Publications:* (jtly) The Leucocyte Antigen Factsbook, 1993, 2nd edn 1997; contribs to scientific jls. *Recreations:* literature, listening to music, writing stories (unpublished). *Address:* Sir William Dunn School of Pathology, Oxford University, South Parks Road, Oxford OX1 3RE. *T:* (01865) 275500.

BARCLAY, Sir David (Rowat), Kt 2000; Joint Proprietor: Littlewoods, since 2002; Woolworths and Ladybird Brands, since 2009; The Daily Telegraph, Sunday Telegraph, Spectator magazine and Apollo, since 2004. Joint Proprietor: Cadogan Hotel, 1968–78; Londonderry Hotel, 1970–80, 1985–87; Kensington Palace Hotel, 1973–77; Howard Hotel, 1975–2000; Mirabeau Hotel, Monte Carlo, 1979–2007; Ellerman Shipping, 1983–87; Tolly Cobold Brewery & JW Cameron Brewery, 1983–89; Howard Hotel, NY, 1984–87; Gotass Larsen Shipping, 1988–97; The European, 1992–98; Scotsman Publications, 1995–2006; Ritz Hotel, 1995–; Cavendish Hotel, London, 2006–; Maybourne Hotel Gp, 2011–15. Mem., Chief Pleas, Sark, 1993–2008. Jt Founder and Trustee, David and Frederick Barclay Foundn. Ambassador Extraordinaire at Large for Econ. Develt of Monaco, 2010. Hon. Dr Glasgow, 1998. KSG 2010. Officier, Ordre de Saint Charles (Monaco), 2000.
See also Sir F. H. Barclay.

BARCLAY, Sir Frederick (Hugh), Kt 2000; Joint Proprietor: Littlewoods, since 2002; Woolworths and Ladybird Brands, since 2009; The Daily Telegraph, Sunday Telegraph, Spectator magazine and Apollo, since 2004. Former estate agent. Joint Proprietor: Cadogan Hotel, 1968–78; Londonderry Hotel, 1970–80, 1985–87; Kensington Palace Hotel, 1973–77; Howard Hotel, 1975–2000; Mirabeau Hotel, Monte Carlo, 1979–2007; Ellerman Shipping, 1983–87; Tolly Cobold Brewery & JW Cameron Brewery, 1983–89; Howard Hotel, NY, 1984–87; Gotass Larsen Shipping, 1988–97; The European, 1992–98; Scotsman Publications, 1995–2006; Ritz Hotel, 1995–; Cavendish Hotel, London, 2006–; Maybourne Hotel Gp, 2011–15. Jt Founder and Trustee, David and Frederick Barclay Foundn. Ambassador Extraordinaire at Large for Econ. Develt of Monaco, 2010. Hon. Dr Glasgow, 1998. KSG 2010. Officier, Ordre de Saint Charles (Monaco), 2000.
See also Sir D. R. Barclay.

BARCLAY, James Christopher, OBE 2006; Chairman, M & G Equity Investment Trust PLC, 1998–2011 (Director, 1996–2011); *b* 7 July 1945; *s* of late Theodore David Barclay and Anne Barclay; *m* 1974, Rolleen Anne, *d* of late Lt-Col Arthur Forbes and Joan Forbes; one *s* one *d*. *Educ:* Harrow. Served 15th/19th The King's Royal Hussars, 1964–67. Dep. Chm., 1981–85, Chm., 1985–98, Cater Allen Hldgs PLC; Chm., Cater Ryder & Co. Ltd, 1981. Director: Abbey National Treasury Services plc, 1997–98; Abbey National Offshore Hldgs Ltd, 1998–2000; Thos Agnew & Sons Ltd, 1998; New Fulcrum Investment Trust plc, 1999–2006; Liontrust Knowledge Economy Trust PLC, 2001–03; Rathbone Brothers PLC, 2003–10. Dir, UK Debt Mgt Office, 2000–05. Chm., London Discount Market Assoc., 1988–90. *Recreation:* fresh air pursuits. *Address:* Rivers Hall, Waldringfield, Woodbridge, Suffolk IP12 4QX. *Clubs:* Boodle's, Pratt's.

BARCLAY, John Alistair; Executive Director, Royal Bank of Scotland Group plc, retired; *b* 5 Dec. 1933; *m* 1963, Mary Tierney (*née* Brown); three *d*. *Educ:* Banff Academy. FCIBS. Joined Royal Bank of Scotland, 1949; Chief City Manager, 1982–84; seconded to Williams & Glyn's Bank (Asst Gen. Manager), 1984–85; Exec. Vice-Pres., NY, 1985–88; Sen. Gen. Manager, UK Banking, 1988–89; Exec. Dir, International, 1989–90; Man. Dir, Corporate and Institutional Banking, 1990–92; Dep. Gp Chief Exec., 1992–94; non-exec. Dir, 1994–96. Chm., Direct Line Financial Services, 1994–2004. *Recreations:* travel, golf, reading, gardening, photography, good food and wine.

BARCLAY, Prof. John Martyn Gurney, PhD; Lightfoot Professor of Divinity, Durham University, since 2003; *b* 31 July 1958; *s* of late Oliver and Dorothy Barclay; *m* 1981, Diana Knox; two *s* one *d*. *Educ:* Queens' Coll., Cambridge (BA 1981; PhD 1986). University of Glasgow: Lectr, 1984–96; Sen. Lectr, 1996–2000; Prof., 2000–03. *Publications:* Obeying the Truth: Paul's ethics in Galatians, 1988; Jews in the Mediterranean Diaspora, 1996; Colossians and Philemon, 1997; Flavius Josephus: translation and commentary, Vol. 10, Against Apion, 2007; Pauline Churches and Diaspora Jews, 2011. *Recreations:* cycling, walking. *Address:* Kimblesworth House, Kimblesworth, Chester-le-Street DH2 3QP. *T:* (0191) 371 0388. *E:* john.barclay@durham.ac.uk.

BARCLAY, Neil; *see* Barclay, A. N.

BARCLAY, Patrick; journalist, author, broadcaster; *b* 15 Aug. 1947; *s* of Guy Deghy and Patricia Wighton; one *s* one *d*. *Educ:* Dundee High Sch. Sub-editor, 1966–77, football writer, 1977–86, The Guardian; football columnist: Today, 1986; The Independent, 1986–91; The Observer, 1991–96; Sunday Telegraph, 1996–2009; Chief Football Commentator, The Times, 2009–12; columnist, Evening Standard, 2012–. *Publications:* Football - Bloody Hell!, 2010; Mourinho: anatomy of a winner, 2011; The Life and Times of Herbert Chapman, 2014. *Recreations:* reading, travel. *Address:* c/o 2 Brydges Place, WC2N 4HP.

BARCLAY, His Honour Paul Robert; a Circuit Judge, 1998–2013; *s* of late John Alexander Barclay and Mabel Elizabeth Barclay; *m* 1972, Sarah Louise Jones; two *s* two *d. Educ:* Nottingham High Sch.; St John's Coll., Cambridge (MA 1971). Called to the Bar, Middle Temple, 1972; in practice at the Bar, 1972–98; an Asst Recorder, 1992–96; a Recorder, 1996–98. *Recreation:* village cricket.

BARCLAY, Sir Robert (Colraine), 15th Bt *cr* 1668 (NS), of Pierston, Ayrshire; *b* 12 Feb. 1950; *e s* of Sir Colville Herbert Sanford Barclay, 14th Bt and Rosamond Grant Renton (*née* Elliott); *S* father, 2010; *m* 1980, Lucilia Saboia (marr. diss. 1986); one *s* one *d. Educ:* Eton; Univ. of East Anglia. Chartered accountant; stockbroker. *Publications:* Brazil: changing course, 1992. *Recreations:* Bach, bromeliads. *Heir: s* Henry William Saboia Barclay, *b* 16 Jan. 1982. *E:* robert.barclay@terra.com.br. *Clubs:* Royal Over-Seas League; Naval (Rio de Janeiro).

BARCLAY, Stephen Paul; MP (C) North East Cambridgeshire, since 2010; an Assistant Government Whip, since 2015; *b* Lytham, Lancs, 1972; *s* of Robert and Janice Barclay; *m* Karen; one *s* one *d. Educ:* King Edward VII Sch., Lancs; Peterhouse, Cambridge (BA Hist. 1994); Coll. of Law, Chester. 2nd Lieut, RRF, 1991. Trainee solicitor, Lawrence Graham, Solicitors, 1996–98; admitted as solicitor, 1998; Solicitor, Axa Insce, 1998–2001; FSA, 2002–06; Dir, Regulatory Affairs, then Hd, Anti-money Laundering and Sanction, Barclays UK Retail Bank, 2006–10. Contested (C): Manchester Blackley, 1997; Lancaster and Wyre, 2001. *Address:* House of Commons, SW1A 0AA.

BARCLAY, Yvonne Fay, (Mrs William Barclay); *see* Minton, Y. F.

BARCLAY-SMITH, Ronald George; Chief Executive, South Square, since 2011; *b* 12 May 1954; *s* of John Hamilton Smith and Jean Lennox Smith (*née* Graeme); *m* 1st, 1978, Elaine Sheila Murdoch (*née* McClure) (marr. diss. 1988); two *s*; 2nd, 2004, Linsey Jane (*née* McDonald). *Educ:* George Heriot's Sch., Edinburgh; Edinburgh Univ. (MA Jt Hons Pol. and Mod. Hist., 1976); Queens' Coll., Cambridge (MPhil Internat. Relns, 1988); Kingston Poly. Business Sch. (MBA 1991). Commnd RAF, 1972; RAF Coll., Cranwell, 1976–77 (Queen's Medal); 51 Sqn RAF Regt, 1977–78; 63 Sqn RAF Regt, Gütersloh, 1978–81; HQ RAF Germany, Rheindahlen, 1981–82; RAF Lyneham, 1982–83; Dep. Sqn Ldr II Sqn (Para) RAF Regt, 1983–84; Sqn Ldr, 1984; Staff Officer, HQ 1 Gp, 1984; OC Short Range Air Defence, Belize, 1984–85; OC 1 (Light Armoured) Sqn RAF Regt, RAF Laarbruch, 1985–87; Wing Comdr, 1988; Desk Officer D Air Plans, 1988–92; retd RAF, 1992; Dep. Regl Dir, Corporate Planning, Trent RHA, 1992–93; Chief Executive: Lincs HA/FHSA, 1993–95; Defence Secondary Care Agency, MoD, 1995–98; mgt and consultancy rôles, 1998–2000; Chief Executive: Common Services Agency, NHS, Scotland, 2000–01; ESPC Gp of Cos (formerly ESPC (UK) Ltd), 2001–09; 9 Gough Square, 2010–11. Chm., Scottish Solicitors' Property Centres Cttee, 2002–04; Mem., Scottish Archæol Finds Allocation Panel (formerly Treasure Trove Adv. Panel for Scotland), 2004–10. Chm., Veterans Scotland, 2006–10. Hon. Pres., RAF Regt Assoc. in Scotland, 2007–. CDir 2004; FCMI 2005; FCIPD 2006; FInstD 2009. Mem., Merchant Co. of Edinburgh, 2002–10. *Publications:* articles in jls. *Recreations:* downhill ski-ing, hillwalking, tennis, philately, fine wine, English landscape paintings. *Address:* c/o New Club, 86 Princes Street, Edinburgh EH2 2BB; South Square, 3–4 South Square, Gray's Inn, WC1R 5HP. *Club:* New (Edinburgh).

BARCROFT, Very Rev. Ian David; Dean of the Diocese of Glasgow and Galloway, since 2010; Rector, St Mary's Episcopal Church, Hamilton, since 1997; *b* Bury, Lancs, 29 Sept. 1960; *s* of Alan and Joyce Barcroft; *m* 1988, Heather Cowe; two *d. Educ:* Bury Grammar Sch.; Univ. of Manchester Inst. of Technol. (BSc Hons 1983); Edinburgh Univ. (BD Jt Hons 1988); Glasgow Univ. (MTh (Res.) 2001). Ordained deacon 1988, priest 1989; Precentor, St Ninian's Cathedral, Perth, 1988–92; Priest, St Clement's, Aberdeen, 1992–97. *Recreations:* football, cricket, theatre, walking. *Address:* St Mary's Rectory, 4C Auchingramont Road, Hamilton ML3 6JT. *T:* (01698) 429895. *E:* ian.barcroft@btinternet.com.

BARDA, Clive Blackmore; freelance photographer, since 1968; *b* 14 Jan. 1945; *s* of Gaston Barda and Marjorie (*née* Blackmore); *m* 1970, Rosalind Mary Whiteley; three *s. Educ:* Bryanston Sch.; Birkbeck Coll., London (BA Hons Modern Langs). Photographer, specialising in performing arts, esp. classical music, opera and theatre. *Exhibitions:* RFH, London, 1979; Science Museum, London, 1985; RNCM, Manchester, 1980; Perth, Australia, 1981; RPS, Bath, 1985; Nat. Mus. of Photography, Film and TV, Bradford, 1988; Nagaoka, Japan, 1996; Tokyo, 1998; Edinburgh, 2001; Paris, 2002; EXPOSURE! (retrospective), China and UK, 2012. FRSA 1996. *Publications:* The Sculpture of David Wynne, 1975; The Complete Phantom of the Opera, 1988; The Complete Aspects of Love, 1990; Celebration!, 1996; Performance!, 2001; The Power of the Ring, 2007. *Recreations:* walking, singing in the church choir, classical music, opera, theatre, cinema, reading, watching cricket. *T:* (020) 8579 5202, *Fax:* (020) 8840 1083. *E:* clivebarda@pobox.com. *Clubs:* Garrick, MCC.

BARDELL, Hannah Mary; MP (SNP) Livingston, since 2015; *b* Craigshill, Livingston. *Educ:* Broxburn Acad.; Univ. of Stirling (BA Hons Film and Media, Politics and English 2005). Researcher, then Asst Producer, GMTV, 2005–07; Office Manager, Rt Hon. Alex Salmond, MSP, 2007–10; Protocol Exec. and Events Manager, American Consulate, Edinburgh, 2010–12; Communications Manager, Subsea 7, 2012; Hd, Communications and Mktg (UK and Africa), Stork Tech. Services, 2013–15. *Address:* House of Commons, SW1A 0AA.

BARDEN, Prof. Laing, CBE 1990; PhD, DSc; Vice-Chancellor, University of Northumbria at Newcastle, 1992–96 (Director, Newcastle upon Tyne Polytechnic, 1978–92); *b* 29 Aug. 1931; *s* of Alfred Eversfield Barden and Edna (*née* Laing); *m* 1956, Nancy Carr; two *s* one *d. Educ:* Washington Grammar Sch.; Durham Univ. (BSc, MSc). R. T. James & Partners, 1954–59. Liverpool Univ., 1959–62 (PhD); Manchester Univ., 1962–69 (DSc); Strathclyde Univ., 1969–74; Newcastle upon Tyne Polytechnic, subseq. Univ. of Northumbria at Newcastle, 1974–96. Director: Microelectronics Applications Res. Inst. Ltd, 1980–90; Tyne and Wear Enterprise Trust Ltd, 1982–96; Newcastle Technology Centre Ltd, 1985–90; Newcastle Initiative, 1988–96. Chm., Bubble Foundn UK, 1997–2006. Mem., Council for Industry and Higher Educn, 1987–96. *Publications:* contribs to Geotechnique, Proc. ICE, Jl Amer. Soc. CE, Qly Jl Eng. Geol. *Recreations:* cricket, soccer, snooker. *Address:* 7 Westfarm Road, Cleadon, Tyne and Wear SR6 7UG. *T:* (0191) 536 2317. *Clubs:* Mid Boldon (Boldon), Boldon Cricket.

BARDER, Sir Brian (Leon), KCMG 1992; HM Diplomatic Service, retired; High Commissioner to Australia, 1991–94; *b* 20 June 1934; *s* of Harry and Vivien Barder; *m* 1958, Jane Maureen Cornwell; two *d* one *s. Educ:* Sherborne; St Catharine's Coll., Cambridge (BA). 2nd Lieut, 7 Royal Tank Regt, 1952–54. Colonial Office, 1957; Private Sec. to Permanent Under-Sec., 1960–61; HM Diplomatic Service, 1965; First Secretary, UK Mission to UN, 1964–68; FCO, 1968–70; First Sec. and Press Attaché, Moscow, 1971–73; Counsellor and Head of Chancery, British High Commn, Canberra, 1973–77; Canadian Nat. Defence Coll., Kingston, Ontario, 1977–78; Head of Central and Southern, later Southern African Dept, FCO, 1978–82; Ambassador to Ethiopia, 1982–86; Ambassador to Poland, 1986–88; High Comr to Nigeria, and concurrently Ambassador to Benin, 1988–91. Mem., Commonwealth Observer Mission for Namibian elections, 1994. ODA Consultant on Diplomatic Trng, Eastern and Central Europe, 1996. Panel of Chairs, CSSB, 1995–96. Member: Bd of Management, Royal Hosp. for Neuro-disability, 1996–2003; Cttee, ESU Centre for Speech and Debate (formerly Internat. Debate and Communication Trng), 1996–2009; Special Immigration Appeals Commn, 1998–2004. Hon. Vis. Fellow, Dept of Politics and Internat. Relns, Univ. of Leicester, 2006–. Editl Consultant, Dictionary of Diplomacy, 2001 and 2003. CON 1989. *Publications:* (contrib.) Fowler's Modern English Usage, 3rd edn 1996; What Diplomats Do: the life and work of diplomats, 2014; contrib. Pol Qly, London Rev. of Books, Guardian, The Hague Jl of Diplomacy, etc. *Recreations:* blogging, email, music, campaigning, writing letters to the newspapers. *Address:* 20 Victoria Mews, Earlsfield, SW18 3PY. *E:* brianbarder@gmail.com. *W:* www.barder.com/ephems. *Club:* Oxford and Cambridge.

See also O. M. Barder, E. L. Wen.

BARDER, Owen Matthew; Senior Fellow and Europe Director, Center for Global Development, since 2011; *b* 20 Feb. 1967; *s* of Sir Brian Leon Barder, *qv*; partner, Grethe Petersen. *Educ:* Sevenoaks Sch.; New Coll., Oxford (BA Hons PPE 1988); London Sch. of Econs (MSc Econs 1991). HM Treasury, 1988–96, Private Sec. to the Chancellor of the Exchequer, 1991–94; Dept of Finance, S Africa, 1997–99; Private Sec., Econ. Affairs, to the Prime Minister, 1999–2000; Department for International Development: Hd, Africa Policy, 2000–02; Dir, Inf., Communications, Knowledge, 2002–04; Center for Global Develt, Washington (on special leave), 2004–06; Dir, Global Develt Effectiveness, then Internat. Finance and Develt Effectiveness, DFID, 2006–08. Dir, aidinfo, 2008–11. Vis. Scholar, Univ. of Calif, Berkeley, 2004–06; Vis. Fellow, Center for Global Develt, 2010–11; Vis. Prof. in Practice, LSE. Non-exec. Dir, One World International, 2000–04. Producer and host, Development Drums podcast, 2008–. *Publications:* Making Markets for Vaccines (jtly), 2004; Running for Fitness, 2002; Get Fit Running, 2004; various articles. *Recreations:* running, information technology, cycling. *T:* 07917 547979. *E:* owen@barder.com. *W:* www.owen.org. *Club:* Serpentine Running.

BAREAU, Peter John, CBE 2002; Chief Executive, National Savings and Investments (formerly National Savings), 1996–2002; *b* 1 June 1942; *s* of late Paul Bareau, OBE and Kitty Bareau (*née* Gibson); *m* 1st, 1967, Irene Nelson (marr. diss.); one *s* one *d*; 2nd, 1976, Karen Giesemann (*d* 2001); one *s* two *d*; 3rd, 2003, Ruth Holyoak (*née* Hardy); two step *s. Educ:* Eton Coll.; Queens' Coll., Cambridge (MA). With Bank of London & S America in UK, USA, Paraguay and Spain, 1966–72; with Lloyds Bank Internat. in UK and Brazil, 1973–84; Lloyds Bank PLC: General Manager: Strategic Planning, 1985–86; Europe, ME and Internat. Pvte Banking, 1987–91; Personnel, 1992–96. Sen. Advr, Corporate Value Associates, 2003–12. Chm., Surrey and Sussex SHA, 2003–06. Ind. Mem., Energy Gp Adv. Bd, DTI, 2004–06. Trustee, Breast Cancer Campaign, 2002–06. Hon. FCMC 2003. *Address:* Red Rose Cottage, Ockham Road South, East Horsley, Surrey KT24 6RL. *T:* (01483) 286814.

BAREHAM, Lindsey Margaret; cookery writer, The Times, since 2006; *b* Chislehurst, 18 Sept. 1948; *s* of Frederick and Jean Bareham; *m* 1977, Ben John (*d* 2006); two *s. Educ:* St Philomena's Convent High Sch., Kent; Chislehurst and Sidcup Grammar Sch. Consumer and Eating-out Ed., Time Out, 1972–87; consumer columnist and restaurant critic, Sunday Telegraph, 1989–91; cookery columnist, Daily Telegraph, 1992–93; Evening Standard cook, 1996–2004; food writer, Saga mag., 2004–12. *Publications:* In Praise of the Potato, 1989; A Celebration of Soup, 1993; (with S. Hopkinson) Roast Chicken and Other Stories, 1994; Onions without Tears, 1995; Supper Won't Take Long, 1997; (with S. Hopkinson) The Prawn Cocktail Years, 1997; The Big Red Book of Tomatoes, 1999; A Wolf in the Kitchen, 2000, new edn as Hungry?, 2008; Just One Pot, 2004; The Fish Store, 2006; Dinner in a Dash, 2007; Pasties, 2008; The Trifle Bowl and Other Tales, 2013; One Pot Wonders, 2014. *Recreations:* Cornish coast walking, dancing, jazz, art, allotmenteering. *Clubs:* Chelsea Arts, Groucho, Union, Quo Vadis.

BARENBLATT, Prof. Grigory Isaakovich, PhD; ScD; Principal Scientist, Institute of Oceanology, Russian Academy of Sciences, Moscow, since 2012; Professor of Mathematics, University of California at Berkeley, 1997–2012, now Emeritus; G. I. Taylor Professor of Fluid Mechanics, University of Cambridge, 1992–94, now Emeritus, and Hon. Fellow, Gonville and Caius College, Cambridge, 1999 (Fellow, 1994–99); *b* 10 July 1927; *s* of Isaak Grigorievich Barenblatt and Nadezhda Veniaminovna (*née* Kagan); *m* 1952, Iraida Nikolaevna Kochina; two *d. Educ:* Moscow Univ. (MSc 1950; PhD 1953; ScD 1957); Univ. of Cambridge (MA 1993). Res. Scientist, Inst. of Petroleum, USSR Acad. of Sci., Moscow, 1953–61; Prof. and Hd, Dept of Mechanics of Solids, Inst. of Mechanics, Moscow Univ., 1961–75; Hd, Theoretical Dept, Inst. of Oceanology, USSR Acad. of Sci., Moscow, 1975–92. Foreign Member: Amer. Acad. of Arts and Scis, 1975; Royal Soc., 2000; Foreign Associate: US Nat. Acad. of Engrg, 1992; US Nat. Acad. of Sci., 1997; MAE, 1993. Hon. DTech Royal Inst. of Technol., Stockholm, 1989; Hon. Dr Civil Engrg Torino Polytechnic Inst., 2005. Laureate, Panetti Gold Medal and Prize, 1995; Lagrange Medal, Accademia dei Lincei, 1995; G. I. Taylor Medal, Amer. Soc. of Engrg Sci., 1999; J. C. Maxwell Prize, Internat. Congress on Industrial and Applied Maths, 1999; S. P. Timoshenko Medal, ASME, 2005; A. M. Obukhov Medal, Inst. of Atmospheric Phys, 2013. *Publications:* Similarity, Self-Similarity, and Intermediate Asymptotics, 1979; Dimensional Analysis, 1987; (jtly) Theory of Fluid Flows in Porous Media, 1990; Scaling, Self-Similarity, and Intermediate Asymptotics, 1996; Scaling, 2003; Self-Similar Phenomena: dimensional analysis and scaling, 2009; Flow, Deformation and Fracture, 2014; contrib. Jl Applied Maths and Mechanics, Physics of Atmosphere and Ocean, Jl Fluid Mechanics, Procs of NAS. *Recreation:* historical reading. *Address:* Institute of Oceanology, Russian Academy of Sciences, 36 Nakhimovsky Prospekt, 119997 Moscow, Russia.

BARENBOIM, Daniel, Hon. KBE 2011; pianist and conductor; Music Director: Berlin State Opera, since 1992; La Scala, Milan, 2011–15 (Principal Guest Conductor, 2006–11); *b* Buenos Aires, 15 Nov. 1942; *s* of Enrique Barenboim and late Aida Barenboim (*née* Schuster); *m* 1st, 1967, Jacqueline du Pré (*d* 1987); 2nd, 1988, Elena Bashkirova; two *s. Educ:* Santa Cecilia Acad., Rome; studied with his father; coached by Edwin Fischer, Nadia Boulanger, and Igor Markevitch. Debut as pianist with: Israel Philharmonic Orchestra, 1953; Royal Philharmonic Orchestra, 1956; Berlin Philharmonic Orchestra, 1963; NY Philharmonic Orchestra, 1964; Music Director: Orchestre de Paris, 1975–88; Chicago SO, 1991–2006; tours include: Australia, North and South America, Far East; regular appearances at Bayreuth, Edinburgh, Lucerne, Prague and Salzburg Festivals; co-founded West-Eastern Divan Orchestra with Edward Saïd, 1998. Many recordings as conductor and pianist. BBC Reith Lectr, 2006. Beethoven Medal, 1958; Paderewski Medal, 1963; subsequently other awards. Grand Officier, Legion of Honour (France), 2011. *Publications:* A Life in Music, 1991; (with Edward Saïd) Parallels and Paradoxes, 2002; Everything is Connected, 2008; (with Patrice Chéreau) Dialoghi su musica e teatro: Tristano e Isotta, 2008. *Address:* c/o Agence de Concerts Cæcilia, 29 rue de la Coulouvrenière, 1204 Genève, Switzerland.

BARFIELD, Julia Barbara, MBE 2000; Director, Marks Barfield Architects, since 1989; *b* 15 Nov. 1952; *d* of Arnold Robert Barfield and Iolanthe Mary Barfield; *m* 1981, David Joseph Marks, *qv*; one *s* two *d. Educ:* Godolphin and Latymer Sch.; AA Sch. of Architecture. Dir, Tetra Ltd, 1978–79; Architectural Asst, Richard Rogers Partnership, 1979–81; Project Architect, Foster Associates, 1981–88; Founding Dir, London Eye Co., 1994–2006. Member: Council, AA, 2001–06; Design Review Panel, CABE, 2004–11; Council, Guy's and St Thomas' Hosp., 2005–10; Gov., Godolphin and Latymer Sch., 2006–. *Recreations:* family, travel, arts. *Address:* Marks Barfield Architects, 50 Bromells Road, SW4 0BG. *T:* (020) 7501 0180. *E:* jbarfield@marksbarfield.com.

BARFIELD, Richard Arthur; Chairman, Standard Life Investments Property Income Trust, since 2014 (non-executive Director, since 2003); *b* 5 April 1947; *s* of Arthur Victor Harold Barfield and Margaret Hilda Barfield; *m* 1969, Alison Helen Hamilton; one *s* one *d. Educ:* Gt Yarmouth Grammar Sch.; Edinburgh Univ. (BSc Maths). Standard Life Assce Co., 1970–96 (Chief Investment Manager, 1988–96). Non-executive Director: Baillie Gifford Japan Trust,

1998–2014 (Chm., 2008–14); Merchants Investment Trust, 1999–2011; Edinburgh Investment Trust, 2001–12; J. P. Morgan Fleming Overseas Investment Trust, 2001–10. Mem., Investment Adv. Panel, Strathclyde Pension Fund, 2004–14; Chm., Investment Sub-Cttee, Rio Tinto Pension Fund, 2007–; Chm. and Trustee, Investment Sub-Cttee, British Coal Staff Superannuation Scheme, 2009–. Member: Public Oversight Bd (formerly Public Oversight Bd for Accountancy), 2004–10; Bd, Pension Protection Fund, 2009–. FFA 1974–2010. *Recreations:* walking, music, good food and wine. *Club:* Sloane.

BARFORD, Prof. David, DPhil; FRS 2006; FMedSci; Team Leader, MRC Laboratory of Molecular Biology, Cambridge, since 2013; *b* 17 Aug. 1963; *s* of Jack and Mai Barford. *Educ:* Univ. of Bristol (BSc 1984); Univ. of Oxford (DPhil 1988). Research Fellow: Univ. of Oxford, 1988–90; Univ. of Dundee, 1990–91; Cold Spring Harbor Lab., NY, 1991–94; Lectr, Univ. of Oxford and Tutorial Fellow, Somerville Coll., Oxford, 1994–99; Prof. of Molecular Biol. and Co-Hd, Div. of Structural Biol., Inst. of Cancer Res., London, 1999–2013. Mem. Scientific Adv. Bd, Ceptyr Corp., Seattle, 1996–2004. Mem. EMBO, 2003. FMedSci 2003. *Publications:* contribs to scientific jls. *Recreations:* classical music, reading. *Address:* MRC Laboratory of Molecular Biology, Cambridge CB2 0QH. *T:* (01223) 267075. *E:* dbarford@mrc-lmb.cam.ac.uk.

BARGERY, (Bruno Philip) Robert; Director: The Georgian Group, since 2002; Royal Fine Art Commission Trust, since 2015; *b* 4 April 1966; *s* of Geoffrey Maxwell Bargery and Barbara Ann Hill. *Educ:* Hinchley Wood Sch.; Kingston Coll.; Exeter Univ.; Exeter Coll., Oxford. DoE, 1991–95; Researcher, Royal Fine Art Commn, 1995–99; Head, Policy and Res., CABE, 1999–2001. Dir, Georgian Enterprises and Trading Ltd, 2008–. FRSA 2003. *Address:* 33 Merganser Court, Star Place, St Katharine Docks, E1W 1AQ. *E:* robert@georgiangroup.org.uk.

BARHAM, His Honour Geoffrey Simon; a Circuit Judge, 1993–2010; *b* 23 Dec. 1945; *s* of late Denis Patrick Barham and Pleasance (*née* Brooke); *m* 1976, Sarah Seebold; one *s* one *d. Educ:* Malvern Coll.; Christ's Coll., Cambridge (MA). Called to the Bar, Lincoln's Inn, 1968; Asst Recorder, 1983; Recorder, 1987. *Recreation:* golf. *Club:* Norfolk (Norwich).

BARI, Dr Muhammad Abdul, MBE 2003; educationalist, parenting consultant, and writer and commentator on social and political issues; *b* 2 Oct. 1953; *s* of Muhammad Manikuddin and Karimunnesa; *m* Sayeda Akhter; three *s* one *d. Educ:* King's Coll., London (PhD; PGCE). Specialist Teacher, London Bor. of Tower Hamlets, 1997–2011. Chm., E London Mosque/London Muslim Centre, 2002–13; Sec. Gen., Muslim Council of GB, 2006–10. Trustee and Sec., Muslim Aid. Non-exec. Dir, LOCOG, 2006–13. Hon. Fellow, Queen Mary, Univ. of London, 2008. Hon. DEd East London, 2012. FRSA 2005. *Publications:* The Greatest Gift: a guide to parenting from an Islamic perspective, 2002; Building Muslim Families: challenges and expectations, 2002; Race, Religion and Muslim Identity in Britain, 2005; Marriage and Family Building in Islam, 2007; A Guide to Parenting in Islam: addressing adolescence, 2011; British, Muslims, Citizens: introspection and renewal, 2012; A Guide to Parenting in Islam: cherishing childhood, 2015. *Recreations:* reading, travelling, writing, youth and community work. *E:* amanaparenting@gmail.com.

BARING, family name of **Earl of Cromer** and **Barons Ashburton, Howick of Glendale, Northbrook,** and **Revelstoke.**

BARING, Sir John (Francis), 3rd Bt *cr* 1911, of Nubia House, Isle of Wight; Director, Camphill Village Copake Foundation, 2007–14; *b* 21 May 1947; *s* of Raymond Alexander Baring (*d* 1967) (2nd *s* of 1st Bt) and Margaret Fleetwood Baring (who *m* 1991, 6th Earl of Malmesbury, TD; she *d* 1994), *d* of late Col R. W. P. C. Campbell-Preston; *S* uncle, 1990; *m* 1st, 1971, Elizabeth Anne (marr. diss. 2004), *yr d* of Robert D. H. Pillitz; two *s* one *d*; 2nd, 2007, Penelope Ann Roberts, *e d* of Cdre John M. Doull, Canada Navy (retd). Citibank NA, 1971–72; Chemical Bank, 1972–84; Kidder, Peabody & Co. Inc., 1984–89; GPA Group Ltd, 1989; Hackman, Baring & Co., 1991–97; PricewaterhouseCoopers Securities LLC, 1997–99; Managing Partner and Mem., Mercator Capital LLC, 1999–2004. Director: Camphill Foundn, 2002–14; Camphill Village USA, 2005–14. Chm. Trustees, Rudolf Steiner Sch., 2002–08. *Recreations:* gardening, fishing. *Heir: s* Julian Alexander David Baring, *b* 10 Feb. 1975. *Address:* (residence) 126 Seacliff Drive, Aptos, CA 95003, USA; (mailing) 500 Cathedral Drive #2814, Aptos, CA 95001, USA.

See also A. H. Buchanan.

BARING, Nicholas Hugo, CBE 2003; *b* 2 Jan. 1934; *er s* of Francis Anthony Baring (killed in action, 1940) and Lady Rose Baring, DCVO; *m* 1972, (Elizabeth) Diana, *d* of late Brig. Charles Crawfurd; three *s. Educ:* Eton (King's Schol.); Magdalene Coll., Cambridge (exhibnr, BA). Nat. service, 2nd Lieut Coldstream Guards, 1952–54. ADC to Governor of Kenya, 1957–58; joined Baring Brothers, 1958; Man. Dir, Baring Brothers & Co., 1963–86; Dir, Barings plc, 1985–94 (Dep. Chm., 1986–89); Mem., 1973–2004, Chm., 1998–2004, Council of Mgt, Baring Foundn. Chm., Baring Archive Trust, 2008–14. Dir, Commercial Union plc, 1968–98 (Chm., 1990–98). Mem., City Capital Markets Cttee, 1983–89 (Chm., 1983–87). Vice Pres., Liverpool Sch. of Tropical Medicine, 1982–89, 1996– (Pres., 1989–96); Chm., Bd of Trustees, Nat. Gall., 1992–96 (Trustee, 1989–96); Trustee, Fitzwilliam Museum Develt Trust (formerly Fitzwilliam Museum Trust), 1997–2011 (Chm., 2004–11). National Trust: Mem. Exec. Cttee, 1965–69 and 1979–2002; Mem. Council, 1978–2002; Chm., Finance Cttee, 1980–91. Mem. Council of Management, Architectl Heritage Fund, 1987–2010. Hon. LLD Liverpool, 1995; Hon. DCL: Kent, 1998; Northumbria, 2004. *Address:* The Old Rectory, Ham, Marlborough, Wilts SN8 3QR. *T:* (01488) 668081. *Clubs:* Brooks's, Beefsteak.

See also P. Baring.

BARING, Peter; *b* 28 Oct. 1935; *yr s* of Francis Anthony Baring (killed in action, 1940) and Lady Rose Baring, DCVO; *m* 1960, Teresa Anne Bridgeman (CBE 1998); three *s. Educ:* Magdalene College, Cambridge (MA English). Joined Baring Brothers & Co., 1959, Director, 1967; Chairman: Barings plc, 1989–95; Baring Asset Management, 1993–95. Dir, Inchcape, 1978–96. Dep. Chm., Provident Mutual Life Assurance Assoc., 1989–95. Chm., London Investment Banking Assoc., 1991–94. Gov., London Business Sch., 1991–95. Chm., Glyndebourne Arts Trust, 1994–96.

See also N. H. Baring.

BARKER, family name of **Baroness Trumpington.**

BARKER, Baroness *cr* 1999 (Life Peer), of Anagach in Highland; **Elizabeth Jean Barker;** Management Consultant, ThirdSectorBusiness, since 2008; Head of Business Development, www.seethedifference.org, since 2009; *b* Outwood, W Yorks, 31 Jan. 1961. *Educ:* Dalziel High Sch., Motherwell; Broadway Sch., Oldham; Univ. of Southampton (BSc(SocSci) Hons Psychology). Pres., Union of Liberal Students, 1982–83. Age Concern England: Project Co-Ordinator, Opportunities for Volunteering Programme, 1983–88; Grants Officer, 1988–92; Field Officer, 1992–2008. Member: Liberal Party Nat. Exec., 1982–83; Liberal Assembly Cttee, 1984–88; Lib Dem Federal Conf. Cttee, 1988– (Chm., 1997–2004); Lib Dem Federal Policy Cttee, 1997–2003. Thought Leader, TheGivingLab, 2009–13. Trustee, Andy Lawson Meml Fund. Patron, Spare Tyre Theatre. Co. *Address:* House of Lords, SW1A 0PW.

BARKER, Prof. Andrew Dennison, PhD; FBA 2005; Professor of Classics, University of Birmingham, 1998–2008, now Emeritus; *b* 24 April 1943; *s* of Edwin Barker and Nancy Ethel Barker; *m* 1st, Susan Margaret Hough (marr. diss. 1976); two *s*; 2nd, 1978, Jill Davida Newman; two *s* one *d. Educ:* Christ's Hosp.; Queen's Coll., Oxford (BA); Australian Nat. Univ. (PhD). Lectr in Philosophy, 1970–87, Sen. Lectr, 1987–92, Univ. of Warwick; Asst Lectr in Classics, Univ. of Cambridge, 1976–78, and Fellow and Dir of Studies in Classics and Philosophy, Selwyn Coll., Cambridge, 1977–78 (on leave from Univ. of Warwick); Sen. Lectr in Classics, 1992–95, Prof., 1995, Univ. of Otago; Reader in Classics, Univ. of Birmingham, 1996–98. *Publications:* Greek Musical Writings, vol. 1, 1984, vol. 2, 1989; Scientific Method in Ptolemy's Harmonics, 2000; Euterpe: ricerche sulla musica Greca e Romana, 2002; Psicomusicologia Nella Grecia Antica, 2005; The Science of Harmonics in Classical Greece, 2007; Ancient Greek Writers on their Musical Past, 2014; articles on ancient Greek music and philosophy. *Recreations:* negotiations with dogs and family; DIY building and land-maintenance, natural history, listening to music. *Address:* Institute of Archaeology and Antiquity, University of Birmingham, Birmingham B15 2TT. *E:* andrewqbarker@hotmail.com.

BARKER, Rt Hon. Dame Anne Judith; *see* Rafferty, Rt Hon. Dame A. J.

BARKER, Barry, MBE 1960; FCIS; Secretary and Chief Executive, Institute of Chartered Secretaries and Administrators (formerly Chartered Institute of Secretaries), 1976–89; *b* 28 Dec. 1929; *s* of late Francis Walter Barker and Amy Barker; *m* 1954, Dr Vira Dubash; two *s. Educ:* Ipswich Sch.; Trinity Coll., Oxford (MA Class. Greats). Secretary: Bombay Chamber of Commerce and Industry, 1956–62; The Metal Box Co. of India Ltd, 1962–67. Dir, Shipbuilding Industry Bd, 1967–71; Consultant at Dept of Industry, 1972; Sec., Pye Holdings Ltd, 1972–76. Chairman: Consultative Council of Professional Management Orgns, 1981–90; Nat. Endorsement Bd, Management Charter Initiative, 1990–94. Member: BTEC, 1985–94; RSA Exams Bd, 1987–94; NCVQ, 1989–92; Bd of Management, Young Vic Co., 1984–90. *Recreation:* the theatre and the arts. *Address:* 82 Darwin Court, Gloucester Avenue, NW1 7BQ. *T:* (020) 7911 0570.

BARKER, His Honour Brian John, CBE 2015; QC 1990; a Senior Circuit Judge, 2000–15; Recorder of London, 2013–15; *b* 15 Jan. 1945; *s* of William Barker and Irene Barker (*née* Gillow); *m* 1977, Anne Judith Rafferty (*see* Rt Hon. Dame A. J. Rafferty); three *d* (and one *d* decd). *Educ:* Strode's School, Egham; Univ. of Birmingham (LLB); Univ. of Kansas (MA). Called to the Bar, Gray's Inn, 1969, Bencher, 1999. A Recorder, 1985–2000; Common Serjeant, City of London, 2005–13. Mem., Senate and Bar Council, 1976–79. A Pres., Mental Health Review Tribunals, 1993–2004. Chm., Criminal Bar Assoc., 1998–2000. Course Dir, Criminal Continuation Seminars, Judicial Studies Bd, 2003–07. Governor: Strode's Coll., Egham, 1992–2003; Sir John Cass Foundn, Aldgate, 2003– (Treas., 2005–07). Freeman, City of London; Liveryman: Coopers' Co., 1989– (Mem., Ct of Assts, 1995; Master, 2008–09); Cutlers' Co., 2006; Curriers' Co., 2013. Hon. LLD City, 2014. *Recreations:* sheep rearing, golf. *Address:* c/o Central Criminal Court, Old Bailey, EC4M 7EH. *Clubs:* Bishopsgate Ward; Rye Golf.

See also P. A. Darling.

BARKER, Caroline; *see* Norbury, C.

BARKER, Rt Rev. Clifford Conder, TD 1970; Bishop Suffragan of Selby, 1983–91; Hon. Assistant Bishop of York, since 1991; *b* 22 April 1926; *s* of Sidney and Kathleen Alice Barker; *m* 1952, Marie Edwards (*d* 1982); one *s* two *d*; 2nd, 1983, Mrs Audrey Gregson; two step *s* one step *d. Educ:* Oriel Coll., Oxford (BA 1950, MA 1955); St Chad's Coll., Durham (Dip. in Theol. 1952). Emergency Commn, The Green Howards, 1944–48; deacon 1952, priest 1953; Curate: All Saints', Scarborough, 1952–55; Redcar, 1955–57; Vicar: All Saints', Sculcoates, Hull, 1957–63; Rudby-in-Cleveland, 1963–70; RD of Stokesley, 1965–70; Vicar, St Olave with St Giles, York, 1970–76; RD of York, 1971–76; Canon of York, 1973–76; Bishop Suffragan of Whitby, 1976–83. CF (TA), 1958–74. *Recreations:* reading, crosswords, music. *Address:* Flat 13, Dulverton Hall, The Esplanade, Scarborough YO11 2AR. *T:* (01723) 340113.

BARKER, Prof. Eileen Vartan, OBE 2000; PhD; FBA 1998; Professor of Sociology with Special Reference to the Study of Religion, London School of Economics, 1992–2003, now Emeritus; Leverhulme Emeritus Fellow, 2004–07; *b* 21 April 1938; *d* of Calman MacLennan and Mary Helen MacLennan (*née* Muir); *m* 1958, Peter Johnson Barker, MBE; two *d. Educ:* Cheltenham Ladies' Coll.; Webber Douglas Sch. of Singing and Dramatic Art; London Sch. of Econs (BSc 1st Cl. Hons Sociol. 1970; PhD 1984; Hon. Fellow, 2011). London School of Economics: Lectr, 1970–85; Sen. Lectr, 1985–90; Reader, 1990–92; Dean, Undergrad. Studies, 1982–86. Leonard Greenberg Distinguished Vis. Fellow, Trinity Coll., Hertford, USA, 2000; William James Guest Prof., Univ. of Bayreuth, 2012. Founder and Chm., INFORM, 1988– (Hon. Dir, 2001–13). President: Soc. for Scientific Study of Religion, 1991–93; Assoc. for Sociol. of Religion, 2001–02. Hon. Pres. for Life, Internat. Study of Religion in Eastern and Central Europe Assoc., 2006. PhD *hc* Copenhagen, 2000. Martin E. Marty Award for Public Understanding of Religion, Amer. Acad. of Religion, 2000; Dist. Scholar Award, Communal Studies Assoc., 2010; George Leslie MacKay Award, Aletheia Univ., Taiwan, 2011; Lifetime Achievement Award, Internat. Cultic Studies Assoc., 2013. *Publications:* (ed) Of Gods and Men, 1982; (ed) New Religious Movements: a perspective for understanding society, 1982; The Making of a Moonie: brainwashing or choice?, 1984 (SSSR Dist. Book Award 1985); New Religious Movements: a practical introduction, 1989; (ed jtly) Secularization, Rationalism and Sectarianism, 1993; (ed jtly) Twenty Years On: changes in new religious movements, 1995; (ed) LSE on Freedom, 1995; (ed jtly) New Religions and New Religiosity, 1998; (ed) Freedom and Religion in Eastern Europe, 2003; (ed) The Centrality of Religion in Social Life, 2008; (ed) Revisionism and Diversification in New Religious Movements, 2013; numerous contribs to scholarly jls and books. *Address:* London School of Economics, Department of Sociology, Houghton Street, WC2A 2AE.

BARKER, Prof. Graeme William Walter, CBE 2015; FSA; FBA 1999; Disney Professor of Archaeology, 2004–14, now Emeritus, and Senior Fellow, since 2014, McDonald Institute for Archaeological Research, University of Cambridge (Director, 2004–14); Fellow, St John's College, Cambridge, since 2004; *b* 23 Oct. 1946; *s* of Reginald Walter Barker and Kathleen (*née* Walton); *m* 1st, 1976, Sarah Miranda Buchanan (marr. diss. 1991); one *d* (and one *s* decd); 2nd, 2008, Annie Grant. *Educ:* Alleyn's Sch., Dulwich; St John's Coll., Cambridge (Henry Arthur Thomas Schol., 1965–67; MA; PhD 1973). FSA 1979. Rome Schol. in Classical Studies, British Sch. at Rome, 1969–71; Lectr, 1972–81, Sen. Lectr, 1981–88, in Prehist. and Archaeol., Sheffield Univ.; Dir, British Sch. at Rome, 1984–88; Leicester University: Prof. and Hd, Sch. of Archaeol Studies, 1988–2000; Graduate Dean, 2000–03; Pro-Vice-Chancellor, 2003–04. Member: Exec. Cttee, UK Council for Graduate Educn, 2001–03; AHRB, subseq. AHRC, 2003–09; Chm., Archaeol. Sub-Panel, RAE, 2008. Pres., Prehistoric Soc., 2001–05. Dan David Prize, 2005. *Publications:* Landscape and Society: Prehistoric Central Italy, 1981, Italian edn 1984; (with R. Hodges) Archaeology and Italian Society, 1981; Prehistoric Communities in Northern England, 1981; (jtly) La Casatico di Marcaria, 1983; (jtly) Cyrenaica in Classical Antiquity, 1984; Prehistoric Farming in Europe, 1985; (with C. S. Gamble) Beyond Domestication in Prehistoric Europe: Investigations in Subsistence Archaeology and Social Complexity, 1985; (with J. A. Lloyd) Roman Landscapes, 1991; (with R. Maggi and R. Nisbet) Archeologia della Pastorizia nell'Europa Meridionale, 1993; A Mediterranean Valley: landscape archaeology and *Annales* history in the Biferno Valley, 1995; The Biferno Valley Survey: the archaeological and geomorphological record, 1995; (jtly) Farming the Desert: the UNESCO Libyan valleys survey, 2 vols, 1996; (with T. Rasmussen) The Etruscans, 1998; (ed) The Companion Encyclopedia of Archaeology, 2 vols, 1999; (with D. Gilbertson) The Archaeology of Drylands: living at the margin, 2000; (ed jtly) The Human Use of Caves in Peninsular and Island Southeast Asia, 2005; The Agricultural Revolution in

Prehistory: why did foragers become farmers?, 2006; (ed jtly) Archaeology and Desertification: the Wadi Faynan landscape survey, Southern Jordan, 2007; (with M. Janowski) Why Cultivate? anthropological and archaeological approaches to foraging-farming transitions in Southeast Asia, 2011; (ed) Foraging and Farming in Island Southeast Asia: the archaeology of the Niah Caves, 2013; contribs to learned jls, esp. on landscape archaeol., ancient agric. and human dispersal. *Address:* McDonald Institute for Archaeological Research, Downing Street, Cambridge CB2 3ER. *T:* (01223) 339622.

BARKER, Rt Hon. Gregory; PC 2012; *b* Sussex, 8 March 1966; *m* 1992, Celeste Harrison (marr. diss. 2008); two *s* one *d. Educ:* Steyning Grammar Sch.; Lancing Coll.; RHBNC (BA 1987). Researcher, Centre for Policy Studies, 1987–88 (Associate, 1988–); Equity Analyst, Gerrard Vivian Gray, 1988–90; Dir, Internat. Pacific Securities, 1990–97; Associate Partner, Brunswick Gp Ltd, 1997–98; Hd, Investor Communications, Siberian Oil Co., 1998–2000. Dir, Daric plc, 1998–2001. MP (C) Bexhill and Battle, 2001–15. An Opposition Whip, 2003–05; Shadow Envmt Minister, 2005–08; Shadow Climate Change Minister, 2008–10; Minister of State, DECC, 2010–14. Mem., H of C Envmtl Audit Select Cttee, 2001–05. Contested (C) Eccles, 1997. Non-exec. Dir, Dragon Harvest Gp, 2015–; Lightsource Renewable Energy Ltd, 2015–.

[Created a Baron (Life Peer) 2015 but title not yet gazetted at time of going to press.]

BARKER, Harold; retired; Keeper, Department of Conservation and Technical Services, British Museum, 1975–79; Member: Council for Care of Churches, 1976–81; Crafts Council, 1979–80; *b* 15 Feb. 1919; *s* of William Frampton Barker and Lily (*née* Pack); *m* 1942, Everilda Alice Whittle; one *s* one *d. Educ:* City Secondary Sch., Sheffield; Sheffield Univ. (BSc). Experimental Asst, 1940, Experimental Officer, 1942, Chemical Inspectorate, Min. of Supply; British Museum: Experimental Officer, Research Lab., 1947; Sen. Experimental Officer, 1953; Chief Experimental Officer, 1960; Principal Scientific Officer, 1966; Acting Keeper, 1975. *Publications:* papers on radiocarbon dating and scientific examination of antiquities in various jls. *Recreations:* music, creative writing (author of novel, Seeking Home). *Address:* 27 Westbourne Park, Falsgrave, Scarborough, N Yorks YO12 4AS. *T:* (01723) 353273.

BARKER, Howard; playwright and poet; *b* 28 June 1946. *Educ:* Univ. of Sussex (MA). Theatre productions, 1970–, include: *Royal Court:* No End of Blame, 1981; Victory, 1983; version of Thomas Middleton's Women Beware Women, 1986; The Last Supper, 1988; Golgo, 1990; Hated Nightfall, 1995; *RSC* at The Pit: The Castle, 1985; Downchild: a fantasy, 1985; The Bite of the Night, 1988; *Leicester:* The Last Supper, 1989; Seven Lears, 1990; Judith, 1995; (Uncle) Vanya, 1996; other productions: A Passion in Six Days, Crucible, Sheffield, 1983; The Power of the Dog, Hampstead, 1985; Possibilities, Almeida, 1988; Scenes from an Execution, NT, 2012; Flesh and Blood, BBC SO, Coliseum, 2013. TV and radio plays include: Scenes from an Execution, Radio 3, 1984 (Best Drama Script, Sony Radio Awards, 1985; Prix Italia, 1985; perf. Almeida, 1990); Pity in History, BBC 2, 1985; A Hard Heart, Radio 3, 1992 (perf. Almeida, 1992); The Early Hours of a Reviled Man, Radio 3, 1992; A House of Correction, Albertina, Radio 3, 1999; Knowledge and a Girl, Radio 4, 2001; The Moving and The Still, Radio 3, 2003; The Road, The House, The Road, Radio 4, 2006. Opera: (with Nigel Osborne) Terrible Mouth, ENO, Almeida, 1992; (with F. M. Einheit) Dead, Dead and Very Dead, 2007. Formed The Wrestling School (company to perform own work), 1989: The Europeans, 1993; Wounds to the Face, 1997; Ursula, 1998; Und, 1999; The Ecstatic Bible, He Stumbled, 2000; A House of Correction, 2001; Gertrude - the Cry, 2002; 13 Objects, 2003; Dead Hands, 2004; The Fence in its Thousandth Year, 2005; The Seduction of Almighty God, 2006; I Saw Myself, The Dying of Today, 2008; Found in the Ground, 2009; Hurts Given and Received, Slowly, 2010. *Publications: plays:* Stripwell, and Claw, 1977; Fair Slaughter, 1978; Love of a Good Man, and All Bleeding, 1981; That Good Between Us, and Credentials of a Sympathiser, 1981; No End of Blame: scenes of overcoming, 1981; Two Plays for the Right: Birth on a Hard Shoulder, and The Loud Boy's Life, 1982; Hang of the Gaol, 1982; Victory: choices in reaction, 1983; The Castle, and Scenes from an Execution, 1984; Crimes in Hot Countries, and Fair Slaughter, 1984; Power of the Dog, 1985; A Passion in Six Days, and Downchild, 1985; The Last Supper: a New Testament, 1988; Lullabies for the Impatient, 1988; Possibilities, 1988; Pity in History, 1989; Seven Lears, and Golgo, 1990; Europeans, and Judith, 1990; Collected Plays, vol. I, 1990, vol. II, 1993, vol. III, 1996, vol. IV, 1997, vol. V, 1999; A Hard Heart, 1992; The Early Hours of a Reviled Man, 1992; Gertrude, and Knowledge and a Girl, 2002; The Ecstatic Bible, 2004; Dead Hands, 2004; The Fence and Its Thousandth Year, 2005; The Seduction of Almighty God, 2006; Collected Plays, vol. 1, 2006, vol. 2, 2006, vol. 3, 2008, vol. 4, 2008, vol. 5, 2009; The Dying of Today, 2008; *poetry:* Don't Exaggerate (Desire and Abuse), 1985; Breath of the Crowd, 1986; Gary the Thief/Gary Upright, 1987; The Ascent of Monte Grappa, 1991; The Tortmann Diaries, 1996; Sheer Detachment, 2009; *essays:* Arguments for a Theatre, 1989; Death, The One and the Art of Theatre, 2004; A Style and Its Origins, 2007. *Address:* c/o Judy Daish Associates Ltd, 2 St Charles Place, W10 6EG.

BARKER, Hon. Sir Ian; *see* Barker, Hon. Sir R. I.

BARKER, Jane Victoria, CBE 2014; FCA; Chairman: Marsh Ltd, since 2013 (non-executive Director, since 2010); Mercer Ltd, since 2014 (non-executive Director, since 2011); *b* Stratford upon Avon, 11 Nov. 1949; *d* of Reginald Badger and Dorothy Badger; *m* 1976, Richard Barker (*d* 1995). *Educ:* Stratford upon Avon Grammar Sch. for Girls; Univ. of Reading (BSc Geol Geophysics 1971). FCA 1980 (ACA 1974). Articled clerk, Supervisor, then Manager, Coopers & Lybrand, 1971–76; various appts, then Chief Financial Officer, C. T. Bowring & Co. Ltd, 1976–90; Finance Dir, 1990–94, Chief Operating Officer, 1993–94, London Stock Exchange; Equitas Ltd: Finance Dir, 1995–2007; Chief Exec., 2007–14; non-exec. Dir, 2014. Non-executive Director: Alliance & Leicester plc, 2004–11; Santander UK plc, 2008–11. Member: Council, Open Univ., 1999–2005; Council, RCM, 2007– (Dep. Chm., 2008–). Mem., Chapter, Salisbury Cath., 2008–. DUniv Open, 2007. *Recreation:* enjoying life. *E:* jane.barker@marsh.com. *Club:* Athenæum.

BARKER, John Alan, CB 2003; CPsychol 1988; Chair, Civil Service Appeal Board, 2012–14 (Deputy Chair, 2007–12); *b* 5 Oct. 1945; *s* of Alan Gilbert Foster Barker and Gwendoline Margery Barker; *m* 1977, Vivienne Frances Cook; one *s* one *d. Educ:* Denstone Coll., Uttoxeter; St Andrews Univ. (MA Econs and Psychol.); Birkbeck Coll., London (MSc Occupational Psychol.). AFBPsS. Sen. Psychologist, CSD, 1974–80; Principal Psychologist, CSSB, 1980–85; Administrative Principal, CSSB, 1985–86; Principal, Personnel Mgt, MPO then HM Treasury, 1986–89; HM Treasury: Head: Allowances Div., 1989–91; Mgt Services, 1991–95; Cabinet Office: Hd, Sen. CS Div., 1995–97; Director: CS Employer Gp, 1997–99; CS Corporate Mgt, 1999–2002; Corporate Develt Gp, 2002–07. NE Dir, Whitehall and Ind. Gp, 2002–09. Associate, Veredus, 2008–12. Chm., Civil Service Retirement Fellowship, 2010–; Treas., Civil Service Club, 2010–. Trustee, Employers' Forum for Age, 2002–05. *Recreations:* choral singing, sport (spectator), reading, wine. *Address:* 42 Hurstdene Avenue, Hayes, Bromley, Kent BR2 7JJ. *E:* johnbarker45@hotmail.co.uk.

BARKER, Dame Katharine (Mary), (Dame Katharine Donovan), DBE 2014 (CBE 2006); Senior Adviser, Credit Suisse, since 2010; *b* 29 Nov. 1957; *d* of Wilfred Barker and Eileen May (*née* Pinhorn); *m* 1982, Peter Richard Donovan; two *s. Educ:* St Hilda's Coll., Oxford (BA Hons PPE). Investment analyst, PO Pension Fund, 1979–81; Res. Officer, NIESR, 1981–85; Chief Economist, Ford of Europe, 1985–94; Chief Econ. Advr, CBI, 1994–2001; Mem. Monetary Policy Cttee, Bank of England, 2001–10; non-exec. Mem., Office for Budget Responsibility, 2011–. Mem., Panel of Independent Advrs, HM Treasury, 1996–97. Non-executive Director: Yorkshire Bldg Soc., 1999–2001, 2010–; Electra Private Equity, 2010–; Taylor Wimpey, 2011–. Member: Bd, Housing Corp., 2005–08; Bd, Homes and Communities Agency, 2008–11. Chairman: Ind. Review of UK Housing Supply, 2003–04; Ind. Review of Land Use Planning, 2005–06; NI Econ. Adv. Gp, 2010–; Commn on the Future of Health and Social Care, King's Fund, 2014; Member: Football Regulatory Authy, 2006–12; Jersey Fiscal Policy Panel, 2014–. Chm., Trustees, British Coal Staff Superannuation Scheme, 2014–. Mem., 1999–2007, Chm., 2007–10, Bd of Govs, Anglia Ruskin (formerly Anglia Poly.) Univ. *Publications:* Housing: where's the plan?, 2014; contribs to jls. *Recreation:* bell-ringing. *T:* 07866 546424.

BARKER, Prof. Kenneth, CBE 1994; Vice-Chancellor, Thames Valley University, 1999–2003; *b* 26 June 1934; *s* of Thomas William and Lillian Barker; *m* 1958, Jean Ivy Pearl; one *s* one *d. Educ:* Royal Coll. of Music (ARCM); King's Coll., London (BMus); Sussex Univ. (MA). GRSM, FTCL, FLCM. Schoolmaster, 1958–62; lectr and university teacher, 1962–75; Principal, Gipsy Hill Coll., 1975; Pro-Dir, Kingston Polytechnic, 1975–86; Dep. Dir/Dir Designate, 1986–87, Dir, 1987–92, Leicester Poly., then Chief Exec. and Vice-Chancellor, De Montfort Univ., 1992–99. Chm., Postgrad. Initial Teacher Trng Bd, 1975–80, Chm., Music Bd and Chm., Cttee for Creative Arts, 1980–90, CNAA. Board Member: London West LSC, 2001–03; London NHS Workforce Confedn, 2001–03. Trustee, Richmond Amer. Internat. Univ. in London, 1997–2004. FRSA; CCMI. Hon. DSc Moscow State Tech. Univ., 1995; DUniv: St Petersburg Univ. of Design and Technology, 1997; De Montfort, 1999; Thames Valley, 2004; Hon. DEd Kingston, 2003. *Publications:* contribs to jls. *Recreations:* music, theatre, watching Rugby. *Address:* Bramshott, Church Road, Surbiton, Surrey KT6 5HH. *T:* (020) 8398 4700. *Club:* Institute of Directors.

BARKER, Ven. Nicholas John Willoughby; Archdeacon of Auckland, since 2007; Priest-in-Charge, Holy Trinity, Darlington, since 2007; *b* 12 Dec. 1949; *s* of Rev. Arthur Barker and Peggy Barker; *m* 1980, Katherine Pritchard; three *s* one *d. Educ:* Sedbergh Sch.; Oriel Coll., Oxford (MA Metallurgy 1973; MA Theol. 1975). Ordained deacon, 1977, priest, 1978; Curate, St Mary's, Watford, 1977–80; Team Vicar, St James & Emmanuel, Didsbury, 1980–86; Team Rector, St George's, Kidderminster, 1986–2007; Rural Dean, Kidderminster, 2001–07. Hon. Canon, Worcester Cathedral, 2003–07; Hon. Supernumerary Canon, Durham Cathedral, 2007–. *Recreations:* bee-keeping, hill-walking, sailing, gardening. *Address:* 45 Milbank Road, Darlington DL3 9NL. *T:* (01325) 480444, *Fax:* (01325) 354027. *E:* archdeacon.of.auckland@durham.anglican.org.

BARKER, Nicolas John, OBE 2002; FBA 1998; FSA; Editor, Book Collector, since 1965; *b* 6 Dec. 1932; *s* of Sir Ernest Barker, FBA, and Olivia Stuart Horner; *m* 1962, Joanna Mary Sophia Nyda Cotton; two *s* three *d. Educ:* Westminster Sch.; New Coll., Oxford (MA; Hon. Fellow, 2011). With Bailliere, Tindall & Cox, 1958 and Rupert Hart-Davis, 1959; Asst Keeper, National Portrait Gallery, 1964; with Macmillan & Co. Ltd, 1965; with OUP, 1971; Dep. Keeper, British Library, 1976–92. William Andrews Clark Vis. Prof., UCLA, 1986–87; Scholar, Getty Center for History of Art and the Humanities, 1996; Sandars Reader in Bibliography, Cambridge Univ., 1999–2000. Panizzi Lectr, BL, 2001; Rosenbach Lectr, Univ. of Pennsylvania, 2002. President: Amici Thomae Mori, 1978–89; Double Crown Club, 1980–81; Bibliographical Soc., 1981–85; Chm., London Liby, 1994–2004 (Mem. Cttee, 1971–2004; a Vice-Pres., 2005–); Member: Publication Bd of Dirs, RNIB, 1969–92; BBC and ITV Appeals Adv. Cttee, 1977–86; Nat. Trust Arts Panel, 1979–91 (Libraries Advr, 1991–99); Liby Cttee, RHS, 1996– (Chm., 1996–2004); Adv. Council, Science Mus., 2006–12. Gov., St Bride Foundn, 1976–; Trustee: The Pilgrim Trust, 1977–2007; York Glaziers Trust, 1990– (Chm., 2004–); Chm., Laurence Sterne Trust, 1984–2010; Chm. Trustees, Type Mus., 1995–. Feoffee, Chetham's Hosp., 2002–10. FSA 2012. DUniv York, 1994. *Publications:* The Publications of the Roxburghe Club, 1962; The Printer and the Poet, 1970; Stanley Morison, 1972; (ed) Essays and Papers of A. N. L. Munby, 1977; (ed) The Early Life of James McBey: an autobiography, 1883–1911, 1977; Bibliotheca Lindesiana, 1977; The Oxford University Press and the Spread of Learning 1478–1978, 1978; (with John Collins) A Sequel to an Enquiry, 1983; Aldus Manutius and the Development of Greek Script and Type, 1985; The Butterfly Books, 1987; Two East Anglian Picture Books, 1988; (ed) Treasures of the British Library, 1989; (ed) S. Morison, Early Italian Writing-Books, 1990; (with Sir Anthony Wagner and A. Payne) Medieval Pageant, 1993; Hortus Eystettensis: the Bishop's Garden and Besler's Magnificent Book, 1994; The Great Book of Thomas Trevilian, 2000; Form and Meaning in the History of the Book, 2002; The Devonshire Inheritance, 2003; The Library of Thomas Tresham and Thomas Brudenell, 2006; The Glory of the Art of Writing: the calligraphic work of Francesco Alunno, 2009; Lady Anne Barnard's Watercolours and Sketches: glimpses of the Cape of Good Hope, 2009; Horace Walpole's Description of the Villa at Strawberry-Hill, 2010; The Roxburghe Club: a bicentenary history, 2012; Esther Inglis's Les Proverbes de Salomon, 2012. *Address:* 22 Clarendon Road, W11 3AB. *T:* (020) 7727 4340. *Clubs:* Garrick, Roxburghe; Roxburghe (San Francisco); Zamorano (Los Angeles).

BARKER, Pamela Gay; *see* Barber, P. G.

BARKER, Patricia Margaret, CBE 2000; novelist, since 1982; *b* 8 May 1943; *d* of Moyra Drake; *m* 1978, Prof. David Faubert Barker (*d* 2009); one *s* one *d. Educ:* Grangefield GS; London School of Economics (BScEcon; Hon. Fellow, 1998); Durham Univ. (DipEd). Teacher, until 1982. Hon. MLitt Teesside, 1994; Hon. DLitt: Napier, 1996; Durham, 1998; Hertfordshire, 1998; London, 2002; DUniv Open, 1997. Author of the Year Award, Booksellers' Assoc., 1996. *Publications:* Union Street (Fawcett Prize), 1982; Blow Your House Down, 1984; The Century's Daughter, 1986 (retitled Liza's England, 1996); The Man Who Wasn't There, 1989; The Regeneration Trilogy: Regeneration, 1991 (filmed 1997; adapted for stage 2014); The Eye in the Door, 1993 (Guardian Fiction Prize, Northern Electric Special Arts Award, 1994); The Ghost Road (Booker Prize), 1995; Another World, 1998; Border Crossing, 2001; Double Vision, 2003; Life Class, 2007; Toby's Room, 2012; Noonday, 2015. *Address:* c/o Aitken Alexander Associates, 291 Gray's Inn Road, WC1X 8EB. *T:* (020) 7373 8672.

BARKER, Paul; writer and broadcaster; Editor, New Society, 1968–86; *b* 24 Aug. 1935; *s* of Donald and Marion Barker; *m* 1960, Sally, *e d* of James and Marion Huddleston; three *s* one *d. Educ:* Hebden Bridge Grammar Sch.; Calder High Sch.; Brasenose Coll., Oxford (Hulme Exhibr), MA. Intell. Corps (commn), 1953–55. Lecteur, Ecole Normale Supérieure, Paris, 1958–59; The Times, 1959–63; The Economist, 1964–65; Staff Writer, 1964, Dep. Ed., 1965–68, New Society; Social Policy Ed., Sunday Telegraph, 1986–88; Associate Ed., The Independent Magazine, 1988–90. Evening Standard: townscape and arts columnist, 1987–92; social commentary, 1992–2007; social and political columnist, Sunday Times, 1990–91; townscape columnist, New Statesman, 1996–99. A Dir, Pennine Heritage, 1978–86. Mem., UK Adv. Cttee, Harkness Fellowships, 1995–97. Vis. Fellow, Centre for Analysis of Social Policy, Univ. of Bath, 1986–2000; Leverhulme Res. Fellow, 1993–95; Res. Fellow in Architecture, Royal Commn for Exhibn of 1851, 2000–02. Institute of Community Studies: Chm., 2000–01 (Trustee, 1991–2001); Fellow, 1992, Sen. Fellow, 1995, Sen. Res. Fellow, 2000–05; Sen. Res. Fellow, Young Foundn, 2005–. FRSA 1990. (Jtly) BPG Award for outstanding radio prog., My Country, Right or Wrong, 1988. *Publications:* (contrib.) Youth in New Society, 1966; (contrib.) Your Sunday Paper, 1967; (contrib. and ed) One for Sorrow, Two for Joy, 1972; (ed) A Sociological Portrait, 1972; (ed) The Social Sciences Today, 1975 (Spanish edn 1979); (contrib. and ed) Arts in Society, 1977, rev. edn 2006; (contrib. and ed) The Other Britain, 1982; (ed) Founders of the Welfare State, 1985; (contrib.) Britain in the Eighties, 1989; (contrib.) Towards a New Landscape, 1993; (contrib.) Young at Eighty, 1995; (contrib. and ed) Gulliver and Beyond, 1996; (contrib. and ed) Living as Equals, 1996 (Spanish edn 2000); (ed jtly) A Critic Writes, 1997; (contrib.) Town and Country, 1998; (contrib.) Non-Plan, 2000; (jtly) The Meaning of the Jubilee, 2002; (contrib.) From Black Economy to Moment of Truth, 2004; (contrib.) Porcupines in Winter, 2006; (contrib.) The Rise and Rise of Meritocracy, 2006; The Freedoms of Suburbia, 2009 (Chinese edn 2012); (contrib.) The Banham Lectures, 2009; (contrib.) William Ralph Turner, 2010; (contrib.) Ordinariness, 2010; (contrib.) David Hepher, 2012; Hebden Bridge, A Sense of Belonging, 2012; A Crooked Smile, 2013; The Dead Don't Die, 2014; Help Me, 2015; numerous essays and articles in magazines and newspapers, incl. TLS, 1960–. *Recreations:* driving to a baroque church, with the radio on. *Address:* 15 Dartmouth Park Avenue, NW5 1JL. *T:* (020) 7485 8861. *Club:* Architecture.

BARKER, Peter William, CBE 1988; DL; Chairman, Fenner (formerly J. H. Fenner (Holdings)) PLC, 1982–93; *b* 24 Aug. 1928; *s* of William Henry George and Mabel Irene Barker; *m* 1961, Mary Rose Hainsworth, MBE, JP, DL; one *s* one *d*. *Educ:* Royal Liberty Sch., Romford; Dorking County High Sch.; South London Polytechnic. CCMI; FInstD; FCIM. J. H. Fenner & Co., 1953–67; Jt Managing Dir, Fenner International, 1967–71; Chief Exec., J. H. Fenner (Holdings), 1971–82. Dir, Neepsend plc, 1984–93. Member: Yorks and Humberside Regional Council, CBI, 1981–94 (Chm., 1991–93); National Council, CBI, 1985–95; Yorks and Humberside Regional Indust. Develt Bd, 1981–95 (Chm., 1992–95). Pro-Chancellor, Univ. of Hull, 1993–2002, now Emeritus. Hon. DSc (Econ) Hull, 1992. FRSA. DL E Yorks (formerly Humberside), 1990; High Sheriff, Humberside, 1993–94. *Recreations:* sailing, ski-ing, tennis, music. *Address:* Swanland Rise, West Ella, East Yorks HU10 7SF. *T:* (01482) 653050. *Clubs:* Royal Yorkshire Yacht, Royal Thames Yacht.

BARKER, Hon. Sir (Richard) Ian, Kt 1994; arbitrator and mediator; Senior Judge, High Court of New Zealand, 1991–97; Chairman, Banking Ombudsman Commission, New Zealand, 1997–2010; *b* 17 March 1934; *s* of Archibald Henry Barker and Kate Dorothy Barker (*née* Humphrys); *m* 1965, Mary Christine Allardyce; two *s* three *d*. *Educ:* Auckland Univ. (BA, LLB, 1958). FAMINZ(Arb/Med). Called to the Bar, NZ, 1958; Partner, Morpeth, Gould & Co., solicitors, Auckland, 1968–80; Barrister, 1968–76; QC (NZ) 1973; Judge, High Court of NZ, 1976–97; Member, Court of Appeal: Cook Is, 1990–; Fiji, 1997–2007; Samoa and Vanuatu, 1998–2001; Pitcairn, 2004–11; Kiribati, 2011–14. Door Tenant, Essex Ct Chambers, London, 1998–. Vis. Fellow, Wolfson Coll., Cambridge, 2006, 2009, 2011. Chancellor, Univ. of Auckland, 1991–99. Nominee of NZ Govt on ICSID Panel of Arbitrators, 1999–. President: Legal Res. Foundn of NZ, 1981–90; Arbitrators' and Mediators' Inst. of NZ, 2000–02. Hon. LLD Auckland Univ., 1999. Ed.-in-Chief, New Zealand Forms and Precedents, 1990–. *Publications:* (Ed.-in-Chief) Law Stories: essays on the New Zealand legal profession, 2003; contrib. articles to NZ and Australian jls. *Recreations:* walking, reading, music, railways. *Address:* 10 Seaview Road, Auckland 1050, New Zealand. *Club:* Northern (Auckland).

BARKER, Dr Richard William, OBE 2012; Director, Oxford-UCL Centre for the Advancement of Sustainable Medical Innovation (formerly Centre for Accelerating Medical Innovation, University of Oxford), since 2012; Chairman: South London Academic Health Science Network, since 2012; South London Genomic Medicine Centre, since 2014; Precision Medicine Catapult, since 2015; *b* 18 Oct. 1948; *s* of late William Barker and Florence Barker; *m* 1st, 1969, Jennifer Ruth (marr. diss. 2000); two *s* one *d*; 2nd, 2008, Michaela. *Educ:* Alleyn's Sch.; Exeter Coll., Oxford (MA; DPhil 1973). Partner, Healthcare Practice Leader, McKinsey & Co., 1980–93; Gen. Manager, Healthcare Solutions, IBM, 1993–96; President: Chiron Diagnostics, 1996–2000; New Medicine Partners, 2001–03; Chm. and CEO, Molecular Staging, 2003–06; Dir-Gen., Assoc. of British Pharmaceutical Industry, 2004–11. Chairman: Stem Cells for Safer Medicines, 2007–; Image Analysis, 2014–; Co-Chair, UK Therapeutic Capability Clusters, 2009–11; non-executive Director: Sunquest, 1997–2001; Exact Scis, 1999–2005; Adlyfe, 2004–09; Internat. Health Partners, 2005–; iCo Therapeutics, 2006–; Celgene Corp., 2012–. Member: Ministerial Industry Strategy Gp, 2005–11; NHS Stakeholder Forum, 2006–; NHS Nat. Leadership Network for Health and Social Care, 2006–10; UK Clin. Res. Consortium, 2006–11 (Vice-Chm., 2009–); e-Health Record Res. Bd, OSCHR, 2007–10; Bd, Academy of Medical Scis Forum, 2009–11. Member: Bd, Eur. Fedn of Pharmaceutical Industry Assocs, 2004–11; Council, Internat. Fedn of Pharmaceutical Manufacturers and Assocs, 2004–11. Hon. Prof., UCL, 2013–; Associate Prof., Univ. of Oxford, 2014–. FRSocMed 2010. *Publications:* 2030: the future of medicine, 2010. *Recreations:* hiking, kayaking, music (especially opera). *Address:* 14 Cottenham Park Road, SW20 0RZ. *T:* 07708 867655. *E:* richard.barker@casmi.org.uk.

BARKER, Ronald Hugh, PhD; BSc; CEng, FIET, FIMechE; Deputy Director, Royal Armament Research and Development Establishment, 1965–75, retired; *b* 28 Oct. 1915; *s* of E. W. Barker and L. A. Taylor; *m* 1943, W. E. Hunt; two *s*. *Educ:* University of Hull. Physicist, Standard Telephones and Cables, 1938–41; Ministry of Supply, 1941–59; Dep. Dir, Central Electricity Research Laboratories, 1959–62; Technical Dir, The Pullin Group Ltd, 1962–65. *Publications:* various, on servomechanisms and control systems.

BARKER, Simon George Harry, FCA; QC 2008; **His Honour Judge Simon Barker;** a Specialist Chancery Circuit Judge, since 2010; *b* London, 1950; *s* of Edgar John Harry and Dorothy Joan Barker; *m* 1972, Eva-Marie; one *s* one *d*. *Educ:* Westminster Sch.; Ealing Tech. Coll. (BA Hons). ACA 1976, FCA 1981. Called to the Bar, Lincoln's Inn, 1979. Recorder, 1995–2010. *Recreations:* rowing, water sports, ski-ing, art, theatre, films, music, football. *Address:* Birmingham Civil Justice Centre, Bull Street, Birmingham B4 6DS. *Club:* London Rowing.

BARKER, Timothy Gwynne; Senior Independent Director, Jefferies International, since 2010; *b* 8 April 1940; *s* of late Lt Col Frank Richard Peter Barker and Hon. Olwen Gwynne (*née* Philipps); *m* 1964, Philippa Rachel Mary Thursby-Pelham; one *s* one *d*. *Educ:* Eton Coll.; McGill Univ., Montreal; Jesus Coll., Cambridge (MA). Dir, 1973–2000 and Hd of Corporate Finance, 1986–90, Kleinwort Benson Ltd; Kleinwort Benson Group plc, subseq. Dresdner Kleinwort Benson: Dir, 1988–93; Dep. Chief Exec., 1990–93; Vice Chm., 1993–2000; Chm., Kleinwort Benson Private Bank Ltd, 1997–2004; Chm., Robert Walters plc, 2001–07. Director-General: City Panel on Take-overs and Mergers, 1984–85; Council for the Securities Industry, 1984–85. Chm., Highview Enterprises Ltd, 2010–; Sen. Ind. Dir, Drax Gp plc, 2004–13; Ind. Dir, 2000–07, Sen. Ind. Dir, 2007–09, Electrocomponents plc; Mem. Bd, Genesis Housing Gp Ltd, 2009–10. Member: Econ. Affairs Cttee, CBI, 1997–2003; Professional Oversight Bd, Financial Reporting Council, 2004–09. *Address:* c/o Jefferies, Vintners Place, 68 Upper Thames Street, EC4V 3BJ.

BARKER, Very Rev. Timothy Reed; Dean of Guernsey, and Rector, St André de la Pommeraye, since 2015; *b* 18 Aug. 1956; *s* of Norman and Marjorie Barker; *m* 1979, Judith Angela Leske; one *s* one *d*. *Educ:* Manchester Grammar Sch.; Queens' Coll., Cambridge (MA 1982); Westcott House, Cambridge. Ordained deacon, 1980, priest, 1981; Asst Curate, St Mary, Nantwich, 1980–83; Vicar: St Berteline and St Christopher, Norton, 1983–88; All Saints, Runcorn, 1988–94; Domestic Chaplain to Bishop of Chester, 1994–98; Vicar, St Mary and St Nicolas, Spalding, 1998–2009; Priest-in-charge, St Paul, Spalding, 2007–09; Rural Dean: Elloe W, 2000–09; Elloe E, 2008–09; Archdeacon of Lincoln, 2009–15. Diocese of Chester: Urban Ministry Officer, 1988–90; Commns Officer, 1991–98; Hon. Priest Asst, Chester Cathedral, 1994–98. Canon and Preb., Lincoln Cathedral, 2003–15 (Mem. Chapter, 2000–08). Mem., Gen. Synod, 2000–05 and 2008–.

BARKER, Trevor; Chairman, Alpha Consolidated Holdings Ltd, 1988–2003; *b* 24 March 1935; *s* of Samuel Lawrence Barker and Lilian Barker (*née* Dawson); *m* 1957, Joan Elizabeth Cross; one *s* one *d*. *Educ:* Acklam Hall Grammar School. FCA. Price Waterhouse & Co. 1957–58; Cooper Brothers, 1958–62; sole practitioner, 1962–70; Chm. and Chief Exec. Gold Case Travel, 1964–77; Dir, Ellerman Wilson Lines, 1977–80; Chairman: John Crowther Gp, 1980–88; William Morris Fine Arts, 1981–88; Micklegate Gp, 1989–95; Drew Scientific Gp, 1993–95; Dep. Chm., Blanchards, 1988–94; Dir, Darlington Bldg Soc., 1994–2000. FRSA 1989. Liveryman, Co. of Woolmen, 1986. *Recreations:* grandchildren, breeding and racing thoroughbred horses, opera, music, literature, the arts.

BARKING, Area Bishop of, since 2014; **Rt Rev. Peter Hill;** *b* Swansea, 4 Feb. 1950; *s* of John and Megan Hill; *m* 1971, Ellen Purvis; one *s* one *d*. *Educ:* UMIST (BSc 1971); Manchester Univ. (PGCE 1973); Wycliffe Hall, Oxford (Cert. Theol 1983); Nottingham Univ. (MTh 1990). Teacher, Manchester and Cheshire, 1972–78; Dep. Head Teacher, The Beaches Primary Sch., Sale Moor, 1978–81; ordained deacon, 1983, priest, 1984; Asst Curate, St James, Porchester, 1983–86; Vicar, All Saints, Huthwaite, 1986–95; Priest-in-charge, St Wilfrid's, Calverton, 1995–2004; Area Dean, Southwell, 1997–2001; Chair, Dio. Bd of Educn, 2001–04, 2012–14; Chief Exec., Dio. of Southwell and Nottingham, 2004–07; Archdeacon of Nottingham, 2007–14. Hon. Canon. Southwell Minster, 2001–14. Mem. Gen. Synod of C of E, 1993–2004 and 2010–14; Vice Chair, Dioceses Commn, 2010–14. *Address:* Barking Lodge, 35A Verulam Avenue, Walthamstow, E17 8ES. *T:* (020) 8509 7377.

BARKING, Archdeacon of; *see* Perumbalath, Ven. J.

BARKLEM, Martyn Stephen; His Honour Judge Barklem; a Circuit Judge, since 2012; *b* Ormskirk, 26 Dec. 1956; *s* of Thomas and Edna Barklem; *m* 2008, Naomi Lisa Ellenbogen, *qv*; two *s* by a former marriage. *Educ:* Dauntsey's Sch.; Univ. of London (LLB Hons ext 1986). Served RN, 1976–78. Royal Hong Kong Police, 1979–88, Detective Chief Inspector, 1983–88. Called to the Bar, Middle Temple, 1989; in practice at the Bar, 1990–2012; a Recorder, 2002–12. *Recreations:* sailing, aviation, IT, cooking. *Address:* Harrow Crown Court, Hailsham Drive, Harrow, Middx HA1 4TU. *T:* (020) 8424 2294. *E:* hhjudge.barklem@judiciary.gsi.gov.uk. *Clubs:* Bar Yacht, Royal Naval Volunteer Reserve Yacht; Hong Kong Cricket.

BARKLEM, Naomi Lisa; *see* Ellenbogen, N. L.

BARKSHIRE, Robert Renny St John, (John), CBE 1990; TD; JP; DL; banker; *b* 31 Aug. 1935; *s* of late Robert Hugh Barkshire, CBE; *m* 1st, 1960, Margaret Elizabeth Robinson (marr. diss. 1990; she *d* 2011); two *s* one *d*; 2nd, 1990, Audrey Mary Anne Witham. *Educ:* Bedford School. ACIB. Served Duke of Wellington's Regt, 2nd Lieut, 1953–55; HAC, 1955–74 (CO, 1970–72; Regtl Col, 1972–74). Joined Cater Ryder & Co., 1955, Jt Man. Dir, 1963–72; Chm., Mercantile House Holdings plc, 1972–87; Non-exec. Dir, Extel Gp PLC, 1979–87 (Dep. Chm., 1986–87); Chairman: CL-Alexanders Laing & Cruickshank Hldgs Ltd, 1984–88; Internat. Commodities Clearing House Ltd, 1986–90. Chm., Financial Futures Wkg Pty, 1980, later LIFFE Steering Cttee, 1981–82; Dir, LIFFE, 1982–91 (Chm., 1982–85). Member: Adv. Bd, Internat. Monetary Market Div., Chicago Mercantile Exchange, 1981–84; London Adv. Bd, Bank Julius Baer, 1988–91. Chairman: Uplink Ltd (EPN Satellite Service), 1988–90; Chaco Investments Ltd, 1994–2001; non-executive Director: Household Mortgage Corp., 1985–94 (Chm., 1993–94); Savills, 1988–95; Sun Life and Provincial Holdings plc, 1988–99; TR Property Investment Trust plc, 1993–2002. Chm., Eastbourne Hosps NHS Trust, 1993–99. Chm., Cttee on Market in Single Properties, 1985–2000. Gen. Comr for Income Tax, City of London, 1981–2009. Chairman: Reserve Forces Assoc., 1983–87; Sussex TA Cttee, 1983–85; SE TAVRA, 1985–91; Dep. Chm., TA Sport Bd, 1983–95 (Mem., 1979–95). Financial Advisor: Victory Services Assoc. (formerly Club), 1981–95; RE Central Mgt Investments Policy Cttee, 1988–2007; Army Central Fund, 1995–2007; Royal Signals Trustees Ltd, 1996–2005; Dir, Officers' Pensions Soc. Investment Co. Ltd, 1982–95; Member: Regular Forces Employment Assoc. Council, 1986–95; SSAFA Council (Trustee and Mem. Exec. and Finance Cttee), 1996–2008; Adv. Bd, Army Common Investment Fund, 2002–04; Chm., Nat. Meml Arboretum, 2003–11; Trustee: Regtl Assoc., Duke of Wellington's Regt, 1990–2011; Army Benevolent Fund, 1999–2010 (Pres., E Sussex Br., 1999–2011); RBL, 2005–10 (Co-opted Mem., Nat. Council, 1991–2005; Chm., Chiddingly and Dist, 1982–87; Pres., Burwash, 2012–); Yorks Regt, 2006–11. Chairman: E Sussex Br. Magistrates' Assoc., 1986–91; E Sussex Magistrates' Courts Cttee, 1993–97 and 1999–2001; Sussex Magistrates' Courts Cttee, 2001–02. Mem., Chiddingly Parish Council, 1979–86; Treas., Burwash PCC, 1999–. Treasurer and Trustee: Sussex Historic Churches Trust, 2003–; Friends of E Sussex Record Office, 2008–; Treas., Wealden, NADFAS, 2010–. Dir, Brighton Philharmonic Orch., 2013–. Governor: Harpur Trust, 1984–89 (Chm., Bedford Sch. Cttee, 1984–89); Eastbourne Coll., 1980–95 (Vice Chm., 1983–92); Roedean Sch., 1984–89; Burwash Primary C of E Sch., 1999–2007 (Chm., 2002–07); Comr, Duke of York's Royal Military Sch., 1986–95. Freeman, City of London, 1973; Liveryman, Worshipful Co. of Farmers, 1981. JP Lewes, 1980; DL E Sussex, 1986. *Recreations:* sailing, shooting. *Address:* Denes House, High Street, Burwash, East Sussex TN19 7EH. *T:* (01435) 882646. *Clubs:* City of London, Cavalry and Guards, MCC; Royal Fowey Yacht (Cornwall).

BARLEY, Nicholas; Director, Edinburgh International Book Festival, since 2009; *b* N Yorks, 22 June 1966; *s* of Anthony and Lesley Barley; *m* 1997, Fiona Bradley; one *s* one *d*. *Educ:* Univ. of Kent, Canterbury (BA Hons Social Psychol.). Publisher, Blueprint mag., 1994–98; Dir, August Publishing, 1998–2003; Ed., The List, 2003–07; Exec. Dir, The Lighthouse, Scotland's Centre for Architecture, Design and the City, 2007–09. *Publications:* Lost and Found: critical voices in new British design, 1999; Breathing Cities: the architecture of movement, 2000. *Address:* Edinburgh International Book Festival, 5A Charlotte Square, Edinburgh EH2 4DR.

BARLING, Hon. Sir Gerald (Edward), Kt 2007; **Hon. Mr Justice Barling;** a Judge of the High Court of Justice, Chancery Division, since 2007; *b* 18 Sept. 1949; *s* of Banks Hubert Barling and Barbara Margarita (*née* Myerscough); *m* 1983, Myriam Frances (*née* Ponsford); three *d*. *Educ:* St Mary's Coll., Blackburn (Peel Foundn Scholar, 1968); New Coll., Oxford (Burnett Open Exhibnr in Classics, 1968; Hons Sch. of Jurisprudence (1st Cl.), 1971; MA). Called to the Bar, Middle Temple, 1972 (Harmsworth Entrance Exhibnr, 1971; Astbury Law Scholar, 1973; Bencher, 2001); called to the Bar, NI, 1992. Practised at Common Law Bar, Manchester, 1973–81; practising in fields of public and competition law, and in all aspects of EC and EU Law, Brick Court Chambers, London, 1981–2007; Asst Recorder, 1990–93; QC 1991; QC (NI) 1992; Recorder, 1993–2007; Dep. High Court Judge, 2007; Actg Deemster, I of M Court of Appeal, 2000–09. Pres., Competition Appeal Tribunal, 2007–13. Lectr in Law, New Coll., Oxford, 1972–77. Chairman: Western European Sub-Cttee, Bar Council, 1991–92; Bar European Gp, 1994–96 (Vice-Chm., 1992–94). Trustee, Develt Fund, New Coll., Oxford, 2003–14. *Publications:* (contrib.) Butterworth's European Court Practice, 1991; (co-ed) Practitioner's Handbook of EC Law, 1998; papers on different aspects of English and EU Law. *Recreation:* country pursuits. *Address:* Royal Courts of Justice, Strand, WC2A 2LL.

BARLOW, Celia Anne; *b* 28 Sept. 1955; two *s* one *d*. *Educ:* King Edward High Sch. for Girls, Birmingham; New Hall, Cambridge (BA 1976); University Coll., Cardiff; Central St Martin's Coll. of Art and Design. Reporter, Telegraph and Argus, Bradford, 1979–82; reporter and Asst Ed., Asia TV HK, 1982–83; journalist and Home News Ed., BBC TV News, 1983–95; freelance video producer, 1998–2000; Lectr in Video Prodn, Chichester Coll. of Arts, Sci. and Technol., 2000–05. Contested (Lab) Chichester, 2001. MP (Lab) Hove, 2005–10; contested (Lab) same seat, 2010. *Publications:* Spray of Pearls, 1993.

BARLOW, Sir Christopher Hilaro, 7th Bt *cr* 1803; architect; *b* 1 Dec. 1929; *s* of Sir Richard Barlow, 6th Bt, AFC, and Rosamund Sylvia, *d* of late F. S. Anderton (she *m* 2nd, 1950, Rev. Leonard Haslet Morrison, MA); *S* father, 1946; *m* 1st, 1952, J. C. de M. Audley (*d* 2002), *e d* of late J. E. Audley, Cheshire; one *s* two *d* (and one *s* decd); 2nd, 2003, Mrs Jeane Gage, *e d* of Douglas Stevens, Hamilton. *Educ:* Eton; McGill Univ., Montreal. BArch. MRAIC. Past Pres., Newfoundland Architects' Assoc. Lt Governor's Silver Medal, 1953. *Heir: s* Crispian John Edmund Audley Barlow, Tech. Advr, Protected Areas Enforcement, WWF, Vietnam [*b* 20 April 1958; *m* 1st, 1981, Anne Waiching Siu (marr. diss. 2005); one *d*; 2nd, 2006, Christi Lane, Philadelphia, Penn]. *Address:* 40 St James Place, Hamilton, ON L8P 2N4, Canada.

BARLOW, Prof. David Hearnshaw, MD; Executive Dean of Medicine, Faculty of Medicine, University of Glasgow, 2005–10, now Emeritus Professor; Director of Women's Services, Hamad Medical Corporation, Qatar, and Chairman, Department of Obstetrics and Gynaecology, Women's Hospital, Doha, Qatar, 2012–15; Professor, Weill-Cornell Medical College, Qatar, since 2014; *b* 26 Dec. 1949; *s* of Archibald and Anne Barlow; *m* 1973, Norma Christie Woodrow; one *s* one *d*. *Educ:* Clydebank High Sch.; Univ. of Glasgow (BSc Hons Biochem. 1971; MB ChB 1975; MD 1982); MA Oxon 1985. FRCOG 1993; MRCP 2005. MRC Trng Fellowship, 1977–78; Hall Tutorial Fellow, Univ. of Glasgow, 1979–81; Sen. Registrar, Queen Mother's Hosp., Glasgow, 1981–84; Oxford University: Clinical Reader in Obstetrics and Gynaecology, 1984–90; Nuffield Professor of Obstetrics and Gynaecology, 1990–2004; Fellow: Green Coll., 1984–90; Oriel Coll., 1990–2004, Hon. Fellow, 2006; Hon. Consultant Obstetrician and Gynaecologist, The Women's Centre, Oxford Radcliffe Hosps NHS Trust (formerly John Radcliffe Hosp.), Oxford, 1984–2004. Lectures: Blair Bell Meml, 1985, Simpson Oration, 2006, RCOG; Howard Jacobs, British Fertility Soc., 2005. Chairman: DoH Adv. Gp on Osteoporosis (report published, 1995); NICE Guideline Develt Gp on Fertility, 2002–04; NICE Guideline Develt Gp on Osteoporosis, 2003–08. Member: Bd, Acad. Medicine for Scotland, 2005–10; Oversight Bd, Scottish Academic Health Scis Collaboration, 2007–10; Univs of Scotland Health Cttee, 2007–10. Mem., HFEA, 1998–2006 (Mem., Scientific and Clinical Advances Adv. Cttee, 2006–). Mem., FIGO Expert Panel on the Menopause, 1998–. Mem. Council, RCOG, 1996–2002. Chm., British Menopause Soc., 1999–2001; Trustee: Nat. Osteoporosis Soc., 1995–2006 (Chm., 2002–04; Mem., Clinical and Scientific Cttee, 2006–); Nat. Endometriosis Soc., 1997–2000. Pres., Eur. Menopause and Andropause Soc., 2007–09 (Vice-Pres., 2004–06). Chm., Oxford NHS R & D Consortium, 2001–04; NHS Greater Glasgow and Clyde Health Board: non-exec. Dir, 2005–10; Chm., Clinical Governance Cttee, 2005–10; Chm., Res. Ethics Governance Cttee, 2005–10; Chm., Glasgow Biomedicine; Mem., Scientific Adv. Bd, Preglem, Geneva, 2008–. Member: Medical Scis Divisional Bd, Univ. of Oxford, 2000–04; RAE 2001 and RAE 2008 Panels, HEFCE; Sen. Investigator, Appts Panel, NIHR, 2008–; Fitness to Practise Panel, GMC, 2011–. Ext. Assessor, Medical Council of Ireland, 2011–. Internat. Trustee, Susan Mubarak Foundn for Women's Health, Egypt, 2006–11. Founder FMedSci 1998; FRSE 2008. Hon. FRCPGlas 2006. Mem., Editl Bd, Best Practice in Obstetrics and Gynaecology, 1995–2004; Ed., Menstrual Disorders & Subfertility Gp, Cochrane Collaboration, 1996–; Editor-in-Chief, Human Reproduction Jl, 2000–06. *Publications:* (ed) Clinical Guidelines on the Prevention and Treatment of Osteoporosis, 1999; over 330 pubns incl. 180 scientific papers in field of reproduction, reproductive medicine and women's health incl. infertility and assisted reproduction, endometriosis and pelvic pain, menopause and osteoporosis. *Recreations:* wide-ranging interest in music, painting.

BARLOW, David John; broadcasting consultant; Adviser on International Relations, BBC, since 1993; *b* 20 Oct. 1937; *s* of Ralph and Joan Barlow; *m* 2001, Stella M. Waterman (*née* Hewer) (*d* 2015); one step *s* one step *d*, and five *s* one *d* of previous marriages. *Educ:* Leighton Park Sch.; The Queen's Coll., Oxford; Leeds Univ. MA, DipEd (Oxon); DipESL (Leeds). British Council, 1962–63; BBC, 1963–: Producer, African Service; Schools Broadcasting, 1965–67; Programme Organiser, Hindi, Tamil, Nepali and Bengali Service, 1967–70; Further Educn Radio, 1970–71; UNESCO, British Council Consultancies, 1970–73; Head of Liaison Internat. Relations, 1974–76; Chief Asst Regions, 1977–79; Gen. Sec., ITCA, 1980–81; BBC: Sec., 1981–84; Controller: Public Affairs and Internat. Relations, 1984–86; Public Affairs, 1986–87; Regional Broadcasting, 1987–90; seconded to EBU as Co-ordinator for Audio Visual Eureka Project, 1990–91; Controller, Information Services and Internat. Relns, 1991–92. Consultant, then Sec. Gen., Public Broadcasters Internat., 1999–2008. Non-exec. Dir, Bedford Hosp. NHS Trust, 2002–04. Mem., RTS, 1980–. Trustee, Children in Need, 1986–92. Chm., Govs, Sharnbrook Upper Sch., 2002–03 (Vice-Chm., 2001–02). *Recreations:* bird watching, mountains, books. *Address:* 6 Rue des Ecoles, 79120 Chenay, France. *T:* (5) 49293899. *E:* davidbarlow@wanadoo.fr.

BARLOW, David Michael Rigby, CB 1996; Under Secretary, Government Legal Service, 1989–96; *b* 8 June 1936; *s* of late Samuel Gordon Barlow and Eunice Hodson Barlow; *m* 1973, Valeree Elizabeth Rush-Smith; one *s*; one *d* by previous marr. *Educ:* Shrewsbury Sch.; Christ Church, Oxford (MA Law). National Service: Midshipman RNVR in Submarine Br. of RN, 1954–56; Sub-Lieut and Lieut in permanent RNR, 1956–61. Solicitor, England and Wales, 1965, NI, 1991. Appointments as a lawyer in the public service, 1965–73; Asst Sec. in Govt Legal Service, 1973–89. *Recreations:* Spanish language and culture, ski-ing, cinema.

BARLOW, Francis; *see* Barlow, R. F. D.

BARLOW, Sir Frank, Kt 1998; CBE 1993; Chairman, Logica, 1995–2002; *b* 25 March 1930; *s* of John and Isabella Barlow; *m* 1950, Constance Patricia Ginns (*d* 2000); one *s* two *d*. *Educ:* Barrow Grammar Sch., Cumbria. Nigerian Electricity Supply Corp., 1952–59; Daily Times, Nigeria, 1960–62; Managing Director: Ghana Graphic, 1962–63; Barbados Advocate, 1963; Trinidad Mirror Newspapers, 1963–64; Gen. Manager, Daily Mirror, 1964–67; Man. Dir, King & Hutchings, 1967–75; Dir and Gen. Manager, Westminster Press, 1975–83; Dir, Economist, 1983–99; Chief Executive: Financial Times Group, 1983–90 (Chm., 1993–96); Westminster Press Group, 1985–90; Man. Dir, Pearson plc, 1990–96; Chairman: BSkyB, 1991–95; Thames Television, 1995–97; Channel 5, 1997. Pres., Les Echos, Paris, 1988–90; Director: Elsevier (UK), 1991–94; Soc. Européene des Satellites SA, 2000–02; Chm., Lottery Products Ltd, 1997–99. Dir, Press Assoc., 1985–93. Chm., Printers' Charitable Corp., 1995–2000, Pres. Emeritus, 2006. Dir, Royal Philharmonic Orch., 1988–93. *Recreations:* golf, fell walking, angling. *Club:* Carlton.

BARLOW, Gavin Galbraith; Director of Strategy, Planning and International, Home Office, since 2015; *b* 5 May 1964; *s* of Peter John Barlow and Elizabeth Findlay Barlow; *m* 1991, Dr Alice Rebecca Chishick; three *s* two *d*. *Educ:* Univ. of Bristol (BSc Soc. Sci. 1986); Imperial Coll., London (MBA, DIC, 1997). Ministry of Defence, 1987–2015: Asst Private Sec. to Minister of State (Armed Forces), 1989–91; Administrative Sec., Sovereign Base Areas Admin, Cyprus, 1999–2002; Dir Policy Planning, 2002–06; Dir Gen. Mgt and Orgn, 2006–07; Dir Prison Population, MoJ, 2007–08; Dir Service Personnel Policy, MoD, 2008–15. *Recreations:* cooking, cycling, books. *Address:* Home Office, 2 Marsham Street, SW1P 4DF.

BARLOW, George Francis, OBE 1998; FRICS; Chairman, London Development Agency, 2000–03; Chief Executive (formerly Director), Peabody Trust, 1987–99; *b* 26 May 1939; *s* of late George and Agnes Barlow; *m* 1969, Judith Alice Newton; one *s* two *d*. *Educ:* Wimbledon Coll.; Hammersmith Sch. of Art and Building; Polytechnic of Central London. Surveyor, Building Design Partnership, 1962–67; Develt Surveyor, GLC Housing Dept, 1967–70; The Housing Develt Officer, London Borough of Camden, 1970–76; Dir/Sec., Metropolitan Housing Trust, 1976–87. External Examiner, Polytechnic of Central London, 1989–90. Mem., Housing Cttee, 1986–91, Chm., Housing Policy Panel, 1996–99, RICS; Chm., London Housing Assocs Council, 1978–82; Dep. Chm., London Develt Partnership, 1998–2000; Member: Central YMCA Housing Assoc., 1982–85; Council, Nat. Fedn of Housing Assocs, 1985–89; Cttee, Community Self Build Agency, 1989–94; Cttee, Broomleigh Housing Assoc., 1989–95; Trustee: Kent Community Housing Trust, 1989–92; William Sutton Trust, 1999–2001; Mem. Bd, East London Partnership, 1991–99. Chm., Youth Homelessness Cttee, Prince's Trust/BITC, 1994–98. Gov., Univ. of E London, 1996–2000. Sen. Associate, King's Fund, 1999–2004. Hon. DLitt: Westminster, 2001; London South Bank, 2004. *Recreations:* theatre, horseracing.

BARLOW, Dr Horace Basil, FRS 1969; Royal Society Research Professor, Physiological Laboratory, Cambridge University, 1973–87; *b* 8 Dec. 1921; *s* of Sir (James) Alan (Noel) Barlow, 2nd Bt, GCB, KBE and Nora Barlow (*née* Darwin); *m* 1st, 1954, Ruthala (marr. diss., 1970), *d* of late Dr M. H. Salaman; four *d*; 2nd, 1980, Miranda, *d* of John Weston Smith; one *s* two *d*. *Educ:* Winchester; Trinity Coll., Cambridge. Research Fellow, Trinity Coll., 1950–54, Lectr, King's Coll., Cambridge, 1954–64. Demonstrator and Asst Dir of Research, Physiological Lab., Cambridge, 1954–64; Prof. of Physiological Optics and Physiology, Univ. of Calif, Berkeley, 1964–73. Australia Prize, 1993; Royal Medal, Royal Soc., 1993; Lashley Award, Amer. Philosophical Soc., 2003. *Publications:* several, on neurophysiology of vision in Jl of Physiology, and elsewhere. *Address:* Trinity College, Cambridge CB2 1TQ.

BARLOW, Ian Edward; Chairman, Racecourse Association, 2009–15; Lead non-executive Director, HM Revenue and Customs, since 2012; *b* Shipley, 30 Sept. 1951; *s* of Sir (George) William Barlow; *m* 1976, Judith Ann Jary; two *s*. *Educ:* Oundle Sch.; Clare Coll., Cambridge (BA Engrg Scis 1973). FCA 1976; CTA 2000, CTA (Fellow). KPMG, 1973–2010: Hd of Tax and Legal UK, 1994–2001; Sen. Partner, London, 2002–08; Sen. Advr, 2008–10. Chm., WSP Gp plc, 2011–12; non-executive Director: Candy & Candy Gp, 2008–11; PA Consulting Gp, 2008–12; Brunner Investment Trust plc, 2009–; Smith & Nephew plc, 2010–; Foxtons plc, 2013–. Dir, China British Business Council, 2008–. Chm., Think London, 2002–11; Dir, London First, 2005–11; Mem. Bd, London Develt Agency, 2008–12. Founder Chm., Safer London Foundn, 2005–08; Trustee, Historic Royal Palaces, 2010–13. *Recreations:* golf, horseracing. *Address:* 7 St Luke's Street, SW3 3RS. *T:* (020) 7349 0649. *E:* ian@ianebarlow.com. *Clubs:* Brooks's; Royal Mid-Surrey Golf, Liphook Golf, St Enodoc Golf, Royal Birkdale Golf.

BARLOW, Sir James (Alan), 4th Bt *cr* 1902, of Wimpole Street, St Marylebone, co. London; Sales Executive, Preston Mobility, since 2014; *b* 10 July 1956; *s* of Sir Thomas Erasmus Barlow, 3rd Bt and of Isabel Barlow (*née* Body); *S* father, 2003; *m* 2004, Sylvia Lois Mann. *Educ:* Highgate Sch.; Manchester Univ. (BSc). US Steel Res. Center, Penn, USA, 1978; The Welding Inst., Cambridge, UK, 1979–82; Harland & Wolff, Shipbuilders, Belfast, 1982–84; Glassdrumman Lodge Hotel, Newcastle, Ire., 1985–92; Galgorm Manor Hotel, Ballymena, 1992–95; Covenant Life Coll., Fort St John, BC, 1996–98; IBM Canada, Vancouver, 1999–2002; Sales Exec. (formerly Communications Consultant), Bell Mobility, 2002–14. Dir, Destiny Encounters, 2010–12. Pres., Interjab Computer Support Services, Vancouver, 2002–12. Mem., Abbotsford Chamber of Commerce, BC, 2001– (Dir, 2007; Vice Pres., 2008; Pres., 2009; Chm., 2010); Dir, British Columbia Chamber of Commerce, 2010–13. Dir, Jimi Hendrix Family Foundn, 2013–. Ambassador, Galapagos Conservation Trust, London, 2005–; Vice Chm., Bd of Trustees, Abbotsford Christ the King, 2006–. *Recreations:* ornithology, the countryside, the Bible, technology, conservation. *Address:* 1652 King Crescent, Abbotsford, BC V2S 7M7, Canada. *T:* (604) 5042412, *Fax:* (604) 5042413. *E:* jabathome@aol.com. *Clubs:* Savile, Royal Over-Seas League.

BARLOW, Jan; Chief Executive: Caxton Foundation, since 2013; Macfarlane Trust, since 2013; *b* 28 Sept. 1965; *d* of Peter and Joan Barlow. *Educ:* Corpus Christi Coll., Cambridge (BA 1989, MA 1992); South Bank Univ., London (MSc 1998). Manager, GP Postgrad. Educn, East Anglian RHA, 1990–92; Jt Planning and Business Manager, Croydon HA and Croydon FHSA, 1992–94; Hd, Corporate Mgt, Croydon HA, 1994–97; Hd, Corporate Affairs, Save the Children, 1997–2001; Chief Executive: Brook Adv. Centres, then Brook, 2001–06; Battersea Dogs & Cats Home, 2006–09; interim consultancy roles, 2009–12. Vice Chair, Nat. Animal Welfare Trust, 2005–11. *Recreations:* dogs and horses, animal welfare.

BARLOW, Sir John (Kemp), 3rd Bt *cr* 1907, of Bradwall Hall, Sandbach; merchant banker and farmer; Director, Majedie Investments plc, 1978–2000; Director of other companies; *b* 22 April 1934; *s* of Sir John Denman Barlow, 2nd Bt and Hon. Diana Helen (*d* 1986), *d* of 1st Baron Rochdale, CB and *sister* of 1st Viscount Rochdale, OBE, TD; *S* father, 1986; *m* 1st, 1962, Susan (marr. diss. 1998), *er d* of Col Sir Andrew Horsbrugh-Porter, 3rd Bt, DSO; four *s*; 2nd, 1998, Mrs Pauline Windsor. *Educ:* Winchester; Trinity Coll., Cambridge (MA 1958). Chm., Rubber Growers' Assoc., 1974. Steward of the Jockey Club, 1988–90. High Sheriff, Cheshire, 1979. *Recreations:* steeplechasing, hunting, shooting. *Heir: s* John William Marshall Barlow [*b* 12 March 1964; *m* 1991, Sarah Nobes; three *s*]. *Clubs:* Brooks's, City of London, Jockey.

BARLOW, Prof. Martin Thomas, ScD; FRS 2005; FRSC 1998; Professor of Mathematics, University of British Columbia, since 1992; *b* 16 June 1953; *s* of late Andrew Dalmahoy Barlow and of Yvonne Rosalind Barlow; *m* 1994, Colleen Patricia McLaughlin. *Educ:* Sussex House Sch., London; St Paul's Sch., London; Trinity Coll., Cambridge (BA 1975; ScD 1993); University Coll. of Swansea (PhD). Fellow, Trinity Coll., Cambridge, 1979–92. *Publications:* contrib. to learned jls. *Address:* Department of Mathematics, University of British Columbia, Vancouver, BC V6T 1Z2, Canada. *T:* (604) 8226377, *Fax:* (604) 8226074.

BARLOW, Patrick; actor, writer, director; *b* 18 March 1947; *s* of Edward Morgan and Sheila Maud Barlow; two *s* one *d*. *Educ:* Uppingham Sch.; Birmingham Univ. (BA 1968). Founder mem., Inter-Action Community Arts, 1968–72; Dir, Lancaster Young People's Theatre, 1972–74; Founder Dir, Solent People's Theatre, 1974–76; created Henrietta Sluggett and appeared nationwide in clubs, streets, theatres, incl. Crucible, Sheffield, Haymarket, Leicester and NT, 1976–79; created *National Theatre of Brent*, 1980, appeared in and wrote jointly: stage: Charge of the Light Brigade, 1980; Zulu!, 1981; Black Hole of Calcutta, 1982; Götterdämmerung, 1982; The Messiah, 1983; Complete Guide to Sex, 1984; Greatest Story Ever Told, 1987; Mysteries of Sex, 1997; Love Upon the Throne, 1998; The New Messiah, 2000; The Wonder of Sex, 2001; television: Messiah, 1983; Mighty Moments from World History, Lawrence of Arabia, Dawn of Man, Boadicea, Arthur and Guinevere, 1985; Revolution!!, 1989; created Royal Dingle Co. for Oh Dear Purcell!, 1995; Massive Landmarks of the Twentieth Century, Queen Victoria, Russian Revolution, Edward VIII and Mrs Simpson, Cuban Missile Crisis, First Man on the Moon, Clinton and Monica, 1999; *other stage appearances* incl.: Truscott, in Loot, Manchester Royal Exchange, 1987; Humphry, in Common Pursuit, Phoenix, 1988; Pseudolus, in A Funny Thing Happened on the Way to the Forum, Manchester Liby Th., 1988; Sidney, in Silly Cow, Haymarket, 1991; Toad, in Wind in the Willows, RNT, 1994; *television* incl.: Talk to Me, 1983; Victoria Wood: As Seen on TV, 1985; All Passion Spent, 1986; Thank You Miss Jones, 1987; Absolutely Fabulous, 1994, 2004; Aristophanes, 1995; Is It Legal?, 1995, 1996, 1998; Cows, 1996; Goodbye Mr Steadman, 1999; The Nearly Complete and Utter History of Everything, 2002; Hans Christian Anderson, 2002; Murder in Suburbia, 2004; Shakespeare's Happy Endings, 2005; Marple: By the Pricking of My Thumbs, 2006; Jam and Jerusalem, 2006, 2008, 2009; Sensitive Skin, 2007; Miranda, 2009; The Queen Mother's Visit, 2010; regular appearances on French & Saunders; *films* incl.: Shakespeare in Love, 1999; Notting Hill, 1999; Girl from Rio, 2001; Bridget Jones's Diary, 2001; Nanny McPhee, 2005; Scoop, 2006; The Riot Club, 2014; *radio* incl.: All the World's a Globe, Midsummer Wedding, 1990; Noah, 1991;

Desmond Dingle's Compleat Life and Works of William Shakespeare, 1995; Rent, 1996, 1997, 1998; The Patrick and Maureen Maybe Music Experience, 1999; Just Plain Gardening, 2002, 2005; National Theatre of Brent's Complete and Utter History of the Mona Lisa, 2004 (Sony Gold for Best Comedy, Gold award, NY Fests, 2005); The Furniture Play, 2004; Volpone, 2004; Small Gods, 2006; National Theatre of Brent's Messiah, 2006; National Theatre of Brent's The Arts and How They Was Done, 6 episodes, 2007; National Theatre of Brent's Iconic Icons: episode 1, Bob Dylan and How He Done the Singing, 2009; episode 2, Tracey Emin and How She Done the Bed, 2010; Joan of Arc, and How She Finally Became a Saint, 2009 (also actor); The Dalai Lama and How He Done The Buddhism, 2011; Giant Ladies That Changed the World, 2011; The Skool Days of Nigel Molesworth, 2014; regular contrib., Looking Forward to the Past, Quote Unquote. Writer: for television: The Ghost of Faffner Hall (jtly), 1989; adaptation, The Growing Pains of Adrian Mole, 1986; screenplay, Van Gogh (Prix Futura, Berlin Film Fest.), 1990; Scarfe on Sex, 1991; The True Adventures of Christopher Columbus (also actor and dir), 1992; Queen of the East, 1994 (also actor); adaptation, The Young Visiters, 2003 (also actor); Marple: Why Didn't They Ask Evans?, 2009; for theatre: libretto, Judgement of Paris, Garden Venture, Royal Opera, 1991; How to Deal with Getting Dumped, GogMagog Theatre Co., 2002; The 39 Steps, W Yorks Playhouse, 2005, transf. Tricycle, then Criterion, 2006 (Best Comedy, Olivier Awards, 2007), transf. NY, 2008–11, UK tour, 2008, 2009–10, US tour, 2009–10, world tour, 2008–13, revived NY, 2015; (jtly) Ben-Hur, Watermill Th., Newbury, 2012 (also co-dir); adaptation, A Christmas Carol, US, 2012, 2013. *Publications:* All the World's a Globe, 1987 (adapted for radio) (Sony Radio award, 1990; Premier Ondas award, 1991); Shakespeare: The Truth, 1993; Love Upon the Throne, 1998; The Messiah, 2001; The Wonder of Sex, 2001; Desmond Olivier Dingle's Complete History of the Whole World, 2002; The 39 Steps (play), 2010; A Christmas Carol (play), 2015. *Address:* (as writer/director) Sayle Screen Ltd, 11 Jubilee Place, SW3 3TD; (as actor) John Altaras Associates Ltd, Covent Garden Hotel, Wellington Street, WC2E 7BB. *Clubs:* Groucho, Two Brydges, Union, Academy.

BARLOW, Phyllida, RA 2011; sculptor; *b* Newcastle upon Tyne, 4 April 1944; *d* of late Erasmus Darwin Barlow and Brigit Ursula Hope Barlow (*née* Black); *m* Fabian Peake; five *c*. *Educ:* Chelsea Coll. of Art, London; Slade Sch. of Fine Art, London. Former Prof. of Fine Art, and Dir, Undergrad. Studies, Slade Sch. of Fine Art, London. Solo exhibitions include: Mus. of Installation, London, 1991, 1995; Baltic Centre for Contemp. Art, Gateshead, 2004; Mead Gall., Warwick Arts Centre, 2008; Hauser & Wirth, London, 2011, NY, 2012; Tate Britain, 2014; group exhibitions include Venice Biennale, 2013; work in public collections: Tate, London; Henry Moore Inst., Leeds. *Address:* c/o Hauser & Wirth, 23 Savile Row, W1S 2ET.

BARLOW, (Richard) Francis (Dudley); QC 2006; barrister; *b* 9 Oct. 1938; *y s* of late Dudley Barlow and Ruby Barlow (*née* Brews); *m* 1966, Helen Mary, *er d* of late Wilfrid Gawthorne and Maureen Gawthorne (*née* Nelson); three *s*. *Educ:* Dauntsey's Sch.; Christ Church, Oxford (BA 1962; MA 1966). Nat. Service, RN, 1957–59; Lt-Comdr RNR. Called to the Bar, Inner Temple, 1965; Bencher, Lincoln's Inn, 1994; in practice at Chancery Bar. *Address:* 10 Old Square, Lincoln's Inn, WC2A 3SU. *T:* (020) 7405 0758. *Club:* Garrick.

BARLOW, Stephen William, FGS, FRCO; conductor, composer and pianist; Artistic Director, Buxton Festival, since 2012; *b* 30 June 1954; *s* of George William Barlow and Irene Catherine Barlow (*née* Moretti); *m* 1986, Joanna Lamond Lumley, *qv*. *Educ:* Canterbury Cathedral Choir Sch.; King's Sch., Canterbury; Trinity Coll., Cambridge (BA 1975); Guildhall Sch. of Music and Drama. FRCO 1971; FGS (FGSM 1986). Associate Conductor, Glyndebourne Fest. Opera, 1980–81; Resident Conductor, ENO, 1980–83; Music Director: Opera 80, 1987–90 (co-founder, 1979); Queensland Philharmonic, 1996–99; Artistic Dir, Opera Northern Ireland, 1996–99. Début as conductor, Royal Opera House, Covent Garden, 1989, then San Francisco, Melbourne, Sydney, Detroit, Miami, Berlin, Auckland, Singapore, Vancouver, Amsterdam, Chicago, Copenhagen, Aarhus, Belgrade, Catania, Toronto, etc. *Publications:* String Quartet, 2000; The Rainbow Bear (for children), 2000; Pas de Deux for Flute and Piano, 2002; King (opera for Canterbury Cathedral), 2004; Nocturne for Clarinet, Marimba and Strings, 2008. *Recreations:* wine, driving, cricket, composing and playing chamber music. *Address:* c/o Musichall, Oast House, Crouch's Farm, Hollow Lane, E Hoathly, E Sussex BN8 6QX. *E:* info@musichall.uk.com.

BARNARD, 11th Baron *cr* 1698; **Harry John Neville Vane,** TD 1960; landowner; Lord-Lieutenant and Custos Rotulorum of County Durham, 1970–88; a Vice-Chairman, Council, British Red Cross Society, 1987–93 (Member Council 1982–85; Hon. Vice President, since 1999); Chairman, Teesdale Mercury Ltd, since 1983; *b* 21 Sept. 1923; *er s* of 10th Baron Barnard, CMG, OBE, MC, TD, and Sylvia Mary (*d* 1993), *d* of Herbert Straker; *S* father, 1964; *m* 1952, Lady Davina Mary Cecil, DStJ (marr. diss. 1992), *e d* of 6th Marquess of Exeter, KCMG; one *s* four *d*. *Educ:* Eton; MSc Durham, 1986. Served War of 1939–45, RAFVR, 1942–46 (Flying Officer, 1945). Northumberland Hussars (TA), 1948–66; Lt-Col Commanding, 1964–66. Vice-Pres., N of England TA&VRA, 1970 and 1977–88, Pres., 1974–77. Hon. Col, 7 (Durham) Bn The Light Infantry, 1979–89. County Councillor, Durham, 1952–61. Member: Durham Co. AEC, 1953–72 (Chm., 1970–72); N Regional Panel, MAFF, 1972–76; CLA Council, 1950–80; Dir, NE Housing Assoc., 1964–77. President: Farmway Ltd (formerly Teesside Farmers), 1965–2003; Durham Co. Br., CLA, 1965–89; Durham Co. St John Council, 1971–88; Durham Co. Scouts Assoc., 1972–88; Durham and Cleveland Co. Br. RBL, 1973–92; Durham Wildlife Trust (formerly Durham Co. Conservation Trust), 1984–95; Durham Co. Fedn of Young Farmers Clubs, 1991–92; Vice-Pres., Game Conservancy Trust, 1997–. Patron: Durham Co. Br., BRCS, 1993– (Pres., 1969–87); Northumbria (formerly Durham Co.) RBL, 2001–12. DL Durham, 1956, Vice-Lieutenant, 1969–70; JP Durham, 1961. Joint Master of Zetland Hounds, 1963–65. Sen. Grand Warden, United Grand Lodge of England, 1970–71; Provincial Grand Master for Durham, 1969–98. Queen's Badge of Honour, BRCS, 1991. KStJ 1971. *Heir: s* Hon. Henry Francis Cecil Vane [*b* 11 March 1959; *m* 1998, Kate, *yr d* of Christopher Robson; one *s* two *d*]. *Address:* Raby Castle, PO Box 50, Staindrop, Darlington, Co. Durham DL2 3AY. *T:* (01833) 660751. *Clubs:* Brooks's; Durham County (Durham); Northern Counties (Newcastle upon Tyne).

See also S. B. Phillips.

BARNARD, Prof. Alan John, PhD; FBA 2010; Professor of the Anthropology of Southern Africa, University of Edinburgh, since 2001; *b* Baton Rouge, Louisiana, 22 Feb. 1949; *s* of John H. Barnard and Doris P. Barnard; *m* 1990, Joy E. Maxwell. *Educ:* George Washington Univ. (BA 1971); McMaster Univ. (MA 1972); PhD London 1976. Jun. Lectr, Univ. of Cape Town, 1972–73; Lectr, UCL, 1976–78; Lectr, 1978–90, Sen. Lectr, 1990–94, Reader, 1994–2001, in Social Anthropol., Univ. of Edinburgh. Hon. Consul of Namibia in Scotland, 2007–. *Publications:* (with A. Good) Research Practices in the Study of Kinship, 1984; A Nharo Wordlist, with Notes on Grammar, 1985; Hunters and Herders of Southern Africa: a comparative ethnography of the Khoisan Peoples, 1992; Kalahari Bushmen, 1993; (ed with J. Spencer) Encyclopedia of Social and Cultural Anthropology, 1996, 2nd edn 2010; History and Theory in Anthropology, 2000; Social Anthropology: a concise introduction for students, 2000, 2nd edn as Social Anthropology: investigating human social life, 2006; Los pueblos cazadores recolectores: tres conferencias dictadas en Argentina (The Hunter-Gatherer Peoples: three lectures presented in Argentina), 2001; (ed) Hunter-Gatherers in History, Archaeology and Anthropology, 2004; Anthropology and the Bushman, 2007; Social Anthropology and Human Origins, 2011; Genesis of Symbolic Thought, 2012; contrib. articles to acad. jls and chapters in books. *Recreations:* black labradors, folk music, watercolour painting. *Address:* Social Anthropology, School of Social and Political Studies, University of Edinburgh, Chrysta Macmillan Building, 15a George Square, Edinburgh EH8 9LD. *E:* a.barnard@ed.ac.uk.

BARNARD, David; *see* Barnard, J. D. W.

BARNARD, Prof. Eric Albert, PhD; FRS 1981; Visiting Professor, Department o Pharmacology, University of Cambridge, 1999–2014; Director, Molecular Neurobiolog Unit, and Professor of Neurobiology, Royal Free and University College Medical Schoo (formerly Royal Free Hospital School of Medicine), London University, 1992–98, Emeritu Professor, since 1999; *m* 1956, Penelope J. Hennessy; two *s* two *d*. *Educ:* Davenant Found Sch. (LCC Schol.); King's Coll., London (BSc Chem.; PhD Molecular Biol.1956). Nat Service, RAF, 1945–48. King's College, London: Nuffield Foundn Res. Fellow, 1956–59 Asst Lectr, 1959–60; Lectr, 1960–64. State University of New York at Buffalo: Associate Prof of Biochemical Pharmacol., 1964–65; Prof. of Biochemistry, 1965–76; Head of Biochemistr Dept, 1969–76; Imperial College of Science and Technology, London: Rank Prof. of Physic Biochemistry, 1976–85; Chm., Div. of Life Sciences, 1977–85; Head, Dept of Biochem. 1979–85; Founder and Dir, MRC Molecular Neurobiol. Unit, Cambridge, 1985–92 Rockefeller Fellow, Univ. of Calif, Berkeley, 1960–61; Guggenheim Fellow, MRC Lab. o Molecular Biol., Cambridge, 1971. Vis. Prof., Univ. of Marburg, Germany, 1965; Vis Scientist, Inst. Pasteur, France, 1973; Vis. Lectr and Res. Leader (Guggenheim Award) Tokyo Univ., 1993. Res. Assessor, CNRS, 1996–2001. UK Rep., Eur. Commn on Internat Decade of the Brain, 1987–89. Member: British Pharmacol Soc.; Biochem. Soc.; Soc. fo Neurosci., USA; Internat. Soc. Neurochem.; EMBO; Central Cttee, Internat. Union o Pharmacology, 1991–2000. Foreign Mem., Polish Acad. of Scis, 2000. Josiah Macy Facult Scholar Award, USA, 1975; Ciba Medal and Prize, 1985; Eastman Kodak Award, USA, 198 Erspamer Internat. Award for Neuroscience and Gold Medal, 1991; ECNP-Synthélab Award for Receptors Res., 1996; Eli Lilly Internat. Prize for Distinguished Res. i Neuropharmacol., 1998; Thudicum Medal and Award for Molecular Neuroscience Biochem. Soc., 2007. Editor-in-Chief, Receptors and Channels, 1993–2000; mem. editl bd three other scientific jls. *Publications:* editor of eight scientific books; several hundred papers i learned biol jls, incl. Nature. *Recreations:* the pursuit of good claret, opera. *Address:* Departmen of Pharmacology, University of Cambridge, Tennis Court Road, Cambridge CB2 1PD. *T* (01223) 847876, 334043. *E:* eb247@cam.ac.uk.

BARNARD, Surg. Rear Adm. Ernest Edward Peter, DPhil; FFCM; Surgeon Rea Admiral, Operational Medical Services, 1982–84; retired 1984; *b* 22 Feb. 1927; *s* of Lione Edward Barnard and Ernestine (*née* Lethbridge); *m* 1955, Dr Joan Barnard (*née* Gunn); one one *d*. *Educ:* schools in England and Australia; Univ. of Adelaide; St Mary's Hosp., Univ. o London (MB, BS 1955); St John's Coll., Univ. of Oxford (student, 1966–68; DPhil 1969) MRCS, LRCP 1955; MFOM 1979; FFCM 1980. After house appts, joined RN, 1956 served, 1957–76: HMS Bulwark, Reclaim and Dolphin; RN Physiol Lab.; RN Med. Sch. Inst. of Naval Medicine; Dept of Med. Dir Gen. (Naval); exchange service with US Navy a Naval Med. Res. Inst., Bethesda, Md, 1976–78; Inst. of Naval Medicine, 1978–80; QH 1980–84; Dep. Med. Dir Gen. (Naval), 1980–82; Surgeon Rear-Adm., Inst. of Nava Medicine, and Dean of Naval Medicine, 1982. FRSocMed 1962. *Publications:* papers o underwater medicine and physiology. *Recreations:* gardening, reading of history an archaeology, photography. *Address:* c/o Barclays Bank, PO Box 6, Portsmouth PO6 3DH.

BARNARD, Dame Hermione; *see* Lee, Dame H.

BARNARD, (John) David (William), CBE 2000; FRCS, FDSRCS; Consultant Oral an Maxillofacial Surgeon, Queen Alexandra Hospital, Portsmouth Hospitals NHS Trust 1979–2005; *b* 5 March 1943; *s* of Dr George Edward Barnard and Gwenllian Mary Barnar (*née* Thomas); *m* 1980, Cheryl Barlow. *Educ:* St Marylebone Grammar Sch.; Guy's Hosp Dental Sch. (BDS London 1966). FDSRCS 1974; FDSRCPSGlas 1974. Hse surgeon, Guy' Hosp., 1967; RN Dental Service, 1967–72; Asst Dental Surgeon, Queen Victoria Hosp., E Grinstead, 1973–75; Sen. Registrar, Oxford Hosps, 1975–79. Civil Consultant, Royal Hosp (formerly Royal Naval Hosp.), Haslar, 1983–2005; Consultant Advr in Oral and Maxillofacia Surgery, RN, 2002–05 Leverhulme Fellow in Oral Surgery, Univ. of California, 1978 Hunterian Prof., RCS, 1978. Clifford Ballard Meml Lecture, Consultant Orthodontists' Gp British Orthodontic Soc., 2004. Member: Central Cttee, Hosp. Dental Services, 1988–9 (Chm., 1995–98); Jt Consultants Cttee, 1995–2001; Central Consultants and Specialists Cttee BMA, 1995–2001; Standing Dental Adv. Cttee, 1998–2004. Mem., GDC, 1998–200 (Chm., Postgrad. Sub Cttee, 2001–03; Chm., Educn Cttee, 2003–04); Hosps Gp Pres., 1985 Chm., Gp Cttee, 1988–99, Mem., Council and Rep. Bd, 1995–98, Fellow, 2004, BDA Mem. Council, 1987–92, Hon. Treas., 1989–92, Pres., 2004, BAOMS; Odontologica Section, Royal Society of Medicine: Mem. Council, 1990–99; Hon. Treas., 1993–96; Vice Pres., 1996–99; Royal College of Surgeons of England: Bd Mem., 1995–2002, Dean 1998–2001, Faculty of Dental Surgery; Mem. Council, 1998–2002; Trustee, Hunteriar Collection, 2008– (Chm of Trustees, 2014–). FDSRCSE (*ad hominem*) 1998; FRCS (by election) 2000; FFGDP(UK) 2008. Hon. Fellow, Amer. Assoc. of Oral and Maxillofacia Surgeons, 2004. Colyer Gold Medal, Faculty of Dental Surgery, RCS, 2004. *Publications* contrib. chapters in books and articles to learned jls. *Recreations:* my border collies, histori motor sport, general aviation, music. *Address:* Squirrels Leap, 59 Warblington Road Emsworth, Hants PO10 7HG. *T:* (01243) 372987. *Clubs:* Army and Navy; Emsworth Sailing Goodwood Road Racing, Goodwood Aero.

BARNARD, Prof. John Michael; Professor of English Literature, School of English University of Leeds, 1978–2001, now Emeritus; *b* Folkestone, 13 Feb. 1936; *s* of John Claud Southard Barnard and Dora Grace Barnard; *m* 1st, 1961, Katherine Duckham (marr. diss 1975); one *s* two *d*; partner, 1975, *m* 2nd, 1991, Hermione Lee (*see* Dame H. Lee). *Educ* Wadham Coll., Oxford (BA (Hons) Eng. Lang. and Lit.; BLitt; MA). Res. Asst, English Dept Yale Univ., 1961–64; Vis. Lectr, English Dept, Univ. of California at Santa Barbara, 1964–65 Post-doctoral Fellow, William Andrews Clark Meml Liby, UCLA, 1965; Leeds University Lectr and Sen. Lectr, Sch. of English, 1965–78; Dir, Inst. of Bibliography and Textua Criticism, Sch. of English, 1996–2001 (Actg Dir, 1982–96). Res. Fellow, William Andrew Clark Meml Liby, UCLA, and Huntington Liby, 1994. Mem., British Cttee, Eighteent Century Short Title Catalogue, 1983–89; Pres., Bibliographical Soc., 2008–10 (Mem Council, 1989–94; Vice-Pres., 1998–2008). Mem., English Panel, 1996 RAE, Chm., Englis Panel, 2001 RAE, HEFCE. Lectures: British Academy Warton, 1989; Friends of Bodleiar Quatercentenary, 2002; D. F. McKenzie, Oxford Univ., 2005; Coffin Meml, London Univ. 2010. Internat. expert Verkenningscommissie Moderne Letteren, Netherlands, 1992–93. FEA 2000. General Editor: Longman Annotated Poets, 1976–, with Paul Hammond, 2001–10 The Cambridge History of The Book, Vols 1–2 and 5–7, 2003–; Member, Editorial Board English Poetry Full Text Database, 1991–93; English Verse Drama Full Text Database 1993–95; English Prose Drama Full Text Database, 1994–96. *Publications:* (ed) Willian Congreve, The Way of the World, 1972; (ed) Pope: The Critical Heritage, 1973; (ed) Johr Keats: the complete poems, 1973, 3rd edn 1988; (ed) Etherege: The Man of Mode, 1979, rev edn 2007; John Keats, 1987; (ed) John Keats: selected poems, 1988; (jtly) The Early Seventeenth-Century York Book Trade and John Foster's Inventory of 1616, 1994; (ed) The Folio Society John Keats, 2001; (ed jtly) The Cambridge History of the Book in Britain, Vol 4 1557–1695, 2002; (ed) Selected Poems: John Keats, 2007; (ed) John Keats: selected letters 2014; chapters in books, articles in Brit. and Amer. learned jls, occasional reviews, etc *Recreations:* travel, walking. *Address:* Lane End, Weeton Lane, Weeton, Leeds LS17 0AN.

BARNARD, Toby Christopher, DPhil; FBA 2007; Lecturer in History, University of Oxford, 1976–2012; Fellow and Tutor in History, 1976–2012, now Emeritus Fellow, and Archivist and Fellow Librarian, 2005–12, Hertford College, Oxford; *b* 17 April 1945; *s* of Robert John Barnard and Gina Barnard (*née* Motta). *Educ:* Torquay Boys' Grammar Sch.; Brighton, Hove and Sussex Grammar Sch.; Queen's Coll., Oxford (BA 1966; DPhil 1972). Bryce Sen. Scholar in Hist., Oxford Univ., 1968–69; Tutor in Hist., Univ. of Exeter, 1969–70; Lectr in Hist., Royal Holloway Coll., Univ. of London, 1970–76. Historical advr, Carroll Inst. of Irish Hist., 1991–94; British Acad. Res. Reader, 1997–99; Vis. Fellow, Archbishop Narcissus Marsh's Liby, Dublin, 2001–02; Leverhulme Sen. Res. Fellow, 2006–09. Dacre Lect., Univ. of Oxford, 2013. Hon. MRIA 2001. FRHistS 1977. *Publications:* Cromwellian Ireland: English government and reform in Ireland 1649–1660, 1975, 2nd edn 2000; The English Republic 1649–1660, 1982, 2nd edn 1997; The Abduction of a Limerick Heiress: social and political relations in mid-eighteenth-century Ireland, 1998; A New Anatomy of Ireland: the Irish protestants 1641–1770, 2003; Making the Grand Figure: lives and possessions in Ireland 1641–1770, 2004; Irish Protestant Ascents and Descents 1641–1770, 2004; The Kingdom of Ireland 1641–1760, 2004; Guide to the Sources for the History of Material Culture in Ireland 1500–2000, 2005; Improving Ireland?: projectors, prophets and profiteers, 1641–1786, 2008; *edited:* (with Jane Clark) Lord Burlington: architecture, art and life, 1995; (with D. Ó. Crónín and K. Simms) A Miracle of Learning: studies in manuscripts and Irish learning: essays in honour of William O'Sullivan, 1998; (with Jane Fenlon) The Dukes of Ormonde 1610–1745, 2000; (with W. G. Neely) The Clergy of the Church of Ireland 1000–2000: messengers, watchmen and stewards, 2006; articles in historical jls and book reviews in TLS, Irish Times, English Historical Review, etc. *Recreations:* pugs (Member, Pug Dog Club), collecting, West Cork. *Address:* 44 High Street, Finstock, Oxon OX7 3DW. *E:* toby.barnard@hertford.ox.ac.uk. *Club:* Oxford and Cambridge.

BARNBROOK, Richard John; private fine art commissions and commercial international fine art and design projects; *b* Catford, London, 24 Feb. 1961; *s* of John and Janet Barnbrook. *Educ:* Immingham Comp. Sch.; Grimsby Sch. of Art (Foundn course); Royal Acad. of Arts (RA Dip; BA 1st Cl. Hons 1985); Limoges Coll. of Art and Design (Minor Schol. 1983); Silipokorn Univ., Bangkok (UNESCO Schol. 1986); Calif Inst. of Art (Interim MA); Greenwich Univ. (PGCE 1995). Practising artist and art lectr, England, Norway, Holland, Germany, France, Thailand and USA, 1985–2003; writer, director and actor, performance art and theatre, 1987–91, film (and film-maker), 1989–92; private commns of art works, 1989–2004; secondary sch. art teacher, 1996–2004. Nat. and internat. exhibns, 1971–2002. Mem. (BNP) Barking and Dagenham LBC, 2006–10 (Leader, 2006–08, Dep. Leader, 2008–10, BNP Gp). Mem., London Assembly, GLA, 2008–12 (BNP, 2008–10, Ind, 2010–12). Contested (BNP) Barking, 2005. Member: Labour Party, 1984–86; BNP, 1999–2010 (Br. Organiser, Lewisham and Bromley, 2000; London Regl Organiser, 2003–05; Mem., Adv. Council, 2004–06). *Recreations:* cycling, Rugby, swimming. *E:* richardbarnbrook2402@hotmail.com.

BARNE, Major Nicholas Michael Lancelot, CVO 2003 (LVO 1996); Extra Equerry to the Duke and Duchess of Gloucester, since 2004 (Private Secretary, Comptroller and Equerry, 1989–2004); *b* 25 Nov. 1943; *m* 1974, Hon. Janet Elizabeth, *d* of Baron Maclean, KT, GCVO, KBE, PC; two *s. Educ:* Eton Coll. Regular officer, Scots Guards, 1965–79; fruit farming, 1979–84. Hon. Col, Norfolk ACF, 1989–2001 (Co. Comdt, 1985–89). Private Sec., Comptroller and Equerry, 1989–2004, Extra Equerry, 2004, to Princess Alice, Duchess of Gloucester. Pres., Broads Soc., 2012–. Freeman, City of London, 2001; Liveryman, Co. of Broderers, 2002–. *Address:* Church Barn, Woodrising, Norfolk NR9 4PJ.

BARNEBY, Col Michael Paul; Clerk to the Salters' Company, 1990–2006; *b* 29 March 1939; *m* 1973, Bridget, *d* of Col A. G. Roberts, DSO, Crickhowell; three *d. Educ:* Radley Coll. Commissioned into 15th/19th King's Royal Hussars, 1958; served Germany, NI, Hong Kong; commanded Royal Hong Kong Regt (Volunteers), 1981–83; retired from Army, 1988; Dir of Planning and Admin, Clark Whitehill, 1988–89. *Recreations:* hunting, shooting, racing. *Address:* Combe House, Titcomb Way, Kintbury, Hungerford RG17 9UG. *Club:* Boodle's.

BARNES; *see* Oppenheim-Barnes.

BARNES, family name of **Baron Gorell**.

BARNES, Adrian Francis Patrick, CVO 1996; DL; Remembrancer of the City of London, 1986–2003; *b* 25 Jan. 1943; *s* of late Francis Walter Ibbetson Barnes and of Heather Katherine (*née* Tamplin); *m* 1980, Sally Eve Whatley; one *s* one *d. Educ:* St Paul's School; Hague Acad. of Internat. Law; Council of Legal Educn; MA City of London Polytechnic 1981. Called to the Bar, Gray's Inn, 1973, Bencher, 2000 (Doyen, Seniors in Hall, 1992–2000); Solicitor's Dept, DTI, 1975; Dep. Remembrancer, Corp. of London, 1982. Chm., Wimbledon Guild of Social Welfare, 2004–08 (Mem., Exec. Cttee, 2003–08; Chairman: Counselling Mgt Cttee, 2004–08; Centenary Cttee, 2004–08). Gov., 1995–, Chm. Govs, 1997–2003, Chm., Res. Cttee, 2014–, The Music Therapy Charity. Freeman: City of London, 1982; Arts Scholars' Co. (formerly Guild of Arts Scholars, Dealers and Collectors), 2007–; Liveryman, Merchant Taylors' Co., 1989–. DL Greater London, 2002. *Recreations:* music, cricket, rowing, chess, biography, City lore. *Clubs:* Garrick, Guildhall, MCC.

BARNES, Anthony Hugh, FSA; Director, Redundant Churches Fund, 1984–92; *b* 16 June 1931; *s* of Sir George Barnes and Anne Barnes; *m* 1st, 1956, Susan Dempsey; one *s* (and one *s* decd) one *d*; 2nd, 1984, Jennifer Carey. *Educ:* King's Coll., Cambridge (MA). FCIPD. Schweppes Ltd, 1954–66; Royal Opera House, 1966–70; ICI, 1970–82; self-employed, 1982–84. Trustee: Norfolk Churches Trust, 1995–2002 (Sec., 1992–95); Norwich Historic Churches Trust, 2001–08. Vice-Pres., Norwich Labour Party, 2000–01. FSA 2004. *Address:* 1 Dixon's Court, 52 Bethel Street, Norwich NR2 1NR. *T:* (01603) 666783.

BARNES, Barbara Lucinda; a District Judge (Magistrates' Courts), since 2004; *b* 28 Nov. 1953; *d* of Arthur Frederick Barnes and Barbara Barnes (*née* Willisford). *Educ:* Blackheath High Sch.; St George's Sch., Harpenden; KCL (LLB 1975). Called to the Bar, Gray's Inn, 1976; Inner London Magistrates' Courts Service: Dep. Chief Clerk, 1979–88; Dep. Trng Officer, 1988–91; Justices' Clerk, Greenwich, 1998–2003. Commng Ed., 2004–07, Ed.-in-Chief, 2007–, Archbold: Magistrates' Courts Criminal Practice. *Recreations:* amateur dramatics, theatre, travel, reading. *Address:* c/o Southwestern Magistrates' Court, 176A Lavender Hill, SW11 1JU.

BARNES, Most Rev. Brian James, GCL 2011; KBE 2003 (MBE 1983); OFM; Archbishop of Port Moresby, (RC), 1997–2008, now Emeritus; Bishop for Disciplinary Forces, 1999–2008; *b* 23 March 1933; *s* of Arthur Keith Barnes and Eileen Victoria (*née* Whereat). *Educ:* Greyfriars, Mornington, Vic; St Paschal's Coll., Box Hill, Vic. Ordained priest, 1958; Missionary, Aitape dio., PNG, 1959–68; Police Chaplain, Port Moresby, 1968–88; Bishop of Aitape, 1988–97. Pres., Catholic Bps' Conf., PNG and Solomon Is, 1993–96; Chm., Heads of Churches' Cttee, 2005–08 (for Service chaplaincies) (Vice Chm., 1998–2005); Member: Nat. Disaster Cttee, 1998–2008; Senate for Priestly Formation, 1999–2008. Chairman: Police Promotion Bd, 1999–2000 and 2006–07; Deputy Chairman: St Mary's Medical Centre Bd, 1999–2010; NCD Commn Liquor Licensing Cttee, 2000–01; Member: NCD Physical Planning Bd, 2003–05; Bd, Envmtl Law Centre, PNG, 2007–10. Chancellor, and Chm. Governing Council, Catholic Theol Inst., 1999–2008; Chairman: Holy Spirit Seminary Bd, 1999–2008; Council, Nat. Res. Inst., 2001–06. *Recreation:* golf. *Address:* Our Lady of Consolation Aged Care Services, 32 Evans Road, Rooty Hill, NSW 2766, Australia. *T:* 98320444, *Fax:* 96258453. *E:* pomarch06@yahoo.com.au, npittorino@franciscans.org.au.

BARNES, Christopher John Andrew, CB 1996; trainer, facilitator, coach and mentor; *b* 11 Oct. 1944; *s* of late Eric Vernon Barnes and Joan Mary Barnes; *m* 1st, 1978, Carolyn Elizabeth Douglass Johnston (*d* 1990); two *s*; 2nd, 1990, Susan Elizabeth Bird; two *s. Educ:* City of London Sch.; London School of Economics (BScEcon). Ministry of Agriculture, Fisheries and Food: Exec. Officer, 1962; Asst Principal, 1967; Private Sec. to Parly Sec., 1969–71; Principal, 1971; Sec. to Northfield Cttee on Agricultural Land Ownership and Occupancy, 1977–79; Asst Sec., 1980; Chief Reg. Officer, Nottingham and Reading, 1980–83; Hd of Personnel and R&D Requirements Divs, 1983–90; 'Barnes Review' of near market R&D, 1988; Under Sec. (Grade 3), 1990–96; Arable Crops and Hort., later Arable Crops and Alcoholic Drinks Gp, 1990–95; Dir of Estabs, 1995–96, retired. A Chm., CSSB, 1995–97. Ind. Accredited Assessor for DEFRA (formerly MAFF), 1996–. Sen. Consultant, Andersons, 1996–98; Associate Dir, Andersons Chamberlain Recruitment, 1996–98; Dir, Drew Associates Ltd, 1996–98; Associate, Nat. Sch. of Govt, 1996–2012; Senior Associate: McNeil Robertson Develt, 1996–2013; Miad UK Ltd, 2001–; Res Consortium, 2003–; Westminster Explained, 2004–; Public Health Action Support Team, 2005–; ISC Medical, 2012–; Exec. Search Consultant, Rundle Brownswood, 2002–12; Mem., Live Academy, 2005–10. Chairman: Assured Produce Ltd, 1999–2001; Chris Barnes Ltd (formerly Modernising Skills Ltd), 1999–; Assured Food Standards Ltd, 2000–03; Man. Dir, Currency Connect UK, 2004–05; Dir, Horticultural Business, Hartington Gp, 2003–05; non-exec. Dir, Booker Food Services, 1987–90. Chm., Governing Bd, CMi plc, 2005–12 (Mem., 2003–12). Mem. Management Cttee, CS Healthcare, 1992–99 (Vice-Chm., 1997–99); Chm., Bucks HA, 1999–2000 (non-exec. Dir, 1996–99). FRSA 1999; FCIHort (FIHort 2002). *Recreations:* competitive off-roading, country living, France.

BARNES, Sir David; *see* Barnes, Sir J. D. F.

BARNES, David John; Head Master, Pate's Grammar School, Cheltenham, 1986–2000; *b* 6 Nov. 1939; *s* of David Alan Barnes and Norah Barnes (*née* Fleming); *m* 1961, Jan Crofts; one *s* one *d. Educ:* The Grammar Sch., Wolstanton, Staffs; Queen's Coll., Oxford (Open Schol.; MA); DipEd London; Post Grad. Cert. in Architectural Hist., Oxford, 2003. Assistant Master: Pocklington Sch., York, 1962–66; Nottingham High Sch., 1966–68; Vice-Principal, Newcastle-under-Lyme Sch., 1968–86. *Publications:* A Parent's Guide to GCSE, 1988; various check-lists and guides to students' reading, 1991. *Recreations:* fly-fishing, Homer, digging holes and other honest labour. *Address:* 32 Gretton Road, Gotherington, Cheltenham, Glos GL52 9QU.

BARNES, (David) Michael (William); QC 1981; a Recorder, since 1985; *b* 16 July 1943; *s* of David Charles Barnes and Florence Maud Barnes; *m* 1970, Susan Dorothy Turner; three *s. Educ:* Monmouth Sch.; Wadham Coll., Oxford. Called to Bar, Middle Temple, 1965, Bencher, 1989. Hon. Research Fellow, Lady Margaret Hall, Oxford, 1979; Vis. Fellow, Univ. of Auckland, NZ, 1995. Chm., Hinckley Point 'C' Public Inquiry, 1988. *Publications:* Leasehold Reform Act 1967, 1967; Hill and Redman's Law of Landlord and Tenant, 15th edn 1970 to 18th edn 1988; Hill and Redman's Guide to Rent Review, 2001; The Law of Compensation and Compulsory Purchase, 2014. *Recreations:* walking, crime fiction. *Address:* Wilberforce Chambers, 8 New Square, WC2A 3QP. *Club:* Beefsteak.

BARNES, Edward Campbell; independent television producer/director and television consultant, 1986–2008; Head of Children's Programmes, BBC Television, 1978–86; *b* 8 Oct. 1928; *s* of Hubert Turnbull Barnes and Annie Mabel Barnes; *m* 1950, Dorothy Smith (*d* 1992); one *s* two *d. Educ:* Wigan Coll. British Forces Network, Vienna, 1946–49; stage management, provincial and West End theatre, 1949–55; BBC Television: studio management, 1955–62; Producer, Blue Peter, 1962–70; Dep. Head of Children's Progs, 1970–78, incl.: original Editor, John Craven's Newsround; Producer: Blue Peter Royal Safari with Princess Anne; 6 series of Blue Peter Special Assignments; Producer and Director: Treasure Houses, 1986; All Our Children, 1987–90; Boxpops, 1992; The Lowdown, 1992. Mem. Bd, Children's Film and Television Foundn Ltd, 1983–97; Dir, Christian Children's Fund, 1995–2002. Consultant, St Paul's Multi-media, 1995–96. Mem., RTS (Mem., Awards Cttee, 1989–91). Trustee, EveryChild, 2002–03. SFTA Award, 1969; RTS Silver Medal, 1986; Pye Television Award, 1986; Special Award as creator of Newsround to celebrate its 40th anniversary, BAFTA, 2012. *Publications:* 25 Blue Peter Books and 8 Blue Peter Mini Books, 1964–; 6 Blue Peter Special Assignment Books, 1973–75; Blue Peter Royal Safari, 1971; Petra: a dog for everyone, 1977; Blue Peter: the inside story, 1989; numerous articles for nat. press. *Recreations:* cricket, music, birding, walking, Venice, Bali.

See also S. J. C. Barnes.

BARNES, Rev. Mgr Edwin Ronald; Bishop Suffragan of Richborough, Episcopal Visitor for the Province of Canterbury, 1995–2001; Hon. Assistant Bishop, Diocese of Winchester, 2001–10; Pastor, Bournemouth Ordinariate Group, since 2012; Assistant Priest, New Forest Pastoral Area; *b* 6 Feb. 1935; *s* of Edwin and Dorothy Barnes; *m* 1963, Jane Elizabeth (*née* Green); one *s* one *d. Educ:* Plymouth College; Pembroke Coll., Oxford (MA). Rector of Farncombe, Surrey, 1967–78; Vicar of Hessle, dio. York, 1978–87; Principal, St Stephen's House, Oxford, 1987–95. Proctor in Convocation, Canterbury 1975–78, York 1985–87; Mem., General Synod of C of E, 1990–95 (Mem. Standing Cttee, 1992–95). Hon. Canon: Christ Church, Oxford, 1994–95; St Albans Cathedral, 1997–2001. Ordained RC priest, 2011. President: Guild of All Souls, 1997–2004; English Church Union, 2005–11. *Address:* 1 Queen Elizabeth Avenue, Lymington, Hants SO41 9HN.

BARNES, Eric Charles, CBE 1992; GBS 2005; High Court Judge, Hong Kong, 1981–91; *b* 12 Sept. 1924; *m* 1st, Estelle Fay Barnes (*née* Darnell); four *s* one *d*; 2nd, 1978, Judianna Wai Ling Barnes (*née* Chang); one *s* one *d. Educ:* Univ. of Queensland (LLB). Chief Adjudicator, Immigration Tribunal, Hong Kong, 1993–2004; Chm., Appeal Bd on Public Meetings and Demonstrations, Hong Kong, 1995–99. Mem., Australian Assoc., Hong Kong, 1994–. *Recreations:* tennis, racing (horse), sports. *Address:* House 52, Manderly Garden, 48 Deep Water Bay Road, Hong Kong. *Clubs:* United Services Recreation, Kowloon Cricket, Hong Kong Jockey (Hong Kong); Tattersall's (Brisbane).

BARNES, Harold, (Harry); *b* 22 July 1936; *s* of late Joseph and Betsy Barnes; *m* 1963, Elizabeth Ann Stephenson; one *s* one *d. Educ:* Ruskin Coll., Oxford (Dip. Econs and Political Science); Hull Univ. (BA Philosophy and Political Studies). National Service, 1954–56. Railway clerk, 1952–54 and 1956–60; adult student, 1960–65; further educn lectr, 1965–66; Lectr, Sheffield Univ., 1966–87. MP (Lab) Derbys NE, 1987–2005. Jt Pres., New Dialogue (Britain), 1992–2005 (Chm., 1990–92); Vice-Pres., Labour Friends of Iraq, 2007–12 (Jt Pres., 2004–06). Mem., National Admin. Council, Ind. Labour Publications, 1977–80 and 1982–85. Writer, http://threescoreyearsandten.blogspot.com. *Publications:* pamphlets on local govt and on the public face of Militant; articles and reviews in Labour Leader, London Labour Briefing, Tribune, Morning Star, Local Socialism, New Socialist, Derbyshire Miner, Leeds Weekly Citizen, Sheffield Forward, Industrial Tutor, Political Studies, Dronfield Miscellany, Post-16 Educator, North East History. *Club:* Dronfield Contact.

BARNES, Ian Colin, PhD; FRCPath; Specialist Advisor to Chief Scientific Officer, NHS England, since 2014; *b* Jersey, CI, 16 Aug. 1950; *s* of Colin Barnes and Margaret Barnes; *m* 1969, Sarah Fraser-Thomson; two *s. Educ:* Hautlieu GS, Jersey; Univ. of Bath (BSc Applied Biochem.); Univ. of London (MSc Clin. Biochem.); Univ. of Bristol (PhD 1978). FRCPath 1996; CSci 2006. Leeds General Infirmary: Consultant Clinical Biochemist, 1987–92; Hd of Clin. Biochem., 1992–96; Dir of Pathol., 1996–98; Hd of Pathol., Leeds Teaching Hosps, 1998–2007. Nat. Pathol. Advr, 2002–09, Nat. Clinical Dir for Pathol., 2009–13, DoH; Chair, Pathol. Quality Assurance Rev. Bd, NHS England (formerly NHS Commng Bd), 2013–14.

Chm., Assoc. of Clin. Biochemists, 1997–2000. *Recreations:* travel, golf, food and wine. *Address:* NHS England, 6th Floor, Skipton House, 80 London Road, SE1 6LH. *T:* (0113) 824 9220. *E:* i.barnes@nhs.net.

BARNES, Jack Henry; Director of Administration, British Society for Allergy and Clinical Immunology, 2002–05; *b* 11 Dec. 1943; *s* of James Barnes and Joan Ivy (*née* Sears); *m* 1966, Nicola Pearse; two *d*. *Educ:* Hatfield Sch., Herts; Univ. of Sussex (BA); LSE (MSc). Dep. Chief Inspector, Social Services Inspectorate, DHSS, 1983–88; Department of Health: Dep. Chief Scientist and Dir, Res. Management, 1988–91; Under Sec. 1991–99; Head: Primary Care Div., NHS Exec., 1991–95; Internat. and Industry Div., 1995–99; Dir of Res. and Policy, Nat. Asthma Campaign, 2000–03. Trustee, Mental Health Foundn, 1997–2003. Non-exec. Dir, E Sussex Downs and Weald PCT, 2006–12; Ind. Mem., Governing Body, Eastbourne, Hailsham and Seaford CCG, 2012–. Gov. and Audit Chair, Goldsmiths, Univ. of London, 2005–10.

BARNES, Sir (James) David (Francis), Kt 1996; CBE 1987; Deputy Chairman, AstraZeneca PLC, 1999–2001; *b* 4 March 1936; *s* of Eric Cecil Barnes, CMG, and of Jean Margaret Barnes; *m* 1963, Wendy Fiona Mary (*née* Riddell); one *s* one *d*. *Educ:* Shrewsbury Sch.; Liverpool Univ. National Service, commnd 'N' Battery (Eagle Troop), 2nd Regt RA, 1958–60 (Malaya). ICI Pharmaceuticals Division: Overseas Dir 1971–77, Dep. Chm. 1977–83; Chm., ICI Paints Div., 1983–86; Exec. Dir, ICI, 1986–93; CEO, Zeneca Group PLC, 1993–99. Non-executive Director: Thorn EMI, 1987–94; Redland, 1994–98; Prudential, 1999–2003; non-exec. Chm., Imperial Cancer Res. Technol., 1999–2002; Dep. Chm., Syngenta AG, 2000–04. Chairman: Pharmaceuticals EDC, NEDO, 1983–92; Biotechnology Industries Working Party, NEDO, 1989–91. Vice-Pres., Thames Valley Hospice, 1986–. Mem. Council, VSO, 1996–99; a Dep. Chm., BITC, 1996–2000 (Chm., Economic Regeneration Leadership Team, 1996–2000). Mem. Bd of Governors, Ashridge (Bonar Law Meml) Trust, 1993–2006; Gov. and Bd Mem., Intellectual Property Inst., 1994–2000; Member: Governing Body, Shrewsbury Sch., 1997–2006; Bd of Trustees, BRCS, 1998–2004. FInstD; CCMI; FRSA 1988; Hon. Associate, 1995, Hon. Mem., 2006, BVA (Wooldridge Meml Medal, 1995). Hon. LLD Liverpool, 1996; Hon. DSc UMIST, 1998. Centenary Medal, SCI, 2000. *Recreations:* fishing, shooting, walking.

BARNES, James Frederick, CB 1982; Deputy Chief Scientific Adviser, and Head of Profession for the Science Group, Ministry of Defence, 1987–89; *b* 8 March 1932; *s* of Wilfred and Doris M. Barnes; *m* 1957, Dorothy Jean Drew; one *s* two *d*. *Educ:* Taunton's Sch., Southampton; Queen's Coll., Oxford. BA 1953, MA 1957. CEng, FRAeS. Bristol Aeroplane Co. (Engine Div.), 1953; Min. of Supply, Nat. Gas Turbine Estabt: Sci. Officer 1955; Sen. Sci. Off. 1957; Principal Sci. Off. 1962; Sen. Principal Sci. Off. (Individual Merit) 1965; Min. of Aviation Supply, Asst Dir, Engine R&D, 1970; seconded to HM Diplomatic Service, Counsellor (Science and Technology), British Embassy, Washington, 1972; Under-Sec., MoD, 1974; Dir Gen. Res. (C), MoD (Procurement Exec.), 1974–77; Dep. Dir (Weapons), RAE, 1978–79; Dep. Chief Scientific Adviser (Projs), MoD, 1979–82; Dep. Controller, Establishments Resources and Personnel, MoD, 1982–84; Dep. Controller, Estabts and Res., MoD, 1984–86. Chm., MoD Individual Merit Promotion Panel, 1990–98. Stewardship Advr, dio. of Monmouth, 1989–96; Dir, Monmouth Diocesan Bd of Finance, 1999–2000; Mem., Monmouth Dio. Trng for Ministry Cttee, 1989–2004; Sec., Monmouth DAC for Care of Churches, 1994–96; Chm., CCBI Stewardship Network, 1993–96; Member: Council on Christian Approaches to Defence and Disarmament, 1980–2006; Member, Church in Wales Working Gps on Ecclesiastical Exemption, Charities Act 1993 and status of PCCs, 1995–96. Lay Member: Guildford Diocesan Synod, 1978–84; Winchester Diocesan Synod, 1985–89; Chm., Deanery Finance Cttee, Alton, Hants, 1987–89; Bishop's Nominee, Monmouth Diocesan Conf., 1990–2004; Member: Hereford Diocesan Bd of Finance, 2007–; Hereford Diocesan Mission and Pastoral Cttee (formerly Hereford Diocesan Pastoral Cttee), 2007–13; Churchwarden, All Saints', Farringdon, 1985–89; Sub-Warden, Trellech PCC, 1997–2003. Chm., Tymawr Convent Appeals Gp, 1997–2003. Member: Monmouth & Llandaff Housing Assoc., 1991–93; Gwerin (Cymru) Housing Assoc., 1993–94; Trustee: Roger Williams & Queen Victoria Almshouses, Newport, 1990–99; Babington Educnl Trust, 1997–2003; Founder Trustee, Friends of Trellech Church & Churchyard, 2002–04. Chm. of Govs, Yateley Manor Prep. Sch., 1981–89. Secretary: Ledbury Ch Stewardship Cttee, 2005–08; Ledbury Deanery, 2007–13; Treas., Ledbury Probus Club, 2006–09. James Clayton Fund Prize, IMechE, 1964. *Publications:* (contrib.) Trellech Millennium book; contrib. books and learned jls on mech. engrg, esp. gas turbine technology, heat transfer and stress analysis. *Recreation:* making things. *Address:* 15 Kempley Brook Drive, Ledbury, Herefordshire HR8 2FJ.

BARNES, Janet, CBE 2014; Chief Executive, York Museums Trust, since 2002; *b* 23 April 1952; *d* of Frederick George Hagan and Margaret Hagan (*née* Wilson); *m* 1970, Philip Barnes. *Educ:* Sheffield Univ. (BA Hons English Lit.); Manchester Univ. (Postgrad. Dip. Mus and Art Gall. Studies). Keeper, Ruskin Gall. and Ruskin Craft Gall., 1985–94; Sen. Curator, Sheffield Galls and Museums, 1995–99; Dir, Crafts Council, 1999–2002. Chm., Yorks, Arts Council England, 2006–13; Mem., Adv. Panel, NHMF, 2014–. Trustee, Anthony Shaw Collection Trust, 2012–. Mem., ICOM UK, 2012. Hon. Curator, Turner Mus. of Glass, Univ. of Sheffield, 1979–99. Dir, Guild of St George, 1994–. Hon. LLD Sheffield, 2000; DUniv Sheffield Hallam, 2001; DUniv York, 2013. *Publications:* Percy Horton: 1897–1970 Artist and Absolutist, 1982; Ruskin and Sheffield, 1985, 3rd edn 2011; Catalogue of the Turner Museum of Glass, 1993. *Recreations:* husband, painting, swimming. *Address:* c/o York Museums Trust, St Mary's Lodge, Museum Gardens, York YO30 7DR.

BARNES, Dr Jennifer Chase, (Mrs R. P. Edgar-Wilson); Pro-Vice-Chancellor, International Strategy, University of Cambridge, since 2010; *b* Massachusetts, 30 July 1960; *d* of Prof. James John Barnes and Patience Plummer Barnes; *m* 1988, Richard Philip Edgar-Wilson; one *s* one *d*. *Educ:* Crawfordsville High Sch., Indiana; Smith Coll., Mass (BA Lit.); Britten Internat. Opera Sch., Royal Coll. of Music (MMus); Univ. of London (PhD 1997); MA Cantab 2008. Founder Mem., Mecklenburgh Opera, 1984–89; Associate Prof., RAM, 1989–91; Dir, Professional Integration Project, RCM, 1995–99; Dean and Asst Principal, Trinity Coll. of Music, 1999–2005; Dir, Global Educn, BP, 2005–08; Pres., New Hall, later Murray Edwards Coll., Cambridge, 2008–12; Lady Margaret Preacher, Univ. of Cambridge, 2013–14. Mem., Exec. Cttee, Centre for Sci. and Policy, Cambridge, 2010–. Trustee, Charles and Julia Henry Fund, 2009–. Mem., Soc. of Authors, 1989–. Hon. Fellow, Trinity Laban Conservatoire of Music and Dance, 2009. FRSA. *Publications:* Television Opera: the fall of opera commissioned for television, 2005; contributor: A Night in at the Opera, 1994; Girls, Girls, Girls, 1996; The New Grove Dictionary of Music and Musicians, 2nd edn 2001; Opera Quarterly. *Recreations:* being with family, coffee shops, walking the dog, reading. *Address:* University of Cambridge, The Old Schools, Trinity Lane, Cambridge CB2 1TN. *T:* (01223) 339664, *Fax:* (01223) 765693. *E:* jennifer.barnes@admin.cam.ac.uk. *Club:* Oxford and Cambridge.

BARNES, John; a Senior Immigration Judge, Asylum and Immigration Tribunal (formerly a Vice-President, Immigration Appeal Tribunal), 2000–06; *b* 13 March 1938; *s* of Frederick Walter John Barnes, MBE, LLB and Phyllis Edna Barnes (*née* Brooks); *m* 1992, Frances (*née* Broadrick); three *s* by a previous marriage. *Educ:* Brentwood Sch., Essex; Univ. of London (LLB Hons ext.). Admitted solicitor, 1961; engaged in private practice, 1961–97. Part-time Chm., Industrial Tribunals, 1993–99; Immigration Adjudicator, part-time, 1995–97, full-time, 1997–2000. International Association of Refugee Law Judges: Mem., 2004–; Mem., Eur. Chapter, 2008–; Rep. to European Asylum Support Office, 2011–. *Publications:* A Manual for Refugee Law Judges, 2007; (with A. R. Mackey) Judicial Criteria and Standarc in Assessment of Credibility, 2013; contrib. to Internat. Jl of Refugee Law. *Recreations* learning to enjoy retirement, theatre, history, art. *Address:* Orchard Place, Triq ta' Sansuna Xaghra XRA 1652, Gozo, Malta. *T:* 21561647. *Club:* Athenæum.

BARNES, John Alfred, CBE 1993; Director-General, City and Guilds of London Institute 1985–93; *b* 29 April 1930; *s* of John Joseph and Margaret Carr Barnes; *m* 1954, Ivy May (*né* Walker); two *d*. *Educ:* Bede Boys Grammar Sch., Sunderland; Durham Univ. (MA, BSc MEd). Teacher, Grangefield Grammar Sch., Stockton-on-Tees, 1953–57; Asst Educn Officer Barnsley, 1957–61; Dep. Dir, then Dir of Educn, City of Wakefield, 1963–68; Chief Educn Officer, City of Salford, 1968–84. Mem. Council, Assoc. of Colls of Further and Highe Educn, 1976–82 (Chm. 1980–81); Chairman: Northern Examining Assoc., 1979–82 Associated Lancs Schs Examg Bd, 1972–84; Member: Associated Examg Bd, Nat. Exams B for Supervisory Studies, 1985–93; Further Educn Unit Management Bd, 1986–89; YT Certification Bd, 1986–89; various ind. trng bds, 1969–78, and MSC cttees, 1978–84; Review of Vocational Qualifications Working Gp, 1985–86; Task Gp on Assessment and Testing 1987–88; Exec. Mem., Standing Conf. on Sch. Sci. and Technol., 1985–89 (Chm., Exec Cttee, 1988–89). Mem., Nat. Exec. Cttee, Soc. of Educn Officers, 1979–84; Sec., Assoc. o Educn Officers, 1977–84; Treas., NFER, 1979–84; Pres., Educnl Develt Assoc., 1980–85 Chm., Sir Isaac Pitman Ltd, 1990–93; Sec., UK Skills, 1990–93. Mem. Council, Cit Technology Colls Trust, 1990–93; Gov., Imperial Coll., 1987–93; Mem. Court, Readin Univ., 1994–97. Mem. (C), Bucks CC, 1993–97 (Chm., Personnel Cttee, 1994–97; Vice Chm., 1994–96, Chm., 1996–97, Educn Cttee). Mem., Thames Valley (formerly Bucks an Oxon) Valuation Tribunals Gp, 1997–2001. Chm., Bournemouth and Poole NT (formerl Bournemouth NT), 2004–09. Trustee, City Parochial Foundn and Trust for London 1993–2005 (Chm., Grants Cttee, 2004–05). Mem., Probus. FRSA 1973; FITD 1986 (Hon FITD 1993); FCollP 1991; Hon. FCGI 1993; Hon. CIPD 1994. *Publications:* occasiona papers in educnl press. *Recreations:* cultural activities, foreign travel. *Address:* 1 Seapoint, Martello Park, Canford Cliffs, Poole, Dorset BH13 7BA. *T:* (01202) 701768. *Club* Athenæum.

BARNES, John Nigel; Conservation & Learning Director, Historic Royal Palaces, sinc 2001; *b* 24 June 1961; *s* of Geoffrey Philip Barnes and Shirley Anne (*née* Eaton); partner Lauren Kathleen Agnew; two *d*. *Educ:* Judd Sch., Tonbridge; S Bank Poly. (BA Hons Postgrad. DipArch). Registered Architect; ARB (ARC 1989); RIBA 1989–2006. In privat practice in architecture, 1984–94; English Heritage: Hd, Architecture and Survey, 1994–95 Director: Professional Services, 1995–98; Major Projects, 1998–2001. *Recreations:* karate, lif drawing. *Address:* Historic Royal Palaces, Hampton Court Palace, Surrey KT8 9AU. *T:* (020 3166 6363, *Fax:* (020) 3166 6365. *E:* john.barnes@hrp.org.uk.

BARNES, Prof. Jonathan, FBA 1987; Professor of Ancient Philosophy, University of Paris Sorbonne, 2002–06; *b* 26 Dec. 1942; *s* of late A. L. Barnes and K. M. Barnes; *m* 1965, Jennife Postgate; two *d*. *Educ:* City of London Sch.; Balliol Coll., Oxford. Oxford University: Fellow Oriel Coll., 1968–78; Fellow, 1978–94, Emeritus Fellow, 1994–, Balliol Coll.; Prof. o Ancient Philosophy, 1989–94; Prof. of Ancient Philosophy, Univ. of Geneva, 1994–2002 Visiting posts at: Inst. for Advanced Study, Princeton, 1972; Univ. of Texas, 1981 Wissenschaftskolleg zu Berlin, 1985; Univ. of Alberta, 1986; Univ. of Zurich, 1987; Istitut Italiano per gli studi filosofici, Naples, 1988, 1998; Ecole Normale Supérieure, Paris, 199 (Condorcet Medal, 1996); Scuola Normale Superiore di Pisa, 2002. John Locke Lectr, Univ of Oxford, 2004. Fellow, Amer. Acad. Arts and Scis, 1999. Hon. Fellow, Oriel Coll., Oxford 2007. Hon. Dr: Geneva, 2010; Humboldt, Berlin, 2012. Hon. Citizen of Velia, 2010 *Publications:* The Ontological Argument, 1972; Aristotle's Posterior Analytics, 1975; Th Presocratic Philosophers, 1979; Aristotle, 1982; Early Greek Philosophy, 1987; The Toils o Scepticism, 1991; The Cambridge Companion to Aristotle, 1995; Logic and the Imperia Stoa, 1997; Porphyry: introduction, 2003; Truth, etc, 2007; Coffee with Aristotle, 2008 Method and Metaphysics, 2011; Zenone e l'infinito, 2011; Logical Matters, 2012; Proof Knowledge and Scepticism, 2014; Mantissa, 2015. *Address:* Les Charmilles, 36200 Ceaulmont France.

See also J. P. Barnes.

BARNES, Joseph Harry George; Chairman, Baxters of Speyside, 1994–98; Director 1969–93, Joint Managing Director, 1988–90, J. Sainsbury plc; *b* 24 July 1930; *s* of Willian Henry Joseph Barnes and Dorothy Eleanor Barnes; *m* 1958, Rosemary Gander; two *s*. *Educ* John Ruskin Grammar Sch., Croydon. FCA 1963. Articled clerk, Lever Honeyman & Co. 1946–52. National Service, 2nd Lieut RAPC, 1953–55. Joined J. Sainsbury plc, 1956 *Recreations:* tennis, fishing. *Address:* Tudor Court, 29 Grimwade Avenue, Croydon, Surrey CR0 5DJ. *T:* (020) 8654 5696.

BARNES, Julian Patrick; writer; *b* 19 Jan. 1946; *m* 1979, Pat Kavanagh (*d* 2008). *Educ:* City of London Sch.; Magdalen Coll., Oxford. Lexicographer, OED Supplement, 1969–72 freelance journalist; Contributing Ed., New Review, 1977; Asst Literary Ed., 1977–79, TV Critic, 1977–81, New Statesman; Dep. Literary Ed., Sunday Times, 1980–82; TV Critic Observer, 1982–86; London correspondent, The New Yorker, 1990–95. E. M. Forste Award, US Acad. of Arts and Letters, 1986; Shakespeare Prize, Germany, 1993; Austrian State Prize for European Literature, 2004; David Cohen Prize for Literature, 2011. Commandeu de l'Ordre des Arts et des Lettres (France), 2004. *Publications:* Metroland, 1980 (Somerse Maugham Award, 1981); Before She Met Me, 1982; Flaubert's Parrot, 1984 (Geoffrey Fabe Meml Prize, 1985; Prix Médicis, 1986; Grinzane Cavour Prize (Italy), 1988); Staring at the Sun, 1986; A History of the World in 10½ Chapters, 1989; Talking it Over, 1991 (Prix Femina, 1992); The Porcupine, 1992; Letters from London (essays), 1995; Cross Channe (short stories), 1996; England, England, 1998; Love, etc, 2000; Something to Declare (essays) 2002; trans. Daudet, In the Land of Pain, 2002; The Pedant in the Kitchen, 2003; The Lemor Table (short stories), 2004; Arthur & George, 2005; Nothing to be Frightened Of (non-fiction), 2008; Pulse (short stories), 2011; The Sense of an Ending, 2011 (Man Booker Prize 2011); Through the Window: seventeen essays (and one short story), 2012; Levels of Life 2013; Keeping an Eye Open: essays on art, 2015; (as Dan Kavanagh): Duffy, 1980; Fiddle City, 1981; Putting the Boot In, 1985; Going to the Dogs, 1987. *Address:* c/o United Agents 12–26 Lexington Street, W1F 0LE.

See also Jonathan Barnes.

BARNES, Kristina Aileen; *see* Montgomery, K. A.

BARNES, Martin; *see* Barnes, N. M. L.

BARNES, Martin; Senior Curator, Photographs, Victoria and Albert Museum, since 2007; *b* Southport, 31 July 1971; *s* of Brian Robinson Barnes and Josephine Barnes; two *d* by Imke Valentien. *Educ:* Univ. of Leicester (BA Combined Arts (Hist. of Art, Eng. Lit., Psychol.) 1994; Courtauld Inst. of Art, Univ. of London (MA Art Mus. Studies 1995). Cataloguer (pt-time), Walker Art Gall., Liverpool, 1994–95; Victoria and Albert Museum: Asst Curator, 1995–2001; Curator, Photographs, 2001–07. J. Dudley Johnston Medal, RPS, 2013. *Publications:* Benjamin Brecknell Turner: rural England through a Victorian lens, 2001 Illumine: photographs by Garry Fabian Miller, 2005; Shadow Catchers: camera-less photography, 2010, 2nd edn 2012; Horst: patterns from nature, 2014. *Recreations:* guitar music, writing, gardens. *Address:* Victoria and Albert Museum, Cromwell Road, South Kensington, SW7 2RL. *T:* (020) 7942 2534. *E:* m.barnes@vam.ac.uk.

BARNES, Melvyn Peter Keith, OBE 1990; MCLIP; Guildhall Librarian and Director of Libraries and Art Galleries, Corporation of London, 1984–2002; *b* 26 Sept. 1942; *s* of Harry and Doris Barnes; *m* 1965, Judith Anne Leicester; two *s*. *Educ:* Chatham House Sch., Ramsgate; North-Western Polytechnic, London. MCLIP (ALA 1965); DMA 1972; FCMI (FBIM 1980). Public library posts in Kent, Herts and Manchester, 1958–68; Dep. Bor. Librarian, Newcastle-under-Lyme, 1968–72; Chief Librarian, Ipswich, 1972–74; Bor. Librarian and Arts Officer, Kensington and Chelsea, 1974–80; City Librarian, Westminster, 1980–84. Hon. Librarian to Clockmakers' Co., and Gardeners' Co., 1984–2002. Member: LA Council, 1974–98 (Chm. Exec. Cttee, 1987–92; Vice-Pres., 1991–93; Pres., 1995); Liby and Inf. Services Council, 1984–89; Brit. Liby Adv. Council, 1986–91; Brit. Liby SRIS Adv. Cttee, 1986–91. Pres., Internat. Assoc. of Metropolitan City Libraries, 1989–92; Dep. Chm., Liby Services Trust and Liby Services Ltd, 1983–93. Hon. Treas., Victoria County History of Inner Middlesex, 1979–90. Gov., St Bride Inst., 1984–2002. Liveryman, Clockmakers' Co., 1990–2002; Hon. Freeman, Gardeners' Co., 1995. Editorial Cons., Journal of Librarianship, 1980–94; Editorial Advr, Librarianship & Information Work Worldwide, 1991–99. *Publications:* Youth Library Work, 1968, 2nd edn 1976; Best Detective Fiction, 1975; Murder in Print, 1986; Dick Francis, 1986; Root and Branch: a history of the Worshipful Company of Gardeners of London, 1994; Francis Durbridge: an appreciation, 2015; (ed) Deerstalker series of classic crime fiction reprints, 1977–82; contributor to numerous books and jls in fields of librarianship and crime fiction criticism. *Recreations:* reading and writing, going to the theatre, studying the history of the movies and stage musicals, performing amateur operatics.

BARNES, Michael; *see* Barnes, D. M. W.

BARNES, Michael Cecil John, CBE 1998; Legal Services Ombudsman for England and Wales, 1991–97; *b* 22 Sept. 1932; *s* of late Major C. H. R. Barnes, OBE and of Katherine Louise (*née* Kennedy); *m* 1962, Anne Mason; one *s* one *d*. *Educ:* Malvern; Corpus Christi Coll., Oxford. Nat. Service, 2nd Lieut, Wilts Regt, served in Hong Kong, 1952–53. MP (Lab) Brentford and Chiswick, 1966–Feb. 1974; an Opposition Spokesman on food and food prices, 1970–71; Chairman: Parly Labour Party Social Security Group, 1969–70; ASTMS Parly Cttee, 1970–71; Jt Hon. Sec., Labour Cttee for Europe, 1969–71; Mem., Public Accounts Cttee, 1967–74. Contested (Lab): Wycombe, 1964; Brentford and Isleworth, Feb. 1974; Mem. Labour Party, 1957–79; helped form SDP, 1981; rejoined Labour Party, 1983–2001. Chm., Electricity Consumers' Council, 1977–83; Dir, UKIAS, 1984–90. Member: Council of Management, War on Want, 1972–77; Nat. Consumer Council, 1975–80; Arts Council Trng Cttee, 1977–83; Energy Commn, 1977–79; Internat. Cttee of Nat. Council for Voluntary Organisations, 1977–83; Advertising Standards Authority, 1979–85; Direct Mail Services Standards Bd, 1983–86; Data Protection Tribunal, 1985–90; Investigation Cttee, Solicitors' Complaints Bureau, 1987–90; Legal Services Commn (formerly Legal Aid Bd), 1998–2001; Financial Ombudsman Service Bd (formerly Financial Services Ombudsman Bd), 1999–2002, Ind. Assessor, 2002–10. Chm., British and Irish Ombudsman Assoc., 1995–98. Chairman: UK Adv. Cttee on EEC Action Against Poverty Programme, 1975–76; Notting Hill Social Council, 1976–79; West London Fair Housing Gp Ltd, 1980–87; Vice Chm., 1980–90, Chm., 2005–, Bangabandhu Soc.; Organising Secretary: Gulbenkian Foundn Drama Trng Inquiry, 1974–75; Music Trng Inquiry, 1976–77; Sec., Nat. Council for Drama Trng, 1976–84; Chm., Hounslow Arts Trust, 1974–82; Trustee, Project Hand Trust, 1974–77; Governor, Internat. Musicians Seminar, Prussia Cove, 1978–81. Friend of Bangladesh Liberation War Honour, 2012. *Recreations:* walking, reading. *Address:* 45 Ladbroke Grove, W11 3AR. *T:* (020) 7727 2533.

BARNES, Prof. Michael Patrick; Professor of Scandinavian Studies, University College London, 1995–2005, now Professor Emeritus (Professor of Scandinavian Philology, 1983–94); *b* 28 June 1940; *s* of William Edward Clement Barnes and Gladys Constance Barnes (*née* Hooper); *m* 1970, Kirsten Heiberg (*née* Røer); one *s* three *d*. *Educ:* University College London (BA, MA); Univ. of Oslo. Asst Lectr, Lectr and Reader in Scandinavian Philology, UCL, 1964–83. Visiting Professor: Tórshavn, Faroe Islands, 1979 and 1990; Uppsala Univ., 1984; Hon. Prof., Centre for Study of the Viking Age, Univ. of Nottingham, 2012–; Hon. Res. Fellow, Univ. of Highlands and Islands, 2012–. Member: Gustav Adolfs Akademien, Uppsala, 1984 (Corresp. Mem., 1977); Det norske Videnskaps-Akademi, Oslo, 1997. Jt Ed., North-Western European Language Evolution, 1989– (Mem. Adv. Bd, 1981–88); Member, Editorial Board: Fróðskaparrit, 1995–; Maal og Minne, 1996–2009; Norsk lingvistisk tidsskrift, 1997–; Nordic Jl of Linguistics, 2000–; Beiträge zur nordischen Philologie, 2000–; Jt Hon. Sec., Viking Soc. for Northern Research, 1983–2006 (Mem. Editl Bd, 1970–76, Chief Editor, 1977–83, Saga Book of the Viking Soc.). Mem., Soc. of Antiquaries of Scotland, 2009. Hon. DPhil Uppsala, 2002. Knight: Order of the Falcon (Iceland), 1992; 1st Cl., Royal Norwegian Order of Merit, 2008; *Publications:* Draumkvæde: an edition and study, 1974; The Runic Inscriptions of Maeshowe, Orkney, 1994; (jtly) The Runic Inscriptions of Viking Age Dublin, 1997; The Norn Language of Orkney and Shetland, 1998; A New Introduction to Old Norse, vol. I: Grammar, 1999; Faroese Language Studies, 2001; (jtly) Introduction to Scandinavian Phonetics, 2005; (jtly) The Scandinavian Runic Inscriptions of Britain, 2006; Runes: a handbook, 2012; articles in learned jls. *Recreations:* badminton, being with family, walking disused railways. *Address:* 93 Longland Drive, N20 8HN. *T:* (020) 8445 4697.

BARNES, Dr (Nicholas) Martin (Limer), CBE 2009; FREng, FICE, FCInstCES; FAPM; project management consultant, since 1971; *b* Sutton Coldfield, 18 Jan. 1939; *s* of Geoffrey and Emily Barnes; *m* 1963, Diana Marion Campbell; one *s* one *d*. *Educ:* King Edward's Sch., Birmingham; Imperial Coll., London (BSc (Eng.) Hons 1960); Univ. of Manchester (PhD 1971). FCInstCES 1974; FICE 1977; FAPM 1984; FREng 1987. Partner: Martin Barnes & Partners, 1971–85; Deloitte, Haskins & Sells, subseq. Coopers & Lybrand Deloitte, then Coopers & Lybrand, 1985–96; Exec. Dir, Major Projects Assoc., 1997–2006. President: Chartered Instn of Civil Engrg Surveyors, 1978–86; Assoc. for Project Mgt, 2003–12. Churchill Fellow, 1973. *Publications:* Measurement in Contract Control, 1977; The CESMM3 Handbook, 1992. *Recreations:* choral singing, railway and canal history. *Address:* Cornbrash House, Kirtlington, Oxon OX5 3HF. *T:* (01869) 350828, *Fax:* (01869) 351314. *E:* cornbrash@aol.com.

BARNES, Prof. Peter John, DM, DSc; FRCP, FMedSci; FRS 2007; Professor of Thoracic Medicine, Imperial College, London (National Heart and Lung Institute) and Hon. Consultant Physician, Royal Brompton Hospital, since 1987; Head of Respiratory Medicine, Imperial College, London, since 1997; *b* 29 Oct. 1946; *s* of late John Barnes and Eileen Gertrude Barnes (*née* Thurman); *m* 1976, Olivia Harvard-Watts; three *s*. *Educ:* Leamington Coll.; St Catharine's Coll., Cambridge (open schol., BA (1st class); MA; Hon. Fellow 2012); Worcester Coll., Oxford (DM, DSc). FRCP 1985. Jun. med. posts, then Registrar, Oxford and UCH, London; MRC fellowships, Univ. of Calif, San Francisco, and RPMS, London; Hammersmith Hospital, London: Sen. Registrar, 1979–82; Sen. Lectr and Consultant Physician, RPMS, 1982–85; Prof. of Clinical Pharmacol., Cardiothoracic Inst., London, 1985–87. NIHR Sen. Investigator, 2008–. Vis. Prof., RSocMed, 1993. Lectures: Linacre, RCP, 1994; Amberson, Amer. Thoracic Soc., 1996; Sadoul, Eur. Respiratory Soc., 1999; Croonian, RCP, 2009. Pres., Eur. Respiratory Soc., 2013–14. Master Fellow, Amer. Coll. Chest Physicians, 2012. MAE 2012. Founder FMedSci 1998. Mem., Assoc. of Amer. Physicians, 2014. Hon. MD: Ferrara, Italy, 1997; Athens, 2001; Leuven, 2010; Maastricht, 2014. Dutch Med. Fedn Prize, 1995; Ariens Prize, Dutch Pharmacol. Soc., 2005; Quintiles Prize, British Pharmacol. Soc., 2005; Presidential Award, Eur. Respiratory Soc., 2007; Medal, British Thoracic Soc., 2007; Galen Medal, Soc. of Apothecaries, 2015. *Publications:* New Drugs for Asthma, 1982, 3rd edn 1998; Asthma: basic mechanisms and clinical management, 1989, 3rd edn 1998; (ed jtly) The Lung: scientific foundations, 1991, 3rd edn 1998; Recent Advances in Respiratory Medicine, 1993; (jtly) Conquering Asthma, 1994; (jtly) Molecular Biology of Lung Disease, 1994; Asthma (2 vols), 1997; (ed jtly) Autonomic Control of the Respiratory System, 1997; (jtly) Asthma Therapy, 1998; Managing Chronic Obstructive Pulmonary Disease, 1999; (jtly) Asthma and Chronic Obstructive Pulmonary Disease, 2002, 2nd edn 2009; over 1,000 pubns on lung pharmacol. and airway disease. *Recreations:* travel, ethnic art collecting, gardening, film and theatre going. *Address:* Airway Disease Section, National Heart and Lung Institute (Imperial College), Dovehouse Street, SW3 6LY. *T:* (020) 7351 8174.

BARNES, Richard Michael; Member (C) Ealing and Hillingdon, 2000–12, and Deputy Mayor of London, 2008–12, London Assembly, Greater London Authority; *b* 1 Dec. 1947; *s* of late John William Barnes and of Kate (Kitty) Barnes (*née* Harper). *Educ:* UWIST, Cardiff (BSc Hons Econs). Mem. (C) Hillingdon BC, 1982– (Leader, Cons. Gp, 1992–2000; Leader, 1998–2000). Mem., Metropolitan Police Authority, 2000–12. London Assembly, Greater London Authority: Chm., Safer London Cttee, 2004–08; Chm., 7 July Rev. Cttee, 2005–12. Contested (C) Ealing and Hillingdon, London Assembly, GLA, 2012. Advr, Book Trust. *Recreations:* gardening, chelonia, opera, bibliophile. *Address:* 280 Northwood Road, Harefield, Middx UB9 6PU. *T:* (020) 7983 4387. *Club:* Hayes and Harlington Conservative.

BARNES, Prof. Robert Harrison, DPhil; Professor of Social Anthropology, University of Oxford, 1996–2012; Fellow, St Antony's College, Oxford, 1987–2012, now Emeritus; *b* Jacksonville, Texas, 11 Oct. 1944; *s* of Robert Harrison Barnes and Edna Ruth Barnes (*née* Farrier); *m* 1968, Ruth Weinlich; one *s* one *d*. *Educ:* Bellaire High Sch., Texas; Reed Coll. (BA 1966, Phi Beta Kappa); St Catherine's Coll., Oxford (BLitt 1969; DPhil 1972). Lecturer in Social Anthropology: Univ. of Edinburgh, 1974–77; Univ. of Oxford, 1978–96; St Antony's College, Oxford: Dean, 1989–92; Dean of Degrees, 2001–02; Sub-Warden, 2005–06. Dir d'Etudes Associé, Ecole des Hautes Etudes en Scis Sociales, Paris, 1980; Vis. Fellow, Dept of Anthropol., Res. Sch. of Pacific Studies, ANU, 1986; Vis. Prof., Dept of Anthropol., Univ. of Michigan, 1986–87; Affiliated Fellow, Internat. Inst. for Asian Studies, Leiden, 2006 and 2007; Vis. Sen. Res. Fellow, Asia Res. Inst., NUS, 2008. FRAI 1969. *Publications:* Kédang: a study of the collective thought of an eastern Indonesian people, 1974; (trans. and ed with Ruth Barnes) Josef Kohler: On the Prehistory of Marriage, Totemism, Group Marriage, Mother Right, 1975; Two Crows Denies It: a history of controversy in Omaha sociology, 1984, 2nd edn 2005; (ed jtly) Contexts and Levels: anthropological essays on hierarchy, 1985; (ed jtly) Indigenous Peoples of Asia, 1995; Sea Hunters of Indonesia: fishers and weavers of Lamalera, 1996; (with U. B. Samely) A Dictionary of the Kedang Language: Kedang-Indonesian-English, 2013; Excursions into Eastern Indonesia: essays on history and social life, 2013; contrib. articles to scholarly jls. *Recreations:* bicycle riding, walking, gardening, mushroom hunting. *Address:* 156 East Rock Road, New Haven, CT 06511, USA. *T:* (203) 7529617; 105 6th Street, SE, Apt 103, Washington, DC 20003, USA. *T:* (202) 5432587.

BARNES, Dr Robert Sandford; Chairman, Robert S. Barnes Consultants Ltd, since 1978; Principal, Queen Elizabeth College, Kensington, London University, 1978–85; *b* 8 July 1924; *s* of William Edward and Ada Elsie Barnes (*née* Sutherst); *m* 1952, Julia Frances Marriott Grant; one *s* three *d*. *Educ:* Univ. of Manchester (BSc Hons 1948, MSc 1959, DSc 1962). FInstP 1961; FIMMM (FIM 1965); CEng 1977; CPhys 1985. Radar Research, Admiralty Signals Estab., Witley, Surrey, 1944–47; AERE, Harwell: Metallurgical Research on nuclear materials, 1948–62; Head of Irradiation Branch, 1962–65; Vis. Scientist, The Science Center, N Amer. Aviation Co., Calif, 1965; Head of Metallurgy Div., AERE, Harwell, 1966–68; Dep. Dir, BISRA, 1968–69; Dir, BISRA, 1969–70; Dir R&D, British Steel Corp., 1970–75; Chief Scientist, BSC, 1975–78. Technical Adviser: Bd of BOC Ltd, 1978–79; Bd of BOC International Ltd, 1979–81; Bd of New Ventures Secretariat, 1978–80. Chm., Ruthner Continuous Crop Systems Ltd, 1976–78. Member: CBI Res. and Technol. Cttee, 1968–75; Adv. Council on R&D for Iron and Steel, 1970–75; Materials Science and Technol. Cttee, SRC, 1975–79; European Industrial Res. Management Assoc., 1970 (Vice-Pres., 1974–78); Parly and Scientific Cttee, 1970–80, 1983–85; Foundn for Science and Technology, 1984– (Mem., Membership Cttee, 1987–98); Chm., Materials Technology Panel, Internat. Tin Res. Inst., 1988–94. Member: Council, Welding Inst., 1970–75; Council, Instn of Metallurgists, 1970–75 and 1979–85 (Vice Pres., 1979; Sen. Vice Pres., 1982; Pres., 1983–85); Council, Metals Soc., 1974–80, 1982–85 (Chm., Coordinating Cttee, 1976–78; Mem., Executive Cttee, 1976–80). Institute of Metals: Mem., Steering Gp, 1983–84; Mem. Council, 1985–92; Mem. Exec. Cttee, 1985–92; Past Pres., 1985–; Chm., Professional Bd, 1985–92; Institute of Materials Members Trust: Trustee, 1984–2003; Mem., 1986–2002; Chm., 1992–99. Chairman: Combined Operations Working Party, 1980–81; European Nuclear Steel-making Club, 1973–76; UK Mem., Conseil d'Association Européenne pour la Promotion de la Recherche Technique en Sidérurgie, 1972–78; Member: Adv. Council on Energy Conservation, Industry Group, 1977–78; Council, Nat. Backpain Assoc., 1979–98. Hon. Mem. Council, Iron and Steel Inst., 1969–73. Governor, Sheffield Polytechnic, 1968–72; Member: Court of Univ. of Surrey, 1968–80; Collegiate Council, Univ. of London, 1978–85; Jt Finance and Gen. Purposes Cttee, Univ. of London, 1978–85; Senate, Univ. of London, 1980–85; Member Council: King's Coll. London, 1982–85; Chelsea Coll., 1983–85; Bd Mem., CSTI, 1984–88. Mem., Supporters of Nuclear Energy, 2003–. Numerous lectures at home and overseas including: Hatfield Meml, Iron and Steel Inst., 1973; John Player, IMechE, 1976. Freeman, City of London, 1984; Liveryman, Worshipful Co. of Engrs, 1985. Rosenhain Medallist, Inst. of Metals, 1964. FRSA 1976; FKC 1985; Life Member: RYA, 1976; Royal Instn, 1986; Nat. Trust, 1986. *Publications:* chapters in specialist books of science; scientific papers in various learned jls on the effects of atomic radiation on materials, on the rôle of energy in the production of engineering materials, etc. *Recreations:* cruising in the Mediterranean on sailing yacht Bombero, coupled with archaeology. *Address:* One The Mansion, Ashwood Place, Woking, Surrey GU22 7JR. *T:* (01483) 761529. *Clubs:* Athenæum, Cruising Association.

BARNES, Roger Anthony; Director, Hambros Bank Ltd, 1993–97; Assistant Director, Bank of England and Head of Banking Supervision Division, 1988–93; *b* 29 May 1937; *s* of Kenneth Ernest Barnes and Lilian Agnes (*née* King); *m* 1961, Tessa Margaret Soundy; two *s* two *d*. *Educ:* Malvern College; St John's College, Oxford (BA). Bank of England, 1961–93. Mem. Council of Management, European Sch. of Management, 1994–2003. Trustee, CAF, 1999–2003. *Recreations:* golf, music. *Address:* 40 Battlefield Road, St Albans, Herts AL1 4DD. *T:* (01727) 851987. *Club:* City of London.

BARNES, Rosemary Susan, (Rosie), OBE 2011; Chief Executive, Cystic Fibrosis Trust, 1996–2010; *b* 16 May 1946; *d* of Alan Allen and Kathleen (*née* Brown); *m* 1967, Graham Barnes; two *s* one *d*. *Educ:* Bilborough Grammar Sch.; Birmingham Univ. (BSocSci Hons). Management Trainee, Research Bureau Ltd, 1967–69; Product Manager, Yardley of London Ltd, 1969–72; primary teacher (briefly), 1972; freelance market researcher, 1973–87. MP Greenwich, Feb. 1987–1992 (SDP, 1987–90, Social Democrat, 1990–92); contested (Soc. Dem.) Greenwich, 1992. Dir, Birthright, subseq. WellBeing, 1992–96. *Recreations:* gardening, cooking, reading, travelling, walking, yoga, my dogs.

BARNES, Scott, FCA; Chairman, Global Board, Grant Thornton, since 2015; *b* Morley, Leeds, 3 Dec. 1955; *s* of Ronald and Sheila Barnes; *m* 1979, Irene Evans; one *s* one *d*. *Educ:* Batley Grammar Sch.; Keble Coll., Oxford (MA Hist.). ACA 1982, FCA 1992. Arthur Andersen, Leeds, 1978–84; Grant Thornton UK LLP: Manager, 1984–87; Partner, Leeds Office, 1987–91; Nat. Hd, Corporate Recovery, 1995–2001; UK Hd of Advisory, 2001–06;

Global Hd of Advisory, 2006–08; CEO, 2008–15. Mem., Adv. Bd, KermaPartners. Pres., Keble Assoc., 2014–. *Recreations:* cricket, watching football and Rugby, theatre, music. *Address:* Grant Thornton UK LLP, Grant Thornton House, Melton Street, Euston Square, NW1 2EP. *E:* scott.c.barnes@uk.gt.com.

BARNES, Shani Estelle; Her Honour Judge Barnes; a Circuit Judge, since 2004; *b* 24 Sept. 1955; *d* of late Sidney Hurst and of Renée Hurst; *m* 1994, David Thomas Howker, *qv*; two *s* three *d. Educ:* Central Foundn Grammar Sch. for Girls; Middlesex Univ. (BA 1st cl. Hons 1984). Called to the Bar, Middle Temple, 1986; Asst Recorder, 1999–2000; Recorder, 2000–04. Hon. Recorder, Brighton and Hove, 2013–. *Address:* c/o The Law Courts, High Street, Lewes, E Sussex BN7 1YB.

BARNES, Simon John Campbell; writer; chief sports writer, 2002–14, wildlife columnist, 2005–14, The Times (sports columnist, 1982–2002); *b* 22 July 1951; *s* of Edward Campbell Barnes, *qv* and late Dorothy Elsie Barnes (*née* Smith); *m* 1983, Cindy Lee Wright; two *s. Educ:* Emanuel Sch.; Bristol Univ. (BA Hons). Surrey and S London Newspapers, 1974–78; contributor to S China Morning Post, Asian Business and Asian Finance, based in Asia, 1978–82; wildlife writer, RSPB Birds magazine, 1994–; sports columnist, The Spectator, 1995–2002. Mem. Council, World Land Trust, 2008–. Patron: Spinal Research, 2000–08; Froglife, 2008–10; Save the Rhino, 2009–. Hon. DLitt Bristol, 2007. Sports Writer of Year: British Press Awards, 1987, What the Papers Say Awards, 2003; Sports Feature Writer of Year, Sports Council, 1988 and 1998; Sports Columnist of the Year: Sports Writers' Assoc., 2001, 2007; Sports Journalists' Assoc., 2007; Football Writer of Year, Football Supporters' Assoc., 1991; Sports Commentator of Year and Olympic Commentator of Year, Comment Awards, 2012. *Publications:* Phil Edmonds: a singular man, 1986; Horsesweat and Tears, 1988; A Sportswriter's Year, 1989; A la Recherche du Cricket Perdu, 1989; Sportswriter's Eye, 1989; Flying in the Face of Nature, 1991; Tiger!, 1994; Planet Zoo, 2000; On Horseback, 2000; How to be a Bad Birdwatcher, 2004; A Bad Birdwatcher's Companion, 2005; The Meaning of Sport, 2006; How to be Wild, 2007; The Horsey Life, 2008; (with Rachel Barnes) The Horse: a celebration of horses in art, 2008; My Natural History, 2010; A Book of Heroes, 2010; Birdwatching With Your Eyes Closed, 2011; Ten Million Aliens: a journey through the entire animal kingdom, 2014; *novels*: Rogue Lion Safaris, 1997; Hong Kong Belongers, 1999; Miss Chance, 2000. *Recreations:* Africa, horses, birdsong, Bach. *Club:* Tewin Irregulars Cricket.

BARNES, Stuart; Rugby Union broadcaster, Sky Television, since 1994; columnist, Sunday Times, since 2005; *b* Grays, Essex, 22 Nov. 1962; *s* of John and Joyce Barnes; *m* 1985, Lesley Patricia; one *s* one *d. Educ:* Bassaleg Comprehensive Sch., Newport, Gwent; St Edmund Hall, Oxford (BA Hons Modern Hist.). England Rugby player, 1984–93; Mem., British and Irish Lions team, 1993; Rugby writer and broadcaster, 1994–. Ambassador, Donald Woods Foundn, 2012–. Mem., RSC. *Publications:* Smelling of Roses: a Rugby autobiography, 1994; The Year of Living Dangerously, 1995; Rugby's New Age Travellers, 1997. *Recreations:* National Hunt horseracing (owner), red wine, literature. *Address:* Sky Sports, British Sky Broadcasting Ltd, Grant Way, Isleworth, Middx TW7 5QD.

BARNES, Prof. Timothy David, DPhil; FBA 2011; FRSC 1985; Hon. Professorial Fellow, School of Divinity and School of History, Classics and Archaeology, University of Edinburgh, 2008–12 and since 2014 (Professorial Fellow in Classics, 2013–14); *b* Ossett, Yorks, 13 March 1942; *e s* of David Barnes and Margaret Barnes (*née* Baxter); *m* 1st, 1965, Anne Jenifer Dixon (marr. diss. 1996); four *s*; 2nd, 1998, Stella Sandahl (marr. diss. 2004); 3rd, 2005, Janet Fairchild Cochrane. *Educ:* Queen Elizabeth Grammar Sch., Wakefield; Balliol Coll., Oxford (Deakin Schol.; BA 1964; MA); Univ. of Oxford (DPhil 1970). Harmsworth Sen. Scholar, Merton Coll., Oxford and Craven Fellow, Univ. of Oxford, 1964–66; Jun. Res. Fellow, Queen's Coll., Oxford, 1966–70; University of Toronto: Asst Prof., 1970–72, Associate Prof., 1972–76, Prof., 1976–2007, of Classics; Associate Chm., 1979–83, 1995–96; Coordinator, Graduate Studies, 1979–83, 1986–89, 1995–96. Vis. Mem. and Herodotus Fellow, Inst. for Advanced Study, Princeton and Leave Fellow, Amer. Council of Learned Socs, 1976–77; Vis. Fellow, Wolfson Coll., Oxford and J. S. Guggenheim Meml Foundn Fellow, 1983–84; Vis. Scholar, ANU, Canberra, 1988; Townsend Lectr and Vis. Prof., Cornell Univ., 1994; Vis. Prof., Univ. di Roma 'La Sapienza' and Vis. Scholar, Amer. Acad. in Rome, 1997; Dist. Vis. Scholar, Princeton Univ., 2000. Connaught Sen. Fellow in Humanities, 1984–85, Fellow, Trinity Coll., 1991, Univ. of Toronto; Killam Sen. Res. Fellow, Humanities and Social Scis Res. Council of Canada, 2001–03. Hon. Res. Fellow, UCL, 2004–08. Ancient Hist. Prize, 1966, Conington Prize, 1974, Univ. of Oxford; Philip Schaff Meml Prize, Amer. Soc. of Ch Hist., 1984; Charles J. Goodwin Award of Merit, Amer. Philol Assoc., 1984. *Publications:* Tertullian: a historical and literary study, 1971, 2nd edn 1985; The Sources of the Historia Augusta, 1978; Constantine and Eusebius, 1981; The New Empire of Diocletian and Constantine, 1982; Early Christianity and the Roman Empire, 1984; Athanasius and Constantius: theology and politics in the Constantinian Empire, 1993; From Eusebius to Augustine: selected papers 1982–1993, 1994; (ed) The Sciences in Greco-Roman Society, 1994; Ammianus Marcellinus and the Representation of Historical Reality, 1998; Early Christian Hagiography and Roman History, 2010; Constantine: dynasty, religion and power in the later Roman Empire, 2011, 2nd edn 2014; (with G. Bevan) The Funerary Speech for John Chrysostom, 2013; over 170 articles and essays; approx. 150 reviews. *Address:* 13 Marchhall Crescent, Edinburgh EH16 5HL. *T:* (0131) 662 0480, *Fax:* (0131) 650 7952. *E:* timothy.barnes@ed.ac.uk.

BARNES, Timothy Paul; QC 1986; a Recorder, since 1987; *b* 23 April 1944; *s* of late Arthur Morley Barnes and Valerie Enid Mary Barnes; *m* 1969, Patricia Margaret Gale; one *s* three *d. Educ:* Bradfield Coll., Berkshire; Christ's Coll., Cambridge (MA). Called to Bar, Gray's Inn, 1968 (Hilbery Exhibn; Bencher, 2004); practises Midland and Oxford Circuit; Asst Recorder, 1983. Chm., Greenwich Soc., 2001. *Recreations:* gardening, theatre. *Address:* The White House, Crooms Hill, SE10 8HH. *T:* (020) 8858 1185, *Fax:* (020) 8858 0788. *Club:* MCC.

BARNES JONES, Deborah Elizabeth Vavasseur; HM Diplomatic Service, retired; Governor, Montserrat, 2004–07; *b* 6 Oct. 1956; *née* Barnes; *m* 1986, Frederick Richard Jones; twin *d.* Joined FCO, 1980; Moscow, 1983–85; First Secretary: on loan to Cabinet Office, 1985–86; (Chancery), Israel, 1988–92; FCO, 1992–96; Dep. Hd of Mission, Uruguay, 1996–2001; Ambassador to Georgia, 2001–04. *Recreation:* choral singing. *Club:* Athenæum.

BARNES THOMPSON, Dame Ingrid Victoria; *see* Allen, Dame I. V.

BARNETT, Alexandra Louise; *see* Marks, A. L.

BARNETT, Andrew; *see* Barnett, J. A.

BARNETT, Andrew Charles Robert; Director, Calouste Gulbenkian Foundation (UK), since 2007; *b* Nowra, NSW, 10 March 1968; *s* of Comdr Kenneth Malcolm Barnett, RAN, and Sheila Margaret Barnett. *Educ:* King's Sch., Bruton, Som; Univ. of St Andrews (MA). Public Affairs Advr, Foyer Fedn, 1992–94; Dep. Hd, Press and Public Affairs, Arts Council of England, 1994–97; Gp Corporate Affairs Manager, HSBC Hldgs plc, 1997–99; Hd, Public Affairs, Nat. Consumer Council, 1999–2001; Director: Communications, UK Sports Council, 2001–05; Policy and Communications, Joseph Rowntree Foundn, 2005–07. Non-exec. Dir, Yorks Metropolitan Housing Assoc., 2000–08. Advr to Jt Chair, All-Party Parly Gp on Homelessness, 1992–94. Mem. Council, Collaborate, 2012–; Mem., Church Council, St Dunstan-in-the-West, 1996–. Chair of Trustees: SPACE Studios, 1998–2003 (Trustee/Dir, 1998–2003); People Can Gp, 2009–12; DV8 Physical Th., 2010–14; Trustee: St Christopher's Fellowship, 1995–98; Addaction, 2006–14; Forces in Mind Trust, 2015–; Founder Trustee Social Innovation Exchange, 2013–. Mem. Cttee, Healthwatch England, 2014–. Gov. Clerkenwell Parochial Primary Sch., 1998–2000. FRSA 1995. *Recreations:* history contemporary dance, aboriginal and modern art, swimming, food and wine, travelling languages. *Address:* c/o Calouste Gulbenkian Foundation, 50 Hoxton Square, N1 6PB. *E* acrbarnett@gmail.com.

BARNETT, Andrew John; His Honour Judge Andrew Barnett; a Circuit Judge, sinc 2004; Liaison Judge, North Hampshire Magistrates, since 2007; Honorary Recorder o Salisbury, since 2010; *b* 19 Sept. 1953; *s* of late Rev. Canon Norman Barnett and of Dorett Barnett; *m* 1978, Gillian Lindsey, *d* of late Patrick Leonard James; three *s* one *d. Educ* Marlborough Coll.; KCL (BD). Called to the Bar, Gray's Inn, 1977; Asst Recorder, 1992–96 Recorder, 1996–2004. Mem. Cttee, Council of Circuit Judges, 2006–; Pres., Wesse Magistrates' Assoc., 2009–. *Recreations:* most outdoor activities, including golf. *Address* Winchester Combined Court Centre, The Law Courts, Winchester, Hants SO23 9DL. *T* (01962) 814100. *Clubs:* Lansdowne; High Post Golf.

BARNETT, Caroline Hannah; Founder and Director, Arts Scape Ltd, since 2013; *b* London 8 Nov. 1966; *d* of Brychan Powell and Noreen Avril Powell (*née* Berry); *m* 2004, Peter Joh Barnett. *Educ:* Lady Margaret Hall, Oxford (BA 1st Cl. Hons Ancient and Modern Hist.) Univ. of Westminster (Legal CPE (Commendation)); Coll. of Law (Dist.). Admitted a solicitor, 1995; Trainee, 1993–95, Solicitor, 1995–99, Slaughter and May; Intellectua Property Counsel, Reuters Gp, 1999–2003; Gen. Counsel, Royal Shakespeare Co., 2003–13 Non-exec. Dir, Belgrade Th. Trust (Coventry) Ltd, 2007–13. *Recreations:* hill walking swimming, theatre, cinema, playing the cello, cooking. *Address:* Orchard House, High Street Longborough, Glos GL56 0QE. *T:* (01451) 833850.

BARNETT, Charles Henry, CVO 2015; Chief Executive, Ascot Racecourse, 2007–14; *b* 1 July 1948; *s* of late Major B. G. Barnett and D. Barnett; *m* 1978, Georgina Greig; one *s* tw *d. Educ:* Eton Coll.; Christ Church, Oxford (BA 2nd Cl. Hons Jurisprudence; MA). Chie Executive: Haydock Park Racecourse, 1984–93; Chester Race Co. Ltd, 1996–2000; Man Dir, Aintree Racecourse Co. Ltd, 1993–2007. *Recreation:* country pursuits.

BARNETT, Dr Christopher Andrew; Headmaster, Whitgift School, Croydon, since 1991 *b* 1 Feb. 1953; *s* of Peter Alan Barnett and Joan Barnett (*née* Cullis); *m* 1976, Hon. Laur Miriam Elizabeth (marr. diss. 2015), *oc* of Baron Weidenfeld, *qv*; three *s* one *d. Educ:* Cedar Sch., Leighton Buzzard; Oriel Coll., Oxford (Exhibnr; BA Hons History 1974; MA 1978 DPhil 1981). Lectr in Econs, Brunel Univ., 1975–77; Head of History Dept, Bradfield Coll. Berks, 1978–87; Second Master, Dauntsey's Sch., Wilts, 1987–91. Fellow Commoner Downing Coll., Cambridge, 1987; Evelyn Wrench Scholar, ESU, 1990. Pres., Croydo Music Fest., 1992–2013. Match Dir, Surrey CCC Festival of Cricket, 2000–11. Exhibn Dir Hidden Treasures from the Mary Rose, 2009. Chevalier, Ordre des Palmes Académique (France), 2012. *Recreations:* opera, political Victoriana, hill-walking, travel, horse-racing *Address:* Whitgift School, Haling Park, South Croydon CR2 6YT. *T:* (020) 8688 9222. *Club* Athenæum.

BARNETT, His Honour Christopher John Anthony; QC 1983; a Circuit Judge 1988–2003, a Deputy Circuit Judge, 2003–10; Designated Family Judge, Suffolk, 1991–2003 *b* 18 May 1936; *s* of Richard Adrian Barnett and Phyllis Barnett (*née* Cartwright); *m* 1959 Sylvia Marieliese (*née* Pritt); two *s* one *d. Educ:* Repton Sch., Derbyshire; College of Law London. Called to the Bar, Gray's Inn, 1965. Volunteer, Kenya Regt, 1954–55; Distric Officer (Kikuyu Guard) and Kenya Government Service, 1955–60; a District Officer in HM Overseas Civil Service, serving in Kenya, 1960–62; in practice as barrister, 1965–88; Recorder, 1982–88; Jt Hd of Chambers, 4 Paper Buildings, 1985–88; a Dep. High Cour Judge, QBD, 1991–97. Led conf. promoting Unified Family Ct, Bermuda, 2010. A Pres. Mental Health Review Tribunal Restricted Patients Panel, 2002–11. Mem., Wine Cttee, SE Circuit, 1984–88; Chm., SE Circuit Area Liaison Cttee, 1985–88; Mem. Cttee, Council o Circuit Judges, 1992–2003; a Chm., Bar Disciplinary Tribunal, 2006–10. Chm., Suffolk Community Alcohol Services, 1993–95; a Patron, Relate, W Suffolk, 1998–. Mem., Cour of Essex Univ., 1983–. Foundn Gov., Colne Engaine C of E Voluntary Assisted Primary Sch. 2009–. Pres., Old Reptonian Soc., 2002. *Recreations:* cricket, tennis, novice golfer, walking travel, gardening under instruction. *Address:* c/o Judicial Secretariat, 2nd Floor, Rose Court 2 Southwark Bridge, SE1 9HS. *Clubs:* MCC (Assoc. Mem.); Kenya Kongonis Cricket.

BARNETT, Cindy; *see* Barnett, L. J.

BARNETT, Clive Durac, MA; HM Inspector of Schools, 2002–09; *b* 22 July 1949; *s* o Edgar Thomas Barnett and Betty Marian Barnett; *m* 1981, Patricia Michelle Morrissey. *Educ* King's Coll. Sch., Wimbledon; Magdalen Coll., Oxford (BA Hons, MA, PGCE). Ass Teacher of History, 1971–79, Hd, Hist. Dept, 1975–79, Kingston GS; Head, History anc Politics Depts, Watford Boys' GS, 1979–86; Dep. Headmaster, Portsmouth GS, 1986–92 Headmaster, Bishop Wordsworth's Sch., Salisbury, 1992–2002. Educnl consultant, 2009–14 Member: Salisbury Diocesan Bd of Educn, 1998–2002; Salisbury Cathedral Chapter 2009–12; Salisbury Cathedral Council, 2012; Lay Canon, Salisbury Cath., 2007–. Trustee Trade Aid, 1996–2006 (Chm., 1996–2002); Mem. Cttee, Bloxham Project, 1998–2005 (Vice-Chm., 1999–2002); Patron, EdUKaid, 2007– (Trustee, 2014–). Governor: Roya Grammar Sch., Guildford, 2009–; Salisbury Cathedral Sch., 2012–. *Publications:* (jtly) Smik (a musical), 1973 (televised 1974). *Recreations:* umpiring and watching cricket, walking, going to the theatre, listening to most forms of music, travelling, spending time with my wife *Address:* Langstone House, Morgans Vale Road, Redlynch, Salisbury, Wilts SP5 2HY. *Club* MCC.

BARNETT, Hon. Colin James; MLA (L) Cottesloe, Western Australia, since 1990; Premie of Western Australia and Minister for State Development, since 2008; *b* Nedlands, WA, 1 July 1950; *s* of James Henry Barnett and Coralle Cross Barnett; *m* 1989, Lynette Kathleen Ashby; one *s*, and three *s* from a previous marriage. *Educ:* Hollywood High Sch.; Univ. o Western Australia (BEc Hons; MEc). Cadet Res. Officer, then Sen. Res. Officer, Aust Bureau of Statistics, 1973–75; Sen. Tutor, then Lectr in Econs, Western Australian Inst. o Technol., 1975–82; Confederation of Western Australian Industry, subseq. Chamber o Commerce and Industry of WA: on secondment, then Economist, and Editor, WA Economic Review, 1982–85; Exec. Dir, 1985–90. Western Australia: Shadow Minister for Housing Works and Services, 1990, for Housing Fuel and Energy, Works and Services, 1991–92, fo State Devel t, 1992, for Resources, Fuel and Energy, 1992; Dep. Leader of the Opposition 1992; Dep. Leader, Parly Liberal Party, 1992–2001; Leader, House of Legislative Assembly 1993–2001; Minister: for Tourism, 1993; for Resources Develt, 1993–2001; for Energy 1993–2001; for Educn, 1995–2001; Leader of the Opposition, 2001–05, 2008; Shadow Minister for the Arts, 2004–05, for Public Sector Mgt, 2004–05; Shadow Treasurer, 2004–05 Shadow Minister for State Develt, 2008; Treasurer, 2008. Centenary Medal (Australia), 2003 *Recreations:* tennis, walking, watching football. *Address:* Office of the Premier of Wester Australia, 1 Parliament Place, Perth, WA 6000, Australia. *T:* (8) 65525000, *Fax:* (8) 65525201 *E:* WA-Gov@dpc.wa.gov.au; (office) Suite 12, 589 Stirling Highway, Cottesloe, WA 6011 Australia. *Clubs:* Claremont Football, Cottesloe Tennis, Peppermint Grove Tennis.

BARNETT, Correlli (Douglas), CBE 1997; author; Fellow, Churchill College, Cambridge since 1977; Keeper of the Churchill Archives Centre, 1977–95; *b* 28 June 1927; *s* of D. A Barnett; *m* 1950, Ruth Murby; two *d. Educ:* Trinity Sch., Croydon; Exeter Coll., Oxford Second class hons, Mod. Hist. with Mil. Hist. and the Theory of War as a special subject; MA

1954. Intell. Corps, 1945–48. North Thames Gas Bd, 1952–57; Public Relations, 1957–63. Vice-Pres., E Arts Assoc., 1978–91 (Chm. Literature Panel, and Mem. Exec. Cttee, 1972–78); Pres., East Anglian Writers, 1969–88; Member: Council, Royal Utd Services Inst. for Defence Studies, 1973–85; Cttee, London Library, 1977–79 and 1982–84. Leverhulme Res. Fellowship, 1976; apptd Lectr in Defence Studies, Univ. of Cambridge, 1980; resigned in order to devote more time to writing, 1983. Winston Churchill Meml Lectr, Switzerland, 1982. Hon. Pres., Western Front Assoc., 1998–2010. FRSL; FRHistS; FRSA. Hon. FCGI 2003. Hon. DSc Cranfield, 1993. Chesney Gold Medal, RUSI, 1991. Contrib., The Times, Daily Mail and The Spectator. *Publications:* The Hump Organisation, 1957; The Channel Tunnel (with Humphrey Slater), 1958; The Desert Generals, 1960, new enlarged edn, 1983; The Swordbearers, 1963; Britain and Her Army, 1970 (RSL award, 1971); The Collapse of British Power, 1972; Marlborough, 1974; Bonaparte, 1978; The Great War, 1979; The Audit of War, 1986 (US edn as The Pride and the Fall, 1987); Engage the Enemy More Closely: the Royal Navy in the Second World War, 1991 (Yorkshire Post Book of the Year Award, 1991); The Lost Victory: British dreams, British realities 1945–1950, 1995; The Verdict of Peace: Britain between her yesterday and the future, 2001; The Lords of War: supreme leadership from Lincoln to Churchill, 2012; (historical consultant and writer to) BBC Television series: The Great War, 1963–64; The Lost Peace, 1965–66; The Commanders, 1972–73; contrib. to: The Promise of Greatness (a symposium on the Great War), 1968; Governing Elites (a symposium), 1969; Decisive Battles of the Twentieth Century, 1976; The War Lords, 1976; The Economic System in the UK, 1985; Education for Capability, 1986; (ed) Hitler's Generals, 1989. *Recreations:* gardening, interior decorating, idling, eating, mole-hunting, travelling through France. *Address:* Catbridge House, East Carleton, Norwich NR14 8JX. *T:* (01508) 570410. *Club:* Royal Over-Seas League.

BARNETT, Prof. David Braham, CBE 2007; MD; FRCP; Professor of Clinical Pharmacology, University of Leicester Medical School, 1984–2009, now Emeritus (Head, Department of Medicine, 1999); *b* 17 July 1944. *Educ:* Sheffield Univ. Med. Sch. (MB ChB Hons 1967; MD 1979). FRCP 1981. Merck Internat. Travelling Fellow, 1975–76; Sen. Lectr, Univ. of Leicester, 1976–84; Hon. Consultant Physician, Leicester Royal Infirmary, 1976–. Non-exec. Dir, Leicester Royal Infirmary NHS Trust, 1993–2000. Chairman: Appraisals Cttee, NICE, 1999–2009. *Publications:* original research, rev. articles and book chapters in fields of molecular pharmacology and general cardiovascular clinical pharmacology, with specialist interest in ischaemic heart disease. *Recreations:* golf, reading, theatre.

BARNETT, Geoffrey Grant Fulton, OBE 2001; Chair (formerly Chair of Council), Barnardo's, 2006–11 (Trustee, 2001–11; Hon. Treasurer, 2002–06); *b* 9 March 1943; *s* of Air Chief Marshal Sir Denis H. F. Barnett, GCB, CBE, DFC; *m* 1968, Fiona Katharine Milligan; two *s* two *d. Educ:* Winchester Coll.; Clare Coll., Cambridge (MA). Courtaulds Ltd, 1964–67; The Economist Intelligence Unit, 1967–70; British Printing Corp., 1970–71; Baring Brothers & Co. Ltd, 1971–95 (Dir, 1979–95); Man. Dir, Baring Brothers Asia, Hong Kong, 1979–83; seconded as Dir Gen., Panel on Takeovers and Mergers, 1989–92. Dir, Language Line Ltd, 1996–99; Trustee: Castelnau Centre Project, 2002–13 (Chm., 2002–13); StartHere, 2000–05; St Michael's Fellowship, 2002–06; Baring Foundn, 2005–13. Hon. Treas., VSO, 1984–2000; Mem., Governing Bd, London and Quadrant Housing Trust, 1985–2000. Lay Chm., Richmond and Barnes Deanery Synod, 2002–07; Lay Reader, C of E, 2003–. FRSA 1992. *Recreations:* Scotland, walking, music, bird watching. *Address:* 2 Mill Hill Road, SW13 0HR. *T:* (020) 8878 6975.

BARNETT, Dame Jenifer W.; *see* Wilson-Barnett.

BARNETT, Jeremy John, OBE 1982; independent tour consultant, since 1999; *b* 26 Jan. 1941; *s* of late Audrey Wickham Barnett and Lt-Comdr Charles Richard Barnett, RN; *m* 1968, Maureen Janet Cullum; one *s* one *d. Educ:* St Edward's Sch., Oxford; St Andrews Univ. (MA); Leeds Univ. (Dip TEFL); SOAS, London Univ. (MA 1994). Joined British Council, 1964; teaching, Victory Coll., Cairo, 1965–67; Lectr, Inst. of Educn, Istanbul, 1967–69; MECAS, Lebanon, 1969–70; Dir of Studies, Turco-British Assoc., Ankara, 1970–72; British Council Rep., Riyadh, 1972–75; Dir, ME Dept, 1975–78; Counsellor for British Council and Cultural Affairs, Ankara, 1978–82; British Council Rep., Warsaw, 1982–85; Dir, E Europe and N Asia Dept, 1985–88; Controller, S and W Asia Div., 1988–89; British Council Rep., later Dir, and Cultural Counsellor, British Embassy, Cairo, 1989–93. Westminster Classic Tours, 1995–99 (Man. Dir, 1998–99). *Recreation:* hill walking. *Address:* Oakdene, Station Road, Groombridge, Tunbridge Wells, Kent TN3 9NB. *T:* and *Fax:* (01892) 864626.

BARNETT, (John) Andrew; Director, The Policy Practice Ltd, since 2004; *b* Repton, 1 Dec. 1946; *s* of William Gordon Barnett and Margaret Acton Barnett (*née* Wain); *m* 1977, Mary Jane Smith; two *d. Educ:* Repton Sch.; Univ. of Sussex (MA Develt Studies 1970). Economist, ODA, 1971–72; University of Sussex: Res. Officer, Inst. of Develt Studies, 1974–77; Prog. Officer, Internat. Develt Res. Centre, Canada, 1977–85; Fellow, 1985–96, Leader, Technol. and Develt Gp, 1987–93, Sci. Policy Res. Unit, subseq. Sci. and Technol. Policy Res. Unit (Hon. Fellow, 1996–); Dir of Res., Intermediate Technol. Develt Gp, 1994–98. Partner, Sussex Development Project Consultants Ltd, 1973–78; Dir, Sussex Research Associates Ltd, 1985–. Specialist Adviser: Select Cttee on Sci. and Technol., H of L, 1989; Select Cttee on Sci. and Technol., H of C, 2003–04; Mem., Tech. Adv. Gp, Energy Sector Mgt Assistance Prog., World Bank, 1996–2007. Member Board: Womankind Worldwide, London, 1999–2007 (Chm., 2006–07); ODI, 2000–11; Small Scale Sustainable Infrastructure Develt Fund, Cambridge, Mass, 2002–08; HEDON Household Energy Network, 2010–. *Publications:* articles in learned jls, books and reports on energy policy, technol. policy and res. policy in developing countries. *Recreations:* walking, cooking, grandson. *Address:* c/o The Policy Practice Ltd, 33 Southdown Avenue, Brighton BN1 6EH. *T:* (01273) 330331.

BARNETT, Joseph Anthony, CBE 1983 (OBE 1975); Director (formerly Representative), British Council, Tokyo, 1983–91, retired; *b* 19 Dec. 1931; *s* of Joseph Edward Barnett and Helen Johnson; *m* 1960, Carolina Johnson Rice (*d* 1998); one *s* one *d. Educ:* St Albans Sch.; Pembroke Coll., Cambridge (BA (Hons) English and Psychology); Edinburgh Univ. (Diploma in Applied Linguistics). Served Army, 1950–51 (2nd Lieut). Teaching, Aylesford House, St Albans, 1954–55; Unilever Ltd, 1955–58; apptd British Council, 1958; Asst Educn Officer, Dacca, Pakistan, 1958; trng at Sch. of Applied Linguistics, Edinburgh Univ., 1960; Educn Officer, Dacca, 1961; seconded to Inst. of Educn, London Univ., 1963; Head, English Language Teaching Inst., London, 1964; Dir of Studies, Regional Inst. of English, Bangalore, India, 1968; Representative, Ethiopia, 1971; Controller, English Language Teaching Div., 1975; Representative, Brazil, 1978–82. *Publications:* (jtly) Getting on in English, 1960; Success with English (language laboratory materials), Books 1–3, 1966–69. *Recreation:* sport (tennis, armchair cricket, Rugby). *Address:* The Thatch, Stebbing Green, Dunmow, Essex CM6 3TE. *T:* (01371) 856014. *Club:* Athenæum.

BARNETT, Kenneth Thomas, CB 1979; Deputy Secretary, Department of the Environment, 1976–80; *b* 12 Jan. 1921; *yr s* of late Frederick Charles Barnett and Ethel Barnett (*née* Powell); *m* 1943, Emily May Lovering; one *d. Educ:* Howard Gardens High Sch., Cardiff. Entered Civil Service (Min. of Transport), 1937; Sea Transport Office, Port Said, 1951–54; Asst Sec., 1965; Under-Sec., Cabinet Office (on secondment), 1971–73; Under-Sec., DoE, 1970–76. Dir, Abbey Data Systems Ltd, 1984–2005. *Recreations:* gardening, watching Rugby football. *Address:* 5 Redan Close, Highcliffe-on-Sea, Christchurch, Dorset BH23 5DJ. *T:* (01425) 276945.

BARNETT, His Honour Kevin Edward; a Circuit Judge, 1996–2014; *b* 2 Jan. 1948; *s* of Arthur and Winifred Barnett; *m* 1972, Patricia Margaret Smith; one *d. Educ:* Wellesbourne Sch.; Tudor Grange Grammar Sch.; London Univ. (LLB Hons ext.). Called to the Bar, Gray's Inn, 1971; Wales and Chester Circuit. *Recreations:* painting, photography, cooking. *Club:* Lansdowne.

BARNETT, Lucinda Jane, (Cindy), OBE 2009; JP; a Vice President, Magistrates' Association, since 2008 (Deputy Chairman, 2002–05; Chairman, 2005–08); *b* 21 March 1951; *d* of late Richard William Gilbert and Margaret Gwenllian Gilbert (*née* Edwards); *m* 1976, William Evans Barnett, *qv*; two *s. Educ:* Croydon High Sch. (GDST); King's Coll. London (Inglis studentship; BA 1st Cl. Hons 1972; MA 1973; PGCE 1974). ARCM 1971. Civil servant, DoE, 1974–77; teacher (pt-time), in schs, and private coaching, 1978–94. Member: Lord Chancellor's Adv. Cttee (SE London), 1993–2001; SE London Probation Cttee, 1998–2001; Magistrates' Courts' Sentencing Guidelines Wkg Party, 2002–03; Magisterial and Family Sub-cttee, 2005–07, Magisterial Cttee, 2007–08, Judicial Studies Bd; Judges' Council, 2005–08; Lay Mem., Council of Inns of Court Disciplinary Pool, 2013–; Jt Chm., Nat. Sentencer/Probation Forum, 2005–08; Mem., Adv. Gp, Sentencing Adv. Panel on Definitive Magistrates' Ct Sentencing Guidelines, 2006–08; Lay Mem., Solicitors' Disciplinary Tribunal, 2009– (Lay Mem. Vice Pres., 2013–); Ind. Mem., Parole Bd, 2010–11. Member, Board of Visitors: HMP Downview, 1994–2002 (Chm., 1997–2000); HMP Wandsworth, 2002. Member: Croydon Area Child Protection Cttee, 1994–2000 (Chm., Registration Appeals Panel); Croydon Magistrates' Courts' Cttee, 1999–2001; Chm., Croydon Family Panel, 2000–02. Panel Chm., Fitness to Practise Cttees, NMC, 2012–. Magistrates' Association: Mem. Council, 2001–13; Chm., Criminal Justice System, subseq. Judicial Policy and Practice, Cttee, 2002–05. JP Croydon, 1986 (Supplemental List, 2015). Gov., Croydon High Sch., 1993–2005 (Chm. Govs, 2000–05). *Publications:* contrib. Magistrate mag. *Recreations:* music, reading, computing. *Address:* c/o Magistrates' Association, 28 Fitzroy Square, W1T 6DD. *T:* (020) 7387 2353, *Fax:* (020) 7383 4020.

BARNETT, Hon. Sir Michael (Lancelot Patrick), Kt 2009; Chief Justice, The Bahamas, 2009–15; *b* Nassau, 21 Aug. 1954; *s* of Arthur Barnett and Beryl Barnett; *m* 1980, Camille Liverpool; two *d. Educ:* Georgetown Univ., Washington, DC (BA). Called to the Bar, Lincoln's Inn, 1978; Partner, Graham Thompson and Co., Nassau, 1983–2008; Attorney Gen., Bahamas, 2008–09.

BARNETT, Rt Rev. Paul William, ThD; Bishop of North Sydney, and an Assistant Bishop, Diocese of Sydney, 1990–2001; *b* 23 Sept. 1935; *s* of William and Edna Barnett; *m* 1963, Anita Janet Simpson; two *s* two *d. Educ:* Univ. of London (BD Hons 1963, PhD 1978); Univ. of Sydney (MA Hons 1975). Deacon, 1963; priest, 1965; Lectr, Moore Theol Coll., 1964–67; Rector, St Barnabas, Broadway, 1967–73; Rector, Holy Trinity, Adelaide, 1973–79; Master, Robert Menzies Coll., Macquarie Univ., 1980–90. Lecturer, part time: Macquarie Univ., 1980–86; Univ. of Sydney, 1982–92. Vis. Prof., 1987, 1991, 1993, 1995, Res. Prof., 1996–, Regent Coll., Vancouver; Vis. Fellow in History, 1987–, Sen. Fellow in Ancient History Documentary Res., 2002–, Macquarie Univ.; Kingham Fellow, Oak Hill Theol Coll., 1996; Fellow, Inst. of Biblical Res., 2000. Hon. ThD Australian Coll. of Theology, 2009. Highly commended author, Christian Booksellers Conf., 1990; Christian Theol Writer's Award, Aust. Christian Lit. Soc., 2009. *Publications:* Is the New Testament History?, 1986; The Message of 2 Corinthians, 1988; Bethlehem to Patmos, 1989; Apocalypse Now and Then, 1990; The Two Faces of Jesus, 1990; The Servant King, 1991; The Truth About Jesus, 1994; Jesus and the Logic of History, 1997; Commentary on 2 Corinthians, 1997; Jesus and the Rise of Early Christianity, 1999; Commentary on 1 Corinthians, 2000; Commentary on Romans, 2003; Birth of Christianity, 2005; Shepherd King, 2005; First Peter, 2006; Paul, Missionary of Jesus, 2008; Messiah, 2009; Finding the Historical Christ, 2009; The Corinthian Question: why the Church opposed her founder, 2011; Paul the Pastor in Second Corinthians, 2012; Galatians: defending the truth, 2012; Following Jesus to Jerusalem, 2012; Gospel Truth: answering new atheist attacks on the Gospels, 2012; Paul in Syria: the background to Galatians, 2014. *Recreations:* tennis, swimming, fishing, fine music. *Address:* 59 Essex Street, Epping, NSW 2121, Australia.

BARNETT, Richard; writer, broadcaster and poet; Faculty Member, Pembroke-King's Programme, University of Cambridge, since 2011; *b* Birmingham, 3 March 1980; *s* of Roy Barnett and Elizabeth Barnett (*née* Clayton); *m* 2006, Caroline Essex (marr. diss. 2013). *Educ:* University Coll. London (BSc 1st Cl. Hons Hist. of Medicine and Basic Med. Scis 2001; MSc Hist. and Philosophy of Sci., Technol. and Medicine (Dist.) 2003; PhD Hist. of Medicine 2007). Lectr in Hist. of Medicine, Wellcome Trust Centre for Hist. of Medicine, UCL, 2007–08 and 2010–11; Teaching Associate in Hist. of Modern Medicine and Biol., Dept of Hist. and Philosophy of Sci., Univ. of Cambridge, 2008–10. Hon. Res. Fellow, Dept of Sci. and Technol. Studies, UCL, 2011–. Wellcome Trust Engagement Fellow, 2011–14. *Publications:* Medical London: city of diseases, city of cures, 2008; The Dedalus Book of Gin, 2011; (contrib.) Natural Death Handbook, 5th edn 2012; (contrib.) Pocket Horizon, 2013; The Sick Rose: disease and the art of medical illustration, 2014; Seahouses, 2015; contribs to Lancet, London Rev. of Books. *Recreations:* walking, cooking, reading, arguing. *E:* richard@richardbarnettwriter.com.

BARNETT, Sir Richard (Robert), Kt 2015; PhD; Vice Chancellor, 2006–15, and Professor of Public Finance and Management, 1990–2015, now Professor Emeritus, University of Ulster; *b* 17 Oct. 1952; *s* of late Sidney Barnett and Joyce Barnett (*née* Stocker). *Educ:* St Ivo Sch., St Ives; Abbey Sch., Ramsey; Univ. of Salford (BSc 1974; PhD 1983). Lecturer in Economics: Univ. of Salford, 1977–78; Univ. of York, 1978–90; University of Ulster: Dean, Faculty of Business and Mgt, 1994–2000; Pro Vice Chancellor, 2000–05; Actg Vice Chancellor, 2004–06. Vivienne Stewart Fellow, Univ. of Cambridge, and Vis. Scholar, Wolfson Coll., Cambridge, 1988; Vis. Prof. of Econs, Queen's Univ., Ontario, 1989–90. Non-exec. Dir, United Hosps HSS Trust, 1996–2004; Director: ILEX Urban Regeneration Co. Ltd, 2005–09; NI Sci. Park Foundn Ltd, 2006–15; non-exec. Dir, Bombadier-Shorts Aerospace (Belfast) Ltd, 2007–. Member: NI Adv. Cttee, British Council, 2000–06; NIHEC, 2004–09; NI Council, CBI, 2006–10; Chm., NI Ind. Review of Economic Policy, 2008–09. Trustee, Daphne Jackson Trust, 2008–11. CCMI 2007; Dist. Fellowship Award, Griffith Coll., Dublin, 2014. *Publications:* contrib. learned jls and chapters in books in area of econ. policy and public finance. *Recreations:* contemporary fiction, motor sport. *Address:* Kidman Farm Cottage, Gravely Way, Hilton, Cambs PE28 9NN. *Club:* Ulster Reform.

BARNETT, Robert William, OBE 1993; HM Diplomatic Service, retired; Head of Science and Technology Unit, Foreign and Commonwealth Office, 2001–02; *b* 25 May 1954; *s* of late Harry Frederick Barnett, Wells-next-the-Sea, Norfolk and Dorothy Anne Barnett (*née* Williamson); *m* 1979, Caroline Sara Weale; two *s. Educ:* Wymondham Coll., Norfolk; St Catharine's Coll., Cambridge (BA Hons Mod. & Med. Langs 1977; MA 1979). Joined FCO, 1977: Japanese lang. trng, 1979; Third Sec., Tokyo, 1980–83; Policy Planning Staff, FCO, 1984; Asst Private Sec. to Minister of State, 1984–86; First Secretary: Western European Dept, FCO, 1986–88; Bonn, 1988–91; seconded to Saxony State Govt as Inward Investment Advr, 1992; Asst Hd, Eastern Adriatic Unit, FCO, 1993–94; Ambassador to Bosnia-Herzegovina, 1994–95; Counsellor (Sci., Technol. and Envmt), Bonn, 1995–99; Counsellor, Review of FCO Internat. Sci. and Technol. Work, 1999–2001. Mem. (Ind.), Cotswold DC, 2003. Trustee: Stow Fund, 2005–; Kate's Home Nursing, 2011–15 (Chm., 2013–15). *Recreations:* walking, sailing, gardening.

BARNETT, Robin Anthony, CMG 2006; HM Diplomatic Service; Ambassador to Poland, since 2011; *b* 8 March 1958; *s* of Bryan Anderson Barnett and Marion Barnett; *m* 1st, 1989, Debra Marianne Bunt (marr. diss. 1999); one *s*, and one step *s*; 2nd, 1999, Tesca Marie Osman; one step *s* one step *d*. *Educ:* Birmingham Univ. (LLB Hons 1979). Joined FCO, 1980: Second Secretary: Warsaw, 1982–85; FCO, 1985–90; First Secretary: UK Delegn to conventional forces in Europe negotiations, Vienna, 1990–91; UK Mission to UN, NY, 1991–95; FCO, 1996–98; Counsellor and Dep. Hd of Mission, Warsaw, 1998–2001; Hd, UKvisas, FCO, 2002–06; Ambassador to Romania, 2006–10; Dir, Business Gp, UK Trade & Investment, 2010–11. *Recreations:* travel, football (Manchester United), reading, film, cooking. *Address:* c/o Foreign and Commonwealth Office, King Charles Street, SW1A 2AH.

BARNETT, Prof. Stephen Mark, PhD; FRS 2006; CPhys; FRSE; Professor of Quantum Theory, University of Glasgow, since 2013; *b* 20 Feb. 1961; *s* of Peter Symon Barnett and Rita Barnett; partner, Dr Claire Rosalie Gilson; one *s* one *d*. *Educ:* Imperial Coll., London (BSc, PhD 1985). Postdoctoral Res. Fellow, Imperial Coll., London, 1985–87; Harwell-Wolfson Res. Fellow, 1987–88; GEC and Fellowship of Engrg Fellow, Univ. of Oxford, 1988–90; Lectr in Physics, KCL, 1990–91; University of Strathclyde: RSE Res. Fellow, 1991–94; Reader, 1994–96; Prof. of Quantum Optics, 1996–2013. FRSE 1996; Fellow, Optical Soc. of America, 2009. Dirac Medal, Inst. of Physics, 2013. *Publications:* Methods in Theoretical Quantum Optics (with Dr P. M. Radmore), 1997; Quantum Information, 2009; (jtly) Phase Space Methods for Degenerate Quantum Cases, 2015. *Recreations:* croquet, playing the viola. *Address:* School of Physics and Astronomy, University of Glasgow, Kelvin Building, University Avenue, Glasgow G12 8QQ.

BARNETT, His Honour William Evans; QC 1984; a Circuit Judge, 1994–2009; a Deputy Circuit Judge, 2009–11; *b* 10 March 1937; *s* of late Alec Barnett and Esmé (*née* Leon); *m* 1976, Lucinda Jane Gilbert (*see* L. J. Barnett); two *s*. *Educ:* Repton; Keble Coll., Oxford (BA Jurisprudence, 1961; MA 1965). National Service, RCS, 1956–58. Called to the Bar, Inner Temple, 1962; Major Scholarship, Inner Temple, 1962. A Recorder, 1981–94. Mem., Personal Injuries Litigation Procedure Wkg Pty, 1976–78; Judicial Mem., Mental Health Rev. Tribunal, 1993–2004. Chm., Ind. Local Rev. Panel into rioting in Croydon in Aug. 2011, 2011–12. Mem., Whitgift Sch. Cttee, 1996–2002; Gov., Whitgift Foundn, 2004–. *Recreations:* photography, gardening. *Address:* c/o Judicial Secretariat for the London and South East Region, City of London Magistrates Court, 3rd Floor, 1 Queen Victoria Street, EC4N 4XY. *Club:* Royal Automobile.

BARNEVIK, Percy; Chairman of the Board: AstraZeneca PLC, 1999–2004; ABB (formerly ABB Asea Brown Boveri) Ltd, Zürich, Switzerland, 1996–2001 (President and Chief Executive Officer, 1988–96); Co-founder and Chairman, Hand in Hand International, 2004–14, now Honorary Chairman; *b* Simrishamn, Sweden, 1941. *Educ:* Sch. of Econs, Gothenburg, Sweden (MBA 1964); Stanford Univ. Johnson Group, 1966–69; Sandvik AB: Group Controller, 1969–75; Pres. of Sandvik, USA, 1975–79; Exec. Vice Pres., 1979–80, Chm., 1983–2002, Hon. Chm., 2002–, Sandvik AB Sweden; Pres. and Chief Exec. Officer, Asea, 1980–87. Chm. Bd, Investor AB, 1997–2002 (Bd Mem., Providentia, subseq. Investor, 1987–2002); Bd Mem., General Motors, 1996–2009. Hon. Fellow London Business Sch., 1996. Hon. FREng 1998. Hon. DTech Linköping, Sweden, 1989; Hon. DEcons Gothenburg, 1991; Hon. DLaws Babson Coll., Mass, USA, 1995; Hon. DSc Cranfield, 1997; Hon. Dr UMIST with Manchester, 1999. *Publications:* Jag Vill Förändra Världen (autobiog.), 2011; Ledarskap, 2013. *Address:* 20 York Street, W1U 6PU.

BARNEWALL, family name of **Baron Trimlestown**.

BARNEWALL, Sir Reginald Robert, 13th Bt *cr* 1622; cattle breeder and orchardist at Mount Tamborine; *b* 1 Oct. 1924; *o s* of Sir Reginald J. Barnewall, 12th Bt and of Jessie Ellen, *d* of John Fry; *S* father, 1961; *m* 1st, 1946, Elsie Muriel (*d* 1962), *d* of Thomas Matthews-Frederick, Brisbane; three *d* (one *s* decd); 2nd, 1962, Maureen Ellen, *d* of William Joseph Daly, South Caulfield, Vic; one *s*. *Educ:* Xavier Coll., Melbourne. Served War of 1939–45, overseas with RAE, AIF. Served with Citizen Military Forces Unit, 8/13 Victorian Mounted Rifles, Royal Australian Armoured Corps, 1948–58 (Lieut, acting Major). Managing Dir, Southern Airlines Ltd of Melbourne, 1953–58; Founder, and Operations Manager, Polynesian Airlines, Apia, Western Samoa, 1958–62; Managing Dir, Orchid Beach (Fraser Island) Pty Ltd, 1962–71; Dir, Island Airways Pty Ltd, Pialba, Qld, 1964–68; owner and operator, Coastal-Air Co. (Qld), 1971–76; Dir and Vice-Chm., J. Roy Stevens Pty Ltd, to 1975. *Publications:* The Orchid Beach Story: tales of Fraser Island and Hervey Bay, 2006; (with B. W. Leamy) Wings over Samoa: a Polynesian story, 2008. *Heir: s* Peter Joseph Barnewall [*b* 26 Oct. 1963; *m* 1988, Kathryn Jane, *d* of Hugh Carroll; two *s* one *d*]. *Clubs:* United Service (Brisbane); RSL (Surfers Paradise); Royal Automobile (Queensland).

BARNICOAT, Thomas Humphry; Chairman, Somethin' Else, since 2008; *b* 21 Oct. 1952; *s* of John Barnicoat and Jane Barnicoat (*née* Selby, now Wright); *m* 1980, Katrina Noelle Chalmers; three *d*. *Educ:* Lycée Français de Londres; St John's Coll., Oxford (BA Hist. and French). Ed., Isis, 1976; joined BBC, 1977: grad. trainee, 1977–79; scriptwriter, TV News, 1979–81; producer and dir, TV Current Affairs, 1981–86; Producer, Crown TV, 1986; Dir, Public Affairs, Sotheby's, 1986–87; Producer, Business TV, 1987–89; Dir, Corporate Develt, 1990–93, Dep. Chief Exec., 1993–95, Broadcast Communications plc; Chief Exec., Broadcast Communications plc, subseq. Endemol UK, 1995–2004; Chief Operating Officer, Endemol Group, 2005–07. *Recreations:* swimming, driving, sleeping, military history. *E:* tbarnicoat@mac.com. *Clubs:* Reform, Hurlingham.

BARNIER, Michel Jean; Officier de la Légion d'honneur; Conseiller d'Etat, since 2005; Member, European Commission, 1999–2004 and 2010–14; *b* 9 Jan. 1951; *m* 1982, Isabelle Altmayer; two *s* one *d*. *Educ:* Ecole Supérieure de Commerce de Paris (Dip. 1972). Govt service, 1973–78. Mem. (RPR) for Savoie, Nat. Assembly, 1978–93; Minister of the Environment, France, 1993–95; Minister of State for European Affairs, 1995–97; Minister of Foreign Affairs, 2004–05; Minister for Agriculture, 2007–09. MEP, 2009–10. Corporate Vice Pres., Internat. Develt, Mérieux Alliance, 2006–07. Mem., 1973–99, Chm., 1982–99, Deptl Council of Savoie; Senator for Savoie, 1997–99; Pres., Senate Delegn for EU, 1998. Jt Pres., Organising Cttee, Olympic Games, Albertville and Savoie, 1987–92. *Publications:* Vive la politique, 1985; Chacun pour tous: le défi écologique, 1990; Atlas des risques majeurs, 1992; Vers une mer inconnue, 1994; Notre contrat pour l'alternance, 2001; Sortir l'Europe des idées reçues, 2005; Atlas for a Sustainable World, 2007; Who will Feed the World: a new agricultural revolution, 2008; Europe, Cards on the Table, 2008.

BARNISH, Alan Joseph; consultant, Cambridgeshire County Council, since 2003 (Chief Executive, 1997–2003); *b* 13 Oct. 1949; *s* of Sydney and Dora Barnish; *m* 1972, Elizabeth Sanders; one *s* one *d*. *Educ:* Leeds Univ. (BCom); IPFA. Mid Glam CC, 1975–90; Chief Exec. and Co. Treas., Powys CC, 1990–93; Chief Exec., Shropshire CC, 1993–97.

BARNSLEY, John Corbitt; company director; Chief Executive Officer, Business Process Outsourcing, PricewaterhouseCoopers, 1998–2001 (Managing Partner, UK, 1995–98); *b* 25 May 1948; *s* of William C. Barnsley, consultant thoracic surgeon, and Hilda C. Barnsley (*née* Robson); *m* (marr. diss.); one *s* one *d* (and one *d* decd); civil partnership 2006, James Ian Mackenzie. *Educ:* Heaton Grammar Sch., Newcastle upon Tyne; Newcastle upon Tyne Univ. (LLB 1st Cl. Hons 1969; Reynoldson Meml Prize). Joined Price Waterhouse, Newcastle, 1970: Sen. Tax Partner, UK, 1990–93; European Leader for Audit and Business Services, 1993–95; Joint Global Dir of Ops, 1996–98. Senior Independent non-executive Director: Northern Investors Co. PLC, 2005– (non-exec. Dir, 2002–); LMS Capital (formerly Leo Capital) plc, 2006–12; Grainger (formerly Grainger Trust) plc, 2011– (non-exec. Dir 2003–11); non-executive Director: American Appraisal Associates, 2003–; Hippodrom Casino, 2013–; Apperley Properties Ltd, 2013–; Chairman: American Appraisal Associate UK, 2005–; Drivestyle Ltd, 2014–; Coverbox Ltd, 2014–. *Recreations:* Chinese porcelain antique furniture. *Address:* Flat 21, Howard Building, Chelsea Bridge Wharf, SW8 4NN.

BARNSLEY, Victoria, (Hon. Mrs Nicholas Howard), OBE 2009; Executive Co Chairman, Castle Howard Estate Ltd, since 2015; *b* 4 March 1954; *d* of late T. E. Barnsley OBE and Margaret Gwyneth Barnsley (*née* Llewellin); *m* 1992, Hon. Nicholas Howard; on *d*, and one step *s*. *Educ:* University Coll. London (BA Hons English; Hon. Fellow, 2005) Univ. of York (MA French and English 19th Century Novel). Founder, and Chm. and Chie Exec., Fourth Estate Ltd, 1984–2000; CEO and Publisher, HarperCollins UK, 2000–13 HarperCollins Internat., 2008–13. Trustee: Tate Gall., 1998–2007; Tate Foundn, 2007–; Dir Tate Enterprises (formerly Tate Gall. Pubns) Ltd, 1998–. Trustee, Nat. Gall., 2004–07; Comr English Heritage, 2014–15. Mem. Council, Publishers' Assoc., 2001– (Pres., 2010–11).

BARNSTAPLE, Archdeacon of; *see* Butchers, Ven. Dr M. A.

BARON, Francine; High Commissioner for Dominica in the United Kingdom, 2012–14; Dominica; two *d*. *Educ:* Univ. of Wolverhampton (LLB). Called to the Bar: Middle Temple 1995; Dominica, 1996; barrister in private practice, 1996–2007, 2010–12; Attorney Gen. Dominica, 2007–10. *Recreations:* hiking, reading. *Club:* Rotary (Dominica).

BARON, Franklin Andrew Merrifield; Permanent Representative of Commonwealth o Dominica to United Nations and to Organisation of American States, 1982–95; Dominica High Commissioner to London, 1986–92; *b* 19 Jan. 1923; *m* 1973, Sybil Eva Francisc McIntyre. *Educ:* Portsmouth Govt Sch., St Mary's Acad., Dominica Grammar Sch. A. A Baron & Co.: entered firm, 1939; Partner, 1945; sole owner, 1978–. Member: Roseau Tow Council, 1945–47 and 1956–58; Legislative and Exec. Councils, 1954–61; Founder an Leader, United People's Party, 1954–56; Minister of Trade and Production, 1956–60; Chie Minister and Minister of Finance, 1960–61. Ambassador to USA, 1982–86. Chairman National Commercial Bank, 1986–90; Fort Young Hotel Co., 1986–89; The New Chronicle 1989–96 (Dir, 1984–96); Proprietor: Paramount Printers Ltd, 1992–; The Chronicle 1996–2013. Member: Public Service Commn, 1976–78; Electoral Commn, 1979–90 Dominica Boundaries Commn, 1979–90; Bd, Dominica Electricity Services, 1981–91 (Chm. 1983–91); Bd, Industrial Develt Corp., 1984–89; Chm., Dominica Public Library, 1985–89 Dominica Award of Honour, 2006. *Recreations:* horticulture, reading, travel. *Address:* 14 Cor Street, Roseau, Dominica. *T:* 4488151, 4480415, *Fax:* 4405295.

BARON, Prof. Jean-Claude, MD, ScD; FMedSci; Professor of Stroke Medicine Department of Clinical Neurosciences (formerly Departments of Medicine and Neurology) University of Cambridge, 2000–10, now Emeritus; Director of Research, INSERM U894 and Deputy Director, Centre for Psychiatry and Neuroscience, Paris 5 University, since 2010 *b* 25 March 1949; *s* of Marcel and Yolaine Baron (*née* Bonan); *m* 1974, Annik Arnette de l Charlonny; one *s* two *d*. *Educ:* Univ. of Paris (MD); Univ. of Cambridge (ScD 2010). Clin Lectr in Biophysics, 1979–82, then in Neurol., 1982–86, Univ. of Paris; Sen. Registrar i Nuclear Medicine, 1979–82, then in Neurol., 1982–86, Salpêtrière Hosp., Paris; Director: o Res., INSERM, France, 1986–2000; INSERM Res. Unit # 320, Caen, 1989–2000 Scientific Dir, CYCERON Neuroimaging Res. Centre, Univ. of Caen, 1987–2000; Hon Consultant in Neurology: Addenbrooke's Hosp., Cambridge, 2000–10; Ste-Anne Hosp. Paris, 2010–. FMedSci 2003. Johann Jacob Wepfer Award, Eur. Stroke Conf., 2005 Mérmain-Pelletier Biomed. Scis Prize, Acad. of Scis, France, 2014. *Publications:* (ed jtly) Th Ischemic Penumbra, 2007; contrib. numerous peer-reviewed articles to learned jls, incl Lancet, Brain, Annals of Neurol., Stroke; numerous book chapters and refereed abstracts *Recreations:* music (playing the guitar), classic blues, J. S. Bach, Mozart. *Address:* INSERM U894, Paris 5 University, 2 ter, rue d'Alésia, 75014 Paris, France.

BARON, John Charles; MP (C) Basildon and Billericay, since 2010 (Billericay, 2001–10); 21 June 1959; *s* of Raymond Arthur Ernest Baron and Kathleen Ruby Baron; *m* 1992, Thali Anne Mayson Laird; two *d*. *Educ:* Jesus Coll., Cambridge (MA). Capt., RRF, 1984–88 Director: Henderson Private Investors, 1988–99; Rothschild Asset Mgt, 1999–2001 Contested (C) Basildon, 1997. Shadow Health Minister, 2002–03; an Opposition Whip 2007–10. *Recreations:* financial journalism, gardening. *Address:* c/o House of Commons SW1A 0AA. *T:* (constituency office) (01268) 520765.

BARON, Dr (Ora) Wendy, OBE 1992; Director (formerly Curator), Government Ar Collection, 1978–97; *b* 20 March 1937; *d* of late Dr S. B. Dimson and Gladys Felicia Dimson CBE; *m* 1st, 1960, Jeremy Hugh Baron (marr. diss.; he *d* 2014); one *s* one *d*; 2nd, 1990, Davi Joseph Wyatt, *qv*. *Educ:* St Paul's Girls' Sch.; Courtauld Institute of Art (BA, PhD). Trustee Public Art Commns Agency, 1990–99; Contemp. Art Soc., 1997–2001; Arts Res. Ltd 1998–2004; NACF, 1998–2010. Has selected, researched and catalogued exhibitions including: Sickert, Fine Art Soc., 1973; Camden Town Recalled, Fine Art Soc., 1976; Th Camden Town Group, New Haven, USA, 1980; Late Sickert, Hayward Gall., 1981; Sickert Royal Acad., 1992, Amsterdam, 1993. FRSA 1993; FSA 2007. *Publications:* Sickert, 1973 Miss Ethel Sands and her Circle, 1977; The Camden Town Group, 1979; Perfect Moderns 2000; Sickert: paintings and drawings, 2006; articles and reviews in professional jls in the fiel of modern British art.

BARON-COHEN, Prof. Simon, PhD; FBA 2009; Professor of Developmenta Psychopathology, since 2001, and Director, Autism Research Centre, since 1997, Universit of Cambridge; Fellow, Trinity College, Cambridge, since 1995; *b* 15 Aug. 1958; *m*; three *c* *Educ:* New Coll., Oxford (BA Human Scis); University Coll. London (PhD Psychol.); Inst of Psychiatry, Univ. of London (MPhil Clin. Psychol.). Lectr, 1987–91, Sen. Lectr, 1991–94 Dept of Psychiatry, Univ. of London; Lectr, 1994–99, Reader, 1999–2001, Dept o Psychiatry, Univ. of Cambridge. *Publications:* (with P. Bolton) Autism: the facts, 1993 Mindblindness: essay on autism and the theory of mind, 1995; (ed jtly) Understanding Othe Minds, 1995; (ed jtly) Synaesthesia: classic and contemporary readings, 1996; (ed) Maladaptec Mind, 1997; (with P. Howlin) Teaching Children with Autism to Mind-read, 1998; (with M Robertson) Tourette Syndrome: the facts, 1998; The Essential Difference, 2003; Prenata Testosterone in Mind, 2004; Zero Degrees of Empathy: a new theory of human cruelty, 2011 contribs to jls incl. Eur. Jl Neurosci., Jl Child Psychol. and Psychiatry, Brain, Jl Amer. Acad Child and Adolescent Psychiatry, Infant Behaviour and Devel, Jl Autism and Develt Disorders. *Address:* Autism Research Centre, Section of Developmental Psychiatry, Universit of Cambridge, Douglas House, 18b Trumpington Road, Cambridge CB2 8AH.

BARÓN CRESPO, Enrique Carlos; lawyer; Member, European Parliament, 1986–200 (President, 1989–92); *b* Madrid, 27 March 1944; *m*; one *s*. *Educ:* Univ. of Madrid (LLL); Inst Católico de Dirección de Empresas (Lic. en Ciencias Empresariales); Ecole Supérieure des Sci Econ. et Commerciales, Paris (Dip.). Lectr in Agricl Econs, Inst. Nacional de Estudio Agrarios, Valladolid, and in Structural Econs, Univ. of Madrid, 1966–70; lawyer in privat practice, 1970–77. Mem. (PSOE), Congress of Deputies, Spain, 1977–87; spokesman o econ. and budgetary affairs, 1977–82; Minister of Transport, Tourism and Communications 1982–85. European Parliament: a Vice-Pres., 1986–89; Pres., Gp of Party of Europea Socialists, 1999–2004. President: Internat. European Movt, 1987–89; European Foundn fo Information Soc. Mem. Adv. Bd, Gold Mercury Internat., 2006–. *Publications:* Población y Hambre en el Mundo; El Fin del Campesinado; La Civilización del Automóvil; Europa 92: e rapto del futuro; Europe at the Dawn of the Millennium, 1997; Más Europa, ¡unida (memoirs), 2013 (Gaziel Prize, 2012); contribs on economic and social questions to major Spanish periodicals.

BARR, Clare Elizabeth; *see* Pelham, C. E.

BARR, David; a Metropolitan Stipendiary Magistrate, 1976–96; *b* Glasgow, 15 Oct. 1925; *s* of late Walter and Betty Barr; *m* 1960, Ruth Weitzman; one *s* one *d*. *Educ:* Haberdashers' Aske's Hampstead Sch.; Largs Higher Grade Sch.; Brookline High Sch., Boston, USA; Edinburgh Univ.; University Coll., London (LLB). Royal Navy, 1943–47. Solicitor, 1953; private practice, 1953–76 (Partner, Pritchard Englefield & Tobin). JP Inner London Area, 1963–76; Chm., Inner London Juvenile Panel, 1969–76; Dep. Chm., N Westminster PSD, 1968–76. Manager, Finnart House Sch., Weybridge, 1955–73 (Trustee, 1973–96, Chm., 1985–96). Mem., Moorfields and Whittington Hosp. NHS Local Regl Ethics Cttee, 2002–10. Pres., David Isaacs Fund, 1986–94. Trustee, London Action Trust, 2001–03. Gov., Haverstock Comp. Sch., 1997–2001; Chm. of Governors, Richard Cobden Primary Sch., 1997–2012. *Recreations:* collecting 'Alice', bridge. *Address:* 19 St Mark's Crescent, NW1 7TU. *Club:* Garrick.

BARR, Maj.-Gen. John Alexander James Pooler, CB 1993; CBE 1989; Engineer-in-Chief (Army), 1991–93; *b* 29 Jan. 1939. 2nd Lieut, RE, 1960; Lt-Col, 1978; GSO1 (DS) SC, 1978; Brig. 1983; Comdt, Royal Sch. of Mil. Engrg, Chatham, 1983–87; Dir of Army Staff Duties, MoD, 1987–89; DCS (Support), HQ Allied Forces Northern Europe, 1989–91; Maj.-Gen., 1991. Col Comdt, RE, 1993–2002. CompICE 1992. *Address:* c/o Lloyds, Cox's & King's Branch, PO Box 1190, 7 Pall Mall, SW1Y 5NA.

BARR, Kenneth Glen; Sheriff of South Strathclyde, Dumfries and Galloway at Dumfries, 1976–2008; *b* 20 Jan. 1941; *o s* of late Rev. Gavin Barr and Catherine McLellan Barr (*née* McGhie); *m* 1970, Susanne Crichton Keir (*d* 1996). *Educ:* Ardrossan Acad.; Royal High Sch.; Edinburgh Univ. (MA, LLB). Admitted to Faculty of Advocates, 1964. *Address:* c/o Sheriff Court House, Dumfries DG1 2AN.

BARR, Prof. Nicholas Adrian, PhD; Professor of Public Economics, European Institute, London School of Economics and Political Science, since 2002; *b* London, 23 Nov. 1943; *s* of Herman and Edith Barr; *m* 1991, Gillian Lee (*née* Audigier); two step *s*. *Educ:* London Sch. of Econs and Political Sci. (BSc (Econ) 1965; MSc (Econ) 1967); Univ. of Calif, Berkeley (PhD 1971). Lectr in Econs, 1971–88, Sen. Lectr in Econs, 1988–2000, Reader, 2000–02, LSE. Vis. Schol., Fiscal Affairs Dept, IMF, 2000. World Bank: Consultant, Europe and Central Asia Reg., Central and Southern Eur. Depts, HR Ops Div., 1990–92; Principal Author, World Develt Report, 1995–96. Gov., LSE, 1993–95, 1999–2005. Trustee, HelpAge Internat., 2004–12. FRSA 1997. *Publications:* (jtly) Self-Assessment for Income Tax, 1977; (with A. Prest) Public Finance in Theory and Practice, 6th edn 1979, 7th edn 1985; The Economics of the Welfare State, 1987, 5th edn 2012 (trans. French, Greek, Hungarian, Korean and Polish); (with J. Barnes) Strategies for Higher Education: the alternative White Paper, 1988; Student Loans: the next steps, 1989; (ed with D. Whynes) Current Issues in the Economics of Welfare, 1993; (ed) Labor Markets and Social Policy in Central and Eastern Europe: the transition and beyond, 1994 (trans. Hungarian, Romanian and Russian); (contrib.) World Development Report 1996: from plan to market, 1996 (trans. Arabic, Chinese, French, German, Japanese, Russian and Spanish); The Welfare State as Piggy Bank: information, risk, uncertainty and the role of the State, 2001 (trans. Japanese); (ed) Economic Theory and the Welfare State, Vol. I: theory, Vol. II: income transfers, Vol. III: benefits in kind, 2001; (with I. Crawford) Financing Higher Education: answers from the UK, 2005; (ed) Labor Markets and Social Policy in Central and Eastern Europe: the accession and beyond, 2005; (with P. Diamond) Reforming Pensions: principles and policy choices, 2008; (with P. Diamond) Pension Reform: a short guide, 2010; contrib. jls incl. Jl Econ. Lit., Econ. Jl, Economica, Oxford Rev. of Econ. Policy, Educn Econs, Econs of Transition, Internat. Social Security Rev., British Tax Rev., Public Money and Mgt, Jl Public Policy, Jl Social Policy, Political Qly. *Recreations:* cricket, computers, grandchildren, photography. *Address:* Economics Department, London School of Economics, Houghton Street, WC2A 2AE. *T:* (020) 7955 7482. *E:* N.Barr@lse.ac.uk. *Club:* Middlesex County Cricket.

BARR, Stephen; Managing Director, SAGE Publications Ltd, since 1996; President, SAGE International, since 2006; *b* Edinburgh, 7 Oct. 1956; *s* of James Barr and Jane Hepburn; partner, Susan Worsey; four *s*. *Educ:* Univ. of Oxford (BA 1st Cl. Hons Mod. Hist. 1978). Europa Publications, 1978–79; Cambridge University Press, 1979–83; Open University Press, 1983–86; SAGE: Sen. Commng Editor, 1986–87; Editl Dir, 1988–96; Exec. Vice Pres., SAGE Inc., 2001–; Director: SAGE India, 2006–; SAGE Asia Pacific, 2006–. Vice Pres., Publishers Assoc., 2015–16. Dir, Phoenix Cinema Trust, 2007– (Chm., 2009–). *Address:* SAGE Publications Ltd, 1 Oliver's Yard, 55 City Road, EC1Y 1SP.

BARR YOUNG, His Honour Gavin Neil; a Circuit Judge, 1988–2005; *b* 14 Aug. 1939; *s* of Dr James Barr Young and Elsie Barr Young (*née* Hodgkinson); *m* 1969, Barbara Elizabeth Breckon; two *d*. *Educ:* Loretto Sch., Musselburgh; Leeds Univ. (LLB). Called to the Bar, Gray's Inn, 1963; Member, North Eastern Circuit, 1964–88 (North Eastern Circuit Junior, 1968); a Recorder of the Crown Court, 1979–88. Part-time Legal Pres., Mental Health Rev. Tribunals (Restricted Patients Panel), 2001–10. *Recreations:* gardening, music. *Address:* Flaxbourne House, Great Ouseburn, York YO26 9RG.

BARRACLOUGH, Richard Michael; QC 2003; *b* 29 April 1953; *s* of Michael Alfred William Barraclough and Doreen Barraclough; *m* 1982, Lindsey Elsa Petronella Taylor; two *s* three *d*. *Educ:* St Michael's Coll., Leeds; St Catherine's Coll., Oxford (MA). Solicitor of the Supreme Court, 1978; called to the Bar, Inner Temple, 1980, Bencher, 2011. Legal Assessor: GMC, 1997–; GDC, 2000–. Chm., Disability Cttee, Bar Council, 2004–08. KHS. *Recreations:* motor-cycling, cellist, opera-singing, morganeering, sailing. *Address:* 6 Pump Court, Temple, EC4Y 7AR. *T:* (020) 7797 8400, *Fax:* (020) 7797 8401. *E:* facutvivas@hotmail.com; Stella Maris, Port Bannatyne, Island of Bute, Scotland. *Clubs:* Royal Automobile; Hog.

BARRADELL, John Bernard, OBE 2008; Town Clerk and Chief Executive, City of London Corporation, since 2012; *b* London, 20 Aug. 1960; *s* of Austin, (Jack), Barradell and Alice Mary Barradell (*née* O'Hara); *m* Marian, (Maggie), Martin; one *d*, and two step *d*. *Educ:* Bishop Challoner Sch.; University Coll. London (BA Hons Geog. 1981). Various tech. and mktg mgt roles in IT and communications industries, 1981–2002; Westminster City Council: Hd of Crime and Disorder Reduction, 2002–03, Asst Dir, 2003–04, Dir, 2004–06, Dept of Community Protection; Dep. Chief Exec., 2006–09; Chief Exec., Brighton and Hove CC, 2009–12. Clerk to Lieutenancy of E Sussex, 2010–13. Special constabulary, Metropolitan Police, 1981–2007: Comdt, Central Area, 1997–99; Chief Comdt, 1999–2007. Member: Adv. Bd, Ind. Police Complaints Commn, 2003–07; London Resilience Partnership, 2012– (Dep. Chm., 2013–); Film London Taskforce, 2012–. Founding Dir, London Apprenticeship Co., 2008–09. Chm., Caterham Barracks Community Trust, 2000–03. FRGS; FRSA. *Recreations:* recreational cycling, philately, social history, National Public Radio. *Address:* City of London Corporation, Guildhall, EC2P 2EJ. *Clubs:* Athenæum, Guildhall.

BARRAN, Sir John Ruthven, 5th Bt *cr* 1895, of Chapel Allerton Hall, Chapel Allerton, West Riding co. York, and of Queen's Gate, St Mary Abbots, Kensington, co. London; *b* 10 Nov. 1971; *o s* of Sir John Napoleon Ruthven Barran, 4th Bt, and Jane Margaret, *d* of Sir Stanley George Hooker, CBE, FRS; *S* father, 2010, but his name does not appear on the Official Roll of the Baronetage; *m* 2005, Helen Elizabeth, *er d* of Robert Ward, Westbury-sub-Mendip, Som; one *s*. *Heir:* *s* John Robert Nicholson Barran, *b* 23 Dec. 2009.

BARRASS, Gordon Stephen, CMG 1992; HM Diplomatic Service, retired; *b* 5 Aug. 1940; *s* of James and Mary Barrass; *m* 1st, 1965, Alice Cecile Oberg (*d* 1984); 2nd, 1992, Dr Kristen Clarke Lippincott, *qv*. *Educ:* Hertford Grammar Sch.; LSE (BSc (Econs)); SOAS (postgrad.). FCO, 1965–67; Chinese Language student, Hong Kong Univ., 1967–69; in Office of HM Chargé d'Affaires, Peking, 1970–72; Cultural Exchange Dept, FCO, 1972–74; UKMIS Geneva, 1974–78; Planning Staff, FCO, 1979–82; RCDS, 1983; seconded to MoD, 1984, Cabinet Office, 1987; Under Sec., 1991–93. Advr, Internat. Affairs, Coopers & Lybrand, then PricewaterhouseCoopers, 1993–2002. Mem., Bd, 2008–, Vis. Prof., 2009–, LSE IDEAS. Guest Curator, Brushes with Surprise exhibn, BM, 2002. *Publications:* The Art of Calligraphy in Modern China, 2002; The Great Cold War, 2009. *Recreations:* Chinese and Western art, classical archaeology, opera, travel, books. *Address:* 3 Mount Vernon, NW3 6QS.

BARRASS, Kristen Clarke; *see* Lippincott, K. C.

BARRATT, Francis Russell, CB 1975; Deputy Secretary, HM Treasury, 1973–82; *b* 16 Nov. 1924; *s* of Frederick Russell Barratt; *m* 1st, 1949, Janet Mary Sherborne (marr. diss. 1978); three *s*; 2nd, 1979, Josephine Norah Harrison (*née* McCririck) (*d* 2005). *Educ:* Durban High Sch., SA; Clifton; University Coll., Oxford. War Service, 1943–46; Captain, Intelligence Corps, 1946. Asst Principal, HM Treasury, 1949; Principal, 1953; First Sec., UK High Commission, Karachi, 1956–58; Asst Sec., 1962, Under Sec., 1968, HM Treasury. Dir, Amdahl (UK), 1983–93; Trustee, Amdahl (UK) Pension Fund, 1984–95. Mem., Rev. Bd for Govt Contracts, 1984–93. *Address:* Little Paddocks, Smallhythe Road, Tenterden, Kent TN30 7LY. *T:* (01580) 763734.

BARRATT, Gilbert Alexander; Master of the Supreme Court, Chancery Division, 1980–97; *b* 7 Aug. 1930; *s* of Arthur Walter Barratt and Frances Erskine Barratt (*née* Scott); *m* 1964, Fiona MacDermott; one *s* one *d*. *Educ:* Winchester; New Coll., Oxford. MA Modern History. Qualified as Solicitor, 1957; Partner: Stitt & Co., 1960–63; Thicknesse & Hull, 1963–67; Lee Bolton & Lee, 1967–78; Winckworth & Pemberton, 1978–80. *Recreation:* travel. *Address:* The Old School House, Clungunford, Craven Arms, Shropshire SY7 0QE. *Club:* Travellers.

BARRATT, Michael Fieldhouse; communications consultant; broadcaster on radio and television; Chairman: Michael Barratt Ltd, 1977–97; Commercial Video Ltd, since 1981; *b* 3 Jan. 1928; *s* of late Wallace Milner Barratt and Doris Barratt; *m* 1st, 1952, Joan Francesca Warner (marr. diss.; she *d* 1995); three *s* three *d*; 2nd, 1977, Dilys Jane Morgan; two *s* one *d*. *Educ:* Rossall and Paisley Grammar Sch. Entered journalism, Kemsley Newspapers, 1944; Editor, Nigerian Citizen, 1956; *television:* Reporter, Panorama, 1963; Presenter: 24 Hours, 1965–69; Nationwide, 1969–77; Songs of Praise, 1977–82; Reporting London, 1983–88; *radio:* Question-Master, Gardeners' Question Time, 1973–79. Dir, Career Best Ltd, 1995–97. Chm. of Trustees, People to Places, 1996–2009; Trustee, Temple Holdings, 1992–96. Rector, Aberdeen Univ., 1973. FRSA. Hon. LLD Aberdeen, 1975. *Publications:* Michael Barratt, 1973; Michael Barratt's Down-to-Earth Gardening Book, 1974; Michael Barratt's Complete Gardening Book, 1977; Golf with Tony Jacklin, 1978; Making the Most of the Media, 1996; Making the Most of Retirement, 1999; Mr Nationwide, 2012. *Recreations:* golf, cricket, listening. *Address:* 9 Andrews Reach, Bourne End, Bucks SL8 5GA. *T:* (01628) 530895. *E:* michael@mbarratt.co.uk.

BARRATT, Michael John; Principal, Priory School, Shrewsbury, since 2015; *b* Lancaster, 12 Oct. 1963; *s* of William Barratt and Muriel Barratt; *m* 1993, Susanna Busi; one *s* two *d*. *Educ:* Lancaster Royal Grammar Sch.; Liverpool Univ. (BA Mgt and Business Studies); Sheffield Poly. (PGCE); Univ. of Worcester (MSc Educn Mgt and Leadership); National Coll. of School Leadership (NPQH). Shrewsbury School: Teacher, 1988–2002; Hd of Business and Econs, 1991–2002; Housemaster, 1999–2003; Dep. Headmaster, 2003–08, Headmaster, 2008–14, Adams' Grammar Sch. Examr, UCLES, 1991–2005. Freeman: Haberdashers' Co., 2015; City of London, 2015. *Publications:* Understanding Industry, 1996; A Level Business Studies, 2001. *Recreations:* cycling (lycra shorts), running (mud preferred), tennis (modest), golf (big handicap), playing traditional jazz bass (no such thing as a wrong note). *Address:* The Yews, Montford Bridge, Shrewsbury, Shropshire SY4 1EB.

BARRATT, Nicholas David, PhD; FRHistS; Associate Director, Collections and Engagement, Senate House Library, University of London, since 2015; *b* Chiswick, London, 16 May 1970; *s* of late David Frank Ernest Barratt and of Daphne June Barratt (*née* Miller). *Educ:* Newland House Prep. Sch.; Hampton Sch.; King's Coll. London (BA 1st cl. Hons Hist. 1991; PhD Medieval Hist. 1996). FRHistS 2013. Reader advr and Co-ordinator of Academic Inductions, PRO, 1996–2000; Specialist Researcher, BBC, 2000–02, incl. House Detectives, House Detectives at Large, Invasion, One Foot in the Past and Britain's Best Buildings; Founder and CEO, Sticks Research Agency, 2000–13; Exec. Dir, FreeBMD, 2010–13; Associate, Ancestral Tourism Partnership, 2011–13; Hd, Medieval and Early Modern, Legal, Maps and Plans Teams, Nat. Archives, 2013–15. Co-Founder, 2005, CEO, 2007–12, Firebird Media. Ed. in Chief, Your Family Hist., 2010–13. Freelance broadcaster; television: on-screen document specialist, House Detectives, 1997–98; presenter: Small Piece of History, 2002; Family History Project, 2003; Secrets From the Attic, 2008; Brit Camp, 2008; specialist researcher: Wreck Detectives, 2003–04; Seven Wonders of the Industrial World, 2003; consultant and specialist researcher: Who Do You Think You Are?, BBC, 2004–07 (and co-presenter, 2004), SBS Australia, 2008–, RTÉ, 2008–09; Not Forgotten, 2007; co-presenter: History Mysteries, 2005; Hidden House History, 2006; So You Think You're Royal, 2007; Live The Dream as Seen on Screen, 2009; Missing Millions, 2011; Find My Past, 2011; radio: co-presenter, Tracing Your Roots, 2007–. Columnist, Daily Telegraph, 2005–08. Co-creator, Nation's Memorybank personal heritage website, 2007; Principal Consultant and Co-founder, National History Show, featuring Who Do You Think You Are? Live, 2007–12. Co-ordinator, Action 4 Archives, 2009–. Pres., Fedn of Family Hist. Socs, 2011– (Member: Exec. Cttee, 2005–06; Educn Cttee, 2010–); Member: Educn Cttee, British Assoc. for Local Hist., 2009–; Cttee for Public Hist., Historical Assoc., 2009–; Knowledge Transfer Adv. Gp, Fine Rolls Project, KCL, 2009–13; Televising History Adv. Bd, Univ. of Lincoln, 2009–10; Educn Cttee, Soc. of Genealogists, 2010–13; Council, Assoc. of Genealogists and Researchers in Archives, 2010–; Cttee, Community Archives and Heritage Gp, 2011–13; Educn Sub-Cttee, Magna Carta Trust, 2013–; Adv. Gp, Within the Walls, York, 2014–. Trustee: Soc. of Genealogists, 2011– (Treas., 2013–); Foundn for Medieval Genealogy, 2011–14; Vice Pres., AGRA, 2011–. Julian Bickersteth Meml Medal, Inst. of Heraldic and Genealogical Studies, 2008. *Publications:* Tracing the History of Your House, 2001, 2nd edn 2006; Receipt Rolls, 4, 5, 6, Henry III, 2003; Receipt Rolls, 7, 8, Henry III, 2007; (jtly) Who Do You Think You Are?, 2, 2005, 3, 2006; The Family Detective, 2006; (jtly) Genealogy Online for Dummies, 2006; The Who Do You Think You Are? Encyclopaedia of Family History, 2008; Lost Voices from the Titanic, 2009; Nick Barratt's Guide to Your Ancestors' Lives, 2010; Greater London: the story of the suburbs, 2012; The Forgotten Spy, 2015; *contributions to:* King John: new interpretations, 1999; Crises, Revolutions and Self-Sustained Growth, 1999; Family and Dynasty in Late Medieval England, 2003; English Government in the Thirteenth Century, 2004; Thirteenth Century X, 2005; The Story of Where You Live, 2005; Henry II: new interpretations, 2007; How to Trace Your Family History on the Internet, 2008; Researching Your Family History Online for Dummies, 2009; contrib. English Historical Rev., Internat. History Rev. *Recreations:* football (playing and managing), running (completed four London marathons), chess. *Address:* c/o HHB Agency Ltd, 6 Warwick Court, WC1R 5DJ. *E:* admin@sra-uk.com.

BARRATT, Peter Frederick; Speaker's Secretary, House of Commons, since 2011; *b* Forest Gate, London, 23 Nov. 1965; *s* of late Frederick Barratt and Mabel Jean Barratt (*née* John). *Educ:* Barking Abbey Comprehensive Sch., Barking. Registrar's Department, Bank of England: Grade 1 Clerk, Chief Registrar's Office, 1982–84, Dividend Office, 1984–86; Computer Officer, Computer Section, 1986–91; House of Commons: Department of Finance and Administration: Sen. Office Clerk, 1991–92; Computer Officer, 1992–93; Payroll Manager, 1993–96; Financial Accountant, 1996–98; Members' Allowances Co-ordinator, 1998–2000; Speaker's Office: Asst Sec. to Speaker, 2000–04 and 2005–11; Actg Speaker's Sec., 2004–05. *Recreations:* reading, theatre, music, genealogy, socialising, regular lager and wine-tasting. *Address:* Speaker's Office, House of Commons, SW1A 0AA. *T:* (020) 7219 4111, *Fax:* (020) 7219 6901. *E:* barrattpf@parliament.uk.

BARRATT, His Honour Robin Alexander; QC 1989; a Circuit Judge, 1998–2011; *b* 24 April 1945; *s* of Harold and Phyllis Barratt; *m* 1st, 1972, Gillian Anne Ellis (marr. diss. 1999); one *s* three *d*; 2nd, 2009, Linda D. Shepley. *Educ:* Charterhouse; Worcester Coll., Oxford (Exhibnr; BA Hons, MA). Harmsworth Entrance Exhibnr, 1965, Schol. 1969; called to the Bar, Middle Temple, 1970. Lectr in Law, Kingston Polytechnic, 1968–71; Western Circuit, 1971; Asst Recorder, 1990; a Recorder, 1993–98. Councillor (C), London Bor. of Merton, 1978–86. Chm., Chichester Cathedral Community Cttee, 2014. *Recreations:* fell walking, music. *Address:* Court Barn, Salthill Park, Fishbourne, Chichester, W Sussex PO19 3PS.

BARRÉ-SINOUSSI, Françoise Claire; Commandeur, Légion d'Honneur, 2009; Director, Regulation of Retroviral Infections Unit (formerly Retrovirus Biology Unit), since 1992 and Professor, since 1996, Institut Pasteur, Paris; *b* Paris, 30 July 1947; *d* of Roger Sinoussi and Jeanine Sinoussi (*née* Fau); *m* 1978, Jean-Claude Barré. *Educ:* Lycée Bergson; Univ. de Paris (DèsSc 1975). Post-doctoral Fellow, NIH, Bethesda, 1975–76; Institut Pasteur, Paris: Res. Asst, 1975–80, Asst Prof., 1980–86, Res. Dir, 1986–, Institut nat. de la santé et de la recherche médicale; Hd, Retrovirus Biology Lab., 1986–91; Mem., Exec. Cttee, 2001–04; Dep. Dir, Scientific Affairs of Internat. Network, 2001–05. Co-discoverer of AIDS virus, 1983. (jtly) Nobel Prize in Physiology or Medicine, 2008. *Address:* Regulation of Retroviral Infections Unit, Virology Department, Institut Pasteur, 25 Rue du Docteur Roux, 75724 Paris Cedex 15, France.

BARRELL, Dr Anthony Charles, CB 1994; FREng; Chief Executive, North Sea Safety, Health and Safety Executive, 1991–94; *b* 4 June 1933; *s* of William Frederick Barrell and Ruth Eleanor Barrell (*née* Painter); *m* 1963, Jean, *d* of Francis Henry Hawkes and Clarice Jean (*née* Silke); one *s* one *d*. *Educ:* Friars Sch., Bangor; Kingston Grammar Sch.; Birmingham Univ.; Imperial Coll. BSc Hons chem. eng. CEng; FREng (FEng 1990); FIChemE 1984; Eur Ing 1988. Chemist, Ministry of Supply, later War Dept, 1959–64; Commissioning Engineer, African Explosives and Chemical Industries, 1964–65; Shift Manager, MoD, 1965–66; Chemical Inspector, then Supt Specialist Inspector, HM Factory Inspectorate, 1966–78; Head of Major Hazards Assessment Unit, HSE, 1978–85; Dir, Technology, HSE, 1985–90; Chief Exec., N Sea Safety, Dept of Energy, 1990–91. Non-executive Director: BAA, 1994–2001; Lloyd's Register (formerly Lloyd's Register of Shipping), 1998–2009; Partner, TBP, 1994–2009; Special Advr, NATS, 2000–09. Member, Council: IChemE, 1989–94 (Pres., 1993–94); Royal Acad. of Engrg, 1994–97. Hon. DEng Birmingham, 1995. *Publications:* papers on assessment and control of major hazards, on offshore safety and on fire and explosion risks. *Recreations:* walking, reading, boating, golf. *T:* (01803) 752266. *Clubs:* Royal Dart Yacht (Cdre, 2000–03; Pres., 2010–); Churston Golf (Chm., 2004–06, 2009–11).

BARRELL, Prof. John Charles, PhD; FBA 2001; Professor of English, Queen Mary University of London, since 2013; *b* 3 Feb. 1943; *s* of John Ellis Barrell and Beatrice Mary Barrell; *m* 1st, 1965, Audrey Jones (marr. diss. 1975); two *s*; 2nd, 1975, Jania Miller (marr. diss. 1978); 3rd, 1992, Prof. Harriet Guest; one *d*. *Educ:* Trinity Coll., Cambridge (BA 1964; MA 1967); Univ. of Essex (PhD 1971). Lectr, Dept of Lit., Univ. of Essex, 1968–72; University of Cambridge: Lectr in English, and Fellow, King's Coll., 1972–85; Lectr, Newnham Coll., 1972–84; Professor of English: Univ. of Sussex, 1986–93; Univ. of York, 1993–2012. British Acad. Reader, 1991–93; Vis. Fellow, Inst. of Advanced Study, Indiana Univ., 2002; Schaffner Vis. Prof., Chicago Univ., 2002; Leverhulme Major Res. Fellow, 2002–04; Dist. Vis. Prof., Carleton Univ., Ottawa, 2009. FEA 2001. Hon. Fellow, King's Coll., Cambridge, 2013. Hon. DHL Chicago, 2008; Hon. DLitt Courtauld Inst. of Art, Univ. of London, 2010; Hon. Dip. Warsaw, 2013. *Publications:* The Idea of Landscape and the Sense of Place 1730–1840: an approach to the poetry of John Clare, 1972; The Dark Side of the Landscape: the rural poor in English painting 1730–1840, 1980; English Literature in History 1730–1780: an equal, wide survey, 1983; The Political Theory of Painting from Reynolds to Hazlitt, 1986; Poetry, Language and Politics, 1988; The Infection of Thomas De Quincey: a psychopathology of imperialism, 1991; The Birth of Pandora and the Division of Knowledge, 1992; Imagining the King's Death: figurative treason, fantasies of regicide 1793–1796, 2000; The Spirit of Despotism: invasions of privacy in the 1790s, 2006; *edited:* S. T. Coleridge, On the Constitution of the Church and State, 1972; (with John Bull) The Penguin Book of Pastoral Verse, 1972; Painting and the Politics of Culture: new essays on British Art 1700–1850, 1992; Exhibition Extraordinary!! Radical Broadsides of the Mid 1790s, 2001; (with Jon Mee) Trials for Treason and Sedition 1792–1794, 8 vols, 2006–07; (with Tim Whelan) The Complete Writings of William Fox, 2011; Edward Pugh of Ruthin, 1763–1813: 'a native artist', 2013. *Recreations:* gardening, print-collecting, walking, watching television. *Address:* School of English and Drama, Queen Mary University of London, Mile End Road, E1 4NS. *T:* (020) 7882 8524.

BARRETT, Angela Jane; illustrator; *b* 23 Aug. 1955; *d* of Donald and Dinah Patricia Barrett. *Educ:* Coborn Sch. for Girls, Bow; Maidstone Coll. of Art; Royal Coll. of Art. Mem., Art Workers' Guild. Illustrator, Jane Austen issue, Royal Mail stamps, 2013. *Publications:* illustrated: The King, the Cat and the Fiddle, by Yehudi Menuhin and Christopher Hope, 1983; Naomi Lewis, The Wild Swans, 1984; Susan Hill, Through the Kitchen Window, 1984; James Riordan, The Woman in the Moon, 1984; Christopher Hope, The Dragon Wore Pink, 1985; Susan Hill, Through the Garden Gate, 1986, Can it be true?, 1988 (Smarties Award); Naomi Lewis, The Snow Queen, 1988; Proud Knight, Fair Lady, trans. Naomi Lewis, 1989; Martin Waddell, The Hidden House, 1990 (W. H. Smith Award 1991); Susan Hill, The Walker Book of Ghost Stories, 1990; Snow White, re-told by Josephine Poole, 1991; Jenny Nimmo, The Witches and the Singing Mice, 1993; Susan Hill, Beware Beware, 1993; Geraldine McCaughrean, The Orchard Book of Stories from the Ballet, 1994; Angela McAllister, The Ice Palace, 1994; Candide, Voltaire, trans. Christopher Thacker, 1996; Naomi Lewis, The Emperor's New Clothes, 1997 (IBBY Award 2000); Josephine Poole, Joan of Arc, 1998; Rocking Horse Land and other classic tales of dolls and toys, compiled by Naomi Lewis, 2000; The Orchard Book of Shakespeare Stories, retold by Andrew Matthews, 2001; Sharon Darrow, Through the Tempests Dark and Wild, 2003; Josephine Poole, Anne Frank, 2005; Beauty and the Beast, re-told by Max Eilenberg, 2006; Paul Gallico, The Snow Goose, 2007; Leo Tolstoy, Anna Karenina, 2008; Tim Binding, Sylvie and the Songman, 2008; Laura Amy Schlitz, The Night Fairy, 2010; Robert Louis Stevenson, The Strange Case of Dr Jekyll and Mr Hyde, 2010 (Parrot Prize for Illustration, Fine Press Book Assoc., 2011); Clement C. Moore, The Night Before Christmas, 2012; Vivian French, The Most Wonderful Thing in the World, 2015; Charles Dickens, A Christmas Carol, 2015. *Recreations:* reading, needlework, roaming about London. *Address:* c/o Caradoc King, A. P. Watt Ltd, 12–26 Lexington Street, W1F 0LE. *T:* (020) 3214 0800. *Club:* Double Crown.

BARRETT, Prof. Ann, OBE 2010; MD; FRCP, FRCR; FMedSci; Professor of Oncology, School of Medicine, University of East Anglia, 2002–08, now Emeritus; *b* 27 Feb. 1943; *d* of Robert Douglas and Elsie Mary Brown. *Educ:* St Bartholomew's Hosp. (MD). Junior posts, St Bartholomew's, UCH, Middlesex, Mount Vernon and Westminster Hosps, 1968–76; Chef de Clinique, Hôpital Tenon, Paris, 1976; Sen. Lectr and Consultant, Royal Marsden Hosp., 1977–86; Prof. of Radiation Oncology, Glasgow Univ., 1986–2002; Dir, Beatson Oncology Centre, Glasgow, 1987–91. Member: Cttee on Med. Aspects of Radiation in the Envmt, NRPB, 1988–93; Molecular and Cellular Med. Bd, MRC, 1991–94; Nat. Radiotherapy Adv Gp, 2005–08; Psychosocial Gp, NCRI, 2005–08. Chm., Standing Scottish Cttee, 1992–95, Registrar, 2000–02, Dean, 2002–04, Faculty of Clin. Oncology, RCR; Pres., Scottish Radiological Soc., 1995–97; Pres., Eur. Soc. for Therapeutic Radiation Oncology, 1997–99. Trustee: The Big C Cancer Charity, 2008–11; Assoc. for Cultural Exchange, Cambridge, 2011–; Read Easy UK, 2014–. Founder FMedSci 1998. *Publications:* Practical Radiotherapy Planning, 1985, 4th edn 2009; Cancer in Children, 1986, 5th edn 2005; (ed jtly) Oxford Desk Reference: Oncology, 2011. *Recreations:* walking, travel, the Arts. *Address:* 23 Blenheim Way, Moreton-in-Marsh GL56 9NA.

BARRETT, Prof. Anthony Gerard Martin, FMedSci; FRS 1999; Glaxo Professor of Organic Chemistry, and Director, Wolfson Centre for Organic Chemistry in Medical Science, since 1993, and Sir Derek Barton Professor of Synthetic Chemistry, since 1999, Imperial College London; *b* Exeter, Devon, 2 March 1952; *s* of Claude E. V. Barrett and Margaret Teresa Barrett (*née* Bannon); naturalised US citizen. *Educ:* Imperial Coll. of Science and Technology (BSc 1st Cl. Hons Chemistry 1973; PhD 1975; DIC 1975; SRC Student 1973–75). Lectr, 1975–82, Sen. Lectr, 1982–83, Imperial Coll. of Science and Technology; Professor of Chemistry: Northwestern Univ., 1983–90; Colorado State Univ., 1990–93. Dir of Chemistry, 1998–2010, Dir of Sci. and Dir, 2000–10, Argenta Discovery (formerly ChemMedICa); Dir, iThemba Pharmaceuticals (S Africa), 2007–. Fellow, Japan Soc. for Promotion of Science, 1989. Mem., Chemicals Panel, Technology Foresight Prog., Office of Sci. and Technology, 1994. FMedSci 2003. Lectureships: Tilden, RSC, 1994; Backer, Univ of Groningen, 1996; Glaxo Wellcome, E Carolina Univ., 1998; Organic Divl Interim, Royal Aust. Chem. Inst., 1999; Eaborn-Cornforth, Sussex Univ., 1999; Allelix Dist., Queens Univ. Ont., 1999; Sir Robert Price, CSIRO, 1999; Novo Nordisk, Tech. Univ. of Denmark, 2000; Upper Rhine, 2001; AstraZeneca Pharmaceuticals, Ohio State Univ., 2002; Pattison, Univ of Western Ont., 2002; Boehringer Ingelheim, Univ. of New Orleans, 2002; Weissberger-Williams, Kodak, NY, 2002; Novartis Chemistry, Basel, 2002; Troisième Cycle, Geneva, Fribourg, Bern and Lausanne, 2002; GlaxoSmithKline and Celltech, Univ. of Bristol, 2003; Pedler, RSC, 2004; Mich Chemistry, 2005; Simonsen, RSC, 2006. Dist. Schol., Hope Coll. Mich, 2003. Meldola Medal, 1980, Harrison Medal, 1982, Corday-Morgan Medal, 1986; Award in Natural Products Chemistry, 2001, RSC; Armstrong Medal, Imperial Coll., 1981; Glaxo Wellcome Award, 2000; Innovation Award, Specialised Organic Sector Assoc., 2000; iAc Award for Applied Catalysis, 2001; Royal Soc. Wolfson Res. Merit Award, 2002; Charles Rees Award, RSC, 2010. *Address:* Department of Chemistry, Imperial College London, SW7 2AZ. *T:* (020) 7594 5766, *Fax:* (020) 7594 5805. *E:* agm.barrett@imperial.ac.uk.

BARRETT, David, OC 2005; OBC 2012; broadcaster, writer and political commentator on national and provincial media, since 1985; Premier and Minister of Finance, Province of British Columbia, Canada, 1972–75; *b* Vancouver, 2 Oct. 1930; *s* of Samuel Barrett and Rose (*née* Hyatt); father a business man in East Vancouver, after war service; *m* 1953, Shirley Hackman, West Vancouver; two *s* one *d*. *Educ:* Britannia High Sch., Vancouver; Seattle Univ (BA (Phil) 1953); St Louis Univ. (Master of Social Work 1956). Personnel and Staff Trng Officer, Haney Correctional Inst., 1957–59; also gained experience in a variety of jobs. Fellow, Inst. of Politics, Harvard Univ., 1987; Adjunct Prof., Simon Fraser Univ.; Visiting Scholar: McGill Univ., 1988; Western Washington Univ. Elected: MLA for Dewdney, Sept 1960 and 1963; to re-distributed riding of Coquitlam 1966, 1969 and 1972; Vancouver East by-election 1976, 1979; New Democratic Party Leader, June 1970–1984 (first Social Democratic Govt in history of Province); Leader, Official Opposition, British Columbia, 1970–72 and 1975–84; MP (NDP) Esquimalt-Juan de Fuca, 1988–93. Chm., BC Royal Commn on the Construction Industry, 1998–99. Dr of Laws, *hc*, St Louis Univ., 1974; Hon DPhil Simon Fraser Univ., BC, 1986. *Publications:* Barrett (memoirs), 1995. *Address:* 1179 Munro Street, Victoria, BC V9A 5P5, Canada.

BARRETT, Prof. Hazel Rose, PhD; Professor of Development Geography, since 2006 and Executive Director, Centre for Communities and Social Justice, since 2014, Coventry University; *b* London, 26 Aug. 1955; *d* of Leslie Peter Edgar Barrett and Hilda May Barrett; partner, Feike Pieter Twijnstra. *Educ:* Plume Comp. Sch., Maldon; Univ. of Sussex (BA Hons Geog. 1976); Univ. of Birmingham (MA W African Studies 1978; PhD Geog./W African Studies 1984); Inst. of Leaning and Teaching (Learning and Teaching Cert. 2001). FRGS 1992; CGeog 2009. Lecturer: in Econ. Geog. (pt-time), Garrett's Green Tech. Coll. Birmingham, 1984–85; in Human Geog. (pt-time), Coventry Poly., 1984–85; in Human Geog., Derbyshire Coll. of Higher Educn, 1985–92; in Develt Geog. (pt-time), Univ. of Sheffield, 1991–92; Coventry University: Sen. Lectr in Human Geog., 1992–98; Reader in Develt Geog., 1998–2005; Head: Geog. Subject Gp, 2001–04; Geog. and Envmtl Sci. Subject Gp, 2004–05; Geog., Envmtl Sci. and Disaster Mgt, 2005–10; Associate Dean for Applied Res., Faculty of Business, Envmt and Society, 2010–14. Geographical Association: Mem. 1991–; Pres., 2013–14; Editor, Geography, 1995–2001. *Publications:* The Marketing of Foodstuffs in The Gambia, 1400–1980: a geographical analysis, 1988; Population Geography, 1992; over 40 papers in academic jls. *Recreations:* gardening, travelling, eating chocolate. *Address:* Centre for Communities and Social Justice, Coventry University, Priory Street, Coventry CV1 5FB. *T:* (024) 7688 7688. *E:* h.barrett@coventry.ac.uk.

BARRETT, Dr Jane Margaret, OBE 2014; FRCP, FRCR, FRCPE; Consultant Oncologist, Royal Berkshire Hospital, Reading, 1991–2013; President, Royal College of Radiologists, 2010–13; Chair, Thames Valley Clinical Senate, since 2014; *b* Pembury, 25 April 1953; *d* of Leonard Sidney Frank Walter and Lilian May Walter (*née* Filson); *m* 1977, Simon Anthony Barrett; two *s* one *d*. *Educ:* Newbury Co. Girls' Grammar Sch.; Bristol Univ (BSc 1974; MB ChB 1977). FRCR 1988; FRCP 1996; FRCPE 2013. Hse Physician and Hse Surgeon, Bristol, 1977–78; Senior House Officer: Accident and Emergency, 1978–79; Pathol., Bristol, 1979–80; Registrar, Medicine, Royal Berks Hosp., 1980–82; Registrar, then Sen. Registrar (pt-time), Oncol., Oxford rotation, 1982–91; Med. Dir, Thames Valley Cancer Network, 2001–07. Registrar, 2006–08, Dean, 2008–10, Royal Coll. of Radiologists. Hon. FFRRCSI 2010; FAMS (Hon.) 2011. *Recreations:* travel, ski-ing, walking, cycling, family history. *E:* janembarrett@me.com.

BARRETT, John; *b* 11 Feb. 1954; *s* of Andrew Barrett and Elizabeth Mary (*née* Benert); *m* 1975, Carol Pearson; one *d*. *Educ:* Forrester High Sch., Edinburgh; Napier Poly., Edinburgh. Director: ABC Productions, 1985–; Edinburgh Internat. Film Fest., 1995–2001; EDI Group, 1997–99; Edinburgh and Borders Screen Industries, 1997–2001; Edinburgh Film House, 1997–2001. Mem. (Lib Dem) Edinburgh CC, 1995–2001. MP (Lib Dem) Edinburgh W 2001–10. Lib Dem spokesman on internat. develt, 2003–05. President: Scottish Liberal Club, 2010–; Edinburgh W Lib Dems, 2013–. Member: Adv. Council, Edinburgh Internat. Film Fest., 2001–; Microfinance Adv. Bd, RBS, 2009–12. *Recreations:* travel, film, theatre, music (playing and listening).

BARRETT, Rev. John Charles Allanson; Headmaster, The Leys School, Cambridge, 1990–2004; Principal, ACS (International), Singapore, 2004–09; Associate Minister, Wesley Methodist Church, Cambridge, 2011–15; *b* 8 June 1943; *s* of Leonard Wilfred Allanson

Barrett and Marjorie Joyce Barrett; *m* 1967, Sally Elisabeth Hatley; one *s* one *d*. *Educ:* Culford Sch.; Univ. of Newcastle upon Tyne (BA Hons); Fitzwilliam Coll., Cambridge; Wesley House, Cambridge. MA Cantab. Ordained Methodist Minister. Chaplain and Lectr in Divinity, Westminster Coll., Oxford, 1968–69; Asst Tutor, Wesley Coll., Bristol, 1969–71; Circuit Minister, Hanley Trinity Circuit, Stoke on Trent, and actg Hd of Religious Studies, Birches High Sch., Hanley, 1971–73; Chaplain and Hd of Religious and Gen. Studies, Kingswood Sch., Bath, 1973–83; Headmaster, Kent Coll., Pembury, 1983–90. Mem., HMC Cttee, 1997–98 (Sec., 1997, Chm., 1998, Eastern Div., HMC; Chm., HMC Working Party on Alcohol and Drug Abuse, 1996–99). World Methodist Council: Mem. Exec. Cttee, 1981– (Vice Chm., 2001–06; Chm., 2006–11; Pres., 2011); Chairman: Educn Cttee, 1991–2001; Prog. Cttee, 1992–96; Brit. Cttee, 1999– (Sec., 1986–97); Mem., Presidium, 1996–. Chm., Educn Commn, Methodist Ch, 2010–12. Vice-Pres., Internat. Assoc. of Methodist Schs, Colls and Univs, 1998–2006. Bloxham Project: Mem. Steering Cttee, 1986–92; Trustee, 2002–. Governor: Queenswood Sch., 1997–2004; Kingswood Sch., 2010–; ACS (Internat.) Singapore, 2010–. FRSA 1996. Hon. DD Florida Southern, 1992. *Publications:* What is a Christian School?, 1981; Family Worship in Theory and Practice, 1983; Methodist Education in Britain, 1990; Methodists and Education: from roots to fulfilment, 2000; (contrib.) Serving God with Heart and Mind, 2001; sections on Methodism in Encyc. Britannica Year Books, 1988–98. *Address:* Tudor Lodge, 151 High Street, Harston, Cambridge CB22 7QD. *T:* (01223) 872842. *E:* jcabarrett@aol.com.

BARRETT, John Edward, MBE 2007; tennis commentator and journalist; *b* 17 April 1931; *s* of Alfred Edward Barrett and Margaret Helen Barrett (*née* Walker); *m* 1967, (Florence) Angela (Margaret) Mortimer; one *s* one *d*. *Educ:* University College Sch., Hampstead; St John's Coll., Cambridge (MA History). National Schoolboy champion, 1948. Joined Slazengers as management trainee, 1957; Tournament Dir, 1975; Dir, 1978; Consultant, 1981–95 (latterly Dunlop Slazenger International). Tennis career: RAF champion, 1950, 1951; Captain of Cambridge, 1954; Nat. Indoor Doubles champion (with D. Black), 1953; Asian Doubles champion (with R. Becker), 1956; Davis Cup, 1956–57, non-playing Captain, 1959–62; Dir, LTA Trng Squad (Barrett Boys), 1965–68; qualified LTA coach, 1969; Founded: BP Internat. Tennis Fellowship, 1968–80 (and directed); BP Cup (21-and-under), 1973–80; Junior Internat. Series, 1975–79. Financial Times: tennis corresp., 1963–2006; crossword contribs, 1986–. TV tennis commentator: BBC, 1971–2006; Australian networks, 1981–2007; USA, 1985–89. Annual Award, Lawn Tennis Writers' Assoc., 2004; Ron Bookman Media Excellence Award, ATP Tour, 2006. *Publications:* Tennis and Racket Games, 1975; Play Tennis with Rosewall, 1975; 100 Wimbledon Championships: a celebration, 1986; (with Dan Maskell) From Where I Sit, 1988; (with Dan Maskell) Oh, I Say, 1989; Wimbledon: the official history of The Championships, 2001, 4th edn as Wimbledon: the official history, 2014; (jt ed and contrib.) Centre Court: the jewel in Wimbledon's crown, 2009 (Best Illustrated Book, British Sports Book Awards, 2010); Wimbledon: the complete singles draws (1877–2012), 2013; (ed and contrib.) World of Tennis, annually, 1969–2001. *Recreations:* music, theatre, reading, bridge. *Address:* All England Lawn Tennis Club, Church Road, Wimbledon, SW19 5AE. *Clubs:* All England Lawn Tennis (Vice-Pres.), International Lawn Tennis (Vice-Pres.), Queen's.

BARRETT, Lorraine Jayne; Member (Lab) Cardiff South and Penarth, National Assembly for Wales, 1999–2011; *b* 18 March 1950; *m* 1972, Paul Franklyn Barrett; one *s* one *d*. *Educ:* Porth County Sch. for Girls. Nursing, 1966–70; secretarial work, 1970–74; Personal and Political asst to Alun Michael, MP, 1987–99. Mem. (Lab), Vale of Glamorgan UA, 1995–99. Patron, Marie Curie Hospice, Penarth, 2006–. Humanist celebrant. *Recreations:* reading horror and thriller books, walking, cinema.

BARRETT, Matthew W., OC 1995; Chairman, Barclays PLC, 2004–06 (Group Chief Executive, 1999–2004); *b* Co. Kerry, 20 Sept. 1944. *Educ:* Christian Brothers Sch., Kells; Harvard Univ. (AMP 1981). Joined Bank of Montreal, 1962; Chief Operating Officer, 1987–89; Chief Exec. Officer, 1989–99; Chm., 1990–99. Dir, Harry Winston Diamond Corp., 2008–13. *Address:* c/o Barclays PLC, One Churchill Place, E14 5HP.

BARRETT, Michael Paul, OBE 1987; Chief Executive Officer, Great Britain Sasakawa Foundation, 2000–06; *b* 30 July 1941; *s* of William James Barrett and Irene (*née* Beynon); *m* 1966, Marie-Thérèse Françoise Juliette Lombard; two *s*. *Educ:* Westminster City Sch.; Univ. of Durham (BA Hons Classics). Asst Tutor in English to Overseas Students, Univ. of Birmingham, 1963–64; British Council: Asst Dir, Port Harcourt, 1964–65; Asst Rep., Addis Ababa, 1966–69; Educnl Television Officer, Tokyo, 1970–72; Dir, Films Dept, 1972–75; Educnl Technologist, Media Dept, 1975–77; Non-Formal Educn Specialist, Nairobi, 1977–80; Dep. Rep., Japan, 1980–84; Cultural Attaché, Washington, 1984–87; Dir, PR, 1987–88; Consultant, Goddard Kay Rogers & Associates Ltd, 1989; Man. Dir, GKR Japan Ltd, 1989–93; Dir, British Council, Japan, 1993–99. Vice-Pres., British Chamber of Commerce in Japan, 1992–99. Non-exec. Dir, S London & Maudsley NHS Trust, 2001–07. Mem. Council, Japan Soc., 2000–06; Mem. Culture Cttee, Asia House, 2001–09; Mem. Mgt Cttee, Sainsbury Inst. for Japanese Art & Culture, 2006–. Trustee: British Sch. in Tokyo, 1992–99 (Chm., 1992–95); Mosaic Clubhouse Internat., 2013–. FRGS 1989. Order of the Rising Sun (Japan), 2006. *Recreations:* music (viola), fishing, sailing, languages. *Address:* 25 Offerton Road, SW4 0DJ; Rosalbert, Roullens 11290, France.

See also P. J. Barrett.

BARRETT, Nicholas James; Chief Executive, Outward Bound Trust, since 2006; *b* 3 Sept. 1960; *s* of Sir Stephen Jeremy Barrett, *qv*; *m* 2001, Fiona Lewis; one *s* four *d*. *Educ:* Christ Church, Oxford (BA Mod. Hist.; PGCE). Volunteer, VSO, Bhutan and Kenya, 1983–87; Regl Organiser, ActionAid, 1987–89; Voluntary Service Overseas: Prog. Dir, W Kenya, 1989–91; Head, New Services, 1991–95; Dir, Recruitment, 1995–2000; Chief Exec., Ramblers' Assoc., 2000–05. *Recreations:* climbing small mountains, family, reading. *Address:* Outward Bound Trust, Hackthorpe Hall, Hackthorpe, Penrith, Cumbria CA10 2HX. *Clubs:* Alpine; Ausable (NY).

BARRETT, Paul Michael, CMG 2001; OBE 1993; Chairman (non-executive): Medreich PLC, 1997–2013; Medreich Ltd, Bangalore, India, 2005–13; *b* 9 Nov. 1945; *s* of Thomas Barrett and Gladys Barrett (*née* Cook); *m* 1970, Mary Elizabeth Tuthill; one *s* one *d*. *Educ:* Sir Roger Manwood's Sch., Sandwich; Grey Coll., Univ. of Durham (BA Hons Modern Hist. 1967); Templeton Coll., Oxford (AMP 1985). VSO, Starene Boys' Centre, Nairobi, 1968–69; Beecham Gp Ltd, 1969–76: Gen. Manager, Nigeria, 1973–74; Regl Mktg Manager, Africa/Caribbean, 1974–76; Nat. Sales Manager, Servier Labs, 1976–78; Manager, Francophone Africa, Beecham Gp, 1978–89, Smithkline Beecham, 1989–93; Dir and Vice-Pres., Africa, Smithkline Beecham, 1993–2000. Chm., Microsulis PLC, 1999–2002. Chm., Tropical Africa Adv. Gp, DTI, 1989–2000. Chm., British Francophone Business Gp, 1981–88. Vice-Chm., Harpsden Hall Trust, 2002–; Chm., John Hodges' Trust for Harpsden Hall, 2005–08; Mem. Cttee, 2001–02, Chm., 2002–, S Oxon Mencap; Mem., Major Gifts Cttee, African Med. and Res. Foundn, 2001–03; Chm., Chiltern Centre for Disabled Children Ltd, 2003–. Churchwarden, St Margaret's Ch, Harpsden, 2001–07. *Recreations:* reading, theatre, opera, walking, keep fit. *Address:* 1 Leicester Close, Henley-on-Thames, Oxon RG9 2LD. *T:* (01491) 578051. *E:* paulandmarybarrett@tiscali.co.uk.

BARRETT, Rt Rev. Peter Francis; Bishop of Cashel and Ossory, 2003–06; *b* 8 Feb. 1956; *s* of Alexander Barrett and Kathleen (*née* Aldred); *m* 1980, Anne (*née* Davidson) (marr. diss. 2011); two *s* one *d*. *Educ:* Avoca Kingstown Sch.; TCD (BA 1978, MA 1981, DipTh 1981, MPhil 1984). Ordained deacon, 1981, priest, 1982; Curate Assistant: Drumachose, 1981–83; St Ann and St Mark with St Stephen, 1983–85; Rector: Conwal Union with Gartan, 1985–90; St George's, Belfast, 1990–94; Dean of Residence and Chaplain, TCD, 1994–98; Dean of Waterford, 1998–2003. Reviews Ed., Search: a C of I Jl, 1994–98. *Publications:* Love's Redeeming Work (Irish Consultant), 2001; The Measure and the Pledge of Love, 2003; Symbols of Service, 2004; contrib. jl Scripture in the Church. *Recreations:* music, ornithology, sport, especially hockey. *Address:* 4 Pembroke Gardens, Ballsbridge, Dublin 4, Ireland. *Club:* Monkstown Hockey.

BARRETT, Dr Peter John, CBE 2006; DL; Chair: NHS Independent Reconfiguration Panel, 2003–12; Nottingham University Hospitals NHS Trust, 2006–13; *b* London, 12 Jan. 1947; *s* of William James and Irene Barrett; *m* 1970, Rosamund Briggs; two *s*. *Educ:* Westminster City Grammar Sch.; King's Coll. Hosp., London Univ. (MB BS 1970). MRCS, LRCP 1970. Principal in Gen. Practice, Nottingham, 1975–2006. Chairman: Nottingham Local Med. Cttee, 1990–98; Nottingham HA, 1998–99; Trent Reg. NHS Exec., 1999–2001. Chm., Regl Employer Engagement Gp (formerly Regl Employer Adv. Bd), E Midlands RFCA, 2012– (Mem., 2009). Chm., Midlands and E Reg., Eur. Inst. of Governance Awards, 2014–. DL Notts, 2010. FRSA. Hon. DM Nottingham, 2014. *Recreations:* playing the 'cello, listening to classical music. *E:* peter@barrett.uk.com.

BARRETT, Richard Martin Donne, CMG 2013; OBE 1992; counter-terrorism and violent extremism consultant; pundit; Senior Vice-President, Special Projects, Soufan Group, New York, since 2013; *b* Taplow, 14 June 1949; *s* of Martin and Joan Barrett; *m* 1st, 1974, Irene Hogg (marr. diss. 2004); two *s* one *d* (and one *s* decd); 2nd, 2008, Lucy Sisman. *Educ:* Ampleforth Coll.; University Coll., Oxford (MA). Served British Govt, incl. in Canada, Turkey, USA and Jordan, 1975–2004; Co-ordinator, Al-Qaida and Taliban Monitoring Team, UN, NY, 2004–13. Board Member: Internat. Centre for Counter Terrorism, The Hague; Global Center on Cooperative Security, Washington; Centre for Res. and Security Studies, Islamabad. Associate Fellow, RUSI, 2013–; Fellow, New America Foundn, Washington, 2013–. *Publications:* book chapters, papers and articles related to counter terrorism, counter radicalisation and reintegration. *E:* rmdbarrett@gmail.com.

BARRETT, Prof. Spencer Charles Hilton, PhD; FRS 2004; FRSC; Professor of Evolutionary Biology (formerly of Botany), since 1977, Canada Research Chair in Evolutionary Genetics, since 2001, and University Professor, since 2008, University of Toronto; *b* 7 June 1948; *s* of Arthur Charles and Doris Barrett; *m* 1973, Suzanne Whittaker; two *s*. *Educ:* Univ. of Reading (BSc Hons (Horticultural Botany) 1971); Univ. of Calif, Berkeley (PhD (Botany) 1977). FRSC 1988. Member, Expert Panel: on Predicting Invasions, Nat. Res. Council, USA, 1999–2001; on Future of Food Biotechnol., RSC, 2000–01. Pres., Canadian Soc. for Ecol. and Evolution, 2010–12; Member: British Ecol Soc.; Soc. for Study of Evolution (Vice Pres. (N America), 2010–12); Botanical Soc. of America; European Evolutionary Biol. Soc. For. Hon. Mem., Amer. Acad. of Arts and Scis, 2009. Ed.-in-Chief, Procs of Royal Soc. Series B, 2015. Sewall Wright Award, Amer. Soc. of Naturalists, 2008; Flavelle Medal, RSC, 2014. *Publications:* (ed) Evolution and Function of Heterostyly, 1992; (ed) Floral Biology: studies on floral evolution in animal-pollinated plants, 1996; (ed) Ecology and Evolution of Flowers, 2006; (ed) Major Evolutionary Transitions in Flowering Plant Reproduction, 2008; numerous book chapters and articles in learned jls. *Recreations:* plant exploration, travel, gardening, photography, music of Brian Eno. *Address:* 182 Humbervale Boulevard, Toronto, ON M8Y 3P8, Canada. *T:* (416) 2341871; Department of Ecology and Evolutionary Biology, University of Toronto, 25 Willcocks Street, Toronto, ON M5S 3B2, Canada. *T:* (416) 9784151, *Fax:* (416) 9785878. *E:* spencer.barrett@utoronto.ca.

BARRETT, Sir Stephen (Jeremy), KCMG 1991 (CMG 1982); HM Diplomatic Service, retired; Ambassador to Poland, 1988–91; *b* 4 Dec. 1931; *s* of late W. P. Barrett and Dorothy Barrett; *m* 1958, Alison Mary Irvine; three *s*. *Educ:* Westminster Sch.; Christ Church, Oxford (MA). FO, 1955–57; 3rd, later 2nd Sec., Political Office with Middle East Forces, Cyprus, 1957–59; Berlin, 1959–62; 1st Sec., FO, 1962–65; Head of Chancery, Helsinki, 1965–68; 1st Sec., FCO, 1968–72; Counsellor and Head of Chancery, Prague, 1972–74; Head of SW European Dept, FCO, later Principal Private Sec. to Foreign and Commonwealth Sec., 1975; Head of Science and Technology Dept, FCO, 1976–77; Fellow, Center for Internat. Affairs, Harvard, 1977–78; Counsellor, Ankara, 1978–81; Head of British Interests Section, Tehran, 1981; Asst Under-Sec. of State, FCO, 1981–84; Ambassador to Czechoslovakia, 1985–88. *Recreations:* family, reading, moderate exercise. *Address:* 9 Redgrave Court, Patron's Way East, Denham Garden Village, Uxbridge UB9 5NT. *Club:* Ausable (St Huberts, NY).

See also N. J. Barrett.

BARRETT-LENNARD, Sir Peter John, 7th Bt *cr* 1801, of Belhus, Essex; *b* 26 Sept. 1942; *s* of Roy Barrett-Lennard and Joyce Christine Elizabeth (*née* Drinkwater); *S* cousin, 2007, but his name does not appear on the Official Roll of the Baronetage; *m* 1979, Sonja (separated), *d* of Vladimir Belačič, Zagreb; one *s*; partner, Phuong Xuan Ho; one *d*. *Heir:* *s* Simon James Barrett-Lennard, *b* 12 Aug. 1980.

BARRICK, Jonathan; Chief Executive Officer, Stroke Association, since 2004; *b* 14 Jan. 1954; *s* of Jack William Barrick and Audrey Joan Barrick (*née* Cook); *m* 1988, Susan Skinner; two *d*; partner, Olivia Belle. *Educ:* Davenant Foundn Grammar Sch.; Bath Univ. (BSc Sociol. 1978); Kent Univ.; Middlesex Univ. (PG Dip. Housing 1993); Henley Mgt Coll. (MBA 2002). FCMI. DHSS, 1979–81; Inspector Taxes, 1981–83; London Bor. of Haringay, 1983–89; RNIB, 1989–2004, Dir, Community Services, 1996–2004. Mem. Bd, World Stroke Orgn, 2009–. Trustee: Pocklington Trust, 1997–2004; Neurological Alliance, 2004–09, 2011–13; AMRC, 2006–10; Stroke Alliance for Europe, 2006–12 (Pres., 2015–). *Publications:* (jtly) Building Sight, 1995; contribs to jls in vision impairment and inclusive access. *Recreations:* Tottenham Hotspur FC, travel, family interests, studying leadership and strategy issues. *Address:* The Stroke Association, Stroke Association House, 240 City Road, EC1V 2PR. *T:* (020) 7566 0305. *E:* Jon.Barrick@stroke.org.uk.

BARRIE, (Charles) David (Ogilvy), CBE 2010; campaigner and author; Project Adviser, Two Temple Place, 2009–13; Chairman, Make Justice Work, 2010–13; *b* 9 Nov. 1953; *s* of late Alexander Ogilvy Barrie and Patricia Mary Tucker; *m* 1978, Mary Emily, *d* of Rt Hon. Sir Ralph Gibson, PC; two *d*. *Educ:* Bryanston Sch.; Brasenose Coll., Oxford (Exp. Psych. and Phil.). HM Diplomatic Service, 1975; served FCO 1975–76; Dublin, 1976–80; seconded to Cabinet Office, 1980–81; FCO, 1981–87; transf. Cabinet Office, 1988; seconded to Japan Festival 1991, as Exec. Dir, 1989–92; resigned from Cabinet Office, 1992. Dir, The Art Fund, 1992–2009. Advr, William Morris Gall. redevelt project, 2009–11. Bd Mem., MLA (formerly Resource: Council for Mus, Archives, and Libraries), 2000–06 (Mem., Acceptance-in-Lieu Panel, 2000–06). Hon. Res. Fellow, Univ. of Leicester, 2010–. Companion, Guild of St George, 1992 (Dir, 1992–2004). Trustee: Civitella Ranieri Foundn, 1995–99; Ruskin Foundn, 1996–; Baltic Centre for Contemporary Art, 2014–; Founder and Chm., Ruskin To-Day, 1999–. Trustee, Butterfly Conservation, 2003–07. FRIN 2015. *Publications:* (ed) John Ruskin's Modern Painters, 1987, 2nd edn 2000; Sextant: a voyage guided by the stars and the men who mapped the world, 2014; numerous articles and reviews. *Recreations:* sailing, entomology, celestial navigation. *Address:* 13 Wingate Road, W6 0UR. *E:* cdobarrie@gmail.com. *Clubs:* Arts; Royal Cruising; Emsworth Sailing.

BARRIE, Herbert, MD, FRCP, FRCPCH; Consultant Paediatrician, Charing Cross Hospital, 1966–84 (Physician in charge, 1984–86); *b* 9 Oct. 1927; *m* 1963, Dinah Barrie, MB, BS, FRCPath; one *s* one *d*. *Educ:* Wallington County Grammar School; University College and Med. Sch., London. MB, BS 1950; MD 1952; MRCP 1957, FRCP 1972; FRCPCH 1997. Registrar, Hosp. for Sick Children, Gt Ormond St, 1955–57; Research Fellow, Harvard

Univ., Children's Med. Center, 1957; Sen. Registrar and Sen. Lectr, Dept of Paediatrics, St Thomas' Hosp., 1959–65. Vis. Prof., Downstate Univ. Med. Center, NY, 1976. Member: British Assoc. of Perinatal Paediatrics; Vaccine Damage Tribunal Panel. *Publications:* contribs to books and jls on paediatric and neonatal topics, esp. resuscitation of newborn and neonatal special care. *Recreations:* tennis, writing, wishful thinking. *Address:* 3 Burghley Avenue, New Malden, Surrey KT3 4SW. *T:* (020) 8942 2836.

BARRIE, Lesley; General Manager and Member, Tayside Health Board, 1993–97, retired; *b* 20 Sept. 1944. *Educ:* Glasgow High Sch. for Girls; Univ. of Glasgow (DPA). MHSM; DipHSM. NHS admin. trainee, 1963–66; hosp. mgt, 1966–77; District General Manager: Inverclyde Dist, 1977–81; Glasgow SE, 1981–83; Dir, Admin Services, Glasgow Royal Infirmary, Royal Maternity Hosp. and Glasgow Dental Hosp., 1983–87; Unit Gen. Manager, Stirling Royal Infirmary, 1987–91; Gen. Manager and Mem., Forth Valley Health Bd, 1991–93. Chm., Social Security Appeal Tribunals, 1978–90; Mem., Industrial Tribunal, 1992–98. Hon. Sen. Lectr, Dept of Epidemiology and Public Health, Dundee Univ., 1994–97. MCMI. *Recreations:* table tennis (Scottish International, 1963–70), badminton, reading.

BARRIE, Peter Anthony Stanfield; His Honour Judge Barrie; a Circuit Judge, since 2010; *b* Oxford, 12 March 1953; *m* 1980, Helen; three *s* one *d*. *Educ:* Kingswood Sch., Bath; New Coll., Oxford. Called to the Bar, Middle Temple, 1976; in practice as barrister, Guildhall Chambers, Bristol, 1976–2010; a Recorder, 1999–2010. *Publications:* Personal Injury Law, 1999, 2nd edn 2005. *Address:* Shrewsbury Crown Court, The Shirehall, Abbey Foregate, Shrewsbury SY2 6LU.

BARRIE, (Thomas) Scott; Member (Lab) Dunfermline West, Scottish Parliament, 1999–2007; *b* 10 March 1962; *s* of William Barrie and Helen McBain Barrie (*née* Scott). *Educ:* Auchmuty High Sch., Glenrothes; Edinburgh Univ. (MA Hons 1983); Stirling Univ. (CQSW 1986). Fife Regional Council: Social Worker, 1986–90; Sen. Social Worker, 1990–91; Team Manager, Social Work Dept, 1991–96; Team Leader, Social Work Service, Fife Council, 1996–99. Mem. (Lab), Dunfermline DC, 1988–92. *Recreations:* hill walking, supporter of Dunfermline Athletic.

BARRINGTON, Sir Benjamin, 8th Bt *cr* 1831, of Limerick; *b* 23 Jan. 1950; *s* of Major John William Barrington and his 1st wife, Annie, *d* of Florian Wetten; *S* cousin, 2003, but his name does not appear on the Official Roll of the Baronetage; *m* 1980, Carola Christel Mogck; one *s* one *d*. *Heir: s* Patrick Benjamin Barrington, *b* 5 May 1988. *Address:* 44 Cherovan Drive SW, Calgary, AB T2V 2P2, Canada.

BARRINGTON, Donal; Judge of the Supreme Court of Ireland, 1996–2000; President, Irish Commission on Human Rights, 2000–02; *b* 28 Feb. 1928; *s* of Thomas Barrington and Eileen Barrington (*née* Bracken); *m* 1959, Eileen O'Donovan; two *s* two *d*. *Educ:* Belvedere Coll.; University Coll., Dublin (MA, LLB). Called to the Bar, King's Inns, 1951, Bencher, 1978; called to Inner Bar, 1968; Judge, High Court of Ireland, 1979–89; Judge, Court of First Instance of European Communities, 1989–96. Chairman: Commn on Safety at Work, 1983–84; Stardust Compensation Tribunal, 1985–86. Chm., Gen. Council of the Bar, Ireland, 1977–79. Pres., Irish Centre for European Law, 1996–2000. Hon. LLD NUI, 2009. *Publications:* contribs to learned jls. *Recreations:* music, gardening. *Address:* 8 St John's Park, Dun Laoghaire, Co. Dublin, Republic of Ireland. *T:* (1) 2841817.

BARRINGTON, Edward John, (Ted); Irish Ambassador to the Court of St James's, 1995–2001; *b* 26 July 1949; *s* of Edward Barrington and Sarah Barrington (*née* Byrne); *m* 1972, Clare O'Brien; one *s*. *Educ:* University College Dublin (BA). Entered Irish Diplomatic Service, 1971; 3rd Sec., 1971, 1st Sec., 1973; Perm. Rep. to EEC, 1975–80; 1st Sec., Press and Information, 1980; Counsellor, Political, 1980–85; Assistant Secretary: Admin, 1985–89; EC Div., 1989–91; Political Div. and Political Dir, 1991–95; Dep. Sec., 1995. Vis. Prof., Res. Inst. for Irish and Scottish Studies, Univ. of Aberdeen; Vis. Res. Fellow, Inst. for British-Irish Studies, UC Dublin. DUniv N London. *Recreations:* bird-watching, cinema, hiking, theatre, jazz, gardening. *Address:* Sun Villa, Mauritiustown, Rosslare Strand, Co. Wexford, Ireland. *T:* (53) 9132880.

BARRINGTON, Jonah, MBE; Consultant, England Squash (formerly Squash Rackets Association), since 1996; *b* 29 April 1941; *m* 1973, Madeline Ibbotson (*née* Wooller); two *s*. *Educ:* Cheltenham Coll.; Trinity Coll., Dublin. Professional squash rackets player, 1969–83; winner: British Open, 1967–68, 1970–73; Egyptian Open, 1968; Canadian Open, 1983. Coach, English Squash Rackets Team; Dir of Excellence, 1988–93, Pres., 1994, Squash Rackets Assoc. *Publications:* On Squash, 1973; (jtly) Tackle Squash, 1977; Murder in the Squash Court, 1982.

BARRINGTON, Sir Nicholas (John), KCMG 1990 (CMG 1982); CVO 1975; HM Diplomatic Service, retired; Ambassador, 1987–89, subsequently High Commissioner, 1989–94, to Pakistan; non-resident Ambassador to Afghanistan, 1994; *b* 23 July 1934; *s* of late Eric Alan Barrington and Mildred (*née* Bill). *Educ:* Repton (Pres., Old Reptonian Soc., 1995–96); Clare Coll., Cambridge (MA 1957; Hon. Fellow 1992). HM Forces, RA, 1952–54. Joined Diplomatic Service, 1957; Tehran (language student), 1958; Oriental Sec., Kabul, 1959; FO, 1961; 2nd Sec., UK Delegn to European Communities, Brussels, 1963; 1st Sec., Rawalpindi, 1965; FO, 1967; Private Sec. to Permanent Under Sec., Commonwealth Office, April 1968; Asst Private Sec. to Foreign and Commonwealth Sec., Oct. 1968; Head of Chancery, Tokyo, 1972–75 (promoted Counsellor and for a period apptd Chargé d'Affaires, Hanoi, 1973); Head of Guidance and Information Policy (subsequently Information Policy) Dept, FCO, 1976–78; Counsellor, Cairo, 1978–81; Minister and Head of British Interests Section, Tehran, 1981–83; Supernumerary Ambassador attached to UK Mission to UN, NY, for Gen. Assembly, autumn 1983; Co-ordinator for London Econ. Summit, 1984; Asst Under-Sec. of State (Public Depts), FCO, 1984–87. Chm., Management Cttee, Southwold Summer Theatre, 1995–2001; Co-Pres., Clare Coll. Develt Prog., 1995–2002; Member: Develt Cttee, Cambridge Univ. Divinity Faculty, 1994–97; Standing Cttee on Schs and Insts, British Acad., 1995–96; Special Projs Cttee, Sadler's Wells Th., 1996–2001; Friends of New River Walk, Islington, 1995–2002; Cttee to restore spire of St Stephen's Ch, Canonbury, 1998–2002. Member: Exec. Cttee, Asia House, 1994–2000 (originator and Exhibn Comr, 50 Years of Painting and Sculpture in Pakistan, Brunei Gall., 2000); Pakistan Soc., 1995–2002 (acting Chm., 2001; Hon. Vice Pres.); Council: Royal Soc. for Asian Affairs, 1995–2000; British Inst. of Persian Studies, 1996–2001 (Mem., Adv. Council, 2002–09); British Assoc. for Cemeteries in S Asia, 1996–2014. Trustee: Ancient India and Iran Trust, 1993–; British Empire and Commonwealth Mus., Bristol, 1996–2013 (first Pres. of Friends, 1996–2002); Patron, Hindu Kush Conservation Assoc., 1995–2000. Mem., Order of St Etheldreda, Ely Cathedral, 1996–. FRSA 1984. 3rd Cl., Order of the Sacred Treasure, Japan, 1975. *Publications:* (foreword and asst ed.) Old Roads, new Highways: 50 years of Pakistan, 1997; (jtly) A Passage to Nuristan, 2005; Envoy, 2013; Nicholas meets Barrington, 2013. *Recreations:* theatre, drawing, prosopography, Persian poetry. *Address:* 2 Banhams Close, Cambridge CB4 1HX. *T:* (01223) 360802. *Clubs:* Athenæum, Nikaean.

BARRINGTON, Ted; *see* Barrington, E. J.

BARRINGTON BROWN, Amanda Margaret; *see* Tincknell, A. M.

BARRINGTON-WARD, Rt Rev. Simon, KCMG 2001; Bishop of Coventry, 1985–97; Hon. Assistant Bishop, Diocese of Ely, since 1998; Prelate of the Most Distinguished Order of St Michael and St George, 1989–2005; *b* 27 May 1930; *s* of Robert McGowan Barrington-Ward and Margaret Adele Barrington-Ward; *m* 1963, Jean Caverhill Taylor; two *d*. *Edu* Eton; Magdalene Coll., Cambridge (MA; Hon. Fellow, 1987). Lektor, Free Univ., Berli 1953–54; Westcott House, Cambridge, 1954–56; Chaplain, Magdalene Coll., Cambridg 1956–60; Asst Lectr in Religious Studies, Univ. of Ibadan, 1960–63; Fellow and Dean Chapel, Magdalene Coll., Cambridge, 1963–69; Principal, Crowther Hall, Selly Oak Coll Birmingham, 1969–74; Gen. Sec., CMS, 1975–85; Hon. Canon of Derby Cathedra 1975–85; a Chaplain to the Queen, 1984–85. Chairman: Partnership for World Missio 1987–91; Internat. Affairs Cttee, Bd for Social Responsibility of Gen. Synod, 1986–96. Pres St John's Coll., Nottingham, 1987–2000. FRAI. Hon. DD Wycliffe Coll., Toronto, 198 Hon. DLitt Warwick, 1998. *Publications:* CMS Newsletter, 1975–85; Love Will O (anthology of news letters), 1988; Why God?, 1993; The Jesus Prayer, 1996, rev. edn 200 (jtly) Praying the Jesus Prayer Together, 2001; The Jesus Prayer and the Great Exchang 2013; *contributor to:* Christianity in Independent Africa (ed Fasholé Luke and others), 197 Today's Anglican Worship (ed C. Buchanan), 1980; Renewal—An Emerging Pattern, b Graham Pulkingham and others, 1980; A New Dictionary of Christian Theology (ed Ala Richardson and John Bowden), 1983; Christianity Today, 1988; The World's Religion 1988; The Weight of Glory (ed D. W. Hardy and P. H. Sedgwick), 1991. *Address:* Magdaler College, Cambridge CB3 0AG; 4 Searle Street, Cambridge CB4 3DB.

BARRITT, Rev. Dr Gordon Emerson, OBE 1979; Principal, National Children's Hom 1969–86; President of the Methodist Conference, 1984–85; *b* 30 Sept. 1920; *s* of Norman an Doris Barritt; *m* 1947, Joan Mary Alway (*d* 1984); two *s* one *d*; *m* 1993, Karen Lesley Wind (marr. diss. 1999); *m* 2003, Eileen Marjorie Smith. *Educ:* William Hulme's Grammar Sch Manchester; Manchester Univ.; Cambridge Univ. (Wesley House and Fitzwilliam Coll. Served War, RAF, 1942–45 (despatches). Methodist Minister: Kempston Methodist Churcl Bedford, 1947–52; Westlands Methodist Church, Newcastle-under-Lyme, 1952–5 Chaplain, Univ. of Keele, 1953–57. Dir, Enfield Counselling Service, 1986–89; Treasure 1969–86, Chm., 1970–72, Nat. Council of Voluntary Child Care Organisations; Membe Home Office Adv. Council on Child Care, 1968–71; Brit. Assoc. of Social Worker 1960–95; Nat. Children's Bureau, 1963–2000 (Treasurer, 1989–95; Vice Pres., 1997–2000 Internat. Union for Child Welfare, 1969–86; Chm., Kids, 1986–93; Gov., CAF, 1996–200 Vice Chm. of Council, Selly Oak Colls, Birmingham, 1991–2000 (Fellow, 1987); Governo Farringtons Sch., 1986–94 (Chm. of Govs, 1986–93); Queenswood Sch., 1986–93. DUni Keele, 1985. *Publications:* The Edgworth Story, 1972; (ed) Many Pieces—One Aim, 197 (ed) Family Life, 1979; Residential Care, 1979; contrib.: Caring for Children, 1969; Givin Our Best, 1982; Thomas Bowman Stephenson, 1996. *Recreations:* music, walking. *Address:* Pitcairne Court, 5 Donovan Place, N21 1RZ. *T:* (020) 8360 8687, *Fax:* (01582) 792658.

BARRON, Prof. Caroline Mary, PhD; FRHistS, FSA; Professor of the History of Londor 2000–05 and Dean of the Graduate School, 1999–2003, Royal Holloway, University c London (Hon. Fellow, 2014); *b* 7 Dec. 1939; *d* of late William David Hogarth, OBE an Grace Allen Hogarth; *m* 1962, Prof. John Penrose Barron (*d* 2008); two *d*. *Educ:* Nort London Collegiate Sch.; Somerville Coll., Oxford (Exhibnr; MA Mod. Hist. 1966; Hor Fellow, 2011); Westfield Coll., London (PhD 1970). Bedford College, subseq. Roy Holloway and Bedford New College, University of London: Asst Lectr, 1967, Lect 1968–83, Sen. Lectr, 1983–91, in Hist.; Dean, Faculty of Arts, 1983–85; Reader in Hist. London, 1991–99. Reader, British Academy, 1988–90. Member: Cttee, Victoria Count Hist., 1970–95; Council, London Record Soc., 1973–76, 1996– (Chm., 2005–); Roy Commn on Historical Manuscripts, 1999–2003; Adv. Council on Nat. Records and Archive 2003–05. Mem. Council, GPDST, 1979–94 (Chm. Educn Cttee, 1992–94); Chm. Gov Wimbledon High Sch., 1985–88; Gov., NLCS, 1985–91. Trustee, St Peter's Coll., Oxfor 2010–. Pres., Assoc. of Senior Mems, Somerville Coll., 1994–99; Chm. Friends, PRC 1999–2002. Mem. Editorial Bd, Hist. of Parliament, 1988–2007. FRHistS (Mem. Counci 1989–94). Corresp. Fellow, Medieval Acad. of America, 2007. *Publications:* (ed and contrib The Reign of Richard II, 1971; The Medieval Guildhall of London, 1974; The Parish of S Andrew Holborn, 1979; Revolt in London 11th to 15th June 1381, 1981; (ed and contrib The Church in the Century before the Reformation, 1985; Hugh Alley's Caveat: markets c London in 1598, 1988; (ed and contrib.) Widows of Medieval London, 1994; (ed an contrib.) England and the Low Countries in the Late Middle Ages, 1995; (ed and contrib The Church and Learning in Later Medieval Society, 2001; London in the Later Middle Age government and people, 2004; *contributions to:* British Atlas of Historic Towns, 1990; Nev Cambridge Medieval History, 1999; Cambridge Urban History of England, 2000; St Paul' the Cathedral Church of London, 2004; contrib. Oxford DNB. *Recreations:* travel, people *Address:* Alhambra Cottage, 9 Boundary Road, NW8 0HE. *Club:* University Women's.

BARRON, Derek Donald; Chairman and Chief Executive, Ford Motor Co. Ltd, 1986–9 Chairman, Ford Motor Credit Co., 1986–91; *b* 7 June 1929; *s* of Donald Frederick Jame Barron and Hettie Barbara Barron; *m* 1963, Rosemary Ingrid Brian; two *s*. *Educ:* Beckenhan Grammar School; University College London. Joined Ford Motor Co. Sales, 1951; Tracto Group, 1961; Tractor Manager, Ford Italiana 1963; Marketing Associate, Ford Motor Co USA, 1970; Gen. Sales Manager, Overseas Markets, 1971; Man. Dir, Ford Italiana, 197 Group Dir, Southern European Sales, Ford of Europe, 1977; Sales and Marketing Dir, For Brazil, 1979; Vice-Pres., Ford Motor de Venezuela, 1982; Dir-Vice-Pres., Operations, For Brazil, 1985. DUniv Essex, 1989.

BARRON, Sir Donald (James), Kt 1972; DL; Chairman, Joseph Rowntree Foundation 1981–96; *b* 17 March 1921; *o s* of Albert Gibson Barron and Elizabeth Macdonald, Edinburgh *m* 1956, Gillian Mary, *o d* of John Saville, York; three *s* two *d*. *Educ:* George Heriot's Sch. Edinburgh; Edinburgh Univ. (BCom). Member, Inst. Chartered Accountants of Scotland Joined Rowntree Mackintosh Ltd, 1952; Dir, 1961; Vice-Chm., 1965; Chm., 1966–81. Di 1972, Vice-Chm., 1981–82, Chm., 1982–87, Midland Bank plc. Dep. Chm., CLCB 1983–85; Chm., Cttee of London and Scottish Bankers, 1985–87. Director: Investors i Industry, subseq. 3i, Gp, 1980–91; Canada Life Assurance Co. of GB Ltd, 1980–96 (Chm 1991–94; Dep. Chm., 1994–96); Canada Life Unit Trust Managers Ltd, 1980–96 (Chm 1982–96); Canada Life Assurance Co., Toronto, 1980–96; Canada Life Assce (Ireland 1992–96; Clydesdale Bank, 1986–87. Mem., Bd of Banking Supervision, 1987–89. Dir, BIM Foundn, 1977–80 and Mem. Council, BIM, 1978–80; Trustee, Joseph Rowntree Fund (formerly Meml Trust), 1966–73, 1975–96 (Chm., 1981–96); Treasurer, 1966–72, a Pro Chancellor, 1982–95, York Univ.; Member: Council of CBI, 1966–81 (Chm., CBI Educ Foundn, 1981–85); SSRC, 1971–72; UGC, 1972–81; Council, PSI, 1978–85; Council, Ins of Chartered Accountants of Scotland, 1980–81; NEDC, 1983–85. Governor, Londo Business Sch., 1982–88. Chm., York Millennium Bridge Trust, 1997–2003. DL N York (formerly WR Yorks and City of York), 1971–96. Hon. doctorates: Loughborough, 1982 Heriot-Watt, 1983; CNAA, 1983; Edinburgh, 1984; Nottingham, 1985; York, 198 *Recreations:* travelling, golf, tennis, gardening. *Address:* Greenfield, Sim Balk Lan Bishopthorpe, York YO23 2QH. *T:* (01904) 705675, *Fax:* (01904) 700183. *Club* Athenæum.

BARRON, Iann Marchant, CBE 1994; Chairman, Division Group plc, 1990–99; *b* 16 Jun 1936; *s* of William Barron; *m* 1962, Jacqueline Almond (marr. diss. 1989); two *s* two *d*; one *s* *Educ:* University College School; Christ's College, Cambridge (exhibitioner; MA). Elliot Automation, 1961–65; Managing Director: Computer Technology Ltd, 1965–72 Microcomputer Analysis Ltd, 1973–78; Exec. Dir, 1978–89, Chief Strategic Officer 1984–89, INMOS International; Man. Dir, INMOS, 1981–88. Vis. Prof., Westfield Coll. London, 1976–78; Vis. Indust. Prof., Bristol Univ., 1985–; Vis. Fellow: QMC, 1976; Scienc

Policy Res. Unit, 1977–78. Exec. Trustee, The Exploratory, 1992–98; Dir, Bristol 2000, 1995–2000. Mem. Council, UCS, 1983–2002. Distinguished FBCS, 1986. FIET (FIEE 1994). Hon. DSc: Bristol Polytechnic, 1988; Hull, 1989. R. W. Mitchell Medal, 1983; J. J. Thompson Medal, IEE, 1986; IEE Achievement Medal for computing and control, 1996. *Publications:* The Future with Microelectronics (with Ray Curnow), 1977; technical papers. *Address:* Barrow Court, Barrow Gurney, Somerset BS48 3RP.

BARRON, Rt Hon. Sir Kevin (John); Kt 2014; PC 2001; MP (Lab) Rother Valley, since 1983; *b* 26 Oct. 1946; *s* of Richard Barron; *m* 1969 (*d* 2008); one *s* two *d*. *Educ:* Maltby Hall Secondary Modern Sch.; Ruskin Coll., Oxford. NCB, 1962–83. PPS to Leader of the Opposition, 1985–87; Opposition spokesman on energy, 1988–92, on employment, 1993–95, on health, 1995–97. Member: Select Cttee on Energy, 1983–85; Select Cttee on Environmental Affairs, 1992–93; Parly Intelligence and Security Cttee, 1997–2005; Liaison Cttee, 2005–15; Chairman: Select Cttee on Health, 2005–10; Standards and Privileges Cttee, 2010– (Mem., 2005–10). Chm., Yorkshire Labour MPs, 1987–. Pres., Rotherham and Dist TUC, 1982–83. Trustee and Dir, Nat. Coal Mining Mus. for England. Vice Pres., RSPH (formerly RSH, then RIPH), 2007–. Hon. FRCP 2008. *Address:* House of Commons, SW1A 0AA.

BARRON, Prof. Laurence David, DPhil; FRS 2005; FRSE; FInstP, FRSC; Gardiner Professor of Chemistry, University of Glasgow, 1998–2008, now Emeritus; *b* 12 Feb. 1944; *s* of Gerald Landon Barron and Stella Barron (*née* Gertz); *m* 1969, Sharon Aviva Wolf; one *s* one *d*. *Educ:* King Edward VI Grammar Sch., Southampton; Northern Poly. (BSc); Lincoln Coll., Oxford (DPhil 1969). FInstP 2005; FRSC 2005. Chemistry Department, University of Cambridge: SRC Fellow, 1969; Res. Asst, 1971; Ramsay Meml Fellow, 1974; University of Glasgow: Lectr in Physical Chem., 1975–80; Reader, 1980–84; Prof. of Physical Chem., 1984–98; EPSRC Sen. Fellow, 1995–2000. Vis. Miller Res. Prof., Univ. of Calif, Berkeley, 1995; Vis. Prof., Univ. Paul Sabatier, Toulouse, 2003; Tetelman Vis. Fellow, Jonathan Edwards Coll., Yale Univ., 2008. Lectures: Schmidt Meml, Weizmann Inst., Israel, 1984; Conover Meml, Vanderbilt Univ., USA, 1987; Schechter Meml, Bar Ilan Univ., Israel, 2012; Zhang Dayu Meml, Dalian Inst. of Chemical Physics, Chinese Acad. of Scis, 2012; Guest Review, Assoc. of Physicians of GB and Ireland, 1997; Chem. Soc. of Zürich, 1998. FRSE 1992. Corday-Morgan Medal and Prize, Chem. Soc., 1977; Sir Harold Thompson Award for Molecular Spectroscopy, 1992; Chirality Medal, Societa Chimica Italiana, 2011. *Publications:* Molecular Light Scattering and Optical Activity, 1982, 2nd edn 2004; contrib. res. papers to chemistry, physics and life sci. jls. *Recreations:* walking, listening to music (classical and jazz), water-colour painting, building and flying radio control model aircraft. *Address:* 84 Erskine Hill, Hampstead Garden Suburb, NW11 6HG.

BARRON, Prof. Nicholas Ian S.; *see* Shepherd-Barron.

BARRON, Peter Scott; Director, Communications and Public Affairs, Europe, Middle East and Africa, Google, since 2013; *b* Belfast, 16 Oct. 1962; *s* of Wilson and Greta Barron; *m* 1996, Julia Stroud; two *s* one *d*. *Educ:* Royal Belfast Academical Instn; Univ. of Manchester Inst. of Sci. and Technol. (BSc Hons Eur. Studies and Mod. Langs). Ed., Algarve News, 1987–88; news trainee, BBC News, 1988–90; Producer, BBC Newsnight, 1990–97; Deputy Editor: Channel 4 News, 1997–2002; Tonight with Trevor McDonald, 2002–03; Editor: If…, BBC Current Affairs, 2003–04; Newsnight, BBC, 2004–08; Google: Hd, Communications and Public Affairs, UK, Ireland and Benelux, 2008–09, N and Central Europe, 2009–11; Dir, Ext. Relns, EMEA, 2011–13. Adv. Chm., Edinburgh TV Fest., 2007. *Recreations:* playing the guitar, collecting records, visiting Spain. *Address:* c/o Google UK Ltd, Central St Giles, 1–13 St Giles High Street, WC2H 8AG.

BARRON, Maj.-Gen. Richard Edward, CB 1993; *b* 22 Nov. 1940; *s* of John Barron and Lorna Frances Barron; *m* 1968, Margaret Ann Eggar; one *s* one *d*. *Educ:* Oundle; RMA. Commissioned Queen's Royal Irish Hussars, 1962; Staff College, 1973; DAA&QMG 7th Armoured Brigade, 1974–76; Instructor, Staff Coll., 1978–81; CO, QRIH, 1981–84; Comdr, 7th Armoured Brigade, 1984–86; RCDS 1987; QMG's Staff, 1988–89; Dir, RAC, 1989–92. Col, Queen's Royal Hussars, 1993–99. *Recreations:* reading, gardening, fishing. *Address:* Willow House, Whistley Road, Potterne, Wilts SN10 5TD. *Club:* Cavalry and Guards.

BARRON, Tanya, (Mrs Gregory Knowles); Chief Executive Officer, Plan International UK, since 2013; *b* London, 18 March 1954; *d* of Donald and Edna Barron; *m* 2000, Gregory Knowles; one *s* one *d*. *Educ:* Dartington Hall Sch.; Poly. of Central London (BA Hons 1985). Dairy worker, 1972–76; Zool Soc. of London, 1976–82; Lectr in Pol Philosophy, Open Univ., 1986–89; Prog. Manager, VSO, 1989–96; Hd of Progs, Eur. Children's Trust, 1996–99; CEO, Home Start Internat., 1999–2004; Internat. Dir, Leonard Cheshire, 2004–13. Chair, UNICEF NGO Cttee for Central and E European States/CIS, 1993–99. Hon Dr Health Scis York St John, 2009. *Publications:* Disability and Inclusive Development, 2007; Poverty and Disability, 2010. *Recreations:* wine-making, grandchildren. *Address:* 135 Whitehall Court, SW1A 2EP. *Club:* Farmers.

BARRONS, John Lawson; Director: Century Newspapers Ltd, Belfast, 1989–98 (Chief Executive, 1989–97); Praxis Care Ltd, Belfast, since 2011; *b* 10 Oct. 1932; *s* of late William Cowper Barrons, MBE and Amy Marie Barrons (*née* Lawson); *m* 1st, 1957, Caroline Anne (marr. diss. 1986), *d* of late George Edward Foster; three *s*; 2nd, 1987, Lauren Ruth, *d* of late Robert Z. Friedman. *Educ:* Caterham Sch. Nat. Service, 1st Bn Northamptonshire Regt, 1952–54. Journalist, UK and USA, 1950–57; Gen. Manager, Nuneaton Observer, 1957; Managing Editor, Northampton Chronicle & Echo, 1959; Gen. Manager, Edinburgh Evening News, 1961; Gen. Manager, 1965–76, Man. Dir, 1976–85, Westminster Press. Director: Pearson Longman, 1979–83; Stephen Austin Newspapers, 1986–91; Northern Press, 1986–91; Lincolnshire Standard Gp plc, 1987–88; President: Westminster (Florida) Inc., 1980–85; Westminster (Jacksonville) Inc., 1982–85. Dir, Evening Newspaper Advertising Bureau, 1978–81 (Chm. 1979–80); Dir, The Press Association Ltd, 1985–86; Chm., Printing Industry Res. Assoc., 1983–85 (Mem. Council, 1978, a Vice-Chm., 1979–83); Mem. Bd of Management, Internat. Electronic Publishing Res. Centre, 1981–85. Member, Council: Newspaper Soc., 1975–87 (Pres., 1981–82; Hon. Vice-Pres., 1983–); CPU, 1970–86. Director: BITC, NI, 1994–2006; City West Action Ltd, Belfast, 1995–2008. *Recreations:* walking, watching wolfhounds, reading. *Address:* 8 Harberton Avenue, Belfast BT9 6PH. *Clubs:* Flyfishers', MCC.

See also Gen. Sir R. L. Barrons.

BARRONS, Gen. Sir Richard (Lawson), KCB 2013; CBE 2003 (OBE 1999; MBE 1993); Commander Joint Forces Command, since 2013; Aide-de-Camp General to the Queen, since 2013; *b* Northampton, 17 May 1959; *s* of John Lawson Barrons, *qv*; *m* 1988, Cherry Louise Dedow; two *d*. *Educ:* Merchant Taylors' Sch., Northwood; Queen's Coll., Oxford (BA; Hon. Fellow 2013); Cranfield Inst. of Technol. (MDA). Psc 1991; COS, 11 Armd Bde, 1992–93; Battery Comdr, B Battery, RHA, 1994–96; MA to CGS, 1997–99; CO, 3rd Regt, RHA, 1999–2001; COS 3(UK) Div., 2002–03; HCSC(J) 2003; Comdr, 39 Infantry Bde, 2004–06; ACOS Commitments, HQ Land, 2006–07; Dep. Comdg Gen. Multinat. Corps (Iraq), 2008–09; COS, HQ ARRC, 2009; Dir, Force Reintegration, HQ ISAF - Afghanistan, 2009–10; Asst Chief of Gen. Staff, 2010–11; DCDS (Military Strategy and Ops), 2011–13. Hon. Col, 3rd Regt RHA, 2013–; Pres. and Col Comdt, HAC, 2013–. Chm., RA Mus. Ltd, 2009–13; Comr, Royal Hosp. Chelsea, 2010–11. Hon. DSc Cranfield, 2014. QCVS 2004 and 2006. Officer, Legion of Merit (USA), 2009. *Publications:* (with Deborah Tom) The Business General, 2006. *Recreations:* ski-ing, cycling, garden labouring, keeping the dog sharp, military history, the search for the perfect cappuccino. *Address:* c/o Military Secretary, Army Personnel Centre, Kentigern House, 65 Brown Street, Glasgow G2 8EX. *E:* richardbarrons825@gmail.com. *Club:* Army and Navy.

BARROS MELET, Cristián; Permanent Representative of Chile to the United Nations, since 2014; *b* 19 Oct. 1952; *s* of Diego Barros and Tencha Melet; *m* 1976, Mary Florence Michell Nielsen; one *s*. *Educ:* St Gabriel's Sch.; Sagrados Corazones Padres Franceses; Sch. of Law, Univ. of Chile; Diplomatic Acad. Andrés Bello; Catholic Univ., Santiago. Entered Diplomatic Service, Consular Div., Chile, 1974; Legal Dept, 1975–78; Protocol Dept, 1978; Admin. Dept, 1978–79; Consul: Mendoza, Argentina, 1979; Bariloche, Argentina, 1980–83; Bilateral Policy Dept, America Div., 1983–85; Consul and Consul Gen., Chicago, 1985–88; First Sec., Canada, 1989–90; Hd of Cabinet for Dir Gen. of Foreign Policy, 1990; Dir of Personnel, 1990–91; Ambassador, Dir Gen., Admin. Dept, 1991–93; Ambassador to Denmark, 1993–96; Dir Gen., Admin. Dept, 1996–98; Dir Gen., Foreign Policy, 1998–99; Ambassador to UK, 2000–02; Vice Minister of Foreign Affairs, 2002–06; Ambassador: to Peru, 2006–08; to Italy, 2008–10; to India, 2010–14. Grand Cross: Order of Merit (Portugal), 1993; Order of Dannebrog (Denmark), 1996; Order of May (Argentina), 1998; Order of El Sol (Peru), 1999; Grand Order, Order of Merit (Brazil), 1999. *Address:* Ministry of Foreign Affairs, Teatinos 180, Santiago, Chile.

BARROSO, José Manuel D.; *see* Durão Barroso.

BARROW, Sir Anthony (John Grenfell), 7th Bt *cr* 1835, of Ulverston, Lancashire; Senior Planning and Budget Officer, Food and Agriculture Organisation of the UN, since 2011; *b* London, 24 May 1962; *o s* of Captain Sir Richard John Uniacke Barrow, 6th Bt and Alison Kate (*née* Grenfell); *S* father, 2009; *m* 1st, 1990, Rebecca Mary Long (marr. diss. 1996); 2nd, 2001, Elisa Isabel Marzo Pérez; one *d*; and one *d*. *Educ:* Edinburgh Univ. (MA Classics 1985). CPFA 1993; Cert. Internat. Risk Mgt, Inst. of Risk Mgt, 2011. Nat. Insce Inspector, DHSS, 1986–88; National Audit Office: Asst Auditor, 1988–91; Auditor, 1991–93; Sen. Auditor, 1993–2000; seconded to Cour des Comptes as Rapporteur, 1998–99; Food and Agriculture Organisation of the UN: Internal Auditor, 2000–02; Regl Auditor, 2002–10; Sen. Auditor, 2010–11. *Publications:* nine published reports to UK and French Parlts. *Heir: cousin* John Lendon Barrow [*b* 1934; *m* 1961, Maureen Ann, *d* of Alfred Stanley Gover; one *s* one *d*].

BARROW, Colin, CBE 2004; Chairman, Alpha Strategic plc, 2005–14; *b* 18 June 1952; *s* of Reginald Barrow and Margaret (*née* Jones); *m* 1994, Angelica Bortis (marr. diss. 2007); two *s*; *m* 2009, Ana Smaldon. *Educ:* Dulwich Coll.; Clare Coll., Cambridge (BA Moral Scis and Law 1974; MA). John Brown Gp, 1974–83; Man. Dir, Funds Mgt Div., ED&F Man, 1983–96; Chm., Sabre Fund Mgt, 1996–2005. Member (C): Suffolk CC, 1997–2002; Westminster CC, 2002–12 (Dep. Leader, 2005–08; Leader, 2008–12). Exec. Mem. for Health, London Councils, 2009–12; Member: Mayor of London's Commn on Health, 2013–14; Expert Adv. Bd, Imperial Coll. Health Partners, 2013–. Chm., Central London Forward, 2009–10. Chm., Improvement and Develt Agency for Local Govt, 2000–04. Director: Rambert Dance Co., 1997–2003; Policy Exchange, 2002–05. Chm., Nat. Autistic Soc., 2005–11 (Treas., 2004). Mem. Council, Sol Price Sch. of Public Policy, USC, 2014–. CEDR Qualified Mediator, 2014–. *Recreations:* inexpert skier, scuba diver, bridge player. *T:* (020) 7222 2223, *Fax:* (01277) 624722. *E:* colin.barrow1@gmail.com.

BARROW, Jill Helen; Director, leadership consultancy, Big Blue Experience, since 2006; *b* 26 April 1951; *d* of Philip Eric Horwood and Mavis Mary (*née* Handscombe); *m* (marr. diss.); two *d*. *Educ:* Durham Univ. (Cert Ed 1972; MA Ed 1993); Open Univ. (BA 1980). Teaching in secondary, special and further educn, 1972–86; educn mgt and inspection, 1986–90; Dep. Dir of Educn, Essex CC, 1990–93; Dir of Educn, Surrey CC, 1993–95; Chief Exec., Lincs CC, 1995–98; Chief Exec., SW of England RDA, 1999–2001; Bd Mem. for England, New Ops Fund, 1999–2004; Dir, Consultancy and Develt, GatenbySanderson, 2004–06. *Recreations:* walking, outdoor activities, travelling, reading.

BARROW, Dame Jocelyn (Anita), DBE 1992 (OBE 1972); Development Director, Focus Consultancy Ltd, 1996–2002; Deputy Chairman, Broadcasting Standards Council, 1989–95; *b* 15 April 1929; *d* of Charles Newton Barrow and Olive Irene Barrow (*née* Pierre); *m* 1970, Henderson Downer. *Educ:* Univ. of London. Mem., Taylor Cttee on School Governors; Gen. Sec., later Vice-Chm., Campaign Against Racial Discrimination, 1964–69; Vice-Chm., Internat. Human Rights Year Cttee, 1968; Member: CRC, 1968–72; Parole Bd, 1983–87. A Governor, BBC, 1981–88. Chairman: Ind. Cttee of Mgt, Optical Consumer Complaints Service, 1992–; Independent Equal Opportunities Inquiry into Ethnicity and Trng and Assessment on Bar Vocational Course, 1993–94; Non-exec. Dir, Whittington Hosp. NHS Trust, 1993–99. Mem., Econ. and Social Cttee, EC, 1990–98. Nat. Vice-Pres., Nat. Townswomen's Guilds, 1978–80, 1987–; Pres. and Founder, Community Housing Assoc.; Governor: Farnham Castle, 1977–93; BFI, 1991–97. Patron: Blackliners, 1989–; Unifem UK, 1998–. FRSA. Hon. DLitt E London, 1992. *Recreations:* theatre, music, cooking, reading. *Address:* c/o Focus Consultancy Ltd, 38 Grosvenor Gardens, SW1W 0EB. *Club:* Reform.

BARROW, Prof. John David, DPhil; FRS 2003; FRAS; CPhys, FInstP; Professor of Mathematical Sciences, Department of Applied Mathematics and Theoretical Physics, University of Cambridge, since 1999; Fellow, Clare Hall, Cambridge, since 1999 (Vice President, 2004–07); Director, Millennium Mathematics Project, Cambridge, since 1999; *b* 29 Nov. 1952; *s* of Walter Henry Barrow and Lois Miriam Barrow (*née* Tucker); *m* 1975, Elizabeth Mary East; two *s* one *d*. *Educ:* Van Mildert Coll., Durham Univ. (BSc Hons 1974); Magdalen Coll., Oxford (DPhil Astrophysics 1977). FRAS 1981; CPhys 1998; FInstP 1998. Res. Lectr, Christ Church and Dept of Astrophysics, Oxford Univ., 1977–80; Lindemann Fellow, Dept of Astronomy, 1977–78, Miller Fellow, Dept of Physics, 1980–81, Univ. of Calif, Berkeley; Astronomy Centre, University of Sussex: Lectr, 1981–88; Sen. Lectr, 1988–89; Prof., 1989–99; Dir, 1989–90 and 1995–99. Gordon Godfrey Vis. Prof., Univ. of NSW, Sydney, 1998, 2000, 2003. Gresham College: Gresham Prof. of Astronomy, 2003–07, now Emeritus; Gresham Prof. of Geometry, 2008–12; Fellow, 2012–15. Hon. Prof., Nanjing Univ., 2005. Lectures: Centenary Gifford, Glasgow, 1989; Scott, Leuven, 1989; Collingwood, Durham, 1990; George Darwin, London, 1992; Spinoza, Amsterdam, 1993; Spreadbury, London, 1994; Benedum, Va, 1997; Kelvin, Glasgow, 1999; Flamsteed, Derby, 2000; Tyndall, Bristol, 2001; Whitrow, London, 2002; Brasher, Kingston, 2002; Newton, Grantham, 2003; Gresham, London, 2003; Hubert James, Purdue, 2004; Carl Von Weizsäcker, Hamburg, 2004; McCrea Centenary, Sussex, 2004; Wood, Newcastle, 2005; Hamilton, Dublin, 2005; Boyle, St Mary-le-Bow, 2007; Roscoe, Liverpool, 2007; Borderlands, Durham, 2007; Källen, Lund, 2007; Si-Wei, Taiwan, 2008; Sciama, Oxford and Trieste, 2008; Phillips, Cardiff, 2008; Sir Henry Tizard, Westminster Sch., 2010; William Herschel, Bath, 2010; Van Mildert Trust, Van Mildert Coll., Durham, 2010; Anile Meml, Catania, 2011; Gregynog, Aberystwyth, 2011; Centenary, Real Sociedad Matemática Española, Paraninfo, Zaragoza, 2011; McCrea, RIA, Cork, 2013; Internat. Maths Olympiad, Cape Town, 2014; Enriques, Milan, 2014. Mem., Internat. Soc. for Sci. and Religion, 2002; Titular Mem., Acad. Internat. de Philosophie des Scis, 2009. Pres., Phys. and Astronomy Sect., 2008–09, Pres., Maths Sect., 2011–12, BAAS. MAE 2009. Forum Fellow, World Econ. Forum, 1999–2000. FRSA 1999. Hon. DSc: Herts, 1999; Szczecin, 2007; Durham, 2008; Sussex, 2010; S Wales, 2014. Locker Prize, Birmingham Univ., 1989; Kelvin Medal, Royal Glasgow Philosophical Soc., 1999; Lacchini Medal, Union Astrofili Italiani, 2005; Templeton Prize, Templeton Foundn, 2006; Queen's Anniversary Prize, 2006; Faraday Prize, Royal Society, 2008; Kelvin Medal, Inst. of Physics, 2009; Gresham Prize, Gresham Coll., 2009; Colletti Sci. Prize, Colletti Foundn, 2010; Merck-Serono Prize for Sci. and Lit., Merck-

Serono, Rome, 2011; Christopher Zeeman Medal, LMS and IMA, 2011. *Publications:* The Left Hand of Creation, 1983, 2nd edn 1995; L'Homme et le Cosmos, 1984; The Anthropic Cosmological Principle, 1986, 2nd edn 1996; The World Within the World, 1988, 2nd edn 1995; Theories of Everything, 1991, 2nd edn 1994; Pi in the Sky, 1992, 2nd edn 1994; Perché il Mondo è Matematico?, 1992, 2nd edn 2001; The Origin of the Universe, 1993, 2nd edn 2001; The Artful Universe, 1995, 2nd edn 1997; Impossibility, 1998, 2nd edn 2000; Between Inner Space and Outer Space, 1999; The Universe that Discovered Itself, 2000; The Book of Nothing, 2000, 2nd edn 2002; The Constants of Nature, 2002; Science and Ultimate Reality, 2004; The Artful Universe Expanded, 2005; The Infinite Book, 2005; New Theories of Everything, 2007; Cosmic Imagery, 2008; 100 Essential Things You Didn't Know You Didn't Know, 2008; The Book of Universes, 2011 (Premio Antico Pignolo Literary Prize, Venice, 2012); 100 Essential Things You Didn't Know You Didn't Know About Sport, 2012; One Hundred Essential Things You Didn't Know about Maths and the Arts, 2014; *theatre script:* Infinities, 2002 (Premi Ubu Italian Theatre Award, 2002; Italgas Prize, 2003); contrib. to works of reference and numerous scientific articles to learned jls. *Recreations:* athletics, books, travelling, throwing things away. *Address:* Centre for Mathematical Sciences, Cambridge University, Wilberforce Road, Cambridge CB3 0WA. *Fax:* (01223) 765900. *E:* J.D.Barrow@damtp.cam.ac.uk.

BARROW, Sir Timothy Earle, (Sir Tim), KCMG 2015 (CMG 2006); LVO 1994; MBE 1994; HM Diplomatic Service; Ambassador to Russia, since 2011; *b* 15 Feb. 1964; *m* Alison; two *s* two *d*. Entered FCO, 1986; Second Sec. (Chancery), Moscow, 1989–93; First Sec., FCO, 1993–94; Pvte Sec. to Minister of State, FCO, 1994–96; First Sec., UK Rep. to EU, Brussels, 1996–98; Pvte Sec. to Sec. of State, FCO, 1998–2000; Hd, Common Foreign and Security Policy Dept, FCO, 2000–03; Asst Dir, EU (Ext.), FCO, 2003–06; Ambassador to Ukraine, 2006–08; UK Rep. to Political and Security Cttee, European Union, 2008–11. *Address:* c/o Foreign and Commonwealth Office, King Charles Street, SW1A 2AH.

BARROW, Ursula Helen, (Viscountess Waverley), PhD; Wisbech Schools Co-ordinator, Cambridgeshire Advisory Service, since 2002; *b* 31 Oct. 1955; *d* of Raymond Hugh and Rita Helen Barrow; *m* 1994, Viscount Waverley, *qv*; one *s*. *Educ:* Newnham Coll., Cambridge (BA Hons 1977; MA 1981; PhD 1988; Fellow, 1999–2000); Jesus Coll., Cambridge (LLM 1992). Econ. Develt Planner, Planning Unit, Govt of Belize, 1978; consultant for small business affairs, urban planning and marketing, Frazier & Assocs, 1979–85; Counsellor and Dep. High Comr, London, 1988–89; Perm. Rep. to UN, 1989–90; Asst Dir (Pol), Commonwealth Secretariat, 1991–93; High Comr for Belize in London, 1993–98, also Ambassador to EU, Belgium, France, Germany and Holy See. Dir, Belize Telecommunications Ltd, 2004–05.

BARRY, Alison Ruth; *see* Pople, A. R.

BARRY, Daniel, CB 1988; Permanent Secretary, Department of the Environment for Northern Ireland, 1983–88; *b* 4 March 1928; *s* of William John Graham Barry and Sarah (*née* Wilkinson); *m* 1951, Florence (*née* Matier); two *s* one *d*. *Educ:* Belfast Mercantile Coll. FCIS, FSCA, FCIHT. Local Government Officer with various NI Councils, 1944–68; Town Clerk, Carrickfergus Borough Council, 1968–73; Asst Sec. (Roads), Dept of the Environment for NI, 1973–76, Dep. Sec., 1976–80; Dep. Sec., Dept of Educn for NI, 1980–83. *Recreations:* golf, gardening, painting.

BARRY, David; *see* Barry, J. D.

BARRY, Sir Edward; *see* Barry, Sir L. E. A. T.

BARRY, Edward Norman, CB 1981; Under Secretary, Northern Ireland Office, 1979–81, retired 1981; *b* 22 Feb. 1920; *s* of Samuel and Matilda (*née* Legge); *m* 1952, Inez Anna (*née* Elliott); one *s* two *d*. *Educ:* Bangor Grammar Sch. Northern Ireland Civil Service: Department of Finance: Establishment Div., 1940–51; Works Div., 1951–60; Treasury Div., 1960–67; Establishment Officer, 1967–72; Min. of Home Affairs, 1972–74; Asst Sec., N Ireland Office, 1974–79. *Recreations:* golf, football (Hon. Treas., 1977–96, and Life Mem., Irish Football Association).

BARRY, Hilary Alice S.; *see* Samson-Barry.

BARRY, Prof. (James) David, PhD; Professor of Molecular Parasitology, 1996, now Honorary Senior Research Fellow, and Director, Wellcome Trust Centre for Molecular Parasitology, 1999–2012, University of Glasgow; *b* Glasgow, 13 Dec. 1949; *s* of James Barry and Helen Barry (*née* Cairns); *m* 1st, 1973, Mary Mowat (*d* 1992); one *s* two *d*; 2nd, 2001, Olwyn Byron; one *d*. *Educ:* Univ. of Glasgow (BSc Combined Biol.; PhD 1977). Res. Fellow, Univ. of Glasgow, 1977–86; Scientist, Internat. Lab. for Res. on Animal Diseases, Nairobi, 1978–80; Sen. Lectr, 1986–92, Reader, 1992–96, Univ. of Glasgow. Consultancy appts with scientific research funding bodies. *Publications:* 100 scientific contribs. *Recreations:* drawing and painting, swimming, reflection. *Address:* c/o Wellcome Trust Centre for Molecular Parasitology, Sir Graeme Davies Building, 120 University Place, Glasgow G12 8TA. *E:* dave.barry@glasgow.ac.uk.

BARRY, Sir (Lawrence) Edward (Anthony Tress), 5th Bt *cr* 1899; Baron de Barry in Portugal *cr* 1876; *b* 1 Nov. 1939; *s* of Sir Rupert Rodney Francis Tress Barry, 4th Bt, MBE, and Diana Madeline (*d* 1948), *o d* of R. O'Brien Thompson; *S* father, 1977; *m* 1st, 1968, Fenella Hoult (marr. diss. 1991); one *s* one *d*; 2nd, 1992, (Elizabeth) Jill Dawe, *d* of G. Bradley, Fishtoft. *Educ:* Haileybury; Imperial Service Coll. Formerly Captain, Grenadier Guards. *Heir:* *s* William Rupert Philip Tress Barry [*b* 13 Dec. 1973; *m* 2004, Diana, d of Antoni Leidner, Germany; one *s* one *d*]. *Address:* Swinstead Cottage, High Street, Swinstead, Grantham NG33 4PA.

BARRY, Rt Rev. (Noel) Patrick, OSB; Abbot of Ampleforth, 1984–97; *b* 6 Dec. 1917; 2nd *s* of Dr T. St J. Barry, Wallasey, Cheshire. *Educ:* Ampleforth Coll.; St Benet's Hall, Oxford. Housemaster, Ampleforth Coll., 1954–64, Headmaster 1964–79. First Asst to Abbot Pres. of English Benedictine Congregation, 1985–97. Chairman: Conference of Catholic Colleges, 1973–75; HMC, 1975; Union of Monastic Superiors, 1989–95. *Publications:* (trans.) Rule of St Benedict, 1981; A Cloister in the World, 2005 (trans. Spanish 2010); various articles. *Address:* Ampleforth Abbey, York YO62 4EN.

BARRY, Peter; *b* Cork, 10 Aug. 1928; *s* of Anthony Barry and Rita Costello; *m* 1958, Margaret O'Mullane (*d* 2013); four *s* two *d*. *Educ:* Christian Brothers' Coll., Cork. Alderman of Cork Corp., 1967–73; Lord Mayor of Cork, 1970–71. TD: Cork City SE, 1969–82; Cork South Central, 1982–97; opposition spokesman on labour and public services, 1972–73; Minister for: Transport and Power, 1973–76; Education, 1976–77; opposition spokesman on finance and economic affairs, 1977–81; Minister for the Environment, 1981–82; opposition spokesman on the environment, 1982; Minister for Foreign Affairs, 1982–87; opposition spokesman on foreign affairs, 1987–91, on industry and commerce, 1991–92. Dep. Leader of Fine Gael Party, 1979–87, 1991; Chm., Nat. Exec., 1982–84. Co-Chm., Anglo-Irish Conf., 1982–87; negotiated Anglo-Irish Agreement, 1986. Established: An Bord Gáis, 1976; Housing Finance Agency, 1982. Freedom, City of Cork, 2010. *Address:* 150 Blackrock Road, Cork, Republic of Ireland.

BARRY, Sebastian; writer, since 1977; *b* Dublin, 5 July 1955; *m* 1992, Alison Deegan; two *s* one *d*. *Educ:* Catholic University Sch., Dublin; Trinity Coll., Dublin (BA Hons). Writer in Association, Abbey Th., Dublin, 1990; Writer Fellow, TCD, 1995; Heimboldt Vis. Prof., Villanova Univ., Philadelphia, 2006. FRSL 2009. Hon. DLitt NUI, Galway, 2012; DUniv Open, 2014. *Publications:* *poetry:* The Water-Colourist, 1983; *plays:* Prayers of Sherkin/Boss Grady's Boys: two plays, 1990; The Steward of Christendom (Lloyds Private Banking Playwright of the Year Award, Ire./America Literary Prize, Christopher Ewart-Biggs Meml Prize), 1995; Our Lady of Sligo, 1998; The Pride of Parnell Street, 2007; *novels:* The Whereabouts of Eneas McNulty, 1998; A Long Long Way, 2005; The Secret Scripture, 2008 (Costa Book of the Year, 2008; James Tait Black Meml Prize, 2009); On Canaan's Side, 2011 (Walter Scott Prize, 2012); The Temporary Gentleman, 2014.

BARSON, Jacqueline Anne, MBE 1995; HM Diplomatic Service; High Commissioner to Papua New Guinea, 2010–14; *b* Walsall, 26 May 1959; *d* of John and Brenda Barson. *Educ:* Arthur Terry Grammar Sch., Sutton Coldfield. Entered FCO, 1979; Desk Officer, Parly Unit, FCO, 1979–81; Archivist, Prague, then Belgrade, 1981–82; Archivist/Registrar: Abu Dhabi, 1982–85; Bandar Seri Begavan, 1985–86; Asst Admin Officer, UKMIS Geneva, 1986–89; Asst Visits Officer, FCO, 1989–91; Desk Officer, Security Coordination Dept, FCO, 1991–92; Presidency Liaison Officer, Copenhagen, Brussels and Athens, 1992–93; Second Sec. (Econ./Trade), Ottawa, 1994–99; Olympic Attaché to Team GB, Sydney, 1999–2000; on secondment to Manchester Organising Cttee, 2002 Commonwealth Games, 2001–02; Sen. Asst to Dir Gen. Corporate Affairs, FCO, 2002–04; Hd, Public Diplomacy Challenge Fund and Hd, London Press Service, FCO, 2004; on secondment to SOCA, 2005; Project Leader, UK/India Educn Initiative, S Asia Gp, FCO, 2005; Dep. Dir, Protocol and Asst Marshal of Diplomatic Corps, FCO, 2005–09; on loan to UK Trade and Investment for Prime Minister's Global Investment Conf., 2009–10. *Recreations:* sport, travel, reading, the arts. *Address:* c/o Foreign and Commonwealth Office, King Charles Street, SW1A 2AH. *E:* Jackie.Barson@fco.gov.uk.

BARSTOW, Dame Josephine (Clare), DBE 1995 (CBE 1985); opera singer, free-lance since 1971; *b* Sheffield, 27 Sept. 1940; *m* 1964, Terry Hands (marr. diss. 1967); *m* 1969, Ande Anderson (*d* 1996); no *c*. *Educ:* Birmingham Univ. (BA). Debut with Opera for All, 1964; studied at London Opera Centre, 1965–66; Opera for All, 1966; Glyndebourne Chorus, 1967; Sadler's Wells Contract Principal, 1967–68, sang Cherubino, Euridice, Violetta; *Welsh National Opera:* Contract Principal, 1968–70, sang Violetta, Countess, Fiordiligi, Mimi, Amelia, Simon Boccanegra; Don Carlos, 1973; Jenufa, 1975; Peter Grimes, 1978, 1983; Tatyana in Onegin, 1980; Tosca, 1985; Un Ballo in Maschera, 1986; The Makropoulos Case, 1994; *Covent Garden:* Denise, world première, Tippett's The Knot Garden, 1970 (recorded 1974); Falstaff, 1975; Salome, 1982; Santuzza, 1982; Peter Grimes, 1988 and 1995; Attila, 1990; Fidelio, 1993; Katya Kabanova, 2000; Queen of Spades, 2001; *Glyndebourne:* Lady Macbeth (for TV), 1972; Idomeneo, 1974; Fidelio, 1981; *English National Opera:* has sung all parts in Hoffman, Emilia Marty (Makropulos Case), Natasha (War and Peace) and Traviata; Der Rosenkavalier, 1975, 1984; Salome, 1975; Don Carlos, 1976, 1986; Tosca, 1976, 1987; Forza del Destino, 1978, 1992; Aida, 1979; Fidelio, Arabella, 1980; The Flying Dutchman, La Bohème, 1982; The Valkyrie, 1983; Don Giovanni, 1986; Lady Macbeth of Mtsensk, 1987, 1991; Street Scene, 1993; Jenufa, 1994; The Carmelites, 1999, 2005; *Opera North:* Gloriana, 1993, 1997, 2001; Jenufa, 1995; Medea, Wozzeck, 1996; Aida, 1997; Falstaff, 2000; Albert Herring, 2002, 2013; Queen of Spades, 2011. Other appearances include: Alice in Falstaff, Aix-en-Provence Festival, 1971; Nitocris in Belshazzar, Geneva, 1972; Jeanne, British première, Penderecki's The Devils, 1973; Marguerite, world première, Crosse's The Story of Vasco, 1974; Fidelio, Jenufa, Scottish Opera, 1977; Gayle, world première, Tippett's The Ice Break, 1977; US début as Lady Macbeth, Miami, 1977; Musetta in La Bohème, NY Met., 1977; Salome, East Berlin, 1979 (Critics Prize), San Francisco, 1982; Abigaille in Nabucco, Miami, 1981; début in Chicago as Lady Macbeth, 1981; new prod. of Jenufa, Cologne, 1981; La Voix Humaine and Pagliacci, Chicago, 1982; The Makropulos Case (in Italian), Florence, 1983; Gutrune, Götterdämmerung, Bayreuth, 1983; Die Fledermaus, San Francisco, 1984; Peter Grimes, 1984, La Traviata, 1985, Salome, 1987, Der Rosenkavalier, 1990, Houston; Benigna, world première, Penderecki's Die Schwarze Maske, Salzburg, 1986, Vienna Staatsoper, 1986; Manon Lescaut, USA, 1986; Tosca, Bolshoi, Tbilisi, 1986; Tosca, and Macbeth, Bolshoi, Riga, 1986; Macbeth, Zurich, 1986, Munich, 1987; Medea, Boston, 1988; Prokofiev's The Fiery Angel, Adelaide, 1988; Un Ballo in Maschera, Salzburg, 1989, 1990; Fanciulla del West, Toulouse, 1991; Chrysothemis, Houston, 1993; Fidelio, 1992, Salome, 1994, Amsterdam; Peter Grimes, Tokyo, 1998; first Jenufa in Czech, Antwerp, 1999; debut at Wigmore Hall, 2007; Mamma Lucia in Cavalleria Rusticana, Liceu, Barcelona, 2011. Sings in other opera houses in USA, Canada and Europe. Recordings include: Un Ballo in Maschera; Verdi arias; scenes from Salome, Médée, Makropulos Case and Turandot; Kiss Me Kate; Kurt Weill's Street Scene, Gloriana; Albert Herring; Wozzeck; Jenufa; The Carmelites. Runs business of Arabian stud farm, Devon. Fidelio medal, Assoc. of Internat. Opera Directors, 1985. *Recreations:* gardening, walking. *Address:* c/o Musichall Ltd, Oast House, Crouch's Farm, Hollow Lane, E Hoathly, E Sussex BN8 6QX.

BARSTOW, Prof. Martin Adrian, PhD; CPhys, FInstP; CSci; FRAS; Professor of Astrophysics and Space Science, since 2003, and Pro Vice-Chancellor and Head of College of Science and Technology, since 2009, University of Leicester; *b* Scunthorpe, 18 May 1958; *s* of Brian Thomas Barstow and Marjorie Anona Barstow (*née* Willans); *m* 1981, Rachel Ann Howes; one *s* one *d*. *Educ:* Carlinghow Primary Sch.; Batley Boys' Grammar Sch.; Univ. of York (BA Physics 1979); Univ. of Leicester (PhD 1983). FRAS 1987; FInstP 1998; CSci 2004. Department of Physics and Astronomy, University of Leicester: Res. Associate, 1983–90; SERC/PPARC Advanced Fellow, 1991–98; Lectr, 1994–98; Reader, 1998–2003; Head of Dept, 2005–09. Member: Public Understanding of Sci. Judges Panel, PPARC, 1996–2000 (Chm., 1997–2000); Public Understanding of Sci. Adv. Panel, PPARC, 1997–2000; STFC, 2009–15. Consultant on Space Educn to BNSC, 2005. Chm., Educn Adv. Bd, Nat. Space Centre, 2001–; Member: Adv. Gp, Near Earth Object Inf. Centre, 2002–12; Mgt Bd, E Midlands Regl Sci. Learning Centre, 2003–12; Astronomy Working Gp, ESA, 2012–14; Sci. Prog. Adv. Cttee, UK Space Agency, 2012–; Adv. Bd, Nat. Space Acad., 2012–. Mem., Time Allocation Cttee, 2001, 2003, 2006, 2012, Users' Cttee, 2004–08, Hubble Space Telescope. Member: Wakeham Panel, Res. Councils UK Rev. of Physics, 2008; Public Engagement with Res. Adv. Panel, Research Councils UK, 2009–15; Physics Panel, HEFCE REF impact pilot exercise, 2010; HEFCE Physics REF 2014 Panel, 2011–14; Chm., Educn, Communication and Outreach Adv. Bd, STFC, 2010–12. Mem., Organizing Cttee, Physics Olympiad 2000, 1997–2000. Mem., 2005–08 and 2013–14, Sec., 2008–13, Pres., 2014–May 2016, Council, RAS. Mem., Div. XI Cttee, IAU, 2009–13. Mem. Adv. Bd, Physics Rev., 1998–2009. *Publications:* (ed) White Dwarfs: advances in observation and theory, 1993; (with J. B. Holberg) Extreme Ultraviolet Astronomy, 2003; (ed jtly) UV Astronomy: stars from birth to death, 2007; contrib. astronomical and instrumentation jls. *Recreations:* choral singing with my family, Morris dancing, allotment and home gardening, church organ playing, folk music. *Address:* Department of Physics and Astronomy, University of Leicester, University Road, Leicester LE1 7RH. *T:* (0116) 252 3492, *Fax:* (0116) 252 3311. *E:* mab@le.ac.uk.

BARTELL, family name of **Baroness Gibson of Market Rasen.**

BARTER, Nicholas Arthur Beamish; theatre director and teacher; Principal, Royal Academy of Dramatic Art, 1993–2007; *b* 12 Sept. 1940; *s* of Paul André Valentine Spencer and Sylvia Theadora Essex Barter; *m* 1961, Brigid Alice Panet (marr. diss. 1981); one *s* one *d*; *m* 1998, Noriko Sasaki; one *d*. *Educ:* Cheltenham Coll.; Pembroke Coll., Cambridge (BA Hons, MA). ABC TV Trainee Directors Award, 1963; Asst Dir, Phoenix Th., Leicester, 1963–65; Dir of Prodns, Lincoln Theatre Royal, 1965–68; Dep. Artistic Dir, RSC Theatregoround, 1968; Dir, Ipswich Arts Th., 1968–71; Asst Drama Dir, Arts Council of GB, 1971–75; Artistic Dir, Unicorn Th., 1977–86 (Best Prodn for Young People Award, Drama mag., 1982, for Beowulf); Children's Th. Consultant, Los Angeles, 1986; Course Dir, and Dep. Principal, RADA, 1988–93. Guest Prof., Toho Gakuen Coll. of Drama and Music, Tokyo, 2007–; Guest Teacher, JOKO Acting Sch., Tokyo, 2007–; Guest Teacher, 2009, Vis. Prof., 2010–, Shanghai Th. Acad. *Productions:* Julius Caesar, 2008, How the Other Half Loves, 2009, Gekidan Subaru, Tokyo; Major Barbara, 2008, Taming of the Shrew, 2011, Midsummer Night's Dream, 2012, Twelfth Night, 2013, The Winter's Tale, 2014, Shanghai Th. Acad.; Pericles, 2009, Merchant of Venice, 2010, Th. du Sygne, Tokyo; A Doll's House, Th. Green, Tokyo, 2012; Doubt, Yorozuya Shouten, Tokyo, 2013; As You Like It, Yunnan Arts Univ., 2014. Chm., Dharma Trust, 1990–97. *Publications:* Playing with Plays, 1979; contrib. Theatre Qly, Theatre Internat.

BARTER, Sir Peter (Leslie Charles), Kt 2001; OBE 1986; *b* Sydney, Australia, 26 March 1940; *s* of late John Frank Barter and of Wyn Emily Barter; *m* 1970 Janet Ellen Carter; one *s*. *Educ:* Newington Coll.; Wellington Coll., Sydney. MP (People's Progress) 1992–97, (Nat. Alliance), 2002–07, Madang, PNG. Gov., Madang Province, 1992–94; Minister for Health, PNG, 1994–96; Minister for Provincial Affairs and Bougainville, 1996–97; Provincial Minister, 1997–98; Minister for Intergovt Relns and Bougainville Affairs, 2002–06; Minister for Health and Bougainville Affairs, 2006–07. Work in aviation and tourism develt in Papua New Guinea: Chairman: Melanesian Foundn, 1980–2008; Mgt Gp, PNG Incentive Fund, 1997–2002; PNG Nat. Events Council, 2000–07; Nat. Aids Council, 2008–; Dep. Chm., PNG Tourist Authy, 1998–2000. Licensed commercial pilot of both fixed and rotary wing, 1967–. Hon. PhD Australian Catholic. *Recreation:* sailing in motor yacht Kalibobo Spirit. *Address:* PO Box 707, Madang 511, Papua New Guinea. *T:* 4222766, *Fax:* 4223543.

BARTFELD, Jason Maurice; QC 2015; *b* St John's Wood, London, 7 Feb. 1972; *s* of Peter Bartfeld and Carol Bartfeld; *m* 2007, Annabel; three *c*. *Educ:* Westminster Sch.; Durham Univ. (BA Philos. and Politics). Called to the Bar, Middle Temple, 1995; in practice as a barrister, 1995–. *Recreations:* cooking, polo, family. *Address:* 187 Fleet Street, EC4A 2AT. *T:* (020) 7430 7430, *Fax:* (020) 7430 7431. *E:* jasonbartfeld@187fleetstreet.com. *Club:* Sussex Polo.

BARTFIELD, Robert; His Honour Judge Bartfield; a Circuit Judge, since 1996; *b* 30 Dec. 1949; *s* of Isaac and Emily Bartfield; *m* 1977, Susan Eleanor Griffin; one *s* one *d*. *Educ:* Leeds Grammar Sch.; Queen Mary Coll., London (LLB). Called to the Bar, Middle Temple, 1971; in practice as barrister, 1971–96; a Recorder, 1993–96. *Recreations:* tennis, football.

BARTHOLOMEW, Prof. David John, PhD; FBA 1987; Professor of Statistics, London School of Economics, 1973–96, then Emeritus (Pro-Director, 1988–91); *b* 6 Aug. 1931; *s* of Albert and Joyce Bartholomew; *m* 1955, Marian Elsie Lake; two *d*. *Educ:* University College London (BSc, PhD). Scientist, NCB, 1955–57; Lectr in Stats, Univ. of Keele, 1957–60; Lectr, then Sen. Lectr, UCW, Aberystwyth, 1960–67; Prof. of Stats, Univ. of Kent, 1967–73. Pres., Royal Statistical Soc., 1993–95 (Hon. Sec., 1976–82; Treas., 1989–93); Vice-Pres., Manpower Soc., 1987–95. Chm., Science and Religion Forum, 1997–2000. *Publications:* (jtly) Backbench Opinion in the House of Commons 1955–1959, 1961; Stochastic Models for Social Processes, 1967, 3rd edn 1982; (jtly) Let's Look at the Figures: the quantitative approach to human affairs, 1971; (jtly) Statistical Inference Under Order Restrictions, 1972; (jtly) Statistical Techniques for Manpower Planning, 1979, 2nd edn 1991; Mathematical Methods in Social Science, 1981; God of Chance, 1984; Latent Variable Models and Factor Analysis, 1987, 3rd edn (jtly) 2011; Uncertain Belief, 1996; The Statistical Approach to Social Measurement, 1996; (jtly) The Analysis and Interpretation of Multivariate Data for Social Scientists, 2002, 2nd edn as Analysis of Multivariate Social Science Data, 2008; Measuring Intelligence: facts and fallacies, 2004; Measurement (4 vols), 2006; God, Chance and Purpose, 2008; Unobserved Variables: models and misunderstandings, 2013; Statistics without Mathematics, 2015; papers in statistical, theological and social science jls. *Recreations:* gardening, steam railways, theology. *Address:* 6 Beaconsfield Close, Sudbury, Suffolk CO10 1JR. *T:* (01787) 372517.

BARTHOLOMEW, Prof. Stuart, CBE 2014; Principal and Vice Chancellor, Arts University Bournemouth (formerly Principal, Arts University College at Bournemouth), since 1997; *b* London, 20 Jan. 1953; *s* of William George and Ada Ellen Bartholomew; *m* 2002, Claire McIntyre; twin *s*. *Educ:* Christ Church Secondary Sch.; Christ Coll. Sch.; Univ. of Hull (BA Hons); Univ. of Nottingham (MEd); Univ. of Leicester (PGCE); McMaster Univ. (MA). Teaching Fellow, Univ. of Calgary, 1973–74; Lectr, Norwich Coll. of Art, 1974–75; Asst Dean, Univ. of Derby, 1975–90; Tutor, Open Univ. (pt-time), 1980–90; Dean of Media, 1990–95, Hd of Coll., 1995–96, Univ. of the Arts, London. Vis. Prof., Univ. of the Arts, London, 2001–04. Dir, Bournemouth SO, 2011–. Chm., UK Assoc. Specialist Colls of Art and Design, 2009–15. FRSA 1999. *Publications:* contrib. articles on specialist educn in arts and design and engagement in promotion of UK creative industries. *Recreations:* being alive, sports, generally using the seated position, the arts. *Address:* Arts University Bournemouth, Wallisdown, Poole BH12 5HH. *T:* (01202) 363203. *Club:* Royal Motor Yacht (Poole).

BARTLE, Philip Martyn; QC 2003; **His Honour Judge Bartle;** a Circuit Judge, since 2012; *b* 24 Dec. 1952; *s* of Leslie Bartle and Zena Bartle (*née* Unger). *Educ:* Manchester Grammar Sch.; Christ Church, Oxford (MA, BCL). Called to the Bar, Middle Temple, 1976, Bencher, 2006; in practice, 1976–2012, specialising in law of professional negligence and mediation. Recorder, 2004–12. Mem. Editl Bd, Jackson ADR Handbook, 2013. *Publications:* (contrib.) ADR and Commercial Disputes, 2002; (consultant ed.) Halsbury's Laws of England, 5th edn, 2008; (contrib.) Security for Costs and Other Court Ordered Security, 2010. *Recreations:* theatre, classical music, travel, reading, Apostrophe Chambers. *Address:* Luton Crown Court, 7 George Street, Luton LU1 2AA.

BARTLE, Ronald David; a Metropolitan Stipendiary Magistrate, 1972–99; Deputy to Chief Magistrate, 1992–99; *b* 14 April 1929; *s* of late Rev. George Clement Bartle and Winifred Marie Bartle; *m* 1st, 1963; one *s* one *d*; 2nd, 1981, Hisako (*née* Yagi) (*d* 2004); 3rd, 2006, Molly. *Educ:* St John's Sch., Leatherhead; Jesus Coll., Cambridge (MA). Nat. Service, 1947–49 (Army Athletic Colours). Called to Bar, Lincoln's Inn, 1954; practised at Criminal Bar, 1954–72; a Dep. Circuit Judge, 1975–79; a Chm., Inner London Juvenile Courts, 1975–79. Member: Home Office Council on Drug Abuse, 1987–; Home Office Cttee on Magistrates' Court Procedure, 1989–. Lectr on Advocacy, Council of Legal Educn, 1984–89. Contested (C) Islington N, 1958, 1959; Mem., Essex CC, 1963–66. Freeman, City of London, 1976; Liveryman, Basketmakers' Co., 1976– (Steward, 1990; Mem. Ct, 1997–; Prime Warden, 2005–06). Patron, Pathway to Recovery Trust. Governor: Corp. of Sons of the Clergy, 1995–; RNLI, 1997–. Church Warden, St Mary the Boltons, Kensington, 1992–95; Church Warden and Trustee, St Margaret Pattens, 1999–; Member: City of London Deanery Synod, 2000–; Friends of City of London Churches, 2001–; Guild of Freemen, City of London; Royal Soc. of St George. *Publications:* Introduction to Shipping Law, 1958; The Police Officer in Court, 1984; Crime and the New Magistrate, 1985; The Law and the Lawless, 1987; Bow Street Beak, 1999; The Police Witness, 2002; The Telephone Murder: the mysterious death of Julia Wallace, 2012; (contrib.) Atkin's Court Forms and Precedents; contrib. to legal jls. *Recreations:* music, reading, swimming. *Clubs:* Garrick, Hurlingham.

BARTLETT, Sir Andrew (Alan), 5th Bt *cr* 1913, of Hardington Mandeville, Somerset; *b* 26 May 1973; *er s* of Sir John Hardington David Bartlett, 4th Bt and of his 2nd wife, Elizabeth Joyce (*née* Raine); *S* father, 1998. *Heir: b* Stephen Mark Bartlett, *b* 5 July 1975.

BARTLETT, Andrew Vincent Bramwell; QC 1993; a Recorder, since 2004; chartered arbitrator; a Deputy High Court Judge, since 2010; *b* 1952; *s* of John Samuel Bartlett and Doris Jean Bartlett; *m* 1974, Elisabeth Jefferis. *Educ:* Jesus Coll., Oxford (BA). Called to the Bar, Middle Temple, 1974, Bencher, 2005. Chm., Technol. and Construction Bar Assoc., 2007–09. FCIArb. *Address:* Crown Office Chambers, 2 Crown Office Row, Temple, EC4Y 7HJ. *T:* (020) 7797 8100.

BARTLETT, Dr Christopher Leslie Reginald, FRCP, FFPH; Director, Public Health Laboratory Service Communicable Disease Surveillance Centre, 1988–2000; *b* 20 Dec. 1940; *s* of Reginald James Bartlett and Dorothea Amelia Bartlett; *m* 1979, Alicia Teresa Tower; one *s* two *d*. *Educ:* Milton Sch., Bulawayo, Southern Rhodesia; Lysses Sch., Hants; St Bartholomew's Hosp. Med. Coll. (MB, BS 1965); MSc LSHTM 1977. MRCS 1965; LRCP 1965, FRCP 1991; MFCM 1978, FFPH (FFPHM 1983). RAF SSC, 1967–72. Registrar, Wessex RHA, seconded to LSHTM, 1975–77; Public Health Laboratory Service: Sen. Registrar, 1977–79; Consultant Epidemiologist, 1979–88. Consultant Med. Epidemiologist, Caribbean Epidemiol. Centre, 1984–85. Hon. Lectr, Dept of Envmtl and Preventative Medicine, St Bartholomew's Hosp. Med. Coll., 1980; Hon. Sen. Lectr, Dept of Epidemiol. and Med. Stats, Royal London Hosp., 1990; Vis. Prof., LSHTM, 1997–. Chm., PHLS Cttee on Legionnaires' Disease, 1989; Member: DHSS Cttee on Aspects and Use of Biocides, 1986; Registrar-Gen's Med. Adv. Cttee, DoH, 1988–90; Expert Gp on Cryptosporidium in Water Supplies, DoE and DoH, 1989–90; Steering Gp on Microbiol Safety of Food, MAFF and DoH, 1991–95; CMO's Health of Nation Cttee, DoH, 1992–2000. Faculty of Public Health Medicine: Member: Bd, 1988–91; Educn Cttee, 1988–94; Pres., Sect. of Epidemiol. and Public Health, RSocMed. 1996 (Mem., Council, 1990–94); Mem. Council, RIPH&H, 1991–94. Member: Scientific Steering Cttee, Réseau Nat. de Santé Publique, France, 1992; Steering Gp, European Prog. for Intervention Epidemiol. Trng, 1994; PROMED Steering Cttee, Fedn of Amer. Scientists, 1995; Communicable Diseases Wkg Gp, G7 Nations Global Healthcare Applications Project, 1995; MRC CJD Epidemiol. Subcttee, 1996; EU/USA Task Force on Communicable Diseases, 1996 (Co-Chm., Surveillance and Response Wkg Gp, 1996); Project Leader, European Surveillance of Travel Associated Legionnaires' Disease, 1993; Jt Project Leader, SALMNET (EU Surveillance of Salmonella Infections), 1994; Chm., Charter Gp of Heads of Instns with responsibilities in nat. surveillance of disease in EU countries, 1994. Specialist Advr, Editl Bd, Jl Infection, 1991–. *Publications:* chapters, articles and papers in med. and scientific texts on aspects of epidemiology and prevention of infectious diseases. *Recreations:* family, walking, ski-ing, travelling. *Club:* Royal Society of Medicine.

BARTLETT, Hon. David John; Chairman, Asdeq Labs, since 2011; Premier of Tasmania, Australia, 2008–11; *b* Hobart, 19 Jan. 1968; *s* of Neil Walker and Grace Lucinda Borella (*née* Bird); *m* 1st, 1994, Jacqui Swee Lan Lim (marr. diss. 1998); 2nd, 2004, Larissa Mary, *d* of Ben and Mary Marriss; one *s* one *d*. *Educ:* Hobart Matriculation Coll.; Univ. of Tasmania (BSc Computer Sci.; Grad. Dip. Business). Manager, SOE Business (Telecom), 1990–95; Dep. Dir, IT, Govt of Tasmania, 1995–97; Dir, IT, Dept of Educn, 1997–99; Manager, Innovation Sci. Technol., Dept of State Develt, 1999–2002; Sen. Private Sec., Office of the Treas., 2002–04; Sen. Advr, Office of the Premier of Tasmania, 2004. MHA (ALP) Denison, Tasmania, 2004–11. Dep. Premier of Tasmania, 2008; Minister for Education, 2006–11, for Planning, 2008, for Workplace Relns, 2008, for Skills, 2008–11. *Address:* Asdeq Labs, Level 5, 29 Elizabeth Street, Hobart, Tas 7000, Australia.

BARTLETT, George Robert; QC 1986; President of the Lands Chamber of the Upper Tribunal (formerly Lands Tribunal), 1998–2012; a Deputy High Court Judge, 1994–2012; *b* 22 Oct. 1944; *s* of late Commander H. V. Bartlett, RN and Angela (*née* Webster); *m* 1972, Dr Clare Virginia, *y d* of G. C. Fortin; three *s*. *Educ:* Tonbridge Sch.; Trinity Coll., Oxford (MA). Called to the Bar, Middle Temple, 1966, Bencher, 1995. A Recorder, 1990–2000; an Asst Parly Boundary Comr, 1992–98. Hon. RICS 2000.

BARTLETT, John Vernon, CBE 1976; MA; FREng, FICE; consulting engineer, retired; *b* 18 June 1927; *s* of late Vernon F. Bartlett and Olga Bartlett (*née* Testrup); *m* 1951, Gillian, *d* of late Philip Hoffmann, Sturmer Hall, Essex; four *s*. *Educ:* Stowe; Trinity Coll., Cambridge. Served 9th Airborne Squadron, RE, 1946–48; Engineer and Railway Staff Corps, TA, 1978; Col 1986. Engineer with John Mowlem & Co. Ltd, 1951–57; joined staff of Mott, Hay & Anderson, 1957; Partner, 1966–88; Chm., 1973–88. Pres., ICE, 1982–83 (Vice-Pres., 1979–82; Mem. Council, 1974–77); Chm., British Tunnelling Soc., 1977–79. Gov., Imperial Coll., 1991–95. FRSA 1975. Hon. Sec., Overseas Affairs, RAEng, 1982–85; Mem. Council, Fellowship of Engrg, 1982–86. Master, Engineers' Co., 1992–93 (Mem., Court of Assts, 1986–2004). Telford Gold Medal, (jointly) 1971, 1973; S. G. Brown Medal, Royal Soc., 1973. *Publications:* Tunnels: Planning Design and Construction (with T. M. Megaw), vol. 1, 1981, vol. 2, 1982; Ships of North Cornwall, 1996; contrib. various papers to ICE, ASCE, etc. *Recreations:* sailing, maritime history (Founder, Bartlett Library, Nat. Maritime Mus. Cornwall, 2002). *Address:* 6 Cottenham Park Road, SW20 0RZ. *T:* (020) 8946 9576. *Clubs:* Hawks (Cambridge); Harlequin Football; Royal Engineers Yacht.

BARTLETT, Neil Vivian, OBE 2000; writer, director; Artistic Director, Lyric Theatre, Hammersmith, 1994–2004; *b* 23 Aug. 1958; *s* of Trevor and Pam Bartlett; partner, James Gardiner. *Educ:* Magdalen Coll., Oxford (BA Hons Eng. Lit.). Works written, adapted and directed include: *theatre:* More Bigger Snacks Now, 1985; A Vision of Love Revealed in Sleep, 1987; Sarrasine, 1990; A Judgement in Stone, 1992; Night After Night, 1993; The Picture of Dorian Gray, 1994; Lady into Fox, 1996; The Seven Sacraments of Nicholas Poussin, 1997; Everybody Loves A Winner, 2009; Or You Could Kiss Me, 2010; For Alfonso, 2011; *television:* That's What Friends are For, 1987; Where is Love?, 1988; Pedagogue, 1989; That's How Strong My Love Is, 1990; *film:* Now That It's Morning, 1992; *major productions directed:* Romeo and Juliet, 1994; The Letter, 1995; Mrs Warren's Profession, A Christmas Carol, 1996; Then Again, Treasure Island, 1997; Cause Célèbre, Seven Sonnets of Michelangelo, Cinderella, 1998; The Dispute, 1999; The Servant, 2001; The Prince of Homburg, The Island of Slaves, 2002; Pericles, 2003; Oliver Twist, Don Juan, 2004; Dido, Queen of Carthage, Amer. Rep. Co., Boston, 2005; The Rake's Progress, Aldeburgh Fest., 2006; The Maids, The Pianist, Twelfth Night, RSC, 2007; An Ideal Husband, Abbey, Dublin, 2008; Romeo and Juliet, RSC, 2008; The Turn of the Screw, Aldeburgh Fest., 2009; The Queen of Spades, Grand Th., Leeds, 2011; The Picture of Dorian Gray, Abbey, Dublin, 2012; Britten's Canticles, Aldeburgh and ROH, 2013; Great Expectations, Bristol Old Vic, 2013; Owen Wingrave, Aldeburgh and Edinburgh Fests, 2014; has performed at RNT, Royal Court, Blackpool Grand and Vauxhall Tavern. Patron, Sussex Beacon, 2011–. Hon. DArts: Oxford Brookes, 2008; Brighton, 2013. *Publications:* Who Was That Man?, 1988; Ready to Catch Him Should He Fall, 1989; A Vision of Love Revealed in Sleep, 1990; (trans.) Berenice/The Misanthrope/School for Wives, 1991; (trans.) The Game of Love and Chance, 1992; Night After Night, 1993; Mr Clive and Mr Page, 1995; (trans.) Splendid's, 1995; (trans.) The Dispute, 1999; (trans.) The Threesome, 2000; In Extremis, 2000; (trans.) The Prince of Homburg, 2002; (trans.) The Island of Slaves, 2002; (trans.) Don Juan, 2005; Solo Voices, 2005; Skin Lane, 2007; Or You Could Kiss Me, 2010; Queer Voices, 2012; The Disappearance Boy, 2014; adaptations for stage: Camille, 2003; A Christmas Carol, 2003; Oliver Twist, 2004; Great Expectations, 2007; The Picture of Dorian Gray, 2012. *Recreations:* weight training, tree peonies, HIV and breast cancer charity work. *Address:* c/o The Agency, 24 Pottery Lane, W11 4LZ. *T:* (020) 7727 1346. *E:* info@theagency.co.uk. *W:* www.neil-bartlett.com.

BARTLETT, Nicholas Michael; Partner, since 2004, and Head, Real Estate Investment, since 2012, Eversheds LLP; *b* Chester, 16 May 1972; *s* of Pierre Nicholas and late Elizabeth Anne Bartlett; *m* 2000, Annabel Sophie Frearson; one *s* one *d*. *Educ:* Eton Coll.; Univ. of Warwick (LLB Hons Law 1993); Coll. of Law, London (Postgrad. DipLP with Commendation 1994). Admitted as solicitor, 1997; Linklaters: trainee solicitor, 1995–97;

Associate, 1997–99; Man. Associate, 1999–2003. Member: Historic Houses Assoc.; Motorsports Assoc.; British Assoc. for Shooting and Conservation; Welsh Rifle Assoc.; Nat. Rifle Assoc. *Recreations:* Captain, Etonian Shooting Club (long range target shooting), motor-racing (owner driver), ski-ing, tennis, scuba diving. *Address:* Eversheds LLP, One Wood Street, EC2V 7WS. *T:* (020) 7919 4570. *E:* nicholasbartlett@eversheds.com. *Clubs:* British Automobile Racing, Lancia Motor; N London Rifle.

BARTLETT, Prof. Philip Nigel, PhD; FRS 2012; Professor of Electrochemistry, University of Southampton, since 1993; *b* Sevenoaks, Kent, 27 July 1956; *s* of Stuart and Edith Bartlett; *m* 2000, Zoë Slattery; one *s* one *d. Educ:* University Coll., Oxford (BA 1978); Imperial Coll. London (PhD 1981). Royal Commn for Exhibn of 1851 Res. Fellow, 1981–83, Asst Dir, Wolfson Unit for Modified Electrodes, 1983–84, Imperial Coll. London; Lectr, Univ. of Warwick, 1984–91; Prof. of Physical Chem., Univ. of Bath, 1991–92. *Recreations:* anything with two wheels, modern literature. *Address:* Chemistry, University of Southampton, Highfield, Southampton SO17 1BJ. *T:* (023) 8059 2373. *E:* p.n.bartlett@soton.ac.uk.

BARTLETT, Prof. Robert John, FBA 1997; FRSE, FSA, FRHistS; Professor of Mediaeval History, University of St Andrews, since 1992; *b* 27 Nov. 1950; *s* of Leonard Frederick Bartlett and Mabel Emily Adams; *m* 1979, Honora Elaine Hickey; one *s* one *d. Educ:* Peterhouse, Cambridge (BA 1972; MA 1976); St John's Coll., Oxford (DPhil 1978). Lectr in History, Edinburgh Univ., 1980–86; Prof. of Medieval History, Univ. of Chicago, 1986–92; British Acad. Reader, 1995–97. Junior Fellow, Univ. of Michigan Soc. of Fellows, 1979–80; Mem., Inst. for Advanced Study and Fellow, Davis Center, Princeton, 1983–84; von Humboldt Fellow, Göttingen, 1988–89; Leverhulme Trust Major Res. Fellow, 2009–12. Presenter: Inside the Medieval Mind, BBC4, 2008; The Normans, BBC2, 2010; The Plantagenets, BBC2, 2014. Corresp. Fellow, Medieval Acad. of America, 2012. *Publications:* Gerald of Wales 1146–1223, 1982; Trial by Fire and Water, 1986; The Making of Europe, 1993; England under the Norman and Angevin Kings, 2000; (ed) Medieval Panorama, 2001; (ed) Geoffrey of Burton, Life and Miracles of St Modwenna, 2002; (ed) The Miracles of St Æbbe of Coldingham and St Margaret of Scotland, 2003; The Hanged Man, 2004; The Natural and the Supernatural in the Middle Ages, 2008; Why Can the Dead Do Such Great Things?: saints and worshippers from the martyrs to the Reformation, 2013; contribs to learned jls. *Address:* Department of Mediaeval History, University of St Andrews, St Andrews, Fife KY16 9AL. *T:* (01334) 463308.

BARTLETT, Timothy Conn; Director, Tourism and Hotel Advisory Services, since 2006; *b* 15 Dec. 1944; *s* of Gordon Thomas Bartlett and Margaret Decima Bartlett; *m* 1st, 1970, Deira Janis Vacher (marr. diss.); one *s* one *d*; 2nd, 1988, Xochitl Alicia Quintanilla; two *d. Educ:* Cranleigh Sch.; Pembroke Coll., Oxford (Hons French and Spanish). Morgan Grampian Books, 1967–68; British Tourist Authority: London, 1968–70 and 1974–77; Sydney, 1970–74; Manager: Mexico, 1977–82; Western USA, based in LA, 1982–87; France, 1987–88; General Manager: S Europe, 1988–91; Asia Pacific, 1991–94; Europe, based in Brussels, 1994–95; Acting Chief Exec., 1995–96, Chief Exec., 1996–99, English Tourist Bd; Chief Exec., British Assoc. of Leisure Parks, Piers and Attractions, 1999–2001; Dir, Tourism Div., 1999–2001 and Dir, Spain, Portugal and Latin America, 2001–05, TRI Hospitality Consulting; Chief Exec., Newcastle-Gateshead Initiative, 2005. *Recreations:* tennis, reading, music, travel. *Address:* Calle 19A No 559 x 24 y 26, Altabrisa, Merida 97130, Yucatan, Mexico. *E:* timcbartlett@hotmail.com.

BARTOLI, Cecilia; mezzo soprano; Artistic Director, Salzburg Whitsun Festival, since 2012; *b* Rome, 4 June 1966; *d* of Pietro Angelo Bartoli and Silvana Bartoli (*née* Bazzoni). *Educ:* Acad. of Santa Cecilia, Rome. Début, Barber of Seville, Teatro dell'opera, Rome, 1986; has performed at La Scala, Milan, Opéra Bastille, Carnegie Hall, Maggio Musicale Fest., Florence, Salzburg Fest., Wigmore Hall, Aix-en-Provence Fest., NY Metropolitan Opera, Royal Opera House, Covent Garden, Zurich Opera, Theater an der Wien, Barbican; also with major orchs, incl. Vienna Philharmonic and Berlin Philharmonic, and major period instrument ensembles. Numerous recordings. Hon. RAM; Hon. Mem., Royal Swedish Acad. of Music; Academician, Santa Cecilia, Rome. Hon. DMus University Coll. Dublin, 2010. Léonie Sonning Music Prize, Denmark, 2010; Handel Prize, Halle, Germany, 2010; Herbert von Karajan Music Prize, Germany, 2012; 5 Grammy Awards. Knight: Order of Merit (Italy); Fine Arts (France); Officer, Order of Merit (France); Medalla de Oro al Mérito en las Bellas Artes (Spain), 2007; Médaille Grand Vermeil de la Ville de Paris, 2010.

BARTON, Alan Burnell; Head of Resource Management and Finance Division (formerly Under Secretary), Department of Health, 1993–98; *b* 2 May 1943; *s* of Charles Henry Barton and Rose Edith Barton; *m* 1969, Jirina Klapstova; one *s* one *d. Educ:* Glyn Grammar Sch., Ewell; Bristol Univ. (BSc Chem.). Operational Research Exec., NCB, 1966–73; Department of Health and Social Security: Principal, 1973–78; Asst Sec., 1979–90; Dir, Medical Devices Directorate, DoH, 1990–93. Advr, Rickmansworth CAB, 2000–; Social Policy Advr, Citizens Advice (formerly NACAB), 2000–12; Mem., Low Incomes Tax Reform Gp, 2005–. *Recreations:* jazz, theatre, country houses, walking. *Address:* 67 Heronsgate Road, Chorleywood, Rickmansworth, Herts WD3 5PA.

BARTON, Amanda Lucy; *see* Foreman, A. L.

BARTON, Ven. (Charles) John Greenwood; Archdeacon of Aston, 1990–2003; Priest-in-charge, St Peter, Bickenhill, 2002–03; *b* 5 June 1936; *s* of Charles William Greenwood Barton and Doris Lilian Leach; *m* 1972 (marr. diss. 1981); one *s. Educ:* Battersea Grammar Sch.; London Coll. of Divinity (ALCD). Asst Curate, St Mary Bredin, Canterbury, 1963–66; Vicar, Whitfield with West Langdon, dio. Canterbury, 1966–75; Vicar, St Luke, South Kensington, 1975–83; Area Dean, Chelsea, 1980–83; Chief Broadcasting Officer, Church of England, 1983–90. Communications Advr, 2005–06, Acting Chief of Staff, 2007–08, Actg Chaplain/Researcher, 2008, to Archbishop of York. Mem., Gen. Synod of C of E, 2000–03. Chm., BBC W Midlands Regl Adv. Council, 1995–98; Mem., English Nat. Forum, 1995–98. Member, Council: Corp. of Church House, 1989–2009; St Luke's Hosp. for Clergy, 2000–03. Chm., 2000–02, Trustee, 2002–03, Midlands Ethnic Albanian Foundn. *Address:* 7 The Spires, Canterbury, Kent CT2 8SD. *T:* (01227) 379688. *E:* johnbarton@greenbee.net. *Club:* National Liberal.

BARTON, Maj.-Gen. Eric Walter, CB 1983; MBE 1966; FRGS; Director, Caravan Club Ltd, 1984–93; *b* 27 April 1928; *s* of Reginald John Barton and Dorothy (*née* Bradfield); *m* 1st, 1955, Rowena Ulrica Riddell (marr. diss. 1960); 2nd, 1963, Margaret Ann (*née* Jenkins) (marr. diss. 1983); two *s*; 3rd, 1984, Mrs Pamela Clare Frimann, *d* of late Reginald D. Mason and of Doris Mason, Winchelsea. *Educ:* St Clement Danes Sch., London; Royal Military Coll. of Science (BScEng 1955). Dip. in Photogrammetry, UCL, 1960. FCMI (FBIM 1979); FRGS 1979. Commnd RE, 1948; served Mid East, 1948–50; Arab Legion, 1951–52; seconded to Dir, Overseas Surveys, E Africa, 1957–59; Sen. Instr, Sch. of Mil. Survey, 1961–63; OC 13 Fd Survey Sqn, Aden, 1965–67; Dir, Surveys and Prodn, Ordnance Survey, 1977–80; Dir of Mil. Survey, 1980–84. Major 1961, Lt-Col 1967, Col 1972, Brig. 1976, Maj.-Gen. 1980. Col Comdt, RE, 1982–87; Hon. Col, Field Survey Sqn, later 135 Ind. Topographic Sqn RE (V) TA, 1984–89. Pres., Defence Surveyors' Assoc. (formerly Field Survey Assoc.), 1991–2004 (Chm., 1984–86); Member: Council, Photogrammetric Soc., 1979–82; Nat. Cttee for Photogrammetry, 1979–84; Council, RGS, 1980–83; Council, British Schs Exploring Soc., 1980–84; Nat. Cttee for Geography, 1981–84. Patron, Aden Veterans Assoc., 2012–13. *Recreations:* swimming, water sports, numismatics. *Address:* Aquarius, Jesters, Rocky Lane, Haywards Heath, W Sussex RH16 4RQ.

BARTON, Fiona; QC 2011; *b* Bromley, Kent, 11 April 1964; *d* of John Barton and Theresa Barton. *Educ:* Stratford House Sch., Bickley; London Univ. (LLB Hons Law ext. 1985) Called to the Bar, Middle Temple, 1986; in practice as a barrister, specialising in police law, 5 Essex Court, Temple, 1986–, Hd of Chambers, 2010–. Mem., Disciplinary Panel, Bar Council, 2003–12. *Publications:* (contrib.) Civil Actions Against the Police, 3rd edn, 2004; regular contrib. to Police Law Reports. *Recreations:* horse riding, walking, travel. *Address:* 5 Essex Court, Temple, EC4Y 9AH. *T:* (020) 7410 2000, *Fax:* (020) 7410 2010. *E:* clerks@5essexcourt.co.uk.

BARTON, Rev. Prof. John, DPhil, DLitt; FBA 2007; Oriel and Laing Professor of the Interpretation of Holy Scripture, University of Oxford, 1991–2014, now Emeritus; Fellow of Oriel College, Oxford, 1991–2014, now Emeritus; *b* 17 June 1948; *s* of Bernard Arthur Barton and Gwendolyn Harriet Barton; *m* 1973, Mary Burn; one *d. Educ:* Latymer Upper Sch., Hammersmith; Keble Coll., Oxford (MA; DPhil 1974; DLitt 1988). Deacon and priest, 1973. University of Oxford: Jun. Res. Fellow, Merton Coll., 1973–74; Official Fellow, St Cross Coll., 1974–91; University Lectr in Theology (OT), 1974–89; Reader in Biblical Studies, 1989–91; Chaplain, St Cross Coll., 1979–91. Canon Theologian, Winchester Cathedral, 1991–2003. Hon. Dr theol. Bonn, 1998. *Publications:* Amos's Oracles against the Nations, 1980; Reading the Old Testament: method in biblical study, 1984, 2nd edn 1996; Oracles of God: perceptions of ancient prophecy in Israel after the Exile, 1986; People of the Book?—the authority of the Bible in Christianity, 1988, 2nd edn 1993; Love Unknown: meditations on the Death and Resurrection of Jesus, 1990; What is the Bible?, 1991, 2nd edn 1997; Isaiah 1–39, 1995; The Spirit and the Letter: studies in the biblical canon, 1997; Making the Christian Bible, 1997; Ethics and the Old Testament, 1998; (ed) The Cambridge Companion to Biblical Interpretation, 1998; (ed jtly) The Oxford Bible Commentary, 2001; Joel and Obadiah, 2001; (ed) The Biblical World, 2002; Understanding Old Testament Ethics, 2003; (with J. L. V. Bowden) The Original Story: God, Israel and the World, 2004; Living Belief: being Christian, being human, 2005; The Nature of Biblical Criticism, 2007; The Old Testament: canon, literature, theology, 2007; The Bible: the basics, 2010; The Theology of the Book of Amos, 2012; Ethics in Ancient Israel, 2014. *Address:* Oriel College, Oxford OX1 4EW. *Club:* Athenæum.

BARTON, John; *see* Barton, R. J. O.

BARTON, John Bernard Adie, CBE 1981; Advisory Director, Royal Shakespeare Company, since 1991 (Associate Director, 1964–91); *b* 26 Nov. 1928; *s* of late Sir Harold Montague Barton and Joyce Wale; *m* 1968, (Barbara) Anne Righter (Prof. Anne Barton, FBA) (*d* 2013). *Educ:* Eton Coll.; King's Coll., Cambridge (BA, MA). Fellow, King's Coll., Cambridge, 1954–60 (Lay Dean, 1956–59). Joined Royal Shakespeare Company, 1960; Associate Dir, 1964. Has adapted texts and directed or co-directed many plays for Royal Shakespeare Company, including: The Taming of the Shrew, 1960; The Hollow Crown, 1961; The Art of Seduction, 1962; The Wars of the Roses, 1963–64; Henry IV, Parts I and II, and Henry V, 1964–66; Love's Labour's Lost, 1965; Coriolanus and All's Well That Ends Well, 1967; Julius Caesar and Troilus and Cressida, 1968; Twelfth Night and When Thou Art King, 1969; Measure for Measure and The Tempest, 1970; Richard II, Henry V, and Othello, 1971; Richard II, 1973; King John, Cymbeline, and Dr Faustus, 1974; Perkin Warbeck, 1975; Much Ado About Nothing, The Winter's Tale, and Troilus and Cressida, 1976; A Midsummer Night's Dream, Pillars of the Community, 1977; The Way of the World, The Merchant of Venice, Love's Labour's Lost, 1978; The Greeks, 1979; Hamlet, 1980; The Merchant of Venice, Titus Andronicus and The Two Gentlemen of Verona, 1981; La Ronde, 1982; Life's a Dream, 1983; The Devils, 1984; Waste, Dream Play, 1985; The Rover, 1986; Three Sisters, 1988; Coriolanus, 1989; Peer Gynt, 1994; Cain, 1995. Directed: The School for Scandal, Haymarket, 1983, Duke of York's, 1983; The Vikings at Helgeland, Den Nationale Scene, Bergen, 1983; Peer Gynt, 1990, Measure for Measure, As You Like It, 1991, Oslo. Wrote and presented Playing Shakespeare, LWT, 1982, Channel 4, 1984; narrated Morte d'Arthur, BBC2, 1984; wrote The War that Never Ends, BBC2, 1990. *Publications:* The Hollow Crown, 1962 (and 1971); The Wars of the Roses, 1970; The Greeks, 1981; Playing Shakespeare, 1982; Tantalus, 2000, 2nd edn 2014. *Recreations:* travel, chess, work. *Address:* 14 de Walden Court, 85 New Cavendish Street, W1W 6XD.

BARTON, Ven. John Greenwood; *see* Barton, Ven. C. J. G.

BARTON, Prof. Leonard Francis; Professor of Inclusive Education, Institute of Education, London University, 2001–05, now Emeritus; *b* 20 April 1941. *Educ:* Liverpool Univ. (BA Hons); Manchester Univ. (MEd). Prof. of Educn, Bristol Poly., 1986–90; Sheffield University: Head of Res. Degrees, and Dir of Inclusive Educn Res. Centre; Prof. of Educn, 1990–2001. Sir Allan Sewell Fellow, Griffiths Univ., Australia, 1995–96. Founder and Editor, Disability and Society, 1985–. *Publications:* (ed) Disability and Society: emerging issues and insights, 1996; (ed) Disability, Politics and the Struggle for Change, 2001. *Recreations:* swimming, walking, listening to music. *Address:* c/o UCL Institute of Education, 20 Bedford Way, WC1H 0AL.

BARTON, Prof. Nicholas Hamilton, PhD; FRS 1994; Professor, Institute of Science and Technology Austria, since 2008. *Educ:* Peterhouse, Cambridge (BA 1976; MA 1980); Univ. of E Anglia (PhD). Cambridge University: Res. Fellow, Girton Coll., 1980; Demonstrator, Dept of Genetics, 1980–82; Lectr, then Reader, Dept of Genetics and Biometry, UCL, 1982–90; Darwin Trust Fellow, 1990, Prof., 1994, Inst. of Cell, Animal and Population Biol., later Inst. for Evolutionary Biol., Edinburgh Univ. FRSE 1995. *Address:* Institute of Science and Technology Austria, Am Campus 1, 3400 Klosterneuburg, Austria.

BARTON, Philip Robert, CMG 2007; OBE 1997; HM Diplomatic Service; High Commissioner to Pakistan, since 2014; *b* 18 Aug. 1963; *s* of late Geoffrey Howard Barton and of Katharine Anne (*née* Stubbings); *m* 1999, Amanda Joy Bowen; one *s* one *d. Educ:* Warwick Univ. (BA Econs and Politics); London Sch. of Econs (MSc Econs). Joined FCO, 1986: Third, then Second, Sec., Caracas, 1987–91; Cabinet Office (on secondment), 1991–93; First Secretary: FCO, 1993–94; New Delhi, 1994–96; Private Sec. to Prime Minister (on secondment), 1997–2000; Dep. High Comr, Cyprus, 2000–04; Dep. Gov., Gibraltar, 2005–08; Dir, S Asia, FCO, 2008–09; Dir, Foreign Policy and Afghanistan, and Pakistan Co-ordinator, Cabinet Office, 2009–11; Dep. Hd of Mission, Washington, 2011–13. *Recreations:* football, tennis, hiking, travel, reading. *Address:* British High Commission, Islamabad, BFPO 5466, HA4 6EP.

BARTON, (Robert) John (Orr); Chairman: Next plc, since 2006 (Director, since 2002; Deputy Chairman, 2004–06); Catlin Group Ltd, since 2012 (Director, since 2011); easyJet plc, since 2013; *b* Lahore, Pakistan, 23 Aug. 1944; *s* of Kenneth Barton and Elizabeth Joan Boyd (*née* Orr); *m* 1972, Anne Marie Coffey; two *s* one *d. Educ:* Gordonstoun Sch., Elgin; Strathclyde Univ. (MBA); CA 1968. CEO, Jardine Insce Brokers Gp plc, 1984–97; Chm., Jardine Lloyd Thompson Gp plc, 1997–2001; Chairman: Wellington Underwriting plc, 2001–06; Brit Insce Hldgs plc, 2008–10; Cable & Wireless Worldwide plc, 2011–12 (Dep. Chm., 2010–11). Non-executive Director: Hammerson plc, 1998–2007; W H Smith plc, 1999–2011; SSP Gp plc, 2014– (Chm., Remuneration Cttee, 2014–). *Recreations:* golf, travelling, ski-ing. *Address:* Next plc, Desford Road, Enderby, Leicester LE9 5AT. *Clubs:* Boodle's, Hurlingham; Sunningdale Golf.

BARTON, Roger; owned and ran Llama Trekking, Sheffield, 2007–10; *b* 6 Jan. 1945; *s* of late Joseph and Doreen Barton; *m* 1965; two *s. Educ:* Burngreave Secondary Modern Sch.; Granville Coll. (Engrg Technician's Cert.). Fitter, 1961–81; Sheffield TUC and Labour Party

Sec., 1981–89. Mem., Sheffield CC, 1971–90. Mem. (Lab) Sheffield, Eur. Parlt, 1989–99; contested (Lab) Yorkshire and the Humber Region, 1999. Former Dir, Insight Dynamics. *Recreations:* walking, gentle cycling, water sports. *Address:* 50 Hartley Brook Avenue, Sheffield S5 0HN. *Clubs:* Trades and Labour, Wortley Hall Labour (Sheffield).

BARTRAM, Christopher John, FRICS; Chairman, Orchard Street Investment Management, 2004–15; *b* Cambridge, 8 April 1949; *s* of John and Irene Bartram; *m* 1974, Carolyn Bates; one *s* one *d.* *Educ:* Oundle Sch.; Downing Coll., Cambridge (BA 1972). FRICS 1989. In private practice, London, 1972–74; Asst Surveyor, Equitable Life Assce, 1974–78; Property Investment Manager, Scottish Amicable Life, 1978–85; Partner, Jones Lang Wootton, 1985–95, Man. Partner, 1991–94; CEO, Haslemere NV, 1995–2004. Non-exec. Dir, Land Securities Gp plc, 2009–. A Crown Estate Comr, 2007–14. Chm., Bank of England Property Forum, 2002–05. Pres., British Property Fedn, 2000–01. Wilkins Fellow, Downing Coll., Cambridge, 2009– (Associate Fellow, 2005–09). *Recreation:* golf. *Clubs:* Reform; Royal West Norfolk Golf, Royal Worlington Golf, Royal and Ancient Golf.

BARTRAM, Prof. Clive Issell, FRCS, FRCP, FRCR; Honorary Professor of Gastrointestinal Radiology, Imperial College School of Medicine, University of London, 1999–2004; *b* 30 June 1943; *s* of Henry George and Muriel Barbara Bartram; *m* 1966, Michele Juliette François; two *s.* *Educ:* Dragon Sch., Oxford; St Edward's Sch., Oxford; Westminster Hosp. Med. Sch. (MB BS 1966). FRCR 1972; FRCP 1985; FRCS 1999. Consultant Radiologist, St Bartholomew's Hosp., 1974–94; Consultant Radiologist, 1974–2004, Clinical Dir, 2001–04, St Mark's Hosp.; Dir, Radiology, Princess Grace Hosp., 1990–2012. Hon. Consultant Radiologist, Hammersmith Hosp., 1994–99. *Publications:* Radiology in Inflammatory Bowel Disease, 1983; Handbook of Anal Endosonography, 1997; Imaging of Pelvic Floor Disorders, 2003; contrib. articles on gastrointestinal radiology and pelvic floor disorders. *Recreations:* walking, photography, music, reading, some gardening. *Address:* Pelhams, Maplefield Lane, Chalfont St Giles, Bucks HP8 4TY. *E:* cibartram@gmail.com. *Club:* Royal Society of Medicine.

BARTTELOT, Col Sir Brian Walter de Stopham, 5th Bt *cr* 1875; OBE 1983; psc; DL; Vice Lord-Lieutenant for West Sussex, 1994–2009; Harbinger, HM Body Guard of the Honourable Corps of Gentlemen at Arms, 2010–11 (Member, 1993–2011); *b* 17 July 1941; *s* of Lt-Col Sir Walter de Stopham Barttelot, 4th Bt, and Sara Patricia (who *m* 2nd, 1965, Comdr James Barttelot, RN retd; she *d* 1998), *d* of late Lieut-Col H. V. Ravenscroft; *S* father, 1944; *m* 1969, Hon. Mary Angela Fiona Weld Forester, (MBE 2001; DL, DStJ), *y d* of 7th Baron Forester, and of Marie Louise Priscilla, CStJ, *d* of Sir Herbert Perrott, 6th Bt, CH, CB; four *d.* *Educ:* Eton; RMA, Sandhurst. Commnd Coldstream Guards, 1961; Temp. Equerry to HM the Queen, 1970–71. Camberley Staff Coll., 1974; GSO2, Army Staff Duties Directorate, MoD, 1975–76; Second in comd, 2nd Bn, Coldstream Guards, 1977–78; Mil. Sec. to Maj.-Gen. comdg London Dist and Household Div., 1978–81; GSO1, MoD, 1981–82; CO 1st Bn Coldstream Gds, 1982–85; GSO1, HQ BAOR, 1985–86; Regtl Lt-Col Comdg Coldstream Guards, 1986–92. Col, Foot Guards, 1989–92; Hon. Col, Sussex ACF, 1996–2007. President: W Sussex Scout Council, 1993–; S of England Agricl Soc., 2001–02; Sussex Br., CLA, 2008–. Chm. Exec. Cttee, Standing Council of the Baronetage, 1996–2001; Chm., Baronets' Trust, 2002–. Liveryman, Gunmakers' Co., 1981. DL W Sussex, 1988, High Sheriff, W Sussex, 1997–98. *Heir:* *b* Robin Ravenscroft Barttelot [*b* 15 Dec. 1943; *m* 1987, Theresa, *er d* of late Kenneth Greenlees; one *s* one *d*]. *Address:* Stopham Park, Pulborough, W Sussex RH20 1DY. *Clubs:* Cavalry and Guards, Pratt's, Farmers, Boodle's.

BARWELL, Charles; *see* Barwell, J. C. F.

BARWELL, Gavin Laurence; MP (C) Croydon Central, since 2010; Comptroller of HM Treasury (Government Whip), since 2015; *b* Cuckfield, W Sussex, 23 Jan. 1972; *s* of David and Jennifer Barwell; *m* 2001, Karen McKenzie; three *s.* *Educ:* Trinity Sch. of John Whitgift, Croydon; Trinity Coll., Cambridge (BA Natural Scis 1993). Conservative Party: Envmt Desk Officer, 1993–95; Special Advr to Sec. of State for Envmt, 1995–97; Press Officer, 1997; Hd of Pol Sect., 1997–98, Hd of Local Govt Dept, 1998–2003, Cons. Campaign HQ; Chief Operating Officer, Cons. Party, 2003–06; consultant, 2006–10. PPS to Minister of State, DCLG, 2012–13; an Asst Govt Whip, 2013–14; a Lord Comr of HM Treasury (Govt Whip), 2014–15. Mem. (C) Croydon LBC, 1998–2010 (Cons. Chief Whip, 2006–07; Cabinet Mem. for Resources and Customer Services, 2007–08, for Community Safety and Cohesion, 2008–10). Mem., Sci. and Technol. Select Cttee, 2010–12. Mem. Exec., 1922 Cttee, 2010–12. Chm. Govs, Trinity Sch. Cons. Backbencher of the Year, Asian Voice, 2011. *Recreations:* sport, particularly football and tennis, military history, travel. *Address:* House of Commons, SW1A 0AA. *E:* gavin.barwell.mp@parliament.uk.

BARWELL, (John) Charles (Fiddian), OBE 2013; Vice-President, Wealth and Investment Management, Barclays, since 2007; *b* Birmingham, 3 Aug. 1968; *s* of late Bryan Fiddian Barwell and of Blanch Barwell; *m* 2010, Juliet Claire Allen; two *s.* *Educ:* Malvern Coll., Worcs; Loomis Chaffee Sch., Windsor, Conn, USA; Univ. of Manchester (BA Amer. Studies 1991); Univ. of Birmingham (DBA 1992). Investment Manager: Albert E Sharp, 1993–98; Capel Cure Sharp, 1998–2005; Associate Dir, Gerrard Investment Mgt Ltd, 2005–07. Vice Pres., 2007–10, Pres., 2010–11, Nat. Cons. Convention. Chm., Birmingham Edgbaston Cons. Assoc., 1999–2002. Conf. Chm., British-American Project, 2005. Trustee: CBSO, 2005– (Dep. Chm., 2012–; Chm., Finance Cttee, 2005–11); CBSO Develt Trust, 2013. Governor: ESU, 1999–2001; Malvern Coll., 2013–; Bilton Grange Sch., 2014. Chartered FCSI (FSI 2000). *Recreations:* singing, the rare sight of a golf ball flying straight!, gardens, sailing, ski-ing, Mahler symphonies, great food, fresh air and sunshine. *Address:* 6 Carpenter Road, Edgbaston, Birmingham B15 2JT. *E:* mail@charlesbarwell.com. *Clubs:* Carlton; MCC, Edgbaston Golf, Edgbaston Priory Lawn Tennis, Royal Cinque Ports Golf.

BARWICK, Brian Robert; Director, Barwick Media & Sport, since 2009; Chairman, Rugby Football League, since 2013; *b* 21 June 1954; *s* of John Leonard Barwick and Jean Ellen Barwick; *m* 1982, Geraldine Lynch; two *s.* *Educ:* Rudston Rd Co. Primary Sch.; Quarry Bank Comprehensive Sch.; Liverpool Univ. (BA Hons Econs). Journalist/sub-editor, North Western Evening Mail, Barrow-in-Furness, 1976–79; BBC Television (Sport): Asst Producer, 1979–84; Producer, Football Focus, 1982–84; Asst Ed., Grandstand, 1984–88; Editor: Match of the Day, 1988–95; Sportsnight, 1990–94; World Cup coverage, 1990 and 1994; Olympics, 1992 and 1996; Sports Rev. of the Year, 1991–95; Hd, Sport (Prodn), 1995–97; Controller, ITV Sport, 1998–2004; Dir of Programming, ITV2, 1998–2001; Chief Exec., FA, 2005–08. Vis. Prof. of Strategic Mgt, Univ. of Liverpool, 2009–. *Publications:* The Great Derbies: Everton *v* Liverpool (with G. Sinstadt), 1988; Anfield Days and Wembley Ways, 2011; Are You Watching the Match Tonight?, 2013. *Recreations:* watching sport, football, Rugby League, boxing and cricket; British TV comedy, sports and comedy memorabilia collecting, contemporary music, holidaying with family.

BARWISE, Stephanie Nicola, (Mrs N. P. O'Donohoe); QC 2006; *b* 17 Feb. 1964; *d* of Frank Barwise and Dorothy Carlyle Barwise (*née* Armstrong); *m* 2003, Nicholas Peter O'Donohoe, *qv*; one *s* two *d*, and two step *d.* *Educ:* Downing Coll., Cambridge (BA Law 1986; LLM 1987). Called to the Bar, Middle Temple, 1988, Bencher, 2010; in practice as barrister, specialising in commercial and construction law, 1989–. Chm., Middle Temple Estates Cttee, 2015– (Vice Chm., 2014). *Recreations:* horse riding, scuba-diving, ski-ing, yoga. *Address:* 1 Atkin Building, Gray's Inn, WC1R 5AT. *Clubs:* Kit Cat; Leander (Henley-on-Thames); Ospreys (Cambridge).

BARWISE, Prof. (Thomas) Patrick, PhD; Professor of Management and Marketing, London Business School, 1990–2006, Emeritus Professor, 2007; *b* 26 June 1946; *s* of (Henry) Balfour and Lily Barwise (*née* Abeles); *m* 1st, 1973, Mary Campbell (separated 2002; marr. diss. 2012); one *s* one *d*; 2nd, 2012, Dr Catherine Horwood (*née* Galitzine). *Educ:* Lincoln Coll., Oxford (Old Members' Scholar; BA Engrg Sci. with Econs 1968; MA 1973); London Business Sch. (MSc with Dist. Business Studies 1973; PhD 1985). Systems Engr, IBM, 1968–71; Asst to Chief Exec., Austin-Hall Gp, 1973–74; Mktg Manager, Graphic Systems Internat., 1974–76; London Business School: Sen. Res. Officer, 1976–82; Lectr, then Sen. Lectr in Mktg, 1982–90. Vis. Fellow, Reuters Inst. for Study of Journalism, Univ. of Oxford, 2011–14; Vis. Sen. Fellow in Media and Communications, LSE, 2015–. Mem. Council, Which? (Consumers' Assoc.), 1995–2000, 2006–15 (Dep. Chm., 1998–2000; Chm., 2010–15); led ind. review of BBC digital television services, DCMS, 2004; Specialist Advr to H of L Select Cttee on Communications inquiry into regulation of TV advertising, 2010–11; expert witness for commercial, tax and competition cases in Brussels, Frankfurt, London, Paris and Washington. Mem., Hansard Soc. Commn on Parlt and the Public, 2004–05. Mem. Cttee of Mgt, Soc. of Authors, 2010–13. Fellow, Sunningdale Inst., 2005–11. Hon. Fellow, Marketing Soc., 2006–. Patron, Market Res. Soc., 2013–. *Publications:* Online Searching, 1979; Television and its Audience, 1988; Accounting for Brands, 1989; Strategic Decisions, 1997; Marketing Expenditure Trends, 2002, 2nd edn 2003; (with S. Meehan) Simply Better, 2004 (Berry-AMA Prize, 2005); (with S. Meehan) Beyond the Familiar: long-term growth through customer focus and innovation, 2011; (with R. G. Picard) The Economics of Television in a Digital World, 2012; (with R. G. Picard) What if There Were No BBC Television?, 2014; numerous publications on mgt, mktg and media. *Recreation:* talking. *Address:* London Business School, Regent's Park, NW1 4SA.

BARYSHNIKOV, Mikhail; dancer, actor, producer; Artistic Director, Baryshnikov Arts Center, since 2005; *b* 27 Jan. 1948; *s* of Nicolai Baryshnikov and Alexandra (*née* Kisselov). *Educ:* Ballet Sch. of Riga, Latvia; Kirov Ballet Sch., Leningrad. Soloist, Kirov Ballet Co., 1969–74; Principal Dancer, NY City Ballet, 1978–79; Artistic Dir, 1980–89, Principal Dancer, 1974–78 and 1980–89, American Ballet Theater; Co-Founder (with Mark Morris) and Dir, White Oak Dance Proj., 1990–2002. Guest Artist, 1974–, with: Royal Ballet; National Ballet of Canada; Hamburg Ballet; Ballet Victoria, Aust.; Stuttgart Ballet; Alvin Ailey Dance Co., and Eliot Feld Ballet, New York; Spoleto Festival. Repertoire includes: Shadowplay (Tudor); Le Jeune Homme et la Morte (Petit); Sacré du Printemps (Tetley); Prodigal Son, Apollo, Theme and Variations (Balanchine); Afternoon of a Faun (Robbins); Romeo and Juliet, Wild Boy (MacMillan); Configurations (Choo San Goh); Les Patineurs, A Month in the Country (Ashton); Spectre de la Rose, Le Pavillon d'Armide, Petrouchka (Fokine); Santa Fe Saga (Feld); La Sylphide, La Bayadère, Coppélia, La Fille mal gardée (Bournonville); Swan Lake (Sergeyev and Bruhn); The Nutcracker, Don Quixote (own choreography). Works created: Medea (Butler), 1975; Push Comes to Shove, and, Once More Frank (Tharp), Connotations on Hamlet (Neumeier), Pas de Duke (Ailey), Other Dances (Robbins), 1976; Variations on America (Feld), 1977; Rubies (Balanchine), Opus Nineteen (Robbins), 1979; Rhapsody (Ashton), 1980. Over 50 works commissioned by White Oak Dance Project and Baryshnikov Dance Foundn including: Waiting for the Sunrise (Lubovitch); Three Preludes (Morris); Punch and Judy (Gordon); Pergolesi (Tharp); Unspoken Territory (Reitz); Journey of a Poet (Hawkins); Heartbeat:mb (Janney and Rudner); Blue Heron (Schlömer); The Good Army (O'Day); Piano Bar (Béjart); See Through Knot (Jasperse); Single Duet (Hay); Chacony (Childs); The Show/Achilles Heels (Move); Yazoo (Feld). Actor: *films:* The Turning Point, 1978; White Nights, 1986; Dancers, 1987; Company Business, 1991; The Cabinet of Dr Ramirez, 1991; *television:* Sex in the City, 2004; *theatre:* Beckett Shorts, NY, 2007; *photography exhibition:* Dancing Away, Contini Art UK, 2014–15. Gold Medal: Varna Competition, Bulgaria, 1966; 1st Internat. Ballet Comp., Moscow, 1968 (also awarded Nijinsky Prize by Paris Acad. of Dance); Dance Magazine Award, NYC, 1978; Kennedy Center Honors, 2000; Nat. Medal of Arts, 2000; Nijinsky Award for choreographic work Past Forward, 2002; Chubb Fellowship Award, Yale Univ., 2003; Liberty Prize, 2004; Jerome Robbins Award, 2004; Nixon Center Award, 2004; Arison Award, 2005. Commandeur, Ordre des Arts et des Lettres (France), 2010; Officier, Légion d'Honneur (France), 2010. *Publications:* (with Charles Engell France, photographs by Martha Swope) Baryshnikov at Work, 1976; (with John Fraser, photographs by Eve Arnold) Private View: inside Baryshnikov's American Ballet Theatre, 1988; Baryshnikov in Black and White, 2002; Merce My Way, 2009. *Recreations:* fishing, golf, photography.

BARZUN, Matthew Winthrop; Ambassador of the United States of America to the Court of St James's, since 2013; *b* NYC, 23 Oct. 1970; *m* 1999, Brooke Lee Brown; two *s* one *d.* *Educ:* St Paul's Sch., New Hampshire; Harvard Univ. (AB Hist. and Lit. 1993). With CNET Networks, 1993–2004: Vice Pres., Software Services, 1995–98; Exec. Vice-Pres., 1998–2000; Chief Strategy Officer, 2000–04; Founder, Brickpath LLC, internet media consultancy, 2004; Mem., Barak Obama's Nat. Finance Cttee for Presidential campaign, 2008; Ambassador to Sweden, 2009–11; Chair, Barak Obama's Nat. Finance Cttee for Presidential re-election campaign, 2012. *Address:* Embassy of the United States of America, 24 Grosvenor Square, W1A 1AE.

BASBAUM, Prof. Allan Irwin, PhD; FRS 2006; Professor, since 1984, and Chairman, Department of Anatomy, since 1977, University of California, San Francisco. *Educ:* McGill Univ. (BS 1968); Univ. of Penn (PhD 1972). Postdoctoral research: in neurophysiol., UCL, 1972–74; in neuroanatomy, UCSF, 1974–76; Associate Prof., Depts of Anatomy and of Physiol., UCSF, 1980–84. Co-founder and Mem., Scientific Adv. Bd, BiPar Sciences Inc. Chm., French American Internat. Sch. (Mem. Bd, 1988–; Pres., until 2004). FMedSci 2007. *Publications:* articles in jls. *Address:* Department of Anatomy, University of California, 1550 4th Street, Rock Hall, San Francisco, CA 94143, USA.

BĂSESCU, Traian; President of Romania, 2004–14; *b* 4 Nov. 1951; *s* of Dimitru and Elena Traian; *m* 1975, Maria; two *d.* *Educ:* Mircea cel Bătrân Naval Inst. (grad 1976); Norwegian Acad. (schol.; advanced courses Mgt in Shipping Ind. 1995). Naval Officer, NAVROM, 1976–81; Captain, Comdr, Arges, Crisana and Biruinta ships, 1981–87; Chief, NAVROM Agency, Belgium, 1987–89; Gen. Manager, State Inspectorate for Civil Navigation, 1989–90, Under-Sec. of State and Chief, Shipping Dept, 1990–91, Min. of Transportation; Minister of Transportation, 1991–92; Deputy (Democratic), Vaslui, 1992–96; Minister of Transportation, 1996–2000; Mayor of Bucharest, 2000–04. Democratic Party (PD): Bucharest Orgn, 2000–01; Pres., 2001–04; Co-Pres., DA (Justice and Truth) Alliance, 2001–04. Hon. Dr Pol Scis Hankuk, Seoul, 2005; Hon. Dr Diplomatic and Strategic Centre of Studies, Paris, 2005. Comdr, Nat. Order of Merit (Romania), 2000; Medal of Renaissance, 1st Cl. (Jordan), 2005. *Recreations:* spending time with my family, taking long walks in nature.

BASHAM, Brian Arthur; *b* 30 July 1943; *s* of late Arthur Edgar Basham and Gladys Florence Alice (*née* Turner); *m* 1st, 1968, Charlotte Blackman; two *d*; 2nd, 1988, Eileen Wise (marr. diss. 1996); 3rd, 1998, Lynne Goodson. *Educ:* Brownhill Road Primary Sch., Catford; Catford Secondary Sch. GEC Export Clerk, 1961; Daily Mail City Office: Stock Exchange prices collector, 1962; City Press reporter, 1963; Prodn Editor, Daily Mail City Page, 1964; Financial Journalist: Daily Telegraph, 1966; The Times, 1968; Fund Man., Regent Fund Managers, 1971; Dir, John Addey Associates, 1973; Founder, 1976, subseq. Dep. Chm., Broad Street Gp; Co-Founder and Dep. Chm., Primrose Care, 1993–98; Founder Chairman: Equity Development, 2006–; ArchOver, 2013–. Founder Trustee, Centre for Investigative Journalism, 2005–. *Publications:* (with Craig Pickering) Tomorrow's Giants, 1998; Thorium:

the eighth element, 2013. *Recreations:* politics, reading, constitutional reform, motorcycling, gardening, walking. *Address:* Nashes Farmhouse, Crowhurst, E Sussex TN33 9BU. *T:* 07771 828828. *Clubs:* Army and Navy, Establishment (Chm., 2012–).

BASHEER, Prof. (Paliakarakadu Assen) Muhammed, PhD, DSc; FREng; Professor of Structural Engineering, since 2014 and Head, School of Civil Engineering, since 2015, University of Leeds; *b* Puramattom, India, 9 Feb. 1959; *s* of Peerukhan Assen and Marium Beevi; *m* 1985, Lulu Bahauddin; one *s* one *d*. *Educ:* Univ. of Kerala (BSc Engrg); Univ. of Calicut (MSc Engrg); Queen's Univ., Belfast (PhD 1991; DSc 2014). CEng 1998. Asst Engr, Kerala Public Health Engrg Dept, 1982; Lectr, Calicut Regl Engrg Coll., 1982–87; Queen's University, Belfast: Lectr, 1993–96; Sen. Lectr, 1996–98; Reader, 1998–99; Prof., 1999–2014. FREng 2014. *Publications:* Resistance of Concrete to Chloride Ingress: testing and modelling, 2012; approx. 85 papers in learned jls. *Recreations:* classical music, driving through countryside, family. *Address:* School of Civil Engineering, University of Leeds, Leeds LS2 9JT. *T:* (0113) 343 2272, *Fax:* (0113) 343 2265. *E:* p.a.m.basheer@leeds.ac.uk.

BASHIR, Amjad Mahmood; Member for Yorkshire and the Humber Region, European Parliament (UK Ind, 2014–15, C, since 2015); *b* Jhelum, Pakistan, 17 Sept. 1952. *Educ:* Thornton Grammar Sch.; Univ. of Bradford (degree in Chem. Engrg). Worked with Kodak; owner, Zouk Tea Bar and Grill, Bradford, 2006, Manchester, 2008. *Address:* European Parliament, 60 Rue Wiertz, 1047 Brussels, Belgium.

BASHIR, Hon. Prof. Dame Marie (Roslyn), AD 2014 (AC 2001; AO 1988); CVO 2005; FRANZCP; Governor of New South Wales, Australia, 2001–14; *d* of M. Bashir; *m* 1957, Sir Nicholas Michael Shehadie, *qv*; one *s* two *d*. *Educ:* Sydney Girls' High Sch.; Univ. of Sydney (MB, BS 1956). Taught at Univs of Sydney and of NSW; Clinical Prof. of Psychiatry, Univ. of Sydney, 1993–2001; Area Dir, Mental Health Services, Central Sydney, 1994–2001; Sen. Consultant, Aboriginal Med. Services, Redfern and Kempsey, 1996–2001. Chancellor, Univ. of Sydney, 2007–. Chevalier, Légion d'Honneur (France), 2009.

BASHMET, Yuri Abramovich; viola player; Principal Conductor, Symphony Orchestra of New Russia, since 2002; *b* 24 Jan. 1953; *m* Natalia Timofeevna; one *s* one *d*. *Educ:* Moscow State Conservatory. Winner, Munich International Viola Competition, 1976; Founder and Dir, Chamber Orchestra Moscow Soloists, 1989–; Artistic Dir, Sviatoslav Richter's December Nights Fest., Moscow. Has performed with the world's major orchestras including: Berlin Philharmonic; Boston Symphony; Concertgebouw; LSO; Los Angeles Philharmonic; Montreal Symphony; first performance of viola concerti by Alfred Schnittke, Aleksander Tchaikovsky, Poul Ruders, Sofia Gubaidulina, Mark-Anthony Turnage, Giya Kancheli and Alexander Raskatov. Founder, Yuri Bashmet Internat. Foundn, 1994. *Address:* c/o International Classical Artists, Dunstan House, 14a St Cross Street, EC1N 8XA. *T:* (020) 7902 0520; Apartment 16, Nezhdanovoy str. 7, 103009, Moscow, Russia.

BASING, 6th Baron *cr* 1887; **Stuart Anthony Whitfield Sclater-Booth;** *b* 18 Dec. 1969; *s* of 5th Baron Basing and of Patricia Ann, *d* of late George Bryan Whitfield, New Haven, Conn; *S* father, 2007; *m* 1997, Kirsten Erica (marr. diss.), *d* of Eric Henry Oxboel; two *s* one *d*. *Educ:* Collegiate Sch.; Vassar Coll.; Boston Univ. (MA). *Heir:* *s* Hon. Luke Waters Sclater-Booth, *b* 1 Sept. 2000.

BASINGSTOKE, Bishop Suffragan of, since 2014; **Rt Rev. David Grant Williams;** *b* Reading, 16 April 1961; *s* of Malcolm Williams and Brenda Williams; *m* 1986, Helen Pacey; one *s* one *d*. *Educ:* Bristol Univ. (BSocSc 1983); Wycliffe Hall, Oxford. Dep. Hd Teacher, St Luke's Yatta, CMS, E Kenya, 1983–85; ordained deacon, 1989, priest, 1990; Asst Curate, All Saints, Ecclesall, 1989–92; Vicar, Christ Church, Dore, 1992–2002; Rural Dean, Ecclesall, 1997–2002; Vicar, Christ Church, Winchester, 2002–14; Hon. Canon, Winchester Cathedral, 2012–14. Elected Gen. Synod, C of E, 2010–; Chair, House of Clergy, Winchester Diocesan Synod, 2012–. *Recreations:* sailing, long distance motorcycle journeys. *Address:* Bishop's Lodge, Colden Lane, Old Alresford, Alresford SO24 9DY. *T:* (01962) 737330. *E:* bishop.david@winchester.anglican.org.

BASKER, Prof. Robin Michael, OBE 2001; DDS; Professor of Dental Prosthetics, University of Leeds, 1978–2000, now Emeritus; Consultant in Restorative Dentistry, United Leeds Teaching Hospitals NHS Trust (formerly Leeds Western Health Authority), 1978–2000; *b* 26 Dec. 1936; *s* of Caryl Ashbourne Basker and Edna Crowden (*née* Russell); *m* 1961, Jacqueline Mary Bowles; two *d*. *Educ:* Wellingborough Sch.; London Hosp. Med. Coll., Univ. of London (BDS 1961); Birmingham Univ. (DDS 1969). LDSRCS 1961, MGDSRCS 1979. General dental practice, 1961–63; Lectr and Sen. Lectr, Univ. of Birmingham, 1963–78; Leeds University: Dean, Sch. of Dentistry, 1985–90; Chm., Bd of Faculty of Medicine and Dentistry, 1990–93. Hon. Scientific Advr, British Dental Jl, 1980–96; British Standards Expert Advr, ISO TC/106, 1982–2005. Mem., Nuffield Foundn Inquiry into trng and educn of personnel auxiliary to dentistry, 1992–93. Member: Dental Cttee, Med. Defence Union, 1985–95; GDC, 1986–99 (Treas., 1992–94; Chm., Registration Sub-Cttee, 1994; Chm., Educn Cttee, 1994–99); President: British Soc. for Study of Prosthetic Dentistry, 1988 (Mem. Council and Sec., 1978–81); Yorks Br., BDA, 1991–92; British Soc. of Gerodontology, 1999; Chm., Lindsay Soc. for the History of Dentistry, 2008–10. Ext. Examr in Dental Subjects, Univs of Birmingham, Bristol, Dundee, London, Manchester, Malaya, Newcastle upon Tyne, Sheffield, Wales, UC, Cork and Univ. Kebangsaan, Malaysia; Examr for Membership of Gen. Dental Surgery, RCS, 1979–84 (Chm. Examrs, 1987–92). Life Mem., British Soc. of Gerodontol., 2001; Hon. Mem., British Soc. for Study of Prosthetic Dentistry, 2001. FRSocMed; Hon. FDSRCSE 2000. John Tomes Medal, BDA, 2000. *Publications:* Prosthetic Treatment of the Edentulous Patient, 1976, 5th edn 2011; Overdentures in General Dental Practice, 1983, 3rd edn 1993; A Colour Atlas of Removable Partial Dentures, 1987; Clinical Guide to Removable Partial Dentures, 2000; Clinical Guide to Removable Partial Denture Design, 2000. *Recreation:* choral singing.

BASS; *see* Hastings Bass, family name of Earl of Huntingdon.

BASS, Rear-Adm. Paul Eric, CB 1981; CEng, FIMechE, MIMarEST; *b* 7 March 1925; *s* of C. H. P. Bass, Ipswich; *m* 1948, Audrey Bruce Tomlinson (*d* 2002); one *s*. *Educ:* Northgate School, Ipswich; Royal Naval Engineering Coll., Keyham. Served as Midshipman in HM Ships Cambrian, Mauritius, Premier and Rodney; Lieut in Belfast, Phoebe and Implacable; Lt Comdr in Ulysses; Comdr in Lion and Tiger; Naval Staff Course, 1962; Captain, Weapons Trials, 1969–72; NATO Defense Course, 1972–73; Asst Chief of Staff (Intelligence), SACLANT, 1973–75; Dir, Naval Manning and Training (Engineering), 1975–78; Flag Officer, Portsmouth and Port Admiral, Portsmouth, 1979–81, retired 1981. *Recreations:* sailing, painting. *Club:* Royal Naval and Royal Albert Yacht (Portsmouth).

BASSAM OF BRIGHTON, Baron *cr* 1997 (Life Peer), of Brighton in the co. of East Sussex; **John Steven Bassam;** PC 2009; *b* 11 June 1953; *s* of late Sydney Stevens and Enid Bassam; partner, Jill Whittaker; one *s* two *d* (and one *s* decd). *Educ:* Univ. of Sussex (BA Hons History 1975; Hon. Fellow, 2001); Univ. of Kent (MA Social Work 1979). Social Worker, E Sussex CC, 1976–77; Legal Advr, N Lewisham Law Centre, 1979–83; Policy Adviser: LB Camden, 1983–84; GLC (Police Cttee), 1984–86; London Strategic Policy Unit (Policing), 1986–87; Asst Sec., Police, Fire, Envmtl Health and Consumer Affairs, AMA, 1988–97; Consultant Advr, KPMG, 1997–99. Parly Under-Sec. of State, Home Office, 1999–2001; a Lord in Waiting (Govt Whip), 2001–08; Captain of Hon. Corps of Gentlemen at Arms (Govt Chief Whip in H of L), 2008–10; Opposition Chief Whip, H of L, 2010–. Member (Lab): Brighton BC, 1983–97 (Leader, 1987–97); Brighton & Hove Unitary Council, 1996–99 (Leader, 1996–99). Fellow, Brighton Coll., 2002–. *Publications:* articles for local govt pubns. *Recreations:* cricket (plays for Preston Village CC), walking, running, watching football, reading, history of churches. *Address:* Longstone, 25 Church Place, Brighton BN2 5JN. *T:* (01273) 609473.

BASSET, Gerard Francis Claude, OBE 2011; Co-owner, Hotel TerraVina Ltd, since 2007; *b* St Etienne, France, 7 March 1957; *s* of Pierre René Basset and Marguerite Basset; *m* 1997, Nina Howe; one *s*. *Educ:* Lycée Albert Camus, Firminy, France. Master Sommelier, 1989; Master of Wine, 1998; Wine MBA, 2007. Maître d'hotel, Crown Hotel, Lyndhurst, 1984–87; Chef Sommelier, Chewton Glen Hotel, New Milton, Hants (one Michelin Star), 1988–94. Co-founder, co-owner and Dir, Hotel du Vin Gp, 1994–2004. Dir, Acad. of Food and Wine Service, 2007–. Gen. Sec., 2010–, Hd, Tech. Commn, Assoc. Sommellerie Internat., 2014–. World Wide Pres., 2008–11, Eur. Pres., 2011–, Court of Master Sommeliers. Hon. Pres., Wine and Spirit Educn Trust, 2014–. Association de la Sommellerie Internationale: Best Sommelier in UK, 1989, 1992; Best Internat. Sommelier for French Wine, 1992; Best Sommelier in Europe, 1996; Best Sommelier in World, 2010; Calvet Cup, Acad. Wine Service, 1989, 1990, 1992; Sommelier Best of the Best, Courvoisier, 1992; Dom Perignon Cup, 1996, Special Achievement Award, 2005, Acad. Food and Wine Service; Catey Awards for Hotel du Vin, 1996, 2001, Special Award, 2010, Caterer and Hotelkeeper mag.; Maître Sommelier, Union de la Sommellerie Française, 2012; Best Ambassador/Communicator for French Wines, Harpers, 2013. *Publications:* The Wine Experience, 2000. *Recreations:* chess, walking in forest with dog, Malmsey. *Address:* c/o Hotel TerraVina, 174 Woodlands Road, Southampton, Hants SO40 7GL. *T:* (023) 8029 3784, *Fax:* (023) 8029 3627.

BASSETT, Claire Elisabeth Rachel; Chief Executive, Electoral Commission, since 2015; *b* Londonderry, 23 Jan. 1974; *d* of Col Keith Whiteman and Jenny Whiteman; *m* 2002, Jason Bassett. *Educ:* Sherborne Sch. for Girls; Univ. of Wales Coll., Cardiff (LLB Hons). Mgt Trainee, SIG plc, 1996–99; Account Manager, Legal Services Commn, 1999–2003; Chief Exec., Connexions Milton Keynes, Oxon and Bucks, 2003–06; Services Dir, NACRO, 2006–09; Chief Executive: Criminal Cases Rev. Commn, 2009–12; Parole Bd for England and Wales, 2012–15. Mem. Bd, Home Gp, 2013–. Mem. Bd, Assoc. of Chief Execs, 2010–. *Recreations:* horse riding, walking, friends and family, pet dachshund. *Address:* Electoral Commission, 3 Bunhill Row, EC1Y 8YZ.

BASSETT, John Anthony Seward, FRICS; Consultant, Jones Lang LaSalle (formerly Jones, Lang, Wootton), since 1997 (Senior Partner, 1991–97); *b* 8 Sept. 1936; *s* of Roger Seward and Marjorie Bassett; *m* 1st, 1960, Jean Margaret Cooper (marr. diss. 1993; remarried 2006); one *s* one *d*; 2nd, 1994, Jennifer David (marr. diss. 2003). *Educ:* Blundell's Sch.; Coll. of Estate Management, London Univ. FRICS 1972. Joined Folkard & Hayward, 1957; Donaldson & Sons, 1960–63; joined Jones, Lang, Wootton, 1963, Partner 1967–97. Chairman: MWB Leisure Funds, 1996–2003; X-Leisure (Gen. Partner) Ltd, 2004–. Hon. Treas., Westminster Property Owners' Assoc., 1989–98. Trustee, Chatham Historic Dockyard Trust, 1997–. *Recreations:* ocean racing, ski-ing, travel, fly fishing. *Address:* 6 Ranelagh Grove, SW1W 8PD. *Clubs:* Pilgrims; Royal Thames Yacht, Royal Ocean Racing.

BASSETT CROSS, Alistair Robert Sinclair; District Judge, 1991–2011, Deputy District Judge, since 2013, Principal Registry, Family Division, High Court of Justice; *b* 25 Aug. 1944; *s* of late Edward Bassett Cross and Marguerite Sinclair Bassett Cross (*née* Mitchell); *m* 1977, Margaret Victoria Janes; one *s* one *d*. *Educ:* Bishop Challoner Sch., Shortlands; Coll. of Law, Lancaster Gate. FInstLEx 1971. Legal Exec. with Lawrence Graham, 1964–77; solicitor, 1980; Legal Exec. and Solicitor, Payne Hicks Beach, 1977–91 (Partner, 1988–91); Dep. County Court and Dist Registrar, 1990. Mem., Solicitors' Family Law Assoc., 1984; Mem., Family Mediators' Assoc., 1989; Accredited Family Mediator, 1990; Mem., Adv. Bd of Mediation Service, Inst. of Family Therapy, 1995–98; Trustee, Mediation for Families (London E and City), 1999–2001; Accredited Civil and Commercial Mediator, 2012; Mem., Civil Mediation Council, 2012–. HAC, 1965, commnd, 1969; Mem., Co. of Pikemen and Musketeers, Lord Mayor's Bodyguard, 1993 (Elder Serjeant, 2003–06; Captain, 2011–14). Freeman, City of London, 1993; Liveryman, Poulters' Co., 1996 (Ct Asst, 2009; Master, 2014–15). Mem., Lime Street Ward Club, 1996 (Master, 2009–10). *Publications:* (ed) Supreme Court Practice, 1994–99; Civil Procedure, 2000–06; (ed) The Family Court Practice, 2004–06. *Recreations:* family, anything and everything. *Address:* c/o Principal Registry (Family Division), First Avenue House, 42–49 High Holborn, WC1V 6NP. *Club:* Victory Services.

BASSEY, Dame Shirley (Veronica), DBE 2000 (CBE 1994); singer; *b* Tiger Bay, Cardiff, 8 Jan. 1937; *d* of late Henry and Eliza Jane Bassey; one *d*; *m* 1st, 1961, Kenneth Hume (marr. diss. 1965; decd); 2nd, 1971, Sergio Novak (marr. diss. 1981); one adopted *s* (one *d* decd). Appeared in Such is Life, 1955; *recordings* include: *singles:* Burn My Candle; Banana Boat Song, 1957; As I Love You, 1959; Kiss Me Honey; Reach for the Stars/Climb Every Mountain, 1961; What Now My Love; I Am What I Am; I (Who Have Nothing); Goldfinger, 1964; Diamonds Are Forever, 1971; Something; For All We Know; Never Never Never; Moonraker, 1979; *albums:* Born to Sing the Blues, 1958; And I Love You So, 1972; Live at Carnegie Hall, 1973; Magic Is You, 1978; Sassy Bassey, 1985; La Mujer, 1989; New York, New York, 1991; Great Shirley Bassey, 1999; The Performance, 2009; Hello Like Before, 2014; numerous concerts and tours; series, BBC TV; appeared in film, La Passione, 1996. Artist for Peace, UNESCO, 2000; Internat. Ambassador, Variety Club, 2001. Britannia Award for Best Female Singer, 1977; Lifetime Achievement Award, Nat. Music Awards, 2003. Légion d'Honneur (France), 2003; Freedom of City of Cardiff, 2012. *Address:* c/o Victoria Settepassi, 31 Avenue Princess Grace, MC 98000, Monaco.

BASSI, (Paramjit) Paul Singh, CBE 2010; DL; Chief Executive, Real Estate Investors plc, since 2007; Founder Chairman, Bond Wolfe, since 1985; Chairman, CP Bigwood (formerly Bigwood) Chartered Surveyors, since 2006; *b* Birmingham, 21 March 1962; *s* of Santokh Singh Bassi and Avtar Kaur (*née* Chaudry); *m* 2008, Priya Paula (*née* Narang); one *d*; one *s* one *d* by a previous marriage. *Educ:* Harlington Comp. Sch., Hayes; Sandwell Coll. Regl Chm., Coutts Bank, 2001–07 (Mem., Exec. Steering Bd, 2006); non-exec. Chm., Corporatewear UK, 2004; Vice Chm., Bigwood Chartered Surveyors, 2006; Chm., Midlands, Kaupthing Singer & Friedlander, 2007–09; Director: Birmingham Hippodrome, 2005–10; InvestBX, 2007–11; Dir, Ind. Financial Advrs, EFG, 2011. Pres., Birmingham Chamber of Commerce, 2009–10 (Vice Pres., 2008–09). DL 2008, High Sheriff 2009, W Midlands. DUniv Birmingham City, 2009; Hon. DSc Aston, 2011. Lifetime Achievement Award, Lloyds TSB, 2005. *Recreations:* sport, reading, travel, prestige cars. *Address:* Real Estate Investors plc, Cathedral Place, 3rd Floor, 42–44 Waterloo Street, Birmingham B2 5QB.

BASSINGTHWAIGHTE, His Honour Keith; a Circuit Judge, 1991–2003; Resident Judge, Guildford Crown Court Centre, 2000–03; a Deputy Circuit Judge, 2003–05; *b* 19 Jan. 1943; *s* of Reginald and Barbara Bassingthwaighte; *m* 1966, Olwyn Burn. *Educ:* Ashford (Middx) County Grammar Sch. Admitted solicitor, 1967. Served RAF Legal Branch as Flt Lt, 1968, Sqdn Ldr 1973, Wing Comdr 1978 and Gp Capt. 1981; retired 1984. Chm., Industrial Tribunals (London Central and S regions), part-time 1984–85, full-time 1985–91; a Recorder of the Crown Court, 1987–91. Pres., Social Security Appeal, Medical Appeal, Disability Appeal, Child Support Appeal and Vaccine Damage Tribunals, 1994–98; a Judge, Employment Appeal Tribunal, 1996. Mem., Parole Bd, 2004–. *Recreations:* golf, bridge, opera. *Address:* c/o Barclays Bank, Sloane Square, SW1W 8AF. *Club:* Oake Manor Golf.

BASSNETT, Prof. Susan Edna, PhD; FRSL; writer; Professor of Comparative Literature, University of Warwick, since 1992 (Pro-Vice-Chancellor, 1997–2003 and 2005–09); *b* 21 Oct. 1945; *d* of Raymond George Bassnett and Anne Eileen Bassnett (*née* Hardwick); one *s* three *d*. *Educ:* Denmark, Portugal, Italy and UK; Univ. of Manchester (BA 1st Cl. Hons

English and Italian 1968); Univ. of Lancaster (PhD French 1975). Lecturer: Univ. of Rome, 1968–72; Univ. of Lancaster, 1972–76; Univ. of Warwick, 1976–: estabd Centre for Translation and Comparative Cultural Studies, 1985; Reader, 1989–92. Has held Vis. Prof. posts at univs worldwide; Vis. Lectr, Michigan State Univ., 1974–75. Member: Arts Adv. Bd, British Council, 2002–06; W Midlands Culture, 2002–09; Arts Council England, W Midlands, 2003–10; QAA, 2003–08. Mem. Bd, SOAS, 2003–08. FCIL (FIL 2000); MAE 2006 (Mem. Council, 2007–); FRSL 2008. *Publications:* Translation Studies, 1980, 4th edn 2013; Luigi Pirandello, 1983; Sylvia Plath: an introduction to the poetry, 1987, 2nd edn 2004; (jtly) The Actress in Her Time: Bernhardt, Terry, Duse, 1988; Magdalena: women's experimental theatre, 1989; (ed) Knives and Angels: Latin American women's writing, 1990; Shakespeare: the Elizabethan plays, 1993; Comparative Literature: a critical introduction, 1993; (jtly) Three Tragic Actresses: Siddons, Rachel, Ristori, 1996; (with A. Lefevre) Constructing Cultures, 1998; (ed with H. Trivedi) Postcolonial Translation: theory and practice, 1999; Exchanging Lives, 2002; (ed with P. Bush) The Translator as Writer, 2006; Ted Hughes, 2009; (with E. Bielsa) Translation in Global News, 2009; Reflections on Translation, 2011; Translation, 2014. *Recreations:* reading, walking with dogs, textiles, writing. *Address:* Modern Languages, University of Warwick, Coventry CV4 7AL. *T:* (024) 7652 3655. *E:* s.bassnett@warwick.ac.uk.

BASTIN, Prof. John Andrew, MA, PhD; FRAS; Professor, 1971–84, now Emeritus, and Head of Department of Physics, 1975–80, Queen Mary College, London University; *b* 3 Jan. 1929; *s* of Lucy and Arthur Bastin; *m*; one *s* one *d*; *m* 1985, Aida Baterina Delfino. *Educ:* George Monoux Grammar Sch., London; Corpus Christi Coll., Oxford (MA, PhD). Univ. of Ibadan, Nigeria, 1952–56; Univ. of Reading, 1956–59; Queen Mary Coll., Univ. of London, 1959–84. Initiated a group in far infrared astronomy at Queen Mary College, 1960–70. *Publications:* papers on far infrared astronomy and lunar evolution. *Recreations:* English water colours, architecture, Renaissance and Baroque music. *Address:* 5 The Clockhouse, Redlynch Park, Bruton, Somerset BA10 0NH.

BASTON, Ven. Caroline; Transition Minister, and Priest-in-charge, St Andrew's, North Swindon, since 2011; *b* 17 Oct. 1956; *d* of Dr John Baston, MB ChB, DPM, FRCGP and Dr Daphne Baston, MB ChB, MRCGP. *Educ:* Birmingham Univ. (BSc 1978); Birmingham Poly. (Cert Ed 1979); Ripon Coll., Cuddesdon (Hon. Fellow 2014). Teacher, Shireland High Sch., Smethwick, 1979–87. Ordained deacon, 1989, priest, 1994; Asst Curate, Thornhill St Christopher, Southampton, 1989–95; Rector, All Saints', Winchester, with St Andrew, Chilcomb, with St Peter, Chesil, 1995–2006; Communications Officer, 1995–98, Dir of Ordinands, 1999–2006, Dio. Winchester; Archdeacon of the Isle of Wight, 2006–11, now Archdeacon Emeritus. Warden, Community of St Mary the Virgin, Wantage, 2013–. Hon. Canon: Winchester Cathedral, 2000–06, now Canon Emeritus; Portsmouth Cathedral, 2006–11. *Address:* 8 Figsbury Close, Taw Hill, Swindon, Wilts SN25 1UA.

BASU, Dijendra Bhushan; QC 2015; a Recorder, since 2010; *b* Solihull, 10 Aug. 1968; *s* of Dr Dipendra Bhushan Basu and late Dr Shashi Kanta Basu; one *d*. *Educ:* Queen Mary's Grammar Sch., Walsall; United Med. and Dental Schs of Guy's and St Thomas's, Univ. of London (MB BS with distinction in Surgery 1991). Called to the Bar, Lincoln's Inn, 1994; in practice as a barrister specialising in police, public and employment law; a Special Advocate, 2009–. *Publications:* technical legal jls. *Recreations:* flying helicopters, sailing, cooking, eating, drinking. *Address:* 5 Essex Court, Temple, EC4Y 9AH. *T:* (020) 7410 2000, *Fax:* (020) 7129 8606. *E:* basu@5essexcourt.co.uk.

BATCHELOR, Prof. (John) Richard; Professor of Immunology, Royal Postgraduate Medical School, Hammersmith Hospital, 1979–94, now Professor Emeritus; *b* 4 Oct. 1931; *s* of B. W. Batchelor, CBE and Mrs C. E. Batchelor; *m* 1955, Moira Ann (*née* McLellan) (*d* 2015); two *s* two *d*. *Educ:* Marlborough Coll.; Emmanuel Coll., Cambridge; Guy's Hospital, London. MB, BChir Cantab, 1955; MD Cantab 1965. FRCPath 1991; FRCP 1995. Nat. Service, RAMC, 1957–59; Dept of Pathology, Guy's Hospital: Res. Fellow, 1959–61; Lectr and Sen. Lectr, 1961–67; Prof. of Transplantation Research, RCS, 1967; Dir, McIndoe Res. Unit, Queen Victoria Hosp., East Grinstead, 1967–78. European Editor, Transplantation, 1964–97. Pres., Transplantation Soc., 1988–90 (Hon. Sec., then Vice-Pres. (E Hemisphere), 1976–80); Member Council, Nat. Kidney Res. Fund, 1979–86; Chm., Scientific Co-ord. Cttee, Arthritis and Rheumatism Council, 1988–96. Trustee: Kennedy Inst. for Rheumatology Trust, 1997– (Dep. Chm., 1997–2014; Hon. Vice Pres., 2014–); Sir Jules Thorn Charitable Trust, 1999–2004. MRSocMed. Mem. Court, Skinners' Company. Hon. Fellow, Faculty of Medicine, Imperial Coll. London, 2002. *Publications:* scientific articles upon tissue transplantation research in various special jls. *Recreations:* Real tennis and lawn tennis, walking. *Address:* Little Ambrook, Nursery Road, Walton-on-the-Hill, Tadworth, Surrey KT20 7TU. *T:* (01737) 812028. *Club:* Queen's.

BATCHELOR, Lance Henry Lowe; Group Chief Executive Officer, Saga plc, since 2014; *b* London, 9 Jan. 1964; *s* of David Henry Lowe Batchelor and Sarah Ann Batchelor; *m* 1989, Wendy Jane Doran; four *s*. *Educ:* Cranleigh Sch.; Univ. of Wales (BSc Econs 1985); Harvard Business Sch. (MBA 1993). Lieut, Submarines, RN, 1985–90; Procter & Gamble: Asst Brand Manager, Health and Beauty Care, 1991–95; Brand Manager, Skincare, 1995–97; Gen. Manager and Mktg Dir, Beauty Care Div., 1997–2000; amazon.com: Gen. Manager and Product Dir, Books, Music/Video, 2000–01; Hd, Worldwide Mktg, 2001–02; Vodafone plc: Mktg Dir and Mem., UK Bd, 2002–04; Global Mktg Dir, Vodafone Consumer, 2004–06; Tesco plc: Mktg Dir, 2007–08; CEO, Tesco Telecoms, 2008–11; CEO, Domino's Pizza Gp plc, 2011–14. Trustee, Nat. Gall., 2011–. Mem., Council of Mgt, White Ensign Assoc., 2014–. Mem., RNSA, 1986. *Recreations:* sailing, fine art. *Address:* Saga plc, Enbrook Park, Sandgate, Kent CT20 3SE. *T:* (01303) 771111, *Fax:* (01303) 771175. *E:* lance.batchelor@saga.co.uk.

BATCHELOR, Paul Anthony; Chairman: Crown Agents, since 2007 (non-executive Director, since 2006); Oxford Policy Management, 2006–13 (non-executive Director, since 2004); *b* Ashford, Kent, 4 July 1946; *s* of Joseph John Batchelor and Irene Margaret Batchelor (*née* Shoobridge); *m* 1969, Janet Rowden King; one *s* one *d*. *Educ:* Ashford Grammar Sch.; St John's Coll., Cambridge (BA 1st Cl. Hons 1968; Postgrad. Dip. Develt Econs). Economist, Swaziland Govt, 1969–72; Sen. Economist, then Actg Chief Economist, Malawi Govt, 1972–74; Coopers & Lybrand, later PricewaterhouseCoopers, 1974–2004: Partner, 1982–2004; Chief Exec., Coopers & Lybrand Europe, 1994–98; Mem., Global Mgt Team, 1998–2004. Mem., UK and Internat. Adv. Councils, Transparency Internat., 1995–. Trustee: Langham Partnership UK and Ireland, 2005–14; OM Ships Internat., 2006–14; Water Aid UK, 2009–15. Chm., Stour Music Fest. Cttee, 2012–; Mem. Bd, Stour Music Fest. Co., 2013–. *Recreations:* classical music, opera, golf, gardening, mountain walking. *Address:* Crown Agents, St Nicholas House, St Nicholas Road, Sutton, Surrey SM1 1EL. *T:* (020) 8643 3311. *E:* pauljanetbatchelor@yahoo.co.uk. *Clubs:* Royal Over-Seas League; Hever Castle Golf.

BATCHELOR, Richard; *see* Batchelor, J. R.

BATE, Sir (Andrew) Jonathan, Kt 2015; CBE 2006; PhD; FBA 1999; FRSL; Professor of English Literature, University of Oxford, since 2011; Provost, Worcester College, Oxford, since 2011; *b* 26 June 1958; *s* of Ronald Montagu Bate and Sylvia Helen Bate; *m* 1st, 1984, Hilary Gaskin (marr. diss. 1995); 2nd, 1996, Paula Jayne Byrne; two *s* one *d*. *Educ:* Sevenoaks Sch., Kent; St Catharine's Coll., Cambridge (MA; PhD 1984; Hon. Fellow, 2000). Harkness Fellow, Harvard Univ., 1980–81; Research Fellow, St Catharine's Coll., Cambridge, 1983–85; Fellow, Trinity Hall, Cambridge and Lectr, Trinity Hall and Girton Coll., 1985–90; King Alfred Prof. of English Lit., Univ. of Liverpool, 1991–2003; Research Reader, British Acad., 1994–96; Leverhulme Personal Res. Prof., 1999–2004; Prof. of Shakespeare and Renaissance Literature, Univ. of Warwick, 2003–11. Vis. Prof., UCLA, 1989, 1996. Vice Pres., Humanities, British Acad., 2011–14. Consultant Curator, Shakespeare: Staging the World, BM, 2012. A Judge, Man Booker Prize, 2014. Mem., AHRC, 2007–11. Gov., 2002–, Mem. Bd, 2003–11, RSC. FRSL 2004. One-man play for Simon Callow, The Man from Stratford, nat. tour, 2010, retitled as Being Shakespeare, Trafalgar Studios, 2011–12, NY and Chicago, 2012, Harold Pinter, 2014. Hon. Fellow, Shakespeare Birthplace Trust, 2013. Patron, Sevenoaks Sch., 2014–. *Publications:* Shakespeare and the English Romantic Imagination, 1986; (ed) Lamb, Essays of Elia, 1987; Shakespearean Constitutions, 1989; Romantic Ecology, 1991; (ed) The Romantics on Shakespeare, 1992; Shakespeare and Ovid, 1993; The Arden Shakespeare: Titus Andronicus, 1995; (ed) Shakespeare: an illustrated stage history, 1996; The Genius of Shakespeare, 1997; The Cure for Love (novel), 1998; The Song of the Earth, 2000; John Clare: a biography, 2003 (Hawthornden Prize, James Tait Black Meml Prize, 2004); (ed) I Am: the selected poetry of John Clare, 2003; (ed) The RSC Shakespeare: complete works, 2007 (individual works, 34 vols, 2009–12); Soul of the Age: the life, mind and world of William Shakespeare, 2008; English Literature: a very short introduction, 2010; (ed) The Public Value of the Humanities, 2011; (with D. Thornton) Shakespeare: staging the world, 2012; (with E. Rasmussen) Shakespeare and Others: collaborative plays, 2013; (with J. Goodman) Worcester: portrait of an Oxford College, 2014; Ted Hughes: the unauthorised life, 2015. *Recreations:* tennis, fine art, opera, walking. *Address:* Worcester College, Oxford OX1 2HB. *Club:* Oxford and Cambridge.

BATE, Anthony John; His Honour Judge Bate; a Circuit Judge, since 2007; *b* Leamington Spa, 30 Nov. 1961; *er s* of Terence and Mary Bate; *m* 1988, Sally Trower; two *s*. *Educ:* Queen Elizabeth's Grammar Sch., Blackburn; Christ's Coll., Cambridge (BA 1983; VetMB 1986). MRCVS 1986. Called to the Bar, Lincoln's Inn (Denning Schol.), 1987; in practice as barrister specializing in criminal and common law, E Anglian Chambers, Norwich, 1988–2007; Mem., Regl Civil Panel of Counsel instructed by Treasury Solicitor, 2000–07; a Recorder, 2003–07. Mem., Parole Bd, 2010–. Trustee, Welfare Fund for Companion Animals, 1999–. *Recreations:* browsing second-hand bookshops, badminton, rambling, railway and military history. *Address:* c/o Norwich Crown Court, Bishopgate, Norwich NR3 1UR.

BATE, Prof. (Christopher) Michael, PhD; FRS 1997; Royal Society Professor of Developmental Neurobiology (formerly Professor of Developmental Neurobiology), University of Cambridge, 1998–2009, now Emeritus; Fellow of King's College, Cambridge, since 1992. *Educ:* Trinity Coll., Oxford (BA 1966); PhD Cantab 1976. Cambridge University: Lectr in Zoology, until 1994; Reader in Develtl Biol., 1994–98. *Address:* Department of Zoology, Downing Street, Cambridge CB2 3EJ. *T:* (01223) 336639, *Fax:* (01223) 336676; King's College, Cambridge CB2 1ST.

BATE, David Christopher; QC 1994; a Recorder, since 1991; *b* 2 May 1945; *s* of late Robert Leslie Bate and Brenda Mabel Bate (*née* Price); *m* 2003, Fiona Adele Graham; three *s* one *d* from previous marriage. *Educ:* Hendon Co. Grammar Sch.; Manchester Univ. (LLB Hons). Called to the Bar, Gray's Inn, 1969; VSO (UNA) with Melanesian Mission, 1969–70; Crown Counsel, British Solomon Is Protectorate, 1971. *Recreations:* swimming, cycling, trying to sing in tune with 'Counterpoint' and Cantemus.

BATE, Jennifer Lucy, OBE 2008; FRCO; classical concert organist, since 1969; composer, since 1972; *b* 11 Nov. 1944; *d* of Horace Alfred Bate and Dorothy Marjorie Alice Bate (*née* Hunt). *Educ:* Bristol Univ. (BA Hons 1966). ARCM 1961; LRAM 1963; FRCO 1967. Shaw Librarian, LSE, 1966–69. Vice-Pres., British Music Soc., 1996–. Vice-Pres., N London Fest., 2003. Has played in over 40 countries, incl. tours in S America, France and Italy; first organist to open a BBC Prom Concert with solo performance, 1974; world expert on organ works of Olivier Messiaen; has lectured worldwide, incl. A Guide to the King of Instruments (an educn prog. for all age gps); masterclasses and teaching projects for British Council; TV appearances and performances; has made numerous recordings, incl. world première recording of Messiaen's Livre du Saint Sacrement, 1987 (Grand Prix du Disque; Record of Year, Sunday Times; Pick of Year, Times), complete organ works of Mendelssohn, 2005, complete organ works of Peter Dickinson, 2008, Messiaen's La Nativité du Seigneurs, 2010. FRSA 2002. Hon. DMus Bristol, 2007. Personnalité de l'Année (France), 1989; Award for Early Instrumental Music, Music Retailers' Assoc., 1991. Officier de l'ordre des Arts et des Lettres (France), 2011; Chevalier, Ordre National de la Légion d'Honneur (France), 2011. *Compositions:* Toccata on a theme of Martin Shaw, 1972; Introduction and Variations on an old French Carol, 1979; Four Reflections: No 3 1981, No 2 1982, No 1 1986, No 4 1986; Homage to 1685, 1985; Lament, 1995; An English Canon, 1996; Variations on a Gregorian Theme, 1998; Four Handel-inspired Miniatures, 2007; Five Hymn-Tune Preludes, 2008; Suite on Veni Creator, for organ, 2010. *Publications:* (contrib.) Grove's Dictionary of Music and Musicians, 6th edn 1974– (incl. New Grove's Dictionary of Music and Musicians, 1998–99). *Recreation:* gardening. *Address:* 35 Collingwood Avenue, Muswell Hill, N10 3EH. *T:* (020) 8883 3811, *Fax:* (020) 8444 3695. *E:* jenniferbate@classical-artists.com.

BATE, Sir Jonathan; *see* Bate, Sir A. J.

BATELY, Prof. Janet Margaret, (Mrs L. J. Summers), CBE 2000; FBA 1990; Sir Israel Gollancz Professor of English Language and Medieval Literature, King's College, University of London, 1995–97, now Emeritus (Professor of English Language and Medieval Literature, 1977–95); *b* 3 April 1932; *d* of late Alfred William Bately and Dorothy Maud Bately (*née* Willis); *m* 1964, Leslie John Summers (*d* 2006), sculptor; one *s*. *Educ:* Greenhead High Sch., Huddersfield; Westcliff High Sch. for Girls; Somerville Coll., Oxford (Shaw Lefevre Scholar; Eileen Gonner Meml Prize, 1953; BA 1st cl. hons English 1954, Dip. in Comparative Philology (with distinction) 1956, MA 1958; Hon. Fellow, 1997); FKC 1986. Asst Lectr in English, Birkbeck Coll., Univ. of London, 1955–58, Lectr, 1958–69, Reader, 1970–76. Lectures: Sir Israel Gollancz Meml, British Acad., 1978; Toller Meml, Manchester Univ., 1987; Dark Age, Univ. of Kent, 1991; Kemble, Trinity Coll., Dublin, 2012. Chm., Scholarships Cttee, Univ. of London, 1988–91. Member: Council, EETS, 1981–; Exec. Cttee, Fontes Anglo-Saxonici, 1985–2008; Adv. Cttee, Internat. Soc. of Anglo-Saxonists, 1986–91; Adv. Cttee, Sources of Anglo-Saxon Lit. and Culture, 1987–; Humanities Res. Bd, British Acad., 1994–95; Adv. Bd, Inst. for Histl Study of Lang., Glasgow Univ., 1998–. Mem. Hon. Develt Bd, Book Trust, 2002–. Governor: Cranleigh Sch., 1982–88; King's Coll. Sch., Wimbledon, 1991–94; Notting Hill and Ealing High Sch., 1998–2002. FRSA 2000. Gen. Ed., King's Coll. London Medieval Studies, 1987–2001. *Publications:* The Old English Orosius, 1980; The Literary Prose of King Alfred's Reign: Translation or Transformation, 1980; (ed) The Anglo-Saxon Chronicle: MS.A, 1986; The Anglo-Saxon Chronicle: texts and textual relationships, 1991; The Tanner Bede, 1992; Anonymous Old English Homilies: a preliminary bibliography, 1993; (ed jtly) Ohthere's Voyages: a late 9th century account of voyages along the coast of Norway and Denmark and its cultural context, 2006; contribs to: England Before the Conquest, 1971; Saints, Scholars and Heroes (ed M. H. King and W. M. Stevens), 1979; Five Hundred Years of Words and Sounds (ed E. G. Stanley and Douglas Grey), 1983; Learning and Literature in Anglo-Saxon England (ed M. Lapidge and H. Gneuss), 1985; Medieval English Studies (ed D. Kennedy, R. Waldron and J. Wittig), 1988; Words for Robert Burchfield's Sixty-Fifth Birthday (ed E. G. Stanley and T. F. Hoad), 1988; From Anglo-Saxon to Early Middle English (ed M. Godden *et al.*), 1994; Medieval English Language Scholarship (ed A. Oizumi and T. Kubouchi), 2005; (ed A. Cowie) Oxford History of English Lexicography, 2008; Companion to King Alfred the Great (ed N. Discenza and P. Szarmach), 2015; The Kemble Lectures on Anglo-Saxon Studies 2009–12 (ed A. Jorgensen *et al.*), 2015; Leeds Studies in English, Reading Medieval Studies, Eichstätter Beiträge, Medium

Aevum, Rev. of English Studies, Anglia, English Studies, Essays and Studies, Classica et Mediaevalia, Scriptorium, Studies in Philology, Mediev. Arch., Notes and Queries, Archaeologia, Anglo-Saxon England, The Dickensian, Jl Soc. of Archivists, Bull. John Rylands Library, etc. *Recreations:* music, gardening. *Address:* 86 Cawdor Crescent, W7 2DD. *T:* (020) 8567 0486.

BATEMAN, Prof. Ian, OBE 2013; PhD; FRSB; Professor of Environmental Sciences, since 2002, and Director, Centre for Social and Economic Research on the Global Environment, since 2010, University of East Anglia; *b* Birmingham, 1961; *s* of Ken and Anne Bateman; *m* Fiona; one *s* two *d*. *Educ:* Handsworth Grammar Sch.; Birmingham Univ. (BSc); Manchester Univ. (MA); Nottingham Univ. (PhD 1997). FRSB (FSB 2014). Principal Investigator: Valuing Nature Network, NERC; Social, Economic and Envmtl Res. Large Grant Award, ESRC. Econs lead, UK Nat. Ecosystem Assessment, DEFRA. Mem., Sci. Adv. Council, DEFRA, 2011–. Mem. Cttee, Natural Capital, 2012–. FRSA 2013. Wolfson Merit Award, Royal Soc., 2011. *Publications:* Applied Environmental Economics, 2003. *Recreation:* family. *Address:* Centre for Social and Economic Research on the Global Environment, School of Environmental Sciences, University of East Anglia, Norwich NR4 7TJ.

BATEMAN, Mary-Rose Christine, (Mrs R. D. Farley), MA; Headmistress, Perse School for Girls, Cambridge, 1980–89; *b* 16 March 1935; *d* of late Comdr G. A. Bateman, RN, and Mrs G. A. Bateman; *m* 1990, Richard Dashwood Farley (*d* 1996). *Educ:* The Abbey, Malvern Wells, Worcs; St Anne's Coll., Oxford (MA); CertEd Cambridge. Assistant English Mistress: Westonbirt Sch., Tetbury, Glos, 1957–60; Ashford Sch., Kent, 1960–61; Lady Eleanor Holles Sch., Middx, 1961–64; Head of English Department: Westonbirt Sch., Glos, 1964–69; Brighton and Hove High Sch., GPDST, 1969–71; Headmistress, Berkhamsted School for Girls, Herts, 1971–80. Administrator, Women's Nat. Cancer Control Campaign, 1989. *Address:* 17 The Moor, Puddletown, Dorchester DT2 8TE. *T:* (01305) 848015.

BATEMAN, Paul Terence; Chairman, JP Morgan Asset Management, since 2007 (Chief Executive Officer, 2002–07); *b* 28 April 1946; *s* of Nelson John Bateman and Frances Ellen (*née* Johnston); *m* 1970, Moira (*née* Burdis); two *s*. *Educ:* Westcliff High Sch. for Boys; Univ. of Leicester (BSc). Save and Prosper Gp Ltd, 1967: graduate, secretarial dept, 1967–68; asst to Gp Actuary, 1968–73; Marketing Manager, 1973–75; Gp Marketing Manager, 1975–80; Gp Marketing and Develt Manager, 1980–81; Exec. Dir, Marketing and Develt, 1981–88; Chief Exec., 1988–95; Chm., Robert Fleming Asset Mgt, 1995–2001; Hd, Asset Mgt for Europe, Asia and Japan, JP Morgan Fleming Asset Mgt, 2001–02. Chm., Barts City Lifesavers, 1998–2011. *Recreation:* yachting. *Address:* JP Morgan Asset Management, 60 Victoria Embankment, EC4Y 0JP.

BATEMAN, Peter; HM Diplomatic Service, retired; Ambassador to Azerbaijan, 2011–13; Clerk and Chief Executive Officer, Armourers and Brasiers' Co., since 2014; *b* 23 Dec. 1955; *s* of Sqdn Ldr Ralph Edwin Bateman, MBE and Alma Bateman (*née* Laws); *m* 1985, Andrea Henriette Subercaseaux; two *s* one *d*. *Educ:* Carre's Grammar Sch., Sleaford, Lincs; St Peter's Coll., Oxford (MA). Conf. interpreter, EC, 1979–84; joined HM Diplomatic Service, 1984: First Secretary: Tokyo, 1986–90; FCO, 1991–93; (Commercial), Berlin, 1993–97; FCO, 1997–98; Commercial Counsellor, Tokyo, 1998–2002; Counsellor, FCO, 2002–03; on secondment as Dep. Chief Exec., Internat. Financial Services, 2003–05; Ambassador to: Bolivia, 2005–07; Luxembourg, 2007–11. *Recreations:* theatre, family life, golf, travel. *Address:* 46 Erpingham Road, SW15 1BG.

BATEMAN, Richard George Saumarez La T.; *see* La Trobe-Bateman.

BATEMAN, Richard Mark, PhD, DSc; Visiting Professor, Reading University, since 2000; Hon. Research Fellow, Royal Botanic Gardens, Kew, since 2003; *b* Bradford, 27 May 1958; *s* of William Horace Roy Bateman and Joan Mary Lund (*née* Laban); *m* (marr. diss. 2002). *Educ:* Luton Coll. of Higher Educn (BSc (Commendation) 1982); Birkbeck Coll., London (BSc 1st Cl. Hons 1984); PhD (Palaeozoic Palaeobotany) London 1988; DSc (Systematic Botany) London 2001. Asst SO, Sect. for Quaternary Studies, Rothamsted Exptl Station, 1977–84; Lindemann Res. Fellow and Vis. Scientist, Dept of Paleobiol., Smithsonian Instn, Washington, 1988–91; Sen. NERC Res. Fellow (Palaeobotany), Depts of Earth and Plant Scis, Oxford Univ., 1991–94; PSO, Royal Botanic Gdn, Edinburgh, and Nat. Museums of Scotland, 1994–96; Dir of Sci. and SPSO, Royal Botanic Gdn, Edinburgh, 1996–99; Keeper of Botany, 1999–2004, Individual Merit Researcher (Evolution), 2005–06, Natural History Mus.; Hd of Policy, Bioscis Fedn, 2006–07 (Mem., Exec. Council, 2004–06); Sen. Res. Fellow, Dept of Geog., Earth and Envmtl Scis, Univ. of Birmingham, 2007–11. Hon. Res. Fellow, Edinburgh Univ., 1997–2002. Member, Council: Systematics Assoc., 1992–2009 (Pres., 2006–09); UK Systematics Forum, 1997–2001; Linnean Soc., 1999–2010 (Vice-Pres., 2004–08); Bot. Soc. Br. Isles, 2002–08 (Vice-Pres., 2004–08); Vice Pres., Eur. Soc. for Evolutionary Develtl Biol., 2009–13. Mem., Awards Cttee III, Royal Soc., 2003–09. Pres., UK Hardy Orchid Soc., 2000–. President's Award, Geol Soc. of GB, 1988; Bicentenary Medal, Linnean Soc., 1994. *Publications:* (jtly) Molecular Systematics and Plant Evolution, 1999; (jtly) Developmental Genetics and Plant Evolution, 2002; contrib. over 140 papers to scientific jls, over 190 other articles. *Recreations:* natural history, travel, film, folk music, pontificating while drinking decent beer. *Address:* c/o Jodrell Laboratory, Royal Botanic Gardens Kew, Richmond, Surrey TW9 3DS. *T:* (020) 8948 2350.

BATEMAN, Richard Montague; Executive Secretary, Geological Society, 1980–97; *b* 27 Nov. 1943; *s* of late Gordon Montague Bateman and Joan Rhoda Bateman (*née* Puddifoot); *m* Gillian Elizabeth, *er d* of late Noel Leslie Costain, OBE; one *d*. *Educ:* Lyme Regis Grammar Sch.; Greenwich Maritime Inst., Univ. of Greenwich (MA 2002). Entered Civil Service, 1964, MoD (Air), 1965–69; Chamber of Shipping of UK, 1969–75, Asst Sec., 1973–75; Gen. Council of British Shipping, 1975–80. Sec., Assoc. of European Geol Socs, 1987–92. Mem., Envmt Council, 1994–97. Mem. Council, Haslemere Educnl Mus., 1998–2010. Member: Ocean Liner Soc., 1992; Sci., Technol., Engrg and Med. PR Assoc., 1993; Geologists' Assoc., 1997–2004, 2008 (Mem. Council, 2008–10); Soc. for Nautical Res., 1997 (Mem. Council, 2003–07, 2008–12 and 2013–); British Titanic Soc., 1998; Steamship Historical Soc. of America, 1999–2010; Council, Greenwich Forum, 2008–. Associate, ACENVO, then ACEVO, 1998–2001. Associate MInstD 1989. *Recreations:* maritime history, classical music. *Club:* Royal Naval and Royal Albert Yacht.

BATES; *see* Baker-Bates.

BATES, family name of **Baron Bates**.

BATES, Baron *cr* 2008 (Life Peer), of Langbaurgh in the County of North Yorkshire; **Michael Walton Bates;** PC 2015; Minister of State, Home Office, since 2015; *b* 26 May 1961; *s* of John Bates and Ruth Walton; *m* 1st, 1983, Carole Whitfield (marr. diss. 2008); two *s*; 2nd, 2012, Xuelin Li. *Educ:* Heathfield Sen. High Sch.; Gateshead Coll.; Wadham Coll., Oxford (MBA 1998). Young Conservatives: Mem., Nat. Adv. Cttee, 1984–87; Chm., Northern Area, 1984–87. Sen. Vice-Pres., later Dir of Consultancy and Res., 1998–2006, Sen. Advr, 2006–07, Oxford Analytica Inc.; Man. Dir, Walton Bates Associates Ltd, 2006–11. Director: estandardsforum.com Inc., 2001–07; Financial Standards Foundn (Bermuda) Ltd, 2001–03; non-executive Director: Congregational & General plc, 2001–06; Vardy Gp of Cos, 2006–10; non-exec. Chm., Scholes & Brown Asset Management, 2008–11. Assoc. Chm., Northern Area Develt Initiative, 1990–92. Contested (C): Tyne Bridge, 1987; Langbaurgh, Nov. 1991. MP (C) Langbaurgh, 1992–97; contested (C) Middlesbrough South and Cleveland East, 1997. PPS to Minister of State, DSS, 1992–93, NI Office, 1994; an Asst Govt Whip, 1994–95; a Lord Comr, HM Treasury, 1995–96; HM Paymaster Gen., 1996–97. Shadow Minister for Cabinet Office, Communities and Local Govt, Energy and Climate Change, Children, Sch. and Families, 2009–10; Dep. Speaker, H of L, 2013; a Lord in Waiting (Govt Whip), 2013–14; Parly Under-Sec. of State, Home Office, 2014–15. Member: Select Cttee on Social Security, 1992; Select Cttee on Health, 1994. Dep. Chm., Cons. Party (North), 2007–10. Shell Fellow, Industry and Parlt Trust, 1997–. Mem., RIIA, 1998–2005. Member: Business Adv. Forum, Saïd Business Sch. (formerly Mem. Council, Sch. of Mgt Studies), Oxford Univ., 2000–10; Caux Round Table, 2001– (Trustee, 2006–08; Fellow, 2008–); European Ideas Network, 2002–05. Vice Chairman: Emmanuel Schs Foundn, 2009–10; Emmanuel Coll., 2008–10; King's Acad., 2008–10; Trinity Acad., 2008–10; Bede Acad., 2008–10. *Address:* House of Lords, SW1A 0PW. *E:* batesm@parliament.uk.

BATES, Anthony John; Executive Vice President, Business Development and Evangelism Group, Microsoft, 2011–14; *b* Isleworth, 29 April 1967; *s* of David Bates and Valerie Bates; *m* 2009, Corica; four *s*. Sen. Network Manager, Univ. of London Computer Centre, 1986–92; Sen. Engr, RIPE Network Coordination Centre, 1992–94; Sen. Network Architect, MCI Telecommunications, 1994–96; Senior Vice President and General Manager, Service Provider Gp, Cisco Systems Inc., 1996–2009; Enterprise, Commercial and Small Business Gp, Cisco, 2009–10; CEO, Skype, 2010–11. Member, Board of Directors, YouTube, 2006–07; LOVEFILM, 2006–08; Bubble Motion, 2008–09; TokBox, 2008–09. *Recreations:* ski-ing, tennis.

BATES, Air Vice-Marshal Brian Lawrence, CBE 2005; Divisional Strategy Director, Tactical Systems Division, Ultra Electronics, since 2013; *b* Nicosia, Cyprus, 15 June 1957; *s* of David Bates and Sylvia Bates (*née* Payne); *m* 1st, 1981, Melinda Lawler (marr. diss. 1998); three *s* two *d*; 2nd, 1998, Joanne Saunders; one *s* one *d*. *Educ:* Wellington Sch., Somerset; Portsmouth Poly. (BA Hons Econs). Navigator and qwi, F4 Phantom, 1980–91; staff duties, HQ UK Air, 1991–92; RAF Staff Coll., 1993; PSO to AOC 11 Gp, 1993–95; staff duties, MoD, 1995–97; OC Ops Wing, RAF Leeming, 1998–2000; Hd RAF Presentation Team, 2000–01; Comdr British Forces Middle E, 2001; OC RAF Leeming, 2002–04; Asst Dir Strategic Plans, MoD, 2004–05; CDS Liaison Officer to Chm. of US Jt Chiefs of Staff, 2005–06; Dir Jt Capability, MoD, 2006–08; ACOS Capability HQ Air Comd, 2008–09; Sen. Directing Staff (Air), RCDS, 2009–12. Chm., RAF Club, 2011–12. *Recreations:* golf, tennis, squash.

BATES, Clive David Nicholas; Director, Counterfactual, since 2013; *b* 16 Feb. 1961; *s* of David and Patricia Bates. *Educ:* Wilmslow Grammar Sch., Cheshire; Emmanuel Coll., Cambridge (BA Hons Engrg 1983); Imperial Coll., London (MSc Envmtl Technol. 1992). Marketing computers for IBM (UK) Ltd, 1983–91; envmtl campaigner, Greenpeace, 1992–95; Programme Manager, Internat. Inst. for Energy Conservation, 1996–97; Dir, ASH, 1997–2003; Team Leader, Prime Minister's Strategy Unit, Cabinet Office, 2003–05; Head, Envmtl Policy, EA, 2005–07; UN Envmt Programme, Sudan, 2007–09; Dir Gen., Sustainable Futures, Welsh Assembly Govt, later Welsh Govt, 2009–12; Special Projects Advr, DECC (on secondment), 2012. *Publications:* reports and papers for campaigning groups. *Recreations:* cycling, mountains. *Address:* 4 Pentney Road, SW12 0NX. *Club:* Black's.

BATES, Daniel; Chief Executive Officer, Sheffield Theatres, since 2009; *b* London, Feb. 1965; *s* of Mark and Barbara Smith; adopted Bates as professional name. *Educ:* Central Sch. of Speech and Drama. Stage Manager, then Exec. Dir, W Yorks Playhouse, 1987–2005; CEO, York Th. Royal, 2005–09. *Recreation:* theatre. *Address:* Sheffield Theatres Trust, 55 Norfolk Street, Sheffield S1 1DA. *T:* (0114) 201 3804. *E:* d.bates@sheffieldtheatres.co.uk.

BATES, Air Vice-Marshal David Frank, CB 1983; RAF retired; *b* 10 April 1928; *s* of late S. F. Bates, MusB, FRCO, and N. A. Bates (*née* Story); *m* 1954, Margaret Winifred (*née* Biles); one *s* one *d*. *Educ:* Warwick Sch.; RAF Coll., Cranwell. Commnd, 1950; served Egypt, Innsworth, UKSLS Australia, HQ Transport Comd, RAF Technical Coll., Staff Coll., Lyneham, El Adem, Staff Coll., Jt Services Staff Coll., Innsworth, and RCDS, 1950–73; Stn Comdr, Uxbridge, 1974–75; Dir of Personnel Ground, 1975–76; Dir of Personnel Management (ADP), 1976–79; AOA, RAF Support Comd, 1979–82. Bursar, Warwick Sch., 1983–85. Pres., Adastrian Cricket Club, 1977–82. *Recreations:* cricket, most sports, gardening, model railways. *Address:* Meadow Cottage, Calf Lane, Chipping Campden, Glos GL55 6JQ.

BATES, Prof. David Richard, PhD; FRHistS, FSA; Professor of Medieval History, University of East Anglia, 2008–10, now Professorial Fellow; *b* 30 April 1945; *s* of Jack Bates and Violet Anne Bates (*née* Swain); *m* 1971, Helen Mary Fryer; one *s* one *d*. *Educ:* King Edward VI Grammar Sch., Nuneaton; Univ. of Exeter (BA 1966; PhD 1970). FRHistS 1985, FSA 1993. Lectr, then Sen. Lectr and Reader in Hist., UC, Cardiff, subseq. Univ. of Wales Cardiff, 1973–94; Edwards Prof. of Medieval Hist., Univ. of Glasgow, 1994–2003; Prof. of Hist. and Dir, Inst. of Historical Res., Univ. of London, 2003–08 (Hon. Fellow, 2008). Huntington Library Fellow, 1984; Prof. Invité, Ecole Nat. des Chartes, Paris, 1999; British Acad. Marc Fitch Res. Reader, 2001–03; Vis. Fellow Commoner, Trinity Coll., Cambridge, 2002–03; Dir d'Etudes Invité, Ecole Pratique des Hautes Etudes, Paris, 2003; Vis. Prof., Univ. de Caen-Basse-Normandie, 2009–12; James Ford Lectr in British Hist., Univ. of Oxford, 2009–10. Dir, Battle Conf. on Anglo-Norman Studies, 2010–13. A Vice-Pres., RHistS, 2003–06. Founding Fellow, Inst. of Contemp. Scotland, 2000; Centenary Fellow, Historical Assoc., 2006; Leverhulme Trust Emeritus Fellow, 2013–15. Life Mem., Clare Hall, Cambridge, 2009. MAE 2009. FRSA 2008. Dr *hc* Caen, 2000. *Publications:* Normandy before 1066, 1982; A Bibliography of Domesday Book, 1986; William the Conqueror, 1989; Bishop Remigius of Lincoln 1067–1092, 1992; (ed jtly) England and Normandy in the Middle Ages, 1994; (ed jtly) Conflict and Coexistence, 1997; Regesta Regum Anglo-Normannorum: the Acta of William I 1066–1087, 1998; Reordering the Past and Negotiating the Present in Stenton's First Century (Stenton Lect.), 2000; (ed jtly) Domesday Book, 2001; (ed jtly) Writing Medieval Biography 750–1250: essays in honour of Frank Barlow, 2006; (ed jtly) Liens personnels, réseaux, solidarités en France et dans les îles britanniques, 2006; (ed jtly) The Creighton Century, 1907–2007, 2009; (ed) Anglo-Norman Studies: XXXIV, proceedings of the Battle conference 2011, 2012, XXXV, proceedings of the Battle conference 2012, 2013, XXXVI, proceedings of the Battle conference 2013, 2014; (ed jtly) East Anglia and its North Sea World in the Middle Ages, 2013; The Normans and Empire, 2013; contribs to various books and many articles in historical jls incl. English Historical Rev., Speculum, Histl Res and Annales de Normandie. *Recreation:* opera. *Address:* 2 Ivy Court, Sleaford Street, Cambridge CB1 2NX.

BATES, Django Leon; jazz keyboardist, E flat hornist and composer; *b* 2 Oct. 1960; *s* of Ralf Bates and Frances Sinker (*née* Roseveare); *m* 2015, Sophie Schudel; one *s* three *d*. *Educ:* ILEA Centre for Young Musicians; Morley Coll. A founder mem., Loose Tubes; band leader: Humans, subseq. Human Chain, 1980–; Delightful Precipice, 1991–; stoRMChaser, 2005–; Belovèd (trio), 2010–. Performances worldwide. Artistic Dir, Fuse Fest., Leeds, March 2004; Prof. of Rhythmic Music, Rhythmic Music Conservatory, Copenhagen, 2005–11; Prof. of Jazz, Bern Univ. of the Arts, 2011–. Resident composer: Molde Internat. Jazz Fest., 1995; European City of Culture, Copenhagen, 1996; Harrogate Internat. Fest., 1997. ALCM; Fellow, Leeds Coll. of Music, 2005; Hon. RAM 2000. Danish Jazzpar Prize, 1997. *Compositions include:* Out There (music theatre prodn), 1993; What it's Like to be Alive (piano concerto), 1996; Interval Song, 1996; 1 in a Million, 1997; 2000 Years Beyond Undo (electronic keyboard concerto), 2000; Umpteenth Violin Concerto, 2004; The Study of Touch, 2013. *Recordings include:* Music for the Third Policeman, 1990; summer fruits (and unrest), 1993; autumn fires (and green shoots), 1994; winter truce (and homes blaze), 1995;

Good Evening…here is the news, 1996; Like Life, 1998; Quiet Nights, 1998; You Live and Learn (apparently), 2004; Spring is Here (Shall We Dance?), 2008; Belovèd Bird, 2010; Confirmation, 2012. *Address:* c/o Jeremy Farnell, 21 St Johns Church Road, E9 6EJ. *E:* management@djangobates.co.uk.

BATES, Prof. Gillian Patricia, PhD; FRS 2007; FMedSci; Professor of Neurogenetics, since 1998, and Head, Division of Genetics and Molecular Medicine, since 2011, King's College London School of Medicine (formerly Guy's, King's College and St Thomas' Hospitals School of Medicine); *b* 19 May 1956; *d* of Alan Richard Bates and Joan Mabel Bates. *Educ:* Kenilworth Grammar Sch.; Sheffield Univ. (BSc 1979); Birkbeck Coll., London (MSc 1984); St Mary's Hosp. Med. Sch., Univ. of London (PhD 1987). Postdoctoral Fellow, ICRF, 1987–93; Sen. Lectr in Molecular Biology, UMDS of Guy's and St Thomas' Hosps, 1994–98. Mem., EMBO, 2002. FMedSci 1999. Hon. DSc Sheffield 2009. Nat. Med. Res. Award, Nat. Health Council, USA, 1993; Milton Wexler Award for Res. into Huntington's Disease, Huntington's Disease Soc. of America, 1998; Glaxo Wellcome Gold Medal, Royal Soc., 1998; Pius XI Medal, 1998; Klaus Joachim Zulch Prize, 2001; Leslie Brenner Gehry Prize for Innovation in Sci., Hereditary Disease Foundn, 2011. *Publications:* papers in genetics, molecular biology, and neurosci. jls; contribs to scientific and med. reference books. *Recreations:* reading, contemporary arts and design. *Address:* Department of Medical and Molecular Genetics, King's College London School of Medicine, 8th Floor Tower Wing, Guy's Hospital, Great Maze Pond, SE1 9RT. *T:* (020) 7188 3722.

BATES, Rt Rev. Gordon; an Hon. Assistant Bishop, Diocese of York, since 2010; *b* 16 March 1934; *s* of Ernest and Kathleen Bates; *m* 1960, Betty (*née* Vaux) (*d* 2014); two *d*. *Educ:* Kelham Theological Coll. (SSM). Curate of All Saints, New Eltham, 1958–62; Youth Chaplain in Gloucester Diocese, 1962–64; Diocesan Youth Officer and Chaplain of Liverpool Cathedral, 1965–69; Vicar of Huyton, 1969–73; Canon Residentiary and Precentor of Liverpool Cathedral and Diocesan Director of Ordinands, 1973–83; Bp Suffragan of Whitby, 1983–99. Hon. Asst Bp, Dios of Carlisle and Blackburn, 1999–2010. Mem., House of Bishops, Gen. Synod, 1988–99. Mem., Central Religious Adv. Council to BBC and ITV, 1990–93. Chm., Cumbria, RSCM, 2002–04. Trustee, Sandford St Martin Trust, 1990–93. *Recreations:* golf, music, writing. *Address:* 19 Fernwood Close, Brompton, Northallerton DL6 2UX. *T:* (01609) 761586.

BATES, Sir James Geoffrey, 7th Bt *cr* 1880, of Bellefield, co. Lancaster; *b* 14 March 1985; *s* of Richard Geoffrey Bates, *yr s* of 5th Bt and Diana Margaret Rankin; *S* uncle, 2007. *Heir: kinsman* Hugh Percy Bates [*b* 9 Jan. 1953; *m* 1977, Angela Roberta Wall; one *s* one *d*].

BATES, John Gerald Higgs; Solicitor, Office of Inland Revenue, 1990–96; *b* 28 July 1936; *o s* of Thomas William Bates and Winifred Alice Higgs; *m* 1971, Antoinette Lotery (*d* 1984); two *s*; *m* 1992, Alba Heather Phyllida Whicher. *Educ:* Kettering Grammar Sch.; St Catharine's Coll., Cambridge (MA); Harvard Law Sch. (LLM). Called to the Bar, Middle Temple, 1959. Practised at the Bar, 1962–66; Office of Solicitor of Inland Revenue, 1966–96: Under Sec. (Legal), 1990. *Recreations:* cooking, wine, music.

BATES, Kenneth; President, Leeds United Football Club, 2013 (Chairman, 2005–13); *b* 4 Dec. 1931; *m* Suzannah. Ready-mix concrete business; dairy farmer; Chairman: Oldham Athletic FC; Wigan Athletic FC, 1981; Chelsea FC, 1982–2004; Wembley Nat. Stadium Ltd, until 2000 (Dir, 1997–2001).

BATES, Laura Carolyn; Founder, Everyday Sexism Project, 2012; *b* Oxford, 27 Aug. 1986; *d* of Adrian Keith Bates and Diane Elizabeth Bates; *m* 2014, Nicholas Taylor. *Educ:* King's Coll., Taunton; St John's Coll., Cambridge (BA Eng. Lit.). Patron, Somerset and Avon Rape and Sexual Abuse Support, 2014. *Publications:* Everyday Sexism, 2014. *E:* laura@everydaysexism.com.

BATES, Meg; *see* Munn, M.

BATES, Michael, (Mick); Member for Montgomeryshire, National Assembly for Wales, 1999–2011 (Lib Dem 1999–2010, Ind 2010–11); *b* 24 Sept. 1947; *s* of George William Bates and Lilly (*née* Stevens); *m* 1972, Buddug Thomas; one *s* one *d*. *Educ:* Open Univ. (BA Educn and Sci. 1970). Science teacher, Humphrey Perkins Jun. High Sch., Barrow on Soar, and Belvidere Secondary Sch., Shrewsbury, 1970–75; Head of Gen. Sci., Grove Sch., Market Drayton, 1975–77; farmer, 1977–99. Mem. (Lib Dem) Powys CC, 1994–95. National Farmers' Union: Chm., Llanfair Caereinion Br., 1983–85; Chm., Co. Livestock Cttee, 1988–91; Mem., Co. Public Affairs Cttee, 1990–97; County Chm., Powys, 1991; NFU delegate, 1995. Lib Dem Br. Sec., 1988, Election Sub Agent, 1992. Mem., Eisteddfod Finance Cttee, 1989. Gov., Llanfair Co. Primary Sch., 1994–95. Chm., Llanfair Forum Community Regeneration Project. *Recreations:* all sports, especially Rugby, charity work, painting, walking, music.

BATES, Michael Charles, OBE 1994; HM Diplomatic Service, retired; Consul-General, Atlanta, 2001–05; *b* 9 April 1948; *s* of late Stanley Herbert Bates and of Winifred (*née* Watkinson); *m* 1971, Janice Kwan Foh Yin; one *s* one *d*. *Educ:* Stratton Grammar Sch. Joined HM Diplomatic Service, 1966: Attaché, New Delhi, 1971–74; Third Sec., Moscow, 1974–77; FCO, 1977–79; Second, later First Sec., Singapore, 1979–83; First Sec., Brussels, 1983–87; Press Officer to Prime Minister, 1987–89; Head, Parly Relns Unit, FCO, 1989–91; Dep. Head of Mission, Riga, 1991–92; Chargé d'Affaires, Bratislava, 1993–94; Ambassador, Slovak Republic, 1994–95; Dep. Head, News Dept, FCO, 1995–96; Dep. High Comr, Bombay, 1996–2001. *Recreations:* music, reading, travel, rambling.

BATES, Patricia Ann; *see* Stewart, P. A.

BATES, Prof. Paul David, PhD; Professor of Hydrology, since 2003, and Head, School of Geographical Sciences, since 2013, University of Bristol; *b* Leamington Spa, 29 May 1967; *s* of Robert John Bates and Joyce Bates; *m* 1995, Dr Alison Matthews; two *s*. *Educ:* Univ. of Southampton (BSc Geog. 1989); Univ. of Bristol (PhD 1993). Postdoctoral Researcher, Univ. of Bristol and Laboratoire Nat. d'Hydraulique, Paris, 1993–95; University of Bristol: Lectr, 1995–2000; on sabbatical at Princeton Univ. and EU Jt Res. Centre, 2000; Reader, 2000–03; on sabbatical at NASA Jet Propulsion Lab. and Univ. of Messina, 2007; Dir, Cabot Inst., 2010–13. Dir, SSBN Ltd, 2013–. *Publications:* (ed jtly) Floodplain Processes, 1996; (ed jtly) High Resolution Flow Modelling in Hydrology and Geomorphology, 2000; (ed jtly) Model Validation: perspectives in hydrological science, 2001; (ed jtly) Computational Fluid Dynamics, 2005; over 150 articles in internat. scientific jls. *Recreations:* running, windsurfing, ski-ing, bass guitarist with the Grateful Dad. *Address:* School of Geographical Sciences, University of Bristol, University Road, Bristol BS8 1SS. *T:* (0117) 928 9954. *E:* paul.bates@bristol.ac.uk.

BATES, Sir Richard (Dawson Hoult), 3rd Bt *cr* 1937, of Magherabuoy, co. Londonderry; *b* 12 May 1956; *er s* of Sir Dawson Bates, 2nd Bt, MC and of Mary Murray (*née* Hoult); *S* father, 1998; *m* 2001, Harriet Domenique, *yr d* of Domenico Scaramella; one *s* one *d*. *Heir: s* Dominic Dawson Bates, *b* 21 Jan. 2006.

BATES, Simon Philip; broadcaster; *b* Birmingham, 17 Dec. 1947; *s* of Henry Edward Bates and Marjorie Joan (*née* Garside); *m* 1978, Carolyn Miller (marr. diss. 2001); one *d*. *Educ:* Adams Grammar Sch., Shropshire. Announcer and commentator, New Zealand Broadcasting Corp., 1966–69; News/Features, Australian Broadcasting Commn, 1969–73; BBC, 1973–93; Breakfast programme presenter: London Broadcasting, 1993–97; Classic FM, 1997–2010; Smooth Radio, 2011–. Commentator, CBS News, 1993–. DUniv Open, 2010. Pater Award for Excellence in Broadcasting, Australia, 1987; Sony Gold Award and NY Fest. Award for Radio series, Around the World in 80 Days, 1989; Radio Personality of Year, Variety Club, 1993; Argiva Commercial Radio Special Award, 2006. *Publications:* Simon Bates, My Tune: an autobiography, 1993. *Recreations:* history, cinema, countryside, travel. *Address:* c/o Qtalent Ltd, 2nd Floor, 161 Drury Lane, Covent Garden, WC2B 5PN. *T:* (020) 7430 5400. *E:* pdale@qtalent.co.uk. *Clubs:* Ivy; Cricketers'.

BATES, Wendy Elizabeth; *see* Sudbury, W. E.

BATESON, John Swinburne, FCIHT; Chairman, Country Holiday Parks Ltd, since 2002; *b* 11 Jan. 1942; *s* of William Swinburne Bateson and Katherine Urquart (*née* Lyttle); *m* Jean Vivien Forsyth; one *s* two *d*. *Educ:* Appleby Grammar Sch.; Lancaster Royal Grammar Sch. FCIHT (FIHT 1986). Family business and associated activities, 1959–61; Harbour & General Works Ltd: Trainee Quantity Surveyor, 1961; Quantity Surveyor, 1966; Site Quantity Surveyor, Marples Ridgway Ltd, 1966–68; Leonard Fairclough Ltd: Site Quantity Surveyor, 1969; Contracts Surveyor, 1971; Chief Quantity Surveyor, Scotland, 1974; Fairclough Civil Engineering Ltd: Asst to Chief Exec., 1977; Man. Dir, Southern Div., 1979; Fairclough Construction Group Ltd: Asst to Chief Exec., 1980; Dir, 1981–95; AMEC plc: Dir, 1982–86; Dep. Chief Exec., 1986–88; Gp Chief Exec., 1988–95. Chairman: Bateson's Hotels (1958) Ltd, 1986–2002; Ind. Radio Gp, 1995–99; Merewood Gp Ltd, 1997–2003. *Recreations:* gardening, aviation, reading, photography, chess, bridge, antiques.

BATESON, Prof. Sir (Paul) Patrick (Gordon), Kt 2003; FRS 1983; Professor of Ethology, University of Cambridge, 1984–2005, now Emeritus Professor; Provost of King's College, Cambridge, 1988–2003 (Fellow, 1964–84; Professorial Fellow, 1984–88; Life Fellow, since 2003); *b* 31 March 1938; *s* of Richard Gordon Bateson and Sölvi Helene Berg; *m* 1963, Dusha Matthews; two *d*. *Educ:* Westminster Sch.; King's Coll., Cambridge (BA 1960, PhD 1963, MA 1965, ScD 1977). Harkness Fellow, Stanford Univ. Medical Centre, Calif, 1963–65; Sen. Asst in Res., Sub-Dept of Animal Behaviour, Univ. of Cambridge, 1965–69; Lectr in Zoology, Univ. of Cambridge, 1969–78; Dir, Sub-Dept of Animal Behaviour, 1976–88; Reader in Animal Behaviour, 1978–84. Pres., Assoc. for the Study of Animal Behaviour, 1977–80; Member: Council for Sci. and Soc., 1989–92; Museums and Galls Commn, 1995–2000 (Vice-Chm., 1998–2000). Biological Sec., Royal Soc., 1998–2003; Pres., Zool Soc. of London, 2004–14 (Mem. Council, 1989–92). Mem., UK Panel for Res. Integrity in Health and Biomed. Scis, 2006–. Trustee, Inst. for Public Policy Research, 1988–95. Rutherford Meml Lect., Australia and NZ, 2007. For. Mem., Amer. Philos. Soc., 2006; Mem., Sigma Xi, 2006. Hon. Fellow, QMW. Hon. FZS; Hon. FRSNZ 2009. Hon. DSc St Andrews, 2001. Scientific Medal, Zool Soc. of London, 1976; Medal Assoc. for Study of Animal Behaviour, 2001. *Publications:* (ed with P. H. Klopfer) Perspectives in Ethology, Vols 1–8, 1973–89; (ed with R. A. Hinde) Growing Points in Ethology, 1976; (ed) Mate Choice, 1983; (contrib.) Defended to Death, 1983; (with Paul Martin) Measuring Behaviour, 1986, 3rd edn 2007; (ed with D. S. Turner) The Domestic Cat: the biology of its behaviour, 1988, 3rd edn 2013; (ed) The Development and Integration of Behaviour, 1991; (with P. Martin) Design for a Life: how behaviour develops, 1999; (with P. Gluckman) Plasticity, Robustness, Development and Evolution, 2011; (with P. Martin) Play, Playfulness, Creativity and Innovation, 2013; reports on ethology and animal welfare. *Recreations:* opera, turning wilderness into garden. *Address:* The Old Rectory, Rectory Street, Halesworth, Suffolk IP19 8BL. *T:* (01986) 873182.

BATH, 7th Marquess of, *cr* 1789; **Alexander George Thynn;** Bt 1641; Viscount Weymouth and Baron Thynne, 1682; Director: Cheddar Caves, 1956–2010; Longleat Enterprises, 1964–2010; *b* 6 May 1932; *s* of 6th Marquess of Bath and his 1st wife, Hon. Daphne Winifred Louise (*d* 1997), *d* of 4th Baron Vivian; *S* father, 1992; *m* 1969, Anna Gael Gyarmathy; one *s* one *d*. *Educ:* Eton College; Christ Church, Oxford (BA, MA). Lieutenant in the Life Guards, 1951–52, and in Royal Wilts Yeomanry, 1953–57. Contested (Wessex Regionalist): Westbury, Feb. 1974; Wells, 1979; contested (Wessex Regionalist and European Federal Party) Wessex, European Election 1979. Permanent exhibn of paintings since 1949 and murals since 1964, first opened to the public in 1962 in private apartments at Longleat House. Record, I Play the Host, singing own compositions, 1974. *Publications:* (as Alexander Thynn) (before 1976 Alexander Thynne) The Carry-cot, 1972; Lord Weymouth's Murals, 1974; A Regionalist Manifesto, 1975; The King is Dead, 1976; Pillars of the Establishment, 1980; The New World Order of Alexander Thynn, 2000; A Plateful of Privilege, vol. 1, the Early Years, vol. 2, Top Hat and Tails, vol. 3, Two Bites of the Apple, 2003, vol. 4, A Degree of Instability: the Oxford years, 2005. *Heir: s* Viscount Weymouth, *qv*. *Address:* Longleat House, Warminster, Wilts BA12 7NN. *T:* (01985) 844300.

BATH, Archdeacon of; *see* Piggott, Ven. A. J.

BATH AND WELLS, Bishop of, since 2014; **Rt Rev. Peter Hancock;** *b* 26 July 1955; *s* of Kenneth and Jean Hancock; *m* 1979, (Elizabeth) Jane Sindall; two *s* two *d*. *Educ:* Price's Sch., Fareham; Selwyn Coll., Cambridge (BA 1976; MA 1979); Oak Hill Theol Coll. (BA 1980); Nottingham Univ. (MA 2008). Ordained deacon 1980, priest 1981; Curate: Christ Church, Portsdown, 1980–83; Radipole and Melcombe Regis Team Ministry, 1983–87; Vicar, St Wilfrid, Cowplain, 1987–99; RD of Havant, 1993–98; Archdeacon of The Meon, 1999–2010; Diocesan Dir of Mission, Portsmouth, 2003–07; Bishop Suffragan of Basingstoke, 2010–14. Hon. Canon, Portsmouth Cathedral, 1997–99. *Recreations:* walking, reading, watching sport. *Address:* The Bishops' Office, The Bishop's Palace, Wells, Som BA5 2PD.

BATHER, Sir John Knollys, KCVO 2009; Lord-Lieutenant of Derbyshire, 1994–2009; *b* 5 May 1934; *m* 1960, Elizabeth Barbara Longstaff; one *s* two *d*. *Educ:* Shrewsbury Sch.; Nat. Foundry Coll. High Sheriff, Derbys, 1990–91. *Recreations:* gardening, shooting, watercolours. *Address:* Longford Grange, Longford, Ashbourne, Derbys DE6 3AH. *T:* (01335) 330429.

BATHERSBY, Most Rev. John Alexius, AO 2008; STD; Archbishop of Brisbane, (RC), 1992–2011, now Archbishop Emeritus; *b* 26 July 1936; *s* of John Thomas Bathersby and Grace Maud Bathersby (*née* Conquest). *Educ:* Pius XII Seminary, Banyo, Qld, Australia; Gregorian Univ., Rome (STL, STD). Priest, 1961; Asst Priest, Goondiwindi, 1962–68; Spiritual Dir, Banyo Seminary, 1973–86; Bishop of Cairns, 1986–92. *Recreation:* bush walking.

BATHO, Sir Peter (Ghislain), 3rd Bt *cr* 1928, of Frinton, Essex; *b* 9 Dec. 1939; *s* of Sir Maurice Benjamin Batho, 2nd Bt and Antoinette Marie (*d* 1994), *d* of Baron d'Udekem d'Acoz; *S* father, 1990; *m* 1966, Lucille Mary, *d* of Wilfrid F. Williamson; three *s*. *Educ:* Ampleforth Coll.; Writtle Agricl Coll. Career in agriculture. Member: Suffolk CC, 1989–93; Suffolk Coastal DC, 2003–15. *Heir: s* Rupert Sebastian Ghislain Batho [*b* 26 Oct. 1967; *m* 1995, Jo-Anne Louise, *e d* of Rodney Frank Hellawell]. *Address:* Park Farm, Saxmundham, Suffolk IP17 1DQ. *T:* (01728) 602132.

BATHURST, family name of **Earl Bathurst** and **Viscount Bledisloe**.

BATHURST, 9th Earl *cr* 1772; **Allen Christopher Bertram Bathurst;** Baron Bathurst, 1712; Baron Apsley, 1771; *b* 11 March 1961; *s* of 8th Earl Bathurst and Judith Mary Bathurst (*née* Nelson); *S* father, 2011; *m* 1st, 1986, Hilary (marr. diss. 1995), *d* of John F. George, Weston Lodge Albury, Guildford; one *s* one *d*; 2nd, 1996, Sara, *d* of Christopher Chapman. *Educ:* Harrow Sch.; Wye Coll., London Univ.; RAC, Cirencester. Gov., 2003–14, Vice Pres., 2014–, Royal Agricl Coll., Cirencester. Chm., NFU, Glos Co., 2003–04; Pres., Glos Farming Wildlife Adv. Gp, 2006–. Patron, Glos CCC. *Heir: s* Lord Apsley, *qv*. *Address:* Cirencester Park, Cirencester, Glos GL7 2BT.

BATHURST, Maj. Gen. Benjamin John, CBE 2015 (OBE 2005); Director, Ministry of Defence Ministerial Advisory Group, Headquarters International Security Assistance Force-Afghanistan, 2014–15; *b* Haslemere, 15 April 1964; *s* of Admiral of the Fleet Sir (David) Benjamin Bathurst, *qv*; *m* 1996, Katherine Ellison; one *s* one *d*. *Educ:* Eton; Univ. of Bristol (BSc 1986); Cranfield Univ. (MA 1996). Commnd Welsh Guards, 1987; CO, 1st Bn Welsh Guards, 2004–06; Dir, Army PR, 2006–08; Dep. Dir, Strategy, Baghdad, Iraq, 2008–09; Comdr, Initial Trng Gp, 2010; Dir, Army Trng, 2011–14; UK Nat. Contingent Comdr, Kabul, Afghanistan, 2014. Comdt, Royal Army Physical Trng Corps, 2011–13. *Recreations:* shooting, fishing, ski-ing. *Address:* c/o Headquarters Welsh Guards, Wellington Barracks, Birdcage Walk, SW1E 6HQ. *Club:* Boodle's.

BATHURST, Admiral of the Fleet Sir (David) Benjamin, GCB 1991 (KCB 1987); First Sea Lord and Chief of Naval Staff, and First and Principal Naval Aide-de-Camp to the Queen, 1993–95; Vice Lord-Lieutenant, Somerset, 1999–2011; *b* 27 May 1936; *s* of late Group Captain Peter Bathurst, RAF and Lady Ann Bathurst; *m* 1959, Sarah Peto; one *s* three *d*. *Educ:* Eton College; Britannia RN College, Dartmouth. Joined RN, 1953; qualified as Pilot, 1960, as Helicopter Instructor, 1964; Fleet Air Arm appts incl. 2 years' exchange with RAN, 723 and 725 Sqdns; Senior Pilot, 820 Naval Air Sqdn; CO 819 Naval Air Sqdn; HMS Norfolk, 1971; Naval Staff, 1973; CO, HMS Ariadne, 1975; Naval Asst to First Sea Lord, 1976; Captain, 5th Frigate Sqdn, HMS Minerva, 1978; RCDS 1981; Dir of Naval Air Warfare, 1982; Flag Officer, Second Flotilla, 1983–85; Dir-Gen., Naval Manpower and Training, 1985–86; Chief of Fleet Support, 1986–89; C-in-C Fleet, Allied C-in-C Channel, and C-in-C Eastern Atlantic Area, 1989–91; Vice Chief of Defence Staff, 1991–93. Younger Brother, Trinity House. Liveryman, Hon. Co. of Air Pilots (formerly GAPAN). DL Somerset, 1996. *Recreations:* gardening, shooting, fishing. *Address:* c/o National Westminster Bank, 9 York Buildings, Cornhill, Bridgwater TA6 3BA. *Clubs:* Boodle's, Army and Navy, MCC.

See also Maj. Gen. B. J. Bathurst.

BATHURST, Sir Frederick William John H.; *see* Hervey-Bathurst.

BATHURST NORMAN, His Honour George Alfred; a Senior Circuit Judge, 1997–2004 (a Circuit Judge, 1986–2004); *b* 15 Jan. 1939; *s* of Charles Phipps Bathurst Norman and Hon. Doreen Albinia de Burgh Norman (*née* Gibbs); *m* 1973, Susan Elizabeth Ball; one *s* one *d*. *Educ:* Harrow Sch.; Magdalen Coll., Oxford (BA). Called to the Bar, Inner Temple, 1961; SE Circuit, 1962; Dep. Circuit Judge, 1975; a Metropolitan Stipendiary Magistrate, 1981–86; a Recorder, 1986. Mem., Home Office Working Party on Coroners Rules, 1976–81. Mem., Gen. Council of the Bar, 1968–70. Mem., Middlesex Probation Cttee, 1994–99. Chm., Lord Chancellor's Adv. Cttee on JPs for Middlesex, 1996–2004 (Dep. Chm., 1994–96). *Publications:* research papers on drugs and drug smuggling. *Recreations:* wildlife, ornithology, cricket, travel. *Address:* c/o 2 Bedford Row, WC1R 4BS. *Club:* MCC.

BATISTE, Spencer Lee; solicitor, since 1970; a Judge of the Upper Tribunal (Immigration and Asylum Chamber) (formerly a Vice-President, Immigration Appeal Tribunal, later a Senior Immigration Judge, Asylum and Immigration Tribunal), 2002–10 (Immigration Adjudicator, 1997–2002); a Fee Paid Upper Tribunal Judge (Immigration and Asylum Chamber), 2010–12; *b* 5 June 1945; *m* 1969, Susan Elizabeth (*née* Atkin); one *s* one *d*. *Educ:* Carmel Coll.; Sorbonne, Paris; Cambridge Univ. (MA). MP (C) Elmet, 1983–97; contested (C) same seat, 1997. PPS to Minister of State for Industry and IT, 1985–87, to Minister of State for Defence Procurement, 1987–89, to Sir Leon Brittan, Vice-Pres. of EC Commn, 1989–97. Member: Select Cttee on Energy, 1985; Select Cttee on Information, 1991–97; Select Cttee on Sci. and Technology, 1992–97; Vice-Chairman: Cons. Space Cttee, 1986–97 (Sec., 1983–85); Cons. Trade and Industry Cttee, 1989–97. Pres., Yorks Cons. Trade Unionists, 1984–87 (Nat. Pres., 1990). Vice-Chm., Small Business Bureau, 1983–92. Law Clerk to Sheffield Assay Office, 1974–2000. Mem., British Hallmarking Council, 1988–2000. *Recreations:* gardening, reading, photography, genealogy. *Address:* c/o Upper Tribunal (Immigration and Asylum Chamber), Field House, 15–25 Bream's Buildings, EC4A 1DZ.

BATLEY-JACKSON, Dame Temuranga, (Dame June), DNZM 2010; QSM 1995; Chief Executive Officer, Manukau Urban Maori Authority, New Zealand, 1986–2009; *b* Te Kuiti, NZ, 24 Aug. 1939; *d* of Barney Ngahrwi Batley and Huinga Batley; *m* 1959, Robert Jackson; two *s* one *d*. *Educ:* Hukarere Coll., Napier, NZ. Mem., Parole Bd, NZ, 1991–. Chairperson: Waitangi Fisheries Commn, Wellington; Family Start, Manukau, Min. of Social Devel, Wellington. Chief Exec., Nga Whare Waateamarae, Mangere. Chm., Te Putea Whakatipu Trust. *Recreations:* outdoor activities, travel. *Address:* c/o Manukau Urban Maori Authority, PO Box 23398, Papatoetoe, Auckland, New Zealand.

BATSON, Philip David; HM Diplomatic Service; Ambassador to the Republic of Moldova, since 2013; *b* Woolwich, 26 June 1968; *s* of David and Margaret Batson; *m* 2006, Joanna Samuels-Watson; one *s*. *Educ:* Dartford Grammar Sch. for Boys. Entered FCO, 1987; Entry Clearance Officer, Bombay, 1991–94; Third Sec. (Pol), Paris, 1995–97; Second, later First Sec., FCO, 1997–2004; Dep. Hd of Mission, Tunis, 2004–08; Dep. Hd, Corporate Services Prog., FCO, 2008–11; Games-time co-ordinator and crisis planner, London 2012 Olympic and Paralympic Games, 2011–12. *Recreations:* cricket, gardening, family. *Address:* c/o Foreign and Commonwealth Office, King Charles Street, SW1A 2AH. *E:* phil.batson@fco.gov.uk.

BATT, Dr Christopher, OBE 1998; Chief Executive, Museums, Libraries and Archives Council, 2003–07; *b* 3 July 1947; *s* of Charles and Ethel Batt; *m* 2004, Adrienne Billcliffe. *Educ:* Henry Thornton Grammar Sch.; Open Univ. (BA 1st Cl. Hons); University Coll. London (PhD 2015). FCLIP (FLA 1985; Hon. Fellow 1998). London Borough of Croydon: Dep. Chief Librarian, 1978–91; Bor. Libraries and Mus Officer, 1991–96; Dir, Leisure Services, 1996–99; Chief Network Advr, Liby and Inf. Commn, 1999–2000; Dir, Libraries and Inf. Soc. Team, Resource: Council for Mus, Archives and Libraries, 2000–03. Dir, Chris Batt Consulting Ltd, 2007–10. FRSA 2001. *Publications:* Information Technology in Public Libraries, 1985, 6th edn 1998; contribs to Public Liby Jl. *Recreations:* flying light aircraft, photography, history of science and technology, music. *E:* cbatt@mac.com.

BATTARBEE, Prof. Richard William, DPhil, DSc; FRS 2006; Professor of Environmental Change, University College London, 1991–2007, now Emeritus; *b* 30 May 1947; *s* of Halstead and Ethel Battarbee; *m* 1972, Gill Parkes. *Educ:* University Coll. London (BA; Hon. Fellow 2011); DPhil NUU 1973; DSc London 1997. Royal Soc. Eur. Res. Fellow, Uppsala Univ., 1971–73; Res. Fellow, NUU, 1973–76; University College London: Lectr, 1976–82, Reader, 1982–91, in Geog.; Dir, Envmtl Res. Centre, 1991–2007. Foreign Mem., Norwegian Acad. of Sci. and Letters, 1991. Hon. Prof., Nanjing Inst. for Geog. and Limnology, 2002–, Einstein Prof., 2012, Chinese Acad. of Scis. Hon. DSc Ulster, 2007. Research medals: (and Rector's Guest) Univ. of Helsinki, 1994; Moscow State Univ., 1995. Back Award, 1989, Victoria Medal, 2010, RGS; Ruth Patrick Award, Amer. Soc. for Limnology and Oceanography, 2009; James Croll Medal, Quarternary Res. Assoc., 2013. *Publications:* Palaeolimnology and Lake Acidification, 1990; Global Change in the Holocene, 2003; Past Climate Variability through Europe and Africa, 2004; Natural Climate Variability and Global Warming, 2008; Climate Change Impacts on Freshwater Ecosystems, 2010. *Recreation:* silent piano playing. *Address:* 9 Main Street, Addingham, W Yorks LS29 0PD. *E:* r.battarbee@ucl.ac.uk.

BATTEN, Gerard; Member (UK Ind) London Region, European Parliament, since 2004; *b* 27 March 1954. Hand bookbinder, 1972–76; Manager, BT, 1976–2004. UK Independence Party: Founder Mem., 1993–; Mem., NEC, 1993–97, 2002–06; Party Sec., 1994–97. Contested (UK Ind) Romford, 2015. *Address:* PO Box 2409, Ilford IG1 8ES; European Parliament, Rue Wiertz, 1047 Brussels, Belgium.

BATTEN, Stephen Duval; QC 1989; a Recorder, 1988–2010; *b* 2 April 1945; *s* of Brig. Stephen Alexander Holgate Batten, CBE and of Alice Joan Batten, MBE, *d* of Sir Ernest Royden, 3rd Bt; *m* 1976, Valerie Jean Trim; one *s* one *d*. *Educ:* Uppingham; Pembroke Coll., Oxford (BA). Called to the Bar, Middle Temple, 1968, Bencher 1998. *Recreations:* planter gardening, kitchen bridge and other puzzles.

BATTEN, Tracey Leigh; Chief Executive, Imperial College Healthcare NHS Trust, since 2014; *b* Melbourne, Australia, 30 April 1966; *d* of Jeffrey and Judith Batten; *m* 2002, Simon Blair; one step *s* one step *d*. *Educ:* Firbank Anglican Sch.; Univ. of Melbourne (MB BS 1989); Univ. of New South Wales (MHA 1995); Harvard Univ. (MBA 2001). CMO, St Vincent's Hosp., Melbourne, 1995–97; Chief of Health Progs, Inner and Eastern Healthcare Network, Vic, 1998–99; Chief Executive: Dental Health Services, Vic, 2001–03; Eastern Health, Melbourne, 2004–08; St Vincent's Health Australia, 2009–13. FRACMA 1996; FAICD 2006. *Recreations:* gourmet cooking, food and wine, travel, paddle boarding. *Address:* Imperial College Healthcare NHS Trust, The Bays, St Mary's Hospital, South Wharf Road, W2 1NY. *T:* (020) 3312 1333. *E:* tracey.batten@imperial.nhs.uk. *Club:* Harvard (Australia).

BATTERBURY, His Honour Paul Tracy Shepherd, TD 1972 (2 bars); DL; a Circuit Judge, 1983–99; *b* 25 Jan. 1934; only *s* of late Hugh Basil John Batterbury and of Inez Batterbury. *Educ:* St Olave's Grammar Sch., Southwark; Univ. of Bristol (LLB). Served RAF, 1952–55, TA, 1959–85 (Major, RA). Called to Bar, Inner Temple, 1959; practising barrister, 1959–83. Councillor: Chislehurst and Sidcup UDC, 1960–62; London Borough of Greenwich, 1968–71 (Chm., Housing Cttee, 1970–71). Founder Trustee, St Olave's Sch., SE9, 1970–2001; Founder Chm., Gallipoli Meml Lects, 1986–89. Vice-Pres., SE London SJAB, 1988–91. DL Greater London, 1986–2001; rep. DL, London Borough of Havering, 1989–95. *Recreations:* walking, caravanning. *Address:* 5 Paper Buildings, Temple, EC4Y 9HB. *T:* (020) 7583 9275.

BATTERHAM, Prof. Robin John, AO 2004; PhD; FREng; FTSE; FAA; Kernot Professor of Engineering, University of Melbourne, since 2009; *b* 3 April 1941; *s* of Maurice Samuel and Marjorie Kate Batterham. *Educ:* Brighton Grammar Sch.; Melbourne Univ. (BEng; PhD 1969). AMusA 1975; FTSE 1988; FAustIMM 1989; FIChemE 1989; FIEAust 1989; FAIM 1999; FAICD 1999; FAA 2001; FREng 2004; CEng; CPEng; CSci. Res. Scientist, later Chief Res. Scientist and Chief of Minerals Res. Div., CSIRO, 1970–88; various positions incl. Man. Dir, R&D, then Global Practice Leader, Innovation, 1988–2006, Gp Chief Scientist, 2006–09, Rio Tinto; Chief Scientist of Australia, 1999–2005. Professorial Fellow, Univ. of Melbourne, 2004–. President: IChemE, 2004; Australian Acad. of Technol Scis and Engrg, 2005–12. Corresp. Mem., Swiss Acad. Engrg Scis, 2002; Foreign Associate: NAE, US, 2004; Chinese Acad. of Engrg, 2013. Hon. DLitt Melbourne, 2004; Hon. DSc Sydney Univ. of Technol., 2006; Hon. DEng Queensland, 2011. Centenary Medal (Australia), 2001. *Publications:* The Chance to Change, 2000; jl, conf. and patent pubns. *Recreations:* music (organist Scots Ch, Melbourne), ski-ing, cycling. *Address:* 153 Park Drive, Parkville, Vic 3052, Australia. *T:* (3) 8344 9737, 0417 351776. *E:* robin.batterham@unimelb.edu.au.

BATTERSBY, Sir Alan (Rushton), Kt 1992; MSc, PhD, DSc, ScD; FRS 1966; Professor of Organic Chemistry, Cambridge University, 1969–92 (1702 Chair, 1988–92), now Emeritus; Fellow of St Catharine's College, Cambridge, 1969–92, Emeritus Fellow, 1992–2000, Hon. Fellow, 2000; *b* Leigh, 4 March 1925; *s* of William and Hilda Battersby; *m* 1949, Margaret Ruth (*d* 1997), *d* of Thomas and Annie Hart, Whaley Bridge, Cheshire; two *s*. *Educ:* Grammar Sch., Leigh; Univ. of Manchester (Mercer and Woodiwiss Schol.; MSc); Univ. of St Andrews (PhD); DSc Bristol; ScD Cantab. Asst Lectr in Chemistry, Univ. of St Andrews, 1948–53; Commonwealth Fund Fellow at Rockefeller Inst., NY, 1950–51 and at Univ. of Illinois, 1951–52; Lectr in Chemistry, Univ. of Bristol, 1954–62; Prof. of Organic Chemistry, Univ. of Liverpool, 1962–69. Mem. Council, Royal Soc., 1973–75. Mem. Deutsche Akademie der Naturforscher Leopoldina, 1967; MAE 1990. Pres., Bürgenstock Conf., 1976. Chm., Exec. Council, 1983–90, Trustee, 1993–2000, Novartis (formerly Ciba) Foundn. Foreign Fellow: Nat. Acad. of Scis, India, 1990; Indian Nat. Science Acad., 1993. Honorary Member: Soc. Royale de Chimie, Belgium, 1987; Amer. Acad. of Arts and Scis, 1988; Soc. Argentina de Investigaciones en Quimica Organica, 1997. Lectures: Treat Johnson, Yale, 1969; Pacific Coast, USA, 1971; Karl Folkers, Wisconsin, 1972; N-E Coast, USA, 1974; Andrews, NSW, 1975; Middle Rhine, 1976; Tishler, Harvard, 1978; August Wilhelm von Hoffmann, Ges. Deutscher Chem., 1979; Pedler, Chem. Soc., 1980–81; Rennebohm, Wisconsin, 1981; Kharasch, Chicago, 1982; Bakerian, Royal Soc., 1984; Baker, Cornell, 1984; Lady Masson Meml, Melbourne, 1987; Atlantic Coast, USA, 1988; Nehru Centenary, Seshadri Meml and Zaheer Meml, India, 1989; Marvel, Illinois, 1989; Gilman, Iowa, 1989; Alder, Cologne, 1991; Dauben, Berkeley, 1994; Alexander Cruickshank, Gordon Confs, 1994; Linus Pauling, Oregon, 1996; IAP, Columbia, 1999; Univ. Lectr, Ottawa, 1993; Visiting Professor: Cornell Univ., 1969; Virginia Univ., 1971; Tohoku Univ., Japan, 1974; ANU, 1975; Technion, Israel, 1977; Univ. of Canterbury, NZ, 1980; Melbourne Univ., 1987; Univ. of Auckland, NZ, 1989, 1993; Univ. of NSW, 1990. Chemical Society: Corday-Morgan Medal, 1959; Tilden Medal and Lectr, 1963; Hugo Müller Medal and Lectr, 1972; Flintoff Medal, 1975; Award in Natural Product Chemistry, 1978; Longstaff Medal, 1984; Robert Robinson Lectr and Medal, 1986. Paul Karrer Medal and Lectr, Univ. Zürich, 1977; Davy Medal, 1977, Royal Medal, 1984, Copley Medal, 2000, Royal Soc.; Roger Adams Award in Organic Chemistry, ACS, 1983; Havinga Medal, Holland, 1984; Antoni Feltrinelli Internat. Prize for Chemistry, Rome, 1986; Varro Tyler Lect. and Award, Purdue, 1987; Adolf Windaus Medal, Göttingen, 1987; Wolf Prize, Israel, 1989; Arun Guthikonda Meml Award, Columbia, 1991; Hofmann Meml Medal, Ges. Deutscher Chem., 1992; Tetrahedron Prize for creativity in org. chem., 1995; Hans Herloff Inhoffen Medal, Univ. Braunschweig, 1997; Robert A. Welch Award in Chemistry, USA, 2000; Robert B. Woodward Award, USA, 2004. Hon. LLD St Andrews, 1977; Hon. DSc: Rockefeller Univ., USA, 1977; Sheffield, 1986; Heriot-Watt, 1987; Bristol, 1994; Liverpool, 1996. *Publications:* papers in chemical jls, particularly Jl Chem. Soc. *Recreations:* music, hiking, camping, sailing, fly fishing, gardening. *Address:* University Chemical Laboratory, Lensfield Road, Cambridge CB2 1EW. *T:* (01223) 336400.

BATTISCOMBE, Christopher Charles Richard, CMG 1992; Director General (formerly Secretary General), Society of London Art Dealers, since 2001; Secretary, British Art Market Federation, since 2001; *b* 27 April 1940; *s* of late Lt-Col Christopher Robert Battiscombe and Karin Sigrid (*née* Timberg); *m* 1972, Brigid Melita Theresa Lunn; one *s* one *d*. *Educ:* Wellington Coll.; New Coll., Oxford (BA Greats). Entered FO, 1963; ME Centre for Arabic Studies, Shemlan, Lebanon, 1963–65; Third/Second Sec., Kuwait, 1965–68; FCO, 1968–71; First Secretary: UK Delegn, OECD, Paris, 1971–74; UK Mission to UN, New York, 1974–78; Asst Head, Eastern European and Soviet Dept, FCO, 1978–80; Commercial Counsellor: Cairo, 1981–84; Paris, 1984–86; Counsellor, FCO, 1986–90; Ambassador to Algeria, 1990–94; Asst Under-Sec. of State, then Dir (Public Depts), FCO, 1994–97; Ambassador to Jordan, 1997–2000. Chm., Anglo Jordanian Soc., 2002–09. JP Wimbledon, 2002–07. *Recreations:* golf, ski-ing, tennis. *Clubs:* Kandahar; Temple Golf.

BATTISHILL, Sir Anthony (Michael William), GCB 1997 (KCB 1989); Chairman, Board of Inland Revenue, 1986–97 (Deputy Chairman, 1985); *b* 5 July 1937; *s* of William George Battishill and Kathleen Rose Bishop; *m* 1961, Heather Frances Lawes; one *d*. *Educ:* Taunton Sch.; Hele's Sch., Exeter; London Sch. of Economics (BSc (Econ); Hon. Fellow

2013). 2nd Lieut, RAEC, 1958–60. Inland Revenue, 1960–63; HM Treasury, 1963–65; Inland Revenue, 1965–76, Asst Sec., 1970; Central Policy Review Staff, 1976–77; Principal Private Sec. to Chancellor of the Exchequer, HM Treasury, 1977–80; Under Sec., HM Treasury, 1980–82, 1983–85, Inland Revenue, 1982–83. Chm., Student Loans Co. Ltd, 1998–2001. Mem. Ct of Governors, LSE, 1987–2012, now Emeritus (Vice-Chm., 2003–09). *Recreations:* gardening, old maps. *Address:* 4 Highfield Close, West Byfleet, Surrey KT14 6QR.

BATTLE, Dennis Frank Orlando; consultant on public sector reform, strategic management and human resource management, since 1998; *b* 17 Dec. 1942; *s* of Frank William Orlando and Marion Kathleen Battle; *m* 1965, Sandra Moule; one *s* one *d*. *Educ:* Bedford Modern School. Joined Customs and Excise as Exec. Officer, 1962; Higher Exec. Officer, NBPI, 1967; Sen. Exec. Officer, CS Coll., 1972; returned to Customs and Excise, 1975: Grade 7 1978, Asst Sec. 1985; Comr, 1990–98; Dir of Personnel, 1990–94, Dir of Personnel and Finance, 1994–98. Non-exec. Dir, Sentinel Housing Assoc. (formerly Sentinel Housing Group), 1998–2010. FCIPD (FIPD 1998). *Recreations:* watching Aldershot FC and Sussex CCC, watercolour painting.

BATTLE, Rt Hon. John Dominic; PC 2002; *b* 26 April 1951; *s* of John and late Audrey Battle; *m* 1977, Mary Meenan; one *s* two *d*. *Educ:* Leeds Univ. (BA Hons (1st cl.) 1976). Training for RC Priesthood, Upholland Coll., 1969–72; Leeds Univ., 1973–77; Res. Officer to Derek Enright, MEP, 1979–83; Nat. Co-ordinator, Church Action on Poverty, 1983–87. MP (Lab) Leeds W, 1987–2010. Opposition front-bench spokesman on housing, 1992–94, on science and technology, 1994–95, on energy, 1995–97; Minister of State: (Minister for Energy and Industry), DTI, 1997–99; FCO, 1999–2001. Mem., Internat. Develt Select Cttee, 2001–10. Chairman, All Party Parliamentary Group: on Overseas Develt, 2005–10 (Vice-Chm., 1992–97); on Poverty, 2006–10. KSG 2009. *Recreations:* walking, poetry, supporting Leeds United FC.

BATTLE, Susan, (Sue), CBE 2006 (OBE 1995); Chief Executive, Birmingham Chamber of Commerce and Industry, 1999–2006; *b* 7 Aug. 1946; *d* of Harry and Beryl Sagar; *m* 1969, George Henry Battle. *Educ:* Old Hall Sch., Norfolk; Newcastle upon Tyne Coll. of Commerce (HND Business Studies). Statistical Asst to Sales Dir, Procter & Gamble Ltd, 1967–72; Adminr, M & R Internat., Riyadh, 1972–75; Birmingham Chamber of Commerce and Industry: Asst Sec., 1977–80; Head of Home and Economic Dept, 1980–84; Asst Dir, 1984–88; Dep. Chief Exec., 1989–99. Hon. Dr Central England in Birmingham, 2007. *Recreations:* ornithology, the countryside, Islamic history and culture. *Address:* 8 Brookfield House, Hackmans Gate Lane, Belbroughton, Stourbridge, Worcs DY9 0DL.

BATTY, Christopher Michael; His Honour Judge Christopher Batty; a Circuit Judge, since 2009; *b* Leeds, 13 Oct. 1966; *s* of Michael Batty and Joyce Batty; *m* 2005, Kate Martha Rayfield; one *s* one *d*. *Educ:* Abbey Grange C of E Sch., Leeds; Liverpool Poly. (LLB Hons). Called to the Bar, Gray's Inn, 1989; in practice as a barrister, 1989–2009; a Recorder, 2005–09. *Recreations:* watching sport, Leeds United, Hunslet Hawks, reading, cooking.

BATTY, Prof. (John) Michael, CBE 2004; PhD; FRS 2009; FBA 2001; FRTPI, FCILT; FAcSS; Bartlett Professor (formerly Professor of Spatial Analysis and Planning, then Bartlett Professor of Planning), since 1995, and Chairman, Centre for Advanced Spatial Analysis, since 2010 (Director, 1995–2010), University College London; *b* 11 Jan. 1945; *s* of Jack Batty and Nell Batty (*née* Marsden); *m* 1969, Susan Elizabeth Howell; one *s*. *Educ:* Quarry Bank Grammar Sch., Liverpool; Univ. of Manchester (BA 1966); UWIST (PhD 1984). FRTPI 1983; FCILT (FCIT 1990). Asst Lectr, Univ. of Manchester, 1966–69; University of Reading: Res. Asst, 1969–72; Lectr, 1972–74 and 1975–76; Reader, 1976–79; Prof. of City and Regl Planning, 1979–90, Dean, Sch. of Envmtl Design, 1983–86, UC Cardiff; Prof. of Geog., 1990–95, Dir, Nat. Center for Geographic Inf. and Analysis, 1990–95, SUNY, Buffalo. Vis. Asst Prof., Univ. of Waterloo, Ont, 1974; Vis. Fellow, Univ. of Melbourne, 1982; Croucher Fellow, Univ. of Hong Kong, 1986; Vis. Prof., Univ. of Illinois at Urbana-Champaign, 1986; Sir Edward Youde Meml Foundn Vis. Prof., Univ. of Hong Kong, 2001. Ed., Envmt and Planning B, 1981–. Mem., Res. Bd, 1980–82, Chm., Planning Cttee, 1980–82, SSRC; Vice-Chm., Envmt and Planning Cttee, ESRC, 1982–84; Mem., Jt Transport Cttee, 1982–85, Mem., Scientific Computing Adv. Panel, 1989–90, SERC; Mem., Cttee on Scientific Computing, NERC, 1988–90; Mem., Computer Bd for Univs and Res. Councils, 1988–90. FAcSS (AcSS 2001). FRSA 1983. Hon. LHD SUNY Buffalo, 2008; Hon. LLD Leicester, 2014. Award for Technol Progress, Assoc. Geographic Inf., 1998; Back Award, RGS, 1999; Alonso Prize, Regl Sci. Assoc., 2011; Univ. Consortium of Geographic Information Sci. Award, 2012; Vautrin-Lud Prize for Geographical Sci., 2013. *Publications:* Urban Modelling, 1976; (ed) Systems Analysis in Urban Policy-Making and Planning, 1983; (ed) Optimization and Discrete Choice in Urban Systems, 1985; (ed) Advances in Urban Systems Modelling, 1986; Microcomputer Graphics, 1987; (ed) Cities of the 21st Century, 1991; Fractal Cities, 1994; (ed) Cities in Competition, 1995; (ed) Spatial Analysis, 1996; (ed) Advanced Spatial Analysis, 2003; Cities and Complexity, 2005; (ed) Virtual Geographic Environments, 2009; (ed) Agent Based Models of Geographical Systems, 2012; The New Science of Cities, 2013. *Recreations:* discovering America, reading, Indian food, Georgian architecture. *Address:* Centre for Advanced Spatial Analysis, University College London, 90 Tottenham Court Road, W1T 4TJ. *T:* (020) 3108 3877; 9 White Horse House, 1 Little Britain, EC1A 7BX. *T:* (020) 7600 8186.

BATTY, Paul Daniel; QC 1995; **His Honour Judge Batty;** a Circuit Judge, since 2003; Honorary Recorder of Carlisle, since 2012; *b* 13 June 1953; *s* of late Vincent Batty and Catherine Batty; *m* 1986, Angela Jane Palmer; one *d*. *Educ:* St Aidan's Grammar Sch., Sunderland; Newcastle upon Tyne Univ. (LLB). Called to the Bar, Lincoln's Inn, 1975, Bencher, 2003; Junior, NE Circuit, 1985; Bar Mess Junior, 1982–85; Asst Recorder, 1991; a Recorder, 1994–2003. *Recreations:* boating, angling, Rugby. *Address:* Carlisle Crown Court, Earl Street, Carlisle CA1 1DJ. *T:* (01228) 882120. *Club:* Northern Counties (Newcastle upon Tyne).

BATTY, Peter Wright; television and film producer, director and writer; Chief Executive, Peter Batty Productions, since 1970; *b* 18 June 1931; *s* of late Ernest Faulkner Batty and Gladys Victoria Wright; *m* 1959, Anne Elizabeth Stringer (*d* 2000); two *s* one *d*. *Educ:* Bede Grammar Sch., Sunderland; Queen's Coll., Oxford. Feature-writer, Financial Times, 1954–56; freelance journalist, USA, 1956–58; Producer, BBC TV, 1958–64: mem. original Tonight team, other prodns incl. The Quiet Revolution, The Big Freeze, The Katanga Affair, Sons of the Navvy Man; Editor, Tonight, 1963–64; Exec. Producer and Associate Head of Factual Programming, ATV, 1964–68: prodns incl. The Fall and Rise of the House of Krupp (Grand Prix for Documentary, Venice Film Fest., 1965; Silver Dove, Leipzig Film Fest., 1965), The Road to Suez, The Suez Affair, Vietnam Fly-in, Battle for the Desert; freelance work for BBC TV, ITV and Channel 4, 1968–. Progs dir., prod and scripted incl. The Plutocrats, The Aristocrats, Battle for Cassino, Battle for the Bulge, Birth of the Bomb, Farouk: last of the Pharaohs, Operation Barbarossa, Superspy, Sunderland's Pride and Passion, A Rothschild and his Red Gold, Search for the Super, Spy Extraordinary, Story of Wine, World of Television, The Rise and Rise of Laura Ashley, The Gospel According to St Michael, Battle for Warsaw, Battle for Dien Bien Phu, Nuclear Nightmares, A Turn Up in a Million, Il Poverello, Swindle!, The Algerian War, Fonteyn and Nureyev: the perfect partnership, The Divided Union, A Time for Remembrance, Swastika over British Soil, Tito: Churchill's man?, Tito: his own man; prod and scripted 6 episodes (incl. pilot) World at War series. *Publications:* The House of Krupp, 1966; (with Peter Parish) The Divided Union, 1987; La Guerre d'Algérie, 1989; Hoodwinking Churchill: Tito's great confidence trick, 2011. *Recreations:* walking, reading, listening to music. *Address:* Claremont House, Renfrew Road, Kingston, Surrey KT2 7NT. *T:* (020) 8942 6304. *E:* peterbatty31@outlook.com. *Club:* Garrick.

BATTY, Wendy; *see* Darke, W.

BATY, Robert John, OBE 2002; CEng, FREng, FICE; Chief Executive, South West Water Ltd, 1996–2006; *b* 1 June 1944; *s* of late Robert George Baty and of Sarah Baty (*née* Hall); *m* 1975, Patricia Fagan; two *d*. *Educ:* Calday Grange Grammar Sch.; Liverpool Coll. of Building. CEng 1970; FCIWEM 1981; FIWO 1990; FICE 1992; FREng 2000. North West Water: Resident Engr, then Principal Engr, 1974–83; Area Manager, 1983–85; Regl Manager, 1985–88; Engrg and Scientific Dir, SW Water Ltd, 1988–96. Exec. Dir, Pennon plc, 1996–2006. Non-exec. Dir, Royal Devon and Exeter NHS Foundn Trust, 2004–10. Registered Comr, Infrastructure Planning Commn, 2010–12. CCMI 2001. *Recreations:* Rugby and sport generally, recreational flying, classic car restoration. *Address:* Hillcot, 78 Oldfield Drive, Heswall, Wirral CH60 9HA. *T:* (0151) 348 4921.

BAUCHER, Heather Anne; Her Honour Judge Baucher; a Circuit Judge, since 2009; *b* Crosby, 2 June 1962; *d* of Keith Robertson and Margaret Patricia Robertson; *m* 1987, Gerald Marsh Baucher (*d* 2012); one *s* one *d*. *Educ:* Formby High Sch., Formby; Sheffield Univ. (LLB 1st Cl. Hons; Jacqueline Falconer Prize); Chester Law Coll. Davis Campbell, later Hill Dickinson: articled clerk, 1984–86; Asst Solicitor, 1986–89; Salaried Partner, 1989–91; Equity Partner/Mem., 1991–2008; Recorder, 2004–09. Mem., Solicitors Disciplinary Tribunal, 2002–09. *Recreations:* walking, swimming, Liverpool FC, St Nicholas Church, Sevenoaks, theatre, art and museum exhibitions. *Address:* County Court at Central London, Royal Courts of Justice, Strand, WC2A 2LL. *T:* (020) 7947 7490. *E:* hhjudge.baucher@judiciary.gsi.gov.uk.

BAUCKHAM, Prof. Richard John, PhD; FBA 1998; FRSE; Professor of New Testament Studies, 1992–2007, and Bishop Wardlaw Professor, 2000–07, St Mary's College, University of St Andrews, now Emeritus Professor; Senior Scholar, Ridley Hall, Cambridge, since 2007; *b* 22 Sept. 1946; *s* of John Robert Bauckham and Stephania Lilian Bauckham (*née* Wells). *Educ:* Enfield GS; Clare Coll., Cambridge (BA Hons Hist. 1st cl. 1969; MA 1972; PhD 1973). FRSE 2002. Fellow, St John's Coll., Cambridge, 1972–75; Lectr in Theol., Leeds Univ., 1976–77; Lectr, 1977–87, Reader, 1987–92, in Hist. of Christian Thought, Manchester Univ. Member: Doctrine Commn, C of E, 1990–2003; Doctrine Cttee, Scottish Episcopal Ch, 1997–2002. *Publications:* Tudor Apocalypse, 1978; Jude, 2 Peter (commentary), 1983; Moltmann: Messianic theology in the making, 1987; The Bible in Politics, 1989, 2nd edn 2010; Word Biblical Themes: Jude, 2 Peter, 1990; Jude and the Relatives of Jesus in the Early Church, 1990; The Theology of the Book of Revelation, 1993; The Climax of Prophecy, 1993; The Theology of Jürgen Moltmann, 1995; The Fate of the Dead, 1998; James: Wisdom of James, Disciple of Jesus the Sage, 1999; God Crucified: monotheism and Christology in the New Testament, 1999; (with Trevor Hart) Hope Against Hope: Christian eschatology in contemporary context, 1999; Gospel Women, 2002; God and the Crisis of Freedom, 2002; Bible and Mission, 2003; The MacBears of Bearloch, 2006; Jesus and the Eyewitnesses, 2006; The Testimony of the Beloved Disciple, 2007; Jesus and the God of Israel, 2008; The Jewish World around the New Testament, 2008; Bible and Ecology: rediscovering the community of creation, 2010; Jesus: a very short introduction, 2011; Living with Other Creatures, 2011; *edited:* (jtly) Scripture, Tradition and Reason, 1988; (jtly) The Nuclear Weapons Debate: theological and ethical issues, 1989; The Book of Acts in its Palestinian Setting, 1995; The Gospels for All Christians, 1997; God will be All in All: the eschatology of Jürgen Moltmann, 1999; many articles in books and learned jls. *Recreations:* novels, poetry, allotment. *Address:* 11 Archway Court, Barton Road, Cambridge CB3 9LW.

BAUGH, John Robert; Headmaster, Dragon School, Oxford, since 2002; *b* Kampala, Uganda, 1956; *s* of Michael Baugh, LVO, MBE, QPM and Iris Baugh; *m* 1984, Wendy; two *d*. *Educ:* Aldenham Sch.; St Luke's Coll., Exeter (BEd 1978). Teacher, Haileybury Coll., 1980–87; Headmaster: Solefield Sch., Sevenoaks, 1987–97; Edge Grove Sch., Herts, 1997–2002. *Recreations:* most sports, music, reading, travel. *Address:* Dragon School, Oxford OX2 6SS. *T:* (01865) 315401. *E:* john.baugh@dragonschool.org.

BAUGH, John Trevor; Director General of Supplies and Transport (Naval), Ministry of Defence, 1986–93; *b* 24 Sept. 1932; *s* of late Thomas Harold Baugh and Nellie Baugh (*née* Machin); *m* 1st, 1956, Pauline Andrews (decd); three *s*; 2nd, 1981, Noreen Rita Rosemary Sykes; two step *s*. *Educ:* Queen Elizabeth's Hospital, Bristol. CMILT (MCIT 1956). Asst Naval Store Officer, Devonport, 1953; Dep. Naval Store Officer, Admiralty, 1959; Armament Supply Officer, Alexandria, 1966; Principal, MoD, Bath, 1970; Supt, RN Store Depot, Copenacre, 1974; Asst Sec., MoD (Navy), 1976, Exec. Dir, 1979; MoD (Army), 1983, Asst Under Sec. of State 1985. *Recreations:* bridge, golf. *Address:* Treetops, North Road, Bath, Avon BA2 6HB. *Clubs:* Athenæum; Bath Golf; Christchurch (NZ).

BAUGH, (John William) Matthew, OBE 2013; HM Diplomatic Service; Head, Africa Department (Central and Southern), Foreign and Commonwealth Office, since 2013; *b* Ndola, Zambia, 24 July 1973; *s* of David Baugh and Nicola Baugh; *m* 2001, Dr Caroline; one *s* two *d*. *Educ:* Oratory Sch.; Univ. of Bristol (BA Hons Hist. 1994; MSc Internat. Policy 1996). Fast Stream, MoD and DFID, 1997–99; Department for International Development: Head: Kosovo Crisis Unit, 1999–2000; Humanitarian Policy and Global Emergencies, 2000–02; Afghanistan Crisis Unit, 2001–02; First Sec., Khartoum, 2002–04; Head: UK Post-Conflict Reconstruction Unit, 2005–06; Iraq Dept, DFID, 2006–07; Principal Private Sec. to the Sec. of State for Internat. Develt, 2008–09; HCSC 2010; UK Rep. to Somalia, 2010–11; Ambassador (non-res.) to Somalia, 2012–13. *Recreations:* ski-ing, walking, mountaineering, family. *Address:* Foreign and Commonwealth Office, King Charles Street, SW1A 2AH. *E:* matt.baugh2@fco.gov.uk.

BAUGHAN, Julian James; QC 1990; a Recorder, since 1985; *b* 8 Feb. 1944; *s* of late Prof. E. C. Baughan, CBE, and Mrs E. C. Baughan. *Educ:* Eton Coll. (King's Schol.); Balliol Coll., Oxford (Brassey Italian Schol.; BA History). Called to Bar, Inner Temple, 1967 (Profumo Schol., Philip Teichman Schol., Major Schol.); Prosecuting Counsel to DTI, 1983–90. *Address:* 13 King's Bench Walk, Temple, EC4Y 7EN.

BAUGHEN, Rt Rev. Michael Alfred; Bishop of Chester, 1982–96; Assistant Bishop, diocese of Guildford, since 2006; *b* 7 June 1930; *s* of Alfred Henry and Clarice Adelaide Baughen; *m* 1956, Myrtle Newcomb Phillips (*d* 2014); two *s* one *d*. *Educ:* Bromley County Grammar Sch.; Univ. of London; Oak Hill Theol Coll. BD (London). With Martins Bank, 1946–48, 1950–51. Army, Royal Signals, 1948–50. Degree Course and Ordination Trng, 1951–56; Curate: St Paul's, Hyson Green, Nottingham, 1956–59; Reigate Parish Ch., 1959–61; Candidates Sec., Church Pastoral Aid Soc., 1961–64; Rector of Holy Trinity (Platt), Rusholme, Manchester, 1964–70; Vicar of All Souls, Langham Place, W1, 1970–75; Rector, 1975–82; Area Dean of St Marylebone, 1978–82; a Prebendary of St Paul's Cathedral, 1979–82; Asst Bp, dio. of London, 1996–2006; Priest-in-charge, St James's, Clerkenwell, 1997–98. Hon. LLD Liverpool, 1994. *Publications:* Moses and the Venture of Faith, 1979; The Prayer Principle, 1981; II Corinthians: a spiritual health-warning to the Church, 1982; Chained to the Gospel, 1986; Evidence for Christ, 1986; Getting through to God, 1992; (with Myrtle Baughen) Your Marriage, 1994; Grace People: rooted in God's covenant love, 2006; The One Big Question: the God of love in a world of suffering, 2010; Centred on Christ: Lent 2014 study guide, 2013; My Beloved Son: Advent study guide, 2015; Editor: Youth Praise, 1966; Youth Praise II, 1969; Psalm Praise, 1973; consultant editor, Hymns for Today's

Church, 1982; gen. ed, Sing Glory, 1999. *Recreations:* music, railways, touring, watercolour painting. *Address:* 23 The Atrium, Woolsack Way, Godalming, Surrey GU7 1EN.

BAULCOMBE, Prof. Sir David (Charles), Kt 2009; PhD; FRS 2001; FMedSci; Regius Professor of Botany, since 2009, and Royal Society Research Professor, since 2007, Department of Plant Sciences, University of Cambridge (Professor of Botany, 2007–09); Fellow of Trinity College, Cambridge, since 2009; *b* 7 April 1952; *s* of William (Jim) and Joan Baulcombe; *m* 1976, Rose Eden; one *s* three *d. Educ:* Leamington Coll., Leamington Spa; Leeds Univ. (BSc Botany); Edinburgh Univ. (PhD 1977). Postdoctoral Fellow: McGill Univ., Montreal, 1977–78; Univ. of Georgia, Athens, 1979–80; res. scientist, Plant Breeding Inst., Cambridge, 1981–88; Sen. Scientist, Sainsbury Lab., John Innes Centre, Norwich, 1988–2007; Prof., Dept of Biological Scis, UEA, 2002–07 (Hon. Prof., 1998–2002). Mem., BBSRC, 2009–. Mem. Bd, NIAB, 2008–. President: Internat. Soc. of Plant Molecular Biology, 2003–04; Biochemical Soc., 2015–. Mem., EMBO, 1998; MAE, 2003; For. Associate Mem., Nat. Acad. of Scis, USA, 2005. Mem., Lawes Agricl Trust, 2009–. For. Fellow, Nat. Acad. of Scis, India, 2011. FMedSci 2010. Corresp. Mem., Royal Acad. of Arts and Scis, Barcelona, 2013. Hon. DSc: Wageningen Agricl Univ., 2008; UEA, 2011; Birmingham, 2011; Edinburgh, 2014; Hon. Dr Helsinki, 2014; Hon. LLD Dundee, 2014. Prix des Céréalières de France, 1990; Kumho Sci. Internat. Award, Kumho Cultural Foundn, S Korea, 2002; (jtly) Wiley Internat. Prize in Biomedicine, 2003; Beijerinck Prize for Virology, Royal Dutch Acad. Arts and Scis, 2004; Royal Medal, Royal Soc., 2006; (jtly) Franklin Medal, Franklin Inst., USA, 2008; (jtly) Albert Lasker Basic Med. Res. Award, 2008; Harvey Prize, Technion Univ., Israel, 2010; Wolf Prize for Agric., Israel, 2010; Balzan Prize, Rome, 2012; (jtly) Gruber Genetics Prize, Gruber Foundn, 2014; McClintock Prize for Plant Genetics and Genome Studies, Maize Genetics Exec. Cttee, 2013. *Publications:* contrib. res. papers and articles on plant genetics, virology and genetic engrg in Nature, Science, Cell, and specialist jls. *Recreations:* sailing, hill-walking, music. *Address:* Department of Plant Sciences, University of Cambridge, Downing Street, Cambridge CB2 3EA. *T:* (01223) 333900. *Club:* Norfolk Punt (Barton, Norfolk).

BAUM, Prof. Michael, ChM; FRCS; Professor of Surgery, 1996–2000, now Emeritus, and Visiting Professor of Medical Humanities, since 2000, University College London; Consultant Surgeon, UCL Hospitals NHS Trust, 1996–2001; *b* 31 May 1937; *s* of Isidor and Mary Baum; *m* 1965, Judith (*née* Marcus); one *s* two *d. Educ:* Univ. of Birmingham (MB, ChB; ChM). FRCS 1965. Lecturer in Surgery, King's College Hosp., 1969–72; Research Fellow, Univ. of Pittsburgh, USA, 1971–72; Reader in Surgery, Welsh National Sch. of Medicine, Cardiff, 1972–78; Hon. Cons. Surgeon, King's College Hosp., 1978–80; Professor of Surgery: KCH Med. Sch., London, 1980–90; Inst. of Cancer Res., Royal Marsden Hosp., 1990–96, Prof. Emeritus, 1996–; Vis. Prof., UCL, 1995–96. Chairman: SE Thames Regional Cancer Organisation, 1988–90; British Breast Gp, 1989–91; Breast Cancer Cttee, UK Co-ordinating Cttee for Cancer Research, 1989–96; Psychosocial Oncology Cttee, Nat. Cancer Res. Network, 2004–06; Mem., Adv. Cttee on Breast Cancer Screening, DHSS, 1987–95; Specialist Advr, Select Cttee on Health, 1996–98. President: British Oncological Assoc., 1996–98; Eur. Breast Cancer Conf., 2000–02. Chm., Med. Cttee, AVMA, 2000–05. Karl Popper Meml Lect., LSE, 2007. FRSA 1998. Hon. FRCR 1998. Hon. MD Göteborg, 1986. Gold Medal, Internat. Coll. of Surgeons, 1994; Celebrating Survival award, Univ. of Texas, San Antonio, 2000; William McGuire Prize, Univ. of Texas, 2002; Internat. Soc. for Breast Cancer Res. Prize, 2003; St Gallen Prize, Switzerland, 2007; Galen Medal for Therapeutics, Soc. of Apothecaries, 2008. *Publications:* Breast Cancer—The Facts, 1981, 3rd edn 1994; Classic Papers in Breast Disease, 2003; Breast Beating: one man's odyssey in the search for the cure for breast cancer, the meaning of life and other easy questions, 2010; The Scepticaemic Surgeon, 2014; *fiction:* The First Tablet of the Holy Covenant, 2013; multiple pubns on breast cancer, cancer therapy, cancer biology and the philosophy of science. *Recreations:* painting, theatre, reading, philosophizing. *Address:* 4 Corringway, NW11 7ED. *Club:* Royal Society of Medicine.

BAUMANN, Paul David; Chief Financial Officer, NHS England, since 2012; *b* Shoreham-by-Sea, 29 May 1962; *s* of Michael David Baumann and Barbara Ellen Baumann; *m* 1985, Diana Rosemary Guthrie (*née* Henderson); two *s* one *d. Educ:* Hardye's Sch., Dorchester; St Catharine's Coll., Cambridge (Posener Schol.; BA Modern and Medieval Langs 1984; MA 1988; Tasker Prize 1984). FCMA 1992; CGMA. Unilever: joined as mgt trainee, latterly Divl Controller, 1984–93; Financial Controller, Langnese-Iglo GmBH, 1993–96; Finance Dir, Unilever Ireland plc, 1996–2000; Finance and IT Dir, UDL GmBH, 2000–01; Vice-Pres., Finance Excellence, Unilever plc, 2001–07; Dir, Finance and Investment, NHS London, 2007–12. Mem., Guildford Cathedral Council, 2009–. *Publications:* (contrib.) Creating Value in a Regulated World: CFO perspectives, 2006. *Recreations:* organist, family accompanist, member of several chamber choirs, concert and opera goer, foreign travel, culture and cuisine. *Address:* NHS England, Skipton House, 80 London Road, SE1 6LH. *T:* (0113) 825 0180. *E:* paul.baumann@nhs.net.

BAUMBERG, Prof. Jeremy John, DPhil; FRS 2011; FInstP; Professor of Nanoscience, University of Cambridge, since 2007; Fellow, Jesus College, Cambridge, since 2007; *b* 14 March 1967; *s* of late Prof. Simon Baumberg, OBE and of Ruth Elizabeth Baumberg; *m* 1994, Melissa Murray; two *d. Educ:* Jesus Coll., Cambridge (BA Hons Natural Scis 1988); Jesus Coll., Oxford (DPhil 1993). FInstP 1999. Jun. Res. Fellow, Jesus Coll., Oxford, 1992–94; IBM Res. Fellow, UCSB, USA, 1994–95; Researcher, Hitachi Cambridge Lab., 1995–98; Prof. of Nano-scale Physics, Univ. of Southampton, 1998–2007. Founder, Mesophotonics Ltd, 2001–. Fellow: Inst. of Nanotechnology, 1999; Optical Soc. of America, 2006. *Recreations:* fell walking, pianist, drinking saké, stone carving, kinetic sculptures, tennis, choral singing, clock making. *Address:* Cavendish Laboratory, University of Cambridge, J. J. Thompson Avenue, Cambridge CB3 0HE. *T:* (01223) 337429. *E:* j.j.baumberg@phy.cam.ac.uk.

BAUME, Jonathan Edward; General Secretary, FDA (formerly Association of First Division Civil Servants), 1997–2012; a Civil Service Commissioner, since 2012; *b* 14 July 1953; *s* of late George Frederick Baume and Mary Louisa Baume (*née* Hardwick). *Educ:* Queen Elizabeth Grammar Sch., Wakefield; Keble Coll., Oxford (BA Hons 1974; MA). Oxfordshire CC, 1974–76; Dept of Employment Gp, 1977–87; Orgn and Indust. Relns Dept, TUC, 1987–89; Asst Gen. Sec., 1989–94, Dep. Gen. Sec., 1994–97, FDA. Member: TUC Gen. Council, 2001–; Council, ACAS, 2011–15. Member: Ministerial Adv. Gp on Openness in Public Sector, 1998–99; Ministerial Adv. Gp on Implementation of Freedom of Information Act, 2001–04; Age Adv. Gp, DTI, 2004–10. *Recreations:* yoga, post-war jazz, world music, rambling. *Club:* Athenæum.

BAUR, Christopher Frank; writer and publisher; Executive Chairman, Editions Publishing Ltd, 2004–12; *b* 28 May 1942; *s* of Mrs Marty Stewart (*née* Sigg) and Frank Baur; *m* 1965, Jaqueline Gilchrist; four *s. Educ:* Dalhousie Prep. Sch.; Strathallan Sch., Perthshire. Joined Scotsman as copy boy, 1960; trained as journalist; Scotsman's Industrial Reporter, 1963, additionally Scottish Politics, 1972; Financial Times, Scottish corresp., 1973; Scottish political corresp., BBC, 1976; The Scotsman: Asst Editor, 1978, writing on politics and economic affairs; Dep. Editor, 1983–85; Editor, 1985–87; Editor, Scottish Business Insider, 1990–94; Dir, Insider Gp, 1994–2003; Man. Dir, Insider Custom Publishing, 1997–99. *Recreation:* creating. *Address:* 4 Roman Court, Pathhead, Midlothian EH37 5AH. *T:* (01875) 320476.

BAVEYSTOCK, Nicholas Guy; Director General, Institution of Civil Engineers, since 2012; *b* Horsham, W Sussex, 14 April 1962; *s* of Robert Harold Baveystock and Anne Mary Baveystock; *m* 1993, Christine Mary Shardlow. *Educ:* Windlesham House Sch., Washington, Sussex; Collyers' Grammar Sch., Horsham; King's Coll. London (MA). Joined Army, 1985; mentioned in despatches, 1989; CO 35 Engr Regt, 2002–04; Comdr, 1st Armd Div., RE, 2004–06; COS Multinat. Div. (S) Iraq, 2005–06; rcds 2007; Comdt, RSME, 2008–11. Non-executive Director: Engrg UK, 2012–; WISE, 2013–. Mem. Bd, E4E, ETF, 2012–. Mem., Construction Industry Council, 2012–. QCVS 2006. *Publications:* Lessons from Post Conflict Reconstruction, 2007; A History of the Royal Engineers in Iraq: 2003–10, 2011. *Recreations:* golf, travel, deputy assistant under-groom to my wife's horse, chief carer to a recalcitrant spaniel. *Address:* Institution of Civil Engineers, One Great George Street, SW1P 3AA. *Clubs:* Army and Navy; Blyth Sappers.

BAVIN, Rt Rev. Timothy John, FRSCM; OSB; Hon. Assistant Bishop: Diocese of Portsmouth, since 2012; Diocese of Winchester, since 2013; *b* 17 Sept. 1935; *s* of Edward Sydney Durrance and Marjorie Gwendoline Bavin. *Educ:* Brighton Coll.; Worcester Coll., Oxford (2nd Cl. Theol., MA); Cuddesdon Coll. Curate, St Alban's Cathedral Pretoria, 1961–64; Chaplain, St Alban's Coll., Pretoria, 1965–68; Curate of Uckfield, Sussex, 1969–71; Vicar of Good Shepherd, Brighton, 1971–73; Dean and Rector of Cathedral of St Mary the Virgin, Johannesburg, 1973–74; Bishop of Johannesburg, 1974–84; Bishop of Portsmouth, 1985–95; monk, OSB, 1996–. Mem., OGS, 1987–97; FRSCM 1991. ChStJ 1975. *Publications:* Deacons in the Ministry of the Church, 1987. *Recreations:* music, gardening. *Address:* Alton Abbey, Alton, Hants GU34 4AP.

BAWDEN, Prof. Charles Roskelly, FBA; Professor of Mongolian, University of London, 1970–84, now Emeritus Professor; *b* 22 April 1924; *s* of George Charles Bawden and Eleanor Alice Adelaide Bawden (*née* Russell); *m* 1949, Jean Barham Johnson; three *s* one *d. Educ:* Weymouth Grammar School; Peterhouse, Cambridge (MA, PhD, Dipl. in Oriental Languages). War Service, RNVR, 1943–46. Asst Principal, German Section, Foreign Office, 1948–49; Lectr in Mongolian, SOAS, 1955; Reader in Mongolian, 1962, and Prof., 1970, Univ. of London; Head of Dept of Far East, SOAS, 1970–84; Pro-Director, SOAS, 1982–84. FBA 1971–80, 1985; Mem. corresp., Soc. Finno-Ougrienne 1975. Hon. Mem., Societas Uralo-Altacia, 2003. Indiana Univ. Prize for Altaic Studies, 2012. Friendship Medal, Mongolia, 1997; Order of the Pole Star, Mongolia, 2007. *Publications:* The Mongol Chronicle Altan Tobči, 1955; The Jebtsundamba Khutukhtus of Urga, 1961; The Modern History of Mongolia, 1968, 2nd edn 1989; The Chester Beatty Library: a catalogue of the Mongolian Collection, 1969; Shamans Lamas and Evangelicals: the English missionaries in Siberia, 1985; Confronting the Supernatural: Mongolian traditional ways and means, 1994; Mongolian-English Dictionary, 1997; Tales of an Old Lama, 1997; Mongolian Traditional Literature: an anthology, 2003; A Tract for the Buryats, 2009; articles and reviews in SOAS Bull., Central Asiatic Jl, Zentralasiatische Studien and other periodicals.

BAWTREE, Rear Adm. David Kenneth, CB 1993; CEng, FIMechE, FIET; Flag Officer, and Naval Base Commander, Portsmouth, 1990–93; *b* 1 Oct. 1937; *s* of Kenneth Alfred Bawtree and Dorothy Constance Bawtree (*née* Allen); *m* 1962, Ann Cummins; one *s* one *d. Educ:* Christ's Hospital; Royal Naval Engineering College. BSc(Eng). Served in HM Ships Maidstone, Jutland, Diamond, Defender, Rothesay, Bristol, and MoD, 1965–76; Staff of C-in-C Fleet, 1979, of DG Weapons, 1981; Dep. Dir, Naval Analysis, 1983; RCDS 1985; Dep. Dir, Op. Requirements (Navy), 1986; Dir, Naval Engrg Training, 1987–90. Civil Emergencies Advr, Home Office, 1993–97. Advr in Civil Emergencies, Visor Consultants, 1998–; Project Manager: MMI (Research), 2001–02; Stargate Technologies, 2002–04; SeaCell, 2004–07. Dir, Portsmouth Healthcare NHS Trust, 1993–96; Chm., Portsmouth Hosps NHS Trust, 1996–2001. Chm. and Chief Exec., 2001–12, Pres., 2012–15, Future Ship Proj. for 21st Century, later UK Flagship, Univ. of the Oceans. Pres., Portsmouth Model Boats Display Team, 1992–. Past President: Royal Naval and Royal Albert Yacht Club, Portsmouth; Naval Home Club; RN & RM Children's Home; Royal Naval Squash Rackets Assoc. Chm., Portsmouth Dockyard Industries, 1997; Past Member: Victory Technical Adv. Cttee; Mary Rose Trust; Royal Naval Mus.; Trustee, HMS Warrior 1860, 1993– (Chm., 1997–2015); Dir, Portsmouth Historic Dockyard (formerly The Flagship Portsmouth Trust), 1997–2012 (Chm., 2000–05). Trustee: St Mary's Music Foundn, 1990–2001 (Chm., 1990–2001); Portsmouth News Snowball Appeal, 1992–94; Chm., Hants Foundn for Young Musicians, 1993–2003. Patron, CP Centre, 2002–13; former Patron, Portsmouth MacMillan Appeal. Almoner, Christ's Hospital, 1998–2004. Governor: Portsmouth Grammar Sch., 1990– (Chm., 1994–2009); Penhale First Sch., 1991–2002. Guildsman, St Bride's, Fleet St, 1997– (Mem. Court, 2013–); Consultant to Bishop of London, 1998–2006. Freeman, City of London; Liveryman, Engineers' Co. (Master, 2007–08). FRSA 2006–09. DL Hants, 1997. City of Portsmouth Merit Award, 2013. *Recreations:* fives (Nat. Masters' Champion, 2003–09, 2011), racket ball, organs and their music, miniature furniture, tropical fish.

BAX, Martin Charles Owen, DM; FRCP; FRSL; Senior Lecturer, Imperial College School of Medicine, 1997–2001, now Emeritus Reader; *b* 13 Aug. 1933; *s* of Cyril E. O. Bax and E. C. M. Bayne; *m* 1956, Judith Mary Osborn; three *s. Educ:* Dauntsey's Sch., Wilts; New Coll., Oxford (MA, BM BCh, DM); Guy's Hosp., London. Lectr, Guy's Med. Sch., 1961–74; Res. Paediatrician, Thomas Coram Res. Unit, St Mary's Hosp., London, 1974–82; Dir, Community Paediatric Res. Unit, St Mary's Hosp. Med. Sch., 1982–85; Med. Dir, Community Paediatric Res. Unit, Westminster Hosp. Med. Sch., later Charing Cross and Westminster Med. Sch., subseq. Imperial Coll. Sch. of Medicine, 1985–2003. Pres., Soc. for the Study of Behavioural Phenotypes, 1978–. Editor, Ambit Literary & Arts Magazine, 1959–; Sen. Ed., Mac Keith Press, 1978–2004. Folke Bernadette Lectr, Sweden, 1984. FRSL 2002. Anderson-Aldrich Award, Amer. Acad. of Paediatrics, 1990; Dist. Service Award, Amer. Acad. for Cerebral Palsy & Develt Medicine, 1994. *Publications:* The Hospital Ship (novel), 1975; Edmond Went Far Away (for children), 1990; (jtly) Child Development and Child Health, 1990; Love on the Borders (novel), 2005; Memoirs of a Gone World (short stories), 2010. *Recreations:* tennis, walking. *Address:* 17 Priory Gardens, Highgate, N6 5QY. *T:* (020) 8340 3566. *Clubs:* Chelsea Arts, Royal Society of Medicine.

BAXENDALE, Leo; freelance artist; *b* 27 Oct. 1930; *s* of Leo Baxendale and Gertrude Baxendale (*née* Dickinson); *m* 1955, Peggy Green; three *s* two *d. Educ:* Preston Catholic Coll. Created: Little Plum, Minnie the Minx and Bash St Kids for The Beano, 1953, drew them and their siblings, Three Bears and Banana Bunch, 1953–64; WHAM! comic (Grimly Feendish, Barmy Army, *et al*), 1964; characters for Fleetway/IPC comics, 1966–75; set up Reaper Books, 1987; created I LOVE You Baby Basil!, The Guardian, 1990; stopped drawing due to repetitive strain injury in drawing hand, 1992. Publisher, The Strategic Commentary, by Terence Heelas, 1965–67. *Publications:* Willy the Kid, Book 1, 1976, Book 2, 1977, Book 3, 1978; A Very Funny Business (autobiog.), 1978; The Encroachment, 1988; On Comedy: the Beano and ideology, 1989, 2nd edn 1993; I LOVE You Baby Basil!, 1991; Pictures in the Mind, 2000; The Worst of Willy the Kid, 2002; The Beano Room, 2005; Hobgoblin Wars: dispatches from the front, 2009 (autobiog.). *Recreation:* seeping into the woodwork and rotting it. *Address:* 11 Brockley Acres, Eastcombe, Stroud, Glos GL6 7DU. *E:* romics@reaper.co.uk.

BAXENDALE, Presiley Lamorna, (Mrs R. K. FitzGerald); QC 1992; *b* 31 Jan. 1951; *d* of late Geoffrey Arthur Baxendale and Elizabeth (*née* Stevenson); *m* 1978, Richard Kieran FitzGerald; one *s* one *d. Educ:* St Mary's Sch., Wantage; St Anne's Coll., Oxford (BA). Called to the Bar, Lincoln's Inn, 1974, Bencher, 1999; Jun. Counsel to Crown, Common Law, 1991. Member: ICSTIS, 1986–90; Council, Justice, 1994–2002. Mem., Ct of Govs, LSE, 1988–2007. Counsel to Scott Inquiry, 1992–95. Hon. Fellow, LSE, 2008. *Club:* CWIL.

BAXENDELL, Sir Peter (Brian), Kt 1981; CBE 1972; FREng; FIC; Director, Shell Transport and Trading Co., 1973–95 (Chairman, 1979–85); *b* 28 Feb. 1925; *s* of Lesley Wilfred Edward Baxendell and Evelyn Mary Baxendell (*née* Gaskin); *m* 1949, Rosemary (*née* Lacey); two *s* two *d*. *Educ:* St Francis Xavier's, Liverpool; Royal School of Mines, London (ARSM, BSc; FIC 1983). FREng (FEng 1978). Joined Royal Dutch/Shell Group, 1946; Petroleum Engr in Egypt, 1947, and Venezuela, 1950; Techn. Dir, Shell-BP Nigeria, 1963; Head of SE Asia Div., London, 1966; Man. Dir, Shell-BP Nigeria, 1969; Chm., Shell UK, 1974–79; Man. Dir, 1973, Chm., Cttee of Man. Dirs, 1982–85, Royal Dutch/Shell Gp of Cos; Chm., Shell Canada Ltd, 1980–85; Dir, Shell Oil Co., USA, 1982–85; Chm., Hawker Siddeley Gp, 1986–91 (Dir, 1984–91; Dep. Chm., Jan.–April 1986); Director: Sun Life Assurance Co. of Canada, 1986–97; Inchcape, 1986–93. Mem., UGC, 1983–89. Mem., Governing Body, Imperial Coll., London, 1983–99 (Vice Chm., 1991–99). Hon. DSc: Heriot-Watt, 1982; QUB, 1986; London, 1986; Loughborough, 1987. Commander, Order of Orange-Nassau, 1985. *Publications:* articles on petroleum engrg subjects in scientific jls. *Recreations:* tennis, fishing. *Address:* c/o Shell Centre, SE1 7NA.

BAXTER, Canon Dr Christina Ann, CBE 2005; Principal, St John's College, Nottingham, 1997–2012 (Dean, 1988–97); Chairman of House of Laity, General Synod of Church of England, 1995–2010 (Vice-Chairman, 1990–95); *b* 8 March 1947; *d* of late Leslie John David and of Madge Adeline Baxter. *Educ:* Walthamstow Hall, Sevenoaks, Kent; Durham Univ. (BA, PhD); Bristol Univ. (Cert Ed). Asst Teacher, 1969–73, Head of Religious Educn, 1973–76, John Leggott Sixth Form Coll., Scunthorpe; part-time tutor, St John's Coll., Durham, and Durham research student, 1976–79; Lectr in Christian Doctrine, St John's Coll., Nottingham, 1979–. Canon Theologian, Coventry Cath., 1996–2006; Lay Canon, Southwell Minster, 2000–13, now Canon Emeritus. Mem., Archbishops' Council, 1998–2010. Hon. DTheol Chester. *Publications:* Wounds of Jesus, 2005. *Recreation:* swimming. *Address:* 18 St Michael's Square, Bramcote, Nottingham NG9 3HG. *T:* (0115) 922 4087.

BAXTER, Glen; artist; *b* 4 March 1944; *s* of Charles Baxter and Florence Baxter; *m* 1991, Carole Suzanne Elsa Agis; one *s* one *d*. *Educ:* Leeds Coll. of Art. *Exhibitions:* Gotham Book Mart, NYC, 1974, 1976, 1979; Anthony Stokes Gall., London, 1978, 1980; ICA, 1981; Mus. of Modern Art, Oxford, 1981; Nigel Greenwood Gall., London, 1983, 1985, 1990; Holly Solomon Gall., NY, 1985; Sydney Biennale, Australia, 1986; Samia Saouma, Paris, 1987, 1991; Musée de l'Abbaye Sainte-Croix, Les Sables d'Olonne, France, 1987; Seita Mus., Paris, 1990; Adelaide Fest., 1992; Tanya Rumpff Galerie, Haarlem, 1992; Ginza Art Space, Tokyo, 1994; Wilkinson Fine Art, London, 1994; Les Entrepôts Laydet, Paris, 1995; Nagy Fine Art, Sydney, 1996; Modernism, San Francisco, 1998, 2002, 2006, 2008; Galerie de la Châme, Paris, 1998, 2004, 2008; Artothèque Gal., Angoulême, and Gal. de la Châtre, Palais de Congrès, Paris, Chris Beetles Gall., and Anthony Wilkinson Gall., London, 1999; Lombard Freid Fine Arts, NY, 2001; Galerie Daniel Blau, Munich, 2001, 2009; Le Salon d'Art, Brussels, 2003, 2008; Wetering Galerie, Amsterdam, 2004; Flowers Central Gall., London, 2004, 2006, 2009, 2011; Galerie Martine et Thibault de la Châtre, Paris, 2006, 2008, 2010–11; Espace Ecureuil Fondation d'Art, Toulouse, 2009; Poitiers, 2010; Advent Calendar, Meymac Contemporary Art Centre, 2010; Cognac, 2011; La Station, Nice, 2013. *Works in collections:* Tate Gall.; De Young Mus., San Francisco; V&A; Arts Council; NY Public Liby; Southampton Univ.; FRAC Poitou-Charentes; FRAC Picardie; Centre Georges Pompidou, Paris; Chase Manhattan Bank, NY. Histl tapestry (commnd by French Min. of Culture, 1999), Contemporary Art Mus., Rochechouart, France. Chevalier des Arts et des Lettres (France), 2013. *Publications:* The Works, 1977; Atlas, 1979; The Impending Gleam, 1981; Glen Baxter: his life, 1983; Jodhpurs in the Quantocks, 1986; The Billiard Table Murders, 1990; Returns to Normal, 1992; The Wonder Book of Sex, 1995; 1936 at the Hotel Furkablick, 1997; Glen Baxter's Gourmet Guide, 1997; Blizzards of Tweed, 1999; Trundling Grunts, 2002; Loomings over the Suet, 2004; (with Clark Coolidge) Speech with Humans, 2007; Ominous Stains, 2009; (with Alberto Manguel) Le safari historico-gastronomique en Poitou Charentes, 2010; Colonel Baxter's Dutch Safari, 2012. *Recreations:* marquetry, snood retrieval. *Clubs:* Groucho, Chelsea Arts, Academy; Ale and Quail (New York).

BAXTER, Gregory David; Managing Director and Global Head, Citi Digital Strategy, since 2011; *b* Australia, 8 Aug. 1967. *Educ:* Monash Univ. (BAppSc); Univ. of Melbourne (MBA). Sen. Project Manager, IBM, 1989–97; Booz Allen Hamilton, later Booz & Co., 1998–2011 (Partner, 2006–11). Guest Lectr, NY Univ. Mem. Council, RIIA, 2011–. *Recreations:* triathlon (Australian representative), running (elite marathon qualification). *Address:* 220 Riverside Boulevard, Apt 41D, New York, NY 10069, USA. *E:* greg.d.baxter@gmail.com.

BAXTER, Maj.-Gen. Ian Stuart, CBE 1982 (MBE 1973); antiques dealer, since 1990; *b* 20 July 1937; *s* of Charles Baxter and Edith (*née* Trinder); *m* 1961, Meg Bullock; three *d*. *Educ:* Ottershaw Sch. Commissioned RASC, 1958; RCT, 1965; regtl and staff appts UK, NI, Kenya, India, Germany and Falkland Is; sc, Camberley, 1970; ndc, Latimer, 1974; DS, Staff Coll., Camberley, 1975–78; CO, 2nd Armoured Div., Regt RCT, 1978–80; Col AQ Commando Forces, RM, 1980–83 (incl. Falklands Campaign); RCDS, 1984; Dir, Army Recruiting, 1985–87; ACDS (Logistics), 1987–90, retd. Col Comdt, RCT, 1989–93. Dir (non-exec.), Cornwall Community Healthcare NHS Trust, 1990–93; Vice-Chm. (non-exec.), Cornwall HealthCare NHS Trust, 1993–95. Dir (non-exec.), Curnow Care, 1995–2001. Pres., RCT/RASC Instn, 1993–98. Chm. Govs, Quethiock Sch., 2001–06. *Recreations:* antique restoration, Rugby. *Address:* Weston House, Callington, Cornwall PL17 7JJ.

BAXTER, (James) Neil; Secretary and Treasurer, Royal Incorporation of Architects in Scotland, since 2008; *b* Bellshill, 3 May 1960; *s* of Andrew Baxter and Elizabeth Baxter (*née* McCardle); civil partnership 2007, John, (Josh), McGuire. *Educ:* Lenzie Acad.; Glasgow Univ. (MA Hons Eng. Lit. and Hist. of Fine Art 1982). Co-ordinator, Thirties Study and Competitions Officer, RIAS, 1982–83; Asst Editor, Architectural Design, 1984; Asst Sec., RIAS, 1984–88; Principal, Neil Baxter Associates, 1988–2008. Tutor (pt-time), Mackintosh Sch. of Architecture, 1987–89; Guest Tutor (pt-time), Sch. of Urban Studies, Glasgow Univ., 2003. Develt Dir (pt-time), Glasgow Building Preservation Trust, 2004–07. Sec., Alexander Greek Thomson Trust, 1998–2008; Vice Chairman: Tron Th., 2002–04; Glasgow Film Th., 2010–14; Dir, St Andrew's in the Square Trust, 2003; Member: Adv. Bd, Common Purpose Glasgow, 2004–07; Glasgow Health Commn, 2008; Trustee: N Highland Connections, 2008–11; Martin Jones Educn Trust, 2008; Scottish Building Contracts Cttee, 2009–. Dir, Cuba Conservation Trust, 2012–13. Life Member: Saltire Soc., 2003 (Mem. Council, 1984–86); Charles Rennie Mackintosh Soc., 1991 (Mem. Bd, 1988–91); Architectural Heritage Soc. of Scotland, 1995. FRSA; MCIPR. Hon. FRIAS 2013. Mem., Eur. Urban Res. Assoc. Glasgow Lord Provost's Medal, 2008. *Publications:* (with Pat Lally) Lazarus Only Done it Once: the story of my lives, 2000; (ed) A Tale of Two Towns: a history of Medieval Glasgow, 2007, 2nd edn 2008; The Wee Green Book: the extraordinary story of Glasgow Green, 2007; Re-Designing Scotland's Cities: the first 25 years of the Burrell Company, 2007; (jtly) Glasgow's Greatest Exhibition, 2008; (ed) A Life in Cities: an architectural autobiography, 2009; (ed) The Architectural Tourist, 2012; (ed) On Life and Architecture, 2013. *Recreations:* reading, writing, running (10 marathons to date), ruins, being walked by the dog. *Address:* Royal Incorporation of Architects in Sotland, 15 Rutland Square, Edinburgh EH1 2BE. *T:* (0131) 229 7545. *E:* nbaxter@rias.org.uk. *Club:* Scottish Arts (Edinburgh) (Hon. Mem.).

BAXTER, Jayne; Member (Lab) Mid Scotland and Fife, Scottish Parliament, since Dec. 2012; *b* Mansfield, 5 Nov. 1955; *d* of Denis and Annabel Knight; two *s*. *Educ:* Napier Univ. (BA Business Studies). Houseparent, Social Work Dept, Fife Regl Council, 1976–81; Chief Exec.'s Unit, Dunfermline DC, 1988–95; Corporate Policy Officer, Fife Council, 1995–2011; Sen. Parly Asst, Office of Rt Hon. Gordon Brown, MP, 2011–12. *Address:* Scottish Parliament, Edinburgh EH99 1SP. *T:* (0131) 348 6753. *E:* jayne.baxter.msp@scottish.parliament.uk.

BAXTER, John, FREng; FRSE; FIMechE, FIET; Group Engineering Director, BP plc, 2004–15; *b* 26 March 1951; *s* of late Robert Baxter and Ruth Baxter (*née* Baxter); *m* 1996, Margaret Helen Carnell; two *s* from a previous marriage. *Educ:* Queen's Park Sch., Glasgow; Strathclyde Univ. (BSc Hons); RNC, Greenwich (Postgrad. Dip.). FIMechE 1993; FIET (FIEE 2001); FREng 2003. Hd, Nuclear Reactors, Harwell, 1988–90; Director: Engrg, UKAEA, 1990–94; Dounreay, 1994–96; Mem., UKAEA, 1994–98; Chief Engr, 1998–2001, Gp Engrg Dir, 2001–04, Powergen plc. President: IMechE, 2007–08; Welding Inst., 2011–14. Vice Pres., RedR, 2010–. Director: Sovereign Living Ltd, 2011–; Florin Living Ltd, 2011–; Thane Ltd, 2012–. FRSE 2008. Hon. FIChemE 2013. Lt Col, 2003–07, Col, 2007–, Engr & Logistic Staff Corps, RE (V). Liveryman: Co. of Engrs, 2001; Tallow Chandlers' Co., 2010; Master, Engineers' Co., 2014. Hon. DTech Robert Gordon, 2008; Hon. DSc Strathclyde, 2011. *Recreations:* sailing, clay pigeon shooting, walking. *Address:* c/o Royal Academy of Engineering, 3 Carlton House Terrace, SW1Y 5DG. *Club:* Institute of Directors.

BAXTER, John Lawson; Vice Lord-Lieutenant of County Londonderry, 2002–14; *b* 25 Nov. 1939; *s* of John Lawson Baxter and Enid Maud Taggart; *m* 1967; three *s*. *Educ:* Trinity Coll., Dublin; Queen's Univ., Belfast; BA, BComm, LLB; LLM Tulane Univ., New Orleans. Solicitor. Mem. (U) N Ireland Assembly, for N Antrim, 1973–75; Minister of Information, N Ireland Executive, 1974. Chm. (part-time), Industrial Tribunals (NI), 1980–83; Member: Northern Health and Social Services Board, 1982–88; Criminal Injury Appeals Panel, 2002–12. Mem. Council, Ulster Univ., 2002–09. DL Co. Londonderry, 1988. *Recreations:* golf, fishing. *Address:* Beardiville, Cloyfin, Coleraine, N Ireland. *T:* (028) 2073 1552.

BAXTER, John Stephen; Head Master, Wells Cathedral School, 1986–2000; *b* 7 Sept. 1939; *s* of George Baxter and Muriel (*née* Firman); *m* 1965, Priscilla Candy; two *s*. *Educ:* Magdalen Coll. Sch., Oxford; Merton Coll., Oxford; Grey Coll., Durham. BA Modern History, Durham; DipEd Oxford. Assistant Master: Cranleigh Sch., 1964–67; Christ's Coll., NZ, 1967–70; Westminster Sch., 1971–86 (Hd of Hist., 1974–79; Hse Master, 1979–86). Educn Consultant, Emergent Dynamics (formerly Breakthrough), 2000–05. Ecclesiastical Insce Gp Scholar, 1993; Korea Foundn Fellow, 1993. Res. Asst, H of C, 1971–79; Reader, Edward Arnold, 1980–83. Mem., Admiralty Interview Bd, 1988–2005. Chairman: SW Div., HMC, 1991; Choir Schs Assoc., 1995–97; Nat. Assoc. of Music and Ballet Schs, 1998–2000; Mem., Music and Dance Scheme Adv. Gp, DfES, 2001–07. Governor: St Aubyn's Sch., 1978–95; Truro Sch., 2000–07 (Chm., 2002–07); Trustee: Commonwealth Linking Trust, 1972–95; Wells Cath. Sch. Foundn, 2007–; Member, Board of Management: MusicSpace, 1988–2000; British Sch. of Brussels, 2000–10 (Trustee, 2006–); Ind. Mem., SW Cttee, NT, 2008–12. Mem. (ex-officio), NYO, 1986–2000. Page Schol., 1998, Chm., Cornwall Br., 2003–10, ESU. Trustee, Cornwall Music Therapy Trust, 2009–. MCMI (MIMgt 1991); FRSA 1990 (Mem., SW Region Cttee, 2001–04). Freeman, City of London, 1991; Liveryman, Musicians' Co., 1991–. *Publications:* (contrib.) History of Lords and Commons Cricket, 1989; The Three Churches of St Minver, 2003, 2nd edn 2013; papers and articles in educn jls. *Recreations:* music, Cornish history, golf, sport (GB Olympic Hockey Squad, Oxon; Capt., Oxon U19 Rugby; Minor Counties Cricket, Cornwall Veterans Cricket). *Address:* Lowerdale, Daymer Lane, Trebetherick, Cornwall PL27 6SA. *T:* (01208) 863613. *Clubs:* MCC (Mem., Indoor Sch. Cttee, 1976–86); Vincent's (Oxford); St Enodoc Golf (Cornwall) (Capt., 2011–13).

BAXTER, Kenneth Peter; Director, Baxter & Associates Pty Ltd, since 2000; Chairman: InfraCo Asia, since 2012; Papua New Guinea Sustainable Infrastructure Ltd; Papua New Guinea Sustainable Energy Development Ltd; XRF Scientific Ltd; *b* 23 Oct. 1943; *s* of P. F. Baxter; *m* 1973, Pamela Annabel Marr; two *s* one *d*. *Educ:* Fort St Boys' High Sch.; Univ. of Sydney (BEc). Industrial Advocate and Research Officer, Graziers' Assoc. of NSW, 1965–70; consultant, 1970–73; farming columnist and press sec., 1972–80; Develt Manager, Versatile Farm Machinery Pty Ltd, 1973–76; Dir, Corporate Affairs and Asst Man. Dir, Philip Morris Aust. Ltd, 1981–82; Manager, Adv. Services, Capel Court Corp. Ltd, 1982–83; Dir, Aust. Egg Bd, 1983–85; Man. Dir, NSW Egg Corp., 1983–88; Advr, Mackay Mill Merger Cttee, 1986–87; Chairman: Aust. Dairy R&D Corp. (formerly Res. Council), 1986–92; Good Food Products Aust. Pty Ltd, 1986–92; Privest Rural Ltd, 1987–88; Darling Harbour Authy, 1989–90; Austdairy Ltd, 1992–98; Aust. Dairy Corp., 1992–98; Thai Dairy Ind. Co. Ltd, 1998–99 (Dir, 1992–98); TFG International Pty Ltd, 2001–12; Director: KPMG Nat. Office, 1996–99; Hydro Tas (formerly Hydro Electric Corp. of Tasmania), 1996–2007; VRI Biomedical Ltd, 2000–03; non-exec. Dir, Air Niugini Ltd, 2002–06. Private Sec. to Hon. K. S. Wriedt, 1976–80; Special Advr, Senate Standing Cttee on Finance and Govt Admin, 1980–81; Dep. Dir-Gen., Premier's Dept, NSW, 1988–92; Sec., Dept of the Premier and Cabinet, Vic, 1992–95 (Chm., Public Service Bd; Mem., State Superannuation Bd); Dir-Gen., Premier's Dept, NSW, 1995–96; Policy Advr to Chief Sec., PNG, 1998–2006. Chairman: Aust. Govt Electricity Industry Supply Cttee; Hunter District Water Bd Corporatisation Cttee; NSW Grain Corp. Privatisation Cttee; Mem., GIO Aust. Ltd Privatisation Cttee. Member: Sydney Org Cttee for 2000 Olympic Games, 1995–96; Audit Cttee, Tasmania HEC, 1999–2007; Chairman: Audit Cttee, Office of Film and Literature Classification, 2002–07; Audit Cttee, Federal Magistrates Court, 2007–08. Dep. Chm., Aust. Nat. Rlys Commn, 2001–03 (Comr, 1997–98). Director: Baker Med. Res. Foundn, 1996–98; Multiple Sclerosis Soc. of NSW. Adjunct Professor: NSW and Sydney Univs, 1999–2003; Macquarie Univ., 2004–05. Dir, Tasmania Symphony Orch., 2006–09. Mem. Cttee, Boston, Melbourne, Oxford Conversazione. Dir, NSW Inst. of Mgt. FAICD 1980; FAIM 1985. *Publications:* Wool Marketing in New Zealand, 1967, 2nd edn 1972; Statutory Marketing Authorities, 1988. *Recreations:* rowing, sailing, surf life-saving, reading. *Address:* Baxter & Associates, Level 18, 25 Bligh Street, Sydney NSW 2000, Australia. *Clubs:* Melbourne (Victoria); Royal Sydney Yacht Squadron (Sydney); Mosman Rowing.

BAXTER, Prof. Murdoch Scott, PhD, CChem, FRSC; FRSE; scientific consultant; Founding Editor: Journal of Environmental Radioactivity, since 1983; Radioactivity in the Environment book series, since 1999; *b* 12 March 1944; *s* of John Sawyer Napier Baxter and Margaret Hastie Baxter (*née* Murdoch); *m* 1968, Janice Henderson; one *s*. *Educ:* Univ. of Glasgow. BSc Hons Chem. 1966, PhD Geochem. 1969. Research Fellow, State Univ. of NY (Noble gas history of lunar rocks and meteorites), 1969–70; Lectr, Dept of Chemistry, Univ. of Glasgow (geochem., radiochem. and envmtl radioactivity), 1970–85; Vis. Consultant, IAEA (nuclear waste disposal), 1981–82; Dir, Scottish Univs Res. and Reactor Centre, 1985–90; Dir, Marine Envmt Lab. (formerly Internat. Lab. of Marine Radioactivity), IAEA, 1990–97; Personal Chair, Univ. of Glasgow, 1985–95. Member: Challenger Soc. for Marine Sci., 1975–; Scottish Assoc. for Marine Sci. (formerly Scottish Marine Biology Assoc.), 1975–. FRSE 1989; Fellow, Internat. Union of Eco-Ethics, 1998; Hon. Mem. and Advr, Internat. Union of Radioecol., 1999–; Advr, Inst. Nuclear Technol., Portugal, 2000–. Mem., Scotch Malt Whisky Soc. Chevalier, Order of St Charles (Monaco), 1997. *Publications:* numerous papers to professional jls. *Recreations:* hill walking, golf, sports, Queen's Park FC, F1, good food, malt whisky, voluntary community driving. *Address:* Ampfield House, Clachan Seil, Argyll PA34 4TL. *T:* (01852) 300351. *E:* baxter@isleofseil.demon.co.uk.

BAXTER, Neil; *see* Baxter, J. N.

BAXTER, Prof. Rodney James, FRS 1982; FAA 1977; Professor in the Department of Theoretical Physics, Institute of Advanced Studies, and in the School of Mathematical Sciences, 1981–2002, Visiting Fellow in the School of Mathematical Sciences, since 2002, Australian National University; *b* 8 Feb. 1940; *s* of Thomas James Baxter and Florence A. Baxter; *m* 1968, Elizabeth Phillips; one *s* one *d*. *Educ:* Bancroft's Sch., Essex; Trinity Coll., Cambridge; Australian National Univ. Reservoir Engineer, Iraq Petroleum Co., 1964–65; Research Fellow, ANU, 1965–68; Asst Prof., Mathematics Dept, Massachusetts Inst. of Technology, 1968–70; Fellow, ANU, 1970–81; Royal Soc. Res. Prof., 1992, Sen. Fellow, 1992–, Isaac Newton Inst. for Mathematical Scis, Cambridge Univ. Pawsey Medal, Aust. Acad. of Science, 1975; Boltzmann Medal, IUPAP, 1980; Heineman Prize, Amer. Inst. of Physics, 1987; Harrie Massey Medal, Inst. of Physics, 1994; Centenary Medal (Australia), 2003; Onsager Prize, Amer. Physical Soc., 2006; Onsager Medal, Norwegian Univ. of Sci. and Technol., 2006; Royal Medal, Royal Soc., 2013. *Publications:* Exactly Solved Models in Statistical Mechanics, 1982; contribs to Proc. Royal Soc., Jl of Physics A, Physical Rev., Statistical Physics, Annals of Physics. *Recreation:* theatre. *Address:* Centre for Mathematics and its Applications, Building 27, Australian National University, Canberra, ACT 0200, Australia. *T:* (2) 61253511.

BAXTER, Roger George, PhD; FRAS; UK boarding school consultant; Partner, Select Education (formerly Select Education and Select Consultants), since 1995; *b* 21 April 1940; *s* of late Rev. Benjamin George Baxter and Gweneth Muriel Baxter (*née* Causer); *m* 1967, Dorothy Ann Cook; one *s* one *d*. *Educ:* Handsworth Grammar Sch., Birmingham; Univ. of Sheffield (BSc, PhD). Junior Research Fellow, Univ. of Sheffield, 1965–66, Lectr, Dept of Applied Mathematics, 1966–70; Asst Mathematics Master, Winchester Coll., 1970–81, Under Master, 1976–81; Headmaster, Sedbergh Sch., 1982–95. Governor: Bramcote Sch., Scarborough, 1982–95; Hurworth Hse Sch., Darlington, 1982–95; Cathedral Choir Sch., Ripon, 1984–95; Mowden Hall Sch., Northumberland, 1984–96; Cundall Manor Sch., York, 1988–98; Durham Sch., 1995–2005; Bow Sch., Durham, 1995–2005; Chetwynde Sch., Barrow, 2003–09 (Chm. Govs, 2005–09). Member: HMC Academic Policy Cttee, 1985–90; Common Entrance Board, 1989–94. Mem. Ct, Univ. of Lancaster, 1994–95. Overseas Mem., British Business Gp Dubai & Northern Emirates, 1999–2008. Church Warden, Cartmel Priory, 1997–. Freeman, City of London, 1992; Liveryman, Gunmakers' Co., 1992–. *Publications:* various papers on numerical studies in magnetoplasma diffusion with applications to the F-2 layer of the ionosphere. *Recreations:* opera, music, cooking, wine. *Address:* The Rivelin, Lindale, Grange-over-Sands, Cumbria LA11 6LJ. *T:* and *Fax:* (01539) 535129. *E:* baxterrg@aol.com.

BAXTER, Sarah April Louise; Editor, Sunday Times Magazine, since 2009; Deputy Editor, Sunday Times, since 2013; *b* London, 25 Nov. 1959; *d* of George Robert Baxter and Virginia Louise Baxter (*née* Cox); *m* 2001, Jez Coulson; one *s* one *d*. *Educ:* N London Collegiate Sch.; St Hilda's Coll., Oxford (BA Hons Modern Hist.). News ed., Time Out, 1988–90; Political ed., New Statesman, 1990–94; Asst Ed., Observer, 1995; Presenter, TV progs, Parliament Prog., 1994, The Midnight Hour, 1995; Sunday Times: Ed., News Rev., 1996–2001; NY corresp., 2001–04; Washington corresp., 2004–09. Non-exec. Dir, Times Newspapers Hlgs Ltd, 2010–. *Recreations:* family and children, juggling work and home life. *Address:* The Sunday Times, 1 London Bridge Street, SE1 9GF. *E:* sarah.baxter@sunday-times.co.uk. *Club:* Soho House.

BAY, Rt Rev. Ross; *see* Auckland (NZ), Bishop of.

BAYCROFT, Rt Rev. John Arthur; Bishop of Ottawa, 1993–99; *b* 2 June 1933; *s* of Robert Baycroft and Mary Alice (*née* Williams); *m* 1955, Joan, *d* of Victor Lake and Dora Lake (*née* Harrison); one *s* two *d*. *Educ:* Sir William Turner Sch.; Christ's Coll., Cambridge (Synge Schol.) (BA 1954; MA 1958); Ripon Hall, Oxford; Trinity Coll., Toronto (BD 1959). Ordained deacon, 1955, priest, 1956; Rector, Loughborough, Ont, 1955–57; Asst Rector, St Matthew's, Ottawa, 1957–62; Rector: Perth, Ont, 1962–67; St Matthias, Ottawa, 1967–84; Christchurch Cathedral, and Dean of Ottawa, 1984–86; Suffragan Bishop of Ottawa, 1985–93; Dir, Anglican Centre in Rome, and Archbp of Canterbury's Rep. to the Holy See, 1999–2001; Dir, Ecumenical Relns and Studies, Anglican Communion, 2002–03. Mem., ARCIC, 1982–2004. Hon. DD: Montreal Diocesan Theol Coll., 1988; Huron Coll., 1997; Wycliffe Coll., Toronto, 2004; DSLitt (*jur. dig.*) Thornloe Univ., 1991; DUniv St Paul, Ottawa, 2002. *Publications:* The Anglican Way, 1980; The Eucharistic Way, 1982; The Way of Prayer, 1983; numerous articles in jls. *Recreations:* theatre, art, ballet. *Address:* 97 Java Street, Ottawa, ON K1Y 3L5, Canada. *Clubs:* National Press, Rideau (Ottawa).

BAYES, Rt Rev. Paul; *see* Liverpool, Bishop of.

BAYFIELD, Rabbi Prof. Anthony Michael, CBE 2011; President, Movement for Reform Judaism, since 2011 (Head of Movement, 2005–10; Chief Executive, Reform Movement and Reform Synagogues of Great Britain, 1994–2005); Professor of Jewish Theology and Thought, Leo Baeck College, since 2014; *b* 4 July 1946; *s* of Ronald Bayfield and Sheila (*née* Mann); *m* 1969, Linda Gavinia (*née* Rose) (*d* 2003); one *s* two *d*. *Educ:* Royal Liberty Sch., Gidea Park; Magdalene Coll., Cambridge (MA (Hons) Law); Leo Baeck Coll., London (Rabbinic degree). Rabbi, NW Surrey Synagogue, 1972–82; Dir, Sternberg Centre for Judaism (Manor House Trust), 1983–. Dir, Advancement of Jewish Educn Trust, 1987–93; Co-ordinator of Supervisors, 1987–93, Lectr in Homiletics, 1992–96, Lectr in Personal Theol., 2002–13, Leo Baeck Coll. Chairman: Assembly of Rabbis, Reform Synagogues of GB, 1980–82; Council of Reform and Liberal Rabbis, 1984–86. Co-Pres., CCJ, 2004–. Founder Editor, Manna (Qly Jl of Progressive Judaism), 1983–2011. DD Lambeth, 2006. *Publications:* Churban: the murder of the Jews of Europe, 1981; (ed) Dialogue with a Difference, 1992; Sinai, Law and Responsible Autonomy: Reform Judaism and the Halakhic tradition, 1993; (ed jtly) He Kissed Him and They Wept, 2001; (ed jtly) Beyond the Dysfunctional Family, 2012; articles in European Judaism, Brit. Jl of Religious Educn, Church Times. *Recreations:* family life, suffering with West Ham United FC. *Address:* Movement for Reform Judaism, Sternberg Centre for Judaism, 80 East End Road, Finchley, N3 2SY. *T:* (020) 8349 5645.

BAYLEY, Hagan; *see* Bayley, J. H. P.

BAYLEY, Sir Hugh, Kt 2015; *b* 9 Jan. 1952; *s* of Michael and Pauline Bayley; *m* 1984, Fenella Jeffers; one *s* one *d*. *Educ:* Haileybury Sch.; Univ. of Bristol (BSc); Univ. of York (BPhil). Dist Officer, 1975–77, Nat. Officer, 1977–82, NALGO; Gen. Sec., Internat. Broadcasting Trust, 1982–86; Lectr in Social Policy, 1986–87, Res. Fellow in Health Econs, 1987–92, Univ. of York. Councillor, London Bor. of Camden, 1980–86. Mem., York HA, 1988–90. MP (Lab) York, 1992–97, City of York, 1997–2010, York Central, 2010–15. PPS to Sec. of State for Health, 1997–98; Parly Under-Sec. of State, DSS, 1999–2001. Dep. Speaker, 2010. Mem., Select Cttee on Health, 1992–97, on Internat. Devclt, 2001–15. Chairman: Public Bill Cttees, 2005–15; Africa All Party Parly Gp, 2003–14 (Vice-Chair, 2014–15). UK delegate to: N Atlantic Assembly, 1997–99; NATO Parly Assembly, 2001–15 (Vice-Pres., 2010–12; Pres., 2012–14; Rapporteur, 2006–08, Chm., 2008–11, Econs and Security Cttee). Chairman: Westminster Foundn for Democracy, 2005–08; UK Br., Commonwealth Parly Assoc., 2006–08; Parly Network on the World Bank, 2008–10. *Publications:* The Nation's Health, 1995. *Address:* 9 Holly Terrace, York YO10 4DS.

BAYLEY, Prof. (John) Hagan (Pryce), PhD; FRS 2011; Professor of Chemical Biology, University of Oxford, since 2003; Fellow, Hertford College, Oxford, since 2003; *b* 13 Feb. 1951; *s* of David and Nora Bayley; *m* 1988, Orit Braha; two *s*. *Educ:* King's Sch., Chester; Uppingham Sch.; Balliol Coll., Oxford (BA, MA); Harvard Univ. (PhD Chem. 1979). Postdoctoral res., Depts of Chem. and Biol., MIT, 1979–81; Asst Prof. of Biochem., Columbia Univ., 1981–84; Lectr in Organic Chem., and Fellow, Brasenose Coll., Oxford Univ., 1984–85; Columbia University: Asst Investigator, Howard Hughes Med. Inst., 1985–88; Associate Prof., Center for Neurobiol. and Behavior, 1987–88; Sen. Scientist, 1988–94, Principal Scientist, 1994–96, Worcester Foundn; Associate Prof. of Biochem. and Molecular Biol., 1991–96, and of Physiol., 1995–96, Univ. of Mass Med. Center; Associate Prof. of Chem., Clark Univ., 1996; Prof. of Chem., Texas A&M Univ., 1997–2003; Prof. and Hd, Dept of Med. Biochem. and Genetics, Texas A&M Univ. System Health Sci. Center, 1997–2003. *Address:* Department of Chemistry, University of Oxford, Chemistry Research Laboratory, Mansfield Road, Oxford OX1 3TA. *T:* (01865) 285100, *Fax:* (01865) 275708. *E:* hagan.bayley@chem.ox.ac.uk.

BAYLEY, Nicola Mary; writer, artist and illustrator; *b* 18 Aug. 1949; *d* of Percy Harold Bayley and Ann Barbara Crowder; *m* 1978, Alan John Howard Hilton, *qv*; one *s*. *Educ:* Farnborough Hill Convent College; St Martin's Sch. of Art (DipAD); Royal College of Art (MA Illus.). *Publications: written and illustrated:* Nicola Bayley's Book of Nursery Rhymes, 1975; One Old Oxford Ox, 1977; Copy Cats (5 books), 1984; As I was Going Up and Down, 1985; Hush-a-bye Baby, 1985; *compiled and illustrated:* The Necessary Cat, 1998; *illustrated:* Tyger Voyage, 1976; Puss in Boots, 1976; La Corona and the Tin Frog, 1979; The Patchwork Cat, 1981; The Mouldy, 1983; Merry Go Rhymes (4 books), 1987; The Mousehole Cat, 1990; (with Jan Mark) Fun with Mrs Thumb, 1993; Katje the Windmill Cat, 2001; The Jungle Book: Mowgli's story, 2005; (with Brian Patten) The Big Snuggle Up, 2011. *Recreations:* watching the garden, opera, sleeping, cats. *Address:* c/o Caroline Sheldon Literary Agency Ltd, 71 Hillgate Place, W8 7SS. *Club:* Art Workers Guild.

BAYLEY, Lt-Comdr Oswald Stewart Morris, (Oscar); RN retd; *b* 15 April 1926; *s* of late Rev. J. H. S. Bayley; *m* 1978, Pamela Margaret Harrison (*d* 2011); one *s* one *d* by a former marriage. *Educ:* St John's Sch., Leatherhead; King James's Grammar Sch., Knaresborough. Called to Bar, Lincoln's Inn, 1959. Entered RN, 1944: Ceylon, 1956–58; Supply Off., HMS Narvik and Sqdn Supply Off., 5th Submarine Div., 1960–62; Sec. to Comdr British Forces Caribbean Area, 1962–65; retd from RN at own request, 1966. Legal Asst (Unfair Competition), The Distillers Co. Ltd, 1966–68; Clerk, Fishmongers' Co., 1968–73; Accountant, Hawker Siddeley Gp, 1978–81, John Lewis Partnership, 1981–82. Dir, Seed Oysters (UK) Ltd. Clerk to Governors of Gresham's Sch., Holt; Hon. Sec., Salmon and Trout Assoc. and of Shellfish Assoc. of Great Britain; Vice-Chm., National Anglers' Council; Secretary: Atlantic Salmon Research Trust; City and Guilds of London Art Sch. Ltd, 1968–73; Nat. Assoc. of Pension Funds Investment Protection Cttee, 1974–75. Dir and Chief Sec., The Royal Life Saving Soc., 1976–78. Reader: All Saints Church, Footscray, 1989; St Andrew's Church, Orpington, Kent, 1994; St Botolph's Ch, Lullingstone, Kent, 1999; Chm., Sidcup Council of Churches, 1990–92. *Address:* 4 Belmont Court, Belmont Hill, St Albans, Herts AL1 1RB.

BAYLEY, Peter Charles; Emeritus Professor, University of St Andrews; Emeritus Fellow, University College, Oxford; *b* 25 Jan. 1921; *y s* of late William Charles Abell Bayley and Irene Evelyn Beatrice (*née* Heath); *m* 1951, Patience (marr. diss. 1980), *d* of late Sir George (Norman) Clark and Lady Clark; one *s* two *d*. *Educ:* Crypt Sch., Gloucester; state scholarship, 1939; University Coll., Oxford (Sidgwick Exhibnr; MA 1st Cl. Hons English, 1947). Served RA (anti-tank) and Intell. Corps (India), 1941–46. Jun. Res. Fellow, University Coll., Oxford, 1947; Fellow and Praelector in English, 1949–72 (at various times Keeper of Coll. Buildings, Domestic Bursar, Tutor for Admissions, Librarian; Editor of University Coll. Record, 1949–70); Univ. Lectr in English, 1952–72; Proctor, 1957–58; Founder Master of Collingwood Coll. and Lectr, Dept of English, Univ. of Durham, 1971–78; Berry Prof. and Head of Dept of English, Univ. of St Andrews, 1978–85. Vis. Reader, Birla Inst., Pilani, Rajasthan, India, 1966; Vis. Lectr, Yale Univ., and Robert Bates Vis. Fellow, Jonathan Edwards Coll., 1970; Brown Distinguished Vis. Prof., Univ. of the South, Sewanee, Tenn, 1978; Brown Distinguished Vis. Lectr in British Studies, Vanderbilt Univ., Univ. of the South, Sewanee, etc, 1985. Oxford Univ. Corresp., The Times, 1960–63. Sen. Mem., OUDS, 1958–69; Chairman: Oxford Univ. Theatre Fund, 1959–61; Oxford Playhouse Mgt Cttee, 1961–65; Founder Mem., Cherwell Family Housing Trust, later Cherwell Housing Trust, Oxford, 1967. *Publications:* Edmund Spenser, Prince of Poets, 1971; 'Casebook' on Spenser's The Faerie Queene, 1977; Poems of Milton, 1982; An ABC of Shakespeare, 1985; University College, Oxford: a guide and brief history, 1992; edited: Spenser, The Faerie Queene: Book II, 1965; Book I, 1966; Loves and Deaths: short stories by 19th century novelists, 1972; contributed to: Patterns of Love and Courtesy, 1966; Oxford Bibliographical Guides, 1971; C. S. Lewis at the Breakfast Table, 1979; Encyclopaedia of Oxford, 1988; Literature East and West, 1995; Sir William Jones 1746–94, 1998; Fancy's Images: 'faerie' and romance in Chaucer, Spenser and Shakespeare, in Festschrift for Prof. V. Kostić, Belgrade Univ., 2000; articles in TLS, Rev. of English Studies, Essays in Criticism, Critical Qly. *Recreations:* nature, art.

BAYLEY, Prof. Peter James; Director of Research, Department of French, University of Cambridge, since 2011 (Drapers Professor of French, 1985–2011, now Professor Emeritus); Fellow of Gonville and Caius College, Cambridge, since 1971; *b* 20 Nov. 1944; *s* of John Henry Bayley and Margaret Burness, Portreath, Cornwall. *Educ:* Redruth County Grammar Sch.; Emmanuel Coll., Cambridge (Kitchener Schol., 1963–66; 1st cl. Hons Mod. and Med. Langs Tripos, 1964 and 1966; MA 1970; PhD 1971); Ecole Normale Supérieure, Paris (French Govt Schol., 1967–68). Cambridge University: Fellow of Emmanuel Coll., 1969–71; Coll. Lectr, Gonville and Caius Coll., 1971–85; Tutor, 1973–79; Praelector Rhetoricus, 1980–86; Univ. Asst Lectr in French, 1974–78; Univ. Lectr, 1978–85; Head, Dept of French, 1983–96; Mem., Gen. Bd of Faculties, 1999–2003; Chm., Sch. of Arts and Humanities, 2001–03. Hon. Sen. Res. Fellow, Inst. of Romance Studies, London Univ., 1990. Vice-Pres., Assoc. of Univ. Profs of French, 1989–97. Pres., Soc. for French Studies, 1990–92; deleg., and Mem. Exec., Univ. Council for Modern Langs, 1994–96. Officier des Palmes Académiques, 1988. *Publications:* French Pulpit Oratory 1598–1650, 1980; (ed with D. Coleman) The Equilibrium of Wit: essays for Odette de Mourgues, 1982; (ed) Selected Sermons of the French Baroque, 1983; (ed) Présences du Moyen Âge et de la Renaissance en France au XVIIe siècle, 2003; contributions to: Critique et création littéraires en France (ed Fumaroli), 1977; Bossuet: la Prédication au XVIIe siècle (ed Collinet and Goyet), 1980; Catholicism in Early Modern History: a guide to research (ed O'Malley), 1988; Convergences: rhetoric and poetic in Seventeenth-Century France (ed Rubin and McKinley), 1989; New Oxford Companion to Literature in French (ed France), 1995; Actes de Tulane, 2001; Actes de Tempe, 2002; Actes de Charlottesville, 2003; Cambridge Rev., Dix-Septième Siècle, French Studies, Mod. Lang. Rev., Studies on Voltaire and the Eighteenth Century, etc. *Recreations:* Spain, food and wine, gardening, English ecclesiastical history. *Address:* Gonville and Caius College, Cambridge CB2 1TA. *T:* (01223) 332439; (vacations) The White House, Hackleton, Northants NN7 2AD. *T:* (01604) 870059.

BAYLEY, Stephen Paul; critic, consultant, curator, commentator and author; *b* 13 Oct. 1951; *s* of late Donald Sydney Staines Bayley and Anne Bayley; *m* 1981, Flo Fothergill; one *s* one *d*. *Educ:* Quarry Bank Sch., Liverpool; Manchester Univ.; Liverpool Univ. Sch. of Architecture. Lecturer: Hist. of Art, Open Univ., 1974–76; Hist. and Theory of Art, Univ. of Kent, 1976–80; Dir, Conran Foundn, 1981–89; Dir, Boilerhouse Project, in V&A Mus., 1982–86; Founding Dir, later Chief Exec., Design Mus., 1986–89 (Mem., Curatorial Cttee, 2012–). Occasional critic and regular contributor to Daily Telegraph, The Times, The

Independent and consumer, technical and professional jls. Mem., Design Cttee, LRT, 1989–91. Chm., Brit Insurance Design Awards, 2011. Has lectured at: Nat. Inst. of Design, Ahmedabad; India Inst. of Technol., Bombay; Art Gall. of WA, Perth; Nat. Gall. of Victoria, Melbourne; Salon de l'Automobile, Geneva; Sony Design Center, Tokyo; Internat. Expo, Nagoya; Art Coll. Center of Design (Europe), La Tour-de-Peilz, Switzerland; École Supérieure des Sciences et Études Commerciales, Paris; RIBA; RSA; RCA; and at univs, colls and museums throughout Britain and Europe. Honorary Fellow: Liverpool Inst. of Performing Arts, 2001; UWIC, 2007; Hon. FRIBA, 2009. Magazine Columnist of the Year, PPA, 1995. Chevalier de l'Ordre des Arts et des Lettres (France), 1989. *Publications:* In Good Shape, 1979; The Albert Memorial, 1981; Harley Earl and the Dream Machine, 1983; The Conran Directory of Design, 1985; Sex, Drink and Fast Cars, 1986; Twentieth Century Style and Design, 1986; Commerce and Culture, 1989; Taste, 1991; Beefeater 2-Day Guide to London, 1993; Labour Camp: the failure of style over substance, 1998; Moving Objects, 1999; General Knowledge, 2000; Sex: an intimate history, 2001; Dictionary of Idiocy (with an Appendix by Gustave Flaubert), 2003; Life's A Pitch, 2007; Intelligence Made Visible, 2007; Cars, 2008; Woman as Design, 2009; La Dolce Vita, 2011; Ugly: the aesthetics of everything, 2012; Charm, 2013; Death Drive: there are no accidents, 2015. *Recreations:* indistinguishable from work, but each involves words, pictures, food, drink, tennis and spending time in sunny places. *Address:* (office) 23 Ganton Street, W1F 9BW. *T:* (020) 7287 5888. *W:* www.stephenbayley.com. *Clubs:* Hurlingham, Chelsea Arts.

BAYLIS, Katharine Mary; *see* Davidson, K. M.

BAYLIS, Prof. Peter Howard, MD; FRCP, FMedSci; Dean of Medicine, 1997–2005, Provost of Faculty of Medical Sciences, 2002–05, University of Newcastle upon Tyne; *b* 9 Sept. 1943; *s* of late Derek Baylis and of Lore Baylis; *m* 1968, Dr Susan Mary While; one *s* two *d*. *Educ:* Wallington Grammar Sch.; Univ. of Bristol (BSc, MB ChB, MD). FRCP 1983. Trng in medicine, endocrinology and research, Queen Elizabeth Hosp., Birmingham, 1970–76; Clinical Endocrinology Fellow, Univ. of Indiana, 1976–78; Lectr in Medicine, Univ. of Birmingham, 1978–80; Consultant Physician and Sen. Lectr in Medicine, Royal Victoria Infirmary, Newcastle, 1980–90; Prof. of Exptl Medicine and Clinical Sub-Dean, Med. Sch., Univ. of Newcastle upon Tyne, 1990–97. Founder FMedSci, 1998. *Publications:* (with P. Padfield) The Posterior Pituitary: hormone secretion in health and disease, 1985; (jtly) Case Presentations in Endocrinology and Diabetes, 1988; Salt and Water Homeostasis in Health and Disease, 1989; book chapters and over 130 original articles. *Recreations:* long-distance running, classical music, reading. *Address:* 53 The Rise, Darras Hall, Ponteland, Newcastle upon Tyne NE20 9LQ.

BAYLIS, Trevor Graham, CBE 2015 (OBE 1997); inventor; President, Trevor Baylis Brands plc, since 2004; *b* 13 May 1937; *s* of Cecil Archibald Walter Baylis and Gladys Jane Brown. *Educ:* Dormers Wells Secondary Modern Sch. Represented Britain in swimming competitions at age of 15; Soil Mechanics Lab., 1953–59; Phys. Trng Instr, NS, 1959–61; Technical Salesman, Purley Pools, 1961 (also designed 50 products for swimming pools); professional swimmer and stuntman; founded Shotline Displays, 1970 (appeared on TV with Peter Cook and Dudley Moore, Dave Allen, and David Nixon); underwater escape artiste, Berlin Circus, Dec. 1970; founded Shotline Steel Swimming Pools, 1971 (built over 300 pools in schs in UK); developed 200 products for the disabled, Orange Aids, 1985; invented clockwork radio, 1990; jt Founder, Baygen, 1995; Co-founded The Electric Shoe Co. and The Personal Power Co. (to power mobile 'phone batteries through walking), 1999. Vis. Prof., Buckingham Univ., 1998–. Vice-President: Techknowlogy charity, 2001–; Women of Achievement Awards, 2002–. Patron: Spelthorne Farm Project for the Handicapped, 2004; Mus. of Sci. and Industry, Manchester, 2004; Dormer Wells Infant Sch., 2004; LEPRA, 2005; Wessex Round Table of Inventors, 2005. Hon. Fellow: UWIST, 1998; Univ. of Wolverhampton, 1999; Hon. Res. Fellow, Sch. of Journalism, Cardiff Univ., 1999. Hon. MSc: Brunel, 1997; UEA, 1997; Teesside, 1998; Hon. DTech: Nottingham Trent, 1998; Southampton Inst., 1998; DUniv: Open, 2001; Middlesex, 2002; Oxford Brookes, 2004; Hon. MBA Luton, 2001; Hon. DSc Heriot-Watt, 2003. Presidential Gold and Silver Medals, IMechE, 1997; Paul Harris Fellow, Rotary Club. *Publications:* Clock This: my life as an inventor, 1999. *Recreations:* swimming, diving, underwater swimming, boating, after dinner speaking; enthusiastic owner of Jaguar E-type. *Address:* Haven Studio, Eel Pie Island, Twickenham TW1 3DY.

BAYLISS, David, OBE 1992; FREng; Director: Halcrow Consulting (formerly Halcrow Fox), 1999–2009; Blackpool Urban Regeneration Co., 2005–10; *b* 9 July 1938; *s* of Herbert and Annie Esther Bayliss; *m* 1961, Dorothy Christine Crohill; two *s* one *d*. *Educ:* Arnold Sch., Blackpool; UMIST (BSc Tech 1961); Manchester Univ. (Dip TP 1966). FRTPI 1970; FCIHT (FIHT 1972); FCILT (FCIT 1972–2008); CEng, FICE, 1980; FITE 1984; FREng (FEng 1993). Manchester Corp., 1961–66; GLC, 1966–68; Centre for Environmental Studies, 1968–69; GLC, 1969–84 (Asst Divl Engr; Head, Transport Studies; Chief Transport Planner); Dir of Planning, London Transport, 1984–99. Chairman: SERC/DoT LINK Transport Infrastructure and Ops Steering Gp, 1991–96, Inland Surface Transport Prog. Adv. Gp, 1996–; UITP Internat. Commn on Transport Econs, 1996–98; Fifth Framework Expert Adv. Gp on Sustainable Mobility and Intermodality, EC, 1998–2002. Vis. Prof., Imperial Coll. London (formerly ICSTM), 1999–2011. Chm., Regional Studies Assoc., 1978–81; Member Council: CIT, 1978–82; IHT, 1992–94; ICE, 1996–98; Royal Acad. of Engrg, 1999–2002. President: British Parking Assoc., 1987–89; Transport Studies Soc., 1989–90; UK Vice Pres., Internat. Union of Public Transport, 1997–98. Chm., Rees Jeffreys Road Fund, 2004–13. Mem., Transit Res. Analysis Cttee, NAE, 2004–09; Mem., Public Policy Cttee, 2005–, Trustee, 2011–, RAC Foundn. TPP 2010. *Recreations:* writing, travel, wine. *Address:* 37 Ledborough Lane, Beaconsfield, Bucks HP9 2DB. *T:* (01494) 673313.

BAYLISS, Frederic Joseph; Special Professor, Department of Continuing Education (formerly Adult Education), University of Nottingham, 1988–97; *b* 15 April 1926; *s* of Gordon and Gertrude Bayliss; *m* 1948, Mary Provost; one *d* (and one *d* decd). *Educ:* Ashby de la Zouch Grammar Sch.; Hertford Coll., Oxford. PhD Nottingham 1960. RAF, 1944–47. Tutor in Economics, Oxford Univ. Tutorial Classes Cttee, 1950–57; Lectr in Industrial Relations, Dept of Adult Education, Univ. of Nottingham, 1957–65; Industrial Relations Advr, NBPI, 1965–69; Asst Sec., CIR, 1969–71; Sen. Economic Advr, Dept of Employment, 1971–73; Under Sec., Pay Board, 1973–74; Sec., Royal Commn on the Distribution of Income and Wealth, 1974–77; Acct Gen., Dept of Employment, 1977–86. Chairman: Campaign for Work, 1988–92; Employment Policy Inst., 1992–95. *Publications:* British Wages Councils, 1962; The Standard of Living, 1965; Making a Minimum Wage Work, 1991; (with S. Kessler) Contemporary British Industrial Relations, 1992, 3rd edn 1998; Does Britain still have a Pay Problem?, 1993. *Recreations:* gardening, walking. *Address:* 42 Greyfriars Court, Court Road, Lewes, East Sussex BN7 2RF. *T:* (01273) 474317.

BAYLISS, Jeremy David Bagot, FRICS; Chief Executive, The Foundation, Royal Botanic Gardens, Kew, 1997–2002; President, Royal Institution of Chartered Surveyors, 1996–97; *b* 27 March 1937; *s* of Edmund Bayliss and Marjorie Clare (*née* Thompson); *m* 1962, Hon. Mary Selina Bridgeman (*see* Hon. M. S. Bayliss); three *s*. *Educ:* Harrow; Sidney Sussex Coll., Cambridge (MA). ARICS 1962, FRICS 1971. 2nd Lieut, Coldstream Guards, 1956–57. Partner, Gerald Eve, Chartered Surveyors, 1967–97 (Sen. Partner, 1988–97); Chm., Gerald Eve Financial Services, 1989–96. Royal Institution of Chartered Surveyors: Chm., various cttees, 1983–; Mem., Gen. Council, 1987–; Pres., Planning and Develt Div., 1989–90. Chm., CBI Land Use Panel, 1992–95. Mem., Adv. Panel to Secs of State for the Envmt and for Wales on Standards for Planning Inspectorate, 1993–96. Hon. Co. Organiser (Berks), Nat. Gardens Scheme, 2002–07. Trustee: Royal Merchant Navy Sch. Foundn, 2003–07; Soc. for Horticl Therapy, 2004–09. Gov., Bearwood Coll., 1999–2008 (Chm., 2003–08). Chm., Reading S Cons. Assoc., 1975–78. *Recreations:* gardening, country pursuits, classic cars. *Address:* Loddon Lower Farm, Swallowfield, near Reading, Berks RG7 1JE. *T:* (0118) 988 3218. *Club:* Boodle's.

BAYLISS, John; Deputy Chairman, Abbey National plc, 1991–93; *b* 22 Jan. 1934; *s* of late Athol Thomas Bayliss and Elizabeth Rose Bayliss; *m* 1954, Maureen (*née* Smith); one *d*. *Educ:* Haberdashers' Aske's, Hatcham. Westminster Bank, 1950; Abbey National Building Society, then Abbey National plc, 1957–93: Regional Man., 1969; Personnel Man., 1972; Asst Gen. Man., 1974; General Manager: Field Operations, 1976; Housing, 1981; Marketing, 1983; Man. Dir (Retail Ops), 1983–91. Chairman: Broomleigh Housing Assoc. Ltd, 1990–96; Richmount Mgt Ltd, 1994–2000; Affinity (formerly Broomleigh Charitable) Trust, 1999–2004; Dir, Downland Affinity Gp Ltd, 2003–04. *Recreation:* France. *Address:* Lyndhurst, Broad Oak, Brenchley, Kent TN12 7NN.

BAYLISS, John Francis Temple; an Assistant Judge Advocate General, 1996–2010; a Recorder, 1999–2015; *b* 11 Aug. 1942; *s* of Capt. Horace Temple Taylor Bayliss, DSO, RN and Patricia Bayliss (*née* Loftus); *m* 1981, Annelize Kors; one *s* one *d*. *Educ:* Ampleforth Coll.; BRNC, Dartmouth. Joined Royal Navy, 1960; called to the Bar, Gray's Inn, 1974, NSW, 1981; Comd Legal Officer, Sydney, RAN, 1980–82; Captain, 1986; Sec. to C-in-C Fleet, 1986–88; IMS, Brussels, 1988–92; Chief Naval Judge Advocate, 1992–95; an Asst Recorder, 1994–99. Liveryman, Glovers' Co., 2014. *Recreations:* golf, fly-fishing. *Address:* Cedarwood, Warwicks Bench Lane, Guildford, Surrey GU1 3TP. *T:* 07711 261869.

BAYLISS, Hon. Mary Selina, CVO 2015; Lord Lieutenant and Custos Rotulorum of Berkshire, 2008–15; *b* Bramham Park, Yorks, 14 Jan. 1940; *d* of 2nd Viscount Bridgeman, KBE, CB, DSO, MC and Mary Kathleen (*née* Lane Fox); *m* 1962, Jeremy David Bagot Bayliss, *qv*; three *s*. *Educ:* St Mary's Sch., Wantage. Gov., Chiltern Nursery Trng Coll., 1970–95; Patron, Reading Mencap, 2006–. President: Swallowfield Horticl Soc., 2006–; Wokingham and Dist Cancer Care Trust, 2013. Berkshire: JP 1978–2010 (Chairman: Family Panel, 1994–97; Bench, 1998–2001); High Sheriff 2005–06; DL 2007. *Recreations:* music, gardening, travel. *Address:* Loddon Lower Farm, Lamb's Lane, Swallowfield, Berks RG7 1JE.

BAYLISS, Rev. Roger Owen; Principal Chaplain, Church of Scotland and Free Churches, and Director, Chaplaincy Services, Royal Air Force, 1998–2001; Chaplain, HM Prison Service; *b* 21 July 1944; *s* of Stanley John Bayliss and Joyce Audrey Bayliss; *m* 1976, Pauline Jones (separated); two *s*. *Educ:* Westminster Coll., Oxford (DTh 1999); MTh Oxon 2007. RMN 1966; SRN 1969; SRN for Mentally Subnormal, 1975; Dip. Counselling. Nurse training: Saxondale Hosp., 1963–66; Nottingham Gen. Hosp., 1966–69; Lea Castle Inst., 1973–75; ordained, 1981; entered Chaplains' Branch, RAF, 1981: served at stations: Lyneham, Marham, Stanley (Falkland Is), Bruggen, N Luffenham, Cottesmore, Leeming, Coningsby; HQ RAF Germany; 2 Gp HQ; RAF Support Comd; HQ PTC. QHC, 1998–2001. *Recreations:* classic cars, fly fishing, squash, music (rock and blues), reading, golf, aerobic fitness, cooking. *Address:* 31 Amelia Way, Ymyl-Yr-Afon, Newport, Gwent NP19 0LQ. *Clubs:* Royal Air Force; Parc Golf Centre (Newport); Players (Doddington).

BAYLISS, Thomas William Maxwell; QC 2003; **His Honour Judge Bayliss;** a Circuit Judge, since 2012; *b* 24 June 1954; *s* of Thomas Maxwell Bayliss and Dorothy Vera Bayliss; *m* 1977, Caroline Jane Allpress; one *s* one *d*. *Educ:* King's Sch., Gloucester; Leeds Univ. (LLB Hons). Called to the Bar, Inner Temple, 1977, Bencher, 2008; Standing Counsel to Inland Revenue, 1991–2003; a Recorder, 2000–12. Mem., Restricted Patients Panel, First-tier Tribunal (Mental Health), 2012–. *Recreations:* bridge, tennis, theatre. *Address:* Leeds Combined Court Centre, The Courthouse, 1 Oxford Row, Leeds LS1 3BG.

BAYLISS, Valerie June, CB 1996; education and training consultant; Associate Professor of Education, University of Sheffield, 1996–2001; *b* 10 June 1944; *d* of George and Ellen Russell; *m* 1971, Derek Andrew Bayliss; one *s*. *Educ:* Wallington County Grammar Sch. for Girls; Univ. of Wales (1st cl. hons History, BA 1965; MA 1967). Research Student, LSE, 1966–68; Dept of Employment, 1968; Manpower Services Commission, subseq. Training Agency: Head of Job Centre Services, 1978–82; Head, YTS Policy, 1982–85; Dir, Field Ops, 1985–87; Under Sec., and Dir, Resources and Personnel, 1987–90; Dir of Educn Progs, later of Youth and Educn Policy, Dept of Employment, subseq. Dept for Educn and Employment, 1991–95. Sheffield University: Mem. Council, 1988–95 and 2002–11 (Chm., Audit Cttee, 2004–11); Dir, Management Sch., 1991–96. Director: Sheffield Futures Ltd (formerly Sheffield Careers Guidance Services Ltd), 1997–2004 (Chm., 1999–2004); Connexions South Yorkshire Ltd, 2001–04. Mem. Bd, Sheffield Develt Corp., 1996–97. Dep. Chm., Nat. Adv. Council for Careers and Educnl Guidance, 1996–2000. Mem. Council, RSA, 2002–07; Director, RSA projects: Redefining Work, 1996–98; Redefining Schooling, 1998–99; Opening Minds, 2000–05. Mem. Council, 1996–2013, Mem. Exec., 1999–2013, Jt Hon. Sec., 2005–09, Vice-Chm., 2009–13, C&G; Gov., Barnsley Coll., 1996–2002. Chm., S Yorks Reg., Victorian Soc., 1997–. Trustee, Brathay Hall Trust, 2001–10; Chair, Friends of Old Town Hall, Sheffield, 2014–. Patron, Nat. Youth Agency, 1996–. Hon. Fellow, Inst. of Careers Guidance, 1996. FRSA 1990; FCGI 2005. *Publications:* Key Views on the Future of Work, 1997; Redefining Work, 1998; Redefining Schooling, 1998; Redefining the Curriculum, 1999; Opening Minds: education for the 21st Century, 1999; What Should Our Children Learn?, 2000; Opening Minds: Taking Stock, 2003. *Recreations:* walking, reading, listening to music. *T:* (0114) 230 7693.

BAYLY, Richard Dion; DL; pig keeper, since 2012; Deputy Regional Director, Government Office for the South West, 2007–11; *b* 25 Feb. 1951; *s* of Edward Hugh Bayly and Denise Bayly (*née* Dudley); *m* 1986, Dr Lea Diane Jones; two *d*. *Educ:* Rugby Sch.; Bristol Univ. (BScEcon). Tutor, Rathkeale Coll., Masterton, NZ, 1970; entered Civil Service, 1974: DoE, 1974–79; Dept of Transport, 1979–97 (on secondment to BRB, as Dir, Privatisation Studies, 1990–91); DETR, 1997–2001 (on secondment to Cabinet Office, 1997–99; Acting Chief Exec., CS Coll., 1998–99); DfT (formerly DTLR), 2001–11; Dir, Devon and Cornwall, Govt Office for SW, 1999–2007. Member: Tavistock Deanery Synod, 2008–13; Plymouth Cultural Bd, 2010–14; Exeter Cathedral Council, 2012–; Dean's Council, Plymouth Univ. Business Sch., 2012–; Bd, Univ. of St Mark and St John (formerly UC of St Mark and St John), 2013–; Client Bd, Plymouth Hist. Centre, 2014–; Dir, Plymouth Barbican Trust, 2012–. Trustee: Peninsula Med. Foundn, 2010–15; SW Film and TV Archive, 2013–. Chair, Sheepstor Welfare Charity, 1980–. Churchwarden, St Leonard's Sheepstor, 2009–. DL Devon, 2012. Hon. DBus Plymouth, 2010. *Recreations:* sailing, gardening, walking, travel, reading, responsibility without power, being a hopeless parent. *Address:* Blowiscombe Barton, Milton Combe, Yelverton, Devon PL20 6HR. *Club:* Hooe Point Sailing (Hooe).

BAYNE, Prof. Brian Leicester, OBE 1998; PhD; FRSB; Visiting Professor, University of Sydney, since 2011 (Research Professor, 1997–2001, Visiting Professor, 2001–11, Centre for Research on Ecological Impacts of Coastal Cities); *b* 24 July 1938; *s* of John Leonard and Jean Leicester Bayne; *m* 1960, Marianne Middleton; two *d*. *Educ:* Ardingly Coll.; Univ. of Wales (BSc, PhD). Post-doctoral res., Univ. of Copenhagen and Fisheries Laboratory, Conwy, 1963–68; Lectr, Sch. of Biology, Univ. of Leicester, 1968–73; Institute for Marine Environmental Research, Plymouth: Res. Scientist, 1973–83; Dir, 1983–88; Plymouth Marine Laboratory, NERC: Dir, 1988–94; Dir, Centre for Coastal and Marine Scis, 1994–97. Fellow, Univ. of Wales, 1996. *Publications:* Marine Mussels: ecology and physiology, 1976; res. papers in marine sci. jls, e.g. Jl of Experimental Marine Biol. and Ecol. *Recreation:* sailing.

BAYNE, Sir Nicholas (Peter), KCMG 1992 (CMG 1984); HM Diplomatic Service, retired; High Commissioner to Canada, 1992–96; *b* 15 Feb. 1937; *s* of late Captain Ronald Bayne, RN and Elisabeth Ashcroft; *m* 1961, Diana Wilde; two *s* (and one *s* decd). *Educ:* Eton Coll.; Christ Church, Oxford (MA, DPhil). Entered Diplomatic Service, 1961; served at British Embassies in Manila, 1963–66, and Bonn, 1969–72; seconded to HM Treasury, 1974–75; Financial Counsellor, Paris, 1975–79; Head of Financial, later Economic Relations, Dept, FCO, 1979–82; attached to RIIA, 1982–83; Ambassador to Zaire, 1983–84, also accredited to the Congo, Rwanda and Burundi, 1984; seconded to CSSB, 1985; Ambassador and UK Perm. Rep. to OECD, Paris, 1985–88; Dep. Under-Sec. of State, FCO, 1988–92. Chm., Liberalisation of Trade in Services Cttee, British Invisibles, 1996–2000. Fellow, Internat. Relns Dept, LSE, 1997–. *Publications:* (with R. D. Putnam) Hanging Together: the Seven-Power Summits, 1984, rev. edn 1987 (trans. German, Japanese, Italian); Hanging in There: the G7 and G8 summit in maturity and renewal, 2000; The Grey Wares of North-West Anatolia and their Relation to the Early Greek Settlements, 2000; (with S. Woolcock) The New Economic Diplomacy, 2003, 3rd edn 2011; Staying Together: the G8 summit confronts the 21st century, 2005; Economic Diplomat (memoirs), 2010. *Recreations:* reading, sightseeing. *Address:* 2 Chetwynd House, Hampton Court Green, East Molesey, Surrey KT8 9BS. *Club:* Travellers.

BAYNE, Shenagh Irvine; a District Judge (Magistrates' Courts), since 2004; *b* 30 April 1953; *d* of David Morton Bayne and Katherine Clementine Bayne; partner, S. A. Gibson. *Educ:* English Sch. of Paris; Berkhamsted Sch. for Girls; Edinburgh Univ. (BA). Admitted solicitor, 1980; Trevor Hamlyn & Co., Solicitors, 1980–82; Deacons, Hong Kong, 1982–84; Simmons & Simmons, Solicitors, 1984–85; EMI Music, 1985–86; Freelance Solicitor Advocate, 1986–92, 1997–2004; CPS, 1992–97; Stipendiary Magistrate, subseq. Dep. Dist Judge, 1998–2004. Immigration Adjudicator (pt-time), 2002–04. *Recreations:* golf, hill-walking, skiing, contemporary literature, film and theatre going, travel. *Address:* South Western Magistrates' Court, Lavender Hill, SW11 1JU. *Club:* Hong Kong Football.

BAYNES, Sir Christopher (Rory), 8th Bt *cr* 1801, of Harefield Place, Middlesex; *b* 11 May 1956; *s* of Sir John Baynes, 7th Bt and of Shirley Maxwell Baynes (*née* Dodds); *S* father, 2005; *m* 1992, Sandra Finuala Merriman; two *s* one *d*. *Heir: s* Alasdair William Merriman Baynes, *b* 3 Dec. 1993.

BAYNHAM, Prof. Alexander Christopher; strategic technical consultant, since 1996; Principal, Cranfield University (formerly Cranfield Institute of Technology) (Shrivenham Campus), 1989–96, now Emeritus Professor; *b* 22 Dec. 1935; *s* of Alexander Baynham and Dulcie Rowena Rees; *m* 1961, Eileen May Wilson; two *s* one *d*. *Educ:* Marling Sch.; Reading Univ. (BSc); Warwick Univ. (PhD); Royal Coll. of Defence Studies (rcds). Joined Royal Signals and Radar Estab., Malvern, 1955; rejoined, 1961 (univ. studies, 1958–61); Head, Optics and Electronics Gp, 1976; RCDS, 1978; Scientific Adviser to Asst Chief Adviser on Projects, 1979; Dep. Dir, 1980–83, Dir, 1984–86, RSRE; Dir, RARDE, 1986–89. *Publications:* Plasma Effects in Semi-conductors, 1971; assorted papers in Jl of Physics, Jl of Applied Physics and in Proc. Phys. Soc. *Recreations:* church activities, music. *Address:* c/o Cranfield University, Shrivenham Campus, Swindon, Wilts SN6 8LA.

BAYS, Rt Rev. Eric; Bishop of Qu'Appelle, 1986–97; *b* 10 Aug. 1932; *s* of Rev. Canon P. C. Bays and Hilda (*née* Harper); *m* 1967, Patricia Ann Earle; one *s* one *d*. *Educ:* Univ. of Manitoba (BSc 1955); Univ. of Saskatchewan (BA 1959): Univ. of Emmanuel College (LTh 1959); Christian Theological Seminary (MMin 1974). Flight Lieut, RCAF (Reserve), 1955. Asst Curate, All Saints', Winnipeg, 1959–61; Lecturer, Emmanuel Coll., 1961–62; Priest-in-charge: Burns Lake, BC, 1962–63; Masset, BC, 1963–64; Novice, Community of the Resurrection, Mirfield, 1964–65; Vicar, St Saviour's, Winnipeg with Bird's Hill, 1965–68; Rector, All Saints', Winnipeg, 1968–76; Professor, Coll. of Emmanuel and St Chad, 1976–86, Vice-Principal, 1981–86. Canon of St John's Cathedral, Winnipeg, 1971–86. Hon. DD Coll. of Emmanuel and St Chad, 1987. *Publications:* Indian Residential Schools: another picture, 2009. *Recreations:* choral music, reading. *Address:* 200 Clearview Avenue, Apt 2327, Ottawa, ON K1Z 8M2, Canada.

BAYTON, Rt Rev. John, AM 1983; Master Iconographer, St Peter's Icon School, since 1999; *b* 24 March 1930; *s* of Ernest Bayton and Jean Bayton (*née* Edwards); *m* 1959, Elizabeth Anne, *d* of Rt Rev. J. A. G. Housden; one *s* two *d*. *Educ:* Aust. Coll. of Theology, ACT (ThL (Hons)); St Francis Theol Coll., Brisbane. Ordained deacon 1956, priest 1957; Rector, Longreach, Qld, 1958–63; Rector and Sub-dean, Thursday Island (Canon in Residence), 1963–65; Rector, Auchenflower, 1965–68; Army Chaplain: CMF, 1967–76; RAA, 1976–84; Dean of St Paul's Cathedral, Rockhampton, 1968–79; Vicar, St Peter's, Eastern Hill, 1980–89; Archdeacon of Malvern, 1986–89; Bishop of Geelong (Asst Bishop, dio. of Melbourne), 1989–95; Episcopal Chaplain, St George's Coll., Jerusalem, 1995–96, 1998 (Chm., Australasian Cttee, 2003–06; Vis. Chaplain and Lectr, 2003–06); Assisting Bishop in Chicago, Chaplain-in-Residence and Vis. Prof., Seabury-Western Seminary, Evanston, 1997; Adminr, St John's Cathedral, Brisbane, 1998–99. Founder, 1981, Patron, 1993–, Inst. for Spiritual Studies, Melbourne; Founder, Rockhampton Regl Art Gall., 1978. Vis. Fellow, Trinity Coll. Theol Sch., Univ. of Melbourne, 2007. Solo Art Exhibitions: Brisbane 1967, 1976, 1978, 1998; Rockhampton 1975, 1976; Melbourne 1981, 1984, 1986, 1987; Jerusalem, 1995, 1996; Chicago, 1997; Raffles Artfolio Gall., Singapore, 1999; Bishopscourt, Melbourne, 2001, 2004, 2006; Malvern Town Hall, 2010. Represented in public and private collections Australia, Chicago, USA, Jerusalem, UK, Singapore, Tokyo, NZ. Prelate, Aust. Priory, Order of St John of Jerusalem and Knights Hospitaler, 1990; GCSJ 1995; ChLJ 2000; OMLJ 2004; Cross of Merit, Order of St John of Jerusalem, 2008. Centenary Medal (Australia), 2001. *Publications:* Cross over Carpentaria, 1965; Coming of the Light, 1971; The Icon, 1980; (ed) Anglican Spirituality, 1982; Stations of the Cross, 2010; Grampy: the life and times of a blacksmith, 2013. *Recreations:* painting, sketching, sculpting, reading, walking. *Address:* 219 Canterbury Road, Blackburn, Vic 3130, Australia. *W:* www.johnbayton.com. *Club:* Melbourne (Melbourne).

BAZALGETTE, Hilary Jane, (Lady Bazalgette); *see* Newiss, H. J.

BAZALGETTE, Sir Peter (Lytton), Kt 2012; Chairman, Arts Council England, since 2013; *b* 22 May 1953; *s* of late (Evelyn) Paul Bazalgette and Diana Muriel Bazalgette (*née* Coffin); *m* 1985, Hilary Jane Newiss, *qv*; one *s* one *d*. *Educ:* Dulwich Coll.; Fitzwilliam Coll., Cambridge (Pres., Cambridge Union, 1975; BA Hons Law 1976). BBC News Trainee, 1977; Man. Dir, Bazal, 1987–98; Creative Dir, GMG Endemol Entertainment, 1998–2002; Chm., Endemol UK plc, 2002–07; Chief Creative Officer, Endemol Gp, 2005–07. Non-exec. Dir, Channel 4, 2001–04. TV formats created, 1984–, incl. Food and Drink, Ready Steady Cook, Changing Rooms, Ground Force; formats sold to 30 countries; UK producer, Big Brother. Dep. Chm., National Film & Television Sch., 2002–09. Chairman: Sony Music Television, 2009–13; Sony Pictures TV UK, 2009–13; MirriAd, 2009–12 (non-exec. Dir, 2013–15). Non-executive Director: YouGov, 2005–15; Base79 (formerly MyVideoRights), 2008–13; Nutopia, 2008–; DCMS, 2011–12; ITV plc, 2013–. Mem., Holocaust Commn, 2014–15 (Chm., Expert Gp on Commemoration, 2014–15). MacTaggart Lectr, Edinburgh TV Fest., 1998; Wheldon Lectr, RTS, 2001. Co-Chm., British Acad. of Gastronomes, 1993–2010. Pres., Crossness Engines Trust, 2009– (Trustee, 1994–; Chm., 1999). Chm., ENO, 2012–13 (Trustee, 2004–09; Dep.-Chm., 2009–12). Mem., English Heritage Blue Plaques Panel, 2014–. Trustee, Debate Mate, 2009–12. Fellow, BAFTA, 2000; FRTS 2002 (Pres., 2010–). Hon. DLitt Warwick, 2015. Judges Award, RTS, 2003. *Publications:* Billion Dollar Game, 2005; (ed) Egon Ronay: the man who taught Britain how to eat, 2011; jointly: BBC Food Check, 1989; The Food Revolution, 1991; The Big Food & Drink Book, 1993; You Don't Have to Diet, 1994. *Recreations:* opera, gluttony. *E:* vikki@newbaz.com. *Club:* Beefsteak.
See also V. P. Bazalgette.

BAZALGETTE, Simon Louis; Group Chief Executive, Jockey Club, since 2008; Chairman, Jockey Club Racecourses, since 2008; *b* Aylesbury, 28 March 1962; *s* of John and Jane Bazalgette; *m* 1990, Elizabeth McInnes; four *s*. *Educ:* Warwick Univ. (BSc Hons Maths). Mem., ICAEW 1987. With KPMG London, 1984–93; Founder Dir, Music Choice Europe plc, Chief Exec., 1999–2003; Founder Exec. Chm., Racing UK, 2004–08. Director: Racecourse Media Gp, 2004–; Turf TV, 2007–09. Chm., Grubb Inst., 2011– (Vice Chm., 2003–11). *Recreations:* family, music, horse racing, Brentford FC, Harlequins Rugby. *Address:* c/o Jockey Club, 75 High Holborn, WC1V 6LS. *T:* (020) 7611 1816. *E:* simon@bazalgette.com.

BAZALGETTE, Vivian Paul; *b* Croydon, 7 May 1951; *s* of late Evelyn Paul Bazalgette and Diana Muriel Bazalgette (*née* Coffin); *m* 1976, Katharine Diana St John-Brooks; one *s* two *d*. *Educ:* Dulwich Coll.; St John's Coll., Cambridge (BA English Lit. 1973; MA 1977). DTI, 1975–79; stockbroker, James Capel, 1979–83; fund manager, S.G. Warburg & Co., 1983–86; Exec. Dir, Gartmore plc, 1986–95; Chief Investment Officer and Exec. Dir, M&G plc, 1996–2002. Advr, BAE Systems Pension Fund, 2003–. Non-executive Director: Brunner Investment Trust plc, 2004–; Henderson High Income Investment Trust plc, 2004–; Perpetual Income & Growth Investment Trust plc, 2007–; St James's Place plc, 2011–14 (Chm., Investment Cttee, 2011–14). Advr, Nuffield Foundn, 2008–. Member: Investment Cttee, St John's Coll., Cambridge, 2000–06; Adv. Bd, Greenwich Hosp., 2008–13. Gov., Dulwich Coll., 2005– (Vice-Chm. Govs, 2009–). Trustee: King's Coll. Hosp. Charity, 2000–10; Dulwich Estate, 2003–12. *Recreations:* classical music, sport, gardening, bridge. *E:* vivian.bazalgette@btinternet.com. *Clubs:* Dulwich, Royal Over-Seas League.
See also Sir P. L. Bazalgette.

BAZLEY, Rt Rev. Colin Frederick; Bishop of Chile, 1977–2000; an Hon. Assistant Bishop, Diocese of Chester, since 2000; *b* 27 June 1935; *s* of Reginald Samuel Bazley and Isabella Davies; *m* 1960, Barbara Helen Griffiths; three *d*. *Educ:* Birkenhead School; St Peter's Hall, Oxford (MA); Tyndale Hall, Bristol. Deacon 1959, priest 1960; Assistant Curate, St Leonard's, Bootle, 1959–62; Missionary of S American Missionary Society in Chile, 1962–69; Rural Dean of Chol-Chol, 1962–66; Archdeacon of Temuco, 1966–69; Assistant Bishop for Cautin and Malleco, Dio. Chile, Bolivia and Peru, 1969–75; Assistant Bishop for Santiago, 1975–77; Bishop of Chile, Bolivia and Peru, 1977; diocese divided, Oct. 1977; Bishop of Chile and Bolivia until Oct. 1981, when diocese again divided; Presiding Bishop of the Anglican Council for South America, 1977–83; Primate, Province of S Cone of America, 1989–95. Warden of Readers, 2000–05, Rural Dean of Wallasey, 2009–11, dio. of Chester. Mem., Inter-Anglican Theol and Doctrinal Commn, 1994–97. *Recreations:* football (Liverpool supporter), fishing on camping holidays. *Address:* 121 Brackenwood Road, Higher Bebington, Wirral CH63 2LU.

BAZLEY, Janet Claire, (Mrs I. F. Airey); QC 2006; a Recorder, since 2000; *d* of John Harold Bazley and Loukia Bazley; *m* 1987, Ian Frank Airey; one *s* two *d*. *Educ:* Lady Eleanor Holles Sch.; University Coll. London (LLB Hons 1979). Called to the Bar, Lincoln's Inn, 1980; in practice as a barrister, 1980–; Asst Recorder, 1998–2000. Member: Family Law Bar Assoc., 1992–; Law Reform Cttee, Bar Council, 2001–. *Publications:* Money Laundering for Lawyers (with David Winch), 2004; (jtly) Applications under Schedule 1 to the Children Act 1989, 2009; contrib. to Halsbury's Laws. *Recreations:* foreign languages and travel, opera, hill walking. *Address:* 1 Garden Court, Temple, EC4Y 9BJ. *T:* (020) 7797 7900, *Fax:* (020) 7797 7929. *E:* bazley@1gc.com.

BAZLEY, Dame Margaret (Clara), ONZ 2012; DNZM 1999; Chair of Commissioners, Canterbury Regional Council, since 2010; Registrar of Pecuniary Interests of Members of New Zealand Parliament, 2006–13; *b* 23 Jan. 1938. *Educ:* Registered Comprehensive Nurse; Dip. Nursing, DoH and Victoria Univ.; Dip. Health Admin, Massey Univ. Nursing, 1956–78, including: Matron, Sunnyside Psych. Hosp., Christchurch, 1965–73; Dep. Matron in Chief, Auckland Hosp. Bd, 1974–75; Chief Nursing Officer, Waikato Hosp. Bd, 1975–78; Dir, Div. of Nursing, NZ Dept of Health, 1978–84; State Services Commission: Comr, 1984–87; Dep. Chm., 1987–88; Sec. for Transport, 1988–93; Dir-Gen., Dept of Social Welfare, 1993–99; Chief Exec., Min. of Social Policy, NZ, 1999–2001. Mem., NZ delegns to OECD, ISSA, WHO, Internat. Council of Nursing, etc, in Australia, USA and Europe. Chair, Foundn for Res., Sci. and Technol., 2004–08 (Dep. Presiding Mem., 2002–04). Chair, NZ Fire Service Commn, 1999–2011. Member: Waitangi Tribunal, 2001–10; Commn of Inquiry into Police Conduct, 2004–07; Royal Commn of Inquiry on Auckland Governance, 2007–09; Chair, Fundamental Rev. of Legal Aid System, 2009; Dep. Chair, Canterbury Earthquake Recovery Commn, 2010–11. Trustee, Westpactrust Stadium, 2000–05. Hon. DLit Massey, 2008. Business Woman of the Year, More/AirNZ, 1987; Blake Medal, Sir Peter Blake Trust, 2011. *Recreations:* gardening, reading, cooking, music. *Address:* 8B Wharenui Apartments, 274 Oriental Parade, Wellington, New Zealand.

BAZLEY, Sir (Thomas John) Sebastian, 4th Bt *cr* 1869, of Hatherop, co. Gloucester; *b* 31 Aug. 1948; *s* of Sir Thomas Bazley, 3rd Bt and of Carmen, *o d* of James Tulla; *S* father, 1997. *Educ:* St Christopher Sch., Letchworth; Magdalen Coll., Oxford (BA Hons Maths). *Heir: b* Anthony Martin Christopher Bazley [*b* 23 Feb. 1958; *m* 1996, Claudia Patricia Montoya Cano; one *s* one *d*].

BEACH; *see* Hicks Beach, family name of Earl St Aldwyn.

BEACH, Prof. David Hugh, PhD; FRS 1996; FMedSci; Professor of Stem Cell Biology, Queen Mary University of London, since 2004; *b* 18 May 1954; *s* of Gen. Sir Hugh Beach, *qv*. *Educ:* Peterhouse, Cambridge (BA); Univ. of Miami (PhD 1977). Postdoctoral Fellow, Univ. of Sussex, 1978–82; Cold Spring Harbor Laboratory: Postdoctoral Fellow, 1982–83; Jun. Staff Investigator, then Sen. Staff Investigator, 1984–89; Tenured Scientist, 1992–; Sen. Staff Scientist, 1989–97; Investigator, Howard Hughes Med. Inst., 1990–97; Adjunct Investigator, Cold Spring Harbour Lab., 1997–2000; Hugh and Catherine Stevenson Prof. of Cancer Biology, UCL, 1997–2002. Adjunct Associate Prof., SUNY, Stony, 1990–97. Founder, Mitotix Inc., 1992; Founder and Pres., Genetica Inc., 1996–2004. FMedSci 2008. Eli Lilly Research Award, 1994; Bristol-Myers Squibb Award, 2000; Raymond Bourgine Award for cancer research, 2001. *Publications:* numerous papers in reviewed jls, incl. Nature and Cell and Science. *Recreations:* flying, scuba diving, ski-ing, shooting, fly fishing, writing fiction. *Address:* Centre for Cutaneous Research, Blizard Institute, Barts and The London School of Medicine and Dentistry, Blizard Building, 4 Newark Street, E1 2AT. *T:* 07799 620947.

BEACH, Gen. Sir Hugh; *see* Beach, Gen. Sir W. G. H.

BEACH, Dr Mark Howard Frances; Director, Blackfriars Settlement, since 2015; *b* Gloucester, 13 Jan. 1962; *s* of John and Frances Beach; *m* 1991, Annabel; one *d*. *Educ:* Univ. of Kent (BA 1983); Univ. of Nottingham (MA 1995); King's Coll. London (DMin 2011). Ordained deacon, 1987, priest, 1988; Rector, All Hallows, Gedling, 1993–2000; Bishop's Chaplain, Dio. of Wakefield, 2000–03; Team Rector, Rugby, 2003–12; Dean of Rochester, 2012–15. Mem., Pewterers' Co., 1986–. *Publications:* Using Common Worship – Holy

Communion, 2000, 2nd edn 2001; (contrib.) Moving on in Ministry, 2013. *Recreation:* music. *Address:* Blackfriars Settlement, 1 Rushworth Street, SE1 0RB. *T:* (020) 7928 9521. *E:* mark.beach@blackfriars-settlement.org.uk.

BEACH, Gen. Sir (William Gerald) Hugh, GBE 1980 (OBE 1966); KCB 1976; MC 1944; *b* 20 May 1923; *s* of late Maj.-Gen. W. H. Beach, CB, CMG, DSO; *m* 1951, Estelle Mary Henry (*d* 1989); three *s* one *d. Educ:* Winchester; Peterhouse, Cambridge (MA; Hon. Fellow 1982). Active service in France, 1944 and Java, 1946; comd: 4 Field Sqn, 1956–57; Cambridge Univ. OTC, 1961–63; 2 Div. RE, 1965–67; 12 Inf. Bde, 1969–70; Defence Fellow, Edinburgh Univ. (MSc), 1971; Dir, Army Staff Duties, MoD, 1971–74; Comdt, Staff Coll., Camberley, 1974–75; Dep. C-in-C, UKLF, 1976–77; Master-Gen. of the Ordnance, 1977–81; Chief Royal Engr, 1982–87; Warden, St George's House, Windsor Castle, 1981–86. Dir, Council for Arms Control, 1986–89. Vice Lord-Lieut for Greater London, 1981–87. Kermit Roosevelt Vis. Lectr to US Armed Forces, 1977; Mountbatten Lectr, Edinburgh Univ., 1981; Gallipoli Meml Lectr, 1985; Wilfred Fish Meml Lectr, GDC, 1986. Colonel Commandant: REME, 1976–81; RPC, 1976–80; RE, 1977–87; Hon. Colonel, Cambridge Univ. OTC, TAVR, 1977–87; Chm., CCF Assoc., 1981–87; Chm., MoD Study Gp on Censorship, 1983. Mem., Security Commn, 1982–91. Chairman: Rochester Cathedral Develt Trust, 1986–99; Winchester DAC for Care of Churches, 1988–97; Hampshire and the Islands Historic Churches Trust, 1993–2003; Winchester Cathedral Fabric Adv. Cttee, 1996–2013; Member, Committee of Management: Council for Christian Approaches to Defence and Disarmament, 1988– (Vice-Chm., 2006–; Co-Chm., 2012–); Verification Res., Trng and Inf. Centre, 1990– (Co-Chm., 2007–12; Pres., 2012–); British Pugwash Gp, 2000–; Acronym Inst., 2004– (Chm., 2008–13). Chairman: SPCK, 1994–99; Foundation Trustees, Church Army, 1996–2001. Chm. Govs, Bedales Sch., 1989–96. CCMI; FRSA. Hon. Fellow CIBSE, 1988. Hon. DCL Kent, 1990. *Publications:* numerous articles, reviews and chapters in books on military matters and arms control. *Address:* College of St Barnabas, Blackberry Lane, Lingfield RH7 6NJ. *T:* (01342) 872879. *Club:* Farmers.
See also D. H. Beach.

BEADLE, (John) Nicholas, CMG 2006; writer and artist; *b* 20 Aug. 1957; *s* of Lt-Col (retd) George Colin Beadle and late Gillian Beadle; *m* 1990, Linda Rose Davidson; one *d. Educ:* Grangefield GS, Stockton; Newcastle upon Tyne Poly. (LLB); Heriot-Watt Univ. (MBA). Thomson Newspapers, 1978–83; Proprietor, Accommodation Ltd, 1984–90; Dir, cos of late Jack Calvert, 1990–97; Ministry of Defence, 1997–2007: UK Hydrographic Office, 1997–2001; RCDS 2002; NATO Policy, 2003; EU and UN Policy, 2004; Sen. Advr to Iraqi MoD, Baghdad, 2004–05; Private Sec. to Sec. of State for Defence, 2005–07; Fellow, Harvard Univ., 2007–08; Dir, Govt Afghanistan Strategy and Communications, Cabinet Office, 2008–09; Sen. Advr to the Prime Minister, 2009–10; Advr on Middle East and N Africa, Cabinet Office, 2011. Partner, Lily Partnership (formerly Lily & Co.), 2011–. Non-executive Director: Region Gp, 2006–; Edinburgh Business Sch., 2013–. Hon. Prof., Univ. of Exeter, 2012–; Sen. Associate Fellow, RUSI, 2012–. Mem. Ct, Heriot-Watt Univ., 2011–. *E:* nicholasbeadle@gmail.com, nicholasbeadle@post.harvard.edu.

BEADLES, Anthony Hugh, MA; Headmaster of Epsom College, 1993–2000; *b* 18 Sept. 1940; *s* of late O. H. R. Beadles, OBE and N. K. Beadles; *m* 1970, Heather Iona McFerran; two *s* one *d. Educ:* Epsom Coll.; Christ Church, Oxford (MA). Head of History, Ellesmere Coll., 1963–67; Head of History and Asst Housemaster, Harrow Sch., 1967–85; Headmaster, King's Sch., Bruton, 1985–93. *Recreations:* cricket, mountains, golf. *Address:* Chaff Barn, Downyard, Compton Pauncefoot, Yeovil, Somerset BA22 7EL. *Clubs:* MCC; Vincent's (Oxford).

BEAKE, Ven. Stuart Alexander; Archdeacon of Surrey, since 2005; *b* 18 Sept. 1949; *s* of Ernest Alexander and Pamela Mary Beake; *m* 1987, Sally Anne Williams; one *s* one *d. Educ:* King's Coll. Sch., Wimbledon; Emmanuel Coll., Cambridge (BA 1972, MA 1975); Cuddesdon Coll., Oxford. Ordained deacon, 1974, priest, 1975; Asst Curate, Hitchin St Mary, 1974–79; Team Vicar, St Mary, Hemel Hempstead, 1979–85; Domestic Chaplain to Bishop of Southwell, 1985–87; Vicar, St Andrew, Shottery, 1987–2000; RD, Fosse Deanery, 1992–99; Diocesan Dir of Ordinands and Hd, Vocations and Trng Dept, Coventry Dio., 1995–2000; Sub-Dean and Canon Residentiary, Coventry Cathedral, 2000–05, now Canon Emeritus, 2005 (Hon. Canon, 1999); Canon Residentiary, Guildford Cathedral, 2010– (Hon. Canon, 2005). *Recreations:* reading, gardening, music, model railway, old jokes. *Address:* Archdeacon's House, Lime Grove, West Clandon, Guildford, Surrey GU4 7UT.

BEAL, Kieron Conrad; QC 2012; *b* Portsmouth, 16 Jan. 1971; *s* of Kerry and Pauline Beal; *m* 2002, Dr Isobel Frisken; two *d. Educ:* Chichester High Sch. for Boys; Phillips Exeter Acad., NH, USA; Selwyn Coll., Cambridge (BA 1993); Harvard Law Sch. (LLM). Called to the Bar, Inner Temple, 1995; in practice as barrister, specialising in EU and competition law, 1995–. Mem., Attorney Gen.'s C Panel, 1999–2002, B Panel, 2002–07, A Panel, 2007–12. *Publications:* (contrib.) EC Competition Procedure, 1996, 3rd edn 2012; (contrib.) Value Added Tax: Commentary & Analysis, 2010; (contrib.) Employee Competition, 2011. *Recreations:* ski-ing, sailing, squash, tennis. *Address:* Blackstone Chambers, Blackstone House, Temple, EC4Y 9BW. *T:* (020) 7583 1770, *Fax:* (020) 7822 7350. *E:* kieronbeal@blackstonechambers.com.

BEAL, Peter George, PhD; FBA 1993; FSA; manuscript expert; Database Compiler, Catalogue of English Literary Manuscripts 1450–1700, since 2005; Consultant, Department of Books and Manuscripts, Sotheby's, London, since 2005; *b* Coventry, 16 April 1944; *s* of William George Beal and Marjorie Ena Owen; *m* 1st, 1974, Gwyneth Morgan (marr. diss. 1980); 2nd, 1982, Sally Josephine Taylor (marr. diss. 1994); one step *s*; 3rd, 1998, Grace Janette Ioppolo. *Educ:* King Henry VIII Grammar Sch., Coventry; Leeds Univ. (BA Hons English, 1966; PhD 1974). Res. editor, Bowker/Mansell Publishing, 1974–79; Manuscript Expert, 1980–2005, Dep. Dir, 1990–95, Dir, 1996–2005, Printed Books and MSS, subseq. Dept of Books and MSS, Sotheby's, London. Lyell Reader in Bibliography, Oxford Univ., 1995–96. Vis. Prof., Dept of English, Reading Univ., 2000–02; Sen. Res. Fellow, Inst. of English Studies, Univ. of London, 2002–. FSA 2007. *Publications:* Index of English Literary Manuscripts, vol. I, parts 1 and 2, 1450–1625 (2 vols), 1980, vol. II, parts 1 and 2, 1625–1700 (2 vols), 1987, 1993; (gen. ed.) English Verse Miscellanies of the Seventeenth Century (5 vols), 1990; In Praise of Scribes: manuscripts and their makers in 17th century England, 1998; A Dictionary of English Manuscript Terminology 1450–2000, 2008; (co-founded and co-ed) English Manuscript Studies 1100–1700, annually, 1989–2013; contribs, mainly on 16th and 17th century literary MSS, to learned jls. *Recreations:* reading, films, travel, swimming. *Address:* Institute of English Studies, Senate House, Malet Street, WC1E 7HU. *E:* Peter.Beal@sas.ac.uk.

BEALE, Prof. Hugh Gurney, FBA 2004; Professor of Law, University of Warwick, since 1987; *b* 4 May 1948; *s* of Charles Beale and Anne Freeland Beale (*née* Gurney-Dixon); *m* 1970, Jane Wilson Cox; two *s* one *d. Educ:* Leys Sch., Cambridge; Exeter Coll., Oxford (BA Jurisp. 1969). Called to the Bar, Lincoln's Inn, 1971 (Hon. Bencher, 1999). Lecturer in Law: Univ. of Connecticut, 1969–71; UCW, Aberystwyth, 1971–73; Univ. of Bristol, 1973–86; Reader, Univ. of Bristol, 1986–87. Visiting Professor: Univ. of N Carolina, 1982–83; Univ. of Paris I, 1995; Univ. of Utrecht, 1996; Univ. of Oxford, 2007–Sept. 2016; Univ. of Amsterdam, 2009–13; Sen. Res. Fellow, Harris Manchester Coll., Oxford, 2014–. A Law Comr, 2000–07. Hon. QC 2002. Hon. LLD: Miskolc, 1995; De Montfort, 2003; Antwerp, 2005. *Publications:* Remedies for Breach of Contract, 1980; (jtly) Contract Cases and Materials, 1985, 5th edn 2007; (ed jtly) Principles of European Contract Law, Part I, 1995, Parts I and II, 2000; (Gen. Ed.) Chitty on Contracts, 28th edn 1999 to 31st edn, 2012; (ed jtly) Casebooks on the Common Law of Europe: Contract Law, 2001, 2nd edn 2010. *Recreations:* fishing, music, walking. *Address:* School of Law, University of Warwick, Coventry CV4 7AL. *T:* (024) 7657 3844.

BEALE, Inga Kristine; Chief Executive, Lloyd's of London, since 2014; *b* Newbury, 15 May 1963; *d* of Raymond John Beale and Astri Beale (*née* Gisholt); *m* 2014, Philippe Henri Pfeiffer. *Educ:* ACII 1987. Underwriter, Prudential Assurance, 1982–92; Pres., Europe, GE Insurance Solutions, 1992–2006; CEO, Converium Gp, 2006–07; Mem., Gp Mgt Bd, Zurich Insurance, 2008–11; CEO, Canopius Gp, 2012–13. *Address:* Lloyd's, One Lime Street, EC3M 7HA. *T:* (020) 7327 6800. *E:* inga.beale@lloyds.com. *Club:* Wasps Rugby.

BEALE, James Patrick; Director, Institutional Funding, Plan International, since 2012; *b* 14 Nov. 1959; *s* of Patrick Ashton Beale and Janet Margaret Beale; *m* 1991, Mary Elizabeth Wilson; two *d. Educ:* Sch. of Oriental and African Studies, Univ. of London (BA Hons Geog.); Univ. of Reading (MSc Agricl Econs 1986). Data analyst, Kestrel Gp, Tripoli, Libya, 1982–84; Project Manager, Agric. and Fisheries Div., Crown Agents, 1986–88; Sight Savers International: Programme Manager, E Asia and Pacific, 1988–93; Regl Dir, Thailand and Bangladesh, 1993–95; Chief Exec., Ockenden Venture, subseq. Ockenden Internat., 1995–2008; Sen. Prog. Manager, Maxwell Stamp plc, 2008; Head, Internat. Partnership Develt, ActionAid Internat., 2008–12. *Address:* Plan International, Block A, Duke Street, Woking, Surrey GU21 5BH.

BEALE, Lt-Gen. Sir Peter (John), KBE 1992; FRCP; Hon. Consultant, British Red Cross, since 2000 (Chief Medical Adviser, 1994–2000); *b* 18 March 1934; *s* of Basil and Eileen Beale; *m* 1st, 1959, Julia Mary Winter, MB BS (*d* 2000); four *s* one *d* (and one *d* decd); 2nd, 2001, Mary Elisabeth Williams. *Educ:* St Paul's Cathedral Choir Sch.; Felsted Sch. (Music Schol.); Gonville and Caius Coll., Cambridge (Choral Schol.; BA); Westminster Hosp. MB BChir 1958. DTM&H; FFCM; FFOM. Commissioned RAMC, 1960; medical training, 1964–71; Consultant Physician, Army, 1971; served Far East, Middle East, BAOR; Community Physician, Army, 1981; served BAOR and UK; Comdr Medical, HQ UKLF, 1987–90; DGAMS, 1990–93; Surg. Gen., MoD, 1991–94. QHP 1987–94. President: Army Squash, 1989–94; Old Felstedian Soc., 1998–2001; Army Officer Golfing Soc., 2001–05; Captain, Old Felstedian Golfing Soc., 2001–03. Gov., Yehudi Menuhin Sch., 1995–2012. OStJ. *Publications:* contribs to professional jls on tropical and military medicine. *Recreations:* music (conductor, tenor, pianist, French Horn player), sport (golf, squash, tennis), bridge. *Address:* The Old Bakery, Avebury, Marlborough, Wilts SN8 1RF. *T:* (01672) 539315. *Club:* Tidworth Garrison Golf (Pres., 1990–2003).
See also S. R. Beale.

BEALE, Simon Russell, (Simon Russell Beale), CBE 2003; actor; *b* 12 Jan. 1961; *s* of Lt-Gen. Sir Peter Beale, *qv. Educ:* St Paul's Cathedral Choir Sch.; Clifton Coll., Bristol; Gonville and Caius Coll., Cambridge (BA 1st Cl. Hons English 1982; Hon. Fellow, 2008); Guildhall Sch. of Music and Drama. Royal Shakespeare Co., 1985–93 (Associate Artist); Royal National Theatre, 1995–98 (Associate Artist). *Theatre:* Look to the Rainbow, Apollo, 1983; Women Beware Women, Royal Court, 1985; Royal Shakespeare Company: A Winter's Tale, The Fair Maid of the West, 1985; Restoration, Man of Mode, 1987; Troilus and Cressida, The Seagull, Edward II, 1989; Richard III, 1990; Ghosts, 1993; The Tempest, 1993–94; Royal National Theatre: Volpone, 1995 (best supporting actor, Olivier Award, 1996); Rosencrantz and Guildenstern are Dead, 1995; Othello, 1997; Candide (best actor in a musical, Olivier Award, 2000), Money, Summerfolk, Battle Royal, 1999; Hamlet (best actor, Evening Standard Award, best Shakespearean perf., Critics' Circle Award), 2000; Humble Boy, 2001; Jumpers, 2003; The Life of Galileo, 2006; The Alchemist, 2006; Much Ado About Nothing, 2007; Major Barbara, 2008; A Slight Ache, 2008; London Assurance, 2010; Collaborators, 2011 (best actor, London Evening Standard Theatre Award, 2012); Timon of Athens, 2012; King Lear, 2014; Uncle Vanya, Twelfth Night, Donmar Warehouse, 2002 (best actor, Evening Standard Award, Critics' Circle Award, and Olivier Award, 2003); Macbeth, Almeida, 2005; Julius Caesar, Barbican, 2005; The Philanthropist, Donmar Warehouse, 2005 (best actor, Evening Standard Theatre Award, and Critics' Circle Award, 2005); Spamalot, NY, 2005, Palace Th., 2007; The Winter's Tale, The Cherry Orchard, Old Vic, 2009; Deathtrap, Noël Coward Th., 2010; Alice's Adventures in Wonderland, Royal Ballet, Covent Garden, 2011; Privates on Parade, Noël Coward Th., 2012; The Hothouse, Trafalgar Studios, 2013; Temple, Donmar Warehouse, 2015; Mr Foote's Other Leg, Hampstead Th., 2015; *television:* Persuasion, 1995; A Dance to the Music of Time, 1997 (best actor, RTS Award, 1997, BAFTA Award, 1998); Spooks, 2010–11; Henry IV, 2012 (best supporting actor, BAFTA, 2013); presenter: Sacred Music, 2008; Symphony, 2011; *films:* Hamlet, 1997; The Temptation of Franz Schubert, 1997; An Ideal Husband, 1999; The Deep Blue Sea, 2011; performances on radio. *Recreations:* music, history, history of religion, crosswords. *Address:* Richard Stone Partnership, Suite 3, De Walden Court, 85 New Cavendish Street, W1W 6XD. *T:* (020) 7497 0849.

BEALES, Prof. Derek Edward Dawson, PhD, LittD; FRHistS; FBA 1989; Professor of Modern History, University of Cambridge, 1980–97, now Emeritus; Fellow of Sidney Sussex College, Cambridge, since 1958; *b* 12 June 1931; *s* of late Edward Beales and Dorothy Kathleen Beales (*née* Dawson); *m* 1964, Sara Jean (*née* Ledbury); one *s* one *d. Educ:* Bishop's Stortford Coll.; Sidney Sussex Coll., Cambridge (MA, PhD, LittD). Sidney Sussex College, Cambridge: Research Fellow, 1955–58; Tutor, 1961–70; Vice-Master, 1973–75; Cambridge University: Asst Lectr, 1962–65, Lectr, 1965–80; Chairman: Faculty Board of History, 1979–81; Mgt Cttee, Internat. Studies, 1992–95; Member: Liby Syndicate, 1982–88; Gen. Bd of Faculties, 1987–89. Vis. Lectr, Harvard Univ., 1965; Lectures: Founder's Meml, St Deiniol's Liby, Hawarden, 1990; Stenton, Univ. of Reading, 1992; Birkbeck, Trinity Coll., Cambridge, 1993. Vis. Prof., Central Eur. Univ., Budapest, 1995–. Fellow, Collegium Budapest, 1995; Leverhulme Emeritus Fellowship, 2000. British rep., Humanities Standing Cttee, ESF, 1994–99. Mem. Council, RHistS, 1984–88. Editor, 1971–75, Mem. Editl Bd, Historical Jl, 1976–2002 (Chm., 1990–97). *Publications:* England and Italy 1859–60, 1961; From Castlereagh to Gladstone, 1969; The Risorgimento and the Unification of Italy, 1971, 2nd edn (with E. F. Biagini), 2002; History and Biography, 1981; (ed with Geoffrey Best) History, Society and the Churches, 1985; Joseph II: in the shadow of Maria Theresa 1741–80, 1987; Mozart and the Habsburgs, 1993; (ed with H. B. Nisbet) Sidney Sussex Quatercentenary Essays, 1996; (Gen. Ed.) Cassell's Companions to 18th and 20th Century Britain, 2001; Prosperity and Plunder: European Catholic monasteries in the Age of Revolution, 2003 (Paolucci/Bagehot Book Award, Intercollegiate Studies Inst., 2004); Enlightenment and Reform in the Eighteenth Century, 2005; Joseph II: against the world 1780–1790, 2009; (contrib.) Quincentenary History of St John's Coll., Cambridge, 2011; (ed with Renato Pasta) Relazione di Pietro Leopoldo sullo stato della Monarchia austriaca (1784), 2013; articles in learned jls. *Recreations:* playing keyboard instruments and bridge, walking, not gardening. *Address:* Sidney Sussex College, Cambridge CB2 3HU. *T:* (01223) 338833. *Club:* Athenæum.

BEALL, Dr Jo; Director, Education and Society, and Member, Executive Board, British Council, since 2011; *b* London, 1952; *d* of Gordon R. Adams and Jeanne C. Adams; one *s. Educ:* La Sagesse Convent, Newcastle upon Tyne; Our Lady of Fatima Convent, Durban, SA; Univ. of Natal (BA Hons; MA); London Sch. of Econs and Pol Sci. (PhD). Prof. of Develt Studies, 2001–09, Dir, Develt Studies Inst., 2004–07, LSE; Dep. Vice Chancellor (Academic, Ext. Relns and Internat.), Univ. of Cape Town, 2009–11. *Publications:* Uniting a Divided City, 2002; Funding Local Governance, 2009; Cities and Development, 2009; Urbanisation and Development: interdisciplinary perspectives, 2010. *Recreations:* walking, reading, music, travel, family. *Address:* British Council, 10 Spring Gardens, SW1A 2BN. *T:* (020) 7389 4238. *E:* jo.beall@britishcouncil.org. *Club:* University Women's.

BEAMISH, Sir Adrian (John), KCMG 1999 (CMG 1988); HM Diplomatic Service, retired; Ambassador to Mexico, 1994–99; *b* 21 Jan. 1939; *s* of Thomas Charles Constantine Beamish and Josephine Mary (*née* Lee); *m* 1965, Caroline Lipscomb (marr. diss. 1991); two *d*; *m* 1994, Antonia Cavanagh (marr. diss. 2011; she *d* 2014); one *d*, and one step *s* one step *d*. *Educ:* Christian Brothers' Coll., Cork; Prior Park Coll., Bath; Christ's Coll., Cambridge (MA); Università per gli Stranieri, Perugia. Third, later Second Secretary, Tehran, 1963–66; Foreign Office, 1966–69; First Sec., UK Delegn, OECD, Paris, 1970–73; New Delhi, 1973–76; FCO, 1976–78; Counsellor, Dep. Head, Personnel Operations Dept, FCO, 1978–80; Counsellor (Economic), Bonn, 1981–85; Hd, Falkland Is Dept, FCO, 1985–87; Ambassador to Peru, 1987–89; Asst Under-Sec. of State (Americas), FCO, 1989–94. Lectr, History Dept, University Coll., Cork, 1999–2009; Consultant, BOC Group, 1999–2001. *Recreations:* books, plants. *Address:* 117 Eton Rise, NW3 2DD.

BEAMISH, David Richard; Clerk of the Parliaments, House of Lords, since 2011; *b* 20 Aug. 1952; *s* of late Richard Ludlow Beamish and Heather Margaret Ensor Beamish (*née* Lock); *m* 1989, (Fiona) Philippa Tudor, *qv*; one *d*. *Educ:* Marlborough Coll.; St John's Coll., Cambridge (MA, LLM). House of Lords: Clerk, 1974; Sen. Clerk, 1979; Chief Clerk, 1987; Principal Clerk, 1993; seconded to Cabinet Office as Private Sec. to Leader of H of L and Govt Chief Whip, 1983–86; Clerk of the Journals, 1993–95 and 2002–05; Clerk of Cttees and Clerk of Overseas Office, 1995–2002; Reading Clerk, 2003–07; Clerk Asst, 2007–11. BBC TV Mastermind Champion, 1988. *Publications:* (ed jtly) The House of Lords at Work, 1993. *Recreations:* church bell ringing, family history. *Address:* House of Lords, SW1A 0PW. *T:* (020) 7219 3181, *Fax:* (020) 7219 0329. *E:* beamishdr@parliament.uk, mail@davidbeamish.uk.

BEAMISH, (Fiona) Philippa; *see* Tudor, F. P.

BEAMISH, Sarah Frances, (Sally); composer and lecturer; *b* 26 Aug. 1956; *d* of William Anthony Alten Beamish and Ursula Mary (*née* Snow); *m* 1988, Robert Irvine (separated 2008); two *s* one *d*. *Educ:* Camden Sch. for Girls; Nat. Youth Orch.; Royal Northern Coll. of Music (GRNCM); Staatliche Hochschule für Musik, Detmold. Viola player, Raphael Ensemble, Acad. of St Martin-in-the-Fields, London Sinfonietta, Lontano, 1979–90; Composer's Bursary, Arts Council, 1989; Composer-in-Residence: Swedish Chamber Orch., 1998–2002; Scottish Chamber Orch., 1998–2002. Co-Dir, St Magnus Composers' Course. Recordings: River ('Cello, Viola and Oboe Concertos); The Imagined Sound of Sun on Stone (Saxophone Concerto, etc); Bridging the Day ('cello and piano), 2001; String Quartets, 2006; The Seafarer, 2008. *Compositions include:* 1st Symphony (first perf., Iceland SO, 1993); Viola Concerto No 2, 2002; Trumpet Concerto, 2003; Percussion Concerto, 2005; Shenachie (stage musical), 2006; Accordion Concerto, 2006; Under the Wing of the Rock (Viola Concerto No 3), 2006; The Song Gatherer (Cello Concerto No 2), 2009; Spinal Chords (Orch.), 2012; Equal Voices (chorus and orch., settings of poems by Sir Andrew Motion), 2014; Song-cycle; Hafez Songs; The Day Dawn; Cage of Doves; Kirschen; Diodati (Orch. and Narrator). Hon. DMus Glasgow, 2001. *Recreations:* painting, writing, walking. *Address:* Scottish Music Centre, City Halls, Candleriggs, Glasgow G1 1NQ. *T:* (0141) 552 5222.

BEAN, Basil, CBE 1985; Vice Chairman, Barratt Developments Plc, 1997–2001; Vice President, National House Building Council, since 1994 (Director General, then Chief Executive, 1985–94 and 1996–97); *b* 2 July 1931; *s* of Walter Bean and Alice Louise Bean; *m* 1956, Janet Mary Brown; one *d*. *Educ:* Archbishop Holgate Sch., York. Mem. CIPFA. York City, 1948–53; West Bromwich Borough, 1953–56; Sutton London Bor., 1957–62; Skelmersdale Develt Corp., 1962–66; Havering London Bor., 1967–69; Northampton Develt Corp., 1969–80 (Gen. Manager, 1977–80); Chief Exec., Merseyside Develt Corp., 1980–85; overseas consultancies. Chm., Admiral Homes Ltd, 1996–97. Mem., British Waterways Bd, 1985–88. Hon. FABE 1980. *Publications:* financial and technical papers. *Recreations:* reading, walking, travel. *Address:* 4 Paget Close, Great Houghton, Northampton NN4 7EF. *T:* (01604) 765135. *Club:* Northampton and County (Northampton).

BEAN, Sir Charles (Richard), Kt 2014; Professor, London School of Economics and Political Science, since 2014; *b* 16 Sept. 1953; *s* of Charles Ernest Bean and Mary (*née* Welsh). *Educ:* Emmanuel Coll., Cambridge (BA 1975); MIT (PhD 1981). Economist, HM Treasury, 1975–79 and 1981–82; London School of Economics: Lectr, 1982–86; Reader, 1986–90; Prof., 1990–2000; Bank of England: Chief Economist and Exec. Dir, 2000–08; Dep. Gov., 2008–14. Visiting Professor: Stanford Univ., 1990; Reserve Bank of Australia, 1999. Pres., Royal Economic Soc., 2013–15. *Publications:* contrib. learned jls. *Recreations:* cricket, opera.

BEAN, Rt Hon. Sir David (Michael), Kt 2004; PC 2014; **Rt Hon. Lord Justice Bean;** a Lord Justice of Appeal, since 2014; Chairman, Law Commission, since 2015; *b* 25 March 1954; *s* of late George Joseph Bean and Zdenka White; *m* 1st, 1986 (marr. diss. 1996); two *s*; 2nd, 2004, Ruth Thompson, *qv*. *Educ:* St Paul's Sch., Barnes; Trinity Hall, Cambridge (1st Cl. Hons Law; Pres., Cambridge Union Soc., 1975). Called to the Bar, Middle Temple, 1976, Bencher, 2001; a Recorder, 1996–2004; QC 1997; a Presiding Judge, SE Circuit, 2007–10; a Judge of the High Court of Justice, QBD, 2004–14. Chairman: Gen. Council of the Bar, 2002 (Vice-Chm., 2001); Employment Law Bar Assoc., 1999–2001; Immigration Services Tribunal, 2001–04. Lay Mem., GMC, 2003–04; Member: Civil Justice Council, 2003–05; Judicial Appts Commn, 2010–14. Pres., Assoc. of Lancastrians in London, 2011. *Publications:* Injunctions, 1979, 12th edn 2015; (with Anthony Nigel Fricker) Enforcement of Injunctions and Undertakings, 1991; (ed) Law Reform for All, 1996. *Recreations:* opera, hill-walking, books. *Address:* Royal Courts of Justice, Strand, WC2A 2LL. *Club:* Reform.

BEAN, Rev. Canon John Victor; Vicar, St Mary, Cowes, Isle of Wight, 1966–91, and Priest-in-charge, All Saints, Gurnard, IoW, 1978–91; Chaplain to the Queen, 1980–95; *b* 1 Dec. 1925; *s* of Albert Victor and Eleanor Ethel Bean; *m* 1955, Nancy Evelyn Evans; two *s* one *d* (and one *d* died in infancy). *Educ:* local schools; Grammar Sch., Gt Yarmouth; Downing Coll., Cambridge (MA); Salisbury Theological Coll., 1948. Served War, RNVR, 1944–46; returned to Cambridge, 1946–48. Assistant Curate: St James, Milton, Portsmouth, 1950–55; St Peter and St Paul, Fareham, 1955–59; Vicar, St Helen's, IoW, 1959–66. Rural Dean of West Wight, 1968–73; Clergy Proctor for Diocese of Portsmouth, 1973–80; Hon. Canon, Portsmouth Cathedral, 1970–91, Canon Emeritus, 1991. *Recreations:* photography, boat-watching, tidying up. *Address:* 23 Queens Road, Ryde, Isle of Wight PO33 3BG. *Club:* Gurnard Sailing (Gurnard).

BEAN, Marisa; *see* Robles, M.

BEAN, Martin George, CBE 2015; Vice-Chancellor and President, RMIT University, since 2015; *b* Melbourne, Australia, 26 Oct. 1964; *s* of Alfred and Margaret Bean; *m* 1987, Mary Murphy; three *d*. *Educ:* Univ. of Technol., Sydney (BEd (Adult)). Assoc. Internat. étudiants en science économique et commerciale, 1985–87; Gen. Manager, Asia Pacific, Drake Trng and Technologies, 1990–93; Area Educn Manager, Australasia, Dir, N Amer. Educn, and Vice-Pres., Educn Worldwide Sales and Mkt Develt, Novell Inc., 1993–97; Exec. Vice-Pres., IT Business Unit and Mktg, Pres., Sylvan Prometric, and Chief IT Business Strategist, Thomson Learning, Thomson Corp./Sylvan Learning Systems, 1997–2001; Chief Operating Officer and Mem. Bd of Dirs, New Horizons Computer Learning Centres Inc., 2001–05; Gen. Manager, Worldwide Educn Products Gp, Microsoft Inc., 2005–09; Vice-Chancellor, Open Univ., 2009–14. Member: Digital Adv. Gp, BM, 2012–; Strategic Adv. Bd, Internat. Unit, UK Higher Educn, 2013–; Leadership Council, Nat. Centre for Univs and Business, 2013–. Mem., Bd of Govs, Commonwealth of Learning, 2010–. Trustee, British Council, 2011–14. Ambassador, UKTI, 2014–. Learning Leadership Award, Masie Center Learning Conf., 2013; Colin Corder Award for Services to Learning, Learning and Perf. Inst., 2014. *Recreations:* sailing, scuba diving, travel. *Address:* Office of the Vice-Chancellor, RMIT University, GPO Box 2476, Melbourne, Vic 3001, Australia. *Club:* Sloane.

BEAN, Prof. Philip Thomas, PhD; Professor of Criminology and Director, Midlands Centre for Criminology and Criminal Justice, Department of Social Sciences, Loughborough University, 1990–2003, now Emeritus Professor; *b* 24 Sept. 1936; *s* of Thomas William Bean and Amy Bean; *m* 1st, 1964, Anne Elizabeth Sellar (marr. diss. 1968); 2nd, 1969, Valerie Winifred Davis (*d* 1999); two *s*. *Educ:* Bedford Modern Sch.; Univ. of London (BSc Soc (ext.), MSc Econ); Univ. of Nottingham (PhD). Probation Officer, Inner London Probation Service, 1963–69; Res. Officer, MRC, 1969–72; Lectr and Sen. Lectr in Social Sci., Univ. of Nottingham, 1972–90; Reader in Criminology, Univ. of Loughborough, 1990. Vis. Prof. at American, Canadian and Australian univs; Vis. Scholar, Univ. of Cambridge, 2014–. Pres., British Soc. of Criminology, 1996–99; Associate, GMC, 2000–05. *Publications:* The Social Control of Drugs, 1974; Rehabilitation and Deviance, 1976; Compulsory Admissions to Mental Hospitals, 1980; Punishment, 1981; Mental Disorder and Legal Control, 1987; Mental Disorder and Community Safety, 2000; Drugs and Crime, 2004, 4th edn 2014; Madness and Crime, 2007; Legalising Drugs, 2010; numerous contribs to learned jls. *Recreations:* poetry, music, esp. New Orleans jazz and opera. *Address:* 41 Trevor Road, West Bridgford, Notts NG2 6FT. *T:* (0115) 923 3895.

BEAN, Richard Anthony; playwright; *b* Kingston-upon-Hull, 11 June 1956; *s* of John and Rita Bean; one *d*. *Educ:* Hull Grammar Sch.; Loughborough Univ. (BSc Hons Social Psychol.). Formerly occupational psychologist and stand-up comedian. Stage plays: Toast, Royal Court, 1999; Mr England, Sheffield Crucible, 2000; The Mentalists, NT, 2002; Under the Whaleback, Royal Court, 2003; Smack Family Robinson, Live, Newcastle, 2003, Rose Th., Kingston-upon-Thames, 2013; The God Botherers, Bush, 2003; Honeymoon Suite, Royal Court, 2004; Harvest, Royal Court, 2005; Up on Roof, Truck, Hull, 2006; The English Game, Yvonne Arnaud, Guildford, 2008; England People Very Nice, NT, 2009; Pub Quiz is Life, Truck, Hull, 2009; The Big Fellah, Lyric, Hammersmith, 2010; The Heretic, Royal Court, 2011; One Man, Two Guvnors, NT, 2011; Great Britain, NT, transf. Th. Royal, Haymarket, 2014; Pitcairn, Minerva Th., Chichester, 2014; Made in Dagenham, Adelphi, 2014. *Publications:* Toast, 1999; Mr England, 2000; The Mentalists, 2002; Under the Whaleback, 2003; Smack Family Robinson, 2003; The God Botherers, 2003; Honeymoon Suite, 2004; Harvest, 2005; Up on Roof, 2006; The English Game, 2008; England People Very Nice, 2009; Pub Quiz is Life, 2009; The Big Fellah, 2010; The Heretic, 2011; One Man, Two Guvnors, 2011. *Recreation:* shouting at the television. *Address:* c/o Rose Cobbe, United Agents, 12–26 Lexington Street, W1F 0LE. *T:* (020) 3214 0800. *Club:* Actors Anonymous Cricket.

BEAN, Shaun Mark, (Sean); actor; *b* Sheffield, 17 April 1959; *s* of Brian and Rita Bean; *m* 1st, 1981, Debra James (marr. diss.); 2nd, 1990, Melanie Hill (marr. diss. 1997); two *d*; 3rd, 1997, Abigail Cruttenden (marr. diss. 2000); one *d*; 4th, 2008, Georgina Sutcliffe (marr. diss.). *Educ:* RADA. Stage début, Tybalt in Romeo and Juliet, Watermill Th., Newbury, 1983; *other theatre includes:* Romeo and Juliet, The Fair Maid of the West, A Midsummer Night's Dream, RSC, 1986–87; Killing the Cat, Royal Court Th., 1990; Macbeth, Albery Th., 2002. *Television includes:* Troubles, 1988; The Fifteen Streets, 1989; Small Zones, Lorna Doone, 1990; Tell Me That You Love Me, My Kingdom for a Horse, Clarissa, Prince, 1991; Fool's Gold, 1992; Lady Chatterley, A Woman's Guide to Adultery, 1993; Sharpe (series), 1993–97; Scarlett, Jacob, 1994; Bravo Two Zero, Extremely Dangerous, 1999; Henry VIII, 2003; Sharpe's Challenge, 2006; Sharpe's Peril, 2008; Red Riding, 2009; Game of Thrones (3 series), 2011–13; Missing, Accused, 2012. *Films include:* Caravaggio, 1986; Stormy Monday, 1988; War Requiem, How to Get Ahead in Advertising, 1989; Windprints, The Field, 1990; In the Border Country, 1991; Patriot Games, 1992; Shopping, Black Beauty, 1994; Goldeneye, 1995; When Saturday Comes, 1996; Anna Karenina, 1997; Airborne, Ronin, 1998; Essex Boys, 2000; The Lord of the Rings: The Fellowship of the Ring, 2001; Don't Say a Word, Tom and Thomas, Equilibrium, 2002; The Big Empty, 2003; Troy, National Treasure, 2004; The Island, Flightplan, 2005; North Country, The Dark, Silent Hill, 2006; Outlaw, The Hitcher, Far North, 2007; Black Death, 2010; Cleanskin, Mirror Mirror, 2012. *Address:* c/o Independent Talent Group Ltd, 40 Whitfield Street, W1T 2RH.

BEANEY, Jan, (Mrs S. Udall); textile artist; author; *b* 31 July 1938; *d* of Jack and Audrey Beaney; *m* 1967, Stephen Udall; one *s* one *d*. *Educ:* Southampton Coll. of Art; W Sussex Coll. of Art (NDD Painting/Lithography); Hornsey Coll. of Art (ATC); City & Guilds of London Inst. (Licentiate). Lecturer in Art and Embroidery: grammar/technical sch., Northolt, 1959–64; Whitelands Coll. of Educn, 1964–68; Associate Lectr in Embroidery and Design, Windsor and Maidenhead Coll., subseq. E Berks Coll., 1976–2000, Artist-in-Residence, 2000–10. Freelance lectr and teacher in design/stitched textiles, UK, USA, Australia, NZ, Canada, Israel and Germany, 1966–. Work exhibited in UK, Europe, Israel and Japan; work in private and public collections, GB and worldwide. Co-founder, Double Trouble Enterprises (publishers), 1997. Presenter, BBC TV series, Embroidery, 1980; contribs to TV progs, 1984–95. Examr, then Jt Chief Examr, Creative Studies, C&G, 1979–95. Member: 62 Gp of Textile Artists, 1962– (Hon. Mem., 1998); Embroiderers' Guild, 1963– (Hon. Mem., 2001; Jt Pres., 2012–); Hon. Mem., C&G, 1996. MUniv Surrey, 1995. *Publications:* The Young Embroiderer, 1966; Fun with Collage, 1970; Fun with Embroidery, 1975; Landscapes in Picture, Collage and Design, 1976; Buildings in Picture, Collage and Design, 1976; Textures and Surface Patterns, 1978; Embroidery: new approaches, 1978; Stitches: new approaches, 1985; The Art of the Needle, 1988; Vanishing Act, 1997; with Jean Littlejohn: A Complete Guide to Creative Embroidery, 1971; Stitch Magic, 1998; Bonding and Beyond, Transfer to Transform, 1999; Gardens and More, Conversations with Constance, 2000; Trees as a Theme, Giving Pleasure, 2001; New Dimensions, Double Vision, 2002; A Tale of Two Stitches, A Sketch in Time, 2003; No Stone Unturned, Connections, 2004; Colour Explorations, Over the Line, 2005; Grids to Stitch, Seductive Surfaces, 2006; Red, Embellish and Enrich, 2007; Location, Location, Seeing Double, 2008; Fragile Fabrics, Constructions, 2009; Stitchscapes, 2010; Stitch Rhythms and Patterns, 2011; contrib. numerous articles on stitching and textile design. *Recreations:* entertaining friends, travel, reading, painting, gardening. *Address:* Double Trouble Enterprises, 233 Courthouse Road, Maidenhead, Berks SL6 6HF.

BEAR, Sir Michael (David), Kt 2012; CEng, FRICS; JP; Managing Director, Michael Bear Developments Ltd, since 1996; Chairman, Regeneration Investment Organisation, UK Trade and Investment, since 2013; UK Special Envoy for Sustainable Urbanisation, China, since 2014; Lord Mayor of London, 2010–11; *b* Nairobi, 21 Jan. 1953; *s* of Lionel Meyer Bear and Rebecca Bear; *m* 1979, Barbara Anne Sandler; one *s* one *d*. *Educ:* Clifton Coll. Sch.; Univ. of Witwatersrand (BSc Eng 1974); Cranfield Inst. of Technol. (MBA 1981). CEng 1978; MICE 1979, Hon. FICE 2008; FRICS 2009. Aid worker, S African Voluntary Service, 1970–74; Project Engineer: Hawkins Hawkins & Osborne, 1974–78; Sir Frederick Snow Ltd, 1978–81; Business Analyst, Taylor Woodrow, 1981–82; Internat. Business Develt Manager, Balfour Beatty Engrg Ltd, 1982–88; Man. Dir, Iberia Develts Ltd, 1988–89; Dir, LET Europe BV, 1989–93; Chief Exec., Spitalfields Develt Gp, 1991–2011; Man. Dir, Balfour Beatty Property Ltd, 1993–2012; Regeneration Dir, Hammerson UK Properties plc, 2007–12. Director: Avatar Ltd, 1993–2000; White City Centre Ltd, 1994–98; British Urban Develt Ltd,

1995–99; Cityside Regeneration Ltd, 1997–2003; non-exec. Dir, Arup Gp Ltd, 2009–. Vis. Prof. in Civil Engrg, City Univ., 2011–. Chm., Bethnal Green City Challenge, 1993–97. Director: Spitalfields Music (formerly Spitalfields Fest.), 1991–2006 (Hon. Advr, 2007–); Spitalfields Mkt Community Trust, 1991–2012; Metropolitan Drinking Fountain and Cattle Trough Assoc., 2005–; CRASH, 2006–11; City Arts Trust, 2007–11. MInstD 1997. Governor: London Metropolitan Univ., 2000–03; London South Bank Univ., 2004–10; Christ's Hosp., 2005–; Sir John Cass Primary Sch., 2006–12; Clifton Coll., 2007–14; Sir John Cass Foundn, 2008–12; Coram, 2008– (Pres., 2012–); City Acad., Hackney, 2008–12. Liveryman: Co. of Paviors, 2002– (Mem., Ct of Assts, 2006–; Master, 2012–13); Co. of Chartered Surveyors, 2006– (Mem., Ct of Assts, 2007–); Co. of Engineers, 2009–. Hon. Liveryman, Co. of Security Professionals, 2010–; Hon. Freeman, Co. of Environmental Cleaners, 2010–. Mem., Guild of Freemen, 2008–. City of London, Portsoken Ward: Councilman, 2003–04; Dep. Alderman, 2004–05; Alderman, 2005–. JP 2005, Sheriff, 2007–08, City of London. Hon. FREng 2010. Hon. DSc: City, 2011; London Southbank, 2012; Cranfield, 2012. KStJ 2011 (SBStJ 2008). *Recreations:* small business ventures, scuba diving, tennis, opera, theatre, international travel, supporting the England Rugby team. *Address:* c/o City of London Corporation, PO Box 270, Guildhall, EC2P 2EJ. *T:* (020) 7887 1145, (01993) 881563, *Fax:* (020) 8346 3991. *E:* michael@thebearsinc.com. *Clubs:* Athenæum, East India.

BEARD, Alexander Charles, CBE 2013; Chief Executive, Royal Opera House, since 2013; *b* London, 14 Oct. 1963; *s* of Charles Henry and Patricia Anne Beard; *m* 1993, Katharine Betty Warde-Aldam; one *s* one *d*. *Educ:* Manchester Grammar Sch.; Westminster Sch.; King's Coll. London (BA Classics). KPMG, London, 1985–86; Arts Council, 1987–93; Tate: Dir, Finance and Admin, 1994–98, Dir, Business, 1998–2002; Dep. Dir, 2002–13. Member: Philanthropy Prog., DCMS, 2010–; WWI Centenary Cultural Prog., 2013–. Trustee: Global Giving UK, 2007–13; Glyndebourne Prodns Ltd, 2008–13. *Recreations:* cricket, visual arts, opera, ballet, music, cycling. *Address:* c/o Royal Opera House, Covent Garden, WC2E 9DD. *E:* alex.beard@roh.org.uk.

BEARD, (Christopher) Nigel; *b* 10 Oct. 1936; *o s* of Albert Leonard Beard, Castleford, Yorks, and Irene (*née* Bowes); *m* 1969, Jennifer Anne, *d* of T. B. Cotton, Guildford, Surrey; one *s* one *d*. *Educ:* Castleford Grammar Sch., Yorks; University Coll. London. BSc Hons, Special Physics. Asst Mathematics Master, Tadcaster Grammar Sch., Yorks, 1958–59; Physicist with English Electric Atomic Power Div., working on design of Hinckley Point Nuclear Power Station, 1959–61; Market Researcher, Esso Petroleum Co., assessing future UK Energy demands and market for oil, 1961; Ministry of Defence: Scientific Officer, later Principal Scientific Officer, in Defence Operational Analysis Estabt (engaged in analysis of central defence policy and investment issues), 1961–68, and Supt of Studies pertaining to Land Ops; responsible for policy and investment studies related to Defence of Europe and strategic movement of the Army, Dec. 1968–72; Chief Planner, Strategy, GLC, 1973–74; Dir, London Docklands Develt Team, 1974–79; Sen. Consultant, ICI, 1979–93; Sen. Man., ICI-Zeneca Ltd, 1993–97. Mem., SW Thames RHA, 1978–86; Mem. Bd, Royal Marsden Hosp., 1982–90. Mem., Lab. Pty Nat. Constitutional Cttee, 1995–98. MP (Lab) Bexleyheath and Crayford, 1997–2005; contested (Lab) same seat, 2005. Member: Select Cttee on Science and Technol., 1997–2000; Ecclesiastical Cttee, 1997–2005; Treasury Select Cttee, 2000–05; Speaker's Panel of Chairmen, 2001–05. Chm., All-Party Gp on the City, 2003–05. Vice-Chm., PLP Defence Cttee, 2001–05. Contested (Lab): Woking, 1979; Portsmouth N, 1983; Erith and Crayford, 1992. FRSA. *Publications:* The Practical Use of Linear Programming in Planning and Analysis, 1974 (HMSO). *Recreations:* reading, walking, the theatre. *Address:* Lanquhart, The Ridgway, Pyrford, Woking, Surrey GU22 8PW. *E:* nigel.beard@btinternet.com. *Club:* Athenæum.

BEARD, Mark John; Headmaster, University College School, since 2013; *b* Carshalton, 27 Jan. 1971; *m* 1998, Jacqueline Aspin; two *s*. *Educ:* Whitgift Sch.; Corpus Christi Coll., Oxford (BA 1994; PGCE 1995; MA); King's Coll. London (MEd 2002). Teacher of Chemistry and CCF Contingent Comdr, King Edward's Sch., Birmingham, 1995–99; Hd of Chemistry, St Paul's Sch., London, 1999–2006; Hd of Sixth Form, 2006–09, Dep. Headmaster, 2009–13, Brighton Coll. *Publications:* contrib. Tetrahedron. *Recreations:* squash, reading, ancient history and the classics. *Address:* University College School, Frognal, Hampstead, NW3 6XH. *T:* (020) 7435 2215.

BEARD, Mary; *see* Beard, W. M.

BEARD, Nigel; *see* Beard, C. N.

BEARD, Peter Hill; American photographer; *b* 22 Jan. 1938; *s* of Anson Beard; *m* 1st, 1967, Minnie Cushing (marr. diss. 1971); 2nd, 1978, Cheryl Tiegs (marr. diss. 1984); 3rd, 1986, Nejma Khanum; one *d*. *Educ:* Yale Univ. (grad 1961). Career of escapism through collage, books, diaries and anthropology. Major exhibitions include: Blum-Helman, NY, 1975 (first exhibn); ICP, NY, 1977 (first one man exhibn); Diary, 1979, African Wallpaper, 1993, Seibu Mus., Japan; Carnets Africains, Paris, 1996–97; Pettiness and Futility, LA, 1998; 50 Years of Portraits, Toronto, LA, New Orleans, 1998–99; Stress and Density, Berlin, Vienna, 1999; 28 Pieces, Paris, 1999; Living Sculpture, London, 2004–05; Time's Up, London, 2006–07. *Publications:* The End of the Game, 1965, 5th edn 2008, 50th Anniv. edn 2015; Eyelids of Morning: the mingled destinies of crocodiles and men, 1973; Longing for Darkness: Kamante's tales from Out of Africa, 1975; Zara's Tales from Hog Ranch, 2004; Peter Beard, art edn 2006, collector's edn 2007, trade edns 2008 and 2013; Ele Portfolio, 2009; exhibition catalogues: Diary, 1993; Photo poche, 1996; Carnets Africains, 1997; Peter Beard: 50 Years of Portraits, 1999; Stress and Density, 1999. *Address:* Peter Beard Studio, 525 West 20th Street, New York, NY 10011, USA. *Club:* White Rhino (Nyeri, Kenya).

BEARD, Philip Charles William; Chief Executive, Queens Park Rangers Football Club, since 2011; *b* Liverpool, 4 Jan. 1961; *s* of Roland and Joan Beard; *m* 1994, Louise; one *s* two *d*. *Educ:* Langley Park Grammar Sch. Founding Partner, Air Miles, 1988–2001; Dir, London 2012 Olympic and Paralympic Bid, 2003–05; Dir, Mktg and Sponsorship, LOCOG, 2005–06; CEO, AEG the O2, 2006–09; Chm., Sport and Partnerships, AEG Europe, 2006–10. *Recreations:* ski-ing, tennis, golf. *Address:* 4 Earlsfield Road, SW18 3DW. *Club:* St George's Hill Golf.

BEARD, Prof. (Winifred) Mary, (Mrs R. S. Cormack), OBE 2013; PhD; FBA 2010; FSA; Professor of Classics, University of Cambridge, since 2004; Fellow, Newnham College, Cambridge, since 1984; Professor of Ancient Literature, Royal Academy, since 2013; *b* 1 Jan. 1955; *d* of Roy Whitbread Beard and Joyce Emily (*née* Taylor); *m* 1985, Robin Sinclair Cormack, *qv*; one *s* one *d*. *Educ:* Newnham Coll., Cambridge (BA Classics 1977, MA 1980; PhD 1982). FSA 2005. Lectr in Classics, KCL, 1979–83; University of Cambridge: Lectr in Classics, 1984–99; Reader in Classics, 1999–2004. Writer and presenter: Pompeii: Life and Death in a Roman Town, BBC2, 2010; A Point of View, BBC Radio 4, 2011, 2012; Meet the Romans with Mary Beard, BBC2, 2012; Caligula with Mary Beard, BBC2, 2013. Mem., First World War Centenary Adv. Gp, 2014–. For. Mem., Amer. Acad. of Arts and Scis, 2011; Internat. Mem., American Philosophical Soc., 2012. Hon. DLitt: Bristol, 2012; St Andrews, 2013; Buckingham, 2014; London, 2014. Classics Ed. (pt-time), TLS, 1992–. *Publications:* (with M. Crawford) Rome in the Late Republic, 1985, 2nd edn 1999; The Good Working Mother's Guide, 1989; (ed jtly) Pagan Priests: religion and power in the ancient world, 1990; (with J. Henderson) Classics: a very short introduction, 1995, 2nd edn 2000; (jtly) Religions of Rome I and II, 1998; The Invention of Jane Harrison, 2000; (with J. Henderson) Classical Art: from Greece to Rome, 2001; The Parthenon, 2002; (with K. Hopkins) The Colosseum, 2005; The Roman Triumph, 2007; Pompeii: the life of a Roman town (Wolfson History Prize), 2008; It's A Don's Life, 2009; All in a Don's Day, 2012; Confronting the Classics, 2013; Laughter in Ancient Rome, 2014. *Address:* Newnham College, Cambridge CB3 9DF. *T:* (01223) 335700. *E:* mb127@cam.ac.uk.

BEARDER, Catherine Zena; Member (Lib Dem) South East Region, European Parliament, since 2009; *b* Broxbourne, Herts, 14 Jan. 1949; *d* of Ernest James Bailey and Joan Irene Clare Bailey; *m* 1974, Prof. Simon Kenneth Bearder; three *s*. *Educ:* Hawthorn Sch., Frinton on Sea; St Christopher's Sch., Letchworth. Work on family farm, Herts, 1964–66; antique dealer, Hertford, 1966–74; field asst to zool field studies on hyenas and bushbabies, S Africa, 1974–78; work in fundraising office, Berks, Bucks and Oxon Wildlife Trust, 1987–90; Manager, Bicester CAB, 1990–94; Development Officer: NFWI, 1994–97; Witness Service, Oxon Victim Support, 1998–99; Regl Dir, SE, Britain in Europe, 2004–05. Member (Lib Dem): Wendlebury PC, 1986–92; Cherwell DC, 1995–99; Oxon CC, 2003–05. Mem., Police Consultative Cttee, Northern Oxfordshire, 1993–95. Chairman: and Co-founder, Bicester Volunteer Link, 1992–95; Bicester Community Educn Council, 1992–95; Banbury Emergency Accommodation Initiative, 1998–2000. Trustee and Board Member: Oxon Rural Community Council, 2000–08; Oxon Victim Support, 2001–02; Thame CAB, 2002–03. Chm., Banbury Lib Dems, 1997; Vice Pres., Green Lib Dems, 2009–; Vice Chm., Lib Dems' Eur. Gp, 2009–. Chm., Lib Dem conf. cttee, S Central Reg., 2003–08. Chm., Oxon Lib Dems Printing Soc., 2000–08. Contested (Lib Dem): Banbury, 1997; SE England, Eur. Parlt, 1999, 2004. Member: IAM; UNA (UK); Amnesty Internat.; Eur. Movt; Women's Envmtl Network. Police Lay Visitor, Bicester and Banbury, 1992–95. Pres., Bicester Friends of the Earth, 1990–96. Gov., St Edburg's C of E Sch., Bicester, 1986–91. FRSA. *Recreations:* painting, gardening. *Address:* (office) 27 Park End Street, Oxford OX1 1HU. *T:* (01865) 249838. *E:* catherine@bearder.eu, catherine.bearder@europarl.europa.eu. *Club:* National Liberal.

BEARDMORE, Prof. John Alec, CBiol, FRSB; Emeritus Professor and Consultant in Aquacultural Genetics, Swansea University (formerly University of Wales, Swansea), since 2000; *b* 1 May 1930; *s* of George Edward Beardmore and Anne Jean (*née* Warrington); *m* 1953, Anne Patricia Wallace; three *s* one *d* (and one *s* decd). *Educ:* Burton on Trent Grammar Sch.; Birmingham Central Tech. Coll.; Univ. of Sheffield. BSc (1st Cl. Botany) 1953, PhD (Genetics) 1956. Research Demonstrator, Dept of Botany, Univ. of Sheffield, 1954–56; Commonwealth Fund Fellow, Columbia Univ., 1956–58; Vis. Asst Prof. in Plant Breeding, Cornell Univ., 1958; Lectr in Genetics, Univ. of Sheffield, 1958–61; Prof. of Genetics and Dir, Genetics Inst., Univ. of Groningen, 1961–66; Nat. Science Foundn Senior Foreign Fellow, Pennsylvania State Univ., 1966; University College of Swansea, subseq. University of Wales, Swansea: Prof. of Genetics, 1966–97; Dean of Science, 1974–76; Vice-Principal, 1977–80; Dir, Inst. of Marine Studies, 1983–87; Hd, Sch. of Biol Scis, 1988–95; Professorial Fellow in Genetics, 1997–2000. Manager, DFID (formerly ODA) Fish Genetics Res. Prog., 1990–2001; Man. Dir, 1995–2005, Chm., 2005–, Fishgen Ltd. Chm., Univ. of Wales Validation Bd, 1994–97; Mem., Univ. of Wales Vice Chancellors' Bd, 1993–96. Vis. Prof., Univ. of Ghent, 1992–2002. Member: NERC Aquatic Life Scis Cttee, 1982–87 (Chm., 1984–87); CNAA: Life Scis Cttee, 1979–85; Cttee for Science, 1985–87; Bd, Council of Sci. and Technology Insts, 1983–85 (Chm., 1984–85); Council, Galton Inst. (formerly Eugenics Soc.), 1980–96, 2002– (Chm., Res. Cttee, 1979–87; Vice-Pres., 2005–08; Treas., 2007–); British Nat. Cttee for Biology, 1983–87; Council, Linnean Soc., 1989–93; Cttee, Heads of Univ. Biol Scis (Treas., 1989–91, Chm., 1991–94); Adv. Bd, Internat. Foundn for Sci., 1992–; Vice-Pres., Inst. of Biol., 1985–87 (Mem. Council, 1976–79; Hon. Sec., 1980–85); UK rep., Council of European Communities Biologists Assoc., 1980–87. Pres., Gower Soc., 2012– (Hon. Treas., 2005–11). FRSA; FAAAS; FRSocMed. Darwin Lectr, Inst. of Biol. and Eugenics Soc., 1984. Univ. of Helsinki Medal, 1980. *Publications:* (ed with B. Battaglia) Marine Organisms: genetics ecology and evolution, 1977; (ed jtly) Artemia: basic and applied biology, 2002; articles on evolutionary genetics, human genetics and applications of genetics to aquaculture. *Recreations:* bridge, walking. *Address:* 153 Derwen Fawr Road, Swansea SA2 8ED. *T:* (01792) 206232.

BEARDMORE, Nicola Ann; Director, Resources and Support, Shropshire Council, since 2013; Chief Operating Officer, Inspiring Partnerships and Enterprise, since 2014; *b* Clatterbridge, 6 Dec. 1970; *d* of Edward Rowlinson and Doreen Rowlinson; *m* 1995, Tim Beardmore; two *s*. *Educ:* Lakelands Sch., Ellesmere. MCIM 1996. Information Officer, 1991–94, Customer Develt and Mktg Manager, 1994–98, British Waterways; Managing Director: Shropshire Bridal Centre, 1997–2006; Borderland Tourism, 2002–07; Hd, Communications, Shropshire Council, 2006–13. Young Entrepreneur of the Yr, Shell, 1999. *Recreations:* painting, art, poetry, creative writing, musical theatre, travel, family, mum, hockey chauffeur and goalkeepers' sandwich maker. *Address:* Shropshire Council, Shirehall, Abbey Foregate, Shrewsbury, Shropshire SY2 6ND. *T:* (01743) 252134. *E:* nicki.beardmore@shropshire.gov.uk.

BEARDSHAW, Christopher Paul; garden designer and television presenter; Director, Chris Beardshaw Ltd, since 2001; *b* Worcs, 11 Jan. 1969; *s* of George and Gillian Beardshaw; partner, Frances Toase; three *d*. *Educ:* Cheltenham and Gloucester Coll. of Higher Educn (BA Hons Landscape Architecture; Postgrad. Landscape Architecture). Landscape architect: Cheltenham Landscape Design, 1992; Andrew Davies Partnership, 1993–97; Lectr, Pershore Coll., Worcs, 1997–2001; presenter, BBC TV and radio, 1998–, including: Gardeners' World, 2001–04; The Flying Gardener, 2001–03; Hidden Gardens, 2002–04; Wild About Your Garden, 2009; Ploughs, Cows and Clover, 2010; Hidcote: a garden for all seasons, 2011; Get Up & Grow, 2011–13; Apples: British to the Core, 2012; British Gardens in Time, 2014; Deep Down & Dirty, 2014. Consultant Lectr, Royal Botanic Gdns, Edinburgh, 2007–. Columnist: The English Garden Mag.; Garden News. Hon. Fellow, Univ. of Glos, 2004. 6 RHS Gold Medals; 5 RHS Best in Show Awards. *Publications:* The Natural Gardener, 2003; How Does Your Garden Grow?, 2007; The Secret Life of the Garden, 2009. *Recreations:* diving, cycling. *Address:* c/o 3rd Floor, One London Square, Cross Lanes, Guildford GU1 1UN. *E:* info@chrisbeardshaw.com.

BEARDSHAW, Virginia Zachry, CBE 2015; Chief Executive Officer, I CAN, since 2005; *b* Manhattan, 15 June 1952; *d* of David Beardshaw and Charlotte Beardshaw (*née* Zachry); *m* 1976, Sir Andrew Thomas Cahn, *qv*; two *s* one *d*. *Educ:* Mount Sch., York; New Hall, Cambridge (BA Hons Soc. Anthropol. 1974); London Sch. of Econs and Pol Sci. (Dip Soc. Admin). Researcher, Dept of Regius Prof. of Medicine, Oxford Univ., 1975–76; Stagiaire, EC, Brussels, 1976–77; Social Audit, London, 1977–82; Eur. Co-ordinator, Health Action Internat., The Hague, 1982–86; Founder Fellow, King's Fund Inst., 1987–89; Director: King's Fund London Initiative, 1989–93; Commissioning, Barnet HA, 1993–99; Modernisation, London Regl Office, NHS, 1999–2002; UK Services, British Red Cross, 2002–05. Vice Chm., ACEVO, 2012–15. Gov., LSE, 2011–. *Recreations:* gardening, choir, walking, theatre, opera. *Address:* I CAN, 8 Wakley Street, EC1V 7QE.

BEARDSWORTH, Maj.-Gen. Simon John, CB 1984; *b* 18 April 1929; *s* of late Paymaster-Captain Stanley Thomas Beardsworth, RN and Pearl Sylvia Emma (Biddy) Beardsworth (*née* Blake); *m* 1954, Barbara Bingham Turner (*d* 2015); two *s* (and one *s* decd). *Educ:* RC Sch. of St Edmund's Coll., Ware; RMA Sandhurst; RMCS. BSc. Commissioned Royal Tank Regt, 1949; Regtl service, staff training and staff appts, 1950–69; CO 1st RTR, 1970–72; Project Manager, Future Main Battle Tank, 1973–77; Student, Royal Naval War College, 1977; Dir of Projects, Armoured Fighting Vehicles, 1977–80; Dep. Comdt, RMCS, 1980–81; Vice

Master Gen. of the Ordnance, 1981–84; consultant in defence procurement, 1984–97. *Recreations:* theatre, sudoku. *Address:* c/o Lloyds Bank, Crewkerne, Somerset TA18 7LR. *Club:* Army and Navy.

BEARE, Stuart Newton; Consultant, Richards Butler, Solicitors, 1996–2002 (Partner, 1969–96, Senior Partner, 1988–91); *b* 6 Oct. 1936; *s* of Newton Beare and Joyce (*née* Atkinson); *m* 1974, Cheryl Wells. *Educ:* Clifton Coll.; Clare Coll., Cambridge (MA, LLB). Nat. Service, commnd Royal Signals, attached RWAFF, 1956–57. Plebiscite Supervisory Officer, N Cameroons, 1960–61; admitted solicitor, 1964. Clerk, Ward of Portsoken, 1993–96 (Hon. Ward Clerk, 1996–2013). Master, City of London Solicitors' Co. and Pres., City of London Law Soc., 1995–96. *Recreations:* mountain walking, ski-ing. *Address:* 24 Ripplevale Grove, N1 1HU. *T:* (020) 7609 0766. *Clubs:* Alpine, Oriental.

BEARMAN, Prof. Peter William, FREng; Professor of Experimental Aerodynamics, Imperial College of Science, Technology and Medicine, 1986–2004, now Emeritus; *b* 8 Oct. 1938; *s* of William Stanley Bearman and Nana Joan Bearman; *m* 1969, Marietta Neubauer; one *s* one *d*. *Educ:* Jesus Coll., Cambridge (MA 1962; PhD 1965). SSO, Nat. Phys. Lab., 1965–69; Department of Aeronautics, Imperial College, London: Lectr, 1969–81; Reader, 1981–86; Head of Dept, 1989–98; Pro-Rector, Projects, 1999–2001, Dep. Rector, 2001–04, ICSTM. FRAeS 1990; FCGI 1997; FREng (FEng 1997). *Publications:* (ed) Flow-induced Vibration, 1995; around 200 sci. papers. *Recreations:* cycling, gardening, ski-ing. *Address:* Imperial College, SW7 2AZ. *T:* (020) 7594 5055.

BEARN, Rev. Hugh William; Vicar, St Anne's Church, Tottington, since 1996; Chaplain to the Queen, since 2006; *b* 31 March 1962; *s* of John Hugh Bearn and Gladys Eileen Bearn (*née* Saint); *m* 1990, Alison Margaret (*neé* Cooper); two *s*. *Educ:* Oxford Sch.; Manchester Univ. (BA 1984; MA 1998); St John's Coll., Durham (CTh 1988). Schoolmaster, St Edmund's Sch., Canterbury; ordained deacon, 1989, priest, 1990; Asst Curate, Christ Church, Heaton, 1989–92; Chaplain, RAF, 1992–96. Chaplain: RAChD, TA, 1996–2002; Bury Hospice, 1999–2004 and 2010–; Manchester County ACF, 2006–; Greater Manchester ACF, 2012–; Chaplain to the Bishop, RBL Fest. of Remembrance, 2002–. Member: Fraternity, CR, Mirfield, 1991–; Sen. Common Room, St Anselm Hall, Univ. of Manchester, 2002– (Hon. Chaplain). Vice-Pres., Manchester Br., Prayer Bk Soc., 2003–. Sec., Old Boys' Soc., Oxford Sch., 1983; Gov., Tottington High Sch., 1996–2001. Freeman: City of London, 2009; Clockmakers' Co., 2009 (Chaplain, 2010–). Bk Reviewer, Contact, 1997. *Publications:* History of Tottington St Anne, 1999; On the Way… a journey into faith, 2007; The Royal College of Chaplains 1912–2012: a photographic register. *Recreations:* family, all things French, marathon running, keep fit, all sport, supporting the varied social, musical and sporting life of my boys, regimental history of the Bearn family. *Address:* The Vicarage, Chapel Street, Tottington, Bury, Lancs BL8 4AP. *T:* (01204) 883713. *E:* hughbearn@aol.com. *Clubs:* Royal Air Force; Royal Irish Officers (Belfast); Manchester Dio. Cricket.

BEARSTED, 5th Viscount *cr* 1925, of Maidstone, Kent; **Nicholas Alan Samuel;** Bt 1903; Baron 1921; *b* 22 Jan. 1950; *s* of 4th Viscount Bearsted, MC, TD and Hon. Elizabeth Adelaide (*d* 1983), *d* of Baron Cohen, PC; *S* father, 1996; *m* 1975, Caroline Jane, *d* of Dr David Sacks; one *s* four *d*. *Educ:* Eton; New Coll., Oxford. *Heir: s* Hon. Harry Richard Samuel, *b* 23 May 1988. *Address:* The Estate Office, Farley Hall, Castle Road, Farley Hill, Berks RG7 1UL.

BEASHEL, His Honour John Francis; DL; a Circuit Judge, 1993–2008; Resident Judge, Dorchester Crown Court, 1994–2006; *b* 3 Aug. 1942; *s* of late Nicholas Beashel and Margaret Rita Beashel, JP; *m* 1966, Kay Dunning; three *s* one *d*. *Educ:* Coll. of Law. Called to the Bar, Gray's Inn, 1970, NSW, 1989; Asst Recorder, 1983–89; Recorder, 1989–93; Liaison Judge to Dorset Justices, 1994–2006. Member: Parole Bd for England and Wales, 2007–; Mental Health Review Tribunal, 2008–12. Pres., Dorset Br., Magistrates' Assoc., 1998–2006. DL Dorset, 2007. *Recreations:* golf, travel, reading, walking, cooking. *Club:* Ferndown Golf (Capt., 2012).

BEASLEY, Ann, (Ann Beasley Manders), CBE 2010; Director General for Finance Assurance and Commercial Group, Ministry of Justice, since 2013; *b* 13 Sept. 1958; *d* of late Albert Beasley and of Joyce Shirley Beasley (*née* Hodgson); marr. diss.; two *s*. *Educ:* Manchester Univ. (BSc Maths, MSc Stats); Kingston Univ. (MBA). CPFA 2008. Asst Statistician, HM Customs & Excise, 1980–82; Sen. Asst Statistician and Statistician, CAA, 1982–88; joined Metropolitan Police Service, 1988; Hd, Performance Inf., 1988–92; Hd, Equal Opportunities, 1992–94; Area Business Manager, 1994–2000; Hd, Business Develt and Support, then Dir, Business Change, 2000–02; Hd, Planning Gp, HM Prison Service, 2002–03; Dir of Finance, HM Prison Service, later Dir of Finance and Perf., Nat. Offender Mgt Service, 2003–10; Dir Gen. for Finance, later Finance and Corporate Services, MoJ, 2010–13. Trustee, Alzheimer's Soc., 2009– (Ind. Mem., Audit Cttee, 2006–09; Vice Chair, 2012–). *Recreations:* theatre, original art, DIY, cats, gardening, chocolate. *Address:* Ministry of Justice, 102 Petty France, SW1H 9AJ.

BEASLEY, Dame Christine (Joan), DBE 2008 (CBE 2002); Chief Nursing Officer, Department of Health, 2004–12; *b* 13 June 1944; *d* of Clifford and Muriel de'Ath; *m* 1st, 1967, John Wills; three *s*; 2nd, 1989, Jack Beasley. *Educ:* Royal London Hosp. (SRN); W London Inst. (Registered Dist Nurse; DMS; DipN). Chief Nurse, Riverside Hosps, 1989–94; Regl Dir of Nursing, N Thames and London, 1994–2002; Partnership Develt Dir, Modernisation Agency, 2002–04. Non-exec. Dir and Vice Chair, NHS Trust Develt Authy, 2012–. Fellow, Queen's Nursing Inst., 2004. Trustee, Marie Curie Cancer Care, 2000–11. Pro-Chancellor, Univ. of W London (formerly Thames Valley Univ.), 2006–12 (Gov., 2000–06); Chairman: Council, Buckinghamshire New Univ., 2012–; Local Educn and Trng Bd of N and E London, 2012–. *Recreations:* theatre, entertaining, travel. *Address:* 80 Mayfield Avenue, Ealing, W13 9UX. *T:* (020) 7210 5598.

BEASLEY, Rt Rev. Noel Michael Roy; *see* Hertford, Bishop Suffragan of.

BEASLEY-MURRAY, Rev. Dr Paul; ministry consultant; Senior Minister, Central Baptist (formerly Baptist) Church, Victoria Road South, Chelmsford, 1993–2014; *b* 14 March 1944; *s* of late Rev. Dr George R. Beasley-Murray; *m* 1967, Caroline (*née* Griffiths); three *s* one *d*. *Educ:* Trinity School of John Whitgift; Jesus Coll., Cambridge (MA); Northern Baptist Coll. and Manchester Univ. (PhD); Baptist Theol Seminary, Rüschlikon and Zürich Univ. Baptist Missionary Soc., Zaire (Professor at National Univ., Theol. Faculty), 1970–72; Pastor of Altrincham Baptist Church, Cheshire, 1973–86; Principal, Spurgeon's Coll., 1986–92. Chairman: Ministry Today (formerly Richard Baxter Inst. for Ministry), 1994–; Coll. of Baptist Ministers, 2013–. Patron: J's Hospice, Essex, 2007–; Soc. of Mary and Martha, Sheldon, Exeter, 2008–. Editor, Ministry Today, 1994–. *Publications:* (with A. Wilkinson) Turning the Tide, 1981; Pastors Under Pressure, 1989; Dynamic Leadership, 1990; (ed) Mission to the World, 1991; Faith and Festivity, 1991; Radical Believers, 1992; (ed) Anyone for Ordination?, 1993; A Call to Excellence, 1995; Radical Disciples, 1996; Happy Every After?: a guide to the marriage adventure, 1996; Radical Leaders, 1997; Power for God's Sake, 1998; The Message of the Resurrection, 2000; Fearless for Truth, 2002; Building for the Future, 2003; A Loved One Dies, 2005; Joy to the World, 2005; Transform Your Church, 2005; Baptism, Belonging and Breaking Bread, 2010; A Retreat Lectionary, 2012; Living Out the Call: rising to the challenges of ministry today, 4 vols, 2015. *Recreations:* music, parties, cooking, entertaining my seven grandchildren. *Address:* The Old Manse, 3 Roxwell Road, Chelmsford, Essex CM1 2LY. *T:* (01245) 352996. *E:* paulbeasleymurray@gmail.com. *W:* paulbeasleymurray.com. *Club:* Chelmsford Rivermead Rotary (Pres., July 2016–).

BEASTALL, John Sale, CB 1995; Head of Local Government Group, HM Treasury, 1993–95; *b* 2 July 1941; *s* of Howard and Marjorie Betty Beastall (*née* Sale). *Educ:* St Paul's School; Balliol College, Oxford (BA 1963). Asst Principal, HM Treasury, 1963–67 (Asst Private Sec. to Chancellor of the Exchequer, 1966–67); Principal: HM Treasury, 1967–68 and 1971–75 (Private Sec. to Paymaster General, 1974–75); CSD, 1968–71; Assistant Secretary: HM Treasury, 1975–79 and 1981–85; CSD, 1979–81; DES, 1985–87; Treasury Officer of Accounts, 1987–93. Receiver, Met. Police Dist, 1995; Develt Dir, St Paul's Sch., 1996–2000. Chairman: Outward Housing, 2002–07; LAMB Health Care Foundn, 2004–10; Feltham Community Chaplaincy Trust, 2008–. Chm., Standards Cttee, Ealing BC, 2010–. Chm. Govs, Green Sch., Isleworth, 2012–. *Club:* Oxford and Cambridge.

BEATH, Prof. John Arnott, OBE 2015; FRSE; Professor, University of St Andrews, 1991–2009, now Emeritus; Secretary General, Royal Economic Society, 2008–15; *b* Thurso, Caithness, 15 June 1944; *s* of James Beath and Marion McKendrick Spence; *m* 1980, Dr Monika Juliana Anna Schröder. *Educ:* Hillhead High Sch., Glasgow; Queen's Coll., Dundee, Univ. of St Andrews (MA 1966); Wye Coll., Univ. of London (MPhil 1968); Univ. of Pennsylvania (AM 1971); St John's Coll., Cambridge (MA 1975). Thouron Scholar, Univ. of Pennsylvania, 1968–71; Res. Officer, Univ. of Cambridge, 1972–79; Lectr, then Sen. Lectr, Univ. of Bristol, 1979–91. Chm., Econ. Res. Inst. of NI, 2003–09; Member: Doctors and Dentists Pay Rev. Body, 2003–09; Prison Service Pay Rev. Body, 2010–; Competition Appeal Tribunal, 2011–. Mem. Council, ESRC, 2009–14. FRSE 2007; FRSA 2003. *Publications:* The Economic Theory of Product Differentiation, 1991; articles in learned jls in econs. *Recreations:* golf, gardening, music, travel, walking. *Address:* School of Economics and Finance, University of St Andrews, St Andrews, Fife KY16 9AL. *T:* (01334) 462421, 462479, *Fax:* (01334) 462444. *Clubs:* Leven Golfing Society; Penn (NY).

BEATON, James Wallace, GC 1974; CVO 1992 (LVO 1987); security manager, now retired; Chief Superintendent, Metropolitan Police, 1985–92; *b* St Fergus, Aberdeenshire, 16 Feb. 1943; *s* of J. A. Beaton and B. McDonald; *m* 1965, Anne C. Ballantyne (*d* 2011); two *d*. *Educ:* Peterhead Acad., Aberdeenshire. Joined Metropolitan Police, 1962: Notting Hill, 1962–66; Sergeant, Harrow Road, 1966–71; Station Sergeant, Wembley, 1971–73; Royalty Protection Officer, 'A' Division, 1973; Police Officer to The Princess Anne, 1973–79; Police Inspector, 1974; Chief Inspector, 1979; Superintendent, 1983; Queen's Police Officer, 1983–92. JP E Yorks, 2004. Director's Honor Award, US Secret Service, 1974. *Recreations:* reading, keeping fit, golf, hill walking. *Address:* 6 Finch Park, Beverley, East Yorkshire HU17 7DW.

BEATON, Prof. Roderick Macleod, PhD; FBA 2013; Koraes Professor of Modern Greek and Byzantine History, Language and Literature, since 1988, and Director, Centre for Hellenic Studies, since 2012, King's College London; *b* Edinburgh, 29 Sept. 1951; *s* of Duncan Beaton and Janet Beaton (*née* Purves); *m* 1978, Fran Downs; two *s*. *Educ:* George Watson's Coll., Edinburgh; Peterhouse, Cambridge (BA Hons English Lit. 1973; PhD Modern Greek 1977). Ouranis Foundn Fellow in Modern Greek, Univ. of Birmingham, 1977–80; King's College London: Lectr in Modern Greek Lang. and Lit., 1981–88; Hd, Dept of Byzantine and Modern Greek Studies, 1988–94, 1995–98. Mem. Council, British Sch. at Athens, 2011–. *Publications:* Ariadne's Children (fiction), 1995; The Medieval Greek Romance, 1996; Introduction to Modern Greek Literature, 1999; George Seferis: waiting for the angel, 2003; Byron's War: romantic rebellion, Greek revolution, 2013. *Recreations:* writing, travel, opera, theatre. *Address:* Centre for Hellenic Studies, King's College London, Strand, WC2R 2LS. *T:* (020) 7848 2517. *E:* rod.beaton@kcl.ac.uk. *Club:* Oxford and Cambridge.

BEATSON, Rt Hon. Sir Jack, Kt 2003; PC 2013; FBA 2001; **Rt Hon. Lord Justice Beatson;** a Lord Justice of Appeal, since 2013; *b* 3 Nov. 1948; *s* of late John James Beatson and Miriam Beatson (*née* White); *m* 1973, Charlotte, *y d* of Lt-Col J. A. Christie-Miller; one *d* (one *s* decd). *Educ:* Whittingehame Coll., Brighton; Brasenose Coll., Oxford (BCL, MA; DCL 2000; Hon. Fellow 2010); LLD Cantab 2001. Called to the Bar, Inner Temple, 1972, Hon. Bencher, 1993; a Law Comr, 1989–94; a Recorder, 1994–2003; QC 1998; a Dep. High Court Judge, 2000–03; a Judge of the High Court of Justice, QBD, 2003–13; Queen's Bench Liaison Judge for Midlands and Wales Circuits, 2009–12. Lectr in Law, Univ. of Bristol, 1972–73; Fellow and Tutor in Law, Merton Coll., Oxford, 1973–94 (Hon. Fellow, 1995); University of Cambridge: Rouse Ball Prof. of English Law, 1993–2003; Fellow, St John's Coll., 1994–2003 (Hon. Fellow, 2005); Dir, Centre for Public Law, 1997–2001; Chm., Faculty of Law, 2001–03. Visiting Professor: Osgoode Hall Law Sch., Toronto, 1979; Univ. of Virginia Law Sch., 1980, 1983; Vis. Sen. Teaching Fellow, Nat Univ. of Singapore, 1987; Vis. Fellow, Univ. of WA, 1988; Dist. Vis. Prof., Univ. of Toronto, 2000. Mem., Competition (formerly Monopolies and Mergers) Commn, 1995–2000. Pres., British Acad. Forensic Scis, 2007–09. *Publications:* (ed jtly) Chitty on Contract, 25th edn 1982 to 28th edn 1999; (with M. H. Matthews) Administrative Law: Cases and Materials, 1983, 2nd edn 1989; The Use and Abuse of Unjust Enrichment, 1991; (ed jtly) Good Faith and Fault in Contract Law, 1995; (ed jtly) European Public Law, 1998; Anson's Law of Contract, 27th edn 1998, (jtly) 29th edn 2010; (jtly) Human Rights: the 1998 Act and the European Convention, 2000; (ed with R. Zimmermann) Jurists Uprooted: German-speaking émigré lawyers in twentieth century Britain, 2004; (jtly) Human Rights: judicial protection in the UK, 2008; articles on administrative law, contract, and restitution in legal jls. *Recreations:* trying to relax, amateur gardening. *Address:* Royal Courts of Justice, Strand, WC2A 2LL.

BEATSON, Mark; Chief Economist, Chartered Institute of Personnel and Development, since 2012; *b* Elsecar, S Yorks, 27 Sept. 1963; *s* of Eric and Brenda Beatson. *Educ:* Swinton Comprehensive Sch.; Univ. of York (BA Hons Econs and Econometrics). Asst Economist, 1985–89, Econ. Advr, 1989–93, Dept of Employment; Econ. Advr, HM Treasury, 1993–95; Chief Economist, HSE, 1995–98; Hd, Employment Mkt Analysis and Res., 1998–2003, Sci. and Innovation Analysis, 2003–08, DTI; Chief Economist, DIUS, 2008–09; Dir of Sci. and Innovation Analysis, BIS, 2009–10; Dir, Econs, FTI Consulting, 2010–12. Hon. Vis. Prof., London Guildhall Faculty of Business and Law, London Metropolitan Univ., 2014–. FRSA. *Recreations:* Arsenal FC, Yorkshire cricket, Spain, music, cinema. *Address:* Chartered Institute of Personnel and Development, 151 The Broadway, SW19 1JQ. *T:* (020) 8612 6364. *E:* mark.beatson@hotmail.com.

BEATTIE, Alan Henry; International Economy Editor, Financial Times, since 2010; *b* Chester, 24 April 1971; *s* of David and Jane Beattie. *Educ:* Christleton Co. High Sch., Chester; Balliol Coll., Oxford (BA Hons Modern Hist. 1993); Jesus Coll., Cambridge (MPhil Econs 1996). Economist, Bank of England, 1996–98; Financial Times: Currency Corresp., 1998–99; Econs Corresp., 1999–2002; Internat. Econs Corresp., 2002–04; Econs Leader Writer, 2004; World Trade Ed., 2004–10. *Publications:* False Economy, 2009; Who's in Charge Here?, 2012. *Recreations:* poetry, cooking, theatre, football, baiting goldbugs. *Address:* Financial Times, 1023 Fifteenth Street NW, Washington, DC 20005, USA. *E:* alan.beattie@ft.com.

BEATTIE, Andrew Watt; Chief Parliamentary Counsel, Scottish Government, since 2012; *b* Aberdeen, 16 Nov. 1972; *s* of Andrew Watt Beattie and Janet Beattie; *m* 1999, Claire Louise Devine; two *s* one *d*. *Educ:* Elgin Acad.; Univ. of Edinburgh (LLB Hons 1994; DipLP 1995). Solicitor, Shepherd & Wedderburn, WS, 1995–99; Depute Scottish Parly Counsel, 1999–2008; Scottish Parly Counsel, 2008–12. *Recreations:* canoeing, camping, hillock-walking. *Address:* 4 Clouds, Duns, Berwickshire TD11 3BB. *T:* (01361) 883745. *E:* andy.beattie@scotland.gsi.gov.uk.

BEATTIE, Basil, RA 2006; artist; *b* W Hartlepool, 9 Jan. 1935. *Educ:* W Hartlepool Coll. of Art; Royal Acad. Schs. Lectr, Goldsmiths' Coll., London, until 1998. *Solo exhibitions* include: Greenwich Th. Gall., 1968; Mayfair Gall., 1971; Goldsmiths' Gall., 1982; Curwen Gall., 1987, 1990; Todd Gall., 1993, 1995, 1996, 1998; Ikon Gall., Birmingham, 1994; Newton Gall., Johannesburg, 1994; Path Galerie, Aalst, Belgium, 1996; Galerie Renate Bender, Munich, 1997; Sadler's Wells Th., 2002; Tate Britain, 2007; Two Rooms Gall., Auckland, NZ, 2008; James Hyman Fine Art, London, 2011; *group exhibitions* include: Whitechapel Art Gall., 1958–61; Walker Art Gall., Liverpool, 1965, 1987, 1989, 1991, 1997; Royal Acad. bicentenary exhibn, 1968; Hayward Gall., 1970, 1974, 1980, 1982, 1996; Jerwood Gall., 1998, 2001, 2009; *work in collections* including: Arts Council; Birmingham City Mus. and Art Gall.; Contemporary Art Soc.; Saatchi; Tate Gall.; Whitworth Art Gall., Manchester. Maj. Arts Council Award, 1976; Athena Award, 1986; Nordstern Print Prize, Royal Acad., 1991.

BEATTIE, Colin; Member (SNP) Midlothian North and Musselburgh, Scottish Parliament, since 2011; *b* Forfar, 17 Oct. 1951; *s* of James Watt Beattie and Catherine Beattie; *m* 1987, Lisa Hallinan. *Educ:* Forfar Acad.; MCIBS 1972. Various internat. banking posts, 1972–92; Regl Hd, Custody, Standard Chartered Bank, 1992–95; Vice-Pres., Citigroup, 1995–2006. Mem. (SNP), Midlothian Council, 2007–12. Nat. Treas., SNP, 2003–. Dir/Trustee, Nat. Mining Mus. of Scotland, 2007–. *Recreations:* history, current affairs, gardening (badly), classical music. *Address:* Eskbank House, Glenesk Crescent, Dalkeith, Midlothian EH22 3BL. *T:* (0131) 660 3242. *E:* colin.beattie1@btinternet.com.

BEATTIE, David, CMG 1989; HM Diplomatic Service, retired; Personnel Assessor, Foreign and Commonwealth Office, 1998–2008; *b* 5 March 1938; *s* of late George William David Beattie and Norna Alice (*née* Nicolson); *m* 1966, Ulla Marita Alha, *d* of late Allan Alha and Brita-Maja (*née* Tuominen), Helsinki, Finland; two *d. Educ:* Merchant Taylors' Sch., Crosby; Lincoln Coll., Oxford (BA 1964, MA 1967). National Service, Royal Navy, 1957–59; Sub-Lieut RNR, 1959; Lieut RNR 1962–67. Entered HM Foreign (now Diplomatic) Service, 1963; FO, 1963–64; Moscow, 1964–66; FO, 1966–70; Nicosia, 1970–74; FCO, 1974–78; Counsellor, later Dep. Head, UK Delegn to Negotiations on Mutual Reduction of Forces and Armaments and Associated Measures in Central Europe, Vienna, 1978–82; Counsellor (Commercial), Moscow, 1982–85; Head of Energy, Science and Space Dept, FCO, 1985–87; Min. and Dep. UK Perm. Rep. to NATO, Brussels, 1987–92; Ambassador to Swiss Confedn, and concurrently (non-resident) to Principality of Liechtenstein, 1992–97. Principal Sec., Royal Stuart Soc., 1997–2002; Vice-Pres., Anglo-Swiss Soc., 2000–06. Hon. Life Mem., British-Swiss Chamber of Commerce, 2000. Trustee, Chiswick House Friends, 1998–2012. Freeman, City of London, 1989; Mem. Ct Assts, Masons' Co., 2000– (Master, 2006–07). Commander's Cross, Order of Merit (Liechtenstein), 2007. *Publications:* Liechtenstein: a modern history, 2004 (trans. German, 2005), 2nd edn 2012 (trans. German, 2015). *Recreations:* bridge, walking, history. *Address:* 19 Riverside Place, Colchester, Essex CO1 2ZG. *Club:* Travellers.

BEATTIE, Dame Heather; *see* Steel, Dame A. H.

BEATTIE, Hon. Peter (Douglas), AC 2012; Queensland Government Trade and Investment Commissioner, The Americas, 2008–10; part-time Lecturer, Clemson University, South Carolina, since 2010; *b* 18 Nov. 1952; *s* of Arthur and Edna Beattie; *m* 1975, Heather Scott-Halliday; twin *s* one *d. Educ:* Atherton High Sch.; Univ. of Queensland (BA, LLB); Qld Univ. of Technol. (MA). Admitted Solicitor, Supreme Court of Qld, 1978. MLA (ALP) Brisbane Central, 1989–2007; Minister for Health, 1995–96; Leader, State Opposition, 1996–98; Premier of Qld, 1998–2007; Minister for Trade, 2001–07. Adjunct Prof. in Biosci. and Nanotechnol., Aust. Inst. for Bioengrg and Nanotechnol. and Inst. for Molecular Biosci., Univ. of Qld, 2010–. Member, Board: Med. Res. Commercialisation Fund, 2010–; Univ. of Queensland in America Inc., 2011–13. Chm., Nat. Assoc. of Cinema Operators, 2011–13. Mem., Amer. Bd, Australian American Dialogue, 2010–13. Columnist, The Australian, 2010–. Hon. DSc Queensland, 2003; DUniv: Griffith, 2004; Qld Univ. of Technol., 2007; Bond, 2007; Hon. DLaws S Carolina, 2007. *Publications:* In the Arena, 1990; The Year of the Dangerous Ones, 1994; Making a Difference: life, leadership and politics, 2006; articles in newspapers. *Recreations:* walking, biotechnology history, reading, swimming, alternative energies, writing.

BEATTIE, Trevor Stephen; Creative Director, Beattie McGuinness Bungay, since 2005; *b* 24 Dec. 1958; *s* of late John Vincent Beattie and Ada Alice Beattie. *Educ:* Wolverhampton Poly. (BA Hons). Copywriter, advertising: ABM 1981–83; BMP, 1987–90; joined TBWA/HKR, 1990; Creative Dir, 1993–2005, Chm., 2001–05, TBWA/London (Advertising). Notable ad campaigns: Labour Party, French Connection (fcuk), Sony PlayStation, Wonderbra. Hon. DA: Wolverhampton, 2000; Birmingham, 2011. *Recreations:* flying, gardening, fighting the forces of conservatism, flying to (and from!) space with Virgin Galactic. *Address:* (office) 16 Shorts Gardens, Covent Garden, WC2H 9AU. *T:* (020) 7632 0400.

BEATTY, 3rd Earl *cr* 1919; **David Beatty;** Viscount Borodale of Wexford, Baron Beatty of the North Sea and of Brooksby, 1919; *b* 21 Nov. 1946; *s* of 2nd Earl Beatty, DSC, and of Dorothy Rita, *d* of late M. J. Furey, New Orleans, USA; *S* father, 1972; *m* 1971, Anne (marr. diss. 1983), *d* of A. Please, Wokingham; two *s*; *m* 1984, Anoma Corinne Wijewardene (marr. diss. 2000). *Educ:* Eton. *Heir:* *s* Viscount Borodale, *qv.*

BEATTY, Hon. (Henry) Perrin; PC (Can) 1979; President and Chief Executive Officer, Canadian Chamber of Commerce, since 2007; *b* 1 June 1950; *m* 1974, Julia Kenny; two *s. Educ:* Upper Canada College; Univ. of Western Ontario (BA 1971). MP (Progressive C) Wellington–Grey–Dufferin–Simcoe, Canada, 1972–93; Minister of State for Treasury Bd, 1979; Minister of Nat. Revenue and for Canada Post Corp., 1984; Solicitor General, 1985; Minister of Nat. Defence, 1986–89; Minister of Nat. Health and Welfare, 1989–91; Minister of Communications, 1991–93; Minister for External Affairs, 1993; Pres. and CEO, Canadian Broadcasting Corp., 1995–99; Pres. and CEO, Canadian Manufacturers and Exporters, 1999–2007. Chancellor, Univ. of Ontario Inst. of Technol., 2008–. Hon. Vis. Prof., Univ. of Western Ontario, 1994–95. *Address:* Canadian Chamber of Commerce, 360 Albert Street, Suite 420, Ottawa, ON K1R 7X7, Canada.

BEAUCHAMP, Sir Christopher Radstock Proctor-, 9th Bt *cr* 1744; solicitor with Gilbert Stephens, Exeter, retired; *b* 30 Jan. 1935; *s* of Rev. Sir Ivor Cuthbert Proctor-Beauchamp, 8th Bt, and Caroline Muriel (*d* 1987), *d* of late Frank Densham; *S* father, 1971; *m* 1965, Rosalind Emily Margot (*d* 2014), 3rd *d* of G. P. Wainwright, St Leonards-on-Sea; two *s* one *d. Educ:* Rugby; Trinity College, Cambridge (MA). *Heir:* *s* Charles Barclay Proctor-Beauchamp [*b* 7 July 1969; *m* 1996, Harriet, *e d* of Anthony Meacock; one *s* twin *d*]. *Address:* The Coach House, 4 Balfour Mews, Sidmouth, Devon EX10 8XL.

BEAUCHAMP, Brig. Vernon John; management consultant, since 2011; International Internal Auditor, World Society for the Protection of Animals, 2008–11; *b* 19 Sept. 1943; *s* of late Herbert George Beauchamp and Vera Helena (*née* Daly); *m* 1971, Annemarie, *d* of Evert Teunis van den Born; two *s. Educ:* Portsmouth Grammar Sch.; RMA Sandhurst. Commnd Royal Warwickshire Fusiliers, 1963; transferred 2nd KEO Gurkha Rifles, 1969; served Germany, Borneo, Hong Kong, Brunei, Malaysia and Nepal; Army Staff Coll., 1976; Bde Major, 20 Armoured Bde, 1977–79; NDC, 1981; Comdt, 2 Bn 2nd KEO Gurkha Rifles, 1981–84; sen. staff appts, MoD and HQ BAOR, 1984–87; Comdr, 48 Gurkha Inf. Bde, 1987–89; RCDS, 1990; Comdt, Sch. of Infantry, 1991–93. Chief Executive: Royal Hosp. for Neuro-disability, 1993–2000; Nat. Autistic Soc., 2000–08. *Recreations:* golf, running, gardening. *Address:* 20 Castle Street, Farnham, Surrey GU9 7JA.

BEAUCLERK, family name of **Duke of St Albans.**

BEAUFORT, 11th Duke of, *cr* 1682; **David Robert Somerset;** Earl of Worcester, 1514; Marquess of Worcester, 1642; Chairman, Marlborough Fine Art Ltd, since 1977; *b* 23 Feb. 1928; *s* of late Captain Henry Robert Somers Fitzroy de Vere Somerset, DSO (*d* 1965) (*ggs* of 8th Duke) and late Bettine Violet Somerset (*née* Malcolm) (*d* 1973); *S* cousin, 1984; *m* 1st, 1950, Lady Caroline Jane Thynne (*d* 1995), *d* of 6th Marquess of Bath and of Hon. Daphne Vivian; three *s* one *d*; 2nd, 2000, Miranda Morley. *Educ:* Eton. Formerly Lieutenant, Coldstream Guards. Pres., British Horse Soc., 1988–90. *Heir:* *s* Marquess of Worcester, *qv. Address:* Badminton, S Glos GL9 1DB.

BEAUFOY, Simon Roger Barton; screenwriter and director; *b* Keighley, 26 Dec. 1966; *s* of Roger and Madeleine Beaufoy; *m* Jane Garwood; one *s* one *d. Educ:* Malsis Prep. Sch., Yorks; Ermysted's Grammar Sch., Skipton; Sedbergh Sch.; St Peter's Coll., Oxford; Bournemouth & Poole Coll. of Art and Design (film course 1992). *Television:* (dir) Shattered Dream, 1993; (dir and writer) Physics for Fish, 1994–95; (writer) Burn Up, 2008; *films:* (co-writer and dir) Yellow, 1996; writer: The Full Monty, 1997 (adapted for stage, 2013); Among Giants, 1998; (and co-dir) The Darkest Light, 1999; This is not a Love Song, 2003; Yasmin, 2004; Miss Pettigrew Lives for a Day, 2008; Slumdog Millionaire (Academy, Golden Globe and BAFTA Awards for Best Adapted Screenplay), 2009; Salmon Fishing in the Yemen, 2012. *Recreations:* barge-driving, ski-touring, climbing, river swimming. *Address:* c/o Charlotte Knight, Knight Hall Agency, Lower Ground Floor, 7 Mallow Street, EC1Y 8RQ. *T:* (020) 3397 2901. *E:* office@knighthallagency.com.

BEAUMONT, family name of **Viscount Allendale.**

BEAUMONT, Bill; *see* Beaumont, W. B.

BEAUMONT, David Colin Baskcomb; HM Diplomatic Service, retired; High Commissioner, Botswana, 1995–98; *b* 16 Aug. 1942; *s* of Colin Baskcomb Beaumont and Denise Heather Smith; *m* 1965, Barbara Enid Morris; two *s* one *d. Educ:* St Benedict's Sch., Ealing. Joined CRO, 1961; Private Sec. to Special Rep. in Africa, Nairobi, 1965; Third Sec., Bahrain, 1967; Second Sec., FCO, 1970; Second Sec. (Commercial), Accra, 1974; First Sec., FCO, 1977; First Sec. (Develt), Kathmandu, 1981; First Sec. and Dep. Head of Mission, Addis Ababa, 1982; First Sec., later Counsellor, FCO, 1986; Head of Protocol Dept, 1989–94, and First Asst Marshal of the Diplomatic Corps, 1993–94, FCO. Dir, Guildford Crossroads Care, 1999–2002. *Recreations:* walking, cooking, playing bridge. *Address:* 42 Harvey Road, Guildford, Surrey GU1 3SE. *T:* (01483) 539577. *Clubs:* MCC; Shalford Bridge.

BEAUMONT, Rt Rev. Gerald Edward; Vicar, Parish of St John's, Camberwell, Diocese of Melbourne, 2004–10; *b* 18 Feb. 1940; *s* of John Beaumont and Marjorie Beaumont; *m* 1967, Elsa Lynette Sampson; two *d. Educ:* Australian Coll. of Theology (LTh); Royal Melbourne Inst. of Technology (BA Fine Arts). Deacon 1968, priest 1969, Melbourne; Curate: St Andrew's, Brighton, Vic., 1968–70; Geelong W, 1970–71; Vicar of Mooroolbark, 1971–74; Priest/Pilot, Carpentaria Aerial Mission, Dio. Carpentaria, Qld, 1974–75; Vicar, Armadale-Hawksburn, Vic., 1975–81; Priest-in-Charge, Kooyong, Vic., 1982–86; Vicar, E Melbourne, 1986–92; Canon Pastor, St George's Cathedral, Perth, WA, 1992–94; Rector, Ascension, Alice Springs, NT, and Hon. Canon, Christ Church Cathedral, Darwin, 1995–98; an Asst Bishop, Dio. of Perth, WA (Bp of Goldfields-Country Region), 1998–2004. *Recreations:* painting (exhibiting professional artist), motorcycling. *Club:* Ulysses (Melbourne).

BEAUMONT, (John) Michael, OBE 2001; Seigneur of Sark, since 1974; *b* 20 Dec. 1927; *s* of late Lionel (Buster) Beaumont and Enid Beaumont (*née* Ripley), and *g s* of Dame Sibyl Hathaway, Dame of Sark; *m* 1956, Diana (*née* La Trobe-Bateman); two *s. Educ:* Loughborough Coll. (DLC). Aircraft Design Engr, 1952–70; Chief Techn. Engr, Beagle Aircraft, 1969–70; Design Engr, BAC GW Div., 1970–75. *Recreations:* theatre, music, gardening. *Heir:* *s* Christopher Beaumont, *b* 4 Feb. 1957. *Address:* La Petite Seigneurie, Sark, Channel Islands GY10 1SF. *T:* (01481) 832017.

BEAUMONT, John Richard; President, Beaumont Partners sprl, since 2007; *b* 24 June 1957; *s* of Jim Beaumont and Betty Marie (*née* Jarratt); *m* 2000, Annie Margaret (*née* Jupp); two *d* by a previous marriage. *Educ:* Univ. of Durham (BA Geog.). Res. Asst, Univ. of Leeds, 1978–80; Lectr, Univ. of Keele, 1980–83; Consultant, Coopers & Lybrand (London and NY), 1983–85; Jt Man. Dir, Pinpoint Analysis Ltd, London, 1985–87; ICL Prof. of Applied Management Information Systems and Dir, European Centre for Inf. Resource Management, Univ. of Stirling, 1987–90; Prof. and Hd of Sch. of Management, Bath Univ., 1990–92. Man. Dir, Stratatech, 1986–93; Energis Communications Ltd: Strategy Planning Manager, 1993–94; Head of Corporate Strategy and Affairs, 1994–95; Dir of Marketing, 1995–96; Dir of Strategy and Business Develt, 1996–99; Man. Dir, Planet Online Ltd, subseq. Energis^2, 1998–2002; Dir, Energis plc, 2001–02; CEO, UK eUniversities Worldwide Ltd, 2002–04; Partner, Beaumont and Beaumont Ltd, 2004–05; CEO, QA plc, 2005–06; Man. Dir and Hd of UK Public Services, BearingPoint Ltd, 2006–07. Chairman: Ision AG, 2001–02; LifeCash Ltd, 2011–14; Dep. Chm. Supervisory Bd, Business Online AG, 1999–2000; Dir, Metro Hldgs Ltd, 1998–2002; non-executive Director: WorldPay Ltd, 1999–2002; European Telecommunications and Technology Ltd, 1999–2003; Novia Financial plc, 2007– (Dep. Chm.); Chm., Novia Global Ltd, 2014–. Non-executive Director: Office of Nat. Statistics, 1996–99; UK Health Educn Partnership, 2003–04; Real Club de Golf Las Brisas, 2012–; Emergent Capital Partners, 2014–. Hon. Professor: QUB, 1990–93; City Univ., 1994–98. Mem. Council, ESRC, 1989–93. *Publications:* (with P. Keys) Future Cities, 1982; (with A. Gatrell) An Introduction to Q-Analysis, 1982; (with S. Williams) Projects in Geography, 1983; An Introduction to Market Analysis, 1991; (with E. Sutherland) Information Resources Management, 1992; (jtly) Managing our Environment, 1993. *Recreations:* family, good wine and food, travel, golf, watching Rugby (League and Union), reading fiction. *Address:* Allée du Bois de Bercuit 129, 1390 Grez-Doiceau, Belgium.

BEAUMONT, John Richard; Regional Chairman of Employment Tribunals (North West Region), 1999–2002; *b* 22 June 1947; *s* of late Stanley and Winifred Beaumont; *m* 1986, Susan Margaret (*née* Blowers); one *s* two *d*, and one step *s. Educ:* Wolverhampton Grammar Sch.; Merton Coll., Oxford (BA 1969; MA 1973). Schoolmaster, Buckingham Coll., Harrow, 1969–71; Regl Organiser, W Midlands, 1971–73, Nat. Dir of Projects, 1973–74, Shelter; Senior Legal Officer: Alnwick DC, 1974; Thurrock BC, 1974–75; called to the Bar, Inner Temple, 1976; in practice at the Bar, Northern Circuit, 1976–94; Chm., Industrial, then Employment, Tribunals, subseq. Employment Judge, 1994–2008 (pt-time, 1992–94); Chm., Reserve Forces Appeal Tribunal, 1999–2008. Gov., Knutsford High Sch., 1999 (Vice-Chm., 2000–02; Chm., 2002–07). *Recreations:* walking, reading (especially Victorian history and literature), family picnics, non-league football (League Rep., Unibond Northern Premier League). *Address:* Carlton House, Seymour Chase, Knutsford, Cheshire WA16 9BY.

BEAUMONT, Martin Dudley, FCA; Chairman, Chester Race Course Co., since 2011 (Director, since 2007); *b* 6 Aug. 1949; *s* of Patrick Beaumont, DL and late Lindesay Beaumont; *m* 1976, Andrea Wilberforce; three *d. Educ:* Stowe Sch.; Magdalene Coll., Cambridge (MA Econs/Land Economy). FCA 1975. Dir, 1980–83, Partner, 1983–87, Thomson McLintock, subseq. KPMG; Gp Finance Dir, Egmont Publishing Gp, 1987–90; Chief Financial Officer, 1990–92, Chief Exec., 1992–2002, United Co-operatives; Dir, 1996–2007, Dep. Chm., 2000–07, Co-operative Bank; Gp Chief Exec., Co-operative Gp, 2002–07; Dep. Chm., Co-operative Financial Services, 2002–07; Dir, CIS, 2002–07. Chairman: Skillsmart Retail Ltd, 2007–12; Kind Consumer Ltd, 2009–. Dir, PBSI Gp, 2010–12. Mem. of Adv. Bd, Kurt

Salmon Associates, 2008–14. Dir, 2005–07, Dep. Chm., 2006–07, NW Business Leadership Team. Mem. Council, Duchy of Lancaster, 2007–. High Sheriff, Cheshire, 2013–14. *Recreations:* family, fishing, shooting, tennis, reading.

BEAUMONT, Michael; *see* Beaumont, J. M.

BEAUMONT, His Honour Peter John Luther, CBE 2013; QC 1986; a Circuit Judge, 1989–2013; *b* 10 Jan. 1944; *s* of S. P. L. Beaumont, OBE, and D. V. Beaumont; *m* 1970, Ann Jarratt; one *s* one *d*. *Educ:* Peterhouse, Zimbabwe; Univ. of Zimbabwe (BScEcon Hons). Called to the Bar, Lincoln's Inn, 1967 (Bencher, 2001); practised South Eastern Circuit; a Recorder, 1986; Common Serjeant, City of London, 2001–04; Recorder of London, 2004–13. Member: Parole Bd, 1992–97; Criminal Cttee, Judicial Studies Bd, 2000–03; Sentencing Guidelines Council, 2004–10. Governor, Felsted Sch., 1990–2002 (Chm., 1993–98). *Recreations:* golf, tennis, gardening. *Address:* 111 Church Street, Orford, Suffolk IP12 2LL. *T:* (01394) 450 967. *Club:* Travellers.

BEAUMONT, Prof. Steven Peter, OBE 2002; PhD; CEng, FREng; FRSE; Professor of Nanoelectronics, since 1989, and Vice Principal for Research and Enterprise, 2005–14, now Emeritus, University of Glasgow; *b* Norwich, 20 Feb. 1952; *s* of Albert Reginald Beaumont and Joyce Margaret Beaumont (later Churchard) and step *s* of Arthur Robert Churchard; *m* 1977, Joanne Mary Beaumont; one *s* two *d*. *Educ:* Norwich Sch.; Corpus Christi Coll., Cambridge (BA 1974; PhD 1979). CEng 1987, MIET 1987; FREng 2007; FRSE 2000. University of Glasgow: Res. Fellow, 1978–83; Barr & Stroud Lectr, then Sen. Lectr, 1983–89; Hd, Dept of Electronics and Electrical Engrg, 1994–98; Dir, Inst. for System Level Integration, 1999–2004. Tech. Dir, Intellemetrics Ltd, 1982–90; Director: Photonix Ltd, 2003–10; GU Hldgs Ltd, 2005–15; Kelvin Nanotechnology Ltd, 2005–; Gold Standard Simulations Ltd, 2011–; Anacail Ltd, 2011–15; Clyde Bioscis Ltd, 2012–15; Cronin 3D Ltd, 2014–; Thermoelectric Conversion Systems Ltd, 2014–. Mem., Scottish Sci. Adv. Cttee, Scottish Govt, 2005–09. Awards Convener, RSE, 2011–. *Publications:* contrib. papers to learned jls and at major academic confs. *Recreations:* crofting, reading, listening to music. *Address:* 11 The Square, University of Glasgow, Glasgow G12 8QQ.

BEAUMONT, William Anderson, CB 1986; OBE (mil.) 1961; AE 1953; Speaker's Secretary, House of Commons, 1982–86; *b* 30 Oct. 1924; *s* of late William Lionel Beaumont and Mrs E. Taverner; *m* 1st, 1946, Kythé (*d* 1988), *d* of late Major K. G. Mackenzie, Victoria, BC; one *d*; 2nd, 1989, Rosalie (*d* 2010), *widow* of Judge Michael Underhill, QC. *Educ:* Terrington Hall, York; Cranleigh Sch. (Entrance Exhibnr); Christ Church, Oxford (MA (Hons) 1950, DipEd (Dist.) 1951). Served RAF, Navigator, 1942–47, 355 Sqdn, 232 Sqdn, SEAC (FO). Asst Master, Bristol Grammar Sch., 1951–54; Beaumont and Smith Ltd, Pudsey, 1954–66 (Man. Dir, 1958–66); Henry Mason (Shipley) Ltd (Man. Dir, 1966–76); Principal, Welsh Office, 1976–79; Asst Sec., Welsh Office, 1979–82. RAuxAF 3507 (Co. of Somerset) FCU, 1948–54; 3609 (W Riding) FCU, 1954–61 (Wing Comdr CO, 1958–61); Observer Comdr, No 18 (Leeds) Gp, Royal Observer Corps, 1962–75 (ROC Medal 1975). A Chm. of Assessors, CSSB, 1988–92. Dir, St David's Forum, 1986–92; Sec., Prince of Wales Award Gp, 1987–90; Mem., Awards Cttee, RAF Benevolent Fund, 1990–2007; Vice-Chm., Franco-British Soc., 1991–98. *Recreations:* pontificating, watching gardening. *Address:* The Royal Star and Garter Home, Upper Brighton Road, Surbiton, Surrey KT6 4JY. *Clubs:* Royal Air Force, Civil Service; United Services Mess (Cardiff); Nothing (Richmond).

BEAUMONT, William Blackledge, (Bill), CBE 2008 (OBE 1982); DL; Rugby Union footballer, retired; sports broadcaster and writer; Managing Director, Bill Beaumont Textiles Ltd, since 1998; *b* 9 March 1952; *s* of Ronald Walton Beaumont and Joyce Beaumont; *m* 1977, Hilary Jane Seed; three *s*. *Educ:* Ellesmere Coll., Shropshire. Joined family textile business, 1971; Dir, J. Blackledge & Son Ltd, 1981–98. First played Rugby Union for England, 1975; 34 caps (20 caps as Captain); Mem., British Lions, NZ tour, 1977; Captain, British Lions, S Africa tour, 1980; played for Lancashire Barbarians, retd 1982. Chm., British Lions, NZ tour, 2005. Television includes A Question of Sport (BBC TV), 1982–96. Mem., Internat. Rugby Bd, 1999– (Vice Chm.); Chm., RFU, 2012–. DL Lancs, 2012. *Publications:* Thanks to Rugby, 1982; Bill Beaumont's Tackle Rugby, 1983; Bill Beaumont's Sporting Year Book, 1984; Bill Beaumont: the autobiography, 2003; (with Mark Baldwin) Beaumont's Up and Under, 2005. *Recreations:* tennis, golf, water ski-ing. *Clubs:* East India, MCC; Fylde Rugby Union Football; Royal Lytham St Anne's Golf.

BEAUREPAIRE, Dame Beryl (Edith), AC 1991; DBE 1981 (OBE 1975); *b* 24 Sept. 1923; *d* of late E. L. Bedggood; *m* 1946, Ian Francis Beaurepaire, CMG (*d* 1996); two *s*. *Educ:* Fintona Girls' Sch., Balwyn, Victoria; Univ. of Melbourne. ASO, WAAAF, 1942–45. Mem. Nat. Exec., YWCA Australia, 1969–77. Liberal Party of Australia: Chm., Victorian Women's Sect., 1973–76; Chm., Federal Women's Sect., 1974–76; Vice-Pres., Victorian Div., 1976–86. Mem., Federal Women's Adv. Cttee Working Party, 1977. Pres., Victorian Assoc. of Order of British Empire, 1988–90. Vice Pres., Citizen's Welfare Service, Vic, 1970–86; Convenor, Nat. Women's Adv. Council, Australia, 1978–82. Member: Council, Australian War Memorial, 1982–93 (Chm., 1985–93; Chm., Fund Raising Cttee, 1993–96); Australian Children's Television Foundation Bd, 1982–88; Bd, Victoria's 150th Authy, 1982–87; Australian Bi-centennial Multicultural Foundn, 1989–92. Chm., Bd of Management, Fintona Girls' Sch., 1973–87; Patron: Portsea (formerly Portsea Children's) Camp, 1996–; Palliative Care Victoria, 1997–; Children First Foundn, 2000–; Child & Family Care Network, 2000–. Silver Jubilee Medal, 1977; Centenary Medal, 2003. *Address:* c/o Beaucorp Pty Ltd, PO Box 2092, North Brighton, Vic 3186, Australia. *Clubs:* Alexandra; Peninsula Country Golf (Frankston).

BEAVER, Dr Sarah Ann; Fellow and Bursar, All Souls College, Oxford, since 2008; *b* 5 Feb. 1952; *d* of John Maurice Wilks and Ida Elizabeth Wilks (*née* Clements); *m* 1979, Rev. Dr William Carpenter Beaver, *qv*; two *s*. *Educ:* Bath High Sch., GPDST; Somerville Coll., Oxford (MA Modern Hist.); Sheffield Univ. (Cert Ed); Wolfson Coll., Oxford (DPhil 1979). Asst Mistress, Lord Williams's Sch., Thame, 1974–76; Jun. Res. Fellow, Wolfson Coll., Oxford, 1978–80; Lectr, Balliol Coll., Oxford, 1979–80; Ministry of Defence, 1980–: Principal, 1985; Hd, Materiel Co-ordination (Navy), 1994; Dir, Procurement Finance, 1995–98; on loan to Nat. Assembly for Wales as Dir, NHS Finance, 1998–2002; Dir, EU and UN, 2002–04; Dir Gen., Internat. Security Policy, 2004–07; Command Sec., Perm. Jt HQ (UK), MoD, 2007–08. Trustee, Marie Curie Cancer Care, 2007–. *Recreations:* cycling, gardening. *Address:* All Souls College, Oxford OX1 4AL. *T:* (01865) 279332. *E:* sarah.beaver@all-souls.ox.ac.uk.

BEAVER, Rev. Dr William Carpenter, II; Officiating Chaplain to Household Division and Household Cavalry Mounted Regiment, 2009–15; Curate, St Mary the Virgin, Iffley, Oxford, since 2011; *b* 17 Sept. 1945; *s* of late William Carpenter Beaver, MD and Margaret Edith Beaver, MD (*née* Nelson); *m* 1979, Sarah Ann Wilks (*see* S. A. Beaver); two *s*. *Educ:* Colorado Coll., USA (BA 1967; Benezet Distinguished Alumnus, 2000); US Army Comd and Staff Coll. (psc 1980); Wolfson Coll., Oxford (Beit Sen. Schol., Rhodes House; DPhil 1976); St Stephen's House, Oxford (CTh 1982). Served US Army, 1967–71 (Bronze Star (valour, thrice); Meritorious Service Medal; Air Medal; Combat Infantry Badge), Reserves, 1971–96. Exec. Dir, Univ. of Oxford Develt Records Project, and Jun. Res. Fellow, Wolfson Coll., Oxford, 1977–80; Dep. Hd, Corporate and Community Communications, J. Walter Thompson, 1980–83; Dir, Publicity, Barnardo's, 1983–89; Group Director: Public Affairs, Pergamon AGB Internat. Res., 1989–90; Corporate Affairs, Nat. Westminster Bank, 1990–92; Dir, Marketing, The Industrial Soc., 1992–97; Dir of Communications, C of E, 1997–2002, BRCS, 2002–03; Office of the Lord Mayor of London, 2003–10. Vice-Chm. (Cadets), Reserve Forces and Cadets Assoc. Gtr London, 2010–15. Ordained deacon, 1982, priest, 1983; Curate: St John the Divine, Kennington, 1982–95; St Mary Redcliffe, Bristol, 1995–2008; St Andrew, Holborn, 2001–04; Univ. Ch of St Mary the Virgin, Oxford, 2010–11; Hon. Priest-in-charge, St Andrew's, Avonmouth, 1995–98. Chaplain, Mercers' Co., 2002–10. Vice Chm., Charles Edward Brooke Sch., Brixton, 1992–2002. Mem., Pilgrim Soc., 2008–. FCIPR (FIPR 2003). Freeman, Art Scholars' Co., 2013–. Editor, Heraldic Craftsman, 2012–. SBStJ 2012. *Publications:* Under Every Leaf, 2012. *Recreation:* bicycling. *Address:* Townsend Close, 50 Church Way, Iffley, Oxford OX4 4EF.

BEAVERBROOK, 3rd Baron *cr* 1917, of Beaverbrook, New Brunswick, and of Cherkley, Surrey; **Maxwell William Humphrey Aitken;** Bt 1916; Chairman, Beaverbrook Foundation, since 1985; *b* 29 Dec. 1951; *s* of Sir (John William) Max Aitken, 2nd Bt, DSO, DFC, and of Violet, *d* of Sir Humphrey de Trafford, 4th Bt, MC; *S* to disclaimed barony of father, 1985; *m* 1974, Susan Angela More O'Ferrall; two *s* two *d*. *Educ:* Charterhouse; Pembroke Coll., Cambridge; RCDS. Beaverbrook Newspapers Ltd, 1973–77; Dir, Ventech, 1983–86; Chm., Ventech Healthcare Corp. Inc., 1986, 1988–92. Govt spokesman for Home Office and DTI, H of L, 1986; a Lord in Waiting (Government Whip), 1986–88; Dep. Treas., 1988–90, Treas., 1990–92, Cons. Party; Treas., European Democratic Union, 1990–92. Chairman: Net Integration Inc., 2000–07; Pine Ventures plc, 2007–10. Chm., Nat. Assoc. of Boys' Clubs, 1989–92. Mem. Council, Homeopathic Trust, 1986–92. Hon. Air Cdre, 4624 Sqn, 2004–09, Hon. Inspector Gen. (Air Vice-Marshal), 2009–, RAuxAF. *Recreations:* motor sport (Eur. GT Champion, 1998), offshore powerboat racing (winner, Harmsworth Trophy, 2004). *Heir:* *s* Hon. Maxwell Francis Aitken [*b* 17 March 1977; *m* 2007, Inés Nieto Gómez-Valencia; one *s* one *d*]. *Address:* Ashlett House, Fawley, Hants SO45 1DT. *Clubs:* White's, Royal Air Force; Royal Yacht Squadron; British Racing Drivers'; British Powerboat Racing (Chm., 2003–).

See also Marquis of Bowmont and Cessford.

BEAVIS, Andrew William, PhD; Chief Scientific Officer, Vertual Ltd, since 2007; Head, Radiation Physics, Hull and East Yorkshire NHS Hospitals Trust, since 2008; *b* Northampton, 1 Jan. 1966; *s* of Colin Beavis and Gillian Beavis; *m* 1990, Sally Andrew; two *s* one *d*. *Educ:* Longcroft Sch., Beverley; Univ. of Newcastle upon Tyne (BSc Hons 1st Cl. 1987; PhD 1990). CPhys 1990; MInstP 1990; CSci 2000; FIPEM 2007; FBIR 2012. Clinical Scientist (Med. Physics), Hull and East Yorks NHS Hosps Trust, 1992–. Vis. Prof., Sheffield Hallam Univ., 2005–; Hon. Prof., Univ. of Hull, 2008–. Member: Amer. Assoc. of Physicists in Medicine, 1998; Inst. of Physics in Medicine, 2000; Eur. Soc. for Radiotherapy and Oncol., 2009. MInstD 2013. *Publications:* scientific articles in jls, 1987–. *Recreations:* music (Hawkwind, Motorhead, etc), Rugby League, Rugby Union, family. *Address:* Vertual Ltd, Logistics Institute, University of Hull, Cottingham Road, Hull, E Yorks HU6 7RX. *T:* (01482) 347572. *E:* andy@vertual.co.uk.

BEAVIS, Air Chief Marshal Sir Michael (Gordon), KCB 1981; CBE 1977 (OBE 1969); AFC 1962; Director, Skye Pharma PLC (formerly Tubular Edgington Group, then Black & Edgington Group), 1989–2006; *b* 13 Aug. 1929; *s* of Walter Erle Beavis and Mary Ann (*née* Sarjantson); *m* 1950, Joy Marion (*née* Jones); one *s* one *d*. *Educ:* Kilburn Grammar Sch. Joined RAF 1947; commnd 1949; served Fighter Comd Squadrons 1950–54, RNZAF 1954–56; flew Vulcan aircraft, Bomber Comd, 1958–62; Staff Coll., 1963; MoD, 1964–66; OC No 10 Squadron (VC10s), 1966–68; Group Captain Flying, Akrotiri, Cyprus, 1968–71; Asst Dir, Defence Policy, MoD, 1971–73; RCDS, 1974; RAF Germany, 1975–77 (SASO 1976–77), Dir Gen. RAF Training, 1977–80; Comdt, RAF Staff Coll., 1980–81; AOC-in-C, RAF Support Comd, 1981–84; Dep. C-in-C, AFCENT, 1984–86. Dir, Alliance Aircraft Co., USA, 2000–03. CCMI. Freeman, City of London, 1980; Liveryman, Hon. Co. of Air Pilots (formerly GAPAN), 1983. *Recreations:* bridge, sociable lunches. *Address:* c/o Lloyds, 202 High Street, Lincoln LN5 7AP. *Club:* Royal Air Force.

BEAZER, Brian Cyril; Chairman and Chief Executive, Beazer (formerly C. H. Beazer (Holdings)) PLC, 1983–91; Chairman, Beazer Homes USA Inc., since 1992; *b* 22 Feb. 1935; *s* of late Cyril Henry George Beazer and of Ada Vera Beazer; *m* 1958, Patricia (*née* White); one *d*. *Educ:* Wells Cathedral School. Joined C. H. Beazer, 1958; Man. Dir, 1968; apptd Chm. and Chief Exec. on death of his father in 1983. *Recreations:* walking, reading. *Address:* The Weavers House, Castle Combe, Wiltshire SN14 7HX.

BEAZLEY, Christopher John Pridham; Member (C) Eastern Region, England, European Parliament, 1999–2009; *b* 5 Sept. 1952; *s* of late Peter George Beazley, CBE; *m* 1978, Christiane Marie Elyane (*née* Dillemann); two *s* one *d*. *Educ:* Shrewsbury; Bristol Univ. Former Nuffield Research Fellow, School of European Studies, Sussex Univ. Vice Chm., Lewes and Eastbourne branch, European Movement, 1980; Wealden DC, 1979–83. MEP (C) Cornwall and Plymouth, 1984–94; contested (C) Cornwall and W Plymouth, Eur. Parly elecns, 1994; European Parliament: spokesman on regl policy, 1984–89, on justice and home affairs, 1992–94, on constitutional affairs, 1999–2001, on educn and culture, 2001; Vice-Chairman: Transport Cttee, 1989–91; Baltic States Delegn, 1991–94; Mem., Foreign Affairs Cttee, 2007–09; Chairman: Estonian Delegn, 2001–04; Baltic States Intergp, 2004–09. Order of the Cross of Terra Mariana (Estonia), 2009; Comdr of the Order of the Three Stars (Latvia), 2009; Cross of Comdr, Order for Merits to Lithuania, 2010.

BEAZLEY, Hon. Kim Christian, AC 2009; Australian Ambassador to the United States of America, since 2010; *b* 14 Dec. 1948; *s* of late Hon. Kim Edward Beazley and of Betty Beazley; *m* 1st, 1974, Mary Paltridge (marr. diss. 1989); two *d*; 2nd, 1990, Susanna Annus; one *d*. *Educ:* Univ. of Western Australia (MA); Oxford Univ. (Rhodes Scholar; MPhil). Tutor in Social and Political Theory, Murdoch Univ., WA, 1976–79, Lectr 1980. MP (ALP) Swan, Perth, 1980–96, Brand, Perth, 1996–2007, Australia; Minister of State for Aviation, and Minister Assisting the Minister for Defence, 1983–84; Special Minister of State, 1983–84; Minister of State for Defence, 1984–90; Minister for Transport and Communications, 1990–91, for Finance, 1991, for Employment, Educn and Training, 1991–93, for Finance, 1993–96; Leader of the House of Representatives, 1988–96 (Vice-Pres., Exec. Council, 1988–91); Dep. Prime Minister, 1995–96; Leader of the Opposition, 1996–2001 and 2005–06. Mem., Jt Parly Cttee on Foreign Affairs and Defence, 1980–83, 2002–05, on Aust Security Intelligence Orgn, ASIS and DSD, 2002–05. Mem. Nat. Exec., ALP, 1991–94, 1996–2001. Member: Bd, Defence S Australia, 2008–10; Council, Aust. Nat. War Meml, 2009. Chancellor, ANU, 2009–10. Professorial Fellow, UWA, 2007–10. Mem. Adv. Bd, Army Jl, 2007–10. Hon. LLD Notre Dame Australia, 2014. *Publications:* (with I. Clark) The Politics of Intrusion: the Super-Powers in the Indian Ocean, 1979. *Recreations:* swimming, reading. *Address:* Australian Embassy, 1601 Massachusetts Avenue, Washington, DC NW 20036–2273, USA.

BEAZLEY, Richard Hugh; Vice Lord-Lieutenant of Hertfordshire, since 2010; *b* Broxbourne, 16 June 1949; *s* of late John Beazley, DFC and Mary Beazley, MBE; *m* 1977, Violet Bradford; two *s*. *Educ:* Cheltenham Coll.; Exeter Univ. (LLB). Lawyer, economist and Chief Exec. of various Mobil Oil Corp. subsidiaries, living in Norway, Indonesia, Canada, USA and UK, 1976–2000. Chm., E and N Herts NHS Trust, 2002–12. Trustee, Florence Nightingale Foundn, 2008– (Vice Chm., 2011–). Chm., Bd of Govs, Univ. of Hertfordshire, 2013–. DL Herts, 2004. Hon. Col, Beds and Herts ACF, 2014–. *Recreations:* cross-country ski-ing, walking, shooting. *Address:* New Hall, Standon, Herts SG11 1NX. *T:* (01279) 842717. *Club:* Travellers.

BEAZLEY, Thomas Alan George; QC 2001; *b* 2 March 1951; *s* of late Derek Edwin George Beazley and of Rosemary Janet Beazley; *m* 1980, Ingrid Ann Marrable; two *d*. *Educ:*

Emmanuel Coll., Cambridge (BA; LLB). Called to the Bar, Middle Temple, 1979; Hd of Chambers, Blackstone Chambers, 2004–12; Hd of Internat. Litigation, Joseph Hage Aaronson LLP, 2013–. *Recreations:* reading, travelling, cooking. *Address:* Hage Aaronson, 7th Floor, 280 High Holborn, WC1V 7EE.

BEBB, Gordon Montfort; QC 2002; a Recorder, since 2001; *b* 1 May 1952; *s* of Simon and Adonia Montfort Bebb; *m* 1978, Rachel Millington; one *s* one *d*. *Educ:* Winchester Coll.; Magdalen Coll., Oxford (MA). Called to the Bar, Middle Temple, 1975; Asst Recorder, 1997–2001. Chm. of Trustees, Blond McIndoe Med. Res. Foundn. *Recreations:* theatre, art, music, sport. *Address:* Outer Temple Chambers, The Outer Temple, 222 Strand, WC2R 1BA. *T:* (020) 7353 6381, *Fax:* (020) 7583 1786. *Clubs:* Boodle's, Jesters.

BEBB, Guto ap Owain; MP (C) Aberconwy, since 2010; *b* Wrexham, 9 Oct. 1968; *s* of Owain Bebb and Helen Gwyn; *m* 1993, Esyllt Penri; three *s* two *d* (incl. twin *s*). *Educ:* Univ. of Wales, Aberystwyth (BA Hist. 1990). Founder, Partneriaeth Egin Partnership, econ. develt consultancy, 1993–2010. Business Develt Dir, Innovas Wales. Contested (C): Ogmore, Feb. 2002; Conwy, 2005. *Recreations:* reading, music. *Address:* House of Commons, SW1A 0AA. *T:* (020) 7219 7002. *E:* guto.bebb.mp@parliament.uk.

BEBBINGTON, Prof. Warren Arthur, PhD; Vice Chancellor, and President, University of Adelaide, since 2012; *b* Caulfield, Vic, 1952; *s* of Arthur and Thelma Bebbington; *m* 1st, 1981 (marr. diss. 1989); 2nd, 1991, Barbara Watson; three *s*. *Educ:* Caulfield High Sch.; Univ. of Melbourne (BMus; MMus); City Univ., NY (MA; MPhil; PhD 1983). Conductor of choirs and opera in Australia, 1979–2005. Lectr, Canberra Sch. of Music, 1979–85; res. asst to Prof. Gustave Reese, NY, 1978; Dean of Music, Univ. of Qld, 1985–91; University of Melbourne: Dean of Music, 1991–2005; Pro Vice Chancellor, 2006–10; Dep. Vice Chancellor, 2010–12. *Publications:* Oxford Companion to Australian Music, 1997; A Dictionary of Australian Music, 1998. *Recreations:* sailing, flying. *Address:* University of Adelaide, North Terrace, SA 5005, Australia. *T:* 883035201. *E:* vice-chancellor@adelaide.edu.au. *Club:* Adelaide.

BECHER, Sir John (William Michael) Wrixon-, 6th Bt *cr* 1831, of Ballygiblin, co. Cork; Chairman, Future Electric Ltd, since 2008; Consultant, Weatherbys Private Bank and Weatherbys Hamilton Insurance Brokers, since 2014; *b* 29 Sept. 1950; *s* of Sir William Fane Wrixon-Becher, 5th Bt, MC and Hon. Vanda Wrixon-Becher (who later *m* 9th Earl of Glasgow), *d* of 4th Baron Vivian; *S* father, 2000. *Educ:* Ludgrove; Harrow; Neuchâtel Univ. G. N. Rouse & Others, 1971–74; Lloyds Broker, Eckersley Hicks Ltd, 1974–82; Hutchison Craft Financial Services Ltd, 1982–87; Dir, Wise Speke Financial Services Ltd, 1987–93; Financial Consultant, HSBC Actuaries and Consultants Ltd, 1993–2000; Partner, Ford Reynolds and Associates Ltd, 2000–05. Director: Old Street Productions Ltd, 2001–03; Wind Energy Ltd, 2002–04. *Recreation:* shooting a line and fishing for compliments. *Address:* The Stables, Garnons, Herefordshire HR4 7JU. *Clubs:* White's, MCC; I Zingari.

BECK, Rev. Brian Edgar, MA; President of the Methodist Conference, 1993–94; Secretary of the Conference, 1984–98; *b* 27 Sept. 1933; *o s* of late A. G. and C. A. Beck; *m* 1958, Margaret Ludlow; three *d*. *Educ:* City of London School; Corpus Christi College, Cambridge (1st Cl. Classical Tripos pts 1 and 2); Wesley House, Cambridge (1st Cl. Theol. Tripos pt 2). BA 1955, MA 1959. Ordained Methodist Minister, 1960; Asst Tutor, Handsworth Coll., 1957–59; E Suffolk Circuit Minister, 1959–62; St Paul's United Theological Coll., Limuru, Kenya, 1962–68; Tutor, Wesley House, Cambridge, 1968–80, Principal 1980–84. Sec., E African Church Union Consultation Worship and Liturgy Cttee, 1963–68; Mem., World Methodist Council, 1966–71, 1981–98; Co-Chm., Oxford Inst. of Methodist Theol. Studies, 1976–2002. Hon. Chaplain, Guild of St Bride, Fleet Street, 1994–. Fernley-Hartley Lectr, 1978; Vis. Prof., Wesley Theol Seminary, Washington, 1999. DD Lambeth, 1998. *Publications:* Reading the New Testament Today, 1977; Christian Character in the Gospel of St Luke, 1989; Gospel Insights, 1998; Exploring Methodism's Heritage, 2004; (ed jtly) Unmasking Methodist Theology, 2004; contributor to: Christian Belief, a Catholic-Methodist statement, 1970; Unity the Next Step?, 1972; Suffering and Martyrdom in the New Testament, 1981; Rethinking Wesley's Theology, 1998; Community-Unity-Communion, 1998; Managing the Church?, 2000; Apostolicity and Unity, 2002; Reflections on Ministry, 2004; A Thankful Heart and a Discerning Mind, 2010; The Ashgate Research Companion to World Methodism, 2013; articles in NT Studies, Epworth Review. *Recreations:* walking, DIY, cross-stitch. *Address:* 26 Hurrell Road, Cambridge CB4 3RH. *T:* (01223) 312260.

BECK, Clive; *b* 12 April 1937; *s* of Sir Edgar Charles Beck, CBE, and Mary Agnes Beck; *m* 1960, Philippa Flood; three *s* three *d*. *Educ:* Ampleforth College. 2nd Lieut, The Life Guards, 1956–57; John Mowlem & Co., 1957–67; SGB Group, 1967–86; Dep. Chm., John Mowlem & Co., 1986–92. Director: London Management Ltd, 1990–; Pioneer Concrete Holdings plc, 1990–97. *Recreation:* golf. *Address:* 8 Atherton Drive, Wimbledon, SW19 5LB. *Clubs:* Royal Wimbledon Golf, Swinley Forest Golf.

See also Sir E. P. Beck.

BECK, Sir (Edgar) Philip, Kt 1988; Chairman: John Mowlem & Co., 1979–95; Railtrack, 1999–2001; *b* 9 Aug. 1934; *s* of Sir Edgar Charles Beck, CBE, and Mary Agnes Beck; *m* 1st, 1957, Thomasina Joanna Jeal (marr. diss.); two *s*; 2nd, 1991, Bridget Cockerell (*née* Heathcoat-Amory). *Educ:* Ampleforth College; Jesus College, Cambridge (MA). Dir, John Mowlem, 1964, Dep. Chm., 1978–79. Chairman: FCEC, 1982–83; Export Group for Constructional Industries, 1986–88. Non-executive Director: Invensys, 1992–2003; Delta, 1993–2004.

See also C. Beck.

BECK, Lydia Helena; *see* Lopes Cardozo Kindersley, L. H.

BECK, Peter, MD; FRCP; Lord-Lieutenant for South Glamorgan, since 2008; *b* Leicester, 4 July 1941; *s* of Frank Beck and Kittie Eileen Beck (*née* Clark); *m* 1964, Lyn Davies; one *s* one *d*. *Educ:* Wyggeston Boys' Sch., Leicester; St Mary's Hosp. Med. Sch., London (MB BS Hons 1965; MD 1976); MA Wales 1989. FRCP 1980. VSO Jordan, 1961–62. Jun. posts, St Mary's and Hammersmith Hosps, 1965–67; SHO, then Registrar, Cardiff Royal Infirmary, 1967–70; Lectr, Welsh Nat. Sch. of Medicine, Cardiff, 1970–71; MRC Clin. Res. Fellow, Cardiff, 1971–73; Wellcome Travelling Fellow, Harvard Med. Sch., 1974–75; Consultant Physician, Cardiff Teaching Hosps, 1974–2003. Surgeon Comdr, RNR, 1975–91. President: Cardiff and Vale of Glamorgan Boy Scouts, 2007–; Cttee, Wales Festival of Remembrance, 2008– (Chm., 2007); Vice President: ABF S Glamorgan, 2008–; RFCA S Glamorgan, 2008–; Chm., Lord Chancellor's Adv. Cttee on JPs, 2008–; Patron, SSAFA, S Glamorgan, 2011–. DL S Glamorgan, 1994–2008. CStJ 2008 (OStJ 2006; Chm., 2006–08, Pres., 2008–, Council, S Glamorgan). *Publications:* contrib. papers on haemophilia, angio-oedema, immuno-assay, diabetes and med. ethics. *Recreations:* golf, Rugby, family, art, ski-ing. *Address:* Tyla Teg, 46 Ty Gwyn Road, Penylan, Cardiff CF23 5JG. *T:* (029) 2048 5982. *E:* pandlbeck@tiscali.co.uk. *Clubs:* Army and Navy; Cardiff and County; Royal Porthcawl Golf.

BECK, Sir Philip; *see* Beck, Sir E. P.

BECKE, Prof. Axel Dieter, PhD; FRS 2006; FRSC; Killam Professor of Computational Science, Dalhousie University, since 2006; *b* Esslingen, Germany, 10 June 1953. *Educ:* Queen's Univ., Kingston, Ont (BSc 1975); McMaster Univ. (MSc 1977; PhD 1981). FRSC 2000. Postdoctoral Fellow, Dalhousie Univ., 1981–84; NSERC Univ. Res. Fellow, Queen's Univ., 1984–94; Prof. of Chemistry, Queen's Univ., until 2006. Killam Res. Fellow, Canada Council for the Arts, 2005–07. Mem., Internat. Acad. of Quantum Molec. Sci. *Publications:* articles in scientific jls. *Address:* Department of Chemistry, Room 212, Chemistry Building, Dalhousie University, 6274 Coburg Road, PO Box 15000, Halifax, NS B3H 4R2, Canada.

BECKER, Boris; former professional tennis player; entrepreneur; *b* 22 Nov. 1967; *s* of late Karl-Heinz and Elvira Becker; *m* 1st, Barbara Feltus (marr. diss. 2001); two *s*; one *d*; 2nd, 2009, Lilly Kerssenberg; one *s*. West German Junior Champion, 1983; wins include: Young Masters' Junior Tournament, 1985; Wimbledon, 1985 (youngest winner), 1986, 1989; US Open, 1989; Australian Open, 1991, 1996; ATP World Champion, 1992, 1995; Davis Cup winner, 1988, 1989; retired as professional tennis player, 1999. Head Coach to Novak Djokovic, 2013–. *Publications:* Boris Becker - The Player: the autobiography, 2004. *Address:* Boris Becker & Co., Ruessenstrasse 6, 6341 Baar, Switzerland.

BECKERLEG, John; Management Consultant, Management Options Ltd, 2004–06 and since 2008; Director of Supporting Services, Chief Fire Officers Association, since 2014; *b* 12 Aug. 1956; *s* of Lewis Beckerleg and Doris (*née* Bundy); *m* 1983, April Cornelia Saunders; two *s* one *d*. *Educ:* Emmanuel Coll., Cambridge (MA 1981); MBA Henley Mgt Coll. 1998. CIPFA 1981. Chief Accountant, Cambs CC, 1985–87; Sen. Asst Co. Treas., Herts CC, 1987–91; Buckinghamshire County Council: Dep. Co. Treas., 1991–93; Dir of Finance, 1993–96; Dir of Corporate Services, 1996–98; Dir of Social Services, 1998–2000; Strategic Manager, 2000–04; Dir of Resources, Nat. Policing Improvement Agency, 2006–08; Hd of Resources, Youth Justice Bd, 2009–10; Director of Corporate Services: S Downs Nat. Park Authy, 2010–11; Hants Fire and Rescue Service, 2011–14. *Recreations:* theatre, genealogy, Rugby, art. *Address:* Daffodil Cottage, Main Street, Grendon Underwood, Bucks HP18 0ST.

BECKERMAN, Wilfred, PhD; Fellow of Balliol College, Oxford, 1975–92, now Emeritus; Hon. Visiting Professor of Economics, University College London, since 2005; *b* 19 May 1925; *s* of Morris and Mathilda Beckerman; *m* 1st, 1952, Nicole Geneviève Ritter (*d* 1979); one *s* two *d*; 2nd, 1991, Joanna Pasek; one *d*. *Educ:* Ealing County Sch.; Trinity Coll., Cambridge (MA, PhD). RNVR, 1943–46. Trinity Coll., Cambridge, 1946–50; Lecturer in Economics, Univ. of Nottingham, 1950–52; OEEC and OECD, Paris, 1952–61; National Inst. of Economic and Social Research, 1962–63; Fellow of Balliol Coll., Oxford, 1964–69; Economic Advr to Pres. of BoT (leave of absence from Balliol), 1967–69; Prof. of Political Economy, Univ. of London, and Head of Dept of Political Economy, UCL, 1969–75; Reader in Economics, Oxford Univ., 1978–92. Mem., Royal Commn on Environmental Pollution, 1970–73. Member: Exec. Cttee, NIESR, 1973–96; Council, Royal Economic Soc., 1990–93. Elie Halévy Vis. Prof. Institut d'Etudes Politiques, Paris, 1977; Resident Scholar, Woodrow Wilson Internat. Center for Scholars, Washington, DC, 1982. Consultant: World Bank; OECD; ILO. Pres., Section F (Economics), BAAS, 1978. *Publications:* The British Economy in 1975 (with associates), 1965; International Comparisons of Real Incomes, 1966; An Introduction to National Income Analysis, 1968; (ed and contrib.) The Labour Government's Economic Record, 1972; In Defence of Economic Growth, 1974; Measures of Leisure, Equality and Welfare, 1978; (ed and contrib.) Slow Growth in Britain: Causes and Consequences, 1979; Poverty and the Impact of Income Maintenance Programmes, 1979; (with S. Clark) Poverty and the Impact of Social Security in Britain since 1961, 1982; (ed and contrib.) Wage Rigidity and Unemployment, 1986; Small is Stupid, 1995; Growth, the Environment and the Distribution of Incomes, 1995; (with J. Pasek) Justice, Posterity and the Environment, 2001; A Poverty of Reason: sustainable development and economic growth, 2003; Economics as Applied Ethics, 2010; articles in Economic Jl, Economica, Econometrica, Review of Economic Studies, Review of Economics and Statistics, World Economics, Oxford Economic Papers, etc. *Recreation:* various. *Address:* 1c Norham Gardens, Oxford OX2 6PS.

BECKETT, family name of **Baron Grimthorpe**.

BECKETT, Maj.-Gen. Denis Arthur, CB 1971; DSO 1944; OBE 1960; *b* 19 May 1917; *o s* of late Archibald Beckett, Woodford Green, Essex; *m* 1946, Elizabeth (marr. diss. 1974), *er d* of late Col Guy Edwards, Upper Slaughter, Glos; one *s*; *m* 1978, Nancy Ann, *d* of late Charles Bradford Hitt, Grosse Pointe, MI. *Educ:* Forest Sch.; Chard Sch. Joined Hon. Artillery Co., 1939; commnd into Essex Regt, 1940; served in W Africa, Middle East, Italy and Greece, 1940–45; DAA & QMG and Bde Major, Parachute Bdes, 1948–50; Instructor, RMA Sandhurst, 1951–53; Directing Staff, Staff Coll., Camberley, 1953–56; Second in Comd 3rd Bn Para. Regt, 1956–58; comd 2nd Bn Para. Regt, 1958–60; Directing Staff, JSSC, 1960–61; comd 19 Bde, 1961–63; idc 1964; DAG, BAOR, 1965–66; Chief of Staff, Far East Land Forces, 1966–68; Dir of Personal Services (Army), 1968–71, retired 1971. Liveryman, Coopers' Co., 1962–. *Address:* 2150 Indian Creek Boulevard E, Apt B324, Vero Beach, FL 32966, USA. *Clubs:* Army and Navy, Lansdowne.

BECKETT, Maj.-Gen. Edwin Horace Alexander, CB 1988; MBE 1974; Head of British Defence Staff, Washington, 1988–91, retired; *b* 16 May 1937; *s* of William Alexander Beckett and Doris Beckett; *m* 1963, Micaela Elizabeth Benedicta, *d* of Col Sir Edward Malet, Bt, OBE; three *s* one *d*. *Educ:* Henry Fanshawe School; RMA Sandhurst; Nat. Defence Coll.; psc, sq. Commissioned 1957 West Yorks Regt; regtl service in Aden (despatches 1968), Gibraltar, Germany and N Ireland; DAA&QMG 11 Armd Brigade, 1972–74; CO 1 PWO, 1976–78 (despatches 1977); GSO1 (DS) Staff Coll., 1979; Comdt Junior Div., Staff Coll., 1980; Comdr UKMF and 6 Field Force, 1981; Comdr UKMF, 1 Inf. Brigade and Tidworth Garrison, 1982; Director: Concepts, MoD, 1983–84; Army Plans and Programmes, MoD, 1984–85; C of S, HQ BAOR, 1985–88. Col Comdt, The King's Div., 1988–94; Col, PWO, 1996–2001. Dir, Corporate Affairs, IDV Ltd, 1991–96; Founder and Chm., British Brands Gp, 1992–96 (Pres., 1997–99). Chairman: Exmoor Trust, 1999–2007; W Somerset Local Action for Rural Communities, 2007–11; Calvert Trust, 2011–12 (Chm., 1994–2000, Trustee, 1994–2003, Calvert Trust Exmoor); Trustee, Directory of Social Change, 2002–08 (Vice-Chm., 2004). *Recreations:* fishing, picture framing, farming for fun, shooting.

BECKETT, Frances Mary, OBE 2006; charity consultant; Chief Executive, Church Urban Fund, 2002–08; *b* 20 Nov. 1951. *Educ:* Trent Poly. (CQSW); LSE (MSc Vol. Sector Orgn). Social Worker, Somerset CC, 1972–76; Student Advr, UCCF, 1976–80; Community Worker, 1981–86; Shaftesbury Society, 1986–2002: Social Work Advr, Community Care Co-ordinator, Urban Action Dir; Chief Exec., 1995–2002. Chairman: ACEVO, 2003–05; Voluntary and Community Sector Adv. Gp, Home Office, 2003–05, Cabinet Office, 2005–08; Get Fair Nat. Poverty Campaign, 2007–10. Member of Board: Faith Based Regeneration Network, 2004–11; NCVO, 2006–07; LDA, 2008–12; Orbit Housing, 2011– (Chm., Orbit SE Assoc., 2011–13; Chm., Orbit Living, 2013–). Trustee: Southwark CAB, 2010–; Action Tutoring, 2014–. Chair: Urban Expression, 2014–; Friends of Brimmington Park, 2014–. FRSA 2000. *Publications:* Called to Action, 1989; Rebuild, 2001. *Recreations:* Church involvement, theatre, cinema, reading. *Address:* 108 Meeting House Lane, SE15 2TT.

BECKETT, Prof. John Vincent, PhD; FRHistS, FSA; Professor of English Regional History, University of Nottingham, since 1990 (on secondment as Director, Victoria County History, University of London, 2005–10); *b* 12 July 1950; *s* of William Vincent Beckett and Kathleen Amelia Beckett (*née* Reed); *m* 1979, Christine Sylvia Campbell; one *s*. *Educ:* Univ. of Lancaster (BA 1971; PhD 1975). FRHistS 1981. Lord Adams Res. Fellow, Univ. of Newcastle upon Tyne, 1974–76; Lectr in Hist., Wroxton Coll. of Fairleigh Dickinson Univ., Banbury, 1976–78; Lectr in Econ. and Social Hist., Univ. of Hull, 1979; University of Nottingham: Lectr in Hist., 1979–87; Reader in English Regl Hist., 1987–90. Chm., Editl Bd, Midland Hist., 2001–. Chm., British Agricl Hist. Soc., 2001–05. Chairman: Hist. of Lincs Cttee, 1988–; Thoroton Soc. of Notts, 1992–. FSA 1992. Hon. Fellow, Inst. of Historical

Res., 2013. *Publications:* Coal and Tobacco: the Lowthers and the economic development of West Cumberland 1660–1760, 1981; The Aristocracy in England 1660–1914, 1986, rev. edn 1989; The East Midlands from AD1000, 1988; A History of Laxton: England's last open-field village, 1989; The Agricultural Revolution, 1990; The Rise and Fall of the Grenvilles, Dukes of Buckingham and Chandos 1710–1921, 1994; (jtly) Agricultural Rent in England 1690–1914, 1997; (ed) A Centenary History of Nottingham, 1997; (jtly) Farm Production in England 1700–1914, 2001; Byron and Newstead: the aristocrat and the Abbey, 2001; (ed) Nottinghamshire Past: essays in honour of Adrian Henstock, 2003; City Status in the United Kingdom 1830–2002, 2005; Writing Local History, 2007; contrib. numerous articles and reviews to jls incl. Agricl Hist., Agricl Hist. Rev., Archives, Bull. Inst. Histl Res., Bull. John Rylands Liby, Byron Jl, Econ. Hist. Rev., English Histl Rev., History Today, Jl British Studies. *Recreations:* sport, walking, local history. *Address:* Department of History, University Park, Nottingham NG7 2RD. *T:* (0115) 951 5936. *E:* John.Beckett@nottingham.ac.uk.

BECKETT, Rear Adm. Keith Andrew, CBE 2014; Chief Strategic Systems Executive, Ministry of Defence, since 2014; *b* Stockport, 7 June 1963; *s* of Charles Beckett and Enid Beckett; *m* 1989, Susan Mary Berry; one *s* three *d*. *Educ:* Holyhead Co. Sec. Sch.; RN Engrg Coll. (BScEng 1985); Royal Mil. Coll. of Sci. (MDA 1999). CEng 2006; FIMarEST 2006. Joined RN, 1981; HMS Trafalgar, 1987–90; HMS Ocelot, 1990–92; Clyde Submarine Base, 1992–94; HMS Triumph, 1994–97; Dept of Naval Sec., 1997–98; Hd, Submarine Nuclear Safety, Defence Procurement, 1999–2002; Devonport Flotilla Submarine Engr, 2002–04; rcds 2004; CSO Engrg (Submarines), 2004–07; UK Tech. Liaison Officer, Naval Sea Systems Comd, Washington, DC, 2007–10; Dir Nuclear Propulsion, Defence Equipment and Support, 2010–13; Naval Base Comdr, Clyde Naval Base, 2013–14. Vice Pres., RNRU, 2011–. *Address:* Office of the Naval Secretary, Navy Command Headquarters, MP 3.1 Leach Building, Whale Island, Portsmouth PO2 8BY. *T:* (023) 9262 5542. *E:* dessmcsse-dir@mod.uk.

BECKETT, Rt Hon. Dame Margaret (Mary), DBE 2013; PC 1993; MP (Lab) Derby South, since 1983; *b* 15 Jan. 1943; *d* of late Cyril and Winifred Jackson; *m* 1979, Lionel A. Beckett; two step *s*. *Educ:* Notre Dame High Sch., Norwich; Manchester Coll. of Sci. and Technol. Formerly: engrg apprentice (metallurgy), AEI, Manchester; exptl officer, Manchester Univ.; Labour Party res. asst, 1970–74; political adviser, Minister for Overseas Develt, 1974; Principal Researcher, Granada TV, 1979–83. Contested (Lab) Lincoln, Feb. 1974; MP (Lab) Lincoln, Oct. 1974–1979; PPS to Minister for Overseas Develt, 1974–75; Asst Govt Whip, 1975–76; Parly Under-Sec. of State, DES, 1976–79; Opposition front bench spokesman on health and social security, 1984–89; Mem., Shadow Cabinet, 1989–97; Shadow Chief Sec. to the Treasury, 1989–92; Shadow Leader, H of C, 1992–94; Campaigns Co-ordinator and Dep. Leader, Lab Party, 1992–94; Actg Leader, Lab Party, May–July 1994; opposition front bench spokesman on health, 1994–95, on trade and industry, 1995–97; Pres., BoT, and Sec. of State for Trade and Industry, 1997–98; Pres. of the Council and Leader, H of C, 1998–2001; Secretary of State: for Envmt, Food and Rural Affairs, 2001–06; for Foreign and Commonwealth Affairs, 2006–07; Minister of State (Minister for Housing and Planning), DCLG, 2008–09. Chair: Intelligence and Security Cttee, 2008; Jt Cttee on Nat. Security Strategy, 2011–. Mem. NEC, Labour Party, 1980–81, 1985–86, 1988–97. *Recreations:* cooking, reading, caravanning. *Address:* c/o House of Commons, SW1A 0AA.

BECKETT, Nikaila Susan; non-executive Chairman, Technetix Group Ltd, since 2008; *b* 16 June 1961; two *s*. IBM, UK, USA and Europe, 1979–95; Founder, 1995, Chief Exec., 1997–2007, NSB Retail Systems Plc; Man. Dir, NSB Ltd (Grenada), 2013–. Non-executive Chairman: Victoria plc, 2010–12 (non-exec. Dir, 2007–12); Kiala SV, 2011–12 (Sen. Ind. Dir, 2009–11); non-exec. Dir, Unit4 Gp, 2013–. *Recreations:* sailing, scuba diving, tennis, eating out.

BECKETT, Sir Richard (Gervase), 3rd Bt *cr* 1921; QC 1988; barrister; *b* 27 March 1944; *s* of Sir Martyn Gervase Beckett, 2nd Bt, MC, RIBA and Hon. Priscilla, *d* of 3rd Viscount Esher, GBE; *S* father, 2001; *m* 1976, Elizabeth Ann, *d* of Major Hugo Waterhouse; one *s* three *d*. *Educ:* Eton. Diploma in Economics (Oxford). Called to the Bar, Middle Temple, 1965; practice at the Bar, 1966–2009. *Recreation:* landscape. *Heir:* *s* Walter Gervase Beckett, *b* 16 Jan. 1987. *Address:* 51 Lennox Gardens, SW1X 0DF. *Clubs:* Pratt's, Portland.

BECKETT, Samantha Mary Constance, (Mrs I. D. Mason), OBE 1999; Director General, Economics and Markets, Department for Business, Innovation and Skills, and Deputy Head, Government Economic Service, since 2013; *b* Camberley, 19 Dec. 1966; *d* of Bill Beckett and Connie Beckett (*née* McKenna); *m* 1994, Ian David Mason; two *d*. *Educ:* St Wilfrid's RC Comprehensive Sch., Crawley; New Coll., Oxford (BA Hons PPE); London Sch. of Econs (MSc Econs). Joined HM Treasury, 1988; Mem., Econ. Briefing and Analysis teams, 1988–96; Chancellor of the Exchequer's Speechwriter, 1996–98; Sec. to Diana, Princess of Wales Meml Cttee, 1998; Head: Productivity Team, 1999–2000; Competition and Econ. Regulation Team, 2000–04; Director: Ops, 2004–07; Policy and Planning, 2007; Fiscal Policy, 2008–12; Dir, Econ. and Domestic Secretariat, Cabinet Office, 2012–13. *Address:* Department for Business, Innovation and Skills, 1 Victoria Street, SW1H 0ET.

BECKETT, Lt Gen. Thomas Anthony, CBE 2010; Defence Senior Adviser to the Middle East, since 2015; *b* Bahrain, 28 July 1962; *s* of Brendan Beckett and Kathleen Beckett; *m* 1992, Fiona Graham; three *d*. *Educ:* Blackrock Coll., Dublin; Cranfield Univ. (MA Military Studies 1994; MSc Global Security 2002). Commnd QRIH, 1984; psc 1994; SO2 DMO, MoD, 1994–96; 2IC 2nd Bn Parachute Regt, 1998–2000; CO 1st Bn Parachute Regt, 2002–04; hcsc 2005; Dep. Dir, HCSC, 2005–07; Dep. C2 Multi-Nat. Forces Iraq, 2007; Comdr 20th Armoured Bde, 2007–09; Dir Commitments HQ Land Forces, 2009–10; Dep. Comdr, NATO Rapid Deployable Corps (Italy), 2010–12; COS ISAF Jt Comd, 2012–13. Col, QRH, 2014–. Officer, Legion of Merit (USA), 2007. *Recreations:* surfing, stalking (deer), military history, cycling, chile sauces. *Club:* Cavalry and Guards.

BECKETT, William Cartwright, CB 1978; LLM; Solicitor to the Corporation of Lloyd's, 1985–93; *b* 21 Sept. 1929; *s* of late William Beckett and Emily (*née* Cartwright); *m* 1st, 1956, Marjorie Jean Hoskin; two *s*; 2nd, 1974, Lesley Margaret Furlonger. *Educ:* Salford Grammar Sch.; Manchester Univ. (LLB 1950, LLM 1952). Called to Bar, Middle Temple, 1952. Joined Treasury Solicitor's Dept, 1956; Board of Trade, 1965; Asst Solicitor, DEP, 1969; Under-Sec., DTI, 1972; Dep.-Sec. 1977; Legal Secretary, Law Officers' Dept, 1975–80; Solicitor, DTI, 1980–84. *Recreations:* music, golf. *Address:* Stocks Farm, New Road, Rayne, Essex CM77 6SY.

BECKFORD, Prof. James Arthur, PhD, DLitt; FBA 2004; Professor of Sociology, University of Warwick, 1989–2007, now Emeritus; *b* 1 Dec. 1942; *s* of late John Henry Beckford and Elisabeth Alice May Beckford; *m* 1965, Julia Carolyn Hanson; one *s* twin *d*. *Educ:* Alma Rd Sch.; Tottenham Grammar Sch.; Univ. of Reading (BA 1965; PhD 1972; DLitt 1985). Lectr in Sociol., Univ. of Reading, 1966–73; Lectr, then Sen. Lectr, Sociol., Univ. of Durham, 1973–87; Prof. of Sociol., Loyola Univ. of Chicago, 1987–89. Directeur d'études invité: Ecole des Hautes Etudes en Sciences Sociales, Paris, 2001; Ecole Pratique des Hautes Etudes, Paris, 2004. F. D. Maurice Lectr, KCL, 2014. Pres., Soc. for the Scientific Study of Religion, 2010–11 Dr Sciences Religieuses *hc*, 2014. *Publications:* The Trumpet of Prophecy: a sociological study of Jehovah's Witnesses, 1975; Religious Organization: a trend report and bibliography, 1975; Cult Controversies: societal responses to new religious movements, 1985; (ed) New Religious Movements and Rapid Social Change, 1986; (ed jtly) The Changing Face of Religion, 1989; Religion and Advanced Industrial Society, 1989; (ed jtly) Secularization, Rationalism and Sectarianism, 1993; (with S. Gilliat) Religion in Prison: equal rites in a multi-faith society, 1998; (ed jtly) Challenging Religion: essays in honour of Eileen Barker, 2003; Social Theory and Religion, 2003; (jtly) Muslims in Prison: challenge and change in Britain and France, 2005; (ed jtly) Theorising Religion: classical and contemporary debates, 2006; (ed jtly) The Sage Handbook of the Sociology of Religion, 2007; numerous scholarly articles and chapters. *Recreations:* owls, Japanese language, playing the clarinet and bagpipes. *Address:* Department of Sociology, University of Warwick, Coventry CV4 7AL. *T:* (home) (01926) 851252, *Fax:* (024) 7652 3497. *E:* j.a.beckford@warwick.ac.uk.

BECKHAM, David Robert Joseph, OBE 2003; professional footballer, 1992–2013; Captain, England Football Team, 2000–06; *b* Leytonstone, 2 May 1975; *s* of Ted and Sandra Beckham; *m* 1999, Victoria Adams; three *s* one *d*. Manchester United Football Club: trainee, 1991; team member, 1992–2003; Premier League début, 1995; member, winning team: FA Premier League, 1996, 1997, 1999, 2000, 2001, 2003; FA Cup, 1996, 1999; Charity Shield, 1996, 1997; UEFA Champions League, 1999; team mem., Real Madrid FC, 2003–07, mem., winning team, La Liga, 2007; team member: Los Angeles Galaxy, 2007–12, mem., winning team, Major League Soccer Championship, 2011; AC Milan, 2009, 2010; Paris Saint-Germain, 2013. Internat. appearances for England, 1996–2006 (115 caps); mem., World Cup team, 1998, 2002 and 2006. Opened David Beckham children's football acad., London and LA, 2005. Bobby Charlton Soccer Skills Award, 1987; Manchester United Player of the Year, 1996–97; Young Player of the Year, PFA, 1996–97; Sky Football Personality of the Year, 1997; Sportsman of the Year, Sport Writers' Assoc., 2001; BBC Sports Personality of the Year, 2001; Lifetime Achievement Award, BBC Sports Personality of the Year, 2010. *Publications:* (with Neil Harman) David Beckham: my story, 1999; David Beckham: my world (autobiog.), 2000; (with Tom Watt) My Side (autobiog.), 2003; David Beckham, 2013.

BECKINGHAM, Peter; HM Diplomatic Service; Governor, Turks and Caicos Islands, since 2013; *b* 16 March 1949; *s* of late Rev. Leslie Beckingham and Eileen Beckingham (*née* Grimsey); *m* 1975, Jill Mary Trotman; two *d*. *Educ:* Chigwell Sch.; Selwyn Coll., Cambridge (MA). MIEx 1998. Argo Record Co., 1970–74; BOTB, 1974–79; Dir, British Inf. Services, NY, 1979–84; News Dept, FCO, 1984 (Hd, Press Centre, G7 Summit); Energy, Sci. and Space Dept, FCO, 1984–86; Hd, Horn of Africa Section, E Africa Dept, FCO, 1986–88; First Sec. (Commercial), Stockholm, 1988–92; Hd, Political Section, Canberra, 1992–96; Dir, Jt Export Promotion Directorate, FCO/DTI, 1996–99; Consul Gen., Sydney, and Dir Gen., Trade and Investment Promotion, Australia, 1999–2004; Ambassador to Philippines, 2005–09; FCO, 2009–10; Dep. High Comr, Mumbai, 2010–13. *Publications:* (ed) Australia and Britain: the evolving relationship, 1993; (ed) Our Shared Future, UK-Australia Dialogue, 2004. *Recreations:* music, golf, tennis. *Address:* c/o Foreign and Commonwealth Office, King Charles Street, SW1A 2AH.

BECKLAKE, (Ernest) John (Stephen), PhD; CEng; Senior Research Fellow, Science Museum, since 1994; *b* 24 June 1943; *s* of Ernest and Evelyn Becklake; *m* 1965, Susan Elizabeth (*née* Buckle), BSc; two *s*. *Educ:* Bideford Grammar Sch.; Exeter Univ. (BSc, PhD). CEng 1988; FRAeS 1992. Engr, EMI Electronics, Wells, 1967–69; Post-Doctoral Fellow, Victoria Univ., BC, Canada, 1969–70; Sen. Scientist, Marconi Space and Def. Systems, Frimley, 1970–72; Science Museum: Asst Keeper, Dept of Earth and Space Sciences, 1972–80; Keeper, Dept of Elect. Engrg, Communications and Circulation, 1980–85; Keeper, Dept of Engrg, subseq. Head of Technology Gp, 1985–94. Member: Internat. Acad. of Astronautics, 1988– (Chm., Hist. Cttee, 1996–); British Interplanetary Soc., 2006. Man. Ed., DERA Hist. Project, DERA Farnborough, 1995–2001. Consultant, German Rocketry, Aerospace Mus., Cosford, 1997–2002. *Publications:* Man and the Moon, 1980; The Climate Crisis, 1989; The Population Explosion, 1990; Pollution, 1990; (ed) History of Rocketry and Astronautics, vol. XVI, 1995; (series editor) Exploration and Discovery, 1980–; technical pubns in Electronics Letters, Jl of Physics D, Jl of British Interplanetary Soc., and Spaceflight. *Recreations:* gardening, golf, Rugby. *Address:* Tree Wood, Robin Hood Lane, Sutton Green, Guildford, Surrey GU4 7QG. *T:* (01483) 766931. *Club:* Puttenham Golf.

BECKMAN, Michael David; QC 1976; *b* 6 April 1932; *s* of Nathan and Esther Beckman; *m*; two *d*. *Educ:* King's Coll., London (LLB (Hons)). Called to the Bar, Lincoln's Inn, 1954. Qualified mediator, CEDR, 2004, ADR, 2006. *Recreation:* various. *Address:* Bullards, Widford, Herts SG12 8SG. *T:* (01279) 842669; (chambers) 11 Stone Buildings, Lincoln's Inn, WC2A 3TG; (chambers) 4 King's Bench Walk, Temple, EC4Y 7DL; 12 North Pallant, Chichester PO19 1TQ.

BECKWITH, Sir John (Lionel), Kt 2002; CBE 1996; FCA; Chairman, Pacific Investments, since 1993; Founder Chairman, London & Edinburgh Trust PLC, 1971–92; *b* 19 March 1947; *s* of Col Harold Beckwith and Agnes Camilla McMichael (*née* Duncan); *m* 1975, Heather Marie Robbins (marr. diss. 2001); two *s* one *d*; one *d* with Hélène Aubry. *Educ:* Harrow Sch. FCA 1970; ATII 1970. Arthur Andersen & Co., 1969–71; with London & Edinburgh Trust PLC, 1971–92. Founder Chm., Rutland Trust plc, 1986–91; Chairman: Riverside PLC, 1993–97; Barbican Healthcare PLC, 1996–98; Red River Capital Hldgs, 2006–11. Director: Frontiers Gp, 1996–; Harlequin FC, 1996–97. Member: Develt Bd, Cancer Relief Macmillan Fund; NCH Action for Children's 125th Anniversary Appeal Cttee. Vice-President: RNIB; Youth Clubs UK; Founder, and Pres., Youth Sport Trust; Patron, Teenage Cancer Trust. Hon. DLitt Loughborough, 2000. Duke of Edinburgh Arthur Bell Trophy, 1999. *Recreations:* sport, music, ballet. *Address:* (office) 124 Sloane Street, SW1X 9BW. *Clubs:* MCC, Annabel's, Queen's, Harry's Bar; Old Harrovian Football; Rosslyn Park Football; Royal Berkshire Golf; Thurlestone Golf; Sunningdale Golf; Riverside Racquets Centre.

See also P. M. Beckwith.

BECKWITH, Peter Michael, OBE 2007; Chairman: PMB Holdings Ltd, since 1992; Aspria Holdings BV, 1992–2012; Director, Ambassador Entertainment Group, 2009–12 (Deputy Chairman, Ambassador Theatre Group Ltd, 1992–2010); *b* 20 Jan. 1945; *s* of Col Harold Andrew Beckwith and Agnes Camilla McMichael Beckwith; *m* 1968, Paula Gay Bateman (*d* 2011); two *d*; *m* 2014, Vivien Louise McLean. *Educ:* Harrow School; Emmanuel College, Cambridge (MA Hons; Hon. Fellow, 1999). Qualified Solicitor, 1970; Asst Solicitor, Norton Rose Botterell & Roche; London & Edinburgh Trust: Joint Founder and shareholder, 1972; Managing Director, 1983–86; Dep. Chm., 1987; Chm., 1992. Pres., Harbour Club, Milan, 1999–. Vice Patron, Cambridge Foundn, 1992– (Trustee, 1997–2002). Gov., Harrow Sch., 1992–2011. Hon. LLD Cantab, 2000. *Recreations:* tennis, ski-ing, Association football, theatre, dogs, cycling. *Address:* PMB Holdings Ltd, Prospect House, SW20 0JP. *Clubs:* Riverside Racquets, Chelsea Football; Downhill Only (Wengen); Harbour (Milan); Austria Haus (Vail).

See also Sir J. L. Beckwith.

BECTIVE, Earl of; Thomas Rupert Charles Christopher Taylour; *b* 18 June 1989; *s* and *heir* of Marquis of Headfort, *qv*. *Educ:* Dragon Sch.; Radley Coll.; Durham Univ. (BA Hons Econs). With Liberum Capital. *Recreation:* rowing (Mem., GB Junior Rowing Team, 2007).

BEDBROOK, Jack Harry, CEng, FRINA; FIMgt; RCNC; Managing Director, HM Dockyard, Devonport, 1979–84; *b* 8 Aug. 1924; *s* of Harry Bedbrook and Emma Bedbrook; *m* (marr. diss. 1989); three *d*; *m* 1996, Sylvia. *Educ:* Technical Coll., Portsmouth; RNC, Greenwich. Dir Gen. Ships Dept, Admiralty, 1946–51; Asst Constructor, Devonport, 1951–54; Dockyard Dept, Bath, 1954–56; Constructor, Gibraltar Dockyard, 1956–58; Admiralty Exptl Works, Haslar, 1958–62; Dir Gen. Ships Dept, 1962–65; Chief Constructor, Portsmouth, 1965–71; Project Manager, Rosyth, 1971–74; Prodn Dir, Devonport, 1974–77; Man. Dir, HM Dockyard, Rosyth, 1977–79. *Recreations:* travelling, theatre, music, gardening. *Address:* Laxtons, Cargreen, Saltash, Cornwall PL12 6PA. *T:* (01752) 844519.

BEDDINGTON, Sir John (Rex), Kt 2010; CMG 2004; PhD; FRS 2001; FRSE; FICE; Chief Scientific Adviser to the Government and Head of the Government Office for Science, Department for Business, Innovation and Skills (formerly Department for Innovation, Universities and Skills), 2008–13; *b* 13 Oct. 1945; *s* of Harry Beddington and Mildred (*née* Weale); *m* 1st, 1968, Sarah West (marr. diss. 1972); one *s*; 2nd, 1973, Prof. Sally Baldwin (marr. diss. 1979); one *d*; 3rd, 1990, Caroline Hiller. *Educ:* Monmouth Sch.; London Sch. of Econs (BSc Econs, MSc); Edinburgh Univ. (PhD). FICE 2010. Res. Asst, Edinburgh Univ., 1968–71; Lectr on Population Biol., York Univ., 1971–84; Imperial College, London: Reader in Applied Population Biol., 1984–91; Prof. of Applied Population Biol., 1991–2007; Dir, Centre for Envmtl Technol., 1994–97; Dir, T. H. Huxley Sch. of Envmt, Earth Scis and Engrg, 1998–2001; Hd, Dept of Envmtl Sci. and Technol., 2001–04. Sen. Fellow, Internat. Inst. for Envmt and Develt, 1980–83; Hd, UK Scientific Delegn, Commn for Conservation of Antarctic Living Marine Resources, 1983–2007; Dir, Fisheries Mgt Sci. Prog., DFID (formerly ODA), 1989–2006; Chairman: Scientific Cttee, Indian Ocean Tuna Commn, 1998; Sci. Adv. Council, DEFRA, 2005–07; Rothamsted Res., 2014–; Mem., NERC, 2000–06 (Mem. Exec. Bd, 2002–05); Pres., Zool Soc. of London, 2014– (Mem. Council, 2003–07). Chairman Trustees: People's Trust for Endangered Species, 1984–2007; Marine Educn and Conservation Trust, 1987–2007; Trustee, Natural History Mus., 2013–. Pres., Resource Modelling Assoc., 1992–94. Sen. Advr, Oxford Martin Sch., 2013–. MAE 2010. FCGI 2011; FRSE 2011. Hon. FREng 2012. DUniv York, 2009; Hon. DSc: Edinburgh, 2011; Aberdeen, 2012; Hon. DCL Newcastle, 2011. Heidelberg Award for Envmtl Excellence, 1997. *Publications:* articles on ecology, population biol. and fisheries mgt. *Recreations:* hill-walking, art, birdwatching. *Club:* Travellers.

BEDDOE; *see* Rowe-Beddoe.

BEDDOE, Martin William Denton; His Honour Judge Beddoe; a Circuit Judge, since 2007; *b* Abyad, Egypt, 7 July 1955; *s* of late Lt Col Arthur Beddoe and of Jane Beddoe; *m* 1993, Prof. Mary Margaret Anne McCabe, *qv*; two *d*. *Educ:* Peterhouse, Cambridge (BA Hons 1977; MA 1982). Called to the Bar, Gray's Inn, 1979; in practice at the Bar, 1980–2007; Recorder, 2002–07; Standing Counsel to HMRC Prosecutions Office, 2005–07. Mem., Parole Bd for England and Wales, 2010–. Tutor Judge, Judicial Coll. (formerly Judicial Studies Bd), 2007–. *Recreations:* golf, cricket, two wheel travel, France. *Address:* c/o Southwark Crown Court, 1 English Grounds (off Battlebridge Lane), Southwark, SE1 2HU. *T:* (020) 7522 7200. *Clubs:* Royal Worlington and Newmarket Golf; Philanderers Cricket.

BEDDOW, Prof. Michael; Professor of German, University of Leeds, 1986–98; *b* 3 Sept. 1947; *s* of Austin Beddow and Ivy Beddow; *m* 1976, Helena Hajzyk; one *s*. *Educ:* West Park Grammar Sch., St Helens; St John's Coll., Cambridge. Trinity Hall, Cambridge: Res. Fellow, 1973–75; Staff Fellow, 1975–79; Lectr in German, KCL, 1979–86. Tech. Consultant, Anglo-Norman Dictionary, 2001–. Vice Chm. Governors, Silcoates Sch., Wakefield, 1993–2001. *Publications:* The Fiction of Humanity, 1982; Goethe's Faust I: a critical guide, 1986; Thomas Mann: Dr Faustus, 1994; articles and reviews in Jl European Studies, London German Studies, MLR, TLS, Publications of English Goethe Soc. *Recreations:* walking, choral singing, photography, computer construction and programming, learning Tagalog and Korean. *Address:* 3 Oakwood Park, Leeds LS8 2PJ. *T:* (0113) 240 1561.

BEDELL, Elaine; Director, Entertainment and Comedy, ITV, since 2009; *d* of Albert and Iris Bedell; *m* 1990, Clive Brill; one *s* one *d*. *Educ:* Valentines High Sch., Ilford; Leeds Univ. (BA 1st Cl. Hons English). Producer, BBC, 1987–93 (productions include: Start the Week (radio); Clive James Talk Shows; Clive James on the 90s (BAFTA award 1991); Postcards; New Year's Eve Shows; Assignment: Bill Clinton's election campaign); Hd, Factual Entertainment, Tiger Aspect Prodns, and Exec. Producer, Bill Hicks, It's Just a Ride, 1993–94; Managing Director: Watchmaker Prodns, 1994–2000; Chrysalis Entertainment, 2000–02; Exec. Dir, Royal Shakespeare Co. Enterprises, 2002–03; Ind. Exec., 2003–04, Commng Ed., Factual Entertainment, 2004–06, Controller, Entertainment Commng, 2007–09, BBC. Trustee, V&A Mus., 2015–. *Recreation:* dancing. *Address:* ITV, London Television Centre, Upper Ground, SE1 9LT. *E:* Elaine.Bedell@ITV.com.

BEDFORD, 15th Duke of, *cr* 1694; **Andrew Ian Henry Russell;** Marquess of Tavistock, 1694; Earl of Bedford, 1550; Baron Russell, 1539; Baron Russell of Thornhaugh, 1603; Baron Howland of Streatham, 1695; Partner, Bloomsbury Stud, since 1985; Director: Tattersalls Ltd, since 1992; Woburn Enterprises Ltd, since 2003; *b* 30 March 1962; *e s* of 14th Duke of Bedford and of Henrietta, *d* of late Henry F. Tiarks; *S* father, 2003; *m* 2000, Louise, *d* of late Donald Crammond and of Dowager Lady Delves Broughton; one *s* one *d*. *Educ:* Heatherdown; Harrow; Harvard. *Recreation:* country pursuits. *Heir: s* Marquess of Tavistock, *qv*. *Address:* Woburn Abbey, Woburn, Beds MK17 9WA. *T:* (01525) 290333, *Fax:* (01525) 290191. *Clubs:* Jockey; AD (Cambridge, Mass).

BEDFORD, Bishop Suffragan of, since 2012; **Rt Rev. Richard William Bryant Atkinson,** OBE 2002; *b* 17 Dec. 1958; *s* of William and Eileen Atkinson; *m* 1984, Helen Valerie Bavister (*see* H. V. Atkinson); one *s* two *d*. *Educ:* St Paul's Sch.; Magdalene Coll., Cambridge (BA 1980; MA 1984); Ripon Coll., Cuddesdon; Birmingham Univ. (MA 2009). Ordained deacon, 1984, priest, 1985; Asst Curate, Abingdon, 1984–87; Team Vicar, 1987–91, Team Rector, 1991–96, Sheffield Manor; Vicar of Rotherham, 1996–2002; Archdeacon of Leicester, 2002–12. Hon. Canon, Sheffield Cathedral, 1998–2002. Mem., Gen. Synod of C of E, 1991–2012; Church Comr, 2001–08. Hon. Tutor, Ripon Coll., Cuddesdon, 1987–92. Mem., Carnegie UK Trust Commn, 2006–09. Dep. Chm., Places for People, 1998–2005; Chairman: Braunstone Community Assoc., 2002–06; Community Resettlement Support Project, 2013–. Chairman: St Philips Centre for Study and Engagement in a Multi Faith Society, 2005–12; St Albans Diocesan Bd of Educn, 2013–; Eastern Reg. Ministry Course, 2014–; Co-Chair: Nat. Hindu Christian Forum, 2009–; Inter Faith Network UK, 2014–; Vice-Chair, C of E Mission and Public Affairs Council, 2012–. Trustee: Church Urban Fund, 2003–08; Near Neighbours, 2010–. *Recreations:* cooking, biography and history, walking, watching Rugby Union, housing and regeneration, The Archers. *Address:* Bishop's Lodge, Bedford Road, Cardington MK44 3SS. *T:* (01234) 831432. *E:* bishopbedford@stalbans.anglican.org.

BEDFORD, Archdeacon of; *see* Hughes, Ven. P. V.

BEDFORD, Robin Steven; His Honour Judge Bedford; a Circuit Judge, since 2013; *b* Heckmondwike, W Yorks, 1 Feb. 1964; *s* of Stanley and Anne Patricia Bedford; *m* 1999, Lynn Janet Ashbee; four *s*. *Educ:* Batley Grammar Sch.; Hatfield Poly. (BA Hons); Univ. of Huddersfield (LLM). Admitted as solicitor, 1988; Partner, 1989–2000, Sen. Partner, 2000–07, Jordans Solicitors; Solicitor-Advocate, Higher Courts (Civil), 2000–07; a Dep. Dist Judge, 2002–07; a Dist Judge, 2007–13. *Recreations:* classic cars, wine, cheese.

BEDFORD, Steuart John Rudolf; freelance conductor; Artistic Director, English Sinfonia, 1981–90; *b* 31 July 1939; *s* of late L. H. Bedford and Lesley Florence Keitley Duff; *m* 1st, 1969, Norma Burrowes, *qv*; 2nd, 1980, Celia, *er d* of Mr and Mrs G. R. Harding; two *d*. *Educ:* Lancing Coll., Sussex; Royal Acad. of Music. Fellow, RCO; FRAM; BA. Royal Acad. of Music, 1965; English Opera Gp, later English Music Theatre Co., 1967–80 (Co-Artistic Dir, 1976–79); Artistic Dir, 1974–98, and Exec. Artistic Dir, 1987–98, Aldeburgh Festival. Debut at Metropolitan, NY, 1974 (Death in Venice); new prodn of The Marriage of Figaro, 1975. Has conducted with English Opera Gp, Welsh National Opera, Florentine Opera, Luxembourg Philharmonic, Royal Scottish Nat. Orch., Bordeaux Opera, Opera Theatre of St Louis, NY City Opera, Canadian Opera; also at Royal Opera House, Covent Garden (operas incl. Owen Wingrave and Death in Venice, by Benjamin Britten, and Così Fan Tutte); also in Santa Fe, Buenos Aires, France, Belgium, Holland, Canada, Vienna, Denmark, etc. Recordings include a series of works by Benjamin Britten. *Recreations:* golf, gardening. *Address:* c/o HarrisonParrott Ltd, 5–6 Albion Court, Albion Place, W6 0QT.

BEDFORD-JONES, Rt Rev. Michael Hugh Harold; a Suffragan Bishop of Toronto, 1994–2008 (Area Bishop of York Scarborough, 1994–2006, of Trent-Durham, 2006–08); *b* 29 Sept. 1942; *s* of Rev. Canon Hugh Bedford-Jones and Gretchen Flagler Bedford-Jones (*née* Gray); *m* 1967, Jeanne Yvonne Soules. *Educ:* Toronto Univ. (BA 1965; MA 1979); Univ. of Trinity Coll., Toronto (STB 1968). Ordained deacon, 1967, priest, 1968; St James' Cathedral, Toronto: Asst Curate, 1968–70; Dir of Christian Educn, 1970–74; Sen. Asst, 1974–75; Rector, Ch. of the Epiphany, Scarborough, 1976–83; Regl Dean, Scarborough, 1980–83; Rector, St Aidan, Toronto, 1983–88; Regl Dean, Toronto East, 1985–88; Exec. Asst to Bishop of Toronto, 1988–91; Canon, St James' Cathedral, 1990; Dean of Dio. of Ontario and Rector of St George's Cathedral, Kingston, Ont, 1991–94. Hon. DD Univ. of Trinity Coll., Toronto, 1997; Hon. STD Thorneloe, 2004. *Recreations:* sailing, music, cottage life. *Address:* 384 Lakebreeze Drive, Newcastle, ON L1B 1P5, Canada. *E:* michaelbj94@hotmail.com.

BEDI, Kirsten Frances; *see* Oswald, K. F.

BEDI, Prof. Raman, DDS; DSc; FDSRCSE, FDSRCS, FFPH, FFGDP(UK); Professor of Transcultural Oral Health, since 2002, and Head, Centre for International Child Oral Health, since 2006, King's College, London; Director, Global Child Dental Health Taskforce, since 2006; *b* 20 May 1953; *s* of Satya-Paul Bedi and Raj Bedi (*née* Kaur); *m* 1986, Kathryn Jane Walter; three *s*. *Educ:* Headlands Sch.; Univ. of Bristol (BDS 1976, DDS 1993; DSc 2003); Trinity Coll., Bristol (DipHE Theol. 1979); Univ. of Manchester (MSc 1986). FDSRCSE 1982; FDSRCS 2002; FFPH 2003; FFGDP(UK) 2004. Lecturer in Paediatric Dentistry: Univ. of Manchester, 1979–82; Univ. of Hong Kong, 1983–86; Univ. of Edinburgh, 1988–91; Sen. Lectr in Paediatric Dentistry, Univ. of Birmingham, 1991–96; Prof. and Head of Dept of Transcultural Oral Health, Eastman Dental Inst., UCL, 1996–2002; Chief Dental Officer for England, DoH, 2002–05. Co-Dir, WHO Collaborating Centre for Disability, Culture and Oral Health, 1998–2008; Chm., Oral Health Gp, World Fedn of Public Health Assocs, 2011–. Member: NHS/DoH Top Team, 2002–05; Strategic Wider Participation Cttee, HEFCE, 2003–09; Bd, Higher Educn Leadership Foundn, 2003–06; Founding Mem., Nat. Health and Social Care Leadership Network, 2004–05. President: British Soc. for Disability and Oral Health, 2002; Educn Res. Gp, Internat. Assoc. for Dental Res., 2002–04 (Chm., Regl Develt Cttee, 2002–04); Chm., British Assoc. of Physicians of Indian Origin, 2006–09; Sec.-Gen., Global Assoc. of Physicians of Indian Origin, 2008–09. Chm., Global Child Dental Fund, 2008–; Trustee, Children's Soc., 2006–09. Mem., Gen. Synod of C of E, 1995–2005. Hon. FDSRCPGlas. Hon. DHL A. T. Still Univ., Arizona, 2009. Public Health Service Medal, USA, 2005. *Publications:* (ed with P. Jones) Betel-quid and Tobacco Chewing Among the Bangladeshi Community in the United Kingdom: usage and health issues, 1995; (with P. Jones) Embracing Goodwill: establishing healthy alliances with black organisations, 1996; (ed jtly) Dentists, Patients and Ethnic Minorities: towards the new millennium, 1996; (with P. A. Lowe) Best Practise in Primary Healthcare: oral healthcare delivery in a multi-ethnic society, 1997; (with J. Sardo Infirri) The Root Cause: oral health care in disadvantaged communities, 1999; (with E. Davidson and J. J. Liu) Health Care Professionals of Indian Origin: a common agenda, 2012; contribs to scientific jls. *Recreations:* chess, tennis, travelling. *Address:* Oak Cottage, 12 Manor Way, Potters Bar, Herts EN6 1EL. *Club:* Athenæum.

BEDINGFELD, Sir Henry (Edgar) Paston-, 10th Bt *cr* 1661, of Oxburgh, Norfolk; Norroy and Ulster King of Arms, 2010–14; *b* 7 Dec. 1943; *s* of Sir Edmund Paston-Bedingfeld, 9th Bt and late Joan Lynette (*née* Rees); *S* father, 2011; *m* 1968, Mary Kathleen, *d* of Brig. R. D. Ambrose, CIE, OBE, MC; two *s* two *d*. *Educ:* Ampleforth College, York. Chartered Surveyor. Rouge Croix Pursuivant of Arms, 1983–93; York Herald of Arms, 1993–2010. Genealogist, British Assoc. of SMO Malta, 1995–2000. Pres., Norfolk Heraldry Soc., 2006–; Vice-President: Cambridge Univ. Heraldic and Genealogical Soc., 1988–; Suffolk Family Hist. Soc., 1991–; Norfolk Record Soc., 2003–; Royal Soc. of St George, 2012–; Mem. Exec. Cttee, Standing Council of the Baronetage, 2012–. Patron, Breckland Soc., 2003–. Hon. Sec., West India Cttee, 2011–. Rep. of Duke of Norfolk, Commn d'Inf. et de Liaison des Assocs Nobles d'Europe, 1994. Mem., Académie Internat. d'Héraldique, 2009. Freeman of the City of London; Liveryman: Scriveners' Co. (Master, 2012–13). Kt of Sovereign Mil. Order of Malta. *Publications:* Oxburgh Hall, The First 500 Years, 1982; (jtly) Heraldry, 1993. *Heir: s* Richard Edmund Ambrose Paston-Bedingfeld, (Father Benedict), *b* 8 Feb. 1975. *Address:* Oxburgh Hall, Norfolk PE33 9PS. *T:* (01366) 328269.

BEDINGFIELD, Julian Peter; HM Diplomatic Service, retired; First Secretary and Deputy Head of Mission, Ljubljana, 1999–2004; *b* 23 July 1945; *s* of Thomas William Bedingfield and Eileen Bedingfield (*née* Neves); *m* 1975, Margery Mary Jones Davies; one *s* two *d*. *Educ:* Sir Joseph Williamson's Mathematical Sch., Rochester. Joined Foreign Office, 1964: lang. trng, 1968; Scientific Attaché, Moscow, 1969–70; FCO, 1970–71; Düsseldorf, 1971–73; Bonn, 1973–75; Second Secretary: (Commercial), Dhaka, 1975–76; Dep. Hd of Mission, Ulan Bator, 1976–78; FCO, 1978–82; (Admin) and Consul, Berne, 1982–86; (Chancery/Inf.), Rabat, 1986–91; First Secretary: FCO, 1991–94; UK Delegn, NATO, Brussels, 1994–99. *Recreations:* gardening, wood turning. *Club:* Rotary (Letchworth).

BEDNORZ, Johannes-Georg, PhD; Physicist at IBM Research Laboratory, Zürich, since 1982; *b* 16 May 1950. *Educ:* Swiss Federal Institute of Technology, Zürich. (Jtly) Nobel Prize for Physics, 1987. *Publications:* papers in learned jls on new super-conducting materials. *Address:* IBM Zürich Research Laboratory, Säumerstrasse 4, 8803 Rüschlikon, Switzerland.

BEECH, Prof. David John, PhD; FMedSci; Professor of Cardiovascular Science, since 2000, and Director, Cardiovascular Research, since 2008, University of Leeds; *b* Chesterfield, 5 March 1964; *s* of John and Valerie Beech; *m* 1989, Maggie Nicol; two *s* one *d*. *Educ:* Silverdale Comprehensive Sch.; Univ. of Manchester (BSc Pharmacol. 1985); St George's Hosp. Med. Sch., Univ. of London (PhD Pharmacol. 1988). Res. Fellow, Univ. of Washington, 1988–90; Wellcome Trust Fellow, Univs of London and Leeds, 1990–93; Lectr in Pharmacol., Univ. of Leeds, 1993–2000. Ed., British Jl Pharmacol., 1997–2001; Ed. and Sen. Ed., Jl Physiol., 1997–2005. Member: Selection Panel, Wellcome Trust-Dept of Biotechnol. India Alliance, 2009–15; Population and Systems Medicine Bd, MRC, 2010–14. FMedSci 2013. *Publications:* contribs to Nature. *Recreation:* running. *Address:* School of Medicine, Garstang Building, University of Leeds, Leeds LS2 9JT. *T:* (0113) 343 4323. *E:* d.j.beech@leeds.ac.uk.

BEECH, Jacqueline Elaine; Her Honour Judge Beech; a Circuit Judge, since 2007; *b* Coventry, 8 Jan. 1958; *d* of Deric Charles Beech and Maureen Mary Beech (*née* Clooney). *Educ:* Wolston High Sch. Sec. Mod.; Tile Hill Coll. of Further Educn; Preston Poly. (BA Hons 1980). Called to the Bar, Middle Temple, 1981; a Recorder, 2002–07. A Judge of the Upper Tribunal (Admin. Appeals Chamber), 2009– (Chairman: Transport Tribunal, 2000–09; London Bus Permits Appeal Panel, 2002–09). *Publications:* (contrib. transport section) Atkins Court Forms, vol. 39, 2nd edn 2006, 3rd edn 2010. *Recreations:* fell walking and all things Cumbrian, arts and literature, fine food and wine (Higher Cert. in Wine and Spirits, Wine & Spirit Education Trust). *Address:* Preston Combined Court Centre, The Law Courts, Openshaw Place, Ringway, Preston, Lancs PR1 2LL. *T:* (01772) 844700. *Club:* Reform.

BEECHAM, family name of **Baron Beecham.**

BEECHAM, Baron *cr* 2010 (Life Peer), of Benwell and Newcastle upon Tyne in the County of Tyne and Wear; **Jeremy Hugh Beecham,** Kt 1994; DL; Member, Newcastle upon Tyne City Council, since 1967 (Leader, 1977–94); Consultant, Beecham Peacock, since 2002; *b* 17 Nov. 1944; *s* of Laurence and Florence Beecham; *m* 1968, Brenda Elizabeth (*née* Woolf) (*d* 2010); one *s* one *d*. *Educ:* Royal Grammar Sch., Newcastle upon Tyne; University Coll., Oxford (First Cl. Hons Jurisprudence; MA). Chm., OU Labour Club, 1964. Admitted Solicitor, 1968; Partner, Allan Henderson Beecham & Peacock, subseq. Beecham Peacock, 1968–2002. Dir, Northern Develt Co., 1986–91. Newcastle upon Tyne City Council: Chairman: Social Services Cttee, 1973–77; Policy and Resources Cttee, 1977–94; Finance Cttee, 1979–85; Develt Cttee, 1995–97; Newcastle City Challenge, 1992–97. Chairman: AMA, 1991–97 (Dep. Chm., 1984–86; Vice Chm., 1986–91); Local Govt Assoc., 1995–2004 (Vice Chm., 2004–10); Review of Local Public Services in Wales, 2005–06; Vice Chm., Northern Regl Councils Assoc., 1986–91. Labour Party: Member: Local and Regl Govt Sub-Cttee, NEC, 1971–83, 1991–; NEC/Shadow Cabinet Wkg Pty on Future of Local Govt, 1984–87; Domestic and Internat. Policy Cttee, 1992–; Jt Policy Cttee, 1992–; NEC, 1998–2010 (Chm., 2005–06). Opposition spokesman on health, 2010–12, on local govt, 2010–, on justice, 2012–, H of L. Member: RTPI Working Party on Public Participation in Planning, 1980–82; Historic Bldgs and Monuments Commn for England, 1983–87; Local and Central Govt Relns Res. Cttee, Joseph Rowntree Meml Trust, 1987–96; President's Cttee, Business in the Community, 1988–; Bd of Trustees, NE Civic Trust, 1989–92; NHS Modernisation Bd, 2000–04; Community Voluntary and Local Services Honours Cttee, 2005–10. Pres., BURA, 1996–2009. Participant, Königswinter Conf., 1986. Member: Council of Management, Neighbourhood Energy Action, 1987–89; Council, Common Purpose, 1989–; President: Age Concern Newcastle, 1995–; Newcastle Choral Soc., 1997–; Newcastle People to People, 1998–2007; Vice President: Community Foundn, 2000–; Newcastle CVS, 2001–. Mem. Adv. Bd, Harold Hartog Sch. of Govt, Tel Aviv Univ., 2005–; Mem. Bd, New Israel Fund, 2007–. Trustee, Trusthouse Charitable Foundn, 1999–2013. Contested (Lab) Tynemouth, 1970. DL Tyne and Wear, 1995. Hon. Freeman Newcastle upon Tyne, 1995. Hon. Fellow, Univ. of Northumbria (formerly Newcastle upon Tyne Poly.), 1989. Hon. DCL Newcastle, 1992. *Recreations:* reading, history, music, very amateur photography, the Northumbrian countryside. *Address:* (office) House of Lords, SW1A 0PW; 39 The Drive, Gosforth, Newcastle upon Tyne NE3 4AJ. *T:* (0191) 285 1888.

BEECHAM, Sir Robert Adrian, 5th Bt *cr* 1914, of Ewanville, Huyton, co. Palatine of Lancaster; *b* 6 Jan. 1942; *yr s* of Sir Adrian Welles Beecham, 3rd Bt and Barbara Joyce (*née* Cohen); *S* brother, 2011, but his name does not appear on the Official Roll of the Baronetage; *m* 1969, Daphne Mattinson; one *s* one *d*. *Educ:* Winchester; Clare Coll., Cambridge (BA 1963; MA 1967). *Heir: s* Michael John Beecham [*b* 1972; *m* 2004, Rachel Smith; two *s*].

BEEDHAM, Brian James, CBE 1989; Associate Editor, The Economist, 1989–2002; *b* 12 Jan. 1928; *s* of James Victor Beedham and Nina Beedham (*née* Zambra); *m* 1960, Barbara Zollikofer. *Educ:* Leeds Grammar Sch.; The Queen's Coll., Oxford. RA, 1950–52. Asst Editor, Yorkshire Post, 1952–55; The Economist, 1955–2002: Washington correspondent, 1958–61; Foreign Editor, 1964–89. Commonwealth Fellowship, 1956–57. Fellow, Royal Geographical Society. *Recreations:* music, Kipling, Wodehouse, cats. *Address:* Coombe Hill Manor, Flat 301, 190–196 Coombe Lane West, Kingston-upon-Thames KT2 7EQ. *Club:* Travellers.

BEEDHAM, Trevor, FRCOG; Consultant Gynaecologist and Obstetrician, The Royal London and St Bartholomew's Hospitals, 1981–2009; Consultant Emeritus, Barts and The London NHS Trust, 2009; Associate Dean, since 2006, and Hon. Professor, since 2008, Barts and the London (formerly Queen Mary) School of Medicine and Dentistry; *b* 30 July 1942; *s* of Herbert and Olive Beedham (*née* Spikings); *m* 1966, Anne Darnbrough-Cameron; two *s* one *d*. *Educ:* High Pavement Grammar Sch., Nottingham; Royal Dental Hosp., and London Hosp. Med. Sch., Univ. of London (BDS 1965; MB BS Hons 1972). MRCOG 1977, FRCOG 1989. Careers Officer, 1994–98, Chm., Contg Med. Educn Cttee, 1998–2002, RCOG; Barts and The London NHS Trust: Clin. Dir, 2003–08; Dep. Med. Dir, 2006–09; Divl Dir, 2008–09; Hon. Sen. Lectr, Queen Mary Sch. of Medicine and Dentistry, 2006–08. Regional Advr and Chm., NE Thames Obs and Gyn. Higher Trng Cttee, 1991–94; Mem., Appeals Panel, Specialist Trng Authy, subseq. Postgraduate Med. Educn and Trng Bd, 1999–. Examr, MB BS, DRCOG, MRCOG, 1981–; PLAB Part 1 Panel and Med. Sch., 2001–09. Visitor, GMC, 2001–. Asst, Soc. of Apothecaries, 1996– (Chm., Exam. Bd, 2004–09; Master, 2009–10; Hon. Registrar, 2010; Dean, 2012–; Chm., Bd of Mgt, Dip. in Forensic and Clin. Aspects of Sexual Assault, 2009–12). Mem., Forensic Adv. Cttee, 2013–. Advr, UK Assoc. of Forensic Nurses, 2012–. Gov., Sons of the Clergy, 2010–. Hon. DSc Buckingham, 2010. *Publications:* contrib. and ed text books in obstetrics and gynaecology; referee for BJOG, Obstetrician and Gynaecologist, Jl of RSM, etc; contrib. British Jl of Hospital Medicine. *Recreations:* swimming, sailing. *Address:* 15 Lawrie Park Crescent, Sydenham, SE26 6HH. *T:* (020) 3252 1024. *Clubs:* Athenæum, City Livery (Mem. Council, 2014–).

BEELS, Jonathan Sidney Spencer, CMG 1998; HM Diplomatic Service, retired; *b* 19 Jan. 1943; *s* of Sidney Beels and Joan Constance Beels (*née* Groves); *m* 1st, 1966, Patricia Joan Mills (marr. diss. 1982); one *s* one *d*; 2nd, 1983, Penelope Jane Aedy (marr. diss. 1998). *Educ:* Ardingly Coll.; St John's Coll., Cambridge (MA 1969). Entered Diplomatic Service, 1965; Prague, 1970–73; FCO, 1973–77; on loan to Northern Ireland Office, 1977–78; resigned from Diplomatic Service, 1979; Govt Service, Sultanate of Oman, 1979–83; Man. Dir, Control Risks (GS) Ltd, 1983–88; rejoined Diplomatic Service, 1988; Counsellor, Nicosia, 1992–93; FCO, 1994–98. Consultant, MoD, 1998–99. *Recreations:* shooting, quad-biking.

BEENSTOCK, Prof. Michael, PhD; Pinchas Sapir Professor of Economics, Hebrew University, Jerusalem, since 1996; *b* 18 June 1946; *s* of Sidney and Taubie Beenstock; *m* 1968, Ruchi Hager; one *s* four *d*. *Educ:* London Sch. of Econs and Political Science (BSc, MSc; PhD 1976). Econ. Advisor, HM Treasury, 1970–76; Economist, World Bank, Washington, DC, 1976–78; Sen. Res. Fellow, London Business Sch., 1978–81; Esmée Fairbairn Prof. of Finance and Investment, City Univ. Business Sch., 1981–87; Prof. of Econs, Hebrew Univ., Jerusalem, 1987–96 (Lady Davis Prof., 1987–89). *Publications:* The Foreign Exchange Market, 1978; A Neoclassical Analysis of Macroeconomic Policy, 1980; Health, Migration and Development, 1980; The World Economy in Transition, 1983, 2nd edn 1984; Work, Welfare and Taxation, 1986; (jtly) Insurance for Unemployment, 1986; (ed) Modelling the Labour Market, 1988; (jtly) Modelling the World Shipping Markets, 1993; Heredity, Family and Inequality, 2012. *Recreation:* music. *Address:* Kefar Etzion 35/4, Jerusalem 93392, Israel. *T:* (2) 6723184.

BEER, Dame Gillian (Patricia Kempster), DBE 1998; FBA 1991; FRSL; King Edward VII Professor of English Literature, University of Cambridge, 1994–2002; President, Clare Hall, Cambridge, 1994–2001 (Fellow, 2001–02, Hon. Fellow, 2002); *b* 27 Jan. 1935; *d* of Owen Kempster Thomas and Ruth Winifred Bell; *m* 1962, John Bernard Beer, *qv*; three *s*. *Educ:* St Anne's Coll., Oxford (MA, BLitt; Hon. Fellow, 1989); LittD Cambridge. Asst Lectr, Bedford Coll., London, 1959–62; part-time Lectr, Liverpool Univ., 1962–64; Cambridge University: Asst Lectr 1966–71, Lectr, subseq. Reader in Literature and Narrative, 1971–89; Prof. of English, 1989–94; Fellow, Girton Coll., 1965–94 (Hon. Fellow, 1994). Andrew W. Mellon Sen. Scholar, Yale Center for British Art, 2009–11. Vice-Pres., British Acad., 1994–96; Pres., Hist. of Science Sect., BAAS, 1998. Trustee, BM, 1992–2002. Chm., Poetry Book Soc., 1992–96; President: British Comparative Lit. Soc., 2003–10; British Lit. and Sci. Soc., 2006–; Modern Humanities Res. Assoc., 2011. Chm. Judges, Booker Prize, 1997. Gen. Ed., Cambridge Studies in Nineteenth Century Lit. and Culture, 1992–. FRSL 2006. Hon. Fellow, Univ. of Wales, Cardiff, 1996. Foreign Hon. Mem., Amer. Acad. of Arts and Scis, 2001; Internat. Mem., Amer. Philosophical Soc., 2010. Hon. LittD: Liverpool, 1995; Anglia Poly., 1997; Leicester, 1999; London, 2001; Sorbonne, 2001; QUB, 2005; Hon. DLitt: Oxford, 2005; Harvard, 2012; St Andrews, 2013. *Publications:* Meredith: a change of masks, 1970; The Romance, 1970; Darwin's Plots, 1983, 3rd edn 2009; George Eliot, 1986; Arguing with the Past, 1989; (ed) The Waves by Virginia Woolf, 1992; Open Fields, 1996; Virginia Woolf: the Common Ground, 1996; (ed) The Origin of Species by Charles Darwin, 1996; (ed) Persuasion by Jane Austen, 1998; (ed) The Wolfman and Other Cases by Sigmund Freud, 2002; (ed) Love and Mr Lewisham by H. G. Wells, 2009; Jabberwocky: collected and annotated edition of the poems of Lewis Carroll, 2012; (ed) Between the Acts by Virginia Woolf. *Recreations:* music, travel, conversation. *Address:* Clare Hall, Herschel Road, Cambridge CB3 9AL. *T:* (01223) 356384 and 332360.

BEER, Ian David Stafford, CBE 1992; MA; Head Master of Harrow, 1981–91; Chairman of Trustees, RFU Injured Players Foundation, 2008–11 (Founder, 1993, Trustee, 1993–2008, and Chairman of Trustees, 2005–08, SPIRE Rugby Trust (formerly SPIRE); Chairman of Trustees, RFU Charitable Trust, 2005–08); *b* 28 April 1931; *s* of late William Beer and Doris Ethel Beer; *m* 1960, Angela Felce, *d* of Col E. S. G. Howard, MC, RA and F. D. Howard; two *s* one *d*. *Educ:* Whitgift Sch.; St Catharine's Coll., Cambridge (Exhibitioner; MA, PGCE). ESU Walter Page Scholar, 1968. Second Lieut in 1st Bn Royal Fusiliers, 1950. Bursar, Ottershaw Sch., 1955; Guinness Ltd, 1956–57; House Master, Marlborough Coll., Wilts, 1957–61; Head Master: Ellesmere Coll., Salop, 1961–69; Lancing Coll., Sussex, 1969–81. Chairman: HMC Academic Cttee, 1977–79; HMC, 1980; Physical Educn Working Gp for Nat. Curriculum, 1990–91; ISJC, then ISC, 1997–2001 (Vice-Chm., 1994–97; Chm., Adv. Cttee, 1988–91); Vice-Chm., GBA, 1994–2001; Founder Mem., Gen. Teaching Council, 2000–01. Mem., Sports Council, 1992–94. Chm. Council, Winston Churchill Meml Trust, 1997–2006 (Mem., 1990–2006; Trustee, 1998–2006); Trustee, RMC Group plc Welfare Trust, 1983–2006. Evelyn Wrench Lectr, ESU, 1988, 1990. Governor: Whitgift Sch., 1986–91; Charterhouse Sch., 1991–93; Malvern Coll., 1991–2001; Mem. Council, Univ. of Buckingham, 1992–96; Chm. of Trustees, Lancing Coll. Chapel Trust, 1996–2008. Chm. Editorial Bd, Rugby World and Post (formerly Rugby World, then Rugby Post), 1977–93. JP Shropshire, 1963–69, W Sussex, 1970–81, Middx, 1981–91, Glos, 1992. Hon. FCP 1990. *Publications:* But Headmaster!, 2001. *Recreations:* Rugby Football Union (Mem. Exec. Cttee, 1984–95; Vice Pres., 1991–93; Pres., 1993–94) (formerly: played Rugby for England; CURFC (Capt.), Harlequins, Bath, Old Whitgiftians), painting, reading, zoology, meeting people. *Address:* c/o RFU Injured Players Foundation, 200 Whitton Road, Twickenham TW2 7BA. *Clubs:* East India, Devonshire, Sports and Public Schools; Hawks (Cambridge).

BEER, Prof. Janet, PhD; Vice-Chancellor, University of Liverpool, since 2015; *b* 1 Aug. 1956; *d* of Derek Stanley John Beer and Jean Patricia Beer; *m* 1996, David Woodman; one *s* one *d*. *Educ:* Univ. of Reading (BA Hons); Univ. of Warwick (MA; PhD 1984). Pt-time Lectr, Univ. of Warwick, 1979–80 and 1981–83; Yale Fellow, Yale Univ., 1980–81; Educn Adminr, ILEA, 1983–89; Sen., then Principal Lectr, Univ. of Surrey, Roehampton, later Roehampton Univ., 1989–97; Hd, Dept of English, 1998–2002, Pro Vice-Chancellor and Dean of Faculty, 2002–07, Manchester Metropolitan Univ.; Vice-Chancellor, Oxford Brookes Univ., 2007–15. Specialist Advr, Educn and Skills Select Cttee, H of C, 2000–07; Member of Board: Higher Educn Acad., 2004–09; Equality Challenge Unit, 2008– (Chair, 2011–); Universities UK, 2009– (Vice-Pres., 2013–); UCAS, 2013–; Nat. Centre for Univs and Business, 2013–; British Council, 2014–; Mem., Adv. Bd, Higher Educn Policy Inst., 2007–; Chairman: Higher Educn Public Information Steering Gp (formerly Teaching Quality Information/Nat. Student Survey Steering Gp), 2009–; University Alliance, 2009–12; Supporting Professionalism in Admissions, 2012–14. Vis. Fellow, Nuffield Coll., Oxford, 2011–. *Publications:* Edith Wharton: traveller in the land of letters, 1990, 2nd edn 1995; Kate Chopin, Edith Wharton and Charlotte Perkins Gilman: studies in short fiction, 1997, 2nd edn 2005; Edith Wharton, 2002; (ed jtly) Special Relationships: Anglo-American antagonisms and affinities 1854–1936, 2002; (jtly) American Feminism: key source documents 1848–1920, 2002; (ed) The Cambridge Companion to Kate Chopin, 2008; (with Avril Horner) Edith Wharton: sex, satire and the older woman, 2011. *Recreations:* swimming, walking, theatre, family. *Address:* Office of the Vice-Chancellor, University of Liverpool, The Foundation Building, Liverpool L69 7ZX. *T:* (0151) 7942003. *E:* J.P.Beer@Liverpool.ac.uk.

BEÉR, Prof. János Miklós, DSc, PhD; FREng; Professor of Chemical and Fuel Engineering, Massachusetts Institute of Technology (MIT), 1976–93, now Emeritus; Scientific Director, MIT Combustion Research Facilities, since 1980; *b* Budapest, 27 Feb. 1923; *s* of Sándor Beér and Gizella Trismai; *m* 1944, Marta Gabriella Csató. *Educ:* Berzsenyi Dániel Gymnasium, Budapest; Univ. of Budapest (Dipl-Ing 1950); PhD Sheffield, 1960, DSc(Tech) Sheffield, 1967. Heat Research Inst., Budapest: Research Officer, 1949–52; Head, Combustion Dept, 1952–56; Princ. Lectr (part-time), University of Budapest, 1953–56; Research Engr, Babcock & Wilcox Ltd, Renfrew, 1957; Research Bursar, University of Sheffield, 1957–60; Head, Research Stn, Internat. Flame Research Foundn, Ijmuiden, Holland, 1960–63; Prof., Dept of Fuel Science, Pa State Univ., 1963–65; Newton Drew Prof. of Chemical Engrg and Fuel Technology and Head of Dept, Univ. of Sheffield, 1965–76; Dean, Faculty of Engineering, Univ. of Sheffield, 1973–75; Programme Dir for Combustion, MIT Energy Lab., 1976–86. Member: Adv. Council on R&D for Fuel and Power, DTI, later Dept of Energy, 1973–76; Adv. Bd, Safety in Mines Research, Dept of Energy, 1974–76; Clean Air Council, DoE, 1974–76; Bd of Directors, The Combustion Inst., Pittsburgh, USA, 1974–86; Mem., Adv. Cttee, Italian Nat. Res. Council, 1974–; Chm., Clean Coal Utilization Project, US Nat. Acad. of Scis, 1987–88; Mem., US Nat. Coal Council (Adv. Council to Energy Sec.), 1993–. Gen. Superintendent of Research, Internat. Flame Research Foundn, 1972–89 (Hon. Supt of Res., 1990–). Editor, Fuel and Energy Science Monograph Series, 1966–. Australian Commonwealth Vis. Fellow, 1972; Fellow ASME, 1978 (Moody Award, 1964; Percy Nicholls Award, 1988); FREng (FEng 1979). Hon. Member: Hungarian Acad. of Scis, 1986; Hungarian Acad. of Engrg, 1991. Foreign Mem., Finnish Acad. of Technology, 1989. Dr *hc* Miskolc, Hungary, 1987; Budapest Tech. Sci., Hungary, 1997. Melchett Medal, Inst. Energy, London, 1985; Coal Science Gold Medal, BCURA, 1986; Alfred Edgerton Gold Medal, Combustion Inst., 1986; Axel Axelson Johnson Medal, Swedish Acad. of Engrg Scis, 1995; Energy System Award, AIAA, 1998; George Westinghouse Gold Medal, ASME, 2001; Homer H. Lowry Award, US Dept of Energy, 2003; Washington Coal Club Lifetime Achievement Award, 2011; Worcester Reed Warner Medal, ASME, 2012. Knight's Cross, Order of Merit (Hungarian Republic), 2008. *Publications:* (with N. Chigier) Combustion Aerodynamics, 1972; (ed with M. W. Thring) Industrial Flames, 1972; (ed with H. B. Palmer) Developments in Combustion Science and Technology, 1974; (ed with N. Afgan) Heat Transfer in Flames, 1975; 324 scientific and technical papers; contribs to Nature, Combustion and Flame, Basic Engrg Jl, Amer. Soc. Mech. Engrg, Jl Inst. F, ZVDI, Internat. Gas Wärme, Proc. Internat. Symposia on Combustion, etc. *Recreations:* swimming, rowing, reading, music. *Address:* Department of Chemical Engineering, Massachusetts Institute of Technology, Cambridge, MA 02139, USA. *T:* (617) 2536661.

BEER, Jason; QC 2011; a Recorder, since 2010; *b* Gillingham, Kent, 11 Nov. 1969; *s* of Barrington Beer and June Patricia Beer; *m* 2007, Samantha Bird; one *s* one *d*. *Educ:* Gillingham Grammar Sch. for Boys; Warwick Univ. (LLB Hons). Called to the Bar, Inner Temple, 1992; Jun. Counsel to the Crown, 2008–11. *Publications:* Public Inquiries, 2011. *Address:* 5 Essex Court, Temple, EC4Y 9AH. *T:* (020) 7410 2000, *Fax:* (020) 7410 2011. *E:* beer@5essexcourt.co.uk.

BEER, Prof. John Bernard, LittD; FBA 1994; Professor of English Literature, University of Cambridge, 1987–93, Professor Emeritus, since 1993; Fellow of Peterhouse, Cambridge, 1964–93, Emeritus Fellow, since 1993; *b* 31 March 1926; *s* of John Bateman Beer and Eva Chilton; *m* 1962, Gillian Patricia Kempster Thomas (*see* Dame G. P. K. Beer); three *s*. *Educ:* Watford Grammar Sch.; St John's Coll., Cambridge (MA, PhD); LittD Cantab 1995. Research Fellow, St John's Coll., Cambridge, 1955–58; Lectr, Manchester Univ., 1958–64; Univ. Lectr, Cambridge, 1964–78; Reader in English Literature, Cambridge, 1978–87. British Acad. Chatterton Lectr, 1964; Vis. Prof., Univ. of Virginia, 1975; Leverhulme Emeritus Fellowship, 1995–96; Stanton Lectureship in Philos. of Religion, 2006–07; numerous lecture tours abroad. Pres., Charles Lamb Soc., 1989–2002. Gen. Ed., Coleridge's Writings, 1990–, Coleridge's Responses, 2007–08. *Publications:* Coleridge the Visionary, 1959; The Achievement of E. M. Forster, 1962; (ed) Coleridge's Poems, 1963, new edn 1999; Blake's Humanism, 1968; Blake's Visionary Universe, 1969; (ed) Coleridge's Variety: bicentenary studies, 1974; Coleridge's Poetic Intelligence, 1977; Wordsworth and the Human Heart, 1978; Wordsworth in Time, 1979; (ed with G. K. Das) E. M. Forster: a human exploration, 1979; (ed) A Passage to India: essays in interpretation, 1985; (ed) Aids to Reflection, 1993; Romantic Influences: contemporary, Victorian, modern, 1993; Against Finality, 1993; (ed) Questioning Romanticism, 1995; (ed) Selected Poems of Arthur Hugh Clough, 1998; Providence and Love: studies in Wordsworth, Channing, Myers, George Eliot and Ruskin, 1998; (ed) Coleridge's Writings: On Religion and Psychology, 2002; Romantic Consciousness: Blake to Mary Shelley, 2003; Post-Romantic Consciousness: Dickens to Plath, 2003; William Blake: a literary life, 2005; Romanticism, Revolution and Language, 2009; Coleridge's Play of Mind, 2010; D. H. Lawrence: nature, narrative, art, identity, 2014; numerous articles and reviews. *Recreations:* music, travel. *Address:* Peterhouse, Cambridge CB2 1RD. *T:* (home) (01223) 356384. *Club:* Royal Over-Seas League.

BEER, Ven. John Stuart; Archdeacon of Cambridge (formerly Ely), 2004–14; Bye Fellow, Fitzwilliam College, Cambridge, since 2001; *b* 15 March 1944; *s* of late John Gilbert Beer and May (*née* Scott); *m* 1970, Susan, *d* of late Gordon and Jessie Spencer; two *s* one *d*. *Educ:* Roundhay Sch.; Pembroke Coll., Oxford (MA (Theol.) 1968); Westcott House, Cambridge (MA 1976). Advertising and Finance, Rowntree & Co. Ltd, York, 1965–69; ordained deacon, 1971, priest, 1972; Asst Curate, St John the Baptist, Knaresborough, 1971–74; Fellow and Chaplain, Fitzwilliam Coll., Cambridge, and Chaplain, New Hall, 1974–80; Rector of Toft with Hardwick, Caldecote and Childerley, 1980–87; Dir of Post Ordination Training and Dir of Studies for Readers, dio. of Ely, and Vicar of Grantchester, 1987–97; Dir of Ordinands, 1987–2002, Co-Dir, 1993–2002, dio. Ely; Archdeacon of Huntingdon, 1997–2004, and of Wisbech, 2003–04. Mem., Ethics Cttee, Dunn Res. Inst., 1987–2001. Chm., Cathedral Pilgrims Assoc. Conf., 1987–97. *Publications:* Who is Jesus?, 1982; (contrib.) Sermons from St Benet's, 2010; contribs to theol jls. *Recreations:* tennis, golf, music, wine.

BEER, Air Vice-Marshal Peter George, CB 1995; CBE 1987 (OBE 1979); LVO 1974; Fellow and Home Bursar, Jesus College, Oxford, 1997–2006, now Emeritus Fellow; *b* 16 July 1941; *s* of Herbert George Beer and Kathleen Mary Beer; *m* 1975, Fiona Georgina Hamilton Davidson; two *s*. *Educ:* Hugh Sexey's Sch., Bruton; MA Oxon 1997. Equerry to HM the Queen, 1971–74; Officer Commanding: No 55 Sqdn, 1977–79; RAF Brize Norton, 1984–86; Dir, RAF Plans and Programmes, 1989–91; Comdr British Forces, Falkland Is, 1991–92; Dir-Gen. Training and Personnel, RAF, 1992–94; COS, Personnel and Training Comd, RAF, 1994–95, retd. Non-exec. Dir, Oxford Radcliffe Hosps NHS Trust, 1997–2003. Vice-Pres., RAF Hockey Assoc. *Recreations:* cricket, opera, travel. *Address:* Southfield, Stonehill Lane, Southmoor, Oxon OX13 5HU. *Clubs:* Royal Air Force, MCC.

BEER, Victoria Louise, CBE 2013; Executive Principal, Ashton on Mersey School, Sale, since 2011; *b* Middlesbrough, 22 Oct. 1966; *d* of Robert Littlefair and Margaret Littlefair; *m* 1998, Roger Beer. *Educ:* Northfield Comp. Sch., Billingham; Nottingham Trent Univ. (BA Hons Communication Studies); Univ. of Leicester (PGCE English). NPQH. Teacher of English, Macmillan Coll., Middlesbrough, 1993–98; Head of English, Wright Robinson Sch., Manchester, 1998–2001; Dep. Head, 2001–07, Head, 2007–11, Ashton on Mersey Sch. *Recreations:* gardening, holidays. *Address:* Ashton on Mersey School, Cecil Avenue, Sale, Cheshire M33 5BP. *E:* vbeer@aom.trafford.sch.uk; Lower Hague Barn, Lower Hague, New Mills, High Peak SK22 3AP. *E:* vickybeer@yahoo.co.uk.

BEERLING, Prof. David John, PhD; FRS 2014; Professor of Palaeoclimatology, University of Sheffield, since 2002; *b* Tunbridge Wells, 1965; *s* of John William Beerling, *qv*; *m* 2011, Juliette Dawn Fraser. *Educ:* University Coll., then Univ. of Wales Coll., Cardiff (BSc Hons 1987; PhD 1990). Post-doctoral research scientist: RHBNC, 1990–91; Univ. of Durham, 1991–93; Royal Soc. Univ. Res. Fellow, 1994–2012. Edward P. Bass Dist. Vis. Envmtl Schol., 2008–09, and Dist. Lectr, 2008, Yale Inst. of Biospheric Studies, Yale Univ. Royal Soc. Wolfson Res. Merit Award, 2009–14. Scientific Consultant, How to Grow a Planet, Life from Light, BBC TV series, 2011–12. Lectures: Eighth Annual Venn, Maths Inst., Univ. of Hull, 2008; Rothamsted, Rothamsted Res., Harpenden, 2012; Holden Botany, Univ. of Nottingham, 2013. Philip Leverhulme Prize in Earth Scis, Leverhulme Trust, 2001. *Publications:* (with F. I. Woodward) Vegetation and the Terrestrial Carbon Cycle: modelling the first 400 million years, 2001; The Emerald Planet: how plants changed Earth's history, 2007, repr. 2012; contribs to learned jls incl. Philosophical Trans Royal Soc. *Recreations:* fishing (coarse, game, sea), fell running, literature, history of science, food, cinema. *Address:* Department of Animal and Plant Sciences, University of Sheffield, Sheffield S10 2TN. *T:* (0114) 222 4359, *Fax:* (0114) 222 0002. *E:* d.j.beerling@sheffield.ac.uk.

BEERLING, John William; freelance media consultant, film director, and writer, since 1994; cruise ship lecturer, since 2008; *b* 12 April 1937; *s* of Raymond Starr and May Elizabeth Julia Beerling; *m* 1st, 1959, Carol Ann Reynolds (marr. diss. 1991); one *s* one *d*; 2nd, 1993, Celia Margaret Potter (marr. diss. 1998); 3rd, 1999, Susan Patricia Armstrong. *Educ:* Sir Roger Manwood's Grammar Sch., Sandwich, Kent. National Service, RAF, 1955–57. Joined BBC, 1957; Studio Manager, 1958; Producer, 1962; Head of Radio 1 Programmes, 1983; Controller, Radio 1, 1985–93. Chairman: Radio Data Systems Forum, Geneva, 1993–2015; Radio Skipton CIC, 2012–14; Dir, Stereo Pair, 1997–98; Partner, The Great Outdoor Picture Co., 1998–2002; Man. Dir, Classic Gold Digital Radio, 2000–02. Gov., Brits Sch. for Performing Arts and Technology, 1995–2006. Pres., TRIC, 1992–93. Fellow, Radio Acad., 2005. *Publications:* Emperor Rosko's D. J. Handbook, 1976; Radio 1—The Inside Scene, 2008. *Recreations:* photography, fishing, ski-ing, watercolour artist. *Address:* Rockfield, 62 Raikeswood Drive, Skipton, N Yorks BD23 1LY. *W:* www.johnnybeerling.com.
See also D. J. Beerling.

BEESLEY, Dr Ian Blake; Official Historian, Cabinet Office, since 2007; Chairman: Wisdom of the Ancients Consulting Ltd, since 2003; Postcode Address File Advisory Board, since 2007; Secretary-General, European Chiropractors' Union, since 2015; *b* 11 July 1942; *s* of Frank and Catherine Beesley; *m* 1st, 1964, Birgitte (*née* Smith) (marr. diss. 1982); 2nd, 1983, Elizabeth (*née* Wigley) (marr. diss. 1998); one *s* two *d*; 3rd, 2000, Edna (*née* Chivers) (CBE 2006); one step *s*. *Educ:* Manchester Grammar School; St Edmund Hall, Oxford (PPE 1963; MA; Cert. in Statistics 1964); Queen Mary, Univ. of London (PhD 2013). Central Statistical Office, 1964–76; Chief Statistician, HM Treasury, 1976–78; Dep. Head, Unit supporting Lord Rayner, PM's adviser on efficiency, 1981–83; Under Sec. and Official Head of PM's Efficiency Unit, 1983–86; Partner, Price Waterhouse, subseq. PricewaterhouseCoopers, 1986–2003. Comr for Nat. Statistics, 2004–08. Alternate Mem., Jarratt Cttee on efficiency in universities, 1984–85; Mem., Croham Cttee to review function and operation of UGC, 1985–87. Member: Employment Service Adv. Gp, 1992–98; Expert Gp advising Govt on Nat. Experience Corps, 2000–01; Home Sec.'s Expert Gp on compilation and publication of crime statistics, 2006. Mem., Council, Surrey Univ., 1986–92. FSS 1966; FRSA 1990. Freeman: Co. of Mgt Consultants, 2003; City of London, 2003. *Publications:* Policy analysis and evaluation in British Government (RIPA seminar papers), 1983; (contrib.) Straight from the CEO, 1998; (contrib.) The Real Iron Lady: working with Mrs T, 2013; contribs to Jl Royal Statistical Soc.; articles on value for money in the arts. *Address:* (office) 15 Park Lane, Southwold IP18 6HL. *Club:* Savile.

BEESLEY, Peter Frederick Barton; Joint Registrar, Faculty Office of the Archbishop of Canterbury, since 2012 (Registrar, 1981–2012); Partner and Consultant, Lee Bolton Monier-Williams, since 2008; *b* 30 April 1943; *s* of Ronald Fitzgerald Barton Beesley and Mary Kurczyn (*née* Parker); *m* 1974, Elizabeth Jane Grahame; one *s* two *d*. *Educ:* King's School, Worcester; Exeter Univ. (LLB); Coll. of Law, Guildford. Articled Clerk and Asst Solicitor, Windeatt & Windeatt, 1965–68; Asst Solicitor, 1968–69, Partner, 1969–2008, Sen. Partner, 2000–08, Lee Bolton & Lee. Jt Registrar, Dio. St Albans, 1969–78; Registrar: Dio. of Guildford, 1981–2013; Woodard Corp., 1987–2011; Dio. of Ely, 2002–13 (Jt, 1978–2002); Dio. of Hereford, 2007–13 (Jt, 1983–2007). Legal Advr, Nat. Soc. (C of E) for Promoting Religious Educn, 1975–2013; Secretary: Ecclesiastical Law Assoc., 1978–98 (Vice-Chm., 1998–2000; Chm., 2000–02); Ecclesiastical Law Soc., 1987–2010; Mem. Legal Adv. Commn, General Synod of C of E, 1992–; Pres., City of Westminster Law Soc., 1991–92. Mem., Glaziers' Trust, 1996– (Vice-Chm., 1998–2000; Chm., 2000–03). Liveryman, Glaziers' and Painters' of Glass Co., 1981 (Mem. Ct Assts, 1995–; Master, 2005–06); Chm., London Stained Glass Repository, 2009–11; Vice Chm., Glaziers Foundn, 2011–. Trustee, Arbory Trust, 2000–14; Bishopsland Educnl Trust, 2002–. Governor: Hampstead Parochial Sch., 1983–2003 (Chm., 1986–95); Sarum Hall Sch., 1997–. *Publications:* (contrib. jtly) Encyclopaedia of Forms and Precedents, Vol. 13, Ecclesiastical Law, 1987; Anglican Marriage in England and Wales, a Guide to the Law for Clergy, 1992. *Address:* (office) 1 The Sanctuary, Westminster, SW1P 3JT. *T:* (020) 7222 5381. *Clubs:* Athenæum, MCC.

BEESON, Andrew Nigel Wendover; company director; *b* 30 March 1944; *s* of Nigel Wendover Beeson (killed in action 1944) and Anne Beeson (*née* Sutherland, now Hodges); *m* 1st, 1971, Susan Gerard (marr. diss. 1983); one *s* one *d*; 2nd, 1986, Carrie Martin; one *d*. *Educ:* Eton Coll. Partner, Capel Cure Myers, 1972–85; Director: ANZ Merchant Bank, 1985–87; ANZ McCaughan, 1987–89; Founder, Beeson Gregory Holdings Ltd, 1989; CEO, 1989–2001, Dep. Chm., 2001, Beeson Gregory Gp; Chm., Evolution Gp plc, 2002–03. Non-executive Director: IP2IPO Gp, 2001–04; Woolworths Gp, 2001–08; NB Real Estate Gp (formerly Nelson Bakewell Hldgs), 2001–10; Schroder Gp plc, 2004– (Sen. Ind. Dir, 2010–12; Chm., 2012–); Queen's Club Ltd, 2007–10; Westhouse Hldgs, 2009–12; DataWind UK, 2007–13 (non-exec. Chm., 2007–12). Founding Chm., City Gp for Small Cos, 1992–95; Director: European Assoc. Securities Dealers, 1995–2002; European Assoc. Securities Dealers Automatic Quotations, 1996–2001; Assoc. of Private Client Investment Managers and Stockbrokers, 2002–03. Trustee, Tennis and Rackets Assoc., 1996–2013. Achievement Award, Coopers & Lybrand, 1995. *Recreations:* Real tennis, shooting, collecting. *Address:* 21 Warwick Square, SW1V 2AB. *T:* (020) 7834 2903. *Clubs:* MCC (Mem. Cttee, 2004–07; Trustee, 2013–), Pratt's, White's; Swinley Golf (Ascot); Royal West Norfolk Golf.

BEESON, Very Rev. Trevor Randall, OBE 1997; writer; Dean of Winchester, 1987–96, now Dean Emeritus; *b* 2 March 1926; *s* of late Arthur William and Matilda Beeson; *m* 1950, Josephine Grace Cope (*d* 1997); two *d*. *Educ:* King's Coll., London (AKC 1950; FKC 1987); St Boniface Coll., Warminster. RAF Met Office, 1944–47. Deacon, 1951; Priest, 1952; Curate, Leadgate, Co. Durham, 1951–54; Priest-in-charge and subseq. Vicar of St Chad, Stockton-on-Tees, 1954–65; Curate of St Martin-in-the-Fields, London, 1965–71; Vicar of Ware, Herts, 1971–76; Canon of Westminster, 1976–87; Treasurer, Westminster, 1978–82; Rector of St Margaret's, Westminster, 1982–87; Chaplain to Speaker of House of Commons, 1982–87. Chaplain of St Bride's, Fleet Street, 1967–84. Television and radio commentator and presenter, 1968–82; Religious Programmes Advr, LWT, 1970–86. Chm., Christian Action, 1988–96. Gen. Sec., Parish and People, 1962–64; Editor, New Christian, and Man. Dir, Prism Publications Ltd, 1965–70; European Corresp. of The Christian Century (Chicago), 1970–83; Chm., SCM Press Ltd, 1978–87. Select Preacher, Oxford, 1980, 1991. Hon. Asst Priest, Romsey Abbey and United Benefice of Braishfield, 1997–. Mem. Council, WWF, 1987–94. MA (Lambeth) 1976; Hon. DLitt Southampton, 1999. *Publications:* New Area Mission, 1963; (jtly) Worship in a United Church, 1964; An Eye for an Ear, 1972; The Church of England in Crisis, 1973; Discretion and Valour: religious conditions in Russia and Eastern Europe, 1974 (trans. French, German, Italian, Finnish, Russian); Britain Today and Tomorrow, 1978; Westminster Abbey, 1981; A Vision of Hope: the churches and change in Latin America, 1984; (contrib.) God's Truth, 1988; A Dean's Diary: Winchester 1987–1996, 1997; Window on Westminster, 1998; Rebels and Reformers, 1999; (contrib.) AD 2000 Years of Christianity, 1999; The Bishops, 2002; (ed) Priests and Prelates, Daily Telegraph Obituaries, 2002; The Deans, 2004; (contrib.) Christianity: a complete guide, 2005; The Canons, 2006; Round the Church in 50 Years: a personal journey, 2007; In Tuneful Accord: the church musicians, 2009; The Church's Folk Songs: a history of hymns ancient and modern, 2011; The Church's Other Half: women's ministry, 2011; Priests and Politics, 2013; contrib. to DNB, Oxford Dictionary of the Church. *Recreation:* gardening. *Address:* 69 Greatbridge Road, Romsey, Hants SO51 8FE. *T:* (01794) 514627.
See also Very Rev. C. W. Taylor.

BEESTON, James, OBE 2004; Consultant (part-time), Invigour Ltd, since 2009 (Chairman, 2001–09); *b* 2 April 1947; *s* of Richard and Mary Beeston; *m* 1971, Christine, *d* of Barry and Enid Thomas; two *s*. *Educ:* King Edward's, Camp Hill; Birmingham Sch. of Planning. DipTP. Birmingham City Council: Public Works Dept, 1965–74; Central Area Planning Officer, 1974–80; Divl Planning Officer, 1980–85; Asst Dir of Develt, 1985–87; Project Controller, National Indoor Arena; Co-ordinator, first phase, Birmingham Olympics bid; Develt Manager and Dep. Chief Exec., Birmingham Heartlands Ltd, 1987–92; Chief Executive: Birmingham Heartlands Develt Corp., 1992–98; Millennium Point Trust Co., 1997–2001. Dir, Beeston Associates Ltd, 2001–11. Mem., Governing Body, Birmingham City Univ., 2007–. Governor: King Edward VI Camp Hill Sch. for Boys, Birmingham, 1996–; Schs of King Edward the Sixth in Birmingham, 2003– (Chm., 2011–15). *Publications:* (jtly) Negotiating with Planning Authorities. *Recreations:* family, cricket, sport, gardening, travel. *Address:* c/o Invigour Ltd, Cornwall Buildings, 45–51 Newhall Street, Birmingham B3 3QR.

BEESTON, Kevin Stanley; Chairman, Taylor Wimpey plc, since 2010; *b* 18 Sept. 1962; *s* of Denis and Patricia Beeston; *m* 1991, Jayne Anne Knowles; two *s* one *d*. *Educ:* Gorleston Grammar Sch. ACMA 1986, FCMA 1990. Serco Group plc, 1985–2010: Finance Dir, 1996–99; Chief Exec., 1999–2002; Exec. Chm., 2002–07; Chm., 2007–10. Chairman: Partnerships in Care, 2007–; Infinitas Learning BV, 2007–10; Domestic & General Hldgs, 2008–; Equiniti, 2011–; non-exec. Dir, IMI plc, 2005–12. *T:* (01784) 410208.

BEETHAM, Geoffrey Howard, CB 1992; Legal Adviser to Department of Transport, 1983–93; Principal Assistant Solicitor, Treasury Solicitor's Department, 1983–93; *b* 9 Jan. 1933; *s* of Reginald Percy Beetham and Hetty Lilian Beetham (*née* Redman); *m* 1st, 1956, Valerie Douglass (marr. diss. 1975); three *d*; 2nd, 1977, Carol Ann Dorrell; two step *s*. *Educ:* City of London Sch.; St John's Coll., Oxford (BA Jurisp.). Nat. Service, RAF, 1951–53. Solicitor, 1960; Assistant Solicitor: Metropolitan Borough of Battersea, 1960–65; London Borough of Wandsworth, 1965–70; Sen. Legal Assistant and Asst Solicitor, DoE, 1970–77; Asst Solicitor, Dept of Transport, 1977–83. Legal Mem., Mental Health Review Tribunal, 1994–2005. *Recreations:* throwing pots, music, countryside.

BEETHAM, Marshal of the Royal Air Force Sir Michael (James), GCB 1978 (KCB 1976); CBE 1967; DFC 1944; AFC 1960; DL; Chief of the Air Staff, 1977–82; Air ADC to the Queen, 1977–82; *b* 17 May 1923; *s* of Major G. C. Beetham, MC; *m* 1956, Patricia Elizabeth Lane; one *s* one *d*. *Educ:* St Marylebone Grammar School. Joined RAF, 1941; pilot trng, 1941–42; commnd 1942; Bomber Comd: 50, 57 and 35 Sqdns, 1943–46; HQ Staff, 1947–49; 82 (Recce) Sqdn, E Africa, 1949–51; psa 1952; Air Min. (Directorate Operational Requirements), 1953–56; CO 214 (Valiant) Sqdn Marham, 1958–60; Gp Captain Ops, HQ Bomber Comd, 1962–64; CO RAF Khormaksar, Aden, 1964–66; idc 1967; Dir Ops (RAF), MoD, 1968–70; Comdt, RAF Staff Coll., 1970–72; ACOS (Plans and Policy), SHAPE, 1972–75; Dep. C-in-C, Strike Command, 1975–76; C-in-C RAF Germany, and Comdr, 2nd Tactical Allied Air Force, 1976–77. Hon. Air Cdre, 2620 (Co. of Norfolk) Sqdn, RAuxAF Regt, 1983–2001; Pres., Bomber Comd Assoc., 1986–. Chm., GEC Avionics Ltd, 1986–90 (Dir, 1984–91); Dir, Brixton Estate PLC, 1983–93. Chm. Trustees, 1983–99, Pres. Soc. of Friends, 1999–, RAF Museum; Pres., RAF Historical Soc., 1993–. Governor: Cheltenham Coll., 1983–89; Wymondham Coll., 1990–98. FRSA 1979. DL Norfolk, 1989. Hon. Liveryman, Hon. Co. of Air Pilots (formerly GAPAN), 1983. Polish Order of Merit, 1998. *Recreations:* golf, tennis. *Clubs:* Royal Air Force (Pres., 1992–2002, Vice Patron, 2003–); Royal West Norfolk Golf.

See also Maj.-Gen. G. Risius.

BEETON, David Christopher, CBE 1998; Chairman, Roman Baths Foundation, since 2015; *b* 25 Aug. 1939; *s* of Ernest Beeton and Ethel Beeton; *m* 1968, Brenda Lomax; two *s*. *Educ:* Ipswich Sch.; King's Coll., London Univ. (LLB). Solicitor. Chief Exec., Bath CC, 1973–85; Sec., National Trust, 1985–89; Chief Exec., Historic Royal Palaces, 1989–99; Dir Gen., British Casino Assoc., 2000–04. Chm., Bath World Heritage Site Steering Gp, 2009–13. Hon. MA Bath, 2003. *Recreations:* swimming, historic buildings, cooking, music. *Address:* 61 Lyncombe Hill, Bath BA2 4PH. *T:* (01225) 317026.

BEEVOR, Antony James, FRSL; historian; *b* 14 Dec. 1946; *s* of John Grosvenor Beevor and Carinthia Jane Beevor (*née* Waterfield); *m* 1986, Artemis Clare Antonia Cooper, *qv*; one *s* one *d*. *Educ:* Winchester Coll.; RMA Sandhurst. Served 11th Hussars (PAO), 1967–70; posts in mktg and advertising, London and Paris, 1971–75; occasional journalism and literary criticism. Mem., Armed Forces into the 21st Century seminars, KCL, 1993–95; Visiting Professor: Sch. of Hist., Classics and Archaeology, Birkbeck Coll., London Univ., 2002–; Sch. of History, Univ. of Kent, 2011–; Lees Knowles Lectr, Cambridge, 2002; Univ. of Kent, 2011–; Boeing Vis. Fellow, Australian War Meml, 2012. Member: Exec. Council, French Theatre Season, 1996–97; Council, Soc. for Army Historical Res., 2000–03; Council, Soc. of Authors, 2005– (Chm., 2003–05); Mem. Mgt Cttee, 2001–05); Cttee, London Library, 2002–04; Cttee, Waterloo 200, 2011–. Dir, Ocito Ltd, 2003–. Judge: Shiva Naipaul Meml Prize, 2000; British Acad. Book Prize, 2004; David Cohen Prize, 2005; Mem., Steering Cttee, Samuel Johnson Prize, 2004–. Patron, Nat. Acad. of Writing, 2000–. FRSL 1999. Hon. DLitt: Kent, 2004; Bath, 2009; UEA, 2014; York, 2015. Chevalier de l'Ordre des Arts et des Lettres (France), 1997; Order of the Cross of Terra Mariana (Estonia), 2008. *Publications:* four novels; The Spanish Civil War, 1982; Inside the British Army, 1990; Crete: the battle and the resistance, 1991 (Runciman Prize); (with Artemis Cooper) Paris After the Liberation, 1994; Stalingrad, 1998 (Samuel Johnson Prize, Wolfson Prize for History, Hawthornden Prize, 1999); (contrib.) The British Army, Manpower and Society, 1999; Berlin: The Downfall 1945, 2002 (Longman-History Today Trustees' Award, 2003); The Mystery of Olga Chekhova, 2004; (ed with L. Vinogradova) A Writer At War: Vasily Grossman with the Red Army 1941–1945, 2005; (contrib.) Russia, War, Peace and Diplomacy: essays in honour of John Erickson, 2005; La Guerra Civil Española, 2005 (La Vanguardia Prize, 2005; UK edn as The Battle for Spain, 2006); D-Day: the battle for Normandy, 2009 (RUSI Duke of Westminster Medal for Mil. Lit., 2010; Prix Henry Malherbe, Assoc. des Écrivains Combattants, 2010); The Second World War, 2012; Ardennes 1944, 2015. *Address:* 54 St Maur Road, SW6 4DP. *W:* www.antonybeevor.com. *Club:* Brooks's.

BEEVOR, Antony Romer, MBE 2010; Senior Advisor, SG Hambros, 2000–03 (Managing Director, 1998–2000); *b* 18 May 1940; *s* of late Miles Beevor and Sybil (*née* Gilliat); *m* 1970, Cecilia Hopton; one *s* one *d*. *Educ:* Winchester; New Coll., Oxford (BA). Admitted Solicitor, 1965. Ashurst Morris Crisp & Co., 1962–72 (on secondment as Sec., Panel on Takeovers and Mergers, 1969–71); joined Hambros Bank, 1972; Dir, 1974–98; Exec. Dir, 1985–98; on secondment, as Dir-Gen., Panel on Takeovers and Mergers, 1987–89 (Dep. Chm., 1999–2013); Director: Hambros plc, 1990–98; (non-exec.), Rugby Gp, 1993–2000; Gerrard Group, 1995–2000; Croda International, 1996–2005 (Chm., 2002–05); Helical Bar, 2000–12; Nestor Healthcare Gp, 2000–03 (Chm., 2002–03). Mem. Council, 1970–2009, Chm., 1999–2009, Fairbridge; Chm., Croda Trustees Ltd, 2006–09. Gov., Francis Holland Schs Trust, 2013–; Mem., Audit Cttee, Compton Verney House Trust, 2013–. *Recreation:* low level golf. *Clubs:* Hurlingham, Brooks's.

BEEVOR, Sir Thomas Agnew, 7th Bt *cr* 1784; *b* 6 Jan. 1929; *s* of Comdr Sir Thomas Beevor, 6th Bt, and Edith Margaret Agnew (who *m* 2nd, 1944, Rear-Adm. R. A. Currie, CB, DSC; she *d* 1985); *S* father, 1943; *m* 1st, 1957, Barbara Clare (marr. diss., 1965), *y d* of Capt. R. L. B. Cunliffe, RN (retd); one *s* two *d*; 2nd, 1966, Carola (marr. diss. 1975), *d* of His Honour J. B. Herbert, MC; 3rd, 1976, Mrs Sally Bouwens, White Hall, Saham Toney, Norfolk. *Heir: s* Thomas Hugh Cunliffe Beevor [*b* 1 Oct. 1962; *m* 1988, Charlotte Louise, *e d* of Keith E. Harvey; two *s* one *d*]. *Address:* The Old Woodyard, Hargham, Norwich NR16 2JW.

BEFFA, Jean-Louis Guy Henri, Hon. CBE 2005; Grand Officier de la Légion d'Honneur; Chairman, Board of Directors, Compagnie de Saint-Gobain, 2007–10, now Hon. Chairman (Chairman and Chief Executive Officer, 1986–2007); *b* 11 Aug. 1941; *m* 1967, Marie-Madeleine Brunel; two *s* one *d*. *Educ:* Ecole Polytechnique (Ing. au Corps des Mines); Dip. de l'Inst d'Etudes Politiques de Paris. Compagnie de Saint-Gobain: Vice-Pres., Corporate Planning, 1974–77; Pres., Pipe Div., 1978–82; Chief Operating Officer, 1982–86. Vice Chm. Bd, BNP Paribas, 2000–10. Mem., Supervisory Bd, Siemens, 2008–13; Dir, ENGIE (formerly GDF Suez), 2008–. Comdr, Order of Merit (Germany). *Recreations:* classical music, opera, ballet. *Address:* c/o Compagnie de Saint-Gobain, Les Miroirs, 18 avenue d'Alsace, 92096 Paris la Défense cedex, France. *T:* 147623310.

BEGBIE, Rev. Prof. Jeremy Sutherland, PhD; Thomas A. Langford Research Professor of Theology, and Director, Duke Initiatives in Theology and the Arts, Duke Divinity School, Duke University, USA, since 2009; *b* Bristol, 15 June 1957. *Educ:* George Watson's Coll., Edinburgh; Univ. of Edinburgh (BA 1977); Univ. of Aberdeen (BD 1980; PhD 1987); Ridley Hall, Cambridge. ARCM 1977; LRAM 1981. Hon. Chaplain, Royal Holloway Coll., Univ. of London, 1982–85; Asst Curate, St John's, Egham, 1982–85; ordained deacon, 1982, priest, 1983; Ridley Hall, Cambridge: Chaplain and Tutor, 1985–87; Lectr in Christian Doctrine, 1987–2008; Dir of Studies, 1987–93; Vice-Principal, 1993–2000; Associate Principal, 2000–08; University of Cambridge: Affiliated Lectr, 1994–2008, Dir, Theol. Through the Arts, Centre for Advanced Religious and Theol Studies, 1997–2000, Faculty of Divinity; Affiliated Lectr, Faculty of Music, 2007–; University of St Andrews: Associate Dir, Inst. of Theol., Imagination and the Arts, 2000–08; Dir, Theol. Through the Arts, 2000–08; Hon. Reader, 2000–08, Hon. Prof., 2003–08, Sch. of Divinity. FRSCM 2006. *Publications:* Music in God's Purposes, 1988; Voicing Creation's Praise: towards a theology of the arts, 1991; Theology, Music and Time, 2000; (ed) Beholding the Glory, 2000; (ed) Sounding the Depths: theology through the arts, 2002; Resounding Truth: Christian wisdom in the world of music, 2007; (ed with S. R. Guthrie) Resonant Witness: conversations between music and theology, 2011; (ed jtly) Art, Imagination and Christian Hope: patterns of promise, 2012; Music, Modernity and God: essays in listening, 2013. *Recreations:* mountain walking, violin making.

BEGENT, Prof. Richard Henry John, MD; FRCP, FMedSci; Professor of Clinical Oncology, UCL Medical School, University College London (formerly Royal Free Hospital Medical School, then Royal Free and University College Medical School), 1990–2010, now Emeritus Professor of Oncology, University College London; *b* 14 Feb. 1945; *s* of Harry Hawley Begent and Doris Ena Begent; *m* 1969, Nicola Ann Thomerson; one *s* two *d*. *Educ:* Haileybury and Imperial Service Coll.; St Bartholomew's Hosp. Medical Coll. (MB BS; MD 1978). FRCP 1986; FRCR 1999. House Officer, Prince of Wales, St Leonard's, Southend and Royal Marsden Hosps, 1967–71; Registrar in Medicine, Royal Marsden, St George's and Chichester Hosps, 1971–75; Clin. Res. Fellow, ICRF, 1975–77; Charing Cross Hospital Medical School: Lectr in Medical Oncology, 1977–80; Sen. Lectr and Hon. Consultant Physician, 1980–86; Gibb Res. Fellow, CRC, 1986–90; Reader in Med. Oncology, Charing Cross and Westminster Med. Sch., 1986–90; Head, Department of Oncology: Royal Free Hosp. Med. Sch., 1990–97; UCL, 1997–2010; Hon. Consultant Physician, Royal Free Hosp., 1990–. Chm., Nat. Cancer Res. Inst. Informatics Task Force, 2004–10. FMedSci 2000. *Publications:* contribs on antibody targeting of cancer and gastrointestinal oncology. *Recreations:* gardening, ski-ing, ancient woodland. *Address:* 6 St Albans Road, NW5 1RD. *E:* r.begent@ucl.ac.uk.

BEGG, Dame Anne; *see* Begg, Dame M. A.

BEGG, Prof. David; Publisher and Contributor, Transport Times, since 2005; Chairman, Tube Lines, 2006–10; *b* 12 June 1956; *m* 2004, Claire Haigh. *Educ:* Portobello Secondary Sch.; Heriot-Watt Univ. Mgt trainee, British Rail, 1979–81; Lectr in Econs, Napier Poly., then Napier Univ., 1981–97; Prof. of Transport Policy and Dir, Centre for Transport Policy Robert Gordon Univ., 1997. Chm., UK Commn for Integrated Transport, 1999–2005. Non-executive Director: BRB, 1997–99; Shadow SRA, 1999–2001; SRA, 2001–05; Manchester Passenger Transport Exec., later Transport for Greater Manchester, 2003–13; First Gp, 2005–14; Heathrow (SP) Ltd (formerly BAA), 2010–; Mem. Bd, Transport for London, 2000–05. Chm., Northern Way Transport Compact, 2006–11. Dir, Portobello Partnership, 2003–. Hd, Heathrow Winter Resilience Enquiry, 2010–11. Vis. Prof., Plymouth Univ., 2006–. Member (Lab): Lothian Regl Council (Chm., Finance Cttee, 1990–94); Edinburgh City Council (Chm., Transport Cttee, 1994–99). *Recreations:* golf, watching football (Hibs). *Address:* Transport Times, Unit 27, Beaufort Court, Admirals Way, E14 8XL.

BEGG, Prof. David Knox Houston, PhD; FRSE; FCGI; Professor of Economics, Imperial College Business School (formerly Tanaka Business School), Imperial College London 2003–12, now Emeritus (Principal, 2003–12); *b* 25 June 1950; *s* of late Robert William Begg, CBE and of Sheena Margaret Begg (*née* Boyd); *m* 2002, Jenny Holland. *Educ:* St John's Coll., Cambridge (BA Econs 1972 (double 1st); Adam Smith Prize 1971); Nuffield Coll., Oxford (MPhil 1974); MIT (PhD 1977; Kennedy Schol.). Oxford University: Fellow in Econs, Worcester Coll., and Lectr, 1977–86; Tutor, 1980–82, Sen. Tutor, 1983–86, Business Summer Sch.; Birkbeck College, London: Prof. of Econs, 1987–2002 (Hd of Dept, 1987–90 and 1996–98); Actg Vice Master, 1997. Res. Dir, Centre for Econ. Forecasting, London Business Sch., 1981–83; Centre for Economic Policy Research: Res. Fellow, 1983–2012; Mem., Exec. Cttee, 2002–08. Vis. Asst Prof., Princeton Univ., 1979; Visiting Professor: MIT, 1994; INSEAD, 1995; Visiting Fellow: IMF, 1999; Reserve Bank of Australia, 2000. Econ. Policy Advr, Bank of England, 1986. Chm., Begg Commn on future of UK outside the euro 2002. Non-executive Director: Trace Gp plc, 2006–07; Imperial Innovations plc, 2012–. FRSE 2004; FCGI 2006. Founding Man. Ed., Econ. Policy, 1985–2000. *Publications:* The Rational Expectations Revolution in Macroeconomics, 1981; (jtly) Economics, 1984, 11th edn 2014 (trans. French, Spanish, Italian, Polish, Vietnamese, Chinese); Monetarism and Macroeconomics: contributions on the UK policy debate, 1987; (jtly) The Impact of Eastern Europe, 1990; (jtly) The Making of Monetary Union, 1991; (jtly) Making Sense of Subsidiarity, 1993; (jtly) EU Enlargement, 1993; (jtly) Independent and Accountable: a new mandate for the Bank of England, 1993; (jtly) EMU: getting the endgame right, 1997; (ed jtly) EMU: prospects and challenges for the Euro, 1998; (jtly) Monetary and Exchange Rate Policies, EMU, and Central and Eastern Europe, 1999; Safe at Any Speed?: monitoring the European Central Bank, 1999; (jtly) Foundations of Economics, 2000, 4th edn 2009; Global Economics: contemporary issues for 2002, 2002; (jtly) Surviving the Slowdown: monitoring the European Central Bank, 2003; (with D. Ward) Economics for Business, 2003, 3rd edn 2010; (jtly) Sustainable Regimes of Capital Movements in Accession Countries, 2003; contribs to learned jls, esp. on exchange rates and monetary policy. *Recreations:* music, crosswords, gardening, all sport. *Address:* Imperial College Business School, Imperial College London, SW7 2AZ. *T:* (020) 7594 9125. *E:* d.begg@imperial.ac.uk.

BEGG, Prof. Hugh MacKemmie, PhD; consultant in private practice; *b* 25 Oct. 1941; *s* of Hugh Alexander Begg and Margaret Neil Begg; *m* 1968, Jane Elizabeth Harrison; two *d*. *Educ:* High Sch., Glasgow; Univ. of St Andrews (MA Hons 1964); Univ. of British Columbia (MA 1966); Univ. of Dundee (PhD 1979); Edinburgh Coll. of Art (DipTP 1981). FRTPI 1991 Lectr in Pol Econ., Univ. of St Andrews, 1966–67; Res. Fellow, Tayside Study, 1967–69, Lectr in Econs, Univ. of Dundee, 1969–76; Asst Dir of Planning and Develt, Tayside Regl Council, 1976–79; Prof. and Hd, Sch. of Town and Regl Planning, and Dean, Fac. of Envmtl Studies, Univ. of Dundee, 1979–93. Vis. Prof. of Econs, Abertay Univ. (formerly Univ. of Abertay Dundee), 2000–. Consultant, UNDP, 1986–2000. Mem., Private Legislation Procedure (Scot.) Extra-Parly Panel, 1993–99; Reporter, Scottish Directorate for Planning and Envmtl Appeals (formerly Scottish Exec. Inq. Reporters Unit), 1995–2014; External Complaints Adjudicator, Scottish Enterprise, 1996–2002; Mem., Local Govt Boundary Commn for Scotland, 1999–2007; Convenor, Standards Commn for Scotland, 2002–03; Assessor, Private Bills Unit, 2006–07, Ind. Assessor, Hybrid and Private Bills, 2009–14 Scottish Parlt. Convenor, RTPI in Scotland, 1991. Mem., Bonnetmaker Craft of Dundee. *Publications:* numerous contribs to academic, professional and tech. jls relating mainly to econs, town and regl planning, and monitoring and evaluation of public policy. *Recreations:* hill walking, Guide Dogs for the Blind (puppy walker), watching Rugby. *Address:* 4 The Esplanade, Broughty Ferry, Dundee DD5 2EL. *T:* (01382) 779642. *E:* HughBegg@blueyonder.co.uk. *Club:* Monifieth and District Rotary.

BEGG, Dame (Margaret) Anne, DBE 2011; *b* 6 Dec. 1955; *d* of David Begg, MBE and Margaret Catherine Begg (*née* Ross). *Educ:* Brechin High Sch.; Univ. of Aberdeen (MA); Aberdeen Coll. of Education. English and History Teacher, Webster's High Sch., Kirriemuir 1978–88; Asst Principal English Teacher, 1988–91, Principal English Teacher, 1991–97, Arbroath Acad. MP (Lab) Aberdeen S, 1997–2015; contested (Lab) same seat, 2015. Member: Scottish Affairs Select Cttee, 1998–2001; Work and Pensions Select Cttee, 2001–15 (Chm., 2010–15); Speaker's Panel of Chairmen, 2002–10. Vice-Chairman: Labour Party Nat. Policy Forum, 2006–10; Speakers' Conf. on Parly Participation, 2008–10. Mem., NEC, Lab Party 1998–99. *Recreations:* reading novels, theatre, cinema, public speaking, watching TV dramas. *E:* anne.annebegg@hotmail.co.uk.

BEGGS, Prof. Jean Duthie, CBE 2006; PhD; FRS 1998; FRSE; Professor of Molecular Biology, since 1999 (SHEFC Professor, 1999–2005), and Royal Society Darwin Trust Research Professor, since 2005, Wellcome Trust Centre for Cell Biology, Institute of Cell Biology, University of Edinburgh; *b* 16 April 1950; *d* of William Renfrew Lancaster and Jean Crawford Lancaster (*née* Duthie); *m* 1972, Dr Ian Beggs; two *s*. *Educ:* Glasgow High Sch. for Girls; Univ. of Glasgow (BSc Hons 1971; PhD 1974). FRSE 1995. Postdoctoral Fellow: Dept of Molecular Biol., Univ. of Edinburgh, 1974–77; Plant Breeding Inst., Cambridge, 1977–79; Beit Meml Fellow for Med. Res., 1976–79; Lectr, Dept of Biochem., ICSTM, 1979–85; University of Edinburgh: Royal Soc. Univ. Res. Fellow, Dept of Molecular Biol., 1985–89; Royal Soc. EPA Cephalosporin Fund Sen. Res. Fellow, 1989–99, Professorial Res. Fellow, 1994–99, Inst. Cell and Molecular Biol. Vice-Pres. for Life Scis, RSE, 2009–12. Wellcome Trust Sen. Investigator, 2014. Mem., EMBO, 1991; MAE 2000. Gabor Medal, Royal Soc., 2003; Novartis Medal, Biochemical Soc., 2004; Chancellor's Award, Univ. of Edinburgh, 2005. *Publications:* research papers and reviews on gene cloning in yeast and molecular biology of RNA splicing. *Recreations:* walking my dogs, yoga, scuba diving, listening to classical music. *Address:* Wellcome Trust Centre for Cell Biology, Institute of Cell Biology, University of Edinburgh, King's Buildings, Mayfield Road, Edinburgh EH9 3JR. *T:* (0131) 650 5351.

BEGGS, John Robert, (Roy); Member (UU), Larne Borough Council, since 1973; *b* 20 Feb. 1936; *s* of John Beggs; *m* 1959, Wilma Lorimer; two *s* two *d. Educ:* Ballyclare High Sch.; Stranmillis Trng Coll. (Certificate/Diploma in Educn). Teacher, 1957–78, Vice-Principal, 1978–83, Larne High Sch. Mem., 1973–, Vice-Chm., 1981–, NE Educn and Library Bd; Pres., Assoc. of Educn and Liby Bds, NI, 1984–85 (Vice-Pres., 1983–84). Mayor of Larne, 1978–83; Mem. for N Antrim, NI Assembly, 1982–86. MP (UU) East Antrim, 1983–2005 (resigned seat Dec. 1985 in protest against Anglo-Irish Agreement; re-elected Jan. 1986); contested (UU) same seat, 2005. Mem., H of C Public Accounts Commn, 1984–2005. Mem., NI Drainage Council, 2006–. Mem., 1973–2009, 2011–, Chm., 2007–09, N Eastern Educn and Liby Bd. *Address:* 171 Carrickfergus Road, Larne, Co. Antrim BT40 3JZ. *T:* and *Fax:* (028) 2827 8976.

See also R. Beggs.

BEGGS, Roy; Member (UU) Antrim East, since 1998, and Deputy Speaker, since 2011, Northern Ireland Assembly; *b* 3 July 1962; *s* of John Robert Beggs, *qv* and Elizabeth Wilhelmina Beggs (*née* Lorimer); *m* 1989, Sandra Maureen Gillespie; two *s* one *d. Educ:* Larne Grammar Sch.; Queen's Univ., Belfast (BEng Hons Industrial Engrg). Hon. Secretary: Ulster Young Unionist Council, 1986 and 1987; E Antrim UU Assoc., 1992–2002. Northern Ireland Assembly: Member: Higher and Further Educn, Trng & Employment Deptl Cttee, subseq. Employment and Learning Cttee, 1999–2002; Public Accounts Cttee, 1999–2003; Cttee of the Centre, 2000–03; Regl Develt Cttee, 2011–12; Assembly and Exec. Review Cttee, 2011–; Health, Social Services and Public Safety Cttee, 2012–14; Vice Chairman: Cttee on Standards and Privileges, 1999–2002; Finance and Personnel Cttee, 2002–03, 2007–08; Public Accounts Cttee, 2007–11, 2014–; Envmt Cttee, 2008–10; Agriculture and Rural Develt Cttee, 2010–11; Assembly and Exec. Rev. Cttee, 2011–; Chm., All Party Assembly Gp on Children and Young People, 2007–09, for Community and Voluntary Sector, 2009–12. Mem. (UU), Carrickfergus BC, 2001–11. Contested (UU) Antrim E, 2015. Vice-Chairman: Carrickfergus Community Safety Partnership, 2004–07; Mem., Carrickfergus Dist Policing Partnership, 2007–11. Mem. Cttee, Raloo Presbyterian Church, 1999–. Gov., Glynn Primary Sch. *Recreations:* walking, cycling; Officer, 1st Raloo Boys' Brigade. *Address:* (office) 3 St Brides Street, Carrickfergus, Northern Ireland BT38 8AF. *T:* (028) 9336 2995. *E:* roybeggs.office@btopenworld.com.

BEGLEY, Kim Sean Robert; tenor; *b* 23 June 1952; *s* of late William Begley and of Elizabeth Begley (*née* Cooke); *m* 1986, Elizabeth Mary, *d* of Charles Collier; two *s. Educ:* Rock Ferry High Sch., Birkenhead; Wimbledon Sch. of Art (costume course); Guildhall Sch. of Music and Drama (theory, piano and voice); Nat. Opera Studio. Early career in theatre: Wardrobe Dept, Gateway Th., Chester; acted in Liverpool, Newbury, London and tours; with RSC, 1977–78; many rôles as principal tenor, Royal Opera House, 1983–89: operas included A Midsummer Night's Dream, King Priam, Florentine Tragedy, Otello, Das Rheingold, Tannhäuser, and Katya Kabanová; début: with Glyndebourne Touring Opera as Don Ottavio in Don Giovanni, 1986; with Glyndebourne Festival Opera as Gastone in La Traviata, 1988; subseq. rôles at Glyndebourne include: Graf Elemer in Arabella, 1989; Boris in Katya Kabanová, 1990; High Priest in Idomeneo, and Pellegrin in New Year, 1991; Laca in Jenůfa, 1992; Albert Gregor in The Makropulos Case, 1995 (also WNO, 1994, and Chicago Lyric Opera (US début), 1995); Florestan in Fidelio, 2001; other rôles include: Male Chorus in The Rape of Lucretia, 1993, Captain Vere in Billy Budd, 2012, ENO; Novagerio in Palestrina, 1997, Drum-Major in Wozzeck, 2002, Edrisi in Król Roger, 2015, Royal Opera House; Laca in Jenufa, 2003, Herod in Salome, 2008, Metropolitan Opera; also appearances at the Proms, at opera houses in Frankfurt, Geneva, Salzburg, Cologne, San Francisco, and at La Scala, Milan. *Address:* c/o HarrisonParrott Ltd, 5–6 Albion Court, Albion Place, W6 0QT.

BEGOVIĆ, Elvira; General Manager, ONASA Independent News Agency, since 2006 (Executive Manager, 2005–06); *b* 28 Jan. 1961; *d* of Arif and Zejna Dizdarević; *m* 1983, Mirza Begović. *Educ:* Univ. Džemal Bijedić Mostar (BA Econs; postgrad. studies in Mgt and Inf. Technologies). Head Office Manager, Zoitours, Olympic Center, Sarajevo, 1983–95; Exec. Manager, 1995–97, Dir, 1997–98, Futura Media, Mktg and Publishing Agency; Exec. Manager of Internat. Mktg, OSSA Mktg Agency, 1998–99; Dep. Gen. Manager, ONASA Ind. News Agency, 1999–2001; Ambassador of Bosnia and Herzegovina to UK, 2001–05, and, non-resident, to Ireland, 2003–05. First Award, MIT Centre, Sarajevo, 1996; Special Recognition, Orgn of Women in Internat. Trade, USA, 1997. *Publications:* (jtly) Let's Buy Domestic Goods, 1998. *Recreations:* music, walking, reading, theatre, art. *Address:* Dženetića Čikma 10/IV, 71000 Sarajevo, Bosnia and Herzegovina.

BEHAGG, Prof. Clive, PhD; Vice-Chancellor, University of Chichester, since 2011; *b* 4 July 1950; *s* of Frederick Arthur Behagg and Freda Winifred Behagg; *m* 1974, Christine Robbins; one *s* two *d. Educ:* West Hatch Technical High Sch., Chigwell; Univ. of Birmingham (BA Hons Medieval and Mod. Hist. 1971; PhD 1982). Lectr, Univ. of Birmingham, 1975–76; Bognor Regis Trng Coll., later West Sussex Inst. of Higher Educn, then Chichester Inst. of Higher Educn, subseq. University Coll. Chichester, then Univ. of Chichester: Lectr, 1976–77; Sen. Lectr, 1977–98; Chair in Hist., 1995; Dep. Principal, 1998–2005; Dep. Vice-Chancellor, 2005–10; Actg Vice-Chancellor, 2010–11. Review Chair, QAA, 1998–2010. Mem., Corp., Central Sussex Coll., 2008–. *Publications:* Politics and Production in the Early Nineteenth Century, 1990; Labour and Reform, 1991, 2nd edn 2001; Years of Expansion, 1991, 2nd edn 2002; Chartism, 1993; contrib. articles in Social History and Business History. *Recreations:* listening to rock, classical music and opera, nineteenth century art, following Tottenham Hotspur. *Address:* University of Chichester, Bishop Otter Campus, College Lane, Chichester PO19 6PE.

BEHAR, His Honour Richard Victor Montague Edward; a Circuit Judge, 2000–11; *b* 14 Feb. 1941; *s* of Edward Behar and Eilleen Behar, *d* of Montague Evans; *m* 1982, Iwona Krystyna (*née* Grabowska); two *s* one *d. Educ:* Stowe Sch. (Schol.); St John's Coll., Oxford (MA). Called to the Bar, Middle Temple, 1965; in practice at the Bar, 1967–2000; SE Circuit; Asst Recorder, 1991–95; a Recorder, 1995–2000; part-time immigration and asylum adjudicator, 1998–2000. Chairman: Bar European Gp, 1988–90; British-Ukrainian Law Assoc., 1993–2000; Co-opted Mem., Internat. Relns Cttee, Gen. Council of Bar, 1988–2000. Freeman, City of London, 2010; Liveryman, Fanmakers' Co., 2011–. *Recreations:* foreign languages and travel, cinema, theatre, reading. *Address:* c/o Judicial Secretariat, 3rd Floor, 1 Queen Victoria Streeet, EC4N 4XY. *Clubs:* Oxford and Cambridge, Hurlingham, Polish Hearth.

BEHARRY, Johnson Gideon, VC 2005; Lance-Corporal, Princess of Wales's Royal Regiment, since 2006; *b* Grenada, 26 July 1979; *s* of Michael Bolah and Florette Beharry; *m* 2013, Mallissa Venice Noel; one *s. Educ:* Samaratin Presbyterian Sch., Grenada. Joined Princess of Wales's Royal Regt, 2001; Private, 2001–06. *Publications:* Barefoot Soldier, 2006. *Address:* c/o RHQ Princess of Wales's Royal Regiment, Howe Barracks, Canterbury, Kent CT1 1JY. *T:* (01227) 818095. *E:* regt1-sec@pwrr.army.mod.uk.

BEHRENS, Clive Owen John; His Honour Judge Behrens; a Circuit Judge, since 1996; *b* 14 Sept. 1948; *s* of late Col William Edward Behrens and Dulcie Bella Behrens; *m* 1974, Clemency Anne Susan Butler; one *s* one *d. Educ:* Eton Coll.; Trinity Coll., Cambridge (BA Hons). Called to the Bar, Gray's Inn, 1972; in practice at the Bar, 1974–96; specialised in Chancery and commercial work; a Recorder, 1992–96. *Recreations:* golf, bridge, tennis, walking. *Address:* Birstwith House, Birstwith, Harrogate HG3 2PN. *Club:* Alwoodley (Leeds).

BEHRENS-ABOUSEIF, Prof. Doris, PhD; Nasser D. Khalili Professor of Islamic Art and Architecture, School of Oriental and African Studies, University of London, 2000–14, now Emerita; *b* 7 Jan. 1946; *d* of Mounir H. Abouseif and Mary Badawy; *m* 1964, Dr Gerhard Behrens; one *s. Educ:* American Univ. of Cairo (MA); Univ. of Hamburg (PhD 1972); Univ. of Freiburg (Habilitation 1992). Privatdozent: Univ. of Freiburg, 1993–95; Univ. of Munich, 1995–2000. Vis. prof. at univs incl. Freie Univ., Berlin, 1995–96, Harvard Univ., 1998, 1999. MAE 2006. *Publications:* The Minarets of Cairo, 1985; Islamic Architecture in Cairo: an introduction, 1989; Egypt's Adjustment to Ottoman Rule: institutions, Waqf and architecture in Cairo (16th & 17th centuries), 1994; Beauty in Arabic Culture, 1999; Cairo of the Mamluks: a history of architecture and its culture, 2007; The Minarets of Cairo, 2010; Practising Diplomacy in the Mamluk Sultanate: gifts and material culture in the Medieval Islamic World, 2014; contrib. articles to Encyclopaedia of Islam, Encyclopaedia of the Quran, Annales Islamologiques, Der Islam, Mamluk Studies Rev., Muqarnas. *Recreation:* reading crime novels. *Address:* Department of Art and Archaeology, School of Oriental and African Studies, University of London, Thornhaugh Street, Russell Square, WC1H 0XG. *T:* (020) 7898 4455, *Fax:* (020) 7898 4477. *E:* da30@soas.ac.uk.

BEIGHTON, Leonard John Hobhouse, CB 1992; Deputy Chairman, Board of Inland Revenue, 1992–94 (Director General, 1988–92); *b* 20 May 1934; *s* of John Durant Kennedy Beighton, OBE and Leonora Hobhouse; *m* 1962, Judith Valerie Bridge (decd); one *s* (one *d* decd). *Educ:* Tonbridge Sch.; Corpus Christi College, Oxford (MA PPE). Inland Revenue, 1957; seconded HM Treasury, 1968–69 (Private Sec. to Chief Sec.), and 1977–79. Dir, World Vision UK, 1997–2007 (Vice Chm., 2002–04, Chm., 2004–07). Mem. Council, Shaftesbury Soc., 1995–2007 (Treas., 1998–99). Trustee, Livability (formerly Grooms-Shaftesbury), 2007–. Hon. Fellow, Chartered Inst. of Taxation, 2011. *Address:* 160 Tilt Road, Cobham, Surrey KT11 3HR.

BEINART, Prof. William J., PhD; FBA 2009; Rhodes Professor of Race Relations, University of Oxford, since 1997 (Director, 2002–06, Director of Graduate Studies, 2009–10, African Studies Centre); Fellow, St Antony's College, Oxford, since 1997. *Educ:* Univ. of Cape Town (BA Hist. 1971); Sch. of Oriental and African Studies, Univ. of London (PhD 1979). Res. Officer, Queen Elizabeth House, Oxford, 1978–83; University of Bristol: Lectr, 1983–90, Reader, 1990–95, in Econ. and Pol Hist.; Prof. of African History, 1995–97. Leverhulme Sen. Res. Fellow, British Acad., 1995–96. Pres., African Studies Assoc., 2008–10. Mem., Editl Bd, Jl of Southern African Studies (Ed., 1982–87; Chm., 1992). *Publications:* The Political Economy of Pondoland 1860–1930, 1982; (jtly) Hidden Struggles in Rural South Africa: politics and popular movements in the Transkei and Eastern Cape 1890–1930, 1987; Twentieth-century South Africa, 1994, 2nd edn 2001; (with Peter Coates) Environment and History: the taming of nature in the USA and South Africa, 1995; The Rise of Conservation in South Africa, 2003; (ed with J. McGregor) Social History and African Environments, 2003; (with Lotte Hughes) Environment and Empire, 2007; (ed with Marcelle Dawson) Popular Politics and Resistance Movements in South Africa, 2010. *Address:* African Studies Centre, University of Oxford, 13 Bevington Road, Oxford OX2 6LH.

BEITH, Rt Hon. Sir Alan (James), Kt 2008; PC 1992; *b* 20 April 1943; *o s* of James and Joan Beith, Poynton, Ches; *m* 1st, 1965, Barbara Jean Ward (*d* 1998); one *d* (one *s* decd); 2nd, 2001, Baroness Maddock, *qv. Educ:* King's Sch., Macclesfield; Balliol and Nuffield Colls, Oxford (BLitt, MA). Lectr, Dept of Politics, Univ. of Newcastle upon Tyne, 1966–73. Member: Gen. Adv. Council of BBC, 1974–84; Hexham RDC, 1969–74; Corbridge Parish Council, 1970–74; Tynedale District Council, 1973–74; NE Transport Users' Consultative Cttee, 1970–74. MP Berwick-upon-Tweed, Nov. 1973–2015 (L 1973–88, Lib Dem 1988–2015). Mem., House of Commons Commn, 1979–97; UK Rep. to Council of Europe and WEU, 1976–84. Liberal Chief Whip, 1976–85; Deputy Leader: Liberal Party, 1985–88; Liberal Democrats, 1992–2003. Member: Select Cttee on Treasury affairs, 1987–94; Intelligence and Security Cttee, 1994–2008; Chairman: Justice Select Cttee (formerly LCD, then Constitutional Affairs), 2003–15; Liaison Cttee, 2010–15; Mem., Speaker's Cttee on Electoral Commn, 2001–10 (Dep. Chm., 2001–03). Trustee, Historic Chapels Trust, 1993–2014 (Chm., 2002–14; Pres., 2014–). Hon. Bencher, Middle Temple, 2014. Hon. DCL: Newcastle upon Tyne, 1998; Northumbria, 2010; Earlham Coll., Indiana, 2013. Methodist Local Preacher. *Publications:* The Case for the Liberal Party and the Alliance, 1983; (jtly) Faith and Politics, 1987; A View from the North, 2008; chapter in The British General Election of 1964, ed Butler and King, 1965. *Recreations:* walking, music. *Address:* 28 Castle Terrace, Berwick-upon-Tweed TD15 1NZ. *Clubs:* Athenæum, National Liberal (Pres.); Northern Counties (Newcastle).

[Created a Baron (Life Peer) 2015 but title not yet gazetted at time of going to press.]

BEKER, Prof. Henry Joseph, PhD; FREng; Chairman: Blackthorn Technologies Ltd, since 2012; CXOWare Inc., since 2013; Visiting Professor of Information Technology, Royal Holloway (formerly Royal Holloway College, then Royal Holloway and Bedford New College), University of London, since 1984; *b* 22 Dec. 1951; *s* of late Jozef and Mary Beker; *m* 1976, Mary Louise (*née* Keilthy); two *d. Educ:* Kilburn Grammar Sch.; Univ. of London (BSc Maths 1973, PhD 1976); Open Univ. (BA 1982). CEng, FIET (FIEE 1997; MIEE 1984); FIS (MIS 1977); CStat 1993; CMath, FIMA 1994 (AFIMA 1978). Sen. Res. Asst, Dept of Statistics, University Coll. of Swansea, 1976–77; Principal Mathematician, Racal-Comsec Ltd, 1977–80, Chief Mathematician, 1980–83; Dir of Research, Racal Research Ltd, 1983–85; Dir of Systems, Racal-Chubb Security Systems Ltd, 1985–86; Man. Dir, Racal-Guardata Ltd, 1986–88; Chm., Zergo Hldgs, then Baltimore Technologies plc, 1989–2000 (Chief Exec., 1988–99). Chairman: Shopcreator plc, 2000–02; Bladerunner Ltd, 2001–10; Director: i-NET VCT plc, 2000–02; Close Finsbury Eurotech Trust plc, 2000–02. Chm., e-Learning Foundn, 2000–03. Mem., Nuffield Health, 2011–14. Mem. Council, British Mycological Soc., 2001–03. Vis. Prof. of IT, Westfield Coll., Univ. of London, 1983–84. Pres., IMA, 1998–99 (Vice Pres., 1988–89). Hon. Fellow: RHBNC, 2000; CABI, 2002; Queen Mary, Univ. of London, 2004. FREng 2000. *Publications:* Cipher Systems, 1982; Secure Speech Communications, 1985; Cryptography and Coding, 1989. *Recreations:* mycology, natural history, travel. *Address:* Rue Père de Deken 19, 1040 Brussels, Belgium. *E:* henry@hjbeker.com.

BEKKER, Althea Enid Philippa D.; *see* Dundas-Bekker.

BEKOE, Dr Daniel Adzei; Chairman, Council of State, Republic of Ghana, 2005–08 (Member, 2001–08); *b* 7 Dec. 1928; *s* of Aristocles Silvanus Adzete Bekoe and Jessie Nadu (*née* Awuletey); *m* 1958, Theresa Victoria Anyisaa Annan (marr. diss. 1983); three *s* (and one *s* decd); *m* 1988, Bertha Augustina Ashia Randolph. *Educ:* Achimota Sch.; University Coll. of Gold Coast (BSc London); Univ. of Oxford (DPhil). Jun. Res. Asst, Univ. of Calif, LA, 1957–58; Univ. of Ghana (formerly University Coll. of Ghana): Lectr, 1958–63; Sen. Lectr, 1963–65; Associate Prof., 1965–74; Prof. of Chemistry, 1974–83; Vice-Chancellor, 1976–83;

Dir, UNESCO Regl Office for Sci. and Technol. for Africa, 1983–85; Regl Dir, Internat. Develt Res. Centre, Nairobi, 1986–92. Chm., Ghana Atomic Energy Commn, 2001–08; Mem., Bd of Govs, IAEA, 2004–06, 2007–08. Sabbatical year, Univ. of Calif, LA, 1962–63; Vis. Associate Prof., Univ. of Ibadan, 1966–67. Member: UN Univ. Council, 1980–83; UN Adv. Cttee on Science and Technology for Develt, 1980–82. Chm., Presbyterian Univ. Council, 2003–05. President: ICSU, 1980–83; Ghana Acad. of Arts and Scis, 1993–96; African Assoc. of Pure and Applied Chem., 1995–98. *Publications:* articles on molecular structures in crystallographic and chemical jls; gen. articles in Proc. Ghana Acad. of Arts and Sciences. *Recreation:* music. *Address:* PO Box CT 3383, Accra, Ghana. *T:* (30) 2774020, (20) 8147622.

BELBEN, Michael John; restaurateur; *b* Swindon, 1952; *s* of John and Rosemary Belben; *m* 1996, Lisa Etherington (marr. diss. 2008); one *s*. *Educ:* Coll. for Distributive Trades, London (HND Business Studies (Advertising and Mktg)). Manager: Peppermint Park Restaurant, 1980–83; Smith's Restaurant, Covent Gdn, 1984–87; Melange Restaurant, Covent Gdn, 1988–90; Proprietor, Eagle Public House, Farringdon, 1991–; Partner: Anchor & Hope, Waterloo, 2003–; Gt Queen St, Covent Gdn, 2007–. London Restaurateur of Year, London Restaurant Awards, 2008. *Recreations:* theatre, contemporary and classical music, art, walking, cycling, car booting! *Address:* 159 Farringdon Road, EC1R 3AL.

BELBIN, Dr (Raymond) Meredith; Founding Partner, Belbin Associates, since 1988; Founder and Chairman, Better Together Ltd, since 2011; *b* W Wickham, Kent, 4 June 1926; *s* of Harold Meredith Belbin and Shirley Agnes Belbin (*née* Herbert); *m* 1st, 1949, Eunice Fellows (*d* 2006); one *s* one *d*; 2nd, 2008, Sheila Munds. *Educ:* Sevenoaks Sch.; Royal Grammar Sch., High Wycombe; Clare Coll., Cambridge (BA 1948; MA; PhD 1952). Res. worker, Nuffield Res. Unit into Problems of Ageing, 1949–52; Res. Fellow, Dept of Econs and Prodn, Coll. of Aeronautics, Cranfield, and Lectr, Work Study Sch., 1952–55; self-employed mgt consultant, 1955–; Chm., Industrial Trng Res. Unit, Cambridge, 1959–69; Dir, Employment Develt Unit, Cambridge, 1969–73. Consultant to OECD, US Dept of Labor and EU Commn. Vis. Prof., Mgt Coll., Univ. of Reading, 2008–13. Has made internat. lecture tours and adv. visits to state orgns in Russia and China. Mem. Court, Univ. of Reading, 2008–13. Hon. Fellow, Henley Mgt Coll., 2005–07. *Publications:* Management Teams: why they succeed or fail, 1981, 3rd edn 2010; The Job Promoters, 1990; Team Roles at Work, 1993, 2nd edn 2010; The Coming Shape of Organization, 1996; Changing the Way We Work, 1997; Beyond the Team, 2000; Managing without Power, 2001; The Evolution of Human Behaviour, 2005; Managing Genetic Diversity, 2011; The Long Road to Civilisation, 2015. *Recreations:* landscape gardening, golf. *Address:* 3–4 Bennell Court, West Street, Comberton, Cambridge CB23 7EN. *T:* (01223) 264975. *E:* meredith@belbin.com.

BELCHER, John William, CBE 2006; PhD; Chief Executive, Anchor Trust, 1995–2009; *b* 1 May 1947; *m* 1973, Norma Wolffberg; one *s* one *d*. *Educ:* Univ. of Western Ontario (BA); London Sch. of Econs and Pol Sci. (PhD 1998). Dept of Nat. Health and Welfare, Canada, 1973–78; Lewisham LBC, 1978; Hd, Prog. Planning Div., Social Services, Bexley LBC, 1979–84; Dir, Social Services Div., Scope, 1984–88; Dir, Social Services, Health, Housing, Envmtl Health, Trading Standards, Redbridge LBC, 1988–94. Mem., Ind. Safeguarding Authy, 2007–11. Sen. Consultant, deVere Gp, São Paulo, 2011–12; Co. Dir, Five Sciences, 2013–.

BELCHER, Penelope Mary; Her Honour Judge Penelope Belcher; a Circuit Judge, since 2006; *b* 27 Aug. 1957; *d* of Arthur John Lucas and Margaret Elizabeth Lucas; *m* 1985, Simon James Belcher; one *s* one *d*. *Educ:* St Hugh's Coll., Oxford (BA, MA Jurisprudence). Called to the Bar, Middle Temple, 1980; barrister, 1980–90; attorney, State Bar of Calif, 1988–89; admitted solicitor, 1993; solicitor: Eversheds, 1993–99, Partner, 1995; Hammonds, 2000–06, Asst Dir for Advocacy. *Recreations:* sailing, racket sports, playing flute, classical music, theatre, reading. *Address:* Leeds Combined Court Centre, The Court House, 1 Oxford Row, Leeds LS1 3BG. *T:* (0113) 306 2800. *E:* HHJudgePenelope.Belcher@judiciary.gsi.gov.uk.

BELCOURT, Norma Elizabeth, (Mrs Emile Belcourt); *see* Burrowes, N. E.

BELDAM, Rt Hon. Sir (Alexander) Roy (Asplin), Kt 1981; PC 1989; a Lord Justice of Appeal, 1989–2000; *b* 29 March 1925; *s* of George William Beldam and Margaret Frew Shettle (formerly Beldam, *née* Underwood); *m* 1st, 1953, Elisabeth Bryant Farr (*d* 2005); two *s* one *d*; 2nd, 2007, Elizabeth Mary Warren. *Educ:* Oundle Sch.; Brasenose Coll., Oxford. Sub-Lt, RNVR Air Branch, 1943–46. Called to Bar, Inner Temple, 1950; Bencher, 1977; QC 1969; a Recorder of the Crown Court, 1972–81; Presiding Judge, Wales and Chester Circuit, Jan.–Oct. 1985; a Judge of the High Court of Justice, QBD, 1981–89. Chm., Law Commn, 1985–89. *Recreations:* sailing, cricket, naval history. *Address:* 16 The Riverside, Graburn Way, East Molesey, Surrey KT8 9BF.

BELFALL, David John; Chairman, Care and Repair Scotland, 2009–15; *b* 26 April 1947; *s* of Frederick Belfall and Ada Belfall (*née* Jacobs); *m* 1972, Lorna McLaughlan; one *s* one *d*. *Educ:* Colchester Royal Grammar Sch.; St John's Coll., Cambridge (BA Hons). Joined Home Office, 1969: Pvte Sec. to Perm. Sec., 1973–74; Sec. to Lord Scarman's Red Lion Square Inquiry, 1974–75; Principal, Police and Prisons Depts, 1975–82; Asst Sec., Police and Immigration Depts, 1982–88; Under-Secretary, Scottish Office: Emergency Services, Home and Health Dept, 1988–91; Health Policy and Public Health Directorate, 1991–95; Head, Housing and Area Regeneration Gp, Scottish Office, then Scottish Exec., Develt Dept, 1995–2002; Chm., Glasgow Council for the Voluntary Sector, 2002–06. Mem., Scottish Criminal Cases Rev. Commn, 2002–09, NHS Lothian Bd, 2004–09.

BELFAST, Earl of; James Chichester; *b* 19 Nov. 1990; *s* and *heir* of Marquess of Donegall, *qv*; *m* 2015, Oilbhe, *d* of late Charles Read and of Dr Mairead Cahill.

BELFAST, Dean of; *see* Mann, Very Rev. J. O.

BELGRAVE, Sir Elliott (Fitzroy), GCMG 2012; CHB 1993; Governor General of Barbados, since 2012; *b* Barbados, 16 March 1931; *s* of Albert Belgrave and Adora Belgrave; *m* 1961, Loretta Rochester; one *d*. *Educ:* Coleridge Secondary Sch., Barbados; University Coll. London (LLB 1962); Darwin Coll., Cambridge (MPhil Criminol. 1979). Called to the Bar, Inner Temple, 1963, Bencher, 2014; Magistrate, Barbados, 1967–69; Sen. Crown Counsel, 1969–76; Principal Crown Counsel, 1976–78; Dep. Dir, Public Prosecutions, 1979–86; Judge, High Court, Barbados, 1987–95. KStJ 2013. *Recreations:* reading, swimming, gardening, travelling. *Address:* Government House, St Michael, Barbados. *T:* 4292962. *E:* elliottfitzroy@caribsurf.com. *Club:* Barbados Yacht.

BELGROVE, David Raymond, OBE 2010; HM Diplomatic Service; Ambassador to Liberia, since 2015; *b* Aylesbury, 18 Jan. 1962; *s* of Raymond and Eunice Belgrove; *m* 1985, Mette Ofstad; two *d*. *Educ:* Aylesbury Grammar Sch. Entered FCO, 1982; Third Secretary: Kuwait, 1986–90; (IT), FCO, 1990–93; (Consular/Immigration), Calcutta, 1993–98; First Secretary: (Media and Public Affairs), Ottawa, 1998–2002; (Caribbean), FCO, 2002–04; Team Leader (Peacekeeping and Peacebuilding), FCO, 2004–07; Head: Counter Narcotics Team, Kabul, 2007–09; Afghan Drugs Unit, FCO, 2009–10; Chargé d'Affaires, Monrovia, 2010–12; Dep. Hd of Mission, Khartoum, 2012–15. *Recreations:* hiking, camping, golf, photography. *Address:* c/o Foreign and Commonwealth Office, King Charles Street, SW1A 2AH.

BELHAVEN and STENTON, 13th Lord *cr* 1647; **Robert Anthony Carmichael Hamilton;** *b* 27 Feb. 1927; *o s* of 12th Lord Belhaven and Stenton; *S* father, 1961; *m* 1st 1952, Elizabeth Ann (*d* 2011), *d* of late Col A. H. Moseley, Warrawee, NSW; one *s* one *d*; 2nd, 1973, Rosemary Lady Mactaggart (marr. diss. 1986), *o d* of Sir Herbert Williams, 1st Bt MP; one *d* (adopted); 3rd, 1986, Malgorzata Maria, *d* of Tadeusz Hruzik-Mazurkiewicz advocate, Krakow, Poland; one *d*. *Educ:* Eton. Commissioned, The Cameronians, 1947 Commander Cross, Order of Merit (Poland), 1995. *Recreation:* cooking. *Heir:* *s* Master of Belhaven, *qv*. *Address:* 710 Howard House, Dolphin Square, SW1V 3PQ. *Club:* Polish Hearth.

BELHAVEN, Master of; Hon. Frederick Carmichael Arthur Hamilton; *b* 27 Sept 1953; *s* of 13th Lord Belhaven and Stenton, *qv*; *m* 1st, 1981, Elizabeth Anne (marr. diss. 1988) *d* of S. V. Tredinnick, Wisborough Green, Sussex; two *s*; 2nd, 1991, Philippa Martha Gause Whitehead (marr. diss. 2010), *d* of Sir Rowland Whitehead, 5th Bt; one *d*; 3rd, 2013, Lorna *d* of James Watson Hurst. *Educ:* Eton.

BELICH, Sir James, Kt 1990; Mayor of Wellington, New Zealand, 1986–92, retired; *b* 25 July 1927; *s* of Yakov Belich and Maria (*née* Batistich); *m* 1951, Valerie Frances Anzulovich one *s* two *d*. *Educ:* Otahuhu Coll.; Auckland Univ.; Victoria Univ. of Wellington (BA Hons Econs); IBM Teaching Fellow, Massey Univ. Consular/Internat. Trade, Auckland, Sydney, Wellington, 1948–56; Economist, Market Res. Manager, Dir, Chief Exec. and Chm. Research, Marketing, Public Relns, Advertising, 1956–86. Member: Wellington Harbour Bd Wellington Regional Council. Director: Air NZ, 1987–89; Lambton Harbour Overview Ltd (Chm.); Wellington Internat. Airport. Pres. and Exec., various orgns incl.: Pres., UNA, Wellington and NZ; Founder Pres., UNICEF, NZ. FInstD; Fellow, Inst. of Advertising. *Recreations:* reading, walking, bowls. *Address:* 4 Indus Street, Khandallah, Wellington 4, New Zealand. *T:* (4) 4793339. *Clubs:* Wellington, Wellington Central Rotary (Wellington).

BELL, family name of **Baron Bell**.

BELL, Baron *cr* 1998 (Life Peer), of Belgravia in the City of Westminster; **Timothy John Leigh Bell,** Kt 1990; Chairman, Bell Pottinger Private (formerly Lowe Bell, then Bell Pottinger Communications), since 1987; *b* 18 Oct. 1941; *s* of Arthur Leigh Bell and Greta Mary Bell (*née* Findlay); *m* 1988, Virginia Wallis Hornbrook; one *s* one *d*. *Educ:* Queen Elizabeth's Grammar Sch., Barnet, Herts. FIPA. ABC Television, 1959–61; Colman Prentis & Varley, 1961–63; Hobson Bates, 1963–66; Geers Gross, 1966–70; Man. Dir, Saatchi & Saatchi, 1970–75; Chm. and Man. Dir, Saatchi & Saatchi Compton, 1975–85; Gp Chief Exec., Lowe Howard-Spink Campbell Ewald, 1985–87; Dep. Chm., Lowe Howard-Spink & Bell, 1987–89; Chm., Chime Communications plc, 1994–2012. Dir, Centre for Policy Studies, 1989–92. Special Adviser to: Chm., NCB, 1984–86; South Bank Bd, 1985–86. Chm., Charity Projects, 1984–93 (Pres., 1993–). Member: Industry Cttee, SCF; Public Affairs Cttee, WWF, 1985–88; Public Relations Cttee, Greater London Fund for the Blind, 1979–86; Council, Royal Opera House, 1982–85; Steering Cttee, Percent Club. Governor, BFI, 1983–86. Council Mem., Sch. of Communication Arts, 1985–87. *Publications:* Right or Wrong (memoirs), 2014. *Address:* (office) 49 Charles Street, Mayfair, W1J 5EN; (office) 6th Floor, Holborn Gate, 330 High Holborn, WC1V 7QD.

BELL, Alan Scott; library and literary consultant; *b* 8 May 1942; *m* 1966, Olivia Butt; one *s* one *d*. *Educ:* Ashville Coll.; Selwyn Coll., Cambridge (MA); MA Oxon 1981. FSA 1996. Asst Registrar, Royal Commn on Historical MSS, 1963–66; Asst Keeper, Nat. Library of Scotland, 1966–81; Librarian: Rhodes House Library, Univ. of Oxford, 1981–93; The London Library, 1993–2002. Vis. Fellow, All Souls Coll., Oxford, 1980. Adv. Editor, Oxford DNB, 1993–. Chm., Marc Fitch Fund, 2001–11. *Publications:* (ed) Scott Bicentenary Essays, 1973; (ed) Sir Leslie Stephen's Mausoleum Book, 1978; (ed) Henry Cockburn, 1979; Sydney Smith, 1980; (contrib.) Illustrated History of Oxford University, 1993; (ed) Letters of Lord Cockburn 2005; (contrib.) History of Oxford University Press, vol. 3, 1896–1970, 2013. *Address:* 38 Danube Street, Edinburgh EH4 1NT. *E:* alan.s.bell@btinternet.com. *Club:* Brooks's.

BELL, Alexander Gilmour, CB 1991; Chief Reporter for Public Inquiries, Scottish Office, 1979–93; Inquiry Reporter (Consultant), 1993–2003; *b* 11 March 1933; *s* of Edward and Daisy Bell; *m* 1966, Mary Chisholm; four *s*. *Educ:* Hutchesons' Grammar Sch.; Glasgow Univ. (BL). Admitted Solicitor, 1954. After commercial experience in Far East and in private practice, entered Scottish Office, as Legal Officer, 1967; Dep. Chief Reporter, 1973. *Recreations:* casual outdoor pursuits, choral music.

BELL, Andrew Montgomery; Sheriff of Lothian and Borders, 1990–2004; *b* 21 Feb. 1940; *s* of James Montgomery Bell and Mary Bell (*née* Cavaye), Edinburgh; *m* 1969, Ann Margaret Robinson; one *s* one *d*. *Educ:* Royal High Sch., Edinburgh; Univ. of Edinburgh (BL). Solicitor, 1961–74; called to Bar, 1975; Sheriff of S Strathclyde, Dumfries and Galloway at Hamilton, 1979–84; Sheriff of Glasgow and Strathkelvin, 1984–90. *Publications:* (contrib.) Stair Memorial Encyclopaedia of Scots Law, 1995. *Recreations:* reading, listening to music. *Address:* 5 York Road, Trinity, Edinburgh EH5 3EJ. *T:* (0131) 552 3859. *Club:* New (Edinburgh).

BELL, Anthony Peter, OBE 1998; independent healthcare consultant, since 2015; Chief Executive Officer, Chelsea and Westminster NHS Foundation Trust, 2012–14; *b* Derby, 28 Oct. 1957; *s* of Douglas Bell and Joyce Bell; partner, Elizabeth Carol Rothwell; three *s* one *d*. *Educ:* St Bede's RC Comp. Sch., Ashby, Scunthorpe; Scunthorpe Sch. of Nursing; Charles Frear Sch. of Nursing, Leicester; Univ. of Huddersfield; Liverpool John Moores Univ. (MBA). RN. Dir, Nursing and Quality, University Hosps Aintree, 1990–93; Dir, Jt Commng, Liverpool HA, 1993–2000; Chief Exec., Royal Liverpool Children's NHS Trust, 2000–07; CEO, Royal Liverpool and Broadgreen Univ. Hosps NHS Trust, 2007–12. Chairman: Standing Nursing and Midwifery Adv. Cttee, 1996–99; Nat. Children's Hosps Alliance, 2003–07. Mem., Adv. Bd, Sch. of Mgt, Univ. of Liverpool, 2008–; Gov., Liverpool John Moores Univ., 2010–. *Publications:* (ed jtly) Placing Ladders: harnessing our leadership potential, 2009. *Recreations:* blues music, guitar, photography, ski-ing, travel. *Address:* 8 Tallow Road, The Island, Brentford TW8 8EU. *E:* tonybellme2@me.com.

BELL, Catherine Elisabeth Dorcas, (Mrs R. J. Weber), CB 2003; PhD; Acting Permanent Secretary, Department of Trade and Industry, 2005; *b* 26 April 1951; *d* of late Frank Douglas Howe and of Phyllis (*née* Walsh); *m* 1993, Richard John Weber; one *s*. *Educ:* Balshaw's Grammar Sch., Leyland, Lancs; Girton Coll., Cambridge (MA); Univ. of Kent (PhD). Joined Department of Trade and Industry, 1975; Pvte Sec. to Sec. of State for Trade and Industry, 1980–81; Principal, 1981; Asst Sec., 1986; Under Sec., 1991; Head of Competition Policy Div., 1991–93; maternity leave, 1993–94; Resident Chm., CSSB, 1994–95; Hd of Central Policy Unit, 1995–97; Dir, Utilities Review Team, 1997–99, and Competition Policy, 1998–99; Dir Gen., Corporate and Consumer Affairs, subseq. Competition and Markets Gp, 1999–2002; Dir Gen., Services Gp, 2002–05. Non-executive Director: Swiss Re (UK), 1999–2008; CAA, 2006–14; Ensus Ltd, 2006–11; United Utilities, 2007–; National Grid Gas plc, 2014–; National Grid Electricity Transmission plc, 2014–. Non-exec. Mem. Bd, DoH, 2011–. Trustee, Charity for Civil Servants (formerly CS Benevolent Fund), 2008– (Chm., Investment Cttee, 2008–14). Gov., LSE, 2008–. *Recreations:* film, ski-ing, gardening.

BELL, (Charles) Trevor; General Secretary, Colliery Officials and Staffs Area of the National Union of Mineworkers, 1979–89; Member, National Executive Committee of the National Union of Mineworkers, 1979–89; *b* 22 Sept. 1927; *s* of Charles and Annie Bell; *m* 1974, Patricia Ann Tappin. *Educ:* state schools; Technical Coll. (City and Guilds Engrg); Coleg

Harlech, N Wales (Trades Union scholarship, 1955). Craftsman in coal mining industry, 1941. Mem., Labour Party, 1946–. *Recreations:* gardening, reading. *Address:* Wakefield, West Yorks.

BELL, Cressida Iras; textile and interior designer; Director, Cressida Bell Ltd, since 1984; *b* 13 April 1959; *d* of late Prof. Quentin Bell, FRSL and of (Anne) Olivier Bell (*née* Popham). *Educ:* St Martin's Sch. of Art (BA Hons Fashion); Royal Coll. of Art (MA). Group exhibitions include: Duncan Grant & Cressida Bell, Sally Hunter Fine Art, 1984; Scarf Show, Liberty's, 1987; Arts & Crafts to Avant-Garde, RFH, 1992; Colour into Cloth, Crafts Council, 1994; Bloomsbury: 3 Generations, NY, 1996. Commissions include: scarf for BM, 1988; scarf for V&A, 1992; book jacket, Song of Love, 1991; interiors, Soho Studios, 1994–; carpet for British Consulate, Hong Kong, 1996. *Publications:* The Decorative Painter, 1996; (illustrated) Arabella Boxer's Book of English Food, 2012; Cressida Bell's Cake Design, 2013. *Recreations:* travel, cookery, dress-making.

BELL, Sir David (Charles Maurice), Kt 2004; Chairman, Financial Times, 1996–2009; Director for People, Pearson plc, 1998–2009; *b* 30 Sept. 1946; *s* of Roderick Martin Bell and Mary Frances Bell (*née* Wade); *m* 1972, Primrose Frances Moran; two *s* one *d*. *Educ:* Worth Sch.; Trinity Hall, Cambridge (BA 2nd Cl. Hons Hist.); Univ. of Pennsylvania (MA Econs and Pol Sci.). Oxford Mail and Times, 1970–72; Financial Times, 1972–2009: Washington Corresp., 1975–78; News Editor, Internat. Edn, 1978–80; Features Editor, 1980–85; Man. Editor, 1985–89; Advertisement Dir, 1989–93; Marketing Dir, 1992–93; Chief Exec., 1993–96. Dir, Pearson plc, 1996–2009. Pres., Les Echos, 2003–07. Mem., UK Council, INSEAD, 1994–2007. Non-exec. Dir, The Economist, 2005–. Chm., Cambridge Univ. Press, 2012–. Trustee: Common Purpose, 1994– (Chm., 2009–11); Bureau of Investigative Journalism, 2010–; Esmée Fairbairn Foundn, 2010–; Chairman: Millennium Bridge Trust, 1997–; Internat. Youth Foundn, 1998–2006; Crisis, 2001–12; Sadler's Wells, 2005–; Internat. Inst. for War and Peace Reporting, 2006–; Transformation Trust, 2009–; Orwell Prize Cttee, 2009–11; London Transport Mus., 2011–; Nat. Equality Standard Bd, 2012–; Media Standards Trust, 2014– (Acting Chm., 2006–11); Chm., Chapel St Community Schools Trust, 2014–. Mem., Leveson Inquiry into culture, practice and ethics of the press, 2011–12. Chm. Council, Roehampton Univ., 2008–. *Recreations:* cycling, theatre, Victorian social history. *Address:* 35 Belitha Villas, N1 1PE. *T:* (020) 7609 4000. *Club:* Garrick.

BELL, David Mackintosh; HM Diplomatic Service, retired; *b* 2 Aug. 1939; *s* of late David Little Bell and Kathleen Bell (*née* McBurnie); *m* 1st, 1963, Ann Adair Wilson (marr. diss.); one *s* one *d*; 2nd, 1996, Dominique Van Hille; two *s*. *Educ:* Ayr Acad.; Glasgow Univ. (MA 1959). Commonwealth Relations Office, 1960; served Karachi, Enugu, Havana and Mexico City; FCO, 1968–71; Budapest, 1971–74; 2nd, later 1st Sec., FCO, 1974–77; Commercial Consul, NY, 1977–81; FCO, 1981–86; Press Sec., Bonn, 1986–90; Consul-General, Lille, 1990–95; Consul-Gen., Zürich, and Dir, British Export Promotion in Switzerland and Liechtenstein, 1995–97. Lectr in Internat. Business Studies, Institut Supérieur Européen de Gestion, Lille, 1997–2002. Chm., British Community Assoc., Lille, 2002–05. *Recreations:* reading, crosswords, cooking. *Address:* 6 rue de Wattignies, 59139 Noyelles-lez-Seclin, France. *T:* (3) 20327910. *E:* david.bell59139@orange.fr.

BELL, Sir David (Robert), KCB 2011; Vice-Chancellor, University of Reading, since 2012; *b* 31 March 1959; *s* of Robert Bell and Marie Blackie Slater Bell; *m* 1981, Louise Caroline Poole; two *d*. *Educ:* Univ. of Glasgow (MA, MEd); Jordanhill Coll. of Educn (PGCE Primary). Teacher, Cuthbertson Primary Sch., Glasgow, 1982–85; Dep. Headteacher, Powers Hall Jun. Sch., Essex, 1985–88; Headteacher, Kingston Primary Sch., Essex, 1988–90; Asst Dir of Educn, Newcastle CC, 1990–93 and 1994–95; Harkness Fellow, Atlanta, Georgia, 1993–94; Chief Educn Officer, 1995–98, Dir of Educn and Libraries, 1998–2000, Newcastle CC; Chief Exec., Beds CC, 2000–02; HM Chief Inspector of Schs, 2002–05; Perm. Sec., DES, later DCSF, then DFE, 2006–11. DUniv Strathclyde, 2004. *Publications:* Parents' Guide to the National Curriculum (Primary), 1991; Parents' Guide to the National Curriculum (Secondary), 1991; Inspirations for History, 1992; Bright Ideas: maths projects, 1992. *Recreations:* reading, football, keeping fit. *Address:* University of Reading, PO Box 217, Whiteknights, Reading RG6 6AH. *T:* (0118) 378 6226. *E:* vc@reading.ac.uk.

BELL, Derek, PhD; independent education consultant, since 2011; Professor of Education, College of Teachers, since 2007; Director, Learnus, since 2013; Head of Education, Wellcome Trust, 2009–11; *b* Hartlepool, 7 Oct. 1950; *s* of Mark Bell and Margaret Bell (*née* Hudson); *m* 1973, Jacqueline Wendy Jackson; twin *d*. *Educ:* Queen Elizabeth's Grammar Sch., Mansfield; Durham Univ. (BSc Hons Botany 1972); Univ. of Liverpool (PGCE 1976; PhD 1976; MEd 1990). Asst teacher, Christleton High Sch., Chester, 1976–80; Hd, Biol. Dept, Grange Comp. Sch., Runcorn, 1980–82; Liverpool Institute of Higher Education, later Liverpool Hope University: Sen. Lectr in Biol., 1983–88, in Professional Studies in Educn, 1988–89 and 1991–92; Admissions Tutor, St Katharine's Coll., 1987–89; on secondment as Res. Fellow, Centre for Res. in Primary Sci., Univ. of Liverpool, 1989–91; Dir, Inservice Educn, 1992–96; Dir, Graduate Studies and Res., 1996–99; Vice Principal, Bishop Grosseteste Univ. Coll., 1999–2002; Chief Exec., Assoc. for Sci. Educn, 2002–08. Co-ordinator, Nuffield Primary Sci. Proj., 1993–99; Chief External Examiner: Modular Prog. in Professional Develt, Bath Spa Univ. Coll., 1998–2000; PGCE Prog., St Martin's Coll. of Higher Educn, Lancaster, 2000–03. Member Board: STEMNET, 2002–; Engrg UK, 2005–11; Sci. Council, 2005–08; IBM Trust, 2010–; Understanding Animal Res., 2010–; Trustee, Centre of the Cell, 2012–14. Hon. DEd Manchester Metropolitan, 2011. Editor, Educn in Science, 2002–09. *Publications:* (ed) Science Co-ordinator's Handbook, 1996; (ed) Understanding Science Ideas: a guide for primary teachers, 1997; (jtly) Science and Literacy: a guide for primary teachers, 1998; (with R. Ritchie) Towards Effective Subject Leadership in the Primary School, 1999; (ed jtly) Teaching the Primary Curriculum, 2002; contrib. chapters in books, articles in jls and res. reports. *Recreations:* ski-ing, walking, theatre-going, active holidays (kayaking, white water rafting and river sledging), resisting growing up. *E:* derek@campanulaconsulting.co.uk.

BELL, Prof. Derek, MD; FRCP, FRCPGlas, FRCPE; Professor of Acute Medicine, Imperial College London, since 2006; Hon. Consultant Physician, Department of Medicine, Chelsea and Westminster Hospital; President, Royal College of Physicians of Edinburgh, since 2014. *Educ:* Univ. of Edinburgh (BSc 1st Cl. Pathol.; MB ChB Medicine; MD Inflammatory Response to Myocardial Infarction). Consultant Chest Physician, Central Middx Hosp., 1990–96; Consultant Physician, Edinburgh Royal Infirmary, 1996–2006; Hon. Sen. Lectr, Univ. of Edinburgh, 1998–2006; Med. Dir, Acute Hosps Div., NHS Lothian, 2005–06; Nat. Clin. Lead for Unscheduled Care, NHS Scotland, 2007–10; Dir, NIHR NW London Collaboration for Leadership in Applied Health Res. and Care, 2008–; R&D Dir and Campus Dean, Chelsea and Westminster Hosp. NHS Trust, 2009–; Acute Care Lead, NHS London, 2011–13. Pres., Soc. of Acute Medicine, 2003–07. Mem. Council, RCPE, 2007–. *Address:* Royal College of Physicians of Edinburgh, 9 Queen Street, Edinburgh EH2 1JQ. *T:* (0131) 247 3638. *E:* president@rcpe.ac.uk.

BELL, Dr Donald Atkinson, CEng; Technical Director, Marchland Consulting Ltd, 1991–2004; *b* 28 May 1941; *s* of late Robert Hamilton Bell and Gladys Mildred Bell; *m* 1967, Joyce Louisa Godber; two *s*. *Educ:* Royal Belfast Academical Instn; Queen's Univ., Belfast (BSc); Southampton Univ. (PhD); Glasgow Univ. (MSc). FIMechE; MIET; FBCS. National Physical Lab., 1966–77; Dept of Industry, 1978–82; Dir, Nat. Engrg Lab., 1983–90; Hd of R&D, Strathclyde Inst., 1990–91. *Address:* 32 Elmfield Avenue, Teddington, Middx TW11 8BS. *T:* (020) 8943 1326. *E:* donald@marchland.org.

BELL, Donald L.; *see* Lynden-Bell.

BELL, Prof. Donald Munro; international concert and opera artist; freelance singer; Professor of Music, Calgary University, 1982–2014; private tutor; *b* 19 June 1934; one *s*; partner, Angela Dowling. *Educ:* South Burnaby High Sch., BC, Canada; Royal Coll. of Music (Associate Bd Scholarship). Made Wigmore Hall (recital) debut, 1958; since then has sung at Bayreuth Wagner Festival, 1958, 1959, 1960; Lucerne and Berlin Festivals, 1959; Philadelphia and New York debuts with Eugene Ormandy, 1959; Israel, 1962; Russia Recital Tour, 1963; Glyndebourne Festival, 1963, 1974, 1982; with Deutsche Oper am Rhein, Düsseldorf, 1964–67; Scottish National Opera, 1974; Scottish Opera, 1978; Basler Kammer Orchestre, 1978; Australian Tour (Musica Viva), 1980. Prof. and Head of Vocal Dept, Ottawa Univ., 1979–82. Worked with mentor, Dr Richard Millar, Oberlin Conservatory, Ohio, 1985–92. Directed Opera Workshop at Univ. of Calgary, 1982–89; Artistic Dir, Univ. of Calgary Celebrity Series, 2004–08; Mem., Univ. of Calgary Senate, 2006–09 (Voting Mem., 2010–14). Member: Nat. Assoc. of Teachers of Singing - Internat., 1985–2014; Nat. Opera Assoc., 1985– (Dir, Alberta Br., 1986–90, for Canada, 1988–90). Has made recordings. Van L. Lawrence Fellowship, Voice Foundn, Philadelphia and NATS, 2009. Judge of various competitions incl. Hynatyshyn and Juno Awards. Arnold Bax Medal, 1955. *E:* tweedlesum@gmail.com.

BELL, Edward; Chairman, Bell Lomax Moreton Agency (formerly Bell Lomax Literary and Sport Agency), 2002–14; *b* 2 Aug. 1949; *s* of Eddie and Jean Bell; *m* 1969, Junette Bannatyne; one *s* two *d*. *Educ:* Airdrie High Sch. Cert. of Business Studies. With Hodder & Stoughton, 1970–85; Man. Dir, Collins General Div., 1985–89; launched Harper Paperbacks in USA, 1989; HarperCollins UK: Publisher, 1990–2000; Dep. Chief Exec., 1990–91; Chief Exec., 1991–92; Chm., 1992–2000; Chm., HarperCollins India, 1994–2000. Non-executive Director: beCogent Ltd, 2000–; Haynes Publishing Gp plc, 2000–; Management Diagnostics Ltd, 2000–; New Century Media, 2009–. *Recreations:* reading, golf, supporting Arsenal, opera, collecting old books. *Clubs:* Royal Automobile; AutoWink (Epsom); Addington Golf (Croydon).

BELL, Prof. Emily Jane; Professor of Professional Practice, and Director, Tow Center for Digital Journalism, Graduate School of Journalism, Columbia University, since 2010; *b* 14 Sept. 1965; *d* of Peter Bell and Bridget Bell; *m* 1994, Edmund Hugh Crooks; three *s*. *Educ:* Christ Church, Oxford (BA Juris. 1987). Reporter: Big Farm Weekly, 1987–88; Campaign, 1988–90; The Observer: reporter, 1990–96; Dep. Business Ed., 1996–98; Business Ed., 1998–2000; Founder and Ed., MediaGuardian.co.uk, 2000; Ed.-in-Chief, Guardian Unlimited, 2001–06; Dir of Digital Content, Guardian News and Media, 2006–10. Columnist, Broadcast, 1999–. Vis. Prof., Univ. College Falmouth, 2009–10. Member: Digital Adv. Bd, Digital First Media, 2010–; Bd of Overseers, Columbia Journalism Review, 2010–. Trustee, Grierson Trust, 2009–. *Publications:* (with Chris Alden) The Media Directory, 2004; contrib. to Guardian and Columbia Journalism Review. *Recreations:* child management, cooking, opera and theatre-going, reading, season ticket holder Arsenal FC. *Address:* Graduate School of Journalism, Pulitzer Hall, MC 3801, Columbia University, 2950 Broadway (at 116th Street), New York, NY 10027, USA. *E:* ebell@columbia.edu.

BELL, Gary Terence; QC 2012; *b* Nottingham, 9 Nov. 1959; *s* of Terence Bell and Maureen Bell; *m* 1992, Sophia Fitzhugh; two *s* one *d*. *Educ:* Toothill Comp. Sch., Bingham, Notts; Univ. of Bristol (LLB Hons 1987). Coal miner, 1976; lawn mower mechanic, 1976; forklift truck driver, 1976–78; fireman, 1978; pork pie prodn line worker, 1978; homeless drifter, 1978–80. Called to the Bar, Inner Temple, 1989; in practice as a barrister, 1989–2012. *Publications:* Toby and the Great Stink, 2010; Toby and the Great Fire, 2012. *Recreations:* golf, football, cricket, fishing. *Address:* No5 Chambers, Fountain Court, Steelhouse Lane, Birmingham B4 6DR. *T:* 07710 472059. *E:* garybell2009@googlemail.com.

BELL, Geoffrey Lakin; President, Geoffrey Bell and Co., New York, since 1982; Chairman, Guinness Mahon Holdings, 1987–93; *b* 8 Nov. 1939; *s* of Walter Lakin Bell and Ann (*née* Barnes); *m* 1973, Joan Abel; one *d*. *Educ:* Grimsby Technical Sch.; London School of Economics and Political Science. Economic Asst, HM Treasury, 1961–63; Vis. Scholar, Fed. Reserve System, principally with Federal Reserve Bank of St Louis, 1963–64; HM Treasury, also Special Lectr at LSE, 1964–66; Economic Advr, British Embassy, Washington, 1966–69; 1969–82: Asst to Chm., J. Henry Schroder Wagg; Dir, Schroder Wagg; Exec. Vice Pres., Schroder Internat. and Sen. Advr, Schroder Bank and Trust Co., NY; Special Columnist on Econs and Finance, The Times, 1969–74; Exec. Sec. and Mem., Gp of Thirty, 1978–. Chairman: Guyana Americas Merchant Bank, 2001–; ProLogis Eur. Properties, 2007–12; Dir, Axis Capital Hldgs Ltd (Bermuda), 2006–. Mem., Court of Govs, LSE, 1994–2014. Cons. Editor, International Reports, 1983–93. *Publications:* The Euro-Dollar Market and the International Financial System, 1973; numerous articles on internat. econs and finance in UK and USA. *Address:* 17 Abbotsbury House, Abbotsbury Road, W14 8EN. *T:* (020) 7603 9408; 455 East 57th Street, New York, NY, USA. *T:* (212) 8381193. *Club:* Reform.

BELL, Graham Andrew; television presenter; Presenter, BBC Ski Sunday, since 2001; *b* Akrotiri, Cyprus, 4 Jan. 1966; *s* of Rod and Jean Bell; *m* 1991, Sarah Edwards; one *s* one *d*. *Educ:* George Watson's Coll. British Alpine Ski Team, 1982–98; British Olympic Team, 1984, 1988, 1992, 1994, 1998; Performance Dir, Snowsport GB, 1999–2003; commentator, Eurosport, 1998–2001. *Recreations:* ski-ing, cycling, triathlon, dangerous stuff, science. *Address:* Champions UK plc, Barrington House, Leake Road, Costock, Loughborough LE12 6XA. *T:* 0845 331 3031. *E:* mail@championsukplc.com. *Club:* Kandahar Ski.

BELL, Howard James; Chief Executive, Provident Financial plc, 1997–2001; *b* 28 March 1944; *m* 1969, Susan Vivienne Fell; one *s* (one *d* decd). *Educ:* Bradford Univ. (MBA). Yorkshire Imperial Metals Ltd, 1963–67; Provident Financial plc, 1967–2001: computer systems analyst, 1967–72; personnel and trng, 1972–80; Line Manager, 1980–89; Dir, 1989–2001. Chm., Invocas Gp plc, 2006–11. Chm., Meningitis Res. Foundn, 1997–2005. *Recreations:* sport, travel.

BELL, Prof. Ian Frederick Andrew, PhD; Professor of American Literature, University of Keele, since 1992; *b* 31 Oct. 1947; *s* of Frederick George Bell and Cecilia Bell; *m* 1983, Elizabeth Mary Tagart (marr. diss. 1989); two *s*; one *s*. *Educ:* West Bridgford Grammar Sch.; Univ. of Reading (BA 1970; PhD 1978). Lectr, Sen. Lectr and Reader in Amer. Lit., Univ. of Keele, 1973–92. *Publications:* Critic as Scientist: the modernist poetics of Ezra Pound, 1981; (ed) Ezra Pound: tactics for reading, 1982; (ed) Henry James: fiction as history, 1984; (ed jtly) American Literary Landscapes: the fiction and the fact, 1988; Henry James and the Past: readings into time, 1991; (ed) The Best of O. Henry, 1993; Washington Square: styles of money, 1993. *Recreations:* visual arts, cinema, ferret wrangling. *Address:* Department of American Studies, University of Keele, Staffs ST5 5BG. *T:* (01782) 733012.

BELL, Rt Rev. James Harold; *see* Ripon, Area Bishop of.

BELL, Janet; *see* Browne, E. J.

BELL, Jason; photographer; *b* London, 19 April 1969; *s* of Peter Alexander Bell and Susan Margaret St Claire Bell (*née* Carruthers, now Laws); civil partnership 2007, Guy Harrington. *Educ:* Westminster Sch.; St Catherine's Coll., Oxford (BA PPE 1990). Self-employed photographer, 1990–. Main editorial clients include Vanity Fair and Vogue UK; work includes numerous film posters. Many photographs in NPG collection. Hon. FRPS 2011. *Publications:* Gold Rush, 2000; Hats Off, 2002; GiveGet, 2004; An Englishman in New York, 2010. *Address:* c/o Soho Management, 17 St Anne's Court, W1F 0BQ; c/o Robbie Feldman, 170 N 11th Street, Suite 6B, Brooklyn, NY 11211, USA. *E:* jason@jasonbellphoto.com.

BELL, Prof. Jeanne Elisabeth, (Mrs D. Rutovitz), CBE 2007; MD; FRCPath, FMedSci; FRSE; Professor of Neuropathology, University of Edinburgh, 1999–2007, now Emeritus; Hon. Consultant in Neuropathology, Western General Hospital, Edinburgh, 1999–2007; *b* 10 Aug. 1942; *d* of Rhys and Joan Hall; *m* 1983, Dr Denis Rutovitz, MBE; two step *s* two step *d*, and one *s* from former marr. *Educ:* Univ. of Newcastle upon Tyne (BSc Hons Anatomy 1963; MD 1972); Univ. of Durham (MB BS 1966). FRCPath 1995. Lectr in Anatomy, Univ. of Newcastle upon Tyne, 1967–70; Res. Officer, MRC Human Genetics Unit, Edinburgh, 1974–79; Sen. Registrar in Paediatric Pathology, Royal Hosp. for Sick Children, Edinburgh, 1979–84; Sen. Lectr in Neuropathol., Univ. of Edinburgh, 1984–99. FRSE 1998; FMedSci 2002. *Publications:* (jtly) Colour Atlas of Neuropathology, 1995; contrib. chapters on develt and forensic, psychiatric and neurol medicine; scientific papers and reviews in neurosci. jls. *Recreations:* travel, handicrafts, films, looking after grandchildren, humanitarian aid work (founded Edinburgh Direct Aid with husband, 1992). *Address:* CJD Surveillance Unit, Bryan Matthews Building, Western General Hospital, Crewe Road, Edinburgh EH4 2XU. *T:* (0131) 537 1955, *Fax:* (0131) 343 1404. *E:* Jeanne.Bell@ed.ac.uk.

BELL, Dame Jocelyn; *see* Bell Burnell, Dame S. J.

BELL, Sir John (Irving), GBE 2015; Kt 2008; DM; FRCP; FRS 2008; Regius Professor of Medicine, University of Oxford, since 2002; Student of Christ Church, Oxford, since 2002; *b* 1 July 1952; *s* of Robert Edward Bell and Mary Agnes (*née* Wholey). *Educ:* Univ. of Alberta, Canada (BSc Medicine); Oxford Univ. (BA Hons Physiol Sci.; BM, BCh; DM 1990). FRCP 1992. Rhodes Scholar, Univ. of Alberta and Magdalen Coll., Oxford, 1975. Postgraduate training in medicine, 1979–82 (John Radcliffe Hosp., Hammersmith Hosp., Guy's Hosp., Nat. Hosp. for Neurol Disease); Clinical Fellow in Immunology, Stanford Univ., USA, 1982–87; University of Oxford: Wellcome Sen. Clin. Fellow, 1987–89; University Lectr, 1989–92; Nuffield Prof. of Clin. Medicine, 1992–2002; Fellow, Magdalen Coll., 1990–2002. Mem., MRC, 1996–2002. Chairman: OSCHR, 2006–; Human Genome Strategy Gp, 2010– (report published 2012); Co-Chm., Centre for Advancement of Sustainable Medical Innovation. UK Life Sciences Champion, 2011. Founder FMedSci 1998 (Pres., 2006–11). Sen. Mem., OUBC, 1996–. *Publications:* scientific papers in immunology and genetics. *Recreations:* rowing, swimming, sailing. *Address:* Christ Church, Oxford OX1 1DP. *Clubs:* Leander (Henley-on-Thames); Vincent's (Oxford).

BELL, Sir John Lowthian, 5th Bt *cr* 1885; *b* 14 June 1960; *s* of Sir Hugh Francis Bell, 4th Bt and Lady Bell (*d* 1990) (Mary Howson, MB, ChB, *d* of late George Howson, The Hyde, Hambledon); *S* father, 1970; *m* 1985, Venetia, *d* of J. A. Perry, Taunton; one *s* one *d*. *Recreations:* shooting, fishing. *Heir:* *s* John Hugh Bell, *b* 29 July 1988.

BELL, Prof. (John) Nigel (Berridge), PhD; Professor of Environmental Pollution, Imperial College London, 1989–2011, now Emeritus; *b* 26 April 1943; *s* of John Edward Donald Bell and Dorothy Elise Bell (*née* White); *m* 1st, 1970, Jennifer Margaret Pollard (marr. diss. 1977); 2nd, 1978, Carolyn Mary Davies (marr. diss. 1992); three *s*; 3rd, 2006, Elinor Margaret Lord. *Educ:* County Grammar Sch. of King Edward VII, Melton Mowbray; Univ. of Manchester (BSc Botany 1964; PhD Plant Ecol. 1969); Univ. of Waterloo, Ont. (MSc Biol. 1965; Science Alumnus of Honour 2007). Teaching Fellow, Univ. of Waterloo, 1964–65; Res. Asst, Bedford Coll., Univ. of London, 1968–70; Imperial College, University of London: Res. Asst, 1970–72; Lectr, 1972–83; Sen. Lectr, 1983–87; Reader in Envmtl Pollution, 1987–89; Dir, 1980–2008, Dir, Careers and Alumni, 2008–13, MSc in Envmtl Technol. (formerly MSc Studies); Dir, Centre for Envmtl Technology, 1986–94; Head, Agricl and Envmtl Mgt Sect., Dept of Biology, 1986–2001. Hon. DES Waterloo, 1998. *Publications:* (ed) Ecological Aspects of Radionuclide Releases, 1983; Air Pollution Injury to Vegetation, 1986; (ed) Acid Rain and Britain's Natural Ecosystems, 1988; Air Pollution and Forest Health in the European Community, 1990; (ed) Air Pollution and Plant Life, 2nd edn 2002; Biosphere Implications of Deep Disposal of Nuclear Waste, 2007; numerous papers in jls on air pollution and radioactive pollution. *Recreations:* classical music, travel, walking, railways. *Address:* Centre for Environmental Policy, 15 Prince's Gardens, Imperial College London, SW7 2AZ. *T:* (020) 7594 9288; 48 Western Elms Avenue, Reading, Berks RG30 2AN. *T:* (0118) 958 0653.

BELL, Rev. Prof. John Stephen, DPhil; FBA 1999; Professor of Law, University of Cambridge, since 2001 (Chair, School of Humanities and Social Sciences, 2005–09); Fellow, Pembroke College, Cambridge, since 2001; *b* 5 May 1953; *s* of Harry Bell and Elsie Bell (*née* Walmsley); *m* 1983, Sheila Brookes; two *s*. *Educ:* Trinity Coll., Cambridge (BA 1974; MA 1978); Gregorian Univ., Rome (Baccalaureus in Philosophy 1976); Wadham Coll., Oxford (DPhil 1980); St Mary's Univ. Coll., London (BA 2013). Asst, Inst de droit comparé, Paris II, 1974–75; Fellow and Tutor in Law, Wadham Coll., Oxford, 1979–89; Leeds University: Prof. of Public and Comparative Law, 1989–2001; Pro-Vice Chancellor for Teaching, 1992–94. Professeur associé: Univs of Paris I and Paris II, 1985–86; Univ. du Maine, 1995–96; Vis. Prof., Katholieke Univ., Brussels, 1993–. Chm., Jt Academic Stage Bd, 2004–09. Mem., Res. Council, Eur. Univ. Inst., Florence, 1997–2003. Pres., SPTL, 1998–99. Ordained deacon, Dio. of East Anglia, 2012. FRSA 1995. Hon. QC 2003. *Publications:* Policy Arguments in Judicial Decisions, 1983; French Constitutional Law, 1992; (with L. N. Brown) French Administrative Law, 4th edn 1993, 5th edn 1998; (with G. Engle) Cross on Statutory Interpretation, 3rd edn 1995; (jtly) Principles of French Law, 1998; (contrib.) New Directions in European Public Law, 1998; French Legal Cultures, 2001; Judiciaries within Europe, 2006; (with D. Ibbetson) European Legal Development: the case of tort, 2012; contribs to learned jls. *Recreation:* learning and speaking foreign languages. *Address:* Faculty of Law, University of Cambridge, 10 West Road, Cambridge CB3 9DZ.

BELL, Dr Jonathan Richard, CB 2006; CChem, FRSC; Director, Jon Bell Associates Ltd, since 2006; *b* 12 Nov. 1947; *s* of late Stanley and Marjorie Bell; *m* 1971, Lynne Trezise; one *s*. *Educ:* Cambridge Grammar Sch. for Boys; Univ. of Hull (BSc 1969; PhD 1972). CChem 1973, FRSC 1992. Post doctoral researcher, Dyon Perrins Lab., Univ. of Oxford, 1973–74; Packaging Chemist, Metal Box Co., 1974–75; Ministry of Agriculture, Fisheries and Food, 1975–2000: Head: Food Sci. Div. I, 1989–92; Food Sci. Div. II, 1992–95; Additives and Novel Food Div., 1995–2000; Food Standards Agency: Dir, Food Safety Policy, Chief Scientific Advr and Dep. Chief Exec., 2000–03; Chief Exec. and Chief Scientific Advr, 2003–06. Consultant on agri-food and health matters, crisis mgt and performance mgt, 2006–. *T:* 0871 855 2988. *E:* jon.bell@jonbellassociates.co.uk.

BELL, Joshua; violinist; Music Director, Academy of St Martin in the Fields, since 2011; *b* Indiana, 9 Dec. 1967; *s* of Alan and Shirley Bell. *Educ:* Sch. of Music, Univ. of Indiana (studied with Josef Gingold). Internat. début with Philadelphia Orch., 1981; performances with orchs in Europe, USA and Canada incl. Royal Philharmonic, London Philharmonic, BBC Symphony, Philharmonia, CBSO, Chicago Symphony, Boston Symphony, LA Philharmonic, NY Philharmonic and Cleveland Orch. Recitals in Europe and USA. Vis. Prof., Royal Acad. of Music, 1997–. Numerous recordings (Grammy Award, 2001). Mercury Music Prize, 2000. *Recreations:* golf, tennis, computers. *Address:* c/o IMG Artists, The Light Box, 111 Power Road, Chiswick, W4 5PY.

BELL, Lindsay Frances; Director, Local Government Finance, Department for Communities and Local Government (formerly Office of the Deputy Prime Minister), 2004–10; *b* 29 April 1950; one *s* one *d*. *Educ:* University Coll. London (BA 1971); St Anne's Coll., Oxford (BPhil 1973). Department of the Environment, later Department of the Environment, Transport and the Regions, subseq. Office of the Deputy Prime Minister, then Department for Communities and Local Govt, 1975–2010: Head: Finance Deptl Services, 1987–89; Water Regulation Div., 1989–90; Local Govt Reorgn Div., 1990–94; Local Authy Grants, 1994–97; Dir, Regl Policy, 1997–2000; Dep. Hd, Domestic Affairs, Cabinet Office (on secondment), 2000–03; Dir, Strategy, Neighbourhood Renewal Unit, 2003–04.

BELL, Marcus David John; Director of Teachers and Teaching (formerly Teachers Group), Department for Education, since 2011; *b* N Tarrytown, NY, 10 Nov. 1966; *s* of Colin James Bell and Kathleen Bell; *m* 1999, Deborah Parkin; twin *s* twin *d*. *Educ:* Winchester Coll. (Schol.); Balliol Coll., Oxford (Markby Schol.; BA Hons Hist. and Mod. Langs). Admin. trainee, DES, 1989–92; Private Sec., Chancellor of Duchy of Lancaster, 1992–93; Principal, DFE, 1993–96; Registrar, Bishop Grosseteste Coll., Lincoln, 1996–98; Principal, DFEE, 1998–2001; Deputy Director: Social Exclusion Unit, Cabinet Office, 2001–04; Young People at Risk Div., DFES, then DCSF, 2004–08; Director of Workforce Strategy, DCSF, 2008–09; Dir of Workforce Gp, DCSF, then DFE, 2009–11. *Recreations:* cooking, cycling. *Address:* Department for Education, Sanctuary Buildings, Great Smith Street, SW1P 3BT. *T:* (020) 7925 5000.

BELL, Marian Patricia, CBE 2005; economist; Member, Monetary Policy Committee, Bank of England, 2002–05; *b* 28 Oct. 1957; *d* of Joseph Denis Milburn Bell and Wilhelmenia Maxwell Bell (*née* Miller). *Educ:* Hertford Coll., Oxford (BA PPE); Birkbeck Coll., London (MSc Econs). Sen. Economist, Royal Bank of Scotland, 1985–89; Econ. Advr, HM Treasury, 1989–91; Sen. Treasury Economist, 1991–97; Hd of Res., Treasury and Capital Mkts, Royal Bank of Scotland, 1997–2000; Consultant, alpha economics, 2000–02, 2005–. Member: Internat. Adv. Council, Zurich Financial Services, 2007–; Fiscal Policy Panel, States of Jersey, 2007–, States of Guernsey, 2010–11, CI. Non-exec. Dir, Emerging Health Threats Forum, 2006–12. Gov., Contemporary Dance Trust, The Place, 2005– (Vice-Chm., 2008–).

BELL, Martin, OBE 1992; Ambassador (formerly Special Representative) for Humanitarian Emergencies, UNICEF, since 2001; *b* 31 Aug. 1938; *s* of late Adrian Hanbury Bell and Marjorie H. Bell; *m* 1st, 1971, Nelly Lucienne Gourdon (marr. diss.); two *d*; 2nd, 1985, Rebecca D. Sobel (marr. diss.); 3rd, 1998, Fiona Goddard. *Educ:* The Leys Sch., Cambridge; King's Coll., Cambridge (MA). BBC TV News: Reporter, 1965–77; Diplomatic Correspondent, 1977–78; Chief Washington Correspondent, 1978–89; Berlin Correspondent, 1989–93; E European Correspondent, 1993–94; Foreign Affairs Correspondent, 1994–96; Special Correspondent, BBC Nine O'Clock News, 1997. Pool TV Reporter, 7th Armoured Bde, Gulf War, 1991. MP (Ind.) Tatton, 1997–2001. Contested (Ind.) Brentwood and Ongar, 2001. Pres., Japanese Labour Camp Survivors' Assoc., 2001–. DUniv Derby, 1996; Hon. MA: East Anglia, 1997; N London, 1997; Hon. DLit Kingston, 2002. RTS Reporter of the Year, 1977, TV Journalist of the Year, 1992. *Publications:* In Harm's Way, 1995; An Accidental MP, 2000; Through Gates of Fire, 2003; The Truth that Sticks: New Labour's breach of trust, 2007; A Very British Revolution, 2009; For Whom the Bell Tolls, 2011. *Address:* 71 Denman Drive, NW11 6RA.

BELL, Martin George Henry; Senior Partner, Ashurst Morris Crisp, 1986–92; *b* 16 Jan. 1935; *s* of Leonard George Bell and Phyllis Bell (*née* Green); *m* 1965, Shirley Wrightson; two *s*. *Educ:* Charterhouse. Nat. Service, 1953–55. Articles, 1956–61, admitted Solicitor, 1961, Assistant, 1961, Partner, 1963, Ashurst Morris Crisp. Dir, Laird Gp, 1994–2002. *Recreation:* walking. *Address:* Mulberry, Woodbury Hill, Loughton, Essex IG10 1JB. *T:* (020) 8508 1188.

BELL, Prof. Martin Guy, PhD; FBA 2009; FSA; Professor of Archaeological Science, University of Reading, since 2002; *b* Brighton, 28 Oct. 1953; *s* of William and Joy Bell; *m* 1981, Dr Jennifer Foster; two *d*. *Educ:* Cardinal Newman Sch., Hove; Inst. of Archaeol., Univ. of London (BSc, PhD). Res. asst, then Res. Fellow, Bristol Univ., 1980–83; Lectr, then Sen. Lectr, Univ. of Wales, Lampeter, 1983–96; Sen. Lectr, Univ. of Reading, 1996–2002. FSA 1984. *Publications:* Brean Down: excavations, 1983–87, 1990; (with M. J. C. Walker) Late Quaternary Environmental Change, 1992, 2nd edn 2005; (ed with J. Boardman) Past and Present Soil Erosion, 1992; (jtly) The Experimental Earthwork Project, 1996; Prehistoric Intertidal Archaeology, 2000; Prehistoric Coastal Communities, 2007; The Bronze Age in the Severn Estuary, 2013. *Recreations:* swimming, walking, natural history. *Address:* Department of Archaeology, University of Reading, Whiteknights, PO Box 227, Reading RG6 6AB. *T:* (0118) 378 7724, *Fax:* (0118) 378 6718. *E:* m.g.bell@reading.ac.uk.

BELL, Mary Elizabeth; *see* Stacey, M. E.

BELL, Prof. Michael, PhD; FBA 2008; Professor of English, University of Warwick, 1994–2008, now Emeritus; *b* Chelmsford, 21 July 1941; *s* of Michael James Bell and Josephine Bell; *m* (marr. diss.); one *s* one *d*. *Educ:* University Coll. London (BA; PhD 1970). English asst, Lyons, France, 1962–63; teacher of English and French, St Stephen's Sch., Welling, 1963–64; English asst, Erlangen, Germany, 1964–65; Instructor, 1965–69, Lectr, 1969–70, Univ. of Western Ontario; Associate Prof., Ithaca Coll., NY, 1970–73; University of Warwick: Lectr, 1973–81; Sen. Lectr, 1981–92; Reader in English, 1992–94. *Publications:* Primitivism, 1972; (ed) Context of English Literature 1900–1930, 1982; The Sentiment of Reality: truth of feeling in the European novel, 1983; F. R. Leavis, 1988; D. H. Lawrence: language and being, 1992; Gabriel García Márquez: solitude and solidarity, 1993; Literature, Modernism and Myth: belief and responsibility in the Twentieth Century, 1997; Sentimentalism, Ethics and the Culture of Feeling, 2001; Open Secrets: literature and education and authority from J.-J. Rousseau to J. M. Coetzee, 2007. *Recreation:* walking. *Address:* 9 Clapham Street, Leamington Spa, Warks CV31 1JJ. *T:* (01926) 312719. *E:* Bell.Michael@talktalk.net.

BELL, Michael John Vincent, CB 1992; Senior Adviser, MK Trade Compliance Group, since 2013; *b* 9 Sept. 1941; *e s* of late C. R. V. Bell, OBE and Jane Bell, MBE; *m* 1983, Mary Shippen, *o d* of late J. W. and Margaret Shippen; one *s* two *d*. *Educ:* Winchester Coll.; Magdalen Coll., Oxford (BA Lit.Hum.). Res. Associate, Inst. for Strategic Studies, 1964; Ministry of Defence: Asst Principal, 1965; Principal, 1969; Asst Sec., 1975; on loan to HM Treasury, 1977–79; Asst Under Sec. of State (Resources and Programmes), 1982–84; Dir Gen. of Management Audit, 1984–86; Asst Sec. Gen. for Defence Planning and Policy, NATO, 1986–88; Dep. Under-Sec. of State (Finance), 1988–92, (Defence Procurement), 1992–95; Dep. Chief of Defence Procurement (Support), 1995–96; Project Dir, European Consolidation, BAe (on secondment), 1996–99; Gp Hd of Strategic Analysis, BAe, subseq. BAE Systems, 1999–2003; Gp Export Controls Consultant, BAE Systems, 2004–12. *Recreation:* military history.

BELL, Nigel; *see* Bell, J. N. B.

BELL, Nigel Christopher, CEng, CITP; Managing Partner, AllChange Business Advisors Ltd; *b* 29 July 1959; *s* of Leonard Norman Bell and Marlene Bell (*née* Gould); *m* 1985, Colette Julia Stein; one *s* one *d*. *Educ:* Kendal Grammar Sch.; Loughborough Univ. (BSc Hons Computer Studies); Sheffield Hallam Univ. (MSc Managing Change). CEng 1990; CITP 2008; FBCS 2008. Analyst Programmer, Comshare, 1981–85; Project Co-ordinator, Honeywell Bull, 1985–87; Project Manager, Boots, 1987–88; Mgt Consultant, Price Waterhouse, 1988–93; Div. Dir, Eur. Inf. Systems, Low & Bonar, 1993–96; Vice-Pres., Inf. Systems and Services, Astra Charnwood, 1996–98; Inf. Systems and Technol. Dir for Drug Develt, Astra AB, 1998–99; Chief Exec., NHS Information Authy, 1999–2001; Dir, Service Transformation, Office of e-Envoy, Cabinet Office, 2001–02; Dir and Principal Consultant, Ophis Ltd, 2002–11; Man. Partner, HP Enterprise Services, 2012–15. *Recreations:* fell-walking, gym, cinema.

BELL, Sir Peter (Robert Frank), Kt 2002; MD; FRCS, FRCSGlas; Professor and Head of Department of Surgery, University of Leicester, 1974–2003, now Emeritus; *b* 12 June 1938; *s* of Frank and Ruby Bell; *m* 1961, Anne Jennings; one *s* two *d*. *Educ:* Univ. of Sheffield (MB,

ChB Hons 1961; MD 1969). FRCS 1965; FRCSGlas 1968. Postgrad. surg. career in Sheffield hosps, 1961–65; Lectr in Surgery, Univ. of Glasgow, 1965–68; Sir Henry Wellcome Travelling Fellow, Univ. of Colorado, 1968–69; Consultant Surgeon and Sen. Lectr, Western Infirm., Glasgow, 1969–74. President: Surgical Res. Soc., 1986–88; European Soc. of Vascular Surgery, 1994; Vascular Soc. of GB and Ireland, 1998–99; Internat. Soc. of Vascular Surgeons, 2003–; Mem. Council, RCS, 1992– (Vice Pres., 2001–04). Pres., Hope Foundn for Cancer Res.; Chm., Circulation Foundn. Founder FMedSci 1998. Hon. DSc Leicester, 2003; Dr *hc* Lisbon, 2009. *Publications:* Surgical Aspects of Haemodialysis, 1974, 2nd edn 1983; Operative Arterial Surgery, 1982; Arterial Surgery of the Lower Limb, 1991; Surgical Management of Vascular Disease, 1992; 596 pubns on vascular disease, transplantation and cancer in med. and surg. jls. *Recreations:* horticulture, oil painting, bowls, reading.

BELL, Robert John; Chief Executive, Royal Brompton and Harefield NHS Foundation Trust, since 2005; *b* Tripoli, Lebanon, 22 July 1950; *s* of Jack R. Bell and May Bell (*née* Dagher); *m* 1973, Patricia L. Neate; one *s* two *d*. *Educ:* Univ. of Toronto (BASc Industrial Engrg 1973); Professional Engr, Ont, 1975; Cornell Univ. (EDP 1978); Queen's Univ., Canada (MPA 1980). Systems engr, Hosp. for Sick Children, Toronto, 1972–74; Planning Officer, Min. of Health, Ont, 1974–75; Treasury Bd Officer, Mgt Bd of Cabinet, Toronto, 1975–76; Exec. Dir, Min. of Health, Ont, 1976–80; Vice President: Extendicare Ltd, London, 1980–83; Hilton Universal Hosps, London, 1983–85; Exec. Dir, Min. of Health, Ont, 1985–86; Partner, KPMG (Peat Marwick), Toronto, 1986–90; Ernst & Young, Toronto: Partner and Nat. Dir (Health Care), 1990–2000; Vice Pres., Cap Gemini, 2000–02; Pres. and CEO, William Osler Health Centre, Ont, 2002–05. Non-executive Director: CORDA, 2008–; Inst. of Cardiovascular Medicine and Sci., 2011–; Imperial Coll. Health Partners, 2012–; Royal Brompton and Harefield Hosps Charity, 2012–. *Recreation:* antique collector (Oriental rugs and carpets, commemorative bronze medallions, coins, model soldiers). *Address:* 8 Salisbury House, 3 Drummond Gate, SW1V 2HJ. *T:* (office) (020) 7351 8652, 07970 296445. *E:* robertbell49@btinternet.com.

BELL, Hon. Sir Rodger, Kt 1993; a Judge of the High Court of Justice, Queen's Bench Division, 1993–2006; a Presiding Judge, South Eastern Circuit, 2001–05; *b* 13 Sept. 1939; *s* of John Thornton Bell and Edith Bell; *m* 1969, (Sylvia) Claire Tatton Brown; one *s* three *d*. *Educ:* Moulsham Sch.; Brentwood Sch.; Brasenose Coll., Oxford (BA). Called to the Bar, Middle Temple, 1963, Bencher, 1989; QC 1982; a Recorder, 1980–93; Chm., NHS Tribunal, 1991–93; Legal Mem., Mental Health Review Tribunals, 1983–93; Mem., Parole Board, 1990–93. *Address:* The Mill House, Upton Hellions, Crediton, Devon EX17 4AE.

BELL, Prof. Ronald Leslie, CB 1988; FREng; FInstP; Director-General, Agricultural Development and Advisory Service and the Regional Organisation, and Chief Scientific Adviser, Ministry of Agriculture, Fisheries and Food, 1984–89; *b* 12 Sept. 1929; *s* of Thomas William Alexander Bell and Annie (*née* Mapleston); *m* 1954, Eleanor Joy (*née* Lancaster); one *s* one *d* (and one *d* decd). *Educ:* The City School, Lincoln; Univ. of Birmingham (BSc, PhD). Research Fellow, Royal Radar Estabt, Malvern, 1954–57; Imperial College, Univ. of London: Lectr in Metallurgy, 1957–62; Reader in Metallurgy, 1962–65; University of Southampton: Prof. of Engrg Materials, 1965–77; Head of Dept of Mech. Engrg, 1968; Dean of Faculty of Engrg and Applied Scis, 1970–72; Dep. Vice Chancellor, 1972–76; Dir, NIAE, 1977–84. Vis. Prof., Cranfield Inst. of Technology, 1979–89. Pres., British Crop Protection Council, 1985–89; Member: AFRC, 1984–89; Council, RASE, 1984–89. Sen. Treas., Methodist Church Div. of Ministries, 1990–96. FREng (FEng 1991). Hon. DSc Southampton, 1985. *Publications:* papers in learned jls dealing with twinning and brittle fracture of metals, grain boundary sliding and creep in metals, dislocations in semi-conductors, agricultural engineering. *Recreations:* the bassoon (Founder and Hon. Pres., St Albans Rehearsal Orch.), musical acoustics, painting, Association football, gardening. *Address:* 3 Old Garden Court, Mount Pleasant, St Albans AL3 4RQ.

BELL, Stephen Ainswood; Associate Conductor, Hallé Pops, since 2013; *b* Bury, Lancs, 13 July 1962; *s* of Frank Bell and Joan Bell; *m* 2007, Charlotte Lines; three *d*. *Educ:* Bacup and Rawtenstall Grammar Sch.; Royal Coll. of Music (GRSM Hons; ARCM). Sub Principal Horn, 1985–92, Principal Horn, 1992–, BBC Concert Orchestra; freelance conductor, 2000–. *Recreations:* travel, cars, food. *Address:* Hallé Concerts Society, Bridgewater Hall, Manchester M1 5HA. *T:* (0161) 237 7000. *E:* stephenabell@btinternet.com.

BELL, Prof. Stephen David, PhD; Professor, Molecular and Cellular Biochemistry Department, Indiana University, since 2012; *b* Glasgow, 10 July 1967; *s* of David and Jean Bell; *m* 2007, Rachel Yvonne Samson; one *d*. *Educ:* Glasgow Univ. (BSc Hons Molecular Biol. 1989; PhD 1992). Post-doctoral res., Wellcome Centre for Molecular Parasitology, 1992–95, Gurdon Inst., Cambridge, 1996–2001; Gp Leader, MRC Cancer Cell Unit, Cambridge, 2001–07; Prof. of Microbiol., Univ. of Oxford, 2007–12; Fellow, Wadham Coll., Oxford, 2007–12. Fellow, EMBO, 2006. Tenovus Medal, Tenovus Scotland, 2006. *Publications:* (with Melvin Depamphilis) Genome Duplication, 2010; contrib. scientific jls in fields of transcription, DNA replication and cell division. *Recreations:* climbing, bird watching. *Address:* Molecular and Cellular Biochemistry Department, Indiana University, Simon Hall MSB, Room 405A, 212 S Hawthorne Drive, Bloomington, IN 47405, USA.

BELL, Steve W. M.; freelance cartoonist and illustrator, since 1977; *b* 26 Feb. 1951; *m* 1977; four *c*. *Educ:* Slough Grammar Sch.; Teesside Coll. of Art; Univ. of Leeds (BA Fine Art 1974); Exeter Univ. (teaching cert.). Teacher of art, Aston Manor Sch., Birmingham, 1976–77. Contribs to Whoopee!, Cheeky, Jackpot, New Statesman, New Society, Social Work Today, NME, Journalist; Maggie's Farm series, Time Out, then City Limits, 1979; IF…series, Guardian, 1981–. Exhibitions of cartoons: Barbican Gall.; Cartoon Gall.; Cartoon Mus.; Lightbox Gall., Woking; Wilhelm Busch Mus., Hanover. Hon. MLit Teesside, 1995; Hon. DLit: Sussex, 1996; Loughborough, 2006; Leeds, 2007; Brighton, 2011. *Publications:* Maggie's Farm, 1981; Further Down on Maggie's Farm, 1982; The If Chronicle, 1983; (with B. Homer) Waiting for the Upturn, 1986; Maggie's Farm: the last round up, 1987; If…Bounces Back, 1987; If…Breezes In, 1988; (with R. Woddis) Funny Old World, 1991; If…Goes Down the John, 1992; If…Bottoms Out, 1993; Big If…, 1995; (with S. Hoggart) Live Briefs: a political sketchbook, 1996; If…Files, 1997; Bell's Eye, 1999; (with B. Homer) Chairman Blair's Little Red Book, 2001; Unstoppable If…, 2001; Unspeakable If…, 2003; Apes of Wrath, 2004; If…Marches On, 2006; My Vision for a New You, 2006; If…Bursts Out, 2010. *Address:* Belltoons, PO Box 5298, Brighton BN50 8AR. *W:* www.belltoons.co.uk.

BELL, Trevor; *see* Bell, C. T.

BELL, William Bradshaw, OBE 2005; JP; Member (UU) Lagan Valley, Northern Ireland Assembly, 1998–2007; *b* 9 Oct. 1935; *s* of Robert Bell and Mary Ann Bell; *m* 1969, Leona Maxwell; one *s* three *d*. *Educ:* Fane Street Primary School, Belfast; Grosvenor High School, Belfast. Member: for N Belfast, NI Constitutional Convention, 1975–76; Belfast City Council, 1976–85 (Unionist spokesman on housing, 1976–79; Lord Mayor of Belfast, 1979–80); for S Antrim, NI Assembly, 1982–86 (Dep. Chm., Finance and Personnel Cttee, 1984–86); Lisburn CC (formerly BC), 1989–2005 (Chairman: Police Liaison Cttee, 1991; Finance Cttee, 1993–95; Economic Develt Cttee, 1996–98; Mayor of Lisburn, 2003–04). Chm., NI Public Accounts Cttee, 1999–2002. Contested (UU) Lagan Valley, NI Assembly, 2007. *Recreations:* music, motoring, writing.

BELL, William Edwin, CBE 1980; Deputy Chairman, Enterprise Oil plc, 1991–97 (Chairman, 1984–91); *b* 4 Aug. 1926; *s* of late Cuthbert Edwin Bell and Winifred Mary Bell (*née* Simpson); *m* 1952, Angela Josephine Vaughan; two *s* two *d*. *Educ:* Birmingham University (BSc Civil Eng.); Royal School of Mines, Imperial College. Joined Royal Dutch Shell Group, 1948; tech. and managerial appts, Venezuela, USA, Kuwait, Indonesia; Shell International Petroleum Co. (Middle East Coordination), 1965–73; Gen. Man., Shell UK Exploration and Production and Dir, Shell UK, 1973; Man. Dir, Shell UK, 1976–79; Middle East Regional Coordinator and Dir, Shell International Petroleum Co., 1980–84, retired; non-exec. Dir, Costain Group, 1982–92. Pres., UK Offshore Operators Assoc., 1975–76. *Publications:* contribs to internat. tech. jls, papers on offshore oil industry develts. *Recreations:* golf, sailing. *Address:* Fordcombe Manor, near Tunbridge Wells, Kent TN3 0SE. *Club:* Nevill Golf.

BELL, Sir William Hollin Dayrell M.; *see* Morrison-Bell.

BELL BURNELL, Dame (Susan) Jocelyn, DBE 2007 (CBE 1999); PhD; FRS 2003; FRSE, FRAS; astronomer; Visiting Professor of Astrophysics, University of Oxford, since 2004; President, Royal Society of Edinburgh, since 2014; *b* 15 July 1943; *d* of G. Philip and M. Allison Bell; *m* 1968, Martin Burnell (separated 1989); one *s*. *Educ:* The Mount Sch., York; Glasgow Univ. (BSc); New Hall, Cambridge (PhD; Hon. Fellow, 1996). FRAS 1969; FRSE 2004. Res. Fellowships, Univ. of Southampton, 1968–73; Res. Asst, Mullard Space Science Lab., UCL, 1974–82; Sen. Res. Fellow, 1982–86, SSO, 1986–89, Grade 7, 1989–91, Royal Observatory, Edinburgh; Prof. of Physics, Open Univ., 1991–2001; Dean, Science Faculty, Univ. of Bath, 2001–04. An Editor, The Observatory, 1973–76. Vis. Fellow, 1999, Vis. Prof. for Distinguished Teaching, 1999–2000, Princeton Univ.; Sackler Vis. Prof., Univ. of Calif, Berkeley, 2000; Philips Visitor, Haverford Coll., Pa, 1999; Tuve Fellow, Carnegie Instn of Washington, 2000; Vainu Bappu Vis. Prof., Indian Inst. of Astrophysics, Bangalore, 2013. Lectures: Marie Curie, Inst. of Physics, 1994; Appleton, Univ., Edinburgh, 1994; Jansky, Nat. Radio Astronomy Observatory, USA, 1995; Royal Instn, 1996; Maddison, Keele Univ., 1997; Flamsteed, Derby Univ., 1997; Royal Soc., 1997; Hamilton, Princeton Univ., 1997; Women in Physics, Aust. Inst. of Physics, 1999; Bishop, Columbia Univ., NY, 1999; Elizabeth Spreadbury, UCL, 2001; Flamsteed, Royal Observatory, Greenwich, 2003; Herschel, Bath, 2003; Robinson (and medal), Armagh, 2004; Nuffield, Assoc. of Sci. Educators, 2005; Inst. of Physics, Ireland, 2005; Campbell, Southampton, 2006; Gordon, Cornell, 2006; Athena, Keele, 2006; Kelvin (and Medal), Royal Philosophical Soc., Glasgow, 2007; Compton, Washington Univ., St Louis, Mo, 2008; Sophia, Newcastle, 2008; Dean's, Melbourne, 2008; Lewis, Assoc. of Sci. Educators, 2010; Faraday, Royal Soc., 2011; de Waard, Groningen Univ., 2011; Wood, Mount Allison Univ., 2012; Edinburgh, Royal Soc. of Edinburgh, 2012; Helen Sawyer Hogg Prize and Lect., Royal Astronomical Soc. of Canada, 2012; Sven Berggren Prize and Lect., Kungl Fysiografiska Sällskapet I Lund, Sweden, 2012; Appleton, Rutherford Appleton Lab., 2012; Lise Meitner, German Physical Soc. and Austrian Physical Soc., 2013; Centenary, Indian Inst. of Sci., Bangalore, 2014. Distinguished Lectr, Internat. Space Univ., 2000, 2002. Mem., IAU, 1979–; Chm., Physics Trng and Mobility of Researchers Fellowships Panel, EC, 1996–98 (Vice Chm., 1995); President: RAS, 2002–04 (Vice-Pres., 1995–97); Inst. of Physics, 2008–11 (Hon. FInstP 2012); British Science Assoc., 2011–12; Mem. Council, Royal Soc., 2004–06; Mem. Panel, Women for Sci., Inter Acad. Council, 2005–06. Mem. Council, Open Univ., 1997–99. Trustee, Nat. Maritime Mus., 2000–09. Chm., Grand Jury, Eur. Commn Marie Curie Excellence Awards, 2005. Foreign Member: Onsala Telescope Bd, Sweden, 1996–2002; Nat. Acad. of Scis, USA, 2005; Hon. Mem., Royal Irish Acad., 2012; Hon. Principal, No 35 Sch., Beijing, 2012; Hon. Prof., Xinjiang Astronomical Observatory, China, 2013. Hon. Mem., Sigma-Pi-Sigma, 2000. FRSA 1999–2011. Honorary Fellow: BAAS, 2006; Glyndwr Univ., 2011. Hon. DSc: Heriot-Watt, 1993; Newcastle, Warwick, 1995; Cambridge, 1996; Glasgow, Sussex, 1997; St Andrews, London, 1999; Leeds, Haverford Coll., Penn, Williams Coll., Mass, 2000; Portsmouth, QUB, 2002; Edinburgh 2003; Keele, 2005; Harvard, Durham 2007; Trinity Dublin, Michigan, Southampton, 2008; Leicester, Loughborough, Lancaster, NUI, 2009; Aberdeen, UCL, 2013; DUniv: York, 1994; Open, 2009. Michelson Medal, Franklin Inst., Philadelphia (jtly with Prof. A. Hewish), 1973; J. Robert Oppenheimer Meml Prize, Univ. of Miami, 1978; Rennie Taylor Award, Amer. Tentative Soc., NY, 1978; (first) Beatrice M. Tinsley Prize, Amer. Astronomical Soc., 1987; Herschel Medal, RAS, 1989; Edinburgh Medal, City of Edinburgh, 1999; Targa Giuseppe Piazzi Award, Palermo, Sicily, 1999; Magellanic Premium, Amer. Philos. Soc., 2000; Joseph Priestly Award, Dickinson Coll., Penn, 2002; Faraday Medal, Royal Soc., 2010; Grote Reber Medal, 2011. Discovered the first four pulsars (neutron stars), 1967–68. *Publications:* Broken for Life, 1989; (ed jtly) Next Generation Infrared Space Observatory, 1992; (ed with Maurice Riordan) Dark Matter: poems of space, 2008; A Quaker Astronomer Reflects, 2013; papers in Nature, Science, Astronomy and Astrophysics, Jl of Geophys. Res., Monthly Notices of RAS. *Recreations:* Quaker interests, walking. *Address:* University of Oxford, Department of Astrophysics, Keble Road, Oxford OX1 3RH.

BELLAK, John George; Chairman, Severn Trent plc (formerly Severn-Trent Water Authority), 1983–94; *b* 19 Nov. 1930; *m* 1960, Mary Prudence Marshall; three *s* one *d*. *Educ:* Uppingham; Clare College, Cambridge. MA (Economics). Sales and Marketing Dir, Royal Doulton, 1968–80, Man. Dir, 1980–83; Chairman: Royal Crown Derby, 1972–83; Lawleys Ltd, 1972–83. President: British Ceramic Manufacturers' Fedn, 1982–83; Fedn of European Porcelain and Earthenware Manufacturers, 1982–83; European Waste Water Group, 1991–93; Dep. Chm., Water Services Assoc., 1992 (Vice-Chm., 1990–91; Chm., 1991). Chm., Aberdeen High Income Trust (formerly Abtrust High Income Investment Trust), 1994–2003; Dir, Ascot Holdings, 1993–96. Mem., Grand Council, CBI, 1984–94. Mem. Court, Keele Univ., 1984–96. *Recreations:* ornithology, field sports, reading. *Address:* 1 Council House Court, Shrewsbury SY1 2AU. *Clubs:* Carlton, Beefsteak.

BELLAMY, Sir Christopher (William), Kt 2000; Senior Consultant, since 2007, and Chairman, Global Competition Practice, since 2011, Linklaters; *b* 25 April 1946; *s* of late William Albert Bellamy, TD, MRCS, LRCP and Vyvienne Hilda, *d* of Albert Meyrick, OBE; *m* 1989, Deirdre Patricia (*née* Turner); one *s* two *d*. *Educ:* Tonbridge Sch.; Brasenose Coll., Oxford (MA). Called to the Bar, Middle Temple, 1968; Bencher, 1994. Taught in Africa, 1968–69; in practice at Bar, 1970–92; QC 1986; Asst Recorder, 1989–92; Judge: Court of First Instance, EC, 1992–99; Employment Appeal Tribunal, 2000–07; a Recorder, 2000–07; a Deputy High Court Judge, 2000–; President: Appeal Tribunals, Competition Commn, 1999–2003; Competition Appeal Tribunal, 2003–07. President: Assoc. of European Competition Law Judges, 2002–06 (Hon. Pres., 2008); UK Assoc. of European Law, 2004–09; Mem., Selection Cttee for Judges of Eur. Civil Service Tribunal, 2004–08. Mem., Council, 2000–06, Adv. Bd, 2007–, British Inst. of Internat. and Comparative Law (Chm., Bingham Appeal, 2008–11; Mem., Adv. Council, Bingham Centre for the Rule of Law, 2011–). Gov., Ravensbourne Coll. of Design and Communication, 1988–92. Liveryman, Broderers' Co., 1995 (Mem., Ct of Assts, 2013–). Commandeur, Ordre Grand-Ducal de la Couronne de Chêne (Luxembourg), 2013. *Publications:* (with G. Child) Common Market Law of Competition, 1973, 7th edn (ed V. Rose and D. Bailey), 2013; public lectures, papers and articles on legal matters. *Recreations:* history, walking, family life. *Address:* Linklaters, 1 Silk Street, EC2Y 8HQ. *T:* (020) 7456 3457. *Clubs:* Athenæum, Garrick.

BELLAMY, Clifford William; His Honour Judge Bellamy; a Circuit Judge, since 2004; Designated Family Judge for Leicester, since 2012; *b* 20 May 1952; *s* of late William Broughton Bellamy and Joan Ernestine Bellamy; *m* 1976, Christine Ann Hughes; two *s*. *Educ:* Burton upon Trent Grammar Sch.; University Coll. London (LLB); Coll. of Ripon and York St John (MA). Admitted solicitor, 1976; Dist Judge, 1995–2004; Designated Family Judge for Warwickshire and Coventry, 2006–12. Ordained Methodist Minister, 2001. *Publications:* Complaints and Discipline in the Methodist Church, 2000, 3rd edn 2008; (contrib.) What is a Minister?, 2002. *Recreations:* reading, opera, walking along the Promenade des Anglais. *Address:* Leicester County Court, 90 Wellington Street, Leicester LE1 6HG. *T:* (0116) 222 5700, *Fax:* (0116) 222 5763.

BELLAMY, David Charles; Chief Executive Officer, St James's Place PLC, since 2007; *b* 15 April 1953; *s* of Percival Leonard Bellamy and Elizabeth Margaret Bellamy; *m* 1970, Janette Godfrey; two *s* one *d*. *Educ:* Sutton High Grammar Sch., Plymouth. Hambro Life Assce, subseq. Allied Dunbar Assce, 1973–91 (Divl Dir, Strategic Res. Unit, 1988–91); Sales Ops, J. Rothschild Assce Gp, 1991–97; Gp Ops Dir, 1997–2000, Man. Dir, 2000–07, St James's Place. Trustee, St James's Place Foundn (Charitable Trust), 1997–. *Recreations:* family, horse racing, horse racing ownership. *Address:* St James's Place PLC, 1 Tetbury Road, Cirencester, Glos GL7 1FP. *T:* (01285) 878005. *E:* david.bellamy@sjp.co.uk.

BELLAMY, David James, OBE 1994; PhD; FLS; CBiol, FRSB; botanist; writer and broadcaster; *b* 18 Jan. 1933; *s* of Thomas Bellamy and Winifred (*née* Green); *m* 1959, Rosemary Froy; two *s* three *d*. *Educ:* London University: Chelsea Coll. of Science and Technology (BSc); Bedford Coll. (PhD). Lectr, then Sen. Lectr, Dept of Botany, Univ. of Durham, 1960–80; Hon. Prof. of Adult and Continuing Educn, 1980–82; Special Prof., then Special Prof. of Geog., Nottingham Univ., 1987–; Vis. Prof. of Natural Heritage Studies, Massey Univ., NZ, 1988–89; Hon. Prof., Univ. of Central Qld, 1999–. Inaugural David Bellamy Lect., 2013. Dir, David Bellamy Associates, envmtl consultants, 1988–95; Associate Dir, P-E Internat., 1993–94; Chm., Greengro Produce Ltd, 2002–; Hon. Dir, Zander Corp., 2004–. Founder Dir, 1982, Pres., 1998, Conservation Foundn; Trustee: WWF, 1985–89; Living Landscape Trust, 1985–; Pensthorpe Conservation Trust Ltd, 2010–; President: WATCH, 1982–2005; YHA, 1983–2004; Population Concern, 1988–2003; Nat. Assoc. Envmtl Educn, 1989–2010; Assoc. of Master Thatchers, 1991–97; Council, Zool Soc. of London, 1991–94, 2002–; Plantlife, 1994–2005; Wildflower Soc., 1995–98; Wildlife Trust Partnership, 1996–2005; British Holiday and Home Parks Assoc., 1996–; Camping and Caravanning Club, 2002–13 (Vice-Pres., 2014–); Vice-Pres., Wild Trout Trust, 2005–. Chair: Welsh Fest. of Countryside, 1999–2002; Abela Conservation Foundn, 2003; Cedrus Ltd, 2003–04; Chair of Govs, Mareeba Wetland Foundn, 2002–. Patron: Te Pua O Whirinaki Regeneration Trust, NZ, 2009–; British Chelonia Gp, 2009–; Lower Mole Countryside Trust, 2013–. Governor, Repton Sch., 1983–89. Chief I Spy, 1983. Contested (Referendum) Huntingdon, 1997. Presenter and script writer for television and radio programmes, BBC and ITV; programmes include Longest Running Show on Earth, 1985; main series: Life in our Sea, 1970; Bellamy on Botany, 1973; Bellamy's Britain, 1975; Bellamy's Europe, 1977; Botanic Man, 1979; Up a Gum Tree, 1980; Backyard Safari, 1981; The Great Seasons, 1982; Bellamy's New World, 1983; You Can't See The Wood, 1984; Discovery, 1985; Seaside Safari, 1985; End of the Rainbow Show, 1985; Bellamy's Bugle, 1986; Turning the Tide, 1986; The End of the Rainbow Show, 1986; Bellamy's Bird's Eye View, 1988; Moa's Ark, 1990; Bellamy Rides Again, 1991, 1992; Wetlands, 1991; England's Last Wilderness, 1992; Blooming Bellamy, 1993; Routes of Wisdom, 1993; Bellamy's Border Raids: the Peak District, 1994; Westwatch, 1996; A Welsh Herbal, 1998; Making Tracks, 1998 and 1999; A Celtic Herbal, 1999; Kite Country, Bellamy and the Argonauts, 2000; The Challenge, 2000; Agrissentials, 2006. FCIWEM 1996; FRIN 2005. Hon. Fellow: BICSc 1997; Royal Entomol Soc. of London; Hon. FLS 1997. Hon. Fellow, Univ. of Lancaster, 1997. DUniv Open, 1984; Hon. DSc: CNAA, 1990; Nottingham, 1993; Dunelm, 1995; Bournemouth, 1999; Kingston, 2000; Oxford Brookes, 2004. Frances Ritchie Meml Prize, Rambler's Assoc., 1989; UNEP Global 500 Award, 1990; Environmental Communicator of the Year, British Assoc. of Communicators in Business, 1996; Guild of Travel Writers Award, 1996; Busk Medal, RGS, 2001. Order of the Golden Ark (Netherlands), 1989. *Publications:* Peatlands, 1974; Bellamy on Botany, 1974; Bellamy's Britain, 1975; Bellamy's Europe, 1977; Life Giving Sea, 1977; Botanic Man, 1978; Half of Paradise, 1979; The Great Seasons, 1981; Backyard Safari, 1981; Discovering the Countryside with David Bellamy: vols I and II, 1982, vols III and IV, 1983; The Mouse Book, 1983; Bellamy's New World, 1983; The Queen's Hidden Garden, 1984; Turning the Tide, 1986; The Vanishing Bogs of Ireland, 1986; Bellamy's Changing Countryside, 4 vols, 1989; (with Brendan Quayle) England's Last Wilderness, 1989; England's Lost Wilderness, 1990; (with Jane Gifford) Wilderness in Britain, 1991; How Green Are You?, 1991; Tomorrow's Earth, 1991; (with Andrea Pfister) World Medicine, 1992; Blooming Bellamy, 1993; Poo, You and the Potoroo's Loo, 1997; (contrib.) The Blue UNESCO, 1999; The English Landscape, 2000; (consultant) The Countryside Detective, 2000; The Jolly Green Giant (autobiog.), 2002; (with Piers Browne) The Glorious Trees of Great Britain, 2002; The Bellamy Herbal, 2003; Conflicts in the Countryside, 2005. *Recreations:* family, gardening, ballet. *Address:* 1 Chapelside Meadows, Hamsterley, Co. Durham DL13 3RG.

BELLAMY, (Kenneth) Rex; Tennis Correspondent, The Times, 1967–89; *b* 15 Sept. 1928; *s* of Sampson Bellamy and Kathleen May Bellamy; *m* 1st, 1951, Hilda O'Shea (*d* 2000); one step *d*; 2nd, 2006, Wendy Elizabeth Matthews. *Educ:* Yeovil; Woodhouse Grammar Sch., Sheffield. National Service, RA and RASC, 1946–49. Sports and Feature Writer, Sheffield Telegraph, 1944–46 and 1949–53; Sports Writer: Birmingham Gazette, 1953–56; The Times, 1956–89. World Championship Tennis award for service to tennis, 1988; International Tennis-writing Awards: 5 from Assoc. of Tennis Professionals, 1975–79 (award discontinued); 2 from Women's Tennis Assoc., 1977–78. *Publications:* Teach Yourself Squash (jtly), 1968; The Tennis Set, 1972; The Story of Squash, 1978 rev. edn as Squash—A History, 1988; The Peak District Companion, 1981; Walking the Tops, 1984; Game, Set and Deadline, 1986; Love Thirty, 1990; The Four Peaks, 1992. *Recreations:* hill-walking, table tennis. *Address:* Ashfield Lodge, 68 Petersfield Road, Midhurst, W Sussex GU29 9JR.

BELLAMY, Martin Clifford, PhD; Director of Information Services, University of Cambridge, since 2014; Fellow, Hughes Hall, University of Cambridge, since 2014; *b* Newcastle, 18 Jan. 1961; *s* of Frank Bellamy and Mildred Bellamy; *m* 1985, Nicola Hammond; one *s* one *d*. *Educ:* Imperial Coll. London (BSc Hons Engrg 1983); London Business Sch. (MSc (Sloan) 1994); Imperial Coll. London (PhD 2014). Marketing Manager, BT, 1983–87; Dir, Real Time Technol., Reuters, 1987–2000; Partner, KPMG, 2000–01; Mem. Faculty, Ashridge Business Sch., 2001–02; Chief Information Officer, Pension Service, DWP, 2002–08; Hd, NHS Connecting for Health, DoH, 2008–09; G Cloud Dir, Cabinet Office, 2009–10; Dir, Change and ICT, Nat. Offender Mgt Service, MoJ, 2010–14; Crown Rep., Cabinet Office, 2011–14. Non-exec. Dir, Group NBT, 2010–12. FBCS; CITP; FAPM; RPP. *Recreations:* theatre, cinema, gym, walking, travel, family. *Address:* University of Cambridge, Roger Needham Building, 7 J J Thomson Avenue, Cambridge CB3 0FB. *T:* (01223) 764224. *E:* martin.bellamy@uis.cam.ac.uk. *Club:* Oxford and Cambridge.

BELLAMY, Prof. Richard Paul, PhD; Professor of Political Science, University College London, since 2005 (Director: School of Public Policy, 2005–10; European Institute, 2010–13); Director, Max Weber Programme, European University Institute, Florence, since 2014; *b* 15 June 1957; *s* of late Edmund Henry Bellamy and of Joan Bellamy (*née* Roberts); one *d*. *Educ:* Trinity Hall, Cambridge (BA 1979; PhD 1982). ESRC Post-doctoral Res. Fellow, Nuffield Coll., Oxford, 1983–86 (Jun. Dean, 1985–86); Lectr, House of Politics, Christ Church, Oxford, 1984–86; Fellow and Coll. Lectr in Hist., Jesus Coll., Cambridge, and Lector, Trinity Coll., Cambridge, 1986–88; Lectr in Politics, Univ. of Edinburgh, 1988–92; Professor: of Politics, UEA, 1992–96; of Politics and Internat. Relns, Univ. of Reading, 1996–2002; of Govt, Univ. of Essex, 2002–05. Acad. Dir, Eur. Consortium for Pol Res., 2002–06; Chair, Britain and Ireland Assoc. for Political Thought, 2009–12. Mem., Politics and Internat. Relns Panel, REF 2014, 2011–. Visiting Fellow: Nuffield Coll., Oxford, 1995; Nat. Europe Centre, ANU, 2005; Jean Monnet Fellow, Social and Pol Sci. Dept, Europea Univ. Inst., Florence, 2000–01; Centre for Advanced Study, Oslo, 2010; Sen. Res. Fellow Hanse Wissenschaft-Kolleg, Delmenhorst, 2013–14. Ed., Critical Rev. of Internat. Social an Political Philosophy, 2002–. FRSA 2002; FAcSS (AcSS 2008). Serena Medal, British Acad 2012. *Publications:* Modern Italian Social Theory: ideology and politics from Pareto to th present, 1987 (trans. Indonesian); Liberalism and Modern Society: an historical argumen 1992 (trans. Portuguese and Chinese); (with D. Schecter) Gramsci and the Italian State, 19 (trans. Japanese); Liberalism and Pluralism: towards a politics of compromise, 199 Rethinking Liberalism, 2000 (trans. Chinese); Political Constitutionalism: a Republica defence of the constitutionality of democracy, 2007 (trans. Spanish; David and Elaine Spi Prize, 2009); A Very Short Introduction to Citizenship, 2008; *editor:* Liberalism and Recer Legal and Social Philosophy, 1989; Victorian Liberalism: nineteenth century political thoug and practice, 1990; Theories and Concepts of Politics: an introduction, 1993; (jtl Democracy and Constitutional Culture in the Union of Europe, 1995; Constitutionalism Democracy and Sovereignty: American and European perspectives, 1996; (with A. Ross) Textual Introduction to Social and Political Thought, 1996; (with D. Castiglion Constitutionalism in Transformation: European and theoretical perspectives, 1996; (with M Hollis) Pluralism and Liberal Neutrality, 1999; (with A. Warleigh) Citizenship an Governance in the European Union, 2001; (with A. Mason) Political Concepts, 2003; (wi T. Ball) The Cambridge History of Twentieth Century Political Thought, 2003 (tran Arabic, Turkish and Chinese); (jtly) Lineages of European Citizenship: rights, belonging an participation in eleven nation states, 2004; The Rule of Law and the Separation of Power 2005; (jtly) Making European Citizens: civic inclusion in a transitional context, 200 Constitutionalism and Democracy, 2006; Introduction to Citizenship, 2008; Public Ethic 2010; Citizenship, 2010; Croce, Gramsci, Bobbio and the Italian Political Tradition, 201 contrib. chapters in books and numerous articles to jls incl. Political Studies, British Jl Pol Sc Philosophical Qly, Eur. Law Jl, Law and Philosophy, Eur. Jl Pol Res., Govt and Oppositio Eur. Jl Pol Theory, Hist. of Pol Thought, Philosophical Forum, Jl Modern Italian Studies, Eur. Public Policy. *Recreations:* listening to and playing music of all kinds, reading and writin walking, talking, cooking, gardening, films and theatre, sex, food and drink. *Address:* Ma Weber Programme, European University Institute, Via dei Roccettini 9, 50014 Sa Domenico di Fiesole, Italy. *T:* (055) 4685809, *Fax:* (055) 4685894. *E:* richard.bellamy@ eui.eu.

BELLAMY-JAMES, Stephen Howard George Thompson; QC 1996; a Recorder, sinc 2000; *b* 27 Sept. 1950; *m* 1988, Rita Margaret Mary James, DCHS; one *d*. *Educ:* The Gramma Sch., Heckmondwike; Trinity Hall, Cambridge (MA Hons Law). ACIArb. Called to the Ba Lincoln's Inn, 1974, Bencher, 2006; Asst Recorder, 1997–2000; Dep. High Court Judg 2000–. Asst Parly Boundary Comr, 2000–10. Accredited Family Mediator, 2007. Membe Cttee, Family Bar Assoc., 1989–96, 2001–02; General Council of the Bar, 1993–96. Chm Bar Council Scholarship Trust, 2000–12. Member: British Inst. of Internat. and Comparativ Law, 1991–97; Family Mediators' Assoc., 2007–. Chm., Public Inquiry into Par Constituencies for Devon, Plymouth, and Torbay, 2003–04. Pres., Nat. Child Safeguardin in Sport Panel, Sport Resolutions (UK), 2012–. Trustee, Wooden Spoon - The Children Charity of Rugby, 2011–. Fellow, Inst. of Advanced Legal Studies, 2000. Freeman: City c London, 2002; City of Glasgow, 2012; Master, Fruiterers' Co., 2016. *Recreations:* music opera, ski-ing, sailing, gardening. *Address:* 1 King's Bench Walk, Temple, EC4Y 7DB. *T* (020) 7936 1500, *Fax:* (020) 7936 1590. *E:* clerks@1kbw.co.uk. *Club:* Oxford an Cambridge.

BELLENGER, Rt Rev. Dr Dominic Terence Joseph, (Dom Aidan Bellenger), OSE FSA; FRHistS; Abbot of Downside, 2006–14; Parish Priest, St Benedict's, Stratton-on-the Fosse, since 1999; *b* 21 July 1950; *s* of Gerald Bellenger and Kathleen Bellenger (*n* O'Donnell). *Educ:* Finchley Grammar Sch.; Jesus Coll., Cambridge (Scholar, MA, PhD Angelicum Univ., Rome. Res. Student in History, 1972–78 and Lightfoot Schol. in Ecc Hist., Cambridge, 1975–78; Assistant Master: St Mary's Sch., Cambridge, 1975–78 Downside Sch., 1978–82; Benedictine Monk, Downside Abbey, 1982; Priest, 198 Housemaster, 1989–91, Head Master, 1991–95, Downside Sch.; Dir of Histl Res., Downsid Abbey, 1995–; Parish Priest: Little Malvern, 1995–99; St Aldhelm's, Chilcompton, 2002–0 Prior, Downside Abbey, 2001–06. Member: Cttee, Eccl. Hist. Soc., 1982–85; Cttee, Englis Benedictine Hist. Commn, 1987–; Council, Catholic Record Soc., 1990–99, 2005–1 2013–; Clifton Diocesan Educn Commn, 1995–2001; Delegate, Benedictine Gen. Chapte 2001–06. Annalist, English Benedictine Congregation, 2009–. Trustee: Catholic Family His Soc., 1990–99; Andrew C. Duncan Catholic History Trust, 1993–; Friends of Somers Churches, 1996–2011; Somerset Record Soc., 1998–; Glastonbury Abbey, 2009–. Presiden English Catholic Hist. Assoc., 1991–; Downside Fisher Club, Bermondsey, 2009–. Governo Moor Park Sch., Ludlow, 1991–99; St Antony's, Leweston, Sherborne, 1991–93; St Mary Sch., Shaftesbury, 1992–96; Moreton Hall, Suffolk, 1995–2001; St Joseph's, Malver 1997–99; Downside Sch., 1999–2015 (Chm.); St Gregory's, Bath, 2001–05; Ammerdow Centre, 2006–09. Chaplain, Kts of Malta, 2004–. Vis. Scholar, Sarum Coll., 2004–. Yor Minster Lecture, 2001. Leverhulme Res. Award, 1986. FRSA; FHEA. Editor: South Wester Catholic History, 1982–2012; The Downside Review, 2011–; English correspondent, Re d'Hist. de l'Eglise de France, 1982–85. *Publications:* English and Welsh Priests 1558–180 1984; The French Exiled Clergy, 1986; (ed) Opening the Scrolls, 1987; (ed jtly) Les Archive du Nord, Calendar of 20 H, 1987; St Cuthbert, 1987; (ed jtly) Letters of Bede Jarrett, 198 (ed) Fathers in Faith, 1991; (ed) The Great Return, 1994; (ed) Downside: a pictorial histor 1998; (jtly) Princes of the Church, 2001; (jtly) Medieval Worlds, 2003; (jtly) The Mitre an the Crown, 2005; (jtly) The Medieval Church, 2006; (ed) Downside Abbey: an architectur history, 2011; Monks with a Mission, 2012; Monastic Identities, 2014; (ed jtly) Davi Knowles, 2014; contributor to many other books; articles in learned jls and periodical *Recreations:* books, church architecture, travel, visual arts, writing. *Address:* Downside Abbe Stratton-on-the-Fosse, Radstock, Bath BA3 4RH. *T:* (01761) 235119.

BELLEW; *see* Grattan-Bellew.

BELLEW, family name of **Baron Bellew**.

BELLEW, 8th Baron *cr* 1848 (Ire.); **Bryan Edward Bellew;** Bt 1688; *b* 19 March 1943; *e* of 7th Baron Bellew and Mary Elizabeth (*d* 1978), *d* of Rev. Edward Eustace Hill; *S* fathe 2010; *m* 1968, Rosemary Sarah, *d* of late Major Reginald Kilner Brasier Hitchcock, MC; on *s* (and one *s* decd). *Educ:* Eton; Royal Military Acad., Sandhurst. Major, Irish Guards, retd *Heir:* *s* Hon. Anthony Richard Brooke Bellew [*b* 9 Sept. 1972; *m* 2001, Ann Elizabeth, *e d* c Peter Plunkett; three *s* one *d*].

BELLEW, Patrick John, RDI 2010; FREng; Principal, Atelier Ten, since 1990; Osmotherly, N Yorks, 12 June 1959; *s* of late James Kevin Bellew and of Judith Ann Bellev (*née* Peckston); *m* 1985, Lois Jane Clay; one *s* two *d*. *Educ:* Stonyhurst Coll.; Univ. of Bat (BSc Hons). Buro Happold, Bath, 1981–87; Dir, Synergy Consulting Engrs, 1988–90. *Majc projects include:* Earth Centre, 2000; Baltic Arts Centre, 2002; Fedn Square, Melbourne, 200 Alpine House, Jodrell Bldg, Shirley Sherwood Gall. and Herbarium, Kew Gardens, 2003–1 Savill Bldg, Savill Gardens, 2005; Grand Rapids Art Mus., 2005; Sculpture Sch., Yale, 2006 Kroon Hall, Yale Univ., 2008; Ashmolean Mus., 2009; British Pavilion, Shanghai Expo 2010; Univ. of the Arts, Kings Cross, 2011; Gardens by the Bay, Singapore, 2011–12; Roya Nat. Th. Renovation, 2012–; WWF HQ, 2013; Türkiye Müteahhitler Birliği HQ, Ankara 2013. Vis. Lectr, Bartlett Sch. of Architecture, 1991–93; Vis. Lectr and Tutor, Sch. o Construction, Reading Univ., 1991–2004; Vis. Lectr, 2001–09, Saarinen Vis. Prof., 2010–

Yale Univ. Sch. of Architecture. Gov., Bldg Centre Trust, 1996–2010; Member: Design Rev. Panel, Design Council (formerly CABE), 1999–2003, 2009–; RIBA Awards Panel, 2011–; Trustee, UK Green Bldg Council, 2008–. FRSA 1997; FEI 2001; FCIBSE 2001; FREng 2004. Hon. FRIBA 2000. Happold Medal, 2008; Silver Medal, CIBSE, 2013. *Publications:* Green:House, Green:Engineering: environmental design at Gardens by the Bay (jtly), 2012; (contrib.) Intelligent Buildings, 2013; articles in Ingenia, Architects Jl, CIBSE Jl, RIBA Jl, Building Design. *Recreations:* guitar, music, cinema, sailing. *Address:* Atelier Ten, 19 Perseverance Works, 38 Kingsland Road, E2 8DD. *T:* (020) 7749 5950. *E:* patrick.bellew@atelierten.com.

BELLINGHAM, Prof. Alastair John, CBE 1997; FRCP, FRCPE, FRCPGlas, FRCPath; Professor of Haematology, King's College London, 1984–97; *b* 27 March 1938; *s* of Stanley Herbert Bellingham and Sybil Mary Milne; *m* 1st, 1963, Valerie Jill Morford (*d* 1997); three *s*; 2nd, 2002, Julia de Quetteville Willott. *Educ:* Tiffin Boys' Sch., Kingston upon Thames; University Coll. Hosp. (MB BS). Research Fellow, Univ. of Washington, 1969–71; Sen. Lectr, UCH, 1971–74; Prof. of Haematology, Univ. of Liverpool, 1974–84; Hon. Consultant Haematologist: Royal Liverpool Hosp., 1974–84; KCH, 1984–97. Transition Dir, Liverpool, Nat. Blood Service, 1997–99; Chairman: Confidentiality Adv. Gp, DoH, 1997–2001; NHS Inf. Authy, 1999–2005; Kennet and N Wilts PCT, 2005–06. Mem. Bd, Inst. of Cancer Res., 1997–2003. Chm. Govs, St Dunstan's Coll., Catford, 1999–2001. Vice-Pres., 1990–93, Pres., 1993–96, RCPath; Past Pres., British Soc. for Haematology; Vice-Pres., Eur. Div., Internat. Soc. Haematology, 1992–98. FFPath, RCPI, 1996. Hon. Fellow, Hong Kong Coll. of Path., 1995. *Publications:* contribs to books and jls on haematol., esp. red cell physiol. and inherited red cell disorders, incl. enzyme deficiencies, sickle cell disorders and thalassaemia. *Recreations:* oenology, viticulture, cricket, photography, Commandeur de la Confrérie de Grande Bretagne des Chevaliers du Sacavin d'Anjou. *Address:* Broadstones, The Street, Teffont Magna, Salisbury SP3 5QP. *T:* (01722) 716267. *Club:* Savage.

BELLINGHAM, Sir Anthony Edward Norman, 8th Bt (2nd creation) *cr* 1796, of Castle Bellingham, co. Louth; Managing Director, City Financial Executive Recruitment, since 1980; *b* 24 March 1947; *yr s* of Sir Roger Carroll Patrick Stephen Bellingham, 6th Bt and of Mary, *d* of William Norman; *S* brother, 1999; *m* 1991, Denise Marie Moity (marr. diss. 1998); one *s*; *m* 1998, Namfon Bellingham (marr. diss. 2001). *Educ:* Rossall. *Heir: s* William Alexander Noel Henry Bellingham, *b* 19 Aug. 1991.

BELLINGHAM, Henry Campbell; MP (C) North West Norfolk, 1983–97 and since 2001; *b* 29 March 1955; *s* of late Henry Bellingham; *m* 1993, Emma, *o d* of P. J. H. Whiteley and Lady Angela Whiteley. *Educ:* Eton; Magdalene Coll., Cambridge (BA 1977). Called to the Bar, Middle Temple, 1978; in practice as barrister, 1978–88. Dir of and consultant to companies, 1998–2010. Contested (C) Norfolk North West, 1997. PPS to Sec. of State for Transport, 1990–92, for Defence, 1992–95, for Foreign and Commonwealth Affairs, 1995–97; Opposition spokesman on Trade and Industry, and Shadow Minister for Small Businesses and Employment, 2002–05; Opposition Whip, 2005–06; Shadow Minister for Justice and Legal Services, 2006–10; Parly Under-Sec. of State (Minister for Africa, UN and Overseas Territories), FCO, 2010–12. Member: Select Cttee on the Environment, 1987–90; NI Select Cttee, 2001–02; Trade and Industry Select Cttee, 2003–04. Chm., Cons. Council on Eastern Europe, 1989–94; officer, Cons. back bench cttees, 1983–90. *Address:* c/o House of Commons, SW1A 0AA. *Club:* White's.

BELLINGHAM, Peter Gordon; Managing Director, Welsh National Opera, since 2009 (Director of Marketing, 1994–2002; Executive Director, 2002–09); *b* 23 Jan. 1956; *s* of Arthur Stanley and Kathleen Bellingham; *m* 1985, Julie Robinson (stage name, Julie Jensen); two *s* one *d*. *Educ:* Royal Northern Coll. of Music. Mgt Trainee, Fulcrum Centre, Slough, 1977–78; Publicity Officer, Torch Th., Milford Haven, 1978–80; PRO, Northern Ballet Th., 1980–81; Festivals Asst, Cheltenham Festivals, 1981–82; Mktg Manager, Northern Ballet Th., 1982–85; Music Officer, 1985–86, Theatres Manager, 1986–87, Bradford CC; Account Dir, sponsorship and events, PRC Communications, 1987–89; Hd, Sales and Mktg, 1989–92, Hd, Planning, 1992–93, Bradford Theatres; freelance arts consultant, 1993–94. *Recreations:* football, tennis (former Chm., Windsor Lawn Tennis Club, Penarth). *Address:* Welsh National Opera, Wales Millennium Centre, Bute Place, Cardiff Bay CF10 5AL. *T:* (029) 2063 5006, *Fax:* (029) 2063 5098. *E:* peter.bellingham@wno.org.uk.

BELLIS, Bertram Thomas; Headmaster, The Leys School, Cambridge, 1975–86; *b* 4 May 1927; *s* of Rev. Thomas J. Bellis and Mary A. Bellis; *m* 1952, Joan Healey; two *s*. *Educ:* Kingswood Sch., Bath; St John's Coll., Cambridge (Exhibr in Maths, MA). Rossall Sch., 1951–55; Highgate Sch., 1955–65; Headmaster, Daniel Stewart's Coll., 1965–72; Principal, Daniel Stewart's and Melville Coll., 1972–75. Founding Dir, Mathematics in Educn and Industry Schools Project, 1963–65. Chm., Scottish Educn Dept Cttee on Computers and the Schools (reports, 1969 and 1972); Member: Council, Inst. of Math., 1975–79; Educational Research Bd, SSRC, 1975–80. Governor: Queenswood Sch., 1980–92; St John's Coll. Sch., 1981–86. Pres., Mathematical Assoc., 1971–72. Schoolmaster Fellow, Balliol Coll., Oxford, 1963; FIMA 1964; FRSE 1972. *Address:* 13 Marlborough Court, Grange Road, Cambridge CB3 9BQ.

BELLOS, Linda Ann, OBE 2007; equality and diversity practitioner, since 2001; Chair, Institute of Equality and Diversity Practitioners, 2009–14; *b* 13 Dec. 1950; *d* of Emmanuel Adebowale and Renee Sackman; *m* 1970, Jonathan Bellos (marr. diss. 1983); one *s* one *d*; civil partnership 2005, Caroline Jones. *Educ:* Silverthorne Girls' Sec. Mod. Sch.; Dick Shephard Comp. Sch.; Univ. of Sussex (BA Hons 1981). HM Inspector of Taxes, Tax Office, 1972–77; finance worker/journalist, Spare Rib, 1981–83; Community Accountant, Lambeth Inner City Consultancy Gp, 1983–84; Team Leader, Women's Unit, GLC, 1984–86; Mem. (Lab), Lambeth LBC, 1985–88 (Leader, 1986–88); Hd, Women's Unit, 1988–90, Actg Asst Dir, Social Services, 1990–91, Hackney LBC; freelance journalist and consultant, 1992–99; Regl Manager, Focus Consultancy Ltd, 1999–2002; self-employed, 2002–03; Dir, Equality Diversity and Human Rights (formerly Diversity Solutions Consultancy) Ltd, 2003–12. Community activist: Queen's Park Community Assoc., Brighton, 1974–81; Women Against Violence Against Women, 1981–86. Vice-Chm., Black Sections, Labour Party, 1984–87; Treas., African Reparations Movt UK, 1994–97; Chairman: New Initiatives Youth and Community Assoc., 1998–2005; Southwark Anti-Homophobic Forum, 1998–2004; Southwark Action for Voluntary Orgns, 2001–07; Southwark Lesbian, Gay, Bisexual and Transgender network, 2002–06; Bronze Woman Proj., 2002–; Co-Chm., LGBT Community Adv. Gp, and Mem., Diversity Bd, Metropolitan Police Service, 2000–03. *Publications:* (contrib.) A Vision Back and Forth, 1995; (contrib.) Making Black Waves, 1995; (contrib.) IC3: the Penguin book of new Black writing in Britain, 2000; contrib. papers, essays and articles in books and magazines. *Recreations:* gardening, reading, music. *Address:* 1 Crown Point Drive, Bixley, Norfolk NR14 8RR. *T:* 0845 260 0028.

BELMAHI, Mohammed; Adviser to Chairman and Chief Executive Officer, since 2009, and Architect General, since 2010, OCP Group; Chairman, OCP Foundation, since 2010; *b* 18 Aug. 1948; *s* of Redouane Belmahi and Aziza Filal Belmahi; *m* 1973, Åse Ask; one *d*. *Educ:* Ecole Nationale d'Architecture, Toulouse (Architect DPLG 1973); New York Univ. (Master of Urban Planning 1975; PhD Prog. in Public Admin 1976; MPhil 1985); Harvard Inst. for Internat. Develt, 1981. London Business Sch. (Sen. Exec. Prog.), 1991. UN Center for Housing, Building and Planning, NY, 1975–76; Min. of Housing and Land Use Planning, and Dir, Land Use Planning, Rabat, 1977–79; Prime Minister's Office, Rabat (Mem., State Owned Enterprise Reform Task Force), 1979–82; Dir of Tourism, Min. of Tourism, 1982–86; Dir Gen., Moroccan Nat. Tourist Bd, 1987–88; Mem., Exec. Cttee, ONA Hldg Gp, Casablanca, 1988–96; Dir Gen. for Real Estate and Tourism, and Dir Gen., Casablanca World Trade Center; Ambassador to India and Nepal, 1996–99; Ambassador to Court of St James's, 1999–2009. Freeman, City of London, 2006. Indira Gandhi Meml Award, 1997; Interfaith Gold Medallion, Three Faiths Forum, 2009. Officer, National Order of Merit (Portugal), 1991; Kt Comdr, Royal Order of Francis I, 2003. *Recreations:* golf, swimming, collecting miniature elephants, drawing portraits. *Address:* OCP Foundation, Rabat Design Center, Rue Mohamed Jazouli, Quatier Al Irfane, 1100 Rabat, Morocco. *E:* mbelmahi@hotmail.com, m.belmahi@ocpgroup.org. *Clubs:* Travellers; Dar Es Salam Golf (Rabat).

BELMONT, Abbot of; *see* Stonham, Rt Rev. Dom P.

BELMORE, 8th Earl of, *cr* 1797; **John Armar Lowry-Corry;** Baron Belmore, 1781; Viscount Belmore, 1789; *b* 4 Sept. 1951; *s* of 7th Earl of Belmore and Gloria Anthea, *d* of late Herbert Bryant Harker, Melbourne, Australia; *S* father, 1960; *m* 1984, Lady Mary Meade, *d* of 6th Earl of Clanwilliam; two *s* one *d*. *Educ:* Lancing; Royal Agricultural Coll., Cirencester. Member: Adv. Bd, PRO, Belfast, 1996–2006; Bd of Govs and Guardians, Nat. Gall. of Ireland, 1998–2003. *Recreation:* fishing. *Heir: s* Viscount Corry, *qv*. *Address:* The Garden House, Castle Coole, Enniskillen, N Ireland BT74 6JY. *T:* (028) 6632 2463.

BELOFF, Hon. Michael Jacob, MA; QC 1981; barrister and writer; President, Trinity College, University of Oxford, 1996–2006; *b* 18 April 1942; *s* of Baron Beloff, FBA and Helen Dobrin; *m* 1969, Judith Mary Arkinstall; one *s* one *d*. *Educ:* Dragon Sch., Oxford; Eton Coll. (King's Schol.; Captain of Sch. 1960); Magdalen Coll., Oxford (Demy; H. W. C. Davis Prizeman, 1962; BA Hist. (1st cl.) 1963, Law 1965; MA 1967). Pres., Oxford Union Soc., 1962 (Trustee, Oldut, 1996); Oxford Union tour of USA, 1964. Called to the Bar, Gray's Inn, 1967 (Gerald Moody Schol., 1963, Atkin Schol., 1967; Bencher, 1988; Treas., 2008); Jt Head of Chambers, 4–5 Gray's Inn Sq., 1993–2000; a Recorder, 1985–95; a Dep. High Court Judge, 1989–99; a Judge of the Courts of Appeal, Jersey and Guernsey, 1995–, Sen. Ordinary Appeal Judge, 2004–14. Vice-Pres., Interception of Communications (Bailiwick of Guernsey) Tribunal, 1998–2014; a Judge of the First-tier Tribunal (Gen. Regulatory Chamber) (formerly Dep. Chm., Information (formerly Data Protection (Nat. Security)) Tribunal), 2000–13; Chm., Interception of Communications (Bailiwick of Jersey) Tribunal, 2003–; Pres., Investigatory Powers Tribunal, Guernsey, 2005–. Lectr in Law, Trinity Coll., Oxford, 1965–66. Legal Correspondent: New Society, 1969–79; The Observer, 1979–81; Columnist, San Diego Law Jl, 1999–2001. First Chm., Administrative Law Bar Assoc., 1986–90, now Chm. Emeritus. Member: Bingham Law Reform Cttee on Discovery of Documents and Disclosure, 1982–; Sen. Salary Review Bd, 1995–2002 (Chm., Judicial Sub-Cttee, 1998–2012); Court of Arbitration for Sport, 1996– (Mem., *ad hoc* Panel, Olympic Games, Atlanta, 1996, Sydney, 2000, Athens, 2004, Beijing, 2008, Commonwealth Games, Kuala Lumpur, 1998, Manchester, 2002, Melbourne, 2006, Football World Cup (Germany), 2006); Singapore Internat. Panel of Mediators, 2009–; Chm., ICC Code of Conduct Commn, 2002– (Mem., Dispute Resolution Panel, Cricket World Cup (Caribbean), 2007); Chm., IAAF Ethics Commn, 2004–12; Judge, Internat. Court of Appeal, Fédn Internat. de l'Automobile, 2010–. Chm., Oxford Univ. Tribunal into Alleged Plagiarism, 1990. Gov., Dragon Sch., Oxford, 1995–2003; Mem. Council, Cheltenham Ladies' Coll., 1996–2002. Chm., Jardine Scholarship Foundn, 2000–06. For. Consultant, Law Counsel (Dacca), 1990–. Visiting Professor: Tulane Univ., 2001, 2003; Buckingham Univ., 2006–. Lectures: Statute Law Soc., 1994; Admin. Law Bar Assoc., 1995; John Kelly Meml, UC Dublin, 1997; Lasok, Univ. of Exeter, 1998; Atkin, Reform Club, 1999; K. Ramamani, Madras, 1999; Margaret Howard, Trinity Coll., Oxford, 2000; Bailiff's, Guernsey, 2002; Espeland, Oslo, 2002; Alexander Howard, RCP, 2003; David Hall Meml, Envmtl Law Foundn, Law Soc., 2004; Neill, All Souls Coll., Oxford, 2006; Ben Kingsley, Warwick Sch., 2008; Barnard's Inn, Reading, 2009; Birkenhead, Gray's Inn, 2010; Sir David Williams, Cambridge, 2010; Lady Hale, Salford, 2012; Edward Grayson Meml, 2012; MacDermott, QUB, 2014. Consultant Ed., Judicial Review Bulletin, 1996; Gen. Ed., Internat. Sports Law Review, 2000–; an Associate Ed., Oxford DNB. Hon. Mem., Internat. Athletes' Club. FRSA 1996. Hon. Fellow, Soc. for Advanced Legal Studies, 1997. FICPD 1998. FAcSS (AcSS 2003). Hon. DLitt Fairleigh Dickinson, 2003; Hon. DLaws De Montfort, 2010. Women's Legal Defence Award (first winner), 1991; Lifetime Achievement Award, Chambers Directory, 2010. *Publications:* A Short Walk on the Campus (ed with J. Aitken), 1966; The Plateglass Universities, 1968; The Sex Discrimination Act, 1976; (jtly) Sports Law, 1999, 2nd edn 2012; contributor to: Halsbury's Laws of England (contribution on Time), 1983, 2nd edn 1999, (contribution on Sports Law) 5th edn 2012; Judicial Safeguards in Administrative Proceedings, 1989; Judicial Review, 1991, 3rd edn 2006; Practitioner's Handbook of EC Law, 1998; Israel Among the Nations, 1998; The Human Rights Act, 1999; The University: international expectations, 2002; Blair's Britain, 1997–2007, 2007; The House of Lords, 2009; Festschriften for: Lord Cooke of Thorndon, 1997; Sir William Wade, 1998; Sir Louis Blom-Cooper, 1999; Sir David Williams, 2000; Lord Slynn of Hadley, 2000; Rolf Ryssdal, 2001; H. M. Seervai, 2002; contrib. Encounter, Minerva, Irish Jurist, Political Qly, Current Legal Problems, Public Law, Statute Law Review, Modern Law Review, British Jl of Sport and Law, Denning Law Jl, Singapore Law Jl, NZ Law Jl, TLS, Spectator, DNB, etc. *Recreation:* running slowly. *Address:* Blackstone Chambers, Blackstone House, Temple, EC4Y 7BW. *T:* (020) 7583 1770. *Clubs:* Reform, Royal Automobile (Steward, 1999–); Vincent's, Gridiron (Oxford); Achilles (Vice Pres., 2013–).

BĚLOHLÁVEK, Jiří, Hon. CBE 2012; Chief Conductor, Czech Philharmonic Orchestra, 1990–92 and since 2012; *b* 24 Feb. 1946; *m* 1971, Anna Fejerova. *Educ:* Prague Conservatory and Acad. of Performing Arts. Chief Conductor, Prague SO, 1977–89; Conductor, Czech Philharmonic Orch., 1981–90; Founder and Music Dir, Prague Philharmonia, 1994–2005, now Music Dir Laureate; Chief Conductor, BBC SO, 2006–12, now Conductor Laureate; Principal Conductor, Slovak Philharmonic Orch., 2003–04; Principal Guest Conductor, BBC SO, 1995–2000; conductor with major orchestras incl. Berlin Philharmonic, Vienna SO, LPO, Japanese Philharmonic and orchestras in N America. Numerous recordings. Prof. of Arts, Acad. of Music Art, Prague, 1997–2008. State Award (Czech Republic) 2001. *Recreations:* gardening, hiking, nature. *Address:* c/o Armstrong Arts Ltd, Unit 3328, China Merchants Tower, Shun Tak Centre, 168 Connaught Road, Central, Hong Kong.

BELPER, 5th Baron *cr* 1856, of Belper, co. Derby; **Richard Henry Strutt;** *b* 24 Oct. 1941; *o s* of 4th Baron Belper and Zara Sophie Kathleen Mary, *y d* of Sir Harry Mainwaring, 5th Bt; *S* father, 1999; *m* 1st, 1966, Jennifer Vivian (marr. diss. 1979), *d* of late Capt. Peter Winser; one *s* one *d*; 2nd, 1980, Judith Mary de Jonge (*née* Twynam). *Educ:* Harrow; RAC Cirencester. *Heir: s* Hon. Michael Henry Strutt [*b* 5 Jan. 1969; *m* 2004, Vanessa Hoare; three *d*]. *Address:* The Park, Kingston on Soar, Nottingham NG11 0DH.

BELSKY, Prof. Jay, PhD; Robert M. and Natalie Reid Dorn Professor of Human and Community Development, University of California, Davis, since 2011; *s* of Irving and Sylvia Belsky; two *s*. *Educ:* Vassar Coll. (BA Psychology 1974); Cornell Univ. (MS Child Develt 1976; PhD Human Develt and Family Studies 1978). Res. Associate, Prenatal/Early Infancy Proj., Elmira, NY, 1977–78; Asst Prof., 1978–83, Associate Prof., 1983–86, Prof., 1986–96, Distinguished Prof., 1996–2001, of Human Develt, Dept of Human Develt and Family Studies, Penn State Univ.; Prof. of Psychology and Dir, Inst. for Study of Children, Families and Social Issues, Birkbeck, Univ. of London, 1999–2010. *Publications:* (ed) In the Beginning: readings on infancy, 1982; (jtly) The Child in the Family, 1984; (ed jtly) Clinical Implications of Attachment, 1988; (with J. Kelly) The Transition to Parenthood, 1994; (jtly) Childhood,

1995; (ed jtly) Evaluating Sure Start: does area-based early intervention work?, 2007. *Recreations:* swimming, travelling. *Address:* University of California, Davis, One Shields Avenue, Hart Hall, Davis, CA 95616, USA.

BELTON, Adrian; Chief Executive, Construction Industry Training Board, since 2014; *b* Cheltenham, 29 June 1956; *s* of Michael and Vera Belton; *m* 2009, Helen Mary Phillips, *qv*; one step *s* one step *d*; one *s* two *d* by a previous marriage. *Educ:* King Edward VII Sch., Sheffield; Univ. of Durham (BSc Hons 1977). ACIB 1979; DipFS 1981. Joined Barclays plc Gp, 1977, Dir, Operational Risk, 1998–2000; Risk Dir, Bradford & Bingley plc, 2000–03; Corporate Dir, Nottingham CC, 2004–05; Exec. Dir, Natural England, 2006–08; Chief Exec., Central Sci. Lab., 2008–09; Chief Exec., Food and Envmt Res. Agency, 2009–14. Chm., Inst. of Envmtl Mgt and Assessment, 2009–13 (Vice Chm., 2007–09). Member: Council, Yorkshire Innovation, 2008–; Bd, Assoc. of Chief Execs, 2009–. *Recreations:* cycling, mountaineering, ski-ing, sailing, fell running, music (playing piano). *Address:* Construction Industry Training Board, 12 Carthusian Street, EC1M 6EZ. *T:* 07920 781797.

BELTON, Prof. Peter Stanley, PhD; Professor of Biomaterials Science, 2001–08, now Emeritus, and Associate Dean, Faculty of Science, 2006–07, University of East Anglia (Head of Chemistry, School of Chemical Sciences and Pharmacy, 2004–06); *b* 19 June 1947; *s* of Stanley Belton and Bertha (*née* Lawrence); *m* 1976, Teresa Stutz; three *s*. *Educ:* Cooper's Sch., Bow; Chelsea Coll., Univ. of London (BSc 1st Cl. Hons Chem. 1968; PhD 1972). University of East Anglia: Open Univ. Fellowship, 1971–72; ICI Fellowship, 1972–74; Res. Leader, Unilever Res., Port Sunlight, 1974–79; AFRC, later BBSRC, Institute of Food Research Norwich Laboratory: Hd, Molecular Spectroscopy Gp, 1979–87; Hd, Chem. Physics Dept, 1987–90; Hd, Food Structure & Biopolymer Technol. Dept, 1990–91; Hd, Food Colloid & Biopolymer Sci. Dept, 1991–92; Hd, Norwich Lab., 1992–99; Dep. Dir, Inst. of Food Res., AFRC, later BBSRC, 1994–99; Hd, Food Materials Div., Inst. of Food Res., BBSRC, 1999–2001. Visiting Professor: Univ. of São Paulo, 1976; Centre d'Etudes Nucléaire, 1989. FIFST 1994 (Vice-Pres., 2001–02; Pres., 2003–05). Series Editor, Monographs in Food Analysis, 1994–. *Publications:* (jtly) From Arms Race to World Peace, 1991; Food, Science and Society, 2002; contrib. books and jls. *Recreations:* coarse fishing, listening to music, making wine. *Address:* School of Chemical Sciences and Pharmacy, University of East Anglia, Norwich NR4 7TJ; 79 The Avenues, Norwich, Norfolk NR2 3QR. *T:* (01603) 465851.

BELTRAMI, Adrian Joseph; QC 2008; *b* Glasgow, 8 Nov. 1964; *s* of late Joseph Beltrami and of Brigid Dolores Beltrami (*née* Fallon); *m* 1991, Charlotte Bentley; one *s* two *d*. *Educ:* Stonyhurst; Downing Coll., Cambridge (BA 1987); Harvard Law Sch. (LLM). Called to the Bar, Lincoln's Inn, 1989; in practice at the Bar, specialising in commercial litigation, banking and financial services, insolvency, professional negligence and civil fraud. *Publications:* (principal contributor) Banking Litigation, 1999, 2nd edn 2005. *Recreations:* family, tennis, Dickens, wine, Wiltshire. *Address:* 3 Verulam Buildings, Gray's Inn, WC1R 5NT. *E:* abeltrami@3vb.com. *Club:* Riverside Racquets.

BEN-TOVIM, Atarah, (Mrs Douglas Boyd), MBE 1980 (for services to children's music); flute course director, adjudicator and concert presenter; *b* 1 Oct. 1940; *d* of Tsvi Ben-Tovim and Gladys Ben-Tovim; *m*; one *d*; *m* 1976, Douglas Boyd. *Educ:* Royal Acad. of Music, London. ARAM 1967. Principal Flautist, Royal Liverpool Philharmonic Orchestra, 1962–75; children's concerts with Atarah's Band, 1973–88; various TV and radio series incl. Atarah's Music Box, Radio 3, 1976–79; Founder and Artistic Dir, Children's Concert Centre, 1975–95; Creator and Presenter, Children's Classic Orchestral Concerts, 1994–2010; Artistic Dir, Children's Music Foundn, 1995–2005. SW France Rep., Associate Bd of Royal Schs of Music, 1996–. Chm., British Flute Soc., 2005–10. Hon. DMus CNAA, 1991. *Publications:* Atarah's Book (autobiog.), 1976, 2nd edn 1979; Atarah's Band Kits (14 published), 1978–; Children and Music, 1979; (jtly) The Right Instrument For Your Child, 1985, 5th edn 2012; You Can Make Music!, 1986; The Young Orchestral Flautist, Books 1–3, 1990; Queen Eleanor's Legacy, 1994; The Flute Book, 1997. *Recreations:* music, writing, building houses, collecting 1200 flute figures. *Address:* 2 Le Bos, Juillac, 33890 Gensac, France. *T:* 557474428. *W:* www.atarah.tv.

BÉNARD, André Pierre Jacques, Hon. KBE 1991; French business executive; Hon. Chairman, Eurotunnel, 1996–2004 (Co-Chairman, 1986–90, Chairman, 1990–94; non-executive Director, 1994–96); *b* 19 Aug. 1922; *s* of Marcel Bénard and Lucie Thalmann; *m* 1946, Jacqueline Preiss; one *s*. *Educ:* Lycée Janson-de-Sailly; Lycée Georges Clémenceau, Nantes; Lycée Thiers, Marseilles; Ecole Polytechnique, Paris. Joined Royal Dutch Shell Group, 1946; with Société Anonyme des Pétroles Jupiter, 1946–49; Société des Pétroles Shell Berre, 1950–59; Shell Française: Pres. Man. Dir, 1967–70; Regional Co-ordinator Europe, 1970; Man. Dir, 1971–83, Mem. Supervisory Bd, 1983–93, Royal Dutch Shell Group. Director: La Radiotechnique SA, Paris, 1980–95; Barclays Bank SA, Paris, 1989–96. Senior Adviser, Lazard Frères, NY, 1983–90. Mem. Bd, INSEAD, Fontainebleau, 1983–99. Hon. Pres., French Chamber of Commerce and Industry, Netherlands, 1980–; Hon. Chm., Autumn Fest., Paris, 1995–2006. Médaille des Evadés; Médaille de la Résistance; Chevalier du Mérite Agricole; Chevalier de l'Ordre National du Mérite; Comdr, Légion d'Honneur; Comdr, Order of Orange Nassau. *Recreations:* music, golf. *Address:* 7 Avenue de Lamballe, 75016 Paris, France.

BENARROCH, Heather Mary; *see* Harper, H. M.

BENDALL, David Vere, CMG 1967; MBE 1945; HM Diplomatic Service, retired; *b* 27 Feb. 1920; *s* of John Manley Bendall; *m* 1941, Eve Stephanie Merrilees Galpin (*d* 2014); one *d*. *Educ:* Winchester; King's Coll., Cambridge (BA). Served Grenadier Guards, 1940–46. Third Sec., Allied Force HQ, Caserta, 1946; Rome, 1947; FO, 1949; First Sec., Santiago, 1952; FO, 1955; seconded to NATO Secretariat, Paris 1957; FO, 1960; NATO Secretariat, Paris as Dep. Head, Economic and Finance Div. and Special Advisor on Defence Policy, 1962; Counsellor, 1962; Counsellor, Washington, 1965–69; Asst Under-Sec. of State for Western Europe, 1969–71. Chairman: Banque Morgan Grenfell en Suisse (formerly Morgan Grenfell Switzerland), 1974–90; Morgan Grenfell Internat. Ltd, 1979–85; Morgan Grenfell Italia, 1982–93; Banca Nazionale del Lavoro Investment Bank, 1986–94. Director: Morgan Grenfell (Holdings) Ltd, 1971–85; Morgan Grenfell France, 1986–90; Dep. Chm., Avon Cosmetics, 1979–90; Member: Morgan Grenfell Internat. Adv. Council, 1986–87; Internat. and London Adv. Bds, Banque de l'Indochine et de Suez, 1974–87. Chm., BRCS, 1980–85 (Vice-Chm., 1979–80); Vice-Chm., Finance Cttee, League of Red Cross Socs, 1981–85. OStJ 1985. *Recreations:* golf, tennis, shooting, languages. *Address:* 3 Eaton Terrace Mews, SW1W 8EU; Ashbocking Hall, near Ipswich, Suffolk IP6 9LG. *T:* (01473) 890262. *Club:* Boodle's.

BENDALL, Dr Eve Rosemarie Duffield; Chief Executive Officer, English National Board for Nursing, Midwifery and Health Visiting, 1981–86; *b* 7 Aug. 1927; *d* of Col F. W. D. Bendall, CMG, MA, and Mrs M. L. Bendall, LRAM, ARCM. *Educ:* Malvern Girls' Coll.; London Univ. (MA, PhD); Royal Free Hosp. (SRN). Ward Sister, Dorset County Hosp., 1953–55; Night Supt, Manchester Babies' Hosp., 1955–56; Nurse Tutor: United Sheffield Hosps Sch. of Nursing, 1958–61; St George's Hosp., London, 1961–63; Principal, Sch. of Nursing, Hosp. for Sick Children, Gt Ormond Street, 1963–69. Registrar, GNC, 1973–77. *Publications:* (jtly) Basic Nursing, 1963, 3rd edn 1970; (jtly) A Guide to Medical and Surgical Nursing, 1965, 2nd edn 1970; (jtly) A History of the General Nursing Council, 1969; So You Passed, Nurse (research), 1975. *Recreation:* auspicious ageing. *E:* evebndll34@gmail.com.

BENDALL, Vivian Walter Hough; chartered surveyor and valuer in private practice, 1956–2014; *b* 14 Dec. 1938; *s* of late Cecil Aubrey Bendall and Olive Alvina Bendall (*née* Hough); *m* 1969, Ann Rosalind Jarvis (marr. diss. 1992). *Educ:* Coombe Hill House, Croydo Broad Green Coll., Croydon. IRRV; FNAEA 1984. Mem. Croydon Council, 1964–7 Mem. GLC, 1970–73; Chm., Greater London Young Conservatives, 1967–68. Contest (C): Hertford and Stevenage, Feb. and Oct. 1974; Ilford North, 1997 and 2001. MP (C) Ilfo North, March 1978–1997. Backbench Committees: Vice-Chm., Transport Cttee, 1982–8 Sec., Foreign and Commonwealth Affairs Cttee, 1981–84; Vice-Chm., Employment Ctte 1984–87 (Jt Sec. 1981–84). Vice Chm., Kensington and Chelsea Cons. Assoc., 2011– (Chm 2009–11). Former Member: Central Council for Care of the Elderly; South Eastern Area Re Assoc. for the Blind; Dr Barnardo's New Mossford Home Fund Raising Cttee. Master, Gla Sellers' Co., 2011–12. AMRSH 1991. Hon. FASI. *Recreations:* cricket, motor sport. *Addres* 57 Basuto Road, SW6 4BL. *T:* (020) 7736 4315. *Club:* Carlton.

BENDER, Sir Brian (Geoffrey), KCB 2003 (CB 1998); PhD; Chairman, London Me Exchange, since 2010; *b* 25 Feb. 1949; *s* of late Prof. Arnold Eric Bender; *m* 1974, Penelo Clark; one *s* one *d*. *Educ:* Greenford Grammar Sch.; Imperial Coll., London Univ. (BSc, PhI FIC 2006). Joined DTI, 1973; Private Sec. to Sec. of State for Trade, 1976–77; First Se (Trade Policy), Office of UK Permanent Rep. to EC, 1977–82; Principal (responsible f internat. steel issues), DTI, 1982–84; Counsellor (Industry), Office of UK Permanent Rep. EC, 1985–89; Under Sec. and Dep. Head of European Secretariat, Cabinet Office, 1990–9 Hd of Regl Devlt Div., DTI, 1993–94; Dep. Sec. and Head of European Secretariat, Cabin Office, 1994–98; Head of Public Service Delivery, Cabinet Office, 1998–99; Permane Secretary: Cabinet Office, 1999–2000; MAFF, 2000–01; DEFRA, 2001–05; DTI, lat BERR, 2005–09. Non-exec. Dir, Financial Reporting Council, 2014–; Trustee, Lloy Register Foundn, 2013–. Gov., Dulwich Coll., 2009–. *E:* brian.bender@btinternet.com.

BENDERSKY, Pamela May H.; *see* Hudson-Bendersky.

BENDIGO, Bishop of, since 2003; **Rt Rev. Andrew William Curnow,** AM 2013; *b* 2 Feb. 1950; *s* of Thomas William Curnow and Esma Jean Curnow (*née* Cook); *m* 1978, Ja Christina Jenkins; two *s* one *d*. *Educ:* Univ. of Melbourne (BComm); Melbourne Coll. Divinity (BD); Presbyterian Sch. of Christian Educn, Richmond, VA, USA, (MA). As Curate, St Alban's, West Coburg, 1973–75; Rector, Parish of Milloo, 1975–79; on leav USA, dios New York and Virginia, 1979–80; Rector of Elmore, 1980–83; Dir, Council f Christian Educn in Schools, Prov. of Victoria, 1983–89; Vicar of St George's, Malver 1989–94; Archdeacon of Kew, 1991–94; Asst Bishop, 1994–2003, Registrar, 2001–03, Di Melbourne. Mem., Standing Cttee, Gen. Synod, 1998–. Chairman: Anglicare Australi 1997–2001; Anglican Superannuation Australia, 2003–06; Dir, Benetas, 2006–11; Presiden Board: St Luke's Anglicare, 2007–14; Anglicare Victoria, 2014–. Exec. Chm., Trinity Co Theol Sch., 1997–2012 (Mem. Bd, 2003–11); Pres., Melbourne Coll. of Divinity, 2001–0 Life Mem., Oxford Business Alumni, 2002–; Mem., Australian Inst. of Co. Dirs, 2012– *Recreations:* reading, theatre, travel. *Address:* PO Box 2, Bendigo, Vic 3552, Australia. *T:* (54434711, *Fax:* (3) 54412173. *Clubs:* Royal Automobile of Victoria (Melbourne); Sandhur (Bendigo).

BENEDETTI, Nicola Joy, MBE 2013; violinist; *b* Irvine, Scotland, 20 July 1987; *d* of G and Francesca Benedetti. *Educ:* Wellington Sch., Ayr; Yehudi Menuhin Sch. Winner, BB Young Musician of Year, 2004; has appeared with LSO, San Francisco SO, Pittsburgh SC Danish Nat. SO, BBC Scottish SO and Scottish Chamber Orch., Orch. Nat. d'Ile de Franc Camerata Salzburg and Melbourne SO; has made recordings; chamber musician, collaboration with cellist, Leonard Elschenbroich and pianist, Alexei Grynyuk, 2008–, inc tours of Scotland and S America and concerts at LSO, St Luke's, Frankfurt Alte Oper, Breme Hong Kong City Hall and at Ravinia Fest., Schloss Elmau Fest., Istanbul Fest. an Cheltenham Fest. Founder, Benedetti Sessions, 2013. Mem. Bd and teacher, Big Noi project, Scotland, 2010–. Hon. DLitt: Glasgow Caledonian, 2007; Heriot-Watt, 2010; Ho LLD Dundee; Hon. DMus: Edinburgh, 2011; Royal Conservatoire of Scotland, 201 Leicester, 2013. Young British Classical Performer, 2008, Best Female Artist, 2012, Fema Artist of Year, 2013, Classic Brit Awards. *Recreations:* cinema, travel, jazz, yoga. *E:* info@ emblemartists.com.

BENEDETTI, Renato Giovanni, RIBA; architect; Partner, McDowell+Benedetti, sinc 1996; Director, McDowell+Benedetti Ltd, since 1998; *b* 30 Nov. 1962; *s* of Giovan Benedetti and Giulia (*née* Fugaccia); *m* 2006, Romy Derman. *Educ:* Cobourg Dist Collegia Inst. East (Ontario Schol. 1981); Univ. of Waterloo Sch. of Architecture, Ontario (BES 198 BArch 1988). RIBA 1996. Stonemason and bricklayer, 1976–81; Associate, Davi Chipperfield Architects, 1989–96; with Jonathan McDowell formed McDowell+Benedett 1996; main projects include: Oliver's Wharf Penthouse, Wapping, 1996; Assoc. c Photographers, New Gall. and HQ, London, 1998; Suncourt House, Islington, 2002; Nursin Home for Merchant Taylors' Co., Lewisham, 2002; Springboard Centre, Stokesley, 200 Castleford Bridge, 2008; Claremont Fan Court Sch., Esher, 2009; Hull Footbridge, 2010; JC Uttoxeter Masterplan, 2010. Dir, The Dance Movement, 1999–2007. Mem. Panel, Art fo Architecture Award, RSA, 1999–2004; Client Design Advr and Competitions Judge, RIBA 2000–; Judge: World Architecture Fest.; Scottish Design Awards; Europan; Leec Architecture Awards; World Architecture News House of the Year. Mem. Ctte Architecture Club, 2001–; Founding Mem. Cttee, London Festival of Architecture, 2003– Mem., Southwark Design Review Panel, 2006–. FRSA 1999. *Recreations:* travel, arts, spor *Address:* (office) 34–35 Hatton Garden, EC1N 8DX. *Clubs:* Architecture, Soho House.

BENEDICT XVI, His Holiness, (Joseph Alois Ratzinger); His Holiness Pope Benedic XVI, 2005–13, now Pope Emeritus; *b* Marktl am Inn, Germany, 16 April 1927; *s* of Josep Ratzinger and Maria Ratzinger (*née* Peintner). *Educ:* St Michael Seminary, Traunstei Ludwig-Maximilian Univ., Munich. Military service, 1943–45. Ordained priest, 1951 Professor: Freising Coll., 1958; Univ. of Bonn, 1959; Univ. of Münster, 1963; Univ. c Tübingen, 1966; Univ. of Regensburg, 1969; Archbishop of Munich and Freising, 1977–8 Prefect, Congregation for the Doctrine of the Faith, 1981–2005. Cardinal Priest, 197 Cardinal Bishop of Velletri-Segni, 1993; Vice-Dean, 1998–2002, Dean, 2002–05, Sacre Coll. of Cardinals; elected Pope, 19 April 2005. *Publications include:* God of Jesus Christ, 197 The Ratzinger Report, 1985; Feast of Faith, 1986; Principles of Christian Morality, 198 Principles of Catholic Theology, 1987; 'In the Beginning'...: a Catholic understanding of th story of the creation and the fall, 1990; To Look on Christ, 1991; The Meaning of Christia Brotherhood, 1993; A Turning Point for Europe?, 1994; The Nature and Mission c Theology, 1995; Called to Communion, 1996; Gospel, Catechesis, Catechism, 1997; *A Tuendam Fidem* - to Protect the Faith, 1998; Milestones: memoirs 1927–1977, 1998; Man Religions, One Covenant, 1999; The Spirit of the Liturgy, 2000; God is Near Us, 200 Truth and Tolerance, 2004; The End of Time?, 2005; Pilgrim Fellowship of Faith, 200 Values in a Time of Upheaval, 2006; Jesus of Nazareth, vol. 1, 2007, vol. 2, 2011, vol. 3, 2012 Great Christian Thinkers: from the Early Church through the Middle Ages, 2011. *Addres* c/o Apostolic Palace, 00120 Vatican City State.

BENEDICTUS, David Henry; critic, book writer, director for stage, television and radic teacher and stamp dealer; *b* 16 Sept. 1938; *s* of late Henry Jules Benedictus and Kathlee Constance (*née* Ricardo); *m* 1971, Yvonne Daphne Antrobus (marr. diss. 2002); one *s* one *d* and one *s* one *d*. *Educ:* Stone House, Broadstairs; Eton College; Balliol College, Oxford (BA English); State Univ. of Iowa. News and current affairs, BBC Radio, 1961; Drama Directo BBC TV, 1962; Story Editor, Wednesday Play and various series, BBC, 1965; Thames TV Trainee Director, at Bristol Old Vic, 1968; Asst Dir, RSC, Aldwych, 1970; Judith E. Wilso Vis. Fellow, Cambridge, and Fellow Commoner, Churchill Coll., Cambridge, 1981–82

Commissioning Editor, Drama Series, Channel 4 TV, 1984–86 (commissions included: The Manageress, 1987; Porterhouse Blue (Internat. Emmy), 1987); BBC Radio: Readings Editor, 1989–95; Editor, Radio 3 Drama, 1992; Sen. Producer, Serial Readings, 1993 (incl. The Bible, 1992; Arcadia, 1993; Macbeth, 1995); also producer of radio series on Cole Porter, Rodgers and Hart, Glenn Miller, film music, etc. Writer in Residence: Sutton Library, Surrey, 1975; Kibbutz Gezer, Israel, 1978; Bitterne Library, Southampton, 1983–84; Snowsfields Sch., Bermondsey, 2001–02; Head of Drama, Putney High Sch., 2003–04; teaching incl. Creative Writing residentially at Oxford for Oxbridge Academics, 2004–; Royal Lit. Fund Fellow, Goldsmiths Coll., 2007; supply teacher variously. Antiques corresp., Standard, 1977–80; reviewer for books, stage, films, records, for major newspapers and magazines, principally The Economist. Dir, Kingston Books, 1988–90. Member: Amnesty International; Soc. of Authors. Plays include: Betjemania, 1976, 1996; The Golden Key, 1982; What A Way To Run A Revolution!, 1985; You Say Potato, 1992; The Happy Hypocrite (music by S. Hodel). *Publications:* The Fourth of June, 1962; You're a Big Boy Now, 1963; This Animal is Mischievous, 1965; Hump, or Bone by Bone Alive, 1967; The Guru and the Golf Club, 1969; A World of Windows, 1971; The Rabbi's Wife, 1976; Junk, how and where to buy beautiful things at next to nothing prices, 1976; A Twentieth Century Man, 1978; The Antique Collector's Guide, 1980; Lloyd George (from Elaine Morgan's screenplay), 1981; Whose Life is it Anyway? (from Brian Clarke's screenplay), 1981; Who Killed the Prince Consort?, 1982; Local Hero (from Bill Forsyth's screenplay), 1983; The Essential London Guide, 1984; Floating Down to Camelot, 1985; The Streets of London, 1986; The Absolutely Essential London Guide, 1986; Uncle Ernie's System, 1988–2009; Little Sir Nicholas, 1990; (with Prof. Hans Kalmus) Odyssey of a Scientist, 1991; Sunny Intervals and Showers, 1992; The Stamp Collector, 1994; How to Cope When the Money Runs Out, 1998; Dropping Names (memoirs), 2005; Return to the Hundred Acre Wood, 2009; numerous short stories for Radio 4 etc. *Recreations:* chess, tennis, cricket, auctions, table tennis, piano playing, horse racing, car boot sales, eating. *Address:* Flat 1, 39 Sackville Gardens, Hove, E Sussex BN3 4GJ. *T:* (01273) 242477, 07986 041386. *E:* davidbenedictus@hotmail.com.

BENEDIKTSSON, Einar, MA; Knight Commander, Order of the Falcon, Iceland; Ambassador of Iceland, retired 2001; *b* Reykjavík, 30 April 1931; *s* of Stefan M. Benediktsson and Sigridur Oddsdóttir; *m* 1956, Elsa Petursdóttir; three *s* two *d.* *Educ:* Colgate Univ., NY; Fletcher Sch. of Law and Diplomacy, Mass; London Sch. of Econs and Pol Science; Inst. des Etudes Européennes, Turin. With OEEC, 1956–60; Head of Section, Mins of Econ. Affairs and Commerce, 1961–64, and Min. of For. Affairs, 1964; Counsellor, Paris, 1964–68; Head of Section, Min. of For. Affairs, 1968–70; Perm. Rep. to Internat. Orgns, Geneva, 1970–76; Chm., EFTA Council, 1975; Ambassador to France, also accredited to Spain and Portugal, and Perm. Rep. to OECD and UNESCO, 1976–82; Ambassador to UK and concurrently to The Netherlands, Nigeria and Ireland, 1982–86; Perm. Rep. to N Atlantic Council, 1986–90, and Ambassador to Belgium and Luxembourg, 1986–91; Ambassador to Norway, also to Poland and Czechoslovakia, 1991–93; Ambassador to USA, also accredited to Canada, Mexico, Chile, Argentina, Uruguay, Venezuela and Costa Rica, 1993–97; Exec. Dir, Leifur Eiriksson Millennium Commn of Iceland, 1997–2001; Advr, Office of the Prime Minister and Min. of Foreign Affairs, Reykjavík, 2001–02, Min. of Foreign Affairs, 2009–. Chm., UNICEF Iceland, 2003–08. Holds foreign decorations. *Publications:* Iceland and European Development—A Historical Account from a Personal Perspective, 2003; Ad skilja heiminn: æviminningar sendiherra (memoir), 2009. *Address:* Hvassaleiti 28, 103 Reykjavík, Iceland. *T:* 5681943. *E:* mason@islandia.is.

BENETTON, Luciano; industrialist; Chairman, Benetton Group SpA; *b* 13 May 1935. Established Fratelli Benetton (with brothers), 1965; founder and Pres., Benetton, 1978; Benetton Holdings, 1981; Vice-Pres. and Man. Dir, Benetton Group SpA; Mem. Board, Edizione Holding SpA; Pres., Benetton Foundn. Mem., Italian Senate, 1992–94. Awards: Civiltà Veneta, 1986; Premio Creatività, 1992. *Publications:* contribs to La Biblioteca di Harvard, economic and business strategies, 1988. *Address:* Benetton Group SpA, via Villa Minelli 1, 31050 Ponzano Veneto (TV), Italy. *T:* (422) 4491.

BENGER, John Stuart, DPhil; Clerk Assistant and Director General, Department of Chamber and Committee Services, House of Commons, since 2015; *b* Stockport, 18 Nov. 1959; *s* of late Kurt Benger and Marian Benger (*née* Hollis); *m* 1986, Susan Elizabeth Irvine; two *s.* *Educ:* Stockport Grammar Sch.; St Catharine's Coll., Cambridge (BA Hons 1982); Worcester Coll., Oxford (PGCE 1983; DPhil 1989). House of Commons: procedural and cttee posts, 1986–90; Clerk: Cttee of Public Accounts, 1990–94; Table Office, 1994–98; Health Cttee, 1998–2004; Public Bill Office, 2004–08; Treasury Cttee, 2008–09; Principal Clerk: Delegated Legislation, 2009–11; Select Cttees, 2011–12; Dir, Service Delivery, Dept of Information Services, 2012–15. *Recreations:* art galleries, Manchester United, coffee, family and friends. *Address:* Department of Chamber and Committee Services, House of Commons, SW1A 0AA. *T:* (020) 7219 3311. *E:* bengerjs@parliament.uk.

BENHAM, George Frederick; Headmaster, Cardinal Hinsley RC High School, 1999–2003; *b* 26 Oct. 1946; *m* 1996, Elizabeth Maria; two *s.* *Educ:* Queen Mary Coll., London (BA 1969; MPhil 1972); Inst. of Educn, London Univ. (DipEd 1978; MA 1980). Lectr, Univ. of Aberdeen, 1971–75; teacher at various schs in London, 1975–85; Educn Advr, 1985–87; London Borough of Brent: Dep. Dir of Educn, 1987–88, Dir, 1989–95; Chief Exec., 1995–98. FRSA 1978; FCMI (FBIM 1978). *Publications:* contribs on education to learned jls in USA, Holland, UK and Switzerland.

BENJAMIN, Baroness *cr* 2010 (Life Peer), of Beckenham in the County of Kent; **Floella Karen Yunies Benjamin,** OBE 2001; DL; actress, independent producer, writer and children's campaigner; Founder, 1987, Chief Executive, since 1998, Floella Benjamin Productions Ltd; *b* 23 Sept. 1949; *d* of Roy Benjamin and Veronica Benjamin (*née* Dryce); *m* 1980, Keith Taylor; one *s* one *d.* *Educ:* Penge Girls' Sch. Chief Accountants Office, Barclays Bank, 1967–69; Actress: *stage:* Hair, Shaftesbury Th., 1970–72; Jesus Christ Superstar, Palace, 1972–74; Black Mikado, Cambridge Th., 1974–75; The Husband-in-Law, Comedy, 1976; *television* includes: Within These Walls, 1973–75; Playschool, 1976–88; Playaway, 1976–82; Angels, 1978–80; Send in the Girls, Waterloo Sunset, 1980; Maybury, 1981; Kids, 1982; Fast Forward, 1983–85; Lay-on-Five, 1986–87; Line of Beauty, 2006; Mama Mirabelle's Home Movies, 2007; Sarah Jane Adventures, 2007–11; Chuggington, 2010–13; CBeebies Bedtime Stories, 2013–; also produced and starred in: Treehouse, 1987; Playabout, 1990–92; Hullaballoo, 1994; Caribbean Light, 1998; Jamboree, 1998–2001; Caribbean Kitchen, 1999; Taste of Barbados, 2000; Taste of Cuba, 2001; Coming to England, 2003 (RTS Award 2004); *films:* Black Joy, 1977; Run Fatboy Run, 2007. Member: Royal Mail Stamp Adv. Cttee, 1994–2001; Video Consultative Council, 1996–2000, Children's Viewing Adv. Gp, 2000–04, BBFC; Foreign and Commonwealth Caribbean Adv. Gp, 1998–2002; Millennium Commn, 1999–2007; Chairman: Women of Year Lunch, 1996–2000; Pegasus Opera Co., 2007–08. Member: BAFTA, 1990–2001 (Vice-Chm., 1998–99; Chm., TV, 1999–2000); Content Bd, Ofcom, 2003–06. Chancellor, Univ. of Exeter, 2006–. Governor: Nat. Film and Television Sch., 1995–; Commonwealth Inst., 1998–2006; Dulwich Coll., 2001–11; Chm. Govs, Isle of Sheppey Acad., 2009–11. Pres., The Ramblers (formerly Ramblers' Assoc.), 2008–10. DL Gtr London, 2008. Hon. Fellow: Shakespeare Birthplace Trust, 2013–; British Kinematograph Sound and Television Soc., 2014–. Hon. DLitt Exeter, 2005. Special Lifetime Achievement Award, BAFTA, 2004; J. M. Barrie Award, Action for Children's Arts, 2012. *Publications:* Caribbean Cookery, 1986; *for children:* Floella's Fun Book, 1984; Why the Agouti Has No Tail, 1984; Floella's Funniest Jokes, 1985; Floella's Favourite Folk Tales, 1986; Fall About with Flo, 1986; Floella's Fabulous Bright Ideas, 1986; Floella's Floorboard Book, 1987; Flo and Aston's Books (series of six books), 1987; Snotty and the Rod of Power, 1987; Floella's Cardboard Box Book, 1987; Exploring Caribbean Food in Britain, 1988; For Goodness Sake, 1994; Skip Across the Ocean, 1995; Coming to England, 1995; My Two Grannies, 2007; The Arms of Britannia, 2010; My Two Grandads, 2010; Sea of Tears (novel), 2011. *Recreations:* singing, golf, cooking, running. *Address:* House of Lords, SW1A 0PW. *W:* www.floellabenjamin.com.

BENJAMIN, George William John, CBE 2010; composer, conductor and pianist; Henry Purcell Professor of Composition, King's College, London University, since 2001; *b* 31 Jan. 1960; *s* of late William Benjamin and Susan Benjamin (*née* Bendon). *Educ:* Westminster School (private tuition with Peter Gellhorn); Paris Conservatoire (Olivier Messiaen); King's College, Cambridge (Alexander Goehr; Hon. Fellow, 2013). MA, MusB. First London orchestral performance, BBC Proms, 1980; research at Institut de Recherche et Coordination Acoustique/Musique, Paris, 1984–87; Prince Consort Prof. of Composition, RCM, 1994–2001 (Vis. Prof., 1987–94); Principal Guest Artist, Hallé Orch., 1993–96; operatic conducting début, Pelléas et Mélisande, La Monnaie, Brussels, 1999; ROH, Covent Garden début, Written on Skin, 2013 (South Bank Sky Arts Award for Opera, 2014). Artistic Dir, contemp. music festivals, USA (San Francisco Symphony Orch.), France (Opéra Bastille), 1992, and London (South Bank), 1993. Artistic consultant, Sounding the Century, BBC R3, 1996–99. Featured composer: Salzburg Fest., 1995; Tanglewood Fest., 1999, 2002, 2003, 2012, 2013; LSO Fest., 2002–03; Deutsches Symphonie Orch., Berlin, 2005; Strasbourg Musica, 2005; Carta Blanca, Madrid, 2005; Fest. d'Automne, Paris, 2006; Lucerne Fest., 2008; San Francisco, 2010; Auftakt Fest., Frankfurt, 2011; Aix-en-Provence Fest., 2012; Southbank London, Cultural Olympiad, 2012; Toronto, 2015. Hon. FRCM 1993; Hon. RAM 2003; Hon. GSMD 2009. Mem., Bavarian Acad. of Arts, 2000; Hon. Mem., Royal Philharmonic Soc., 2011. Lili Boulanger Award, USA, 1985; Koussevitzky Internat. Record Award, 1987; Gramophone Contemp. Music Award, 1990, 2014; Edison Award, Holland, 1998; Schönberg Prize, Berlin, 2002; Royal Philharmonic Soc. Awards, 2003, 2004, 2009, 2014; Composer of the Year, Musical America, 2014. Commandeur, Ordre des Arts et des Lettres (France), 2014 (Chevalier, 1996). *Publications: include: orchestral:* Altitude, 1977; Ringed by the Flat Horizon, 1980; A Mind of Winter, 1981; At First Light, 1982; Jubilation, 1985; Antara, 1987; Sudden Time, 1993; Three Inventions for Chamber Orchestra, 1995; Sometime Voices, 1996; Palimpsests, 2002; Olicantus, 2002; Dance Figures, 2004; Duet, for piano and orch., 2008; A Dream of the Song, 2015; *chamber music:* Violin Sonata, 1977; Piano Sonata, 1978; Octet, 1978; Flight, 1979; Sortilèges, 1981; Three Studies for Solo Piano, 1985; Upon Silence, 1990, 1991; Viola, Viola, 1997; Shadowlines, for solo piano, 2001; Three Miniatures for Violin, 2001; Piano Figures, 2004; *opera:* Into the Little Hill, 2006; Written on Skin, 2012. *Address:* c/o Faber Music Ltd, Bloomsbury House, 74–77 Great Russell Street, WC1B 3DA.

BENJAMIN, Jon; *see* Benjamin, M. J.

BENJAMIN, Jonathan, (Jon); HM Diplomatic Service; High Commissioner to Ghana and non-resident Ambassador to Togo, Burkina Faso and Benin, since 2014; *b* London, 19 Jan. 1963; *s* of late Arthur Benjamin and of Edith Benjamin (*née* Landau). *Educ:* Univ. of Surrey (BSc 1st Cl. Hons German, Swedish and Internat. Relns 1985). Telex operator, Skandinaviska Enskilda Banken, Gothenburg, 1983, 1985; joined FCO, SE Asia Section, 1986; Second Sec. (Pol), Jakarta, 1987–91; Hd, Central Asia and Caucasus Section, Eastern Dept, FCO, 1992–93; Private Sec. to Minister for Europe, 1993–95; Hd, Pol Section, Ankara, 1996–99; Hd, Human Rights Policy Dept, FCO, 2002–05; Dep., then Actg Consul Gen., NY, 2005–08; on secondment to AIG, then to Eurasia Gp, NY, 2008–09; Ambassador to Chile, 2009–14. Ed.-in-Chief, Human Rights Annual Report, FCO, 2002–04. Pres., Alexander Selkirk Foundn, 2010–13. *Recreations:* football, world music, learning languages. *Address:* c/o Foreign and Commonwealth Office, King Charles Street, SW1A 2AH. *E:* Jon.Benjamin@fco.gov.uk.

BENJAMIN, Leanne Faye, OBE 2005; AM 2015; Principal, Royal Ballet Company, 1993–2013; *b* Australia, 13 July 1964; *m* 2001, Tobias Round; one *s.* *Educ:* Royal Ballet Sch. (Adeline Genée Gold Medal). Joined Sadler's Wells Royal Ballet, 1983: Soloist, 1985–87; Principal, 1987–88; Principal: English Nat. Ballet, 1988–90; Deutsche Oper Ballet, Berlin, 1990–92; joined Royal Ballet Co., 1992. Numerous leading rôles; *created roles:* Greta in Metamorphosis; Earth in Homage to the Queen; Mr Worldly Wise; Two-Part Invention; Masquerade; Qualia; Tanglewood; Despite; DGV; Children of Adam. Prix de Lausanne, 1981. *Address:* c/o Royal Ballet, Royal Opera House, Covent Garden, WC2E 9DD.

BENJAMIN, Marc Jonathan, (Jon); Chief Operating Officer, World ORT, since 2014; *b* 31 Oct. 1964; *s* of Alan and Barbara Benjamin; *m* 1990, Suzanne Nicola Taylor; one *s* one *d.* *Educ:* Dulwich Coll.; Univ. of Manchester (LLB Hons); Coll. of Law (Dist.). With Denton Hall, 1988–92; admitted solicitor, 1990; solicitor, Teacher Stern Selby, 1993–96; Hd, Business Div., United Jewish Israel Appeal, 1996–99; Chief Exec., British ORT, 1999–2004; Dir Gen. and Chief Exec., Bd of Deputies of British Jews, 2005–13. *Recreations:* family, travel, cycling, reading (histories in particular), ski-ing, Crystal Palace FC, music. *Address:* World ORT, ORT House, 126 Albert Street, NW1 7NE. *T:* (020) 7446 8500. *E:* jon.benjamin@ort.org.

BENJAMIN, Dr Ralph, CB 1980; DSc(Eng), PhD, BSc, FCGI, FREng, FIET; consultant; Visiting Professor, University College, London, since 1988; *b* 17 Nov. 1922; *s* of Charles Benjamin and Claire Benjamin (*née* Stern); *m* 1951, Kathleen Ruth Bull, BA; one *s* (and one *s* decd). *Educ:* in Germany and Switzerland; St Oswald's Coll., Ellesmere; Imperial Coll. of Science and Technology, London. DSc(Eng) London, 1970; FREng (FEng 1983); FCGI 1982. Joined Royal Naval Scientific Service, 1944; Senior Scientific Officer, 1949; Principal Scientific Officer, 1952; Senior Principal Scientific Officer (Special Merit), 1955; Deputy Chief Scientific Officer (Special Merit), 1960; Head of Research and Deputy Chief Scientist, Admiralty Surface Weapons Establishment, 1961; Dir and Chief Scientist, Admiralty Underwater Weapons Estab., 1964–71, and Dir, Underwater Weapons R&D (Navy), 1965–71; Certified RN Diving Officer, 1970; Chief Scientist, GCHQ, 1971–82; Head of Communications Techniques and Networks, SHAPE (NATO) Technical Centre, The Hague, 1982–87. Hon. consultant: Univ. of Illinois; US Office of Naval Research, 1956. Mem. Council, IEE, 1994–97 (Chm., Bristol Area, 1992–93; Chm., Western Centre, 1995–96). Council Mem., Brit. Acoustical Soc., 1971. Visiting Professor: Dept of Electrical and Electronic Engineering, Univ. of Surrey, 1973–80; ICSTM, Univ. of London, 1988–2001; Cranfield Univ., 1991–95; Univ. of Bristol, 1993–2012. Mem. Court, Brunel Univ., 1997–2003. FRSA 1984. Hon. DEng Bristol, 2000. IEE Marconi Premium, 1964; IERE Heinrich Hertz Premium, 1980, 1983; Clark Maxwell Premium, 1995; Innovation in Electronics, 2006, Oliver Lodge Medal, 2007, IET. Led first ascent of Cima Moro, Bregaglia Alps, 1955. Judo Black Belt, 1974. *Publications:* Modulation, Resolution and Signal Processing for Radar Sonar and Related Systems, 1966; Five Lives in One (autobiog.), 1996; contribs to various advisory cttees, working parties, symposia, etc; articles in various professional jls. *Recreations:* work, hill-walking, swimming. *Address:* 13 Bellhouse Walk, Rockwell Park, Bristol BS11 0UE. *Club:* Athenæum.

BENN, family name of **Viscount Stansgate**.

BENN, Rt Hon. Hilary (James Wedgwood); PC 2003; MP (Lab) Leeds Central, since June 1999; *b* 26 Nov. 1953; *s* of Rt Hon. Tony Benn, PC; *m* 1st, 1973, Rosalind Caroline Retey (*d* 1979); 2nd, 1982, Sally Christina Clark; three *s* one *d.* *Educ:* Holland Park Comprehensive Sch.; Sussex Univ. (BA Hons Russian and East European Studies). Res. Asst, Nat. Referendum Campaign, 1975; Res. Officer, 1975–93, Head of Res., 1993–96, Head of Policy and Communications, 1996–97, ASTMS, then MSF; Jt Sec., Finance Panel, Labour

Party Commn of Inquiry, on secondment, 1980; Special Advr to Sec. of State for Educn and Employment, 1997–99. MSF Rep., Labour Party Nat. Policy Forum, 1994–97; Chair: Educn Cttee, ALA, 1988–90; Unions 21, 1995–99; Member: Educn Cttee, AMA, 1986–90; Envmt Policy Commn, Labour Party, 1994–97; Party into Power Task Force on Labour Party's Democracy, 1996–97. Parliamentary Under-Secretary of State: DFID, 2001–02; Home Office, 2002–03; Minister of State, DFID, 2003; Secretary of State: for Internat. Develt, 2003–07; for Envmt, Food and Rural Affairs, 2007–10; Shadow Sec. of State for Envmt, Food and Rural Affairs, 2010; Shadow Leader, H of C, 2010–11; Shadow Sec. of State for Communities and Local Govt, 2011–15; Shadow Foreign Sec., 2015–. Member: Envmt, Transport and the Regions Select Cttee, 1999–2001; H of C Commn, 2010–11. Vice-Chair, PLP Educn and Employment Cttee, 2000–01; Mem., Sustainable Communities Policy Commn, Labour Party, 2007–; Pres., Acton CLP, 1979–82. Mem. (Lab) Ealing LBC, 1979–99 (Dep. Leader, 1986–90; Chair, Educn Cttee, 1986–90; Dep. Leader, Labour Gp, 1984–94). Vice-Chm., Commn for Africa, 2004–05. Contested (Lab) Ealing N, 1983, 1987. *Publications:* (contrib.) Beyond 2002: long-term policies for Labour, 1999; (contrib.) Men Who Made Labour, 2006. *Recreations:* watching sport, gardening. *Address:* House of Commons, SW1A 0AA.

See also Viscount Stansgate.

BENN, Sir (James) Jonathan, 4th Bt *cr* 1914; Chairman, SCA Pension Trusts Ltd, 1988–98; *b* 27 July 1933; *s* of Sir John Andrews Benn, 3rd Bt, and Hon. Ursula Lady Benn, *o d* of 1st Baron Hankey, PC, GCB, GCMG, GCVO, FRS; *S* father, 1984; *m* 1960, Jennifer Mary, *e d* of late Dr Wilfred Howells, OBE; one *s* one *d*. *Educ:* Harrow; Clare College, Cambridge (MA). Various positions with Reed International PLC (formerly A. E. Reed & Co.), 1957–88; Dir, Reed Paper & Board (UK) Ltd, 1971, Man. Dir 1976; Dir, Reed Group Ltd, 1976; Chm. and Chief Exec., Reed Paper & Board (UK) Ltd, 1977–90; Chm., Reedpack Paper Gp, 1988–90; Dir, Reedpack Ltd, 1988–90. Pres., British Paper and Board Industries Fedn, 1985–87. Dir, Broomhill Trust, 1991–96. *Recreations:* golf, ski-ing, music. *Heir: s* Robert Ernest Benn [*b* 17 Oct. 1963; *m* 1985, Sheila Margaret (marr. diss. 2014), 2nd *d* of Dr Alastair Blain; one *s* one *d*]. *Address:* Fielden Lodge, Tonbridge Road, Ightham, Kent TN15 9AN.

See also T. J. Benn.

BENN, Jeremy Richard, CEng, FREng, FICE, CWEM, FCIWEM; Executive Chairman, JBA Group Ltd, since 2013 (Chief Executive, 2006–13); *b* Stockton-on-Tees, Co. Durham, 30 April 1962; *s* of Selwyn Benn and Joan Margaret Benn (*née* Blamires); *m* 1998, Caroline Louise Storey. *Educ:* Archbishop Holgate's Grammar Sch., York; Girton Coll., Cambridge (BA Geog. 1983; MA); Univ. of Newcastle upon Tyne (MSc Engrg Hydrol. 1984). CEng 1995; FICE 1996; CWEM, FCIWEM 1996; CEnv 2000; FREng 2010. Grad. Engr, Hydraulics Research Ltd, 1984–85, Hydraulic Engr, Hydraulic Analysis Ltd, 1985–87; Hydrologist, Bullen and Partners, 1987–93; Associate, Bullen Consultants, 1993–95; Dir, JBA Consulting, 1996–2006; Dir, JBA Consulting Engrs and Scientists (Ireland), 2006–. Vis. Prof. in Flood Risk Mgt, Univ. of Sheffield, 2008–. Mem., Modelling and Risk R&D Theme Tech. Adv. Gp, DEFRA/Envmt Agency, 2005–. Advr to NZ Earthquake Commn, 2013. Mem., Scour at Foundns panel, Internat. Assoc. of Hydraulic Engrg, 2001–. Member: British Hydrol Soc., 1997; British Dam Soc., 2004; Engrs Ireland, 2010; MASCE 1997. *Publications:* Floodplain Modelling using HEC-RAS, 2003; Managing Scour and Flood Risk to Railway Infrastructure, 2013; contribs to Jl Forensic Engrg, Jl ICE, Jl Flood Risk Mgt. *Recreations:* walking, industrial history. *Address:* JBA Consulting, South Barn, Broughton Hall, Skipton, N Yorks BD23 3AE. *T:* (01756) 799919, *Fax:* (01756) 799449. *E:* jeremy.benn@jbaconsulting.com.

BENN, Sir Jonathan; *see* Benn, Sir J. J.

BENN, Timothy John; Chairman, Timothy Benn Publishing Ltd, 1983–97, and other companies; *b* 27 Oct. 1936; *yr s* of Sir John Andrews Benn, 3rd Bt, and Hon. Ursula Helen Alers Hankey; *m* 1982, Christina Grace Townsend. *Educ:* Harrow; Clare Coll., Cambridge (MA); Princeton Univ., USA; Harvard Business Sch., USA (National Marketing Council Course; Scholarship Award). FInstM. 2nd Lieut Scots Guards, 1956–57. Benn Brothers Ltd: Board Member, 1961–82; Managing Director, 1972–82; Dep. Chm., 1976–81; Chm., Benn Brothers plc, 1981–82; Ernest Benn: Board Member, 1967–82; Managing Director, 1973–82; Chairman and Managing Director, 1974–82; Proprietor and Publisher, Creel Press, 1991–. Chairman: Bouverie Publishing Co., 1983–2003; Buckley Press, 1984–97; Henry Greenwood and Co., 1987–98; Dalesman Publishing Co., 1989–2004; The Countryman Publishing Co., 2000–04; Dir, Huveaux plc, 2001–06. Chairman: Council, PPA, 1970–73; Nat. Advertising Benevolent Soc., 1970–71; Member: Council, Advertising Assoc., 1962; Special Projects Cttee, Crafts Council, 1979–82. President: Thirty Club of London, 1982–83; Tonbridge Civic Soc., 1982–87. Chm., Kennel Appeal Bd, Battersea Dogs and Cats Home, 2012–14. *Publications:* The (Almost) Compleat Angler, 1985; Images of Angling, 2010. *Recreations:* writing, gardening, flyfishing, toymaking. *Address:* Chase Cottage, Chase Lane, Blackdown, Haslemere, Surrey GU27 3AG. *Clubs:* Flyfishers', Third Guards.

See also Sir J. J. Benn.

BENN, Rt Rev. Wallace Parke; Bishop Suffragan of Lewes, 1997–2012; *b* 6 Aug. 1947; *s* of William and Lucinda Jane Benn; *m* 1978, Lindsay Develing; one *s* one *d*. *Educ:* St Andrew's Coll., Dublin; UC, Dublin (BA); Trinity Coll., Bristol (external DipTheol London Univ.). Ordained deacon, 1972, priest, 1973; Assistant Curate: St Mark's, New Ferry, Wirral, 1972–76; St Mary's, Cheadle, 1976–82; Vicar: St James the Great, Audley, Stoke-on-Trent, 1982–87; St Peter's, Harold Wood, and part-time Chaplain, Harold Wood Hosp., 1987–97. President: Fellowship of Word and Spirit, 1998–; Church of England Evangelical Council, 2000–. *Publications:* The Last Word, 1996; Jesus our Joy, 2000; The Heart of Christianity, 2004; (contrib.) Preach the Word, 2007; articles in theol jls. *Recreations:* reading, walking with my wife, Rugby, motor sports. *Club:* National.

BENNATHAN, Joel Nathan; QC 2006; a Recorder, since 2009; *b* 15 July 1961; *s* of Esra Bennathan and Marion Bennathan, OBE; *m* 2004, Melanie Gingell; one *s* two *d*. *Educ:* Bristol Grammar Sch.; Queen Mary Coll., Univ. of London (LLB). Called to the Bar, Middle Temple, 1985; specialising in criminal law. *Publications:* legal articles in The Times, Solicitors' Jl and New Statesman. *Recreations:* art, theatre, family, socialism. *Address:* Doughty Street Chambers, 54 Doughty Street, WC1N 2LS.

BENNER, Michael Peter; Managing Director, Society of Independent Brewers, since 2014; *b* Rotherham, 6 July 1966; *s* of Peter and Anita Benner; *m* 1997, Helen; three *s* one *d*. *Educ:* McAuley Sch., Doncaster; Middlesex Univ. (BA Hons). Lectr in Mktg and Econs, 1992–94; Press Manager, 1994–97, Hd of Campaigns and Communications, 1997–2004, Chief Exec., 2004–14, CAMRA. *Recreations:* running, music, Jaguar cars. *Address:* Society of Independent Brewers, National Brewery Centre, Horninglow Street, Burton-Upon-Trent DE14 1NG.

BENNER, Patrick, CB 1975; Deputy Secretary, Department of Health and Social Security, 1976–84; *b* 26 May 1923; *s* of Henry Grey and Gwendolen Benner; *m* 1952, Joan Christabel Draper; two *d*. *Educ:* Ipswich Sch.; University Coll., Oxford. Entered Min. of Health as Asst Princ., 1949; Princ., 1951; Princ. Private Sec. to Minister, 1955; Asst Sec., 1958; Under-Sec., Min. of Health, 1967–68, DHSS, 1968–72; Dep. Sec., Cabinet Office, 1972–76. Chm., Rural Dispensing Cttee, 1987–91; Member: Exec. Council, Hosp. Saving Assoc., 1984–99; Exec. Cttee, Musicians Benevolent Fund, 1985–99 (Dep. Chm., 1996–99). *Address:* 12 Manor Gardens, Hampton, Middx TW12 2TU. *T:* (020) 8783 0848.

BENNET, family name of **Earl of Tankerville**.

BENNET, Dr Carey Louise; National Delivery Director (North and East) (formerl Regional Lead for the East of England), Achievement for All 3As, since 2011; *b* 10 Jan. 1958 *d* of Robin Bennet and Ann-Marie Bennet; *m* 1989, Peter James Cunningham; two *s*. *Edu* Froebel Inst., Roehampton; Jesus Coll., Oxford; Linacre Coll., Oxford (DPhil). Educatio Officer: Leics CC, 1987–90; Cambs CC, 1990–2000; Asst Dir of Educn, Northants CC 2000–03; Dir for Schs, 2003–06, Dir for Schs, Children and Families, 2007–08, Essex CC 2003–06; Dir of Delivery Support, Together for Disabled Children, 2008–10; Strategic Advr Children and Learners Div., DCSF, later DFE, 2010; Dir, Carey Bennet Associates Ltd 2010–11. *Publications:* (with P. J. Downes) Help Your Child Through Secondary Schoo 1997. *Recreations:* art, travel, cinema, theatre. *Address:* 21 Halifax Road, Cambridge CB4 3QB

BENNETT, Alan; dramatist and actor; *b* 9 May 1934; *s* of Walter Bennett and Lilian Mar Peel; civil partnership 2006, Rupert Thomas. *Educ:* Leeds Modern Sch.; Exeter Coll., Oxfor (BA Modern History, 1957; Hon. Fellow, 1987). Jun. Lectr, Modern History, Magdale Coll., Oxford, 1960–62. Trustee, National Gall., 1993–98. Hon. Freeman: Leeds, 2005 Rousham, 2009. Hon. FRA 2000. Hon. DLitt Leeds, 1990. Co-author and actor, Beyond th Fringe, Royal Lyceum, Edinburgh, 1960, Fortune, London, 1961 and Golden, NY, 1962 author and actor, On the Margin (TV series), 1966; *stage plays:* Forty Years On, Apollo, 1968 Getting On, Queen's, 1971; Habeas Corpus, Lyric, 1973; The Old Country, Queen's, 1977 Enjoy, Vaudeville, 1980; Kafka's Dick, Royal Court, 1986; Single Spies (double bill: A Question of Attribution; An Englishman Abroad (also dir)), NT, 1988; The Wind in th Willows (adapted), NT, 1990; The Madness of George III, NT, 1991; Talking Heads Comedy, 1992 and 1996; The Lady in the Van, Queen's, 1999; Hymn, Harrogate Fest., 2001 The History Boys, NT, 2004, NY, 2006; The Habit of Art, NT, 2009; People, NT, 2012 Cocktail Sticks, NT, 2012; *BBC TV films:* A Day Out, 1972; Sunset Across the Bay, 1975 *TV Plays for LWT*, 1978–79: Doris and Doreen; The Old Crowd; Me! I'm Afraid of Virgini Woolf; All Day on the Sands; Afternoon Off; One Fine Day; *BBC TV plays:* A Little Outing A Visit from Miss Prothero, 1977; Intensive Care, Say Something Happened, Our Winnie Marks, A Woman of No Importance, Rolling Home; An Englishman Abroad, 1983; Th Insurance Man, 1986; Talking Heads (series), 1988 (adapted for stage comedy, 1992); 10 Boulevard Haussmann, 1991; A Question of Attribution, 1991; Talking Heads 2 (series) 1998; Telling Tales (series), 2000; *BBC TV documentaries:* Dinner at Noon, 1988; Portrait o Bust, 1994; The Abbey, 1995; *Channel 4:* Poetry in Motion, 1990; Poetry in Motion 2, 1992 *feature films:* A Private Function, 1984; Prick Up Your Ears, 1987; The Madness of Kin George, 1995; The History Boys, 2006; *radio play:* Denmark Hill, 2014. *Publications:* (wit Cook, Miller and Moore) Beyond the Fringe, 1962; Forty Years On, 1969; Getting On, 1972 Habeas Corpus, 1973; The Old Country, 1978; Enjoy, 1980; Office Suite, 1981; Objects o Affection, 1982; A Private Function, 1984; The Writer in Disguise, 1985; Prick Up Your Ear (screenplay), 1987; Two Kafka Plays, 1987; Talking Heads, 1988 (Hawthornden Prize, 1989) Single Spies, 1989; The Lady in the Van, 1990; Poetry in Motion, 1990; The Wind in th Willows (adaptation), 1991; The Madness of George III, 1992; (jtly) Poetry in Motion 2 1992; Writing Home, 1994 (collected articles); The Madness of King George (screenplay) 1995; The Clothes They Stood Up In, 1998; The Complete Talking Heads, 1998; Father Father! Burning Bright, 2000; Telling Tales (autobiog.), 2000; The Laying On of Hands 2001; The History Boys, 2004, screenplay, 2006; Untold Stories, 2005; The Uncommo Reader, 2007; A Life Like Other People's (memoir), 2009; The Habit of Art, 2009; Smut two unseemly stories, 2011; Hymn and Cocktail Sticks, 2012; People, 2012; Six Poets: Hard to Larkin (anthology), 2014. *Address:* c/o Chatto & Linnit, Worlds End Studios, 132–134 Lot Road, SW10 0RJ. *T:* (020) 7349 7222.

BENNETT, Cdre Alan Reginald Courtenay, DSC 1982; FRAeS; Chief Executive, Roya College of Surgeons of England, 2009–13; *b* Gosport, 11 Feb. 1954; *s* of late Peter Bennet and Joan Bennett; *m* 1979, Sarah Anne Shaw; two *s* one *d*. *Educ:* Bradfield Coll., Berk BRNC Dartmouth. Royal Navy: officer trng, 1972–75; Warfare Officer, HMS Amazon 1976–77; helicopter flying trng, 1978–79; pilot, 846 Cdo Sqdn, HMS Bulwark and HMS Hermes, 1979–82; Lynx Flight Comdr, HMS Arrow, 1982–84; RNSC 1985; Principa Warfare Officer, HMS Danae, 1986–87; Sen. Pilot, 846 Cdo Sqdn, 1988–90; CO, HMS Alacrity, 1990–92; Directing Staff, JSDC, Greenwich, 1993; Commander: RN Air Office Appts, MoD, 1994–95; Air Wing, HMS Illustrious, 1996–97; Hd, Policy and Plans Div. Internat. Mil. Staff, NATO HQ, Brussels, 1997–99; Dir, Personnel/Plans/Communications Jt Helicopter Comd, Wilton, 1999–2002; JSCSC 2003; CO, RN Air Station Yeovilton 2003–05; British Naval Attaché, Washington, DC, 2006–08. Comdr 1990; Capt. 1997; Cdre 2003. RYA Yachtmaster Offshore Instructor (pt-time), 2008–. FRAeS 2003. Mem., RNSA *Recreations:* family, cruising a Sweden Yachts 390, enjoying the countryside.

BENNETT, (Albert) Edward; Director, G24 Nuclear Safety Assistance Co-ordinatior Centre, 1992–95, and Directorate of Nuclear Safety, Industry and the Environment, and Civi Protection (formerly of Nuclear Safety and Control of Chemical Pollution), 1987–95 European Commission; *b* 11 Sept. 1931; *s* of Albert Edward and Frances Ann Bennett; *m* 1957, Jean Louise Paston-Cooper; two *s*. *Educ:* University Coll. Sch., Hampstead; London Hosp. Med. Coll. MB BS London; FFCM 1972, FFOM 1984. Surgeon Lieut, RN, 1957–60 Senior Lectr, Dept of Clinical Epidemiology and Social Medicine, St Thomas's Hosp. Med Sch., 1964–70; Dir, Health Services Evaluation Gp, Univ. of Oxford, 1970–77; Prof. and Head of Dept of Clinical Epidemiology and Social Medicine, St George's Hosp. Med. Sch. Univ. of London, 1974–81; Director: Health and Safety Directorate, EEC, 1981–87. Hon Editor, Internat. Jl of Epidemiology, 1977–81. *Publications:* Questionnaires in Medicine, 1975 (ed) Communications between Doctors and Patients, 1976; (ed) Recent Advances in Community Medicine, 1978; numerous sci. reports and contribs on epidemiology of chronic disease and evaluation of health services. *Recreations:* opera, gardening, browsing.

See also N. E. F. Bennett.

BENNETT, Andrew Francis; retired teacher; *b* Manchester, 9 March 1939; *m*; two *s* one *d* *Educ:* Birmingham Univ. (BSocSc). Joined Labour Party, 1957; Member, Oldham Borough Council, 1964–74. Member, National Union of Teachers. Contested (Lab) Knutsford, 1970 MP (Lab) Stockport North, Feb. 1974–1983, Denton and Reddish, 1983–2005. Ar Opposition spokesperson on educn, 1983–88. Jt Chm., Select Cttee on Envmt, Transport and Regl Affairs, 1997–2005 (Chm., Envmt Sub-Cttee, 1997–2005). Interested especially in environment and education. *Recreations:* photography, walking, climbing. *Address:* 28 Brownsville Road, Stockport SK4 4PF.

BENNETT, Andrew John, CMG 1998; Director, Syngenta Foundation for Sustainable Agriculture, since 2002 (Executive Director, 2002–07); *b* 25 April 1942; *s* of Leonard Charle Bennett and Edna Mary Bennett (*née* Harding); *m* 1996, Yin Yin Jackson. *Educ:* St Edward's Sch., Oxford; University Coll. of N Wales (BSc Agr Scis 1965); Univ. of West Indies Trinidad (DipTA 1967); Univ. of Reading (MSc Crop Protection 1970). VSO Kenya 1965–66; Agricl Officer (Research), Govt of St Vincent, 1967–69; Maize Agronomist, Govt of Malawi, 1971–74; Crop Develt Manager, 1976–78, Chief Research Officer, 1978–79, S Region, Sudan; Asst Agricl Adviser, ODA, 1980–83; Natural Resources Adviser (ODA), SE Asia Develt Div., Bangkok, 1983–85; Head, British Develt Div. in Pacific (ODA), Fiji, 1985–87; Chief Natural Resources Advr, ODA, FCO, subseq. DFID, 1987–2002. Dir and Sec., Eynesbury Estates, 1990–2008. Non-executive Director: CABI, 2009–; IBO UK, 2009–. Pres., Tropical Agric. Assoc., 2003–. Chm., Bd of Trustees, Sci. Develt Network, 2008–14; Chair, Alliance Bd, Consultative Gp on Internat. Agricl Res., 2010–11; Member: Bd Trustees, Centre for Internat. Forestry Res., 2002–10 (Chm., 2006–10); Council, ODI

2003–08; Interim Panel, Global Crop Diversity Trust, 2003–06; Bd Trustees, Internat. Network on Bamboo and Rattan, 2011–; Trustee, Crop Innovations (formerly Eur. Centre for Underutilised Crops), 2012–. Dir, Doyle Foundn, 2002–. FRSA 2000. Hon. DSc Cranfield, 1999. *Recreations:* walking, gardening. *Address:* Chroyle, Gloucester Road, Bath BA1 8BH. *T:* (01225) 851489. *E:* andrewj.bennett@btinternet.com.

BENNETT, Brian Maurice; HM Diplomatic Service, retired; Ambassador to Belarus, 2003–07; Administrator, Humphrey Richardson Taylor Charitable Trust, since 2008; *b* 1 April 1948; *s* of Valentine and Dorothy Bennett; *m* 1969, Lynne Skipsey; three *s*. *Educ:* Totton Grammar Sch.; Sheffield Univ. (BA Hons Russian). AIL 1988. Joined HM Diplomatic Service, 1971; Prague, 1973–76; Helsinki, 1977–79; Bridgetown, Barbados, 1983–86; Vienna, 1986–88; The Hague, 1988–92; Dep. Hd of Mission, Tunis, 1997–2000. Chm., Anglo-Belarusian Soc., 2014–. *Publications:* The Last Dictatorship in Europe: Belarus under Lukashenko, 2011. *Recreations:* singing, walking, table tennis.

BENNETT, Catherine Elizabeth; *see* O'Leary, C. E.

BENNETT, Clive Ronald Reath, CBE 2007; CEng; Managing Director, Imago Services Ltd, 2008–13; *b* 20 Dec. 1947; *s* of Ron and Betty Bennett; *m* 1970, Pauline Weeks; two *d*. *Educ:* Hatfield Poly. (BSc). CEng 1971. Design Engr, Norton Abrasives Ltd, 1970–71; Industrial Engr, Radiomobile (Smiths Industries), 1971–73; Rank Xerox (UK) Ltd: Technical Service and Supply Dir, 1973–83; Gen. Manager, Supplies Distribn, 1983–84; Gen. Manager, Distribn, Polycell Products, 1984–87; Business Excellence Dir, Sara Lee Household and Personal Care, 1987–94; Gp Ops Dir, Norton Health Care, 1994–99; Chief Exec., DVLA, 2000–07. *Recreations:* music, swimming. *T:* (01243) 261904. *E:* clivebennett20@btinternet.com.

BENNETT, David John, CBE 2015; FCA; Group Chief Executive (formerly Managing Director), Sanctuary Group (formerly Sanctuary Housing Group), since 1992; *b* 16 April 1951; *s* of Wing Comdr Donald Albert Bennett, MBE and Eva Mary Bennett; *m* 1987, Katrina Momcilovic; two *d*. *Educ:* De Aston Sch. FCA 1975; CCMI 2007. Payne Stone Fraser, Chartered Accountants, 1969–74; Management Accountant, Beecham Pharmaceuticals, 1974–76; Chief Accountant, Heurtey Petrochem, 1976–80; Financial Controller: Samuel Lewis Trust, 1980–82; Peabody Trust, 1982–85; Finance Dir, 1985–86, Chief Exec., 1986–89, Spiral Housing Assoc.; Dep. Chief Exec., Sanctuary Housing Assoc., 1989–92. Gov., Sutton Community Sch., 2003–08. *Recreations:* music, photography, game fishing. *Address:* c/o Sanctuary House, Chamber Court, Castle Street, Worcester WR1 3ZQ. *T:* (01905) 334198, *Fax:* (01905) 334959. *E:* davidbt@sanctuary-housing.co.uk.

BENNETT, David Jonathan; Chairman, HomeServe Membership Ltd, since 2012; *b* 26 March 1962; *m* 1991, Sue Moss; two *s*. *Educ:* King's Coll. Sch., Wimbledon; Queens' Coll., Cambridge (BA Hons Econs 1983). Grindlays Bank, 1983–85; Money Market Dealer: Chemical Bank, 1985–86; Abbey Nat. Building Soc., 1986–88; Cheltenham & Gloucester plc: Gen. Mgr (Treasury and Investments), 1988–93; Head: of Strategic Planning, 1994; of Sales and Marketing, 1994–95; Finance Dir, 1995–96; Exec. Dir, NBNZ, 1996–98; CEO, Countrywide Bank, Lloyds TSB Gp, 1999; Alliance & Leicester plc: Gp Treas., 1999–2000; Exec. Dir, 2000–01; Gp Finance Dir, 2001–07; Gp Chief Exec., 2007–08; Exec. Dir, Abbey, 2008–09. Dir, David Bennett Adv. Ltd, 2011–. Non-executive Director: easyJet plc, 2005–; Pacnet Ltd, 2009–; Clarity Commerce Solutions Ltd, 2010–11; CMC Markets, 2010–12; Jerrold Hldgs Ltd, 2011–; Bank of Ireland (UK) plc, 2013–; PayPal Europe, 2014–. *Recreations:* travel, Rugby supporter.

BENNETT, Dr David William; Chief Executive, Monitor, Independent Regulator of NHS Foundation Trusts, since 2012 (Interim Chief Executive, 2010–12; Chairman, 2011–14); *b* Wolverhampton, 3 Aug. 1955; *s* of William Edwin Bennett, Halesowen and Irene Joan Bennett (*née* Davis). *Educ:* Halesowen GS; Univ. of Birmingham (BSc; S. W. J. Smith Prize); Trinity Coll., Oxford (DPhil); London Business Sch. (Cert. Corporate Finance). Manager: Shell Research Ltd, 1979–82; Shell Internat. Petroleum Co., 1982–86; Dir, McKinsey & Co. Inc., 1986–2004; Hd, Prime Minister's Policy Directorate and Prime Minister's Strategy Unit, 2005–07; Chm., 10 Partnership Ltd, 2007–10. Non-exec. Dir, GHK Hldgs Ltd, 2008–12. Associate Fellow, Inst. for Govt, 2008–. *Publications:* contrib. res. papers to Nuclear Physics, 1977–80. *Recreations:* motor sports, cycling, squash. *Address:* Monitor, Wellington House, 133–155 Waterloo Road, SE1 8UG. *E:* david@bennetts-online.net.

BENNETT, Douglas Simon; trainee child and adolescent psychotherapist; Chief Executive, North London Hospice, 2002–14; *b* 18 Aug. 1958. *Educ:* Bristol Univ. (LLB); Brunel Univ. (MA Public Sector Mgt 1989). Trainee Solicitor, Slaughter & May, 1980–82; admitted Solicitor, 1982; Society of Voluntary Associations: Inner London Co-ordinator, 1982–84; Asst Dir, 1984–86; Dep. Dir, 1986–88; Dir, Age Concern, Brent, 1989; Head of Planning, British Red Cross, 1989–97; Chief Exec., Nat. Soc. for Epilepsy, 1997–2000; Univ. of Salamanca, 2000–01. *Recreations:* meals with friends, walking, concerts, opera, going to cinema and theatre. *E:* londonchildtherapy@hotmail.com.

BENNETT, Edward; *see* Bennett, A. E.

BENNETT, Elizabeth Martin; *see* Allen, E. M.

BENNETT, Air Vice Marshal Sir Erik Peter, KBE 1990; CB 1984; CVO 2010; retired from RAF, 1991; Commander, Sultan of Oman's Air Force (in the rank of Air Marshal), 1974–90; *s* of Robert Francis and Anne Myra Bennett. *Educ:* The King's Hospital, Dublin. Air Adviser to King Hussein, 1958–62; RAF Staff College, 1963; Jt Services Staff Coll., 1968; RAF Coll. of Air Warfare, 1971. Order of Istiqlal (Jordan), 1960; Order of Oman, 1980; Order of Merit (Oman), 1989; Order of Sultan Qaboos (Oman), 1985; Medal of Honour (Oman), 1989. *Recreations:* riding, sailing, big game fishing. *Address:* Al Hail Farm, Seeb-Hail Al Awahir, PO Box 1751, Postal Code 111, Sultanate of Oman. *Clubs:* Royal Air Force, Beefsteak, Pratt's.

BENNETT, Hon. Sir Hugh (Peter Derwyn), Kt 1995; DL; Deputy Judge of the High Court of Justice, since 2010 (a Judge of the High Court of Justice, Family Division, 1995–2010); Nominated Administrative Court Judge, 2004–10; *b* 8 Sept. 1943; *s* of late Peter Ward Bennett, OBE, and Priscilla Ann Bennett; *m* 1969, Elizabeth (*née* Landon); one *s* three *d*. *Educ:* Haileybury and ISC; Churchill College, Cambridge (MA). Called to the Bar, Inner Temple, 1966, Bencher, 1993; an Assistant Recorder, 1987; QC 1988; a Recorder, 1990–95; Family Law (finance) Facilitator, 2010–; arbitrator, 2012–. Presiding Judge, NE Circuit, 1999–2002; a Judge, Courts of Appeal of Jersey and Guernsey, 2010–15. Mem., Supreme Court Rule Cttee, 1988–92; Chm. (part-time), Betting Levy Appeal Tribunal, 1989–95. Hon. Legal Advr, Sussex County Playing Fields Assoc., 1988–95. Chm., Sussex Assoc. for Rehabilitation of Offenders, 1998–2004. Fellow of Woodard Corp., 1987–99; Mem. Council, Lancing Coll., 1981–95. MCIArb 2012. DL W Sussex, 2003. *Recreations:* cricket, tennis, shooting, fishing. *Clubs:* Garrick, Pilgrims, MCC; Sussex.

See also Sir H. J. F. S. Cholmeley, Bt.

BENNETT, Hywel Thomas; actor; director; *b* Wales, 8 April 1944; *s* of Gordon Bennett and Sarah Gwen Bennett (*née* Lewis); *m* 1st, 1967, Cathy McGowan (marr. diss. 1988); one *d*; 2nd, 1996, Sandra Elayne Fulford. *Educ:* Henry Thornton Grammar School, Clapham; RADA (scholarship). *Stage:* Nat. Youth Theatre for 5 years; repertory, Salisbury and Leatherhead; first major roles in The Screwtape Letters and A Smashing Day, Arts Th., 1966; Shakespeare at Mermaid, Young Vic, Shaw Theatres; repertory, 1972–77 (roles included Jimmy Porter, in Look Back in Anger, Belgrade, and Hamlet, S Africa); Otherwise Engaged, Comedy, 1977; Night Must Fall, Shaw Th., 1977; Levantine, Her Majesty's, 1979; Terra Nova, Chichester, 1980; Fly Away Home, Lyric, Hammersmith, 1983; She Stoops to Conquer, Nat. Theatre, 1985; Toad of Toad Hall; Three Sisters, Albery, 1987; Edinburgh Festival, 1967 and 1990 (Long John Silver, in Treasure Island); *directed:* plays at provincial theatres incl. Lincoln, Leatherhead, Birmingham, Coventry, Sheffield and Cardiff; *films:* The Family Way, 1966; Twisted Nerve, 1968; The Virgin Soldiers, 1969; Loot, 1970; The Buttercup Chain, 1971; Endless Night, 1971; Alice in Wonderland, 1972; Twilight Zone, 1987; Murder Elite, 1990; War Zone, 1990; Age Unknown, 1992; Deadly Advice, 1994; Married to Malcolm, 1997; Misery Harbour, 1998; Nasty Neighbours, 1998; Vatel, 1999; Mary of Nazareth, 1999; *TV plays and films* include: Romeo and Juliet; The Idiot; A Month in the Country; Trust Me; Artemis 81; Frankie and Johnnie; The Other Side of Paradise; Murder Most Horrid; The Quest; Lloyd and Hill; One for the Road; *TV series:* Malice Aforethought; Pennies from Heaven; Tinker, Tailor, Soldier, Spy; Shelley (10 series); Where the Buffalo Roam; Death of a Teddy Bear; The Consultant; Absent Friends; Myself a Mandarin; The Secret Agent; A Mind to Kill; Casualty; Virtual Murder; Neverwhere; Lock Stock; Frontiers; Karaoke; Last of the Summer Wine; Time Gentlemen Please; The Bill; Eastenders, 2002; The Quest 1–3, 2002–04; many radio plays, commercial voiceovers and film narrations. Hon. Fellow, Cardiff Univ., 1996. *Recreations:* fishing, golf, reading, walking. *Club:* Savile.

BENNETT, Prof. James Arthur, PhD; Director, Museum of the History of Science, 1994–2012, and Professor, 2010–12, now Emeritus, University of Oxford; Fellow of Linacre College, Oxford, 1994–2012, now Emeritus; Visiting Keeper, The Science Museum, 2013–15, now Emeritus; *b* 2 April 1947; *s* of James Hutchinson Bennett and Margaret Anna Bennett (*née* McCune); *m* 1st, 1971, France Annie Ramette (marr. diss. 2002); two *d*; 2nd, 2005, Sylvia Sumira. *Educ:* Grosvenor High Sch., Belfast; Clare Coll., Univ. of Cambridge (BA 1969; PhD 1974). FRAS 1976; FSA 1989. Lectr, Univ. of Aberdeen, 1973–74; Archivist, Royal Astronomical Soc., 1974–76; Curator of Astronomy, Nat. Maritime Mus. 1977–79; Curator, Whipple Mus. of Hist. of Sci., Cambridge, 1979–94; Sen. Res. Fellow, 1984–94, Sen. Tutor, 1992–94, Churchill Coll., Cambridge. Member: Cttee, Sci. Mus., 2004–10; Astronomical Heritage Cttee, RAS, 2009–; Bd, Nobel Mus., Stockholm, 2011–14; Council, Hakluyt Soc., 2012–; Council, Belfast Natural Hist. and Philosophical Soc., 2015–. President: Scientific Instrument Commn, IUHPS, 1998–2002; British Soc. for History of Sci., 2000–02; Vice Pres., Internat. Acad. of History of Sci., 2013–. Paul Bunge Prize, German Chemical Soc., 2001. Member, Editorial Board: Jl for History of Astronomy, 1990–2004; Notes and Records, Royal Soc., 2000–06; Isis, 2001–03; Nuncius, 2001–12; Chm., Editl Bd, Sci. Mus. Gp Jl, 2013–. *Publications:* The Mathematical Science of Christopher Wren, 1982; The Divided Circle, 1987; Church, State and Astronomy in Ireland, 1990; (ed jtly) Making Instruments Count, 1993; (with S. Johnston) The Geometry of War, 1996; (with S. Mandelbrote) The Garden, the Ark, the Tower, the Temple, 1998; (jtly) London's Leonardo, 2003; (ed jtly) Oxford Companion to the History of Modern Science, 2003; (ed jtly) Cabinets of Experimental Philosophy in Eighteenth-Century Europe, 2013; articles in books and jls, and exhibition catalogues. *Recreations:* music, Rugby, cooking. *Address:* 20 Alma Place, Oxford OX4 1JW. *T:* (01865) 203883.

BENNETT, Jana Eve, OBE 2000; President, FYI and LMN channels, A+E Networks LLC, since 2013; *b* 6 Nov. 1956; *d* of Gordon Willard Bennett and Elizabeth (*née* Cushing); *m* 1996, Richard Clemmow; one *s* one *d*. *Educ:* Bognor Regis Comprehensive Sch.; St Anne's Coll., Oxford (BA PPE); London Sch. of Econs (MSc with dist. Internat. Relns); Wharton Sch., Univ. of Penn (AMP). Co-editor, Millennium, jl internat. relns; British Broadcasting Corporation: news trainee, 1978; news daily editor; series producer, then Ed., Antenna, 1987; Ed., Horizon, 1990; Head, BBC Science, 1994–97; Dir and Dep. Chief Exec., BBC Prodn, 1997–99; Exec. Vice-Pres., Learning Channel, US Discovery Communications Inc., 1999–2002; Dir, Television and Mem., Exec. Bd, BBC, 2002–11; Pres., Worldwide Networks and Global iPlayer, and Man. Dir for Latin America, BBC Worldwide, 2011–12 (Mem., Exec. Bd, 2003–11). Member: Bd, UKTV, 2011–12; Bd, Women in Film and TV, 2011–13 (Chm., 2012–13); Exec. Cttee, Internat. Emmys, 2010–13; Bd, Pew Res. Center, 2013–. Trustee, Natural Hist. Mus., 1999–2004; Mem., Visitors Bd, Oxford Univ. Mus. of Natural History, 2013–. Gov., RSC, 2005–. Gov., LSE, 2002–07. FRTS 1999. *Publications:* (jtly) The Disappeared: Argentina's dirty war, 1986. *Recreations:* exploration, travel literature, family, Brazil. *Address:* (office) 235 E 45th Street, 5th Floor, New York, NY 10017, USA.

BENNETT, Jeremy John Nelson; independent producer; Director, 3BM Television, 1995–2004 (Managing Director and Chairman, 1995–2001); *b* 1 Dec. 1939; *s* of Denis Pengelley Bennett and Jill (*née* Nelson); *m* 1963, Tine Langkilde; three *s*. *Educ:* Haileybury; Clare Coll., Cambridge (Open Schol. in Hist.; MA); Copenhagen Univ. (Churchill Fellow). With British Council, 1963–65; BBC European Service, 1966–68; Producer/Dir, BBC TV documentaries, 1968–89; Producer, Richard Dimbleby Lecture, 1983–87; Exec. Producer, Contemporary Hist. Unit, 1989–92; freelance, 1993–95. *Productions* include: Cry Hungary, 1986 and 1996 (Blue Ribbon Award, American Film Fest.); Juan Carlos, King of All the Spaniards, 1980 and 1986; Alphabet: the Story of Writing (Silver Award, NY Film and TV Fest., 1980; Times Newcomer Award); Monty: in Love and War, 1987 (Blue Ribbon Award, American Film Fest.); Churchill, 1992; The Cuban Missile Crisis, 1992 (US Nat. Emmy Award); Chairman Mao: The Last Emperor, 1993; Hiroshima, 1995; The Suez Crisis, 1996; The Berlin Airlift, 1998; The Illuminator, 2003; *TV histories of the BBC:* What Did You Do in the War, Auntie?, 1995; Auntie: The Inside Story, 1997. Associate Fellow, Centre for Cultural Policy Studies, Warwick Univ., 2003–10. Chairman: Camberwell Soc., 1979–85 (Pres., 2007–); Southwark Envmt Trust, 1987–95; Groundwork Southwark and Lambeth (formerly Southwark), 1995–2007; Groundwork London, 2007–09; Groundwork South East, 2010–12; Member, Board: Cross River Partnership, 1995–2006; Groundwork Nat. Fedn, 1999–2014; Southwark Alliance, 2006–08; Groundwork South, 2012–. Southwark Citizen of the Year, Southwark LBC, 2003. Cross of Merit, Order of Vitéz (Hungary), 1987. *Publications:* British Broadcasting and the Danish Resistance Movement 1940–45, 1966; The Master-Builders, 2004. *Address:* 30 Grove Lane, Camberwell, SE5 8ST. *T:* (020) 7703 9971.

BENNETT, Jonathan Simon; a District Judge (Magistrates' Courts), since 2003; a Recorder, since 2009; *b* 13 July 1957; *s* of late Leonard Arthur Covil Bennett and Edith Irene Bennett; *m* 1982, Sarah Jayne Blackmore; three *s* one *d*. *Educ:* City of London Sch.; Reading Univ. (LLB Hons). Admitted solicitor, 1982; Dep. Dist Judge, 1998–2003. Chm. (pt-time), Appeals Service, 1997–2003. Chm. of Trustees, Open Hands Project, 2007–. *Recreations:* following Charlton Athletic, lay leader within St Thomas' Church, Philadelphia, Sheffield. *Address:* The Law Courts, College Road, Doncaster, S Yorks DN1 3HT. *E:* jonathan.bennett57@sky.com.

BENNETT, Linda Kristin, OBE 2007; Chief Executive, L. K. Bennett, 1990–2008 (non-executive Director, since 2008); *b* 8 Sept. 1962; *d* of Peter and Hafdis Bennett; *m* 2000, Philip W. Harley; one *d*. *Educ:* Haberdashers' Aske's Sch. for Girls; Univ. of Reading (BSc). Founded L. K. Bennett, 1990. Hon. Fellow, Univ. of Arts, London, 2004. Hon. LLD Reading, 2005. Veuve Clicquot Business Woman of Year Award, 2004. *Recreations:* architectural history, British 20th century art, walking, travel, cinema. *Address:* c/o Anthony Pins, Nyman Libson Paul, Regina House, 124 Finchley Road, NW3 5JS. *T:* (020) 7433 2427. *E:* linda.bennett@lkbennett.com.

BENNETT, Margaret Joan; freelance mentor and consultant, since 2011; Finance and Human Resources Director, Tinder Foundation (formerly Online Centres Foundation), since 2011; *b* 22 Dec. 1960; *d* of Rev. Canon Ian Frederick Bennett and Dr Rachel Bennett; *m*

1987, David Hill (marr. diss. 1994); one *s*. *Educ:* St Anne's Coll., Oxford (BA Hons PPE 1983). Chartered Accountant, KPMG, 1983–87; Finance Officer, West Midlands Arts, 1987–89; Asst Dir, North West Arts, 1989–91; Central Services Dir, Nottingham Community Housing Assoc., 1992–96; Chief Exec., Nat. Liby for the Blind, 1996–2001; Head, Lifelong Learning and Technologies Div., then Lifelong Learning Directorate, DCSF, later DFES, subseq. Dep. Dir, Further Educn and Skills Directorate, DIUS, then BIS, 2001–06; Dep. Chief Exec. and Exec. Dir, Finance and Resources, Learning and Skills Improvement Service, 2006–11. *Recreations:* the arts, reading, walking, music, cooking. *Address:* 23 Endcliffe Rise Road, Sheffield S11 8RU. *T:* (0114) 268 3053.

BENNETT, Prof. Martin Arthur, FRS 1995; FRSC, FRACI, FAA; Professor, Research School of Chemistry, Australian National University, 1991–2000, Emeritus Professor, since 2001; *b* 11 Aug. 1935; *s* of late Arthur Edward Charles Bennett and Dorothy Ivy Bennett; *m* 1964, Rae Elizabeth Mathews; two *s*. *Educ:* Haberdashers' Aske's Hampstead Sch.; Imperial Coll. of Science and Technology, London (BSc 1957; PhD 1960; DSc 1974). FRACI 1977; FAA 1980; FRSC 1997. Postdoctoral Fellow, Univ. of S California, 1960–61; Turner and Newall Fellow, 1961–63, Lectr, 1963–67, UCL; Fellow, 1967–70, Sen. Fellow, 1970–79, Professorial Fellow, 1979–91, Res. Sch. of Chem., ANU. Adjunct Prof., RMIT, 2000–. Vis. Prof. and Vis. Fellow, univs in Canada, Germany, USA, Japan, China and NZ. Corresp. Mem., Bayerische Akademie der Wissenschaften, 2005. Numerous awards, Aust. learned instns; Nyholm Medal, RSC, 1991; Max Planck Soc. Res. Award, 1994; Centenary Medal (Australia), 2001. *Publications:* chapters on Ruthenium in Comprehensive Organometallic Chemistry; contribs to learned jls. *Recreations:* golf, reading, foreign languages. *Address:* Research School of Chemistry, Australian National University, Canberra, ACT 2601, Australia. *T:* (2) 61253639; 21 Black Street, Yarralumla, ACT 2600, Australia. *T:* (2) 62824154.

BENNETT, Prof. Martin Richard, PhD; FRCP; FAHA; British Heart Foundation Professor of Cardiovascular Sciences, University of Cambridge, since 2000; Hon. Consultant Cardiologist, Cambridge University Hospitals NHS Trust, since 2000; *b* Northampton, 30 Aug. 1962; *s* of Peter and Beryl Bennett; *m* 1991, Catherine Margaret Blaymires; two *s*. *Educ:* Northampton Sch. for Boys; Welsh Nat. Sch. of Medicine, Cardiff (BSc 1st Cl. Hons Anatomy 1983; MB BCh 1st Cl. Hons 1986); PhD Wales 1993; MA Cantab 2001. FRCP 2001. Registrar in Cardiology, Gen. and Sandwell Hosps, Birmingham, 1988–90; BHF Clinician Scientist, 1990–97; BHF Sen. Fellow and Hon. Consultant Cardiologist, Univ. of Cambridge, 1997–2000. Vis. Scientist, Univ. of Washington, Seattle, 1993–95. FAHA 2001; FMedSci 2007. *Publications:* contrib. scientific papers and book chapters on cardiovascular disease, with specialist interest in atherosclerosis, apoptosis, restenosis and cellular senescence. *Recreations:* cricket, classic cars, contemporary film and books, travelling. *Address:* Division of Cardiovascular Medicine, Box 110, Addenbrooke's Centre for Clinical Investigation, Addenbrooke's Hospital, Cambridge CB2 0QQ. *T:* (01223) 331504, *Fax:* (01223) 331505. *E:* mrb@mole.bio.cam.ac.uk.

BENNETT, Natalie Louise; Leader, Green Party, since 2012; *b* Sydney, Australia, 10 Feb. 1966; *d* of John and Joy Bennett. *Educ:* Univ. of Sydney (BAgrSc Hons); Univ. of New England, Armidale (BA Hons Asian Studies); Univ. of Leicester (MA Mass Communications). Reporter and sub-editor, Northern Daily Leader, Cootamunda Herald, Eastern Riverina Observer, Australia; volunteer, Office of Nat. Commn on Women's Affairs, Thailand, 1995–96; sub-editor: Bangkok Post, 1996–99; The Times, 2000–04; Independent, 2004–05; Ed., Guardian Weekly, 2007–12. Blogger, 2006–. Founder, Carnival of Feminists, 2005–09. Trustee, Fawcett Soc., 2010–14. Gov., Netley Primary Sch., 2008–. *Recreations:* women's history, enjoying the London Library, cycling and walking, playing cricket, baking and conserve making. *Address:* Green Party, Development House, St Leonard Street, EC2A 4LT. *T:* (020) 7549 0310. *E:* leader@greenparty.org.uk.

BENNETT, Neil Edward Francis; Chief Executive, Maitland, since 2010 (Managing Partner, 2004–08; Vice Chairman, 2008–10); *b* 15 May 1965; *s* of Albert Edward Bennett, *qv*; *m* 1992, Carole Kenyon; two *d*. *Educ:* Westminster Sch.; University Coll. London (BA Medieval Archaeol.); City Univ. (Dip. Journalism). Staff writer, Investors Chronicle, 1987–89; The Times: Banking Corresp., 1989–92; Ed., Tempus column, 1992–94; Dep. Business Editor, 1994–95; City Editor, Sunday Telegraph, 1995–2002; Chief Exec., Gavin Anderson & Co. Ltd, 2002–04. Principal financial columnist, jagnotes-euro.com, 1999–2000. Mem. Bd of Advrs, London Capital Club, 2004–. Trustee, John Schofield Trust, 2011–. FRSA 2008. Jun. Wincott Foundn Award, 1992; Business Journalist of the Year, British Press Awards, 1998, 1999. *Recreations:* running, antiquarian book collecting, Irish Terriers. *Address:* Maitland, 125 Shaftesbury Avenue, WC2H 8AD.

BENNETT, Nicholas; Public Services Ombudsman for Wales, since 2014; *b* St Asaph, 29 April 1969; *s* of Nicholas Bennett and Catherine Ellen Bennett (*née* Roberts); *m* 1994, Nia Gwenllian Thomas; one *s* two *d*. *Educ:* Llangefni Comprehensive Sch.; University Coll. of Wales, Aberystwyth (BSc Econ Politics 1990; MBA 1991). Wales Eur. Centre, Brussels, 1995–99; Special Advr to Dep. First Minister of Wales, Welsh Assembly Govt, 2000–02; Dir, Bute Communications, 2004–06; Gp Chief Exec., Community Housing Cymru, 2006–14. Member: All Wales Convention, Welsh Lang. Bd; Ofcom Adv. Panel, Williams Commn. *Recreations:* running, indie rock, Laugharne, walking. *Address:* (office) 1 Ffordd yr Hen Gae, Pencoed, Bridgend, Glamorgan CF35 5LJ. *T:* (01656) 641152. *E:* nick.bennett@ombudsman-wales.org.uk. *Club:* Glamorganshire Golf.

BENNETT, Nicholas Jerome; JP; Managing Director, Kent Refurbishment Ltd, since 2002; *b* 7 May 1949; *s* of late Peter Ramsden Bennett and Antonia Mary Flanagan; *m* 1995, Ruth, *er d* of late Andrew and Alma Whitelaw, Barnham Broom, Norfolk. *Educ:* Sedgehill Sch.; Polytechnic of North London (BA Hons Philosophy); Univ. of London Inst. of Educn (PGCE Distinction); Univ. of Sussex (MA). Educnl publishing, 1974; schoolmaster, 1976–85; educn officer, 1985–87; Advr on public affairs, Price Waterhouse, 1993–98; Chief Exec., ACE, 1998–2002. Member (C): Lewisham LBC, 1974–82 (Leader of the Opposition, 1979–81); co-opted Mem., ILEA Educn Cttee, 1978–81; Bromley LBC, 2006– (Chm., Educn Cttee). Mem., FEFCE, 1992–97. Contested (C): St Pancras N, 1973 and Greenwich, by-elecn 1974, GLC elections; Hackney Central, 1979. MP (C) Pembroke, 1987–92; contested (C): Pembroke, 1992; Reading W, 1997. PPS to Minister of State, Department of Transport, 1990; Parly Under-Sec. of State, Welsh Office, 1990–92. Member: Select Cttee on Welsh Affairs, 1987–90; Select Cttee on Procedure, 1988–90; Vice-Chm. (Wales), Cons. backbench Party Organisation Cttee, 1990. Chm., Beckenham Cons. Assoc., 2006–09. Chm., Nat. Council for Civil Protection, 1990. Mem., Western Front Assoc. JP, SW Div., Greater (formerly Inner) London, 1998. *Publications:* (contrib.) Primary Headship in the 1990s, 1989; (contrib.) 100 Buildings, 100 Years, 2014. *Recreations:* swimming, history, transport, browsing in second-hand bookshops, cinema, small scale gardening, visiting battlefields of First and Second World War, architecture. *Address:* 18 Upper Park Road, Bromley, Kent BR1 3HT. *T:* and *Fax:* (020) 8466 1363. *E:* md@kentrefurbishment.co.uk.

BENNETT, Nicholas John, CB 2008; Director General, Strategic Technologies, Ministry of Defence, 2005–09; *b* 30 Sept. 1948; *s* of John Douglas Bennett and Betty Yvonne Bennett (*née* Harker); *m* 1st, 1971, Susan Mary Worthington (*d* 1997); one *s* one *d*; 2nd, 2000, Lesley Ann Davie (*née* Thorpe). *Educ:* Bishop Wordsworth Sch., Salisbury; Brunel Univ. (BTech Hons Electronic Engrg 1971). Ministry of Defence: HQ No 90 (S) Gp, 1971–77; A&AEE, 1977–80; Hd, Engrg Design, RAF Signals Engrg Estabt, 1980–83; Principal D Air Radio, 1983–84; Asst Chief Design Engr, RAF Signals Engrg Estabt, 1984–86; Asst Dir, European Fighter Aircraft, 1986–89; rcds 1990; Hd, Civilian Mgt (Specialists) 2, 1991–92; Dir, Ops an Engrg, NATO European Fighter Aircraft Mgt Agency, 1992–96; Chief Exec., Specialis Procurement Services, 1996–99; Dir Gen., Human Resources, Defence Logistics Orgr 1999–2001; Dir Gen., Scrutiny and Analysis, 2001–05. *Recreations:* cricket, ski-ing, practica study of wine.

BENNETT, Rear Adm. Paul Martin, OBE 2007; Chief of Staff Joint Forces Command since 2013; *b* Newcastle-under-Lyme, 3 Aug. 1964; *s* of John and Helen Bennett; *m* 198 Kay Sutherland; two *d*. *Educ:* Hymers Coll., Hull; Univ. of Newcastle upon Tyne (BA Hon Hist. 1985). BRNC, Dartmouth, 1985–86; HMS Hermione, 1986–87; HMS Cygnet 1987–88; Dep. Ops Officer (Sen. Naval Officer), NI, 1988–89; HMS Birmingham, 1989–92 Commanding Officer: HMS Biter and Manchester Univ. RN Unit, 1992–93; HMS Dryad 1993–94; HMS Atherstone, 1996–98; HMS Exeter, 1998–2000; Fleet Ops Officer, 2000–02 Hd Maritime, Directorate of Operational Capability, 2002–03; Dep. ACOS, Above Water 2003–06; hcsc 2007; Multi-nat. Security Transition Team, Baghdad, 2007; Comdg Officer HMS Daring, 2008–09; Comdr, Amphibious Task Gp, 2009–11; Dir, Naval Personne Strategy, 2011–13; Dir, Develt Concepts and Doctrine Centre, MoD, 2013. Younge Brother, Trinity Hse, 2010–. Liveryman, Carpenters' Co., 2012–. *Recreations:* mountai biking, road biking, traditional rowing, sailing. *Address:* Headquarters Joint Forces Command Northwood Headquarters, Sandy Lane, Northwood, Middx HA6 3HP. *E:* paul.bennett531@ mod.uk.

BENNETT, Penelope Anne; Commissioner for Health and Social Care, South Wes Region, Appointments Commission (formerly NHS Appointments Commission), 2003–12 *b* 5 June 1956; *d* of late Peter Atherton Pettican-Runnicles and of Dorothy Isabel Pettican Runnicles (*née* Grover); *m* 1982, John David Bennett; three *d*. *Educ:* West Hatch, Chigwell Hatfield Poly. (BSc Hons); Open Univ. (MBA). Admitted as solicitor, 1982; solicitor i private practice, 1982–95; non-exec. Dir and Vice Chm., 1995–98, Chm., 1998–2002, Glos NHS Trust; non-exec. Dir and Vice Chm., Avon, Glos and Wilts Strategic HA 2002–04. Ind. Mem., Standards Cttee, Cotswold DC, 2001–10. Gp Bd Dir, Chm., Audi Cttee and Trustee, Hanover Housing Assoc., 2004–11. *Recreations:* family life, travel, walking reading, gardening. *Address:* 11 St Peters Road, Cirencester, Glos GL7 1RE. *T:* (01285 640691.

BENNETT, Peter Gordon, FRICS; City Surveyor, City of London Corporation, sinc 2008; *m* 1973, Janetta Hall; two *s* one *d*. *Educ:* Fitzwilliam Coll., Cambridge (BA Geog. 1970) Chartered Surveyor, 1977. FRICS 1989. Res. Officer, Wool, Jute and Flax Trng Bc 1970–72; Valuer, Valuation Office, Bd of Inland Revenue, 1972–76; Valuer, then Sen. Mg Surveyor, Bradford CC, 1976–85; Dep. City Estate Agent, 1985–88, City Estate Agent an Valuer, 1988–90, Swansea CC; Dep. City Surveyor, Corp. of London, subseq. City c London Corp., 1990–2008. Perm. Mem., Bank of England Property Forum, 2002–. Mem. London Council, CBI, 2004–08. First Chm., London Reg., RICS, 2001–04. Charit Trustee, Royal Grammar Sch., High Wycombe, 2003–. Liveryman, Chartered Surveyors Co., 2009–. *Recreations:* Rugby, opera, gardening. *Address:* City of London Corporation, PC Box 270, Guildhall, EC2P 2EJ. *T:* (020) 7332 1502, *Fax:* (020) 7322 3955. *E:* peter.bennett@ cityoflondon.gov.uk.

BENNETT, Gen. Sir Phillip (Harvey), AC 1985 (AO 1981); KBE 1983; DSO 1969 Chairman, Australian War Memorial Foundation, 1996–2003; National President, Order o Australia Association, 1997–2000; *b* 27 Dec. 1928; *m* 1955, Margaret Heywood; two *s* one *d* *Educ:* Perth Modern Sch.; Royal Mil. Coll.; jssc, rcds, psc (Aust.). Served, 1950–57: 3rd Bn RAR, Korea (despatches 1951), Sch. of Infantry (Instr), 25 Cdn Bde, Korea, 1952–53, Pacifi Is Regt, PNG, and 16th Bn Cameron Highlanders of WA; Commando training, Roya Marines, England, Malta and Cyprus, 1957–58; OC 2 Commando Co., Melb., 1958–61 Aust. Staff Coll., 1961–62; Sen. Instr, then Chief Instr, Officer Cadet Sch., Portsea, 1962–65 AAG Directorate of Personal Services, AHQ, 1965–67; Co. 1 RAR, 1967–69 (serve Vietnam; DSO); Exchange Instr, Jt Services Staff Coll., England, 1969–71; COL Directorat of Co-ordination and Organization, AHQ, 1971–73; COS HQ Fd Force Comd, 1974–75 RCDS, England, 1976; Comdr 1st Div., 1977–79; Asst Chief of Def. Force Staff, 1979–82 Chief of General Staff, 1982–84; Chief of Defence Force, Australia, 1984–87; Governor Tasmania, 1987–95. Hon. Col, Royal Tasmania Regt, 1987–95. KStJ 1988. Hon. LLD: Nev South Wales, 1987; Tasmania, 1992. *Recreations:* reading, golf. *Address:* c/o Commonwealt Club, ACT 2600, Australia. *Clubs:* Commonwealth, University House (Canberra).

BENNETT, Ralph Featherstone; *b* 3 Dec. 1923; *o s* of late Mr and Mrs Ralph J. P. Bennett Plymouth, Devon; *m* 1948, Delia Marie, *o d* of late Mr and Mrs J. E. Baxter, Franklyns Plymouth; two *s* two *d*. *Educ:* Plympton Grammar Sch.; Plymouth Technical Coll. Article pupil to City of Plymouth Transport Manager, 1940–43; Techn. Asst, Plymouth City Transp. 1943–54; Michelin Tyre Co., 1954–55; Dep. Gen. Man., City of Plymouth Transp. Dept 1955–58; Gen. Manager: Gt Yarmouth Transp. Dept, 1958–60; Bolton Transp. Dept 1960–65; Manchester City Transp., 1965–68; London Transport Executive (formerly Londo Transport Board): Mem., 1968–71; Dep. Chm., 1971–78; Chief Exec., 1975–78; Chairman London Transport Executive, 1978–80; London Transport International, 1976–80. Pres. Confedn of Road Passenger Transport, 1977–78; Vice-President: Internat. Union of Publi Transport, 1978–81; CIT, 1979–82. CEng; FIMechE; FCILT; FRSA. *Address:* 12 The Beeches, Harrowbeer Lane, Yelverton, Devon PL20 6EF. *T:* (01822) 853269.

BENNETT, His Honour Raymond Clayton Watson; a Circuit Judge, 1989–2004; *b* 2 June 1939; *s* of Harold Watson and Doris Helena Bennett (previously Watson); *m* 1965, Elain Margaret Haworth; one *s* one *d*. *Educ:* Bury Grammar Sch.; Manchester Univ. (LLB) Solicitor, 1964–72; called to the Bar, Middle Temple, 1972; practising barrister, 1972–89; a Asst Recorder, 1984; a Recorder, 1988. Hon. Recorder, Burnley, 1998–2004. *Recreations* reading, painting, golf.

BENNETT, Richard Charles; Deputy Director, High Speed Rail programme, Departmen for Transport, since 2013; *b* 8 Sept. 1958; *s* of Ben and Cynthia Bennett. *Educ:* Bristo Grammar Sch.; Christ's Coll., Cambridge (MA). Joined Dept of Transport, 1983; variou roles, incl. internat. aviation, streetworks and investigation into King's Cross fire; Private Sec to Minister of State for Transport, 1984–85; Railways Div., 1993–96, Finance Div., 1996–99 Dept of Transport, later DETR; Divl Manager, 1999–2001, Dir, 2001–03, London Underground Task Gp, DTLR, later DfT; Corporate Dir, Highways Agency, 2003–05 Department for Transport: Shared Services Prog. Manager, 2006–07; Hd of Ports Div. 2007–10; Hd of Maritime Commerce and Infrastructure, 2011–12. *Address:* High Speed Rail Department for Transport, Zone 3/13, Great Minster House, 33 Horseferry Road, SW1P 4DR. *E:* richard.bennett@dft.gsi.gov.uk.

BENNETT, Richard Ernest Tulloch; Group General Counsel, HSBC Holdings plc, since 2010; *b* at sea on SS Corfu, 20 Sept. 1951; *s* of Norman Bennett and June Bennett; *m* 1977 Helen M. Tailby; two *s*. *Educ:* Haileybury; Univ. of Bristol (LLB 1973). Admitted solicitor England and Wales, 1976, Hong Kong, 1979, Victoria, Australia, 1984; Asst Solicitor Stephenson Harwood, 1976–79; Hongkong and Shanghai Banking Corporation, later HSBC Holdings plc: Asst Gp Legal Advr, 1979–88; Dep. Gp Legal Advr, 1988–92; Hd, Legal and Compliance, Asia Pacific, 1993–97; Gp Gen. Manager, Legal and Compliance, 1998–2010 Treas., Assoc. of Gen. Counsel and Co. Secs of FTSE 100, 2005–10. Member, Organising Committee: Hong Kong Sevens, 1983–96; Rugby World Cup Sevens, 1997; Pres., Penguins Internat. RFC, 2010. *Recreations:* sport (Rugby and golf), wine. *Address:* HSBC Holdings plc

8 Canada Square, E14 5HQ. *Clubs:* Liphook Golf; Hong Kong (Chm., 1996–97), Hong Kong Golf, Sheko Country (Hong Kong).

BENNETT, Prof. Robert John, PhD; FBA 1991; Professor of Geography, University of Cambridge, 1996–2010, now Emeritus; Fellow of St Catharine's College, Cambridge, 1996–2010, now Emeritus; *b* 23 March 1948; *s* of Thomas Edward Bennett and Kathleen Elizabeth Robson; *m* 1971, Elizabeth Anne Allen; two *s*. *Educ:* Taunton's Sch., Southampton; St Catharine's Coll., Cambridge (BA 1970; PhD 1974). Lecturer: University Coll. London, 1973–78; Univ. of Cambridge, 1978–85; Fellow and Dir of Studies, 1978–85, Tutor, 1981–85, Fitzwilliam Coll., Cambridge; Prof. of Geography, LSE, 1985–96. Leverhulme Personal Res. Prof., 1996–2000. Vis. Prof., Univ. California at Berkeley, 1978; Guest Schol., Brookings Instn, Washington DC, 1978, 1979, 1981; Hubert Humphrey Inst. Fellow, Univ. Minnesota, 1985; Univ. Fellow, Macquarie, 1987; Snyder Lectr, Toronto, 1988. Treas., IBG, 1990–93; Vice Pres., RGS, 1993–95 and 1998–2001 (Mem. Council, 1990–2001); Chm., Council of British Geography, 1995–2000; Vice Pres. and Res. Chm., British Acad., 2001–08. Vice Pres., Inst. of Small Business and Entrepreneurship, 2004–07. Mem., Res. Awards Adv. Panel, Leverhulme Trust, 2000–07. MInstD. Murchison Award, 1982, Founder's Medal, 1998, RGS. Co-editor, Government and Policy, 2008– (Gen. Editor, 1982–2008); European Co-Editor, Geographical Analysis, 1985–88. *Publications:* Environmental Systems (with R. J. Chorley), 1978; Spatial Time Series, 1979; Geography of Public Finance, 1980; (ed) European Progress in Spatial Analysis, 1981; (ed with N. Wrigley) Quantitative Geography, 1981; Central Grants to Local Government, 1982; (with K. C. Tan) Optimal Control of Spatial Systems, 1984; Intergovernmental Financial Relations in Austria, 1985; (with A. G. Wilson) Mathematical Methods in Human Geography and Planning, 1985; (ed with H. Zimmermann) Local Business Taxes in Britain and Germany, 1986; (with G. Krebs) Die Wirkung Kommunaler Steuern auf die Steuerliche Belastung der Kapitalbildung, 1987; (with G. Krebs) Local Business Taxes in Britain and Germany, 1988; (ed) Territory and Administration in Europe, 1989; (ed) Decentralisation, Local Governments and Markets, 1990; (with G. Krebs) Local Economic Development Initiatives in Britain and Germany, 1991; (ed with R. C. Estall) Global Change and Challenge, 1991; (with A. McCoshan) Enterprise and Human Resource Development, 1993; (jtly) Local Empowerment and Business Services, 1994; (with G. Krebs and H. Zimmermann) Chambers of Commerce in Britain and Germany, 1994; (ed) Trade Associations in Britain and Germany, 1997; (with D. Payne) Local and Regional Economic Development, 2000; The Voice of Liverpool Business: the first chamber of commerce 1774–1796, 2010; Local Business Voice: the history of chambers of commerce 1760–2011, 2011; Entrepreneurship, Small Business and Public Policy: evolution and revolution, 2014. *Recreations:* the family, genealogy. *Address:* c/o Department of Geography, University of Cambridge, Downing Place, Cambridge CB2 3EN.

BENNETT, Robin; adult educator; *b* 6 Nov. 1934; *s* of James Arthur Bennett, Major RA, and Alice Edith Bennett, Ipswich; *m* 1st, 1962, Patricia Ann Lloyd (marr. diss. 1991); one *s* one *d*; 2nd, 1992, Margaret Jane Allen. *Educ:* Northgate Grammar School, Ipswich; St John's Coll., Univ. of Durham (BA 1958); Queen's Coll., and Univ. of Birmingham (Dip Th 1960); MEd Birmingham 1987. Ordained deacon, 1960, priest, 1961; curate, Prittlewell, Essex and Plaistow, 1960–65; incumbencies in Canning Town and Loughton, Essex, 1966–75, and Bletchingdon, Oxon, 1976–79; appts in C of E adult educn, incl. Dir, Oxford Inst. for Church and Soc. and Urban Ministry Project, 1974–78, Principal, Aston Training Scheme, 1977–82, Adult Educn Officer, Gen. Synod Bd of Educn, 1983–85; Archdeacon of Dudley, 1985–86; left C of E, 1986. Vice-Principal, Clapham Battersea Adult Educn Inst., ILEA, 1986–89; Dep. Principal, Wandsworth Adult Coll., 1989–95; Teacher, HMP Belmarsh, 1995–97. Joined Soc. of Friends, 1988. Mem. (Lab), Ludlow Town Council, 1999–2003. Clerk: Quaker Cttee for Racial Equality, 1998–2004, Quaker Cttee for Christian and Interfaith Relations, 2009–12 (Mem., 2007–12); Quaker Liby Cttee, 2010–12 (Trustee, 2008–12); Quaker Mem., Churches Commn for Racial Justice, 1998–2005; Mem., Meeting for Sufferings, 2009–12. Governor: Fircroft Coll., 1983–99; Ludlow County Jun. Sch., 1999–2010. Trustee: Woodbrooke Quaker Study Centre, 1998–2000; Rockspring Trust, Ludlow, 1998–2004; Ludlow and Dist Community Assoc., 1999–2005 (Chm., 2001–05); Gallows Bank Millennium Green, Ludlow, 1999–2014 (Chm., 2000–07); S Shropshire Furniture Scheme, 2011–14. *Recreations:* travel, music, football, family. *Address:* 115 Kings Road, Bury St Edmunds, Suffolk IP33 3DS. *T:* (01284) 719299. *E:* robinsuffolk@icloud.com.

BENNETT, Sir Ronald (Wilfred Murdoch), 3rd Bt *cr* 1929; *b* 25 March 1930; *o s* of Sir Wilfred Bennett, 2nd Bt, and Marion Agnes, OBE (*d* 1985), *d* of late James Somervell, Sorn Castle, Ayrshire, and step *d* of late Edwin Sandys Dawes; *S* father, 1952; *m* 1st, 1953, Rose-Marie Audrey Patricia, *o d* of Major A. L. J. H. Aubépin, France and Co. Mayo, Ireland; two *d*; 2nd, 1968, Anne, *d* of late Leslie George Tooker; *m* 3rd. *Educ:* Wellington Coll.; Trinity Coll., Oxford. *Heir: cousin* Mark Edward Francis Bennett [*b* 5 April 1960; *m* 1995, Jayne M. Jensen (marr. diss. 1998)]. *Clubs:* Kampala, Uganda (Kampala).

BENNETT, Timothy Mark; Acting Chairman, Food Standards Agency, since 2013 (Board Member, since 2007; Deputy Chairman, 2012–13); *b* Old Hill, Staffs, 18 July 1953; *s* of Roy Bennett and Betty Bennett; *m* 1976, Susan Elizabeth Davies; one *s* one *d*. *Educ:* Halesowen Grammar Sch.; Seale Hayne Agricultural Coll. (Dip. 1973). Farmer, nr Carmarthen, 1978–. Pres., NFU, 2004–06 (Dep. Pres., 1998–2004); Vice Pres., COPA, 2005–06; Chm., DairyCo, 2007–14. Member: Agricl Land Tribunal (Wales), 1990–; Policy Issues Council, Inst. of Grocery Distribution, 2004–06; Agricl and Horticl Develt Bd, 2007–13; Trustee, Farming and Wildlife Adv. Gp, 2008–10. FRAGS 2010. *Recreations:* reading, gardening, walking, West Bromwich Albion Football Club. *Address:* Derwendeg Farm, Maesybont, Llanelli, Carmarthenshire SA14 7HG. *T:* (01558) 668238. *E:* bennett-tim@btconnect.com. *Club:* Farmers.

BENNETT, Vivienne Jane; Chief Nurse, Public Health England, and Principal Adviser to Government on Public Health Nursing, since 2015; *b* London, 24 Sept. 1957; *d* of Anthony and Jean Willis; *m* 1978, Timothy Bennett; one *s* one *d*. *Educ:* Wheatley Park Sch.; Oxford Sch. of Nursing (RGN); Oxford Poly. (HVCert); Open Univ. (BA); Sch. of Advanced Urban Studies, Bristol Univ. (MSc Health and Social Policy). Nurse, 1979–; Health Visitor, 1981–; Dir of Nursing, S Warks Combined Care Trust, 2000–02, S Warks PCT, 2002–07; Dep. Chief Nursing Officer, 2007–12, Dir of Nursing, 2012–15, DoH; Dir of Nursing, PHE, 2013–15. Vis. Prof., KCL, 2011–. Fellow: Queen's Nursing Inst., 2009; Inst. of Health Visiting, 2013. Hon. FKC 2013. Hon. DBA Coventry, 2012; Hon. LLD Bristol, 2015. *Recreations:* power walking, travel. *Address:* Public Health England, Wellington House, 133–155 Waterloo Road, SE1 8UG.

BENNETT, Hon. William Richards, OBC 2007; PC (Can.) 1982; Premier of British Columbia, 1975–86; *b* 14 April 1932; *y s* of late Hon. William Andrew Cecil Bennett, PC (Can.) and of Annie Elizabeth May Richards; *m* 1955, Audrey Lyne, *d* of late Jack James; four *s*. Began a business career. Elected MP for Okanagan South (succeeding to a constituency which had been held by his father), 1973; Leader of Social Credit Group in Provincial House, 1973; formed Social Credit Govt after election of Dec. 1975. Hon. Dr Justice Inst. of British Columbia, 2011.

BENNETT, Zai; Director, Sky Atlantic, since 2014; *b* London, 5 May 1974; *s* of Alan Bennett and Raesa Nursey (*née* Lycholit); *m* 2007, Penny White; one *s* one *d*. *Educ:* Goffs Sch., Cheshunt; Queen Mary Coll., Univ. of London (BA Hist. and Politics; MA Contemp. British Hist.). Scheduler: Carlton TV, 1996–97; Channel 5, 1997–98; Planning Manager, ITV2, 1998–2001; Hd of Programme Strategy Digital Channels, ITV, 2001–06; Controller, ITV2, 2006–09; Dir, Digital Channels and Acquisitions, ITV, 2009–11; Controller, BBC Three, 2011–14. *Recreation:* impersonating primates for children. *Address:* c/o Sky Broadcasting, 1st Floor, The Hub, Grant Way, Isleworth TW7 5QD.

BENNETT-JONES, Peter, CBE 2014; Chairman: PBJ Management, since 1988; KBJ Management, since 2000; Burning Bright Productions, since 2012; *b* 11 March 1955; *s* of late Dr Nicholas and of Ruth Bennett-Jones; *m* 1990, Alison E. Watts; two *s* one *d*. *Educ:* Winchester Coll.; Magdalene Coll., Cambridge (MA Law). Director: Oxford and Cambridge Shakespeare Co. Ltd, 1977–82; Pola Jones Assocs, 1977–82; Managing Director: Talkback, 1982–86; Corporate Communications Consultants Ltd, 1986–88; Chairman: Tiger Television, 1988–2011; Tiger Aspect Prodns, 1993–2011; Tiger Aspect Pictures, 1999–2011. Production credits include: Mr Bean; The Vicar of Dibley; Harry Enfield; Billy Elliot; Our House (Olivier Award, 2003). Chm., Comic Relief, 1998–2013. Member: Council, RADA, 2007–10; Bd, RNT, 2010–. Gov., Rugby Sch., 2009–; Trustee: Arnold Foundn, 2007– (Chm., 2009–); Liverpool Playhouse-Everyman, 2014–; Save the Children (UK), 2015–. FRTS 2009. Hon Fellow, Bangor Univ., 2008. Special Award, BAFTA, 2011; Lifetime Achievement Award, RTS, 2011. Hon. Golden Rose of Montreux, 1999. *Recreation:* simply messing about in boats. *Address:* (office) 22 Rathbone Street, W1T 1LG; 8 Rawlinson Road, Oxford OX2 6UE. *T:* (01865) 515414. *Clubs:* Oxford and Cambridge, Groucho, Soho House.

BENNETTS, Denise Margaret Mary; Co-Founder and Director, Bennetts Associates Architects, since 1987; *b* 26 Jan. 1953; *d* of James and Agnes Smith; *m* 1974, Robert John, (Rab), Bennetts, *qv*; one *s* one *d*. *Educ:* Heriot-Watt Univ./Edinburgh Coll. of Art (BArch Hons 1976; DipArch 1977). RIBA 1979. Casson Conder Partnership, 1978–88. Major projects include: Brighton Central Liby; Wessex Water Operations Centre, Bath; BT Headquarters, Edinburgh; Hampstead Th., London. Assessor: Civic Trust Awards, 1997–; RIBA Awards, 2005. *Address:* Bennetts Associates Architects, 1 Rawstorne Place, EC1V 7NL. *T:* (020) 7520 3300, *Fax:* (020) 7520 3333. *E:* denise.bennetts@bennettsassociates.com.

BENNETTS, Philip James; QC 2011; a Principal Crown Advocate, since 2009; *b* Weiburg, Germany, 10 June 1962; *s* of Col Michael Bennetts and Bridget Bron-Bennetts; *m* 1994, Jill Mathews; one *s* one *d*. *Educ:* Kingswood Sch.; Brunel Univ. (LLB Hons). Called to the Bar, Lincoln's Inn, 1986; in practice as a barrister, QEB Hollis Whiteman Chambers, 1988–2009. *Recreations:* riding, shooting, long distance running. *E:* philip.bennetts@cps.gsi.gov.uk.

BENNETTS, Robert John, (Rab), OBE 2003; Co-Founder and Director, Bennetts Associates Architects, since 1987; *b* 14 April 1953; *s* of Frank Vivian Bennetts and Frances Mary Bennetts; *m* 1974, Denise Margaret Mary Smith (*see* D. M. M. Bennetts); one *s* one *d*. *Educ:* Heriot-Watt Univ./Edinburgh Coll. of Art (BArch Hons 1976; DipArch 1977). RIBA 1979. Architect, Arup Associates, 1977–87. Major projects include: Powergen HQ, 1994; Wessex Water Offices, 2000; Hampstead Th., 2003; Brighton Central Liby, 2005; New Street Square, City of London, 2003; Royal Shakespeare Th., Stratford upon Avon, 2005; Edinburgh Univ. Informatics Forum. Member: Movt for Innovation Bd, DTI, 1999–2002; Planning Cttee, Islington LBC, 2000–03; Strategic Forum for Construction, Olympic Task Gp, 2005–; Bd, UK Green Bldg Council, 2007–; CABE, 2010–11; Trustee, Design Council CABE, 2011–. Chm., Competitions Cttee, RIBA, 1995–98. Dir, Sadler's Wells Th., 2006–15. Contribs to BBC Radio culture progs. *Publications:* (contrib.) The Commercial Offices Handbook, 2003; Bennetts Associates - Four Commentaries, 2005. *Recreations:* travel (especially with family), drawings, arts generally, watching football (Arsenal) and attempting to play. *Address:* Bennetts Associates Architects, 1 Rawstorne Place, EC1V 7NL. *T:* (020) 7520 3300, *Fax:* (020) 7520 3333. *E:* rab.bennetts@bennettsassociates.com. *Club:* Architecture.

BENNION, Phillip; Member (Lib Dem) West Midlands Region, European Parliament, Feb. 2012–2014; *b* Tamworth, 7 Oct. 1954; *m* 2000, Penny Foord. *Educ:* Queen Elizabeth Grammar Sch.; Aberdeen Univ. (BSc Agricl Botany); Newcastle Univ. (PhD Agronomy); Birmingham Univ. (BA 1st Cl. Hist. and Econ. and Social Hist.). Arable farmer, Staffs, 1985–. Member (Lib Dem): Lichfield DC, 1999–2011; Staffs CC, 2002–05. Mem., Oilseeds R&D Cttee, 1996–2002, Combinable Crops R&D Cttee, 2005–11, Cereals and Oilseeds Div., Agriculture and Horticulture Develt Bd. Vice Chm., Staffs Rural Forum, 2003–09; Founding Chm., Staffs Rural Hub, 2004–09. Contested (Lib Dem): W Midlands, EP, 2014; Birmingham Hodge Hill, 2015.

BENSBERG, Mark; HM Diplomatic Service; Ambassador to Côte d'Ivoire, since 2014; *b* 19 July 1962; *s* of Anthony Charles Bensberg and Ann Bensberg; *m* 1991, Jacqueline Margaret Campbell; one *d*. *Educ:* Tiffin Sch. Entered FCO, 1980; Paris, 1982–85; Africa/ME floater, 1985–88; Vice-Consul, Vienna, 1988–91; FCO, 1991–94; Accra, 1994–97; Second Sec., Brussels, 1997–2000; FCO, 2000–04; Dep. Hd of Mission, Kinshasa, 2004–06; High Commissioner, Namibia, 2007–11; Dep. Dir, Estates and Security Directorate, FCO, 2011–14. *Recreations:* cooking, photography, shooting, ski-ing. *Address:* c/o Foreign and Commonwealth Office, King Charles Street, SW1A 2AH.

BENSON, Charles Jefferis Woodburn; QC 2010; barrister; Proprietor: Benson Ingram Law LLP; Praxis Professional Services Ltd; *b* Salisbury, Wilts, 28 Feb. 1962; *s* of Sir Christopher (John) Benson, *qv*. *Educ:* Cheltenham Coll.; Dundee Univ. (BBA Hons 1985); Wolfson Coll., Cambridge (BA Tripos 1987; LLM 1988). Called to the Bar, Middle Temple, 1990; in practice as barrister, specialising in commercial and quasi criminal law, civil and criminal recovery. Member: Amnesty Internat.; Liberty; Bar Pro Bono Unit. Freeman: City of London; Watermen and Lightermen's Co., 2006. *Publications:* Marine Environmental Law (with John Bates), 1993. *Recreations:* fishing, river restoration, Greek language and culture, boating, travel, literature and poetry (especially Russian), film, cinema, cat lover, being outdoors. *Address:* Benson Ingram Law LLP, 42–44 Bishopsgate, EC2N 4AH; Goldsmith Chambers, Goldsmith Building, Temple, EC4Y 7BL. *E:* charles.bensonqc@bensoningram.com.

BENSON, Sir Christopher (John), Kt 1988; DL; FRICS; Chairman: Cross London Rail Links Ltd, 2001–04; Salisbury Vision, 2009–13; Director, Eredene Capital plc, 2006–13; *b* 20 July 1933; *s* of Charles Woodburn Benson and Catherine Clara (*née* Bishton); *m* 1960, Margaret Josephine, OBE, JP, DL, *d* of Ernest Jefferies Bundy; two *s*. *Educ:* Worcester Cathedral King's Sch.; Thames Nautical Trng Coll., HMS Worcester. FRICS. Cadet, Union Castle Mail Steamship Co. (Midshipman, RNR, 1949–51); Ordinary Seaman, RN, 1951–52; Sub-Lieut, RNVR, 1952–56. Chartered surveyor and agricl auctioneer, Worcs, Herefords, Wilts, Dorset, Hants, 1953–64; Dir, Arndale Develts Ltd, 1965–69; Chm., Dolphin Develts Ltd, 1969–71; Man. Dir, 1976–88, Chm., 1988–93, MEPC; Chairman: The Boots Company, 1990–94 (Dir, 1989–94); Sun Alliance Gp, 1993–96 (Dir, 1988; Dep. Chm., 1992–93); Costain plc, 1993–96; Albright & Wilson, 1995–99; Dep. Chm., Thorn Lighting Gp, 1994–98. Dir, House of Fraser plc, 1982–86; Chm., Reedpack Ltd, 1989–90. Chairman: LDDC, 1984–88; Housing Corp., 1990–94; Funding Agency for Schs, 1994–97. Pres., British Property Fedn, 1981–83; Chm., Property Adv. Gp to DoE, 1988–90; Pres., London Chamber of Commerce and Industry, 2000–01 (Hon. Vice Pres., 2001–); Mem. Council, CBI, 1990–97. Mem., Adv. Bd, Cathedral plc, 2013–. Dir, Royal Opera House, 1984–92. Chm., Britain-Australia Soc., 2007–09 (Chm., Educn Trust, 2012–). Chm., Civic Trust, 1985–90; Trustee: Metropolitan Police Museum, 1986–2011; Sea Cadets Assoc., 2002–05; Marine Soc. and Sea Cadets, 2005–09 (Hon. Vice Pres., 2009–); Vice Pres., Macmillan Cancer Relief (formerly Cancer Relief Macmillan Fund), 1991–; Pres.'s Rep. Vice Pres., RSA, 1992–97; Pres., Nat. Deaf Children's Soc., 1995–; Chm., Coram (formerly Coram Family), 2005–08

(Hon. Vice Pres., 2008–). Patron: Changing Faces, 1993–; River Bourne Community Farm, 2010–; Friends of Erlestoke Prison, 2012–. Mem. Council, Marlborough Coll., 1982–90; Gov., Inns of Court Sch. of Law, 1996–2001 (Principal, 2000–01). Freeman: City of London, 1975; Co. of Watermen and Lightermen, 1985 (Master, 2004–05); Liveryman: Co. of Gold and Silver Wyre Drawers, 1975; Hon. Co. of Air Pilots (formerly GAPAN), 1981; Co. of Chartered Surveyors, 1984; Associate, Co. of Master Mariners, 2012–. High Sheriff of Wilts, 2002. DL Greater London, 2005. Lay Canon, Salisbury Cathedral, 2000–10. FRSA 1984. Hon. FRCPath 1992; Hon. FCIOB 1992. Hon. Fellow: Wolfson Coll., Cambridge, 1990; Univ. of Southampton, 2014. Hon. Bencher, Middle Temple, 1984. Hon. DSc: City, 2000; Bradford, 2001. *Recreations:* farming, aviation, opera, ballet. *Address:* 2, 50 South Audley Street, W1K 2QE. *T:* (020) 7629 2398. *E:* sircjbenson@me.com. *Clubs:* Garrick, Oxford and Cambridge.

See also C. J. W. Benson.

BENSON, David Holford; Senior Adviser, Fleming Family & Partners, since 2002; *b* 26 Feb. 1938; *s* of Sir Rex Benson, DSO, MVO, MC, and Lady Leslie Foster Benson; *m* 1964, Lady Elizabeth Mary Charteris, *d* of 12th Earl of Wemyss and March, KT; one *s* two *d*. *Educ:* Eton Coll.; Madrid. CIGEM (CIGasE 1989). Shell Transport & Trading, 1957–63; Kleinwort Benson Gp, subseq. Dresdner Kleinwort Benson Gp, 1963–2004: Vice-Chm., 1989–92; non-exec. Dir, 1992–98; Chm., Charter European Trust, 1992–2003. Non-executive Director: Rouse Co., 1987–2004; BG Group plc (formerly British Gas), 1988–2004; Dover Corp., 1995–2014; Daniel Thwaites plc, 1998–2006; Murray Internat. Investment Trust, 2000–09; Vice Chm., Leach Internat. (formerly Leach Relais), 1992–2004. Chairman: COIF Charities Funds (formerly Charities Official Investment Fund), 1984–2005; Trustees, Edward James Foundn, 2002–11 (Trustee, 1996–2011); Fleming-Wyfold Art Foundn, 2010–; Trustee, UK Historic Bldg Preservation Trust, 1996–2001. *Recreation:* painting. *Address:* Fleming Family & Partners, 15 Suffolk Street, SW1Y 4HG; Cucumber Farm, Singleton, Chichester, W Sussex PO18 0HG. *Clubs:* White's, English-Speaking Union.

BENSON, Ven. George Patrick; Archdeacon of Hereford, since 2011; *b* Derby, 26 June 1949; *s* of George and Barbara Benson; *m* 1974, Eleanor Silver; one *s* two *d*. *Educ:* Bemrose Sch., Derby; Leighton Park Sch., Reading; Christ Church, Oxford (BA 1970); Trinity Coll., Bristol (BD Univ. of London 1977); All Nations Christian Coll., St John's Coll., Nottingham; Open Univ. (MPhil 1994). Editl Asst, Marcham Manor Press, 1971–74; Dir of Academic Studies, St Andrew's Coll., Kabare, Kenya, 1979–86; Publications Sec. and Dir of Communications, Dio. of Mt Kenya East, 1987–89; ordained deacon, 1991, priest, 1992; Curate, St Mary Upton, Wirral, 1991–95; Vicar, Christ Church, Barnston, Wirral, 1995–2010. Hon. Canon, Chester, 2009, Emeritus, 2011. *Publications:* (ed) Origen as Apologist by Dora Pym; numerous chapters in works on mission theology and politics in Kenya; contrib. to Expository Times, Evangelical Fellowship in the Anglican Communion Bulletin. *Recreations:* gardening, walking, following Derby County and Tranmere Rovers. *Address:* Diocesan Office, The Palace, Hereford HR4 9BL. *T:* (01432) 373300. *E:* archdeacon@hereford.anglican.org.

BENSON, Glenwyn; Creative Lead, BBC response to OFCOM review of Public Service Broadcasting, 2007–09; *b* 23 Nov. 1947; *d* of late Tudor David, OBE and Nancy David; *m* 1973, Dr Ian Anthony Benson; one *s* one *d*. *Educ:* Nonsuch County Grammar Sch. for Girls, Cheam; Girton Coll., Cambridge (MA); Harvard Univ. (Frank Knox Fellow). Dep. Editor, Weekend World, LWT, 1986–88; BBC: Editor: On the Record, 1990–92; Panorama, 1992–95; Head: of Commng, Adult Educn, 1995–97; of Science, 1997–2000; Controller, Specialist Factual, 2000–01; Jt Dir, Factual and Learning, 2001–03; Mem., Exec. Cttee, 2001–03; Controller, BBC Knowledge (formerly Factual TV), 2003–07. Mem., RTS, 2005–. Gov., Nat. Film and Television Sch., 2001–09. FRSA. Hon. FRTS 2008. *Recreations:* gardening, music.

BENSON, Gordon Mitchell, OBE 2000; RA 2000; FRIAS; Partner, Benson+Forsyth, architects, established 1978; *b* 5 Oct. 1946; *s* of William Benson and Gavina Dewar (*née* Mitchell); one *s* one *d*. *Educ:* Univ. of Strathclyde; Architectural Assoc. Sch. of Architecture (AA Dip). SADG; FRIAS; ARIBA. London housing projects, Camden Council, 1968–78. Prof. of Architecture, Strathclyde Univ., 1986–90; Vis. Prof., Edinburgh Univ., 1991–96. Mem., Royal Fine Art Commn for Scotland, 1993. *Built work:* Branch Hill Housing, 1974; Mansfield Rd Housing, 1975; Lambie St Housing, 1975; Maiden Lane, 1976; Marico Furniture Workshop and Residence, 1979; Boarbank Oratory, 1985; Physio Room, Cumbria, 1986; Pavilion, Glasgow Garden Fest., 1989; Machi Nakao: The Divided House, Jyohanna Mus., Japan, 1994; Gall. 22 Admin Bldg, Mus. of Scotland, 1997; Mus. of Scotland, 1998; extension, Nat. Gall. of Ireland, 2000. Has won numerous awards and competitions incl. Lifetime Achievement Award, Scottish Design Awards, 2011. *Publications:* contribs to Scotsman, Daily Telegraph, Sunday Times and professional jls incl. Architectural Rev., Architects Jl, Bldg Design, RIBA Jl, RSA Jl and overseas architectural jls. *Address:* (office) 37D Mildmay Grove North, N1 4RH. *T:* (020) 7359 0288.

BENSON, James, OBE 2003; President, James Benson Associates Inc., since 1987; *b* 17 July 1925; *s* of Henry Herbert Benson and Olive Benson (*née* Hutchinson); *m* 1950, Honoria Margaret Hurley; one *d*. *Educ:* Bromley Grammar Sch., Kent; Emmanuel Coll., Cambridge (MA). RN, 1943–46 (Midget Subs (X-craft) and Minesweepers). Manager, Res. and Promotion, Kemsley Newspapers, 1948–58; Dir, Mather & Crowther, 1959–65; Man. Dir, 1966–69, Chm., 1970–71 and 1975–78, Ogilvy & Mather Ltd; Vice-Chm., The Ogilvy Group (formerly Ogilvy & Mather Internat.) Inc., 1971–87. Chm. Emeritus, American Associates of the Royal Acad. Trust, 2001– (Chm., 1983–2001); Trustee, Royal Medical Benevolent Fund, 2001–. *Publications:* Above Us The Waves, 1953; The Admiralty Regrets, 1956; Will Not We Fear, 1961; The Broken Column, 1966; Silent Unseen, 1995. *Recreations:* swimming, walking, painting, reading. *Address:* 64 Harley House, Regent's Park, NW1 5HL.

BENSON, Jeremy Keith; QC 2001; a Recorder, since 1997; *b* 17 Jan. 1953; *s* of Jack Henry Benson and Renee Esther Benson; *m* 1985, Dr Karen Judith Silkoff; two *s* one *d*. *Educ:* City of London Sch.; Essex Univ. (BA Hons 1973); St Peter's Coll., Saltley, Birmingham (PGCE 1974). Hd of Econs Dept, King's Heath Boys' Sch., 1974–76; called to the Bar, Middle Temple, 1978, Bencher, 2002. Asst Recorder, 1993–97. Member: Cttee, Criminal Bar Assoc., 1997–2003; Qualifications Cttee, Bar Standards Bd, 2006–. Mem., Political Cartoon Soc., 2001–. *Recreations:* cricket, collecting political cartoons. *Address:* 18 Red Lion Court, EC4A 3EB. *T:* (020) 7520 6000.

BENSON, John Trevor; QC 2001; a Recorder, since 1998; *b* 22 Jan. 1955; s of Trevor Benson and Ruth (*née* Oliver); *m* 1984, Sheila Patricia Riordan; one *s* two *d*. *Educ:* Liverpool Univ. (LLB Hons). Called to the Bar, Middle Temple, 1978. *Recreations:* cookery, Liverpool FC, music, Italy. *Address:* Atlantic Chambers, 4/6 Cook Street, Liverpool L2 9QU. *T:* (0151) 236 4421; 1 Mitre Court Chambers, Mitre Court, Temple, EC4Y 7BS.

BENSON, Hon. Michael D'Arcy; Chairman, Ashmore Group, since 2006; *b* Windsor, 23 May 1943; *s* of Baron Benson, GBE; *m* 1969, Rachel Woods; one *s* two *d*. *Educ:* Eton. Dir, Lazard Bros, 1979–85; CEO, Scimitar Asset Mgt, 1985–92; Dir, Capital House, 1992–94; CEO, Invesco Asia, 1994–97; CEO, 1997–2003, Chm., 2003–05, Invesco Global; Vice Chm., Amvescap, 2001–05. Chm., Hayaat Gp, 2012–; Director: Border Asset Mgt, 2006–11; Morse plc, 2007–09; Trinity Street Asset Mgt, 2011–. Dir, York Minster Fund, 2007–; Chief Exec., York Minster Revealed, 2010–. *Recreations:* sailing, shooting, gardening. *Address:* Grange Farm, Westow, York YO60 7NJ. *T:* (01653) 658296. *E:* mdbenson@btinternet.com. *Clubs:* Brooks's; Newport Sailing (S Wales).

BENSON, Neil Winston, OBE 2004; FCA; Senior Partner, Lewis Golden & Co., Chartere Accountants, since 1980; *b* 17 Oct. 1937; *s* of late John William Benson and Rebecca (*n* Winston); *m* 1960, Ann Margery Licht; one *s* one *d*. *Educ:* Clifton Coll. FCA 1961. Article clerk with Hartleys, Wilkins and Flew, 1955–60; qualified as chartered accountant, 196 Lewis Golden & Co.: Sen. Clerk, 1961–63; Partner, 1963–. Director: Davis Service G (formerly Godfrey Davis) Plc, 1981–2005 (Chm., 1990–2001); Shaftesbury Plc, 1986–200 Moss Bros Gp Plc, 1989–2001 (Chm., 1990–2001); Business Post Gp Plc, 1993–2001 (Chm 1995–2001). Royal Shakespeare Company: Gov. and Main Bd Dir, 1997–2008; Hon. Gov 2011–; Corp. of London Assessor, 1995–97. Hon. Treasurer and Trustee: Cystic Fibrosis Re Trust, 1990–99; Foundn for Liver Res. (formerly Liver Res. Trust), 1991–2005. *Recreation* Real tennis, golf, watching Rugby, theatre, my Alvis. *Address:* 40 Queen Anne Street, W1 9EL. *T:* (020) 7580 7313. *Clubs:* Garrick, MCC, Saints and Sinners (Chm., 1979 and 200 Life Pres.); Highgate Golf, Lake Nona Golf (Orlando, Fla).

BENSON, Peter Charles; His Honour Judge Peter Benson; a Circuit Judge, since 200 *b* 16 June 1949; *s* of Robert Benson and Dorothy Benson (*née* Cartman). *Educ:* Bradfor Grammar Sch.; Birmingham Univ. (Schol.; BSocSc). Called to the Bar, Middle Templ 1975; in practice at the Bar, Leeds, 1975–2001. A Recorder of the Crown Court, 1995–200 Liaison Judge: for Calderdale Magistrates' Ct, 2003–; for Huddersfield Magistrates' C 2003–12. Mem., Parole Bd, 2003–09. *Recreations:* golf, wine, travel. *Address:* c/o Bradfor Crown Court, Exchange Square, Bradford BD1 1JA. *T:* (01274) 840274. *Clubs:* East Indi Bradford; Ilkley Golf, Ganton Golf, Ilkley Bowling.

BENSON, Maj.-Gen. Peter Herbert, CBE 1974 (MBE 1954); Member, Lord Chancellor Panel of Independent Inspectors, Planning Inspectorate, Departments of Environment an Transport, 1981–88; *b* 27 Oct. 1923; *s* of Herbert Kamerer Benson and Edith Doris Bensor *m* 1949, Diana Betty Ashmore (*d* 2011); one *s* one *d*. Joined Army, 1944; commnd into Wales Borderers, 1945; transf. to RASC, 1948, and Royal Corps of Transport, 1965; serve Palestine, Cyprus, Germany, Malaya and Singapore (three times), Borneo, Africa an Australia; Comdr, 15 Air Despatch Regt, 1966–68; GSO1 (DS) Staff Coll., Camberley, an Australian Staff Coll., 1968–70; Col Q (Movements), MoD (Army), 1971–72; Comdr, Transport Gp RCT (Logistic Support Force), 1972–73; Comdr, ANZUK Support G Singapore, Sen. British Officer Singapore, and Leader, UK Jt Services Planning Tean 1973–74; Chief Transport and Movements Officer, BAOR, 1974–76; Dir Gen. of Transpo and Movements (Army) (formerly Transport Officer in Chief (Army)), MoD, 1976–7 Chm., Grants Cttee, Army Benevolent Fund, 1980–92. Col Comdt, RCT, 1978–90. Chm Abbeyfield Soc., Beaminster, 1982–92. Pres., Army Officers' Golfing Soc., 1993–9 Liveryman, Co. of Carmen, 1977. *Club:* Lyme Regis Golf (Captain, 1993).

BENSON, Richard Anthony; QC 1995; a Recorder, since 1995; *b* 20 Feb. 1946; *s* c Douglas Arthur Benson and Muriel Alice Benson (*née* Fairfield); *m* 1st, 1967, Katherine Ann Smith (marr. diss. 1997); one *s* two *d*; 2nd, 2000, Sarah Levina Gaunt (marr. diss. 2004); thre *s* one *d*; 3rd, 2006, Prof. Alison Jane Simmons; twin *s*. *Educ:* St Piran's Prep. Sch.; Wreki Coll.; Coll. of Law; Inns of Court Sch. of Law. Sailing and overland expedition to Afric 1964–65; articled to Bircham & Co. (Solicitors), 1965–67; joined Inner Temple as studen 1968; adventuring in Sudan, 1969–70; called to the Bar, Inner Temple, 1974, Bencher, 201 in practice on Midland (formerly Midland and Oxford) Circuit, specialising in defendin heavyweight criminal cases and courts martial; Asst Recorder, 1991–95. Mem., Steering Ctte for tape recording of police interviews, 1983–84. Consultant, Justice for Agricultur Zimbabwe, 2003; Personal aide to Roy Bennett, MP, Zimbabwe, 2003; Inter Univ. Moc advocacy consultant, 2007–; part-time Chm. of disciplinary cttees for political parties, 2014 *Recreations:* restoring wooden boats, writing letters to The Times, flying (flew Atlantic vi Greenland 1983), off-shore cruising, aviation, military and nautical history, drama, writing an performing in reviews, after-dinner speaking, the company of friends! *Address:* Cornwa Street Chambers, 85–87 Cornwall Street, Birmingham B3 3BY. *T:* (0121) 233 7500. *Clu* Bar Yacht.

BENSON, His Honour Richard Stuart Alistair; a Circuit Judge, 1993–2004; *b* 23 Nov 1943; *s* of late Frank Benson and of Jean Benson; *m* 1st, 1980, Susan (marr. diss. 1998); 2nd 2008, Linda Radford (*née* Duckett); one step *s* one step *d*. *Educ:* Clapham Coll.; Univ. c Nottingham (BA Politics). Called to the Bar, Gray's Inn, 1968; in practice at the Bar, firstl Midland Circuit, later Midland and Oxford Circuit, Nottingham, 1968–92; a Recorde 1991–93. Member, Court of Appeal: St Helena, 1997–2005; Falkland Is, 2000–; Britis Antarctic Territory, 2000–; British Indian Ocean Territories, 2002–. Chm., Nottinghar Cons. Fedn, 2005–07. Mem. (C), Nottingham CC, 2007–11. Dir, Nottingham Racecours 2007–11. *Recreations:* steeplechasing, horses (formerly Joint Master, Trent Valle Draghounds), books, France, whiskey and wine. *Address:* 1 High Pavement, Nottinghar NG1 1HF. *T:* (0115) 941 8218. *Clubs:* Beeston Fields Golf; Notts CC.

BENT, Margaret (Hilda), CBE 2008; PhD; FBA 1993; musicologist; Senior Researc Fellow, All Souls College, Oxford, 1992–2008, now Emeritus Fellow; *b* 23 Dec. 1940; *d* c late Horace Bassington and Miriam (*née* Simpson); *m*; one *s* one *d*; partner, Myles Fredri Burnyeat, *qv*. *Educ:* Haberdashers' Aske's Acton Sch.; Girton Coll., Cambridge (organ schol BA 1962; MusB 1963; MA; PhD 1969; Hon. Fellow 2007). Lectr, then Sen. Lectr, Musi Dept, Goldsmiths' Coll., London Univ., 1972–75; Vis. Prof., then full Prof. and Chm., Musi Dept, Brandeis Univ., 1975–81; Prof., later Chm., Music Dept, Princeton Univ., 1981–92 Guggenheim Fellow, 1983–84; Dist. Sen. Fellow, Sch. of Advanced Studies, London Univ. 2010. Visiting Professor: Univ. of Chicago, 2005; Harvard Univ., 2009; Univ. of Base 2009–10. Pres., Amer. Musicological Soc., 1984–86 (Corresp. Mem., 1995). MAE 199 FRHistS 1995; FSA 2002. For. Hon. Mem., Amer. Acad. of Arts and Scis, 1994; Corresp Fellow, Medieval Acad. of America, 2004; Internat. Mem., Amer. Philosophical Soc., 201 Hon. DMus Glasgow, 1997; Hon. DFA Notre Dame, 2002; Dr *hc* Montreal, 2010. F. L Harrison Medal, Soc. for Musicol. in Ireland, 2007; Claude V. Palisca Award, Amer. Music Soc., 2009. *Publications:* (ed jtly) Old Hall Manuscript, vols I and II 1969, vol III 1973; (ed jtly John Dunstable, Complete Works, 1970; (ed) Four Anonymous Masses, 1979; Dunstapl 1981; (ed jtly) Ciconia, 1985; (ed) Rossini, Il Turco in Italia, 1988; Fauvel Studies, 199 Counterpoint, Composition and Musica Ficta, 2002; Bologna Q15: the making and remakin of a musical manuscript, 2008; (ed jtly) A Veneto Liber Cantus, 2012; (contrib.) New Grov Dictionary of Music and Musicians, 1980; contrib. Musica Disciplina, Jl of Amer. Music Soc., Early Music Hist. etc. *Address:* All Souls College, Oxford OX1 4AL. *T:* (01865) 279379

BENTALL, (Leonard) Edward; DL; FCA; Chairman, Bentalls, 1982–2001; *b* 26 May 193 *s* of late Leonard Edward Rowan Bentall and Adelia Elizabeth Bentall (*née* Hawes); *m* 196 Wendy Ann Daniel; three *d*. *Educ:* Stowe School. Articled Clerk, Dixon Wilson Tubbs Gillett, 1958–64. Bentalls, 1965–2001: Management Accountant, Merchandise Controlle Merchandise Dir, Man. Dir, Chm. and Man. Dir, Chm. and Chief Exec. Non-exec. Dir Associated Independent Stores, 1979–82. Pres., Textile Benevolent Assoc., 1991–95. Non exec. Director: Kingston Hosp. Trust, 1990–98 (Dep. Chm., 1998); Riverside Radic 1996–99. Governor: Brooklands Tech. Coll., 1981–90; Kingston Coll., 1990; Kingsto Grammar Sch., 1992–2002; Patron, Bedelsford Sch. Assoc., 1997–2008. Trustee: Kingsto and Dist Sea Cadet Corps TS Steadfast, 1966– (Chm., Unit Mgt Cttee, 1994–2004); Spirit o Normandy Trust, 2000–; Chm. Bd of Trustees, Shooting Star Trust Children's Hospic Appeal, 2000–03. Vice-Pres., Surrey PGA, 1995–. Steward, Nat. Greyhound Racing Club 1998–2007 (Sen. Steward, 2005–07). Hon. Life Mem., Tamesis Sailing Club, 1997. FInstD

DL Greater London, 1999. *Address:* Heneage Farm, Windlesham Road, Chobham, Woking, Surrey GU24 8QR. *T:* (01276) 858256. *Clubs:* Naval, MCC, Saints and Sinners; Surrey Cricket.

ENTHALL, Jonathan Charles Mackenzie; social researcher; Hon. Research Fellow, Department of Anthropology, University College London, since 1994; Director, Royal Anthropological Institute, 1974–2000; *b* Calcutta, 12 Sept. 1941; *s* of Sir Arthur Paul Benthall, KBE and Mollie Pringle; *m* 1975, Zamira, *d* of Baron Menuhin, OM, KBE; two *s* and one step *s*. *Educ:* Eton (KS); King's Coll., Cambridge (MA). Sec., Inst. of Contemporary Arts, 1971–73. Ed., Anthropol. Today, 1985–2000. Member: UK Adv. Cttee, 1981–87, Overseas Adv. Cttee, 1985–86, 1990–96, Council, 1987–90, Assembly, 1990–98, SCF; Assoc. of Social Anthropologists, 1983; Trustee: Internat. NGO Trng and Res. Centre, 1997–2006 (Chm., 1998–2003); Alliance of Religions and Conservation, 1997–2004. Associate Fellow, Humanitarian and Conflict Response Inst., Univ. of Manchester, 2010–. Co-Dir, Gulf Charities Workshop, Univ. of Cambridge, 2012. Advr, Islamic Charities Project (formerly Montreux Initiative), Swiss Federal Dept of Foreign Affairs, 2005–13. Expert testimony in legal cases, 2006–. Anthropology in Media Award, Amer. Anthropol Assoc., 1993; Patron's Medal, RAI, 2001. Chevalier de l'Ordre des Arts et des Lettres (France), 1973. *Publications:* Science and Technology in Art Today, 1972; (ed) Ecology: the Shaping Enquiry, 1972; (ed) The Limits of Human Nature, 1973; (ed jtly) The Body as a Medium of Expression, 1975; The Body Electric: patterns of western industrial culture, 1976; Disasters, Relief and the Media, 1993, 2nd edn 2010; (ed) The Best of Anthropology Today, 2002; (jtly) The Charitable Crescent: politics of aid in the Muslim world, 2003, 2nd edn 2009; Returning to Religion: why a secular age is haunted by faith, 2008; (ed jtly) Gulf Charities and Islamic Philanthropy in the "Age of Terror" and Beyond, 2014; Islamic Charities and Islamic Humanism in Troubled Times, 2015. *Recreations:* listening to music, swimming, mountain walking, books, writing light verse. *Address:* Downingbury Farmhouse, Pembury, Tunbridge Wells, Kent TN2 4AD. *Club:* Athenæum.

ENTHAM, Howard Lownds; QC 1996; a Recorder, since 1988; *b* 26 Feb. 1948; *s* of William Foster Bentham and Elsie Bentham; *m* 1978, Elizabeth Anne Owen; one *s*. *Educ:* Malvern Coll.; Liverpool Univ. (LLB). Called to the Bar, Gray's Inn, 1970; Asst Recorder, 1985–88. *Recreations:* motor racing, scuba diving, watching wildlife. *Address:* c/o St Johns Buildings, 24a–28 St John Street, Manchester M3 4DJ. *T:* (0161) 214 1500.

ENTHAM, Prof. Richard Walker; Professor of Petroleum and Mineral Law, and Director of the Centre for Petroleum and Mineral Law Studies, University of Dundee, 1983–90; Professor Emeritus, since 1991; *b* 26 June 1930; *s* of Richard Hardy Bentham and Ellen Walker (*née* Fisher); *m* 1956, Stella Winifred Matthews; one *d*. *Educ:* Campbell Coll., Belfast; Trinity Coll., Dublin (BA, LLB). Called to the Bar, Middle Temple, 1955. Lecturer in Law: Univ. of Tasmania, 1955–57; Univ. of Sydney, 1957–61; Legal Dept, The British Petroleum Co. PLC, 1961–83 (Dep. Legal Advisor, 1979–83). Founder Mem., Scottish Council for Internat. Arbitration (formerly Scottish Council for Arbitration), 1988–99; Mem. Council, Inst. of Internat. Business Law and Practice, ICC, 1988–94; British nominated Mem., Panel of Arbitrators, Dispute Settlement Centre, IEA, 1989–96. Mem. and consultant, Russian Petroleum Legislation Project (sponsored by Univ. of Houston, World Bank and ODAS), 1991–96. FRSA 1986–2013. *Publications:* articles in learned jls in UK and overseas. *Recreations:* cricket, military history, military modelling. *Address:* Earlham, 41 Trumlands Road, St Marychurch, Torquay, Devon TQ1 4RN. *T:* (01803) 314315.

ENTHAM-MacLEARY, Donald Whyte, OBE 2004; Guest Principal Répétiteur to the Principal Artists, Royal Ballet (Répétiteur, 1981–94; Senior Répétiteur, 1994–99; Principal Répétiteur, 1999–2002); *b* Glasgow, 22 Aug. 1937; *s* of Donald Herbert MacLeary, MPS, and Jean Spiers (*née* Leslie); adopted surname Bentham-MacLeary, 2006; civil partnership 2006, Trevor Bentham. *Educ:* Inverness Royal Academy; The Royal Ballet School. Principal male dancer, 1959–78, Ballet Master, 1978–81, Royal Ballet. *Classical Ballets:* (full length) Swan Lake, Giselle, 1958; Sleeping Beauty, Cinderella, Sylvia, 1959; Ondine, La Fille Mal Gardée, 1960; (centre male rôle) in Ashton's Symphonic Variations, 1962; Sonnet Pas de Trois, 1964; Romeo and Juliet, 1965; Eugene Onegin, Stuttgart, 1966; Apollo, 1966; Nutcracker, 1968; Swan Lake with N. Makarova, 1972. *Creations:* (1954–74): Solitaire, The Burrow, Danse Concertante, Antigone, Diversions, Le Baiser de la Fée, Jabez and the Devil, Raymonda Pas de Deux (for Frederick Ashton), two episodes in Images of Love; Song of the Earth; Lilac Garden (revival); Jazz Calendar; Raymonda (for Nureyev); The Man in Kenneth MacMillan's Checkpoint; leading rôle in Concerto no 2 (Balanchine's Ballet Imperial, renamed); Elite Syncopations, 1974; Kenneth MacMillan's Four Seasons Symphony; the Prince in Cinderella; Catalabutte in Sleeping Beauty, 2003. Toured Brazil with Royal Ballet, Spring 1973. Guest dancer, Scottish Ballet, 1979. *Recreations:* reading, theatre, records (all types), riding, swimming.

See also A. R. MacLeary.

ENTINCK, Timothy; *see* Portland, Earl of.

ENTINCK van SCHOONHETEN, Baron Willem Oswald; Ambassador of the Netherlands to the Court of St James's, 1999–2003 (and concurrently to Iceland, 1999–2002); *b* 9 March 1940; *s* of late Baron Oswald François Bentinck van Schoonheten and Meta Hendrica Bentinck van Schoonheten (*née* van der Slooten); *m* 1974, Corinne C. Elink Schuurman; two *s* one *d*. *Educ:* Univ. of Utrecht (Master of Law). Entered Netherlands Foreign Service, 1968; Buenos Aires, 1968–71; Rome, 1971–73; Internat. Relns Dept, Min. of Foreign Affairs, 1973–76; Perm. Rep., NY, 1976–79; Economic Counsellor, Moscow, 1979–81; Counsellor and Dep. Hd of Mission, Ottawa, 1981–84; Hd of Political Affairs Section and Dep. Dir, Atlantic Co-operation and Security Affairs Dept, Min. of Foreign Affairs, 1984–87; Minister and Deputy Head of Mission: Moscow, 1987–90; Washington, 1990–94; Ambassador to Madrid, 1994–98. Officer, Order of Orange Nassau (Netherlands), 1992; Kt, Order of Merit (Italy), 1972; Grand Cross, Order of Isabella la Católica (Spain), 1999. *Recreations:* shooting, golf, bridge. *Address:* Delistraat 59, 2585 VX Den Haag, The Netherlands. *Clubs:* Haagsche (Plaats Royaal); Royal Haagsche Golf and Country.

ENTLEY, (Anthony) Philip; QC 1991; Barrister, McDermott Will & Emery/Stanbrook (formerly Stanbrook & Hooper), Brussels, since 1980; *b* 5 Dec. 1948; *s* of late Kenneth Bentley and of Frances Elizabeth (*née* Scott); *m* 1980, Christine Anne-Marie Odile Bausier; two *s* two *d*. *Educ:* St George's Coll., Weybridge; St Catharine's Coll., Cambridge (MA); Faculté de droit d'Aix-en-Provence (Dip.). Called to the Bar, Lincoln's Inn, 1970. With ICI, 1973–77; Dilley & Custer, 1977–80. Dir, Bar Mutual Indemnity Fund, 1989–2003. Mem., Fondation Universitaire, Brussels. Oboist and Librarian, Orch. symphonique des étudiants, Catholic Univ. of Louvain. *Publications:* (with C. Stanbrook) Dumping and Subsidies, 2nd edn 1996; (with A. Silberston) Anti-Dumping and Countervailing Action: limits imposed by economic and legal theory, 2007. *Address:* (office) Avenue des Nerviens 9–31, 1040 Brussels, Belgium. *T:* (2) 2305059.

ENTLEY, Rt Rev. David Edward; Bishop of Gloucester, 1993–2003; Hon. Assistant Bishop, Lichfield Diocese, since 2004; *b* 7 Aug. 1935; *s* of William Bentley and Florence (*née* Dalgleish); *m* 1962, Clarice Lahmers; two *s* two *d*. *Educ:* Gt Yarmouth Grammar School; Univ. of Leeds (BA English); Westcott House, Cambridge. Deacon 1960, priest 1961; Curate: St Ambrose, Bristol, 1960–62; Holy Trinity with St Mary, Guildford, 1962–66; Rector: Headley, Bordon, 1966–73; Esher, 1973–86; RD of Emly, 1977–82; Suffragan Bishop of Lynn, 1986–93; Warden, Community of All Hallows, Ditchingham, 1989–93. Hon. Canon of Guildford Cathedral, 1980. Chairman: Guildford dio. House of Clergy, 1977–86; Guildford dio. Council of Social Responsibility, 1980–86; ACCM Candidates Cttee, 1987–91; ABM Recruitment and Selection Cttee, 1991–93; ABM Ministry Develt and Deployment Cttee, 1995–98; Deployment, Remuneration and Conditions of Service Cttee, Ministry Div., Archbishops' Council, 1999–2002. Hon. PhD Gloucestershire, 2002. *Recreations:* music; sport, especially cricket; theatre, travel. *Address:* 19 Gable Croft, Lichfield WS14 9RY. *T:* (01543) 419376. *Clubs:* MCC; Warwickshire CC.

BENTLEY, David Jeffrey, CB 1993; Legal Counsellor, Foreign and Commonwealth Office, 1995–97; *b* 5 July 1935; *s* of late Harry Jeffrey Bentley and Katherine (*née* Barnett). *Educ:* Watford Boys' Grammar School; New College, Oxford (BCL, MA). Called to the Bar, Lincoln's Inn, 1963; University teaching, 1957–79; Asst Parly Counsel, 1965–67; Legal Adviser's Branch, Home Office, 1979–95, Principal Asst Legal Advr, 1988–95. *Recreations:* reading, listening to music, walking. *Address:* 192 Randolph Avenue, W9 1PE. *Club:* Oxford and Cambridge.

BENTLEY, Ven. Frank William Henry; Archdeacon of Worcester and Canon Residentiary of Worcester Cathedral, 1984–99, now Emeritus; Chaplain to the Queen, 1994–2004; *b* 4 March 1934; *s* of Nowell and May Bentley; *m* 1st, 1957, Muriel Bland (*d* 1958); one *s*; 2nd, 1960, Yvonne Wilson (*d* 2000); two *s* one *d*; 3rd, 2006, Kathleen M. Gibbs. *Educ:* Yeovil School; King's College London (AKC). Deacon 1958, priest 1959; Curate at Shepton Mallet, 1958–62; Rector of Kingsdon with Podymore Milton and Curate-in-charge, Yeovilton, 1962–66; Rector of Babcary, 1964–66; Vicar of Wiveliscombe, 1966–76; Rural Dean of Tone, 1973–76; Vicar of St John-in-Bedwardine, Worcester, 1976–84; Rural Dean of Martley and Worcester West, 1979–84. Hon. Canon of Worcester Cathedral, 1981. *Recreations:* gardening, local history. *Address:* Willow Cottage, Station Road, Fladbury, Pershore, Worcs WR10 2QW. *T:* (01386) 861847.

BENTLEY, Prof. George, ChM; DSc; FRCS, FMedSci; Professor of Orthopaedic Surgery at University College London (formerly at Postgraduate Medical Federation), University of London, 1982–2002, now Emeritus Professor and Director, Institute of Orthopaedics; Hon. Consultant Orthopaedic Surgeon, Royal National Orthopaedic Hospital, Stanmore, since 1982; *b* 19 Jan. 1936; *s* of George and Doris Bentley; *m* 1960, Ann Gillian Hutchings; two *s* one *d*. *Educ:* Rotherham Grammar Sch.; Sheffield Univ. (MB, ChB, ChM; DSc 2002). FRCS 1964. House Surgeon, Sheffield Royal Infirmary, 1959–61; Lectr in Anatomy, Birmingham Univ., 1961–62; Surg. Registrar, Sheffield Royal Infirm., 1963–65; Orthopaedic Registrar, Orthopaedic Hosp., Oswestry, 1965–67; Sen. Registrar in Orthopaedics, Nuffield Orthopaedic Centre and Radcliffe Infirm., Oxford, 1967–69; Instructor in Orth., Univ. of Pittsburgh, USA, 1969–70; Lectr, 1970–71, Sen. Lectr and Reader in Orth., 1971–76, Univ. of Oxford; Prof. of Orth. and Accident Surgery, Univ. of Liverpool, 1976–82; Dir, Inst. of Orthopaedics, UC and Middx Sch. of Medicine, Univ. of London, 1982–2002. Hon. Consultant Orthopaedic Surgeon, Middlesex Hosp., 1984–2001. Eur. Ed.-in-Chief, Jl Arthroplasty, 2001–; Member, Editorial Board: Jl Bone and Jt Surgery, 1974–76, 2006–; The Knee, 1993–2004; Clinical Materials, 1993–98; Orthopaedics Internat., 1997–. Numerous lectures including: Hunterian Prof., RCS, 1972; Watson-Jones, 1996, Alan Apley Meml, 2006, Robert Jones, 2007, RCS and BOA. Chairman: Scientific Cttee, EFORT, 1995–2002; Intercollegiate Bd, Exam. in Orthopaedics UK, 1996–99. Vice-Pres., RCS, 2003–04 (Mem. Council); Mem. Council, British Orthopaedic Assoc. (Pres., 1991–92); Pres., British Orthopaedic Res. Soc., 1985–87; Vice-Pres., 2002–03, Pres., 2004–06, European Fedn of Nat. Assocs of Orthopaedics and Traumatology; Member Council: Orthopaedic Association: Australia; NZ; SA; Eastern; Argentina; Amer. Orthopaedic and Res. Assoc.; Eur. Orthopaedic Res. Soc.; SICOT; ESSKA; ISAKOS. Pres., Seddon Soc., 1996–. FMedSci 1999. FRCSE ad hominem 1999; Hon. FRSocMed 2009. Hon. Mem., French Soc. of Trauma and Orthopaedics, 1999; Hon. Fellow: Educnl Council for Foreign Medical Graduates, 1969; British Orthopaedic Assoc., 2004; Czech Orthopaedic Assoc., 2004; Eur. Fedn of Nat. Assocs of Orthopaedics and Traumatol., 2007. *Publications:* (ed) 3rd edn vols I and II, Rob and Smith Operative Surgery—Orthopaedics, 1979, 4th edn 1991; (ed) Mercer's Orthopaedic Surgery, 8th edn, 1983, 9th edn 1996; (ed) European Surgical Orthopaedics and Traumatology, 2014; papers on cell-engineered cartilage grafting of joints, arthritis, accident surgery and scoliosis in leading med. and surg. jls. *Recreations:* golf, tennis, music, horology. *Address:* Royal National Orthopaedic Hospital, Stanmore, Middx HA7 4LP. *T:* (020) 8909 5532.

BENTLEY, John Ransome; writer and novelist; *b* 19 Feb. 1940; *m* 1st, 1960, Dorothy (marr. diss. 1969; decd); one *s* one *d*; two *d*; 2nd, 1982, Katherine Susan (marr. diss. 1986; she *d* 2011), *d* of Gerald Percy and the Marchioness of Bute; 3rd, 1990, Honore (marr. diss. 1992); 4th, 2002, Janet. *Educ:* Harrow Sch. Media entrepreneur and financier. Chairman: Barclay Securities plc, 1969–73; Intervision Video (Holdings) plc, 1980–83; Viewcall America Inc., 1995–97; Electronic Game Card Inc., 2002–05. Inventor of Internet TV (Viewcall America, 1996) and digital gaming (Electronic Game Card, 2004). *Recreations:* living, writing, travel, politics, history. *E:* j.bentley2@btinternet.com. *W:* www.johnbentley.biz.

BENTLEY, Julie; Chief Executive, Girlguiding, since 2012; *b* Chelmsford, Essex, 21 March 1969; *d* of Donald and Pamela Bentley; partner, Sean Murphy. *Educ:* Open Univ. (MBA). Dir, Corporate Services, ARP, 2000–04; Chief Executive Officer: Suzy Lamplugh Trust, 2004–08; FPA, 2008–12. Member: Internat. Women's Forum; Fawcett Soc. *Recreations:* theatre, cinema, walking, cycling. *Address:* Girlguiding, 17–19 Buckingham Palace Road, SW1W 0PT. *T:* (020) 7828 8317. *E:* Julie.bentley@girlguiding.org.uk. *W:* www.twitter.com/JulieBentley.

BENTLEY, Philip; *see* Bentley, A. P.

BENTLEY, Robert Paul, FDSRCS, FRCS, FRCS (OMFS); Consultant Craniofacial Surgeon, since 2000, Clinical Director for Major Trauma, since 2007 and Clinical Director for Surgery, since 2013, King's College Hospital; Clinical Director for South East London, Kent and Medway Major Trauma Network, since 2013; *b* Cardiff, 16 Feb. 1963; *s* of Thomas Hamilton Bentley and Dorothy Irene Bentley; *m* 2008, Madelene Jerlmyr; one *s* one *d*. *Educ:* Whitchurch High Sch., Cardiff; Univ. of Wales Coll. of Medicine (BDS 1985; MB ChB 1992). FDSRCS 1988; FRCS 1995; FRCS (OMFS) 1999. Hse Surgeon, University Hosp. of Wales, 1992–93; SHO, Royal Gwent Hosp., 1993–94; Registrar, Queen Elizabeth Hosp., Birmingham, 1994–99; Craniofacial Fellow: Birmingham Children's Hosp., 1999–2000; Univ. of Heidelberg, 2000. *Publications:* over 20 articles in peer-reviewed jls; four book chapters. *Recreations:* cycling, tennis, sailing, football. *Address:* Department of Maxillofacial Surgery, King's College Hospital, Denmark Hill, SE5 9RS. *T:* (020) 3299 1753, *Fax:* (020) 3299 3754. *E:* robert.bentley@nhs.net.

BENTLEY, Sarah Rosamund Irvine; *see* Foot, S. R. I.

BENTLY, Prof. Lionel Alexander Fiennes; Herchel Smith Professor of Intellectual Property Law, and Director, Centre of Intellectual Property and Information Law, University of Cambridge, since 2004; Professorial Fellow, Emmanuel College, Cambridge, since 2004; *b* 2 July 1964; *s* of Lionel Charles Warwick Bently and Helen Joy Bently (*née* Wright); partner, Clair Milligan. *Educ:* Pembroke Coll., Cambridge (BA Law). Prof. of Law, KCL, 2002–04. Called to the Bar, Inner Temple, 2009. Door Tenant: Hogarth Chambers, Lincoln's Inn, 2004–11; 11 South Square, Gray's Inn, 2011–. *Publications:* with Brad Sherman: The Making of Modern Intellectual Property Law, 1999; Intellectual Property Law, 2001, 3rd edn 2008. *Recreations:* football (Mem., Arsenal FC), punk rock, industrial and related music. *Address:*

Centre of Intellectual Property and Information Law, Faculty of Law, University of Cambridge, 10 West Road, Cambridge CB3 9DZ. *T:* (01223) 330081, *Fax:* (01223) 330086. *E:* lb329@cam.ac.uk.

BENTON, David Michael; Partner, since 1997, and Global Co-Head, International Capital Markets, since 2014, Allen & Overy LLP; *b* Leeds, 4 March 1966; *s* of Alan and Jean Benton; *m* 1991, Mary Bull; one *s* one *d*. *Educ:* Monmouth Sch.; Bradford Grammar Sch.; Corpus Christi Coll., Cambridge (BA Hons Law 1987). Admitted as solicitor, 1990; Allen & Overy LLP: Associate, 1990–97; Hd, Derivatives and Structured Finance, 2010–14. Legal Advr to Credit Derivatives Determinations Cttee, Internat. Swaps and Derivatives Assoc., 2009–. *Recreations:* running and cycling, Leeds Rhinos and New York Rangers. *Address:* Allen & Overy LLP, One Bishops Square, E1 6AD. *T:* (020) 3088 3118. *E:* david.benton@allenovery.com.

BENTON, Joseph Edward; JP; *b* 28 Sept. 1933; *s* of Thomas and Agnes Benton; *m* 1959, Doris Wynne; four *d*. *Educ:* St Monica's Primary and Secondary Sch.; Bootle Technical Coll. Nat. Service, RAF, 1955. Apprentice fitter and turner, 1949; former Personnel Manager, Pacific Steam Navigation Co.; Girobank, 1982–90. Councillor, Sefton Borough Council, 1970–90 (Leader, Labour Gp, 1985–90). MP (Lab) Bootle, Nov. 1990–2015. An Opposition Whip, 1994–97. Mem., Speaker's Panel of Chairmen, 1992–94, 1997–2015. Member: Select Cttee on Educn, 1997–98; NI Affairs Cttee, 2010–15; Sec., All Party Parly Pro-Life Gp, 1992–2015; Member: British/Spanish Parly Gp, 1997–2015; British/Irish Parly Gp, 1997–2015; Parly Assembly of Council of Europe, 2010–. Mem., Bd Visitors, Liverpool Prison (Walton), 1974–81. Chm. of Govs, Hugh Baird Coll. of Technology, 1972–93. Assoc. Mem., IPM, 1965; MIL 1963. JP South Sefton, 1969. KSG 2014.

BENTON, Margaret Carole; arts consultant, since 2013; *b* 14 April 1943; *d* of late Lawrence and Mary Benton; *m* Stephen Green. *Educ:* The Red Maids Sch., Bristol; Univ. of Wales (BA Hons French). British Broadcasting Corporation: Radio, 1966–67; News, Paris Office, 1967–69; Schools Television, 1969–70; Gen. Features Television, 1970–71; COI (Overseas Documentaries/Co-prodns), 1971–75; BBC Television, Bristol, 1975–85; Nat. Museum of Photography, Film and Television, 1985–90; Director: Theatre Mus., V&A, 1990–2003; The Making, 2003–12. Young People's Mentor, Surrey Care Trust, 2013–. Estab. Nat. Video Archive of Performance, V&A, 1992. Member: Theatres Adv. Council, 1991–2002; Council of Management (British Centre), Internat. Theatre Inst.; Museums Assoc.; Pres., Société Internationale des Bibliothèques et des Musées des Arts du Spectacle, 1992–96. Trustee, New Ashgate Gall., 2013–; Patron, Stroud Internat. Textiles, 2013–. Prod and dir. numerous television documentaries and other progs for BBC. *Recreations:* rural "idylling", theatre, opera, cinema, visual arts, gardening. *Address:* Summerden South, Waggoners Wells, Grayshott GU26 6DN.

BENTON, Prof. Michael James, PhD; FRS 2014; FGS, FLS; FRSE; Professor of Vertebrate Palaeontology, University of Bristol, since 1997; *b* 8 April 1956; *s* of Alexander Charles Benton and Elsie Christine Benton (*née* Taylor); *m* 1983, Mary Monro; one *s* one *d*. *Educ:* Univ. of Aberdeen (BSc Hons Zool. 1978); Univ. of Newcastle upon Tyne (PhD Geol. 1981). FLS 1983; FGS 1987. SO, NCC, 1981–82; Jun. Res. Fellow, Trinity Coll., Oxford, 1982–84; Lectr, QUB, 1984–89; University of Bristol: Lectr, Dept of Geol., 1989–92; Reader in Vertebrate Palaeontol., 1992–97; Hd, Dept of Earth Scis, 2001–08. President: Geologists' Assoc., 2006–08; Internat. Palaeontol Assoc., 2010–14; Palaeontol Assoc., 2012–14. Edward Bass Dist. Vis. Scholar, Yale Univ., 2009; Dist. Prof., Chinese Acad. of Scis, 2012. FRSE 2008. Lyell Medal, Geol Soc. of London, 2005; T. Neville George Medal, Geol Soc. of Glasgow, 2006. *Publications:* The Phylogeny and Classification of the Tetrapods, 1988; Vertebrate Palaeontology, 1990, 4th edn 2015; Fossil Record 2, 1993; Fossil Reptiles of Great Britain, 1995; The Penguin Historical Atlas of Dinosaurs, 1996; (with D. A. T. Harper) Basic Palaeontology, 1997; Walking with Dinosaurs: the facts, 2000; (jtly) The Age of Dinosaurs in Russia and Mongolia, 2001; (jtly) Permian and Triassic Red Beds and the Penarth Group of Great Britain, 2002; When Life Nearly Died: the greatest mass extinction of all time, 2003, 2nd edn 2015; Mesozoic and Tertiary Fossil Mammals and Birds of Great Britain, 2005; Very Short Introduction to the History of Life, 2008; The Seventy Great Mysteries of the Natural World, 2008; (with D. A. T. Harper) Introduction to Paleobiology and the Fossil Record, 2009; 43 popular books and over 280 scientific papers. *Recreations:* reading, travelling, swimming, crosswords. *Address:* School of Earth Sciences, University of Bristol, Bristol BS8 1RJ. *T:* (0117) 954 5433, *Fax:* (0117) 925 3385. *E:* mike.benton@bristol.ac.uk.

BENTON, Peter Faulkner, MA; Director-General, British Institute of Management, 1987–92; *b* 6 Oct. 1934; *s* of late S. F. Benton and Mrs H. D. Benton; *m* 1959, Ruth, *d* of late R. S. Cobb, MC, FRIBA and Mrs J. P. Cobb; two *s* three *d*. *Educ:* Oundle; Queens' Coll., Cambridge (MA Nat. Sciences). 2nd Lieut RE, 1953–55. Unilever Ltd, 1958–60; Shell Chemicals Ltd, 1960–63; Berger Jenson and Nicholson Ltd, 1963–64; McKinsey & Co. Inc., London and Chicago, 1964–71 (led reorgn of British gas industry, 1967–71); Gallaher Ltd, 1971, Dir, 1973–77; Man. Dir, Post Office Telecommunications, 1978–81; Dep. Chm., British Telecom, 1981–83. Advr, Stern Stewart Inc., 1995–2002. Chairman: Saunders Valve Ltd, 1972–77; Mono Pumps Group, 1976–77; European Practice, Nolan, Norton & Co., 1984–87; Identica Ltd, 1992–93; Director: Singer and Friedlander, 1983–89; Woodside Communications, 1995–96; Mem., Supervisory Bd, Hiross Holdings AG, Austria, 1992–94. Dir, Turing Inst., 1985–94. Chairman: Enfield Dist HA, 1986–92; Enterprise Support Gp, 1993–96. Chm., Heating, Ventilating, Air Conditioning and Refrigerating Equipment Sector Working Party, NEDO, 1976–79; Member: Electronics Industry EDC, 1980–83; Econ. and Financial Policy Cttee, CBI, 1979–83; Special Adviser to EEC, 1983–84; Nat. Curriculum Science Wkg Gp, 1987–88; Indust. Develt Adv. Bd, DTI, 1988–94; Ind. Mem., British Liby Adv. Council, 1988–93; Internat. Adv. Bd for Science and Technology to Govt of Portugal, 1996–2003. Adviser, Arthur Andersen Société Coopérative, 1993–98. Vice-President: British Mech. Engrg Confedn, 1974–77; European Council of Management, 1989–93. Chairman: Ditchley Conf. on Inf. Technol., 1982; Financial Times Conf., World Electronics, 1983; World Bank Conf. on Catastrophe Avoidance, Washington, 1988, Karlstad, 1989; Vis. Gp, Inst. for Systems Engrg and Informatics, Italy, 1993; Inst. for Systems, Informatics and Safety, 1996; Euromoney Conf., New Delhi, 1998; Jt Chm., European Mgt Congress, Prague, 1990. Royal Signals Instn Lectr, London, 1980; ASLIB Lectr, 1988; Adam Smith Lectr, 1991. Pres., Highgate Literary and Scientific Instn, 1981–88. Chm., N London Hospice Gp, 1985–89. Governor, Molecule Club Theatre, 1985–91. CCMI. *Publications:* Riding the Whirlwind, 1990; articles on management, science and IT. *Recreations:* reading, baroque music, sailing, conversation, looking at buildings. *Address:* Northgate House, 130 Highgate Hill, N6 5HD. *T:* (020) 8341 1122; Dolphins, Hockens Lane, Polruan, Fowey, Cornwall PL23 1PP. *Clubs:* Athenæum, Oxford and Cambridge, The Pilgrims; Blythe Sappers; Royal Fowey Yacht.

BENTON JONES, Sir Simon Warley Frederick; *see* Jones, Sir S. W. F. B.

BENYON, Richard Henry Ronald; MP (C) Newbury, since 2005; *b* 21 Oct. 1960; *s* of Sir William Richard Benyon; *m* 2004, Zoe Robinson; two *s*, and three *s* from previous marriage. *Educ:* Bradfield Coll.; Royal Agricl Coll. MRICS. Served Army, 1980–84: commnd RGJ; served NI and Far East. Land Agent, 1987–90; farmer, Englefield, Berks, 1990–; Chm., Englefield Estate Trust Corp. Ltd (Rural and Urban Land Hldgs), 2001–10. Parly Under Sec. of State, DEFRA, 2010–13. *Recreations:* walking, conservation, shooting, cooking. *Address:* House of Commons, SW1A 0AA. *Club:* Beefsteak.

BENYON, Thomas Yates, OBE 2010; Founder and Director, ZANE: Zimbabwe A National Emergency, since 2000; Co-Founder and Trustee, Community Emergency Foodbank, since 2006; Founder, Zimbabwe Charity Alliance, since 2013; Director of vario companies; *b* 13 Aug. 1942; *s* of late Thomas Yates Benyon and Joan Ida Walters; *m* 196 Olivia Jane (*née* Scott Plummer); two *s* two *d*. *Educ:* Wellington Sch., Somerset; RM Sandhurst; Wycliffe Hall, Oxford (DBTS 2002). Lieut, Scots Guards, 1963–67. Insuran broking and banking, 1967–79. Chm., Milton Keynes HA, 1989–94; Dir, Bucks Purchasi Auth, 1994–96. Councillor, Aylesbury Vale DC, 1976–79. Contested (C): Huyton, Fe 1974; Haringey (Wood Green), Oct. 1974; MP (C) Abingdon, 1979–83; Vice Chm., Heal and Social Services Cttee, 1982–83; Mem., Social Services Select Cttee, 1980–83. Found Chm., Assoc. of Lloyd's Members, 1982–87; Founder: Soc. of Names, 1990–; Insuran Insider Publishing plc, 1997–; Guild Acquisitions plc, 2006–; Co-founder, Trendwatch Ass Mgt, 2009. Mem., Gen. Synod of C of E, 2005–10. *Recreations:* family, music. *Addres* Rectory Farm House, Bladon, Oxon OX20 1RS. *Clubs:* Royal Automobile, Pratt's; Thi Guards.

BERAL, Dame Valerie, DBE 2010; AC 2010; MD; FRCP; FRS 2006; Director, Canc Epidemiology Unit (formerly ICRF Clinical Trials and Epidemiology, then Canc Epidemiology, Unit), Oxford, since 1989; Fellow of Green Templeton College (former Green College), Oxford, since 1989; Professor of Epidemiology, University of Oxford, sin 1996; *b* 28 July 1946; partner, Prof. Paul E. M. Fine; two *s*. *Educ:* Univ. of Sydney (MB E 1969; MD 2001). MRCP 1971, FRCP 1992. Lectr, Sen. Lectr, then Reader in Epidemio LSHTM, 1970–88. Chm., DoH Adv. Cttee on Breast Cancer Screening, 2000–. Hon. FFP (Hon. FFPHM 2000); Hon. FRCOG 2001. *Publications:* articles on causes of breast and oth cancers in women. *Address:* 193 Morrell Avenue, Oxford OX4 1NF; Cancer Epidemiolog Unit, Richard Doll Building, Roosevelt Drive, Oxford OX3 7LF.

BERASATEGUI, Vicente Ernesto; Ambassador of the Argentine Republic to the Court St James's, 2000–03; *b* 13 May 1934; *s* of Miguel Bernardo Gabriel Berasategui and Mar Luisa Rivanera Carles; *m* 1960, Teresita Mazza. *Educ:* Univ. of Buenos Aires (degree in Law American Univ., Washington (Master in Internat. Relns and Orgn). Joined Argentine Foreig Service, 1954: Attaché, 1954–59; Hd, OAS Div., Foreign Min., 1960–61; Third, lat Second, Sec., USA, 1961–65; Sec., Policy Making Cttee, Minister for Foreign Affair 1967–69; Dep. to Dir Gen. for Political Affairs, Foreign Min., 1970–72; Dep. Perm. Rep. UN, Geneva, 1972–76; Minister, 1973; Ambassador, 1985; Dir for Western Eur. Affai Foreign Min., 1994–96; Ambassador to Denmark, 1997–2000. Rep., and Hd of delegns, internat. confs, 1959–76 (Hd, Delegn to Conf. of Cttee on Disarmament, 1974–76); Mem. and Hd for meeting of delegns with heads of state and political consultations, 1971–98. Unite Nations posts include: Consultant, Centre for Disarmament, 1977–78; Sec., First Cttee Gen. Assembly and Dep. Sec., Cttee on Disarmament, 1980; Dir, Geneva Br., Dept f Disarmament Affairs, 1983; Dep. Sec.-Gen., 1984–92, Sec.-Gen., 1992–93, Conf. c Disarmament (also Personal Rep. of Sec.-Gen. of UN); Chm., Adv. Bd of Sec.-Gen. c disarmament, 2005. Dir, Sch. of Internat. Relns and Prof. of Theory of Internat. Relns an Contemp. Internat. Politics, Univ. of Salvador, 1967–70; Visiting Professor: of Foreig Policy, Sch. of Law, Univ. of Buenos Aires, 1971; Prog. of Diplomatic Studies, Grad. Inst. Internat. Studies, Geneva, 1987–93; lectures on subjects concerning internat. relns, main disarmament, in Argentina, France and USA. Mem., Argentine Council for Internat. Reln 2014. Grand Cross, Order of Dannebrog (Denmark), 2000; Grand Officer: Order of Di Services (Peru), 1968; Order of Merit (Italy), 1995; Commander: Order Bernardo O'Higgi (Chile), 1971; Order of Condor of the Andes (Bolivia), 1971; Order of Civil Merit (Spai 1995; Order of Merit (France), 1999. *Address:* Avenida Alvear 1494, 1014 Buenos Aire Argentina. *T:* (11) 48159811.

BERCOW, Rt Hon. John (Simon); PC 2009; MP Buckingham; Speaker of the House c Commons, since June 2009; *b* 19 Jan. 1963; *s* of late Charles Bercow and of Brenda Berco (*née* Bailey); *m* 2002, Sally Illman; two *s* one *d*. *Educ:* Finchley Manorhill Sch.; Univ. of Ess (BA 1st Cl. Hons Govt 1985). Nat. Chm., Fedn of Cons. Students, 1986–87; Credit Analys Hambros Bank, 1987–88; Public Affairs Consultant, Sallingbury Casey, later Rowlan Sallingbury Casey, 1988–95; Dir, Rowland Co., 1994–95; Special Adviser to: Chief Sec. t Treasury, 1995; Sec. of State for Nat. Heritage, 1995–96; free-lance consultant, 1996–9 Councillor (C), Lambeth BC, 1986–90 (Dep. Leader, Opposition Gp, 1987–89). Vice-Chm Cons. Collegiate Forum, 1987. MP Buckingham, 1997– ((C) 1997–June 2009, when elect Speaker). Opposition spokesman: on educn and employment, 1999–2000; on home affair 2000–01; Shadow Chief Sec. to HM Treasury, 2001–02; Shadow Minister for Work an Pensions, 2002; Shadow Sec. of State for Internat. Develt, 2003–04. Member: Trade an Industry Select Cttee, 1998–99; Internat. Develt Select Cttee, 2004–09; Chairmen's Pane 2005–09. Chair: (ex officio) H of C Commn, 2009–; Speaker's Cttee on Electoral Comm 2009–; Speaker's Cttee for indep. Parly Standards Authy, 2009–; Speaker's Commn on Digit Democracy, 2014–. President: All-Party Parly Gp for America, 2009–; All-Party Parly Gp f Internet and Communications Technol., 2011–. Contested (C): Motherwell S, 1987; Brist S, 1992. Leader, Review of Services for Children and Young People with Speech, Languag and Communication Needs, 2007–08 (report published 2008). Pres., UK Br., CPA, 2009 Hon. President: Hansard Soc. for Parly Govt, 2009–; IPU British Gp, 2009–. Co-Di Advanced Speaking and Campaigning Course, 1989–97. Chancellor, Bedfordshire Univ 2014–. DUniv Essex, 2010; Hon. Dr of Laws: Buckingham, 2013; De Montfort, 2014; DS City, 2014. Backbencher to Watch, Spectator Mag., 1998; Opposition MP of the Year, C4 Hansard Soc. Political Awards, 2005; Backbencher of the Year, House Mag., 2005; ePolitix Dods Health Champion, 2006, Disability Champion, 2007, Internat. Champion, 200 Politician of the Year, Stonewall Awards, 2010. *Publications:* Tennis Maestros, 201 *Recreations:* tennis, swimming, reading, cinema. *Address:* Speaker's House, Westminste SW1A 0AA.

BERESFORD, family name of **Baron Decies** and **Marquess of Waterford**.

BERESFORD, Sir (Alexander) Paul, Kt 1990; dental surgeon; MP (C) Mole Valley, sinc 1997 (Croydon Central, 1992–97); *b* 6 April 1946; *s* of Raymond and Joan Beresford; *m* Jul Haynes; three *s* one *d*. *Educ:* Richmond Primary Sch., Richmond, Nelson, NZ; Waim Coll., Richmond; Otago Univ., Dunedin. Mem. (C), Wandsworth BC, 1978–94 (Leader c Council, 1983–92). Mem., Audit Commn, 1991–92. Parly Under-Sec. of State, DoI 1994–97. *Address:* c/o House of Commons, SW1A 0AA.

BERESFORD, Marcus de la Poer, CBE 2003; Chairman, Ricardo plc, 2004–09; non executive Director, Cobham plc, 2004–13; *b* 15 May 1942; *s* of late Anthony de la Po Beresford and Mary (*née* Canning); *m* 1965, Jean Helen Kitchener; two *s*. *Educ:* Harrow Sch St John's Coll., Cambridge (MA Mech. Sci.). FIET (FIEE 1986). Man. Dir, Automotiv Instrumentation Gp, Smiths Industries, 1978–83; Dir and Gen. Manager, Lucas Electroni Ltd, 1983–85; Man. Dir, Siemens Plessey Controls Ltd, 1985–92; Dir, Siemens plc, 1991–9 Man. Dir, GKN Industrial Services, 1992–2001; Dir, 1992–2002, Chief Exec., 2001–0 GKN plc. Non-executive Director: Camas, then Aggregate Industries, plc, 1994–200 Spirent plc, 1999–2006. Non-exec. Dir, Engrg and Technol. Bd, 2002–05. Mem. Counci Open Univ., 1997–2000. Freeman, City of London, 1963; Liveryman, Skinners' Co., 197 *Recreations:* golf, tennis, gardening. *Club:* Royal Over-Seas League.

BERESFORD, Meg; Manager, Wiston Lodge (formerly YMCA Centre, Wiston Lodge since 1997 (Assistant Director, 1994–97); *b* 5 Sept. 1937; *d* of late John Tristram Beresford an of Anne Stuart-Wortley; *m* 1959, William Tanner; two *s*. *Educ:* Sherborne School for Girl Seale Hayne Agricultural Coll., Newton Abbot; Univ. of Warwick. Community worke Leamington Spa; Organising Sec., European Nuclear Disarmament, 1981–83; Gen. Sec

CND, 1985–90; gardener, 1991–92, Staff Co-ordinator, 1992–94, Iona Community. Mem. Bd, Wiston Lodge, 2014–; Founder Mem., Tinto Music and Arts, 2014–. *Publications:* Into the Twenty First Century, 1989; contributor to End Jl, Sanity. *Recreations:* walking, reading, camping, music. *Address:* Wiston Lodge, Millrigg Road, Wiston, Biggar ML12 6HT.

BERESFORD, Sir Paul; *see* Beresford, Sir A. P.

BERESFORD-PEIRSE, Sir Henry (Njerš de la Poer), 7th Bt *cr* 1814, of Bagnall, Waterford; *b* London, 25 March 1969; *er s* of Sir Henry Grant de la Poer Beresford-Peirse, 6th Bt and of Jadranka Beresford-Peirse (*née* Njerš); *S* father, 2013; *m* 2005, Joanna Tamlyn; two *s* one *d*. *Educ:* Harrow Sch. *Recreation:* cricket. *Heir: s* Harry Tamlyn de la Poer Beresford-Peirse, *b* 23 Feb. 2007. *Address:* Bedale Manor, Bedale, N Yorkshire DL8 1EP. *T:* (01677) 422811. *Club:* White's.

BERG, Alan; District Judge (Magistrates' Courts) (formerly Stipendiary Magistrate), Greater Manchester, 1994–2010; Deputy District Judge, 2010–14; *b* 17 Feb. 1943; *s* of Simon and Esther Berg; *m* 1967, Lorna Lewis; two *s*. *Educ:* King George V Grammar Sch., Southport; Law Coll., Liverpool. Solicitor in private practice, Liverpool, 1967–94; Sen. Partner, Canter Levin & Berg, 1980–93; Asst Stipendiary Magistrate, 1991–94. *Recreations:* grandchildren, reading, worrying, voluntary work.

BERG, Eddie; Director, Eddie Berg Projects, since 2014; *b* 25 Aug. 1958; *s* of Francis and Edith Hollingsworth; *m* 1986, Karen Berg (marr. diss.); one *s*. *Educ:* Open Univ. House Manager, Everyman Th., Liverpool, 1984–87; Dir, Moviola, Liverpool, 1988–96; Chief Exec., Foundn for Art and Creative Technol., Liverpool, 1996–2005; Artistic Dir, BFI Southbank, 2005–11; Dir of Partnerships, BFI, 2011–14. Consultant, Employability and Ind. Engagement, Sch. of Arts and Digital Industries, Univ. of E London, 2014–. Exec. Chm., Gtr Birmingham Film Strategy Bd, 2014–. Chair: Puppetry Develt Steering Cttee, Arts Council England, 2014–; Ext. Adv. Bd, Inst. for Creative Enterprise, Edge Hill Univ., 2014–. Trustee, Culture24, 2014–. FRSA. *Publications:* (contrib.) Empire, Ruins and Networks: the transcultural agenda in art, 2005; Factors: 1988–2005. *Recreations:* films, media art, music, cooking, eating out, discovering new ideas/places/people, football, travel, thinking, soaking up the sun, reading.

BERG, Geoffrey, MVO 1976; HM Diplomatic Service, retired; *b* 5 July 1945; *s* of Bertram Lionel Berg and Irene Amelia Berg (*née* Hunt); *m* 1970, Sheila Maxine Brown; one *s*. *Educ:* Woking County Grammar Sch. for Boys. Joined CRO, 1963; Diplomatic Service Admin, 1965–68; Latin American floater duties, 1968–70; Third Sec. (Vice-Consul), Bucharest, 1970–72; FCO, 1972–75; Second, later First Sec. (Inf.), Helsinki, 1975–79; FCO, 1979–84; First Sec. (Commercial), Madrid, 1984–88; FCO, 1988–90; Counsellor on secondment to DTI, 1990–93; Dep. Head of Mission, Mexico City, 1993–96; Dep. Consul-Gen. and Dir of Trade, NY, 1997–2001; Consul-Gen., Toronto and Dir, Trade and Investment, Canada, 2002–05. Chevalier First Cl., Order of Lion (Finland), 1976; Official Cross, Order of Civil Merit (Spain), 1988. *Recreations:* travel, photography. *Club:* Royal Over-Seas League.

BERG, Rev. John J.; *see* Johansen-Berg.

BERG, Prof. Maxine Louise, DPhil; FBA 2004; FRHistS; Professor of History, University of Warwick, since 1998; *b* 22 Feb. 1950; *m* 1977, Prof. John Charles Robertson, *qv*; three *d*. *Educ:* Simon Fraser Univ., BC (BA); Univ. of Sussex (MA); Univ. of Oxford (DPhil 1976). Sir Lewis Namier Jun. Res. Fellow in Hist., Balliol Coll., Oxford, 1974; University of Warwick, 1978–: Lectr, then Sen. Lectr, Dept of Econs; Sen. Lectr, then Reader, Dept of History; Director: Eighteenth Century Centre, 1998–2007; Global History and Culture Centre, 2007–10. Associate Fellow, Centre for Hist. and Econs, Univ. of Cambridge, 2010–. Sen. Mem., Robinson Coll., Cambridge, 2010–. Hon. Fellow, Balliol Coll., Oxford, 2009. *Publications:* (ed) Technology and Toil in Nineteenth Century Britain, 1979; Machinery Question and the Making of Political Economy 1815–48, 1982; (ed jtly) Manufacture in Town and Country Before the Factory, 1983; The Age of Manufactures: industry, innovation and work in Britain 1700–1820, 1985, 2nd edn 1994; Political Economy in the Twentieth Century, 1989; (ed) Markets and Manufacture in Early Industrial Europe, 1991, new edn 2013; A Woman in History: Eileen Power 1889–1940, 1996; (ed with Kristine Bruland) Technological Revolutions in Europe 1760–1860, 1997; (ed with Helen Clifford) Consumers and Luxury in Europe 1650–1850, 1999; (ed with Elizabeth Eger) Luxury in the Eighteenth Century: debates, desires and delectable goods, 2002; Luxury and Pleasure in Eighteenth-Century Britain, 2005; (ed) Writing the History of the Global: challenges for the twenty-first century, 2013; (ed jtly) Goods from the East: trading Eurasia 1600–1800, 2014; contrib. learned jls. *Address:* Department of History, University of Warwick, Coventry CV4 7AL.

BERG, Prof. Paul, PhD; Cahill Professor in Cancer Research (Biochemistry), 1994–2000, now Professor Emeritus, and Director, Beckman Center for Molecular and Genetic Medicine, 1985–2000, Stanford University School of Medicine; *b* New York, 30 June 1926; *m* Mildred Levy; one *s*. *Educ:* Pennsylvania State Univ. (BS); Western Reserve Univ. (PhD). Pre-doctoral and post-doctoral med. research, 1950–54; scholar in cancer research, American Cancer Soc., Washington Univ., 1954; Asst to Associate Prof. of Microbiology, Washington Univ., 1955–59; Stanford Univ. Sch. of Medicine: Associate Prof. of Biochem., 1959–60; Prof., Dept of Biochem., 1960, Chm. 1969–74; Willson Prof. of Biochem., 1970–93; Non-resident Fellow, Salk Inst., 1973–83. Editor, Biochemical and Biophysical Res. Communications, 1959–68; Member: NIH Study, Sect. on Physiol Chem.; Editorial Bd, Jl of Molecular Biology, 1966–69; Bd of Sci. Advisors, Jane Coffin Childs Foundn for Med. Res.; Adv. Bds to Nat. Insts of Health, Amer. Cancer Soc., Nat. Sci. Foundn, MIT and Harvard, 1970–80; Council, Nat. Acad. of Scis, 1979. Former Pres., Amer. Soc. of Biological Chemists; Foreign Member: Japan Biochem. Soc., 1978; French Acad. of Scis, 1981; Royal Soc., 1992; Pontifical Acad. of Scis, 1996. Lectures: Harvey, 1972; Lynen, 1977; Weizmann Inst., 1977; Univ. of Pittsburgh, 1978; Priestly, Pennsylvania State Univ., 1978; Shell, Univ. of California at Davis, 1978; Dreyfus, Northwestern Univ., 1979; Jesup, Columbia Univ., 1980; Karl-August-Förster, Univ. of Mainz, 1980; David Rivett Meml, CSIR, Melb., 1980. Hon. DSc: Rochester and Yale Univs, 1978; Washington Univ., St Louis, 1986; Pennsylvania State Univ., 1995; numerous awards include: Eli Lilly Award, 1959; Calif. Scientist of the Year, 1963; Nat. Acad. of Scis, 1966, 1974; Amer. Acad. of Arts and Scis, 1966; Henry J. Kaiser, Stanford Univ. Sch. of Med., 1969, 1972; V. D. Mattia Prize of Roche Inst. for Molec. Biol., 1972; Gairdner Foundn Award, Nobel Prize in Chemistry, New York Acad. of Scis and Albert Lasker Med. Res. awards, 1980; National Medal of Science, 1983. *Publications:* (jtly) Genes and Genomes: a changing perspective, 1990; (jtly) Dealing with Genes: the language of heredity, 1992; (jtly) George Beadle: an uncommon farmer, 2003; many scientific articles and reviews. *Address:* Beckman Center-BO62, Stanford University Medical Center, Stanford, CA 94305–5301, USA.

BERGANZA, Teresa; singer (mezzo-soprano); *b* Madrid, Spain; *d* of Guillermo and Maria Ascension Berganza; *m*; three *c*. Début in Aix-en-Provence, 1957; début in England, Glyndebourne, 1958; appeared at Glyndebourne, 1959; Royal Opera House, Covent Garden, 1959, 1960, 1963, 1964, 1976, 1977, 1979, 1981, 1984, 1985; Royal Festival Hall, 1960, 1961, 1962, 1967, 1971; appears regularly in Vienna, Milan, Aix-en-Provence, Holland, Japan, Edinburgh, Paris, Israel, America; Carmen, opening ceremonies, Expo 92, Seville; participated opening ceremonies, Barcelona Olympics, 1992. Mem. (first elected woman), Spanish Royal Acad. of Arts, 1994. Prizes: Lucretia Arana; Nacional Lírica, Spain; Lily Pons, 1976; Acad. Nat. du Disque Lyrique; USA record award; Harriet Cohen Internat. Music Award, 1974; Grand Prix Rossini; Médaille d'or, Ville Aix-en-Provence; International Critic Award, 1988. Charles Cross (6 times); Grand Cross, Isabel la Católica, Spain; Gran Cruz al Mérito en las Bellas Artes, Spain; Commandeur, l'Ordre des Arts et des Lettres, France. *Publications:* Flor de Soledad y Silencio, 1984. *Recreations:* music, books, the arts. *Address:* Avenida de Juan de Borbón y Battenberg 16, 28200 San Lorenzo del Escorial, Madrid, Spain.

BERGER, John; author and art critic; *b* London, 5 Nov. 1926; *s* of late S. J. D. Berger, OBE, MC, and Mrs Miriam Berger (*née* Branson). *Educ:* Central Sch. of Art; Chelsea Sch. of Art. Began career as a painter and teacher of drawing; exhibited at Wildenstein, Redfern and Leicester Galls, London. Art Critic: Tribune; New Statesman. Vis. Fellow, BFI, 1990–. Numerous TV appearances, incl.: Monitor; two series for Granada TV. Scenario: (with Alain Tanner) La Salamandre; Le Milieu du Monde; Jonas (New York Critics Prize for Best Scenario of Year, 1976); Play me Something (also principal rôle) (Europa Prize, Barcelona Film Fest., 1989). George Orwell Meml Prize, 1977; Lannan Foundn Lit. Award for Fiction, USA, 1989; State Prize for Artistic Achievement, Austria, 1990; Petrarca Award, Germany, 1991. *Publications: fiction:* A Painter of Our Time, 1958; The Foot of Clive, 1962; Corker's Freedom, 1964; G (Booker Prize, James Tait Black Meml Prize), 1972; Into their Labours (trilogy), 1992: Pig Earth, 1979; Once in Europa, 1989; Lilac and Flag, 1991; To The Wedding, 1995; Photocopies, 1996; King: a street story, 1999; Here is Where We Meet, 2005; From A to X: a story in letters, 2008; *theatre:* with Nella Bielski: Question of Geography, 1986 (staged Marseilles, 1984, Paris, 1986 and by RSC, Stratford, 1987); Francisco Goya's Last Portrait, 1989; *non-fiction:* Marcel Frishman, 1958; Permanent Red, 1960; The Success and Failure of Picasso, 1965; (with J. Mohr) A Fortunate Man: the story of a country doctor, 1967; Art and Revolution, Moments of Cubism and Other Essays, 1969; The Look of Things, Ways of Seeing, 1972; The Seventh Man, 1975 (Prize for Best Reportage, Union of Journalists and Writers, Paris, 1977); About Looking, 1980; (with J. Mohr) Another Way of Telling, 1982 (televised, 1989); And Our Faces, My Heart, Brief as Photos, 1984; The White Bird, 1985 (USA, as The Sense of Sight, 1985); Keeping a Rendezvous (essays and poems), 1992; Pages of the Wound (poems), 1994; (with K. Berger-Andreadakis) Titian: nymph and shepherd, 1996; (with J. Christie) I Send You This Cadmium Red, 2000; The Shape of a Pocket (essays), 2001; Selected Essays (ed G. Dyer), 2001; Hold Everything Dear: dispatches on survival and resistance, 2007; Bento's Sketchbook, 2011; *translations:* (with A. Bostock): Poems on the Theatre, by B. Brecht, 1960; Return to My Native Land, by Aime Cesaire, 1969; (with Lisa Appignanesi): Oranges for the Son of Alexander Levy, by Nella Bielski, 1982; The Year is '42, by Nella Bielski, 2004. *Address:* Quincy, Mieussy, 74440 Taninges, France.

BERGER, Luciana Clare; MP (Lab Co-op) Liverpool, Wavertree, since 2010; *b* Wembley, 13 May 1981. *Educ:* Haberdashers' Aske's Sch. for Girls, Elstree; Univ. of Birmingham (BCom); Birkbeck Coll., Univ. of London (MSc Govt). Govt Strategy Unit, Accenture, 2005–06; Govt and Parly Manager, NHS Confedn, 2006–07. Shadow Minister: for Energy and Climate Change, 2010–13; of Public Health, 2013–15; for Mental Health, 2015–. Dir, Labour Friends of Israel, 2007–10. FRSA. *Address:* House of Commons, SW1A 0AA.

BERGHUSER, Sir Hugo (Erich), Kt 1989; MBE 1981; *b* Germany, 25 Oct. 1935; *m* Christa; one *s* one *d*. *Educ:* Volksschule, Stiepel; Trade School, Bochum. Cabinet-maker. Embarked on ship to emigrate to Australia, 1958; ship (Skaubryn) caught fire and sank in the Indian Ocean; arrived in Papua New Guinea in 1959; active in the building industries, meat trade and timber sawmilling trade, employing over 700. MP, PNG, 1987–92; Minister for Civil Aviation, Tourism and Culture, 1987. Independence Medal, PNG, 1975; Silver Jubilee Medal, 1977; Service Medal, PNG, 1980; Long Service Medal, PNG, 1985. Distinctive Cross, 1st Cl. (Germany), 1986; Grand Cross (Germany), 1991; Hon. Consulate Gen. (Turkey). *Address:* PO Box 1785, Boroko, NCD, Papua New Guinea. *Club:* Papua.

BERGIN, Prof. Joseph, LittD; FBA 1996; Professor of History, University of Manchester, 1996–2011, now Emeritus; *b* Kilkenny, 11 Feb. 1948; *s* of Cornelius Bergin and Brigid (*née* Phelan); *m* 1978, Sylvia Papazian; one *s* one *d*. *Educ:* Rockwell Coll., Co. Tipperary; University Coll., Dublin; Peterhouse, Cambridge; LittD Manchester 2004. Lectr in History, Maynooth Coll., 1976–78; Manchester University: Lectr in History, 1978–88; Sen. Lectr, 1988–92; Reader, 1992–96. Visiting Professor: Lyon Univ., 1991–92; Ecole des Chartes, Paris, 1995; Nancy Univ., 1999; Montpellier, 2004; Sorbonne, 2005. Leverhulme Major Res. Fellow, 2000–03; Fellow, Wissenschaftskolleg, Berlin, 2006–07. Resident, Inst. for Advanced Study, Nantes, 2012–13. Corresp. étranger, Acad. des Inscriptions et Belles-Lettres, Paris, 2011; MAE 2011. Prix Richelieu, Rueil-Malmaison, France, 1995; Medal of Antiquities of France, Acad. Inscriptions et Belles-Lettres, Paris, 2010; Médaille Richelieu, Sorbonne, 2010. Officier, Ordre des Palmes Académiques (France), 2010. *Publications:* Cardinal Richelieu: power and the pursuit of wealth, 1985; Cardinal La Rochefoucauld, 1987; The Rise of Richelieu, 1991; The Making of the French Episcopate 1589–1661, 1996; Seventeenth Century Europe, 2000; Crown, Church and Episcopate under Louis XIV, 2004; Church, Society and Religious Change in France 1580–1730, 2009; The Politics of Religion in Early Modern France, 2014. *Recreations:* sports, book hunting, music, walking. *Address:* 9 Sibley Road, Heaton Moor, Stockport, Cheshire SK4 4HH. *T:* (0161) 432 4650.

BERGIN, Thomas; correspondent, since 2001, and investigative journalist, since 2012, Reuters; *b* Dublin, 24 Oct. 1971; *s* of Charles J. Bergin and Mary Rose Bergin (*née* O'Doherty); *m* 2005, Sophy Tonder; two *s*. *Educ:* Clongowes Wood Coll., Ireland; University Coll. Dublin (BA Philosophy and Econs 1992); University Coll., Galway (Dip. Business Studies 1993). Researcher, Foreign Trade Bank of Mexico, 1994–95; Fund Adminr, ING Barings, 1995–97; Energy Broker, HOB (Ireland) Ltd, 1997–98; reporter, Futures & Options World, 1999–2001. Orwell Prize for Journalism, Orwell Trust, 2013; Gerald Loeb Award, UCLA Anderson Sch. of Mgt, 2013; Business Reporter of Year, British Press Awards, 2013; Business Journalist of Year, London Press Club, 2013; Business Reporting Award, NY Press Club, 2013; Business Feature Award, Deadline Club, 2013; Soc. of American Business Editors and Writers Award, 2013. *Publications:* Spills & Spin: the inside story of BP, 2011. *Address:* c/o Reuters, 30 South Colonnade, E14 5EP. *T:* (020) 7542 1111. *E:* tom.bergin@reuters.com.

BERGONZI, Prof. Bernard, FRSL; Professor of English, University of Warwick, 1971–92, now Emeritus; *b* 13 April 1929; *s* of late Carlo and Louisa Bergonzi; *m* 1st, 1960, Gabriel Wall (*d* 1984); one *s* two *d*; 2nd, 1987, Anne Samson. *Educ:* Wadham Coll., Oxford (BLitt, MA). Asst Lectr in English, Manchester Univ., 1959–62, Lectr, 1962–66; Sen. Lectr, Univ. of Warwick, 1966–71, Pro-Vice-Chancellor, 1979–82. Vis. Lectr, Brandeis Univ., 1964–65; Visiting Professor: Stanford Univ., 1982; Univ. of Louisville, 1988; Nene Coll., 1994–2000; Vis. Fellow, New Coll., Oxford, 1987. FRSL 1984. *Publications:* Descartes and the Animals (verse), 1954; The Early H. G. Wells, 1961; Heroes' Twilight, 1965; The Situation of the Novel, 1970; Anthony Powell, 1971; T. S. Eliot, 1972; The Turn of a Century, 1973; Gerard Manley Hopkins, 1977; Reading the Thirties, 1978; Years (verse), 1979; The Roman Persuasion (novel), 1981; The Myth of Modernism and Twentieth Century Literature, 1986; Exploding English, 1990; Wartime and Aftermath, 1993; David Lodge, 1995; War Poets and Other Subjects, 1999; A Victorian Wanderer, 2003; A Study in Greene, 2006. *Recreations:* conversation, retrospection. *Address:* 19 St Mary's Crescent, Leamington Spa CV31 1JL. *T:* (01926) 883115.

BERGQUIST, Mats Fingal Thorwald, Hon. CMG 1983; PhD; Ambassador of Sweden to the Court of St James's, 1997–2004; *b* 5 Sept. 1938; *s* of Thorwald and Ingrid Bergquist; *m* 1st, 1968, Marianne Lübeck (*d* 1979); two *s*; 2nd, 1991, Agneta Lorichs; two *s*. *Educ:* Univ. of Lund (MA 1960; PhL 1964; PhD 1970). Joined Swedish Diplomatic Service, 1964: served:

London, 1964–66; Perm. Mission to UN, NY, 1966–68; First Sec., subseq. Counsellor, Foreign Ministry, 1970–76; Counsellor, Washington, 1976–81; Asst Dep. Under Sec., 1981–85; Dep. Under Sec. for Political Affairs, 1985–87; Ambassador to: Israel, 1987–92; Finland, 1992–97. Chm., Swedish Inst. for Internat. Affairs, 2006–12. Chancellor, Växjö Univ., 2005–09. Commander: Légion d'Honneur (France), 1983; Order of Orange-Nassau (Netherlands), 1987; Grand Cross, Finnish Lion (Finland), 1994. *Publications:* Sweden and the EEC, 1970; War and Surrogate War, 1976; Balance of Power and Deterrence, 1988; Conflict Without End?, 1993; From Cold War to Lukewarm Peace, 1998; The Blair Experiment, 2007. *Recreations:* music, tennis. *Address:* Bergsgatan 16, 11223 Stockholm, Sweden.

BERINGER, Guy Gibson; Chairman, Export Credits Guarantee Department (UK Export Finance), since 2010; *b* 12 Aug. 1955; *s* of Lt Col Frederick Richard Beringer and Hazel Margaret Beringer (*née* Orr); *m* 1979, Margaret Catherine Powell; three *d. Educ:* Campbell Coll., Belfast; St Catharine's Coll., Cambridge (MA). Admitted Solicitor, 1980; joined Allen & Overy, 1980: Asst Solicitor, 1980–85; Partner, 1985–2008; Managing Partner, Corporate Dept, 1994–99; Sen. Partner, 2000–08. Non-exec. Chm., ATC Gp, 2010–13; non-executive Director: Fleming Family & Partners Ltd, 2008–15; London Irish Hldgs Ltd, 2009–14; BCKR Ltd, 2012–. Non-exec. Mem. Bd, HM Courts Service, 2008–11. Mem., Law Soc., 1980–. Adjunct Prof., Imperial Coll. Business Sch. (formerly Tanaka Business Sch.), Imperial Coll., London, 2008–. Chm., City Music Services, 2012–. Gov. and Dep. Chm., Coll. of Law, 2009–12; Chm., Legal Educn Foundn, 2012–. Co-Chm., Appeal Bd, Bingham Centre for the Rule of Law, 2012–. Fellow Commoner, St Catharine's Coll., Cambridge, 2008. Hon. QC 2006; Hon. Bencher, Inner Temple, 2009. *Recreations:* choral singing, golf, boating. *Address:* The River House, Wey Road, Weybridge, Surrey KT13 8HR. *T:* (01932) 844868. *Clubs:* Athenæum; Hawks (Cambridge).

BERINGER, Prof. Sir John (Evelyn), Kt 2000; CBE 1993; Professor of Molecular Genetics, 1984–2005, now Professor Emeritus, and Pro-Vice-Chancellor, 2001–05, University of Bristol; *b* 14 Feb. 1944; *s* of late Group Captain William Beringer and of Evelyn Joan Beringer; *m* 1970, Sheila Murray; three *s. Educ:* Univ. of Edinburgh (Scottish Dip. in Agric. 1965; BSc 1970); Univ. of East Anglia (PhD 1973). Microbial Geneticist, John Innes Inst., 1970–80; Head, Dept of Microbiology, Rothamsted Exptl Station, Harpenden, 1980–84; University of Bristol: Dir, Molecular Genetics Unit, 1984–88; Head, Dept of Microbiology, 1986–90; Head, Dept of Botany, 1990–93; Dean of Science, 1996–2001. Chairman, advisory committees: Genetic Manipulation Planned Release Sub-Cttee, 1987–90; Releases to Envmt, 1990–99; Chm., Main Panel D, 2008 RAE. Member: NERC, 1996–2001; Council for Sci. and Technol., 2004–08. Chairman: Governing Council, John Innes Centre, 2000–09; Inst. of Garden and Landscape History, 2006–08. Fleming Lectr, Soc. for Gen. Microbiology, 1979. Hon. DSc: Exeter, 2006; East Anglia, 2011. *Publications:* sci. contribs to biological jls and proceedings. *Recreations:* gardening, reading, classic cars, golf.

BERKELEY, family name of **Baron Berkeley of Knighton**.

BERKELEY, 18th Baron *cr* 1421; **Anthony Fitzhardinge Gueterbock,** OBE 1989; Baron Gueterbock (Life Peer) 2000; Chairman, Rail Freight Group, since 1996; *b* 20 Sept. 1939; *o s* of Brig. E. A. L. Gueterbock (*d* 1984) and Hon. Cynthia Ella Gueterbock (*d* 1991), *sister* of Baroness Berkeley, 17th in line; *S* aunt, 1992; *m* 1st, 1965, Diane Christine (marr. diss. 1998), *e d* of Eric William John Townsend; two *s* one *d*; 2nd, 1999, Julia Rosalind (marr. diss. 2011), *d* of Michael Clarke. *Educ:* Eton; Trinity Coll., Cambridge (MA). CEng, MICE. Engineering, construction and planning, Sir Alexander Gibb & Partners, 1961–65; multi-disciplinary engineering and construction, planning and business develt, George Wimpey PLC, 1965–81; The Channel Tunnel Group/Eurotunnel, 1981–96. Chm., Piggyback Consortium, 1992–98. Chm., UK Marine Pilots' Assoc., 1998–; Mem. Bd, Eur. Rail Freight Assoc., 2007– (Pres. 2009–11). Trustee, Plymouth Marine Laboratories Ltd, 2011–. Harbour Comr, Port of Fowey, 2006–13. Hon. DSc Brighton, 1996. *Recreations:* ski-ing, sailing. *Heir: s* Hon. Thomas Fitzhardinge Gueterbock [*b* 5 Jan. 1969; *m* 1995, Helen Ruth, *er d* of Lt-Comdr Brian Walsh, RN retd]. *Address:* c/o House of Lords, SW1A 0PW.

BERKELEY OF KNIGHTON, Baron *cr* 2013 (Life Peer), of Knighton in the County of Powys; **Michael Fitzhardinge Berkeley,** CBE 2012; composer and broadcaster; *b* 29 May 1948; *s* of late Sir Lennox Randal Berkeley and of Elizabeth Freda (*née* Bernstein); *m* 1979, Deborah Jane Coltman-Rogers; one *d. Educ:* Westminster Cathedral Choir Sch.; The Oratory Sch.; Royal Acad. of Music (ARAM 1984; FRAM 1996). FRWCMD 2003; FRNCM 2004. Studied privately with Richard Rodney Bennett; rock musician; phlebotomist, St Bartholomew's Hosp., 1969–71; Presentation Asst, LWT, 1973; Announcer, BBC Radio 3, 1974–79; regular presenter of arts programmes for BBC (Meridian, World Service, Private Passions, Radio 3); introduces proms, concerts and festivals for BBC2 and Radio 3, BBC television documentaries and Glyndebourne for C4. Associate Composer: to Scottish Chamber Orch., 1979; to BBC Nat. Orch. of Wales, 2001–08. Jt Artistic Dir, Spitalfields Fest., 1994–97; Artistic Dir, Cheltenham Fest., 1995–2004. Member: Exec. Cttee, Assoc. of Professional Composers, 1982–84; Central Music Adv. Cttee, BBC, 1986–90; Gen. Adv. Council, BBC, 1990–95; New Music Sub-Cttee, Arts Council of GB, 1984–86; Music Panel Adviser to Arts Council, 1986–90; Mem., Bd of Dirs, Royal Opera House, Covent Gdn, 1996–2001 (Mem., 1994–98, Chm., 1998–99, Opera Bd). Vis. Prof., Huddersfield Univ. (formerly Poly.), 1991–94. Governor: NYO, 1994–96; Royal Ballet, 2001– (Chm., 2003–12); Dir, Britten-Pears Foundn, 1996–2009. Hon. DMus UEA, 2007. *Compositions: orchestral music:* Fanfare and National Anthem, 1979; Primavera, 1979; Flames, 1981; Gregorian Variations, 1982; Daybreak and a Candle End, 1985; Gethsemane Fragment, 1990; Secret Garden, 1998; The Garden of Earthly Delights, 1998; Tristessa, 2003; Concerto for Orchestra, 2005; Slow Dawn, 2008; *for chamber or small orchestra:* Meditations, 1977 (Guinness Prize for Composition); Fantasia Concertante, 1978; Uprising: Symphony in one movement, 1980; Suite: the Vision of Piers the Ploughman, 1981; The Romance of the Rose, 1982; Coronach, 1988; Entertaining Master Punch, 1991; Abstract Mirror, 2002; *concertos:* Concerto for Oboe and String Orch., 1977; Concerto for Cello and Small Orch., 1983; Concerto for Horn and String Orch., 1984; Organ Concerto, 1987; Clarinet Concerto, 1991; Viola Concerto, 1994; *chamber music:* String Trio, 1978; American Suite, 1980; Chamber Symphony, 1980; String Quartet No 1, 1981; Nocturne, 1982; Piano Trio, 1982; Music from Chaucer, 1983; Quintet for Clarinet and Strings, 1983; String Quartet No 2, 1984; The Mayfly, 1984; Pas de deux, 1985; For the Savage Messiah, 1985; Quartet Study, 1987; Catch Me if You Can, 1993; Torque and Velocity, 1997; Piano Quintet, 2009; Into the Ravine (oboe quintet), 2011; *strings:* Etude de Fleurs, 1979; Sonata for Violin and Piano, 1979; Iberian Notebook, 1980; Variations on Greek Folk-Songs, 1981; Funerals and Fandangos, 1984; A Mosaic for Father Popieluszko, 1985; *guitar:* Lament, 1980; Worry Beads, 1981; Sonata in One Movement, 1982; Impromptu, 1985; Magnetic Field, 1995; *keyboard:* Passacaglia, 1978; Strange Meeting, 1978; Organ Sonata, 1979; Dark Sleep, 1994; *woodwind:* Three Moods, 1979; American Suite, 1980; Fierce Tears, 1984; Flighting, 1985; Keening, 1987; *vocal music for solo voice:* The Wild Winds, 1978; Rain, 1979; Wessex Graves, 1981; Songs of Awakening Love, 1986; Speaking Silence, 1986; Three Cabaret Sons, 2012 (words by Ian McEwan); *vocal/orchestral:* Love Cries, 1999 (adaptation from the Second Mrs Kong by Harrison Birtwistle); *vocal/chamber:* Three Rilke Sonnets for Soprano and Ensemble, 2011; *choral music:* At the Round Earth's Imagin'd Corners, 1980; The Crocodile and Father William, 1982; Easter, 1982; As the Wind Doth Blow, 1983; Hereford Communion Service, 1985; Pasce Oves Meas, 1985; Verbum Caro Factum Est, 1987; The Red Macula, 1989; Night Song in the Jungle, 1990; Winter Fragments, 1996; Farewell, 1999; Torch Light, 2006; Gabriel's Lament (chorus and orch.), 2009; Anthem: Advent Carol (words by Rowan Williams), 2010; Listen, Listen, O My Child (anthem for Archbishop of Canterbury's enthronement), 201 Build This House, 2014 (for King's Coll., Cambridge); Magna Carta Te Deum, 2015 (fo 800th Anniv. of Magna Carta, Lincoln Cathedral); *oratorio:* Or Shall We Die?, 1983 (text b Ian McEwan; filmed for Channel 4); *opera:* libretti by David Malouf: Baa Baa Black Shee 1993; Jane Eyre, 2000; libretto by Ian McEwan: For You, 2008; *ballet:* Bastet, 1988; Rushe - Fragments from a Lost Story, 2008 (adapted from Prokofiev's film music and subseq. pub and recorded as Symphonic Suite from The Queen of Spades, 2009); Tetractys - The Art Fugue (arranged and orchestrated from Bach's Art of Fugue), 2014; *film music:* Captive, 198 Twenty-one, 1990; Goldeneye, 1991. *Publications:* The Music Pack, 1994; music compositions; articles in The Observer, The Guardian, The Listener, The Sunday Telegrap and Vogue. *Recreations:* looking at paintings, reading, walking and hill farming in mid-Wale tennis, ski-ing. *Address:* c/o Ralph Blackbourn, Artist Manager, Rayfield Allied, Southban House, Black Prince Road, SE1 7SJ. *T:* (020) 3176 5502.

BERKHOUT, Prof. Frans, DPhil; Professor of Environment, Society and Climate, King College London, since 2013; Interim Director, Future Earth Programme, Internation Council for Science, Paris, since 2013; *b* Dar-es-Salaam, Tanganyika, 21 Oct. 1961; *s* of Joo Berkhout and Katherine Berkhout-Heim; *m* 1992, Diane Moody; one *s* one *d. Educ:* Univ of Leeds (BSc Geog. 1983); Sussex Univ. (DPhil Sci. and Technol. Policy Studies 1989). Re Fellow, Sci. Policy Res. Unit, Sussex Univ., 1989–92 and 1994–96; Res. Associate, Cent for Energy and Envmtl Studies and Lectr, Woodrow Wilson Sch., Princeton Univ., 1992–9 Sen. Fellow, and Leader, Envmt Prog., SPRU-Sci. and Technol. Policy Res., Univ. Sussex, 1996–2004; Co-Dir, Global Envmtl Change Prog., 1999–2000, Dir, Sustainab Technologies Prog., 2002–04, UK ESRC; VU University, Amsterdam: Prof. of Innovatio and Sustainability, 2004–; Director: Inst. for Envmtl Studies, 2004–12; Amsterdam Glob Change Inst., 2010–13. *Publications:* (with S. M. MacGill) The Politics of Anxiety: Sellafield cancer-link controversy, 1987; Radioactive waste: politics and technology, 1991; (jtly) Worl Inventory of Plutonium and Highly-Enriched Uranium, 1992; (ed jtly) Industrial Ecology an Global Change, 1994; (jtly) Plutonium and Highly Enriched Uranium 1996: worl inventories, capabilities and possibilities, 1997; (ed jtly) Managing a Material World perspectives in industrial ecology, 1998; (ed jtly) Negotiating Environmental Change: ne perspectives from social science, 2003; (ed jtly) Climate Change Governance in Europe confronting dilemmas of mitigation and adaptation, 2010; contrib. articles to learned jl *Recreations:* distance running, golf, walking. *Address:* King's College London, Strand Campu WC2R 2LS. *T:* (020) 7848 1306. *E:* frans.berkhout@kcl.ac.uk.

BERKLEY, David Nahum; QC 1999; a Recorder, since 2001; *b* 3 Dec. 1955; *s* of Elchana Berkovitz and Doreen Berkley (*née* Wacks); *m* 1978, Deborah Fay Haffner; one *s* four *d. Edu* Manchester Jewish Grammar Sch.; Gateshead Yeshiva; Univ. of Manchester (LLB (Hons)) Litigation Asst, Halliwell Landau, 1978–79; called to the Bar, Middle Temple, 1979 Founding Head, Merchant Chambers, Northern Circuit, 1996; Hd, Commercial Gp, St John Bldgs, 2004–. Dep. Dist Judge, 1998–2001. Chm., N Circuit Commercial Bar Assoc 2003–08 (Sec. 1997–2003). Hon. Teaching Fellow, Sch. of Law, Manchester Metropolita Univ., 2012–14. *Recreation:* books. *Address:* St Johns Buildings, 24A–28 St John Stree Manchester M3 4DJ. *T:* (0161) 214 1500, *Fax:* (0161) 835 3929. *E:* david.berkley@ stjohnsbuildings.co.uk; 1 Gray's Inn Square, Gray's Inn, WC1R 5AA. *T:* (020) 7405 0001.

BERKOFF, Steven; actor, director and writer; *b* 3 Aug. 1937; *s* of Polly and Al Berk (formerly Berkovitch); *m* (marr. diss.). *Educ:* Raine's Foundation Grammar School, Stepney Grocers' Co. Sch., Hackney. *Plays acted,* 1965–: Zoo Story; Arturo Ui; Dinner with Saddam *plays directed/acted/wrote,* 1969–: Metamorphosis (also directed on Broadway, 1989, Japan 1992); Macbeth (directed and acted); Agamemnon; The Trial; The Fall of the House o Usher; East; Kvetch (Evening Standard Comedy of the Year Award, 1991); season of 3 plays NT; Hamlet (directed and acted); Decadence (filmed, 1993); Brighton Beach Scumbags Greek; West; One Man; Shakespeare's Villains (one-man show), Haymarket, 1998; Messia Old Vic, 2003; *wrote and directed:* Sink the Belgrano, Mermaid, 1986, Acapulco, 1992; Si Actors in Search of a Director, 2012; *wrote and co-directed:* Religion and Anarchy, Jermyn S Th., 2013; *directed:* Coriolanus, NY, 1988, Munich, 1991; Salomé, Edinburgh Festival, N (and acted), 1989, Phoenix (and acted), 1990; The Trial, NT, 1991; Coriolanus, Mermai (and acted), 1996; Massage, LA (and acted), 1997; East, Vaudeville, 1999; Messiah, 2000; Th Secret Love Life of Ophelia, 2001; Sit and Shiver, New End, 2006; On the Waterfront Nottingham Playhouse (and adapted), 2008, transf. Th. Royal, Haymarket, 2009; Oedipus Liverpool Playhouse (and adapted), 2011; *films acted:* A Clockwork Orange, 1971; Barr Lyndon, The Passenger, 1975; McVicar, 1980; Outland, 1981; Octopussy, 1983; Beverly Hill Cop, 1984; Rambo, Underworld, Revolution, 1985; Under the Cherry Moon, Absolut Beginners, 1986; Prisoner of Rio, 1988; The Krays, 1990; Decadence, 1994; Fair Game 1995; Another 9½ Weeks (Love in Paris), 1997; Legionnaire, 1998; The Big I Am, Drop Dea Gorgeous, The Tourist, 2010; The Girl with the Dragon Tattoo, 2012. Hon. DLitt Brune 2010. *Publications:* East, 1977; Gross Intrusion (short stories), 1979; Decadence, 1982; Greek 1982; West, 1985; Lunch, 1985; Harry's Xmas, 1985; Kvetch, 1987; Acapulco, 1987; Sin the Belgrano, 1987; Massage, 1987; America, 1988; I Am Hamlet, 1989; A Prisoner in Rio 1989; The Theatre of Steven Berkoff (photographic), 1992; Coriolanus in Deutschland, 1992 Meditations on Metamorphosis, 1995; Free Association (autobiog.), 1996; Graft: tales of a actor (short stories), 1998; Shopping in the Santa Monica Mall, Ritual in Blood, Messia Oedipus, 2000; The Secret Love Life of Ophelia, 2001; Tough Acts, 2003; Richard II in Ne York, 2007; My Life in Food, 2008; You Remind Me of Marilyn Monroe, 2009; Diary of Juvenile Delinquent (memoir), 2010; Tales from an Actor's Life, 2011; One-Act Plays, 2012 East-End Photographs, 2012; *play adaptations:* The Fall of the House of Usher, 1977 Agamemnon, 1977; The Trial, 1981; Metamorphosis, 1981; In the Penal Colony, 1988 *Recreations:* ping-pong, photography, travelling. *Address:* c/o Joanna Marston, 1 Clarevill Grove Mews, SW7 5AH. *T:* (020) 7370 1080. *W:* www.stevenberkoff.com.

BERKOVIC, Prof. Samuel Frank, AC 2014 (AM 2005); MD; FRS 2007; FRACP; FAA neurologist and clinical researcher; Laureate Professor, Department of Medicine, Universit of Melbourne, since 2007 (Australia Fellow, 2007–12); *b* Melbourne, 13 Oct. 1953; *s* o Alexander and Eva Clara Berkovic; *m* 1977, Helena Makowski; one *s* two *d. Educ:* Univ. o Melbourne (MB BS 1977; BMedSci 1977; MD 1985). FRACP 1985. Department o Medicine, University of Melbourne: Sen. Lectr, 1989–94; Associate Prof., 1995–98; Prof. 1998–2007; Scientific Dir, Brain Res. Inst., Melbourne, 2001–; Dir, Epilepsy Res. Centre 1998–. Adjunct Prof., Dept of Neurol. and Neurosurgery, Faculty of Medicine, McGil Univ., Canada, 1989–. FAA 2005. Epilepsy Res. Recognition Award, Amer. Epilepsy Soc. 1995; Novartis Prize for Epilepsy Res., 2001; GlaxoSmithKline Australia Award for Res Excellence, 2002; Zulch Prize for Basic Neurol Res., Max Planck Soc., Germany, 2005 Curtin Medal, ANU, 2005; Clive and Vera Ramaciotti Medal for Excellence in Biomed Res., 2006; Bethlehem Griffiths Res. Foundn Medal, 2009; Samuel Gershon Medal fo Translational Neurosci., S Australian Health and Med. Res. Inst., 2014; (jtly) Prime Ministe of Australia's Award for Sci., 2014; Sen. Australian of Year, Vic, 2015. *Address:* Departmen of Medicine, Melbourne Brain Centre, 245 Burgundy Street, Heidelberg, Vic 3084, Australia *T:* (3) 90357093, *Fax:* (3) 94962291. *E:* s.berkovic@unimelb.edu.au.

BERKSHIRE, Archdeacon of; *see* Graham, Ven. O. J.

BERLINS, Marcel Joseph; journalist and broadcaster; *b* 30 Oct. 1941; *s* of Jacques and Pear Berlins; *m* 2005, Lisa Forrell. *Educ:* schools in France and South Africa; Univ. o Witwatersrand (BComm, LLB); LSE (LLM). Legal Asst, Lord Chancellor's Dept, 1969–71 Legal Corresp. and leader writer, The Times, 1971–82; freelance writer and TV presenter

1982–86; crime fiction reviewer, The Times, 1983–; Editor, Law Magazine, 1987–88; presenter, Radio 4 Law in Action, 1988–2004; columnist, The Guardian, 1988–2010; panellist, Round Britain Quiz, Radio 4, 1997–. Visiting Professor: Queen Mary, London Univ., 2004–09; UCL; City Univ., 2005–10. *Publications:* Barrister behind Bars, 1974; (with Geoffrey Wansell) Caught in the Act, 1974; (with Clare Dyer) Living Together, 1982; (with Clare Dyer) The Law Machine, 1982, 5th edn 2000; (ed) The Law and You, 1986; numerous articles for large variety of newspapers, magazines and legal jls. *Recreations:* cinema, jazz. *Address:* 83 Bedford Court Mansions, Bedford Avenue, WC1B 3AE. *T:* (020) 7323 9981.

BERLUSCONI, Silvio; Senator, Italian Parliament, 2013; Prime Minister of Italy, 1994, 2001–06 and 2008–11; *b* 29 Sept. 1936; *s* of late Luigi Berlusconi and Rosella Berlusconi (*née* Bossi); *m* 1st, 1965, Carla Elvira Dall'Oglio (marr. diss. 1985); one *s* one *d*; 2nd, 1990, Veronica Lario (marr. diss. 2014), actress; one *s* two *d*. *Educ:* Univ. of Milan (law degree 1961). Founder: Edilnord construction co., 1962; Telemilano, cable TV station, 1974; Fininvest, 1975–94, hldg co. with interests in commercial TV, printed media, publishing, advertising, insurance, financial services, retailing and football; companies created/acquired include: TV networks, Canale 5, 1980, Italia 1, 1982, Rete 4, 1984, La Cinq, 1986, Telefünf, 1987, Telecinco, 1989; cinema chain, Cinema 5, 1985; dept store chain, La Standa, 1988; publg co., Arnoldo Mondadori Editore, 1990; newspaper, Il Giornale; Chm., AC Milan FC, 1986–2004 and 2006–. MP Italy, 1994 and 1996–2013 (Forza Italy, 1994 and 1996–2009; Popolo della Libertà, 1996–2013). Leader: Forza Italia, 1993–2009, 2013–; Popolo della Libertà, 2009–13; Leader of the Opposition, Italy, 1996–2001; Minister of Foreign Affairs, 2002.

BERMAN, Charlotte Allegra; Managing Director, Global Head of Public Sector Banking, HSBC, since 2013; *b* London, 12 Aug. 1971; *d* of late Nestor Montague Berman and Ursula Anne Berman (*née* Sharp); civil partnership 2006, J. E. M. Arnold; one *d*. *Educ:* Wellington Sch., Som; Rugby Sch.; Magdalen Coll., Oxford (MA Modern Langs). Associate, CS First Boston, 1994–97; Dir, Barclays Capital, 1997–2001; Exec. Dir, 2001–03, Man. Dir, 2003–13, UBS. Mem. Bd, Internat. Capital Mkts Assoc., 2011–13. Trustee: NPG, 2011–; Magdalen Coll. Develt Trust, 2014–. *Recreations:* the arts, travel, scuba diving, ski-ing. *Address:* c/o HSBC, 8 Canada Square, E14 5HQ. *T:* (020) 7992 2651. *Clubs:* Oxford and Cambridge, Royal Automobile, Soho House; Victoria Racing.

BERMAN, Edward David, (ED Berman), MBE 1979; social entrepreneur and activist, playwright, theatre director and producer; educationalist; Founder, Chief Executive and Artistic Director, Inter-Action, since 1968; *b* 8 March 1941; 2nd *s* of Jack Berman and Ida (*née* Webber); naturalized British citizen, 1976. *Educ:* Harvard (BA Hons); Exeter Coll., Oxford (Rhodes Schol.); Dept of Educnl Studies, Oxford (1978–). *Plays:* 8 produced since 1966; *director: theatre:* (premières) *inter alia* Dirty Linen (London and Broadway), 1976, and The Dogg's Troupe (15 minute) Hamlet, (ed) by Tom Stoppard, 1976 (also filmed, 1976); Dogg's Hamlet, Cahoot's Macbeth, 1979, by Tom Stoppard; *producer: theatre:* 125 stage premières for adults and 170 new plays for children, London, 1967–89; *maker of films:* (educational) The Head, 1971; Two Weeler, 1972; Farm in the City, 1977; Marx for Beginners Cartoon (co-prod., voice dir), 1978; *actor:* over 1200 performances as Prof. Dogg, Otto Première Check, Super Santa. Editor: 18 community arts, action and constructive leisure handbooks, 1972–; 2 anthologies of plays, 1976–78. Trustee and Founder, Inter-Action Trust, 1968; Director and Founder: Ambiance Lunch-Hour Th. Club, 1968; Prof. Dogg's Troupe for Children, 1968; Labrys Trust, 1969; Inter-Action Advisory Service, 1970; Infilms, 1970; The Almost Free Th., 1971; Inprint Publishing Unit, 1972; City Farm 1, 1972; Alternative Education Project, 1973–84; Inter-Action Trust Ltd, 1974; Town and Country Inter-Action (Milton Keynes) Ltd, 1975; Ambiance Inter-Action Inc., 1976; Talacre Centre Ltd, 1977; Co-Founder: Inter-Action Housing Trust Ltd, 1970; NUBS, Neighbourhood Use of Bldgs and Space; Community Design Centre, 1974; Beginners Books Ltd, 1978; Inter-Action Housing Co-operative, 1978; Founder and Artistic Dir, Fun Art Bus I, 1972–73. Founder, Artistic Dir, BARC, British Amer. Rep. Co., 1978. Devised: Inter-Action Creative Game Method, 1967; Super Santa, Father Xmas Union, 1967–82; Chairman: Save Piccadilly Campaign, 1971–80; Talacre Action Gp, 1972; Nat. Assoc. of Arts Centres, 1975–79; Dir, Islington Bus Co., 1974–76; Treas., Fair Play for Children Campaign, 1975–77; Hd of campaign to re-open blocked Thames Walkway, Isle of Dogs, 2010–. Founder: Nat. Fedn of City Farms, 1976; WAC—Weekend Arts Coll., 1979; co-founder: Sport-Space, 1976; FUSION—London and Commonwealth Youth Ensemble, 1981. Founder and Co-Director: Internat. Inst. for Social Enterprise, 1980; Country Wings, 1981; OPS, Occupation Preparation Systems, 1982; Options Training Ltd, 1983; Social Enterprise Projects Ltd, 1984; Founder and Trustee: Inter-Action Social Enterprise Trust Ltd, Social Enterprise Foundn of Inter-Action, 1984; Inter-Action Trust, South Africa, 2001–04; Cdre, Ships-in-the-City, 1988; Pres., HMS President (1918), 1988–2004; Founder and Director: Network Inter-Action; Youth-Tech; Star Dome, 1989; Marketing and Business Services International Ltd, 1992; Artistic Dir, Inter-Action Fun Art Bus II, 2010–. Public Service Special Adviser: on inner city matters to Sec. of State for the Environment, 1982–83; Ministry of Labour, Russia, 1992–94, Min. of Economy, 1993–95. Visiting Professor: of Social Enterprise, Great Lakes Inst. of Mgt, Chennai, 2006–07; in Community Develt, Rose Bruford Coll., 2011–12. Consultant, Res. Books, UEL, 2009–. Founding Chairman: Rhodes Scholars in Britain, 2014–15 (Trustee, 2014–); FAB Foundn UK, 2015–. Co-Chm., Isle of Dogs Neighbourhood Planning Forum, 2015–. As community artist: created 17 formats for participatory theatre, 1968–85; Community Media Van, 1983; Community Cameos, 1977–83; MIY—Make It Yourself, 1978; RIY—Raise It Yourself, 1981; IES—Instant Enterprise Systems, 1981; Learning Domes, 1993; Public Art Workshop, 1994. Mayor's Community Champion for Canary Wharf Ward, 2014–. Torchbearer, London 2012 Olympics. FRSA 2015. Freeman, City of London, 2003; Mem. Guild of Freemen, City of London. Pearly King of River Thames, 2002–. *Publications:* Prof. R. L. Dogg's Zoo's Who I and II, 1975; Selecting Business Software, 1984; Make a Real Job of It, Breaks for Young Bands, 1985; How to Set Up a Small Business, 1987; Healthy Learning Songs & Activities, 1989; New Game Songs & Activities, 1989; (research paper) The Democracy Handbook, 1999. *Recreations:* solitude, conversation, work, music. *Address:* Inter-Action, 55 Anchorage Point, Chandlers Mews, Isle of Dogs, E14 8NF. *T:* and *Fax:* (020) 7515 4449.

BERMAN, Sir Franklin (Delow), KCMG 1994 (CMG 1986); HM Diplomatic Service, retired; barrister and international arbitrator; Visiting Professor of International Law: University of Oxford, since 2000; University of Cape Town, since 2000; *b* 23 Dec. 1939; *s* of Joshua Zelic Berman and Gertrude (*née* Levin); *m* 1964, Christine Mary Lawler; two *s* three *d* (triplets). *Educ:* Rondebosch Boys' High Sch., Cape Town; Univ. of Cape Town; Wadham and Nuffield Colls, Oxford (Hon. Fellow, Wadham Coll., 1995). BA, BSc Cape Town; MA Oxford. Rhodes Scholar, 1961; Martin Wronker Prizeman, 1963; called to Bar, Middle Temple, 1966 (Hon. Bencher, 1997). HM Diplomatic Service, 1965–99: Asst Legal Adviser, FO, 1965; Legal Adviser: British Military Govt, Berlin, 1971; British Embassy, Bonn, 1972; Legal Counsellor, FCO, 1974; Counsellor and Legal Adviser, UK Mission to UN, NY, 1982; FCO, 1985, Dep. Legal Advr, 1988, Legal Advr, 1991–99. *Ad hoc* Judge, Internat. Court of Justice, 2003–05; Member: Perm. Court of Arbitration, The Hague, 2010–; Court of Arbitration under Indus Waters Treaty, 2010–. Chairman: Diplomatic Service Assoc., 1979–82; Appeals Bd, Internat. Oil Pollution Compensation Fund, 1986–2004; Claims Cttee, General Settlement Fund, Austria, 2001–; Diplomatic Service Appeal Bd, 2002–06; Appeals Bd, WEU, 2002–05. Member: Council of Mgt, then Bd of Trustees, British Inst. of Internat. and Comparative Law, 1992–2011 (Chm., 2012–); Council, British Br., Internat. Law Assoc., 1993–; Adv. Council, Centre for Advanced Study of European and Comparative Law, Oxford, 1995–; Adv. Council, Oxford Univ. Law Foundn, 1998–2004; Gov., Inst. of Advanced Legal Studies, Univ. of London, 1992–98. J. C. Smith Vis. Fellow, Nottingham Univ., 1993. Hon. Fellow, Soc. of Advanced Legal Studies, 1997. Trustee: Greenwich Foundn for RNC, 1997–2005; Univ. of Cape Town Trust, 2001– (Chm., 2010–). Hon. QC 1992. Mem. Editl Bd, British Yearbook of Internat. Law, 1994–. Grand Decoration of Honour in Gold with Star (Austria), 2007; Grand Croix, Ordre Royal (Cambodia), 2014. *Recreations:* walking, reading, music, choral singing. *Address:* Essex Court Chambers, 24 Lincoln's Inn Fields, WC2A 3EG.

BERMAN, Lawrence Sam, CB 1975; retired; *b* 15 May 1928; *yr s* of late Jack and Violet Berman; *m* 1954, Kathleen D. Lewis (*d* 1996); one *s* one *d*. *Educ:* St Clement Danes Grammar Sch.; London Sch. of Economics. BSc (Econ) 1st cl. hons 1947; MSc (Econ) 1950. Res. Asst, LSE, 1947; Nuffield Coll., Oxford, 1948; Econ. Commn for Europe, 1949; Central Statistical Office: Asst Statistician 1952; Statistician 1955; Chief Statistician 1964; Asst Dir 1968; Dir of Statistics, Depts of Industry and Trade, 1972–83. Statistical Advr, Caribbean Tourism R&D Centre, Barbados, 1984–85. Editor, National Income Blue Book, 1954–60; Member: Council, Royal Statistical Soc., 1970–74 (Vice-Pres., 1973–74); Council, Internat. Assoc. for Research in Income and Wealth, 1980–85; ISI. *Publications:* Caribbean Tourism Statistical Reports; articles and papers in Jl of Royal Statistical Soc., Economica, Economic Trends, Statistical News, etc. *Recreations:* bridge, travel, theatre. *Address:* 10 Carlton Close, Edgware, Middx HA8 7PY. *T:* (020) 8958 6938.

BERMAN, Paul Richard; HM Diplomatic Service; Director, Legal Service, Council of the European Union, since 2012; *b* London, 23 Nov. 1964; *s* of Prof. David Solomon Berman and Patricia Denise Berman (*née* Clayman). *Educ:* Westminster Sch. (Queen's Schol.); Balliol Coll., Oxford (BA 1st Cl. Hons PPE); Grad. Inst. of Internat. Studies, Geneva (DES Relns Internationales); City Univ. (DipLaw). Called to the Bar, Gray's Inn, 1990 (Holt Schol.); joined HM Diplomatic Service, 1991; Asst Legal Advr, FCO, 1991–95; Legal Advr, Adv. Service on Internat. Humanitarian Law, Internat. Cttee of Red Cross, Geneva, 1996–98; Sen. Asst Legal Advr, FCO, 1998–2000; Counsellor, Attorney Gen.'s Chambers, 2000–02; Legal Counsellor: UK Perm. Representation to EU, Brussels, 2002–07; FCO, 2007–08; Cabinet Office Legal Advr and Dir, European Div., Treasury Solicitor's Dept, 2008–12. Member: Adv. Bd, Centre for Eur. Law, KCL, 2008–; Internat. Inst. of Humanitarian Law, San Remo, 2009–. Vis. Prof., Coll. of Europe, Bruges, 2013–. *Publications:* (contrib.) Satow's Diplomatic Practice, 6th edn 2009; (contrib.) EU Law after Lisbon, 2012. *Recreations:* hiking, sailing, music, theatre. *Address:* Council of the European Union, rue de la Loi 175, 1048 Brussels, Belgium. *Club:* Royal Over-Seas League.

BERMINGHAM, Gerald Edward; barrister; *b* Dublin, 20 Aug. 1940; *s* of late Patrick Xavier Bermingham and Eva Terescena Bermingham; *m* 1st, 1964, Joan (marr. diss.); two *s*; 2nd, 1978, Judith (marr. diss.); 3rd, 1998, Jilly; one *s*. *Educ:* Cotton College, N Staffs; Wellingborough Grammar School; Sheffield University (LLB Hons). Admitted Solicitor, 1967; called to the Bar, Gray's Inn, 1985. Councillor, Sheffield City Council, 1975–79, 1980–82. Contested (Lab) SE Derbyshire, 1979. MP (Lab) St Helens South, 1983–2001. *Recreations:* sport, reading, TV. *Address:* 5 Fountain Court, Steelhouse Lane, Birmingham B4 6DR.

BERNARD, Beverley Amari; *see* Blaize, B. A.

BERNARD, Sir Dallas (Edmund), 2nd Bt *cr* 1954; Director: Morgan Grenfell (Holdings) Ltd, 1972–79; Italian International Bank plc, 1978–89; *b* 14 Dec. 1926; *o s* of Sir Dallas Gerald Mercer Bernard, 1st Bt, and Betty (*d* 1980), *e d* of late Sir Charles Addis, KCMG; *S* father, 1975; *m* 1st, 1959, Sheila Mary Gordon Robey (marr. diss. 1979; she *d* 2009); two *d* (and one *d* decd); 2nd, 1979, Mrs Monica Montford (*née* Hudson) (marr. diss. 2003); one *d*; 3rd, 2003, Mrs Graciela Scorza, *d* of late Francisco Scorza Fúster and Celmira Leguizamón O'Higgins. *Educ:* Eton Coll.; Corpus Christi Coll., Oxford (MA). FCIS. Director: Dreyfus Intercontinental Investment Fund NV, 1970–91; Morgan Grenfell & Co. Ltd, 1964–77; Dominion Securities Ltd, Toronto, 1968–79; Nat. & Foreign Securities Trust Ltd, 1981–86; Dreyfus Dollar Internat. Fund Inc., 1982–91; Chm., Thames Trust Ltd, 1983–86. Mem. Monopolies and Mergers Commn, 1973–79. Mem. Council, GPDST, 1988–93 (Finance Cttee, 1975–92). *Heir:* none. *Address:* Ivery House, Church Hill, Wroughton, Wilts SN4 9JS. *T:* (01793) 813854. *Club:* Army and Navy.

BERNARD, Daniel Camille; Chairman: Kingfisher plc, since 2009 (Joint Deputy Chairman, 2006–07; Deputy Chairman, 2007–09); Majid Al Futtaim Retail Group, since 2010; Senior Advisor, Towerbrook Capital Partners, since 2010; *b* 18 Feb. 1946; *s* of Paul Bernard and Simone (*née* Doise); *m* 1968, Chantal Leduc; one *s* two *d*. *Educ:* Lycée Camille Desmoulins, Cateau; Lycée Faidherbe, Lille; HEC Business Sch.; Univ. of Paris. Divl Manager, Mammouth, 1976–81; Chief Exec. Officer, Metro France, 1981–89; Mem. Bd and Chief Operating Officer, Metro Internat., 1989–92; Carrefour Group: CEO, 1992–98; Chm. and CEO, 1998–2005. Pres., Provestis; non-executive Director: Alcatel-Lucent (formerly Alcatel), 1997–; Cap Gemini, 2005–. Chm., HEC Foundn, 2008–. *Recreations:* mountains, ski-ing, opera. *Address:* c/o Kingfisher plc, 3 Sheldon Square, W2 6PX.

BERNARD, Ralph Mitchell, CBE 2002; Chairman: Classic FM plc, 2007–12 (Director, 1991–2012; Chief Executive, 1997–2005); British Lung Foundation, 2009–11; Quidem Productions Ltd, since 2011; *b* 11 Feb. 1953; *s* of Reginald and Irene Bernard; *m* 1977, Lisa Anne Susan Kiené; four *d*. *Educ:* Caterham High Sch., Ilford. Copy boy, London News Service, 1970–71; Reporter: Express and Independent, Leytonstone, 1971–72; Stratford Express, 1972–73; Cambridge Evening News, 1973–75; radio journalist, 1975–78, Documentaries Ed., 1978–80, Radio Hallam, Sheffield; News Ed., Hereward Radio, Peterborough, 1980–82; Prog. Controller, 1982–83, Man. Dir, 1983–85, Wiltshire Radio; Pre-launch Manager, Classic FM, 1991; Exec. Chm., GWR Gp plc, 2001–05; Chief Exec., GCap Media plc, 2005–07. Chairman: London News Radio (LBC and News Direct), 1996–2001; Digital One Ltd, 1998–2009; USP Content Ltd, 2015–; Director: Ind. Radio News, 1994–2011; Watermill Th., Newbury, 2005–; Touch Broadcasting Ltd, 2009–. Chm., Broadcast Journalists' Trng Council, 2014–. Chm., Central Sch. of Ballet, 2008–. Chm., Campaign Bd, Great Western Hosp., Swindon, 2000–02. Trustee, Shakespeare Birthplace Trust, 2013–. Gov., Dauntsey's Sch., 2007–. Fellow, Radio Acad., 1999. Sony Gold Award, 2000. *Recreations:* music (most), walking, newspaper originals, cricket. *Address:* Quidem Productions Ltd, Spittleborough Farmhouse, Old Swindon Road, Royal Wootton Bassett, Swindon SN4 8ET.

BERNAYS, Robert Edward John, OBE 2010; Vice Lord-Lieutenant of Gloucestershire, since 2011; *b* Bristol, 7 Oct. 1944; *s* of Robert Hamilton Bernays, MP and Nancy Bernays (*née* Britton); *m* 1975, Alison Urquhart; three *d*. *Educ:* Eton Coll.; Wye Coll., Univ. of London (Dip. Farm Business Admin). Farmer, 1963–2005. Man. Trustee, Berkeley Estates, 1999–. Chm., Tender LifeCare Ltd, 2015. Dir, Fertility Focus, 2008. Pres. and Chm., St Monica Trust, 1999–2010. Gov., Dauntsey's Sch., 1995–2005 (Chm., 1999–2005); Chm., Colston's Sch., Bristol, 2013–. Master, Merchant Venturers' Soc., Bristol, 1996–97. High Sheriff Avon, 1987; DL Glos, 1988. *Recreations:* sailing, ski-ing, walking, gardening and most of all, family. *Address:* Kilcot House, Kilcot, Wotton-under-Edge, Glos GL12 7RL. *E:* robert@kilcot.com.

BERNAYS, Rosamund; *see* Horwood-Smart, R.

BERNBAUM, Prof. Gerald; Vice-Chancellor and Chief Executive, South Bank University, 1993–2001; *b* 25 March 1936; *s* of Benjamin Bernbaum and Betty (*née* Sack); *m* 1959, Pamela Valerie Cohen (marr. diss. 1987); two *s*. *Educ:* Hackney Downs Grammar Sch.; LSE (BSc

Econ 1957); London Inst. of Educn (PGCE 1958). Mitcham Grammar School for Boys: Asst Master, 1958–59; Head of Dept, 1959–62; Head of Dept, Rutherford Comprehensive Sch., 1962–64; University of Leicester School of Education: Lectr, 1964–70; Sen. Lectr, 1970–74; Prof. of Educn, 1974–93; Dir, 1976–85; Pro-Vice-Chancellor, 1985–87; Exec. Pro-Vice-Chancellor and Registrar, 1987–93. Chm. of Govs, Morley College, 2004–06. Hon. LLD Leicester, 2000; Hon. DLitt Assumption Univ., Bangkok, 1997; Hon. DEd: E London, 2002; South Bank, 2004. *Publications:* Social Change and the Schools, 1967; Knowledge and Ideology in the Sociology of Education, 1977; (ed) Schooling in Decline, 1978; (with H. Patrick and M. Galton) Educational Provision in Small Primary Schools, 1990; articles in Sociol Rev., Brit. Jl Educnl Studies. *Recreations:* public affairs, professional sport, music. *Address:* c/o London South Bank University, 103 Borough Road, SE1 0AA. *T:* (020) 7815 6004.

BERNER, Roger Francis; a Judge of the Upper Tribunal (Tax and Chancery Chamber), since 2011; *b* London, 16 March 1952; *s* of John and Doreen Berner; *m* 1st, 1979, Susan Gibbons (marr. diss. 1995); one *s* one *d*; 2nd, 2011, Gay Bateman. *Educ:* Southgate Sch.; Coll. of Law, Guildford (Clements Inn Prizeman 1975). Admitted as solicitor, 1976; Asst Solicitor, Freshfields, 1976–79; Solicitor, 1979–82, Partner, 1982–90, Stevens & Bolton; Solicitor, Freshfields, 1990–93; Partner, Freshfields Bruckhaus Deringer, 1993–2007; Gp Hd of Tax, N. M. Rothschild & Sons Ltd, 2007–09; a Judge, First-tier Tribunal (Tax Chamber), 2009–11. *Publications:* (contrib.) Tolley's Company Law, 1983. *Recreations:* family, sport, theatre, opera, ballet, cinema. *Address:* HM Courts and Tribunal Service, 45 Bedford Square, WC1B 3DN.

BERNERD, Elliott; Co-founder and Chairman, Chelsfield Partners, since 2006; *b* 23 May 1945; *s* of late Geoffrey Bernerd and of Trudie Malawer (*née* Melzack); *m* 1st, 1968, Susan Elizabeth Lynton (marr. diss. 1989); two *d*; 2nd, 1992, Sonia Ramsay (*née* Ramalho) (marr. diss. 2009). Chairman: Chelsfield plc, 1987–2004; Wentworth Group Holdings Ltd, 1990–2004. Chairman: London Philharmonic Trust, 1987–94; South Bank Foundn, 1996–2007; South Bank Bd Ltd, 1998–2002. Chm. Trustees, Facial Surgery Res. Foundn, 2004–. *Recreations:* tennis, ski-ing. *Clubs:* Savile, Cavalry and Guards, Royal Automobile; Wentworth.

BERNERS, Baroness (16th in line), *cr* 1455; **Pamela Vivien Kirkham;** *b* 30 Sept. 1929; *er d* of Harold Williams and Baroness Berners, 15th in line (*d* 1992); *S* to Barony of mother (called out of abeyance, 1995); *m* 1952, Michael Joseph Sperry Kirkham; two *s* one *d*. *Educ:* Bredenbury Court, Hereford; Stonar Sch., Wilts. Radcliffe Infirmary, Oxford (SRN 1951). *Recreations:* painting, drawing, gardening, reading. *Heir:* *s* Hon. Rupert William Tyrwhitt Kirkham [*b* 18 Feb. 1953; *m* 1994, Lisa Carol Judy Lipsey; one *s*].

BERNERS-LEE, Sir Timothy (John), OM 2007; KBE 2004 (OBE 1997); RDI 2009; FRS 2001; FREng; 3Com Founders Professor, since 1999, Director, World Wide Web Consortium, and Professor of Engineering, Computer Science and Artificial Intelligence Laboratory, Massachusetts Institute of Technology; Professor of Computer Science, University of Southampton, since 2004; *b* London, 8 June 1955. *Educ:* Emanuel Sch., London; Queen's Coll., Oxford (BA 1976; Hon. Fellow, 1999). Plessey Telecommunications Ltd, 1976–78; software engr, D. G. Nash Ltd, 1978; ind. consultant, 1978–80, incl. software consultancy, CERN, Geneva (wrote unpublished prog., Enquire, forerunner of World Wide Web); Founding Dir, responsible for tech. design, Image Computer Systems Ltd, 1981–84; Fellowship, CERN, 1984–94: global hypertext project, 1989, became World Wide Web, 1990 (available on Internet, 1991); designed URL (universal resource locator) and HTML (hypertext markup lang.); joined Lab. for Computer Sci., MIT, 1994. Founder Dir, Web Science Trust, 2009–. Co-Dir, Open Data Inst., Shoreditch, 2011–. MacArthur Fellow, John D. and Catherine T. MacArthur Foundn, 1998. Distinguished FBCS; FREng 2001. Hon. FBA 2011. Hon. DSc Oxon, 2001. (Jtly) Queen Elizabeth Prize for Engrg, Royal Acad. of Engrg, 2013. *Publications:* Weaving the Web, 2000. *Address:* Computer Science and Artificial Intelligence Laboratory, 77 Massachusetts Avenue, Cambridge, MA 02139, USA.

BERNEY, Sir Julian (Reedham Stuart), 11th Bt *cr* 1620; Director and Proprietor, Consulting South East Ltd, since 2010; *b* 26 Sept. 1952; *s* of Lieut John Reedham Erskine Berney (killed on active service in Korea, 1952), Royal Norfolk Regt, and Hon. Jean Davina, *d* of 1st Viscount Stuart of Findhorn, PC, CH, MVO, MC; *S* grandfather, 1975; *m* 1976, Sheena Mary, *yr d* of late Ralph Day and Ann Gordon Day; two *s* one *d*. *Educ:* Wellington Coll.; North East London Polytechnic. FRICS 1992. Formerly Internat. Dir, Jones Lang LaSalle. Freeman, Fishmongers' Co. *Recreation:* sailing. *Heir:* *s* William Reedham John Berney, *b* 29 June 1980. *Address:* Reeds House, 40 London Road, Maldon, Essex CM9 6HE. *T:* (01621) 853420. *Clubs:* Royal Ocean Racing; Royal Cruising; Royal Yacht Squadron.

BERNIE, Philip Robert; Head of Sport, BBC Television, since 2009; *b* Maidenhead, 22 Feb. 1962; *s* of Ronald Bernie and Yetta Bernie (*née* Zurich); *m* 2010, Pamela Hunnisett. *Educ:* St Paul's Sch., London; University Coll., Oxford (MA Hist.). BBC Sport: asst producer, 1986–90; asst ed., 1990–96; ed., 1996–2005; progs edited incl. Match of the Day, Grandstand, Match of the Day 2, Sports Personality of the Year, Wimbledon, World Cup, Olympics; Head: of Progs, 2005–06; of TV Sport Editorial, 2006–09. *Recreations:* finding and eating good food, time with our dog and cat, playing football and tennis, watching comedy, reading. *Address:* BBC Television, Quay House, Media City UK, Salford M50 2BH. *T:* (0161) 335 6261. *E:* philip.bernie@bbc.co.uk. *Clubs:* MCC; Tottenham Hotspur Football.

BERNSTEIN, David, CBE 2014; Chairman, Ted Baker plc, since 2013 (non-executive Director, since 2003); Chairman of Trustees, British Red Cross, since 2014; *b* St Helens, Lancs, 22 May 1943; *s* of Henry Bernstein and Anne Bernstein; *m* 1966, Gillian Davis; four *s*. *Educ:* Christ's Coll. Finchley. FCA 1966. Joined Bright Grahame Murray, chartered accountants, 1968; admitted Partner, 1969; Jt Sen. Partner, 1980–88; Man. Dir, Gp Develt, Pentland Gp plc, 1988–94; Dir, 1994–2003, Chm., 1998–2003, Manchester City plc; Dir, 2003–11, Chm., 2008–11, Wembley National Stadium; Chm., FA, 2011–13. Non-executive Chairman: French Connection Gp plc, 1995–2001; Blacks Leisure Gp plc, 1996–2011; Adams Childrenswear Ltd, 2000–05; Sport and Leisure Gp Ltd, 2006–11; Chm., Orchid Gp Ltd, 2010–12; non-exec. Dir, Carluccio's plc, 2005–10. Pres., Level Playing Field, 2007–; Chm., Centre for Access to Football in Europe, 2008–; Trustee, Sharre Zadek Hosp., Jerusalem. *Recreations:* tennis (Chm., Chandos Lawn Tennis Club), running (completed two London Marathons), golf, theatre, modern history. *Address:* Ted Baker plc, Ugly Brown Building, 6a St Pancras Way, NW1 0TB.

BERNSTEIN, Sir Howard, Kt 2003; Chief Executive, Manchester City Council, since 1998; *b* 9 April 1953; *s* of Maurice and Miriam Bernstein; *m* 1980, Yvonne Selwyn (marr. diss. 2004); one *s* one *d* (and one *s* decd); *m* 2004, Vanessa. *Educ:* Ducie High Sch., Manchester; London Univ. (ext.). Manchester City Council: Head of Urban Policy, 1980–86; Asst Chief Exec., 1986–90; Dep. Chief Exec., 1990–98; Dep. Clerk, 1986–98, Clerk, 1998–, Gtr Manchester PTA; Chief Exec., Manchester City Centre Task Force, 1996–. Sec., Commonwealth Games Organising Cttee, 1996–2002; Mem. Bd, Olympic Delivery Authy, 2006–08. Chm., ReBlackpool, 2008–. Hon. FRIBA 2003. Hon. RNCM 2005. Hon. DLitt UMIST, 2003; Hon. LLD Manchester, 2004; Hon. DBA Manchester Metropolitan, 2005. *Recreations:* sport, particularly football and cricket. *Address:* Manchester City Council, Town Hall, Manchester M60 2LA. *T:* (0161) 234 3006.

BERNSTEIN, Her Honour Ingeborg, (Inge); a Circuit Judge, 1991–2001; *b* 24 Feb. 1931; *d* of Sarah and Eli Bernstein; *m* 1967, Eric Geoffrey Goldrein; one *s* one *d*. *Educ:* Peterborough County School; St Edmund's College, Liverpool; Liverpool University. Called to the Bar, Inner Temple, 1952; practice on Northern Circuit; a Recorder, 1978–91. Chm., Ment Health Review Tribunal, 1968–91 and 1992–2007; Mem., Mental Health Act Comm 1984–86. *Recreation:* the domestic arts.

BERNSTEIN, Ingrid Ann; *see* Simler, Hon. Dame I. A.

BERRAGAN, Maj.-Gen. Gerald Brian, CB 1988; Chief Executive, Institute of Packagin 1988–98; *b* 2 May 1933; *s* of William James and Marion Beatrice Berragan; *m* 1956, An Helen Kelly; three *s*. Commissioned REME 1954; attached 7th Hussars, Hong Kon 1954–55; transf. RAOC 1956; served UK, Belgium, Germany and with 44 Para Bde (TA Staff College, 1966; Nat. Defence Coll., 1972–73; Comdr RAOC 3 Div., 1973–76; AQM HQ N Ireland, 1976–78; HQ DGOS, 1978–80; Comdt Central Ordnance Depot, Chilwe 1980–82; Sen. Management Course, Henley, 1982; Comdt COD Bicester, 1982–83; D Supply Ops (Army), 1983–85; Sen. Internat. Defence Management Course, USA, 1985; D Gen. of Ordnance Services, 1985–88. Col Comdt, RAOC, 1988–93, RLC 1993–98. U Dir, World Packaging Orgn, 1988–98. FInstPkg. *Recreation:* tennis.

BERRAGAN, Lt Gen. Sir Gerald William, (Sir Gerry), KBE 2015; CB 2011; Adjuta General, 2012–15. Commnd RA, 1979; Chief Targeting and Information Ops, HQ ARR(2002–04; COS Field Army, 2004–06; Dep. Comdr Multi-Nat. Corps Iraq, 2007; Dir Ge Army Recruiting and Trng, 2007–11; Dir Gen. Personnel, HQ Land Forces, 2011–1 Legion of Merit (USA), 2007.

BERRESFORD, James Whistler; Chief Executive Officer, VisitEngland, since 2009; Chesterfield, 29 April 1956; *s* of Michael and Mary Berresford; *m* 1995, Dawn Mary; one *Educ:* Abbotsholme Sch.; Huddersfield Poly. (BA Hons Humanities); City of London Uni (Postgrad. Arts). Mktg Manager, Nottingham Playhouse, 1979–82; Nottinghamshire Coun Council: Tourism Officer, 1982–90; Asst Dir, Leisure, 1990–99; Dir (E), Heart of Englar Tourist Bd, 1999–2002; Dir, Tourism, NW Regl Develt Agency, 2002–08. Associat Liverpool Inst. Performing Arts, 2007–. Hon. DBA Chester, 2011. *Recreations:* walkin cycling, English holidays, theatre, football. *E:* james.berresford@ntlworld.com.

BERRIDGE, Baroness *cr* 2011 (Life Peer), of the Vale of Catmose in the County of Rutlan **Elizabeth Rose Berridge;** *b* Oakham, Rutland, 22 March 1972. *Educ:* Catmose Coll Rutland Coll.; Emmanuel Coll., Cambridge (BA 1995); Inns of Court Sch. of Law, Londo Called to the Bar, Inner Temple, 1996; barrister, Kings Chambers, Manchester, 1996–200 Exec. Dir, Conservative Christian Fellowship, 2005–11 (Patron, 2011–). Mem., Jt Cttee c Human Rights, H of L, 2011–; Founding Chair, All Party Parly Gp on Internat. Religio Freedom, 2012–. Member, Advisory Council: Foundn for Relief and Reconciliation in th Middle East, 2011–; Theos, 2012–. Trustee: Kainos Community, 2006; British Future, 2012 Contested (C) Stockport, 2005. *Recreations:* swimming, Ghana, church. *Address:* House Lords, SW1A 0PW. *T:* (020) 7219 8943. *E:* oneilldm@parliament.uk.

BERRIDGE, Sir Michael (John), Kt 1998; PhD; FRS 1984; Fellow of Trinity Colleg Cambridge, since 1972; Head of Signalling Programme, Babraham Institute Laboratory Molecular Signalling, 1996–2003, now Emeritus Babraham Fellow; *b* 22 Oct. 1938; *s* George Kirton Berridge and Stella Elaine Hards; *m* 1965, Susan Graham Winter; one *s* one *Educ:* University Coll. of Rhodesia and Nyasaland (BSc); Univ. of Cambridge (PhD). Pos doctoral Fellow: Univ. of Virginia, 1965–66; Case Western Reserve Univ., Cleveland, Ohi 1966–69; AFRC Lab. of Molecular Signalling (formerly Unit of Insect Neurophysiology ar Pharmacology), Dept of Zoology, Univ. of Cambridge, 1969–90; Babraham Inst. Lab. Molecular Signalling, 1990–2003. Founder FMedSci 1998. King Faisal Internat. Prize in Sci 1986; Jeantet Prize in Medicine, 1986; Gairdner Foundn Internat. Award, 1988; Lasker Basi Med. Res. Award, 1989; Dr H. P. Heineken Prize for Biochemistry and Biophysics, 199 Wolf Foundn Prize in Medicine, 1995; Shaw Prize in Life Sci. and Medicine, Shaw Priz Foundn, 2005. *Publications:* papers in Jl Exptl Biol., Biochem. Jl and Nature. *Recreations:* gol gardening. *Address:* The Babraham Institute, Babraham Hall, Babraham, Cambridge CB2 3AT. *T:* (01223) 496621.

BERRIEDALE, Lord; Alexander James Richard Sinclair; *b* 26 March 1981; *s* and *heir* Earl of Caithness, *qv*. *Educ:* St David's Coll., Llandudno. Studying to be a commercial pilo *Recreation:* outdoor pursuits.

BERRIMAN, Sir David, Kt 1990; FCIB; Chairman, Association of Lloyd's Member 1994–98 (Committee Member, 1993–98); *b* 20 May 1928; *s* of late Algernon Edwar Berriman, OBE and late Enid Kathleen Berriman (*née* Sutcliffe); *m* 1st, 1955, Margaret Lloy (*née* Owen) (marr. diss. 1970; she *d* 1995); two *s*; 2nd, 1971, Shirley Elizabeth (*née* Wright) 1993); 3rd, 1995, Patricia Ann Salter (*née* Walker) (*d* 2013); 4th, 2014, Caryl Ann Ayscoug (*née* Spinks). *Educ:* Winchester; New Coll., Oxford (MA, Dip. Econ. and Pol Sci.); Harvar Business Sch. PMD course, 1961. First National City Bank of New York, 1952–56; For Motor Co. Ltd, 1956–60; AEI Hotpoint, 1960–63; Gen. Manager, United Leasin Corporation Ltd, 1963–64; Morgan Grenfell & Co. Ltd: Manager, 1964; Exec. Dir, 1968–7 Dir, Guinness Mahon & Co. Ltd, 1973–87 (Exec. Dir, 1973–85). Chairman: Bunzl Texti Holdings Ltd, 1981–88 (Dep. Chm., 1980); Alban Communications Ltd, 1988–90 (Di 1983–; Dep. Chm., 1987–88); Privatised Public Service Pension Plan Trustees Ltd, 1994–97 Director (non-exec.): Cable and Wireless, 1975–88; Sky Television (formerly Satelli Television), 1981–89 (Chm., 1981–85); Bahrain Telecommunications Corp., 1982–8 Britannia Building Soc., 1983–93; Ashenden Enterprises Ltd, 1983–2001; Videotron Hld plc, 1989–97; KDB Bank (UK) Ltd, 1991–98. Chairman: Lewisham and N Southwark DHA 1981–84; NE Thames RHA, 1984–90. Member: Govt review body on Harland and Wol diversification, 1980; Corp. of Lloyd's Disciplinary Bd, 1996–2001; Bd of Trade's Interir Action Cttee for the Film Industry, 1977–85; British Screen Adv. Council, 1985–91 Director: British Screen Finance Ltd, 1985–91; Nat. Film Develt Fund, 1985–91. Dep. Chm Nat. Film and Television School, 1988–92 (Gov., 1977–92). Chairman: MacIntyre Car 1978–92 (Gov., 1977–92); MacIntyre Charitable Trust, 1986–92; MacIntyre Found 1993–95; Member, Council: Internat. Hosp. Fedn, 1985–86; King Edward's Hosp. Fund fc London, 1985–90. Trustee: New Coll., Oxford Development Fund, 1983–95; Ker Community Housing Trust, 1990–2008 (Dep. Chm., 1998–2008). CCMI. *Recreations:* gol lawn tennis. *Club:* Royal Automobile (Mem., Sen. One Hundred Roll).

BERRUYER, Guy; Chief Executive, Sage Group plc, 2010–14; *b* France, 12 Aug. 1951; 1986, Pascale Laroche; two *s* one *d*. *Educ:* Ecole Poly. Fédérale de Lausanne; Harvard Univ (MBA). Dir, Mktg and Sales Distribution, Groupe Bull, 1984–89; S Eur. Man. Dir, Clari 1989–94; Eur. Man. Dir, Intuit, 1994–97; Sage Group plc: joined 1997 to run Frenc operation; Mem. Bd of Dirs and CEO, Mainland Europe business, 2000–10, Asian Op 2005–10. *Recreations:* golf, theatre.

BERRY, family name of **Viscounts Camrose** and **Kemsley**.

BERRY, Amanda Sonia, OBE 2009; Chief Executive, British Academy of Film an Television Arts, since 2000; *b* Darlington, 20 Aug. 1961; *d* of Thomas and Anita Berry. *Edu* Richmond Sch.; York Coll. of Art and Technol.; Newcastle upon Tyne Poly. Co-di Duncan Health Associates, later ICM, 1982–88; researcher, light entertainment and currer affairs, LWT, 1989–90; Producer and Develt Exec., Scottish Television Enterprises, 1990–98 Dir, Develt and Events, 1998–99, Dep. Exec. Dir, 1999–2000, BAFTA. *Recreations:* filn music, art, cycling, holidays. *Address:* British Academy of Film and Television Arts, 19 Piccadilly, W1J 9LN. *T:* (020) 7734 0022.

BERRY, Anthony Charles; QC 1994; *b* 4 Oct. 1950; *s* of Geoffrey Vernon Berry and Audrey Millicent Berry (*née* Farrar); *m* 1977, Susan Carmen Traversi; three *s* one *d*. *Educ:* Downside Sch.; Lincoln Coll., Oxford (BA Phil. and Psychol.). Called to the Bar, Gray's Inn, 1976, Bencher, 2002. Sec., Criminal Bar Assoc., 1991–93; Mem., Bar Council, 1993–95. *Recreations:* tennis, golf. *Address:* 9 Bedford Row, WC1R 4AZ. *T:* (020) 7489 2727.

BERRY, (Anthony) Scyld (Ivens); cricket correspondent, The Telegraph, since 2014; Editor, Wisden Cricketers' Almanack, 2007–11; *b* 28 April 1954; *s* of late Prof. Francis Berry; *m* 1984, Sunita Ghosh; two *s* one *d*. *Educ:* Westbourne School, Sheffield; Ampleforth College; Christ's College, Cambridge (MA Oriental Studies). Cricket correspondent: The Observer, 1978–89; The Sunday Correspondent, 1989–90; The Independent on Sunday, 1991–93; Sunday Telegraph, 1993–2014. *Publications:* Cricket Wallah, 1982; Train to Julia Creek, 1984; (ed) The Observer on Cricket, 1987; Cricket Odyssey, 1988; (with Phil Edmonds) 100 Great Bowlers, 1989; (with Rupert Peploe) Cricket's Burning Passion, 2006. *Recreations:* playing village cricket, being at home. *Address:* c/o The Telegraph, 111 Buckingham Palace Road, SW1W 0DT. *Club:* Hinton Charterhouse Cricket.

BERRY, Cicely Frances, (Mrs H. D. Moore), CBE 2009 (OBE 1985); Advisory Director, Royal Shakespeare Co. (Voice Director, 1969); *b* 17 May 1926; *d* of Cecil and Frances Berry; *m* 1951, Harry Dent Moore (*d* 1978); two *s* one *d*. *Educ:* Eothen Sch., Caterham, Surrey; Central Sch. of Speech and Drama, London. Teacher, Central Sch. of Speech and Drama, 1948–68; 4-week Voice Workshops: Nat. Repertory Co. of Delhi, 1980; Directors and Actors in Australia (org. by Aust. Council), 1983; Directors, Actors, Teachers in China, Chinese Min. of Culture, 1984; text-based workshops: Theatre Voice, Stratford, 1992; Actors in Croatia, Poland, Bulgaria and the Netherlands, 1993, in Colombia and Croatia, 1998, and in Brazil; workshops: Writers in Stratford, 1993; Eur. League of Insts of Arts, Berlin, 1994; Theatre For A New Audience, NY, 1997, 1998, 2001, 2007–11 (Artistic Associate, 1997); Theatre Lab., Sydney, 2001; Shakespeare in translation, for Javier Ortiz Arraiza, Madrid, 2009; various Hip Hop groups, London, 2010; work with Nos Do Morro theatre co., Vidigal, Rio, 2005, 2006 and 2007–11. Hon. Prof., de Montfort Univ.; Vis. Fellow, Royal Central Sch. of Speech and Drama (formerly Central Sch. of Speech and Drama), 1994–. Organised: Internat. Voice Conf., Stratford, 1995, 1998; debate, Theatre and Citizenship, Barbican, 1997. Plays directed: Hamlet, Educn Dept, NT, 1985; King Lear, The Other Place, Stratford and Almeida Theatre, 1989. Patron of Northumberland and Leicester Youth Theatres. FRSAMD 1987. Hon. Dr, Nat. Acad. of Theatre Studies, Bulgaria, 1997; Hon. DLitt Birmingham, 1999; DUniv Open, 2001. Sam Wanamaker Award, Globe Theatre, 2000; Samuel H. Scripps Award, Theatre for a New Audience, NY, 2007. *Publications:* Voice and the Actor, 1973, 7th edn 2000; Your Voice and How to Use it Successfully, 1975, 2nd edn as Your Voice and How to Use it, 1994, 3rd edn 2000; The Actor and the Text, 1987, 2nd edn 2000; Text in Action, 2001; From Word to Play, 2008.

BERRY, Sir Colin (Leonard), Kt 1993; DSc; FRCPath; Professor of Morbid Anatomy, University of London, at The London Hospital Medical College, 1976–2002, now Emeritus; Warden of Joint Medical and Dental School, St Bartholomew's and Royal London Hospitals, and Vice-Principal for Medicine and Dentistry, Queen Mary and Westfield College, London University, 1995–96; *b* 28 Sept. 1937; *s* of Ronald Leonard Berry and Peggy-Caroline (*née* Benson); *m* 1960, Yvonne Waters; two *s*. *Educ:* privately, and Beckenham Grammar Sch.; Charing Cross Hosp. Med. Sch. (MB, BS; Governors' Clinical Gold Medal, Llewellyn Schol., Pierera Prize in Clinical Subjects, Steadman Prize in Path.); trained in Histopath., Charing Cross Hosp., 1962–64. MD 1968, PhD 1970, DSc 1993 (London). FRCPath 1979; FFPM 1991; FRCP 1993; FFOM 1995; FRCPE 1997. Lectr and Sen. Lectr, Inst. of Child Health, London, 1964–70; Reader in Pathology, Guy's Hosp. Med. Sch., 1970–76; Dean, London Hosp. Med. Coll., 1994–95. Gillson Scholar, Worshipful Soc. of Apothecaries, 1967–68 and 1970–72; Arris and Gail Lectr, RCS, 1973; Lectures: Bawden, BCPC, 1990; John Hull Grundy, Royal Army Med. Coll., 1992; Simonides, European Soc. of Pathology, 1993; Lucas, RCP, 1994; Sir Michael Davies, Expert Witness Inst., 2005; Sir Roy Cameron, RCPath, 2009; Sir William Paton, British Toxicol. Soc., 2014. Chairman: Cttee on Dental and Surgical Materials, 1982–92 (Vice-Chm., 1979–82); Scientific Sub-Cttee on Pesticides, MAFF, 1984–87; Adv. Cttee on Pesticides, MAFF/DHSS, 1988–99 (Mem., 1982–87); Bd in Histology and Cytology, Union Européenne des Médecins Spécialistes, 1993–99; Member: Toxicology Review Panel, WHO, 1976–84, 1987–; Scientific Adv. Cttee on Pesticides, EEC, 1981–88; Cttee on Toxicity of Chemicals in Food, Consumer Products and the Environment, 1982–88; Cttee on Safety of Medicines, Dept of Health, 1990–92; Ownership Bd, Pesticides Safety Directorate, 1994–99; Steering Gp on Envmt and Health, ESF, 1995–; Radical Review of Coroner Service, Home Office, 2001–03; MRC, 1990–94; GMC, 1993–96 and 1998–2003; Chm., Physiological Systems and Disorders Bd, MRC, 1990–92 (Mem., 1988–). Member, Advisory Board: Sci. and Policy, American Council on Sci. and Health, 2001–; Sense about Science, 2003–; Scientific Alliance, 2003–; Fundação para Ciência e a Tecnologia, Portugal, 2005–; Agência de Acreditação e Avaliação do Ensino Superior, Portugal, 2008–. Chm., Programme Cttee, Eur. Sci. Open Forum, 2006, 2008. President: Developmental Path. Soc., 1976–79; European Soc. of Pathology, 1989–91 (Pres. elect, 1987–89); British Acad. of Forensic Scis, 2003–05 (Pres. elect, 2001–02). Sec., Fedn of Assocs of Clinical Profs, 1987– (Hon. Fellow, 2007); Chm. Council, 1993–99, Hon. Vice-Pres., 2000–, Res. Defence Soc.; Hon. Sec., ACP, 1982–85 (Meetings Sec., 1979–82). Scientific Advr, BIBRA, 1987–90. Hon. Curator, Deutsches Mus., Munich, 2006–10. Treasurer, RCPath, 1988–93 (Asst Registrar, 1981–84). Asst to Court, Apothecaries' Soc., 1990– (Master, 2003–04; Treas., 2004–14). Knight Principal, Imperial Soc. of Knights Bachelor, 2012– (Mem. Council, 1997–; Treas., 2006–12). Founder FMedSci 1998. Hon. Fellow, British Toxicol. Soc., 2006. Corresp. Member: Deutsche Akad. der Naturforscher Leopoldina, 1993 (Hon. Mem., 2005); Nordrhein-Westfälische Akademie, 1993; German Pathol Soc., 2000 (Hon. Mem., 2005). Hon. MD Ioannina, Greece, 2003. *Publications:* Teratology: trends and applications, 1975; Paediatric Pathology, 1981, 3rd edn 1995; Diseases of the Arterial Wall, 1988; contrib. to many texts; numerous pubns in Jl of Path., Circulation Res. and other path. jls. *Recreations:* fishing, pond building, golf. *Clubs:* Reform, Farmers; Dulwich and Sydenham Golf.

BERRY, Graham; freelance advisor and consultant on the arts, Singapore, 2007–11; Director, Scottish Arts Council, 2002–07; *b* 12 Jan. 1945; *s* of Alexander and Émélie Berry; *m* 2007, Irene Ng; one *s* one *d* by a previous marriage. *Educ:* Royal High Sch., Edinburgh. ICAS. Chartered accountant, Price Waterhouse, 1968–70; Divl Chief Accountant, Trust House Forte, 1970–74; Company Secretary, 1974–86: Scottish Film Council; Scottish Council for Educn and Technol.; Glasgow Film Th.; Filmhouse, Edinburgh; Scottish Film Prodn Fund; Finance Officer, Univ. of Stirling, 1986–89; Hd of Funding and Resources, Scottish Arts Council, 1989–2002. *Recreations:* mountaineering, photography.

BERRY, (Gwenda) Lynne, OBE 2006; Chair: Public Benefit, since 2011; Commission on the Voluntary Sector and Ageing, since 2013; Breast Cancer Now, since 2015; *b* 27 Jan. 1953. Social Worker, Wandsworth LBC, 1976–79; Community Worker, Camden Council of Social Service, 1979–81; Lecturer: PCL, 1981–84; NISW, 1984–88; Social Services Inspector, DoH, 1988–90; Chief Exec., Family Welfare Assoc., 1990–96; Exec. Dir, Charity Commn, 1996–99; Chief Executive: EOC, 1999–2001; Gen. Social Care Council, 2001–07; WRVS, 2007–11. Non-exec. Dir, Europe Div., DTI, 1998–2001. Chm., CPAG, 2001–05; Member: Better Regulation Commn (formerly Better Regulation Task Force), 2005–07; Risk and Regulation Commn, 2007–09; Adv. Bd, Office of Third Sector, 2008–12; Lifting the Burdens of Red Tape on Charities and Social Enterprises, Cabinet Office/BIS Task Force, 2010; Bd, Internat. Women's Forum UK, 2012–. Associate, Civil Exchange, 2011–. Vis. Prof., Cass Business Sch., City Univ., 2014– (Sen. Fellow, 2011); Fellow Commoner, Lucy Cavendish Coll., Cambridge, 2015–. Mem. Bd, British Waterways, 2011–12; Vice Chm., Canal and River Trust, 2012–; Chm., Glandŵr Cymru, 2015–. Trustee: Tomorrow Project, 2001–06; Nat. Centre for Social Res., 2002–09; Cumberland Lodge, 2008–; Anne Frank Trust, 2010–; Pro-Bono Economics, 2011–. Non-exec. Dir, Cambridge Univ. Hosp. Trust, 2012–. Former Member of Council: Inst. of Educn, London Univ.; Franco-British Council. FRSA. Hon. Fellow, Cardiff Univ., 2012. Hon. Dr Health Scis Anglia Ruskin, 2010; Hon. DSc Bedfordshire, 2011. Merit Award, Social Care Assoc., 2006. *Publications:* contrib. books on Europe and social policy, complaints procedures and consumer rights, and jls on social policy and women's issues. *T:* (020) 7697 8446. *E:* lynne@lynneberry.co.uk.

BERRY, James; *see* Berry, M. J. E.

BERRY, James Jacob Gilchrist, (Jake); MP (C) Rossendale and Darwen, since 2010; *b* Liverpool, 29 Dec. 1978; *s* of John David Gilchrist Berry and Ann Elizabeth Berry (*née* Curtis); *m* 2009, Charlotte Piroska Alexa. *Educ:* Liverpool Coll.; Sheffield Univ. (BA Hons); Coll. of Law, Chester. Admitted solicitor, 2003; Solicitor: Bremner Sons and Corlett, 2001–02; City Law Partnership, 2002–04; DWF Solicitors, 2004–07; Halliwells, 2007–10. PPS to Minister of State for Housing and Local Govt, 2010–12, to Minister without Portfolio, Cabinet Office, 2012–15, to Chief Secretary to the Treasury, 2015–. Mem., Downing Street Policy Unit, 2013–. Consultant Solicitor, Squire Sanders (UK) LLP, 2011–. *Recreations:* sailing, ski-ing, fishing. *Address:* House of Commons, SW1A 0AA. *E:* jake.berry.mp@parliament.uk. *Clubs:* Carlton; St James's (Manchester); Rawtenstall Conservative.

BERRY, Dr James William; Director General (formerly Director) of Scientific and Technical Intelligence, 1982–89; *b* 5 Oct. 1931; *s* of Arthur Harold Berry and Mary Margaret Berry; *m* 1960, Monica Joan Hill; three *d*. *Educ:* St Mary's Coll., Blackburn; Municipal Technical Coll., Blackburn; Manchester Univ. (BSc); Leeds Univ. (PhD). FIET. Royal Signals and Radar Estab., Malvern, 1956–60; Admiralty Surface Weapons Estab., Portsdown, 1960–76 (Head of Computer Div., 1972–76); Dir of Long Range Surveillance and Comd and Control Projs, MoD (PE), 1976–79; Dir Gen. Strategic Electronic Systems, MoD (PE), 1979–82. Organist, St Michael's RC Church, Leigh Park, Havant. *Recreations:* music (organ, 'cello, piano), walking, watching wild life. *Clubs:* Civil Service; Probus (Havant).

BERRY, Janette Susan, QPM 2006; Independent Bureaucracy Advocate, Home Office, 2008–10; *b* Carshalton, 29 Aug. 1954; *d* of Ralph Cooke and Marian (*née* Hook); *m* 1980, Graham Berry; one *s* one *d*. *Educ:* Fosse Bank Girls' Sch., Tonbridge; Open Univ. (BA). Kent County Constabulary, 1971–2008: Cadet, 1971–73; Constable, 1973–75; Detective Constable, 1975–77; Sergeant, 1977–79; Sergeant (Instructor), 1979–81; Patrol Sergeant, 1981–84; Inspector, 1984–97; Force Crime Prevention Officer, 1986–2000; Chief Inspector, 1987–2008. Chairman: Kent Police Fedn, 1991–97; Police Fedn of England and Wales, 2002–08. Sec., Inspectors' Central Cttee, 1987–2001. FRSA. Police Long Service and Good Conduct Medal, 1996; Golden Jubilee Medal, 2002. *Recreations:* family, theatre, current affairs, travel, supporting Crystal Palace Football Club, armchair sports fan.

BERRY, Lynne; *see* Berry, G. L.

BERRY, Mary Rosa Alleyne, (Mrs P. J. M. Hunnings), CBE 2012; cookery writer, since 1966, and television cook, since 1970; *b* Bath, 24 March 1935; *d* of Alleyne and Margery Berry; *m* 1966, Paul John March Hunnings; one *s* one *d* (and one *s* decd). *Educ:* Bath High Sch.; Bath Coll. of Home Econs; C&G Teaching; Paris Cordon Bleu. Cookery Editor: Housewife mag., 1966–70; Ideal Home mag., 1970–73; radio and TV series and appearances, 1970–, including: (as judge) The Great British Bake Off, BBC TV, 2010–; Desert Island Discs, BBC Radio 4, 2012; The Mary Berry Story, BBC TV, 2013; Mary Berry Cooks, BBC TV, 2014; Mary Berry's Absolute Favourites, BBC TV, 2015. *Publications:* Cook Book, 1970; Popular Freezer Cookery, 1972; Popular French Cookery, 1972; Good Afternoon Cookery Book, 1976; One Pot Cooking, 1978; Family Recipes, 1979; Television Cook Book, 1979; Glorious Puds, 1980; Home Cooking, 1980; Cooking with Cheese, 1980; Day by Day Cooking, 1981; Mary Berry's Main Course, 1981; Recipes from Home and Abroad, 1981; New Book of Meat Cookery, 1981; Fruit Fare, 1982; County Cooking, 1982; The Perfect Sunday Lunch, 1982; Crockery Cookery, 1983; Cooking at Home, 1983; Complete Television Cook Book, 1983; Food as Presents, 1983; Fast Desserts, 1983; Family Cooking, 1984; Iceland Guide to Cooking from your Freezer, 1985; Kitchen Wisdom, 1985; Feed Your Family the Healthier Way, 1985; New Freezer Cook Book, 1985; Cooking for Celebrations, 1986; Chocolate Delights, 1987; Mary Berry's Favourite Microwave Recipes, 1988; Mary Berry's Favourite Recipes, 1990; Mary Berry's Desserts and Confections, 1991; Mary Berry's Food Processor Cookbook, 1992; Hamlyn All Colour Cookbook, 1992; Fast Cakes, 1992; Mary Berry's Cookery Course, 1993; Mary Berry's Quick and Easy Cakes, 1993; Mary Berry's Freezer Cookbook, 1994; More Fast Cakes, 1994; Fast Suppers, 1994; Ultimate Cakes, 1994, 2nd edn as Mary Berry's Ultimate Cake Book, 2003; Favourite French Recipes, 1995; Classic Home Cooking, 1995; Mary Berry's Complete Cookbook, 1995, 2nd edn 2003; Mary Berry's Perfect Sunday, 1996; The Aga Book, 1996; Mary Berry Cooks Puddings and Desserts, 1997; The New Cook, 1997; Favourite Cakes, 1997; Mary Berry Cooks Cakes, 1998; Mary Berry's New Aga Cookbook, 1999; Mary Berry at Home, 2001; Mary Berry's Cakes, Puddings and Breads, 2001; Mary Berry's Classic Meat Dishes, 2001; Mary Berry's Soups, Salads and Starters, 2001; Cook Now, Eat Later, 2002; Mary Berry's Foolproof Cakes, 2004; Real Food Fast, 2005; Mary Berry's Christmas Collection, 2006; One Step Ahead with Mary Berry, 2007; Mary Berry's Stress-free Kitchen, 2008; Mary Berry's Baking Bible, 2009; Mary Berry and Lucy Young Cook up a Feast, 2010; Sunday Lunches, 2011; Mary Berry and Lucy Young At Home, 2013; Mary Berry Cooks, 2014; Mary Berry's Absolute Favourites, 2015. *Recreations:* gardening, tennis, walking. *E:* info@maryberry.co.uk. *W:* www.maryberry.co.uk.

BERRY, (Michael) James (Ellwood); MP (C) Kingston and Surbiton, since 2015; *b* Canterbury, 4 Aug. 1983; *s* of Dr Michael Berry and Margaret Berry; *m* 2013, Nehali Shah. *Educ:* King's Sch., Canterbury; University Coll. London (LLB 1st Cl. Hons 2005); Harvard Law Sch. (LLM 2007). Called to the Bar, Lincoln's Inn, 2006; barrister, specialising in healthcare and police law. Associate, Coll. of Policing, 2014–. *Recreations:* walking, cooking. *Address:* House of Commons, SW1A 0AA. *E:* james.berry.mp@parliament.uk.

BERRY, Sir Michael (Victor), Kt 1996; FRS 1982; Professor of Physics, Bristol University, 1978–88 and 2006–08, now Emeritus (Royal Society Research Professor, 1988–2006); *b* 14 March 1941; *s* of Jack and Marie Berry; *m* 1st, 1961, Eveline Ethel Fitt (marr. diss. 1970); two *s*; 2nd, 1971, Lesley Jane Allen (marr. diss. 1984); two *d*; 3rd, 1984, Monica Suzi Saiovici; one *s* one *d*. *Educ:* Univ. of Exeter (BSc; Hon. PhD 1991); Univ. of St Andrews (PhD). Bristol University: Res. Fellow, 1965–67; Lectr, 1967–74; Reader, 1974–78. Bakerian Lectr, Royal Soc., 1987. Mem., Royal Scientific Soc., Uppsala, 1988; Foreign Member: US Nat. Acad. of Sci., 1995; Royal Netherlands Acad. of Arts and Scis, 2000. Hon. FInstP 1999. Maxwell Medal and Prize, Inst. of Physics, 1978; Dirac Medal and Prize, Inst. of Physics, 1990; Lilienfeld Prize, Amer. Physical Soc., 1990; Royal Medal, Royal Soc., 1990; Naylor Prize and Lectureship in Applied Maths, London Math. Soc., 1992; Science for Art Prize, LVMH, Paris, 1994; Hewlett Packard Europhysics Prize, 1995; Dirac Medal, Internat. Centre for Theoretical Physics, 1996; Kapitsa Medal, Russian Acad. of Scis, 1997; Wolf Prize for Physics, Wolf Foundn, Israel, 1998; Ig Nobel Prize for Physics, 2000; Onsager Medal, Norwegian Technical Univ., 2001; 1st and 3rd prizes, Visions of Sci., Novartis/Daily Telegraph, 2002; Polya Prize, London Mathematical Soc., 2005; Chancellor's Medal, Univ. of Bristol, 2005;

Richtmyer Award, Amer. Assoc. of Physics Teachers, 2014; Lorentz Medal, Royal Netherlands Acad. Arts and Scis, 2015. *Publications:* Diffraction of Light by Ultrasound, 1966; Principles of Cosmology and Gravitation, 1976; about 480 research papers, book reviews, etc, on physics. *Recreation:* anything but sport. *Address:* H. H. Wills Physics Laboratory, Royal Fort, Tyndall Avenue, Bristol BS8 1TL. *T:* (0117) 928 8778. *W:* http://michaelberryphysics.wordpress.com.

BERRY, Nicholas (William); Chairman, Stancroft Trust Ltd, since 1972; *b* 3 July 1942; *yr s* of Baron Hartwell, MBE, TD; *m* 1977, Evelyn Prouvost; two *s*. *Educ:* Eton; Christ Church, Oxford. Publisher and investor; former Chairman: Harrap Publg; Manchester Ship Canal; Director: Blackwells, 1997–2003; Sibir Energy, 2000–03; Daily Mail Gp, 2007–, and other cos. Controlling shareholder: Mintel International Ltd; Intersport PSC Holding AG. *Address:* Stancroft Trust, 20 Bride Lane, EC4Y 8JP. *T:* (020) 7583 3808. *Club:* White's.

See also Viscount Camrose.

BERRY, Paul L.; Member (Ind Unionist), Armagh City and District Council; *b* 3 June 1976. *Educ:* Craigavon Coll. of Further Educn. Sales person, hardware warehouse, 1994–96; examr, shoe firm, 1996–98. Northern Ireland Assembly: Mem. (DUP, 1998–2006, Ind., 2006–07) Newry and Armagh; contested (Ind) same seat, 2007; Mem., Health Cttee and Standards and Privileges Cttee. Mem., Health Action Zone. Member: Loyal Orange Instn; Royal Black Perceptory; Apprentice Boys of Derry. Contested (DUP) Newry and Armagh, 2005. *Recreation:* interest in football.

BERRY, Very Rev. Peter Austin; Provost of Birmingham, 1986–99, now Emeritus; *b* 27 April 1935; *s* of Austin James Berry and Phyllis Evelyn Berry. *Educ:* Solihull Sch.; Keble Coll., Oxford (BA English, BTh, MA); St Stephen's House, Oxford. Intelligence Corps, 1954–56. Ordained deacon, 1962, priest, 1963; Chaplain to Bishop of Coventry, 1963–70; Midlands Regl Officer, Community Relations Commn, 1970–73; Canon Residentiary, Coventry Cathedral, 1973–86, Canon Emeritus 1987; Vice-Provost of Coventry, 1977–85. Mem., Gen. Synod of C of E, 1990–99; Church Comr, 1994–99. Chaplain to High Sheriff of W Midlands, 2005–06 and 2006–07. Chairman: Standing Adv. Cttee for Religious Educn, Birmingham, 1987–93; Birmingham Internat. Council, 1987–99 (Vice Pres., 1999–); Birmingham/Pakistan Friendship Assoc., 1995–99 (Vice Pres., 1999); Pre-Raphaelite Soc., 1986–2000 (Life Pres., 2000). Pres., Birmingham and Midland Inst., 2005–06. Vice-Chm., Iqbal Acad. Life Fellow, Coventry Univ. (Fellow, Lanchester Coll., Coventry, 1985). FRAS 2006. Hon. DD Birmingham, 1997. *Recreations:* music, theatre, architecture. *Address:* Reed Lodge, D5 Kenilworth Court, Hagley Road, Birmingham B16 9NU. *T:* (0121) 454 0021.

BERRY, Peter Fremantle, CMG 1999; Chairman, Crown Agents for Oversea Governments and Administrations, 1998–2007; President, Crown Agents Foundation, 2003–11; *b* St Andrews, Fife, 17 May 1944; *s* of late John Berry, CBE and Hon. Bride Berry, *d* of 3rd Baron Cottesloe, CB; *m* 1972, Paola Padovani; one *s* two *d*. *Educ:* Eton Coll.; Lincoln Coll., Oxford (MA Hons Mod. History). Harrisons & Crosfield, London, 1966–73: Manager: Kuala Belait, Brunei, 1968; Indonesia, 1970; Anglo Indonesian Corp., London: Gen. Man., 1973; Dir, 1974–82; Crown Agents for Oversea Governments and Administrations, 1982–2007: Director: Asia and Pacific, based Singapore, 1982–84; ME, Asia and Pacific, based London, 1984–88; Man. Dir and Crown Agent, 1988–2002; Chm. of Crown Agents' banking and asset mgt subsidiaries. Director: Thomas Tapling Ltd, 1987– (Chm., 2007–); Anglo-Eastern Plantations Plc, 1991–93; Henderson TR Pacific Investment Trust, 1994–2008; Scottish Eastern Investment Trust, 1995–98; Kier Group plc, 1997–2007; Martin Currie Portfolio Investment Trust plc, later Martin Currie Global Portfolio Trust, 1999–2012 (Chm., 2000–12); Martin Currie Capital Return Trust plc, 1999–2000; Mylnfield Res. Services, 2007– (Chm., 2008–11). Member: Management Bd, Resource, 1989–92; Internat. Bd, Transparency Internat., 1993–; Pres., Transparency Internat. (UK), 2003–. Member: Rubber Growers Assoc., 1978–82; UK Task Force on Kuwait, 1991; UK-Japan 21st Century (formerly UK-Japan 2000) Gp, 1992–2007 (Dir, 2000–03); Whitehall Export Promotion Cttee, 1992–98; Internat. Cttee, CBI, 1997–2003; British Trade Internat. Sectors and Projects, subseq. Business Adv., Gp, 1998–2004; Council: Malaysia, Singapore and Brunei Assoc., 1982–87; Indonesia Assoc., 1974–93 (Chm., 1986–89). Advr on econ. develt, City of London Corp., 2003–14. Trustee: CAF, 2000–09 (Chm., Internat. Cttee, 2000–09); Mylnfield Trust, 2007–11; Dir and Trustee, Charity Bank, 2003–09. Mem., Adv. Council, Sch. of Mgt, RHUL, 2005–. Governor, Scottish Crop Res. Inst., 2007–11 (Chm., 2008–11). Liveryman, Musicians' Co., 2008–. FRSA. Order of the Rising Sun (Japan), 2008. *Recreations:* wildlife and country pursuits in Britain and Italy, travel and international development. *Address:* 58 Pyrland Road, N5 2JD. *Club:* Royal Automobile.

BERRY, Prof. Peter Jeremy, FRCP, FRCPath; Professor of Paediatric Pathology, University of Bristol, 1991–2001, now Emeritus; *b* 21 March 1950; *s* of Peter Berry and Marjorie Berry (*née* Lang). *Educ:* Epsom Coll.; Magdalene Coll., Cambridge (BA, MB, BChir); London Metropolitan Univ. (MA Music Technol. 2010). Kent and Canterbury Hosp., 1975–77; Sen. Registrar in Histopathology, Addenbrooke's Hosp., 1977–81; Research Fellow, Children's Hosp., Denver, 1981–83; Consultant Paediatric Pathologist, Bristol Royal Hosp. for Sick Children, 1983–2001. Hon. FRCPH 2007. *Publications:* chapters and papers on cot death and children's tumours. *Recreations:* walking, fishing, music, canal boating, making period woodwind instruments. *Club:* Royal Society of Medicine.

BERRY, Prof. Robert James, (Sam), FRSE 1981; FRSB; Professor of Genetics in the University of London, 1974–2000, then Emeritus; *b* 26 Oct. 1934; *o s* of Albert Edward James Berry and Nellie (*née* Hodgson); *m* 1958, Anne Caroline Elliott, *d* of Charles Elliott and Evelyn Le Cornu; one *s* two *d*. *Educ:* Shrewsbury Sch.; Caius Coll., Cambridge (MA); University Coll. London (PhD; DSc 1976). Lectr, subseq. Reader, then Prof., in Genetics, at Royal Free Hospital Sch. of Medicine, 1962–78; Prof. of Genetics at University Coll. London, 1978–2000. Leverhulme Emeritus Fellow, 2001–04. Gifford Lectr, Glasgow Univ., 1997–98; Hooker Lectr, Linnean Soc., 2008 Mem., Human Fertilization and Embryology Authy, 1990–96. Member: Gen. Synod, 1970–90; Board of Social Responsibility of the General Synod, 1976–91; Natural Environment Research Council, 1981–87; Council, Zoological Soc. of London, 1986–90 (Vice-Pres., 1988–90); President: Linnean Soc., 1982–85; British Ecological Soc., 1987–89; Christians in Science (formerly Research Scientists' Christian Fellowship), 1993–95 (Chm., 1968–88); Mammal Soc., 1995–97; Chm., Environmental Issues Network, 1992–2008. Hon. Mem., Nat. Biodiversity Trust, 2010–. Trustee, Nat. Museums and Galleries, Merseyside, 1986–94. Governor: Monkton Combe Sch., 1979–91; Walthamstow Hall Sch., 2001–05. FRSA. Templeton UK Award, 1996; Marsh Award for Ecology, Marsh Trust, 2001. *Publications:* Teach Yourself Genetics, 1965, 3rd edn 1977; Adam and the Ape, 1975; Inheritance and Natural History, 1977; (jtly) Natural History of Shetland, 1980; (ed) Biology of the House Mouse, 1981; Neo-Darwinism, 1982; (ed) Evolution in the Galapagos, 1984; (jtly) Free to be Different, 1984; Natural History of Orkney, 1985; (ed jtly) The People of Orkney, 1986; (ed jtly) Nature, Natural History and Ecology, 1987; (ed jtly) Changing Attitudes to Nature Conservation, 1987; God and Evolution, 1988; (ed jtly) Evolution, Ecology and Environmental Stress, 1989; (ed) Real Science, Real Faith, 1991; (ed jtly) Genes in Ecology, 1992; (ed) Environmental Dilemmas, 1993; God and the Biologist, 1996; (jtly) Science, Life and Christian Belief, 1998; Orkney Nature, 2000; (ed) The Care of Creation, 2000; God's Book of Works, 2003; (ed) Environmental Stewardship, 2006; (ed) When Enough is Enough, 2007; Islands, 2009; (ed) Real Scientists, Real Faith, 2009; (ed jtly) Darwin, Creation and the Fall, 2009; (ed jtly) Theology After Darwin, 2009; Ecology and the Environment, 2012; (ed) Lion Handbook of Science & Christianity, 2012; (ed) Real Scientists, Real Faith, 2014; (ed) Christians and Evolution, 2014. *Recreations:* remembering hill-walking (especially Munros), dreaming, the resting. *Address:* Quarfseter, Sackville Close, Sevenoaks, Kent TN13 3QD. *T:* (01732) 451907.

BERRY, Prof. Roger Julian, RD 1987; FRCP; FRCR; FFOM; Director, Westlake Research Institute, Cumbria, 1992–95; Chairman, British Committee on Radiation Units and Measurements, 1995–2000 (Member, 1978–2000; Vice-Chairman, 1984–95); *b* 6 April 1935; *s* of Sidney Norton Berry and Beatrice (*née* Mendelson); *m* 1960, Joseline Valerie Joan (*née* Butler). *Educ:* Stuyvesant High Sch., New York; New York Univ. (BA); Duke Univ. (BSc, MD); Magdalen Coll., Oxford (MA, DPhil). MRC External Staff and Hd, Radiobiol. Lab, Churchill Hosp., Oxford, also Hon. Cons. Med. Radiobiologist, Oxford AHA, and Clin. Lectr, Univ. of Oxford, 1969–74; Hd, Neutrons and therapy-related effects gp, MRC Radiobiol. Unit, Harwell, 1974–76; Sir Brian Windeyer Prof. of Oncology, Middx Hosp. Med. Sch., 1976–87; Dir, Health, Safety and Environmental Protection, British Nuclear Fuels, 1987–92. Vis. Prof., Inst. of Envmtl and Natural Scis, Lancaster Univ., 1993–2003. Member: Internat. Commn on Radiological Protection, 1985–89; Nat. Radiological Protection Bd, 1982–87; MRC Cttee on Effects of Ionizing Radiation, and Chm., Radiobiol. Sub-Cttee, 1983–87; DoE Radioactive Waste Management Cttee, 1984–87; DHSS Cttee on Med. Aspects of Radiation in the Environment, 1985–87, Black Enquiry on Windscale; HSC Adv. Cttee on Safety of Nuclear Installations, 1992–96; CBI Health and Safety Policy Cttee, 1988–92; CIA Health, Safety and Envmt Council, 1990–92. President: BIR, 1986–87; Radiology Sect., RSM, 1985–86; Chm., Sci. Adv. Cttee, Thames Cancer Registry, 1985–87. RNR, 1971–92: recall to sea service in HM Submarines, 1975, 1977, 1979; Surg. Captain RNR, 1986, and PMO (Reserves), 1987–89. QHP 1987–89. Chm., St John Ambulance, IoM, 2008–12 (County Comdr, 2005–08). Gov., King William's Coll., IOM and Trustee, Bishop Barrow's Charity, 2000–. Hon. Fellow, Amer. Coll. of Radiology, 1983. KStJ 201. (CStJ 2005). Editor, Cell and Tissue Kinetics, 1976–80. *Publications:* Manual on Radiation Dosimetry (jtly), 1970; contributor to Oxford Textbook of Medicine, Florey's Textbook of Pathology; over 190 sci. papers in Brit. Jl of Radiology, etc. *Recreations:* sailing, music, naval history. *Address:* 59 Quay West, Bridge Road, Douglas, Isle of Man IM1 5AG. *T:* (01624) 617959. *E:* rogerberry@iom.com. *Clubs:* Royal Over-Seas League, Royal Naval Sailing Association.

BERRY, Dr Roger Leslie; *b* 4 July 1948; *s* of Mary Joyce Berry and Sydney Berry; *m* 1996, Alison Delyth. *Educ:* Dalton County Jun. Sch.; Huddersfield New Coll.; Univ. of Bristol (BSc); Univ. of Sussex (DPhil). Lectr in Econs and Associate Fellow, IDS, Univ. of Sussex, 1973–74; Lecturer in Economics: Univ. of Papua New Guinea, 1974–78; Univ. of Bristol, 1978–92. Avon County Council: Mem., 1981–93; Chm., Finance and Admin Cttee, 1981–84; Dep. Leader of Council, 1985–86; Leader, Labour Group, 1986–92. Contested (Lab): Weston-super-Mare, 1983; Kingswood, 1987. MP (Lab) Kingswood, 1992–2010; contested (Lab) same seat, 2010. Mem., Trade and Industry Select Cttee, 1995–2010; Sec., 1994–2009, Co-chair, 2009–10, All-Party Disability Gp. Vice-Chair, 2004–07, Chair, 2007–10, British Gp, Occasional Consultant, 2013–, IPU. Chair, Full Employment Forum, 1994–99. Dir, Tribune Publications Ltd, 1997–2003. Vice Pres., Disabled Drivers Assoc., 1997–2010; Trustee: Disabled Law Service, 1997–99; Snowdon Award Scheme, 1997–2003; Disability Alliance, 2010–12; Action on Disability and Work UK (formerly Vassall Centre Trust), 2010–; Disability Rights UK, 2011–; Avon and Bristol Law Centre, 2014–. Chair, Connecting Kingswood, 2013–. *Publications:* contribs to learned jls; newspaper articles and pamphlets. *Recreations:* travel, cooking, reading, cinema, theatre. *Address:* 9 Manor Road, Bristol BS16 2JD. *T:* 07748 965655.

BERRY, (Roger) Simon; QC 1990; a Recorder, 2000–05; a Deputy High Court Judge, 2001–05; *b* 9 Sept. 1948; *e s* of Kingsland Jutsum Berry and Kathleen Margaret Parker; *m* 1974, Jennifer Jane, *d* of Jonas Birtwistle Hall and Edith Emilé Vester; three *s*. *Educ:* St Brendan's Coll., Bristol; Manchester Univ. (LLB). Admitted Solicitor, 1973; Partner, Stanley Wasbrough & Co., Solicitors, Bristol (later Veale Wasbrough), 1975–77; removed from Roll 1977, at own request, in order to seek call to the Bar; called to the Bar, Middle Temple, 1977; Mem., Middle Temple and Lincoln's Inn; Harmsworth Benefactor's Law Schol.; Mem. Western Circuit, 1978–2005; in practice at Chancery Bar, 1978–2005; Asst Recorder 1996–2000; Ordinary Bencher, Lincoln's Inn, 1998. Member: Bar Council, 1996–99 (Mem. Professional Conduct Cttee, 1996–99, and Practice Mgt and Develt Cttee, 1998–99) Chancery Bar Assoc., 1978–2005 (Mem. Cttee, 1984, 1985); Professional Negligence Bar Assoc., 1991–2005; Property Bar Assoc., 2001–05. Mem., Theatre Panel of Judges, Olivier Awards, 2000. *Publications:* (contrib.) Professional Negligence and Liability, 2000. *Recreations:* family, the performing arts, keeping fit, climbed Mt Kilimanjaro in Tanzania, walked Inca Trail in Peru. *Club:* Riverside.

BERRY, Sam; *see* Berry, R. J.

BERRY, Scyld; *see* Berry, A. S. I.

BERRY, Simon; *see* Berry, R. S.

BERRY, Simon George Francis; Chairman, Berry Bros & Rudd Ltd, since 2005; *b* London 26 Nov. 1957; *s* of late Antony Arthur Berry and Sonia Alice Berry (*née* Graham-Hodgson) *m* 2005, Lucy Hamilton; one step *s* one step *d*. *Educ:* Eton Coll.; Harvard Business Sch (OPM). With Berry Bros & Rudd, 1977–. Chm., Wine and Spirit Benevolent Soc., 2008 Clerk to Royal Cellars, 2008–. Mem. Council, 2010–, Chm., Develt Bd, 2014–, RADA *Recreation:* choosing Desert Island Discs while waiting patiently for the BBC to call. *Address* 3 St James's Street, SW1A 1EG. *E:* simon.berry@bbr.com. *Clubs:* Boodle's, Pratt's.

BERRY, Thomas Henry Seager S.; *see* Seager Berry.

BERTHOIN, Georges Paul; Officier, Légion d'Honneur, 2006; Médaille militaire, Croix de Guerre, Médaille de la Résistance avec Rosette, France, 1945; Executive Member of the Trilateral Commission (Japan, N America, W Europe), 1973–75, and since 1993 (Chairman 1975–92, Hon. European Chairman, since 1992); Honorary International Chairman, the European Movement, since 1981 (Chairman, 1978–81); *b* Nérac, France, 17 May 1925; *s* of Jean Berthoin and Germaine Mourgnot; *m* 1st, 1950, Ann White Whittlesey (decd); three *d* (and one *d* decd); 2nd, 1965, Pamela Jenkins (decd); two *s*. *Educ:* Grenoble Univ.; École des Sciences Politiques, Paris; Harvard Univ. Licencié ès Lettres (Philosophie), Licencié en Droit, Laureate for Economics (Grenoble). Lectr, McGill Univ., Montreal, 1948; Private Sec. to French Minister of Finance, 1948–50; Head of Staff of Superprefect of Alsace-Lorraine-Champagne, 1950–52. Joined High Authority of European Coal and Steel Community, and then Principal Private Sec. to its Pres. (Jean Monnet), 1952–53–55. Dep. Chief Rep. of ECSC in UK, 1956–67; Chargé d'Affaires for Commission of the European Communities (ECSC Euratom-Common Market), 1968; Principal Adviser to the Commission, and its Dep. Chief Rep. in London, 1969–70, Chief Representative, 1971–73. Member: Nine Wise Men Gp on Africa, 1988–89; Bd, Aspen Inst., Berlin; Adv. Bd, Johns Hopkins Univ. Bologna Center Sch of Advanced Studies. Hon. Chm., Jean Monnet Assoc., 2001–. Regular Lectr, RCDS, London. *Recreations:* art, theatre, walking, collecting objects. *Address:* 67 Avenue Niel, 75017 Paris, France.

BERTHOUD, Sir Martin (Seymour), KCVO 1985; CMG 1985; HM Diplomatic Service retired; *b* 20 Aug. 1931; *s* of Sir Eric Berthoud, KCMG and late Ruth Tilston, *d* of Sir Charles Bright, FRSE; *m* 1960, Marguerite Joan Richarda Phayre (*d* 2009); three *s* one *d*. *Educ:* Rugby Sch.; Magdalen Coll., Oxford (MA). Served with British Embassies in: Tehran, 1956–58,

Manila, 1961–64; Pretoria/Cape Town, 1967–71; Tehran, 1971–73; Counsellor, Helsinki, 1974–77; Inspector, HM Diplomatic Service, 1977–79; Head of N. American Dept, FCO, 1979–81; Consul-General, Sydney, 1982–85; High Comr, Trinidad and Tobago, 1985–91. EC Monitor, Croatia, 1991. Dir, The Wates Foundn, 1993–2001. Patron: Green Light Trust, 2001–10; Prisoners Abroad, 2002–; Church Housing Trust, 2002–. EC Monitoring Mission Service Medal, 1994. Commander, Order of the Lion (Finland), 1976; Keys of City of San Fernando (Trinidad), 1991. *Recreations:* writing, golf, tennis, bird-watching, cooking, grandchildren, grappling with IT. *Address:* Gillyflower Cottage, Stoke by Nayland, Suffolk CO6 4RD. *T:* (01206) 263237. *Club:* Oxford and Cambridge.

ERTIE, family name of **Earl of Lindsey and Abingdon**.

ERTRAM, Dr Brian Colin Ricardo; Special Projects Co-ordinator, Bristol Zoo Gardens, 1995–2003; *b* 14 April 1944; *s* of late Dr Colin Bertram and Dr (Cicely) Kate Bertram; *m* 1975, Katharine Jean Gillie; one *s* two *d*. *Educ:* Perse School, Cambridge; St John's Coll., Cambridge (BA 1965; MA 1968); PhD Cambridge, 1969. FRSB (FIBiol 1981). Research Fellow, Serengeti Res. Inst., Tanzania, 1969–73; Sen. Res. Fellow, King's Coll., Cambridge, 1976–79; Curator of Mammals, 1980–87, and Curator of Aquarium and Invertebrates, 1982–87, Zoological Society of London; Dir-Gen., Wildfowl and Wetlands Trust, 1987–92. Zoo Inspector, Sec. of State's List, 1983–. Mem., Zoos Expert Cttee (formerly Zoos Forum), 2005–15. Vice-Pres., World Pheasant Assoc., 1990–97 (Mem. Council, 2010–); Mem. Council, Zool Soc. of London, 1993–97, 1999–2002, 2004–07, 2010–14 (Vice Pres., 2011–12). *Publications:* Pride of Lions, 1978; The Ostrich Communal Nesting System, 1992; Lions, 1998. *Recreations:* family, friends, zoology, garden, travel. *Address:* Fieldhead, Amberley, Stroud, Glos GL5 5AG. *T:* (01453) 872796. *Club:* Zoological.

ERTRAM, (Charles) William, RIBA; Founder and Managing Director, William Bertram of Bath Ltd, 2006–13; *b* 2 Oct. 1939; *s* of Lt Col Richard Bertram and Elizabeth Florence Oriana Bertram (*née* Bedwell); *m* 1963, Victoria Harriette Ingle; one *s* two *d*. *Educ:* Sherborne Sch.; AA Sch. of Architecture (AA Dip. Hons 1964). RIBA 1965. Founder: William Bertram Fell (architectural practice), 1970; William Bertram, Consulting Architect, 1996–2006. Architect to the Prince of Wales, 1987–2010; Consultant Architect: to Strangways Estate, 1972–96; to Duchy of Cornwall Eastern Reg., 1987–2014; to RNLI, 2002–08; Architect to Churchill Graves Trust, 1996–2009; Advr to Theatre Royal, Bath, 2005–13. Major projects include: *conversions and restorations:* Nos 15 and 16 into Royal Crescent Hotel, Bath, 1979; Abbotsbury Village, Dorset, 1980 (UK Council EAHY Award, 1987); St Anne's Place, Bath, 1985 (Bath Conservation Area Adv. Cttee Envmtl Award, 1987); Dower House, Bath (Civic Trust Award for Conservation), 1986; Cliveden into hotel, 1986–89; farm buildings and visitor's extension, Highgrove, Glos, 1988; Perrystone Court, Herefordshire, 1996; Shooting Lodge, Easter Auchintoul, 1998 (Inverness Civic Trust Biennial Award, 1999); Dinmore Manor, 2000–05; Rockley Manor, Wilts, 2000–03; Parnham House, Dorset (re-ordering), 2005; Encombe House, Dorset, 2005 (Georgian Group Award, 2006); Old Rectory, Combe Hay, 2009 (Design Quality Award, Bath and NE Som Council, 2010); *new work:* Stradling House, Somerset, 1979; Angmering Park, Sussex, 1983–85; Cavendish Lodge, Bath, 1986–97 (Stone Fedn Award, 1997); tree house, Highgrove, 1988; Dunley Farmhouse, Hants, 1996; South Kenwood, Devon, 1997; Nos 25, 1997, 57, 1999, 79, 2009, and 53, 2010, Winnington Rd, Hampstead; *gardens:* Highgrove, Camerton Court, Dinmore Manor, Albemarle House, Va, USA. Trustee, Bath Preservation Trust, 1966–68. Chm., Compton Dando Ch Estate Trust, 1981–2005. *Publications:* An Appreciation of Abbotsbury, 1973; The Architect's Tale, 2009. *Recreations:* garden designing, tennis, golf (badly), walking, writing, sketching. *Address:* Woodrising, Loves Hill, Timsbury, Bath BA2 0EU. *T:* (01761) 470718. *E:* william@bertramofbath.fsnet.co.uk.

ERTRAM, Dr Christoph; Partner, Bernzen Sonntag Attorneys, Hamburg, since 2008; Steven Müller Chair in German Studies, School of Advanced International Studies, Bologna Center, Johns Hopkins University, 2005–06; *b* 3 Sept. 1937; German national; *m* 1st, 1967, Renate Edith Bergemann (marr. diss. 1980); 2nd, 1980, Ragnhild Lindemann; two *s* two *d*. *Educ:* Free Univ. Berlin and Bonn Univ. (law); Institut d'Etudes Politiques, Paris (political science). Dr of Law 1967. Joined Internat. Inst. for Strategic Studies as Research Associate, 1967, Asst Dir, 1969–74, Dir, 1974–82; Mem. Planning Staff, West German Min. of Defence, 1969–70. Political and Foreign Editor, 1982–85, Diplomatic Correspondent, 1986–98, Die Zeit; Dir, Stiftung Wissenschaft und Politik (Foundn Sci. and Policy), 1998–2005. Chm. of Bd, Berlin Inst. for Population and Develt, 2007–12. *Publications:* (with Alastair Buchan *et al.*) Europe's Futures—Europe's Choices, 1969; Mutual Force Reductions in Europe: the political aspects, 1972; (ed, with Johan J. Holst) New Strategic Factors in the North Atlantic, 1977; Arms Control and Technological Change, 1979; Europe in the Balance, 1995; Rethinking Iran—from Confrontation to Cooperation, 2008. *Recreations:* clocks, sailing.

ERTRAM, George, CB 1999; Director, National Services, Board of Inland Revenue, 2000–01; *b* 19 Sept. 1944; *s* of late George Bertram and of Muriel Bertram; *m* 1969, Jean Swales. *Educ:* Houghton-le-Spring Grammar Sch. Nat. Assistance Bd, Sunderland, 1964–70; Department of Health and Social Security, then Department of Social Security: Staff Trng, Billingham, 1970–73; Sunderland, 1973–76; Regl Office, Newcastle upon Tyne, 1976–80; South Shields, 1980–83; Manager: Peterlee, 1983; Hartlepool, 1983–84; Middlesbrough, 1984–89; Sunderland, 1989; Contributions Agency: Head of Field Ops, 1989–92; Dep. Chief Exec., and Dir of Compliance and Educn, 1992–94; actg Chief Exec., 1994–95; Dep. Chief Exec., and Dir of Ops, 1995–97; Chief Exec., 1997–99; Dir, Nat. Insce Contribns, Bd of Inland Revenue, 1999–2000. Mem., CSAB, 2001–12. *Recreations:* golf, Sunderland AFC, cricket, gardening, travel. *Address:* 8 Holmewood Drive, Rowlands Gill, Tyne and Wear NE39 1EL. *Club:* Garesfield Golf.

ERTRAM, Robert David Darney; Member, Competition (formerly Monopolies and Mergers) Commission, 1998–2005; *b* 6 Oct. 1941; *s* of late D. N. S. Bertram; *m* 1967, Patricia Joan Laithwaite; two *s*. *Educ:* Edinburgh Academy; Oxford Univ. (MA); Edinburgh Univ. (LLB (Hons), Berriedale Keith Prize). An Assistant Solicitor, Linklaters & Paines, London, 1968–69; Partner: Dundas & Wilson, CS, 1969–92; Shepherd & Wedderburn, WS, 1992–98. Associate, Institute of Taxation, 1970 (Mem., Technical Cttee, 1986); Examiner (pt-time), Law Society of Scotland, 1972–75; Member: Scottish Law Commn, 1978–86; VAT Tribunal, Scotland, 1984–92; Council, UKCC (later Nurses' and Midwives' Council), 1988–2002 (Chm., Audit Cttee, 1998–2002; Lay Panellist, 2002–); Insolvency Practices' Council, 2000–; Audit Adv. Bd, Scottish Parlt Corporate Body, 2002–. Assessor, Edinburgh Univ. Ct, 2000–03. Vis. Prof., Edinburgh and Heriot-Watt Univs, 2000–. Non-exec. Dir, The Weir Group plc, 1983–2000. Trustee, David Hume Inst., 1998–2011. *Publications:* contribs to professional jls. *Recreations:* books, jazz, browsing. *Clubs:* Royal Over-Seas League; Scottish Arts, New (Edinburgh).

ERTRAM, William; *see* Bertram, C. W.

ERTSCHINGER, Dame Claire, DBE 2010; DL; Director, Tropical Nursing course, London School of Hygiene and Tropical Medicine, since 2003; author and public speaker, since 2005; *b* Herts; *d* of John William Bertschinger and Rene Bertschinger (*née* White). *Educ:* St Nicholas Prim. Sch., Old Harlow; Fawbert and Barnard Prim. Sch., Sawbridgeworth; Chantry Mount Sch., Bishops Stortford; Loughton Coll. of Further Educn (Pre-Nursing Course); St Mary's Hosp., Paddington (RGN 1975); Hosp. for Tropical Diseases, London (Cert. Tropical Nursing 1978); ICRC (Cours d'Intégration and Cours de Détention 1991); Brunel Univ. (MSc Med. Anthropol. 1998). Nursing appts, UK; medic, Scientific Exploration Soc., Panama, PNG and Sulawesi; work in emergency disaster relief, primarily war zones, with ICRC incl. Afghanistan, Kenya, Lebanon, Sudan, Sierra Leone, Ivory Coast and Liberia; trng officer, Health Div., ICRC, Geneva. Hon. DSSc Brunel, 2008; Hon. DSc De Montfort, 2009; Hon. DEd Robert Gordon, Aberdeen, 2010; DUniv Stafford, 2011; Hon. Dr Health Scis Anglia Ruskin, 2012. Bish Medal, Scientific Exploration Soc., 1985; Florence Nightingale Medal, ICRC, 1991; Window to the World Award, Woman of the Year, 2005; Internat. Human Rights and Nursing Award, Internat. Centre for Nursing Ethics, Univ. of Surrey, 2007; Commemorative Medal, Soka Gakki Internat., 2010. DL Herts, 2012. *Publications:* Moving Mountains (autobiog.), 2005. *Address:* Department of Infectious and Tropical Diseases, London School of Hygiene and Tropical Medicine, Keppel Street, WC1E 7HT. *E:* claire.bertschinger@lshtm.ac.uk.

BERWICK, Sir George (Thomas), Kt 2013; CBE 2007; Executive Principal, Ravens Wood School, 2011–13; Chief Executive Officer, Ravens Wood Learning Trust, 2012–13; *b* Folkestone, 10 Oct. 1948; *m* 1973, Maria; two *d*. *Educ:* Duke of York's Mil. Sch., Dover; Univ. Coll. of Wales, Aberystwyth (BA); Leeds Univ. (MA); Carnegie Sch. of Physical Educn (PGCE); Anglia Univ. (Advanced Dip.); Cambridge Univ. (PhD). Plymouth Coll.; Deanes Sch., Thundersley; Hassenbrook Sch., Stanford-le-Hope; Epping Forest High Sch.; Sen. Educn Officer, Essex LEA, 1989–93; Headteacher, Ravens Wood Sch., Bromley, 1993–2011. Educn Advr to Cabinet Office, 2001–05. Dir, London Leadership Strategy, 2003–08. Chief Exec., Nat. Teaching Schs, 2008–11. Chief Executive Officer: Olevi Ltd, 2005–; Challenge Partners, 2011–. Vis. Professorial Fellow, Inst. of Educn, Univ. of London, 2011–. *Publications:* Building Success, 2001; Engaging in Excellence, Vol. 1, The Approach, 2011, Vol. 2, Moral Capital, 2012. *Recreations:* family life, cycling, piano, gardening, wine.

BĒRZIŅŠ, Andris; President of Latvia, since 2011; *b* 10 Dec. 1944. *Educ:* Nītaure Elementary Sch.; Sigulda No 1 High Sch.; Faculty of Mechanics, Rīga Poly. Inst.; Faculty of Radio Engrg, Rīga Poly. Inst.; Faculty of Econs, Univ. of Latvia. Served Soviet military, 1963–66. Radio engr, then Man. Dir, R/A Elektrons, 1971–88; Dep. Minister for Community Services, 1988–89. Chm., Valmira Dist, Council of People's Deputies, 1989–93; Member: Supreme Council, Republic of Latvia, 1990–93; Saeima, Republic of Latvia, 2010–11; Chm., Econ., Agricl, Envmtl and Regl Policy Cttee, 2010–11. Mem., Supervisory Council, Bank of Latvia, 1990–92; Pres., A/S Latvijas Unibanka, 1993–2004; Chm., Supervisory Council, A/S Latvenergo, 2007–09. Pres., Latvian Chamber of Commerce and Industry, 2006–10. Commemorative pin for participants in 1991 barricades, Latvia, 1996. Comdr, 2000, First Grade, with Chain, 2011, Order of Three Stars (Latvia); Cross of Recognition, First Grade (Latvia), 2011; Order of Viesturs, First Grade (Latvia), 2011. *Address:* Chancery of the President of Latvia, Rātslaukums 7, Rīga 1900, Latvia.

BESGROVE, Maj.-Gen. Peter Vincent Ronald, CBE 1992; CEng, FIET, FCMI; Chief Executive, Haig Homes, 2002–14; *b* 23 Oct. 1948; *s* of Ronald Alfred Besgrove and Josephine Besgrove (*née* Buckley); *m* 1971, Eileen McEwan; two *d*. *Educ:* Magdalen Coll. Sch.; Welbeck Coll.; Royal Military Coll. of Sci. (BSc Eng Hons). CEng 1985; FIET (FIEE 1997). Commnd REME, 1968: served BAOR, NI and England, 1968–79; Staff Coll., 1980; Dep. COS, 6 Armd Bde, 1981–83; Comd, 5 Armd Workshop, BAOR, 1983–84; jsdc 1985; DS, Staff Coll., 1985–87; Comd Maintenance 3 Armd Div., BAOR, 1987–89; Asst COS, HQ NI, 1989–91; Comdt, Sch. of Electrical and Mechanical Engrg, 1991–92; Comd, REME Trng Gp, 1992–93; rcds 1994; Dir of Manning (Army), 1995–97; Dir Gen. Equipment Support (Army), 1997–99; Asst COS J1, HQ Allied Forces S, 1999–2001. Col Comdt, REME, 1999–2004. Co. Sec., Haig Housing Trust, 2008–14. Non-exec. Dir, SCS Ltd, 2002–06. Mem. Bd of Trustees, Treloar Trust, 2002–12; Chm. of Govs, Treloar Coll., 2003–10. Dir, United Services Trustee, 2007–11. FCMI (FIMgt 2001). *Recreations:* fishing, shooting, sailing, DIY. *Address:* c/o Regimental HQ REME, MoD Lyneham, Lyneham, Chippenham SN15 9HB. *Club:* Army and Navy.

BESLEY, Morrish Alexander, (Tim), AC 2002 (AO 1992); FTSE; Chairman: Australian Research Council, 2002–06; Co-operative Research Centre for greenhouse gas technology, 2003–09; Wheat Export Authority, 2005–07; *b* New Plymouth, NZ, 14 March 1927; *s* of Hugh Morrish Besley and Isabel (*née* Alexander); *m* 1st, 1952, Nancy Cave (marr. diss. 2001); three *s*; 2nd, 2001, Sarah Harrington; one *s* one *d*. *Educ:* Univ. of New Zealand (BE Civil); Macquarie Univ. (BLegS). Hon. FIEAust 2005 (FIEAust 1982); FTSE (FTS 1985). Engr, Ministry of Works, NZ, 1950; Snowy Mts Hydro-Electric Authy, Australia, 1950–67; First Assistant Secretary: Dept of External Territories, Australia, 1967–73; Dept of Treasury, Australia, 1973–76 (Exec. Mem., Foreign Investment Rev. Bd, 1975–76); Sec., Commonwealth Dept of Business and Consumer Affairs, and Comptroller General of Customs, Australia, 1976–81; Monier Ltd: Man. Dir, 1982–87; Chm. and Chief Exec., 1987; Chairman: Monier Redland Ltd, 1988; Redland Australia, 1988–95; CIG Gp, 1988–93; Commonwealth Banking Corp., 1988–91; Leighton Hldgs Ltd, 1990–2001; Commonwealth Bank of Australia, 1991–99. Director: Amcor Ltd, 1985–97; Fujitsu Australia Ltd, 1988–97; O'Connell Street Associates Pty Ltd, 1990–; Clyde Industries Ltd, 1991–96. Chm., NSW Transport Adv. Bd, 2013–15. Mem., NSW Council and Nat. Exec., Metal Trades Industry Assoc. (Pres., 1991–92). Chancellor, Macquarie Univ., 1994–2001. Mem. Bd, Australian Learning and Teaching Council (formerly Carrick Inst. for Teaching and Learning in Higher Educn), 2006–11; Chm., Sci. and Engrg Challenge, Univ. of Newcastle, 2005–15. Chm., Sydney Royal Botanic Gardens Trust, 1988–92; Trustee, Royal Botanic Gdns Sydney Foundn, 1992–99; Governor, Australian Nat. Gall. Foundn, 1992–; Chm., Centenary Inst. Med. Res. Foundn, 1992–96; Mem., Aust. Bd of Reference, World Vision, 1992–. Pres., AATSE, 1998–2002. Mem., Red Shield Appeal Cttee, 1988–99, Sydney Adv. Bd, 1994–99, Salvation Army. Hon. DSc Macquarie, 2002. *Recreations:* golf, fishing. *Address:* PO Box 304, Cammeray, NSW 2062, Australia. *Clubs:* Australian, Union (Sydney); Royal Sydney Yacht Squadron.

BESLEY, Prof. Timothy John, CBE 2010; DPhil; FBA 2001; School Professor of Economics and Political Science, London School of Economics, since 2012 (Professor of Economics and Political Science, 1995–2007; Kuwait Professor of Economics and Political Science, 2007–11); *b* 14 Sept. 1960; *s* of John Besley and June Besley (*née* Turton); *m* 1993, Gillian Nicola Paull; two *s*. *Educ:* Keble Coll., Oxford (BA PPE 1983); All Souls Coll., Oxford (MPhil; DPhil 1987). Prize Fellow, All Souls Coll., Oxford, 1984–91 and 1995–2000; Asst Prof., Princeton Univ., 1988–95; Dir, Suntory Toyota Internat. Centres for Econs and Related Disciplines, LSE, 2001–11. Research Fellow: Inst. for Fiscal Studies, 1995–; Inst. for Econ. and Social Res., 1995–2011. Mem., Monetary Policy Cttee, Bank of England, 2006–09. Co-Ed., Amer. Econ. Rev., 1999–2004. Chm., Council of Mgt, NIESR, 2008–. Pres., Internat. Economic Assoc., 2014–. Fellow, Econometric Soc., 2000. Foreign Hon. Mem., Amer. Acad. of Arts and Scis, 2011. *Publications:* contribs to Amer. Econ. Rev., Jl Political Econ., Econometrica, Qly Jl Econs and other scholarly jls. *Recreations:* Fulham FC, squash, playing violin, reading. *Address:* London School of Economics, Houghton Street, WC2A 2AE. *T:* (020) 7955 6702.

BESSANT, Rev. Canon Simon David; Vicar, St Saviour, High Green, Sheffield, since 2012; Priest in Charge, St Mark, Grenoside, Sheffield, since 2014; *b* 16 Feb. 1956; *s* of Ernest and Joan Bessant; *m* 1978, Ruth Margaret Hadfield; three *d*. *Educ:* Sheffield Univ. (BMus 1977; MA 2000); Nottingham Univ. (DipTh 1979). Ordained deacon, 1981, priest, 1982; Curate, St John and St James, Liverpool, 1981–84; Vicar: Emmanuel Ch, Holloway, 1984–91; Ch of the Redeemer, Blackburn, 1991–98; RD, Blackburn, 1997–98; Diocesan Dir for Mission, Dio. of Blackburn, 1998–2007; Vicar, All Saints, Ecclesall, Sheffield, 2007–12. Member: Gen. Synod of C of E, 2001–15; Archbishops' Council, 2006–07. Hon. Canon, Blackburn Cathedral, 2006–07, now Canon Emeritus. *Recreations:* listening to Schoenberg, reading counterfactuals, experimental fish cookery. *Address:* The Vicarage, Mortomley Lane, High Green, Sheffield S35 3HS. *T:* (0114) 4182036. *E:* simon.bessant@sheffield.anglican.org.

BESSBOROUGH, 12th Earl of, *cr* 1739 (Ire.); **Myles Fitzhugh Longfield Ponsonby;** Baron Bessborough (Ire.) 1721; Viscount Duncannon (Ire.) 1722; Baron Ponsonby (GB) 1749; Baron Duncannon (UK) 1834; *b* 16 Feb. 1941; *e s* of 11th Earl of Bessborough and his 1st wife, Patricia, *d* of Col Fitzhugh Minnigerode; *S* father, 2002; *m* 1972, Alison, *d* of William Storey, OBE; two *s* one *d*. *Heir: s* Viscount Duncannon, *qv*. *Address:* Broadreed, Stansted Park, Rowlands Castle, Hants PO9 6DZ.

BESSBOROUGH, Madeleine, Countess of; Madeleine Lola Margaret Ponsonby, OBE 2010; owner and Director, New Art Centre Sculpture Park and Art Gallery, Roche Court and Roche Farm; *b* Aldershot, 8 Nov. 1935; *d* of Maj. Gen. Laurence Douglas Grand, CB, CIE, CBE and Irene Grand (*née* Mathew); *m* 1963, Arthur Mountifort Longfield Ponsonby, 11th Earl of Bessborough; two *s*. *Educ:* St Mary's Sch., St Leonards-on-Sea; Prior's Field, Godalming. Founder: New Art Centre, London, 1957; Roche Court Sculpture Park, 1995; Roche Court Educnl Trust, 2005. Mem. Council, RCA, 1963–72 (Hon. Fellow, 1979). Lay Canon, Salisbury Cathedral, 2008. Patron, Salisbury Hospice, 1999–2007; Vice-Pres., Wilts Historic Churches Trust, 2009. FRSA. *Recreations:* contemporary architecture, small working farm, gardening. *Address:* Roche Court, East Winterslow, Salisbury, Wilts SP5 1BG. *T:* (01980) 862244, *Fax:* (01980) 862447. *E:* nac@sculpture.uk.com.

BESSER, Prof. (Gordon) Michael, MD, DSc; FRCP, FMedSci; Professor of Medicine and Head of Department of Endocrinology and the Medical Professorial Unit, St Bartholomew's and the Royal London School of Medicine and Dentistry, Queen Mary and Westfield College (formerly St Bartholomew's Hospital Medical College), London University, at St Bartholomew's Hospital, 1992–2001, and at Royal London Hospital, 1994–2001, now Professor Emeritus, Queen Mary University of London; Consultant and Lead Clinician, Department of Endocrinology, Bart's and the London (formerly Royal Hospitals) NHS Trust, 1994–2001, now Hon. Consultant Physician; *b* 22 Jan. 1936; *s* of Hyman Besser and Leah Besser (*née* Geller); *m* 1972; one *s* one *d*. *Educ:* Hove County Grammar Sch.; Bart's Med. Coll., Univ. of London (BSc, MB BS, MD, DSc). FRCP 1973. St Bartholomew's Hospital: Lectr in Medicine, 1966–70; Sen. Lectr and Hon. Consultant Physician, 1970–74; Prof. of Endocrinology, Med. Coll., 1974–92; Consultant and Physician i/c Dept of Endocrinology, 1974–2001; Dir of Medicine, 1989–93; Chief Exec., 1992–94. Consultant Endocrinologist: to RN, 1989–2001; The London Clinic Centre for Endocrinology, 2001–14. Vis. Prof., univs and med. estabts in Australasia, Canada, China, Hong Kong, Italy, Malta, S Africa, USA, Yugoslavia. Cttee work for RCP, RSocMed, Soc. for Endocrinology, Jt Cttee on Higher Med. Training; Medical Research Council: former Mem., Physiol. Systems Bd and Grants Cttee (Chm., 1984–86); Chm., Working Party on Hormone Replacement Therapy, 1992–95. Royal College of Physicians: Lectr, 1974, 1993, 1999; Censor, 1990–92; Sen. Vice-Pres. and Sen. Censor, 1995–97; Chm. Clinical Examng Bd, MRCP (UK), 1999–2003. Founder FMedSci 1998. Hon. MD Turin, 1985. Mem. Editl Bd, Clinics in Endocrinology and Metabolism, 1977–92; former Mem. Editl Bd, Jl of Endocrinol., Neuroendocrinol., and Clinical Endocrinol. Trustee: Barts Foundn for Res., 1985–2005; Barlow Collection of Chinese Ceramics, Univ. of Sussex, 2004–11; William Harvey Res. Foundn, 2005–11; St Bartholomew's Hosp. Med. Coll., 2005–; Willoughby Trust for Inflammatory Res., 2012–. *Publications:* Fundamentals of Clinical Endocrinology (with R. Hall and J. Anderson), 2nd edn 1978, 3rd edn 1980, (ed with R. Hall) 4th edn 1989; Clinical Neuroendocrinology, 1977; Recent Advances in Medicine, 3 edns, 1981–87; (ed jtly) Endocrinology, 2nd edn 1989, 3rd edn 1994; Clinical Endocrinology, 1986, 3rd edn 2002; Clinical Diabetes, 1988; contribs to learned jls. *Recreations:* early Chinese ceramics, modern European art, opera, ballet, theatre, making ceramics, keeping fit. *Address:* 5 Devonshire Place, W1G 6HL. *Club:* Garrick.

BEST, family name of **Barons Best** and **Wynford**.

BEST, Baron *cr* 2001 (Life Peer), of Godmanstone in the County of Dorset; **Richard Stuart Best,** OBE 1988; DL; *b* 22 June 1945; *s* of Walter Stuart Best, DL, JP and Frances Mary Chignell; *m* 1st, 1970, Ima Akpan (marr. diss. 1976); one *s* one *d*; 2nd, 1978, Belinda Janie Tremayne Stemp; one *s* one *d*. *Educ:* Shrewsbury School; University of Nottingham (BA). British Churches Housing Trust, 1968–73 (Dir, 1971–73); Director: Nat. Fedn of Housing Assocs, 1973–88; Joseph Rowntree Foundn, 1988–2006. Pres., LGA, 2005–15; Chairman: Hanover Housing Assoc., 2006–14; Hull Partnership Liaison Bd, 2002–04; Westminster Housing Commn, 2004–05; The Giving Forum, 2005–11; Commn on Future of Housing in NI, 2009–10; DCLG/LGA Housing Commn, 2010; The Glazing Ombudsman, 2012–14; Dep. Chm., Westminster CC Standards Cttee, 2008–13; Sec., Duke of Edinburgh's Inquiry into British Housing, 1984–91. Chm., UK Nat. Council for UN City Summit, 1995–96. Trustee: Sutton Housing Trust, 1971–84 (Dep. Chm., 1983–84); Internat. Year of Shelter for the Homeless 1987 Trust; RSA, 2006–12 (Treas., 2009–12); Committee Member: UK Housing Trust, 1976–88; Sutton Hastoe Housing Assoc., 1982–2000. House of Lords: Chm., Audit Cttee, 2005–10; Mem., Econ. Affairs Cttee, 2007–12; Chm., All Party Parly Gp on Housing and Care for Older People, 2009–; Dep. Chm., All Party Gp on Urban Develt, 2007–; Chm., Select Cttee on Communications, 2014–. Member: Social Policy Cttee, C of E Bd for Social Responsibility, 1986–91; BBC/IBA Central Appeals Cttee, 1989–91; Cttee, Assoc. of Charitable Foundns, 1989–92; Council for Charitable Support, 1995–2005; Housing Minister's Sounding Bd, DETR, 1999–2001; DTI Foresight Panel on Built Envmt, 1999–2001; Minister for Local Govt's Sounding Bd, DTLR/ODPM, 2001–05; NCVO Adv. Council, 2001–; Commn on Future of Birmingham's Council Housing, 2002; Comr, Rural Develt Commn, 1989–98. Trustee, 2020 Public Services Trust, 2008–11. Mem. Council, Ombudsman for Estate Agents, 2007–09; Chm., The Property Ombudsman, 2009–. Vice Pres., TCPA, 2007–. Pres., Continuing Care Conf., 2002–. Patron: Nat. Family and Parenting Inst., 2001–; Housing Assocs Charitable Trust, 2007–; Vice-Patron, Servite Houses, 2001–. DL N Yorks, 2012. FAcSS. Hon. FRIBA, 2001. Hon. LittD Sheffield, 2003; DUniv York, 2007. *Publications:* Rural Housing: problems and solutions, 1981; Housing Associations 1890–1990, 1991; Housing After 2000 AD, 1992; The Inclusive Homes of the Future, 1999; Housing Shortages: what councils can do, 2010; (with Jeremy Porteus) Housing our Ageing Population: plan for implementation, 2012. *Address:* House of Lords, SW1A 0PW. *Clubs:* Travellers, Farmers.

See also J. L. S. Best.

BEST, Dr Anthony Bernard, OBE 2010; Chief Executive, Percy Hedley Foundation, 2008–11; *b* 1 June 1947. *Educ:* Univ. of Leeds (Teacher's Cert.); Univ. of Newcastle upon Tyne (Dip. Special Ed.); Univ. of Birmingham (MEd; PhD 1993). Lectr in Special Educn, Univ. of Birmingham, 1978–90; Educn Develt Consultant, Hilton Perkins, USA, 1990–93; Principal, RNIB, 1993–2001; Chief Exec., Sense, 2001–08. European Rep., Internat. Council for Visually Impaired, 1997–99; Chm., Strategy Cttee, Deafblind International, 2006–09; Mem., Diversity Panel, ITV, 2009–. Trustee: Sightsavers, 1984–87; Signature (Council for Advancement of Communication with Deaf People), 2008–12. Ext. Examr, deafblind studies, Open Univ., 2009–; Educn Consultant, Scope, 2011–. Trustee, Henshaws Soc. for Blind People, 2014–. Gov., Whitefields Sch., Waltham Forest, 2005–12. *Publications:* Steps to Independence, 1987; Teaching Children with Visual Impairment, 1992; The Management of Visually Impaired Children, 1993; An International Research Agenda for Conductive Education, 2011. *E:* tonybest987@gmail.com.

BEST, David William; Chairman, Medical Marketing International Group plc (formerly Medical Marketing International Ltd), 1996–2008; *b* 1 Dec. 1949; *s* of William Robertson Best and Frances Best; *m* 1972, Margaret Smart Mitchell; one *s* one *d*. *Educ:* North Manchest Grammar Sch.; Univ. of Edinburgh. Mgt posts in pharmaceutical industry, 1973–88; C Founder, Man. Dir, 1988–96, Chief Exec., 1995–96, Medical Marketing Internat. Ltd (fi private sector technology mgt co. in Europe); Founder and CEO, Bioscience Innovati Centre plc, 1996–2008; Chairman: BioStarter Initiative, 2001–08; Oncosense Ltd, 2003–0 Viratis Ltd, 2003–08; Genvax Ltd, 2004–08; Founder, Bioscience Venture Capital Trust p 2001. Mem., AIM Adv. Panel, London Stock Exchange, 2002–08. Gold Friend, Duke Edinburgh's Internat. Award, 2000–; Mem., Internat. Fundraising Cttee, British Red Cro 2001–. Founder Mem., Global Scots, 2003. Ambassador, Med. Emergency Relief Interna 2002–. *Recreations:* running, alpine climbing. *E:* best.david@btinternet.com.

BEST, Dr Geoffrey Francis Andrew, FBA 2003; Senior Associate Member, St Anton College, Oxford, 1988–2004; *b* 20 Nov. 1928; *s* of Frederick Ebenezer Best and Catheri Sarah Vanderbrook (*née* Bultz); *m* 1955, Gwenllyan Marigold Davies; two *s* one *d*. *Educ:* Paul's Sch.; Trinity Coll., Cambridge (MA, PhD). Army (RAEC), 1946–47; Choate Fello Harvard Univ., 1954–55; Fellow of Trinity Hall and Asst Lectr, Cambridge Univ., 1955–6 Lectr, Edinburgh Univ., 1961–66; Sir Richard Lodge Prof. of History, Edinburgh Uni 1966–74; Prof. of History, Sch. of European Studies, 1974–85 (Hon. Prof., 1982–85), Dea 1980–82, Univ. of Sussex; Academic Visitor, Dept of Internat. Relations, LSE, 1985–8 Visiting Professor: Chicago Univ., 1964; York Univ., Toronto, 1968; Visiting Fellow: A Souls Coll., Oxford, 1969–70; LSE, 1983–85; ANU, 1984; Fellow, Woodrow Wils Internat. Center, Washington, DC, 1978–79. Lees Knowles Lectr, Cambridge, 1970; Joan Goodman Lectr, Univ. of Western Ontario, 1981; Cyril Foster Lectr, Univ. of Oxford, 199 Mem. Council, British Red Cross Soc., 1981–84, Hon. Consultant, 1985–91. Emery Rev Award, Churchill Centre, Washington, 2002. Editor, Cambridge Review, 1953–54; Jt Edito Victorian Studies, 1958–68; Editor, War and Society Newsletter, 1973–82. Paul Reuter Priz ICRC, 1997. *Publications:* Temporal Pillars, 1964; Shaftesbury, 1964; Bishop Westcott and t Miners, 1968; Mid-Victorian Britain, 1971; (ed) Church's Oxford Movement, 1971; (jt e War, Economy and the Military Mind, 1976; Humanity in Warfare, 1980; War and Socie in Revolutionary Europe, 1982; Honour Among Men and Nations, 1982; Nuremberg an After: the continuing history of war crimes and crimes against humanity, 1984; (ed jtl History, Society and the Churches, 1985; (ed) The Permanent Revolution: the Frenc Revolution and its legacy, 1789–1989, 1988; War and Law since 1945, 1994; Churchill: study in greatness, 2001; Churchill and War, 2005; contrib. various jls. *Address:* 1 Buckingham Street, Oxford OX1 4LH.

BEST, Harold; *b* 18 Dec. 1937; *s* of Fred and Marie Patricia Best; *m* 1960, Mary Glyn; two two *d*. *Educ:* Meanwood County Sch.; Leeds Coll. of Technol. Electrical technician; worke for Co-op. Movt, in electrical contracting industry, and in educn (technical support). M (Lab) Leeds North West, 1997–2005. *Address:* 19 Wynmore Avenue, Bramhope, Leeds LS1 9DD.

BEST, James Leigh Stuart; Director, DDB Worldwide, 1991–2008 (Chief Strategy an People Officer, 2002–07); *b* 1 April 1954; *s* of Walter Stuart Best, DL, JP and Frances Ma Best (*née* Chignell); *m* 1979, Priscilla Mary Rose McNeile; two *s* one *d*. *Educ:* Shrewsbu Sch.; New Coll., Oxford (BA, MA). Dir, Boase Massimi Pollitt plc, 1985–89; Chm., BM DDB, 1989–2000; Gp Chm., DDB UK, 2000–05. Chairman: UK Advertising Asso 1997–2002; Credos, 2010–; Cttee of Advertising Practice and Broadcast Cttee of Advertisi Practice, 2011–; Mem. Council, ASA, 2007–11. Pres., Eur. Assoc. Communicatio Agencies, 2003–05. Vice-Chm., Deborah Hutton campaign, 2009–. Trustee, Hist. Advertising Trust, 2013–. FIPA 1996; FRSA 2007. *Publications:* (ed) Scottish Advertisi Works, vol. 3 2003, vol. 4 2005. *Recreations:* farming, wildlife. *Address:* Manor Farm Hous Godmanstone, Dorset DT2 7AQ.

See also Baron Best.

BEST, (Katherine) Jane; *see* Humphries, K. J.

BEST, Keith (Lander), TD 1981; Chief Executive, Freedom from Torture (formerly Medic Foundation for the Care of Victims of Torture), 2010–14; *b* 10 June 1949; *s* of late Pet Edwin Wilson Best and Margaret Louisa Best; *m* 1990, Elizabeth Margaret Gibson; two *Educ:* Brighton Coll.; Keble Coll., Oxford (BA (Hons) Jurisprudence; MA). Assistant Maste Summerfields Sch., Oxford, 1967; called to the Bar, Inner Temple, 1971; Lectr in Law, 197 Served: 289 Parachute Battery, RHA (V), 1970–76; with RM on HMS Bulwark, 1976; Nav Gunfire Liaison Officer with Commando Forces (Major). Councillor, Brighton Boroug Council (Chm. Lands Cttee, Housing Cttee), 1976–80. Dir, Prisoners Abroad, 1989–9 Chief Exec., Immigration Adv. Service, 1993–2009. MP (C): Anglesey, 1979–83; Ynys Mô 1983–87. PPS to Sec. of State for Wales, 1981–84. Former Chm., All Party Alcohol Poli and Services Gp; former Mem., Select Cttee on Welsh Affairs. Chairman: Bow Gp Defen Cttee; British Cttee for Vietnamese Refugees; Internat. Council of Parliamentarians' Glob Action; World Federalist Movement, 1987–; Conservative Action for Electoral Refor 1992–; Vauxhall Conservative Assoc., 1997–99; Electronic Immigration Networ 1998–2008; Electoral Reform Soc., 1998–2003 (Mem. Council, 1996–2013; Chm., M Cttee, 1997–2003); Assoc. of Regulated Immigration Advrs, 2003–09; Electoral Refor Internat. Services, 2007–14 (Dir, 2004–); Wyndham Place Charlemagne Trust, 2013–; Vi Chm., European Council on Refugees and Exiles, 2011–14; Mem., Foreign Secretary's Ad Sub-Gp on Prevention of Torture, 2010–14. Chm., Charity 2020, 2015–. Hon. Sec., Lond for Europe (Eur. Movement), 2015–. Member: Conservative Gtr London Area Exec. Ctte 1997–99; UN Disarmament Cttee. Mem., Young Conservative Nat. Adv. Cttee, 1978. Me Cttee, Assoc. of Lloyd's Mems. Pres., Holyhead Leisure Fest. Ltd, 1981–2012. Truste Cranstoun Drug Services (formerly Odyssey Trust), 2003–09. Chm. and Trustee, Banglades Female Acad., 2009–11. Founder Member: Two Piers Housing Co-operative, 197 Brighton Housing Trust, 1976; school manager, Downs County First Sch. and Downs Midd Sch., 1976. *Publications:* Write Your Own Will, 1978 (paperback); The Right Way to Pro a Will, 1980 (paperback); contrib. District Councils Rev. *Recreations:* parachuting, walkin photography, travel. *Address:* 15 St Stephen's Terrace, SW8 1DJ; 7 Alderley Terrac Holyhead, Anglesey LL65 1NL. *Clubs:* New Cavendish; Royal Artillery Mess (Woolwich Holyhead Conservative.

BEST, Matthew Robert; opera singer, conductor, composer, arranger, teacher; Founde Musical Director, Corydon Singers, since 1973, Corydon Orchestra, since 1991, Artist Director, since 1996; *b* 6 Feb. 1957; *s* of late Peter Best and of Isabel Mary Best; *m* 198 Rosalind Sandra Mayes; one *s* one *d*. *Educ:* Sevenoaks Sch.; King's Coll., Cambridge (Chor Schol.; MA Hons Music). Singer: Nat. Opera Studio, 1979–80; Principal bass, Royal Oper 1980–86; Guest Artist, Royal Opera, Opera North, WNO, ENO, Scottish Oper Netherlands Opera, Florida Grand Opera, Théâtre du Châtelet (Paris), Opéra de Nanc Staatstheater Stuttgart, Théâtre de la Monnaie, Brussels, Opéra de Lyon, Santa Fé Opera, Op Frankfurt, Royal Swedish Opera, Oper Leipzig, Ópera de Bilbao and others, 1982–; princip operatic rôles incl. Flying Dutchman, Scarpia, Pizarro, Wotan (complete Ring Cycl Edinburgh Internat. Fest., 2003), King Mark, Rocco, Commendatore, Amfortas, Kurwena King Heinrich, Orest, Jochanaan, Peneios, La Roche; created rôles: Vairochana in Jonath Harvey's Wagner Dream (world premiere); Tiresias in Julian Anderson's Thebans (wor premiere); Tsargo in Kaija Saariaho's Adriana Mater (US premiere); has performed in concer worldwide and at major European and American fests. Conductor: concert appearances wit Corydon Singers and Corydon Orch. at fests throughout UK and Europe, at South Bank an BBC Promenade concerts; Prin. Conductor, The Hanover Band, 1998–99; Guest Conduct with English Chamber Orch., London Mozart Players, City of London Sinfonia, Roy

Seville SO, English Northern Philharmonia, New Queen's Hall Orch., Manchester Camerata, RTE Concert Orch., Northern Sinfonia, BBC Nat. Orch. of Wales, Sønderjyllands Symfoniorkester and Royal Liverpool Philharmonic Orch.; has made numerous recordings of choral/orchestral music and opera. *Compositions* include: Alice (operetta) performed at Aldeburgh Fest., 1979; choral and orchestral works performed by King's Coll. Choir, Cambridge, Corydon Singers. Teacher, Sch. of Vocal Studies and Opera, RNCM, 2014–. *Recreations:* reading, hill-walking, crosswords, gardening. *Address:* c/o Intermusica Artists' Management Ltd, Crystal Wharf, 36 Graham Street, N1 8GJ. *T:* (020) 7608 9900.

BEST, Prof. Serena Michelle, (Mrs A. I. Jaunzens), PhD; CEng, FREng; Professor of Materials Science, University of Cambridge, since 2009; Fellow, St John's College, Cambridge, since 2000; *b* 24 Jan. 1964; *d* of Anthony and Barbara Best; *m* 1986, Allan Imants Jaunzens; two *s*. *Educ:* Univ. of Surrey (BSc); Queen Mary and Westfield Coll., Univ. of London (PhD 1990). CEng 1995; FREng 2012. Lectr, 1994–99, Reader, 1999–2000, QMW; Lectr, 2000–06, Reader, 2006–09, Univ. of Cambridge. *Publications:* contribs to learned jls incl. Jl Royal Soc. Interface, Advanced Materials and Biomaterials. *Address:* Department of Materials Science and Metallurgy, University of Cambridge, 27 Charles Babbage Road, Cambridge CB3 0FS. *E:* smb51@cam.ac.uk.

BEST-SHAW, Sir Thomas (Joshua), 11th Bt *cr* 1665, of Eltham, Kent; *b* Maidstone, 7 March 1965; *s* of Sir John Michael Robert Best-Shaw, 10th Bt and of Jane Best-Shaw (*née* Guthrie); *S* father, 2014; *m* 1992, Emily Susan (*née* Rubin); two *s*. *Educ:* Maidstone Grammar Sch.; Univ. of Reading (BSc Hons Bldg Surveying). Local govt, 1992–2014; portrait artist, 2014–. Liveryman, Vintners' Co., 1994. *Recreations:* walking, classical music. *Heir: s* Joshua John Kirkland Best-Shaw, *b* 17 Jan. 1995. *Address:* 1 School Cottages, The Street, Sissinghurst, Cranbrook, Kent TN17 2JJ. *E:* bestshaw1@gmail.com.

BESTERMAN, Tristram Paul; freelance adviser, speaker and writer on museums and cultural studies; *b* 19 Sept. 1949; *s* of late Dr Edwin Melville Mack Besterman and Audrey (*née* Heald); *m* 1977, Perry Garceau; two *s* one *d*. *Educ:* Stowe Sch.; Trinity Coll., Cambridge (BA 1971, MA 1979). FGS 1978; AMA 1979, FMA 1986. Studio Manager, BBC, 1971–73; Preparator's Asst, Geological and Mining Mus., Sydney, NSW, 1974; jackeroo, cattle station, Qld, 1974; Educn Asst, Sheffield City Museums, 1974–78; Dep. Curator and Keeper of Geology, Warwickshire Museums, 1978–85; City Curator, Plymouth City Museums and Art Gall., 1985–93; Dir, Manchester Mus., 1994–2005. Civil mediator, CMC accredited, 2010. Chm., Ethics Cttee, Museums Assoc., 1994–2001; Mem., Ministerial Working Gp on Human Remains, 2001–03. Trustee, Centre for Contemporary Art and the Natural World, 2008–13 (Chm., 2012–13). Mem. Cttee, Cornwall Butterfly Conservation, 2015–. FRSA 2001. *Publications:* contribs to museological literature. *Recreations:* music, photography, industrial archaeology, grandchildren and other forms of natural history. *Address:* Hollywell House, Lodge Hill, Liskeard, Cornwall PL14 4EH. *T:* (01579) 349146.

BETEGH, Prof. Gábor Sándor, PhD; Laurence Professor of Ancient Philosophy, University of Cambridge, since 2014; Fellow, Christ's College, Cambridge, since 2014; *b* Budapest, Hungary, 20 June 1968; *s* of Sándor Betegh and Katalin Soltész; *m* 1997, Ágnes Sándor; two *d*. *Educ:* Eötvös Univ., Budapest (MA); École des Hautes Études en Sciences Sociales, Paris (Dip. d'études approfondies; PhD 1999). Jun. Res. Fellow, Center for Hellenic Studies, Harvard Univ., 2000–01; Prof., Central European Univ., 2001–14. Vis. Prof., Cornell Univ., 2007; Fellow, Wissenschaftskolleg Berlin, 2004–05; Topoi Sen. Res. Fellow, 2009–10. *Publications:* The Derveni Papyrus, 2004, 2nd edn 2007. *Recreations:* climbing, music. *Address:* Christ's College, Cambridge CB2 3BU.

BETHEL, Dr Archibald Anderson, CBE 2008 (OBE 1996); CEng, FREng; FIMechE; FRSE; Executive Director, Babcock International Group plc, since 2004; *b* High Blantyre, Lanarkshire, 9 Feb. 1953; *s* of Jack and Margaret Bethel; *m* 1984, Doreen; one *s* one *d*. *Educ:* Hamilton Acad.; Univ. of Strathclyde (BSc, MBA, DSc). FREng 2003. Chief Exec., Scottish Enterprise Lanarkshire, 1991–96; Chief Operating Officer, Motherwell Bridge Gp, 1996–2003; Chm., Scottish Enterprise Lanarkshire, 2003–08. Vice Pres., IMechE, 2005–13; Pres., Soc. of Maritime Industries, 2010–. Lay Mem. Court, Univ. of Strathclyde, 2012–. FRSE 2010. *Recreations:* golf, guitar, travel, science. *Address:* 2 Birch Grove View, Newton Mearns, Glasgow G77 6NJ. *T:* (0141) 639 0285. *E:* aabethel@btinternet.com, archie.bethel@babcockinternational.com.

BETHEL, Martin; QC 1983; a Recorder of the Crown Court, 1979–2015; *b* 12 March 1943; *o s* of late Rev. Ralph Bethel and Enid Bethel; *m* 1974, Kathryn Denby; two *s* one *d*. *Educ:* Kingswood Sch.; Fitzwilliam Coll., Cambridge (MA, LLM). Called to the Bar, Inner Temple, 1965; North-Eastern Circuit (Circuit Junior, 1969); a Dep. High Court Judge, 1995–2015. Member: Criminal Injuries Compensation Bd, 1999–2000; Criminal Injuries Compensation Tribunal (formerly Appeals Panel), 2000–10. Governor, Ashville Coll., Harrogate, 1989–2001. Pres., Runswick Bay Rescue Boat, 2001–04. *Recreations:* family, boating, ski-ing, golf. *Address:* (chambers) St Pauls Chambers, Trafalgar House, 29 Park Place, Leeds LS1 2SP. *T:* 0844 272 2322.

BETHEL, Robert George Hankin; Registered Medical Practitioner, since 1972; *b* London, 7 June 1948; *s* of Horace Hankin Bethel and Eileen Maude, (Mollie), Bethel (*née* Motyer). *Educ:* Eastbourne Grammar Sch.; Pembroke Coll., Cambridge (BA 1969; MA 1973); St Mary's Hosp. Med. Sch., London (MB BChir 1972). MRCGP 1979. Hse Physician, Queen Elizabeth II Hosp., Welwyn Garden City, 1972; Hse Surgeon, Nottingham Gen. Hosp., 1973; SHO, Northwick Park Hosp. and Clin. Res. Centre, Harrow, 1974; Registrar, W Middx Univ. Hosp., 1974–76; GP, Englefield Green and Old Windsor, 1976–2005 (Sen. Partner, Runnymede Med. Practice, 1997–2005); Rheumatologist (pt-time), Heatherwood Hosp., Ascot, 1976–92; Hosp. Practitioner, Windsor (Geriatrics), 1980–91. Course Tutor, Open Univ., 1979–80; Approved Trainer for Gen. Practice (Oxford Deanery), 1984–2005; Associate Teacher, ICSTM (formerly St Mary's Hosp. Med. Sch.), 1989–2004; Med. Officer, Brunel Univ., 1993–98. GP Appraiser, Thames Valley Primary Care Agency (formerly Berks E PCT), 2004–. GMC Associate (Performance Assessor and Professional and Linguistic Assessments Bd Examr), 2002–. Adv. Ed., Horizons, 1988–91. Member: Exec. Cttee, E Berks BMA, 1977–93 (Divl Sec., 1983–85); Bd, SW Thames Faculty, RCGP, 1983–92; Med. Mem., Ind. Tribunal Service (disability), 1991–99. Vice Chm., Old Windsor Day Centre, 1989–94. Vice Chm., Middx Province Relief Fund, 2010–. Life FRSocMed 1975 (Sec., 1993–95; Vice Pres., Sect. of Gen. Practice, 1995–97); FRSPH (FRSH 1990); Fellow, Med. Soc. of London, 1995. Member: Council, Royal Masonic Trust for Girls and Boys, 2002–; Matthew Wren Soc., 2009–. Cambridge Society: Sec., 1982–85; Chm., 1988–95; Mem. Council, 1991–2009; Vice Pres., Surrey Br., 1995–. Freeman, City of London, 1977 (Mem., Guild of Freemen, 1978–). Society of Apothecaries of London: Freeman, 1977–; Liveryman, 1981–; Court Asst, 1998–; Chm., Charity Cttee, 2007–10; Warden, 2008–10; Master, 2010–11; Hon. Treas., 2014–; Liveryman and Freeman, Curriers' Co., 2011– (Trustee, Millennium Trust, 2003–; Mem., Charity Cttee, 2014–). Governor: Corp. of Sons of the Clergy 2011–; Royal Humane Soc., 2011–14 (Life Gov., 2014). Wandsman, St Paul's Cath., 1987–. *Publications:* contrib. scientific papers to med. jls with special ref. to rheumatol. and gen. practice. *Recreations:* genealogy, books, travel. *T:* (01753) 540411. *E:* robert.bethel@virgin.net. *Clubs:* United Oxford and Cambridge; Windsor Constitutional.

BETHELL, family name of **Barons Bethell** and **Westbury**.

BETHELL, 5th Baron *cr* 1922, of Romford, co. Essex; **James Nicholas Bethell;** Bt 1911; Founder and Director, Westbourne Communications, since 2009; *b* 1 Oct. 1967; *e s* of 4th Baron Bethell and Cecilia Lothian Bethell (*née* Honeyman); *S* father, 2007; *m* 2004, Melissa, *d* of Douglas Wong, Newport Beach, Calif; one *s* two *d*. *Educ:* Harrow; Edinburgh Univ. (MA Hons History). Legislative aide, Office of Sec. of State, US Senate, 1985; Stagière, DG IV, EC, 1989; reporter, Sunday Times, 1990–93; correspondent, The Independent, 1993–94; Ministry of Sound, 1995–2001 (latterly Man. Dir); Capital Radio plc, 2001–05; Man. Partner, Portland, 2005–08; Dir of Communications, Policy Exchange, 2008. Contested (C) Tooting, 2005. *Publications:* (ed) A Pub Guide to Edinburgh, 1989; (jtly) Blue Skies Ahead, 1997. *Recreations:* hunting, shooting, clubbing. *Heir: s* Hon. Jacob Nicholas Douglas Bethell, *b* 17 Oct. 2006. *Address:* Lockeridge Down, Lockeridge, near Marlborough, Wilts SN8 4EL. *T:* (01672) 861 192. *Clubs:* Pratt's, Soho House.

BETHELL, Prof. Leslie Michael; Director, Centre for Brazilian Studies, University of Oxford, 1997–2007; Fellow, St Antony's College, Oxford, 1997–2007, now Emeritus; *b* 12 Feb. 1937; *s* of late Stanley Bethell and Bessie Bethell (*née* Stoddart); *m* 1961 (marr. diss. 1983); two *s*. *Educ:* Cockburn High Sch., Leeds; University Coll. London (BA, PhD). Lectr in History, Univ. of Bristol, 1961–66; Lectr 1966–74, Reader 1974–86, in Hispanic Amer. and Brazilian History, UCL; Prof. of Latin Amer. Hist., 1986–92, now Emeritus, and Dir, Inst. of Latin Amer. Studies, 1987–92, London Univ.; Sen. Res. Fellow, St Antony's Coll., Oxford, 1993–97. Visiting Professor: Instituto Universitário de Pesquisas do Rio de Janeiro, 1979; Univ. of California at San Diego, 1985; Woodrow Wilson Internat. Center for Scholars, Washington, 1987, 1996–97, 2008–09, 2010 and 2011 (Sen. Scholar, 2009–); Univ. of Chicago, 1992–93; Centro de Pesquisa e Documentação de História, Fundação Getúlio Vargas, Rio de Janeiro, 2008–; Univ. Federal da Integração Latino-Americana, Foz do Iguaçu, 2011–; KCL, 2011–; Univ. São Paulo, 2012. Member: Acad. Brasileira de Ciencias, 2004; Acad. Brasileira de Letras, 2010. Grand Officer, Nat. Order of the Southern Cross (Brazil), 1999 (Comdr, 1994); Comdr, Nat. Order of Scientific Merit (Brazil), 2010. *Publications:* The Abolition of the Brazilian Slave Trade, 1970; (ed) The Cambridge History of Latin America: vols I and II, Colonial Latin America, 1984; vol. III, From Independence to *c* 1870, 1985; vols IV and V, From *c* 1870 to 1930, 1986; vol. VII, Mexico, Central America and the Caribbean since 1930, 1990; vol. VIII, Spanish South America since 1930, 1991; vol. VI, Economy, Society and Politics since 1930, Part 1, Economy and Society, Part 2, Politics and Society, 1994; vol XI, Bibliographical Essays, 1995; vol. X, Ideas, Culture and Society since 1930, 1995; vol. IX, Brazil since 1930, 2008; (jtly) Latin America between the Second World War and the Cold War 1944–48, 1992; (jtly) A Guerra do Paraguai, 1995; (ed) Brasil. Fardo do Passado, Promessa do Futuro: dez ensaios sobre política e sociedade brasileira, 2002; Brazil by British and Irish authors, 2003; (jtly) Joaquim Nabuco e os abolicionistas ingleses, 2008; Joaquim Nabuco: British abolitionists and the end of slavery in Brazil, 2009; Charles Landseer: Desenhos e aquarelas de Portugal e do Brasil 1825–1826, 2010; (ed) Joaquim Nabuco, My Formative Years, 2012; (jtly) Joaquim Nabuco, correspondente internacional, 1882–91, 2 vols, 2013, vol. 3, Joaquim Nabuco na Europa e nos Estados Unidos, 2015; articles and chapters on Latin American history, Brazilian history, culture, politics and internat. relns. *Address:* Avenida Aquarela do Brasil 333, Bloco 1, apto 1302, São Conrado, 22610-010 Rio de Janeiro, Brazil. *E:* leslie.bethell@sant.ox.ac.uk; c/o St Antony's College, Oxford OX2 6JF.

BETHLEHEM, Sir Daniel (Lincoln), KCMG 2010; QC 2003; Director: Legal Policy International Ltd, since 2011; Palantir Technologies UK Ltd, since 2013; Consulting Senior Fellow for Law and Strategy, International Institute for Strategic Studies, since 2011; *b* London, 16 June 1960. *Educ:* Univ. of Witwatersrand (BA 1981); Univ. of Bristol (LLB Hons 1985); Queens' Coll., Cambridge (LLM 1990). Called to the Bar, Middle Temple, 1988, Bencher, 2008; in practice as a barrister specialising in public internat. law, 1990–2006 and 2011–. Lectr in Internat. Law, LSE, 1992–98; Dep. Dir, 1998–2003, Dir, 2003–06, Lauterpacht Res. Centre for Internat. Law, subseq. Lauterpacht Centre for Internat. Law, Univ. of Cambridge; Legal Advr, FCO, 2006–11. *Publications:* (ed jtly) The Kuwait Crisis: basic documents, 1991; (ed) The Kuwait Crisis: sanctions and their economic consequences (2 vols), 1991; (ed jtly) The Yugoslav Crisis in International Law: general issues, 1997; (Gen. Ed.; jtly) International Environmental Law Reports, (5 vols), 1999–2007; (ed jtly) The Oxford Handbook of International Trade Law, 2009; contribs to Cambridge Jl of Internat. Law, Am. Jl of Internat. Law, Eur. Jl of Internat. Law. *Address:* 20 Essex Street, WC2R 3AL.

BETT, Sir Michael, Kt 1995; CBE 1990; MA; *b* 18 Jan. 1935; *s* of Arthur Bett, OBE and Nina Daniells; *m* 1959, Christine Angela Reid; one *s* two *d*. *Educ:* Aldenham Sch.; Pembroke Coll., Cambridge (Hon. Fellow, 2004). Dir, Industrial Relations, Engrg Employers' Fedn, 1970–72; Personnel Dir, General Electric Co. Ltd, 1972–77; Dir of Personnel, BBC, 1977–81; British Telecom: Bd Mem. for Personnel, 1981–84; Corporate Dir, Personnel and Corporate Services, 1984–85; Man. Dir Local (Inland) Communications Services, 1985–87; Man. Dir, UK Communications, 1987–88; Man. Dir, British Telecom UK, 1988–91; Vice-Chm., 1990–91; Dep. Chm., 1991–94; non-exec. Dir, 1994–96. Chairman: Cellnet, 1991–99; Workhouse Ltd, 1992–95; J2C plc, 2000–02; Pace Micro Technology Plc, 2000–06; Director: Compel Gp plc, 1993–2005 (Chm., 2000–05); KMG Financial Services, 1994–99; Eyretel plc, 1996–2003; non-exec. Dir, Ordnance Survey, 2002–06. Chairman: Nurses Pay Rev. Body, 1990–95; Social Security Adv. Cttee, 1993–95; Armed Forces Ind. Review on Manpower, 1994–95; Nat. Council, TEC, 1994–95; Inspectorate of the Security Industry, 1994–2000; Nat. Security Inspectorate, 2000–07; Pensions Protection and Investment Accreditation Bd, 2000–06; Ind. Review of Pay and Conditions of Service in Higher Educn; Co-Chm., British N Amer. Cttee, 1997–99; Member: Pay Bd, 1973–74; Training Levy Exemption Referee, 1975–82; Civil Service Arbitration Tribunal, 1977–83; Cttee of Inquiry into UK Prison Services, 1978–79; Cttee of Inquiry into Water Service Dispute, 1983; NHS Management Inquiry, 1983; Armed Forces Pay Review Body, 1983–87; Civil Service Coll. Adv. Council, 1983–88; Trng Commn (formerly MSC), 1985–89; First Civil Service Comr, 1995–2000. Member Council: St Christopher's Hospice, 1993–99; Royal Hosp. for Neurodisability, 1996–2005 (Chm., 1998–2005); Cranfield Inst. of Technology, 1982–87; Pro-Chancellor, 1993–2003, Chancellor, 2004–11, Aston Univ.; Vice-Pres., Roffey Park Mgt Inst., 1999–. Chairman: Bromley CABx, 1985–93; SCF, 1992–98. Chm. of Govs, Cranbrook Sch., 1992–2000. Dir, English Shakespeare Co., 1988–95; Chairman: One World Broadcasting Trust, 1996–2002; English Shakespeare Internat., 1997–2000. Chm., Sevenoaks Volunteer Develt Agency, 2005–07. CCIPD (Pres., 1992–98); CCMI; FRSA. Hon. Col, 81 Signal Sqn (Vols), RCS, 1990–96. DBA (*hc*): IMCB, 1986; CNAA/Liverpool Poly., 1991; Hon. DSc Aston, 1996; DUniv Kent, 2013. *Recreations:* television and radio, theatre, music, cooking, gardening, golf. *Address:* Colets Well, The Green, Otford, Kent TN14 5PD.

BETTEL, Xavier; Prime Minister of Luxembourg, since 2013; Minister of State, Minister of Communications and Media and Religious Affairs Minister, since 2013; *b* Luxembourg, 3 March 1973; *s* of Claude and Aniela Bettel; *m* 2015, Gauthier Destenay. *Educ:* Univ. of Nancy (MA Public and Eur. Law; Postgrad. Dip. Advanced Studies in Pol Scis and Public Law). Lawyer, 2001–13. Parliament of Luxembourg: Mem. (Dem) Chamber of Deputies, 1999–2013; Vice Chairman: Legal Affairs Cttee, 2004–13; Cttee of Inquiry into Intelligence Service, 2012–13. Mem. Council, 2000–05, Alderman, 2005–11, Mayor, 2011–13, Luxembourg City. Chm., Democratic Party, 2013– (Chm., Parly Gp, 2009–11). Grand Officier, Order of Orange Nassau (Netherlands), 2012; Grand Cross, Order of Oak Crown (Luxembourg), 2014. *Address:* Office of the Prime Minister, 4 rue de la Congrégation, 1352 Luxembourg. *E:* bureau.premierministre@me.etat.lu.

BETTERIDGE, Prof. (Denis) John, MD, PhD; FRCP; Consultant Physician, University College Hospital, London, since 1981; Professor of Endocrinology and Metabolism,

University College London, 1994–2010, now Emeritus; Dean, Royal Society of Medicine, since 2011; *b* Ashby-de-la-Zouch, Leics, 24 Sept. 1948; *s* of Winston and Annie Betteridge; *m* 1989, Christine Martin; one *s* one *d*. *Educ:* Ashby-de-la-Zouch Boys' Grammar Sch.; King's Coll. Med. Sch. and Guy's Hosp. Med. Sch., London (BSc 1st Cl. Hons Biochem. 1969; MB BS 1972; MD 1979); Bath Univ. (PhD 1981). FRCP 1985. House posts, King's Coll. Hosp., 1972–73; SHO, Hammersmith, Brompton and St Bartholomew's Hosps, 1973–75; Registrar and Res. Registrar, St Bartholomew's Hosp. (Aylwen Bursary); R. D. Lawrence Fellowship, British Diabetic Assoc.; Sen. Registrar, Royal United Hosp., Bath; UK Prin. Investigator and Mem., Internat. Steering Cttee, PROactive. Member: taskforce gp on diabetes and vascular disease, Jt Eur. Soc. Cardiol. and Eur. Assoc. for Study of Diabetes; Steering Cttee for UK Prospective Diabetes Study, MRC. Mem., Grants Cttee, BHF, 2005–09. Past Pres., Council on Lipids in Clin. Medicine, RSocMed. Formerly Chm., Heart UK. Dist. Fellow, Internat. Atherosclerosis Soc. (Sen. Advr to Bd); FAHA. Member: Eur. Diabetes Assoc.; Amer. Diabetes Assoc.; Eur. Atherosclerosis Soc. Governor: City of London Sch. for Girls; City Acad. Islington. *Publications:* Sport for Diabetics, 1987; Lipids: current perspectives, 1996; Lipoproteins in Health and Disease, 1999; Diabetes: current perspectives, 2000; Lipids in Vascular Disease, 2000; Clinicians Guide to Lipids and Coronary Disease, 2003; Case Studies in Diabetes, 2003; Case Studies in Lipid Management, 2007. *Recreations:* music, gardening, cricket, fly fishing, shooting. *Address:* 88 Harley Street, W1G 7HR. *T:* (020) 7079 4348; Royal Society of Medicine, 1 Wimpole Street, W1G 0AE. *T:* (020) 7290 2900. *E:* j.betteridge@ucl.ac.uk. *Club:* MCC.

BETTISON, Sir Norman (George), Kt 2006; QPM 2000; Chief Constable, West Yorkshire Police, 2007–13; *b* 3 Jan. 1956; *s* of George and Betty Bettison; *m* 2004, Gillian. *Educ:* Queen's Coll., Oxford (MA Psychol. and Philosophy); Sheffield Hallam Univ. (MBA). Police officer, 1972–2004: S Yorks Police, 1972–93; W Yorks Police, 1993–98; Chief Constable, Merseyside Police, 1998–2004; Chief Exec., Centrex (nat. trng body to Police Service), 2004–06. Independence Medal (Rhodesia), 1980.

BETTLEY-SMITH, Robert, FRICS; chartered surveyor; consultant and company director; consultant, Unipol Student Homes, since 2012; *b* 27 July 1953; *s* of late Dr Neville Smith and Joyce Bettley, BA; *m* 1980, Judith, (Judy), Patricia Naylor, MA (Cantab); two *s* one *d*. *Educ:* Royal Wolverhampton Sch.; Royal Agricl Coll., Cirencester (Prizeman); Queens' Coll., Cambridge. Surveyor, 1980–83, Sen. Surveyor, 1983–85, ADAS; Principal, 1985–91, Regl Dir, 1992–98, MAFF; Chief Exec., FWAG (on secondment), 1998–2002; Dir, Project Team, DEFRA, 2003–05; Chief Exec., Govt Decontamination Service, DEFRA, 2005–09; Chief Exec. and Sec., Strategic Adv. Bd for Intellectual Property Policy, 2009–10; Sen. Civil Servant, DEFRA, 2010–11. Director: Mercian Mktg Ltd, 1997–2002; Peak Produce Ltd, 2001–05; Camley Estates Ltd, 2002–; Ryan Housing Ltd, 2012–; Betley and District Heritage Ltd, 2013–. Chm., Betley, Balterley and Wrinehill PC, 2007– (Vice Chm., 2005–07). Trustee, Newcastle-under-Lyme Rural Parishes' Transport Scheme, 2010–. FCMI. *Publications:* Capital Investment by Landowners 1972–1977; contribs to RASE Jl, Chartered Surveyor, and other professional jls. *Recreations:* Christian faith, village activities, Association Football (referee and spectator), our boat, fruit growing, ski-ing, steam engines, keeping my children in a manner to which they aspire to be accustomed whilst working on heritage railways as a trainee fireman. *Address:* Estate Office, Beech Wood, Betley, Crewe, Cheshire CW3 9AB. *T:* (01270) 820137. *E:* r.bettley-smith@talk21.com. *Club:* Farmers.

BETTRIDGE, Brig. John Bryan, CBE 1983; Principal, Emergency Planning College (formerly Civil Defence College), 1984–93; *b* 16 Aug. 1932; *s* of Henry George Bettridge and Dorothy Bettridge; *m* 1959, one *s* one *d*. *Educ:* Eastbourne Grammar School. Commissioned RA, 1951; regimental duty, 4 RHA and 52 Locating Regt, 1952–59; Instructor, RMA Sandhurst, 1959–61; Student, Staff Coll., Camberley, 1962; War Office, 1964–66; Bty Comd, 1 RHA, 1968–70; Comd, 3 RHA, 1973–75, Hong Kong; Chief Instructor, Tactics, RSA, 1976; Comd RA 2 Div., 1977–78; RCDS 1979; Dep. Comdt, Staff Coll., 1980–82; Comdt, RSA Larkhill, 1983–84. *Recreations:* golf, carpentry. *Address:* Cherry Garth, Main Street, Bishopthorpe, York YO23 2RB. *T:* (01904) 704270.

BETTS, Charles Valentine, CB 1998; FREng, FRINA; Director General Submarines, and Deputy Controller of the Navy, Ministry of Defence, 1994–98; Head, Royal Corps of Naval Constructors, 1992–98; *b* 10 Jan. 1942; *s* of late Harold Blair Betts and Mary Ellis Betts (*née* France); *m* 1965, Rev. Patricia Joyce Bennett; two *s*. *Educ:* St Catharine's Coll., Cambridge (BA Hons, MA Mech. Scis); Royal Naval Coll., Greenwich (Prof. Cert., Naval Arch.); Univ. of London (MPhil Naval Arch.). CEng; FREng (FEng 1991). Asst Constructor, MoD, 1966–71; Lectr in Naval Arch., UCL, 1971–74; Constructor, HM Dockyard, Portsmouth, 1974–77; Constructor and Chief Constructor, MoD, Bath, 1977–83; Chief Constructor, MoD, London, 1983–85; Prof. of Naval Arch., UCL, 1985–89; Dir, Surface Ships B, MoD, Bath, 1989–92; Dir Gen., Surface Ships, MoD, 1992–94. Director (non-executive): BMT Group Ltd, 1999–2001; BMT Reliability Consultants Ltd, 2000–01; BMT Gp Ltd (formerly British Maritime Technology Ltd, later BMT Ltd), 2001–12. Mem., Nat. Historic Ships Cttee, 2000–06. Mem. Council, RINA, 1985–2002, 2003–09 (Vice-Pres., 2003–09). Trustee: Alpha Internat. Ministries, 1993–2001; The Coverdale Trust, 2001–04 (Vice-Chm.); BMT Gp Employee Benefit Trust, 2006–12 (Chm., 2010–12); Chm. Trustees, BMT Pension and Life Assurance Scheme, 2006–12. Mem. Court, Univ. of Bath, 2007–. FRSA 1994. *Publications:* (jtly) The Marine Technology Reference Book, 1990; papers in professional jls. *Recreations:* supporting my wife in her rôle as Church of England priest, cruising together under sail, listening to music, amusing our grandchildren, walking, reading. *Clubs:* Royal Naval Sailing Association; Royal Victoria Yacht (IoW).

BETTS, Clive James Charles; MP (Lab) Sheffield South East, since 2010 (Sheffield Attercliffe, 1992–2010); *b* 13 Jan. 1950; *s* of late Harold and Nellie Betts. *Educ:* Longley Sch., Sheffield; King Edward VII Sch., Sheffield; Pembroke Coll., Cambridge (BA Econ). Sheffield City Council: Councillor (Lab), 1976–92; Chm., Housing Cttee, 1980–86; Chm., Finance Cttee, 1986–88; Dep. Leader, 1986–87; Leader, 1987–92. Chm., S Yorks Pension Authority, 1989–92; Dep. Chm., AMA, 1988–91 (Chm., Housing Cttee, 1985–89). An Asst Government Whip, 1997–98; a Lord Comr of HM Treasury (Govt Whip), 1998–2001. Member, Select Committee on: HM Treasury, 1995–96; Selection, 1997–2001; Transport, Local Govt and the Regions, 2001–02; DCLG (formerly ODPM), 2002– (Chm., 2010–); Finance and Services, 2005–. Member: Parly Contributory Pension Fund, 2005–; H of C Members' Fund, 2005–. Chm., 1995–96, Sec., 1995–97, Labour's Treasury Deptl Cttee; Labour Ldr's Campaign Team, 1995–96. *Recreations:* Sheffield Wednesday FC, football, squash, walking, real ale. *Address:* House of Commons, SW1A 0AA.

BETTS, Jane Margaret; *see* Mordue, J. M.

BETTS, Lily Edna Minerva, (Mrs John Betts); *see* Mackie, L. E. M.

BETTS, Peter George, CBE 2010; Director, International Climate Change, Department of Energy and Climate Change, since 2010; *b* 3 March 1959; *s* of George Frank Betts and Joyce Ann Betts (*née* Pedder); *m* 2006, Fiona Jane MacGregor. *Educ:* Emanuel Sch., Battersea; Mansfield Coll., Oxford (BA Hist. 1982); Ecole Nationale d'Administration, Paris. Joined Civil Service, 1984; First Sec. (Envmt), Office of UK Permt Rep. to EU, Brussels, 1994–98; Head, Global Atmosphere Div., DETR, 1998–2001; Head, Work and Pensions Team, 2001–02, Pension and Savings Team, 2002–04, Budget and Public Finances Directorate, HM Treasury; Principal Private Sec. to Dep. Prime Minister and Hd, Ministerial Gp, ODPM, 2004–05; Dir, Regl Policy, ODPM, subseq. DCLG, 2005–06; Dir, Fire and Resilience, DCLG, 2006–08; Dir, Internat. Climate Change, DEFRA, later DECC, 2008–09; Actg Dir-Gen., Energy and Climate Change Internat., DECC, 2009–10. *Address:* International Climat Change, Department of Energy and Climate Change, 3 Whitehall Place, SW1A 2AW.

BETTS, Ven. Steven James; Archdeacon of Norfolk, since 2012; *b* Nottingham, 22 Nov 1964; *s* of Ronald and Mary Betts; *m* 1992, Sarah Taylor; three *s*. *Educ:* Nottingham Bluecoa Grammar Sch.; Univ. of York (BSc Chemistry 1986); Univ. of Oxford (CTh 1990). Ordaine deacon, 1990, priest, 1991; Curate, Holy Cross, Bearstead, with St Mary's, Thurnham 1990–94; Chaplain to Bishop of Norwich, 1994–97; Vicar, Old Catton, Norwich 1997–2005; Bishop's Officer for Ordinands and Initial Trng, 2005–12. *Recreations:* family walking (especially in Austria), European travel. *Address:* 8 Boulton Road, Thorpe St Andrew Norwich NR7 0DF. *T:* (01603) 559199. *E:* archdeacon.norfolk@dioceseofnorwich.org *Club:* Norfolk (Norwich).

BEUTLER, Prof. Bruce Alan, MD; Regental Professor, Director, Center for Genetics o Host Defense, and Raymond and Ellen Willie Distinguished Chair in Cancer Research University of Texas Southwestern Medical Center, since 2011; *b* Chicago, Ill, 29 Dec. 1957 *s* of Ernst Beutler and Brondelle May Beutler (*née* Fleisher); *m* 1980, Barbara Lanzl (marr diss.); three *s*. *Educ:* Polytechnic Sch., Pasadena, Calif; Univ. of Calif, San Diego (BA 1976) Univ. of Chicago (MD 1981). Residency, Univ. of Texas Southwestern Med. Center 1981–83; Postdoctoral Fellow, 1983–85, Asst Prof., 1985–86, Rockefeller Univ.; Universit of Texas Southwestern Medical Center: Asst Prof., 1986–90; Associate Prof., 1990–96; Prof. 1996–2000; Investigator, Howard Hughes Med. Inst., 1986–2000; Prof., Scripps Res. Inst. 2000–11. Member: NAS, 2008; Inst. of Medicine, 2008. Fellow, Amer. Acad. of Arts an Scis, 2013. (Jtly) Robert Koch Prize, 2004; (jtly) Balzan Prize, Internat. Balzan Prize Foundn 2007; (jtly) Shaw Prize in Life Sci. and Medicine, 2011; (jtly) Nobel Prize for Physiology o Medicine, 2011. *Publications:* over 300 papers. *Address:* Beutler Lab, University of Texa Southwestern Medical Center, 5323 Harry Hines Boulevard, Dallas, TX 75390–8505, USA.

BEVAN, Alison Claire, BEM 2013; Director, Royal West of England Academy, since 2013 *b* Singapore, 1 Jan. 1965; *d* of John Edbrooke Lloyd and Barbara Lloyd; *m* 2004, Vince Bevan *Educ:* Tasker Milward Sch.; Univ. of Nottingham (BA Hons Hist. of Art 1986). Res. Asst Graham Sutherland Gall., 1987; Gall. Asst, Henry Thomas Gall., 1987–89; Glynn Vivian Ar Gallery: Exhibns Asst, 1989–91; Exhibns Officer, 1991–97; Actg Curator, 1997–99; Dir Penlee House Gall. and Mus., 1999–2013. *Recreations:* walking (ideally by the sea), co parenting delinquent border collie, holidaying in Ireland. *Address:* Royal West of Englan Academy, Queens Road, Bristol BS8 1PX. *T:* (0117) 906 7603. *E:* Alison.Bevan@ rwa.org.uk.

BEVAN, Anthony Richard Van, RA 2007; artist (painter); *b* Bradford, 22 July 1951; *s* o Adrian Van Christkarken Bevan and Margaret Betty Bevan (*née* Pemberton); *m* 1991, Gleny Johnson; one *d*. *Educ:* Bradford Sch. of Art; Goldsmiths Coll., London (DipAD); Slade Sch of Fine Art (HDFA). *Solo exhibitions:* Tony Bevan: Paintings 1980–87, ICA, London, Orcharc Gall., Londonderry, Kettle's Yard, Cambridge and Cartwright Hall, Bradford, 1987–88; Hau der Kunst, Munich, 1989; Whitechapel Art Gall., 1993; (retrospective) Inst. Valencia d'Ar Modern, Valencia, 2005–06; (retrospective) Long Mus., Shanghai, 2014. *Relevant publication* Tony Bevan, 2006. *Recreation:* food and wine. *Address:* 20 Blackheath Park, Blackheath, SE3 9RP. *T:* (020) 8852 0250, *Fax:* (020) 8469 0856. *E:* glenys.johnson@btconnect.com.

BEVAN, Dianne; Deputy Clerk, 2003–12, and Chief Operating Officer, 2007–12, Nationa Assembly for Wales; *b* 31 Oct. 1958; *d* of Alan and Brenda Roe; *m* 1986, Nigel Bevan; one one *d*. *Educ:* Selby Grammar Sch., N Yorks; Univ. of Hull (LLB Hons); Chester Coll. of Law (Solicitors' Finals); Cardiff Univ. (MPA). Articled clerk, Surrey CC, 1981–83; admittec solicitor, 1983; Solicitor: W Sussex CC, 1983–85; S Glamorgan CC, 1985–88; Chie Solicitor, 1988–91, Asst Co. Sec., 1991–93, W Glamorgan CC; Director, Legal anc Administrative Services: S Glamorgan CC, 1993–96; Cardiff CC, 1996–99; Corporat Manager, Cardiff CC, 1999–2003. *Recreations:* travel, theatre, cinema, visual arts.

BEVAN, (Edward) Julian; QC 1991; *b* 23 Oct. 1940; *m* 1966, Bronwen Mary Windso Lewis; two *s* two *d*. *Educ:* Eton. Called to the Bar, Gray's Inn, 1962, Bencher, 1989; Standing Counsel for the Inland Revenue, 1974; Jun. Treasury Counsel, 1977, Sen. Treasury Counsel 1985, First Sen. Treasury Counsel, 1989–91, Central Criminal Court.

BEVAN, Prof. Hugh Keith; JP; Professor of Law, University of Hull, 1969–89; *b* 8 Oct 1922; *s* of Thomas Edward Bevan and Marjorie Avril Bevan (*née* Trick); *m* 1950, Mary Harris one *d* (one *s* decd). *Educ:* Neath Grammar Sch.; University Coll. of Wales, Aberystwyth. LLB 1949, LLM 1966. Called to the Bar, Middle Temple, 1959. Served RA, 1943–46. University of Hull: Lectr in Law, 1950–61; Sen. Lectr in Law, 1961–69; Pro Vice-Chancellor, 1979–82 Wolfson College, Cambridge: Vis. Fellow, 1986 and 1989–90; Fellow, 1990–92; Hon Fellow, 1992. Chm., Rent Assessment Cttees, 1982–92. Pres., Soc. of Public Teachers o Law, 1987–88. JP Kingston-upon-Hull, 1972 (Chm. of Bench, 1984–89). Hon. Fellow Swansea Univ., 2007. Hon. LLD: Hull, 1990; Sheffield, 2000. *Publications:* Source Book o Family Law (with P. R. H. Webb), 1964; Law Relating to Children, 1973; (with M. L. Parry) The Children Act 1975, 1978; Child Law, 1988; numerous articles. *Recreations:* music, golf *Address:* Wolfson College, Cambridge CB3 9BB. *T:* (01223) 335900.

BEVAN, Sir James (David), KCMG 2012 (CMG 2006); HM Diplomatic Service, retired Chief Executive, Environment Agency, since 2015; *b* 13 July 1959; *s* of late Douglas Bevar and of Diana Bevan; *m* 1984, Janet Purdie; three *d*. *Educ:* Univ. of Sussex (BA Hons Socia Anthropology). Joined FCO, 1982; Kinshasa, 1984–86; UK Delegn to NATO, Brussels, 1986–90; FCO, 1990–92; Paris, 1993; Washington, 1994–98; Hd, Africa Dept (Equatorial) FCO, 1998–2000; Hd, EU Dept (Internal), FCO, 2000–01; Director: SE Europe and Gibraltar, FCO, 2002; Africa, FCO, 2003–06; Dir Gen., Change and Delivery, then Chie Operating Officer, FCO, 2007–11; High Comr to India, 2011–15. FCO Vis. Fellow, Harvard Univ., 2006. *Recreations:* music, not worrying.

BEVAN, John Penry Vaughan; QC 1997; **His Honour Judge Bevan;** a Circuit Judge since 2004; a Senior Circuit Judge, since 2011; *b* 7 Sept. 1947; *s* of late Llewellyn Vaughar Bevan and Hilda Molly Bevan; *m* 1st, 1971, Dinah Nicholson; two *d*; 2nd, 1978, Veronica Aliaga-Kelly; one *s* one *d*. *Educ:* Radley Coll.; Magdalene Coll., Cambridge (BA). Called to the Bar, Middle Temple, 1970, Bencher, 2001. A Recorder, 1988–2004; Sen. Treasury Counsel, CCC, 1989–97. *Recreation:* sailing. *Clubs:* Leander (Henley-on-Thames); Aldeburgh Yacht; Orford Sailing.

BEVAN, John Stuart, OBE 1995; Further Education Funding Council for Englanc Ombudsman, 1996–2001; *b* 19 Nov. 1935; *s* of Frank Oakland and Ruth Mary Bevan; *m* 1960, Patricia Vera Beatrice (*née* Joyce); two *s* two *d*. *Educ:* Eggars Grammar Sch.; Jesus Coll. Oxford; St Bartholomew's Hosp. Med. Coll. MA, MSc; FInstP. Health Physicist, UK Atomic Energy Authority, 1960–62; Lectr, then Sen. Lectr in Physics, Polytechnic of the South Bank (previously Borough Polytechnic), 1962–73; Inner London Education Authority: Asst Educn Officer, then Sen. Asst Educn Officer, 1973–76; Dep. Educn Officer, 1977–79; Dir of Educn 1979–82; Sec., NAB, 1982–88; Dir of Educn Services, London Residuary Body, 1989–92 Chief Exec., ACFHE, 1992–93; Sec., Assoc. for Colls, 1993–94. Former Member, National Executive Committees: Nat. Union of Teachers; Assoc. of Teachers in Technical Instns (Pres., 1972–73). Chm., Nat. Youth Agency, 1996–2002. Scout Association: Asst, later Dep. Comr, Kent, 1982–99; Chm., Nat. Activities Bd, 1988–93; Nat. Comr for Activities, 1994–95; Chm., Programme and Trng, 1995–96; Chm., Cttee of Council, 1996–2001; Skills Instructor, Eden Dist, 2000–. Mem., Adventure Activities Industry Adv. Cttee, CCPR (formerly HSC), 1997–2007 (Chm., 2004–07). Co. Sec., Great Asby Broadband CIC, 2007–; Vice-Chm., Cumbria Local Access Forum, 2001–12. Treas., Appleby Deanery, Carlisle Dio., 2002–13. Hon. Fellow: S Bank Univ. (formerly Poly of the S Bank), 1987; Westminster Coll., Oxford, 1990. DUniv Surrey, 1990; Hon. LLD CNAA, 1992. *Recreations:* Scouting, foreign travel, hill-walking. *Address:* The Hollies, Great Asby, Appleby, Cumbria CA16 6HD. *T:* (01768) 353433.

See also R. M. Bevan.

BEVAN, Julian; *see* Bevan, E. J.

BEVAN, Sir Martyn Evan E.; *see* Evans-Bevan.

BEVAN, Prof. Michael John, PhD; FRS 1991; Investigator, Howard Hughes Medical Institute, and Professor, Department of Immunology, University of Washington, Seattle, since 1990; *b* 20 Sept. 1945; *s* of Thomas John and Doris Mary Bevan; *m* 1985, Pamela Jean Fink; two *s*. *Educ:* Pontypridd Boys' Grammar Sch.; University Coll. London (BSc Zool. 1967; MSc Biochem. 1968); Nat. Inst. for Med. Research, London (PhD 1972). Postdoctoral Fellow, Salk Inst. for Biol Studies, La Jolla, Calif, 1973–76, Asst Res. Prof., 1976–77; Asst, then Associate, Prof., Dept of Biology, MIT, 1977–82; Associate, then Member, Dept of Immunology, Scripps Res. Inst., La Jolla, Calif, 1982–90. *Publications:* numerous original res. pubns in scientific jls incl. Nature, Science, Cell, Jl Exptl Medicine. *Recreations:* hiking, reading. *Address:* Howard Hughes Medical Institute, Department of Immunology, University of Washington, Room E-441, 750 Republican Street, Seattle, WA 98109, USA. *T:* (206) 6853610.

BEVAN, Prof. Michael Webster, PhD; FRS 2013; Project Leader, Cell and Developmental Biology Department, and Deputy Director, John Innes Centre, Biotechnology and Biological Sciences Research Council, since 2010 (Acting Director, 2009–10); Professor, University of East Anglia, since 1997; *b* Otorohanga, NZ, 5 June 1952; *s* of John Vernon Bevan and Sue (*née* Webster); *m* 1982, Jane Foster; two *s*. *Educ:* Univ. of Auckland (BSc 1973; MSc Hons 1974); Univ. of Cambridge (PhD 1979). Res. Fellow, Washington Univ., St Louis, Mo, 1980; Higher Scientific Officer, 1982–84, SSO, 1984–86, PSO, 1986–88, Plant Breeding Inst., Cambridge; Hd, Dept of Molecular Genetics, then Cell and Develtl Biol., Inst. of Plant Sci. Res., AFRC, subseq. John Innes Centre, BBSRC, 1988–2009. Mem., EMBO, 2001. Rank Prize, Rank Foundn, 1986; Kumho Science Internat. Award in Plant Molecular Biol. and Biotechnol., Kumho Cultural Foundn of Korea, 2001. *Publications:* contrib. numerous chapters in books and articles to learned jls. *Recreations:* reading modern literature, gardening, walking. *Address:* 329 Unthank Road, Norwich NR4 7QA. *T:* (01603) 504181.

BEVAN, Sir Nicolas, Kt 2001; CB 1991; Speaker's Secretary, House of Commons, 1993–2003; *b* 8 March 1942; *s* of late Roger Bevan, BM, and Diana Mary Bevan (*née* Freeman); *m* 1982, Christine, *d* of N. A. Berry. *Educ:* Westminster Sch. (Hon. Fellow 2003); Corpus Christi Coll., Oxford (MA LitHum). Ministry of Defence: Asst Principal, 1964; Principal, 1969; Private Sec. to Chief of Air Staff, 1970–73; Cabinet Office, 1973–75; Asst Sec., 1976; RCDS 1981; Asst Under Sec. of State, 1985; Under Sec., Cabinet Office, 1992–93. Freeman, City of London, 2008; Liveryman, Woolmen's Co., 2009. *Recreation:* gardening. *Clubs:* National Liberal, Lansdowne.

BEVAN, Rev. Canon Richard Justin William, PhD; ThD; Chaplain to the Queen, 1986–92; Canon Emeritus, Carlisle Cathedral, since 1989 (Canon Residentiary, Carlisle Cathedral, 1982–89, Treasurer and Librarian, 1982–89, Vice-Dean, 1986–89); *b* 21 April 1922; *s* of Rev. Richard Bevan, Vicar of St Harmon, Radnorshire and Margaret Bevan; *m* 1948, Sheila Rosemary Barrow, Fazakerley, Liverpool; three *s* one *d* (and one *s* decd). *Educ:* St Edmund's Sch., Canterbury; St Augustine's Coll., Canterbury; Lichfield Theol Coll.; St Chad's Coll., Univ. of Durham (Theol. Prizeman; BA, LTh). ThD: Geneva Theol Coll., 1972; Greenwich Univ., USA, 1990; PhD Columbia Pacific Univ., 1980. Ordained deacon, Lichfield Cathedral, 1945, priest, 1946; Asst Curate, Stoke-on-Trent, 1945–49; Chaplain, Aberlour Orphanage and licence to officiate, dio. of Moray, Ross and Caithness, 1949–51; Asst Master, Burnley Tech. High Sch., 1951–60; Asst Curate, Church Kirk, 1951–56, Whalley, 1956–60; Rector, St Mary-le-Bow, Durham and Chaplain to Durham Univ., 1960–74; Vicar, St Oswald's United Benefice, 1964–74; Convener of Chaplains, Univ. of Durham, 1964–74; Rector of Grasmere, 1974–82. Examg Chaplain to Bishop of Carlisle, 1970–2008; Chaplain, Durham Girls' High Sch., 1966–74; Vice-President: Friends of St Chad's Coll., 1990– (Governor, St Chad's Coll., 1969–89); Greenwich Sch. of Theology, 1977–2003 (Hon. Vice-Pres. and Hon. Governor, 2003–). First Pres., and Founder Mem., Grasmere Village Soc., 1976–78; Dove Cottage Local Cttee, 1974–82. Chancellor's medal, North-West Univ. (Potchefstroom campus), S Africa, 2004. *Publications:* (ed) Steps to Christian Understanding, 1959; (ed) The Churches and Christian Unity, 1964; (ed) Durham Sermons, 1964; Unfurl the Flame (poetry), 1980; A Twig of Evidence: does belief in God make sense?, 1986; (contrib.) John Cosin: from priest to prince bishop, 1997; articles on ethics and culture. *Recreations:* poetry reading, musical appreciation. *Address:* 15 Solway Park, Carlisle CA2 6TH. *T:* (01228) 631428. *Club:* Victory Services.

BEVAN, Robert, MBE 2004; after-dinner speaker (as Bob "The Cat" Bevan), author, broadcaster, presenter, interviewer, comedian, journalist, poet, scriptwriter; *b* 26 Feb. 1945; *s* of Eric and Iris Rose Bevan; *m* 2012 Laura Collins. *Educ:* Wilson's Grammar Sch., Camberwell. MCIPR 1974. Trainee sales rep., Nicholls & Clarke, 1961–62; Asst Chief Reporter, Lloyd's List and Shipping Gazette, 1962–66; PR Manager, Shorthorn Soc. of GB and Ireland, 1966; Dep. Ed., Travel Agency Mag., 1967–69; Hertford Public Relations Ltd: Account Exec., 1969–70; Dir, 1970–72; Man. Dir, 1972–74; Gp Dir of PR, European Ferries Plc, 1974–83; Chm., Bevan PR Ltd, 1983–92. Member: NUJ, 1967–; Soc. of Authors. Hon. Barker, Variety Club of GB, 1990–; Mem., Grand Order of Water Rats, 2001–. Ambassador for County of Kent, 2011–. President: Old Wilsonians' Assoc., 1995 (Life Mem.); Bells Yew Green CC, 1996–2009; Kent CCC, 2013–14; Nat. Sporting Club, 2014; Vice President: Old Wilsonians' FC, 1970–; Crystal Palace FC, 1986–2006; Frant CC, 1993–; Middlesex Wanderers FC, 1996–; Dulwich Hamlet FC, 2000–; Tonbridge Angels FC, 2002–. Trustee, Lord's Taverners, 1995–2004, 2009–11, 2015–. *Publications:* Nearly Famous, 2003. *Recreations:* football, cricket, reading, travel, food, drink. *Address:* Barelands Oast, Bells Yew Green, Kent TN3 9BD. *E:* Bob@bobthecatbevan.co.uk. *W:* www.bobthecatbevan.com. *Clubs:* Les Ambassadeurs; Kent CC.

BEVAN, Dr Robin Meredith; Headteacher, Southend High School for Boys, since 2007; *b* Tonbridge, Kent, 14 Aug. 1966; *s* of John Stuart Bevan, *qv*; *m* 1991, Marion Jones; one *s* two *d*. *Educ:* Judd Sch., Tonbridge (Stamp Leaving Schol.); Jesus Coll., Oxford (MA Maths 1987); Nottingham Univ. (PGCE Secondary Maths 1989); Trinity Hall, Cambridge (MEd Curriculum 1999; PhD Educn (Computerised Knowledge Mapping) 2007). Teacher of Mathematics: Mill Hill Co. High Sch., Mill Hill, 1989–91; Friends Sch. (Soc. of Friends), Gt Ayton, 1991–94; Hd of Maths, 1994–99, Asst Dir of Studies, 1998–99, Westcliff High Sch. for Boys, Westcliff on Sea; Dep. Headteacher, King Edward VI GS, Chelmsford, 1999–2007. Pubns Ed. and Cttee Chair, Managing Maths, Mathematical Assoc., 2001–05. Mem., Adv. Gp, Support Staff Res., DfES, 2004–07. Member: Res. Rev. Gps, Evidence for Policy and Practice Information Centre, 2001–07; Res. Bulletin Steering Gp, Nat. Educnl Res. Foundn, 2003–05; Nat. Teacher Res. Panel, 2003– (Vice Chair, 2008–13; Chair, 2014–); Steering Gp, Nat. Assoc. of Sch. Partnerships, 2012–; Association of Teachers and Lecturers: Member, National Executive: for Essex, Southend, Thurrock and Germany, 2005–14; representing UK Sch. and Coll. Leadership; Mem., Nat. Council, Assoc. of Managers in Educn, 2010–. Trustee, Pension Scheme, 2012–. Chair, Consortium for Selective Schs in Essex, 2011–12 (Advr, 1999–; Mem., 2007–). Mem., Fabian Soc., 1995–. Trustee, Southend Educn Trust, 2008–. *Publications:* (contrib.) Graded Exercises in Pure Mathematics for AS and A2, 2001; (ed) Managing Mathematics: handbook for heads of mathematics, 2005; contribs to Teacher Develt, Reflecting Educn. *Recreations:* competitive cycling (qualified coach and active competitor, time triallist representing Cambridge University Cycling Club in national student events, 2004, 2005); running half-marathons and duathlons, with mid-life triathlon delusions. *Address:* Southend High School for Boys, Prittlewell Chase, Southend on Sea, Essex SS0 0RG. *T:* (01702) 606200. *E:* enquiries@shsb.org.uk.

BEVAN, Stephen Mark; Director, Centre for Workforce Effectiveness, The Work Foundation, since 2011; *b* Maidstone, 21 Aug. 1959; *s* of Keith Bevan and Janet Bevan; *m* 1983, Jennifer Karen Bray; three *s* one *d*. *Educ:* Oakwood Park Grammar Sch., Maidstone; Aston Univ. (BSc Hons Mgt 1981); Inst. of Educn, London Univ. (PGCE 1982). Associate Dir, Inst. of Employment Studies, 1983–2001; Dir, Res., 2002–08, Man. Dir, 2008–11, The Work Foundn. Hon. Prof., Lancaster Univ., 2011–. Global Alliance of Mental Illness Advocacy Networks-Europe Personality Award, 2014. *Publications:* Cracking the Performance Code, 2005; Fit for Work: musculoskeletal disorders in the European workforce, 2009; reviewer for Lancet and Jl of Occupational and Organisational Psychol. *Recreations:* walking, reading, current affairs, cycling with Chris. *Address:* The Work Foundation, 21 Palmer Street, SW1H 0AD. *T:* (020) 7976 3546. *E:* sbevan@theworkfoundation.com.

BEVAN, Tim, CBE 2005; film producer; Co-Founder and Co-Chairman, Working Title Films, since 1984; Chairman, UK Film Council, 2009–11; *m* 1st, 1992, Joely Richardson, *qv* (marr. diss. 2001); one *d*; 2nd, Amy Gadney; one *s* one *d*. Formerly runner, Video Arts; co-founder, Aldabra, 1984. Film producer (jointly): A World Apart, 1988; Fools of Fortune, 1990; Drop Dead Fred, 1991; Bob Roberts, 1992; with Sarah Radclyffe: My Beautiful Laundrette, 1986; Sammy and Rosie Get Laid, Personal Services, 1987; Paperhouse, For Queen and Country, 1989; Dark Obsession, The Tall Guy, Chicago Joe and the Showgirl, 1990; London Kills Me, Rubin and Ed, 1992; with Eric Fellner: Posse, Romeo is Bleeding, 1993; Four Weddings and a Funeral, The Hudsucker Proxy, 1994; Loch Ness, Panther, French Kiss, Moonlight & Valentino, Dead Man Walking, 1995; Fargo, 1996; Bean, The Matchmaker, The Borrowers, The Hi-Lo Country, 1997; Elizabeth, The Big Lebowski, What Rats Won't Do, 1998; Notting Hill, Plunkett & Macleane, 1999; O Brother, Where Art Thou?, Billy Elliot, 2000; Bridget Jones's Diary, Captain Corelli's Mandolin, The Man Who Wasn't There, Long Time Dead, 2001; 40 Days and 40 Nights, About a Boy, Ali G Indahouse, The Guru, My Little Eye, 2002; Love Actually, Calcium Kid, Ned Kelly, Shape of Things, Johnny English, Thirteen, 2003; Thunderbirds, Inside I'm Dancing, Wimbledon, Shaun of the Dead, Bridget Jones: The Edge of Reason, 2004; Mickybo and Me, Pride and Prejudice, Nanny McPhee, The Interpreter, 2005; United 93, Hot Stuff, 2006; The Golden Age, Atonement, Mr Bean's Holiday, Hot Fuzz, Gone, Smokin' Aces, 2007; Definitely Maybe, Wild Child, Burn After Reading, 2008; Frost/Nixon, State of Play, The Soloist, The Boat That Rocked, Hippie Hippie Shake, A Serious Man, 2009; Green Zone, Nanny McPhee and the Big Bang, 2010; Paul, Senna, Johnny English Reborn, Tinker, Tailor, Soldier, Spy, 2011; Anna Karenina, Les Misérables, 2012; I Give it a Year, Closed Circuit, About Time, Rush, 2013; Two Faces of January, 2014; The Theory of Everything, Trash, 2015; sole producer, High Fidelity, 2000. Television includes: Tales of the City, 1993; The Borrowers, 1993; More Tales of the City, 1998; The Borrowers, Birdsong, 2011; Yonderland, 2013. *Address:* Working Title Films, 26 Aybrook Street, W1U 4AN.

BEVAN, Sir Timothy (Hugh), Kt 1984; Deputy Chairman, Foreign & Colonial Investment Trust plc, 1993–98 (Director, 1988–98); *b* 24 May 1927; *y s* of late Hugh Bevan and Pleasance (*née* Scrutton); *m* 1952, Pamela, *e d* of late Norman and Margaret Smith; two *s* two *d*. *Educ:* Eton. Lieut Welsh Guards. Called to Bar, 1950. Joined Barclays Bank Ltd, 1950; Dir, 1966–93; Vice-Chm., 1968–73; Dep. Chm., 1973–81; Chm., 1981–87. Dir, BET, 1987–92 (Chm., 1988–91). Chm., Cttee of London Clearing Bankers, 1983–85. Mem., NEDC, 1986–87. *Recreations:* sailing, gardening. *Address:* c/o Barclays Bank, 1 Churchill Place, E14 5HP. *Clubs:* Cavalry and Guards, Royal Ocean Racing; Royal Yacht Squadron.

BEVAN, Rear-Adm. Timothy Michael, CB 1986; Assistant Chief of Defence Staff (Intelligence), 1984–87; *b* 7 April 1931; *s* of Thomas Richard and Margaret Richmond Bevan; *m* 1970, Sarah Knight; three *s*. *Educ:* Eton College. psc(n), jssc. Entered RN, 1949; commanded: HMS Decoy, 1966; HMS Caprice, 1967–68; HMS Minerva, 1971–72; HMS Ariadne, 1976–78; HMS Ariadne, and Captain of 8th Frigate Sqdn, 1980–82; Britannia Royal Naval Coll., 1982–84; retd 1987. Dep. Dir, ACRE, The Rural Communities Charity, 1990–95; Chm., SSAFA Glos, 1996–2000.

BEVAN, Dame Yasmin (Prodhan), DBE 2007; Chief Executive, Chiltern Learning Trust, 2013–14 (Executive Principal and Headteacher: Denbigh High School and Challney High School for Boys, 2008–14; Dallow Primary School, 2014; Headteacher, Denbigh High School, 1991–2014); *b* 3 Dec. 1953; *d* of Badiuzzaman and Selima Prodhan. *Educ:* London Sch. of Econs (BSc Hons Govt 1976); Roehampton Inst. (PGCE 1977); Open Univ. (BA 1983); Inst. of Educn, Univ. of London (MA 1990). Teacher of Maths, Greenford High Sch., Ealing, 1977–78; Hd of Sixth Form and Hd of Maths, Pen Park Girls' Sch., Bristol, 1979–86; Dep. Hd, Canons High Sch., Harrow, 1987–91; Adv. headteacher, DCSF (on secondment), 2007–08. Nat. Leader of Educn, 2008–; Member: Practitioners' Gp on Sch. Behaviour and Discipline, DfES, 2005; Sure Start Stakeholders' Gp, DfES, 2006; Ministerial Task Force on Gifted and Talented Educn, 2007–08; Expert Gp on Assessment, 2008–; Ministerial Adv. Gp, DfE, on Role of Local Authy in relation to children and educnl services, 2010–, Nat. Curriculum Review, 2010–; Ofsted Access and Achievement Expert Panel, 2012. Mem., Governing Council, 2000–04, Adv. Gp on Nat. Leaders of Educn, 2006, Nat. Coll. for Sch. Leadership. Trustee, United Learning, 2014–. Hon. DEd Bedfordshire, 2008. Headteacher of the Year in a Secondary Sch., Eastern Region, Teaching Awards, 2005. *Recreations:* reading, keeping fit, cinema, opera, gardening, spending time with family and friends.

BEVERIDGE, Bruce Cameron; non-executive Chairman, thinkWhere Ltd, since 2015; President, Law Society of Scotland, 2013–14 (Vice President, 2012–13); *b* Edinburgh, 1966; *s* of Alec Beveridge and Sandra Margaret Moncrieff. *Educ:* High Sch. of Dundee; Edinburgh Acad.; Univ. of Edinburgh (LLB; DipLP). Legal Sec. to Lord Pres. of Court of Session, 2000–04; Dep. Keeper, Registers of Scotland, 2004–09; Dep. Dir, Rural Affairs and Envmt, Scottish Govt, 2009–11; Chair, Centre for Rural Develt, Scottish Land and Estates, 2012. Chair, Professional Services, WS Soc., 2012– (formerly Vice Chair). Chm., Edinburgh Academy Foundn, 2014–. Mem., Editl Bd and Wise Owl, LBC Wise Counsel, 2008–. *Publications:* contrib. articles to Jl Law Soc. of Scotland. *Recreations:* golf, music and the arts, motorsport (spectating). *Clubs:* Western (Glasgow); Royal and Ancient Golf (St Andrews), Golf House (Elie).

BEVERIDGE, Crawford William, CBE 1995; Chairman, Autodesk Inc., since 2009; *b* 3 Nov. 1945; *s* of William Wilson Beveridge and Catherine Crawford Beveridge; *m* 1977, Marguerite DeVoe; one *s* one *d*. *Educ:* Edinburgh Univ. (BSc); Bradford Univ. (MSc). Appts with Hewlett Packard in Scotland, Switzerland, USA, 1968–77; European Personnel Manager, Digital Equipment Corp., 1977–81; Vice-Pres., Human Resources, Analog Devices, 1982–85; Vice-Pres., Corporate Resources, Sun Microsystems, 1985–90; Chief Exec., Scottish Enterprise, 1991–2000; Exec. Vice-Pres., People and Places, and Chief Human Resources Officer, 2000–06, Chm., 2006–10, Sun Microsystems Inc. Mem., Scottish Parlt Ind. Budget Review Panel, 2010; Chm., Council of Econ. Advrs, Scotland, 2011–. *Recreations:* music, cooking, paperweights.

BEVERIDGE, John Caldwell; QC 1979; Recorder, Western Circuit, 1975–96; *b* 26 Sept. 1937; *s* of late Prof. William Ian Beardmore Beveridge; *m* 1st, 1972, Frances Ann Clunes Grant Martineau (marr. diss. 1988); 2nd, 1989, Lilian Adamson (marr. diss. 2003); 3rd, 2005, Rebecca Rosemary Amara Boulos-Hanna. *Educ:* Jesus Coll., Cambridge (MA, LLB). Called to the Bar, Inner Temple, 1963, Bencher, 1985; Western Circuit; called to the Bar, NSW, 1975, QC (NSW), 1980. Mem. (C), Westminster City Council, 1968–72. Trustee: Dogs Trust (formerly Nat. Canine Defence League), 1998–; Manchester Dogs Home, 2003–07 (Vice-Pres., 2007–14). Partner, Perfect Pitch, 2008–. Chm., 2003–14, Vice Pres., 2013–14, Patron, 2014–, St James's Conservation Trust. Freeman, City of London; Liveryman, Goldsmiths' Co. Jt Master, Westmeath Foxhounds, 1976–79. Comdr, Star of Honour (Ethiopia), 1992. *Recreations:* conversation, travelling. *Address:* Tilden Farm, Hawkhurst, Kent TN18 5AY. *T:* (01760) 444444. *Clubs:* Beefsteak, Pratt's, Turf; Brook (New York).

BEVERLEY, Bishop Suffragan of, since 2013; **Rt Rev. Glyn Hamilton Webster;** Episcopal Visitor for the Northern Province, since 2013; an Honorary Assistant Bishop: Diocese of Chester, since 2013; Diocese of Sheffield, since 2013; Diocese of Liverpool, since 2013; Diocese of Durham, since 2014; Diocese of Manchester, since 2014; *b* 1951. *Educ:* Cranmer Hall, Durham. SRN, Blackburn Royal Infirmary, 1973; ordained deacon, 1977, priest, 1978; Asst Curate, All Saints, Huntingdon, 1977–81; Vicar, St Luke, York, 1981–92; Sen. Chaplain, York Hosps NHS Foundn Trust, 1992–99; Rural Dean, City of York, 1997–2004; Dir of Ordinands, Dio. of York, 2005–10. Canon and Preb., 1994–99, Canon Res., 1999–2013, York Minster. Member: Gen Synod, 1995–; Crown Nominations Commn; Archbishops' Council. *Address:* Holy Trinity Rectory, Micklegate, York YO1 6LE. *T:* (01904) 628155.

BEVERLEY, Lt-Gen. Sir Henry (York La Roche), KCB 1991; OBE 1979; Commandant General Royal Marines, 1990–93; Director-General, Winston Churchill Memorial Trust, 1993–2002; *b* 25 Oct. 1935; *s* of Vice-Adm. Sir York Beverley, KBE, CB, and Lady Beverley; *m* 1963, Sally Anne Maclean; two *d*. *Educ:* Wellington College. DS Staff Coll., 1976–78; CO 42 Cdo RM, 1978–80; Comdt CTC RM, 1980–82; Director RM Personnel, MoD, 1983–84; Comd 3 Cdo Bde RM, 1984–86; Maj.-Gen. Trng and Reserve Forces RM, 1986–88; COS to CGRM, 1988–90. Chm. Trustees, Royal Marines Mus., 1997–2007. Pres., Corps of Commissionaires, 2008–11. *Club:* Royal Thames Yacht.

BEVERLEY, Prof. Peter Charles Leonard, FMedSci; Scientific Head, Edward Jenner Institute for Vaccine Research, 1995–2005; Emeritus Professor, University of Oxford, 2011 (Principal Research Fellow, 2005–11); Visiting Professor, Imperial College London, since 2014; *b* 7 March 1943; *s* of Samuel and Elinor Beverley; *m* 1967, Elisabeth A. Copleston (separated); two *s*; one *d* with Prof. Elizabeth Simpson, *qv*. *Educ:* University Coll. London (BSc, MB BS; DSc 1987). Research Fellow: NIMR, London, 1969–72; Sloan-Kettering Inst., NY, 1972–73; ICRF Tumour Immunology Unit, UCL, 1973–78; permanent staff mem., ICRF, 1978–95; Prof. of Tumour Immunology, UCL, 1988–95; Dep. Dir, 1988–92, Dir, 1992–95, Tumour Immunology Unit, UCL. FMedSci 2003. *Publications:* contribs to immunological, biological and med. jls. *Recreations:* music, reading, writing.

BEVERSTOCK, Rear Adm. Mark Alistair; Assistant Chief of Defence Staff (Nuclear and Chemical, Biological), Ministry of Defence, since 2015; *b* Dumfries, 8 Feb. 1964; *s* of Alistair Beverstock and Jane Beverstock; *m* 1984, Morag Hazlett; two *s* one *d*. *Educ:* RNEC Manadon (BScEng 1985). CEng 1996; FIET 2006. Tactical Weapons Engr Officer, 1986–88; Tenth Submarine Sqn, 1988–92; Weapon Engr Officer, HMS Vanguard, 1992–96; Ministry of Defence: Defence Equipment and Support, 1996–98; Naval Staff, 1998–2000; Strategic Systems Proj., Defence Equipment and Support, 2000–03; rcds 2004; MoD, 2005–07; CO HMS Neptune, 2007–09; Ministry of Defence: Dep. Chief Strategic Systems Exec., Defence Equipment and Support, 2009–10; Hd, Underwater Capability, 2010–12; Chief Strategic Systems Exec., Defence Equipment and Support, 2012–15. Pres., RN and RM Cycling Assoc., 2002–15. *Address:* Ministry of Defence, Whitehall, SW1A 2HB. *T:* (020) 7807 8853. *E:* ACDSNUCCB-ACDS@mod.uk.

BEVINGTON, Adrian; Owner, Adrian Bevington Sport & PR Ltd, since 2015; *b* Middlesbrough, 14 July 1971; *s* of Graham Bevington and Barbara Bevington; *m* 1996, Andrea Rounce; one *s*. *Educ:* Hustler Sch., Middlesbrough. Trainee reporter, C&P News, ICI Wilton, 1987–89; Clerk: Langbaurgh on Tees BC, 1989–94; Middlesbrough BC, 1994–95; Press Officer, Middlesbrough FC, 1995–97; Football Association: Media Officer, 1997–2000; Sen. Media Officer, 2000–03; Hd, Media, 2003–04; Dir, Communications, 2004–10; Man. Dir, 2010–14, Dir of Communications, 2011–14, Club England. Pt-time writer, Middlesbrough FC, and various pubns, 1989–95. *Publications:* (jtly) Doom to Boom: the most dramatic decade in the life of Middlesbrough FC 1986–1996, 1996; (jtly) Boro's Best: the players' and fans' fabulous fifty, 1997; (jtly) Don't Call Me Happy—John Hendrie: the autobiography, 1997. *Recreations:* reading, football, golf, travelling. *Address:* Adrian Bevington Sport & PR Ltd, Cambridge House, 16 High Street, Saffron Walden, Essex CB10 1AX.

BEVINGTON, Her Honour Christian Veronica; a Circuit Judge, 1998–2009; a Deputy Circuit Judge, since 2009; *b* 1 Nov. 1939; *d* of late Michael Falkner Bevington and Dulcie Marian Bevington (*née* Gratton); *m* 1961, David Levitt, OBE (marr. diss. 1973); one *s* two *d*. *Educ:* St James's, W Malvern; London Sch. of Econs (LLB Hons). Called to the Bar: Inner Temple, 1961 (Bencher, 1994); Lincoln's Inn, *ad eundem* 1971. Co-Founder, Charitable Housing Trust, 1966: Company Sec. and Housing Manager, Circle 33 Housing Trust, 1966–76; joined Peat Marwick & Co., 1976; returned to full-time practice at the Bar, 1980; Head of Chambers, 1981–98; Recorder, 1994–98. Chm., Independent Inquiry for City and County of Cardiff, 1997. Mem., Mental Health Review Tribunals, 2002–03. Dir, Veronica Grant Centre for Spoken English and Culture Ltd, 2014. *Publications:* The Bevington Report, 1997. *Recreations:* music, travel.

See also A. F. J. Levitt.

BEW, family name of **Baron Bew**.

BEW, Baron *cr* 2007 (Life Peer), of Donegore in the County of Antrim; **Paul Anthony Elliott Bew,** PhD; Professor of Irish Politics, Queen's University of Belfast, since 1991; *b* 22 Jan. 1950; *s* of Dr Kenneth Bew and Dr Mary Bew (*née* Leahy); *m* 1977, Prof. Greta Joyce Jones; one *s*. *Educ:* Brackenber House Sch.; Campbell Coll., Belfast; Pembroke Coll., Cambridge (MA; PhD 1974; Hon. Fellow, 2007). Lectr, Sch. of Humanities, Ulster Coll., 1975–79; Queen's University, Belfast: Lectr in Eur. and American Hist., 1979–84; Lectr, 1984–87, Reader, 1987–91, Dept of Politics. Vis. Lectr, Univ. of Pennsylvania, 1982–83; Parnell Fellow, Magdalene Coll., Cambridge, 1996–97; Vis. Prof., Surrey Univ., 1997–; Burns Vis. Schol., Boston Coll., 1999–2000. Historical Advr to Bloody Sunday Tribunal. Chm., Key Stage 2 Assessment Rev., 2010–11. Mem., British/Irish Interparly Assembly, 2011. Chm., Cttee on Standards in Public Life, 2013–. Mem., Select Cttee on London Local Authy Bill, 2008, on Draft Defamation Bill, 2011, on Parly Privilege (both Houses), 2013; Co-Chm., Speaker's Adv. Cttee, 2015; Sec., All Party Gp on Archives and Hist., 2007–. Pres., Irish Assoc. for Econs and Cultural Relns, 1990–92; Exec. Mem., British Irish Assoc., 1995– (Chm., 2007–); Mem., Anglo Israel Assoc. (Chm., 2011). MRIA 2004. Mem., Editl Bd, Parliamentary Affairs, 2012–. Special Recognition Award, Pol Studies Assoc., 2012. *Publications:* Land and the National Question in Ireland 1858–82, 1978; (jtly) The State in Northern Ireland, 1979, 2nd edn 1996; C. S. Parnell, 1980, 2nd edn 1991; (jtly) Seán Lemass and the Making of Modern Ireland, 1983; (jtly) The British State and the Ulster Crisis, 1985; Conflict and Conciliation in Ireland 1890–1910, 1987; (jtly) The Dynamics of Irish Politics, 1989; (ed jtly) Passion and Prejudice, 1993; (jtly) Northern Ireland: a chronology of the Troubles, 1993, rev. edn 1999; Ideology and the Irish Question, 1994; John Redmond, 1996; (jtly) The Northern Ireland Peace Process 1993–96, 1996; (jtly) Between War and Peace 1997; Ireland: the politics of enmity 1789–2006, 2007; The Making and Re-making of the Good Friday Agreement, 2007; Enigma: a new life of Parnell, 2011; David Gray: a Yankee in de Valera's Ireland, 2012; Churchill and Ireland, 2015; contrib. numerous articles and reviews. *Recreations:* soccer, cinema, theatre. *Address:* Department of Politics, Queen's University of Belfast, 21 University Square, Belfast BT7 1NN. *T:* (028) 9024 5133.

BEWES, Rev. Preb. Richard Thomas, OBE 2005; Rector, All Souls Church, Langham Place, 1983–2004; Prebendary of St Paul's Cathedral, 1988–2005, now Prebendary Emeritus; *b* 1 Dec. 1934; *s* of late Rev. Canon Cecil and Sylvia Bewes; *m* 1st, 1964, Elisabeth Ingrid Jaques (*d* 2006); two *s* one *d*; 2nd, 2012, Pamela Joy Wright. *Educ:* Marlborough Sch.; Emmanuel Coll., Cambridge (MA); Ridley Hall, Cambridge. Deacon, 1959; priest, 1960; Curate of Christ Church, Beckenham, 1959–65; Vicar: St Peter's, Harold Wood, 1965–74; Emmanuel, Northwood, 1974–83. *Publications:* God in Ward 12, 1973; Advantage Mr Christian, 1975; Talking about Prayer, 1979; The Pocket Handbook of Christian Truth, 1981; John Wesley's England, 1981, 2nd edn as Wesley Country, 2003; The Church Reaches Out, 1981; The Church Overcomes, 1983; On The Way, 1984; Quest for Truth, 1985; Quest for Life, 1985; The Church Marches On, 1986; When God Surprises, 1986; The Resurrection, 1989; A New Beginning, 1989; Does God Reign?, 1995; Speaking in Public—Effectively, 1998; Great Quotations of the 20th Century, 1999, 2nd edn as Words that Circled the World, 2002; The Lord's Prayer, 2000; The Lamb Wins, 2000; The Bible Truth Treasury, 2000; The Stone that became a Mountain, 2001; The Top 100 Questions, 2002; Beginning the Christian Life, 2004; 150 Pocket Thoughts, 2004; The Goodnight Book, 2009; Equipped to Serve, 2013. *Recreations:* tennis, photography, hosting TV and DVD Bible studies/sermons. *Address:* 2 Home Close, Virginia Water GU25 4DH. *W:* www.richardbewes.com.

BEWICK, Dr Michael, FRCGP, FRCP; Deputy Medical Director, NHS England, since 2013; *b* Workington, Cumbria, 11 Sept. 1956; *m* 1978, Patricia; two *d*. *Educ:* Workington Grammar Sch.; St Mary's Med. Sch., Univ. of London (MB BS 1980). MRCPE 1985; MRCP 1988, FRCP 2010; FRCGP 2004. Jun. hse posts, St Mary's Hosp., Paddington; Asst Lectr, Dept of Oncol., St Bartholomew's Hosp.; SHO, Stoke Mandeville Hosp.; Registrar then Sen. Registrar, Ninewells Hosp., Dundee, until 1987; GP trng, Cumbria, 1987–89; Principal, Beech Hse Med. Centre, Cumbria, 1987–2007; Medical Director: for Primary Care, NHS Cumbria, 2007–12; N of England, 2012–13. Teacher and Examr, RCGP (Chair of Assessment, 2005–12). *Recreations:* cycling (slowly), theatre, travel, pursuit of the best taste in food and wine. *Address:* Moat Barn, 17 Redgates Lane, Sewards End, Saffron Walden, Essex CB10 2LW.

BEWICKE-COPLEY, family name of **Baron Cromwell**.

BEWLEY, Dame Beulah (Rosemary), DBE 2000; MD; FRCP, FFPH, FRCPCH; Reader in Public Health Sciences, St George's Hospital Medical School, University of London 1992–93, now Emeritus; *b* 2 Sept. 1929; *d* of John B. Knox and Ina E. (*née* Charles); *m* 1955 Thomas Henry Bewley, *qv*; one *s* three *d* (and one *d* decd). *Educ:* Alexandra Sch. and Coll. Dublin; Trinity Coll., Dublin (MA); LSHTM, Univ. of London (MSc Social Medicine 1971) MD 1974. FRCP 1992; FFPH (FFPHM 1980). Qualified TCD, 1953; trained at Queen Elizabeth Hosp. for Children, London, Maudsley Hosp., London and Children's Hosp., Cincinatti; postgrad. trng at LSHTM and St Thomas' Hosp. Med. Sch.; Consultant, St Thomas' Hosp., 1974–79; Senior Lecturer and Hon. Consultant: KCH Med. Sch., 1979–83; LSHTM, 1979–86; St George's Hosp. Med. Sch., 1987–93; Undergrad. and postgrad teacher/examr, Univ. of London, 1973–93; Chm., Bd of Studies in Public Health Medicine London Univ., 1987–89; Postgrad. Acad. Tutor, SW Thames Reg., 1987–93. Mem., GMC 1979–99 (Treas., 1992–99). Pres., Med. Women's Fedn, 1986. Mem. and Mem. Exec. Cttee Women's Nat. Commn, 1992–99. FRSocMed 1969 (Vice Pres. and Past Pres., Section of Epidemiology and Public Health); FRCPCH (Mem., BPA 1985). Hon. LLD TCD, 2002. *Publications:* Choice not Chance, 1975; contrib. numerous articles and papers on research on children's smoking, adolescence, med. educn, women doctors and women's health. *Recreations:* piano, opera, travel. *Address:* 4 Grosvenor Garden Mews North, SW1W 0JP. *T:* (020) 7730 9592. *Clubs:* Reform, London Chapter of Irish Georgian Society.

BEWLEY, Thomas Henry, Hon. CBE 1988; MA; MD; FRCP, FRCPI, FRCPsych; Consultant Psychiatrist, Tooting Bec and St Thomas' Hospitals, 1961–88, now Emeritus Consultant, St Thomas' Hospital; *b* 8 July 1926; *s* of Geoffrey Bewley and Victoria Jane Wilson; *m* 1955, Beulah Rosemary Knox (*see* Dame B. R. Bewley); one *s* three *d* (and one *d* decd). *Educ:* St Columba's College, Dublin; Trinity College, Dublin University (MA; MD 1958). FRCPsych 1972, Hon. FRCPsych 1989. Hon. MD Dublin, 1987. Qualified TCD 1950; trained St Patrick's Hosp., Dublin, Maudsley Hosp., Univ. of Cincinnati. Hon. Sen. Lectr, St George's Hosp. Med. Sch., 1968–96. Member: Standing Adv. Cttee on Drug Dependence, 1966–71; Adv. Council on Misuse of Drugs, 1972–84; Consultant Adviser on Drug Dependence to DHSS, 1972–81; Consultant, WHO, 1969–88. Pres., RCPsych, 1984–87 (Dean, 1977–82); Jt Co-founder and Mem. Council, Inst. for Study of Drug Dependence, 1967–96. *Publications:* Handbook for Inceptors and Trainees in Psychiatry, 1976, 2nd edn 1980; Madness to Mental Illness, 2008; papers on drug dependence, medical manpower and side effects of drugs. *Address:* 4 Grosvenor Gardens Mews North, SW1W 0JP. *T:* (020) 7730 9592. *Clubs:* Reform, London Chapter of Irish Georgian Society.

BEWSEY, Jane, (Mrs Robert Mocatta); QC 2010; *b* Malaysia, 12 Feb. 1964; *d* of Jack and Audrey Bewsey; *m* 1992, Robert Mocatta; two *s* one *d*. *Educ:* Rosebery Sch., Epsom; Jesus Coll., Cambridge (BA 1985). Called to the Bar, Inner Temple, 1986; in practice as barrister specialising in crime. *Publications:* The Law of Investor Protection, 1996, 2nd edn 2003. *Recreations:* reading, walking. *Address:* 18 Red Lion Court, EC4A 3EB. *T:* (020) 7520 6000.

BEY, Patricia Mary Alice, (Mrs R. S. L. Woodward); Founder and Owner, Barwheys Dairy, since 2009; *b* Lagos, Nigeria, 18 Nov. 1957; *d* of Alex and Mary Bey; *m* 2009, Robert Stanley Laurence Woodward, *qv*. *Educ:* St Joan of Arc Sch., Rickmansworth; Durham Univ. (BSc Hons Engrg Sci. 1979); London Business Sch. (MBA 1987). Editor, Derwent Pubns, 1979–85; Touche Ross, subseq. Deloitte and Touche, then Deloitte Consulting: consulting roles, 1987–94; Partner, 1994–2001; Man. Partner, Deloitte Consulting Netherlands, 1999–2001; Man. Dir, Sch. of Coaching, 2003–07; freelance consultant, 2008. Member: Ayrshire Cattle Soc., 2008–; Specialist Cheesemakers Assoc., 2009–. Trustee: Friends of V&A, 2010–; Nat. Galleries of Scotland, 2012–. *Recreations:* breeding pedigree Ayrshire cattle, gardening, cooking. *Address:* Crawfordston Farm, Maybole, Ayrshire KA19 7JS. *E:* tricia@pmab.co.uk. *Club:* Scottish Arts.

BEYER, John Charles; HM Diplomatic Service, retired; Senior Associate Member, St Antony's College, Oxford, since 2009; *b* 29 April 1950; *s* of William Herbert Beyer and Doris Irene Beyer (*née* Tomline); *m* 1971, Letty Marindin Minns; one *s* one *d*. *Educ:* Abingdon Sch.; Queens' Coll., Cambridge (MA). Vis. Schol., Université de Paris VII, 1973–74; British Council Schol., Beijing Langs Inst., 1974–75; Lectr, Dept of Oriental Langs, Univ. of Calif. Berkeley, 1979–80; Researcher, Dept of Chinese Studies, Leeds Univ., 1980–82; Missions Exec., Sino-British Trade Council, 1983–85; Editor, China-Britain Trade Rev., 1985–90; Dir, Sino-British Trade Council, 1990–91; Dir, China-Britain Trade Gp, 1991–98; Head, Mediterranean Section, EU Dept, FCO, 1999–2002; Dep. Hd of Mission, Luxembourg, 2002–05; Ambassador to Moldova, 2006–09. *Recreation:* family. *Address:* 44 South Hill Park, NW3 2SJ. *T:* (020) 7435 4795.

BEYFUS, Drusilla Norman; writer, editor, broadcaster; Tutor, Central St Martin's College of Art, 1989–2007; *d* of Norman Beyfus and Florence Noel Barker; *m* 1956, Milton Shulman (*d* 2004); one *s* two *d*. *Educ:* Royal Naval Sch.; Channing Sch. Woman's Editor, Sunday Express, 1950; columnist, Daily Express, 1952–55; Associate Editor, Queen magazine, 1956; Home Editor, The Observer, 1963; Associate Editor, Daily Telegraph magazine, 1966; Editor, Brides and Setting Up Home magazine, 1972–79; Associate Editor, 1979–87, Contributing Editor, 1987–88, Vogue magazine; Editor, Harrods Magazine, 1987–88; columnist, Sunday Telegraph, 1990–91; Contributing Editor, Telegraph Magazine, 1991–2009; columnist, You magazine (Mail on Sunday), 1994–2002. TV and radio appearances, incl. Call My Bluff, The Big Breakfast and talks programmes. Hon. MA London Inst., 2002. *Publications:* (with Anne Edwards) Lady Behave, 1956, rev. edn 1969; The English Marriage, 1968; The Brides Book, 1981; The Art of Giving, 1987; Modern Manners, 1992; The Done Thing (series): Courtship, 1992; Parties, 1992; Business, 1993; Sex, 1993; The You Guide to Modern Dilemmas, 1997; Vogue on Hubert de Givenchy, 2013; Vogue On Valentino, 2015; contrib. to Sunday Times, Punch, New Statesman, Daily Telegraph, Daily Mail. *Recreations:* walking, modern art, cooking. *Address:* 51G Eaton Square, SW1W 9BE. *T:* (020) 7235 7162.

See also Marchioness of Normanby, A. Shulman.

BEYNON, Ann, OBE 2008; Director, Wales, BT, since 2004 (National Manager, 1998–2004); *b* 14 April 1953; *d* of Roger Talfryn Jones and Margaret Rose Beynon Jones; name changed to Beynon by deed poll, 1981; *m* 1st, 1976, John Trefor (marr. diss. 1983); 2nd, 1986, William Gwenlyn Parry (*d* 1991); one *s* one *d*; 3rd, 1996, Leighton Russell Andrews, *qv*. *Educ:* UCNW, Bangor (BA Hons). Pres., Students' Union, UCNW, 1974–75. Administrator, Yr Academi Gymreig (Welsh Acad.), 1977–81; S4C, 1981–95: Press Officer, 1981–83; Head of Press and PR, 1983–91; Head, Political and Internat. Affairs, 1991–95; Dir of Business Develt, Cardiff Bay Develt Corp., 1995–98. Mem. Bd, BITC UK, 2006–10; Chm., BITC Wales Cttee, 2006–10. Member: Royal Commn on H of L Reform, 1999; Welsh Lang. Bd, 1995–2000; Wales Cttee, EOC, 2000–07; Wales Comr, Equality and Human Rights Commn, 2009–. Gov., Nat. Film and TV Sch., 1995–2002; Mem. Council, Bangor Univ. (formerly Univ. of Wales, Bangor), 2004–10. Chm., Sgript Cymru Theatre Co., 1999–2007. *Recreations:* reading, languages, tapestry, managing my late husband's literary estate. *Address:* 11 Waungron Road, Llandaff, Cardiff CF5 2JJ. *T:* (029) 2055 5425.

BEYNON, Prof. Huw, DSocSc; Professor of Sociology, 1999–2010, Research Professor, 2010–14, now Professor Emeritus, and Founding Director, Wales Institute of Social and Economic Research, Data and Method, 2008–10, Cardiff University; *b* 10 Dec. 1942; *s* of Dewi and Megan Beynon; *m* 1994, Helen Anne Sampson; one *s* from previous *m*. *Educ:* University Coll. of Wales, Aberystwyth (BA 1964); Univ. of Liverpool (Dip. Industrial Admin); Univ. of Manchester (DSocSc 1999). Lectr, Univ. of Bristol, 1968–73; Simon Marks Res. Fellow, Univ. of Manchester, 1973–75; Lectr, then Reader, Durham Univ., 1975–87; Prof. and Res. Dean, Univ. of Manchester, 1987–99; Dir, Sch. of Social Scis, Cardiff Univ., 1999–2009. FAcSS (AcSS 2000); Founding FLSW 2010. Hon. DLitt Durham, 2013. *Publications:* (with R. M. Blackburn) Perceptions of Work: variations within a factory, 1972; Working for Ford, 1973, 2nd edn 1985; (with T. Nichols) Living with Capitalism: class relations in the modern factory, 1977; (with H. Wainwright) The Workers' Report on Vickers Ltd, 1978; (with N. Hedges) Born to Work, 1980; (ed) Digging Deeper: issues in the 1984 miners' strike, 1987; (jtly) A Tale of Two Industries: the decline of coal and steel in the North East of England, 1991; (jtly) A Place Called Teesside: a locality in a global economy, 1994; (with T. Austrin) Masters and Servants: class and patronage in the making of a labour organisation, 1994; (ed with P. Glavanis) Patterns of Social Inequality, 1999; (jtly) Digging Up Trouble: protest and the environment on the coal-fields, 2000; (jtly) Coalfield Regeneration: dealing with the consequences of industrial decline, 2000; (ed with S. Rowbotham) Looking at Class, 2002; (jtly) Managing Employment Change: the new reality of work, 2002; (jtly) Exploring the Tomato: transformations of nature, society and economy, 2002; (ed with T. Nichols) The Fordism of Ford and Modern Management: Fordism and post-Fordism, vols 1 and 2, 2006; (ed with T. Nichols) Patterns of Work in the post-Fordist Era: Fordism and post-Fordism, vols 1 and 2, 2006. *Recreations:* hill-walking, gardening. *Address:* Orchard Farm, Llanellen, Abergavenny NP7 9BU. *T:* (01873) 858307. *E:* beynonh@cardiff.ac.uk.

BEYNON, Dr John David Emrys, FREng, FIET; Principal, King's College London, 1990–92; *b* 11 March 1939; *s* of John Emrys and Elvira Beynon; *m* 1964, Hazel Janet Hurley; two *s* one *d*. *Educ:* Univ. of Wales (BSc); Univ. of Southampton (MSc, PhD). FIERE 1977; FIET (FIEE 1978); FREng (FEng 1988). Scientific Officer, Radio Res. Station, Slough, 1962–64; Univ. of Southampton: Lectr, Sen. Lectr and Reader, 1964–77; Prof. of Electronics, UWIST, Cardiff, 1977–79; University of Surrey: Prof. of Elec. Engrg, 1979–90; Head of Dept of Electronic and Elec. Engrg, 1979–83; Pro-Vice-Chancellor, 1983–87; Sen. Pro-Vice-Chancellor, 1987–90. Vis. Prof., Carleton Univ., Ottawa, 1975; Cons. to various cos, Govt estabts and Adviser to British Council, 1964–. Member: Accreditation Cttee, IEE, 1983–89; Adv. Cttee on Engrg and Technology, British Council, 1983–92; Technology Sub-Cttee, UGC, 1984–89; Nat. Electronics Council, 1985–91; Cttee 1, 1990–92, Main Cttee, 1991–94, CICHE; Adv. Cttee, Erasmus, 1990–92; Standing Cttee on Educn and Trng, Royal Acad. of Engrg, 1992–95; Adv. Council, British Liby, 1994–99; ITC, 1995–2000. Engrg Professors' Conference: Hon. Sec., 1982–84; Vice-Chm., 1984–85 and 1987–88; Chm., 1985–87. Chm., Westminster Christian Council, 1998–2000; Sec., Bloomsbury Central Baptist Church, 2000–14. FRSA 1982; FKC 1990. Hon. Fellow, UC Swansea, 1990. *Publications:* Charge-Coupled Devices and Their Applications (with D. R. Lamb), 1980; papers on plasma physics, semiconductor devices and integrated circuits, and engrg educn. *Recreations:* music, photography, travel. *Address:* 13 Great Quarry, Guildford, Surrey GU1 3XN.

BEYNON, Timothy George, MA; President, British Dragonfly Society, 2000–04; *b* 13 Jan. 1939; *s* of George Beynon and Fona I. Beynon; *m* 1973, Sally Jane Wilson; two *d*. *Educ:* Swansea Grammar Sch.; King's Coll., Cambridge (MA). City of London Sch., 1962–63; Merchant Taylors' Sch., 1963–78; Headmaster: Denstone Coll., 1978–86; The Leys Sch., Cambridge, 1986–90. Sen. Warden, Saltwells Local Nature Reserve, Dudley, 1992–99. *Recreations:* odonatology, ornithology, fishing, sport, music, expeditions. *Address:* 34 Church Lane, Checkley, Stoke-on-Trent ST10 4NJ.

BEZOS, Jeffrey Preston; Founder, and Chairman, since 1994, Chief Executive Officer, since 1996, Amazon.com Inc., internet retailer, since 1994; founder, Blue Origin, Seattle, 2000; *b* 12 Jan. 1964; *m* 1993, MacKenzie Tuttle; four *c*. *Educ:* Princeton Univ. (degree in elec. engrg and computer sci., *summa cum laude*, 1986). Mem. staff, FITEL, NY, 1986–88; Bankers Trust Co., 1988–90 (Vice-Pres., 1990); D. E. Shaw & Co., 1990–94 (Sen. Vice-Pres., 1992–94). Owner, Washington Post, 2013–. *Address:* Amazon.com Inc., 410 Terry Avenue North, Seattle, WA 98109–5210, USA.

BHADESHIA, Sir Harshad (Kumar Dharamshi Hansraj), Kt 2015; PhD; FRS 1998; FREng; TATA Steel Professor of Metallurgy, since 2008, and Director, SKF Steel Technology Centre, since 2009, University of Cambridge; Fellow of Darwin College, Cambridge, since 1993; *b* 27 Nov. 1953; *s* of Dharamshi Hansraj Bhadeshia and Narmda Dharamshi Bhadeshia; *m* 1978 (marr. diss. 1992); two *d*. *Educ:* City of London Poly. (BSc 1976); Univ. of Cambridge (PhD 1979). CEng. Technician: British Oxygen Co., 1970–72; Murex Welding Processes, 1972–73; University of Cambridge: engaged in res., 1976–79; SERC Res. Fellow, 1979–81; Demonstrator, 1981–85; Lectr in Physical Metallurgy, 1985–93; Reader in Physical Metallurgy, 1993–99; Prof. of Physical Metallurgy, 1999–2008. FREng 2002. *Publications:* Geometry of Crystals, 1987; Bainite in Steels, 1992; (with R. W. K. Honeycombe) Steels, 1995; more than 260 res. papers. *Recreation:* squash.

BHALOO, Zia Kurban, (Mrs P. L. Arden); QC 2010; *b* Dar es Salaam, Tanzania, 3 Aug. 1967; *d* of Malek and Kurban Bhaloo; *m* 1999, Peter Leonard Arden, *qv*; one *d*. *Educ:* Banda Prep. Sch.; Cheltenham Ladies' Coll.; University Coll. London (LLB, LLM). Called to the Bar, Middle Temple, 1990, Bencher, 2014; in practice as barrister, specialising in commercial chancery, property and landlord and tenant; Hd of Chambers, 2013–. Chm., Property Bar Assoc., 2014–. *Address:* Enterprise Chambers, 9 Old Square, Lincoln's Inn, WC2A 3SR.

BHANJI, Abdul Fazal, FCA; Special Advisor to the Senior Partner, PricewaterhouseCoopers, since 2001; Director, Hanson Green, since 2012; *s* of Fazal Bhanji Jessa and Jenabai Karmali Jinah; *m* 1980, Arzina Dhalla; three *s*. *Educ:* Kelly Coll., Tavistock; Univ. of Kent, Canterbury (BA Hons Accounting). FCA 1980. Coopers & Lybrand, then PricewaterhouseCoopers, 1972–: work in audit, accountancy and adv. practice in London, Canada, India and Switzerland; estabd Business Develt practice in UK, 1986–2001; Partner, 1988; Partner-in-Charge, Business Develt in UK, 1988–2001; Chairman: India Desk, 1995–2001; Charity Focus Gp, 1995–2001. Non-exec. Dir, Whitehead Mann plc, 2005–06. Member: FEFC for Gtr London, 1993–99; City of London Early Years Develt and Childcare Partnership, 1999–2000. Mem., Europe Cttee, 2002–, London Reg. Council, 2006–, CBI. Mem. and Chm., Finance Cttee, Marshall Aid Commemoration Commn, 2001–. Member: Governing Body, SOAS, 2000–10; Council, Open Univ., 2001–02; Trustee, 2008–, Dep. Chm., 2009–, Univ. of London. Mem., Develt Cttee, Asia House, 2000–02. Charter Mem., Indus Entrepreneurs (TiE), 2000–04. Chairman: Aga Khan Econ. Planning Bd, UK, 1990–93; Nat. Cttee, Aga Khan Foundn (UK), 1997–2006; Mem., HH Prince Aga Khan Shia Imami Ismaili Council, UK, 1990–93; Trustee, Prince's Foundn for Children and the Arts, 2008–14. FRSA. Freeman, City of London, 1987; Liveryman: Co. of Glaziers and Painters of Glass, 2003; Barbers' Co., 2009. *Recreations:* cricket, bridge, squash, golf, chess, ski-ing, backgammon. *Address:* PricewaterhouseCoopers LLP, 1 Embankment Place, WC2N 6RH. *Clubs:* Brooks's, Farmers, Mosimann's, Walbrook.

BHARDWAJA, Neelam; Management Consultant, Neelam Management Consultancy Ltd, since 2012; Corporate Director, Adult and Children's Social Services, Education and Lifelong Learning (formerly Corporate Director, Opportunities), Cardiff Council, 2005–12; one *s*. *Educ:* Univ. of E Anglia (BSc Hons 1978; MA; CQSW 1982). Social worker, Birmingham CC, 1978–80 and 1982–83; various appts, Cambs CC, 1983–2001; Service Manager, Peterborough CC, 2001–03; Hd, Children's and Families, Bor. of Poole, 2003–05. Mem., Children and Families Cttee, ADSS, 2003–05; Vice Pres., 2008–09, Pres., 2009–10, ADSS Cymru. *Publications:* various articles. *Recreations:* enjoying Welsh countryside and beaches, enjoying success and achievements to date. *T:* 07837 491589. *E:* n.mc@outlook.com.

BHARUCHA, Chitra, MBE 2009; FRCPath; Vice-Chairman, BBC Trust, 2006–10 (Acting Chairman, 2007); Trustee, Marie Curie Cancer Care, since 2007; *b* 6 April 1945; *d* of late George Gnanadickam and Mangalam Gnanadickam (*née* Ramaiya); *m* 1967, Hoshang Bharucha; two *d*. *Educ:* Ewart Sch., Madras; Christian Med. Coll., Vellore, India (MB BS); Queen's Univ. Belfast (Cert. Commercial Law 1993). Nuffield Schol., 1967; Council of Europe Fellow, 1980. Dep. Dir, NI Blood Transfusion Service, 1981–2000; Consultant Haematologist, Belfast City Hosp., 1981–2000. Non-exec. Dir, UK Transplant, 2000–01. Chm., Adv. Cttee on Animal Feeding Stuffs, Food Standards Agency, 2002–08; Mem. Council, ASA, 2004–07. Mem., Lab. Services Adv. Cttee, DHSS NI, 1995–2000. Mem., Partners' Council, NICE, 1999–2000. UK Blood Transfusion Service: Mem., Standing Adv. Cttee for Selection of Blood Donors, 1995–98; Chm., Standing Adv. Cttee for Transfusion Transmitted Infections, 1998–2000. Member: WHO Expert Adv. Panel for Blood Products, 1988–2000; Blood Safety Adv. Cttee, NI, 1998–2000; Standing Adv. Cttee for Pathology, NI, 1998–2000. Mem., Scientific Cttee, Eur. Sch. of Blood Transfusion, 1996–2000; Co-ordinator of Standardisation for Eur. Cord Blood Banking, 1996–2000. Chm., Adjudication Panels, Med. Practitioners Tribunal Service, 2010–. Mem., Appts Cttee, Bd of Recognition Panel, 2014–. Mem., 1999–2003, Associate Mem., 2004–07, GMC. Royal College of Pathologists: Mem. Council, 1996–2000; Chm., NI Affairs Cttee, 1998–2000; Mem., Patient Liaison Gp, 1998–2001. Pres., Med. Women's Fedn, 1994–95. Mem. Council, Internat. Soc. of Blood Transfusion, 1996–2000. Vice-Chm., NI Council for Postgrad. Med. Educn, 1999–2000. Member: Council, BBC NI, 1996–99; ITC, 2001–03. Member: Adv. Forum (NI), Sargent Cancer Care for Children, 2000–03; NI Council, Leprosy Mission, 1994–2003. Gov., Methodist Coll., Belfast, 1990–93; Mem., Exec. Cttee, Assoc. of Governing Bodies of Voluntary Grammar Schs, 1990–95. FRSA 2002–08; FCGI 2009. Hon. DMedSci QUB, 2008. *Recreations:* opera, theatre, classical music, hill walking. *Club:* Reform.

BHASKAR, Sanjeev, OBE 2006; actor and writer; *b* 31 Oct. 1963; *s* of Inderjit and Janak Bhaskar; *m* 2005, Meera Syal, *qv*; one *s*, and one step *d*. *Educ:* Springwell Primary Sch., Heston; Cranford Community Coll.; Univ. of Hertfordshire (BA Hons Business Studies (Mktg)). Mktg Exec., IBM, 1987–88; Tour Manager, Arts Council (GB) Project, 1990–92; Mktg Officer, Tom Allen Arts Centre, Stratford, London, 1993–95. Performer and writer: Goodness Gracious Me, Radio 4, 1996–98, BBC TV, 1998–2000; The Kumars at No 42, BBC TV, 2001–06, The Kumars, Sky 1, 2014; Mumbai Calling, ITV, 2009; actor: Life Isn't All Ha Ha Hee Hee, BBC TV, 2005; The Indian Doctor, BBC TV, 2010, 2012, 2013; actor in films: Notting Hill, 1999; The Mystic Masseur, 2001; The Guru, 2002; Anita and Me, 2002; actor in play, Dinner with Saddam, Menier Chocolate Factory, 2015. Presenter, India with Sanjeev Bhaskar, BBC TV series, 2007. Ambassador, Prince's Trust, 2000–. Chancellor, Univ. of Sussex, 2009–. Hon. DLitt, 2004. *Publications:* India with Sanjeev Bhaskar, 2007. *Recreations:* dreaming, chatting, collecting and watching movies, staying in, anything relating to Elvis Presley/Beatles/film trivia/gadgets. *Address:* c/o United Agents, 12–26 Lexington Street, W1F 0LE.

BHATIA, Baron *cr* 2001 (Life Peer), of Hampton in the London Borough of Richmond-upon-Thames; **Amirali Alibhai Bhatia,** OBE 1997; Chairman, Forbes Trust, since 1985; *b* 18 March 1932; *s* of Alibhai Bhatia and Fatma Alibhai Bhatia; *m* 1954, Nurbanu Amersi Kanji; three *d*. Career in manufacturing, Tanzania, 1960–72; Dir, Casley Finance Ltd and Forbes Campbell (Internat.) Ltd, 1973–2001. Chm., SITPRO, 1998–2004; Board Member: E London TEC, 1991–2001; Nat. Lottery Charities Bd, 1995–2000; Local Investment Fund, 1997–; Project Fullemploy, 1997–99 (Chm., 1994–97); Mem., Prime Minister's Adv. Cttee for Queen's Award, 1999–. Chairman: Council of Ethnic Minority Vol. Sector Orgns, 1999–; Ethnic Minority Foundn, 1999–2009; Hon. Treas., Mem. Bd and Exec. Cttee, Internat. Alert, 1994–2000; Trustee: Oxfam, 1985–99 (Chm., Trading Bd, 1986–92); Community Develt Foundn, 1988–97 (Mem., Budget and Finance Cttee); Charities Evaluation Services, 1989–90; Water Aid, 2000–03; St Christopher's Hospice, 1997–2003 (Mem., Audit Cttee); Bd, Diana, Princess of Wales Meml Fund, 2001–03. Trustee, High/Scope Educn Res. Foundn, Mich, 1985–97; Bd Mem., Tower Hamlets Coll., 1991–98. MInstD. Personality of the Year, UK Charity Awards, 2001; Beacon Prize for Leadership, Beacon Fellowship, 2003. *Recreations:* reading, cricket, voluntary work.

BHATT, Raju; Partner, Bhatt Murphy Solicitors, since 1998; *b* Kampala, Uganda, 24 Oct. 1957; *s* of Manjula and Batukrai Bhatt; *m* 1987, Pragna Patel; two *d*. *Educ:* Shimoni Primary Sch., Kampala; Kololo Secondary Sch., Kampala; Christ's Coll., Finchley; Worcester Coll., Oxford (BA Hons Oriental Studies (Sanskrit)); City of London Poly. BM Birnberg & Co.: trainee, 1986–88; admitted Solicitor, 1988; Solicitor, 1988–98. Mem., Hillsborough

Ind. Panel, 2010–12. *Recreations:* music, walking, reading, family. *Address:* Bhatt Murphy, 27 Hoxton Square, N1 6NN. *T:* (020) 7729 1115, *Fax:* (020) 7729 1117. *E:* r.bhatt@bhattmurphy.co.uk.

BHATTACHARYA, Satyajit, FRCSE, FRCS; Consultant Surgeon, Royal London Hospital, Barts Health NHS Trust (formerly Royal London Hospital and St Bartholomew's Hospital), since 1999 (specialist in liver, biliary and pancreatic surgery); Surgeon to the Royal Household, since 2006; *b* Mumbai, 22 Nov. 1962; *s* of Durga Prasanna and Kalpana Bhattacharya; *m* 1988, Dr Shanti Vijayaraghavan; one *d. Educ:* Don Bosco Sch. and St Xavier's Coll., Mumbai; Grant Med. Coll., Mumbai (MB BS 1984, MS 1988); Royal Free Hosp. Sch. of Medicine (MPhil 1995). FRCSE 1991; FRCS 1998. Registrar and Lectr, Royal Free and University Coll. Hosps, 1989–95 and 1996–98. Member: Ct of Examrs, RCS, 2005–11; Jt Inter-Collegiate Exam. Bd in Gen. Surgery, 2014–. *Publications:* contrib. chapters to med. textbooks; papers in med. jls incl. Nature Clin. Practice, Hepatology, British Jl Surgery, British Jl Cancer. *Address:* HPB Surgery Unit, Royal London Hospital, Whitechapel, E1 1BB. *T:* (020) 3594 2747, *Fax:* (020) 3594 3255. *E:* satya.bhattacharya@bartshealth.nhs.uk.

BHATTACHARYA, Prof. Shoumo, MD; FRCP, FMedSci; Professor of Cardiovascular Medicine, since 2004, and British Heart Foundation Professor of Cardiovascular Medicine, since 2009, University of Oxford; Fellow, Green Templeton College (formerly Green College), Oxford, since 2004; *b* 24 Feb. 1960; *s* of Cdre Asoke Kumar Bhattacharya and Jayashri Bhattacharya; *m* 1989, Dr Jane Caldwell; two *s. Educ:* All India Inst. of Med. Sci., New Delhi (MD 1985); King's Coll. London (MSc). FRCP 2003. Jun. Resident in Medicine, All India Inst. of Med. Scis, New Delhi, 1983–85; Registrar in Cardiology and Medicine, Northwick Park Hosp., Harrow, 1987–90; MRC Trng Fellow and Hon. Sen. Registrar, Northwick Park Hosp., Harrow and Hammersmith Hosp., London, 1990–94; BHF Internat. Res. Fellow, 1994–96, Instructor in Medicine, 1996–98, Dana-Farber Cancer Inst. and Harvard Med. Sch., Boston, Mass; Wellcome Trust Sen. Fellow in Clinical Sci., 1998–2008 and Hon. Consultant Cardiologist, 1998–, Dept of Cardiovascular Medicine and Wellcome Trust Centre for Human Genetics, Univ. of Oxford. FMedSci 2006. *Publications:* articles in Nature, Nature Genetics, Cell, Genes & Develt, Jl Biol Chem. *Recreations:* science, history, theory and practice of the culinary arts. *Address:* Wellcome Trust Centre for Human Genetics, Roosevelt Drive, Oxford OX3 7BN. *T:* (01865) 287771. *E:* sbhattac@well.ox.ac.uk.

BHATTACHARYYA, family name of **Baron Bhattacharyya**.

BHATTACHARYYA, Baron *cr* 2004 (Life Peer), of Moseley in the County of West Midlands; **Sushantha Kumar Bhattacharyya,** Kt 2003; CBE 1997; FRS 2014; FREng, FIMechE; Professor of Manufacturing (formerly of Manufacturing Systems Engineering), since 1980, Director, WMG (formerly Warwick Manufacturing Group), since 1980, University of Warwick; *b* 6 June 1940; *s* of Sudhir Bhattacharyya and Hemanalini (*née* Chakraborty); *m* 1981, Bridie Rabbitt; three *d. Educ:* IIT, Kharagpur (BTech); Univ. of Birmingham (MSc, PhD). MIMechE, FIMechE 2005; FIET; FREng (FEng 1991). CAV Ltd, 1960–63; Prodn Engr, Joseph Lucas Ltd, 1964–68; Lectr, Dept of Engrg Prodn, Univ. of Birmingham, 1970. Advr, nat. and multinat. cos, UK and abroad. Non-exec. Dir, Technology Rover Gp, 1986–92; Mem. Bd, Transnet Ltd, S Africa, 2003–04. Member: Nat. Consumer Council, 1990–93; Council for Sci. and Technology, 1993–2003; UK Technol. Foresight Panel on Manufg, 1994–97; Indo-British Partnership Area Adv. Gp, 1994–2000; W Midlands Regl Develt Agency, 1999–2003; Competitiveness Council, 1999–2000; Rover Task Force, 2000; Trade Partners UK: India Advisors, 2000–03. Mem., Scientific Adv. Bd, Singapore Inst. of Manufg Technol., 2002–07. Trustee, IPPR, 1998–2010. Hon. Professor: Hong Kong Poly. Univ., 1992; Univ. of Technol., Malaysia, 1993; Min. of Machinery, Beijing, 1994. Mem. Council, Edgbaston High Sch. for Girls, Birmingham, 2007–. Fellow: World Acad. of Productivity, 1999; NAE, India, 1999. CCMI (CIMgt 1996). Hon. FILog 1996. DUniv Surrey, 1992; Hon. DEng Univ. of Technol., Malaysia; Hon. DBA Hong Kong Polytechnic Univ., 2003; Hon. DSc: Birmingham, 2004; Kharagpur, 2008; Indian Inst. of Technol. Bhubaneswar, 2013. Dist. Alumnus Award, IIT, Kharagpur, 2005. Mensforth Internat. Gold Medal, IEE, 1998; Sir Robert Lawrence Award, Inst. of Logistics and Transport, 2000. Padma Bhushan (India), 2002. *Publications:* numerous, on operational and technological change in manufacturing industry. *Recreations:* family, flying, cricket. *Address:* WMG, International Manufacturing Centre, University of Warwick, Coventry CV4 7AL. *T:* (024) 7652 3155. *Club:* Athenæum.

BHOGAL, Rev. Inderjit Singh, OBE 2005; Officer, Methodist Discipleship and Ministries Learning Network, since 2014; President, Methodist Conference, 2000–01; *b* Nairobi, 17 Jan. 1953; *m* 1986, Kathryn Anne; one *s* one *d. Educ:* Khalsa Sikh Sch., Nairobi; Blue Coat C of E Sch., Dudley; Dudley Tech. Coll.; Hartley Victoria Coll., Manchester (BA Manchester Univ. 1979); Westminster Coll., Oxford (MA 1991). Minister: Darlington Street Circuit, 1979–87; Carver Street Circuit, Sheffield, 1987–94; Sheffield Inner City Ecumenical Mission, 1994–2004. Co-ordinator, Wolverhampton Inter-Faith Gp, 1984–87; Mem., Sheffield Chaplaincy to Higher Educn, 1987–94 (Chm., 1990–94); Dir of Studies, 1994–97, Dir, 1997–2004, Urban Theol. Unit, Sheffield; Consultant Theologian, Christian Aid, 2004–05; CEO (formerly Dir), Yorks and Humber Faiths Forum, 2005–11; Leader, Corrymeela Community, 2011–14. Mem., Home Office Race Equality Adv. Panel, 2003–07. Patron, Race Equality in Employment Prog., 2003–10. Founder, 2005, Pres., 2011–, City of Sanctuary (Chm., 2005–12). DUniv: Oxford Brookes, 2001; Sheffield Hallam, 2002. *Publications:* A Table for All, 2000; On the Hoof: theology in transit, 2001; Unlocking the Doors, 2002; Becoming a City of Sanctuary, 2009; West Highland Way: diary of a walker, 2009; (with Satwant Kaur Rait) Understanding Sikhism, 2010. *Recreations:* walking, cooking, sport, writing.

BHOWMICK, Prof. Bimal Kanti, OBE 2001; DL; MD; FRCP; Professor (personal chair), Cardiff University, 2004; Consultant Physician, now Emeritus, Care of the Elderly, 1976–2005, Intermediate Care, since 2006, Glan Clwyd Hospital, Rhyl; Consultant Physician, Community Care: Isle of Anglesey, since 2011; Powys Teaching Hospital, since 2013; *b* 13 Feb. 1940; *s* of late Jamini Mohan Bhowmick and of Ashalata Bhowmick; *m* 1969, Dr Aparna Banerjee; two *s* one *d. Educ:* Calcutta Univ. (MB BS; MD 1968). FRCP 1987. SHO, Victoria Hosp., Blackpool, 1969–71; SHO, 1971–72, Registrar, 1972–74, Burton Rd Hosp., Dudley; Sen. Registrar, H. M. Stanley Hosp., St Asaph, 1974–76; Clin. Dir, 1993–2004, Clin. Dir of Integrated Medicine, 2001–02, Care of the Elderly, Glan Clwyd Hosp., Rhyl. Associate Dean for Overseas Doctors in Wales, Sch. of Postgrad. Med. and Dental Educn, Univ. of Wales Coll. of Med., 1997–2006; Hon. Sen. Lectr, Inst. of Res., Univ. of Wales, Bangor, 1998–. Mem. Council, 1998–2001, Censor, 2001–03, RCP. Mem., Bevan Commn, 2011–. Fellow: UWCM, 2003; Glyndwr Univ., Wrexham, 2006. DL Clwyd, 2009. Lifetime Achievement Award, NHS, 2009; Recognition Achievement Award, Welsh Govt, 2011. *Publications:* (contrib.) Parkinson's Disease and Parkinsonism in the Elderly, 2000; numerous contribs to learned jls. *Recreations:* reading, gardening, cinema. *Address:* Jamini, Allt Goch, St Asaph, Denbighshire LL17 0BP.

BHUGRA, Prof. Dinesh Kumar Makhan Lal, CBE 2012; PhD; FRCP, FRCPsych; Professor of Mental Health and Cultural Diversity, Institute of Psychiatry, King's College London, 2004–14, now Emeritus; President, World Psychiatric Association, since 2014 (President-elect, 2011–14); President, Mental Health Foundation, since 2014 (Chair, 2011–14); *b* Yamuna Nagar, India, 8 July 1952; *s* of Makhan Lal and Shanta Bhugra; partner, Michael Bryn Thacker. *Educ:* Univ. of Poona (MB BS 1976); Univ. of Leicester (MPhil Psychiatry 1990); S Bank Univ. (MSc Sociol. 1991); Univ. of London (MA Social Anthropol. 1996; PhD Psychiatry 1999). LMSSA 1980; MRCPsych 1985, FRCPsych 1997, Ho FRCPsych 2012; FRCP 2010; FFPH 2011; FRCPE 2012. Registrar, then SHO, Leic Rotation Scheme, 1981–86; Sen. Registrar, Maudsley Trng Scheme, 1986–89; Lectr, MR(Social Psychiatry Unit, 1989–92; Sen. Lectr, Maudsley Hosp., 1992–2002; Reader, S Londo and Maudsley NHS Trust, 2002–04; Hon. Consultant, S London and Maudsley Foundn NH Trust (formerly Maudsley Hosp., then S London and Maudsley NHS Trust), 2004–. Pres RCPsych, 2008–11 (Dean, 2003–08). Hon. Fellow: Am. Coll. of Psychiatrists, 2010; Hon Kong Coll. of Psychiatrists, 2012. Lifetime Achievement Award, Pakistan Psychiatric Soc 2012. *Publications:* Mad Tales from Bollywood: portrayal of mental illness in convention Hindi cinema, 2006; (ed with K. Bhui) Culture and Mental Health: a comprehensiv textbook, 2007; (ed with K. Bhui) Textbook of Cultural Psychiatry, 2007; (ed jtly) A Selecte Annotated Bibliography of Public Attitudes to Mental Health, 1975–2005, 2007; (ed jtly Workplace-based Assessments in Psychiatry, 2007, 2nd edn 2011; (ed jtly) Management fc Psychiatrists, 3rd edn 2007; (ed with O. Howes) Handbook for Psychiatric Trainees, 200 (ed jtly) Principles of Social Psychiatry, 2010; (ed jtly) Clinical Topics in Cultural Psychiatry 2010; (ed jtly) Mental Health of Refugees and Asylum Seekers, 2010; (ed jtly) Migration an Mental Health, 2011; (ed jtly) Professionalism in Mental Health Care, 2011; (ed jtly Workplace-Based Assessments in Psychiatric Training, 2011; (ed jtly) Troublesome Disguise 2015. *Recreations:* reading crime novels and fiction by Indian authors, cinema (Hitchcock an Billy Wilder), theatre, Hindi film music. *Address:* PO 25, HSPRD, Institute of Psychiatry Psychology and Neuroscience, King's College London, De Crespigny Park, SE5 8AF. *T* (020) 7848 0500, *Fax:* (020) 7848 0333. *E:* dinesh.bhugra@dineshbhugra.net. *Club:* Reform

BIAGI, Marco; Member (SNP) Edinburgh Central, Scottish Parliament, since 2011; Ministe for Local Government and Community Empowerment, since 2014; *b* Alexandria, W Dunbartonshire, 31 July 1982; *s* of Antonio Biagi and Mary Biagi. *Educ:* Hermitage Acad Wadham Coll., Oxford; Univ. of Calif, Berkeley; Univ. of St Andrews (MA Hons Internat Relns 2005); Univ. of Glasgow (MSc Pol Communication 2010). Vice-Pres (Representation), Students' Assoc., Univ. of St Andrews, 2002–03. Parly Asst to Keit Brown, MSP, 2007–09; Parly Researcher, SNP Central Staff, 2009–11. Trustee, Nat. Liby c Scotland, 2011–13. *Recreations:* amateur drama, running, retro music, science fiction, musica theatre, real ciders. *Address:* Scottish Parliament, Edinburgh EH99 1SP. *T:* (0131) 348 6482 *E:* marco.biagi.msp@scottish.parliament.uk.

BIANCHI, Adrian, MOM 1995; MD; FRCS, FRCSE; Consultant Specialist Paediatric an Neonatal Surgeon, Manchester and North Western Region, 1984–2010; *b* 19 Jan. 1948; *s* c Loris and Yvonne Bianchi (*née* Ganado); *m* 1970, Claire (*née* Sammut); two *s* one *d. Edu* Medical Sch., Royal Univ. of Malta (MD 1969). FRCS 1975; FRCSE 1975. Specialised i paediatric and neonatal surgery through surgical progs, Liverpool and Manchester; Dir Neonatal Surgery, and Mem., Bd of Mgt, St Mary's Hosp., Manchester, 1987–2002 Paediatric Surgical Rep., Mgt Bd, Royal Manchester Children's Hosp., 1984–90; ha developed orig. surgical techniques and new surgical approaches incl. surgical mgt of childre with short bowel. *Publications:* contrib. chapters in paediatric surgical operative and gen surgical textbooks; 70 articles in medical jls. *Recreations:* reproduction of antique furniture marquetry, ancient civilizations, swimming, gardening (bonsai, carnations). *Address:* 1 Elleray Road, Middleton, Manchester M24 1NY. *T:* (0161) 643 6406. *E:* bianchi54@gmail.com.

BIBB, Prof. Mervyn James, PhD; FRS 2013; Project Leader, Molecular Microbiology, John Innes Centre, since 1982; *m*; two *d. Educ:* Univ. of East Anglia (BSc; PhD Streptomyce Genetics 1978). Postdoctoral res., Stanford Univ., Calif, 1978–82; on leave of absence from John Innes Centre with biotechnol. co. in San Diego. Co-founder: Novacta Biosystems Procarta Biosystems. Heatley Medal and Prize, Biochem. Soc., 2013. *Address:* Department o Molecular Microbiology, John Innes Centre, Norwich Research Park, Colney, Norwich NR4 7UH.

BIBBY, Benjamin; *see* Bibby, J. B.

BIBBY, Dame Enid, DBE 2004; expert consultant; school improvement adviser Headteacher, Wood Green High School College of Sport, Maths and Computing Wednesbury, 1998–2006; Chief Executive Officer, DEB Consultants Ltd, since 2006; *b* 8 Feb 1951; *d* of Fred and Ivy Kemp; *m* 1999, Dr Bob Bibby; two step *d. Educ:* Lancaster Univ. (BA Hons English); Liverpool Univ. (PGCE); Univ. of Cambridge (AdvDip. Ed). Deputy Headteacher: Lealands Community Sch., Luton, 1986–89; Leon Community Sch., Bletchley 1989–95; Headteacher, Silverdale Sch., Sheffield, 1995–98. Mem. Council, Specialist Schs and Acads (formerly Special Schs) Trust, 2002–05; Mem. Bd, 2004–05, Lead Nat. Challenge Advr, W Midlands, British Educnl Communications and Technol. Agency; Nat. Challenge Advr, 2008–10. Gov., Ofsted, 2007–08. Unilever Fellow, London Leadership Centre, 2002 FRSA 1997; FCMI (FIMgt 1998). JP Milton Keynes, 1989–94. Vol. driver, Bridgnorth Community Cars, 2012–; Chair, Shropshire Rural Community Council, 2013–. Editor, W Shropshire Talking Newspaper, 2012–. *Recreations:* sailing (ocean and dinghy), fell walking modern literature, Bridgnorth's Theatre on the Steps (mem.), Van Morrison, Crete. *Address* Sabrina House, 2 Southwell Riverside, Bridgnorth, Shropshire WV16 4AS. *T:* (01746) 768956. *E:* dameenid@me.com.

BIBBY, (John) Benjamin; Director, 1961–94, Chairman, 1970–78, J. Bibby & Sons PLC; *b* 19 April 1929; *s* of late J. P. and D. D. Bibby; *m* 1956, Susan Lindsay Paterson; two *s* one *d. Educ:* Oundle Sch.; St Catharine's Coll., Cambridge (MA). Nat. Service, 2nd Lieut, King's Regt, 1948–49. Called to the Bar, Gray's Inn, 1981. Held various positions in J. Bibby & Sons PLC, 1953–94. Mem. Council, Univ. of Liverpool, 1978–81; Mem. Exec. Cttee, West Kirby Residential Sch., 1978–87. Mem. Cttee, 1982–2001, Chm., 1983–87, Hon. Treas., 1987–2001, Hon. Membership Sec., 2002–04, Nat. Squib Owners' Assoc.; Pres., Merseyside and Deeside Br., STA (formerly STA Schooners), 1992–2003. Fellow Commoner, St Catharine's Coll., Cambridge, 1996–. JP Liverpool 1975–81. *Publications:* (with C. L. Bibby) A Miller's Tale, 1978; A Birthday Ode and Other Verse, 1994; A Letter to a Grandson and Other Verse, 1994; Taking Life as it Comes, 2011. *Recreations:* sailing, gardening. *Address* Ty'n Cae, Brynsiencyn, Llanfairpwll, Anglesey LL61 6HJ. *T:* (01248) 430491. *Clubs:* Royal Thames Yacht; Royal Mersey Yacht; Royal Anglesey Yacht.

BIBBY, Sir Michael (James), 3rd Bt *cr* 1959, of Tarporley, Co. Palatine of Chester; DL; Managing Director, Bibby Line Group Ltd, since 2000; *b* 2 Aug. 1963; *e s* of Sir Derek Bibby, 2nd Bt and Christine Maud, *d* of Rt Rev. F. J. Okell, Bishop Suffragan of Stockport; *S* father 2002; *m* 1994, Beverley, *o d* of Donald Graham; two *s* (twins). *Educ:* Rugby; Trinity Coll., Oxford Univ. DL Merseyside, 2013. *Heir: s* Alexander James Bibby, *b* 24 Aug. 1997. *Address:* Bibby Line Group Ltd, 105 Duke Street, Liverpool L1 5JQ.

BIĆANIĆ, Prof. Nenad Josip Nikola, PhD; FICE, FIACM; Regius Professor of Civil Engineering, University of Glasgow, 1994–2011, now Emeritus Professor and Honorary Senior Research Fellow (Head of Department of Civil Engineering, 1997–2001); *b* Zagreb, Croatia, 6 Sept. 1945; *s* of Vladimir Bićanić and Elizabeta (*née* Kostial-Živanović); *m* 1969, Jasna Babić; one *s* one *d. Educ:* Zagreb Univ., Croatia (Dip. Ing 1968); Univ. of Wales, Swansea (PhD 1978). Structural Engr, Zagreb, 1968–69; Consulting Engr, Arnhem, Netherlands, 1969–72; Zagreb University: Lectr and Researcher, 1972–76; Docent, Prof., 1978–83; Prof., 1984–85; Lectr, Sen. Lectr, then Reader, Univ. of Wales, Swansea, 1985–94. Vis. Prof., Univ. of Colo, Boulder, 1983–84. FICE 1998; FIACM 1998. *Publications:* Computer Aided Analysis and Design of Concrete Structures, 1990; (ed) Computational

Modelling of Concrete Structures, 1994, revd edn 1998, 2003; papers in learned and professional jls. *Recreations:* international folk-dancing, ski-ing, tennis. *Club:* College (Glasgow).

BICESTER, 4th Baron *cr* 1938, of Tusmore, co. Oxford; **Hugh Charles Vivian, (Hugo) Smith;** *b* 8 Nov. 1934; *yr s* of late Lt-Col Hon. Stephen Edward Vivian Smith and Elenor Anderson (*née* Hewitt); *S* brother, 2014. *Educ:* Eton; Worcester Coll., Oxford. Late 2nd Lt, RAC. *Heir: cousin* Charles James Vivian Smith [*b* 7 Sept. 1963; *m* 2006, Deborah Michelle James; two *s*].

BICHARD, Baron *cr* 2010 (Life Peer), of Nailsworth in the County of Gloucestershire; **Michael George Bichard,** KCB 1999; Chairman: Design Council, 2008–11; National Audit Office, since 2015; *b* 31 Jan. 1947. *Educ:* Manchester Univ. (LLB); Birmingham Univ. (MSocSci). Chief Executive: Brent BC, 1980–86; Gloucestershire CC, 1986–90; Social Security Benefits Agency, 1990–95; Perm. Sec., Employment Dept Gp, April–July 1995; Jt Perm. Sec., July–Dec. 1995, Perm. Sec., 1996–2001, DfEE. Rector, London Inst., subseq. Univ. of the Arts London, 2001–08. Dir, 2008–10, Sen. Fellow, 2010–, Inst. for Govt. Chm., Soham Murders Inquiry, 2004. Chm., Legal Services Commn, 2005–08. Chairman: Rathbone Training Ltd, 2001–08; RSe Consulting, 2003–08; non-exec. Dir, Reed Exec. plc, 2002–04. Mem., ESRC, 1989–92. Chm. Bd Dirs, ARTIS, 2003–06. Chm. Trustees, Social Care Inst. for Excellence, 2013–; Dir, River and Rowing Mus. Foundn, 2002–. Governor: Henley Mgt Coll., 2002–; Council, Dyslexia Inst., 2003–06. Hon. Fellow, Inst. of Local Govt Studies, Birmingham Univ. FIPD; CCMI; FRSA. DUniv: Leeds Metropolitan, 1992; Middlesex, 2001; Southampton Inst., 2002; Hon. LLD: Birmingham, 1999; Bradford, 2004.

BICK; *see* Moore-Bick.

BICKELL, Brian; Chief Executive, Shaftesbury plc, since 2011; *b* London, 6 Aug. 1954; civil partnership 2007, Kevin Keogh. *Educ:* FCA 1976. Audit dept, F. W. Stephens, Chartered Accts, 1972–77, Stoy Hayward, Chartered Accts, 1977–82; Gp Financial Accountant, Stock Conversion plc, 1983–86; joined Shaftesbury plc, 1986: Dir, 1987; Finance Dir, 1987–2011. *Address:* Shaftesbury plc, 22 Ganton Street, W1F 7BY. *T:* (020) 7333 8118, *Fax:* (020) 7333 0660. *E:* brian.bickell@shaftesbury.co.uk.

BICKERSTETH, Rt Rev. John Monier, KCVO 1989; Clerk of the Closet to the Queen, 1979–89; *b* 6 Sept. 1921; *yr s* of late Rev. Canon Edward Monier, OBE and Inez Katharine Bickersteth; *m* 1955, Rosemary (*d* 2009), *yr d* of late Edward and Muriel Cleveland-Stevens, Gaines, Oxted; three *s* one *d*. *Educ:* Rugby; Christ Church, Oxford (MA 1953); Wells Theol College; Open Univ. 1997. Captain, Buffs and Royal Artillery, 1941–46. Priest, 1951; Curate, St Matthew, Moorfields, Bristol, 1950–54; Minister, Conventional District of St John's, Hurst Green, Oxted, 1954–62; Vicar, St Stephen's, Chatham, 1962–70; Hon. Canon of Rochester, 1968–70; Bishop Suffragan of Warrington, 1970–75; Bishop of Bath and Wells, 1975–87. A C of E delegate to 4th Assembly, WCC, 1968. Chaplain and Sub-Prelate, OStJ, 1977–96. Chairman: Royal Sch. of Church Music, 1977–88; Bible Reading Fellowship, 1978–90; Vice Chm., Central Bd of Finance of Church of England, 1981–84. Member: Marlborough Coll. Council, 1980–91; Wilts Wildlife Trust Council, 1989–95. Freeman of the City of London, 1979. *Publications:* (jtly) Clerks of the Closet in the Royal Household, 1991; (ed) The Bickersteth Diaries 1914–1918, 1995, 3rd edn 1998; Run o' the Mill Bishop (autobiog.), 2005. *Address:* 10 Elizabeth Court, Crane Bridge Road, Salisbury, Wilts SP2 7UX. *T:* (01722) 238804. *E:* johnbickersteth@waitrose.com.

BICKET, Harry Alexander Clarence; Artistic Director, The English Concert, since 2007; Chief Conductor, Santa Fe Opera, since 2013; *b* Liverpool, 15 May 1961; *s* of late Henry Bicket and Katharine Bicket; *m* 2011, Audrey du Cauzé de Nazelle; one *s* one *d*. *Educ:* Radley Coll.; Royal Coll. of Music; Christ Church, Oxford (BA 1983; MA 1985). FRCO 1980. Duke of Edinburgh's Organ Scholar, St George's Chapel, Windsor Castle, 1978–80; Christopher Tatton Organ Scholar, Christ Church, Oxford, 1980–83; Sub-Organist, Westminster Abbey, 1984–88; Chorus Master, ENO, 1988–93; freelance conductor, 1993–. *Address:* c/o The English Concert, West Wing, Somerset House, Strand, WC2R 1LA. *T:* (020) 7759 1100.

BICKFORD, James David Prydeaux, CB 1995; Chairman, Bickford Associates; author and scriptwriter; *b* 28 July 1940; *s* of late William A. J. P. Bickford and Muriel Bickford (*née* Smythe); *m* 1965, Carolyn Jane, *d* of late Major W. A. R. Sumner, RHA; three *s*. *Educ:* Downside; Law Society's College of Law, London. Admitted to Roll of Solicitors, 1963; Solicitor of the Supreme Court. In practice, J. J. Newcombe, Solicitors, Okehampton, 1963–69; Crown Counsel and Legal Advr to Govt of Turks and Caicos Islands, BWI, 1969–71; Asst Legal Advr, FCO, 1971–79 and 1982–84; Legal Advr, British Mil. Govt, Berlin, 1979–82; Legal Counsellor, FCO, 1984–87; Under Sec., MoD, and Legal Advr to Security and Intelligence Services, 1987–95. Judge Ben C. Green Lectr in Law, Case Western Reserve Univ., USA; Vis. Prof. of Law, Cleveland State Univ., USA. Mem., Panel of Legal Experts, Internat. Telecommunications Satellite Orgn, 1985–87; Chm., Assembly of Internat. Maritime Satellite Orgn, 1985–87. Mem., Law Soc. Hon. Mem., Nat. Security Cttee, Amer. Bar Assoc. Scriptwriter (with wife), infomercial for SOCA, Was Any of This Your Fault?, 2008 (Internat. Visual Commns Silver Award for Best Drama). *Publications:* Land Dealings Simplified in the Turks and Caicos Islands, 1971; *fiction*: The Face of Tomorrow, 2004; contribs on intelligence, organised crime and money-laundering issues to symposia, jls, media and internet. *Recreations:* the family, sailing, fishing. *Address:* c/o National Westminster Bank, Torrington, Devon EX38 8HP.

BICKFORD-SMITH, Margaret Osborne; QC 2003; a Recorder, since 1997; *b* 4 June 1950; *d* of James Maclean Todd and Janet Gillespie Todd (*née* Holmes); *m* 1970, Stephen William Bickford-Smith; one *s*. *Educ:* Headington Sch.; Lady Margaret Hall, Oxford (MA). MCIArb 2006. Called to the Bar, Inner Temple, 1973, Bencher, 1993; in practice as barrister and mediator. Chair: Inns' Conduct Cttee, 2012–14 (Vice Chair, 2009–12); London Br., CIArb, 2012–15. Mem., Hounslow LBC, 1974–82. *Recreations:* Italy, art, music. *Address:* Crown Office Chambers, 2 Crown Office Row, Temple, EC4Y 7HJ. *T:* (020) 7797 8100, *Fax:* (020) 7797 8101. *Club:* Royal Automobile.

BICKLE, Prof. Michael James, DPhil; FRS 2007; Professor, Department of Earth Sciences, University of Cambridge, since 2000; *b* 26 Feb. 1948; *s* of Ronald Stancliffe Bickle and René Florence Bickle; *m* 1978, Hazel Joan Chapman; two *d*. *Educ:* Queens' Coll., Cambridge (BA 1970); DPhil Oxon. Lectr, then Sen. Lectr, Univ. of Western Australia, 1978–83; Lectr, 1983–95, Reader, 1995–2000, in Earth Scis, Univ. of Cambridge. *Recreations:* orienteering, sailing. *Address:* Department of Earth Sciences, Downing Street, Cambridge CB2 3EQ. *T:* (01223) 333400, *Fax:* (01223) 333450. *E:* mb72@esc.cam.ac.uk.

BICKLER, Simon Lloyd; QC 2011; a Recorder, since 2012; *b* Leeds, 19 July 1964; *s* of David Bickler and Ruth Bickler; *m* 1990, Tracy Coburn; three *s* one *d*. *Educ:* Allerton High Sch.; Sheffield Univ. (BA Hons Law). Called to the Bar, Inner Temple, 1988; in practice as a barrister, specialising in family and criminal law, 1988–. *Recreations:* Leeds United, golf, reading. *Address:* St Pauls Chambers, 2nd Floor, Trafalgar House, 29 Park Place, Leeds LS1 2SP.

BICKLEY, Susan Rochford; mezzo soprano, since 1982; *b* Liverpool, 27 May 1955; *d* of Alan Rochford Bickley and Mabel Bickley (*née* Owens); *m* 1984, Anthony Castro; two *s*. *Educ:* Quarry Bank Comp. Sch., Liverpool; City Univ., London (BSc Hons Music 1980); Guildhall Sch. of Music (Cert. Postgrad. Studies 1981, Gold Medal 1981). Mem. (Alto 1), Swingle Singers, 1982–84. *Operatic roles* include: Kostelnicka in Jenufa, Glyndebourne, WNO, New Israeli Opera; Kabanicha in Katya Kabanova, Glyndebourne, ENO, Paris Opera; Cassandra in Les Troyens, ENO; Dorabella in Così fan tutte, ENO; Marcellina in Figaro, Glyndebourne, ENO; Donna Elvira in Don Giovanni, Glyndebourne Touring Opera; Dido in Dido and Aeneas, ENO, Opera North; Mrs Sedley in Peter Grimes, Glyndebourne; Florence Pike in Albert Herring, Glyndebourne; Mrs Grose in Turn of the Screw, Glyndebourne; Baba the Turk in Rake's Progress, Glyndebourne, Garsington; Fyodor in Boris Godunov, ROH; Aksinya in Lady Macbeth of Mtsensk, ROH; Babulenka in The Gambler, ROH; Mistress Quickly in Falstaff, Opera North; Meg Page in Falstaff, ENO; Irene in Theodora, Glyndebourne; Storge in Jeptha, WNO, ENO; Juno in Semele, ENO, Scottish Opera; Andromache in King Priam, ENO; Nan in New Year, Glyndebourne; Jezibaba in Rusalka, Opera North; Herodias in Salome, San Francisco Opera; Brangane in Tristan und Isolde, WNO; Ghost in The Last Supper, Berlin Stadtsoper Unter den Linden, Glyndebourne; Mescalina in Grand Macabre, ENO; Countess Geschwitz in Lulu, de Vlaamse Oper; Die Kurfurstin in Prinz vom Homburg, de Vlaamse Oper; Sarah in Roberto Devereux, Buxton Opera; Romeo in i Capuleti e i Montecchi, Grange Opera; Waltraute in Götterdämmerung, Halle Orch.; Josefa Miranda in Of Love and Other Demons, Opera National du Rhin; Louise Michel in Al Gran Sole Carico d'Amore, Salzburg Fest. and Berlin Staatsoper; Fricka in Die Walküre, Halle Orch.; La Nourrice in Ariane et Barbe Bleu, Frankfurt Oper; Tzippy/Mama in Where the Wild Things Are, Aldeburgh Fest. and with LA Phil.; La Messagiera in Orfeo, Royal Opera Hse; Mother in Between Worlds, ENO; Kostelnicka in Jenufa, Opera North; multiple roles, Julietta, ENO; Ortrud in Lohengrin, WNO; Witch in Hänsel und Gretel, Garsington Opera; Eduige in Rodelinda, ENO; Jocasta in Thebans, ENO; Herodias in Salome, Dallas Opera; Waltraute in Götterdämmerung, Opera North; created rôles: Virgie in Anna Nicole, ROH; Anne in Two Boys, ENO; concerts with all major British ensembles, orchs, etc; frequent broadcasts and recitals. Over 40 commercial recordings. RPS Singer's Award, 2010. *Recreations:* walking in Britain, reading, theatre, playing Snatch, planning Xmas parties. *Address:* c/o Intermusica, Unit 2, Crystal Wharf, 36 Graham Street, N1 8GJ. *T:* (020) 7608 9900, *Fax:* (020) 7490 3263. *E:* jmaynard@intermusica.co.uk.

BIDDER, Neil; QC 1998; **His Honour Judge Bidder;** a Circuit Judge, since 2004; a Deputy High Court Judge, since 2007; *b* 22 July 1953; *s* of Glyn Turner Bidder and Constance Mabel Bidder; *m* 1978, Madeleine Thomas; two *s*. *Educ:* Ogmore Grammar Sch.; Queens' Coll., Cambridge (BA 1974; MA 1977); Dalhousie Univ., Canada (LLM 1977). Called to the Bar, Lincoln's Inn, 1976, Additional Bencher, 2008; in practice at the Bar, 1976–; an Asst Recorder, 1991–94; a Recorder, 1994–2004; Hd of Chambers, 2001–04. Judicial Mem., Parole Bd, 2007–12. Hon. Sec., Council of HM's Circuit Judges, 2012–. Founder Chm., Welsh Personal Injury Lawyers Assoc., 1999–2002. *Recreations:* choral singing, opera, gardening, sport. *Address:* Cardiff Crown Court, Cathays Park, Cardiff CF10 3PG.

BIDDLE, Prof. Martin, CBE 2014 (OBE 1997); FBA 1985; FSA; Professor of Medieval Archaeology, University of Oxford, 1997–2002, now Emeritus; Astor Senior Research Fellow in Medieval Archaeology, Hertford College, Oxford, 1989–2002, now Emeritus; Director, Winchester Research Unit, since 1968; *b* 4 June 1937; *s* of Reginald Samuel Biddle and Gwladys Florence Biddle (*née* Baker); *m* 1966, Birthe (*d* 2010), *d* of Landsretssagfører Axel Th. and Anni Kjølbye of Sønderborg, Denmark; two *d*, and two *d* by previous marriage. *Educ:* Merchant Taylors' Sch., Northwood; Pembroke Coll., Cambridge (MA 1965; Hon. Fellow 2006); MA Oxon 1967; MA Pennsylvania 1977. FSA 1964. Second Lieut, 4 RTR, 1956; 1 Ind. Sqn, RTR, Berlin, 1956–57. Asst Inspector of Ancient Monuments, MPBW, 1961–63; Lectr in Medieval Archaeology, Univ. of Exeter, 1963–67; Vis. Fellow, All Souls Coll., Oxford, 1967–68; Dir, University Museum, and Prof. of Anthropology and of History of Art, Univ. of Pennsylvania, 1977–81; Lectr of The House, Christ Church, Oxford, 1983–86. Directed excavations and investigations: Nonsuch Palace, 1959–60; Winchester, 1961–71; (with Birthe Kjølbye-Biddle): Repton, 1974–88, 1993; St Alban's Abbey, 1978, 1982–84, 1991, 1994–95, 2003, 2006; Holy Sepulchre, Jerusalem, 1989–90, 1992, 1993, 1998; Qasr Ibrim, Egypt, 1990, 1992, 1995, 2000. Archaeological Consultant: Canterbury Cathedral; St Alban's Abbey and Cathedral Church; Eurotunnel, etc. Mem., Faculty Adv. Cttee, Winchester Cathedral, 2011– (Chm., 2013–). Chm., Rescue, Trust for British Archaeology, 1971–75. Mem., Royal Commn on Historical Monuments of England, 1984–95. Chm., Historic Towns Atlas Cttee, 1994–2013; Pres., Soc. for Medieval Archaeology, 1995–98; Vice-Pres., Soc. of Antiquaries, 2006–09. Hon. Mem., British Numismatic Soc., 2008. Hon. Freeman, Winchester, 2010. General Editor, Winchester Studies, 1976–. Hon. DLitt Southampton, 2003. (With Birthe Biddle) Frend Medal, Soc. of Antiquaries, 1986. *Publications:* (with C. Heighway) The Future of London's Past, 1973; (with F. Barlow and others) Winchester in the Early Middle Ages, 1976; (with H. M. Colvin, J. Summerson and others) The History of the King's Works, vol. iv, pt 2, 1982; Object and Economy in Medieval Winchester, 1990; The Tomb of Christ, 1999 (German edn, 1998; Italian edn, 2002); King Arthur's Round Table, 2000; (jtly) Henry VIII's Coastal Artillery Fort at Camber Castle, Rye, Sussex, 2001; Nonsuch Palace: the material culture of a noble restoration household, 2005; (ed) The Winchester Mint, 2012; papers on archaeological, historical and art-historical subjects in learned jls. *Recreations:* travel, esp. Hellenic travel, reading. *Address:* 19 Hamilton Road, Oxford OX2 7PY. *T:* and *Fax:* (01865) 559017.

BIDDLECOMBE, Henrietta Catherine; *see* Knight, H. C.

BIDDLESTONE, Prof. Anthony Joseph, (Joe), PhD; CEng, FIChemE; Professor of Chemical Engineering, 1993–2004, now Professor Emeritus, and University Foundation Fellow, since 2005, University of Birmingham; *b* 8 Aug. 1937; *s* of William Albert and Ivy Evelyn Biddlestone; *m* 1973, Marion Summers; two *s*. *Educ:* George Dixon Grammar Sch., Birmingham; Univ. of Birmingham (BSc 1958; PhD 1961). CEng 1964; FIChemE 1973. University of Birmingham: Lectr, 1965–85; Sen Lectr, 1985–93; Hd, Sch. of Chem. Engrg, 1993–98; Dean of Engrg, 1998–2002. Chm., Accreditation Bd, IChemE, 1992–99. FRSA 1999. *Publications:* numerous contribs to refereed learned jls on aerobic biodegradation of organic wastes. *Recreations:* church music, organist, conductor. *Address:* School of Chemical Engineering, University of Birmingham, Edgbaston, Birmingham B15 2TT. *T:* (0121) 414 5290.

BIDDULPH, family name of **Baron Biddulph.**

BIDDULPH, 5th Baron *cr* 1903; **Anthony Nicholas Colin Maitland Biddulph;** interior designer; sporting manager; *b* 8 April 1959; *s* of 4th Baron Biddulph and of Lady Mary, *d* of Viscount Maitland (killed in action, 1943) and *gd* of 15th Earl of Lauderdale; *S* father, 1988; *m* 1993, Hon. Sian Diana (marr. diss. 2001), *y d* of Baron Gibson-Watt, MC; two *s*. *Educ:* Cheltenham; RAC, Cirencester. Liveryman, Armourers' and Brasiers' Co., 1995. *Recreations:* shooting, fishing, painting. *Heir: s* Hon. Robert Julian Maitland Biddulph, *b* 8 July 1994. *Address:* 8 Orbel Street, SW11 3NZ; Makerstoun House, Kelso TD5 7PA. *Clubs:* Cavalry and Guards, White's.

BIDDULPH, Sir Ian D'Olier, (Jack), 11th Bt *cr* 1664, of Westcombe, Kent; *b* 28 Feb. 1940; *s* of Sir Stuart Royden Biddulph, 10th Bt and Muriel Margaret (*d* 1995), *d* of Angus Harkness, Hamley Bridge, S Australia; *S* father, 1986; *m* 1967, Margaret Eleanor, *o d* of late John Gablonski, Oxley, Brisbane; one *s* two *d*. *Heir: s* Paul William Biddulph [*b* 30 Oct. 1967; *m* 2000, Susan, *d* of late James Adkins; two *d*]. *Address:* 17 Kendall Street, Oxley, Qld 4075, Australia.

BIDE, Rev. Mary Elizabeth; Team Rector, St Mary's Church, Wimbledon, since 2007; a Chaplain to the Queen, since 2013; *b* Oxford, 10 Feb. 1953; *d* of Norman Ellis and Phyllis Ellis; *m* 1975, Mark Bide; one *s* two *d*. *Educ:* Oxford High Sch. for Girls (GPDST); St Anne's Coll., Oxford (BA 1st Cl. Hons Botany 1974). Teacher of Biol., St Paul's Girls' Sch., 1974–75; Ed., W. B. Saunders, 1976–78; Teacher of Sci., St Bede's, 1978–82; Teacher of Maths, St Catherine's Sch., Bramley, 1989–95; ordained deacon, 1994, priest, 1995; Asst Curate, St Nicholas, Gt Bookham, 1994–98; Vicar, Frimley Green, 1998–2003; Precentor, Christ Church Cath., Oxford, 2003–07. Chair, Oxford Diocesan Liturgical Cttee, 2006–07; Member: Guildford Diocesan Adv. Cttee, 2001–03; Guildford Diocesan Synod, 2002–03; Gen. Synod of C of E, 2005–07; Diocesan Bd of Finance, 2009–12. Tutor, Guildford Diocesan Ministry Course, 1996–2003. *Recreations:* walking, singing, wildlife, theatre, music. *Address:* The Rectory, 14 Arthur Road, SW19 7DZ. *T:* (020) 8946 2830. *E:* rector.wimbledon@gmail.com.

BIDEN, Joseph Robinette, Jr; JD; Vice-President of the United States of America, since 2009; *b* Scranton, Penn, 20 Nov. 1942; *s* of late Joseph Robinette Biden and Jean Biden; *m* 1st, 1966, Neilia Hunter (*d* 1972); one *s* (and one *s* one *d* decd); 2nd, 1977, Jill Jacobs; one *d*. *Educ:* Univ. of Delaware (AB 1965); Syracuse Univ. Coll. of Law, NY (JD 1968). Admitted to Delaware Bar, 1968; Trial Attorney, Public Defender's Office, Delaware, 1968; Founding Partner, Biden & Walsh, law firm, Wilmington, 1968–72. Mem. (Democrat), New Castle CC, 1970–72; US Senator (Democrat) from Delaware, 1973–2009. US Senate: Member: Judiciary Cttee, 1981–87 and 1995–97 (Chm., 1987–95); Foreign Relns Cttee, 1997–2009 (Chm., 2001–03 and 2007–09); Chm., Caucus on Internat. Narcotics Control, 2007–09; Co-Chm., NATO Observer Gp. Adjunct Prof., Widener Univ. Sch. of Law, 1991– (on leave of absence). *Publications:* Promises to Keep: on life and politics (autobiog.), 2007. *Address:* c/o The White House, Washington, DC 20501, USA.

BIDWELL, James Richard Philip; Chairman and Chief Executive Officer, Springwise Intelligence Ltd, 2015; *b* 19 Jan. 1965; *s* of Sir Hugh Charles Philip Bidwell, GBE; *m* 1995, Rebecca Mathiesen (marr. diss. 2014); three *d*. *Educ:* Eton Coll.; Univ. of Bristol (BA Hons French). Account Mgr, Lowe Howard-Spink Advertising, 1987–92; Marketing Mgr, Walt Disney Attractions, 1992–97; Head of Marketing, Segaworld, 1997–98; Marketing Dir, Carland LP, 1998–99; Marketing Director: eToys Inc., 1999–2001; Selfridges plc, 2001–05; Chief Executive Officer: Visit London, 2005–08; London Unlimited, 2005–08; Man. Dir, Anthropologie, Europe, 2009–11; Man. Dir, subseq. CEO, Cass Art, 2012–13 (non-exec. Dir, 2011–12, 2013–14); non-exec. Chm., 2013, CEO, 2013–14, Easyart Hldgs Ltd. Non-executive Director: Natural Mat Co., 2007–; Goodwood Estate, 2011–12. Trustee, Cass Sculpture Foundation 2008–13. Liveryman, Co. of Grocers, 1999–. *Recreations:* mountain biking, fly fishing, ski-ing, tennis, sea kayaking. *E:* bidwelljames1@gmail.com. *Clubs:* Ivy; Frensham Flyfishers.

BIDWELL, Robin O'Neill, CBE 1999; PhD; Chairman, LOC Holdings Ltd, since 2014; *b* 15 Sept. 1944; *s* of late Philip John Bidwell and Ellen O'Neill Bidwell; *m* 1st, 1970, Caroline Margaret Budd (marr. diss. 1993); one *s* one *d*; 2nd, 1995, Veronica Rosemary Lucia Verey. *Educ:* Charterhouse; Christ Church, Oxford (BA 1966; MA 1970); Bradford Mgt Centre (PhD 1974). Founder ERL, now ERM, 1973: Dir, 1974–2011; Man. Dir, 1977–93; Chm., ERM Internat., 1993–2001; Exec. Chm., 2001–08; Gp Pres., 2008–11. Non-executive Director: CU Envmtl Trust plc, 1992–2002; ICE Organisation Ltd, 2010–; Chm., Insitor Impact Fund. Authy Mem., Ofgem, 2003–10. Advr, Prince of Wales Business Leaders Forum, 1993–2007; Trustee, Heritage Trust, 1987–96; Chm., Adv. Cttee, ZSL Field Conservation, 2009–. Member: Task Force on envmtl implications of 1992, EC, 1989–90; Bd, Sustainability Challenge Foundn, Netherlands, 1993–2003; NERC, 1996–2002; Adv. Cttee on Business and the Envmt, 1999–2003; Member Council: World Business Council for Sustainable Devlt, 1997–2012; UK Roundtable on Sustainable Devlt, 1998–2000; Chairman: Low Carbon Enterprise Fund, 2008–; Ofgem Low Carbon Network Fund Expert Panel, 2011–. Chm., Green Alliance, 2008–14 (Trustee, 1995–). Chm., Woodchester Trust, 2012–. *Recreations:* conservation, ski-ing, reading, theatre. *Address:* Woodchester Park House, Nympsfield, Glos GL10 3UN. *T:* (office) (020) 3206 5331.

BIELBY, Catherine Mary; *see* Markus, C. M.

BIENZ, Dr Mariann, (Lady Pelham), FRS 2003; Senior Scientific Staff Member, since 1991, Joint Head of Cell Biology, since 2007, and Joint Head of Protein and Nucleic Chemistry, since 2008, MRC Laboratory of Molecular Biology; *b* 21 Dec. 1953; *d* of Jürg Bienz and Lilly Bienz (*née* Gubler); *m* 1996, Hugh Reginald Brentnall Pelham (*see* Sir Hugh Pelham); one *s* one *d*. *Educ:* Gymnasium Winterthur; Univ. of Zürich (Dip. Zool. and Molecular Biol.; PhD 1981). Postdoctoral res. at MRC Lab. of Molecular Biol., Cambridge; Asst Prof., 1986–90, Associate Prof., 1990–91, Univ. of Zürich. Mem., EMBO, 1989. FMedSci 2006. Friedrich Miescher Prize, Swiss Biochemical Soc., 1990. *Publications:* contribs on cell and molecular biol. to various internat. jls. *Recreations:* music, mountain walking. *Address:* MRC Laboratory of Molecular Biology, Francis Crick Avenue, Cambridge CB2 0QH.

BIERMAN, James; Producer, Michael Grandage Co., since 2012; *b* London, 1971; *m* 2014, Kate Mitchell; one *s* two *d*. Actor; Gen. Manager, Aldwych Th., 2002–06; Gen. Manager, 2006–08, Exec. Producer, 2008–11, Donmar Warehouse. *Recreations:* theatre, film, family, Liverpool FC. *Address:* Michael Grandage Co., Fourth Floor, Gielgud Theatre, Shaftesbury Avenue, W1D 6AL. *T:* (020) 3582 7210.

BIGG, Sally; *see* Gunnell, S. J. J.

BIGGAM, Sir Robin (Adair), Kt 1993; Chairman, Independent Television Commission, 1997–2003; *b* 8 July 1938; *s* of Thomas and Eileen Biggam; *m* 1962, Elizabeth McArthur McDougall; one *s* two *d*. *Educ:* Lanark Grammar Sch. Chartered accountant. Peat Marwick Mitchell, 1960–63; ICI, 1964–81; Director: ICL, 1981–84; Dunlop Holdings plc, 1984–85; Man. Dir, 1986–87, Chief Exec., 1987–91, Chm., 1992–96, BICC plc; Chm., Spectris (formerly Fairey Gp), 1996–2001. Non Executive Director: Chloride Group plc, 1985–87; Lloyds Abbey Life plc (formerly Abbey Life Gp), 1985–90; Redland Gp plc, 1991–97; BAE Systems (formerly British Aerospace) plc, 1994–2003; Foreign & Colonial German Investment Trust plc, 1995–98; British Energy plc, 1996–2002. Pres., German-British Chamber of Commerce, 1995–97. Chancellor, Univ. of Bedfordshire (formerly Univ. of Luton), 2001–09. *Recreations:* golf, fishing.

BIGGAR, Rev. Canon Prof. Nigel John, PhD; Regius Professor of Moral and Pastoral Theology, since 2007 and Director, McDonald Centre for Theology, Ethics and Public Life, since 2008, University of Oxford; Canon of Christ Church, Oxford, since 2007; *b* 14 March 1955; *s* of Francis and Jeanne Biggar; *m* 1982, Virginia Dunn. *Educ:* Monkton Combe Sen. Sch., Bath; Worcester Coll., Oxford (BA Modern Hist. 1976; MA 1988); Regent Coll., Vancouver (Master of Christian Studies 1981); Univ. of Chicago (AM Religious Studies 1980; PhD Christian Theol. 1986). Librarian, Latimer Hse, Oxford, 1985–91; Lectr in Christian Ethics, Wycliffe Hall, Oxford, 1987–94; ordained deacon, 1990, priest, 1991; Fellow and Chaplain, Oriel Coll., Oxford, 1990–99; Prof. of Theol., Dept of Theol. and Religious Studies, Univ. of Leeds, 1999–2004; Prof. of Theol., Sch. of Religions and Theol., 2004–07, Fellow, 2005–07, TCD; Canon, Christ Ch Cathedral, Dublin, 2004–07. Lectr, Leeds Parish Ch, 1999–2003. Mem., Cttee on Ethical Issues in Medicine, RCP, 2000–14. Pres., Soc. for Study of Christian Ethics, 2003–06. *Publications:* (ed jtly) Cities of Gods: faith, politics and pluralism in Judaism, Christianity and Islam, 1986; (ed) Reckoning with Barth: essays in commemoration of the 100th anniversary of the birth of Karl Barth, 1988; Theological Politics: a critique of Faith in the City, the report of the Archbishop of Canterbury's Commission on Urban Priority Areas (1985), 1988; The Hastening that Waits: Karl Barth's Ethics, 1993, rev. edn 1995; Good Life: reflections on what we value today, 1997; (ed with Rufus Black) The Revival of Natural Law: philosophical, theological and ethical responses to the Finnis-Grisez School, 2000; (ed) Burying the Past: making peace and doing justice after civil conflict, 2001, rev. edn 2003; Aiming to Kill: the ethics of suicide and euthanasia, 2004; (ed with Linda Hogan) Religious Voices in Public Places, 2009; Behaving in Public: how to do Christian ethics, 2011; In Defence of War, 2013; Between Kin and Cosmopolis: an ethic of the nation, 2014. *Recreations:* reading history, walking battlefields, visiting historic cemeteries, playing cards. *Address:* Christ Church, Oxford OX1 1DP. *Club:* Athenæum.

BIGGART, (Thomas) Norman, CBE 1984; WS; Partner, Biggart Baillie & Gifford, WS Solicitors, Glasgow and Edinburgh, 1959–95; *b* 24 Jan. 1930; *o s* of Andrew Stevenson Biggart, JP and Marjorie Scott Biggart; *m* 1956, Eileen Jean Anne Gemmell; one *s* one *d*. *Educ:* Morrison's Acad., Crieff; Glasgow Univ. (MA 1951, LLB 1954). Served RN, 1954–56 (Sub-Lt RNVR). Law Society of Scotland: Mem. Council, 1977–86; Vice-Pres., 1981–82; Pres., 1982–83. Mem., Council on Tribunals, and Chm., Scottish Cttee, 1990–98. Pres., Business Archives Council, Scotland, 1977–86. Member: Exec. Cttee, Scottish Council (Development and Industry), 1984–93; Scottish Tertiary Educn Adv. Council, 1984–87; Scottish Records Adv. Council, 1985–91. Director: Clydesdale Bank, 1985–97; Independent (formerly New Scotland) Insurance Gp, 1986–2000 (Chm., 1989–93); Beechwood Glasgow, 1989–97 (Chm., 1989–97). Trustee, Scottish Civic Trust, 1989–97. Hon. Mem., American Bar Assoc. 1982. OStJ 1968. *Recreations:* golf, hill walking. *Address:* Gailes, Kilmacolm, Renfrewshire PA13 4LZ. *T:* (01505) 872645. *Club:* The Western (Glasgow).

BIGGS, Dr John, CChem, FRSC; Moderator, 1992–93, Chairman, 1993–97, Free Church Federal Council; *b* 3 Jan. 1933; *s* of Horace James Biggs and Elsie Alice Biggs, Leicester; *m* 1965, Brenda Muriel Hicklenton. *Educ:* Wyggeston Grammar Sch. for Boys, Leicester; Downing Coll., Cambridge (Graystone Scholar). MA, PhD (Cantab). FRSC (FCS 1958); CChem 1979. DSIR Res. Fellow, Cambridge, 1958–60; Lectr in Chemistry, Univ. of Hull, 1960–87. President: Baptist Students' Fedn, 1955–56; Yorkshire Baptist Assoc., 1973–74; Vice-Pres., Baptist Men's Movement, 1995–97, Pres., 1997–98; Baptist Union of GB: Chm., Home Mission Working Gp, 1981–88; Mem. Council, 1978–2013, Chm., 1990–94; Pres., 1989–90; Mem., Scholarships and Ministerial Trng Bursary Cttee, 1978–2001 (Chm., 1995–2001). Examnr in Chem., Cambridge Assessment (formerly UCLES), 1958–2014 (Consultant and Prin. Examnr, 1983–2011). Governor, Northern Baptist Coll., Manchester, 1989–2000; Chm., Relocation Steering Cttee, Baptist Theol Seminary, Prague, 1994–96 (Mem. Bd of Trustees, Rüschlikon, Zürich, 1989–94, Vice-Chm., 1992–94). Member: Envmtl Issues Network, CTBI (formerly CCBI), 1990–2007 (Mem. Steering Cttee and Adv. Panel, Eco-Congregation Prog., 1999–2004); Envmt Gp, Churches Together in Cumbria, 1997–2012; Chm., Sustainable Communities (Cumbria), 2004–08. Dir and Chm., Ambleside Parish Centre, 2012– (Mem., 2005–, Vice Chm., 2009–12, Chm., 2012–, Mgt Cttee); Trustee, Ambleside with Brathay Trust, 2008–. *Publications:* (contrib.) Energy, 2003. *Recreations:* fell-walking, opera, photography. *Address:* Fellcroft, Easedale Road, Grasmere, Ambleside, Cumbria LA22 9QR.

BIGGS, John; Member (Lab) City and East, London Assembly, Greater London Authority, since 2000; Mayor of Tower Hamlets, since 2015; *b* 19 Nov. 1957; *s* of late Robert Edmund Biggs and of Mary Jeanette Biggs (*née* Phillips); *m* 1993, Christine Sibley (marr. diss. 2015); one *d*. *Educ:* Queen Elizabeth's Boys' Sch., Barnet; Bristol Univ. (BSc Hons Chem. 1979); Birkbeck Coll., London Univ. (Postgrad. Dip. Computer Sci. 1984); Westminster Univ. (Postgrad. Dip. Law 1996, Legal Practice Course 1998). Operating theatre orderly, 1979–80; lab. technician, 1980–83; systems analyst, 1984–91; self-employed computer consultant, 1991–92. Mem. (Lab), Tower Hamlets BC, 1988–2002 (Leader of Opposition, 1991–94; Leader, 1994–95). Non-exec. Dir, Tower Hamlets HAT, 1996–2004 (Vice-Chm. 1999–2004); Vice Chm., London Devlt Agency, 2004–08; Dep. Chm., London Thames Gateway Devlt Corp., 2004–08; Member: London Health Commn, 2008–11; Metropolitan Police Authy, 2000–03, 2009–12; London Legacy Devlt Corp., 2015–. Dir, Socialist Health Assoc., 1997–2000. Gov., Birkbeck, Univ. of London, 2009–. Hon. Fellow, QMUL, 2009. *Recreations:* reading, walking. *Address:* Greater London Authority, City Hall, Queen's Walk, SE1 2AA. *T:* (020) 7983 4350; Flat 30, Stepney City Apartments, 49 Clark Street, E1 3HS. *T:* 07974 918322.

BIGGS, John Sydney Grainge, MD; FRCOG, FRANZCOG; Postgraduate Medical Dean, University of Cambridge, and Eastern Region, NHS Executive, 1991–2001; Consultant Emeritus, Canberra Hospital, 2014; *b* 16 Dec. 1935; *s* of Charles V. G. Biggs and Leah M Biggs (*née* Price); *m* 1960, T. Glyndon Daley; three *s* two *d*. *Educ:* Carey Grammar Sch. Melbourne; Univ. of Melbourne (MB BS 1960); MD Aberdeen 1973; MA Cantab 1994 MRCOG 1966, FRCOG 1980; FRANZCOG 1979; DHMSA 1993. House Officer, Royal Melbourne Hosp., 1961; RMO, Royal Children's Hosp., Melbourne, 1962; RMO and Registrar, Royal Women's Hosp., Melbourne, 1963–64; Lecturer in Obstetrics and Gynaecology: Univ. of Qld, 1965; Univ. of Aberdeen, 1966–69; University of Queensland Sen. Lectr, 1969–72; Reader, 1973–82; Dean of Medicine and Prof., 1983–91. Vis. Fellow, ANU, 2010–. Adjunct Prof. of Medical Educn, 2008–, Invited Lectr, 2011, Univ. of Health Scis, Lahore, Pakistan. Chairman: Bd, Coast City Country Trng, 2006–10; ACT Health Human Res. Ethics Cttee, 2010–14. Conducted evaluation of postgrad. med. trng for Higher Educn Commn, Pakistan, 2006–07 and survey of performance in hospitals, Lahore for Govt of Punjab, Pakistan, 2008. Hon. Prof., UEA, 1997–2001. Pres., ASME, 1999–2002 (Chm., 1996–99). *Publications:* contrib. to learned jls on ovarian structure and function, 1996–82, and medical educn, 1983–2013. *Recreations:* gardening, walking, reading. *Address:* 21 Conyers Street, Hughes, ACT 2605, Australia. *T:* (2) 61616643. *Club:* Royal Society of Medicine.

BIGGS, Lewis, OBE 2011; curator, writer and cultural consultant; Director/Chief Executive Liverpool Biennial of Contemporary Art, 2000–11 (Trustee and non-executive Director, 1998–2000); *b* 22 April 1952; *s* of Lewis Ian Biggs and Penelope Torre Biggs (*née* Torr); *m* 1983, Ann Margaret Compton (marr. diss. 2002); one *s* one *d*; *m* 2011, Lisa Katharine Milroy, *qv*. *Educ:* New Coll., Oxford (MA Mod. Hist. 1974); Courtauld Inst., Univ. of London (MA Hist. of Art 1979). Gallery Co-ordinator, Arnolfini Gall., Bristol, 1979–84; Exhibns Officer, British Council, 1984–87; Curator of Exhibns, Tate Gall., Liverpool, 1987–90; Curator, then Dir, Tate Gall., Liverpool, 1990–2000. Director: Oriel Mostyn Gall., Llandudno, 1991–98; Art Transpennine Ltd, 1996–2002; Culture Campus Ltd, 2006–11; Another Place Ltd, 2006–. Member: Visual Arts Adv. Cttee, British Council, 1991–2007; Visual Arts Panel, Arts Council of England, 1996–99; NW Arts Bd, 1997–2002; Liverpool Cath. Fabric Adv. Cttee, 1995–98; Liverpool Urban Design and Conservation Panel, 2003–09; Cass Sculpture Foundn, Goodwood, 2010–11; Internat. Council, Rockbund Art Mus., Shanghai, 2011–13. Trustee: Liverpool Architecture and Design Trust, 1997–99; John Moores Liverpool Exhibn Trust, 2011–; Foundn for Art and Creative Technol., 2011–14; Centre for Chinese Contemporary Art (formerly Chinese Arts Centre), Manchester, 2011–; Situations, Bristol, 2011–13. Dir and Chm., Inst. of Public Art, Hong Kong, 2013–. Dir, Internat. Award for Art Criticism Ltd, 2014–. Vis. Prof. of Contemporary Art, Liverpool Art Sch., Liverpool John Moores Univ., 2001–04 and 2011– (Hon. Fellow, 1998); Hon. Prof., Glasgow Sch. of Art, 2011–14. Advr, Coll. of Arts, Shanghai Univ., 2011–. Curator: Aichi Triennale Nagoya, 2013; Folkestone Triennal, 2014. Associate Fellow, Univ. of Liverpool, 1992. FRSA. Gen. series Ed., Tate Modern Artists, 2001–14. Hon. MA Univ. for Creative Arts, 2014.

BIGGS, Matthew John; gardener, writer and broadcaster; *b* Leicester, 2 June 1960; *s* of Ivan and Marion Biggs; *m* 1991, Gillian Mastemaker; one *s* two *d. Educ:* City of Leicester Boys' Grammar Sch.; Charles Keene Coll. of Further Educn (ONC Public Admin 1978); Pershore Coll. of Horticulture (Nat. Cert. Horticulture Nursery and Ornamental 1979); Royal Botanic Gdns, Kew (Dip. Hort. 1986). Educnl guide, Royal Botanic Gdns, Kew, 1986–94; researcher and presenter, Garden Club, Channel 4, 1991–96; expert tour leader, Gardening Cruises, 1994–; guest expert, Gardening Phone-In, LBC Radio, 1994–2008; Dir, Grass Roots, Meridian TV, 1997–2002; Panel Mem., Gardeners' Question Time, BBC Radio 4, 2003–; Course Dir, Plants and Plantsmanship, English Gardening Sch., 2009–12. Feature gardens at Hampton Court Flower Show, 2009, BBC Gardeners' World Live, 2011; conceptual artist, Hampton Court Flower Show, 2014. Journalist: RHS The Garden mag., 1993–; BBC Gardeners' World mag., 1994–. *Publications:* (contrib.) RHS Dictionary of Gardening, 1990; Practical Guide to Healthy Houseplants, 1996; Matthew Biggs' Complete Book of Vegetables, 1997; (with R. Lancaster) What Houseplant, Where, 1998; (contrib.) Gardeners' Question Time: plant chooser, 2003; (contrib.) Gardeners' Question Time: Gardening Techniques, 2005; Gardening at Eden and how to do it at home, 2006; Allotment Days, 2007. *Recreations:* supporting Leicestershire sport, making cider (badly!), church visiting. *Address:* 40 Singlets Lane, Flamstead, St Albans, Herts AL3 8EP. *T:* (01582) 849020. *E:* matthew-biggs@btconnect.com.

BIGGS, Michael Nicholas; Chairman, Direct Line Insurance Group plc, since 2012; *b* 14 Aug. 1952; *s* of Eric Peter and Hilda May Biggs; two *s. Educ:* Alleyne's Grammar Sch.; Worcester Coll., Oxford (MA 1974). ACA 1979. Arthur Andersen & Co., 1976–84; HSBC, 1984–87; Gp Financial Controller, Morgan Grenfell & Co., 1987–91; Norwich Union: Gp Financial Controller, 1991–95; Gen. Manager Internat., 1995–97; Gp Finance Dir, 1997–2000; Gp Exec. Dir, 2000–01, Gp Finance Dir, 2001–03, CGNU, subseq. Aviva; Gp Finance Dir, 2005–07, Gp Chief Exec., 2007–08, Chm., 2008–13, Resolution plc. *Recreations:* gardening, history, antiques. *Club:* Royal Automobile.

BIGGS, Prof. Peter Martin, CBE 1987; PhD, DSc; FRS 1976; Director of Animal Health (formerly Animal Disease Research), Agricultural and Food Research Council, 1986–88, retired; Visiting Professor of Veterinary Microbiology, Royal Veterinary College, University of London, 1982–2008, now Honorary Professor; *b* 13 Aug. 1926; *s* of Ronald Biggs and Cécile Biggs (*née* Player); *m* 1950, Alison Janet Molteno; two *s* one *d. Educ:* Bedales Sch.; Cambridge Sch., USA; Queen's Univ., Belfast; Royal Veterinary Coll., Univ. of London (BSc 1953, DSc 1975); Univ. of Bristol (PhD 1958). FRCVS, FRCPath, FRSB, CBiol. Served RAF, 1944–48; Research Asst, Univ. of Bristol, 1953–55, Lectr, 1955–59; Houghton Poultry Research Station: Head of Leukosis Experimental Unit, 1959–74; Dep. Dir, 1971–74; Dir, 1974–86. Andrew D. White Prof.-at-Large, Cornell Univ., 1988–94. Sir William Dick Meml Lectr, Univ. of Edinburgh, 1974 and 1987; E. H. W. Wilmott Guest Lectr, Univ. of Bristol, 1977; Leeuwenhoek Prize Lectr, Royal Soc., 1997. Member: Veterinary Products Cttee, 1973–98; Management Bd, AFRC, 1986–88. President: BVPA, 1974–75; World Vet. Poultry Assoc., 1981–85 (Hon. Life Pres., 1985); Internat. Assoc. for Comparative Res. on Leukemia and Related Diseases, 1981–83; Inst. of Biol., 1990–92; Vice Pres., BVA, 1996–98. Founder FMedSci 1998. Hon. FRASE 1986. Hon. DVM Ludwig-Maximilians Univ., 1976; Dr *hc* Liège, 1991. Tom Newman Meml Award, 1964; Poultry Science Award, British Oil and Cake Mills, 1968; J. T. Edwards Meml Medal, 1969; Dalrymple-Champneys Cup and Medal, 1973; Bledisloe Veterinary Award, 1977; Wooldridge Meml Medal and Lecture, 1978; Joszef Marek Meml Medal, Vet. Univ. of Budapest, 1979; Victory Medal, Central Vet. Soc., 1980; Gordon Meml Medal and Lecture, Robert Fraser Gordon Meml Trust, 1989; Wolf Foundn Prize in Agric., 1989; Chiron Award, BVA, 1999; Poultry Industry Special Merit Award, British Poultry Council, 2011. *Publications:* scientific papers on viruses and infectious disease. *Recreations:* music making, natural history. *Address:* Willows, London Road, St Ives PE27 5ES. *T:* and *Fax:* (01480) 463471. *Clubs:* Athenæum, Farmers.

BIGGS, Prof. Simon Richard, PhD; FREng; Executive Dean, Faculty of Engineering, Architecture and Information Technology, University of Queensland, since 2014; *b* Butleigh, Som, 22 Jan. 1965; *s* of Alan Michael Biggs and Shirley Anne Biggs; *m* 1999, Sarah Jane Gardiner; two *d. Educ:* Crispin Comprehensive Sch.; Strode Coll.; Univ. of Bristol (BSc 1986; PhD 1990). FREng 2011. Research Fellow: CNRS, Strasbourg, 1990–92; Univ. of Melbourne, 1992–94; University of Newcastle, New South Wales: Lectr, 1994–97; Sen. Lectr, 1998–99; Associate Prof., 2000–02; Prof. of Particle Sci. and Engrg, Univ. of Leeds, 2002–14. CSO, Chamelic Ltd, 2006–14; Mem. Bd, Escubed Ltd, 2009–. *Address:* Faculty of Engineering, Architecture and Information Technology, Level 2, Hawken Engineering Building, University of Queensland, Brisbane, Qld 4072, Australia.

BIGHAM, family name of **Viscount Mersey**.

BIGLAND, Brenda, CBE 2006; education consultant, adviser, trainer and coach, since 2011; *b* 6 June 1951; *d* of Edwin and Sylvia Francis; *m* 1972, Paul Bigland; one *s. Educ:* Calcot Primary Sch., Reading; St Joseph's Convent, Reading; St Osyth's Coll., Essex; British Dyslexia Inst. (Associate Mem.); Bulmershe Coll. (BEd Hons 1989); Reading Univ. (MA Instnl Mgt and Educnl Admin 1993). Teacher: Garland Primary Sch., Berks, 1972–74; Aldermaston Sch., Berks, 1974–75; Francis Bailey Sch., Berks, 1975; Dep. Hd, St John Bosco (Ind.) Sch., Reading, 1978–80; Hd, Prep. Sch., Presentation Coll. (Indep.), Reading, 1980–88; Dep. Hd, Marish Sch., Berks, 1988–92; Headteacher, Lent Rise School, Burnham and Nat. Leader of Educn, 1993–2011. Consultant/Adviser, DFE (formerly DES, then DFES, subseq. DCSF), 2002–; Nat. Coll. of Sch. Leadership, 2002–; Specialist Schs and Academies Trust, 2002–; Consultant, Implementation Rev. Gp (Educn), 2009– (Mem., 2006). Member: Bd, Trng and Develt Agency, 2002–09; Nat. Educn Leadership Gp for Business in the Community, 2002–; Task Force Gp on Employer Engagement in Educn, 2008–10. Ambassador for British Council promoting internat. collaboration across schs nationally and internationally. Judge, Teaching Awards Trust, 2004– (Fellow, 2006); Lifetime Fellow, ICT Register, Schools Network Trust, 2010. Consultant, Bentley Priory Battle of Britain Trust (Trustee, 2008–09). FBCS 2009. *Publications:* articles on educn subjects, incl. 21st Century learning, employer engagement in educn, internat. collaboration, community cohesion, leadership in educn, inspections and accountability in educn, etc. *Recreations:* travel, theatre, music, reading, spending time with family and friends, Rotarian. *E:* b.bigland@btinternet.com. *W:* www.askbrenda.co.uk.

BIGLOU, Liliana, OBE 2003; Director, Ghana, British Council, since 2013; *b* Jaworzno, Poland, 25 Feb. 1957; *d* of Józef Sztejnbis and Henryka Kowalska; *m* 1977, Conrad Biglou; two *d. Educ:* Sch. of Slavonic and E Eur. Studies, Univ. of London (BA Russian and Polish Studies; DipLib; MA Liby and Information Sci.). MCLIP 1991. British Council: Asst Dir, Malawi, 1992–95; Dep. Dir, Ghana, 1995–97; Director: Kazakhstan, 1997–2001; Ukraine, 2001–05; Romania, 2005–09; Kenya, 2009–10; Canada, 2010–13. Medal, Supreme Council of Ukraine, 2005. *Recreations:* gardening, travel, herbal medicine. *Address:* British Council, PO Box GP 771, Accra, Ghana. *E:* liliana.biglou@britishcouncil.org.

BIGNELL, (Francis) Geoffrey; Founder and Chairman, Just Employment Ltd, Solicitors, 1999–2015; *b* 7 March 1949; *s* of Ernest Francis John Bignell and Olive Ethel Bignell (*née* Peatson); *m* 1978, Susan Rachel Harrison; two *s* one *d. Educ:* Isleworth Grammar Sch.; Trinity Hall, Cambridge (MA); Coll. of Law. Social work in Basildon and Worksop, 1971–74; articled to Notts CC, 1975–78; admitted Solicitor, 1977; Prosecuting Solicitor, Notts Police Authy, 1978–80; Asst and Sen. Asst Solicitor, Leics CC, 1980–83; Prin. Solicitor, Warwicks CC, 1983–87; Asst Sec.-Gen. (Management), Law Soc., 1987–95; Chief Executive: Law Soc. Services Ltd, 1995–97; Solicitors Property Centres Ltd, 1997–98. Non-executive Director: Cheviot Financial Services (formerly Cheviot Personal Pensions) Ltd, 1992–2005; Ambersham Holdings Ltd, 1998–2001; Lawyers Defence Union Ltd, 1999–2002; Peter Honey Publications Ltd, 2000–02. Member: Rail Passengers' (formerly Rail Users' Consultative) Cttee for Southern England, 1997–2005 (Vice-Chm., 2002–05); SW Trains Passenger Panel, 2002– (Chm., 2015–). Gov., George Abbot Sch., 1995–2001 (Vice-Chm., 1998–2001); Mem., Corp. of Guildford Coll., 1997–2001 (Vice-Chm., 1998–2001). *Publications:* contribs to learned jls. *Recreations:* faith, family, friendship and fun. *Address:* Roseland, 13 Lower Edgeborough Road, Guildford, Surrey GU1 2DX.

BIGNELL, Janet Susan; QC 2015; a Recorder, since 2009; *b* Shrewsbury, 31 Jan. 1968; *d* of Richard Bignell and Rosemary Bignell (*née* Jones). *Educ:* King Edward VI Coll., Nuneaton; Downing Coll., Cambridge (BA Hons Law 1990; MA 1994); Hertford Coll., Oxford (BCL Hons 1991); Inns of Court Sch. of Law. FCIArb 2014. Called to the Bar, Lincoln's Inn, 1992. Exec. Ed., The Lawyers' Factbook, Landlord and Tenant, 2001–04; Mem., Editl Bd and contributor, Landlord and Tenant Rev., 1999–. *Publications:* contrib. Auctioneers, Estate Agents and Valuers, in Encyclopaedia of Forms and Precedents, 5th edn, 1985, 1995 and 1999 reissues; The Carers Directory, 1987; (contrib.) Fisher and Lightwood's Law of Mortgage, 11th edn 2000; (with C. Harpum) Registered Land: the new law, 2002; (with C. Harpum) Registered Land, Law and Practice under the Land Registration Act 2002, 2004; Lewison's Drafting Business Leases, 7th edn 2007, 8th edn 2013. *Recreations:* theatre, travel. *Address:* Falcon Chambers, Falcon Court, EC4Y 1AA. *E:* bignell@falcon-chambers.com.

BIGSBY, Prof. Christopher William Edgar, PhD; FRSL; Professor of American Studies, 1984, now Emeritus, and Founder and Director, Arthur Miller Centre for American Studies, since 1989, University of East Anglia; *b* Dundee, 27 June 1941; *s* of Edgar and Ivy Bigsby; *m* 1965, Pamela Lovelady; two *s* two *d. Educ:* Univ. of Sheffield (BA English 1962; MA 1964); Univ. of Nottingham (PhD 1966). FRSL 2000. Lectr, UC of Wales, Aberystwyth, 1966–69; Lectr, 1969–73, Sen. Lectr, 1973–76, Reader, 1976–84, UEA. Fulbright Schol. *TV plays*: (with Malcolm Bradbury): The After Dinner Game, 1975; Stones, 1976; *BBC radio plays*: (with Malcolm Bradbury): Patterson, 1983; Long Days Journey, 1988; Presenter: BBC Radio: Kaleidoscope, 1982–90; Present Voices, Past Words, 1991; The Index, 1999; First Night; Third Ear; The Archive Hour; Off the Page, 2000–02; Meridian; BBC TV: Bookmark; Edith Wharton; Of Mice and Men. FRSA. *Publications:* Confrontation and Commitment, 1967; Albee, 1969; (ed) Three Negro Plays, 1969; The Black American Writer, 2 vols, 1971; Dada and Surrealism, 1972; (ed) Edward Albee, 1975; (ed) Superculture, 1975; (ed) Approaches to Popular Culture, 1976; Tom Stoppard, 1980; The Second Black Renaissance, 1980; (ed) Contemporary English Drama, 1981; A Critical Introduction to 20th Century American Drama, vol. 1, 1982, vol. 2, 1984, vol. 3, 1985; Joe Orton, 1982; (ed) The Radical Imagination and the Liberal Tradition, 1982; David Mamet, 1985; (ed) Cultural Change in the United States since World War II, 1986; (ed) Plays by Susan Glaspell, 1987; (ed) File on Miller, 1987; (ed) Arthur Miller and Company, 1990; Modern American Drama 1945–1990, 1992; (ed) Nineteenth Century American Short Stories, 1995; (ed) The Portable Arthur Miller, 1995; (ed) The Cambridge Companion to Arthur Miller, 1997; (ed with D. B. Wilmeth) The Cambridge History of American Theatre, vol. 1, 1998, vol. 2, 1999, vol. 3, 2000; Contemporary American Playwrights, 1999; Modern American Drama 1945–2000, 2000; (ed) Writers in Conversation with Christopher Bigsby, vol. 1, 2000, vol. 2, 2001, vols 3 and 4, 2011, vol. 5, 2013; (ed) The Cambridge Companion to David Mamet, 2004; Arthur Miller: a critical study, 2004; (ed) Remembering Arthur Miller, 2005; (ed) A New Introduction to American Studies, 2005; Remembering and Imagining the Holocaust: the chain of memory, 2006; (ed) The Cambridge Companion to Modern American Culture, 2006; Neil La Bute, 2007; (ed) The Cambridge Companion to August Wilson, 2007; Arthur Miller: 1915–1962, 2009; Arthur Miller: 1962–2005, 2011; Viewing America: 21st century television drama, 2013; *novels*: Hester, 1994; Pearl, 1995; Still Lives, 1996; Beautiful Dreamer, 2002; One Hundred Days: One Hundred Nights, 2007; Poe, or the Revenant, 2012; Ballygoran, 2014. *Recreations:* still looking, avoiding questionnaires. *Address:* Department of American Studies, University of East Anglia, Norwich NR4 7TJ. *E:* c.bigsby@uea.ac.uk; 3 Church Farm, Watton Road, Colney, Norwich NR4 7TX.

BIJUR, Peter Isaac; Chairman of the Board and Chief Executive Officer, Texaco Inc., 1996–2001; *b* 14 Oct. 1942; *m* 2000, Kjestine M. Anderson; two *s* one *d* from former marriage. *Educ:* Univ. of Pittsburgh (BA Pol Sci. 1964); Columbia Univ. (MBA 1966). Texaco, 1966–2001: Manager, Buffalo sales dist, 1971–73; Asst Manager to Vice-Pres. for public affairs, 1973–75; Staff Co-ordinator, dept of strategic planning, 1975–77; Asst to Exec. Vice-Pres., 1977–80; Manager, Rocky Mountain Refining and Marketing, 1980–81; Asst to Chm. of Bd, 1981–83; Pres., Texaco Oil Trading & Supply Co., 1984; Vice-Pres., special projects, 1984–86; Pres. and Chief Exec., Texaco Canada, 1987–89; Chm., Pres. and Chief Exec., Texaco Canada Resources, Calgary, 1988–89; Chm., Texaco Ltd, 1989–91; Pres., Texaco Europe, 1990–92; Sen. Vice Pres., 1992–96, Vice Chm. Bd, 1996, Texaco Inc. Director: GulfMark Offshore, Inc., 2003–; AB Volvo, 2006–14.

BIKAS, Konstantinos; Grand Commander, Order of the Phoenix (Greece); Ambassador of Greece to the Court of St James's, since 2012; *b* Athens, 14 March 1955; *s* of Konstantinos Bikas and Aphrodite Gana; *m* 1987, Maria Goga; one *s* one *d. Educ:* Varvakeion Exemplary High Sch.; Univ. of Athens (Law degree with Hons 1978); Univ. of Hamburg (Grad. studies in Private Shipping Law and Internat. Law). Mil. Service, Hellenic Navy, 1978–79. Diplomatic Cabinet of Dep. Minister of Foreign Affairs, 1984–85, and of Minister of Foreign Affairs, 1985–88; Consul, Vancouver, 1988–92; First Sec., Algeria, 1992–93; spokesman of Greek Foreign Ministry and Counsellor, 1993–98; Hd of Mission (as Chargé D'Affaires en pied), Baghdad, 1998–2002; Consul Gen., Boston, 2002–05; Dir, Private Office of Pres. of Greece and Minister Plenipotentiary 2nd Cl., 2005–09; Head (Dir Gen.), Nat. Intelligence Service and Minister Plenipotentiary 1st Cl., 2009–12. Pres., Varvakeion Foundn, 2006–09. Founder and Ed., Thesis (Min. of Foreign Affairs foreign policy pubn), 1996–98. Grand Officer, Order of Merit (Italy); Commander 1st Class: Royal Order of Polar Star (Sweden); Order of Dannebrog (Denmark); Order of Lion (Finland); Comdr, Order of Merit (Germany); Grand Decoration of Honour in Gold with Star (Austria). *Address:* Embassy of Greece, 1a Holland Park, W11 3TP.

BILDT, Carl, Hon. KCMG 1998; Minister of Foreign Affairs, Sweden, 2006–14; *b* Halmstad, 15 July 1949; *s* of Daniel B. Bildt and Kerstin Bildt (*née* Andersson); *m* 1984, Mia Bohman; one *s* one *d*; *m* 1998, Anna Maria Corazza. *Educ:* Stockholm Univ. Mem., Stockholm CC, 1974–77; MP (Moderate Party), Sweden, 1979–2001; Under-Sec. of State for Co-ordination and Planning, Cabinet Office, 1979–81; Member: Parly Standing Cttee in Foreign Affairs, 1982–86; Adv. Council on Foreign Affairs, 1982–99; Submarine Defence Commn, 1982–83; 1984 Defence Cttee, 1984–87; Prime Minister of Sweden, 1991–94; EU Special Rep. to Conflict in Former Yugoslavia, and Co-Chm., Internat. Conf. on Former Yugoslavia, 1995; High Rep. for Peace Implementation in Bosnia and Herzegovina, 1996–97; Special Envoy of UN Sec. Gen., Balkans, 1999–2001. Chm., Moderate Party, 1986–99. Chm., Kreab Gp, Sweden; Sen. Advr, IT Provider, Stockholm; Director: Legg Mason Inc.; HiQ; Lundin Petroleum; Vostok Nafta; Öhmans. Trustee, RAND Corp. Mem., IISS, 1981–. Mem., Nordic Council, 1986 (Chm., Conservative Gp, 1988–91). Chm., Nordic Venture Network. Chm., Internat. Democratic Union, 1992–99. Chm., Global Commn on Internet Governance, 2014–. *Publications:* Landet Som Steg ut i Kylan, 1972; Framtid i Frihet, 1976; Hallänning, Svensk, Europé, 1991; Peace Journey, 1998.

BILGIÇ, Abdurrahman; Ambassador of Turkey to the Court of St James's, since 2014; *b* Adiyaman, Turkey, 1963; *m* Esra; one *s* one *d*. *Educ:* Ankara Univ. Dir Gen., Press and Information Dept, Prime Ministry, Turkey, 2003–05; Consul Gen., Munich, 2005–07; Ambassador to Japan, 2011; Dep. Undersec., Prime Ministry, 2011–14. *Address:* Embassy of Turkey, 43 Belgrave Square, SW1X 8PA. *T:* (020) 7393 0202, *Fax:* (020) 7393 0066. *E:* embassy.london@mfa.gov.tr. *Club:* Travellers.

BILIMORIA, family name of **Baron Bilimoria**.

BILIMORIA, Baron *cr* 2006 (Life Peer), of Chelsea in the Royal Borough of Kensington and Chelsea; **Karan Faridoon Bilimoria,** CBE 2004; DL; FCA; Chairman, Cobra Beer Partnership Ltd (formerly Cobra Beer), since 2007 (Founder, 1989; Chief Executive, 1989–2007); *b* 26 Nov. 1961; *s* of late Lt Gen. Faridoon Noshir Bilimoria, PVSM, ADC and of Yasmin Bilimoria; *m* 1993, Heather Walker; two *s* two *d*. *Educ:* Indian Inst. of Mgt and Commerce, Osmania Univ., Hyderabad (BCom Hons); City of London Poly. (Dip. Acctg 1982); Sidney Sussex Coll., Cambridge (BA Law 1988; half blue polo; MA; Hon. Fellow 2007); Cranfield Univ. (Business Growth Prog. 1998); London Business Sch. (Entrepreneurial Growth Prog. 2008); Harvard Business Sch. (President's Leadership Prog. 2011). ACA 1986, FCA 2002. Trainee articled chartered accountant, Ernst & Young, 1982–86, qualified chartered accountant, 1987; Consulting Accountant, Cresvale Ltd, London, 1988–89; Sales and Mktg Dir, Eur. Accounting Focus Mag., 1989; Founder, Gen. Bilimoria Wines, 1989. Non-executive Director: Brake Bros Ltd, 2004–07; Booker Gp plc, 2007–; Mem., Adv. Bd, Seven Hills, 2013–. Vis. Entrepreneur, Centre for Entrepreneurial Learning, Cambridge Univ., 2004–; Guest Lecturer: Judge Business Sch., Cambridge; Cranfield Univ. Sch. of Mgt; London Business Sch. UK Chm., Indo-British Partnership, UK Trade and Investment, DTI and FCO, 2003–09; Chairman: Indo-British Partnership Network, 2005–07; UK India Business Council, 2007–09 (Pres., 2009–12); Member: UK India Consultative Gp, FCO, 2002–03; Chancellor's Asia Task Force, 2005–10; UK-India Round Table, 2005–; Member: Nat. Employment Panel, DWP, 2001–07 (Chm., Small and Med. Size Enterprise Bd, 2001–05); New Deal Task Force, DfEE, 1999–2001; Neighbourhood Renewal Private Sector Panel, ODPM, 2003–05; RE Council of England and Wales, 2013–. Mentor, Metropolitan Police Jt Mentoring Initiative, 2002–04. Vice-Chm., Asian Business Assoc., 2003–08, Dep. Pres., 2008–10, LCCI; Mem., LCCI/Asian Business Assoc. Panel, Bank of England, 2000–03; Charter Mem., Indus Entrepreneurs, 2002–; Mem. Bd, Indus Entrepreneurs, UK, 2003–06; Founding Pres., UK Zoroastrian Chamber of Commerce, 2003–06. Member: Young Presidents' Orgn, 2000–12 (Chm., London Chapter, 2004–05); Birmingham Business Sch. Adv. Bd, 2005–; Adv. Council, CIDA Foundn UK, 2006–; Duke of York's Business Adv. Council, 2006–10; World Presidents' Orgn, 2012–; CEO World Presidents' Orgn, 2012–; E20 Steering Gp, 2013–; Enterprise Leader, Prince's Trust, 2008–. Mem., Meml Gates Cttee, 2009– (Chm., 2003–09; Vice Patron, Meml Gates Trust, 1999–2004). Mem., Pres.'s Cttee, London First, 2002–06; Ambassador: London 2012 Olympic Bid, 2005; Interactive Univ., UK, 2005–; British Liby Business and IP Centre, 2013–. Nat. Champion, Nat. Council for Grad. Entrepreneurship, 2004–. Chancellor: Thames Valley Univ., 2005–10 (Gov., 2001–04); Univ. of Birmingham, 2014–; Mem., Adv. Bd, Judge Business Sch., Univ. of Cambridge, 2008–. Comr, Royal Hosp. Chelsea, 2006–12. Gov., Ditchley Foundn, 2004– (Mem. Council, 2011–). Trustee, British Cardiovascular Res. Trust, 2006–. Patron: Rethink severe mental illness, 2003–; Children in Need Inst. UK, 2008–; Pratham UK, 2008–; British Consultancy Charitable Trust, 2008–; founding Patron, Oxford Entrepreneurs, 2004–; Member, Advisory Board: Adab Trust, 2007–; Roundhouse Trust, 2008–; Gov., Jawaharlal Nehru Meml Trust, 2013–. Trustee, St Paul's Cathedral Foundn, 2011–13. Vice-Pres., Cambridge Union. FInstD 2005; CCMI 2005. Hon. Life FRSA 2004 (Council Mem., 2004–07). Freeman, City of London; Liveryman: Drapers' Co., 2005; Brewers' Co., 2008; Chartered Accountants' Co., 2010. DL Gtr London, 2001–; Rep. DL Hounslow, 2005–10. Hon. DBus: Brunel, 2005; London Metropolitan, 2008; Hon. DLitt: Heriot-Watt, 2005; Univ. of W London, 2012; DUniv Staffs, 2006; Hon. DSc Cranfield, 2009. Numerous awards, including: Outstanding Achievement Award: Execs Assoc. of GB, 2002; ICAEW, 2005; Asian of the Year, Asian Who's Who, 2002; Entrepreneur of the Year: Asian Achievers Awards, 2003; LCCI, 2003; Nat. Business Awards, London and SE England, 2004; Business Person of the Year, LCCI, 2004; Albert Medal, RSA, 2004; Leadership Award, Dir Mag., IoD, 2008; Special Recognition Award, UK Trade and Investment India; Gold Medal, CMI, 2009. Pravasi Bharti Samman (India), 2008. *Publications:* (jtly) Bottled for Business: the less gassy guide to entrepreneurship, 2007; (jtly) Against the Grain: lessons in entrepreneurship from the founder of Cobra Beer, 2009. *Recreations:* reading, current affairs, travel, art, music, theatre, tennis, horse riding, golf, scuba diving, sailing. *Address:* Welken House, 10–11 Charterhouse Square, Barbican, EC1M 6EH. *T:* (020) 7788 2880. *E:* bilimoria@parliament.uk. *Clubs:* Carlton; Hawks, University Pitt (Cambridge); Guards' Polo; Delhi Gymkhana, Delhi Golf; Secunderabad; Kelvin Grove (Cape Town).

BILL, Lt Gen. Sir David (Robert), KCB 2011 (CB 2006); Strategy Director, FSI Europe Ltd, since 2014; *b* 17 Nov. 1954; *s* of late Robert Bill, DSO, RN and Wendy Jean Bill (*née* Booth); *m* 1981, Gabrielle Catherine Thunder; two *s* one *d*. *Educ:* Charterhouse; Welbeck Coll.; RMA Sandhurst; RMCS (BA Hons Eng 1978). Maj., Dir Mil. Ops, 1987–88; 33 Ind. Field Sqn, RE, 1989–90; DS Staff Coll., 1991–92; in Comd, 39 Engr Regt, 1992–94; Col, Army Staff Duties, 1994–97; Comdr Engr, 1997–99, BGS, 1999–2001, HQ Land Comd; rcds, 2002; GOC UK Support Comd (Germany), 2003–06; Dep. Comdr, NATO Rapid Deployable Corps, Italy, 2006–08; UK Mil. Rep. to NATO and EU, 2008–11; Comdt, RCDS, 2012–14. Col, Queen's Gurkha Engrs, 2006–13. Pres., Gurkha Bde Assoc., 2013–. *Recreations:* alpine ski-ing, golf, hockey, bridge. *Address:* Stourcastle Lodge, Gough's Close, Sturminster Newton, Dorset DT10 1BU. *E:* david.gay@the-bills.co.uk. *Club:* MCC.

BILL, Peter Anthony; author; columnist: London Evening Standard (formerly Evening Standard), since 2007; Estates Gazette, since 2009; *b* 14 March 1947; *s* of John Samuel Bill and Margaret Mary Bill; *m* 1969, Elizabeth Allen; one *s* one *d*. *Educ:* St Bartholomew's Grammar Sch., Newbury; Oxford Poly. Surveyor, construction industry: Bance & Sons, Newbury, 1962–64; Kingerlee of Oxford, 1964–69; George Wimpey, Bristol, 1969–75, and Kent, 1977–83; Anglo-American (Zambia), 1975–77; journalist: Contract Jl, 1983–85; Building mag., 1985–96 (Ed., 1990–96); Hd of Pubns, Fleming Securities, 1996–97; Ed., Estates Gazette, 1998–2009. Pres., Internat. Bldg Press, 1991–95 and 1997–2000. Mem., Develt Cttee, Duke of Edinburgh's Award, 2013–. *Publications:* Planet Property, 2013; monographs for Smith Institute on housing, building sustainable communities, and environmental policies. *Recreations:* reading, writing. *Address:* Flat 29, 43 Bartholomew Close, EC1A 7HN. *T:* (020) 7600 2871. *E:* peter.bill@me.com. *Club:* Reform.

BILLARI, Prof. Francesco Candeloro, FBA 2014; Professor of Sociology and Demography and Head, Department of Sociology, University of Oxford, since 2012; Fellow, Nuffield College, Oxford, since 2012; *b* Milan, 13 Oct. 1970; *s* of Giovanni Billari and Vera Billari (*née* Pullara); *m* 1996, Chiara de Florio la Rocca; five *c*. *Educ:* Univ. Bocconi (Laurea Economia Politica 1994); Univ. di Padova (Dottorato di Ricerca (Demografia) 1998). Hd, Res. Gp, Max Planck Inst. for Demographic Res., 1999–2002; Prof. of Demography, 2002–12, Vice-Rector of Develt, 2009–12, Univ. Bocconi. Dist. Res. Schol., Univ. of Pennsylvania, 2008–09. Ed.-in-Chief, Advances in Life Course Res., 2008–. *Recreations:* family, ski-ing, football. *Address:* Department of Sociology, University of Oxford, Manor Road Building, Manor Road, Oxford OX1 3UG. *T:* (01865) 281933, *Fax:* (01865) 286171. *E:* francesco.billari@nuffield.ox.ac.uk.

BILLER, Prof. Peter Paul Arpad, DPhil; FBA 2012; FRHistS; Professor of Medieval History, University of York, since 2001; *b* Stanmore, Middx, 9 April 1945; *s* of Victor and Klara Biller; *m* 1973, Margherita, (Miggy), Minio-Paluello; two *d*. *Educ:* St Benedict's, Ealing; Oriel Coll., Oxford (BA Modern Hist. 1966; MA 1970; DPhil 1974). FRHistS 1987. Temp. Lectr, Univ. of Keele, 1969–70; University of York: Temp. Lectr, 1970–71; Lectr, 1971–93; Sen. Lectr, 1993–2001. Vis. Fellow, All Souls Coll., Oxford, 1990; British Acad. Marc Fitch Sen. Res. Reader, 1993–95; Vis. Prof., Écoles des Hautes Études en Sci. Sociale, Paris, 2001. Antiquary Essay Prize, Denys Hay Seminar in Medieval and Renaissance Hist., Univ. of Edinburgh, 1986–87. *Publications:* (ed with A. Hudson) Heresy and Literacy, 1000–1530, 1994; (ed with A. Minnis) Medieval Theology and the Natural Body, 1997; (ed with A. Minnis) Handling Sin: confessions in the Middle Ages, 1998; (ed with R. B. Dobson) The Medieval Church: universities, heresy and the religious life: essays in honour of Gordon Leff, 1999; The Measure of Multitude: population in Medieval thought, 2000 (Longman/History Today Best Hist. Book of Year (jtly), 2001); (ed with J. Ziegler) Religion and Medicine in the Middle Ages, 2001; The Waldenses 1170–1530: between a religious order and a church, 2001; (ed with C. Bruschi) Texts and the Repression of Medieval Heresy, 2003; (ed jtly) Inquisitors and Heretics in Thirteenth-Century Languedoc: edition and translation of Toulouse inquisition depositions, 1273–1282, 2011; contribs to learned jls incl. Past and Present, Jl Ecclesiastical Hist. *Recreations:* grandchildren, cooking and entertaining, art, cinema, music, theatre. *Address:* Department of History, University of York, Heslington, York YO10 5DD. *T:* (01904) 624783, *Fax:* (01904) 322955. *E:* pete.biller@york.ac.uk.

BILLETT, Paul Rodney, CB 1981; *b* 19 Feb. 1921; *s* of late Arthur William and Grace Hilda Billett; *m* 1st, 1945, Muriel Gwendoline Marsh (*d* 1977); one *s*; 2nd, 1985, Eileen May Nourse. *Educ:* Commonweal and College Grammar Schools, Swindon. Entered Exchequer and Audit Dept, 1939. Served RASC, 1941–46. Deputy Secretary, Exchequer and Audit Dept, 1975–81 (retired). *Address:* Wynthorpe, Cornsland, Brentwood, Essex CM14 4JL. *T:* (01277) 224830.

BILLEY, Emma Marion; *see* Ward, E. M.

BILLINGHAM, family name of **Baroness Billingham**.

BILLINGHAM, Baroness *cr* 2000 (Life Peer), of Banbury in the co. of Oxfordshire; **Angela Theodora Billingham;** JP; *b* 31 July 1939; *d* of late Theodore Vincent Case and Eva Case (*née* Saxby); *m* 1962, Anthony Peter Billingham (*d* 1992); two *d*. *Educ:* Aylesbury GS; London Univ. Teacher, 1960–90; Examiner, 1990–95. Mayor of Banbury, 1976; Member (Lab): Banbury BC, 1970–74; Cherwell DC, 1974–84; Oxfordshire CC, 1993–94. Contested (Lab) Banbury, 1992. MEP (Lab) Northants and Blaby, 1994–99; contested (Lab) E Midlands Reg., 1999. Chief Whip, Party of European Socialists, EP, 1995–99. Opposition spokesman for sport, H of L, 2013–. Member: Cttee on Olympic and Paralympic Legacy, H of L, 2013–; Eur. Sub-Cttee C, EU Russia Relns, H of L, 2014–. Chm., Lords and Commons Tennis Club, 2002–; Mem., H of L Bridge Team, 2001–. Chm., Corby Urban Regeneration Bd, 2001–07. JP N Oxfordshire and Bicester, 1976. *Recreations:* tennis, gardening, bridge, cinema, grandchildren. *Address:* 6 Crediton Hill, NW6 1HP; c/o House of Lords, SW1A 0PW. *Clubs:* All England Lawn Tennis, Cumberland Lawn Tennis (W Hampstead).

See also Z. A. Billingham, S. A. Jones.

BILLINGHAM, Mark Philip David; writer and comedian; crime novelist, since 2001; *b* Birmingham, 2 July 1961; *s* of Jeff Billingham and Patricia Billingham (*née* Grice, now Thompson); *m* 1994, Claire Winyard; one *s* one *d*. *Educ:* King Edward VI Camp Hill Grammar Sch. for Boys; Birmingham Univ. (BA Hons Drama and Th. Arts). Stand-up comedian, 1987–2012; television actor: Boon, 1984; Dempsey and Makepeace, 1985; Juliet Bravo, 1985; Maid Marian and Her Merry Men, 1989–92 (also writer, 1992); Harry's Mad, 1993–96 (also writer, 1993); Knight School (also writer), 1997–98; writer for television: What's That Noise?, 1995–96 (also presenter); The Cramp Twins, 1998–2000. *Publications:* Knight School, 1998; Sleepyhead, 2001; Scaredy Cat, 2002; Lazybones, 2003; The Burning Girl, 2004; Lifeless, 2005; Buried, 2006; Death Message, 2007; In the Dark, 2008; Bloodline, 2009; From the Dead, 2010; Good As Dead, 2011; Rush of Blood, 2012; The Dying Hours, 2013; The Bones Beneath, 2014; Great Lost Albums, 2014; Time of Death, 2015; *as Will Peterson:* Triskellion, 2008; Triskellion 2: The Burning, 2009; Triskellion 3: The Gathering, 2010. *Recreations:* music, especially country (alt and cheesy), playing the guitar badly, movies, poker, tennis, food, embarrassing my children, supporting Wolverhampton Wanderers in spite of everything, trying to smuggle examples of Victorian taxidermy into the house. *Address:* c/o Lutyens & Rubinstein, 21 Kensington Park Road, W11 2EU. *T:* (020) 7792 4855. *E:* mail@markbillingham.com. *Clubs:* One Alfred Place, Union.

BILLINGHAM, Zoe Ann, (Mrs Dennis Skinner); HM Inspector of Constabulary, since 2009; *b* Kings Lynn, Norfolk, 31 Dec. 1964; *d* of late Anthony Peter Billingham and of Baroness Billingham, *qv*; *m* 1997, Dennis Skinner, *s* of Dennis Edward Skinner, *qv*; one *s*. *Educ:* Banbury Comprehensive Sch.; St Hugh's Coll., Oxford (BA Hons PPE 1986); Coll. of Law, London. Policy Advr, London Bor. of Brent, 1987–90; Policy Advr, 1990–93, Solicitor, 1993–2000, London Bor. of Camden; Develt Manager, 2000–02, Dep. Dir, Prime Minister's Office of Public Services Reform, 2002–04, Cabinet Office; Dir, Community Safety and Sustainability, Audit Commn, 2004–09. *Recreations:* losing to 13 year old son at tennis, photography, travel. *Address:* c/o HM Inspectorate of Constabulary, 6th Floor, Globe House, 89 Eccleston Square, SW1V 1PN. *T:* (020) 7802 1800. *Club:* Cumberland Lawn Tennis.

BILLINGS, Rev. Canon Dr Alan Roy; Police and Crime Commissioner for South Yorkshire, since 2014; *b* Leicester, 7 Oct. 1942; *s* of Paul William Stanley Billings and Dorothy May Billings (*née* Siddons); *m* 1966, Daphne Thomas (marr. diss. 1993); two *s*; *m* 1994, Linda Woodhead (marr. diss. 2002); *m* 2007, Veronica Mary Hardstaff, *qv*. *Educ:* Wyggeston Grammar Sch., Leicester; Emmanuel Coll., Cambridge (BA Theol Tripos 1965; MA 1969); Bristol Univ. (PGCE); Leicester Univ. (MEd); New York Theol Seminary (DMin 1987); Lincoln Theol Coll. Ordained deacon, 1968, priest, 1969; Curate, St Mary, Knighton, Leicester, 1968–72; Vicar, St Silas, Broomhall, Sheffield, 1972–76; Vicar, St Mary the Virgin, Beighton, 1976–77; Hd of RE, Broadway Sch., Barnsley, 1977–81; Vicar, St Mary, Walkley, Sheffield, 1981–86; Vice Principal, and Dir, Oxford Inst. for Church and Society, Ripon Coll., Cuddesdon, Oxford, 1986–92; Principal, W Midlands Ministerial Trng Course, and Actg Principal, Queen's Coll., Birmingham, 1992–94; Vicar, St George, Kendal and St John, Grayrigg, 1994–2007; Hon. Sen. Res. Fellow, and Dir, Centre for Ethics and Religion, Lancaster Univ., 1996–2007. Schs Adjudicator, 1999–2006. Member: Bd, Funding Agency for Schs, 1997–99; Community Cohesion Panel, Home Office, 2002–04; Youth Justice Bd for England and Wales, 2004–10; England Cttee, Big Lottery Fund, 2007–13. Hon. Canon, Carlisle Cathedral, 2005–07, now Canon Emeritus. Mem. (Lab), Sheffield CC, 1975–86 (Dep. Leader, 1980–86). FRSA. *Publications:* Dying and Grieving, 2002; Secular Lives, Sacred Hearts, 2004; God and Community Cohesion, 2009; Making God Possible, 2010; Lost Church, 2013; The Dove, the Fig Leaf and the Sword, 2014. *Recreation:* writing stories for grandchildren. *Address:* 43 Northfield Court, Sheffield S10 1QR. *T:* (0114) 267 6549. *E:* alanbillingsuk@yahoo.co.uk. *Clubs:* Travellers; Trades and Labour (Sheffield).

BILLINGTON, Brenda May, OBE 2012; FRCS, FRCOphth; Consultant Ophthalmic Surgeon, Royal Berkshire Hospital, Reading, 1985–2011; President, Royal College of Ophthalmologists, 2006–09; *b* 19 Jan. 1951; *d* of Gwynn and Leslie Billington; *m* 1987, James (marr. diss. 1997); one *s*. *Educ:* Queen Anne's Sch., Caversham; Univ. of Birmingham (MB ChB 1974). FRCS 1980; FRCOphth 1989. Resident Surgical Officer, Moorfields Eye Hosp., 1978–81; Sen. Registrar in Ophthalmology, St Thomas' Hosp. and Moorfields Eye Hosp.,

1982–85. Liveryman, Soc. of Apothecaries, 1989–. Fellow, European Bd of Ophthalmology, 2003. *Publications:* contribs to ophthalmic scientific jls, mainly clinical studies of treatment for patients with retinal detachment. *Recreations:* returning purchases to clothes shops, excursions with nieces and nephew, walking with the dog. *Club:* Royal Society of Medicine.

BILLINGTON, Brian John, (Bill); consultant on roads and transport, since 1998; *b* 25 Feb. 1939; *s* of late Kenneth Jack Billington and Doris Violet Billington; *m* 1965, Gillian Elizabeth Annis; two *d*. *Educ:* Slough Grammar Sch.; The Polytechnic, Regent Street (BSc(Econ)); LSE (MSc). Lectr, The Polytechnic, Regent Street, 1966–68; Min. of Power, later Dept of Energy, 1969–74; Dept of Transport, later Dept of Envmt, Transport and the Regions, 1974–98; Highways Agency, 1994–98; Under Sec., 1991–98. *Address:* 100 Fox Lane, N13 4AX. *T:* (020) 8886 0898.

BILLINGTON, Dr James Hadley; Librarian of Congress, USA, since 1987; *b* 1 June 1929; *s* of Nelson Billington and Jane Coolbaugh; *m* 1957, Marjorie Anne Brennan; two *s* two *d*. *Educ:* Princeton Univ.; Balliol College, Oxford (Rhodes Scholar; DPhil 1953). Served US Army, 1953–56. Harvard University: Instructor in History, 1957–58; Asst Prof. of History and Res. Fellow, Russian Res. Center, 1958–59; Asst Prof. of History, 1958–61; Associate Prof. of History, 1962–64, Prof., 1964–73, Princeton; Dir, Woodrow Wilson Internat. Center for Scholars, Washington, 1973–87. Chm., Bd of Foreign Scholarships, 1971–73. Visiting Research Professor: Inst. of History, Acad. of Scis, USSR, 1966–67; Univ. of Helsinki, 1960–61; Ecole des Hautes Etudes en Scis Sociales, Paris, 1985, 1988; Vis. Lectr, USA, Europe, Asia; Guggenheim Fellow, 1960–61. Writer and host, The Face of Russia, TV series, 1998. Member: Amer. Acad. of Arts and Scis; Amer. Philosophical Soc.; Russian Acad. of Scis; numerous hon. degrees; Hon. DLitt Oxon, 2002. Chevalier and Comdr, Ordre des Arts et des Lettres. *Publications:* Mikhailovsky and Russian Populism, 1958; The Icon and the Axe: an interpretive history of Russian culture, 1966; The Arts of Russia, 1970; Fire in the Minds of Men: origins of the Revolutionary Faith, 1980; Russia Transformed: breakthrough to hope, Moscow, August 1991, 1992; The Face of Russia, 1998; Russia in Search of Itself, 2004; contribs to learned jls. *Address:* Office of the Librarian, Library of Congress, 101 Independence Avenue, Washington, DC 20540–1000, USA. *T:* (202) 7075205.

BILLINGTON, Kevin; film, theatre and television director; *b* 12 June 1934; *s* of Richard and Margaret Billington; *m* 1967, Lady Rachel Mary Pakenham (*see* Lady Rachel Billington); one *s* two *d* (and one *s* decd). *Educ:* Bryanston Sch.; Queens' Coll., Cambridge (BA); Open Univ. (MusDip 1999; BA Hons 2002; MA (Mus) 2007). Film dir, BBC prog., Tonight, 1960–63; documentary film dir, BBC, 1963–67; films include: A Sort of Paradise; Many Mexicos; The Mexican Attitude; Twilight of Empire; Mary McCarthy's Paris; These Humble Shores; Matador; A Few Castles in Spain; The English Cardinal; A Socialist Childhood; Madison Avenue, USA; ATV documentary, All The Queen's Men. *Feature Film Director:* Interlude, 1967; The Rise and Rise of Michael Rimmer, 1969; The Light at the Edge of the World, 1970; Voices, 1974; Reflections, 1984. *Television Director:* And No One Can Save Her, 1973; Once Upon a Time is Now (documentary), 1978; The Music Will Never Stop (documentary), 1979; Henry VIII, 1979; The Jail Diary of Albie Sachs, 1980; The Good Soldier, 1981; Outside Edge, 1982; The Sonnets of William Shakespeare, 1984; Heartland, 1989; Small Doses, 1990; A Time to Dance, 1992. *Theatre Director:* Find Your Way Home, 1970; Me, 1973; The Birthday Party, 1974; The Caretaker, 1975; Bloody Neighbours, 1975; Emigrés, 1976; The Homecoming, 1978; Quartermaine's Terms, 1982; The Deliberate Death of a Polish Priest, 1985 (Channel Four, 1986); The Philanthropist, 1986; The Lover, and A Slight Ache (double bill), 1987; The Breadwinner, 1989; Veterans Day, 1989; Quartermaine's Terms, 1993; Old Times, 1994; Six Characters in Search of an Author, 1999; Our Country's Good, 1999; Victory, 2001; Wild Honey, 2002. *Screenplays:* Bodily Harm, 2000; Loving Attitudes, 2001. Chm., BAFTA, 1989–90 and 1990–91. Screenwriters' Guild Award, 1966 and 1967; Guild of TV Producers and Directors Award, 1966 and 1967. *Recreation:* swimming. *Address:* The Court House, Poyntington, Sherborne, Dorset DT9 4LF. *Club:* Garrick.

BILLINGTON, Michael, OBE 2013; Drama Critic of The Guardian, since 1971; *b* 16 Nov. 1939; *s* of Alfred Billington and Patricia (*née* Bradshaw); *m* 1978, Jeanine Bradlaugh. *Educ:* Warwick Sch.; St Catherine's Coll., Oxford (BA; Hon. Fellow 2005). Trained as journalist with Liverpool Daily Post and Echo, 1961–62; Public Liaison Officer and Director for Lincoln Theatre Co., 1962–64; reviewed plays, films and television for The Times, 1965–71. Film Critic: Birmingham Post, 1968–78; Illustrated London News, 1968–81; London Arts Correspondent, New York Times, 1978–; Drama Critic, Country Life, 1987–. Contributor to numerous radio and television Arts programmes, incl. Kaleidoscope, Critics' Forum, The Book Programme, Arena. Presenter, The Billington Interview and Theatre Call, BBC World Service. Writer and Presenter, television profiles of Peggy Ashcroft, Peter Hall and Alan Ayckbourn. Prof. of Drama, Colorado Coll., 1981; Vis. Prof., KCL, 2002–. FKC 2009. Hon. DLitt Warwick, 2009. IPC Critic of the Year, 1974; Pragnell Shakespeare Birthday Award, 2009. *Publications:* The Modern Actor, 1974; How Tickled I Am, 1977; (ed) The Performing Arts, 1980; The Guinness Book of Theatre Facts and Feats, 1982; Alan Ayckbourn, 1983; Tom Stoppard, 1987; Peggy Ashcroft, 1988; (ed) Twelfth Night, 1990; One Night Stands, 1993; The Life and Work of Harold Pinter, 1996; (ed) Stage and Screen Lives, 2001; State of the Nation, 2007. *Recreations:* work, travel, cricket. *Address:* 15 Hearne Road, W4 3NJ. *T:* (020) 8995 0455.

BILLINGTON, Lady Rachel (Mary), OBE 2012; writer; *b* 11 May 1942; *d* of 7th Earl of Longford, KG, PC, and Elizabeth, Countess of Longford, CBE; *m* 1967, Kevin Billington, *qv*; one *s* two *d* (and one *s* decd). *Educ:* London Univ. (BA English). Work includes: short stories; four BBC radio plays; two BBC TV plays, Don't be Silly, 1979, Life After Death, 1981. Reviewer and feature writer. Co-editor, Inside Time, 1991–. Trustee: Tablet Trust, 1991–; Longford Trust, 2002–; Siobhan Dowd Trust, 2008–. *Publications:* All Things Nice, 1969; The Big Dipper, 1970; Lilacs out of the Dead Land, 1971; Cock Robin, 1973; Beautiful, 1974; A Painted Devil, 1975; A Woman's Age, 1979; Occasion of Sin, 1982; The Garish Day, 1985; Loving Attitudes, 1988; Theo and Matilda, 1990; Bodily Harm, 1992; The Family Year, 1992; The Great Umbilical: mother, daughter, mother, 1994; Magic and Fate, 1996; Perfect Happiness: the sequel to Emma, 1996; Tiger Sky, 1998; A Woman's Life, 2002; The Space Between, 2004; One Summer, 2006; Lies and Loyalties, 2008; The Missing Boy, 2010; Maria and the Admiral, 2012; *for children:* Rosanna and the Wizard-Robot, 1981; The First Christmas, 1983; Star-Time, 1984; The First Easter, 1987; The First Miracles, 1990; Life of Jesus, 1996; Life of St Francis, 1999; Far-out, 2002; There's More to Life, 2006; Poppy's Hero, 2012; Poppy's Angel, 2013; Glory: a story of Gallipoli, 2015. *Recreations:* nature, painting. *Address:* The Court House, Poyntington, near Sherborne, Dorset DT9 4LF. *Clubs:* Society of Authors, PEN (Pres., 1997–2000).

BILSLAND, Christopher Nigel, OBE 2014; Chamberlain, City of London Corporation, 2007–14; *b* 5 May 1954; *s* of John Bilsland and Dallas Aileen Bilsland; *m* 1980, Gillian Smith; one *s* one *d*. *Educ:* Doncaster Grammar Sch.; Chesterfield Coll. of Technol. CPFA 1976. Accountant, Doncaster MBC, 1972–79; Chief Auditor, Derby CC, 1979–82; Sen. Manager, Deloitte Haskins & Sells, 1982–87; Asst County Treas., Hampshire CC, 1987–91; County Treas., Somerset CC, 1991–2006. Mem. Council, CIPFA, 1998–2011 (Pres., 2011–12). Chm., Lewisham and Southwark Coll., 2014–. *Recreations:* high handicap golfer, horseracing, taking credit for children's achievements. *Address:* Alpenhaus, 3 Laurel Drive, Oxted, Surrey RH8 9DT.

BILTCLIFFE, Moira Elizabeth; *see* Buffini, M. E.

BINDMAN, Sir Geoffrey (Lionel), Kt 2007; Consultant, Bindmans LLP (formerly Bindman & Partners), Solicitors, since 2004 (Senior Partner, 1974–2004); *b* 3 Jan. 1933; *s* of Dr Gerald and Lena Bindman; *m* 1961, Lynn Janice Winton; two *s* one *d*. *Educ:* Newcastle upon Tyne Royal Grammar Sch.; Oriel Coll., Oxford (BCL 1956; MA 1959). Admitted Solicitor, 1959; Teaching Fellow, Northwestern Univ., Ill, 1959–60; Partner, Lawford & Co., 1965–74. Legal adviser: Race Relations Bd, 1966–76; CRE, 1976–83. Visiting Professor of Law: UCLA, 1982; UCL, 1990–; London South Bank Univ., 2003–. Hon. Pres., Discrimination Law Assoc., 1999–; Chm., Soc. of Labour Lawyers, 1999–2001. Chm., British Inst. of Human Rights, 2005–13. Pres., Client Interviewing Comp. for England and Wales, 1990–. Columnist, New Law Journal, 2006–. Trustee: Wordsworth Trust, 1997–2013; Helen Bamber Foundn, 2006–13; ATG Trust (Pres., 2010–); Lawyers for Palestinian Human Rights, 2011–; Vice-Pres., One World Trust, 2006–; Pres., John Thelwall Soc., 2012–. Hon. QC 2011. Hon. LLD: De Montfort, 2000; Kingston, 2006. Liberty Award for Lifetime Human Rights Achievement, 1999; Centenary Award for Human Rights, Law Soc. Gazette, 2003. *Publications:* (jtly) Race and Law, 1972; (ed) South Africa: human rights and the rule of law, 1988. *Recreations:* walking, music, book collecting. *Address:* (office) 236 Gray's Inn Road, WC1X 8HB. *T:* (020) 7833 4433.

BING, His Honour Inigo Geoffrey; a Circuit Judge, 2000–12; *b* 1 April 1944; *s* of late Geoffrey Henry Cecil Bing, QC and Crystal Frances Bing; *m* 1st, 1980, Shirley-Anne Holmes (*née* Benka) (*d* 2003); three step *c*; 2nd, 2004, Judith Caroline Anne Hughes, *qv*. *Educ:* St Olave's Grammar Sch., Southwark; Birmingham Univ. (LLB). Called to the Bar, Inner Temple, 1967, Bencher, 2012; practised London and SE Circuit; a District Judge (Magistrates' Courts) (formerly a Metropolitan Stipendiary Magistrate), 1989–2000; a Recorder, 1996–2000. Mem., Parole Bd, 2002–09. Mem. (Lab) London Borough of Lambeth, 1971–78 (Chm., F and GP Cttee, 1974–78); Co-founder, Lambeth Community Law Centre. Contested Braintree: (SDP) 1983; (SDP/Alliance) 1987. *Publications:* Criminal Procedure and Sentencing in the Magistrates' Court, 1990, 5th edn 1999. *Recreations:* music, travel, studying history and philosophy. *Club:* Reform (Chm., 2006–07).

BING, Judith Caroline Anne; *see* Hughes, J. C. A.

BINGHAM, family name of **Earl of Lucan** and **Baron Clanmorris**.

BINGHAM, Lord; George Charles Bingham; *b* 21 Sept. 1967; *s* and *heir* of 7th Earl of Lucan, *qv*. *Educ:* Eton; Trinity Hall, Cambridge. *Clubs:* Turf, White's, Pratt's.
See also Lady C. Bingham.

BINGHAM, Andrew Russell; MP (C) High Peak, since 2010; *b* Buxton, 23 June 1962; *s* of late Anthony Russell Bingham and of Mary Dorothea Bingham; *m* 1986, Jayne Elizabeth Dranfield. *Educ:* Long Lane Sec. Sch., Chapel-en-le-Frith; High Peak Coll. of Further Educn. Company Dir, A.R.B. Sales Ltd, 1983–2004. Mem. (C) High Peak BC, 1999– (Chm., Social Inclusion Cttee, 2003–07). Contested (C) High Peak, 2005. *Recreations:* cricket, football, cooking. *Address:* House of Commons, SW1A 0AA. *T:* (020) 7219 7086. *E:* andrew.bingham.mp@parliament.uk.

BINGHAM, Lady Camilla; QC 2013; *b* London, 30 June 1970; *yr d* of 7th Earl of Lucan, *qv* and of Veronica Mary (*née* Duncan); *m* 1998, Michael Gordon Bloch, *qv*; four *s*. *Educ:* St Swithun's Sch., Winchester; Balliol Coll., Oxford (BA Lit. Hum. 1992). Called to the Bar, Inner Temple, 1996; in practice as barrister, specialising in commercial litigation and arbitration. *Address:* One Essex Court, Temple, EC4Y 9AR. *T:* (020) 7583 2000. *E:* cbingham@oeclaw.co.uk.
See also Lord Bingham.

BINGHAM, Hon. Charlotte Mary Thérèse; playwright and novelist; *b* 29 June 1942; *d* of 7th Baron Clanmorris (John Bingham) and of Madeleine Mary, *d* of late Clement Ebel; *m* 1964, Terence Brady, *qv*; one *s* one *d*. *Educ:* The Priory, Haywards Heath; Sorbonne. *TV series* with Terence Brady: Boy Meets Girl; Take Three Girls; Upstairs Downstairs; Away From It All; Play for Today; No—Honestly; Yes—Honestly; Pig in the Middle; Thomas and Sarah; The Complete Lack of Charm of the Bourgeoisie; Nanny; Oh Madeline! (USA TV); Father Matthew's Daughter; Forever Green; The Upper Hand; *TV films:* Love With a Perfect Stranger, 1986; Losing Control, 1987; The Seventh Raven, 1987; This Magic Moment, 1988; screenwriter with Terence Brady, Riders, 1993; *stage:* with Terence Brady: (contrib.) The Sloane Ranger Revue, 1985; I Wish, I Wish, 1989; (adaptation) The Shell Seekers, 1999; *radio* with Terence Brady: Hear Hear! The Victoria Line. *Publications:* Coronet among the Weeds, 1963; Lucinda, 1965; Coronet among the Grass, 1972; Belgravia, 1983; Country Life, 1984; At Home, 1986; To Hear A Nightingale, 1988; The Business, 1989; In Sunshine or In Shadow, 1991; Stardust, 1992; By Invitation, 1993; Nanny, 1993; Change of Heart, 1994 (Romantic Novel of the Year Award, 1995, Romantic Novelists' Assoc.); Debutantes, 1995; The Nightingale Sings, 1996; Grand Affair, 1997; Love Song, 1998; The Kissing Garden, 1999; The Love Knot, 2000; The Blue Note, 2000; The Season, 2001; Summertime, 2001; Distant Music, 2002; The Chestnut Tree, 2002; The Wind off the Sea, 2003; The Moon at Midnight, 2003; Daughters of Eden, 2004; House of Flowers, 2004; The Magic Hour, 2005; Friday's Girl, 2005; Out of the Blue, 2006; In Distant Fields, 2006; The White Marriage, 2007; Goodnight Sweetheart, 2007; The Enchanted, 2008; The Land of Summer, 2008; The Daisy Club, 2009; Mums on the Run, 2010; A Dip before Breakfast, 2011; The Light on the Swan, 2014; with Terence Brady: Victoria, 1972; Rose's Story, 1973; Victoria and Company, 1974; Yes—Honestly, 1977. *Recreations:* horses, watching other people garden. *Address:* United Authors Ltd, 11–15 Betterton Street, WC2H 9BP. *Club:* Society of Authors.

BINGHAM, Sir (Eardley) Max, Kt 1988; QC (Tas.) 1974; Chairman, Queensland Criminal Justice Commission, 1989–92; *b* 18 March 1927; *s* of Thomas Eardley and Olive Bingham; *m* 1952, Margaret Garrett Jesson; three *s* one *d*. *Educ:* Univ. of Tasmania (LLB (Hons)); Lincoln Coll., Oxford (BCL; Rhodes Schol., 1950); Univ. of California at Berkeley (Harkness Commonwealth Fund Fellow, 1963). RANR, 1945–46. Legal practice, and teaching, Univ. of Tasmania, 1953–69. MHA Tasmania, 1969–84; Attorney-General, 1969–72; Leader of the Opposition, 1972–79, Dep. Leader of the Opposition, 1982; Dep. Premier of Tas., 1982–84. Mem., Nat. Crime Authority, 1984–87. Hon. LLD Tasmania, 1998. *Publications:* contribs to jls. *Recreations:* reading, music. *Address:* Unit 8, Queenborough Rise, Peel Street, Sandy Bay, Tas 7005, Australia. *Clubs:* Tasmanian, Royal Yacht of Tasmania (Hobart).

BINGHAM, James Stewart, TD 1982; FRCP, FRCPE, FRCOG; Consultant Physician in Genitourinary and HIV Medicine, Guy's and St Thomas' NHS Foundation Trust (formerly St Thomas' Hospital, then Guy's and St Thomas' Hospital Trust), 1992–2011; *b* 31 July 1945; *s* of Dr William Bingham and Nora Mary Bingham (*née* Beckett); *m* 1974, Elizabeth Eleanor Stewart; one *s*. *Educ:* Campbell Coll., Belfast; Queen's Univ., Belfast (MB BCh BAO 1969). MRCOG 1974, FRCOG 1989; FRCPE 1994; FRCP 1999. Initial career in obstetrics and gynaecology in NI, Rhodesia and Canada, 1970–75; Middlesex Hospital: Sen. Registrar in Venereology, 1975–77; Consultant in Genitourinary Med., 1977–92; Consultant Physician in Genitourinary Med., Bromley Hosps, 1992–94. Hon. Consultant in Genitourinary Medicine to the Army, 2000–09. Pres. Exec. Cttee, Internat. Union against Sexually Transmitted Infections, 2001–03 (Mem., 1995–; Hon. Treas., 1995–99; Mem. jt initiative with WHO Europe and Open Soc. Inst. to introduce protocols to Central Asia, 2004–06; Sen. Counsellor, 2005–12); Member: Council, Med. Soc. for Study of Venereal Diseases, 1979–82, 1983–97, 1999–2001 (Hon. Treas., 1986–93; Pres., 1993–95; Hon. Life Fellow, 2007); Cttee, Assoc. for Genitourinary Medicine, 1993–2003 (Chm., 1999–2001); Specialist Adv. Cttee in Genitourinary Medicine, Jt Cttee for Higher Med. Trng, 1988–95, 2003–09 (Sec., 1989–93;

Chm., 1993–95); Working Party on Med. Audit in Genitourinary Medicine, 1989–94; Dermatology and Venereology sub-cttee, Central Consultants' and Specialists' Cttee, BMA, 1992–2008 (Chm., 1998–2000); Working Gp on Read Codes (Genitourinary Medicine), 1993–94; Exec. Cttee, British HIV Assoc., 1996–2000 (Founding Hon. Treas., 1996–2000; Hon. Fellow, 2002). Examiner in Genitourinary Medicine: Soc. of Apothecaries, 1982–2007 (Convenor, 1992–95); Univ. of Liverpool, 1996–98; Prince of Songkla Univ., Thailand, 2000–02; UCL, 2005–07. WHO: Consultant, Bulgaria, 1993; Advr, STD interventions for preventing HIV infection, Geneva, 1998; UK rep., Dermatovenereology cttee, Union of European Monospecialties, 2003–09 (Treas., 2005–09). Mem., Editl Bd, Eur. S&D Guidelines, 2008–09. Trustee: BMA Foundn for AIDS, subseq. Med. Foundn for AIDS and Sexual Health, 2000–06; River House, 1996–2002. 257 (NI) Field Ambulance and 217 General Hosp. RAMC(V), TA, 1969–83. Life FRSocMed, 2009. Hon. Life Fellow Oration, 2009, Harrison Lect., 2010, BASHH. Silver Medal Oration, Inst. of Venereology, India, 2000. Freeman, City of London, 2013; Yeoman, Apothecaries' Soc., 2012. *Publications:* Sexually Transmitted Diseases: a pocket picture guide, 1984, 2nd edn 1989; articles and chapters on aspects of genital tract and HIV infections. *Recreations:* military and medical history, gardening. *E:* james.bingham@btinternet.com. *Clubs:* Army and Navy, City Volunteer Officers, Royal Automobile.

BINGHAM, Col Jeremy David S.; *see* Smith-Bingham.

BINGHAM, John, CBE 1991; FRS 1977; Plant Breeding International, Cambridge, 1981–91; *b* 19 June 1930; *s* of Thomas Frederick Bingham and Emma Maud Lusher; *m* 1983, Jadwiga Anna Siedlecka; one *s.* Mem. of staff, Plant Breeding Inst. of Cambridge, subseq. Plant Breeding Internat. Cambridge Ltd, 1954–91. Has researched in plant breeding, culminating in production of improved winter wheat varieties for British agriculture. Pres., Royal Norfolk Agricl Assoc., 1991. Hon. FRASE, 1983. Hon. ScD UEA, 1992. Res. Medal, RASE, 1975; Mullard Medal of Royal Society, 1975; Massey Ferguson Nat. Award for Services to UK Agric., 1984. *Recreations:* farming, conservation of wild life. *Address:* Hereward Barn, Church Lane, Mattishall Burgh, Dereham, Norfolk NR20 3QZ. *T:* (01362) 858354.

BINGHAM, Judith Caroline; composer; *b* 21 June 1952; *d* of Jack Bingham and Peggy (*née* McGowan); *m* 1985, Andrew Petrow (marr. diss. 2011). *Educ:* High Storrs Grammar Sch., Sheffield; Royal Acad. of Music (Principal's Prize for Music, 1972; ARAM 1997). Mem., BBC Singers, 1983–95. *Major works:* The Divine Image, 1976; Cocaine Lil, 1977; Flynn, 1979; Chamouni, 1982; Cradle Song of the Blessed Virgin, Scenes From Nature, 1983; Just Before Dawn, 1985; A Cold Spell, 1987; Christmas Past, Christmas Present, 1988; Chartres, 1988; Dove Cottage by Moonlight, 1989; Four Minute Mile, 1991; The Stars Above, The Earth Below, 1991; Unpredictable But Providential, 1991; Irish Tenebrae, The Uttermost, 1992; O Magnum Mysterium, Santa Casa, Beyond Redemption, 1994; Evening Canticles, Epiphany, Salt in the Blood, The Red Hot Nail, 1995; The Mysteries of Adad, The Temple at Karnak, No Discord, 1996; Gleams of a Remoter World, The Waning Moon, Below the Surface Stream, Chapman's Pool, 1997; Missa Brevis, The Clouded Heaven, Bassoon Concerto, Unheimlich, Vorarlberg, Shelley Dreams, 1998; The Shooting Star, Walzerspiele, The Cathedral of Trees, Water Lilies, Otherworld, 1999; Necklace of Light, Annunciation, The Shepherd's Gift, St Bride, Assisted by Angels, These are Our Footsteps, 2000; 50 Shades of Green; The Shadow Side of Joy Finzi, 2001; Beneath these alien stars, 2001; Bright Spirit, 2001; My Father's Arms, 2002; Ave Verum Corpus, enter GHOST, The Mystery of Boranup, Aquileia, Uppon the First Sight of New England, Incarnation with Shepherds Dancing, 2002; Missa Brevis No 2, The Road to Emmaeus, The Moon over Westminster Cathedral, Ancient Sunlight, The Christmas Truce, Bach's Tomb, O Clap Your Hands, 2003; The Ivory Tree, The Secret Garden, The Yearning Strong, Limehouse Nocturne, Lo in the Silent Night, Our Faith is a Light, Margaret Forsaken, Down and Out, Touch'd by Heavenly Fire, In Nomine, 2004; Ghost Towns of the American West, A Formal Order, Down and Out, We Two, Edington Canticles, The Shepheardes Calender, 2005; Hidden City, La Boiteuse, An Ancient Music, Winter's Pilgrimage, My Heart Strangely Warm'd, The Cruelty of the Gods, The Flying Hours, The Morning-Watch, Capriccio, 2006; Missa Brevis, Awake My Soul, The Hired Hand, Ziggurat, Jacob's Ladder, Fantasia, Shakespeare Requiem, 2007; She Walks in Beauty, Byron, violent progress, Harvest, Shadow Aspect, 2008; See and Keep Silent, Billingbear, Actaeon, Annunciation II, Distant Thunder, Tomkat Murr, 2009; Wells Service, A Bird is Singing, The Pilgrims Travels, Mary Anning, Annunciation III, Now the Magi Arrive, Holy of Holies, 2010; The Everlasting Crown, Corpus Christi Carol, Ave Virgo Sanctissimi, Eden, Celticity, 2011; London Haiku, The Hythe, Leonardo (Bassoon Concerto 2), 2012; In Mary's Love, Angel Fragments, My Heart Laid Bare, 2013; Hymn to St Paul, A Walk with Ivor Gurney, Dürer Portrait, Tableaux Vivants, The Very Distant Days, Altartavla, Les Saintes Maries de la Mer, Oboe Concerto, Solomon and Love, Arcadia, Missa Brevis IV, Ghostly Grace, Glass Beatitude, Fa La Ninna, 2014; Zodiack, 2015. BBC Young Composer, 1977; Barlow Prize for choral music, 2004; BASCA British Composer Awards for liturgical music, 2004, for choral music, 2004, 2006 and for Instrumental Music, 2008. FRNCM 2005; FRSCM 2007; FGCM 2014. *Recreations:* films, art, books, friends. *Address:* c/o Peters Edition, 2–6 Baches Street, N1 6DN. *T:* (020) 8660 4766.

BINGHAM, Sir Max; *see* Bingham, Sir E. M.

BINI SMAGHI, Lorenzo, PhD; President, Snam, since 2012; Chairman, Société Générale, since 2015 (Director, since 2014); *b* Florence, 29 Nov. 1956. *Educ:* Univ. Catholique de Louvain (Lic. Scis Econs 1978); Univ. of Southern Calif (MA Econs 1980); Univ. of Chicago (PhD Econs 1988). Research Department, Banca d'Italia: Economist, Internat. Section, 1983–88; Hd of Exchange Rate and Internat. Trade Div., 1988–94; Hd of Policy Div., EMI, Frankfurt, 1994–98; Dep. Dir Gen. for Res., ECB, Frankfurt, 1998; Dir Gen. for Internat. Financial Relns, Min. of the Economy and Finance, Italy, 1998–2005; Mem., Exec. Bd, European Central Bank, 2005–11. Vis. Scholar, Center for Internat. Affairs, Harvard Univ., 2012–. Pres., Fondazione Palazzo Strozzi, Florence, 2006–. Grande Ufficiale al Merito della Repubblica Italiana, 2006. *Publications:* L'Euro, 1998, 3rd edn 2001; (with D. Gros) Open Issues in European Central Banking, 2000; Chi Ci Salva dalla Prossima Crisi Finanziaria?, 2000; Il Paradosso dell'euro, 2008; Austerity: European democracies against the wall, 2013; 33 false verità sull'Europa, 2014. *Address:* Via Giuseppe Cuboni 2, Rome 00197, Italy.

BINLEY, Brian Arthur Roland; *b* 1 April 1942; *s* of Frank Binley and Phyllis Binley (*née* Underwood); *m* 1985, Jacqueline Denise Gibbs; one *s*, and one *s* by a previous marriage. *Educ:* Finedon Mulso (C of E) Sch. Chairman and Founder: BCC Mktg Services Ltd, 1989–; Beechwood House Publishing Ltd, 1993–2001 (publishers of Binley's Directories). Mem. (C) Northants CC, 1997–2009. MP (C) Northampton S, 2005–15. FRSA 1996. *Recreations:* golf, Association football, cricket, opera. *Clubs:* Carlton; Northampton Town and County.

BINMORE, Prof. Kenneth George, CBE 2001; PhD; FBA 1995; Professor of Economics, University College London, 1991–2003, now Emeritus; *b* 27 Sept. 1940; *s* of Ernest George Binmore and Maud Alice (*née* Holland); *m* 1968, Josephine Ann Lee; two *s* two *d. Educ:* Imperial Coll., London (BSc; PhD 1964). Lectr, Reader and Prof. of Maths, LSE, 1969–88; Prof. of Econs, LSE and Univ. of Michigan, 1988–93; Dir, ESRC Centre for Econ. Learning and Social Evolution, 1994–2002. *Publications:* Mathematical Analysis, 1977, 2nd edn 1982; Logic, Sets and Numbers, 1980; Topological Ideas, 1981; Calculus, 1982; Economic Organizations as Games, 1986; Economics of Bargaining, 1986; Essays on the Foundations of Game Theory, 1991; Fun and Games, 1992; Frontiers of Game Theory, 1993; Game Theory and the Social Contract: vol. I, Playing Fair, 1994; vol. II, Just Playing, 1998; Natural Justice, 2005; Playing for Real, 2007; Does Game Theory Work?, 2007; Very Short Introduction to Game Theory, 2007; Rational Decisions, 2008; papers. *Recreation:* philosophy. *Address:* Newmills, Whitebrook, Monmouth NP25 4TY. *T:* (01600) 860691.

BINNEY, Prof. James Jeffrey, DPhil; FRS 2000; FRAS, FInstP; Professor of Physics, University of Oxford, since 1996; Fellow, Merton College, Oxford, since 1981; *b* 12 April 1950; *s* of Harry Augustus Roy Binney and Barbara Binney (*née* Poole); *m* 1993, Lucy Elliot Buckingham; one *s* one *d. Educ:* King's Coll. Sch., Wimbledon; Churchill Coll., Cambridge (BA 1971, MA 1975); Albert Ludwigs Univ., Freiburg im Breisgau; Christ Church and Magdalen Coll., Oxford (DPhil 1976). Fellow, Magdalen Coll., Oxford, 1975–79; Vis. Asst Prof., Princeton Univ., 1979–81; Lectr in Theoretical Physics, 1981–90, Reader, 1990–96, Oxford Univ. Lindemann Fellow, Princeton Univ., 1975–76; Fairchild Dist. Schol., CIT 1983–84; Visiting Fellow: Univ. of Arizona, 1989; Princeton Univ., 1992; ANU, 1995. FRAS 1973; FInstP 2000. Maxwell Medal and Prize, 1986, Dirac Medal, 2010, Inst. of Physics; Brouwer Award, American Astronomy Soc., 2003; Eddington Medal, RAS, 2013. *Publications:* jointly: Galactic Astronomy: structure and kinematics, 1981; Galactic Dynamics, 1987; PICK for Humans, 1990; The Theory of Critical Phenomena, 1992; Galactic Astronomy, 1998; The Physics of Quantum Mechanics, 2008. *Recreations:* carpentry, stone and metalwork, walking. *Address:* Rudolf Peierls Centre for Theoretical Physics, Keble Road, Oxford OX1 3NP. *T:* (01865) 273979.

BINNEY, Marcus Hugh Crofton, CBE 2006 (OBE 1983); FSA; writer, journalist, conservationist; Founder, 1975, and President, since 1984, Save Britain's Heritage (Chairman, 1975–84); *b* 21 Sept. 1944; *s* of late Lt-Col Francis Crofton Simms, MC and of Sonia, *d* of Rear-Adm. Sir William Marcus Charles Beresford-Whyte, KCB, CMG (she *m* 2nd, Sir George Binney, DSO); *m* 1st, 1966, Hon. Sara Anne Vanneck (marr. diss. 1976), *e d* of 6th Baron Huntingfield; 2nd, 1981, Anne Carolyn, *d* of Dr T. H. Hills, Merstham, Surrey; two *s. Educ:* Magdalene Coll., Cambridge (BA 1966). Architectural writer, 1968–77, Architectural Editor, 1977–84, Editor, 1984–86, Country Life; Ed., Landscape, 1987–88; envmt correspondent, Harpers & Queen, 1989–90; architecture correspondent, The Times, 1991–. Sec., UK Cttee, Internat. Council on Monuments and Sites, 1972–81; Mem., Montagu Cttee (report, Britain's Historic Buildings, published 1980); Director: Rly Heritage Trust, 1985–; HMS Warrior; Chm., Save Europe's Heritage, 1995–; President: Friends of City Churches, 1998– (Chm., 1995–98); Save Jersey's Heritage, 1990–. Television series: Co-Presenter, Great Houses of Europe, 1993, 1996, 1997. Exhibitions: (joint organizer) The Destruction of the Country House, V&A Mus., 1974; Change and Decay: the future of our churches, V&A Mus., 1977. FSA 1989. Hon. FRIBA 2004. London Conservation Medal, 1985. *Publications:* (with Peter Burman): Change and Decay: the future of our churches, 1977; Chapels and Churches: who cares?, 1977; (with Max Hanna) Preservation Pays, 1978; (ed jtly) Railway Architecture, 1979; (ed jtly) Satanic Mills, 1979; (ed jtly) Our Past Before Us, 1981; (with Kit Martin) The Country House: to be or not to be, 1982; (with Max Hanna) Preserve and Prosper, 1983; The Architecture of Sir Robert Taylor, 1984; Our Vanishing Heritage, 1984; Country Manors of Portugal, 1987; (jtly) Bright Futures: the reuse of industrial buildings, 1990; Palace on the River, 1991; (with M. Watson-Smyth) The Save Action Guide, 1991; Châteaux of the Loire, 1992; (with R. Runciman) Glyndebourne: building a vision, 1994; The Châteaux of France: photographs by Frederick Evans 1906–7, 1994; Railway Architecture: the way ahead, 1995; (with Patrick Bowe) Houses and Gardens of Portugal, 1998; Town Houses: 800 years of evolution and innovation in urban design, 1998; Airport Builders, 1999; The Ritz Hotel, London, 1999, Centenary edn 2006; (with Graham Byfield) London Sketchbook: a city observed, 2001; Women Who Lived for Danger, 2002; Great Houses of Europe, 2003; Secret War Heroes, 2005; Save Britain's Heritage 1975–2005: thirty years of campaigning, 2005; In Search of the Perfect House: 500 of the best buildings in Britain and Ireland, 2007; The Blandys of Madeira: 1811–2011, 2011. *Address:* Domaine des Vaux, St Lawrence, Jersey JE3 1JG. *T:* (01534) 864424, *Fax:* (01534) 862612. *E:* mbinney@msn.com.

BINNIE, David Stark, OBE 1979; General Manager, British Rail, London Midland Region, 1977–80; *b* 2 June 1922; *s* of Walter Archibald Binnie and Helen (*née* Baxter), Bonkle, Lanarkshire; *m* 1947, Leslie Archibald; one *s* one *d. Educ:* Wishaw High School. British Railways: Gen. and Signalling Asst to Gen. Manager Scottish Region, 1955; Asst District Operating Supt 1961, District Operating Supt 1963, Glasgow North; Divisional Movements Manager, Glasgow Div., 1965; Movements Manager, Scottish Region, 1967; Divisional Manager, SE Div., Southern Region, 1969; Asst Gen. Manager, Southern Region, 1970; Gen. Manager, 1972; Exec. Dir, Freight, BR Board, 1974–76. Lt-Col Engineer and Railway Staff Corps, RE (T&AVR). OStJ. *Recreation:* Dartmoor and Highland life. *Address:* Above Ways, Lower Knowle Road, Lustleigh, Devon TQ13 9TR. *T:* (01647) 277386.

BINNIE, Frank Hugh, FCSD; Chairman and Chief Executive, Binnie International, since 1998; Founder and Director, Rainbow Cloud Ltd, since 2014; *b* 1 March 1950; *s* of Dr Hugh Lawson Binnie and Isobel May Van Dijk (*née* Nairn); *m* 1996, Fiona Margaret Maclean Nicolson (*née* Hart); one *s* one *d*; and three *s* by previous marriage. *Educ:* Loughborough GS; De Montfort Univ., Leicester (Dip. Textile Technol. 1970). ATI. FCSD 1992. Mgt trainee, Corah Textiles, Leicester, 1970–73; Founder Manager, Floreal Knitwear, Mauritius, 1973–76; Sales Manager, Kemptons Knitwear, Leicester, 1976–79; Gen. Manager, Texport Unilever, 1979–82; Manager, Kilspindie Knitwear, Haddington, 1982–85; Dir and Co. Sec., Midlothian Enterprise, 1985–88; Man. Dir, Perkins, Hodgkinson & Gillibrand, 1988–90; Chief Exec., Design Council, Scotland, then Scottish Design, 1990–96. Chief Exec., Caledonian Foundn, 1996–97; Chief Executive Officer: Internet Soc. Scotland, 1998–2003; ScotlandIS, 2000–03; Executive Chairman: Scottish Internet Exchange, 1999–2003; Scotnom Ltd, 2000–05; Broadband Scotland Ltd, 2001–04; Chm., EBusiness Scotland Ltd, 1999–2004; Co-Founder, Ecommerce Exchange (Scotland) Ltd, 1999–2004; Sen. Consultant, Career Associates, 1998–2014. Vis. Prof., Strathclyde Univ., 1990–96; External Assessor: MBA, Westminster Univ., 1995–97; Design Mgt, De Montfort Univ., 1996–99. Chm., Sector Gp for Design, Scotvec, 1995–96. Mem. Exec. Council, Scottish Council of Develt and Industry, 2001–. Gen. Manager, Kenilworth Court Assoc., 2005–. Formerly Mem. Bd, 1996 UK City of Architecture and Design. Trustee, Flatfeet Dance Co. Ltd, 2013–14. FRSA 1992; MInstD. *Recreations:* sailing (RYA Yachtmaster), motor boating, weightlifting, global travel. *Clubs:* Winchester House (Sec., 2009–10); Hurlingham Yacht.

BINNIG, Prof. Dr Gerd Karl; IBM Fellow, since 1986; Honorary Professor of Physics, University of Munich, since 1987; Founder and Chief Technology Officer (formerly Head of Research), Definiens AG, since 1994; *b* 20 July 1947; *m* 2003, Renate; one *s* one *d* by former marriage. *Educ:* J. W. Goethe Univ., Frankfurt/M (DipPhys; PhD). Research staff mem., IBM Zurich Res. Lab., in fields of superconductivity of semiconductors and scanning tunnelling microscopy, 1978–, Gp Leader 1984–; IBM Almaden Res. Center, San José, and collab. with Stanford Univ., 1985–86; Vis. Prof., Stanford Univ., 1985–86. Member: Technology Council, IBM Acad., 1989–92; Supervisory Bd, Mercedes Automobil Holding AG, 1989–95. For. Associate Mem., Acad. of Scis, Washington, 1987. Hon. FRMS 1988. Scanning Tunnelling Microscopy awards: Physics Prize, German Phys. Soc., 1982; Otto Klung Prize, 1983; (jtly) King Faisal Internat. Prize for Science and Hewlett Packard Europhysics Prize, 1984; (jtly) Nobel Prize in Physics, 1986; Elliot Cresson Medal, Franklin Inst., Philadelphia, 1987; Minnie Rosen Award, Ross Univ., NY, 1988. Grosses Verdienstkreuz mit Stern und Schulterband des Verdienstordens (FRG), 1987; Bayerischer Verdienstorden, 1992. *Recreations:* music, tennis, soccer, golf. *Address:* Definiens AG, Bernhard-Wicki-Strasse 5, 80636 Munich, Germany.

BINNING, Lord; George Edmund Baldred Baillie-Hamilton; *b* 27 Dec. 1985; *s* and *heir* of Earl of Haddington, *qv*. *Educ:* Eton; Glasgow Univ.

BINNS, Benjamin Edward Noël L.; *see* Lyster-Binns.

BINNS, David John, CBE 1989; Trust Board Secretary, Halton General Hospital NHS Trust, 1995–99 (non-executive Director, 1992–94); *b* 12 April 1929; *s* of Henry Norman Binns, OBE and Ivy Mary Binns; *m* 1957, Jean Margaret Evans; one *s* (one *d* decd). *Educ:* Fleetwood Grammar Sch.; Rossall Sch.; Sheffield Univ. LLB 1951. Solicitor 1954. Articled Clerk, Sheffield City Council, 1949; Asst Solicitor, Warrington County Borough Council, 1954; Dep. Town Clerk, Warrington County Borough Council, 1958; General Manager: Warrington Develt Corp., 1969–81; Warrington and Runcorn Develt Corp., 1981–89. Mem., Warrington DHA, 1990–92. *Recreations:* walking, gardening, music. *Address:* 4 Cedarways, Appleton, Warrington, Cheshire WA4 5EW.

BINNS, Gareth Ian; Director, Learning and Content, London Children's Museum, since 2011; *b* 6 Feb. 1958; *s* of Ian Binns and Mavis Eleanor Binns (*née* Jones); partner, Sally Bacon; one *s*. *Educ:* Southampton Univ. (BA Hons Archaeol. and Geog.); Durham Univ. (MA Anglo-Saxon and Viking Archaeol.); Nottingham Univ. (PGCE Geog. and Hist.); Birkbeck Coll., London (Dip. Multimedia Mgt). Actg Hd of Dept, and Div. Leader, Bilborough Sixth Form Coll., 1984–88; Educn Officer, Council for British Archaeol., 1988–91; Countryside and Envmtl Educn Officer, 1991–98, Hd of Educn and Interpretation, 1998–2000, NT; Educn Dir, NESTA, 2000–03; Keeper of Learning and Inf., BM, 2003–06; Dir of Ops, Personal Finance Educn Gp, 2006–09; Chief Exec., Sorrell Foundn, 2009–10. *Recreations:* museums and galleries, hill-walking, art appreciation and collecting, historic buildings, landscape history, running. *Address:* London Children's Museum, 18 Broadwick Street, W1F 8HS.

BINNS, Jacqueline Sukie, (Mrs W. A. T. Hills); artist, embroiderer and sculptor, since 1986; *b* 24 May 1963; *d* of Dennis Binns and Eileen (*née* Andrews); *m* 1986, Warwick Alan Theodore Hills. *Educ:* Goldsmiths' Coll., London (BA Textiles 1986). Exhibitions include: Southwark Cathedral, Leicester Mus., Salisbury Cathedral, 1987 and 2007; Gawthorpe Hall, Peterborough Cathedral, 1988; St Alban's Abbey, 1989, 1992; St Paul's Cathedral, 1990; Royal Sch. of Needlework, 1993; Sheffield Cath., Goldsmiths' Coll., 1997; Shrewsbury Abbey, 1998; Wimpole Hall, Cambridge, Winchester Cath., 1999; Guildford Cath., Portsmouth Cath., Alexandra Palace, 2000; De Morgan Centre, 2003; Guildford Cathedral, 2008; works of art in private collections and cathedrals and churches in America, Australia, Europe and UK; works include: St Alban Cope, 1988, and embroideries for 12 copes in St Albans Abbey; Anniversary Cope for St Paul's Cathedral, 2004; lifesize Crucifixion sculpture for St Peter's Ch, Plymouth, 2007; Virgin and Child Sculpture, All Hallows by the Tower, London, 2011; The Unity Sculptures for St Mary the Virgin Ch and Christopher Rawlins Sch., Adderbury, 2013; Coffin Pall for King Richard III, 2015. *Recreations:* walking, the arts, costume. *Address:* 1 Cargill Road, Earlsfield, SW18 3EF. *T:* (020) 8874 0895. *E:* jb@jacquiebinns.com.

BINNS, James Wallace, PhD, DLitt; FBA 2004; Lecturer, 1984–91, Reader, 1991–2002, in Latin Literature, Honorary Fellow, since 2002, University of York; *b* 1 Sept. 1940; *s* of Wallace William and Madge Binns. *Educ:* Univ. of Birmingham (BA 1964; MA 1965; PhD 1969; DLitt 1992). Exec. Officer, War Office, 1958–61; Lectr in Later Latin, Univ. of Birmingham, 1965–84. Hon. Lectr, Univ. of Leeds, 1987–. *Publications:* Intellectual Culture in Elizabethan and Jacobean England, 1990; (ed with S. E. Banks) Gervase of Tilbury: Otia Imperialia, 2002. *Recreations:* travel, films, military history. *Address:* Centre for Medieval Studies, University of York, King's Manor, York YO1 7EP. *T:* (01904) 433910, *Fax:* (01904) 433918.

BINNS, Rev. John Richard, PhD; Vicar, St Mary the Great with St Michael, Cambridge, since 1994; Rural Dean of North Cambridge, 2007–11; *b* 10 Jan. 1951. *Educ:* St John's Coll., Cambridge (MA 1976); King's Coll., London (PhD 1989); Coll. of the Resurrection, Mirfield. Ordained deacon, 1976, priest, 1977; Assistant Curate: Holy Trinity, Clapham, 1976–78; Clapham Old Town, 1978–80; Team Vicar, Mortlake with E Sheen, 1980–87; Vicar, Holy Trinity, Upper Tooting, 1987–94. Dir, Inst. for Orthodox Christian Studies, 1996–. Hon. Canon, Ely Cathedral, 2007–. Chm. Trustees, Partners for Change Ethiopia (formerly St Matthew's Children's Fund, Ethiopia), 2004–. *Publications:* Cyril of Scythopolis: lives of the Monks of Palestine, 1991; Ascetics and Ambassadors of Christ, 1994; Great St Mary's, Cambridge's University Church, 2000; An Introduction to the Christian Orthodox Churches, 2002. *Address:* Great St Mary's Vicarage, 39 Madingley Road, Cambridge CB3 0EL. *T:* (01223) 355285.

BINNS, Malcolm; concert pianist; *b* 29 Jan. 1936; *s* of Douglas and May Binns. *Educ:* Bradford Grammar Sch.; Royal Coll. of Music (ARCM, Chappell Gold Medal, Medal of Worshipful Co. of Musicians). London début, 1957; Henry Wood Proms début, 1960; Royal Festival Hall début, 1961; Festival Hall appearances in London Philharmonic Orchestra International series, 1969–; toured with Scottish Nat. Orch., 1989; concerts at Aldeburgh, Leeds, Three Choirs (1975), Bath and Canterbury Festivals; regular appearances at Promenade concerts and broadcasts for BBC Radio; celebrated 60th birthday with series of concerts, 1996; series of recitals for BBC linking Clementi and Beethoven, 1997. First complete recording of Beethoven piano sonatas on original instruments, 1980; première recordings of Sir William Sterndale Bennett's piano concertos with London Philharmonic and Philharmonia Orchs, 1990; première recording of Stanford's re-discovered Third Piano Concerto, with RPO, 1996. *Recreation:* collecting antique gramophone records. *Address:* 233 Court Road, Orpington, Kent BR6 9BY. *T:* (01689) 831056.

BINNS, Hon. Patrick George; Consul General of Canada to Boston, USA, since 2010; *b* Saskatchewan, 8 Oct. 1948; *s* of Stan and Phyllis Binns; *m* 1971, Carol MacMillan; three *s* one *d*. *Educ:* Univ. of Alberta (BA, MA 1971). Rural Develt Council, PEI, 1974–78; MLA (PC) 4th Kings, PEI, 1978–84; Minister: of Municipal Affairs, Labour, and Envmt, 1979–80; of Community Affairs, 1980–82; of Fisheries and of Industry, 1982–84; MP (PC) Cardigan, 1984–88; Parly Sec. to Minister of Fisheries and Oceans, 1984–88; MLA (PC) Dist 5, Murray River-Gaspereaux, PEI, 1996–2007; Premier and Pres. of Exec. Council, PEI, 1996–2007; Leader, PC Party, PEI, 1996–2007; Minister responsible for Intergovtl Affairs, 1996–2007; Minister of Agriculture, Fisheries and Aquaculture, 2006–07; Ambassador of Canada to Ireland, 2007–10. President: Island Bean Ltd, 1988–96; Pat Binns & Associates, 1988–96. Silver Jubilee Medal, 1977; Golden Jubilee Medal, 2002; Diamond Jubilee Medal, 2012. *Recreations:* hockey, ski-ing. *Address:* Canadian Consulate General, Three Copley Place, Suite 400, Boston, MA 02116, USA; (home) Hopefield, Murray River RR#4, PE C0A 1W0, Canada. *T:* (902) 9622196.

BINNS, Susan May; Director, Information Society and Media, European Commission, 2005–08; *b* 22 April 1948; *d* of Jack and Mollie Binns. *Educ:* Harrogate Coll.; LSE (BSc Econ Internat. Relations). HM Diplomatic Service, 1968–80: served FCO and Brussels; New Delhi, 1978–80; Cabinet of Ivor Richard, EC Member, Brussels, 1981–84; Counsellor, EC Delegations: Washington, 1985–88; Belgrade, 1988; Dep. Chef de Cabinet of Bruce Millan, EC Mem. resp. for regl policies, 1989–91, Chef de Cabinet, 1991–95; Dir, Internal Market, EC, 1995–2004. *Recreations:* gardening, golf. *Address:* 18 rue du Charnois, 1342 Limelette, Belgium.

BINSKI, Prof. Paul, PhD; FSA; FBA 2007; Professor of the History of Medieval Art, since 2006, and Head, Department of History of Art, 2014–Sept. 2016, University of Cambridge; Fellow, Gonville and Caius College, Cambridge, 1983–87 and since 1996; *b* 9 Nov. 1956; *s* of late Eugene and Pamela Binski. *Educ:* Harrow Sch.; Gonville and Caius Coll., Cambridge (BA 1979, MA); PhD 1984. Asst Prof., Dept of History of Art, Yale Univ., and Fellow, Saybrook Coll., 1988–91; Lecturer, Department of History of Art: Univ. of Manchester, 1991–95; Cambridge Univ., 1996–2002 (Hd of Dept, 1999–2001); Reader in Hist. of Medieval Art, Cambridge Univ., 2002–06. Slade Prof. of Fine Art, Univ. of Oxford, 2007. Vis. Mem., IAS, Princeton, 1987–88; Getty Postdoctoral Fellow, Dept of Art and Archaeol., Princeton Univ., 1987–88; Ailsa Mellon Bruce Vis. Sen. Fellow, Center for Advanced Study in Visual Arts, Nat. Gall. of Art, Washington, 1992; British Acad./Leverhulme Trust Sen. Res. Fellow, 2003–04; Leverhulme Trust Major Res. Fellowship, 2011–14. Associate Ed., Art History, 1992–97; Mem., Res. and Pubn Cttee, British Acad. *Corpus Vitrearum Medii Aevi*, 1995–; Mem., Editl Bd, British Art Jl, 1999–. Member: Peterborough Cathedral Fabric Adv. Cttee, 1996–2006; Westminster Abbey Fabric Commn, 1998–. Mem., Exec. Cttee, Walpole Soc., 1999–2003. Foreign Advr, Internat. Center of Medieval Art, The Cloisters, NY, 2004–07. Presenter, Divine Designs, Channel 5, 2002–04. FSA 1998. Gov., Harrow Sch., 2011–. *Publications:* The Painted Chamber at Westminster, 1986; (jtly) Dominican Painting in East Anglia: the Thornham Parva Retable and the Musée de Cluny Frontal, 1987; (ed with J. Alexander) Age of Chivalry: art in Plantagenet England 1200–1400, 1987; Westminster Abbey and the Plantagenets: kingship and the representation of power 1200–1400, 1995; Medieval Death: ritual and representation, 1996; (ed with W. Noel) New Offerings, Ancient Treasures: essays in medieval art in honour of George Henderson, 2001; Becket's Crown: art and imagination in Gothic England 1170–1300, 2004; (ed with S. Panayotova) The Cambridge Illuminations: ten centuries of book production in the Medieval West, 2005; (with P. Zutshi) Western Illuminated Manuscripts: a catalogue of the collection in Cambridge University Library, 2011; Gothic Wonder: art, artifice and the decorated style 1290–1350, 2014; contrib. articles to learned jls. *Recreations:* organ music, old churches and houses, conversation. *Address:* Gonville and Caius College, Cambridge CB2 1TA. *Club:* Athenæum.

BINTLEY, David Julian, CBE 2001; choreographer; Artistic Director: Birmingham Royal Ballet, since 1995; National Ballet of Japan, 2010–14; *b* 17 Sept. 1957; *s* of David Bintley and Glenys Bintley (*née* Ellinthorpe); *m* 1981, Jennifer Catherine Ursula Mills; two *s*. *Educ:* Holme Valley Grammar School. Royal Ballet School, 1974; Sadler's Wells Royal Ballet, 1976; first professional choreography, The Outsider, 1978; first three act ballet, The Swan of Tuonela, 1982; Company Choreographer, 1983–85, Resident Choreographer, 1985–86, Sadler's Wells Royal Ballet; Resident Choreographer and Principal Dancer, Royal Ballet, 1986–93. Ballets created include: Carmina Burana, 1995; Far From the Madding Crowd, 1996; The Nutcracker Sweeties; The Protecting Veil, 1998; The Shakespeare Suite; Arthur, Part One, 2000; Arthur, Part Two, 2001; Beauty and the Beast, 2003; Take Five, 2007; Aladdin, 2008; E=mc², 2009; Cinderella, 2010; The Prince of the Pagodas (new version), 2011; Hobson's Choice, Faster, 2012; The King Dances, 2015. Evening Standard Award for Ballet, for Choros and Consort Lessons, both 1983; Laurence Olivier Award for Petrushka, 1984; Manchester Evening News Award for Dance, for Still Life at the Penguin Café, 1987, for Edward II, 1998. *Address:* Birmingham Royal Ballet, Birmingham Hippodrome, Thorp Street, Birmingham B5 4AU.

BIRBALSINGH, Katharine; Headmistress, Michaela Community School, Brent, since 2014; *b* Auckland, NZ, 16 Sept. 1973; *d* of Frank and Norma Birbalsingh; one *s*. *Educ:* Victoria Park Collegiate Inst., Toronto; Univ. of Oxford (MA French and Philosophy). Secondary sch. teacher, schs in Brixton, 2000–10; Teacher of French and Dep. Head Teacher, St Michael and All Angels Acad., Camberwell, 2010. *Publications:* To Miss with Love, 2011. *Recreation:* cinema. *Address:* Michaela Community School, North End Road HA9 0UU. *E:* kbirbalsingh@mcsbrent.co.uk.

BIRCH, family name of **Baroness Young of Hornsey**.

BIRCH, Prof. Bryan John, FRS 1972; Professor of Arithmetic, University of Oxford, 1985–98, now Emeritus; Fellow of Brasenose College, Oxford, 1966–98, now Emeritus; *b* 25 Sept. 1931; *s* of Arthur Jack Benjamin Birch and Mary Edith Birch; *m* 1961, Gina Margaret Christ (*d* 2005); two *s* one *d*. *Educ:* Shrewsbury Sch.; Trinity Coll., Cambridge (MA, PhD). Harkness Fellow, Princeton, 1957–58; Fellow: Trinity Coll., Cambridge, 1956–60; Churchill Coll., Cambridge, 1960–62; Sen. Lectr, later Reader, Univ. of Manchester, 1962–65; Reader in Mathematics, Univ. of Oxford, 1966–85. Deleg., OUP, 1988–98. Ed., Proc. London Math. Soc., 2001–03. Sen. Whitehead Prize, 1993, De Morgan Medal, 2007, LMS. *Publications:* articles in learned jls, mainly on number theory; various editorships. *Recreations:* gardening (theoretical), opera, hunting wild flowers and watching marmots. *Address:* Green Cottage, Boars Hill, Oxford OX1 5DQ. *T:* (01865) 735367; Mathematical Institute, University of Oxford, Radcliffe Observatory Quarter, Woodstock Road, Oxford OX2 6GG. *E:* birch@maths.ox.ac.uk.

BIRCH, Prof. Dinah Lynne, DPhil; Professor of English Literature, since 2003, and Pro-Vice Chancellor, since 2011, University of Liverpool; *b* Melton Mowbray, Leics, 4 Oct. 1953; *d* of Edward Neil Baggaley and Rowena Iris Baggaley (*née* Hempshall); *m* 1976, Sidney Ian Birch; one *s* one *d*. *Educ:* King Edward VII Upper Sch., Melton Mowbray; St Hugh's Coll., Oxford (BA, MA; DPhil 1980). Jun. Res. Fellow, Merton Coll., Oxford, 1980–82; Fixed-term Tutorial Fellow in English, St Hugh's Coll., Oxford, 1982–85; Lectr in Lit., Open Univ., 1986–90; Lectr, Univ. of Oxford, 1990–2003; Stirling Boyd Fellow in English Lit., 1990–2003, Vice-Pres., 2002–03, Trinity Coll., Oxford. Vis. Prof., Lancaster Univ., 2003–; Chancellor's Dist. Lectr, Louisiana State Univ., 2002. Mem., RAE 2008 Sub-Panel 57, English Lang. and Lit., 2008; Chair, Sub-Panel 29, English Lang. and Lit., 2014, Dep. Chair, Main Panel D, Arts and Humanities, 2014, REF 2014. Mem., Judging Panel for Man Booker Prize, 2012. Richard Hillary Trust, 1990–. Companion, Guild of St George, 2002–. FEA 2003. *Publications:* Ruskin's Myths, 1988; Ruskin on Turner, 1990; (ed) Anthony Trollope's The Duke's Children, 1995; (ed) George Eliot's The Mill on the Floss, 1996; (ed) Ruskin and the Dawn of the Modern, 1999; (ed) John Ruskin's Fors Clavigera, 2000; (ed jtly) Ruskin and Gender, 2002; (ed) John Ruskin: selected writings, 2004; Our Victorian Education, 2008; (gen. ed.) Oxford Companion to English Literature, 2009; (ed jtly) Conflict and Difference in Nineteenth-Century Literature, 2010; (ed) Elizabeth Gaskell's Cranford, 2011; (ed) Anthony Trollope's Can You Forgive Her?, 2012; (ed jtly) Concise Oxford Companion to English Literature, 2012; (ed) Anthony Trollope's The Small House at Allington, 2014; contrib. articles to essay collections and learned jls; contrib. reviews to London Rev. of Books, TLS, The Times, Guardian, Independent. *Recreations:* reading, music, cinema. *Address:* University of Liverpool, Foundation Building, 765 Brownlow Hill, Liverpool L69 7ZX. *T:* (0151) 794 2220.

BIRCH, Sir John (Allan), KCVO 1993; CMG 1987; HM Diplomatic Service, retired; Ambassador to Hungary, 1989–95; *b* 24 May 1935; *s* of late C. Allan Birch, MD, FRCP and Marjorie (*née* Bold); *m* 1960, Primula Haselden; three *s* one *d*. *Educ:* Leighton Park Sch.; Corpus Christi Coll., Cambridge (MA). Served HM Forces, Middlesex Regt, 1954–56. Joined HM Foreign Service, 1959; served: Paris, 1960–63; Singapore, 1963–64; Bucharest, 1965–68; Geneva, 1968–70; Kabul, 1973–76; Royal Coll. of Defence Studies, 1977; Comprehensive Test Ban Treaty Negotiations, Geneva, 1977–80; Counsellor, Budapest, 1980–83; Hd of East European Dept, FCO, 1983–86; Ambassador and Dep. Perm. Rep. to UN, NY, 1986–89. Pres., UN Trusteeship Council, 1987–89. Dir and Chief Exec., British Assoc. for Central and Eastern Europe, 1995–2004. Dir, Schroder Emerging Countries Fund plc, 1996–2004; Directing Staff, RCDS, 2004–15. Chairman, Advisory Board: SSEES, 2006–; UCL European Inst., 2014–; Member Council: Chatham House (RIIA), 1997–2003; UCL, 1999–2008 (Vice-Chm., 2005–08; Chm., Research Ethics Cttee, 2003–12; Hon. Fellow, 2009). Trustee, Wytham Hall for the Homeless, 1999–2014. Comdr, Order of Merit (Hungary), 2004. *Recreations:* tennis, ski-ing, carpentry. *Address:* 185 Ashley Gardens, Emery Hill Street, SW1P 1PD. *Club:* Athenæum.

BIRCH, Peter Gibbs, CBE 1992; Chairman, Land Securities PLC, 1998–2007; Chairman, Legal Services Commission, 2000–03; *b* 4 Dec. 1937; *m* 1962, Gillian (*née* Benge); three *s* one *d*. *Educ:* Allhallows Sch., Devon. Royal West Kent Regt, seconded to Jamaica Regt, 1957–58 (2nd Lieut). Nestlé Co., UK, Singapore and Malaysia, 1958–65; Sales and Mkting Manager, Gillette, 1965; Gen. Sales Manager, Gillette Australia, 1969; Man. Dir, Gillette, NZ, 1971; Gen. Manager, Gillette, SE Asia (based Singapore), 1973; Gp Gen. Manager, Gillette, Africa, ME, Eastern Europe, 1975; Man. Dir, Gillette UK, 1981; Dir and Chief Exec., Abbey Nat. Building Soc., then Abbey Nat. plc, 1984–98. Chairman: Trinity plc, 1998–99; UCTX, 2000–01; Kensington Gp, 2000–07; Trigold plc, 2007–; Sen. non-exec. Dir, Trinity Mirror plc, 1999–2007; non-executive Director: Hoskyns Gp, 1988–93; Argos, 1990–98; Scottish Mutual Assurance, 1992–98; N. M. Rothschild & Sons, 1998–2004 (Advr, 2004–08); Dalgety, 1993–98; Dah Sing Financial Services, 1997–2011; PIC, 1998–2000; Coca-Cola Beverages, 1998–2000; Travelex plc, 1999–2009; Sainsbury's Bank plc, 2002–06; Lamprell Energy Ltd, 2006–08 (Chm., 2007–08); Banco Finantia, 2007–08; Advr, Cambridge Place Investment Mgt LLP, 2004–. Chm., Council of Mortgage Lenders, 1991–92. Trustee, Cap Gemini, 1993–. FCBSI. Pres., Middlesex Young People's (formerly Middlesex Assoc. of Boys') Clubs, 1988–; Chm., Clubs for Young People, 2010–. *Recreations:* active holidays, swimming.

BIRCH, Robin Arthur, CB 1995; voluntary worker; civil servant, retired; *b* 12 Oct. 1939; *s* of late Arthur and Olive Birch; *m* 1962, Jane Marion Irvine Sturdy; two *s*. *Educ:* King Henry VIII Sch., Coventry; Christ Church, Oxford (MA). Entered Min. of Health as Asst Principal, 1961; Private Sec. to Charles Loughlin, MP (Parly Sec.), 1965–66; Principal, 1966; seconded to: Interdeptl Social Work Gp, 1969–70; Home Office (Community Develt Project), 1970–72; Asst Sec., DHSS, 1973; Chm., Working Party on Manpower and Trng for Social Services, 1974–76 (HMSO Report, 1976); Principal Private Sec. to Leader of the House of Commons, 1980–81; Under Sec., DHSS, 1982; Asst Auditor Gen., Nat. Audit Office, 1984–86, on secondment; Dir, Regl Orgn, 1988–90; Dep. Sec. (Policy), 1990–95, DSS. Hon. Sec., Friends of Christ Church Cathedral, Oxford, 1978–2006. Vice-Pres., Age Concern England, 1998–2008 (Chm., 1995–98). Chairman: Response Organisation (formerly Oxfordshire Gp Homes), 1995–2014 (Chm., Finance Cttee, 2014–); Low Vision Services Implementation Gp for England, 1999–2005 (Chm. Working Gp, 1998–99; Report, 1999); City of Oxford Charity, 2004–; Oxford Credit Union, 2005–10; Buildings and Glebe Cttees, Dio. of Oxford, 2009–; Oxford Develt Bd, Crisis UK, 2011–. Trustee: Oxford CAB, 1996–2004 (Chm., 1997–2002); Oxfordshire Community Foundn, 1996–2002; Age Concern Oxfordshire, 1998–2005; Wyndham Housing Assoc., 2001–09; Roman Research Trust, 2002–; Lady Nuffield Home (Oxford), 1996–. Jt Patron, Oxfordshire Assoc. for the Blind, 2010–. Mem., Order of St Frideswide, Dio. Oxford, 2015. DL Oxfordshire, 1996. *Recreations:* family and friends, travel, music, byways of classical antiquity, garden railway. *Clubs:* Oxford Rotary (Pres., 2008–09); Warwickshire CC.

BIRCH, Sir Roger, Kt 1992; CBE 1987; QPM 1980; Chief Constable, Sussex Police, 1983–93; *b* 27 Sept. 1930; *s* of John Edward Lawrence Birch and Ruby Birch; *m* 1st, 1954, Jeanne Margaret Head (*d* 2006); one *s*; 2nd, 2011, Susan Elizabeth Raine. *Educ:* King's Coll., Taunton. Cadet, Royal Naval Coll., Dartmouth, 1949–50; Pilot Officer, RAF, 1950–52. Devon Constabulary, 1954–72: Constable, uniform and CID; then through ranks to Chief Supt; Asst Chief Constable, Mid-Anglia Constab., 1972–74; Dep. Chief Constable, Kent Constab., 1974–78; Chief Constable, Warwickshire Constab., 1978–83. Dir, Police Extended Interviews, 1983–91; Pres., Assoc. of Chief Police Officers, 1987–88 (Vice-Pres., 1986–87; Chm., Traffic Cttee, 1983–86; Chm., Internat. Affairs Adv. Cttee, 1988–92); Vice Chm., Internat. Cttee, Internat. Assoc. of Chiefs of Police, 1989–93; Trustee: Police Dependants' Trust, 1981–93; Police Gurney Fund, 1983–91. Mem., St John Ambulance Council, Sussex, 1986–93. UK Vice-Pres., Royal Life Saving Soc., 1985–93 (Chm., SE Region, 1983–93). Mem. Council, IAM, 1984–93. Hon. Fellow, Centre for Legal Studies, 1993. Hon. LLD Sussex, 1991. *Publications:* articles on criminal intelligence, breath measuring instruments and on the urban environment, in learned jls. *Recreations:* walking, music. *Club:* Royal Air Force.

BIRCH, Prof. Sarah, DPhil, PhD; FBA 2013; Professor of Comparative Politics, University of Glasgow, since 2013; *b* Boston, Mass, 5 Dec. 1963; *d* of David and Louisa Birch. *Educ:* Dartmouth Coll. (AB); Somerville Coll., Oxford (MPhil; DPhil 1992); Univ. of Essex (MA; PhD 1998). Lectr, 1996–2003, Reader, 2003–12, Prof., 2012–13, Univ. of Essex. Ed., British Jl Political Sci., 2002–11. *Publications:* Elections and Democratization in Ukraine, 2000; Electoral Systems and Political Transformation in Post-communist Russia, 2003; Full Participation: a comparative study of compulsory voting, 2009; Electoral Malpractice, 2011; Ethics and Integrity in British Politics: how citizens judge their politicians' conduct and why it matters, 2015. *Recreation:* photography. *Address:* School of Social and Political Sciences, University of Glasgow, Glasgow G12 8QQ.

BIRCH, Hon. Dame Sue (Lascelles); *see* Carr, Hon. Dame S. L.

BIRCH, Rt Hon. Sir William (Francis), GNZM 1999; PC 1992; consultant in public policy and affairs; company director; Minister of Finance, 1993–99, Treasurer, 1998–99, New Zealand; *b* 9 April 1934; *s* of Charles William Birch and Elizabeth Alicia (*née* Wells); *m* 1953, Rosa Mitchell; three *s* one *d*. Surveyor. Borough Councillor 1965–74, Dep. Mayor 1968–74, Pukekohe. MP (Nat.) Pukekohe, NZ, 1972–99; Jun. Opposition Whip, 1973–75; Sen. Govt Whip, 1975–78; Minister of: Energy, Science and Technol. and Nat. Develt, 1978–81; Energy, Regl Develt and Nat. Develt, 1981–84; Labour, Immigration and State Services, 1990–93; Employment, 1991–93; Health, 1993; Minister for Pacific Island Affairs, 1990–91. Chm., Internat. Energy Agency, 1983. *Recreations:* fishing, gardening. *Address:* 420 Bremner Road, RD2, Drury, New Zealand. *Clubs:* Rotary; Jaycee International.

BIRCHALL, Prof. Martin Anthony, FRCSI; FMedSci; Professor of Laryngology, University College London, since 2009; Programme Director, UCL-Partners, since 2010; *b* Wigan, Lancs, 13 Aug. 1961; *s* of Gerrard and Ruth Birchall; *m* 1989, Tina Pike; three *s* two *d*. *Educ:* St Edward's Coll., Liverpool; Jesus Coll., Cambridge (BA 1982; BChir 1984; MB 1985; MA Hons 1986; MD 1994). FRCSI 1988; FRCS (Otolaryngol.) 1989; FRCS (Otorhinolaryngol.) 1989. Sen. Lectr and Reader, Univ. of Bristol; Professor: of Head and Neck Surgery, Univ. of Liverpool, 2004–05; of Surgery, Univ. of Bristol, 2006–08. FMedSci 2010. *Publications:* contrib. scientific papers to jls incl. Lancet, BMJ and Nature. *Recreations:* running, reading, films. *Address:* Professorial Unit, Royal National Throat, Nose and Ear Hospital, 330 Gray's Inn Road, WC1X 8DA. *T:* (020) 7915 1300, 7915 1308. *E:* m.birchall@ucl.ac.uk.

BIRD, Sir Adrian (Peter), Kt 2014; CBE 2005; PhD; FMedSci; FRS 1989; FRSE; Buchanan Professor of Genetics, Edinburgh University, since 1990; Director, Wellcome Trust Centre for Cell Biology, 1999–2011; *b* 3 July 1947; *s* of Kenneth George Bird and Aileen Mary Bird; *m* 1st, 1976; one *s* one *d*; 2nd, 1993, Prof. Catherine Mary Abbott; one *s* one *d*. *Educ:* Queen Elizabeth's Grammar School, Hartlebury; Univ. of Sussex (BSc(Hons)); Univ. of Edinburgh (PhD 1971). Damon Runyan Fellow, Yale Univ., 1972–73; postdoctoral fellowship, Univ. of Zurich, 1974–75; Medical Research Council, Edinburgh: scientific staff, Mammalian Genome Unit, 1975–87; Sen. Scientist, Inst. for Molecular Pathol., Vienna, 1988–90. Mem. Bd of Govs, Wellcome Trust, 2000–10. Trustee, Cancer Research UK, 2011–. FRSE 1994; FMedSci 2001. Louis Jeantet Prize for Med. Res., Switzerland, 1999; Gabor Medal, 1999, GlaxoSmithKline Prize, 2012, Royal Soc.; Novartis Medal, Biochem. Soc., 2007; Charles Leopold Mayer Prize, French Acad. of Scis, 2008; Gairdner Internat. Award, Gairdner Foundn, Canada, 2011; Frontiers of Knowledge Award, Banco Bilbao Vizcaya Argentaria, Spain, 2014. *Publications:* articles in Nature, Cell and other jls. *Recreations:* sport, music, food. *Address:* Wellcome Trust Centre for Cell Biology, University of Edinburgh, Michael Swann Building, Max Born Crescent, Edinburgh EH9 3BF. *T:* (0131) 650 5670.

BIRD, Anthony Patrick Michael, OBE 1991; Chairman, Bird Group of Companies Ltd, since 2002 (Director, since 1958); *b* 28 Dec. 1935; *s* of William Thomas Bird and May Frances Bird; *m* 1985, Janet Eleanor Burns; one *s* six *d*. *Educ:* Ratcliffe Coll., Leics. Served 4th RTR. Jt Man. Dir, Bird Gp of Cos, 1973–2002. Chm., Nuclear Services Gp Ltd, 1982–91. Member: Minerals, Metals, Materials and Chemicals Requirements Cttee, 1983–85, Industrial Materials and Vehicles Mkt Adv. Cttee, 1985–86, DTI; Lead Waste Cttee, DoE, 1984–85; Adv. Gp on Decommng of North Sea Oil Platforms, 1985–90 (Chm.); Adv. Cttee on Business and the Envmt, 1990–93; Bd, Envmtl Mgt Agency, Welsh Office, 1991–93. Mem. Bd, Warwickshire Police Authy, 1995–2003. Bureau International de la Récupération: Pres., Ferrous Div., 1976–95; Pres., 1995–99 (Pres. of Honour, 1999); Treas., 2000–08; Life Mem. of Honour, 2008. President: Midwest Metals Assoc., 1975–76; British Metals Fedn, 1979–80 (Life Pres., 1992); Fedn of Eur. Recycling Industry, 1981–89 and 2001–03 (Pres. of Honour, 2003). Chm. Trustees, Stoneleigh Abbey Ltd, 1998–. Gov., 2002–, Chm. Trustees, 2004–, King Edward VI GS, Stratford-upon-Avon. Prince of Wales Award for Prodn and Innovation, 1986. *Recreations:* field sports, Rugby football, agriculture, architecture, fine arts. *Address:* c/o Bird Group of Companies Ltd, The Hunting Lodge, Billesley Road, Stratford-upon-Avon, Warwicks CV37 9RA. *Club:* Carlton.

BIRD, Rev. Dr Anthony Peter; General Medical Practitioner, since 1979; Principal of The Queen's College, Edgbaston, Birmingham, 1974–79; *b* 2 March 1931; *s* of late Albert Harry Bird and Noel Whitehouse Bird; *m* 1962, Sabine Boehmig; two *s* one *d*. *Educ:* St John's Coll., Oxford (BA LitHum, BA Theol., MA); Birmingham Univ. (MB, ChB, 1970; DipMus 2001). Deacon, 1957; Priest, 1958; Curate of St Mary's, Stafford, 1957–60; Chaplain, then Vice-Principal of Cuddesdon Theological Coll., 1960–64. General Medical Practitioner, 1972–73. Member: Home Office Policy Adv. Cttee on Sexual Offences, 1976–80; Parole Board, 1977–80. Hon. Lectr in Theol., Univ. of Birmingham, 1974–82. Freedom of Information Campaign Award, 1986. *Publications:* The Search for Health: a response from the inner city, 1981; The God Who Says Sorry, 2010. *Recreations:* sailing, walking, music—J. S. Bach, innovation in primary health care, Wolverhampton Wanderers FC.

BIRD, Prof. Colin Carmichael, CBE 2000; PhD; FRCPath, FRCPE, FRCSE, FMedSci; FRSE; Dean, Faculty of Medicine and Provost, Faculty Group of Medicine and Veterinary Medicine, University of Edinburgh, 1995–2002; *b* 5 March 1938; *s* of John and Sarah Bird; *m* 1964, Ailsa M. Ross; two *s* one *d*. *Educ:* Lenzie Acad.; Glasgow Univ. (MB ChB 1961; PhD 1967). FRCPath 1978 (MRCPath 1968); FRCPE 1989; FRCSE 1995; FRSE 1992. Research Fellow and Lectr in Pathology, Univ. of Glasgow, 1962–67; Lectr in Pathology, Univ. of Aberdeen, 1967–72; Sen. Lectr in Pathology, Univ. of Edinburgh, 1972–75; Professor of Pathology: Univ. of Leeds, 1975–86; Univ. of Edinburgh, 1986–2002, now Emeritus. Founder FMedSci 1998. Dr *hc* Edinburgh, 2004. Knight's Cross, Order of Merit (Poland), 2006. *Publications:* contribs to various scientific jls on cancer and cancer genetics. *Recreations:* golf, walking, music, reading. *Address:* 45 Ann Street, Edinburgh EH4 1PL. *T:* (0131) 332 5568. *Club:* New (Edinburgh).

BIRD, Dickie; *see* Bird, H. D.

BIRD, Drayton Charles Colston; Founder, 1991, Chairman, since 1992, Drayton Bird Associates (formerly Partnership); *b* 22 Aug. 1936; *s* of George Freeman Bird and Marjorie Louise Bird; *m* 1st, 1957, Pamela Bland (marr. diss.); two *s* one *d*; 2nd, 1971, Anna Te Paora (marr. diss.); 3rd, 1982, Cece Topley (marr. diss.). *Educ:* Trent Coll.; Manchester Univ. Asst Sec., Manchester Cotton Assoc., 1955–57; with sundry advertising agencies, 1957–68; Founder, Small Business Inst., 1968; publisher, Business Ideas newsletter, 1968–70; Co-Founder, then Man. Dir, Trenear-Harvey, Bird & Watson, 1977–85; Vice Chm., Ogilvy & Mather Direct Worldwide, 1985–91. Inaugural Fellow, Inst. Direct Mktg, 1996. *Publications:* Some Rats Run Faster, 1964; Commonsense Direct Marketing: the printed shop, 1982, 5th edn 2007; How To Write Sales Letters That Sell, 1994, 2nd edn 2002; Marketing Insights and Outrages, 1999; How to Make Direct Marketing Work for Your Law Firm, 2009. *Recreations:* music, reading, wine, writing. *Address:* Drayton Bird Associates, Moyle House, Fleet Hill, Finchampstead, Wokingham, Berks RG40 4LJ.

BIRD, Harold Dennis, (Dickie), OBE 2012 (MBE 1986); umpire of first-class cricket, 1970–98, and of Test cricket, 1970–96; foundation Member, Independent International Panel of Umpires, 1993; Founder and Trustee, Dickie Bird Foundation, since 2004; *b* 19 April 1933; *s* of James Harold Bird and Ethel Bird; unmarried. *Educ:* Burton Road Primary Sch.; Raley Sch., Barnsley. Played county cricket for Yorkshire, 1956–60 (highest first-class score, 181 not out *v* Glamorgan, 1959), and Leicestershire, 1960–66; qualified MCC Advanced Cricket Coach, 1966; umpired 159 international matches (world record in 1996): 67 Tests (world record in 1994), incl. Queen's Silver Jubilee Test, Lord's, 1977, Centenary Test, Lord's, 1980, Bi-Centenary Test, Lord's, 1987, 3 in Zimbabwe, and WI *v* Pakistan series, 1993, in NZ, Pakistan and India, 1994, and Australia *v* Pakistan series, 1995; 92 one-day internationals, 1973–96 (world record in 1994); 4 World Cup tournaments, 1975–87, and Final at Lord's, 1975, 1979, 1983; Women's World Cup, and Final, NZ, 1982; finals of Gillette, NatWest, and Benson & Hedges competitions, Lord's, 1974–98; Rest of the World XI *v* World XI, Wembley Stadium, 1983; Centenary of Test Cricket, England *v* WI, Old Trafford, 1984; Rothmans Cup, 1983, 1985, Asia Cup, 1984, 1985, Champion's Cup, 1986, and Sharjah Tournament, 1993, UAE. Has travelled worldwide. Guest appearances on TV and radio progs include Down Your Way, Question of Sport, This is Your Life, Breakfast with Frost and Desert Island Discs; subject of BBC2 documentary, 1996; participant, The Young Ones, 2010. Freeman of Barnsley, 2000. Subject of life-size bronze statue, Barnsley, 2009. Hon. Life Mem., Assoc. of Cricket Officials, 2012. DUniv Sheffield Hallam, 1996; Hon. LLD Leeds, 1997; Hon. DCL Huddersfield, 2008. Yorkshire Personality of the Year, 1977; Yorkshire Man of the Year, 1996; People of the Year Award, RADAR/Abbey Nat., 1996; Special Sporting Award, Variety Club of GB, 1997; Cricket Writer's Award, 1997; English Sports Council (Yorks Reg.) Award, 1998; Special Merit Award, Professional Cricketers' Assoc., 1998; Barnsley Millennium of Merit Award, 2000; Yorkshire Hall of Fame, BBC Yorkshire Sports Awards, 2006. *Publications:* Not Out, 1978; That's Out, 1985; From the Pavilion End, 1988; Dickie Bird, My Autobiography, 1997; White Cap and Bails, 1999; Dickie Bird's Britain, 2002. *Recreations:* watching football, listening to Barbra Streisand, Nat King Cole, Diana Ross and Shirley Bassey records. *Address:* White Rose Cottage, 40 Paddock Road, Staincross, Barnsley, Yorks S75 6LE. *T:* (01226) 384491. *Clubs:* MCC (Hon. Life Mem., 1996), Lord's Taverners; Yorkshire CC (Hon. Life Mem., 1994; Pres., 2014–); Leicestershire CC (Hon. Life Mem., 1996); Cambridge University Cricket (Hon. Life Mem., 1996); Barnsley Football (Hon. Life Mem., 2003).

BIRD, John Anthony, MBE 1995; Founder, and Editor-in-Chief: The Big Issue, since 1991; ITTIA, since 2004; Wedge Card, since 2007; *b* 30 Jan. 1946; *s* of Alfred Ernest Bird and Eileen Mary (*née* Dunne); *m* 1st, 1965, Linda Stuart Haston (marr. diss.); one *d*; 2nd, 1973, Isobel

Theresa (marr. diss.), *d* of Sir Robert Ricketts, 7th Bt; one *s* one *d*; 3rd, 2004, Parveen Sodhi; one *s* one *d*. *Educ:* St Thomas More's Secondary Mod. Sch.; Ealing Coll. (BA Hons Hum.). Gardening asst, Royal Borough of Kensington and Chelsea, 1963–64; printer, Acrow Engrg, 1964–73; bean canner, H. J. Heinz, 1973–74; printer: Pictorial Charts Educnl Trust, 1974–75; Broadoak Press, 1978–83; print and publishing consultant, 1983–91. Contested Mayor of London, 2008. Hon. Fellow, Liverpool John Moores Univ., 2000. Hon. Dr Oxford Brookes, 2001. *Publications:* Some Luck (autobiog.), 2003; How to Change Your Life in 7 Steps, 2006; Change Your Life: 10 steps to get what you want, 2008; Necessity of Poverty, 2012; Why Drawing Naked Women is Good for the Soul, 2013. *Recreations:* swimming, cycling, running, drawing, talking, educating. *Address:* c/o The Big Issue, 1–5 Wandsworth Road, SW8 2LN.

BIRD, John Michael; actor and writer; *b* 22 Nov. 1936; *s* of Horace George Bird and Dorothy May Bird (*née* Haubitz); *m* Libby Crandon, musician. *Educ:* High Pavement Grammar Sch., Nottingham; King's Coll., Cambridge (BA 1958). Asst Artistic Dir, 1959–61, Associate Artistic Dir, 1961–63, Royal Court Theatre; writer and performer, The Establishment, 1961–64; Joint Founder: New York Establishment, 1963; New Theatre, NY, 1963. *Stage* includes: Luv, tour, 1971; Who's Who?, Arnaud, Guildford, 1972; Habeas Corpus, Lyric, 1973; The Ball Game, Open Space, 1978; Bremner, Bird and Fortune, Albery, 2002; *films:* Take a Girl Like You; The Seven Per Cent Solution; Yellow Pages; A Dandy in Aspic; *television* includes: Not so much a Programme, 1965–66; The Late Show, 1966; BBC3; A Series of Birds; With Bird Will Travel; John Bird/John Wells; Blue Remembered Hills; A Very Peculiar Practice; Travelling Man; El C.I.D., 1990, 1991, 1992; Rory Bremner… Who Else?, 1992–99 ((jtly) BAFTA Award for best light entertainment performance, 1997); The Long Johns, 1996–99; In the Red, 1998; Bremner, Bird and Fortune, 1999–2007; Chambers, 2000, 2001; Absolute Power, 2003, 2005; South Bank Show, 2007; Silly Money, 2008. Hon. DLitt Nottingham, 2002. *Publications:* (with John Fortune) The Long Johns, 1996; (with Rory Bremner and John Fortune) You Are Here, 2004. *Address:* c/o Chatto & Linnit Ltd, Worlds End Studios, 132–134 Lots Road, SW10 0RJ. *T:* (020) 7349 7222.

BIRD, Judith Pamela; *see* Kelly, Judith Pamela.

BIRD, Julian Piers; Chief Executive: Society of London Theatre, since 2010; UK Theatre Association (formerly Theatrical Management Association), since 2010; *b* Epsom, 3 April 1974; *s* of Colin Miles Dudley Bird and Veronica Mary Bird. *Educ:* Epsom Coll.; Univ. of Exeter (BA Hons Econs). Bank of England, 1995–97; FSA, 1997–2007; Chief Operating Officer, Tate, 2007–10; Exec. Producer, Olivier Awards, 2011–. Chair, Drama UK, 2013–. Mem., Adv. Cttee, American Theatre Wing, NY, 2012–. Trustee: Yvonne Arnaud Th., Guildford, 2005– (Chair, 2013–); De La Warr Pavilion, Bexhill on Sea, 2008–; Southwold and Aldeburgh Th. Trust, 2010–. *Recreations:* theatre, cinema, art, overseas travel, watching Spurs. *Address:* Society of London Theatre, 32 Rose Street, WC2E 9ET. *T:* (020) 7557 6702. *E:* julian@soltukt.co.uk. *Clubs:* Ivy, Groucho, Adam Street.

BIRD, Rt Rev. Michael; *see* Niagara, Bishop of.

BIRD, Michael George, OBE 2000; Director, Russia, British Council, since 2015; *b* 5 Jan. 1960; *s* of George Bird and Margaret Bird; *m* 2003, Simone Lees. *Educ:* Bedales Sch.; Emmanuel Coll., Cambridge (BA 1982); Voronezh Univ. (Dip. Russian Studies). Kennedy Schol., Harvard Univ., 1982–83. Teacher, Vienna, 1983–85; British Council: London, 1985–87; Asst Dir, Moscow, 1987–91; Eur. Liaison Officer, Brussels, 1991–93; Director: St Petersburg, 1993–97; Ukraine, 1997–2001; Scotland, 2001–05; Germany, 2005–09; Regional Director: SE Europe, 2009–11; Wider Europe, 2012–15. *Recreations:* music, travel, mountaineering. *Address:* British Council, Moscow, Russia. *T:* 4952871810. *E:* Michael.Bird@britishcouncil.org.

BIRD, Michael James; Regional Employment Judge (formerly Chairman of Industrial, later Employment Tribunals) for Wales, 1992–2008; *b* 11 Nov. 1935; *s* of Walter Garfield and Ireen Bird; *m* 1963, Susan Harris (*d* 2008); three *d*. *Educ:* Lewis Sch., Pengam; King's Coll., Univ. of London (LLB Hons). Solicitor (Hons) 1961. Assistant solicitor, 1961–62; Partner, T. S. Edwards & Son, 1962–67, Sen. Partner, 1967–84. Deputy Registrar of County and High Court, 1976–77; Chairman of Industrial Tribunal, Cardiff (part-time), 1977–83; Chm. of Industrial Tribunal, Bristol, 1984–87, Cardiff, 1987–92. Chm., Gwent Italian Soc., 1978–86 (Sec., 1976–78); Member: Royal Life Saving Soc., 1976– (President's Commendation, 1984); Amateur Swimming Assoc. (Advanced Teacher, 1981–); Newport and Maindee ASC; Crawshays Welsh RFC. *Recreations:* water sports, opera. *Address:* 17 Allt-yr-yn Avenue, Newport, Gwent NP20 5DA. *T:* (01633) 252000.

BIRD, Richard; Executive Director, UK Major Ports Group, 2007–14; *b* 12 Feb. 1950; *s* of late Desmond and Betty Bird; *m* 1973, Penelope Anne Frudd; one *s* one *d*. *Educ:* King's Sch., Canterbury; Magdalen Coll., Oxford. Admin. Trainee, DoE, 1971–73; Asst Private Sec. to Minister for Planning and Local Govt, 1974–75; Principal, Dept of Transport, 1975–78; First Sec., UK Rep. to EC, Brussels, 1978–82; Principal Private Sec. to Sec. of State for Transport, 1982–83; Asst Sec., 1983, Under Sec., 1990, Dept of Transport; Cabinet Office, 1992–94; Dir of Personnel, Dept of Transport, 1994–97; Dir, Urban (later Integrated) and Local Transport, DETR, 1997–2001; Dir of Energy, Envmt and Waste, 2001–03, of Water, 2003–07, DEFRA. Non-exec. Dir, United Utilities Water, 2008–11. Mem., Oxford Univ. Fencing Club, 1969–71 (represented Britain at World Youth Fencing Championship, 1970). FRSA 2006. *Recreations:* choral singing, summer sports. *Address:* c/o UK Major Ports Group, 30 Park Street, SE1 9EZ.

BIRD, Sir Richard (Geoffrey Chapman), 4th Bt *cr* 1922; *b* 3 Nov. 1935; *er* surv. *s* of Sir Donald Bird, 3rd Bt, and Anne Rowena (*d* 1969), *d* of late Charles Chapman; *S* father, 1963; *m* 1st, 1957, Gillian Frances (*d* 1966), *d* of Bernard Haggett, Solihull; two *s* four *d*; 2nd, 1968, Helen Patricia, *d* of Frank Beaumont, Pontefract; two *d*. *Educ:* Beaumont. *Heir:* *s* John Andrew Bird [*b* 19 Jan. 1964; *m* 1988, Winifred Dixon; two *s* one *d*]. *Address:* 20 Milcote Road, Solihull, W Midlands B91 1JN.

BIRD, Richard Herries, CB 1983; Deputy Secretary, Department of Education and Science, 1980–90; *b* 8 June 1932; *s* of late Edgar Bird and Armorel (*née* Dudley-Scott); *m* 1963, Valerie, *d* of Edward and Mary Sanderson; two *d*. *Educ:* Winchester Coll.; Clare Coll., Cambridge. Min. of Transport and Civil Aviation, 1955; Principal Private Sec. to Minister of Transport, 1966–67; CSD 1969; DoE 1971; DES 1973. *Address:* 15 Pinehurst, Sevenoaks, Kent TN14 5AQ.

BIRD, Prof. Richard Simpson, PhD; Professor of Computation, University of Oxford, 1996–2008; Fellow, Lincoln College, Oxford, since 1988; *b* 13 Feb. 1943; *s* of John William Bird and Martha (*née* Solar); *m* 1967, Norma Christine Lapworth. *Educ:* St Olave's Grammar Sch.; Gonville and Caius Coll., Cambridge (MA); Inst. of Computer Sci., Univ. of London (MSc; PhD 1973). Lecturer: in Computer Sci., Reading Univ., 1972–83; Oxford Univ., 1983–88; Dir, Computing Lab., Oxford Univ., 1998–2003. *Publications:* Programs and Machines, 1977; Introduction to Functional Programming, 1988, 2nd edn 1998; Algebra of Programming, 1996; Pearls of Functional Algorithm Design, 2010; Thinking Functionally with Haskell, 2014. *Recreations:* swimming, bridge, poker. *Address:* Stocks, Chapel Lane, Blewbury, Oxon OX11 9PQ. *T:* (01235) 850258; Lincoln College, Oxford OX1 3DR.

BIRD, Roger Charles; District Judge, Bristol County Court and District Registry of High Court, 1987–2005; *b* 28 April 1939; *s* of late Bertram Charles Bird and Olive Mary Bird; *m* 1964, Marie-Christine Snow; two *s*. *Educ:* Millfield Sch.; Univ. of Bristol (LLB Hons). Admitted solicitor, 1965; asst solicitor with various firms, 1965–69; Partner, Wilmot Thompson and Bird, Bristol, 1969–79; Registrar, Yeovil County Court, 1979–86. Member: Matrimonial Causes Rule Cttee, 1986–90; President's Adoption Cttee, Family Div., 1990–2002; Children Act Adv. Cttee, 1993–97; Lord Chancellor's Adv. Gp on Ancillary Relief, 1993–2004; Judicial Adv. Gp, Children and Family Court Adv. Support Service, 2000–01. Chm., Child Protection (later Safeguarding) Commn, dio. of Clifton, 2002–12; Mem., Nat. Catholic Safeguarding Council, 2008–12. Pres., Assoc. of Dist Judges, 1995–96. *Publications:* (with C. F. Turner) Bird and Turner's Forms and Precedents, 1985, 3rd edn 1992; (editor-in-chief) Sweet and Maxwell's Family Law Manual, 1985–96; Child Maintenance: the new law, 1992, 6th edn 2008; Domestic Violence, 1996, 6th edn 2015; (with S. M. Cretney) Divorce: the new law, 1996; Ancillary Relief Handbook, 1998, 9th edn as Ancillary Relief and Financial Orders Handbook, 2013, 10th edn as Financial Orders Handbook, 2015; Pension Sharing: the new law, 2000; (editor-in-chief) Emergency Remedies in the Family Courts, 2000–09; (editor-in-chief) Jordan's Precedents Service, 2002–09; numerous articles in legal jls. *Recreations:* wine, listening to music, gardens and gardening, rural walks. *Address:* c/o Jordans Publishing, 21 St Thomas Street, Bristol BS1 6JS.

BIRD, Rufus Benedict Godfrey; Deputy Surveyor of the Queen's Works of Art, since 2010; *b* Berlin, 16 April 1974; *s* of Derek and Jacina Bird; *m* 2004, Arabella Venetia Jane Hardy; three *d*. *Educ:* Eton Coll.; Peterhouse, Cambridge (BA Hons Hist. of Art 1996). Furniture Specialist, Christie, Manson & Woods Ltd, 1999–2010 (Dir, 2007–10). *Recreations:* yachting, shooting, music, music dramas of Richard Wagner. *Address:* The Royal Collection, York House, St James's Palace, SW1A 1BQ. *Clubs:* Beefsteak; University Pitt (Cambridge).

BIRD, Sheila Macdonald, OBE 2011; PhD; FRSE; Programme Leader, MRC Biostatistics Unit, Cambridge, since 1996; Visiting Professor, Department of Mathematics and Statistics, University of Strathclyde, since 2002; *b* Inverness, 18 May 1952; *d* of Herbert Gore and Isabella Agnes Gordon Gore (*née* Macdonald); *m* 1999, Dr Angus Graham Bird (*d* 2000); one step *s*. *Educ:* Elgin Acad.; Aberdeen Univ. (MA 1974; PhD 1981). CStat 1993; FFPH (by dist.) 2005. Res. Asst in Med. Stats, Edinburgh Univ., 1974–76; Lectr in Stats, Aberdeen Univ., 1976–80; Statistician, 1980–90, Sen. Statistician, 1990–96, MRC Biostats Unit, Cambridge; Statistical Dir, MRC-Biostatistical Initiative for AIDS and HIV Studies in Scotland, 1991–96. Vice-Pres. for Ext. Affairs, Royal Statistical Soc., 2005–09. FRSE 2012. Guy Medal in Bronze, 1989, Bradford Hill Medal, 2000, Chambers Medal, 2010, Howard Medal, 2015, Royal Statistical Soc.; Glaxo Medal, Soc. of Apothecaries, 2001. *Publications:* (with D. G. Altman) Statistics in Practice, 1982; (with B. A. Bradley) Renal Transplantation: sense and sensitization, 1988; contribs to learned jls, incl. Jl Royal Statistical Soc., Lancet, Addiction, BMJ, Jl Statistical Methods in Med. Res. *Recreations:* hill walking, antiques, Scottish paintings, culinary essays. *Address:* MRC Biostatistics Unit, Cambridge Institute of Public Health, Robinson Way, Cambridge CB2 0SR. *T:* (01223) 330368, *Fax:* (01536) 712451. *E:* sheila.bird@mrc-bsu.cam.ac.uk; Department of Mathematics and Statistics, University of Strathclyde, Livingstone Tower, 26 Richmond Street, Glasgow G1 1XH.

BIRD, Simon Christopher; QC 2009; *b* Felixstowe, 9 Oct. 1963; *s* of John and Christine Bird. *Educ:* Univ. of Reading (LLB). Called to the Bar, Middle Temple, 1987; a Dep. Principal Judge, First-tier Tribunal, Local Govt Standards in England (formerly Dep. Pres., Adjudication Panel for England), 2006–12; a Judge, First-tier Tribunal, General Regulatory Chamber (Envmt), 2012–. *Recreations:* gardening, golf, fly-fishing. *Address:* Francis Taylor Building, Inner Temple, EC4Y 7BY. *Clubs:* East India, MCC.

BIRD, Steven David; Managing Director, Birds Solicitors, since 2000; *b* Billericay, 9 Dec. 1963; *s* of David Roy Bird and Diane Christine Rena Bird (*née* Bugg); *m* 1993, Cathryn Mary Williams; two *s* two *d*. *Educ:* Royal Liberty Sch.; Univ. of Birmingham (LLB Hons Law and French 1986; LLM 1988); Univ. de Limoges (Dip. d'Etudes Juridiques Françaises 1985); Coll. of Law, Guildford. Admitted solicitor, 1990. With Simons Muirhead & Burton, 1988–2000. Member, Committee: London Criminal Courts Solicitors' Assoc., 2006–; Criminal Appeal Lawyers' Assoc., 2002– (Chm., 2014–). *Publications:* Police Station Advisers Index, 1995, 4th edn 2010; (contrib.) The Criminal Cases Review Commission: hope for the innocent?, 2010; (contrib.) Taylor on Criminal Appeals, 2nd edn 2012. *Recreations:* football (still playing), Arsenal FC, music, theatre, golf. *Address:* Birds Solicitors, 61 Wandsworth High Street, SW18 2PT. *T:* (020) 8874 7433, *Fax:* (020) 8870 4770. *E:* s.bird@birds.eu.com.

BIRD, Vivien Mary; Chief Executive, Booktrust, 2007–15; Senior Policy Adviser and Member, Management Board, European Literacy Policy Network, since 2015; *b* Jersey, CI, 29 Nov. 1950; *d* of late Jurat Lester Vivian Bailhache (sometime Lieut Bailiff of Jersey), and Nanette Ross Bailhache (*née* Ferguson); *m* 1974, Brendan John Bird; one *d* (and one *d* decd). *Educ:* Jersey Coll. for Girls; Southbank Poly. (HND Business Studies with Langs). DipM; Dip. Adult Literacy Teaching, RSA; Trainer Dip. (IT) Adult Educn, RSA. Mktg Exec., United Newspapers, 1971–74; Information Officer, Res. Unit, COI, 1974–78; volunteer adult literacy tutor, CRE community literacy project, Hammersmith Reading Centre, 1979–83; Community Outreach Worker, 1983–87 and 1990–94; National Literacy Trust, 1994–2007, posts include: Partnerships Develt Manager, 1999–2002; Ed., Literacy Today, 1995–2002; Project Dir, Literacy and Social Inclusion, 2002–05; Dir, Reading is Fundamental, 2005–07. Contrib. to TV, radio and print media debates on literacy and reading promotion, 2004–; keynote speaker for British Council at confs in Cairo, China and Taiwan, 2009–12. Chair, EU Read, 2009–14. Governor: Horder Rd Nursery Sch., 1980–83 (Chair, 1981–83); Langford Primary Sch., 1980–83; Sulivan Primary Sch., 1983–89 (Chair, 1984–88); Jack Tizard Special Sch., 1985–88; Sacred Heart High Sch., 1989–94; Phoenix High Sch., 1995–2006 (Special Gov.; Vice Chair of Govs, 1995–97, Chair, 1997–2006). FRSA. JP W London, 1989–96. *Publications:* A Literacy Guide for School Governors, 1998; (contrib. with P. Hannon) Handbook of Family Literacy, 2004, repr. 2011; Literacy and Social Inclusion: the handbook, 2005; (contrib.) Literacy and Social Inclusion: closing the gap, 2007. *Recreations:* tennis (player in Middlesex League), reading (especially translated fiction), music (Bruce Springsteen and Mary Black), family, promotion of reading in UK and internationally. *Address:* 1 Sulivan Road, SW6 3DT. *T:* (020) 7736 8722. *E:* viv.bird1@icloud.com. *Club:* Parsons Green Tennis.

See also Sir P. M. Bailhache, W. J. Bailhache.

BIRDS, Prof. John Richard; Professor of Commercial Law, University of Manchester, 2006–10, now Emeritus; Hon. Professor, University of Sheffield, since 2011; *b* 20 June 1948; *s* of John Sidney Birds and Katharine Charlotte Birds; *m* 1st, 1973, Margaret Rhona Richardson (marr. diss. 2008); two *s* one *d*; 2nd, 2009, Rachel Jane Williams. *Educ:* Chesterfield Grammar Sch.; University College London (LLB, LLM). Lectr in Law: Newcastle Polytechnic, 1970; QMC, Univ. of London, 1972; University of Sheffield: Lectr in Law, 1978–82; Sen. Lectr, 1982–85; Reader, 1985–89; Hd, Dept of Law, 1987–99 and 2002–05; Prof. of Commercial Law, 1989–2006. Hon. Prof. of Law, Univ. of Manchester, 2010–11. FRSA. Pres., Soc. of Legal Scholars, 2003–04. *Publications:* Modern Insurance Law, 1982, 9th edn 2013; (with A. J. Boyle) Company Law, 1983, 9th edn 2014; (jtly) Secretarial Administration, 1984; (ed jtly) MacGillivray and Parkington on Insurance Law, 8th edn 1988, 9th edn (as MacGillivray on Insurance Law) 1997 to 12th edn 2012; General Editor: Encyclopedia of Insurance Law, 2006; Annotated Companies Acts, 2007, 3rd edn 2013; Annotated Companies Legislation, 2010, 2nd edn 2012; articles in learned jls. *Recreations:* music, gardening, walking.

BIRDSALL, Derek Walter, RDI; freelance graphic designer; *b* 1 Aug. 1934; *s* of Frederick Birdsall and Hilda Birdsall (*née* Smith); *m* 1954, Shirley Thompson; three *s* one *d*. *Educ:* King's Sch., Pontefract, Yorks; Wakefield Coll. of Art, Yorks; Central Sch. of Arts and Crafts,

London (NDD). National Service, RAOC Printing Unit, Cyprus, 1955–57. Lectr in Typographical Design, London Coll. of Printing, 1959–61; freelance graphic designer, working from his studio in Covent Garden, later Islington, 1961–; Founding Partner, Omnific Studios Partnership, 1983. Vis. Prof. of Graphic Art and Design, RCA, 1987–88. Consultant designer, The Independent Magazine, 1989–93; Tutor and designer of house-style for Prince of Wales's Inst. of Arch., 1991; Design Consultant, NACF, 1992–97; Consultant Designer to C of E, 1999–. Has broadcast on TV and radio on design subjects and his work; catalogue designs for major museums throughout the world have won many awards, incl. Gold Medal, New York Art Directors' Club, 1987. Mem., AGI, 1968–96; FCSD (FSIAD 1964); RDI 1982; FRSA; Hon. FRCA 1988; Hon. FISTD 2005. Prince Philip Designers Prize, 2005; D&AD President's Award, 2012. *Publications:* (with C. H. O'D. Alexander) Fischer *v* Spassky, 1972; (with C. H. O'D. Alexander) A Book of Chess, 1974; (with Carlo M. Cippola) The Technology of Man—a visual history, 1978; (with Bruce Bernard) Lucian Freud, 1996; Notes on Book Design, 2004. *Recreations:* chess, poker. *Address:* 8 Compton Terrace, Islington, N1 2UN. *Club:* Chelsea Arts.

BIREEDO, Omer Yousif; National Adviser, Republican Palace, Sudan, since 2004; *b* 1 Jan. 1939; *s* of Yousif Bireedo and Fatima Hasan; *m* 1978, Kalthoum M. E. Barakat; one *s* two *d.* *Educ:* Univ. of Khartoum (BA); Delhi Univ. (MA). Sudanese Diplomatic Service: Third Sec., New Delhi, 1963–66; London, 1966–69; Dep. Dir, Consular Dept, Min. of Foreign Affairs, Khartoum, 1969–71; Uganda, 1971–73; Mission to UN, NY, 1973–76; Dir, Dept of Internat. Orgns, Min. of Foreign Affairs, Khartoum, 1976–78 and 1986–89; Ambassador and Perm. Rep. to UN and Internat. Orgns, Geneva and Vienna, 1978–83, NY, 1983–86; Ambassador to Saudi Arabia, 1989–92; 1st Under-Sec., Min. of Foreign Affairs, Khartoum, 1992–95; Ambassador to UK, 1995–99; Dir, Political Dept, Palace of Pres. of Sudan, Khartoum, 1999–2004. Mem., UN Admin. Tribunal, 2001–04; Pres., UN Assoc. of Sudan, 2009. Pres., Council, Sinnar Univ., 2009–. Republican Order (Sudan), 1972. *Recreations:* walking, reading. *Address:* c/o Ministry of Foreign Affairs, Khartoum, Sudan.

BIRGENEAU, Dr Robert Joseph, FRS 2001; FRSC 2002; Arnold and Barbara Silverman Distinguished Professor of Physics, Materials Science and Engineering, and Public Policy, University of California, Berkeley, since 2013 (Chancellor, 2004–13); *b* Toronto, 25 March 1942; *m* 1964, Mary Catherine Ware; one *s* three *d.* *Educ:* Univ. of Toronto (BSc 1963); Yale Univ. (PhD 1966). Grad. Student, 1963–66, Instructor, 1966–67, Dept of Engrg and Applied Sci., Yale Univ.; Nat. Res. Council of Canada Postdoctoral Fellow, Oxford Univ., 1967–68; Bell Laboratories, Murray Hill, NJ: Mem., Tech. Staff, Physical Res. Lab., 1968–74; Res. Hd, Scattering and Low Energy Physics Dept, 1975; Consultant, 1977–80; Massachusetts Institute of Technology: Prof. of Physics, 1975–2000; Cecil and Ida Green Prof. of Physics, 1982–2000; Associate Dir, Res. Lab. of Electronics, 1983–86; Head: Solid State, Atomic and Plasma Physics, 1987–88; Dept of Physics, 1988–91; Dean, Sch. of Sci., 1991–2000; Pres. and Prof. of Physics, Univ. of Toronto, 2000–04. Consultant: IBM Res. Labs, NY, 1980–83; Sandia Nat. Labs, Albuquerque, 1985–90. Guest Sen. Physicist, Brookhaven Nat. Lab., NY, 1968–2004; Vis. Scientist, Riso Nat. Lab., Roskilde, Denmark, 1971, 1979. Numerous lectures at univs in USA, Canada, UK and Israel, incl. A. W. Scott Lecture, Cambridge Univ., 2000. Co-Chm., Polaroid Sci. and Technol. Bd, 1998–2002. Mem., Ext. Adv. Cttee, Physics Dept, Oxford Univ., 2000. FAAAS 1982; Fellow: APS, 1980; Amer. Acad. Arts and Scis, 1987 (Co-Chm., Lincoln Project, 2013–). Trustee, Boston Mus. of Sci., 1992–2001; Gov., Argonne Nat. Lab., 1992–2001; Mem., Adv. Council, Nippon Electric Co. Res. Inst., 1995–2000. Holds numerous awards and prizes. *Publications:* numerous contribs to learned jls on phases and phase transition behaviour of novel states of matter. *Address:* c/o University of California, Berkeley, 366 Le Conte Hall, Berkeley, CA 94720–7300, USA.

BIRKENHEAD, Bishop Suffragan of, since 2007; **Rt Rev. (Gordon) Keith Sinclair;** *b* 3 Dec. 1952; *s* of Donald and Joyce Sinclair; *m* 1989, Rosemary Jones; two *s* one *d.* *Educ:* Christ Church, Oxford (BA, MA 1975); Cranmer Hall, Durham (BA 1984). Ordained deacon, 1984, priest, 1985; Asst Curate, Christ Church, Summerfield, 1984–88; Vicar, St Peter and St Paul, Aston, 1988–2001; Area Dean, Aston, 2000–01; Vicar, Holy Trinity, Coventry, 2001–07. Hon. Canon, Birmingham Cathedral, 2000–01. *Recreations:* walking, cinema, theatre. *Address:* Bishop's Lodge, 67 Bidston Road, Prenton CH43 6TR. *T:* (0151) 652 2741, *Fax:* (0151) 651 2330. *E:* bpbirkenhead@chester.anglican.org.

BIRKETT, family name of **Baron Birkett.**

BIRKETT, 3rd Baron *cr* 1958, of Ulverston; **Thomas Birkett;** *b* 25 July 1982; *o s* of 2nd Baron Birkett and Gloria Birkett (*née* Taylor); *S* father, 2015.

BIRKETT, Sir Peter, Kt 2012; founder, and education and skills consultant, Passion 5 Excellence, since 2013; *b* Scunthorpe, 6 Nov. 1959; *s* of John and Sylvia Birkett; *m* 1997, Julie Nicola Doe; one *s* one *d.* *Educ:* Frederick Gough Comprehensive Sch.; Huddersfield Poly. (Cert Ed 1985); Univ. of Reading (MA). Apprentice engr, 1976–82; engrg work, Australia, 1982–84; Lectr, Basingstoke Coll. of Technol., 1985–96; Dir of Technol., Bristol Coll., 1996–2001; Dep. Principal, Sheffield Coll., 2002–05; Founder and Chief Exec., then Dir Gen., Barnfield Fedn, 2005–13. Mem. Bd, Young People's Learning Agency, 2009–12. *Recreations:* fitness, gym, golf. *Address:* Coles House, Coles Lane, Kinsbourne Green, Harpenden, Herts AL5 3PX. *T:* 07765 182948. *E:* spbirkett@outlook.com. *Club:* Luton Hoo.

BIRKETT, Peter Vidler; QC 1989; a Recorder, since 1989; *b* 13 July 1948; *s* of late Neville Lawn Birkett, MA, MB BCh, FRES and Marjorie Joy Birkett; *m* 1976, Jane Elizabeth Fell; two *s.* *Educ:* Sedbergh School; Univ. of Leicester. Called to the Bar, Inner Temple, 1972, Bencher, 1996; practice on SE Circuit, 1973–77, on N Circuit, 1977– (Leader, 1999–2001). Asst Recorder, 1986–89; Deemster, High Ct, IOM, 2000. Mem., General Council of the Bar, 1999–2001. Vice-Chm., Advocacy Trng Council of Eng. and Wales, 2004–08. Hon. Fellow, Manchester Metropolitan Univ., 2007. *Recreations:* golf, conversation, playing the piano. *Address:* 18 St John Street, Manchester M3 4EA. *T:* (0161) 834 9843. *Clubs:* Wilmslow Golf; Seniors Golf Soc.

BIRKHEAD, Prof. Timothy Robert, DPhil, DSc; FRS 2004; Professor of Zoology, Department of Animal and Plant Sciences, University of Sheffield, since 1992; *b* 28 Feb. 1950; *s* of Robert Harold and Nancy Olga Birkhead; *m* 1976, Miriam Enid Appleton; one *s* two *d.* *Educ:* Univ. of Newcastle upon Tyne (BSc; DSc 1989); Wolfson Coll., Oxford (DPhil 1976). Department of Animal and Plant Sciences, University of Sheffield: Lectr, 1976–86; Sen. Lectr, 1986–89; Reader, 1989–92. Nuffield Res. Fellow, 1990–91; Leverhulme Res. Fellow, 1995–96. Elliot Coues Medal, Amer. Ornithologists' Union, 2011; Medal, Assoc. for Study of Animal Behaviour, 2012; Silver Medal, Zool Soc. of London, 2014. *Publications:* (with C. M. Perrins) Avian Ecology, 1983; (with M. E. Birkhead) The Survival Factor, 1989; The Magpies: the ecology and behaviour of black-billed and yellow-billed magpies, 1991; (with A. P. Møller) Sperm Competition in Birds: evolutionary causes and consequences, 1992; Great Auk Islands, 1993; (with A. P. Møller) Sperm Competition and Sexual Selection, 1998; Promiscuity, 2000; The Red Canary, 2003; The Wisdom of Birds, 2008; (ed jtly) Sperm Biology: an evolutionary perspective, 2009; Bird Sense: what it's like to be a bird, 2012; (jtly) Ten Thousand Birds: ornithology since Darwin, 2014. *Recreations:* art, music, walking. *Address:* 47 Whiteley Wood Road, Sheffield S11 7FF. *T:* (0114) 222 4622, *Fax:* (0114) 222 0002. *E:* t.r.birkhead@sheffield.ac.uk.

BIRKIN, Sir Derek; *see* Birkin, Sir J. D.

BIRKIN, Sir John (Christian William), 6th Bt *cr* 1905, of Ruddington Grange, Notts; *b* 1 July 1953; *s* of Sir Charles Lloyd Birkin, 5th Bt and Janet (*d* 1983), *d* of Peter Johnson; *S* father 1985; *m* 1994, Emma Gage; one *s* one *d.* *Educ:* Eton; Trinity Coll., Dublin; London Film School. *Heir:* *s* Benjamin Charles Birkin, *b* 4 Nov. 1995. *Address:* Place Barton, Ashton, Exeter, Devon EX6 7QP.

BIRKIN, Sir (John) Derek, Kt 1990; TD 1965; Chairman, The RTZ Corporation PLC (formerly Rio Tinto-Zinc Corporation), 1991–96 (Chief Executive and Deputy Chairman 1985–91); *b* 30 Sept. 1929; *s* of Noah and Rebecca Birkin; *m* 1952, Sadie Smith; one *s* one *d.* *Educ:* Hemsworth Grammar Sch. Managing Director: Velmar Ltd, 1966–67; Nairn Williamson Ltd, 1967–70; Dep. Chm. and Man. Dir, Tunnel Holdings Ltd, 1970–75; Chm. and Man. Dir, Tunnel Holdings, 1975–82; Dir, Rio Tinto-Zinc, then RTZ, Corp., 1982–96; Dep. Chief Exec., 1983–85. Director: Smiths Industries, 1977–84; British Gas Corp. 1982–85; George Wimpey, 1984–92; CRA Ltd (Australia), 1985–94; Rio Algom Ltd (Canada), 1985–92; The Merchants Trust PLC, 1986–99; British Steel plc (formerly BSC) 1986–92; Barclays PLC, 1990–95; Merck & Co. Inc. (USA), 1992–2000; Carlton Communications Plc, 1992–2001; Unilever PLC, 1993–2000; Chm., Watmoughs (Holdings) PLC, 1996–98. Member: Review Body on Top Salaries, 1986–89; Council, Industrial Soc. 1985–97. Dir, Royal Opera House, 1993–97 (Trustee, 1990–93). CCMI (CBIM 1980) FRSA 1988. Hon. LLD Bath, 1998. *Recreations:* opera, Rugby, cricket.

BIRKINSHAW, Prof. Julian Mark, PhD; FBA 2012; Professor of Strategy and Entrepreneurship, London Business School, since 2004; *b* Hexham, 16 Oct. 1964; *s* of John (Ian) and Susan Birkinshaw; *m* 1994, Laura Maclellan; two *s* one *d.* *Educ:* Perse Sch. for Boys; Manchester Grammar Sch.; Durham Univ. (BSc); Univ. of Western Ontario (MBA; PhD 1995). Asst Prof., Stockholm Sch. of Econs, 1995–99; London Business School: Asst Prof. 1999–2000; Associate Prof., 2000–04; Dep. Dean, Progs, 2007–10. Vis. Schol., INSEAD Business Sch., 2006–07. *Publications:* Becoming a Better Boss: why good management is so difficult, 2013. *Recreations:* running, triathlons, orienteering, piano. *Address:* London Business School, Regents Park, NW1 4SA. *T:* (020) 7000 8718. *E:* jbirkinshaw@london.edu.

BIRKMYRE, Sir James, 4th Bt *cr* 1921, of Dalmunzie, County of Perth; Director of Championship Management (formerly Tournament Development), PGA European Tour since 1994; *b* 29 Feb. 1956; *s* of Sir Archibald Birkmyre, 3rd Bt and of Gillian Mary (*née* Downes); *S* father, 2001; *m* 1st, 1990 (marr. diss. 2010); one *s*; 2nd, 2012, Kim Jean Andreolli *d* of George and Jane Florek, Florida, USA. *Educ:* Radley Coll.; Ecole Supérieure de Commerce, Neuchâtel; Ealing Tech. Coll. (BA Hons). Account Mgr, Collet Dickenson & Pearce Advertising, 1978–82; Account Dir, TBWA Advertising, 1982–87; Sponsorship Dir The Wight Co., 1987–93; Man. Dir, Birchgrey, 1993–94. Mem., RGS. *Recreations:* tennis fly-fishing, golf, ski-ing, shooting, mountaineering. *Heir:* *s* Alexander Birkmyre, *b* 24 May 1991. *Address:* 1 Parsonage Farm Cottage, Frilsham, Berks RG18 9UY. *T:* (01635) 201282 *Clubs:* MCC, Lord's Taverners; Sunningdale Golf; Reading Football; Dalmunzie Golf (Hon. Mem.).

BIRLEY, Prof. Susan Joyce, (Mrs David Norburn); Professor of Entrepreneurship, The Business School (formerly Professor of Management), Imperial College, London, 1990–2003 Director, Entrepreneurship Centre, 2000–03; *m* 1st, 1964, Arwyn Hopkins (marr. diss. 1970) 2nd, 1975, Prof. David Norburn, *qv.* *Educ:* Nelson Grammar Sch.; University College London (BSc 1964; Fellow, 2004); PhD London 1974. FSS. Teacher, Dunsmore Sch. 1964–66; Lectr, Lanchester Polytechnic, 1966–68; Lectr and Sen. Lectr, Poly. of Central London, 1968–72; Sen. Res. Fellow, City Univ., 1972–74; London Business School: Sen. Res. Fellow, 1974–79; Lectr in Small Business, 1979–82; University of Notre Dame, USA Adjunct Associate Prof., 1978–82; Associate Prof. of Strategy and Entrepreneurship, 1982–85 Philip and Pauline Harris Prof. of Entrepreneurship, Cranfield Inst. of Technol., 1985–90 Academic Dir, European Foundn for Entrepreneurship Res., 1988–91. Member: CNAA 1987–90; NI Economic Council, 1988–94; PCFC, 1988–92; Adv. Panel on Deregulation DTI, 1989–91; Bd, LEDU, NI, 1992–93. Founder Director and Shareholder: Guidehouse Group, 1980–85; Greyfriars Ltd, 1982–85; Newchurch & Co., 1986–97 (Chm.); Director NatWest Bank, 1996–2000; Process Systems Enterprise Ltd, 1997–2003; IC Innovations Ltd 1997–2003; BAE Systems, 2000–07. Mem. Panel, Foresight Steering Gp, 1997–2001 Governor, Harris City Technol. Coll., 1990–92. FCGI 2001; Fellow, British Acad. of Mgt 1996. Freeman, City of London, 1964. Mem. Editl Bds, various business jls. *Publications:* From Private to Public (jtly), 1977; The Small Business Casebook, 1979; The Small Business Casebook: teaching manual, 1980; New Enterprises, 1982; (contrib.) Small Business and Entrepreneurship, ed Burns and Dewhurst, 1989; (jtly) Exit Routes, 1989; (jtly) The British Entrepreneur, 1989; (ed) European Entrepreneurship: emerging growth companies, 1989; (ed jtly) International Perspectives on Entrepreneurship, 1992; Entrepreneurship Research: global perspectives, 1993; Mastering Enterprise, 1997; Mastering Entrepreneurship, 2000 Franchising: pathway to wealth creation, 2004; numerous contribs to learned jls. *Recreation* gardening.

BIRMINGHAM, Archbishop of, (RC), since 2009; **Most Rev. Bernard Longley;** *b* 5 April 1955; *s* of Frederick and Audrey Longley. *Educ:* Xaverian Coll., Manchester; RNCM New Coll., Oxford (MA); St John's Seminary, Wonersh. Ordained priest, 1981; Asst Priest St Joseph's, Epsom, 1982–85; English Coll., Rome, 1985–87; Theol. Tutor, St John's Seminary, Wonersh, 1987–96; Catholic Bishops' Conference: Nat. Ecumenical Officer 1996–2003; Asst Gen. Sec. (responsible for Ecumenism and Inter Faith Affairs), 2000–03 Auxiliary Bishop of Westminster, (RC), 2003–09; Titular Bishop of Zarna, 2003–09. Hon Canon, Worcester Cathedral, 2013–. Co-chair, Anglican RC Internat. Commn, 2011– Mem., Pontifical Council for Promoting the New Evangelism, 2011–; RC Co-Chm., English Anglican-Roman Catholic Cttee, 2011–; Chairman: Bishops' Conference Dept for Dialogue and Unity, 2009–; Commn for Overseas Seminaries, 2012–. Surrey Chm., Diocesan Commn for Christian Unity, 1991–96; Moderator, Steering Cttee, CTBI, 1999–2003. *Address* Archbishop's House, 8 Shadwell Street, Birmingham B4 6EY.

BIRMINGHAM, Bishop of, since 2006; **Rt Rev. David Andrew Urquhart;** Prelate of the Most Distinguished Order of St Michael and St George, since 2005; *b* 14 April 1952; *s* of late Hector Maconochie Urquhart, FRCSE and of Elizabeth Mary Florence Urquhart (*née* Jones). *Educ:* Croftinloan; Rugby Sch.; Ealing Business Sch. (BA Hons); Wycliffe Hall, Oxford. Volunteer in Uganda, 1971; BP plc, 1972–82; ordained deacon, 1984, priest, 1985 Curate, St Nicholas, Kingston upon Hull, 1984–87; Team Vicar, Drypool, 1987–92; Vicar Holy Trinity, Coventry, 1992–2000; Bp Suffragan of Birkenhead, 2000–06. Hon. Canon, Coventry Cathedral, 1999–2000. Chairman: Hull and E Yorks Faith in the City Gp, 1985–90; CMS, 1994–2007; Chester Dio. Bd of Educn, 2001–06; Wirral Local Strategic Partnership, 2002–06; Council, Ridley Hall, Cambridge, 2010–; Birmingham Social Inclusion Process, 2012–; Univ. of Birmingham Commn on Wealth Distribution, 2012–13. Director: Coventry City Centre Co., 1997–2000; Hippodrome Theatre, Birmingham, 2009–; Be Birmingham Strategic Partnership, 2009–12. Archbp of Canterbury's Episcopal Link with China, 2006– Chm. Governors, Craven (LEA) Primary Sch., 1988–92; Gov., Rugby Sch., 1999–. Entered House of Lords, 2010. Hon. Freeman, Metropolitan Borough of Wirral, 2006. Tallow Chandlers Medal, BP, 1977. Hon. DD Birmingham, 2009; DUniv Birmingham City, 2014. *Recreations:* squash, fives (half blue, Rugby fives, 1984), watching films, collecting books on red deer. *Address:* Bishop's Croft, Old Church Road, Harborne, Birmingham B17 0BG. *T:* (0121) 427 1163. *E:* bishop@birmingham.anglican.org. *Club:* Athenæum.

BIRMINGHAM, Auxiliary Bishops of, (RC); *see* Byrne, Rt Rev. R. J.; Kenney, Rt Rev. W.; McGough, Rt Rev. D.

BIRMINGHAM, Dean of; *see* Ogle, Very Rev. C.

BIRMINGHAM, Archdeacon of; *see* Osborne, Ven. H. J.

BIRNBAUM, Michael Ian; QC 1992; a Recorder, since 1995; *b* 26 Feb. 1947; *s* of Samuel Birnbaum and Anne (*née* Zucker); *m* 1984, Aimee Dara Schachter. *Educ:* Southgate County Grammar Sch.; Christ Church, Oxford (BA Jurisp.). Called to the Bar, Middle Temple, 1969; practice mainly in criminal law, extradition and human rights; Asst Recorder, 1990–95. Chm., W Africa Sub-Cttee, Bar Human Rights Cttee, 2002–07; Mem., Bar Internat. Relns Cttee, 2001–07. Trustee, Redress Trust, 2007–. *Publications:* two reports on the case in Nigeria of Ken Saro-Wiwa and others. *Recreations:* singing, opera, reading. *Address:* 9–12 Bell Yard, WC2A 2JR. *T:* (020) 7400 1800.

BIRNEY, Dr Ewan, FRS 2014; Joint Associate Director and Senior Scientist, European Molecular Biology Laboratory - European Biometrics Institute, since 2012; *b* Paddington, 1972; *s* of Jack and Joy Birney; *m* 2003, Barley Laycock; one *s* one *d*. *Educ:* Eton Coll.; Balliol Coll., Oxford (BA Biochem. 1996); St John's Coll., Cambridge (PhD 2000). Res. at Sanger Inst., Univ. of Cambridge, 1996–2000; Team leader, Eur. Bioinformatics Inst., 2000–10; Mem., Associate Faculty, Wellcome Trust Sanger Inst., 2012–. Francis Crick Award, Royal Soc., 2003; Overton Prize, Internat. Soc. for Computational Biol., 2005; Benjamin Franklin Award, Bioinformatics Orgn, 2005. *Publications:* contribs to learned jls, incl. Nature, Science, Genome Res. *Recreations:* science, cookery. *Address:* European Bioinformatics Institute, Wellcome Trust Genome Campus, Hinxton, Cambridge CB10 1SD.

BIRNIE, Dr Esmond; Chief Economist, Northern Ireland, PricewaterhouseCoopers, since 2010; *b* 6 Jan. 1965; *s* of Dr James Whyte Birnie and Ruth Alexandra Birnie (*née* Bell). *Educ:* Gonville and Caius Coll., Cambridge (BA 1st Cl. Hons Econs 1986); Queen's Univ., Belfast (PhD Econs 1994). Res. Asst, NI Econ. Res. Centre, 1986–89; Lectr in Econs, 1989–2000, Sen. Lectr in Econs and Mgt, 2000–07, QUB. Northern Ireland Assembly: Mem. (UU) Belfast S, 1998–2007; contested same seat, 2007; Ministerial Special Advr, Dept for Employment and Learning, NI, 2007–10. Chm., Cttee for Higher and Further Educn, Trng and Employment, then for Employment and Learning, 1999–2002. UU Party spokesman: on North-South affairs and British-Irish Council, 1999–2003; on Dept of Finance and Family, 2006–07; Talks negotiator, 2006–07. *Publications:* Without Profit or Prophets, 1997; *jointly:* Closing the Productivity Gap, 1990; East German Productivity, 1993; The Competitiveness of Industry in Ireland, 1994; Competitiveness of Industry in the Czech Republic and Hungary, 1995; An Economics Lesson for Irish Nationalists and Republicans, 1995; Environmental Regulation, the Firm and Competitiveness, 1998; The Northern Ireland Economy, 1999; Environmental Regulation and Competitive Advantage, 2000; Can the Celtic Tiger Cross the Border?, 2001; A Brighter Future for Northern Ireland: the case against the Euro, 2002; Government Futures (pamphlet series), 2010–12. *Recreations:* cycling, jogging, art, architecture, music, church choir, active church member. *Address:* 32 Finaghy Road South, Finaghy, Belfast BT10 0DR.

BIRRELL, Sir James (Drake), Kt 1993; FCA; FCBSI; Chief Executive, Halifax Building Society, 1988–93; *b* 18 Aug. 1933; *s* of James Russell Birrell, MA and Edith Marion Birrell, BSc (*née* Drake); *m* 1958, Margaret Anne Pattison; two *d*. *Educ:* Belle Vue Grammar School, Bradford. FCA 1955; FCBSI 1989. Boyce Welch & Co. (articled clerk), 1949–55; Pilot Officer, RAF, 1955–57; chartered accountant, Price Waterhouse, 1957–60; Accountant, ADA Halifax, 1960–61; Management Accountant, Empire Stores, 1961–64; Dir and Co. Sec., John Gladstone & Co., 1964–68; Halifax Building Society, 1968–93. Non-executive Director: Securicor, 1993–2003; Wesleyan Gen. Assce Soc., 1993–2004. Mem., Building Societies Commn, 1994–2001. *Recreations:* golf, gardening, archaeology, local history. *Address:* 4 Marlin End, Berkhamsted, Herts HP4 3GB.

BIRSE, Peter Malcolm; Chairman, Birse Group, 1999–2001 (Chairman and Chief Executive, 1970–99); *b* 24 Nov. 1942; *s* of Peter A. M. Birse and Margaret C. Birse; *m* 1969, Helen Searle; two *s* one *d*. *Educ:* Arbroath High Sch.; St Andrews Univ. (BScEng). MICE. Engineer, John Mowlem, 1963–66; Site Manager: Cammon (Ghana), 1966–68; Cammon (UK), 1968–69; Engineer, Foster Wheeler, 1969–70; founded Birse Group, 1970. *Recreations:* sailing, ski-ing. *Address:* c/o Birse Group, Humber Road, Barton-on-Humber, N Lincs DN18 5BW. *Club:* Royal Ocean Racing.

BIRSS, Hon. Sir Colin (Ian); Kt 2013; **Hon. Mr Justice Birss;** a Judge of the High Court of Justice, Chancery Division, since 2013; *b* Thurso, 28 Dec. 1964; *s* of Ian and Davina Birss; *m* 1987, Kathryn Squibbs; two *s* one *d*. *Educ:* Downing Coll., Cambridge (BA Natural Sci. 1986); City Univ. (Dip. Law 1989). Called to the Bar, Middle Temple, 1990, Bencher, 2011; in practice at the Bar, 1990–2010; QC 2008; a Specialist Circuit Judge, Patents County Ct, 2010–13. Standing Counsel to Comptroller-Gen. of Patents, 2003–08; Mem., Bar Standards Bd Professional Conduct and Complaints Cttee, 2003–09; Dep. Chm., 2009–10, Chm., 2010–13, Copyright Tribunal. *Publications:* Terrell on the Law of Patents, 15th edn, 2000 to 17th edn, 2011. *Recreation:* beekeeping. *Address:* Royal Courts of Justice, Rolls Building, 7 Rolls Buildings, Fetter Lane, EC4A 1NL.

BIRT, family name of **Baron Birt**.

BIRT, Baron *cr* 2000 (Life Peer), of Liverpool in the County of Merseyside; **John Birt,** Kt 1998; Prime Minister's Strategy Adviser, 2001–05; *b* 10 Dec. 1944; *s* of Leo Vincent Birt and Ida Birt; *m* 1965, Jane Frances (*née* Lake) (marr. diss. 2006); one *s* one *d*; *m* 2006, Eithne Victoria Wallis, *qv*. *Educ:* St Mary's Coll., Liverpool; St Catherine's Coll., Oxford (MA; Hon. Fellow 1992). Producer, Nice Time, 1968–69; Joint Editor, World in Action, 1969–70; Producer, The Frost Programme, 1971–72; Executive Producer, Weekend World, 1972–74; Head of Current Affairs, LWT, 1974–77; Co-Producer, The Nixon Interviews, 1977; Controller of Features and Current Affairs, LWT, 1977–81; Dir of Programmes, LWT, 1982–87; Dep. Dir-Gen., 1987–92, Dir-Gen., 1992–2000, BBC. Adviser: McKinsey & Co., 2000–05; Terra Firma, 2005–; Capgemini, 2006–10. Chairman: Lynx New Media, subseq. Lynx Capital Ventures, 2000–04; Waste Recycling Gp, 2006; Infinis, 2006–07 (non-exec. Dir, 2007–13); Maltby Capital Ltd, 2008–10 (non-exec. Dir, 2007–08); Novera Energy plc, 2010; PayPal (Europe) Ltd, 2010–14 (non-exec. Dir, 2004–10); Vice-Chm. Dir, Eutelsat, 2012 (non-exec. Dir, 2006–12); non-exec. Dir, Shopvolution, 2012–; Chm., HEG (formerly Host Europe Gp), 2013–. Advr to Prime Minister on Criminal Justice, 2000–01; Mem., Cabinet Office Strategy Bd, 2003–05. Vis. Fellow, Nuffield Coll., Oxford, 1991–99. Member: Wilton Park Academic Council, 1980–83; Media Law Gp, 1983–94; Opportunity 2000 (formerly Women's Economic) Target Team, BITC, 1991–98; Internat. Council, Mus. of TV and Radio, NY, 1994–2000; Broadcasting Research Unit: Mem., Working Party on the new Technologies, 1981–83; Mem., Exec. Cttee, 1983–87. Mem. Adv. Bd, GovernUp, 2013–. Vice-Pres., RTS, 1994–2000 (Fellow, 1989). FIET (CompIEE 1998). Hon. Fellow, Univ. of Wales Cardiff, 1997. Hon. DLitt: Liverpool John Moores, 1992; City, 1998; Bradford, 1999; Westminster, 2010. Emmy Award, US Nat. Acad. of Television, Arts and Scis, 1995. *Publications:* The Harder Path (autobiog.), 2002; various articles in newspapers and journals. *Recreations:* football, walking, cinema. *Address:* c/o House of Lords, SW1A 0PW.

BIRT, Sir Michael (Cameron St John), Kt 2012; QC 1995; a Judge of the Court of Appeal of Guernsey, since 2009; a Commissioner, Royal Court of Jersey, since 2015; Deemster, Appeal Division, High Court of Isle of Man, since 2015; *b* 25 Aug. 1948; *s* of late St John Michael Clive Birt, OBE, FRCS and Mairi Araminta Birt (*née* Cameron); *m* 1973, Joan Frances Miller; two *s* one *d*. *Educ:* Marlborough Coll.; Magdalene Coll., Cambridge (MA Law). Called to the Bar, Middle Temple, 1970, Bencher, 2009, to Jersey Bar, 1977; in practice: London, 1971–75; as Jersey advocate, with Ogier & Le Cornu, St Helier, 1976–93; Crown Advocate of Jersey, 1987–93; HM Attorney General, Jersey, 1994–2000; Dep. Bailiff, 2000–09, Bailiff, 2009–15, of Jersey. *Recreations:* ski-ing, yachting, golf. *Address:* Bailiff's Chambers, Royal Court House, St Helier, Jersey JE1 1BA. *T:* (01534) 441100, *Fax:* (01534) 441137. *Clubs:* Royal Channel Islands Yacht; Royal Jersey Golf.

BIRT, Simon Christopher; QC 2015; *b* Farnborough, Kent, 5 March 1975; *s* of Derek and Theresa Birt; *m* 1999, Gemma Lau; one *s* three *d*. *Educ:* Solihull Sch.; Brasenose Coll., Oxford (MA; BCL). Called to the Bar, Gray's Inn, 1998; in practice as barrister, specialising in commercial litigation, 1998–. *Recreations:* music, family. *Address:* Brick Court Chambers, 7–8 Essex Street, WC2R 3LD.

BIRTLES, His Honour William Jack; a Circuit Judge, 2002–14; *b* 27 Oct. 1944; *s* of William George Birtles and Dorothy Louisa Birtles (*née* Martin); *m* 1981, Rt Hon. Patricia Hope Hewitt, *qv*; one *s* one *d*. *Educ:* King's Coll. London (LLB, AKC 1967; LLM 1968); Harvard Law Sch. (Kennedy Schol.; LLM 1971); New York Univ. Law Sch. (Robert Marshall Fellow). Called to the Bar: Gray's Inn, 1970, Bencher, 2008; Lincoln's Inn, 1986; NI, 1998; Lecturer in Law: KCL, 1968–70; UCL, 1972–74; in practice as barrister, 1974–2002. Vis. Fellow, 1993–94, Sen. Associate Mem., 1996–2014, St Antony's Coll., Oxford. Liveryman, Tallow Chandlers' Co., 2011. *Publications:* (with R. Stein) Planning and Environmental Law, 1994; (with A. Forge) Local Government Finance Law, 2000; (jtly) Environmental Liability, 2004; contrib. legal jls. *Recreations:* listening to opera and classical music, reading fiction and poetry, collecting European travel books, international relations, theatre, being in Norfolk. *Club:* Travellers.

BIRTS, Peter William; His Honour Judge Birts; QC 1990; QC (NI) 1996; a Circuit Judge, since 2005; *b* 9 Feb. 1946; *s* of late John Claude Birts and Audrey Lavinia Birts; *m* 1st, 1971, Penelope Ann Eyre (marr. diss. 1997); two *d* one *s*; 2nd, 1997, Mrs Angela Forcer-Evans. *Educ:* Lancing College; St John's College, Cambridge (choral scholarship; MA). Called to the Bar, Gray's Inn, 1968, Bencher 1998; a Recorder, 1989–2005; a Dep. High Ct Judge, 2000–05; Mem., Gen. Council of the Bar, 1989–95 (Chm., Legal Aid and Fees Cttee, 1994–95). Member: Judicial Studies Bd (Main Bd and Civil and Family Cttee), 1991–96; County Court Rules Cttee, 1991–99; Legal Member: Mental Health Review Tribunals, 1994–; Parole Bd, 2006–. Asst Parly Boundary Comr, 1992–95. Freeman, City of London, 1967; Liveryman, Carpenters' Co., 1967–. *Publications:* Trespass: summary procedure for possession of land (with Alan Willis), 1987; Remedies for Trespass, 1990; (ed and contrib.) Butterworths Costs Service, 1999–2009. *Recreations:* music, tennis, country pursuits. *Address:* Kingston Crown Court, 6–8 Penrhyn Road, Kingston upon Thames, Surrey KT1 2BB. *T:* (020) 8240 2500. *Club:* Hurlingham.

BIRTWISTLE, Gordon; *b* Oswaldwistle, 6 Sept. 1943; *m* 1986, Kathleen; one *s* one *d*. *Educ:* Accrington Coll. (HNC Prodn Engrg; HNC Mech. Engrg). Apprentice, Howard and Bullough, Accrington; work in engrg industry; owner, Stuart Engrg, 1996–2002. Councillor (Lab), Gt Harwood, Lancs, 1970–74; Mem. (Lib Dem) Burnley BC, 1983– (Mayor, 2002–03; Leader, 2006–10). Contested (Lib Dem) Burnley, 1992, 1997. MP (Lib Dem) Burnley, 2010–15; contested (Lib Dem) same seat, 2015.

BIRTWISTLE, Sir Harrison, CH 2001; Kt 1988; composer; Henry Purcell Professor of Composition, King's College London, 1994–2001; *b* 1934; *m* Sheila; three *s*. *Educ:* Royal Manchester Coll. of Music; RAM (Hon. FRAM). Dir of Music, Cranborne Chase Sch., 1962–65. Composer-in-residence, London Philharmonic Orch., 1993–. Vis. Fellow, Princeton Univ., 1966–68; Cornell Vis. Prof. of Music, Swarthmore Coll., 1973; Vis. Slee Prof., State Univ. of NY at Buffalo, 1974–75. An Associate Dir, NT, 1975–88. Mem., Akademie der Kunst, Berlin. FKC 1998. Hon. DMus: Sussex; Cambridge, 2010; Hon. DLitt Salford. Evening Standard Award for Opera, 1987, 1991; Ernst von Siemens Foundn Prize, 1995. Chevalier des Arts et des Lettres (France), 1986. *Publications:* Refrains and Choruses, 1957; Monody for Corpus Christi, 1959; Précis, 1959; The World is Discovered, 1960; Chorales, 1962, 1963; Entre'actes and Sappho Fragments, 1964; Three Movements with Fanfares, 1964; Tragoedia, 1965; Ring a Dumb Carillon, 1965; Carmen Paschale, 1965; The Mark of the Goat, 1965, 1966; The Visions of Francesco Petrarca, 1966; Verses, 1966; Punch and Judy, 1966–67 (opera); Three Lessons in a Frame, 1967; Linoii, 1968; Nomos, 1968; Verses for Ensembles, 1969; Down by the Greenwood Side, 1969; Hoquetus David (arr. of Machaut), 1969; Cantata, 1969; Ut Hermita Solvs, 1969; Medusa, 1969–70; Prologue, 1970; Nenia on the Death of Orpheus, 1970; An Imaginary Landscape, 1971; Meridian, 1971; The Fields of Sorrow, 1971; Chronometer, 1971; Epilogue—Full Fathom Five, 1972; Tombeau, 1972; The Triumph of Time, 1972; La Plage: eight arias of remembrance, 1972; Dinah and Nick's Love Song, 1972; Chanson de Geste, 1973; The World is Discovered, 1973; Grimethorpe Aria, 1973; 5 Chorale Preludes from Bach, 1973; Chorales from a Toyshop, 1973; Interludes from a Tragedy, 1973; The Mask of Orpheus, 1973–84 (opera) (Grawemeyer Award, Univ. of Louisville, 1987); Melencolia I, 1975; Pulse Field, Bow Down, Silbury Air, 1977; For O, for O, the Hobby-horse is forgot, 1977; Carmen Arcadiae Mechanicae Perpetuum, 1978; agm, 1979; On the Sheer Threshold of the Night, 1980; Quintet, 1981; Pulse Sampler, 1981; Deowa, 1983; Yan Tan Tethera, 1984; Still Movement, 1984; Secret Theatre, 1984; Songs by Myself, 1984; Earth Dances, 1986; Fanfare for Will, 1987; Endless Parade, 1987; Gawain, 1990 (opera); Four Poems by Jaan Kaplinski, 1991; Gawain's Journey, 1991; Antiphonies, 1992; The Second Mrs Kong, 1994 (opera); Cry of Anubis, 1995; Panic, 1995; Pulse Shadows, 1996; Slow Frieze, 1997; Exody, 1997; Harrison's Clocks, 1998; The Silk House Antiphonies, 1999; The Woman and the Hare, 1999; The Last Supper (opera), 2000; The Axe Manual, 2001; The Shadow of Night, 2002; Theseus Game, 2003; 26 Orpheus Elegies, 2003; Ring Dance of the Nazarene, 2003; The Gleam, 2003; The Io Passion, 2004; Night's Black Bird, 2004; Neruda Madrigales, 2005; The Minotaur, 2008; The Tree of Strings, 2008; The Corridor (opera), 2009; Angel Fighter, 2010, Violin Concerto, 2011; Oboe Quartet, 2011; Piano Trio, 2011; Moth Requiem, 2012; In Broken Images, 2012; Songs from the Same Earth, 2013; Fantasia Upon All the Notes, 2013; Construction with Guitar, 2013; Responses, 2014; The Cure (opera), 2015. *Address:* c/o Rayfield Allied, Southbank House, Black Prince Road, SE1 7SJ.

BIRTWISTLE, Susan Elizabeth, (Lady Eyre); film and television producer; writer; *d* of late Frank Edgar Birtwistle and Brenda Mary Birtwistle (*née* Higham); *m* 1973, Richard Charles Hastings Eyre (*see* Sir Richard Eyre); one *d*. Theatre director: Royal Lyceum Th. in Educn Co., 1970–72; Nottingham Playhouse Roundabout Co., 1973–78; freelance TV producer, 1980–: work includes: Hotel du Lac, 1986 (BAFTA Award; Cable/Ace Award); Scoop; 'v' (RTS Award); Or Shall We Die?; Dutch Girls; Ball Trap on the Côte Sauvage; Anna Lee, 1993; Pride and Prejudice, 1995 (TRIC Award, TV Critics of Britain Award, 1995; TV Critics of America Award, Peabody Award, Voice of the Listener and Viewer Award, 1996; BVA Award, English Heritage Award, Banff Award, Banff Victor Ludorum Award); Emma, 1996; King Lear, 1998; Wives and Daughters, 1999; Armadillo, 2001; Cranford, 2007, 2009. Mem., Arts Council Drama Panel, 1975–77. *Publications:* The Making of Pride and Prejudice, 1995; The Making of Jane Austen's Emma, 1996; The Cranford Companion, 2010. *Recreations:* music, books, theatre, gardening. *Address:* c/o Nick Marston, Curtis Brown, 4th Floor, Haymarket House, 28–29 Haymarket, SW1Y 4SP. *T:* (020) 7396 6600.

BISCHOFF, Dr Manfred; Chairman, Supervisory Board, Daimler (formerly DaimlerChrysler) AG, since 2007; *b* Calw, Germany, 22 April 1942. *Educ:* Univ. of Tubingen; Univ. of Heidelberg (MEc; Dr rer. pol. 1973). Asst Prof. for Econ. Politics and Internat. Trade, Alfred Weber Inst., Univ. of Heidelberg, 1968–76; joined Daimler-Benz AG, 1976; Project Co-ordinator for Mercedes Benz Cross Country Cars, Corporate Subsids, M & A Dept, 1976–81; Internat. Projects, M & A, Finance Dept, 1981–88 (Vice-Pres., Finance Cos and Corporate Subsids); Member, Board of Management: and Chief Financial Officer, Mercedes do Brasil, 1988–89; and Chief Financial Officer, Deutsche Aerospace AG, later Daimler-Benz Aerospace AG, 1989–95; Daimler-Benz AG, later Daimler Chrysler AG, 1995–2003; and Pres. and CEO, DASA, 1995–2000; Mitsubishi Motors Corp., 2000–03; Chm. Supervisory Bd, MTU Aero Engines, 2000–03; Chm., EADS (European Aeronautic Defence and Space Co.), 2000–07; Mem. several supervisory bds. President: Eur. Assoc. Aerospace Industries, 1995–96; Fedn of German Aerospace Industries, 1996–2000. *Address:* Daimler AG, 70546 Stuttgart, Germany.

BISCHOFF, Sir Winfried Franz Wilhelm, (Sir Win), Kt 2000; Chairman: Financial Reporting Council, since 2014; J. P. Morgan Securities plc, since 2015; *b* 10 May 1941; *s* of late Paul Helmut Bischoff and Hildegard (*née* Kühne); *m* 1972, Rosemary Elizabeth, *d* of Hon. Leslie Leathers; two *s*. *Educ:* Marist Brothers, Inanda, Johannesburg, S Africa; Univ. of the Witwatersrand, Johannesburg (BCom). Man. Dir, Schroders Asia Ltd, Hong Kong, 1971–82; Dir, 1978–2000, Chm., 1983–94, J. Henry Schroder & Co. Ltd; Dir, 1983–2000, Gp Chief Exec., 1984–95, Chm., 1995–2000, Schroders plc. Dep. Chm., Cable and Wireless, 1995–2003 (non-exec. Dir, 1991–2003); Chairman: Citigroup Europe, 2000–07; Citigroup Inc., 2007–09; non-executive Director: Land Securities plc, 1999–2008; McGraw-Hill Cos, Inc., 1999–; IFIL, Finanziaria di Partecipazioni SpA, 2000–04; Eli Lilly & Co., 2000–14; Siemens Hldgs plc, 2001–03; Prudential plc, 2007–09; Akbank AS, 2007–08 (Mem., Internat. Adv. Bd, 2009–); Lloyds Banking Gp, 2009–14. Chm., Adv. Council, TheCityUK, 2009–14. *Recreations:* opera, music, golf. *Address:* Financial Reporting Council, 125 London Wall, EC2Y 5AS. *Clubs:* Swinley Forest Golf, Frilford Heath Golf, Loch Lomond Golf; Blind Brook Golf (US).

BISCOE, Prof. Timothy John; Visiting Professor, University of Bristol, since 2006; Pro-Provost, China, University College London, 1996–2001; *b* 28 April 1932; *s* of late Rev. W. H. Biscoe and Mrs M. G. Biscoe; *m* 1st, 1955, Daphne Miriam (*née* Gurton) (*d* 2005); one *s* two *d*; 2nd, 2008, Sarah Neale Lawson. *Educ:* Latymer Upper School; The London Hospital Medical College. BSc (Hons) Physiology, 1953; MB, BS 1957; DSc London, 1993; FRCP 1983. London Hospital, 1957–58; RAMC Short Service Commission, 1958–62; Physiologist, CDEE, Porton Down, 1959–62; ARC Inst. of Animal Physiology, Babraham, 1962–65; Res. Fellow in Physiology, John Curtin Sch. of Med. Res., Canberra, 1965–66; Associate Res. Physiologist, Cardiovascular Res. Inst., UC Medical Center, San Francisco, 1966–68; University of Bristol: Res. Associate, Dept of Physiology, 1968–70; 2nd Chair of Physiology, 1970–79; Head of Dept of Physiology, 1975–79. University College London: Jodrell Prof. of Physiology, 1979–92; Vice Provost, 1990–92; Hon. Fellow, 1996; Dep. Vice-Chancellor, Univ. of Hong Kong, 1992–95. McLaughlin Vis. Prof., McMaster Univ., Ont, 1986; Hooker Distinguished Vis. Prof., McMaster Univ., 1990. Hon. Sec., Physiological Soc., 1977–82; Member Council: Harveian Soc., 1983–86; Research Defence Soc., 1983–90 (Hon. Sec., 1983–86). Mem., Academia Europaea, 1991. *Publications:* papers on neurophysiology in Journal of Physiology, etc. *Recreations:* looking, listening, reading. *Address:* c/o Physiology Department, University of Bristol, Bristol BS8 1TD. *Club:* Garrick.

BISH-JONES, Trevor Charles; Co-founder, mypeoplebiz.com, 2009; Chief Operating Officer, United Electronics, 2010–14; *b* 23 April 1960; *m* 1990, Amanda Zeil; two *d*. *Educ:* Varndean Grammar Sch., Brighton; Portsmouth Sch. of Pharmacy (BSc Hons Pharmacy). Res. Chemist, Tosco Corporate, Colorado, 1980–81; Boots plc: Store Manager, 1981–84; EPOS Project Manager, 1984–86; Buying and Marketing Controller for Photo/Sound/Vision/Home, 1987–94; Dixons Group: Marketing Dir, PC World and Dixons, 1994–97; Man. Dir, The Link, then Dixons, then Currys, 1997–2002; CEO, Woolworths Gp plc, 2002–08. *Recreation:* horse riding.

BISHKO, Roy Colin; Founder and Chairman, Tie Rack Ltd, 1981–99 (Co-Chairman, 1999–2007); *b* 2 March 1944; *s* of Isidore Bishko and Rae Bishko; *m* 1969, Barbara Eileen (*née* Hirsch); one *s* one *d*. *Educ:* Grey Coll., Bloemfontein, SA; Univ. of S Africa (Attorney's Admission 1967). With Schlesinger Orgn, 1969–74; Dir, Dorrington Investment Co. Ltd, 1974–76; Man. Dir, Chaddesley Investments, London, 1976–78. FRSA 1992. *Recreations:* golf, history.

BISHOP, family name of **Baroness O'Cathain**.

BISHOP, Alan Henry, CB 1989; HM Chief Inspector of Prisons for Scotland, 1989–94; *b* 12 Sept. 1929; *s* of Robert Bishop and May Watson; *m* 1959, Marjorie Anne Conlan; one *s* one *d*. *Educ:* George Heriot's Sch., Edinburgh; Edinburgh Univ. (MA Hons Econ. Sci., 1951, History, 1952). Served RAF Educn Br., 1952–54. Asst Principal, Dept of Agric. for Scotland, 1954; Private Sec. to Parly Under-Secs of State, 1958–59; Principal, 1959; First Sec., Agric. and Food, Copenhagen and The Hague, 1963–66; Asst Sec., Commn on the Constitution, 1969–73; Asst Under-Sec. of State, 1980–84, Principal Establishment Officer, 1984–89, Scottish Office. *Recreations:* contract bridge (Pres., Scottish Bridge Union, 1979–80), theatre. *Address:* Beaumont Court, 19/8 Wester Coates Gardens, Edinburgh EH12 5LT. *T:* (0131) 346 4641. *Clubs:* New (Edinburgh); Melville Bridge.

BISHOP, Alan John; Chief Executive, Southbank Centre, since 2009; *b* 2 Aug. 1953; *s* of Ronald and Betty Bishop. *Educ:* Queen's Coll., Oxford (BA Hons). With various advertising agencies, incl. Bates & FCB, 1974–85; joined Saatchi & Saatchi, 1985; Chairman: N America, 1994–97; UK, 1997–98; International, 1998–2002; Chief Exec., COI, 2003–09. *Recreations:* bridge, music. *Address:* Southbank Centre, Belvedere Road, SE1 8XX. *Club:* Soho House.

BISHOP, Ven. (Anthony) Peter, CB 2001; Associate Priest, Tewkesbury with Walton Cardiff and Twyning, 2001–06; *b* 24 May 1946; *s* of Geoffrey Richard Bishop and Dora Annie Bishop; *m* 1970, Ruth Isabel Jordan; two *s*. *Educ:* London Coll. of Divinity; St John's Coll., Nottingham (LTh 1971; MPhil 1983). Civil Servant, MoT, 1963–67; ordained deacon 1971, priest 1972; Curate, Beckenham, 1971–75; RAF Chaplain, 1975–2001: Asst Chaplain-in-Chief, 1991–98; Chaplain-in-Chief, and Archdeacon, RAF, 1998–2001. QHC 1996–2001. Canon of Lincoln, 1998–2001. Mem., Gen. Synod of C of E, 1998–2001. Mem. Council, RAF Benevolent Fund, 1998–2001; Vice-Pres., RAFA, 1998–. Vice-Pres., Friends of St Clement Danes, 1998–. FRSA 1983; FRAeS 1999. *Recreations:* walking, history, biography, cookery, living in France. *Address:* La Croix Blanche, 50810 St Germain d'Elle, France.

BISHOP, Dr Arthur Clive; Deputy Director, British Museum (Natural History), 1982–89, and Keeper of Mineralogy, 1975–89; *b* 9 July 1930; *s* of late Charles Henry Bishop and Hilda (*née* Clowes); *m* 1st, 1962, Helen (*née* Bennison) (*d* 2005); one *d*; 2nd, 2008, Kathleen Martha Renfrew (*née* Hope). *Educ:* Wolstanton County Grammar Sch., Newcastle, Staffs; King's Coll., Univ. of London (Shell Scholar; FKC 1985). BSc 1951, PhD 1954. Geologist, HM Geological Survey, 1954; served RAF Educn Br., 1955–57; Lectr in Geology, Queen Mary Coll., Univ. of London, 1958; Principal Sci. Officer, British Museum (Natural History), 1969, Deputy Keeper 1972. Geological Society: Daniel Pidgeon Fund, 1958; Murchison Fund, 1970; Vice-Pres., 1977–78; Mineralogical Society: Gen. Sec., 1965–72; Vice-Pres., 1973–74; Pres., 1986–87; Pres., Geologists' Assoc., 1978–80 (Halstead Medallist, 1999); Vice-Pres., Inst. of Science Technology, 1973–82. Mem. d'honneur, La Société Jersiaise, 1983. *Publications:* An Outline of Crystal Morphology, 1967; (with W. R. Hamilton and A. R. Woolley) Hamlyn Guide to Minerals, Rocks and Fossils, 1974, rev. edn as Philip's Minerals, Rocks and Fossils, 1999; papers in various jls, mainly on geology of Channel Is and Brittany and on dioritic rocks. *Recreation:* drawing and painting.

BISHOP, Hon. Bronwyn Kathleen; MHR (L) Mackellar, New South Wales, since 1994; Speaker, House of Representatives, Australia, 2013–15; *b* Sydney, NSW, 19 Oct. 1942; *d* of Thomas Francis Setright and Kathleen Setright (*née* Congreve); *m* 1966, Alan Bishop (marr. diss. 1992; he *d* 2010); two *d*. *Educ:* Univ. of Sydney (LLB). Admitted as solicitor, NSW, 1967. Senator (L), NSW, 1987–94. Shadow Minister: for Urban and Regl Strategy, 1994; for Health, 1994–95; for Privatisation and for Commonwealth and State Relns, 1995–96. Minister: for Defence Industry, Sci. and Personnel, 1996–98; for Aged Care, 1998–2001. Shadow Minister: for Veterans' Affairs, 2007–08; for Seniors, 2009–13; Shadow Special Minister of State, 2010–13. Chair: Standing Cttee on Legal and Constitutional Affairs, 2002–04; Hse of Reps Standing Cttee on Family and Human Services, 2004–07; Mem., Speaker's Panel, House of Reps, 2004–07. Dep. Chm., Pacific Democratic Union, 1993–98. Mem., Australian Cttee, Pacific Basin Econ. Council. NSW Division, Liberal Party of Australia: Mem., State Exec., 1980–; Vice-Pres., 1982–85; Pres., 1985–87; Mem., Jt Parly Public Accounts Cttee, 1987–94. Vice-Pres., Asthma Foundn, NSW, 1975–78; Life Member: Royal NSW Inst. for Deaf and Blind Children (former Vice-Pres.); Art Gall. Soc. of NSW. Centenary Medal, 2003. *Recreations:* family, music, art, football. *Address:* Parliament House, Canberra, ACT 2600, Australia. *T:* (2) 62774000. *E:* Bronwyn.bishop.mp@aph.gov.au. *Clubs:* Commonwealth (ACT); Union University and Schools (Sydney).

BISHOP, Prof. Christopher Michael, PhD; FREng; FRSE; Distinguished Scientist, Microsoft Research, Cambridge, since 2010 (Deputy Director, 1997–2008; Chief Research Scientist, 2008–10); Professor of Computer Science (part-time), University of Edinburgh, since 1997; *b* Norwich, 7 April 1959; *s* of Leonard Bishop and Joyce Bishop; *m* 1988, Jennifer Mary Morris; two *s*. *Educ:* Earlham Sch., Norwich; St Catherine's Coll., Oxford (BA Hons Physics 1980; MA 1984); Univ. of Edinburgh (PhD Theoretical Physics 1983). FREng 2004; FRSE 2007. Res. Physicist, Culham Lab., UKAEA, 1983–93; Prof. of Computer Sci., Aston Univ., 1993–97. Vice Pres., Royal Instn of GB, 2010–. *Publications:* Neural Networks for Pattern Recognition, 1995; Pattern Recognition and Machine Learning, 2006. *Recreations:* flying light aircraft, including aerobatics. *Address:* Microsoft Research, 21 Station Road, Cambridge CB1 2FB. *E:* Christopher.Bishop@microsoft.com.

BISHOP, Prof. David Hugh Langler, PhD, DSc; FRSB; Fellow, St Cross College, Oxford, 1984–98, now Emeritus; Director, Natural Environment Research Council Institute of Virology and Environmental Microbiology (formerly Institute of Virology), 1984–95; *b* 31 Dec. 1937; *s* of late Reginald Samuel Harold Bishop and of Violet Rosina May Langler; *m* 1st, 1963, Margaret Duthie (marr. diss.); one *s* one *d*; 2nd, 1971, Polly Roy (marr. diss.); one *s*; 3rd, 1999, Margreta Buijs; one *s* two *d*. *Educ:* Liverpool Univ. (BSc Hons Biochem. 1959, PhD 1962); MA 1984, DSc 1988, Oxon. FRSB (FIBiol 1989). Postdoctoral Fellow, CNRS, Gif-sur-Yvette, 1962–63; Research Associate, Univ. of Edinburgh, 1963–66, Univ. of Illinois, 1966–69; Asst Prof., 1969–70, Associate Prof., 1970–71, Columbia Univ.; Associate Prof., 1971–75, Prof., 1975, Rutgers Univ.; University of Alabama at Birmingham: Prof., 1975–84; Sen. Scientist, Comprehensive Cancer Center, 1975–84; Chm., Dept of Microbiology, 1983–84; Adjunct Prof., Dept of Internat. Health, 1996–99. Vis. Fellow, Lincoln Coll., Oxford, 1981–82; Vis. Prof. of Virology, Oxford Univ., 1984–97; Hon. Prof., Dept of Microbiol., Univ. of Qld, 1997–2000. Nathaniel A. Young Award in Virology, 1981. *Publications:* Rhabdoviruses, 1979; numerous contribs to books and jls. *Recreation:* hill walking. *Address:* 12 Chemin du Haut Morier, 41000 Blois Les Grouets, Loir et Cher, France.

BISHOP, Prof. Dorothy Vera Margaret, DPhil; FBA 2006; FRS 2014; FMedSci; Professor of Developmental Neuropsychology, since 1999, and Wellcome Principal Research Fellow, since 1998, University of Oxford; *b* 14 Feb. 1952; *d* of Aubrey Francis Bishop and Annemarie Sofia Bishop (*née* Eucken); *m* 1976, Patrick Michael Anthony Rabbitt, *qv*. *Educ:* St Hugh's Coll., Oxford (BA Hons 1973; MA; DPhil 1978); Inst. of Psychiatry, Univ. of London (MPhil 1975). Res. Officer, Neuropsychology Unit, Dept of Clinical Neurology, Univ. of Oxford, 1975–82; Sen. Res. Fellow, MRC, at Univs of Newcastle upon Tyne and Manchester, 1982–91; Sen. Res. Scientist, MRC Applied Psychology Unit, Cambridge, 1991–98. Adjunct Prof., Univ. of Western Australia, 1998. Mem., ESRC, 1996–2000. FMedSci 2000; Fellow, Assoc. for Psychol Sci., 2010. Hon. DM Lund, 2004; Hon. DSc: Newcastle upon Tyne, 2012; Western Australia, 2012. *Publications:* (ed with K. Mogford) Language Development in Exceptional Circumstances, 1988; Handedness and Developmental Disorders, 1990; Uncommon Understanding: development and disorders of language comprehension in children, 1997; (ed with L. B. Leonard) Speech and Language Impairments in Children, 2000. *Recreations:* Victorian novels, pre-1945 films, blogging (http://deevybee.blogspot.com), Twitter (www.twitter.com/deevybee), writing crime fiction under pen-name Deevy Bishop (two Kindle e-books, The Case of the Fremantle Fingers, The Case of the Brothel in the Bush, 2011). *Address:* Department of Experimental Psychology, South Parks Road, Oxford OX1 3UD. *T:* (01865) 271386.

BISHOP, Edward James; QC 2011; *b* London, 13 Sept. 1960; *s* of James Drew Bishop, *qv*; *m* 1994, Sarah Paneth. *Educ:* King's Sch., Canterbury; Pembroke Coll., Cambridge (BA 1982); Poly. of Central London (DipLaw). Called to the Bar, Middle Temple, 1985; in practice as a barrister, specialising in clinical negligence, 1 Chancery Lane, 1986–. *Publications:* (contrib. ed.) Kemp and Kemp on the Quantum of Damages, 2008–; contribs to various other legal books and jls. *Recreations:* travel, travel writing, football, cricket, music (fiddle player and singer in country folk band Police Dog Hogan). *Address:* 1 Chancery Lane, WC2A 1LF. *T:* 0845 634 6666, *Fax:* 0845 634 6667. *E:* ebishop@1chancerylane.com. *Club:* MCC.

BISHOP, Ven. Ian Gregory; Archdeacon of Macclesfield, since 2011; *b* Devizes, 13 Nov. 1962; *s* of John and Lorna Bishop; *m* 1986, Sue Winton; three *s*. *Educ:* Devizes Sch.; Portsmouth Poly. (BSc Urban Land Admin. 1984; ARICS 1986); Oak Hill Theol Coll. (BA Theol and Pastoral Studies 1991). Ordained deacon, 1991, priest, 1992; Curate, Christ Church, Purley, 1991–95; Rector: Tas Valley Team Ministry, 1995–2001; St Michael and All Angels, Middlewich, and St John the Evangelist, Byley, 2001–11. *Address:* 57A Sandbach Road, Congleton, Cheshire CW12 4LH. *E:* ian.bishop@chester.anglican.org.

BISHOP, James Drew; writer and editor; Chairman, National Heritage, 1998–2012 (Trustee, 1995–2012); *b* 18 June 1929; *s* of late Sir Patrick Bishop, MBE, MP, and Vera Drew; *m* 1959, Brenda Pearson; two *s*. *Educ:* Haileybury; Corpus Christi Coll., Cambridge. Reporter, Northampton Chronicle & Echo, 1953; joined editorial staff of The Times, 1954; Foreign Correspondent, 1957–64; Foreign News Editor, 1964–66; Features Editor, 1966–70; Editor, Illustrated London News, 1971–87; Editor-in-Chief, Illustrated London News Publications, 1987–94. Director: Illustrated London News & Sketch Ltd, 1973–94; International Thomson Publishing Ltd, 1980–85. Chm., Assoc. of British Editors, 1987–96. Mem., 1970–2012, Chm., 2000–12, Adv. Bd, Annual Register (contributor, Amer. sect., 1960–88); Chm. Editl Bd, Natural World, 1981–97. *Publications:* A Social History of Edwardian Britain, 1977; Social History of the First World War, 1982; (with Oliver Woods) The Story of The Times, 1983; (ed) The Illustrated Counties of England, 1985; The Sedgwick Story, 1998. *Recreations:* reading, walking, looking and listening. *Address:* Black Fen, Scotland Street, Stoke by Nayland, Suffolk CO6 4QD. *T:* (01206) 262315. *E:* jamesbishop.3@btinternet.com. *Clubs:* Oxford and Cambridge, MCC.

See also E. J. Bishop.

BISHOP, His Honour John Edward; a Circuit Judge, 1993–2004; *b* 9 Feb. 1943; *s* of Albert George Bishop and Frances Marion Bishop; *m* 1968, Elizabeth Ann Grover; two *d. Educ:* St Edward's Sch., Oxford. Articled to P. F. Carter-Ruck at Messrs Oswald Hickson Collier & Co., WC2, 1962–66; admitted solicitor, 1966; Partner: Messrs Copley Clark & Co., Sutton, 1969–81; Messrs Tuck & Mann, Epsom, 1981–85; Registrar: Woolwich County Court, 1985–88; Croydon County Court, 1988–93 (District Judge, 1992–93); an Asst Recorder, 1987–90; a Recorder, 1990–93. Pres., Mid-Surrey Law Soc., 1980–81. *Recreations:* golf, walking, music, reading, garden, family. *Clubs:* East India; Walton Heath Golf.

BISHOP, Prof. (John) Michael, MD; Professor of Microbiology and Immunology, since 1972, and of Biochemistry and Biophysics, since 1982, University Professor, since 1994, Director, G. W. Hooper Research Foundation, since 1981, and Chancellor, 1998–2009, now Chancellor Emeritus, University of California, San Francisco; *b* 22 Feb. 1936; *s* of John and Carrie Bishop; *m* 1959, Kathryn Putman; two *s. Educ:* Gettysburg Coll., Gettysburg (AB); Harvard Univ., Boston (MD). Intern/Asst Resident in Internal Med., Mass. Gen. Hosp., 1962–64; Res. Associate, NIAID, NIH, 1964–67; Vis. Scientist, Heinrich-Pette Inst., Hamburg, 1967–68; Asst Prof., Microbiology, 1968–70, Associate Prof., Microbiology, 1970–72, Univ. of California. Member: Nat. Acad. of Scis, 1980–; Amer. Acad. of Arts and Scis, 1984–. Foreign Mem., Royal Soc., 2008. Hon. DSc: Gettysburg, 1983; KCL, 2008. Albert Lasker Award for Basic Med. Res., 1982; Passano Foundn Award, 1983; Warren Triennial Prize, 1983; Armand Hammer Cancer Res. Award, 1984; Gen. Motors Cancer Res. Award, 1984; Gairdner Foundn Internat. Award, 1984; ACS Medal of Honor, 1985; (jtly) Nobel Prize in Physiology or Medicine, 1989. *Publications:* The Rise of the Genetic Paradigm, 1995; Proto-oncogenes and Plasticity in Cell Signaling, 1995; How to Win the Nobel Prize: an unexpected life in science, 2003; over 400 pubns in refereed sci. jls. *Recreations:* music, reading, theatre. *Address:* G. W. Hooper Research Foundation, Box 0552, 1542 HSW, University of California, 513 Parnassus Avenue, San Francisco, CA 94143–0552, USA. *T:* (415) 4763211.

BISHOP, Kathryn Ann, (Mrs Mark Carden); a Civil Service Commissioner, since 2012; Associate Fellow, Saïd Business School, University of Oxford, since 2004; *b* Binghamton, NY, 2 Aug. 1958; *d* of Geoffrey and Marjorie Bishop; *m* 1990, Mark Carden; two *s. Educ:* City of Worcester Grammar Sch. for Girls; Wellesley Coll., USA (BA Hons *summa cum laude* 1979); Jesus Coll., Oxford (MPhil 1981). Sen. Manager, Accenture, 1981–90; Asst Dir, 1990–91, Personnel Develt Dir, 1992–94, Allied Dunbar; Change Manager, Eagle Star Life, 1994–96; Prog. Dir, Allied Dunbar/Eagle Star Life, 1996–98; Dir, Business Transformation, Eagle Star, Allied Dunbar and Zurich Gp, 1998–99; Dir, Naughton Consulting Ltd, 1999–; Hd, Planning and Projects, UWE, 2001–04. Non-executive Director: UK Intellectual Property Office, 2000–09; Welsh Assembly Govt, 2003–10; UK Border Agency, 2010–12. Mem., Phi Beta Kappa, 1979. Gov., Horsley C of E (Aided) Primary Sch., 1996–2012; Chairman: Bd of Trustees, Dean Close Sch., 2014–; Horsley Free Sch. Charities Trust, 1996–. *Recreations:* singing in choirs, theatre, reading. *Address:* Saïd Business School, University of Oxford, Egrove Park, Kennington, Oxford OX1 4DY. *Club:* Lansdowne.

BISHOP, Malcolm Leslie; QC 1993; a Recorder, since 2000; *b* 9 Oct. 1944; *s* of late John Bishop and Irene Bishop (*née* Dunn); civil partnership 2006, Anthony Patrick Vander Woerd, *e s* of Surg. Comdr Dirk Jan Albert Vander Woerd, Royal Dutch Navy, and Anne Patricia Venise Bowen Vander Woerd (now Kennard). *Educ:* Ruabon Grammar Sch.; Regent's Park Coll., Oxford Univ. (Samuel Davies Prizeman; Hon. Mods in Theology, BA Jurisprudence, MA). Chm., OU Dem. Lab. Club, 1966. Called to the Bar, Inner Temple, 1968, Bencher, 2003; in practice on Wales and Chester Circuit. A Dep. High Court Judge, Family Div., 1997; an Asst Recorder, 1998–2000. Chm., I of M Legal Services Commn, 2002. Circuit Rep., Bar Council, 1987–92; Mem., Exec. Cttee, Family Law Bar Assoc., 1985–. Contested (Lab), Bath, Feb. and Oct. 1974. Hon. Standing Counsel, Regent's Park Coll., Oxford Univ., 2007–. *Recreations:* politics, wine. *Address:* Ely Place Chambers, 30 Ely Place, EC1N 6TD. *T:* (020) 7400 9600; 30 Park Place, Cardiff CF10 3BS. *T:* (029) 2039 8421. *Clubs:* Oxford and Cambridge; Cardiff and County (Cardiff).

BISHOP, Mark Andrew; His Honour Judge Bishop; a Circuit Judge, since 2009; *b* Cambridge, 12 July 1958; *s* of Robin Bishop and Joyce Bishop; *m* 1986, Christine Smart; three *d. Educ:* Leys Sch., Cambridge; Downing Coll., Cambridge (MA 1984). Called to the Bar, Middle Temple, 1981 (Astbury Schol.); in practice as a barrister, 1 Temple Gardens, 1982–2009; Recorder, 2001–09; Fee-paid Tribunal Judge, Mental Health Rev. Tribunal, 2007–, Restricted Patients Panel, 2009–. Dep. Chancellor, Dio. of Rochester, 2000–; Chancellor, Dio. of Lincoln, 2007–; Chm., Bishops' Disciplinary Tribunals, 2015–. Ordained deacon, 2002, priest, 2003; Asst Curate, 2002–05, Asst Priest, 2005–, Little St Mary, Cambridge. Pres., Cambridge Union Soc., 1980; ESU debating tour of USA, 1981. Gov., Leys Sch., Cambridge, 1989–. *Recreations:* family, holidays, music. *Address:* Inner London Crown Court, Sessions House, Newington Causeway, SE1 6AZ. *T:* (020) 7234 3100, *Fax:* (020) 7234 3287.

BISHOP, Mark John; Headmaster, Trinity School, Croydon, since 2006; *b* Wimbledon, 4 Feb. 1962; *s* of John and Jean Bishop; *m* 2004, Tymian Brown; one *s* and one step *d. Educ:* Charterhouse Sch.; St Edmund Hall, Oxford (MA); Henley Mgt Coll. (MBA). Teacher of Religious Studies and Philosophy, Royal Grammar Sch., Guildford, 1985–96; Dep. Hd, Caterham Sch., 1996–2005; Dir, Perrett Laver, 2005. *Recreations:* mountain walking, diving, cycling, golf. *Address:* Trinity School, Shirley Park, Croydon CR9 7AT. *T:* (020) 8656 9541. *E:* mjb@trinity.croydon.sch.uk.

BISHOP, Michael; *see* Bishop, J. M.

BISHOP, Michael William; JP; Chairman, Heritage Care Ltd, 2001–08; *b* 22 Oct. 1941; *s* of Ronald Lewis William and Gwendoline Mary Bishop; *m* Loraine Helen Jones; two *s* one *d. Educ:* Manchester Univ. (BA (Econs) IIi Hons); Leicester Univ. (CertAppSocStudies). Director of Social Services: Cleveland CC, 1981–89; Manchester City Council, 1989–95. Mem., Derbys Probation Bd, 2004–10. Non-exec. Dir, Derbys NHS PCT, 2007–09. Chm., Derbys Assoc. for Blind People, 2004–08; Trustee, RNID, 1996–2004 (Dep. Chm., 2002–04); Mem., Hearing Aid Council, 2004–10. Mem. Bd, Community Transport for Town and Country, 2011–. JP Manchester City, 1996–2000, High Peak, 2000. *Address:* The Brambles, Hemming Green, Old Brampton, Chesterfield S42 7JQ.

BISHOP, Patrick Joseph; military historian and author, since 2007; *b* Ashford, Kent, 17 Oct. 1952; *s* of Ernest Bishop and Kathleen Bishop (*née* Kelly); *m* 2008, Henrietta Miers; one *d. Educ:* Wimbledon Coll.; Corpus Christi Coll., Oxford (Exhibnr; BA Hons Modern Hist.). Reporter, The Observer, 1979–84 (corresp. with British Forces in Falkland Is War, 1982); reporter and Diplomatic Corresp., Sunday Times, 1985–87; Daily Telegraph: ME Corresp., 1988–92; Sen. Foreign Corresp., 1992–95; Foreign Ed., 1995–97; Associate Ed. (Foreign), 1997–99; Paris Corresp., 1999–2001; Special Corresp., 2002–07. Dir, Médecins sans Frontières UK, 1992–2002 (Chm., 1995–2000). *Publications:* Famous Victory, 1992; The Irish Empire, 1999; Fighter Boys, 2003; Bomber Boys, 2007; 3 Para, 2007; A Good War (novel), 2008; Ground Truth, 2009; The Battle of Britain, 2009; Follow Me Home (novel), 2011; Target Tirpitz, 2012; Wings, 2012; The Reckoning, 2014. *Recreations:* fishing, painting, family. *E:* patrickbishop2001@hotmail.com. *Club:* Savile.

BISHOP, Ven. Peter; *see* Bishop, Ven. A. P.

BISHOP, Prof. Peter Antony; Professor of Urban Design, Bartlett School of Architecture, University College London, since 2012; Director, Allies and Morrison Urban Practitioners, since 2011; *b* 15 Sept. 1953; *s* of Jack and Audrey Bishop; *m* 1998, Lesley Williams; one *s* one *d. Educ:* Trinity Sch. of John Whitgift; Univ. of Manchester (BA 1st Cl. Hons). Hd of Planning, London Bor. of Tower Hamlets, 1985–87; Dir, Engrg and Property, London Bor. of Haringey, 1987–97; Director of Environment: London Bor. of Hammersmith & Fulham, 1997–2001 (projects included: develt of White City, the BBC, Fulham FC); London Bor. of Camden, with resp. for redevelt of King's Cross, 2001–06; London Development Agency: Dir, Design for London, 2006–09; Gp Dir, Design Develt and Envmt, and Dep. Chief Exec., 2009–11. Mem., London Adv. Cttee, English Heritage, 2007–. Chm., Architecture Centre Network, 2010–. Has lectured and taught extensively. Vis. Prof., Nottingham Trent Univ., 2007–. Hon. Fellow, UCL, 2008; Hon. FRIBA, 2008. Hon. Dr Kingston, 2011. *Publications:* (with Lesley Williams) The Temporary City, 2012. *Recreations:* rock climbing, squash, collecting antiquarian books, European cinema. *Address:* Bartlett School of Architecture, University College London, Wates House, 22 Gordon Street, WC1H 0QB. *E:* peter.bishop@ucl.ac.uk.

BISHOP, Stephen; *see* Kovacevich, S.

BISHOP, Timothy Harper Paul; QC 2011; *b* Horsham, 16 June 1969; *s* of Hedley Paul Bishop and Marian Dorothy Bishop (*née* German); *m* 1993, Claire Louise Brind; three *s* one *d. Educ:* Maidstone Grammar Sch.; Trinity Coll., Cambridge (BA 1990; MA 1993). Called to the Bar, Inner Temple, 1991; in practice as a barrister specialising in matrimonial finance, 1992–. *Publications:* (with Gavin Smith) Enforcing Financial Orders in Matrimonial Proceedings, 2000. *Recreations:* Rugby coaching, ski-ing, tennis. *Address:* 1 Hare Court, Temple, EC4Y 7BE. *T:* (020) 7797 7070, *Fax:* (020) 7797 7435. *E:* bishop@1hc.com. *Club:* Royal Automobile.

BISHOP-KOVACEVICH, Stephen; *see* Kovacevich, S.

BISHOPP, Colin Philip; a Judge of the Upper Tribunal, since 2009 (Special Commissioner of Income Tax, 2001–09; Chairman, VAT and Duties Tribunal, 2001–09 (part-time Chairman, 1990–2001)); President, Tax Chamber of the First-tier Tribunal, since 2011; *b* 10 Oct. 1947; *s* of late Clement Walter Bishopp and of Alison Moray Bishopp (*née* Stewart); *m* 1st, 1970 (marr. diss. 1987); one *s* one *d*; 2nd, 1988 (marr. diss. 2010); three *s. Educ:* Manchester Grammar Sch.; St Catharine's Coll., Cambridge (BA 1968, MA 1971). Admitted solicitor, 1971; Partner: A. W. Mawer & Co., Solicitors, 1973–88; Lace Mawer, Solicitors, 1988–97; Berrymans Lace Mawer, Solicitors, 1997–2001. Chairman: Financial Services and Markets Tribunal, 2001–10; Pensions Regulator Tribunal, 2005–10; Claims Mgt Services Tribunal, 2007–09. *Recreations:* walking, classical music, travel. *Address:* Tax Tribunals, Royal Courts of Justice, Strand, WC2A 2LL. *T:* (020) 7612 9660. *E:* colin.bishopp@judiciary.gsi.gov.uk.

BISIGNANI, Giovanni; Director General and Chief Executive Officer, International Air Transport Association, 2002–11, now Emeritus (Member, Executive Committee, 1991–94); Chairman, Global Agenda Council on Aviation, Travel and Tourism, World Economic Forum, 2011–12 (Member, since 2012); *b* 10 Dec. 1946; *s* of Renato Bisignani and Vincenza Carpano; *m* 1975, Elena Pasanisi; one *d. Educ:* Rome Univ. (Master of Law); Harvard Business Sch. First National City Bank, NY, 1970; Manager, Res. and Econ. Planning Dept, Ente Partecipazioni e Finanziamento Industria Manifatturiera, Rome, 1973–76; COS to Chair, ENI, Rome, 1976–79; Istituto Ricostruzione Industriale, Rome: COS to Chm., 1979–81, and Rep. on Bds of Finsider, Italstat, SME and Fincantieri, 1979–89; Exec. Vice Pres., Internat., 1981–89; Man. Dir and CEO, Alitalia, Rome, 1989–94; Chm., Galileo Internat., Chicago, 1993–94; Pres., Tirrenia di Navigazione SpA, Rome, 1994–98; SM Logistics-Gruppo Serra Merzario SpA, 1998–2001: Man. Dir and CEO, Milan; Chm., Merzario USA, Inc., NY; Bd Mem., Merzario UK, London; Opodo, 2001–02: CEO, London; Man. Dir, Berlin; Man. Dir, Paris. Vis. Prof., Sch. of Engrg, Cranfield Univ., 2012–. Chm., AEA, 1991; Member: Bd, Assolombarda, Milan, 1998–2000; European Adv. Bd, Pratt & Whitney, United Technologies, 1998–2001; Bd, UK NATS Ltd, 2002–12; Bd, Safran, 2011–; Bd, Aircastle Ltd, 2012–; Bd, Alitalia, 2015–. FRAeS 2009. Hon. DSc Cranfield, 2008. *Recreations:* golf, tennis, riding. *Address:* International Air Transport Association, Route de l'Aéroport 33, PO Box 416, 1215 Geneva 15 Airport, Switzerland. *E:* bisignanig@gmail.com.

BISS, Adele, (Mrs R. O. Davies); businesswoman; a Civil Service Commissioner, since 2010; *b* 18 Oct. 1944; *d* of Robert and Bronia Biss; *m* 1973, Roger Oliver Davies, *qv*; one *s. Educ:* Cheltenham Ladies' Coll.; University Coll. London (BSc Econ; Fellow, 2008). Unilever, 1968; Thomson Holidays, 1970; Chief Exec., Biss Lancaster, 1978–88; Chm., BTA and English Tourist Bd, 1993–96; Chm., A. S. Biss & Co., 1996–2007. Director: Aegis plc, 1985–90; BR, 1987–92; European Passenger Services, subseq. Eurostar (UK) Ltd, 1990–2010; Bowthorpe plc, 1993–97; Harry Ramsden's, 1995–99; Engine Gp, 2005–10. Gov., Middx Univ., 1995–2007; Member Council: GDST (formerly GPDST), 1996–2003; UCL, 1997–2007. Hon. DBA Lincoln, 2002. *Recreation:* friends and family.

BISSELL, Frances Mary; freelance writer; *b* 19 Aug. 1946; *d* of Robert Maloney and Mary Maloney (*née* Kelly); *m* 1970, Thomas Emery Bissell; one step *d. Educ:* Univ. of Leeds (BA Hons French). VSO Nigeria, 1965–66; Assistante, Ecole Normale, Albi, 1968–69; British Council, 1970–87; The Times, 1987–2000; food and cookery writer, cook and consultant, 1983–, TV presenter, 1995–. Guest cook: Mandarin Oriental, Hong Kong, 1987, 1990, 1995; London Intercontinental, 1987, 1988 and 1996; Manila Peninsula, 1989; Colombo Hilton, Sri Lanka, 1991; The Dusit Thani, Bangkok, 1992; George V, Paris, 1994; The Mark, NY, 1997, 1999 and 2000; Rio Suites Hotel, Las Vegas, 1997; guest teacher: Bogotá Hilton, Colombia, 1988; Ballymaloe Cooking Sch., Ireland, 1990; The Times cookery evenings at Leith's Sch. of Food and Wine, 1991; Learning for Pleasure, Spain, 1995 and 1996; Consultant: Ta' Frenc, Gozo, 2004–; Sloane Club, 2006–13; Guest Lecturer: Swan Hellenic, 2001–; Hebridean Internat. Cruises, 2005–09; Hebridean Island Cruises, 2010–. Member judging panel: THF Hotels Chef of the Year, 1988 and 1990; Annual Catey Award Function Menu, 1989–94; A Fresh Taste of Britain, Women's Farming Union, 1989; UK Finals, Prix Taittinger, 1993, 1994; Roux Diners Club Scholarship, 1995–98; Roux Scholarship, 2000–02; Slow Food, 2003–; Gourmet Voice, 2006–; Shackleton Fund Fellowship, 2001. Founder Mem., Guild of Food Writers, 1985. Chef Mem., Acad. of Culinary Arts (formerly Académie Culinaire de France), 1997, Fellow, 2008. Columnist: Caterer & Hotelkeeper, 1988–94; Hampstead and Highgate Express, 1999–; Sunday Times of Malta, 2003–; Malta Taste, 2005–. Glenfiddich Cookery Writer of the Year, 1994; James Beard Foundn Award, USA, 1995. *Television:* Frances Bissell's Westcountry Kitchen, 1995; Frances Bissell's Christmas Cooking, 1996. *Publications:* A Cook's Calendar, 1985; The Pleasures of Cookery, 1986; Ten Dinner Parties for Two, 1988; Sainsbury's Book of Food, 1989 (US edn, as The Book of Food, 1994); Oriental Flavours, 1990; The Real Meat Cookbook, 1992; The Times Cookbook, 1993; Frances Bissell's West Country Kitchen, 1996; (with Tom Bissell) An A–Z of Food and Wine in Plain English, 1999; The Organic Meat Cookbook, 1999; Modern Classics, 2000; Entertaining, 2002; Preserving Nature's Bounty, 2006; The Scented Kitchen, 2007, 2nd edn 2012; The Floral Baker, 2014; The Fragrant Pantry, 2016; contrib. to Caterer and Hotelkeeper, Sunday Times Mag., Homes and Gardens, House & Garden, Country Living, Decanter, Country Life. *Recreations:* travelling, reading. *Address:* 2 Carlingford Road, Hampstead, NW3 1RX.

BISSON, (Anthony) Nicholas, PhD; Director, HS2 Phase 2 and Northern Transport, Department for Transport, since 2014; *b* Manchester, 7 July 1972; *s* of Anthony Bisson and

Anne Bisson; *m* 2002, Sally Rickards; one *s* one *d*. *Educ:* St Albans Sch.; Univ. of Durham (BSc Maths 1993); Univ. of Warwick (PhD Stats 1996). Department of the Environment, later DETR, then DTLR, subseq. DfT, 1996–: EC (on secondment), 1999; Downing Street Policy Directorate, 2001–02; Hd, London Transport, 2002–05; Asst Hd, Highways and Transport, W Sussex CC (on secondment), 2006–07; Dir, Regl and Local Transport, 2007–11; Dir, Rail Policy, subseq. Rail Strategy and Funding, 2011–14. *Address:* Department for Transport, 33 Horseferry Road, SW1P 4DR. *T:* (020) 7944 4250. *E:* nick.bisson@dft.gsi.gov.uk.

BISSON, Hon. Claude, OC 1999; Counsel, McCarthy Tétrault, Montreal, since 1996; a Judge of the Court of Appeal, Quebec, 1980–96; Chief Justice of Quebec, 1988–94; *b* 9 May 1931; *m* 1957, Louisette Lanneville; two *s* one *d*. *Educ:* Univ. de Laval, Quebec (BA 1950; LLL 1953). Called to Bar, Quebec, 1954. Superior Court Judge, Montreal, 1969–80. *Address:* (office) 1000 de La Gauchetière Street West, Montreal, QC H3B 0A2, Canada.

BISSON, Nicholas; *see* Bisson, A. N.

BISZTYGA, Jan; Officer's Cross of the Order of Polonia Restituta 1970; Order of Merit 1973; Senior Advisor to President, Bartimpex, since 2003; *b* 19 Jan. 1933; *s* of Kazimierz Biszytyga; *m* 1956, Otylia; one *s*. *Educ:* Jagiellonian Univ. (MSc Biochemistry). Asst Professor, Jagiellonian Univ., Cracow, 1954–57; political youth movement, 1956–59; Min. for Foreign Affairs, 1959–63; Attaché, New Delhi, 1963–64; Min. for Foreign Affairs, 1964–69; Head of Planning Dept, Min. for Foreign Affairs, 1969–71; Dep. Foreign Minister, 1972–75; Ambassador in Athens, 1975–78, to UK, 1978–81; Ideology Dept, Polish United Workers' Party; expert in Office of Pres. of Polish Republic, 1990–91; Advr on Foreign Trade Enterprise, Euroamer, 1991–94; Advr to PM's Office, 1994–97; Pol Advr to Minister of Interior and Admin, 1997–2001; Advisor: to PM of Poland, 2001–03; The Foreign Trade Enterprise Bartimpex, 2003–06. *Recreations:* game shooting, fishing, history. *Address:* (home) Jaworzyńska 11–18, Warsaw 00634, Poland; (office) Bartimpex, Al. Szucho 9, Warsaw, Poland. *T:* (622) 2757, 0604 787878, *Fax:* (621) 0943. *E:* biuro@bartimpex.com.pl.

BITEL, Nicholas Andrew; Consultant, Kerman & Co., since 2012; Chief Executive, London Marathon, since 1995; Director, London Legacy Development Corporation (formerly Olympic Park Legacy Company), since 2009; Chairman, Sport England, since 2013; *b* 31 Aug. 1959; *s* of Max and Cecilia Bitel; *m* 1982, Sharon Levan; three *s*. *Educ:* St Paul's Sch., London; Davidson Coll., NC (Dean Rusk Schol.); Manchester Univ. (LLB). Admitted solicitor, 1983; Partner, Max Bitel Greene, 1983–2011. Member: Council, UK Sport, 2003–08 and 2013–; Bd, Sport England, 2010–. Vice-Chm., Wigan Athletic, 1991–95. *Publications:* contribs to Sport and the Law Jl. *Recreations:* sports, theatre. *Address:* Kerman & Co., 200 Strand, WC2R 1DJ. *T:* (020) 7539 7272, *Fax:* (020) 7240 5780. *Club:* MCC.

BJERREGAARD, Ritt Jytte; Lord Mayor, City of Copenhagen, 2006–09; *b* Copenhagen, 19 May 1941; *d* of Gudmund Bjerregaard and Rita (*née* Hærslev); *m* 1966, Prof. Søren Mørch. Qualified as teacher, 1964. MP (Social Dem.), Denmark: Otterup (Fyn), 1971–95; Lejre, 1999–2005; Minister for: Educn, 1973 and 1975–78; Social Affairs, 1979–81; Mem., EC, 1995–99; Minister for Food, Agric. and Fisheries, 2000–01. Chm., Social Dem. Parly Gp, 1981–82 and 1987–92 (Dep. Chm., 1982–87). Pres., Danish European Movt, 1992–94. Mem., Trilateral Commn, 1982–2001. Vice-Pres., Danish delegn, CSCE, 1992–94. Vice-Pres., Socialist Internat. Women, 1992–94. *Publications:* books on educn and politics in Denmark, including: Strid, 1979; Til venner og fjender, 1982; I opposition, 1987; (with S. Mørch) Fyn med omliggende oor, 1989; Verden er saa stor, saa stor, 1990; Mine Æbler, 2003; Mit København, 2005; (jtly) Min mor er død, 2010; articles in Danish jls. *Recreation:* growing apples. *Address:* Stestrup Old 17, 4360 Kirke Eskilstrup, Denmark.

BLACK OF BRENTWOOD, Baron *cr* 2010 (Life Peer), of Brentwood in the County of Essex; **Guy Vaughan Black;** Executive Director (formerly Corporate Affairs Director), Telegraph Media Group, since 2005; *b* 6 Aug. 1964; *s* of Thomas Black and Monica Black (*née* Drew); civil partnership 2006, *m* 2015, Mark William Bolland, *qv*. *Educ:* Brentwood Sch., Essex; Peterhouse, Cambridge (John Cosin Schol.; Sir Herbert Butterfield Prize for History, 1985; MA). Graduate Trainee, Corporate Banking Div., BZW, 1985–86; Desk Officer, Conservative Res. Dept, 1986–89; Special Advr to Sec. of State for Energy, 1989–92; Account Dir, Westminster Strategy, 1992–94; Associate Dir, Lowe Bell Good Relns, 1994–96; Dir, Press Complaints Commn, 1996–2003; Press Sec. to Leader of the Opposition, and Dir of Media, Conservative Central Office, 2004–05. Dir, Advertising Standards Bd of Finance, 2005–; Chm., Press Standards Bd of Finance, 2009–15. Mem. (C), Brentwood DC, 1988–92. President: London Press Club, 2012–; Soc. of Old Brentwoods, 2012–13; Printing Charity, 2013–14; Eur. Newspaper Publishers Assoc., 2014–15. Patron: Peterhouse Politics Soc., 2004–; Rory Peck Trust, 2014–; Vice-President: NI Schools Debating Competition, 2011–; Journalists' Charity, 2014–. Chairman: Commonwealth Press Union Trust, 2009–; Hanover Band Foundn, 2014–; Trustee: Sir Edward Heath's Charitable Foundn, 2006–10; Imperial War Museum, 2007–15; Mayor of London's Fund for Young Musicians, 2011–12; Treas., Imperial War Mus. Foundn, 2015–. Member: Council, RCM, 2009–; Guild of St Bride's, Fleet Street, 2010–. Gov., Brentwood Sch., 2013–. Churchwarden, St Bride's, 2014–. FRSA 1997; MCIPR 2007. *Recreations:* music, cats, reading, Umbria. *Address:* House of Lords, SW1A 0PW. *T:* (office) (020) 7931 3806. *Club:* Athenæum.

BLACK OF CROSSHARBOUR, Baron *cr* 2001 (Life Peer), of Crossharbour in the London Borough of Tower Hamlets; **Conrad Moffat Black;** PC (Can.) 1992; Chairman, Conrad Black Capital Corporation, since 1975; Chairman and Chief Executive Officer, Hollinger International Inc., 1990–2003; *b* 25 Aug. 1944; *m* 1st, 1978, Joanna Catherine Louise Hishon (name changed by deed poll in 1990 from Shirley Gail Hishon) (marr. diss., 1992); two *s* one *d*; 2nd, 1992, Barbara Amiel. *Educ:* Carleton Univ. (BA); Laval Univ. (LLL); MA History McGill, 1973. Chm. and Chief Exec., Ravelston Corp., 1979–2005; Chm., 1979, Chief Exec., 1985–2005, Argus Corp.; Chm., The Telegraph Gp Ltd, 1987–2005 (Dir, 1985–2005). Mem., Editl Bd, Nat. Interest, Washington, 1997. Hon. LLD: St Francis Xavier, 1979; McMaster, 1979; Carleton, 1989; Hon. LittD Univ. of Windsor, 1979. KLJ; KCSG 2001. *Publications:* Duplessis, 1977, rev. edn as Render Unto Caesar, 1998; A Life in Progress (autobiog.), 1993; Franklin Delano Roosevelt: champion of freedom, 2003; The Invincible Quest: the life of Richard Milhous Nixon, 2007; A Matter of Principle, 2011; Flight of the Eagle: a strategic history of the United States, 2013; Rise to Greatness, The History of Canada - from the Vikings to the Present, 2014.

BLACK, Dr Aline Mary; Headteacher, Colchester County High School for Girls, 1987–98; *b* 2 July 1936; *d* of Maurice and Harriet Rose; *m* 1972, David Black. *Educ:* Manchester Univ.; Birkbeck and King's Colls, London (BSc Hons Physics 1957; PGCE 1959; BSc Hons Chemistry 1970; PhD 1973). Res. Physicist, Richard, Thomas & Baldwins, 1957–58; Physics Teacher, Sir William Perkins' Sch., 1959–61; Head of Physics, City of London Sch. for Girls, 1961–71; Science Advr, Waltham Forest LBC, 1973–75; Science and Maths Advr, Bexley LBC, 1975–77; Headteacher: Leyton Sen. High Sch. for Girls, 1977–82; Gravesend Grammar Sch. for Girls, 1982–87. *Recreations:* archaeology, flying, sailing. *Address:* 11 Winchester Road, Frinton on Sea, Essex CO13 9JB. *T:* (01255) 852794.

BLACK, Col Anthony Edward Norman, OBE 1981; Chief Executive Commissioner, Scout Association, 1987–95; *b* 20 Jan. 1938; *s* of late Arthur Norman Black and Phyllis Margaret Ranicar; *m* 1963, Susan Frances Copeland; two *s*. *Educ:* Brighton College; RMA Sandhurst. Commissioned RE, 1957; served Kenya, Aden, Germany, Cyprus; Army Staff Course, Camberley, 1970; GSO1 Ghana Armed Forces Staff Coll., 1976–78; CO 36 Engr Regt, 1978–80; Col GS MGO Secretariat, 1980–82; Comd Engrs Falkland Islands, 1983; Comdt, Army Apprentices Coll., Chepstow, 1983–86; retired 1987. *Recreations:* gardening, bird watching. *Address:* National Westminster Bank, 50 High Street, Egham, Surrey TW20 9EU.

BLACK, His Honour Barrington (Malcolm); a Circuit Judge, 1993–2005; a Deputy Circuit Judge, 2005–07; a Justice of Supreme Court of Gibraltar, 2012–14; *b* 16 Aug. 1932; *s* of Louis and Millicent Black; *m* 1962, Diana Heller, JP; two *s* two *d*. *Educ:* Roundhay Sch.; Leeds Univ. (Pres. of Union, 1952; Vice-Pres., NUS, 1953–54; LLB). Admitted Solicitor, 1956. Served Army, 1956–58, commnd RASC. Partner, Walker, Morris & Coles, 1958–69; Sen. Partner, Barrington Black, Austin & Co., 1969–84. An Asst Recorder, 1987–91, a Recorder, 1991–93; a Metropolitan Stipendiary Magistrate, 1984–93. Chairman: Inner London Juvenile Court, 1985–93; Family Court, 1991–93. Mem. Court and Council, Leeds Univ., 1979–84. Councillor, Harrogate Bor. Council, 1964–67; contested (L) Harrogate, 1964. *Recreations:* writing, opera, music.

BLACK, Benjamin; *see* Banville, J.

BLACK, Dame Carol (Mary), DBE 2005 (CBE 2002); FRCP, FMedSci; Principal, Newnham College, Cambridge, since 2012; *b* 26 Dec. 1939; *d* of Edgar and Annie Herbert; *m* 1st, 1973, James Black (marr. diss. 1983); 2nd, 2002, Christopher Morley. *Educ:* Univ. of Bristol (BA Hist. 1962; Dip. Med. Social Studies 1963; MB ChB 1970; MD 1974). FRCP 1988; FRCSGlas 2003; FRCPI 2003; FRCPE 2003; FRCPCH 2003. Res. Fellow, Univ. of Bristol Sch. of Medicine, 1971–73; Consultant Rheumatologist: W Middx Univ. Hosp., 1981–89; Royal Free Hampstead NHS Trust, 1989–94; Prof. of Rheumatol., Royal Free and University Coll. Med. Sch., Univ. of London, 1994–2006, now Emeritus; Med. Dir, Royal Free Hampstead NHS Trust, 2000–02; Nat. Dir for Health and Work, DoH and DWP, 2006–11. Member: Nat. Specialist Commng Adv. Gp, DoH, 2000–06; Appraisal Cttee, NICE, 1999–2002; NHS Modernisation Bd, DoH, 2002–04; non-exec. Dir, NHS Inst. for Innovation and Improvement, 2006–. Public Appts Ambassador, Govt Equalities Office, Cabinet Office, 2009–; Chm., Centre for Workforce Intelligence, 2010–; Member: Employee Engagement Task Force, BIS, 2011–; Life Scis Skills Strategy Bd, Cogent, 2011–. Chm., Nuffield Trust, 2006–; Mem., Clin. Interest Gp, Wellcome Trust, 1996–2003 (Vice-Chm., 1997); Mem., Scientific Co-ordinating Cttee, Arthritis Res. Campaign, 1999–2004; Founder Member and Chairman: UK Scleroderma Gp, 1985–; Eur. Scleroderma Club, 1989–2003; President: Scleroderma Soc., 2006–; Raynaud's and Scleroderma Assoc., 2007–; British Lung Foundn, 2007–; Treat Trust, Wales, 2009–. Member Council: Section of Clin. Immunol. and Allergy, RSocMed, 1998–2000 (Pres., 1997–99); Acad. Med. Sci. Vice-Pres., 1998–2002, Pres., 2002–06, RCP; Vice-Chm., 2003–05, Chm., 2006–09, Acad. of Med. Royal Colls. Pro-Chancellor, Univ. of Bristol, 2007–. Vice Chm., Imperial Coll. Healthcare Charity, 2008– (Chm., Res. Cttee, 2008–). Trustee: St Mary's and Hammersmith Hosps NHS Charitable Trust, 2008–; NPG, 2010–; Mem., Main Awards Cttee, Queen's Award for Voluntary Service, 2009–. FMedSci 1999; FRCS; FACP 2002; FRACP 2003; FAMM 2003; FAMS 2003; Mem., Assoc. Physicians, 1997; CCMI 2002. Hon. Member: Italian Soc. Rheumatol., 1995; Turkish Soc. Rheumatol., 1995–. Hon. Fellow: UCL, 2003; Lucy Cavendish Coll., Cambridge, 2004; Hon. FRCPsych 2012. Hon. DSc Bristol, 2003; Leicester, 2006; Sheffield, 2006; Hertfordshire, 2006; Glasgow, 2007; Exeter, 2007; Southampton, 2007; Imperial Coll. London, 2008; Hon. MD Nottingham, 2004. Mem., editl bds, various scientific jls. *Publications:* (with A. R. Myers) Systemic Sclerosis, 1985; (with J. Jayson) Scleroderma, 1988; contrib. scientific and med. papers in learned jls. *Recreations:* music, walking, travel, theatre. *Address:* 28 Cornwall Terrace Mews, NW1 5LL.

BLACK, Charles Stewart Forbes; a District Judge (Magistrates' Courts) (formerly a Metropolitan Stipendiary Magistrate), 1993–2012 (Chairman, Youth Courts, 1994–2012); *b* 6 Feb. 1947; *s* of Roger Bernard Black and Mary Agnes (*née* Murray); *m* 1976, Mhairi Shuna Elspeth McNab; one *d*. *Educ:* Kent Coll., Canterbury; Council of Legal Educn. Called to the Bar, Inner Temple, 1970; *ad eundem* Gray's Inn, 1973; Head of Chambers, 1981–93. *Recreations:* reading, playing with computers.

BLACK, Colin Hyndmarsh; Chairman: Kleinwort Benson Investment Management Ltd, 1988–95; Merchants Trust, 1993–2000 (Director, 1992–2000); *b* 4 Feb. 1930; *s* of Daisy Louise (*née* Morris) and Robert Black; *m* 1955, Christine Fleurette Browne; one *s* one *d*. *Educ:* Ayr Acad.; Fettes Coll.; St Andrews Univ. (MA); Edinburgh Univ. (LLB). Subaltern, RA, 1954–56; Brander and Cruickshank, Aberdeen, 1957–71 (Partner in charge of investment management); Globe Investment Trust, 1971–90, Dep. Chm., 1983–90. Chairman: Scottish Widows' Fund and Life Assurance Soc., 1987–95; Assoc. of Investment Trust Cos, 1987–89; non-executive Director: Temple Bar Investment Trust, 1963–2000; Clyde Petroleum, 1976–96; Electra Investment Trust, 1975–94; Kleinwort Benson Gp plc, 1988–95; Scottish Power plc, 1990–95; East German Investment Trust, 1990–96; Govett Asian Smaller Cos Investment Trust, 1994–2000 (Chm., 1994–2000); Postern Fund Management Ltd, 1996–99; PFM Carried Interest Ltd, 1996–2000. *Recreations:* travel, watching cricket, walking Labradors. *Address:* Patney House, Bath Road, Fyfield, Wilts SN8 1PU. *T:* (01672) 861451.

BLACK, Sir David; *see* Black, Sir R. D.

BLACK, Don, OBE 1999; lyric writer; *b* 21 June 1938; *s* of Betsy and Morris Blackstone; *m* 1958, Shirley Berg; two *s*. *Educ:* Hackney Central Sch. Professional lyric writer, 1960–; collaborates with Andrew Lloyd Webber, John Barry, Jule Styne, Elmer Bernstein and other leading composers; musicals include: Billy, 1974; Tell Me on a Sunday, 1979; Song and Dance, 1982; Aspects of Love, 1989; Sunset Boulevard, 1993; The Goodbye Girl, 1997; Bombay Dreams, 2002; Dracula, 2002; Romeo and Juliet: The Musical, 2002; Brighton Rock, 2004; Bonnie and Clyde, NY, 2011; Stephen Ward, 2013; Mrs Henderson Presents, 2015; films include: Thunderball, 1965; Diamonds Are Forever, 1971; The Man with the Golden Gun, 1974; Tomorrow Never Dies, 1997; The World is Not Enough, 1999. Fellow, BASCA, 2009. Hon. DArts City, 2005. Numerous awards, UK and USA, including: Academy Award, 1966, for song Born Free; Tony Award, 1995, for Sunset Boulevard (Best Book for a musical, and Best Score, lyrics). *Recreations:* snooker, swimming. *Address:* c/o John Cohen, Clintons, 55 Drury Lane, WC2B 5SQ. *T:* (020) 7379 6080. *Clubs:* Royal Automobile, Groucho.

BLACK, Gavin MacFarlane, CBE 2010; FRICS; DL, JP; Senior Partner, Gavin Black & Partners, since 2003; Vice Lord-Lieutenant for Tyne and Wear, since 2013; *b* Gosforth, Newcastle upon Tyne, 19 July 1949; *s* of Joseph Gavin Landells Black and Mildred Mabel Black (*née* Johnston); *m* 1974, Christine Lynne Smith; two *d*. *Educ:* Rossall Sch., Lancs. FRICS 1986. Founding Partner, Swaisland Black & Partners, 1973–79; Sen. Partner, Gavin Black & Partners, 1979–87; Partner, 1987–94, Dep. Chm., 1994–2003, Chesterton Internat. Chm. Govs, Univ. of Northumbria, 1997–2010. High Sheriff, 2009–10, DL, 2010, Tyne & Wear. *Recreations:* walking, Rugby football, golf, family. *Address:* Garden House, Hawkwell, Stamfordham, Newcastle upon Tyne NE18 0QT. *T:* (01661) 886406. *E:* gavinmblack@gmail.com. *Clubs:* Sloane; Northern Counties.

BLACK, Air Vice-Marshal George Philip, CB 1987; OBE 1967; AFC 1962 (Bar 1971); FRAeS; Royal Air Force, retired 1987; Defence Consultant: BAE SYSTEMS, 2001–05; SELEX Galileo Ltd (formerly SELEX (Sensors and Airborne Systems)), 2000–11; *b* 10 July 1932; *s* of William and Elizabeth Black; *m* 1954, Ella Ruddiman (*née* Walker); two *s*. *Educ:* Hilton Acad., Aberdeen. Joined RAF, 1950; flying trng in Canada, 1951; served, 1952–64: fighter pilot; carrier pilot (on exchange to FAA); Flying Instr; HQ Fighter Comd; commanded

No 111 (Fighter) Sqdn, 1964–66; Mem., Lightning Aerobatic Team, 1965; commanded Lightning Operational Conversion Unit, 1967–69; commanded No 5 (Fighter) Sqdn, 1969–70 (Huddleston Trophy); JSSC, 1970; Air Plans, MoD, 1971–72; Stn Comdr, RAF Wildenwrath, and Harrier Field Force Comdr, RAF Germany, 1972–74; Gp Captain Ops HQ 38 Gp, 1974–76; RCDS, 1977; Gp Captain Ops HQ 11 (Fighter) Gp, 1978–80; Comdr Allied Air Defence Sector One, 1980–83; Comdt ROC, 1983–84; DCS (Ops), HQ AAFCE, 1984–87. Air ADC to the Queen, 1981–83. Sen. Defence Advr, subseq. Dir, Mil. Marketing, GEC-Ferranti, 1987–93; Dir, Mil. Business Develt, Marconi Electronic Systems, subseq. BAE SYSTEMS, 1993–2000. Pres., ROC Seaborne Assoc., 1990–. FCMI (FBIM 1977). FRAeS 2001. *Recreations:* military aviation history, railways. *Club:* Royal Air Force.

BLACK, Helen Mary; Her Honour Judge Black; a Circuit Judge, since 2007; *b* 14 June 1959; *d* of Dennis and Carole Clifford; *m* 1981, Jonathan Stuart Winterhalter Black, *qv*; two *s*. *Educ:* Ashburton High Sch.; Coll. of Law, Chester. Admitted solicitor, 1982; Partner, Addison Madden, Portsmouth, 1982–2000; Dep. Dist Judge, 1995–2000, Dist Judge, 2000–07, Principal Registry of Family Div.; Recorder, 2005–07. Family Tutor Team Mem., Judicial Studies Bd, 2004–. *Publications:* (ed) Butterworth's Family Law Service: vol. 21, Atkins Court Forms: Husband and Wife and Cohabitation, and civil partnerships, 2004–, new edn, vol. 20, as Family: relationships and their breakdowns, and financial remedies, 2012. *Recreations:* marathon running, ski-ing, mountain biking, having fun, Crystal Palace FC, golf. *Address:* Portsmouth Combined Court Centre, The Courts of Justice, Winston Churchill Avenue, Portsmouth, Hants PO1 2EB. *Club:* Ladies' Ski (Chichester).

BLACK, His Honour James Walter; QC 1979; Judge, District Court of New South Wales, 2000–13; *b* 8 Feb. 1941; *s* of Dr James Black and Mrs Clementine M. Black (*née* Robb); *m* 1st, 1964, Jane Marie Keyden; two *s* one *d*; 2nd, 1985, Diana Marjorie Day (*née* Harris); one *d*. *Educ:* Harecroft Hall, Gosforth, Cumbria; Trinity Coll., Glenalmond, Perthshire; St Catharine's Coll., Cambridge (MA). Called to the Bar, Middle Temple, 1964, NSW Bar, 1986; a Recorder, 1976–87. *Recreations:* fishing, sailing, golf.

BLACK, Adm. Sir Jeremy; *see* Black, Adm. Sir J. J.

BLACK, Prof. Jeremy Martin, MBE 1999; PhD; Professor of History, University of Exeter, since 1996; *b* 30 Oct. 1955; *s* of Cyril Alfred Black and Doreen Black (*née* Ellis); *m* 1981, Sarah Elizabeth Hollis; one *s* one *d*. *Educ:* Haberdashers' Aske's Sch.; Queens' Coll., Cambridge (Entrance Schol.; Foundn Schol.; BA Starred First 1978; MA); St John's Coll., Oxford (MA); Merton Coll., Oxford (Harmsworth Schol.); PhD Dunelm 1983. University of Durham: Lectr, 1980–90; Sen. Lectr, 1990–91; Reader, 1991–94; Prof., 1994–95; Dir, Res. Foundn and Soc. of Fellows, 1990–95. Sen. Fellow, Foreign Policy Res. Inst., 2002–. Member, Council: British Records Assoc., 1989–2005; Royal Historical Soc., 1991–95 and 1996–2000. Mem., Council, Univ. of Exeter, 1999–2003. Ed., Archives, 1989–2005. *Publications:* The British and the Grand Tour, 1985; British Foreign Policy in the Age of Walpole, 1985; Natural and Necessary Enemies: Anglo-French relations in the eighteenth century, 1986; The English Press in the Eighteenth Century, 1987; The Collapse of the Anglo-French Alliance 1727–31, 1987; Culloden and the '45, 1990; The Rise of the European Powers 1679–1793, 1990; Robert Walpole and the Nature of Politics in Early-Eighteenth Century Britain, 1990; Europe in the Eighteenth Century, 1990, 2nd edn 2000; A System of Ambition?: British foreign policy 1660–1793, 1991; A Military Revolution?: military change and European society 1550–1800, 1991; War for America: the fight for independence 1775–1783, 1991; The British Abroad: the Grand Tour in the eighteenth century, 1992; Pitt the Elder, 1992; The Politics of Britain 1688–1800, 1993; History of England, 1993; British Foreign Policy in an Age of Revolution, 1994; European Warfare 1660–1815, 1994; Convergence or Divergence? Britain and the Continent, 1994; A History of the British Isles, 1996, 2nd edn 2003; Illustrated History of Eighteenth Century Britain, 1996; Warfare Renaissance to Revolution 1492–1792, 1996; America or Europe: British foreign policy 1739–63, 1997; Maps and History, 1997; Maps and Politics, 1997; War and the World: military power and the fate of continents 1450–2000, 1998; Why Wars Happen, 1998; From Louis XIV to Napoleon: the fate of a great power, 1999; Britain as a Military Power 1688–1815, 1999; A New History of England, 2000; Historical Atlas of Britain: the end of the Middle Ages to the Georgian era, 2000; War: past, present and future, 2000; Modern British History, 2000; A New History of Wales, 2000; British Diplomats and Diplomacy 1688–1800, 2001; The Politics of James Bond, 2001; War in the New Century, 2001; Eighteenth Century Britain, 2001; The English Press 1621–1861, 2001; Western Warfare 1775–1882, 2001; Western Warfare 1882–1975, 2001; Walpole in Power, 2001; The Making of Modern Britain. The Age of Edinburgh to the New Millennium, 2001; Europe and the World 1650–1830, 2001; European Warfare 1494–1660, 2002; The World in the Twentieth Century, 2002; America as a Military Power 1775–1882, 2002; France and the Grand Tour, 2003; Italy and the Grand Tour, 2003; World War Two: a military history, 2003; Visions of the World: a history of maps, 2003; Britain Since the Seventies: politics and society in the consumer age, 2003; Georgian Devon, 2003; The Hanoverians, 2004; The British Seaborne Empire, 2004; Parliament and Foreign Policy in the Eighteenth Century, 2004; Kings, Nobles and Commoners: states and societies in early modern Europe, 2004; War and the New Disorder in the 21st Century, 2004; Rethinking Military History, 2004; War since 1945, 2004; Using History, 2005; Introduction to Global Military History, 2005; A Subject for Taste: culture in eighteenth century England, 2005; The Continental Commitment: Britain, Hanover and interventionism 1714–1793, 2005; The European Question and the National Interest, 2006; George III, 2006; The Age of Total War 1860–1945, 2006; The Dotted Red Line: Britain's defence policy in the modern world, 2006; A Military History of Britain, 2006; The Slave Trade, 2006; Altered States: America since the Sixties, 2006; War in European History 1494–1660, 2006; Trade, Empire and British Foreign Policy 1689–1815, 2007; European Warfare in a Global Context 1660–1815, 2007; George II, 2007; A Short History of Britain, 2007, 2nd edn 2015; The Holocaust, 2008; The Curse of History, 2008; Great Powers and the Quest for Hegemony: the world order since 1500, 2008; What If?: counterfactualism and the problem of history, 2008; War Since 1990, 2009; Europe Since the Seventies, 2009; War in the Nineteenth Century, 2009; War: a short history, 2009; The War of 1812 in the Age of Napoleon, 2009; Geopolitics, 2009; Ideas for the Universities, 2009; Defence Policy Issues for a New Government, 2009; The Politics of World War Two, 2009; London: a history, 2009; Naval Power, 2009; The Battle of Waterloo, 2010; A History of Diplomacy, 2010; A Brief History of Britain 1851–2010, 2010; The Cold War, 2011; The Great War and the Making of the Modern World, 2011; Beyond the Military Revolutions: war in the seventeenth century world, 2011; A Brief History of Slavery, 2011; Debating Foreign Policy in Eighteenth-Century Britain, 2011; Historiography: contesting the past; claiming the future, 2011; War in the World: a comparative history 1450–1600, 2011; Fighting for America: the struggle for mastery in North America, 2011; War and the Cultural Turn, 2011; Empire Reviewed, 2012; Avoiding Armageddon: from the Great War to the fall of France, 1918–1940, 2012; War in the Eighteenth-Century World, 2012; War and Technology, 2013; The Reign of King George II, 2014; Politics and Foreign Policy in the Age of George I: 1714–1727, 2014; British Politics and Foreign Policy 1727–1744, 2014; A Century of Conflict, War 1914–2014, 2014; The Power of Knowledge: how information technology made the modern world, 2014; Contesting History: narratives of public history, 2014; War in the Modern World 1990–2014, 2015; Rethinking World War Two, 2015; The Cold War, A Military History, 2015; Clio's Battles, 2015; The Atlantic Slave Trade in World History, 2015. *Recreations:* pub lunches, country walks, reading detective novels in a hot bath, talking, family and friends, travel to the USA. *Address:* Department of History, University of Exeter, Amory Building, Rennes Drive, Exeter EX4 4RJ. *T:* and *Fax:* (01392) 254567. *Club:* Athenæum.

BLACK, Rt Hon. Dame Jill (Margaret), DBE 1999; PC 2010; **Rt Hon. Lady Justice Black;** a Lady Justice of Appeal, since 2010; *b* 1 June 1954; *d* of Dr James Irvine Currie and late Dr Margaret Yvonne Currie; *m* 1978, David Charles Black (marr. diss. 2013); one *s* one *d*; *m* 2013, Rt Hon. Sir Richard George Bramwell McCombe, *qv*. *Educ:* Penrhos Coll., Colwyn Bay; Durham Univ. (BA Hons Law). Called to the Bar, Inner Temple, 1976; QC 1994; a Recorder, 1999; a Judge of the High Ct of Justice, Family Div., 1999–2010; Family Div. Liaison Judge, N Circuit, 2000–04. Chm., Family Cttee, Judicial Studies Bd, 2004–. Comr, Judicial Appts Commn, 2008–. *Publications:* Divorce: the things you thought you'd never need to know, 1982, 8th edn 2004; A Practical Approach to Family Law, 1986, 9th edn 2012; (jtly) The Working Mother's Survival Guide, 1988; (jtly) The Family Court Practice, annually, 1993–2011; (jtly) Family Law: Legal Practice Course guide, 2009. *Address:* Royal Courts of Justice, Strand, WC2A 2LL.

BLACK, John Alexander; QC 1998; *b* 23 April 1951; *s* of late John Alexander Black and Grace Gardiner Black (*née* Cornock); *m* 1st, 1977, Penelope Anne Willdig (marr. diss. 2007); one *s* two *d*; 2nd, 2008, Fiona, *d* of Dr and Mrs G. Jackson. *Educ:* St James' Choir Sch., Grimsby; Hull Univ. (LLB 1974). Called to the Bar, Inner Temple, 1975. *Recreations:* classical music, motor cars, political history. *Address:* 33 Chancery Lane, WC2A 1EN.

BLACK, Adm. Sir (John) Jeremy, GBE 1991 (MBE 1963); KCB 1987; DSO 1982; Stia Negara Brunei 1963; Vice Admiral of the United Kingdom and Lieutenant of the Admiralty, 2001–03 (Rear Admiral of the United Kingdom, 1997–2001); *b* 17 Nov. 1932; *s* of Alan H. Black and G. Black; *m* 1958, Alison Pamela Barber; two *s* one *d*. *Educ:* Royal Naval College, Dartmouth (entered 1946). Korean War and Malayan Emergency, 1951–52; qualified in gunnery, 1958; commanded HM Ships: Fiskerton, 1960–62 (Brunei Rebellion, 1962); Decoy, 1969 (Comdr 1969, Captain 1974); Fife, 1977; RCDS 1979; Director of Naval Operational Requirements, Naval Staff, 1980–81; commanded HMS Invincible (Falklands), 1982–83; Flag Officer, First Flotilla, 1983–84; ACNS (Policy), Oct.–Dec. 1984; ACNS, 1985–86; Dep. CDS (Systems), 1986–89; C-in-C Naval Home Comd, 1989–91; Flag ADC, 1989–91. Chairman: Remy and Associates (UK) Ltd, 1992–96; Applied Visuals Ltd, 1998–2000; Berry Birch & Noble, 1999–2002; Director: Devonport Management Ltd, 1992–97; Macallan-Glenlivet plc, 1993–96; Global Emerging Markets Europe Ltd, 1993–96; St Davids Investment Trust, 1996–98; Gosport Seaport Ltd, 1993–96; Consultant: Shorts, 1992–98; British Aerospace, 1993–97; Krug Champagne, 1996–99. Trustee, Imperial War Mus., 1991–97; Chm., Britain at War Mus., 1999–2010; Dir, Nat. Army Mus., 2004–10. Mem. Council, RUSI, 1987–89. Gov., Wellington Coll., 1992–2003; Chm. Govs, Eagle House, 1998–2003. Chairman: Whitbread Round the World Race Cttee, 1990–94; Royal Navy Club of 1765 and 1785, 1992–95; Governor, Ocean Youth Club, 1991–95 (Chm., World Voyage, 1994–97). Life Vice Cdre, RNSA, 1991 (Cdre, 1989–91). *Publications:* There and Back (autobiog.), 2005. *Recreations:* sailing, history. *Clubs:* Boodle's; Royal Yacht Squadron.

BLACK, John Newman, CEng, FICE, FIMarEST; FRGS; Partner, Robert West and Partners, Chartered Consulting Engineers, 1988–90; *b* 29 Sept. 1925; *s* of late John Black and late Janet Black (*née* Hamilton); *m* 1952, Euphemia Isabella Elizabeth Thomson; two *d*. *Educ:* Cumberland and Medway Technical Colls. Civil and marine engrg naval stations and dockyards, UK and abroad, incl. Singapore, Hong Kong, Colombo, Gibraltar and Orkney Isles, 1941–64; joined PLA as Civil Engr, 1964; Planning and Construction, Tilbury Docks, 1964–66; Planning Manager, 1967; seconded to Thames Estuary Develt Co. Ltd, for work on Maplin Airport/Seaport Scheme, 1969; Asst Dir Planning, PLA, 1970; Director: Maplin, 1972; Tilbury Docks, 1974; all London Docks, 1977; Man. Dir, 1978–81; Bd Mem., 1978–86, Chief Exec., 1982–86, and Dep. Chm., 1985–86, PLA. Dep. Chm., PLA (Met. Terminals) Ltd, 1974; Director: PLACON Ltd (PLA's cons. subsid. co.), 1972; Orsett Depot Ltd, 1974; Port Documentation Services Ltd (Chm.), 1978; Chairman: Thames Riparian Housing Assoc., 1974; PLA Group Property Holdings, 1984. Member: Exec. Council, British Ports Assoc., 1982–86; Exec. Cttee, Nat. Assoc. of Port Employers, 1982–86 (Vice-Chm., 1984–86); British Nat. Cttee, Permt Internat. Assoc. of Navigation Congresses, 1981–; London Maritime Assoc., 1975; Council, ICHCA Internat., 1985–86; Nat. Exec. Cttee, ICHCA (UK), 1985–88. Co-Adviser to Indian Govt on port ops and potential, 1968; lectures: for UN, Alexandria, 1975; for ESCAP (UN), Bangkok, 1983. Freeman: City of London, 1977; Watermen and Lightermen of River Thames, 1977. *Publications:* numerous articles and papers in Geographical Jl, Civil Engr and other learned jls. *Recreations:* shooting, fishing. *Address:* Westdene Cottage, Tanyard Hill, Shorne, near Gravesend, Kent DA12 3EN.

BLACK, John Nicholson, MA, DPhil, DSc; FRSE; Principal, Bedford College, University of London, 1971–81; *b* 28 June 1922; *e s* of Harold Black, MD, FRCP, and Margaret Frances Black (*née* Nicholson); *m* 1st, 1952, Mary Denise Webb (*d* 1966); one *s* one *d*; 2nd, 1967, Wendy Marjorie Waterston; two *s*. *Educ:* Rugby Sch.; Exeter Coll., Oxford. MA 1952, DPhil 1952, Oxford; DSc 1965, Adelaide; FRSE 1965. Served War, RAF, 1942–46. Oxford Univ., 1946–49; BA Hons Cl. 1 (Agric.) 1949; Agricl Research Council Studentship, 1949–52; Lectr, Sen. Lectr, Reader, Univ. of Adelaide (Waite Agricl Research Inst.), 1952–63; André Mayer Fellowship (FAO), 1958; Prof. of Forestry and Natural Resources, Univ. of Edinburgh, 1963–71. Dir and Sec., The Wolfson Foundn, 1981–87; Dir, The Wolfson Family Charitable Trust, 1987–89. Tutor in Ceramic Restoration, Missenden Abbey, 1993–98. Mem., NERC, 1968–74; Mem. Council and Finance Cttee, RAF Benevolent Fund, 1989–97. Conductor, City of Burnside Symphony Orch., SA, 1956–63; Chm., Donizetti Soc., 1984–87. Hon. Pres., Oxford Ceramic Gp, 2007–. *Publications:* The Dominion of Man, 1970; Donizetti's Operas in Naples, 1983; The Italian Romantic Libretto, 1984; (contrib. entries (26) on Italian librettists) The New Grove Dictionary of Opera, 1992; British Tinglazed Earthenware, 2001; papers on: ecological subjects in scientific jls (60); Italian opera libretti (25); history of ceramics (12). *Recreations:* music, repair and restoration of porcelain and pottery, collecting English delftware and Dutch maiolica. *Address:* Paddock House, Pyrton, Watlington, Oxford OX49 5AP. *T:* (01491) 612600.

BLACK, Jonathan Stuart Winterhalter; His Honour Judge Jonathan Black; a Circuit Judge, since 2010; *b* Radcliffe, Lancs, 2 March 1957; *s* of Stuart James Black and Dorothy Mildred Black; *m* 1981, Helen Mary Black, *qv*; two *s*. *Educ:* Burnley Grammar Sch.; Manchester Poly. (Law Soc. Pt 1 1975); Coll. of Law, Chester; Univ. of Portsmouth (Post Graduate Dip. Personnel Mgt 1984); Univ. of Staffordshire (LLM Dist. 1992). Admitted solicitor, 1980; Clerk to the Justices: for NE Hants, 1989–99; for Hants and IoW, 1999–2010; a Dep. District Judge (Magistrates' Courts), 2004–10; a Recorder, 2005–10. Member: Youth Justice Bd for England and Wales, 1998–2002; Criminal Justice Consultative Council, 2001–02. *Publications:* Drinking and Driving: a decade of development, 1999; Drinking and Driving Offences: law and practice, 2004, 2nd edn 2007; (ed jtly) Atkin's Court Forms, Vol. 21, 3rd edn 2012; articles in Criminal Law Rev., New Law Jl, Solicitors Jl. *Recreations:* ski mountaineering, climbing, cricket, Burnley Football Club. *Address:* Basildon Combined Court Centre, The Gore, Basildon, Essex SS14 2BU. *T:* (01268) 458000, *Fax:* (01268) 458100. *E:* hhjudgejonathan.black@judiciary.gsi.gov.uk. *Clubs:* MCC, Alpine.

BLACK, Prof. Julia, DPhil; FBA 2015; Professor of Law, since 2006 and Pro Director for Research, since 2014, London School of Economics and Political Science; *b* Waterloo, Lancs, 29 Jan. 1967; *d* of Peter Black and Marilyn Black; *m* 1999, Tim Cross; one *s* one *d*. *Educ:*

Lincoln Coll., Oxford (BA Hons Juris. 1st Cl. 1988; DPhil 1994). Lectr, LSE, 1994–2006. Ind. Mem. Bd, Solicitors Regulation Authy, 2014– (Chm., Standards Cttee, 2015–). Gen. Editor, Modern Law Rev., 2013–. *Publications:* Rules and Regulators, 1997; (ed jtly) Regulatory Innovation, 2005; articles in Modern Law Rev., Oxford Jl of Legal Studies, Regulation and Governance, Jl of Law and Society, Law and Policy. *Recreations:* marathon running, downhill and cross-country ski-ing, mountain walking. *Address:* London School of Economics and Political Science, Houghton Street, WC2A 2AE. *T:* (020) 7955 7684. *E:* j.black@lse.ac.uk.

BLACK, Rev. Leonard Albert; Catholic Priest of the Ordinariate of Our Lady of Walsingham in Scotland, since 2011; *b* 19 March 1949; *s* of James Morrison Black and Mary Cruickshanks Black (*née* Walker); *m* 1975, Ruth Catherine (*née* Morrison); two *s* one *d*. *Educ:* Bernard Gilpin Soc., Durham; Edinburgh Theol Coll. (Luscombe Schol. 1972). Ordained deacon, 1972, priest, 1973; Curate, St Margaret of Scotland, Aberdeen, 1972–75; Chaplain, St Paul's Cathedral, and St Martin's, Dundee, with All Souls, Invergowrie, 1975–77; Priest i/c, St Ninian's, Aberdeen, 1977–80; Rector: St John the Evangelist, Inverness, and Priest i/c, Culloden Mission, 1980–87; St Michael and All Angels, Inverness, 1980–2011; ordained RC deacon and priest, 2011, to serve the Ordinariate Gp in Scotland; Gp Pastor, Scotland Ordinariate Gp, 2011–; Ordinariate Cluster Co-ord., 2012–; webmaster, Ordinariate of Our Lady of Walsingham, 2014–. Canon, St Andrew's Cathedral, Inverness, 1992–2011. Area Chaplain (Scotland), Actors' Church Union, 1987–2003; Northern Area Regional Chaplain, Missions to Seamen (Scotland), 1991–2002; Synod Clerk, Dio. of Moray, Ross and Caithness, 1992–2003; Dean of Moray, Ross and Caithness, 2003–09. Mem., SSC, 1979–2011. Regional Dean (Scotland), Forward in Faith, 2001–11. Commissary to Bishop of the Murray, Anglican Church of Australia, 2006–11; permission to officiate, dio. of the Murray, 2006–11. Religious Affairs and Community Progs Producer, 1987–2004, Religious Progs Producer, 2004–14, Moray Firth Radio, Inverness; Religious Progs Producer, Nevis Radio, Fort William, 2007–. Ed., Diocese of Moray, Ross and Caithness Diocesan Directory, 1985–2003; Mem., Editl Bd, Portal Mag., 2011–. *Publications:* Churches of Diocese of Moray, Ross and Caithness, annually, 1992–2004; Sir Ninian Comper - Liturgical Architect, 1999; The Church that Moved Across the Water, 2003. *Recreations:* visiting Baroque churches and ancient archaeological sites, music, theatre, real ale, good food and fine wines. *Address:* 49 Laurel Avenue, Inverness IV3 5RR. *T:* (01463) 235597. *E:* fr.len@angelforce.co.uk.

BLACK, Liam; Co-Founder, Wavelength Companies Ltd, since 2008; *b* Reading, 24 Jan. 1961; *s* of John Black and Anne Black (*née* Delaney); *m* 1981, Maggie Sheehan; two *s* one *d*. *Educ:* Roehampton Inst. (BA Hons Eng. and Religious Studies). Volunteer overseas, 1982–84; Archdio. of Liverpool, 1985–91; Crisis, 1991–94; Big Issue, 1995–96; Chief Executive Officer: FRC Gp, Liverpool, 1996–2004; Fifteen Foundn, 2004–08. Trustee, NESTA, 2008–12. *Publications:* There's No Business Like Social Business, 2004. *Recreations:* drinking, tennis, arguing. *E:* liam@thesamewavelength.com.

BLACK, Mhairi; MP (SNP) Paisley and Renfrewshire South, since 2015; *b* Paisley, 1994; *d* of Alan Black. *Educ:* Univ. of Glasgow (BA 1st Cl. Hons Politics 2015). *Address:* House of Commons, SW1A 0AA.

BLACK, Hon. Michael Eric John, AC 1998; Chief Justice, Federal Court of Australia, 1991–2010; *b* 22 March 1940; *s* of Col E. R. E. Black, OBE; *m* 1963, Margaret Dungan; one *s* one *d*. *Educ:* St John's on the Hill, Chepstow; Wesley Coll., Melbourne; Univ. of Melbourne (LLB). Practice, Victorian Bar, 1964–90, ACT Bar, 1974–90; QC Victoria 1980, QC Tasmania 1984. Mem. Board, Royal Melbourne Hosp., 1986–90 (Chm., Ethics Cttee); The Defence Force Advocate, 1987–90; Chm., Attorney General's Steering Cttee, Courts Exec. Service, 2011–12. Mem., Dispute Resolution Panels for Nat. Gas and Electricity Mkt Rules, 2012–13. Co-Pres., Internat. Assoc. of Supreme Admin. Jurisdictions, 2007–10. Sen. Fellow, Law Sch., Melbourne Univ., 2011–14. Chair, Australian Law Schs Standards Cttee, 2011–; Legal Services Council, 2014–. Mem., Adv. Bd, Social Equity Inst., Melbourne Univ., 2013–. Hon. LLD Melbourne, 2010. *Address:* PO Box 728, Kew, Vic 3101, Australia.

BLACK, Michael Jonathan; QC 1995; a Recorder, 1999–2013; *b* 31 March 1954; *s* of Samuel and Lillian Black; *m* 1984, Ann, *e d* of Keith and Rosa Pentol; two *s*. *Educ:* Stand Grammar Sch.; University College London (LLB). FCIArb 1991. Called to the Bar, Middle Temple, 1978, Bencher, 2006; an Asst Recorder, 1995–99; a Dep. Judge, Technology and Construction Court, 1999–2013; Dep. High Court Judge, 2008–13. Asst Comr, Parly Boundary Commn for England, 2000–. Admitted to Bar: of Dubai Internat. Financial Centre Court, 2006; of Eastern Caribbean Supreme Court, 2007. Member: Civil Procedure Cttee, 2000–04; Panel of Mediators, Court of Appeal, 2001–03; Civil Justice Council, 2005–09. Vis. Res. Fellow, UMIST, 1996–2002; Vis. Prof. of Construction and Engrg Law, Sch. of Mech., Aerospace and Civil Engrg, Manchester Univ. (formerly Manchester Centre for Civil and Construction Engrg), 2002–. FCInstCES (FInstCES 2001). Liveryman, Arbitrators' Co., 2002 (Freeman, 2000). *Publications:* (contrib.) New Horizons in Construction Law, 1998; (contrib.) The Law and Practice of Compromise, 5th edn 2002, 7th edn 2010; (contrib.) Discovery Deskbook for Construction Disputes, 2006; (contrib.) International Construction Law, 2009. *Address:* 24 Old Buildings, Lincoln's Inn, WC2A 3UP. *T:* (020) 7691 2424, *Fax:* (0845) 280 1950; 11 rue du General-Dufour, 1204 Geneva, Switzerland. *T:* (22) 3222500, *Fax:* (22) 3222515. *E:* mbqc@xxiv.co.uk. *Clubs:* Athenæum; Capital (Dubai).

BLACK, Neil; Performance Director, UK Athletics, since 2012; *b* Ashington, Northumberland, 23 May 1959; *s* of Neville and Mary Ann Black; *m* 1988, Ruth Carlyle. *Educ:* Ashington High Sch.; Northumbria Univ. Chartered SRP 1981. Nat. Lead Physiotherapist, English Inst. of Sport, 2003; UK Athletics: Chief Physiotherapist, 2004–12; Lead for Medicine and Sports Sci., 2006–12. *Publications:* (jtly) Sports Injuries Management. *Recreations:* biking, running. *Address:* UK Athletics, Athletics House, Alexander Stadium, Walsall Road, Perry Barr, Birmingham B42 2BE.

BLACK, Neil Cathcart, OBE 1989; Principal Oboist, English Chamber Orchestra, 1970–98; *b* 28 May 1932; *s* of Harold Black and Margaret Frances Black; *m* 1st, 1960, Jill (*née* Hemingsley); one *s* two *d*; 2nd, 1984, Janice Mary (*née* Knight). *Educ:* Rugby; Exeter College, Oxford (BA History). Entered musical profession, 1956; Principal Oboist: London Philharmonic Orch., 1959–61; in various chamber orchs, incl. London Mozart Players, Acad. of St Martin-in-the-Fields, 1965–72; Musical Dir, Kirckman Concert Soc., 1997–; oboe soloist internationally. Hon. RAM 1969. *Recreations:* wine, travel.

BLACK, Prof. Nicholas Andrew, MD; FRCS, FFPH, FRCPE; Professor of Health Services Research, London School of Hygiene and Tropical Medicine, since 1995; *b* Bristol, 21 May 1951; *s* of Joseph and Margaret Black; *m* 2005, Philippa Gough. *Educ:* Bristol Grammar Sch.; Univ. of Birmingham (MB BS 1974; MD 1983). DCH 1976; DRCOG 1976; FFPH 1990; FRCS 2002; FRCPE 2013. MO, Save the Children Fund, Nepal, 1977–78; Registrar in Public Health, Oxon, 1978–83; Lectr, Open Univ., 1983–85; Sen. Lectr, 1985–93, Reader, 1993–95, LSHTM. Hon. Consultant in Public Health, NHS London, 2006–13, NHS England, 2013–. Co-ed., Jl Health Services Res. and Policy, 1995–. Chair, Nat. Adv. Gp on Clin. Audit and Enquiries, NHS England (formerly DoH), 2007–. Founding Chair, UK Health Services Res. Network, 2005–08. Trustee, Intensive Care Nat. Audit and Res. Centre, 2002–. *Publications:* Understanding Health Services, 2005; Walking London's Medical History, 2006, 2nd edn 2012. *Recreations:* Arsenal, cooking, gardening, contemporary art, history of healthcare. *Address:* Department of Health Services Research and Policy, London School of Hygiene and Tropical Medicine, 15–17 Tavistock Place, WC1H 9SH. *T:* (020) 7927 2228. *E:* nick.black@lshtm.ac.uk.

BLACK, Prof. Paul Joseph, OBE 1983; PhD; FInstP; Professor of Science Education, University of London, 1976–95 (in School of Education, King's College, 1985–95), now Emeritus Professor; *b* 10 Sept. 1930; *s* of Walter and Susie Black; *m* 1957, Mary Elaine Weston; four *s* one *d*. *Educ:* Rhyl Grammar Sch.; Univ. of Manchester (BSc); Univ. of Cambridge (PhD). FInstP 1986. Royal Society John Jaffé Studentship, 1953–56. Univ. of Birmingham: Lectr in Physics, 1956–66; Reader in Crystal Physics, 1966–74; Prof. of Physics (Science Education), 1974–76; Dir, Centre for Science and Maths Educn, Chelsea Coll., Univ. of London, 1976–85; subseq., following merger of colls, Head, Centre for Educn Studies, KCL, 1985–89 (FKC 1990); Dean, Faculty of Educn, Univ. of London, 1978–82. Vis. Prof., Stanford Univ., 1999–2002. Educnl Consultant: to Nuffield Chelsea Curriculum Trust, 1978–93 (Chm., 1992–93); to OECD, 1988–96; Consultant to: World Bank, 1991; US Nat. Sci. Foundn, 1992. Vice-Pres., Royal Instn of Great Britain, 1983–85; Chairman, National Curriculum Task Gp on Assessment and Testing, DES, 1987–88; Internat. Commn on Physics Educn, 1993–99 (Mem., 1987–93); S London Cttee, RC Archdio. of Southwark Schs' Commn, 1996–2006; Dep. Chm., Grubb Inst. for Behavioural Studies, 1990–2003 (Mem. Council, 1983–2002; Chm., 1985–90; Hon. Vice-Pres., 1997); Member: School Curriculum Develt Cttee, 1984–88; Nat. Curriculum Council, 1988–91 (Dep. Chm., 1989–91); Exec., Univs Council for Educn of Teachers, 1982–86; Res. Grants Bd, ESRC, 1987–90; Exec., Editl Cttee for Nat. Sci. Educn Standards, Nat. Res. Council, USA, 1994–95; US Nat. Acad. of Scis Bd on Testing and Assessment, 1995–99. President: Groupe Internat. de la Recherche sur l'Enseignement de la Physique, 1984–91; Educn Section, British Assoc., 1992–93; Vice Pres. and Mem. Council, IUPAP, 1997–99; Member: US Nat. Acad. of Educn, 2010; Phi Delta Kappan, 2010; Hon. Pres., Assoc. for Science Educn, 1986 (Hon. Life Mem., 1986); Hon. Mem., Standing Conf. on Sch. Science and Technol., 1989. Trustee, Nat. Energy Foundn, 1992–2000; One Plus One Marriage and Partnership Research, 1996– (Chair of Trustees, 1996–2013). Hon. Mem., CGLI, 1989. FRSA 1990; Osher Fellow, San Francisco Exploratorium, 1993. DUniv: Surrey, 1991; Open, 2002; Hon. DEd Kingston, 2003. Bragg Medal, Inst. of Physics, 1973; Medal, Internat. Commn on Physics Educn, 2000; Dist. Contribs to Sci. Educn Res. Award, Nat. Assoc. for Res. in Sci. Teaching, USA, 2004; Lifetime Achievement Award: Assoc. for Sci. Educn, 2005; Internat. Soc. for Design and Develt in Educn, 2009; John Nisbet Fellowship Award, British Educnl Res. Assoc., 2014. KSG of St Gregory, 1973. *Publications:* (jtly) Nuffield Advanced Physics Project, 1972; (contrib.) Higher Education Learning Project Books, 1977; (jtly) Open Work in Science, 1992; Nuffield Primary Science books (for Key Stages 1 and 2), 1993; (ed jtly) Children's Informal Ideas in Science, 1993; (ed jtly) Teachers Assessing Pupils: lessons from science classrooms, 1995; (jtly) Primary SPACE Project Research Reports: Light, 1990, Electricity, 1991, Processes of Life, 1992, The Earth in Space, 1994; (ed jtly) Changing the Subject, 1996; Testing: friend or foe, 1998; (jtly) Inside the Black Box, 1998; (ed jtly) Classroom Assessment and the National Science Education Standards, 2001; (jtly) Working Inside the Black Box, 2002; (jtly) Standards in Public Examinations, 2002; (jtly) Inside Science Education Reform, 2003; (jtly) Assessment for Learning, 2003; (jtly) Science Inside the Black Box, 2004; (jtly) Inside the Black Box of Assessment, 2013; papers on crystallography, physics and science, technology education, and assessment in education. *Address:* 16 Wilton Crescent, SW19 3QZ. *T:* (020) 8542 4178.

BLACK, Peter Malcolm; Member (Lib Dem) South Wales West, National Assembly for Wales, since 1999; *b* 30 Jan. 1960; *s* of John Malcolm and Joan Arlene Black; *m* 1st, 1984, Patricia Mary Hopkin (marr. diss. 1995); 2nd, 2000, Angela Lynette Jones. *Educ:* Wirral Grammar Sch. for Boys; University Coll. of Swansea (BA Hons English and History). Exec. Officer, Land Registry for Wales, 1983–99. Member: (L) Swansea City Council, 1984–96; (Lib Dem) City and County of Swansea Unitary Council, 1996–. Chm., Lib Dem Wales, 1995–97 (Sec., Finance and Admin Cttee, 1996–99). *Recreations:* theatre, poetry, films. *Address:* 115 Cecil Street, Manselton, Swansea SA5 8QL.

BLACK, Prof. Richard, PhD; Pro-Director (Research and Enterprise), School of Oriental and African Studies, University of London, since 2013; *b* Cambridge, 10 Aug. 1964; *s* of Harold and Dorothy Black; *m* 1998, Martha Walsh; one *s*. *Educ:* Perse Sch., Cambridge; Hertford Coll., Oxford (BA Geog. 1986); Royal Holloway and Bedford New Coll., Univ. of London (PhD 1990). Lectr in Geog., KCL, 1989–95; University of Sussex: Lectr, 1995–99; Sen. Lectr, 1999–2001, Reader, 2001–02, in Human Geog.; Prof. of Human Geog., 2003–13; Hd, Sch. of Global Studies, 2009–13. *Publications:* Crisis and Change in Rural Europe, 1992; Geography and Refugees, 1993; Refugees, Environment and Development, 1998; The End of the Refugee Cycle?, 1999; Targeting Development, 2004. *Recreations:* walking, theatre, football, banjo, family. *Address:* School of Oriental and African Studies, University of London, Thornhaugh Street, Russell Square, WC1H 0XG. *T:* (020) 7898 4002. *E:* r.black@soas.ac.uk.

BLACK, Prof. Robert; QC (Scot.) 1987; FRSE; Professor of Scots Law, University of Edinburgh, 1981–2004, now Emeritus; *b* 12 June 1947; *s* of James Little Black and Jeannie Findlay Lyon. *Educ:* Lockerbie Acad.; Dumfries Acad.; Edinburgh Univ. (LLB); McGill Univ., Montreal (LLM); Lord Pres. Cooper Meml Prize, Univ. of Edinburgh, 1968; Vans Dunlop Scholarship, Univ. of Edinburgh, 1968; Commonwealth Scholarship, Commonwealth Scholarship Commn, 1968. Advocate, 1972; Lectr in Scots Law, Univ. of Edinburgh, 1972–75; Sen. Legal Officer, Scottish Law Commn, 1975–78; in practice at Scottish Bar, 1978–81; Temp. Sheriff, 1981–95. Chm., Inquiry into operations of Monklands DC, 1994–95. Dir, Gannaga Lodge, Agterkop, South Africa, 2005–. Gen. Editor, The Laws of Scotland: Stair Memorial Encyclopaedia, 1988–96 (Dep., then Jt, Gen. Editor, 1981–88). FRSA 1991; FRSE 1992; Founding Fellow, Inst. of Contemporary Scotland, 2000. *Publications:* An Introduction to Written Pleading, 1982; Civil Jurisdiction: the new rules, 1983; articles in UK, US, German and S African legal jls. *Recreation:* seeking to overturn the Lockerbie conviction. *Address:* 6/4 Glenogle Road, Edinburgh EH3 5HW. *T:* (0131) 557 3571. *E:* rblackqc@gmail.com; 4 Vygie Street, Middelpos 8193, Northern Cape, South Africa. *T:* (087) 8026467. *Club:* Royal Over-Seas League.

BLACK, Sir (Robert) David, 3rd Bt *cr* 1922; *b* 29 March 1929; *s* of Sir Robert Andrew Stransham Black, 2nd Bt, ED, and Ivy (*d* 1980), *d* of late Brig.-Gen. Sir Samuel Wilson, GCMG, KCB, KBE; *S* father, 1979; *m* 1st, 1953, Rosemary Diana (marr. diss. 1972), *d* of Sir Rupert John Hardy, 4th Bt; two *d* (and one *d* decd); 2nd, 1973, Dorothy Maureen (*d* 2011), *d* of Major Charles R. Eustace Radclyffe and *widow* of A. R. D. Pilkington. *Educ:* Eton. Lieut, Royal Horse Guards, 1949; Captain 1953; Major 1960; retired, 1961. Served with Berkshire and Westminster Dragoons, TA, 1964–67, and Berkshire Territorials, TAVR III, 1967–69; Vice-Chm., Berkshire, Eastern Wessex TAVRA, 1985–92. Joint Master, Garth and South Berks Foxhounds, 1965–73. Hon. Col, 94 (Berks Yeo.) Signal Sqn (TA), 1988–98. DL Caithness, 1991–2004; High Sheriff, Oxfordshire, 1993. *Recreations:* shooting, gardening, fishing. *Heir:* none. *Address:* Beech Farm House, Woodcote, near Reading, Berks RG8 0QB. *T:* (01491) 682234. *Clubs:* Flyfishers', Cavalry and Guards.

BLACK, Robert William, CBE 2012; FRSE; Auditor General for Scotland, 2000–12; *b* 6 Nov. 1946; *s* of Robert G. Black and Nell Black (*née* Gray); *m* 1970, Doreen Mary Riach, MBE; three *s* one *d*. *Educ:* Univ. of Aberdeen (MA Hons Econs); Heriot-Watt Univ. (MSc Town Planning); Univ. of Strathclyde (MSc Public Policy). Planner, Notts CC, 1971–73; Supervisory Planner, Glasgow CC, 1973–75; Gp Leader, Res. and Intelligence, 1975–80, Sen. Exec., Chief Exec.'s Dept, 1980–85, Strathclyde Regl Council; Chief Executive: Stirling DC, 1985–90; Tayside Regl Council, 1990–95; Controller of Audit, Accounts Commn for Scotland, 1995–2000. Chm., Shelter Commn on Housing and Wellbeing in Scotland, 2013–; Chair, Fiscal Affairs Scotland, 2014–. Public Interest Mem., ICAS, 2012–. Mem. Bd, BL 2012–. Lay Mem. Ct, Univ. of Edinburgh, 2012–. FSS 1984–2012; FRSE 2006; FRSA 2007

Hon. LLD Aberdeen, 2004; Hon. DBA Queen Margaret UC, Edinburgh, 2006. *Recreations:* the outdoors, the arts. *Address:* Backcroft Cottage, Backcroft, Dunblane FK15 0BL. *E:* robertwblack@me.com. *Club:* New (Edinburgh).

BLACK, Roger Anthony, MBE 1992; former athlete; presenter, BBC Television, since 1998; corporate motivational speaker; *b* 31 March 1966; *s* of late David Black and of Thelma Black; one *d*; *m* 2002, Julia Burgess; twin *s*. *Educ:* Portsmouth Grammar Sch. Commonwealth Games: gold medal for 400m and 4 × 400m, 1986; European Championships: gold medal for 400m and 4 × 400m, 1986, 1990; silver medal for 400m, 1994; World Championships: gold medal for 4 × 400m, silver medal for 400m, 1991; Olympic Games: bronze medal for 4 × 400m, 1992; silver medal for 400m and 4 × 400m, 1996. Hon. MA Southampton, 1992. *Publications:* How Long's the Course? (autobiog.), 1998. *Recreations:* guitar, football, dog. *Address:* (office) 7 Stratfield Park, Elettra Avenue, Waterlooville, Hants PO7 7XN. *T:* (023) 9226 8866, *Fax:* (023) 9226 8777. *E:* roger@rogerblack.co.uk.

BLACK, Rona McLeod, (Lady Black); *see* MacKie, R. McL.

BLACK, Stewart; *see* Black, C. S. F.

BLACK, Prof. Susan Margaret, (Sue), OBE 2001; PhD; FRSE; FRCPE; Professor of Anatomy and Forensic Anthropology, since 2003, and Deputy Principal for Public Engagement, since 2013, University of Dundee; *b* 7 May 1961; *d* of Alasdair John Gunn and Isabel Ann Gunn (*née* Bailey); *m* 1993, Thomas William Black; three *d*. *Educ:* Univ. of Aberdeen (BSc Hons 1982; PhD 1987). FRCPE 2013. Lectr in Anatomy, UMDS, 1987–92; Consultant Forensic Anthropologist, Univ. of Glasgow, 1995–2001. Hd, Forensic Anthropol., Kosovo Mission, FCO, 1999–2000. Founder, 2001, and Pres., 2009, British Assoc. for Human Identification. Director: Centre for Internat. Forensic Assistance, 2001–; Nat. Advanced Training in Disaster Victim Identification, 2007–10. FRSE 2005; FRAI 2009; Hon. FRCPSGlas 2007. Hon. DSc: Robert Gordon, 2003; Abertay, 2009. Police Commendation, Disaster Victim Identification, 2008; Lucy Mair Medal, RAI, 2008. *Publications:* Developmental Juvenile Osteology, 2000; The Juvenile Skeleton, 2004. *Recreations:* writing, family. *Address:* Centre for Anatomy and Human Identification, College ofArt, Science and Engineering, University of Dundee, Dundee DD1 5EH. *T:* (01382) 385776, *Fax:* (01382) 385893. *E:* s.m.black@dundee.ac.uk.

BLACKADDER, Dame Elizabeth (Violet), DBE 2003 (OBE 1982); RA 1976; RSA 1972; artist; Her Majesty's Painter and Limner in Scotland, since 2000; *b* 24 Sept. 1931; *m* 1956, John Houston. *Educ:* Falkirk High Sch.; Univ. of Edinburgh; Edinburgh Coll. of Art. Lectr, Sch. of Drawing and Painting, Edinburgh Coll. of Art, 1962–86. Exhibns, Mercury Gall., London, 1965–; retrospective exhibitions: Scottish Arts Council, 1981; Aberystwyth Arts Centre, 1989; Talbot Rice Gall., Edinburgh, 2000. Work in collections including: Scottish Nat. Gall. of Modern Art; Scottish Nat. Portrait Gall.; Nat. Portrait Gall.; Government Art Collection; Kettle's Yard, Cambridge; Hunterian Art Gall., Glasgow. Hon. FRIAS 1986; Hon. FRSE 1994. Hon. DLitt: Heriot-Watt, 1989; Strathclyde, 1998; Glasgow, 2001; St Andrews, 2003; Dr (*hc*): Edinburgh, 1990; London, 2004; Hon. LLD Aberdeen, 1997; Hon. Dr Stirling, 2002. *Relevant publications:* Elizabeth Blackadder, by Judith Bumpus, 1988; Elizabeth Blackadder, by Duncan Macmillan, 1999; Elizabeth Blackadder Prints, by Christopher Allan, 2003. *Address:* c/o Royal Scottish Academy, The Mound, Edinburgh EH2 2EL.

BLACKBEARD, Roy Warren; High Commissioner for Botswana in the United Kingdom, since 1998; *b* 16 April 1953. *Educ:* Kimberley Boys' High Sch. Official Learner, Metallurgy, De Beers, 1972–79; Audit Clerk, Price Waterhouse, 1973–74; CEO, Blackbeard & Co. (Pty) Ltd, 1974–89; ranch manager, 1974–96. MP, Serowe N, 1989–98; Asst Minister, 1992–94, Minister, 1994–97, of Agriculture, Botswana. Mem., Central DC, 1979–89 (Member: Gen. Purposes and Finance Cttee, 1979–89; Livestock Industry Adv. Cttee, 1979–89). Treas., Youth Wing, Botswana Democratic Party, 1980–96. Dir, Air Botswana, 1979–89. *Recreations:* sporting, skeet shooting, theatre, cinema, tennis. *Address:* Botswana High Commission, 6 Stratford Place, W1C 1AY. *T:* (020) 7499 0031, *Fax:* (020) 7495 8595; 34 Winnington Road, Hampstead, N2 0UB.

BLACKBOURN, Prof. David Gordon, PhD; FRHistS; Cornelius Vanderbilt Distinguished Professor of History, Vanderbilt University, since 2012; *b* 1 Nov. 1949; *s* of Harry Blackbourn and Pamela Jean (*née* Youngman); *m* 1st, 1985, Deborah Frances Langton (marr. diss. 2013); one *s* one *d*; 2nd, 2014, Celia Stewart Applegate. *Educ:* Leeds Modern Grammar Sch.; Christ's Coll., Cambridge (BA Hons Hist. 1970); MA 1974, PhD 1976, Cambridge. Res. Fellow, Jesus Coll., Cambridge, 1973–76; Lectr in History, QMC, Univ. of London, 1976–79; Birkbeck College, University of London: Lectr, 1979–85; Reader, 1985–89; Prof. of Mod. European History, 1989–92; Harvard University: Prof. of Hist., 1992–97; Coolidge Prof. of Hist., 1997–2012; Dir, Center for Eur. Studies, Harvard, 2007–12. Research Fellow: Inst. of European Hist., Mainz, 1974–75; Alexander von Humboldt Foundn, Bonn-Bad Godesberg, 1984–85; John Simon Guggenheim Meml Foundn, NY, 1994–95; Vis. Kratter Prof. of European Hist., Stanford Univ., 1989–90; Walter Channing Cabot Fellow, Harvard Univ., 2003–04. Lectures: Annual, German Histl Inst., London, 1998; Malcolm Wynn, Stetson Univ., Fla, 2002; George C. Windell Meml, Univ. of New Orleans, 2006; Crayenborgh, Leiden, Netherlands, 2007; Jakob and Wilhelm Grimm, Univ. of Waterloo, Ont, 2010. Mem., Editl Bd, Past and Present, 1988–. Sec. 1979–81, Mem. Cttee 1981–86, German Hist. Soc.; Member, Academic Advisory Board: German Hist. Inst., London, 1983–92; Inst. for European Hist., Mainz, 1995–2006; Lichtenbergkolleg, Univ. of Goettingen, 2007–; German Histl Inst., Washington, 2008– (Mem., 2004–, Pres., 2008–, Bd of Friends); Mem., Vis. Cttee for the Social Scis, MIT, 2009–13; Vice-Pres., 2002, Pres., 2003, Conference Gp on Central European Hist., American Hist. Assoc. Mem. Adv. Bd, Edmund Spevack Meml Foundn, 2003–06. FRHistS 1987; Fellow, American Acad. of Arts and Scis, 2007. Corresp. FBA 2011. *Publications:* Class, Religion and Local Politics in Wilhelmine Germany, 1980; (with Geoff Eley) Mythen Deutscher Geschichtsschreibung, 1980 (Japanese edn 1983); (with Geoff Eley) The Peculiarities of German History, 1984; Populists and Patricians, 1987; (ed with Richard J. Evans) The German Bourgeoisie, 1991; Marpingen: apparitions of the Virgin Mary in Bismarckian Germany, 1993 (Amer. Historical Assoc. prize for best book in German history); The Fontana History of Germany: the long nineteenth century 1780–1918, 1997, 2nd edn as A History of Germany 1780–1918: the long nineteenth century, 2003; The Conquest of Nature: water, landscape and the making of modern Germany, 2006 (George L. Mosse Prize, Weyerhaeuser Prize, H-Soz-u-Kult Prize); (ed with James Retallack) Localism, Landscape and the Ambiguities of Place, 2007. *Recreations:* reading, jazz and classical music, walking. *Address:* Department of History, Vanderbilt University, PMB 351802, 2301 Vanderbilt Place, Nashville, TN 37235, USA. *E:* david.blackbourn@vanderbilt.edu.

BLACKBURN, Bishop of, since 2013; **Rt Rev. Julian Tudor Henderson;** *b* 23 July 1954; *s* of Ian Tudor Henderson and Susan Blundell Henderson; *m* 1984, Heather Gwenllian Lees; one *s* one *d*. *Educ:* Radley Coll.; Keble Coll., Oxford (MA Theol.). Ordained deacon, 1979, priest, 1980; Curate, St Mary's, Islington, 1979–83; Vicar: Emmanuel and St Mary in the Castle, Hastings, 1983–92; Holy Trinity, Claygate, 1992–2005; Archdeacon of Dorking, 2005–13. Hon. Canon, Guildford Cathedral, 2001–13. *Recreations:* gardening, reading, walking. *Address:* Bishop's House, Ribchester Road, Clayton Le Dale, Blackburn BB1 9EF. *T:* (01254) 248234. *E:* bishop@bishopofblackburn.org.uk.

BLACKBURN, Dean of; *see* Armstrong, Very Rev. C. J.

BLACKBURN, Archdeacon of; *no new appointment at time of going to press.*

BLACKBURN, Dr Bonnie Jean, FBA 2005; freelance editor, since 1990; *b* 15 July 1939; *d* of John Hall Blackburn and Ruth Blackburn; *m* 1st, 1971, Edward E. Lowinsky (*d* 1985); one *d*; 2nd, 1990, Leofranc Holford-Strevens. *Educ:* Wellesley Coll., Mass (BA 1961); Univ. of Chicago (MA 1963, PhD 1970). Vis. Associate Prof., Univ. of Chicago, 1986; Lectr, Sch. of Music, Northwestern Univ., 1987; Vis. Associate Prof., State Univ. of NY, Buffalo, 1989–90; Mem., Common Room, Wolfson Coll., Oxford, 1993–. Hon. Mem., Faculty of Music, Oxford Univ., 1999–. *Publications:* (ed) Johannis Lupi Opera omnia, 3 vols, 1980–89; (ed jtly) A Correspondence of Renaissance Musicians, 1991; (with L. Holford-Strevens) The Oxford Companion to the Year, 1999; Composition, Printing and Performance: studies in Renaissance music, 2000; (with L. Holford-Strevens) The Oxford Book of Days, 2000; (ed) New Josquin Edition, 21–22: Motets on Non-biblical Texts De Domino Jesu Christo, 2003–07; (ed with L. Holford-Strevens) Florentius de Faxolis, Book on Music, 2010; contribs to volumes of essays and Festschriften; contrib. articles to Basler Jahrbuch für historische Musikpraxis, Early Music Hist., Early Music, Jl Alamire Foundn, Jl Musicol., Jl Amer. Musicol. Soc., Musica disciplina, Musical Qly, Studi musicali, Tijdschrift van de Koninklijke Vereniging voor Nederlandse Muziekgeschiedenis. *Recreation:* travel. *Address:* 67 St Bernard's Road, Oxford OX2 6EJ. *T:* (01865) 552808, *Fax:* (01865) 512237. *E:* bonnie.blackburn@wolfson.ox.ac.uk.

BLACKBURN, Vice Adm. Sir David Anthony James, (Sir Tom), KCVO 2004 (LVO 1978); CB 1999; Master of HM Household, 2000–05; an Extra Equerry to the Queen, since 2000; *b* 18 Jan. 1945; *s* of late Lieut J. Blackburn, DSC, RN, and late Mrs M. J. G. Pickering-Pick; *m* 1973, Elizabeth Barstow; three *d*. *Educ:* Taunton Sch. RNC Dartmouth, 1963; HMS Kirkliston (in comd), 1972–73; Equerry-in-Waiting to the Duke of Edinburgh, 1976–78; Exec. Officer, HMS Antrim, 1978–81; MoD (Navy), 1981–83; Comdr, HMS Birmingham, 1983–84; MoD (Navy), 1984–86; HMS York (in comd) and Captain Third Destroyer Sqn, 1987–88; Dir, Naval Manpower and Trng (Seamen), MoD, 1988–90; Cdre, Clyde, and Naval Base Comdr, Clyde, 1990–92; HMS Cornwall (in comd) and Captain, Second Frigate Sqn, 1992–93; Defence Attaché and Hd of British Defence Staff, Washington, 1994–97; COS to Comdr Allied Naval Forces Southern Europe, 1997–99. Mem., Pensions Appeal Tribunal, 2005–15. Chairman: St John Ambulance (London Dist), 2006–10; Marine Soc. & Sea Cadets, 2006–10; Dep. Chm., RYA, 2007–10. Trustee: Mission to Seafarers, 2005–15; Order of St John, 2007–15. *Club:* Royal Cruising.

BLACKBURN, David Michael; property project consultant, since 1986, and commercial mediator, since 2004; *b* London, 23 Dec. 1937; *s* of Rudolph Isaac Blackburn and Esther Sybil Blackburn; *m* 1970, Janice Brown (OBE 2011); three *s* one *d*. *Educ:* City of London Sch.; St John's Coll., Cambridge (BA 1959; LLM 1960; MA 1962). Registered Mediator, CEDR, 2006–. Admitted solicitor 1962; Partner, Courts & Co., solicitors, 1962–81. Director: Rosehaugh plc, 1979–85; Rosehaugh Stanhope Developments plc, 1983–92; Blackburn Associates Ltd, 1986–2010; QVS Developments Ltd, 1998–2004. Member Board: Nat. Opera Studio, 1994–2012; Design Mus., 2006–11; Olivebrook Ltd, 2011–. *Recreations:* opera, contemporary arts, architecture and design, lively discussion, Indian and other travel. *Address:* 3 Norland Place, W11 4QG. *T:* (020) 7792 8288, *Fax:* (020) 7792 3334. *E:* db@blackburnuk.net.

BLACKBURN, Elizabeth; QC 1998; *b* 5 Oct. 1954; *d* of Robert Arnold Parker and Edna Parker (*née* Baines); *m* 1979, John Blackburn, *qv*; two *s*. *Educ:* City of London Sch. for Girls; Manchester Univ. (BA Hons English 1976). Called to the Bar, Middle Temple, 1978 (Harmsworth Schol.), Bencher, 2008; in practice at the Bar, 1978–, specialising in commercial and admiralty law, 1980–; Examr, High Court, 1987–90; Jt Hd of Chambers, Stone Chambers, Gray's Inn, 2014–. Mem., Exec. Cttee, British Maritime Law Assoc., 2003–. Mem., UK delegn, Internat. Oil Pollution Compensation Supplementary Fund Protocol Diplomatic Conf., 2003; Legal Mem., DCMS Adv. Cttee on Historic Wreck Sites, 2004–; Mem. Panel, Lloyd's Form Salvage Arbitrators, 2009–. *Recreations:* cinema, travel. *Address:* Stone Chambers, 4 Field Court, Gray's Inn, WC1R 5EF. *T:* (020) 7440 6900.

See also R. S. Parker.

BLACKBURN, Prof. Elizabeth Helen, (Mrs J. W. Sedat), AC 2010; PhD; FRS 1992; Morris Herzstein Professor in Biology and Physiology, University of California, San Francisco (Professor of Biochemistry and Biophysics, 1990; Chair, Department of Microbiology and Immunology, 1993–99); *b* 26 Nov. 1948; *d* of Harold Stewart Blackburn and Marcia Constance (*née* Jack); *m* 1975, John William Sedat; one *s*. *Educ:* Univ. of Melbourne (BSc Hons 1970; MSc 1972); Cambridge Univ. (PhD 1975). University of California, Berkeley: Asst Prof., Dept of Molecular Biol., 1978–83; Associate Prof., 1983–86; Prof. of Molecular Biology, 1986–90. Pres., Amer. Soc. for Cell Biol., 1998. Mem., Amer. Acad. Arts and Scis; For. Associate, Nat. Acad. of Scis, USA, 1993. Hon. DSc: Yale, 1991; Cambridge, 2009. Award for Molecular Biol., Nat. Acad. Scis, USA, 1990; Australia Prize, 1998; Gairdner Prize, Gairdner Foundn, 1998; General Motors Sloan Prize, 2001; Lasker Prize, 2006; (jtly) Nobel Prize in Physiology or Medicine, 2009. *Publications:* research and review articles in Nature, Science, Cell. *Recreation:* music. *Address:* Department of Biochemistry and Biophysics, University of California, Mission Bay Campus, 600 16th Street, Room GH–S312F, Box 2200, San Francisco, CA 94158–2517, USA. *T:* (415) 4764912.

BLACKBURN, (Jeffrey) Michael, CVO 2009; Chief Executive, Halifax Building Society, then Halifax plc, 1993–98; *b* 16 Dec. 1941; *s* of Jeffrey and Renee Blackburn; *m* 1987, Louise Clair Jouny; two *s*, and one *s* one *d* from a previous marriage. *Educ:* Northgate Grammar Sch., Ipswich. FCIB. Chief Manager, Lloyds Bank Business Adv. Service, 1979–83; Dir and Chief Exec., Joint Credit Card Co. Ltd, 1983–87; Dir and Chief Exec., Leeds Permanent Building Soc., 1987–93. Director: DFS Furniture plc, 1999–2004; George Wimpey PLC, 1999–2005; Town Centre Securities plc, 1999–2002; In Kind Direct, 1999–2009 (Dep. Chm., 2001–09); Freeport plc, 2003–07; Chm., Fairpoint (formerly Debt Free Direct) Gp plc, 2005–08. Pres., CIB, 1998–99. Mem. Court, Leeds Univ., 2001–07. Gov., NYO, 1999–2007; Trustee, Duke of Edinburgh's Award, 1998–2009. DUniv Leeds Metropolitan, 1998; Hon. DLitt Huddersfield, 1998. *Recreations:* music, theatre, opera, sport. *Club:* Oriental.

See also T. M. Blackburn.

BLACKBURN, John; QC 1984; arbitrator; *b* 13 Nov. 1945; *s* of Harry and Violet Blackburn; *m* 1st, 1970, Alison Nield (marr. diss. 1978); 2nd, 1979, Elizabeth Parker (*see* E. Blackburn); two *s*. *Educ:* Rugby Sch.; Worcester Coll., Oxford (Scholar, 1967; Gibbs Prize in Law, 1967). Called to the Bar, Middle Temple, 1969 (Astbury Law Scholar), Bencher, 1993. Practising barrister, 1970–2006. *Recreations:* cricket, golf, paintings, wine. *Address:* 1 Atkin Building, Gray's Inn, WC1R 5AT.

BLACKBURN, Ven. John, CB 2004; Vicar of Risca, Gwent, 2004–13; *b* 3 Dec. 1947; *m* 1970, Anne Elisabeth Woodcock; two *d*. *Educ:* University Coll., Cardiff (DipTh); St Michael's Coll., Llandaff (DPS 1971); Open Univ. (BA Hons 1988; AdvDipEd; BSc 2004). Deacon 1971, priest 1972; Curate, Risca, 1971–76; Chaplain, HM Forces, 1976–2004: Dep. Chaplain-Gen., 1999–2000, Chaplain-Gen., 2000–04; Archdeacon of HM Land Forces, 1999–2004, now Emeritus. QHC 1996–2004. Hon. Canon, Ripon Cathedral, 2001–04, now Canon Emeritus. Chm., Gwent Br., SSAFA, 2006–. Trustee, League of Mercy, 2013. FRSA 1999. *Recreations:* travelling, game shooting, reading, English watercolours. *Address:* St Hilary, 11 Gelliz Avenue, Risca, Newport, Gwent NP11 6QF. *Club:* National.

BLACKBURN, Michael; *see* Blackburn, J. M.

BLACKBURN, Michael John, FCA; Chairman, Touche Ross & Co., 1990–92 (Managing Partner, 1984–90); *b* 25 Oct. 1930; *s* of Francis and Ann Blackburn; *m* 1955, Maureen (*née* Dale); one *s* two *d*. *Educ:* Kingston Grammar Sch. Joined Touche Ross, 1954; Partner, 1960. Chm., GEI International, 1990–95; Deputy Chairman: Aerostructures Hamble Hldgs, 1992–95; Blue Arrow Hldgs, 1992–96; Director: Chubb Security, 1992–97; William Hill Gp, 1992–99; Steel, Burrill Jones, 1992–99; Wolverhampton Wanderers FC, 1995–97. Chm., Voices for Hospices, 1990–2001. *Recreations:* horse racing, the garden.

BLACKBURN, Peter Hugh, CBE 2003; FCA; Chairman, Northern Foods, 2002–05; *b* 17 Dec. 1940; *s* of Hugh Edward Blackburn and Sarah Blackburn (*née* Moffatt); *m* 1967, Gillian Mary Popple; three *d*. *Educ:* Douai Sch., Reading; Leeds Univ. (BA Hons Philosophy and French); Poitiers Univ. (Dipl. French); Inst. of Chartered Accts; AMP, Harvard Business Sch., 1976. R. S. Dawson & Co., Bradford (articles), 1962–66; various positions within John Mackintosh and Rowntree Mackintosh, 1966–91; Chm., Rowntree UK, 1985–91; Head, Nestlé Chocolate, Confectionery and Biscuit Strategy Group, 1989–90; Chm. and Chief Exec., Nestlé UK, 1991–96 and 1997–2001; Pres. and Dir Gen., Nestlé France, 1996–97. Non-executive Director: SIG, 2001–09; Compass Gp, 2002–07. President: ISBA, 1998–2000; FDF, 2000–02. Nat. Pres., Modern Languages Assoc., 1987–89; Chm., Council, Festival of Languages Young Linguist Competition, 1985–89; Chm., Harrogate Internat. Fest., 2004–11 (Trustee, 2011–). Mem., Council of Industry and Higher Educn, 1990–92. Mem. Council, York Univ., 1989–92, 2001–03. York Merchant Adventurers, 1989–2006. FIGD 1991. Hon. FCIL (Hon. FIL 1989). Hon. DLitt Bradford, 1991; Hon. DBA Leeds Metropolitan, 2005. Chevalier du Tastevin, 1984. *Recreations:* fell walking, photography.

BLACKBURN, Rt Rev. Richard Finn; *see* Warrington, Bishop Suffragan of.

BLACKBURN, Prof. Robert, PhD, LLD; Professor of Constitutional Law, King's College London, since 1997; *b* London; *s* of Lt Comdr Richard, (Dick), Blackburn and Dulcie Blackburn; *m* 1985, Paula Summerhayes; one *s* two *d*. *Educ:* Rugby Sch.; Univ. of Leeds (BA Hist.; PhD; LLD Law); Coll. of Law (law diplomas); London Sch. of Econs and Political Sci. (MSc Govt). Admitted solicitor, 1979; King's College London: Lectr, 1981–92; Sen. Lectr, 1992–94; Reader in Public Law, 1994–97; Actg Hd, Law Sch., 2006–07; Leverhulme Res. Fellow, 2007–09; Hd of Dept, Inst. of Contemporary British Hist., 2010–14. UK Nat. Corresp., Council of Europe Directorate of Human Rights, 1983–2008. Special Counsel, Inq. into Codifying the UK Constitution, Political and Constitutional Reform Cttee, H of C, 2010–15. FRHistS 1989. *Publications:* The Meeting of Parliament, 1990; (ed jtly) Human Rights for the 1990s: legal, political and ethical issues, 1991; (ed) Constitutional Studies: contemporary issues and controversies, 1992; (ed) Rights of Citizenship, 1993; (jtly) A Written Constitution for the United Kingdom, 1993; The Electoral System in Britain, 1995; (ed jtly) Human Rights for the 21st Century, 1997; Towards a Constitutional Bill of Rights for the United Kingdom, 1999; (ed jtly) Constitutional Reform: the Labour government's constitutional reform agenda, 1999; (ed jtly) Fundamental Rights in Europe, 2001; (ed jtly) Griffith and Ryle on Parliament: functions, practice and procedures, 2nd edn 2003; King and Country: monarchy and the future King Charles III, 2006; (contrib.) Halsbury's Laws of England: Parliament, Vol. 78, 5th edn 2010; Constitutional and Administrative Law, Vol. 20, 5th edn 2014; Crown and Crown Proceedings, Vol. 29, 2014. *Recreations:* playing guitar, picnics in Richmond Park, holidaying in the French Alps. *Address:* School of Law, King's College London, Strand, WC2R 2LS. *T:* (020) 7848 2516.

BLACKBURN, Prof. Simon Walter, PhD; FBA 2002; Bertrand Russell Professor of Philosophy (formerly Professor of Philosophy), University of Cambridge, 2001–11; *b* 12 July 1944; *s* of Cuthbert and Edna Blackburn; *m* 1968, Angela Bowles; one *s* one *d*. *Educ:* Trinity Coll., Cambridge (BA 1965; PhD 1970). Research Fellow, Churchill Coll., Cambridge, 1967–70; Fellow and Tutor in Philosophy, Pembroke Coll., Oxford, 1970–90; Edna J. Koury Dist. Prof. of Philosophy, Univ. of N Carolina, 1990–2000. Visiting Professor: Princeton Univ., 1987; Ohio State Univ., 1988; Adjunct Prof., ANU, 1993–2001. Fellow, Amer. Acad. of Arts and Scis, 2008. Editor, Mind, 1984–90. *Publications:* Reason and Prediction, 1973; Spreading the Word, 1984; Essays in Quasi Realism, 1993; Oxford Dictionary of Philosophy, 1994; Ruling Passions, 1998; Think, 1999; Being Good, 2001; Lust, 2004; Truth: a guide for the perplexed, 2005; Plato's Republic, 2006; How to Read Hume, 2008; The Big Questions: philosophy, 2009; Practical Tortoise Raising, 2011; Mirror, Mirror: the uses and abuses of self-love, 2014. *Recreations:* hill-walking, sailing, photography. *Address:* 141 Thornton Road, Cambridge CB3 0NE. *T:* (01223) 528278.

BLACKBURN, Prof. Timothy Michael, DPhil; Professor of Invasion Biology, University College London, since 2014; *b* Chelmsford, 3 July 1966; *s* of (Jeffrey) Michael Blackburn, *qv* and Jill I. Firth; *m* 2010, Noëlle F. Kümpel; one *d*. *Educ:* St Albans Sch.; Leeds Grammar Sch.; Univ. of Manchester (BSc 1st Cl. Hons Zool.); DPhil Zool. Oxon 1990. Lectr, 2000–05, Prof. of Macroecol., 2005–07, Univ. of Birmingham; Dir, Inst. of Zool., 2007–14. *Publications:* with K. J. Gaston: Pattern and Process in Macroecology, 2000; Macroecology: concepts and consequences, 2003; (jtly) Avian Invasions: the ecology and evolution of exotic birds, 2009. *Recreations:* birding, running, epicureanism, photography. *Address:* Department of Genetics, Evolution and Environment, Centre for Biodiversity and Environment Research, Darwin Building, University College London, Gower Street, WC1E 6BT.

BLACKBURN, Vice Adm. Sir Tom; *see* Blackburn, Vice Adm. Sir D. A. J.

BLACKBURNE, Alison; HM Diplomatic Service; High Commissioner to Uganda, since 2012; *b* 20 June 1964. *Educ:* Leeds Univ. (BA Hons French/Russian). Entered FCO, 1987; Third, later Second, Sec. (Chancery), Warsaw, 1989–92; First Secretary: FCO, 1992–96; UKMIS, NY, 1996–2000; (Political), Stockholm, 2000–03; Counsellor and Dep. Hd of Mission, Harare, 2003–06; Political Counsellor, UK Perm. Representation to EU, Brussels, 2006–08; Principal Private Sec. to Lord Chancellor and Sec. of State, MoJ, 2008–10; Dep. Hd of Mission, Indonesia, 2011; Consul-Gen., Washington, DC, 2011–12.

BLACKBURNE, Hon. Sir William (Anthony), Kt 1993; a Judge of the High Court of Justice, Chancery Division, 1993–2009; *b* 24 Feb. 1944; *m* 1996, Vivien, *d* of A. C. Webber. Vice-Chancellor of the County Palatine of Lancaster, 1998–2002. Treasurer: Gen. Council of the Bar, 1988–90; Lincoln's Inn, 2015. Mem., Haringey LBC, 1974–78, 1986–93. Chm., Pakistan Soc., 2012–. Mem., Bomber Comd Meml Trust, 2010–15. Pres., Madrigal Soc., 2011–13. *Clubs:* Garrick, Alpine.

BLACKER, Captain Derek Charles, RN; Director of Personnel, Orion Royal Bank Ltd, 1984–88; *b* 19 May 1929; *s* of Charles Edward Blacker and Alexandra May Farrant; *m* 1952, Brenda Mary Getgood (*d* 2001); one *s* one *d*. *Educ:* County Sch., Isleworth; King's Coll., Univ. of London (BSc Hons 1950). Entered RN, 1950; specialisations: navigation, meteorology, oceanography; HMS Birmingham, HMS Albion, BRNC Dartmouth, HMS Hermes, 1966–69; Comdr 1965; NATO Commands: SACLANT, 1969; CINCHAN, 1972; SACEUR, 1974; Captain 1975; Dir of Public Relations (RN), 1977–79; Bd Pres., Admiralty Interview Bd, 1980; staff of C-in-C, Naval Home Comd, 1980–81; Dir of Naval Oceanography and Meteorology, MoD, 1981–84. Naval ADC to the Queen, 1983–84. Chm., Teignbridge DFAS, 2006–09 (Visits Sec., 1997–2003; Hon. Treas., 2003–06). Hon. Treas., 2005–09, Vice-Chm., 2009–11, Exeter Br., ESU. Hon. Rep., Officers' Assoc., 2006–. *Recreations:* gardening, music, golf, country pursuits. *Address:* Frenchacre, 16 Coach Road, Newton Abbot, Devon TQ12 1EW. *T:* (01626) 330120, 07988 760303. *Club:* Army and Navy.

BLACKER, Norman; Executive Director, British Gas, 1989–95; *b* 22 May 1938; *m* 1st, 196 Jennifer Mary Anderson (*d* 1992); 2nd, 1994, Carol Anderson. *Educ:* Wolverton Gramma School. CPFA. British Gas: Dir of Finance, Northern Reg., 1976–80; Dir of Finance 1980–84; Chm., N Eastern Region, then British Gas N Eastern, 1985–89; Managin Director: Eastern Regions, 1989–91; Regl Services, 1991–92; Gas Business, 1992–94. Chm. Nat. Council for Hospice and Specialist Palliative Care Services, 1994–2000. *Address:* 4 Whit Heather Court, Hythe Marina Village, Hythe SO45 6DT.

BLACKETT, Sir Hugh Francis, 12th Bt *cr* 1673, of Newcastle, Northumberland; *b* 11 Feb 1955; *e s* of Major Sir Francis Hugh Blackett, 11th Bt and his 1st wife, Elizabeth Eily Barri (*née* Dennison) (*d* 1982); *S* father, 1995; *m* 1982, Anna, *yr d* of J. St G. Coldwell; one *s* thre *d*. *Educ:* Eton. High Sheriff, Northumberland, 2007–08. *Heir:* *s* Henry Douglas Blackett, *b* Feb. 1992.

BLACKETT, Jeffrey; His Honour Judge Blackett; Judge Advocate General of the Arme Forces, since 2004; a Senior Circuit Judge, since 2005; a Deputy High Court Judge, sinc 2013; *b* 20 May 1955; *s* of Lt Comdr William Blackett and Gwendoline Blackett; *m* 1981 Sally Anne Fulford; one *s* one *d*. *Educ:* Portsmouth Grammar Sch.; University Coll. Londo (LLB 1976); Council of Legal Educn; St Antony's Coll., Oxford (MSt 2000). Called to th Bar, Gray's Inn, 1983, Bencher, 2008. Served RN, Supply and Secretariat Br., 1973–2004 Comdr, HMS Collingwood, 1995–97; Dir, Pay and Pensions, 1997–99; Chief Naval Judg Advocate, 2000–04. Actg Metropolitan Stipendiary Magistrate, 1995–99; a Recorde 2000–04. Chm., Inns Conduct Cttee, 2009–12. Special Prof., Univ. of Nottingham, 201 Mem., Bd of Dirs, RFU, 2014– (Hon. Discipline Officer, 2003–13). Trustee, Help fo Heroes. *Publications:* (with J. W. Rant) Courts-Martial, Discipline and the Criminal Process i the Armed Services, 2003; Rant on the Court Martial and Service Law, 2009. *Recreations* Rugby, squash, golf. *Address:* Room TM9.06, Thomas More Building, Royal Courts o Justice, Strand, WC2A 2LL. *T:* (020) 7218 8095, *Fax:* (020) 7218 8094. *E* HHJudgeJeff.Blackett@judiciary.gsi.gov.uk. *Club:* Royal Automobile.

BLACKFORD, Ian; MP (SNP) Ross, Skye and Lochaber, since 2015; *b* Edinburgh, 1961; *n* Ann. *Educ:* Royal High Sch., Edinburgh. Dir, UBS Philips and Drew, 1989–93; Man. Dir Nat West Mkts, 1993–99; Man. Dir, Deutsche Bank, 1999–2003; Man. Dir, First Seer, 2003– Hd, Investor Relns, CSM, 2005–12. Non-executive Director: Edinburgh Bicycl Cooperative, 2008–13; Commsworld, 2006– (Chm., 2014–). Chm., NW Skye Recreationa Assoc. Dir, Cuillin FM (community radio stn). Mem. Bd, Golden Charter Trust, 2008– Contested (SNP): Ayr, 1997; Paisley, Nov. 1997. *Address:* House of Commons, SW1A 0AA.

BLACKHAM, Vice-Adm. Sir Jeremy (Joe), KCB 1999; Chairman: Atmaana Ltd, 2005–0 (Director, 2003–10); Sarnmere, since 2006; *b* 10 Sept. 1943; *s* of Rear-Adm. Joseph Lesli Blackham, CB; *m* 1971, Candy Carter. *Educ:* Bradfield Coll., Berks; Open Univ. (BA 1st Cl Hons 1979; MA 2009); RN Staff Course, 1974. Joined RN, 1961; Spanish Interpreter, 1966 commanded HM Ships Beachampton, 1969–70, Ashanti, 1977–79, Nottingham, 1984–85 rcds 1986; Commandant, RN Staff Coll., Greenwich, 1987–89; Dir of Naval Plans, 1989–92 Captain, HMS Ark Royal, 1992–93 (Comdr RN Task Group, Adriatic); DG, Nava Personnel Strategy and Plans, 1993–95; ACNS and Adm. Pres., RNC, Greenwich, 1995–97 Dep. Comdr, Fleet, 1997–99; DCDS (Progs and Personnel), 1999; DCDS (Equipmen Capability), MoD, 1999–2002. Mem., CDS Strategic Adv. Panel, 2012–. Lectr, RUSI an defence orgns; Visiting Lecturer: KCL, 2008–; Kingston Univ., 2014–. UK Pres., EADS 2003–06; Chm., EADS Defence Systems UK, 2004–06. Director: Condor PM, 2006–; Airbu Helicopters UK (formerly Eurocopter UK), 2008–. Ext. Examr, Kingston Univ., 2013– Chm., Academic Adv. Bd, Aeronautical Engrg Faculty, City Univ., 2004–07; Member Council, RUSI (Vice Pres., 2003–); RIIA; MInstD. Pres., HMS Cavalier Assoc., 2010– Chm., Blackheath Conservatoire of Music and Arts, 2000–07. Liveryman, Shipwrights' Co. 1999–. Ed., Naval Review, 2003–; Mem., Editorial Adv. Bd, Defence Procurement Analysis 2004–06. Mem., Adv. Bd, City Forum, 2005–08. MInstD. Member: NT; English Heritage *Publications:* numerous articles on defence, strategic affairs and walking. *Recreations:* cricket music, theatre, language, travel, walking. *Address:* Monk Frith, Bell Green, Cratfield, Suffolk IP19 0DH. *Clubs:* MCC; Kent County Cricket.

BLACKHURST, Christopher Charles; journalist and commentator, since 2015; Grou Editorial Director, 2012–14, Group Content Director, 2013–15, and Multi-media Head o Business, 2014–15, The Independent and Evening Standard; *b* Barrow-in-Furness, 24 Dec 1959; *s* of Donald Blackhurst and Rose Bestwick Blackhurst (*née* Wood); *m* 1st, 1986, Lynett Dorothy Wood Grice (marr. diss. 2003); two *s* one *d*; 2nd, 2004, Annabelle Sara Fisher; on *s* one *d*. *Educ:* Barrow-in-Furness Grammar Sch. for Boys; Trinity Hall, Cambridge (BA Hon Law 1982). With Cameron Markby Solicitors, 1983–84; Asst Ed., 1984–85, Dep. Ed. 1985–86, Internat. Financial Law Rev.; Sen. Writer, Business Mag., 1986–89; Busines Feature Writer and Dep. Insight Ed., Sunday Times, 1989–90; City Ed., Sunday Express 1990–92; Sen. Business Writer, Independent on Sunday, 1992–93; Westminster corresp. Independent, 1993–96; Asst Ed., Independent on Sunday, 1996–97; Deputy Editor Independent and Independent on Sunday, 1997–98; Daily Express and Sunday Express 1998–2001; City Ed., Evening Standard, 2002–11; Ed., The Independent, 2011–13. Truste and Dir, Kingston Th. Trust, 2004–11; Mem., Develt Bd, The Sixteen, 2009–11. Mem., Arts & Business Adv. Bd, 2010–11. Mem., Fund Raising Bd, Maggie's Cancer Care Charity 2005–07. *Recreations:* golf, tennis, theatre. *Address:* The Independent, Northcliffe House, 2 Derry Street, W8 5HF. *T:* (020) 3615 2002, *Fax:* (020) 3615 2635. *Clubs:* Reform, Soh House, Roehampton (Chm., 2011).

BLACKIE, Jonathan Adam, CBE 2010; Regional Director, Government Office for th North East, 2002–11; Culture Partnership Manager, Association of North East Councils, sinc 2013; *b* 29 April 1953; *s* of late James Blackie and of Nansie Blackie; *m* 1983, Julie; four *d* *Educ:* Heriot-Watt Univ./Edinburgh Coll. of Art (BSc Hons Town and Country Planning 1976). Res. Associate, Univ. of Edinburgh, 1976–81; Sen. Policy Officer, Newcastle CC 1981–87; Principal Policy Officer, Kirklees MDC, 1987–89; Regl Projects Manager, Audi Commn, 1989–92; Dir, Newcastle City Challenge, 1992–96; Regl Dir, English Partnership (NE), 1996–99; Dir, One NorthEast RDA, 1999–2002. Vis. Prof., Univ. of Northumbria 2012–. Peer Reviewer, Study of Central and Southern Denmark, OECD, 2011–12. Chair New Writing North, 2008–; Governing Body, St Chad's Coll., Univ. of Durham, 2009– River Tyne Steering Gp, 2014–; Trustees, Alnwick Garden, 2011–. *Recreations:* arts, golf tennis. *Address:* The Coach House, Prestwick Whins Farm, Northumberland NE20 9UD. *E* jonathanblackie@hotmail.co.uk.

BLACKLEY, Air Vice-Marshal Allan Baillie, CBE 1983; AFC; BSc; Principal, Emergency Planning College, 1993–97; *b* 28 Sept. 1937. Flight Lieut, 1961; Sqn Leader, 1968; Wing Comdr, 1974; Directorate of Air Staff Plans, Dept of CAS, Air Force Dept, 1977; Gp Capt. 1980; OC RAF Valley and ADC to the Queen, 1980–82; Gp Capt. (Air Defence) RAF Strik Comd, 1982–83; Dir (Air Defence), MoD, 1984–85; Air Cdre, 1985; Comdt, RAF CFS Scampton, 1985–87; SASO, No 11 Gp, 1987–89; Dep. COS (Ops), HQ AFCENT 1989–91; AO Scotland and NI, 1991–93. Chm., Lincs and Notts Air Ambulance Charitable Trust, 1998–2001. *Address:* Benameer, 40a Horncastle Road, Woodhall Spa, Lincs LN10 6UZ.

BLACKLEY, Ian Lorimer; HM Diplomatic Service, retired; *b* 14 Dec. 1946; *s* of late Joh Lorimer Blackley and Christina Ferrier (*née* Aitken); *m* 1981, Pamela Ann Helena Belt; one *s* *Educ:* Sedbergh Sch.; St Catharine's Coll., Cambridge (MA). Joined Diplomatic Service, 1969 MECAS, Lebanon, 1971–72; Third Sec., Tripoli, 1972–73; Second Sec., Berlin, 1973–74

First Sec., Damascus, 1974–77; FCO, 1977–80; Head of Chancery and HM Consul, Beirut, 1980–82; First Sec. (Agric.), The Hague, 1982–86; Asst Head, ME Dept, FCO, 1986–88; Counsellor, Kuwait, 1988–90; British Rep. to Govt of Occupied Kuwait in Exile, Aug. 1990–March 1991; Counsellor, Damascus, 1991–93; Spokesman, EU Electoral Mission, Palestinian Elections, 1995–96; Sen. Observer, British Mission to Yemeni Elections, 1997. *Recreations:* fly fishing, Islamic art. *Address:* 63 Northumberland Street, Edinburgh EH3 6JQ.

BLACKMAN, Elizabeth Marion; *b* 26 Sept. 1949; *m* Derek Blackman (marr. diss.); one *s* one *d*. *Educ:* Carlisle County Sch. for Girls; Prince Henry's Grammar Sch., Otley; Clifton Coll., Nottingham (BEd Hons). Teacher, 1972–93, Hd, 1993–97, Upper Sch., Bramcote Park Comp., Nottingham. Mem. (Lab) Broxtowe BC, 1991–98 (Dep. Leader, 1995–97). MP (Lab) Erewash, 1997–2010. PPS to Sec. of State for Defence, 2000–05, to Leader of the H of C, 2005–06; an Asst Govt Whip, 2006–07; Vice-Chamberlain of HM Household, 2007–08. Mem., Treasury Select Cttee, 1997–2000. Chm., All-Pty Parly Gp on Autism, 2004–06.

BLACKMAN, Sir Frank (Milton), KA 1985; KCVO 1985 (CVO 1975); OBE 1969 (MBE 1964); Ombudsman for Barbados, 1987–93; *b* 31 July 1926; *s* of late A. Milton Blackman and Winnifred Blackman (*née* Pile); *m* 1st, 1958, Edith Mary Knight (*d* 1994); one *s*; 2nd, 1995, Norma Cox Astwood. *Educ:* Wesley Hall Boys' Sch., Barbados; Harrison Coll., Barbados. Clerical Officer, Colonial Secretary's Office, 1944–56; Sec., Public Service Commn, 1956–57; Asst Sec., Colonial Sec.'s Office, 1957; Cabinet Office/Premier's Office, 1958–66: Clerk of the Legislative Council, 1958–64; Perm. Sec./Cabinet Sec., 1966–86; Head of CS, 1981–86. *Address:* Lausanne, Rendezvous Hill, Christ Church, BB 15115, Barbados. *T:* 4273463.

BLACKMAN, Gilbert Albert Waller, CBE 1978 (OBE 1973); FREng, CEng, FIMechE; Chairman, Central Electricity Generating Board, Jan.–March 1990, retired; *b* 28 July 1925; *s* of Ernest Albert Cecil Blackman and Amy Blackman; *m* 1948, Lilian Rosay. *Educ:* Wanstead County High Sch.; Wandsworth Tech. Coll. CEng, FIMechE 1967; Hon. FInstE (FInstF 1964). Commnd RE, 1945–48. Trainee Engr, London Div., Brit. Electricity Authority, 1948–50; various appts in power stns, 1950–63; Central Electricity Generating Board: Stn Supt, Belvedere, 1963–64; Asst Reg. Dir, E Midlands Div., 1964–67; Asst Reg. Dir, Midlands Reg., 1967–70; Dir of Generation, Midlands Reg., 1970–75; Dir Gen., N Eastern Reg., 1975–77; Mem., 1977–90; Dep. Chm. and Prodn Man. Dir, 1986–89; Chm., British Electricity Internat. Ltd, 1988–90; Dir, Nat. Power, 1990–94. *Recreations:* music, photography, art.

See also L. C. F. Blackman.

BLACKMAN, Kirsty; MP (SNP) Aberdeen North, since 2015; *b* Aberdeen; *m* Luke Blackman; one *s* one *d*. *Educ:* Robert Gordon's Coll. Adminr, Planning Dept, Aberdeen Council. Mem. (SNP) Aberdeen CC, 2007–15. *Address:* House of Commons, SW1A 0AA.

BLACKMAN, Dr Lionel Cyril Francis; Director, British American Tobacco Co. Ltd, 1980–85 (General Manager, Group Research and Development, 1978–80); *b* 12 Sept. 1930; *s* of Mr and Mrs Ernest Albert Cecil Blackman; *m* 1955, Susan Hazel Peachey (marr. diss. 1983); one *s* one *d*. *Educ:* Wanstead High Sch.; Queen Mary Coll., London. BSc 1952; PhD 1955. Scientific Officer, then Senior Research Fellow, RN Scientific Service, 1954–57; ICI Research Fellow, then Lectr in Chemical Physics of Solids, Imperial Coll., London, 1957–60; Asst Dir (London), then Dir, Chemical Research Div., BR, 1961–64; Dir of Basic Research, then Dir Gen., British Coal Utilisation Research Assoc., 1964–71; Director: Fibreglass Ltd (subsid. of Pilkington Bros Ltd), 1971–78; Compocem Ltd, 1975–78; Cemfil Corp. (US), 1975–78; Vice-Pres., Cementos y Fibras SA (Spain), 1976–78. Chm., Hockering Residents Assoc., 1995–2003. CEng; CChem; FRSC; DIC; Sen. FEI. *Publications:* (ed) Modern Aspects of Graphite Technology, 1970; Athletics World Records in the 20th Century, 1988; Four histories of the development of the Hockering Estate, Woking, 2000, 2004, 2007, 2009; papers in various scientific and technical jls on dropwise condensation of steam, ferrites, sintering of oxides, graphite and its crystal compounds, glass surface coatings, glass reinforced cement. *Recreations:* gardening, glass, music, wine (Founder Chm., Epping Forest Wine Soc. (Pres., 1971–)). *Address:* Griffin House, Knowl Hill, The Hockering, Woking, Surrey GU22 7HL. *T:* (01483) 766328.

See also G. A. W. Blackman.

BLACKMAN, Malorie, OBE 2008; FRSL; author, since 1990; *b* London, 8 Feb. 1962. *Educ:* Honor Oak Grammar Sch.; Thames Poly. (HNC Computer Sci.); Nat. Film and Television Sch. (Screenwriting). Documentation Asst, 1981–82, Jun. Programmer, 1982–83, Scicon; Systems Programmer, Reuters, 1983–85; Project Manager, Digital Equipt, 1985–87; Database Manager, Reuters, 1987–90. Children's Laureate, 2013–15. FRSL 2009. Eleanor Farjeon Award, Children's Book Circle, 2006. *Publications: for young adults:* Not So Stupid, 1990; Trust Me, 1997; Impact: Horror, 1997; Words Last Forever, 1998; The Stuff of Nightmares, 2007; (ed) Unheard Voices, 2007; Boys Don't Cry, 2010; Noble Conflict, 2013; Jon for Short, 2013; Dr Who: the ripple effect, 2013; Heart Break Girl, 2014; Noughts & Crosses series: Noughts & Crosses, 2001; An Eye For An Eye, 2003; Knife Edge, 2004; Checkmate, 2005; Double Cross, 2008; Callum, 2012; (ed) Love Hurts, 2015; *for children:* That New Dress, 1992; Hacker, 1992; Operation Gadgetman!, 1993; Jack Sweettooth the 73rd, 1995; Whizziwig, 1995; The Space Stowaway, 1995; Thief!, 1996; A.N.T.I.D.O.T.E., 1997; Pig Heart Boy, 1997 (televised 1999); Forbidden Game, 1999; Animal Avengers, 1999; Don't Be Afraid, 1999; Whizziwig Returns, 1999; Hostage, 1999; Tell Me No Lies, 1999; Dangerous Reality, 1999; Dead Gorgeous, 2002; Cloud Busting, 2004; Robot Girl, 2015; Deadly Dare Mystery series: The Computer Ghost, 1997; Deadly Dare, 1998; Lie Detectives, 1998; *for new readers:* Elaine, You're a Brat, 1991; Girl Wonder and the Terrific Twins, 1991; Girl Wonder's Winter Adventures, 1992; Betsey Biggalow is Here!, 1992; Betsey Biggalow the Detective, 1992; Hurricane Betsey, 1993; Magic Betsey, 1994; Girl Wonder to the Rescue, 1994; My Friend's a Gris-Quok!, 1994; Rachel versus Bonecrusher the Mighty, 1994; Rachel and the Difference Thief, 1994; (jtly) Crazy Crocs, 1994; Betsey's Birthday Surprise, 1996; Grandma's Haunted Handbag, 1996; The Mellion Moon Mystery, 1996; Peril on Planet Pelia, 1996; Quasar Quartz Quest, 1996; Secret of the Terrible Hand, 1996; Space Race, 1997; Fangs, 1998; Snow Dog, 2001; The Monster Crisp-Guzzler, 2002; Sinclair, Wonder Bear, 2003; Amazing Adventures of Girl Wonder, 2003; Ellie and the Cat, 2005; *picture books:* That New Dress, 1991; Mrs Spoon's Family, 1995; Marty Monster, 1999; Dizzy's Walk, 1999; I Want a Cuddle, 2002; Jessica Strange, 2002. *Recreations:* music, reading, theatre, cinema, computer games. *Address:* c/o The Agency (London) Ltd, 24 Pottery Lane, Holland Park, W11 4LZ. *T:* (020) 7727 1346. *E:* hd-office@theagency.co.uk.

BLACKMAN, Robert; MP (C) Harrow East, since 2010; *b* 26 April 1956; *m* 1988, Nicola Jennings. *Educ:* Univ. of Liverpool (BSc). Sales trng, 1991–98, Regulatory Compliance Manager, 1998–2010, BT. Mem. (C) Brent BC, 1986–2010 (Leader, 1991–96; Dep. Leader, 2006–10). Mem. (C) Brent and Harrow, London Assembly, GLA, 2004–08. Contested (C): Brent S, 1992; Bedford, 1997; Brent N, 2005. *Address:* House of Commons, SW1A 0AA.

BLACKMAN-WOODS, Roberta C., PhD; MP (Lab) City of Durham, since 2005; *b* 16 Aug. 1957; *d* of Charles and Eleanor Woods; *m* Prof. Timothy J. Blackman; one *d*. *Educ:* Univ. of Ulster (BSc Combined Soc. Scis 1979; PhD 1989). Welfare Rights Officer, Newcastle CC, 1982–85; Lectr in Social Policy, Univ. of Ulster, then Univ. of Newcastle upon Tyne, 1985–95; Dean of Social and Labour Studies, Ruskin Coll., Oxford, 1995–2000; Prof. of Social Policy and Dep. Dean, Sch. of Arts and Social Scis, Univ. of Northumbria, 2000–05. Mem., Child Poverty Action Gp. PPS to Minister of State for Innovation, Univs and Skills, 2008–10; Asst Regl Minister for NE; Shadow Minister: Cabinet Office, 2010–11; BIS, 2010–11; DCLG, 2011–15. Chair, Parly Univ. Gp, 2011–; Vice Chair, All Party Parly Gp on Sch. Food, 2010–. *Recreation:* music. *Address:* (office) The Miners' Hall, Redhills, Durham DH1 4BD. *T:* (0191) 374 1915, *Fax:* (0191) 374 1916. *E:* mail@roberta.org.uk; House of Commons, SW1A 0AA.

BLACKMORE, Prof. Stephen, CBE 2011; PhD; FRSE; CBiol, FRSB; FLS; FRSE; Her Majesty's Botanist in Scotland, since 2010; Chair, Botanic Gardens Conservation International, since 2014; *b* 30 July 1952; *s* of Edwin Arthur and Josephine Blackmore; *m* 1973, Patricia Jane Melrose Hawley; one *s* one *d*. *Educ:* Univ. of Reading (BSc 1973; PhD 1976). CBiol, FRSB (FIBiol 1993); FLS 1976. Botanist and Administrator, Royal Society Aldabra Research Station, Indian Ocean, 1976–77; Head of Nat. Herbarium and Lectr in Botany, Univ. of Malaŵi, 1977–80; Head of Palynology Section, Dept of Botany, BM (Natural Hist.), 1980–90; Keeper of Botany, 1990–99, Associate Dir, 1992–95, Natural Hist. Mus.; Regius Keeper, Royal Botanic Garden Edinburgh, 1999–2013 (Hon. Fellow, 2014). Visiting Professor: Reading Univ., 1995–; Glasgow Univ., 1999–; Kunming Inst. of Botany, 2004–; Hon. Prof., Univ. of Edinburgh, 2004–. Chm., Darwin Adv. Cttee, DEFRA, 2013–. Pres., Systematics Assoc., 1994–97; Chm., UK Systematics Forum, 1993–99. Trustee: Little Sparta Trust, 2001–10; Botanic Gardens Conservation Internat., 2000–; Seychelles Islands Foundn, 2007–; Mem., Bd of Govs, Edinburgh Coll. of Art, 2004–10. FRSE 2000. Hon. Fellow, 48 Gp Club 'The Icebreakers', 2005. Scottish Horticl Medal, Royal Caledonian Horticl Soc., 2008; Victoria Medal of Honour, RHS, 2012; Linnean Medal, Linnean Soc. of London, 2012. *Publications:* Bee Orchids, 1985; Buttercups, 1985; (ed jtly) Pollen and Spores: form and function, 1986; (ed jtly) Evolution, Systematics and Fossil History of the Hamamelidae, 2 vols, 1989; (ed jtly) Microspores: evolution and ontogeny, 1990; (ed jtly) Pollen and Spores: patterns of diversification, 1991; (ed jtly) An Atlas of Plant Sexual Reproduction, 1992; (ed jtly) Systematics Agenda 2000: The Challenge For Europe, 1996; Pollen and Spores: morphology and biology, 2000; Gardening the Earth: gateways to a sustainable future, 2009; Green Universe, 2012; (ed jtly) Plants of China, 2013; contribs to professional jls. *Recreations:* hill walking, photography, blues guitar music. *Address:* Botanic Gardens Conservation International, Descanso House, 199 Kew Road, Richmond, Surrey TW9 3BW. *T:* (020) 8332 5953.

BLACKMORE, Timothy John, MBE 1999; Consultant Editorial Director, UBC Media Group, since 2004; *b* Hull, 3 July 1944; *s* of Rev. Harry J. Blackmore and Marjorie Blackmore; *m* 1967, Margaret Hughes; one *s* one *d*. *Educ:* King's Sch., Pontefract; Blyth Grammar Sch. Producer, Radio One, 1967–77; Hd of Programmes, Capital Radio, 1977–83; freelance producer and artist manager, 1983–87; Dir, Radio Acad., 1987–89; Prog. Dir, Unique Broadcasting, 1989–2004. Manager, Alan, (Fluff), Freeman, 1983–2006; Producer, Ivor Novello Awards, 1986–2005; Chm., Sony Radio Academy Awards, 1999–2011. Chm., Charles Parker Archive Trust, 2008–. Chm., Lydiard Millicent Parish Council, 2013– (Vice Chm., 2011–13). Fellow, Radio Acad., 1994. *Recreations:* DIY, grandchildren, music, food and wine. *Address:* Manor House, Church Place, Lydiard Millicent, Wilts SN5 3LS. *E:* tim@timblackmore.com.

BLACKSELL, Henry Oliver; QC 1994; **His Honour Judge Blacksell;** a Circuit Judge, since 1996; *b* 28 Nov. 1948; *s* of James Edward Blacksell, MBE and Joan Simmons Yates Blacksell (*née* Yates); *m* 1st, 1971, Diana Frances Mary Burton (marr. diss. 1985; she *d* 2005); 2nd, 1986, Miranda Jane, *d* of His Honour W. A. L. Allardice; one *s* one *d*. *Educ:* Barnstaple Grammar Sch.; Exeter Univ. (LLB). Called to the Bar, Inner Temple, 1972; a Recorder, 1993–96. *Recreations:* family, theatre, ancient humour. *Address:* Blackfriars Crown Court, 1–15 Pocock Street, SE1 0BJ. *Club:* Harlequin Rugby Football.

BLACKSHAW, William Simon; Headmaster of Brighton College, 1971–87; *b* 28 Oct. 1930; *s* of late C. B. Blackshaw, sometime Housemaster, Cranleigh School and Kathleen Mary (who *m* 1965, Sir Thomas McAlpine, 4th Bt); *m* 1956, Elizabeth Anne Evans; one *s* one *d* (and one *s* decd). *Educ:* Sherborne Sch.; Hertford Coll., Oxford. 2nd cl. hons Mod. Langs. Repton School: Asst Master, 1955–71; Head of Modern Languages Dept, 1961–66; Housemaster, 1966–71. Chm., Bankside Gall., 1994–2000. Chm., Sussex Schs Cricket Assoc., 1994–96. Hon. RWS 2000. *Publications:* Regardez! Racontez!, 1971; A History of Bilton Grange School, 1997; 100 Not Out: chronicles of the cryptics cricket club, 2010. *Recreations:* painting, cricket, golf. *Address:* Squash Court, The Green, Rottingdean, East Sussex BN2 7HA.

BLACKSTONE, Baroness *cr* 1987 (Life Peer), of Stoke Newington in Greater London; **Tessa Ann Vosper Blackstone;** PC 2001; PhD; Vice-Chancellor, University of Greenwich, 2004–11; Chairman, Orbit Group, since 2013; *b* 27 Sept. 1942; *d* of late Geoffrey Vaughan Blackstone, CBE, GM, QFSM and Joanna Blackstone; *m* 1963, Tom Evans (marr. diss.; he *d* 1985); one *s* one *d*. *Educ:* Ware Grammar Sch.; London School of Economics (BScSoc, PhD; Hon. Fellow, 1995). Associate Lectr, Enfield Coll., 1965–66; Asst Lectr, then Lectr, Dept of Social Administration, LSE, 1966–75; Adviser, Central Policy Review Staff, Cabinet Office, 1975–78; Prof. of Educnl Admin, Univ. of London Inst. of Educn, 1978–83; Dep. Educn Officer (Resources), then Clerk and Dir of Education, ILEA, 1983–87; Master, Birkbeck Coll., London Univ., 1987–97 (Fellow, 1998). Fellow, Centre for Studies in Social Policy, 1972–74; Special Rowntree Visiting Fellow, Policy Studies Inst., 1987. Vis. Prof., LSE, 2003–05. Chm., Gen. Adv. Council of BBC, 1987–91; First Chm., Inst. for Public Policy Research, 1988–97. Non-executive Director: Project Fullemploy, 1984–91; Royal Opera House, 1987–97 and 2009–14 (Chm., Ballet Bd, 1991–97); Thames Television, 1991–92; Granada Learning, 2003–06; VT Gp plc, 2004–10; Mott McDonald, 2005–07. Member: Planning Bd, Arts Council of GB, 1986–90; Management Cttee, King Edward's Hosp. Fund for London, 1990–95; Marshall Aid Commemoration Commn, 2005–09; Gov. and Mem. of Council, Ditchley Foundn, 1990–97; Gov., Royal Ballet, 1991–2001. Vice Pres., VSO, 1992–. Co-Chm., Franco-British Council, 2013–. Chm., RIBA Trust, 2003–10. Opposition spokesman, House of Lords: on educn and science, 1988–92; on foreign affairs, 1992–97; Minister of State, DfEE, 1997–2001; Minister of State (Minister for Arts), DCMS, 2001–03. Trustee: Architecture Foundn, 1991–97; Nat. Hist. Mus., 1992–97. Chairman: Great Ormond St Hosp. Trust Bd, 2009–; British Library, 2010–. Hon. DLitt: Bradford, 1990; Bristol Poly., 1991; Kent, 2011; DUniv: Middlesex, 1993; Strathclyde, Leeds Metropolitan, 1996; QUB, 2007; Greenwich, 2012; Hon. LLD: Aberdeen, 1994; St Andrews, 1995; Hon Dr Sorbonne, 1998; Rome, 2004; Hon. Fellow, Canterbury Christchurch, 2009; Hon. FRIBA 2005. *Publications:* Students in Conflict (jtly), 1970; A Fair Start, 1971; Education and Day Care for Young Children in Need, 1973; The Academic Labour Market (jtly), 1974; Social Policy and Administration in Britain, 1975; Disadvantage and Education (jtly), 1982; Educational Policy and Educational Inequality (jtly), 1982; Response to Adversity (jtly), 1983; Testing Children (jtly), 1983; Inside the Think Tank (jtly), 1988; Prisons and Penal Reform, 1990; Race Relations in Britain, 1997. *Address:* House of Lords, SW1A 0PW.

BLACKWELL, family name of **Baron Blackwell**.

BLACKWELL, Baron *cr* 1997 (Life Peer), of Woodcote in the co. of Surrey; **Norman Roy Blackwell;** Chairman: Interserve plc, since 2006; Lloyds Banking Group, since 2014 (non-executive Director, since 2012); *b* 29 July 1952; *s* of Albert Blackwell and Frances Blackwell (*née* Lutman); *m* 1974, Brenda Clucas; three *s* two *d*. *Educ:* RAM (Jun. Exhibnr); Trinity Coll., Cambridge (MA); Wharton Business Sch., Univ. of Pennsylvania (AM, MBA; PhD 1976). With Plessey Co., 1976–78; Partner, McKinsey & Co., 1978–95, elected Partner, 1984; Special Advr, Prime Minister's Policy Unit, 1986–87 (on leave of absence); Head, Prime Minister's Policy Unit, 1995–97; Dir, Gp Develt, NatWest Gp, 1997–2000; Special Advr, KPMG Corp. Finance, 2000–08. Chm., Scottish Widows Gp, 2012–14; non-executive

Director: Dixons Gp, 2000–03; Corporate Services Gp, 2000–06; Centre for Policy Studies, 2000–13 (Chm., 2000–09); Segro (formerly Slough Estates), 2001–10; SmartStream Technologies Ltd, 2001–06; Standard Life Assurance, 2003–12; OFT, 2003–10; OFCOM, 2009–14; Halma, 2010–14; Comr, Postcomm, 2010–11. *Recreations:* classical music, walking. *Address:* c/o House of Lords, SW1A 0PW. *E:* blackwelln@parliament.uk. *Clubs:* Carlton, Royal Automobile.

BLACKWELL, Rt Rev. Douglas Charles; an Area (formerly Suffragan) Bishop of Toronto (Area Bishop of Trent-Durham), 1988–2003; *b* 3 June 1938; *s* of late William John Blackwell and Ethel N. Blackwell (*née* Keates); *m* 1963, Sandra Dianne Griffiths; one *s* two *d*. *Educ:* Wycliffe Coll., Univ. of Toronto (DipTh, LTh). Deacon 1963, priest 1964; Asst Curate, St Stephen's, Calgary, 1964; Vicar, Cochrane Mission, Diocese of Calgary, 1966; Rector, St Paul's, North Battleford, Diocese of Saskatoon, 1969; Regional Dean of Battleford, 1970; Archdeacon of Battlefords-Lloydminster, 1973; Asst Director, Aurora Conf. Centre, Diocese of Toronto, 1974; Executive Asst to Archbishop of Toronto, 1977; Canon of St James's Cathedral, Toronto, 1978; Archdeacon of York, 1986. Hon. DD Wycliffe Coll., Toronto, 1990. *Address:* 63 Glen Dhu Drive, Whitby, ON L1R 1K3, Canada. *T:* (905) 4308460.

BLACKWELL, Prof. Jenefer Mary; Professor of Genetics and Health, Telethon Kids Institute (formerly Telethon Institute for Child Health Research), University of Western Australia, since 2007; Affiliated Principal Investigator, Cambridge Institute for Medical Research, since 2007; Professorial Fellow, Newnham College, Cambridge, since 1993; *b* 8 Dec. 1948; *d* of Frank Blackwell and Elsie Winifred Broadhurst; *m* 1973, Simon John Miles; one *s* one *d*. *Educ:* Univ. of Western Australia (BSc 1969 (1st Cl. Hons Zoology); PhD 1974 (Population Genetics)); DSc Cantab, 2010. Cons. Biologist and Res. Officer, WA Govt Depts, 1973–74; Lectr in Biol., Avery Hill Coll. of Educn, London, 1975–76; London School of Hygiene and Tropical Medicine: Res. Fellow, Ross Inst. of Tropical Hygiene, 1976–82; Wellcome Trust Sen. Lectr, Dept of Trop. Hygiene, 1982–88, Dept of Med. Parasitology, 1988–91 (and Head, Immunobiol. of Parasitic Diseases Unit); Reader, Univ. of London, 1989–91; Glaxo Prof. of Molecular Parasitology, Univ. of Cambridge, 1991–2007; Dir, Cambridge Inst. for Med. Res., 1998–2001. Faculty Mem., Molecular Biol. of Parasitism Course, Marine Biol. Labs, Wood's Hole, Mass, 1988. Hon. DSc Khartoum, 2009. *Publications:* (with D. Wakelin) Genetics of Resistance to Bacterial and Parasitic Infection, 1988. *Recreations:* music, walking. *Address:* Genetics and Health Laboratory, Telethon Kids Institute, PO Box 855, West Perth, WA 6872, Australia. *T:* (8) 94897910.

BLACKWELL, Julian, (Toby); DL; President, since 1995, and Chairman, 1996–99, Blackwell Ltd; Chairman, The Blackwell Group Ltd, 1980–94; *b* 10 Jan. 1929; *s* of Sir Basil Henry Blackwell and late Marion Christine, *d* of John Soans; *m* 1953, Jennifer Jocelyn Darley Wykeham; two *s* one *d*. *Educ:* Winchester; Trinity Coll., Oxford. Served 5th RTR, 1947–49; 21st SAS (TA), 1950–59. Dir and Chm., various Blackwell companies, 1956–2003. Chm. Council, ASLIB, 1966–68 (Vice-Pres., 1982); Co-founder and Chm., Mail Users' Assoc., 1975–78 and 1987–90; Pres., Booksellers' Assoc., 1980–82; Chairman: Thames Business Advice Centre, 1986–97; Heart of England TEC, 1989–94; Fox FM, 1989–98. Chm., Son White Meml Trust, 1991–. DL Oxon 1987, High Sheriff, 1991–92. Hon. DLitt Robert Gordon, 1997; DUniv Sheffield Hallam, 1998; Hon. DBA Oxford Brookes, 1999. *Recreations:* thinking, fighting the Eurocrats. *Address:* c/o 50 Broad Street, Oxford OX1 3BQ. *T:* (01865) 792111. *Clubs:* Special Forces; Royal Yacht Squadron; Leander (Henley); Rock and District Sports.

BLACKWELL, Nigel Stirling; Chairman, Blackwell Publishing Ltd, 2001–07; *b* 18 March 1947; *s* of late Richard Blackwell, DSC and Marguerite Brook Blackwell (*née* Holliday); *m* 1st, 1984, Eliza Pumpelly Mauran (*d* 1995), *d* of Frank Mauran III; one *s* one *d*; 2nd, 2005, Christina Lowry, *d* of Rolf Pasold. *Educ:* Dragon Sch., Oxford; Winchester; St Edmund Hall, Oxford (MA). Dep. Chm. and CEO, Blackwell N America, 1979–86; Jt Man. Dir, B. H. Blackwell Ltd, 1980–83 (Dir, 1974–89); Man. Dir, Blackwell Gp, 1983–89; Chm. and Man. Dir, Blackwell Retail Gp, 1983–89; Chairman: Basil Blackwell Ltd, subseq. Blackwell Publishers, 1985–2001; Blackwell Scientific, subseq. Blackwell Science, 1990–2001; Munksgaard Publishers, Copenhagen, 1992–2001. Dir, 1990–2004, Vice Pres., 2003–, Western Provident Assoc.; Chm., Richard Blackwell Scholarship Trust, 1984–2001; Sen. Trustee, Pharsalia Charitable Trust, 2007–. Mem., York Harbor Volunteer Veteran Fireman's Assoc., Maine, 2001. *Recreations:* country pursuits, swimming, boats, collecting. *Clubs:* White's; Vincent's (Oxford); Leander; York Harbor Reading Room (Maine); Dunes (Narragansett, RI).

BLACKWOOD, family name of **Baron Dufferin and Clandeboye**.

BLACKWOOD, (Andrew) Guy; QC 2014; *b* 5 April 1970; *s* of Roger Arthur Blackwood and Carolyn Mary Blackwood (*née* Crichton, later Markham); *m* 2003, Francesca Muscau; one *d*. *Educ:* Stowe Sch.; University Coll. London (LLB Laws). Called to the Bar, Inner Temple, 1997; in practice as barrister, specialising in commercial law, insurance, energy and banking, 1997–. *Publications:* (jtly) Chalmers' Marine Insurance Act 1906, 11th edn, 2015. *Recreations:* Italian culture, reading, travel, antique books. *Address:* Quadrant Chambers, Quadrant House, 10 Fleet Street, EC4Y 1AU.

BLACKWOOD, Nicola; MP (C) Oxford West and Abingdon, since 2010; *b* Johannesburg, 1979. *Educ:* home schooled; Trinity Coll. of Music; St Anne's Coll., Oxford (BA 1st Cl. Music); Emmanuel Coll., Cambridge (MPhil Musicology). Political Unit, Cons. Res. Dept, Gen. Election, 2005; Parly researcher to Andrew Mitchell, MP, 2007; PPS to Minister for Skills and Enterprise, 2013–14, for Energy, 2014–15. Mem., Home Affairs Select Cttee, 2010–15; Chm., Sci. and Technol. Select Cttee, 2015–; Chair, All Party Gp on Women, Peace and Security, 2010–. Vice Chm., Cons. Party, 2010–13. *Address:* House of Commons, SW1A 0AA.

BLAGDEN, Emma Rosemary; *see* Read, E. R.

BLAHNIK, Manolo, Hon. CBE 2007; designer of shoes and furniture, since 1973; Director, Manolo Blahnik International Ltd, since 1973; *b* Canary Is, 28 Nov. 1942; *s* of late E. Blahnik and of Manuela Blahnik. *Educ:* Univ. of Geneva; Louvre Art Sch., Paris. Hon. RDI 2001. Hon. DArts RCA, 2001; Hon. Dr Bath Spa, 2012. Retrospective exhibn, Design Mus., London, 2003. Fashion Council of America Award, 1987, 1990, 1997; Balenciaga Award, 1989; Antonio Lopez Award, Hispanic Inst., Washington, 1990; British Fashion Council Award, 1990, 1999; American Leather New York Award, 1991; Silver Slipper Award, Houston Mus. of Fine Art, 1999 (first awarded to a shoe designer); Neiman Marcus Award, USA, 2000; Golden Needle Award, Spain, 2001; Medalla de Oro al Mérito en las Bellas Artes, Spain, 2002; Medalla de Oro de Canarias, Spain, 2003; Shoe Designer of the Year, Footwear News, 2003; Accessory Designer of the Year, Lycra British Style Awards, 2003; Pinnacle in Art and Design Award, Pratt Inst., NY, 2005; Rodeo Drive Walk of Style Award, Beverly Hills, 2008; Best Internat. Professional Aim Prix, Marie Claire Prix de la Mode, Spain, 2008; Felicidad Duce Fashion Prize, Spain, 2010; André Leon Talley Lifetime Achievement Award, Savannah Coll. of Art and Design, 2011; Lifetime Achievement Award, Footwear News, 2011; Outstanding Achievement in Fashion Award, British Fashion Awards, 2012; Premio Nacional de Diseño de Moda, Spain, 2012. *Publications:* Manolo Blahnik: Drawings, 2003; Manolo's New Shoes, 2010; (illustrator) Manolo Blahnik and the Tale of the Elves and the Shoemaker, by Camilla Morton; *relevant publications:* Manolo Blahnik, by Colin McDowell, 2000; Blahnik by Boman: a photographic conversation, by Eric Boman, 2005. *Recreations:* travel, painting. *Address:* (office) 49–51 Old Church Street, SW3 5BS. *T:* (020) 7352 8622.

BLAIN, Prof. Peter George, CBE 2002; PhD; FRCP, FRCPE, FFOM; CBiol, FRSB, FBTS; Professor of Environmental Medicine, University of Newcastle upon Tyne, and Consultant Physician, Newcastle Hospitals NHS Trust, since 1986; Director: Medical Toxicology Centre, since 2006; Health Protection Research Unit in Chemical and Radiation Threats and Hazards, National Institute of Health Research, since 2014; Consultant in Emergency Response Medicine, Public Health England (formerly Health Protection Agency), since 2009; *b* 15 March 1951; *s* of Reginald Blain and Margaret (*née* Graham); *m* 1977, Patricia Anne Crawford; two *s* one *d*. *Educ:* Univ. of Newcastle upon Tyne (BMedSci, MB, BS; PhD 1988). MFOM 1990, FFOM 1997; FRCP 1990; FRCPE 1991; CBiol 1986, FRSB (FIBiol 1989). Jun. hosp. doctor, Royal Victoria Infirmary, Newcastle upon Tyne, 1975–79; University of Newcastle upon Tyne: Lectr in Clinical Pharmacol., 1979–80; Wellcome Res. Fellow in Clinical Pharmacol. and Neurology, 1980–81; First Asst in Clinical Pharmacol., 1981–85; Hd, Biomed. Scis and Human Toxicol. Res., ICI plc, 1985–86; Consultant Physician: Freeman Gp of Hosps NHS Trust (formerly Freeman Hosp.), 1988–; Royal Victoria Infirmary NHS Trust (formerly Royal Victoria Inf.), 1988–; Newcastle Hosps NHS Trust, 1998–; Consultant in Envmtl Medicine and Toxicol., Northern and Yorks RHA, 1992–. Hd, Med. Toxicol., HPA, 2004–10. UK Expert Advr on Weapons of Mass Destruction to Sec. Gen. of UN, 2010–; UK Delegate to G8 Global Health Security Gp, 2011–. Medical Advisor: to ICRC, 2012–; to WHO, 2013–. Chairman: Chem., Biol, Radio and Nuclear Defence and Human Scis Bd (formerly Chem., Biol and Human Technologies Bd), MoD, 1994–; Adv. Gp on Military Medicine (formerly Med. Countermeasures), MoD, 1998–; Member: Defence Scientific Adv. Council, MoD, 1994–; Scientific Adv. Gp on the Medical Implications of Less-Lethal Technologies, 2011–. FBTS 2007. *Publications:* contribs to textbooks in toxicol. and medicine; res. papers in acad. jls in toxicol. *Recreations:* hill walking, extreme tourism. *Address:* Medical Toxicology Centre, Wolfson Building, Medical School, Newcastle upon Tyne NE2 4AA. *T:* (0191) 222 7195, *Fax:* (0191) 222 6442. *E:* p.g.blain@ncl.ac.uk.

BLAIN, Sophie Clodagh Mary; *see* Andreae, S. C. M.

BLAIR, family name of **Baron Blair of Boughton**.

BLAIR OF BOUGHTON, Baron *cr* 2010 (Life Peer), of Boughton in the County of Cheshire; **Ian Warwick Blair,** Kt 2003; QPM 1999; Chairman, Thames Valley Partnership, since 2009; Commissioner, Metropolitan Police, 2005–08 (Deputy Commissioner, 2000–05); *b* 19 March 1953; *yr s* of late Francis James Blair and Sheila Kathleen Blair; *m* 1980, Felicity Jane White; one *s* one *d*. *Educ:* Wrekin Coll.; Harvard High Sch., LA; Christ Church, Oxford (MA; Hon. Student, 2005). Joined Metropolitan Police, 1974; uniform and CID posts, 1974–91; Chief Supt, SO to HM Chief Inspector of Constabulary, 1991–93; Asst Chief Constable, 1994–97, des. Dep. to Chief Constable, 1997, Thames Valley Police; Chief Constable, Surrey Police, 1998–2000. Mem., Commn on Assisted Dying, 2010–12. Visiting Fellow: Internat. Centre for Advanced Studies, NY Univ., 1998; Nuffield Coll., Oxford, 2001; John Jay Coll., NY, 2009; Hon. Vis. Prof., Univ. of Northampton, 2015–. Trustee: St Paul's Cathedral Foundn, 2010–13; Shakespeare's Globe Theatre, 2010–; Woolf Inst. of Abrahamic Faiths, 2010–; Longford Trust, 2010–. Freeman, City of London, 2009. Hon. DLaws Lincoln, 2013. *Publications:* Investigating Rape: a new approach for police, 1985; Policing Controversy (memoir), 2009. *Recreations:* ski-ing, tennis, golf, theatre. *Club:* Athenæum.

See also R. D. Blair.

BLAIR, Rt Hon. Anthony Charles Lynton, (Tony); PC 1994; Senior Advisor, JPMorgan Chase, since 2008; Chairman, European Council on Tolerance and Reconciliation, since 2015; *b* 6 May 1953; *s* of late Leo Charles Lynton Blair and Hazel Blair; *m* 1980, Cherie Booth, *qv*; three *s* one *d*. *Educ:* Durham Choristers School; Fettes College, Edinburgh; St John's College, Oxford. Called to the Bar, Lincoln's Inn, 1976; Hon. Bencher, 1994. MP (Lab) Sedgefield, 1983–June 2007. Leader of the Opposition, 1994–97; Prime Minister and First Lord of the Treasury, 1997–2007, Leader of the Labour Party, 1994–2007. Quartet Representative, 2007–15. Founder and Patron: Tony Blair Sports Foundn, 2007–; Tony Blair Faith Foundn, 2008–; Africa Governance Initiative, 2008–. US Presidential Medal of Freedom, 2009. *Publications:* New Britain: my vision of a young country, 1996; The Third Way, 1998; A Journey (memoirs), 2010. *Address:* PO Box 60519, London, W2 7JU. *Club:* Fishburn Working Men's.

See also Hon. Sir W. Blair.

BLAIR, Bruce Graeme Donald; QC 1989; a Deputy High Court Judge, since 1990; *b* 12 April 1946; *s* of late Dr Donald Alexander Sangster Blair, MA, MD, DPM and Eleanor Violet Blair (*née* Van Ryneveld); *m* 1970, Susanne Blair (*née* Hartung); three *d* (and one *s* decd). *Educ:* Harrow School; Magdalene College, Cambridge. Called to the Bar, Middle Temple, 1969; Bencher, 1997; Hd of Chambers, 1 Hare Court, 1997–2007. *Publications:* Practical Matrimonial Precedents (jtly), 1989. *Recreations:* bridge, golf, turf. *Address:* 1 Hare Court, Temple, EC4Y 7BE. *T:* (020) 7797 7070. *Club:* MCC.

BLAIR, Cherie; *see* Booth, C.

BLAIR, Hew David; Chairman, Justerini & Brooks, since 2007 (Director of Buying, 1986–2012); *b* Surrey, 10 Feb. 1951; *s* of David Arthur Blair and Elizabeth Blair (*née* Morton); *m* 1980, Joanna McCorquodale; three *d*. *Educ:* Harrow Sch.; Bordeaux Univ. Pres., Vignobles Internationaux, 2010–. Mem., Royal Household Wine Cttee, 2007–; Pres., Royal Warrant Holders Assoc., 2012 (Vice Pres., 2011–12). Mem., Queen's Body Guard for Scotland, Royal Co. of Archers. *Recreations:* fishing, shooting, golf, garden design, wine. *Address:* Leadervale House, Earlston, Berwickshire TD4 6AJ; 15 Thurloe Court, SW3 6SB. *T:* (office) (020) 7484 6400. *E:* hew.blair@justerinis.com. *Clubs:* White's; Honourable Company of Edinburgh Golfers.

BLAIR, Ian Charles; public finance consultant, 2002–12; *b* 31 Aug. 1947; *s* of John Blair and Robina Poppy Blair (*née* Carr); *m* 1974, Jennifer Mary Hodgson (*d* 2007); one *s* one *d*. *Educ:* Liberton High Sch., Edinburgh; Open Univ. (BA 1995). CPFA (IPFA 1969). Accountant, Midlothian CC, 1964–72; Sen. Accountant, Scottish Special Housing Assoc., 1972–75; Sen. Asst Treas., Lothian Health Bd, 1975–81; City Treasurer: Bath CC, 1981–91; Nottingham CC, 1991–2002; Chm., Ian and Jennifer Blair & Co. Ltd, 2002–. Treas., Derbys Probation Bd, 2005–11. Advr, ADC, 1992–97. Non-exec. Dir, Rushcliffe Clinical Commng Gp, 2012–. Chm., S Wales and West, CIPFA, 1991; Pres., Audit Cttee, Eurocities, 1999–2002; Mem., Exec., Soc. Municipal Treasurers, 1999–2002. Sen. Res. Associate, Warwick Business Sch., 2007–13. Mem., Probus, 2014–. *Publications:* contribs to prof. jls, govt research papers. *Recreations:* family, sports (Hearts FC and Bath RFC), theatre. *Address:* 24 Purbeck Drive, West Bridgford, Notts NG2 7UA. *T:* (0115) 982 2802.

BLAIR, John; *see* Blair, W. J.

BLAIR, Michael Campbell; barrister in independent practice; *b* 26 Aug. 1941; *s* of Sir Alastair Campbell Blair, KCVO and Catriona Hatchard Blair (*née* Orr); *m* 1966, Halldóra Isabel (*née* Tunnard); one *s*. *Educ:* Rugby Sch.; Clare Coll., Cambridge (MA, LLM); Yale Univ., USA (Mellon Fellow; MA). Called to the Bar, Middle Temple, 1965 (Harmsworth Law Scholar); Bencher, 1995, Dep. Treas., 2007, Treas., 2008. Lord Chancellor's Dept, 1966–87: Private Sec. to the Lord Chancellor, 1968–71; Sec., Law Reform Cttee, 1977–79; Under Sec., 1982–87; Circuit Administrator, Midland and Oxford Circuit, 1982–86; Hd, Courts and Legal Services Gp, 1986–87. Securities and Investments Board: Dir of Legal Services,

1987–91; General Counsel, 1991–93; Head of Policy and Legal Affairs, 1993–95; Dep. Chief Exec. and Gen. Counsel, 1996–98; Gen. Counsel to Bd, FSA, 1998–2000; Chairman: PIA, 2000–02; IMRO, 2000–02; SFA, 2001–02. Dep. Chm., 2007–08, Chm., 2008–09, SWX Swiss Exchange Europe Ltd. Dir, Financial Services Compensation Scheme Ltd, 2000–05. Mem., Competition Appeal Tribunal, 2000–13; Chm., Review Body on Doctors' and Dentists' Remuneration, 2001–07; Pres., Guernsey Financial Services Tribunal, 2002–08; Member, Board: Dubai FSA, 2003–13; Chicago Mercantile Exchange (London) Ltd, 2013–. Chairman: Bar Assoc. for Commerce, Finance and Industry, 1990–91; Bar Conf., 1993; Member: Gen. Council of the Bar, 1989–98 (Chm., Professional Standards Cttee, 1994; Treas., 1995–98); Council of Legal Educn, 1992–97. Hon. QC 1996. FRSA 1992. *Publications:* Sale of Goods Act 1979, 1980; Financial Services: the new core rules, 1991; (ed) Blackstone's Guide to the Bank of England Act 1998, 1998; (ed) Blackstone's Guide to the Financial Services and Markets Act 2000, 2001, 2nd edn, 2009; (ed) Butterworths Financial Regulation Service, 2002–07; (ed) Financial Services, Halsbury's Laws of England, vol. 18(i), 4th edn, 2003; (ed jtly) Financial Services Law, 2006, 3rd edn 2013; (ed jtly) Financial Markets and Exchanges Law, 2007, 2nd edn 2012; legal articles in jls. *Address:* 3 Burbage Road, SE24 9HJ. *T:* (020) 7274 7614. *Club:* Athenæum.

See also R. O. Blair.

BLAIR, Capt. Neil; *see* Blair, Capt. R. N.

BLAIR, Neil Lyndon Marc; Founding Partner, The Blair Partnership, since 2011; *b* London, 21 Sept. 1966; *s* of Dennis and Cynthia Blair; *m* Debra; two *s*. *Educ:* Exeter Coll., Oxford (MA Juris. 1989); Coll. of Law, Guildford. Admitted solicitor, 1990; Solicitor, Linklaters & Paines, 1992–96; Hd, Business Affairs, Europe, Warner Bros Prodns, 1996–2001; Partner and Literary Agent, Christopher Little Literary Agency, 2001–11. Dir, Pottermore Ltd, 2011–. Trustee, Lumos, 2010–. *Address:* The Blair Partnership, PO Box 7828, W1A 4GE. *T:* (020) 7504 2520. *E:* neil.blair@theblairpartnership.com.

BLAIR, Sir Patrick David H.; *see* Hunter Blair.

BLAIR, Peter Michael; QC 2006; **His Honour Judge Blair;** a Circuit Judge, since 2014; *b* 24 Aug. 1961; *s* of Michael Blair and Joan (*née* Goodwin); *m* 1984, Sharon Atherton; one *s* two *d*. *Educ:* Princess Sophie Primary Sch., Addis Ababa; Brocksford Hall; Monkton Combe Sch.; Univ. of Oxford (BA Juris.). Called to the Bar, Inner Temple, 1983; in practice as barrister, Guildhall Chambers, Bristol, 1984–2014; Hd of Chambers, 2006–14. Asst Recorder, 1998–2000; Recorder, 2000–14. Mem., Western Circuit Cttee, 1991–97. Mem., Bath CC, 1988–92. *Recreations:* landscape oil painting, poultry and pig keeping, gadgets. *Address:* Swindon Combined Court, The Law Courts, Islington Street, Swindon SN1 2HG.

BLAIR, Richard David, (Sandy), CBE 2005; DL; Chair, Remuneration Board, National Assembly for Wales, since 2013 (Member, since 2010); *b* Hull, 15 Aug. 1946; *s* of late Francis James Blair and Sheila Kathleen Blair (*née* Law); m 1971, Susan Elizabeth Crump; two *s* one *d*. *Educ:* Bromsgrove Sch.; Durham Univ. Admitted as solicitor, 1969; private solicitor, 1969–74; local govt solicitor, 1974–77, local govt manager, 1977–84, Knowsley MBC; Chief Executive: Bassetlaw DC, 1984–92; Newport BC, 1992–96; Newport CC, 1995–2000; Dir, Welsh Local Govt Assoc., 2001–04. Non-exec. Dir, HSE, 2006–12. Interim Local Govt Boundary Comr for Wales, 2011. Chair, Monmouth Diocesan Bd of Finance, 2006–; Mem., Governing Body and Representative Body, Church in Wales, 2006–. Gov., UWIC, 2004–10. Pres., Solace, 1999–2000. Mem., Cardiff Business Club. DL Gwent, 2014. *Recreations:* minor charity trusteeships, watching Rugby. *Address:* Orchard House, Llantrisant, Usk NP15 1LG. *T:* (01291) 673239. *E:* rd_sandyblair@hotmail.com. *Club:* Newport Rugby.

See also Baron Blair of Boughton.

BLAIR, Capt. (Robert) Neil, RN; CVO 2001 (LVO 1997); Private Secretary, Treasurer and Extra Equerry to the Duke of York, 1990–2001; Private Secretary to Princess Alexandra, the Hon. Lady Ogilvy, 1995–2001; *b* 14 July 1936; *s* of Harley Blair and Jane Blair (*née* Tarr); *m* 1960, Barbara Jane, *d* of Ian and Monica Rankin; two *s* one *d*. *Educ:* St John's Coll., Johannesburg; RNC, Dartmouth. Joined RN, 1954: served HMY Britannia, 1958–59 and 1970–71; FAA, 1961–70; in command: HMS Shavington, 1965–67; HMS Ashanti, 1972–74; HMS Royal Arthur, 1978; Comdr, BRNC, Dartmouth, 1979–80; Naval and Air Attaché, Athens, 1982–85; Defence and Naval Attaché, The Hague, 1986–89. Younger Brother, Trinity House, 1991. *Recreations:* photography, cricket, hill-walking. *Clubs:* Army and Navy, MCC.

BLAIR, Robin Orr, CVO 2008 (LVO 1999); Lord Lyon King of Arms and Secretary of the Order of the Thistle, 2001–08, Angus Herald Extraordinary, since 2008; *b* 1 Jan. 1940; *s* of Sir Alastair Campbell Blair, KCVO and Catriona Hatchard Blair (*née* Orr); *m* 1st, 1972, Elizabeth Caroline McCallum Webster (*d* 2000); two *s* one *d*; 2nd, 2005, Lel Simpson. *Educ:* Cargilfield; Rugby; St Andrews Univ. (MA); Edinburgh Univ. (LLB). WS 1965. Partner: Davidson & Syme WS, 1967–72; Dundas & Wilson CS, 1972–97 (Managing Partner, 1976–83, 1988–91); Turcan Connell WS, 1997–2000. Chm., Top Flight Leisure Gp, 1987–98 (non-exec. Dir, 1977–98); non-exec. Dir, Tullis Russell & Co. Ltd, 1977–98. Chm., Scottish Solicitors' Staff Pension Scheme, 1985–91. Hon. Sec., Assoc. of Edinburgh Royal Tradesmen, 1966–91. Purse Bearer to Lord High Comr to Gen. Assembly, C of S, 1988–2002. Chairman: Scotland's Churches Scheme, 1997–2013; Scotland's Churches Trust, 2013–15. Gen. Council Assessor, Ct of Edinburgh Univ., 2003–07. Mem., Royal Co. of Archers. *Address:* 2 Blacket Place, Edinburgh EH9 1RL. *T:* (0131) 667 2906. *Clubs:* New (Edinburgh); Hon. Company of Edinburgh Golfers.

See also M. C. Blair.

BLAIR, Sandy; *see* Blair, R. D.

BLAIR, Rt Hon. Tony; *see* Blair, Rt Hon. A. C. L.

BLAIR, Hon. Sir William (James Lynton), Kt 2008; **Hon. Mr Justice Blair;** a Judge of the High Court of Justice, Queen's Bench Division, since 2008; *b* 31 March 1950; *s* of late Leo Charles Lynton Blair and Hazel Elizabeth (*née* Corscadden); *m* 1982, Katy Tse. *Educ:* Fettes Coll., Edinburgh; Balliol Coll., Oxford (BA 1971). Called to the Bar, Lincoln's Inn, 1972, Bencher, 2003; QC 1994; Asst Recorder, 1996–98; Recorder, 1998–2008; Dep. High Court Judge, 2003–08. Vis. Prof. of Law, LSE, 1994–. Part-time Chm., Financial Services and Mkts Tribunal, 2001–10; Chm., Qatar Financial Centre Regulatory Tribunal, 2006–11. Member: Internat. Monetary Law Cttee, 1996– (Chm., 2004–), Council, British Br., 2000–, Internat. Law Assoc.; Financial Mkts Law Cttee, 2008–; Jt Bd of Appeal, European Supervisory Authorities, 2011– (Pres., 2012–). Trustee, British Inst. of Internat. and Comparative Law, 2009–. Hon. Fellow, Soc. for Advanced Legal Studies, 1997. *Publications:* (ed) Encyclopaedia of Banking Law, 1982; (jtly) Banking and the Financial Services Act, 1993, 3rd edn, as Banking and Financial Services Regulation, 2002; (ed) Bullen, Leake and Jacob's Precedents of Pleading, 16th edn, 2008; (ed) Banks and Financial Crime, 2008; contrib. other legal books and jls. *Recreations:* travel, walking. *Club:* Athenæum.

See also Rt Hon. A. C. L. Blair.

BLAIR, Prof. (William) John, DPhil; FBA 2008; FSA; historian and archaeologist; Fellow and Praelector in History, Queen's College, Oxford, since 1981; Professor of Medieval History and Archaeology, University of Oxford, since 2006; *b* Woking, 4 March 1955; *s* of late Claude Blair, CVO, OBE and Joan Mary Greville Blair (*née* Drinkwater); *m* 2005, (Terttu) Kanerva Heikkinen; one *s* one *d*. *Educ:* St John's Sch., Leatherhead; Brasenose Coll., Oxford (BA 1st Cl. 1976; DPhil 1983). FSA 1983. Freeman, Cutlers' Co., 2004, Liveryman, 2009. *Publications:* (ed) Minsters and Parish Churches, 1988; (ed with N. Ramsay) English Medieval Industries, 1991; Early Medieval Surrey, 1991; (ed with R. Sharpe) Pastoral Care before the Parish, 1992; Anglo-Saxon Oxfordshire, 1994; (ed with B. Golding) The Cloister and the World, 1996; (ed jtly) The Blackwell Encyclopaedia of Anglo-Saxon England, 1999; The Church in Anglo-Saxon Society, 2005; (ed) Waterways and Canal-Building in Medieval England, 2007; contribs to books and jls. *Recreations:* travel, landscape and architecture, reading, listening to music. *Address:* Queen's College, Oxford OX1 4AW. *T:* (01865) 279120. *E:* john.blair@queens.ox.ac.uk.

BLAIS, Hon. Jean Jacques; PC (Can.) 1976; QC (Can.) 1978; Counsel, MBM Intellectual Property Law LLP (formerly Marusyk, Miller & Swain), Ottawa, since 1999; *b* 27 June 1940; *m* 1968, Maureen Ahearn; two *s* one *d*. *Educ:* Secondary Sch., Sturgeon Falls; Univ. of Ottawa (BA, LLB, LLM). Professional lawyer. MP (L) Nipissing, Ontario, 1972, re-elected 1974, 1979, 1980; defeated Sept. 1984; Parliamentary Sec. to Pres. of Privy Council, 1975; Post Master General, 1976; Solicitor General, 1978; Minister of Supply and Services, and Receiver General, 1980; Minister of Nat. Defence, 1983–84. Lectr in Private Internat. Law, Ottawa Univ., 1986–88. Dir, Canada Israel Industrial R & D Foundn, 1994–2008. Mem., Security and Intelligence Review Cttee, 1984–91; Dep. Chm., Provisional Election Commn, Bosnia and Herzegovina, 1998; Head of Mission: Elections Canada/Internat. Foundn of Election Systems mission to Afghanistan, 2003; Internat. Foundn for Electoral Systems, Iraq, 2003. Chm., Canadian Inst. of Strategic Studies, 1993–2003, 2004–05; Chm. Emeritus, Pearson Internat. Peacekeeping Center, 2003– (Chm., 1994–2003); Director: Canadian Parly Center, 2005–13 (Vice-Pres., 2010–13); Conference of Defence Assocs Inst., 2008–12. Chm., Heart Inst., Univ. of Ottawa, 2005–11 (Dir, 1995–2003). Hon DLitt Nipissing, 2007. *Recreations:* golf, snooker. *Address:* (office) 285 Slater Street, 14th Floor, Ottawa, ON K1P 5H9, Canada. *T:* and *Fax:* (613) 5670762. *E:* jjblais@mbm.com.

BLAIZE, Beverley Amari; health practitioner; Deputy Chair, Commission for Racial Equality, 2000–03; *b* 9 Aug. 1949; *d* of Edmund Blaize and Jane John-Baptist; *m* 1974, Leslie Bernard; one *d*. *Educ:* Univ. of Westminster (BA Hons); De Montfort Univ. (MA). Founder Trustee and CEO, Windsor Fellowship, 1985–95; Advr to Kagiso Trust, 1995–96, Man. Trustee, Nations Trust, 1995–98, RSA. Trustee, Esmée Fairbairn Foundn, 2003–06. *Publications:* The Homecoming: journey of the orphan child, 2006. *Recreations:* writing, yoga, cooking. *Address:* 1 Hydeside Gardens, Lower Edmonton, N9 9RP.

BLAKE, Prof. Andrew, PhD; FRS 2005; FREng, FIET, FIEEE; Laboratory Director, Microsoft Research, since 2010 (Deputy Managing Director, Microsoft Research Cambridge, 2008–10); Fellow Clare Hall, Cambridge, since 2000; *b* 12 March 1956; *s* of Alan Geoffrey Blake and Judith Anne Blake (*née* Hart); *m* 1982, Fiona Anne-Marie Hewitt; one *s* one *d*. *Educ:* Rugby Sch.; Trinity Coll., Cambridge (MA); Univ. of Edinburgh (PhD 1983). FIET (FIEE 1994); FREng (FEng 1998); FIEEE 2008. Kennedy Meml Fellow, MIT, 1977–78; Research Scientist, Ferranti Edinburgh, 1978–80; University of Edinburgh: Res. Associate, 1980–83; Lectr in Computer Sci., 1983–87; Royal Soc. Res. Fellow, 1984–87; University of Oxford: Lectr in Image Processing, 1987–96; Fellow, Exeter Coll., 1987–99; Prof. of Engrg Sci., 1996–99; Royal Soc. Sen. Res. Fellow, 1998–99; Vis. Prof. of Engrg, 1999–; Principal Res. Scientist (formerly Sen. Res. Scientist), Microsoft Research Ltd, 1999–2008. Honorary Professor: of Informatics, Univ. of Edinburgh, 2006–07; of Machine Intelligence, Univ. of Cambridge, 2007–. Gibbs Lect., Amer. Math. Soc., 2014. Mem., EPSRC, 2012–. Mem. Council, Royal Soc., 2010–. Hon. DSc Edinburgh, 2012; Hon. DEng Sheffield, 2013. Marr Prize, IEEE, 2001; Silver Medal, 2006, (jtly) MacRobert Award, 2011, RAEng; Mountbatten Medal, IET, 2007. *Publications:* (with A. Zisserman) Visual Reconstruction, 1987; (with T. Troscianko) AI and the Eye, 1990; (with A. Yuille) Active Vision, 1992; (with M. Isard) Active Contours, 1998; (jtly) Markov Random Fields for Vision and Image Processing, 2011; articles on machine vision, robotics, visual psychology. *Address:* Microsoft Research Ltd, 21 Station Road, Cambridge CB1 2FB.

BLAKE, Andrew Nicholas Hubert; His Honour Judge Blake; a Circuit Judge, since 1999; *b* 18 Aug. 1946; *s* of late John Berchmans Blake and Beryl Mary Blake; *m* 1978, Joy Ruth Shevloff; one *s*. *Educ:* Ampleforth Coll.; Hertford Coll., Oxford (MA Hist.). Called to the Bar, Inner Temple, 1971; in practice in Manchester, 1972–99. Mem. Cttee, Council of Circuit Judges, 2004–08. *Recreations:* ski-ing, fishing, cycling, the Turf. *Address:* Manchester Crown Court, Crown Square, Manchester M3 3FL. *Club:* Norbury Fishing.

BLAKE, Sir Anthony Teilo Bruce, 18th Bt *cr* 1622, of Menlough; *b* 5 May 1951; *s* of Major Charles Anthony Howell Bruce Blake (killed in action, Korea, 1951) and Elspeth, *d* of late Lt-Col A. M. Arnott; *S* kinsman, 2008, but his name does not appear on the Official Roll of the Baronetage; *m* 1988, Geraldine, *d* of Cecil Shnaps; one *s* two *d*. *Educ:* Wellington Coll. *Heir:* *s* Charles Valentine Bruce Blake, *b* 13 July 1994.

BLAKE, Carole Rae; Joint Managing Director, Blake Friedmann Literary Agency Ltd, since 1983; *b* 29 Sept. 1946; *née* Blake; *d* of Maisie Lock and step *d* of Gilbert Lock; *m* 1st, 1970, David Urbani (marr. diss. 1982); 2nd, 1983, Julian Friedmann (marr. diss. 1996). *Educ:* Pollards Hill Co. Secondary Sch. Rights Manager, George Rainbird Ltd, 1963–70; Rights and Contracts Manager: Michael Joseph Ltd, 1970–74; W. H. Allen Ltd, 1974–75; Marketing Dir, Sphere Books Ltd, 1975–76; founded Carole Blake Literary Agency Ltd, subseq. Blake Friedmann Literary Agency Ltd, 1976. Pres., Assoc. of Authors' Agents, 1991–93. Mem., Soc. of Bookmen, 1991– (Chm., 1997–98); Dir, Book Trade Benevolent Soc., 1999–2007 (Chm., 2004–07; Patron, 2007–; Pres., 2010–). Member, Advisory Board: Publishing Studies, City Univ., 2000–; UCL Centre for Publishing, 2006–. Patron, Chipping Norton Literary Fest., 2015–. Hon. Vice Pres., Romantic Novelists' Assoc., 2015–. Pandora Award, Women in Publishing UK, 2013. *Publications:* From Pitch to Publication, 1999. *Recreations:* reading, classical music, wildlife, Medieval and Ancient Egyptian history, collecting dollshouse miniatures. *Address:* Blake Friedmann Literary Agency Ltd, First Floor, Selous House, 5–12 Mandela Street, NW1 0DU. *T:* (020) 7387 0842. *E:* carole@blakefriedmann.co.uk. *W:* www.twitter.com/caroleagent.

BLAKE, Prof. Christopher, CBE 1991; FRSE; Chairman, Glenrothes Development Corporation, 1987–96; *b* 28 April 1926; *s* of George Blake and Eliza Blake; *m* 1951, Elizabeth McIntyre (*d* 2009); two *s* two *d*. *Educ:* Dollar Academy; St Andrews Univ. (MA 1950; PhD 1965). Served in Royal Navy, 1944–47. Teaching posts, Bowdoin Coll., Maine, and Princeton Univ., 1951–53; Asst, Edinburgh Univ., 1953–55; Stewarts & Lloyds Ltd, 1955–60; Lectr and Sen. Lectr, Univ. of St Andrews, 1960–67; Sen. Lectr and Prof. of Economics, 1967–74, Bonar Prof. of Applied Econs, 1974–88, Univ. of Dundee. Dir, Alliance Trust plc, 1974–94; Chm., William Low & Co. plc, 1985–90 (Dir, 1980–90). Member: Council for Applied Science in Scotland, 1978–86; Royal Commn on Envmtl Pollution, 1980–86. Treasurer, RSE, 1986–89. *Publications:* articles in economic and other jls. *Recreation:* golf. *Address:* 7 Provost Niven Close, St Andrews, Fife KY16 9BL. *T:* (01334) 473840. *Club:* Royal and Ancient (St Andrews).

BLAKE, Clifford Douglas, AO 2002 (AM 1988); PhD; FAIAS; Vice-Chancellor, University of Adelaide, 2001–02; *b* 27 Aug. 1937; *s* of William Oscar Blake and Isobel Florence Blake (*née* Keown). *Educ:* Muswellbrook High Sch.; Univ. of Sydney (BScAgr 1st Cl. Hons; Univ. Medal); Univ. of London (PhD). University of Sydney: Sir Benjamin Fuller Travelling Schol., 1959–61; Lectr and Sen. Lectr in Plant Pathology, 1963–70; Wilson Fellow, St Andrew's Coll., 1963–71; foundation Principal, Riverina College of Advanced Educn, subseq. renamed Riverina-Murray Inst. of Higher Educn, 1971–90; Vice-Chancellor, Charles Sturt Univ., 1990–2001. Chm., Bd of Dirs, S. P. Jain Sch. of Global Mgt, 2012–. Pres., Aust. Higher

Educn Industrial Assoc., 1992–99; Member, Board of Directors: Open Learning Agency of Australia Pty, 1993–96; Australian Vice Chancellors' Cttee, 1994–99; Convenor, NSW Vice Chancellors' Cttee, 1996–98. Member: NSW Bd, Vocational and Tech. Educn, 2001–02; NSW Admin. Appeals Tribunal, 2002–10. Gov., Commonwealth of Learning, 1992–2000; Chm., Nat. Cttee on Distance Educn, 1994–95. Freeman, City of Wagga Wagga, 1996; Hon. Citizen, City of Bathurst, 1998. Hon. Fellow, Commonwealth Learning, 2002. Hon. DEd Admin, Sydney, 2001; DUniv Charles Sturt, 2001. Farrer Medallist for contribn to Aust. agriculture, Farrer Meml Trust, 1996; Paul Harris Fellow, Rotary Club, 2001. *Publications:* (ed) Fundamentals of Modern Agriculture, 1967, 3rd edn 1971. *Recreation:* travel. *Address:* 55 Waratah Road, Wentworth Falls, NSW 2782, Australia. *Clubs:* Union, University and Schools (Sydney).

BLAKE, David Charles, Eur Ing, CEng, FIMechE; Partner, Bee Services, since 1996; *b* 23 Sept. 1936; *s* of Walter David John Blake and Ellen Charlotte Blake; *m* 1st, 1959, Della Victoria Stevenson (marr. diss. 1996); two *s*; 2nd, 1996, Christine Emmett; one *d*. *Educ:* South East Essex Technical Sch.; South East Essex Technical Coll. British Transport Commn, later British Railways Board, 1953–96: Engrg apprentice, Stratford Locomotive Works, 1953–57; Technical Management, BR Eastern Reg., 1957–69; Construction Engr, W Coast Main Line Electrification, 1969–74; Area Maintenance Engineer: Motherwell Scottish Reg., 1974–75; Shields Scottish Reg., 1975–76; Rolling Stock Engr, Scottish Reg., 1976–78; Electrical Engr, E Reg., 1978–80; Chief Mechanical and Electrical Engr, Southern Reg., 1980–82; Director: Manufacturing and Maintenance Policy, BRB, 1983–87; Mech. and Elec. Engrg, BRB, 1987–90; Man. Dir, King's Cross Projects Gp, BRB, 1990–93; Man. Dir, Vendor Unit, BRB, 1993–96. Non-executive Director: Engineering Link Ltd, 1999–2003; Leics County and Rutland PCT, 2006–09; Chm., Leics County and Rutland Community Health Services, 2009–11. Gov., St Mary & St John C of E Voluntary Aided Primary Sch., North Luffenham, 2004–08. *Recreations:* gardening, hill walking. *Address:* The Windmill, Morcott, Rutland LE15 9DQ. *T:* (01572) 747000, *Fax:* (01572) 747373.

BLAKE, Prof. David Leonard; Professor of Music, University of York, 1976–2001, now Emeritus; *b* 2 Sept. 1936; *s* of Leonard Blake and Dorothy Blake; *m* 1960, Rita Muir; two *s* one *d*. *Educ:* Latymer Upper School; Gonville and Caius College, Cambridge (BA 1960, MA 1963); Deutsche Akademie der Künste, Berlin, GDR. School teacher: Ealing Grammar Sch., 1961–62; Northwood Secondary Sch., 1962–63; University of York: Granada Arts Fellow, 1963–64; Lectr in Music, 1964; Sen. Lectr, 1971–76. *Recordings* (own compositions): Violin Concerto: In Praise of Krishna; Variations for Piano; The Almanack. *Compositions* include: String Quartet No 1, 1962; It's a Small War (musical for schools), 1962; Chamber Symphony, 1966; Lumina (text from Ezra Pound's Cantos) (cantata for soprano, baritone, chorus and orch.), 1969; Metamorphoses, for large orch., 1971; Nonet, for wind, 1971; The Bones of Chuang Tzu (cantata for baritone and piano), 1972; In Praise of Krishna: Bengali lyrics, 1973; String Quartet No 2, 1973; Violin Concerto, 1976; Toussaint (opera), 1974–77; From the Mattress Grave (song cycle), 1978; Nine Songs of Heine, 1978; Clarinet Quintet, 1980; String Quartet No 3, 1982; Rise Dove, for bass and orch., 1983; The Plumber's Gift (opera), 1985–88; Cello Concerto, 1992; Three Ritsos Choruses, 1992; The Griffin's Tale, for baritone and orch., 1994; Diversions on Themes of Hanns Eisler, for alto sax. and piano, 1995; The Fabulous Adventures of Alexander the Great, for chorus and orch. of young people, 1996; Scoring a Century (entertainment), 1999; The Shades of Love (Cavafy), for bass and small orch., 2000; The Lonely Wife I and II (poems from the Chinese for soprano and mezzo), 2003; String Quartet No 4, 2004; Rings of Jade (poems by Ho Chi Minh), for medium voice and orch., 2005; The Coming of the Year 'Carol' for SATB chorus and piano, 2008; Four Cabaret Songs for female voice and piano, 2008; On the Autumn Air for oboe, 2009; Ten Gallows Songs of Christian Morgenstern, 2009; String Quartet No 5, 2010; Fanny and Alexander (operatic drama with text by Keith Warner), 2013; Songs and Epigrams, 2014. *Publications:* (ed) Hanns Eisler: a miscellany, 1995. *Recreation:* land management. *Address:* Mill Gill, Askrigg, Leyburn, North Yorks DL8 3HR. *T:* (01969) 650364. *E:* dl.blake@tiscali.co.uk.

BLAKE, Sir Francis Michael, 3rd Bt *cr* 1907; *b* 11 July 1943; *o s* of Sir F. Edward C. Blake, 2nd Bt and Olive Mary (*d* 1946) *d* of Charles Liddell Simpson; *S* father, 1950; *m* 1968, Joan Ashbridge, *d* of F. C. A. Miller; two *s*. *Educ:* Rugby. High Sheriff, Northumberland, 2002. *Heir: s* Francis Julian Blake [*b* 17 Feb. 1971; *m* 1st, 2000, Dr Jennifer Armstrong (marr. diss. 2007), *o d* of Peter Armstrong; 2nd, 2009, Claire Louise, *d* of James Donald; one *s*]. *Address:* The Dower House, Tillmouth Park, Cornhill-on-Tweed, Northumberland TD12 4UR. *T:* (01890) 882443.

BLAKE, Howard David, OBE 1994; FRAM; composer; *b* 28 Oct. 1938; *s* of Horace C. Blake and Grace B. Blake (*née* Benson); two *s* one *d*. *Educ:* Brighton, Hove and Sussex Grammar Sch.; Royal Acad. of Music. FRAM 1989. Dir, PRS, 1978–87; Co-founder, Assoc. of Professional Composers, 1980. *Compositions: concert works:* The Song of St Francis, 1976; Benedictus, 1979; Sinfonietta for brass ensemble, 1981; Clarinet Concerto, 1984; Shakespeare Songs, 1987; Festival Mass, 1987; Diversions for Cello and Orchestra, 1989; Four Songs of the Nativity, 1990; Piano Concerto for Princess of Wales, 1990; Violin Concerto for City of Leeds, 1993; The Land of Counterpane, 1995; Charter for Peace (commissioned by FCO for 50th anniv. of UN), 1995; All God's Creatures, 1995; Lifecycle for solo piano, 1996; Flute Concerto, 1996; Still Falls the Rain, 1998; The Passion of Mary, 2002, revised 2006; The Rise of the House of Usher, 2003; Songs of Truth and Glory, 2005; Winterdream, 2006; Violin Sonata, 2007; Spieltreib (String Quartet), 2008; Sleepwalking, 2009; Bassoon Concerto, 2009; Speech after Long Silence (piano), 2010; Cello Sonata, 2010; James Joyce Songs, 2012; Prelude for Vova (for Vladimir Ashkenazy), 2012; *stage works:* Henry V, 1984, As You Like It, 1985, RSC; The Snowman Stageshow (ballet in two acts), 1993; Eva (ballet), Gothenburg Opera House, 1996; *film and television scores include:* The Duellists, 1977; The Snowman (TV), 1982; A Month in the Country, 1986 (BFI Anthony Asquith Award); Granpa (TV), 1987; A Midsummer Night's Dream (RSC and Channel 4), 1996; The Bear (TV), 1998; My Life So Far, 1999. *Recreations:* reading, walking, swimming. *Address:* Studio 6, 18 Kensington Court Place, W8 5BJ. *E:* howard@howardblake.com. *Clubs:* Groucho, Chelsea Arts, Ivy.

BLAKE, John Michael; Managing Director: Blake Publishing, since 1991; John Blake Publishing, since 2000; Metro Publishing, since 2001; *b* 6 Nov. 1948; *s* of late Major Edwin Blake, MBE, and of Joyce Blake; *m* 1968, Diane Sutherland Campbell; one *s* two *d*. *Educ:* Westminster City Grammar Sch.; North-West London Polytechnic. Reporter: Hackney Gazette, 1966; Evening Post, Luton, 1969; Fleet Street News Agency, 1970; Columnist: London Evening News, 1971; London Evening Standard, 1980; The Sun, 1982; Asst Editor, Daily Mirror, 1985; Editor, The People, 1988–89; Pres., Mirror Group Newspapers (USA), 1989; Exec. Producer, Sky Television, 1990. *Publications:* Up and Down with The Rolling Stones, 1978; All You Needed Was Love, 1981. *Recreations:* messing about in boats, distance running. *Address:* John Blake Publishing Ltd, 3 Bramber Court, 2 Bramber Road, W14 9PB. *Clubs:* Groucho, Chelsea Arts; Cruising Association.

BLAKE, Jonathan Elazar; Partner, since 1982, and Head, International Private Funds Department, since 2012, King & Wood Mallesons SJ Berwin (formerly SJ Berwin) LLP (Senior Partner, 2006–12); *b* 7 July 1954; *s* of late Asher Blake and Nomi Blake; *m* Isabel Horovitz; three *s* one *d*. *Educ:* Haberdashers' Aske's Sch.; Queens' Coll., Cambridge (BA 1975; LLB 1976). CTA; CF. Stephenson Harwood, 1977–82. Former Mem. Council, British Venture Capital Assoc.; former Chm., Tax and Legal Cttee, European Private Equity and Venture Capital Assoc. *Recreations:* ski-ing, walking, theatre, travel, family. *Address:* King & Wood Mallesons SJ Berwin LLP, 10 Queen Street Place, EC4R 1BE. *T:* (020) 7111 2317. *Fax:* (020) 7111 2000. *E:* jonathan.blake@eu.kwm.com.

BLAKE, Mary Netterville, MA; Headmistress, Manchester High School for Girls, 1975–83; *b* 12 Sept. 1922; *d* of John Netterville Blake and Agnes Barr Blake. *Educ:* Howell's Sch. Denbigh; St Anne's Coll., Oxford (MA). Asst Mistress, The Mount Sch., York, 1945–48; Head of Geography Dept, King's High Sch., Warwick, 1948–56; Associate Gen. Sec., Student Christian Movement in Schools, 1956–60; Head Mistress, Selby Grammar Sch., 1960–75; Pres., Assoc. of Headmistresses, 1976–77; first Pres., Secondary Heads Assoc., 1978. *Address:* 11 Baldenhall, Hall Green, Malvern, Worcs WR14 3RZ. *T:* (01684) 564359.

BLAKE, Hon. Sir Nicholas (John Gorrod), Kt 2007; **Hon. Mr Justice Blake;** a Judge of the High Court of Justice, Queen's Bench Division, since 2007; a President, Upper Tribunal (Immigration and Asylum Chamber), 2010–13; *b* 21 June 1949; *s* of Leslie Gorrod Blake and Jean Margaret (*née* Ballinger); *m* 1986, Clio Whittaker; one *s* two *d* (and one *s* decd). *Educ:* Cranleigh Sch.; Magdalene Coll., Cambridge (BA Hons Hist.); Inns of Court Sch. of Law. Called to the Bar, Middle Temple, 1974, Bencher, 2002. QC 1994; Asst Recorder, 1999–2000; Recorder, 2000–07; Dep. Judge of the High Court, 2003–07. Chm. Immigration Lawyers Practitioners Assoc., 1994–97. Mem. Council, Justice, 1995–2007. Trustee, NPG, 2005–13. FRSA. *Publications:* Police, Law and the People, 1974; (jtly) Wigs and Workers, 1980; (jtly) New Nationality Law, 1983; (ed jtly) Immigration Law and Practice, 3rd edn 1991, 4th edn 1995; Immigration Asylum and Human Rights, 2002; The Deepcut Review, 2006. *Recreation:* the visual arts. *Address:* Royal Courts of Justice, Strand, WC2A 2LL.

BLAKE, Sir Peter (Thomas), Kt 2002; CBE 1983; RDI 1987; ARCA; painter; *b* 25 June 1932; *s* of Kenneth William Blake; *m* 1963, Jann Haworth (marr. diss. 1982); two *d*; *m* 1987, Chrissy Wilson; one *d*. *Educ:* Gravesend Tech. Coll.; Gravesend Sch. of Art; RCA. ARA 1974; RA 1980, resigned 2005; Prof. of Drawing, Royal Acad., 2002–04. Works exhibited: ICA, 1958, 1960; Guggenheim Competition, 1958; Cambridge, 1959; RA, 1960; Musée d'Art Moderne, Paris, 1968; Waddington Galls, 1970, 1972, 1977 and 1990; Stedelijk Mus. Amsterdam, 1973; Kunstverein, Hamburg, 1973; Gemeentemuseum, Arnhem, 1974; Palais des Beaux-Arts, Brussels, 1974; Galleria Documenta, Turin, 1982; Paul Stolper Gall., London, 2007; Waddington Custot Galleries, 2012; retrospective exhibitions: Tate Gall., 1983; Gal. Claude Bernard, Paris, 1984, 2009; Nishimura Gall., Tokyo, 1988; Nat. Gall., 1996; London Inst. Gall., 2003; Wetterling Gall. Stockholm, 2006; Tate Liverpool, 2007; Paul Morris Gall. NY, 2007; Galerie Thomas Levy, Hamburg, 2008; works in public collections: Trinity Coll. Cambridge; Carlisle City Gall.; Tate Gall.; Arts Council of GB; Mus. of Modern Art, NY; V & A Mus.; Mus. Boymans-van Beuningen, Rotterdam; Calouste Gulbenkian Foundn, London; RCA; Whitworth Art Gall., Univ. of Manchester; Baltimore Mus. of Art, Md; Pallant House Gall., Chichester. Third Associate Artist, Nat. Gall., 1994. *Publications:* Peter Blake's ABC, 2009; Venice Fantasies, 2009; illustrations for: Oxford Illustrated Old Testament, 1968; Roger McGough, Summer with Monica, 1978; cover illustration, Arden Shakespeare: Othello, 1980; Anthony and Cleopatra, 1980; Timon of Athens, 1980; contrib. to: Times Educnl Supp.; Ark; Graphis 70; World of Art; Architectural Rev.; House and Garden; Painter and Sculptor; relevant publication: Peter Blake: one man show, by Marco Livingstone, 2009. *Recreations:* sculpture, wining and dining, going to rock and roll concerts, boxing and wrestling matches; living well is the best revenge. *Address:* c/o Waddington Galleries Ltd, 11 Cork Street, W1S 3LT.

BLAKE, Sir Quentin (Saxby), Kt 2013; CBE 2005 (OBE 1988); RDI 1981; freelance artist and illustrator, since 1957; Honorary Professor, Royal College of Art, since 1989; first Children's Laureate, 1999–2001; *b* 16 Dec. 1932; *s* of William Blake and Evelyn Blake. *Educ:* Chislehurst and Sidcup Grammar Sch.; Downing Coll., Cambridge (MA; Hon. Fellow 2000); Inst. of Education, Univ. of London (PGCE 1957). Royal College of Art: Tutor 1965–77; Head, Dept of Illustration, 1978–86; Vis. Tutor, 1986–89; Sen. Fellow, 1988. Exhibitions of watercolour drawings, Workshop Gallery: Invitation to the Dance, 1972; Runners and Riders, 1973; Creature Comforts, 1974; Water Music, 1976; exhibitions of illustration work: Chris Beetles Gall., 1993, 1996, 2004, 2007, 2010, 2011, 2012, 2013; Dulwich Picture Gall., 2004; South Kensington and Chelsea Mental Health Care Centre: The Kershaw Pictures, 2006; Sixty New Drawings, 2006; Our Friends in the Circus, 2009; New Drawings, Etchings and Lithographs, Marlborough Fine Art, 2012; Drawn by Hand, Fitzwilliam Mus., Cambridge, 2013; Quentin Blake: Life Under Water - A Hastings Celebration, Jerwood Gall., 2015; retrospective: Nat. Theatre, 1984; Paris, 1995, 1999; Somerset House, 2003; Museo Luzzati, Genoa, 2009; As Large as Life, Compton Verney 2011; Quentin Blake et les Ages de la Vie, Municipal Liby, Angers, France, 2011; Inside Stories, House of Illustration, 2014. Curator: Tell Me A Picture, Nat. Gall., 2001; A Baker's Dozen, Bury St Edmunds, 2001; Magic Pencil, British Council, 2001; In All Directions, Arts Council, 2005; Quentin Blake et les Demoiselles des Bords de Seine, Paris, 2005. Freeman, City of London, 2015. Hon. Fellow, Brighton Univ. Hon. FRA 2001. Hon. Dr: London Inst., 2000; RCA, Northumbria, 2001; Anglia Ruskin, 2007; Inst. of Educn, London, 2008. Hon. LittD Cambridge, 2004; DUniv Open, 2006; Hon. DLitt Loughborough, 2007. Hans Christian Andersen Award, 2002; Prince Philip Designers' Prize, Design Council, 2011; Eleanor Farjeon Award, 2012. Officier, l'Ordre des Arts et des Lettres (France), 2007; Chevalier de la Légion d'Honneur (France), 2014. *Publications:* (author and illustrator) for children: Patrick, 1968; Jack and Nancy, 1969; Angelo, 1970; Snuff, 1973; The Adventures of Lester, 1977; Mr Magnolia, 1980 (Fedn of Children's Bk Gps Award; Kate Greenaway Medal, 1981); Quentin Blake's Nursery Rhyme Book, 1983; The Story of the Dancing Frog, 1984; Mrs Armitage on Wheels, 1987; Quentin Blake's ABC, 1989; All Join In, 1990; Cockatoos, 1991; Simpkin, 1993; Clown, 1995 (Bologna Ragazzi Prize, 1996); Mrs Armitage and the Big Wave, 1997; Dix Grenouilles, 1997; The Green Ship, 1998; Zagazoo, 1998; Fantastic Daisy Artichoke, 1999; Un Bateau dans le Ciel, 2000; Loveykins, 2002; Mrs Armitage Queen of the Road, 2003; Angel Pavement, 2004; Angelica Sprocket's Pockets, 2010; The Five of Us, 2014; (editor and illustrator) for children: Custard and Company, by Ogden Nash, 1979; The Quentin Blake Book of Nonsense Verse, 1994; The Quentin Blake Book of Nonsense Stories, 1996; Promenade de Quentin Blake au Pays de la Poésie Française, 2003; (illustrator) for children: Russell Hoban: How Tom Beat Captain Najork and his Hired Sportsmen, 1974 (Whitbread Lit. Award, 1975; Hans Andersen Honour Book, 1975); A Near Thing for Captain Najork, 1976; The Rain Door, 1986; Rosie's Magic Horse, 2012; Hilaire Belloc: Algernon and Other Cautionary Tales, 1991; Michael Rosen: Mind Your Own Business, 1974; Wouldn't You Like to Know, 1977; You Can't Catch Me, 1981; Quick Let's Get Out of Here, 1982; Don't Put Mustard in the Custard, 1985; Michael Rosen's Sad Book, 2005; Roald Dahl: The Enormous Crocodile, 1978; The Twits, 1980; George's Marvellous Medicine, 1981; Revolting Rhymes, 1982; The BFG, 1982; The Witches, 1983; Dirty Beasts, 1984; The Giraffe and the Pelly and Me, 1985; Matilda, 1988; Rhyme Stew, 1989; Esio Trot, 1990; Dahl Diary, 1991; My Year, 1993; Danny the Champion of the World, 1994; Roald Dahl's Revolting Recipes, 1994; Charlie and the Chocolate Factory, 1995; Charlie and the Great Glass Elevator, 1995; James and the Giant Peach, 1995; The Magic Finger, 1995; Fantastic Mr Fox, 1996; Even More Revolting Recipes, 2001; Boy, 2012; John Yeoman: Featherbrains, 1993; The Singing Tortoise, 1993; The Family Album, 1993; The Do-It-Yourself House that Jack Built, 1994; Mr Nodd's Ark, 1995; Up with Birds!, 1997; The Princes' Gifts, 1997; The Heron and the Crane, 1999; Joan Aiken, The Winter Sleepwalker, 1994; books by Clement Freud, Sid Fleischman, Sylvia Plath, Margaret Mahy, Dr Seuss, Michael Morpurgo and David Walliams; (illustrator) for adults: Aristophanes, The Birds, 1971; Lewis Carroll, The Hunting of the Snark, 1976; Stella Gibbons, Cold Comfort Farm

1977; Evelyn Waugh, Black Mischief, 1980, Scoop, 1981; George Orwell, Animal Farm, 1984; Cyrano de Bergerac, Voyages to the Sun and Moon, 1991; Cervantes, Don Quixote, 1995; Charles Dickens, A Christmas Carol, 1995; Victor Hugo, The Hunchback of Notre Dame, 1998; Voltaire, Candide, 2011; Fifty Fables of La Fontaine, 2013; The Golden Ass of Lucius Apuleius, 2015; *non-fiction:* (author) La Vie de la Page, 1995; Woman with a Book (drawings), 1999; (jtly) Drawing for the Artistically Undiscovered, 2000; Words and Pictures, 2000; The Laureate's Party, 2000; Tell me a Picture, 2001; Laureate's Progress, 2002; In All Directions, 2005; Quentin Blake et les Demoiselles des Bords de Seine, 2005; The Life of Birds (drawings), 2005; Vive Nos Vieux Jours!, 2007; Beyond the Page, 2012. *Address:* 30 Bramham Gardens, SW5 0HF. *T:* (020) 7373 7464.

BLAKE, Richard Andrew; a District Judge (Magistrates' Courts), Camberwell Green, since 2011 (Lincolnshire, 2006–11); *b* 14 March 1955; *s* of late Lionel Henry Blake and of Betty Blake; civil partnership 2006, Jonathan Neil Langston. *Educ:* Magistrates Law Dip. 1980; Poly. of Central London (Dip. Law 1981); Inns of Court Sch. of Law (Bar. Dip. 1982). Magistrates' Courts Service, 1974–83, Sen. Ct Clerk, Willesden Magistrates' Ct, 1982–83; called to the Bar, Gray's Inn, 1982; Avon and Somerset Prosecuting Solicitor's Office, 1983–86; Sen. Crown Prosecutor, Kingston, 1986–89, Principal Crown Prosecutor, 1989–90, CPS; in private practice as a barrister, One Inner Temple Lane, 1990–2006; apptd Dep. Stipendiary Magistrate, later Dist Judge, 1999. *Recreations:* boating, Jaguar motor cars, Isle of Wight, walking the dog. *Address:* Camberwell Green Magistrates' Court, 15 D'Eynsford Road, Camberwell, SE5 7UP. *T:* (020) 7805 9802. *Club:* Island Sailing (Cowes).

BLAKE, Richard Frederick William; Editor, Whitaker's Almanack, 1981–86; *b* 9 April 1948; *s* of late Frederick William Blake and Doris Margaret Blake; *m* 1973, Christine Vaughan; one *d. Educ:* Archbishop Tenison's Grammar School. Joined J. Whitaker & Sons, Ltd (Whitaker's Almanack Dept), 1966; apptd Asst Editor of Whitaker's Almanack, 1974. *Recreation:* listening to music. *Address:* 60 Woodview Road, Dunmow, Essex CM6 1BU.

BLAKE, Robert John William F.; *see* ffrench Blake.

BLAKE, Simon Anthony, OBE 2011; Chief Executive, Brook, since 2006; *b* 28 Jan. 1974; *s* of John and Margaret Blake; civil partnership 2010, Dr John Swift. *Educ:* Univ. of Wales Coll. of Cardiff (BA Psychol.); Univ. of Wales Coll., Newport (Postgrad. Cert. Counselling); London South Bank Univ. (Postgrad. Dip. Social Res. Methods). Develt Officer, FPA, 1996–99; Dir, Sex Educn Forum, 1999–2002; Asst Dir, Nat. Children's Bureau, 2002–06; on secondment to DoH as Children's Policy Advr, 2004. Chairman: Compact Voice, 2008–15; Diversity Role Models, 2012–15; Vice Chair, Black Health Agency, 2009–11. FCMI. *Publications:* (with J. Laxton) Strides: a practical guide to sex and relationships education with young men, 1998; A Whole School Approach to PSHE and Citizenship, 2000, 2nd edn 2006; (with G. Frances) Just Say No to Abstinence Education!, 2001; (with M. Biddulph) Moving Goalposts: setting a training agenda for sexual health work with boys and young men, 2001; (with Z. Katrak) Faith, Values and Sex and Relationships Education, 2002; Sex and Relationships Education: a step-by-step guide for teachers, 2002; (with P. Power) Teaching and Learning About HIV: a resource for Key Stages 1 to 4, 2003; (with J. Lynch) Sex, Alcohol and Other Drugs: exploring the links in young people's lives, 2004; (with A. Shutt) Be Aware: young people, alcohol and other drugs, 2004; Cards for Life: promoting emotional and social development, 2005; (with S. Plant) Addressing Inequalities and Inclusion through Personal, Social, Health Education and Citizenship, 2005; (with S. Muttock) Assessment and Evaluation in Sex and Relationships Education, 2005; (jtly) Promoting Emotional and Social Development in Schools: a practical guide, 2007; (with P. Baraitser) Involving Young Men in Chlamydia Screening: a practical guide, 2009; (with T. Lloyd) Young Men, Sex and Pregnancy: best practice guidance, 2010. *Recreations:* swimming, running, horseriding. *Address:* Brook, 50 Featherstone Street, EC1Y 8RT. *T:* (020) 7284 6065, *Fax:* (020) 7284 6050. *E:* simon.blake@brook.org.uk.

BLAKE-JAMES, Linda Elizabeth; *see* Sullivan, L. E.

BLAKELEY, Trevor, CEng; FRINA; FIMarEST; FIMechE; Chief Executive, Royal Institution of Naval Architects, since 1997; *b* 22 Nov. 1943; *m* 1965, Patricia Challenger; one *s* one *d. Educ:* Goole Grammar Sch.; BRNC Dartmouth; RNEC Manadon (BSc 1968); BA Open Univ. 1995. CEng 1973; FIMarEST (FIMarE 1996); FIMechE 1996; FRINA 1997. Joined RN, 1963; served as engineering specialist; retired 1996. Chm., Confedn of Eur. Maritime Technology Socs, 2006–. Mem. Ct, Cranfield Univ., 1999–; Gov., Horndean Technol. Coll., 2002–. Mem., Shipwrights' Co., 1999–. *Recreations:* theatre, music, horse riding. *Address:* Royal Institution of Naval Architects, 8–9 Northumberland Street, WC2N 5DA. *T:* (020) 7235 4622.

BLAKEMORE, Sir Colin (Brian), Kt 2014; FRS 1992; Professor of Neuroscience, Oxford University, 2007–12, now Emeritus; Fellow of Magdalen College, Oxford, 1979–2012, now Emeritus; Emeritus Professor, Duke-National University of Singapore Graduate Medical School, since 2008; Professor of Neuroscience and Philosophy, School of Advanced Study, University of London, since 2012; *b* 1 June 1944; *s* of Cedric Norman Blakemore and Beryl Ann Smith; *m* 1965, Andrée Elizabeth Washbourne; three *d. Educ:* King Henry VIII Sch., Coventry; Corpus Christi Coll., Cambridge (Smyth Scholar; BA 1965; MA 1969; ScD 1988; Hon. Fellow, 1994); Univ. of Calif, Berkeley (PhD 1968); Magdalen Coll., Oxford (MA 1979; DSc 1989). FIBiol, CBiol 1996, Hon. FRSB (Hon. FIBiol 2004). Harkness Fellow, Neurosensory Lab., Univ. of Calif, Berkeley, 1965–68; Cambridge University: Fellow and Dir of Medical Studies, Downing Coll., 1971–79; Univ. Demonstr in Physiol., 1968–72; Univ. Lectr in Physiol., 1972–79; Leverhulme Fellow, 1974–75; Royal Soc. Locke Res. Fellow, 1976–79; Oxford University: Waynflete Prof. of Physiology, 1979–2007 (on leave of absence, 2003–07); Prof. of Neuroscience, Univ. of Warwick, 2007–11; Director: McDonnell-Pew Centre for Cognitive Neuroscience, 1990–2003; MRC IRC for Cognitive Neurosci., 1996–2003. Chief Exec., MRC, 2003–07 (Chm., Neurobiology and Mental Health Bd Grants Cttee, 1977–79). Non-exec. Dir, BTG plc, 2007–10. Agency for Science, Technology and Research, Singapore: Mem., Biomed. Scis Internat. Adv. Cttee, 2005–08; Mem., Neurosci. Adv. Cttee, 2006–07; Chairman: UK Stem Cell Funders Forum, 2003–07; Internat. Stem Cell Forum, 2003–07; Hds of Internat. Res. Orgns, 2003–07; Duke-Nat. Univ. of Singapore Grad. Med. Sch. Partnership in Neurosci., 2007–10 (Ext. Scientific Advr, 2010–); Gen. Adv. Cttee on Sci., Food Standards Agency, 2007–; Sci. Skills Working Gp, 2009–; Rev. Panel for Neuroscis, Swedish Res. Council, 2009; Inst. of Medicine Workshop on US and Eur. Animal Res. Regulations, 2010–11. Visiting Professor: NY Univ., 1970; Bell Telephone Labs, 1970; MIT, 1971; Royal Soc. Study Visit, Keio Univ., Tokyo, 1974; Lethaby Prof., RCA, 1978–79; Storer Vis. Prof., Univ. of Calif, Davis, 1980; Royal Soc. Exchange Visit, Inst. of Biophysics, Beijing, 1980; Vis. Scientist, Salk Inst., 1982, 1983, 1992; Macallum Vis. Lectr, Univ. of Toronto, 1984; McLaughlin Vis. Prof., McMaster Univ., Ont, 1992; Regents' Prof. and Vis. Prof., Univ. of Calif, Davis, 1995–97; Spinoza Prof., Univ. of Amsterdam, 1996; Dist. Visitor, BioMed. Res. Council, Singapore, 2005. Chm. Council, BAAS, 2001–04 (Pres., Gen. Section, 1989; Pres., 1997–98, Vice-Pres., 1990–97, 1998–2001; Hon. Fellow, 2001); President: British Neurosci. Assoc., 1997–2000; Physiological Soc., 2001–03 (Mem. Council and Exec. Cttee, 2001–03); Bioscis Fedn, 2002–04 (Mem. Exec. Cttee and Council, 2001–04); Assoc. of British Sci. Writers, 2004– (Chm., Judging Panel, Assoc. of British Sci. Writers and Irish Sci. Writer Awards, 2010–11); British Biol. Olympiad, 2005–; Internat. Scientific Council, Fondation Neurodis, Lyon, 2009–. Hon. Pres., World Cultural Council, 1983–. Mem., World Fedn of Scientists, 1988–; Fellow: World Econ. Forum, 1994–98; World Innovation Foundn, 2002–. Chairman: Council, Research Defence Soc., 2007–08; Selection Cttee, Brain Prize, 2010–; Founding Chm. of Council, Understanding Animal Res., 2008–09. Founder Mem., Bd of Govs, Internat. Brain Injury Assoc. (Nat. Head Injury Foundn Inc., Washington), 1993–; Mem. Professional Adv. Panel, and Patron, Headway (Nat. Head Injuries Assoc.), 1997–; Member: BBC Science Consultative Group, 1975–79; Scientific Cttee, Bristol Exploratory, 1983–99; British Nat. Cttee for Physiol. Scis, 1985–86; Professional Adv. Cttee, Schizophrenia: A National Emergency, 1989–95 (Trustee, 2001–03; Vice-Patron, 2003–); Adv. Gp on Non-Ionising Radiation, NRPB, 1992–2003 (Chm., Weak Electrical Fields Gp, 2008–09; Mem., Sub-Cttee on MRI, 2003, Working Party on melatonin, 2003); Council, European Neuroscience Assoc., 1998–2000; Council, Fedn of European Neuroscience Socs, 1998–2000; Nat. Cttee for 2000 Forum for European Neurosci., Brighton, 1998–2000; Home Office/DSTL TETRA Health and Safety Study Mgt Cttee, 2002–05; AlphaGalileo Foundn, 2003–; Adv. Bd, Cable Sci. Network, 2003–; Public Educn and Communication Cttee, Soc. for Neurosci., 2004–08; UK Drug Policy Commn, 2006–; Royal Instn, 2008–; Wilton Park Adv. Council, FCO, 2010–. Member: Department of Health: Ind. Expert Gp on Mobile Phones, 1999–2000; Prog. Mgt Cttee, UK Telecoms Health Res. Prog., 2000–03; Res. for Patient Benefits Working Party, 2003–04; Bd, UK Clinical Res. Collaboration, 2004–07; UK Stem Cell Initiative Panel, 2005–07; Department for Business, Innovation and Skills: Co-ordinating Cttee, Foresight project on Cognitive Systems, 2001–04; Stakeholder Gps for Foresight projects on Brain Sci., Addiction and Drugs, 2004–06, and Obesity, 2005–07; Expert Gp on Sci. and Media, Govt Office for Sci., 2009–10; Mem. Bd, OSCHR, 2007. International Brain Research Organization: Member: Council, 1973–2001; Exec. Cttee, 1985–91; Nominating Cttee, 1993–2001 (Chm., 1997–2001); Publications Cttee, 1992–99; Cttee on By-Laws, 1999–2001; Chm., Special Cttee, 1984–86; Ed.-in-Chief, IBRO News and website, 1993–2001. Co-Founder, 1992, Mem., 1992–2003, Boyd Gp. Dana Foundation: Mem. Exec. Cttee, Dana Alliance for Brain Initiatives, NY, 1996–; Mem. Adv. Gp for Dana Centre, Sci. Mus., London, 2002–03; Vice-Chm., European Dana Alliance for the Brain, 1996–. Royal Society: Chairman: Wkg Gp, Public Prog., 2001–03; Partnership Grants Cttee, 2001–03; Steering Cttee for Brain Waves project on policy implications of advances in neurosci., 2010–; Member: Hooke Cttee, 1992–2001; Council, COPUS, 2001–02; Sci. in Soc. Cttee, 2001–04; Michael Faraday Prize Cttee, 2001–05; Jt Acad. Med. Scis Wkg Gp on Sci. of Transmissible Spongiform Encephalopathies, 2000; Editl Bd, Phil Trans Royal Soc. B, 2010–; Member: Scientific Adv. Bd, Cognitive Neurosci. Inst., NY, 1981–95; Adv. Bd, WNET TV, NY, 1986–88; Organising Cttee, Child Vision Res. Soc., 1986–; Cttee of Scientific Direction, CNRS Lab de Neuroscis, Marseille, 1989; Review Cttee, Human Sci. Frontier Prog., 1992–95; Scientific Adv. Cttee, Volkswagen Stiftung, 1997–2003; Strategic Adv. Cttee, ProSeed Capital Hldgs, 2000–; Adv. Council, Sense about Science, 2002–; Exec. Council, Novartis Foundn, 2002–; Sci., Engrg and Envmt Adv. Cttee, British Council, 2003–; Bd, Coalition for Med. Progress, 2003–07 (Chm., 2005–07; Trustee, 2005–07); Adv. Bd, Imaging Sci. Centre, Imperial Coll. London, 2005–; Adv. Gp for Health Res., EC Framework Prog. 7, 2006–08; Council, Med. Genetics Sect., RSocMed, 2007–; Adv. Council, ABPI, 2007–09; Sci. Adv. Bd, Agence Nationale de Recherche, France, 2008–; RIKEN Adv. Council, Japan, 2008– (Vice Chm., 2011); Adv. Bd, Eur. Neuroethics Soc., 2008–; Longevity Sci. Adv. Panel, Legal & General, 2009–; Adv. Council, Campaign for Sci. and Engrg, 2011–; Adv. Bd, RedHill Biopharma Ltd, 2011–; Scientific and Strategic Adv. Gp, ReNeuron, 2011–; Sci. and Technol. Advr, Technol. Develt Cttee, Abu Dhabi, 2010–. Hon. Associate: Rationalist Press Assoc., 1986–; Rationalist Internat., 2000–; Cheltenham Fest. of Sci., 2001–; Nat. Secular Soc., 2010–; Mem. Jury, Sci. Book Prizes, 1989; Founder Mem. Cttee, Dir and Trustee, Harkness Fellowships Assoc., 1997–; Patron: Assoc. for Art, Sci., Engrg and Technol., 1997–; At-Bristol Science Centre, 1997– (Scientific Advr, 1997–; Mem., Adv. Council, 2007–); Clifton Scientific Trust, Bristol, 1999–; Oxford Univ. Scientific Soc., 2000–; Oxford Literary Fest., 2002–; Wrexham Sci. Fest., 2002–; Humanists for a Better World, 2011–. Distinguished Supporter, British Humanist Assoc., 1996–. President: Science Soc., Dulwich Coll., 1983; Brain Tumour UK, 2010–. Motor Neurone Disease Association: Pres., Oxon Br., 2004–; Patron, 2005–; Pres., 2008–; Hon. Mem., 2005; Vice-Pres., Progressive Supranuclear Palsy Assoc., 2004–; Trustee: Brain Child, 1991–; Bhopal Med. Appeal, 2003–; Pilgrim Trust, 2009–; Patron: Corpal, 1989–; Saferworld, 1991–; Member: Med. Panel, Patients' Voice for Med. Advance (formerly Seriously Ill for Med. Res.), 2002–; Internat. Adv. Council, Louise T. Blouin Foundn, 2005–; Scientific Adv. Bd, Lifeboat Foundn, 2006–; Neurosci. Adv. Bd, Peter and Patricia Gruber Foundn, 2006–09; Supporter, Sense, 2009–; Scientific Advr, Beckley Foundn, 2001–; Consultant: ASPEX Ltd, 1987–89; MMCO Ltd, 1988–95; Bébé Vision Tropique, Paris, 1993–94; Hall of Human Biol., Natural Hist. Mus., 1989; USAF Spatial Orientation Prog., 1994; WHO, 2002–03; Thriving Child Project, Jabadao (Centre for Study of Movt, Learning and Health), 2002–; Adv. Cttee, Progress Educnl Trust, 2008–; Tandent Vision Science, Inc., 2010–. Judge: Debating Matters Competition, Inst. of Ideas, 2008; Grierson Awards, 2009; Nat. Young Scientist and Young Technologist of the Year, 2009–. BBC Reith Lectr, 1976; Presenter: BBC Radio programmes: Science in China, 1981; From Molecules to Mind, 1982; Machines with Minds, 1982; Science in Japan, 1987; You Know it Makes Sense, 1992; BBC TV series: Common Sense, 1982; The Mind Machine, 1988; Imagina, 1995; Moments of Genius, 2000; The Next Big Thing, 2000–02; God and the Scientists, Channel 4, 2009; The Evidence, Vaccine Disputes, BMJ Video series, 2009; Lectures include: Aubrey Lewis, Inst. of Psych., 1979; Lord Charnwood, Amer. Acad. of Optometry, 1980; Vickers, Neonatal Soc., 1981; Harveian, Harveian Soc. of London, 1982; Christmas, Royal Instn, 1982; George Frederic Still, BPA, 1983; Edridge-Green, RCS, 1984; Halliburton, KCL, 1986; Cairns Meml (also Medal), Cambridge Univ., 1986; Bertram Louis Abrahams, RCP, 1986; Norman McAlister Gregg (also Medal), RACO, 1988; Dietrich Bodenstein, Univ. of Va, 1989; Charnock Bradley, Univ. of Edinburgh, 1989; Boda Meml, Oxford Soc., Bombay, 1989; Doyne, Oxford Ophthalmol Congress, 1989 (also Medal); G. L. Brown, Physiol Soc., 1990; Sir Douglas Robb, Univ. of Auckland, 1991; Montgomery (also Medal), RCSI and Irish Ophthalmol Soc., 1991; T. T. Cozzika Foundn, Patras, 1992; Osler (also Medal), RCP, 1993; James Law, Cornell, 1994; Newton, Cos of Spectacle Makers, and Clockmakers and Scientific Instrument Makers, 1997; Cockcroft, UMIST, 1997; David Oppenheimer Meml, Oxford, 2000; Alfred Meyer Meml (also Medal), British Neuropathol Soc., 2001; Dorothy J. Killam, Dalhousie Univ., 2001; Menzies Foundn (and Medal), 2002; F. C. Donders, Nijmegen, 2003; Miller Com, Univ. of Illinois, 2003; Gordon Holmes, Cambridge Univ., 2004; Lord David Sainsbury, Bristol Univ., 2005; Harveian Oration, RCP, 2005; Kenneth Myer, Howard Florey Inst., Univ. of Melbourne, 2006 (also Medal); IBM Hursley, Southampton Univ., 2006; Kavli Distinguished, Yale Univ., 2008; Chief Scientist's, Food Standards Agency, 2008; Bristol, Bristol Univ., 2008; Foundn, RCPath, 2008; Max Cowan, Dana Foundn, 2010; Ida Mann (also Medal), Oxford Eye Hosp., 2010; Humphreys, Univ. of Birmingham, 2011. Hon. Professor: China Acad. of Mgt Sci., 1990–; Peking Union Med. Coll., 2005; Univ. of Warwick, 2010–. Mem., Academia Rodinensis Pro Remediatione, 1988; MAE 1995; Founder FMedSci 1998; FRSocMed 2003. Hon. FRCP 2004. Foreign Member: Royal Netherlands Acad. of Arts and Scis, 1993; Chinese Acad. of Engrg, 2009. Hon. Member: Alpha Omega Alpha Honor Med. Soc., USA, 1996; Physiol Soc., 1998; Internat. Assoc. of Sci. Clubs, 2002–; Cambridge Union Soc., 2003. Freeman, City of London, 1998; Mem., Co. of Spectacle Makers, 1997, Liveryman, 1998–. Foreign Fellow, Nat. Acad. Scis, India, 2008. Hon. Fellow: Cardiff Univ., 1998; Downing Coll., Cambridge, 1999; Indian Acad. of Neuroscis, 2007; Hon. FBPhS (Hon. FBPharmacolS 2007). Hon. DSc: Aston, 1992; Salford, 1994; Manchester, 2005; Aberdeen, 2005; KCL, 2007; Hon. DM Nottingham, 2008; DUniv: Open, 2011; York, 2011. Silver Award, BMA Film Competition, 1972; Silver Award, Padua Internat. Film Fest., 1973; Robert Bing Prize, Swiss Acad. of Med. Sciences, 1975; Copeman

Medal, Corpus Christi Coll., Cambridge, 1977; Richardson Cross Medal, S Western Ophthalmol Soc., 1978; Man of the Year, Royal Assoc. for Disability and Rehabilitation, 1978; Phi Beta Kappa Award in Sci., 1978; John Locke Medal, Apothecaries' Soc., 1983; Prix du Docteur Robert Netter, Acad. Nat. de Médecine, Paris, 1984; Norman McAlister Gregg Award, RACO, 1988; Michael Faraday Prize, Royal Soc., 1989; John P. McGovern Science and Soc. Medal, Sigma Xi, USA, 1990; G. L. Brown Prize, Physiol Soc., 1990; Ellison-Cliffe Medal, RSM, 1993; Annual Review Prize, Physiol Soc., 1994; Charles F. Prentice Award, Amer. Acad. of Optometry, 1994; Alcon Prize, Alcon Res. Inst., 1996; Meml Medal, Charles Univ., Prague, 1998; Charter Award, IBiol, 2001; Baly Medal, RCP, 2001; Outstanding Contribn to Neurosci. Award, British Neurosci. Assoc., 2001; BioIndustry Assoc. Award, 2004; Lord Crook Gold Medal, Spectacle Makers' Co., 2004; Edinburgh Medal, City of Edinburgh, 2005; Sci. Educator Award, Soc. for Neurosci., 2005; Kenneth Meyer Medal, Howard Florey Inst., Melbourne, 2006; James Bull Gold Medal, British Soc. of Neuroradiologists, 2009; Ferrier Prize, Royal Soc., 2010; Prize for Sci. Documentaries, Fest. de Film CinéGlobe, Geneva, 2010. *Publications:* Handbook of Psychobiology (with M. S. Gazzaniga), 1975; Mechanics of the Mind, 1977; (with S. A. Greenfield) Mindwaves, 1987; The Mind Machine, 1988, 2nd edn 1994; (with H. B. Barlow and M. Weston-Smith) Images and Understanding, 1990; Vision: coding and efficiency, 1990; (with S. D. Iversen) Gender and Society, 2000; (with S. Jennett) Oxford Companion to the Body, 2001; (with A. Parker and A. Derrington) The Physiology of Cognitive Processes, 2003; (with C. A. Heywood and A. D. Milner) The Roots of Visual Awareness, 2003; res. reports in Jl of Physiol., Jl of Neuroscience, Nature, Lancet, etc; opinion columns in The Times, Guardian, Independent, Daily Telegraph, Sunday Times, Observer, etc. *Recreation:* wasting time. *Address:* Magdalen College, Oxford OX1 4AU. *Club:* Chelsea Arts (Hon. Mem., 1992).

See also S.-J. Blakemore.

BLAKEMORE, Michael Howell, AO 2003; OBE 2003; freelance director; *b* Sydney, NSW, 18 June 1928; *s* of late Conrad Blakemore and Una Mary Blakemore (*née* Litchfield); *m* 1st, 1960, Shirley (*née* Bush); one *s*; 2nd, 1986, Tanya McCallin; two *d*. *Educ:* The King's Sch., NSW; Sydney Univ.; Royal Academy of Dramatic Art. Actor with Birmingham Rep. Theatre, Shakespeare Memorial Theatre, etc, 1952–66; Co-dir, Glasgow Citizens Theatre (1st prod., The Investigation), 1966–68; Associate Artistic Dir, Nat. Theatre, 1971–76. Dir, Players, NY, 1978. Resident Dir, Lyric Theatre, Hammersmith, 1980. Best Dir, London Critics, 1972. *Productions include:* A Day in the Death of Joe Egg, Comedy, 1967, Broadway 1968; Arturo Ui, Saville, 1969, Israel, 1969; Forget-me-not Lane, Apollo, 1971; Separate Tables, Apollo, 1976; Privates on Parade, Aldwych (RSC), transf. Piccadilly, 1977; Candida, Albery, 1977; Design for Living, Phoenix, 1977; Knuckle, Comedy, 1978; All My Sons, Wyndham's, 1981; Benefactors, Vaudeville, 1984, NY, 1986; Made in Bangkok, Aldwych, 1986; Lettice and Lovage, Globe, 1987, NY, 1990 (Outer Critics Circle Award, NY, 1990); Uncle Vanya, Vaudeville, 1988; City of Angels, Broadway, 1989 (Outer Critics Circle Award, NY, 1990), Prince of Wales Th., 1993; The Ride Down Mount Morgan, Wyndhams, 1991; Tosca, WNO, 1992; Here, Donmar Warehouse, 1993; The Sisters Rosensweig, Old Vic, 1994; Now You Know, Hampstead, 1995; Alarms and Excursions, Gielgud, 1998; Mr Peter's Connections, Almeida, 2000; Life After George, Duchess, 2002; The Three Sisters, Playhouse, 2003; Embers, Duke of York, 2006; Blithe Spirit, Gielgud Th., 2014; *National Theatre:* The National Health, 1969; Long Day's Journey Into Night, 1971; The Front Page, Macbeth, 1972; The Cherry Orchard, 1973; Grand Manoeuvres, 1974; Plunder, 1976; After the Fall, 1990; Copenhagen, 1998, transf. Duchess, then Montparnasse, Paris, 1999 (Molière Award, Tony Award, Drama Desk Award, 2000); Democracy, 2003 (Helpman Award, Australia), transf. Wyndham's, then NY, 2005; Afterlife, 2008; *Royal Court Theatre:* Widowers' Houses, 1968; Don's Party, 1973; *Lyric Theatre, Hammersmith:* Make and Break, 1980, transf. Haymarket, 1980; Travelling North, 1980; The Wild Duck, 1980; Noises Off, 1982 (transf. to Savoy, 1982, NY, 1983 (Drama Desk Award, NY, 1983–84; Outer Critics Circle Award, NY, 1983; Hollywood Drama-League Award, LA, 1984)); *foreign productions include:* The White Devil, Minneapolis, 1976; Hay Fever, 1976, The Seagull, 1979, Aarhus; Mourning Becomes Electra, Melbourne, 1980; Death Defying Acts, NY, 1995; The Life (musical), Broadway, NY, 1997; Kiss Me Kate, Broadway, NY, 1999 (Tony Award, Drama Desk Award, 2000), transf. Victoria Palace, 2001; Deuce, Is He Dead?, Broadway, NY, 2007; Blithe Spirit, Broadway, NY, 2009, US tour 2015. *Films:* A Personal History of the Australian Surf, 1981 (Standard film award, 1982); Privates on Parade, 1983; The Old Reliable, 1988; Country Life, 1995 (Film Critics Circle of Australia Award, 1994). *Publications:* Next Season (novel), 1969; Australia Fair, 1985; Arguments with England (memoir), 2005; Stage Blood (memoir), 2013 (Sheridan Morley Prize, 2013); contrib. The New Yorker. *Recreation:* surfing. *Fax:* (020) 7209 0141.

BLAKEMORE, Prof. Sarah-Jayne, PhD; Royal Society University Research Fellow, 2007–Jan. 2016, and Professor of Cognitive Neuroscience, since 2010, University College London; *b* Cambridge, 11 Aug. 1974; *d* of Sir Colin Brian Blakemore, *qv*; *m* 2002, Dr James Kilner; two *s*. *Educ:* St Philip's and St James's Primary Sch., Oxford; Crescent Prep. Sch., Oxford; Oxford High Sch. (GDST), Oxford; St John's Coll., Oxford (BA 1st Cl. Hons Exptl Psychol. 1996); University Coll. London (PhD Neurosci. 2000). Wellcome Trust Internat. Res. Fellow, Neurosci. Res. Centre, Inserm, Lyon, 2001–02; University College London: Wellcome Trust Res. Fellow, 2002–03; Gp Leader, Develtl Cognitive Neurosci. Lab., 2004; Reader in Cognitive Neurosci., 2006; Royal Soc. Dorothy Hodgkin Res. Fellow, 2004–08. *Publications:* (with U. Frith) The Learning Brain: lessons for education, 2005; Section Ed., The Cognitive Neurosciences, 5th edn, 2014; contrib. papers to scientific jls. *Recreations:* family, friends, travel, restaurants, music, swimming, mindfulness, tweeting. *Address:* Institute of Cognitive Neuroscience, University College London, 17 Queen Square, WC1N 3AR. *E:* s.blakemore@ucl.ac.uk.

BLAKENHAM, 2nd Viscount *cr* 1963, of Little Blakenham; **Michael John Hare;** farmer; *b* 25 Jan. 1938; *s* of 1st Viscount Blakenham, PC, OBE, VMH, and Hon. Beryl Nancy Pearson (*d* 1994), *d* of 2nd Viscount Cowdray; *S* father, 1982; *m* 1965, Marcia Persephone, *d* of late Hon. Alan Hare, MC; one *s* two *d*. *Educ:* Eton College; Harvard Univ. (AB Econ.). National Service, 1956–57. English Electric, 1958; Harvard, 1959–61; Lazard Brothers, 1961–63; Standard Industrial Group, 1963–71; Royal Doulton, 1972–77; Pearson, 1977–97 (Chief Exec., 1978–90; Chm., 1983–97). Chairman: The Financial Times, 1983–93; MEPC plc, 1993–98; UK Chm., Japan 2001 Fest., 1999–2002; Partner, Lazard Partners, 1984–97; Director: Lazard Bros, 1975–97; Sotheby's Holdings Inc., 1987–2013; Lafarge, 1997–2007; Mem., Internat. Adv. Gp, Toshiba, 1997–2002. Member, House of Lords Select Committee: on Science and Technol., 1985–88; on Sustainable Develt, 1994–95. Chairman: RSPB, 1981–86; Bd of Trustees, Royal Botanic Gardens, Kew, 1997–2003; Governance Review Report, NT, 2003; Mem., Nature Conservancy Council, 1986–90; President: Sussex Wildlife Trust, 1983–2003; British Trust for Ornithology, 2001–05; Suffolk Wildlife Trust, 2014–. Order of Merit of Republic of Italy, 1988; Gold and Silver Star, Order of Rising Sun (Japan), 2002. *Address:* Cottage Farm, Little Blakenham, Ipswich, Suffolk IP8 4LZ.

BLAKER, Gary Mark; QC 2015; *b* London, 20 June 1970; *s* of Marshall Blaker and Philippa Blaker; *m* 1998, Sharon Horwitz; one *d*. *Educ:* Haberdashers' Aske's Sch. for Boys, Elstree; Christ's Coll., Cambridge (BA Law 1992; MA). Called to the Bar, Middle Temple, 1993, Bencher, 2015; in practice as a barrister, specialising in property and chancery, Selborne Chambers. Vice Pres., POhWER, 2012–. Liveryman, Fan Makers' Co., 1992– (Mem., Ct of Assts, 2014–). *Recreations:* opera, theatre, travel, collecting historical autograph letters, watching Arsenal FC. *Address:* Selborne Chambers, 10 Essex Street, WC2R 3AA. *T:* (020) 7420 9500. *E:* gary.blaker@selbornechambers.co.uk.

BLAKER, Sir John, 3rd Bt *cr* 1919; *b* 22 March 1935; *s* of Sir Reginald Blaker, 2nd Bt, TD and Sheila Kellas, *d* of Dr Alexander Cran; *S* father, 1975; *m* 1st, 1960, Catherine Ann (marr. diss. 1965), *d* of late F. J. Thorold; 2nd, 1968, Elizabeth Katherine (*d* 2012), *d* of late Col John Tinsley Russell, DSO. *Address:* Stantons Farm, East Chiltington, near Lewes, East Sussex BN7 3BB.

BLAKESLEY, Rosalind Polly, DPhil; Reader in Russian and European Art, University of Cambridge, since 2013; Fellow of Pembroke College, Cambridge, since 2002; *b* Purley, London, 30 March 1970; *d* of Peter Gray and Mavis Gray (*née* Donaldson); *m* 2001, Patrick James Blakesley; one *s* one *d*. *Educ:* Beacon Hill Sch., Hong Kong; Cheltenham Ladies' Coll.; Gonville and Caius Coll., Cambridge (BA 1992); Christ Church, Oxford (DPhil 1997). Leverhulme Study Abroad Student, Moscow State Univ., 1994–95; Laming Jun. Fellow, Queen's Coll., Oxford, 1996–98, Affiliated Res. Fellow, Russian Inst. of Art Hist., Moscow, 1997; Lecturer in History of Art: Univ. of Newcastle upon Tyne, 1998–2000; Univ. of Kent, 2001–02; University of Cambridge: Asst Lectr, 2002–03, Lectr, 2003–05, Sen. Lectr, 2005–13, in Hist. of Art; Leverhulme Res. Fellow, 2009–10; Founder and Co-Dir, Cambridge Courtauld Russian Art Centre, 2011–. Curator, Images of Persuasion: an Exhibn of Soviet Posters, Barbican Centre, London, 1993; Consultant to: A Style of Life, a Style of Art: Nat. Romantic Movements in Eur. Art, State Tretyakov Gall., Moscow, 1999; International Arts and Crafts, V&A Mus., 2005; Consultant Curator, An Imperial Collection: Women Artists from the State Hermitage Mus., Nat. Mus. of Women in Arts, Washington DC. Ind. Assessor, Reviewing Cttee on Export of Works of Art, DCMS, 2000–01. Trustee, NPG, 2010–. Gov., Shrewsbury Sch., 2008–12. *Publications:* Russian Genre Painting in the Nineteenth Century, 2000; (ed jtly) An Imperial Collection: women artists from the State Hermitage Museum, 2003; The Arts and Crafts Movement, 2006; (ed jtly) Russian Art and the West, 2007; (ed jtly) From Realism to the Silver Age: new studies in Russian artistic culture, 2014; contribs to books, exhibn catalogues and learned jls; book and exhibn reviews. *Recreations:* boats, brunch. *Address:* Pembroke College, Cambridge CB2 1RF.

BLAKEWAY, Richard Anthony; Deputy Mayor for Housing, Land and Property, Greater London Authority, since 2012; *b* Wales, 14 Oct. 1978; *s* of John and Maureen Blakeway; *m* 2011, Joanna Tudor. *Educ:* Univ. of Hull (BA Hons British Politics and Legislative Studies). Parly researcher, 2001–08; Ed., Internat. Develt Mag., 2004–08; Mayoral Advr on Housing, 2008–12. Election Observer: Somaliland, 2005; Ukraine, 2006. Trustee, Chartered Inst. of Housing. Chm., Homes for London. FRSA. *Recreations:* opera, collecting art and artefacts, travel, architecture, writing, Rugby, Victorian politics. *Address:* Greater London Authority, City Hall, The Queen's Walk, SE1 2AA. *T:* (020) 7983 4000. *E:* richard.blakeway@london.gov.uk. *Club:* Savile.

BLAKEY, David Cecil, CBE 1998; QPM 1993; DL; HM Inspector of Constabulary, 1999–2004; *b* 1943; *s* of Cecil and Elsie Jane Blakey; *m* 1966, Wendy Margaret Cartwright; one *s* one *d*. *Educ:* Jarrow Grammar Sch.; Univ. of Newcastle upon Tyne (MBA). VSO, Sarawak, 1962; Constable, Durham Constabulary, 1963; Police National Computer, 1972–76; Supt, Durham, 1979; Chief Supt, Northumbria, 1984; Asst Chief Constable, West Mercia, 1986; RCDS, 1989; Deputy Chief Constable: Leics, 1989–90; West Mercia, 1990–91; Chief Constable, W Mercia, 1991–99. Pres., ACPO, 1997–98. DL Worcs, 1999. *Recreations:* books, history. *Address:* c/o HM Inspectorate of Constabulary, Bartleet House, 165a Birmingham Road, Bromsgrove, Worcs B61 0DJ.

BLAKEY, (Diana) Kristin; *see* Henry, D. K.

BLAKISTON, Sir Ferguson Arthur James, 9th Bt *cr* 1763; entrepreneur and writer; *b* 19 Feb. 1963; *er s* of Sir Arthur Norman Hunter Blakiston, 8th Bt, and Mary Ferguson (*d* 1982), *d* of late Alfred Ernest Gillingham, Cave, S Canterbury, NZ; *S* father, 1977; *m* 1993, Linda Jane, *d* of late Robert John Key, Queenstown, NZ; two *d*. *Educ:* Lincoln Coll., NZ (Diploma in Agriculture 1983); Auckland Inst. of Technology (Cert. in Marketing, 1993); NZ Inst. of Business Studies (Diploma in Travel Writing). *Heir: b* Norman John Balfour Blakiston, Executive Officer [*b* 7 April 1964; *m* 1994, Rhonda Maree Hart; three *s* one *d*]. *Address:* 8 Coulter Place, Geraldine, S Canterbury, New Zealand.

BLAKSTAD, Michael Björn; External Professor of Digital Media, University of Glamorgan, 2002–12; *b* 18 April 1940; *s* of late Clifford and Alice Blakstad; *m* 1965, Patricia Marilyn Wotherspoon; one *s* twin *d*. *Educ:* Ampleforth Coll.; Oriel Coll., Oxford (MA Lit. Hum.). General trainee, BBC, 1962–68; Producer, Yorkshire Television, 1968–71; freelance TV producer, 1971–74; Programme Editor, BBC, 1974–80; Dir of Programmes, TV South, 1980–84. Founder and Managing Director, Blackrod, 1980 (Chm., 1981–84); Chairman and Chief Executive: Workhouse Productions, 1984–88; Chrysalis Television Ltd, 1988–90 (Chm., 1990–2003, Chief Exec., 1990–94, Workhouse Ltd; Chairman: Filmscreen Internat. Ltd, 1984–86; Friday Productions, 1984–88; Blackrod Interactive Services, 1988–90; Winchester Independent Radio Ltd, 1995–98; Moviola, 2009–11; Jt Chief Exec., Videodisc Co., 1984–88; Dir, Chrysalis Gp, 1988–90. Director: IPPA, 1986–90; Internat. Video Communications Assoc., 1988–90, 1999–2001; Winchester Theatre Royal, 1988–95 (Chm. 1990–95). Chairman: Southern Screen, 1998–2004; Exec. Steering Gp, broadbandshow, 2002–04. Chm. Govs, Bedales Schs, 2001–05. Hampshire Ambassador, 2005–13. Chm., East Meon History Gp. Awards include: Radio Industries Club, 1975, 1977, 1979; RTS, 1976; BAFTA/Shell Prize, 1976; BIM/John Player, 1976; Nyon, 1978. Hon. MSc Salford, 1983. FRSA; MRI. *Publications:* The Risk Business, 1979; Tomorrow's World looks to the Eighties, 1979; (with Aldwyn Cooper) The Communicating Organisation, 1995; The Liphook Story, 2004. *Recreations:* writing, interactive design and print layout, opera. *Address:* 15 The Green, East Meon, Petersfield, Hants GU32 1QT.

BLAMEY, Marjorie Netta, MBE 2007; botanical illustrator and wildlife artist, since 1970; *b* 13 March 1918; *d* of Dr Arthur Percival Day and Janetta Day; *m* 1941, Philip Bernard Blamey (*d* 2014); two *s* two *d*. *Educ:* private schools; Italia Conti Stage Sch.; RADA. Actress and part-time photographer, prior to 1939; farmer, Cornwall, 1948–70. *Publications:* include: wrote and illustrated: Learn to Paint Flowers in Watercolour, 1986; Painting Flowers, 1997; illustrated: R. Mabey, Food for Free, 1972; R. Fitter: Handguide to Wild Flowers, 1979; Collins Gem Guide to Wild Flowers, 1980; R. and A. Fitter: Wild Flowers of Britain and Northern Europe, 1974, 5th edn 1996 (trans. 8 langs); Wild Flowers of Britain and Ireland, 2003 (Botanical Soc. and Wild Flower Soc. Prize, 2003); C. Grey-Wilson: Alpine Flowers of Europe, 1979, 2nd edn 1995; The Illustrated Flora of Britain and Northern Europe, 1989; Mediterranean Wild Flowers, 1993; Cassell's Wild Flowers of Britain and Europe, 2003; P. Blamey: Collins Gem Guide to Fruits, Nuts and Berries, 1984; Wild Flowers by Colour, 1997. *Recreations:* bird watching, gardening, travel, walking, cooking, my family, painting!

BLANC, Christian; Deputy (Allied UDF, then New Centre) for Yvelines, French National Assembly, 2002–08 and 2010–12; Secretary of State for Development of the Greater Paris Area, 2008–10; *b* Talence, Gironde, 17 May 1942; *s* of Marcel Blanc and Encarna (*née* Miranda); *m* 1st, 1973, Asa Birgitta Hagglund (marr. diss.); two *d*; 2nd, 2003, Ingrid Arion. *Educ:* Institut d'Etudes Politiques, Bordeaux (Dip.). Asst Dir, Sopexa Scandinave, 1969; Dep. to Controller, Mission for Territorial Equipment, 1970–74; Hd of Bureau, Sec. of State for Youth and Sports, 1974–76; Asst Gen. Delegate, Tech. Interministerial Agency for Leisure and Fresh Air, 1976–80; Dir of Cabinet, Commn of EC, Brussels, 1981–83; Prefect: Commune of Haute-Pyrénées, 1983–84; Govt of New Caledonia, 1985; Seine and Marne, 1985–89; without portfolio, 1989. Pres. and Dir-Gen., Régie Autonome des Transports Parisiens, 1989–92; Pres., Air France, 1993–97; Vice-Chm., Merrill Lynch Europe, 2000–02; Chm., Merrill Lynch France SA, 2000–02. Director: Middle East Airlines, 1998–99;

Carrefour; Cap Gemini. Dir, Chancery, Univs of Paris, 1991–2001. Pres. External Selection Cttee for Recruitment of Sen. Treasury Officials, 2000–02. Officer, Légion d'Honneur (France), 1988; Officier, Ordre National du Merite (France), 1994. *Publications:* Pour un Etat Stratège garant de l'intérêt général, 1993; Le Lièvre et la Tortue, 1994; La Croissance ou le Chaos, 2006; Le Grand Paris du XXIe siècle, 2010.

BLANC, Raymond René, Hon. OBE 2007; chef; Patron and Chairman, Blanc Restaurants Ltd, since 1984; Culinary Director, Eurostar, since 2012; *b* 19 Nov. 1949; *m*; two *s. Educ:* CEG de Valdahon; Lycée technique de horlogerie, Besançon. Chef de rang, 1971; Manager and chef de cuisine, 1976; proprietor and chef, Les Quat' Saisons, Summertown, 1977; Dir and Chm., Maison Blanc, 1978–88; proprietor, Le Petit Blanc, 1984–88; Chef/patron and Chairman, Le Manoir aux Quat' Saisons, 1984–; co-owner: Brasserie Blanc (formerly Le Petit Blanc) restaurants: Oxford, 1996–; Cheltenham, 1998–; Birmingham, 1999–; Manchester, 2000–09; Tunbridge Wells, 2004–09; Bristol, 2008–; Portsmouth, 2009–; Milton Keynes, 2010–; Chichester, 2010–; Winchester, 2010–; Berkhamsted, 2012–; Beaconsfield, 2014–. TV series: Blanc Mange, 1994; The Restaurant, 2007, 2008, 2009; Raymond Blanc's Kitchen Secrets, 2010, 2011; Raymond Blanc: the very hungry Frenchman, 2012; Raymond Blanc: how to cook well, 2013. Academicien Mentor, Académie Culinaire de France. Master Chef Great Britain. Hon. DBA Oxford Brookes Univ., 1999. Personnalité de l'année, 1990. Commandeur de l'Assoc. Internat. des Maîtres Conseils en Gastronomie Française. Chevalier: Légion d'Honneur (France), 2013; Ordre du Mérite agricole (France), 2013. *Publications:* Recipes from Le Manoir aux Quat' Saisons, 1988; Cooking for Friends, 1991; Blanc Mange, 1994; A Blanc Christmas, 1996; Blanc Vite, 1998; Foolproof French Cookery, 2002; A Taste of My Life, 2008; Kitchen Secrets, 2011. *Recreations:* reading, tennis, riding, classical and rock music. *Address:* Le Manoir aux Quat' Saisons, Church Road, Great Milton, Oxford OX44 7PD.

BLANCH, Sir Malcolm, KCVO 1998 (CVO 1992; LVO 1981; MVO 1968); Clerk Comptroller to Queen Elizabeth the Queen Mother, 1967–98; *b* 27 May 1932; *s* of late John and Louie Blanch; *m* 1957, Jean Harding Richardson (*d* 2007); two *s. Educ:* Dinnington Sch., Yorks. Served RN, 1949–56. Asst Keeper and Steward in Royal Yachts, Victoria & Albert, 1953, Britannia, 1954–56; Queen Elizabeth the Queen Mother's Household, 1957–98: Clerk Accountant, 1960–67. Freeman, City of London, 1989. *Recreations:* gardening, music. *Address:* 12 Bishop's Drive, East Harnham, Salisbury, Wilts SP2 8NZ. *T:* (01722) 329862.

BLANCH, Rev. Dr Michael Dennis, TD and bar 1990; public sector management consultant, since 2003; non-stipendiary Church of England priest; *b* 22 Oct. 1946; *s* of Harold Clement Blanch and Jane Emily Blanch; *m* 1973, Penelope Ann Worthington; two *s. Educ:* William Ellis Sch.; Univ. of Birmingham (BScSoc 1969; DipEd 1970; PhD 1975). AMA 1979. Keeper of Education, Nat. Army Mus., 1973–77; Sen. Museums Keeper, Rotherham MBC, 1977–79; Asst Dir, Libraries, Oldham MBC, 1979–81; Dir of Museums, 1981–84, Dir of Leisure Services, 1984–88, Calderdale MBC; County Leisure Services Officer, Shropshire CC, 1988–91; Chief Executive: Eastbourne BC, 1991–95; London Borough of Bromley, 1995–2000; Falkland Is Govt, 2000–03 and 2007. Ordained Priest (C of E), 2010; Priest in Charge, St Mary's, Hampden Park and St Peter's The Hydneye, 2013–. Mem. (Lib Dem), E Sussex CC, 2013–. FCMI (FIMgt 1985). *Publications:* War and Weapons, 1976; Soldiers, 1980. *Recreations:* mountain biking, hill walking, sailing, previously Territorial Army. *Address:* 4 Ashburnham Road, Eastbourne, E Sussex BN21 2HU. *T:* (01323) 747944.

BLANCHARD, Claire; QC 2010; *b* Louth, 11 Aug. 1969; *d* of Jeffrey and Judith Blanchard. *Educ:* Liverpool Poly. (LLB Hons 1991). Called to the Bar, Gray's Inn, 1992, Bencher, 2014; in practice as barrister specialising in commercial law. *Recreation:* Arsenal FC. *Address:* Essex Court Chambers, 24 Lincoln's Inn Fields, WC2A 3EG.

BLANCHARD, Rt Hon. Sir Peter, KNZM 2009 (DCNZM 2005); PC 1998; **Rt Hon. Justice Blanchard;** a Judge of the Supreme Court, New Zealand, 2004–12, Acting Judge, since 2012; *b* 2 Aug. 1942; *s* of Cyril Francis Blanchard and Zora Louis Blanchard (now Parkinson); *m* 1968, Judith Isabel Watts; one *s* one *d. Educ:* King's Coll., Auckland; Univ. of Auckland (LLM 1968); Harvard Univ. (Frank Knox Fellow, 1968; Fulbright Fellow, 1968; LLM 1969). Admitted barrister and solicitor, Supreme Court of NZ, 1966; Partner: Grierson Jackson & Partners, 1968–83; Simpson Grierson, 1983–92; Judge: High Court of NZ, 1992–96; Court of Appeal of NZ, 1996–2003. Comr, Law Commn, 1990–94. *Publications:* Handbook on Agreements for Sale and Purchase of Land, 1978, 4th edn 1987; Company Receiverships in Australia and New Zealand, 1982, 2nd edn (jtly) 1994; (jtly) Private Receivers of Companies in New Zealand, 2008. *Recreations:* reading, music, theatre, walking. *Address:* 1/2 Marine Parade, Herne Bay, Auckland 1011, New Zealand.

BLANCHET, Pauline; *see* Marois, P.

BLANCHETT, Catherine Elise, (Cate); actress; Joint Artistic Director, Sydney Theatre Company, 2008–13; *b* 1969; *d* of late Bob Blanchett and of June Blanchett; *m* 1997, Andrew Upton; three *s* one adopted *d. Educ:* Methodist Ladies' Coll., Melbourne; Melbourne Univ.; Nat. Inst. of Dramatic Art, Sydney. *Theatre includes:* Top Girls, Sydney Th. Co., 1992; Kafka Dances (Newcomer Award, Sydney Th. Critics Circle, 1993); Oleanna, Sydney Th. Co. (Rosemont Best Actress Award); Hamlet, Belvoir Th. Co., 1995; Sweet Phoebe, Sydney Th. Co.; The Tempest, The Blind Giant is Dancing, Belvoir Street Th. Co.; The Seagull, 1996; Plenty, Almeida, 1999; A Streetcar Named Desire, Sydney Th. Co., Sydney, transf. NY, 2009; Gross und Klein, Sydney Th. Co., Sydney, 2011, transf. Barbican, 2012. *Television includes:* Heartland, GP, Police Rescue, 1994; Bordertown, 1995. *Films include:* Parkland, 1996; Paradise Road, Thank God He Met Lizzie, Oscar and Lucinda, 1997; Elizabeth, 1998 (Best Actress, BAFTA, and Best Actress in a Drama, Golden Globe Awards, 1999); An Ideal Husband, Pushing Tin, 1999; Dreamtime Alice (also co-prod.), The Talented Mr Ripley, The Man Who Cried, 2000; The Fellowship of the Ring, The Gift, Bandits, 2001; Heaven, The Shipping News, Charlotte Gray, Chasing the Dragon, The Two Towers, 2002; Veronica Guerin, The Return of the King, 2003; The Missing, Coffee & Cigarettes, 2004; The Aviator (Academy Award for Best Supporting Actress), The Life Aquatic with Steve Zissou, 2005; Little Fish, Babel, 2006; Notes on a Scandal, The Good German, I'm Not There, The Golden Age, 2007; Indiana Jones and the Kingdom of the Crystal Skull, 2008; The Curious Case of Benjamin Button, 2009; Robin Hood, 2010; Hanna, 2011; The Hobbit: An Unexpected Journey, 2012; Blue Jasmine, 2013 (Best Actress in a Motion Picture, Drama, Golden Globe Awards and Screen Actors Guild Awards, Best Actress, BAFTA and Independent Spirit Awards, Leading Actress, Academy Awards, 2014); The Monuments Men, How to Train Your Dragon 2, 2014; Cinderella, Carol, Truth, 2015. Hon. DLitt Macquarie, 2014. *Address:* c/o RGM Artist Group, PO Box 128, Surry Hills, NSW 2010, Australia.

BLANCKENHAGEN, Jane Maureen; *see* Kelly, Jane Maureen.

BLAND, Christopher Donald Jack; Lord-Lieutenant of the Isle of Wight, 1995–2006; Chairman, Hovertravel Ltd, 1965–2010; *b* 8 Oct. 1936; *s* of Christopher Donald James Bland and Iris Raynor Bland; *m* 1962, Judith Anne Louise Maynard; one *s* three *d. Educ:* Sandroyd Prep. Sch.; Clayesmore Public Sch. Nat. Service, Gordon Highlanders, later Lieut RE, 1955–57. Rolls Royce Ltd, 1957–61; Britten Norman Aircraft Co., 1961–65; Hovertravel Ltd (world's first hovercraft operator), 1965; Sen. Partner, Norwood, 1981–; Dir, Red Funnel Gp PLC, 1986–2006; Chm., Vectis Transport PLC, 1988–2006. Mem., Albany Prison Bd, 1978–88; Chm., IoW HA, 1988–90. High Sheriff, IoW, 1989–90. *Recreations:* flying vintage aircraft, vintage sports cars, tinkering with water mills. *Address:* Yafford House, Shorwell, Isle of Wight PO30 3LH. *T:* (01983) 740428. *Clubs:* Isle of Wight County; Royal Yacht Squadron (Cowes).

BLAND, Sir (Francis) Christopher (Buchan), Kt 1993; Chairman, British Telecommunications plc, 2001–07; *b* 29 May 1938; *e s* of James Franklin MacMahon Bland and Jess Buchan Bland (*née* Brodie); *m* 1981, Jennifer Mary, Viscountess Enfield, *er d* of late Rt Hon. W. M. May, PC, FCA, MP, and of Mrs May, Mertoun Hall, Holywood, Co. Down; one *s*, and two step *s* two step *d. Educ:* Sedbergh; The Queen's Coll., Oxford (Hastings Exhibnr; Hon. Fellow, 2001). 2nd Lieut, 5th Royal Inniskilling Dragoon Guards, 1956–58; Lieut, North Irish Horse (TA), 1958–69. Dir, NI Finance Corp., 1972–76; Dep. Chm., IBA, 1972–80; Chairman: Sir Joseph Causton & Sons, 1977–85; LWT (Hldgs), 1984–94; Century Hutchinson Group, 1984–89; Phicom, subseq. Life Sciences Internat., 1987–97; NFC, 1994–2000; Director: Nat. Provident Instn, 1978–88; Storehouse plc, 1988–93. Chairman: Bd of Govs, BBC, 1996–2001; RSC, 2004–11. Mem. GLC, for Lewisham, 1967–70; Chm., ILEA Schs Sub-Cttee, 1970; Mem. Burnham Cttee, 1970; Chm., Bow Group, 1969–70; Editor, Crossbow, 1971–72; Mem., Prime Minister's Adv. Panel on Citizen's Charter, 1991–94; Chm., Chancellor's Private Finance Panel, 1995–96 (Mem., 1994–96). Chairman: NHS Rev. Gp on Nat. Trng Council and Nat. Staff Cttees, 1982; Hammersmith and Queen Charlotte's Hosps (formerly Hammersmith) SHA, 1982–94; Hammersmith Hosps NHS Trust, 1994–96. Vis. Fellow, Nuffield Coll., Oxford, 2000. William Pitt Fellow, Pembroke Coll., Cambridge, 2005. Governor, Prendergast Girls Grammar Sch. and Woolwich Polytechnic, 1968–70; Mem. Council: RPMS, 1982–96 (Hon. Fellow, 1997); St Mary's Med Sch., 1984–88. Hon. LLD South Bank, 1994; DUniv York, 2006. *Publications:* Bow Group pamphlet on Commonwealth Immigration; (with Linda Kelly) Feasts, 1987; Ashes in the Wind (novel), 2014. *Recreations:* fishing, ski-ing; formerly: Captain, OU Fencing Team, 1961; Captain, OU Modern Pentathlon Team, 1959–60; Mem. Irish Olympic Fencing Team, 1960. *Address:* Blissamore Hall, Clanville, Andover, Hants SP11 9HL. *T:* (01264) 772274; 10 Catherine Place, SW1E 6HF. *T:* (020) 7834 0021. *Club:* Beefsteak.

BLAND, Dr Roger Farrant, OBE 2008; Keeper, Department of Britain, Europe and Prehistory, British Museum, since 2013 (Keeper: Department of Portable Antiquities and Treasure, 2005–13; Department of Prehistory and Europe, 2012–13); *b* London, 3 April 1955; *s* of David Farrant Bland and Mary Elmore Bland; *m* 1987, Dr Lucilla Mary Burn; one *d. Educ:* St Paul's Sch., London; King's Coll. London (BA 1978); Magdalen Coll., Oxford; University Coll. London (PhD 1991). Curator, 1979–2001, Dep. Keeper, 2001–05, Dept of Coins and Medals, BM. Advr, DNH, then DCMS, 1994–2003. Pres., British Numismatic Soc., 2011–; Vice Pres., Royal Numismatic Soc., 2009–; Mem. Council, Soc. of Antiquaries of London, 1995–98, 2011–. Joint Editor: Portable Antiquities: Annual Reports, 1997–2006; Reports on the Operation of the Treasure Act, 1997–2006; Portable Antiquities and Treasure: Annual Reports, 2007–09. Prix de l'Académie des Inscriptions et Belles-Lettres, 2011; Medal, Royal Numismatic Soc., 2014. *Publications:* Coin Hoards from Roman Britain III: the Blackmoor hoard, 1982; (with E. M. Besly) The Cunetio Treasure, 1983; (ed jtly) Coin Hoards from Roman Britain VI, 1986, and VII, 1987; (with A. M. Burnett) The Normanby Hoard and Other Roman Coin Hoards, 1988; (ed) The Chalfont Hoard and Other Roman Coin Hoards, 1992; (with C. Johns) The Hoxne Treasure: an illustrated introduction, 1993; Portable Antiquities: a discussion document, 1996; (ed jtly) Coin Hoards from Roman Britain X, 1997; The Treasure Act 1996: Code of Practice (England and Wales), 1997; (with K. Leahy) The Staffordshire Hoard, 2009, 2nd edn 2014; (with X. Loriot) Roman and Early Byzantine Gold Coins Found in Britain and Ireland, 2010; (jtly) The Frome Hoard, 2010. *Recreations:* being out of London, walking, sailing, bird watching, Norfolk churches. *Address:* British Museum, Great Russell Street, WC1B 3DG. *T:* (020) 7323 8209. *E:* rbland@britishmuseum.org.

BLAND, Lt-Col Sir Simon (Claud Michael), KCVO 1982 (CVO 1973; MVO 1967); Extra Equerry to the Duke and Duchess of Gloucester, since 1989 (Comptroller, Private Secretary and Equerry, 1972–89); Extra Equerry to Princess Alice Duchess of Gloucester, 1989–2004 (Private Secretary and Comptroller, 1974–89); *b* 4 Dec. 1923; *s* of late Sir Nevile Bland, KCMG, KCVO, and Portia (*née* Ottley); *m* 1954, Olivia (DStJ 1999) (*d* 2013), *d* of late Major William Blackett, Arbigland, Dumfries; one *s* three *d. Educ:* Eton College. Served War of 1939–45, Scots Guards, in Italy; BJSM, Washington, 1948–49; 2nd Bn, Scots Guards, Malaya, 1949–51; Asst Mil. Adviser at UK High Commn, Karachi, 1959–60; Comptroller and Private Sec. to late Duke of Gloucester, 1961–74 and Private Sec. to late Prince William, 1968–72. Dir, West End Bd, Commercial Union, 1964–95; Vice-Pres., Raleigh Internat. (formerly Operation Raleigh), 1989–96. Chm., Coll. of St Barnabas, 1993–97; Member Council: Pestalozzi Children's Village Trust, 1989–2006, Vice-Pres., 2006–; Elizabeth Finn Trust (formerly DGAA Homelife), 1990–; Order of St John for Kent, 1990–; Pres., Friends of Edenbridge Hosp., 1990–2013. Freeman, City of London, 1988. KStJ 1988. *Address:* Blossoms, Mill Hill, Edenbridge, Kent TN8 5DD. *T:* (01732) 865489. *Club:* Buck's.

BLANDFORD, Marquess of; George John Godolphin Spencer-Churchill; *b* 28 July 1992; *er s* and *heir* of Duke of Marlborough, *qv. Educ:* Harrow.

BLANDFORD, Jacqueline Leigh, (Jay); *see* Hunt, J. L.

BLANDFORD, Prof. Roger David, FRS 1989; Professor of Physics, since 2003, and Luke Blossom Professor, School of Humanities and Sciences, since 2005, Stanford University; *b* 28 Aug. 1949; *s* of Jack George and Janet Margaret Blandford; *m* 1972, Elizabeth Denise Kellett; two *s. Educ:* King Edward's Sch., Birmingham; Magdalene Coll., Cambridge Univ. (BA, MA, PhD; Bye Fellow 1973). Res. Fellow, St John's Coll., Cambridge, 1973–76; Inst. for Advanced Study, Princeton, 1974–75; CIT, 1976–2003, Richard Chace Tolman Prof. of Theoretical Astrophysics, 1989–2003; Pehong and Adele Chen Prof. of Particle Astrophysics and Cosmology, 2003–05, Dir, Kavli Inst. for Particle Astrophysics and Cosmology, 2003–13, Stanford Univ. Mem., Nat. Acad. of Scis, 2005–. Fellow, Amer. Acad. of Arts and Scis, 1993. Gold Medal, RAS, 2013. *Address:* Department of Physics, Stanford University, 382 Via Pueblo Mall, Stanford, CA 94305–4060, USA. *T:* (650) 7234233. *E:* rdb3@stanford.edu.

BLANEY, Dr David McAllister; Chief Executive, Higher Education Funding Council for Wales, since 2012; *b* Loughton, Essex, 5 March 1964; *s* of Prof. Walter Blaney and Jane Blaney; *m* 1991, Julia Mallett; two *d. Educ:* St John's Sch., Epping; Manchester Poly. (BA Hons Business Studies); Univ. of Wolverhampton (MBA); Cardiff Univ. (EdD 2006). Lectr, Humberside Coll. of HE, 1986–89; Lectr, 1989–90, Sen. Lectr, 1990–92, Principal Lectr, 1992–93, Univ. of Wolverhampton; University of Wales, Newport: Academic Develt Officer, 1993–95; Hd, Academic Develt, 1995–97; Dep. Asst Principal, 1997–99; Asst Principal, 1999–2003; Dir of Quality, 2003–04; Hd, Funding and Reconfiguration, 2005–08, Dir, Strategic Develt, 2008–12, HEFCW. *Recreations:* music, motor sports, war histories, malt whisky. *Address:* Higher Education Funding Council for Wales, Linden Court, The Orchards, Ilex Close, Llanishen, Cardiff CF14 5DZ. *T:* (020) 2068 2251. *E:* david.blaney@hefcw.ac.uk.

BLANK, Sir (Maurice) Victor, Kt 1999; Chairman, Lloyds Banking Group (formerly Lloyds TSB Group) plc, 2006–09; *b* 9 Nov. 1942; *s* of Joseph Blank and Ruth Blank (*née* Levey); *m* 1977, Sylvia Helen (*née* Richford); two *s* one *d. Educ:* Stockport Grammar Sch.; St Catherine's Coll., Oxford (MA; Domus Fellow, 1998; Hon. Fellow 2002). Solicitor of the Supreme Court. Joined Clifford-Turner as articled clerk, 1964: Solicitor, 1966; Partner, 1969; Charterhouse Bank: Dir, and Head of Corporate Finance, 1981; Chief Exec., 1985–96; Chm., 1985–97; Chief Exec., 1985–96, Chm., 1991–97, Charterhouse plc; Dir, Charterhouse Eur. Hldg, 1993– (Chm., 1993–97); Chairman: Mirror Group plc, 1998–99; Trinity Mirror PLC, 1999–2006; GUS (formerly The Great Universal Stores) plc, 2000–06 (Dir, 1993–2006; Dep.

Chm., 1996–2000). Non-executive Director: Coats Viyella, subseq. Coats, plc, 1989 (Dep. Chm., 1999–2003); Williams (formerly Williams Hldgs) plc, 1995–2000; Sen. Ind. Dir, Chubb plc, 2000–03; Sen. Advr, Texas Pacific Gp. Mem., 1998–2004, Chm., 1998–2004, Industrial Develt Adv. Bd; Mem., Financial Reporting Council, 2003–07; Mem., Adv. Bd, Global Leadership Foundn, 2011–; Chm., Eur. Adv. Bd, Cheung Kong Graduate Sch. of Business, 2012–. UK Business Ambassador, 2008–12. Chairman: Wellbeing, subseq. Wellbeing of Women, 1989–; Social Mobility Foundn, 2013–. Mem. Council, Oxford Univ., 2000–07; Trustee, Saïd Business Sch., Univ. of Oxford, 2005–. Mem., RSA. CCMI (CIMgt 2000). Hon. FRCOG 1998. *Publications:* (jtly) Weinberg and Blank on Take-Overs and Mergers, 3rd edn 1971 to 5th edn 1989. *Recreations:* family, cricket, tennis, theatre.

BLANNING, Prof. Timothy Charles William, LittD; FBA 1990; Professor of Modern European History, University of Cambridge, 1992–2009, now Emeritus; Fellow, Sidney Sussex College, Cambridge, since 1965; *b* 21 April 1942; *s* of Thomas Walter Blanning and Gwendolyn Marchant (*née* Jones); *m* 1988, Nicky Jones; one *s* one *d. Educ:* King's Sch., Bruton, Somerset; Sidney Sussex Coll., Cambridge (BA, MA; PhD 1967; LittD 1998). University of Cambridge: Res. Fellow, Sidney Sussex Coll., 1965–68; Asst Lectr in History, 1972–76; Lectr in History, 1976–87; Reader in Modern European History, 1987–92. *Publications:* Joseph II and Enlightened Despotism, 1970; Reform and Revolution in Mainz 1740–1803, 1974; The French Revolution in Germany, 1983; The Origins of the French Revolutionary Wars, 1986; The French Revolution: aristocrats versus bourgeois?, 1987 (trans. Italian, 1989, Portuguese, 1991, 2005); Joseph II, 1994; The French Revolutionary Wars 1787–1802, 1996; (ed) The Oxford Illustrated History of Modern Europe, 1996 (trans. Japanese, 2000, Korean, 2003, Greek, 2013); (ed) The Rise and Fall of the French Revolution, 1996; (ed) History and Biography: essays in honour of Derek Beales, 1996; The French Revolution: class war or culture clash?, 1998 (trans. Japanese, 2005); (ed) Reform in Great Britain and Germany 1750–1850, 1999; (ed) The Short Oxford History of Europe: the eighteenth century, 2000 (trans. Polish, 2000, Spanish, 2002); (ed) The Short Oxford History of Europe: the nineteenth century, 2000 (trans. Polish, 2000, Spanish, 2002); The Culture of Power and the Power of Culture: old regime Europe 1660–1789, 2002; (ed) Unity and Diversity in European Culture *c* 1800, 2006; The Pursuit of Glory: Europe 1648–1815, 2007 (trans. Italian, 2011); The Triumph of Music: composers, musicians and their audiences, 1700 to the present, 2008 (trans. German, 2010, Portuguese, 2011, Spanish, 2011); The Romantic Revolution, 2009 (trans. Croatian, 2012, Arabic, 2014). *Recreation:* music. *Address:* Sidney Sussex College, Cambridge CB2 3HU. *T:* (01223) 338854. *Club:* Athenæum.

BLANTERN, Dr Paul Jonathan; Chief Executive, Northamptonshire County Council, since 2010; *b* Ketton, Rutland, 10 Feb. 1966; *s* of Edward John and Cynthia Blantern; *m* 1991, Georgina Jane Findlay; two *s. Educ:* Stamford Sch.; Southampton Univ. (BSc Hons Envmtl Sci.); Exeter Univ. (PhD 1991); Cass Business Sch. (MBA 1997); Chartered Instn of Water and Envmtl Mgt (Dip. Water and Envmtl Mgt). Prodn Manager, Anglian Water, 1991–98; Business Perf. and Transformation Manager, AWG plc, 1998–2000; Strategy Manager, Fountain GB Ltd, 2000–01; Principal Consultant, 2001–03, Man. Dir, 2003–05, Severn Trent Utility Services; Man. Dir, Complete Credit Mgt, 2003–05; Dir, Customer Services, Solihull MBC, 2005–07; Corporate Dir, Customer and Community Services, Northants CC, 2008–10; Man. Dir, Local Govt Shared Services, 2010. Clerk to Lieutenancy of Northants, 2010–. Pres., Northants County Assoc. of Local Councils, 2010–. *Recreations:* table tennis, skiing, canoeing. *Address:* Northamptonshire County Council, County Hall, Northampton NN1 1ED. *T:* (01604) 367100. *E:* pblantern@northamptonshire.gov.uk. *Club:* Thrapston Table Tennis.

BLASHFORD-SNELL, Col John Nicholas, OBE 1996 (MBE 1969); author, lecturer and broadcaster; Ministry of Defence consultant (on staff, 1983–91); *b* 22 Oct. 1936; *s* of late Rev. Prebendary Leland John Blashford Snell and Gwendolen Ives Sadler; *m* 1960, Judith Frances (*née* Sherman); two *d. Educ:* Victoria Coll., Jersey, CI; RMA, Sandhurst. Commissioned Royal Engineers, 1957; 33 Ind. Fd Sqdn RE Cyprus, 1958–61; comd Operation Aphrodite (Expedition) Cyprus, 1959–61; Instructor: Junior Leaders Regt RE, 1962–63; RMA Sandhurst, 1963–66; Adjt 3rd Div. Engineers, 1966–67; comd Great Abbai Expedn (Blue Nile), 1968; sc RMCS Shrivenham and Camberley, 1968–69; comd Dahlak Quest Expedn, 1969–70; GSO2 MoD, 1970–72; comd British Trans-Americas Expedn, 1971–72; OC 48 Fd Sqdn RE, service in Belize, Oman, Ulster, 1972–74; comd Zaire River Expedn, 1974–75; CO Junior Leaders Regt RE, 1976–78; Dir of Operations, Operation Drake, 1977–81; on staff (GSO1), MoD, 1978–82; in command, The Fort George Volunteers, 1982–83. Operation Raleigh: Operations Dir, 1982–88; Dir Gen., 1989–91; Leader, Kota Mama expedn, 1995–, and numerous other expedns. Hon. Chm., 1969–2008, Pres., 2008–, Scientific Exploration Soc.; Hon. Chm., Scientific Exploration Soc. Jersey, 2002–; Pres., Just A Drop, 2004– (Hon. Chm., 2001–04); Appeal Dir, Trinity Sailing Trust, 2004–09 (Hon. Vice-Pres., 2009–); Trustee, Operation New World, 1995–. Hon. Pres., The Vole Club, 1996–; Hon. Life Pres., Centre for Fortean Zoology, 2003–. Hon. Keeper of the Quaich, 2013. Chm., Liverpool Construction Crafts Guild, 2003–05 (Pres., 2005–). FRSGS 1975. Freeman, City of Hereford, 1984. Hon. Fellow, Liverpool John Moores Univ., 2010. Hon. DSc Durham, 1986; Hon. DEng Bournemouth, 1997. Darien Medal (Colombia), 1972; Segrave Trophy, 1974; Livingstone Medal, RSGS, 1975; Paul Harris Fellow, Rotary Internat., 1981; Patron's Medal, RGS, 1993; Gold Medal, Instn of RE, 1994; La Paz Medal (Bolivia), 2000. *Publications:* Weapons and Tactics (with Tom Wintringham), 1970; (with Richard Snailham) The Expedition Organiser's Guide, 1970, 2nd edn 1976; Where the Trails Run Out, 1974; In the Steps of Stanley, 1975, 2nd edn 1975; (with A. Ballantine) Expeditions the Experts' Way, 1977, 2nd edn 1978; A Taste for Adventure, 1978; (with Michael Cable) Operation Drake, 1981; Mysteries: encounters with the unexplained, 1983; Operation Raleigh, the Start of an Adventure, 1987; (with Ann Tweedy) Operation Raleigh, Adventure Challenge, 1988; (with Ann Tweedy) Operation Raleigh, Adventure Unlimited, 1990; Something lost behind the Ranges, 1994, rev. edn 2014; (with Rula Lenska) Mammoth Hunt, 1996; (with Richard Snailham) Kota Mama, 2000; (with Richard Snailham) East to the Amazon, 2002. *Recreations:* motoring, shooting, food, wine. *Clubs:* Buck's, Travellers; Artists' (Liverpool); Galley Hill Shooting (Hon. Pres.); Explorers (New York); Jersey Pistol.

BLATCHFORD, Ian; Director and Chief Executive, Science Museum Group, and Director, Science Museum, since 2010; *b* Plymouth, 17 Aug. 1965; *s* of late David George Blatchford and of Elizabeth Jayne Cole. *Educ:* Mansfield Coll., Oxford (MA Law); Birkbeck Coll., Univ. of London (MA Renaissance Studies). Bank of England, 1986–88; Barclays de Zoete Wedd, 1988; Dep. Finance Dir, Arts Council, 1989–94; Financial Controller, Cricket Communications, 1994–96; Dir, Finance, RA, 1996–2002; Dir, Finance and Resources, 2002–04, Dep. Dir, 2004–10, V&A Mus. Chm. of Govs, De Montfort Univ., 2011–. Mem., CIMA. FSA. *Recreations:* collecting English porcelain, classical music. *Address:* Science Museum, Exhibition Road, SW7 2DD. *E:* ian.blatchford@sciencemuseum.ac.uk. *Club:* Athenæum.

BLATCHLEY, Geraldine; *see* James, G.

BLATCHLY, John Marcus, MBE 2007; MA, PhD; FSA 1975; Headmaster, Ipswich School, 1972–93; *b* 7 Oct. 1932; *s* of late Alfred Ernest Blatchly and Edith Selina Blatchly (*née* Giddings); *m* 1955, Pamela Winifred, JP, *d* of late Major and Mrs L. J. Smith; one *s* one *d. Educ:* Sutton Grammar Sch., Surrey; Christ's Coll., Cambridge (Natural Scis Triposes; BA, MA, PhD). Instr Lieut RN, 1954–57. Asst Master and Head of Science Dept: King's Sch., Bruton, 1957–62; Eastbourne Coll., 1962–66; Charterhouse, 1966–72 (PhD awarded 1967 publication of work carried out with Royal Society grants at these three schools). Sen. Vis. Fellow in History, 2011–14, Hon. Wolsey Prof. of History, 2014–, Univ. Campus Suffolk Pres., Suffolk Inst. of Archaeology and History, 1975–2001; Chm., Suffolk Records Soc 1988–2013. Editor, Conference and Common Room (Journal of HMC Schools), 1987–9 Hon. Treas., 1990–92, Hon. Associate Mem., 1993, HMC; lead inspector to HMC sch 1994–2000. Co-ed., Bookplate Jl, 1994–98. Hon. Res. Associate, Oxford DNB, 2001. Gov of several schs, 1993–2005. President: Old Ipswichian Club, 2011; Bookplate Soc., 2012– Hon. LittD UEA, 1993. *Publications:* Organic Reactions, vol. 19, 1972 (jtly, with J. F. W McOmie); The Topographers of Suffolk, 1976, 5th edn 1988; (with Peter Eden) Isaa Johnson of Woodbridge, 1979; Eighty Ipswich Portraits, 1980; (ed) Davy's Suffolk Journa 1983; The Town Library of Ipswich: a history and catalogue, 1989; The Bookplates o Edward Gordon Craig, 1997; Some Suffolk and Norfolk Ex-Libris, 2000; (jtly) The Journa of William Dowsing, 2001; The Bookplates of George Wolfe Plank, 2002; A Famous Antien Seed-Plot of Learning: a history of Ipswich School, 2003; John Kirby's Suffolk: his maps an roadbooks, 2004; (with Peter Northeast) Decoding Flint Flushwork on Suffolk and Norfol Churches, 2005; East Anglian Ex-Libris, 2008; (with Martin Sanford) Thomas Fella's Book o Divers Devices, 2012; (with Diarmaid MacCulloch) Miracles in Lady Lane: the Ipswic Shrine at the Westgate, 2013; Isaac Johnson of Woodbridge, Georgian Surveyor and Artis 2014; many papers in chemical, educnl, archaeological and antiquarian jls. *Recreations:* Eas Anglian history, music, books. *Address:* 11 Burlington Road, Ipswich, Suffolk IP1 2HS. *Club* East India.

BLATHERWICK, Sir David (Elliott Spiby), KCMG 1997 (CMG 1990); OBE 1973; HM Diplomatic Service, retired; Chairman, British Egyptian Chamber of Commerce, 1999–2015 *b* 13 July 1941; *s* of Edward S. Blatherwick; *m* 1964, (Margaret) Clare Crompton; one *s* one *d. Educ:* Lincoln Sch.; Wadham Coll., Oxford. Entered FO, 1964; Second Sec., Kuwait, 1968 First Sec., Dublin, 1970; FCO, 1973; Head of Chancery, Cairo, 1977; Head, Pol Affairs Dept NI Office (Belfast), 1981; Hd, Energy, Science and Space Dept, FCO, 1983; sabbatical leav at Stanford Univ., Calif, 1985–86; Counsellor and Hd of Chancery, UK Mission to UN, NY 1986–89; Prin. Finance Officer and Chief Inspector, FCO, 1989–91; Ambassador to Republic of Ireland, 1991–95; Egypt, 1995–99. *Publications:* The International Politics o Telecommunications, 1987. *Recreations:* music, sailing, walking. *Club:* Athenæum.

BLATT, Prof. Michael Robert, PhD; FRSE; Regius Professor of Botany, University o Glasgow, since 2001; *b* 9 Sept. 1953; *s* of Frank Blatt and Gloria Blatt (*née* Freeman); *m* 198(Jane Stroh; one *s* one *d. Educ:* Univ. of Wisconsin-Madison (BSc Biochem. and Botany 1975 Univ. Erlangen-Nürnberg (Matricula Natural Scis 1979); Stanford Univ. (PhD Biol Sci 1981). NRSA Res. Fellow, Dept of Physiol., Yale Univ. Sch. of Medicine, 1980–83; NATO Fellow and Sen. Res. Associate, Botany Sch., Univ. of Cambridge, 1983–90; Lectr an Reader in Plant Cell and Membrane Biol., 1990–97, Prof. of Plant Membrane Biol 1997–2000, Wye Coll., Univ. of London; Prof. of Plant Physiol. and Biophysics, Imperia Coll., London, 2000–01. Ed.-in-Chief, Jl Plant Physiol., 2013–. FRSE 2003. *Publications* numerous res. articles in fields of biol membrane transport, plant and fungal cell biol. an sensory physiol. *Recreations:* ski-ing, mountaineering, sailing, music. *Address:* Institute o Molecular Cell and Systems Biology, University of Glasgow, Glasgow G12 8QQ. *T:* (0141 330 4451, *Fax:* (0141) 330 4447. *E:* michael.blatt@glasgow.ac.uk.

BLATTER, Joseph Sepp; President, Fédération Internationale de Football Associatior 1998–Feb. 2016; *b* 10 March 1936; *s* of Joseph and Berta Blatter-Nellen; *m* (marr. diss.); on *d. Educ:* Univ. of Lausanne (BA Business Admin and Econs). Gen. Sec., Swiss Ice-Hocke Fedn, 1964–66; Press Officer, Swiss Sports Orgn, 1966–68; Dir, Sports Timing and PR Longines SA, 1968–75; Technical Dir, 1975–81, Gen. Sec. and CEO, 1981–98, FIFA. Mem IOC, 1999–2015. Hon. Mem., Swiss FA. Hon. PhD Nelson Mandela Metropolitan, SA 2006. Olympic Order, 1994; American Global Peace Award, 2003. Kt, Sultanate of Pahang 1990; Order of Good Hope (S Africa), 1998; Chevalier, Légion d'Honneur (France); Gross Verdienstkreuz (Germany), 2006. *Recreations:* crosswords, tennis, books (detective stories) *Address:* (until Feb. 2016) FIFA, FIFA Strasse 20, PO Box, 8044 Zurich, Switzerland. *T:* (43 2227777.

BLAYNEY, David James; QC 2013; *b* 1969; *s* of Robert and Ann Blayney; *m* 1995 Katherine; two *c. Educ:* St Michael's Sch., Jersey; Canford Sch., Dorset; Lincoln Coll., Oxfor (BA Juris.). Called to the Bar, Lincoln's Inn, 1992; Intern, Legal Resources Centre, Cap Town, 1992–93; Pupil, 13 Old Sq., Lincoln's Inn, 1993–94; in practice as barrister, 1994– Trustee, Reigate and Banstead CAB, 2012–. *Recreations:* family, music, windsurfing, running *Address:* 6 New Square, Lincoln's Inn, WC2A 3QS. *T:* (020) 7242 6105. *E:* dblayney@ serlecourt.co.uk.

BLAZE, Robin Peter; countertenor; Professor, Royal College of Music, since 1999; *b* 11 Jan 1971; *s* of Peter Michael and Christine Margaret Blaze; *m* 1999, Lisa Jane Beckley; one *s. Educ* Magdalen Coll., Oxford (MA Hons); Royal Coll. of Music (Postgrad. Dip.). First professiona engagements, 1995; recital broadcasts BBC Radio 3, 1999–2002; Proms solo début, 2000 début recital Wigmore Hall, 2001; opera débuts: Glyndebourne Touring Opera, 200 (Bertarido, in Rodelinda); ENO, 2002 (Arsamene, in Xerxes); Glyndebourne Fest. Oper (Didymus, in Theodora), and Royal Opera, Covent Gdn (Athamus, in Semele), 2003; concer appearances in Australia (Sydney Opera House), Japan (Tokyo Opera City), Argentina, Brazil USA (Kennedy Centre) and across Europe. Solo recital recordings, 1999– incl. complete Bac series with Bach Collegium Japan. *Recreations:* golf, reading, cricket.

BLAZWICK, Iwona Maria Anna, OBE 2008; Director, Whitechapel Art Gallery, sinc 2001; *b* 14 Oct. 1955; *d* of Wojciech Blaszczyk and Danuta Mondry-Blaszczyk; *m* 2003, D Richard Noble; one *d. Educ:* Exeter Univ. (BA 1977). Curator, 1980–85, Dir of Exhibns 1987–93, Inst. of Contemporary Arts, London; Dir, A.I.R. Gall., 1985–87; Commng Editor Phaidon Press, 1993–97; Curator, then Hd of Exhibns, Tate Gall. of Modern Art, subseq. Tat Modern, 1997–2001. Art critic, lectr and broadcaster on contemporary art, 1985–; Vis. Lectr RCA, 1993–97. Curator: Ha-Ha: Contemporary British Artists in an 18th Century Park Univ. of Plymouth and Nat. Trust, 1993; (jtly) On Taking a Normal Situation, Mus. o Contemporary Art, Antwerp, 1993; Now Here, Louisiana Mus., Denmark, 1996; New Tendencies in British and Japanese Art, Toyama Mus. of Modern Art, Japan, 1996. FRCA Hon. Fellow, Goldsmiths, 2009. Hon. MA London Metropolitan, 2003; Hon. DPh Plymouth, 2006; Hon. Dr Univ. of the Arts, 2011. *Publications:* An Endless Feast: on Britis situationism, 1988; Lawrence Weiner, 1993; Ilya Kabakov, 1998; (ed jtly) Tate Modern: th handbook, 2000; (ed) Century City, 2001; Faces in the Crowd, 2004; Alex Katz, 2006 Revolutions: forms that turn, 2008; Elizabeth Peyton, 2008; Gary Hume, 2009; exhib catalogues; contribs to jls. *Recreations:* cinema, dancing, travel, photography. *Address:* 77–8 Whitechapel High Street, E1 7QX. *Club:* Blacks.

BLEAKLEY, Rt Hon. David Wylie, CBE 1984; PC (NI) 1971; President, Church Missio (formerly Church Missionary) Society, 1983–97; *b* 11 Jan. 1925; *s* of John Wesley Bleakle and Sarah Bleakley (*née* Wylie); *m* 1949, Winifred Wason; three *s. Educ:* Ruskin Coll. Oxford; Queen's Univ., Belfast. MA, DipEconPolSci (Oxon). Belfast Shipyard, 1940–46 Oxford and Queen's Univ., 1946–51; Tutor in Social Studies, 1951–55; Principal, Belfas Further Educn Centre, 1955–58; Lectr in Industrial Relations, Kivukoni Coll., Dar-es Salaam, 1967–69; Head of Dept of Economics and Political Studies, Methodist Coll., Belfast 1969–79; Chief Exec., Irish Council of Churches, 1980–92. MP (Lab) Victoria, Belfast Parliament of N Ireland, 1958–65; contested: (Lab) East Belfast, General Elections, 1970, Feb and Oct. 1974. Minister of Community Relations, Govt of NI, March–Sept. 1971; Membe (NILP), E Belfast: NI Assembly, 1973–75; NI Constitutional Convention, 1975–76

Contested (Lab) Belfast E, NI Assembly, 1998. Mem., Cttee of Inquiry on Police, 1978. Chm., NI Standing Adv. Commn on Human Rights, 1980–84. Mem., Labour Delegn, NI Peace Talks, 1996–. Irish Deleg. to ACC, 1976; Delegate to WCC, to Conf. of European Churches. WEA and Open Univ. tutor; Vis. Sen. Lectr in Peace Studies, Univ. of Bradford, 1974–. Mem., Press Council, 1987–90. Hon. MA Open, 1975. *Publications:* Ulster since 1800: regional history symposium, 1958; Young Ulster and Religion in the Sixties, 1964; Peace in Ulster, 1972; Faulkner: a biography, 1974; Saidie Patterson, Irish Peacemaker, 1980; In Place of Work, 1981; The Shadow and Substance, 1983; Beyond Work—Free to Be, 1985; Will the Future Work, 1986; Europe: a Christian vision, 1992; Ageing and Ageism in a Technological Society, 1994; Peace in Ireland: two states, one people, 1995; Europe: obligations and opportunities for Christians, 1997; C. S. Lewis: at home in Ireland, 1998; regular contribs to BBC and to press on community relations and industrial studies. *Address:* 8 Thornhill, Bangor, Co. Down, Northern Ireland BT19 1RD. *T:* (028) 9145 4898.

BLEARS, Rt Hon. Hazel Anne; PC 2005; *b* 14 May 1956; *d* of Arthur and Dorothy Blears; *m* 1989, Michael Halsall. *Educ:* Wardley Grammar Sch.; Trent Poly. (BA Hons Law). Trainee Solicitor, Salford Council, 1978–80; in private practice, 1980–81; Solicitor: Rossendale Council, 1981–83; Wigan Council, 1983–85; Principal Solicitor, Manchester City Council, 1985–97. Mem. (Lab) Salford City Council, 1984–92. MP (Lab) Salford, 1997–2010, Salford and Eccles, 2010–15. Parly Under-Sec. of State, DoH, 2001–03; Minister of State, Home Office, 2003–06; Minister without Portfolio and Chair, Labour Party, 2006–07; Sec. of State for Communities and Local Govt, 2007–09. Contested (Lab): Tatton, 1987; Bury S, 1992. *Recreations:* dance, motorcycling.

BLEASDALE, Alan; writer and producer; *b* 23 March 1946; *s* of George and Margaret Bleasdale; *m* 1970, Julia Moses; two *s* one *d*. *Educ:* St Aloysius RC Jun. Sch., Huyton; Wade Deacon Grammar Sch., Widnes; Padgate Teachers Trng Coll. (Teacher's Cert.). Schoolteacher, 1967–75. *TV series: writer:* Boys from the Blackstuff, 1982 (BPG TV Award for Best Series, 1982; Best British TV Drama of the Decade, ITV Achievement of the Decade Awards, 1989); Scully, 1984; The Monocled Mutineer, 1986; (also prod) GBH, 1991 (BPG TV Award for Best Drama Series, 1992); (also prod) Jake's Progress, 1995 (Best Writer Award, Monte Carlo Internat. TV Fest., 1996); (also prod) Melissa, 1997; (adapt.) Oliver Twist, 1999 (Best TV Drama Series, TRIC Award, 2000); The Sinking of the Laconia, 2010; *producer:* Alan Bleasdale Presents, 1994; Soft Sand, Blue Sea, 1997. Hon. DLitt Liverpool Poly., 1991. BAFTA Writers Award, 1982; RTS Writer of the Year, 1982. *Publications: novels:* Scully, 1975; Who's been sleeping in my bed, 1977; *play scripts:* No more sitting on the Old School Bench, 1979; Boys from the Blackstuff, 1982; Are you lonesome tonight?, 1985 (Best Musical, London Standard Drama Awards, 1985); Having a Ball, 1986; It's a Madhouse, 1986; The Monocled Mutineer, 1986; On the Ledge, 1993; *film script:* No Surrender, 1986. *Recreation:* rowing. *Address:* c/o The Agency, 24 Pottery Lane, Holland Park, W11 4LZ. *T:* (020) 7727 1346.

BLEASDALE, Cyril, OBE 1988; FCILT; Managing Director, Railnews Ltd, since 1996; *b* 8 July 1934; *s* of Frederick and Alice Bleasdale; *m* 1970, Catherine; two *d*. *Educ:* Evered High Sch., Liverpool; Stanford Univ., Calif (Sen. Exec. Program). Man. Dir, Freightliner Ltd, 1975–82; Dir, Inter City British Rail, 1982–86; Gen. Manager, BR London Midland Region, 1986–90; Dir, Scotrail, 1990–94. Dir, 1997–2009, Chm., 2003–09, Hertfordshire Business Incubation Centre Ltd. Dir Gen., Internat. Council, Chartered Inst. (formerly Inst.) of Logistics and Transport, 1999–2009. FCMI. *Recreations:* music, fitness. *Address:* 22 Trafalgar Street, Cheltenham GL50 1UH. *Club:* Royal Automobile.

BLEASDALE, Marcus; documentary photographer, since 1998; human rights activist; *b* Kendal, Cumbria, 7 March 1968; *s* of Terence and Helen Bleasdale; *m* 2007, Karin Beate Nøsterud. *Educ:* Univ. of Huddersfield (BA Hons Business Econs and Finance); London Inst. (London Coll. of Printing Postgrad. Photojournalism). Investment banker: Schroders, 1990–94; ABN, 1994–96; Bank of America, 1996–98. Member and owner, VII Photo, 2007– (Vice Chair, 2007–09). *Publications:* One Hundred Years of Darkness, 2002; The Rape of a Nation, 2009; contribs to Nat. Geographic Mag., New Yorker. *Recreations:* ski-ing, running, photography. *E:* marcusbleasdale@gmail.com. *Club:* Frontline.

BLEASDALE, Paul Edward; QC 2001; a Recorder of the Crown Court, since 1996; *b* 18 Dec. 1955; *s* of late William Arthur Bleasdale and Dorothy Elizabeth Bleasdale; *m* 1991, Dr Sarah Alexandra Nicholson; one *s* one *d*. *Educ:* Langley Park Sch. for Boys, Beckenham; Queen Mary Coll., London (LLB 1977). Called to the Bar, Inner Temple, 1978, Bencher, 2011; Asst Recorder, 1992–96. Fee Paid Judge, First-tier Tribunal (Property Chamber) (formerly Dep. Chm., Agricl Lands Tribunal), 1994–. Hon. Prof. of Law, Birmingham Univ., 2012–15. *Recreations:* holidays abroad, outdoor sports. *Address:* No 5 Chambers, Fountain Court, Steelhouse Lane, Birmingham B4 6DR.

BLEDISLOE, 4th Viscount *cr* 1935; **Rupert Edward Ludlow Bathurst;** portrait artist, since 1989; *b* London, 13 March 1964; *s* of 3rd Viscount Bledisloe, QC, and Elizabeth Mary Thompson; *S* father, 2009; *m* 2001, Shera, *d* of Rohinton and Irma Sarosh; one *s* two *d*. *Educ:* Eton (Oppidan Schol.); Univ. of Exeter. *Heir: s* Hon. Benjamin Rohinton Ludlow Bathurst, *b* 28 March 2004. *Address:* The Old Coach House, Lydney Park Estate, Lydney, Glos GL15 6BT. *Club:* St Moritz Tobogganing.

BLELLOCH, Sir John (Niall Henderson), KCB 1987 (CB 1983); Permanent Under-Secretary of State, Northern Ireland Office, 1988–90; *b* 24 Oct. 1930; *s* of late Ian William Blelloch, CMG and Leila Mary Henderson; *m* 1958, Pamela, *d* of late James B. and E. M. Blair; one *s* (and one *s* decd). *Educ:* Fettes Coll.; Gonville and Caius Coll., Cambridge (MA). Nat. Service, RA, 1949–51 (commnd 1950). Asst Principal, War Office, 1954; Private Sec. to successive Parly Under Secs of State, 1956–58; Principal, 1958; MoD, 1964–80; London Business Sch. (EDP 3), 1967; Asst Sec., 1968; RCDS, 1974; Asst Under-Sec. of State, 1976; Dep. Sec., NI Office, 1980–82; Dep. Under-Sec. of State (Policy and Programmes), MoD, 1982–84; Second Permanent Under-Sec. of State, MoD, 1984–88. Mem., Security Commn, 1991–2001; Jt Chm., Sentence Review Commn, NI, 1998–2010. Comr, Royal Hosp. Chelsea, 1988–94. Mem. Cttee, 1993–99, Vice-Chm., 1995–99, Automobile Assoc.; Pres., Emergency Planning Soc., 1993–2005. Trustee: RAF Mus., 1993–2002; Cheshire Foundn, 1996–2005; Gov., Fettes Coll., 1992–2002. *Recreations:* golf, music, books. *Club:* Sherborne Golf.

BLENCATHRA, Baron *cr* 2011 (Life Peer), of Penrith in the county of Cumbria; **David John Maclean;** PC 1995; *b* 16 May 1953. MP (C) Penrith and the Border, July 1983–2010. Asst Govt Whip, 1987–88; a Lord Comr of HM Treasury (Govt Whip), 1988–89; Parly Sec., MAFF, 1989–92; Minister of State: DoE, 1992–93; Home Office, 1993–97; Opposition Chief Whip, 2001–05. *Address:* House of Lords, SW1A 0PW.

BLENKINSOP, Dorothy, CBE 1990; Regional Nursing Officer, Northern Regional Health Authority, 1973–89, retired; *b* 15 Nov. 1931; *d* of late Joseph Henry Blenkinsop, BEM, and Thelma Irene (*née* Bishop). *Educ:* South Shields Grammar Sch. for Girls. MA (Dunelm) 1978. SRN 1953; SCM 1954; Health Visitors Cert. 1962. Ward Sister, Royal Victoria Infirmary, Newcastle upon Tyne, 1955–61; Health Visitor, S Shields, 1962–64; Dep. Matron, Gen. Hosp., S Shields, 1964–67; Durham Hospital Management Committee: Prin. Nurse, Durham City Hosps, 1967–69; Prin. Nursing Officer (Top), 1969–71; Chief Nursing Officer, 1971–73. Chm., S Tyneside Health Care Trust, 1992–96. Local Preacher, Methodist Church. Hon. MSc CNAA, 1990. *Publications:* (with E. G. Nelson): Changing the System, 1972; Managing the System, 1976; articles in nursing press. *Address:* 143 Temple Park Road, South Shields, Tyne and Wear NE34 0EN. *T:* (0191) 456 1429.

BLENKINSOP, Thomas Francis; MP (Lab) Middlesbrough South and East Cleveland, since 2010; *b* Middlesbrough, 14 Aug. 1980; *s* of William Blenkinsop and Barbara Blenkinsop; *m* 2007, Victoria Emtage. *Educ:* Teesside Univ. (BSc PPE); Warwick Univ. (MA Continental Philos.). Constituency Researcher for Dr Ashok Kumar, MP, 2002–08; full-time Regl Official, Community Trade Union, 2008–10. An Opposition Whip, 2011–. *Recreation:* football (playing and watching Middlesbrough Football Club). *Address:* (office) Harry Tout House, 8 Wilson Street, Guisborough TS14 6NA. *T:* (01287) 610878. *E:* info@tomblenkinsop.com.

BLENKINSOPP, Prof. Alison, OBE 2010; PhD; Professor of the Practice of Pharmacy, University of Bradford, since 2011; *b* 22 June 1959; *d* of Ron and Margaret Morley; *m* 1988, John Blenkinsopp. *Educ:* Bradford Univ. (BPharm 1st Cl. Hons); Aston Univ. (PhD 1988). Lecturer in Pharmacy Practice: Aston Univ., 1982–88; Univ. of Bradford, 1988–91; Dir, NHS Centre for Pharmacy Postgrad. Educn, 1991–95; Sen. Lectr, Health Services Res., 1995–99, Prof. of Practice of Pharmacy, 1999–2011, Keele Univ. Ed., Internat. Jl Pharmacy Practice, 1998–2005. Mem., Cttee on Safety of Medicines, 1999–2005. Mem., Jt Nat. Formulary Cttee, 1989– (Dep. Chm., 2008–). Charter Gold Medal, RPSGB, 2001. *Publications:* Symptoms in the Pharmacy, 1989, 7th edn 2014; Health Promotion for Community Pharmacists, 1991, 2nd edn 2000; Over the Counter Medication, 2005; Supporting Self Care in Primary Care, 2006; Evaluation of Nurse and Pharmacist Independent Prescribing in England, 2011. *Recreations:* travel, reading, contemporary music, Chicago Cubs supporter. *Address:* School of Pharmacy, University of Bradford, Richmond Road, Bradford BD7 1DP. *T:* (01274) 236040. *E:* a.blenkinsopp@bradford.ac.uk.

BLENNERHASSETT, Sir (Marmaduke) Adrian (Francis William), 7th Bt, *cr* 1809; *b* 25 May 1940; *s* of Lieut Sir Marmaduke Blennerhassett, 6th Bt, RNVR (killed in action, 1940), and Gwenfra (*d* 1956), *d* of Judge Harrington-Morgan, Churchtown, Co. Kerry, and of Mrs Douglas Campbell; *S* father 1940; *m* 1972, Carolyn Margaret, *yr d* of late Gilbert Brown; one *s* one *d*. *Educ:* Michael Hall, Forest Row; McGill Univ.; Imperial Coll., Univ. of London (MSc); Cranfield Business Sch. (MBA). FRGS 2000. *Recreations:* sailing, ski-ing, adventure travelling. *Heir: s* Charles Henry Marmaduke Blennerhassett, *b* 18 July 1975. *Address:* 38 Hugon Road, SW6 3EN. *Club:* Travellers.

BLESSED, Brian; actor, author and climber; *b* 9 Oct. 1936; *s* of William Blessed and Hilda Blessed (*née* Wall); *m* 1st, Anne Bomann (marr. diss.); one *d*; 2nd, 1978, Hildegard Neil (*née* Zimmermann); one *d*. *Educ:* Bolton-on-Dearne Sch.; Bristol Old Vic Theatre Sch. *Stage:* worked in rep., Nottingham, Birmingham, etc; Incident at Vichy, Phoenix, 1966; The Exorcism, Comedy, 1967; State of Revolution, NT, 1977; The Devil's Disciple, 1979 and The Eagle has Two Heads, Chichester; Hamlet, Richard III, and Henry V, RSC, 1984–85; The Relapse, RNT, 2001; King Lear, Guildford, 2015; dir, The Glass Menagerie, tour 1998; one-man show, An Evening with Brian Blessed, tours 1992–93, 1995–96; musicals: Old Deuteronomy, in Cats, New London, 1981; Metropolis, Piccadilly, 1989; Hard Times, Haymarket, 2000; Chitty Chitty Bang Bang, Palladium, 2002; narrator, Morning Heroes (Arthur Bliss), with LSO, 1991, and other works; *films include:* The Trojan Women, 1971; Man of La Mancha, 1972; Flash Gordon, 1980; Henry V, 1989; Robin Hood, Prince of Thieves, 1991; Much Ado About Nothing, 1993; Hamlet, 1997; Star Wars—The Phantom Menace, 1998; Walt Disney's Tarzan, 1999; Mumbo Jumbo, 2000; Alexander, 2004; As You Like It, The Conclave, The Day of Wrath, 2006; Back in Business, 2007; As You Like It, 2008; *television includes:* series: Fancy Smith, in Z Cars, 1962–78; The Little World of Don Camillo, 1980; The Black Adder, 1983; My Family and Other Animals, 1987; serials: The Three Musketeers, 1966; I, Claudius, 1976; Return to Treasure Island, 1986; War and Remembrance, 1988; Catherine the Great, 1995; Tom Jones, 1997; documentary, Ascent of Mars Mountain, 2005. Has made expeditions to: Mt Everest, 1991 (film, Galahad of Everest, won Canadian Grand Prix, Banff Fest., 1992), 1993, 1996; N Pole, Mt Aconcagua, 2002; Chile, 1993; Mt Ararat, Turkey, 2004; Mt Kuiten and Malkin, Mongolia; Mt Kilimanjaro, Africa. *Publications:* The Turquoise Mountain, 1991; The Dynamite Kid, 1992; Nothing's Impossible, 1994; Quest for the Lost World, 1999. *Address:* c/o AIM, 4th Floor, 6–7 Hatton Garden, EC1N 8AD.

BLESSLEY, Andrew Charles; Clerk to the Clothworkers' Co. of the City of London and Chief Executive (formerly Secretary), Clothworkers' Foundation, since 2001; *b* 20 May 1951; *s* of late Kenneth Harry Blessley, CBE, ED and Gwendeline Blessley; *m* 1979, Linda Kristine Marr; one *s* one *d*. *Educ:* Haberdashers' Aske's Sch., Elstree; St John's Coll., Cambridge (MA); Harvard Business Sch. (AMP). Joined National Westminster Bank, 1972: appointments in UK and USA, including: Dir, Energy and Natural Resources Gp, 1989–90; COS to Gp Chief Exec., 1990–92; Regl Dir, Central London, 1992–94; Dir, Gp Strategy, 1994–95; Vice-Chm. and Chief Operating Officer, NatWest Bancorp USA, 1995–96; Dir, Retail Mktg and Distribution, 1996–2001. Director: Fleet Bank NA, 1996–97; Lombard NatWest Commercial Services, 1996–98. Dir, Banking Ombudsman Bd, 1996–2000. Member: Regeneration Leadership Team, BITC, 1997–2001; HM Treasury Credit Union Taskforce, 1999–2000. Trustee: NatWest Gp Charitable Trust, 1996–2001; South Square Trust, 2009–. Dir, Prostate Centre, 2004–13; Trustee: Prostate Cancer Charity, 2006–12; Gtr London Fund for the Blind, 2013–14 (Vice Chm., 2014–). Director: Brooklyn Acad. of Music, 1995–96; Corporate Culture, 2006–07. Member: Court, Univ. of Leeds, 2001–; Council, Blind Aid (formerly Metropolitan Soc. for the Blind), 2001–. FRSA 1993. *Recreations:* art, theatre, cinema, jazz, family, walking. *Address:* Clothworkers' Hall, Dunster Court, Mincing Lane, EC3R 7AH. *T:* (020) 7623 7041, *Fax:* (020) 7397 0107. *E:* clerk@clothworkers.co.uk.

BLETHYN, Brenda Anne, OBE 2003; actress; *b* 20 Feb. 1946; *d* of William Charles Bottle and Louisa Kathleen Bottle; partner, 1977, *m* 2011, Michael Mayhew. *Educ:* St Augustine's RC Sch., Ramsgate; Thanet Tech. Coll., Ramsgate; Guildford Sch. of Acting. *Theatre* includes: work with NT, 1975–90, incl. Mysteries, 1979, Double Dealer, 1982, Dalliance, 1987, Beaux' Stratagem, 1989, Bedroom Farce; A Doll's House, 1987, Born Yesterday, 1988, An Ideal Husband, 1992, Royal Exchange, Manchester; Steaming, Comedy, 1981; Benefactors, Vaudeville, 1984; Wildest Dreams, RSC, 1993; The Bed Before Yesterday, Almeida, 1994; Habeas Corpus, Donmar Warehouse, 1996; Absent Friends, NY; Mrs Warren's Profession, Strand, 2002; Haunted, Royal Exchange, Manchester, 2009, 59E59 St Th., NY, 2010, Sydney Opera Hse, 2011; *films* include: The Witches; A River Runs Through It, 1992; Secrets and Lies, 1996; Remember Me, 1996; Music From Another Room, 1997; Girls' Night, In the Winter Dark, 1998; Little Voice, Daddy and Them, 1999; Night Train, Saving Grace, 2000; Anne Frank - The Whole Story, 2001; Lovely and Amazing, 2002; Pumpkin, Yellow Bird, Plots with a View, Blizzard, Sonny, A Way of Life, 2003; Piccadilly Jim, Beyond the Sea, 2004; On a Clear Day, Pride and Prejudice, 2005; Atonement, Clubland, 2007; London River, The Calling, Dead Man Running, 2010; *television* includes: Henry VI Part I, 1981; King Lear, 1983; Chance in a Million (3 series), 1983–85; The Labours of Erica, 1987; The Bullion Boys, 1993; The Buddha of Suburbia, 1993; Sleeping with Mickey, 1993; Outside Edge (3 series), 1994–96; First Signs of Madness (Mona), 1996; Between the Sheets (series), 2003; Belonging, 2004; Mysterious Creatures, 2006; War and Peace, 2007; Vera (5 series), 2011–; King of the Teds, 2012; Mary & Martha, 2013. Hon. DLitt: Kent, 1999; Surrey, 2008. Numerous awards incl. Best Actress Awards for Secrets and Lies: Cannes Film Fest., 1996; Boston Film Critics, 1997; LA Film Critics, 1997; Golden

Globe, 1997; London Film Critics, 1997; BAFTA, 1997. *Publications:* Mixed Fancies (memoir), 2006. *Recreations:* reading, swimming, cryptic crosswords. *Address:* c/o Independent Talent Group Ltd, 40 Whitfield Street, W1T 2RH. *T:* (020) 7636 6565.

BLEWETT, Hon. Neal, AC 1995; DPhil; FRHistS; FASSA; High Commissioner for Australia in the United Kingdom, 1994–98; *b* 24 Oct. 1933; *s* of James and Phyllis Blewett; *m* 1962, Jill Myford (*d* 1988); one *s* one *d*; partner, 1998, Robert John Brain, *s* of Joseph Linley Brain and Dorothy Eleanor Pierce. *Educ:* Launceston High Sch.; Univ. of Tasmania (Dip Ed, MA); Jesus Coll., Oxford (MA; Hon. Fellow, 1998); St Antony's Coll., Oxford (DPhil). FRHistS 1975. Oxford University: Sen. Schol., St Antony's Coll., 1959–61; Lectr, St Edmund Hall, 1961–63; Lectr in Politics, Univ. of Adelaide, 1964–69; Flinders University, S Australia: Reader, 1970–74; Prof., Dept of Pol Theory and Instns, 1974–77. MP (Lab) Bonython, SA, 1977–94; Mem., Jt Hse Cttee on Foreign Affairs and Defence, 1977–80; Deleg. to Australian Constitutional Convention, 1978; Opposition Spokesman on health and Tasmanian affairs, 1980–83; Minister for: Health, 1983–87; Community Services and Health, 1987–90; Trade and Overseas Develt, 1990–91; Social Security, 1991–93. Vis. Prof., Faculty of Medicine, Univ. of Sydney, 1998–2002. Member Council: Univ. of Adelaide, 1972–74; Torrens Coll. of Advanced Educn, 1972–78. Exec. Bd Mem., WHO, 1995–98. Nat. Pres., Australian Inst. of Internat. Affairs, 1998–2005; Pres., Alcohol and other Drugs Council of Australia, 2002–06; Chair, Rev. of Food Labelling Law and Policy, 2010–11. Chm., NSW Film and Television Office, 2006–09. Life Gov., Kirby Inst., Sydney, 2014. Hon. LLD: Tasmania, 1998; ANU, 2003; Hon. DLitt: Hull, 1999; Flinders, 2009; Univ. of Technol., Sydney, 2010. *Publications:* The Peers, the Parties and the People, 1972; (jtly) Playford to Dunstan: the politics of transition, 1971; A Cabinet Diary, 1999. *Recreations:* bush-walking, reading, cinema, gardening. *Address:* 32 Fitzroy Street, Leura, NSW 2780, Australia.

BLEWITT, Major Sir Shane (Gabriel Basil), GCVO 1996 (KCVO 1989; CVO 1987; LVO 1981); Keeper of the Privy Purse and Treasurer to the Queen, 1988–96; an Extra Equerry to the Queen, since 1996; *b* 25 March 1935; *s* of late Col Basil Blewitt; *m* 1969, Julia Morrogh-Bernard, *widow* of Major John Morrogh-Bernard, Irish Guards, and *d* of late Mr Robert Calvert; one *s* one *d* (and one step *s* one step *d*). *Educ:* Ampleforth Coll.; Christ Church, Oxford (MA Hons Mod. Languages). Served Irish Guards, 1956–74 (BAOR, NI, Aden, HK); Antony Gibbs and Sons, 1974; Asst Keeper, 1975–85, Dep. Keeper, 1985–88, of the Privy Purse; Receiver-General, Duchy of Lancaster, 1988–96. Gov., King Edward VII Hosp. Sister Agnes, 1988–2010; Mem. Gen. Council, King's Hosp. Fund, 1988–2010. *Address:* South Corner House, Duncton, Petworth, W Sussex GU28 0LT. *T:* (01798) 342143. *E:* blewittshane@aol.com.

BLIGH, family name of **Earl of Darnley**.

BLIGH, Stephen Ernest; Director and Head of Maritime Services UK, DNV GL Group (formerly Det Norske Veritas), since 2008 (Principal Consultant, 2006–08); *b* 13 May 1953; *s* of George and Doreen Bligh; *m* 1977, Susan Jane Duncan; two *d*. *Educ:* Fullbrook Co. Secondary Sch.; Hull Nautical Coll. Master Mariner 1987. Served at sea with various cos, 1970–85; joined P&O, 1985; Fleet Ops Manager, P&O Containers Ltd, 1989–97; Fleet Marine Manager, P&O NedLloyd, 1997–2003; Chief Exec., Maritime and Coastguard Agency, 2003–06. *Recreations:* Rugby, sailing, flying. *Address:* DNV GL, Palace House, 3 Cathedral Street, SE1 9DE. *E:* stephen.bligh@dnv.com.

BLIGHT, Dr Denis Geoffrey, AO 2004; Executive Director, Crawford Fund, since 2008; *b* 20 Feb. 1945; *s* of Geoffrey Ivan Blight and Bernice Ethel Janet Blight; *m* 1970, Sharon Hill; one *s* one *d*. *Educ:* Univ. of Western Australia (BSC Hons; PhD). Third, then Second Sec., Australian Embassy, Ankara, 1972–73; First Sec., Australian High Commn, Nairobi, 1976–78; First Sec., Australian High Commn, London, 1980–82; Centre Sec., Australian Centre for Internat. Agricultural Res., 1982–84; Asst Dir Gen., AusAID, 1984–86; Dep. Chief Exec., 1986–91, Chief Exec., 1991–2000, IDP Education Australia; Dir Gen., CAB Internat., 2000–05; Chm., LIS Pty Ltd, 2006–10. Advr, India-Australia Grand Challenge Fund, 2010–; Mem., Adv. Cttee, Australia India Strategic Res. Fund, Australian Dept of Industry Innovation, Sci., Res. and Tertiary Educn, 2011–. Member: Commonwealth Scholarship Commn, 2006–09; Commonwealth Round Table (Australia), 2009–; Mem., ACT Br., Royal Commonwealth Soc., 2007–. FRSA. *Publications:* (with Alec Lazenby) Thirty years in International Education and Development: the IDP story, 1999; History of CAB International: 100 years of scientific endeavour, 2011; Doing Well by Doing Good: how Australia benefits from international agricultural research, 2013. *Recreations:* writing, bicycle riding, travelling.

BLISHEN, Anthony Owen, OBE 1968; HM Diplomatic Service, retired; Counsellor, Foreign and Commonwealth Office, 1981–87; *b* 16 April 1932; *s* of Henry Charles Adolphus Blishen, MBE and Joan Cecile Blishen (*née* Blakeney); *m* 1st, 1963, Sarah Anne Joscelyne (marr. diss. 1994); three *s* one *d*; 2nd, 1994, Elizabeth Appleyard (*née* West). *Educ:* Clayesmore Sch., Dorset; SOAS, London Univ. Commnd Royal Hampshire Regt, 1951; Lt 1st Bn: BAOR, 1953; Malaya, 1953–55; Captain, GSO3 HQ 18 Inf. Bde, Malaya, 1955–56; attached HQ Land Forces, Hong Kong (language trng), 1957–59; GSO3 HQ Far East Land Forces, Singapore, 1960–62; FO, 1963–65; First Sec. and Consul, Peking, 1965–67; First Sec., FCO, 1968–70; Chargé d'Affaires (ad interim), Ulan Bator, 1970; Trade Comr (China trade), Hong Kong, 1971–73; First Sec., FCO, 1973–77; First Sec., 1977–78, Counsellor, 1978–81, Tokyo. *Publications:* translations: The Art of Attainment, 2011; The Art of Self Cultivation, 2011; All the Tea in China, 2012; Chinese Jade: the spiritual and cultural significance of jade in China, 2012; Chinese Zen: a path to peace and happiness, 2013; The New Analects: Confucius reconstructed, 2013; The Power of Enlightenment: Chinese Zen poems, 2014; Memory and Oblivion, 2014; No Sail on the Western Sea, 2015; A Journey to Inner Peace and Joy: tracing contemporary Chinese hermits, 2015; contrib. Oxford DNB; contribs to Asian Affairs. *Recreations:* Renaissance music (founded Aragon Consort, 1990), oriental languages. *Address:* 5 Beechrow, Ham Common, Richmond, Surrey TW10 5HE.

BLISS, Prof. Christopher John Emile, PhD; FBA 1988; Nuffield Professor of International Economics, Oxford University, 1992–2007; Fellow of Nuffield College, Oxford, 1977–2007, now Emeritus; *b* 17 Feb. 1940; *s* of John Llewlyn Bliss and Patricia Paula (*née* Dubern); *m* 1983, Ghada (*née* Saqf El Hait); one adopted *s*, and one *s* two *d* by previous marr. *Educ:* Finchley Catholic Grammar Sch.; King's Coll., Cambridge (BA 1962, MA 1964, PhD 1966). Fellow of Christ's Coll., Cambridge, 1965–71; Asst Lectr, 1965–67, and Lectr, 1967–71, Cambridge Univ.; Prof. of Econs, Univ. of Essex, 1971–77; Nuffield Reader in Internat. Econs, Oxford Univ., 1977–92. Dir, General Funds Investment Trust Ltd, 1980–87. Fellow, Econometric Soc., 1978–96. Editor or Asst Editor, Rev. of Econ. Studies, 1967–71; Managing Editor: Oxford Economic Papers, 1989–96; Economic Jl, 1996–2000. *Publications:* Capital Theory and the Distribution of Income, 1975; (with N. H. Stern) Palanpur: the economy of an Indian village, 1982; Economic Theory and Policy for Trading Blocks, 1994; Trade, Growth, and Inequality, 2007; papers and reviews in learned jls. *Recreation:* music. *Address:* Nuffield College, Oxford OX1 1NF. *T:* (01865) 278500.

BLISS, Dr Timothy Vivian Pelham, FRS 1994; Head, Division of Neurophysiology, National Institute for Medical Research, 1988–2006, Visiting Worker, since 2006; *b* 27 July 1940; *s* of Pelham Marryat Bliss and Elizabeth Cotton Bliss (*née* Sproule); *m* 1st, 1975, Virginia Catherine Morton-Evans (*née* O'Rorke); one step *s* two step *d*; one *d* by Katherine Sarah Clough; 2nd, 1994, Isabel Frances Vasseur (*née* Wardrop); two step *s*. *Educ:* Dean Close Sch.; McGill Univ. (BSc 1963; PhD 1967). Mem., scientific staff, MRC, 1967–2006. Vis. Prof., Dept of Physiology, UCL, 1993–. Croonian Lectr, Royal Soc., 2012. Trustee, Sir John Soane Mus., 2005–09. Founder FMedSci 1998. Hon. LLD Dalhousie, 2012; Hon. DSc Herts, 2014. Bristol Myers Squibb Award for Neuroscience, 1991; Feldberg Prize, 1994; British Neurosci. Assoc. Award for outstanding services to British neurosci., 2003; Ipsen Prize for Neural Plasticity, Ipsen Foundn, 2013. *Publications:* (ed jtly) Long-term Potentiation, 2004; The Hippocampus Book, 2006; numerous papers on the neural basis of memory and other aspects of the neurophysiology of the brain. *Recreations:* wine, Shakespeare, church architecture. *Address:* Holman House, 18 Market Place, Aylsham, Norwich NR11 6EH. *T:* (01263) 734216. *E:* tbliss@nimr.mrc.ac.uk. *Club:* Academy.

BLIX, Hans, PhD, LLD; Chairman, Weapons of Mass Destruction Commission, 2004–09; Executive Chairman, UN Monitoring, Verification and Inspection Commission for Iraq, 2000–03; *b* 28 June 1928; *s* of Gunnar Blix and Hertha Blix (*née* Wiberg); *m* 1962, Eva Margareta Kettis; two *s*. *Educ:* Univ. of Uppsala; Columbia Univ.; Univ. of Cambridge (PhD); Stockholm Univ. (LLD). Associate Prof. in International Law, 1960; Ministry of Foreign Affairs, Stockholm: Legal Adviser, 1963–76; Under-Secretary of State, in charge of internat. development co-operation, 1976; Minister for Foreign Affairs, 1978; Under-Secretary of State, in charge of internat. development co-operation, 1979. Dir Gen., IAEA, 1981–97, now Dir Gen. Emeritus. Member: Sweden's delegn to UN General Assembly, 1961–81; Swedish delegn to Conference on Disarmament in Geneva, 1962–78. Hon. doctorates: Moscow State Univ., 1987; Bucharest Univ., 1994; Univ. of Managua, 1996; Vrije Univ. Brussel, 2003; Padova Univ., 2004; Gothenburg Univ., 2004; Cambridge, 2007. Foratom Award, 1994; Fulbright Award, 2014. *Publications:* Treaty Making Power, 1959; Statsmyndigheternas Internationella Förbindelser, 1964; Sovereignty, Aggression and Neutrality, 1970; The Treaty-Maker's Handbook, 1974; Disarming Iraq, 2004; Why Nuclear Disarmament Matters, 2008. *Recreation:* antique rugs.

BLIZZARD, Robert John; parliamentary researcher, since 2011; *b* 31 May 1950; *s* of late Arthur Blizzard and Joan Blizzard; one *s* one *d*. *Educ:* Univ. of Birmingham (BA Hons 1971). Head of English: Crayford Sch., Bexley, 1976–86; Lynn Grove High Sch., Gorleston, 1986–97. Mem. (Lab), Waveney DC, 1987–97 (Leader, 1991–97). MP (Lab) Waveney, 1997–2010; contested (Lab) same seat, 2010, 2015. PPS to Minister of State, MAFF, 1999–2001, to Minister of State for Work, DWP, 2001–03, to Minister of State for Europe, FCO, 2005–06, to Sec. of State for Transport, 2006–07; an Asst Govt Whip, 2007–08; a Lord Comr of HM Treasury (Govt Whip), 2008–10. Mem., Envmtl Audit Select Cttee, 1997–99; Chairman: British-Brazilian All Pty Gp, 1997–2007; British Offshore Oil and Gas Industry All Pty Gp, 1999–2007; British-Latin America All Pty Gp, 2004–07; British-Chile All Pty Gp, 2005–07; Sec., Jazz Appreciation All Pty Gp, 2004–07. Prospective Parly Cand. (Lab) for Waveney, 2011–. Chm., Jazz Services Ltd, 2010–13. Gov., Lowestoft Coll., 2010–14. *Recreations:* walking, ski-ing, travel, listening to jazz, watching Lowestoft Town FC. *E:* bob@waveney.co.

BLOBEL, Prof. Günter, MD, PhD; John D. Rockefeller Jr Professor, since 1992, and Head of Laboratory of Cell Biology, since 1976, Rockefeller University, New York; Investigator, Howard Hughes Medical Institute, since 1986; *b* Waltersdorf, Germany (now Poland); US citizen 1982; *m* 1978, Laura Maioglio. *Educ:* Univ. of Tübingen (MD 1960); Univ. of Wisconsin (PhD 1967). Intern, German hosps, 1960–62; Laboratory of Cell Biology, Rockefeller University, New York: Fellow, 1967–69; Asst Prof., 1969–73; Associate Prof., 1973–76; Prof., 1976–92. Member: US Nat. Acad. of Scis, 1983; Amer. Acad. of Arts and Scis. Founder and Pres. Bd of Dirs, Friends of Dresden Inc. Nobel Prize for Physiology or Medicine, 1999. *Publications:* contribs to books and jls. *Address:* Laboratory of Cell Biology, Rockefeller University, 1230 York Avenue, New York, NY 10021–6399, USA; Apt 10D, 1100 Park Avenue, New York, NY 10128, USA.

BLOCH, Lady Camilla; *see* Bingham, Lady C.

BLOCH, Prof. Maurice Émile Félix, PhD; FBA 1990; Professor of Anthropology, University of London at London School of Economics, 1984–2005, now Emeritus; *b* 21 Oct. 1939; *s* of late Pierre Bloch and of Claude Kennedy; step *s* of John Stodart Kennedy, FRS; *m*; one *s* one *d*. *Educ:* Lycée Carnot, Paris; Perse Sch., Cambridge; LSE (BA 1962); Fitzwilliam Coll., Cambridge (PhD 1968). Asst Lectr, Univ. of Wales, Swansea, 1968; Lectr, LSE, 1969; Reader, London Univ., 1977. Prof., Collège de France, 2005–06. Corresp. Mem., Académie Malgache, Madagascar, 1965. *Publications:* Placing the Dead, 1971; Marxism and Anthropology, 1983; From Blessing to Violence, 1986; Ritual, History and Power, 1989; Prey into Hunter, 1992; How We Think They Think, 1998. *Recreation:* book binding. *Address:* Department of Anthropology, London School of Economics, Houghton Street, WC2A 2AE.

BLOCH, Dame Merle Florence; *see* Park, Dame M. F.

BLOCH, Michael Gordon; QC 1998; *b* 18 Oct. 1951; *s* of John and Thelma Bloch; *m* Caroline Williams (marr. diss.); two *d*; *m* 1998, Lady Camilla Bingham, *qv*; four *s*. *Educ:* Bedales Sch.; Corpus Christi Coll., Cambridge (MA); UEA (MPhil). Called to the Bar, Lincoln's Inn, 1979; in practice as a barrister, 1979–. Trustee, ChildLine. *Recreations:* squash, cinema. *Address:* Blackstone Chambers, Blackstone House, Temple, EC4Y 9BW. *Club:* Royal Automobile.

BLOCH, Selwyn Irving; QC 2000; *b* 23 Feb. 1952; *s* of Rev. Cecil Maurice Bloch and Esther Bloch; *m* 1983, Brenda Igra; three *d*. *Educ:* Potchefstroom Boys' High Sch.; Witwatersrand Univ. (BA); Stellenbosch Univ. (LLB). Attorney, S Africa, 1977–; called to the Bar, Middle Temple, 1982; in practice at the Bar, 1983–. *Publications:* (jtly) Employment Covenants and Confidential Information, 1993, 3rd edn 2009. *Recreations:* listening to music, walking, reading, theatre. *Address:* Littleton Chambers, 3 King's Bench Walk North, EC4Y 7HR. *T:* (020) 7797 8699.

BLOCK, David Greenberg, AC 1988 (AO 1983); *b* 21 March 1936; *s* of Emanuel Block and Hannah Greenberg; *m* 1959, Naomi Denfield; one *s* three *d*. *Educ:* King Edward VII Sch., Johannesburg; Univ. of Witwatersrand (BJuris cum laude). Joined Schroder-Darling & Co., 1964, Dir, 1967–72; Chairman: David Block & Associates, 1972–81; Trinity Properties, 1984–90; George Ward Group, 1986–89; Dep. Chm., Concrete Constructions, 1990; Director: CSR, 1977–88; Kalamazoo Holdings, 1986–94; Dep. Chm., Pacific Magazines & Publishing, 1991–95; Dir, Lloyds Bank NZA, Chm., Lloyds Internat., Dir, Lloyds Merchant Bank (UK) and Adviser, Lloyds Merchant Bank Holdings, 1981–86; Consultant, Coudert Brothers, 1986–91; Adviser: Coopers & Lybrand, 1986–93; S. G. Warburg Group, 1987–95. Consultant: to Prime Minister and Cabinet, 1986–89; to govts, cos and instns, 1986–96; to Premier's Dept, NSW, 1987–88; Mem., Cttee of Enquiry into inflation and taxation, 1975; Chm., Efficiency Scrutiny Unit and Admin. Reform Unit, 1986–88. Comr, Aust. Film Commn, 1978–81; Chm., Sydney Opera House Trust, 1981–89; Trustee, Japanese Friends of Sydney Opera House Foundn, 1992–96; Councillor: Asia-Australian Inst., 1991–96; Nat. Heart Foundn, 1994–96; Gov., Aust. Nat. Gall. Foundn, 1992–96. Dir, Univ. of NSW Foundn, 1989–96. Fellow, Senate of Univ. of Sydney, 1983–87. FAICD; FAIM; FSIA. Hon. LLD New South Wales, 1992. *Recreations:* swimming, squash, music, theatre. *Address:* 30 Clarke Street, Vaucluse, NSW 2030, Australia. *T:* (2) 93376211. *Club:* University (Sydney).

BLOCK, Neil Selwyn; QC 2002; *b* 24 May 1957; *s* of Ronald Sydney Block and Barbara Block; *m* 1988, Amanda Jane Hatton; four *s*. *Educ:* E Barnet Grammar Sch.; City of London Poly. (BA Hons Law); Exeter Univ. (LLM); Inns of Court Sch. of Law. Called to the Bar, Gray's Inn, 1980, Bencher, 2008; in practice, specialising in law of professional negligence (incl. clinical negligence), personal injury, product liability, material loss claims, insurance related disputes and contract/commercial litigation; Hd of Chambers, 2013–. Accredited mediator, 2006. *Recreations:* tennis, golf, family, friends. *Address:* Naphill House, Naphill, Bucks HP14 4RL; (chambers) 39 Essex Street, WC2R 3AT.

BLOCK, Simon Jonathan; Honorary Secretary, Commonwealth Boxing Council, since 1980; General Secretary, British Boxing Board of Control, 2000–08; *b* 13 Feb. 1950; *s* of Michael Abraham Hyman Block and Winifred Joy Block (*née* Harris); *m* 1998, Annette Mary Clements (*née* Dunphy); one *s*, and one step *d. Educ:* Sunbury Grammar Sch.; East Grinstead Grammar Sch.; Crawley Coll. of Further Educn. Boxed, Crawley Amateur Boxing Club, 1965–68; British Boxing Board of Control: joined, 1979; Sec., S Area Council, 1981–96; Asst Gen. Sec., 1986–99. Company Sec., European Boxing Union, 2000–07; Mem. Bd Governors, World Boxing Council, 2000–03 and 2007–09. Vice President: Kent and Sussex Ex-Boxers' Assoc.; Hastings Ex-Boxers' Assoc.; Lynn Athletic Club; Hon. Mem., London Ex-Boxers' Assoc.; Member: St George's Day Club; Soc. of Friends of Ashdown Forest. *Recreations:* walking, running (London Marathon, 1987, 1995), horse riding, songwriting (record 'He's the Guy' released 1975). *Address:* 22 Bis, Rue du Charme, Ricarville du Val, Normandie 76510, France. *T:* (9) 61052534. *E:* sblock@commboxing.com.

BLOEMBERGEN, Prof. Nicolaas; Gerhard Gade University Professor, Harvard University, 1980–90, now Emeritus; *b* 11 March 1920; *m* 1950, Huberta Deliana Brink; one *s* two *d. Educ:* Univ. of Utrecht (BA, MA); Univ. of Leiden (PhD). Research Associate, Leiden, 1947–48; Harvard University: Associate Prof., 1951; Gordon McKay Prof. of Applied Physics, 1957; Rumford Prof. of Physics, 1974. Hon. Prof. of Optical Scis, Univ. of Arizona, 2001–. Hon. DSc: Laval Univ., 1987; Connecticut Univ., 1988; Univ. of Hartford, 1990; Univ. of Massachusetts at Lowell, 1994; Moscow State Univ., 1997; N Carolina State Univ., 1998; Harvard Univ., 2000. Stuart Ballantine Medal, Franklin Inst., 1961; Nat. Medal of Science, 1974; Lorentz Medal, Royal Dutch Acad. of Science, 1978; Alexander von Humboldt Senior US Scientist Award, Munich, 1980; (jtly) Nobel Prize in Physics, 1981; IEEE Medal of Honor, 1983; Dirac Medal, Univ. of NSW, 1983; Byvoet Medal, Univ. of Utrecht, 2001. Commander, Order of Orange Nassau (Netherlands), 1983. *Publications:* Nuclear Magnetic Relaxation, 1948 (New York 1961); Nonlinear Optics, 1965, reprinted 1996; Encounters in Magnetic Resonance, 1996; Encounters in Nonlinear Optics, 1996; over 370 papers in scientific jls. *Address:* College of Optical Sciences, University of Arizona, PO Box 210094, Tucson, AZ 85721–0094, USA. *T:* (520) 6263479. *E:* nbloembergen@optics.arizona.edu.

BLOFELD, Sir John (Christopher Calthorpe), Kt 1991; DL; a Judge of the High Court of Justice, Queen's Bench Division, 1990–2001; *b* 11 July 1932; *s* of late T. R. C. Blofeld, CBE; *m* 1961, Judith Anne (*d* 2013), *er d* of Alan Mohun and Mrs James Mitchell; two *s* one *d. Educ:* Eton; King's Coll., Cambridge. Called to Bar, Lincoln's Inn, 1956, Bencher, 1990; QC 1975; a Recorder of the Crown Court, 1975–82; a Circuit Judge, 1982–90; Presiding Judge, SE Circuit, 1993–96. Inspector, Dept of Trade, 1979–81. Chancellor: Dio. St Edmundsbury and Ipswich, 1973–2009; Dio. of Norwich, 1998–2007. DL Norfolk, 1991. *Recreations:* watching test cricket, gardening.

BLOHM, Helen; *see* Mifflin, H.

BLOHM, Leslie Adrian; QC 2006; a Recorder, since 2003; a Deputy High Court Judge, since 2008; *b* 27 Feb. 1959; *s* of Albert Blohm and Ann Blohm; *m* 1986, Helen Mifflin, *qv*; two *d. Educ:* Christ's Hospital, Horsham; Keble Coll., Oxford (MA 1981). Called to the Bar, Lincoln's Inn, 1982 (Hardwicke and Jenkins Scholar, 1982), Bencher, 2013; barrister, St John's Chambers, Bristol, 1984–; in practice, specialising in Chancery, esp. Real Property law. *Recreations:* cycling, chess, restoring British motor cars of the sixties. *Address:* St John's Chambers, 101 Victoria Street, Bristol BS1 6PU. *T:* (0117) 921 3456, *Fax:* (0117) 921 4821. *E:* leslie.blohm@stjohnschambers.co.uk.

BLOIS, Sir Charles (Nicholas Gervase), 11th Bt *cr* 1686; farming since 1965; *b* 25 Dec. 1939; *s* of Sir Gervase Ralph Edmund Blois, 10th Bt and Mrs Audrey Winifred Blois (*née* Johnson) (*d* 1997); *S* father, 1968; *m* 1967, Celia Helen Mary Pritchett (marr. diss. 2004); one *s* one *d. Educ:* Harrow; Trinity Coll., Dublin; Royal Agricultural Coll., Cirencester. Australia, 1963–65. FRGS 1992. *Recreations:* motor cycle adventure travel, RIB cruising. *Heir: s* Andrew Charles David Blois [*b* 7 Feb. 1971; *m* 2002, Judith, *d* of John Hardy]. *Address:* Red House Farm, Westleton, Saxmundham, Suffolk IP17 3EQ. *Clubs:* Cruising Association; Ocean Cruising.

BLOKH, Alexandre, PhD, (pen-name **Jean Blot**); writer, since 1956; Vice President, PEN Club, since 1998 (International Secretary, 1982–98); *b* Moscow, 31 March 1923; *s* of Arnold Blokh, man of letters, and Anne (*née* Berlinrote); *m* 1956, Nadia Ermolaiev. *Educ:* Bromsgrove Public Sch., Worcester; Univ. of Paris (PhD Law, PhD Letters). International Civil Servant, United Nations, 1947–62: New York, until 1956; Geneva, 1956–62; Director, Arts and Letters, UNESCO, Paris, 1962–81. Critic, arts and letters, in reviews: Arche, Preuves, NRF. Prix des Critiques, 1972; Prix Valéry Larbaud, 1977; Prix Cazes, 1982; Grand Prix de la Critique, 1986; Prix International de la Paix, 1990. Citizen of Honour, City of St Petersburg. Officier, Ordre des Arts et des Lettres (France), 1997; Bogwan Order of Cultural Merit (Korea). *Publications: novels:* Le Soleil de Cavouri, 1956; Les Enfants de New York, 1959; Obscur Ennemi, 1961; Les Illusions Nocturnes, 1964; La Jeune Géante, 1969; La Difficulté d'aimer, 1971; Les Cosmopolites, 1976; Gris du Ciel, 1981; Tout l'été, 1985; Sainte Imposture, 1988; Le Juif Margolin, 1998; Roses d'Amérique, 2003; Une vie à deux, 2007; *essays:* Marguerite Yourcenar; Ossip Mandelstam; Là où tu iras; Sporade; Ivan Gontcharov; La Montagne Sainte; Albert Cohen; Si loin de Dieu et autres voyages; Bloomsbury; Retour en Asie; Vladimir Nabokov; Moïse, notre contemporain; Le Soleil se couche à l'Est, 2005; Alexandre Blok: poète de la perspective Nevski, 2007; Mozart, 2008; Le roman poésie de la prose, 2010; Affaire de coeur, 2012; À Saint-Pétersbourg, nous nous retrouverons, 2013; Le rendez-vous de la Marquise, 2014. *Address:* 34 Square Montsouris, 75014 Paris, France. *T:* (1) 45893416.

BLOM-COOPER, Sir Louis (Jacques), Kt 1992; QC 1970; Independent Commissioner for the Holding Centres, Northern Ireland, 1993–2000; a Judge of the Courts of Appeal, Jersey and Guernsey, 1989–96; *b* 27 March 1926; *s* of Alfred Blom-Cooper and Ella Flesseman, Rotterdam; *m* 1952 (marr. diss. 1970); two *s* one *d*; *m* 1970, Jane Elizabeth (*d* 2006), *e d* of Maurice and Helen Smither, Woodbridge, Suffolk; one *s* two *d. Educ:* Port Regis Prep. Sch.; Seaford Coll.; King's Coll., London (FKC 1994); Municipal Univ. of Amsterdam; Fitzwilliam Coll., Cambridge. LLB London, 1952; Dr Juris Amsterdam, 1954. HM Army, 1944–47: Capt., E Yorks Regt. Called to Bar, Middle Temple, 1952, Bencher, 1978, Reader, 1998. Mem., Home Secretary's Adv. Council on the Penal System, 1966–78. Chairman: Panel of Inquiry into circumstances surrounding the death of Jasmine Beckford, 1985; Cttee of Inquiry into complaints about Ashworth Hosp., 1991–92; Commissioner of Inquiry: into allegations of arson and political corruption in the Turks and Caicos Is, 1986 (report published, 1986); into the N Creek Develt Project, Turks and Caicos Is, 1986–87. Chairman: Ind. Cttee for the Supervision of Standards of Telephone Information Services, 1986–93; Mental Health Act Commn, 1987–94; Commn on the future of Occupational Therapy, 1988–89; Press Council, 1989–90; Review of Mental Health Services in S Devon, 1994; Georgina Robinson Inquiry Cttee, 1994; Jason Mitchell Inquiry Panel, 1996. Vice-Pres., Howard League for Penal Reform, 1984– (Chm., 1973–84); Mem., Prison Reform Trust, 1982–2003; Chm., Expert Witness Inst., 1998–2004. Chm., BBC London Local Radio Adv. Council, 1970–73. Jt Dir, Legal Res. Unit, Bedford Coll., Univ. of London, 1967–82; Vis. Prof., QMC, London Univ., 1983–88. Trustee, Scott Trust (The Guardian Newspaper), 1982–88. Joint Editor, Common Market Law Reports. JP Inner London, 1966–79 (transf. City of London, 1969). FRSA 1984. Hon. DLitt: Loughborough, 1991; Ulster, 1994; UEA, 1998. *Publications:* Bankruptcy in Private International Law, 1954; The Law as Literature, 1962; The A6 Murder (A Semblance of Truth), 1963; (with T. P. Morris) A Calendar of Murder, 1964; Language of the Law, 1965; (with O. R. McGregor and Colin Gibson) Separated Spouses, 1970; (with G. Drewry) Final Appeal: a study of the House of Lords in its judicial capacity, 1972; (ed) Progress in Penal Reform, 1975; (ed with G. Drewry) Law and Morality, 1976; The Birmingham Six and Other Cases, 1997; (with T. P. Morris) With Malice Aforethought, 2004; (ed jtly) The Judicial House of Lords 1876–2009, 2009; Fine Lines and Distinctions, 2011; Power of Persuasion: essays from a very public lawyer, 2015; contrib. to Modern Law Review, Criminal Law Review, Public Law, Brit. Jl of Criminology, Brit. Jl of Sociology. *Recreations:* watching and reporting on Association football, reading, music, writing, broadcasting. *Address:* 1 Bayes House, Augustas Lane, N1 1QT. *T:* (020) 7607 3127; Southminster Hall, Southminster, Essex CM0 7EH. *T:* (01621) 772416. *E:* louisblomcooper@gmail.com. *Clubs:* Athenæum, MCC.

See also D. C. Tierney.

BLOMEFIELD, Sir (Thomas) Charles (Peregrine), 6th Bt *cr* 1807; fine art and philatelic consultant; *b* 24 July 1948; *s* of Sir Thomas Edward Peregrine Blomefield, 5th Bt, and of Ginette, Lady Blomefield; *S* father, 1984; *m* 1975, Georgina Geraldine, *d* of late Commander C. E. Over, Lugger End, Portscatho, Cornwall; one *s* two *d. Educ:* Wellington Coll., Berks; Mansfield Coll., Oxford. Christie's, 1970–75; Wildenstein and Co., 1975–76; Director: Lidchi Art Gallery, Johannesburg, 1976–78; Direct Import Ltd, 1985–2012; Man. Dir, Charles Blomefield and Co., 1980–. *Heir: s* Thomas William Peregrine Blomefield, *b* 16 July 1983. *Address:* 42 Simpson Street, SW11 3HW.

BLOMFIELD, Paul; MP (Lab) Sheffield Central, since 2010; *b* Chatham, Kent, 25 Aug. 1953; *s* of Henry and Mabel Blomfield; *m* 2000, Linda McAvan, *qv*; one *s* by a previous marriage. *Educ:* Abbeydale Boys' Grammar Sch.; Tadcaster Grammar Sch.; St John's Coll., York (Cert Ed). Mem., NEC and Vice-Pres., NUS, 1976–78. Various roles, Sheffield Univ., 1978–2003; Gen. Manager, Sheffield Univ. Students' Union, 2003–10. Mem. Bd, Sheffield City Trust, 1994–2008 (Chair, 1997–2008). Gov., Sheffield City Poly., 1982–92. Chm., Sheffield Lab Party, 1993–2008. Mem., Exec. Cttee, Anti-Apartheid Movement, 1978–94. *Recreations:* walking, cycling, watching Sheffield United. *Address:* House of Commons, SW1A 0AA. *E:* paul.blomfield.mp@parliament.uk; Unit 4, Edmund Road Business Centre, 135 Edmund Road, Sheffield S2 4ED. *T:* (0114) 272 2882, *Fax:* (0114) 272 2442.

BLONDEL, Prof. Jean Fernand Pierre; Professor of Political Science, European University Institute, Florence, 1985–94; *b* Toulon, France, 26 Oct. 1929; *s* of Fernand Blondel and Marie Blondel (*née* Santelli); *m* 1st, 1954, Michèle (*née* Hadet) (marr. diss. 1979); two *d*; 2nd, 1982, Mrs Theresa Martineau. *Educ:* Collège Saint Louis de Gonzague and Lycée Henri IV, Paris; Institut d'Etudes Politiques and Faculté de Droit, Paris; St Antony's Coll., Oxford. Asst Lectr, then Lectr in Govt, Univ. of Keele, 1958–63; Vis. ACLS Fellow, Yale Univ., 1963–64; Prof. of Government, 1964–84, and Dean, Sch. of Comparative Studies, 1967–69, Univ. of Essex. Visiting Professor: Carleton Univ., Canada, 1969–70; Univ. of Siena, 1995–; Vis. Schol., Russell Sage Foundn, NY, 1984–85. Exec. Dir, European Consortium for Political Res., 1970–79. Member: Royal Swedish Acad. of Scis, 1990; Academia Europaea, 1993; Amer. Acad. of Scis, 2005. Hon. DLitt Salford, 1990; Dr *hc* Essex, 1992; Univ. Catholique de Louvain, 1992; Turku, 1995; Macerata, 2007; Siena, 2008. Johan Skytte Prize, Johan Skytte Foundn, 2004. *Publications:* Voters, Parties and Leaders, 1963; (jtly) Constituency Politics, 1964; (jtly) Public Administration in France, 1965; An Introduction to Comparative Government, 1969; (jtly) Workbook for Comparative Government, 1972; Comparing Political Systems, 1972; Comparative Legislatures, 1973; The Government of France, 1974; Thinking Politically, 1976; Political Parties, 1978; World Leaders, 1980; The Discipline of Politics, 1981; The Organisation of Governments, 1982; (jtly) Comparative Politics, 1984; Government Ministers in the Contemporary World, 1985; Political Leadership, 1987; (ed jtly) Western European Cabinets, 1988; Comparative Government, 1990, 2nd edn 1995; (ed jtly) The Profession of Cabinet Minister in Western Europe, 1991; (ed jtly) Governing Together, 1993; (ed jtly) Party and Government, 1996; (jtly) People and Parliament in the European Union, 1998; (ed jtly) Democracy, Governance and Economic Performance, 1999; (ed jtly) The Nature of Party Government, 2000; (jtly) Cabinets in Eastern Europe, 2001; (jtly) Political Cultures, 2006; (jtly) Governing New Democracies, 2007; (jtly) Citizens and the State, 2007; (jtly) Personalisation of Leadership, Parties and Citizens, 2010; (jtly) Political Parties and Democracy, 2012; articles in: Political Studies, Parliamentary Affairs, Public Administration, Revue Française de Science Politique, European Jl of Political Research, etc. *Recreation:* holidays in Provence. *Address:* 3 Thornhill Bridge Wharf, Caledonian Road, N1 0RU; 10 Piazza Pitti, 50125 Florence, Italy.

BLOOD, Baroness *cr* 1999 (Life Peer), of Blackwatertown in the county of Armagh; **May Blood,** MBE 1995; Information Officer, Great Shankhill Partnership Co. Ltd, since 1994; Founding Member, Northern Ireland Women's Coalition, since 1996; *b* 26 May 1938; *d* of William and Mary Blood. *Educ:* Donegall Road Primary Sch.; Linfield Secondary Sch. Cutter/Supervisor, Blackstaff Linen Mill Co. Ltd, 1952–90; Manager, Cairn Martin Wood Products, 1991–94. DUniv: Ulster, 1998; QUB, 2000; Open, 2001. *Recreations:* home decorating, reading, gardening. *Address:* 7 Black Mountain Place, Belfast BT13 3TT. *T:* (028) 9032 6514.

BLOOM, Adrian Jonathan Richard, VMH; Chairman, Blooms Nurseries Ltd, since 2003; *b* Oakington, Cambridge, 22 May 1940; *s* of Alan Bloom, MBE and Doris Bloom; *m* 1966, Rosemary Vaughan; three *s. Educ:* Diss Grammar Sch. Jt Man. Dir, 1970–90, Man. Dir, 1995–2003, Blooms Nurseries Ltd; Jt Man. Dir, 1984–90, Chm., 1990–99, Blooms of Bressingham plc. Owner, Foggy Bottom garden, Bressingham. VMH 1985. *Publications:* Conifers for your Garden, 1972; A Year Round Garden, 1979; Blooms of Bressingham Garden Plants, 1992; Winter Garden Glory, 1993; Summer Garden Glory, 1996; Gardening with Conifers, 2001; Blooms Best Perennials and Grasses, 2010. *Recreations:* gardening, walking, ski-ing, travelling, cinema. *Address:* Foggy Bottom, Bressingham, Diss, Norfolk IP22 2AA.

BLOOM, Anthony Herbert; Chairman, Cineworld (formerly CINE-UK Ltd), since 1995; *b* 15 Feb. 1939; *s* of Joseph Bloom and Margaret Roslyn Bloom; *m* 1973, Gisela von Mellenthin; two *s* two *d. Educ:* Univ. of Witwatersrand (BCom, LLB); Harvard Law Sch. (LLM); Stanford Graduate Sch. of Business (Sloan Fellow, 1970). Hayman Godfrey and Sanderson, S Africa, 1960–64; joined Premier Gp Ltd, S Africa, 1966, Dir, 1969; Dep. Chm., 1975–79, Chm., 1979–88; Director: Barclays Nat. Bank, later First Nat. Bank of Southern Africa Ltd, 1980–88; Liberty Life Assoc., 1982–88; South African Breweries Ltd, 1983–89; CNA Gallo Ltd, 1983–88; RIT Capital Partners plc, 1988–97; Dir and Dep. Chm., Sketchley, 1990–95; Director: Rio Narcea Gold Mines Ltd, 1995–2007; Orthoworld plc, 1999–2007. Director: Ballet Rambert, 1995–2001; LSO, 2008–; Mem., British Library Bd, 1995–2000. Hon. LLD Witwatersrand, 2002. *Recreations:* opera, ballet, theatre, music. *Address:* 8 Hanover Terrace, NW1 4RJ. *T:* (020) 7723 3422.

BLOOM, His Honour Charles; QC 1987; a Circuit Judge, 1997–2012; *b* 6 Nov. 1940; *s* of Abraham Barnett Bloom and Freda Bloom (*née* Craft); *m* 1967, Janice Rachelle Goldberg; one *s* one *d. Educ:* Manchester Central Grammar School; Manchester University. LLB Hons 1962. Called to the Bar, Gray's Inn, 1963; practised on Northern Circuit, 1963–97; a Recorder, 1983–97; a Dep. High Ct Judge, Family Div., 1990–2012. Chm., Medical Appeal Tribunals,

1979–97. Tutor Judge, Judicial Coll., 2004–11. Member: Larner Vinifloral Soc., 1996–; Rhodes Sabbatical Debating Soc., 2007–. *Recreations:* tennis, creative writing, reading. *Club:* Friedland Postmusaf Tennis (Cheadle).

BLOOM, Claire, CBE 2013; *b* London, 15 Feb. 1931; *d* of late Edward Bloom and Elizabeth Bloom; *m* 1st, 1959, Rod Steiger (marr. diss. 1969; he *d* 2002); one *d*; 2nd, 1969; 3rd, 1990, Philip Roth (marr. diss. 1995). *Educ:* schs in UK and USA. First work in England, BBC, 1946. Stratford: Ophelia, Lady Blanche (King John), Perdita, 1948; The Damask Cheek, Lyric, Hammersmith, 1949; The Lady's Not For Burning, Globe, 1949; Ring Round the Moon, Globe, 1949–50. Old Vic: 1952–53: Romeo and Juliet; 1953: Merchant of Venice; 1954: Hamlet, All's Well, Coriolanus, Twelfth Night, Tempest; 1956: Romeo and Juliet (London, and N American tour). Cordelia, in Stratford Festival Company, 1955 (London, provinces and continental tour); Duel of Angels, Apollo, 1958; Rashomon, NY, 1959; Altona, Royal Court, 1961; The Trojan Women, Spoleto Festival, 1963; Ivanov, Phoenix, 1965; A Doll's House, NY, 1971; Hedda Gabler, 1971; Vivat! Vivat Regina!, NY, 1971; A Doll's House, Criterion, 1973 (filmed 1973); A Streetcar Named Desire, Piccadilly, 1974; Rosmersholm, Haymarket, 1977; The Cherry Orchard, Chichester Fest., 1981, Cambridge, Mass, 1994; When We Dead Waken, Almeida, 1990; A Long Day's Journey into Night, ART, Cambridge, Mass, 1996; Electra, McCarter Th., Princeton, NJ, 1998, transf. NY, 1999; Conversations After a Burial, Almeida, 2000; A Little Night Music, Seattle, 2001, NY, 2003; Whistling Psyche, Almeida, 2004; Six Dance Lessons in Six Weeks, Haymarket, 2006. One-woman performances: These Are Women, 1981– (US tour, 1981–82); Enter the Actress, 1998–. First film, Blind Goddess, 1947; *films include:* Limelight; The Man Between; Richard III; Alexander the Great; The Brothers Karamazov; The Buccaneers; Look Back in Anger; Three Moves to Freedom; The Brothers Grimm; The Chapman Report; The Haunting; 80,000 Suspects; Alta Infedelta; Il Maestro di Vigevano; The Outrage; The Spy Who Came in From The Cold; Charly; Three into Two won't go; A Severed Head; Red Sky at Morning; Islands In The Stream; The Clash of the Titans, 1979; Always, 1984; Sammy and Rosie Get Laid, 1987; Crimes and Misdemeanors, 1989; Daylight, 1997; The Book of Eve, 2001; Imagining Argentina, 2002; Daniel and the Superdogs, 2003; The King's Speech, 2011; Max Rose, 2013. *Television:* first appearance on television programmes, 1952, since when she has had frequent successes on TV in the US: In Praise of Love, 1975; Anastasia, 1986; Queenie, 1986; BBC: A Legacy, 1975; The Ghost Writer, 1983; Shadowlands, 1985 (BAFTA award Best TV Actress); Time and the Conways, 1985; Oedipus the King, 1986; What the Deaf Man Heard, 1997; Doctor Who, 2009; BBC Shakespeare: Katharine in Henry VIII, 1979; Gertrude in Hamlet, 1980; the Queen in Cymbeline, Lady Constance in King John, 1983; ITV: series: Brideshead Revisited, 1981; Intimate Contact, 1987; Shadow on the Sun, 1988; play, The Belle of Amherst, 1986; Channel Four: series, The Camomile Lawn, 1992; The Mirror Crack'd, 1992; Remember, 1993; A Village Affair, 1994; Family Money, 1996; series, Imogen's Face, 1998; The Lady in Question, 1999; Law and Order, 2003; Doc Martin, 2005 and 2013. Many appearances as narrator in both contemporary and classic repertoire. Distinguished Vis. Prof., Hunter Coll., NY, 1989. *Publications:* Limelight and After (autobiog.), 1982; Leaving a Doll's House (autobiog.), 1996. *Recreations:* opera, music. *Address:* c/o Conway van Gelder Grant, Third Floor, 8/12 Broadwick Street, W1F 8HW.

BLOOM, Godfrey, TD and bar 1988; Member for Yorkshire and North Lincolnshire, European Parliament, 2004–14 (UK Ind, 2004–13; Ind, 2013–14); *b* 22 Nov. 1949; *s* of Alan Bloom and Phylis Bloom; *m* 1986, Katryna Skowronek. *Educ:* St Olave's Sch.; Royal Military Acad. Sandhurst; Royal Coll. of Defence Studies. Fund Manager, Mercury Asset Mgt, 1988–93; Econ. Res. Dir, TBO Gp of Cos, 1993–2004. European Parliament: Member: Women and Gender Equality Cttee, 2004–14; Econ. and Monetary Affairs Cttee, 2009–14; Reserve Mem., Envmt Cttee, 2009–14. Econ. Advr, Educational Research Associates, 2008–. Member: Campaign against Political Correctness, 2005–; Surtees Soc., 2012–; British Charolais Cattle Soc. Life Mem., War Memls Trust, 2001. Associate Mem., RCDS, 2011. Hon. Life Mem., Cambridge Univ. Women's RFC, 2003. Patron: Drivers' Union, 2013–; Victoria Cross Trust, 2013–. Micropal Award for Fund Mgt, 1992. Graduate, 2005, Postgraduate, 2009, Armed Forces Parly Scheme. Resident Author, Libertarian Alliance. *Publications:* Beyond the Fridge, 2007; War Aims and the Economic Consequences for the UK, 2010; Billy Nomates: or what he really said, 2013; Guinea a Minute, 2013; A Dinosaur's Guide to Libertarianism, 2014; contribs to Financial Times pubns and Army Review. *Recreations:* hunting and shooting, cricket, military history, fell walking. *E:* gbloom@outlook.com. *Clubs:* East India, Royal Over-Seas League, New Frontier; Bentley Drivers, MG Owners'; Royal Cornish (Hawkedon); Diogenes, Pocklington Rugby; Horsehouse Formals Cricket (Londesborough Park); Brocklesbury Tumblers (Brocklesbury Hunt, N Lincs); Gadflys (Strasbourg).

BLOOM, Louise Anne Harris; Member: (Lib Dem) Eastleigh Borough Council, since 2002 (Cabinet Member for Environment and Sustainability, since 2002); Liberal Democrat Federal Policy Committee, 2011–15; Assistant Director, Options Wellbeing Trust, Southampton, since 2013; *b* 7 April 1964; *d* of Christopher George Harris and Patricia Rose Harris (*née* Fray, now Cherrill); *m* 1987, Charles Neil Bloom (marr. diss.); two *d*. *Educ:* Kingston Poly. (BA Hons Applied Soc. Sci. 1985). Worked for various advertising agencies, 1985–90; freelance orgn mgt of press and publicity events, 1991–97; res. and admin assistant to Lib Dem councillors, Royal Bor. of Kingston upon Thames, 1991–93; Asst to Co-ordinator of Ind. Living Scheme, Kingston Assoc. of Disabled People, 1997; Inf. and Volunteer Develt Officer, Richmond Advice and Inf. on Disability, 1998–2000; Advocacy Service Manager (formerly Advocacy Project Manager), Solent Mind, Southampton, 2002–13. Mem. (Lib Dem), London Assembly, GLA, 2000–02; Vice Chair: SE England Regl Assembly, 2006–10 (Exec. Mem., 2002–10); SE England Councils, 2010–11. Mem., Standards Bd for England, 2004–06. *Recreations:* theatre, music, reading, travelling, history. *Address:* 25 Mescott Meadows, Hedge End, Southampton SO30 2JT.

BLOOM, Margaret Janet, (Lady Bloom), CBE 2003; Visiting Professor, Dickson Poon School of Law (formerly School of Law), King's College London, since 2003; Senior Consultant, Freshfields Bruckhaus Deringer, since 2003; *b* 28 July 1943; *d* of John Sturrock and Jean Elizabeth Sturrock (*née* Ranken); *m* 1965, Stephen Robert Bloom (*see* Prof. Sir S. R. Bloom); two *s* two *d*. *Educ:* Sherborne Sch. for Girls; Girton Coll., Cambridge (MA). Economist, then Dep. Gp Economist, John Laing and Son, 1965–69; Gp Economist, Tarmac, 1969–70; Sen. Project Manager, NEDO, 1970–86; Sci. and Technol. Secretariat, Cabinet Office, 1986–89; Res. and Technol. Policy Div., 1989–91, Competition Policy Div., 1991–93, Finance and Resource Mgt Div., 1993–95, DTI; Head, Agencies Privatisation Team, 1995–96, Dir, Agencies Gp B, 1996, Cabinet Office; Dir of Competition Policy, subseq. Competition Enforcement, OFT, 1997–2003. Dir, Lending Standards Bd, 2012–. Mem., LINK Consumer Council, 2006–. Vice Chair, Professional Standards Council, Asset Based Finance Assoc., 2013–. Pt-time Lectr, 1977–80, Ext. Examr, 1985–88, for MSc in Architecture, UCL. Dep. Chm., Money Advice Trust, 2007– (Trustee, 2003–). *Recreations:* family, foreign travel, eating out, rambling. *Address:* Dickson Poon School of Law, King's College London, Strand, WC2R 2LS. *T:* (020) 7848 2324, *Fax:* (020) 7848 2443. *E:* margaret.bloom@kcl.ac.uk.

BLOOM, Prof. Sir Stephen (Robert), Kt 2012; MD, DSc; FRCP, FRCPath, FMedSci; FRS 2013; FRSB; Professor of Medicine, since 1982, and Head of Division of Diabetes, Endocrinology and Metabolism, since 1994, Imperial College Faculty of Medicine (formerly Royal Postgraduate Medical School), London University; Chief of Service for Pathology, Imperial College Healthcare NHS Trust, since 1994; Consultant Physician, Hammersmith Hospital, since 1982; *b* 24 Oct. 1942; *s* of Arnold and Edith Bloom; *m* 1965, Margaret Jan Sturrock (*see* M. J. Bloom); two *s* two *d*. *Educ:* Queens' Coll., Cambridge (MA 1968; M 1979); Middlesex Hosp. Med. Sch.; DSc London 1982. FRCP 1978; FRCPath 1993; FRS (FInstBiol 2008). Middlesex Hospital: Gastro House Physician, 1967–68; Cardiology Hous Physician, 1968; Casualty Med. Officer, 1969; Leverhulme Res. Schol., Inst. of Clin. Res 1970; Med. Unit Registrar, 1970–72; MRC Clin. Res. Fellow, 1972–74; House Surgeo Mount Vernon Hosp., 1968–69; Endocrinology House Physician, Hammersmith Hosp 1969–70; Sen. Lectr, 1974–78, Reader in Medicine, 1978–82, RPMS, Hammersmith Hosp Dir, Endocrinol. Clin. Service, 1982–, and Head of Div. of Investigative Sci., 1997–200 Imperial Coll., London (formerly RPMS). CSO, Thiakis, 2006–09. Lectures: Copp, Ame Diabetes Assoc.; Goulstonian, and Lumleian, RCP; Amer. Endocrine Soc. Transatlanti Lawrence, and Arnold Bloom, British Diabetic Assoc.; Wellcome, RSM. Sen. Censor, RC 1999–2001. Chm., Soc. for Endocrinology, 2002–06 (Sec., 1999–2002). Founder FMedSc 1998. Dale Medal, Soc. for Endocrinology, 2003. *Publications:* Toohey's Medicine, 15th ed 1994; (with J. Lynn) Surgical Endocrinology, 1993. *Recreations:* walking, jogging, travellin opera. *Address:* Department of Investigative Medicine, Imperial College Faculty of Medicin 6th Floor Commonwealth Building, Hammersmith Campus, Du Cane Road, W12 0NN. (020) 8383 3242.

BLOOMER, Giles; *see* Bloomer, R. J. G.

BLOOMER, Jonathan William, FCA; Chairman: Arrow Global Group plc, since 2013; JL Employee Benefits Group, since 2013; *b* 23 March 1954; *s* of Derick William Bloomer an Audrey Alexandra Bloomer; *m* 1977, Anne Elizabeth Judith May; one *s* two *d*. *Edu* Halesowen Grammar Sch.; Imperial Coll., London (BSc, ARCS 1974). FCA 1982. Partne Arthur Andersen, 1987–94; Gp Finance Dir, Prudential Corp. plc, 1995–99; Prudential pl Dep. Gp Chief Exec., 1999–2000; Chief Exec., 2000–05; Partner, Cerberus European Capit Advrs LLP, 2006–12; Chief Exec. (formerly Exec. Chm.), Lucida plc, 2006–12. Chm Scottish Re, 2007–12; Sen. Ind. Dir, Hargreaves Lansdown plc, 2006–13; non-exec. Di Autonomy, 2010–11. Bd Mem., ABI, 2001–05; Chm., Financial Services Practitioner Pane 2003–05 (Dep. Chm., 2001–03). CCMI (CIMgt 1996). Trustee and Treas., NSPCC, 2009– Chm. Trustees, Caterham Sch., 2010–. *Recreations:* sailing, watching Rugby, gardening.

BLOOMER, Dr (Robert John) Giles, OBE 1998; Vice Lord-Lieutenant of Sout Yorkshire, since 2010; *b* Barnsley, 1943; *s* of Robert and Aileen Bloomer; *m* 1967, Elizabet Broughton; two *s* one *d*. *Educ:* Rotherham Grammar Sch.; Univ. of Birmingham (BSc 196 PhD 1967). MICE 1969. Water engr, Cornwall River Authy and Water Resources B 1967–72; Dir, Bramall Construction, later Keepmoat plc, 1972–85; Chm., Aizlewoods Bld Materials, 1985–2002. Dir, Rotherham Chamber of Commerce and Industry, 1988–200 (Pres., 1990). Non-exec. Dir, Rotherham Hosp. NHS Foundn Trust, 2005–11. Truste Magna Trust, 1998–2013; S Yorks Community Foundn, 2006–. Feoffee, Common Lands Rotherham, 1995–. Liveryman, Builders Merchants' Co., 1991–. DL 1999, High Sheri 2008–09, S Yorks. *Publications:* (with J. R. Sexton) Generation of Synthetic River Flow Dat 1972. *Club:* Rotary (Rotherham).

BLOOMFIELD, Keith George, CMG 2007; HM Diplomatic Service, retired; Ambassad to Nepal, 2002–06; *b* 2 June 1947; *s* of George William Bloomfield and Edith Jo Bloomfield; *m* 1976, Genevieve Charbonneau; three *d*. *Educ:* Kilburn Grammar Sch.; Lincol Coll., Oxford (MA). Home Civil Service, 1969–80; Office of UK Rep. to EC, Brussel 1980–85; FCO, 1985–87; Head of Chancery, Cairo, 1987–90; Dep. Head of Mission, Algier 1990–94; Counsellor (Political and Mgt), Rome, 1994–96; Minister and Dep. Head Mission, Rome, 1997–98; Hd, Counter Terrorism Policy Dept, FCO, 1998–200 *Recreations:* music, tennis, reading.

BLOOMFIELD, Sir Kenneth Percy, KCB 1987 (CB 1982); Joint Internation Commissioner, Commission for Location of Victims Remains, since 1999; President, AQE since 2011 (Chairman, AQE Ltd, 2008–11); *b* 15 April 1931; *oc* of late Harry Percy Bloomfiel and Doris Bloomfield, Belfast; *m* 1960, Mary Elizabeth Ramsey (MBE 2013); one *s* one *Educ:* Royal Belfast Academical Instn; St Peter's Coll., Oxford (MA; Hon. Fellow, 1991 Min. of Finance, N Ireland, 1952–56; Private Sec. to Ministers of Finance, 1956–60; De Dir, British Industrial Develt Office, NY, 1960–63; Asst and later Dep. Sec. to Cabinet, N 1963–72; Under-Sec., Northern Ireland Office, 1972–73; Sec. to Northern Irelan Executive, Jan.–May 1974; Permanent Secretary: Office of the Executive, NI, 1974–75; De of Housing, Local Govt and Planning, NI, 1975–76; Dept of the Environment, NI, 1976–8 Dept of Commerce, NI, 1981–82; Dept of Economic Develt, 1982–84; Head, NICS, an Second Perm. Under Sec. of State, NI Office, 1984–91. Nat. Gov. and Chm. of Broadcastin Council for NI, BBC, 1991–99. Review of Dental Remuneration, 1992; Consultant, Crow Appts Review Gp, 1999–2001. Comr, NI Victims Commn, 1997–98 (report publishe 1998). Chairman: Chief Executives' Forum for NI Public Services, 1991–97; NI High Educn Council, 1993–2001; Review of Criminal Injuries Compensation in NI, 1998–9 Bangor and Holywood Town Centre Mgt Ltd, 2000–06; Legal Services Commn for N 2003–04; Vice-Chm., Mus and Galls of NI, 2002–06. Pres., NI Council, Stationery Offic 1998–2000. Mem., NI Adv. Bd, Bank of Ireland, 1991–; Member of Board: Co-operatio North, 1991–93; Opera, NI, 1992–97. Member: Statute Law Adv. Cttee, 1993–97; Na Steering Cttee, Give as You Earn, 1992–93; Adv. Cttee, Constitution Unit, 1997; Jerse Review of Machinery of Govt, 1999–2000. Chm., Children in Need Trust, 1992–98; Mem Bd, Green Park Hosp. Trust, 1993–2001; Patron, NI Council for Integrated Educn, 1998– Senator (Crown nominee), QUB, 1991–93. Bass Ireland Lectr, Univ. of Ulster, 1991. Gov Royal Belfast Academical Instn, 1984–2011 (Chm., 2004–11). MRIA 2008. Hon. LL QUB, 1991; DUniv Open, 2000; Hon. DLitt Ulster, 2002. Dr Ben Wilson Trophy f Individual or Corporate Excellence, NI Chamber of Commerce and Industry, 199 *Publications:* Stormont in Crisis (a memoir), 1994; A Tragedy of Errors, 2007; A New Lif 2008; The BBC at the Watershed, 2008; *contributions to:* Hope and History, 199 Broadcasting in a Divided Community, 1996; People and Government: questions f Northern Ireland, 1997; Cool Britannia, 1998; various jls and periodicals. *Recreations:* histor travel, swimming, authorship and public speaking. *Address:* 16 Larch Hill, Holywood, C Down BT18 0JN. *T:* (028) 9042 8340.

BLOOR, Prof. David; Scientific Adviser, Peratech Ltd, 2003–14; Professor of Applie Physics, University of Durham, 1989–2002, now Emeritus (Chairman, Department Physics, 1993–96); *b* 25 July 1937; *s* of Alfred Edwin Bloor and Gladys Ellen Bloor (*n* Collins); *m* 1960, Margaret E. A. Avery; four *s* (and one *s* decd). *Educ:* Queen Mary Colleg London (BSc, PhD). CPhys, FInstP. Lectr, Dept of Physics, Univ. of Canterbury, N 1961–64; Queen Mary College London: Lectr, Dept of Physics, 1964; Reader, 1980–8 Prof. of Polymer Physics, 1984–89. Humboldt Fellow: Univ. of Stuttgart, 1975–76; Univ. Bayreuth, 1997–98; Erskine Fellow, Univ. of Canterbury, NZ, 1983; Royal Society SER Indust. Fellow, GEC Marconi Res. Centre, 1985–86; Sir Derman Christopherson Found Fellow, Univ. of Durham, 1996–97. Co-ordinator, DTI/SERC Molecular Electroni Initiative, 1987–93. Mem., Exec. Cttee, Canon Foundn in Europe, 2000–09 (Chm Selection Cttee, 2005–09; Hon. Mem., 2009–). *Publications:* over 300 articles in profession jls. *Recreations:* cycling, gardening. *Address:* Department of Physics, Durham University, Sout Road, Durham DH1 3LE. *T:* (0191) 334 3581.

BLOSSE, Sir Richard Hely L.; *see* Lynch-Blosse.

BLOT, Jean; *see* Blokh, A.

ɜLOW, Bridget Penelope, CBE 2014; Chairman (non-executive), City of Birmingham Symphony Orchestra, since 2012; Deputy Chairman (non-executive), Coventry Building Society, since 2009 (Director, since 2007); non-executive Director, Birmingham Hippodrome Theatre Trust, since 2006; *b* 2 June 1949; *m* Rod Blow (marr. diss.); one *d*. *Educ:* Caistor Grammar Sch. Systems Develt, Grimsby BC, 1968–79; Human Resources Dir, Divl Dir, Dir of Technol., then Exec. Dir, FI Gp, 1979–92; Systems Dir, 1992–94, Chief Exec., 1994–2005, ITNET; Gp Technol. Dir, Serco Gp plc, 2005–06. Dir, Bank of England, 2000–05. Non-executive Chairman: Trustmarque Solutions, 2006–13; Harvard Internat. plc (formerly Alba plc), 2007–12 (Dir, 2005–12). Non-exec. Chm., Gtr Birmingham and Solihull Local Enterprise Partnership Develt Bd, 2010–11. Pres., Birmingham Chamber of Commerce and Industry, 2008–09. Mem. Council, Univ. of Birmingham, 2005–10. CCMI. NatWest Midlands Business Woman of the Year, 1996. *Recreations:* golf, gym, tennis, theatre.

ɜLOW, Prof. (John) Julian, PhD; FRSE; FMedSci; Professor of Chromosome Maintenance, since 2001, and Dean of Research, College of Life Sciences, since 2014, University of Dundee; *b* Cambridge, 23 Feb. 1961; *s* of Prof. David Mervyn Blow, FRS, and of Mavis Blow; *m* 1988, Margret Michalski; one *s* one *d*. *Educ:* Univ. of Edinburgh (BSc Pathol. 1984); Trinity Coll., Cambridge (PhD 1987). Post-doctoral Fellow: Univ. of Cambridge, 1987–88; Univ. of Oxford, 1988–91; Res. Scientist, 1991–96, Sen. Scientist, 1996–97, ICRF Clare Hall Labs; University of Dundee: Sen. Lectr, Dept of Biochem., 1997–2000; Reader, 2000–01; Dep. Hd, Div. of Gene Regulation and Expression, Sch. of Life Scis, 1998–2008; Dep. Dir, 2008–12, Dir, 2012–14, Wellcome Trust Centre for Gene Regulation and Expression; Associate Dean, Coll. of Life Scis, 2010–12. FRSE 2002; FMedSci 2012. *Publications:* peer-reviewed pubns, mainly in field of DNA replication. *Recreations:* mountaineering, orienteering, progressive rock. *Address:* Centre for Gene Regulation and Expression, College of Life Sciences, University of Dundee, Dow Street, Dundee DD1 5EH. *T:* (01382) 385136, *Fax:* (01382) 388072. *E:* j.j.blow@dundee.ac.uk.

ɜLOW, Joyce; *see* Blow Darlington, J.

ɜLOW, Julian; *see* Blow, J. J.

ɜLOW DARLINGTON, Joyce, OBE 1994; Chairman, Child Accident Prevention Trust, 1996–2002; *b* 4 May 1929; *d* of late Walter Blow and Phyllis (*née* Grainger); *m* 1974, Lt-Col J. A. B. Darlington, RE retd (*d* 2011). *Educ:* Bell Baxter Sch., Cupar, Fife; Edinburgh Univ. (MA Hons). John Lewis Partnership, 1951–52; FBI, 1952–53; Press Officer, Council of Indust. Design, 1953–63; Publicity and Advertising Manager, Heal & Son Ltd, 1963–65; entered Civil Service on first regular recruitment of direct entry Principals from business and industry: BoT, 1965–67; Monopolies Commn (gen. enquiry into restrictive practices in supply of prof. services), 1967–70; DTI, 1970, Asst Sec. 1972; Dept of Prices and Consumer Protection, 1974–77; Under-Secretary: OFT, 1977–80; DTI, 1980–84; Chairman: Mail Order Publishers' Authy, 1985–92; Direct Marketing Assoc. Authy, 1992–97. Chm., E Sussex FHSA, 1990–96. Pres., Assoc. for Quality in Healthcare, 1991–94; Vice-Pres., Trading Standards Inst., 1985–; Bd Mem., BSI, 1987–97 (Chm., Consumer Policy Cttee, 1987–93). Founder Mem. and Past Pres., Women in Public Relations. Trustee, Univ. of Edinburgh Develt Trust, 1990–94; Chm., PR Educn Trust, 1992–97. Freeman, City of London. Hon. FCIPR (FIPR 1964); FCMI; FRSA. *Publications:* Consumers and International Trade: a handbook, 1987. *Recreations:* music, art, architecture, travel, France. *Address:* 17 Fentiman Road, SW8 1LD. *Clubs:* Arts, Reform.

BLOXHAM, Prof. Jeremy, PhD; FRS 2007; Mallinckrodt Professor of Geophysics, since 2004, and Dean of Science, since 2008, Harvard University; *b* 29 April 1960; *s* of Lawrence Bloxham and Christine Bloxham; *m* 1985, Katharine Jane Everist; two *s*. *Educ:* Portsmouth Grammar Sch.; Pembroke Coll., Cambridge (BA 1982; PhD 1985). Harvard University: Asst Prof. of Geophysics, 1987–90; John L. Loeb Associate Prof. of Natural Scis, 1990–93; Prof. of Geophysics, 1993–2004; Chair, Dept of Earth and Planetary Scis, 2000–06; Prof. of Computational Sci., 2006; Dean of Physical Scis, 2006–08. *Publications:* over 60 articles in learned jls. *Recreations:* sailing, ski-ing, flying. *Address:* 14 Washington Square, Marblehead, MA 01945, USA. *T:* (office) (617) 4959517, *Fax:* (617) 4957660. *E:* jeremy_bloxham@harvard.edu. *Club:* Eastern Yacht (Marblehead, Mass).

BLOXHAM, Thomas Paul Richard, MBE 1999; Chairman and Co-Founder, Urban Splash Group, since 1993; *b* 20 Dec. 1963; *m* 1987, Jo Speakman; two *s*. *Educ:* Manchester Univ. (BA Hons Politics and Mod. History). Founder, Urban Splash (Properties), 1992; Baa Bar Ltd, 1991–2006 (Chm.). Mem., Property Adv. Gp, DTLR. Chm., Arts Council England (North West) (formerly NW Arts Bd), 1999–2008; Mem., Arts Council England, 2003–08. Dir, Liverpool Cultural Co. Ltd, 2001–08; Chairman: Manchester Internat. Arts Fest., 2005–; IPPR Centre for Cities Think Tank, 2005–. Chancellor, Manchester Univ., 2008–15. Trustee, Tate Gall., 2009–. Trustee, Manchester Utd Foundn. Hon. RIBA; FRSA. Hon. Fellow: Liverpool John Moores Univ., 2001; Univ. of Central Lancashire, 2003. Hon. DDes: Oxford Brookes, 2004; Bristol, 2007; Hon. LittD Manchester, 2007; Hon. DBus Plymouth, 2009. UK Property Entrepreneur of the Year, 1998; Nat. Young Entrepreneur of the Year, 1999; North Region Young Entrepreneur of the Year, 1999; Northwest Young Entrepreneur of the Year, IoD, 1999. *Address:* (office) Timber Wharf, 16–24 Worsley Street, Castlefield, Manchester M15 4LD. *E:* tombloxham@urbansplash.co.uk.

ɜLUCK, Duncan Robert Yorke, CBE 1990 (OBE 1984); Chairman: British Tourist Authority, 1984–90; English Tourist Board, 1984–90; Director, John Swire & Sons, 1984–99; *b* 19 March 1927; *s* of Thomas Edward Bluck and Ida Bluck; *m* 1952, Stella Wardlaw Murdoch; one *s* three *d*. *Educ:* Taunton Sch. RNVR, 1944–47. Joined John Swire & Sons, 1948; Dir, 1964–99, Chief Exec., 1971–84, Chm., 1980–84, Cathay Pacific Airways; Chairman: John Swire & Sons (HK) Ltd, 1980–84; Swire Pacific Ltd, 1980–84; Swire Properties Ltd, 1980–84. Dir, Hongkong and Shanghai Banking Corp., 1981–84. Chairman: English Schools Foundn (Hongkong), 1978–84; Hongkong Tourist Assoc., 1981–84; Kent Economic Develt Bd, 1986–91; Cystic Fibrosis Trust, 1996–2003 (Pres., 2003–11). Governor, Marlborough House Sch., 1986–2007; Mem. Ct, Univ. of Kent, 1991–2001. JP Hong Kong, 1981–84. *Recreation:* sailing. *Address:* 2 West Cross, Tenterden, Kent TN30 6JL. *T:* (01580) 766729. *Clubs:* Hong Kong, Sheko (Hong Kong).

ɜLUCK, Rt Rev. John William; Bishop of Waiapu, 2002–08; *b* 22 July 1943; *m* 1969, Elizabeth Anne Frost; one *s* one *d*. *Educ:* Univ. of Canterbury, NZ (MA 1966); Episcopal Theol Sch., Cambridge, Mass, USA (BD *cum laude* 1969). Ordained deacon, 1970, priest, 1971; served Holy Trinity parish, Gisborne, 1970–72; Editor: NZ Methodist, 1972–77; One World, WCC, 1977–80; Dir of Communications, WCC, 1980–84; Prof. of Pastoral Theol. and Communication, Knox Theol Hall, 1984–90; Dean of Christchurch Cathedral, NZ, 1990–2002. *Publications:* Everyday Ecumenism, 1987; Christian Communication Reconsidered, 1989; Canberra Takeaways, 1991; Long, White and Cloudy, 1998; Waking Up in Strange Places, 1999; Killing Us Softly, 2001; The Giveaway God, 2001; Credible Christianity: finding faith here and now, 2008; Praying the Lord's Prayer, 2010; Hidden Country: finding faith in Aotearoa, 2011; Wai Karekare—Turbulent Waters: the Anglican bicultural journey 1814–2014. *E:* bluck@vodafone.co.nz.

ɜLUE, Rabbi Lionel, OBE 1994; former broadcaster and author; Lecturer, Leo Baeck College, 1967–2013; Convener of the Beth Din (Ecclesiastical Court) of the Reform Synagogues of Great Britain, 1971–88; *b* 6 Feb. 1930; *s* of late Harry and Hetty Blue. *Educ:* Balliol Coll., Oxford (MA History); University Coll. London (BA Semitics); Leo Baeck Coll., London (Rabbinical Dip). Ordained Rabbi, 1960; Minister to Settlement Synagogue and Middlesex New Synagogue, 1960–63; European Dir, World Union for Progressive Judaism, 1963–66; Co-Editor, Forms of Prayer, 1967–; broadcaster, 1967–; Feature Writer: The Universe, 1979–; The Standard, 1985–86; The Tablet, 1994–. Scriptwriter and presenter, TV series, In Search of Holy England, 1989. Templeton (UK) Prize, 1993. Vis. Fellow, Grey Coll., Univ. of Durham, 2005. DUniv Open; Hon. DD Durham, 2007. *Publications:* To Heaven with Scribes and Pharisees, 1975; (jtly) A Taste of Heaven, 1977; (ed jtly) Forms of Prayer (Sabbath and Daily), 1977; A Backdoor to Heaven, 1979, revd edn 1985; (ed jtly) Forms of Prayer (Days of Awe), 1985; Bright Blue, 1985; (jtly) Simply Divine, 1985; Kitchen Blues, 1985; Bolts from the Blue, 1986; Blue Heaven, 1987; (jtly) Daytrips to Eternity, 1987; (jtly) The Guide to the Here and Hereafter, 1988; Blue Horizons, 1989; (jtly) How to Get Up When Life Gets You Down, 1992; (jtly) The Little Blue Book of Prayer, 1993; Tales of Body and Soul, 1994; (jtly) Kindred Spirits: a year of readings, 1995; My Affair with Christianity (autobiog.), 1998; (jtly) Sun, Sand and Soul, 1999; Blue's Jokes, 2001; A Little Book of Blue Thoughts, 2001; Hitchhiking to Heaven (autobiog.), 2004; The Best of Blue, 2006; The Godseeker's Guide, 2010. *Recreations:* window shopping, package holidays, monasteries, cooking. *Address:* Leo Baeck College, 80 East End Road, N3 2SY. *T:* (020) 8349 4525.

BLUGLASS, Prof. Robert Saul, CBE 1995; MD; FRCP, FRCPsych; Professor of Forensic Psychiatry, University of Birmingham, 1979–96, now Emeritus; Hon. Consultant, Reaside Clinic, Birmingham, since 1995; *b* 22 Sept. 1930; *s* of Henry Bluglass and Fay (*née* Griew); *m* 1962, Dr Jean Margaret Kerry (*née* Montgomery); one *s* one *d*. *Educ:* Warwick Sch., Warwick; Univ. of St Andrews (MB, ChB 1957, MD 1967). DPM 1962; MRCPsych 1971, FRCPsych 1976; MRCP 1994, FRCP 1997. Formerly, Sen. Registrar in Psych., Royal Dundee Liff Hosp. and Maryfield Hosp., Dundee; Consultant in Forensic Psychiatry: W Midlands RHA and the Home Office, 1967–94; S Birmingham Mental Health NHS Trust, 1994–95 (Med. Dir, 1995–96); Consultant i/c Midland Centre for For. Psych., All Saints Hosp., Birmingham, 1967–93; Clinical Dir, Reaside Clinic, Birmingham, 1986–95. Birmingham University: Hon. Lectr, 1968–75, Sen. Clin. Lectr in For. Psych., 1975–79; Regl Postgrad. Tutor in Forensic Psych., 1967–95; Jt Dir, Midland Inst. of For. Medicine, 1975–87. Dep. Regional Advr in Psychiatry, W Midlands RHA, 1985–87, Regional Advr, 1987–92; Specialist Advr, H of C Select Cttee on Social Services, 1985–87, on Health, 2000–01; Consultant Advr in Psych., RAF, 1992–2001, now Hon. Consultant; Advr in For. Psych., Bd of Corrections, Health Service, NSW, 1996–97. Member: Adv. Cttee on Alcoholism, DHSS, 1975–80; Adv. Council on Probation, Home Office, 1974–77; Mental Health Review Tribunal, 1979–2004; Mental Health Act Commn, 1983–85; Forensic Psych. Res. Liaison Gp, DHSS; Rev. of Services for Mentally Disordered Offenders (Reed Cttee), DoH, 1991–94; Inquiry into care and mgt of Christopher Edwards and Richard Linford, 1996–98; Judicial Inquiry into Personality Disorder Unit at Ashworth Special Hosp., 1997–99. Royal College of Psychiatrists: Mem., Ct of Electors, 1976–79; Mem. Council, Exec. and Finance Cttees, 1973–76, 1976–78, 1980–86, 1986–91; Vice-Pres., 1983–85; Chm., For. Psych. Specialist Section, 1978–82; Chm., Midlands Div., 1986–91; Chm., Midlands Soc. of Criminology, 1981–95 (Sec., 1970–81); Past Pres., Sect. of Psych., Birmingham Med. Inst.; Vice-Pres., RAF Psych. Soc.; Mem., Brit. Acad. of For. Sciences; Associate Mem., GMC, 1991–2009. FRSocMed 1975. Baron ver Heyden de Lancey Law Prize, RSocMed, 1983. *Publications:* Psychiatry, The Law and The Offender, 1980; A Guide to the Mental Health Act 1983, 1983; (ed with Prof. Sir Martin Roth) Psychiatry, Human Rights and the Law, 1985, repr. 2009; (ed with Dr Paul Bowden) The Principles and Practice of Forensic Psychiatry, 1990; articles in Brit. Jl of Hosp. Med., BMJ, Brit. Jl of Psych., and Med., Science and the Law. *Recreations:* water-colour painting, cooking, gardening, travelling, genealogy, supporter of St James's Singers, Compton Verney Gallery, RSC. *E:* robert.bluglass@gmail.com.

BLUM, Heather Anne Elise Lilian M.; *see* Munroe-Blum.

BLUME, Dame Hilary (Sharon Braverman), DBE 2008; Founder and Director, Charities Advisory Trust (formerly Charity Trading Advisory Group), since 1979; *b* 9 Jan. 1945; *d* of Henry and Muriel Braverman; *m* 1st, 1965, Prof. Stuart Blume (marr. diss. 1977); two *s*; 2nd, 1977, Michael Aslan Norton, *qv*; one *d*. *Educ:* London Sch. of Econs (BSc Econ.); Univ. of Sussex (MPhil). Fund raiser: War on Want, 1971–74; SHAC, 1975–79. Dir, Card Aid, 1984–. Comr, Nat. Lottery Commn, 1999–2000. Creator, Good Gifts Catalogue, 2003. Chm. (formerly Co-Chm.), Finnart House Sch. Trust, 2007– (Vice-Chm., 1996–2007). Patron, Trees for London, 2000–. FRSA 2002 (Mem. Council, 2004–07). Creator, Peace Oil, 2006; Founder and Trustee, UK Disaster Relief, 2010; Founder, Knit for Peace, 2007; Knit for Peace UK, 2010. Mem., St Pancras Cruising Club, 2015–. *Publications:* Fund-raising: a comprehensive handbook, 1977; (jtly) Accounting and Financial Management for Charities, 1979, 2nd edn 1985; Charity Trading Handbook, 1981; Charity Christmas Cards, 1984; Museum Trading Handbook, 1987; Charity Shops Handbook, 1995. *Address:* Charities Advisory Trust, Radius Works, Back Lane, Hampstead, NW3 1HL.

BLUMENTHAL, Heston, OBE 2006; Chef Proprietor, The Fat Duck, Bray, since 1995; *b* 27 May 1966; *s* of Stephen Jeffrey Blumenthal and Celia Blumenthal; *m* 1991, Susanna Gage; one *s* two *d*. Credit controller, Team Leasing, 1987–95. Proprietor: The Hinds Head, Bray, 2004– (Michelin Star); Dinner by Heston Blumenthal, Mandarin Oriental Hotel, Knightsbridge, 2011– (2 Michelin Stars). Chef of the Year: Good Food Guide, 2001; AA Guide, 2002; GQ Mag., 2004; Catey Awards, Caterer & Hotelkeeper Magazine: Restaurateur of the Year, 2003; Chef of the Year, 2004; Food and Wine Personality of Year Award, GQ/Glenfiddich Awards, 2004; The Fat Duck has also received numerous best restaurant awards, incl. 3rd Michelin Star, 2004. BBC TV programmes: In Search of Perfection, 2006; Further Adventures in Search of Perfection, 2007; Channel 4: Heston's Mission Impossible, 2011; How to Cook like Heston, 2012; Heston's Fantastical Food, 2012; Heston's Great British Food, 2013. Hon. DSc Reading, 2006; Hon. MSc Bristol, 2007. Hon. FRSC 2006. *Publications:* Family Food, 2002, 2nd edn 2004; In Search of Perfection, 2006; Further Adventures in Search of Perfection, 2007; The Big Fat Duck Cookbook, 2008, new edn 2009; In Search of Total Perfection, 2009; Heston Blumenthal at Home, 2011; Historic Heston, 2013. *Recreations:* the study of historical food, nutrition and exercise, sport. *Address:* The Fat Duck, High Street, Bray, Berks SL6 2AQ. *T:* (01628) 580333, *Fax:* (01628) 776188. *E:* heston@thefatduck.co.uk.

BLUMENTHAL, W(erner) Michael, PhD; US Secretary of the Treasury, 1977–79; Director, Jewish Museum Berlin, since 1997; *b* Germany, 3 Jan. 1926. *Educ:* Univ. of California at Berkeley; Princeton Univ. Research Associate, Princeton Univ., 1954–57; Vice-Pres., Dir, Crown Cork Internat. Corp., 1957–61; Dep. Asst Sec. of State for Econ. Affairs, Dept of State, 1961–63; Dep. Special Rep. of the President (with rank Ambassador) for Trade Negotiations, 1963–67; Pres., Bendix Internat., 1967–70; Bendix Corp.: Dir, 1967–77; Vice-Chm., 1970–71; Pres. and Chief Operating Officer, 1971–72; Chm. and Chief Exec. Officer, 1972–77; Burroughs Corp. subseq. Unisys: Chief Exec. Officer, 1980–90; Vice-Chm., 1980; Chm., 1981–90; Lazard Frères & Co. LLC, 1990–96. *Publications:* The Invisible Wall: three hundred years of a German Jewish family, 1998; In achtzig Jahren um die Welt: mein Leben, 2010; From Exile to Washington: a memoir of leadership in the twentieth century, 2013. *Address:* Princeton, NJ 08540, USA; Jewish Museum Berlin, Lindenstrasse 9–14, 10969 Berlin, Germany.

BLUMER, Rodney Milnes, (Rodney Milnes), OBE 2002; Chief Opera Critic, The Times, 1992–2002; *b* 26 July 1936; *s* of Charles Eric Milnes Blumer and Kathleen Bertha Croft. *Educ:* Rugby School; Christ Church, Oxford (BA Hons Hist.). Editorial Dir, Rupert Hart-Davis Ltd, 1966–68; Music Critic, Queen magazine, later Harpers and Queen, 1968–87; Opera

Critic: The Spectator, 1970–90; Evening Standard, 1990–92; Opera magazine: contribs, 1971–; Editl Bd, 1973; Associate Editor, 1976; Editor, 1986–99. Pres., Critics' Circle, 1988–90. Trustee, British Youth Opera, 2010–12. Hon. RAM 2002. Kt, Order of White Rose (Finland). *Publications:* numerous opera translations. *Recreation:* travel. *Address:* c/o Opera Magazine, 36 Black Lion Lane, W6 9BE.

BLUMGART, Prof. Leslie Harold, MD; FRCS, FRCSE, FRCSGlas, FACS; Enid A. Haupt Professor of Surgery, Memorial Sloan-Kettering Cancer Center, New York, since 1991 (Chief, Section of Hepato-Biliary Surgery, and Director, Programme on Hepato-Biliary Diseases, 1995–2007); Professor of Surgery, Cornell University Medical Center, since 1992; *b* 7 Dec. 1931; of S African parentage; *m* 1955, Pearl Marie Navias (decd); *m* 1968, Sarah Raybould Bowen; two *s* two *d*. *Educ:* Jeppe High Sch., Johannesburg, SA; Univ. of Witwatersrand (BDS); Univ. of Sheffield (MB, ChB Hons; MD 1969). Prize Medal, Clin. Med. and Surg.; Ashby-de-la-Zouche Prize, Surg., Med., Obst. and Gynaecol. FRCS 1966; FRCSGlas 1973 (Hon. FRCSGlas 2001); FRCSE 1976. General dental practice, Durban, SA, 1954–59; Sen. Surgical Registrar, Nottingham Gen. Hosp. and Sheffield Royal Infirmary, 1966–70; Sen. Lectr and Dep. Dir, Dept of Surgery, Welsh Nat. Sch. of Med., also Hon. Cons. Surg., Cardiff Royal Inf., 1970–72; St Mungo Prof. of Surgery, Univ. of Glasgow, and Hon. Cons. Surg., Glasgow Royal Inf., 1972–79; Prof. of Surgery, Royal Postgrad. Sch. of London and Dir of Surgery, Hammersmith Hosp., 1979–86; Prof. of Surgery, Univ. of Bern, 1986–91. Moynihan Fellow, Assoc. of Surgs of Gt Brit. and Ire., 1972; Mayne Vis. Prof., Univ. of Queensland, Brisbane, 1976; Vis. Prof., Univ. of Lund, Sweden, 1977; Nimmo Vis. Prof., Adelaide Univ., 1982; Oliver Beahrs Vis. Prof., Mayo Clinic, 2002; Purvis Oration, 1974; President's Oration, Soc. for Surgery of Aliment. Tract, Toronto, 1977; Lectures: Honyman Gillespie, Univ. of Edinburgh, 1978; Walton, RCPGlas, 1984; Monsarrat, Univ. of Liverpool, 1985; Legg Meml, KCH, 1985; Philip Sandblom, Lund Univ., Sweden, 1986; T. E. Jones Meml, Cleveland Clinic, USA, 1986; L. W. Edwards, Vanderbilt Univ., USA, 1987; Ernest Miles, British Assoc. Surg. Oncology, 1995; DeQuervain, Insespital Bern, Switzerland, 2006; Dallas B. Phemister, Univ. of Chicago, 2007; Sabiston, Univ. Hosp., Zurich, 2007; Davis Foundn, RCPSG, 2007; Lumpkin Lect. in Surgery, Dallas, Texas, 2008; Bevan, Chicago Surgical Soc., 2008; William Longmire, UCLA, 2014. Pres., Internat. Biliary Assoc., 1987. Member: BMA, 1963–; Assoc. of Surgs of GB and Ire., 1971–; Surgical Research Soc., 1971–; Brit. Soc. of Gastroenterology, 1972–; Swiss Surg. Soc., 1987–; Internat. Hepato-Pancreato-Biliary Assoc., 1992–; Amer. Surgical Assoc., 1993–; Soc. Surgical Oncology, 1994–. Hon. Member: Soc. for Surgery of Aliment. Tract, USA, 1977; Soc. Amer. Endoscopic Surgs, 1986–; Danish Surg. Soc., 1988; Yugoslavian Surg. Soc., 1988; French Surg. Soc., 1990; Austrian Surg. Soc., 2007; Hon. Fellow: Italian Surg. Soc., 2002; French Acad. of Surgery, 2008. Hon. FRCSI 2002. Hon. DSc Sheffield, 1998. Acral Medal, Swedish Soc. Surgery, 1990; Alumnus of the Year, Meml Sloan-Kettering Cancer Center, 2012; Lifetime Achievement Award, European Soc. of Surgical Oncology, 2014. Order of Prasidda, Prabala-Gorkha-Dakshin Bahu, Nepal, 1984. *Publications:* (ed with A. C. Kennedy), Essentials of Medicine and Surgery for Dental Students, 3rd edn 1977, 4th edn 1982; (ed) The Biliary Tract, 1982; (ed) Surgery of the Liver and Biliary Tract, vols 1 and 2, 1988, 5th edn as Surgery of the Liver, Biliary Tract and Pancreas, 2012; Video Atlas of Liver, Billiary and Pancreatic Surgery, 2010; (ed) Surgical Management of Hepatobiliary and Pancreatic Disorders, 2003; chapters in books; numerous publications concerned with medical educn, gastrointestinal surgery and aspects of oncology with particular interests in surgery of the liver, pancreas and biliary tract and hepatic pathophysiology in med. and surgical jls. *Recreations:* water colour painting, wood carving, sculpture. *Address:* Memorial Sloan-Kettering Cancer Center, 1275 York Avenue, New York, NY 10021, USA. *T:* (212) 6395526; 447 E 57th Street #3E, New York, NY 10022, USA. *T:* (917) 9727850.

BLUNDELL, Prof. Derek John; Professor of Environmental Geology, University of London, 1975–98, now Emeritus Professor of Geophysics; Dean of Research and Enterprise, Royal Holloway, University of London, 1995–98; *b* 30 June 1933; *s* of Frank and Mollie Blundell; *m* 1960, Mary Patricia, *d* of Archibald and Mildred Leonard. *Educ:* Univ. of Birmingham (BSc); Imperial Coll., London (DIC, PhD). Res. Fellow 1957, Lectr 1959, in Geology, Univ. of Birmingham; Sen. Lectr 1970, Reader 1972, in Geophysics, Univ. of Lancaster; Royal Soc. Vis. Prof., Univ. of Ghana, 1974; Prof. of Environmental Geol., Univ. of London, first at Chelsea Coll. (Hd of Geol. Dept), 1975, then at Royal Holloway and Bedford New Coll., 1985–98; Hd of Geol. Dept, 1992–97; Hon. Fellow, Royal Holloway, 2004. Leverhulme Emeritus Fellow, 1998–2000. Pres., Geological Soc., 1988–90. Mem., Academia Europaea, 1990. Coke Medal, Geological Soc., 1993. *Publications:* (jtly) A Continent Revealed: the European geotraverse, 1992; Lyell: the past is the key to the present, 1998; The Timing and Location of Major Ore Deposits in an Evolving Orogen, 2002; Geodynamics and Ore Deposit Evolution in Europe, 2005; contribs to learned jls mainly relating to seismic exploration of the earth's crust, to earthquake hazards and, early on, to palæomagnetism. *Recreation:* travel. *Address:* Earth Sciences Department, Royal Holloway, University of London, Egham, Surrey TW20 0EX. *Club:* Athenæum.

BLUNDELL, Sir Richard (William), Kt 2014; CBE 2006; FBA 1997; Professor of Economics, since 1984, and Ricardo Professor of Political Economy, since 2006, University College London; Director of Research, Institute for Fiscal Studies, since 1986; *b* 1 May 1952; *s* of Horace Leon and Marjorie Blundell; *m* 1984, Anne Gaynor Aberdeen; one *s* one *d*. *Educ:* Univ. of Bristol (BSc 1st cl. Hons Econs with Stats); LSE (MSc Econometrics). Lectr in Econometrics, Univ. of Manchester, 1975–85; University College London: Head, Dept of Economics, 1988–92; Leverhulme Personal Res. Prof., 1999–2004; Dir, ESRC Centre for Microecon. Analysis of Public Policy, Inst. Fiscal Studies, 1991–. Visiting Professor: Univ. of BC, 1980–81; MIT, 1993; Univ. of Calif at Berkeley, 1994, 1999. Member, Council: Econometric Soc., 1991– (Fellow, 1991; Yrjö Jahnsson Prize, 1995; Frisch Medal, 2000; Mem. Exec. Cttee, 2001–; Pres., 2006); European Econ. Assoc., 1997– (Pres., 2004; Fellow 2004); NRC Panel Mem., Nat. Acad. of Scis, 1999–2000; Pres., REconS, 2010–13. Associate Editor: Rev. Econ. Studies, 1984–88; Jl of Human Resources, 1995–97; Co-Editor: Jl of Econometrics, 1991–97 (Mem., Exec. Council, 1997–); Econometrica, 1997–2001. Hon. For. Mem., Amer. Acad. of Arts and Science, 2002; Hon. Mem., AEA, 2001; Hon. FIA 2003. Hon. Dr: St Gallen, Switzerland, 2003; Mannheim, Germany, 2011; Norges Handelshøyskole, Bergen, Norway, 2011. Laffont Prize, Toulouse, 2008; IZA Prize in Labour Econs, Inst. for Study of Labour, Bonn, 2012. *Publications:* Unemployment, Search and Labour Supply, 1986; The Measurement of Household Welfare, 1994; Mirrlees Review of Tax Reform, 2010; contrib. Econometrica, Rev. Econ. Studies, Econ. Jl, Jl Econometrics. *Recreations:* saxophone, guitar, jazz music, travel. *Address:* Department of Economics, University College London, Gower Street, WC1E 6BT. *T:* (020) 7679 5863. *E:* r.blundell@ucl.ac.uk.

See also Sir T. L. Blundell.

BLUNDELL, Sir Thomas Leon, (Sir Tom), Kt 1997; FRS 1984; FRSC; FMedSci; Emeritus Professor and Director of Research, Department of Biochemistry, Cambridge University, since 2009 (Sir William Dunn Professor of Biochemistry, 1995–2009); Fellow of Sidney Sussex College, Cambridge, since 1995; Chairman, Biotechnology and Biological Sciences Research Council, 2009–15; President, Science Council, since 2011; *b* 7 July 1942; *s* of Horace Leon Blundell and Marjorie Blundell; one *s*; *m* 1987, Bancinyane Lynn Sibanda; two *d*. *Educ:* Steyning Grammar Sch.; Brasenose Coll., Oxford (BA, DPhil; Hon. Fellow, 1989). FRSC 2006. Postdoctoral Res. Fellow, Laboratory of Molecular Biophysics, Oxford Univ., 1967–72; Jun. Res. Fellow, Linacre Coll., Oxford, 1968–70; Lectr, Biological Scis, Sussex Univ., 1973–76; Prof. of Crystallography, Birkbeck Coll., Univ. of London, 1976–90; Dep. Chm. and Dir Gen., AFRC, 1991–94; Chief Exec. and Dep. Chm., BBSRC, 1994–96 (on secondment); Hd, Dept of Biochem., 1996–2009, Chm., Sch. of Biol Scis, 2003–09, Univ. of Cambridge. Director: International Sch. of Crystallography, 1981–; Babraham Inst., Cambridge, 1997–2002. Founder, non-exec. Dir and Chm., Scientific Adv. Bd, Astex Therapeutics (formerly Astex Technol.), 1999–2011; Chm., Scientific Adv. Bd, Astex Pharmaceuticals, 2011–13; non-exec. Dir and Chm., Scientific Adv. Bd, Astex Therapeutics (Otsuka), 2013–. Chm., Royal Commn on Envmtl Pollution, 1998–2005. Dep. Chm., Inst. of Cancer Res., 2007–15. Member: Council, AFRC, 1985–90; MRC AIDS Res. Steering Cttee, 1987–90; ACOST, 1988–90; Council, SERC, 1989–90 (Mem., 1979–82, Chm., 1983–87, Biological Scis Cttee; Mem., Science Bd, 1983–87); ABRC, 1991–94; Council, Royal Soc., 1997–99; R&D Bd, SmithKline Beecham, 1997–2000; Bd, Parly OST, 1998–2007. Hon. Dir, ICRF Unit of Structural Molecular Biology, 1989–96. Councillor, Oxford CBC, 1970–73 (Chm. Planning Cttee, 1972–73). Scientific Consultant, Oxford Molecular Ltd, 1996–99; Chm., Scientific Adv. Bd, Bioprocessing Ltd, 1997–2000; Member: UCB Sci. Adv. Bd, 2005–; Utek Sci. Adv. Bd, 2005–09; Industrial Consultant: Celltech, 1981–86 (non-exec. Dir, 1997–2004; Chm., Scientific Adv. Bd, 1998–2004); Pfizer Central Res., Groton, USA and Sandwich, UK, 1984–90, 2015–; Abingworth Management Ltd, 1988–90, 1996–. President: UK Bioscis Fedn, 2004–08; UK Biochemical Soc., 2009–11. Dir, Lawes Agricl Trust, 1998–2010; Trustee, Daphne Jackson Trust, 1996–11. Governor, Birkbeck Coll., 1985–89. Founder FMedSci 1998. Hon. Fellow, Linacre Coll., Oxford, 1991. Hon. FRASE 1993; Hon. FIChemE 1995; Hon. Fellow, Biochem. Soc., 2011; Hon. FRSB (Hon. FSB 2012). Hon. Mem., British Biophysics Soc., 2006. Associate Mem., Third World Acad. of Scis, 2009–; Corresponding Mem., Chilean Acad. of Scis, 2011–. Hon. DSc: Edinburgh, East Anglia, 1993; Sheffield, Strathclyde, 1994; Warwick, Antwerp, 1995; Nottingham, 1996; UWE, 1997; Stirling, 2000; Sussex, Pavia, 2002; St Andrews, 2002; London, 2003; Dundee, 2007; Liverpool, 2011; Chile, 2011. Alcon Award for Dist. Work in Vision Research, 1985; Gold Medal, Inst. of Biotechnological Studies, 1987; Sir Hans Krebs Medal, Fedn of European Biochemical Socs, 1987; Ciba Medal, UK Biochemical Soc., 1988; Feldberg Prize for Biology and Medicine, 1988; Gold Medal, SCI, 1995; Pfizer Eur. Award for Innovation, 1998; Bernal Medal, Royal Soc., 1998; Biochem. Soc. Award, 2013. Joint Editor: Progress in Biophysics and Molecular Biology, 1979–; Current Opinion in Structural Biology, 1996–; Member Editorial Advisory Board: Biochemistry, 1986–89; Protein Engineering, 1986–2003; Protein Science, 1992–98; Structure, 1993–. *Publications:* Protein Crystallography, 1976; papers in jls incl. Nature, Science, Structure, Jl Molecular Biol. *Recreations:* playing jazz, listening to opera, walking, international travel. *Address:* Department of Biochemistry, Tennis Court Road, Cambridge CB2 1GA.

See also Sir R. W. Blundell.

BLUNDEN, Sir Hubert (Chisholm), 8th Bt *cr* 1766, of Castle Blunden, Kilkenny; *b* 9 Aug. 1948; *s* of Sir Philip Overington Blunden, 7th Bt and Jeannette Francesca Alexandra, *d* of Captain D. Macdonald, RNR; *S* father, 2007; *m* 1975, Ellish O'Brien; one *s* one *d*. *Educ:* Avoca Sch., Blackrock. 1st Bn, Irish Guards. *Heir:* *s* Edmond Blunden, *b* 31 July 1982.

BLUNDY, Prof. Jonathan David, PhD; FRS 2008; Professor of Petrology, University of Bristol, since 2004; *b* Wallingford, 7 Aug. 1961; *s* of Peter Desmond Blundy and late Jean Dorothy Blundy; *m* 1992, Katharine Melanie Fawcett (separated 2003); one *s* one *d*, and one step *d*. *Educ:* St Paul's Sch., São Paulo; Giggleswick Sch.; Leeds Grammar Sch.; University Coll., Oxford (BA Hons 1983); Trinity Hall, Cambridge (PhD 1989). Jun. Res. Fellow, Hertford Coll., Oxford, 1990–91; University of Bristol: NERC Res. Fellow, 1991–95; Royal Soc. Univ. Res. Fellow, 1995–2002; NERC Sen. Res. Fellow, 2002–07. *Publications:* over 80 articles in scientific jls. *Recreations:* rambling, cooking, public transport, Leeds United FC. *Address:* c/o School of Earth Sciences, Wills Memorial Building, University of Bristol, Queens Road, Bristol BS8 1RJ.

BLUNKETT, family name of **Baron Blunkett**.

BLUNKETT, Baron *cr* 2015 (Life Peer), of Brightside and Hillsborough in the City of Sheffield; **David Blunkett;** PC 1997; *b* 6 June 1947; *m* (marr. diss.); three *s*; one *s*; *m* 2009, Dr Margaret Williams. *Educ:* night sch. and day release, Shrewsbury Coll. of Technol. and Richmond Coll. of Further Educn, Sheffield; Nat. Cert. in Business Studies, E Midlands Gas Bd; Sheffield Univ. (BA Hons Pol Theory and Instns); Huddersfield Holly Bank Coll. of Educn (Tech.) (PGCFE). Tutor in Industrial Relns, Barnsley Coll. of Technol., 1974–87. Elected to Sheffield City Council (at age of 22), 1970; Chm., Family and Community Services Cttee, 1976–80; Leader, 1980–87; Dep. Chm., AMA, 1984–87. Joined Labour Party at age of 16; Chm., Labour Party NEC, 1993–94 (Dep. Chm., 1992–93; Mem., 1983–98); Chm., Labour Party Cttee on Local govt, 1984–92. MP (Lab) Sheffield, Brightside, 1987–2010, Sheffield, Brightside and Hillsborough, 2010–15. Front bench spokesman on the environment, with special responsibility for local govt and poll tax, 1988–92, on health, 1992–94, on educn, 1994–95, on educn and employment, 1995–97 (Mem., Shadow Cabinet, 1992–97); Secretary of State: for Educn and Employment, 1997–2001; for Home Dept, 2001–04; for Work and Pensions, 2005. Prof. of Politics in Practice, Univ. of Sheffield, 2015–. Chair, Bd of Governance, Univ. of Law, 2015–. *Publications:* (jtly) Local Enterprise and Workers' Plans, 1981; (jtly) Building from the Bottom: the Sheffield Experience, 1983; (jtly) Democracy in Crisis: the town halls respond, 1987; On a Clear Day, 1995; Politics and Progress, 2001; The Blunkett Tapes: my life in the bear pit, 2006. *Address:* House of Lords, SW1A 0PW.

BLUNSDON, His Honour Alan James; a Circuit Judge, 2010–13; Deputy Coroner, North West Kent, since 2004; *b* 22 Aug. 1949. Admitted solicitor, 1973; a Dep. Dist Judge, 1983–91, Dist Judge, 1991–2010.

BLUNT, Charles William; Executive Chairman, Carmichael Carrol, since 2005. *Educ.* Sydney Univ. (BEcon). AASA; CPA. Exec. appts in mining, finance and agricultural industries. MP (Nat. Party) Richmond, NSW, 1984–90; Leader, Parly Nat. Party, 1989–90, opposition Minister, 1984–90, variously for: Sport, Recreation and Tourism; Social Security, Transport and Communications; Community Services and Aged Care; Trade and Resources. Former Mem., parly cttees and official delegns. Chm., Permo-Drive Technologies Ltd, 2001–05; Man. Dir, American Business Services Pty Ltd, 2003–13; CEO, American Chamber of Commerce in Australia, 1990–2013. *Recreations:* tennis, reading. *Address:* PO Box 66, Wahroonga, NSW 2076, Australia. *Clubs:* Union, American (Sydney).

BLUNT, Crispin Jeremy Rupert; MP (C) Reigate, since 1997; *b* 15 July 1960; *s* of Maj. Gen. Peter Blunt, CB, MBE, GM and Adrienne (*née* Richardson); *m* 1990, Victoria Ainsley Jenkins (separated 2010); one *s* one *d*. *Educ:* Wellington Coll.; RMA, Sandhurst; Durham Univ. (BA 1984); Cranfield Inst. of Technology (MBA 1991). Commnd, 13th/18th Royal Hussars (QMO), 1980; Troop Leader: UK and Cyprus, 1980–81; BAOR, 1984–85; Regtl Signals Officer/Ops Officer, BAOR/UK, 1985–87; Sqn Leader, 2IC UK, 1987–89; resigned commn, 1990; Rep., Forum of Private Business, 1991–92; Consultant, Politics Internat., 1993; Special Advr to Sec. of State for Defence, 1993–95, to Foreign Sec., 1995–97. Opposition spokesman on NI, 2001–02, on trade, energy and science, 2002–03; on security and counter terrorism, 2009–10; Opposition Whip, 2004–09; Parly Under-Sec. of State, MoJ, 2010–12. Member: Select Cttee on Defence, 1997–2000, 2003–04; Select Cttee on Envmt Transport and the Regions, 2000–01; Chm., Select Cttee on Foreign Affairs, 2015–. Sec. Cons. Foreign and Commonwealth Affairs Cttee, 1997–2001; Chm., Cons. Middle East Council, 2004–08. Co-Chm., Council for Advancement of Arab-British Understanding

2004–09. *Recreations:* cricket, ski-ing, bridge, gardening. *Address:* House of Commons, SW1A 0AA. *T:* (020) 7219 2254. *Clubs:* MCC; Reigate Priory Cricket.

See also O. S. P Blunt.

BLUNT, David Graeme, CVO 2001 (LVO 1986); HM Diplomatic Service, retired; Managing Director UK, Gamesa, since 2013; *b* 19 Jan. 1953; *s* of Daryl and Deidre Blunt; *m* 1975, Geirid Bakkeli; three *s*. *Educ:* Cranleigh Sch.; Manchester Univ. (BA Hons). Teacher, Blairmore Sch., Aberdeenshire, 1976–78; joined HM Diplomatic Service, 1978; FCO, 1978–79; Second, later First, Sec., Vienna, 1979–83; First Secretary: Peking, 1983–87; FCO, 1987–89; Canberra, 1989–94; Counsellor, FCO, 1994–97; Dep. Hd of Mission and Consul-Gen., Oslo, 1997–2001; Dep. Gov., Gibraltar, 2002–05; Hd of Office, then Ambassador, Pristina, Kosovo, 2006–08; Ambassador to Croatia, 2008–11. Dir, Public Policy UK and EU Instns, Gamesa Wind UK, 2012–13. *Recreations:* choral music, sailing, cross-country ski-ing. *Address:* Gamesa, 5th Floor, 16 Palace Street, SW1E 5JD.

BLUNT, David John; QC 1991; a Recorder of the Crown Court, since 1990; writer; *b* 25 Oct. 1944; *s* of late Vernon Egerton Rowland Blunt and of Catherine Vera Blunt; *m* 1976, Zaibonessa Ebrahim; one *s* one *d*. *Educ:* Farnham Grammar Sch.; Trinity Hall, Cambridge (MA Hons). Called to the Bar, Middle Temple, 1967, Bencher, 2001. Asst Recorder, 1985–90. Contested (L): Lambeth Central, 1978, 1979; Cornwall SE, 1983. First TV play broadcast, 1976. *Recreations:* walking, running, cycling, reading, writing, old cars. *Address:* 4 Pump Court, Temple, EC4Y 7AN. *T:* (020) 7842 5555.

BLUNT, Sir David Richard Reginald Harvey, 12th Bt *cr* 1720; *b* 8 Nov. 1938; *s* of Sir Richard David Harvey Blunt, 11th Bt and Elisabeth Malvine Ernestine, *d* of Comdr F. M. Fransen Van de Putte, Royal Netherlands Navy (retd); *S* father, 1975; *m* 1969, Sonia Tudor Rosemary (*née* Day) (*d* 2008); one *d*. *Heir: kinsman* Robin Anthony Blunt, CEng, MIMechE [*b* 23 Nov. 1926; *m* 1st, 1949, Sheila Stuart (marr. diss. 1962), *d* of C. Stuart Brindley; one *s*; 2nd, 1962, June Elizabeth, *d* of Charles Wigginton; one *s*].

BLUNT, Oliver Simon Peter; QC 1994; a Recorder, since 1995; *b* 8 March 1951; *s* of Maj.-Gen. Peter Blunt, CB, MBE, GM and Adrienne (*née* Richardson); *m* 1979, Joanna Margaret Dixon; one *s* three *d*. *Educ:* Bedford Sch.; Southampton Univ. (LLB 1973). Called to the Bar, Middle Temple, 1974; Asst Recorder, SE Circuit, 1991–95. *Recreations:* cricket, golf, ski-ing, swimming, mini-rugby coach. *Address:* Furnival Chambers, 32 Furnival Street, EC4A 1JQ. *T:* (020) 7405 3232. *Clubs:* Roehampton; Bank of England Sports; Barnes Cricket; Rosslyn Park Rugby.

See also C. J. R. Blunt.

BLY, John; antique dealer, since 1956; *b* Tring, 27 May 1939; *s* of Frank John and Nina Bly; *m* 1967, Virginia Fisher; two *s*. *Educ:* Berkhamsted Sch. Lectr, TV presenter, public speaker, restorer, valuer, fund raiser, editor and columnist, 1956–. Presenter, TV series: Looking At Antiques, 1971–72; Heirloom, 1975–92; Heirs and Graces, 1989–90; furniture expert, Antiques Roadshow, BBC, 1979–. Columnist, Antiques Monthly (USA), 1975–; contribs to magazines incl. Collectors' Guide, Antique Collecting, Chic Chat and lifestyle mags for Fishmedia Gp. Lectures include: Dupont Winterthur Mus.; Art Inst. of Chicago; Univ. of Birmingham, Alabama; New York Histl Soc.; San Francisco Histl Soc.; Mus. of Art Milwaukee; Governor's Mansion, Springfield, Ill; Key West Mus.; Rosary Coll., Chicago; Galesburg Univ., Ill; V&A Mus.; lectr on cruise ships. FRSA. Liveryman, Goldsmiths' Co. Hon. Citizen, New Orleans; Kentucky Squire. *Publications:* Discovering Hallmarks on English Silver, 1969, 3rd edn 2000; Discovering English Furniture, 1971, 3rd edn 2010, Japanese edn 1993; Discovering Victorian and Edwardian Furniture, 1973; (ed and compiled) Is It Genuine?, 1986, Italian edn 1983, reissued as Miller's Is It Genuine?, 2002; Antiques Guide for the Collector, 1986; (ed and compiled) Heirloom, 1989; Antique Furniture Expert, 1991; Silver and Sheffield Plate Marks, 1993, 2nd edn 2008; (ed and contrib.) Treasures in Your Home, 1993; (jtly) The Pocket Guide to Antiques and Collectables, 1999; John Bly's Antiques Masterclass, 2005; English Furniture, 2010. *Recreations:* jazz historian, playing drums, cooking, mixing proper martinis and manhattans and drinking same. *Address:* Chelsea Gallery, 533 Kings Road, Chelsea, SW10 0TZ. *Club:* Lansdowne.

BLYTH, family name of **Barons Blyth** and **Blyth of Rowington**.

BLYTH, 5th Baron *cr* 1907; **James Audley Ian Blyth;** Bt 1895; *b* 13 Nov. 1970; *s* of 4th Baron Blyth and of Oonagh Elizabeth Ann, *yr d* of late William Henry Conway, Dublin; *S* father, 2009; *m* 2003, Elodie Bernadette Andrée Odette, *d* of Jean-Georges Cadet de Fontenay; one *s* one *d*. *Educ:* Newtown Sch., Waterford. *Heir: s* Hon. Hugo Audley Jasper Blyth, *b* 9 May 2006.

BLYTH OF ROWINGTON, Baron *cr* 1995 (Life Peer), of Rowington in the County of Warwickshire; **James Blyth,** Kt 1985; Chairman: Diageo plc, 2000–08 (Director, 1998–2008); Greycastle Holdings Ltd, since 2014; Senior Advisor, Greenhill & Co., 2000–02 and 2007–14 (Vice Chairman and Partner, 2002–07); *b* 8 May 1940; *s* of Daniel Blyth and Jane Power Carlton; *m* 1967, Pamela Anne Campbell Dixon; one *d* (one *s* decd). *Educ:* Spiers Sch.; Glasgow Univ. Mobil Oil Co., 1963–69; General Foods Ltd, 1969–71; Mars Ltd, 1971–74; General Manager: Lucas Batteries Ltd, 1974–77; Lucas Aerospace Ltd, 1977–81; Head of Defence Sales, MoD, 1981–85; Man. Dir, Plessey Electronic Systems, 1985–86; Chief Exec., The Plessey Co. plc, 1986–87; The Boots Co.: Chief Exec., 1987–98; Dep. Chm., 1994–98; Chm., 1998–2000; Vice Chm., Middlebrook Pharmaceuticals Inc., 2009–10. Non-executive Director: Imperial Gp PLC, 1984–86; Cadbury-Schweppes PLC, 1986–90; British Aerospace, 1990–94; Anixter Internat. Inc., 1995–; NatWest Gp, 1998–2000; Avoca Capital Hldgs, 2013–14. Chm., Adv. Panel on Citizen's Charter, 1991–97. Pres., ME Assoc., 1988–93; Patron, Combined Services Winter Sports Assoc., 1997–2002. Gov., London Business Sch., 1987–96 (Hon. Fellow, 1997). Liveryman, Coachmakers' and Coach Harness Makers' Co. Hon. LLD Nottingham, 1992. *Recreations:* ski-ing, tennis, paintings, theatre, horse racing, golf. *Address:* House of Lords, SW1A 0PW. *Clubs:* East India, Royal Automobile, Caledonian.

BLYTH, Sir Charles, (Sir Chay), Kt 1997; CBE 1972; BEM 1967; Chairman, First ScotRail Stakeholder Advisory Board, 2007–15; *b* 14 May 1940; *s* of Robert and Jessie Blyth; *m* 1st, 1962, Maureen Margaret Morris (marr. diss. 1992); one *d*; 2nd, 1995, Felicity Rayson. *Educ:* Hawick High School. HM Forces, Para. Regt, 1958–67. Cadbury Schweppes, 1968–69; Dir, Sailing Ventures (Hampshire) Ltd, 1969–73; Managing Dir, The Challenging Business Ltd (formerly Crownfields Ltd), 1989–2006. Chm. and Dir, First Gt Western Ltd, 2006–07. Organiser: British Steel Challenge Round World Yacht Race 1992–93, 1989–93; BT Global Challenge Round the World Yacht Race 1996–97, 1994–97. Rowed North Atlantic with Captain John Ridgway, June–Sept. 1966; circumnavigated the world westwards solo in yacht British Steel, 1970–71; circumnavigated the world eastwards with crew of paratroopers in yacht Great Britain II, and Winner, Elapsed Time Prize Whitbread Round the World Yacht Race, 1973–74; Atlantic sailing record, Cape Verde to Antigua, 1977; won Round Britain Race in yacht Great Britain IV, 1978 (crew Robert James); won The Observer/Europe 1 doublehanded transatlantic race in record time, 1981 (crew Robert James); Number One to Virgin Atlantic Challenge II successful attempt on the Blue Riband, 1986. Pres., Inst. of Professional Sales, 1998. Yachtsman of the Year, 1971, Special Award for outstanding services to yachting, Yachting Journalists Assoc., 1994; Chichester Trophy, RYS, 1971. Freeman of Hawick, 1972. *Publications:* A Fighting Chance, 1966; Innocent Aboard, 1968; The Impossible Voyage, 1971; Theirs is the Glory, 1974; The Challenge, 1993. *Recreations:* sailing, horse-riding, hunting. *Address:* Tandlaw Steading, Stouslie, Hawick, Scottish Borders TD9 7NY. *Clubs:* Royal Ocean Racing; Royal Southern Yacht.

BLYTHE, His Honour James Forbes, TD 1946; a Circuit Judge, 1978–92; solicitor; *b* Coventry, 11 July 1917; *s* of J. F. Blythe and Dorothy Alice (*née* Hazlewood); *m* 1949, Margaret, *d* of P. D. Kinsey; two *d*. *Educ:* Wrekin Coll.; Birmingham Univ. (LLB). Commissioned TA, Royal Warwickshire Regt, 1936–53 (Major); served War of 1939–45 with BEF in France (Dunkirk), 1939–40; Central Mediterranean Force (Tunisia, Sicily, Italy, Corsica, S France and Austria), 1942–45; Air Liaison Officer GSO II (Ops) with RAF (despatches); GSO II (Ops) 10 Corps, 1945; GSO II (Ops) HQ Polish Repatriation Gp, 1945–46. Admitted solicitor, 1947; private practitioner in partnership in Coventry and Leamington Spa, 1948. HM Deputy Coroner for City of Coventry and Northern Dist of Warwickshire, 1954–64; HM Coroner for City of Coventry, 1964–78; a Recorder of the Crown Court, 1972–78. Pres., Warwicks Law Soc., 1978–79. Trustee, Samuel Smith's Charity, 1963–2014. *Recreations:* sport, music, domesticity. *Address:* Hazlewood, Upper Ladyes' Hill, Kenilworth, Warwickshire CV8 2FB. *Clubs:* Army and Navy; Leamington Tennis Court.

BLYTHE, Mark Andrew, CB 1999; Principal Assistant Solicitor, Treasury Solicitor's Department, 1989–2003, and Legal Adviser, HM Treasury, 1993–2003; *b* 4 Sept. 1943; *s* of John Jarratt Blythe and Dorothy Kathleen Blythe; *m* 1972, Brigid Helen Frazer (*née* Skemp); two *s* one *d*. *Educ:* King Edward VII Grammar Sch., Sheffield; University Coll., Oxford (BCL, MA; Open Schol. in Classics, 1961; Gibbs Prize in Law, 1963). Called to the Bar, Inner Temple, 1966; Attorney, NY Bar, 1980. Teaching Associate, Univ. of Pennsylvania Law Sch., 1965–66; Chancery Bar, 1967–77; Legal Consultant, NY, 1978–80; Treasury Solicitor's Dept, 1981–2003: Assistant Solicitor, European Div., 1986–89; Hd, Central Adv. Div., 1989–93.

BLYTHE, Moira; *see* Gibb, Dame M.

BLYTHE, Rex Arnold; Under-Secretary, Board of Inland Revenue, 1981–86, retired; *b* 11 Nov. 1928; *s* of late Sydney Arnold Blythe and Florence Blythe (*née* Jones); *m* 1953, Rachel Ann Best (*d* 2008); one *s* two *d*. *Educ:* Bradford Grammar Sch.; Trinity Coll., Cambridge (MA Classics). Entered Inland Revenue as Inspector of Taxes, 1953; Sen. Inspector, 1962; Principal Inspector, 1968; Asst Sec., 1974. *Recreations:* photography, travel. *Address:* 18A Kirkwick Avenue, Harpenden, Herts AL5 2QX. *T:* (01582) 715833.

BLYTHE, Ronald George; writer, since 1953; *b* 6 Nov. 1922; *s* of Albert George Blythe and Matilda Elizabeth (*née* Elkins). *Educ:* St Peter's and St Gregory's Sch., Sudbury, Suffolk. Librarian, 1943–54. Soc. of Authors' Travel Scholarship, 1969. Editor, Penguin Classics, 1966–87. Assistant, Aldeburgh Fest., 1955–57; Member: Eastern Arts Lit. Panel, 1975–85; Cttee, Centre of E Anglian Studies, UEA, 1975–80; Soc. of Authors' Management Cttee, 1980–85; Chm., Essex Fest., 1981–84. President: John Clare Soc., 1981–; Robert Bloomfield Soc., 2001–; Kilvert Soc., 2006–. Reader, C of E, 1984–; Lay Canon, St Edmundsbury Cathedral, 2003–. FRSL 1969. Hon. MA UEA, 1990; Hon. DLitt: Anglia Poly. Univ., 2001; Essex, 2002; MLitt Lambeth, 2001. Benson Medal for Literature, RSL, 2006. *Publications:* A Treasonable Growth, 1960; Immediate Possession, 1961; The Age of Illusion, 1963; William Hazlitt: selected writings, 1970; Akenfield (Heinemann Award), 1969; Aldeburgh Anthology, 1972; (ed jtly) Works of Thomas Hardy, 1978; The View in Winter, 1979, 2nd edn 2005; (ed) Writing in a War: stories, essays and poems of 1939–45, 1982; Places, 1982; From the Headlands, 1982; The Stories of Ronald Blythe (Angel Prize for Literature), 1985; Divine Landscapes, 1986; Each Returning Day: the pleasure of diaries, 1989; Private Words: letters and diaries of the Second World War, 1991; First Friends, 1998; Going to Meet George and other outings, 1999; Talking About John Clare, 1999; The Circling Year, 2001; Talking to the Neighbours, 2002; (ed) George Herbert, A Priest to the Temple or The Country Parson, 2003; Eight Poems, 2004; A Country Boy, 2004; The Assassin, 2004; A Writer's Day-Book, 2006; A Year At Bottengoms Farm, 2006; Field Work: selected essays, 2007; Outsiders: a book of garden friends, 2008; The Bookman's Tale, 2009; Aftermath: selected writings 1960–2010, 2010; At the Yeoman's House, 2011; At Helpston: meetings with John Clare, 2011; The Time by the Sea: Aldeburgh 1955–1958, 2013; Village Hours, 2012; Under a Broad Sky, 2013; Wormingford Trilogy: Word from Wormingford, 1997; Out of the Valley, 2000; Borderland, 2005; Decadal. *Recreations:* walking, looking, listening. *Address:* Bottengoms Farm, Wormingford, Colchester, Essex CO6 3AP. *T:* (01206) 271308.

BLYTHMAN, Joanna; journalist and author specialising in food issues. Mem. Council, Soil Assoc., 2013–. Caroline Walker Award, Caroline Walker Trust, 1993; Derek Cooper Award, BBC Radio 4 Food and Farming Awards, 2004; Good Housekeeping Award for Outstanding Contribn to Food, 2007. *Publications:* The Food We Eat, 1996, 2nd rev. edn 1998 (Glenfiddich Special Award, 1997); The Food Our Children Eat, 1999; How to Avoid GM Food, 1999; Shopped, 2004 (Glenfiddich Food Book of Year, 2005); Bad Food Britain, 2006; What to Eat, 2013; Swallow This: serving up the food industry's darkest secrets, 2015. *Address:* c/o Publicity, Fourth Estate, 77–85 Fulham Palace Road, W6 8JB. *T:* (020) 8307 4247. *E:* rebecca.mcewan@harpercollins.co.uk.

BOA, Prof. Elizabeth Janet, PhD; FBA 2003; Professor of German and Head of Department of German, University of Nottingham, 1996–2001, now Emeritus Professor; *b* 20 March 1939. *Educ:* Univ. of Glasgow (MA 1961); Univ. of Nottingham (PhD). Lectr, Sen. Lectr, then Reader in German, Univ. of Nottingham, 1965–94; Prof. of Modern German Literature, Univ. of Manchester, 1994. *Publications:* (with James H. Reid) Critical Strategies: German fiction in the twentieth century, 1972; Sexual Circus: Wedekind's theatre of subversion, 1987; Kafka: gender, class and race in the letters and fictions, 1996; (with Rachel Palfreyman) Heimat—A German Dream: regional loyalties and national identity in German culture 1890–1990, 2000. *Address:* c/o Department of German, University of Nottingham, University Park, Nottingham NG7 2RD.

BOADEN, Helen; Director, BBC Radio, since 2013; *b* 1 March 1956; *d* of William John Boaden and Barbara Mary Boaden; *m* 1994, Stephen Burley. *Educ:* Univ. of Sussex (BA Hons English 1978). Care Asst, Hackney Social Services, 1978; Reporter: Radio WBAI, NY, 1979; Radio Tees and Radio Aire, 1980–83; Producer, BBC Radio Leeds, 1983–85; Reporter: File on 4, Radio 4, 1985–91; Brass Tacks, BBC 2, 1985–91; Presenter: Woman's Hour, Radio 4, 1985–91; Verdict, Channel 4, 1991; Editor, File on 4, Radio 4, 1991–94; Head: Network Current Affairs, BBC Manchester, 1994–97; Business Progs, BBC News, 1997; Current Affairs and Business Progs, BBC, 1998–2000; Controller: BBC Radio 4, 2000–04; BBC7, 2002–04; Director: BBC News, 2004–13; BBC News Group, 2011–13. Chm., Radio Acad., 2003–. Pres., Holiday Fellowship, 2014–. Trustee: Alcohol Res. UK; Stephen Joseph Th., Scarborough. Hon. Fellow, Univ. of the Arts, 2011. Hon. Dr: UEA (Suffolk Coll.); Sussex, 2003; York, 2004; DUniv Open, 2011. *Recreations:* walking, food, travel. *Address:* c/o BBC, Broadcasting House, Portland Place, W1A 1AA.

BOAG, Shirley Ann; *see* Robertson, S. A.

BOAL, His Honour (John) Graham; QC 1993; a Senior Circuit Judge, and Permanent Judge at Central Criminal Court, 1996–2005; *b* 24 Oct. 1943; *s* of late Surg. Captain Jackson Graham Boal, RN, and late Dorothy Kenley Boal; *m* 1978, Elizabeth Mary East; one *s*. *Educ:* Eastbourne Coll.; King's Coll. London (LLB). Called to the Bar, Gray's Inn, 1966, Bencher, 1991; Junior Treasury Counsel, 1977–85; Sen. Prosecuting Counsel to the Crown, 1985–91; First Sen. Counsel to the Crown at CCC, 1991–93; a Recorder, 1985–96. Vice Chm.,

Criminal Bar Assoc., 1991–93. Judicial Mem., Parole Bd, 2001–05. Chairman: Orchid Cancer Appeal, 1999–2005; Seventy4, 2012–13. Trustee, Westminster Drug Project/Seventy4 Foundn, 2013–. *Recreations:* theatre, golf, walking, watching cricket. *Clubs:* Garrick, MCC; Royal West Norfolk Golf; Old Bailey Judges Golfing Society; New Zealand Golf.

BOAM, Maj.-Gen. Thomas Anthony, CB 1987; CBE 1978 (OBE 1973); Vice President, Leonard Cheshire, since 2003 (Trustee and Chairman, South Region, 1997–2003); *b* 14 Feb. 1932; *s* of late Lt-Col T. S. Boam, OBE, and of Mrs Boam; *m* 1961, Penelope Christine Mary Roberts; one *s* two *d*. *Educ:* Bradfield Coll.; RMA Sandhurst. Commissioned Scots Guards, 1952; Canal Zone, Egypt (with 1SG), 1952–54; GSO3, MO4 War Office, 1959–61; psc 1962; Kenya (with 2 Scots Guards), 1963–64; DAA&QMG 4 Guards Bde, 1964–65; Malaysia (with 1SG), 1966–67; BM 4 Guards Bde, 1967–69; GSO1 (DS) Staff Coll., Camberley, 1970–71; CO 2SG, 1972–74; RCDS 1974–75; Comd BAAT Nigeria, 1976–78; BGS (Trng) HQ UKLF, 1978; Dep. Comdr and COS Hong Kong, 1979–81; Hd of British Defence Staff Washington, and Defence Attaché, 1981–84, Mil. Attaché, 1981–83; Comdr, British Forces Hong Kong, and Maj.-Gen., Brigade of Gurkhas, 1985–87. MEC, Hong Kong, 1985–87. Dir, British Consultants Bureau, 1988–95. Chm., 4Sight, W Sussex Assoc. for the Blind, 2003–06. Gov., Hayes Dashwood Foundn, 1992–2006. Vice-Patron, Queen Alexandra Hosp. Home, 2006– (Gov., 1996–2006; Vice-Chm., 1998–2006). *Recreations:* shooting, gardening, sport. *Address:* Bury Gate House, Pulborough, W Sussex RH20 1HA. *Clubs:* MCC; Sussex.

BOARDMAN, Christopher Miles, MBE 1993; professional cyclist, retired 2000; Founder, 2004, and Director of Research and Development, Boardman Bikes; *b* 26 Aug. 1968; *s* of Keith and Carole Boardman; *m* 1988, Sally-Ann Edwards; four *s* two *d*. Gold Medal, Individual Pursuit, Olympic Games, Barcelona, 1992; World Champion: Pursuit, 1994; Time Trial, 1994; Yellow Jersey Holder, Tour de France, 1994, 1997, 1998; Silver Medal, Time Trial, World Championship, 1996; Bronze Medal, Time Trial, Olympic Games, Atlanta, 1996; World Champion, 4,000 Pursuit, 1996; World One Hour Record Holder: 52.270 km, 1993; 56.375 km, 1996; (under new regulations) 49.441 km, 2000. Policy Advr, British Cycling (Elite Coach, 2005–08; Dir of R&D, 2009–12). Mem., Sports Council for England, 1995–96, English Sports Council, 1996. Hon. DSc Brighton, 1997; Hon. MSc Liverpool, 1995. Man of Year Award, Cheshire Life mag., 1997. *Publications:* (with Andrew Longmore) The Complete Book of Cycling, 2000. *Address:* c/o British Cycling, Stuart Street, Manchester M11 4DQ.

BOARDMAN, Faith Rosemary; independent consultant, since 2005; non-executive Director, King's College Hospital NHS Foundation Trust, since 2012; *b* 21 Aug. 1950; *d* of Kenneth Mills and Vera Mills (*née* Waterson); *m* 1974, David Boardman; one *s* one *d*. *Educ:* Lady Margaret Hall, Oxford (MA Modern Hist.). Sen. Civil Service trainee, 1972–77, VAT Policy, 1977–79, HM Customs and Excise; Fiscal Policy, HM Treasury, 1979–83; HM Customs and Excise: Tobacco Taxation, 1983–86; Personnel Policy, 1986–89; Chief Exec. (Collector), London Central, 1989–95; Chief Exec. (Grade 3), Contributions Agency, DSS, 1995–97; Chief Exec. (Grade 2), CSA, 1997–2000; Exec. Mem., Deptl Bd, DSS, then DWP, 1995–2000; Chief Exec., London Borough of Lambeth, 2000–05. Ind. Mem., Metropolitan Police Authy, 2007–12; non-exec. Advr, Mayor of London's Office for Policing and Crime, 2012–. Non-exec. Mem., Audit Cttee, Nat. Offenders Mgt Service, 2005–11. Mem. Bd, Public Mgt and Policy Assoc. (interim Develt Dir, 2010–13). Non-exec. Dir, HM Courts Service, 2006–08; Associate: Whitehall and Industry Gp; Major Projects Authy; SOLACE; College of Policing. Treas., Vauxhall Business Improvement Dist, 2012–. Chair of Trustees: Vauxhall City Farm, 2005–; London Ecumenical Aids Trust, 2005–13. Financial Services Woman of Year Award, 1990. *Recreations:* family, friends, community, music, history, public speaking, travelling.

BOARDMAN, Sir John, Kt 1989; FSA 1957; FBA 1969; Lincoln Professor of Classical Archaeology and Art, and Fellow of Lincoln College, University of Oxford, 1978–94 (Hon. Fellow, 1995); *b* 20 Aug. 1927; *s* of Frederick Archibald Boardman; *m* 1952, Sheila Joan Lyndon Stanford (*d* 2005); one *s* one *d*. *Educ:* Chigwell Sch.; Magdalene Coll., Cambridge (BA 1948, MA 1951, Walston Student, 1948–50; Hon. Fellow 1984). 2nd Lt, Intell. Corps, 1950–52. Asst Dir, British Sch. at Athens, 1952–55; Asst Keeper, Ashmolean Museum, Oxford, 1955–59; Reader in Classical Archaeology, Univ. of Oxford, 1959–78; Fellow of Merton Coll., Oxford, 1963–78, Hon. Fellow, 1978. Geddes-Harrower Prof., Aberdeen Univ., 1974; Vis. Prof., Australian Inst. of Archaeology, 1987; Prof. of Ancient History, Royal Acad., 1989–; Lectures: Andrew W. Mellon, Washington, 1993; Myres Meml, Oxford, 1993. Editor: Journal of Hellenic Studies, 1958–65; Lexicon Iconographicum, 1972–99; Cambridge Ancient History, 1978–94. Conducted excavations on Chios, 1953–55, and at Tocra in Libya, 1964–65. Delegate, OUP, 1979–89. Pres. Fédn Internat. des Assocs d'Etudes Classiques, 1994–97. Corresponding Fellow: Bavarian Acad. of Scis, 1969; Athens Acad., 1997; Fellow, Inst. of Etruscan Studies, Florence, 1983; Hon. Fellow, Archaeol Soc. of Athens, 1989 (Vice Pres., 1998–); Member: Amer. Philosophical Soc., 1999; Accad. dei Lincei, Rome, 1999; Foreign Member: Royal Danish Acad., 1979; Russian Acad. of Scis, 2003; Mem. associé, Acad. des Inscriptions et Belles Lettres, Institut de France, 1991 (Correspondant, 1985); Hon. Mem., Archaeol Inst. of America, 1993. Pres., Soc. of Jewellery Historians, 2010–12. Hon. MRIA, 1986. Hon. Dr: Dept of Archaeology and History, Univ. of Athens, 1991; Sorbonne, 1994. Cromer Greek Prize, 1959, Kenyon Medal, 1995, British Acad.; Onassis Prize for Humanities, 2009. *Publications:* Cretan Collection in Oxford, 1961; Date of the Knossos Tablets, 1963; Island Gems, 1963; Greeks Overseas, 1964, rev. edn 1999; Greek Art, 1964, rev. edns 1973, 1984, 1996; Excavations at Tocra, vol. I 1966, vol. II 1973; Pre-Classical, 1967, repr. 1978; Greek Emporio, 1967; Engraved Gems, 1968; Archaic Greek Gems, 1968; Greek Gems and Finger Rings, 1970, repr. 2001; (with D. Kurtz) Greek Burial Customs, 1971; Athenian Black Figure Vases, 1974; Athenian Red Figure Vases, Archaic Period, 1975; Intaglios and Rings, 1975; Corpus Vasorum, Oxford, vol. 3, 1975; Greek Sculpture, Archaic Period, 1978; (with M. Robertson) Corpus Vasorum, Castle Ashby, 1978; (with M. L. Vollenweider) Catalogue of Engraved Gems, Ashmolean Museum, 1978; (with D. Scarisbrick) Harari Collection of Finger Rings, 1978; (with E. La Rocca) Eros in Greece, 1978; Escarabeos de Piedra de Ibiza, 1984; La Ceramica Antica, 1984; Greek Sculpture, Classical Period, 1985; (with D. Finn) The Parthenon and its Sculptures, 1985; (jtly) The Oxford History of the Classical World, 1986; Athenian Red Figure Vases, Classical Period, 1989; (jtly) The Oxford History of Classical Art, 1993; The Diffusion of Classical Art in Antiquity, 1994 (Runciman Prize, 1995); Greek Sculpture, Later Classical, 1995; Early Greek Vase Painting, 1998; Persia and the West, 2000; Greek Vases, 2001; Archaeology of Nostalgia, 2002 (Runciman Prize, 2003); Classical Phoenician Scarabs, 2003; A Collection of Classical and Eastern Intaglios, 2003; The World of Ancient Art, 2006; (with K. Piacenti) Gems and Jewels: the Royal Collection, 2008; The Marlborough Gems, 2009; The Relief Plaques of Eastern Eurasia and China, 2010; The Triumph of Dionysos, 2014; The Greeks in Asia, 2015; articles in jls. *Address:* 11 Park Street, Woodstock, Oxford OX20 1SJ. *T:* (01993) 811259. *Club:* Athenæum.

BOARDMAN, Hon. Nigel Patrick Gray; Partner, Slaughter and May, since 1982; *b* Northampton, 19 Oct. 1950; *s* of Baron Boardman, MC, TD; one *s* five *d*. *Educ:* Ampleforth Coll.; Bristol Univ. (BA Hons). Joined Slaughter and May, 1973. Trustee, British Mus., 2013–. *Recreations:* my children, grandchildren, dog, watching sport and digging up golf courses. *Address:* Slaughter and May, 1 Bunhill Row, EC1Y 8YY. *T:* (020) 7090 3418, *Fax:* (020) 7090 5000. *E:* nigel.boardman@slaughterandmay.com.

BOARDMAN, Norman Keith, AO 1993; PhD, ScD; FRS 1978; FAA; FTSE; Chi Executive, Commonwealth Scientific and Industrial Research Organization, 1986–90 (pos retirement Fellow, 1990–99); *b* 16 Aug. 1926; *s* of William Robert Boardman and Marga Boardman; *m* 1952, Mary Clayton Shepherd; two *s* five *d*. *Educ:* Melbourne Univ. (BSc 194 MSc 1949); St John's Coll., Cambridge (PhD 1954, ScD 1974). FAA 1972; FTSE (FTS 198 ICI Fellow, Cambridge, 1953–55; Fulbright Scholar, Univ. of Calif, LA, 1964–66. R Officer, Wool Res. Section, CSIRO, 1949–51; CSIRO Div. of Plant Industry: Sen. R Scientist, 1956; Principal Res. Scientist, 1961; Sen. Prin. Res. Scientist, 1966; Chief R Scientist, 1968; Mem. Exec., 1977–85, Chm. and Chief Exec., 1985–86, CSIRO. Membe Aust. Res. Grants Cttee, 1971–75; Council, ANU, 1979–89 and 1990–91; Bd, Aust. Cent for Internat. Agricl Research, 1982–88; Nat. Water Research Council, 1982–85; Prin Minister's Science Council, 1989–90. Director: Sirotech Ltd, 1986–90; Landcare Aust. Lt 1990–98. Pres., Aust. Biochem. Soc., 1976–78; Sec. of Sci. Policy, Aust. Acad. of Sc 1993–97 (Treas., 1978–81). Corresp. Mem., Amer. Soc. of Plant Physiologists; Forei Mem., Korean Acad. of Sci. and Technology. Hon. DSc Newcastle, NSW, 1988. Dav Syme Res. Prize, Melbourne Univ., 1967; Lemberg Medal, Aust. Biochem. Soc., 196 *Publications:* scientific papers on plant biochemistry, partic. photosynthesis and structur function and biogenesis of chloroplasts; papers on science and technology policy. *Recreation* reading, tennis, listening to music. *Address:* 6 Somers Crescent, Forrest, ACT 2603, Austral *T:* (2) 62951746. *Club:* Commonwealth (Canberra).

BOARDMAN, Rev. Canon Philippa Jane, MBE 2011; Canon Treasurer, St Pau Cathedral, since 2013; *b* Harrow, 24 March 1963; *d* of Lionel Boardman and Audr Boardman. *Educ:* Haberdashers' Aske's Sch. for Girls; Jesus Coll., Cambridge (BA 198 Ridley Hall, Cambridge. Ordained deacon, 1990, priest, 1994; Parish Deacon, St Mary a St Stephen, Walthamstow, 1990–93; Curate, St Mary of Eton, Hackney Wick, 1993–9 Priest-in-charge, 1996–2003, Vicar, 2003–13, St Paul and St Mark, Old Ford. Member: Ge Synod of C of E, 1994–; Church Bldgs Council, C of E, 2010–14. Chaplain to Sheriff of t City of London, 2014–; Honorary Chaplain: Chartered Accountants' Co., 2013–; Coal Tra Benevolent Assoc., 2013–. Gov., Old Ford Sch., 1997–2013. *Recreations:* travel, cinem walking, sports, history. *Address:* Chapter House, St Paul's Churchyard, EC4M 8AD. *T:* (02 7248 3312. *E:* treasurer@stpaulscathedral.org.uk.

BOAS, John Robert Sotheby, (Bob); Chairman, Federation of British Artists (M Galleries), 2001–07; *b* 28 Feb. 1937; *s* of Edgar Henry Boas and Mary Katherine Boas; *m* 196 Elisabeth Gersted; one *s* one *d* (and one *s* decd). *Educ:* Corpus Christi Coll., Cambridge (B Maths (Sen. Optimes)). FCA 1964. Price Waterhouse, 1960–65; ICI, 1965–66; S. Warburg, 1966–95; Dir, 1971–95; Vice Chm., 1990–95; Man. Dir, SBC Warburg, 1995–9 Non-executive Director: Chesterfield Properties, 1978–99; ENO, 1990–99; Norwich Unio 1998–2000; Invesco Continental Smaller Cos Trust, 1998–2004; Trident Safeguards Lt 1998–2003; Land Command Mgt Bd, 1998–2001; Prospect Publishing Co. Ltd, 2000 Telecom Italia, 2004–07. Dir, SFA, 1988–96. Trustee: Nat. Life Stories Collection, 1998 Nat. Heritage Meml Fund and Heritage Lottery Fund, 1998–2002; Guildhall Sch. Trus 2000–09; Internat. Musicians Seminar, Prussia Cove, 2002–; Paul Hamlyn Foundn, 2002–0 Architectural Heritage Fund, 2003–08; UCL Cancer Inst. Res. Trust, 2005–; London Stri Quartet Foundn, 2006–10; Hatfield House Chamber Music Fest., 2013–. *Recreations:* musi art, theatre, reading, travelling. *Address:* 22 Mansfield Street, W1G 9NR.

BOASE, Martin; Chairman, Omnicom UK plc, 1989–95; *b* 14 July 1932; *s* of Prof. Al Martin Boase and Elizabeth Grizelle Boase; *m* 1st, 1960, Terry Ann Moir (marr. diss. 1971 one *s* one *d*; 2nd, 1974, Pauline Valerie Brownrigg; one *s* one *d*. *Educ:* Bedales Sch Rendcomb Coll.; New Coll., Oxford. MA; FIPA 1976. Executive, The London Pre Exchange, Ltd, 1958–60; Pritchard Wood and Partners, Ltd: Manager, 1961–65; Dir, th Dep. Man. Dir, 1965–68; Founding Partner, The Boase Massimi Pollitt Partnership, Lt 1968; Chm., Boase Massimi Pollitt plc, 1977–89 (Jt Chm., 1977–79). Chairman: Maide Outdoor, 1993–2006; Kiss 100 FM, 1993–2000; Herald Investment Trust, 1994–200 Investment Trust of Investment Trusts, 1995–2005; Heal's, 1997–2000; Global Profession Media plc, 1999–2005; Jupiter Dividend & Growth Investment Trust, 1999–; Directo Omnicom Gp Inc., 1989–93; EMAP plc, 1991–2000; Matthew Clark plc, 1995–98; New St Investment Trust, 2000–06. Chairman: Advertising Assoc., 1987–92; British Televisio Advertising Awards Ltd, 1993–2000. Dir, Oxford Playhouse Trust, 1991–97. *Recreation:* th Turf. *Address:* (office) 12 Bishop's Bridge Road, W2 6AA.

BOATENG, family name of **Baron Boateng**.

BOATENG, Baron *cr* 2010 (Life Peer), of Akyem in the Republic of Ghana and of Wembl in the London Borough of Brent; **Paul Yaw Boateng;** PC 1999; British High Commission in South Africa, 2005–09; barrister-at-law; *b* 14 June 1951; *s* of Eleanor and Kwaku Boaten *m* 1980, Janet Alleyne; two *s* three *d*. *Educ:* Ghana Internat. Sch.; Accra Acad.; Apsl Grammar Sch.; Bristol Univ. (LLB Hons); Coll. of Law. Admitted Solicitor, 1976; Solicito Paddington Law Centre, 1976–79; Solicitor and Partner, B. M. Birnberg and Co., 1979–8 called to the Bar, Gray's Inn, 1989. Legal Advr, Scrap Sus Campaign, 1977–81. Great London Council: Mem. (Lab) for Walthamstow, 1981–86; Chm., Police Cttee, 1981–8 Vice-Chm., Ethnic Minorities Cttee, GLC, 1981–86. Chairman: Afro-Caribbean Educ Resource Project, 1978–86; Westminster CRC, 1979–81. Contested (Lab) Herts W, 198 MP (Lab) Brent South, 1987–2005. Opposition frontbench spokesman: on treasury an economic affairs, 1989–92; on legal affairs, LCD, 1992–97; Parly Under-Sec. of State, DoH 1997–98; Minister of State, 1998–2001, and Dep. Home Sec., 1999–2001, Home Offic Financial Sec., 2001–02, Chief Sec., 2002–05, HM Treasury. Mem., H of C Environme Cttee, 1987–89. Member: Home Sec.'s Adv. Council on Race Relations, 1981–86; WC Commn on prog. to combat racism, 1984–91; Police Training Council, 1981–85; Exec NCCL, 1980–86. Co-Chm., Africa Intellectual Property Trust, 2012–; non-exec. Dir an Mem., Adv. Bd of various cos. Chairman: Book Aid Internat., 2014–; In Their Lifetim Appeal, Christian Aid, 2014–. Chm. Governors, Priory Park Sch., 1978–84; Governor: Poli Staff Coll., Bramshill, 1981–84; LSE, 2012–; Mem. Ct, Bristol Univ., 1994–2001. Interna Trustee, Duke of Edinburgh's Internat. Youth Award, 2009–; Global Trustee, Unified B Food for the Hungry Inc., 2010–; Governor: Ditchley Park, 2009–12; Mus. of Londo 2009–; ESU, 2010– (Chm., 2015–). Mem. Bd, ENO, 1984–97. Broadcaster. Hon. DLaw Lincoln, Penn, 2004; Hon. LLD Bristol, 2007. *Publications:* (contrib.) Reclaiming the Groun 1993; (contrib.) Complete Novels of Jane Austen, 1993. *Recreations:* opera, swimmin *Address:* House of Lords, SW1A 0PW. *E:* boatengp@parliament.uk. *Club:* none.

BOATENG, Ozwald, OBE 2006; Managing Director, Bespoke Couture Ltd, since 1991; London, 22 Feb. 1967. *Educ:* Southgate Coll. First studio, Portobello Rd, 1991; first sto opened London, 1995. Best Menswear Designer, British Fashion Awards, 2000. *Addres* Bespoke Couture Ltd, 30 Savile Row, W1S 3PT. *T:* (020) 7440 5242. *E:* Anne.marie(bespokecoutureltd.co.uk.

BOBROW, Prof. Martin, CBE 1995; FRS 2004; FRCP, FRCPath, FMedSci; Professor Medical Genetics, Cambridge University, 1995–2005, now Emeritus; *b* 6 Feb. 1938; *s* of J and Bessie Bobrow; *m* 1963, Lynda Geraldine Strauss; three *d*. *Educ:* Univ. of th Witwatersrand (BSc Hons 1958; MB BCh 1963; DSc Med 1979). MRCPath 1978, FRCPat 1990; FRCP 1986. Consultant in Clin. Genetics, Oxford, and Mem., MRC Ext. Sci. Sta Genetics Lab., Oxford Univ., 1974–81; Prof. of Human Genetics, Univ. of Amsterda 1981–82; Prince Philip Prof. of Paediatric Res., UMDS of Guy's and St Thomas' Hosp London Univ., 1982–95. Mem. Council, 1988–92, 1993–94, Chm., Molecular and Cellul

Medicine Bd, 1992–95, MRC; Chairman: Cttee on Med. Aspects of Radiation in the Envmt, 1985–92; Unrelated Live Donor Transplant Regulatory Authy, 1990–99; Nat. Council, Muscular Dystrophy Gp, 1995–2011; Expert Adv. Gp on Data Access, 2012–; Member: Black Adv. Gp on Possible Increased Incidence of Cancer in West Cumbria, 1983–84; Cttee to examine the ethical implications of gene therapy, 1989–93; NHS Central R&D Cttee, DoH, 1991–97; Nuffield Council on Bioethics, 1996–2003; Human Genetics Adv. Commn, 1997–99; Steering Cttee, Global Alliance for Genomics and Health, 2013–. Non-exec. Dir, Cambridge Univ. NHS Foundn Trust, 2004–13. Governor, Wellcome Trust, 1996–2007 (Dep. Chm., 2004–07). *Publications:* papers in sci. books and jls. *Address:* The Old School, 38 High Street, Balsham, Cambridge CB21 4DJ.

BOBZIEN, Prof. Susanne, DPhil; FBA 2014; Professor of Philosophy, University of Oxford, since 2013; Senior Research Fellow, All Souls College, Oxford, since 2013; *b* Hamburg, Germany, 6 June 1960; *d* of Hans and Hannelore Bobzien; *m* 2012, Nathan A. Schatz. *Educ:* Univ. of Bonn (MA 1985); Univ. of Oxford (DPhil 1993). Tutorial Fellow in Philosophy, Balliol Coll., Oxford, 1989–90; Official Fellow and Praelector in Philosophy, Queen's Coll., Oxford, 1990–2002; Lectr in Philosophy, Univ. of Oxford, 1993–2002; Prof. of Philosophy, Yale Univ., 2002–10. Erasmus Visiting Professor: Padua, 1992; Bern, 1998; British Acad. Res. Reader, 2000–02; Sen. Vis. Fellow, 2001–02, Sen. Res. Scholar, 2010–13, Yale Univ. Mem., Inst. for Advanced Study, Princeton, 2008–09. *Publications:* Die Stoische Modallogik, 1986; (jtly) Alexander of Aphrodisias: on Aristotle prior Analytics 1.1–7, 1991; Determinism and Freedom in Stoic Philosophy, 1998. *Recreations:* piano playing, walking, nature photography, concerts, cinema. *Address:* All Souls College, Oxford OX1 4AL. *E:* susanne.bobzien@all-souls.ox.ac.uk.

BOCKMUEHL, Prof. Markus Nikolaus Andreas, PhD; Dean Ireland's Professor of the Exegesis of Holy Scripture, University of Oxford, since 2014; Fellow, Keble College, Oxford, since 2007; *b* Dueren, 29 Dec. 1961; *s* of Klaus Erich and Elisabeth Bockmuehl; *m* 1994, Celia Rosamund Withycombe; two *s* three *d*. *Educ:* St George's Sch., Vancouver; Univ. of British Columbia (BA Classical Studies 1981); Regent Coll., Vancouver (MA Theol Studies, MDiv 1984); Univ. of Cambridge (PhD 1987); MA Oxon 2007. Res. Asst in Ancient Hebrew Inscriptions, Univ. of Cambridge, 1987–88; Asst Prof., Regent Coll., Vancouver and Sessional Lectr in Hebrew, Univ. of BC, 1988–89; University of Cambridge: Asst Lectr, 1989–94; Lectr, 1994–2000; Reader, 2000–04; Prof. of Biblical and Early Christian Studies, 2004–06; Professor of Biblical and Early Christian Studies: Univ. of St Andrews, 2006–07; Univ. of Oxford, 2007–14. *Publications:* Revelation and Mystery in Ancient Judaism and Pauline Christianity, 1990; This Jesus: Martyr, Lord, Messiah, 1994; The Epistle to the Philippians, 1997; (ed with M. B. Thompson) A Vision for the Church: studies in early Christian ecclesiology in honour of J. P. M. Sweet, 1997; Jewish Law in Gentile Churches, 2000; (ed) The Cambridge Companion to Jesus, 2001; (ed with D. A. Hagner) The Written Gospel, 2005; Seeing the Word: refocusing New Testament study, 2006; (ed with J. Carleton Paget) Redemption and Resistance: the messianic hopes of Jews and Christians in antiquity, 2007; (ed with A. J. Torrance) Scripture's Doctrine and Theology's Bible: how the New Testament shapes Christian dogmatics, 2008; The Remembered Peter in Ancient Reception and Modern Debate, 2010; (ed with G. G. Stroumsa) Paradise in Antiquity: Jewish and Christian views, 2010; Simon Peter in Scripture and Memory, 2012 (Spanish edn 2014, Italian edn 2015); contribs to jls incl. Expository Times, Horizons in Biblical Theol., Jl Jewish Studies, Jl for Study of New Testament, Jl for Study of Paul and His Letters, Jl Theol Studies, New Testament Studies, Nova et Vetera, Pro Ecclesia, Revue Biblique, Revue de Qumran, Scottish Jl Theol., Theology. *Recreations:* ski-ing, Italy, Mozart, jazz, spy novels, biographies. *Address:* Keble College, Oxford OX1 3PG. *T:* (01865) 272727. *E:* Markus.Bockmuehl@keble.ox.ac.uk.

BODDINGTON, Caroline Elizabeth; Archbishops' Secretary for Appointments, since 2004; *b* 23 Feb. 1964; *d* of David Gamgee Boddington and Marianne Boddington; *m* 2006, Rt Rev. Dr Alastair Llewellyn John Redfern (*see* Bishop of Derby). *Educ:* Malvern Girls' Coll.; Keble Coll., Oxford (MA). MCIPD 1989. BG Gp plc, 1986–2003: Human Resources Manager, Learning and Develt, 1997–99; Business Analyst, Mediterranean Region, 2000; Head: Learning and Develt, 2000–01; Human Resources Ops, 2002–03. *Recreations:* music, travel. *Address:* The Wash House, Lambeth Palace, SE1 7JU. *T:* (020) 7898 1876. *E:* caroline.boddington@churchofengland.org.

BODDINGTON, Ewart Agnew; JP; DL; Chairman, The Boddington Group PLC (formerly Boddingtons' Breweries), 1970–88 (President, 1989–95); *b* 7 April 1927; *m* 1954, Vine Anne Clayton (*d* 1989); two *s* one *d*. *Educ:* Stowe Sch., Buckingham; Trinity Coll., Cambridge (MA). Jt Man. Dir, Boddingtons', 1957. Dir, Northern Bd, National Westminster Bank, 1977–92. Pres., Inst. of Brewing, 1972–74; Chm., Brewers' Soc., 1984–85; Mem., Brewers' Co., 1980–. JP Macclesfield, 1959; High Sheriff of Cheshire, 1978–79; DL Cheshire 1993. Chetham's School of Music: Feoffee, 1953–2009 (Chm., 1969–92; Hon. Feoffee, 2009); Gov., 1953–99 (Chm., 1969–83). Trustee, NSPCC, 1993–2002. Hon. MA Manchester, 1977. *Recreations:* bridge, fishing, music. *Address:* Fanshawe Brook Barn, Henbury, Macclesfield, Cheshire SK11 9PP. *T:* (01260) 224387.

BODEN, Prof. Margaret Ann, OBE 2002; ScD, PhD; FBA 1983; Research Professor in Cognitive Science, University of Sussex, since 2002 (Professor of Philosophy and Psychology, 1980–2002); *b* 26 Nov. 1936; *d* of late Leonard Forbes Boden, OBE, LLB and Violet Dorothy Dawson; *m* 1967, John Raymond Spiers, *qv* (marr. diss. 1981); one *s* one *d*. *Educ:* City of London Sch. for Girls; Newnham Coll., Cambridge (Major schol. in Med. Scis; Sarah Smithson Scholar in Moral Scis; MA; Associate, 1981–93; ScD 1990); Harvard Grad. Sch. (Harkness Fellow; AM; PhD in Cognitive and Social Psychology). Asst Lectr, then Lectr, in Philosophy, Birmingham Univ., 1959–65; Sussex University: Lectr, 1965–72; Reader, 1972–80; Founding Dean, Sch. of Cognitive Sciences, later Cognitive and Computing Sciences, 1987. Vis. Scientist, Yale Univ., 1979. Co-founder, Dir, 1968–85, Sec., 1968–79, Harvester Press. Scientific Advr, Cambridge Centre for Study of Existential Risk, 2012–. Founding Chm., Hist. and Philosophy of Psychology Sect., BPsS, 1983; Pres., Sect. X, BAAS, 1993; Vice-Pres., and Chm. of Council, Royal Instn of GB, 1993–95 (Mem. Council, 1992–95). Member: Council for Science and Society, 1986–91 (Trustee, 1990–91); ABRC, 1989–90 (Chm., Working Gp on Peer-Review, 1989–90); Animal Procedures Cttee, Home Office, 1994–98; Council, Royal Inst. of Philosophy, 1987–; Council, British Acad., 1988–91 (Vice-Pres., 1989–91). Mem., Bd of Curators, Sch. of Advanced Study, Univ. of London, 1995–99. Mem., Soc. of Authors, 1982–98. Trustee, Eric Gill Trust, 1993–. Mem., Academia Europaea, 1993; Fellow, Amer. Assoc. for Artificial Intelligence, 1993; Life Fellow, Assoc. for Study of Artificial Intelligence and Simulation of Behaviour, 1997; Fellow, European Co-ord. Cttee for Artificial Intelligence, 1999. FRSA 1992. Hon. DSc: Sussex, 2001; Bristol, 2002; DUniv Open, 2004. Leslie McMichael Premium, IERE, 1977; 50th Anniv. Gold Medal, Univ. of Sussex, 2013; Covey Award, Internat. Assoc. of Computing and Philosophy, 2013. *Publications:* Purposive Explanation in Psychology, 1972; Artificial Intelligence and Natural Man, 1977; Piaget, 1979; Minds and Mechanisms, 1981; Computer Models of Mind, 1988; Artificial Intelligence in Psychology, 1989; (ed) The Philosophy of Artificial Intelligence, 1990; The Creative Mind: myths and mechanisms, 1990, 2nd edn 2004; (ed) Dimensions of Creativity, 1994; (ed) The Philosophy of Artificial Life, 1996; (ed) Artificial Intelligence, 1996; Mind as Machine, 2006; Creativity and Art, 2010; General Editor: Explorations in Cognitive Science; Harvester Studies in Cognitive Science; Harvester Studies in Philosophy; contribs to philosophical and psychological jls. *Recreations:* dress-making, dreaming about the South Pacific. *Address:* Centre for Cognitive Science, University of Sussex, Brighton BN1 9QJ. *T:* (01273) 678386. *Club:* Reform.

BODEN, Martin James; Headmaster, King Edward's School, Bath, since 2008; *b* Bolton, Lancs, 6 Feb. 1970. *Educ:* Bolton Sch.; Jesus Coll., Cambridge (BA 1992; MA; PGCE). Teacher of Modern Foreign Langs, Bolton Sch., 1993–97; Head: of German, Cheadle Hulme Sch., 1997–2001; of Modern Foreign Langs, Bradford Grammar Sch., 2001–05; Dir of Studies, King Edward's Sch., Bath, 2005–08. *Recreations:* football, cricket, art, music and film appreciation. *Address:* King Edward's Senior School and Sixth Form, North Road, Bath BA2 6HU. *T:* (01225) 464313, *Fax:* (01225) 481363. *E:* headmaster@kesbath.com.

BODEY, Hon. Sir David (Roderick Lessiter), Kt 1999; **Hon. Mr Justice Bodey;** a Judge of the High Court of Justice, Family Division, since 1999; *b* 14 Oct. 1947; *s* of late Reginald Augustus Bodey, FIA and Betty Francis Bodey; *m* 1976, Ruth (*née* MacAdorey); one *s* one *d*. *Educ:* King's Sch., Canterbury; Univ. of Bristol (LLB Hons 1969). Called to the Bar, Middle Temple, 1970 (Harmsworth Scholar, 1970), Bencher, 1998; QC 1991; an Asst Recorder, 1989; a Recorder, 1993–98; a Dep. High Court Judge, 1994–98; Family Div. Liaison Judge for London, 1999–2001, for N Eastern Circuit, 2001–07. Mem., Family Justice Council, 2008; Dir of Family Trng, Judicial Coll. (formerly Judicial Studies Bd), 2008–. Legal Assessor, 1983–94, Sen. Legal Assessor, 1994–98, UKCC. Mem., Supreme Court Procedure Cttee, 1995–97. Chm., Family Law Bar Assoc., 1997–98 (Sec., 1995–97); Mem., Family Cttee, Justice, 1995–98. Fellow, Internat. Acad. of Matrimonial Lawyers, 1995. *Recreations:* music, sometime marathon running, attempting to keep on road Triumph TR3. *Address:* Royal Courts of Justice, Strand, WC2A 2LL. *Club:* Lansdowne.

BODGER, Michael Roland S.; *see* Steele-Bodger.

BODINETZ, Gemma, (Mrs R. Reddrop); Artistic Director, Liverpool Everyman and Playhouse Theatres, since 2003; *b* 4 Oct. 1966; *d* of Shirley McCarthy and Tony Bodinetz and adopted *d* of Terry Brown; *m* 1995, Richard Reddrop; one *s*. *Educ:* Trinity Coll., Dublin (BA Hons). Assistant Director: Royal Court Th., 1991–92; NT, 1992–93; freelance director, 1993–: major productions include: Chimps, Hampstead Th., 1997; Caravan, Bush Th., 1997; Guiding Star, Liverpool, transf. NT, 1998; Bristol Old Vic: Hamlet; Yard Girl, Royal Court; Shopping and Fucking, NYT Workshop; Luminosity, RSC, 2001; at Liverpool Everyman and Playhouse: Mayor of Zalamea, The Kindness of Strangers, 2004; Ma Rainey's Black Bottom; Yellowman, 2004, nat. tour 2006; Who's Afraid of Virginia Woolf?, 2005; The Lady of Leisure, 2006; All My Sons, 2006; Intemperance, 2007; Tartuffe, 2008; The Hypochondriac, 2009; The Misanthrope, 2013; Twelfth Night, 2014; Juno and the Paycock, 2014, transf. Bristol Old Vic; Educating Rita, 2015; also at W Yorks Playhouse, Plymouth Th. Royal, and other theatres. Mem. Bd, Headlong Th. Co. Hon. Fellow, Liverpool John Moores Univ., 2014. Merseyside Woman of the Year, 2004. *Recreations:* cinema, reading, building theatres, running, West Ham Utd. *Address:* 40 Alderley Road, Hoylake, Wirral CH47 2BA. *T:* (0151) 632 4990. *E:* g.bodinetz@everymanplayhouse.com.

BODINHAM, Susan; *see* Sowden, S.

BODMER, Sir Walter (Fred), Kt 1986; FRCPath; FRS 1974; FRSB; Principal, Hertford College, Oxford, 1996–2005; Consulting Professor, Department of Medicine (Oncology), Stanford University, since 2007; President, Galton Institute, since 2008; *b* 10 Jan. 1936; *s* of late Dr Ernest Julius and Sylvia Emily Bodmer; *m* 1956, Julia Gwynaeth Pilkington, FMedSci (*d* 2001); two *s* one *d*; partner, Dr Ann Ganesan. *Educ:* Manchester Grammar Sch.; Clare Coll., Cambridge (BA 1956; MA, PhD 1959). FRCPath 1984; FRSB (FIBiol 1990). Research Fellow 1958–61, Official Fellow 1961, Hon. Fellow 1989, Clare Coll., Cambridge; Demonstrator in Genetics, Univ. of Cambridge, 1960–61; Asst Prof. 1962–66, Associate Prof. 1966–68, Prof. 1968–70, Dept of Genetics, Stanford Univ.; Prof. of Genetics, Univ. of Oxford, 1970–79; Dir of Res., 1979–91, Dir Gen., 1991–96, ICRF. Non-exec. Dir, Fisons plc, 1990–96. Chm., BBC Sci. Consultative Gp, 1981–87; Member: BBC Gen. Adv. Council, 1981–91 (Chm., 1987); Council, Internat. Union Against Cancer, 1982–90; Adv. Bd for Res. Councils, 1983–88; Council, Found for Sci. and Technol., 1995–; Chairman: COPUS, 1990–93; Orgn of European Cancer Insts, 1990–93; NRPB, 1998–2003; Med. and Scientific Adv. Panel, Leukaemia Res. Fund, 2003–09; President: Royal Statistical Soc., 1984–85 (Vice-Pres., 1983–84; Hon. Fellow, 1997); BAAS, 1987–88 (Vice-Pres., 1989–2001; Chm., Council, 1996–2001; Hon. Fellow, 2001); ASE, 1989–90; Human Genome Orgn, 1990–92; British Soc. for Histocompatibility and Immunogenetics, 1990–91 (Hon. Mem. 1992); EACR, 1994–96; British Assoc. for Cancer Res., 1998–2002; first Pres., Internat. Fedn of Assocs for Advancement of Sci. and Technol., 1992–94; Vice-President: Royal Instn, 1981–82; Parly and Scientific Cttee, 1990–93; Hon. Vice-Pres., Res. Defence Soc., 1990–2008. Trustee: BM (Natural History), 1983–93 (Chm., Bd of Trustees, 1989–93); Sir John Soane's Mus., 1982–2003; Foulkes Foundn, 2002–; Porter Foundn, 2006–. Chancellor, Salford Univ., 1995–2005. Chm. Bd of Dirs, Laban Centre, 1998–2005; Mem. Bd, Trinity Laban, 2005–08 (Companion, 2008); Mem. Bd of Patrons, St Mark's Hosp. and Academic Inst., 1996. Founder FMedSci 1998. Hon. MRIA 1998; Hon. Member: British Soc. of Gastroenterology, 1989; Amer. Assoc. of Immunologists, 1985; St Mark's Assoc., 1995; British Transplantation Soc., 2002; British Soc. Immunol., 2006; For. Associate, US Nat. Acad. of Scis, 1981; For. Mem., Amer. Philosophical Soc., 1989; For. Hon. Mem., Amer. Acad. Arts and Scis, 1972; Fellow, Internat. Inst. of Biotechnology, 1989; Hon. Fellow: Keble Coll., Oxford, 1982; Green Coll., Oxford, 1993; Hertford Coll., Oxford, 2005; Hon. FRCP 1985; Hon. FRCS 1986; Hon. FRSE 1992; Hon. FRSocMed 1994. Liveryman, Drapers' Co., 2008–. Hon. DSc: Bath, Oxford, 1988; Hull, Edinburgh, 1990; Bristol, 1991; Loughborough, 1993; Lancaster, Aberdeen, 1994; Plymouth, 1995; London, Salford, 1996; UMIST, 1997; Witwatersrand, 1998; DUniv Surrey, 1990; Laurea *hc* in Medicine and Surgery, Univ. of Bologna, 1987; Dr *hc*: Leuven, 1992; Masaryk, 1994; Haifa, 1998; Hon. MD Birmingham, 1992; Hon. LLD Dundee, 1993. William Allan Meml Award, Amer. Soc. Human Genetics, 1980; Conway Evans Prize, RCP/Royal Soc., 1982; Rabbi Shai Shacknai Meml Prize Lectr, 1983; John Alexander Meml Prize and Lectureship, Univ. of Pennsylvania Med. Sch., 1984; Rose Payne Dist. Scientists Lectureship, Amer. Soc. for Histocompatibility and Immunogenetics, 1985; Bernal Lectr, 1986, Faraday Award, 1994, Royal Medal, 2013, Royal Soc.; Neil Hamilton-Fairley Medal, RCP, 1990; Romanes Lectr, Univ. of Oxford, 1995; Harveian Orator, RCP, 1996; Dalton Medal, Manchester Lit. and Philos. Soc., 2002; D. K. Ludwig Award, 2002; Seroussi Foundn Res. Award, 2003. *Publications:* The Genetics of Human Populations (with L. L. Cavalli-Sforza), 1971; (with A. Jones) Our Future Inheritance: choice or chance?, 1974; (with L. L. Cavalli-Sforza) Genetics, Evolution and Man, 1976; (with Robin McKie) The Book of Man, 1994; research papers in genetical, statistical and mathematical and medical jls, etc. *Recreations:* playing the piano, riding, swimming, scuba diving. *Address:* Cancer and Immunogenetics Laboratory, Weatherall Institute of Molecular Medicine, John Radcliffe Hospital, Oxford OX3 9DS. *T:* (01865) 222356. *Clubs:* Athenæum, Oxford and Cambridge.

BODMIN, Archdeacon of; *see* Elkington, Ven. A. A.

BODY, Sir Richard (Bernard Frank Stewart), Kt 1986; *b* 18 May 1927; *s* of Lieut-Col Bernard Richard Body, formerly of Hyde End, Shinfield, Berks; *m* 1959, Marion, *d* of late Major H. Graham, OBE; one *s* one *d*. *Educ:* Reading Sch.; Inns of Court Sch. of Law. RAF (India Comd), 1945–48. Called to the Bar, Middle Temple, 1949; Chm., E London Poor Man's Lawyer Assoc., 1952–59. Contested (C) Rotherham, 1950; Abertillery bye-election, 1950; Leek, 1951; MP (C): Billericay Div., Essex, 1955–Sept. 1959: Holland with Boston, 1966–97, Boston and Skegness, 1997–2001. Member: Jt Select Cttee on Consolidation of

Law, 1975–91; Commons Select Cttee on Agric., 1979–87 (Chm., 1986–87). Jt Chm., Council, Get Britain Out referendum campaign, 1975. Chm. Trustees, Centre for European Studies, 1991–; Trustee, Leopold Kohr Inst., 2004–. President: William Cobbett Soc., 1996–2010; Ruskin Soc., 2002– (Chm., 1997–2002). Internat. Assoc. of Masters of Bloodhounds, 1997–2003. Dir, New European Publications Ltd, 1986–. Editor, World Review, 1996–2001. *Publications:* The Architect and the Law, 1954; (contrib.) Destiny or Delusion, 1971; (ed jtly) Freedom and Stability in the World Economy, 1976; Agriculture: The Triumph and the Shame, 1982; Farming in the Clouds, 1984; Red or Green for Farmers, 1987; Europe of Many Circles, 1990; Our Food, Our Land, 1991; The Breakdown of Europe, 1998; England for the English, 2001; A Democratic Europe: the alternative to the European Union, 2006. *Recreation:* trying to catch trout. *Address:* Jewell's Farm, Stanford Dingley, near Reading, Berks RG7 6LX. *T:* (0118) 9744295. *Clubs:* Athenæum, Carlton, Pratt's.

BOE, Norman Wallace; Deputy Solicitor to Secretary of State for Scotland, 1987–96; *b* 30 Aug. 1943; *s* of late Alexander Thomson Boe and Margaret Wallace Revans; *m* 1968, Margaret Irene McKenzie; one *s* one *d*. *Educ:* George Heriot's Sch., Edinburgh; Edinburgh Univ. LLB Hons 1965. Admitted Solicitor, 1967. Legal apprentice, Lindsays, WS, 1965–67; Legal Asst, Menzies & White, WS, 1967–70; Office of Solicitor to Sec. of State for Scotland, 1970–96. Volunteer with Volunteer Stroke Service, Chest, Heart and Stroke, Scotland, 1996–. *Recreations:* golf, gardening, travelling.

BOEHMER, Prof. Elleke Deirdre, DPhil; Professor of World Literature in English, University of Oxford, since 2007; Fellow, since 2007 and Deputy Director, Oxford Life Writing Centre, since 2011, Wolfson College, Oxford; *b* Durban, SA, 14 Nov. 1961; *d* of Antony Gerhardus Boehmer and Fredrika Boehmer (*née* ten Tusschedé); *m* 1994, Steven John Matthews; two *s*. *Educ:* Rhodes Univ. (BA Hons 1984); St John's Coll., Oxford (MPhil 1987; DPhil 1990). Jun. Lectr in English, Vista Univ., Mamelodi Township, SA, 1984–85; Rhodes Scholar, 1985–88; Lecturer: in Commonwealth Lit., Amer. and Commonwealth Arts Studies, Univ. of Exeter, 1987–88; in Nineteenth- and Twentieth-Century Eng. Lit., St John's Coll., Oxford, 1988–90; in Eng. Lit., Univ. of Leeds, 1990–2000; Prof. in Colonial and Postcolonial Studies, Nottingham Trent Univ., 2000–04; Hildred Carlile Prof. in Lits in English, Royal Holloway, Univ. of London, 2004–07. Vis. Prof., Univ. of Adelaide, 2004; Distinguished Visiting Professor: Univ. of the Witwatersrand, 2009; Monash Univ., 2011; Dist. Vis. Fellow, Univ. of Barcelona, 2010; Dist. Scholar in Residence, Univ. of Virginia, 2014. Mem. Jury, Internat. Man Booker Prize, 2014–15. Trustee, Charlie Perkins Scholarships, 2010–. FEA 2004. Hon. DHum Linnaeus, 2009. *Publications: fiction:* Screens Against the Sky (novel), 1990 (trans. German, 1994); An Immaculate Figure (novel), 1993; Bloodlines (novel), 2000; Nile Baby (novel), 2008; Sharmilla and Other Portraits (stories), 2010; The Shouting in the Dark (novel), 2015 (trans. Dutch, 2015); *non-fiction:* (ed jtly) Altered State?: writing and South Africa, 1994; Colonial and Postcolonial Literature: migrant metaphors, 1995 (trans. Mandarin 1998), 2nd edn 2005; (ed) Empire Writing: an anthology of colonial literature 1870–1918, 1998, 2nd edn 2009; Empire, the National, and the Postcolonial, 1890–1920: resistance in interaction, 2002; (ed with Naella Grew) India Calling by Cornelia Sorabji, 2004; (ed) Scouting for Boys by Robert Baden-Powell, 2004; Stories of Women: gender and narrative in the postcolonial nation, 2005; Nelson Mandela: postcolonial thinker, 2008, US edn as Nelson Mandela, 2010 (trans. Arabic, Thai, 2011; Brazilian Portuguese, 2012; Portuguese, 2014); (ed jtly) J. M. Coetzee in Context and Theory, 2009; (ed with Stephen Morton) Terror and the Postcolonial, 2010; (ed with Rosinka Chaudhuri) The Indian Postcolonial: a critical reader, 2010; (ed with Sarah de Mul) The Postcolonial Low Countries: literature, colonialism, multiculturalism, 2012; Indian Arrivals: networks of British Empire 1870–1915, 2015; articles in jls incl. Papers of Modern Langs Assoc., Interventions, Jl of Postcolonial Writing, Jl of Commonwealth Lit. *Recreations:* swimming, walking, family, theatre, friends. *Address:* English Faculty, University of Oxford, St Cross Building, Oxford OX1 3UL. *T:* (01865) 271040/055, 07881 623840. *E:* elleke.boehmer@ell.ox.ac.uk.

BOEL, (Else) Mariann Fischer; *see* Fischer Boel.

BOEVEY, Sir Thomas (Michael Blake) C.; *see* Crawley-Boevey.

BOFFEY, Christopher John; News Editor, Guardian News and Media, 2010–11; media consultant, since 2011; columnist, The Drum, since 2012; *b* Manchester, 23 Nov. 1951; *s* of William and Nora Boffey; *m* 1972, Shirley Edwards; two *s*. *Educ:* Xaverian Coll., Manchester. Reporter, Winsford Guardian, Newcastle Jl, Daily Star, Today, News of the World, The Sun, 1971–94; News Ed., Sunday Mirror, 1994–97; Asst Ed., News, Sunday Telegraph, 1998–2001; Special Advr to Sec. of State for Educn, 2001–02; News Ed., Daily Mirror, 2004–05; media consultant, 2005–07; News Ed., The Observer, 2007–10. Treas., Journalists' Charity, 2014– (Chm., 2008–10; Life Vice-Pres., 2011). *Recreations:* walking, reading, travelling, exploring London pub architecture. *Address:* 7 Berkeley Road, Crouch End, N8 8RU. *T:* 07860 959450. *E:* chris@boffey.london.

BOGAN, Paul Simon; QC 2011; *b* London, 6 Oct. 1957; *s* of Ralph Bogan and Jean Bogan; *m* 1991, Kate Rohde; two *s*. *Educ:* Sevenoaks Sch.; City of London Poly. (BA). Called to the Bar, Gray's Inn, 1983; in practice as barrister, specialising in criminal defence. Mem., Bar Council, 2006–11. Mem. Council, Liberty, 2000–06. *Publications:* Identification: investigation, trial and scientific evidence, 2004, 2nd edn 2011; (jtly) Butterworth's Guide to the Proceeds of Crime Act, 2003, 3rd edn 2008; (jtly) Human Rights in the Investigation and Prosecution of Crime, 2009. *Recreations:* theatre, literature, bridge, football. *Address:* 23 Essex Street Chambers, WC2R 3AA. *T:* (020) 7413 0353, *Fax:* (020) 7413 0374. *E:* paulbogan@23es.com.

BOGDANOR, Prof. Vernon Bernard, CBE 1998; FBA 1997; Professor of Government, Oxford University, 1996–2010, now Emeritus; Fellow, Brasenose College, Oxford, 1966–2010, now Emeritus; Research Professor, Institute of Contemporary British History, King's College London, since 2010; *b* 16 July 1943; *s* of Harry Bogdanor and Rosa (*née* Weinger); *m* 1st, 1972, Judith Evelyn Becket t (marr. diss. 2000); two *s*; 2nd, 2009, Sonia Margaret Robertson. *Educ:* Bishopshalt Sch.; The Queen's College, Oxford (BA 1st Cl. PPE 1964; MA 1968; Hon. Fellow, 2009). Brasenose College, Oxford: Sen. Tutor, 1979–85, 1996–97; Vice-Principal, 2001–02; Reader in Government, Oxford Univ., 1990–96. Gresham Prof. of Law, 2004–07; Vis. Prof. of Law, KCL, 2009–10. Special Advr, H of L Select Cttee on European Communities, 1982–83; Advr on Constitutional and Electoral Matters to Czechoslovak, Hungarian, and Israeli Govts, 1988–; Special Advr, H of C Public Service Cttee, 1996; Mem., UK Delegn to CSCE Conf., Oslo, 1991. Mem. Council, Hansard Soc. for Parly Govt, 1981–97. Mem., Internat. Adv. Council, Israel Democracy Inst., 2010. FAcSS (AcSS 2009). Hon. Fellow, Soc. for Advanced Legal Studies, 1997. Hon. Bencher, Middle Temple, 2010. Hon. DLitt Kent, 2010. FRSA 1992. Sir Isaiah Berlin Prize for Lifetime Contribn to Pol Studies, Pol Studies Assoc., 2008. Chevalier de la Légion d'Honneur (France), 2009. *Publications:* (ed) Disraeli: Lothair, 1975; Devolution, 1979; The People and the Party System, 1981; Multi-Party Politics and the Constitution, 1983; (ed) Democracy and Elections, 1983; (ed) Coalition Government in Western Europe, 1983; What is Proportional Representation?, 1984; (ed) Parties and Democracy in Britain and America, 1984; (ed) Constitutions in Democratic Politics, 1988; (ed) The Blackwell Encyclopaedia of Political Science, 1992; (jtly) Comparing Constitutions, 1995; The Monarchy and the Constitution, 1995; Politics and the Constitution: essays on British Government, 1996; Power and the People: a guide to constitutional reform, 1997; Devolution in the United Kingdom, 1999; (ed) The British Constitution in the 20th century, 2003; (ed) Joined-up Government, 2005; The New British Constitution, 2009; (ed) From the New Jerusalem to New Labour: British Prime Ministers from Attlee to Blair, 2010; The Coalition and the Constitution, 2011; contribs to learned jls. *Recreations:* music, walking, talking. *Address:* 21 Edmunds Walk, Ea Finchley, N2 0HU.

BOGDANOV, Michael; Founder and Artistic Director, Wales Theatre Company, sinc 2003; *b* 15 Dec. 1938; *s* of Francis Benzion Bogdin and Rhoda Rees Bogdin; *m* 1st, 196 Patsy Ann Warwick (marr. diss. 2000); two *s* one *d*; 2nd, 2000, Ulrike Engelbrecht; one *s* on *d*. *Educ:* Lower School of John Lyon, Harrow; Univ. of Dublin Trinity Coll. (MA); Univs o the Sorbonne, and Munich. Writer, with Terence Brady, ATV series, Broad and Narrow 1965; Producer/Director with Telefis Eireann, 1966–68; opening production of Theat Upstairs, Royal Court, A Comedy of the Changing Years, 1969; The Bourgeo Gentilhomme, Oxford Playhouse, 1969; Asst Dir, Royal Shakespeare Theatre Co., 1970–7 Associate Dir, Peter Brook's A Midsummer Night's Dream, Stratford 1970, New York 197 World Tour 1972; Dir, Two Gentlemen of Verona, São Paulo, Brazil, 1971; Associate to Jea Louis Barrault, Rabelais, 1971; Associate Director: Tyneside Th. Co., 1971–73; Haymark Th., Leicester; Director: Phoenix Th., Leicester, 1973–77; Young Vic Th., London 1978–80; an Associate Dir, Royal Nat. Theatre, 1980–88; Artistic Dir, English Shakespear Co., 1986–98; Intendant (Chief Exec.), Deutsches Schauspielhaus, Hamburg, 1989–9 National Theatre productions: Sir Gawain and the Green Knight, The Hunchback of Notr Dame, 1977–78; The Romans in Britain, Hiawatha, 1980; One Woman Plays, The Mayor o Zalamea, The Hypochondriac, 1981; Uncle Vanya, The Spanish Tragedy, 1982; Lorenzacci 1983; You Can't Take it With You, 1983; Strider, 1984; Royal Shakespeare Co. production The Taming of the Shrew, 1978 (SWET Dir of the Year award, 1979); Shadow of a Gunmar 1980; The Knight of the Burning Pestle, 1981; The Venetian Twins, 1993; The Hostag 1994; Faust Parts I and II, 1995; English Shakespeare Co. productions: Henry IV (Parts I an II), Henry V, UK tour, European tour, Old Vic, and Canada, 1986–87; The Wars of th Roses (7 play history cycle), UK, Europe and world tour, 1987–89 (Laurence Olivier Awar Dir of the Year, 1989); Coriolanus, The Winter's Tale, UK and world tour, 1990–91 Macbeth, UK tour, 1992; The Tempest, 1992; Beowulf, 1997; As You Like It, 1998; Anton and Cleopatra, 1998; Wales Theatre Co. productions: Under Milk Wood, 2003; Twelft Night, Cymbeline, The Merchant of Venice, 2004; Amazing Grace The Musical, Haml (Welsh/English), 2005; Contender, The Musical, 2007; The Servant of Two Masters, 2007 The Thorn Birds – A Musical, 2009; also directed: The Seagull, Toho Th. Co., Tokyo, 198 Hamlet, Dublin, 1983; Romeo and Juliet, Tokyo, 1983, RSC, 1986, Lyric, Hammersmith 1993; The Mayor of Zalamea, Washington, 1984; Measure for Measure, Stratford, Ont, 1985 Mutiny (musical), 1985; Donnerstag aus Licht, Royal Opera House, 1985; Julius Caesar, 198 (also filmed by ZDF TV), Reineke Fuchs, 1987, Hamlet, 1989, Schauspielhaus, Hamburg The Canterbury Tales, Prince of Wales, 1987; Montag, Stockhausen Opera, La Scala, Milan 1988 (world première); Hair, Old Vic, 1993; Peer Gynt, Munich, 1995; Timon of Athens Chicago, 1997; Troilus and Cressida, Olympic Arts Fest., Sydney Opera House, 2000; Lon Star Love, NY, 2001; The Winter's Tale, Chicago, 2003; The Servant of Two Masters Hamburg, 2004; The Dresser, Hamburg, 2005; Waiting for Godot, Hamburg, 2007 (Rolp Mares Preis, Best Dir, 2007); UK Holocaust Meml Day Event, Wales Millennium Centre 2006; Abolition of Slave Trade Bicentennial Event, St David's Hall, Cardiff, 2007; Elling Hamburg, 2008; Ein Bisschen Ruhe vor dem Sturm, Frost/Nixon, Hamburg, 2009; A Midsummer Night's Dream, Ohnsorg, Hamburg, Frost/Nixon, Ein Bisschen Ruhe vor den Sturm, Kammerspiele, Hamburg, Bred in Heaven, Swansea Grand, 2011; Vier Maenner in Nebel, Kammerspiele, Hamburg, Uncle Vanya, Ohnsorg, The King's Speech, St Paul Hamburg (Pegasus Prize, Rolf-Mares Prize, Nachkritik Online Award), Elwyn, Swanse Grand, 2012; Rot, Kammerspiele, Hamburg, Mephisto (world premiere), Altonaer Hamburg, Langen Na Leev (A Moon for the Misbegotten), Ohnsorg, Jetzt oder Nie – Zeit is Geld, Kammerspiele, Hamburg, 2013; Oeffentliches Eigentum, Schlossparktheater, Berlin 2014; Goetz von Berlichingen, Burgfestspiele, Jagsthausen, 2014; The Dylathon, Grand Swansea (36 hr non-stop reading of works of Dylan Thomas), 2014; Ludlow Festival: Merr Wives of Windsor, 2002; The Winter's Tale, The Merchant of Venice, 2003; Twelfth Night Cymbeline, 2004. *Television:* deviser and presenter, Shakespeare Lives, series, 1983; director Shakespeare on the Estate (documentary), Bard on the Box series, 1995 (BAFTA, RTS, an Banff Film Fest. Awards); films: The Tempest in Butetown, 1996; Macbeth, 1997; Light i the Valley, 1998 (RTS Award); Light on the Hill, 1999; A Light in the City, 2001; The Wels in Shakespeare, 2003. Co-author, plays, adaptations and children's theatre pieces. Hon. Prof. Univ. of Wales, 1993; Sen. Fellow, De Montfort Univ., 1992; Fellow: Sunderland Univ. 1997; Univ. of S Wales (formerly Univ. of Glamorgan), 2008; Hon. FRWCMD (Hon FWCMD 1994); Hon. Fellow: in Drama, TCD, 1997; Swansea Univ., 2008; Shakespear Birthplace Trust, 2011. Hon. DLitt TCD, 2005. *Publications:* (jtly) The English Shakespear Company, 1990; Shakespeare The Director's Cut, vol. 1, 2003, vol. 2, 2004, vol. Compilation, 2013; Theatre The Director's Cue: thoughts and reminiscences, 2013 *Recreations:* cricket, wine, music, Dylan Thomas, Georgian glass. *Address:* 9 Farleigh Road Cardiff CF11 9JT. *E:* mbogdin@hotmail.com.

BOGDANOVICH, Peter; American film director, writer, producer, actor; *b* Kingston, NY 30 July 1939; *s* of Borislav Bogdanovich and Herma (*née* Robinson); *m* 1962, Polly Platt (marr diss. 1970; she *d* 2011); two *d*; *m* 1988, L. B. Straten (marr. diss. 2001). Owner: Crescen Moon Productions, Inc., LA, 1986; Holly Moon Co. Inc., LA, 1992. Mem. Faculty, Sch. o Filmmaking, Univ. of N Carolina Sch. of the Arts, 2010. Member: Dirs Guild of America Writers' Guild of America; Acad. of Motion Picture Arts and Sciences. *Theatre:* Actor, Amer Shakespeare Fest., Stratford, Conn, 1956, NY Shakespeare Fest., 1958; Dir and producer, off Broadway: The Big Knife, 1959; Camino Real, Ten Little Indians, Rocket to the Moon 1961; Once in a Lifetime, 1964. *Films include:* The Wild Angels (2nd-Unit Dir, co-writer actor), 1966; Targets (dir, co-writer, prod., actor), 1968; The Last Picture Show (dir, co-writer), 1971 (NY Film Critics' Award for Best Screenplay, British Acad. Award for Bes Screenplay); Directed by John Ford (dir, writer, interviewer), 1971; What's Up, Doc? (dir co-writer, prod.), 1972 (Writers' Guild of America Award for Best Screenplay); Paper Moor (dir, prod.), 1973 (Silver Shell Award, Spain); Daisy Miller (dir, prod.), 1974 (Brussels Festiva Award for Best Director); At Long Last Love (dir, writer, prod.), 1975; Nickelodeon (dir, co-writer), 1976; Saint Jack (dir, co-writer, actor), 1979 (Pasinetti Award, Critics' Prize, Venice Festival); They All Laughed (dir, writer), 1981; Mask (dir), 1985; Illegally Yours (dir, prod.) 1988; Texasville (dir, prod., writer), 1990; Noises Off (dir, exec. prod.), 1992; The Thing Called Love (dir), 1993; The Cat's Meow (dir), 2002; Hustle (dir), 2004; She's Funny Tha Way, 2015. *Television:* The Great Professional: Howard Hawks, BBC, 1967; CBS Thi Morning (weekly commentary), 1987–89; Prowler, CBS, 1995; Blessed Assurance, To Si With Love II, CBS-MOW, 1996; (actor) The Sopranos, 2000–07. *Publications:* The Cinema of Orson Welles, 1961; The Cinema of Howard Hawks, 1962; The Cinema of Alfrec Hitchcock, 1963; John Ford, 1968; Fritz Lang in America, 1969; Allan Dwan: the last pioneer 1971; Pieces of Time: Peter Bogdanovich on the Movies 1961–85, 1973, enlarged 1985; The Killing of the Unicorn: Dorothy Stratten, 1960–1980, a Memoir, 1984; (ed with introd.) A Year and a Day Engagement Calendar, annually, 1991–; This is Orson Welles, 1992; Whc The Devil Made It, 1997; Who the Hell's in It?, 2004; features on films in Esquire, New York Times, Village Voice, Cahiers du Cinema, Los Angeles Times, New York Magazine, Vogue Variety etc, 1961–. *Address:* c/o William Peiffer, Victor Building. One Market Street Camden, NJ 08102, USA.

BOGER, Prof. David Vernon, PhD; FRS 2007; FAA, FTSE; Professor of Chemical Engineering, 1982–2009, Laureate Professor, 2000–09, Emeritus Professor, 2010, University of Melbourne; Professor of Engineering, Monash University, since 2011; *b* Kutztown, Penn

13 Nov. 1939; *s* of Charles and Edna Boger; *m* 2003, Reba Angstadt; one *s* two *d* by a previous marriage. *Educ:* Bucknell Univ. (BSc 1961; MSc 1964); Univ. of Illinois (PhD 1965). Monash University: Lectr, 1965–71; Sen. Lectr, 1971–80; Reader, 1980–82; University of Melbourne: Dep. Dean Engrg, 1988–90; Associate Dean (Res.) Engrg, 1990–92; Hd, Dept of Chemical Engrg, 1997–99; Dir, Particulate Fluids Res. Centre, 2000–04. Member: Amer. Soc. of Rheology, 1970–; Australian Soc. of Rheology, 1983–; British Soc. of Rheology, 1989–; Inst. of Non-Newtonian Fluid Mechanics, Univ. of Wales, 1996–. FTSE 1989; FAA 1993; FRSV 2008. *Publications:* Thermodynamics: an introduction, 1976, rev. edn 1987; Rheology and Flow of Non-Newtonian Systems, 1976; An Introduction to the Flow Properties of Polymers, 1980; Rheology and Non-Newtonian Fluid Mechanics, 1983; Rheological Phenomena in Focus, 1993; over 360 articles. *Recreations:* fly fishing, farming. *Address:* Department of Chemical and Biomolecular Engineering, University of Melbourne, Parkville, 3010 Vic, Australia. *T:* (home) (3) 97072407, (mobile) 61459323239. *E:* dvboger@unimelb.edu.au.

BOGGIS, Andrew Gurdon, MA; Warden of Forest School, 1992–2009; *b* 1 April 1954; *s* of Lt-Col (Edmund) Allan (Theodore) Boggis and Myrtle (Eirene) Boggis (*née* Donald); *m* 1983, Fiona Mary Cocke; two *d* one *s*. *Educ:* Marlborough Coll.; New Coll., Oxford (MA); King's Coll., Cambridge (PGCE). Asst Master, Hitchin Boys' Sch., 1978–79; Eton College: Asst Master, 1979–92; Master-in-College, 1984–92. Chm., HMC, 2006 (Mem., Cttee, 2001–07); Member: Ind. Schs Exam. Bd, 1992–2001 (Chm., Langs Cttee, 1997–2001); Educn Cttee, ESU, 2004–10. Liveryman, Skinners' Co., 1990– (Extra Mem. Ct, 2004–06; Mem. Ct, 2009–; Master, 2011–12; Chm., Educn Cttee, 2013–). Dir, HMC Projects in Central and Eastern Europe, 2012–. Governor: King's Coll. Sch., Cambridge, 1994–99; Skinners' Co.'s Sch. for Girls, 1997–2009; Purcell Sch. for Music, 2008–11; Skinners' Grammar Sch., 2009–13; Skinners' Kent Acad., 2009–13 (Chm., 2009–13); Canford Sch., Dorset, 2012–; W Buckland Sch., Devon, 2013–. Mem. Ct, Essex Univ., 1997–2004. Trustee, Dorset Historic Churches Trust, 2012–. *Publications:* articles and reviews. *Recreations:* music, cookery, reading, Austria, rearing pigs, playing the organ, old gramophones. *Address:* Church Cottages, Hooke, Beaminster, Dorset DT8 3PA. *T:* (01308) 861176. *Club:* East India.

BOGGIS, Emma Louise; Chief Executive Officer, Sport and Recreation Alliance, since 2014; *b* Guildford, 1 April 1973; *d* of Christopher Woodhams and Susan Woodhams; *m* Mark Boggis. *Educ:* Chelmsford County High Sch. for Girls; Oriel Coll., Oxford (BA Hons Philos. and Theol. 1995). Officer, British Army, 1996–2001; Ofsted: Private Sec. to HM Chief Inspector of Schs, 2002–05; Hd, Strategic Communications, 2006–07; Dep. Dir, Cabinet Office, 2007–09; Dep. Hd of Mission, Madrid, 2009–11; Private Sec. to the Prime Minister, 2011–12; Hd, Olympic and Paralympic Legacy Unit, Cabinet Office, 2012–14. Non-exec. Dir, British Paralympic Assoc., 2013–. *Recreations:* running, cycling, swimming, travelling by pedal power, good food. *Address:* Sport and Recreation Alliance, 4th Floor, Burwood House, 14–16 Caxton Street, SW1H 0QT.

BOGGIS, His Honour John Graham; QC 1993; a Circuit Judge, 1996–2010; *b* 2 April 1949; *s* of Robert Boggis and Joyce (*née* Meek); *m* 2011, Jill Fairall. *Educ:* Whitgift Sch.; Univ. of London (LLB); Univ. of Keele (MA). Called to the Bar, Lincoln's Inn, 1972; a Recorder, 1994–96; a Chancery Circuit Judge, 1997–2001. Asst Boundary Comr, 1993–95. Member: Chancery Bar Assoc., 1982–84; Senate of the Inns of Court and Bar, 1984–85. Staff Rep. Gov., Sherborne Sch., 1993–98. *Recreation:* boating (Cdre, Fairey Owners' Club, 2006–08).

BOGGIS-ROLFE, Richard; Chairman, Odgers Berndtson, since 2001; *b* Bury St Edmunds, 5 April 1950; *s* of Paul Boggis-Rolfe and (Anne) Verena Boggis-Rolfe (*née* Collins); *m* Lucy Elizabeth, *d* of Lt Col Stephen Jenkins, MC, DL; one *s* two *d*. *Educ:* Eton; Trinity Coll., Cambridge (MA); London Business Sch. Commnd Coldstream Guards, 1970; retd as Hon. Major, 1980. Dir, Russell Reynolds Associates, 1983; Dir, Norman Broadbent Internat., 1984–97; Man. Dir, Norman Broadbent Hong Kong, 1985–86; Man. Dir, then Chm., NB Selection Ltd, 1987–95; Chm., Barkers Human Resources, 1992–97; Gp Man. Dir, BNB Resources plc, 1995–97. Chm., Nat. Employer Adv. Bd, 2011–. Chm., Holfords of Westonbirt Trust, 2007–. Master, Pewterers' Co., 2011. Vice Patron, Poppy Factory, 2013–. *Address:* The Glebe House, Shipton Moyne, Tetbury, Glos GL8 8PW; L'Hermitage, Basse Neuailette, Hautfort, France. *E:* richard.boggis-rolfe@odgersberndtson.com. *Clubs:* Brooks's, Pratt's, Beefsteak.

BOGLE, Ellen Gray, CD 1987; consultant on international trade matters, Lascelles de Mercado Co. Ltd, since 2002; *d* of late Victor Gray Williams and Eileen Avril Williams; *m* (marr. diss.); one *s* one *d*. *Educ:* St Andrew High Sch., Jamaica; Univ. of the West Indies, Jamaica (BA). Dir of For. Trade, Min. of For. Affairs, Jamaica, 1978–81; Dir, Jamaica Nat. Export Corp., 1978–81; High Comr to Trinidad and Tobago, Barbados, E Caribbean and Guyana, and Ambassador to Suriname, 1982–89; High Comr, UK, 1989–93, and Ambassador to Denmark, Norway, Sweden, Spain and Portugal, 1990–93; Perm. Sec., Min. of Industry, Tourism and Commerce, subseq. Industry, Investment and Commerce, Jamaica, 1993–96; Min. of Foreign Affairs and Foreign Trade, 1996–2002. Special Envoy of Jamaica to Assoc. of Caribbean States and CARICOM, 1997–2001. *Recreations:* gardening, reading, cooking, table tennis.

BOGLE, Sir Nigel (Peter Cranston), Kt 2013; Founding Partner, since 1982, and non-executive Group Chairman, Bartle Bogle Hegarty Ltd; *b* 1947. Trainee, then Manager, Leo Burnett, 1967–73; Founding Partner, TBWA, London, 1973–82; former Chief Exec., Bartle Bogle Hegarty Ltd. *Address:* Bartle Bogle Hegarty Ltd, 60 Kingly Street, W1B 5DS.

BOGORODSK, Bishop of; *see* Sourozh, Archbishop of, (Russian Orthodox).

BOHUON, Olivier Jean; Chief Executive Officer, Smith & Nephew plc, since 2011; *b* Paris, 3 Jan. 1959; *s* of Claude Jean Joseph Bohuon and Odile Germaine Bohuon (*née* Guinnebault); *m* 1981, Alexandra Florence Michelle Marie Polliot; two *s* one *d*. *Educ:* Univ. of Paris XI (Dr Pharmacy 1982); HEC (MBA 1985). Mktg Dir, then Ops Dir, Glaxo France, 1991–95; CEO, then Pres., SmithKline Beecham Labs, 1995–2001; Sen. Vice Pres., Eur. Commercial Ops, GlaxoSmithKline, 2001–03; Hd of Eur., Abbott Labs, 2003–06; Pres., Abbott Internat., 2006–09; Exec. Vice Pres., Abbott Pharmaceuticals, 2009–10; Chief Exec., Pierre Fabre, 2010. Non-exec. Dir, Shire, 2015–. Chevalier, Légion d'Honneur (France), 2007. *Recreations:* golf, sailing. *Address:* Smith & Nephew plc, 15 Adam Street, WC2N 6LA. *T:* (020) 7960 2201, *Fax:* (020) 7930 3426. *Clubs:* Royal Automobile; Saint Cloud Golf, Dinard Golf.

BOILEAU, Sir Nicolas Edmond George, 9th Bt *cr* 1838, of Tacolnestone Hall, Norfolk; *b* 17 Nov. 1964; *s* of Sir Guy Francis Boileau, 8th Bt, and of Judith Frances, *d* of George Conrad Hannan; *S* father, 2013. *Heir:* *b* Christopher Guy Boileau [*b* 1969; *m* 2002, Helen Baker; one *d*].

BOISSIER, Martin Scobell; Vice Lord-Lieutenant of Derbyshire, 1992–2001; *b* 14 May 1926; *s* of Ernest Gabriel Boissier, DSC and Doris Mary Boissier (*née* Bingham); *m* 1955, Margaret Jean Blair, JP; one *s* one *d*. *Educ:* Bramcote Prep. Sch., Scarborough; Royal Naval Coll., Dartmouth. Service in RN, 1943–58; qualified as Pilot, 1947; Lt-Comdr, retired 1958. Aiton & Co., Derby, 1958, Dir, 1976, retired 1988; Gp Personnel Controller and local Dir, Whessoe, 1980–88; former Director: Silkolene; ATV (Midlands). Mem., East Reg. Bd, Central ITV, 1982–92. Chm., Derbys FHSA, 1990–97. Pres., Royal Sch. for the Deaf, Derby, 1977–; Patron, Arkwright Soc., Cromford, 2002–. Freeman, City of London, 1978; Liveryman, Tinplate Workers alias Wire-workers' Co., 1978 (Mem., Ct of Assts, 1994–2005). DL 1977, High Sheriff, 1978–79, Derbys. *Recreations:* gardening; appreciation of art, music and wine; needlework, charity work. *Address:* Ithersay Cottage, Idridgehay, Belper, Derbyshire DE56 2SB. *T:* (01773) 550210. *Clubs:* MCC; County (Derby).

See also R. H. Boissier.

BOISSIER, Vice Adm. Robin Paul, CB 2007; Chief Executive, Royal National Lifeboat Institution, since 2009; *b* 14 Oct. 1953; *s* of late Peter Clement Boissier and Joan Rosemary Boissier; *m* 1980, Susan Jane Roxanna Stocker. *Educ:* Harrow Sch.; Emmanuel Coll., Cambridge (MA); London Business Sch. (MSc). Joined RN, 1974; in command: HMS Onyx, 1985; HMS Trafalgar, 1989; HMS Chatham, 1994; Asst Dir, Navy Staff Duties, 1996–97; Dir, Navy Plans and Progs, MOD, 1998–99; Portsmouth Naval Base, 2000–02; ADC to the Queen, 2000–02; Dep. Comdr, NATO Striking Forces, Southern Reg., 2002–04; Dep. Chief Exec., Warship Support Agency, 2004–05; Dir Gen. Logistics (Fleet), MoD, 2005–06; Dep. C-in-C Fleet and Chief Naval Warfare Officer, 2006–09. Younger Brother, Trinity House, 2007. *Publications:* Understanding the Rule of the Road, 2003; Learn the Nautical Rules of the Road, 2010; How to Read a Nautical Chart, 2010. *Recreations:* sailing, gardening. *Address:* c/o Royal National Lifeboat Institution, Head Office, West Quay Road, Poole, Dorset BH15 1HZ. *Clubs:* MCC; Royal Yacht Squadron (Cowes).

BOISSIER, Roger Humphrey, CBE 1992; Chairman, Royal Crown Derby Porcelain Co. Ltd, 2000–07 (non-executive Director, 2000–08); *b* 30 June 1930; *y s* of late Ernest Boissier, DSC, CEng, FIEE and Doris Boissier (*née* Bingham), of Bingham's Melcombe; *m* 1965, (Elizabeth) Bridget (Rhoda), *e d* of Sir Gerald Ley, Bt, TD and Rosemary, Lady Ley; one *s* one *d*. *Educ:* Harrow. International Combustion Ltd, 1950–52; Cooper-Parry, Hall, Doughty & Co., 1952–53; Merz & McLellan, 1953–55; Aiton & Co., 1955–83, Man. Dir, 1975–83; Exec. Dir, Whessoe plc, 1975–83. Chm., Pressac Hldgs PLC, then Pressac plc, 1990–2002 (non-exec. Dir, 1984); non-executive Director: Derbyshire BS, 1972–81; Simmonds Precision NV, 1976–82; Ley's Foundries & Engrg, 1977–82; Allott & Lomax Ltd, 1984–2000; Severn Trent Water Authy, then Severn Trent plc, 1986–98; British Gas plc, 1986–96 (pt-time Mem., British Gas Corp., 1981–86); T & N plc, 1987–98; Edward Lumley Ltd, 1988–2004; Kalon Gp plc, 1992–99 (Chm., 1992–95). Mem. Exec., British Energy Assoc. (formerly Brit. Nat. Cttee, World Energy Council), 1975–2005 (Chm., 1977–80; Hon. Mem., 2009); Mem. Council, 1991–2007, Mem. Court, 1991–, a Pro-Chancellor and Dep. Chm. Council, 2000–07, Loughborough Univ.; Mem. Court, Univ. of Derby, 1998–; Governor: Harrow Sch., 1976–96 (Dep. Chm., 1988–96); Landau Forte Coll., Derby, 1995–2011. Pres., Harrow Assoc., 2006–11. Mem. Cttee, Canadian War Meml, London, 1990–94. High Sheriff of Derbyshire, 1987–88. Freeman, City of London, 1971; Master, Co. of Tin Plate Workers alias Wire Workers, 1988–89. CIGEM (CIGasE 1983); FRSA 1987–2010; Hon. FEI 1991. Hon. DTech Loughborough, 2001. *Recreations:* cars, reading, meeting people. *Address:* Low Baronwood, Armathwaite, Carlisle, Cumbria CA4 9TW. *T:* (01697) 472347. *E:* rogerboissier@btinternet.com. *Clubs:* Brooks's, MCC.

See also M. S. Boissier.

BOIZOT, Peter James, MBE 1986; DL; founded PizzaExpress Ltd, 1965; President, PizzaExpress Plc, since 1996 (Chairman, 1993–96); *b* 16 Nov. 1929; *s* of late Gaston Charles and Susannah Boizot. *Educ:* King's Sch., Peterborough (chorister, Peterborough Cathedral); St Catharine's Coll., Cambridge. MA (BA (Hons) History). Captain, MV Yarvic, 1951. Various jobs, predominantly in sales field, 1953–64; Chm. and Man. Dir, PizzaExpress Ltd, 1965–93; Dir, Connoisseur Casino, 1970–82. Publisher, monthly magazines: BOZ (formerly Jazz Express), 1983–; Hockey Sport (formerly Hockey Digest), 1995–; World Hockey, 1995. Proprietor: Pizza on the Park, 1976–2005; Kettners Restaurant, Soho, 1980–2002; Great Northern Hotel, Peterborough, 1993–. Founder and Chm., Soho Restaurateurs Assoc., 1980–. Founder and Dir, Soho Jazz Fest., 1986–. Dir, CENTEC, 1990–93. Chm., Westminster Chamber of Commerce, 1992–95. Founder, Venice in Peril Charity. Mem., Royal Acad. Adv. Bd, 1988–91. Fellow Commoner, St Catharine's Coll., Cambridge, 1996. Contested (L) Peterborough, Feb. and Oct. 1974. Founder Mem., Soho Soc., 1972. Pres., Hampstead and Westminster Hockey Club, 1986–; a Vice-Pres., Hockey Assoc., 1990–; Chm., Peterborough United FC, 1997–. DL Cambs, 1998. FIH (FHCIMA 1989). Hon. LLD Westminster, 1995; Hon. DLitt Loughborough, 2000. Freeman of Peterborough, 2007. Bolla Award, 1983; Hotel and Caterer Food Service Award, 1989. Commendatore, Al Merito della Repubblica Italiana, 1996 (Cavaliere Ufficiale, 1983). *Publications:* PizzaExpress Cook Book, 1976, rev. edn 1991; Mr Pizza and All That Jazz (autobiog.), 2014. *Recreations:* hockey, presenting jazz, cabaret, dining out. *Clubs:* National Liberal; Hawks (Cambridge); Vincent's (Oxford).

BOK, Prof. Derek; Professor of Law, since 1961, 300th Anniversary University Professor, since 1991, President, 1971–91, now President Emeritus, and Interim President, 2006–07, Harvard University; *b* Bryn Mawr, Pa, 22 March 1930; *s* of late Curtis and Margaret Plummer Bok (later Mrs William S. Kiskadden); *m* 1955, Sissela Ann Myrdal, *d* of late Prof. Karl Gunnar Myrdal and Alva Myrdal; one *s* two *d*. *Educ:* Stanford Univ. (BA); Harvard Univ. (JD); Inst. of Political Science, Univ. of Paris (Fulbright Scholar); George Washington Univ. (MA Economics). Served AUS, 1956–58. Asst Prof. of Law, Harvard Univ., 1958–61, Dean of Law Sch., 1968–71. Chairman: Common Cause, 1998–; Bd, Spencer Foundn, 2002–. *Publications:* The First Three Years of the Schuman Plan, 1955; (ed with Archibald Cox) Cases and Materials on Labor Law, 5th edn 1962, 6th edn 1965, 7th edn 1969, 8th edn 1977; (with John Dunlop) Labor and the American Community, 1970; Beyond the Ivory Tower, 1982; Higher Learning, 1986; Universities and the future of America, 1990; The Cost of Talent, 1993; The State of the Nation, 1996; The Shape of the River, 1998; The Trouble with Government, 2001; Universities in the Marketplace, 2003; Our Underachieving Colleges, 2006; The Politics of Happiness, 2010. *Recreations:* gardening, tennis, ski-ing. *Address:* c/o Kennedy School of Government, Harvard University, Mailbox 50, 79 JFK Street, Cambridge, MA 02138–5801, USA.

BOKHARY, Syed Kemal Shah; Hon. Mr Justice Bokhary; a Non-Permanent Judge, Hong Kong Court of Final Appeal, since 2013 (a Permanent Judge, 1997–2013); *b* 25 Oct. 1947; *s* of Syed Daud Shah Bokhary and Halima Bokhary (*née* Arculli); *m* 1977, Verina Saeeda Chung (*see* V. S. Bokhary); three *d*. *Educ:* King George V Sch., Hong Kong. Called to the Bar, Middle Temple, 1970 (Hon. Bencher, 2001); QC (Hong Kong) 1983; practised in Hong Kong and before the Judicial Cttee of the Privy Council, London, 1971–89; Judge of High Court, Hong Kong, 1989–93; Justice of Appeal, Supreme Court of Hong Kong, 1993–97. Mem., Law Reform Commn of Hong Kong, 2000–. Mem. Bd, Law Faculty, 1994–, and Chm., Law and Professional Legal Educn Depts Adv. Cttee, 1997–, City Univ., Hong Kong; Chm., Adv. Bd, Centre for Criminology, Dept of Sociology, Univ. of Hong Kong, 1999–; Chm. Academic Bd, Sch. of Law, 2006–, Chm., Adv. Bd, Faculty of Law, Chinese Univ. of Hong Kong. University of Hong Kong: Hon. Lectr, Dept of Professional Legal Educn, 2000–; Hon. Prof., 2012–; Affiliate, Centre of Near and Middle Eastern Studies, SOAS, 2001–. Mem., Acad. of Experts' Judicial Cttee, 2003–. Mem., RSAA, 1988–. FRAI 1998; Fellow, Hong Kong Inst. of Arbitrators, 2012. Patron, Advocacy and Mooting Soc., Univ. of Hong Kong, 2003–. Chm., Welsh and W of England Bullmastiff Soc.; Life Mem., Southern Bullmastiff Soc. Mem., Editl Adv. Bd, Halsbury's Laws of Hong Kong, 1993– (Chm., 2011–); Editor-in-Chief: Tort Law and Practice in Hong Kong, 2005–; Archbold Hong Kong, 2008–; Bullen & Leake & Jacobs, Hong Kong vol., 2013–; General Editor: Hong Kong Court of Final Appeal Reports, 2013–; Hong Kong Law Reports and Digest, 2013–; Internat. Adv. Ed., Malaysian Civil Procedure, 2013–. Hon. LLD: Hong Kong, 2012; Hong Kong Shue Yan, 2014. Grand Bauhinia Medal (Hong Kong), 2013. *Publications:* Recollections, 2013; The Law is a Crocodile, 2013; Crocodile at Law, 2014; articles in Hong Kong Law Jl and other learned jls. *Recreations:* dogs, opera, anthropology, reading, walking, travel, shooting. *Address:* Court of Final Appeal, 1 Battery Path, Hong Kong. *Clubs:* Hong Kong Jockey, Hong Kong Country, Aberdeen Marina, Hong Kong Clay Target Shooting Association, Hong Kong Rifle Association, Hong Kong Kennel (President).

BOKHARY, Verina Saeeda; a Judge of the Court of First Instance of the High Court (formerly Judge of the High Court), Hong Kong, 1996–2015, now Deputy Judge; *b* 5 Feb. 1950; *d* of Chung Hon-Wing and Hung Shui-Chan; *m* 1977, Syed Kemal Shah Bokhary, *qv*; three *d*. Called to the Bar, Lincoln's Inn, 1971; Temp. Asst Registrar, Royal Courts of Justice, Chancery Div., 1972; Legal Asst, HM Customs & Excise, 1972–76; Legal Officer, Unofficial Mems of the Exec. and Legislative Council Office, Hong Kong, 1976–78; in private practice, Hong Kong, 1978–85; Hong Kong Judiciary: Magistrate, 1985–87; Adjudicator, 1987–89; Dist Court Judge, 1989–95. Chm., Release under Supervision Bd, 1998–2003; Dep. Pres., Long-term Prison Sentences Rev. Bd, 1997–2003. Mem., Updating Gp, High Court Criminal Manual Specimen Directions, 1998–2004. Adv. Ed. and reviewer, Archbold HK, 2003–05. *Recreations:* homelife, antiques, reading. *Address:* High Court, 38 Queensway, Hong Kong. *T:* 28254312, 92856766.

BOKOVA, Irina Gueorguieva; Director General, UNESCO, since 2009; *b* 12 July 1952; *d* of Georgi and Nadezhda Bokov; *m* Kalin Mitrev; one *s* one *d*. *Educ:* English Secondary Sch., Sofia; Moscow State Inst. of Internat. Relns (MBA Internat. Relns); Sch. of Public Affairs, Univ. of Maryland, Washington; John F. Kennedy Sch. of Govt, Harvard Univ. (Exec. Prog. in Leadership and Econ. Devlt 1999). Third Sec., Min. of Foreign Affairs, Sofia, 1977–82; Perm. Mission of Bulgaria to UN, NY, 1982–84; Second Sec., UN Dept, 1984–86, Advr to Minister, 1986–90, Min. of Foreign Affairs; Ford Foundn Fellow, 1989; Mem., Constituent Nat. Assembly, 1990–91; First Sec., Eur. Security Dept, Min. of Foreign Affairs, 1991–92; NATO Fellow, Prog. for Central and Eastern Europe on democratic instns, 1992–94; State Sec., Eur. Integration, 1995–97; Minister of Foreign Affairs, 1996–97; Advr to Minister of Foreign Affairs, 1997; MP, 2001–05; Ambassador to France and Monaco, Perm. Delegate of Bulgaria and Rep. on Exec. Bd, UNESCO, 2005–09. Hon. doctorates incl. Edinburgh, 2011. Numerous state distinctions. *Publications:* contribs to Mediterranean Qly, Eur. Policy Forum annual pubns, Jl SE and Black Sea Studies and articles on foreign policy and Eur. integration issues, culture, heritage, educn and sci. *Address:* UNESCO, 7 place de Fontenoy, 75352 Paris 07 SP, France. *T:* 0145681310, *Fax:* 0145685555. *E:* dg@unesco.org.

BOKSENBERG, Prof. Alexander, CBE 1996; PhD; FRS 1978; FInstP; FRAS; Hon. Professor of Experimental Astronomy, Institute of Astronomy, University of Cambridge, since 1991; Research Professor and PPARC Senior Research Fellow, Universities of Cambridge and London, 1996–99; Extraordinary Fellow, Churchill College, Cambridge, since 1996; Director, Royal Observatories, 1993–96: Royal Greenwich Observatory, Cambridge; Royal Observatory, Edinburgh; Isaac Newton Group of optical telescopes, Canary Islands; Joint Astronomy Centre, Hawaii; Chairman, UK National Commission for UNESCO, since 2004; *b* 18 March 1936; *s* of Julius Boksenberg and Ernestina Steinberg; *m* 1960, Adella Coren; one *s* one *d*. *Educ:* Stationers' Co.'s Sch.; Univ. of London (BSc, PhD); MA Cantab. Dept of Physics and Astronomy, University Coll. London: SRC Res. Asst, 1960–65; Lectr in Physics, 1965–75; Head of Optical and Ultraviolet Astronomy Res. Group, 1969–81; Reader in Physics, 1975–78; SRC Sen. Fellow, 1976–81; Prof. of Physics and Astronomy, 1978–81; Dir, Royal Greenwich Observatory, 1981–93. Sherman Fairchild Dist. Schol., CIT, 1981–82; Visiting Professor: Dept of Physics and Astronomy, UCL, 1981–; Astronomy Centre, Univ. of Sussex, 1981–89. Chm., New Industrial Concepts Ltd, 1969–81. UK Project Scientist: ESA astronomical satellite TD-1A, 1969–73; NASA-ESA-SERC Internat. Ultraviolet Explorer satellite observatory, 1969–79. Inventor, photon camera system, ESA-NASA Hubble Space Telescope, 1974–76. USA-UK-Canada Gemini Telescopes Project: UK Dir, 1993–96; Chm., Internat. Expert Cttee, 1992; Chm., UK Steering Cttee, 1992–93; Mem., USA Oversight Cttee, 1993–94. Chairman: SRC Astronomy II Cttee, 1980–81; UK-Japan N+N Bd on Co-operation in Astronomy, 1997–2005; PPARC VISTA Review Bd, 1999–2000; Pres., Internat. Scientific Cttee, Canary Is Observatories, 1984–95 (Mem., 1981–96). Member: ESA Hubble Space Telescope Instrument Definition Team, 1973–95; S African Astronomical Observatory Adv. Cttee, 1978–85; British Council Science Adv. Cttee, 1987–91; Anglo-Australian Telescope Bd, 1989–91 (Dep. Chm., 1991–92); Hubble Space Telescope Users Cttee, 1990–91; Fachbeirat, Max Planck Inst. für Astronomie, 1991–95; European Southern Observatory Vis. Cttee, 1993–95; Finance Cttee, IAU, 1997–2000; Wkg Gp on Basic Scis and Basic Res., ICSU, 2004; Mgt Cttee, Language Centre, Univ. of Cambridge, 2003–07; Steering Cttee, Universe Awareness, 2005–; Scientific Cttee, Starlight Initiative, 2007–; formerly mem. or chm. of more than 40 other councils, boards, cttees, panels or courts, 1970–. Exec. Ed., Experimental Astronomy, 1995–2007. Mem. Council and Trustee, Royal Soc., 1995–97 (Mem., Technical Support Steering Gp, 1997–98; Chm., Internat. Exchanges Far East Panel, 2000–06; Hughes Medal, 1999); Mem. Council, Trustee and Vice-Pres., Royal Astronomical Soc., 2000–03 (Chm., Awards Cttee A, 2002–03; Mem., Astronomical Heritage Cttee, 2005–; Jackson-Gwilt Medal, 1998); Mem. Council, Inst. of Physics, 2001–03 (Mem., Women in Physics Cttee, 2002–03; Chm., Ethics Cttee, 2004–08; Glazebrook Medal and Prize, 2000). UK National Commission for UNESCO: Mem., Foundn Cttee, 1999–2000; Mem. Council, 2000–03; Chm., Sci. Cttee, 2000–03; Chm., Steering Cttee, Campaign Gp, 2003–04; Chm. Bd, 2004–10; Chm., Nat. Sci. Cttee, 2004–11; UNESCO Regional Bureau for Science in Europe: Mem., Scientific Council, 2000–08; Mem., Task Force for Reconstruction of Scientific Co-operation in SE Europe, 2000–03; Chm., Wkg Gp on Restoring Human Potential in SE Europe, 2002–03. UNESCO: Mem., Sci. Sector Cttee of Experts on Internat. Basic Scis Prog., 2002–04; Mem., World Heritage Centre Cttee of Internat. Experts on Archaeo-Astronomical Sites and Observatories, 2004–05; Mem., Internat. Rev. Cttee of Experts for Overall Review of UNESCO Sci. Sectors, 2006–08. Mem., Adv. Cttee, Commonwealth Day 2010, 2009–10. Member: Internat. Juries of the UNESCO Science Prize, Javed Husain Prize for Young Scientists, and Kalinga Prize for Popularisation of Science, 2004–; Jury, UNESCO-L'Oreal Fellowships for Women in Science (UK and Ireland), 2006–; Chm., Internat. Jury for Latsis Prize, ESF, 2008. Pres., W London Astronomical Soc., 1978–; Hon. Pres., Astronomical Soc. of Glasgow, 1995–. Pres., British Horological Inst., 2000–01. Royal Soc. lecture tours: Russia, 1989; China, 1995; Japan, 1999; British Council lect. tour, India, 1999. Founding Member: Academia Europaea, 1989; European Astronomical Soc., 1990; Mem., Cambridge Philosophical Soc., 1996–; Titular Mem., Eur. Acad. of Arts, Scis and Humanities, 2007. Patron, Hanwell Community Observatory, 2009–. Member: Council, Churchill Coll., Cambridge, 1998–2003; Council, Winston Churchill Meml Trust, 2010–; Bd of Trustees, Future Univ., Sudan, 2011–. Fellow, UCL, 1991. FRAS 1965; FInstP 1998; FRSA 1984. Clockmakers' Co.: Freeman, 1984; Liveryman, 1989; Mem., Court of Assts, 1994–; Master, 2000. Asteroid (3205) Boksenberg, named 1988. Dr *hc* l'Observatoire de Paris, 1982; DSc *hc* Sussex, 1991. Golden Diploma, Eur. Forum of Experts, 2007. *Publications:* (ed jtly) Modern Technology and its Influence on Astronomy, 1990; (dedicatee and contrib.) Hubble Space Telescope and High Redshift Universe, Procs of 37th Herstmonceux Conf., 1996; (ed jtly) The Role of Astronomy in Society and Culture, Procs of 260th Symposium of Internat. Astronomical Union, 2011; over 240 contribs to learned jls. *Recreation:* ski-ing. *Address:* University of Cambridge, Institute of Astronomy, The Observatories, Madingley Road, Cambridge CB3 0HA. *T:* (01223) 337548. *Club:* Athenæum.

BOLADUADUA, Emitai Lausiki; Director, Institute of Indigenous (Fijian) Studies, since 2009; *b* 13 April 1944; *s* of Naibuka Lausiki and Mere Turavono; *m* 1973, Asinate U. Taleaua; four *d*. *Educ:* Queen Victoria Sch., Fiji; Suva Grammar Sch., Fiji; Univ. of New England, Armidale, NSW (BSc, DipEd); Univ. of Reading. Ratu Kadavulevu School: asst teacher 1968–73; Vice Principal, 1973–81; Principal, 1981–84; Principal: Labasa Coll., 1984–87; Fij Inst. of Technol., 1988–90; Deputy Secretary: for Educn, Youth and Sport, 1990–93; fo Foreign Affairs and Civil Aviation, 1993–97; Permanent Secretary: for Inf., Broadcasting, TV and Telecommunications, 1997; for Home Affairs and Immigration, 1997–99; for Educn 1999; for Foreign Affairs and External Trade, 1999–2000. Mem., Land Transport Authy, Fiji 2002. High Comr of Fiji in UK, also accredited to Republic of Ireland, Denmark, Germany the Holy See, Israel and Egypt, 2002–06. Chm., Cakaudrove Provincial Council, 2008–13 Chm. Council, Fiji Inst. of Technol., 1999; Mem. Council, Univ. of S Pacific, 1990–92 an 1999. CS Medal (Fiji), 1995. *Publications:* Na Vuku ni Vanua - Wisdom of the Land: aspect of Fijian knowledge, culture and history, 2013. *Recreations:* watching cricket, tennis, Rugb Union, reading. *Address:* PO Box 4528, Samabula, Fiji Islands.

BOLAM, James, MBE 2009; actor; *b* Sunderland, 16 June 1938; *s* of Robert Alfred Bolam and Marion Alice Bolam (*née* Drury); *m* Susan Jameson, actress. *Educ:* Bede Grammar Sch. Sunderland; Bemrose Sch., Derby. First stage appearance, The Kitchen, Royal Court, 1959 later plays include: Events While Guarding the Bofors Gun, Hampstead, 1966; In Celebration Royal Court, 1969; Veterans, Royal Court, 1972; Treats, Royal Court, 1976; Who Kille 'Agatha' Christie?, Ambassadors, 1978; King Lear (title rôle), Young Vic, 1981; Run for You Wife!, Criterion, 1983; Arms and the Man, Cambridge; Who's Afraid of Virginia Woolf? Birmingham, 1989; Victory, Chichester, 1989; Jeffrey Bernard is Unwell, Apollo, 1990 Glengarry Glen Ross, Donmar Warehouse, 1994; Wild Oats, National, 1995; Endgame Nottingham Playhouse, 1999; Semi-Detached, 1999, How to Succeed in Business Withou Really Trying, 2005, Chichester. *Films:* A Kind of Loving, 1962; The Loneliness of the Lon Distance Runner, 1962; Half a Sixpence, 1967; Otley, 1969; Crucible of Terror, 1971 Straight on till Morning, 1972; In Celebration, 1974; Murder Most Foul; The Likely Lads 1976; The Great Question; Seaview Knights; Clockwork Mice; Stella Does Tricks; Island o Bird Street; End of the Affair, 1999; It Was an Accident, 2000. *Television series:* The Likel Lads, 1965–69; Whatever Happened to the Likely Lads?, 1973; When the Boat Comes In 1975–77; The Limbo Connection (Armchair Thriller Series); Only When I Laugh; The Beiderbecke Affair; Room at the Bottom; Andy Capp; The Beiderbecke Tapes; Th Beiderbecke Connection; Second Thoughts; Eleven Men Against Eleven; Have your Cake The Missing Postman, 1997; Pay and Display, Dirty Tricks, Close and True, 2000; Born an Bred, Shipman, 2002; New Tricks (9 series), 2003–12; The Plot Against Harold Wilson 2006; Grandpa In My Pocket, 2009–; also As You Like It, Macbeth, in BBC Shakespeare *Address:* c/o Jane Brand, Independent Talent Group Ltd, 40 Whitfield Street, W1T 2RH.

BOLAND, Leo; Chief Executive, Greater London Authority, 2009–11; *b* 1 Aug. 1952; *s* c Stephen and Ellen Boland; *m* 1981, Margaret Gibbons; one *s*. *Educ:* Ushaw Coll., Durham Bristol Univ. (BSc Hons Social Scis); Open Univ. Business Sch. (MBA). Grad. trainee, Ealin BC, 1974–75; Community Worker, Newham Rights Centre, 1975–79; Improvemer Officer, Housing Dept, Islington BC, 1979–89; Newham Borough Council: Capital Prog Manager, 1989–91; Asst Dir of Social Services, 1991–98; Asst Chief Exec., 1998–2001; Chie Exec., London Borough of Barnet, 2001–09. *Recreations:* walking, reading, film, eating out.

BOLEAT, Mark John; company director and consultant; *b* 21 Jan. 1949; *s* of Paul Boleat an Peggy Boleat (*née* Still); *m* 1991, Elizabeth Ann Baker (*née* Barker). *Educ:* Victoria College Jersey; Lanchester Polytechnic and Univ. of Reading (BA Econs, MA Contemp. Europea Studies). FCIB. Asst Master, Dulwich College, 1972; Economist, Indust. Policy Group, 197 The Building Societies Association: Asst Sec., 1974; Under Sec., 1976; Dep. Sec., 1979; De Sec.-Gen., 1981; Sec.-Gen., 1986; Dir-Gen., 1987. Sec.-Gen., Internat. Union of Housin Finance Instns (formerly Internat. Union of Building Socs and Savings Assocs), 1986–8 Mem. Bd, Housing Corp., 1988–93; Chm., Circle 33 Housing Trust, 1990–93; Dir-Gen ABI, 1993–99; Director: Comino Gp, 2000–06; Countryside Properties, 2001–05. Mem Regulatory Policy Cttee, 2009–12; Chairman: Jersey Competition Regulatory Authy, 2010– States of Jersey Development Co., 2011–. Chairman: Hillingdon Community Trus 2003–08; Green Corridor, 2008–11. Member: NCC, 2000–05; Gibraltar Financial Service Commn, 2000–09; Chm., Assoc. of Labour Providers, 2004–12. Mem., Ct of Commo Council, City of London Corp., 2002– (Chm., Mkts Cttee, 2008–; Dep. Chm., 2009–12 Chm., 2012–, Policy and Resources Cttee). *Publications:* The Building Society Industry, 1982 National Housing Finance Systems: a comparative study, 1985; Housing in Britain, 198 (with Adrian Coles) The Mortgage Market, 1987; Building Societies: the regulator framework, 1988, 3rd edn 1992; Trade Association Strategy and Management, 1996; Mode of Trade Association Co-operation, 2000; Good Practice in Trade Association Governance 2001; Managing Trade Associations, 2003; Housing Development and Housing Finance i Britain, 2008; An Agenda for Better Regulation, 2009; Jersey's Population—a history, 201 articles on housing, insurance and finance. *Recreation:* golf. *Address:* 26 Westbury Roa Northwood, Middx HA6 3BU. *Clubs:* Moor Park Golf, La Moye Golf.

BOLES, Nicholas Edward Coleridge; MP (C) Grantham and Stamford, since 201 Minister of State, Department for Business, Innovation and Skills and Department fo Education, since 2014; *b* 2 Nov. 1965; *s* of Sir John Dennis, (Sir Jack), Boles, MBE. *Edu* Winchester; Magdalen Coll., Oxford (BA PPE); John F. Kennedy Sch. of Govt, Harvar Univ. (MPP 1989). Founder, 1995, Chief Exec., 1995–2000, non-exec. Chm., 2000–0 Longwall Hldgs Ltd. Founder and Dir, Policy Exchange, 2002–07; COS to Mayor of Londo 2008. Mem. (C) Westminster CC, 1998–2002 (Chm., Housing Cttee, 1999–2001 Contested (C) Hove, 2005. PPS to Minister of State, DfE, 2010–12; Parly Under-Sec. of Stat (Minister for Planning), DCLG, 2012–14. Sen. Fellow, Inst. for Govt, 2010–12. *Publication* Which Way's Up?: the future for coalition Britain and how to get there, 2010. *Address:* Hous of Commons, SW1A 0AA.

See also J. D. Fishburn.

BOLES, Sir Richard Fortescue, 4th Bt *cr* 1922, of Bishop's Lydeard, Somerset; *b* 12 De 1958; *er s* of Sir Jeremy John Fortescue Boles, 3rd Bt and Dorothy Jane Boles (*née* Worswick *S* father 2014, but his name does not yet appear on the Official Roll of the Baronetage; 1990, Allison Beverley, *d* of Brian MacDonald; one *s* one *d*. *Heir:* *s* James Alexander Fortescu Boles, *b* 25 May 1993.

BOLGER, Rt Hon. James Brendan, (Jim), ONZ 1997; PC 1991; Chairman: Kiwiban Ltd, 2001–10; KiwiRail, 2008–10; *b* 31 May 1935; *s* of Daniel Bolger and Cecilia (*née* Doyle *m* 1963, Joan Maureen Riddell; six *s* three *d*. *Educ:* Opunake High Sch. Sheep and catt farmer, Te Kuiti, 1965–72. Federated Farmers: Br. Chm., 1967–72; sub-provincial Chm 1970–72; Vice-Pres., Waikato, 1971–72; Mem., Dominion Exec., 1971–72. MP (Nat. Party King Country, 1972–98; Parly Under-Sec., Min. of Agric. and Fisheries, Min. of Mao Affairs, then Minister i/c of Rural Banking Finance Corp., 1975–77; Minister of Fisheries an Associate Minister of Agric., 1977–78; Minister of Labour, 1978–84; Minister of Immigratio 1978–81; Leader of Nat. Party, 1986–97; Leader of the Opposition, 1986–90; Prime Ministe of NZ, 1990–97; NZ Ambassador to USA, 1998–2002. Chairman: Adv. Bd, World Agric Foundn, 2002–; Ian Axford (NZ) Fellowship in Public Policy, 2002–. Chairman: New Zealan Post Ltd, 2002–10; Gas Industry Co., 2004–; Express Couriers Ltd, 2004–; Trustees Executo Ltd, 2006–; Parcels Direct Gp. Chancellor, Waikato Univ., 2007–. Pres., ILO, 1983. Hon Dr Agricl Econs Khon Kaen, 1994; Hon. DLitt Massey, 2002. Silver Jubilee Medal, 1977; N Commemoration Medal, 1990; NZ Suffrage Centennial Medal, 1993. *Recreations:* hikin fishing, reading, Rugby, cricket. *Address:* Somerville Road, PO Box 406, Te Kuiti, Ne Zealand.

OLINGBROKE, 9th Viscount *cr* 1712, **AND ST JOHN,** 10th Viscount *cr* 1716; **Nicholas Alexander Mowbray St John;** Bt 1611; Baron St John of Lydiard Tregoze, 1712; Baron St John of Battersea, 1716; *b* 20 June 1974; *s* of 7th Viscount Bolingbroke and 8th Viscount St John and of Jainey Anne (*née* McRae); *S* half-*b* 2011; *m* 2012, Helen McDougall. *Heir: kinsman* Walter Warren St John [*b* 14 Feb. 1921; *m* 1949, Lida Amelia Goicoechea; one *s* one *d*]. *Address:* New Zealand.

OLITHO, Col Edward Thomas, OBE 1994; Lord-Lieutenant of Cornwall, since 2011; *b* Penzance, 30 Dec. 1955; *s* of Maj. Simon Edward Bolitho, MC and Elizabeth Margaret Bolitho (*née* Creswell); *m* 1985, Alexandra Laura Melissa, *d* of Rear-Adm. Sir Morgan Charles Morgan-Giles, DSO, OBE, GM; one *s* twin *d*. *Educ:* Eton Coll.; Pembroke Coll., Cambridge (BA 1977). Commnd Grenadier Guards, 1978; Comd 1 Bn, 1993–95; Staff Coll., 1995–98. Chairman: CLA Cornwall, 2007–09; CLA SW, 2009–12. Mem., Newlyn Harbour Commn, 2007–10. Regtl Lt Col, Grenadier Guards, 2000–07. Hon. Air Cdre 2625 (Co. of Cornwall) Sqdn, RAuxAF, 2000–06. Mem., HM Bodyguard, Hon. Corps of Gentlemen at Arms, 2008–. Vice Pres., Royal Cornwall Agricl Assoc., 2014–. Trustee, Duke of Cornwall's Benevolent Fund, 2014–. DL 2008, High Sheriff, 2011–12, Cornwall. *Address:* Trengwainton, Penzance, Cornwall TR20 8SA.

OLKESTEIN, Frederik, (Frits); Member, European Commission, 1999–2004; runs one-person political and economic think tank; *b* 4 April 1933; *m* 1988, Femke Boersma; one *s* one *d* (and one *s* decd). *Educ:* Oregon State Coll., USA; Gemeentelijke Univ., Amsterdam; Univ. of Leiden (Master of Law). Shell Group, 1960–76: posts in E Africa, Honduras, El Salvador, UK, Indonesia and France; Dir, Shell Chimie, Paris, 1973–76. Mem. Parliament (VVD), Netherlands, 1978–82, 1986–88 and 1989–99; Minister for Foreign Trade, 1982–86; Minister of Defence, 1988–89; Chm., VVD Parly Gp, 1990–98. Pres., Liberal Internat., 1996–99. Visiting Professor: Univ. of Leiden, 2005–10; Univ. of Delft, 2005–. Member Supervisory Board: Central Bank of the Netherlands, 2005–11; AF/KLM, 2005–. MRIIA. *Publications:* The Limits of Europe, 2004; De twee lampen van de staatsman, 2006; (with Michel Rocard) Peut-on réformer la France?, 2006; Overmoed en Onverstand, 2008; De Intellectuele Verleiding, 2011 (The Intellectual Temptation, 2013). *W:* www.fritsbolkestein.com.

OLLAND, Alexander; QC (Scot.) 1992; *b* 21 Nov. 1950; *s* of James Bolland and Elizabeth Agnes (*née* Anderson); *m* 1973, Agnes Hunter, *d* of Dr George Pate Moffat, Crookedholm; one *s* two *d*. *Educ:* Kilmarnock Acad.; Univ. of St Andrews (BD 1973); Glasgow Univ. (LLB 1976). Admitted to Faculty of Advocates, 1978; Capt., Directorate of Army Legal Services, later Army Legal Corps, 1978–80; Standing Jun. Counsel to Dept of Employment in Scotland, 1988–92; Temp. Sheriff, 1988–99; part-time Judge (formerly Chm.), Employment (formerly Industrial) Tribunals, 1993–2013; Legal Chm., Pensions Appeal Tribunal (Scotland) (War Pensions), 2008–; Chm., Dentists' Vocational Trng Appeal Tribunal, 2013–; Mem., Judicial Proceedings Panel, C of S, 2013–. *Recreations:* Hellenistics, walking, reading. *Address:* The Old Dairy, 60 North Street, St Andrews, Fife KY16 9AH. *T:* (01334) 474599. *Club:* New (Edinburgh).

OLLAND, (David) Michael; broadcast consultant, 2007–15; *b* 27 Feb. 1947; *s* of Allan Bolland and Eileen Lindsay; *m* 1987, Katie Lander; one *s* one *d*, and one *s* two *d* by former marrs. *Educ:* Hillhead High School, Glasgow. Film editor, BBC Scotland, 1965–73; TV Producer, BBC TV, 1973–81; Channel Four Television: Commissioning Editor, Youth, 1981–83; Senior Commissioning Editor, Entertainment, 1983–87; Asst Dir of Programmes, and Head of Art and Entertainment Gp, 1987–88; Controller Arts and Entertainment, and Dep. Dir of Progs, 1988–90; Man. Dir, Initial Films and Television, 1990; Man. Dir, Channel X Ltd, 1990–96; Project Dir, Channel X Broadcasting (Scotland) Ltd, 1991–95; BBC Scotland: Hd of Arts and Entertainment, 1996–2001; Hd of Comedy and Entertainment, 2001–04; Dir of Television, 2004–07, Creative Dir, 2006–07, Nat. Film and Television Sch. Chairman: Edinburgh Internat. TV Fest., 1990; Producers' Alliance for Film and Television, 1995. Member: RTS; BAFTA. *Recreation:* catching up with the world. *Address:* 1 Westbourne Gardens, Glasgow G12 9XE.

OLLAND, Hugh Westrope; Vice Chairman, Schroder Investment Management Ltd, 1999–2000; *b* 14 May 1946; *s* of late Gp Capt. Guy Alfred Bolland, CBE; *m* 1972, Marian Wendy Elton; two *s* one *d*. *Educ:* St Edward's Sch., Oxford; Univ. of Exeter (BA (Hons) Econs). Joined Schroders, 1970; Man. Dir, Schroders Asia Ltd, Hong Kong, 1984–87; Chief Exec., Schroders Australia Ltd, 1987–90; Chm., Schroder Unit Trusts Ltd, 1990–92; Jt Chief Exec., 1995–96, Chief Exec., 1997–99, Schroder Investment Management Ltd (Dir, 1990–2000); Director: Schroder Split Fund plc, 1993–2002; Fidelity Asian Values plc, 2004–14; JP Morgan Indian Investment Trust, 2004–15; Alliance Trust plc, 2007–12. Mem. Supervisory Bd, Eurocommercial Properties NV, 1998–2013. Gov., St Edward's Sch., Oxford, 1999–2012. *Recreations:* sailing, golf, music. *Clubs:* Hong Kong, Hong Kong Jockey (Hong Kong); Woking Golf, Royal Motor Yacht.

OLLAND, Marc J.; Chief Executive Officer, Marks & Spencer plc, since 2010; *b* Netherlands, 28 March 1959; *s* of J. Bolland and M. Bolland-Bronsvoort. *Educ:* Univ. of Groningen (Masters of Business Admin). Heineken: various mktg roles, 1987–95; Man. Dir, Slovakia and E Europe, 1995–99, Heineken Export Worldwide, 1999–2001; Mem. Bd, 2001–05, Chief Finance Officer, 2005–06, Heineken, NV, Netherlands; CEO, Wm Morrison Supermarkets plc, 2006–10. Non-executive Director: Manpower Inc., 2004–15; Coca-Cola Co., 2015–. *Address:* Marks & Spencer plc, Waterside House, 35 North Wharf Road, W2 1NW.

OLLAND, Mark William; communications consultant, since 2002; *b* 10 April 1966; *s* of late Robert Arthur Bolland and of Joan Bolland (*née* Barker); civil partnership 2006, *m* 2015, Guy Vaughan Black (*see* Baron Black of Brentwood). *Educ:* Kings Manor Sch., Middlesbrough; Univ. of York (BSc). Res. Manager, and Advr to Dir Gen., Advertising Standards Authy, 1988–91; Exec. Asst to Chm., 1991–92, Dir, 1992–96, Press Complaints Commn; Asst Private Sec., 1996–97, Dep. Private Sec., 1997–2002, to HRH the Prince of Wales. Columnist, London Evening Standard, 2006–09; Contributing Editor, Tatler, 2011–. Vice Pres., Journalists' Charity, 2007–. Trustee: Helen Hamlyn Trust, 2008–14; Open Futures Trust, 2010–13; David Ross Foundn, 2011–; Middlesbrough and Teesside Philanthropic Foundn, 2011–14; David Ross Educn Trust, 2012–15; Dir, Bertarelli Foundn, 2013–. *Address:* 34 Cannon Court, 5 Brewhouse Yard, EC1V 4JQ. *E:* mark@markbolland.com. *Club:* Garrick.

OLLAND, Michael; *see* Bolland, D. M.

OLLOBÁS, Prof. Béla, PhD, DSc; FRS 2011; Fellow of Trinity College, Cambridge, since 1971; Honorary Professor of Pure Mathematics, University of Cambridge, since 2006; Distinguished Professor of Excellence in Combinatorics, University of Memphis, Tennessee, since 1995; *b* 3 Aug. 1943; *s* of Béla Bollobás and Emma Varga; *m* 1969, Gabriella Farkas; one *s*. *Educ:* Univ. of Budapest (BA 1966; Dr rer. nat. 1967); Univ. of Cambridge (PhD 1972; DSc 1984). Res. Scientist, Hungarian Acad. of Scis, 1966–69; Vis. Scientist, Soviet Acad. of Scis, 1967–68; Vis. Fellow, Oxford, 1969; Cambridge University: Res. Fellow, 1970–72, Dir of Studies in Maths, 1972–96, Trinity Coll.; Asst Lectr, 1971–74, Lectr in Maths, 1974–85; Reader in Pure Maths, 1985–96. Foreign Mem., Hungarian Acad. of Scis, 1990. Hon. Dr Adam Mickiewicz Univ., Poznan, 2013. *Publications:* Extremal Graph Theory, 1978; Graph Theory, 1979; Random Graphs, 1985, 2nd edn 2001; Combinatorics, 1986; Linear Analysis, 1990; Modern Graph Theory, 1998; (with O. M. O'Riordan) Percolation Theory, 2006; The Art of Mathematics, 2006; over 450 papers in learned jls. *Recreations:* books, opera, theatre, tennis, swimming, jogging, windsurfing, riding, ski-ing. *Address:* Trinity College, Cambridge CB2 1TQ; 5 Selwyn Gardens, Cambridge CB3 9AX. *T:* (01223) 354872; 1644 Neshoba Trace Cove, Germantown, TN 38138, USA. *T:* (901) 7514162.

BOLLOM, Air Marshal Simon John, CB 2011; FREng, FRAeS; Chief of Materiel (Air), Defence Equipment and Support, Ministry of Defence, since 2012; *b* London, 22 Jan. 1960; *s* of John and Mary Bollom; *m* 1988, Kathryn Megraw; one *s* one *d*. *Educ:* Grove Sch., Hastings; Hastings Grammar Sch.; Southampton Univ. (BSc Hons Mech. Engrg). MIMechE 1991; CEng 2009; FREng 2013. Joined RAF, 1981; Sen. Engrg Officer, 72 Sqn, 1992–94; OC Engrg Wing, RAF Odiham, 1998–99; Dir, Tactical Mobility, 2001–03; Team Leader, Tornado project, 2005–08; Dir, Combat Air, 2008–12. *Recreations:* hockey, cricket coach. *Address:* Defence and Equipment Support, Ministry of Defence, Abbey Wood, Bristol BS34 8JH.

BOLSOVER, George William, (Bill), CBE 2011; non-executive Chairman, Aggregate Industries (HOLCIM), 2010–14; Director, B2 Consulting Ltd, since 2010; *b* Oxford, 10 Aug. 1950; *s* of Derrick and Yoma Bolsover; *m* 1972, Bridget Lynne Hopkin; one *s* two *d*. *Educ:* Dragon Sch., Oxford; Worksop Coll., Notts. FRICS 2012. Grad. trainee, Amey plc, 1972–74; Tarmac plc: Prodn Manager, 1974–82; Engrg and Technical Manager, 1982–84; Gen. Manager, 1984–88; Man. Dir, Topmix, 1988–92; Man. Dir, Roadstone East, 1992–95; Chief Operating Officer, Quarry Products, 1995–98; Exec. Dir, Tarmac plc, 1998–2000; Man. Dir, 2000–03, Gp CEO, Eur. and USA, 2003–05, Aggregate Industries plc; CEO, Aggregate Industries (HOLCIM) and Area Manager, HOLCIM Gp, 2005–10. Chm., Natural World Safaris, 2007–; non-exec. Dir, Robert Brett & Sons Ltd, 2013–. Vice Pres., Wildlife Trusts, 2010–. Lt Col, RE and Logistics Staff Corps, RE (V), 2003. Hon. LLD Leicester, 2009. *E:* B2consulting@me.com. *Club:* Worcester Rugby (Dir, 2012–).

BOLSOVER, John Derrick; Chairman and Chief Executive, Baring Asset Management Holdings Ltd, 1995–2002; Corporate Adviser, Silver Heritage Group; *b* 21 June 1947; *m* 1st, 1971, Susan Elizabeth Peacock; two *s* one *d*; 2nd, 1994, Kate Woollett. *Educ:* Repton Sch.; McGill Univ., Canada (BA). Director: Baring Internat. Investment Mgt Ltd (Hong Kong), 1973–85; Baring Asset Mgt (Japan) Ltd, 1986–2002; Baring Asset Mgt Ltd, 1994–2002; Dep. Chm., Baring Hldgs Ltd, 1995–97; Dir, Baring Asset Mgt Hldgs Inc., 1996–98. Chm., Vpar Ltd, 2011–. *Recreation:* sport. *Clubs:* Boodle's, City; Sunningdale Golf; Valderrama Golf.

BOLT, (Mohan) Paul; non-executive Director, Horserace Betting Levy Board, 2011–14; *b* 8 Feb. 1954; *s* of Sydney Bolt and Jaya Bolt (*née* Chandran); *m* 1991, Carol Spekes. *Educ:* Trinity Coll., Cambridge (BA 1975); Open Univ. (MBA 1995). Joined Home Office as admin trainee, 1975: Principal, 1980–89; Hd, Mgt Div., 1989–92; Department of National Heritage, then Department for Culture, Media and Sport, 1992–2001: Head: Libraries Div., 1992–94; Fundamental Expenditure Rev., 1994–95; Broadcasting Bill Team, 1995–96; Broadcasting Policy Div., 1996–98; Dir, Strategy and Communications, 1998–2001; Dir, Broadcasting Standards Commn, 2001–03; Dir, Olympic Games Unit, DCMS, 2003–05; Interim Dir, Olympic Bd Secretariat, 2005–06; Dir, Capability Reviews Team, Cabinet Office, 2006–07; Dir, Sport and Leisure, DCMS, 2008–11. *Recreations:* cricket, theatre, reading, bridge. *Clubs:* Reform; Lancashire County Cricket.

See also R. R. Bolt.

BOLT, Ranjit Ralph, OBE 2003; writer and translator, since 1988; *b* Manchester, 10 Jan. 1959; *s* of Sydney Bolt and Jaya Bolt (*née* Chandran). *Educ:* Perse Sch., Cambridge; Balliol Coll., Oxford (BA Lit. Hum. 1982). Fund Manager: S. G. Warburg, 1982–88; Smith & Williamson, 1988–90; writer and translator, mainly of French verse plays, including: The Liar, 1989, The Illusion, 1990, Old Vic; Arturo Ui, NT 1991; Tartuffe, Playhouse Th., 1991; The Sisterhood, Chichester, 1991; The Venetian Twins, RSC, 1993; Lysistrata, Old Vic, 1993; Le Cid, NT, 1994; The School for Wives, Piccadilly Th., 1996; Cyrano de Bergerac, NY, 2012; co-writer, Hard Times (musical), 2002; lyricist, Merry Wives, The Musical, RSC, 2006. *Publications:* Losing It (novel in verse), 2001, 2nd edn 2012; The Art of Translation, 2010; translations: Corneille, The Liar, The Illusion and Le Cid, 1995; Tartuffe, 1995, 2nd version, 2001; The Sisterhood, 1995; The Venetian Twins, 1996; The School for Wives, 1997; Lysistrata, 2006; La Fontaine, The Hare and the Tortoise, 2006. *Recreations:* fishing, poker.

See also M. P. Bolt.

BOLTON, 8th Baron *cr* 1797, of Bolton Castle, co. York; **Harry Algar Nigel Orde-Powlett;** *b* 14 Feb. 1954; *s* of 7th Baron Bolton and of Hon. Christine, *e d* of 7th Baron Forester; *S* father, 2001; *m* 1977, Philippa, *d* of Major Peter Tapply; three *s*. *Educ:* Eton. *Heir: s* Hon. Thomas Peter Algar Orde-Powlett, MC [*b* 16 July 1979; *m* 2008, Katie, *d* of Edward Gribble; two *s* two *d*]. *Address:* Bolton Hall, Wensley, Leyburn, N Yorks DL8 4UF. *T:* (01969) 623674.

BOLTON, Bishop Suffragan of, since 2008; **Rt Rev. Christopher Paul Edmondson;** *b* Carlisle, 25 June 1950; *s* of Jack and Margaret Edmondson; *m* 1973, Susan Heap; two *s*. *Educ:* St John's Coll., Durham Univ. (BA 1971, MA 1981); Cranmer Hall, Durham (DipTh 1972). Ordained deacon, 1973, priest, 1974; Asst Curate, Kirkheaton, Huddersfield, 1973–79; Vicar, St George's, Halifax, 1979–86; Diocesan Officer for Evangelism, Dio. of Carlisle, 1986–92; Vicar, St Peter's, Shipley, 1992–2002; Warden, Lee Abbey, Devon, 2002–08. Occasional Lecturer: Trinity Coll., Bristol; Cliff Coll., Derbyshire. Mem., British Inst. of Innkeepers, 2004. *Publications:* Strategies for Rural Evangelism, 1989; How Shall They Hear?, 1994; Minister, Love Thyself, 2000; Fit to Lead, 2002, 3rd edn 2009; (contrib.) Vicar's Guide, 2004; (jtly) Celebrating Community, 2006; Leaders Learning to Listen, 2010. *Recreations:* cricket, football, playing piano, guitar and organ (former organ scholar), walking. *Address:* Bishop's Lodge, Walkden Road, Worsley, Manchester M28 2WH. *T:* (0161) 790 8289, *Fax:* (0161) 703 9157. *E:* bishopchrisedmondson@manchester.anglican.org.

BOLTON, Archdeacon of; *see* Bailey, Ven. D. C.

BOLTON, Anthony John; President - Investment, Fidelity Worldwide Investment (formerly Fidelity International), 2008–14, Adviser, since 2014 (Director, 1979–2014); *b* London, 7 March 1950; *s* of Alwyn and Betty Bolton; *m* 1979, Sarah Boyce; two *s* one *d*. *Educ:* Stowe Sch.; Trinity Coll., Cambridge (BA 1971; MA). Keyser Ullmann, 1971–76; Schlesinger Investments, 1976–79; Portfolio Manager, Fidelity Worldwide Investment (formerly Fidelity Internat.), 1979–2008, 2010–14. *Publications:* Investing Against the Tide, 2009. *Recreation:* classical music (listening and writing).

See also E. J. Bolton.

BOLTON, Her Honour Beatrice Maud; a Circuit Judge, 2001–12; *b* 26 July 1953; *d* of late Arthur Henry Bolton and of Freda Bolton; divorced; one *s*. *Educ:* Newcastle upon Tyne Church High Sch.; Sheffield Univ. (LLB Hons). Called to the Bar, Gray's Inn, 1975; Asst Recorder, 1994–98; a Recorder, 1998–2001. *Recreations:* playing tennis, gardening, watching football, horse riding.

BOLTON, Catriona; *see* Jarvis, C.

BOLTON, Group Captain David; Director, Royal United Services Institute, 1981–94 (Deputy Director, 1980–81); *b* 15 April 1932; *o s* of late George Edward and Florence May Bolton; *m* 1955, Betty Patricia Simmonds; three *d*. *Educ:* Bede Sch., Co. Durham. Commnd RAF Regt, 1953; subsequent service in Egypt, Jordan, Singapore, Aden, Cyprus, Malta and Germany; RAF Staff Coll., 1969; National Def. Coll., 1972; Central Planning Staff, MoD, 1973–75; OC 33 Wing RAF Regt, 1975–77; Comdt RAF Regt Depot, Catterick, 1977–80;

retd 1980. Chm., Macbeth Associates, 1994–2000; Vice-Chm., TASC Eur., 1994–97; Dir, Project Constant Endeavour, 2000–04. Member: RUSI Council, 1973–79; IISS, 1964–90; RIIA, 1975–92; Council, British Atlantic Cttee, 1981–91; Bd of War Studies, Univ. of London, 1984–92; a founding Mem., Adv. Bd, British-American Project, 1985–99. Hon. Steward, Westminster Abbey, 1981–2004. Trench Gascoigne Essay Prize, RUSI, 1972. Editor: Brassey's Defence Year Bk, 1982–92; MacMillan-RUSI Defence Studies, 1982–94; RUSI Internat. Security Review, 1992–94. *Publications:* contrib. learned jls. *Recreations:* choral music, international affairs. *Address:* Churchfield House, Churchfield Lane, Benson, Wallingford, Oxon OX10 6SH. *Club:* Royal Air Force.

BOLTON, David Michael William; education consultant; Head Master, Dame Alice Owen's School, 1981–94; *b* 29 Feb. 1936; *s* of William Benedict Bolton and Edith Phyllis Bolton; *m* 1961, Janet Christine Fleming; two *s* one *d*. *Educ:* St Francis Xavier's Coll., Liverpool; St Edmund Hall, Oxford (BA 1960; MA 1964); DipEd London 1971. Nat. Service, RAF (Coastal Command), 1955–57. Reckitt & Colman Ltd, 1960–62; Alleyn's Sch., Dulwich, 1962–63; Housemaster, Highgate Sch., 1963–72; Dep. Head, Chancellor's Sch., Herts, 1972–74; Headmaster, Davenant Foundn Grammar Sch., 1974–81. OFSTED Inspector, 1995–. Mem. Council, Secondary Heads Assoc., 1991–94 (Chm., Area Five). Governor, St Albans High School for Girls, 1997–. FRSA 1993. Freeman, City of London, 1994. *Publications:* articles and reviews in TES. *Recreations:* reading, music, travel, walking, family history. *Address:* Mayfield, 8 Wykeham Gate, Haddenham, Bucks HP17 8DF.

BOLTON, Eric James, CB 1987; Deputy Chairman, New Opportunities Fund, 2001–04 (Member Board, 1998–2004); *b* 11 Jan. 1935; *s* of late James and Lilian Bolton; *m* 1960, Ann Gregory; one *s* twin *d*. *Educ:* Wigan Grammar Sch.; Chester Coll.; Lancaster Univ. MA. English teacher at secondary schs, 1957–68; Lectr, Chorley Teacher Training Coll., 1968–70; Inspector of Schs, Croydon, 1970–73; HM Inspector of Schs, 1973–79; Staff Inspector (Educnl Disadvantage), 1979–81; Chief Inspector of Schools, DES, 1981–83, Sen. Chief Inspector of Schools, 1983–91; Prof. of Teacher Educn, Inst. of Educn, London Univ., 1991–96. Chairman: Book Trust, 1997–2000 (Vice Chm., 1996–97); ITC Schs Adv. Cttee, 1997–2000; Member: Educn Adv. Cttee, LSO, 1997–2013; Educn Cttee, NESTA, 1999–2002; Trustee, Foundn of Young Musicians, 1992–2010. *Publications:* Verse Writing in Schools, 1964; various articles in educnl jls. *Recreations:* reading, music and opera, fly fishing. *Address:* 50 Addington Road, Sanderstead, South Croydon, Surrey CR2 8RB.

BOLTON, Erica Jane, OBE 2014; Director, Bolton & Quinn Ltd, since 1981; *b* 29 June 1953; *d* of Alwyn Bolton and Betty Bolton (*née* Pile); *m* 1986, Robert Alwyn Petrie Hewison, *qv*; two *d*. *Educ:* Westonbirt Sch.; Westfield Coll., Univ. of London (BA Hist. and Hist. of Art 1974). Established Erica Bolton and Jane Quinn Ltd, 1981. Trustee, Parasol Unit. *Recreations:* walking, going to museums. *Address:* c/o Bolton & Quinn Ltd, 6 Addison Avenue, W11 4QR. *T:* (020) 7221 5000.

See also A. J. Bolton.

BOLTON, Prof. Geoffrey Curgenven, AO 1984; DPhil; Chancellor, Murdoch University, 2002–06 (Pro-Chancellor, 2000–02); Professor of History, Edith Cowan University, 1993–96, now Emeritus; *b* 5 Nov. 1931; *s* of Frank and Winifred Bolton, Perth, W Australia; *m* 1958, (Ann) Carol Grattan; two *s*. *Educ:* North Perth State Sch.; Wesley Coll., Perth; Univ. of Western Australia; Balliol Coll., Oxford, (DPhil). FRHistS 1967; FAHA 1974; FASSA 1976. Res. Fellow, ANU, 1957–62; Sen. Lectr, Monash Univ., 1962–65; Prof. of Modern Hist., Univ. of Western Australia, 1966–73; Prof. of History, 1973–82 and 1985–89, and Pro-Vice-Chancellor, 1973–76, Murdoch Univ.; Prof. of Australian Studies, Univ. of London, 1982–85; Prof. of Australian Hist., Univ., of Queensland, 1989–93. Vis. Fellow, All Souls Coll., Oxford, 1995; Sen. Scholar in Residence, Murdoch Univ., 1997–. Mem. Council, Australian Nat. Maritime Museum, Sydney, 1985–91; Trustee, Western Australian Mus., 2005–12. Boyer Lectr, Australian Broadcasting Corp., 1992. FRSA. General Editor, Oxford History of Australia, 1987–91. DUniv Murdoch, 1995. Western Australia Citizen of the Year, 2003. *Publications:* Alexander Forrest, 1958; A Thousand Miles Away, 1963; The Passing of the Irish Act of Union, 1966; Dick Boyer, 1967; A Fine Country to Starve In, 1972; Spoils and Spoilers: Australians Make Their Environment, 1981; Oxford History of Australia, vol. 5, 1990; Daphne Street, 1997; Claremont: a history, 1999; Edmund Barton, 2000; May It Please Your Honour, 2005; Land of Vision and Mirage: Western Australia since 1826, 2008; Paul Hasluck: a life, 2014; articles in learned jls. *Recreation:* sleep. *Address:* PO Box 792, Claremont, WA 6910, Australia. *Club:* Athenæum.

BOLTON, Ivor; conductor; Chief Conductor (formerly Music Director), Salzburg Mozarteum Orchestra, since 2004; *b* 17 May 1958; *s* of Cyril John Bolton and Elsie Bolton (*née* Worthington); *m* 1984, Tessa Wendy Knighton, *qv*; one *s*. *Educ:* Queen Elizabeth's GS, Blackburn; Clare Coll., Cambridge (MusB, MA); Royal Coll. of Music (schol.); Nat. Opera Studio. FRCO (CHM) 1976; LRAM 1976. Conductor, Schola Cantorum of Oxford, 1981–82; Music Dir, St James's, Piccadilly, 1982–90; Chorus Master, Glyndebourne, 1985–88; Music Director: English Touring Opera, 1990–93; Glyndebourne Touring Opera, 1992–97; Chief Conductor, Scottish Chamber Orchestra, 1993–96. Founder Dir, St James's Baroque Players, 1984–; Founder and Music Dir, Lufthansa Fest. of Baroque Music, 1985–. Bayerische Staatsoper début, 1994; Royal Opera début, world première of Goehr's Arianna, 1995; Salzburg Fest. début, 2000. Has made several recordings. Bayerische Theaterpreis, Bavarian Govt, 1998; Seal of City of Salzburg, 2010. *Recreation:* football (keen follower of Arsenal and Blackburn Rovers). *Address:* 171 Goldhurst Terrace, NW6 3ES. *Club:* Garrick.

BOLTON, John Robert, JD; Senior Fellow, American Enterprise Institute, since 2007; Senior Adviser, Kirkland and Ellis, since 2008; *b* 20 Nov. 1948; *s* of Edward Jackson Bolton and Virginia Bolton (*née* Godfrey); *m* 1986, Gretchen Brainerd; one *d*. *Educ:* Yale Coll. (BA 1970); Yale Law Sch. (JD 1974). Associate, 1974–81, Partner, 1983–85, Covington & Burling, Washington; Gen. Counsel, 1981–82, Asst Adminr, 1982–83, US Agency for Internat. Develt; Asst Attorney Gen., Legislative Affairs, 1985–88, Civil Div., 1988–89, US Dept of Justice; Asst Sec. of State, Internat. Orgn, 1989–93; Partner, Lerner, Reed Bolton & McManus, Washington, 1993–99; Of Counsel, Kutak Rock LLP, 1999–2001; Under Sec. of State, Arms Control and Internat. Security, 2001–05; US Perm. Rep. to UN, 2005–06. Pres., Nat. Policy Forum, 1995–96; Mem., US Commn on Internat. Religious Freedom, 1999–2001. Adjunct Prof., George Mason Univ., Virginia, 1994–2001. Sen. Vice Pres., American Enterprise Inst., 1997–2001; Sen. Fellow, Manhattan Inst., 1993. *Publications:* Surrender is Not an Option: defending America at the United Nations and Abroad, 2007; contributor: The Bush Presidency, 1997; Delusions of Grandeur: the United Nations and global intervention, 1997; US International Leadership in the 21st Century, 2000; The Oxford Companion to Politics of the World, 2nd edn 2001; contrib. numerous articles to Wall Street Jl, Washington Post, Washington Times, LA Times, and to jls incl. Foreign Policy, Foreign Affairs, Eur. Jl, National Interest, Legal Times. *Address:* American Enterprise Institute, 1150 Seventeenth Street NW, Washington, DC 20036–4600, USA.

BOLTON, Tessa Wendy; *see* Knighton, T. W.

BOMBAY, Archbishop of, (RC), since 2006; **His Eminence Cardinal Oswald Gracias;** *b* 24 Dec. 1944; *s* of Jervis and Aduzinda Gracias. *Educ:* St Xavier's Coll., Ranchi (BA 1976); Urban Univ., Rome (DCL 1982); Gregorian Univ., Rome (Dip. Jurisprudence 1982). Ordained priest, 1970; Sec. and Chancellor, Dio. of Jamshedpur, 1971–76; Sec. to Archbp of Bombay, 1982–86; Chancellor, Archdio. of Bombay, 1982–97; Aux. Bishop of Bombay, 1997–2000; Archbishop of Agra, 2000–06. Cardinal, 2007. Judicial Vicar, 1988–98, Vicar Gen., 1998–2000, Archdio. of Bombay. President: Canon Law Soc. of India, 1987–91 and 1993–97; Catholic Bishops' Conf. of India, 2005– (Sec. Gen., 1998–2002). *Address:* Archbishop's House, 21 Nathalal Parekh Marg, Mumbai 400 001, India.

BOMFORD, David Robert Lee; Chairman, Department of Conservation, since 2012, and Head of European Art, since 2015, Museum of Fine Arts, Houston, Texas; Secretary-General, International Institute for Conservation, 1994–2003; *b* 31 March 1946; *s* of Donald James Bomford and Margaret Vanstone Bomford (*née* Spalding); *m* 1st, 1969, Helen Graham (marr. diss. 1989); one *s* two *d*; 2nd, 1990, Zahira Véliz; one *s* one *d*. *Educ:* Merchant Taylors' Sch.; Univ. of Sussex (BSc 1967; MSc 1968). Asst Restorer, 1968–74, Sen. Restorer of Paintings, 1974–2007, National Gall.; Associate Dir for Collections, 2007–10, Acting Dir, 2010–12, J. Paul Getty Mus., LA (Guest Scholar, 2005). Editor, Studies in Conservation, 1981–91. Vis. Prof., Churubusco Nat. Inst. of Conservation, Mexico City, 1987; Slade Prof. of Fine Art, Univ. of Oxford, 1996–97. FIIC 1979. *Publications:* Art in the Making: Rembrandt, 1988; Art in the Making: Italian painting before 1400, 1989; Art in the Making: Impressionism, 1990; Conservation of Paintings, 1997; Venice through Canaletto's Eyes, 1998; Colour, 2000; Art in the Making: underdrawings in Renaissance paintings, 2002; Art in the Making: Degas, 2004; Readings in Conservation, 2004. *Recreations:* walking, travel, theatre. *Address:* Museum of Fine Arts, 1001 Bissonnet, Houston, TX 77005, USA. *E:* dbomford@mfah.org.

BOMFORD, Nicholas Raymond, MA; Head Master of Harrow, 1991–99; *b* 27 Jan. 1939; *s* of late Ernest Raymond Bomford and Patricia Clive Bomford (*née* Brooke), JP; *m* 1966, Gillian Mary Reynolds; two *d*. *Educ:* Kelly Coll.; Trinity Coll., Oxford (MA, Mod. History). Teaching appts, 1960–64; Lectr in History and Contemp. Affairs, BRNC, Dartmouth, 1964–66, Sen. Lectr, 1966–68; Wellington Coll., 1968–76 (Housemaster, 1973–76); Headmaster: Monmouth Sch., 1977–82; Uppingham Sch., 1982–91. Chm., Jt Standing Cttee, HMC/IAPS, 1986–89; Nat. Rep., HMC Cttee, 1990–91; Mem., Exec. Cttee, Assoc. Governing Bodies of Ind. Schs, 2003–08. Mem. Navy Records Soc. (Councillor, 1967–70, 1973–76, 1984–88). Governor: Sherborne Sch. for Girls, 1994–2007 (Chm., 2000–07); Elstree Prep. Sch., 1996–2009 (Chm., 2001–09); Lord Wandsworth Coll., 1999–2006; Kelly Coll., 1999–2008; Malvern Coll., 2000–06. Chm., Usk Rural Life Mus., Monmouthshire, 2002–11 (Vice-Pres., 2011–); Pres., Tregate Anglers, 2010–14. Freeman, Haberdashers' Co., 1992. *Publications:* Documents in World History, 1914–70, 1973; (contrib.) Dictionary of World History, 1973; Brothers in War: letters from the Western Front, 2013; The Long Meadow: a life in schools, 2013. *Recreations:* shooting (Captain OURC, 1959–60; England VIII (Elcho match), 1960), fishing, gardening, music, enjoying Welsh border country and travel in the USA. *Address:* Long Meadow House, Millend, Newland, Glos GL16 8NF.

BOMPAS, (Anthony) George; QC 1994; *b* 6 Nov. 1951; *s* of Donald George Bompas, CMG; *m* 1981, Donna Linda, *d* of J. O. Schmidt; two *s* one *d*. *Educ:* Merchant Taylors' Sch., Northwood; Oriel Coll., Oxford (Schol., MA). Called to the Bar, Middle Temple, 1975; Bencher, Lincoln's Inn, 2001. Junior Counsel (Chancery), DTI, 1989–94; Ordinary Judge of Courts of Appeal of Guernsey and Jersey, 2014–. Liveryman, Merchant Taylors' Co., 1982–. *Address:* 4 Stone Buildings, Lincoln's Inn, WC2A 3XT. *T:* (020) 7242 5524.

BOMPAS, George; *see* Bompas, A. G.

BON, Michel Marie; Chairman: Editions du Cerf, since 1997; Devoteam, 2006–13; *b* 5 July 1943; *s* of Emmanuel Bon and Mathilde (*née* Aussedat); *m* 1971, Catherine de Sairigné; one *s* three *d*. *Educ:* Lycée Champollion, Grenoble; Ecole supérieure des scis économiques et commerciales, Paris; Inst. d'Etudes Politiques, Paris; Ecole Nat. d'Administration, Paris. Insp. of Finance, Min. of Finance, 1971–75; Crédit National, 1975–78; Caisse Nat. de Crédit Agricole, 1978–85; Carrefour, 1985–93 (Chm. and CEO, 1990–93); Dir, Agence Nationale pour l'Emploi, France, 1993–95; Chm. and CEO, France Telecom, 1995–2002; Chm., Institut Pasteur, 2003–05. Chairman: Fondation Nat. pour l'Enseignement de la Gestion des Entreprises, 2008–; Fondact, 2009–. *Address:* 4 avenue de Camoëns, 75116 Paris, France.

BONA, Sir Kina, KBE 1993; Judge of the National and Supreme Court, Papua New Guinea, since 2014; Resident Judge, Bougainville, since 2015; *b* 14 Feb. 1954; *m* 1990, Judith Lilian Sharples; one *d*. *Educ:* Univ. of Papua New Guinea (LLB 1976). Legal Officer, PNG, 1976–78; Teaching Fellow, Univ. of PNG, 1979; Sen. Legal Officer, 1980–82; Asst Sec., Dept of Justice, 1985–87; Public Prosecutor, PNG, 1988–94; High Comr for PNG in the UK, 1996–2002; lawyer in private practice, 2002–07 and 2012; Dep. Registrar, 2007–08; Registrar, 2009–12, Integrity of Political Parties and Candidates Commn, PNG. Pres., PNG Law Soc., 2012–. *Address:* PO Box 58, Waigani, National Capital District, Papua New Guinea.

BONALLACK, Sir Michael (Francis), Kt 1998; OBE 1971; Director, The Old Course Ltd (St Andrews), since 1990; *b* 31 Dec. 1934; *s* of Sir Richard (Frank) Bonallack, CBE; *m* 1958, Angela Ward; one *s* three *d*. *Educ:* Chigwell; Haileybury. National Service, 1953–55 (1st Lieut, RASC). Joined family business, Bonallack and Sons Ltd, later Freight Bonallack Ltd, 1955, Dir, 1962–74; Dir, Buckley Investments, 1976–84. Sec., 1983–99, Captain, 1999, Royal and Ancient Golf Club of St Andrews. Non-exec. Dir, PGA European Tour, 2000–. Chairman: Golf Foundn, 1977–83 (Pres., 2000–); Professional Golfers' Assoc., 1976–82; President: English Golf Union, 1982; PGA of Europe, 2003–04. Hon. Fellow, Myerscough Coll., 2000. DUniv Stirling, 1994; Hon. LLD: Abertay, Dundee, 2000; St Andrews, 2003. *Recreation:* golf (British Amateur Champion, 1961, 1965, 1968, 1969, 1970; English Amateur Champion, 1962–63, 1965–67 and 1968; Captain, British Walker Cup Team, 1971; Bobby Jones Award for distinguished sportsmanship in golf, 1972). *Address:* The Croft, Blebo Craigs, Cupar, Fife KY15 5UF. *T:* (01334) 850600. *Clubs:* Royal and Ancient Golf (St Andrews); Golf House (Elie); Pine Valley, Ocean Forest (USA); Hermanus (RSA); Chantilly (France).

BOND, Andrew, CEng; Executive Chairman, Euro Garages, since 2011; Director, Pepkor UK, since 2014; *b* Grantham, 16 March 1965; *s* of Terence and Christine Bond; *m* 1997, Susan Stringfellow; one *s* one *d*. *Educ:* King's Grammar Sch., Grantham; Salford Univ. (BSc 1st Cl Hons 1987); Cranfield Sch. of Mgt (MBA 1993); CEng 1992. Grad. prog., British Gas, 1987–88; Product Dir and Mktg Manager, Hopkinsons Plc, 1988–92; Mktg Manager, 1994–97, Corporate Mktg Dir, 1997–99, Asda; Eur. Own Label Dir, Asda and Wal-Mart Germany, 1999–2000; Man. Dir, George at Asda, 2000–04; Chief Operating Officer, Asda, and Man. Dir, Global George, 2004–05; Pres. and CEO, 2005–10, Chm., 2010–11, Asda. Exec. Vice Pres., Walmart, 2010–11; Exec. Chm., Republic, 2011–13. *Recreations:* running, cycling. *E:* andy@woodcliffeassociates.com.

BOND, Prof. Brian James, FRHistS; Professor of Military History, King's College, University of London, 1986–2001, now Emeritus; *b* 17 April 1936; *s* of Edward Herbert Bond and Olive Bessie Bond (*née* Sartin); *m* 1962, Madeleine Joyce Carr. *Educ:* Sir William Borlase's Sch., Marlow; Worcester Coll., Oxford (BA Hist. 1959); King's Coll. London (MA Hist. 1962; FKC 1996). FRHistS 1978. Nat. Service, 1954–56, commnd RA. Tutor in Mod. Hist. Univ. of Exeter, 1961–62; Lectr, Univ. of Liverpool, 1962–66; King's College London: Lectr in War Studies, 1966–78; Reader, 1978–86. Vis. Prof., Univ. of Western Ontario, 1972–73. Visiting Fellow: Brasenose Coll., Oxford, 1992–93; All Souls Coll., Oxford, 2000. Liddell Hart Lectr, KCL, 1997; Lees Knowles Lectr, Cambridge Univ., 2000; War Studies Lectr, KCL, 2001. Mem. Council, RUSI, 1972–84. Pres., British Commn for Mil. Hist. 1986–2006. Member Editorial Board: Jl Contemp. Hist., 1988–2004; Jl Strategic Studies, 1978–2005; Jl Mil. Hist. (USA), 1992–96; War in Hist., 1994–; an Associate Editor, Oxford DNB, 1996–2002. *Publications:* (ed) Victorian Military Campaigns, 1967, 2nd edn 1994; The Victorian Army and the Staff College, 1972; (ed) Chief of Staff: the diaries of Lt-Gen. Sir Henry Pownall 1933–1944, vol. 1, 1972, vol. 2, 1974; Britain, France and Belgium

1939–1940, 1975, 2nd edn 1990; Liddell Hart: a study of his military thought, 1977, 2nd edn 1991; British Military Policy between the Two World Wars, 1980; War and Society in Europe 1870–1970, 1984; (ed with S. Robbins) Staff Officer: the diaries of Lord Moyne 1914–1918, 1987; (ed) The First World War and British Military History, 1991; (ed) Fallen Stars: eleven studies of twentieth century military disasters, 1991; The Pursuit of Victory: from Napoleon to Saddam Hussein, 1996; (ed with N. Cave) Haig: a reappraisal 70 years on, 1999; The Unquiet Western Front: Britain's role in literature and history, 2002; (ed) War Memoirs of Earl Stanhope 1914–1918, 2006; Survivors of a Kind: memoirs of the Western Front, 2008; Liddell Hart and the Western Front, 2010; Britain's Two World Wars Against Germany: myth, memory and the distortions of hindsight, 2014. *Recreations:* gardening, visiting country houses, observing and protecting wild animals (especially foxes). *Address:* Olmeda, Ferry Lane, Medmenham, Marlow, Bucks SL7 2EZ. *T:* (01491) 571293.

BOND, Rt Rev. (Charles) Derek; appointed Bishop Suffragan of Bradwell, 1976, Area Bishop, 1984–92; Hon. Assistant Bishop: Dioceses of Gloucester and Worcester, 1992–2006; Diocese of Chelmsford, since 2006; *b* 4 July 1927; *s* of Charles Norman Bond and Doris Bond; *m* 1951, Joan Valerie Meikle; two *s* two *d*. *Educ:* Bournemouth Sch.; King's Coll., London. AKC (2nd hons). Curate of Friern Barnet, 1952; Midlands Area Sec. of SCM in Schools and Public Preacher, dio. Birmingham, 1956; Vicar: of Harringay, 1958; of Harrow Weald, 1962; Archdeacon of Colchester, 1972–76. Nat. Chm., CEMS, 1983–86; Chm., Retired Clergy Assoc., 1998–2003. *Recreation:* travel. *Address:* 52 Horn Book, Saffron Walden, Essex CB11 3JW. *T:* (01799) 521308. *E:* derekbond@greenbee.net.

BOND, David James; Director, Milltown Partners, since 2014; *b* London, 6 Aug. 1973; *s* of George and Jacqueline Bond; *m* 2006, Lucy Edwards; one *s*. *Educ:* Wallington High Sch. for Boys; Univ. of Southampton (BA Hons 1995); King's Coll. London (Postgrad. Cert. Sports Law 2004). Sports news reporter: Evening Standard, 1998–2002; Sunday Times, 2002–04; Dep. Sports Ed., Evening Standard, 2004–06; Daily Telegraph: sports news corresp., 2006–08; Sports Ed., 2008–10; Sports Ed., BBC, 2010–14. *Recreations:* running, cricket, reading. *Club:* Frontline.

BOND, Rt Rev. Derek; *see* Bond, Rt Rev. C. D.

BOND, Edward; playwright and director; *b* 18 July 1934; *m* 1971, Elisabeth Pablé. Northern Arts Literary Fellow, 1977–79. Hon. DLitt Yale, 1977. George Devine Award, 1968; John Whiting Award, 1968; Obie Award, 1976; City of Lyon Medal, 2007. *Opera Libretti:* We Come to the River (music by Hans Werner Henze), 1976; The English Cat (music by Hans Werner Henze), 1982; *ballet libretto:* Orpheus, 1982; *translations:* Chekhov, The Three Sisters, 1967; Wedekind, Spring Awakening, 1974; Wedekind, Lulu—a monster tragedy, 1992. Hon. DLitt Newman, 2013. *Publications:* Theatre Poems and Songs, 1978; Collected Poems 1978–1985, 1987; Notes on Post-Modernism, 1990; Notes on Imagination, 1995; Selected Letters (5 vols), 1994–2004; Selected Notebooks, vol. 1, 2000, vol. 2, 2001; The Hidden Plot: notes on theatre and the state, 2000; My Day, a song cycle for young people, 2005; The Playwright Speaks: interviews with David Tuallion, 2015; *plays:* The Pope's Wedding, 1962; Saved, 1965; Narrow Road to the Deep North, 1968; Early Morning, 1968; Passion, 1971; Black Mass, 1971; Lear, 1972; The Sea, 1973; Bingo, 1974; The Fool, 1976; A-A-America! (Grandma Faust, and The Swing), 1976; Stone, 1976; The Woman, 1978; The Bundle, 1978; The Worlds with The Activist Papers, 1980; Restoration, 1981; Summer: a play for Europe, and Fables (short stories), 1982; Derek, 1983; Human Cannon, 1984; The War Plays (part 1, Red Black and Ignorant; part 2, The Tin Can People; part 3, Great Peace), 1985; Jackets, 1989; In The Company of Men, 1990; September, 1990; Olly's Prison, 1993; Tuesday, 1993; Coffee: a tragedy, 1995; At the Inland Sea: a play for young people, 1996; Eleven Vests, 1997; The Crime of the Twenty-first Century, 1998; The Children: a play for two adults and sixteen children, 2000; Chair, 2000; Have I None, 2000; Existence, 2002; The Balancing Act, 2003; The Short Elektra, 2004; The Under Room, 2005; Born, 2006; People, 2006; Arcade, 2006; Tune, 2007; Innocence, 2009; A Window, 2009; There Will Be More, 2010; The Edge, 2011; The Broken Bowl, 2011; The Angry Roads, 2014; The Testament of This Day, 2014; Collected Plays (9 vols), 1977–2011. *Address:* c/o Casarotto Ramsay, Waverley House, 7–12 Noel Street, W1F 8GQ. *E:* mel@casarotto.co.uk. *W:* www.edwardbond.org.

BOND, Geoffrey Charles, OBE 2008; DL; FSA; heritage consultant; Chairman, Geoffrey Bond Consultancy, since 1996; *b* 14 Oct. 1939; *s* of Frederick Richard Bond and Dorothy Bond (*née* Gardner); *m* 1963, Dianora Dunnet; one *s* one *d*. *Educ:* Becket Sch., Nottingham; Univ. of Hull (BSc Econ Hons 1963). FSA 2008. Baring Bros, London, 1963–64; admitted solicitor, 1969; articled to Ashton Hill & Co., Nottingham, later Ashton Bond Gigg, 1964–68, Partner, 1970–85, Sen. Partner, 1985–96. Chairman: Linpack Packaging plc, 1982–89; Old Market Square Securities, 1984–99; non-executive Director: Charles Lawrence Gp plc, 1973–2013; Hooley Gp of Cos, 1976–; Regl Bd, Central Ind. TV plc, 1982–92. Hon. Solicitor to: British Sporting Art Trust, London, 1977–2008; Derby Internat. Porcelain Soc., 1985–2011. Dep. Chm., Nat. Mus. of Law and Nat. Centre for Citizenship and the Law, 1993–2015; Chairman: Arts & Business Midlands, 1999–2003; Gp for Educn in Museums, 2001–07; London Livery Cos Collections Adv. Gp, 2008–14; Member: Council, MLA, 2006–12 (Chm., MLA London, 2002–09); London Cultural Strategy Gp, 2010–; Acceptance in Lieu Panel, MLA, then Arts Council England, 2006–12; Council, Soc. of Antiquaries, 2013–. Mem., Editl Bd, Byron Jl (Chm., 1996–2003); Chairman: London Byron Soc., 1996–2003 (Vice Pres., 2004–); Scottish Byron Soc., 2008–. Founder Trustee, Papplewick Pumping Stn Trust, 1976–2015 (Chm., 1999–2015); Norwegian Business Scholars Trust, Bridge Ward Club, 2002–; Chairman: Water Educn Trust, 2005–15; Chizel Trust, 2013–; Founder, 2010, and Chm., Lord Mayor of London's Cultural Scholarships Scheme, 2010–; Chairman: Curatorial Adv. Panel, Guildhall Art Gall., 2010–15; Rolls Bldg Art and Educn Trust, 2011–; Livery Cos King James Bible Educn Project, 2011. Patron, British Red Cross, Notts, 2010–; Trustee of Council, Liby and Mus. of Freemasonry, 2009–. President: Southwell Archaeology Gp, 2013–; Notts County Show, 2015–16. Sponsor, Southwell Music Fest., 2014–. Mem., City of London Gp, St John Ambulance (formerly City of London Cttee, St John Ambulance (Prince of Wales') Dist), 2003–12. Hon. Consul for Norway in Midlands, 1981–2007; Chm., Assoc. of Hon. Norwegian Consuls in British Isles and Ireland, 1997–99. *Radio:* presenter, The Antiques Shop, Radio Nottingham, 1973–80; *television:* Mem., team of experts, Antiques Roadshow, 1979–84; presenter, Something to Treasure (series), 1985–91; *television films:* producer, Byron's Mine, 1994; assistant producer: The Heart of Shelley, 1992; The Sweet Life, 1997. Sheriff, 2003–04, Dep. Gauger, 2004, City of London; Chm., Livery Cttee, 2007–10; Liveryman: Co. of Glaziers and Painters of Glass, 1973 (Mem., Ct of Assts, 1992; Master, 1997); Co. of Clockmakers, 2010; Member: Guild of Freemen, 2003–; City of London Sheriffs' Soc., 2004–; Hon. Liveryman (formerly Mem.), Co. (formerly Guild) of Educators, 2002–; Master, Guild of Arts Scholars, Dealers and Collectors, 2006–08; Founder Liveryman, Co. of Arts Scholars, 2014–; Mem. Court, City of London Solicitors' Co., 2006–08. Hon. DLaws Nottingham, 2013. DL Notts, 1998. OStJ 2004. Lifetime Award, City Livery Club, 2014. Kt First Class, Royal Norwegian Order of Merit, 1989. *Publications:* (contrib.) Byron: the image of the poet, 2008; (contrib.) Sir Walter Scott Club Celebration Edinburgh Edition Waverley novels, 2010; Lord Byron's Best Friends: from bulldogs to Boatswain and beyond, 2013; articles for learned jls incl. Byron Jl, Newstead Byron Soc. Rev., Studies in Romanticism, Sir Walter Scott Club Rev., Keats-Shelley Jl, Collectors Guide, Trans Thoroton Soc. *Recreations:* antiquarian book collecting, gardening, entertaining, music, giving lectures, rowing. *Address:* Burgage Manor, Southwell, Notts NG25 0EP. *T:* (01636) 816855. *E:* consultancy@gbond.demon.co.uk. *Clubs:* Garrick, Athenæum, Bridge Ward, City Pickwick.

See also Sir M. R. Bond.

BOND, Maj.-Gen. Henry Mark Garneys, OBE 1993; JP; Vice Lord-Lieutenant of Dorset, 1984–99; *b* 1 June 1922; *s* of W. R. G. Bond, Tyneham, Dorset; unmarried. *Educ:* Eton. Enlisted as Rifleman, 1940; commnd in Rifle Bde, 1941; served Middle East and Italy; seconded to Parachute Regt, 1947–50; ADC to Field Marshal Viscount Montgomery of Alamein, 1950–52; psc 1953; served in Kenya, Malaya, Cyprus and Borneo; Comd Rifle Bde in Cyprus and Borneo, 1964–66; Comd 12th Inf. Bde, 1967–68; idc 1969; Dir of Defence Operational Plans and Asst Chief of Defence Staff (Ops), 1970–72; retd 1972. President: Dorset Natural History and Archaeological Soc., 1972–75; Dorset Br., CPRE, 1990–95; Dorset Community Council, 1988–97; Dorset Assoc. of Parish Councils, 1990–97; Chm., Dorset Police Authy, 1980–92. Mem., Dorset CC, 1973–85 (Vice-Chm., 1981–85). JP Dorset, 1972 (Chm., Wareham Bench, 1984–89). High Sheriff of Dorset, 1977, DL Dorset, 1977. Chm., Governors of Milton Abbey Sch., 1982–94 (Visitor, 1994–98). *Recreations:* forestry, reading. *Address:* Moigne Combe, Dorchester, Dorset DT2 8JA. *T:* (01305) 852265.

BOND, Ian Andrew Minton, CVO 2006; Director, Foreign Policy, Centre for European Reform, since 2013; *b* 19 April 1962; *s* of Roy and Joan Bond; *m* 1987, Kathryn Joan Ingamells; two *s* one *d*. *Educ:* King Edward VI Sch., Birmingham; Phillips Acad., Andover, Mass; Balliol Coll., Oxford (BA Hons). Joined Diplomatic Service, 1984; FCO, 1984–87; Mem., UK Delegn to NATO, 1987–90; FCO, 1990–93; First Secretary: Moscow, 1993–96; FCO, 1996–2000; Counsellor and Dep. Hd of Mission, UK Delegn to OSCE, Vienna, 2000–04; Ambassador to Latvia, 2005–07; Counsellor, Washington, 2007–12. *Recreations:* music, opera, choral singing, travel, reading. *Address:* Centre for European Reform, 14 Great College Street, Westminster, SW1P 3RX.

BOND, Jennie, (Mrs James Keltz); broadcaster and professional speaker; television presenter, since 2003; *b* 19 Aug. 1950; *d* of late Kenneth Bond and of Pamela Bond; *m* 1982, James Keltz; one *d*, and one step *s* one step *d*. *Educ:* St Francis' Coll., Letchworth; Univ. of Warwick. Reporter: Richmond Herald, 1972–75; Evening Mail, Uxbridge, 1975–77; News Producer, BBC, 1977–86; News Corresp., 1986–89, Court Corresp., 1989–2003, BBC. *Publications:* Reporting Royalty (autobiog.), 2001; Elizabeth, Fifty Glorious Years, 2002; Elizabeth, 80 Glorious Years, 2006; Elizabeth: a Diamond Jubilee portrait, 2012. *Recreations:* country life, coastal walks, entertaining friends and family, bopping to bands in our local pub. *Address:* c/o Knight Ayton, 35 Great James Street, WC1N 3HB.

BOND, Jeremy Viktor, (Jez); Founder, 2010, and Artistic Director, since 2013, Park Theatre; *b* Kingston upon Thames, Surrey, 25 May 1977; *s* of Jeremy Bond and Viktoria Bond (*née* Lengyel Rheinfuss); partner, Awsa Bergstrøm. *Educ:* Oundle Sch.; Dulwich Coll.; Univ. of Hull (BA Hons Drama). Freelance th. dir, 1998–2009; trained at Watford Palace Th. (Channel Four Th. Dir Bursary), 2002–04; plays directed include: A Season in South Africa, Old Vic, 2000; Big Boys, Warehouse, Croydon, 2002; Canaries Sometimes Sing, Kings Head and France, 2003; Misconceptions, Hong Kong Arts Centre, 2004; I Have Been Here Before, Watford Palace, 2005; Oliver!, Oxford, 2005; Sleeping Beauty, Salisbury Playhouse, 2006; Shot of Genius, Leicester Sq., 2006; The Twits, Switzerland tour, 2007; The Fame Game, tour of Austria, 2010; Adult Supervision, Sleeping Beauty (also co-wrote), Park Th., 2013. *Recreations:* singing, composing, dog training, comedy, never having enough time to play tennis. *Address:* Park Theatre, Clifton Terrace, N4 3JP. *T:* (020) 7870 6876. *E:* info@parktheatre.co.uk. *Club:* Hospital.

BOND, Sir John (Reginald Hartnell), Kt 1999; Chairman: Glencore Xstrata plc (formerly Xstrata), 2011–13; Vodafone, 2006–11 (non-executive Director, 2005–11); *b* 24 July 1941; *s* of late Capt. R. H. A. Bond, OBE and of E. C. A. Bond; *m* 1968, Elizabeth Caroline Parker; one *s* two *d*. *Educ:* Tonbridge Sch., Kent; Cate Sch., Calif, USA (E-SU Scholar). Joined Hongkong & Shanghai Banking Corp., 1961; worked in Hong Kong, Thailand, Singapore, Indonesia and USA; Chief Exec., Wardley Ltd (Merchant Banking), 1984–87; Hongkong & Shanghai Banking Corporation: Exec. Dir, 1988–91; responsible for: Americas, 1988–89; commercial banking, based in Hong Kong, 1990–91; Pres. and Chief Exec., Marine Midland Banks Inc., Buffalo, USA, 1991–92. Chairman: Hongkong Bank of Canada, 1987–98; HSBC Americas Inc., 1997–2003; Marine Midland Bank, then HSBC Bank USA, 1997–2003; British Bank of the Middle East, then HSBC Bank Middle East, 1998–2004; Midland Bank, then HSBC Bank Plc, 1998–2004; Gp Chief Exec., 1993–98, Gp Chm., 1998–2006, HSBC Hldgs plc; Director: Hang Seng Bank Ltd, 1990–96; HSBC Hldgs, 1990–2006; HSBC Bank plc (formerly Midland Bank), 1993–2004 (Dep. Chm., 1996–98); Bank of England, 2001–04; HSBC N Amer. Hldgs Inc., 2005–06; Chm., KKR Asia, 2009– (Advr, 2006–); non-executive Director: London Stock Exchange, 1994–99; British Steel, 1994–98; Orange plc, 1996–99; Ford Motor Co., 2000–08; Shui On Land Ltd, Hong Kong, 2006–; A P Moller-Maersk A/S, 2008–; non-executive Advisory Director: Northern Trust Corp., 2009–; Northern Trust Co., 2009–; Mem., Adv. Cttee, Mitsubishi, 2007–. Member: Mayor of Shanghai's Internat. Business Leaders' Adv. Council, 1999– (Chm., 2006–07); China Develt Forum, Beijing, 2001–; Council of Internat. Advrs, China Banking Regulatory Cttee, 2010–14. Mem., Bd of Dirs, Qatar Foundn, 2009–14. Chm., Inst. of Internat. Finance, Washington, 1998–2003. FCIB (FIB 1982). Hon. Fellow, London Business Sch., 2003. Hon. DEc Richmond, American Univ. in London, 1998; Hon. DLitt: Loughborough, 2000; Sheffield, 2002; Hon. DCL South Bank, 2000; Hon. DSc City, 2004; Hon. DBA London Metropolitan, 2004; Hon. LLD: Nottingham, 2005; Bristol, 2005. Foreign Policy Assoc. Medal, NY, 2003; Magnolia Gold Award, Shanghai Municipal People's Govt, 2003. *Recreations:* golf, ski-ing, reading biography. *Clubs:* MCC; Royal Ashdown Forest Golf; Hong Kong (Hong Kong); John's Island (Florida).

BOND, Prof. (John) Richard, OC 2004; OOnt 2008; PhD; FRS 2001; FRSC; Professor, since 1987, and University Professor, since 1999, Canadian Institute for Theoretical Astrophysics (Director, 1996–2006); *b* 15 May 1950; *s* of Jack Parry Bond and Margaret Bond. *Educ:* Univ. of Toronto (BSc); Calif Inst. of Technol. (MS, PhD 1979). FRSC 1996. Res. Asst, Kellogg Lab., CIT, 1973–78; Postdoctoral Fellow, Univ. of Calif, Berkeley, 1978–81; Res. Fellow, Inst. of Astronomy, Cambridge, 1982–83; Asst Prof., 1981–85, Associate Prof., 1985–87, Stanford Univ.; Associate Prof., 1985–87, Actg Dir, 1990–91, Canadian Inst. for Theoretical Astrophysics. Fellow, 1988–, Dir, 2002–, Cosmology and Gravity Prog., Canadian Inst. for Advanced Research. Fellow, APS, 1996. Foreign Hon. Mem., American Acad. of Arts and Scis, 2003; Foreign Associate, NAS, 2011. *Address:* Canadian Institute for Theoretical Astrophysics, University of Toronto, 60 St George Street, Toronto, ON M5S 3H8, Canada. *T:* (416) 9786874.

BOND, Dr Martyn Arthur; consultant on European affairs, since 2003; Visiting Lecturer, London Academy of Diplomacy, University of Stirling, since 2014; *b* 10 Oct. 1942; *s* of Jack Bond and Muriel Caroline Janet (*née* Webb); *m* 1965, Dinah Macfarlane; two *s* one *d*. *Educ:* Portsmouth Grammar Sch.; Peter Symonds Sch.; Winchester Coll.; Queens' Coll., Cambridge (MA); Univ. of Sussex (DPhil 1971); Univ. of Hamburg. Producer, BBC, 1966–70; Lectr in W European Studies, NUU, 1970–73; Press Officer, Gen. Secretariat, Council of Ministers of EC, 1974–81; BBC Rep., Berlin, 1981–83; Principal Adminr, Gen. Secretariat, Council of Ministers of EC, 1983–88; Dir, UK Office of EP, 1989–99; Dir, Federal Trust, 1999–2002; Dir, Information Europe Ltd, 1999–; UK Press Correspondent for Council of Europe, 2006–13. Mem. Bd, Europe-China Assoc., 1976–82; Founder Mem., Quaker Council for European Affairs, 1979–. Contested (SDP/Alliance) Hull W, 1987.

Chm., Internat. Adv. Council, 1987–94, Sen. Fellow, 1995–, Salzburg Seminar in American/ Global Studies. Vis. Prof. of European Politics, RHUL (formerly RHBNC), 1999–2014; Dist. Vis. Fellow, Eur. Business Sch., 2009, Sen. Hon. Fellow, 2014–, Regent's Univ. (formerly Regent's Coll.), London. Dir, 2000–05, Dep. Chm., 2005–, London Press Club. FAcSS (AcSS 2009). Dir, English Coll. Foundn, 1993–; Gov., English Coll. in Prague, 1995–. FRSA 1992. *Publications:* A Tale of Two Germanies, 1991; (ed) Eminent Europeans, 1996; (ed) The Treaty of Nice Explained, 2001; (ed) Europe, Parliaments and the Media, 2003; The Council of Europe and the European Convention on Human Rights, 2010; The Council of Europe, 2011; (ed) The UK and Europe: costs, benefits, options, 2013; (ed) The EU and the US: the Transatlantic relationship, 2014; Europe and its Neighbours, 2015; contrib. to Jl Legislative Studies, German Life and Letters, Parliament Mag., House Mag., Diplomat mag., The World Today. *Recreations:* Europe, travel, chess, fly-fishing.

BOND, Michael, OBE 1997; author; *b* 13 Jan. 1926; *s* of Norman Robert and Frances Mary Bond; *m* 1950, Brenda Mary Johnson (marr. diss. 1981); one *s* one *d*; *m* 1981, Susan Marfrey Rogers. *Educ:* Presentation College, Reading. RAF and Army, 1943–47; BBC Cameraman, 1947–66; full-time author from 1966. Paddington TV series, 1976. Hon. DLitt Reading, 2007. *Publications: for children:* A Bear Called Paddington, 1958; More About Paddington, 1959; Paddington Helps Out, 1960; Paddington Abroad, 1961; Paddington at Large, 1962; Paddington Marches On, 1964; Paddington at Work, 1966; Here Comes Thursday, 1966; Thursday Rides Again, 1968; Paddington Goes to Town, 1968; Thursday Ahoy, 1969; Parsley's Tail, 1969; Parsley's Good Deed, 1969; Parsley's Problem Present, 1970; Parsley's Last Stand, 1970; Paddington Takes the Air, 1970; Thursday in Paris, 1970; Michael Bond's Book of Bears, 1971, 1992; Michael Bond's Book of Mice, 1972; The Day the Animals Went on Strike, 1972; Paddington Bear, 1972; Paddington's Garden, 1972; Parsley the Lion, 1972; Parsley Parade, 1972; The Tales of Olga da Polga, 1972; Olga Meets her Match, 1973; Paddington's Blue Peter Story Book, 1973; Paddington at the Circus, 1973; Paddington Goes Shopping, 1973; Paddington at the Sea-side, 1974; Paddington at the Tower, 1974, rev. edn 2011; Paddington on Top, 1974; Windmill, 1975; How to make Flying Things, 1975; Eight Olga Readers, 1975; Paddington's Loose End Book, 1976; Paddington's Party Book, 1976; Olga Carries On, 1976; Paddington's Pop-up Book, 1977; Paddington Takes the Test, 1979; Paddington's Cartoon Book, 1979; J. D. Polson and the Liberty-Head Dime, 1980; J. D. Polson and the Dillogate Affair, 1981; Paddington on Screen, 1981; Olga Takes Charge, 1982; The Caravan Puppets, 1983; Paddington at the Zoo, 1984; Paddington and the Knickerbocker Rainbow, 1984; Paddington's Painting Exhibition, 1985; Paddington at the Fair, 1985; Oliver the Greedy Elephant, 1985; Paddington at the Palace, 1986; Paddington Minds the House, 1986; Paddington's Busy Day, 1987; Paddington and the Marmalade Maze, 1987; Paddington's Magical Christmas, 1988; Paddington and the Christmas Surprise, 1997; Paddington at the Carnival, 1998; Paddington's Scrap Book, 1999; Paddington - a classic collection, 1999; Paddington in Hot Water, 2000; Paddington's Party Tricks, 2000; Olga Moves House, 2001; Olga Follows Her Nose, 2002; Paddington's Grand Tour, 2003; Love From Paddington, 2014; with Karen Bond: Paddington Posts a Letter, 1986; Paddington at the Airport, 1986; Paddington's London, 1986; Paddington Goes to Hospital, 2001; Paddington Rules the Waves, 2008; Paddington Here and Now, 2008; Paddington: my book of marmalade, 2008; Paddington and the Disappearing Sandwich, 2009; Paddington King of the Castle, 2009; Paddington at the Rainbow's End, 2009; Paddington - a treasury, 2010; The Paddington Treasury for the Very Young, 2011; Paddington's London Treasury, 2011; Paddington's Guide to London, 2011; Paddington's Cookery Book, 2011; Paddington Goes for Gold, 2012; Paddington Races Ahead, 2012; *for adults:* Monsieur Pamplemousse, 1983; Monsieur Pamplemousse and the Secret Mission, 1984; Monsieur Pamplemousse on the Spot, 1986; Monsieur Pamplemousse Takes the Cure, 1987; The Pleasures of Paris, 1987; Monsieur Pamplemousse Aloft, 1989; Monsieur Pamplemousse Investigates, 1990; Monsieur Pamplemousse Rests His Case, 1991; Monsieur Pamplemousse Stands Firm, 1992; Monsieur Pamplemousse on Location, 1992; Monsieur Pamplemousse takes the Train, 1993; Monsieur Pamplemousse Afloat, 1998; Monsieur Pamplemousse on Probation, 2000; Monsieur Pamplemousse on Vacation, 2002; Monsieur Pamplemousse Hits the Headlines, 2003; Monsieur Pamplemousse and the Militant Midwives, 2006; Monsieur Pamplemousse and the French Solution, 2007; Monsieur Pamplemousse and the Carbon Footprint, 2010; Monsieur Pamplemousse and the Tangled Web, 2014; *autobiography:* Bears and Forebears: a life so far, 1996. *Recreations:* photography, travel, food and wine. *Address:* The Agency, 24 Pottery Lane, W11 4LZ. *T:* (020) 7727 1346.

BOND, Sir Michael (Richard), Kt 1995; FRCPsych, FRCPGlas, FRCSE; Professor of Psychological Medicine, University of Glasgow, 1973–98, now Emeritus (Vice Principal, 1986–97; Administrative Dean, Faculty of Medicine, 1991–97); *b* 15 April 1936; *s* of Frederick Richard Bond and Dorothy Bond (*née* Gardner); *m* 1961, Jane Issitt; one *s* one *d*. *Educ:* Magnus Grammar Sch., Newark, Notts; Univ. of Sheffield (MD, PhD). FRSE 1998. Ho. Surg./Ho. Phys., Royal Inf., Sheffield, 1961–62; Asst Lectr/Res. Registrar, Univ. Dept of Surgery, Sheffield, 1962–64; Res. Registrar/Lectr, Univ. Dept of Psychiatry, Sheffield, 1964–67; Sen. Ho. Officer/Res. Registrar, Registrar/Sen. Registrar, Inst. of Neurological Scis, Glasgow, 1968–71; Lectr in Neurosurgery, Univ. Dept of Neurosurgery, Glasgow, 1971–73. Locum Cons. Neurosurgeon, Oxford, 1972; Hon. Cons. Psychiatrist, Greater Glasgow Health Bd, 1973–98. Member: UGC, 1982–91; UFC, 1991–93; SHEFC, 1992–96; Chm., Jt Med. Adv. Cttee, 1992–95. Pres., 1999–2001, Interim Pres., 2009–10, British Pain Soc.; Member Council: Internat. Assoc. for Study of Pain, 1981–93, 1996–2008 (Pres. 2002–05); St Andrews Ambulance Assoc., 1995–2000. Dir, Prince and Princess of Wales Hospice, Glasgow, 1997–2002. Chm., Head Injuries Trust for Scotland, 1989–99; Mem., The London Inquiry, 1991–92. Trustee, Lloyds TSB Foundn, 1999–2005. Gov., High Sch., Glasgow, 1990–2006 (Chm., 2001–06). Member: Incorpn of Bakers of Glasgow, 2006– (Mem., Master Ct, 2007–; Collector, 2009–; Deacon, 2011–12); Merchants House of Glasgow, 2014–. Chm., Bearsden Art Club, 2014–. FRSA 1992. Hon. DSc Leicester, 1996; DUniv Glasgow, 2001. *Publications:* Pain, its nature, analysis and treatment, 1979, 2nd edn 1984; (co-ed) Rehabilitation of the Head Injured Adult, 1983, 2nd edn 1989; (with K. H. Simpson) Pain: its nature and treatment, 2006; papers on psychological and social consequences of severe brain injury, psychological aspects of chronic pain and cancer pain, 1963–, and others on similar topics. *Recreations:* painting, collecting antique books, forest walking, ornithology, gardening. *Address:* 33 Ralston Road, Bearsden, Glasgow G61 3BA. *T:* (home) (0141) 942 4391, (work) (0141) 330 3692. *E:* m.bond@admin.gla.ac.uk. *Clubs:* Athenæum; Glasgow Arts.

See also G. C. Bond.

BOND, Richard; *see* Bond, J. R.

BOND, Richard Douglas; Senior Partner, Herbert Smith, 2000–05; *b* 23 July 1946; *s* of Douglas Charles Bond and Vera Eileen Bond; *m* 1st, 1973, Anthea Mary Charrington (*d* 1996); two *d*; 2nd, 2007, Julie Ann Nicholls. *Educ:* Berkhamsted Sch. Articled Clerk, Halsey, Lightly & Hemsley, 1964–69; joined Herbert Smith, 1969; seconded to BNOC, 1976–78; Partner, 1977; Head of Corporate, 1993–2000. *Recreations:* golf, cricket, theatre. *Club:* MCC.

BOND, Richard Henry; His Honour Judge Bond; a Circuit Judge, since 1997; *b* 15 April 1947; *s* of Ashley Raymond Bond and Hester Mary Bond (*née* Bowles); *m* 1987, Annabel Susan Curtis; one *s* one *d*. *Educ:* Sherborne Sch. Called to the Bar, Inner Temple, 1970. *Recreations:* architecture, walking, gardening. *Address:* Combined Court Centre, Deansleigh Road, Bournemouth BH7 7DS.

BOND, Richard Ian Winsor; His Honour Judge Richard I. W. Bond; a Circuit Judg since 2013; *b* Lapworth, 22 July 1965; *s* of Ian Charles Winsor Bond and Audrey Kathlee Bond; *m* 1997, Emma-Jane Parsons; one *s* two *d*. *Educ:* Warwick Sch.; Manchester Uni (LLB Hons 1986); Inns of Court Sch. of Law. Called to the Bar, Middle Temple, 1988; Recorder, 2009–13. Gov., Welcombe Hills Sch., Stratford upon Avon, 2011–. *Recreation* family, walking, racquet sports, cinema, theatre. *Address:* Birmingham Crown Court, Newton Street, Birmingham B4 7NA.

BOND, Samantha; actress; *b* 27 Nov. 1961; *d* of Philip Bond and late Pat Bond (then Sandys *m* 1989, Alexander Hanson; one *s* one *d*. *Educ:* Godolphin and Latymer Sch.; Bristol Old V Theatre Sch. *Theatre* includes: Juliet in Romeo and Juliet, Lyric, Hammersmith, 198 Beatrice in Much Ado About Nothing, Phoenix, 1988; Hermione in The Winter's Tal 1992–93, Rosalind in As You Like It, 1992–93, RSC; C in Three Tall Women, Wyndham' 1995; Amy in Amy's View, RNT, transf. Aldwych, then NY, 1997; Mary in Memory Water, Vaudeville, 1998; Lady Macbeth in Macbeth, Albery, 2002; title rôle in A Woman No Importance, Th. Royal, Haymarket, 2003; Lady Driver in Donkey's Years, Comed 2006; Arcadia, Duke of York's, 2009; An Ideal Husband, Vaudeville, 2010; What the Butl Saw, Vaudeville, 2012; Passion Play, Duke of York's, 2013; Dirty Rotten Scoundrels, Savo 2014; *television* includes: The Ginger Tree, Emma, Family Money, Tears Before Bedtim Morse, Manhunt, The Hunt, Donovan, Distant Shores, Clapham Junction, Wolfende Fanny Hill, Midsomer Murders, Outnumbered, Downton Abbey, Home Fires; *films* includ Eric The Viking, 1989; What Rats Won't Do, 1998; Blinded, 2005; Yes, 2005; A Bunch Amateurs, 2008; rôle of Moneypenny in: Goldeneye, 1995; Tomorrow Never Dies, 199 The World is Not Enough, 1999; Die Another Day, 2002. Ambassador: The Prince's Trus 1997–; Macmillan Cancer Support, 2006–; Patron, Shooting Star Children's Hospice, 2006- *Recreations:* Scrabble, crosswords, gardening, dancing, watching cricket. *Address:* c/o Conwa Van Gelder Grant Ltd, 8–12 Broadwick Street, W1F 8HW. *T:* (020) 7287 0077, *Fax:* (02 7287 1940.

BONDEVIK, Rev. Kjell Magne; President, Oslo Center for Peace and Human Rights, sinc 2006; *b* Molde, Norway, 3 Sept. 1947; *s* of Johannes and Margit Bondevik; *m* 1970, Bjø Rasmussen; two *s* one *d*. *Educ:* Free Faculty of Theology, Oslo (*Candidatus Theologiae* 1975 Ordained priest, Lutheran Church of Norway, 1979. State Sec., Prime Minister's Offic 1972–73; MP (KrF) Møre og Romsdal, Norway, 1973–2005; Minister of Church and Educ 1983–86; Minister of Foreign Affairs, 1989–90; Prime Minister of Norway, 1997–2000 an 2001–05. UN Special Humanitarian Envoy for the Horn of Africa, 2006–07. *Publications:* E liv i spenning (memoir), 2006. *Address:* c/o Oslo Center for Peace and Human Rights, Øv Slottsgt. 11, 0157 Oslo, Norway.

BONDY, Rupert Mark; Group General Counsel, BP plc, since 2008; *b* London, 30 Jun 1961; *s* of Ivo Bondy and Shuna Bondy (*née* Black); one *s* three *d*. *Educ:* King's Coll Cambridge (BA 1983); Stanford Law Sch. (JSM 1989). Harkness Fellow, Harvard Univ 1984–85; called to the Bar, Middle Temple, 1987; admitted California Bar, 1990; lawye Morrison & Foerster, 1989–94; Lovells, 1994–95; Smith Kline Beecham, late GlaxoSmithKline: Counsel, 1995–2000; Sen. Vice Pres. and Gen. Counsel, 2001–08. *Addres* BP plc, 1 St James's Square, SW1Y 4PD. *T:* (020) 7496 4000, *Fax:* (020) 7496 4242. *E* rupert.bondy@bp.com.

BONE, Charles, PPRI, ARCA; President, Royal Institute of Painters in Water Colour 1979–89; Governor, Federation of British Artists, 1976–81 and since 1983 (Membe Executive Council, 1983–84 and 1986–88); *b* 15 Sept. 1926; *s* of William Stanley an Elizabeth Bone; *m* Sheila Mitchell, FRBS, ARCA, sculptor; two *s*. *Educ:* Farnham Coll. Art; Royal Coll. of Art (ARCA). FBI Award for Design. Consultant, COSIRA, 1952–7 Craft Adviser, Malta Inds Assoc., Malta, 1952–78; Lecturer, Brighton Coll. of Art, 1950–8 Director, RI Galleries, Piccadilly, 1965–70. Many mural paintings completed, including tho in Eaton Square and Meretea, Italy; oils and water colours in exhibns of RA, London Grou NEAC and RBA, 1950–; 50 one-man shows, 1950–; works in private collections in Franc Italy, Malta, America, Canada, Japan, Australia, Norway, Sweden, Germany. Designer Stourhead Ball, 1959–69; produced Ceramic Mural on the History of Aerial Photograph Critic for Arts Review. Mem. Council, RI, 1964– (Vice-Pres. 1974). Hon. Member: Medic Art Soc.; Soc. Botanical Artists. Hon. FCA (Can.). Hunting Gp Prize for a Britis Watercolour, 1984. *Film:* Watercolour Painting: a practical guide, 1990. *Publications:* autho and illustrator: Waverley, 1991; Authors Circle, 1998; Cathedrals, 2000. *Address:* Winte Farm, Puttenham, Guildford, Surrey GU3 1AR. *T:* (01483) 810226.

BONE, Sir (James) Drummond, Kt 2008; Master, Balliol College, Oxford, since 2011; *b* 1 July 1947; *s* of William Drummond Bone, ARSA, RSW and Helen Bone (*née* Yuill); *m* 197 Vivian Clare Kindon. *Educ:* Ayr Acad.; Univ. of Glasgow (MA); Balliol Coll., Oxford (Sne Exhibnr, 1968–72). Lectr, English and Comparative Literature, Univ. of Warwick, 1972–8 University of Glasgow: Lectr, 1980–89, Sen. Lectr, 1989–95, in English Literature; Dea Faculty of Arts, 1991–95; Vice-Principal, 1995–99; Prof. of English Literature, 1995–200 Principal, RHBNC, London Univ., 2000–02 (Hon. Fellow, 2004); Pro-Vice-Chancello London Univ., 2001–02; Vice-Chancellor, Univ. of Liverpool, 2002–08. Pres., UUK 2005–07. Chairman: Foundn for Arts and Creative Technol., 2004–10; Liverpool Capital Culture Bd, 2005–07; UK Library Research Reserve, 2007–; Internat. Adv. Bd, Laureat Inc., 2008–11; Observatory on Borderless Higher Educn, 2008–10; i-graduate, 2009- AHRC, 2014–; Vice Chm., The Northern Way, 2004–08 (Chm., Innovation and Industr Gp, 2007–10). Mem. Council, 2009–13, Hon. Rector, 2015–, City Univ.; Mem., Adv Council, UK NARIC, 2010–. Pres., British and Irish Assoc. of Zoos and Aquaria, 2008–1 Mem., Editl Bd, THE (formerly Times Higher Educn Supplement), 2008–; Jt Edito Romanticism jl, 1993–. FRSA 1995; FRSE 2008. Freeman, Coachmakers' Co., 2007. Ho DLitt: Chester, 2008; Liverpool, 2008; Lancaster, 2009; DUniv Glasgow, 2010; Hon. DE Edinburgh, 2014. *Publications:* Writers and their Work: Byron, 2000; Cambridge Companio to Byron, 2004. *Recreations:* music, ski-ing, Maseratis. *Address:* Balliol College, Oxford OX 3BJ. *Club:* Athenæum.

BONE, Peter William, FCA; MP (C) Wellingborough, since 2005; *b* 19 Oct. 1952; *m* 198 Jeanette Sweeney; two *s* one *d*. *Educ:* Westcliff-on-Sea Grammar Sch. FCA 1976. Financi Dir, Essex Electronics and Precision Engrg Gp, 1977–83; Chief Exec., High Tech Electroni Co., 1983–90; Man. Dir, Palm Travel (West) Ltd, 1990–2002. Mem. (C), Southend-on-Se BC, 1977–86. Contested (C): Islwyn, 1992; Pudsey, 1997; Wellingborough, 2001. *Addres* House of Commons, SW1A 0AA; (office) 21 High Street, Wellingborough, Northants NN 4JZ.

BONE, Quentin, MA, DPhil; FRS 1984; zoologist; Honorary Research Fellow, Marin Biological Association UK; *b* 17 Aug. 1931; *s* of late Stephen Bone (landscape painter) an Mary Adshead (mural painter); *m* 1958, Susan Elizabeth Smith; four *s*. *Educ:* Warwick Sch St John's Coll., Oxon (Hon. Fellow, 1998). Naples Scholarship, 1954; Fellow by examinatio Magdalen Coll., Oxford, 1956. Zoologist at Plymouth Laboratory, Marine Biol Assoc 1959–91. *Publications:* Biology of Fishes (with N. B. Marshall), 1983, 2nd edn (with J. S Blaxter also), 1994, 3rd edn (with R. Moore), 2008; (ed) Biology of Pelagic Tunicates, 199 papers on fish and invertebrates, mainly in Jl of Mar. Biol Assoc. UK. *Address:* Marchan House, 98 Church Road, Plymstock, Plymouth PL9 9BG.

BONE, Sir Roger (Bridgland), KCMG 2002 (CMG 1996); HM Diplomatic Service retired; President, Boeing UK, 2005–14; *b* 29 July 1944; *s* of late Horace Bridgland Bone an Dora R. Bone (*née* Tring); *m* 1970, Lena M. Bergman; one *s* one *d*. *Educ:* William Palmer

Sch., Grays; St Peter's Coll., Oxford (MA). Entered HM Diplomatic Service, 1966; UK Mission to UN, 1966; FCO, 1967; 3rd Sec., Stockholm, 1968–70; 2nd Sec., FCO, 1970–73; 1st Secretary: Moscow, 1973–75; FCO, 1975–78; 1st Sec., UK Perm. Representation to European Communities, Brussels, 1978–82; Asst Private Sec. to Sec. of State for Foreign and Commonwealth Affairs, 1982–84; Vis. Fellow, Harvard Univ. Center for Internat. Affairs, 1984–85; Counsellor, 1985–89, and Head of Chancery, 1987–89, Washington; Counsellor, FCO, 1989–91; Asst Under Sec. of State, FCO, 1991–95; Ambassador to Sweden, 1995–99; Ambassador to Brazil, 1999–2004. Non-exec. Chm., Boeing Commercial Air Services UK Ltd, 2012–14; non-executive Director: Foreign and Colonial Investment Trust plc, 2008–; Continental Data Graphics Ltd, 2010–14; ITM Power plc, 2014–. Mem. Council, Brazilian Chamber of Commerce, 2005–12. UK Trade & Investment Ambassador for British Business, 2009–. Mem., Exec. Council, RUSI, 2007– (Trustee, 2012–); Dir and Trustee, Nat. Centre for Univs and Businesses (formerly Mem., Council for Industry and HE), 2011–. Chm., Anglo-Latin America Foundn, 2005–10; Trustee, Nobrega Foundn, 2005–09; Mem. Council, Air League, 2007– (Pres., 2015–). Freeman, City of London, 2011; Liveryman, Coachmakers' and Coach Harness Makers' Co., 2011–. Hon. FIED, 2014. Hon DEng Sheffield, 2015. *Recreations:* music, wine. *Address:* 5 Roxburghe Mansions, 32 Kensington Court, W8 5BQ. *Club:* Oxford and Cambridge.

ONE, Prof. Thomas Renfrew, CBE 1987; Deputy Principal, University of Strathclyde, 1992–96; *b* 2 Jan. 1935; *s* of James Renfrew Bone and Mary Williams; *m* 1959, Elizabeth Stewart; one *s* one *d. Educ:* Greenock High Sch.; Glasgow Univ. MA 1st cl. English 1956, MEd 1st cl. 1962, PhD 1967. Teacher, Paisley Grammar Sch., 1957–62; Lecturer: Jordanhill Coll. of Educn, 1962–63; Glasgow Univ., 1963–67; Jordanhill College of Education: Hd of Educn Dept, 1967–71; Principal, 1972–92. FCCEA 1984; FRSGS 1997; FSES 2011. *Publications:* Studies in History of Scottish Education, 1967; School Inspection in Scotland, 1968; *chapters in:* Whither Scotland, 1971; Education Administration in Australia and Abroad, 1975; Administering Education: international challenge, 1975; European Perspectives in Teacher Education, 1976; Education for Development, 1977; Practice of Teaching, 1978; World Yearbook of Education, 1980; The Management of Educational Institutions, 1982; The Effective Teacher, 1983; Strathclyde: changing horizons, 1985; The Changing Role of the Teacher, 1987; Teacher Education in Europe, 1990; Educational Leadership: challenge and change, 1992. *Recreations:* golf, bridge. *Address:* 7 Marchbank Gardens, Paisley PA1 3JD. *Clubs:* Western Gailes Golf, Buchanan Bridge; Paisley Burns.

ONELL, Carlos Antonio; guitarist; concert artist since 1969; *b* London, 23 July 1949; *s* of Carlos Bonell and Ana Bravo; two *s* by a former marriage. *Educ:* William Ellis Sch., Highgate; Royal Coll. of Music (Hon. RCM 1973). Lectr, City Lit, 1970; Prof., RCM 1972. Artistic Dir, London Internat. Guitar Fest., 2005. Début as solo guitarist, Purcell Room, 1971; GLAA Young Musician, 1973; resident guitarist, London Contemp. Dance Theatre, 1974; concert tours and recording with John Williams & Friends, 1975; first solo album, 1975; concerto début, RFH, 1977; NY début, 1978; Carlos Bonell Ensemble début, QEH, 1983, and tours in Europe and Far East; soloist with all major UK orchestras; commissioned and first performed Sonata by Stephen Oliver, 1981; first performance of: guitar concertos by Bryan Kelly, 1979, Barrington Pheloung, 1994, Armand Coeck, 1997; recorded Rodrigo's Concierto de Aranjuez, 1981; first recording of Carlos Bonell Ensemble, The Sea in Spring, 1997; interactive DVD, Classical Guitar Performance, 2004; (with Sir Paul McCartney) composition of concerto for guitar and orchestra, 2006–; recording based on music of rock group Queen, 2008; recording of music by Maltese composer Gordon Mizzi, 2010; recording of arrangements of Beatles' songs, 2011; numerous other solo records and awards. Trujamán Prize, Spain, 2008. *Publications:* Spanish folk songs and dances, 1975; Gaspar Sanz airs and dances, 1977; A Tarrega collection, 1980; First Pieces for solo guitar, 1980; The romantic collection, 1983; The classical collection, 1983; Spanish folk songs for 3 guitars, 1984; Purcell: 3 pieces, 1984; Tarrega Fantasia, 1984; Technique Builder, 1998; Carlos Bonell Guitar Series, 1998; Essential Classics for Guitar, 2004. *Recreations:* cinema, reading, history, playing the guitar, listening to music. *E:* info@carlosbonell.com. *W:* www.carlosbonell.com.

ONES, Prof. Christopher John; Professor, University of Manchester, since 2011; Founding Partner: Hammersley and Bones Ltd, since 2010; Good Growth Ltd, since 2010; *b* 12 June 1958; *s* of James C. E. and Sydness M. Bones; *m* 1984, Pamela Gail Fawcett; one *s* one *d. Educ:* Dulwich Coll.; Aberdeen Univ. (MA Hons). Advr, Employee Relns, 1982–84, Industrial Relns, 1985–87, Shell; Group Management Development Manager: Grand Met Brewing, 1987–89; Grand Met Retailing, 1989; Personnel and Admin Dir, GME, 1990–92; United Distillers: Orgn Develt Manager, 1992–95; HR Dir, Internat., 1995–97; HR Dir, Europe, 1997–99; Gp Compensation and Benefits Dir, Diageo, 1999; Gp Orgn Effectiveness and Develt Dir, Cadbury Schweppes plc, 1999–2004; Principal, Henley Mgt Coll., 2005–08; Dean, Henley Business Sch., 2008–10, now Dean Emeritus; Prof., Univ. of Reading, 2008–10. Member, Advisory Board: Savile plc, 2008–10; Norman Broadbent, 2014–. Mem. Bd, Govt Skills, 2005–10; non-exec. Ind. Dir, Agric. and Horticulture Develt Bd UK, 2007–13; non-executive Director: The Working Manager Ltd, 2010–12; MK-LF Partnership, 2013–. Chm., Lib Dem Party Reform Commn, 2008. Contrib., Human Resources mag., 2003–10. Trustee, Terrence Higgins Trust, 2010–15 (Dep. Chair, 2012–13; Chair, 2013–15). CCMI 2007; FCIPD 2002; FRSA 2001. Dr *hc* Aberdeen, 2012. *Publications:* The Self-Reliant Manager, 1993; The Cult of the Leader, 2010 (CMI/British Liby Mgt Bk of the Year, 2012); (with J. Hammersley) Leading Digital Strategy, 2015. *Recreations:* gardening, theatre, eradicating bullshit. *Club:* Reform.

ONEY, His Honour Guy Thomas Knowles; QC 1990; a Circuit Judge, 2003–14; *b* 28 Dec. 1944; *oc* of Thomas Knowles Boney, MD and Muriel Hilary Eileen Long, FRCS; *m* 1976, Jean Harris Ritchie, *qv*; two *s. Educ:* Winchester College; New College, Oxford (BA 1966; MA 1987). Called to the Bar, Middle Temple, 1968 (Harmsworth Scholar), Bencher, 1997; in practice on Western Circuit, 1969–2003; Asst Recorder, 1982–85; Head of Pump Court Chambers, 1992–2001; Recorder, 1985–2003; a Dep. High Court Judge, 1994–2003. Chm., Friends of Winchester Coll., 2001–09. Freeman, Clockmakers' Co., 1996 (Liveryman, 2010–). Lord of the Manor, Stockbridge, 2003–. *Publications:* The Road Safety Act 1967, 1971; contribs to: Halsbury's Laws of England, 4th edn (Road Traffic); horological jls. *Recreations:* horology, history, music (Organist, King's Somborne Parish Church, 1980–), amateur theatre, walking Archie. *Address:* c/o Winchester Combined Court Centre, Winchester SO23 9EL. *Club:* Garrick.

ONEY, Jean Harris, (Mrs G. T. K. Boney); *see* Ritchie, J. H.

ONFIELD, Andrew Robert John; Executive Director, Finance, National Grid plc, since 2010; *b* Wimbledon, 17 Aug. 1962; *s* of Terence and Roberta Bonfield; *m* Sandra Ann Peel; two *s. Educ:* Westville Boys High Sch.; Univ. of Natal (BCom; Postgrad. Dip. Accountancy). CA (SA). Price Waterhouse, 1984–90; SmithKline Beecham plc: Exec. Corporate Planning, 1990–91; Dir and Vice Pres., Corporate Accts, 1991–95; Corporate Controller, 1995–97; Dep. Finance Dir and Sen. Vice Pres., 1997–98; Chief Financial Officer, 1999–2000; Exec. Dir, Finance, BG Gp plc, 2001–02; Chief Financial Officer: Bristol Myers Squibb Co., 2002–08; Cadbury plc, 2009–10. Director: BOC Gp, 2003–06; ImClone Systems, 2007–08; Kingfisher plc, 2010– (Chm., Audit Cttee, 2010–). *Recreations:* golf, watching sports. *Address:* National Grid plc, 1–3 Strand, WC2N 5EH. *Club:* Wentworth Golf.

ONFIELD, Dr Astrid Elizabeth, CBE 2014; Chief Executive, Queen Elizabeth Diamond Jubilee Trust, since 2012; *b* Welwyn Garden City, 21 May 1969; *d* of Prof. William Bonfield, *qv*; partner, 2006, David Godwin; one *s* one *d. Educ:* Bishop's Hatfield Girls Sch.; Southampton Univ. (BA Hons Archaeol. 1990); Univ. of Manchester (MA (Econ) Social Anthropol. 1991; PhD Social Anthropol. 1996). Dir, Inter-Country People's Aid (Zimbabwe), 1997–2001; Prog. Develt Specialist, Bernard van Leer Foundn, 2001–04; Dir of Policy, Aga Khan Foundn, 2004–05; Chief Exec., Diana Princess of Wales Meml Fund, 2005–12. Chair, Eur. Funders Gp for HIV/AIDS, 2005–11. Trustee: Assoc. of Charitable Foundns, 2007–10; Big Lottery Fund, 2012–; Internat. Agency for Prevention of Blindness, 2014–. *Recreations:* contemporary dance, gardening. *Address:* Queen Elizabeth Diamond Jubilee Trust, 128 Buckingham Palace Road, SW1W 9SA. *T:* (020) 3358 3370. *E:* astrid.bonfield@qejubileetrust.org.

BONFIELD, Sir Peter (Leahy), Kt 1996; CBE 1989; FREng; international business executive; *b* 3 June 1944; *s* of George and Patricia Bonfield; *m* 1968, Josephine Houghton. *Educ:* Hitchin Boys' Grammar School; Loughborough Univ. (BTech Hons; Hon. DTech, 1988). FIET (FIEE 1990), FBCS 1990, FCIM 1990; FREng (FEng 1993). Texas Instruments Inc., Dallas, USA, 1966–81; Group Exec. Dir, ICL, 1981–84; Chm. and Man. Dir, STC Internat. Computers Ltd, 1984–90; Chm. and Chief Exec., 1985–96, Dep. Chm., 1997–2000, ICL plc; Dep. Chief Exec., STC plc, 1987–90; Chief Exec., BT plc, 1996–2002. Director: BICC PLC, 1992–96; Ericsson, 2002–; Mentor Graphics Corp., 2002–; Taiwan Semiconductor Manufacturing, 2002–; Sony Corp., Japan, 2005–14; GlobalLogic Inc., USA; Member: Internat. Adv. Bd, Citigroup (formerly Salomon Smith Barney), 1999–2009; Adv. Bd, Sony Corp., 2004–14; New Venture Partners LLP, 2006–; Adv. Bd, Apax, 2007–13; Adv. Bd, Longreach Gp, Hong Kong; Adv. Bd, Silent Circle; Chm. Supervisory Bd, NXP Semiconductors, 2006–; non-exec. Mem., Supervisory Bd, Actis LLP, 2005–12; non-exec. Dir, Dubai Internat. Capital, 2007–09; Sen. Advr, Rothschild London, 2010–; Bd Mentor, CMI, Belgium. Chm., Small Business Charter; Dir, EastWest Inst., USA; Chm. Bd, EastWest Inst., UK. Member: European Round Table, 1996–2002; EU-Japan Business Dialogue Round Table, 1999–2002; Ambassador for British Business. Mem., British Quality Foundn, 1993–2012 (Vice-Pres.). Mem., CS Coll. Adv. Council, 1993–97. Chm. Council, Loughborough Univ., 2012–. FRSA 1992. Freeman, City of London, 1990; Liveryman, Information Technologists' Co., 1992. Hon. Citizen, Dallas, Texas, 1994. Hon. doctorates from univs of Loughborough, Surrey, Mid Glamorgan, Nottingham Trent, Brunel, Open, Northumbria at Newcastle, Kingston, Cranfield, Essex and London. Mountbatten Medal, Nat. Electronics Council, 1995; Gold Medal, Inst. of Mgt, 1996. Comdr, Order of the Lion (Finland), 1995. *Recreations:* music, sailing, ski-ing. *Address:* PO Box 129, Shepperton, Middx TW17 9WL. *W:* www.sirpeterbonfield.com. *Clubs:* Royal Automobile, Royal Thames Yacht.

BONFIELD, Prof. William, CBE 1998; PhD; FRS 2003; FREng; FMedSci; Professor of Medical Materials, University of Cambridge, 2000–05, now Professor Emeritus; Director, Pfizer Institute for Pharmaceutical Materials Science, 2002–05; *b* 6 March 1937; *s* of Cecil William Bonfield and Ellen Gertrude Bonfield; *m* 1960, Gillian Winifred Edith Cross; one *s* two *d. Educ:* Letchworth GS; Imperial College, London (Perry Meml and Bessemer Medals; BScEng, PhD, DIC, ARSM). CEng, FIMMM; FREng (FEng 1993); CPhys 2003; FInstP 2003; FRSC 2005; FMedSci 2010. Honeywell Res. Center, Hopkins, Minn, USA, 1961–68; Queen Mary, later Queen Mary and Westfield College, London: Reader in Materials Science, 1968; Prof. of Materials, 1974–99; Head, Dept of Materials, 1980–90; Chm., Sch. of Engineering, 1981–88; Dean of Engineering, 1985–89; Dir, Univ. of London IRC in Biomedical Materials, 1991–99. Visiting Professor: Chulalongkorn Univ., Bangkok, 1988–98; Henry Ford Hosp., Detroit, 1992; Nat. Univ. of Singapore, 2007; OCMR Dist. Vis. Prof., Univ. of Toronto, 1990; Honorary Professor: Univ. of Sichuan, 1992–; UCL, 2007–. Lectures: Royal Microscopical Soc., 1992; Mellor Meml, Inst. of Materials, 1993; Prof. Moore Meml, Univ. of Bradford, 1994; Dist. Scholar, QUB, 1994; C. W. Hall Meml, SW Res. Inst., San Antonio, Texas, 1996; Hatfield Meml, Univ. of Sheffield, 1996; CSE Internat., Royal Acad. of Engrg, 1998; Hawksley Meml, IMechE, 1999; William Mong Dist., Univ. of Hong Kong, 2002; Robert Warner, Founders' Co., 2005; Furlong Christmas, RCS, 2008; Plenary Lectr, World Biomaterials Congress, Chengdu, 2012; R. W. Thomson, Scottish Assoc. Metals, 2012. Project Leader, EEC Concerted Action in Skeletal Implants, 1989–96. Chm., Med Engrg Cttee, 1989, Mem., Materials Cttee, later Materials Commn, 1983–88, SERC; Institute of Materials: Chairman: Biomaterials Cttee, 1989–96; Biomedical Applications Div., 1996–2005; Vice-Pres., 1998–2002; Member: Materials Sci. Bd, 1989–95; Council, 1996–2005; Member: Jt Dental Cttee, 1984–89; DoH Cttee on Dental and Surgical Materials, 1986–90; Directive Council, Internat. Soc. for Bio-analoging Skeletal Implants, 1988–95; Jl Cttee, Internat. Fedn for Med. and Biol Engrg, 1989–2001; Tech. Cttee, BSI, 1992–; Metallurgy and Materials Res. Assessment Panel, HEFC, 1995–96 and 2001–02; Materials Foresight Panel, OST, 1995–98; Chm., UK Focus on Med. Engrg, Royal Acad. of Engrg, 1998–2001. Chm., London Metallurgical Soc., 1991; Sec. Gen., Internat. Soc. for Ceramics in Medicine, 1998–2005. Mem., Adv. Bd, Royal Soc., 2013–. Director: Abonetics Ltd, 1996–; Biocompatibles plc, 2000–02; Apatech Ltd, 2001–10; OrthoMimetics Ltd, 2007–10; AtoCap Ltd, 2011–. Chm., Editl Bd, Materials in Electronics, 1990–2005; Mem., Editl Bd, Jl of Applied Polymer Sci., 1992–2005; Editor: Jl of Materials Science, 1973–2002; Jl Royal Soc.: Interface, 2004–10; Founding Editor: Jl of Materials Science Letters, 1981–2002; Materials in Medicine, 1990–2006. Freeman: Armourers' and Brasiers' Co., 1994 (Liveryman, 1999; Mem., Ct of Assts, 2001–; Master, 2007–08); City of London, 1998; Engrs' Co., 2013. Hon. Member: Canadian Ortho. Res. Soc., 1983; Materials Res. Soc. of India, 1993. FBSE 1995; FCGI 2012. Hon. FIPEM 2003; Hon. Fellow, Queen Mary, Univ. of London, 2007. Hon. DSc: Aberdeen, 2002; Turku, 2011. Griffith Medal, Inst. of Metals, 1991; Royal Soc. Armourers' and Brasiers' Co. Medal, 1991; George Winter Award, Eur. Soc. for Biomaterials, 1994; Kelvin Medal, ICE, 1995; Acta Metallurgica J. Herbert Hollomon Award, 2000; Chapman Medal, Inst. of Materials, Minerals, and Mining, 2003; Japanese Soc. for Biomaterials Medal, 2003; Prince Philip Gold Medal, Royal Acad. Engrg, 2004; President's Prize, UK Soc. for Biomaterials, 2004; Award of Merit, Internat. Union for Physical and Engrg Scis in Medicine, 2009. *Publications:* Bioceramics, 1991; over 450 research papers on biomaterials, biomechanics and physical metallurgy in sci. jls. *Recreation:* cycling. *Address:* Department of Materials Science and Metallurgy, University of Cambridge, 27 Charles Babbage Road, Cambridge CB3 0FS. *Clubs:* Athenæum; North Road Cycling.

See also A. E. Bonfield.

BONGERS de RATH, Paul Nicholas; Director, Local Government International Bureau, 1988–95; international relations consultant in urban affairs, 1996–2002; *b* 25 Oct. 1943; *s* of late Henry Bongers and Marjorie Bongers (*née* Luxton); *m* 1968, Margaret Rennie Huddleston Collins; one *s* two *d. Educ:* Bradfield Coll.; New Coll., Oxford (MA); DPA Univ. of London (external), 1968. Administrative Trainee, City of Southampton, 1965–68; Personal Asst to Chief Exec., City of Nottingham, 1968–69; Administrator, Council of Europe, 1969–71; Assistant Secretary: AMC, 1971–74; AMA, 1974–78; Exec. Sec., British Sections, IULA/CEMR, 1978–88. Special Advr, CEMR, 1996–2001; Consultant: World Assocs of Cities and Local Authorities Co-ordination, 1996–99; UN Human Settlements Prog., 2001–02; Special Rep., Bremen Initiative, 1999–2001. Hon. Sec. and Develt Officer, Local Govt Gp for Europe, 1999–2005; Mem., Exec. Cttee, 2005–07, Chm., Som and Dorset Br., 2010–11, European Movt. Mem., Aldeburgh Town Planning Steering Cttee, 2013–14. Volunteer: Aldeburgh Music, 2012–; Britten-Pears Foundn, 2012–. *Publications:* Local Government and 1992, 1990, 2nd edn as Local Government and the European Single Market, 1992; articles in local govt jls. *Recreations:* family, music, countryside, travel, the arts. *Address:* South House, Church Close, Aldeburgh, Suffolk IP15 5DY.

BONHAM, Sir (George) Martin (Antony), 5th Bt *cr* 1852; *b* Cirencester, 18 Feb. 1945; *e s* of Major Sir Antony Lionel Thomas Bonham, 4th Bt and Felicity (*d* 2003), *o d* of late Col. Frank L. Pardoe, DSO; *S* father, 2009; *m* 1st, 1979, Nenon Baillieu (marr. diss. 1992), *e d* of R. R. Wilson and Hon. Mrs Wilson; one *s* three *d*; 2nd, 2011, Pamela Elizabeth, *d* of late Reginald Ernest Harding and of Mrs Elizabeth Hazeldine Hyde Clarke (*née* Bent). *Educ:* Heatherdown Prep. Sch.; Eton Coll.; Aston Univ. Area Manager, Calor Gas Ltd, 1987–91; Consultant, Industrial Soc., 1998–2004; Clerk, Firefighters' Co., 2005–14. *Recreations:* sailing, tennis, ski-ing, golf. *Heir: s* Michael Francis Bonham [*b* 24 May 1980; *m* 2008, Louise Gregory; two *s* one *d*]. *Address:* 21 Tonsley Place, Wandsworth, SW18 1BH. *T:* (020) 8874 8896. *E:* martin.bonham@icloud.com. *Clubs:* Telford Park Tennis; Bembridge Sailing.

BONHAM, Nicholas; Director, Nicholas Bonham Consultancy, since 2004; *b* 7 Sept. 1948; *s* of late Leonard Charles Bonham and Diana Maureen (*née* Magwood); *m* 1st, 1977, Kaye Eleanor (*née* Ivett) (marr. diss. 1999); two *d*; 2nd, 2003, Susan Angela Chester. *Educ:* Trent College. Joined W. & F. C. Bonham & Sons Ltd, Fine Art Auctioneers, 1966; Dir, 1970; Man. Dir, 1975–87; Dep. Chm., W. & F. C. Bonham & Sons Ltd, subseq. Bonhams & Brooks, then Bonhams, 1987–2004. Chairman: Noble Investments (UK) plc, 2004–08; Corporate Communication Ltd, 2006–08; Sugar Collection Ltd, 2006–12. Director: Montpelier Properties, 1970–95; Bonhams Gp, 1995–2004; Hodie Ltd, 2001–. Master, Pewterers' Co., 2009–10. *Recreations:* sailing, tobogganing, ski-ing, swimming, scuba. *Clubs:* Kennel; Royal Yacht Squadron, Royal Thames Yacht, Seaview Yacht, South West Shingles Yacht; St Moritz Tobogganing.

BONHAM-CARTER OF YARNBURY, Baroness *cr* 2004 (Life Peer), of Yarnbury in the County of Wiltshire; **Jane Mary Bonham Carter;** Deputy Convenor, Liberal Democrat Peers, since 2010; Prime Minister's Trade Envoy for Mexico, since 2012; *b* 20 Oct. 1957; *d* of Baron Bonham-Carter and Leslie Adrienne, *d* of Condé Nast. *Educ:* St Paul's Girls' Sch.; University Coll. London (BA Philosophy). Producer, Panorama and Newsnight, BBC, 1988–93; Ed., A Week in Politics, Channel 4, 1993–96; Dir of Communications, Lib Dem Party, 1996–98; ind. producer, 1998–2004, Associate, 2004–09, Brook Lapping Productions. Member: Lib Dem Campaigns and Communications Cttee, 1998–2006; Council, Britain in Europe, 1998–2005; Referendum Campaign Team, 2004–05. Member: Adv. Cttee, Centre Forum (formerly Centre for Reform), 1998–; RAPt (Rehabilitation for Addicted Prisoners Trust), 1999–. Member: H of L sub-cttee on Home Affairs, 2004–07; H of L Select Cttee on BBC Charter Review, 2005–06, on Communications, 2007–10; EU Sub-cttee C on Foreign Affairs, Defence and Develt Policy, 2010–. Mem. Bd, Nat. Campaign for the Arts, 2010–12; Trustee, The Lowry, 2011–. Vis. Parly Fellow, St Antony's Coll., Oxford, 2013–14. *Address:* House of Lords, SW1A 0PW. *Clubs:* Groucho, Electric House.

BONHAM CARTER, Edward Henry; Executive Vice-Chairman, Jupiter Fund Management plc, since 2014 (Joint Chief Executive, 2000–07; Chief Executive Officer, 2007–14); *b* London, 24 May 1960; *s* of late Raymond Henry Bonham Carter and of Elena Bonham Carter (*née* Propper de Callejón); *m* 1994, Victoria Studd; two *s* one *d*. *Educ:* Harrow Sch.; Manchester Univ. (BA Econs and Politics). With Schroder Investment Mgt; Electra Investment, 1986–94; Jupiter Investment Management, 1994–: Manager, Jupiter UK Growth Fund, 1995–99; Chief Investment Officer, 1999–2010. Non-exec. Dir, Land Securities, 2014–. *Recreations:* yoga, table tennis. *Address:* Jupiter Fund Management plc, 1 Grosvenor Place, SW1X 7JJ. *T:* (020) 7412 0703. *Club:* Brooks's.

See also H. Bonham Carter.

BONHAM CARTER, Helena, CBE 2012; actress; *b* 26 May 1966; *d* of late Hon. Raymond Henry Bonham Carter and of Elena Bonham Carter (*née* Propper de Callejón); one *s* one *d* with Tim Burton, *qv*. *Educ:* Hampstead High Sch. for Girls; Westminster Sch. *Films include:* Lady Jane, 1985; A Room with a View, 1986; A Hazard of Hearts, The Mask, 1988; St Francis of Assisi, Getting it Right, 1989; Hamlet, Where Angels Fear to Tread, 1990; Howard's End, 1992; Fatal Deception, 1993; Mary Shelley's Frankenstein, 1994; Mighty Aphrodite, Twelfth Night, 1996; Margaret's Museum, Portraits Chinois, Keep the Aspidistra Flying, 1997; The Wings of the Dove, The Theory of Flight, 1998; The Revengers' Comedies, Fight Club, 1999; Planet of the Apes, Women Talking Dirty, 2001; Novocaine, 2002; Til Human Voices Wake Us, Heart of Me, Big Fish, 2003; Charlie and the Chocolate Factory, 2005; Sixty Six, 2006; Conversations With Other Women, Harry Potter and the Order of the Phoenix, 2007; Sweeney Todd: The Demon Barber of Fleet Street, 2008; Terminator Salvation, Harry Potter and the Half-Blood Prince, 2009; Alice in Wonderland, Harry Potter and the Deathly Hallows, Pt 1, 2010, Pt 2, 2011; The King's Speech (Best Supporting Actress, BAFTA), 2011; Great Expectations, Les Misérables, 2012; The Lone Ranger, 2013; The Young and Prodigious T. S. Spivet, 2014; Cinderella, 2015; *television includes:* Miami Vice, 1987; The Vision, 1988; Arms and the Man, 1988; Dancing Queen, 1993; A Dark Adapted Eye, 1994; Live from Baghdad, 2002; Henry VIII, 2003; Enid, 2009 (Best Actress, Internat. Emmy Awards, 2010); Burton and Taylor, 2013; Turks & Caicos, Salting the Battlefield, 2014; *theatre includes:* Woman in White, Greenwich, 1988; The Chalk Garden, Windsor, 1989; House of Bernarda Alba, Nottingham Playhouse, 1991; The Barber of Seville, Palace, Watford, 1992; Trelawney of the Wells, Comedy, 1992; *radio:* The Reluctant Debutante; Marie Antoinette; The Seagull. Fellow, BFI 2012. *Recreation:* reading. *Address:* c/o Conway van Gelder Grant Ltd, 8–12 Broadwick Street, W1F 8HW. *T:* (020) 7287 0077.

See also E. H. Bonham Carter.

BONINGTON, Sir Christian (John Storey), Kt 1996; CVO 2010; CBE 1976; DL; mountaineer, writer and photographer; *b* 6 Aug. 1934; *s* of Charles Bonington, journalist, and Helen Anne Bonington (*née* Storey); *m* 1962, Muriel Wendy Marchant (*d* 2014); two *s* (and one *s* decd). *Educ:* University Coll. Sch., London. RMA Sandhurst, 1955–56; commnd Royal Tank Regt, 1956–61. Unilever Management Trainee, 1961–62; writer and photographer, 1962–. Climbs: Annapurna II, 26,041 ft (1st ascent) 1960; Central Pillar Freney, Mont Blanc (1st ascent), 1961; Nuptse, 25,850 ft (1st ascent), 1961; North Wall of Eiger (1st British ascent), 1962; Central Tower of Paine, Patagonia (1st ascent), 1963; Mem. of team, first descent of Blue Nile, 1968; Leader: successful Annapurna South Face Expedition, 1970; British Everest Expedition, 1972; Brammah, Himalayas (1st ascent), 1973; co-leader, Changabang, Himalayas (1st ascent), 1974; British Everest Expedition (1st ascent SW face), 1975; Ogre (1st ascent), 1977; jt leader, Kongur, NW China (1st ascent), 1981; Shivling West (1st ascent), 1983; Mt Vinson, highest point of Antarctica (1st British ascent), 1983; reached Everest summit, 1985; Panch Chuli II (W Ridge), Kumaon, Himalayas (1st ascent), 1992; Mejslen, Greenland (1st ascent), 1993; Rang Rik Rang, Kinnaur, Himalayas (1st ascent), 1994; Drangnag Ri (1st ascent), 1995; Danga II (1st ascent), 2000. President: British Mountaineering Council, 1988–91 (Vice-Pres., 1976–79, 1985–88); British Orienteering Fedn, 1985–; NT Lake Dist Appeal, 1989–; Council for National Parks, 1992–2000 (Life Vice-Pres., 2000); Vice-President: Army Mountaineering Assoc., 1980–; YHA, 1990–. Non-exec. Chm., Berghaus Ltd, 1998–. Chm., Mountain Heritage Trust, 2000–04; Dep. Patron, Outward Bound, 2010– (Trustee, 1998–2010; Chm., Risk Mgt Cttee, 1998–2007). Ambassador, Cumbrian Scouts, 2012–. Chancellor, Lancaster Univ., 2005–14. Pres., LEPRA, 1983. DL Cumbria, 2004. MInstD 1992. FRGS (Founders' Medal, 1974); FRPS 1991; FRSA 1996. Hon. Fellow: UMIST, 1976; Lancashire Polytechnic, 1991; Univ. of Cumbria, 2010. Hon. MA Salford, 1973; Hon. DSc: Sheffield, 1976; Lancaster, 1983; Hon. DCL Northumbria, 1996; Hon. Dr Sheffield Hallam, 1998; Hon. DLitt Bradford, 2002. Lawrence of Arabia Medal, RSAA, 1986; Livingstone Medal, RSGS, 1991. *Publications:* I Chose to Climb (autobiog.), 1966; Annapurna South Face, 1971; The Next Horizon (autobiog.), 1973; Everest, South West Face, 1973; Everest the Hard Way, 1976; Quest for Adventure, 1981, rev. edn 2000; Kongur: China's elusive summit, 1982; (jtly) Everest: the unclimbed ridge 1983; The Everest Years, 1986; Mountaineer (autobiog.), 1989; The Climbers, 1992; (with Robin Knox-Johnston) Sea, Ice and Rock, 1992; Chris Bonington's Lake District, 1997 (with Charles Clarke) Tibet's Secret Mountain, 1999; Boundless Horizons (autobiog.), 2000 Chris Bonington's Everest, 2002. *Recreations:* mountaineering, ski-ing, orienteering. *Address* Badger Hill, Nether Row, Hesket Newmarket, Wigton, Cumbria CA7 8LA. *T:* (01697 478286. *E:* chris@bonington.com. *Clubs:* Travellers (Hon. Mem., 2004–09), Alpine (Pres. 1996–99), Alpine Ski, Army and Navy; Climbers' (Hon. Mem.), Fell and Rock Climbing (Hon. Mem.), Border Liners, Carlisle Mountaineering (Hon. Mem.), Keswick Mountaineering; American Alpine (Hon. Mem.), Himalayan (Hon. Mem.), East India (Hon. Mem.).

BONINO, Emma; Minister of Foreign Affairs, Italy, since 2013; *b* 9 March 1948. *Educ* Bocconi Univ., Milan (BA 1972). Mem., Italian Chamber of Deputies, 1976–94 and 2006–08; Minister for Internat. Trade and European Affairs, 2006–08; Vice-Pres., Italian Senate, 2008–13; other posts include: Chm., Radical Party Gp, 1979–81; Mem., Bureau o Parlt, 1992–94. MEP, 1979–94 and 1999–2006; Mem., European Commn, 1994–99 Transnational Radical Party: Pres., 1991–93; Sec., 1993–95. *Recreations:* snorkelling, scuba-diving. *Address:* Ministry of Foreign Affairs, Piazzale della Farnesina 1, 00135 Rome, Italy.

BONNAR, Anne Elizabeth; Co-founder and Director, Bonnar Keenlyside, since 1991; *b* St Andrews, 9 Oct. 1955; *d* of George and Patricia Bonnar; two *s* two *d*. *Educ:* Dumbarton Acad. Glasgow Univ. (MA); Jordanhill Coll. of Educn (DipEd); City Univ., London (Dip. Arts Admin). Th. Manager, Young Vic, 1979–80; Publicity Officer, Glasgow Citizens' Th. 1980–83; Gen. Manager, Traverse Th., 1986–91. Transition Dir, Creative Scotland, 2008 Non-executive Director: Nat. Galls of Scotland, 2002–10; NT of Scotland, 2005–07; Neuro Foundn, 2007–12. FRSA. *Recreations:* arts, running, pilates. *E:* anne@b-k.co.uk.

BONNER, Mark; Founder and Creative Director, GBH Design, since 1999; *b* 24 June 1970 *s* of John and Joan Bonner; *m* 2008, Janice Davison; one *s* one *d*. *Educ:* Hounslow Coll. (Nat Dip. BTEC (Dist.)); Kingston Univ. (BA 1st Cl. Hons 1991); Royal Coll. of Art (MA 1993) The Partners, 1993–95; Carter Wong & Partners, 1995–96; SAS Design, 1997–99. Tutor in Graphic Design: W Bucks Coll., 1995–; Kingston Univ., 1999–; London Coll. o Communication, 2012. Chm., Consort Royal Awards, 2004. Mem., D&AD, 2000– (Mem. Exec. Cttee, 2011–13; Vice Pres., 2014). D&AD Annual Award, 1991, 1993, 1994, 1995 1996, 1997, 1998, 1999, 2001, 2002, 2003, 2004, 2005, 2007, 2008, 2009, 2011, Silver Award, 2003, 3 Yellow Pencils, 2011; One Show Gold, Silver and Bronze, 2011, NY Art Dirs Club; Design Week Award, 2003, 2005, 2007, 2008, 2011, 2013, and Best of Show, 2003 Benchmark Award, 2007. *Address:* GBH Design, Chiswick Station House, Burlington Lane Chiswick, W4 3HB. *T:* (020) 8742 2277. *E:* mark@gregorybonnerhale.com.

BONNER, Paul Max, OBE 1999; writer; Director, Secretariat, ITV Network Centre 1993–94; *b* 30 Nov. 1934; *s* of late Jill and Frank Bonner; *m* 1956, Jenifer Hubbard (*d* 2013) two *s* one *d*. *Educ:* Felsted Sch., Essex. National Service commission, 1953–55. Local journalism, 1955; Radio production, BBC Bristol, 1955–57; Television production, BBC Bristol, 1957–59, BBC Lime Grove, 1959–62; Television Documentary prodn and direction BBC Lime Grove and Kensington House, 1962–74; Editor, Community Programmes for BBC, 1974–77; Head of Science and Features Programmes for BBC, 1977–80; Channel Controller, Channel Four TV, 1980–83; Exec. Dir and Programme Controller, Channel Four TV, 1983–87; Dir, Programme Planning Secretariat, ITVA, 1987–93. A Manager, Royal Instn, 1982–85; Governor, Nat. Film and TV School, 1983–88; Director: Broadcasting Support Services, 1982–93; House of Commons Broadcasting Unit Ltd, 1989–91; Parly Broadcasting Unit, 1991–94; Chm., Sponsorship and Advertising Cttee, EBU, 1991–94 Member: Bd, Children's Film Unit, 1989–97; COPUS, 1986–92 (Chm., Broadcast Trust 1995–98). FRTS 1989. *Publications:* Independent Television in Britain: Vol. 5, ITV and the IBA 1981–1992, 1998, Vol. 6, New Developments in Independent Television 1981–92 Channel Four, TV-am, cable and satellite, 2002; *documentaries include:* Strange Excellency 1964; Climb up to Hell, 1967; Lost: Four H Bombs, 1967; Search for the Real Che Guevara 1971; Who Sank the Lusitania?, 1972. *Recreations:* photography, the theatre, listening to good conversation. *Address:* Alan Road, Wimbledon, SW19 7PT. *Clubs:* Reform, Chelsea Arts Garrick.

BONNET, Maj.-Gen. Peter Robert Frank, CB 1991; MBE 1975; Colonel Commandant Royal Regiment of Artillery, 1990–2000; *b* 12 Dec. 1936; *s* of James Robert and Phyllis Elsie Bonnet; *m* 1961, Sylvia Mary Coy; two *s*. *Educ:* Royal Military Coll. of Science, Shrivenham BSc (Engrg). Commnd from RMA Sandhurst, 1958; RMCS Shrivenham, 1959–62; apptd to RHA, 1962; Staff trng, RMCS and Staff Coll., Camberley, 1969–70; Comd (Lt-Col), 26 Field Regt, RA, 1978–81; Comd RA (Brig.) 2nd Div., 1982–84; attendance at Indian Nat Defence Coll., New Delhi, 1985; Dir RA, 1986–89 (Maj.-Gen. 1986); GOC Western Dist 1989–91, retd 1992. Mem., Exec. Cttee, ABF, 1993–99; Gen. Sec., Officers' Pensions Soc. 1995–2000; Dir, OPS Investment Co. Ltd, 1995–2000; Man. Trustee, OPS Widows' Fund 1995–2000; Vice Patron, Council Officers' Assoc., 1995–. Hon. Col, 26 Field Regt RA 1992–99. Vice-Pres., Nat. Artillery Assoc., 1989–99. Trustee: Kelly Holdsworth Meml Trust 1996–2004; Council, Age Concern, 1998–99. *Publications:* International Terrorism, 1985; A Short History of the Royal Regiment of Artillery, 1994. *Recreations:* tennis, sculpture, painting. *T:* (01398) 341324. *Club:* Army and Navy.

BONNETT, Prof. Raymond, CChem, FRSC; Professor of Organic Chemistry, Queen Mary, then Queen Mary and Westfield, College, University of London, 1974–94, now Professor Emeritus; *b* 13 July 1931; *s* of Harry and Maud Bonnett; *m* 1956, Shirley Rowe; two *s* one *d*. *Educ:* County Grammar Sch., Bury St Edmunds; Imperial Coll. (BSc, ARCS) Cambridge Univ. (PhD); DSc London 1972. Salters' Fellow, Cambridge, 1957–58; Res Fellow, Harvard, 1958–59; Asst Prof., Dept of Chemistry, Univ. of British Columbia 1959–61; Queen Mary, subseq. Queen Mary and Westfield, College, London: Lectr in Organic Chem., 1961–66; Reader in Organic Chem., 1966–74; Hd of Dept of Chemistry 1982–87; Scotia Res. Prof., 1994–2000. George and Christine Sosnovsky Award in Cancer Therapy, RSC, 2012. *Publications:* sci. papers, esp. in Jls of Royal Soc. of Chemistry and Biochemical Soc. *Recreations:* theatre, bookbinding, gardening. *Address:* Elmbank, 19 Station Road, Epping, Essex CM16 4HG. *T:* (01992) 573203.

BONNEVILLE, Hugh; *see* Williams, H. R. B.

BONNEY, Barbara; soprano; *b* Montclair, NJ, 14 April 1956; *d* of Alfred Bonney III and Janet Gates; *m* 1989, Håkan Hagegård; *m* Maurice Whitaker. *Educ:* Univ. of New Hampshire Mozarteum, Salzburg. Performances include: Sophie in Der Rosenkavalier, Royal Opera Covent Garden, 1984; Pamina in Die Zauberflöte, La Scala, Milan, 1985; Nyade in Ariadne auf Naxos, Falstaff, 1990, Metropolitan Opera, NY; Susanna in The Marriage of Figaro, Royal Opera, 1995; Les Boréades, Salzburg Fest., 1999; Idomeneo, San Francisco, 1999; Orlando 2003, Zdenka in Arabella, 2004, Royal Opera. Regular lied recitals and concert perfs numerous recordings. Prof., Mozarteum, Salzburg, 2007–; Jt Dir, Young Singers Prog. Salzburg Festival, 2008. Vis. Prof., Royal Acad. of Music. *Address:* c/o Michael Storrs Music Ltd, 211 Piccadilly, W1J 9HF.

BONNEY, Very Rev. Mark Philip John; Dean of Ely, since 2012; *b* Welwyn Garden City, 2 March 1957; *s* of John and Patricia Bonney; *m* 1991, Katherine Jarvis; two *d*. *Educ.* Northgate Grammar Sch. for Boys, Ipswich; St Catharine's Coll., Cambridge (PGCE 1979; MA 1981); St Stephen's House, Oxford (MA 1988). Asst Dir of Music, Durham Sch.

1979–82; ordained deacon, 1985, priest, 1986; Asst Curate, St Peters, Stockton on Tees, 1985–88; Chaplain, 1988–90, Precentor, 1990–92, Cath. and Abbey Church of St Alban; Vicar, Eaton Bray with Edlesborough, 1992–96; Rector, Gt Berkhamstead, 1996–2004; Canon Treas., Salisbury Cath., 2004–12. *Recreations:* golf, cooking, art, family, music. *Address:* The Deanery, The College, Ely, Cambs CB7 4DN. *T:* 07811 466517. *E:* mpjbonney@gmail.com. *Club:* Hawks.

ONNICI; *see* Mifsud Bonnici.

ONO; *see* Hewson, P. D.

ONOMY, Rt Hon. Lord; Iain Bonomy; PC 2010; a Senator of the College of Justice in Scotland, 1997–2012; a Judge of the International Criminal Tribunal for the former Yugoslavia, 2004–09; *b* 15 Jan. 1946; *s* of late John Bonomy and of Mary Gray Bonomy (*née* Richardson); *m* 1969, Janet (*née* Gray); two *d. Educ:* Dalziel High Sch., Motherwell; Univ. of Glasgow (LLB Hons). Apprentice solicitor, East Kilbride Town Council, 1968–70; Asst solicitor, then Partner, Ballantyne & Copland, solicitors, Motherwell, 1970–83; admitted Faculty of Advocates, 1984; Advocate Depute, then Home Advocate Depute, 1990–96; QC (Scot.) 1993. Surveillance Comr, under Pt III Police Act 1997 and Pt II Regulation of Investigatory Powers Act 2000, 1998–2004, 2010–; Chair: Infant Cremation Commn, 2013–14; Post-Corroboration Safeguards Review, 2014–. Hon. Bencher, Inner Temple, 2010. Hon. LLD Strathclyde, 2006. *Recreations:* golf, travel, football terraces (now stands). *Address:* Parliament House, Parliament Square, Edinburgh EH1 1RQ. *Clubs:* Glasgow Art (Glasgow); Torrance House Golf, East Kilbride Golf, Motherwell Football and Athletic.

ONSEY, Martin Charles Brian, AO 2005; CVO 2003 (LVO 2000); Official Secretary to the Governor-General of Australia, 1998–2003; *b* 2 May 1948; *s* of late Thory Richmond Bonsey and of Frances Mary Bonsey; *m* 1971, Joan Hair. *Educ:* Univ. of Melbourne (BA Hons Hist. and Pol Sci.); Australian Nat. Univ. (LLB). Public servant, Australia, 1974–2003. Secretary: Order of Australia, 1998–2003; Australian Bravery Decorations Council, 1998–2003. CStJ 1999.

ONSOR, Sir Nicholas (Cosmo), 4th Bt *cr* 1925; DL; barrister; *b* 9 Dec. 1942; *s* of Sir Bryan Cosmo Bonsor, 3rd Bt, MC, TD, and of Elizabeth, *d* of late Captain Angus Valdimar Hambro; *S* father, 1977; *m* 1969, Hon. Nadine Marisa Lampson, *d* of 2nd Baron Killearn; two *s* three *d* (including twin *d*). *Educ:* Eton; Keble College, Oxford (MA). Served Royal Buckinghamshire Yeomanry, 1964–69. Called to the Bar, Inner Temple, 1967; in practice at the Bar, 1967–75, 2003–10. Mem., CLA Legal and Parly Sub-Cttee, 1978–82. MP (C) Nantwich, 1979–83, Upminster, 1983–97; contested (C) Upminster, 1997. Minister of State, FCO, 1995–97. Chm., Select Cttee on Defence, 1992–95; Sec., Cons. Tourism Sub-Cttee, 1979–80; Vice-Chairman: Cons. Foreign Affairs Cttee, 1981–83; Cons. Defence Cttee, 1987–90. Mem. Council, RUSI, 1992–95, 1997–2000. Chm., Food Hygiene Bureau, later Checkmate Plc, 1986–95; Pres. and non-exec. Dir, Liscombe Hldgs, 1997–2000; Chairman: Egerton International Ltd, 2005–; Metallon Corp. plc, 2011–; Director: London Mining plc, 2007– (Dep. Chm., 2010–); Blue Note Mining Inc., 2007–09. Chairman: Cyclotron Trust for Cancer Treatment, 1984–92 (Pres., 1992–); British Field Sports Soc., 1987–93; Standing Council of the Baronetage, 1990–93 (Vice-Chm., 1987–90); Baronets' Trust, 1993–95 (Trustee, 1986–95); Verdin Home for Mentally Handicapped, 1981–85. Mem., Council of Lloyd's, 1987–92. MCIArb 2004. Hon. Col, 60 Signals Sqdn, Royal Bucks Hussars (V), 2000–10; Vice Chm., SE RFCA, 2000–10. FRSA 1970. Freeman, City of London, 1988. DL Bucks, 2007. *Publications:* political pamphlets on law and trades unions and defence. *Recreations:* sailing, shooting, military history. *Heir: s* Alexander Cosmo Walrond Bonsor [*b* 8 Sept. 1976; *m* 2006, Jane, *d* of James Troughton; one *s*]. *Address:* c/o Brunswick Chambers, 2 Middle Temple Lane, EC4Y 7AA. *Clubs:* White's, Pratt's; Royal Yacht Squadron.

BONVIN, Her Honour Jane Anne Marie, (Mrs S. M. Poulter); DL; a Circuit Judge, 1995–2008; *b* 15 Dec. 1946; *d* of Jean Albert Bonvin and Phyllis Margaret (*née* Boyd); *m* 1972, Sebastian Murray Poulter (*d* 1998). *Educ:* Putney High Sch.; Bristol Univ. (LLB Hons). Law Lectr, IVS, Lesotho, 1969–71; called to the Bar, Gray's Inn, 1971; barrister, Western Circuit, 1972–77 and 1979–95. Trustee, St Cross Hospital, Winchester, 2008–13. Editor, Lesotho Law Reports, 1977–79. DL Hampshire, 2003. *Recreations:* gardening, walking, travel, music, breeding and racing thoroughbred horses. *Address:* Old Dairy Cottage, 7 Southdowns, Old Alresford, Hants SO24 9UR.

BONYNGE, Richard, AC 2012 (AO 1983); CBE 1977; opera conductor; *b* Sydney, 29 Sept. 1930; *s* of C. A. Bonynge, Epping, NSW; *m* 1954, Dame Joan Sutherland, OM, AC, DBE (*d* 2010); one *s. Educ:* Sydney Conservatorium (pianist). Official debut, as Conductor, with Santa Cecilia Orch. in Rome, 1962; conducted first opera, Faust, Vancouver, 1963. Has conducted in most leading opera houses in world, and in Edinburgh, Vienna and Florence Fests. Has been Princ. Conductor and Artistic/Musical Dir of cos, incl. Sutherland/Williamson Internat. Grand Opera Co., Aust., 1965; Vancouver Opera, 1974–77; Australian Opera, 1976–85. Many opera and ballet recordings; also recital discs with Sutherland, Tebaldi, Tourangeau and Pavarotti, and many orchestral and ballet anthologies. Socio d'onore, Regia Accademia Filarmonica di Bologna, 2007. Comdr, Ordre des Arts et des Lettres (France), 1989. *Publications:* (with Dame Joan Sutherland) The Joan Sutherland Album, 1986. *Address:* c/o Ingpen & Williams, 7 St George's Court, 131 Putney Bridge Rccoad, SW15 2PA.

BOOBIS, Prof. Alan Raymond, OBE 2003; PhD; Professor of Biochemical Pharmacology, since 1996, and Director, Health Protection Agency Toxicology Unit, since 2003, Imperial College London (formerly Royal Postgraduate Medical School, London); *b* Glasgow, 15 Jan. 1949; *s* of Samuel Boobis and Esther Boobis; *m* 1975, Susan Wallace; one *s* one *d. Educ:* Bellahouston Acad., Glasgow; Univ. of Glasgow (BSc Hons Pharmacol. 1971; PhD Pharmacol. 1974). CBiol 1991; FRSB (FIBiol 1991). Fogarty Vis. Fellow, Nat. Inst. of Child Health and Human Develt, NIH, Bethesda, 1974–76; Royal Postgraduate Medical School, London, later Imperial College London: MRC Postdoctoral Res. Fellow, 1976–79, Lectr, 1979–83, Sen. Lectr, 1983–88, Reader, 1988–96, Dept of Clin. Pharmacol.; Dep. Dir, DoH Toxicology Unit, 1998–2003. Member: Sub-cttee on Pesticides, MAFF, 1992–96; UK Adv. Cttee on Pesticides, 1997–2002 (Dep. Chm., 2000–02; Chm., Med. and Toxicol. Panel, 2000–03); Vet. Residues Cttee, 2001–04; Cttee on Carcinogenicity, 2003–13; Cttee on Toxicity, 2003–12, 2015– (Chm., 2015–); HPA Bd Sub-Cttee for Radiation, Chem. and Envmtl Hazards, 2005–10. Member: WHO Expert Adv. Panel on Food Safety, 1997–; Jt FAO/WHO Expert Cttee on Food Additives (Residues of Vet. Drugs), 1997– (Chm., 2011, 2013); Jt FAO/WHO Meeting on Pesticide Residues, 1999– (Chm./Vice-Chm., 2003–07, 2011, 2013); Scientific Panel on Plant Health, Plant Protection Products and their Residues, 2003–09 (Vice-Chm., 2006–09), Scientific Panel on Contaminants in the Food Chain, 2009–12, Eur. Food Safety Authy. Medical Research Council: Member: Physiol Medicine and Infections Bd, Res. Cttee A, 1992–95; Adv. Bd, 2000–04; Coll. of Experts, 2004–09. Mem. Scientific Adv. Cttee, Assoc. for Internat. Cancer Res., 2001–05. European Cooperation in the field of Scientific and Technical Research: UK Rep., Mgt Cttee, Action B1, 1986–98; UK Rep. and Vice-Chm., Mgt Cttee, Action B15, 1998–2004; UK Rep. and Chm., Action B25, 2005–09. Mem. Bd of Trustees, Internat. Life Scis Inst., 2009– (Chm., 2015); Mem. Bd of Trustees, Health and Envmtl Scis Inst., 2001–11 (Chm., 2008–10); Mem. Bd of Trustees, Internat. Life Scis Inst. Europe, 2010– (Vice-Pres., 2012–). Member: Biochem. Soc., 1971–2011; British Toxicology Soc., 1982– (Chm., 1994–96; Fellow, 2006; John Barnes Prize Lectureship, 2013); British Pharmacol Soc., 1997–; Soc. of Toxicology, USA, 2007–; Pres., Fedn of Eur. Toxicologists and Eur. Socs of Toxicol., 2000–02 (Hon. Mem. 2006; Merit Award, 2009). Toxicol. Award, RSC, 2013. Jt Ed.-in-Chief, 2004–10, Emeritus Ed., 2011–, Food and Chemical Toxicology. *Publications: edited jointly:* Microsomes and Drug Oxidations, 1985; European Consensus Conference on Pharmacogenetics, 1990; Therapeutic Drugs, 1991, 2nd edn 1998; Therapeutic Drugs, Supplement 1, 1992; Therapeutic Drugs, Supplement 2, 1994; Proceedings of the Third International Conference on Practical In Vitro Toxicology, 1994; European Conference on Specificity and Variability in Drug Metabolism, 1995; European Symposium on Prediction of Drug Metabolism in Man: progress and problems, 1999; Proceedings of EUROTOX 2000, 2000; approx. 150 book chapters, reviews, procs of meetings, etc; contrib. over 230 articles in scientific jls. *Recreations:* listening to music (classical, jazz, rock, world), reading (especially science fiction), photography, computers. *Address:* Centre for Pharmacology and Therapeutics, Division of Experimental Medicine, Department of Medicine, Imperial College London, Hammersmith Campus, Ducane Road, W12 0NN. *T:* (020) 7594 6805, *Fax:* (020) 7594 7393. *E:* a.boobis@imperial.ac.uk.

BOOKBINDER, Alan Peter; Director, Sainsbury Family Charitable Trusts, since 2006; *b* 16 March 1956; *s* of Geoffrey Ellis Bookbinder and Bridget Mary Bookbinder; *m* 2005, Vicki Ambery-Smith; one *s* one *d. Educ:* Manchester Grammar Sch.; St Catherine's Coll., Oxford (BA Modern Hist. and Modern Langs); Harvard Univ. (MA Regl Studies). Producer, 1986–92, Exec. Producer, 1992–2001, BBC Television; Head of Religion and Ethics, BBC, 2001–06. *Publications:* Comrades, 1985; contribs to Spectator, Listener, The Tablet. *Address:* 5 Wilton Road, SW1V 1AP. *T:* (020) 7410 7035.

BOOKER, Christopher John Penrice; journalist and author; *b* 7 Oct. 1937; *s* of late John Booker and Margaret Booker; *m* 1979, Valerie, *d* of late Dr M. S. Patrick, OBE and Alla Petrovna Patrick; two *s. Educ:* Dragon Sch., Oxford; Shrewsbury Sch.; Corpus Christi Coll., Cambridge (History scholar). Liberal News, 1960; jazz critic, Sunday Telegraph, 1961; Editor, Private Eye, 1961–63, and regular contributor, 1965–; resident scriptwriter, That Was The Week That Was, 1962–63, and Not So Much A Programme, 1963–64; contributor to Spectator, 1962–, Daily Telegraph, 1972– (Way of the World column, as Peter Simple II, 1987–90), and to many other newspapers and jls; columnist, Sunday Telegraph, 1990–. Wrote extensively on property develt, planning and housing, 1972–77 (with Bennie Gray, Campaigning Journalist of the Year, 1973); City of Towers—the Rise and Fall of a Twentieth Century Dream (TV prog.), 1979. Mem., Cowgill enquiry into post-war repatriations from Austria, 1986–90. *Publications:* The Neophiliacs: a study of the revolution in English life in the 50s and 60s, 1969; (with Candida Lycett-Green) Goodbye London, 1973; The Booker Quiz, 1976; The Seventies, 1980; The Games War: a Moscow journal, 1981; (with Lord Brimelow and Brig. A. Cowgill) The Repatriations from Austria in 1945, 1990; (with Richard North) The Mad Officials: how the bureaucrats are strangling Britain, 1993; (with Richard North) The Castle of Lies: why Britain must leave the European Union, 1996; A Looking Glass Tragedy: the controversy over the repatriations from Austria in 1945, 1997; Nice and Beyond, 2000; Britain and Europe: the culture of deceit, 2001; The Seven Basic Plots: why we tell stories, 2004; (with Richard North) The Great Deception: can the European Union survive?, 2005; (with Richard North) Scared to Death: from BSE to global warming, why scares are costing us the Earth, 2007; The Real Global Warming Disaster: is the obsession with 'climate change' turning out to be the most costly scientific blunder in history?, 2009; The BBC and Climate Change: a triple betrayal, 2011; contrib. Private Eye anthologies, 1962–, incl. The Secret Diary of John Major, 1992–97, St Albion Parish News, 1998–2007, Not the Foot and Mouth Report, 2001. *Recreations:* the psychology of storytelling, nature, music, playing village cricket, teasing global warmists. *Address:* The Old Rectory, Litton, Bath BA3 4PW. *T:* (01761) 241263. *E:* cblitton@aol.com.

BOOKER, Gordon Alan, FIWEM; utility adviser; Deputy Director General of Water Services, 1990–98; *b* 17 Feb. 1938; *s* of Frederick William Booker and Beryl Booker; *m* 1957, Anne Christine Pike; two *s* one *d. Educ:* Dronfield Grammar Sch.; Sheffield Univ. (BEng (Hons) 1960). MICE 1963; FIWEM 1966. Sheffield Water, 1960–65; Birmingham Water, 1965–70; W Glam Water, 1970–74; Welsh Water, 1974–80; Chief Exec., E Worcester Water, 1980–89; Managing Director: Biwater Supply, 1987–90; Bournemouth and W Hants Water Cos, 1989–90. Mem., Council, Water Res. Centre, 1985–90; mem. and chm. of several water industry cttees on automation and leakage control. *Publications:* Water Distribution Systems, 1984; Telemetry and Control, 1986; contrib. Procs of ICE and of IWSA, reports for DoE and NWC, and Jls of IWEM and IAWPRC. *Recreations:* walking, painting. *Address:* 106 The Holloway, Droitwich, Worcs WR9 7AH. *T:* (01905) 772432; Sheplegh Court, Blackawton, Devon TQ9 7AH.

BOOKER, Pamela Elizabeth; *see* Alexander, P. E.

BOOMGAARDEN, Georg; Ambassador of Germany to the Court of St James's, 2008–13; political consultant; *b* Emden, Germany, 24 June 1948; *m* 1972, Christiane von Blücher; two *s* one *d. Educ:* Univ. of Kiel (Geophysics Dip. 1973). Entered Foreign Service, Germany, 1974; Desk Officer, Cultural Section, Moscow, 1976–80; Press Officer, Buenos Aires, 1980–83; Federal Foreign Office: Desk Officer, Central America Div., 1983–86; Hd, Information Processing Div., 1986–89; Ambassador to Nicaragua, 1989–92; Hd, Economic Service, Moscow, 1992–95; Federal Foreign Office: Hd, Div. responsible for S Latin America, 1995–99; Dir for Latin American Affairs, 1999–2003; Ambassador to Spain, 2003–05; State Sec., Fed. For. Office, 2005–08. Cross, Order of Merit (Germany), 2001; numerous foreign decorations. *Address:* Berlin.

BOON, (George) Peter (Richard); HM Diplomatic Service, retired; High Commissioner to Cameroon and non-resident Ambassador to Chad, Central African Republic, Gabon and Equatorial Guinea, 1998–2002; *b* 2 Nov. 1942; *s* of late George Alan James Boon and Enid Monica Boon (*née* Smith); *m* 1971, Marie Paule Calicis; one *s. Educ:* Repton Sch., Derbys. Joined CRO, later FCO, 1963; Bombay, 1966–69; Brussels, 1969–71; Vienna, 1971–74; on secondment to DTI, 1974–75; FCO, 1975–78; The Hague, 1978–81; Spokesman, BMG, Berlin, 1981–86; FCO, 1986–90; First Sec. (Political), Dhaka, 1990–93; FCO, 1994–97. Hon. Sec., BACSA, 2014–. *Address:* Barn End, London Road, Blewbury, Didcot, Oxon OX11 9PB.

BOORD, Sir Nicolas (John Charles), 4th Bt *cr* 1896; scientific translator; English training specialist; *b* 10 June 1936; *s* of Sir Richard William Boord, 3rd Bt, and of Yvonne, Lady Boord, *d* of late J. A. Hubert Bird; *S* father, 1975; *m* 1965, Françoise Renée Louise Mouret. *Educ:* Eton (Harmsworth Lit. Prize, 1952); Sorbonne, France; Societa Dante Alighieri, Italy; Univ. of Santander, Spain. *Publications:* (trans. jtly) The History of Physics and the Philosophy of Science—Selected Essays (Armin Teske), 1972; numerous translations of scientific papers for English and American scientific and technical jls. *Recreation:* English and French literature and linguistics. *Heir: b* Antony Andrew Boord [*b* 21 May 1938; *m* 1960, Anna Christina von Krogh; one *s* one *d*]. *Address:* 61 Traverse Le Mée, 13009 Marseille, France. *T:* (4) 91731395.

BOORMAN, Anthony John; Deputy Chief Ombudsman and Deputy Chief Executive, Financial Ombudsman Service, 2012–14 (Principal Ombudsman and Decisions Director, 2000–12); *b* 14 Nov. 1958; *s* of William Harry and Margaret Boorman; *m* 1984, Alison Drury; two *s. Educ:* Kent Coll., Canterbury; New Coll., Oxford (BA). Various posts, Electricity Consumers' Council, 1985–90, Dir, 1989–90; Dir, Office of Electricity Regulation, 1990–98; Dep. Dir Gen., Office of Gas and Electricity Mkts, 1998–2000. Non-exec. Dir, S Warwicks NHS Foundn Trust, 2007–. Mem., Commn for Judicial Appts, 2001–06.

BOORMAN, Lt-Gen. Sir Derek, KCB 1986 (CB 1982); Chairman, Health Care Projects Ltd, 1998–2010; *b* 13 Sept. 1930; *s* of late N. R. Boorman, MBE, and Mrs A. L. Boorman (*née* Patman); *m* 1st, 1956, Jennifer Jane Skinner (*d* 1991); two *d* (one *s* decd); 2nd, 1992, Mrs Nicola Cox. *Educ:* Wolstanton Grammar Sch.; RMA Sandhurst. Commnd N Staffords, 1950; Adjt 1 Staffords, 1958–59; Staff Coll., 1961; HQ 48 Gurkha Inf. Bde, 1962–64; Jt Services Staff Coll., 1968; CO 1 Staffords, 1969–71; Instr, Staff Coll., 1972–73; Comdr 51 Inf. Bde, 1975–76; RCDS, 1977; Dir, Public Relations (Army), 1978–79; Director of Military Operations, 1980–82; Comdr, British Forces Hong Kong, and Maj.-Gen. Bde of Gurkhas, 1982–85; Chief of Defence Intelligence, 1985–88. Lieut, Tower of London, 1989–92. Colonel: 6th Queen Elizabeth's Own Gurkha Rifles, 1983–88; Staffordshire Regt (Prince of Wales's), 1985–90. Director: Tarmac Construction, 1988–95. Chairman: KCH Trust, 1992–93; Royal Hosps NHS Trust, 1994–97. Mem., Security Commn, 1991–96. Dep. Pro-Chancellor, Univ. of Kent, 2000–05. *Recreations:* gardening, music, taking wife out to dinner.

BOORMAN, John, CBE 1994; film director; *b* 18 Jan. 1933; *m* 1st, 1956, Christel Kruse; one *s* three *d*; 2nd, 1997, Isabella Weibrecht; one *s* two *d*. *Educ:* Salesian Coll., Chertsey. Film Editor, ITN, 1955–58; Dir and Producer, Southern TV, 1958–60; Head of Documentaries, BBC Bristol. *Films include:* Catch us if you Can, 1965; Point Blank, 1967; Hell in the Pacific, 1968; Leo the Last, 1969; Deliverance, 1972; Zardoz, 1973; The Heretic, 1976; Excalibur, 1981; The Emerald Forest, 1985; Hope and Glory, 1987; Where the Heart Is, 1989; I Dreamt I Woke Up, 1991; Beyond Rangoon, 1995; Two Nudes Bathing, 1995; The General, 1998; The Tailor of Panama, 2001; The Tiger's Tail, 2007; Queen and Country, 2014. Gov., BFI, 1983–94. BAFTA Fellow, 2004; BFI Fellow, 2011. Commandeur, Ordre des Arts et des Lettres (France), 2014. *Publications:* The Legend of Zardoz, 1973; Money into Light, 1985; Hope and Glory, 1987; Projections: (ed) no 1, 1992; (joint editor): no 2, 1993; no 3, 1994; nos 4 and 4½, 1995; nos 5 and 6, 1996; no 7, 1997; no 8, 1998; nos 9–12; no 13, 2004; Adventures of a Suburban Boy, 2003. *Address:* Merlin Films Group, 33 Fitzwilliam Place, Dublin 2, Ireland.

BOORMAN, Steven Robert, CBE 2013; specialist occupational health physician, since 1990; Chief Medical Officer, Optima Health and Nutrition, since 2015; *b* London, 10 July 1959; *s* of John Thomas and Joy Theresa Boorman; *m* 1984, Sharon Mary Griffiths; two *d*. *Educ:* Middlesex Hosp. Med. Sch. (MB BS 1983). MRCGP 1988; FRCP 2008; FRSPH 2013. House Officer, then SHO, Middx Hosp., 1983–84; Anatomy Demonstrator and A&E SHO, 1984–85; GP trainee in London and Warwicks, 1985–90; Med. Advr to Sec. of State for Transport, 1988–90; Royal Mail: Occupational Physician, 1990–92; Prin. Med. Officer, 1992–2000; CMO, 2000–03; Dir, Corporate Responsibility, 2003–11; Med. Dir for UK occupational Health Services, Abermed, 2011–13; Chief Med. Advr, Capita PIP Assessment Services, 2013–14. Author, Report of Ind. NHS Health and Well-being Rev., 2009. Hon. Sen. Clinical Lectr, Univ. of Birmingham, 1990–2014; Hon. Sen. Lectr, Robert Gordon Univ., Aberdeen, 2011–. Chief Examr, Dip. Occupational Medicine, 1998–. FFOM 2000. Hon. FRCN 2011. *Publications:* (contrib.) Fitness for Work, 2014. *Recreations:* DIY, car mechanics, RC modelling. *Address:* 3 Queens Lane, Farnham, Surrey GU9 0LU. *E:* steven.boorman@gmail.com.

BOOTE, Robert Edward, CVO 1971; first Director General, Nature Conservancy Council, 1973–80; *b* 6 Feb. 1920; *s* of Ernest Haydn Boote and Helen Rose Boote; *m* 1949, Vera (*née* Badian); one *s* one *d*. *Educ:* London Univ. (BSc Econ Hons). DPA; FREconS 1953–61; AIPR 1957–61; FCIS 1960–81. War service, 1939–46, Actg Lt-Col, Hon. Major. Admin. Officer, City of Stoke-on-Trent, 1946–48; Chief Admin. Officer, Staffs County Planning and Develt Dept, 1948–54; Principal, 1954–64, Dep. Dir, 1964–73, Nature Conservancy. Sec. 1965–71, formerly Dep. Sec., Countryside in 1970 Confs, 1963, 1965, 1970 and numerous study groups; a Chief Marshal to the Queen, 1970. Mem., Pesticides Cttee, 1958–73; Chm., Broadland Report, 1963–65; UK Deleg. to Council of Europe Cttee for Conservation of Nature and Natural Resources, 1963–71; Mem., Countryside Review Cttee, 1977–79; Various posts in meetings of UN, UNESCO, EEC and OECD, 1968–81; Member, UK Delegations: USA, 1978; USSR, 1978; China, 1982; Chm. Preparatory Gp for Eur. Conservation Year 1970; Chm. Organising Cttee for European Conservation Conf. 1970 (Conf. Vice-Pres.); Chm. European Cttee, 1969–71; Consultant for European Architectural Heritage Year 1975; Advr, H of L Select Cttee on Eur. Communities, 1980–81. A Vice-Pres. and Chm., Euro Fedn of Nature and Nat. Parks, 1980–81; International Union for Conservation of Nature and Natural Resources: Treas., 1975–78; Mem., Governing Council and Bureau, 1975–81; a Vice-Pres., 1978–81; Rep., Internat. Conf. on Antarctic Marine Living Resources, 1980; Chm., Antarctica Resolution, 1981; Election Officer, 1984; Founder and Chm., 1974–80, Mem., 1980–85, UK Cttee. Council Member: FFPS, 1979–83; RGS, 1983–86; BTCV (Vice-Pres.) 1980–; RSNC (Vice-Pres.) 1980–99; RSNC Wildlife Appeal, 1983–87; WWF, 1980–86; Ecological Parks Trust, 1980–85; YPTES (Chm.), 1982–87; Friends of ENO, 1980–87; Common Ground Internat., 1981–85; Cttees for UK Conservation and Develt Prog., 1980–83; HGTAC, Forestry Commn, 1981–87; Conservator, Wimbledon and Putney Commons, 1981–97; Patron, CSV, 1978–85; Chairman: Instn of Environmental Sciences, 1981–84; Seychelles Appeal Cttee, Royal Soc., 1980–87; Chm., Gp A, Ditchley Foundn Anglo/Amer. Conf. on Environment, 1970; Lead Speaker: Eurogespracht, Vienna, 1970; Internat. Conf., Rehovot, Israel, 1971; Mem., Entretiens Ecologiques de Dijon, 1981; UK Officer Rep., Eur. Environment Ministers Conf., 1976; Judge, Berlin world agro/environ films and TV competitions, 1970, 1972, 1974 and 1980. Initiator and Chm., Age Resource, 1988–98, now Chm. Emeritus; a Vice-Pres., Age Concern, later Age UK, 1990–. Trustee and Hon. Treas., New Renaissance Gp, 1995–2002. FRSA 1971–2010. Hon. Vice-Pres., Landscape Inst., 1971; Hon. MRTPI, 1978, Lifetime Hon. MRTPI, 2014. Greek Distinguished Service Medal, 1946; van Tienhoven European Prize, 1980; Merit Award, IUCN, 1984; Alfred Toepfer Prize for European nature protection, Goethe Foundn, 1995. Adviser: Macmillan Guide to Britain's Nature Reserves, 1980–94; Shell Better Britain Campaign, 1980–91. Member Editorial Boards: Internat. Jl of Environmental Studies, 1975–2002; Town Planning Review, 1979–85; Internat. Jl Environmental Educn and Information, 1981–83. Helped to prepare: Pacemaker (film), 1970 (also appeared in); Man of Action, BBC Radio, 1977. *Publications:* (as Robert Arvill) Man and Environment, 1967, 5th edn 1983; numerous papers, articles, addresses, TV and radio broadcasts, over 4 decades in UK and internat. professional confs in 50 countries. *Recreations:* theatre, music. *Address:* 3 Leeward Gardens, Wimbledon, SW19 7QR. *T:* (020) 8946 1551.

BOOTE, Sarah Joan; *see* Thomas, S. J.

BOOTH; *see* Sclater-Booth, family name of Baron Basing.

BOOTH, Alan James; His Honour Judge Booth; a Circuit Judge, since 2009; *b* Stockport, 18 Jan. 1955; *s* of His Honour James Booth and of Joyce Doreen Booth; *m* 1983, Anne Lesley Binns; one *s* one *d*. *Educ:* Bolton Sch. (Boys Div.), Bolton; Selwyn Coll., Cambridge (BA 1977). Called to the Bar, Gray's Inn, 1978; in practice, Deans Court Chambers, Manchester, 1978–2009; Asst Recorder, 1996–2000; Recorder, 2000–09. Mem. Bd, NW Reg., 2005–13, Chm., Technical Water Polo Cttee, 2008–13, Amateur Swimming Assoc.; Mem., Water Polo Cttee, 2008–13, Chm., GB Men's Water Polo Mgt Gp, 2013–14, British Swimming. *Recreation:* sport. *Clubs:* Hawks (Cambridge); Sale Harriers; City of Manchester Water Polo.

BOOTH, Prof. Alison Lee, PhD; FASSA; Professor of Economics, since 2002, and ANU Public Policy Fellow, since 2012, Australian National University; *b* Melbourne, Australia; *d* of Norman Booth and Marjorie Booth; *m* 1986, Timothy James Hatton; two *d*. *Educ:* Pymble Ladies' Coll., Sydney; Univ. of NSW (BArch); Univ. of Sydney (Master of Town and Country Planning); London Sch. of Econs and Pol Sci. (MSc 1980; PhD 1984). Teaching Asst, LSE, 1981–83; Lecturer in Economics: Univ. of Bristol, 1983–84; City Univ., 1984–88; Brunel Univ., 1988–90; Lectr in Econs, 1990–91, Sen. Lectr in Econs, 1991–94, Birkbe Coll., Univ. of London; Prof. of Econs, Univ. of Essex, 1995–2013. Mem., Exec. Ctte Royal Econ. Soc., 1999–2003. Pres., Eur. Assoc. of Labour Economists, 2005–08. FASS 2005. Ed.-in-Chief, Labour Economics, 1999–2004. *Publications:* The Economics of Tra Unions, 1995; (ed with D. Snower) Acquiring Skills: market failures, their symptoms ar policy responses, 1996; (ed) The Economics of Labor Unions (2 vols), 2002; *fiction:* Stillwat Creek, 2010; The Indigo Sky, 2011; A Distant Land, 2012; articles in learned jls. *Recreation* writing and reading fiction, walking, sleeping. *Address:* Research School of Economics, AN College of Business and Economics, Australian National University, Canberra, ACT 020 Australia. *E:* alison.booth@anu.edu.au.

BOOTH, Anthony John, CBE 1993; CEng, FIET; Director, RB Phusion Ltd, since 2001; 18 March 1939; *s* of Benjamin and Una Lavinia Booth; *m* 1965, Elspeth Marjorie (*née* Frase one *s* one *d*. *Educ:* Bungay Grammar Sch.; London Univ. (BScEng, DMS). Joined Post Offi Res. Dept, 1957; Exec. Engr and Sen. Exec. Engr, Telecom HQ, 1965–71; Asst Staff Eng Central HQ Appointments, 1971–74; Head of Section and Div., External Telecom Exe 1974–78; Head of Div., THQ, 1978–79; Dir, Internat. Networks, 1979–80; Regional D London Region, 1980–83; Corporate Dir, British Telecommunications PLC, 1984–9 Managing Director: BT International, 1983–91; Business Communications, 1991–92; Speci Businesses and Internat. Affairs Div., 1992–94; Chm., Ericsson Ltd, 1994–2002. Dir, Prot Network Mgt Ltd, 2001–04; Dir and Trustee, AQA (Assessment and Qualifs Alliance Ltd 2000–06 (Vice-Chm., 2003–06); Trustee, AQA Pension Scheme, 2006–11. Mem., HEFC 1996–2001. Gov., and Chm. Finance Cttee, Polytechnic of W London, 1991–92; Chm. Govs, Thames Valley Univ., 1993–96; Mem. Council, Univ. of Surrey, 1998–2004. Membe Guild of Freemen of City of London, 1982–. Chm., SE Reg., RLSS, 1997–2001. FInst 1997 (Chm., 1999–2002, Pres., 2002–11, W Surrey); CCMI (CBIM 1986; Mem. Bd Companions, 1999–2006); FRSA 1991. Hon. DPhil Thames Valley, 1998. *Recreations:* oper golf. *Club:* Caledonian.

BOOTH, Cherie, (Mrs A. C. L. Blair), CBE 2013; QC 1995; Founder and Chair, Omn Strategy LLP, since 2011; *b* 23 Sept. 1954; *d* of Anthony and Gale Booth; *m* 1980, Rt Ho Anthony Charles Lynton Blair, *qv*; three *s* one *d*. *Educ:* St Edmund's RC Primary Sch Liverpool; Seafield Grammar Sch., Crosby; London Sch. of Economics (LLB; Hon. Fellov 1999). Called to the Bar, Lincoln's Inn, 1976, Bencher, 1999; an Asst Recorder, 1996–99; Recorder, 1999–2015; barrister specialising in public, employment and EC law; accredit advanced mediator, ADR Chambers/Harvard Legal Project. Dir, Renault Gp, 2015 Contested (Lab) Thanet North, 1983. Hon. Vice Pres., Barnardo's, 2007–; Vice Pres 4Children (formerly Kids Club Network), 1998–; Vice Chair, Internat. Council on Women Business Leadership, 2011; Founder: Cherie Blair Foundn for Women, 2008–; Africa Justi Foundn, 2011–; Patron: Refuge, 1995–; Home Start, Islington, 1997–; Sargent Cancer Ca for Children, subseq. CLIC Sargent, 1998–; Breast Cancer Care, 1998–; Islington Mus Centre, 1999–; Victim Support, London, 1999–; Patron, SCOPE, 2002–. Truste Citizenship Foundn, 1995–. Fellow: Inst. of Advanced Legal Studies, 1998; Internat. Soc. Lawyers for Public Service, 1999; FRSA. Chancellor Emeritus, Liverpool John Moores Uni (Fellow, 1997; Chancellor, 1999–2006); Chancellor, Asian Univ. for Women, Banglades 2011–. Hon. Bencher, King's Inns, Dublin, 2002. DUniv Open, 1999; Hon. LLI Westminster, 1999; Liverpool, 2003; Hon. DLitt UMIST, 2003. Der Steiger, Germany, 201 Commonwealth Award for Public Service, Delaware, USA, 2011; Trinity Justitia Omnib Award, Dublin Univ. Law Society, 2012. *Publications:* (with Cate Haste) The Goldfish Bow married to the Prime Minister, 2004; (contrib.) Evidence, 2004; The Negligence Liability Public Authorities, 2006; Speaking for Myself (autobiog.), 2008. *Recreations:* theatre, the ar keeping fit, enjoying my children. *Address:* Omnia Strategy LLP, PO Box 60519, W2 7JU.

BOOTH, Sir Clive, Kt 2003; PhD; Trustee, Lloyds TSB Foundation for England and Wal since 2011; Chair, Berkshire, Buckinghamshire and Oxfordshire Wildlife Trust, since 20 (Trustee, since 2010); *b* 18 April 1943; *s* of Henry Booth and Freda Frankland; *m* 196 Margaret Sardeson. *Educ:* King's Sch., Macclesfield; Trinity Coll., Cambridge (1st cl. Ho Nat Scis Tripos; MA 1969); Univ. of California, Berkeley (Harkness Fellow, 1973; MA 197 PhD 1976). Joined DES, 1965; Prin. Pvte Sec. to Sec. of State for Educn and Scienc 1975–77; Asst Sec., 1977–81; Dep. Dir, Plymouth Polytechnic, 1981–84; Mem., H Inspectorate, DES, 1984–86; Dir, Oxford Poly., 1986–92; Vice-Chancellor, 1992–97, Pr Emeritus, 1997, Oxford Brookes Univ. Asst Comr, Nat. Commn on Educn, 1992–9 Chairman: TTA, 1997–2003; Pay Review Body for Nurses, Midwives and Professions Alli to Medicine, 1998–2005; Big Lottery Fund, 2004–10; Dep. Chm., SEEDA, 1999–200 Chairman: Central Police Trng and Develt Authy, 2002–07; SE Reg. Bd for Reduci Reoffending, 2005–. Member: Governing Council, SRHE, 1981–90; Adv. Cttee, Brun Univ. Educn Policy Centre, 1986–91; Computer Bd for Univs and Res. Councils, 1987–9 CNAA Cttee for Information and Develt Services, 1987–92; Fulbright Academ Administrators Selection Cttee, 1988–97; British Council Cttee for Internat. Co-operation Higher Educn, 1988–96 (Chm., 1994–96); Council for Industry and Higher Educn, 1990–9 Fulbright Commn, 1992–97; Royal Soc. Study Gp on Higher Educn, 1991–97; UFC In Systems Cttee, 1991–93; Oxford Science Park Adv. Cttee, 1990–97; Oxford Inst. of Nursi Bd, 1991–95; Commonwealth Scholarships Commn, 1992–96; UK ERASMUS Counc 1992–97 (Chm., 1993–97); Oxford Trust Adv. Council, 1992–97; Bd, British Inst., Pari 1997–2005; Know How Fund Mgt Cttee, DFID, 1998–2000. Chairman: PCFC Steering G on Statistical Information, 1989–93; Heart of England Educn Forum, 1997–2002; Vic Chm., CVCP, 1992–97. Chairman: Oxfordshire Learning Partnership, 1999–2004; M Cttee, Oxfordshire Connexions, 2000–03; Director: Thames Action Resource Gp for Educ and Trng, 1986–2000; Thames Valley Technology Centre, 1989–93; British Counc 1995–97 (Sen. Advr, 1997–2005). Leverhulme Res. Fellow, 1983. Governor: Headingt and Wheatley Park Schs; Westminster Coll., Oxford, 1997–2000. Vice-Chair, Oxford Civ Soc., 2012–; Concert Manager, Summertown Choral Soc., 2012–. Jt Ed., Higher Educn Ql 1986–97; Member: Editorial Bd, Oxford Review of Educn, 1990–2015; Editorial Adv. Ctte Peabody Jl of Educn, Vanderbilt Univ., USA, 2005–15. DUniv Oxford Brookes, 2000; Ho DEd Sunderland, 2002. *Recreations:* gardening, cycling, walking, bridge, opera. *Address:* 43 John Street, Oxford OX1 2LH. *T:* (01865) 557762. *E:* boothclive99@gmail.com.

BOOTH, Sir Douglas Allen, 3rd Bt *cr* 1916; writer and producer for television, writer f films; Associate, Barak Realty, New York City, since 2007; *b* 2 Dec. 1949; *s* of Sir Phil Booth, 2nd Bt, and Ethel, *d* of Joseph Greenfield, NY, USA; *S* father 1960; *m* 1991, Yolan Marcela (*née* Scantlebury); two *d*. *Educ:* Beverly Hills High Sch.; Harvard Univ. (Harvard N Scholarship, Nat. Merit Scholarship, 1967); BA (*magna cum laude*) 1975. *Recreations:* musi back-packing. *Heir:* *b* Derek Blake Booth [*b* 7 April 1953; *m* 1st, 1981, Elizabeth Dreisba (marr. diss. 2000); one *s* one *d*; 2nd, 2006, Stephanie Louise Moret, MS, PhD]. *Address:* Ne York City, NY, USA.

BOOTH, Edmund Dwight, FREng; Principal, Edmund Booth Consulting Engineer, sin 1995; *b* Richmond, Surrey, 16 May 1948; *s* of Edmund Booth and Henrietta Booth; *m* 1s 1983, Sheena Jean Collison (*d* 2002); 2nd, 2009, Anna Mary Le Hair. *Educ:* King's Colleg Sch., Wimbledon; King's Coll., Cambridge (BA Engrg and Econs 1969). CEng 1975; FIC 1992; FIStructE 1993; FREng 2010. Volunteer, VSO, Sierra Leone, 1975–77; joined O Arup & Partners, 1977, Associate, 1992–95. Vis. Prof., Univ. of Oxford, 1997–2002; Ho Sen. Lectr, Imperial Coll. London, 2010. Chairman: Soc. for Earthquake and Civil Engr Dynamics, 1985–87; Cttee B/525/8: Eurocode 8, BSI, 2011–. Chm., Sheena Booth Mus Trust, 2003–10. Mem., Oxford and Cambridge Music Club. *Publications:* (ed) Concre

Structures in Earthquake Regions, 1994; Earthquake Design Practice for Buildings, 2nd edn, 2006, 3rd edn 2014. *Recreations:* violin, opera, house and garden. *Address:* 2 Miswell Cottages, Icknield Way, Tring HP23 4JU. *T:* (01442) 891007. *E:* edmund@booth-seismic.co.uk. *W:* www.booth-seismic.co.uk.

BOOTH, Fiona Irene; Chief Executive, Association of Independent Healthcare Organisations, since 2013; *b* London, 8 July 1970; *d* of David Carvosso and Marlene Donovan; *m* 1st, 1993, Paul Booth (marr. diss. 1997); 2nd, 2009, Christopher Moody. *Educ:* Curtin Univ., WA (BEd 1993). Science teacher, Bunbury Cathedral Grammar Sch., 1994–95; Regl Co-ordinator, Australian Red Cross, 1996–97; Services Manager, QUIT, 1998–2000; Science teacher, Grey Coat Hospital, 2000–01; Educn Welfare Officer, Royal Bor. of Kensington and Chelsea, 2001–02; Hd of Educn, Help the Aged, 2002–03; Hansard Society: Dir, Citizenship Educn Prog., 2003–07; Dep. Chief Exec., 2006–07; Chief Exec., 2007–12. FRSA 2007. *Recreations:* reading, cinema, travelling, wine tasting, gourmet cooking. *Address:* (office) 1 King Street, EC2V 8AU. *T:* (020) 3713 1740.

BOOTH, Hartley, OBE 2010; Chairman, Uzbek British Trade and Industry Council, UK Trade & Investment (formerly British Trade International), 1999–2012; *b* 17 July 1946; *s* of late V. W. H. Booth and Eilish (*née* Morrow); *m* 1977, Adrianne Claire Cranefield; two *s* one *d. Educ:* Queen's Coll., Taunton; Bristol Univ. (LLB); Downing Coll., Cambridge (LLM, PhD). Called to the Bar, Inner Temple, 1970 (Scholar); in practice, 1970–84; Special Advr to Prime Minister and Mem., 10 Downing Street Policy Unit, 1984–88; Chief Exec., British Urban Develt, 1988–90; Consultant: Berwin Leighton (Solicitors), 1991–99; Maclay Murray Spens (Solicitors), 2003–06; Pinsent Masons, 2006–08; Dentons (formerly SNR Denton), 2008–. Director: Canford Gp plc, 1978–; Edexcel, 1999–2001. MP (C) Finchley, 1992–97. PPS to Minister of State, FCO, 1992–94, to Minister of State for Educn, 1995–97. Mem. Select Committees: Home Affairs, 1992; European Legislation, 1992; Public Service, 1995–97; Chm., Urban Affairs Select Cttee, 1994–97. Chm., British Uzbek Soc., 2001–. Vice President: Royal Life Saving Soc., 1990–; British Urban Regeneration Assoc., 1991–94 (Chm., 1990–91); AMA, 1992. Pres., Resources for Autism, 2004– (Chm., 1996–2004). European Editor, Current Law Year Books, 1974–84. Dostlik Medal (Uzbekistan), 2011. *Publications:* British Extradition Law and Procedure, vol. I 1979, vol. II 1980; Return Ticket, 1994. *Recreations:* writing, swimming, delving into history, poetry. *Address:* c/o Dentons, One Fleet Place, EC4M 7WS.

BOOTH, Prof. Ian Westerby, MD; FRCP, FRCPCH; Sir Leonard Parsons Professor of Paediatrics and Child Health, University of Birmingham, 1996–2010, now Emeritus; Honorary Consultant Paediatric Gastroenterologist, Birmingham Children's Hospital, since 1985; *b* 15 Aug. 1948; *s* of William Westerby Booth and Audrey Iris (*née* Corless). *Educ:* Sir George Monoux Grammar Sch., London; King's Coll. Hosp. Med. Sch., Univ. of London (BSc Hons Physiol. 1969; MB BS 1972; MSc with Dist. Biochem. 1982; MD 1987). DRCOG 1974; DCH 1975; MRCP 1977, FRCP 1991; Founder FRCPCH 1997. Eden Res. Fellow, RCP, 1980–83; Lectr, Inst. Child Health, London, 1983–85; University of Birmingham: Sen. Lectr in Paediatrics and Child Health, 1985–92; Prof. of Paediatric Gastroenterology and Nutrition, 1992–96; Dir, Inst. of Child Health, 1993–2010; Associate Dean, 2000–06, Dean, 2007–10, Medical Sch.; Dir of Educn, 1998–2002, Mem. Exec. Bd, 1995–2002, Children's Hosp., Birmingham. Department of Health: Vice-Chm., Adv. Cttee on Borderline Substances, 1990–97; Member: Panel on Novel Foods, 1992–98; Wkg Gp on Nutritional Adequacy of Infant Formulas, 1994–96. Member: Med. and Res. Adv. Gp, HEA, 1994–99; Specialised Health Services Commn for Wales Wkg Gp on Tertiary Services for Children, 2000–02; Food Standards Agency Expert Gp on Choking Hazards, 2002–04; Ind. Drug Monitoring Cttee, MRC/Food Standards Agency, 2009–. Pres., British Soc. Paediatric Gastroenterology and Nutrition, 1995–98 (Sec., 1985–89); Royal College of Paediatrics and Child Health: Chairman: Standing Cttee on Nutrition, 1996–2002; Academic Bd, 1998–2003; Wkg Gp on Intestinal Failure, 1998–2002; Mem., Safety and Efficiency Register of New Interventional Procedures, Acad. of Med. Royal Colls, 1996–2001. GMC Visitor for Quality Assuring Basic Med. Educn, 2004–08. Non-exec. Dir, Birmingham Women's Healthcare Foundn Trust Bd, 2005–11 (Vice Chm., 2008–11). Trustee, Sir Arthur Thomson Charitable Trust, Univ. of Birmingham, 2011– (Chm., 2014–). Associate Ed., Archives of Diseases of Childhood, 1993–96; Member, Editorial Board: Gut, 1996–2000; Internat. Jl of Gastroenterology, 1996–2011. *Publications:* (with E. Wozniak) Pocket Picture Guides in Clinical Medicine: Paediatrics, 1984; (with D. A. Kelly) An Atlas of Paediatric Gastroenterology and Hepatology, 1996; contribs to learned jls on paediatric gastroenterology and nutrition. *Recreations:* walking to restaurants, hill-walking in France. *Address:* 17 Custom House Quay, Weymouth, Dorset DT4 8BG. *T:* (01305) 786284. *E:* i.w.booth@bham.ac.uk. *Club:* Athenæum.

BOOTH, Jonothan H.; *see* Hammond Booth, J.

BOOTH, Sir Josslyn Henry Robert G.; *see* Gore-Booth.

BOOTH, Prof. Ken, PhD; FBA 2006; E. H. Carr Professor of International Politics, 1999–2008, Senior Research Associate, Department of International Politics, since 2009, and President, David Davies Memorial Institute of International Studies, since 2013 (Director, 2010–13), Aberystwyth University (formerly University of Wales, Aberystwyth); Editor, International Relations, since 2003; *b* 29 Jan. 1943; *s* of Fred and Phyllis Booth; *m* 1967, Eurwen Jones; two *s. Educ:* King's Sch., Pontefract; University Coll. of Wales, Aberystwyth (BA 1st Cl. Hons; PhD 1982). Lectr, Sen. Lectr, then Reader, 1967–99, Hd of Dept, 1999–2005, Dept of Internat. Politics, UC of Wales, Aberystwyth, then Univ. of Wales, Aberystwyth. Scholar-in-Residence, US Naval War Coll., Newport, RI, 1977; Sen. Res. Fellow, Dalhousie Univ., Canada, 1979–81; Vis. Fellow, Cambridge Univ., 1992–93. Chm., British Internat. Studies Assoc., 1995–96. FAcSS (AcSS 2002). FRSA 2006. Susan Strange Award, Internat. Studies Assoc., 2004. *Publications:* (ed jtly and contrib.) Soviet Naval Policy, 1975; (jtly) Contemporary Strategy: Vol. I: Theories and Concepts, 1975, 2nd edn 1987, Vol. II: The Nuclear Powers, 1987; Navies and Foreign Policy, 1977; (ed jtly and contrib.) American Thinking About Peace and War, 1978; Strategy and Ethnocentrism, 1979; Law, Force and Diplomacy at Sea, 1985; (with J. Baylis) Britain, NATO and Nuclear Weapons, 1989; (ed and contrib.) Strategic Power: USA/USSR, 1990; (ed and contrib.) New Thinking About Strategy and International Security, 1991; (with E. Herring) Strategic Studies: keyguide to information sources, 1994; (ed jtly and contrib.) International Relations Theory Today, 1995; (ed jtly and contrib.) International Theory: positivism and beyond, 1996; (ed and contrib.) Statecraft and Security: the Cold War and beyond, 1998; (ed jtly) The Eighty Years' Crisis, 1998; (ed jtly and contrib.) Strategic Cultures in the Asia-Pacific Region, 1999; (ed jtly) The Interregnum: controversies in world politics 1989–1999, 1999; (ed and contrib.) The Kosovo Tragedy, 2001; (ed jtly) How Might We Live?, 2001; (ed jtly) Great Transformations, 2001; (ed jtly and contrib.) Worlds in Collision, 2002; (ed and contrib.) Critical Security Studies in World Politics, 2005; Theory of World Security, 2007 (jt winner of Foster Watson Prize, 2008); (with N. J. Wheeler) The Security Dilemma, 2008; Realism and World Politics, 2011; (with T. Dunne) Terror in Our Time, 2011; International Relations: all that matters, 2014; contrib. articles to Internat. Affairs, Rev. Internat. Studies, Political Qly, etc. *Recreations:* sport, literature, hill-walking. *Address:* Department of International Politics, Aberystwyth University, Penglais, Aberystwyth SY23 3FE. *T:* (01970) 622694, *Fax:* (01970) 622709. *E:* kob@aber.ac.uk.

BOOTH, Dame Margaret (Myfanwy Wood), DBE 1979; President, Family and Parenting Institute, since 2004 (Chairman, 1999–2004); a Judge of the High Court, Family Division, 1979–94; *b* 11 Sept. 1933; *d* of late Alec Wood Booth and Lilian May Booth; *m* 1st, 1982, Joseph Jackson, QC (*d* 1987); 2nd, 1993, Peter Glucksmann (*d* 2002). *Educ:* Northwood Coll.; University Coll., London (LLM; Fellow, 1982). Called to the Bar, Middle Temple, 1956; Bencher, 1979. QC 1976. Chairman: Family Law Bar Assoc., 1976–78; Matrimonial Causes Procedure Cttee, 1982–85; Inner London Adv. Cttee on Justices of the Peace, 1990–93; Children Act Procedure Adv. Cttee, 1990; Children Act 1989 Adv. Cttee, 1991–93 (report published, 1996); Bar Central Selection Bd, 1993–96; Family Law Cttee, Justice, 1993–98. Pres., Family Mediators Assoc., 1994–95; Chm. Govs, UK Coll. of Family Mediators, 1996–99. Vis. Prof. of Law, Liverpool Univ., 1994–99. Trustee: Rowntree Foundn, 1996–2003; Apex Charitable Trust Ltd, 1996–2003 (Chm., 1997–2003; Pres., 2003–06); Trustee and Chm., Communities That Care (UK), 1997–2003 (Pres., 2003–07). Pres., Alone in London, 1998–; Vice-Pres., Catch 22 (formerly Rainer), 2007–10; Patron, The Place to Be, 1999–; Governor, Northwood Coll., 1975–96; Member, Council: UCL, 1980–84; Liverpool Univ., 1994–99 (Vice-Pres., 1996–99). Hon. LLD Liverpool, 1992; DUniv Open, 2007. *Publications:* (co-ed) Rayden on Divorce, 10th edn 1967, (cons. ed.) 17th edn 1997; (co-ed) Clarke Hall and Morrison on Children, 9th edn 1977, (cons. ed.) 10th edn 1985. *Address:* 15 Wellington House, Eton Road, NW3 4SY. *Club:* Reform.

BOOTH, Sir Michael Addison John W.; *see* Wheeler-Booth.

BOOTH, Michael John; QC 1999; *b* Salford, 24 May 1958; *s* of Eric Charles Booth and Iris Booth (*née* Race); *m* 1987, Sarah Jane Marchington; two *s* one *d. Educ:* Manchester Grammar Sch. (Schol.); Trinity Coll., Cambridge (Open Schol.; MA Hons Law). Pres., Cambridge Union Soc., Michaelmas, 1979. Called to the Bar, Lincoln's Inn, 1981, Bencher, 2008. Mem., Manchester GS's winning team, ESU Nat. Schools Public Speaking Comp., 1975. *Recreations:* walking, swimming, reading, watching football, wine. *Address:* New Square Chambers, 12 New Square, Lincoln's Inn, WC2A 3SW.

BOOTH, Peter John Richard; National Organiser, Manufacturing, 1999–2007, and Textile National Trade Group Secretary, 1986–2007, T&G Section of Unite (formerly Transport and General Workers' Union); *b* 27 March 1949; *s* of Eric Albert and Edith Booth; *m* 1970, Edwina Ivy; three *s. Educ:* Little London Infant Sch.; Rawdon Littlemore Junior Sch., Rawdon; Benton Park Secondary Modern School. Dyers' Operative, 1964; National Union of Dyers, Bleachers and Textile Workers: District Officer, 1973; Nat. Research Officer, 1975; Nat. Organiser, 1980; transf. to TGWU, 1982; Nat. Trade Group Organiser, 1982. Member: Yorks and Humberside Regl Innovation Strategy, 1998–2000; Manufg Forum, DTI, 2005–; Manufg Task Gp, TUC, 2005–; Exec., Gen. Fedn of Trade Unions. Director: Man-Made Fibres Industry Trng Adv. Bd, 1986–98; Apparel, Knitting & Textiles Alliance, 1989–96; Nat. Textile Trading Orgn, 1998–2000; Skill-Fast UK, 2002–; Member: Internat. Textile, Garment and Leather Workers Fedn, 1986–2008 (Pres., 1996–2004); Confedn of British Wool Textiles Trng Bd, 1986–98; Carpet Industry Trng Council, 1986–95 (Chm.); Nat. Textile Trng Gp, 1989–2000 (Vice Pres.); Textile, Clothing and Strategy Gp; Presidium, European TU Cttee, 1990–2007; Textiles Industry Adv. Cttee, 1994–2007; Cotton & Allied Textiles Industry Adv. Cttee, 1986–94; Chairman: Wool Textile and Clothing Industry Action Cttee, 1996–98; Cotton Industry War Meml Trust, 2010– (Sec., 2014–). FRSA; CCMI 2006–10. *Publications:* The Old Dog Strike, 1985. *Recreations:* walking, gardening, dominoes, chess. *Address:* Unite (T&G Section), Unite House, 128 Theobalds Road, Holborn, WC1X 8TN.

BOOTH, Richard George William Pitt, MBE 2004; bookseller, since 1961; Chairman, Welsh Booksellers Association, since 1987; *b* 12 Sept. 1938; *m* 1987, Hope Estcourt Stuart (*née* Barrie). *Educ:* Rugby; Univ. of Oxford. Founding father of following towns as centres of bookselling: Hay-on-Wye, 1961; Redu, 1984; Becherel, 1988; Montolieu, 1989; Bredevoort, 1992; Fjaerland, 1996; Kam Pung Buku, 2006. Life Pres., Internat. Orgn of Book Towns (formerly Internat. Book Town Movement), 2000. *Publications:* Country Life Book of Book Collecting, 1976; Independence for Hay, 1977. *Recreations:* creating a monarchy in Hay because democracy has vanished and the divine right of kings is an effective opposition to the divine right of the officials, gardening. *Address:* Brynmelin, Cusop, Hay-on-Wye, via Hereford HR3 5RQ.

BOOTH, Richard John; QC 2013; a Recorder, since 2008; *b* Newport, Mon, 30 May 1969; *s* of Lyndon Parry Booth and Judith Eleanor Booth (*née* Blandford); *m* 1995, Jo Cooper; one *s* one *d. Educ:* Monmouth Sch.; Michaelhouse, Kwazulu Natal; Fitzwilliam Coll., Cambridge (BA 1991); Univ. Libre de Bruxelles (Lic.Spec.Dr.Eur.). Called to the Bar, Middle Temple, 1993; in practice as barrister, specialising in medical law, professional discipline and sports law, 1993–; Jun. Counsel to the Crown, Attorney Gen.'s Regl Panel, 2000–12. *Recreations:* sport (especially Rugby), live music. *Address:* 1 Crown Office Row, Temple, EC4Y 7HH. *T:* (020) 7797 7500, *Fax:* (020) 7797 7550. *E:* richard.booth@1cor.com. *Clubs:* East India; Monmouth Rugby Football; Old Monmothian (Pres., 2011–13).

BOOTH, Roger Hignett; Royal Academy of Engineering Visiting Professor, Department of Engineering Science, University of Oxford, 1998–2006; *b* 3 May 1940; *s* of David and Elsie Booth; *m* 1st, 1968, Maureen (*née* Howell) (marr. diss. 1996); two *s*; 2nd, 1997, Thelly (*née* Price). *Educ:* Bentham Grammar Sch.; Birmingham Univ. (BSc Chem. Engrg). MIChemE 1966; CEng 1973. Royal Dutch/Shell Gp (posts in UK, Indonesia, USA, Netherlands, Pakistan), 1961–96; Dir, Solar Century Hldgs Ltd, 1999–2003. Mem., Newnham Parish Council, 2004–12. *Publications:* articles on renewable energy and sustainable develt. *Recreations:* golf, walking, dining with friends, listening to music. *Address:* Firtree Cottage, Newnham Road, Newnham, Hook RG27 9AE. *T:* (01256) 762456.

BOOTH, Sarah Ann; *see* Hinkley, S. A.

BOOTH, Vernon Edward Hartley; *see* Booth, H.

BOOTHBY, Sir Brooke (Charles), 16th Bt *cr* 1660, of Broadlow Ash, Derbyshire; Vice Lord-Lieutenant, South Glamorgan, since 2011; Chairman: Adventure Activities Licensing Service, since 2007; Adventure Activities Licensing Authority, 1996–2007; *b* 6 April 1949; *s* of Sir Hugo Robert Brooke Boothby, 15th Bt and (Evelyn) Ann (*d* 1993), *d* of late H. C. R. Homfray; *S* father, 1986; *m* 1976, Georgiana Alexandra, *o d* of late Sir John Wriothesley Russell, GCVO, CMG; two *d. Educ:* Eton; Trinity Coll., Cambridge (BA Econs). Chm., Associated Quality Services, 1994–2008; Man. Dir, 1979–95, Vice Chm., 1995–2003, Chm., 2004–, Fontygary Parks Ltd (formerly Fontygary Leisure); Dir, Bradford Rural Estates Ltd, 2001–. Chm., Capital Region Tourism, 2002–03; Dir, Wales Tourism Alliance, 2002–09. Chairman: Nat. Caravan Council Parks Div., 1987–90; Historic Houses Assoc. for Wales, 2009–13. President: Glamorgan Br., CLA, 1992–94; Vale of Glamorgan Nat. Trust, 1998–. Hon. Treas., Consular Assoc. in Wales, 2010–12. Hon. Consul for the Republic of Malta in Wales, 2007–. High Sheriff, 1986–87, DL, 2007, South Glamorgan. Gov., United World Coll. of the Atlantic, 2003–06. *Recreation:* gardening. *Heir: kinsman* George William Boothby [*b* 18 June 1948; *m* 1977, Sally Louisa Thomas; three *d*]. *Address:* Church House, Penllyn, Cowbridge, Vale of Glamorgan CF71 7RQ. *T:* (01446) 775666. *E:* sirbrookeboothby@hotmail.com.

BOOTHMAN, His Honour Campbell Lester; a Circuit Judge, 1988–2003; *b* 3 Sept. 1942; *s* of Gerald and Ann Boothman; *m* 1966, Penelope Evelyn Pepe; three *s. Educ:* Oundle; King's College, London. Called to the Bar, Inner Temple, 1965. A Recorder, 1985–88. *Recreations:* ski-ing, squash. *Address:* 13 The Keg Store, Bath Street, Bristol BS1 6HL.

BOOTHMAN, Nicholas, CEng; Director of Technology, Metropolitan Police Service, 1992–2000; *b* 16 Dec. 1941; *s* of late Frederick Boothman and Sarah Ellen (*née* Kirk); *m* 1964, Ernestine Carole Jane Billings; one *d*. *Educ:* Threshfield Sch.; Ermysted's Grammar Sch., Skipton; Univ. of Birmingham (BSc Physics). CEng, MIET (MIEE 1972). Research at GEC Hirst Res. Centre, Wembley, 1963–72; project management of communication systems for RAF, MoD (PE), 1972–77; Project Manager, Metropolitan Police Office, 1977–88; Chief Engr, Metropolitan Police, 1988–92. *Recreations:* amateur musician, watching cricket, railways, unavoidable gardening. *Address:* 57A Wensleydale Road, Hampton, Middx TW12 2LP.

BOOTHROYD, Baroness *cr* 2000 (Life Peer), of Sandwell in the co. of West Midlands; **Betty Boothroyd,** OM 2005; PC 1992; Speaker of the House of Commons, 1992–2000; *b* Yorkshire, 8 Oct. 1929; *d* of Archibald and Mary Boothroyd. *Educ:* Dewsbury Coll. of Commerce and Art. Personal/Political Asst to Labour Ministers. Delegate to N Atlantic Assembly, 1974. MP (Lab) West Bromwich, May 1973–1974, West Bromwich West, 1974–92 (when elected Speaker); MP West Bromwich West, 1992–2000. An Asst Govt Whip, Oct. 1974–Nov. 1975; Dep. Chm. of Ways and Means, and Dep. Speaker, 1987–92. Member: Select Cttee on Foreign Affairs, 1979–81; Speaker's Panel of Chairmen, 1979–87; House of Commons Commn, 1983–87. Mem., European Parlt, 1975–77. Mem., Labour Party NEC, 1981–87. Contested (Lab): SE Leicester (by-elec.), 1957; Peterborough (gen. elec.), 1959; Nelson and Colne (by-elec.), 1968; Rossendale (gen. elec.), 1970. Chancellor, Open Univ., 1994–2007. Hon. Bencher, Middle Temple, 2011. Hon. FCOptom 2005. Freeman: Borough of Sandwell, 1992; Borough of Kirklees, 1992; City of London, 1993; Hon. Freeman: Lightmongers' Co., 2003; Grocers' Co., 2005; Hon. Liveryman: Feltmakers' Co., 1993; Glovers' Co., 1997. Hon. LLD: Birmingham, 1992; South Bank, 1992; Leicester, 1993; Cambridge, 1994; St Andrews, 2001; Hon. DLitt Bradford, 1993; DUniv: Leeds Metropolitan, 1993; North London, 1993; Hon. DCL Oxford, 1995. *Publications:* Betty Boothroyd: the autobiography, 2001. *Address:* House of Lords, SW1A 0PW.

BOOTLE, Roger Paul; Managing Director, since 1999, and Executive Chairman, since 2014, Capital Economics Ltd; *b* 22 June 1952; *s* of David Bootle and Florence (*née* Denman); *m* 1st, 1993, Sally Broomfield (marr. diss. 2007); one *s* two *d*; 2nd, 2011, Alya Samokhvalova. *Educ:* Merton Coll., Oxford (BA PPE 1973); Nuffield Coll., Oxford (BPhil Econs 1975). Chief Economist: Capel-Cure Myers, 1982–86; Lloyds Merchant Bank, 1986–89; Greenwell Montagu, 1989–92; HSBC Markets, 1992–96; Gp Chief Economist, HSBC, 1996–98. Vis. Prof., Manchester Business Sch., 1995–2003. Mem., Chancellor of the Exchequer's Panel of Ind. Econ. Advrs, 1997; Specialist Advr, H of C Treasury Cttee, 1998–. Econ. Advr, Deloitte, 1999–2011. Columnist: The Times, 1997–99; Sunday Telegraph, 1999–2006; Daily Telegraph, 2006–. Wolfson Prize for Econs, 2012. *Publications:* (with W. T. Newlyn) Theory of Money, 1978; Index-Linked Gilts, 1985; The Death of Inflation, 1996; Money for Nothing, 2003; The Trouble with Markets, 2009; The Trouble with Europe, 2014. *Recreations:* squash, horse-racing, classical music, bridge. *Address:* 150 Buckingham Palace Road, SW1W 9TR. *T:* (020) 7823 5000.

BOOTLE-WILBRAHAM, family name of **Baron Skelmersdale**.

BOPA RAI, Aprampar Apar Jot Kaur, (Joti), (Mrs W. F. Casey); a District Judge (Magistrates' Courts), since 2004; *b* 18 Feb. 1957; *d* of Manjit Singh Bopa Rai and Swaran Kaur Bopa Rai; *m* 1993, William Francis Casey. *Educ:* Wolverhampton Polytech. (LLB (Law) 1980); Coll. of Law, Guildford. Admitted solicitor, 1984; Asst Solicitor, Partner, Elgoods, Cheltenham, 1984–89; Partner, Tarlings, Cheltenham, 1989–93; sole practitioner, 1993–2004; Dep. Dist Judge, 2000–04. *Recreations:* walking, ski-ing, reading, visiting historic sites.

BORBIDGE, Hon. Robert Edward, AO 2006; Chairman: Rotec Design Ltd, since 2003; Cedar Creek Cellars, since 2007; ATM, since 2012; CareFlight Group (Qld), since 2013; Trinity Health Services, since 2013; Senior Counsel, Govstrat, since 2011; consultant; *b* Ararat, Vic, 12 Aug. 1954; *s* of Edward A. Borbidge and Jean, (Jane), Borbidge; *m* 1984, Jennifer Gooding; one *s* one *d*. *Educ:* Ararat High Sch., Vic; Overberg High Sch., S Africa. Mem. Bd, Gold Coast Visitors' Bureau, 1980. MLA (Nat.) Surfers Paradise, Qld, 1980–2001; formerly Mem., Qld Parly Delegn, Qld Govt Cttees on Transport, Tourism, Nat. Parks, Sport and Arts, Ind. and Commerce, Local Govt, Main Roads and Police; Minister: for Industry, Small Business, Communications and Technol., 1987–89; for Ind., Small Business, Technol. and Tourism, then for Police, Emergency Services and Corrective Services, and subseq. for Tourism and for Envmt, Conservation and Forestry, 1989; Opposition spokesman on Small Business, Manufg and Regl Develt and Assisting Leader on Econ. and Trade Develt, 1990–91; Dep. Leader of Opposition, 1989–91, Leader, 1991–95 and 1998–2001; Premier of Qld and Minister responsible for Ethnic Affairs, 1996–98; Leader, Qld Nat. Party-Lib. Party Coalition, 1992–2001. Chair, Study Gold Coast, 2013–. Chairman: Asset Loan Co., 2004; CEC Gp, 2004–08; Early Learning Services, 2007–08. Chairman: Australian Sports Coll.; Australian Acad. of Sport Ltd. Griffith University: Chm., Bd of Advice (formerly Exec. Task Force), Inst. for Glycomics, 2003–; Member: Univ. Council, 2006–; Univ. Foundn, 2006–; Trustee, Friends of Griffith Univ., USA, 2004–. DUniv Griffith, 2004. Centenary Medal (Australia), 2001. *Recreations:* travel, reading, tourism, swimming. *Address:* 294 Ron Penhaligon Way, Robina, Qld 4226, Australia.

BORCHERDS, Prof. Richard Ewen, FRS 1994; Professor of Mathematics, University of California at Berkeley, 1993–96 and since 1999; *b* 29 Nov. 1959; *s* of Dr Peter Howard Borcherds and Margaret Elizabeth Borcherds; *m* Ursula Gritsch. *Educ:* Trinity Coll., Cambridge (BA, MA; PhD 1985). Research Fellow, Trinity Coll., Cambridge, 1983–87; Morrey Asst Prof., Univ. of California, Berkeley, 1987–88; Cambridge University: Royal Soc. Univ. Res. Fellow, 1988–92; Lectr, 1992–93; Royal Soc. Prof., Dept of Maths, 1996–99. Fields Medal, Internat. Mathematical Union, 1998. *Publications:* papers in math. jls. *Address:* Department of Mathematics, University of California, 927 Evans Hall # 3840, Berkeley, CA 94720–3840, USA.

BORDEN, Prof. Iain Michael, PhD; Professor of Architecture and Urban Culture, Bartlett School of Architecture, since 2002, and Vice-Dean for Communications, Bartlett Faculty of the Built Environment, since 2010, University College London; *b* 9 Nov. 1962; *s* of Anthony Ian Borden and Shelagh Mary Borden; *m* 2001, Claire Haywood; one *s*. *Educ:* Univ. of Newcastle upon Tyne (BA Hist. of Art, Arch. and Ancient Hist. 1985); Bartlett Sch., University Coll. London (MSc Hist. of Modern Arch. 1986); Univ. of Calif, LA (MA Hist. of Arch. and Planning 1989); PhD London 1998. Bartlett School of Architecture, University College London: Lectr, 1989–97, Sen. Lectr, 1997–99, in Architectural Hist.; Reader in Arch. and Urban Culture, 1999–2002; Dir, 2001–05; Head, 2005–09; Sub-Dean and Vice-Dean, Faculty of Built Envmt, UCL, 1996–2001. Hon. FRIBA 2003. *Publications:* (ed with D. Dunster) Architecture and the Sites of History: interpretations of buildings and cities, 1995; (ed jtly) Strangely Familiar: narratives of architecture in the city, 1996; (ed jtly) Gender Space Architecture: an interdisciplinary introduction, 1999; (ed jtly) The City Cultures Reader, 2000, 2nd edn 2003; (ed with J. Rendell) InterSections: architectural histories and critical theories, 2000; (with K. Rüedi) The Dissertation: an architecture student's handbook, 2000, 3rd edn as The Dissertation: a guide for architecture students, 2014; (ed jtly) The Unknown City: contesting architecture and social space, 2001; Skateboarding, Space and the City: architecture and the body, 2001; Manual: the architecture and office of Alford Hall Monaghan Morris, 2003; (ed jtly) Bartlett Works, 2004; (ed jtly) Transculturation: cities, spaces and architectures in Latin America, 2005; (ed jtly) Bartlett Designs: speculating with architecture, 2009; Drive: journeys through film, cities and landscapes, 2012; (ed jtly) Forty Ways To Thin About Architecture, 2014. *Recreations:* driving, photography, skateboarding, wanderin around cities. *Address:* Bartlett School of Architecture, University College London, 14 Hampstead Road, NW1 2BX. *T:* (020) 3108 9646. *E:* i.borden@ucl.ac.uk.

BORDER, Allan Robert, AO 1989 (AM 1986); journalist and sports commentator; Directo Queensland Cricket, since 2001 (Life Member, since 2010); Cricket Australia, 2002–09; *b* 2 July 1955; *s* of John and Sheila Border; *m* 1980, Jane, *d* of John and Eve Hiscox; two *s* two *d*. *Educ:* N Sydney Tech. Sch.; N Sydney High Sch. First class cricket début, for NSW, 1976 professional cricketer, Queensland State, 1977–96 (Captain, 1983–84); Test début, 1978 Captain, Australian cricket team, 1984–94; played 156 Test matches for Australia, with recor of 93 as Captain, scored 27 centuries and 2 double centuries, record total of 11,174 Test runs also took 39 wickets and record 156 catches; in all first-class cricket matches to 1994, ha scored 25,551 runs incl. 68 centuries, and taken 102 wickets and 345 catches. Mem., Nat Cricket Selection Panel, Aust., 1998–2005 and 2006. With Ronald McConnell Hldgs 1980–84; with Castlemaine Perkins, 1984–98. Columnist, Courier Mail; commentator, Fo Sports TV. *Publications:* Beyond Ten Thousand: my life story, 1994; Cricket As I See It, 2014 *Address:* c/o Cricket Australia, 60 Jolimont Street, Jolimont, Vic 3002, Australia.

BORE, Sir Albert, Kt 2002; Member (Lab), since 1980, and Leader, 1999–2004 and sinc 2012, Birmingham City Council; Chairman, University Hospital Birmingham NHS Foundation Trust, 2006–13. Former Lectr in Physics, Aston Univ. Chairman: Birminghar Econ. Develt Cttee, 1984–93; Member: Bd, Advantage West Midlands, 1999–2002 Birmingham Marketing Partnership. Director: Aston Sci. Park; Nat. Exhibition Centre Ltd Birmingham Technol. Ltd; NEC Finance plc; Optima Community Assoc.; non-exec. Dir Colliers CRE, 2005–. Pres., EU Cttee of the Regions, 2002–04 (Mem., 1994–). *Address:* c/o Birmingham City Council, Council House, Victoria Square, Birmingham B1 1BB.

BOREEL, Sir Stephan Gerard, 14th Bt *cr* 1645, of Amsterdam; *b* 9 Feb. 1945; *s* of Gerar Lucas Boreel and Virginia Rae Bright; *S* kinsman, Sir Francis Boreel, 13th Bt, 2001, but hi name does not appear on the Official Roll of the Baronetage; *m* 1972, Francien P. Kooijman one *s*. *Heir:* *s* Jacob Lucas Cornelis Boreel, *b* 29 Sept. 1974.

BORELAND-KELLY, Dame Lorna (May), DBE 1998; JP; Chief Executive Officer Bokell Associates, since 2013; Strategic Advisor, Management and Social Work Development Social Work Academy, Medway Councils, since 2013; *b* 9 Aug. 1952; *d* of James Borelan and late Hortence Boreland Swaby (*née* Boyd); *m* Anthony Owen Kelly; three *s* three *d*. *Educ* North London Univ. (CQSW 1991). Sen. Practitioner, Social Work Children and Families St Thomas' Hosp., 1997–2000; Team Manager, 2001–01, Hospital Manager, Children an Families, 2001–07, Mayday Hosp., Croydon; Mayday and Permanence Manager, Dept o Children, Young People and Learners, Mayday NHS Trust, Croydon, 2008–09; Strategi Advr, Social Work Acad., Children, Young People and Learners, Croydon Council 2010–13. Chair, Professional Capabilities Framework Quality Assurance Gp, Coll. of Socia Work, 2013– (Mem., Professional (formerly Transitional Professional) Assembly, 2012–13) Mem., Judicial Appts Commn, 2006–12. Chair of Govs, Lambeth Coll., 1992–2013. Mem. Editl Bd, Community Care Inform, 2010–. Mem., Coll. of Social Work, 2011. Mem., Union of Catholic Mothers. FRSA 2000. JP S Westminster, 1991. *Recreations:* reading, writing shor stories (never to be published), walking, boxing, swimming. *Address:* c/o Bokell Associate Ltd, 34 Upper Close, Forest Row RH18 5DX.

BORG, Alan Charles Nelson, CBE 1991; PhD; FSA; Director, Victoria and Albert Museum 1995–2001; *b* 21 Jan. 1942; *s* of late Charles John Nelson Borg and Frances Mary Olive Hughes; *m* 1st, 1964, Anne (marr. diss.), *d* of late Dr William Blackmore; one *s* one *d*; 2nd 1976, Lady Caroline, *d* of late Captain Lord Francis Hill, *yr s* of 6th Marquess of Downshire two *d*. *Educ:* Westminster Sch.; Brasenose Coll., Oxford (MA); Courtauld Inst. of Art (PhD) Lecteur d'anglais, Université d'Aix-Marseille, 1964–65; Lectr, History of Art, Indiana Univ. 1967–69; Asst Prof. of History of Art, Princeton Univ., 1969–70; Asst Keeper of the Roya Armouries, HM Tower of London, 1970–78; Keeper, Sainsbury Centre for Visual Arts, Univ of E Anglia, 1978–82; Dir Gen., Imperial War Mus., 1982–95. Vis. Prof., Univ. of Reading 2010–. Member: British Nat. Cttee for Hist. of Second World War, 1982–95; Bd of Wa Studies, KCL, 1982–95; COPUS, 1992–95; Council, Museums Assoc., 1992–95; Adv. Cttee on Public Records, 1993–99; Court of Advisers, St Paul's Cathedral, 1996–2000; Bd of Mgt Courtauld Inst. of Art, 1998–2002; Chm., Nat. Inventory of War Memls, 1988–95; Admin Council, Louvre Mus., 1999–2001. Chm., Nat. Mus. Dirs' Conf., 1998–2000. President Elizabethan Club, 1994–2000; Meyrick Soc., 1994–. Trustee: Foundling Museum 1998–2010 (Chm. Trustees, 2006–09; Vice Pres., 2010–); Handel House, 2002–06; St Paul's Cathedral Foundn, 2002–05; Topolski Memoir, 2007–10. Governor: Thomas Coram Foundn for Children, 1995–2005; Westminster Sch., 1998–. Freeman, City of London, 1997 Hon. Liveryman, Painter Stainers' Co., 1997; Hon. Freeman, Cooks' Co., 2011. Librarian and Trustee, Priory of England and the Islands, Order of St John, 2007–. KStJ 2012 (OStJ 2007). Hon. FRCA 1991; Hon. FRIBA 2001. DUniv Sheffield Hallam, 2000. *Publications* Architectural Sculpture in Romanesque Provence, 1972; European Swords and Daggers in the Tower of London, 1974; Torture and Punishment, 1975; Heads and Horses, 1976; Arms and Armour in Britain, 1979; (ed with A. R. Martindale) The Vanishing Past: studies presented to Christopher Hohler, 1981; War Memorials, 1991; The History of the Worshipfu Company of Painter-Stainers, 2005; A History of the Worshipful Company of Cooks, 2011 (with D. Coke) Vauxhall Gardens, 2011; articles in learned jls. *Recreations:* fencing (Oxford blue, 1962, 1963), music, travel. *Address:* Telegraph House, 36 West Square, SE11 4SP. *Clubs* Beefsteak, Special Forces.

BORG, Björn Rune; professional tennis player, 1972–83 and 1991–93, now playing on ATP Champions Tour; *b* 6 June 1956; *s* of late Rune Borg and of Margaretha Borg; *m* 1st, 1980, Mariana Simionescu (marr. diss. 1984); one *s* by Jannike Björling; 2nd, 1989, Loredana Berte (marr. diss. 1992); 3rd, 2002, Patricia Östfeldt; one *s*. *Educ:* Blombacka Sch., Södertälje. Started to play tennis at age of 9; won Wimbledon junior title, 1972; became professional player in 1972. Mem., Swedish Davis Cup team, annually 1972–80 (youngest player ever in a winning Davis Cup team, 1975). Championship titles: Italian, 1974, 1978; French, 1974, 1975, 1978, 1979, 1980, 1981; Wimbledon, record of 5 consecutive singles titles, 1976–80; World Champion, 1978, 1979, 1980; Masters, 1980, 1981. Owner, fashion label, Björn Borg. *Publications:* (with Eugene Scott) Björn Borg: my life and game, 1980. *Address:* c/o IMG, McCormack House, Hogarth Business Park, Chiswick, W4 2TH.

BORG, Joseph, LLD; Senior Lecturer, 1988–2004, and since 2010, and Chairman Mediterranean Academy of Diplomatic Studies, since 2010, University of Malta; *b* 19 March 1952; *m* Isabelle Agius; one *s* one *d*. *Educ:* Univ. of Malta (NP 1974; LLD 1975); University Coll. of Wales, Aberystwyth (LLM 1988). Legal advr to cos and corporate bodies, Malta and abroad, 1976–98; Lectr in Law, Univ. of Malta, 1979–88. Dir, Central Bank of Malta, 1992–95. MP (Nationalist), Malta, 1995–2004; Parly Sec., Min. of Foreign Affairs, 1998–99; Minister of Foreign Affairs, 1999–2004; Mem., EC, 2004–10. Consultant, Fipra, 2010–13. Non-exec. Dir, AgriBank plc, 2012– (Chm., 2013–).

BORINGDON, Viscount; Mark Lionel Parker; *b* 22 Aug. 1956; *s* and *heir* of 6th Earl of Morley, *qv*; *m* 1983, Carolyn Jill, *d* of Donald McVicar, Meols, Wirral, Cheshire; three *d*. *Educ:* Eton. Commissioned, Royal Green Jackets, 1976. *Address:* Pound House, Yelverton, Devon PL20 7LJ.

BÖRJESSON, Rolf Libert; Chairman: Rexam PLC, 2004–08 (Chief Executive, 1996–2004); Ahlsell AB, 2006–12; *b* 27 Sept. 1942; *s* of Stig Allan Börjesson and Brita Ahlström; *m* 1969, Kristina Ivarsson; two *d. Educ:* Chalmers Univ., Gothenburg (MSc Chem. Engrg). With Steenberg & Flygt, 1968–71; ITT Europe, Brussels, 1971–74; President: Sund Akesson/Sundpacma, 1974–77; AB Securitas Industrier, 1977–81; Wayne Europe, 1981–87; PLM AB: Exec. Vice Pres., 1987–88; Chief Operating Officer, 1988–90; Pres. and CEO, 1990–96. Chm., Biolight AB, 2011–; non-executive Director: SCA AB, 2003–; Avery Dennison, 2005–; Huhtamaki Gp, 2008–. *Recreations:* shooting, ski-ing, riding.

BORLAND, Polly; photographic artist; *b* E Melbourne, Australia; *d* of Kevin William Borland and Margaret Agnes Aitken; *m* 1989, John Anthony Hillcoat; one *s. Educ:* Primary Sch., Preshil; Mitcham High Sch., Tenaden; Royal Melbourne Inst. of Technol. (Dip. Photography with Hons). Self-employed photographic portraiturist and editorial photographic-based artist. Hon. FRPS 2002. *Publications:* (jtly) Australians, 2000; The Babies, 2001; (jtly) Polly Borland: Everything I Want to Be When I Grow Up, 2012. *Address:* 7523 Mulholland Drive, Los Angeles, CA 90046, USA. *T:* (323) 3887657. *E:* pollyborland@hotmail.com. *Club:* Blacks.

BORLEY, Lester, CBE 1993; Secretary General, 1993–96, Member Council, since 1990, Europa Nostra, The Hague; Chairman, Europa Nostra UK, since 2009; *b* 7 April 1931; *er s* of Edwin Richard Borley and Mary Dorena Davies; *m* Mary Alison, *e d* of Edward John Pearce and Kathleen Florence Barratt; three *d. Educ:* Dover Grammar Sch.; Queen Mary Coll. and Birkbeck Coll., London Univ. Pres. of Union, QMC, 1953; Dep. Pres., Univ. of London Union, 1954; ESU debating team tour of USA, 1955. Joined British Travel Assoc., 1955; Asst to Gen. Manager, USA, 1957–61; Manager: Chicago Office, 1961–64; Australia, 1964–67; West Germany, 1967–69; Chief Executive: Scottish Tourist Bd, 1970–75; English Tourist Bd, 1975–83; Dir, Nat. Trust for Scotland, 1983–93 (Mem. Council, 2002–07). Member: Exec. Cttee, Scotland's Garden Scheme, 1970–75, 1983–93; Council, Nat. Gardens Scheme, 1975–83; Park and Gardens Cttee, Zool Soc. of London, 1979–83; Internat. Cultural Tourism Cttee, ICOMOS, 1990–; Chm., Cultural Tourism Cttee, ICOMOS (UK), 1993–2003. Adviser: World Monuments Fund, NY, 1995–; UNESCO World Heritage Centre, Paris, 2002–; Mem., Scotland Cttee, Nat. Commn, UNESCO UK, 2008–. Governor, Edinburgh Film House, 1987–96 (Hon. Vice Pres., 1996–2007); Trustee: Cromarty Arts Trust, 1995–2006; Hopetoun House Preservation Trust, 1998–2002. Visiting Lecturer: Acad. Istropolitana Nova, Bratislava, 1993–; Coll. of New Europe, Krakow, 1998–; Faculty Mem., Salzburg Seminar, 1996. Organiser of and speaker at many internat. confs on conservation and cultural heritage. Founder Fellow, Tourism Soc., 1978. FRSA 1982. Hon. FRSGS 1989. DLitt *hc* Robert Gordon Inst. of Technology, Aberdeen, 1991. Honorable Kentucky Col, 1963. *Publications:* English Cathedrals and Tourism, 1979; Historic Cities and Sustainable Tourism, 1995; Sustaining the Cultural Heritage of Europe, 1998; (ed) Dear Maurice: Culture and Identity in late 20th Century Scotland, 1998; (ed) To be a Pilgrim: meeting the needs of visitors to cathedrals and great churches in the UK, 2001; (ed) Hugh Miller in Context, 2002; (ed) Celebrating The Life and Times of Hugh Miller: Scotland in the early 19th century, 2003; (ed) The Grand Tour and its Influence on Architecture, Artistic Taste and Patronage, 2008; contributor to: Patronage of the Arts by Foundations and NGOs in Europe, 1991; Universal Tourism, 1992; Cultural Tourism, 1994; Manual of Heritage Management, 1994; Tourism and Culture, 1996; Il Paesaggio Culturale nelle strategia europea, 1996; Preserving the Built Heritage, 1997. *Recreations:* reading, listening to music, visiting exhibitions, collecting glass and ceramics, gardening. *Address:* 4 Belford Place, Edinburgh EH4 3DH. *Club:* New (Edinburgh).

BORN, Gary Brian; Partner, Wilmer Cutler Pickering Hale and Dorr (formerly Wilmer Cutler & Pickering) LLP, since 1988; *b* New York, 14 Sept. 1955; *s* of Clyde Raymond and Eleanor Born; *m* 1986, Beatrix von Wedel; one *s* one *d. Educ:* Haverford Coll., Pennsylvania (BA *summa cum laude* 1978); Univ. of Pennsylvania Law Sch. (JD *summa cum laude* 1981). Rapporteur, Cttee on Extraterritorial Application of Nat Laws, ICC, 1985–90; Associate Prof. of Law, Univ. of Arizona Coll. of Law, 1987–88; Adjunct Prof. of Law, Georgetown Law Sch., 1987–91; Lectr, Stanford Law Sch., 2007–09; Adjunct Prof., Sch. of Transnat. Law, Peking Univ., 2010; Vis. Prof. of Law and Kwa Geok Choo Dist. Visitor, Nat. Univ. of Singapore, 2011; Lectr, Harvard Law Sch., 2011–12; Hon. Prof. of Law, Univ. of St Gallen, Switzerland, 2012–; Bok Internat. Law Prof., Univ. of Pennsylvania Law Sch., 2013–14; Vis. Prof. of Law, Tsinghua Univ. Sch. of Law, 2014–. Member: Singapore Internat. Arbitration Centre Court of Arbitration, 2013–; Court of Arbitration, Jerusalem Arbitration Center, 2014–. Co-Chair, Cttee on Internat. Aspects of Litigation, Internat. Section, ABA, 1989–92. Member: Bd, Inst. for US Studies, 1996–2001; Amer. Law Inst., 1999–; Acad. Council, Inst. for Transnat. Arbitration, 2009–. Member: Exec. Council, Amer. Soc. of Internat. Law, 1991–94 (Exec. Vice-Pres., 2014–); Adv. Cttee, Amer. Law Inst. Project on Internat. Commercial Arbitration Law of US, 2009–; Adv. Bd, Africa Internat. Legal Awareness, 2011–; Adv. Cttee, Amer. Law Inst. Restatement (Fourth) Foreign Relations Law of US, 2013–; Internat. Arbitration Cttee, Korean Commercial Arbitration Bd, 2014–; Internat. Adv. Bd, Hong Kong Internat. Arbitration Centre, 2014–; Global Adv. Bd, NY Internat. Arbitration Center, 2014–. Chm., Bd of Trustees, Haverford Coll. Foundn (UK) Ltd, 2012–; Mem., Bd of Trustees, British Inst. of Internat. and Comparative Law, 2010–. Hon. LLD Wayne State, 2012. Member: Adv. Bd, Indian Jl of Arbitration Law, 2012–; Editl Adv. Bd, Jl of World Investment and Trade, 2013–. *Publications:* (jtly) The Extraterritorial Application of National Laws, 1987; International Civil Litigation in United States Courts, 1990, 5th edn 2011; International Commercial Arbitration: commentary and materials, 1996, 2nd edn 2000; International Arbitration and Forum Selection Agreements: drafting and enforcing, 1999, 3rd edn 2010; International Commercial Arbitration, 2009, 2nd edn 2014; International Arbitration: cases and materials, 2011, 2nd edn 2014; International Arbitration: law and practice, 2012. *Recreation:* my children. *Address:* Wilmer Cutler Pickering Hale and Dorr LLP, 49 Park Lane, W1K 1PS. *T:* (020) 7872 1000, *Fax:* (020) 7872 1699. *E:* gary.born@wilmerhale.com.

BORN, Prof. Georgina Emma Mary, PhD; FBA 2014; FRAI; Professor of Music and Anthropology, and Senior Research Fellow, University of Oxford, since 2010; Fellow, Mansfield College, Oxford, since 2012; *b* Wheatley, Oxon, 15 Nov. 1955; *d* of Prof. Gustav Victor Rudolf Born, *qv* and Dr Wilfrida Ann Born (later Mully); partner, Prof. Andrew M. Barry; one *s* one *d. Educ:* Godolphin and Latymer Sch.; Purcell Sch., London; Dartington Hall Sch., Devon; Royal Coll. of Music (Jun. Exhibnr); Chelsea Sch. of Art; University Coll. London (BSc 1st Cl. Hons Anthropol. 1982; PhD Anthropol. 1989). Cellist and bass guitarist, Henry Cow, Mike Westbrook's Orch., Derek Bailey's Co., 1976–89; Lecturer: Dept of Human Scis, Brunel Univ., 1986–89; Dept of Media and Communications, Goldsmiths' Coll., Univ. of London, 1989–97; Sen. Res. Fellow, King's Coll., Cambridge, 1997–98; Fellow and Dir of Studies in Social and Pol Scis, Emmanuel Coll., Cambridge, 1998–2006; University of Cambridge: Lectr in Social and Pol Scis, 1998–2003; Reader, 2003–06; Prof. of Sociol., Anthropol. and Music, 2006–10; Fellow, Girton Coll., Cambridge, 2008–10. Vis. Prof., Inst. of Musicol., Aarhus Univ., 1996–97; Hon. Prof., Dept of Anthropol., UCL, 2006–11; Schulich Dist. Vis. Prof. and Dean's Chair in Music, McGill Univ., 2013–15; Bloch Dist. Vis. Prof. in Music, Univ. of Calif, Berkeley, 2014; Vis. Prof., Dept of Musicol., Univ. of Oslo, 2014–; Fellow, Humanities Res. Inst., Univ. of Calif, 2002–03; Vis. Fellow, Centre for Critical and Cultural Studies, Univ. of Qld, 2006. Radcliffe-Brown Lectr in Social Anthropol., British Acad., 2015. Advr, H of L Select Cttee on review of BBC's Charter, 2005. Consultant, NESTA, 2005. FRAI 1998. Dent Medal, Royal Musical Assoc., 2007. *Publications:* Rationalizing Culture: IRCAM, Boulez, and the institutionalization of the musical avant-garde, 1995; (ed with D. Hesmondhalgh) Western Music and its Others: difference, representation and appropriation in music, 2000; Uncertain Vision: Birt, Dyke and the reinvention of the BBC, 2004, 2nd edn 2005; (ed with A. Barry) Interdisciplinarity: reconfigurations of the social and natural sciences, 2013; (ed) Music, Sound and Space, 2013; (ed jtly) Improvisation and Social Aesthetics, 2016. *Recreations:* family, reading, politics, music and sound, film and television, art, walking, travel. *Address:* Faculty of Music, St Aldate's, University of Oxford, Oxford OX1 1DB. *T:* (01865) 286079. *E:* georgina.born@music.ox.ac.uk.

BORN, Prof. Gustav Victor Rudolf, FRCP 1976; FRS 1972; FKC; Professor of Pharmacology, King's College, University of London, 1978–86, now Emeritus; Research Professor, The William Harvey Research Institute, Barts and The London School of Medicine and Dentistry, Queen Mary University of London (formerly St Bartholomew's Hospital Medical College, then St Bartholomew's and the Royal London School of Medicine and Dentistry), since 1989; *b* 29 July 1921; *s* of late Prof. Max Born, FRS; *m* 1st, 1950, Wilfrida Ann Plowden-Wardlaw (marr. diss., 1961); two *s* one *d*; 2nd, 1962, Dr Faith Elizabeth Maurice-Williams; one *s* one *d. Educ:* Oberrealschule, Göttingen; Perse Sch., Cambridge; Edinburgh Academy; University of Edinburgh. Vans Dunlop Scholar; MB, ChB, 1943; DPhil (Oxford), 1951, MA 1956. Med. Officer, RAMC, 1943–47; Mem. Scientific Staff, MRC, 1952–53; Research Officer, Nuffield Inst. for Med. Research, 1953–60 and Deptl Demonstrator in Pharmacology, 1956–60, University of Oxford; Vandervell Prof. of Pharmacology, RCS and Univ. of London, 1960–73; Sheild Prof. of Pharmacology, Univ. of Cambridge, and Fellow, Gonville and Caius Coll., Cambridge, 1973–78. Vis. Prof. in Chem., NW Univ., Illinois, 1970; William S. Creasy Vis. Prof. in Clin. Pharmacol., Brown Univ., 1977; Prof. of Fondation de France, Paris, 1982–84. Hon. Dir, MRC Thrombosis Res. Gp, 1964–73. Scientific Advr, Vandervell Foundn, 1967–2001; Pres., Internat. Soc. on Thrombosis and Haemostasis, 1977–79; Adviser, Heineman Med. Res. Center, Charlotte, NC, 1981–2010; Patron, Alzheimer Res. UK (formerly Alzheimer Res. Trust), 1997–. Member: Editl Board, Handbook of Experimental Pharmacology; Cttee of Enquiry into Relationship of Pharmaceut. Industry with Nat. Health Service (Sainsbury Cttee), 1965–67; Kuratorium, Lipid Liga, Munich; Kuratorium, Ernst Jung Foundn, Hamburg, 1983–91; Kuratorium, Shakespeare Prize, Hamburg, 1991–98; Forensic Science Adv. Gp, Home Office. Hon. Life Mem., New York Acad. of Scis. Lectures: Beyer, Wisconsin Univ., 1969; Sharpey-Schäfer, Edinburgh Univ., 1973; Cross, RCS, 1974; Wander, Bern Univ., 1974; Johnson Meml, Paris, 1975; Lo Yuk Tong Foundn, Hong Kong Univ., and Heineman Meml, Charlotte, NC, 1978; Carlo Erba Foundn, Milan, 1979; Sir Henry Dale, RCS, 1981; Rokitansky, Vienna, and Oration to Med. Soc., London, 1983. Mem., Akad. Leopoldina; Hon. Mem., German Physiological Soc.; Corresp. Member: German Pharmacological Soc.; Royal Belgian Acad. of Medicine; Rheinisch-Westfälische Akad. der Wissenschaften, Düsseldorf. Hon. Fellow, St Peter's Coll., Oxford, 1972; FKC 1988. Hon. FRCS 2002. Hon. D de l'Univ.: Bordeaux, 1978; Paris, 1987; Hon. MD: Münster, 1980; Leuven, 1981; Edinburgh, 1982; Munich, 1989; Düsseldorf, 2001; Hon. DSc: Brown, 1987; Loyola, 1995; London, 2006. Albrecht von Haller Medal, Göttingen Univ., 1979; Ratschow Medal, Internat. Kur. of Angiology, 1980; Auenbrugger Medal, Graz Univ., 1984; Royal Medal, Royal Soc., 1987; Morawitz Prize, German Soc. for Cardiovascular Res., 1990; Pfleger Prize, Robert Pfleger Foundn, Bamberg, 1990; Alexander von Humboldt Award, 1995; Internat. Sen. Aspirin Prize, 1995; Gold Medal for Medicine, Ernst Jung Foundn, Hamburg, 2001; Wellcome Gold Medal and Prize, British Pharmacol Soc., 2009. Chevalier de l'Ordre National de Mérite, France, 1980. *Publications:* articles in scientific jls and books. *Recreations:* music, social history past and future, being in the country. *Address:* 5 Walden Lodge, 48 Wood Lane, N6 5UU. *T:* (020) 8341 7681.

See also G. E. M. Born.

BORODALE, Viscount; Sean David Beatty; *b* 12 June 1973; *s* and *heir* of 3rd Earl Beatty, *qv*; *m* 2002, Susan Jane Hill; two *s. Publications:* Bee Journal (poetry), 2012. *Heir: s* Hon. Orlando Thomas Beatty, *b* 17 Nov. 2003.

BORRELL, Roger; Group Editor, Archant Life magazines (North), since 2010; Editor, Lancashire Life magazine, since 2006; *b* 26 May 1954; *s* of Henry and Joy Borrell; *m* 1st, Anne Youngman (marr. diss.); one *s* one *d*; 2nd, 2010, Barbara Waite. *Educ:* Falmouth Grammar Sch. Dep. Ed., Newcastle Evening Chronicle, 1995–99; Editor: Lancs Evening Post, 1999–2001; Birmingham Evening Mail, 2001–05; Ed.-in-Chief, Trinity Mirror Midlands, 2003–05. *Recreations:* fly-fishing, hill-walking. *Address:* Archant Life, Cinnamon House, Crab Lane, Fearnhead, Warrington WA2 0XP. *T:* (01253) 795584. *E:* roger.borrell@lancashirelife.co.uk.

BORRELL FONTELLES, Josep; President, European University Institute, 2010–12; *b* 24 April 1947. *Educ:* Univ. Politécnica, Madrid; Complutense Univ., Madrid (DEconSc); Inst. français du Pétrole, Paris; Stanford Univ. Engr and Dir, Dept of Systems, Compañía Española de Petróleos, 1972–81. Councillor, Madrid, 1979–82; Hd of Finance, Madrid Regl Govt, 1979–82; Under Sec., Budget and Public Spending, 1982–84; Treasury Minister, 1984–91; Mem. (PSOE) for Barcelona, Congress of Deputies, 1986–2004; Minister of Public Works and Transport, 1991–96, of the Envmt, 1993–96. Mem. (PSOE), 2004–09, Pres., 2004–07, Eur. Parlt.

BORRETT, Neil Edgar; non-executive Chairman, Forentech Ltd, 2004–11; *b* 10 March 1940; *m* 1965; two *d. Educ:* Coll. of Estate Management. FRICS 1969. Dir of property cos, 1963–90; Dir, Property Hldgs, DoE, 1990–96; Chief Exec., Property Advisers to the Civil Estate, 1996–97; Dir, Urban Estate, Crown Estate, 1997–2000. Chm., Matek Business Media, 1994–2004. Governor: London South Bank (formerly S Bank) Univ., 1996–2004; Hillcroft Coll., Surbiton, 2005–14.

BORRIE, Baron *cr* 1995 (Life Peer), of Abbots Morton in the County of Hereford and Worcester; **Gordon Johnson Borrie,** Kt 1982; QC 1986; Chairman of the Council, Ombudsman for Estate Agents, 2007–09; *b* 13 March 1931; *s* of Stanley Borrie, Solicitor; *m* 1960, Dorene (*d* 2010), *d* of Herbert Toland, Toronto, Canada; no *c. Educ:* John Bright Grammar Sch., Llandudno; Univ. of Manchester (LLB, LLM). Barrister-at-Law and Harmsworth Scholar of the Middle Temple; called to Bar, Middle Temple, 1952; Bencher, 1980. Nat. Service: Army Legal Services, HQ Brit. Commonwealth Forces in Korea, 1952–54. Practice as a barrister, London, 1954–57; Lectr and later Sen. Lectr, Coll. of Law, 1957–64; University of Birmingham: Sen. Lectr in Law, 1965–68; Prof. of English Law and Dir, Inst. of Judicial Admin, 1969–76; Dean of Faculty of Law, 1974–76; Hon. Prof. of Law, 1989–2010; Dir Gen. of Fair Trading, 1976–92. Chm., Advertising Standards Authy, 2001–07. Member: Parole Bd for England and Wales, 1971–74; CNAA Legal Studies Bd, 1971–76; Circuit Adv. Cttee, Birmingham Gp of Courts, 1972–74; Council, Consumers' Assoc., 1972–75; Consumer Protection Adv. Cttee, 1973–76; Equal Opportunities Commn, 1975–76; Chm., Commn on Social Justice, 1992–94. Director: Woolwich plc (formerly Woolwich Building Soc.), 1992–2000; Three Valleys Water, 1992–2003; Mirror Group, 1993–99; UAPT/Infolink, 1993–94; TeleWest Communications Group, 1994–2001; General Utilities, 1998–2003. Chm., Accountancy Foundn, 2000–03. Mem., H of L Select Cttee on the EC, 1996–2000, 2004–07. Pres., Inst. of Trading Standards Admin, 1992–96 (Vice-Pres., 1985–92, and 1996–). Sen. Treasurer, Nat. Union of Students, 1955–58. Hon. Mem., SPTL, 1989. Contested (Lab): Croydon, NE, 1955; Ilford, S, 1959. Gov., Birmingham Coll. of Commerce, 1966–70. FRSA 1982. Hon. LLD: City of London Poly., 1989; Manchester, 1990; Hull, 1991; Dundee, 1993; W of England, 1997; Nottingham, 2005; DUniv Nottingham Trent, 1996. *Publications:* Commercial Law, 1962, 6th edn 1988; The Consumer, Society and the Law (with Prof. A. L. Diamond), 1963, 4th edn 1981; Law of

Contempt (with N. V. Lowe), 1973, 4th edn 2010; The Development of Consumer Law and Policy (Hamlyn Lectures), 1984. *Recreations:* gastronomy, piano playing, travel. *Address:* Manor Farm, Abbots Morton, Worcestershire WR7 4NA. *T:* (01386) 792330; 4 Brick Court, Temple, EC4Y 9AD. *T:* (020) 7353 4434. *Clubs:* Garrick, Pratt's, Reform (Chm., 1990–91).

BORRIELLO, Prof. (Saverio) Peter, PhD; Chief Executive, Veterinary Medicines Directorate, since 2011; *b* 29 Oct. 1953; *s* of Pasquale Borriello and Margaret Rose (*née* Taylor); partner, Helen Georgina Archer; one *s* one *d*. *Educ:* Oldbury Grammar Sch., W Midlands; University Coll. London (BSc; Fellow 1998); Central Public Health Lab. and St Thomas's Hosp. Med. Sch. (PhD 1981). MRCPath 1987, FRCPath 1998; FFPH 2004–09. MRC Clinical Research Centre: Upjohn Res. Fellow, 1979–82; Res. Scientist, 1982–86; Head of Gp, 1986–92; University of Nottingham: Head of Gp, Dept of Microbiol., 1992–93; personal chair, 1993; Founding Dir, Inst. of Infections and Immunity, 1993–95; Special Prof., 1996–2004; Dir, Central Public Health Lab., 1995–2006, when integrated with Communicable Diseases Surveillance Centre to form Centre for Infections, HPA; Health Protection Agency: Dir, Centre for Infections, 2006–08; Dir, Specialist and Ref. Microbiology Div. and R&D, 2003–08; CEO, Veterinary Laboratories Agency, 2008–11. Vis. Prof., LSHTM, 1997–2004; Hon. Professor: RVC, 2009–; Nottingham Univ., 2013–. Hon. Mem., Soc. of Applied Microbiol., 2009. Oakley Lectr, Pathol Soc. of GB and Ireland, 1990; J. D. Williams Lectr, Fedn of Infection Socs, 2013. Proctor & Gamble Applied Healthcare Microbiol. Award, Soc. of Applied Microbiol., 2010. *Publications:* Antibiotic Associated Diarrhoea and Colitis, 1984; Clostridia in Gastro-intestinal Disease, 1985; Clinical and Molecular Aspects of Anaerobes, 1990; (ed) Topley & Wilson's Microbiology and Microbial Infections, 10th edition, 2005; papers in scientific jls. *Recreations:* antiques and bric a brac, interesting facts, questioning. *Address:* Veterinary Medicines Directorate, Woodham Lane, New Haw, Addlestone, Surrey KT15 3LS. *T:* (01932) 338302.

BORROW, David Stanley; Member (Lab): Preston City Council, since 2011; Lancashire County Council, since 2013 (Deputy Leader, since 2013); *b* 2 Aug. 1952; *s* of James Borrow and Nancy (*née* Crawshaw); civil partnership 2006, John Garland. *Educ:* Mirfield Grammar Sch., W Yorks; Lanchester Poly. (BA Hons Econs). Trainee, Yorkshire Bank, 1973–75; Lancashire Valuation Tribunal: Asst Clerk, 1975–78; Dep. Clerk, 1978–81; Dep. Clerk, Manchester S Valuation Tribunal, 1981–83; Clerk to Tribunal, Merseyside Valuation Tribunal, 1983–97. Pres., Soc. of Clerks of Valuation Tribunals, 1990–92 and 1996–97. Mem. (Lab) Preston BC, 1987–97 (Leader, 1992–94, 1995–97). MP (Lab) S Ribble, 1997–2010; contested (Lab) same seat, 2010. *E:* davidsborrow@hotmail.com.

BORROWS, Simon Alexander; Chief Executive, 3i Group plc, since 2012 (Director, since 2011); *b* Taplow, Bucks, 24 Jan. 1959; *s* of Kenneth Ambrose Borrows and Ailsa Nancy Borrows; *m* 1987, Sally Ann Weston; one *s* two *d*. *Educ:* Rossall Sch.; Queen Mary Coll., Univ. of London (LLB Hons); London Business Sch. (MBA 1985). Executive: Credit Dept, HSBC, Hong Kong, 1980–83; Corporate Finance Div., Morgan Grenfell and Co Ltd, 1985–88; Dir, Baring Bros & Co. Ltd, 1988–98 (Hd, Mergers and Acquisitions, 1995–98); Partner, Greenhill & Co. Inc., 1998–2011: Founding Partner, London Office, 1998; Co-Pres., 2004–07; Co-Chief Exec., 2007–10; Chm., Greenhill Europe, 2010–11. Director: British Land plc, 2011–; Inchcape plc, 2011–. *Recreations:* running, golf, ski-ing, theatre. *Address:* 3i Group plc, 16 Palace Street, SW1E 5JD. *T:* (020) 7975 3280, *Fax:* (020) 7975 3543. *E:* simon.borrows@3i.com. *Clubs:* Queenwood Golf, Rye Golf, St George's Hill Golf.

BORTHWICK, family name of **Baron Borthwick**.

BORTHWICK, 24th Lord *cr* 1450 (Scot.); **John Hugh Borthwick of That Ilk;** DL; Baron of Heriotmuir and Laird of Crookston, Midlothian; Hereditary Falconer of Scotland to the Queen; landowner; *b* 14 Nov. 1940; *er twin s* of 23rd Lord Borthwick and Margaret Frances (*d* 1976), *d* of Alexander Campbell Cormack; *S* father, 1996; *m* 1974, Adelaide, *d* of A. Birkmyre; two *d*. *Educ:* Gordonstoun; Edinburgh School of Agriculture (SDA, NDA). DL Midlothian, 2001. *Recreations:* wild trout fishing, stalking, stamp and cigarette card collecting. *Heir: twin b* Hon. James Henry Alexander Borthwick, Master of Borthwick [*b* 14 Nov. 1940; *m* 1972, Elspeth, *d* of Lt-Col A. D. MacConachie; one *s*]. *Address:* The Garden Flat, Crookston House, Heriot, Midlothian EH38 5YS. *T:* (01875) 835236. *Club:* New (Edinburgh).

BORTHWICK, Prof. Alistair George Liam, PhD, DSc; FREng; FRSE; Professor of Applied Hydrodynamics, University of Edinburgh, since 2013; *b* Meriden, 7 Feb. 1957; *s* of Max and Pamela Borthwick; *m* 2014, Gillian Parsons. *Educ:* Univ. of Liverpool (BEng Civil Engrg 1978; PhD 1982); Univ. of Oxford (MA 1990; DSc 2007). FREng 2014. Engr, Brown & Root (UK) Ltd, 1982–83; Lectr, Univ. of Salford, 1984–90; Lectr, 1990–96, Reader, 1996–2002, Prof., 2002–11, Univ. of Oxford; Fellow, St Edmund Hall, Oxford, 1990–2011, now Emeritus; Hd, Dept of Civil and Envmtl Engrg, UC Cork, 2011–13. Adjunct Professor: Peking Univ., 2010–; of Marine Energy, NUI Galway, 2014–. FRSE 2015. *Publications:* contribs to scientific jls incl. Water, Bioresource Technol., Jl Hydrol. *Recreations:* literature, art, contemporary music, walking, football (Plymouth Argyle), history of science. *Address:* School of Engineering, University of Edinburgh, King's Buildings, Edinburgh EH9 3JL. *T:* (0131) 650 5588. *E:* alistair.borthwick@ed.ac.uk.

BORTHWICK, Sir Antony Thomas, 4th Bt *cr* 1908, of Whitburgh, Humbie, Co. Haddington; *b* 12 Feb. 1941; *e s* of Sir John Borthwick, 3rd Bt and his 1st wife, Irene Sophie (*née* Heller); *S* father, 2002; *m* 1966, Gillian Deirdre Broke Thurston (marr. diss.); one *s* two *d*; *m* 2002, Martha Wheeler Donner. *Educ:* Eton. *Heir: s* Matthew Thomas Thurston Borthwick, *b* 2 July 1968.

BORTHWICK, Kenneth W., CBE 1980; JP; DL; Rt Hon. Lord Provost of the City of Edinburgh, 1977–80; Lord Lieutenant of the City and County of Edinburgh, 1977–80; *b* 4 Nov. 1915; *s* of Andrew Graham Borthwick; *m* 1942, Irene Margaret Wilson (*d* 2009), *d* of John Graham Wilson, Aberdeen; one *s* one *d* (and one *s* decd). *Educ:* George Heriot's Sch., Edinburgh. Served War of 1939–45: Air Crew Officer, RAF. Elected Edinburgh Town Council, 1963; Lothian Regional Council, 1974–77; Edinburgh District Council, 1976. Judge of Police, 1972–75. Member: Lothians River Bd, 1969–73; Organising Cttee, Commonwealth Games, Edinburgh, 1970; Edinburgh and Lothian Theatre Trust, 1975–76; Lothian and Borders Police Bd, 1975–77; British Airports Authorities Consultative Cttee, 1977–80; Convention of Scottish Local Authorities, 1977; Scottish Council Develt and Industry, 1977; Chairman: Edinburgh Dist. Licensing Court, 1975–77; Edinburgh Internat. Festival Soc., 1977–80; Edinburgh Military Tattoo Policy Cttee, 1977–80; Queen's Silver Jubilee Edinburgh Appeal Fund, 1977; Organising Cttee, XIII Commonwealth Games, Scotland 1986, 1983–86. Dean, Consular Corps, Edinburgh and Leith, 1991–92. Curator of Patronage, Univ. of Edinburgh, 1977–80. Governor, George Heriot Sch., 1965–73. Vice-President (ex officio): RZS of Scotland, 1977–80; Lowland TA&VRA, 1977–80. DL City of Edinburgh, 1980. Hon. Consul for Malaŵi, 1982, Hon. Consul Gen., 1993–94. OStJ. Commander, Order of the Lion (Malaŵi), 1993. *Recreations:* golf, gardening. *Address:* 17 York Road, Edinburgh EH5 3EJ.

BORWICK, family name of **Baron Borwick**.

BORWICK, 5th Baron *cr* 1922, of Hawkshead, co. Lancaster; **Geoffrey Robert James, (Jamie), Borwick;** Bt 1916; Chairman, Federated Trust Corporation Ltd, since 1987; *b* 7 March 1955; *s* of Hon. Robin Sandbach Borwick (*d* 2003), 3rd *s* of 3rd Baron Borwick, and Hon. Patricia Garnett Borwick (*d* 2009), *d* of Baron McAlpine of Moffat (Life Peer); *S* uncle, 2007; *m* 1981, Victoria Lorne Peta (*née* Poore) (*see* V. L. P. Borwick); three *s* one *d*. *Educ:* Eton Coll. Sir Robert McAlpine & Sons Ltd, 1972–81; Manganese Bronze Holdings plc 1981–2003 (CEO, 1987–2001; Chm., 2001–03); non-exec. Dir, Hansa Trust plc, 1984–2012 Trustee: Federated Foundn, 1985–; British Lung Foundn, 2001–08, 2011–; Royal Brompton and Harefield Hosps Charity, 2012–. Elected Mem., H of L, 2013–. *Recreations:* travel swimming, walking. *Heir: s* Hon. Edwin Dennis William Borwick, *b* 14 April 1984. *Address:* 33 Phillimore Gardens, W8 7QG. *T:* (020) 7776 9000, *Fax:* (020) 7776 9001; 1 Love Lane EC2V 7JN. *E:* jamie@borwick.com. *Club:* Garrick.

BORWICK, Lady; Victoria Lorne Peta Borwick; MP (C) Kensington, since 2015 Member (C), London Assembly, Greater London Authority, since 2008; *b* London, 26 April 1956; *d* of late R. Dennis and Peta Poore; *m* 1981, Geoffrey Robert James Borwick (*see* Baron Borwick); three *s* one *d*. *Educ:* Wispers Sch. Dir, Clarion Events, 1976–2002; Dir, Treasurer's Dept, Conservative Central Office, 2002–04; Commercial Dir, ACI, 2004–06; Mem., Adv Council, Open Europe, 2007–. Mem. (C), RBK&C Council, 2002–. Greater London Authority: Member: Transport Cttee, 2008–; Police and Crime Cttee, 2012–; Chm., Health Cttee, 2011–12; Dep. Mayor of London, 2012–15; Chm., Civil Liberties Panel, Metropolitan Police Authy, 2009–12. Gov., Golborne Children's Centre (formerly Ainsworth Nursery Sch.), 1990–. Trustee, Federated Foundn, 1985–. FRSA 1989. Freeman, City of London 1999; Liveryman, Clockmakers' Co., 2000. *Publications:* The Cost of the London Mayor 2007; Streets Ahead: relieving congestion on Oxford Street, Regent Street and Bond Street 2010; Responding to G20, 2010. *Recreations:* making fudge, ski-ing, tennis. *Address:* 33 Phillimore Gardens, W8 7QG. *T:* (020) 7376 9262, *Fax:* (020) 7937 2656; House of Commons, SW1A 0AA. *E:* cllr.borwick@rbkc.gov.uk.

BORYSIEWICZ, Sir Leszek (Krzysztof), Kt 2001; PhD; FRCP, FRCPath, FMedSci; FRS 2008; DL; Vice-Chancellor, Cambridge University, since 2010; *b* 13 April 1951; *s* of Jan Borysiewicz and Zofia Helena Woloszyn; *m* 1976, Gwenllian Sian Jones; two *d*. *Educ:* Cardiff High Sch.; Welsh Nat. Sch. of Medicine (BSc, MB BCh 1975); Univ. of London (PhD 1986) MRCP 1979, FRCP 1989; FRCPath 2002. Hosp. appts at University Hosp. of Wales Hammersmith Hosp., Nat. Hosp. for Nervous Diseases and Ealing Hosp., 1975–79; Registrar Dept of Medicine, Hammersmith Hosp., 1979–80; Royal Postgraduate Medical School MRC Clinical Trng Fellow, 1980–82; Lister Res. Fellow and Sen. Lectr, 1982–86; Wellcome Trust Sen. Lectr in Infectious Diseases, Addenbrooke's Hosp., Cambridge, 1987–88; Lectr in Medicine, Univ. of Cambridge, 1988–91; Prof. of Medicine, Univ. of Wales Coll. of Medicine, 1991–2001; Principal, Faculty of Medicine, 2001–04, Dep. Rector, 2004–07 Imperial Coll.; Chief Exec., MRC, 2007–10 (Mem., Technol. Bd, 2007–10). Chm., R&D Grants Cttee, NHS (Wales), 1994–98. Non-exec. Dir, NW London Strategic HA, 2003–05 Member: MRC, 1995–2000 (Chm., Molecular and Cell Bd, 1996–2000; Chm., Jt MRC/DoH Spongiform Encephalopathies Cttee, 1996–2002); Cancer Res. UK, 2004– (Mem Council and Trustee, 2002–05; Chm., Sci. Cttee, 2002–04); Lister Inst., 2004–; Health Innovation Council, 2008–; Global Sci. and Innovation Forum, 2008–10; Singapore Biomed Scis Internat. Adv. Council, 2008–; Chairman: Sci. Council, Internat. Agency for Res. on Cancer, WHO, 2002–04; UK Stem Cell Funders' Forum, 2007–10; Hds of Internat (Biomed.) Res. Orgns, 2007–10. Harveian Orator, RCP, 2009. Gov., Wellcome Trust 2006–07; Trustee, Nuffield Trust, 2002–07. Founder FMedSci 1998 (Mem. Council 1997–2002); FCGI 2004. Mem., Polish Acad. Arts and Scis, Krakow, 1996. Hon. Prof. Shanghai Jiao Tong Univ., 2011. DL Cambs, 2012. Fellow, Cardiff Univ., 2006; Hon Fellow: Wolfson Coll., Cambridge, 2002; Univ. of Wales Inst., Cardiff, 2011. Hon. DSc Southampton, 2008; Hull, 2008; Glasgow, 2011; Hong Kong, 2012; Peking, 2012; Aberdeen 2014; Hon. MD Sheffield, 2010. Moxon Trust Medal, RCP, 2002; Jephcott Medal, RSM 2007; Galen Medal in Therapeutics, Soc. of Apothecaries, 2011; Inserm Internat. Prize, 2014 *Publications:* papers on immunology and pathogenesis of virus infection and viral induced cancer. *Recreations:* Rugby football, cricket, painting. *Address:* Office of the Vice-Chancellor The Old Schools, Trinity Lane, Cambridge CB2 1TN. *T:* (01223) 332290, *Fax:* (01223) 339669. *Clubs:* Athenæum, Oxford and Cambridge.

BOSANQUET, Prof. Nicholas; Professor of Health Policy, Imperial College London (formerly Imperial College, University of London), since 1993; *b* 17 Jan. 1942; *s* of late Lt Col Neville Richard Gustavus Bosanquet and Nancy Bosanquet; *m* 1st, 1974, Anne Connolly (marr. diss. 1993); two *d*; 2nd, 1996, Anna Zarzecka. *Educ:* Winchester Coll.; Clare Coll. Cambridge (BA Hist.); Yale Univ. (Mellon Fellow); London Sch. of Econs (MSc Econs) Econ. Advr, NBPI, 1967–69; Lecturer in Economics: LSE, 1969–72; King's Fund Coll. 1973–86; City Univ., 1977–84; Sen. Research Fellow, Centre for Health Econs, Univ. of York, 1984–88; Prof. of Health Policy, RHBNC, Univ. of London, 1988–93. Special Advr Health Cttee, H of C, 1988–90, 2000–. Consultant: WHO, 1989; World Bank, 1993 Arbitrator, ACAS, 1983–90. Non-executive Director: Abbey Health, 1998–2000; Richmond and Twickenham Primary Care Trust, 2001–07; Associate, Volterra Consulting, 2012–. Health Policy Advr, Care UK plc, 1995–2003; Health Policy Advr, 2003–15, Dir, 2015–, Sussex Health Care; Advr on NHS Business Relns, Hosp. Corp. of America, 2002–04 Consultant Dir, Reform, 2005–; Chm., 2006–12, Dir, 2012–, TBS (GB). Chm., Health Service Rev. for Cornwall, 2007–08; Mem. Adv. Bd, Cancer Reform Strategy, 2007; Chief Investigator, GlaxoSmithKline, Salford Lung Study, 2013–. Mem., York Central Lib Dems *Publications:* Industrial Relations in the NHS: the search for a system, 1980; After the New Right, 1983; Family Doctors and Economic Incentives, 1989; (with K. Sikora) The Economics of Cancer Care, 2006; Our Land at War: Britain's key First World War sites, 2014 contrib. to econ. and med. jls. *Recreations:* visiting battlefields, brainstorming with Americans and others about military history. *Address:* 40 Bishophill Senior, York YO1 6DZ.

BOSCAWEN, family name of **Viscount Falmouth**.

BOSE, Mihir, FICA; freelance writer and broadcaster; *b* 12 Jan. 1947; *s* of Kiran Chandra Bose and Sova Rani Bose; *m* 1st, 1986, Kalpana (marr. diss. 1999); one *d*; 2nd, 2002, Caroline Alison Gascoyne-Cecil. *Educ:* St Xavier's High Sch.; St Xavier's Coll., Bombay (BSc Physics and Maths). Cricket Corresp., LBC, 1974–75; For. Corresp., Sunday Times, Spectator, New Society, 1975–78; freelance writer, 1979; Editor: Property Guide, 1980–81; International Fund Guide, 1980–81; Pensions, 1981–83; Financial Planning Ed. 1983–84, City Ed. 1984–86, Dep. Ed. 1985–86, Financial Weekly; City Features Ed., London Daily News 1986–87; freelance writer, mainly on regular contract basis, specialising in finance, sports and feature writing for Sunday Times, Spectator, Mail on Sunday, Independent, The Times Guardian, Daily Telegraph, 1987–2006; Sports Ed., BBC News, 2007–09; columnist, London Evening Standard, Insideworldfootball.biz, 2009–; contributor: Sunday Times, Independent 2009–; Financial Times, PlayUp, 2011–. Mem., Gambling Review Body, Home Office 2000–01. Mem. Council, Nat. Army Mus., 2007–13. Trustee, Sporting Equals, 2009–. Hon DLitt Loughborough, 2012. *Publications:* Keith Miller, 1979, 2nd edn 1980; The Lost Hero 1982; All in a Day's Work, 1983; The Aga Khan, 1984; A Maidan View, 1986; The Crash 1988, 3rd edn 1989, incl. Jap. edn; Insurance: are you covered?, 1988, 2nd edn 1991; Crash – a new money crisis, 1989; (jtly) Fraud, 1989; Cricket Voices, 1990; How to Invest in a Bear Market, 1990; History of Indian Cricket, 1990, 2nd edn 2002; Michael Grade: screening the image, 1992; (jtly) Behind Closed Doors, 1992; Sporting Colours, 1994; False Messiah: the life and times of Terry Venables, 1996; Sporting Alien, 1996; Sporting Babylon, 1999 Manchester Unlimited: the rise and rise of the world's premier football club, 1999; Raj, Spies Rebellion, 2004; The Magic of Indian Cricket, 2006; Bollywood – a history, 2006 Manchester Disunited: trouble and takeover at the world's richest football club, 2007; The World Cup: all you need to know, 2010; The Spirit of the Game: how sport has changed the modern world, 2012; Game Changer: how the English Premier League came to dominate the world, 2012; The Lost Hero, 2014; (jtly) William Hill: the man and the business, 2014. *Recreations:* running his own cricket team, walking, reading, films, travelling. *Clubs:* Reform, MCC.

BOSHER, Sir Robin, Kt 2012; Regional Director, South East and Director of Quality and Training, Ofsted, since 2014; *b* Oxford, 30 Jan. 1957; *s* of Frederick A. and Eileen A. D. Bosher; *m* 1978, Anna Maria Davey; two *d. Educ:* Gosford Hill Sch., Oxford; Culham Coll., Abingdon (Cert Ed, BEd Oxon). Teacher, 1978–88: Primary Teacher, Oaklands Junior, Biggin Hill, then New Ash Green First Sch.; Dep. Hd, Wickham Common Sch., Bromley; Headmaster: Clare Hse Primary Sch., Bromley, 1988–93; Perry Hall Primary Sch., Orpington, 1993–99; Hd of Access, Bromley Local Authy, 1999–2002; Headmaster, Fairlawn Primary Sch., Lewisham, 2002–12; Exec. Head, Fairlawn, Kilmorie and Haseltine Primary Schs, Lewisham, 2009–12; Dir, Primary Educn, Harris Fedn, 2012–14. Operational Dir (Primary), London Challenge, 2005–10. *Recreations:* theatre, cinema, travel. *Address:* 64 Constance Crescent, Hayes, Bromley, Kent BR2 7QQ. *T:* (020) 8402 7297, 07909 687959. *E:* robinbosher@hotmail.com.

BOSHOFF, Dr Christoffer, FRCP; Vice-President, Early Development and Immuno-Translational Oncology, Pfizer Inc., since 2013; *b* 22 June 1965. *Educ:* Pretoria Univ. (MB ChB 1987); PhD London 1998. MRCP 1991. University College London: Glaxo Wellcome Res. Fellow, 1998–2004; Prof. of Cancer Medicine, 2001–13; Dir, Cancer Inst., 2006–13; Consultant Physician, Dept of Oncology, UCL and University Coll. London Hosps, 2000–13. Adjunct Prof., Yale Univ., 2014–. FMedSci 2005. *Address:* Pfizer Inc., 10555 Science Center Drive, La Jolla, CA 92121, USA. *E:* chris.boshoff@pfizer.com.

BOSONNET, Paul Graham, CBE 1995; Deputy Chairman, BOC Group, 1985–92; *b* 12 Sept. 1932; *s* of Edgar Raymond Bosonnet and Sylvia Gladys Cradock; *m* 1958, Joan Colet Cunningham; one *s* two *d. Educ:* St John's College, Southsea. FCA. Accountant, British Oxygen Co., 1957; Dir, BOC International, 1976; Dep. Chm., British Telecommunications plc, 1991–95. Chairman: Logica, 1990–95; G. A. Day, 1996–2001; Director: MAM Gp, 1991–98; Lucas Varity (formerly Lucas Industries), 1993–97. Vice Chm., Council, Royal Holloway (formerly RHBNC), Univ. of London, 1986–95 (Hon. Fellow, 2003). *Recreations:* genealogy, walking. *Address:* 2 The Green, Charters Village Drive, East Grinstead, W Sussex RH19 2GX. *T:* (01342) 870717.

BOSSANO, Hon. Joseph John; MP (Gibraltar Socialist Labour Party); Leader of the Opposition, Gibraltar, 1984–88 and 1996–2011; *b* 10 June 1939; *s* of Maria Teresa and Oscar Bossano; *m* (marr. diss.); three *s* one *d*; *m* 1988, Rose Torrilla. *Educ:* Gibraltar Grammar School; Univ. of London (BScEcon); Univ. of Birmingham (BA). Factory worker, 1958–60; Seaman, 1960–64; Health Inspector, 1964–68; student, 1968–72; building worker, 1972–74; Union leader, 1974–88; MP, Gibraltar, 1972–; Chief Minister, 1988–96. *Recreations:* thinking, cooking, gardening. *Address:* 2 Gowlands Ramp, Gibraltar.

BOSSOM, Hon. Sir Clive, 2nd Bt *cr* 1953; *b* 4 Feb. 1918; *s* of late Baron Bossom (Life Peer); *S* to father's Baronetcy, 1965; *m* 1951, Lady Barbara North, *sister* of 9th Earl of Guilford; three *s* one *d. Educ:* Eton. Regular Army, The Buffs, 1939–48; served Europe and Far East. Kent County Council, 1949–52; Chm. Council Order of St John for Kent, 1951–56; Mem. Chapter General, Order of St John (Mem., Jt Cttee, 1961–93; Chm., Ex-Services War Disabled Help and Homes Dept, 1973–87; Almoner, 1987–93). Contested (C) Faversham Div., 1951 and 1955. MP (C) Leominster Div., Herefordshire, 1959–Feb. 1974; Parliamentary Private Secretary: to Jt Parly Secs, Min. of Pensions and Nat. Insce, 1960–62; to Sec. of State for Air, 1962–64; to Minister of Defence for RAF, 1964; to Home Secretary, 1970–72. Chm., Europ Assistance Ltd, 1973–88. President: Anglo-Belgian Union, 1970–73, 1983–85 (Vice-Pres., 1974–82); Anglo-Netherlands Soc., 1978–89 (Vice Pres., 1989–); BARC, 1985–91; Vice-President: Industrial Fire Protection Assoc., 1981–88; Fédération Internationale de L'Automobile, 1975–81 (Vice-Pres. d'Honneur, 1982–); Internat. Social Service, 1989– (Internat. Pres., 1984–89); Chairman: RAC Motor Sports Council, 1975–81; RAC Motor Sports Assoc. Ltd, 1979–82; Iran Soc. 1973–76; Mem. Council, RGS, 1982–86. Trustee, Brooklands Museum Trust, 1987–95; Vice-Pres., First Gear Foundn, 1996–2006. Liveryman of Worshipful Company of Grocers (Master, 1979). FRSA (Mem. Council, 1971–77). KStJ 1961. Badge of Honour, British Red Cross, 1993. Comdr, Order of Leopold II; Order of Homayoun III (Iran), 1977; Comdr, Order of the Crown (Belgium), 1977; Kt Comdr, Order of Orange Nassau (Netherlands), 1980. *Recreation:* travel. *Heir: s* Bruce Charles Bossom [*b* 22 Aug. 1952; *m* 1985, Penelope Jane, *d* of late Edward Holland-Martin and of Mrs Holland-Martin, Overbury Court, Glos; one *s* two *d*]. *Address:* 97 Cadogan Lane, SW1X 9DU. *T:* (020) 7245 6531; Rotherdown, Grove Lane, Petworth, Sussex GU28 0BT. *T:* (01798) 342329. *Clubs:* Royal Automobile (Chm., 1975–78; Vice Pres., 1998–), Carlton.

BOSSY, Prof. John Antony, PhD; FRHistS; FBA 1993; Professor of History, University of York, 1979–2000, now Emeritus; *b* 30 April 1933; *s* of Frederick James Bossy and Kate Louise Fanny Bossy (*née* White). *Educ:* St Ignatius Coll., London; Queens' Coll., Cambridge (BA 1954; PhD 1961). FRHistS 1975. Res. Fellow, Queens' Coll., Cambridge, 1959–62; Lectr in Hist., Goldsmiths' Coll., London, 1962–66; Lectr, then Reader, in Mod. Hist., QUB, 1966–78. Mem., Editl Bd, Past and Present, 1972–2003. *Publications:* The English Catholic Community 1570–1850, 1976; Christianity in the West 1400–1700, 1984; Giordano Bruno and the Embassy Affair, 1991; Peace in the Post-Reformation, 1998; Under the Molehill, 2001. *Recreations:* chess, piano. *Address:* 80 Stockton Lane, York YO31 1BS. *T:* (01904) 424801.

See also Rev. M. J. F. Bossy.

BOSSY, Rev. Michael Joseph Frederick, SJ; Assistant Priest, St Ignatius Church, South Tottenham, since 2005; Rector, Stonyhurst College, 1993–97 (Headmaster, 1972–85); *b* 22 Nov. 1929; *s* of F. J. Bossy and K. Bossy (*née* White). *Educ:* St Ignatius Coll., Stamford Hill; Heythrop Coll., Oxon (STL); Oxford Univ. (MA). Taught at: St Ignatius Coll., Stamford Hill, 1956–59; St Francis Xavier's Coll., Liverpool, 1963–64; Stonyhurst Coll., 1965–85; Asst Priest, 1986–88, Rector and Parish Priest, 1988–92, Parish of St Aloysius, Glasgow; Actg Parish Priest, St Mary of the Angels, Liverpool, 1998; Asst Priest, Corpus Christi Church, Brixton, 1998–2005. *Recreation:* watching games. *Address:* St Ignatius Church, 27 High Road, N15 6ND.

See also J. A. Bossy.

BOSTOCK, Prof. Christopher John, PhD; Director, BBSRC Institute for Animal Health, 1997–2002; *b* 29 May 1942; *s* of John Major Leslie Bostock and Mildred Lilian Bostock; *m* 1st, 1963, Yvonne Pauline Kendrick (marr. diss. 1990); one *s* two *d*; 2nd, 1992, Patricia Roberts. *Educ:* Univ. of Edinburgh (BSc Hons; Sir Ramsay Wright Post-Grad. Schol., 1965; PhD 1968). Univ. Demonstr, Univ. of Edinburgh, 1965–69; Vis. Fellow, Univ. of Colorado, 1969–71; Res. Fellow, Univ. of St Andrews, 1971–72; Res. Scientist, MRC Clin. and Population Cytogenetics Unit, Edinburgh, 1972–77; Res. Scientist, 1977–83, Asst Dir, 1983–85, MRC Mammalian Genome Unit; Head of Molecular Biology: Animal Virus Res. Inst., AFRC, 1985–89; Inst. for Animal Health, AFRC, then BBSRC, 1989–97. Visiting Professor: Univ. of Wisconsin, 1985; Dept of Clin. Veterinary Sci., Univ. of Bristol, 1998–; Sch. of Animal and Microbial Scis, Univ. of Reading, 2000–. Hon. FRAgS 2002. *Publications:* (with Adrian Sumner) The Eukaryotic Chromosome, 1978; scientific res. papers on chromosomes, tumour cell drug resistance, infectious disease agents. *Recreations:* French country life, walking, building.

BOSTOCK, Sir David (John), KCMG 2015 (CMG 1998); Member, European Union Court of Auditors, 2002–13; *b* 11 April 1948; *s* of John C. Bostock and Gwendoline G. (*née* Lee); *m* 1975, Beth Ann O'Byrne; one *s* one *d. Educ:* Cheltenham Grammar Sch.; Balliol Coll., Oxford (BA Mod. Hist. 1969); University Coll. London (MSc Econs of Public Policy 1978). VSO, Indonesia, 1970. Joined HM Treasury, 1971; Second Sec., Office of UK Permanent Rep. to EC, 1973–75; Principal: HM Treasury, 1975–81; Cabinet Office (Economic Secretariat), 1981–83; Asst Sec., HM Treasury, 1983–85; Financial and Econ. Counsellor, Office of UK Permanent Rep. to EC, 1985–89; Under Sec. and Head of EC Gp, HM Treasury, 1990–94; UK Dep. Perm. Rep. to EU, 1995–98; Head of European Secretariat, Cabinet Office, 1999–2000; Vis. Fellow, LSE, 2000–01; Practitioner Fellow, European Inst., Univ. of Sussex, 2001–10. Trustee, YHA (England and Wales), 2003–11. *Recreations:* choral singing, walking, looking at old buildings, reading.

BOSTOCK, Prof. Hugh, PhD; FRS 2001; Professor of Neurophysiology, Institute of Neurology, University College London, 1996–2009, now Emeritus; *b* 25 Aug. 1944; *s* of Edward and Alice Bostock; *m* 1975, Kate Shaw; two *s* one *d. Educ:* Merton Coll., Oxford (BA); University Coll. London (MSc, PhD 1974). Institute of Neurology, London University, 1974–2009: Lectr, 1976–87; Sen. Lectr, 1987–92; Reader, 1992–96. *Publications:* contrib. papers to Jl Physiol., Brain and similar jls. *Address:* Newton House, 24 Bridge Street, Olney, Bucks MK46 4AB.

BOSTOCK, Kate Margaret; Chief Executive, Coast, since 2013; founder and owner, Angel & Rocket, since 2014; *b* Burton-on-Trent, 8 Sept. 1956; *d* of George and Ruth Parker; *m* 1991, Neil Andrew Bostock; two *s. Educ:* Ashby Grammar Sch. Work in design, 1982–92; Dir, Buying to Buying, 1992–95; Product Dir, Next, 1995–2001; Clothing Dir, George @ Asda, 2001–04; Womenswear Dir, 2004–08, Exec. Dir, Clothing, 2008–09, Exec. Dir, Gen. Merchandise, 2009–12, Marks & Spencer; Exec. Dir, Product and Trading, ASOS plc, 2013. Hon. DA De Montfort, 2008; Hon. Dr Business Studies Manchester, 2008; Hon. DArts Leicester, 2008. *Recreations:* music, art, theatre, travel, shopping!

BOSTON, 11th Baron *cr* 1761; **George William Eustace Boteler Irby;** Bt 1704; derivatives broker, since 1993; *b* 1 Aug. 1971; *s* of 10th Baron Boston and Rhonda Anne (*née* Bate); *S* father, 2007; *m* 1998, Nicola Sydney Mary (*née* Reid); two *s* two *d. Educ:* Eton; Bristol Univ. (BSc Hons Psychology). *Heir: s* Hon. Thomas William George Boteler Irby, *b* 9 Dec. 1999. *Address:* Hookers Farm, Hartley Wespall, Hook, Hants RG27 0AP.

BOSTON, Archdeacon of; *see* Allain Chapman, Ven. J. P. H.

BOSTON, David Merrick, OBE 1976; MA; Director (formerly Curator), Horniman Public Museum and Public Park Trust (formerly Horniman Museum and Library), London, 1965–93; Hon. Curator, and tenant, 1996–2006, Hon. Archivist and Librarian, since 2006, Quebec House, National Trust; *b* 15 May 1931; *s* of late Dr H. M. Boston, Salisbury, Wilts; *m* 1961, Catharine, *d* of late Rev. Prof. (Edward) Geoffrey (Simons) Parrinder; one *s* two *d. Educ:* Rondebosch, Cape Town; Bishop Wordsworth's, Salisbury; Selwyn Coll., Cambridge; Univ. of Cape Town. BA History Cantab 1954; MA 1958. RAF, 1950–51; Adjt, Marine Craft Trng School. Field survey, S African Inst. of Race Relations, 1955; Curator, King's Regt Collection, and Keeper of Ethnology, Liverpool Museums, 1956–62; Asst Keeper, British Museum, New World archaeology and ethnography, 1962–65. Chm., British Nat. Cttee of Internat. Council of Museums, 1976–80; Vice-Chm., Internat. Cttee for Museums of Ethnography, 1989–95; Member, Council: Museums Assoc., 1969–70; Royal Anthropological Inst., 1969 and 1998–2001 (Vice-Pres., 1972–75, 1977–80, 1995–98, Hon. Sec., 1985–88, Hon. Librarian, 1992–2001). Visiting Scientist: National Museum of Man, Ottawa, 1970; Japan Foundation, Tokyo, 1986. Consultant, Prog. for Belize, 1994–. Gov., Dolmetsch Foundn, 1983–. Vice President: Dulwich Decorative & Fine Arts Soc., 1987–2001; Friends of the Horniman, 1995–2002; Mem. Cttee, Wolfe Soc., 1999–. Trustee, Haslemere Museum, 1996–2012. FMA; FRAI; FRGS; FRSA. Ordenom Jugoslavenske Zastave sa zlatnom zvezdom na ogrlici (Yugoslavia), 1981. *Publications:* Pre-Columbian Pottery of the Americas, 1980; contribs to learned jls and encyclopaedias and on Pre-European America, in World Ceramics (ed R. J. Charleston). *Address:* 14 The Green, Westerham, Kent TN16 1AS. *T:* (01959) 565812. *Club:* Royal Air Force.

BOSTON, Kenneth George, AO 2001; PhD; Chief Executive, Qualifications and Curriculum Authority, UK, 2002–09; *b* 9 Sept. 1942; *s* of Kenneth Frances and Enid Beatrice Boston; *m* 1978, Yvonne Roep; one *d. Educ:* Univ. of Melbourne (MA; PhD 1981). Director-General: of Educn, SA, 1988–91; of Educn and Trng, NSW, 1991–2002. Pres., Australian Coll. of Educn, 2001–02. Member: Expert Panel for School Funding Review, Australia, 2010–11; Australian Qualifications Framework Council, 2010–12. Member, Board: Musica Viva Australia, 2012–14; Stewart House, 2012–. *Club:* Sydney Cricket.

BOSTRIDGE, Dr Ian Charles, CBE 2004; singer and writer; *b* 25 Dec. 1964; *s* of late Leslie John Bostridge and of Lilian Winifred (*née* Clark); *m* 1992, Lucasta Miller; one *s* one *d. Educ:* Dulwich Coll. Prep. Sch.; Westminster Sch. (Queen's Schol.); St John's Coll., Oxford (MA, DPhil Hist. 1990; Hon. Fellow, 2010); St John's Coll., Cambridge (MPhil Hist. and Philosophy of Sci.). North Sen. Schol., St John's Coll., Oxford, 1988–90; Jun. Res. Fellow, and British Acad. Postdoctoral Res. Fellow, Corpus Christi Coll., Oxford, 1992–95 (Hon. Fellow, 2001). Humanitas Vis. Prof. of Classical Music and Music Educn, Univ. of Oxford, 2014–15; Vis. Prof., Univ. of California, Berkeley, 2015. Professional début as Young Sailor in Tristan, RFH/LPO, 1993; operatic stage début as Lysander, Midsummer Night's Dream, Australian Opera at Edinburgh Fest., 1994; Royal Opera House début, in Salome, 1995; début: with ENO, as Tamino, 1996; with Munich State Opera, as Nerone in Poppaea, 1998; Vienna State Opera, as Ottavio, 2006; other rôles include: Belmonte, Die Entführung aus dem Serail; Vasek, The Bartered Bride; Quint, The Turn of the Screw; title rôle, Orfeo (Monteverdi); Caliban, The Tempest (world première, 2004); Jupiter, Semele; Vere, Billy Budd; Aschenbach, Death in Venice. Wigmore Hall recital début, 1995; Carnegie Hall début, 1999; recitals include: Edinburgh Fest., Aldeburgh Fest., Munich, Salzburg, Schubertiade Fests; Vienna Konzerthaus and Musikverein; Châtelet; Champs Elysées; Lincoln Center; Carnegie Hall; La Scala; own Carte Blanche series, Concertgebouw, 2005; own Perspectives series, Carnegie Hall, 2006 and Barbican Centre, 2007–08; programmed own series at Schubertiade, Vienna Konzerthaus and Wigmore Hall; première (Cologne) and dedicatee, Hans Werner Henze, Sechs Gesänge aus dem Arabischen. Television includes: Schubert's Winterreise, Channel 4, 1997 (Prague TV Award); Britten Serenade, and as presenter, Janacek documentary, BBC; subject of S Bank Show profile. Has made numerous recordings. Patron: Music Libraries Trust; Macmillan Carol Concert; Ambassador, Youth Music. Edinburgh Fest. Univ. Lect., 2000; Breakspear Lect., Univ. of Trondheim, 2015; Lect., Bristol Inst. for Res. in Humanities and Arts, Univ. of Bristol, 2015. Hon. RAM 2002. Hon. DMus St Andrews, 2003. NFMS award, 1990; Young Concert Artists' Trust award, 1992; Début Award, Royal Philharmonic Soc., 1995; Solo Vocal Award, Gramophone, 1996, 1998; Classical Music Award, South Bank Show, 1996; Echo Award, 1997, 1999, 2013, 2014; Munich Fest. Prize, 1998; Choc de l'Année Award, 1998, 2004; Edison Award, 1999, 2002; Grammy Award (opera), 1999, 2010; Brit Critics Award, 2000; Preis der Deutschen Schallplattenkritik, 2001, 2006; Acad. Charles Cros, Grand Prix du Disque, 2001; Japanese Recording Acad. Prize, 2004, 2007. *Publications:* Witchcraft and its Transformations c. 1650–c. 1750, 1997; (contrib.) Civil Histories: essays presented to Sir Keith Thomas, 2000; A Singer's Notebook, 2011; Schubert's Winter Journey: anatomy of an obsession, 2014; reviews and articles in The Times,

TLS, Wall St Jl, Guardian, etc. *Recreations:* reading, cooking, looking at pictures. *Address:* c/o Askonas Holt Ltd, Lincoln House, 300 High Holborn, WC1V 7JH. *T:* (020) 7400 1700, *Fax:* (020) 7400 1799. *Club:* Garrick.

BOSTRIDGE, Mark Andrew; writer; *b* London, 28 June 1961; *s* of late Leslie John Bostridge and of Lilian Winifred, (Sandy), (*née* Clark). *Educ:* Dulwich College Prep. Sch.; Westminster Sch.; St Anne's Coll., Oxford (Gladstone Meml Prize; BA). Political res. asst, 1985–86; researcher/asst producer, BBC, 1990–94; Literary Executor, Vera Brittain Estate, 1999–. Consultant on feature film, Testament of Youth, 2008–14. *Publications:* Vera Brittain: a life (with Paul Berry), 1995; (ed jtly) Letters from a Lost Generation, 1998; (ed) Lives for Sale, 2004; Florence Nightingale: the woman and her legend, 2008 (Elizabeth Longford Prize for Histl Biog., 2009); (ed) Because You Died, 2008; The Fateful Year: England 1914, 2014; Vera Brittain and the First World War, 2014; articles and reviews in nat. press. *Recreations:* diary-keeping, ghost-watching. *Address:* c/o United Agents, 12–26 Lexington Street, W1F 0LE. *T:* (020) 3214 0800.
See also I. C. Bostridge.

BOSVILLE MACDONALD OF SLEAT, Sir Ian Godfrey, 17th Bt *cr* 1625; Premier Baronet of Nova Scotia; DL; MRSPH; 25th Chief of Sleat; *b* 18 July 1947; *er s* of Sir (Alexander) Somerled Angus Bosville Macdonald of Sleat, 16th Bt, MC, 24th Chief of Sleat and Mary, Lady Bosville Macdonald of Sleat; *S* father 1958; *m* 1970, Juliet Fleury, *o d* of late Maj.-Gen. J. M. D. Ward-Harrison, OBE, MC; one *s* one *d* (and one *d* decd). *Educ:* Pinewood Sch.; Eton Coll.; Royal Agricultural Coll. ARICS 1972; FRICS 1986. Member (for Bridlington South), Humberside CC, 1981–84. MRSPH (MRSH 1972); Mem., Econ. Res. Council, 1979–. Chairman: Rural Develt Commn, Humberside, 1988–95; Rural Partnership ER of Yorks Council, 2000–; President: Humber and Wolds Rural Community Council, 1996–2012; British Food and Farming in Humberside, 1989; Humberside Young Farmers, 1989–96; British Red Cross: Mem. Council and Trustee, 1995–97; Nat. Trustee, 2001–06; Chairman: N of England Reg., 2000–04; Nat. Assembly, 2002–07; Chm., Clan Donald Lands Trust, Armadale Castle, Isle of Skye, 2008–. President: Humberside Br., 1988–96; Hull and ER Br., 1996–2003. High Sheriff, Humberside, 1988–89; DL ER of Yorks, 1997. *Recreation:* ornithology. *Heir: s* Somerled Alexander Bosville Macdonald, younger of Sleat [*b* 30 Jan. 1976; *m* 2003, Charlotte, *yr d* of Richard Perkins; two *s*]. *Address:* Hazel Bush House, Hazel Bush Lane, York YO32 9TR. *T:* (01904) 468239, 07733 413527. *Clubs:* Lansdowne, White's; New, Puffin's (Edinburgh).

BOSWALL, Sir (Thomas) Alford H.; *see* Houstoun-Boswall.

BOSWELL, family name of **Baron Boswell of Aynho**.

BOSWELL OF AYNHO, Baron *cr* 2010 (Life Peer), of Aynho in the County of Northamptonshire; **Timothy Eric Boswell;** DL; *b* 2 Dec. 1942; *s* of late Eric New Boswell and of Joan Winifred Caroline Boswell; *m* 1969, Helen Delahay, *d* of Rev. Arthur Rees; three *d*. *Educ:* Marlborough Coll.; New Coll., Oxford (MA; Dip. Agricl Econs). Conservative Res. Dept, 1966–73 (Head of Econ. Section, 1970–73); managed family farming business, 1974–87; part-time Special Adviser to Minister of Agriculture, Fisheries and Food, 1984–86. Chm., Leics, Northants and Rutland Counties Br., NFU, 1983; Mem. Council, 1966–90, Pres., 1984–90, Perry Foundn (for Agricl Res.); Mem., AFRC, 1988–90. MP (C) Daventry, 1987–2010. PPS to Financial Sec. to the Treasury, 1989–90; an Asst Govt Whip, 1990–92; a Lord Comr of HM Treasury (a Govt Whip), 1992; Parly Under-Sec. of State, DFE, 1992–95; Parly Sec., MAFF, 1995–97; Opposition frontbench spokesman on Treasury matters, 1997, on trade and industry, 1997–99, on further and higher educn and disabilities, 1999–2001, 2002–03, on pensions and disabilities, 2001–02, on home, constitutional and legal affairs, 2003–04; Shadow Minister for Work, 2004–07; PPS to Chm., Cons. Party, 2005–07. Member Select Cttee for: Agriculture, 1987–89; Innovation, Univs and Skills, 2007–09; for Sci. and Technol., 2009–10; Sec., Cons. Backbench Cttee on Agriculture, 1987–89; Chm., All-Party Charity Law Review Panel, 1988–90. Treas., 1976–79, Chm., 1979–83, Daventry Constituency Cons. Assoc. Contested (C) Rugby, Feb. 1974. Principal Dep. Chm. of Cttees, H of L, 2012–; Chair, EU Select Cttee, H of L, 2012–. Pres., Nat. Energy Action, 2012–13. Chairman: Friends of Torres Vedras, 2011–12; Northants VCH Trust, 2011–. Governor: Cardiff Metropolitan Univ. (formerly Univ. of Wales Inst.), 2007–12 (Vice-Chm., 2010–12); Northampton Univ., 2010–12 (Hon. Fellow, 2010). DL Northants, 2010. *Recreations:* the countryside, shooting, snooker, poetry. *Address:* House of Lords, SW1A 0PW. *Club:* Farmers.
See also Hon. V. M. B. Prentis.

BOSWELL, Alexander; Vice Lord-Lieutenant for Buckinghamshire, since 2011; *b* North Crawley, 26 Jan. 1951; *s* of Ian Boswell and Vera Boswell; *m* 1977, Jane Elizabeth Ratcliffe; one *s* one *d*. *Educ:* Radley Coll.; Corpus Christi, Oxford (MA Mod. Hist.). Working landowner and farmer, 1977–; small business entrepreneur, 1977–. Dir, BW Foods Ltd, 1996–. Country Land & Business Association: Chairman: London Council, 2011; London Policy Cttee, 2011; Bucks Br., 2012. Chm., Bucks Honours Cttee, 2014. Pres., Milton Keynes Community Foundn, 2009; Patron: Willen Hospice, 2007; Bletchley Park, 2011; Trustee, Milton Keynes Parks Trust, 2009; organiser, Treasures in MK art exhibn, 2014. Bucks Ambassador, 2005. High Sheriff 2006–07, DL 2008, Bucks. *Recreations:* beautiful places, collecting and racing historic cars, wildlife conservation, game shooting, art, music, Italy. *Address:* Quakers House, North Crawley MK16 9HW. *T:* (01234) 391203. *E:* ab@quakershouse.com. *Club:* Royal Automobile.

BOSWELL, Lt-Gen. Sir Alexander (Crawford Simpson), KCB 1982; CBE 1974 (OBE 1971; MBE 1962); DL; Lieutenant-Governor and Commander-in-Chief, Guernsey, 1985–90; *b* 3 Aug. 1928; *s* of Alexander Boswell Simpson Boswell and Elizabeth Burns Simpson Boswell (*née* Park); *m* 1956, Jocelyn Leslie Blundstone Pomfret, *d* of Surg. Rear-Adm. A. A. Pomfret, CB, OBE; five *s*. *Educ:* Merchiston Castle Sch.; RMA, Sandhurst. Enlisted in Army, 1947; Commnd, Argyll and Sutherland Highlanders, Dec. 1948; regimental appts, Hong Kong, Korea, UK, Suez, Guyana, 1949–58; sc Camberley, 1959; Mil. Asst (GSO2) to GOC Berlin, 1960–62; Co. Comdr, then Second in Comd, 1 A and SH, Malaya and Borneo, 1963–65 (despatches 1965); Directing Staff, Staff Coll., Camberley, 1965–68; CO, 1 A and SH, 1968–71; Col GS Trng Army Strategic Comd, 1971; Brig. Comdg 39 Inf. Bde, 1972–74; COS, 1st British Corps, 1974–76; NDC (Canada), 1976–77; GOC 2nd Armd Div., 1978–80; Dir, TA and Cadets, 1980–82; GOC Scotland and Governor of Edinburgh Castle, 1982–85. Chairman: Scottish Veterans' Residences, 1991–2001; Officers Assoc. (Scottish Br.), 1991–98. Col, Argyll and Sutherland Highlanders, 1972–82; Hon. Col, Tayforth Univs OTC, 1982–86; Col Comdt, Scottish Div., 1982–86; Hon. Col, Scottish Transport Regt RLC(V), 1993–96. Captain of Tarbet, 1974–82. Pres., Friends of St Mary's Haddington, 1992–2003. KStJ 1985. DL East Lothian, 1993. *Address:* c/o Bank of Scotland, 44 Court Street, Haddington EH41 3NP.

BOSWELL, Lindsay Alice; QC 1997; *b* Nairobi, 22 Nov. 1958; *d* of Graham Leonard William Boswell and Erica Boswell (*née* Mayers); *m* 1987, Jonathan James Acton Davis, *qv*; one *s*. *Educ:* St Mary's, Ascot; Brooke House; University Coll. London (BSc Econ Hons); City Univ. (Dip. Law). Called to the Bar, Gray's Inn, 1982, Bencher, 2004. *Recreations:* walking, beekeeping, counting sheep. *Address:* Quadrant Chambers, 10 Fleet Street, Temple, EC4Y 1AU. *Club:* Royal Air Force.

BOSWELL, Philip John; MP (SNP) Coatbridge, Chryston and Bellshill, since 2015; *b* Bellshill, 23 July 1963; *s* of Peter and Joan Boswell; *m* Anne; one *s* two *d*. *Educ:* Glasgow Caledonian Univ. (BSc Quantity Surveying 1989); Univ. of Reading (Dip. Arbitration 2007). FCIArb 2007. Sen. Contracts Engr, Qatar Petroleum, 2003–06; Sen. Contracts Engr and Project Services Engr, 2006–08, Lead Contracts Engr, 2008–11, BP; Contracts and Procurement Specialist, Shell, 2011–14; Contracts Engr, Premier Oil, 2014–15. *Recreations:* family, music, cycling, walking, reading. *Address:* House of Commons, SW1A 0AA. *E:* phil.boswell.mp@parliament.uk.

BOSWOOD, Anthony Richard; QC 1986; international arbitrator; *b* 1 Oct. 1947; *s* of late Noel Gordon Paul Boswood and of Cicily Ann Watson; *m* 1973, Sarah Bridget Alexander; three *d*. *Educ:* St Paul's Sch.; New Coll., Oxford (BCL, MA). Called to Bar, Middle Temple, 1970, Bencher, 1995. *Recreations:* opera, riding, racing, gardening, theology. *Address:* Fountain Court, Temple, EC4Y 9DH. *T:* (020) 7583 3335; Podere Casanuova, Pieveasciata, Castelnuovo Berardenga (SI), Italy; South Hay House, Binsted, Alton, Hants GU35 9NR. *E:* aboswood@fountaincourt.co.uk. *Club:* Athenæum.

BOTHA, Roelof Frederik, (Pik), DMS 1981; MP (National Party), 1977–96; Minister of Energy, South Africa, 1994–96; Leader, Transvaal National Party, 1992–96; *b* 27 April 1932; *m* 1953, Helena Susanna Bosman; two *s* two *d*; *m* 1998, Ina Joubert. *Educ:* Volkskool, Potchefstroom; Univ. of Pretoria (BA, LLB). Dept of Foreign Affairs, 1953; diplomatic missions, Europe, 1956–62; Mem. team from S Africa, in SW Africa case, Internat. Court of Justice, The Hague, 1963–66, 1970–71; Agent for S African Govt, Internat. Court of Justice, 1965–66; Legal Adviser, Dept of Foreign Affairs, 1966–68; Under-Sec. and Head of SW Africa and UN Sections, 1968–70. National Party, MP for Wonderboom, 1970–74. Mem., SA Delegn to UN Gen. Assembly, 1967–69, 1971, 1973–74. Served on select Parly Cttees, 1970–74. South African Permanent Representative to the UN, NY, 1974–77; South African Ambassador to the USA, 1975–77. Minister of Foreign Affairs, 1977–94; Minister of Information, 1978–86. Grand Cross, Order of Good Hope, 1980; Order of the Brilliant Star with Grand Cordon, 1980. *Address:* PO Box 59492, Karen Park, 0118, South Africa.

BOTHAM, Sir Ian (Terence), Kt 2007; OBE 1992; broadcaster, commentator and writer; *b* 24 Nov. 1955; *s* of Leslie and Marie Botham; *m* 1976, Kathryn Waller; one *s* two *d*. *Educ:* Milford Junior Sch.; Buckler's Mead Secondary Sch., Yeovil. Bowler and batsman for County Cricket Clubs: Somerset, 1974–87 (Captain, 1983–85; Hon. Life Mem., 1993); Worcestershire, 1987–91; Durham, 1992–93 (Hon. Life Mem.); England Test cricketer, 1977–92 (Captain, 1980–81); scored 1,000 runs and took 100 wickets in 21 Tests at age 23, 1979; scored 3,000 runs and took 300 wickets in Tests to 1982; first player to score a century and take 10 wickets in a Test match, Bombay, 1979; made 100 runs and took 8 wickets in 3 Tests, 1978, 1980, 1984; made 5,200 runs, took 383 wickets and 120 catches in 102 Tests; played cricket for Queensland, football for Scunthorpe and Yeovil. Chm., Mission Sports Mgt (formerly Mission Logistics) Ltd, 2000–12. Marathon walks for leukaemia research incl. Land's End to John o'Groats and Alps; Pres., Leukaemia and Lymphoma Res. (formerly Leukaemia Res. Fund), 2003–. Columnist, Daily Mirror. Team captain, A Question of Sport, BBC, 1989–96. Mem., Sky cricket commentary team, 1995–. *Publications:* Ian Botham on Cricket, 1980; (with Ian Jarrett) Botham Down Under, 1983; (with Kenneth Gregory) Botham's Bedside Cricket Book, 1983; (with Peter Roebuck) It Sort of Clicks, 1986, rev. edn 1987; (with Jack Bannister) Cricket My Way, 1989; Botham: my autobiography, 1994; (with Peter Hayter) The Botham Report, 1997; Botham's Century, 2001; My Illustrated Life, 2007; Head On: the autobiography, 2007; Ian Botham on Fishing, 2008; My Sporting Heroes, 2009; Beefy's Cricket Tales, 2013. *Address:* North Yorkshire. *Club:* MCC (Hon. Mem. 1994).

BOTHAMLEY, John Peter, CBE 2013; Managing Director, John Newlands Ltd, since 1970; *b* Bramley, Guildford, 31 May 1944; *s* of Stanley Vincent Bothamley and Ethel Florence Bothamley (*née* Ingall); partner, Elizabeth Lloyd. *Educ:* Purley Grammar Sch.; Thames Poly. (BA Hons Architecture). Res. Exec., Economist Intelligence Unit, 1962–65; Econ. Researcher, Transport Hldg Co., 1965–66; Man. Dir's Asst, Ayling Industries Ltd, 1967–69. Associate, Creating Buildings, 1991–. Founder Trustee: Four Acre Trust, 1996–; Talk the Talk, 2013–; Trustee, Assoc. of Charitable Foundns, 2002–06. Member: Hereford Civic Soc.; Twentieth Century Soc. *Recreations:* contemporary architecture, education, drawing, cycling, democracy research, travel, journalism. *Address:* Treferanon, St Weonards, Hereford HR2 8QF. *T:* (01981) 580002. *E:* john@johnbothamley.co.uk.

BOTHROYD, Shirley Ann; barrister. Called to the Bar, 1982; Second Prosecuting Counsel, 1989–91, First Prosecuting Counsel, 1991–93, to Inland Revenue at CCC and Inner London Crown Ct. *Recreations:* wine, organizing others. *Address:* Littleton Chambers, 3 King's Bench Walk North, Temple, EC4Y 7HR. *T:* (020) 7797 8600.

BOTÍN-SANZ DE SAUTUOLA Y O'SHEA, Ana; Executive Chairman, Banco Santander, since 2014; *b* Santander, Spain, 4 Oct. 1960; *d* of late Emilio Botín and of Paloma O'Shea, 1st Marquise of O'Shea; *m* 1983, Guillermo Morenès Mariátegui; three *s*. *Educ:* St Mary's, Ascot; Bryn Mawr Coll. (BA Econs). JP Morgan, 1981–88 (Vice Pres., 1985–88); Banco Santander, 1988–99: Dep. Man. Dir, then Man. Dir, Banco Santander, later Chief Exec., Banco Santander de Negocios; Founder and CEO, Suala, private equity fund and IT web consultancy firm, 1999–2002; Chair, Banesto, 2002–10; CEO, Santander UK, 2010–14. Non-exec. Dir, Coca Cola Co., 2013–. *Recreations:* family, golf, reading, music, social responsibility and philanthropic work as a Founder and Chair of CyD Foundn for higher education and Empieza por Educar (Spanish affiliate of Teach for All). *Address:* Santander Group City, Av. de Cantabria s/n 28660, Boadilla del Monte, Madrid, Spain.

BOTT, Catherine Jane; singer and broadcaster; *b* 11 Sept. 1952; *d* of Maurice Bott and Patricia Bott (*née* Sherlock). *Educ:* King's High Sch. for Girls, Warwick; Guildhall Sch. of Music and Drama (GGSM). Concert, oratorio and recital singer; worldwide concert engagements, incl. world premières of Francis Grier's Five Joyful Mysteries, 2000, Joe Duddell's Not Waving but Drowning, 2002; first public performance of Jonathan Dove's Five Am'rous Sighs, 2002; radio broadcasts; numerous recordings with leading ensembles and orchestras, recital recordings and recordings of operatic roles, incl. Purcell's Dido, Messaggiera (l'Orfeo), Drusilla (l'Incoronazione di Poppaea), and Mandane (Artaxerxes). Co-Presenter, The Early Music Show, BBC Radio 3, 2003–13; presenter, Everything You Ever Wanted to Know About Classical Music, Classic FM, 2013–; regular contribs to music and arts progs on Radio 3 and Radio 4. Gov., Trinity Laban Conservatoire of Music and Dance, 2008–12 (Hon. Fellow, 2013); Patron: Portsmouth Festivities, 2005–; Isleworth Baroque, 2006–. FGS (FGSM 2009). *Recreations:* exploring London, going to the ballet, learning Spanish rather slowly. *Address:* c/o MAS, Ranmore House, 19 Ranmore Road, Dorking, Surrey RH4 1HE.

BOTT, Dr David Charles, FRSC; Chairman, Oxford Biomaterials, since 2004; Director of Innovation Programmes and Communications, Technology Strategy Board, since 2007; *b* Gosport, Hants, 25 Nov. 1953; *s* of Kenneth Charles and Mary Lewis Bott; *m* 1981, Connie Ramsay; three *s*. *Educ:* Univ. of Sussex (BSc 1975; PhD 1979). Res. scientist, British Petroleum Res., 1979–87; Res. Manager, Courtaulds, 1987–95; Res. Dir, ICI Acrylics, 1995–99; Divl Vice Pres. of Res., National Starch, 1999–2001; Dir of Res., ICI, 2001–04; CEO, Materials UK, 2004–07. Dir, Oxford Advanced Surfaces, 2010–. FRSA. Hon. PhD Sheffield, 2011. *Publications:* contrib. chapters in books and papers to jls. *Recreations:* keeping an old car on the roads, trying to play guitar. *Address:* High House, High Street, Inkberrow, Worcs WR7 4DT. *T:* (01386) 793591. *E:* david.bott@mac.com.

BOTT, Ian Bernard, FREng; Director, Admiralty Research Establishment, Ministry of Defence, 1984–88, retired; consultant engineer, since 1988; *b* 1 April 1932; *s* of late Edwin Bernard and Agnes Bott; *m* 1955, Kathleen Mary (*née* Broadbent); one *s* one *d*. *Educ:* Nottingham High Sch.; Southwell Minster Grammar Sch.; Stafford Technical Coll.;

Manchester Univ. BSc Hons Physics. FIEE, FInstP; FREng (FEng 1985). Nottingham Lace Industry, 1949–53. Royal Air Force, 1953–55. English Electric, Stafford, 1955–57; Royal Radar Estabt, 1960–75 (inventor of terahertz Electron Cyclotron Maser, patent applied for 1963; Head of Electronics Group, 1973–75); Counsellor and Dep. Hd of Defence Research and Development Staff, British Embassy, Washington DC, 1975–77; Ministry of Defence: Dep. Dir Underwater Weapons Projects (S/M), 1977–79; Asst Chief Scientific Advr (Projects), 1979–81; Dir Gen., Guided Weapons and Electronics, 1981–82; Principal Dep. Dir, AWRE, MoD, 1982–84. Mem. Council, Fellowship of Engrg, 1987–90. Hon. Chm., Portsmouth Area Hospice, 1989–94 (Hon. Life Vice Pres., 1998). Trustee, Panasonic Trust, 1993–96. Freeman, City of London, 1985; Liveryman, Co. of Engineers, 1985. *Publications:* papers on physics and electronics subjects in jls of learned socs. *Recreations:* golf, horology, music. *Address:* The Lodge, Brand Lane, Ludlow, Shropshire SY8 1NN. *E:* ianbbott@tiscali.co.uk. *Club:* Royal Automobile.

BOTT, Prof. Martin Harold Phillips, FRS 1977; Professor, 1966–88, Research Professor, 1988–91, in Geophysics, University of Durham, now Professor Emeritus; *b* 12 July 1926; *s* of Harold Bott and Dorothy (*née* Phillips); *m* 1961, Joyce Cynthia Hughes; two *s* one *d.* *Educ:* Clayesmore Sch., Dorset; Magdalene Coll., Cambridge (Scholar). MA, PhD. Nat. Service, 1945–48 (Lieut, Royal Signals). Durham University: Turner and Newall Fellow, 1954–56; Lectr, 1956–63; Reader, 1963–66. Anglican Reader, 1959–. Mem. Council, Royal Soc., 1982–84. Murchison Medallist, Geological Soc. of London, 1977; Clough Medal, Geol Soc. of Edinburgh, 1979; Sorby Medal, Yorkshire Geol Soc., 1981; Wollaston Medal, Geol Soc. of London, 1992. *Publications:* The Interior of the Earth, 1971, 2nd edn 1982; papers in learned jls. *Recreations:* walking, mountains (Scottish Munros completed in 2002), garden slavery.

BOTT, Susan Mary, CBE 2014; Director, Policy and Development, Disability Rights UK, since 2012; *b* Faversham, Kent, 23 Aug. 1956; *d* of E. R. Bott and E. Bott; one *s* one *d.* *Educ:* Exhall Grange Special Sch., Coventry; Univ. of Sheffield (BSc); Aston Univ. (MSc). Shropshire Disability Consortium: devolt worker; Chief Exec., 1995–2005; Chief Exec., Nat. Centre for Independent Living, 2006–12. Chm., Think Local Act Personal Partnership, 2011–13. *Recreations:* enjoying the great outdoors, especially the sea. *T:* 07725 511562. *E:* suembott@gmail.com.

BOTTAI, Bruno; President, Società Dante Alighieri, since 1996; Chairman, Fondazione Premio Balzan, 1999–2013, now Chairman Emeritus; *b* 10 July 1930; *s* of Giuseppe Bottai and Cornelia Ciocca. *Educ:* Univ. of Rome (law degree). Joined Min. for For. Affairs, 1954; Vice Consul, Tunis, 1956; Second Sec., Perm. Representation to EC, Brussels, 1958; Gen. Secretariat, Co-ord. Service, Min. for For. Affairs, 1961; Counsellor, London, 1966; Dep. Chef de Cabinet, Min. for For. Affairs, 1968; Minister-Counsellor, Holy See, 1969; Diplomatic Advr to Pres., Council of Ministers, 1970; Hd of Press and Inf. Dept 1972, Dep. Dir-Gen. of Political Affairs 1976, Min. for For. Affairs; Ambassador to Holy See and Sovereign Mil. Order of Malta, 1979; Dir-Gen. Pol Affairs, Min. for For. Affairs, 1981; Ambassador to UK, 1985–87; Sec. Gen., Min. of Foreign Affairs, Italy, 1987–94; Ambassador of Italy to the Holy See, 1994–97. Numerous decorations from Europe, Africa, Latin Amer. countries, Holy See, Malta. *Publications:* political essays and articles. *Recreations:* modern paintings and modern sculpture, theatre, reading, walking. *Address:* Società Dante Alighieri, Piazza Firenze 27, 00186 Rome, Italy.

BOTTING, Maj.-Gen. David Francis Edmund, CB 1992; CBE 1986; Director General of Ordnance Services, Ministry of Defence, 1990–93; *b* 15 Dec. 1937; *s* of Leonard Edmund Botting and Elizabeth Mildred Botting (*née* Stacey); *m* 1962, Anne Outhwaite; two *s.* *Educ:* St Paul's School, London. National Service, RAOC, 1956; commissioned Eaton Hall, 1957; Regular Commission, 1958; regtl appts, Kineton, Deepcut, Borneo, Singapore and Malaya, 1957–67; sc 1968; BAOR, 1972–74; 1 Div., 1974–75; 3rd Div., 1981–82; Col AQ 1 Div., 1982–85; Comd Sup. 1 (BR) Corps, 1987; ACOS HQ UKLF, 1987–90. Rep. Col Comdt, RAOC, 1993; Col Comdt, RLC, 1993–2002. Trustee, Army Benevolent Fund, 1997–2007; Chm., RLC Mus. Trust, 2000–04; Pres., RAOC Charitable Trust, 2002–07. FILDM 1991; MInstPS 1991. Freeman, City of London, 1990; Liveryman, Co. of Gold and Silver Wyre Drawers, 1991–2008. *Recreations:* golf, philately, furniture restoration. *Clubs:* Army and Navy; Tidworth Golf.

BOTTING, (Elizabeth) Louise, CBE 1993; Chairman, Douglas Deakin Young, 1988–2005 (Managing Director, 1982–88); *b* 19 Sept. 1939; *d* of Robert and Edith Young; marr. diss.; two *d*; *m* 1989, Leslie Arthur Carpenter, *qv.* *Educ:* Sutton Coldfield High School; London Sch. of Economics (BSc Econ.). Kleinwort Benson, 1961–65; Daily Mail, 1970–75; British Forces Broadcasting, 1971–83; Douglas Deakin Young, financial consultancy, 1975–2005. Director: Trinity International, 1991–99; CGU (formerly General Accident), 1992–2000; London Weekend Television, 1992–94; 102, Stratford-upon-Avon Radio Station, 1996–2001; Camelot plc, 1999–2010. Presenter, BBC Moneybox, 1977–92. Mem. Top Salaries Review Body, 1987–94. *Address:* Duncan Lawrie Private Bank, 1 Hobart Place, SW1W 0HU. *T:* (020) 7201 3030.

See also J. R. C. Young.

BOTTO DE BARROS, Adwaldo Cardoso; Director-General, International Bureau of Universal Postal Union, 1985–94; *b* 19 Jan. 1925; *s* of Julio Botto de Barros and Maria Cardoso Botto de Barros; *m* 1951, Neida de Moura; one *s* two *d.* *Educ:* Military Coll., Military Engineering Inst. and Higher Military Engineering Inst., Brazil. Railway construction, 1952–54; Dir, industries in São Paulo and Curitiba, 1955–64; Dir, Handling Sector, São Paulo Prefecture, Financial Adviser to São Paulo Engrg Faculty and Adviser to Suzano Prefecture, 1965–71; Regional Dir, São Paulo, 1972–74; Pres., Brazilian Telegraph and Post Office, Brasília-DF, 1974–84. Mem. and Head, numerous delegns to UPU and other postal assocs overseas, 1976–84. Numerous Brazilian and foreign hons and decorations. *Recreations:* philately, sports.

BOTTOMLEY, family name of **Baroness Bottomley of Nettlestone**.

BOTTOMLEY OF NETTLESTONE, Baroness *cr* 2005 (Life Peer), of St Helens, in the county of Isle of Wight; **Virginia Hilda Brunette Maxwell Bottomley;** PC 1992; JP; DL; *b* 12 March 1948; *d* of late W. John Garnett, CBE and of Barbara (*née* Rutherford-Smith); *m* Sir Peter James Bottomley, *qv*; one *s* two *d.* *Educ:* London Sch. of Econs and Pol Science (MSc). Research for Child Poverty Action Gp, 1971–73; behavioural scientist, 1973–84. Partner, Odgers Berndtson, 2000– (Dir, Odgers Gp Ltd); Member: Supervisory Bd, Akzo Nobel NV, 2000–12; Internat. Adv. Council, Chugai Pharmaceutical Co. Ltd, 2012–. Non-executive Director: BUPA, 2007–12; Smith & Nephew, 2012–. Mem., MRC, 1987–88. Contested (C) IoW, 1983. MP (C) Surrey SW, May 1984–2005. PPS: to Minister of State for Educn and Science, 1985–86; to Minister for Overseas Develt, 1986–87; to Sec. of State for Foreign and Commonwealth Affairs, 1987–88; Parly Under-Sec. of State, DoE, 1988–89; Minister for Health, 1989–92; Secretary of State: for Health, 1992–95; for Nat. Heritage, 1995–97. Fellow, Industry Parlt Trust, 1987 (Trustee, 2002–05); Ind. Trustee, Economist newspaper, 2005–. Vice-Chm., British Council, 1998–2001. Pro-Chancellor, Univ. of Surrey, 2005–; Chancellor, Univ. of Hull, 2006–. Mem. Bd, Prince of Wales Internat. Business Leaders Forum, 2002–; Pres., Farnham Castle, Centre for Internat. Briefing, 2003–. Mem., UK Adv. Bd, ICC, 2005–. Nat. Pres., Abbeyfield Soc., 2003–09. Mem., Court of Govs, LSE, 1985–; Mem. Council, Ditchley Foundn, 2005– (Gov., 1991–2005); Gov., Univ. of the Arts (formerly London Inst.), 2000–06. JP Inner London, 1975 (Chm., Lambeth Juvenile Court, 1981–84). DL Surrey, 2006. Sheriff, Kingston-upon-Hull, 2013–. Freeman, City of London, 1988. Lay Canon, Guildford Cathedral, 2002–. *Recreations:* work, grandchildren. *Address:* House of Lords, SW1A 0PW. *Clubs:* Athenæum; Seaview Yacht.

BOTTOMLEY, Sir Peter (James), Kt 2011; MP (C) Worthing West, since 1997 (Greenwich, Woolwich West, June 1975–1983, Eltham, 1983–97); *b* 30 July 1944; *er s* of Sir James Reginald Alfred Bottomley, KCMG; *m* 1967, Virginia Garnett (*see* Baroness Bottomley of Nettlestone); one *s* two *d.* *Educ:* comprehensive sch.; Westminster Sch.; Trinity Coll., Cambridge (MA). Driving, industrial sales, industrial relations, industrial economics. Contested (C) GLC elect., Vauxhall, 1973; (C) Woolwich West, gen. elecns, 1974. PPS to Minister of State, FCO, 1982–83, to Sec. of State for Social Services, 1983–84, to Sec. of State for NI, 1990; Parly Under Sec. of State, Dept of Employment, 1984–86, Dept of Transport, 1986–89, NI Office, 1989–90. Member: Transport Cttee, 1992–97; Ecclesiastical Cttee, 2002–05, 2010–15; Select Cttee on HS2. Sec., Cons. Parly For. and Commonwealth Cttee, 1979–81; Leader, UK Delegn to Parly Assembly, OSCE, 2010–. Pres., Cons. Trade Unionists, 1978–80; Vice-Pres., Fedn of Cons. Students, 1980–82. Chairman: British Union of Family Orgns, 1973–80; Family Forum, 1980–82; Church of England Children's Soc., 1983–84. Member Council: MIND, 1981–82; NACRO, 1997–2004; Trustee, Christian Aid, 1978–84. Parly Swimming Champion, 1980–81, 1984–86; Captain, Parly Football Team; occasional Parly Dinghy Sailing Champion; Parly Warden, St Margaret's Church, Westminster, 2010–. Mem., Ct of Assts, Drapers' Co. Castrol/Inst. of Motor Industry Road Safety Gold Medal, 1988. *Recreations:* children, book reviewing, canoeing. *Address:* House of Commons, SW1A 0AA. *E:* bottomleyp@parliament.uk.

BOTTOMS, Sir Anthony Edward, Kt 2001; FBA 1997; Wolfson Professor of Criminology, 1984–2006, now Emeritus, and Director of the Institute of Criminology, 1984–98, University of Cambridge; Fellow of Fitzwilliam College, Cambridge, 1984–2006, now Life Fellow (President, 1994–98); Professorial Fellow in Criminology, University of Sheffield, 2002–07, now Honorary Professor; *b* 29 Aug. 1939; *yr s* of James William Bottoms, medical missionary, and Dorothy Ethel Bottoms (*née* Barnes); *m* 1962, Janet Freda Wenger; one *s* two *d.* *Educ:* Eltham Coll.; Corpus Christi Coll., Oxford (MA; Hon. Fellow, 2012); Corpus Christi Coll., Cambridge (Dip. Criminol. 1962; MA); Univ. of Sheffield (PhD). Probation Officer, 1962–64; Research Officer, Inst. of Criminology, Univ. of Cambridge, 1964–68; Univ. of Sheffield: Lecturer, 1968–72; Sen. Lectr, 1972–76; Prof. of Criminology, 1976–84; Dean of Faculty of Law, 1981–84. Canadian Commonwealth Vis. Fellow, Simon Fraser Univ., BC, 1982; Vis. Prof., QUB, 1999–2000. Member: Parole Bd for England and Wales, 1974–76; Home Office Res. and Adv. Gp on Long-Term Prison System, 1984–90. Specialist Advr, NI Cttee, H of C, 1998, 2003–04, 2007. Chm. of Trustees, Westminster Coll., Cambridge, 2008–14. Editor, Howard Journal of Penology and Crime Prevention, 1975–81. Hon. LLD: QUB, 2003; Sheffield, 2009; Hedersdoktor, Malmö, 2014. Sellin-Glueck Award, Amer. Soc. of Criminology, 1996; Eur. Criminology Award, Eur. Soc. of Criminology, 2007. *Publications:* (jtly) Criminals Coming of Age, 1973; (jtly) The Urban Criminal, 1976; (jtly) Defendants in the Criminal Process, 1976; The Suspended Sentence after Ten Years (Frank Dawtry Lecture), 1980; (ed jtly) The Coming Penal Crisis, 1980; (ed jtly) Problems of Long-Term Imprisonment, 1987; (jtly) Social Inquiry Reports, 1988; (jtly) Intermediate Treatment and Juvenile Justice, 1990; Crime Prevention facing the 1990s (James Smart Lecture), 1990; Intensive Community Supervision for Young Offenders, 1995; (jtly) Prisons and the Problem of Order, 1996; (jtly) Criminal Deterrence and Sentence Severity, 1999; (ed jtly) Community Penalties, 2001; (ed jtly) Ideology, Crime and Criminal Justice, 2002; (ed jtly) Alternatives to Prison, 2004; (ed jtly) Hearing the Victim, 2010; (ed jtly) Young Adult Offenders, 2012; various articles and reviews. *Address:* Institute of Criminology, Sidgwick Avenue, Cambridge CB3 9DA. *T:* (01223) 335360.

BOTTONE, Bonaventura; tenor; *s* of Bonaventura Bottone and Kathleen; *m* Jennifer Dakin; two *s* two *d.* *Educ:* Lascelles Secondary Mod. Sch., Harrow; Royal Acad. Music (ARAM 1984; FRAM 1998). Has appeared at numerous international venues, including: Nice Opera (début 1982); Houston Opera (début 1987); Royal Opera House, Covent Garden (début 1987); London Coliseum; Glyndebourne Fest. (début 1990); Bavarian State Opera, Munich (début 1991); Fundação de São Carlos, Lisbon (début 1994); Chicago Lyric Opera (début 1994); New Israeli Opera, Tel Aviv (début 1995); Metropolitan Opera, NY (début 1998); Opera del Teatro Municipal, Santiago (début 1998); Paris Opéra Bastille (début 2000); Atlanta Opera (début 2001); Brisbane SO (début 2002); Deutsches SO Berlin (début 2002); La Fenice, Venice (début 2003); La Scala, Milan (début 2007); Los Angeles Opera (début 2008). Has performed with Philharmonia Orch., Edmonton SO, ENO, Royal Opera Co., Scottish Opera, Opera North and Welsh Opera; rôles include: Alfredo in La Traviata, Italian Tenor in Der Rosenkavalier, Governor General in Candide, Nanki-Poo in Mikado, Lenski in Eugene Onegin, Alfred in Die Fledermaus, Narraboth in Salome, Duke of Mantua in Rigoletto, Pinkerton in Madam Butterfly, Turridù in Cavalleria Rusticana, title rôle, Damnation of Faust, title rôle, Doctor Ox's Experiment (world première), Rodolfo in La Bohème, Riccardo in Un Ballo in Maschera, Troilus in Troilus and Cressida, Loge in Das Rheingold, Torquemada in L'heure Espagnole, Nick in La Fanciulla del West, L'Abate in Adriana Lecouvreur, Basilio in Le Nozze di Figaro, Benda in The Jacobin. Has made numerous recordings. *Recreations:* gardening, boating. *Address:* c/o Rayfield Allied, Southbank House, Black Prince Road, SE1 7SJ. *T:* (020) 3176 5500, *Fax:* 0700 602 4143. *E:* info@rayfieldallied.com.

BOTWOOD, Richard Price; Director-General, Chartered Institute of Transport, 1989–98; *b* 1 June 1932; *s* of Allan Bertram and Hilda Amelia Botwood; *m* 1964, Victoria Sanderson; one *s* one *d.* *Educ:* Oundle School. Sec., Tozer Kemsley & Millbourn, 1952–56; Dir, International Factors, 1956–61; Asst Man. Dir, Melbray Group, 1961–73; Chm. and Man. Dir, W. S. Sanderson (Morpeth), wine and spirit merchants, 1973–85; Dir-Gen., Air Transport Users' Cttee, 1986–89. *Recreations:* opera, gardening, embroidery, golf. *Address:* 54 Bute Gardens, W6 7DX. *T:* (020) 8748 8875.

BOUCHARD, Hon. Lucien; GOQ 2008; PC (Can.) 1988; Senior Partner, Davies Ward Phillips & Vineberg LLP, since 2001; President, Quebec Oil and Gas Association, since 2011; *b* 22 Dec. 1938; *m* 1989, Audrey Best (marr. diss; she *d* 2011); two *s.* *Educ:* Collège de Jonquière; Université Laval (BA, BSocSc, LLB 1964). Called to the Bar, Quebec, 1964; in private practice, Chicoutimi, 1964–85. Pres., Saguenay Bar, 1978; Mem., Admin Cttee and Chm., Specialisation Cttee, Quebec Bar. Ambassador to France, 1985–88; MP (C), 1988–90, (Ind), 1990–91, (Bloc Québécois), 1991–96, Lac-St-Jean; Secretary of State, 1988–89; Minister of the Envmt, 1989–90; Chm. and Leader, Bloc Québécois, 1991–96; Leader of Federal Opposition, 1993–96; Mem. for Jonquière, Quebec Nat. Assembly, 1996–2001; Prime Minister of Quebec, 1996–2001; Leader, Parti Québécois, 1996–2001. Director: Transcontinental Inc.; Saputo Inc.; TransForce Inc. Commandeur, Légion d'Honneur (France), 2002. *Publications:* (jtly) Martin-Bouchard Report, 1978; A visage découvert, 1992 (trans. English 1994); specialised articles in legal and labour relns jls. *Address:* Davies Ward Phillips & Vineberg LLP, 1501 McGill College Avenue, 26th Floor, Montreal, QC H3A 3N9, Canada.

BOUCHIER, Prof. Ian Arthur Dennis, CBE 1990; Professor of Medicine, University of Edinburgh, 1986–97; Chief Scientist, Scottish Office Department of Health (formerly Home and Health Department), 1992–97; *b* 7 Sept. 1932; *s* of E. A. and M. Bouchier; *m* 1959, Patricia Norma Henshilwood; two *s.* *Educ:* Rondebosch Boys' High Sch., Cape Town; Univ. of Cape Town. MB, ChB, MD, FRCP, FRCPE, FFPH; FRSE, FRSB. Groote Schuur Hospital: House Officer, 1955–58; Registrar, 1958–61; Asst Lectr, Royal Free Hosp., 1962–63; Instructor in Medicine, Boston Univ. Sch. of Medicine, 1964–65; Sen. Lectr

1965–70, Reader in Medicine 1970–73, Univ. of London; Prof. of Medicine, 1973–86, and Dean, Faculty of Medicine and Dentistry, 1982–86, Univ. of Dundee. Pres., World Organisation of Gastroenterology, 1990–98 (Sec. Gen., 1982–90); British Society of Gastroenterology: Mem. Council, 1987–90; Chm. Educn Cttee, 1987–90; Pres., 1994–95. Member: Chief Scientist Cttee, Scotland, 1980–97; MRC, 1982–86; Council, RCPE, 1984–90. Goulstonian Lectr, RCP, 1971; Sydney Watson Smith Lectr, RCPE, 1991. Visiting Professor of Medicine: Michigan Univ., 1979; McGill Univ., 1983; RPMS, 1984; Shenyang Univ., Hong Kong Univ., 1988. FRSA. Hon. FCP (SoAf); Founder FMedSci 1998. Hon. Mem., Japanese Soc. Gastroenterology; Corresp. Member: Soc. Italiana di Gastroenterologia; Royal Catalonian Acad. of Medicine. Chm., Editl Bd, Current Opinion in Gastroenterology, 1987–91; Member, Editorial Board: Baillière's Clinical Gastroenterology, 1987–98; Hellenic Jl of Gastroenterology, 1988–98; Internat. Gastroenterology, 1988–98. Hon. MD Iasi, 2001. *Publications:* (ed jtly) Bilirubin Metabolism, 1967; (ed) Clinical Investigation of Gastrointestinal Function, 1969, 2nd edn 1981; (ed) Seventh Symposium on Advanced Medicine, 1971; (ed) Diseases of the Biliary Tract, vol. 2, 1973; Gastroenterology, 1973, 3rd edn 1982; (jtly) Aspects of Clinical Gastroenterology, 1975; (ed jtly) Clinical Skills, 1976, 2nd edn 1982; (ed) Recent Advances in Gastroenterology 3, 1976, 4, 1980, 5, 1983; (ed jtly) Textbook of Gastroenterology, 1984; (ed jtly) Inflammatory Bowel Disease, 1986, 2nd edn 1993; (ed jtly) Davidson's Principles and Practice of Medicine, 15th edn 1987 to 17th edn 1995; (ed jtly) Clinical Investigations in Gastroenterology, 1988; (ed) Jaundice, 1989; (ed jtly) Infectious Diarrhoea, 1993; (ed jtly) Gastroenterology Clinical Science and Practice, vols 1 and 2, 2nd edn 1993; (ed jtly) Quality Assurance in Medical Care, 1993; (ed jtly) French's Index of Differential Diagnosis, 13th edn 1996; 600 scientific papers and communications. *Recreations:* history of whaling, music of Berlioz, cooking.

BOUGH, Francis Joseph; broadcaster; *b* 15 Jan. 1933; *m*; three *s*. *Educ:* Oswestry; Merton College, Oxford (BA). With ICI, 1957–62; BBC, 1962–89; presenter of Sportsview, 1964–67, of Grandstand, 1967–82, of Nationwide, 1972–83, of breakfast television, 1983–87, of Holiday, 1987–88; presenter: 6 o'clock Live, LWT, 1989–92; Sky TV, 1989–90; LBC Radio, 1992–96; Travel Live, on Travel TV (cable and satellite), 1996–. Richard Dimbleby Award for Factual Television, BAFTA, 1976. Former Oxford soccer blue, Shropshire sprint champion. *Publications:* Cue Frank! (autobiog.), 1980; Frank Bough's Breakfast Book, 1984.

BOUGHEY, Sir John (George Fletcher), 11th Bt *cr* 1798; medical practitioner; *b* 12 Aug. 1959; *s* of Sir Richard James Boughey, 10th Bt, and of Davina Julia (now Lady Loch), *d* of FitzHerbert Wright; *S* father, 1978; *m* 2004, Hebote Bishaw (marr. diss. 2006). *Educ:* Eton; Univ. of Zimbabwe (MB ChB 1984); LRCPE; LRCSE; LRCPSGlas 1990; MRCPI 1994. *Heir: b* James Richard Boughey [*b* 29 Aug. 1960; *m* 1989, Katy Fenwicke-Clennell; two *s* two *d*].

BOULDING, Hilary; Principal, Royal Welsh College of Music & Drama, since 2007; *b* 25 Jan. 1957; *d* of James Frederick Boulding and Dorothy Boulding (*née* Watson). *Educ:* Heaton Sch., Newcastle upon Tyne; St Hilda's Coll., Oxford (BA Hons Music). TV Dir, 1981–85, TV Producer, 1985–92, BBC Scotland; Head of Arts and Music, BBC Wales, 1992–97; Commissioning Editor, Music (Policy), BBC Radio 3, 1997–99; Dir of Music, Arts Council of England, subseq. Arts Council England, 1999–2007. Mem. Bd, WNO, 2008–; Chm., Conservatoires UK, 2014–. *Recreations:* music, gardening. *Address:* Royal Welsh College of Music & Drama, Castle Grounds, Cathays Park, Cardiff CF10 3ER. *T:* (029) 2039 1333.

BOULDING, Philip Vincent; QC 1996; *b* 1 Feb. 1954; *s* of Vincent Fergusson Boulding and Sylvia Boulding; *m* 1988, Helen Elizabeth Richardson; one *s* one *d*. *Educ:* Downing Coll., Cambridge (Scholar; BA Law 1st Cl. Hons 1976; LLM 1977; MA 1979; Rugby Blue). Called to the Bar, Gray's Inn, 1979, Bencher, 2004; practice in London and South East; internat. arbitration practice in FE, based in Hong Kong; regular arbitrator, adjudicator and mediator in commercial contract disputes, esp. in engrg and construction law; admitted to Hong Kong Bar, 1997. Pres., Cambridge Univ. Amateur Boxing Club, 1990–94 (Vice-Pres., 1994–2000); Sen. Pres., Downing Coll. Griffins' Club, Cambridge, 2004–. Gov., Hills Road VI Form Coll., Cambridge, 1997–2000. Consultant Ed., Construction Law Reports, 2007–. *Publications:* (contrib.) Keating on Construction Contracts, 8th edn, 2008, 9th edn, 2012, (contrib.) Keating Supplement, 2013. *Recreations:* Rugby, tennis, swimming, shooting. *Address:* c/o Keating Chambers, 15 Essex Street, WC2R 3AA. *Clubs:* Royal Automobile; Hawks (Cambridge).

BOULEZ, Pierre, Hon. CBE 1979; composer, conductor; Honorary Director, Institut de Recherche et de Coordination Acoustique/Musique, since 1992 (Founding Director, 1976–91); *b* Montbrison, Loire, France, 26 March 1925. *Educ:* Saint-Etienne and Lyon (music and higher mathematics); Paris Conservatoire. Studied with Messiaen and René Leibowitz. Theatre conductor, Jean-Louis Barrault Company, Paris, 1948; visited USA with French Ballet Company, 1952. Has conducted major orchestras in his own and standard classical works in Great Britain, Europe, USA, S America and Asia; also conducted Wozzeck in Paris and Frankfurt; Parsifal at Bayreuth, 1966–70; The Ring, at Bayreuth, 1976–80; Chief Conductor, BBC Symphony Orch., 1971–75; Music Dir, NY Philharmonic, 1971–77; Principal Guest Conductor, Chicago Symphony Orch., 1995–2006, now Emeritus. Interested in poetry and aesthetics of Baudelaire, Mallarmé and René Char. *Compositions include:* Sonata No 1 (piano), 1946; Sonatine for flute and piano, 1946; Sonata No 2 (piano), 1947; Polyphonie X for 18 solo instruments, 1951; Visage nuptial (2nd version), 1951, rev. version, 1989; Structures for 2 pianos, 1952; Le Marteau sans Maître (voice and 6 instruments), 1954; Sonata No 3 (piano), 1957; Deux Improvisations sur Mallarmé for voice and 9 instruments, 1957; Doubles for orchestra, 1957; Pli selon Pli Hommage à Mallarmé, for voice and orchestra, 1957–62; Poésie pour Pouvoir for voices and orchestra, 1958; Soleil des Eaux (text by René Char) for chorus and orchestra, 1965; Eclat, 1965; Domaines for solo clarinet, 1968; Cummings ist der Dichter (16 solo voices and instruments), 1970; Eclat/Multiples, 1970; Explosante Fixe (8 solo instruments), 1972, rev. 1986; Rituel, for orchestra, 1975; Messagesquisses (7 celli), 1976; Notations, for orch., 1980; Répons, for orch. and live electronics, 1981–84; Dérive, 1984; Mémoriale, 1985; Dialogue de l'Ombre Double, 1985; Anthèmes 1, for violin solo, 1991; …explosante/fixe…, for 3 flutes, large ensemble and electronics, 1993; Incises, 1994; Anthèmes 2, for violin solo and electronics; Sur Incises, 1998; Notation VII, 1998; Dérive 2, 2006. Hon. doctorates include: Cambridge, 1980; UCLA, 1984; Bristol, 1986; Oxford, 1987; Brussels, 1988; Montreal, 1993; RCM, 1997; Birmingham, 2008; Brno Tchéquie, 2009; London Univ./Royal Academy, 2010. Knight, Order of Merit (Germany). Awards include: Grand Prix de la Musique, Paris, 1982; Charles Heidsieck Award for Outstanding Contribution to Franco-British Music, 1989; Polar Music Prize, Stockholm, 1996; Royal Philharmonic Soc. Award, 1999; Wolf Prize, Israel, 2000; Grawemeyer Award, Univ. of Louisville, 2001; Glenn Gould Prize, Glenn Gould Foundn, 2002; Kyoto Prize, Japan, 2009; De Gaulle-Adenauer Prize, 2011; Giga-Hertz Prize, 2011; Golden Lion for Lifetime Achievement, Venice Biennale, 2012; Gloria Artis Gold Medal, 2012; Robert Schumann Prize for Poetry and Music, 2012; Karol Szymanowski Prize, Foundn Karol Szymanowski, 2012; Frontiers of Knowledge Award, BBVA Foundn, 2013. *Publications:* Penser la musique d'aujourd'hui, 1966 (Boulez on Music Today, 1971); Relevés d'apprenti, 1966; Par volonté et par hasard, 1975; Points de Repère, 1981; Orientations, 1986; Jalons, 1989; Le pays fertile—Paul Klee, 1989; Pierre et John/Boulez et Cage, 1991; Imaginer/Points de repère I, 1995; Eclats 2002, 2002; L'écriture du geste, 2002; Regards sur autrui/Points de repère II, 2005; Leçons de musique/Points de repère III, 2005. *Address:* IRCAM, 1 place Igor Stravinsky, 75004 Paris, France. *Fax:* (1) 44781540.

BOULT, Geoffrey Pattisson; education consultant, since 2014; Headmaster, Giggleswick School, 2001–14; *b* 6 June 1957; *s* of late Peter and Jane Boult; *m* 1984, Katharine Goddard; four *d*. *Educ:* Durham Univ. (BA Hons; PGCE). Teacher, Canford Sch., Dorset, 1980–87; Hd of Humanities, Geelong GS, 1984–85; Hd of Geog., Cranleigh Sch., 1987–92; Housemaster, St Edward's Sch., Oxford, 1992–2001. Sec., Oxford Conf. in Educn, 1982–86; Dir, Boarding Schs Assoc., 2003–09 (Chm., 2007–08); Sec. and Chm. (NE), HMC, 2010–12. *Recreations:* golf, fireworks, reading, visiting Southwold.

BOULTON, Adam; *see* Boulton, T. A. B.

BOULTON, Sir Clifford (John), GCB 1994 (KCB 1990; CB 1985); DL; Clerk of the House of Commons, 1987–94; *b* 25 July 1930; *s* of Stanley Boulton and Evelyn (*née* Hey), Cocknage, Staffs; *m* 1955, Anne, *d* of Rev. E. E. Raven, Cambridge; one adopted *s* one adopted *d*. *Educ:* Newcastle-under-Lyme High School; St John's Coll., Oxford (exhibnr). MA (Modern History). National Service, RAC, 1949–50; Lt Staffs Yeomanry (TA). A Clerk in the House of Commons, 1953–94: Clerk of Select Cttees on Procedure, 1964–68 and 1976–77; Public Accounts, 1968–70; Parliamentary Questions, 1971–72; Privileges, 1972–77; Clerk of the Overseas Office, 1977–79; Principal Clerk, Table Office, 1979–83; Clerk Asst, 1983–87. A school Governor and subsequently board mem., Church Schools Company, 1965–79; Trustee, Oakham Sch., 1998–2010. Trustee, Industry and Parliament Trust, 1991–95. Mem., Standing Cttee on Standards in Public Life, 1994–2000. Chairman: Standards Cttee, Rutland CC, 2000–05; Rutland Historic Churches Preservation Trust, 2004–12. DL Rutland, 1997. Hon. LLD Keele, 1993. *Publications:* (ed) Erskine May's Parliamentary Practice, 21st edn, 1989; contribs to Halsbury's Laws of England, 4th edn, and Parliamentary journals. *Recreations:* visual arts, the countryside. *Address:* 2 Main Street, Lyddington, Oakham LE15 9LT. *T:* (01572) 823487.

See also R. E. S. Boulton.

BOULTON, His Honour David John; a Circuit Judge, 2001–12; Liaison Judge, St Helens Justices, 2004–11; *b* 2 July 1945; *s* of late John Ellis and Hilda May Boulton; *m* 1971, Suzanne Proudlove. *Educ:* Quarry Bank High Sch., Liverpool; Liverpool Univ. (LLB). Called to the Bar, Middle Temple, 1970; specialised in crime; Standing Counsel for DTI, 1989–99, Customs and Excise, 1993–99, Inland Revenue, 1997–99; an Asst Recorder, 1984–89; a Recorder, 1989–2001. Mem., Bar Council, 1995–2001. Tutor Judge, Judicial Studies Bd, 2007–12. *Recreations:* wine, gardens, travel. *Address:* c/o Queen Elizabeth II Law Courts, Derby Square, Liverpool L2 1XA. *Clubs:* Athenæum (Liverpool); Lancashire CC.

BOULTON, Fiona Jane; Headmistress, Guildford High School, since 2002; *b* 11 April 1964; *d* of Michael Harry Lockton and (Elizabeth) Iona Lockton; *m* 1994, Richard Edward Stanley Boulton, *qv*; one *s* two *d*. *Educ:* University Coll., Cardiff (BSc Hons); Exeter Coll., Oxford (PGCE); Inst. of Educn, Univ. of London (MA; NPQH). Housemistress: Stowe Sch., 1989–91; Marlborough Coll., 1991–95; Dep. Head, Guildford High Sch., 1996–2002. Nat. Leader of Educn. *Recreations:* cooking, walking, art, theatre, reading. *Address:* Waterton, Cleardown, The Hockering, Woking, Surrey GU22 7HH. *E:* fiona.boulton@church-schools.com. *Club:* Lansdowne.

BOULTON, Prof. Geoffrey Stewart, OBE 2000; FRS 1992; FRSE; Regius Professor of Geology and Mineralogy, 1986–2008, and Vice-Principal, 1999–2008, University of Edinburgh, now Senior Hon. Professorial Fellow and Regius Professor of Geology Emeritus; General Secretary, Royal Society of Edinburgh, 2007–11; *b* 28 Nov. 1940; *s* of George Stewart and Rose Boulton; *m* 1964, Denise Bryers Lawns; two *d*. *Educ:* Longton High Sch.; Birmingham Univ. BSc, PhD, DSc. FGS 1961; FRSE 1989. British Geol Survey, 1962–64; Demonstrator, Univ. of Keele, 1964–65; Fellow, Univ. of Birmingham, 1965–68; Hydrogeologist, Kenya, 1968; Lectr, then Reader, Univ. of E Anglia, 1968–86; Provost and Dean, Faculty of Sci. and Engrg, Univ. of Edinburgh, 1994–99. Prof., Amsterdam Univ., 1980–86. Mem., Royal Commn on Envmtl Pollution, 1994–2000. NERC: Chairman: Polar Sci. Bd, 1992–95; Earth Sci. and Technol. Bd, 1994–98; Mem. Council, 1993–98; Royal Society: Chm., Sect. Cttee 5 for Earth Sci. and Astronomy, 1993–95; Mem., Council, 1997–99, 2013–; Chair, Policy Advisory Gp, 2012–. Member: NCC Scotland, 1991–92; SHEFC, 1997–2003 (Chm., Res. Policy Cttee, 2000–03); Council, Scottish Assoc. for Marine Sci., 1997–2003 (Pres., 2013–); Scottish Sci. Adv. Cttee, 2003–07; Council for Sci. and Technol., 2004–; Pres., Cttee on Data for Sci. and Technol., Internat. Council for Sci., 2014–. UK Deleg. to IUGS, 1996–99. President: Geol Soc. of Edinburgh, 1991–93; Quaternary Res. Assoc., 1991–94; Chm., Council, Univ. of Heidelberg, 2007–; Mem., Strategic Council, Univ. of Geneva, 2009–. Hon. DTech Chalmers, Sweden, 2002; Hon. DSc: Birmingham, 2007; Keele, 2007; Heidelberg, 2008. Kirk Bryan Medal, Geol Soc. of America, 1976; Seligman Crystal, Internat. Glaciol. Soc., 2001; Lyell Medal, Geol Soc., 2006; Tedford Sci. Medal, Inst. for Contemp. Scotland, 2006; James Croll Medal, Quaternary Res. Assoc., 2011; Polar Medal, 2015. Commandeur, Ordre des Palmes Académiques (France), 2009. *Publications:* numerous articles in learned jls on glaciology, quaternary, marine and polar geology. *Recreations:* violin, mountaineering, sailing. *Address:* 19 Lygon Road, Edinburgh EH16 5QD.

BOULTON, Sir John Gibson, 4th Bt *cr* 1944, of Braxted Park, co. Essex; *b* 18 Dec. 1946; *o s* of Sir William Whytehead Boulton, 3rd Bt, CBE, TD, and of Margaret Elizabeth, *o d* of late Brig. H. N. A. Hunter, DSO; *S* father, 2010. *Educ:* Stowe. *Heir:* none.

BOULTON, Richard Edward Stanley; QC 2011; FCA; *b* London, 3 May 1959; *s* of Sir Clifford (John) Boulton, *qv*; *m* 1994, Fiona Jane Lockton (*see* F. J. Boulton); one *s* two *d*. *Educ:* Marlborough Coll.; Oriel Coll., Oxford (MA Modern Hist.); Coll. of Law, Guildford (Postgrad. DipLaw (Dist.) 2002); BPP Law Sch. (BVC (Outstanding) 2003). ACA 1986, FCA 1996. With Arthur Andersen, 1981–2001: Partner, 1990–2001; UK Head of Econ. and Financial Consulting Gp, 1994–95, of Business Consulting, 1995–97; Worldwide Managing Partner: Strategy and Service Categories, 1997–2000; Business Consulting, 2000–01; Chief Information Officer, 2000–01; LECG LLC: Global Hd of Finance and Accounting Services, 2002–11; Sen. Man. Dir, 2007–11; Bd Mem., 2008–10. Called to the Bar, Inner Temple, 2003; in practice as barrister, specialising in commercial litigation, 2004–. Treas., Tate Members, 1993–2006. Fellow, Academy of Experts, 1994. *Publications:* (jtly) Cracking the Value Code: how successful businesses are creating wealth in the new economy, 2000. *Recreations:* running, golf, theatre, wine, cricket, travel. *Address:* One Essex Court, Temple, EC4Y 9AR. *E:* rboulton@oeclaw.co.uk; Waterton, Cleardown, Woking, Surrey GU22 7HH. *T:* (01483) 760258, 07785 396954. *E:* richardeboulton@hotmail.com. *Clubs:* MCC; Wisley Golf.

BOULTON, (Thomas) Adam (Babington); broadcaster; Editor at Large, Sky News, since 2014; *b* 15 Feb. 1959; *s* of Dr Thomas B. Boulton and Helen C. Boulton; *m* 1st, 1985, Kerena Mond (marr. diss. 2004); three *d*; 2nd, 2006, Angela Margaret Jane Hunter, *qv*. *Educ:* Tower Hse Sch., Sheen; St Andrew's Sch., Pangbourne; Westminster Sch.; Christ Church, Oxford (MA); Sch. of Advanced Internat. Studies, Johns Hopkins Univ. (MA). Stringer, Inter Press, Washington, 1981–82; Talks Writer, BBC External Services, 1982; TV Journalist, 1982–84, Political Editor, 1984–89, TV-am; Political Ed. and Presenter, Sky News, 1989–2014. Columnist, Sunday Times, 2013–. Chm., Parly Lobby, 2007. Gov., Sevenoaks Sch., 2013–. Mem. Council, KCL, 2004–13; FKC 2013. Hon. Dr Sheffield Hallam, 2008; Hon. DBus Plymouth, 2013. *Publications:* (contrib.) Political Communications: why Labour won the general election of 1997, 2000; (contrib.) Political Communications: the general election campaign of 2005, 2007; Tony's Ten Years, 2008; (contrib.) 20 Years of Breaking News, 2009; (with Joey Jones) Hung Together, 2010; (contrib.) Political Communication in Britain,

2011. *Recreations:* arts, gardening. *Address:* c/o Sky News, 2nd Floor, 4 Millbank, SW1P 3JA. *T:* (020) 7032 2820, *Fax:* (020) 1900 7028. *E:* adam.boulton@sky.uk. *W:* www.twitter.com/adamboultonsky. *Club:* Beefsteak.

BOUNDS, (Kenneth) Peter, CBE 2013; Chief Executive, Liverpool City Council, 1991–99; *b* 7 Nov. 1943; *s* of Rev. Kenneth Bounds and Doris Bounds; *m* 1965, Geraldine Amy Slee; two *s. Educ:* Ashville College, Harrogate. Admitted Solicitor, 1971. Dir of Admin, Stockport MBC, 1973–82; Chief Exec., Bolton MBC, 1982–91. A Civil Service Comr, 2001–07. Pres., Assoc. of Dist Secs, 1980–81; Chm., Soc. of Metropolitan Chief Execs, 1997; Company Secretary: Greater Manchester Econ. Develt Ltd, 1986–91; NW Tourist Bd, 1986–91; Royal Liverpool Philharmonic Soc., 2000–07, 2008–11 (Dir, 1993–2000; Dep. Chm., 1997–2000; Chm., 2007–08). Chairman: Liverpool City Challenge, 1991–95; Liverpool City of Learning, 1994–97; Liverpool Partnership Gp, 1994–99; Renew N Staffs (Housing Market Renewal Partnership), 2002–11; Liverpool Cathedral Council, 2004–; Centre of Refurbishment Excellence Ltd, 2011–13. Non-executive Director: Mgt Bd, Government Office for SE, 2008–09, for NW, 2009–11; N Staffs Regeneration Partnership, 2007–10. Chm., Relate Cheshire and Merseyside, 2010–. Member: President's Council, Methodist Church, 1981–84; Bd of Trustees for Methodist Church Purposes, 1983–2008. Mem. Council, Liverpool Inst. of Performing Arts, 2009–11. Patron, Centre for Tomorrow's Company, 1997–. Hon. Fellow, Bolton Inst. of Higher Educn, 1991. FRSA 1994. Hon. LLD Liverpool, 2009; DUniv Bolton, 2010. *Recreations:* music, theatre. *Address:* 44 Reynolds Court, Vale Road, Woolton, Liverpool L25 7RZ.

BOURDEAUX, Rev. Canon Michael Alan; Director, 1969–99, President, since 2003, Keston Institute, Oxford (formerly Keston College, Kent); *b* 19 March 1934; *s* of Richard Edward and Lillian Myra Bourdeaux; *m* 1st, 1960, Gillian Mary Davies (*d* 1978); one *s* one *d*; 2nd, 1979, Lorna Elizabeth Waterton; one *s* one *d. Educ:* Truro Sch.; St Edmund Hall, Oxford (MA Hons Mod. Langs); Wycliffe Hall, Oxford (Hons Theology); BD Oxon 1969. Moscow State Univ., 1959–60; Deacon, 1960; Asst Curate, Enfield Parish Church, Middx, 1960–64; researching at Chislehurst, Kent, on the Church in the Soviet Union, with grant from Centre de Recherches, Geneva, 1965–68. Vis. Prof., St Bernard's Seminary, Rochester, NY, 1969; Vis. Fellow, LSE, 1969–71; Research Fellow, RIIA, Chatham House, 1971–73; Dawson Lectr on Church and State, Baylor Univ., Waco, Texas, 1972; Chavasse Meml Lectr, Oxford Univ., 1976; Kathryn W. Davis Prof. in Slavic Studies, Wellesley Coll., Wellesley, Mass, 1981; Moorhouse Lectr, Melbourne, 1987; Vis. Fellow, St Edmund Hall, Oxford, 1989–90; Vis. Prof., Inst. for Econ., Political and Cultural Develt, Notre Dame Univ., Ind., 1993; Croall Lectr, Univ. of Edinburgh, 2002; Paul G Manolis Dist. Lectr, Patriarch Athenagoras Inst., Berkeley, CA, 2009. Mem., High-Level Experts' Gp on For. Policy and Common Security, EC, 1993–94. Hon. Canon, Rochester Cathedral, 1990–99, now Canon Emeritus; Artistic Dir (formerly Hon. Dir), Iffley Music Soc., 1996–2013. Founded Keston College, a research centre on religion in the Communist countries, 1969. Founder of journal, Religion in Communist Lands, 1973, retitled Religion, State and Society: the Keston Jl, 1992. Mem. Council, Britain-Russia Centre, 1991–2000. DD Lambeth, 1996; Hon. DHL Wittenberg, Ohio, 2009; Hon. DD Evangelical Theol Faculty, Osiek, Croatia, 2009. Templeton Prize for Progress in Religion, 1984. Order of Grand Duke Gediminas, 1999, Order of Vytautas the Great, 2005 (Lithuania). *Publications:* Opium of the People, 1965, 2nd edn 1977; Religious Ferment in Russia, 1968; Patriarch and Prophets, 1970, 2nd edn 1975; Faith on Trial in Russia, 1971; Land of Crosses, 1979; Risen Indeed, 1983; (with Lorna Bourdeaux) Ten Growing Soviet Churches, 1987; Gorbachev, Glasnost and the Gospel, 1990, rev. US edn, The Gospel's Triumph over Communism, 1991; (ed) The Politics of Religion in Russia and the New States of Eurasia, 1995; (ed jtly) Proselytism and Orthodoxy in Russia, 1999; Religion and Society: essays on religious life in Russia today, 2002; (ed jtly) Contemporary Religious Life in Russia, vol. 1, 2003, vol. 2, 2003, vol. 3, 2005; (ed jtly) Atlas of Contemporary Religious Life in Russia, vol. 1, 2005, vol. 2, 2006, vol. 3, 2008, vol. 4, 2009. *Recreations:* choral singing, Member, Assoc. of British Tennis Officials. *Address:* 101 Church Way, Iffley, Oxford OX4 4EG. *T:* (01865) 777276. *Club:* Athenæum.

BOURDILLON, Peter John, FRCP; Medical Awards Administrator, Association of Commonwealth Universities, since 2001; *b* 10 July 1941; *s* of John Francis Bourdillon and Pamela Maud Bourdillon (*née* Chetham); *m* 1964, Catriona Glencairn-Campbell, FGA, *d* of Brig. W. Glencairn-Campbell, OBE and Lady Muir-Mackenzie; one *s* two *d. Educ:* Rugby Sch.; Middlesex Hosp. Med. Sch. (MB BS 1965). MRCP 1968, FRCP 1983. House physician and surgeon posts in London, 1965–68; Med. Registrar, Middlesex Hosp., 1969–70; Hammersmith Hospital: Med. Registrar, 1970–72; Sen. Registrar in Cardiol., 1972–74; Consultant in Clin. Physiol. (Cardiol.), subseq. in Cardiovascular Disease, 1975–2006. Part-time MO, 1975–81, part-time SMO, 1981–91, Hd of Med. Manpower and Educn Div., 1991–93, DHSS, then DoH; Head (Grade 3), Health Care (Med.), then Specialist Clin. Services, Div., DoH, 1993–97; on secondment from DoH to Academy of Med. Royal Colls, 1997–2001. Cardiologist (part-time), Hertford Cardiology (formerly Quantum Res.) Ltd, 2002–07. Medical Awards Administrator, ACU, 2001–. Hon. Sen. Lectr, RPMS, later ICSM, London Univ., 1979–. QHP 1996–99. *Publications:* contrib. to med. jls incl. Drug Information Jl and Annals of Noninvasive Electrocardiol. *Recreations:* writing software, walking, ski-ing, renaissance art history. *Address:* 13 Grove Terrace, NW5 1PH. *T:* (020) 7485 6839. *E:* pbourdillon@msn.com.

BOURDON, Derek Conway, FIA; Director, 1981–84, and General Manager, 1979–84, Prudential Assurance Co. Ltd; Director, London and Manchester Group PLC, 1986–94; *b* 3 Nov. 1932; *s* of late Walter Alphonse Bourdon and Winifred Gladys Vera Bourdon; *m* Uta Margrit Bourdon. *Educ:* Bancroft's School. FIA 1957. RAF Operations Research (Flying Officer), 1956–58. Joined Prudential, 1950; South Africa, 1962–65; Dep. General Manager, 1976–79. Chairman, Vanbrugh Life, 1974–79. Member, Policyholders Protection Board, 1980–84; Chm., Industrial Life Offices Assoc., 1982–84 (Vice-Chm., 1980–82). *Recreations:* golf, bridge. *Club:* Barton-on-Sea Golf.

BOURKE, family name of **Earl of Mayo**.

BOURKE, Dame (Elizabeth) Shân (Josephine) L.; *see* Legge-Bourke, Hon. Dame E. S. J.

BOURKE, Martin; HM Diplomatic Service, retired; Deputy High Commissioner, New Zealand, 2000–04; *b* 12 March 1947; *s* of late Robert Martin Bourke and Enid Millicent Bourke (*née* Love); *m* 1973, Anne Marie Marguerite Hottelet; four *s. Educ:* Stockport Grammar Sch.; University Coll. London (BA Hons 1969); King's Coll. London (MA 1970). Joined FCO, 1970; Brussels, 1971–73; Singapore, 1974–76; Lagos, 1978–80; on loan to DTI, 1980–84; Consul (Commercial), Johannesburg, 1984–88; Asst Head, Envmt, Sci. and Energy Dept, FCO, 1990–93; Gov., Turks and Caicos Islands, 1993–96; Area Manager, Prince's Trust (on secondment), 1996–99. *Recreations:* walking, reading, theatre, amateur dramatics.

BOURKE, Rt Rev. Michael Gay; Bishop Suffragan of Wolverhampton, 1993–2006; *b* 28 Nov. 1941; *s* of Gordon and Hilda Bourke; *m* 1968, Elizabeth Bieler; one *s* one *d. Educ:* Hamond's Grammar Sch., Swaffham, Norfolk; Corpus Christi Coll., Cambridge (Mod. Langs, MA); Univ. of Tübingen (Theology); Cuddesdon Theological Coll. Curate, St James', Grimsby, 1967–71; Priest-in-charge, Panshanger Conventional Dist (Local Ecumenical Project), Welwyn Garden City, 1971–78; Vicar, All Saints', Southill, Beds, 1978–86; Archdeacon of Bedford, 1986–93. Course Dir, St Albans Diocese Ministerial Trng Scheme, 1975–87. Anglican Co-Chm., Meissen Commn, 1997–2006. Hon. Canon, Lichfield Cathedral, 1993–2006. *Recreations:* astronomy, railways, European history, Welsh language. *Address:* The Maltings, Little Stretton, Church Stretton SY6 6AP.

BOURKE, Patrick Francis John O'D.; *see* O'Donnell Bourke.

BOURN, Sir John (Bryant), KCB 1991 (CB 1986); Comptroller and Auditor General, 1988–2008; Independent Adviser to Prime Minister on Ministers' Interests, 2006–08; *b* 21 Feb. 1934; *s* of late Henry Thomas Bryant Bourn and Beatrice Grace Bourn; *m* 1959, Ardita Ann Fleming; one *s* one *d. Educ:* Southgate County Grammar Sch.; LSE. 1st cl. hons BScEcon 1954, PhD 1958. Air Min. 1956–63; HM Treasury, 1963–64; Private Sec. to Perm. Under-Sec., MoD, 1964–69; Asst Sec. and Dir of Programmes, Civil Service Coll., 1969–72; Asst Sec., MoD, 1972–74; Under-Sec., Northern Ireland Office, 1974–77; Asst Under-Sec. of State, MoD, 1977–82; Dep. Sec., Northern Ireland Office, 1982–84; Dep. Under Sec. of State (Defence Procurement), MoD, 1985–88; Auditor General for Wales, 1999–2005. Visiting Professor: LSE, 1983–2013; Bournemouth Univ., 2009–. Chairman: Accountancy Foundn Review Bd, 2000–03; Professional Oversight Bd (formerly Professional Oversight Bd for Accountancy), 2003–08. Chm., Multi-Lateral Audit Adv. Gp, World Bank, 1999–2008; Member: Financial Reporting Council, 1990–2008; Financial Reporting Review Panel, 1991–2008; Foundn for Governance Res. and Educn, 2008–. FCIPS 1995; CCMI (CIMgt 1994). Freeman, City of London, 1996. Hon. Fellow: Brighton Univ., 1989; LSE, 1995. Hon. LLD Brunel, 1995; DUniv Open, 1998; Hon. DBA West of England, 2011. *Publications:* Public Sector Audit: is it value for money, 2007; articles and reviews in professional jls. *Recreations:* swimming, tennis.

BOURNE OF ABERYSTWYTH, Baron *cr* 2013 (Life Peer), of Aberystwyth in the County of Ceredigion and of Wethersfield in the County of Essex; **Nicholas Henry Bourne;** a Lord in Waiting (Government Whip), since 2014; Parliamentary Under-Secretary of State, Department for Energy and Climate Change and Wales Office, since 2015; *b* 1 Jan. 1952; *s* of late John Morgan Bourne and Joan Edith Mary Bourne. *Educ:* King Edward VI Sch., Chelmsford; UCW, Aberystwyth (LLB 1st Cl. Hons; LLM 1976); Trinity Coll., Cambridge (LLM). Called to the Bar, Gray's Inn, 1976. Supervisor in Law: Corpus Christi Coll., Cambridge, 1974–80; St Catharine's Coll., Cambridge, 1974–82; LSE, 1975–77; Principal, Chart Univ. Tutors Ltd, 1979–88; Co. Sec. and Dir, Chart Foulks Lynch plc, 1984–88; Dir, Holborn Gp Ltd, 1988–91; Swansea Institute: Prof. of Law, 1991–96; Dean of Law, 1992–96; Asst Principal, 1996–98. Lectr in Co. Law, Univ. of London Ext. Degree Prog. at UCL, 1991–96; Sen. Lectr in Law, South Bank Univ., 1991–92; Vis. Lectr, Hong Kong Univ., 1996–2008. Member: Editl Bd, Malaysian Law News, 1991–2008; Editl Adv. Bd, Business Law Rev., 1991–. Member: NE Thames RHA, 1990–92; W Glamorgan HA, 1994–97; Doctors' and Dentists' Review Body, 1998–99. Mem. (C) Mid and W Wales, and Leader of Conservatives, Nat. Assembly for Wales, 1999–2011; contested (C) same seat, 2011. Mem., Delegated Powers and Regulatory Reform Cttee, H of L, 2014. *Publications:* Duties and Responsibilities of British Company Directors, 1982; British Company Law and Practice, 1983; Business Law for Accountants, 1987; Lecture Notes for Company Law, 1993, 3rd edn 1998; Essential Company Law, 1994, 2nd edn 1997; Business Law and Practice, 1994; (with B. Pillans) Scottish Company Law, 1996, 2nd edn 1999; Bourne on Company Law, 1993, 6th edn 2013; contrib. to business and co. law jls. *Recreations:* walking, tennis, badminton, squash, theatre, cricket, travel, cinema. *Address:* House of Lords, SW1A 0PW. *Club:* Oxford and Cambridge.

BOURNE, Charles Gregory; QC 2014; a Recorder, since 2009; *b* London, 4 July 1964; *s* of Stanford Bourne and Judith Bourne; *m* 1995, Catherine Chadwick; one *s* one *d. Educ:* University College Sch., Hampstead; Trinity Coll., Cambridge (BA English 1986); Université de Paris IV (Maîtrise Lettres Modernes 1987). Called to the Bar, Middle Temple, 1991; in practice as barrister, specialising in public and employment law, 11 King's Bench Walk, 2012–. Mediator, CEDR, 2000–. *Publications:* (jtly) Civil Advocacy: a practical guide, 1997, 2nd edn 2001; Going Back, 2013; (contrib.) The Civil Court Practice, 2007–; (contrib.) Tolley's Employment Handbook, 2013–. *Recreations:* literature, music, tennis, cookery. *Address:* 11 King's Bench Walk, Temple, EC4Y 7EQ. *T:* (020) 7632 8500, *Fax:* (020) 7583 9123. *E:* clerks@11kbw.com.

BOURNE, Prof. (Frederick) John, CBE 1995; Professor of Animal Health, University of Bristol, 1988–2007, now Emeritus; *b* 3 Jan. 1937; *s* of Sidney John Bourne and Florence Beatrice Bourne; *m* 1959, Mary Angela Minter; two *s. Educ:* Univ. of London (BVetMed); Univ. of Bristol (PhD). MRCVS 1961. Gen. vet. practice, 1961–67; University of Bristol: Lectr in Animal Husbandry, 1967–76; Reader in Animal Husbandry, 1976–80; Prof. and Hd of Dept of Veterinary Medicine, 1980–88; Dir, AFRC, subseq. BBSRC, Inst. for Animal Health, 1988–97. Vis. Prof., Univ. of Reading, 1990–97. Chm., Govt Ind. Scientific Gp for Control of Cattle TB, 1998–2007. For. Mem., Polish Acad. of Sci., 1994. Hon. Fellow, Edward Jenner Inst. for Vaccine Res., 2001. *Publications:* over 250 contribs to variety of jls, incl. Immunology, Vet. Immunology and Immunopath., Res. in Vet. Sci., Infection and Immunity, Nature, Procs of US Nat. Acad. of Scis, Internat. Jl of Infectious Diseases, Animal Welfare, Jl of Applied Ecology, Jl of Zoology. *Recreations:* gardening, fishing, golf, cricket, music. *Address:* Westlands, Jubilee Lane, Langford, Bristol BS40 5EJ. *T:* (01934) 852 464.

BOURNE, Gordon Lionel, FRCS, FRCOG; Hon. Consultant, Department of Obstetrics and Gynæcology, St Bartholomew's Hospital, London (Consultant Gynæcologist and Obstetrician, 1961–84); Hon. Consultant Gynæcologist to Royal Masonic Hospital (Consultant Gynæcologist, 1965–89); *b* 3 June 1921; *s* of Thomas Holland Bourne and Lily Anne (*née* Clewlow); *m* 1948, Barbara Eileen Anderson; three *s* one *d. Educ:* Queen Elizabeth Grammar Sch., Ashbourne; St Bartholomew's Hosp.; Harvard Univ. MRCS, LRCP 1945, FRCS 1954; MRCOG 1956, FRCOG 1962; FRSocMed. Hertford Hosp., 1945; Highlands Hosp., 1946; Derbs Royal Infirm., 1947–50; Anatomy Demonstrator, St Bartholomew's Hosp., 1951; City of London Mat. Hosp., 1951–53; Hosp. for Women, Soho, 1954–55; Gynæcol Registrar, Middlesex Hosp., 1956–57; Sen. Registrar, Obsts and Gyn., St Bartholomew's Hosp., 1958–59; Nuffield Trav. Fellow, 1959; Res. Fellow and Lectr, Harvard, 1959–60; Cons. Gynæcol., St Luke's Hosp., 1963–84. Arris and Gale Lectr, RCS, 1962; Mem. Bd of Professions Suppl. to Medicine, 1964–73; Regional Assessor in Maternal Deaths, 1974–83; Examr in Obsts and Gyn., Univs of London, Oxford and Riyadh, Jt Conjt Bd and RCOG, Central Midwives Bd; Mem. Ct of Assts, Haberdashers' Co., 1968, Master, 1984; Mem. Bd of Governors, 1971–83, Chm., 1980–83, Haberdashers' Aske's Schs, Hatcham; Mem., 1983–95, Chm., 1987–95, Bd of Governors, Haberdashers' Aske's Schs, Elstree. United Grand Lodge of England: Grand Superintendent Middx, 1986–96; Past Jun. Grand Warden, 1987; Pro Provincial Grand Master Middx, 1987–96; Mem. Cttee, New Samaritan Fund, 1990–93; Rose Croix, Inspector Gen. Middx, 1996–2001. Mem., Masonic Fishing Charity for disadvantaged and disabled children, 2001– (Pres., 2003–). Liveryman, Soc. of Apothecaries, 2005–. *Publications:* The Human Amnion and Chorion, 1962; Shaw's Textbook of Gynæcology, 8th edn, 1962 to 9th edn, 1970; Recent Advances in Obstetrics and Gynæcology, 11th edn, 1966 to 13th edn, 1979; Modern Gynæcology with Obstetrics for Nurses, 4th edn, 1969 and 5th edn, 1973; Pregnancy, 1972, 8th edn 2006; Bourne - The History of a Family 1647–2001, 2002; numerous articles in sci. and professional jls. *Recreations:* fishing, swimming, writing, golf. *Address:* Little Reuters, Common Road, Ightham, Kent TN15 9AY. *T:* (01732) 885746. *Clubs:* Carlton, Royal Soc. of Medicine, MCC, English Twenty (shot for England, 1947).

BOURNE, Ian Maclean; QC 2006; a Recorder, since 2000; *b* 19 Jan. 1954; *s* of late Ian Bourne and of Jean Talbot (*née* Scarrott); *m* 1993, Lucy Pollock; one *s* three *d. Educ:* Marlborough; Exeter Univ. (LLB). Called to the Bar, Inner Temple, 1977; in practice, S

Eastern Circuit. Member: Criminal Bar Assoc., 1983–; CCC Bar Mess, 1985–. *Recreations:* cricket, gardening, photography. *Address:* Charter Chambers, 33 John Street, WC1N 2AT. *T:* (020) 7618 4400. *E:* ian.bourne@charterchambers.com. *Club:* Hurlingham.

BOURNE, John; *see* Bourne, F. J.

BOURNE, Lisa; *see* Roberts, L.

BOURNE, Margaret Janet, OBE 1982; Chairman, CORDA Ltd, 1992–2001; *b* 18 Aug. 1931; *d* of Thomas William Southcott and Nora Annie Southcott (*née* Pelling); *m* 1960, George Brian Bourne. *Educ:* Twickenham Grammar Sch.; Royal Holloway Coll. (BSc). MRAeS 1962; CEng, FIET (FIEE 1997). Fairey Engineering, 1953–62; Army Operational Res. Estabt, 1962–65; Defence Operational Analysis Estabt, 1965–76; Asst Dir, Scientific Adv. Gp Army, 1976–80; Hd of Assessments Div., ASWE, 1980–82; Hd of Weapon Dept, ASWE, 1982–84; Dep. Dir, Admiralty Res. Estabt, 1984–87; Asst Chief Scientific Advr (Capabilities), MoD, 1987–91. *Recreations:* playing early music, gardening, natural history. *T:* (01428) 714329.

BOURNE, Matthew Christopher, OBE 2001; director and choreographer; Founder Director, New Adventures, since 2002; *b* 13 Jan. 1960; *s* of Harold Jeffrey, (Jim), Bourne and June Lillian Bourne (*née* Handley). *Educ:* Laban Centre for Movement and Dance (BA Hons Dance and Theatre 1986; Hon. Fellow 1997). Artistic Dir and Jt Founder Mem., Adventures in Motion Pictures, 1987–2002. Dir, Spitfire Trust, 1996–; Mem. Bd, Laban Centre for Movt and Dance, 1999–; Mem., Hon. Cttee, Dance Cares, 1995–. *Works* include: *for Adventures in Motion Pictures,* created and directed: Overlap Lovers, 1987; Spitfire, 1988; The Infernal Galop, 1989; Green Fingers, 1990; Town and Country, 1991; Deadly Serious, 1992; Nutcracker, 1992 (revised 2002); The Percys of Fitzrovia, 1992; Highland Fling, 1994 (revised 2005); Swan Lake, 1995 (Olivier Award, 1996; LA Drama Critics Award, 1997; 2 Tony Awards, 1999; 3 Drama Desk Awards, 1999; 2 Outer Critics' Circle Awards, 1999; Astaire Award, 1999); Cinderella, 1997; The Car Man (Evening Standard Award), 2000; Lord of the Flies, 2014 *for other companies,* choreographed: As You Like It, RSC, 1989; Leonce and Lena, Crucible, Sheffield, 1989; Children of Eden, Prince Edward Theatre, 1991; A Midsummer Night's Dream, Aix-en-Provence Fest., 1991; The Tempest, NYT, 1991; Show Boat, Malmö Stadsteater, 1991; Peer Gynt, Ninagawa Co., Oslo, Barbican, 1994; Watch with Mother, Nat. Youth Dance Co., 1994; Oliver!, London Palladium, 1994, (and co-dir) Th. Royal, 2009; My Fair Lady, South Pacific, RNT, 2001; dir, Play Without Words, NT, 2002, Sadler's Wells, 2012; co-dir and choreographer, Mary Poppins, Prince Edward Th., 2004; director and choreographer: Edward Scissorhands, Sadler's Wells, 2005; Dorian Gray (tour), 2009; Lord of the Flies, Th. Royal, Glasgow, 2011; Sleeping Beauty, Sadler's Wells, 2012; as performer, created numerous rôles in AMP prodns on stage and in films; *films choreographed* include: Late Flowering Lust, 1993; Drip: a narcissistic love story, 1993; *television film*: Matthew Bourne's Christmas, 2011. *Recreations:* old movies, theatre and music, reading obituaries. *Address:* c/o Jessica Sykes, Independent Talent Group Ltd, 40 Whitfield Street, W1T 2RH. *T:* (020) 7636 6565; New Adventures, Sadler's Wells, Rosebery Avenue, EC1R 4TN. *Club:* Soho House.

BOURNE, (Rowland) Richard, OBE 2002; Head, Commonwealth Policy Studies Unit, Institute of Commonwealth Studies, London University, 1999–2005, Senior Research Fellow, since 2006; *b* 27 July 1940; *s* of late Arthur Brittan and Edith Mary Bourne; *m* 1966, Juliet Mary, *d* of John Attenborough, CBE; two *s* one *d*. *Educ:* Uppingham Sch., Rutland; Brasenose Coll., Oxford (BA Mod. Hist.). Journalist, The Guardian, 1962–72 (Education correspondent, 1968–72); Asst Editor, New Society, 1972–77; Evening Standard: Dep. Editor, 1977–78; London Columnist, 1978–79; Founder Editor, Learn Magazine, 1979; Dep. Dir, Commonwealth Inst., 1983–89; Dir, Commonwealth Human Rights Initiative, 1990–92 (Chm., Trustee Cttee, 1994–2003); consultant, 1993–94; Co-Dir, Commonwealth Values in Educn Project, Inst. of Educn, London Univ., 1995–98; Dir, Commonwealth Non-Govtl Office for S Africa and Mozambique, 1995–97; Sec., Ramphal Inst. (formerly Ramphal Centre), 2007–14. Chm., Editl Bd, Round Table, 2005–11. Consultant: Internat. Broadcasting Trust, 1980–81; Adv. Council for Adult and Continuing Educn, 1982. Chm., Survival Internat., 1983–98. Chm., Brazilian Contemporary Arts, 1995–98; Acting Chair of Corporation, Greenwich Community Coll., 2014–15. Treas., Anglo-Portuguese Foundn, 1985–87. Dep. Chm., Royal Commonwealth Soc., 2001–07. *Publications:* Political Leaders of Latin America, 1969; (with Brian MacArthur) The Struggle for Education, 1970; Getulio Vargas of Brazil, 1974; Assault on the Amazon, 1978; Londoners, 1981; (with Jessica Gould) Self-Sufficiency, 16–25, 1983; Lords of Fleet Street, 1990; News on a Knife-Edge, 1995; Britain in the Commonwealth, 1997; (ed) Universities and Development, 2000; (ed) Where Next for the Group of 54?, 2001; Invisible Lives, 2003; Lula of Brazil: the story so far, 2008; (ed) Shridath Ramphal: the Commonwealth and the world, 2008; (ed with Mark Collins) From Hook to Plate, 2009; Catastrophe: what went wrong in Zimbabwe, 2011. *Recreations:* theatre, fishing, supporting Charlton Athletic. *Address:* 26 Bennett Park, SE3 9RB. *T:* (020) 8297 4182. *Club:* Royal Automobile.

BOURNE, Sam; *see* Freedland, J. S.

BOURNE, Stephen Robert Richard, FCA; Chapter Clerk and Administrator, Ely Cathedral, since 2013; Fellow, since 2001, and Vice-President, since 2015, Clare Hall, Cambridge; *b* 20 March 1952; *s* of Colyn M. Bourne and Kathleen Bourne (*née* Turner); *m* 1978, Stephanie Ann Bickford; one *s* one *d*. *Educ:* Berkhamsted Sch.; Univ. of Edinburgh (MA 1974); MA Cantab 2001. FCA 1977. Deloitte Haskins and Sells, London and Hong Kong, 1974–80; Exxon Chemical Asia-Pacific, Hong Kong, 1980–86; Dow Jones Telerate, Hong Kong and London: Financial Dir Asia, 1986–89; Gen. Manager, N Europe, 1989–94; Man. Dir, Financial Printing Div., St Ives plc, 1994–96; Cambridge University Press: Development Dir, 1997–2000; Chm., Printing, 2000–02; University Printer and Chief Exec., 2002–12; Pres., 2012–13; Pres., Cambridge Internat. Connections, 2012–. Director: Britten Sinfonia, 2003– (Chm., 2010–); Wine Soc., 2004–; Th. Royal, Bury St Edmunds, 2012– (Chm., 2012–). Mem. Council, CBI East, 2007–14 (Chm., 2010–12). Prince of Wales' Ambassador, E of England, BITC, 2009. Governor: Perse Sch. for Girls, 1998–2004; Berkhamsted Sch., 2010–12. Treas. and Vice-Chm., RSPCA Hong Kong, 1981–86. Chm., Hong Kong Water Ski Assoc., 1980–85. Hon. Vice-President: Cambridge Univ. Lawn Tennis Club, 2005–; Exning Cricket Club, 2006–. Pres., Old Berkhamstedians, 2011–13. Liveryman, Stationers' Co.. FRSA 2002. *Recreations:* performing arts, ski-ing, cricket-watching, fine wines. *Address:* Falmouth Lodge, Snailwell Road, Newmarket CB8 7DN. *T:* (01353) 660308. *E:* stephenrrbourne@gmail.com. *Clubs:* Athenæum; Kent CC, Cambridge University Cricket; Hong Kong, Aberdeen Boat (Hong Kong).

BOURNE, Dame Susan (Mary), DBE 2013; Headteacher, The Avenue School, Reading, since 2003; *b* Penwortham, 2 Feb. 1953; *d* of William Fiddler and Ruth Fiddler; *m* 1987, Roger Bourne; one *s* one *d*. *Educ:* Balshaw's Grammar Sch., Leyland; Bath Coll. of Educn (Cert Ed Home Econs); Reading Coll. (Dip. Special Educn). NPQH. Nat. Leader of Educn, 2009–. *Recreations:* sailing, sewing, cooking, art, bonsai.

BOURNE, Thomas Holland, PhD; FRCOG; Consultant Gynaecologist, Queen Charlotte's and Chelsea Hospital, Imperial College NHS Trust, London, since 2008; Consultant, Department of Obstetrics and Gynaecology, University Hospitals Leuven, since 2007; Adjunct Professor, Imperial College London, since 2013; *b* Kendal, 19 Dec. 1959; *s* of Douglas Holland Bourne and Lilian Anne Bourne; *m* 2010, Vicky Cripps; two step *d*. *Educ:* Cheadle Hulme Sch.; Middlesex Hosp. Med. Sch., London (MS BS 1984); Univ. of Göteborg (PhD 1995). MRCOG 1990, FRCOG 2003. House Officer: Gen. Medicine, Cheltenham Gen. Hosp., 1984–85; Surgery, Middlesex Hosp., London, 1984; Senior House Officer: Accident and Emergency and Orthopaedics, Bristol Royal Inf., 1985; Obstetrics and Gynaecol., St Mary's Hosp., Manchester, 1986; (and Registrar) Obstetrics and Gynaecol., Gloucester Royal Hosp., 1987; Neonatal Unit, John Radcliffe Hosp., Oxford, 1988; Sen. Clin. Res. Fellow in Gynaecol., 1989–91, Lectr and Hon. Sen. Registrar in Obstetrics and Gynaecol., 1991–95, King's Coll. Hosp., London; Swedish MRC Vis. Scientist Fellow, Sahlgrenska Univ. Hosp., Univ. of Göteborg, 1995–96; St George's, University of London: Sen. Lectr in Obstetrics and Gynaecol., 1996–99; Reader in Acute Gynaecol. and Gynaecol Ultrasound, 2005–07; Consultant Obstetrician and Gynaecologist, St George's Hosp., London, 1999–2007. Visiting Professor: Katholieke Univ. Leuven, 2007–; Imperial Coll. London, 2008–. Dir, Women's Ultrasound Centres Ltd, 1998–. Member: Steering Cttee, Internat. Ovarian Tumor Analysis trial, 1993–; consensus gp on pregnancy viability, Soc. of Radiologists in Ultrasound, USA, 2012; consensus panel on criteria to diagnose ovarian cancer, American Inst. of Ultrasound in Medicine, 2014–15; world conference cttee, RCOG, 2014–. Trustee and Med. Advr, Ectopic Pregnancy Trust, 2005–; Mem. Bd, Assoc. of Early Pregnancy Units, 2005–11. Expert Advr to NICE, 2011–. Mem. Bd and Dir, Internat. Soc. of Ultrasound in Obstetrics and Gynaecol., 2006–14 (Dir, ISUOG Courses and Conferences Ltd, 1997–2003); Pres., UK Assoc. of Early Pregnancy Units, 2015–; Treas., Internat. Soc. of Ultrasound in Obstetrics and Gynaecol., 2015–. Mem., Chelsea Clinical Soc. Hon. Fellow, Amer. Inst. of Ultrasound in Medicine, 2015. *Publications:* (ed) Transvaginal Colour Doppler: a scientific basis to the use of transvaginal colour Doppler in gynaecology, 1995; (ed) Ultrasound and Endoscopic Surgery in Obstetrics and Gynaecology: a combined approach to diagnosis and treatment, 2002; (ed) Ultrasound in Gynaecology, 2004; (ed) Handbook of Early Pregnancy Care, 2006; (ed) Acute Gynaecology: early pregnancy complications, 2009; (ed) Acute Gynaecology: infection, uterine and ovarian pathology, 2009; over 300 articles in academic jls; h-index of 57. *Recreations:* family, cricket, cycling, drumming, sailing, theatre, cinema, visual arts. *Address:* 86 Harley Street, W1G 7HP. *T:* (020) 7636 6765. *E:* womensultrasound@btinternet.com. *Clubs:* MCC; Armadillos Cricket; Bembridge Sailing, Royal Solent Sailing.

BOURNE, Valerie Iris; organic gardener; garden writer, since 1995; *b* Southall, Middx, 28 July 1950; *d* of Albert Edward Teall and Iris Mary Teall (*née* Bosanquet); partner, Dr Jolyon Kirby; two *d* by a previous marriage. *Educ:* Greenford Co. Grammar Sch.; Bordesley Coll. of Educn (Teaching Cert. 1971). Vegetable res., Nat. Vegetable Res. Stn, Wellesbourne, 1971–75; teacher specialising in literacy, 1971–95; internat. lectr and photographer, 1995–; freelance writer for newspapers and jls, incl. Daily Telegraph, Oxford Times, Saga Gdns Illustrated, 1995–. Mem. Cttee, RHS, 2006–. Journalist of the Year, Garden Media Guild, 2014. *Publications:* Seeds of Wisdom, 2004; The Natural Gardener, 2005; The Winter Garden, 2006; Ten Minute Gardener's Vegetable Growing Diary, 2011; Ten Minute Gardener's Flower Growing Diary, 2011; Colour in the Garden, 2011; Ten Minute Gardener's Fruit Diary, 2011. *Recreations:* cricket, gardening, crosswords, children, grandchildren, conservation. *Address:* Spring Cottage, Cold Aston, Cheltenham, Glos GL54 3BJ. *E:* info@valbourne.co.uk. *W:* www.valbourne.co.uk.

BOURNE-ARTON, Simon Nicholas; QC 1994; **His Honour Judge Bourne-Arton;** a Senior Circuit Judge, since 2012; *b* 5 Sept. 1949; *s* of late Major Anthony Temple Bourne-Arton, MBE; *m* 1974, Diana Carr-Walker; two *s* one *d*. *Educ:* Aysgarth Prep. Sch.; Harrow; Teesside Poly. (HND Bus. Studies); Leeds Univ. (LLB Hons). Called to the Bar, Inner Temple, 1975, Bencher, 2003. A Recorder, 1993–2012; Leader, North Eastern Circuit, 2006–09; Hon. Recorder of Middlesbrough, 2012–. *Recreations:* living in the country, golf, tennis, being with family and friends, drinking wine. *Address:* c/o Teesside Combined Court Centre, Russell Street, Middlesbrough, Cleveland TS1 2AE.

BOURNE-MAY, Jonathan James Seaburne; Clerk to Vintners' Company, since 2012; *b* Dumfries, 4 July 1958; *s* of late Geoffrey and Josephine Bourne-May; *m* 1986, Karen Laver; two *s*. *Educ:* Eton; RMA, Sandhurst. Joined Coldstream Guards, 1977; psc 1990; jsdc 1996; MA to C-in-C, 1997–98; i/c 1st Bn Coldstream Guards, 1998–2001; COS HQ London Dist, 2004–06; i/c 143 (W Midlands) Bde, 2006–09; Brig., HQ Land, 2009–12. Regtl Lieut Col, Coldstream Guards, 2002–12. Chm., Mgt Bd, Guards Mus., 2013– (Mem., 2012–). Dir, Livery Cos' Mutual Ltd, 2014–. *Recreations:* music, history, travel, hill walking. *Address:* Vintners' Company, Upper Thames Street, EC4V 3BG. *T:* (020) 7651 0744. *E:* theclerk@vintnershall.co.uk.

BOURNEMOUTH, Archdeacon of; *see* Rouch, Ven. P. B.

BOURNS, Prof. Arthur Newcombe, OC 1982; FRSC 1964; FCIC; President and Vice-Chancellor, 1972–80, Professor of Chemistry 1953–81, now Emeritus, McMaster University; *b* 8 Dec. 1919; *s* of Evans Clement Bourns and Kathleen Jones; *m* 1943, Marion Harriet Blakney; two *s* two *d*. *Educ:* schs in Petitcodiac, NB; Acadia Univ. (BSc); McGill Univ. (PhD). Research Chemist, Dominion Rubber Co., 1944–45; Lectr, Acadia Univ., 1945–46; Asst Prof. of Chemistry, Saskatchewan Univ., 1946–47; McMaster University: Asst Prof., 1947–49; Associate Prof., 1949–53; Dean, Faculty of Grad. Studies, 1957–61; Chm., Chemistry Dept, 1965–67; Vice-Pres., Science and Engrg Div., 1967–72; Actg Pres., 1970. Nuffield Trav. Fellow in Science, University Coll., London, 1955–56. Chm., Gordon Res. Conf. on Chem. and Physics of Isotopes (Vice-Chm. 1959–60; Chm., 1961–62); Nat. Res. Council of Canada: Mem. Chem. Grant Selection Cttee, 1966–69 (Chm. 1968–69); Mem. Council, 1969–75; Mem. Exec. Cttee, 1969–75; Mem. or Chm. various other cttees; Natural Scis and Engrg Res. Council: Member: Council, 1978–85; Exec. Cttee, 1978–85; Allocations Cttee, 1978–86; Cttee on Strategic Grants, 1978–83; Chm., Grants and Scholarships Cttee, 1978–83; Mem., Adv. Cttee on University/Industry Interface, 1979–83; Vis. Res. Officer, 1983–84. Member: Ancaster Public Sch. Bd, 1963–64; Bd, Royal Botanic Gdns, 1972–80 (Vice-Chm.); Cttee on Univ. Affairs, Prov. Ontario; Canadian Cttee for Financing Univ. Res., 1978–80; Council of Ontario Univs, 1972–80; Bd of Dirs and Exec. Cttee, Assoc. of Univs and Colleges of Canada, 1974–77; Mohawk Coll. Bd of Dirs, 1975–82; Council, Canadian Inst. for Advanced Research, 1983–89; Chm., Internat. Adv. Cttee, Chinese Univ. Develt Project, 1985–92; Pres. and Chm. Exec. Cttee, Canadian Bureau for Internat. Educn, 1973–76. McMaster Univ. Med. Centre: Member: Bd of Trustees, 1972–80; Exec. Cttee, 1972–80. Director: Nuclear Activation Services, 1978–80; Slater Steel Industries Ltd, 1975–79. British Council Lectr, 1963. Assoc. Editor, Canadian Jl Chemistry, 1966–69; Mem. Editorial Bd, Science Forum, 1967–73. FCIC 1954 (Chm. Hamilton Section, 1952–53; Mem. Educn Cttee, 1953–59; Mem. Council, 1966–69; Montreal Medal, 1976). Hon. Prof., Jiangxi Univ., China, 1989. Hon. DSc: Acadia, 1968; McGill, 1977; New Brunswick, McMaster, 1981; Hon. LLD Brock, 1980. *Address:* No 1411, 100 Burloak Drive, Burlington, ON L7L 6P6, Canada. *T:* (905) 6396964. *E:* abourns2@cogeco.ca.

BOURNS, Robert Henry Glanville; DL; Partner, TLT LLP, since 2000 (Senior Partner, 2002–15); Vice-President, 2015–July 2016, President, from July 2016, Law Society of England and Wales; *b* Bristol, 11 May 1956; *s* of Herbert Kitchener Bourns and (Grace) Joan (Valerie) Bourns; *m* 1983, Fiona Mary Spencer; three *s* one *d*. *Educ:* Clifton Coll., Bristol; University Coll., Cardiff (LLB). Admitted as solicitor, 1980; solicitor, Osborne Clarke, 1980–83; solicitor, 1983–86, Partner, 1986–96, Man. Partner, 1996–2000, Trumps; Man. Partner, TLT LLP, 2000–02. Pres., Bristol Law Soc., 2005–06. Trustee: St Peter's Hospice, 2005–11 (Chm., 2011–14); ABLAZE (Bristol Learning Action Zone), 2009–; Dir, Friends of Room 13 (Hareclive) Ltd, 2011–; Chm., Quartet Community Foundn, 2014–; Pres., Dolphin Soc., 2014–15; Mem., Soc. of Merchant Venturers, 2015–. DL Bristol, 2014.

Recreations: walking, ski-ing, gardening. *Address:* TLT LLP, 20 Gresham Street, EC2V 7JE. *T:* 0333 006 0266. *E:* robert.bourns@tltsolicitors.com, robert.bourns@lawsociety.org.uk.

BOURS, Louise; Member (UK Ind) North West Region, European Parliament, since 2014; *b* Congleton, Cheshire, 23 Dec. 1968; *d* of Terence Bours and Mavis Bours; two *d*. *Educ:* Mountview Conservatoire for the Performing Arts. Actor in TV progs, Grown Ups, 1996, Peak Practice, 1997, Band of Gold, 1997, Brookside, 2000; Mem., D'Oyly Carte Opera Co., 2000. Mem., Congleton Town Council, 2003–15 (Mayor, 2006–07); Mem. (C, then Ind, later UKIP) Congleton BC, 2007–09. Contested (UK Ind) Knowsley, 2015. *Address:* European Parliament, Rue Wiertz, Brussels 1047, Belgium. *W:* www.louiseboursmep.co.uk.

BOUSHER, Stephen; Principal Assistant Solicitor, HM Revenue and Customs (formerly Board of Inland Revenue), 2000–13; barrister, Joseph Hage Aaronson, since 2014; *b* 13 Feb. 1952; *s* of Leslie Arthur and Clare Bousher; *m* 1974, Jan Townsend; one *s* one *d*. *Educ:* Bec Grammar Sch., Tooting; Southampton Univ. (LLB). Called to the Bar, Gray's Inn, 1975; Board of Inland Revenue (later HM Revenue and Customs), 1976–: Asst Solicitor, 1988–2000; Team Leader, Tax Simplification, then Tax Law Rewrite, Project, 1996–2000. *Recreations:* cinema, watching sport, arguing with Holden, listening to The Grateful Dead, travelling.

BOUSTED, Dr Mary Winefride; General Secretary, Association of Teachers and Lecturers, since 2003; *b* 15 Sept. 1959; *d* of Edward and Winefride Bleasdale; *m* 1983, Donald Bousted; one *d*. *Educ:* Hull Univ. (BA Hons); Inst. of Educn, London Univ. (MA Dist.); York Univ. (PhD 1999). English teacher, Bentley Wood High Sch., Harrow, 1982–87; Hd of English, Whitmore High Sch., Harrow, 1988–91; Lectr, 1991–95, Dir, Initial Teacher Trng, 1995–97, Univ. of York; Head: Secondary Educn, Edge Hill Coll., 1997–99; Sch. of Educn, Kingston Univ., 1999–2003. *Publications:* contrib. English in Educn, Changing English, Educnl Rev. *Recreations:* walking, reading, film, music. *Address:* Association of Teachers and Lecturers, 7 Northumberland Street, WC2N 5RD. *T:* (020) 7930 6441, *Fax:* (020) 7930 1359.

BOUTROS-GHALI, Boutros, PhD; President, Egyptian Human Rights Commission, 2004–12; Secretary-General, United Nations, 1992–96; *b* Cairo, 14 Nov. 1922; *m* Maria Leia Nadler. *Educ:* Cairo Univ. (LLB 1946); Paris Univ. (PhD 1949). Prof. of Internat. Law and Internat. Relns, and Head, Dept of Political Scis, Cairo Univ., 1949–77; Minister of State for Foreign Affairs, Egypt, 1977–91; Dep. Prime Minister for Foreign Affairs, 1991–92. Mem., Secretariat, Nat. Democratic Party, 1980–92; MP 1987–92. Sec.-Gen., Orgn Internat. de la Francophonie, 1997–2002. Pres., Curatorium, Hague Acad. of Internat. Law, 2004–. Mem., UN Commn of Internat. Law, 1979–92. Founder and Editor: Al Ahram Iktisadi, 1960–75; Al-Siyassa Dawlya, 1965–91. *Publications:* Contribution à l'étude des ententes régionales, 1949; Cours de diplomatie et de droit diplomatique et consulaire, 1951; (jtly) Le problème du Canal de Suez, 1957; (jtly) Egypt and the United Nations, 1957; Le principe d'égalité des états et les organisations internationales, 1961; Contribution à une théorie générale des Alliances, 1963; Foreign Policies in a World of Change, 1963; L'Organisation de l'unité africaine, 1969; Le mouvement Afro-Asiatique, 1969; Les difficultés institutionelles du panafricanisme, 1971; La ligue des états arabes, 1972; Les Conflits de frontières en Afrique, 1973; Unvanquished: a US-UN saga, 1999; En attendant la prochaine lune: carnets: 1997–2002, 2004; 60 ans de Conflit Israélo-Arabe: entretiens croisés avec Shimon Peres et André Versaille, 2006; also many books in Arabic and numerous contribs to periodicals and learned jls. *Address:* Giza, Cairo, Egypt.

BOUVERIE; *see* Pleydell-Bouverie, family name of Earl of Radnor.

BOVEY, Kathleen Margaret; *see* Wales, K. M.

BOVEY, Philip Henry; Director, Company Law Reform Project, Department of Trade and Industry, 2004–07; *b* 11 July 1948; *s* of late Norman Henry Bovey and Dorothy Yvonne Kent Bovey; *m* 1974, Jenet Alison, *d* of late Rev. Canon J. M. McTear and Margaret McTear; one *s* one *d*. *Educ:* Rugby; Peterhouse, Cambridge (schol.; MA). Solicitor. 3rd Sec., FCO, 1970–71; with Slaughter and May, 1972–75; Legal Assistant, 1976; Sen. Legal Assistant, 1976; Depts of Trade and Industry, 1976–77; Cabinet Office, 1977–78; Depts of Trade, Industry, Prices and Consumer Protection, later DTI, 1978–2007; Asst Solicitor, 1982; Under-Sec., 1985; Dir, Legal Services, 1996–2004. Companies Act Inspector, 1984–88 (report published 1988); Legal Advr to Deregulation, subseq. Better Regulation, then Regulatory Impact Unit, Cabinet Office, 1995–2002. ARPS 2008. *Recreation:* photography. *Address:* 102 Cleveland Gardens, Barnes, SW13 0AH. *T:* (020) 8876 3710.

BOWATER, Sir Euan David Vansittart, 3rd Bt *cr* 1939, of Friston, Suffolk; *b* 9 Sept. 1935; *s* of Sir Noël Vansittart Bowater, 2nd Bt, GBE, MC, and Constance Heiton, *d* of David Gordon Bett; *S* father, 1984; *m* 1964, Susan Mary Humphrey, *d* of late A. R. O. Slater, FCA; two *s* two *d*. *Educ:* Eton; Trinity Coll., Cambridge (BA). *Recreations:* travel, golf, music. *Heir:* *s* Moray David Vansittart Bowater [*b* 24 April 1967; *m* 1993, Mandana Firoozan; two *d*].

BOWATER, Sir Michael Patrick, 5th Bt *cr* 1914, of Hill Crest, Croydon; *b* 18 July 1949; *s* of Sir J(ohn) Vansittart Bowater, 4th Bt, and Joan Kathleen Bowater (*née* Scullard); *S* father, 2008; *m* 1968, Alison, *d* of Edward Wall; four *d*. *Heir:* none.

BOWCOCK, John Brown, FICE; consulting engineer; Senior Consultant, Sir Alexander Gibb & Partners Ltd, 1996–99 (Director, 1989–96; Chairman, 1993–95); *b* 25 Oct. 1931; *s* of John Brown Bowcock and Mabel Bowcock; *m* 1955, Pauline Mary Elizabeth Dalton; three *d*. *Educ:* Hastings Grammar Sch.; St Catherine's Coll., Oxford (MA). FICE 1971. Nat. service, RAF, 1954–56. Joined Sir Alexander Gibb & Partners, 1957: worked on water resource projects overseas incl. Kariba (Zimbabwe), Roseires (Sudan) and Latiyan (Iran), 1957–70; responsible for major dam projects and Drakensberg pumped storage project, SA, 1970–78; Partner, 1978–89; Chief Exec., 1989–93. Chairman: British Dam Soc., 1992–93; British Consultants Bureau, 1991–92; ACE, 1995–96. *Recreations:* golf, music, reading. *Address:* Lothlorien, Crowsley Road, Shiplake, Oxon RG9 3JU. *T:* (0118) 940 4443. *Clubs:* Royal Air Force; Huntercombe Golf (Henley).

BOWDEN, Rev. Canon Andrew; *see* Bowden, Rev. Canon R. A.

BOWDEN, Sir Andrew, Kt 1994; MBE 1961; International Consultant, Global Equities Corp., 2004–10; *b* 8 April 1930; *s* of William Victor Bowden, Solicitor, and Francesca Wilson; *m* 1970, Benita Napier; one *s* one *d*. *Educ:* Ardingly College. Paint industry, 1955–68; Man. Dir, Personnel Assessments Ltd, 1969–71; Man. Dir, Haymarket Personnel Selection Ltd, 1970–71; Director: Sales Education & Leadership Ltd, 1970–71; Jenkin and Purser (Holdings) Ltd, 1973–77. Mem., Wandsworth Borough Council, 1956–62. Contested (C): N Hammersmith, 1955; N Kensington, 1964; Kemp Town, Brighton, 1966. MP (C) Brighton, Kemptown, 1970–97; contested (C) same seat, 1997. Jt Chm., All Party Old Age Pensioners Parly Gp, 1972–97; Chm., All Party BLESMA Gp, 1975–97; Mem. Select Cttee on Expenditure, 1973–74, on Abortion, 1975, on Employment, 1979–83. Mem., Council of Europe, 1987–97. Nat. Chm., Young Conservatives, 1960–61. Internat. Chm., People to People, 1981–83. Nat. Pres., Captive Animals Protection Soc., 1978–98. Mem., Chichester Dio. Synod, 1998–2003. Mem. School Council, Ardingly Coll., 1982–97. *Publications:* (jtly) Dare We Trust Them? - a new vision for Europe, 2005. *Recreations:* birdwatching, chess, poker. *Address:* 35 Wanderdown Road, Ovingdean, Brighton BN2 7BT. *T:* (01273) 552136. *Club:* Carlton.

BOWDEN, Gerald Francis, TD 1971; barrister, chartered surveyor and university lecturer; *b* 26 Aug. 1935; *s* of Frank Albert Bowden and Elsie Bowden (*née* Burrill); *m* 1967, Heather Elizabeth Hill (*née* Hall) (*d* 1984); two *d*, and one step *s* one step *d*. *Educ:* Battersea Grammar School; Magdalen College, Oxford (MA); Coll. of Estate Mgt, London. FRICS 1984. Called to the Bar, Gray's Inn, 1962. Worked in advertising industry, 1964–68; property marketing and investment, 1968–72; Principal Lecturer in Law, Dept of Estate Management, Polytechnic of the South Bank, 1972–83; Vis. Lectr, Kingston Univ., 1993–2004. Chm. Panel, Examination in Public of Suffolk Co. Structure Plan, 1993. Mem. of Delegacy, KCL, 1978–84. Mem. GLC for Dulwich, 1977–81; a co-opted Mem., ILEA, 1981–84. MP (C) Dulwich, 1983–92; contested (C) Dulwich, 1992. PPS to Minister for Arts, 1990–92. Mem., Select Cttee on Educn, Sci. and Arts, 1990–92. Vice-Chairman: Cons. Backbench Educn Cttee, 1987–89; Cons. Backbench Arts and Heritage Cttee, 1987–92. Pres., Greater London Conservative Trade Unionists, 1985–88. Pres., Southwark Chamber of Commerce, 1986–89. Chairman: Walcot Educn Foundn, 1978–2001; Lambeth and Southwark Housing Assoc. (formerly Soc.), 1973–84; London Rent Assessment Panel, 1994–2006; Leasehold Valuation Tribunal, 1994–2006; Pres., Appeal Tribunal on Building Regulation, 1995–2005. Chm., Magdalen Soc., 1991–2001; Trustee, Magdalen Develt Trust, 1991–2009. Mem. Council, Royal Albert Hall, 1994–. Estates Gov., Alleyn's Coll. of God's Gift, Dulwich, 1992–2003 (Chm.). After Nat. Service, continued to serve in TA until 1984 (Lt-Col). Vice Pres., London City Hall Br., RBL, 2010–. *Publications:* An Introduction to the Law of Contract and Tort, 1977; The Housing Act, 1988. *Recreations:* gardening, books, pictures, renovating old houses. *Address:* 130 Kennington Park Road, SE11 4DJ. *T:* (020) 7582 7361. *Clubs:* Oxford and Cambridge (Trustee, 2002–11), Chelsea Arts, Garrick.

BOWDEN, James Nicholas Geoffrey, CMG 2012; OBE 2002; HM Diplomatic Service; Deputy Private Secretary to the Prince of Wales and the Duchess of Cornwall, since 2014; *b* 27 May 1960; *s* of Geoffrey Bowden and Gillian (*née* Mathieson); *m* 1st, 1986, Alison Hulme (marr. diss. 1999); one *s* one *d*; 2nd, 1999, Sarah Peaslee; twin *s* one *d*. *Educ:* Eton. Served RGJ, 1980–86. Entered HM Diplomatic Service, 1986; Second Sec., FCO, 1986–90; Dep. Consul Gen., Aden, 1990–91; Second Sec., Khartoum, 1991–93; First Secretary: FCO, 1993–96; Washington, 1996–99; Riyadh, 1999–2000; FCO, 2000–03; Deputy Head of Mission: Kuwait, 2003–04; Baghdad, 2004–05; Kuwait, 2005–06; Ambassador: to Bahrain, 2006–11; to Oman, 2011–14. *Recreations:* hunting, walking. *Address:* Clarence House, SW1A 1BA.

BOWDEN, Sir Nicholas Richard, 4th Bt *cr* 1915, of City of Nottingham; farmer, now retired; *b* 13 Aug. 1935; *s* of Sir Frank Bowden, 3rd Bt and his 1st wife, Marie-José Stiénon De Messey; *S* father, 2001. *Educ:* Millfield Sch. Asst to horse-trainer; farmer. *Recreation:* riding. *Heir:* *half-nephew* Alexander Gordan Houston Bowden [*b* 14 May 1972; *m* 2009, Nicola Judy Fleming; one *s* two *d*]. *Address:* 4 Hensting Farm Cottages, Fishers Pond, Eastleigh, Hants SO50 7HH. *Club:* Lansdowne.

BOWDEN, Rev. Canon (Robert) Andrew; Chaplain to the Queen, 1992–2008; Associate Priest, Thameshead benefice, diocese of Gloucester, 2004–08; *b* 13 Nov. 1938; *s* of Charles Bowden and Miriam (*née* Howard-Tripp); *m* 1966, Susan (*née* Humpidge); three *d*. *Educ:* Clifton Coll., Bristol; Worcester Coll., Oxford (Scholar; BA 1962; DipTh 1963; MA 1967; BDQ 1968); Cuddesdon Coll., Oxford. Ordained deacon, 1965, priest, 1966. Curate: St George, Wolverhampton, 1965–69; St Luke's, Duston, 1969–72; Rector: Byfield, 1972–79; Coates, Rodmarton and Sapperton with Frampton Mansell, 1979–2004. Chaplain, Royal Agricl Coll., Cirencester, 1979–93; Rural Advr, 1981–93, Local Ministry Officer, 1993–2004, dio. of Gloucester; Mem., Archbp's Commn on Rural Areas, 1988–90; Chm., Churches Rural Gp, 2004–07. Hon. Canon, Gloucester Cathedral, 1990–2008, Canon Emeritus, 2008–. *Publications:* Ministry in the Countryside, 1994; (with M. West) Dynamic Local Ministry, 2000; (ed) Ordained Local Ministry in the Church of England, 2012. *Recreation:* breeding old breeds of poultry and Shetland sheep. *Address:* Washbrook Cottage, Caudle Green, Cheltenham, Glos GL53 9PW. *T:* (01285) 821067. *E:* randrewbowden@gmail.com.

BOWDERY, Martin Howard; QC 2000; a Recorder, since 2003; Deputy Judge, Technology and Construction Court, since 2004; *b* 2 July 1956; *s* of Ray Bowdery and Beryl Bowdery (*née* Porter); *m* 1st, 1982 (marr. diss. 1999); two *s* four *d*; 2nd, 2002, Lindsay Moffat, *d* of Ted and Joan Moffat. *Educ:* Trinity Sch. of John Whitgift; Pembroke Coll., Oxford (BA PPE 1978). Called to the Bar, Inner Temple, 1980; practising Barrister, 1982–. Ed., Internat. Construction Law Rev., 1983–87. *Publications:* contributor to: Construction Contract Reform: a plea for sanity, 1999; Construction Law Handbook, 2000; Hudson's Building and Engineering Contracts, 12th edn, 2010. *Address:* 1 Atkin Building, Gray's Inn, WC1R 5AT. *T:* (020) 7404 0102. *Clubs:* Garrick; Isle of Purbeck Golf.

BOWDLER, Timothy John, CBE 2006; company director; Chairman, Laidlaw Interiors Group, since 2012; *b* 16 May 1947; *s* of Henry Neville Bowdler and Barbara Mary Bowdler (*née* Richardson); *m* 1976, Brita Margaretha Eklund; two *d*. *Educ:* Wrekin Coll.; Birmingham Univ. (BSc Engrg Prodn 1969); London Business Sch. (MBA 1975). Graduate mgt trainee, subseq. branch admin. manager, GKN Sankey Ltd, 1969–73; General Bearings Division, RHP Bearings Ltd: Commercial Manager, 1975–77; Gen. Manager, Business Ops, 1977–81; Sandvik Ltd: Dir and Gen. Manager, Sandvik Steel, 1981–84; Man. Dir, Spooner Industries Ltd, 1984–87; Man. Dir, Chloride Motive Power, Chloride Gp plc, 1987–88; Dir N Div., Tyzack & Partners Ltd, 1989–90; Divl Man. Dir, Cape Architectural Products, 1990–92, Cape Building and Architectural Products, 1992–94, Cape plc; Gp Man. Dir, 1994–97, Chief Exec., 1997–2009, Johnston Press plc. Chm., Press Standards Bd of Finance Ltd, 2005– (Dir, 2000–); non-executive Director: ABP Hldgs plc, 2001–06; PA Group, 2001–10 (non-exec. Chm., 2009–10); Miller Gp, 2004–12; Tullis Russell, 2010–. Council Mem., Newspaper Soc., 1994–2008 (Pres., 2002–03). *Recreations:* golf, ski-ing, fishing, Swedish summerhouse. *E:* timbowdler@gmail.com. *Clubs:* Bruntsfield Links Golfing Society, Hon. Company of Edinburgh Golfers.

BOWDON, Humphrey Anthony Erdeswick B.; *see* Butler-Bowdon.

BOWE, Dame Colette, DBE 2014; PhD; Chairman: Banking Standards Board (formerly Banking Standards Review Council), since 2014; Associated Board of the Royal Schools of Music, since 2012; *b* 27 Nov. 1946; *d* of Philip Bowe and Norah (*née* Hughes). *Educ:* Notre Dame High Sch., Liverpool; Queen Mary Coll., Univ. of London (BSc Econs, PhD); LSE (MSc Econs). Research Officer, LSE, 1969–70; Econ. Advr, Nat. Ports Council, 1971–73; Department of Industry: Econ. Advr, 1975–78; Principal, 1979–81; Department of Trade and Industry: Asst Sec., 1981–84; Dir of Information, 1984–87; Controller of Public Affairs, IBA, 1987–89; Dir, SIB, 1989–93; Chief Exec., PIA, 1994–97; Exec. Chm., Save & Prosper and Fleming Fund Mgt (Luxembourg), 1998–2001; Chm., Telecoms Ombudsman Service Council, 2002–03. Chm., OFCOM, 2009–14 (Chm., Consumer Panel, 2003–07; non-exec. Dir, 2008–09); Member: Statistics Commn, 2000–08; UK Statistics Authy, 2010–; non-exec. Dir, DfT, 2014–. Chm., Electra Private Equity plc, 2010–14 (non-exec. Dir., 2007–14); non-executive Director: Thames Water Utilities Ltd, 2001–06 (Dep. Chm., 2002–06); Yorkshire Building Soc., 2003–06; Framlington Gp, 2003–05; Axa Framlington, 2005–09; Morgan Stanley Bank Internat., 2005–10; Morgan Stanley Internat., 2010–11; Goldfish Bank, 2007–08; London and Continental Railways, 2008–11; Mem., Supervisory Bd, Axa Deutschland GmbH, 2009–; Mem. Bd, Axa IM, 2012–14. Chm., Alcohol Concern, 2002–06. Chm. Council, Queen Mary, Univ. of London, 2003–09; Gov. and Mem. Council of Mgt, NIESR, 2002–10. Gov., Bancroft's Sch., 2009. Trustee: Camden People's Theatre, 2002–11; Wincott Foundn, 2004–11; Tablet Trust, 2010–; Nuffield Foundn, 2012–. Liveryman, Drapers' Co., 2008–. Hon. Fellow, Liverpool John Moores Univ., 1995. Hon. DSc QMUL, 2010. *Recreations:* music, London, watching football. *E:* office@redrock23.com.

BOWE, David Robert; public affairs consultant; Member (Lab) Yorkshire and the Humber Region, European Parliament, 1999–2004 (Cleveland and Yorkshire North, 1989–94; Cleveland and Richmond, 1994–99); *b* Gateshead, 19 July 1955; *m* 1978, Helena Scattergood; one *s* one *d*. *Educ:* Sunderland Polytechnic; Bath Univ. BSc; PGCE. Former science teacher. Mem., Middlesbrough Borough Council, 1983–89 (Chm., Monitoring and Review Cttee). European Parliament: Mem., Cttee on Envmt, Public Health and Consumer Protection, 1989–2004; substitute Member: Cttee on Econ. and Monetary Affairs, 1994–99; Industry Cttee, 1999–2004. Mem., UNISON. *Address:* 4 Silverdale Mount, Guiseley, Leeds LS20 8PY. *E:* mail@davidbowe.demon.co.uk.

BOWEN, Anthony John; Lector, Faculty of Classics, 1990–2003, and Orator, 1993–2007, University of Cambridge; Fellow, Jesus College, Cambridge, 1995–2007, now Emeritus Fellow (President, 2003–05); *b* 17 May 1940; *s* of Dr Reginald Bowen and Dorothy Bowen (*née* Jinks). *Educ:* Bradfield Coll., Berks; St John's Coll., Cambridge. Teacher: Bradfield Coll., 1963–67 (producer of Greek play, 1961, 1964, 1967); Shrewsbury Sch., 1967–90. Contested (L/Alliance) Shrewsbury and Atcham, 1983. Member: (L, then Lib Dem) Shropshire CC, 1981–89; (Lib Dem) Cambridgeshire CC, 1997–2005. *Publications:* Aeschylus, Cheophori, 1986; The Story of Lucretia, 1987; Plutarch, the Malice of Herodotus, 1992; Xenophon, Symposium, 1998; (with Peter Garnsey) Lactantius, Divine Institutes, 2003; Cambridge Orations 1993–2007: a selection, 2008; Aeschylus, Suppliant Women, 2013. *Recreations:* travel, politics, music, food and wine. *Address:* Jesus College, Cambridge CB5 8BL. *T:* (01223) 323722.

BOWEN, Maj.-Gen. Bryan Morris, CB 1988; Paymaster-in-Chief and Inspector of Army Pay Services, 1986–89, retired; *b* 8 March 1932; *s* of Frederick Bowen and Gwendoline Bowen (*née* Morris); *m* 1955, Suzanne Rowena (*née* Howell); two *d*. *Educ:* Newport High Sch.; Exeter Univ. FCMA; ndc, psc†, sq, pfc. Joined RE, 1953, served UK and BAOR; transf. RAPC, 1958; Paymaster 1/6 QEO Gurkha Rifles, Malaya and UK, 1960–63; Army Cost and Management Accounting Services, 1963–68; DAAG, MoD, 1968–70; Exchange Officer, US Army, Washington, DC, 1970–72; Nat. Defence Coll., 1972–73; DS, RMCS Shrivenham, 1973–76; AAG, MOD, 1976–79; Col (Principal), MoD F4(AD), 1979–81; Chief Paymaster, Army Pay Office (Officers Accounts), 1981–82; Dep. Paymaster-in-Chief, 1982–85. Col Comdt, RAPC, 1990–92; Dep. Col Comdt, AGC, 1992–93. Mem. Council, CIMA, 1990–94; Chm., Oxfordshire Cttee, Army Benevolent Fund, 1990–92; Special Comr, Duke of York's Royal Mil. Sch., Dover, 1990–2000 (Chm., 1992–2000); Dir, United Services Trustee, 1990–2000; Pres., Nat. Service Veterans' Assoc., 2003–15. Freeman, City of London, 1987. *Address:* Foxlea, Yew Tree Farm, Goodworth Clatford, Andover, Hants SP11 7QY.

BOWEN, Carolyn Elizabeth Cunningham; *see* Sinclair, C. E. C.

BOWEN, Prof. (David) Keith, DPhil; FRS 1998; FREng; Visiting Professor of Physics, University of Durham, since 2003; Professor of Engineering, University of Warwick, 1989–97, now Emeritus; consultant in X-ray science and technology and in technical due diligence for investors and M&A, since 2010; *b* 10 May 1940; *s* of Harold Lane Bowen and Muriel Bowen; *m* 1968, Beryl Lodge; one *s*. *Educ:* Christ's Hosp.; St Edmund Hall, Oxford (MA 1966; DPhil Metallurgy 1967; Hon. Fellow 2006); Open Univ. (Dip. Music 2006; MA Music 2009). FREng (FEng 1997); FIMMM (FIM 1983); CPhys 1998, FInstP 1998. SRC Res. Fellow, Oxford Univ., 1966–68; Department of Engineering, University of Warwick: Lectr, 1968–78; Sen. Lectr, 1978–85; Reader, 1985–89. Vis. Prof., MIT, 1987. Pres., Bede Scientific Inc., 1996–2002; Gp Dir of Technology, 2000–05, Chief Scientist, 2005–08, Bede plc. Pres., Kammermusik Workshops Inc., USA, 2004–15; Chm., Spires Music Ltd, 2007–15. Non-exec. Dir, Circadian Solar (formerly AdvanceSis) Ltd, 2005–10; Chm., goHDR, 2011–15 (non-exec. Dir, 2010–15). Royal Coll. of Music Scholar (Pamela Weston Award, 2012). *Publications:* (with C. R. Hall) Microscopy of Materials, 1975; (with B. K. Tanner) High Resolution X-Ray Diffractometry and Topography, 1998; X-Ray Metrology in Semiconductor Manufacturing, 2006; more than 130 articles in learned jls; 8 patents; pubns in clarinet organology. *Recreations:* music (orchestral and chamber clarinet player, conductor and coach), clarinet restoration, woodwork, gardening. *E:* keith.bowen@gmx.com.

BOWEN, Desmond John, CB 2009; CMG 2002; Staff Counsellor, Security and Intelligence Services, since 2009; *b* 11 Jan. 1949; *s* of John and Deborah Bowen; *m* 1979, Susan Brandt; one *s* one *d*. *Educ:* Charterhouse; University Coll., Oxford (MA). Parachute Regt, 1970–73; joined MoD, 1973; seconded to FCO, 1978–81, 1987–91; Private Sec. to Permanent Under Sec. of State, 1982–85; Dir Gen. of Mktg, Defence Export Services Orgn, 1995–97; Fellow, Center for Internat. Affairs, Harvard Univ., 1997–98; Asst Under Sec. of State (Service Personnel Policy), 1998–99; Dir, Private Office of Sec. Gen., NATO, 1999–2001; Dir Gen. Operational Policy, MoD, 2001–02; on secondment as Dep. Dir, Overseas and Defence Secretariat, Cabinet Office, 2002–04; Policy Dir, MoD, 2004–08. Mem., UN Sec.-Gen.'s Adv. Bd on Disarmament Matters, 2009–13. Vis. Prof., Reading Univ., 2010–. *Publications:* (contrib.) British Generals in Blair's Wars, 2013; contrib. Conflict and Terrorism jl, Survival jl, RUSI's Afghan Papers. *Recreation:* mountains. *Address:* c/o Cabinet Office, SW1A 2AS.

BOWEN, Edward Farquharson, CBE 2010; TD 1976; QC (Scot.) 1992; Temporary Judge, Court of Session, since 2000; *b* 1 May 1945; *s* of late Stanley Bowen, CBE; *m* 1975, Patricia Margaret Brown, *y d* of Rev. R. Russell Brown, Perth; two *s* two *d*. *Educ:* Melville Coll., Edinburgh; Edinburgh Univ. (LLB 1966). Enrolled as Solicitor in Scotland, 1968; admitted to Faculty of Advocates, 1970. Standing Jun. Counsel: to Scottish Educn Dept, 1977–79; to Home Office in Scotland, 1979; Advocate-Depute, 1979–83; Sheriff of Tayside Central and Fife, 1983–90; Partner, Thorntons, WS, 1990–91; Sheriff-Principal of Glasgow and Strathkelvin, 1997–2005, of Lothian and Borders, 2005–11. Chm. (part-time), Industrial Tribunals, 1995–97; Mem. Criminal Injuries Compensation Bd, 1996–97. Chm., Ind. Rev. of Sheriff and Jury Procedure, 2009–10. Chm., Northern Lighthouse Bd, 2003–05 (Comr of Northern Lights, 1997–2011). Chancellor's Assessor, Edinburgh Univ. Court, 2011–. Served RAOC (TA and T&AVR), 1964–80. *Recreation:* golf. *Address:* The Old Manse, Lundie, Angus DD2 5NW. *Clubs:* New (Edinburgh); Royal & Ancient Golf (St Andrews); Hon. Company of Edinburgh Golfers; Panmure Golf.

BOWEN, Sir George Edward Michael, 6th Bt *cr* 1921, of Colworth, Co. Bedford; *b* 27 Dec. 1987; *s* of Sir Mark Edward Mortimer Bowen, 5th Bt and of Kerry Tessa Bowen (*née* Moriarty); *S* father 2014. *Heir: cousin* Michael Edward Bowen [*b* 14 Dec. 1944; *m* 1968, Gillian Margaret Garside; three *d*].

BOWEN, Geraint Robert Lewis, FRCO; Organist and Director of Music, Hereford Cathedral, since 2001; *b* 11 Jan. 1963; *s* of Kenneth John Bowen and Angela Mary Bowen (*née* Evenden); *m* 1987, Catherine Lucy Dennis; two *s*. *Educ:* Haverstock Sch.; William Ellis Sch.; Jesus Coll., Cambridge (organ schol.; BA 1986, MA 1989); Trinity Coll., Dublin (MusB 1987). FRCO 1987. Assistant Organist: Hampstead Parish Ch and St Clement Danes Ch, 1985–86; St Patrick's Cathedral, Dublin, 1986–89; Hereford Cathedral, 1989–94; Organist and Master of the Choristers, St Davids Cathedral, and Artistic Dir, St Davids Cathedral Fest., 1995–2001. Conductor, Hereford Choral Soc., 2001–; Associate Conductor, Three Choirs Fest. at Gloucester and Worcester, 2002–; Conductor, Three Choirs Fest. at Hereford, 2003–. Hon. FGCM 2012. *Recreations:* growing vegetables, railways, travel, typography, walking. *Address:* 7 College Cloisters, The Close, Hereford HR1 2NG. *T:* (01432) 374238. *E:* organist@herefordcathedral.org.

BOWEN, Janet Margaret; Lord-Lieutenant of Ross and Cromarty, Skye and Lochalsh, since 2007; *b* 12 July 1944; *d* of Capt. Alexander Matheson, RN and Mary Matheson; *m* 1972, Christopher Richard Croasdaile Bowen; one *s* one *d*. *Educ:* Butterstone House Sch.; North Foreland Lodge. Sec., British Red Cross HQ and volunteer, British Red Cross VSO scheme, 1965–68; Sec., Church Soc., 1969–72; Mem., Children's Panel, 1986–2004. Pres., Red Cross, Highland and Western Isles, 2007–12 (Chm., Volunteer Council, 2000–07). *Recreations:* cherishing temperamental husband, gardening, cooking, succeeding in life without formal qualifications, five grandchildren. *Address:* Kinellan House, Strathpeffer, Ross-shire IV14 9ET. *T:* (01997) 421476. *E:* janet@kinellan.org.

BOWEN, Jeremy Francis John; Middle East Editor, BBC, since 2005; *b* 6 Feb. 1960; *s* of (David) Gareth (Francis) Bowen and (Margaret Frances) Jennifer Bowen (*née* Delany); partner, Julia Williams; one *s* one *d*. *Educ:* Cardiff High Sch.; University Coll. London (BA Hons Hist.; Fellow 2005); Johns Hopkins Univ. Sch. of Advanced Internat. Studies, Washington and Bologna, Italy (MA Internat. Affairs). Joined BBC, 1984: news trainee, 1984–85; financial news reporter, 1986–87; Foreign Correspondent, 1987–2000: Radio Corresp., Geneva, 1987; Foreign Affairs Corresp., TV, 1988–95; Middle East Corresp., 1995–2000; Presenter, BBC Breakfast, 2000–02; foreign correspondent and television presenter, 2002–05; Rome Corresp., 2005. Hon. Fellow: Cardiff Univ., 2009; Univ. of S Wales, 2013; Cardiff Metropolitan Univ., 2015; Aberystwyth Univ., 2015. Hon. DSocSci Nottingham Trent, 2014. Journalism award: NY TV Fest., 1993; Monte Carlo TV Fest., 1994; RTS, 1996; BAFTA Award for BBC team coverage of Kosovo Crisis, 1999; Sony Gold Award for coverage of Saddam Hussein's arrest, 2004; Internat. Emmy, BBC Team Award for coverage of 2006 war in Lebanon and Israel, 2007; Bayeux war corresp. prize for coverage of Gaza war, 2009, for radio report covering Syrian war, 2012; Charles Wheeler Award for excellence in broadcast journalism, British Journalism Rev., 2010; (jtly) Peace Through Media Award, Next Century Foundn, 2012; Specialist Journalist of the Year, 2013, Television Journalist of the Year, 2014, RTS; BAFTA Cymru Siân Phillips Award, 2014; Emmy Award, 2014, Peabody Award, 2014, for Syria coverage. *Publications:* Six Days: how the 1967 war shaped the Middle East, 2003; War Stories, 2006; The Arab Uprisings: the people want the fall of the regime, 2012. *Recreations:* sport, cooking, not travelling. *Address:* c/o BBC News, Broadcasting House, Portland Place, W1A 1AA.

See also N. J. H. Bowen.

BOWEN, John Griffith; playwright and novelist; freelance drama producer for television; *b* 5 Nov. 1924; *s* of Hugh Griffith Bowen and Ethel May Cook; unmarried. *Educ:* Queen Elizabeth's Grammar Sch., Crediton; Pembroke Coll., Oxford; St Antony's Coll., Oxford. Frere Exhibition for Indian Studies, Oxford, 1951–52 and 1952–53. Asst Editor, The Sketch, 1954–57; Advertising Copywriter and Copy Chief, 1957–60; Consultant on TV Drama, Associated TV, 1960–67; productions for Thames TV, LWT, BBC. *Publications:* The Truth Will Not Help Us, 1956; After the Rain, 1958; The Centre of the Green, 1959; Storyboard, 1960; The Birdcage, 1962; A World Elsewhere, 1965; The Essay Prize, 1965; Squeak, 1983; The McGuffin, 1984 (filmed for TV, 1986); The Girls, 1986; Fighting Back, 1989; The Precious Gift, 1992; No Retreat, 1994; *plays:* I Love You, Mrs Patterson, 1964; After the Rain, 1967; Fall and Redemption, 1967; Little Boxes, 1968; The Disorderly Women, 1968; The Corsican Brothers, 1970; The Waiting Room, 1970; Robin Redbreast, 1972; Heil Caesar, 1973; Florence Nightingale, 1975; Which Way Are You Facing?, 1976; Singles, 1977; Bondage, 1978; The Inconstant Couple (adaptation of Marivaux, L'Heureux Stratagème), 1978; Uncle Jeremy, 1981; The Geordie Gentleman (adaptation of Molière's Le Bourgeois Gentilhomme), 1987; Cold Salmon, 1998. *Address:* Old Lodge Farm, Sugarswell Lane, Edgehill, Banbury, Oxon OX15 6HP.

BOWEN, Keith; *see* Bowen, D. K.

BOWEN, Most Rev. Michael George; Archbishop and Metropolitan of Southwark, (RC), 1977–2003, now Archbishop Emeritus; *b* 23 April 1930; *s* of late Major C. L. J. Bowen and Maisie Bowen (who *m* 1945, Sir Paul Makins, 4th Bt). *Educ:* Downside; Trinity Coll., Cambridge; Gregorian Univ., Rome. Army, 1948–49, 2nd Lieut Irish Guards; Wine Trade, 1951–52; English Coll., Rome, 1952–59; ordained 1958; Curate at Earlsfield and at Walworth, South London, 1959–63; taught theology, Beda Coll., Rome, 1963–66; Chancellor of Diocese of Arundel and Brighton, 1966–70; Coadjutor Bishop with right of succession to See of Arundel and Brighton, 1970–71; Bishop of Arundel and Brighton, 1971–77. Pres., Bishops' Conf. of England and Wales, 1999–2000 (Vice-Pres., 1996–98). *Recreations:* golf, tennis. *Address:* c/o Archbishop's House, St George's Road, SE1 6HX. *T:* (020) 7928 2495.

BOWEN, Nicholas James Hugh; QC 2009; *b* Cardiff, 18 Aug. 1961; *s* of (David) Gareth (Francis) Bowen and (Margaret) Jennifer Bowen (*neé* Delany); *m* 1990, Maryanne St Clare; two *s* one *d*. *Educ:* Cardiff High Sch.; Univ. of Sussex (BA Law 1983); Council of Legal Educn. Called to the Bar, Gray's Inn, 1984; in practice as a barrister, 29 Bedford Row, 1988–2005, Doughty Street, 2005–, specialising in public and admin. law, human rights and civil liberties, state liability in tort, actions against the police, inquest law and professional negligence. *Recreations:* gardening, sailing, walking the Black Mountains, building sheds. *Address:* 53–54 Doughty Street, WC1N 2LS. *T:* (020) 7404 1313, *Fax:* (020) 7404 2283/4.

See also J. F. J. Bowen.

BOWEN, Paul Edward; QC 2012; *b* Oslo, 17 July 1967; *s* of Brig. Derek Harvey Bowen, OBE and Juliet Aymée Bowen; *m* 2000, Michèle, (Mimi), Spencer; one *s* one *d*. *Educ:* Tonbridge Sch.; Univ. of Exeter (LLB 1989). Called to the Bar, Inner Temple, 1993; in practice as a barrister, specialising in human rights and public law, Doughty Street Chambers, 1993–2014, Brick Court Chambers, 2014–. Mem., Adv. Bd, Children's Comr, 2010–. Gov., Wildlesham House Sch., 2007–10. *Publications:* Blackstone's Guide to the Mental Health Act 2007, 2008. *Recreations:* family life, sailing, the great outdoors. *Club:* Penn.

BOWEN, Thomas Edward Ifor L.; *see* Lewis-Bowen.

BOWEN, William G(ordon), PhD; President, The Andrew W. Mellon Foundation, 1988–2006, now Emeritus; President, Princeton University, 1972–88, now Emeritus; *b* 6 Oct. 1933; *s* of Albert A. and Bernice C. Bowen; *m* 1956, Mary Ellen Maxwell; one *s* one *d*. *Educ:* Denison Univ. (AB); Princeton Univ. (PhD). Princeton University: Asst Prof. of Economics, Associate Prof. of Economics; Prof. of Econs, 1958–88; Provost, 1967–72; Sen. Fellow, Woodrow Wilson Sch. of Public and Internat. Affairs, 1988. Director: NCR, 1975–91; Reader's Digest, 1985–97; Merck, 1986; DeWitt and Lila Wallace-Reader's Digest Funds, 1986–97; American Express, 1988; Teachers' Insce and Annuity Assoc., 1995–; Coll. Retirement Equities Fund, 1995–; JSTOR (first Chm., 1995). Trustee: Center for Advanced Study in the Behavioral Sciences, 1986–92; Ithaka; Regent, Smithsonian Instn, 1980–92; Mem. Bd of Dirs, Denison Univ., 1992 (Trustee, 1992–2000). Hon. LLD: Denison, Rutgers, Pennsylvania and Yale, 1972; Harvard, 1973; Jewish Theol Seminary, 1974; Seton Hall Univ., 1975; Dartmouth and Princeton, 1987; Brown, 1988; Michigan, 1995; Hon. DHL: Morehouse Coll., 1992; Hartwick Coll., 1992; Hon. DSc Lafayette Coll., 1992; Hon. DEconSc Cape Town, 1996; Hon. DCL Oxford, 2001. Nat. Humanities Medal (USA), 2012. *Publications:* Economic Aspects of Education, 1964; (with W. J. Baumol) Performing Arts: the Economic Dilemma, 1966; (with T. A. Finegan) Economics of Labor Force Participation, 1969; Ever the Teacher, 1987; (with Julie Ann Sosa) Prospects for Faculty in the Arts & Sciences, 1989; (with N. L. Rudenstine) In Pursuit of the PhD, 1992; Inside the Boardroom: governance by directors and trustees, 1994; (jtly) The Charitable Nonprofits, 1994; (with Derek Bok) The Shape of the River: long-term consequences of considering race in college and university admissions, 1998; (with James Shulman) The Game of Life: college sports and educational values, 2001; (with Sarah A. Levin) Reclaiming the Game: college sports and educational values, 2003; (jtly) Equity and Excellence in American Higher Education, 2005; Crossing the Finish Line: completing college at America's public universities, 2009; Lessons Learned: reflections of a university President, 2010; contribs to Amer. Econ. Review, Economica, Quarterly Jl of Economics, etc. *Address:* c/o Andrew W. Mellon Foundation, 140 E 62 Street, New York, NY 10065, USA. *T:* (212) 8268114.

BOWEN-BRAVERY, Katy Louise; Editor, Saga Magazine, since 2008 (Deputy Editor, 2002–08); *b* Cosford, Salop, 27 June 1959; *d* of late Kenyon Bowen-Bravery and of Mary Bowen-Bravery; *m* (marr. diss.); one *s*. *Educ:* Francis Bacon Sch., St Albans; Univ. of Wales Inst. of Sci. and Technol. (BA Hons); Cardiff Sch. of Journalism (Dip. Journalism); PPA Dip. Publishing. Reporter, sub-ed., Western Daily Press, 1983–85; freelance feature writer, Daily Mail and sub-ed., Mail on Sunday, 1985; Mem., launch team, Today newspaper, then Ed., Saturday mag., Male and Female, 1985–89; Commng Ed., Good Weekend mag., Sydney Morning Herald, 1989–94; Editor: Boulevard, subseq. Express on Sunday Mag., Sunday Express, 1994–96; Sunday Mirror mag., 1996–2002. *Recreations:* lepidoptery, windsurfing, VW campervanning. *Address:* Saga Publishing Ltd, The Saga Pavilion, Enbrook Park, Folkestone, Kent CT20 3SE. *T:* (01303) 771523, *Fax:* (01303) 776699. *E:* editor@saga.co.uk. *Club:* Union.

BOWEN-SIMPKINS, Peter, FRCOG; Consultant Obstetrician and Gynaecologist: Singleton Hospital, Swansea, 1979–98; Swansea NHS Trust, 1999–2002; Medical Director, London Women's Clinic at Singleton Hospital (formerly Cromwell IVF and Fertility Centre), Swansea, since 1992; Executive Medical Director, JD Healthcare, since 2005; *b* 28 Oct. 1941; *s* of late Horace John Bowen-Simpkins and of Christine Dulce Bowen-Simpkins (*née* Clarke); *m* 1967, Kathrin Ganguin; two *d*. *Educ:* Malvern Coll.; Selwyn Coll., Cambridge (BA 1963); MA 1966, MB BChir 1966, Cambridge; Guy's Hosp. Med. Sch. LRCP, MRCS 1966; FRCOG 1985; FFSRH (FFFP 2005; MFFP 1993). Leader, Cambridge expedn to Eritrea, 1963; Resident MO, Queen Charlotte's Maternity Hosp., London, 1971; Resident Surg. Officer, Samaritan Hosp. for Women, London, 1972; Sen. Registrar and Lectr, Middlesex Hosp. and Hosp. for Women, Soho Square, 1972–78; Inspector of Nullity for Wales, 1980–. Lectr, Margaret Pyke Centre for Family Planning, 1973–2003. Royal College of Obstetricians and Gynaecologists: Mem. Council, 1993–2005; Hon. Treas., 1998–2005; Mem. Foundn Bd, Fac. of Family Planning, 1995–98; Trustee and Bd Mem., WellBeing, 1998–2012. Chm. Mgt Bd, BJOG, 1998–2005. Pres., Victor Bonney Soc., 2002–05. Hon. Treas., Royal Med. Benevolent Fund, 2008–14. Freeman, City of London, 1980; Liveryman: Soc. of Apothecaries, 1976; Livery Co. of Wales (formerly Welsh Livery Guild), 1995. Handcock Prize for Surgery, RCS, 1966. *Publications:* Pocket Examiner in Obstetrics and Gynaecology, 1983, 2nd edn 1992; A Practice of Obstetrics and Gynaecology, 2000; papers on obstetrics and gynaecol. in BMJ, BJOG, BJA, Fertility and Sterility, etc. *Recreations:* flyfishing, walking, ski-ing, sailing. *Address:* Cysgod-y-Bryn, Brynview Close, Reynoldston, Swansea SA3 1AG. *E:* pbs@reynoldston.com. *Clubs:* Athenæum; Gynaecological Travellers.

BOWER, Cynthia; Chief Executive, Care Quality Commission, 2009–12; *b* Worksop, Notts, 6 July 1955; *d* of Harold and Clariss Bower; one *s* by Roger William Shannon. *Educ:* Univ. of Birmingham (BA Hons English Lang. and Lit. 1976; DipSW 1979; MScSoc 1994). Various posts with Birmingham CC, 1979–95, incl. Asst Dir of Social Services, 1992–95; Chief Executive: Birmingham Specialist Community Health Trust, 2000–02; S Birmingham PCT, 2002–05; NHS W Midlands, 2006–08. Chm., Gateway Family Services, 2006–08; Mem. Bd, Skills for Health, 2007–13. Mem., Lunar Soc. Hon. PhD: Birmingham, 2009; Aston, 2009. *Recreations:* music, literature, art, cinema, running, swimming, dining, recent Londonophile.

BOWER, Thomas Michael; writer and journalist; *b* 28 Sept. 1946; *s* of George Bower and Sylvia Bower; *m* 1st, 1971, Juliet Ann Oddie (marr. diss. 1981); two *s*; 2nd, 1985, Veronica Judith Colleton Wadley, *qv*; one *s* one *d*. *Educ:* William Ellis Sch.; London Sch. of Econs (LLB). Called to the Bar, Gray's Inn, 1969; with BBC TV, 1970–95: researcher, 24 Hours, 1970–72; producer, Midweek, 1972–76; Dep. Ed. and Producer, Panorama, 1976–86; Producer, Documentaries, 1986–95; contributor, Daily Mail, 1996–2014. Queen Victoria Bronze Medal, RSPCA, 1975; Award for Excellence in Broadcasting, Ohio State Univ., 1979; Best TV Documentary, Fest. dei Popoli, 1987; Fipa d'Or, Cannes, for best TV documentary, The Confession, 1991; Chairman's Award, BPA, 1991; Special Award, Outstanding Achievement for a Body of Work, Spear's Book Awards, 2011. *Publications:* Blind Eye to Murder, a Pledge Betrayed, 1981; Klaus Barbie, Butcher of Lyons, 1984; The Paperclip Conspiracy, 1987; Maxwell the Outsider, 1988; The Red Web, 1989; Tiny Rowland, a Rebel Tycoon, 1993; The Perfect English Spy, Sir Dick White, 1995; Heroes of World War 2, 1995; Maxwell: the Final Verdict, 1995; Blood Money: the Swiss, the Nazis and the looted billions, 1997; Fayed: the unauthorised biography, 1998; Branson, 2000, reissued, 2008; The Paymaster: Geoffrey Robinson, Maxwell and New Labour, 2001; Broken Dreams: vanity, greed and the souring of British football (William Hill Sports Book of the Year), 2003; Gordon Brown, 2004, reissued as Gordon Brown, Prime Minister, 2007; Conrad & Lady Black: dancing on the edge, 2006; The Squeeze: oil, money and greed in the twenty-first century, 2009; No Angel: the secret life of Bernie Ecclestone, 2011; Sweet Revenge: the intimate life of Simon Cowell, 2012; Branson: behind the mask, 2014. *Recreations:* walking, ski-ing, shooting. *Address:* 10 Thurlow Road, NW3 5PL. *T:* (020) 7435 9776. *Clubs:* Garrick, Beefsteak.

BOWER, Veronica Judith Colleton; *see* Wadley, V. J. C.

BOWERING, Christine, DL; MA; Chairman, Nottingham City Hospital NHS Trust, 1998–2006; Headmistress, Nottingham High School for Girls (GPDST), 1984–96; *b* 30 June 1936; *d* of Kenneth Soper and Florence E. W. Soper; *m* 1960, Rev. John Anthony Bowering (*d* 2014); one *s* one *d*. *Educ:* St Bernard's Convent, Westcliff-on-Sea; Newnham Coll., Cambridge (MA). Assistant Teacher: St Bernard's Convent; Ursuline Convent, Brentwood; Sheffield High Sch. (GPDST). Mem., Engineering Council, 1988–91. Dir, Queen's Med. Centre, Nottingham, 1993–98. Chairman: Educn Cttee, GSA, 1989–93; Ind. Schs Curriculum Cttee, 1992–94; Mem., Educn Cttee, Goldsmiths' Co., 1992–2009. Governor: Nottingham Trent Univ. (formerly Nottingham Poly.), 1989–96 (Mem., 1990–, Chm., 1990–96, Employment Cttee); Minster Sch., Southwell, 2004–. Assoc. Mem., Newnham Coll., Cambridge, 1991–2002. Trustee, Southwell Dio. Council for Family Care, 1998– (Chm., 2007–12). FRSA 1994. DL Notts, 2000. Freeman, Goldsmiths' Co., 2005. Hon. DLitt Nottingham, 1996. *Address:* Linthwaite Cottage, Main Street, Kirklington, Newark NG22 8ND. *T:* (01636) 816995.

BOWERS, John Simon; QC 1998; a Recorder, since 2003; a Deputy High Court Judge, since 2010; Principal, Brasenose College, Oxford, since 2015; *b* 2 Jan. 1956; *s* of Alfred and Irene Bowers; *m* 1982, Prof. Suzanne Franks; one *s* two *d*. *Educ:* Matthew Humberstone Comp. Sch., Cleethorpes; Lincoln Coll., Oxford (MA, BCL). Called to the Bar, Middle Temple, 1979, Bencher, 2004; in practice at the Bar, 1979–. Chairman: Employment Appeal Tribunal Users' Gp, 1995–99; (part-time), Employment Tribunals, 2001–02; Mediator, Centre for Dispute Resolution, 1998–. Chairman: Employment Law Bar Assoc., 2001–03; Bar Disciplinary Tribunal, 2001–; Member: Liaison Cttee, Govt Human Rights Task Force, 1999–2001; Bar Council Race Relations Cttee, 1999–2002; Standards Bd for England, 2000–05; Standards Bd, Metropolitan Police Authy, 2010–12. Mem. Council, Univ. of Kent, 2012–. Member: Bd of Friends, Neve Shalom village, 2009–; Bd, Kessler Foundn, 2011–. *Publications:* Bowers on Employment Law, 1980, 8th edn 2009; (jtly) Atkin's Court Forms, vol. 38, 1986, 2003; (jtly) Modern Law of Strikes, 1987; Industrial Tribunal Procedure, 1987, 2nd edn, as Employment Tribunal Procedure, 1998; (jtly) The Employment Act 1988, 1988; Termination of Employment, 1988, 3rd edn 1995; (jtly) Transfer of Undertakings: the legal pitfalls, 1989, 6th edn 1996; (jtly) Basic Procedure in Courts and Tribunals, 1990; (jtly) Textbook on Employment Law, 1990, 9th edn 2006; (jtly) Employment Law Update, 1991; Transfer of Undertakings Encyclopaedia, 1998; Whistleblowing: the new law, 2000, 2nd edn 2007; Employment Law and Human Rights, 2000; The Law of Industrial Action and Trade Union Recognition, 2011; (contrib.) Bullen & Leake on Pleadings; many articles in legal jls. *Recreations:* football, tennis. *Address:* Brasenose College, Radcliffe Square, Oxford OX1 4AJ.

BOWERS, His Honour Peter Hammond; a Circuit Judge, 1995–2015; *b* 22 June 1945; *s* of Edward Hammond Bowers and Elsie Bowers; *m* 1970, Brenda Janet Burgess; two *s* one *d*. *Educ:* Acklam Hall, Middlesbrough. Admitted solicitor, 1966; in private practice, 1966–70; Prosecuting Solicitor, 1970–72; called to the Bar, Inner Temple, 1972; barrister, N Eastern Circuit, 1972–95. *Recreations:* cricket, aspiring artist, antiques, paintings, armchair sportsman.

BOWERS, Roger George, CMG 1997; OBE 1984; PhD; Chief Executive, Trinity College, London, 1998–2006 (Member Council, 1997–98); *b* 23 May 1942; *s* of George Albert Bowers and Hilda Mary Bowers (*née* Wells); *m* 1st, 1963, Gweneth Iris Pither (marr. diss.); one *s* one *d*; 2nd, 2009, Jennifer Ann Pugsley. *Educ:* Royal Grammar Sch., Guildford; Wadham Coll., Oxford (BA); Reading Univ. (MPhil; PhD). Joined British Council, 1964; Tutor to Overseas Students, Univ. of Birmingham, 1965; Asst Regl Dir, Cape Coast, Ghana, 1965–69; seconded to Eng. Lang. Trng Inst., Allahabad, 1971–73; Asst Regl Educ. Advr, Calcutta, 1973–76; Eng. Lang. Consultancies Dept, 1978–80; seconded to Ain Shams Univ., Cairo, 1980–84; Dir, Eng. Lang. Services Dept, 1984–85; Dep. Controller, 1985–89, Controller, then Dir, 1989–93, Eng. Lang. and Lit. Div.; Asst Dir-Gen. (Manchester), and Dir of Professional Services, 1993–96. Director: R. G. Bowers & Associates, 1996–2009; World of Language Ltd, 1997–2009. Jt Editor, Cambridge Handbooks for Language Teachers, 1985–92; Member: Editorial Cttee, ELT Documents, 1984–93; Bd of Management, ELT Jl, 1985–96. Mem. Corp., Trinity Coll. of Music, 1999–2006. Trustee, A. S. Hornby Educnl Trust, 1997– (Chm., 2007–14). FRSA 1993. Hon. FTCL 2007. *Publications:* In Passing, 1976; Talking About Grammar, 1987; Word Play, 1990. *Recreations:* fishing, cooking, eating. *Address:* 25 Hillbrow, Richmond Hill, Surrey TW10 6BH.

BOWERS, Rupert John; QC 2015; *b* New York, 29 Jan. 1971; *s* of John Robert Bowers and Patricia Ann Maureen Bowers; *m* 1999, Olivia Charlotte Eliott Lockhart; three *d*. *Educ:* Oundle Sch.; Univ. of Newcastle upon Tyne (BA Hons Psychol. 1992); Coll. of Law, London (DipLaw); Inns of Court Sch. of Law. Called to the Bar, Gray's Inn, 1995; in practice as barrister, specialising in search and seizure, white collar crime, extradition and sports law. *Publications:* Blackstone's Guide to the Terrorism Act 2006, 2006. *Recreations:* mountaineering, ski-ing, playing football (knees permitting), attending the village pub and La Grange in St Gervais. *Address:* Doughty Street Chambers, 53/54 Doughty Street, WC1N 2LS. *T:* (020) 7404 1313. *E:* r.bowers@doughtystreet.co.uk. *Club:* Offham Tennis.

BOWERS-BROADBENT, Christopher Joseph St George; organist and composer; *b* 13 Jan. 1945; *s* of late Henry W. Bowers-Broadbent and Doris E. Bowers-Broadbent (*née* Mizen); *m* 1970, Deirdre Ann Cape; one *s* one *d*. *Educ:* King's Coll., Cambridge (Chorister); Berkhamsted Sch.; Royal Acad. of Music (Rec.Dip.; FRAM 1983). Organist and Choirmaster, St Pancras Parish Church, 1965–88; début recital, 1966; Organist, 1973–, and Dir of Music, W London Synagogue, 2012–; Organist and Choirmaster, Hon. Soc. of Gray's Inn, 1983– (Fellow, 2012). Prof., RAM, 1975–92. Numerous recordings. *Publications:* numerous sacred and secular compositions; chamber operas: The Pied Piper, 1972; The Seacock Bane, 1979; The Last Man, 1983, 2nd edn 2003; The Face, 2012. *Recreations:* sketching, silence. *Address:* 94 Colney Hatch Lane, N10 1EA. *T:* (020) 8883 1933.

BOWERY, Prof. Norman George, PhD; DSc; FBPhS; Professor Emeritus, University of Birmingham, since 2004; *b* 23 June 1944; *s* of George Bowery and Olga (*née* Beevers); *m* 1970, Barbara Joyce (*née* Westcott); one *s* two *d*. *Educ:* Christ's Coll., Finchley; NE Surrey Coll. of Technology; St Bartholomew's Med. Coll., Univ. of London (PhD 1974; DSc 1987). MRSB (MIBiol 1970). Res. Asst, CIBA Labs, 1963–70; Res. Student, St Bart's Med. Coll., London, 1970–73; Postdoctoral Res. Fellow, Sch. of Pharmacy, London Univ., 1973–75; Lectr in Pharmacology, 1975–82, Sen. Lectr in Pharm., 1982–84, St Thomas's Hosp. Med. Sch.; Section Leader, Neuroscience Res. Centre, Merck, Sharp & Dohme, Harlow, 1984–87; Wellcome Prof. of Pharmacol., Sch. of Pharmacy, London Univ., 1987–95: Prof. of Pharmacol., 1995–2004, Head of Neurosci., 1999–2001, Birmingham Univ. Vice Pres., Biology Verona, GlaxoSmithKline SpA, Italy, 2004–06. Pres., British Pharmacol Soc., 1999–2000, now Pres. Emeritus. Laurea ad honorem in pharmacy *hc* Florence, 1992. Biological Council Medal, 1991; Gaddum Meml Medal, British Pharmacol Soc., 2004. Ed.-in-Chief, Current Opinion in Pharmacol., 2000–12. *Publications:* Actions and Interactions of GABA and Benzodiazepines, 1984; GABAergic Mechanisms in the Mammalian Periphery, 1986; GABA: basic mechanisms to clinical applications, 1989; $GABA_B$ Receptors in Mammalian Function, 1990; GABA: transport, receptors and metabolism, 1996; The GABA Receptors, 1996; Allosteric Receptor Modulation in Drug Targetting, 2006. *Recreations:* gardening, socializing, family life.

BOWES, Michael Anthony; QC 2001; a Recorder, since 2000; Deputy High Court Judge, since 2010; *b* 22 Dec. 1956; *s* of late Michael Philip Bowes and of Patricia Bowes; *m* 1987, Amanda Wissler; two *d*. *Educ:* St George's Coll., Weybridge; Manchester Univ. (LLB). Called to the Bar, Middle Temple, 1980, Bencher, 2007; in practice, Western Circuit, 1996–; specialising in criminal law, fraud and financial regulatory work; Jt Hd, Outer Temple Chambers, 2012–. Fellow, Goodenough Coll., 2015–. Trustee, Bloomsbury Art Fair Ltd, 2011–. Gov., Knighton House Sch., Dorset, 2008–15. *Recreations:* ski-ing, riding, sailing. *Address:* Outer Temple Chambers, 222 Strand, WC2R 1BA. *T:* (020) 7353 6381.

BOWES, Roger Norman; Managing Director and Proprietor, Global Information Management Services Ltd, 2005–10; *b* 28 Jan. 1943; *s* of late Russell Ernest Bowes and Sybil Caroline Rose Bowes (*née* Bell); *m* 1st, 1961, Denise Hume Windsor (marr. diss. 1974); one *d*; 2nd, 1977, Ann Rosemary O'Connor (*née* Hamstead) (marr. diss. 1988). *Educ:* Chiswick and Dorking Grammar Schools. Advertisement Executive: Associated Newspapers, 1962–67; IPC/Mirror Gp Newspapers, 1967–70; Marketing Exec./Sales Manager, Mirror Gp, 1970–75; Media Dir, McCann Erickson Advertising, 1976–78; Mirror Gp Newspapers: Adv. Dir, 1978–81; Dep. Chief Exec., 1982–83; Chief Exec., 1984; Man. Dir, Guinness Enterprises, 1985; Chief Executive: Express Gp Newspapers, 1985–86; Aslib, 1989–2004; Chm., Citybridge, 1987–97. *Recreations:* political and military history, cookery, architectural restoration, classic cars.

BOWES LYON, family name of **Earl of Strathmore**.

BOWES LYON, Sir Simon (Alexander), KCVO 2005; FCA; director of investment companies; farmer; Lord-Lieutenant of Hertfordshire, 1986–2007; *b* 17 June 1932; *s* of Hon. Sir David Bowes Lyon, KCVO, and Rachel Bowes Lyon (*née* Spender Clay) (*d* 1996); *m* 1966, Caroline, *d* of Rt Rev. Victor Pike, CB, CBE, DD, and of Dorothea Pike; three *s* one *d*. *Educ:* Eton; Magdalen Coll., Oxford (BA). Hon. LLD Herts, 2007. KStJ 1997. *Recreations:* botany, gardening, shooting, music. *Address:* St Paul's Walden Bury, Hitchin, Herts SG4 8BP. *T:* (01438) 871218, *Fax:* (01438) 871341. *E:* spw@boweslyon.demon.co.uk.

BOWEY, Prof. Angela Marilyn, PhD; Director, Glassencyclopedia.com and Glass-time.com, since 1997; Professor of Business Administration, Strathclyde Business School, University of Strathclyde, Glasgow, 1976–87; *b* 20 Oct. 1940; *d* of Jack Nicholas Peterson and Kathleen (*née* Griffin); *m* 1st, 1960, Miklos Papp; two *s* one *d*; 2nd, 1965, Gregory Bowey (marr. diss. 1980); one *s* one *d*; 3rd, 2001, Prof. Andrew William John Thomson, OBE (*d* 2014). *Educ:* Withington Girls' Sch., Manchester; Univ. of Manchester (BA Econs, PhD). Technical Asst, Nuclear Power Gp, 1961–62; Asst Lectr, Elizabeth Gaskell Coll. of Educn, 1967–68; Manchester Business School: Res. Associate, 1968–69; Res. Fellow, 1969–72; Lectr, 1972–76; Dir, Pay Advice Res. Centre, Glasgow, 1977–86, Gibraltar, 1987–97. Vis. Professor: Admin. Staff Coll. of India, 1975; Western Australian Inst. of Technology, 1976; Univ. of WA, 1977; Prahran Coll. of Advanced Educn, Australia, 1978; Massey Univ., NZ, 1978. ACAS Arbitrator, 1977–92; Dir, Pay and Rewards Res. Centre, 1978–85; Comr, Equal Opportunities Commn, 1980–86; Member: Scottish Econ. Council, 1980–83; Police Adv. Bd (Scotland) (formerly Adv. Panel on Police), 1983–88. Gov., Scottish Police Coll., 1985–88. Dir, Paihia Gym Ltd, 1993–; Chair, Rotary Oceania Med. Aid for Children, NZ, 2014–. Editor, Management Decision, 1979–82. Website Ed., Paperweight Collectors' Assoc. Inc., USA, 2007–. *Publications:* Job and Pay Comparisons (with Tom Lupton), 1973, 2nd edn 1974; A Guide to Manpower Planning, 1974, 2nd edn 1977; (with Tom Lupton) Wages and Salaries, 1974, 2nd edn 1982; Handbook of Salary and Wage Systems, 1975, 2nd edn 1982; The Sociology of Organisations, 1976; (with Richard Thorpe and Phil Hellier) Payment Systems and Productivity, 1986; Managing Salary and Wage Systems, 1987; (jtly) Bagley Glass, 2004, 3rd edn 2010; New Zealand Glass, 2005, 2nd edn 2013; London Lampworkers: Pirelli, Bimini and Komaromy glass, 2013; articles in Brit. Jl of Indust. Relations, Jl of Management Studies, and Management Decision. *Address:* Paihia, Bay of Islands, New Zealand. *Clubs:* Rotary (Bay of Islands), Waitangi Golf (New Zealand).

BOWEY, Olwyn, RA 1975 (ARA 1970); practising artist (painter); *b* 10 Feb. 1936; *o d* of James and Olive Bowey. *Educ:* West Hartlepool Sch. of Art; Royal Coll. of Art. One-man shows: Zwemmer Gall., 1961; New Grafton Gall., 1969; also exhibited at Leicester Gall., Royal Academy; work purchased through Chantrey Bequest for Tate Gall., Royal Academy, Min. of Works, etc.

BOWHAY, Rosalind Louise; *see* Smyth, R. L.

BOWIE, Rev. (Alexander) Glen, CBE 1984; Principal Chaplain (Church of Scotland and Free Churches), Royal Air Force, 1980–84, retired; *b* 10 May 1928; *s* of Alexander Bowie and Annie (*née* McGhie); *m* 1st, 1952, Mary McKillop (*d* 1991); two *d*; 2nd, 2002, Jean Lawson (*d* 2012). *Educ:* Stevenston High Sch.; Irvine Royal Acad.; Glasgow Univ. (BSc 1951; Dip Theol 1954); BA Open Univ., 1977. Nat. Service, RAF, 1947–49. Assistant, Beith High Church, 1952–54; ordained, 1954; entered RAF Chaplains' Br., 1955; served: RAF Padgate, 1955–56; Akrotiri, 1956–59; Stafford, 1959–61; Butzweilerhof, 1961–64; Halton, 1964–67; Akrotiri, 1967–70; RAF Coll., Cranwell, 1970–75; Asst Principal Chaplain, 1975; HQ Germany, 1975–76; HQ Support Comd, 1976–80. Officiating Chaplain, RAF Brampton and RAF Wyton, 1985–2009; Acting Chaplain to Moderator of Church of Scotland, in London, 1985–99; Moderator, Ch of Scotland Presbytery of England, 1988–89. QHC 1980–84; Hon. Chaplain, Royal Scottish Corp., 1981–2001. Editor, Scottish Forces Bulletin, 1985–95. *Recreations:* oil painting, travel, leading Holy Land tours. *Address:* 16 Weir Road, Hemingford Grey, Huntingdon, Cambs PE28 9EH. *T:* (01480) 381425. *Club:* Royal Air Force.

BOWIE, David; international recording artist and performer; film and stage actor; video and film producer; graphic designer; *b* 8 Jan. 1947; *s* of Hayward Stenton Jones and late Margaret Mary Burns; *né* David Robert Jones; *m* (marr. diss.); one *s*; *m* 1992, Iman Abdul Majid; one *d*. *Educ:* Stansfield Road Sch., Brixton. Artiste from age of 16; many major recordings, 1970–, and video productions, 1979–; numerous live musical stage performances; guest appearances on television shows. Actor: *films:* The Man who Fell to Earth, 1976; Just a Gigolo, 1978; The Hunger, 1982; Merry Christmas, Mr Lawrence, 1983; Ziggy Stardust and the Spiders from Mars, 1983; Absolute Beginners, 1986; Labyrinth, 1986; Into the Night; The Last Temptation of Christ, 1988; The Linguini Incident, 1990; Basquiat, 1997; The Prestige, 2006; *stage:* The Elephant Man, New York, 1980; *television:* Baal, 1982. Recipient of internat. music and entertainment awards. *Recreations:* painting, ski-ing. *Address:* c/o Isolar, 270 Lafayette Street, Suite 600, New York, NY 10012, USA.

BOWIE, Rev. Glen; *see* Bowie, Rev. A. G.

BOWIE, Graham Maitland, CBE 1992; Chief Executive, Lothian Regional Council, 1986–94; *b* 11 Nov. 1931; *s* of John Graham Bowie and Agnes Bowie; *m* 1962, Maureen Jennifer O'Sullivan; one *s* two *d*. *Educ:* Alloa Academy; Univ. of St Andrews (MA); Univ. of Glasgow (LLB). National Service, 1956–58. Asst Sec., Glasgow Chamber of Commerce, 1958–60; Product Planner, Ford Motor Co., 1960–64; Edinburgh Corp. Educn Dept, 1964–69; ILEA, 1969–75; Dir of Policy Planning, Lothian Regional Council, 1975–86. Mem., Nat. Lotteries Charities Bd, 1994–97. *Recreations:* walking, travel, the arts. *Address:* 8 Keith Crescent, Edinburgh EH4 3NH.

BOWIS, John Crocket, OBE 1981; Chairman, Health First Europe, since 2009; adviser and consultant on health, since 2009; *b* 2 Aug. 1945; *s* of late Thomas Palin Bowis and Georgiana Joyce (*née* Crocket); *m* 1968, Caroline May (*née* Taylor); two *s* one *d*. *Educ:* Tonbridge Sch.; Brasenose Coll., Oxford (MA). Tutor, Cumberland Lodge, Windsor Great Park, 1966–67; Cons. Party Agent, Peterborough, Derby, Harborough and Blaby, 1968–72; Conservative Central Office: National Organiser, Fedn of Cons. Students, 1972–75; Nat. Organiser, Cons. Trade Unionists, 1975–79; Dir of Community Affairs, 1979–81; Campaign Dir, 1981–82, Public Affairs Dir, 1983–87, British Insurance Brokers Assoc.; Press and Parly Consultant, Nat. Fedn of Self-employed and Small Firms, 1982–83. Councillor (C) Royal Bor. of Kingston upon Thames, 1982–86 (Chm. of Educn, 1985–86). MP (C) Battersea, 1987–97; contested (C) same seat, 1997. PPS to Minister for Local Govt and Inner Cities, DoE, 1989–90, to Sec. of State for Wales, 1990–93; Parly Under-Sec. of State, DoH, 1993–96, Dept of Transport, 1996–97. Mem., Select Cttee on Members' Interests, 1987–90; Vice-Chm., All Party Gp on Social Sci., 1988–93; Chm., All Party Somali Gp, 1991–97. Secretary: Cons. Inner Cities Cttee, 1987–89; Cons. Educn Cttee, 1988–89; Cons. Arts and Heritage Cttee, 1988–89; Parliamentary Adviser to: ACFHE, 1987–93; Assoc. for Coll. Management, 1990–93; ATL (formerly AMMA), 1992–93. MEP (C) London Region, 1999–2009. European Parliament: Party spokesman on envmt, health and consumer affairs, 1999–2009; Rapporteur: on food safety, 2000–01; on health and enlargement, 2000–04; on European Centre for Disease Control, 2005–09; on patient mobility, 2005–09; on mental health, 2006–09; on cross border healthcare, 2007–09; Dep. Leader, Cons. MEPs, 2002–04. Special Advr, FIPRA Internat., 2009–; Member, Advisory Board: Hanover, 2010–; Policy Action, 2010–; Chm., Health Adv. Bd, GlaxoSmithKline, 2009–; Vice-Pres., Eur. Health Forum Gastein, 2009–. Chm., Nat. Council for Civil Protection, 1992–93. Internat. Policy Advr to WHO at Inst. of Psychiatry, 1997–2009; Board Member: Inst. of Psychiatry, 1997–99; Internat. Social Service, 1997–2000; Internat. Inst. for Special Needs Offenders, 1998–2008; Churches Educn and Develt Partnership for SA, 1998–2005; SANE and Saneline, 2000–; European Men's Health Forum, 2001–; Mental Disability Advocacy Center - UK, 2008–; Global Initiative on Psychiatry, 2009–; Gamian Europe, 2009–; TB Vaccine Initiative, 2009–; World Fedn for Mental Health, 2011–. Trustee and Vice-Pres., Share Community, 1990–; Ambassador: Nat. Aids Trust, 1997–; Alzheimer's Soc., 2009–; Patron: Epilepsy Res. UK, 1997–; Dame Vera Lynn Trust, 2009–; President: Torche, 1999–2009; Battersea Cons. Assoc., 2000–; Kingston and Surbiton Cons. Assoc., 2011–; Vice Pres., Parkinson's Disease Soc., 2003–. Director: Battersea Arts Centre, 1991–99; Royal Nat. Theatre, 1992–95; South Bank Centre, 1992–95; Royal Acad. of Dancing, 1992–99. Fellow, Industry and Parlt Trust, 1992. Hon. FRCPsych 2003; Hon. FRCP 2009. Eur. Public Health Alliance Award for Service to Public Health, 2009. *Recreations:* theatre, music, art, sport, watching AFC Wimbledon. *Address:* 44 Howard Road, New Malden KT3 4EA. *E:* johnbowis@aol.com.

BOWKER, Prof. John Westerdale; Hon. Canon of Canterbury Cathedral, since 1985; Adjunct Professor of Religion, North Carolina State University, since 1986; Adjunct Professor of Religious Studies, University of Pennsylvania, since 1986; *b* 30 July 1935; *s* of Gordon Westerdale Bowker and Marguerite (*née* Burdick); *m* 1963, Margaret Roper; one *s*. *Educ:* St John's Sch., Leatherhead; Worcester Coll., Oxford (MA); Ripon Hall, Oxford. National Service, RWAFF, N Nigeria, 1953–55. Henry Stephenson Fellow, Sheffield Univ., 1961; Deacon, St Augustine's, Brocco Bank, Sheffield, 1961; Priest and Dean of Chapel, Corpus Christi Coll., Cambridge, 1962; Asst Lectr, 1965, Lectr, 1970, Univ. of Cambridge; Prof. of Religious Studies, Univ. of Lancaster, 1974–85; Dean, 1984–91 and Fellow, 1984–93, Trinity Coll., Cambridge. Gresham Prof. of Divinity, 1992–97; Fellow, Gresham Coll., London, 1997. Lectures: Wilde, Univ. of Oxford, 1972–75; Staley, Rollins Coll., Florida, 1978–79; Public, Univ. of Cardiff, 1984; Riddell, Newcastle Univ., 1985; Boutwood, Univ. of Cambridge, 1985; Harris Meml, Toronto, 1986; Boardman, Univ. of Pa, 1988; Montefiore, Univ. of Southampton, 1989; Scott Holland, London Univ., 1989; Bicentenary, Univ. of Georgetown, Washington, 1989; Heslington, York, 1997; Member: Durham Commn on Religious Educn, 1967–70; Root Commn on Marriage and Divorce, 1967–71; Archbps' Commn on Doctrine, 1977–86; Patron, Marriage Research Inst.; Hon. Pres., Stauros; Vice-President: Inst. on Religion in an Age of Science, 1980; Culture and Animals Foundn, 1984–92; Pres., Christian Action on AIDS, 1987–91. *Publications:* The Targums and Rabbinic Literature, 1969, 2nd edn 1979; Problems of Suffering in Religions of the World, 1970, 3rd edn 1987; Jesus and the Pharisees, 1973; The Sense of God, 1973, 2nd edn 1995; The Religious Imagination and the Sense of God, 1978; Uncle Bolpenny Tries Things Out, 1973; Worlds of Faith, 1983; (ed) Violence and Aggression, 1983; Licensed Insanities: religions and belief in God in the contemporary world, 1987; The Meanings of Death, 1991 (HarperCollins Religious Book Prize, 1993); A Year to Live, 1991; Hallowed Ground: the religious poetry of place, 1993; (ed jtly) Themes in Religious Studies, 1994; Voices of Islam, 1995; Is God a Virus? Genes, Culture and Religion, 1995; World Religions, 1997; The Oxford Dictionary of World Religions, 1997; The Complete Bible Handbook: an illustrated companion, 1998 (Benjamin Franklin Award, 1999); The Concise Oxford Dictionary of World Religions, 2000; The Cambridge Illustrated History of Religions, 2002; God: a brief history, 2002; The Sacred Neuron, 2005; Beliefs that Changed the World, 2007; The Aerial Atlas of the Holy Land, 2008; Conflict and Reconciliation: the contribution of religions, 2008; Knowing the Unknowable: science and religions on God and the universe, 2008; An Alphabet of Animals, 2009; Before the Ending of the Day, 2010; The Message and the Book, 2011; God: a very short introduction, 2014; Why Religions Matter, 2015. *Recreations:* books, painting, poetry. *Address:* 14 Bowers Croft, Cambridge CB1 8RP.

BOWKER, (Steven) Richard, CBE 2005; FCILT; FCMA; independent non-executive Director: Football League Ltd, since 2012; Super League (Europe) Ltd, since 2014; Member, Football Association Council, since 2012; Commissioner, Football Regulatory Authority, since 2013; Member, International Committee, Football Association, since 2014; *b* 23 April 1966; *s* of Roger William Bowker and Dr Sylvia Grace Bowker; *m* 2002, Madeline Victoria Ivemy; two *s* one *d*. *Educ:* Queen Elizabeth's Grammar Sch., Blackburn; Univ. of Leicester (BA Upper 2nd Cl. Hons Econs and Econ. and Social Hist. 1988). ACMA 1993, FCMA 2003; FCILT (FCIT, FILT 2001); CGMA 2012. Professional musician, 1988–89; Manager, London Underground Ltd, 1989–96; Principal, Babcock & Brown Ltd, 1996–99; Dir, Quasar Associates Ltd, 1999–2000; Gp Commercial Dir, Virgin Gp, 2000–01; Co-Chm., Virgin Rail Gp Ltd, 2000–01 (non-exec. Dir, 1999–2001); Dir, Virgin Atlantic Airways, 2000–01; Chm. and Chief Exec., Strategic Rail Authy, 2001–04; Chief Executive: Partnerships for Schs, 2005–06; Etihad Rail (formerly Union Railway), UAE, 2009–12; Gp Chief Exec., Nat. Express Gp plc, 2006–09. Sen. Advr, EC Harris, 2013–. Non-exec. Dir, British Waterways, 2004–09 (Vice Chm., 2008–09); Dir, Criterium Cycles, 2013–. Mem., Internat. Adv. Council, Assoc. of MBAs, 2003–07. Mem. Bd, Countryside Alliance, 2006–09. Vice-President: London Internat. Piano Competition, 2002–; Settle & Carlisle Railway Trust, 2009– (Trustee, 2004–09); Dep. Pres., Heritage Railway Assoc., 2005–; Vice-President: Friends of Nat. Railway Mus., York, 2009–; Settle and Carlisle Railway Trust, 2009–. *Recreations:* hill walking, piano, canal boating, wine, Blackburn Rovers FC, running, cycling.

BOWKETT, Alan John; venture capitalist and organic farmer; *b* 6 Jan. 1951; *er s* of John and Margaret Bowkett; *m* 1975, Joy Dianne Neale; three *s* two *d*. *Educ:* King Charles I Grammar Sch., Kidderminster; University College London (BSc Econ); London Business Sch. (MSc Econ). Corporate Planning Manager, Lex Service, 1977–83; Corporate Develt Manager, BET, 1983–85; Man. Dir, Boulton & Paul, 1985–87; Chief Executive: United Precision Industries, 1987–91; Berisford Internat., then Berisford plc, 1992–99. Director: Anglian Group, 1992–94; Pallasinvest SA (Luxembourg), 1992–98; Greene King, 1993–2006 (Chm., Audit Cttee, 1997–2006); Chairman: Calder Gp Ltd, 1994–96; Acordis BV, 2000–04; Metzeler APS SA, 2000–05; Doncaster Gp Ltd, 2003–06; Britax plc, 2004–08; Redrow plc, 2007–09; Strix Ltd, 2008–; Gladedale Ltd, 2009–12; Norwich City FC plc, 2009–; McCarthy & Stone plc, 2010–13; Avio Gp SpA, 2010–; Euromedic Bv, 2012–. Councillor (C) London Borough of Ealing, 1978–82 (Chm., Social Services); Dep. Chm., Ealing Acton Cons. Assoc., 1982–84. Chm., Univ. of Law, 2012–; Council Mem., UEA, 1988–94 (Treasurer, 1990–94; Hon. Fellow, 1997). FRSA 1993. *Recreations:* growing vegetables, shooting, opera, Italy, listening to Archers, salmon fishing, watching Norwich City. *Clubs:* Carlton, Royal Automobile.

BOWLBY, Prof. Rachel Helena, FBA 2007; Professor of Comparative Literature and English, University College London, since 2014; Professor of Comparative Literature, Princeton University, since 2013; *b* 29 Jan. 1957; *d* of Rt Rev. Ronald Oliver Bowlby, *qv*; two *d*. *Educ:* St Anne's Coll., Oxford (1st Cl. Hon. Mods Latin and Greek Lit. 1977; BA 1st Cl. Hons English 1979); Yale Univ. (PhD Comparative Lit. 1983). University of Sussex: Lectr in English, 1984–90; Sen. Lectr, 1990–92; Reader, 1992–94; Prof., 1994–97; Oxford University: Fellow, St Hilda's Coll., 1997–99; Prof. of English, 1998–99; Prof. of English and Related Lit., Univ. of York, 1999–2004; Lord Northcliffe Prof. of Modern English Lit., UCL, 2004–14. Leverhulme Major Res. Fellow, 2011–13. Lectures: Bateson, Oxford, 2006; Gauss Seminars, Princeton Univ., 2008; Churchill, Univ. of Bristol, 2013. *Publications:* Just Looking, 1985; Virginia Woolf, 1988; Still Crazy After All These Years: women, writing and psychoanalysis, 1992; Shopping with Freud, 1993; Feminist Destinations and Further Essays on Virginia Woolf, 1997; Carried Away: the invention of modern shopping, 2000; Freudian Mythologies: Greek tragedy and modern identities, 2007; A Child of One's Own: parental stories, 2013. *Address:* Department of English, University College London, Gower Street, WC1E 6BT. *T:* (020) 7679 3138. *E:* r.bowlby@ucl.ac.uk.

BOWLBY, Sir Richard Peregrine Longstaff, 3rd Bt *cr* 1923, of Manchester Square, St Marylebone; *b* 11 Aug. 1941; *s* of Edward John Mostyn Bowlby, CBE, MD (*d* 1990), 2nd *s* of Sir Anthony Alfred Bowlby, 1st Bt, KCB, KCMG, KCVO, and Ursula, *d* of Dr T. G. Longstaff; *S* uncle, 1993; *m* 1963, Xenia, *o d* of R. P. A. Garrett; one *s* one *d*. *Heir: s* Benjamin Bowlby [*b* 2 Nov. 1966; *m* 1992, Mylanna Sophia, *er d* of M. C. Colyer; two *s* one *d*]. *Address:* Boundary House, Wyldes Close, NW11 7JB.

BOWLBY, Rt Rev. Ronald Oliver; Bishop of Southwark, 1980–91; *b* 16 Aug. 1926; *s* of Oliver and Helena Bowlby; *m* 1956, Elizabeth Trevelyan Monro; three *s* two *d*. *Educ:* Eton Coll.; Trinity College, Oxford (MA; Hon. Fellow, 1991); Westcott House, Cambridge. Curate of St Luke's, Pallion, Sunderland, 1952–56; Priest-in-charge and Vicar of St Aidan, Billingham, 1956–66; Vicar of Croydon, 1966–72; Bishop of Newcastle, 1973–80; Asst Bishop, Dio. of Lichfield, 1991–2010. Chairman: Hospital Chaplaincies Council, 1975–82; Social Policy Cttee, Bd for Social Responsibility, 1986–90; Mem., Anglican Consultative Council, 1977–85. President: Nat. Fedn of Housing Assocs, 1988–94; Churches' Nat. Housing Coalition, 1991–94. Hon. Fellow, Newcastle upon Tyne Polytechnic, 1980. *Publications:* contrib. Church without Walls, ed Lindars, 1969; contrib. Church and Politics Today, ed Moyser, 1985. *Recreation:* reading. *Address:* Swan Hill House, Swan Hill, Shrewsbury SY1 1NQ.

See also R. H. Bowlby.

BOWLER, Prof. Peter John, PhD; FBA 2004; Professor of the History of Science, Queen's University, Belfast, 1992–2009, now Emeritus; *b* 8 Oct. 1944; *s* of Wallace Bowler and Florence Edith Bowler (*née* Moon); *m* 1966, Sheila Mary Holt; one *s* one *d*. *Educ:* King's Coll., Cambridge (BA 1966, MA 1971); Univ. of Sussex (MSc 1967); Univ. of Toronto (PhD 1971). Lectr in Humanities, Science Univ. of Malaysia, Penang, 1972–75; Asst Prof. of Hist., Univ. of Winnipeg, 1975–79; Lectr, 1979–87, Reader, 1987–92, in Hist. and the Philos. of Sci., Queen's Univ., Belfast. MRIA 1993. *Publications:* The Eclipse of Darwinism, 1983, 2nd edn 1992; The Non-Darwinian Revolution, 1988; The Invention of Progress, 1990; Charles Darwin: the man and his influence, 1990; The Fontana History of the Environmental Sciences, 1992; Life's Splendid Drama, 1996; Reconciling Science and Religion, 2001; Monkey Trials and Gorilla Sermons, 2007; Science for All, 2009; Darwin Deleted, 2013. *Recreations:* collecting antiquarian science books, walking (when I can find the time). *Address:* School of History and Anthropology, Queen's University, Belfast BT7 1NN. *E:* p.bowler@qub.ac.uk.

BOWLER, Tim(othy); novelist and writer; *b* 14 Nov. 1953; *yr s* of Norman and Doreen Bowler; *m* 1977, Rachel. *Educ:* Chalkwell Hall Primary Sch.; Westcliff High Sch. for Boys; Univ. of E Anglia (BA Hons Swedish and Scandinavian Studies); Kingston Poly. (PGCE French and German). Forester, 1977; EFL teacher, 1978–79; timber salesman, 1979–82; French and German teacher, 1983–90; Swedish translator, 1990–97; full-time writer, 1997–. Speaker on writing at confs, fests, schs, writers' circles and on radio. Mem., Judging Panel, Costa Book Award, 2010. 15 book awards, both regl and from USA and Europe. *Publications:* Midget, 1994; Dragon's Rock, 1995; River Boy, 1997 (Carnegie Medal, 1998); Shadows, 1999; Storm Catchers, 2001; Starseeker, 2002; Apocalypse, 2004; Blood on Snow, 2004; Walking with the Dead, 2005; Frozen Fire, 2006; Bloodchild, 2008; Buried Thunder, 2011; Sea of Whispers, 2013; Night Runner, 2014; Game Changer, 2015; Blade series: Playing Dead, Book 1, 2008; Closing In, Book 2, 2008; Breaking Free, Book 3, 2009; Running Scared, Book 4, 2009; Fighting Back, Book 5, 2009; Mixing It, Book 6, 2010; Cutting Loose, Book 7, 2010; Risking All, Book 8, 2010; Blade series re-issued as four book series: Enemies, Book 1, 2012; Flight, Book 2, 2012; Firestorm, Book 3, 2012; Endgame, Book 4, 2012. *Recreations:* reading, music, theatre, ballet, cinema, yoga, squash, walking, thinking, dreaming, meditating, holding hands with my wife. *Address:* c/o David Higham Associates, 7th Floor, Waverley House, 7–12 Noel Street, W1F 8GQ. *E:* tim@timbowler.co.uk. *W:* www.timbowler.co.uk.

BOWLES, Prof. Dianna Joy, OBE 2003; PhD; Professor of Biochemistry, Centre for Novel Agricultural Products, University of York, 2008–12, now Emerita; *b* 1 May 1948; *d* of Bertie James Bowles and Cicely (*née* Mee). *Educ:* Univ. of Newcastle upon Tyne (BSc Hons 1970); New Hall, Cambridge (PhD 1973). Research Fellow: Univ. of Kaiserslautern, 1973–75; Univ. of Regensburg, 1975; Weizmann Inst., 1976; Univ. of Cambridge, 1976–77; EMBL, 1978; University of Leeds, 1979–93, Prof., 1991–93; University of York: Prof. of Biochemistry and Co-Founder, Plant Lab., 1994–2000; Weston Prof. of Biochem. and Dir, Centre for Novel Agricultural Products, 2001–08. Scientific Advr, Ownership Bd, MAFF Central Science Lab., 1995–2001. Member: ODA Scientific Adv. Gp, Plant Scis Prog., 1993–97; BBSRC Cttees, 1995–2000; EU Framework 5 External Adv. Gp, 1998–2002. Founder, 2001, Chm. Bd of Trustees, 2002–, Heritage GeneBank, subseq. Sheep Trust. Founding Ed., and Ed.-in-Chief, Plant Jl, 1991–2002. *Publications:* articles in jls. *Recreations:* Upper Nidderdale, Wasdale Head, Herdwick sheep. *Address:* Department of Biology (Area 9), University of York, Heslington, York YO10 5DD.

BOWLES, Huw Martin Richard; non-executive Finance Director and Growth Coach, Trecelyn Ltd, since 2012; *b* Tredegar, 27 Nov. 1966; *s* of late Donald Bowles and of Pauline Bowles (now Milner); *m* 1999, Emma Foster; two *s*. *Educ:* Newbridge Comp. Sch.; Pontypool Coll.; Univ. of Reading (BSc Agric. 1989). Mem., ICAEW, 1993. Auditor: Hays Allan, 1990–95; KPMG, 1995–96; Sen. Consultant, KPMG Financial Mgt, 1996–2000; Finance Director: bEurope Ltd, 2000–01; Investis Ltd, 2001–03; Corporate Affairs and Finance Dir, Organic Milk Suppliers Co-operative Ltd, 2004–12; Finance Dir, Eccentric Gin Co. Ltd, 2014–. Chm., 2009–12, Co. Sec., 2013–, Organic Trade Bd; Mem. Council, Soil Assoc., 2009–12. Mem., Glos Referees Soc. Gov., Sherston C of E Primary Sch., 2008–11. *Recreations:* Rugby coaching, refereeing and watching, family, cycling, music. *E:* huw@bowles.net.

BOWLES, Peter; actor; *b* 16 Oct. 1936; *s* of Herbert Reginald Bowles and Sarah Jane (*née* Harrison); *m* 1961, Susan Alexandra Bennett; two *s* one *d*. *Educ:* High Pavement Grammar Sch., Nottingham; RADA (schol.; Kendal Prize 1955). London début in Romeo and Juliet, Old Vic, 1956; *theatre* includes: Happy Haven, Platonov, Royal Court, 1960; Bonne Soupe, Wyndham's, 1961; Afternoon Men, Arts, 1962; Absent Friends, Garrick, 1975; Dirty Linen, Arts, 1976; Born in the Gardens, Globe, 1980; Some of My Best Friends Are Husbands, nat. tour, 1985; The Entertainer, Shaftesbury, 1986; Canaries Sometimes Sing, Albery, 1987; Man of the Moment, Globe, 1990; Otherwise Engaged (also dir), nat. tour, 1992; Separate Tables, Albery, 1993; Pygmalion, Chichester, 1994; Present Laughter, nat. tour, 1994, Aldwych, 1996; In Praise of Love, Apollo, 1995; Gangster No 1, Almeida, 1995; The School for Wives, Piccadilly, 1997; Major Barbara, The Misanthrope, Piccadilly, 1998; Sleuth, tour, 1999; Hedda Gabler, tour, 1999; The Beau, The Royal Family, Th. Royal, Haymarket, 2001; Sleuth, Apollo, 2002; Our Song, nat. tour, 2003; Wait Until Dark, Garrick, 2003; The Old Masters, Comedy, 2004; The Unexpected Man, nat. tour, 2005; Joe & I, King's Head, 2005; Hay Fever, Th. Royal, Haymarket, 2006; The Waltz of the Toreadors, Chichester, 2007; Relatively Speaking, nat. tour, 2008; Loves Labour's Lost, Rose Th., Kingston, 2008; Swan Song, The Browning Version, Bath Th. Royal, 2009; The Rivals, Bath Th. Royal, 2010, transf. Th. Royal, Haymarket, 2011; The Governess, UK tour, 2013; *films* include: Blow Up, 1966; The Charge of the Light Brigade, 1967; Laughter in the Dark, 1968; A Day in the Death of Joe Egg, 1970; The Steal, 1994; The Hollywood Ten, 2000; Gangster No 1 (Exec. Producer); Colour Me Kubrick, 2004; Freebird, 2008; The Bank Job, 2008; Lilting, 2014; *TV films* include: Shadow on the Sun, 1988; Running Late (also co-prod), 1992; Little White Lies, 1998; Love and War in the Apennines, 2001; Ballet Shoes, 2007; *television series* include: Rumpole of the Bailey, 1976–92; To the Manor Born, 1979–82, 2007; Only when I Laugh, 1979–82; The Bounder, 1982–83; The Irish RM, 1983–85; Lytton's Diary, 1984–86 (also co-created series); Executive Stress, 1987–88; Perfect Scoundrels, 1990–92 (also co-created series); Jericho, 2005. Comedy Actor of the Year, Pye Awards, 1984; ITV Personality of the Year, Variety Club of GB, 1984. Hon. DLitt Nottingham Trent, 2002. *Publications:* (autobiog.) Ask Me If I'm Happy, 2010; Behind the Curtain: the job of acting, 2012. *Recreations:* British art, physical jerks. *Address:* c/o Conway Van Gelder Grant Ltd, 3rd Floor, 8–12 Broadwick Street, W1F 8HW.

BOWLES, Sharon Margaret; Member (Lib Dem) South East Region, European Parliament, May 2005–2014; non-executive Director, London Stock Exchange Group, since 2014; *b* 12 June 1953; *d* of late Percy Bowles and Florence Bowles; *m* 1981, Andrew Horton; two *s*. *Educ:* Our Lady's Convent, Abingdon; Univ. of Reading (BSc Hons Chem. Physics with Maths 1974); Lady Margaret Hall, Oxford (res. into semiconductors). Chartered Patent Attorney; European Patent Attorney. Trng as patent agent, 1978–81; in practice as Patent Attorney and Trade Mark Attorney, 1981–2014, founded professional practice, subseq. Bowles Horton partnership, 1981. Contested (Lib Dem): Aylesbury, 1992, 1997, Parly elecns; Buckinghamshire and Oxford East, 1994, South East Reg., 1999, 2004, EP elecns. European Parliament: Member: Cttee on Econ. and Monetary Affairs, 2005–14 (Chm., 2009–14); Cttee of Inq. into collapse of Equitable Life Assce Soc., 2006–07; Cttee for Legal Affairs, 2007–14; Special Cttee on Financial and Econ. Crisis, 2009–11; Delegn for relns with countries of SE Asia and ASEAN, 2005–09; Delegn for relns with USA, 2009–14. Liberal Democrats: Sec., Chilterns Reg., 1990–95; Co-Chm., Internat. Relns Cttee, 2002–06. Vice President: ELDR, 2004–10; Liberal Internat., 2005–07. *Recreation:* music. *Club:* National Liberal (Trustee, 2014–).

[Created a Baroness (Life Peer) 2015 but title not yet gazetted at time of going to press.]

BOWLES, Timothy John; Master of the Senior (formerly Supreme) Court, Chancery Division, since 1999; *b* 20 March 1951; *s* of late Arthur Ernest Bowles and of Elizabeth Mary Bowles. *Educ:* Downside Sch.; Durham Univ.; Inns of Ct Sch. of Law. FCIArb 1994. Called to the Bar, Gray's Inn, 1973 (Mould Schol.); in practice at the Bar, 1973–99; Dep. Chancery Master, 1996–99. Legal Chairman: South and South Eastern Rent Assessment Panel, 1994–2001; London Rent Assessment Panel, 1997–2001; Dep. Chm., Agricl Land Tribunal, 1995–2013. Regl Judge, First-tier Property Chamber, Agric. and Drainage Div., 2013–. Gov., King Edward VI Grammar Sch. (The Royal Grammar Sch.), Guildford, 2001–04. *Publications:* (ed) Civil Court Practice, annually 2001–. *Recreations:* sailing, cricket. *Address:* Rolls Building, Fetter Lane, EC4A 1NL. *Clubs:* Bar Yacht; St Mawes Sailing; Merrow Cricket, Buccaneers Cricket.

BOWLEY, Martin Richard; QC 1981; a Recorder of the Crown Court, 1979–88; *b* 29 Dec. 1936; *s* of late Charles Colin Stuart Bowley and Mary Evelyn Bowley; partner, 1976, Julian Marquez Bedoya (*d* 1990). *Educ:* Magdalen Coll. Sch., Oxford; Queen's Coll., Oxford (Styring Exhibnr, 1955; MA; BCL 1961). National Service, 1955–57: commnd Pilot Officer as a Fighter Controller; served 2nd Tactical Air Force, 1956–57. Called to the Bar, Inner Temple, 1962 (Bencher, 1994; Master of the Revels, 2002–10); Midland and Oxford Circuit, 1963–2002; Member: Senate and Bar Council, 1985–86; Gen. Council of Bar, 1987–88, 1989–94 (Treas., 1992–94); Chm., Bar Cttee, 1987. Dir, Barco, 2001–05. Member: Lord Chancellor's Standing Commn on Efficiency, 1986–87; Marre Cttee on Future of Legal Profession, 1987–88; Home Office Steering Gp on Sexual Offences Law Reform, 1999–2000; CPS Wkg Pty on Prosecuting Homophobic Hate Crimes, 2002. Pres., Bar Lesbian and Gay Gp, 1994–. Stonewall Lectr, 1994. Trustee, Bar Representation Unit, 1997–2001. Chm., Questors Theatre, 1972–84 and 1988–93 (Sec., 1963–72; Hon. Life Mem., 1986); Mem. Standing Cttee, Little Theatre Guild of GB, 1974–84 (Vice-Chm., 1979–81, Chm., 1981–84; Hon. Associate, 1997). Mem., Stonewall Gp, 1999–. Mem. Editl Bd, Counsel, 1992–2009. *Publications:* (contrib.) Advising Gay and Lesbian Clients, 1999; Friends and Families (memoir), 2009; contrib. to nat. and legal periodicals. *Recreations:* playing at theatre, watching cricket, island hopping, supporting Stonewall and Terrence Higgins Trust. *Address:* Flat E, 23/24 Great James Street, WC1N 3ES. *T:* (020) 7831 1674. *Clubs:* Garrick, MCC, Surrey CC.

BOWLING, Frank, OBE 2008; RA 2005; artist; *b* 29 Feb. 1936; *s* of Richard Sheridan Bowling and Agatha Elizabeth Franklin Bowling; *m* 2013, Rachel Scott; two *s* (and one *s* decd). *Educ:* Royal Coll. of Art (ARCA); Slade Sch., Univ. of London. Tutor, Camberwell Sch. of Arts and Crafts, 1968–83; Lectr, Reading Univ., 1964–66; Instructor, Columbia Univ., NY, 1968–69; Assistant Professor: Douglass Coll., Rutgers Univ., NJ, 1969–70; Massachusetts Coll. of Art, Boston, 1970–71; Artist-in-residence, Rhode Is. Sch. of Design, 1974–75; Lectr, Sch. of Visual Arts, NY, 1975–76; Tutor, Byam Shaw Sch. of Painting and Sculpture, 1975–86; Artist-in-residence, Skowhegan Sch. of Painting and Sculpture, Maine, 1984. John Simon Guggenheim Meml Fellow, 1967 and 1973. *Solo exhibitions:* Grabowski Gall., London, 1962, 1963; Whitney Mus. of Amer. Art, NY, 1971; Gall. Center for Inter-Amer. Relations, 1973–74; Tibor de Nagy, NY, freq. exhibns 1976–89; Serpentine Gall., 1986; Bowling Through the Decade, RWEA, 1989; Nat. Acad. of Scis, Washington, 1993; Bowling Through the Century, De La Warr Pavilion, Bexhill, 1997; Center for Art and Culture, Brooklyn, 1997; Aljira Center for the Arts, Newark, 2003; Frank Bowling: 4 Decades with Color, Phillips Mus. of Art, Lancaster, Pa, 2004; Arts Club, London, 2007; Rollo Contemporary Art, 2010; Tate Britain, 2012; Spanierman Gall., NY, 2012; Hales Gall., London, 2012; Traingone, Spritmuseum, Stockholm, 2014; Map Paintings, Dallas Mus. of Arts, Texas, 2015. Contributing Ed., Artsmagazine, 1969–72. Jt Founder, Young Commonwealth Artists Gp, 1958–63; Chm., London Gp, 1962–66. Shakespeare Quarto Centenary Commn, 1963. Hon. Fellow: Arts Inst., Bournemouth, 2006; UAL, 2013. Hon. DA Wolverhampton, 2007. Grand Prize for Contemporary Art, First World Fest. of Negro Art, Dakar, Senegal, 1966; Pollock Krasner Award, 1992, 1998. *Recreations:* cricket, athletics. *Address:* 8A John Islip Street, SW1P 4PY. *T:* (020) 7821 7065; PO Box 023703, Brooklyn, NY 11202, USA. *T:* (718) 6252579. *Clubs:* Chelsea Arts, Royal Over-Seas League.

BOWMAN, Prof. Alan Keir, PhD, DLitt; FBA 1994; FSA; Camden Professor of Ancient History, University of Oxford, 2002–10; Fellow, 2002–10, Emeritus Fellow, 2015, and Principal, 2011–15, Brasenose College, Oxford (Acting Principal, 2010–11); *b* Manchester, 23 May 1944; *s* of late Cyril Bowman and Freda (*née* Bowman); *m* 1966, Jacqueline Frayman; one *s* one *d*. *Educ:* Manchester Grammar Sch.; Queen's Coll., Oxford (MA; Hon Fellow, 2006); Univ. of Toronto (MA, PhD 1969); DLitt Oxon 2012. Canada Council Postdoctoral Fellow, 1969–70; Asst Prof. of Classics, Rutgers Univ., 1970–72; Lectr in Ancient Hist., Manchester Univ., 1972–77; Oxford University: Official Student, Christ Church, 1977–2002, Emeritus Student, 2002; Sen. Censor, Christ Church, 1988–90; Lectr in Ancient Hist., 1977–2002; Dir, Centre for Study of Ancient Documents, 1995–. Vis. Mem., Inst. for Advanced Study, Princeton, 1976, 1981; British Acad. Res. Reader, 1991–93. Chm., Roman Res. Trust, 1990–2009; Pres., Soc. for the Promotion of Roman Studies, 2001–05; Vice-Pres. (Humanities), British Acad., 2014–. FSA 1999. *Publications:* The Town Councils of Roman Egypt, 1971; (with J. D. Thomas) The Vindolanda Writing-Tablets, 1983, vol. II 1994, vol. III 2003; Egypt after the Pharaohs, 1986, 3rd edn 1996; Life and Letters on the Roman Frontier: Vindolanda and its people, 1994, 2nd edn 1998 (British Archaeological Book Award, 1998), 3rd edn 2003; (jtly) Literacy and Power in the Ancient World, 1994; (ed jtly) The Cambridge Ancient History, 2nd edn, Vol. X 1996, Vol. XI 2000, Vol. XII 2005; (ed jtly) Agriculture in Egypt from Pharaonic to modern times, 1998; (ed jtly) Quantifying the Roman Economy, 2009; (ed jtly) Settlement, Urbanization and Population, 2011; (ed jtly) The Roman Agricultural Economy, 2013; contrib. learned jls. *Recreations:* photography, music, cricket, tennis, walking. *Address:* Brasenose College, Oxford OX1 4AJ. *T:* (01865) 277820, 277821. *Club:* Oxford and Cambridge.

BOWMAN, Claire Margaret; *see* Makin, C. M.

BOWMAN, Edward Thomas K.; *see* Kellett-Bowman.

BOWMAN, Sir (Edwin) Geoffrey, KCB 2004 (CB 1991); First Parliamentary Counsel, 2002–06; *b* Blackpool, Lancs, 27 Jan. 1946; *er s* of late John Edwin Bowman and Lillian Joan Bowman (*née* Nield); *m* 1969, Carol Margaret, *er d* of late Alexander Ogilvie and Ethel Ogilvie; two *s* one *d*. *Educ:* Roundhay Sch., Leeds; Trinity Coll., Cambridge (Senior Scholar; BA 1st cl., LLB 1st cl., MA, LLM). Called to Bar, Lincoln's Inn (Cassel Scholar), 1968, Bencher, 2002; in practice, Chancery Bar, 1969–71; joined Parliamentary Counsel Office, 1971 (seconded to Law Commission, 1977–79, 1996–98); Dep. Parly Counsel, 1981–84; Parly Counsel, 1984–2002. Hon. QC 2006. Hon. LLD London, 2007. *Publications:* The Elements of Conveyancing (with E. L. G. Tyler), 1972; contrib. legal jls. *Recreations:* music (bassoon, curtal, recorder), history. *Address:* c/o Parliamentary Counsel Office, 1 Horse Guards Road, SW1A 2HQ. *T:* (020) 7276 6572. *Club:* Les Amis du Basson Français (Paris).

BOWMAN, Eric Joseph; consultant, since 1986; *b* 1 June 1929; *s* of late Joseph John Bowman and Lilley Bowman; *m* 1951, Esther Kay; one *d*. *Educ:* Stationers' Company's School; College of Estate Management. FRICS. Private practice, 1945–51; Royal Engineers, 1951–53; private practice, 1953–54; Min. of Works, 1954–63; Min. of Housing and Local Govt, 1963–73; Directorate of Diplomatic and Post Office Services, MPBW, later DoE, 1973–80; Directorate of Quantity Surveying Services, DoE, 1980–83; Dir of Building and Quantity Surveying Services, PSA, DoE, 1983–86. *Recreations:* fly fishing, walking, swimming, gardening, reading, crown green bowls. *Address:* Mearsons Farm, Hubbersty Head, Crosthwaite, near Kendal, Cumbria LA8 8JB. *T:* (01539) 568400.

BOWMAN, Sir Geoffrey; *see* Bowman, Sir E. G.

BOWMAN, James Thomas, CBE 1997; counter-tenor; *b* Oxford, 6 Nov. 1941; *s* of Benjamin and Cecilia Bowman (*née* Coote). *Educ:* Ely Cathedral Choir Sch.; King's Sch., Ely; New Coll., Oxford (MA (History) 1967; DipEd 1964; Hon. Fellow, 1998). Lay Vicar, Westminster Abbey, 1969–75; Teacher of Voice, GSM, 1983–92; Gentleman in Ordinary, HM Chapel Royal, St James's Palace, 2000–09 (Hon. Epiphany Usher, 2010). Many concert performances with Early Music Consort, 1967–76; operatic performances with: English Opera Gp, 1967; Sadler's Wells Opera, 1970–; Glyndebourne Festival Opera, 1970–; Royal Opera, Covent Gdn, 1972; Sydney Opera, Australia, 1978; Opéra Comique, Paris, 1979; Le Châtelet, Paris, 1982; Geneva, 1983; Scottish Opera, 1985; La Scala, Milan, 1988, 1991; La Fenice, Venice, 1991; Paris Opera, 1991; Badisches Staatstheater, Karlsruhe, 1984; in USA at Santa Fe and Wolf Trap Festivals, Dallas and San Francisco Operas; at Aix-en-Provence Fest., 1979; operatic roles include: Oberon, in A Midsummer Night's Dream; Endymion, in La Calisto; the Priest, in Taverner; Polinesso, in Ariodante; Apollo, in Death in Venice; Astron, in The Ice Break; Ruggiero in Alcina; title rôles: Giulio Cesare; Tamerlano; Xerxes; Scipione; Giustino; Orlando; Ottone. Extensive discography of opera, oratorio and contemporary music. Pres., Holst Singers, 1997–; Vice-Pres., Bach Choir, 2006–. Mem., Royal Soc. of Musicians, 2004. Hon. FRSCM 2012. Hon. DMus Newcastle, 1996. Medal, City of Paris, 1992. Officier, Ordre des Arts et des Lettres (France), 1995. *Recreations:* ecclesiastical architecture, collecting records. *Address:* 4 Brownlow Road, Redhill RH1 6AW. *Club:* Athenæum.

BOWMAN, Sir Jeffery (Haverstock), Kt 1991; FCA; Chairman: Mid Essex Hospital Services NHS Trust, 1993–99; Masthead Insurance Underwriting PLC, 1993–99; *b* 3 April 1935; *s* of Alfred Haverstock Bowman and Doris Gertrude Bowman; *m* 1963, Susan Claudia Bostock; one *s* two *d*. *Educ:* Winchester Coll. (schol.); Trinity Hall, Cambridge (major schol.; BA Hons 1st cl. in Law). Served RHG, 1953–55 (commnd, 1954). Price Waterhouse: articled in London, 1958; NY, 1963–64; admitted to partnership, 1966; Mem., Policy Cttee, 1972–91; Dir of Tech. Services, 1973–76; Dir, London Office, 1979–81; Sen. Partner, 1982–91; Chm., Price Waterhouse Europe, 1988–93; Jt Chm., Price Waterhouse World Firm, 1992–93. Dir, Gibbs Mew, 1995–97. Auditor, Duchy of Cornwall, 1971–93. Vice-Pres., Union of Ind. Cos, 1983–93; Member: Council, ICAEW, 1986–90 (Mem., Accounting Standards Cttee, 1982–87); Council, Industrial Soc., 1985–93; Economic and Financial Policy Cttee, CBI, 1987–93; City Capital Markets Cttee, 1989–93; Council, Business in the Community, 1985–91. Chairman: Court of Appeal (Civil Div.) Review, 1996–97; Crown Office Review, 1999–2000. Trustee, 1995–2003, Queen's Trustee, 1998–2003, Royal Botanic Gdns, Kew. Gov., Brentwood Sch., 1985–97. FRSA 1989. Hon. Bencher, Inner Temple, 1998. *Recreations:* golf, opera, gardening, sailing. *Address:* The Old Rectory, Church Road, Boreham, Chelmsford, Essex CM3 3EP. *T:* (01245) 467233. *Club:* Garrick.

BOWMAN, Dr John Christopher, CBE 1986; PhD; FRSB; independent environmental consultant, 1993–2001; Managing Director (Europe and Africa), Brown & Root Environmental, 1991–93; *b* 13 Aug. 1933; *s* of M. C. Bowman and C. V. Simister; *m* 1961, S. J. Lorimer; three *d*. *Educ:* Manchester Grammar Sch.; Univ. of Reading (BSc); Univ. of Edinburgh (PhD). Geneticist, later Chief Geneticist, Thornbers, Mytholmroyd, Yorks, 1958–66. Post-doctoral Fellow, North Carolina State Univ., Raleigh, NC, USA, 1964–65; University of Reading: Prof. of Animal Production, 1966–81; Head of Dept of Agric., 1967–71; Dir, Univ. Farms, 1967–78; Dir, Centre for Agricl Strategy, 1975–81; Sec., NERC, 1981–89; Chief Exec., NRA, 1989–91. Dir, Certa Foundn, 1998–2001. Chm., Sonning Parish Council, 1994–98. Mem., Cannington Coll. Corp., 2002–04. Trustee, Somerset Community Foundn, 2005–14. FRSA 1976 (Chair, Forum for Envmtl and Sustainable Develt Awards, 2005–11). Hon. DSc Cranfield, 1990. *Publications:* An Introduction to Animal Breeding, 1974; Animals for Man, 1977; (with P. Susmel) The Future of Beef Production in the European Community, 1979; (jtly) Hammond's Farm Animals, 1983. *Recreations:* golf, gardening, bridge. *Address:* 3 Nut Tree Farm, 2 Lower Street, Merriott, Som TA16 5NG.

BOWMAN, Mark; Director General, International Finance, HM Treasury, since 2013; *b* Chelmsford, 23 Sept. 1970; *s* of Jeffery and Susan Bowman; *m* 2004, Tabitha Jay; two *s* one *d*. *Educ:* Winchester Coll.; Univ. of Bristol (BSc); Univ. of Warwick (MSc). ODI Fellow, Min. of Planning and Finance, Mozambique, 1993–95; HM Treasury, 1995–2011: Principal Private Sec. to Chancellor of Exchequer, 2001–04; Hd, Internat. Poverty Reduction Team, 2005; Director: Internat. Finance, 2006–08; Budget and Tax, 2008–10; Strategy, Planning and Budget, 2010–11; Dir Gen., W Africa, ME, Security and Humanitarian Response, then Humanitarian, Security, Conflict and Internat. Finance, DFID, 2011–13. *Recreations:* sailing, tennis, photography, family. *Address:* 34 Boscombe Road, W12 9HU; HM Treasury, 1 Horse Guards Road, SW1A 2HQ. *E:* mark.bowman@hmtreasury.gsi.gov.uk.

BOWMAN, Pamela Margaret Munro; Sheriff at Glasgow, 2003–10; *b* 1 Aug. 1944; *d* of late James M. Wright and Jean Wright; *m* 1967, Bernard Neil Bowman; two *d*. *Educ:* Beacon Sch., Bridge of Allan; St Andrews Univ. (LLB). Admitted as solicitor and NP, 1967; Partner, Bowman, Solicitors, Dundee and Forfar, 1980–97; Temp. Sheriff, 1995–97; Floating Sheriff, 1997–99; Sheriff of Glasgow and Strathkelvin, 1999–2001; Sheriff of Grampian, Highland and Islands at Aberdeen, 2001–03. Mem. Bd, Scottish Children's Reporter Admin, 2003–10. *Recreations:* theatre, dancing.

BOWMAN, Penelope Jill; *see* Watkins, P. J.

BOWMAN, Philip, FCA; Chief Executive, Smiths Group plc, 2007–15; *b* Melbourne, Australia, 14 Dec. 1952; *s* of late Thomas Patrick Bowman and Norma Elizabeth (*née* Deravin). *Educ:* Westminster Sch.; Pembroke Coll., Cambridge (MA). FCA 1983. Price Waterhouse, London, 1974–78; Gibbs Bright & Co. Pty Ltd, Melbourne, 1978–83; Granite Industries Inc., Atlanta, 1983–85; Bass plc, London, 1985–95: Finance Dir, 1991–94; Chief Exec., Retail Div., 1994–95; Finance Dir, Coles Myer Ltd, Melbourne, 1995; Chm., Liberty plc, 1998–2000; Chief Executive: Allied Domecq plc, 1999–2005; Scottish Power plc, 2006–07. Chairman: Coral Eurobet Hldgs, 2004–05; Miller Gp Ltd, 2012–14; Miller Gp (UK) Ltd, 2014–; non-executive Director: BSkyB Gp plc, 1994–2003; Berry Bros & Rudd, 2006–; Better Capital Ltd, 2009–; Sen. Ind. Dir, Burberry Gp plc, 2002–; Dir, Scottish & Newcastle plc, 2006–08. Mem. Adv. Bd, Alchemy Partners, 2000–09. *Recreations:* scuba diving, entomology, opera, computers and electronics. *Clubs:* Victoria Racing, Royal Automobile of Victoria, National Golf (Vic).

BOWMAN, Richard Alan; Master of the Supreme Court, Chancery Division, 1996–2004; *b* 3 Oct. 1943; *s* of Harry Bowman and Gladys Bowman (*née* Croft); *m* 1970, Joanna Mary Lodder; two *s* one *d*. *Educ:* Clifton; St George's Sch., Newport, RI; Keble Coll., Oxford (MA). FCIArb 1995. Admitted solicitor, 1970; Dep. Chancery Master, 1988–96. Chm., Legal Aid Commn, General Synod of C of E, 1996–2011. Accredited Mediator, 2005–12. *Recreations:* Trollope, lunch. *Address:* Smithy House, Tormarton, Badminton, S Glos GL9 1HU.

BOWMAN, Sarah Meredith; District Judge, Principal Registry (Family Division), 1993–2014; *b* 24 May 1949; *d* of late Alexander Dennis Bowman and Jean Bowman; *m* 1984, Jake Downey (marr. diss. 2012); three *s*. *Educ:* Notting Hill and Ealing High Sch.; Leeds Univ. (BA). Called to the Bar, Middle Temple, 1976; Barrister, 1976–93. *Recreations:* my sons, my grandchildren, walking, bridge.

BOWMAN, Dr Sheridan Gail Esther, FSA; Keeper, Department of Conservation, Documentation and Science, British Museum, 2002–05; *b* Westlock, Alta, Canada, 11 March 1950; *o d* of late Otto Michael Bowman and of Eva (*née* McKnight). *Educ:* Whitehaven County Grammar Sch., Cumbria; St Anne's Coll., Oxford (Open Scholar; MA; DPhil Physics, 1976); Chelsea Coll., London (MSc Maths, 1981); (extramural) London Univ. (Dip. in Archaeol., 1985). FSA 1987 (a Vice Pres., 1993). British Museum: Scientific Officer, 1976; Keeper, Dept of Scientific Res., 1989–2002. *Publications:* Radiocarbon Dating, 1990; (ed) Science and the Past, 1991; papers on scientific techniques, particularly dating, applied to archaeology. *Recreations:* heath and fell walking, gardening, theatre.

BOWMAN, Victoria Jane, (Vicky); HM Diplomatic Service; Director, Myanmar Centre for Responsible Business, since 2013; *b* 12 June 1966; *d* of Dr Frank Neville Hosband Robinson and Daphne Isabel (*née* Coulthard); *m* 1st, 1991, Mark Andrew Bowman (marr. diss. 2001); 2nd, 2006, Htein Lin; one *d*. *Educ:* Oxford High Sch. for Girls; Pembroke Coll., Cambridge (BA Hons Natural Scis); Univ. of Chicago. Entered FCO, 1988; Third, later Second, Sec., Rangoon, 1990–93; FCO, 1993–96; Spokeswoman, UK Repn to EU, 1996–99; Mem., Cabinet of Eur. Comr for Ext. Relns, 1999–2002; Ambassador to Burma (Union of Myanmar), 2002–06; Hd, Africa Dept (Southern), FCO, 2006–08; Jt Dir, Global and Econ. Issues, FCO, 2008–11; Global Practice Leader Ext. Affairs, Rio Tinto, 2011–13. *Publications:* On the Road to Mandalay: translation of writings by Mya Than Tint, 1996. *Recreations:* cycling, diving, travel, learning languages, translating Burmese fiction and poetry, bridge. *Address:* Myanmar Centre for Responsible Business, 15 Shan Yeiktha Street, Yangon, Myanmar.

BOWMONT AND CESSFORD, Marquis of; Charles Robert George Innes-Ker; *b* 18 Feb. 1981; *s* and *heir* of Duke of Roxburghe, *qv* and of Lady Jane Dawnay, *qv*; *m* 2011, Hon. Charlotte Susanna Aitken (marr. diss. 2013), *e d* of Baron Beaverbrook, *qv*. *Educ:* Eton Coll.; Newcastle Univ. (BSc); RMA Sandhurst. Commnd Blues and Royals (RHG and 1st Dragoons), 2004. *Recreations:* motor racing, golf, tennis, fishing. *Address:* Floors Castle, Kelso TD5 7RW.

BOWN, Prof. Lalage Jean, OBE 1977; FRSE; FEIS; CCIPD; Director, Department of Adult and Continuing Education, University of Glasgow, 1981–92, now Professor Emeritus; *b* 1 April 1927; *d* of late Arthur Mervyn Bown, MC and Dorothy Ethel (*née* Watson); two foster *d*. *Educ:* Wycombe Abbey Sch.; Cheltenham Ladies' Coll.; Somerville Coll., Oxford (MA); Oxford Post-grad. Internship in Adult Education. FEIS 1990; FRSE 1991; CCIPD (FIPD 1993). Resident Tutor: University Coll. of Gold Coast, 1949–55; Makerere University Coll., Uganda, 1955–59; Asst Dir, then Dep. Dir, Extramural Studies, Univ. of Ibadan, Nigeria, 1960–66; Dir, Extramural Studies and Prof. (*ad personam*), Univ., of Zambia, 1966–70; Prof. of Adult Educn, Ahmadu Bello Univ., Nigeria, 1971–76, Univ. of Lagos, Nigeria, 1977–79; Dean of Educn, Univ. of Lagos, 1979–80; Vis. Fellow, Inst. of Development Studies, 1980–81. Hon. Professor: Internat. Centre for Educn in Develt, Warwick Univ., 1992–97; Inst. of Educn, Univ. of London, 1998–99; James Coleman Meml Lectr, UCLA, 1991; UNESCO Internat. Literacy Lectr, 2009. Member: Bd, British Council, 1981–89; Scottish Community Educn Council, 1982–88; Exec. Cttee, Scottish Inst. of Adult and Continuing Educn, 1982–88; Bd, Network Scotland, 1983–88; Bd of Trustees, Nat. Museums of Scotland, 1987–97; Council, Insite Trust, 1987–95; Bd of Trustees, Womankind Worldwide, 1988–96; Interim Trustee, Books for Develt, 1987–90; British Mem., Commonwealth Standing Cttee on Student Mobility and Higher Educn Co-operation, 1989–94; Trustee, Education Action (formerly World Univ. Service, UK), 1997–2003; Mem. Bd, Council for Educn in the Commonwealth, 2000–07 (Chm., Wkg Gp on Student Mobility, 1998–2000; Jt Dep. Vice-Chair, 2003–06). Governor, Inst. of Develt Studies, 1982–91; President: Develt Studies Assoc., 1984–86; British Comparative and Internat. Educn Soc., 1985–86; Vice-President: WEA, 1989–95 (Hon. Vice-Pres., 1984–88); Commonwealth Assoc. for Educn and Trng of Adults, 1990–93; Hon. Pres., British Assoc. for Literacy in Develt, 1993–98. Patron, African Families Foundn, 2001–; Trustee, Britain Nigeria Educnl (formerly Alhaji Tafawa Balewa Meml) Trust, 2005–. Hon. Vice-Pres., Townswomen's Guilds, 1984–2005. Hon. Life Member: People's Educnl Assoc., Ghana, 1973; African Adult Educn Assoc., 1976; NIACE, 2007. FAcSS (AcSS 2002). DUniv: Open, 1975; Paisley, 1993; Stirling, 1994; Dr (*hc*) Edinburgh, 1993; Hon. DLitt Glasgow, 2002. William Pearson Tolley Medal, Syracuse Univ., USA, 1975; Meritorious Service Award, Nigerian Nat. Council for Adult Educn, 1979; Symons Medal, ACU, 2001; World Teachers' Day Award, Commonwealth Secretariat, 2003; Internat. Adult and Continuing Educn Hall of Fame, 2009; Distinguished Africanist Award, African Studies Assoc. (UK), 2012. *Publications:* Report of the Tongu Rural Survey, 1953; (ed with Michael Crowder) Proceedings of First International Congress of Africanists, 1964; (ed) Two Centuries of African English, 1973; (ed) Adult Education in Nigeria: the next 10 years, 1975; A Rusty Person is Worse than Rusty Iron, 1976; Lifelong Learning: prescription for progress, 1979; (ed with S. H. O. Tomori) A Handbook of Adult Education for West Africa, 1980; (ed with J. T. Okedara) An Introduction to Adult Education: a multi-disciplinary and cross-cultural approach for developing countries, 1980; Preparing the Future: women, literacy and development, 1991; (ed) Towards a Commonwealth of Scholars, 1994; (ed) Education in the Commonwealth: the first 40 years, 2003; (ed) Maintaining Universal Primary Education: lessons from Commonwealth Africa, 2009; numerous articles in academic jls. *Recreations:* travel, reading, entertaining friends. *Address:* 1 Dogpole Court, Dogpole, Shrewsbury SY1 1ES. *T:* (01743) 356155, *Fax:* (01743) 233626. *Club:* Royal Over-Seas League (Life Mem.).

BOWNE, Anthony Doran; lighting designer; Director, Laban, since 2003; Principal, Trinity Laban Conservatoire of Music and Dance, since 2010 (Joint Principal, 2006–10); *b* 23 April 1956; *s* of Tony Alfred Bowne and Kathleen Bowne (*née* Doran); *m* 2005, Emma Redding; one *s* one *d*. *Educ:* Princethorpe Coll.; Kenilworth Grammar Sch.; Univ. of Southampton (BSc Econs 1977); Bartlett Sch. of Architecture, University Coll. London (MSc Arch. 1992). Sen. Financial Analyst, Rover Cars, 1978–81; Laban: Lectr in Lighting Design, 1983–86; Sen. Lectr, 1987–94; Exec. Dir, Transitions Dance Co., 1992–2002; Dep. Chief Exec.,

1994–2003. Dep. Chair, Conservatoires UK, 2011–. Sen. Lectr in Th. Lighting Design, Hong Kong Acad. for Performing Arts, 1996–98; Prof. of Dance, Lasalle Coll., Singapore, 2004–; Hon. Vis. Prof., City Univ., London, 2010–. Mem., Teaching Quality and Student Experience Strategic Cttee, HEFCE, 2013–. Lighting Designer, 1993–: Carmina Burana, Taiwan, Silent Tongues, Set the Night on Fire, RFH, 1993; Metalcholica, Forgotten Voices, Silence the Pestle Sound, Taiwan, 1994; Swinger, Car, Fierce/Pink/House, 1995; Spring Dance, Hong Kong, 1996; Una Cosa Rara (opera), Dance!! Dance!! Dance!!, Hong Kong, 1997; Vast Desert, Taiwan, 2000; Rite of Spring, Hong Kong, 2001; Now Blind Yourself, Place, London, 2002; Slow-Still-Divided, Place, London, Rite of Spring, Hong Kong Ballet tour, 2003; architectural: G's Club, Shanghai, 1997; Joyce, Dusk 'til Dawn, Hong Kong, 1998; World Finance Centre, Shanghai, 1999; Chijmes, Singapore, 2001. Chair, Cholmondeleys and Featherstonehaughs Dance Co., 2000–08; Board Member: Bonnie Bird Choreography Fund, 1995–; Dance Forum, DCMS, 2006–; Mem., London Cultural Strategy Gp, 2013–. Board Member: Deptford Creative Village Consortium, 2007–; Creative Process, 2008–. Board Member: Granada/Univ. of Calif Davis, 2002–07; Bird Coll., 2006–; London Higher, 2008–; Gov., Finnish Inst., London, 2006–. FRSA 2002. Designer for the 90s, Lighting Dimensions mag., USA, 1990; London Dance and Performance Award, Time Out mag., 1992. *Recreations:* wine, food, ski-ing, theatre. *Address:* Trinity Laban Conservatoire of Music and Dance, King Charles Court, Old Royal Naval College, Greenwich, SE10 9JF. *T:* (020) 8305 4444. *E:* a.bowne@trinitylaban.ac.uk.

BOWNES, Prof. Mary, OBE 2007; DPhil; CBiol, FRSB, FRES; FRSE; Professor of Developmental Biology, since 1994, and Vice Principal, 2003–12 and since 2015, University of Edinburgh (Senior Vice Principal 2012–14); *b* Drewsteignton, 14 Nov. 1948; *d* of Frederick and Florence Bownes; *m* 1973, Michael John Greaves; one *d*. *Educ:* Univ. of Sussex (BSc 1970; DPhil 1973); CBiol, FRSB (FIBiol 2001); FRES 2001; FRSE 2004. Postdoctoral Associate, Univ. of Freiberg and Univ. of Calif, Irvine, 1973–76; Lectr in Genetics and Develt Biol., Univ. of Essex, 1976–79; University of Edinburgh: Lectr, 1979–89, Sen. Lectr, 1989–91, Reader, 1991–94, in Molecular Biol.; Associate Dean for Postgrads, Faculty of Sci. and Engrg, 1997–98; Hd, Inst. of Cell and Molecular Biol., 1998–2001; mem. of numerous univ. cttees and gps. Dir, Scottish Initiative for Biotechnol. Educn, 2002–. External Examiner: Univ. of Sussex, 1996–2000; Univ. of Oxford, 2001–03; Univ. of York, 2004–06; Univ. of Glasgow, 2005–09; Univ. of Leicester, 2007–09. Chairman: Steering Cttee, Sci. and Plants for Schs Biotechnol. Scotland Proj., 2000–09 (Mem., 1998–); Bd, Edinburgh Consortium for Rural Res., 2003–11 (Mem., 1999–; Mem. Exec. Cttee, 2000–03); Strategy Bd, BBSRC, 2004–07; Studentships and Fellowships Strategy Panel, BBSRC, 2004–07; Young People's Cttee, RSE, 2008–11 (Mem., 2004–07); Member: Bd, Genetics Soc., 1980–83; Cttee, Brit. Soc. for Develtl Biol., 1982–87 (Treas., 1984–89); Adv. Bd, MRC, 2002–03; Cell and Molecular Biol. Section Cttee, 2004–07, Meetings Cttee, 2004–07, RSE; Skills Cttee, SFC, 2006–10; Bd, Scottish Assoc. for Marine Scis, 2009–14; Dir, Edinburgh Beltane, 2008–14. Mem. Bd, Highlands and Is Enterprise, 2007–11. FRSA. Mem., Editl Bd, Jl of Endocrinol., 2000–. *Publications:* (ed jtly) Metamorphosis, 1985; (ed) Ecdysone: from metabolism to regulation of gene expression, 1986; (with J. Grier) Private Giving, Public Good: the impact of philanthropy at the University of Edinburgh, 2014; over 100 papers in scientific jls and numerous book chapters. *Recreations:* photography, walking. *Address:* University of Edinburgh, Charles Stewart House, Room 1.9, 9–16 Chambers Street, Edinburgh EH1 1HT. *E:* mary.bownes@ed.ac.uk.

BOWNESS, family name of **Baron Bowness**.

BOWNESS, Baron *cr* 1995 (Life Peer), of Warlingham in the County of Surrey and of Croydon in the London Borough of Croydon; **Peter Spencer Bowness,** Kt 1987; CBE 1981; DL; NP; Consultant, Streeter Marshall, Solicitors, Croydon, Purley and Warlingham, 2002–11; *b* 19 May 1943; *s* of Hubert Spencer Bowness and Doreen (Peggy) Bowness; *m* 1969, Marianne Hall (marr. diss.); one *d*; *m* 1984, Mrs Patricia Jane Cook; one step *s*. *Educ:* Whitgift Sch., Croydon. Admitted Solicitor, 1966; NP 1977; Partner, Horsley, Weightman, Richardson and Sadler, subseq. Weightman, Sadler, then Streeter Marshall, 1970–2002. Croydon Council: Mem. (C), 1968–98: Leader, 1976–94; Leader of the Opposition, 1994–96; Mayor of Croydon, 1979–80; Chm., London Boroughs Assoc., 1978–94; Dep. Chm., Assoc. of Metropolitan Authorities, 1978–80. Opposition spokesman on the envmt, transport and the regions, H of L, 1997–98; Member: H of L Select Cttee on EU, 2003–07, 2009– (Chairman: Foreign Affairs, Defence and Develt Policy Sub Cttee, 2003–06; Law and Instnl Sub Cttee, 2009–13); Jt Cttee on Human Rights, 2003–07, 2008–12; Agric., Fisheries, Envmt and Energy Sub-cttee, 2013–; Co-Chm., All-Party Parly Gp on Lithuania, 2001–12; Vice-Chm., All-Party Parly Gp on Romania, 2006–; Sec., All-Party Parly Gp on Moldova, 2007–; Mem., All-Party Parly Gp on Kosovo, 2012–, on Serbia, 2012–; Mem., Ministerial Bd on Deaths in Custody, 2009–12. Member: Audit Commn, 1983–95; London Residuary Body, 1985–93; Nat. Training Task Force, 1989–92; UK Delegn, CLRAE (Council of Europe), 1990–98; UK Mem., Mem. Bureau, and Mem. Transportation and Telecommunications Commn, EC Cttee of the Regions, 1994–98; Member: UK Delegn to EU Charter of Fundamental Rights Drafting Convention, 1999–2000; Parly Assembly, OSCE, 2007– (Leader of Delegn, 2014–). Gov., Whitgift Foundn, 1982–94. Hon. Col, 151 (Greater London) Transport Regt RCT (V), 1988–93. DL Greater London, 1981; Freeman, City of London, 1984; Hon. Freeman, London Borough of Croydon, 2002. *Recreations:* travel, gardening, our two dachshunds. *Address:* House of Lords, SW1A 0PW.

BOWNESS, Sir Alan, Kt 1988; CBE 1976; Director of the Tate Gallery, 1980–88; Director, Henry Moore Foundation, 1988–94 (Member, Committee of Management, 1984–88 and 1994–2003); *b* 11 Jan. 1928; *er s* of George Bowness and Kathleen (*née* Benton); *m* 1957, Sarah Hepworth-Nicholson, *d* of Ben Nicholson, OM, and Dame Barbara Hepworth, DBE; one *s* one *d*. *Educ:* University Coll. Sch.; Downing Coll., Cambridge (Hon. Fellow 1980); Courtauld Inst. of Art, Univ. of London (Hon. Fellow 1986). Worked with Friends' Ambulance Unit and Friends' Service Council, 1946–50; Reg. Art Officer, Arts Council of GB, 1955–57; Courtauld Inst., 1957–79, Dep. Dir, 1978–79; Reader, 1967–78, Prof. of Hist. of Art, 1978–79, Univ. of London. Vis. Prof., Humanities Seminar, Johns Hopkins Univ., Baltimore, 1969. Exhibitions arranged and catalogued include: 54:64 Painting and Sculpture of a Decade (with L. Gowing), 1964; Dubuffet, 1966; Sculpture in Battersea Park, 1966; Van Gogh, 1968; Rodin, 1970; William Scott, 1972; French Symbolist Painters (with G. Lacambre), 1972; Ceri Richards, 1975; Courbet (with M. Laclotte), 1977. Mem. Internat. Juries: Premio Di Tella, Buenos Aires, 1965; São Paulo Bienal, 1967; Venice Biennale, 1986; Lehmbruck Prize, Duisburg, 1970; Rembrandt Prize, 1979–88; Heiliger Prize, 1998. Arts Council: Mem., 1973–75 and 1978–80; Mem., Art Panel, 1960–80 (Vice-Chm., 1973–75, Chm., 1978–80); Mem., Arts Film Cttee, 1968–77 (Chm., 1972–75). Member: Fine Arts Cttee, Brit. Council, 1960–69 and 1970–92 (Chm., 1981–92); Exec. Cttee, Contemp. Art Soc., 1961–69 and 1970–86; Kettle's Yard Cttee, Univ. of Cambridge, 1970–99; Cultural Adv. Cttee, UK National Commn for UNESCO, 1973–82. Governor, Chelsea Sch. of Art, 1965–93; Hon. Sec., Assoc. of Art Historians, 1973–76; Dir, Barbara Hepworth Museum, St Ives, Cornwall, 1976–88. Mem. Council, RCA, 1978–99 (Hon. Fellow 1984). Trustee: Yorkshire Sculpture Park, 1979–; Handel House, 1994–2001 (Chm., 1997–2001). Hon. Fellow, Bristol Polytechnic, 1980. Hon. FRIBA 1994. Hon. DLit Liverpool, 1988; Hon. DLitt: Leeds, 1995; Exeter, 1996. Chevalier, l'Ordre des Arts et des Lettres, France, 1973. *Publications:* William Scott Paintings, 1964; Impressionists and Post Impressionists, 1965; (ed) Henry Moore: complete sculpture 1955–64 (vol. 3) 1965, 1964–73 (vol. 4) 1977, 1974–80 (vol. 5) 1983, 1949–54 (vol. 2) 1987, 1980–86 (vol. 6) 1988; Modern Sculpture, 1965; Barbara Hepworth Drawings, 1966; Alan Davie, 1967; Recent British Painting, 1968; Gauguin, 1971; Barbara Hepworth: complete sculpture 1960–70, 1971; Modern European Art, 1972; Ivon Hitchens, 1973; (contrib.) Picasso 1881–1973, ed R. Penrose, 1973; (contrib.) The Genius of British Painting, ed D. Piper, 1975; The Conditions of Success, 1989; Bernard Meadows, 1994; articles in Burlington Magazine, TLS, Observer, and Annual Register. *Recreations:* going to concerts, theatre, opera. *Address:* 91 Castelnau, SW13 9EL. *T:* (020) 8846 8520; 16 Piazza, St Ives, Cornwall TR26 1NQ. *T:* (01736) 795444.

BOWRING, Prof. Richard John; Professor of Japanese Studies, University of Cambridge, 1985–2012, now Emeritus; Master, Selwyn College, Cambridge, 2000–13, now Emeritus Fellow; *b* 6 Feb. 1947; *s* of late Richard Arthur Bowring and Mabel Bowring (*née* Eddy); *m* 1970, Susan (*née* Povey); one *d*. *Educ:* Blundell's Sch.; Downing Coll., Cambridge (PhD 1973; LittD 1997). Lectr in Japanese, Monash Univ., 1973–75; Asst Prof. of Japanese, Columbia Univ., NY, 1978–79; Associate Prof. of Japanese, Princeton Univ., NJ, 1979–84; Cambridge University: Lectr in Japanese, 1984; Chm., Faculty Bd of Oriental Studies, 1987–89, 1998–2000; Fellow, Downing Coll., 1985–2000; Hon. Fellow, 2000; Chm., Bd of Scrutiny, 2010–11; Hd, Dept of E Asian Studies, 2010–12. British Acad. Reader, 1995–97. Trustee: Cambridge Foundn, 1989–98; Daiwa Anglo-Japanese Foundn, 2013–. Advr, UFC, subseq. HEFCE, 1992–94. Gov., SOAS, 1994–99. Order of Rising Sun, 3rd Cl. (Japan), 2013. *Publications:* Mori Ogai and the Modernization of Japanese Culture, 1979; trans., Murasaki Shikibu: her diary and poetic memoirs, 1982; Murasaki Shikibu: The Tale of Genji, 1988, 2nd edn 2004; (jtly) An Introduction to Modern Japanese, 1992; (ed) Cambridge Encyclopedia of Japan, 1993; The Diary of Lady Murasaki, 1996; (jtly) Cambridge Intermediate Japanese, 2002; The Religious Traditions of Japan 500–1600, 2005.

BOWRON, Margaret Ruth, (Mrs A. T. Davy); QC 2001; *b* 8 July 1956; *d* of late John Lewis Bowron, CBE and of Patricia (*née* Cobby); *m* 1988, Anthony Tallents Davy; two *d*. *Educ:* Convent of Our Lady of Sion, Worthing; Brighton and Hove High Sch., Brighton; King's Coll., London (LLB 1977). Called to the Bar, Inner Temple, 1978, Bencher, 2008; in practice as barrister, specialising in clinical negligence and related work, 1978–. *Recreations:* walking, theatre, travel. *Address:* (chambers) 1 Crown Office Row, Temple, EC4Y 7HH. *T:* (020) 7797 7500.

BOWRON, Michael, QPM 2007; Chief Officer of Police, States of Jersey Police, since 2011; *b* 8 Sept. 1957; *s* of Ronald and Christina Bowron; *m* 1994, Karen Elizabeth Purkiss. *Educ:* Ernest Bevin Comprehensive Sch., Tooting; Sussex Univ. (BA Hons (Sociol.) 1989); Nat. Exec. Inst., FBI Acad. 2007. Sussex Police: Constable 1980; Sergeant 1984; Insp. 1985; Bramshill Schol., Sussex Univ., 1986–89; Chief Insp. 1990; Supt 1991; Asst Chief Constable, Kent Police, 1997–2002; Asst Comr, 2002–06, Comr, 2006–11, City of London Police. Comr of Lieutenancy, City of London, 2007–11. FRSA. Hon. DSc City, 2008. OStJ 2012. *Recreations:* athletics, cross-country running, horse riding, travel. *Address:* States of Jersey Police, Police Headquarters, PO Box 789, St Helier, Jersey JE4 8ZD. *T:* (01534) 612502, *Fax:* (01534) 612503. *E:* chief.officer@jersey.pnn.police.uk.

BOWSHER, Brian Robert, PhD; FRSC, FInstP; Managing Director, National Physical Laboratory, 2009–15; *b* Birmingham, 12 July 1957; *s* of Robert Newman Bowsher and Patricia Mary Bowsher; *m* 1987, Sally Smith; one *s*. *Educ:* Handsworth Grammar Sch., Birmingham; Fosters Grammar Sch., Sherborne; Univ. of Southampton (BSc Hons 1978; PhD Chem. 1981). FRSC 2003; CSci 2004; FInstP 2009. Proj. and Sect. Manager, UKAEA, 1981–96; Dept Manager, AEA Technology, 1996–2002; AWE: Hd, Materials Sci., 2002–03; Dir, Res. and Applied Sci., 2003–07; Dir, Systems Engrg, 2007–09. Mem., STFC, 2013–. Mem., Comité internat. des poids et mesures, 2012–. MInstD. *Publications:* approx. 200 tech. articles. *Recreations:* fly fishing, ski-ing, walking, gardening, playing piano.

BOWSHER, Michael Frederick Thomas; QC 2006; *b* 22 Nov. 1963; *s* of His Honour Peter Charles Bowsher, *qv*; *m* 1990, Haylee Fiona, *d* of Terrence and Mary O'Brien, Aberdare; two *s* one *d*. *Educ:* St George's Sch., Windsor Castle; Radley Coll.; Brasenose Coll., Oxford (BA). FCIArb 2000; Chartered Arbitrator, 2002. Called to the Bar: Middle Temple, 1985, Bencher, 2014; NI, 2000; Republic of Ireland, 2012; in practice, Chambers of Donald Keating, QC, then Keating Chambers, 1986–88 and 1992–2001; Associate, Cleary, Gottlieb, Steen & Hamilton (Brussels), 1988–92; in practice, Monckton Chambers, 2001–. Vis. Lectr in EU Public Procurement Law, KCL, 2013–. Co-Chm., ICC Task Force on Public Procurement, 2007–13. Mem., Bar Council, 2010–14 (Chair, EU Law Cttee, 2012–14; Mem., Gen. Mgt Cttee, 2012–14). Fellow: Eur. Law Inst., 2012–; Centre of Eur. Law, KCL, 2014–. Freeman, Arbitrators' Co., 2011– (Liveryman, 2014–). *Publications:* (contrib.) Keating on Building Contracts, 5th edn 1991 to 7th edn 2001; (contrib.) Ward & Smith, Competition Litigation in the UK, 2005; (contrib.) Current Competition Law, 2005; (contrib.) Public Procurement Law, 2011; articles on public procurement and competition law in Public Procurement Law Rev., Current Competition Law and Internat. Construction Law Rev. *Address:* Monckton Chambers, 1 & 2 Raymond Buildings, Gray's Inn, WC1R 5NR. *T:* (020) 7405 7211, *Fax:* (020) 7405 2084. *E:* mbowsher@monckton.com. *Clubs:* Brooks's; Leander (Henley-on-Thames).

BOWSHER, His Honour Peter Charles; QC 1978; FCIArb; arbitrator; a Judge of the Technology and Construction Court of the High Court, 1998–2003 (an Official Referee, 1987–98); *b* 9 Feb. 1935; *s* of Charles and Ellen Bowsher; *m* 1960, Deborah Ann, *d* of Frederick Wilkins and Isobel Wilkins (*née* Copp), Vancouver; two *s*. *Educ:* St George's Sch., Windsor Castle; Ardingly; Oriel Coll., Oxford (MA). FCIArb 1990; Chartered Arbitrator, 2000–. Commnd Royal Artillery, 1954; Territorial Army XX Rifle Team, 1957. Called to the Bar, Middle Temple, 1959, Bencher, 1985. Harmsworth Scholar; Blackstone Entrance Scholar. A Legal Assessor to GMC and GDC, 1979–87; a Recorder, 1983–87; a Deputy High Court Judge, Queen's Bench and Chancery Divs, 1985–87. Ind. Review Body, Modified Colliery Review Procedure, 1986–87; Adjudicator, Crown Prosecution Service (Transfer of Staff) Regulations, 1985, 1986–87. Member: IT and the Courts Cttee, 1991–2003; Judicial Cttee, British Acad. of Experts, 1992–2003; Arbrix, 2004–. Member: Soc. for Computers and Law, 1990–; Soc. of Construction Arbitrators, 2005–. Liveryman, Arbitrators' Co., 2010–. *Recreations:* photography, music. *Address:* 150 Clifford's Inn, Fetter Lane, EC4A 1BY. *Clubs:* Brooks's, Royal Automobile.

See also M. F. T. Bowsher.

BOWTELL, Dame Ann (Elizabeth), DCB 1997 (CB 1989); PhD; Permanent Secretary, Department of Social Security, 1995–99; *b* 25 April 1938; *d* of John Albert and Olive Rose Kewell; *m* 1961, Michael John Bowtell; two *s* two *d*. *Educ:* Kendrick Girls' Sch., Reading; Girton Coll., Cambridge (MA; Hon. Fellow, 2000); Royal Holloway, Univ. of London (MA 2001; PhD 2010). Asst Principal, Nat. Assistance Board, 1960; Principal: Nat. Assistance Board, 1964; Min. of Social Security, 1966; DHSS, 1968; Asst Sec., 1973, Under Sec., 1980, DHSS; Dep. Sec., DHSS, later DSS, 1986; Principal Establishment and Finance Officer, DoH (on secondment), 1990–93; First Civil Service Comr and Dep. Sec., Cabinet Office, 1993–95; Dep. Sec., DSS, 1995. Trustee: Joseph Rowntree Foundn, 2001–11; Research Autism, 2012–. Hon. Dr Middlesex, 1996. *Recreations:* bird watching, medieval history, music, walking. *Address:* 26 Sidney Road, Walton-on-Thames, Surrey KT12 2NA.

BOWYER, family name of **Baron Denham**.

BOWYER, Gordon Arthur, OBE 1970; RIBA; FCSD; Partner, Bowyer Langlands Batchelor (formerly Gordon Bowyer & Partners), Chartered Architects, 1948–92; *b* 21 March 1923; *s* of Arthur Bowyer and Kathleen Mary Bowyer; *m* 1950, Ursula Meyer; one *s* one *d*. *Educ:* Dauntsey's Sch.; Polytechnic of Central London. Architect and designer in private practice, in partnership with Ursula Bowyer, Iain Langlands and Stephen Batchelor, 1948–92. Practice started with design of Sports Section, South Bank Exhibn, Fest. of Britain, 1951; schs and hostel for handicapped children in Peckham, Bermondsey and Dulwich, 1966–75; housing for Southwark, GLC, Family Housing Assoc., London & Quadrant Housing Assoc. and Greenwich Housing Soc., 1969–83; numerous office conversions for IBM (UK), 1969–89; Peckham Methodist Church, 1975; new offices and shops for Rank City Wall at Brighton, 1975 and Folkestone, 1976; Treasury at Gloucester Cathedral, 1976; conservation at Vanbrugh Castle, Greenwich, 1973, Charlton Assembly Rooms, 1980, Hill Hall, Essex, 1982; lecture theatre, library and accommodation, Jt Services Defence Coll., RNC, Greenwich, 1983; Cabinet War Rooms Museum, Whitehall (with Alan Irvine), 1984; refurbishment of Barry Rooms at Nat. Gall., Stuart & Georgian Galls at Nat. Portrait Gall. and East Hall of Science Museum; new Prints & Drawings and Japanese Gall. at BM; gall. for Japanese prints, Fitzwilliam Mus. Advisory architect: Science Mus., 1992–96; Trustees' Buildings Cttee, Nat. Maritime Mus., 1993–96. Hon. Sec., SIAD, 1957–58. Mem. Council, Friends of the Nat. Maritime Mus., 1985–2003; Trustee, Nat. Maritime Museum, 1977–93. *Address:* 111 Maze Hill, SE10 8XQ.

BOWYER, (Sir) Thomas Weyland, (15th Bt *cr* 1661); *b* 25 June 1960; *s* of Captain Sir Philip Weyland Bowyer-Smyth, 14th Bt, RN, and Veronica Mary, *d* of Captain C. W. Bower, DSC, RN; relinquished surname of Smyth by deed poll, 1997; *S* father, 1978, but does not use the title; *m* 1st, 1992, Sara Louise Breinlinger (marr. diss. 1997); 2nd, 1998, Mary Rose Helen Giedroyc; one *s* one *d*, and one step *s*. *Heir: kinsman* John Jeremy Windham, MBE [*b* 22 Nov. 1948; *m* 1976, Rachel Mary Finney; one *s* two *d*].

BOXALL, Barbara Ann, (Mrs Lewis Boxall); *see* Buss, B. A.

BOXER, Anna; *see* Ford, Anna.

BOXER, Charles Ian; *b* 11 Feb. 1926; *s* of Rev. William Neville Gordon Boxer and Margaret Boxer; *m* 1968, Hilary Fabienne Boxer. *Educ:* Glasgow High Sch.; Edinburgh Univ. (BL). Church of England ministry, 1950–54; apprentice to solicitors, 1954–58; Mem., Dominican Order (RC), 1958–67; Sen. Community Relations Officer for Wandsworth, 1967–77; Dir, Community Affairs and Liaison Div., Commn for Racial Equality, 1977–81. Communicator of the Year, BAIE Awards, 1976. *Recreation:* music. *Address:* Parish Farmhouse, Hassell Street, Hastingleigh, near Ashford, Kent TN25 5JE. *T:* (01233) 750219.

BOXER, Prof. David Howell, PhD; Director, Institute of Food Research, 2009–15; Professor of Microbial Metabolism, University of East Anglia, since 2009; *b* Aberdare, 11 June 1947; *s* of W. H. S. Boxer and S. M. Boxer; *m* 1978, Maureen; one *s* two *d*. *Educ:* Aberdare Boys' Grammar Sch.; Bristol Univ. (BSc Hons Biochem. 1969; PGCE 1973; PhD Biochem. 1974). Dundee University: Nuffield Res. Fellow, 1983–84; Hd, Biochem. Dept, 1988–94; Dean, Sci. Engrg Faculty, 1994–99; Dep. Principal, 2000–02; Vice Principal (Res. and Enterprise), 2002–09. Chm., Scottish Inst. for Res. in Policing, 2007–09; Mem. Bd, Scottish Crop Res. Inst., 2004–. *Publications:* numerous scientific articles. *Recreations:* ski-ing, cycling.

BOXER, Graham; Director, Imperial War Museum North, since 2012; *b* Chingford, London, 26 Aug. 1957; *s* of Charles Boxer and Kathleen Boxer (*née* Webber); *m* 1992, Angela Scholes; two *s*. *Educ:* Univ. of Nottingham (BA Jt Hons Ancient Hist. and Hist.); Univ. of Leicester (Grad. Cert. Mus. Studies); Univ. of Lancaster (Postgrad. Dip. Public Service Collaborative Leadership). Liverpool City Council: Curator, King's Regiment Collection, Regl Hist. Dept, 1990–93, HM Customs and Excise Nat. Mus., 1993–98, Hd, Regl Hist., 1998–2000, Nat. Mus Liverpool; Dir, St George's Hall, 2000–04; Hd, Heritage Develt, Liverpool Culture Co., 2004–09; Hd, Arts, Heritage and Participation, 2009–12. Parent Gov., Ellenbrook Community Prim. Sch., 2003–10; Chm., Interim Exec. Bd, Marlborough Rd Prim. Sch., 2009–11; Foundn Gov., St Andrew's Prim. Sch., 2013–. Mem., St Mary's Dist Church Council, 2013–. *Address:* Imperial War Museum North, Trafford Wharf Road, Trafford Park, Manchester M17 1TZ. *T:* (0161) 836 4010. *E:* gboxer@iwm.org.uk.

BOXSHALL, Dr Geoffrey Allan, FRS 1994; Merit Researcher (Band 1), Natural History Museum, since 2014; *b* 13 June 1950; *s* of John Edward Boxshall and Sybil Irene Boxshall (*née* Baker); *m* 1972, Roberta Gabriel Smith; one *s* three *d*. *Educ:* Churcher's Coll., Petersfield; Leeds Univ. (BSc, PhD). British Museum (Natural History), subseq. Natural History Museum: Higher SO, 1974–76; SSO, 1976–80; PSO, 1980–91; SPSO, 1991–97; DCSO, 1997–2014. *Publications:* (jtly) Dictionary of Ecology, Evolution and Systematics, 1982, 2nd edn 1998; (jtly) Cambridge Illustrated Dictionary of Natural History, 1987; (ed jtly) Biology of Copepods, 1988; (jtly) Copepod Evolution, 1991; (ed jtly) Pathogens of Wild and Farmed Fish: sea lice, 1993; An Introduction to Copepod Diversity, 2004; numerous papers in scientific jls. *Recreations:* tennis, reading, lexicography, travel. *Address:* Department of Life Sciences, Natural History Museum, Cromwell Road, SW7 5BD. *T:* (020) 7942 5749.

BOYACK, Sarah; Member (Lab) Lothian, Scottish Parliament, since 2011 (Edinburgh Central, 1999–2011); *b* 16 May 1961; *d* of late Jim Boyack. *Educ:* Royal High Sch., Edinburgh; Glasgow Univ. (MA); Heriot-Watt Univ. (DipT&CP). MRTPI. Planning Asst, London Borough of Brent, 1986–88; Sen. Planning Officer, Central Regl Council, 1988–92; Lectr in Planning, Edinburgh Coll. of Art, 1992–99. Scottish Executive: Minister for Transport and the Envmt, 1999–2000, for Transport, 2000–01, for Transport and Planning, 2001; Dep. Minister for Envmt and Rural Develt, 2007. Scottish Parliament: shadow spokesperson on rural affairs, environment and climate change, 2008–11; Shadow Cabinet Sec. for Local Govt and Planning, 2011–14; Shadow Cabinet Sec. for Rural Affairs, Food, Climate Change and Envmt, 2014–; Convener, Envmt and Rural Develt Cttee, 2003–07. *Address:* Scottish Parliament, Edinburgh EH99 1SP.

BOYCE, family name of **Baron Boyce**.

BOYCE, Baron *cr* 2003 (Life Peer), of Pimlico in the City of Westminster; **Admiral of the Fleet Michael Cecil Boyce,** KG 2011; GCB 1999 (KCB 1995); OBE 1982; DL; Lord Warden and Admiral of the Cinque Ports, and Constable of Dover Castle, since 2004; Bath King of Arms, since 2009; *b* 2 April 1943; *s* of late Comdr Hugh Boyce, DSC, RN and Madeleine Boyce (*née* Manley); *m* 1st, 1971, Harriette Gail Fletcher (separated 1994; marr. diss. 2005); one *s* one *d*; 2nd, 2006, Fleur Margaret Anne (*née* Smith), *widow* of Vice Adm. Malcolm Rutherford, CBE. *Educ:* Hurstpierpoint Coll.; BRNC, Dartmouth. Joined RN, 1961; qualified Submarines, 1965 and TAS, 1970; served in HM Submarines Anchorite, Valiant, and Conqueror, 1965–72; commanded: HM Submarines: Oberon, 1973–74; Opossum, 1974–75; Superb, 1979–81; HMS Brilliant, 1983–84; Captain (SM), Submarine Sea Training, 1984–86; RCDS, 1988; Sen. Naval Officer, ME, 1989; Dir Naval Staff Duties, 1989–91; Flag Officer: Sea Training, 1991–92; Surface Flotilla, 1992–95; Comdr, Anti-Submarine Warfare Striking Force, 1992–94; Second Sea Lord, and C-in-C Naval Home Comd, 1995–97; C-in-C Fleet, C-in-C Eastern Atlantic Area and Comdr Naval Forces N Western Europe, 1997–98; First Sea Lord and Chief of Naval Staff, and First and Principal Naval ADC to the Queen, 1998–2001; Chief of the Defence Staff, 2001–03; ADC to the Queen, 2001–03. Col Comdt, SBS, 2003–. Non-executive Director: VT Gp plc, 2004–10; W. S. Atkins plc, 2004–13. Chm., HMS Victory Preservation Co., 2012–. President: Officers' Assoc., 2003–12; London Br., St John Ambulance, 2003–11; RN Submarine Mus., 2005–; Pilgrims' Soc., 2010–; Member of Council: White Ensign Assoc., 2003–13 (Chm., 2007–10); RNLI, 2004–13 (Trustee, 2006–13; Chm., 2008–13); Chm. Adv. Bd, RBL Centre for Blast Injury Studies, 2011–; Trustee, Nat. Maritime Mus., 2005–13; Patron: Sail4Cancer, 2003–; Submariners Assoc., 2003–; Forces in Mind Trust, 2012–. Gov., Alleyn's Sch., 1995–2005. Freeman, City of London, 1999; Master, Drapers' Co., 2013–14 (Hon. Freeman, 2005; Liveryman, 2009–; Mem. Ct, 2011). Elder Brother, Trinity House, 2006 (Yr Brother, 1999–2006). Hon. Bencher, Middle Temple, 2012. DL Greater London, 2003. KStJ 2002. Hon. LLD Portsmouth, 2005; Hon. Dr Canterbury Christ Church, 2011; Hon. DCL Kent, 2013. Comdr, Legion of Merit (US), 1999 (Bronze Oak Leaf, 2003). *Recreations:* squash, tennis, Real tennis, sailing, windsurfing, opera. *Address:* House of Lords, SW1A 0PW. *Clubs:* Garrick, Naval and Military (Dir, 2003–08; Vice Chm., 2005–08; Trustee, 2012–), Queen's.
See also Sir G. H. Boyce.

BOYCE, Frank C.; *see* Cottrell-Boyce.

BOYCE, Sir Graham (Hugh), KCMG 2001 (CMG 1991); HM Diplomatic Service, retired; Senior Adviser, Bank of America Merrill Lynch, since 2013; *b* 6 Oct. 1945; *s* of late Comdr Hugh Boyce, DSC, RN and Madeleine Boyce (*née* Manley); *m* 1970, Janet Elizabeth Spencer; one *s* three *d*. *Educ:* Hurstpierpoint Coll.; Jesus Coll., Cambridge (MA). VSO, Antigua, 1967; HM Diplomatic Service, 1968; Ottawa, 1971; MECAS, 1972–74; 1st Sec., Tripoli, Libya, 1974–77; FCO, 1977–81; Kuwait, 1981–85; Asst Hd of ME Dept, FCO, 1985–86; Counsellor and Consul-Gen., Stockholm, 1987–90; Ambassador and Consul-Gen., Doha, 1990–93; Counsellor, FCO, 1993–96; Ambassador to Kuwait, 1996–99; Ambassador to Egypt, 1999–2001. Chairman, Middle East Board: Invensys, 2005–10; Lehman Brothers, 2006–08; MEC Internat., 2011–13; Chm., Common Purpose Internat., 2012–; Vice Chairman: VT Internat. Services, 2002–06; EMEA Adv. Bd, Nomura Internat., 2009–13; Adviser: to Emir of Qatar, 2001–02; to Shell, 2001–06; to Air Products, 2003–14; Mem., Adv. Bd, Kuwait Investment Office, 2004–; Senior Adviser: Nomura, 2009–13; DLA Piper, 2009–14; various consultancies. Trustee, Dakhleh Oasis Trust, 2001–14. Global Ambassador, SOAS, 2011–13. *Recreations:* tennis, golf, walking. *Club:* Oxford and Cambridge.
See also Baron Boyce.

BOYCE, Peter John, AO 1995; PhD; Vice-Chancellor, Murdoch University, Western Australia, 1985–96, now Emeritus Professor; Hon. Research Fellow, University of Tasmania, since 2004 (Visiting Professor, 1996–2000; Hon. Professor of Political Science, 2000–04); *b* 20 Feb. 1935; *s* of Oswald and Marjorie Boyce; *m* 1962, Lorinne Peet; one *s* two *d*. *Educ:* Wesley Coll., Perth, WA; Univ. of Western Australia (MA); Duke Univ., USA (PhD). Res. Fellow, then Fellow, Dept of Internat. Relns, ANU, 1964–66; Nuffield Fellow, St Antony's Coll., Oxford, 1966–67; Sen. Lectr, then Reader, in Political Science, Tasmania Univ., 1967–75; Prof. of Pol Science and Hd, Dept of Govt, Queensland Univ., 1976–79; Prof. of Politics and Hd of Dept, Univ. of W Australia, 1980–84. Visiting Fellow: Corpus Christi Coll., Cambridge, 1989; Merton Coll., Oxford, 1996; Christ Church, Oxford, 1997. Interim Principal, Aust. Maritime Coll., 2005–06. Exec. Mem., Aust.-NZ Foundn, 1979–83; Member: Aust. Human Rights Commn, 1981–86; Consultative Cttee on Relns with Japan, 1983–85; Asia Business Council of WA, 1993–96. Lay Canon of St George's Cath., Perth, 1986–96. Editor, Australian Outlook, 1973–77. Hon. LLD Tasmania, 2006. *Publications:* Malaysia and Singapore in International Diplomacy, 1968; Foreign Affairs for New States, 1977; (co-ord. ed.) Dictionary of Australian Politics, 1980; (co-ord. ed.) Politics in Queensland, 1980; (co-ord. ed.) The Torres Strait Treaty, 1981; (ed) Independence and Alliance, 1983; Diplomacy in the Market Place, 1991; Honest and Unsullied Days, 2001; The Queen's Other Realms, 2008; God and the City, 2012. *Recreations:* gardening, walking, church music. *Address:* #1, 13 Rose Court, Lower Sandy Bay, Tas 7005, Australia. *T:* (03) 62252009.

BOYCE, Most Rev. Philip; *see* Raphoe, Bishop of, (RC).

BOYCE, Sir Robert (Leslie), 3rd Bt *cr* 1952; FRCSEd (Ophth); Consultant Ophthalmic and Oculoplastic Surgeon, Sunderland Eye Infirmary, since 2003; Managing Director, Minor Ops Ltd, since 2007; *b* 2 May 1962; *s* of Sir Richard (Leslie) Boyce, 2nd Bt, and of Jacqueline Anne (who *m* 2nd, 1974, Christopher Boyce-Dennis), *o d* of Roland A. Hill; *S* father, 1968; *m* 1985, Fiona, second *d* of John Savage, Whitmore Park, Coventry; one *s* one *d*. *Educ:* Cheltenham Coll.; Salford Univ. (BSc 1984, 1st cl. hons); Nottingham Univ. (BMedSci 1991, 1st cl. hons; BM BS 1993). FRCSEd (Ophth) 1998. Sen. House Officer, Manchester Royal Eye Hosp., 1995–98; Specialist Registrar in Ophthalmology, Royal Victoria Infirmary, Sunderland Eye Infirmary and N Riding Infirmary, 1998–2003. *Heir: s* Thomas Leslie Boyce, *b* 3 Sept. 1993.

BOYCE, Walter Edwin, OBE 1970; Director of Social Services, Essex County Council, 1970–78; *b* 30 July 1918; *s* of Rev. Joseph Edwin Boyce and Alice Elizabeth Boyce; *m* 1942, Edna Lane (*née* Gargett) (*d* 2001); two *d*. *Educ:* High Sch. for Boys, Trowbridge, Wilts. Admin. Officer, Warwickshire CC, 1938–49. Served war, commnd RA; Gunnery sc, 1943; demob. rank Major, 1946. Dep. County Welfare Officer: Shropshire, 1949–52; Cheshire, 1952–57; Co. Welfare Officer, Essex, 1957–70. Adviser to Assoc. of County Councils, 1965–78; Mem., Sec. of State's Adv. Personal Social Services Council, 1973 until disbanded, 1980 (Chm., People with handicaps Gp); Mem., nat. working parties on: Health Service collaboration, 1972–74; residential accommodation for elderly and mentally handicapped, 1974–78; boarding houses, 1981. Pres., County Welfare Officers Soc., 1967–68. Governor, Queen Elizabeth's Foundn for the Disabled, 1980–91. *Recreations:* sailing, golf, in sports, particularly Rugby and athletics, voluntary services, travel.

BOYCE, William; QC 2001; a Recorder, since 1997; *b* 29 July 1951. *Educ:* St Joseph's Acad. Grammar Sch., Blackheath; Univ. of Kent (BA). Called to the Bar, Gray's Inn, 1976, Bencher, 2007; Jun. Treasury Counsel, 1991–97, Sen. Treasury Counsel, 1997–2001, CCC. *Address:* QEB Hollis Whiteman Chambers, 1–2 Laurence Pountney Hill, EC4R 0EU.

BOYCOTT, Geoffrey; cricket commentator; *b* 21 Oct. 1940; *s* of late Thomas Wilfred Boycott and Jane Boycott; *m* 2003, Rachael Swinglehurst; one *d*. *Educ:* Kinsley Modern Sch.; Hemsworth Grammar Sch. Played cricket for Yorkshire, 1962–86, received County Cap, 1963, Captain of Yorkshire, 1970–78. Played for England, 1964–74, 1977–82; scored 100th first-class hundred, England v Australia, 1977, 150th hundred, 1986; passed former world record no of runs scored in Test Matches, Delhi, Dec. 1981. Mem., General Cttee, 1984–93, Bd, 2005–11, Yorks CCC. Commentator: BBC TV; Trans World Internat.; Channel 9; SABC; Talk Radio; ESPN Star; Channel 4, 2004–05; BBC Radio, 2004–; Ten Sports, 2006–; Five (formerly Channel 5), 2006–. Columnist, Daily Telegraph. Pres., Yorks CCC, 2012–14. *Publications:* Geoff Boycott's Book for Young Cricketers, 1976; Put to the Test: England in Australia 1978–79, 1979; Geoff Boycott's Cricket Quiz, 1979; On Batting, 1980; Opening Up, 1980; In the Fast Lane, 1981; Master Class, 1982; Boycott, The Autobiography, 1987; Boycott on Cricket, 1990; Geoffrey Boycott on Cricket, 1999; The Best XI, 2008; Play Cricket the Right Way, 2010; Corridor of Certainty, 2014. *Recreation:* golf. *Address:* c/o Yorkshire County Cricket Club, Headingley Cricket Ground, Leeds, Yorks LS6 3DP.

BOYCOTT, Kay Elizabeth; Chief Executive, Asthma UK, since 2013; *b* Manchester, 3 Dec. 1969; *d* of Alan Boycott and Elizabeth Boycott; one *s* one *d*. *Educ:* Manchester High Sch. for Girls; Univ. of Durham (BA Econs and Hist. 1991). Brand Asst, Nestlé Rowntree, 1991–93; Brand and Account Manager, Johnson & Johnson, 1994–99; Management Consultant, Oxford Strategic Mktg, 1999–2009; Dir, Communications, Policy and Campaigns, Shelter, 2009–13. Non-exec. Dir, Hammersmith and Fulham PCT, 2004–09. Trustee, Gingerbread, 2011–. *Address:* Asthma UK, 18 Mansell Street, E1 8AA. *T:* (020) 7786 4900. *E:* kboycott@asthma.org.uk.

BOYCOTT, Rosie; Chair, London Food, since 2008; *b* 13 May 1951; *d* of late Charles Boycott and of Betty Boycott; *m* 1983, David Leitch (marr. diss. 1998; he *d* 2004); one *d*; *m*

1999, Charles Anthony Frederick Howard, *qv*. *Educ:* Cheltenham Ladies' Coll.; Kent Univ. (pure maths). Has worked on: Frendz mag., 1971; Spare Rib (Founder and Editor), 1971–72; Luka (Buddhist Jl of America), 1973–75; Osrati (Kuwait), 1976–79; Honey mag., 1979–81 (Dep. Ed.); Daily Mail, 1984–85; Sunday Telegraph, Harpers & Queen, 1989–92; Editor: Esquire, 1992–96; Independent on Sunday, 1996–98; The Independent, 1998; The Express, 1998–2001. Regular appearances on Newsnight Review (BBC2) and The Moral Maze (BBC Radio 4). Dir, Dillington Park Nurseries, 2005–09; non-exec. Dir, Eden Project. Bd Mem., Old Vic, 2002–05; Trustee, Hay-on-Wye Literary Fest., 2000–. Trustee, Street Smart. Editor of Year (Magazines), 1994, 1995. *Publications:* Batty, Bloomers & Boycott, 1982; A Nice Girl Like Me, 1984; All for Love, 1987; Our Farm, 2007. *Recreations:* riding, ski-ing, tennis, reading, arts. *Club:* Groucho.

BOYD; *see* Lennox-Boyd.

BOYD, family name of **Barons Boyd of Duncansby** and **Kilmarnock**.

BOYD OF DUNCANSBY, Baron *cr* 2006 (Life Peer), of Duncansby in Caithness; **Colin David Boyd;** PC 2000; a Senator of the College of Justice in Scotland, since 2012; *b* 7 June 1953; *s* of Dr David Hugh Aird Boyd and Betty Meldrum Boyd; *m* 1979, Fiona Margaret MacLeod; two *s* one *d*. *Educ:* Wick High Sch.; George Watson's Coll., Edinburgh; Manchester Univ. (BA Econ); Edinburgh Univ. (LLB). WS 2007. Solicitor, 1978–82 and 2007–12; called to the Bar, Scotland, 1983; Legal Associate, Royal Town Planning Inst., 1990; Advocate Depute, 1993–95; QC (Scot.) 1995; Solicitor Gen. for Scotland, 1997–99; Solicitor Gen., 1999–2000, Lord Advocate, 2000–06, Scottish Exec. Consultant, Dundas & Wilson LLP, 2007–12. Mem., Commn on Scottish Devolution, 2008–09. Hon. Prof. of Law, Univ. of Glasgow, 2008–12. Chm., Northern Lighthouse Heritage Trust, 2009–13. FRSA 2000. *Publications:* (contrib.) The Legal Aspects of Devolution, 1997. *Recreations:* walking, reading, watching Rugby. *Address:* Supreme Courts, Parliament Square, Edinburgh EH1 1RQ. *T:* (0131) 225 2595.

BOYD OF MERTON, 2nd Viscount *cr* 1960, of Merton-in-Penninghame, Co. Wigtown; **Simon Donald Rupert Neville Lennox-Boyd;** *b* 7 Dec. 1939; *e s* of 1st Viscount Boyd of Merton, CH, PC, and Lady Patricia Guinness, *d* of 2nd Earl of Iveagh, KG, CB, CMG, FRS; *S* father, 1983; *m* 1962, Alice Mary (JP, DL, High Sheriff of Cornwall, 1987–88), *d* of late Major M. G. D. Clive and of Lady Mary Clive; two *s* two *d*. *Educ:* Eton; Christ Church, Oxford. Dep. Chm., Arthur Guinness & Sons, 1981–86. Chairman: SCF, 1987–92 (Vice-Chm., 1979–82); Stonham Housing Assoc., 1992–99; Iveagh Trustees Ltd, 1992–2003; Trustee, Guinness Trust, 1974–2004. *Heir: s* Hon. Benjamin Alan Lennox-Boyd [*b* 21 Oct. 1964; *m* 1993, Sheila Carroll; two *s* one *d*]. *Address:* Ince Castle, Saltash, Cornwall PL12 4QZ. *T:* (01752) 842672.

See also Baron Spens.

BOYD, Alan Robb; Consultant, Pinsent Masons LLP (formerly McGrigors LLP, solicitors), 2010–14 (Director, Public Law, 1997–2010, McGrigor Donald, subseq. McGrigors LLP, solicitors); *b* 30 July 1953; *er s* of Alexander Boyd and Mary Herd Boyd; *m* 1973, Frances Helen Donaldson; two *d*. *Educ:* Irvine Royal Acad.; Univ. of Dundee (LLB 1974); Open Univ. (BA 1985). Admitted solicitor, 1976; Principal Legal Asst, Shetland Is Council, 1979–81; Principal Solicitor, Glenrothes Develt Corp., 1981–84; Legal Advr, Irvine Develt Corp., 1984–97. Mem. Council, Law Soc. of Scotland, 1985–97 (Vice-Pres., 1994–95; Pres., 1995–96); Bd Mem., 1988–94, Pres., 1992–94, European Company Lawyers' Assoc.; Chm., Assoc. for Scottish Public Affairs, 1998–2000. *Recreations:* golf, music, gardening. *Address:* 26 Hannah Wynd, St Quivox, Ayr KA6 5HB. *T:* (01292) 521936. *Club:* Turnberry Golf.

BOYD, Sir Alexander Walter, 3rd Bt *cr* 1916; *b* 16 June 1934; *s* of late Cecil Anderson Boyd, MC, MD, and Marjorie Catharine, *e d* of late Francis Kinloch, JP, Shipka Lodge, North Berwick; *S* uncle, 1948; *m* 1958, Molly Madeline, *d* of late Ernest Arthur Rendell; one *s* three *d* (and one *s* decd). *Heir: g s* Kyle Robert Rendell Boyd, *b* 15 Feb. 1987.

BOYD, Andrew Jonathan Corrie, CMG 2005; OBE 1992; HM Diplomatic Service, retired; Director, Special Projects, QinetiQ plc, 2005–11; Flick Research Fellow, University of Buckingham, since 2012; *b* 5 May 1950; *s* of John Ronald Boyd and Jane Rhiain Boyd (*née* Morgan); *m* 1979, Ginette Anne Vischer; two *s* one *d*. *Educ:* Tonbridge Sch.; BRNC Dartmouth; St John's Coll., Oxford (BA Hons PPE). Served RN, Submarine Service, 1968–80. Entered FCO, 1980; First Secretary: FCO, 1980; (Econ.), Accra, 1981–84; (Chancery), Mexico City, 1988–91; Political Counsellor, Islamabad, 1996–99; Counsellor, FCO, 1999–2005. Dir, Special Projects, QinetiQ plc, 2005–11. *Recreations:* mountain walking, sea swimming, military history. *Address:* c/o Foreign and Commonwealth Office, King Charles Street, SW1A 2AH.

BOYD, Atarah, (Mrs Douglas Boyd); *see* Ben-Tovim, A.

BOYD, (David) John; QC 1982; arbitrator; accredited mediator; Chairman, Axxia Systems Ltd, 1995–2008; *b* 11 Feb. 1935; *s* of David Boyd and Ellen Jane Boyd (*née* Gruer); *m* 1960, Raija Sinikka Lindholm, Finland (*d* 2011); one *d* (one *s* decd). *Educ:* Eastbourne Coll.; St George's Sch., Newport, USA (British-Amer. schoolboy schol.); Gonville and Caius Coll., Cambridge (MA). FCIArb 1979. Various secretarial posts, ICI, 1957–62; Legal Asst, Pfizer, 1962–66; called to the Bar, Gray's Inn, 1963, Bencher, 1988; Sec. and Legal Officer, Henry Wiggin & Co., 1966; Asst Sec. and Sen. Legal Officer (UK), Internat. Nickel, 1968; Dir, Impala Platinum, 1972–78; Sec. and Chief Legal Officer, 1972–86, and Dir, 1984–86, Inco Europe; practising barrister, 1986; Director: Legal Services, 1986–93, Public Affairs and Communications, 1993–95, Digital Equipment Co.; Digital Equipment Scotland, 1987–95. Gen. Comr of Income Tax, 1978–83; Immigration Adjudicator, 1995–2005; Immigration Judge, 2005–08; Vice-Pres., Council of Immigration Judges, 1998–2000. Chm., Bar Assoc. for Commerce, Finance and Industry, 1980–81; Mem., Senate of Inns of Court and Bar, 1978–81. Sec. Gen., Assoc. des Juristes d'Entreprise Européens (European Company Lawyers Assoc.), 1983–84. Dir, Centre for European Dispute Resolution, 1991–94. Legal Advisor to Review Bd for Govt Contracts, 1984–91. Chm., CBI Competition Panel, 1988–93; Mem., Electricity Panel, Monopolies and Mergers Commn, 1991–98. Mem., Exec. Cttee, Royal Acad. of Dancing, 1991–98; Chm., The Place Th. and Contemp. Dance Trust, 1995–98; Dir, Oxford Orch. da Camera, 1996–2001. Treas., Upton Bishop PCC, 2003–. *Recreations:* holidaying in France, viticulture. *Address:* Beeches, Upton Bishop, Ross-on-Wye, Herefordshire HR9 7UD. *T:* (01989) 780214. *E:* boyd456@btinternet.com.

BOYD, Prof. Ian Lamont, DSc; FRSB; FRSE; Professor of Biology, since 2001, and Adviser to the Principal's Office, since 2012, University of St Andrews; Chief Scientific Adviser, Department for Environment, Food and Rural Affairs, since 2012; *b* 9 Feb. 1957; *s* of late Dr John Morton Boyd, CBE, FRSE and of Winifred Isobel Boyd; *m* 1982, Sheila M. E. Aitken; one *s* two *d*. *Educ:* George Heriot's Sch., Edinburgh; Univ. of Aberdeen (BSc 1st Cl. Hons 1979; DSc 1996); St John's Coll., Cambridge (PhD 1983). FRSB (FSB 2011). RAF Volunteer Reserve, 1975–78. Churchill Fellow, 1980; SSO, Inst. of Terrestrial Ecol., 1982–87, SPSO, British Antarctic Survey, 1987–2001, NERC; Dir, NERC Sea Mammal Res. Unit, 2001–12, Dir, Scottish Oceans Inst., 2009–12, Univ. of St Andrews; Chief Exec., SMRU Ltd, 2006–09. Chief Scientist, US Navy Behavioral Response Study, 2007–08. Mem., Scottish Govt Enquiry into future of Common Fisheries Policy, 2008–10. Hon. Prof., Univ. of Birmingham, 1997–2001. Chairman: Alliance for Marine Sci. and Technol. for Scotland, 2005–10; UK Food Res. Partnership, 2014–; Member, Council of Management: Hebridean Trust, 1990–2012; Seamark Trust, 1993–2012; Scottish Assoc. for Marine Sci., 2004–08; Scottish Sustainable Seas Task Force, 2008; Member: Adv. Council, Nat. Oceanography Centre, Southampton, 2008–10; Lenfest Forage Fish Task Force, 2009–11; Scottish Science Adv. Council, 2010–; Adv. Cttee, British Geological Survey, 2012–; NERC, 2013–; Chm., Scientific Adv. Bd on Decommissioning, Oil & Gas UK, 2010–12; Co-Chm., Internat. Quiet Oceans Experiment, 2010–12. Ed., 2000–06, Ed.-in-Chief, 2006–07, Jl of Zoology; Mem. Bd, Reviewing Eds, Science, 2011–. FRSE 2002. US Antarctic Medal, 1995; Bruce Medal, RSE, 1996; Scientific Medal, Zool Soc. of London, 1998; Marsh Award for Marine & Freshwater Conservation, Zool Soc. of London, 2006. *Publications:* The Hebrides: a natural history, 1990; Marine Mammals: advances in behavioural and population biology, 1993; The Hebrides: a mosaic of islands, 1996; The Hebrides: a natural tapestry, 1996; The Hebrides: a habitable land, 1996; Conserving Nature: Scotland and the wider world, 2005; Top Predators in Marine Ecosystems, 2006; Marine Mammal Ecology and Conservation: a handbook of techniques, 2010; contrib. numerous papers to scientific jls. *Recreations:* walking, sailing, photography, Rugby. *Address:* University of St Andrews, College Gate, North Street, St Andrews, Fife KY16 9LB. *T:* (01334) 463230. *E:* ilb@st-andrews.ac.uk; Department for Environment, Food and Rural Affairs, Nobel House, 17 Smith Square, SW1P 3JR. *T:* (020) 7238 1645. *E:* ian.boyd@defra.gsi.co.uk.

BOYD, John; *see* Boyd, D. J.

BOYD, Sir John (Dixon Iklé), KCMG 1992 (CMG 1985); HM Diplomatic Service, retired; Fellow, Churchill College, Cambridge, since 2006 (Master, 1996–2006); Chairman: Trustees, Joseph Needham Research Institute, since 2008 (Trustee, since 2005); Asia House, since 2010 (Member, International Advisory Council, 2001–10); *b* 17 Jan. 1936; *s* of Prof. James Dixon Boyd and late Amélie Lowenthal; *m* 1st, 1968, Gunilla Kristina Ingegerd Rönngren; one *s* one *d*; 2nd, 1977, Julia Daphne Raynsford; three *d*. *Educ:* Westminster Sch. (Hon. Fellow, 2003); Clare Coll., Cambridge (BA; Hon. Fellow, 1994); Yale Univ. (MA). Joined HM Foreign Service, 1962; Hong Kong, 1962–64; Peking, 1965–67; Foreign Office, 1967–69; Washington, 1969–73; 1st Sec., Peking, 1973–75; secondment to HM Treasury, 1976; Counsellor: (Economic), Bonn, 1977–81; (Economic and Soc. Affairs), UK Mission to UN, 1981–84; Asst Under-Sec. of State, FCO, 1984; Political Advr, Hong Kong, 1985–87; Dep. Under-Sec. of State, FCO, 1987–89; Chief Clerk, FCO, 1989–92; Ambassador to Japan, 1992–96. Non-exec. Dir, BNFL, 1997–2000. UK Rep., ASEM Vision Gp, 1998–2000; Mem., All Nippon Airways Adv. Gp, 2003–09. Co-Chm., Nuffield Langs Inquiry, 1998–2000. Syndic, Fitzwilliam Mus., 1997–2002. Advr, Iran Heritage Foundn, 2008–. Trustee: Sir Winston Churchill Archive Trust, 1996–2006; Wordsworth Trust, 1997–2013 (Fellow, 2014–); Margaret Thatcher Archive Trust, 1997–2006; Cambridge Foundn, 1997–2005; GB Sasakawa Foundn, 2001–; RAND Europe (UK), 2001–; Huang Hsing Foundn, 2001–; British Mus., 1996–2006, now Trustee Emeritus (Chm., 2002–06). Gov., RSC, 1996–2005. Member: Council, Cambridge Univ. Senate, 2001–04; Bd, and Advr, E Asia Inst., Cambridge Univ., 1998–2006; Bd, UK-Japan 21st Century Gp, 2006–; Adv. Council, LSO, 2008–. Emeritus Fellow, British Assoc. for Japanese Studies, 2007–. Chairman: Bd of Govs, Bedales Sch., 1996–2001; David Davies Meml Inst., 1997–2001; Trustees, Cambridge Union Soc., 1997–2006. Vice-Chm., Menuhin Competition (formerly Yehudi Menuhin Internat. Violin) Trust Ltd, 1996–. Vice Pres., Lakeland Housing Trust, 2007–. Hon. Fellow, Inst. of Linguistics, 1998–. Fellow, 48 Gp Club, 2008–. Grand Cordon, Order of the Rising Sun (Japan), 2007. *Recreations:* music, fly fishing. *Clubs:* Athenæum, Beefsteak.

See also Sir R. D. H. Boyd.

BOYD, John MacInnes, CBE 1990; QPM 1984; HM Chief Inspector of Constabulary for Scotland, 1993–96; *b* 14 Oct. 1933; *s* of late F. Duncan Boyd and M. Catherine MacInnes; *m* 1957, Sheila MacSporran; two *s*. *Educ:* Oban High School. Paisley Burgh Police, 1956–67; Renfrew and Bute Constabulary, 1967–75; Strathclyde Police, 1975–84 (Asst Chief Constable, 1979–84); Chief Constable, Dumfries and Galloway Constabulary, 1984–89; HM Inspector of Constabulary for Scotland, 1989–93. Pres., Scotland, ACPO, 1988–89. *Address:* Beechwood, Lochwinnoch Road, Kilmacolm PA13 4DZ.

BOYD, Sir (John) Michael, Kt 2012; Artistic Director, Royal Shakespeare Company, 2002–12 (Associate Director, 1996–2002); *b* 6 July 1955; *s* of John Truesdale Boyd and Sheila Boyd; one *s* one *d* by Marcella Evaristi; one *d* by Caroline Hall. *Educ:* Latymer Upper Sch.; Daniel Stewart's Coll.; Univ. of Edinburgh (MA English Lit.). Trainee Dir, Malaya Bronnaya Th., Moscow, 1980; Asst Dir, Belgrade Th., Coventry, 1980–82; Associate Dir, Crucible Th., Sheffield, 1982–84; Founding Artistic Dir, Tron Th., Glasgow, 1985–96. Hon. Prof., Univ. of Michigan, 2001–04. *Productions:* for Tron Theatre: The Guid Sisters, 1989, Tremblay's The Real World, 1991 (also Toronto, NY and Montreal); (with I. Glen) Macbeth, 1993; The Trick is to Keep Breathing (also Royal Court and World Stage Fest., Toronto), 1995; for Royal Shakespeare Co.: The Broken Heart, 1994; The Spanish Tragedy, 1996; Measure for Measure, 1997; Troilus and Cressida (also Tel Aviv and USA), 1999; A Midsummer Night's Dream (also NY), 1999; Romeo and Juliet, 2000; Henry VI, Parts 1, 2 and 3, and Richard III (also USA), 2001; The Tempest, 2002; Hamlet, transf. Albery, 2004; Twelfth Night, transf. Novello, 2005; The Histories, 2006–08, transf. Roundhouse, 2008; As You Like It, 2009, transf. Roundhouse, 2010 (also NY, 2011); The Grain Store, 2009; Antony and Cleopatra, 2010, transf. Roundhouse, 2010, Swan, 2011; Macbeth, 2011; Boris Godunov, 2012; West End: Miss Julie, Haymarket, 2000; other productions: The Big Meal, Ustinov Studio, Bath Th. Royal, 2014. Hon. DLitt Edinburgh, 2009. *Recreations:* cooking, walking, swimming, reading, music. *Address:* c/o Casarotto Ramsay & Associates, Waverley House, 7–12 Noel Street, W1F 8GQ. *T:* (020) 7287 4450.

BOYD, Morgan Alistair, CMG 1990; Adviser, Commonwealth Development Corporation, 1994–2000; *b* 1 May 1934; *s* of Norman Robert Boyd and Kathleen Muriel Boyd; *m* 1959, Judith Mary Martin. *Educ:* Marlborough College; Wadham College, Oxford (BA, MA 1955). FRGS 1957. Commonwealth Development Corporation: Management trainee, 1957; Exec., Malaysia, 1958–66; Manager, East Caribbean Housing, Barbados, 1967–70; Gen. Manager, Tanganyika Develt Finance Co., 1970–74; Advr, Industrial Develt Bank, Kenya, 1975; Regl Controller, Central Africa, 1976–80, East Africa, 1981–82; Dep. Gen. Manager, Investigations, London, 1983–84; Dir of Ops, 1985–89; Dep. Gen. Manager, 1989–91; Dep. Chief Exec., 1991–94. Director: EDESA Management, Switzerland, 1995–97; Laxey (formerly Tea Plantations) Investment Trust PLC, 1998–2009; AMREF UK, 1999–2007 (Chm., 2001–07); Douglas Bay Capital PLC, 2009–12; Chm., Gateway to Growth Ltd, 2005–08. Chm., Southern Africa Business Assoc., 1995–2007. Member: RSA, 1990–; Council, Royal African Soc., 1992– (Vice-Chm., 1996–); Management Council, Africa Centre, 1995–2002; Trustee, African Fellowship Trust, 2009–. *Publications:* Royal Challenge Accepted, 1962; Get Up and Go, 2009. *Recreations:* music, sailing, travel. *Address:* 7 South Hill Mansions, South Hill Park, NW3 2SL. *T:* (020) 7435 1082. *Clubs:* Naval, English-Speaking Union.

BOYD, Norman Jonathan; Member, Antrim South, Northern Ireland Assembly, 1998–2003 (UKU, 1998–99, NIU, 1999–2003); *b* 16 Oct. 1961; *s* of William and Jean Boyd; *m* 1984, Sylvia Christine (*née* Brindley); one *s* one *d*. *Educ:* Belfast High Sch.; Newtownabbey Technical Coll. (BEC Nat. Cert. in Business Studies with Distinction, 1982). Joined Halifax Bldg Soc., later Halifax plc, 1980: posts included Deptl Manager, Asst Branch Manager, and Manager. NIUP Whip, NI Assembly, 1999–2002. Member: Kilroot True Blues Loyal Orange Lodge, 1988–; Kilroot Royal Arch Purple Chapter, 1989–; Royal Black Instn, Carrickfergus, 1993–. Formerly Mem., Boys' Bde (President's Badge, 1979; Queen's Badge, 1980). *Recreations:* sport - soccer, caravanning, theatre, cinema, programme collecting. *Address:* 18

Woodford Park, Newtownabbey, Co. Antrim BT36 6TJ. *T:* (028) 9084 4297, *Fax:* (028) 9083 6644.

BOYD, Sir Robert (David Hugh), Kt 2004; FRCP, FFPH, FRCPCH, FMedSci; Principal, St George's Hospital Medical School, University of London, 1996–2003; Professor of Paediatrics, 1996–2003, Pro-Vice Chancellor (Medicine), 2000–03, and Deputy Vice-Chancellor, 2002–03, University of London; *b* 14 May 1938; *s* of James Dixon Boyd and Amélie Boyd; *m* 1966, Meriel Cornelia Talbot; one *s* two *d*. *Educ:* Leys Sch.; Clare Coll., Cambridge (MA; MB, BChir); University Coll. Hosp., London. FRCP 1977; FFPH (FFPHM 1997); FRCPCH 1997, Hon. FRCPCH 2004. Jun. med. posts, Hosp. for Sick Children, Gt Ormond St, Brompton Hosp., UCH, 1962–65; Sir Stuart Halley Res. Fellow and Sen. Registrar, UC Hosp. and Med. Sch., 1966–71; Goldsmith's MRC Travelling Fellow, Univ. of Colo Med. Center, 1971–72; Sen. Lectr and Hon. Consultant, UCH Med. Sch., 1972–80; Asst Registrar, RCP, 1980–81; University of Manchester Medical School: Prof. of Paediatrics, 1981–96; Dean, 1989–93; Vis. Prof., 1996–; Hon. Consultant: St Mary's Hosp., Manchester and Booth Hall Children's Hosp., Manchester, 1981–96; St George's Healthcare NHS Trust, 1996–2003. Chm., Nat. Primary Care R&D Centre, Manchester, Salford and York Univs, 1994–96. Vis. Prof., Oregon Health Sci. Univ., 1988. Ed., Placenta, 1989–95. Chm., Manchester HA, 1994–96. Member: Standing Med. Adv. Cttee, 1988–92; Standing Cttee on Postgrad. Med. and Dental Educn, 1995–99; Jt Med. Adv. Cttee, HEFCs, 1994–99; Univs UK (formerly CVCP), 1997–2003 (Mem. Health Cttee, 1997–2003); Scientific Adv. Cttee, AMRC, 1996–2003; Council, RVC, 1999–2004; Chm., Council of Heads of UK Med. Schs, 2001–03; Dir, Gtr Manchester Res. Alliance, 2004–08. Chair: Lloyds TSB Foundn for England & Wales, 2003–09; Council for Assisting Refugee Academics, 2004–10. Non-exec. Chm., Nuovoprobe, 2007–. Mem., Taskforce supporting R & D in NHS (Culyer Cttee), 1994. Sec., 1977–80, Chm., 1987–90, Acad. Bd, BPA. Co-opted Gov., Kingston Univ., 1998–2003; Gov., Univ. of Manchester, 2004–09. Pres., 1942 Club, 1998–99. Hon. Mem., Amer. Pediatric Soc., 2006. Founder FMedSci 1998. Hon. DSc: Kingston, 2003; Keele, 2005. *Publications:* (jtly) Paediatric Problems in General Practice, 1982, 3rd edn 1996; contribs to Placental and Fetal Physiol. and Paediatrics. *Recreations:* flute, cooking, reading, holidays. *Address:* The Stone House, Adlington, Macclesfield, Cheshire SK10 4NU. *T:* (01625) 872400.

See also Sir J. D. I. Boyd.

BOYD, Robert Stanley, CB 1982; Solicitor of Inland Revenue, 1979–86; *b* 6 March 1927; *s* of Robert Reginald Boyd (formerly Indian Police) and Agnes Maria Dorothea, *d* of Lt-Col Charles H. Harrison; *m* 1965, Ann, *d* of Daniel Hopkin. *Educ:* Wellington; Trinity Coll., Dublin (BA, LLB). Served RN, 1945–48. Called to Bar, Inner Temple, 1954. Joined Inland Revenue, 1959; Prin. Asst Solicitor, 1971–79. *Address:* Great Beere, North Tawton, Devon EX20 2BS.

BOYD, Stewart Craufurd, CBE 2005; QC 1981; a Recorder, since 1994; *b* 25 Oct. 1943; *s* of late Leslie Balfour Boyd, CBE, and Wendy Marie Boyd; *m* 1970, Catherine Jay; one *s* three *d*. *Educ:* Winchester Coll.; Trinity Coll., Cambridge (MA). Called to the Bar, Middle Temple, 1967, Bencher, 1989. Dep. Chm., FSA, 1999–2005. *Publications:* (ed) Scrutton, Charterparties, 18th edn, 1972 to 21st edn, 2009; (with Sir Michael Mustill) The Law and Practice of Commercial Arbitration, 1982, 1989, 2001; contrib. Civil Justice Rev., Arbitration Internat., Lloyd's Commercial and Maritime Law Qly. *Recreations:* boats, pianos, gardens. *Address:* 1 Gayton Crescent, NW3 1TT. *T:* (020) 7431 1581.

BOYD, William Andrew Murray, CBE 2005; FRSL; author; *b* 7 March 1952; *s* of Dr Alexander Murray Boyd and Evelyn Boyd; *m* 1975, Susan Anne (*née* Wilson). *Educ:* Gordonstoun Sch.; Glasgow Univ. (MA Hons English and Philosophy); Jesus Coll., Oxford (Hon. Fellow, 2007). Lecturer in English, St Hilda's Coll., Oxford, 1980–83; Television Critic, New Statesman, 1981–83. *Screenplays:* Good and Bad at Games (TV), 1983; Dutch Girls (TV), 1985; Scoop (TV), 1987; Stars and Bars, 1988; Aunt Julia and the Scriptwriter, 1990; Mr Johnson, 1990; Chaplin, 1992; A Good Man in Africa, 1994; The Trench, 1999 (also Dir); Sword of Honour (TV), 2001; Armadillo (TV), 2001; Man to Man, 2005; A Waste of Shame (TV), 2005; The Three Kings (TV), 2009; Any Human Heart (TV), 2010; Restless (TV), 2012. *Plays:* Longing, 2013, the Argument, 2015, Hampstead Th. FRSL 1983. Hon. DLitt: St Andrews, 1997; Stirling, 1997; Glasgow, 2000; Dundee, 2008. Officier de l'Ordre des Arts et des Lettres (France), 2005. *Publications:* A Good Man in Africa, 1981 (Whitbread Prize 1981, Somerset Maugham Award 1982); On the Yankee Station (short stories), 1981; An Ice-Cream War, 1982 (John Llewellyn Rhys Prize, 1982); Stars and Bars, 1984; School Ties (screenplays: Good and Bad at Games; Dutch Girls), 1985; The New Confessions, 1987; Brazzaville Beach, 1990 (James Tait Black Meml Prize, 1990; McVitie's Prize, 1991); The Blue Afternoon, 1993 (Sunday Express Book of the Year Award, 1993; LA Times Book Award for Fiction, 1995); The Destiny of Nathalie X (short stories), 1995; Armadillo, 1998; Nat Tate: an American artist, 1998; Any Human Heart, 2002 (Prix Jean Monnet, 2003); Fascination (short stories), 2004; Bamboo, 2005; Restless (Costa Novel Award), 2006; The Dream Lover (short stories), 2008; Ordinary Thunderstorms, 2009; Waiting for Sunrise, 2012; Longing (play), 2013; Solo, 2013; The Vanishing Game (novella), 2014; Sweet Caress, 2015. *Recreation:* strolling. *Address:* c/o The Agency, 24 Pottery Lane, Holland Park, W11 4LZ.

BOYD-CARPENTER, Sir (Marsom) Henry, KCVO 2002 (CVO 1994); Senior Partner, Farrer & Co., Solicitors, 2000–02 (Partner, 1968–2002); Private Solicitor to the Queen, 1995–2002; *b* 11 Oct. 1939; *s* of Francis Henry Boyd-Carpenter and Nina Boyd-Carpenter (*née* Townshend); *m* 1971, Lesley Ann Davies; one *s* one *d*. *Educ:* Charterhouse; Balliol Coll., Oxford (BA 1962; MA 1967). Admitted solicitor, 1966; Solicitor to Duchy of Cornwall, 1976–94; Private Solicitor: to Prince of Wales, 1994–96; to Queen Elizabeth the Queen Mother, Duke of York and Prince Edward, later Earl of Wessex, 1995–2002. Law Society: Mem., 1966–; Hon. Auditor, 1979–81. Member: Council, Prince of Wales's Inst. of Architecture, 1995–99; Bd, British Library, 1999–2007 (Dep. Chm., 2003–07; Mem. Council, Friends, 2005–07). Hon. Steward, Westminster Abbey, 1980–; Hon. Legal Advr, Canterbury Cathedral Trust Fund, 1994–2001. Mem. Governing Body, Charterhouse, 1981–2004 (Chm., 2000–04); Governor: St Mary's Sch., Gerrards Cross, 1967–70; Sutton's Hosp. in Charterhouse, 1994–2005. Member: RHS Governance Wkg Party, 2000–01; Council, Chelsea Physic Garden, 1983–2002; Trustee: Nat. Gardens Scheme, 1998–2003; Merlin Trust, 1998–2003; BL Trust, 2012–; UK Flagship Project, 2012–13. Mem., Bd of Trustees, Inst. of Cancer Res., 2001–07. Pres., Wood Green, The Animals Charity (formerly Wood Green Animal Shelters), 2001–. Ritterkreuz des Herzoglich Sachsen-Coburg und Gotha'schen Hausordens, 2010. *Recreations:* reading, gardening, listening to music, hill-walking. *Address:* Georgian Wing, Williamscot House, Williamscot, Oxon OX17 1AE.

BOYD-CARPENTER, Hon. Sir Thomas (Patrick John), KBE 1993 (MBE 1973); Chairman, Moorfields Eye Hospital NHS Foundation Trust, 2001–08; senior consultant, 1996–2010, and Director, 1997–2010, People in Business; *b* 16 June 1938; *s* of Baron Boyd-Carpenter, PC; *m* 1972, Mary-Jean (*née* Duffield); one *s* two *d*. *Educ:* Stowe. Commnd 1957; served UK, Oman, Malaya, Borneo and Germany; Instr, Staff Coll., 1975–77; Defence Fellowship, Aberdeen Univ., 1977–78; CO 1st Bn Scots Guards, 1979–81; Comdr 24 Inf. Brigade, 1983–84; Dir, Defence Policy, 1985–87; COS, HQ BAOR, 1988–89; ACDS (Programmes), 1989–92; DCDS (Progs and Personnel), 1992–96; retd in rank of Lt-Gen. Chairman: Social Security Adv. Cttee, 1995–2004; Kensington & Chelsea and Westminster HA, 1996–2001; Adv. Bd on Family Law, 1997–2002. *Publications:* Conventional Deterrence: into the 1990s, 1989. *Recreations:* reading, gardening.

See also Baroness Hogg.

BOYD-LEE, Paul Winston Michael; Director, Bible Truth Publishers, since 1974; *b* 3 May 1941; *s* of Harry William Lee and Violet Cynthia (*née* Cabrera); *m* 1962, Jean Warburton; one *s*. *Educ:* Brighton Coll.; Open Univ. (BA); Exeter Univ. (DipTh). Entertainments manager 1963–66; credit controller, 1966–72; farmer, 1973–88; publisher, 1988–. Member: Dir's Bd Church Army, 1999–2012; Church Army Investment Cttee, 2000–. Member: Gen. Synod of C of E, 1991–; Archbp's Council, 2006–; Audit Cttee, C of E, 2006–; Ethical Investment Adv. Gp, C of E, 2006–. *Publications:* Israel and the New Testament, 1981, 2nd edn 1996; Bible Study Guide to the Israel Peoples, 2012; The Significance of Biblical Israel Today, 2013. *Recreations:* fruit culture, canal drawing, travel. *Address:* Manor Barn, Horsington, Som BA8 0ET. *T:* (01963) 371137, 07710 604777. *E:* pbl2@btinternet.com.

BOYDE, Prof. Patrick, PhD; FBA 1987; Serena Professor of Italian, 1981–2002, and Fellow of St John's College, since 1966, University of Cambridge; *b* 30 Nov. 1934; *s* of late Harry Caine Boyde and Florence Colonna Boyde; *m* 1956, Catherine Taylor; four *s*. *Educ:* Braintree County High Sch.; Wanstead County High Sch.; St John's Coll., Cambridge. BA 1956, MA 1960, PhD 1963. Nat. service, commnd RA, 1956–58. Research, St John's Coll., Cambridge 1958–61; Asst Lectr in Italian, Univ. of Leeds, 1961–62; Asst Lectr, later Lectr, Univ. of Cambridge, 1962–81. Corresp. Fellow, Accademia Nazionale dei Lincei, 1986. *Publications:* Dante's Lyric Poetry (with K. Foster), 1967; Dante's Style in his Lyric Poetry, 1971; Dante Philomythes and Philosopher: Man in the Cosmos, 1981; Perception and Passion in Dante's Comedy, 1993; Human Vices and Human Worth in Dante's Comedy, 2000. *Recreations:* staging plays in Ancient Greek, music.

BOYE-ANAWOMAH, Margo Ciara Essi; Her Honour Judge Boye; a Circuit Judge since 2013; *b* Bromsgrove, 10 Nov. 1963; *d* of Michael and Marjorie Boye-Anawomah; *m* 2008, Martin Soorjoo. *Educ:* Ghana Internat. Sch., Ghana; Greycoats, Westminster; South Bank Univ. (LLB Hons); Inns of Court Sch. of Law. Called to the Bar, Inner Temple, 1989; in practice as barrister, 1989–2013; Dep. Dist Judge, Principal Registry of Family Div. 2003–13; a Family Recorder, 2009–13. Member: Bd, CAFCASS, 2003–10; Professional Adv Gp, Nat. Youth Advocacy Service, 2007–; Children's Adv. Panel, BBFC, 2010–. *Recreations:* cinema, theatre, music, travel. *Address:* Central London Family Court, First Avenue House 42–49 High Holborn, WC1V 6NP. *T:* (020) 7421 8594.

BOYER, Prof. Paul Delos, PhD; Professor of Biochemistry, University of California at Los Angeles, 1963–89, now Emeritus; *b* 31 July 1918; *s* of Dell Delos Boyer and Grace Guymon; *m* 1939, Lyda Whicker; one *s* two *d*. *Educ:* Brigham Young Univ.; Univ. of Wisconsin (PhD 1943). Res. Asst, Univ. of Wisconsin, 1939–43; Instructor, Stanford Univ., 1943–45; University of Minnesota: Associate Prof., 1946–53; Prof., 1953–56; Hill Prof. of Biochemistry, 1956–63; Dir, Molecular Biology Inst., 1965–83, Biotechnology Prog. 1985–89, UCLA. Editor, Annual Biochemistry Review, 1964–89. ACS Award, 1955; Tolman Medal, ACS, 1981; Rose Award, Amer. Soc. of Biochemistry and Molecular Biology, 1989; (jtly) Nobel Prize for Chemistry, 1997. *Publications:* (ed jtly) The Enzymes, vol 2, 1970 to vol. 20, 1992; papers on biochem. and molecular biology. *Address:* Molecular Biology Institute, University of California, Los Angeles, Paul Boyer Hall, 611 Charles E Young Drive East, Los Angeles, CA 90095, USA; 1033 Somera Road, Los Angeles, CA 90077–2625, USA.

BOYLAN, Prof. Patrick John, PhD; FMA; FGS; Professor of Heritage Policy and Management, Department of Cultural Policy and Management, City University, 1996–2004 now Emeritus; *b* 17 Aug. 1939; *s* of Francis Boylan and Mary Doreen (*née* Haxby), Hull Yorks; *m* 1st, Ann Elizabeth, *o d* of late Alfred William and Elizabeth Worsfold (marr. diss.) four *s*; 2nd, Pamela Mary, *o d* of late Rev. Robert William Jack and Mary Inder; three *s*. *Educ:* Marist Coll., Hull; Univ. of Hull (BSc 1960; PGCE 1961); Univ. of Leicester (PhD 1985) Museums Diploma (with Distinction), Museums Assoc., 1966. FMA 1972; FGS 1973; FCMI (FBIM 1990; MBIM 1975). Asst Master, Marist Coll., Hull, 1961–63; Keeper of Geology and Natural History, Kingston upon Hull Museums, 1964–68; Dir of Museums and Art Gallery Exeter City Council, 1968–72; Dir of Museums and Art Gall., Leicester City Council 1972–74; Dir of Museums and Arts, Leics County Council, 1974–90; Prof. of Arts Policy Mgt and Hd, Dept of Cultural Policy and Mgt, City Univ., 1990–96. International Council of Museums: Chm., Internat. Cttee for Training of Personnel, 1983–89 and 1998–2004; Chm. UK Nat. Cttee, 1987–93; Mem., Adv. Cttee, 1983–93; Chm., Ethics Cttee, 1984–90; Mem. Exec. Council, 1989–92; Vice-Pres., 1992–98; Chm., Legal Affairs Cttee, 2004–08; Hon Mem., 2004. Councillor, Museums Assoc., 1970–71 and 1986–92 (Centenary Pres. 1988–90); Sec., Soc. of County Museum Dirs, 1974–78; Chm., Library Cttee, Geol Soc. 1984–87. Chm., William Pengelly Cave Studies Trust, 2007–15 (Hon. Pres., 2015–); Pres. Yorks Geol Soc., 2012–14. Consultant: UNESCO; Jt UN/UNESCO World Commn on Culture and Devlt; Council of Europe; World Bank; British Council, etc. Freeman, City of London, 1991; Liveryman, Framework Knitters' Co., 1991–. FCMI (FBIM 1990; MBIM 1975). Advocacy Award, Internat. Inst. of Conservation, 2012. High Order of Merit 'Danica (Croatia) 1997. Ed.-in-Chief, Internat. Jl of Intangible Heritage, 2005–09. *Publications:* Ice Age in Yorkshire and Humberside, 1983; The Changing World of Museums and Art Galleries, 1986; Museums 2000: politics, people, professionals and profit, 1991; Review of Convention on Protection of Cultural Property in the Event of Armed Conflict, 1993 Running a Museum: a practical handbook, 2005 (trans. Arabic, French, Spanish, Russian Chinese, Vietnamese); (with A. V. R. Woollard) Trainer's Manual: for use with Running a Museum: a practical handbook, 2006 (trans. Arabic, French, Spanish, Chinese, Vietnamese) Exchanging Ideas Dispassionately and without Animosity: the Leicester Literary and Philosophical Society 1835–2010, 2010; over 200 papers in learned jls, professional pubns and chapters in books on museums, cultural policy, mgt, prof. training, geology, natural history history of science and history of music. *Recreations:* the arts (especially opera and contemporary arts and crafts), research on history of science and music, Rotary (Pres., Rotary Club of Leicester, 2009–10; Paul Harris Fellow, 2012). *Address:* 2A Compass Road, Leicester LE5 2HF. *T:* (0116) 220 5496. *E:* p.boylan@city.ac.uk.

BOYLE, family name of **Earls of Cork, Glasgow,** and **Shannon**.

BOYLE, Alan Gordon; QC 1991; *b* 31 March 1949; *s* of late Dr Michael Morris Boyle and of Hazel Irene Boyle; *m* 1981, Claudine-Aimée Minne-Vercruysse; two *d*. *Educ:* Royal Shrewsbury Sch.; St Catherine's Coll., Oxford (MA). Called to the Bar, Lincoln's Inn, 1972 Bencher, 2003; Head of Chambers, 2008–. *Recreations:* walking, music. *Address:* Serle Court Chambers, 6 New Square, Lincoln's Inn, WC2A 3QS. *T:* (020) 7242 6105.

See also Sir R. M. Boyle.

BOYLE, (Anthony) Mark; non-executive Chairman: Land Registry, since 2011; The Pensions Regulator, since 2014; *b* Caerleon, 5 July 1960; *s* of Anthony Boyle and Rosemary Boyle; *m* 1990, Laura Peckham; one *s* one *d*. *Educ:* St Joseph's High Sch., Newport Mon; Durham Univ. (BA Hons Econ. Hist. 1981). Lloyds Bank Internat., 1982–86 Kleinwort Benson Ltd, 1986–96; Gp Corporate Develt Dir, Compass Gp plc 1996–2004; Gp Strategy and Develt Dir, Rentokil Initial plc, 2004–08; Chief Operating Officer, Shareholder Exec., BIS, 2008–13. *Recreations:* golf, tennis, classical music. *Address* The Pensions Regulator, Napier House, Trafalgar Place, Brighton BN1 4DW. *E* mark.boyle@thepensionsregulator.gov.uk. *Club:* Royal Mid-Surrey Golf.

BOYLE, Christopher Alexander David; QC 2013; *b* Helensburgh, Scotland, 1970; *s* of Paul Boyle and Helen Boyle (later Jones); *m* 1998, Ilona Scrymsoure, *d* of Robert Steuart Fothringham of Pourie, DL; two *s* one *d*. *Educ:* Sedbergh Sch.; Merton Coll., Oxford (BA Hons Juris.). Called to the Bar, Lincoln's Inn, 1994; in practice as barrister, specialising in town and country planning, envmtl and infrastructure. Dep. Commissary Gen. and Dep. Vicar Gen., Dio. Canterbury, 2012–13. Sec., Planning and Envmtl Bar Assoc., 2006–13. Chm., Georgian Group, 2015–. Mem., Founding Cttee, Compulsory Purchase Assoc., 2005. Trustee: Prince's Foundn for Building Community, 2009–14 (Chm., Adv. Bd, 2014–); Cumbria Building Preservation Trust, 2012–. Mem. Council, 2007–12, Mem., Rural Enterprise Panel, 2009–15, Nat. Trust. *Recreations:* farming, restoring ruins, designing gardens. *Address:* Mallsgate Hall, Roweltown, Carlisle CA6 6LX; Landmark Chambers, 180 Fleet Street, EC4A 2HG. *T:* (020) 7430 1221. *Club:* Oxford and Cambridge.

BOYLE, Rt Rev. Christopher John; Assistant Bishop of Leicester, since 2009; *b* Birmingham, 8 Nov. 1951. *Educ:* King's Coll. London (AKC). Ordained deacon, 1976, priest, 1977; Asst Curate, Emmanuel, Wylde Green, 1976–80; Bishop's Chaplain, Dio. of Birmingham, 1980–83; Rector, St Mary and St Margaret, Castle Bromwich, 1983–2001; Bishop of N Malawi, 2001–09. Area Dean, Coleshill, 1992–99; Priest-in-charge, All Saints, Shard End, 1996–97; Hon. Canon, Birmingham Cathedral, 1996–2001. *Address:* St Martin's House, 7 Peacock Lane, Leicester LE1 5PZ. *T:* (0116) 261 5311.

BOYLE, Danny; director and producer; Artistic Director, Isles of Wonder, opening ceremony of London Olympic Games 2012, 2010–12; *b* Bury, Lancs, 20 Oct. 1956; one *s* two *d.* With Joint Stock Th. Co.; Artistic Dir, Royal Court Th., 1982–87; also dir prodns for RSC; dir, Frankenstein, NT, 2011. *Films* include: director: Shallow Grave, 1994; Trainspotting, 1996; A Life Less Ordinary, 1997; The Beach, 2000; Alien Love Triangle, 2002; 28 Days Later, 2002; Millions, 2005; Sunshine, 2007; Slumdog Millionaire, 2008 (Academy, BAFTA and Golden Globe Awards for Best Dir, 2009); 127 Hours, 2010; Trance, 2013; executive producer: Twin Town, 1996; 28 Weeks Later, 2007; *television* includes: producer, Elephant, 1989; director: Inspector Morse (2 episodes), 1990–92; The Greater Good, 1991; Arise and Go Now, 1991; Not Even God is Wise Enough, 1993; Mr Wroe's Virgins, 1993; Vacuuming Completely Nude in Paradise, 2001; Strumpet, 2001; Babylon, 2014. Beyond Theatre Award, London Evening Standard Theatre Award, 2012. *Address:* c/o Independent Talent Group Ltd, 40 Whitfield Street, W1T 2RH.

BOYLE, Gillian Anne McGregor; *see* Watson, G. A. McG.

BOYLE, James; Founder and Trustee, Edinburgh UNESCO City of Literature, 2004–12 (Chairman, 2004–07); *b* 29 March 1946; *s* of James Boyle and Margaret Halliday Crilly; *m* 1969, Marie Teresa McNamara; three *s. Educ:* Strathclyde Univ. (BA Hons (1st cl.) 1969); Univ. of East Anglia (MA 1971). Adult educn lectr, 1971–75; BBC: Educn Officer, 1975–83; Head of Educnl Broadcasting, then Sec. and Head of Press, Scotland, 1983–93; Hd, BBC Radio Scotland, 1992–96; Chief Advr, Editorial Policy, 1996; Controller, Radio 4, 1996–2001; Chm., Scottish Arts Council, 2001–04. A CS Comr, 2001–04, 2007–08. Non-exec. Dir, Franklin Rae Communications, 2004–. Hon. Lectr, Stirling Univ., 1994. Founder Mem., Glasgow UNESCO City of Music, 2008. Chm., Adv. Cttee, British Council Scotland, 2009–14; Trustee, British Council, 2011–13; Chm., Bd of Trustees, Nat. Library of Scotland, 2012–. Hon. DArts: Napier, 2002; Edinburgh, 2005; Hon. LLD Aberdeen, 2005. *Publications:* extensive writing for newspapers; six TV plays for school children; radio scripts. *Recreations:* collecting modern first editions, World War I memorabilia. *Address:* 69 Morningside Drive, Edinburgh EH10 5NJ. *T:* (0131) 447 2121. *E:* james@theboylefamily.com.

BOYLE, Mark; *see* Boyle, A. M.

BOYLE, Michael David; Director of Strategy, National Probation Directorate, Home Office, 2002–04; *b* 23 Jan. 1954; *s* of Robert Brian Boyle and Kathleen Boyle; *m* 1977, Clare Gillard. *Educ:* Regent House Grammar Sch., Newtownards, Co. Down; Univ. of St Andrews (MA 1976). Home Office, 1976–2004: Private Sec. to Parly Under-Sec. of State, 1980–81; Prison Dept, 1981–85; Immigration and Nationality Dept, 1985–89; Criminal Policy Dept, 1989–90; Grade 5, Police Dept, 1990–93; Estabt Dept, 1993–96; Criminal Dept, 1996–2001; Actg Dir, Community Policy, 2001; Dir, Criminal Law and Policy, 2001–02. *Recreations:* dog-walking, foreign travel, Crystal Palace Football Club. *Address:* 4 Drydales, Kirk Ella, Hull, E Yorks HU10 7JU.

BOYLE, Prof. Nicholas, LittD; FBA 2001; Schröder Professor of German, University of Cambridge, 2006–13, now Emeritus (Director of Research, 2013); Fellow of Magdalene College, Cambridge, since 1968 (President, 2006–11); *b* 18 June 1946; *e s* of late Hugh Boyle and Margaret Mary Faith (*née* Hopkins, then Mrs R. G. Boothroyd); *m* 1983, Rosemary Angela Devlin; one *s* three *d. Educ:* King's Sch., Worcester; Magdalene Coll., Cambridge (schol.; BA 1967; MA; PhD 1976; LittD 2004). University of Cambridge: Res. Fellow in German, Magdalene Coll., 1968–72; Lectr in German, Magdalene and Girton Colls, 1972–74; Univ. Asst Lectr in German, 1974–79; Lectr, 1979–93; Reader, 1993–2000; Hd of Dept, 1996–2001; Prof. of German Literary and Intellectual History, 2000–06; Sec., Faculty Bd of Mod. and Medieval Langs, 1982–85; Tutor, Magdalene Coll., 1984–93. Scholar, Alexander von Humboldt Foundn, 1978, 1980–81; British Acad. Res. Reader in Humanities, 1990–92; Res. Fellow, John Rylands Res. Inst., Univ. of Manchester, 1993; Fellow, Wissenschaftskolleg, Berlin, 1994–95; Erasmus Lectr, Univ. of Notre Dame, 2002–03. Corresp. Fellow, Göttingen Acad. of Scis, 2010. Hon. DHL Georgetown, 2004. W. Heinemann Prize, RSL, 1992; J. G. Robertson Meml Prize, Univ. of London, 1994; Goethe Medal, 2000; Annibel Jenkins Prize, Amer. Soc. for Eighteenth Century Studies, 2002; Friedrich Gundolf Prize, Deutsche Akademie für Sprache und Dichtung, 2009. *Publications:* (ed with M. Swales) Realism in European Literature: essays in honour of J. P. Stern, 1986; Goethe: Faust, Part One, 1987; Goethe: the poet and the age, Vol. 1, 1991 (trans. German 1995), Vol. 2, 2000 (trans. German, 1999); Who Are We Now?: Christian humanism and the global market from Hegel to Heaney, 1998; (ed) Goethe: selected works, 1999; (ed with J. Guthrie) Goethe and the English-Speaking World, 2002; Sacred and Secular Scriptures: a Catholic approach to literature, 2004; German Literature: a very short introduction, 2008, enlarged German edn 2009; 2014: how to survive the next world crisis, 2010; (Gen. Ed.) The Impact of Idealism: the legacy of post-Kantian German thought (4 vols), 2013; articles in The Tablet, New Blackfriars, German Life and Letters, French Studies, etc. *Recreation:* enjoying other people's gardens. *Address:* Magdalene College, Cambridge CB3 0AG. *T:* (01223) 332137; 20 Alpha Road, Cambridge CB4 3DG. *T:* (01223) 364310.

BOYLE, Prof. Paul, PhD; FBA 2013; FRSE; President and Vice-Chancellor, University of Leicester, since 2014; *b* Felixstowe, Suffolk, 16 Nov. 1964. *Educ:* Deben High Sch., Felixstowe; Lancaster Univ. (BA Hons Geog. 1986; PhD 1991); Univ. of Colorado, Boulder. Lecturer: Univ. of Wales, Swansea, 1991–95; Univ. of Leeds, 1995–99; Prof. of Human Geog., 1999–2014, and Hd, Sch. of Geog. and Geosciences, 2007–10, Univ. of St Andrews; Chief Exec., ESRC, 2010–14. Hon. Prof., Univ. of Dundee, 2003–. Founding Dir, Social Dimensions of Health Inst., 2003–07. Dep. Dir, Census Interaction Data Service, 2001–05; Dir, ESRC Longitudinal Studies Centre, Scotland, 2001–10; Co-Dir, ESRC Centre for Population Change, 2009–10; Co-Investigator: Wellcome Trust Scottish Health Informatics Prog., 2008–10; ESRC Admin. Data Liaison Service. Pres., Science Europe, 2011–14. Pres., British Soc. for Population Studies, 2007–09 (Vice-Pres., 2005–07). FRSE 2006. *Publications:* contribs to learned jls. *Address:* University of Leicester, University Road, Leicester LE1 7RH.

BOYLE, Paul Vincent, OBE 2010; CA; Chief Audit Officer, Aviva plc, since 2010; *b* Glasgow, 27 July 1959; *s* of Gerrard Boyle and Joan Boyle (*née* O'Donnell); *m* 1991, Claire Andrews; two *d* and one step *s. Educ:* Univ. of Glasgow (BAcc 1st Cl. Hons 1980). CA 1983. Coopers & Lybrand, 1980–88; Gp Financial Controller, W H Smith Gp plc, 1988–90; posts with Cadbury Schweppes plc, 1991–98; Chief Operating Officer, FSA, 1998–2004; Chief Exec., Financial Reporting Council, 2004–09. Non-exec. Dir, Plus500 Ltd, 2015–. Hon. Prof., Accounting and Finance, Univ. of Glasgow, 2010–. *Recreations:* golf, tennis. *Clubs:* Caledonian; Denham Golf.

BOYLE, Dr Peter, PhD, DSc; FRCPSGlas, FFPH, FRCPE, FMedSci; FRSE; President, International Prevention Research Institute, since 2009; Director, University of Strathclyde Institute for Global Public Health at International Prevention Research Institute, since 2013; President, World Prevention Alliance, since 2011; *b* 8 June 1951; *s* of Simon and Brigid Boyle; *m* 1976, Helena Mary McNicol; three *d. Educ:* Glasgow Univ. (BSc 1974; PhD 1985, DSc (Med) 2006). FRCPSGlas 2003; FFPH 2004; FRCPE 2006. Res. Asst, Dept of Medicine, Univ. of Glasgow, 1974–77; Sen. Statistician, W Scotland Cancer Surveillance Unit, Glasgow, 1977–84; Instructor and Asst Prof., Depts of Biostats and Epidemiol., Harvard Sch. of Public Health, 1984–86; Sen. Scientist, Internat. Agency for Res. on Cancer, Lyon, 1986–91; Dir, Div. of Epidemiol. and Biostats, Eur. Inst. Oncology, Milan, 1991–2004; Dir, Internat. Agency for Res. on Cancer, WHO, 2004–09. Hon. Professor: of Cancer Epidemiol., Birmingham Univ., 1996–; of Cancer Prevention and Control, Oxford Univ., 2003–; Dundee Univ., 2009–; Vis. Prof., Glasgow Univ., 2000–; Adjunct Prof., Yale Univ., New Haven, 2010–. Mem., Eur. Acad. of Cancer Sci., 2010. MAE 2013. Hon. Mem., Hungarian Acad. of Sci., 2010. FRSE 2000; FMedSci 2006. Hon. DSc Aberdeen, 2006; Hon. LLD Dundee, 2012. Kt's Cross, Order of Merit (Poland), 2000. *Publications: jointly:* Cancer Incidence in Scotland: atlas and epidemiological perspective, 1985; Textbooks for General Practitioners, II: Breast Cancer, 1990; Cancer Mortality Atlas in Central Europe, 1996; Nutrition and Cancer, 1996; Tobacco: science, policy and public health, 2004, 2nd edn 2010; *edited jointly:* Cancer Mapping, 1989; Cancer Epidemiology: vital statistics through prevention, 1990; Cancer Mortality Atlas of EEC, 1993; Statistical Methods in Cancer Research, 1996; Textbook of Benign Prostatic Hyperplasia, 1996 (Ipertrofia Prostatica Benigna, vol. I–II, 1997); Monographs in Oncology, vol. I, Colorectal Cancer, 2000; Cancer Incidence in Five Continents, 2008; World Cancer Report 2008, 2008; Cancer Mortality Atlas of Europe, 1993–98, 2009; Textbook of Epidemiology and Biostatistics, 2011; World Breast Cancer Report, 2013; Alcohol: science, policy and public health, 2013; State of Oncology 2013, 2013; contribs to scientific jls. *Recreations:* family, music, football. *Address:* International Prevention Research Institute, 95 cours Lafayette, 69006 Lyon, France. *T:* (4) 72171180. *E:* peter.boyle@i-pri.org. *Clubs:* Celtic (Glasgow); LYINC (Lyon).

BOYLE, Dr Philip David; HM Diplomatic Service; Deputy Head, Intelligence Policy Department, since 2014; *b* Birkenhead, 7 May 1976; *s* of David and Valerie Boyle. *Educ:* Whitby High Sch., Ellesmere Port; Univ. of Manchester Inst. of Sci. and Technol. (BSc 1st Cl. Hons Chem. 1997; PhD Inorganic Chem. 2000). Postdoctoral researcher, Inorganic Chem. Lab., Univ. of Oxford, 2001–02; entered FCO, 2002; Desk Officer for Falkland Is, FCO, 2002–03; Arabic trng, FCO, 2004–05; Second Sec. (Pol), Sana'a, 2005–08; Consul Gen., Lille, 2008–11; First Sec. (Pol), Islamabad, 2011–12; Ambassador to Mali and (non-resident) to Niger, 2012–14. *Publications:* contrib. papers to peer-reviewed chem. jls. *Recreations:* Land Rovers, hiking, photography, Mölkky. *Address:* c/o Foreign and Commonwealth Office, King Charles Street, SW1A 2AH. *E:* philip.boyle@fco.gov.uk.

BOYLE, Sir Roger (Michael), Kt 2011; CBE 2004; FRCP, FRCPE, FESC, FACC; Consultant Cardiologist, York District Hospital, 1983–2011; National Director for Heart Disease, 2000–11, and for Stroke, 2006–11; *b* 27 Jan. 1948; *s* of late Dr Michael Maurice Boyle and of Hazel Irene Boyle; *m* 1975, Susan Scutt (marr. diss.); three *s*; *m* 2002, Margo Bispham Cox; one *d. Educ:* Shrewsbury Sch.; London Hosp. Med. Sch., London Univ. (MB BS 1972). House physician and surgeon, then SHO, London Hosp., 1972–75; Registrar, Chelmsford Hosp., 1975–78; Res. Fellow, Wythenshawe Hosp., Manchester, 1978–80; Lectr in Cardiovascular Studies, Univ. of Leeds, 1980–83. Co-Dir, Nat. Centre for Cardiovascular Prevention and Outcomes, UCL, 2011–13. Hon. Prof., Dept of Surgery, UCH, 2005–08; Hon. Prof. of Cardiol., UCL, 2007. Hon. Consultant Cardiologist, St Mary's Hosp., London, 2004–07. FRSA. Hon. FFPH. *Publications:* contribs to cardiovascular jls on coronary heart disease and trng in cardiology. *Recreations:* sailing, playing the piano, walking. *Address:* Lanhoose Barn, Portscatho, Truro TR2 5EP. *Clubs:* Percuil Sailing, St Mawes Sailing.
See also A. G. Boyle.

BOYLE, Sir Simon Hugh Patrick, KCVO 2015; Lord-Lieutenant for Gwent, since 2001; *b* 22 March 1941; *s* of late Lt Col P. J. S. Boyle (killed in action 1944) and Mary Elizabeth Boyle (later Mrs Charles Floyd); *m* 1970, Catriona Gordon; four *d. Educ:* Eton Coll. Industrial career with: Stewarts & Lloyds, Australia and UK, 1959–65; Avon Rubber Co. Ltd, 1966–69; British Steel, 1970–2001. Chm., Gwent Criminal Justice Bd, 2003–05. Chm., Monmouth Diocesan Parsonage Bd, 1997–2008; Vice Chm., Monmouth Diocesan Bd of Finance, 2001–12. Vice Chm. of Trustees, St David's Hospice, 1999–. DL 1997, JP 2002, Gwent. CStJ 2002. *Recreations:* gardening, sailing. *Address:* Penpergwm Lodge, Abergavenny, Gwent NP7 9AS. *T:* (01873) 840208. *E:* boyle@penpergwm.co.uk.

BOYLE, Sir Stephen Gurney, 5th Bt *cr* 1904; *b* 15 Jan. 1962; *s* of Sir Richard Gurney Boyle, 4th Bt, and of Elizabeth Ann, *yr d* of Norman Dennes; *S* father, 1983. Chm., Co-operative property services. *Recreations:* play, make, fix, and set up guitars, singing, playing piano and synthesizers, making/listening to music, watching cricket and football, cooking, reading, writing (lyrics mainly). *Heir: b* Michael Desmond Boyle, *b* 16 Sept. 1963. *Address:* 38 Partridge Court, Barn Mead, Harlow, Essex CM18 6SH.

BOYLING, Very Rev. Mark Christopher; Dean of Carlisle, since 2004; *b* 14 Oct. 1952; *s* of Denis and Margaret Boyling; *m* 1991, Helen Mary (*née* Enoch); one *s* one *d. Educ:* Keble Coll., Oxford (BA (Modern Hist.) 1974, BA (Theol.) 1976; MA 1978); Cuddesdon Theol Coll. Ordained deacon, 1977, priest, 1978; Asst Curate, Kirkby, 1977–79; Priest i/c, 1979–80, Team Vicar, 1980–85, St Mark, Kirkby; Chaplain to Bp of Liverpool, 1985–89; Vicar, St Peter, Formby, 1989–94; Canon Residentiary, Liverpool Cathedral, 1994–2004. *Recreations:* travel, cooking. *Address:* The Deanery, Carlisle CA3 8TZ. *T:* (01228) 523335, *Fax:* (01228) 547049. *E:* dean@carlislecathedral.org.uk.

BOYNE, 11th Viscount *cr* 1717 (Ire.); **Gustavus Michael Stucley Hamilton-Russell;** DL; Baron Hamilton 1715; Baron Brancepeth (UK) 1866; *b* 27 May 1965; *o s* of 10th Viscount Boyne and of Rosemary Anne, *d* of Sir Dennis Stucley, 5th Bt; *S* father, 1995; *m* 1st, 1991, Lucy (marr. diss. 2012), *d* of George Potter; three *s* one *d* (incl. twin *s*); 2nd, 2013, Julia Howard, *d* of Sir John Philip Howard-Lawson, Bt, *qv. Educ:* Harrow; RAC Cirencester. Dip. Rural Estate Management; MRICS (ARICS 1991). Chartered Surveyor with Carter Jonas. DL Shropshire, 2009. *Recreations:* country sports, tennis, ski-ing. *Heir: s* Hon. Gustavus Archie Edward Hamilton-Russell, *b* 30 June 1999. *Address:* Burwarton House, Bridgnorth, Shropshire WV16 6QH. *T:* (01746) 787221. *Club:* Turf.

BOYNE, Maj.-Gen. John, CB 1987; MBE 1965; CEng, FIMechE; company director, since 1988; *b* 7 Nov. 1932; *s* of John Grant Boyne and Agnes Crawford (*née* Forrester); *m* 1956, Norma Beech (*d* 2002); two *s. Educ:* King's Sch., Chester; Royal Military Coll. of Science, Shrivenham (BScEng 1st Cl. Hons). CEng, FIMechE 1975. Served in Egypt, Cyprus, Libya and UK, 1951–62; Staff Coll., Camberley, 1963; DAQMG(Ops) HQ MEC, Aden, 1964–66; OC 11 Infantry Workshop, REME, BAOR, 1966–67; Jt Services Staff Coll., 1968; GSO2 MoD, 1968–70; GSO1 (DS), Staff Coll., 1970–72; Comdr REME, 2nd Div., BAOR, 1972–73; AAG MoD, 1973–75; CSO (Personnel) to CPL, MoD, 1975–76; Dep. Dir Elec. and Mech. Engrg, 1st British Corps, 1976–78; RCDS, 1979; Dep. Dir Personal Services (Army), MoD, 1980–82; Vice Adjutant Gen. and Dir of Manning (Army), MoD, 1982–85; Dir Gen., Electrical and Mechanical Engrg, Logistic Executive (Army), MoD, 1985–88. Col

Comdt, REME, 1988–93 (Rep. Col Comdt, 1989–90). Trustee, Army Benevolent Fund, 1986–2005. Vice Pres., Army Football Assoc., 1988–. FCMI (FBIM 1975). *Recreations:* music, philately, football. *Address:* c/o HSBC, 48 High Street, Runcorn, Cheshire WA7 1AN.

BOYS, Rt Hon. Sir Michael H.; *see* Hardie Boys.

BOYS, Penelope Ann, (Mrs D. C. H. Wright), CB 2005; Member: Water Services Regulation Authority, 2006–14; Membership Selection Panel, Network Rail, since 2011; Consumers' Committee, National House Builders Council, since 2013; *b* 11 June 1947; *d* of late Hubert John Boys and Mollie Blackman Boys; *m* 1977, David Charles Henshaw Wright. *Educ:* Guildford County Sch. for Girls. Exec. Officer, DES, 1966–69; Asst Principal, Min. of Power, 1969–72; Private Sec., Minister without Portfolio, 1972–73; Principal, Dept of Energy, 1973–78; seconded to BNOC, 1978–80; Head of Internat. Unit, Dept of Energy, 1981–85; seconded to HM Treasury as Head, ST2 Div., 1985–87; Dir of Personnel, Dept of Energy, 1987–89; Dep. Dir Gen., Office of Electricity Regulation, 1989–93; Head of Personnel, DTI, 1993–96; Sec., Monopolies and Mergers, later Competition, Commn, 1996–2000 (Mem. Council, 2012–14); Dep. Dir Gen., 2000–03, Exec. Dir, 2003–05, OFT. Mem., 2006–08, Dep. Chm., 2008–11, Horserace Betting Levy Bd. *Recreations:* entertaining, racing, music.

BOYS-GREENE, Jenny; *see* Greene, J.

BOYS SMITH, Stephen Wynn, CB 2001; Joint Secretary, Independent Monitoring Commission, Northern Ireland, 2004–11; *b* 4 May 1946; *s* of late Rev. Dr John Sandwith Boys Smith and Gwendolen Sara Boys Smith (*née* Wynn); *m* 1971, Linda Elaine Price; one *s* one *d*. *Educ:* Sherborne Sch.; St John's Coll., Cambridge (MA); Univ. of British Columbia (MA). Home Office, 1968; Asst Private Sec. to Home Sec., 1971–73; Central Policy Review Staff, Cabinet Office, 1977; Home Office, 1979; Private Sec. to Home Sec., 1980–81; NI Office, 1981; Principal Private Sec. to Sec. of State for NI, 1981–82; Home Office, 1984; Principal Private Sec. to Home Sec., 1985–87; Asst Under Sec. of State, Ho me Office, 1989–92; Under Sec., HM Treasury, 1992–95; Home Office: Dep. Sec. and Head of Police Dept, 1995–96; Dir, Police Policy, 1996–98; Dir-Gen., Immigration and Nationality Directorate, 1998–2002; Dir-Gen., Organised Crime, Drugs and Internat. Gp, 2002–03. Mem., Civil Service Appeal Bd, 2004–12. Associate Consultant, Public Admin Internat., 2009–12. *Recreations:* gardening, reading, history of the Levant. *Address:* 23 Church Street, Ampthill, Beds MK45 2PL. *T:* (01525) 403800. *E:* boyssmith@ntlworld.com.

BRABAZON, family name of **Earl of Meath**.

BRABAZON OF TARA, 3rd Baron *cr* 1942; **Ivon Anthony Moore-Brabazon;** PC 2013; DL; *b* 20 Dec. 1946; *s* of 2nd Baron Brabazon of Tara, CBE, and Henriette Mary (*d* 1985), *d* of late Sir Rowland Clegg; *S* father, 1974; *m* 1979, Harriet Frances, *o d* of Mervyn P. de Courcy Hamilton, Salisbury, Zimbabwe; one *s* one *d*. *Educ:* Harrow. Mem., Stock Exchange, 1972–84. A Lord in Waiting (Govt Whip), 1984–86; Parly Under-Sec. of State, Dept of Transport, 1986–89; Minister of State: FCO, 1989–90; Dept of Transport, 1990–92; Opposition spokesman on Transport, H of L, 1998–2001; elected Mem., H of L, 1999; Principal Dep. Chm. of Cttees, 2001–02, Chm. of Cttees, 2002–12, H of L; Chm., EU Select Cttee, H of L, 2001–02. Mem., RAC Public Policy Cttee, 1992–99. Dep. Chm., Foundn for Sport and the Arts, 1992–. President: UK Warehousing Assoc., 1992–; British Internat. Freight Assoc., 1997–99; Inst. of the Motor Industry, 1998–2004. DL Isle of Wight, 1993. *Recreations:* golf, sailing, Cresta Run. *Heir: s* Hon. Benjamin Ralph Moore-Brabazon [*b* 15 March 1983; *m* 2011, Molly Claire Parish; one *s*]. *Address:* House of Lords, SW1A 0PW. *Clubs:* Royal Yacht Squadron; Bembridge Sailing, St Moritz Tobogganing.

BRABBINS, Martyn Charles; freelance orchestral and opera conductor; Chief Conductor, Nagoya Philharmonic Orchestra, since 2013; Principal Guest Conductor, Royal Flemish Philharmonic Orchestra, since 2009; *b* 13 Aug. 1959; *s* of Herbert Henry Brabbins and Enid Caroline Brabbins; *m* 1985, Karen Maria Evans; two *s* one *d*. *Educ:* Goldsmiths' Coll., Univ. of London (BMus, MMus; Hon. Fellow, 2004); Leningrad State Conservatoire. Professional début with Scottish Chamber Orch., 1988; Associate Conductor, 1992–94, Associate Prin. Conductor, 1994–2005, BBC Scottish SO; Principal Conductor, Sinfonia 21, 1994–2001; Conducting Consultant, RSAMD, 1996–2002; Huddersfield Choral Society: Principal Conductor, 1998–2006; Conductor Laureate, 2006–13; Music Dir, 2013–; Artistic Dir, Cheltenham Fest., 2005–07; has conducted most major British orchestras, and orchestras abroad, incl. Lahti SO, Tapiola Sinfonietta, St Petersburg Philharmonic, Bergen Philharmonic, Ensemble Intercontemporain, Amsterdam Concertgebouw; Tokyo Metropolitan SO, Deutsches SO Berlin, Adelaide SO; also conducted: Don Giovanni, Kirov Opera, 1988; Magic Flute, ENO, 1995; Montpellier Opera, 1999; Netherlands Opera, 2001; Deutsche Oper, 2001; Frankfurt Opera, 2003, 2007, 2011; Hamburg State Opera, 2006; The Pilgrim's Progress, ENO, 2012; Bavarian State Opera, 2013. Founding Dir, Orkney Conducting Course, 2002–. Has made over 100 recordings. Hon. DMus Bristol, 2013. Winner, Leeds Conductors Competition, 1988. *Recreation:* family. *Address:* c/o Intermusica, Crystal Wharf, 36 Graham Street, N1 8GJ. *T:* (020) 7608 9900.

BRABEN, David John, OBE 2014; Founder and Chief Executive Officer, Frontier Developments plc, since 2013 (Founder and Chairman, Frontier Developments Ltd, 1994–2013); *b* 2 Jan. 1964; *s* of Prof. Don Braben and Shirley Braben; *m* 1st, 1993, Kathy Dickinson (marr. diss. 1996); 2nd, 2014, Wendy Irvin. *Educ:* Stockton Heath Primary Sch.; Royal Kent Primary Sch.; Buckhurst Hill Co. High Sch.; Jesus Coll., Cambridge (BA 1985; MA Hons Electrical Scis; Dip. Computer Sci.). FIET 2012; FREng 2012. Freelance software designer and writer, 1982–94; Elite, Zarch, Virus, Frontier. Non-exec. Dir, Phonetic Arts Ltd, 2008–10. Chm., Skillset Univ. Accreditation Panel, 2009–14; Mem. Bd, BAFTA Games Cttee, 2009–13. Mem., Cambridge Angels, 2006–. Founder Trustee and Mem. Bd, Raspberry Pi, 2008–. Hon. DTech Abertay, 2013; Hon. PhD Open, 2014. *Recreations:* sailing, movies, board games, computer games, the family, I loved walking my dog before she died. *Address:* c/o Frontier Developments plc, 306 Science Park, Milton Road, Cambridge CB4 0WG. *T:* (01223) 394300. *E:* dbraben@frontier.co.uk.

BRABOURNE, 8th Baron *cr* 1880; **Norton Louis Philip Knatchbull;** Bt 1641; *b* 8 Oct. 1947; *s* of 7th Baron Brabourne, CBE and of Countess Mountbatten of Burma, *qv*; *S* father, 2005; *m* 1979, Penelope M. M. Eastwood; one *s* one *d* (and one *d* decd). *Educ:* Dragon School, Oxford; Gordonstoun; University of Kent (BA Politics). *Heir: s* Hon. Nicholas Louis Charles Norton Knatchbull, *b* 15 May 1981. *Address:* Broadlands, Romsey, Hants SO51 9ZD.

BRACADALE, Rt Hon. Lord; Alastair Peter Campbell; PC 2013; a Senator of the College of Justice in Scotland, since 2003; *b* 18 Sept. 1949; *s* of Rev. Donald Campbell and Margaret Campbell (*née* Montgomery); *m* 1973, Flora Beaton; one *s* two *d*. *Educ:* George Watson's Coll.; Aberdeen Univ. (MA); Strathclyde Univ. (LLB). Teacher of English, 1973–75; Solicitor, Procurator Fiscal Service, 1979–84; Advocate, 1985; Advocate Depute, 1990–93; called to the Bar, Inner Temple, 1990; QC (Scot.) 1995; Standing Jun. Counsel in Scotland to HM Customs and Excise, 1995; Home Advocate Depute, 1997–98; Crown Counsel, Scottish Court in the Netherlands, 2000–02. Member: Criminal Justice Forum, 1996–97; Scottish Criminal Rules Council, 1996–98; Criminal Injuries Compensation Bd, 1997. Hon. LLD: Strathclyde, 2005; Aberdeen, 2012. *Recreations:* walking, sailing, golf. *Address:* Cerna, 69 Dirleton Avenue, North Berwick EH39 4QL. *T:* (01620) 894288; Court of Session, Parliament House, Edinburgh EH1 1RQ.

BRACE, Christopher James; Chief Executive, Magistrates' Association, since 2012; *b* Wimbledon, 21 Dec. 1975; *s* of Paul Spencer Brace and Lisa Anne Brace (*née* Corteen); *m* 2004, Jennifer Elinor Walters; three *d*. *Educ:* King's Coll., Sch., Wimbledon; Univ. of York (MSc Hons Psychol.); Goldsmith's Coll., Univ. of London (MA Hons Contemp. British Politics). Policy and Communications Manager, Centre for Econ. and Social Inclusion, 2002–05; Campaigns Dir, RADAR, 2005–08; Chief Exec., Peter Bedford Housing Assoc., 2008–11. *Publications:* (jtly) Counselling in Schools, 2002; (ed with W. Somerville) Welfare to Work Handbook, 2004. *Recreations:* current affairs, reading, family. *Address:* Magistrates' Association, 28 Fitzroy Square, W1T 6DD. *T:* (020) 7387 2353. *E:* chris.brace@magistrates-association.org.uk.

BRACE, Gary; Chief Executive, General Teaching Council for Wales, 2000–14; *b* Cardiff, 4 Feb. 1954; *s* of Eric and Irene Brace; *m* 2003, Dawn Morley; two *s* one *d*. *Educ:* Canton High Sch.; University Coll., Cardiff (BA Hons Hist. 1975; PGCE 1976). Teacher: Lady Mary High Sch., Cardiff, 1976–87; St David's Sixth Form Coll., Cardiff, 1987–91; Curriculum Field Officer, Curriculum Council for Wales, 1991–94; Hist. Subject Officer, Curriculum and Assessment Authy for Wales, 1994–97; Asst Chief Exec., Qualifications, Curriculum and Assessment Authy for Wales, 1997–2000. Mem. Bd, UK Nat. Commn for UNESCO, 2011– (Vice Chm., 2013–). Gov., Herbert Thompson Primary Sch., 2009– (Vice Chm., 2014–). Writer: BBC and Channel 4 Teachers' Guides; Official Guidance for National Curriculum and Assessment. Trustee, Cynnal Cymru-Sustain Wales, 2014–. FRSA. Chancellor's Medal, Univ. of Glamorgan. *Recreations:* rowing (Pres., Llandaff Rowing Club), travel, music, general aviation flying.

BRACE, Michael Thomas, CBE 2009 (OBE 2005); Chief Executive: VISION 2020 UK, 2001–12; OPSIS, 2002–09; Chairman, British Paralympic Association, 2001–08; *b* 19 June 1950; *s* of Thomas Brace and Rosina Brace (now Taylor); *m* 1972, Maureen Browne. *Educ:* Poly. of North London (DipSW 1976); CETSW (CQSW 1976); Inst. of Management (DipMgt 1996). Tower Hamlets BC, 1976–81; Hackney BC, 1981–83; Area Manager, Islington BC, 1983–89; Service Manager, RBK&C, 1989–2001. Non-exec. Dir, Nemisys, 2008–. Mem. Bd, London 2012, 2003–08; Dir, UK Anti Doping, 2009–; Chm., City of London Sport and Physical Activity Network, 2010–12. Trustee: Primary Club, 1998–; British Judo Council Foundn, 2010–. Gov., UEL, 2006–. Hon. FCOptom 2005; Hon. FRCOphth 2011. Hon. DPhil London Metropolitan, 2009; Hon. DBA Anglia Ruskin, 2011. *Publications:* Where There's a Will, 1980. *Recreations:* playing cricket, after dinner speaking, ski-ing, reading, music, keep fit (gym), assistive technology. *Address:* 80 Elms Farm Road, Hornchurch, Essex RM12 5RD. *T:* (01708) 456832. *E:* mike@mikebrace.co.uk.

BRACEGIRDLE, Dr Brian, FSA, FRPS, FRSB; Research Consultant in microscopy, and Fellow, Science Museum, 1990–2005; *b* 31 May 1933; *oc* of Alfred Bracegirdle; *m* 1st, 1958, Margaret Lucy Merrett (marr. diss. 1974); one *d*; 2nd, 1975, Patricia Helen Miles; no *c*. *Educ:* King's Sch., Macclesfield; Univ. of London (BSc); PhD 1975 (UCL). DipRMS 1975. FRPS 1969; FBIPP (FIIP 1970); FRSB (FIBiol 1976); FSA 1981. Technician in industry, 1950–57; Biology Master, Erith Grammar Sch., 1958–61; Sen. Lectr in Biol., S Katharine's Coll., London, 1961–64; Head, Depts of Nat. Science and Learning Resources, Coll. of All Saints, London, 1964–77; Science Museum: Keeper, Wellcome Mus. of Hist. of Medicine, 1977; Head of Dept of Med. Scis, and Head of Collections Management Div., 1987–89; Asst Dir, 1987–89. Hon. Lectr in History of Medicine, UCL, 1978–90; Hon. Res. Fellow in Hist. of Sci., Imperial Coll., 1990–93. Hon. Treasurer, ICOM (UK), 1978–89. Chm., Inst. of Medical and Biological Illustration, 1973–74; President: Assoc. Européenne de Musées de l'Histoire des Sciences Médicales, 1983–90; Quekett Microscopical Club, 1985–88; Vice-Pres., Royal Microscopical Soc., 1988–90. Ed., Quekett Jl of Microscopy, 1998–2012. *Publications:* Photography for Books and Reports, 1970; The Archaeology of the Industrial Revolution, 1973; The Evolution of Microtechnique, 1978, 1987; (ed) Beads of Glass: Leeuwenhoek and the early microscope, 1984; Scientific Photomacrography, 1995; Notes on Modern Microscope Manufacturers, 1996; Microscopical Mounts and Mounters, 1998; A Catalogue of the Microscopy Collections at the Science Museum, 2005; A History of Photography with the Light Microscope, 2010; The Quekett Microscopical Club 1865–2015, 2016; (with W. H. Freeman): An Atlas of Embryology, 1963, 1978; An Atlas of Histology, 1966; An Atlas of Invertebrate Structure, 1971; An Advanced Atlas of Histology, 1976; (with P. H. Miles): An Atlas of Plant Structure, vol. I, 1971; An Atlas of Plant Structure, Vol. II, 1973; Thomas Telford, 1973; The Darbys and the Ironbridge Gorge, 1974; An Atlas of Chordate Structure, 1977; (with J. B. McCormick) The Microscopic Photographs of J. B. Dancer, 1993; (with S. Bradbury): Modern Photomicrography, 1995; Introduction to Light Microscopy, 1998; papers on photography for life sciences, on scientific topics, and on history of science/medicine. *Recreations:* walking, music, travel, shouting at the television set. *Address:* 22 Montpellier Spa Road, Cheltenham, Glos GL50 1UL. *T:* (01242) 517478.

BRACEWELL, Julia Helen, OBE 1999; Director, British Fencing, 2012–13; *b* 26 April 1964; *d* of Herbert and Joan Bracewell; one *s* one *d*. *Educ:* Bristol Univ. (LLB). Called to the Bar, Lincoln's Inn, 1997 (non-practising barrister); admitted solicitor, 1998. Partner, Brobeck Hale & Dorr, 1997–2000; Morrison & Forester, 2000–02; Counsel, WilmerHale, 2013–. Mem., Sports Council, GB, 1993–96, Sport England, 1996–2001; Chair, sportscotland, 2005–08; Chm., Scottish Steering Gp for 2012 Olympic Games, 2005–08; Board Director: Scottish Inst. of Sport, 2005–08; UK Sport, 2005–08; Dep. Chair, Scottish Athletics, 2009–13. Fencing competitor: Commonwealth Championships, 1986 (Bronze Medal), 1990 (Bronze Medal); Olympic Games, Barcelona, 1992. Sailed across Atlantic, 1995. *Recreations:* ski-ing, sailing, racket sports, fencing. *Club:* British Olympians.

BRACEWELL-SMITH, Sir Charles, 4th Bt *cr* 1947, of Keighley; *b* 13 Oct. 1955; *s* of Sir George Bracewell Smith, 2nd Bt, MBE, and Helene Marie (*d* 1975), *d* of late John Frederick Hydock, Philadelphia, USA; *S* brother, 1983; *m* 1977, Carol Vivien Hough (*d* 1994); *m* 1996, Nina Kakkar. Former Dir, Park Lane Hotel Ltd. Founder, Homestead Charitable Trust, 1990. *Recreations:* mysticism, theology, philosophy, psychology, poetry, writing, music. *Heir:* none. *Address:* The Hermitage, 7 Clarence Gate Gardens, Glentworth Street, NW1 6AY. *Clubs:* Royal Automobile, Arsenal Football.

BRACK, Rodney Lee, CBE 2006; Chief Executive, Horserace Betting Levy Board, 1993–2005; *b* 16 Aug. 1945; *s* of Sydney William Brack and Mary Alice Brack (*née* Quested); *m* 1973, Marilyn Carol Martin; two *s* one *d*. *Educ:* Whitgift Sch. FCA 1979. Chartered Accountant, 1963–68; Finance Manager, Daily Mirror Gp, 1969–75; Man. Dir, Leisure Div., EMI, 1976–80; Dir, Leisure Div., Lonrho, 1981–84; Financial Controller and Dep. Chief Exec., Horserace Betting Levy Bd, 1985–92. Dir, Horseracing Forensic Lab., 1986–2005. Mem., Lord Donoughue's Future Funding of Racing Review Gp, 2005–06. *Recreations:* music, theatre, cricket, golf. *Address:* 2 Dempster Close, Long Ditton, Surbiton, Surrey KT6 5EZ. *T:* (020) 3624 5047. *E:* rodneybrack@hotmail.com. *Clubs:* MCC, Royal Automobile.

BRACK, Terence John, CB 1994; Assistant Under-Secretary of State (General Finance), Ministry of Defence, 1989–94; *b* 17 April 1938; *s* of late Noël D. J. Brack and Tertia Brack; *m* 1983, Christine Mary, *d* of late Douglas and Evelyn Cashin. *Educ:* Bradfield Coll., Berkshire; Caius Coll., Cambridge Univ. (BA Hist. (1st cl. Hons), MA). Pilot Officer, Secretarial Br., RAF, 1956–58. Entered Air Ministry, subseq. MoD, 1961; Private Sec. to Parly Under-Sec. of State for Defence (RAF), 1964–66; Principal, 1966; seconded to HM Treasury, 1968–72; Asst Sec., 1973; Head, Finance and Sec. Div. for Controller of the Navy, 1975–78; Head, Defence Secretariat Div. for Equipment Requirements, 1978–81; RCDS, 1982; Head, Finance and Sec. Div. (Air Launched Guided Weapons and Electronics),

1983–84; Asst Under-Sec. of State (Naval Personnel), 1985–89. Vice-Chm., Management Bd, Royal Hosp. Sch., Holbrook, 1985–89. Pres., London Manx Soc., 2001–02. *Recreations:* walking, travel, family history projects.

BRACKEN, Michael Thomas, CBE 2014; Chief Digital Officer, Co-operative Group, since 2015; *b* St Helens, 10 Dec. 1968; *s* of Thomas Francis and Valerie Bracken; *m* 2009, Abigail Susan Billinghurst; two *d. Educ:* W London Inst., Brunel Univ. (BA American Studies and Hist. 1991); Liverpool Univ. (MA Latin American Studies 1993); Henley Mgt Coll. (MBA 2006). Internet researcher, journalist and entrepreneur, 1994–97; Vice Pres., Interactive Products, UPC Media/Chello, 1999–2002; Dir, mySociety.org, 2002–05; Commercial Dir, Wavex Technol., 2005–08; Dir, Digital Develt, Guardian News and Media, 2008–11; Exec. Dir, Digital, Cabinet Office, 2011–15. *Recreations:* changing nappies mostly, supporting the mighty Sporting Hackney FC. *Address:* 86 Oldfield Road, N16 0RP. *E:* mike@mikebracken.com. *W:* www.twitter.com/mtbracken. *Clubs:* Liverpool Football, Sporting Hackney Football (Chm., 2007–); Hadley Wood Golf.

BRACKENBURY, (Frederick Edwin) John (Gedge), CBE 2000; Chairman, Brackenbury Leisure Ltd, since 1996; Vice Chairman, Avanti Communications Group, since 2014 (Chairman, 2007–14); *b* 9 Feb. 1936; *s* of Claude Russell Brackenbury and Florence Edna Brackenbury; *m* 1st, 1958, Pauline Hinchliffe (marr. diss. 1977); one *s* two *d*; 2nd, 1978, Desiree Sally Taylor; one *s. Educ:* Mercers' Sch., London. Justerini & Brooks Ltd, 1954–62 (Dir, 1958–62); Man. Dir, City Cellars, 1962–65; Chm., Morgan Furze, 1965–67; Dir, IDV Ltd, 1967–72; Founder, Brackenbury consultancy co., 1972–75; Exec. Dir, G. & W. Walker, 1975–83 (Gp Operational Dir, Brent Walker, 1976–83); Man. Dir, All Weather Sports Activities Ltd, 1983–88; Exec. Dir, Brent Walker Gp Plc, 1988–96. Chm., 1991–2002, Dep. Chm., 2002–03, Pubmaster Gp Ltd; Chairman: Active Media Capital Ltd, 2000–07; Avanti Screenmedia Gp plc, 2003–07; non-executive Director: Western Wines Ltd, 1997–2002; Aspen Gp Plc, 1997–99; Hotel and Catering Trng Co., 1998–2002; SFI Gp Plc, 1998–2005; Holsten (UK) Ltd, 2000–04; Isle of Capri Casinos Inc. (USA), 2004–10; The Isle Casinos Ltd, 2004–09 (Chm.); Blue Chip Casinos, 2006–09. Chairman: Business in Sport & Leisure, 1985–2005 (Life Pres., 2005–13); Hospitality Trng Foundn, 1997–2004; People 1st, 2004–05; Dir, Springboard (formerly Tourism & Hospitality) Educn Trust, 1999–; Trustee and Vice Pres., GamCare, 2009–. *Recreations:* golf, tennis, viticulture, shooting. *Address:* 8 Moore Street, SW3 2QN. *Clubs:* Carlton, Hurlingham.

BRACKENBURY, Air Vice-Marshal Ian, CB 2000; OBE 1987; CEng, FIMechE; Director, Rolls-Royce Defence Aerospace (Europe), 2001–06; *b* 28 Aug. 1945; *s* of late Capt. D. E. Brackenbury and of R. Brackenbury (*née* Grant). Directorate of Aircraft Engrg, 1975; Engrg Staff, Strike Comd, 1981; joined Dept for Supply and Orgn, 1986, Dir of Support Mgt, 1993; Dir of Support Mgt, HQ Logistics Comd, 1994; Dir, Helicopter Support, Chief of Fleet Support, 1995–97; Air Officer Engrg and Supply, Strike Comd, 1997–98; Dir Gen. Defence Logistics (Ops and Policy), MoD, 1998–2000. Trustee, Cornwall Air Ambulance Trust, 2009–. *Club:* Royal Air Force.

BRACKENBURY, John; *see* Brackenbury, F. E. J. G.

BRACKENBURY, Ven. Michael Palmer; Archdeacon of Lincoln, 1988–95, now Emeritus; *b* 6 July 1930; *s* of Frank Brackenbury and Constance Mary (*née* Palmer); *m* 1953, Jean Margaret, *d* of Oscar Arnold Harrison and May (*née* Norton). *Educ:* Norwich School; Lincoln Theological Coll. ACII 1956. RAF, 1948–50. Asst Curate, South Ormsby Group, 1966–69; Rector of Sudbrooke with Scothern, 1969–77; RD of Lawres, 1973–78; Diocesan Dir of Ordinands, Lincoln, 1977–87; Personal Assistant to Bishop of Lincoln, 1977–88; Canon and Prebendary of Lincoln, 1979–95; Diocesan Lay Ministry Adviser, Lincoln, 1986–87. Mem., Gen. Synod of C of E, 1989–95. Mem., Ecclesiastical Law Soc., 1988–. Chm. Lincs Award Bd, Prince's Trust, 1996–2001. *Recreations:* music, reading, travel. *Address:* 18 Lea View, Ryhall, Stamford, Lincs PE9 4HZ. *T:* (01780) 752415.

BRACKLEY, Rt Rev. Ian James; Bishop Suffragan of Dorking, 1996–2015; *b* 13 Dec. 1947; *s* of Frederick Arthur James Brackley and Ivy Sarah Catherine (*née* Bush); *m* 1971, Penny Saunders; two *s. Educ:* Westcliff High Sch.; Keble Coll., Oxford (MA); Cuddesdon Coll., Oxford. Ordained deacon, 1971, priest, 1972; Asst Curate, Lockleaze, Bristol, 1971–74; Asst Chaplain, 1974–76, Chaplain, 1976–80, Bryanston Sch., Dorset; Vicar, East Preston with Kingston, 1980–88; Team Rector, St Wilfrid, Haywards Heath, 1988–96. Rural Dean: Arundel and Bognor, 1982–87; Cuckfield, 1989–95. Commissary Bishop of Guildford, 2003–04, 2013–14, of Portsmouth, 2009–10. *Recreations:* golf, cricket, classical music, pipe organs. *Address:* 1 Bepton Down, Petersfield, Hants GU31 4PR. *T:* (01730) 266465. *E:* ijbrackley@gmail.com.

BRACKS, Hon. Stephen (Phillip), AC 2010; Senior Adviser: to Prime Minister of East Timor, since 2007; to KPMG, 2007–12; Premier of Victoria, and Minister for Multicultural Affairs, 1999–2007; *b* 15 Oct. 1954; *m* 1983, Terry Horsfall; two *s* one *d. Educ:* St Patrick's Coll., Ballarat; Ballarat Univ. (Dip. Business Studies, Grad. DipEd). Secondary commerce teacher, 1976–81; employment project worker and municipal recreation officer, 1981–85; Exec. Dir, Ballarat Educn Centre, 1985–89; Statewide Manager, Victoria's Employment Progs, 1989–93 (on secondment as Ministerial Advr to Premiers of Victoria, 1990); Principal Advr to Fed. Parly Sec. for Transport and Communications, 1993; Exec. Dir, Victorian Printing Industry Trng Bd, 1993–94. MLA (ALP) Williamstown, Vic, 1994–2007; Shadow Minister for Employment, Industrial Relns and Tourism, 1994–96; Shadow Treas. and Shadow Minister for Finance and Industrial Relns, 1996–99; Dep. Chm., Public Accounts and Estimates Cttee, 1996–99; Shadow Treas. and Shadow Minister for Multicultural Affairs, March–Oct. 1999; Treas., 1999–2000. Leader, State Parly Labor Party, March–Oct. 1999. Chm., United Super Pty Ltd, 2009–; Non-exec. Dir, Jardine Lloyd Thompson Australia, 2007–; Vice Chm., Adv. Bd, AIMS Financial Gp, 2007–09. Aust. Automotive Industry Envoy, 2009–13. Chm., Aust. Subscription TV and Radio Assoc., 2009–13. Hon. Professorial Fellow, Univ. of Melbourne, 2007. Hon. Dr Ballarat. *Recreations:* camping, distance swimming, tennis, football supporter, cycling. *Address:* Old Treasury Building, 20 Spring Street, Melbourne, Vic 3000, Australia. *E:* info@stevebracks.com.au.

BRADBEER, Sir (John) Derek (Richardson), Kt 1988; OBE 1973; TD 1965; DL; Partner, Wilkinson Maughan (formerly Wilkinson Marshall Clayton & Gibson), 1961–97; President of the Law Society, 1987–88; *b* 29 Oct. 1931; *s* of late William Bertram Bradbeer and Winifred (*née* Richardson); *m* 1962, Margaret Elizabeth Chantler (DL Northumberland); one *s* one *d. Educ:* Canford Sch.; Sidney Sussex Coll., Cambridge (MA). Nat. Service, 2nd Lieut RA, 1951–52; TA, 1952–77: Lt-Col Comdg 101 (N) Med. Regt RA(V), 1970–73; Col, Dep. Comdr 21 and 23 Artillery Bdes, 1973–76; Hon. Col, 101 (N) Field Regt, RA(V), 1986–91. Admitted Solicitor, 1959. Member: Criminal Injuries Compensation Bd, 1988–2000; Criminal Injuries Compensation Appeals Panel, 1996–2008. Member: Disciplinary Cttee, Inst. of Actuaries, 1989–96; Insurance Brokers Registration Council, 1992–96. Mem. Council, 1973–94, Vice-Pres., 1986–87, Law Soc.; Pres., Newcastle upon Tyne Incorp. Law Soc., 1981–82; Gov., Coll. of Law, 1983–2002 (Chm., 1990–99). Director: Newcastle and Gateshead Water plc, 1978–90; Sunderland and South Shields Water plc, 1990–2002; Chm., North East Water, 1992–2002; Dep. Chm., Northumbrian Water Gp, 1996–2002. UK Vice-Pres., Union Internationale des Avocats, 1988–92. Chm., N of England TA&VRA, 1990–96 (Vice-Chm., 1988–90). DL Tyne and Wear, 1988. DUniv Open, 2000; Hon. DLaws Coll. of Law, 2007. *Recreations:* reading, gardening, sport. *Address:* Forge Cottage, Shilvington, Newcastle upon Tyne NE20 0AP. *T:* (01670) 775214. *Clubs:* Army and Navy, Garrick.

BRADBURY, family name of **Baron Bradbury.**

BRADBURY, 3rd Baron *cr* 1925, of Winsford, Co. Chester; **John Bradbury;** *b* 17 March 1940; *s* of 2nd Baron Bradbury and of his 1st wife, Joan, *o d* of W. D. Knight; *S* father, 1994; *m* 1968, Susan, *d* of late W. Liddiard; two *s. Educ:* Gresham's Sch.; Univ. of Bristol. *Heir: s* Hon. John Timothy Bradbury, *b* 16 Jan. 1973.

BRADBURY, Anita Jean, (Mrs Philip Bradbury); *see* Pollack, A. J.

BRADBURY, His Honour Anthony Vincent; a Circuit Judge, 1992–2006; Resident Judge, Bow County Court, 1998–2006; *b* 29 Sept. 1941; *s* of late Alfred Charles Bradbury, OBE and Noreen Vincent Bradbury; *m* 1966, Rosalie Anne Buttrey; one *d. Educ:* Kent College, Canterbury; Univ. of Birmingham (Sir Henry Barber Law Scholar; LLB). Solicitor 1965; Principal, Bradbury & Co., 1970–81; Registrar, then Dist Judge, Ilford County Court, 1981–91, Chelmsford County Court, 1991–92; a Recorder of the Crown Court, 1990–92; authorised to sit as a Judge of the High Court, Queen's Bench, Chancery and Family Divs, 1998–2006. Chm., SE Circuit Dist Judges, 1989–92. Wandsworth Mem., GLC and ILEA, 1967–70. Contested (C): N Battersea, 1970; S Battersea, Feb. 1974. Chairman of Governors: Putney Coll. for Further Educn, 1968–74; St John's C of E Sch., Buckhurst Hill, 1989–96. Hon. Treas., British Assoc. for Cemeteries in S Asia, 2010–. *Publications:* Early London County Courts: a brief account of their history and buildings, 2010; Frank Mitchell - Imperial Cricketer, 2014; contribs to cricketing periodicals. *Recreations:* walking, Yorkshire cricket, writing for pleasure, travelling. *Clubs:* Reform, MCC; Yorkshire CC (Chm., Southern Gp, 1985–87); Cricket Writers'.

BRADBURY, David Anthony Gaunt; Director of Libraries, Archives and Guildhall Art Gallery, City of London Corporation (formerly Corporation of London), 2005–09; *b* 1 Nov. 1947; *s* of late Peter Bradbury and Iris Bradbury (*née* Tweedale); *m* 1974, Ellen Williams; three *s* one *d. Educ:* Repton Sch.; Univ. of Sussex (BA Russian Studies 1970, MA Contemp. Eur. Studies 1972). MCLIP. Grad. trainee, BM liby, 1972–73; British Library: Lending Div., 1975–86; Dep. Dir (Services), 1986–89, Dir, 1989–95, Document Supply Centre; Dir-Gen., Collections and Services, 1996–2001; Mem. Bd, 1996–2001; Dir, Libraries and Guildhall Art Gall., Corp. of London, 2002–05. Member: Bd, London Univ. Sch. of Advanced Study, 2000–01; Adv. Cttee, Univ. of London Centre for Metropolitan Hist., 2005–09. Mem. Conseil, Projet d'Etablissement de la Bibliothèque nationale de France, 1999–2000. Chm., Saga Trust, 1996–2001. Trustee, London Jl, 2005–09. *Publications:* contrib. jl articles on future of libraries, library co-operation, publishing, digital information. *Recreations:* languages, walking, Scrabble, history of Saddleworth. *Address:* 25 Britton Street, EC1M 5NY. *T:* (020) 7250 3907.

BRADBURY, Julia Michelle; television presenter and broadcaster; *b* Dublin, 24 July 1970; *d* of Michael Bradbury and Chrissi Bradbury; partner, Gerard Cunningham; one *s* two *d* (incl. twin *d*). *Educ:* King Edward VII Sch., Sheffield. Reporter, Live TV, 1995; LA Corresp., GMTV, 1996–97; anchor and launch face, Channel 5 TV, 1997, presenter, Exclusive, 1997–99; Presenter: Top Gear, 1998–99; Moral Dilemmas, 2000; Wish You Were Here, 2001–03; Moto GP, Speedway, 2002–04; Watchdog, 2004–09; Wainwright Walks, 2007; Kill It, Cook It, Eat It, 2007–11; Rough Guide To…, 2008; Railway Walks, 2008; Countryfile, 2009–14; Coast to Coast, 2009; South Africa Walks, German Wanderlust, 2010; Canal Walks, 2011; Planet Earth Live, 2013; Take on the Twisters, 2013; Wonders of Britain, 2015. Pres., Camping and Caravanning Club, 2013–; Ambassador: Scouts, 2011–; Outdoor Trust, 2013–. DUniv Sheffield Hallam, 2013. *Publications:* Railway Walks, 2010; Canal Walks, 2011; Julia Bradbury's Wainwright Walks, 2012; Julia Bradbury's Wainwright Walks, Coast to Coast, 2013. *Recreations:* walking, travel, dancing, family, charity. *Address:* PO Box 18612, NW3 2GH. *T:* (020) 7431 7454. *E:* info@juliabradbury.com.

BRADBURY, Richard Edward, CBE 2008; Chief Executive, River Island, 2008–11; non-executive Director, Boden, since 2012; *b* Bedford, 4 Feb. 1956; *s* of Albert Edward and Lily Bradbury; *m* 1981, Susan Price; two *d. Educ:* Bedford Modern Sch.; Luton Poly. Mgt trainee, Barnaby Rudge, 1975–76; Merchandiser, Harry Fenton Menswear, 1977–79; Burton Group: Merchandiser, 1979–81; Buyer, 1981–84; Buying and Merchandising Controller, 1984–86; Buying Dir, 1986–89; River Island: Man. Dir, Womenswear, 1989–98; Gp Man. Dir, 1998–2007. Mem., Develt Bd, Chickenshed, 2014–; Patron, Scope, 2012– (Chm., Appeal Bd). Worked with NHS on Patient Revolution Initiative, 2012. Beacon Fellowship for Pioneering Philanthropy, 2013. *Recreations:* travel, golf, music, wine, eating out, retail.

BRADBURY, Susan Alison, (Mrs J. C. Whitley), OBE 2010; Director, Folio Holdings Ltd, since 2010; *b* 15 June 1947; *d* of John Donovan and Mary Alison Bradbury; *m* 1984, John Christopher Whitley (*d* 2014); one step *s. Educ:* Nottingham High Sch. for Girls (GPDST); Bretton Hall Coll. of Educn; Leeds Univ. (BEd Hons). Teacher: British Sch., Gran Canaria, Canary Is, 1969–71; Haydon Rd Jun. Sch., Nottingham, 1971–72; Governess, Seville, 1972–73; Folio Society: Membership Sec., Production Asst, Picture Researcher, Asst Editor, then Sen. Editor, 1973–83; Associate Editl Dir, 1983–84; Editl Dir, 1984–2006; Dep. Man. Dir, 1991–2006; Acting Man. Dir, 1992–96; Ed.-in-Chief, 2006–09. Trustee: John Hodgson Theatre Trust, 2005–; Keats-Shelley Meml Assoc., 2010–; Bankside Gall., 2010–. Hon. Sec., Soc. of Bookmen, 2000–04 and 2007–13. Freeman, 2010, Liveryman, 2013, Barbers' Co. *Publications:* (trans.) Three Tragedies, by Federico Garcia Lorca, 1977; (ed and transcribed) Sir Thomas Malory's Chronicles of King Arthur, 1982; (with Urgunge Onon) Chinngis Khan, 1993; Midnight Madonna (novel), 1995; anthologies: (with John Letts) A Few Royal Occasions, 1977; Fifty Folio Epigrams, 1996; Christmas Crime Stories, 2004; Christmas Ghost Stories, 2005; A Traveller's Christmas, 2006; (with Robert Fox) Eyewitness to History, 2008; Joanna, George and Henry: a Pre-Raphaelite novel of art, love and friendship, 2012; selected and introduced: Short Stories by Somerset Maugham, 1985; Dream Street: short stories by Damon Runyan, 1989; Love Poems by Robert Graves, 1990. *Recreations:* travel, drawing, reading, opera, playing flamenco guitar, riding elderly motorbike. *Address:* 9 Edna Street, SW11 3DP. *T:* (020) 7228 9534. *E:* suewhitley44@gmail.com.

BRADBURY, Rear-Adm. Thomas Henry, CB 1979; *b* 4 Dec. 1922; *s* of Thomas Henry Bradbury and Violet Buckingham; *m* 1st, 1945, Beryl Doreen Evans (marr. diss. 1979; she *d* 1985); one *s* one *d*; 2nd, 1979, Sarah Catherine, *d* of Harley Hillier and Mrs Susan Hillier. *Educ:* Christ's Hosp. CO HMS Jufair, 1960–62; Supply Officer, HMS Hermes, 1965–67; Sec. to Controller of Navy, MoD, 1967–70; CO HMS Terror, 1970–71; RCDS, 1972; Dir, Naval Admin. Planning, MoD, 1974–76; Flag Officer, Admiralty Interview Bd, 1977–79. Gp Personnel Dir, Inchcape Gp of Cos, 1979–86; Gp Personnel Exec., Davy Corp., 1987–91. Non-exec. Dir, Eastbourne HA, 1990–93. *Address:* Padgham Down, Dallington, Heathfield, E Sussex TN21 9NS. *T:* (01435) 830208.

BRADBY, Thomas; Presenter, ITV News at Ten, since 2015; *b* 13 Jan. 1967; *s* of Daniel James Bradby and late Sarah Ley Bradby; *m* 1994, Claudia Hill-Norton; two *s* one *d. Educ:* Sherborne Sch.; Edinburgh Univ. (MA Hons Hist.). ITN trainee, 1990–92; ITV News: political producer, 1992–93; Ireland Corresp., 1993–96; Political Corresp., 1996–98; Asia Corresp., 1998–2001; Royal Corresp., 2001–03; UK Ed., 2003–05; Political Ed., 2005–15. Scriptwriter, TV series, The Great Fire, 2014. *Publications: novels:* Shadow Dancer, 1998 (screenplay for film, 2012); The Sleep of the Dead, 2001; The Master of Rain, 2002; The White Russian, 2003; The God of Chaos, 2005; Blood Money, 2009. *Recreations:* ski-ing, writing, walking, soccer. *Address:* c/o ITV News, Press Gallery, House of Commons, SW1A 0AA. *T:* (020) 7430 4991. *E:* tom.bradby@itn.co.uk. *Club:* Royal Automobile.

BRADDICK, Prof. Michael Jonathan, PhD; FBA 2013; Professor of History, University of Sheffield, since 2001; *b* Hayling Island, Hants, 29 Aug. 1962; *s* of William and Ann Braddick; *m* 2002, Karen Louise Harvey; two *d. Educ:* Ashlyns Sch., Berkhamsted; King's Coll., Cambridge (BA Hons 1984; PhD 1988). FRHistS 1995. Asst Prof., Birmingham Southern Coll., Ala, 1988–90; University of Sheffield: Temp. Lectr, 1990–91; British Acad. Postdoctoral Fellow, 1991–92; Lectr, 1992–98; Sen. Lectr, 1998–2001; Pro-Vice-Chancellor, 2009–13. Vis. Fellow, Max Planck Inst. for Eur. Legal Hist., Frankfurt, 1999; Mem., Sch. of Histl Studies, Inst. for Advanced Study, Princeton, 2006; Prof. associé, École des Hautes Études en Sciences Sociales, Paris, 2011; Dist. Vis. Fellow, Aust. Res. Council Centre for Hist. of Emotions, Univ. of Adelaide, 2013. *Publications:* Parliamentary Taxation in Seventeenth-Century England: local administration and response, 1994; The Nerves of State: taxation and the financing of the English State, 1558–1714, 1996 (trans. Japanese 2000); (ed with M. Greengrass) The Letters of Sir Cheney Culpeper, 1641–1657, 1996; State Formation in Early Modern England, c. 1550–1700, 2000; (ed with J. Walter) Negotiating Power in Early Modern Society: order, hierarchy and subordination in Britain and Ireland, 2001; (ed with D. Armitage) The British Atlantic World, 1500–1800, 2002, 2nd edn 2009; Political Culture in Later Medieval England: essays by Simon Walker, 2006; God's Fury, England's Fire: a new history of the English civil wars, 2008; The Politics of Gesture: historical perspectives, 2009; The Experience of Revolution in Stuart Britain and Ireland: essays for John Morrill, 2011; contrib. articles to jls and edited vols. *Recreations:* walking, cinema, football, cricket, Rugby, family. *Address:* Department of History, University of Sheffield, Jessop West, 1 Upper Hanover Street, Sheffield S3 7RA. *E:* m.braddick@sheffield.ac.uk.

BRADDICK, Prof. Oliver John, PhD; FBA 2012; FMedSci; Professor of Psychology and Head, Department of Experimental Psychology, Oxford University, 2001–11, now Emeritus Professor; Fellow, Magdalen College, Oxford, since 2001; *b* 16 Nov. 1944; *s* of Henry John James Braddick and Edith Muriel Braddick; *m* 1979, Prof. Janette Atkinson; two *s* two *d. Educ:* Trinity Coll., Cambridge (MA; PhD 1968). Cambridge University: Lectr, 1969–86; Reader in Vision, 1986–93; Fellow, Trinity Coll., 1968–72; University College London: Prof. of Psychol., 1993–2001; Hd of Dept, 1998–2001. Associate, Brown Univ., USA, 1968–69. FMedSci 2001. MAE 2008. Trustee, Assoc. for Res. in Vision and Ophthalmol., 1999–2004. Koffka Medal, Univ. of Giessen, 2009. Ed.-in-Chief, Oxford Res. Encyclopaedia of Psychol., 2014–. *Publications:* numerous articles on vision and its develt in scientific jls and books. *Recreations:* family life, the arts. *Address:* Department of Experimental Psychology, University of Oxford, South Parks Road, Oxford OX1 3UD. *T:* (01865) 512025.

BRADES, Susan Deborah F.; *see* Ferleger Brades.

BRADFORD, 7th Earl of, *cr* 1815; **Richard Thomas Orlando Bridgeman;** Bt 1660; Baron Bradford, 1794; Viscount Newport, 1815; *b* 3 Oct. 1947; *s* of 6th Earl of Bradford, TD, and Mary Willoughby (*d* 1986), *er d* of Lt-Col T. H. Montgomery, DSO; *S* father, 1981; *m* 1st, 1979, Joanne Elizabeth (marr. diss. 2006), *d* of B. Miller; three *s* one *d*; 2nd, 2008, Dr Penelope Law. *Educ:* Harrow; Trinity College, Cambridge. Owner of Porters English Restaurant of Covent Garden, 1979–2015, and Covent Garden Grill, until 2015. Chm., Restaurant Assoc., 2010–14; Bd Mem., Nat. Restaurant Assoc. (USA), 2006–14. *Publications:* (compiled) My Private Parts and the Stuffed Parrot, 1984; The Eccentric Cookbook, 1985; Stately Secrets, 1994; (with Carol Wilson) Porters English Cookery Bible: Ancient and Modern, 2004; (with Carol Wilson) Porters Seasonal Celebrations, 2007. *Heir: s* Viscount Newport, *qv. Address:* 46 Sutton Court Road, Chiswick, W4 4NL. *T:* (020) 8994 4846. *E:* bradfordr@porters.uk.com.

BRADFORD, Area Bishop of, since 2014; **Rt Rev. Toby Matthew Howarth;** *b* 1962; *m* Henriette; three *d. Educ:* Yale Univ. (BA 1986); Wycliffe Hall, Oxford; Birmingham Univ. (MA 1991); Free Univ. of Amsterdam (PhD 2001). Ordained deacon, 1992, priest, 1993; Curate, St Augustine, Derby, 1992–95; Res. Student, Henry Martyn Centre for Reconciliation and Inter Faith Relns, Hyderabad, India, 1995–2000; Evangelist, Pilgrim Father's Church, Rotterdam, 2000–02; Vice Principal and Tutor, Crowther Hall CMS Trng Coll., Selly Oak, 2002–04; Priest-in-charge, St Christopher, Springfield, 2004–11; Bishop's Advr on Inter-faith Relns, 2005–11; Archbishop of Canterbury's Sec. for Inter-religious Affairs, 2011–14. Hon. Canon, All Saints Cathedral, Cairo. *Address:* 47 Kirkgate, Shipley, W Yorks BD18 3EH.

BRADFORD, Dean of; *see* Lepine, Very Rev. J. J.

BRADFORD, Archdeacon of; *see* Lee, Ven. D. J.

BRADFORD, Barbara Taylor, OBE 2007; author; *b* Leeds, 10 May; *d* of late Winston and Freda Taylor; *m* 1963, Robert Bradford. Jun. Reporter, 1949–51, Women's Editor, 1951–53, Yorkshire Evening Post; Fashion Editor, Woman's Own, 1953–54; columnist, London Evening News, 1955–57; Exec. Editor, London American, 1959–62; moved to USA, 1964; Editor, National Design Center Magazine, 1965–69; syndicated columnist, 1968–81. Member, Board of Directors: Police Athletic League, NY; Literacy Partners of NY; Reporters Without Borders, Washington DC. Hon. Ambassador, Nat. Literacy Trust (UK). Hon. DLitt: Leeds, 1989; Bradford, 1995; Hon. DHL Teikyo Post, Conn, 1996. *Publications:* Complete Encyclopedia of Homemaking Ideas, 1968; A Garland of Children's Verse, 1968; How to be the Perfect Wife, 1969; Easy Steps to Successful Decorating, 1971; How to Solve Your Decorating Problems, 1976; Decorating Ideas for Casual Living, 1977; Making Space Grow, 1979; Luxury Designs for Apartment Living, 1981; *novels:* A Woman of Substance, 1979 (televised, 1985); Voice of the Heart, 1983; Hold the Dream, 1985 (televised, 1986); Act of Will, 1986; To Be the Best, 1988; The Women in His Life, 1990; Remember, 1991; Angel, 1993; Everything to Gain, 1994; Dangerous to Know, 1995; Love in Another Town, 1995; Her Own Rules, 1996; A Secret Affair, 1996; Power of a Woman, 1997; A Sudden Change of Heart, 1999; Where You Belong, 2000; The Triumph of Katie Byrne, 2001; Emma's Secret, 2003; Unexpected Blessings, 2004; Just Rewards, 2005; The Ravenscar Dynasty, 2006; Heirs of Ravenscar, 2007; Being Elizabeth, 2008; Breaking the Rules, 2009; Playing the Game, 2010; Letter from a Stranger, 2011; Cavendon Hall, 2014; The Cavendon Women, 2015. *Address:* Bradford Enterprises, 505 Park Avenue, New York, NY 10022–2605, USA. *T:* (212) 308 7390, *Fax:* (212) 935 1636.

BRADFORD, (Sir) Edward Alexander Slade, 5th Bt, *cr* 1902 (but does not use the title); *b* 18 June 1952; *s* of Major Sir Edward Montagu Andrew Bradford, 3rd Bt (*d* 1952) and his 2nd wife, Marjorie Edith (*née* Bere); *S* half-brother, Sir John Ridley Evelyn Bradford, 4th Bt, 1954; *m* 1990, Jacqueline W. Bolton. *Heir: cousin* Andrew Edward Hanning Bradford [*b* 6 Jan. 1955; *m* 1978, Nicola Barbara Smythe; two *s* one *d*].

BRADFORD, Hon. Max(well Robert); World Bank consultant and economic consultant, since 2002; Principal, since 2001, and Director, since 2005, Bradford & Associates Ltd; *b* 19 Jan. 1942; *s* of Robert and Ella Bradford; *m* 1st, 1967, Dr Janet Grieve (marr. diss. 1988); 2nd, 1991, Rosemary Young; two step *d. Educ:* Christchurch Boys' High Sch.; Univ. of Canterbury, NZ (MCom Hons); Melbourne Business Sch. (AMP 1978). NZ Treasury, 1966–69, 1973–78; Economist, IMF, Washington, 1969–73; Dir of Advocacy, Employers' Fedn, 1978–85; Chief Exec., Bankers Assoc., 1985–87; Sec.-Gen., Nat. Party, 1987–89; MP (Nat. Party): Tarawera, 1990–96; Rotorua, 1996–99; List, 1999–2002; Minister of Defence, Enterprise, Commerce, Business Develt, Labour, Energy, Revenue, and Immigration, 1996–99; Minister of Defence, 1997–99; Minister for Tertiary Educn, 1999. Dir, Castalia Advisors, 2001–05. Associate, Oxford Policy Mgt Ltd, UK, 2012–14. *Recreations:* sailing, music, reading, fishing, ski-ing, boatbuilding. *Club:* Wellington.

BRADFORD, Sarah Mary Malet Ward, (Viscountess Bangor); historian and biographer, critic, broadcaster and journalist; *b* 3 Sept. 1938; *d* of late Brig. Hilary Anthony Hayes, DSO, OBE, and Mary Beatrice de Carteret (*née* Malet), who *m* 2nd, Keith Murray; *m* 1st, 1959, Anthony John Bradford (marr. diss. 1976); one *s* one *d*; 2nd, 1976, Viscount Bangor, *qv. Educ:* St Mary's Convent, Shaftesbury; Lady Margaret Hall, Oxford (schol.). Manuscript Expert, Christies, 1974–78; Consultant, Manuscript Dept, Sotheby's, 1979–81. *Publications:* The Englishman's Wine, 1969, new edn as The Story of Port, 1978, 2nd edn 1983; Portugal and Madeira, 1969; Portugal, 1973; Cesare Borgia, 1976, 2nd edn 2001; Disraeli, 1982, 2nd edn 1996; Princess Grace, 1984; King George VI, 1989, revised edn 2001; Sacheverell Sitwell, 1993; Elizabeth, A Biography of Her Majesty The Queen, 1996, revised edn 2001; America's Queen, The Life of Jacqueline Kennedy Onassis, 2000, 2nd edn 2013; Lucrezia Borgia: life, love and death in Renaissance Italy, 2004; Diana, 2006; Queen Elizabeth II: her life in our times, 2011. *Recreations:* reading biographies, diaries and letters, gardening, travelling, watching Liverpool FC. *Address:* c/o Aitken Alexander Associates, 291 Gray's Inn Road, WC1X 8EB. *T:* (020) 7373 8672, *Fax:* (020) 7373 6002.

BRADING, Prof. David Anthony, PhD, LittD; FBA 1995; Professor of Mexican History, University of Cambridge, 1999–2004; Fellow of Clare Hall, Cambridge, 1995–2004; *b* 26 Aug. 1936; *s* of Ernest Arthur Brading and Amy Mary (*née* Driscoll); *m* 1966, Celia Wu; one *s. Educ:* Pembroke Coll., Cambridge (BA 1960; LittD 1991; Hon. Fellow 2008); UCL (PhD 1965). Asst Prof., Univ. of Calif, Berkeley, 1965–71; Associate Prof., Yale Univ., 1971–73; Cambridge University: Lectr, 1973–92; Reader in Latin American Hist., 1992–99. Hon. Prof., Univ. of Lima, 1993. Order of the Aztec Eagle (Mexico), 2003; Medal of the Congress (Peru), 2011. *Publications:* Miners and Merchants in Bourbon Mexico, 1971; Haciendas and Ranchos in the Mexican Bajío, 1979; The Origins of Mexican Nationalism, 1985; The First America, 1991; Church and State in Bourbon Mexico, 1994; Mexican Phoenix, 2001. *Recreations:* music, walking. *Address:* 28 Storey's Way, Cambridge CB3 0DT. *T:* (01223) 352098. *Club:* Oxford and Cambridge.

BRADLEY, family name of **Baron Bradley**.

BRADLEY, Baron *cr* 2006 (Life Peer), of Withington in the County of Greater Manchester; **Keith John Charles Bradley;** PC 2001; *b* 17 May 1950; *m* 1987, Rhona Graham; two *s* one *d. Educ:* Manchester Polytechnic (BA Hons); York Univ. (MPhil). Former health service administrator, North West RHA. Mem., Manchester City Council, 1983–88. MP (Lab) Manchester, Withington, 1987–2005; contested (Lab) same seat, 2005. Opposition spokesman on social security, 1991–96, on transport, 1996–97; Parly Under-Sec. of State, DSS, 1997–98; Treasurer of HM Household (Dep. Chief Whip), 1998–2001; Minister of State, Home Office, 2001–02. Joined Labour Party, 1973; Mem., Manchester Withington Co-op Party. Mem., Unite. Ind. Review of Mental Health, Learning Disabilities and Criminal Justice System, 2009. Chm., Christie NHS Foundn Trust, 2011–14; Trustee: Centre for Mental Health, 2012–; Prison Reform Trust, 2012–. Associate Vice-Pres., 2010–13, Hon. Special Advr, 2013–, Univ. of Manchester. *Address:* House of Lords, SW1A 0PW.

BRADLEY, Prof. Allan, PhD; FRS 2002; Director, Wellcome Trust Sanger Institute (formerly The Sanger Centre), Hinxton, Cambridge, 2000–10, now Director Emeritus. *Educ.* Trinity Coll., Cambridge (BA Hons 1981; PhD 1986). Baylor College of Medicine, Houston, Texas: Asst Prof., 1987–92, Associate Prof., 1992–95, Cullen Prof. of Genetics, 1995–2000, Dept of Molecular and Human Genetics; Associate Investigator, Howard Hughes Med. Inst., 1993–2000. Mem., EMBO, 2006. *Publications:* articles in jls. *Address:* Wellcome Trust Sanger Institute, Genome Campus, Hinxton, Cambridge CB10 1SA.

BRADLEY, Andrew; *see* Bradley, J. A.

BRADLEY, Andrew, PhD; Chief Engineer, Hawk Advanced Jet Trainer Aircraft, BAE Systems, 2004–13; *b* Blackburn, Lancs, 20 Jan. 1955; *s* of John Bradley and Margaret Elizabeth Bradley; one *s* two *d*; *m* 2012, Kairen Dods. *Educ:* St Mary's Coll., Blackburn; Durham Univ. (BSc Jt Hons Maths and Phys; PhD Particle Physics 1978). CEng 2009; FIET 2009; FRAeS 2009; FREng 2010. Res. Fellow, Univ. of Manchester, 1978–81; Systems Engr, Nat. Nuclear Corp., 1981–87; British Aerospace, subseq. BAE Systems, 1987–2013: Hd, Software Engrg, 1989–95; Dir, Systems Engrg, 1995–2004. RAEng Vis. Prof. in Applied Systems Engrg, Univ. of Loughborough, 2008–15. *Publications:* articles on particle physics in learned jls. *Recreations.* computer games—writing software (games published from 1980 onwards), golf, squash, music. *Address:* Sandrigg Laithe, Gildersleets Lane, Giggleswick, N Yorks BD24 0JZ. *T.* (01729) 822395. *E:* drandrewbradley@msn.com.

BRADLEY, Anna Louise; Chair, Healthwatch England, since 2012; *b* 29 July 1957; *d* of Donald Bradley and Angela Lucy Bradley (*née* Bradley, now Ratcliffe); *m* 1995, Norman Howard Jones; one *s* one *d. Educ:* Camden Sch. for Girls; Warwick Univ. (BA Phil, 1978; MBA 1994). Sen. Sub-Editor, Marshall Cavendish Partworks Ltd, 1978–82; Consumers' Association: Sen. Project Leader, 1982–87; Project Manager, Food and Health, 1987–88; Head, Food and Health, 1988–91; Dep. Research Dir, 1991–93; Exec. Dir and Co. Sec., Inst. for the Study of Drug Dependence Ltd, 1993–98; Dir, Nat. Consumer Council, 1999–2002; Dir of Consumer Affairs, then of Retail Themes and Consumer Sector Leader, Financial Services Authy, 2002–05. Chair: Organic Standards Bd, 2006–10; Soil Assoc. Certification Ltd, 2010–13 (non-exec. Dir, 2007–10); Consumer Panel, Office of Communications, 2008–11; Gen. Optical Council, 2010–12 (Mem., 2009–10); Council of Licensed Conveyancers, 2010–15; Southern Water Customer Challenge Gp, 2012–; Rail Safety Standards Bd, 2015–; Comr, Care Quality Commn, 2012–. Member: Adv. Council on the Misuse of Drugs, 1996–98; Agriculture, Envmt and Biotechnol. Commn, 2000–05; Sci. Adv. Council, 2004–05; Ind. Governance Cttee, Zurich Insurance, 2015–. Adv. Consultant, Fishburn Hedges, 2006–10. Trustee, Addaction, 2006–12; non-exec. Dir, Life Trust Foundn, 2008–09. Non-exec. Mem. Bd, Colchester Univ. Foundn Trust, 2010–12. Mem., Mgt Cttee, Patients' Assoc., 1985–88. *Publications:* Healthy Eating, 1989; (ed) Understanding Additives, 1988; acad. and research papers in Lancet, Jl Human Nutrition, Dietetics, etc.

BRADLEY, Anne; *see* Smith, Anne.

BRADLEY, Prof. Anthony Wilfred; constitutional lawyer; *b* 6 Feb. 1934; *s* of David and Olive Bradley (*née* Bonsey); *m* 1959, Kathleen Bryce; one *s* three *d. Educ:* Dover Grammar Sch.; Emmanuel Coll., Cambridge (BA 1957, LLB 1958, MA 1961). Solicitor of the Supreme Court, 1960 (Clifford's Inn Prize); called to the Bar, Inner Temple, 1989; in practice as a barrister, 1990–2010. Asst Lectr, 1960–64, Lectr, 1964–68, Cambridge, and Fellow of Trinity Hall, 1960–68; Prof. of Constitutional Law, 1968–89, Dean, Faculty of Law, 1979–82, Prof Emeritus, 1990, Univ. of Edinburgh. Vis. Reader in Law, UC, Dar es Salaam, 1966–67; Vis. Prof. of Public Law, Univ. of Florence, 1984; Res. Fellow, Inst. of European and Comparative Law, Univ. of Oxford, 2003–. Chairman: Edinburgh Council for Single Homeless, 1984–88; Social Security Appeal Tribunal, 1984–89; Member: Wolfenden Cttee on Voluntary Orgns, 1974–78; Social Scis and Law Cttee, SSRC, 1975–79; Social Studies Sub-Cttee, UGC, 1985–89; Cttee of Inquiry into Local Govt in Scotland, 1980; Cttee to review local govt in Islands of Scotland, 1983–84. Mem. Exec. Cttee, Internat. Assoc. of Constitutional Law, 1999–2007. Legal Advr, H of L Select Cttee on the Constitution, 2002–05; Alternate Mem. (UK), Venice Commn for Democracy Through Law, 2003–10. Ed., Public Law, 1986–92. Hon. QC 2011. Hon. LLD: Staffordshire, 1993; Edinburgh, 1998. *Publications:* (ed with M. Adler) Justice, Discretion and Poverty, 1976; (ed) Wade and Bradley, Constitutional and Administrative Law, 9th edn 1978 to 11th edn 1993, subseq. Bradley and Ewing, Constitutional and Administrative Law, 12th edn 1997 to 16th edn 2014; (with D.

Christie) The Scotland Act 1978, 1979; Administrative Law (in Stair Meml Encyc. of the Laws of Scotland), 1987, 2nd edn (with C. Himsworth) 2000; (ed with J. S. Bell) Governmental Liability, 1991; (with M. Janis and R. Kay) European Human Rights Law: text and materials, 1995, 3rd edn 2008; (ed with K. S. Ziegler and D. Baranger) Constitutionalism and the Role of Parliaments, 2007; contrib. to legal jls and collaborative books. *Recreation:* music (playing and listening). *Address:* 20 Abingdon Road, Cumnor, Oxford OX2 9QN.

BRADLEY, Averil Olive, (Mrs J. W. P. Bradley); *see* Mansfield, A. O.

BRADLEY, Prof. Benjamin Arthur de Burgh, PhD; FRCP, FRCPath; Professor of Transplantation Sciences, and Director, Department of Transplantation Sciences, University of Bristol, 1992–2004; *b* 17 Sept. 1942; *s* of Reuben Stephen Bradley and Elsie Marjorie Bradley (*née* Burke); *m* 1968, Anne White; four *d. Educ:* Silcoates Sch., Wakefield; Bilston Grammar Sch.; Birmingham Univ. Med. Sch. (MB ChB 1965); Birmingham Univ. (MSc 1967; PhD 1970). FRCPath 1986 (MRCPath 1974); FRCP 1999. House surgeon and house physician, United Birmingham Hosps, 1965–66; MRC Res. Fellow, Dept of Surgery and Exptl Pathology, Univ. of Birmingham, 1967–70; Asst Dir of Res., Dept of Surgery, Univ. of Cambridge, 1970–75; Asst Prof., Dept of Immunohaematology, Univ. of Leiden, 1975–79; Dir, UK Transplant Service, 1979–92. Prof. of Transplantation Immunology, Univ. of Bristol, 1988. Dir of Immunol., Ximerex Inc., 2006–07. Dir, Shannon Applied Biotechnol. Centre, Ireland, 2008–10. Member: Scientific Policy Adv. Cttee, Nat. Inst. for Biol Standards, 1991–96; Bd, Jenner Educnl Trust, 1992–2000; Scientific Cttee, Foundn for Nephrology, 1992–2004. President: Eur. Foundn for Immunogenetics, 1988–89; British Soc. for Histocompatibility and Immunogenetics, 1996–98. Hon. Consultant in Transplantation Scis, N Bristol NHS Trust, 1979–; Hon. Prof., Faculty of Medicine, Nat. Univ. of Ireland, Galway, 2013–. Chm., Editl Bd, European Jl Immunogenetics, 1989–2004. Hon. MA Cantab, 1974. Thomas Pocklington Meml Lect. and Medal, 1985. *Publications:* (with S. M. Gore) Renal Transplantation: sense and sensitization, 1986; Editor and contributor to annual reports of: UK Transplant Service, 1979–90; Transplantation Services and Statistics in UK and Eire, 1991; contrib. textbooks and med. jls on clinical organ and tissue transplantation and immunology, genetics of transplantation and blood transfusion and post-traumatic immunosuppression; articles in scientific jls, chapters in books and papers in conf. procs. *Recreations:* mountain walking, cycling, motorhoming, singing, swimming. *Address:* East Barn, The Pound, Lower Almondsbury, Bristol BS32 4EF. *T:* (01454) 201077. *E:* benjaminbzone-whoswho2009@yahoo.co.uk.

BRADLEY, Dr (Charles) Clive; Managing Director, 1990–99, and Consultant, 1999–2000, Sharp Laboratories of Europe Ltd; *b* 11 April 1937; *s* of late Charles William Bradley and Winifred Smith; *m* 1965, Vivien Audrey Godley; one *s* one *d. Educ:* Longton High Sch.; Birmingham Univ. (BSc Hons in Physics, 1958); Emmanuel Coll., Cambridge (PhD 1962). CPhys 1997; FInstP 1997. Nat. Phys. Lab., 1961–67; MIT, USA, 1967, 1969; Nat. Bureau of Standards, USA, 1968; Nat. Phys. Lab., 1969–75; DoI, 1975–82, SPSO and Head of Energy Unit, 1978–82; Counsellor (Science and Technology), British Embassy, Tokyo, 1982–88; DCSO and Head of Secretariat, ACOST, Cabinet Office, 1988–90. Dir, Birds Hill Oxshott Estate Co., 2000–08. Vis. Prof., Univ. of Oxford, 1999–2002. Chm., Industrial Energy Conservation Cttee, Internat. Energy Agency, 1980–82. Dep. Comr Gen. for Britain, Sci. Expo Tokyo, 1985. Mem., Oxford Univ. Adv. Council on Continuing Educn, 1993–2001. Treas. and Mem. Council, Japan Soc., 2001–07. A. F. Bulgin Prize, IERE, 1972. Japanese Ambassador's Commendation, 2010. *Publications:* High Pressure Methods in Solid State Research, 1969; contribs to jls on lasers, metals and semiconductors. *Recreations:* tennis, gardening. *Address:* 39B The Ridgeway, Fetcham, Leatherhead, Surrey KT22 9BE. *Clubs:* Athenæum; St George's Hill Lawn Tennis.

BRADLEY, (Charles) Stuart, CBE 1990; Managing Director, Associated British Ports, 1988–95; Director, Associated British Ports Holdings, 1988–2001; *b* 11 Jan. 1936; *s* of Captain Charles Bradley, OBE and Amelia Jane Bradley; *m* 1959, Kathleen Marina (*née* Loraine); one *s* one *d* (and one *s* decd). *Educ:* Penarth County Sch.; University Coll. Southampton (Warsash). Master Mariner, 1961; FCILT (FCIT 1978). Deck Officer, P&OSN Co., 1952–64; joined British Transport Docks Bd, subseq. Associated British Ports, 1964; Dock and Harbour Master, Silloth, 1968–70; Dock Master, 1970–74, Dock and Marine Superintendent, 1974–76, Plymouth; Docks Manager, Lowestoft, 1976–78; Port Manager, Barry, 1978–80; Dep. Port Manager, 1980–85, Port Manager, 1985–87, Hull; Asst Man. Dir (Resources), 1987–88; Chm., Red Funnel Gp, 1989–2000. Younger Brother, Trinity House, 1994–. *Recreations:* Welsh Rugby football, cycling, walking, theatre. *Clubs:* Oriental, Honourable Company of Master Mariners.

BRADLEY, Clive; *see* Bradley, Charles C.

BRADLEY, Clive, CBE 1996; Chief Executive, The Publishers Association, 1976–97; Convenor, Confederation of Information Communication Industries, 1984–2014; *b* 25 July 1934; *s* of late Alfred and Kathleen Bradley. *Educ:* Felsted Sch., Essex; Clare Coll., Cambridge (Scholar; MA); Yale Univ. (Mellon Fellow). Called to the Bar, Middle Temple. Current Affairs Producer, BBC, 1961–63; Broadcasting Officer, Labour Party, 1963–64; Political Editor, The Statist, 1965–67; Gp Labour Adviser, IPC, 1967–69; Dep. Gen. Man., Daily and Sunday Mirror, 1969–71; Controller of Admin, IPC Newspapers, 1971–72; i/c IPC local radio applications, 1972–73; Dir i/c new prodn arrangements, The Observer, 1973–75. Dep. Chm., Central London Valuation Tribunal, 1973–2006. Chairman: Soc. of Bookmen, 1998–2000; Book Power Ltd, 2009–11. Director: Organising Cttee, World Congress on Books, London, 1982; Don't Tax Reading campaign, 1984–85; Organiser, IPA Congress, London, 1984; Mem., DTI Inf. Age Partnership, 1997–2001. Vice Pres., Richmond upon Thames Arts Council, 2010– (Chair, 2003–09); Pres., U3A Richmond upon Thames, 2011–. Trustee: Age Concern, Richmond, 1998–2011 (Chm., 2001–03; Treas., 2010–11); Garrick's Temple to Shakespeare, Hampton, 2006–. Gov., Felsted Sch., 1973–2008. *Publications:* Which Way?, 1970; (ed) The Future of the Book, 1982; articles on politics, economics, the press, television, industrial relations. *Recreations:* reading, travel, walking. *Address:* 8 Northumberland Place, Richmond, Surrey TW10 6TS. *T:* (020) 8940 7172. *E:* bradley_clive@btopenworld.com.

BRADLEY, Prof. David John, DM; FRCP, FRCPath, FFPH, FMedSci; FRSB; Director, Ross Institute, London School of Hygiene and Tropical Medicine, and Professor of Tropical Hygiene, University of London, 1974–2000, now Ross Professor Emeritus of Tropical Public Health; *b* 12 Jan. 1937; *s* of late Harold Robert and of Mona Bradley; *m* 1961, Lorne Marie, *d* of late Major L. G. Farquhar and Marie Farquhar; two *s* two *d. Educ:* Wyggeston Sch., Leicester; Selwyn Coll., Cambridge (Scholar); University Coll. Hosp. Med. Sch. (Atchison Schol., Magrath Schol., Trotter Medal in Surgery, Liston Gold Medal in Surgery, BA Nat. Scis Tripos, Med. Scis and Zoology, 1st cl. Hons, Frank Smart Prize Zool.; MB, BChir, MA 1960); DM Oxon 1972. FRSB (FIBiol 1974); FFPH (FFCM 1979); FRCPath 1981; FRCP 1985. Med. Res. Officer, Ross Inst. Bilharzia Res. Unit, Tanzania, 1961–64; Lectr, 1964–66, Sen. Lectr, 1966–69, Makerere Univ. of East Africa, Uganda; Trop. Res. Fellow of Royal Soc., Sir William Dunn Sch. of Pathology, Oxford, 1969–73; Sen. Res. Fellow, Staines Med. Fellow, Exeter Coll., Oxford, 1971–74; Clinical Reader in Path., Oxford Clinical Med. Sch., 1973–74; Chm., Div. of Communicable and Tropical Diseases, LSHTM, 1982–88. Vis. Prof., Univ. of Wales Coll. of Medicine, 1994–. Co-Director, Malaria Ref. Lab., HPA (formerly PHLS), 1974–2003; Hon. Consultant in Public Health Medicine, HPA (formerly PHLS) and to Westminster PCT (formerly to Kensington, Chelsea and Westminster), 1974–; Hon. Consultant in Trop. and Communicable Diseases, Bloomsbury DHA, 1983–2001; Dir, WHO Collaborating Centre Envmtl Control of Vectors, 1983–; Mem., Bd of Trustees, Internat. Centre for Diarrhoeal Disease Res., Bangladesh, 1979–85 (Chm., 1982–83); Consultant Advisor to Dir, Royal Tropical Inst., Amsterdam, 1980–90; Advr, Ind. Internat. Commn on Health Res.; Member: WHO Expert Adv. Panel on Parasitic Diseases, 1972–; Tech. Adv. Gp, Diarrhoea Programme, 1979–85; Panel of Experts on Envmtl Management, 1981–; External Review Gp on Trop. Diseases Programme, 1987; Task Force on Health Res. for Develt, 1991–93; Chm., Rev. Cttee, Swiss Tropical Inst., 1994–. Editor, Jl of Trop. Med. and Hygiene, 1981–; Founding Ed., Tropical Medicine and Internat. Health. Pres., RSTM&H, 1999–2001. FMedSci 1999; For. Corresp. Mem., Royal Belgian Acad. of Medicine, 1984; Corresp. Mem., German Tropenmediziningesellschaft, 1980; Hon. FIWEM (Hon. FIPHE, 1981). Hon. DSc Leicester, 2004. Chalmers Medal, 1980, Macdonald Medal, 1996, RSTM&H; Harben Gold Medal, RIPH, 2002. *Publications:* (with G. F. and A. U. White) Drawers of Water, 1972; (with E. E. Sabben-Clare and B. Kirkwood) Health in Tropical Africa during the Colonial Period, 1980; (with R. G. Feachem, D. D. Mara and H. Garelick) Sanitation and Disease, 1983; (jtly) Travel Medicine, 1989; (jtly) The Impact of Development Policies on Health, 1990; (jtly) The Malaria Challenge, 1999; papers in learned jls. *Recreations:* natural history, landscape gardens, travel. *Address:* London School of Hygiene and Tropical Medicine, Keppel Street, WC1E 7HT. *T:* (020) 7927 2216.

BRADLEY, David John; actor, since 1968; Associate Artist, Royal Shakespeare Co., since 1992; *b* York, 17 April 1942; *s* of George and Hilda Bradley; *m* 1978, Rosanna Baldaccini; two *s* one *d. Educ:* St George's Secondary Modern Sch., York; Royal Acad. of Dramatic Art. Joined National Theatre Co., Old Vic, 1972: The Front Page, Tis a Pity She's a Whore, Twelfth Night, The Cherry Orchard; Royal Shakespeare Co., 1978–, including: The Merchant of Venice, 1979; The Merry Wives of Windsor, 1986; Twelfth Night, Cymbeline, 1988; Dr Faustus, 1989; The Alchemist, 1992; Henry IV, Part 2, 1992; Hamlet, 1993 (Clarence Derwent Award, Equity); The Tempest, 1993; (title rôle) Titus Andronicus, 2003; Royal National Theatre, includes: Richard III, 1990; King Lear, 1990 (Laurence Olivier Award, 1991); Mother Courage; The Homecoming, 1997; The Mysteries, 1999; The Night Season, 2004; Henry IV, Parts 1 and 2, 2005; other performances include: York Mystery Plays, 1976; Britannicus/Phaedra (double-bill) Albery, 1998, transf. NY; Twelfth Night, Donmar, 2004, transf. NY; Vanya, Donmar, 2004, transf. NY; The Caretaker, Crucible Th., Sheffield, 2007, transf. Tricycle; No Man's Land, Duke of York's, 2009; Moonlight, Donmar, 2011; *television* includes: A Family at War, 1971; Martin Chuzzlewit, 1994; Our Friends in the North, 1996; Reckless, 1997; Our Mutual Friend, 1998; Vanity Fair, 1998; The Way We Live Now, 2002; Wild West, 2002–04; Blackpool, 2004; Ideal, 2006–08; True Dare Kiss, 2007; Game of Thrones, 2011–13; World Without End, 2012; Dr Who, 2012; Mount Pleasant, 2012–13; Prisoner's Wives, 2012–13; Broadchurch, 2013 (BAFTA Award for Best Supporting Actor, 2014); The Strain, 2014; *films* include: Tom's Midnight Garden, 1999; The King is Alive, 2000; Harry Potter and the Sorcerer's Stone, 2001; Harry Potter and the Chamber of Secrets, 2002; Nicholas Nickleby, 2002; Harry Potter and the Prisoner of Azkaban, 2004; Harry Potter and the Goblet of Fire, 2005; Harry Potter and the Order of the Phoenix, 2007; Hot Fuzz, 2007; Harry Brown, 2009; Harry Potter and the Half-Blood Prince, 2009; Another Year, 2010; Harry Potter and the Deathly Hallows: Part 2, 2011; Captain America: the First Avenger, 2011; The World's End, 2013; An Adventure in Space and Time, 2013. Pres., Shakespeare Hospice, Stratford-upon-Avon, 2010–. Hon. DLitt Warwick, 2012. *Recreations:* ski-ing, football (watching), family dinners, singing (frontman for The Crisps), all things Italian. *Address:* c/o Ruth Young, United Agents, 12–26 Lexington Street, W1F 0LE. *T:* (020) 3214 0800.

BRADLEY, David Rice; Director of Development, King's College School, Wimbledon, 2000–07; *b* 9 Jan. 1938; *s* of George Leonard Bradley and Evelyn Annie Bradley; *m* 1962, Josephine Elizabeth Turnbull Fricker (*née* Harries); two *s. Educ:* Christ Coll., Brecon; St Catharine's Coll., Cambridge (Exhibnr; MA English); Edinburgh Univ. (Dip. in Applied Linguistics). Nat. service commn, S Wales Borderers. British Council: served: Dacca, 1962–65; Allahabad, 1966–69; New Delhi, 1969–70; Dir of Studies, British Inst., Madrid, 1970–73; Department of the Environment: Principal, Res. Admin, 1973–76; Planning, Develt Control, 1976–78; Inner Cities, 1978–79; Rayner Study (develt of Management Inf. System for Ministers), 1979–80; Central Policy Planning Unit, 1980–81; Study of Local Govt Finance (Grade 5), 1981–82; on special leave, Gwilym Gibbon Res. Fellow, Nuffield Coll., Oxford, 1982–83; Finance, Envmtl Servs, 1983–86; London Urban Develt, sponsorship of LDDC, 1986–88; Dir (G3), Merseyside Task Force, DoE, 1988–90; Chief Exec., London Borough of Havering, 1990–95; Mgt Consultant, CSC Computer Scis Ltd, 1995–96; Head, Corporate Funding, Univ. of Oxford, 1997–2000. Vis. Fellow, Nuffield Coll., Oxford, 1993–2001. Mem., DoE Adv. Panel on appointments to Sponsored Bodies, 1996–98; non-exec. Dir, E Thames Housing Gp, 1997–98. Mem. Mgt Bd, Bankside Gall., 2002–03. Mem. Council, Sch. of Mgt Studies, Oxford Univ., 1995–98. Hon. Sec., London Planning and Develt Forum, 1990–2003. *Recreations:* painting, gardening. *Address:* 29 York Court, Albany Park Road, Kingston upon Thames, Surrey KT2 5ST. *T:* (020) 8547 1573.

BRADLEY, Prof. Denise Irene, AC 2008 (AO 1995); Vice Chancellor and President, University of South Australia, 1997–2007, now Emeritus Professor; *b* 23 March 1942; *d* of Richard Francis Haren and Lillian Irene (*née* Ward); *m* 1st, 1962, Michael Charles Bradley (marr. diss. 1985); four *s*; 2nd, 1987, Bruce Simpson King. *Educ:* Sydney Univ. (BA); Adelaide Univ. (DipEd 1964); Univ. of NSW (DipLib 1973); Flinders Univ. (MSocAdmin 1986). Women's Advr, Dept of Educn, S Australia, 1977–80; South Australia College of Advanced Education: Dean, Faculty of Educn and Humanities, 1983–86; Dir (Academic), 1986–88; Dep. Principal, 1988–90; Principal, 1990; University of South Australia: Dep. Vice Chancellor, 1991–92; Dep. Vice Chancellor (Academic), 1992–95; Dep. Vice Chancellor and Vice Pres., 1995–96. Chairman: Expert Panel, Nat. Rev. of Higher Educn, 2008; Aust. Health Workforce Adv. Council, 2010–12; Interim Chief Comr, Tertiary Educn Quality and Standards Agency, 2010–11; Member: UNESCO Nat. Commn, 2008–13; Educn Infrastructure Fund Adv. Council, 2009–14; NSW Skills Bd, 2013–. Chm., VERNet Pty Ltd, 2008–; Dir, SEEK Ltd, 2010–. SA Great, 2005 South Australian of the Year. *Recreation:* reading. *Address:* University of South Australia, GPO Box 2471, Adelaide, SA 5001, Australia.

BRADLEY, Dominic; Member (SDLP) Newry and Armagh, Northern Ireland Assembly, since 2003; *b* 18 Nov. 1954; *s* of William J. Bradley and Sarah McKeown; *m* Mary McManus; one *s. Educ:* St Paul's High Sch., Bessbrook; Abbey Christian Brothers Grammar Sch., Newry; Queen's Univ. Belfast (BA Hons); Univ. of Ulster (MA). Teacher, St Paul's High Sch., Bessbrook, 1978–89 and 1991–2003; Southern Educn and Library Bd, 1989–91. Northern Ireland Assembly: SDLP spokesperson on finance; Mem., Culture, Arts and Leisure Cttee, 2006–; Mem., Finance and Personnel Cttee, 2011–. Contested (SDLP) Newry and Armagh, 2010. *Recreations:* walking, swimming, reading. *Address:* (office) 15 Trevor Hill, Newry BT34 1DN. *T:* (028) 3026 7933, *Fax:* (028) 3026 7828. *E:* dominicobrolchain@btinternet.com. *Club:* St Patrick's Gaelic Athletic (Carrickcruppen, Co. Armagh).

BRADLEY, Prof. Donal Donat Conor, CBE 2010; PhD; FRS 2004; CPhys, CEng; Professor of Engineering Science and Physics, and Head, Mathematical, Physical and Life Sciences Division, University of Oxford, since 2015; *b* 3 Jan. 1962; *s* of Prof. Daniel Joseph Bradley, FRS and of Winefride Marie-Therese Bradley; *m* 1989, Beverley Diane Hirst; one *s* two *d. Educ:* Wimbledon Coll., London; Imperial Coll., Univ. of London (BSc 1st Cl. Hons 1983; ARCS); Cavendish Lab., Univ. of Cambridge (PhD 1987). MInstP 1990, FInstP 2005; FIET 2013; CEng 2015. Unilever Res. Fellow in Chem. Physics, Corpus Christi Coll., Cambridge, 1987–89; Toshiba Res. Fellow, Toshiba R&D Center, Kawasaki, Japan,

1987–88; Asst Lectr in Physics, Univ. of Cambridge, 1989–93; Churchill College, Cambridge: Lectr and Fellow, 1989–93; Dir of Studies, 1992–93; Tutor, 1992–93; University of Sheffield: Reader in Physics, 1993–95; Warden, Tapton Hall, 1994–99; Prof. of Physics, 1995–2000; Dir, Centre for Molecular Materials, 1995–2000; Royal Soc. Amersham Internat. Sen. Res. Fellow, 1996–97; Leverhulme Trust Res. Fellow, 1997–98; Imperial College, University of London: Prof. of Exptl Solid State Physics, 2000–06; Lee-Lucas Prof. of Experimental Physics, 2006–15; Dep. Dir, Centre for Electronic Materials and Devices, and Hd of Exptl Solid State Gp, 2001–05; Hd, Dept of Physics, 2005–08; Dir, Centre for Plastic Electronics, 2009–15; Dep. Principal, Faculty of Natural Scis, 2008–11; Pro-Rector (Res.), 2011–13; Vice-Provost (Res.), 2013–15; Vis. Prof. of Physics, 2015–. Adjunct Prof., Hong Kong Baptist Univ., 2012–; Hon. Prof., Nanjing Univ. of Technol., 2013–; 1000-talent Plan Researcher, Key Lab. for Organic Electronics and Inf. Display, Nanjing Univ. of Posts and Telecoms, 2014–. Member: SERC/EPSRC Laser Facility Cttee Panel, 1991–95; EPSRC Functional Materials Coll., 1995–; ESF EUROCORES Cttee, 2006; Jury Cttee, Degussa European Sci. to Business Award, 2006; RCUK Rev. of UK Physics Panel, 2008; Optoelectronics Adv. Cttee, Rank Prize Funds, 2010–13 (Chair and Trustee, 2013–); Sub-panel 9: Physics, 2014 REF, 2010–14; Special Advr to UK Parlt IUSS cttee inquiry on plastic electronics engrg, 2008–09. Co-inventor, conjugated polymer electroluminescence; co-founder: Cambridge Display Technol. Ltd; Molecular Vision Ltd (Dir, 2001–12); C-Change llp, 2008–; Director: Imperial Coll. London Consultants Ltd, 2005–06; Solar Press UK Ltd, 2009–. Lectures: Weissberger-Williams, Eastman Kodak, 2004; Frolich, Univ. of Liverpool, 2009; Chau Wai-yin Meml, Hong Kong Poly. Univ., 2009; Mott, Inst. of Physics, 2009; Bakerian, Royal Soc., 2010; Dist. Lect. in Physics, Hong Kong Baptist Univ., 2011; Global Vision, Nanjing Univ. of Technol., 2013; Founders Prize Lect., Polymer Physics Gp, 2013. Ed., Organic Electronics, 2000–05. Member: Physical Soc. Club, 2005–; Royal Soc. Club, 2009–. FRSA 1983. Hon. DSc Sheffield, 2014. RSA Silver Medal, Outstanding Grad., RCS, 1983; Daiwa Award for Anglo-Japanese Collaboration, 1994; Descartes Prize, EU, 2003; Jan Rajchman Prize, Soc. for Inf. Display, 2005; European Latsis Prize, ESF, 2005; Res. Excellence Award, Imperial Coll., London, 2006; Brian Mercer Award for Innovation, 2007, Bakerian Medal, 2010, Royal Soc.; Faraday Medal, Inst. of Physics, 2009; Faraday Medal, IET, 2010; Founders Prize, Polymer Physics Gp (Inst. of Physics/RSC/IMMM), 2013. *Publications:* numerous papers in learned jls and 16 patents on polymer optoelectronics. *Recreations:* DIY, cinema, music, military history. *Address:* Division of Mathematical, Physical and Life Sciences, University of Oxford, 9 Parks Road, Oxford OX1 3PD.

BRADLEY, Edgar Leonard, OBE 1979; Metropolitan Stipendiary Magistrate, 1967–83; *b* 17 Nov. 1917; 2nd *s* of Ernest Henry and Letitia Bradley, W Felton, Oswestry; *m* 1942, Elsa, *o d* of Colin and Elizabeth Matheson, Edinburgh; two *s* three *d*. *Educ:* Malvern Coll.; Trinity Hall, Cambridge. BA 1939; MA 1942. Called to Bar, Middle Temple, 1940. Served 1940–46, RA; Capt. and Adjt, 1943–45; Major, GSO2, Mil. Govt of Germany, 1946. Practised at Bar, 1946–51, SE Circuit, Central Criminal Ct, S London and Surrey Sessions. Legal Dept of Home Office, 1951–54. Sec., Departmental Cttee on Magistrates' Courts Bill, 1952; Sec. of Magistrates' Courts Rule Cttee, 1952–54; Clerk to Justices: Wrexham and Bromfield, 1954–57; Poole, 1957–67. Justices' Clerks Society: Mem. Council, 1957–67; Hon. Sec., 1963–67. Mem., Nat. Adv. Council on Trng of Magistrates, 1965–67; Magistrates' Association: Vice Pres., 1984–; Mem. Council, 1968–84; Chm. Legal Cttee, 1973–82. Adv. tour of Magistrates' Courts in Ghana, 1970. *Publications:* (with J. J. Senior) Bail in Magistrates' Courts, 1977; articles in legal jls. *Recreations:* visiting Perthshire, music. *Address:* 55 St Germains, Bearsden, Glasgow G61 2RS. *T:* (0141) 942 5831.

BRADLEY, Prof. (John) Andrew, PhD; FRCSGlas; Professor of Surgery, University of Cambridge, since 1997; Hon. Consultant Surgeon, Addenbrooke's Hospital, Cambridge, since 1997; *b* 24 Oct. 1950; *s* of Colin Bradley and Christine Bradley (*née* Johnstone Miller); *m* 1987, Eleanor Mary Bolton; two *s*. *Educ:* Salendine Nook Secondary Sch., Huddersfield; Huddersfield Coll. of Technol.; Univ. of Leeds (MB ChB 1975); Univ. of Glasgow (PhD 1982). FRCSGlas 1979. Lectr in Surgery, Glasgow Univ., 1978–84; Cons. Surgeon, Western Infirmary, Glasgow, 1984–94; Prof. of Surgery, Univ. of Glasgow, 1994–97; Hon. Cons. Surgeon, Western Infirmary, Glasgow, 1994–97. President: British Transplantation Soc., 1999–2002; Soc. of Academic and Res. Surgery, 2011–13. Founder FMedSci 1998; FRCS *ad eundem* 1999. *Publications:* articles in sci. jls, mainly in the field of organ transplantation and immunology. *Recreations:* ski-ing, mountaineering. *Address:* University Department of Surgery, Box 202, Level 9, Addenbrooke's Hospital, Cambridge CB2 0QQ.

BRADLEY, Karen Anne; MP (C) Staffordshire Moorlands, since 2010; Parliamentary Under-Secretary of State, Home Office, since 2014; *b* Newcastle-under-Lyme, 12 March 1970; *d* of Kenneth and Olive Howarth; *m* 2001, Neil Austin Bradley; two *s*. *Educ:* Buxton Girls' Sch., Derbys; Imperial Coll., London (BSc Hons Maths). Tax Manager, Deloitte & Touche (formerly Touche Ross), 1991–98; Sen. Tax Manager, KPMG, 1998–2004; self-employed fiscal and economic consultant, 2004–07; Sen. Tax Manager, KPMG, 2007–10. An Asst Govt Whip, 2012–13; a Lord Comr of HM Treasury (Govt Whip), 2013–14. Associate Mem., ICAEW, 1995; Mem., Chartered Inst. of Taxation, 1996. *Recreations:* travel, wine tasting, cooking, puzzles. *Address:* House of Commons, SW1A 0AA. *T:* (020) 7219 7215. *E:* karen.bradley.mp@parliament.uk.

BRADLEY, Martin Eugene Joseph, OBE 2013; FRCN; DL; Chairman, Northern Ireland Association for Mental Health, 2011–14; *b* Belfast, 23 June 1950; *s* of Edward and Elizabeth Bradley; *m* 1986, Nuala Mooney; one *s* one *d*. *Educ:* Univ. of London (Dip. Nursing 1976); Univ. of Ulster (BSc Hons Educn 1981; MSc Educn 1985); Queen's Univ. Belfast (Dip. Health Econs 1996). Nursing student, St Olave's and Guy's Hosps, 1968–71; Postgrad. nursing student, Maudsley Hosp., 1973–74; Staff Nurse, 1974–75, Charge Nurse, 1975–76, Whiteabbey Hosp.; Nurse Tutor, Central Sch. of Psychiatric and Special Care Nursing, 1977–80; Sen. Tutor, Belfast Northern Gp Sch. of Nursing, 1980–82; Sen. Tutor, 1982–86, Dir of Nurse Educn, 1986–89, Belfast Northern Coll. of Nursing; Dir of Nurse Educn, Eastern Area Coll. of Nursing, Belfast, 1989–91; Dep. Chief Nursing Officer, Dept of Health and Social Services, NI, 1991–97; Chief Nurse, 1997–2000, Dir of Health Care, 2000–03, Western Health and Social Services Bd, Londonderry; Dir, RCN, NI, 2003–05; Chief Nursing Officer, DoH, Social Services and Public Safety, NI, 2005–11. Chair, Ministerial Review of Undergraduate Nursing and Midwifery Educn, Dept of Health and Children, Ireland, 2011–. Mem. Bd, UK Bd of Healthcare Chaplaincy, 2011–. Vis. Prof. of Nursing, Univ. of Ulster, 1998–. Mem. Council, Pharmaceutical Soc. of NI, 2012–. Trustee, Florence Nightingale Foundn, 2010–. FQNI 2011. DL Belfast, 2015. *Recreations:* gardening, music, theatre, opera, walking, reading. *E:* martinbradley06@hotmail.com.

BRADLEY, Prof. Patrick James, FRCSI, FRCSE, FRCS; Consultant Head and Neck Oncologic Surgeon, Nottingham University Hospitals, Queen's Medical Centre Campus, 1982–2009, now Emeritus Consultant; Special Professor of Head and Neck Oncologic Surgery, University of Nottingham Medical School, 2007–09, now Emeritus Hon. Professor; *b* Thurles, Co. Tipperary, 10 May 1949; *s* of Gerry Bradley and Nan Bradley (*née* O'Leary); *m* 1974, Sheena Kelly; three *s* two *d*. *Educ:* Glenstal Abbey Sch., Limerick; University Coll. Dublin (MB BCh, BAO 1973; DCH 1975); Univ. of Nottingham (MBA Public Health 2002). FRCSI 1977; FRCSE 1979; FRCS (*ad eundem*) 1999, Hon. FRCS 2015. Registrar, then Sen. Registrar, Royal Liverpool Hosp., 1977–82. Nat. Clinical Lead for Head and Neck Cancer (NHS England and Wales), 2003–08. Hon. Sen. Lectr, 2003–07, Hon. Prof., Faculty of Medicine and Social Scis, 2007–, Middlesex Univ. Ed., Oncol. News (UK), 2008–11 (Associate, Editl Bd, 2006–11); Jt Ed., Current Opinions ORL-HNS (USA), 2008– (Ed., Head and Neck Cancer Section, 1999–2008; Mem., Editl Bd, 2007–08); Member, Editorial Board: Jl Laryngology and Otology (UK), 1996–2011; ENT News (UK), 1997–2011 (Chm., 2002–11); Head and Neck (USA), 2001–; ORL Otolaryngol. (USA), 2003–; Oral Oncol. (UK), 2003–07 (Sen. Advr to Bd, 2007–); Clin. Otolaryngol. (UK), 2006–11; Acta Otolaryngologica (Scandinavia), 2006–; Eur. Archives ORL-HNS, 2008–. Hunterian Prof., RCS, 2007–08. British Association of Head and Neck Oncologists: Mem., Nat. Council, 1986–93 and 2001–06; Hon. Sec., 1989–93; Pres., 2003–05; British Association of Otorhinolaryngologists, Head and Neck Surgeons: Mem. Council, 1994–95; Chm., Educnl Cttee, 1999–2002, Cancer Cttee, 1999–2009; Mem., Nat. Exec. Council, British Assoc. Surgical Oncologists, 1998–2000; Pres., 2004–06, Hon. Pres., 2008–, Eur. Laryngological Soc.; Founding Mem. Bd, Eur. Head and Neck Soc., 2004–11; Mem., Foundn Exec. Bd, 2005–11, Vice-Pres., 2006–09, Eur Acad. of Otorhinolaryngology, Head and Neck Surgery; Founding Mem. Bd, 2006, Pres., 2007–09, Eur. Salivary Gland Soc.; Founding Mem., 2005, Chm., Nominating Cttee, 2009–11, Internat. Acad. Oral Oncol. Trustee and Chm. Bd, Head and Neck Foundn, 1998–; Trustee, Nottingham Rhinological Res. Fund, 1999–. FACS 2007. Hon. FRCSLT 2006; Hon. FRACS 2007; Hon. Fellow, Hong Kong Coll. of Otolaryngol., Head and Neck Surgery, 2007. *Publications:* contrib. book chapters and articles to learned jls on topics related to clin. activity, head and neck cancers, salivary gland diseases and disorders, rehabilitation, hosp. mgt and med. educn. *Recreations:* golf, wine tasting, travel. *Address:* 10 Chartwell Grove, Mapperley Plains, Nottingham NG3 5RD. *T:* (0115) 920 1611. *E:* pjbradley@zoo.co.uk. *Clubs:* Royal Automobile, Royal Society of Medicine; Skellig Bay Golf (Waterville, Co. Kerry).

BRADLEY, Peadar John; Member (SDLP) South Down, Northern Ireland Assembly, 1998–2011; *b* 28 April 1940; *s* of William T. Bradley and Annie E. Barry; *m* 1962, Leontia Martin; three *s* five *d*. *Educ:* Carrick Primary Sch.; St Colman's Coll., Newry, Co. Down; Warrenpoint Tech. Centre. Mem., Irish Auctioneers and Valuers Inst., 1986 (Fellow, 2000). Salesman, 1958–65; Agricl Rep., 1965–78; Property Negotiator, 1978–81; self-employed Estate Agent, 1981–99. Mem., Newry and Mourne DC, 1981–2005. *Recreations:* Gaelic games, part-time farming, travel. *Address:* 10 Carrogs Road, Newry, Co. Down BT34 2NJ. *T:* (028) 3026 2062. *Clubs:* Naomh Mhuire, Cumann Luth Chleas Gael (Boireann).

BRADLEY, Peter Charles Stephen; Director, Speakers' Corner Trust, since 2007; *b* 12 April 1953; *s* of Fred and Trudie Bradley; *m* 2000, Annie Hart; one *s* one *d* (twins). *Educ:* Abingdon Sch.; Univ. of Sussex (BA Hons 1975); Occidental Coll., LA. Res. Dir, Centre for Contemporary Studies, 1979–85; Dir, Good Relations Ltd, 1985–93; Man. Dir, Millbank Consultants Ltd, 1993–97. Mem. (Lab), Westminster CC, 1986–96 (Dep. Leader, Labour Gp, 1990–96). MP (Lab) The Wrekin, 1997–2005; contested (Lab) same seat, 2005. PPS to Minister of State for Rural Affairs, 2001–05. Mem., Select Cttee on Public Admin, 1997–99; Chm., Rural Gp of Labour MPs, 1997–2001. Member: Affordable Rural Housing Commn, 2005–06; Rural Housing Adv. Gp, 2007–09. Hon. Patron, AFC Telford Utd, 2004–. FRSA. *Recreations:* playing/watching cricket, supporting Aston Villa, walking and reading (both slowly). *Address:* Old Roslyn House, Roslyn Road, Wellington, Telford TF1 3AX. *Club:* Warwickshire County Cricket.

BRADLEY, Ven. Peter David Douglas; Archdeacon of Warrington, 2001–15; *b* 4 June 1949; *m* 1970, Pat Dutton; three *s*. *Educ:* Brookfield Comp. Sch., Kirkby; Lincoln Theol Coll.; Ian Ramsey Coll., Brasted; Nottingham Univ. (BTh 1979). Ordained deacon, 1979, priest, 1980; Curate, Upholland Team, 1979–83; Vicar, Holy Spirit, Dovecot, Liverpool, 1983–94; Dir, Continuing Ministerial Educn, dio. Liverpool, 1989–2001; Team Rector, Upholland, 1994–2011. Mem., Gen. Synod of C of E, 1990–2010. Hon. Canon, Liverpool Cathedral, 2000–15. *Recreations:* walking, reading. *Address:* 30 Sandbrook Road, Orrell, Wigan WN5 8UD. *T:* (01695) 624131.

BRADLEY, Very Rev. Peter Edward; Dean of Sheffield, since 2003; *b* 26 June 1964; *s* of William Charles Basil Bradley and Elizabeth Alexandra Bradley. *Educ:* Royal Belfast Academical Instn; Trinity Hall, Cambridge (BA Theol. and Religious Studies 1986, MA 1989); Ripon Coll., Cuddesdon. Ordained deacon, 1988, priest, 1989; Chaplain, Gonville and Caius Coll., Cambridge, 1990–95; Team Vicar: St Michael and All Angels, Abingdon, 1995–98; All Saints', High Wycombe, 1998–2003; Team Rector, High Wycombe, 2003. Chair: Church and Community Fund, 2014–; Open Coll. of the Arts, 2014–; Finance for Sheffield, 2015–. *Recreations:* sculpture, contemporary art, being Irish, hypochondria. *Address:* The Cathedral, Church Street, Sheffield S1 1HA. *T:* (0114) 263 6063, *Fax:* (0114) 279 7412. *E:* enquiries@sheffield-cathedral.org.uk.

BRADLEY, Peter Richard, CBE 2005; Chief Executive, St John Ambulance Service, New Zealand, since 2012; *b* 28 Dec. 1957; *s* of John and Mary Bradley; *m* 1978, Mary Elisabeth Verhoeff (marr. diss.); one *s* two *d*. *Educ:* Temple Moor Grammar Sch., Leeds; Otago Univ., NZ (MBA). With Commercial Bank of Australia, Auckland, 1973–76; St John Ambulance Service, Auckland, 1976–95; qualified paramedic, 1986; Chief Ambulance Officer, 1993–95; joined London Ambulance Service NHS Trust, 1996; Dir of Ops, 1998–2000; Chief Exec., 2000–12, and Nat. Ambulance Dir, DoH, 2004–12. FNZIM 1999. OStJ 1994 (SBStJ 1992). *Recreations:* reading, sport, music. *Address:* St John National Headquarters and Northern Region HQ, 2 Harrison Road, Private Bag 14902, Panmore, Auckland 1741, New Zealand.

BRADLEY, Prof. Richard John, FSA, FSAScot; FBA 1995; Professor of Archaeology, Reading University, 1987–2014, now Emeritus; *b* 18 Nov. 1946; *s* of John Newsum Bradley and Margaret Bradley (*née* Saul); *m* 1976, Katherine Bowden. *Educ:* Portsmouth Grammar Sch.; Magdalen Coll., Oxford (MA). MCIfA. Lectr in Archaeology, 1971–84, Reader, 1984–87, Reading Univ. Mem., Royal Commn on Historical Monuments of England, 1987–99. Hon. FSAScot 2007. Hon. Dr Univ. of Lund, 2002. *Publications:* (with A. Ellison) Rams Hill: a Bronze Age Defended Enclosure and its Landscape, 1975; The Prehistoric Settlement of Britain, 1978; (ed with J. Barrett) Settlement and Society in the British Later Bronze Age, 1980; The Social Foundations of Prehistoric Britain, 1984; (ed with J. Gardiner) Neolithic Studies, 1984; The Passage of Arms: an archæological analysis of prehistoric hoards and votive deposits, 1990, rev. edn 1998; (with J. Barrett and M. Green) Landscape, Monuments and Society, 1991; (ed with J. Barrett and M. Hall) Papers on the Prehistoric Archaeology of Cranborne Chase, 1991; Altering the Earth: the origins of monuments in Britain and Continental Europe, 1993; (with M. Edmonds) Interpreting the Axe Trade: production and exchange in Neolithic Britain, 1993; (jtly) Prehistoric Land Divisions on Salisbury Plain: the work of the Wessex Linear Ditches Project, 1994; Rock Art and the Prehistory of Atlantic Europe, 1997; The Significance of Monuments, 1998; An Archaeology of Natural Places, 2000; The Good Stones: a new investigation of the Clava Cairns, 2000; The Past in Prehistoric Society, 2002; The Moon and the Bonfire: an investigation of three stone circles in north-east Scotland, 2004; Ritual and Domestic Life in Prehistoric Europe, 2005; The Prehistory of Britain and Ireland, 2007; Image and Audience: rethinking prehistoric art, 2009; Stages and Screens: an investigation of four henge monuments in northern and north-eastern Scotland, 2011; (ed jtly) Development-led Archaeology in Northwest Europe, 2012; The Idea of Order: the circular archetype in Prehistoric Europe, 2012; contribs to learned jls. *Recreations:* literature, contemporary classical music, watercolours, antiquarian bookshops. *Address:* Department of Archaeology, University of Reading, Whiteknights, Reading RG6 6AB. *T:* (0118) 378 8130.

BRADLEY, Robin Alistair, CBE 2000; CEng; Chief Executive, Atomic Weapons Establishment, Aldermaston, 1997–2000; *b* 3 Aug. 1938; *s* of Cyril Robert Bradley and Phyllis Mary (*née* Stalham); *m* 1964, Marguerite Loftus; one *s* two *d*. MIMechE 1972; CEng 1972.

MoD, 1962–65; Hunting Engrg, Ampthill, 1965–72; Manager, Defence Progs (Australia), Hunting Systems, S Australia, 1972–75; Chief Project Engr, Project Manager, then Divl Manager Engrg, Hunting Engrg, Ampthill, 1975–90; Ops Director, AWE/Hunting Brown Root/AEA, Aldermaston (originally on secondment), 1990–96. *Recreations:* athletics, climbing, gardening. *Address:* c/o Hunting plc, 3 Cockspur Street, SW1Y 5BQ.

BRADLEY, Roger Thubron, FICFor; FIWSc; Chairman, Loch Lomond and Trossachs National Park Fisheries Forum, since 2005; *b* 5 July 1936; *s* of Ivor Lewis Bradley and Elizabeth Thubron; *m* 1959, Ailsa Mary Walkden; one *s* one *d*. *Educ:* Lancaster Royal Grammar Sch.; St Peter's Coll., Oxford (MA). FICFor 1980; FIWSc 1985. Asst District Officer, Kendal, 1960; Mensuration Officer, Alice Holt, 1961; Working Plans Officer, 1967; District Officer, North Argyll, 1970; Asst Conservator, South Wales, 1974; Conservator, North Wales, 1977; Forestry Commission: Dir, and Sen. Officer for Wales, 1982–83; Dir, Harvesting and Marketing, Edinburgh, 1983–85; Forestry Comr, 1985–95; Hd of Forestry Authy, 1992–95; Dir, Scottish Greenbelt Foundn, 1996–2006. Chairman: UK Forestry Accord, 1996–2002; Forth Dist Salmon Fishery Bd, 1998–2003. Chm., Edinburgh Centre for Tropical Forestry, 1996–99. Chm., Commonwealth Forestry Assoc., 1988–90; Pres., Inst. of Chartered Foresters, 1996–98. *Publications:* Forest Management Tables, 1966, 2nd edn 1971; Forest Planning, 1967; Thinning Control in British Forestry, 1967, 2nd edn 1971; various articles in Forestry, etc. *Recreation:* sailing. *Club:* 1970 (Edinburgh).

BRADLEY, Stanley Walter; business consultant, 1988–2014; Director, W. Hart & Son (Saffron Walden) Ltd, 1991–2014; Director General, British Printing Industries Federation, 1983–88; *b* 9 Sept. 1927; *s* of Walter Bradley; *m* 1955, Jean Brewster; three *s* one *d*. *Educ:* Boys' British Sch., Saffron Walden. Joined Spicers Ltd, 1948: held posts in prodn, marketing and gen. management; Personnel Dir, 1973–83; Dir, Capital Spicers Ltd, Eire, 1971–83. Dir, Harman Gp, 1988–91. Chm., BPIF Manufg Stationery Industry Gp, 1977–81; Pres., E Anglian Printing Industries Alliance, 1978–79; Mem., Printing Industries Sector Working Party, 1979–87, Chm., Communications Action Team, 1980–85, NEDC. *Recreations:* painting, golf, fishing. *Address:* 5 Edward Bawden Court, Park Lane, Saffron Walden, Essex CB10 1FP. *T:* (01799) 529209.

BRADLEY, Stephen Edward; HM Diplomatic Service, retired; Vice Chairman, Wanlian Development, Beijing; Senior Consultant, ICAP (Asia Pacific); *b* 4 April 1958; *s* of Maj.-Gen. Peter Edward Moore Bradley, CB, CBE, DSO; *m* 1982, Elizabeth Gomersall (marr. diss. 2011); one *s* one *d*; *m* 2013, Tara Wang. *Educ:* Marlborough Coll.; Balliol Coll., Oxford; Fudan Univ., Shanghai. South Asian Dept, FCO, 1982; Tokyo, 1983–87; Guinness Peat Aviation, 1987–88; Dep. Political Advr, Hong Kong Govt, 1988–93; Lloyd George Investment Management, 1994–95; Near East and North Africa Dept, FCO, 1995–97; West Indian and Atlantic Dept, FCO, 1997–98; New Millennium Experience Co., 1998–99; Paris, 1999–2002; Minister, Beijing, 2002–03; Consul-Gen., Hong Kong, 2003–08. Director: Husky Energy Inc., 2010–; Swire Properties Ltd, 2011–; China Heritage Fund; Broad Lea Gp. *Recreations:* books, gardens, travel. *Address:* PO Box 10153, General Post Office, Hong Kong, China. *Clubs:* Athenæum; Hong Kong.

BRADLEY, Stuart; *see* Bradley, C. S.

BRADLEY-JONES, Luke; Brand Director, TV, BSkyB, since 2012; *b* Malmesbury, 1 April 1976; *s* of Rhodri and Sue Bradley-Jones; *m* 2007, Charlotte; two *d*. *Educ:* Malvern Coll., Worcs; Balliol Coll., Oxford. Manager, Spectrum Strategy Consultants, 1999–2006; BBC Worldwide: Hd of Strategy, 2006–07; Exec. Vice Pres., Digital Media, US, 2007–09; Man. Dir, BBC.com and Global iPlayer, 2009–11. Gov., Haverstock Sch., 2010–. *Recreations:* golf, squash, watching cricket, art, hanging out with my wife and daughters. *E:* lbj1476@yahoo.co.uk.

BRADLEY GOODMAN, Michael; *see* Goodman, His Honour M. B.

BRADMAN, Godfrey Michael, FCA; company director; *b* 9 Sept. 1936; *s* of William I. Bradman and Anne Bradman (*née* Goldsweig); *m* 1975, Susan Bennett; two *s* three *d*. FCA 1961. Sen. Partner, Godfrey Bradman and Co. (Chartered Accountants), 1961–69; Chm. and Chief Exec., London Mercantile Corp. (Bankers), 1969; Chm., Rosehaugh plc, 1979–91; Joint Chairman: Broadgate Develts, 1984–91; Victoria Quay Ltd, 1993; Chairman: Eur. Land & Property Corp. plc, 1992; Ashpost Finance, 1993; Pondbridge Europe Ltd, 1994; Dep. Chm., Kyp Hldgs plc, 2003–10; Director: Property & Land Investment Corp. plc, 2001–11; Midatech Ltd, 2004–13; Metropolitan & Suburban, 2006–09. Founder and Mem., CLEAR (Campaign for Lead-Free Air) Ltd, 1981–91; Jt Founder, 1983, and Hon. Pres., Campaign for Freedom of Information, 1983; Founder and Chm., Citizen Action and European Citizen Action, 1983–91 (Dir, AIDS Policy Unit, 1987–90); Chm., Friends of the Earth Trust, 1983–91; Council Mem., UN Internat. Year of Shelter for the Homeless, 1987; Pres., Soc. for the Protection of Unborn Children Educnl Res. Trust, 1987; Trustee, Right To Life Charitable Trust; Founder and Jt Chm., Parents Against Tobacco Campaign; Founder, Opren Victims Campaign. Mem. governing body, LSHTM, 1988–91. Hon. Fellow, Downing Coll., Cambridge, 1997 (Wilkins Fellow, 1999); Hon. FKC. Hon. DSc Salford. *Recreation:* reading. *Address:* 1 Berkeley Street, W1J 8DJ. *T:* (020) 7706 0189. *E:* gb@godfreybradman.com.

BRADNEY, John Robert; HM Diplomatic Service, retired; *b* 24 July 1931; *s* of Rev. Samuel Bradney, Canon Emeritus of St Alban's Abbey, and Constance Bradney (*née* Partington); *m* 1st, Jean Marion Halls (marr. diss. 1971); one *s* two *d*; 2nd, 1974, Sandra Cherry Smith, JP, *d* of Richard Arthur Amyas Smith, MC. *Educ:* Christ's Hospital. HM Forces, 1949–51, Herts Regt and RWAFF; Colonial Police, Nigeria, 1953–65; HM Diplomatic Service, 1965–86: First Sec., Lagos, 1974; FCO, 1977–86 (Counsellor, 1985); Advr, Govt of Oman, 1986–89. Trustee, Carlisle Cathedral Develt Trust, 2007–13 (Chm., 2007–09). DSM Oman, 1989. *Recreations:* salmon and trout fishing, gardening, ornithology. *Address:* Barclays Bank PLC, Penrith, Cumbria CA11 7YB. *Clubs:* Royal Over-Seas League; Yorks Fly Fisher's.

BRADSHAW, family name of **Baron Bradshaw**.

BRADSHAW, Baron *cr* 1999 (Life Peer), of Wallingford in the county of Oxfordshire; **William Peter Bradshaw;** Senior Visiting Research Fellow, Centre for Socio-Legal Studies, Wolfson College, Oxford, 1985–2000; Honorary Fellow, Wolfson College, Oxford, since 2004 (Supernumerary Fellow, 1988–2003); *b* 9 Sept. 1936; *s* of Leonard Charles Bradshaw and Ivy Doris Bradshaw; *m* 1st, 1957, Jill Hayward (*d* 2002); one *s* one *d*; 2nd, 2003, Diana Mary Ayris. *Educ:* Univ. of Reading (BA Pol Economy, 1957; MA 1960). FCIT 1987 (MCIT 1966). Joined Western Region of British Railways as Management Trainee, 1959; various appts, London and W of England Divs; Divl Manager, Liverpool, 1973; Chief Operating Man., LMR, 1976, Dep. Gen. Man. 1977; Chief Ops Man., BR HQ, 1978; Dir, Policy Unit, 1980; Gen. Man., Western Region, BR, 1983–85; Prof. of Transport Mgt, Univ. of Salford, 1986–92; Chm., Ulsterbus and Citybus Ltd, 1987–93. Member: Thames Valley Police Authority, 1997–2008 (Vice Chm., 1999–2003); BRB, later Strategic Rail Authy, 1999–2001; Commn for Integrated Transport, 1999–2001; Chm., Bus Appeals Body, 1998–2000. Mem. (Lib Dem) Oxfordshire CC, 1993–2008. Special Advr to Transport Select Cttee, H of C, 1992–97; Lib Dem spokesman on transport, H of L, 2001–. *Recreation:* growing hardy plants. *Address:* House of Lords, SW1A 0PW. *Club:* National Liberal.

BRADSHAW, Gen. Sir Adrian (John), KCB 2013 (CB 2009); OBE 1998; Deputy Supreme Allied Commander Europe, since 2014; *b* 1958; *m* Sally; two *s* one *d*. *Educ:* Univ. of Reading (BSc Agric. 1979); King's Coll. London (MSc Defence Studies 1991; MA Internat. Relns 2005). Oxford Univ. OTC, 1977–79; RMA, 1979–80; Tank Troop Leader, 14/20th King's Hussars, 1980–82; Intelligence Officer, Nuclear, Biol, Chem. Warfare Officer, 1982–84; army pilots course, 1984; helicopter pilot and AAC Flight Sqdn Dep. Comd, 1984–87; Troop Comdr, 1987–89; acsc, 1990; Ops Officer, UK Special Forces Gp, 1990–92; Sqdn Comdr, 1992–94; Armd Sqdn Leader, 1994–95, CO, Armd Regt, 1995–97, King's Royal Hussars; Instructor, JSCSC, 1998–2000; Dep. Comdr, Combined Jt Special Ops Task Force, Kosovo, 2000; Col, Mil. Ops, MoD, 2000–01; hcsc 2001; Mil. Advr, 3rd (US) Army, Kuwait, 2002–03; Dep. Comdr, US Task Force W, Iraq theatre of ops, 2003; Comdr, 7th Armd Bde, Iraq and Germany, 2003–05; rcds, 2005; Dir Special Forces, MoD, 2005–09; GOC, 1st (UK) Armd Div., 2009–11; US Army Strategic Leadership Prog. (Advanced), 2011; Dep. Comdr, ISAF and UK Nat. Contingent Comdr, Afghanistan, 2011–13; Comdr, Land Forces, 2013. Vis. Defence Fellow, Balliol Coll., Oxford, 2011. Chief of Gen. Staff's Liaison Officer and Advr to Jordan. Col Comdt, AAC. Officer, Legion of Merit (US), 2003; Bundeswehr Cross of Honour (Germany), 2011.

BRADSHAW, Prof. Alexander Marian, CBE 2007; PhD; FRS 2008; Scientific Member, Max-Planck-Institut für Plasmaphysik, Garching and Greifswald, since 1999 (Scientific Director, 1999–2008); *b* 12 July 1944. *Educ:* Queen Mary Coll., London (BSc 1965; PhD 1969). Scientific Mem., Fritz-Haber Institute of Max-Planck Soc., Berlin, 1980–98. Adjunct Professor of Physics: Technical Univ. of Berlin, 1997; Technical Univ. of Munich, 2000. Pres., German Physical Soc., 1998–2000. Fellow, German Nat. Acad. of Scis (formerly German Acad. of Scis Leopoldina), 2002. Hon. FInstP 2006. *Publications:* articles in learned jls. *Address:* Max-Planck-Institut für Plasmaphysik, Boltzmannstrasse 2, 85748 Garching, Germany. *T:* (89) 32992123, (30) 84134860, *Fax:* (89) 32991001. *E:* alex.bradshaw@ipp.mpg.de.

BRADSHAW, Rt Hon. Benjamin (Peter James); PC 2009; MP (Lab) Exeter, since 1997; *b* 30 Aug. 1960; *s* of late Canon Peter Bradshaw and Daphne Bradshaw (*née* Murphy); civil partnership 2006, Neal Thomas Dalgleish. *Educ:* Thorpe St Andrew Sch., Norwich; Univ. of Sussex (BA Hons). Reporter: Express and Echo, Exeter, 1984–85; Eastern Daily Press, Norwich, 1985–86; BBC Radio Devon, Exeter, 1986–89; BBC Radio Corresp., Berlin, 1989–91; reporter, World At One and World This Weekend, BBC Radio 4, 1991–97. Parly Under-Sec. of State, FCO, 2001–02; Parly Sec., Privy Council Office, 2002–03; Parly Under-Sec. of State, 2003–06, Minister of State, 2006–07, DEFRA; Minister of State, DoH, 2007–09; Minister for the SW, 2007–09; Sec. of State for Culture, Media and Sport, 2009–10; Shadow Sec. of State for Culture, Media and Sport, 2010. Member: European Legislation Select Cttee, 1997–2001; Ecclesiastical Cttee, 1997–2001, 2010–15; Culture, Media and Sport Select Cttee, 2012–15. Member: Christians on the Left (formerly Christian Socialist Movement), 1997–; Lab. Campaign for Electoral Reform, 1997–. Mem., Inst. of Internat. and Foreign Affairs. Consumer Journalist of Year, Argos, 1988; Journalist of Year, Anglo-German Foundn, 1990; Sony News Reporter Award, 1993. *Recreations:* cycling, walking in Devon, classical music, cooking, gardening. *Address:* House of Commons, SW1A 0AA. *T:* (020) 7219 6597, (constituency office) (01392) 424464. *Club:* Whipton Labour (Exeter).

See also J. R. Bradshaw.

BRADSHAW, Prof. Jonathan Richard, CBE 2005; DPhil; FBA 2010; Professor of Social Policy: University of York, 1981–2013, now Emeritus; Durham University (part-time), since 2013; *b* Windsor, 15 Feb. 1944; *s* of late Canon Peter Bradshaw and Daphne Jessica Bradshaw (*née* Murphy); *m* 1st, 1967, Nora Cook (marr. diss. 1986); two *s* one *d*; 2nd, 1995, Carol Stimson (*d* 1997); two step *s*; 3rd, 2004, Prof. Karen Bloor. *Educ:* Lancing Coll.; Trinity Coll., Dublin (BSS 1st Cl. 1967; MA 1967); Univ. of York (MPhil 1969; DPhil 1978). University of York: Lectr, 1968–73; Founding Dir, Social Policy Res. Unit, 1973–88; Hd, Dept of Social Policy and Social Work, 1988–94 and 2003–07; Dir, Inst. for Res. in the Social Scis, 1994–98. Hon. Vis. Prof., Univ. of Oxford, 2008–; Hon. Res. Fellow, Human Scis Res. Council, SA, 2008–. Chair, Mgt Cttee, York Welfare Benefits Unit, 1969–2014; Dir, Family Budget Unit, 2001–11. Pres., Foundn for Internat. Studies in Social Security, 1999–2003. Member: Res. Cttee, Internat. Social Security Assoc., 1998–; Bd, Internat. Soc. for Child Indicators, 2007–13; Bd, Child Poverty Action Gp, 2012–. FAcSS (AcSS 1996). Hon. FFPHM 1996. DUniv Turku, 2011. *Publications:* The Financial Needs of Disabled Children, 1975; Found Dead, 1978; (jtly) Issues in Social Policy, 1979; Equity and Family Incomes, 1980; The Family Fund: an initiative in social policy, 1980; (jtly) Child Support in the European Community, 1980; (jtly) Energy and Social Policy, 1983; (jtly) Reserved for the Poor: the means test in British social policy, 1983; (jtly) Lone Mothers, Paid Work and Social Security, 1984; (jtly) Budgeting on Benefits, 1987; (jtly) Public Support for Private Residential Care, 1988; Social Security Parity in Northern Ireland, 1989; Lone Parents: policy in the doldrums, 1989; (jtly) Living on the Edge, 1989; Child Poverty and Deprivation in the UK, 1990; (jtly) Lone Parent Families in the UK, 1990; (ed) Budget Standards for the United Kingdom, 1993; (jtly) Support for Children: a comparison of arrangements in fifteen countries, 1993; (jtly) The Employment of Lone Parents: a comparison of policy in 20 countries, 1996; (jtly) Social Assistance in OECD Countries, 1996; (jtly) Using Child Benefit in the Family Budget, 1997; (jtly) Comparative Social Assistance: localisation and discretion, 1997; (jtly) Absent Fathers?, 1999; (ed jtly) Experiencing Poverty, 2000; (ed jtly) Researching Poverty, 2000; (jtly) Poverty and Social Exclusion in Britain, 2000; (ed) Poverty: the outcomes for children, 2001; (jtly) A Comparison of Child Benefit Packages in 22 Countries, 2001; (ed) The Well-being of Children in the UK, 2002, 3rd edn 2011; (jtly) Gender and Poverty in Britain, 2003; (jtly) The Drivers of Social Exclusion, 2004; (jtly) Routes out of Poverty, 2004; (ed jtly) Social Policy, Family Change and Employment in Comparative Perspective, 2006; (jtly) Child Poverty in Large Families, 2006; (jtly) A Minimum Income Standard for Britain, 2008; (jtly) Understanding Children's Well-being, 2010; (jtly) The Measurement of Extreme Poverty in the European Union, 2011; contrib. articles to Jl Social Policy, Jl Eur. Social Policy, Poverty, Jl Poverty and Social Justice, Jl Child Indicators Res., Jl Social Indicators, Children and Youth Services Rev., Children and Society, Jl Children's Services, Family Matters. *Recreation:* gardening. *Address:* Department of Social Policy and Social Work, University of York, Heslington, York YO10 5DD. *T:* (01904) 321329. *E:* jrb1@york.ac.uk. *W:* http://php.york.ac.uk/inst/spru/profiles/jrb.php.

See also Rt Hon. B. P. J. Bradshaw.

BRADSHAW, Martin Clark; Planning consultant, MB Consultants, 1995–2005; Director, Civic Trust, 1987–95; *b* 25 Aug. 1935; *s* of late Cyril Bradshaw and Nina Isabel Bradshaw; *m* 1st, 1959, Patricia Anne Leggatt (*d* 1981); two *s* one *d*; 2nd, 1986, Gillian Rosemary Payne; three step *s* one step *d*. *Educ:* King's Sch., Macclesfield; St John's Coll., Cambridge (MA); Univ. of Manchester (DipTP); MRTPI. Staff Surveyor, Lands and Surveys Dept, Uganda Protectorate, 1958–63; Asst Planning Officer, Planning Dept, City of Manchester, 1963–67; Asst Dir, City of Toronto Planning Bd, 1967–70; Asst Chief Planner, Cheshire CC, 1970–72; Asst County Planning Officer, Leics CC, 1972–73; Exec. Dir, Planning and Transport, 1973–81, Dir of Planning, 1981–86, W Yorks MCC; DoE Local Plans Inspectorate, 1986–87. Mem. Council, 1989–2001, Pres., 1993, RTPI. Gen. Comr for Income Tax, Bedford, 1987–96, Oxford, 2000–09. Hon. FRIBA 1995. *Recreations:* theatre, art, golf.

BRADSHAW, Prof. Peter, FRS 1981; Thomas V. Jones Professor of Engineering, Department of Mechanical Engineering, Stanford University, 1988–95, now Emeritus; *b* 26 Dec. 1935; *s* of Joseph W. N. Bradshaw and Frances W. G. Bradshaw; *m* 1968, Sheila Dorothy (*née* Brown). *Educ:* Torquay Grammar Sch.; St John's Coll., Cambridge (BA). Scientific Officer, Aerodynamics Div., National Physical Lab., 1957–69; Imperial College, London: Sen. Lectr, Dept of Aeronautics, 1969–71; Reader, 1971–78; Prof. of Experimental Aerodynamics, 1978–88. *Publications:* Experimental Fluid Mechanics, 1964, 2nd edn 1971; An

Introduction to Turbulence and its Measurement, 1971, 2nd edn 1975; (with T. Cebeci) Momentum Transfer in Boundary Layers, 1977; (ed) Topics in Applied Physics: Turbulence, 1978; (with T. Cebeci and J. H. Whitelaw) Engineering Calculation Methods for Turbulent Flow, 1981; (with T. Cebeci) Convective Heat Transfer, 1984; author or co-author of over 100 papers in Jl of Fluid Mechanics, AIAA Jl, etc. *Recreations:* ancient history, walking. *Address:* c/o Department of Mechanical Engineering, Stanford University, Stanford, CA 94305–3030, USA.

BRADSHAW, Peter Nicholas; film critic, The Guardian, since 1999; *b* 19 June 1962; *s* of late Albert Desmond Bradshaw and of Mollie Bradshaw (*née* Fine); *m* 2007, Dr Caroline Hill; one *s*. *Educ:* Haberdashers' Aske's Sch., Elstree; Pembroke Coll., Cambridge (BA 1st Cl. Hons 1984; PhD 1989). Evening Standard: reporter, Londoner's Diary, 1989–92; leader writer and columnist, 1992–99. Radio: The Skivers, 1995; For One Horrible Moment, 1999; Heresy, 2003; Listener, They Wore It, 2011; In Praise of Powell and Pressburger, 2013; From Fact to Fiction, 2014; television: What The Papers Say; BBC Breakfast; Baddiel's Syndrome, 2001. *Publications:* Not Alan Clark's Diaries, 1998; Lucky Baby Jesus, 1999; Dr Sweet and His Daughter, 2003; Night Of Triumph, 2013. *Recreation:* swimming. *Address:* The Guardian, Kings Place, 90 York Way, N1 9AG. *Clubs:* Soho House, Century.

BRADTKE, Hon. Robert Anthony; United States Ambassador to Croatia, 2006–09; Senior Advisor for Partner Engagement on Syria Foreign Fighters, US Department of State, since 2014; *b* 11 Oct. 1949; *s* of Albert Bradtke and Lucille Bradtke (*née* Gale); *m* 1983, Marsha Barnes. *Educ:* Univ. of Notre Dame; Bologna Center; Johns Hopkins Univ.; Univ. of Virginia. Joined Foreign Service, US Dept of State, 1973; served in: Georgetown, 1973–75; Zagreb, 1976–78; Office of Eastern European Affairs, Dept of State, 1978–81; Moscow, 1983–86; Bonn, 1986–90; Office of Congressional Affairs, Dept of State, 1990–94 (Dep. Asst Sec. of State, 1992–94); Exec. Asst to Sec. of State, 1994–96; Minister and Dep. Chief of Mission, London, 1996–99; Exec. Sec., Nat. Security Council, 1999–2001; Dep. Asst Sec. of State for European and Eurasian Affairs, 2002–05. Co-Chair, Minsk Gp, OSCE, 2009–12. Superior Honor Award, Dept of State, 1988, 1996. *Recreations:* hiking, reading, baseball.

BRADWELL, Area Bishop of, since 2011; **Rt Rev. John Michael Wraw;** *b* 4 Feb. 1959; *s* of Peter and Betty Wraw; *m* 1981, Gillian Webb; one *s* three *d*. *Educ:* Lincoln Coll., Oxford (BA Hons (Jurisprudence) 1981); Fitzwilliam Coll., Cambridge (BA Hons (Theol. and Religious Studies) 1984); Ridley Hall, Cambridge. Ordained deacon, 1985, priest, 1986; Curate, St Peter's, Bromyard, 1985–88; Team Vicar, Sheffield Manor, 1988–92; Vicar, St James, Clifton, 1992–2001; Area Dean, Rotherham, 1998–2004; Priest-in-charge, St Alban, Wickersley, 2001–04; Archdeacon of Wilts, 2004–11. Hon. Canon, Sheffield Cathedral, 2001–04. *Recreations:* walking, reading, sailing. *Address:* Bishop's House, Orsett Road, Horndon-on-the-Hill, Stanford-le-Hope SS17 8NS. *T:* (01375) 673806.

BRADY, Baroness *cr* 2014 (Life Peer), of Knightsbridge in the City of Westminster; **Karren Rita Brady,** CBE 2014; Vice Chairman, West Ham United Football Club, since 2010; *b* 4 April 1969; *d* of Terry and Rita Brady; *m* 1995, Paul Peschisolido; one *s* one *d*. *Educ:* Aldenham Sch. Saatchi & Saatchi, 1987–88; LBC, 1988–89; Sport Newspapers Ltd, 1989–93; Man. Dir, Birmingham City FC, 1993–2009. Non-executive Director: Kerrang! Radio Ltd, 2001–08; Mothercare, 2003–12; Arcadia, 2010–; Advr, Syco Entertainment. Co-presenter, The Apprentice, BBC TV, 2010–. Mem., Women in Sport Adv. Bd, DCMS. Small Business Ambassador, Cons. Party. DUniv Birmingham, 2010. *Publications:* Brady Plays the Blues, 1997; Playing to Win, 2004; Strong Woman (autobiog.), 2012. *Address:* c/o West Ham United Football Club, Boleyn Ground, Green Street, Upton Park, E13 9AZ.

BRADY, Angela Maria, RIBA; Director (formerly Partner), Brady Mallalieu Architects Ltd, since 1987; architect and television broadcaster; President, Royal Institute of British Architects, 2011–13; *d* of late Peter Gerard Brady, FRCSI and of Deirdre (*née* Rowan); *m* 1987, Robin Mallalieu, *s* of late Edward Mallalieu and Rita Mallalieu (*née* Shaw); one *s* one *d*. *Educ:* Dublin Sch. of Architecture (BArch Sc; DipArch); Royal Danish Acad., Copenhagen; Univ. of Westminster. MRIAI 1984 (Hon. FRIAI 1999); RIBA 1986; ARB 1986. Work with: William Strong and Associates, Toronto, 1981; Arthur Erikson Architects, Toronto, 1982; Brady, Shipman Martin Architects, Dublin, 1983–84; GMW Partnership, 1983–85; Lewis and Hickey Architects, London, 1985–87; Shepherd, Epstein and Hunter, 1987–91. Brady Mallalieu projects include: 200 homes in sustainable develt by Ballymore Property, London E14 (RIAI Award, Evening Standard award, 2010); Barra Park Open Air Th. (RIAI Award); new Sch. of Architecture for Metropolitan Univ., London (RIAI Award); St Catherine's Foyer and sports centre, Dublin (Brick Award, Brick Develt Assoc.) housing and healthcare projects for the private and public sector in UK and Ireland. Curator, DiversCity Exhibn, touring UK and world cities, 2003–10. Designer and co-presenter, Building the Dream, ITV, 2004; presenter, The Home Show, Channel 4, 2008–09. Member: CABE/English Heritage Urban Panel, 2001–08; Bd, London Develt Agency, 2006–08 (Design Champion); CABE Enabler, 2009–11. Chair, Women in Architecture, RIBA, 2000–05; Co-Founder, 1986, Chair, 2007–, RIAI London Forum; Mem. Council, RIAI, 2007–11. Chm., Finsbury Park Community Forum, 2001–03. Trustee Dir, Building Exploratory, Hackney, 1998–2008. STEMnet Ambassador, 2004–10; Ambassador, Govt Equalities Office, 2009–11. Vice Chair, Civic Trust Awards, 2000–10. Ext. Examr, Brighton Univ., Liverpool Univ., Dublin Sch. of Architecture and Mackintosh Sch. of Architecture, 2009–10. Mem., Women's Irish Network, 2003–10. Hon. PhD Dublin Sch. of Architecture, 2011. Hon. FRSA 2003. Greenwich Business Partnership Award, 2008; Women of Outstanding Achievement, WISE Awards, 2012; Lifetime Achievement Award, Women in Construction, 2012. *Publications:* (with R. Mallalieu) Dublin: a guide to recent architecture, 1997; articles on architecture and sustainable architecture; contribs to RIBA Jl. *Address:* Brady Mallalieu Architects Ltd, 90 Queen's Drive, N4 2HW. *E:* bma@bradymallalieu.com. *W:* www.angelabradydesigns.com, www.bradymallalieu.com, www.twitter.com/AngelaBradyRIBA, www.linkedin.com/AngelaBrady, www.facebook.com/AngelaBrady.

BRADY, Graham Stuart; MP (C) Altrincham and Sale West, since 1997; *b* 20 May 1967; *s* of John Brady and Maureen Brady (*née* Birch); *m* 1992, Victoria Anne Lowther; one *s* one *d*. *Educ:* Altrincham Grammar Sch.; Univ. of Durham (BA Hons Law 1989); Chm., Durham Univ. Cons. Assoc., 1987; Chm., Northern Area Cons. Collegiate Forum, 1987–89. Shandwick plc, 1989–90; Centre for Policy Studies, 1990–92; Public Affairs Dir, Waterfront Partnership, 1992–97. PPS to Chm. Cons. Party, 1999–2000; an Opposition Whip, 2000; Opposition frontbench spokesman on educn and employment, 2000–01, on educn, 2001–03; PPS to Leader of the Opposition, 2003–04; Shadow Minister for Europe, 2004–07. Member: Educn and Employment Select Cttee, 1997–2001; Treasury Select Cttee, 2007–10; Select Cttee on Parly Reform, 2009–10; Jt Chm., All Party Railfreight Gp, 1998–99; Vice-Chm., All Party Gp on Advertising, 1999–2008. Sec., Cons. backbench Educn and Employment Cttee, 1997–2000; Chm., 1922 Cttee, 2010– (Mem. Exec., 1998–2000, 2007–10). Vice-Chm., E Berks Cons. Assoc., 1992–95. Patron, Counselling and Family Centre (formerly Family Contact Line), 2006–; Vice Patron, Friends of Rosie, 1997–; Trustee, Jubilee Centre, 2008–. Associate: GMC, 2011–12; Medical Practitioners' Tribunal Service, 2012–. Vice Pres., Gtr Altrincham Chamber of Commerce, 1997–. Ind. Gov., Manchester Metropolitan Univ., 2008–11. *Recreations:* family, friends, garden. *Address:* House of Commons, SW1A 0AA.

BRADY, Sir (John) Michael, Kt 2004; FRS 1997; FREng; FMedSci; BP Professor of Information Engineering, Oxford University, 1985–2010, now Emeritus Professor of Oncological Imaging; Fellow of Keble College, Oxford, since 1985; *b* 30 April 1945; *s* of late John and of Priscilla Mansfield; *m* 1967, Naomi Friedlander; two *d*. *Educ:* Manchester Univ. (BSc (1st Cl. Hons Mathematics) 1966; Renold Prize 1967; MSc 1968); Australian Nation Univ. (PhD 1970). FREng (FEng 1992); FIET (FIEE 1992), Hon. FIET; FInstP 1997. Lect Computer Science, 1970, Sen. Lectr 1979, Essex Univ.; Sen. Res. Scientist, MIT, 198 EPSRC Sen. Fellow, 1994–99. Member: ACOST, 1990–93; Bd, UKAEA, 1994–95; Na Technology Foresight Steering Gp, 1994–97; Royal Commn for Exhibn of 1851, 2007– Chm., IT Adv. Bd, 1989–94. Member Board: Guidance Ltd, 1991–; Oxford Instrument 1995–2014; AEA Technology, 1995–2003; Surgister, 1997–2002; Mirada Solutions, 2001–0 (Oxford Med. Image Analysis, 1997–2001; OXIVA, 1999–2001); IXICO, 2006–11; Dexel 2006–11; Matakina, 2008–; Mirada Medical, 2008–; Acuitas Medical, 2009–; Colwiz, 2010– IRISS Medical Technologies, 2012–; ScreenPoint bv, 2014–. FMedSci 2008. DU Esse 1996; Hon. DSc: Manchester, 1998; Southampton, 1999; Hon. DEng Liverpool, 1999; D (*hc*) Univ. Paul Sabatier, Toulouse, 2000; Oxford Brookes, 2006. Faraday Medal, IEE, 200 Millennium Medal, IEEE, 2000. *Publications:* Theory of Computer Science, 1975; Compute Vision, 1981; Robot Motion, 1982; Computational Theory of Discourse, 1982; Robotic Research, 1984; Artificial Intelligence and Robotics, 1984; Robotics Science, 198 Mammographic Image Analysis, 1999; Images and Artefacts of the Ancient World, 200 Digital Mammography, 2006; contribs to jls on computer vision, medical image analysi robotics, artificial intelligence, computer science. *Recreations:* hiking, music, wine tasting.

BRADY, Mickey; MP (SF) Newry and Armagh, since 2015; *b* Ballybot, Newry. Projec Manager and worker, Newry Welfare Rights Centre. Mem. (SF) Newry and Armagh, N Assembly, 2007–15. Mem. Bd, Confederation of Community Gps. Gov., Abbey Primary Sc *Address:* (office) 1 Kilmorey Terrace, Patrick Street, Ballinlare, Newry BT35 8DW.

BRADY, Dr Paul A.; Head of International Communications Group, Scottish Executiv 2004–05; *b* 28 July 1949; two *s* one *d*. *Educ:* St Mungo's Acad., Glasgow; Univ. of Glasgo (BSc Hons; PhD 1974). Joined Scottish Office, 1974; Hd, electricity privatisation tean 1988–90; leader, higher educn reforms, 1991–92; Dir of Policy, SHEFC, 1992–93; H Finance Div., Scottish Office, 1993–94; Dir, Finance and Planning, Scottish Enterpris 1994–98; Dir of Finance, Mgt Exec., NHS in Scotland, 1998–99; Hd, Fisheries and Rur Develt Gp, Envmt and Rural Affairs Dept, Scottish Exec., 1999–2003. Various non-exe positions incl. Registers of Scotland and Glasgow Univ., 2006–10. *Recreations:* walking, musi family. *Address:* 32 Grange Road, Edinburgh EH9 1UL. *E:* pabrady@gmail.com.

BRADY, Robin James; non-profit consultant, since 2009; Chief Executive, Crusaic 2003–09; *b* 26 June 1971; *s* of Peter Robin Brady and Brenda Patricia Brady (*née* Worth *Educ:* Univ. of Witwatersrand, Johannesburg (BA (Dramatic Art) 1992). Singer and dance 1990–94; Asst Dept Manager, Harrods, 1994–96; retail consultant, 1996–99; Capital Service Officer, Arts Council England, 2000–03. Consultant (pt-time), Crusaid, 2001–03. Di Robin's Trading Co. Ltd, 2009–; Mem., Adv. Bd, Galeforce Capital, 2009–. Certified Mem Inst. of Fundraising, 2006; Mem., SROI Network, 2010–. FRSA 2003. *Recreations:* theatr opera, film, literature, wine. *E:* robinbrady@me.com.

BRADY, Scott; QC (Scot.) 2000; *b* 31 Oct. 1962; *s* of late John Brady and Miriam Camero Brady (*née* Brown). *Educ:* Ardrossan Acad., Ayrshire; Edinburgh Univ. (LLB); Glasgow Univ (DipLP). Admitted Advocate, Scottish Bar, 1987; Advocate Depute, 1993–97; called to th Bar, Middle Temple, 1998. *Address:* c/o Advocates' Library, Parliament House, Edinburg EH1 1RF. *T:* (0131) 226 5071; 3 Temple Gardens, EC4Y 9AU. *Clubs:* Caledonia Lansdowne; Scottish Arts (Edinburgh).

BRADY, His Eminence Cardinal Seán; Archbishop of Armagh, (RC), and Primate of A Ireland, 1996–2014; *b* 16 Aug. 1939. *Educ:* St Patrick's Coll., Cavan; St Patrick's Coll Maynooth (BA 1960; HDipEd 1967); Irish Coll., Rome; Lateran Univ., Rome (STB 196 DCL 1967). Ordained priest, 1964; teacher, High Sch., St Patrick's Coll., Cavan, 1967–8 Vice Rector, 1980–87, Rector, 1987–93, Pontifical Irish Coll., Rome; Parish Pries Castletara, Co. Cavan, 1993–95; Coadjutor Archbishop of Armagh, 1995–96. Cardinal, 200 *Address:* c/o Ara Coeli, Armagh, Ireland BT61 7QY.

BRADY, Stephen Christopher, CVO 2011; AO 2015; Ambassador of Australia to Franc and (non-resident) to Morocco, Monaco, Algeria and Mauritania, since 2014; *b* London, 1 June 1959; *s* of Geoffrey Brady and Susanne Brady; partner, Peter Stephens. *Educ:* Canber Grammar Sch.; Australian National Univ. (BA Hons Internat. Relns). Joined Australia Foreign Service as diplomatic trainee, 1982; Foreign Policy Advr to Leader of the Oppositio 1986–90; Chargé d'Affaires, Dublin, 1990–91; Sen. Advr to Prime Minister of Australi 1996–98; Ambassador to Sweden and (non-resident) to Finland, Estonia, Latvia and Lithuani 1998–2003, to Denmark, Norway and Iceland, 1999–2001; Sen. Advr to Prime Minister c Australia, 2003–04; Ambassador to the Netherlands, and Perm. Rep. to OPCW, The Hague 2004–08; Diplomatic Rep. to Internat. Ct of Justice, Internat. Criminal Ct, Internat. Ct o Former Yugoslavia, and Perm. Ct of Arbitration, 2004–08; Official Sec. to Gov.-Gen. c Australia, 2008–14; Secretary: Council, Order of Australia, 2008–14; Australian Braver Decorations Council, 2008–14. Kt Comdr, Order of Orange Nassau (Netherlands), 200 Comdr, Order of the Crown (Tonga), 2010. CStJ 2010. *Address:* Australian Embassy, 4 ru Jean Rey, 75724 Paris Cedex 15, France. *Club:* Commonwealth (Canberra).

BRADY, Terence Joseph; playwright, novelist, artist and actor, since 1962; *b* 13 March 193 *s* of late Frederick Arthur Noel and Elizabeth Mary Brady; *m* Charlotte Mary Thérès Bingham, *qv*; one *s* one *d*. *Educ:* Merchant Taylors', Northwood; TCD (BA Moderatorshi History and Pol Sci. 1961; MA Moderatorship, History and Pol Sci. 2011). Actor: Woul Anyone who saw the Accident?, The Dumb Waiter, Room at the Top, 1962; Beyond th Fringe, 1962–64; Present from the Corporation, In the Picture, 1967; Quick One 'Ere, 196 films include: Baby Love; Foreign Exchange; TV appearances include plays, comedy series an shows, incl. Dig This Rhubarb, 1963–64; Barty in Pig in the Middle, 1980–82; Nanny, 198 Writer for *radio:* Lines from my Grandfather's Forehead (BBC Radio Writers' Guild Awar Best Radio Entertainment, 1972); Thank Goodness It's Saturday; Hear Hear! The Victor Line (with Charlotte Bingham); *television:* Broad and Narrow; TWTWTW; with Charlott Bingham: TV series: Boy Meets Girl; Take Three Girls; Upstairs Downstairs; Away From All; Play for Today; Plays of Marriage; No—Honestly; Yes—Honestly; Thomas and Sara Pig in the Middle; The Complete Lack of Charm of the Bourgeoisie; Nanny; Oh Madelin (USA TV); Father Matthew's Daughter; Forever Green; adapted for television: Love with Perfect Stranger; Losing Control, 1987; The Seventh Raven, 1987; This Magic Momen 1988; Lorna Doone, 1997; The Lost Domain (film), 1999; screenwriter with Charlott Bingham, Riders, 1993; *stage:* Anyone for Tennis?, 2003; A Change of Heart, 2005; Belo Stairs, 2006; Adam and Eve, 2008; Noel and Cole, 2010; D.L., 2011; with Charlott Bingham: (contrib.) The Sloane Ranger Revue, 1985; I wish I wish, 1989; The Shell Seeke (adapted 1999); Four Hearts, 2013; exhibitions include: The Actors' Picture Show, NT 1984–85; Wykenham Gall., 1992; Teddy House Gall., 2009–. Member: Soc. of Author 1988–; Point to Point Owners Assoc., 1988–. Dir, Wincanton Racecourse, 1995–200 *Publications:* Rehearsal, 1972; The Fight Against Slavery, 1976; Blueprint, 1998; The Whit Horse, 2013; with Charlotte Bingham: Victoria, 1972; Rose's Story, 1973; Victoria an Company, 1974; Yes—Honestly, 1977; A View of Meadows Green, 2013; (with Micha Felton) Point-to-Point, 1990; regular contribs to Daily Mail, Living, Country Homes an Interiors, Punch, Sunday Express, Mail on Sunday. *Recreations:* painting, music, gardenin *Address:* c/o United Authors Ltd, 11–15 Betterton Street, WC2H 9BP. *T:* (020) 7470 888 *Club:* PEN.

BRAGG, family name of **Baron Bragg**.

BRAGG, Baron *cr* 1998 (Life Peer), of Wigton in the co. of Cumbria; **Melvyn Bragg;** DL; writer; Presenter and Editor, The South Bank Show, for Sky Arts, since 2011 (for ITV, 1977–2010); Controller of Arts, London Weekend Television, 1990–2010 (Head of Arts, 1982–90); *b* 6 Oct. 1939; *s* of late Stanley Bragg and of Mary Ethel (*née* Parks); *m* 1st, 1961, Marie-Elisabeth Roche (*d* 1971); one *d*; 2nd, 1973, Catherine Mary Haste; one *s* one *d*. *Educ:* Nelson-Thomlinson Grammar Sch., Wigton; Wadham Coll., Oxford (MA; Hon. Fellow, 1995). BBC Radio and TV Producer, 1961–67; writer and broadcaster, 1967–. Novelist, 1964–. Presenter: BBC TV series: 2nd House, 1973–77; Read all About It (also editor), 1976–77; Reel History of Britain, 2011; Melvyn Bragg on Class and Culture, 2012; The Mystery of Mary Magdalene, 2013; ITV series: Two Thousand Years, 1999; Who's Afraid of the Ten Commandments?, 2000; The Apostles, 2001; (also writer) The Adventure of English, 2003; Not Just on Sunday, 2004; The Big Idea, Channel 4 series, 2001; BBC Radio 4: writer/presenter: Start the Week, 1988–98; On Giants' Shoulders, 1998; In Our Time, 1998–; Routes of English, 1999–; Voices of the Powerless, 2002. Dep. Chm., 1985–90, Chm., 1990–95, Border Television. Mem. Arts Council, and Chm. Literature Panel of Arts Council, 1977–80. President: Northern Arts, 1983–87; Nat. Campaign for the Arts, 1986–; Nat. Acad. of Writing, 2000–. Pres., MIND, 1999–; Appeal Chm., RNIB Talking Books Appeal, 2000–. Chancellor, Leeds University, 1999–. Governor, LSE, 1997–. Domus Fellow, St Catherine's Coll., Oxford, 1990. DL Cumbria, 2003. FRSL; FRTS; Fellow, BAFTA, 2010. Hon. FCLIP (Hon. FLA 1994); Hon. FRS 2010; Hon. FBA 2010. Hon. Fellow: Lancashire Polytechnic, 1987; Univ. of Wales, Cardiff, 1996. Hon. DLitt: Liverpool, 1986; Lancaster, 1990; CNAA, 1990; South Bank, 1997; DUniv Open, 1987; Hon. LLD St Andrews, 1993; Hon. DCL Northumbria, 1994. *Plays:* Mardi Gras, 1976 (musical); Orion (TV), 1977; The Hired Man, 1984 (musical); King Lear in New York, 1992; *screenplays:* Isadora; Jesus Christ Superstar; The Music Lovers; Clouds of Glory; Play Dirty. *Publications:* Speak for England, 1976; Land of the Lakes, 1983 (televised); Laurence Olivier, 1984; Rich: the life of Richard Burton, 1988; The Seventh Seal: a study on Ingmar Bergman, 1993; On Giants' Shoulders, 1998; The Adventure of English 500AD–2000, 2003; 12 Books that Changed the World, 2006; In Our Time, 2009; The South Bank Show: final cut, 2010; The Book of Books: the radical impact of the King James Bible 1611–2011, 2011; *novels:* For Want of a Nail, 1965; The Second Inheritance, 1966; Without a City Wall (John Llewellyn Rhys Award), 1968; The Hired Man, 1969 (Time/Life Silver Pen Award, 1970); A Place in England, 1970; The Nerve, 1971; Josh Lawton, 1972; The Silken Net, 1974; A Christmas Child, 1976; Autumn Manoeuvres, 1978; Kingdom Come, 1980; Love and Glory, 1983; The Maid of Buttermere, 1987; A Time to Dance, 1990 (televised 1992); Crystal Rooms, 1992; Credo, 1996; The Soldier's Return, 1999 (W. H. Smith Lit. Award, 2000); A Son of War, 2001; Crossing the Lines, 2003; Remember Me, 2009; Grace & Mary, 2013; articles for various English jls. *Recreations:* walking, books. *Address:* 12 Hampstead Hill Gardens, NW3 2PL. *Clubs:* Garrick, PEN.

BRAGG, Billy; *see* Bragg, S. W.

BRAGG, Heather Jean; *see* Williams, H. J.

BRAGG, Stephen William, (Billy); singer and songwriter; *b* Barking, Essex, 20 Dec. 1957; partner, Juliet de Valero Wills; one *s*. *Educ:* Barking Abbey Comprehensive Sch. Singer with Riff Raff, 1977–81, The Blokes, 1999–2008; perf. Pressure Drop, Wellcome Collection, 2010. *Recordings include:* Life's a Riot with Spy vs Spy, 1983; Brewing Up with Billy Bragg, 1984; Between the Wars, 1985; Talking with the Taxman about Poetry, 1986; Back to Basics, 1987; Workers Playtime, 1988; Help Save the Youth of America, 1988; The Internationale, 1990; Don't Try This at Home, 1991; William Bloke, 1996; (with Wilco) Mermaid Avenue, vol. 1, 1998, vol. 2, 2000; Reaching to the Converted, 1999; (with The Blokes) England, Half English, 2002; Mr Love & Justice, 2008; The Complete Mermaid Avenue Sessions, 2012; Tooth & Nail, 2013. *Publications:* The Progressive Patriot: a search for belonging, 2006. *Recreations:* reading, beachcombing, reforming the House of Lords. *Address:* c/o Bragg Office, PO Box 6830, Bridport, Dorset DT6 9BH. *W:* www.billybragg.co.uk.

BRAGGE, Nicolas William; Master of the Senior (formerly Supreme) Court, Chancery Division, 1997–2014; Acting Chief Chancery Master, 2013–14; *b* Ashford, Kent, 13 Dec. 1948; *o s* of late Norman Bragge and Nicolette Hilda Bragge (*née* Simms); *m* 1973, Pamela Elizabeth Brett; three *s*. *Educ:* S Kent Coll. of Technol., Ashford; Holborn Coll. of Law and Inns of Court Sch. of Law (LLB Hons London). Called to the Bar, Inner Temple, 1972; in practice, Intellectual Property and Chancery Bars, 1974–97; Dep. Chancery Master, 1993–97. Chm. (part-time), Social Security and Disability Appeal Tribunals, 1990–97; Dep. Social Security Comr, 1996–98. Mem. Cttee, Barristers' Benevolent Assoc., 1995–2008. Mem. Council, City of London Br., Royal Soc. of St George, 2008–12. Master, Cutlers' Co., 2003–04; Mem. Court, Guild of Freemen, City of London, 2005–14. Jt Ed., Civil Procedure, 2001–14; an Ed., Atkin's Court Forms, 2011. *Address:* The Towers, Brabourne, Ashford, Kent TN25 6RA.

RAGGINS, Peter Charles Deverell; Senior Lecturer, and Professional Tutor for Teach First, Canterbury Christ Church University, since 2006; *b* 10 July 1945; *s* of Charles and Hilda Braggins; *m* 1968, Julia Cox; three *d*. *Educ:* Bedford Sch.; Christ's Coll., Cambridge (Open Award; BA Hons Hist. 1967). Teacher, Royal Grammar Sch., Newcastle upon Tyne, 1968–72; Head of History: Bootham Sch., York, 1972–77; Bedford Sch., 1977–82; Dep. Headmaster, Wilson's Sch., Sutton, 1982–91; Headmaster, Skinners' Sch., Tunbridge Wells, 1991–2005. Cadet Force Medal, 1998; Golden Jubilee Medal, 2002. *Recreations:* walking, swimming, music, historical research, football.

RAHAM, Edward Charles; Partner, Freshfields Bruckhaus Deringer LLP (formerly Freshfields), since 1995 (Global Corporate Practice Group Leader, 2009–14); *b* 17 July 1961; *s* of late David Gerald Henry Braham, QC and of (Margaret) Louise Hastings (*née* Treves); *m* 1988, Isabel Dorothy Gurney; two *s* one *d*. *Educ:* Worcester Coll., Oxford (BA 1983; BCL 1984; Vinerian Scholar 1984). Freshfields: articled clerk, 1985; admitted solicitor, 1987. Mem., Lowtonian Soc., 2006–. Trustee, Goldsmiths' Centre, 2012–. Liveryman, Goldsmiths' Co., 2004 (Asst, 2011). *Recreations:* riding, photography, ski-ing, wine, bird watching, shooting. *Address:* Fittleworth House, Fittleworth, Pulborough, W Sussex RH20 1JH. *T:* (01798) 865305. *E:* edward.braham@freshfields.com. *Club:* Athenæum.

RAIDEN, Prof. Paul Mayo, PhD; FREng, FIMechE, FIET; CPhys; Sir James Woodeson Professor of Manufacturing Engineering, 1983–2006, now Emeritus Professor of Engineering, and Head, Department of Mechanical, Materials and Manufacturing Engineering, 1992–97, University of Newcastle upon Tyne (Postgraduate Dean, Faculty of Engineering, 1985–88); *b* 7 Feb. 1941; *s* of late Isaac Braiden and of Lilian Braiden (*née* Mayo); *m* 1st, 1967, Elizabeth Marjorie Spensley (marr. diss. 1993); 2nd, 1993, Lesley Howard. *Educ:* Univ. of Sheffield (BEng, MEng, PhD). CEng, FIMechE 1978; FIET (FIEE 1983); FREng (FEng 1994); CPhys, MInstP 1973. Asst Prof., Carnegie Mellon Univ., Pittsburgh, 1968–70; Atomic Energy Research Establishment, Harwell: SSO, 1970–73; PSO, 1973–76; Lectr, then Sen. Lectr, Dept of Engrg, Univ. of Durham, 1976–83. Science and Engineering Research Council: Chm., Engrg Design Cttee, 1990–94; Member: Engrg Bd, 1990–91; Engrg Res. Commn, 1991–94; Cttee on Electro-Mechanical Engrg, 1989–91; Automotive Design Prog., 1989–91; Panel on the Innovative Manufg Initiative, 1993–94. Chm., DTI Working Party on Advanced Mfg Technol., 1987–89. Chm., Northern Reg. and Council Mem., IProdE, 1988–90; Hon. Sec. for Mechanical Subjects, Royal Acad. Engrg, 1997–2000. Mem. Bd, Entrust, 1984–91. Mem., Nat. Cttee for Revision of Methodist Hymn Book, 1979–82. *Publications:* articles on materials behaviour, stress analysis, manufacturing technol. and systems in various jls. *Recreations:* music, especially opera/oratorio (trained singer, tenor voice), cycling, ski-ing. *Address:* 34 Eastern Way, Ponteland, Northumberland NE20 9PF. *T:* (01661) 871810.

BRAILSFORD, Hon. Lord; (Sidney) Neil Brailsford; a Senator of the College of Justice in Scotland, since 2006; *b* 15 Aug. 1954; *s* of Sidney James Brailsford and Jean Thelma Moar Leighton or Brailsford; *m* 1984, Elaine Nicola Robbie; three *s*. *Educ:* Daniel Stewart's Coll., Edinburgh; Stirling Univ. (BA); Edinburgh Univ. (LLB). Admitted Faculty of Advocates, 1981, Treasurer, 2000; QC (Scot.) 1994; called to the Bar, Lincoln's Inn, 1990. DUniv Stirling, 2010. *Recreations:* travel, food and wine, American history, fishing. *Address:* Court of Session, Parliament House, Parliament Square, Edinburgh EH1 1RQ; 29 Warriston Crescent, Edinburgh EH3 5LB. *T:* (0131) 556 8320; Kidder Hill Road, Grafton, VT 05146, USA. *T:* (802) 8432120. *Club:* New (Edinburgh).

BRAILSFORD, Sir David (John), Kt 2013; CBE 2009 (MBE 2005); National Performance Director, British Cycling, 2003–14; Team Principal, Team Sky, since 2010; *b* Derby, 29 Feb. 1964; *s* of John and Barbara Brailsford; partner, Lisa Buckle; one *d* and one step *d*. *Educ:* Liverpool Univ. (BA Hons Sports Sci. and Psychol.); Sheffield Business Sch. (MBA). Dir, Planet X, 1998–2000; Commercial and Mktg Consultant, BDJ Consultancy Ltd, 1999–2003. Coach of the Year, BBC Sports Personality of the Year Awards, 2008, 2012. *Recreations:* cycling, music, family. *Address:* c/o Team Sky, National Cycling Centre, Stuart Street, Manchester M11 4DQ.

BRAILSFORD, (Sidney) Neil; *see* Brailsford, Hon. Lord.

BRAIN, family name of **Baron Brain**.

BRAIN, 3rd Baron *cr* 1962, of Eynsham; **Michael Cottrell Brain,** FRCP, FRCPC; Bt 1954; Professor of Medicine, McMaster University, Canada, 1969–94, now Emeritus; *b* 6 Aug. 1928; *yr s* of 1st Baron Brain, DM, FRS, FRCP and Stella Brain (*née* Langdon-Down); *S* brother, 2014; *m* 1960, Dr the Hon. Elizabeth Ann Herbert, *e d* of Baron Tangley, KBE; one *s* two *d*. *Educ:* Leighton Park Sch., New Coll., Oxford (BA 1950; BM BCh 1953; MA 1955; DM 1963). MRCP 1955, FRCP 1968; FRCPC 1972. Hon. Prof. of Biochemistry and Molecular Biol., Calgary Univ., 1995–. *Heir:* *s* Hon. Thomas Russell Brain, *b* 23 Oct. 1965.

BRAIN, Charlotte; *see* Atkins, C.

BRAIN, David; President and Chief Executive Officer, Edelman Asia-Pacific, since 2011; *b* Worcs, 15 June 1962; *s* of Denis Brain and Hilda Brain; *m* 1997, Susan Fraser; one *s* one *d*. *Educ:* Univ. of East Anglia (BA Eng. Lit.). Man. Dir, Baldwin Boyle Shand, Singapore, 1994–96; Strategic Planner, Batey ADS, Singapore, 1996–98; Man. Dir, Burson-Marsteller, UK, 1998–2000; Jt CEO, Weber Shandwick, UK, 2000–03; Pres. and CEO, Edelman EMEA, 2003–10. *Publications:* Crowd Surfing, 2008. *Recreations:* sailing, following Manchester City. *Address:* Edelman, 701 Central Plaza, 18 Harbour Road, Nanchai, Hong Kong. *E:* david.brain@edelman.com. *Clubs:* Ivy, Groucho.

BRAIN, Dame Margaret Anne, DBE 1994 (OBE 1989); FRCOG; President, Royal College of Midwives, 1987–94 (Member Council, 1970–96); *b* 23 April 1932; *d* of late Charles and Leonora Brain; *m* 1985, Peter Wheeler (*d* 1988), MBE, FRCS, FRCOG. *Educ:* Northampton High Sch.; Westminster Hosp. (SRN 1953); Northampton and Epsom Hosps (SCM 1956); Sheffield Hosp. (MTD 1966). FRCOG *ad eund* 1991. Med. Missionary, USPG St Columba's Hosp., Hazaribagh, Bihar, India, 1959–65; Dep. Matron, Barratt Maternity Home, Northampton, 1966–68; Prin. Midwifery Officer, Reading HMC, 1968–73; Dist Nursing Officer, W Berks DHA, 1974–77; Chief Admin. Nursing Officer, S Glamorgan HA, 1977–88, retd. Member: Nat. Staff Cttee for Nurses and Midwives, 1978–86; Maternity Services Adv. Cttee, 1981–85; Standing Midwifery Cttee, Welsh Nat. Bd, 1982–87; Perinatal Mortality Initiative Steering Gp for Wales, 1983–85; Standing Nursing and Midwifery Adv. Cttee, 1987–93; Women's Nat. Commn, 1990–92; Alternate Treas., 1972–78, Treas., 1978–90, Internat. Confedn of Midwives. Reader, C of E, 2001–. Hon. DSc City, 1995. *Address:* Squirrels, Castle Farm, Lower Broad Oak Road, West Hill, Ottery St Mary, Devon EX11 1UF. *T:* (01404) 812958.

BRAIN, Rt Rev. Dr Peter Robert; Bishop of Armidale, 2000–12; Rector, Rockingham - Safety Bay, Perth, since 2012; *b* 2 April 1947; *s* of Paul W. and Doris J. Brain; *m* 1973, Christine Charlton; three *s* one *d*. *Educ:* North Sydney Tech. High Sch.; Moore Theol Coll. (ThL, DipA, DipRE); Fuller Seminary, Pasadena (DMin 1994). Worked in Accounts, and Investments, Australian Mutual Provident Soc., 1963–70. Ordained deacon and priest, 1975; Curate: Sans Souci, Sydney, 1975–76; Holy Trinity, Adelaide, 1977–80; Rector: Maddington, Perth, 1980–88; Wanneroo, Perth, 1988–99. *Publications:* Going the Distance in Ministry, 2004; Jesus, Only and Always: studies in Hebrews, 2004; Jesus Hope Realised, 2011. *Recreations:* golf, walking, woodwork. *Address:* 48 Abingdon Crescent, Wellard, WA 6170, Australia. *T:* (8) 94393793.

BRAIN, Rt Rev. Terence John; *see* Salford, Bishop of, (RC).

BRAITHWAITE, Julian Nicholas; HM Diplomatic Service; UK Permanent Representative to the United Nations and Other International Organisations in Geneva (with rank of Ambassador), since 2015; *b* Rome, 25 July 1968; *s* of Sir Rodric (Quentin) Braithwaite, *qv*; *m* 1999, Biljana Njagulj; two *d*. *Educ:* Bryanston Sch.; St Catharine's Coll., Cambridge (BA Hist. and Nat. Scis 1990); Harvard Univ. (MPA). Bank of England, 1992–94; joined HM Diplomatic Service, 1994; First Sec., Belgrade, 1996–98; Press Officer, then speechwriter, 10 Downing Street (on secondment), 1998–2002; Special Advr to Supreme Allied Comdr Europe, NATO, 1999; Dir of Communications for High Rep. of Internat. Community, Bosnia and Herzegovina, 2002–04; Counsellor for Global Issues, Washington, DC, 2004–08; Dir, Consular Services, FCO, 2008–11; Hd, Libya Communications Team, 10 Downing Street, 2011; Ambassador to Pol and Security Cttee, EU, 2011–15. *Recreations:* cycling, ski-ing, Montenegro, my family. *Address:* c/o Foreign and Commonwealth Office, King Charles Street, SW1A 2AH.

BRAITHWAITE, Sir Rodric (Quentin), GCMG 1994 (KCMG 1988 CMG 1981); HM Diplomatic Service, retired; freelance writer; Senior Advisor and Managing Director, Deutsche Bank (formerly Deutsche Morgan Grenfell), 1994–2002; *b* 17 May 1932; *s* of Henry Warwick Braithwaite and Lorna Constance Davies; *m* 1961, Gillian Mary Robinson (*d* 2008); three *s* one *d* (and one *s* decd). *Educ:* Bedales Sch.; Christ's Coll., Cambridge (1st cl. Mod. Langs, Pts I and II; Hon. Fellow, 1989). Mil. Service, 1950–52. Joined Foreign (subseq. Diplomatic) Service, 1955; served Djakarta, Warsaw and FO, 1957–63; Moscow, 1963–66; Rome, 1966–69; FCO, 1969–72; Vis. Fellow, All Souls Coll., Oxford, 1972–73; Head of European Integration Dept (External), FCO, 1973–75; Head of Chancery, Office of Permanent Rep. to EEC, Brussels, 1975–78; Head of Planning Staff, FCO, 1979–80; Asst Under Sec. of State, FCO, 1981; Minister Commercial, Washington, 1982–84; Dep. Under-Sec. of State, FCO, 1984–88; Ambassador to Russia, 1988–92; Prime Minister's foreign policy advr, and Chm., Jt Intelligence Cttee, 1992–93. Member: European Strategy Bd, ICL plc, 1994–99; Adv. Bd, Sirocco Aerospace, 1999–2003; Bd, OMZ (Moscow), 2002–03. Vis. Fellow, Wilson Center, Washington, 2005; Sen. Res. Fellow, Univ. of Buckingham, 2012–. Mem., Adv. Council on Nat. Records and Archives, 2005–09. Chm. Council, Britain-Russia Centre, 1995–99; Mem. Council, VSO, 1994–99. Dir, ENO, 1992–99. Chm., Internat. Adv. Bd, Moscow Sch. of Political Studies, 1998–2012. Governor: RAM, 1993–2002 (Chm. of Govs, 1998–2002; Hon. FRAM 1996); Wilton Park, 2002–09; Ditchley Park, 2003–.

Trustee, BBC Marshall Plan for the Mind, 1995–98. Hon. LLD, 1997, Hon. Prof., 1999, Birmingham; Hon. LLD Buckingham, 2014. *Publications:* (jtly) Engaging Russia, 1995; Russia in Europe, 1999; Across the Moscow River, 2002; Moscow 1941: a city and its people at war, 2006; Afgantsy: the Russians in Afghanistan 1979–1989, 2011; Coming of Age in Warsaw: a Cold War story, 2014; various articles.

See also J. N. Braithwaite.

BRAITHWAITE, William Thomas Scatchard; QC 1992; a Recorder, 1993–99; *b* 20 Jan. 1948; *s* of late John Vernon Braithwaite and Nancy Phyllis Braithwaite; *m* 1972, Sheila Young; one *s* one *d*. *Educ:* Gordonstoun Sch.; Liverpool Univ. (LLB Hons). Called to the Bar, Gray's Inn, 1970; joined chambers in Liverpool, 1970; Asst Recorder of the Crown Court, 1990. Consultant Editor, Kemp and Kemp, The Quantum of Damages, 1995–2004. *Publications:* Medical Aspects of Personal Injury Litigation (ed jtly), 1997; Brain and Spine Injuries: the fight for justice, 2001, 2nd edn 2010. *Recreations:* cars, wine, photography. *Address:* Exchange Chambers, Pearl Assurance House, 1 Derby Square, Liverpool L2 9XX; Exchange Chambers, 7 Ralli Court, West Riverside, Manchester M3 5FT; Exchange Chambers, Oxford House, Oxford Row, Leeds LS1 3BE.

BRAKA, Ivor Isaac; art dealer in 20th century and contemporary art; *b* Manchester, 19 Dec. 1954; *s* of Joseph Braka and Elizabeth Braka (*née* Dodds); *m* 1st, 1991, Camilla Mary Davidson (marr. diss. 1998); one *s*; one *s* by former partner, Elizabeth de Stanford; 2nd, 2009, Sarah Caroline Graham. *Educ:* Oundle Sch.; Pembroke Coll., Oxford (BA Hons English). *Recreations:* historic landscape restoration, planting trees, breeding red deer, ski-ing, squash, watching Manchester United, impersonating Alice Cooper. *Address:* 63 Cadogan Square, SW1X 0DY. *Club:* Chelsea Arts.

BRAKE, Rt Hon. Thomas (Anthony); PC 2011; MP (Lib Dem) Carshalton and Wallington, since 1997; *b* 6 May 1962; *s* of Michael and Judy Brake; *m* 1998, Candida Goulden; one *s* one *d*. *Educ:* Imperial Coll., London (BSc Hons Physics); Lycée International, France (Internat. Baccalauréat). Formerly Principal Consultant, Cap Gemini, (IT services). Lib Dem spokesman: on envmt, 1997–2001; on transport, local govt and the regions, 2001–02; on transport and London, 2002–03; on internat. develt, 2003–05; on transport, 2005–06; on local govt, 2006–07; on the Olympics, 2007–10; on London, 2007–10; on foreign affairs, 2015–; a Lib Dem Whip, 2000–01; Parly Sec. (Dep. Leader), Office of the Leader of the H of C, 2012–15; an Asst Govt Whip, 2014–15; Lib Dem Chief Whip, 2015–. Mem., Select Cttee on Transport, 2002–03. Mem., Accommodation and Works Cttee, H of C, 2001–02; Co-Chair, Lib Dem backbench cttee on Home Affairs, Justice and Equalities, 2010– (Lib Dem spokesman on home affairs, 2008–10). *Publications:* (jtly) Costing the Earth, 1991. *Recreations:* running, swimming, cycling. *Address:* House of Commons, SW1A 0AA.

BRAKEFIELD, Prof. Paul Martin, PhD; FRS 2010; Professor of Zoology, and Director, University Museum of Zoology, University of Cambridge, since 2010; Fellow, Trinity College, Cambridge, since 2011; *b* Woking, 31 May 1952. *Educ:* Univ. of Oxford (BSc Hons Zool.); Univ. of Liverpool (PhD 1979). Formerly Prof. of Evolutionary Biol., Univ. of Leiden. Hon. Prof., Univ. of Sheffield. Pres., Linnean Soc. of London, 2015–. *Publications:* contribs to jls incl. Amer. Naturalist, Proc. Royal Soc., Proc. NAS, Evolution and Develt, Ecol Entomology. *Address:* Department of Zoology, University of Cambridge, Downing Street, Cambridge CB2 3EJ.

BRAMALL, family name of **Baron Bramall**.

BRAMALL, Baron *cr* 1987 (Life Peer), of Bushfield in the County of Hampshire; **Field Marshal Edwin Noel Westby Bramall,** KG 1990; GCB 1979 (KCB 1974); OBE 1965; MC 1945; JP; HM Lord-Lieutenant of Greater London, 1986–98; Chief of the Defence Staff, 1982–85; *b* 18 Dec. 1923; *s* of late Major Edmund Haselden Bramall and Mrs Katherine Bridget Bramall (*née* Westby); *m* 1949, Dorothy Avril Wentworth Vernon (*d* 2015); one *s* one *d*. *Educ:* Eton College. Commnd into KRRC, 1943; served in NW Europe, 1944–45; occupation of Japan, 1946–47; Instructor, Sch. of Infantry, 1949–51; psc 1952; Middle East, 1953–58; Instructor, Army Staff Coll., 1958–61; on staff of Lord Mountbatten at MoD, 1963–64; CO, 2 Green Jackets, KRRC, Malaysia during Indonesian confrontation, 1965–66; comd 5th Airportable Bde, 1967–69; idc 1970; GOC 1st Div. BAOR, 1971–73; Lt-Gen., 1973; Comdr, British Forces, Hong Kong, 1973–76; Gen., 1976; C-in-C, UK Land Forces, 1976–78; Vice-Chief of Defence Staff (Personnel and Logistics), 1978–79; Chief of the General Staff, 1979–82; Field Marshal, 1982. ADC (Gen.), 1979–82. Mem., H of L, 1987–2013. Col Comdt, 3rd Bn Royal Green Jackets, 1973–84; Col, 2nd Goorkhas, 1976–86; President: Greater London TAVRA, 1986–98; Gurkha Bde Assoc., 1987–97. Hon. Life Vice Pres., MCC, 1997 (Mem. Cttee, 1985–94; Pres., 1988–89; Trustee, 1994–97). A Trustee, Imperial War Museum, 1983–98 (Chm., 1989–98). JP London 1986. KStJ 1986. *Publications:* (jtly) The Chiefs, 1993. *Recreations:* cricket, painting, travel. *Address:* House of Lords, SW1A 0PW. *Clubs:* Travellers, Army and Navy, Pratt's, MCC, I Zingari, Free Foresters.

BRAMLEY, Prof. Sir Paul (Anthony), Kt 1984; FRCS, FDSRCS; Professor of Dental Surgery, University of Sheffield, 1969–88, now Emeritus; *b* 24 May 1923; *s* of Charles and Constance Bramley; *m* 1952, Hazel Morag Boyd, MA, MB ChB; one *s* three *d*. *Educ:* Wyggeston Grammar Sch., Leicester; Univ. of Birmingham. MB ChB, BDS. FDSRCS 1953; FRCS 1982. HS, Queen Elizabeth Hosp., Birmingham, 1945; Capt., RADC, 224 Para Fd Amb., 1946–48; MO, Church of Scotland, Kenya, 1952; Registrar, Rooksdown House, 1953–54; Consultant Oral Surgeon, SW Region Hosp. Bd, 1954–69; Dir, Dept of Oral Surgery and Orthodontics, Plymouth Gen. Hosp. and Truro Royal Infirmary, 1954–69; Civilian Consultant, RN, 1959–88, now Emeritus; Dean, Sch. of Clinical Dentistry, Univ. of Sheffield, 1972–75. Consultant Oral Surgeon, Trent Region, 1969–88. Chm., Dental Protection Ltd, 1989–95. Member: General Dental Council, 1973–89; Council, Medical Protection Soc., 1975–95; Council, RCS, 1975–83 (Tomes Lectr, 1980; Dean of Faculty of Dental Surgery, 1980–83; Colyer Gold Medal, 1988); Royal Commission on NHS, 1976–79; Dental Strategy Review Group; Chm., Standing Dental Adv. Cttee; Consultant Adviser, DHSS, 1970–80; Hon. Sec., British Assoc. of Oral Surgeons, 1968–72, Pres., 1975; President: S Yorks Br., British Dental Assoc., 1975; Oral Surgery Club of GB, 1985–86; Inst. of Maxillofacial Technol., 1987–89; Nat. Pres., BDA, 1988–89. Adviser, Prince of Songkla Univ., Thailand, 1982–94; External Examiner to RCS, RCSI, RCSG, RACDS, Univs of Birmingham, Baghdad, Hong Kong, London, Singapore, Trinity College Dublin, Cardiff, NUI. Pres., Norman Rowe Educnl Trust, 1993–95; Chm., Cavendish Br., NADFAS, 1996–99. Lay Reader, dio. of Winchester, 1953–68. Hon. FRACDS. Hon. DDS: Birmingham, 1987; Prince of Songkla Univ., 1989; Hon. MD Sheffield, 1994. Fellow, Internat. Assoc. of Oral and Maxillofacial Surgeons. Bronze Medal, Helsinki Univ., 1990. *Publications:* (with J. Norman) The Temporomandibular Joint: disease, disorders, surgery, 1989; (ed) Doing Anything After Work?... What About Retirement?, 2010; chapters in textbooks; scientific articles in British and foreign medical and dental jls. *Recreation:* 12 grandchildren and 2 great-grandchildren. *Address:* 7 The Roost, Heather Lane, Hathersage S32 1DQ.

BRAMLEY, Steven Michael Stuart, CBE 2014; Director of Legal Services, Department for Communities and Local Government, since 2014; *b* 18 March 1961; *s* of Michael Frank Rayner Bramley and Patricia Anne Bramley (*née* Easter); *m* 1990, Ann Weir; three *s*. *Educ:* Royal Grammar Sch., High Wycombe; UCL (LLB Hons). Called to the Bar, Gray's Inn, 1983, Bencher, 2013; Legal Advr's Br., Home Office, 1986–93 and 1996–2003 (Asst Legal Advr, 1997–2003); NI Office, 1993–96; Dep. Legal Sec. to the Law Officers, 2003–04; Dep. Legal Advr, Home Office, 2004–14. *Address:* Department for Communities and Lo[cal] Government, 2 Marsham Street, SW1P 4DF.

BRAMMA, Harry Wakefield, FRCO; Organist and Director of Music, All Saints', Marga[ret] Street, 1989–2004; Director, Royal School of Church Music, 1989–98; *b* 11 Nov. 1936; *s* [of] late Fred and Christine Bramma. *Educ:* Bradford Grammar Sch.; Pembroke Coll., Oxf[ord] (MA). FRCO 1958 (Harding Prize). Organist, All Saints, Bingley, WR Yorks, 1954–55; [D]ir of Music, King Edward VI Grammar Sch., Retford, Notts, 1961; Asst Organist, Worces[ter] Cathedral, 1963; Dir of Music, The King's Sch., Worcester, 1965; Organist, Southw[ark] Cathedral, 1976. Vis. Music Supervisor, King's Coll., Cambridge, 1998–2000; Vis. Mu[sic] Tutor, Christ Church, Oxford, 2000–05. Organist, St Saviour's, E Retford and St Michael[,] W Retford, 1961; Asst Conductor and Accompanist, Worcester Fest. Choral Soc., 196[–]; Organist, Worcester Three Choirs Fest., 1966, 1969, 1972 and 1975; Conduct[or,] Kidderminster Choral Soc., 1972–79. Examr, Associated Bd of Royal Schs of Mus[ic,] 1978–89. Mem. Council, RCO, 1979–96, Hon. Treas., 1987–96; Mem., Archbisho[p's] Commn on Church Music, 1989–92; Organ Advr, Dio. of Southwark, 1976–93 and 199[–]; Mem., Ct of Advrs, St Paul's Cathedral, 1993–99. Hon. Sec., Cathedral Organists' Asso[c.,] 1989–98; Pres., Southwark and S London Soc. of Organists, 1976–; Vice Pres., Church Mu[sic] Soc.; Mem. Cttee, Organists Charitable Trust (formerly Organists' Benevolent Leagu[e]) 1989–2011. Patron, Herbert Howells Soc., 1987–. Liveryman, Musicians' Co., 198[–]; FGCM 1988; FRSCM 1994. Hon. Mem., Assoc. of Anglican Musicians, USA. Hon. DL[itt] Bradford, 1995. *Recreations:* travel, walking. *Address:* c/o The Parish Office, 7 Margaret Stre[et,] W1W 8JG. *Club:* Athenæum.

BRAMPTON, Sally Jane; novelist; *b* 15 July 1955; *d* of Roy and Pamela Brampton; *m* 1[st,] 1981, Nigel Cole (marr. diss. 1990); 2nd, 1990, Jonathan Leslie Powell, *qv* (marr. diss. 200[–];) one *d*; 3rd, 2007, Tom Wnek. *Educ:* Ashford Sch., Ashford, Kent; St Clare's Hall, Oxford; [St] Martin's School of Art, London. Fashion Writer, Vogue, 1978; Fashion Editor, Observ[er,] 1981; Editor, Elle (UK), 1985–89; Associate Editor, Mirabella, 1990–91; Editor, Red, 20[–]; Contrib. Ed., Easy Living, 2005–13; columnist: Saga mag., 2005–; Sunday Times, 2006–. V[is.] Prof., Central St Martin's Coll. of Art and Design, 1997–. TV documentary: Undressed: t[he] history of 20th century fashion, C4, 1998. *Publications: novels:* Good Grief, 1992; Lovesic[k,] 1995; Concerning Lily, 1998; Love, Always, 2000; *non-fiction:* Shoot The Damn Dog[:] memoir of depression, 2008.

BRAMSON, David; Consultant, Nabarro Nathanson, 2001–06 (Senior Partner, 1995–200[1]); *b* 8 Feb. 1942; *s* of late Israel Bramson and Deborah Bramson (*née* Warshinsky); *m* 1966, Lili[an] de Wilde; one *s* one *d*. *Educ:* Willesden Co. Grammar Sch.; University Coll. London (LL[B]). Solicitor: Mobil Oil Co. Ltd, 1966–68; Nabarro Nathanson, 1968–2006 (Partn[er,] 1969–2001). Member, Policy Cttee, British Property Fedn, 1995–2001; Trustee, Investme[nt] Property Forum Educnl Trust, 1997–2001. Lectr on commercial property, 1996–2000. No[n-]exec. Dir, Liberty Internat. plc, 2001–06. Gov. and Vice Chm., Coram Family, 2002–[–]; Chairman: Home-Start Camden, 2003–08; Westminster Advocacy Service for S[enior] Residents, 2006–10; Advocacy Plus (London) Ltd, 2010–13. Trustee, U3A London, 2014[–]. *E:* dbramson@blueyonder.co.uk.

BRAMWELL, Richard Mervyn; QC 1989; *b* 29 Sept. 1944; *s* of Clifford and Dorot[hy] Bramwell; *m* 1968, Susan Green (decd); one *d*. *Educ:* Stretford Grammar Sch.; LSE (LL[B,] LLM). Called to the Bar, Middle Temple, 1967. *Publications:* Taxation of Companies a[nd] Company Reconstructions, 1973, 9th edn 2009; Inheritance Tax on Lifetime Gifts, 198[–]. *Recreations:* hunting, tennis. *Address:* 3 Temple Gardens, EC4Y 9AU.

BRANAGH, Sir Kenneth (Charles), Kt 2012; actor and director; *b* 10 Dec. 1960; *s* [of] William and Frances Branagh; *m* 1st, 1989, Emma Thompson, *qv* (marr. diss. 1997); 2n[d,] 2003, Lindsay Brunnock. *Educ:* Meadway Comprehensive Sch., Reading; Royal Academy [of] Dramatic Art (Bancroft Gold Medalist). *Theatre:* Another Country, Queen's, 1982 (SWE[T] Award, Most Promising Newcomer; Plays and Players Award); The Madness; Francis; Hen[ry] V, Golden Girls, Hamlet, Love's Labours Lost, 1984–85; Tell Me Honestly (also autho[r]); Across the Roaring Hill; The Glass Maze; Hamlet, RSC, 1992; Edmond, NT, 2003; Ivano[v,] Wyndham's, 2008; The Painkiller, Lyric Th., Belfast, 2011; Macbeth (also dir), Manchest[er] Internat. Fest., 2013, NY 2014; directed: The Play What I Wrote, Wyndham's, 2001, N[Y] 2003; Ducktastic, Albery, 2005; founder dir, Renaissance Theatre Company, 1987–[9]; Romeo and Juliet (also dir); Public Enemy (also author); Much Ado About Nothing; As Y[ou] Like It; Hamlet; Look Back in Anger (also televised); A Midsummer Night's Dream (also di[r]); King Lear (also dir); Coriolanus; Richard III; directed: Twelfth Night (also televised); T[he] Life of Napoleon; (with Peter Egan) Uncle Vanya; actor-manager, Kenneth Branagh Th. C[o.,] Garrick Th., 2015–. *Films include:* A Month in the Country, 1987; High Season, 1987; Hen[ry] V (also dir), 1989 (Evening Standard Best Film of the Year, 1989; Oscar, Best Costu[me] Design, 1990; BFI Award, Best Film and Technical Achievement, 1990; Young Europe[an] Film of the Year, 1990; NY Critics Circle Award, Best New Dir; European Actor of the Ye[ar,] 1990); Dead Again (also dir), 1991; Peter's Friends (also dir), Swan Song (dir), 1992; Swi[ng] Kids, Much Ado About Nothing (also dir), 1993; Mary Shelley's Frankenstein (also dir), 19[9–;] (writer and dir) In the Bleak Midwinter, 1995; Othello, 1995; Hamlet (also dir), 1997; T[he] Proposition, 1997; The Gingerbread Man, 1998; The Theory of Flight, 1998; Celebri[ty,] 1999; Wild Wild West, 1999; Love's Labour's Lost (also dir), 2000; How to Kill Yo[ur] Neighbor's Dog, 2002; Rabbit-Proof Fence, 2002; Harry Potter and the Chamber of Secre[ts,] 2002; Five Children and It, 2004; As You Like It (dir), 2006; The Magic Flute (dir), 20[0–;] Sleuth (dir), 2007; Valkyrie, 2009; The Boat that Rocked, 2009; Thor (dir), 2011; My We[ek] with Marilyn, 2011 (Best Supporting Actor, London Critics' Circle Film Awards, 2012); Ja[ck] Ryan (also dir), 2013; Cinderella (dir), 2015; *television includes:* Billy Trilogy, 1982; Fortun[es] of War, 1987; Boy in the Bush; To the Lighthouse; Strange Interlude; Ghosts, 1987; T[he] Lady's Not for Burning; Shadow of a Gunman, 1995; Shackleton, Conspiracy (Em[my] Award), 2002; Warm Springs, 2005; Wallander, 2008, 2010, 2012 (Best Actor, BAFT[A,] 2010); *radio includes:* Hamlet, and Romeo and Juliet (both also co-dir); King Lear; Anthem f[or] the Doomed Youth; Diaries of Samuel Pepys; Mary Shelley's Frankenstein; Bequest to t[he] Nation, 2005; Cyrano De Bergerac, 2008; Life and Fate, 2011; Antony and Cleopatra, 201[–]. *Publications:* Public Enemy (play), 1988; Beginning (autobiog.), 1989; *screenplays:* Henry [V;] Much Ado About Nothing; Hamlet; In the Bleak Midwinter. *Recreations:* reading, playi[ng] guitar. *Address:* Pinewood Studios, Pinewood Road, Iver Heath, Bucks SL0 0NH.

BRANCH, Prof. Michael Arthur, CMG 2000; PhD; Director, School of Slavonic and E[ast] European Studies, 1980–2001, and Professor of Finnish, 1986–2001, London University, [now] University College London; Fellow, University College London, since 2001; *b* 24 Mar[ch] 1940; *s* of Arthur Frederick Branch and Mahala Parker; *m* 1963, Ritva-Riitta Hannele, *d* [of] Erkki Kari, Heinola, Finland; three *d*. *Educ:* Shene Grammar Sch.; Sch. of Slavonic and E[ast] European Studies, Univ. of London (BA 1963; PhD 1967). School of Slavonic and E[ast] European Studies: Asst Lectr and Lectr in Finno-Ugrian Studies, 1967–72; Lectr, 1972–7[–] and Reader in Finnish, 1977; Chm., Dept of East European Language and Literatu[re,] 1979–80. Corresponding Member: Finno-Ugrian Soc., 1977; Finnish Literature S[oc.] (Helsinki), 1980. Hon. PhD Oulu (Finland), 1983. Comdr, Lion of Finland, 1980; Com[dr,] Polish Order of Merit, 1992; Comdr, Estonian Terra Mariana Cross, 2000; Officer, Order [of] Lithuanian Grand Duke Gediminas, 2002. *Publications:* A. J. Sjögren, 1973; (jtly) Finnish F[olk] Poetry: Epic, 1977; (jtly) A Student's Glossary of Finnish, 1980; (ed) Kalevala, 1985; (jt[ly]) Edith Södergran, 1992; (jtly) The Great Bear, 1993; (jtly) Uses of Tradition, 1994; (jt[ly]) Finland and Poland in the Russian Empire, 1995; (ed) The Writing of National History a[nd]

Identity, 1999; (ed) Defining Self: essays on emergent identities in Russia, seventeenth to nineteenth centuries, 2010. *Recreations:* forestry, walking. *Address:* 33 St Donatt's Road, SE14 6NU.

BRANCH, Sonya Judith Clara; General Counsel, Bank of England, since 2015; *b* Essex, 19 June 1974; *d* of David and Martina McNulty; *m* 2003, David Henry Branch; two *s* one *d*. *Educ:* St Paul's Girls Sch., Hammersmith; Magdalen Coll., Oxford (MA Hons Juris.); Coll. of Law, London (DipLP); King's Coll. London (Postgrad. Dip. Eur. Competition Law). Corporate Partner, Clifford Chance LLP; Sen. Dir, OFT, 2007–12; Dir, Triennial Rev., DEFRA, 2012; Exec. Dir, Enforcement and Mergers, and Mem. Bd, OFT, 2012–14; Exec. Dir, Enforcement, CMA, 2014–15. Trustee, Target Ovarian Cancer, 2011–. *Recreations:* wishing for more time to enjoy literature, running and theatre, but focussed now on family, fundraising and fine wine. *Address:* Bank of England, Threadneedle Street, EC2R 8AH. *E:* sonya.branch@bankofengland.co.uk.

BRAND, family name of **Viscount Hampden**.

BRAND, Prof. Andrea Hilary, PhD; FRS 2010; FMedSci; Herchel Smith Professor of Molecular Biology, Wellcome Trust/Cancer Research UK Gurdon Institute and Department of Physiology, Development and Neuroscience, University of Cambridge, since 2007; Fellow, Jesus College, Cambridge, since 2009; *b* 9 March 1959; *d* of Howard and Marlene Brand (*née* Nykerk); partner, Dr Jim Haseloff; one *d*. *Educ:* UN Internat. Sch., NY; Brasenose Coll., Oxford (BA Hons Biochem. 1981); MRC Lab. of Molecular Biol. and King's Coll., Cambridge (PhD Molecular Biol. 1986). SERC Post Doctoral Fellow, 1986–87, Helen Hay Whitney Fellow, 1987–89, Harvard Univ.; Leukemia Soc. Special Fellow, Harvard Med. Sch., 1990–93; Cancer Research Campaign Gurdon Institute, subseq. Wellcome Trust/Cancer Research UK Gurdon Institute, University of Cambridge: Wellcome Trust Sen. Fellow in Basic Biomed. Res., 1993–2003; Dir of Res. in Develtl Neurobiol., 2003–07; Sen. Gp Leader, 2005–; Res. Fellow, King's Coll., Cambridge, 1999–2003. Invited Prof., Ecole Normale Supérieure, Paris, 2002; Dietrich Bodenstein Lectr, Univ. of Virginia, 2002. Member, Editorial Board: Bioessays, 2003–07; Neural Develt, 2006–; Fly, 2006–. Mem., Internat. Scientific Adv. Bd, Promega Corp., 1999–2004. Mem., Academic Careers Cttee, 2003–06, Sectional Cttee, 2008–10, Acad. Med. Scis. Founding Bd Mem., Rosalind Franklin Soc., 2006–. Mem., EMBO, 2000. FMedSci 2003. Hooke Medal, British Soc. for Cell Biol., 2002; (jtly) William Bate Hardy Prize, Cambridge Philosophical Soc., 2004; Rosalind Franklin Award, Royal Soc., 2006. *Publications:* contrib. articles on cell and develtl biol. in scientific jls. *Recreations:* contemporary dance, decorative arts, reading. *Address:* Wellcome Trust/Cancer Research UK Gurdon Institute, University of Cambridge, Tennis Court Road, Cambridge CB2 1QN.

BRAND, Dr Carlton Michael; Corporate Director (Head of Paid Service, Electoral Registration Officer, Returning Officer), Wiltshire Council, since 2011 (Corporate Director, Resources, 2007–11); Owner and Coach, LeadershipMentor.co.uk (Executive Coaching), since 2011; *b* Maldon, Essex, 12 Oct. 1966; *s* of Michael Brand and Gloria Brand; *m* 2000, Tracy; two *s*. *Educ:* Plume Sch., Maldon; Univ. of East London (BA Hons Business Studies 1993); Univ. of Hertfordshire (MSc Advanced Automotive Engrg, Manuf. and Mgt 1998; EngD 2005); Univ. of West of England (Adv. Cert. Exec. Coaching 2011); Inst. of Leadership and Mgt (Level 7 Exec. Coaching and Leadership Mentoring, 2011). Ford Motor Company: apprentice, 1983–87; test engr, 1987–89; develt engr, 1989–92; Manager: Powertrain Systems Engrg, 1993–95; Strategy Planning, 1995–97; Body Engrg, 1997–2003; Dir, Resources, St Edmundsbury BC, 2004–06. Member: SOLACE, 2005–; Assoc. for Coaching, 2011–. Chartered Manager 2011. FCMI 2010; FRSA 2013. *Publications:* contribs to Mgt Jl for local govt, Local Govt Chronicle, Jl of Automotive Engrg and Public Money and Management. *Recreations:* executive coaching and leadership mentoring, fishing, cricket, road cycling, motorsport, challenging public sector thinking through systems thinking, being a frustrated academic, amateur astronomy (observing), researching the history of big telescopes. *Address:* Wiltshire Council, County Hall, Trowbridge, Wilts BA14 8JN. *T:* 07500 808307. *E:* drcarltonbrand@aol.co.uk.

BRAND, Prof. Charles Peter, FBA 1990; Professor of Italian, 1966–88, and Vice-Principal, 1984–88, University of Edinburgh; *b* 7 Feb. 1923; *er s* of Charles Frank Brand and Dorothy (*née* Tapping); *m* 1948, Gunvor (*d* 2010), *yr d* of Col I. Hellgren, Stockholm; one *s* three *d*. *Educ:* Cambridge High Sch.; Trinity Hall, Cambridge. War Service, Intelligence Corps, 1943–46. Open Maj. Scholar, Trinity Hall, 1940; 1st Class Hons Mod. Languages, Cantab, 1948; PhD Cantab, 1951. Asst Lecturer, Edinburgh Univ., 1952; Cambridge University: Asst Lecturer, subsequently Lecturer, 1952–66; Fellow and Tutor, Trinity Hall, 1958–66. Pres., MHRA, 1995. Cavaliere Ufficiale, 1975, Commendatore, 1988, al Merito della Repubblica Italiana. General Editor, Modern Language Review, 1971–77; Editor, Italian Studies, 1976–81. *Publications:* Italy and the English Romantics, 1957; Torquato Tasso, 1965; Ariosto: a preface to the Orlando Furioso, 1974; (ed) Cambridge History of Italian Literature, 1996; contributions to learned journals. *Recreations:* sport, travel, gardening.

BRAND, Geoffrey Arthur; Under-Secretary, Department of Employment, 1972–85; *b* 13 June 1930; *s* of late Arthur William Charles Brand and Muriel Ada Brand; *m* 1954, Joy Trotman; two *d*. *Educ:* Andover Grammar Sch.; University Coll., London. Entered Min. of Labour, 1953; Private Sec. to Parly Sec., 1956–57; Colonial Office, 1957–58; Private Sec. to Minister of Labour, 1965–66; Asst Sec., Industrial Relations and Research and Planning Divisions, 1966–72. Mem., Archbishop of Canterbury's (later Bishops') Adv. Gp on Urban Priority Areas, 1986–98. FRSA 1985. *Address:* Cedarwood, Seer Green, Beaconsfield, Bucks HP9 2UH. *T:* (01494) 676637.

BRAND, Helen Joanna, OBE 2011; Chief Executive, Association of Chartered Certified Accountants, since 2008; *b* Rawtenstall, 22 April 1965; *d* of Colin Anthony and Judith Anne Brand; two *d*. *Educ:* Rainford High Sch.; Univ. of Exeter (BA Hons Politics). Pres., Exeter Univ. Guild of Students, 1986–87. Dir, Internat. Affairs, CIMA, 1987–96; Association of Chartered Certified Accountants: Hd of Corporate Develt, 1996–2002; Chief Operating Officer, 2002–07; Man. Dir, Strategy, 2007–08. *Recreations:* family activities, cooking, beach life in N Devon, Liverpool FC, modern literature. *Address:* Association of Chartered Certified Accountants, 29 Lincoln's Inn Fields, WC2A 3EE. *T:* (020) 7059 5731.

BRAND, Jo; writer and comedian; *m*; two *d*. Formerly psychiatric nurse. Comedy includes stand-up. Television series: Jo Brand Through the Cakehole, 1995; A Big Slice of Jo Brand, 1996; Jo Brand's Commercial Breakdown, 1999; Head on Comedy with Jo Brand, 2000; Nobody Likes a Smartass, 2003; QI, 2003–; Getting On, 2009, 2010, 2012 (Best Female Performance in a Comedy Role, BAFTA, 2011); Jo Brand's Big Splash, 2011; Jo Brand's Winter Warm Up, 2012; The Great British Bake Off - An Extra Slice, 2014–. Radio series: Windbags (with Donna McPhail); Seven Ages of Man, 2000. Theatre, The Pirates of Penzance, Gielgud, 2008. Pantomime début as the Genie of the Lamp, Aladdin, New Wimbledon Th., 2013. Former columnist, The Independent; columnist, Nursing Times, 2000. Best Comedy Club Performer, 1992, Best Female Comedian, 2010, British Comedy Awards. *Publications:* Load of Old Balls: ranking of men in history, 1995; Load of Old Ball Crunchers: women in history, 1996; (with Helen Griffin) Mental (play), 1996; Sorting Out Billy (novel), 2004; It's Different for Girls (novel), 2005; The More You Ignore Me (novel), 2009; Look Back in Hunger (autobiog.), 2009; Can't Stand Up for Sitting Down (autobiog.), 2010. *Address:* c/o Vivenne Clore, Richard Stone Partnership, Suite 3, De Walden Court, 85 New Cavendish Street, W1W 6XD.

BRAND, Dr Michael; Director, Art Gallery of New South Wales, Sydney, since 2012; *b* 9 Jan. 1958; *s* of Lindsay and Betty Brand; *m* 1988, Tina Gomes; two *d*. *Educ:* Canberra Grammar Sch.; Maret Sch., Washington, DC; Emerson Prep. Sch., Washington; Australian Nat. Univ. (BA Hons Asian Studies); Harvard Univ. (MA; PhD 1987). Curator, Asian Art, Mus. of Art, Rhode Is. Sch. of Design, 1985–87; Res. Fellow, Arthur M. Sackler Gall., Smithsonian Instn, 1987; Co-Dir, Smithsonian Instn Mughal Garden Project, Lahore, Pakistan, 1988–93; Curator, Asian Art, Nat. Gall., Australia, 1988–96; Asst Dir, Qld Art Gall., Brisbane, 1996–2000; Director: Virginia Mus. of Fine Arts, USA, 2000–05; J. Paul Getty Mus., 2005–10; Consulting Dir, Aga Khan Mus., Toronto, 2010–12. *Publications:* (ed with G. D. Lowry) Fatehpur-Sikri: a sourcebook, 1985; (with G. D. Lowry) Akbar's India: art from the Mughal City of Victory, 1985; (ed with G. D. Lowry) Studies on Fatehpur-Sikri, 1987; (jtly) Shalamar Garden Lahore: landscape, form and meaning, 1990; (with C. Phoeurn) The Age of Angkor: treasures from the National Museum of Cambodia, 1992; (ed and contrib.) Traditions of Asian Art (traced through the Collection of the National Gallery of Australia), 1995; The Vision of Kings: art and experience in India, 1995; (ed with C. Roberts) Earth, Spirit, Fire: Korean masterpieces of the Choson Dynasty, 2000; contrib. numerous articles to art catalogues, books and jls. *Address:* Art Gallery of New South Wales, Art Gallery Road, Sydney, NSW 2000, Australia. *T:* (2) 92251725.

BRAND, Prof. Paul Anthony, DPhil; FBA 1998; Professor of English Legal History, University of Oxford, 2010–14; Senior Research Fellow, 1999–2014 and Senior Dean, 2011–14, now Emeritus Fellow, All Souls College, Oxford; *b* 25 Dec. 1946; *s* of Thomas Joseph Brand and Marjorie Jean Brand (*née* Smith); *m* 1970, Vanessa Carolyn Alexandra Rodrigues (*d* 2009). *Educ:* Hampton Grammar Sch.; Magdalen Coll., Oxford (BA 1967; DPhil 1974). Asst Keeper, Public Record Office, 1970–76; Lectr in Law, UCD, 1976–83; research, 1983–93; Res. Fellow, Inst. of Historical Res., Univ. of London, 1993–99; Fellow, All Souls Coll., Oxford, 1997–99. Vis. Fellow, All Souls Coll., Oxford, 1995; Vis. Prof., Columbia Univ. Law Sch., 1995, 2003; Dist. Vis. Prof., Arizona Center for Medieval and Renaissance Studies and Merriam Vis. Prof. of Law, Arizona State Univ., 2000; Cook Global Law Prof., Univ. of Michigan Law Sch., 2013. Hon. Bencher, Middle Temple, 2014. *Publications:* The Origins of the English Legal Profession, 1992; The Making of the Common Law, 1992; The Earliest English Law Reports, vol. I, vol. II, 1996, vol. III, 2005, vol. IV, 2007; Kings, Barons and Justices: the making and enforcement of legislation in thirteenth century England, 2003; The Parliament Rolls of Medieval England, vols I and II, 2005; Plea Rolls of the Exchequer of the Jews, vol. VI, 2005. *Recreations:* travelling, visiting old buildings and interesting cities. *Address:* All Souls College, Oxford OX1 4AL. *T:* (01865) 279286; 155 Kennington Road, SE11 6SF. *T:* (020) 7582 4051.

BRAND, Dr Peter; General Practitioner, Brading, Isle of Wight, 1977–2006; *b* 16 May 1947; *s* of L. H. Brand and J. Brand (*née* Fredricks); *m* 1972, Jane Vivienne Attlee; two *s*. *Educ:* Thornbury Grammar Sch., Glos; Birmingham Univ. Med. Sch. MRCS; LRCP; DObstRCOG; MRCGP. Chm., IoW Div., BMA, 1980–84. Contested (Lib Dem) Isle of Wight, 1992, 2001; MP (Lib Dem) Isle of Wight, 1997–2001. *Recreations:* boating, building, choral singing (Mem., Ryde Chorus). *Address:* Chain Ferry House, 3 Ferry Road, East Cowes, Isle of Wight PO32 6RA. *Clubs:* National Liberal; Island Sailing, E Cowes Sailing.

BRANDON, Prof. Nigel Peter, OBE 2011; PhD; CEng, FREng; Professor of Sustainable Development in Energy, since 2004 (Shell Professor, 2004–09), and Director, Sustainable Gas Institute, since 2014, Imperial College London (Director, Energy Futures Laboratory, 2005–14); *b* Birmingham, 3 May 1960; *s* of Jeffrey Brandon and Anne Elizabeth Brandon; *m* 1986, Janet Mary Reeves; two *s*. *Educ:* Arthur Terry Sch.; Imperial Coll., London (BSc Engr 1981; PhD 1984). CEng 2006; FREng 2008. Res. Scientist, BP, 1984–92; Staff Technologist, Rolls-Royce, 1992–98; Sen. Lectr, Imperial Coll. London, 1998–2004. Ceres Power: Founder and CEO, 2001–03; Chief Tech. Officer, 2003–06; Chief Scientist, 2006–09. Sen. Fellow to Res. Councils UK Energy Prog., 2006–14. BIS (formerly DIUS) UK Focal Point in climate change, energy and envmt with China, 2007–11. FEI 2006; FIMMM 2006; FRSA 2007; FHEA 2007; FCGI 2008. Silver Medal, Royal Acad. of Engrg, 2007; Francis Bacon Medal, ASME, 2014. *Publications:* Fuel Cells Compendium, 2005; papers on fuel cell science, energy storage science and engrg and hydrogen systems in jls. *Recreations:* reading science fiction, rolling icosahedra. *Address:* Imperial College London, SW7 2AZ. *T:* (020) 7594 5704, *Fax:* (020) 7594 7444. *E:* n.brandon@imperial.ac.uk.

BRANDON, Prof. Peter Samuel, OBE 2010; FRICS; Professor of Quantity and Building Surveying, University of Salford, 1985–2010, now Emeritus; *b* 4 June 1943; *s* of Samuel Brandon and Doris Eileen Florence Brandon (*née* Downing); *m* 1968, Mary Ann Elizabeth Canham; one *s* two *d*. *Educ:* Bournemouth Grammar Sch.; Bristol Univ. (MSc Architecture); DSc Salford 1996. Private practice and local govt, 1963–69; Lectr, Portsmouth Poly., 1969–73; Prin. Lectr, Bristol Poly., 1973–81; Head of Dept, Portsmouth Poly., 1981–85; Salford University: Chm., Surveying Dept, 1985–93; Pro-Vice-Chancellor, 1993–2001; Dir, Res. and Grad. Coll., 1993–2001; Dir of Strategic Progs, 2001–10. Royal Institution of Chartered Surveyors: Chm., Res. Cttee, 1987–91; Mem. Gen. Council representing Gtr Manchester, 1989–93; Mem., Exec. Bd, QS Div., 1991–; Science and Engineering Research Council: Chm., Construction Cttee, 1991–94; Chm., Building Design Technology and Management Sub-Cttee, 1990–91; Member: Engrg Res. Commn, 1991–94; DTI Technology Foresight Panel for Construction, 1994; Chm., Built Envmt Panel for HEFCE RAE, 1996 and 2001. Hon. Mem., ASAQS, 1994. Hon. DEng Heriot-Watt, 2006. *Publications:* Cost Planning of Buildings, 1980, 8th edn 2007; (ed) Building Cost Techniques, 1982; Microcomputers in Building Appraisal, 1983; (ed) Quality and Profit in Building Design, 1984; Computer programs for Building Cost Appraisal, 1985; Building, Cost Modelling and Computers, 1987; Expert Systems: the strategic planning of construction projects, 1988; (ed) Investment, Procurement & Performance in Construction, 1991; (ed) Management, Quality and Economics in Building, 1991; (ed) Integration of Construction Information, 1995; (ed) Client Centered Approach to Knowledge Based Systems, 1995; Evaluation of the Built Environment Sustainability, 1997; (ed) Cities and Sustainability, 2000; (ed) Evaluating Sustainable Development in the Built Environment, 2005, 2nd edn 2010; (ed) Virtual Futures for Design, Construction and Procurement, 2008; (ed) Clients Driving Innovation, 2008. *Recreations:* mountain biking alongside canals, walking, travel, modern art. *Address:* School of the Built Environment, Maxwell Building, University of Salford, Salford M5 4WT. *T:* (0161) 295 5164.

BRANDON-BRAVO, Martin Maurice, OBE 2002; *b* 25 March 1932; *s* of late Isaac, (Alfred), and Phoebe Brandon-Bravo; *m* 1964, Sally Anne Wallwin; two *s*. *Educ:* Latymer Sch.; Nottingham Poly. FCMI (FBIM 1980). Joined Richard Stump Ltd, later Richard Stump (1979), 1952; successively Floor Manager, Factory Manager, Production Dir and Asst Man. Dir; Man. Dir, 1979–83; non-exec. Dir, 1983–87; Dir, Hall & Earl Ltd, 1970–83. Mem., Nottingham City Council, 1968–70 and 1976–87; Chm., 1970–73, Pres., 1975–83, Nottingham West Cons. Party Orgn; Dep. Chm., City of Nottingham Cons. Fedn. Contested (C): Nottingham East, 1979; Nottingham South, 1992. MP (C) Nottingham South, 1983–92; PPS to Minister of State for Housing and Urban Affairs, 1985–87, to Minister of State, Home Office, 1987–89, to Home Sec., 1989–90, to Lord Privy Seal and Leader of the House of Lords, 1990–92. Mem., Notts CC, 1993–2009 (Hon. Alderman, 2009). Contested (C) Nottingham and Leicestershire NW, Eur. Parly elecns, 1994. Mem., Nat. Water Sport Centre Management Cttee, 1972–83; Pres., 1993–2001, Hon. Life Vice Pres., 2001–, British Rowing (formerly Amateur Rowing Assoc.); Pres. and Trustee, Nottingham and Union Rowing Club, 1983–; Vice Pres., Henley River and Rowing Mus.,

2006– (Trustee, 1993–2006). Hon. Alderman, City of Nottingham, 2012. *Recreation:* rowing (held Internat. Umpire licence, now retired). *Address:* The Old Farmhouse, 27 Rectory Place, Barton-in-Fabis, Nottingham NG11 0AL. *T:* (0115) 983 0459. *Clubs:* Leander; Nottingham and Union Rowing.

BRANDRETH, Gyles Daubeney; author, broadcaster; *b* 8 March 1948; *s* of late Charles Brandreth and Alice Addison; *m* 1973, Michèle Brown; one *s* two *d*. *Educ:* Lycée Français de Londres; Betteshanger Sch., Kent; Bedales Sch., Hants; New Coll., Oxford (Scholar). Pres. Oxford Union, Editor of Isis. Chairman: Archway Productions Ltd, 1971–74; Victorama Ltd, 1974–93; Complete Editions Ltd, 1988–93; Director: Colin Smythe Ltd, 1971–73; Newarke Wools Ltd, 1988–92; J. W. Spear & Sons, 1992–95. Dep. Chm., Unicorn Heritage, 1987–90; children's publisher, André Deutsch Ltd, 1997–2000; consultant ed., Whitaker's Almanack, 1997–2002. Freelance journalist, 1968–: contrib. Observer, Guardian, Express, Daily Mail, Daily Mirror, Daily Telegraph, Evening Standard, Spectator, Punch, Homes & Gardens, She, Woman's Own; Columnist: Honey, 1968–69; Manchester Evening News, 1971–72; Woman, 1972–73, 1986–88; TV Times, 1989–92; Press Assoc. weekly syndicated column in USA, 1981–85; Ed., Puzzle World, 1989–92; Ed.-at-Large, Sunday Telegraph Review, 1999–2004. MP (C) City of Chester, 1992–97; contested (C) same seat, 1997. PPS to Financial Sec. to Treasury, 1993–94, to Sec. of State for Nat. Heritage, 1994–95, to Sec. of State for Health, 1995; an Asst Govt Whip, 1995–96; a Lord Comr, HM Treasury, 1996–97. Sponsor, 1994 Marriage Act. Broadcaster, 1969–: TV series incl.: Child of the Sixties, 1969; Puzzle Party, 1977; Chatterbox, 1977–78; Memories, 1982; Countdown, 1983–90 and 1997–; TV-am, 1983–90; Railway Carriage Game, 1985; Catchword, 1986; Discovering Gardens, 1990–91; CBS News, 1992–2002; Have I Got News For You, 1997–; Home Shopping Network, 2002–05; This Is Your Life, 2003; Public Opinion, 2004; The One Show, 2007–; (with Hinge and Bracket) Dear Ladies (TV scripts); radio: A Rhyme in Time, Radio 4, 1971; Just A Minute, Radio 4, 1981–; Wordaholics, Radio 4, 2012–; theatrical producer, 1971–86: Through the Looking-Glass, 1972; Oxford Theatre Fest., 1974, 1976; The Dame of Sark, Wyndham's, 1974; The Little Hut, Duke of York's, 1974; Dear Daddy, Ambassador's, 1976; Cambridge Fest., 1986; also Son et Lumière; writer: (with Julian Slade) Now We Are Sixty (play), 1986; (and performer) Zipp! (musical), Edinburgh Fest., 2002 (Most Popular Show award), Duchess, 2003, UK tour, 2004; (with Susannah Pearse) Wonderland (play), 2010; performer: Baron Hardup in Cinderella, Guildford, 1989, Wimbledon, 1990; Malvolio in Twelfth Night The Musical!, Edinburgh Fest., 2005; The One to One Show, Edinburgh Fest., 2010, tour, 2010–11; Lady Bracknell in The Importance of Being Earnest (musical), Riverside Studios, 2011; Looking for Happiness, Edinburgh Fest., 2013, tour, 2013–14; Word Power!, Edinburgh Fest., 2015, tour 2016. Founder: National Scrabble Championships, 1971; British Pantomime Assoc., 1971; Teddy Bear Mus., 1988. Dir, Eur. Movement's People for Europe campaign, 1975; Mem., Better English Campaign, 1995–97. Appeals Chm., 1983–89, Chm., 1989–93, Vice-Pres., 1993–, NPFA. Co-curator, NPG exhibition of children's writers, 2002. Three times holder, world record for longest-ever after-dinner speech (4 hrs 19 mins, 1976; 11 hrs, 1978; 12 hrs 30 mins, 1982). *Publications:* over fifty books since Created in Captivity, 1972; most recent: Under the Jumper (autobiog.), 1993; Who is Nick Saint? (novel), 1996; Venice Midnight (novel), 1998; Breaking the Code (diaries), 1999; John Gielgud, 2000; Brief Encounters: meetings with remarkable people, 2001; Philip and Elizabeth: portrait of a marriage, 2004; Charles and Camilla: portrait of a love affair, 2005; Oscar Wilde and the Candlelight Murders (novel), 2007; Oscar Wilde and the Ring of Death, 2008; Oscar Wilde and the Dead Man's Smile, 2009; Something Sensational to Read in the Train: the diary of a lifetime, 2009; Oscar Wilde and the Nest of Vipers, 2010; Oscar Wilde and the Vatican Murders, 2011; Oscar Wilde and the Murders at Reading Gaol, 2012; (ed) Oxford Dictionary of Humorous Quotations, 2013; The 7 Secrets of Happiness, 2013; (with S. Brandreth) The Lost Art of Having Fun, 2013; (with Saethryd Brandreth) Novelty Knits, 2014; Breaking the Code: 1990–2007, 2014; Word Play, 2015; over seventy books for children. *Address:* c/o Ed Victor Ltd, 6 Bayley Street, WC1B 3HB. *W:* www.gylesbrandreth.net.

BRANDRICK, David Guy, CBE 1981; Secretary, British Coal Corporation (formerly National Coal Board), 1972–89, retired; Director: Coal Staff Superannuation Scheme Trustees Ltd (formerly British Coal Staff Scheme Superannuation Trustees Ltd), 1989–2002; CMT Pension Trustee Services Ltd, 1993–2002; *b* 17 April 1932; *s* of Harry and Minnie Brandrick; *m* 1956, Eunice Fisher (*d* 1999); one *s* one *d*. *Educ:* Newcastle-under-Lyme High Sch.; St John's Coll., Oxford (MA). Joined National Coal Board, 1955; Chairman's Office, 1957; Principal Private Secretary to Chairman, 1961; Departmental Sec., Production Dept, 1963; Dep. Sec. to the Bd, 1967. *Recreation:* walking.

BRANDT, Peter Augustus; Chairman, Atkins Fulford Ltd, 1977–2006; *b* 2 July 1931; *s* of late Walter Augustus Brandt and late Dorothy Gray Brandt (*née* Crane); *m* 1962, Elisabeth Margaret (*née* ten Bos); two *s* one *d*. *Educ:* Eton Coll.; Trinity Coll., Cambridge (MA). Joined Wm Brandt's Sons & Co. Ltd, Merchant Bankers, 1954; Mem. Bd, 1960; Chief Executive, 1966; resigned, 1972. Director: London Life Assoc., 1962–89; Corp. of Argentine Meat Producers (CAP) Ltd and affiliates, 1970; Edward Bates (Holdings) Ltd, 1972–77; Edward Bates & Sons Ltd, 1972–77 (Chm., 1974–77). Mem., Nat. Rivers Authy (formerly Nat. Rivers Adv. Cttee), 1988–95. *Recreations:* sailing, rowing, steam engines, wild fowl, English water colours. *Address:* Spout Farm, Boxford, Suffolk CO10 5HA. *Clubs:* Boodle's; Leander (Henley-on-Thames).

BRANIGAN, Kate Victoria; QC 2006; *b* 3 Sept. 1961; *d* of late Cyril and of Patricia Branigan; *m* 1983, Robert Solomon; one *s* one *d*. *Educ:* Coopers' Company and Coborn Sch., Upminster; Univ. of Southampton (LLB 1983). Called to the Bar, Inner Temple, 1984; in practice as a barrister specialising in family law, 1984–. Family Mediator, 2011–. *Recreations:* church, entertaining, classical music, reading, theatre, France, walking, ski-ing, being with my family. *Address:* 4 Paper Buildings, Temple, EC4Y 7EX. *T:* (020) 7583 0816, *Fax:* (020) 7353 4979. *E:* kb@4pb.com.

BRANKIN, Rhona; Member (Lab) Midlothian, Scottish Parliament, 1999–2011; *b* 19 Jan. 1950; *d* of Edward and Joyce Lloyd; *m* 1998, Peter Jones; two *d* by former marriage. *Educ:* Aberdeen Univ. (BEd 1975); Moray House Coll. (Dip. Special Educnl Needs 1989). Teacher, 1975–94; Lectr in Special Educnl Needs, Northern Coll., Dundee, 1994–99. Scottish Executive: Deputy Minister: for Culture and Sport, 1999–2001; for Envmt and Rural Develt, 2000–01 and 2005–07; for Health and Community Care, 2004–05; Minister for Communities, 2007; Shadow Cabinet Sec. for Educn and Lifelong Learning, 2007–09. Former Chair, Scottish Labour Party. Mem. Bd, Arts and Business Scotland, 2011–; Public Interest Mem., ICAS, 2011–. Trustee: Leuchie House Respite Centre, 2011–; Mavisbank House, 2011–. Hon. FRIBA. *Recreations:* the arts, golf, France.

BRANNAN, Micheline Hadassah; Head, Civil and International Group, Scottish Executive Justice Department, 2005–07; Head, Social Justice Group, Scottish Executive Development Department, 2006–07; staff nurse, NHS Lothian, since 2011; *b* 23 Oct. 1954; *d* of Israel and Halina Moss; *m* 1986, Michael Neilson Brannan (*d* 2008); two *s*. *Educ:* St Hilda's Coll., Oxford (BA 1976, MA Lit. Hum. 1978); Edinburgh Napier Univ. (BNSc 2011). Scottish Office: admin. trainee, 1976–78; HEO(D), 1978–82; Principal, 1982–91; Head: Parole and Lifer Rev. Div., 1991–95; Civil Law Div., 1995–2001; Hd, Criminal Justice Gp, Scottish Exec. Justice Dept, 2001–05. Chair, BEMIS (formerly Black and Ethnic Minority Infrastructure in Scotland), 2014– (Co. Sec., 2011–14). Mem. Bd, Barony Housing Assoc., 2008–12. Board Member: Scottish Council of Jewish Communities, 2007– (Vice-Chair, 2013–); Edinburgh Inter Faith Assoc., 2007–10; Mem., Bd of Mgt, Edinburgh Hebrew Congregation, 2013–. Editor, Edinburgh Star, mag. for Edinburgh Jewish community, 2011–. *Recreations:* Jewish cultural activities, India. *Address:* 31/3 Rattray Grove, Edinburgh EH1[illegible] 5TL. *E:* michelinehbrannan@msn.com.

BRANNEN, Paul; Member (Lab) North East Region, European Parliament, since 2014; *b* Peterborough, 13 Sept. 1962; *s* of Colin and Joyce Brannen; *m* 1999, Angela Acton Davis; one *s* one *d* and one step *d*. *Educ:* Walbottle Comprehensive Sch., Newcastle upon Tyne; Leeds Univ. (BA Theol. and Religious Studies); Durham Univ. (MBA). Pres., Leeds Univ. Students' Union, 1987–88; Campaigns Officer, Anti-Apartheid Movt, London, 1988–91; press officer, Labour Party, 1991–92; Hd of Campaigns, Christian Aid, 1992–97; Sen. Manager, Hobsbawm Macaulay Communications, 1997–98; Campaigns and Press Officer, Labour Party, 1998–99; Sen. Prog. Dir, Sunderland and Durham Co., Common Purpose, 1999–2005; Hd, Company and Sector Communications, Global Res. Corporate, HSBC, 2005–06; Hd of Advocacy, 2006–12, Hd of England N and Central, 2012–14, Christian Aid. Mem. (Lab), Newcastle upon Tyne CC, 1999–2004. Contested (Lab): Berwick upon Tweed, 1997; Hexham, 2001. *Address:* Labour Central, Kings Manor, Newcastle upon Tyne NE1 6PA. *T:* (0191) 620 0105. *E:* office@northeastlabour.eu.

BRANNEN, Peter; Visiting Professor in Management, Southampton University, 2000–09; Director, International Labour Office, London, 1992–2003; *b* 1 Dec. 1941; *s* of Joseph Brannen and Monica Brannen (*née* Cairns); *m* 1966, Julia Mary Morgan; two *s*. *Educ:* Ushaw Coll., Durham; Univ. of Manchester (BA Hons Econs 1964). Account Exec., McCann Erickson Advertising, 1964; Sen. Res. Asst, Univ. of Durham, 1966–69; Senior Research Fellow: Univ. of Bradford, 1969–72; Univ. of Southampton Med. Sch., 1973; Department of Employment: Special Advr, 1974; Chief Res. Officer, 1975–86; Head of Internat. Relns, 1989–91. Visiting Fellow: ANU, 1987; Nuffield Coll., Oxford, 1988; Sen. Vis. Fellow, PSI, 1988. Advr, Solidar, Sri Lanka, 2005–10. Mem., Mgt, Indust. Relns and other cttees, SSRC, 1975–81; Chm., British Workplace Indust. Relns Surveys, 1980–89; Member: Admin. Bd, European Foundn, 1986–92 (Dep. Chm., 1991); Employment Labour and Social Affairs Cttee, OECD, 1990–92; Employment Cttee, Council of Europe, 1990–92. FRSA 2000. Edit. Bd, Work, Employment and Society, 1986–90. *Publications:* Entering the World of Work, 1975; The Worker Directors, 1976; Authority and Participation in Industry, 1983; various contribs to anthologies and learned jls on economic sociology. *Recreations:* sailing, gardening, music. *Club:* Royal Southampton Yacht.

BRANSON, Sir Richard (Charles Nicholas), Kt 2000; Founder and Chairman, Virgin Retail Group, Virgin Communications, Virgin Travel Group, Virgin Hotels Group, Virgin Direct Ltd, Virgin Bride Ltd, Virgin Net Ltd, Virgin Express Holdings Plc and Virgin Mobile; Life President, Virgin Music Group (sold to Thorn-EMI, 1992); *b* 18 July 1950; *s* of late Edward James Branson and of Evette Huntley Branson (*née* Flindt); *m* 1st, 1969 (marr. diss.); 2nd, 1989, Joan Templeman; one *s* one *d*. *Educ:* Stowe. Editor, Student magazine, 1968–69; set up Student Advisory Centre (now Help), 1970. Founded Virgin Mail-Order Co., 1969, followed by Virgin Retail, Virgin Record Label, Virgin Music Publishing, Virgin Recording Studios; estabd Virgin Record subsids in 25 countries, 1980–86; founded Virgin Atlantic Airways, 1984; Voyager Gp Ltd formed 1986, encompassing interests in travel, clubs and hotels; Virgin Records launched in US, 1987; founded: Virgin Radio, 1993; Virgin Rail Gp Ltd, 1996; Virgin Games, 2004; Virgin Sport, 2015. Pres., UK 2000, 1988– (Chm., 1986–88); Dir, Intourist Moscow Ltd, 1988–90. Launched charity, The Healthcare Foundn, 1987. Captain, Atlantic Challenger II, winner Blue Riband for fastest crossing of Atlantic by a ship, 1986; with Per Lindstrand, first to cross Atlantic in hot air balloon, 1987, and Pacific, 199[illegible] (longest flight in hot air balloon, 6700 miles, and fastest speed, 200 mph, 1991). *Publications:* Losing My Virginity: the autobiography, 1998; Business Stripped Bare: adventures of a global entrepreneur, 2008; The Virgin Way, 2014. *Address:* c/o Virgin Group Ltd, The Battleship Building, 179 Harrow Road, W2 6NB.

BRANSTON, Gareth Philip; a District Judge (Magistrates' Courts), since 2013; a Recorder, since 2012; *b* Leicester, 25 March 1973; *s* of Julian Rex Branston and Patricia Mary Branston (*née* Spencer); *m* 2008, Patricia Anne Louise Travers; one *d*. *Educ:* Loughborough Grammar Sch.; Episcopal High Sch., Baton Rouge; Queens' Coll., Cambridge (BA Law 1995; MA 1999); Inns of Court Sch. of Law. Called to the Bar, Gray's Inn, 1996 (Prince of Wales Schol. Lionel Blundell Award); in practice as a barrister specialising in criminal law and regulatory law, 1997–2013; Tenant, 23 Essex St, 1999–2013 (Sec. of Chambers, 2005–12); Dep. Dist Judge (Magistrates' Courts), 2009–13. Pegasus Schol., NZ, 2001. Member, Cttee, Criminal Bar Assoc., 2001–04; Inns' Conduct Cttee, 2013–; Panel Mem. of Bar Tribunals and Adjudication Service, 2013; Treas., Thames Valley Bar Mess, 2007–13. *Recreations:* cycling, swimming, cricket, Leicester Tigers, arm wrestling with Chas & Dave, trance, dance, France. *Address:* c/o Thames Magistrates' Court, 58 Bow Road, E[illegible] 4DJ. *E:* DistrictJudgeGareth.Branston@judiciary.gsi.gov.uk. *Club:* Leicester Tigers Rugby Football.

BRANT, Colin Trevor, CMG 1981; CVO 1979; HM Diplomatic Service, retired; *b* 2 June 1929; *m* 1954, Jean Faith Walker; one *s* two *d*. *Educ:* Christ's Hospital, Horsham; Sidney Sussex Coll., Cambridge (MA). Served Army, 4th Queen's Own Hussars, active service Malaya, 1948–49; Pilot, Cambridge Univ. Air Squadron, 1951–52. Joined Sen. Br., Foreign Office, 1952; MECAS, Lebanon, 1953–54; Bahrain, 1954; Amman, 1954–56; FO, 1956–59; Stockholm, 1959–61; Cairo, 1961–64; Joint Services Staff Coll., Latimer, Bucks, 1964–65 (jssc); FO, 1965–67; Head of Chancery and Consul, Tunis, 1967–68; Asst Head, Oil Dept, FCO, 1969–71; Counsellor (Commercial), Caracas, 1971–73; Counsellor (Energy), Washington, 1973–78; Ambassador to Qatar, 1978–81; FCO Fellow, St Antony's Coll., Oxford, 1981–82; Consul Gen., and Dir Trade Promotion for S Africa, Johannesburg, 1982–87. Internat. business consultant, 1990–96. Donation Governor, Christ's Hosp., 1980–; Almoner, 1989–95; Cttee Mem., Oxfordshire Sect., Christ's Hosp. Club, 1999–2010 (Chm. 2002–04). *Recreations:* music, painting, history. *Address:* Apt 4, 15 Vittoria Walk, Montpellier, Cheltenham, Glos GL50 1TL. *Club:* Royal Over-Seas League.

BRASH, Dr Donald Thomas; economic policy consultant, since 2007; *b* 24 Sept. 1940; *s* of late Rev. Alan Anderson Brash, OBE and Eljean Ivory Brash; *m* 1st, 1964, Erica Beatty; one *s* one *d*; 2nd, 1989, Je Lan Lee; one *s*. *Educ:* Christchurch Boys' High Sch.; Canterbury Univ. NZ (BA Hist. and Econs 1961; MA 1st Cl. Hons Econs 1962); Australian Nat. Univ. (PhD 1966). IBRD, Washington, 1966–71; Gen. Manager, Broadbank Corp. Ltd, 1971–81; Managing Director: NZ Kiwifruit Authy, 1982–86; Trust Bank Gp, 1986–88; Gov., Reserve Bank of NZ, 1988–2002. MP (Nat.) NZ, 2002–07. Leader of Opposition, and Leader, Nat. Party, NZ, 2003–06. Director: ANZ Nat. Bank, 2007–11; Oceania Dairy, 2009–1[illegible]; Transpower NZ, 2009–11; Chm., Industrial and Commercial Bank of China (NZ), 2013–. Adjunct Prof. of Banking, Auckland Univ. of Technol., 2009–11. Chm., 2025 Taskforce, 2009–11. Member: Monetary and Econ. Council, 1974–76; NZ Planning Council, 1976–8[illegible]; Cttee of Inquiry on Inflation Accounting, 1976–77; chaired tax cttees incl. cttee which designed NZ's Goods and Services Tax. Hon. Dr Canterbury, 1999. NZIER-Qantas Econ. Award, 1999. *Publications:* New Zealand's Debt Servicing Capacity, 1964; American Investment in Australian Industry, 1966; Incredible Luck, 2014. *Recreation:* growing kiwifruit. *Address:* Apt 311, 184 Symonds Street, Auckland 1010, New Zealand. *W:* www.donbrash.com.

BRASLAVSKY, Dr Nicholas Justin; QC 1999; a Recorder, since 2001; a Deputy High Court Judge, since 2008; *b* 9 Feb. 1959; *s* of late Rev. Cyril and of Stella Braslavsky; *m* 1990, Jane Margolis; two *s* one *d*. *Educ:* Blackpool Grammar Sch.; High Pavement Grammar Sch.

Nottingham; Univ. of Birmingham (LLB Hons 1979; PhD 1982). Called to the Bar, Inner Temple, 1983; in practice at the Bar, 1983–; Hd, Kings Chambers, Manchester, 2010–. Accredited Mediator, 2013. Mem., Sports Resolutions Panel of Arbitrators and Mediators, 2012–. Hon. Lectr of Law, Univ. of Manchester, 2012–. *Address:* Kings Chambers, 36 Young Street, Manchester M3 3FT; 5 Park Square East, Leeds LS1 2NE; 3 Paper Buildings, Temple, EC4Y 7EU; Embassy House, 60 Church Street, Birmingham B3 2DJ.

BRASNETT, John, CMG 1987; HM Diplomatic Service, retired; Deputy High Commissioner, Bombay, 1985–89; *b* 30 Oct. 1929; *s* of late Norman Vincent Brasnett and of Frances May Brasnett (*née* Hewlett); *m* 1956, Jennifer Ann Reid; one *s* one *d.* *Educ:* Blundell's Sch.; Selwyn Coll., Cambridge (BA). Served Royal Artillery, 1948–49. Colonial Administrative Service, Uganda, 1953–65; retired from HM Overseas CS as Dep. Administrator, Karamoja District, 1965; entered HM Diplomatic Service, 1965; 1st Sec., OECD Delegn, 1968; Dep. High Comr, Freetown, 1970; FCO, 1973; Olympic Attaché, Montreal, 1975–76; Dep. High Comr, Accra, 1977–80; Counsellor (Econ. and Commercial), Ottawa, 1980–85. *Recreations:* reading, photography. *Address:* 8 Croft Way, Sevenoaks, Kent TN13 2JX.

BRASON, Paul, PPRP (RP 1994); RWA 2001; artist, portrait painter; President, Royal Society of Portrait Painters, 2000–02; *b* 17 June 1952; *s* of John Ainsley Brason and Audrey (*née* Wheldon). *Educ:* King James I Grammar Sch., Newport, IoW; Camberwell Coll. of Art. Work in many public and private collections incl. NPG, Royal Collection, Windsor Castle, Bodleian Library, Eton Coll., Mus and Galls Commn, Duke of Westminster, Goodwood House, etc. *Recreation:* early period houses and gardens. *Address:* Blakeleys House, Beechen Cliff, Bath BA2 4QT. *T:* 07799 417255. *Clubs:* Arts, Chelsea Arts.

BRASSARD, Prof. Gilles, OC 2013; PhD; FRS 2013; FRSC; Professor of Computer Science, since 1988, and Canada Research Chair in Quantum Information Processing, since 2001, University of Montréal; *b* Montréal, 1955. *Educ:* Univ. of Montréal (BSc Computer Sci. 1972; MSc Computer Sci. 1975); Cornell Univ. (PhD Computer Sci. 1979). University of Montréal: Asst Prof., 1979–83; Associate Prof., 1983–88; Founding Dir, Transdisciplinary Inst. for Quantum Information. E. W. R. Steacie Meml Fellow, Chem. Inst. Canada, 1992; Killam Res. Fellow, 1997; Sen. Fellow, Canadian Inst. for Advanced Res., 2002. Ed.-in-Chief, Jl Cryptol., 1991–97. FRSC 1996; Fellow, Internat. Assoc. Cryptologic Res., 2006. Hon. Dr ETH Zurich, 2010. Steacie Prize, E. W. R. Steacie Meml Fund, Canada, 1994; Prix Marie-Victorin, 2000; (jtly) Rank Prize in Optoelectronics, 2006; Award of Excellence, Natural Scis and Energy Res. Council of Canada, 2006; Gerhard Herzberg Canada Gold Medal for Sci. and Engrg, 2009; Killam Prize for Natural Scis, 2011. *Publications:* (with P. Bratley) Algorithmics: theory and practice, 1987; Modern Cryptology, 1988; (with P. Bratley) Fundamentals of Algorithmics, 1996; contribs to learned jls, incl. Physical Rev. Letters, Jl Cryptol., Jl Computer and Systems Scis, Scientific American, Science. *Address:* Department of Computer Science and Operations Research, University of Montréal, PO Box 6128, Centre-Ville STN, Montréal, QC H3C 3J7, Canada.

BRASSE, Gillian Denise; Her Honour Judge Gillian Brasse; a Circuit Judge, since 2008; *b* London, 19 June 1953; *d* of late Robert Brasse and Iris Brasse; *m* 1986, Patrick Michael Joseph O'Connor, *qv*; two *d.* *Educ:* Varndean Sch. for Girls, Brighton; Liverpool Univ. (BA Hons 1975). Called to the Bar, Gray's Inn, 1977; Dep. Dist Judge, 1996–2004; Recorder, 2002–08. Jt Hd of Chambers, 14 Gray's Inn Sq., 2004–08. *Recreations:* cinema, theatre, music, pilates, travel. *Address:* Principal Registry of the Family Division, First Avenue House, 42–49 High Holborn, WC1V 6NP.

BRASSE, Glenn Clifford; His Honour Judge Brasse; a Circuit Judge, since 2006; *b* 16 June 1949; *s* of late Robert Brasse and Iris Brasse; *m* 1974, Valerie Hauser, PhD; three *s.* *Educ:* Brighton, Hove and Sussex Grammar Sch.; LSE (LLB Hons). Called to the Bar, Middle Temple, 1972; Actg Stipendiary Magistrate, 1989–94; a Dep. Dist Judge, 1995; a Dist Judge, Principal Registry, Family Div., High Ct of Justice, 1995–2006; a Recorder, SE Circuit, 2002–06. *Publications:* (contrib.) Evidence in Family Proceedings, 1999; (contrib.) Family Law in Practice, 2006; contrib. numerous articles to Family Law. *Recreations:* sport (cycling, squash, mountain walking, ski-ing), classical guitar, drawing and painting, reading, cinema, opera. *Address:* Clerkenwell and Shoreditch County Court, The Gee Street Court House, 29–41 Gee Street, EC1V 3RE.

BRASSEY, family name of **Baron Brassey of Apethorpe**.

BRASSEY OF APETHORPE, 4th Baron *cr* 1938, of Apethorpe; **Edward Brassey;** Bt 1922; *b* 9 March 1964; *o s* of 3rd Baron Brassey of Apethorpe, OBE and Myrna Elizabeth Brassey (*née* Baskervyle-Glegg); *S* father, 2015; *m* 2003, Joanna Clare Pardoe; one *s* one *d.* *Educ:* Eton. Grenadier Guards. *Heir: s* Hon. Christian Brassey, *b* 23 Dec. 2003.

BRATHWAITE, James Everett, CBE 2001; Executive Chairman, DRENL Ltd, since 2011; *b* 31 March 1953; *s* of James and Louise Brathwaite; *m* 1977, Barbara Worby; one *s* four *d.* *Educ:* Sheffield Univ. (BSc Hons Physiol. and Zool.); Open Univ. (Dip. Competent Mgt). Graduate trainee acct, then Sales Trainer, Beecham Pharmaceuticals UK Ltd, 1975–79; a Product Manager, then a Mktg Manager, Antibiotic Mktg Strategy gp, Bayer Pharmaceuticals UK Ltd, 1979–82; founder and Chief Exec., VPS, subseq. Epic Multimedia Group plc, 1982–97; founder Dir and Chief Exec., XL Entertainment plc, 1997–2012; consultant and CEO, Future Gp Ltd, 1997–98; Chairman: Floella Benjamin Productions Ltd, 1997–2002 (Dir, 1997–2002); Renga Media Ltd, 2001–09; SE England Develt Agency, 2002–09; Community Alerts Ltd, 2002–12; Morgan Everett Ltd, 2003–12; Splash FM, 2004–; Brighton and Hove Radio Ltd, 2005–12; non-exec. Chairman: Business Link Sussex Ltd, 1995–2002; X-Tension Ltd, 1996–98 (Dir); Citizen TV Ltd, 1998–2002; BookLines plc, 2000–01; SEAL Ltd, 2000–08; consultant and non-exec. Dir, Amplicon LiveLine Ltd, 1997–99; non-executive Director: Sussex TEC Ltd, subseq. Sussex Enterprise Ltd, 1994–2002; Nat. Business Angels Network, 2003–04; Dir, RSTV, 2007–. Advr on multimedia industry to DTI, 1989; Member: Caribbean Adv. Gp, FCO, 1998–2003 (Treas., 1998–2003); Nat. Business Link Accreditation Adv. Bd, 1999–2000; Small Business Council, 2000–04; Americas Advrs Gp, Trade Partners UK, subseq. UK Trade and Investment, 2001–03; Bd, Envmt Agency, 2005–11. Founder Director: Brit. Interactive Media Assoc. (formerly Brit. Interactive Video Assoc.), 1985–90 (Chm., 1989–90); Wired Sussex, 1996–2002; Dir, Internat. CD-i Assoc., 1993–96. Council Member: Univ. of Sussex, 1995–2001 (Mem. of Ct, 2002–07); Univ. of Greenwich, 2002–12; C&G, 2006–; Business Rep., Bd, Brighton & Hove Sixth Form Coll., 1995–99 (Chm., Finance Cttee, 1995–99). Board Member: Rockinghorse Charity, 1994–96; Arundel Fest., 1998–2002 (Chm., 1999–2002); Farnham Castle Trustees Ltd, 2004–13; Bd of Trustees, Public Catalogue Foundn, 2006–10. Mem., World Traders' Co., 2007–. Hon. Consul for S Africa in SE England, 2007–. Hon. Fellow, UC Chichester, 2003. Mem., BAFTA; MInstD. Hon. FCGI 2006. Hon. Dr Business Southampton Solent, 2008. *Recreations:* the arts, music, ski-ing, watching cricket, football (Manchester United) and Rugby. *Address:* Church Farm House, Rectory Lane, Angmering, W Sussex BN16 4JU. *T:* (01903) 772648, *Fax:* (01903) 859863. *E:* james@brathwaite.net.

BRATHWAITE, Rt Hon. Sir Nicholas (Alexander), Kt 1995; OBE 1975; PC 1994; Prime Minister of Grenada, 1990–95; *b* Carriacou, 8 July 1925; *s* of Charles and Sophia Brathwaite; *m*; three *s* one *d.* *Educ:* Univ. of W Indies (BEd 1967). Formerly: teacher; Sen. Tutor, then Principal, Teachers' Coll.; Chief Educn Officer, Min. of Social Affairs, Grenada; Regl Dir, Commonwealth Youth Prog., Caribbean Centre, 1974–83; Chm., Interim Council, Grenada, 1983–84; Leader, Nat. Democratic Congress, 1989–95; formerly Minister of: Finance; Home Affairs; Nat. Security; Foreign Affairs; Personnel and Mgt; Carriacou and Petit Martinique Affairs. *Address:* Villa A, St George's, Grenada.

BRATTON, Prof. Jacqueline Susan, DPhil; Professor of Theatre and Cultural History, Royal Holloway, University of London, 1992–2013, now Emeritus (Head of Drama and Theatre, 1994–2001); *b* 23 April 1945; *d* of Jack Stanley Bratton and Doris Nellie Bratton (*née* Reynolds); partner, Gillian Bush-Bailey. *Educ:* St Anne's Coll., Oxford (BA 1966; DPhil 1969). Lectr, 1969–83, Reader in English Literature, 1983–84, Bedford Coll., Univ. of London; Reader in Theatre and Cultural History, RHBNC, 1984–92. Series Editor, Shakespeare in Production, 1994–2009; Editor, Nineteenth Century Theatre, 1996–2001. *Publications:* The Victorian Popular Ballad, 1975; The Impact of Victorian Children's Fiction, 1981; (ed) Music Hall: Performance and Style, 1986; King Lear: a stage history edition, 1987; Acts of Supremacy, 1991; (ed) Melodrama: stage picture screen, 1994; New Readings in Theatre History, 2003; The Victorian Clown, 2006; The Making of the West End Stage: marriage, management and the mapping of gender in London, 1830–1870, 2011. *Address:* Department of Drama, Royal Holloway, University of London, Egham TW20 0EX.

BRATZA, Hon. Sir Nicolas (Dušan), Kt 1998; a Judge of the High Court, Queen's Bench Division, 1998–2012; Judge, 1998–2012, and President, 2011–12, European Court of Human Rights (Section President, 1998–2000, and 2001–07; Vice-President of the Court, 2007–11); *b* 3 March 1945; *s* of late Milan Bratza, concert violinist, and Hon. Margaret Bratza (*née* Russell). *Educ:* Wimbledon Coll.; Brasenose Coll., Oxford (BA 1st Cl. Hons, MA; Hon. Fellow 2011). Instructor, Univ. of Pennsylvania Law Sch., 1967–68; called to Bar, Lincoln's Inn, 1969 (Hardwicke and Droop Schol.), Bencher, 1993; Jun. Counsel to the Crown, Common Law, 1979–88; QC 1988; a Recorder, 1993–98; UK Mem., European Commn of Human Rights, 1993–98. Member: Adv. Council, British Inst. of Human Rights, 2004– (Gov., 1985–2004; Vice-Chm., 1989–98; Pres., 2013–14; Chm. Bd, 2014–); Adv. Bd, British Inst. of Internat. and Comparative Law, 2006– (Mem., Bd of Mgt, 1999–2006); Bd, Internat. Service for Human Rights, 2013–; Internat. Commn of Jurists, 2013–. Patron: Peace Brigade Internat. UK, 2013–; Centre for Study of Human Rights, Univ. of Strathclyde, 2014–. Member Editorial Board: European Human Rights Law Review, 1996–; European Law Review, 2004–. Hon. Bencher, King's Inns, Dublin, 2012. Hon. Prof., Sch. of Law, Univ. of Nottingham, 2013–. Mem. Bd, Surrey Hills Internat. Music Fest., 2013–. Ambassador, Toynbee Hall 2013–. DU Essex, 2005; Hon. LLD Glasgow, 2007. *Publications:* (jtly) Contempt of Court, and Crown Proceedings, in Halsbury's Laws of England, 4th edn. *Recreations:* music, cricket. *Clubs:* Garrick, MCC.

BRAUDE, Prof. Peter Riven, OBE 2015; PhD; FRCOG; FMedSci; FRSB; Professor and Head of Department of Women's Health (formerly Division of Women's and Children's Health), King's College London School of Medicine (formerly Guy's, King's and St Thomas' School of Medicine, King's College, London) (formerly Head of Department of Obstetrics and Gynaecology, United Medical and Dental Schools of Guy's and St Thomas' Hospitals), 1991–2011, now Professor Emeritus of Obstetrics and Gynaecology; *b* Johannesburg, 29 May 1948; *s* of Dr Barnett Braude and Sylvia (*née* Grumberg); *m* 1973, Beatrice Louise Roselaar; two *s.* *Educ:* Univ. of Witwatersrand (BSc 1968; MB BCh 1972); Jesus Coll., Cambridge (MA 1975; PhD 1981). DPMSA 1983; MRCOG 1982, FRCOG 1993; FRSB (FSB 2011). Lectr in Physiology and Pharmacology, Univ. of Witwatersrand Med. Sch., 1973; Demonstrator, Dept of Anatomy, Univ. of Cambridge, 1974–79; sen. house officer appts, St Mary's Hosp., London and Addenbrooke's Hosp., Cambridge, 1979–81; Sen. Res. Associate, Dept of Obstetrics and Gynaecol., Univ. of Cambridge, 1981–83; Registrar in Obstetrics and Gynaecol., Rosie Maternity Hosp., Cambridge, 1983–85; University of Cambridge: Clinical Lectr in Obstetrics and Gynaecol., 1985–88; MRC Clinical Res. Consultant, Clinical Sch., 1988–89; Consultant and Sen. Lectr, Dept of Obstetrics and Gynaecol., 1989–90; Clinical Dir for Women's Services, 1993–94, Dir, Assisted Conception Unit and Fertility Service, 1993–99, Dir, Centre for Pre-implantation Genetic Diagnosis, 1999–2011, Guy's and St Thomas' Hosp. NHS Trust. Member: HFEA, 1999–2004 (Inspector, 1991–99; Mem., expert panel review of scientific methods to avoid mitochondrial disease, 2011, 2013, 2014); Mgt Cttee, UK Stem Cell Bank, 2008–10; Adv. Bd on the Safety of Blood Tissues and Organs, DoH, 2008–; Nuffield Council on Bioethics wkg gp on Novel techniques for prevention of mitochondrial DNA disorders, 2012; Internat. Panel of Experts, Bioethics Adv. Cttee, Singapore, 2014–; Chairman: Sci. Adv. Cttee, 2004–07, Expert Gp on Umbilical Cord Blood Banking, 2006, RCOG; Expert Adv. Gp on multiple births after IVF, HFEA (report, One Child at a Time), 2006. Exec. Sec., Assoc. Profs of Obstetrics and Gynaecol., 1993–95. Mem., Med. Adv. Bd, Tommy's Campaign, 1993–99. Member, Editorial Board: Molecular Human Reproduction, 1992–98; Stem Cells, 2005–08. FMedSci 2006. *Publications:* Obstetric and Gynaecologic Dermatology, 1995, 2nd edn 2002; ABC of Subfertility, 2004; (jtly) Preimplantation Genetic Diagnosis in Clinical Practice, 2014; contribs to scientific jls on develt of the human embryo *in vitro*, assisted conception techniques, treatment of infertility, ethics and politics of new reproductive technologies and preimplantation diagnosis, human embryonic stem cells. *Recreations:* narrowboater (The Slowgoose), Egyptology, geology, ski-ing, music, Apple Macs. *Address:* King's College London Division of Women's Health, 10th Floor NW, St Thomas' Hospital, Westminster Bridge Road, SE1 7EH. *T:* (020) 7188 4138. *E:* peter.braude@kcl.ac.uk.

BRAVERY, Katy Louise B.; *see* Bowen-Bravery.

BRAVINER ROMAN, Stephen Thomas; Director General, Government Legal Department (formerly Treasury Solicitor's Department), since 2014; *b* Leeds, 25 Oct. 1968; *s* of Dennis Braviner and Elizabeth Ann Braviner (*née* Kench); *m* 2001, Veronica Roman; two *d.* *Educ:* Harrington High Sch., Leeds; Bradford Coll. (BA Hons 1st Cl. Orgn Studies); Leeds Poly. (CPE (Law)); London Sch. of Econs (LLM). Called to the Bar, Gray's Inn, 1992; Legal Advr, EC Litigation, Treasury Solicitor's Dept, 1994–96, DfT, then DETR, 1996–99; Legal Advr, 1999–2001, Dep. Dir, NI Office Team, 2001–02, Legal Advrs' Br., Home Office; Sen. Legal Advr, Attorney Gen's Office, 2002–05; Dep. Dir, Border Control and Counter-terrorism, Legal Advrs' Br., Home Office, 2005–08; Dir of Legal Services (Business, Consumers, Employment and Skills), BERR, later BIS, 2008–11; Legal Adviser: SOCA, 2011–13; DCLG, 2013–14. Co. Sec. and Trustee, Bliss, 2009–13. *Recreations:* (rediscovering) children's literature, history, detective novels, music. *Address:* Government Legal Department, One Kemble Street, WC2B 4TS.

BRAVO, Martin Maurice B.; *see* Brandon-Bravo.

BRAY, Angela Lavinia; *b* 13 Oct. 1953; *d* of Benedict and Patricia Bray. *Educ:* Downe House, Newbury; St Andrews Univ. (MA Hons Medieval Hist.). Presenter, British Forces Broadcasting, Gibraltar, 1979–80; presenter, producer and reporter, LBC Radio, 1980–88; Hd, Broadcasting Unit, Cons. Central Office, 1989–91; Press Officer, Rt Hon. John Major's Leadership Campaign, Nov. 1990; Press Sec. to Chm., Conservative Party, 1991–92; Public Affairs Consultant, 1992–2000. Mem. (C) West Central, London Assembly, GLA, 2000–08. Contested (C) E Ham, 1997. MP (C) Ealing Central and Acton, 2010–15; contested (C) same seat, 2015. PPS to Minister for Cabinet Office and Paymaster Gen., 2010–12. Mem., Culture, Media and Sport Select Cttee, 2012–15. Pres., Kensington and Chelsea Cons. Pol Forum, 2000–03; Vice Pres., Hammersmith and Fulham Cons. Assoc., 2000–08. *Recreations:* tennis, music, history, walking my dogs.

BRAY, Prof. Julia Margaret, DPhil; FRAS; Laudian Professor of Arabic, University of Oxford, since 2012; Fellow, St John's College, Oxford, since 2012; *b* Cambridge, 28 Sept. 1952; *yr d* of John Bray and Barbara Bray (*née* Jacobs). *Educ:* Coll. Sévigné, Paris; St Hilda's

Coll., Oxford (BA Oriental Studies 1974); St Cross Coll., Oxford (DPhil 1984). Archivist, India Office Liby and Records, British Acad. Oriental Documents Cttee, 1976–82; Lecturer in Arabic: Univ. of Manchester, 1983–87; Univ. of Edinburgh, 1989–92; Sen. Lectr in Arabic, Univ. of St Andrews, 1996–2003; Professeur de littérature arabe médiévale, Univ. Paris 8 Vincennes-St Denis, 2003–12. Vis. Lectr, St Antony's Coll. ME Centre, Oxford, 1994–95; James Mew Sen. Res. Fellow in Arabic, Faculty of Oriental Studies, Univ. of Oxford, 1994–96; Dir de Recherches invitée, Ecole des Hautes Etudes en Sciences Sociales, Paris, 2003. Member and Associate Member: UMR 8167 Orient et Méditerranée, 2004–; EA 1571 Centre de recherches historiques: histoire des pouvoirs, savoirs, sociétés, 2009–. Mem., Union Européenne des Arabisants et Islamisants; Sch. of 'Abbasid Studies. FRAS 1976; Fellow, Amer. Oriental Soc. *Publications:* The Arabic Documents in the Archives of the British Political Agency, Kuwait, 1904–1949, 1982; (ed jtly) The Cambridge History of Arabic Literature: 'Abbasid Belles-Lettres, 1990; Media Arabic, 1993; (ed) Writing and Representation in Medieval Islam, 2006. *Recreations:* the arts, the country, family and friends, Middle Eastern textiles. *Address:* St John's College, Oxford OX1 3JP.

BRAY, Prof. Kenneth Noel Corbett, PhD; FRS 1991; CEng; Hopkinson and Imperial Chemical Industries Professor of Applied Thermodynamics, 1985–97, now Emeritus, and Fellow of Girton College, 1985–97, Cambridge University; *b* 19 Nov. 1929; *s* of Harold H. Bray and Effie E. Bray; *m* 1958, Shirley Maureen Culver; two *s* one *d*. *Educ:* Univ. of Cambridge (BA); Univ. of Southampton (PhD); MSE Princeton; CEng; MRAeS; MAIAA. Engr in Research Dept, Handley Page Aircraft, 1955–56; University of Southampton, 1956–85: Dean, Faculty of Engrg and Applied Science, 1975–78; Head, Dept of Aeronautics and Astronautics, 1982–85. Vis. appt, Avco-Everett Res. Lab., Mass, USA, 1961–62; Vis. Prof., MIT, 1966–67; Vis. Res. Engr, Univ. of California, San Diego, 1975, 1983. *Publications:* on topics in gas dynamics, chemically reacting flows, molecular energy transfer processes and combustion. *Recreations:* walking, wood carving, gardening. *Address:* 23 De Freville Avenue, Cambridge CB4 1HW.

BRAY, Michael Peter; Consultant, Clifford Chance, since 2012 (Partner, 1976–2012; Chief Executive Officer, 2000–03); *b* 27 March 1947; *s* of William Charles Bray and Ivy Isobel (*née* Ellison); *m* 1st, 1970, Elizabeth Ann Harrington (marr. diss. 2007); two *d*; 2nd, 2010, Gabrielle Taylor. *Educ:* Caterham Sch.; Liverpool Univ. (LLB 1969). Joined Coward Chance, subseq. Clifford Chance, 1970, Partner, 1976; Global Head, Clifford Chance Finance Practice, 1995–2000. *Recreations:* golf, ski-ing, opera, theatre. *Address:* Clifford Chance, 10 Upper Bank Street, E14 5JJ. *T:* (020) 7600 1000. *E:* Michael.Bray@cliffordchance.com.

BRAY, Richard Winston Atterton; a Circuit Judge, 1993–2014; *b* 10 April 1945; *s* of late Winston Bray, CBE and Betty Atterton Bray (*née* Miller); *m* 1978, Judith Elizabeth Margaret Ferguson; one *s* three *d*. *Educ:* Rugby Sch.; Corpus Christi Coll., Oxford (BA). Called to the Bar, Middle Temple, 1970; practised on Midland and Oxford Circuit; Asst Recorder, 1983–87; Recorder, 1987–93. *Recreations:* cricket, Real tennis, gardening, golf. *Clubs:* MCC; Leamington Real Tennis; Aspley Guise Golf.

BRAYBROOKE, 10th Baron *cr* 1788; **Robin Henry Charles Neville;** Lord-Lieutenant of Essex, 1992–2002; Hereditary Visitor of Magdalene College, Cambridge; Patron of three livings; farmer and landowner; *b* 29 Jan. 1932; *s* of 9th Baron Braybrooke and Muriel Evelyn (*d* 1962), *d* of William C. Manning; *S* father, 1990; *m* 1st, 1955, Robin Helen Brockhoff (marr. diss. 1974); four *d* (inc. twins) (and one *d* decd); 2nd, 1974, Linda Norman (marr. diss. 1998); three *d*; 3rd, 1998, Mrs Perina Fordham. *Educ:* Eton; Magdalene Coll., Cambridge (MA); RAC Cirencester. Commnd Rifle Bde, 1951; served 3rd Bn King's African Rifles in Kenya and Malaya, 1951–52. Dir of Essex and Suffolk Insurance Co. until amalgamation with Guardian Royal Exchange. Member: Saffron Walden RDC, 1959–69; for Stansted, Essex CC, 1969–72; Council of CLA, 1965–83; Agricl Land Tribunal, Eastern Area, 1975. Chairman: Price Trust, 1983–95; Rural Develt Commn for Essex, 1984–90. Pres., Essex Show, 1990. DL Essex, 1980. DU Essex, 2000. *Recreations:* railway and airfield operating, photography, motorcycling. *Heir: kinsman* Richard Ralph Neville, *b* 10 June 1977. *Address:* Abbey House, Audley End, Saffron Walden, Essex CB11 4JB. *T:* (01799) 522484, *Fax:* (01799) 542134. *Club:* Farmers.

See also Earl of Derby.

BRAYBROOKE, Rev. Marcus Christopher Rossi; President, World Congress of Faiths, since 1997 (Chairman, 1978–83 and 1992–99; Vice-President, 1986–97); *b* 16 Nov. 1938; *s* of late Lt-Col Arthur Rossi Braybrooke and Marcia Nona Braybrooke; *m* 1964, Mary Elizabeth Walker, JP, BSc, CQSW; one *s* one *d*. *Educ:* Cranleigh School; Magdalene College, Cambridge (BA, MA); Madras Christian College; Wells Theological College; King's College, London (MPhil). Curate, St Michael's, Highgate, 1964–67; Team Vicar, Strood Clergy Team, 1967–73; Rector, Swainswick, Langridge, Woolley, 1973–79; Dir of Training, Dio. of Bath and Wells, 1979–84; Hon. priest-in-charge, Christ Church, Bath, 1984–91; Exec. Director, Council of Christians and Jews, 1984–87; Preb., Wells Cathedral, 1990–93; Chaplain, Chapel of St Mary Magdalene, Bath, 1992–93; non-stipendiary priest, Marsh and Toot Baldon, Dorchester Team Ministry, Oxford, 1993–2005. Chm., Internat. Cttee, 1988–93, Internat. Interfaith Orgns Co-ordinating Cttee, 1990–93, World Congress of Faiths. Trustee: Interfaith Centre, 1993–2000 (Patron, 2001–12); Internat. Peace Council, 1995–2000; Council for Parlt of World Religions, 1995–2001; Three Faiths Forum, 2001–; Patron, Utd Religions Initiative, 2001–12. Peace Councillor, 2000–. Examng Chaplain to Bishop of Bath and Wells, 1984–88. Editor: World Faiths Insight, 1976–91; Common Ground, 1987–93. DD Lambeth, 2004. Sir Sigmund Sternberg Award for contributions to Christian-Jewish relations, 1992; Kashi Humanitarian Award, Kashi Ashram, Fla, 2001; Interfaith Visionary Award, Temple of Understanding, NY, 2010; Man of the Year Award, Ramanuja Mission Trust, 2013. *Publications:* Together to the Truth, 1971; The Undiscovered Christ of Hinduism, 1973; Interfaith Worship, 1974; Interfaith Organizations: a historical directory, 1980; Time to Meet, 1990; Wide Embracing Love, 1990; Children of One God, 1991; Pilgrimage of Hope, 1992; Stepping Stones to a Global Ethic, 1992; Be Reconciled, 1992; (ed with Tony Bayfield) Dialogue with a Difference, 1992; Love Without Limit, 1995; Faith in a Global Age, 1995; How to Understand Judaism, 1995; A Wider Vision: a history of the World Congress of Faiths, 1996; The Wisdom of Jesus, 1997; (contrib.) The Miracles of Jesus, 1997; (ed with Jean Potter) All in Good Faith, 1997; (contrib.) The Journeys of St Paul, 1997; The Explorers' Guide to Christianity, 1998; (ed with Peggy Morgan) Testing the Global Ethic, 1999; Christian-Jewish Dialogue: the next steps, 2000; Learn to Pray, 2001; (ed) Bridge of Stars, 2001; What Can We Learn from Hinduism, 2002; What Can We Learn from Islam, 2002; (ed) Lifelines, 2002; (ed) One Thousand World Prayers, 2003; 365 Meditations for a Peaceful Heart and a Peaceful World, 2004; (with Kamran Mofid) Sustaining the Common Good, 2005; A Heart for the World: the interfaith alternative, 2006; (ed) 365 Meditations and Inspirations on Love and Peace, 2006; Beacons of the Light, 2009; Meeting Jews, 2010; Peace in our Hearts, Peace in our World, 2012; Hinduism: a Christian approach, 2012; Islam: a Christian approach, 2012; Christians and Jews Building Bridges, 2012; Widening Vision: the World Congress of Faiths and the Interfaith Movement, 2013; Christianity: an explorer's guide, 2014; contrib. to various theol books and jls incl. Theology, Modern Believing (formerly The Modern Churchman), The Tablet, Expository Times, Church Times, Church of England Newspaper, Faith and Freedom, Interreligious Insight, The Interfaith Observer. *Recreations:* gardening, swimming, travel, photography. *Address:* 17 Courtiers Green, Clifton Hampden, Abingdon OX14 3EN.

BRAYE, Baroness (8th in line), *cr* 1529, of Eaton Braye, Co. Bedford; **Mary Penelope Aubrey-Fletcher;** DL; *b* 28 Sept. 1941; *d* of 7th Baron Braye and Dorothea (*d* 1994), *yr d* of late Daniel C. Donoghue, Philadelphia; *S* father, 1985; *m* 1981, Lt-Col Edward Hen[ry] Lancelot Aubrey-Fletcher, Grenadier Guards. *Educ:* Assumption Convent, Hengrave Ha[ll]; Univ. of Warwick. Pres., Blaby Cons. Assoc., 1986–; Dep. Pres., Northants Red Cros[s], 1983–92; Chm. School Cttee, St Andrew's Occupational Therapy School, 1988–9[.]; Governor: St Andrew's Hosp., Northampton, 1978–; Three Shires Hosp., Northampto[n], 1983–. High Sheriff of Northants, 1983; JP South Northants, 1981–86; DL Northants 199[.]. *Heir: cousin* Linda Kathleen Fothergill [*b* 2 May 1930, *née* Browne; *m* 1965, Com[.] Christopher Henry Fothergill (*d* 2014), RN; two *s*]. *Address:* The Garden House, Th[e] Avenue, Flore, Northampton NN7 4LZ.

BRAYFIELD, Celia Frances; author; Reader in Creative Writing, Brunel University, sinc[e] 2007 (Senior Lecturer, 2005–06); Senior Lecturer in Creative Writing, Bath Spa Universit[y] since 2010; *d* of Felix Francis Brayfield and Helen (Ada Ellen) Brayfield; one *d*. *Educ:* St Paul[']s Girls' Sch.; Univ. of Grenoble. Feature writer, Daily Mail, 1969–71; media columnis[t], Evening Standard, 1974–82; TV critic, The Times, 1984–88; columnist, Sunday Telegrap[h], 1988–90; feature writer, The Times, 1998–; contrib. to other pubns. Mem., Cttee of Mg[t], NCOPF, 1989–2006. Mem., Cttee of Mgt, Soc. of Authors, 1995–98; Dir, Nat. Aca[d.] Writing, 1999–2003. *Publications:* Glitter: the truth about fame, 1985; Bestseller, 1996; Dee[p] France, 2004; Arts Reviews, 2008; Writing Historical Fiction, 2013; *fiction:* Pearls, 1986; Th[e] Prince, 1990; White Ice, 1993; Harvest, 1993; Getting Home, 1998; Sunset, 199[.]; Heartswap, 2000; Mister Fabulous and Friends, 2003; Wild Weekend, 2004. *Recreation[s]:* family life, the arts. *Address:* c/o Curtis Brown Ltd, Haymarket House, 28/29 Haymarke[t], SW1Y 4SP. *T:* (020) 7396 4400. *Club:* Chelsea Arts.

BRAYNE, Prof. Carol Elspeth Goodeve, MD; FRCP, FFPH, FMedSci; Professor [o]f Public Health Medicine, since 2001, and Director, Cambridge Institute of Public Healt[h], since 2008, University of Cambridge; Fellow, Darwin College, Cambridge, since 1995; *b* [.] July 1957; *d* of Thomas and Audrey Brayne; *m* 1984, Paul Calloway; two *s* two *d*. *Educ:* Roy[al] Free Hosp. Sch. of Medicine, London Univ. (MB BS, MD); London Sch. of Hygiene an[d] Tropical Medicine (MSc). FFPH (FFPHM 1998); FRCP 2000. Lectr in Epidemiolog[y], Cambridge Univ., 1991–2001. Hon. Consultant in Public Health Medicine: Cambs H[A], 1991–2002; Cambs (formerly Hunts) PCT, 2002–13; Public Health England, 2013–. FMedSci 2014. *Address:* Cambridge Institute of Public Health, Forvie Site, Cambrid[ge] Biomedical Campus, Cambridge CB2 0SR; Darwin College, Cambridge CB3 9EU.

BRAZIER, Helen; Head of RNIB National Library Service, 2007–13; *b* 15 Feb. 1957; *d* [of] late John David Brazier and Nancy (*née* Lloyd); partner, Paul Sutcliffe. *Educ:* Newnham Coll[.], Cambridge (MA); Sheffield Univ. (MA). MCLIP. Various posts, 1981–97, incl. U[K] Volunteer Librarian, 1990–92; Liby Services Dir, 1997–2001, Chief Exec., 2002–06, Na[t.] Liby for the Blind. Co-ordinator, Share the Vision, 2007–13 (Dir, 2001–07). Non-exec. D[ir], Henshaws Soc. for Blind People, 2014–. *Publications:* contrib. various articles to jls. *Recreation[s]:* walking, studio pottery, travel, reading.

BRAZIER, Julian William Hendy, TD; MP (C) Canterbury, since 1987; Parliamenta[ry] Under-Secretary of State, Ministry of Defence, since 2014; *b* 24 July 1953; *s* of Lt-Col P. H[.] Brazier; *m* 1984, Katharine Elizabeth, *d* of Brig. P. M. Blagden; three *s* (incl. twins). *Edu[c:]* Wellington Coll.; Brasenose Coll., Oxford (schol. in maths; MA); London Business Sc[h.] Chm., Oxford Univ. Cons. Assoc., 1974. Charter Consolidated, 1975–84, Sec., Exec. Ctte[e] of Bd, 1981–84; management consultant to industry, H. B. Maynard, internat. manageme[nt] consultants, 1984–87. Contested (C) Berwick-upon-Tweed, 1983. PPS to Minister of Stat[e], HM Treasury, 1990–92, to Sec. of State for Employment, 1992–93; an Opposition Whi[p], 2001–02; Opposition front bench spokesman: for work and pensions, 2002–03; for interna[t.] develt and overseas trade, 2004–05; for transport (aviation and shipping), 2005–10. Mem[.], Defence Select Cttee, 1997–2001 and 2010–14; Chm., All-Party Reserves and Cadets G[p], 2008–14; Co-Chm., All-Party Ports and Maritime Gp, 2010–14; Vice Chm., Con[s.] Backbench Defence Cttee, 1993–97; Sec., Cons. Backbench Finance Cttee, 1990. Vic[e] Chm., Ind. Commn on Reserve Forces, 2010–11. Served 13 yrs as an officer in TA, incl. [.] yrs with 21 SAS. *Publications:* pamphlets on defence, economic policy, social security an[d] family issues. *Recreations:* science, philosophy, cross-country running. *Address:* House [o]f Commons, SW1A 0AA.

BRAZIER, Prof. Margaret Rosetta, OBE 1997; FMedSci; FBA 2014; Professor of La[w], University of Manchester, since 1990; *b* 2 Nov. 1950; *d* of Leslie Jacobs and Mary Jacobs (*n*[ée] Pickering); *m* 1974, Rodney John Brazier, *qv*; one *d*. *Educ:* Univ. of Manchester (LLB 1971[)]. Called to the Bar, Middle Temple, 1973. University of Manchester: Lectr, 1971–83, Se[n.] Lectr, 1983–89, Reader, 1989–90, in Law; Dir of Legal Studies, Centre for Social Ethics an[d] Policy, 1987; a founder Dir, Inst. of Medicine, Law and Bioethics, 1996. Chairman: Anim[al] Procedures Cttee, 1993–98; Review of Surrogacy, DoH, 1997–98; Chair: NHS Retain[ed] Organs Commn, 2001–04; Nuffield Council Working Pty Critical Care Decision Making [in] Fetal and Neonatal Medicine, 2004–06; Mem., Nuffield Council on Bioethics, 199[.]. FMedSci 2007. Hon. QC 2008. *Publications:* Medicine, Patients and the Law, 1987, (with [E.] Cave) 5th edn 2011; (jtly) Protecting the Vulnerable: autonomy and health care, 1991; (Ge[n.] Ed.) Clerk & Lindsell on Torts, 17th edn 1995; (ed) Street on Torts, 8th edn to 10th edn 199[.]; (jtly) Bioethics and Medicine in the Theatre of the Criminal Process, 2013. *Recreation[s]:* literature, theatre, cooking. *Address:* School of Law, University of Manchester, Manchest[er] M13 9PL. *T:* (0161) 275 3593.

BRAZIER, Dr Patrick Charles; International Director, CfBT Education Trust, since 201[.]; *b* 2 Aug. 1960; *s* of Kenneth and Judith Brazier. *Educ:* Univ. of Liverpool (MSc (Microbio[l.] 1981); PCL (PhD (Microbial Genetics) 1987). Consultant in Biotechnol., Inst. of Technol[.] Bandung, Indonesia, 1987–88; Sci. Policy Res. Officer, Royal Soc., London, 1989–9[.]; British Council, 1990–: Project Officer, London, 1990–91; Dep. Dir, Uganda, 1991–9[.]; Director: Swaziland, 1994–96; Durban, 1996–97; Dep. Regl Dir, Southern Afric[a], Johannesburg, 1997–2001; Director: Syria, 2001–03; Indonesia, 2003–04; Governance an[d] Develt, Manchester, 2004–07; Contracts and Projects, Manchester, 2007–08; Middle Ea[st] 2008–11; Mem. Mgt Bd, 2011–13; Regl Dir, ME and N Africa, 2011–13. *Address:* CfB[T] Education Trust, 60 Queens Road, Reading, Berks RG1 4BS. *T:* (0118) 902 1689. [E:] pbrazier@cfbt.com.

BRAZIER, Rev. Canon Raymond Venner; Vicar, St Matthew and St Nathana[el], Kingsdown, Bristol, 1984–2005; Chaplain to the Queen, 1998–2010; *b* 12 Oct. 1940; *s* [of] Harold and Doris Brazier; *m* 1964, Elizabeth Dawn Radford; three *d*. *Educ:* Brockley Coun[ty] Sch., London; Bishop Otter Coll., Chichester; Wells Theol Coll. Assistant teacher: St Martin[']s County Secondary Boys' Sch., Shenfield, Essex, 1963–66; Kingswood Secondary Boys' Sch[.], Kingswood, Bristol, 1966–68; ordained deacon 1971, priest 1972; Curate, St Gregory th[e] Great, Horfield, Bristol, 1971–75; Priest-in-charge, 1975–79, Vicar, 1979–84, St Nathana[el] with St Katharine, Bristol; also Priest-in-charge, St Matthew, Kingsdown, Bristol, 1980–8[.]; Rural Dean of Horfield, 1985–91; Priest-in-charge, Bishopston, Bristol, 1993–97. Asst Ad[v.] for Licensed Ministry, Bristol, 2007–. Canon Emeritus, Bristol Cathedral, 2006 (Hon. Cano[n] 1994–2006); Hon. Chaplain, Colston's Girls Sch., Bristol, 1976–2005; Supplementa[l] Chaplain, HM Prison Bristol, 2006–10. *Recreations:* reading, listening to music, watchi[ng] sport, cooking, walking. *Address:* 51 Chalks Road, St George, Bristol BS5 9EP. *T:* (0117) 3[.] 4611.

BRAZIER, Prof. Rodney John, MVO 2013; LLD; FRHistS; Professor of Constitution[al] Law, University of Manchester, since 1992; *b* 13 May 1946; *s* of late Eric Brazier and Mildre[d] Brazier (*née* Davies); *m* 1974, Margaret Rosetta Jacobs (*see* M. R. Brazier); one *d*. *Edu[c:]*

Buckhurst Hill County High Sch.; Univ. of Southampton (LLB 1968; LLD 2008). Called to the Bar, Lincoln's Inn, 1970, Bencher, 2000, Emeritus Bencher, 2011. University of Manchester: Asst Lectr, 1968–70; Lectr, 1970–78; Sen. Lectr in Law, 1978–89; Reader in Constitutional Law, 1989–92; Dean, Faculty of Law, 1992–94. Chm., Consumer Credit Appeals Tribunal, 1992–2006. Specialist Adviser: H of C Public Admin Select Cttee, 2003–04; Jt Select Cttee on Draft Constitnl Renewal Bill, 2007–08. Mem., Lord Chancellor's Adv. Council on Nat. Records and Archives, 2014–. JP Manchester, 1982–89. FRHistS 1994. *Publications:* Constitutional Practice, 1988, 3rd edn 1999; Constitutional Texts, 1990; Constitutional Reform: reshaping the British political system, 1991, 3rd edn 2008; Ministers of the Crown, 1997; (jtly) Constitutional & Administrative Law, 8th edn 1998; articles in legal jls. *Address:* School of Law, University of Manchester, Oxford Road, Manchester M13 9PL. *T:* (0161) 275 3575.

BREADALBANE AND HOLLAND, Earldom of, *cr* 1677; dormant since 1995.

BREADEN, Very Rev. Robert William; Priest-in-charge, St Columba's, Portree, Isle of Skye, 2007–12; licence to officiate, Diocese of Moray, Ross and Caithness; *b* 7 Nov. 1937; *s* of Moses and Martha Breaden; *m* 1970, Glenice Sutton Martin; one *s* four *d*. *Educ:* The King's Hospital, Dublin; Edinburgh Theological Coll. Deacon 1961, priest 1962; Asst Curate, St Mary's, Broughty Ferry, 1961–65; Rector: Church of the Holy Rood, Carnoustie, 1965–72; St Mary's, Broughty Ferry, 1972–2007; Canon of St Paul's Cathedral, Dundee, 1977; Dean of Brechin, 1984–2007. OStJ 2001. *Recreations:* gardening, horse riding, Rugby enthusiast. *Address:* 6 Chapel Road, Evanton, Dingwall IV16 9XT. *T:* (01349) 830490. *E:* ateallach@gmail.com.

BREAKWELL, Prof. Dame Glynis (Marie), DBE 2012; DL; Vice Chancellor and Professor, University of Bath, since 2001; *b* 26 July 1952; *d* of Harold and Vera Breakwell; partner, Colin Rowett. *Educ:* Univ. of Leicester (BA Hons 1973); Univ. of Strathclyde (MSc 1974); Univ. of Bristol (PhD 1976); Nuffield Coll., Oxford (MA 1978; DSc 1995). FBPsS 1987 (Hon. FBPsS 2006); CPsychol 1988. Prize Fellow, Nuffield Coll., Oxford, 1978–82; University of Surrey: Lectr in Psychol., 1981–87; Sen. Lectr, 1987–88; Reader, 1988–91; Prof., 1991–2001; Pro-Vice Chancellor, 1994–2001. Res. Advr to MAFF and Food Standards Agency, 1991–2001. Member: Coll. of Postgrad. Trng Assessors, 1996–2001, Council, 2011–, ESRC (Chm., Res. Cttee, 2011–); CVCP/HEFCE Steering Gp on costing and pricing, 1997–2001; HEFCE Leadership Governance and Mgt Cttee, 2004–14; Social Scis Panel, Finnish RAE, 2005; Bd, Higher Educn Career Services Unit, 2007–10; Financial Sustainability Strategy Gp, HEFCE, 2008–; HEFCE Accountability Burden Proj. Steering Gp, 2008–10; Task Force on HE, CBI, 2009; Res Councils UK Panel on Public Engagement in Sci., 2009–; Bd, Leadership Foundn for Higher Educn, 2013– (Chair, Res. Panel, 2013–); Chairman: Nat. Cataloguing Unit for Archives of Contemp. Scientists, 2001–09; HEFCE Widening Participation Rev. Gp, 2004–06; Director: UUK, 2005– (Chm., Funding Policy Network (formerly Funding and Mgt Policy Gp), 2008–; Chm., HE Funding Task Gp, 2010–11); Universities Superannuation Scheme, 2009–; Student Loans Co. Ltd, 2011–; Chm., HERDA-SW, 2006–08. Pres., Psychol. Section, BAAS, 1994–95. Mem. Bd, 2001–12, Exec. Cttee, 2010–12, 1994 Gp. Royal Society: Mem., Internat. Policy Cttee, 2002–05, Fruits of Curiosity Report, 2009–10; Advr, Res. on Public Communication of Sci., 2005; Mem., Royal Soc./Acad. of Med. Scis Cttee on Pandemic Influenza, 2006. Member: SW Sci. and Industry Council, 2006–10; West of England Local Econ. Partnership, 2011–14. Dir, New Swindon Co., 2002–07. Dir, Theatre Royal, Bath, 2001–06; Trustee, Holburne Mus., Bath, 2001–04; Chairman: Bath Fests, 2006–09; Daphne Jackson Trust, 2009–15. Mem. Council, Cheltenham Ladies' Coll., 2009–15. Mem., Cttee, World Cultural Council, Mexico, 2010–; Chm., Adv. Bd, Inst. of Social Scis, Univ. of Lisbon, 2010–14. DL Somerset, 2010. FRSA 1997; FAcSS (AcSS 2002). Hon. Prof., Univ. of Shandong, China, 2004. Hon. Fellow, Soc. of Sports and Exercise Medicine Malaysia, 2013. Hon. LLD Bristol, 2004. *Publications:* (jtly) Social Work: the social psychological approach, 1982; The Quiet Rebel, 1985; Coping with Threatened Identities, 1986, reprint 2015; Facing Physical Violence, 1989; Interviewing, 1990; (jtly) Managing Violence at Work, 1992; (jtly) Careers and Identities, 1992; (jtly) Basic Evaluation Methods, 1995; Coping with Aggressive Behaviour, 1997; The Psychology of Risk, 2007, 2nd edn 2014; *edited:* (jtly) Social Psychology: a practical manual, 1982; Threatened Identities, 1983; (jtly) Doing Social Psychology, 1988; Human Behavior: encyclopedia of personal relationships, vol. 17, shaping your life, vol. 18, coping with change, 1990; Social Psychology of Political and Economic Cognition, 1991; Social Psychology of Identity and the Self Concept, 1992; (jtly) Empirical Approaches to Social Representations, 1993; (jtly) Changing European Identities: social psychological analyses of change, 1996; (jtly) Research Methods in Psychology, 2000, 4th edn 2012; Doing Social Psychology Research, 2004; (jtly) Identity Process Theory: identity, social action and social change, 2014. *Recreations:* racket sports, painting. *Address:* University of Bath, Bath BA2 7AY. *T:* (01225) 386262. *E:* g.breakwell@bath.ac.uk. *Club:* Athenæum.

BREALEY, Maj. Gen. Bruce, CB 2012; Director General Capability, 2011–13; *b* Burton upon Trent, Staffs, 8 Feb. 1959; *s* of Trevor Graham Brealey and Judith Brealey; *m* 1986, Susan Margaret Harrison; one *d*. *Educ:* St Olave's Grammar Sch.; RMA, Sandhurst. Various sen. military command and staff appts; Dep. Comdg Gen., Multi Nat. Corps, Iraq, 2007–08; GOC Theatre Troops, 2008–11. *Recreations:* golf, travel, theatre, gardening. *Clubs:* Wentworth, Salisbury and S Wilts Golf.

BREALEY, Mark Philip; QC 2002; barrister; *b* 26 Jan. 1960; *s* of Leonard and Shirley Brealey. *Educ:* Reading Univ. (LLB); University Coll. London (LLM). Called to the Bar, Middle Temple, 1984. *Publications:* (with M. Hoskins) Remedies in EC Law, 1994, 2nd edn 1998. *Address:* Brick Court Chambers, 7–8 Essex Street, WC2R 3LD. *T:* (020) 7379 3550. *Clubs:* Royal Ascot Racing; Tottenham Hotspur Football.

BREALEY, Prof. Richard Arthur, FBA 1999; Special Adviser to the Governor, Bank of England, 1998–2001; Professor of Finance, London Business School, 1974–98, Professor Emeritus, since 2001; *b* 9 June 1936; *s* of late Albert Brealey and of Irene Brealey; *m* 1967, Diana Cecily Brown Kelly; two *s*. *Educ:* Queen Elizabeth's, Barnet; Exeter Coll., Oxford (MA, 1st Cl. Hons PPE). Sun Life Assce Co. of Canada, 1959–66; Keystone Custodian Funds of Boston, 1966–68; London Business School: Prudential Res. Fellow, 1968–74; Sen. Lectr, 1972–74; Barclaytrust Prof. of Investment, 1974–82; Midland Bank Prof. of Corporate Finance, 1982–91; Tokai Bank Prof. of Finance, 1993–98; Dep. Prin., 1984–88; Governor, 1984–88. Director: Swiss Helvetia Fund Inc., 1987–96, 2009–; Sun Life Assurance Co. of Canada UK Hldgs plc, 1994–97; Tokai Derivative Products, 1995–97. Trustee, HSBC Investor Family of Funds, 2005–08. Pres., European Finance Assoc., 1975; Dir, Amer. Finance Assoc., 1979–81. *Publications:* An Introduction to Risk and Return from Common Stocks, 1969, 2nd edn 1983; Security Prices in a Competitive Market, 1971; (with J. Lorie) Modern Developments in Investment Management, 1972, 2nd edn 1978; (with S. C. Myers) Principles of Corporate Finance, 1981, (with S. C Myers and F. Allen) 11th edn 2013; (with S. C. Myers and A. J. Marcus) Fundamentals of Corporate Finance, 1995, 8th edn 2015; articles in professional jls. *Recreations:* trekking, horse riding. *Address:* Haydens Cottage, The Pound, Cookham, Berks SL6 9QE. *T:* (01628) 520143.

BREAM, Julian, CBE 1985 (OBE 1964); guitarist and lutenist; *b* 15 July 1933; *e s* of Henry G. Bream; *m* 1st, Margaret Williamson; one adopted *s*; 2nd, 1980, Isabel Sanchez. *Educ:* Royal College of Music (Junior Exhibition Award, 1945 and Scholarship, 1948). Began professional career at Cheltenham, 1947; London début, Wigmore Hall, 1951; subsequently has appeared in leading world festivals in Europe, USA, Australia and Far East. A leader in revival of interest in Elizabethan Lute music, on which he has done much research; has encouraged and commissioned many contemporary compositions for the guitar including works by Walton, Britten, Tippett, Henze and Takemitsu. Formed Julian Bream Consort, 1960; inaugurated Semley Festival of Music and Poetry, 1971. DUniv Surrey, 1968. Villa-Lobos Gold Medal, 1976; Gramophone Lifetime Achievement Award, 2013. *Recreations:* walking, gardening, cricket, table tennis, backgammon. *Address:* c/o Hazard Chase, 25 City Road, Cambridge CB1 1DP.

BREARLEY, Christopher John Scott, CB 1994; DL; Lead Governor, Hertfordshire Partnership University NHS Foundation Trust (formerly Hertfordshire Partnership Foundation Trust), since 2013 (Governor, since 2011); *b* 25 May 1943; *s* of Geoffrey Brearley and Winifred (*née* Scott); *m* 1971, Rosemary Stockbridge; two *s*. *Educ:* King Edward VII Sch., Sheffield; Trinity Coll., Oxford. MA 1964, BPhil 1966. Entered Ministry of Transport, 1966; Private Sec. to Perm. Sec., 1969–70; Principal, DoE, 1970; Sec. to Review of Develt Control Procedures (Dobry), DoE, 1973–74; Private Sec. to the Secretary of the Cabinet, Cabinet Office, 1974–76; Asst Sec., 1977; Under Sec., 1981; Dir of Scottish Services, PSA, 1981–83; Cabinet Office, 1983–85; Department of the Environment, 1985–97: Deputy Secretary: Local Govt, 1990–94; Local Govt and Planning, 1994–95; Local and Regl Develt, 1996–97; Dep. Sec., later Dir Gen., Planning, Roads and Local Transport, DETR, 1997–2000. Mem. (Lib Dem), Three Rivers DC, 2003–07; Chm., SW Herts Lib Dems, 2005–08, 2009–11. Sec., Review of Child Protection in the Catholic Ch, 2000–01. Chm., Nat. Retail Planning Forum, 2005–13. Member: Policy Cttee, CPRE, 2001–07 (Chm., Herts Soc., CPRE, 2004–09); Chiltern Conservation Bd, 2005–07. Governor, Watford Grammar Sch. for Boys, 1988–2004 (Chm. of Govs, 1998–2004); Trustee, Watford Grammar Schs, 1992–2004, 2011–. Trustee: Motability Tenth Anniv. Trust, 2001–; Motorway Archive Trust, 2001–09; Gov., Oxfordshire and Bucks Mental Health Foundn Trust, 2008–11. Freeman, City of London, 1998. DL Herts, 2007. Hon. Fellow, Sch. of Public Policy, Birmingham Univ., 2001–03. *Recreations:* crosswords, sudoku, vernacular architecture. *Address:* Middlemount, 35 South Road, Chorleywood, Herts WD3 5AS. *T:* (01923) 283848. *Club:* Oxford and Cambridge.

BREARLEY, (John) Michael, OBE 1978; psychoanalyst; *b* 28 April 1942; *s* of late Horace and Midge Brearley; lives with Mana Sarabhai; two *c*. *Educ:* City of London Sch.; St John's Coll., Cambridge (MA; Hon. Fellow, 1998). Lectr in Philosophy, Univ. of Newcastle upon Tyne, 1968–71. Middlesex County Cricketer, intermittently, 1961–82, capped 1964, Captain, 1971–82; played first Test Match, 1976; Captain of England XI, 1977–80, 1981. Fellow, British Psychoanalytical Soc. (Associate Mem., 1985; Mem., 1991; Pres., 2008–10). Hon. LLD Lancaster, 1999; DUniv Oxford Brookes, 2006. *Publications:* (with Dudley Doust) The Return of the Ashes, 1978; (with Dudley Doust) The Ashes Retained, 1979; Phoenix: the series that rose from the ashes, 1982; The Art of Captaincy, 1985, 2nd edn 2001; (with John Arlott) Arlott in Conversation with Mike Brearley, 1986; articles for The Times. *Club:* MCC (Hon. Life Mem.; Pres., 2007–08).

BREARLEY, Jonathan; Director, Brearley Economics, since 2013; *b* Buckie, Scotland, 23 July 1973; *s* of David William Brearley and Gillian Rose Brearley; *m* 2009, Sumita Dutta. *Educ:* Gillingham Comprehensive Sch., Dorset; Sexey's Sch., Bruton; Glasgow Univ. (BSc Hons Maths and Physics 1995); Girton Coll., Cambridge (MPhil Econs 2000). Analyst, Bain & Co., 2000–02; Sen. Policy Advr, Prime Minister's Strategy Unit, 2002–06; Hd, Local Govt White Paper, DCLG, 2006; Director: Office of Climate Change, 2006–09; Energy Strategy and Futures, then Energy Markets and Networks, DECC, 2009–13. *Recreations:* walking, travel, scuba diving, refurbishing houses, home swapping, reading, cooking, watching DVD box sets. *Address:* Hill Meadows, Radnage, High Wycombe, Bucks HP14 4BU. *T:* 07961 441081. *E:* contactjbrearley@gmail.com.

BREARLEY, Michael; *see* Brearley, J. M.

BREARLEY-SMITH, Anne Margaret; *see* Luther, A. M.

BREARS, Peter Charles David, FMA, FSA; writer and museums consultant, since 1994; *b* 30 Aug. 1944; *s* of Charles Brears and Mary (*née* Fett). *Educ:* Castleford Technical High Sch.; Leeds Coll. of Art (DipAD 1967). FMA 1980; FSA 1980. Hon. Asst, Wakefield City Museum, 1957–66; Keeper of Folk Life, Hampshire CC, 1967–69; Curator: Shibden Hall, Halifax, 1969–72; Clarke Hall, Wakefield, 1972–75; Castle Museum, York, 1975–79; Dir, Leeds City Museums, 1979–94. Founder, 1975, and Mem., 1975–, Group for Regional Studies in Museums, subseq. Social Hist. Curators Gp, 1975; Mem., Social History and Industrial Classification Wkg Party, 1978–; Pres., Soc. for Folk Life Studies, 1995–96. Sophie Coe Prize for food writing, Oxford Symposium for Food History, 1997. *Publications:* The English Country Pottery, 1971; Yorkshire Probate Inventories, 1972; The Collectors' Book of English Country Pottery, 1974; Horse Brasses, 1981; The Gentlewoman's Kitchen, 1984; Traditional Food in Yorkshire, 1987; North Country Folk Art, 1989; Of Curiosities and Rare Things, 1989; Treasures for the People, 1989; Images of Leeds, 1992; Leeds Describ'd, 1993; Leeds Waterfront, 1994; The Country House Kitchen, 1996; Ryedale Recipes, 1998; A Taste of Leeds, 1998; The Old Devon Farmhouse, 1998; All the King's Cooks, 1999, 2nd edn 2011; The Compleat Housekeeper, 2000; The Boke of Kervynge, 2003; A New and Easy Method of Cookery, 2005; Cooking and Dining in Medieval England, 2008 (Andre Simon Award, 2009); Traditional Food in Shropshire, 2009; Jellies and their Moulds, 2010; Cooking and Dining with the Wordsworths, 2011; Traditional Food in Northumbria, 2013; A Leeds Life, 2013; Traditional Food in Yorkshire, 2014; Cooking and Dining in Tudor and Early Stuart England, 2015; articles in Folk Life, Post-Medieval Archaeology, etc; museum guides and catalogues. *Recreations:* hill walking, drawing, cookery. *Address:* 4 Woodbine Terrace, Headingley, Leeds LS6 4AF. *T:* (0113) 275 6537.

BRECHIN, Bishop of, since 2011; **Rt Rev. Dr Nigel Peyton;** JP; *b* 5 Feb. 1951; *s* of Hubert Peyton and Irene Louise Peyton (*née* Ellis); *m* 1981, Anne Marie Thérèse (*née* McQuillan), *widow* of Colin Campbell; one *s* one *d* (and one *d* decd). *Educ:* Latymer Upper Sch.; Univ. of Edinburgh (MA 1973; BD 1976); Edinburgh Theol Coll.; Union Theol Seminary, NY (Scottish Fellow, 1976; STM 1977); Univ. of Lancaster (PhD 2009). Deacon 1976, priest 1977; Chaplain, St Paul's Cathedral, Dundee, 1976–82; Dio. Youth Chaplain, Brechin, 1976–85; Priest-in-charge, All Souls, Invergowrie, 1979–85; Vicar, All Saints, Nottingham, 1985–91; Priest-in-charge, Lambley, 1991–99; Dio. Ministry Develt Advr, Southwell, 1991–99; Archdeacon of Newark, 1999–2011. Hon. Canon: Southwell Minster, 1999–2011; Des Moines, Iowa, 2012–. Chaplain: University Hosp., Dundee, 1982–85; Nottingham Bluecoat Sch., 1990–92; Bishop, Mission to Seafarers Scotland, 2013–. Bishops' Selector, 1992–2000, Sen. Vocational Selector, 2001–11. Proctor in Convocation, 1995–2010. Dir, Ecclesiastical Insce Gp, 2005–12. Gov., Abertay Univ. (formerly Univ. of Abertay, Dundee), 2013–. Hon. Teaching Fellow, Univ. of Lancaster, 2010–. Columnist, Dundee Courier, 2012–. JP Nottingham, 1987. *Publications:* Dual Role Ministry, 1998; (jtly) Managing Clergy Lives, 2013. *Recreations:* grandparenting, music, reading, gardening, walking, real ale. *Address:* Bishop's House, 5 Glamis Drive, Dundee DD2 1QG. *T:* (home) (01382) 641586, (office) (01382) 562244, 07974 402449. *E:* bishop@brechin.anglican.org. *Clubs:* Royal Scots (Edinburgh); Nottingham Forest Football.

BRECHIN, Dean of; *see* Bridger, Very Rev. F. W.

BRECHT, Air Vice-Marshal Malcolm Andrew Brian, CBE 2009; Chief of Staff Capability, Headquarters Air Command, since 2012; *b* Pembroke, 19 Feb. 1965; *s* of Terence Brian Brecht and Hazel Mary Brecht (*née* Fletcher); *m* 1987, Barbara Joan Corrigan; two *s*.

Educ: Kingham Hill Sch., Oxfordshire; Univ. of Hull (BA Hons Operational Res. and Mgt Scis 1986); King's Coll. London (MA Defence Studies 2000). Joined RAF, 1983; pilot on HS125, BAe146 and Tristar with 32 Sqdn, Queen's Flight and 216 Sqdn, 1988–98; PSO to AOC 2 Gp, 1998–99; OC 99 Sqdn, introducing Boeing C-17 into service, 2000–03; Air Resources and Plans, 2003–05; Comdr Basrah Air Station, 2005–06; Station Comdr, RAF Brize Norton, 2006–08; Comdr, Kandahar Airfield, 2009–10; on secondment to Cabinet Office to lead Strategic Defence and Security Rev. Defence Team, 2010; Air Staff, MoD, 2010–12. Mem. Council, Dean Close Sch., Cheltenham, 2010–. Mem., Gen. Synod, 2014–. FRAeS 2006. Freeman, Coachmakers' and Coach Harness Makers' Guild, 2012–. QCVS 2006. *Recreations:* cycling and keeping fit, keen Rugby follower, member of local church. *Address:* RAF High Wycombe, Bucks HP14 4UE. *T:* (01494) 496239.

BRECKELL, Paul Anthony; Chief Executive, Action on Hearing Loss, since 2012; *b* Rugby, Warks, 18 Jan. 1971; *s* of Trevor Harry Breckell and Janice Marion Breckell; *m* 1995, Chantal Phillips; one *s*. *Educ:* Ashlyn's Sch., Berkhamsted; Univ. of Sheffield (BA 1st Cl. Hons Econs); London South Bank Univ. (MSc with Dist. Charity Accounting and Financial Mgt). CPFA 1997. Sen. Auditor, Audit Commn, 1992–97; Hd of Finance, Mildmay, 1997–2000; Finance Dir, Church Mission Soc., 2000–07; Man. Dir, Action on Hearing Loss, 2007–12. Chm., Charity Finance Gp, 2003–07. Trustee: CIPFA, 2009–13; Roffey Park Inst., 2013–. FRSA. *Recreations:* reading, gardening, watching and playing sport. *Address:* Action on Hearing Loss, 19–23 Featherstone Street, EC1Y 8SL. *T:* (020) 7296 8014. *E:* paul.breckell@hearingloss.org.uk.

BRECKENRIDGE, Sir Alasdair (Muir), Kt 2004; CBE 1995; MD; FRCP, FRCPE; FRSE; FMedSci; Chairman, Medicines and Healthcare Products Regulatory Agency, 2003–12; Professor of Clinical Pharmacology, University of Liverpool, 1974–2002; *b* 7 May 1937; *s* of Thomas and Jane Breckenridge; *m* 1967, Jean Margaret Boyle; two *s*. *Educ:* Bell Baxter Sch., Cupar, Fife; Univ. of St Andrews (MB, ChB Hons 1961); Univ. of London (MSc 1968); Univ. of Dundee (MD Hons 1974). FRCP 1974; FRCPE 1988; FRSE 1991. House Phys. and Surg., Dundee Royal Infirm., 1961–62; Asst, Dept of Medicine, Univ. of St Andrews, 1962–63; successively House Phys., Registrar, Sen. Registrar, Tutor, Lectr and Sen. Lectr, Hammersmith Hosp. and RPMS, 1964–74. Non-exec. Dir, 1990–94, Vice Chm., 1993–94, Mersey RHA (Chm., Jan.–July 1993; Chm., Res. Cttee, 1987–91); Vice Chm., NW RHA, 1994–96 (Dir of R & D, 1994–96); Chm., NW Reg., NHS Exec., 1996–99. NHS Advr in Clin. Pharm. to CMO, 1982–94; Mem., NHS Adv. Cttee on Drugs, 1985–98 (Vice Chm., 1986–98). Committee on Safety of Medicines: Mem., 1982–2003 (Vice Chm., 1996–98; Chm., 1999–2003); Chm., Adverse Reactions Subgroup, 1987–92; Chm., Adverse Reactions to Vaccination and Immunisation Sub Cttee, 1989–92; Chm., Sub Cttee on Safety and Efficacy, 1993–95. Medical Research Council: Mem., 1992–96; Member: Clin. Trials Cttee, 1983–; Physiol Systems and Disorders Bd, 1987–91 (Vice Chm., 1990–91); AIDS Therapeutic Cttee, 1989– (Chm., 1993–). Royal College of Physicians: Mem. Council, 1983–86; Mem., Res. Cttee, 1983–88; Mem., Clin. Pharm. Cttee, 1990–95; Mem. Adv. Res. Cttee, 1993–98; Goulstonian Lectr, 1975; William Withering Lectr, 2006. British Pharmacological Society: Mem., 1972–; Foreign Sec., 1984–91; Chm., Clin. Section, 1988–93; Lilly Medal, 1994; Chm. Editl Bd, British Jl of Clin. Pharmacol., 1983–87. Member: Panel on Tropical and Infectious Disease, Wellcome Trust, 1984–87; Res. Cttee, British Heart Foundn, 1977–82; Steering Cttee for Chemotherapy of Malaria, WHO, 1987–91; Exec. Cttee, Internat. Union of Pharm., 1981–87; Central R&D Cttee, NHS, 1991–94; Jt Med. Adv. Cttee, HEFCE, 1995–2002 (Chm., 1998–2002); Cttee on Proprietary Medicinal Products of EU, 2001–02. Mem., Assoc. of Physicians, 1975–. Founder FMedSci 1998. Hon. DSc: St Andrews, 2005; Keele, 2005; Hon. LLD Dundee, 2005; Hon. MD Liverpool, 2007. Paul Martini Prize in Clin. Pharm., Paul Martini Foundn, 1974; Poulson Medal, Norwegian Pharmacol Soc., 1988. Exec. Editor, Pharmacology and Therapeutics, 1982–98. *Publications:* papers on clinical pharmacology in various jls. *Recreations:* hill-walking, golf, music. *Address:* Cree Cottage, Feather Lane, Heswall, Wirral CH60 4RL. *Club:* Athenæum.

BRECKNOCK, Earl of; James William John Pratt; *b* 11 Dec. 1965; *s* and *heir* of Marquess Camden, *qv*. *Educ:* Eton; Univ. of Edinburgh.

BRECON, Dean of; *see* Shackerley, Very Rev. A. P.

BREED, Colin Edward; *b* 4 May 1947; *s* of Alfred Breed and Edith Violet Breed; *m* 1968, Janet Courtiour; one *s* one *d*. *Educ:* Torquay GS. ACIB. Junior, to Area Manager, Midland Bank plc, 1964–81; Manager, Venture Capital Fund, later Man. Dir, Dartington & Co. Ltd, 1981–91; Consultant, Corporate Finance, Allied Provincial Stockbrokers, 1991–92; Dir, Gemini Abrasives Ltd, 1992–97. MP (Lib Dem) SE Cornwall, 1997–2010. Mem., GMC, 1999. *Recreations:* golf, watching live sport. *Address:* 10 Dunheved Road, Saltash, Cornwall PL12 4BW.

BREEDON, Timothy James, CBE 2013; Group Chief Executive, Legal & General Group plc, 2006–12; *b* 14 Feb. 1958; *s* of Peter and Ruth Breedon; *m* 1982, Susan Hopkins; three *s*. *Educ:* Worcester Coll., Oxford (MA); London Business Sch. (MSc). Standard Chartered Bank, 1981–85; Legal & General Group, 1987–2012: Gp Dir (Investments), 2002–05; Dep. Chief Exec., 2005. Non-exec. Chm., Apax Global Alpha, 2015–; non-exec. Dir, Barclays Bank plc, 2012–; Lead non-exec. Dir, MoJ, 2012–15. Dir, Financial Reporting Council, 2004–07; Chm., ABI, 2010–12. Hon. Treas., Marie Curie Cancer Care, 2014–.

BREEN, His Honour Geoffrey Brian; a Circuit Judge, 2000–08; *b* 3 June 1944; *s* of Ivor James Breen and late Doreen Odessa Breen; *m* 1978, Lucy Bolaños (marr. diss. 1999); one *s* one *d*; *m* 2014, Carmen Gabriela Rodriguez Lozada. *Educ:* Harrow High School. Articled to Stiles Wood & Co., Harrow, 1962–67; admitted Solicitor, 1967; Partner, Stiles, Wood, Head & Co., 1970–75; Sen. Partner, Stiles, Breen & Partners, 1976–86; Partner, Blaser Mills & Newman, Bucks and Herts, 1976–86; a Metropolitan Stipendiary Magistrate, subseq. Dist Judge (Magistrates' Courts), 1986–2000; Asst Recorder, 1989–93; Recorder, 1993–2000. Chairman: Youth Courts, 1989–93; Family Proceedings Courts, 1991–2000; a Judge of (formerly Pres.), Mental Health Tribunals, 2006–14; Mem., Parole Bd, 2007–10. Mem., British Acad. of Forensic Scis, 1989–2012. *Recreations:* classical guitar, reading, relaxing in Spain. *Club:* Travellers.

BREEN, Mary; Headmistress, St Mary's School Ascot, since 1999; *b* Lancs, 4 Jan. 1964; *d* of Gerard Hayes and Mary Hayes; *m* 1988, James Breen. *Educ:* Univ. of Exeter (BSc Hons 1985); Univ. of Manchester (MSc 1987). Teacher of Physics: Wellington Coll., 1988–89; Abbey Sch., Reading, 1989–91; Eton Coll., 1991–92; St Mary's Sch. Ascot, 1992; Eton Coll., 1992–98, Head of Physics, 1996–98. *Recreations:* travel, cooking, reading, racing, walking, wine. *Address:* St Mary's School Ascot, St Mary's Road, Ascot, Berks SL5 9JF. *T:* (01344) 296600. *E:* mbreen@st-marys-ascot.co.uk. *Club:* Athenæum.

BREEN, Prof. Richard James, PhD; FBA 1999; William Graham Sumner Professor of Sociology, Yale University, since 2010 (Professor of Sociology, since 2007); *b* 25 Aug. 1954; *s* of Edward Francis Breen and Emily Breen (*née* Wolstenholme); *m* 1st, 1981, Eleanor Burgess (marr. diss. 1993); 2nd, 1997, Mary Christine O'Sullivan. *Educ:* St Thomas Aquinas Grammar Sch., Leeds; Fitzwilliam Coll., Cambridge (BA 1976; MA 1979; PhD 1981). Research Officer, then Sen. Research Officer, Economic and Social Research Inst., Dublin, 1980–91; Professor of Sociology: QUB, 1991–2000; European Univ. Inst., Florence, 1997–2001; Official Fellow, Nuffield Coll., Oxford, 2000–06. MRIA 1998. *Publications:* Understanding Contemporary Ireland, 1990; Social Class and Social Mobility in the Republic of Ireland, 1996; Social Mobility in Europe, 2005; numerous contribs to learned jls. *Recreations:* music chess, reading, hill walking. *Address:* Department of Sociology, Yale University, PO Bo 208265, New Haven, CT 06520–8265, USA. *T:* (203) 4323324.

BREEZE, Alastair Jon, CMG 1990; HM Diplomatic Service, retired; Counsellor, Foreig and Commonwealth Office, 1987–94; *b* 1 June 1934; *s* of Samuel Wilfred Breeze and Glady Elizabeth Breeze; *m* 1st, 1960, Helen Burns Shaw (*d* 2011); two *s* one *d*; 2nd, 2011, Sarah Elizabeth Fausset. *Educ:* Mill Hill School; Christ's College, Cambridge (Scholar; MA 1959) Served Royal Marines, 1953–55. Foreign Office, 1958; 3rd Sec., Jakarta, 1960–62; FO 1962–64; 2nd Sec., seconded to Colonial Office for service in Georgetown, 1964–66; 1st Sec. Tehran, 1967–71; FCO, 1971–72; 1st Sec., Islamabad, 1972–75, Lagos, 1976–79; FCO 1979–83; Counsellor, UK Mission to UN, NY, 1983–87. *Recreations:* sailing, ornithology *Address:* La Vieille Boucherie, Puntous 65230, France.

BREEZE, Dr David John, OBE 2009; FSA, FSAScot, FRSE; Chief Inspector of Ancien Monuments, 1989–2005, Head, Special Heritage Projects, 2005–08, Historic Scotland; Co ordinator, Antonine Wall World Heritage Site, 2008–09; *b* Blackpool, 25 July 1944; *s* o Reginald C. Breeze and Marian (*née* Lawson); *m* 1972, Pamela Diane Silvester; two *s*. *Educ* Blackpool Grammar Sch.; University Coll., Durham Univ. (BA; PhD 1970). FSAScot 197 (Hon. FSAScot 2005); FSA 1975; FRSE 1991; MIFA 1990; Hon. MCIfA (Hon. MIFA 2006) Inspector of Ancient Monuments, Scotland, 1969–88, Principal Inspector, 1988–89. Vis Prof., Durham Univ., 1994–; Hon. Professor: Edinburgh Univ., 1996–; Newcastle Univ. 2003–. Chairman: Hadrian's Wall Pilgrimage, 1989, 1999 and 2009; Internat. Congress o Roman Frontier Studies, 1989–; British Archaeol Awards, 1993–2009; Mem., Hadrian's Wa Adv. Cttee, English Heritage, 1977–97; President: South Shields Archaeol and Historical Soc. 1983–85; Soc. of Antiquaries of Scotland, 1987–90; Soc. of Antiquaries of Newcastle upo Tyne, 2008–11; Royal Archaeol Inst., 2009–12 (Vice-Pres., 2002–07); Cumberland an Westmorland Antiquarian and Archaeol Soc., 2011–14 (Vice-Pres., 2003–11). Trustee Senhouse Museum Trust, 1985– (Chm., 2013–). Corresp. Mem., German Archaeol Inst. 1979. Hon. DLitt Glasgow, 2008. Eur. Archaeol Heritage Prize, Eur. Assoc. o Archaeologists, 2010. *Publications:* (with Brian Dobson) Hadrian's Wall, 1976, 4th edn 2000 (with D. V. Clarke and G. Mackay) The Romans in Scotland, 1980; The Northern Frontier of Roman Britain, 1982; Roman Forts in Britain, 1983, 2nd edn 2002; (ed) Studies in Scottis Antiquity, 1984; Hadrian's Wall, a Souvenir Guide, 1987, 2nd edn 2003; A Queen's Progress 1987; The Second Augustan Legion in North Britain, 1989; (ed) Service in the Roman Army 1989; (with Anna Ritchie) Invaders of Scotland, 1991; (with Brian Dobson) Roman Officer and Frontiers, 1993; Roman Scotland: frontier country, 1996, 2nd edn 2006; (with G Munro) The Stone of Destiny, 1997; Historic Scotland, 1998; Historic Scotland: peoples an places, 2002; (ed with R. Welander and T. Clancy) The Stone of Destiny: artefact and icon 2003; (with Sonja Jilek and Andreas Thiel) Frontiers of the Roman Empire, 2005; Handboo to the Roman Wall, 14th edn, 2006; The Antonine Wall, 2006; Roman Frontiers in Britain 2007; Edge of Empire, Rome's Scottish frontier, The Antonine Wall, 2008; (ed with Sonj Jilek) Frontiers of the Roman Empire: the European dimension of a world heritage site, 2008 Frontiers of the Roman Empire: the Antonine Wall, 2009; Frontiers of the Roman Empire Hadrian's Wall, 2011; The Frontiers of Imperial Rome, 2011; (ed) The First Souvenirs enamelled vessels from Hadrian's Wall, 2012; (ed) 200 Years: the Society of Antiquaries o Newcastle upon Tyne 1813–2013, 2013; (with M. C. Bishop) The Crosby Garrett Helmet 2013; Hadrian's Wall: a history of archaeological thought, 2014; contribs to British and foreig jls. *Recreations:* reading, walking, travel.

BREEZE, Stevan William; Chief Executive, BSI Group, 2002–08; *b* 4 June 1951; *s* o William and Gwendoline Breeze; *m* 1973, Diana Julie Farthing; one *s* one *d*. Man. Dir, Tefa UK Ltd, 1984–87; Divl Dir, Polly Peck Internat., 1987–90; Divl Gp Man. Dir, BTR plc 1990–98; Divl Man. Dir, Jarvis plc, 1999–2002. *Recreations:* tennis, ski-ing, travel. *E* stevanbreeze@yahoo.co.uk.

BREHONY, Dr John Albert Noel, CMG 1991; Chairman, Menas Associates, since 2001 *b* 11 Dec. 1936; *s* of Patrick Paul Brehony and Agnes Maher; *m* 1961, Jennifer Ann (*née* Cox) one *s* one *d*. *Educ:* London Oratory Sch.; Univ. of Durham (BA, PhD). Tutor, Durham Univ. 1960; Economist Intell. Unit, 1961; Res. Fellow, Jerusalem (Jordan), 1962; Lectr, Univ. o Libya, 1965–66; FO, 1966; Kuwait, 1967–69; Aden, 1970–71; Amman, 1973–77; Cairo 1981–84; Counsellor, FCO, 1984–92; Dir of Middle East Affairs, 1992–99, Advr to Bd o ME Affairs, 1999–2013, Rolls-Royce PLC. Chm., Middle East Assoc., 1996–97; Pres., Britis Soc. of ME Studies, 2000–06; Mem. Council, Brit. Egyptian Soc., 2003–; Chairman: Anglo Jordanian Soc., 2009–13; British Yemeni Soc., 2010–15. Chairman: British Inst. at Amma for Archaeol. and Hist., 1992–99; Council for British Res. in the Levant, 2004–09, 2013– Mem. Council, British Foundn for the Study of Arabia, 2011–. Mem. Adv. Bd, Londo Middle East Inst., SOAS, 1999–; Internat. Advr to Gaza 2010 Project, Harvard Univ. 2005–08. Mem., Algerian British Business Council, 2013–. Trustee, Altajir Trust, 2009– *Publications:* (ed with Ayman El-Desouky) British-Egyptian Relations from Suez to th Present Day, 2007; Yemen Divided: a failed state in South Arabia, 2011. *Recreations:* Middl Eastern history, theatre, opera. *Address:* (office) 31 Southampton Row, WC1B 5HJ. *Club* Athenæum.

BREHONY, Rosemary; *see* Deem, R.

BREMER de MARTINO, Juan José, Hon. CVO 1975; Ambassador of Mexico to Cuba since 2013; *b* 22 March 1944; *s* of Juan José Bremer Barrera and Cristina de Martino Noriega *m* Marcela Sánchez de Bremer Science; two *s*. *Educ:* Nat. Autonomous Univ. of Mexico (la degree 1966). Private Sec. to Pres. of Mexico, 1972–75; Dep. Sec., Ministry of the Presidency 1975–76; Hd, Nat. Fine Arts Inst., Mexico, 1976–82; Dep. Sec. for Cultural Affairs, Ministry of Educn, 1982; Ambassador to Sweden, 1982; Mem., Mexican Legislature, 1985–88 (Pres. Foreign Affairs Cttee, Chamber of Deputies); Ambassador to: Soviet Union, 1988–90; FRG 1990–98; Spain, 1998–2000; USA, 2000–04; Court of St James's, 2004–09. Mem., Comm to Study the Future of Mexican-Amer. Relns, 1986–88. Pres., Cervantino Internat. Fest. 1983; guest lectr at US, Mexican and European univs. *Address:* c/o Mexican Embassy, Call 12 No. 518, esq. Avenida 7ma, Reparto Miramar, Municipio Playa, Habana, Cuba.

BREMNER, Myles Ironside; Director, School Food Plan, since 2013 (Member, Exper Panel, 2012–13); *b* London, 9 Nov. 1971; *s* of Andrew Bremner and Elaine Bremner (*né* Arkle); *m* 2001, Stephanie Turner; one *s*. *Educ:* Haileybury Coll.; Univ. of Leeds (BA Hon Hist. 1993). Mktg contracts, 1993–97; Appeals Manager, RNLI, 1997–99; Mktg Manager British Olympic Assoc., 1999–2001; Hd, Ops, St John Ambulance, 2001–03; Dir Fundraising, CLIC Sargent Cancer Care for Children, 2003–06; Interim Dir, Fundraising NCH (Action for Children), 2006–07; Chief Exec., Garden Organic, 2007–13. Chairman Capital Growth, 2008–12; Food Growing in Schs Taskforce, 2012; Member: London Foo Bd, 2010–; Warwickshire Local Nature Partnership, 2012–13; Trustee, Sustain, 2008–13 FRSA. *Recreations:* cooking, vegetable growing, amassing my bicycle collection. *Address* Fighting House, Fighting Close, Kineton, Warwicks CV35 0LS. *T:* 07985 170737. *E* mylesbremner@mac.com.

BREMNER, Rory Keith Ogilvy; satirical impressionist, writer and presenter; *b* 6 April 1961 *s* of late Major Donald Stuart Ogilvy Bremner and Anne Ulithorne Bremner (*née* Simpson) *m* 1987, Susan Shackleton (marr. diss. 1994); *m* 1999, Tessa Campbell Fraser; two *d*. *Educ* Wellington Coll.; King's Coll. London (BA Hons French and German 1983; FKC 2005 Hon. Fellow 2006). Television: Now… Something Else, 1986–87; Rory Bremner, 1988–92 Rory Bremner… Who Else?, 1993–99; Bremner, Bird and Fortune, 1999–2010 (also stag version, Albery, 2002); Between Iraq and a Hard Place, 2003; Rory Bremner's Coalition Report, 2015; Rory Bremner's Election Report, 2015. Opera translations: Silver Lake (Weill), 1999; Carmen (Bizet), 2001; Orpheus in the Underworld (Offenbach), 2011; trans. Brecht, A Respectable Wedding, Young Vic, 2007. Theatre, Relative Values, Th. Royal, Bath, 2013, transf. Harold Pinter Th., 2014. British Comedy Award, 1993; BAFTA Award for Best Light Entertainment Performance, 1995, 1996; RTS Awards for Best Television Perf., 1995, 1999, 2000; Channel 4 political humorist of the year, 1998, 2000. *Publications:* (with John Bird and John Fortune) You Are Here, 2004. *Recreations:* cricket, opera, travel. *Address:* c/o PBJ Management, 22 Rathbone Street, W1T 1LG. *T:* (020) 7287 1112. *Club:* Lord's Taverners.

BRENDEL, Alfred, Hon. KBE 1989; writer and poet; concert pianist, 1948–2008; *b* 5 Jan. 1931; *s* of Albert Brendel and Ida Brendel (*née* Wieltschnig); *m* 1960, Iris Heymann-Gonzala (marr. diss. 1972); one *d*; *m* 1975, Irene Semler (marr. diss. 2012); one *s* two *d*. *Educ:* Studied piano with: S. Deželić, 1937–43; L. V. Kaan, 1943–47; also under Edwin Fischer, P. Baumgartner and E. Steuermann; composition with Artur Michl, harmony with Franjo Dugan, Zagreb. Vienna State Diploma, 1947; Premio Bolzano Concorso Busoni, 1949. Concerts: most European countries, North and Latin America, Australia and New Zealand, also N and S Africa and Near and Far East. Many appearances Vienna and Salzburg Festivals, 1960–. Other Festivals: Athens, Granada, Bregenz, Würzburg, Aldeburgh, York, Cheltenham, Edinburgh, Bath, Puerto Rico, Barcelona, Prague, Lucerne, Dubrovnik, etc. Many long playing records (Bach to Schoenberg) incl. first complete recording of Beethoven's piano works (Grand Prix du Disque, 1965). Cycle of Beethoven Sonatas: London, 1962, 1977, 1982–83, 1992–95; Copenhagen, 1964; Vienna, 1965–66; Puerto Rico, 1968; BBC and Rome, 1970; Munich and Stuttgart, 1977; Amsterdam, Paris and Berlin, 1982–83; New York, 1983; 14 Eur. and 4 N Amer. cities, 1992–96; Cycle of Schubert piano works 1822–28 in 19 cities, incl. London, Paris, Amsterdam, Berlin, Vienna, New York, Los Angeles, 1987–88. *Television (series):* Schubert Piano Music (13 films), Bremen, 1978; Alfred Brendel Masterclass, BBC, 1983; Liszt Années de Pèlerinage, BBC, 1986; Schubert Last Three Sonatas, BBC, 1988. Hon. RAM; FRNCM 1990; Hon. RCM 1999; Hon. Mem., Amer. Acad. of Arts and Sciences, 1984; Korrespondierendes Mitglied, Bayer. Akad. der Wissenschaften (Orden pour le Mérite für Wissenschaften und Künste, 1991); Hon. Fellow, Exeter Coll., Oxford, 1987; Hon. DMus: London, 1978; Sussex, 1981; Oxford, 1983; Warwick, 1991; Yale, 1992; Dublin UC, 1997; Exeter, 1998; RCM, 1999; Southampton, 2002; Boston New England Conservatoire, 2009; Hochschule Franz Liszt Weimar, 2009; Sheffield, 2010; Bucharest Musikuniv., 2011; McGill, 2011; Peterhouse Coll., Cambridge, 2012; Juilliard Sch., 2013; DPhil Cologne, 1995; DLit Bari, 2011. Busoni Foundn Award, 1990; Hans von Bülow Medal, Kameradschaft der Berliner Philharmoniker eV, 1992; Gold Medal, Royal Philharmonic Soc., 1993; Ehrenmitgliedschaft der Wiener Philharmoniker, 1998; Léonie Sonnings Musikpris, Denmark, 2002; Ernst von Siemens Musikpreis, 2004; A Life for Music, Artur Rubinstein Prize, Venice, 2007; South Bank Show Award, 2009; Praemium Imperiale, Japan Art Assoc., 2009; Herbert von Karajan Music Prize, 2008; Musikpreis Duisburg, 2010; Franz Liszt Ehrenpreis Weimar, 2011; Goldene Mozart-Medaille Salzburg, 2014. Commandeur des Arts et des Lettres, 2004. *Publications:* Musical Thoughts and Afterthoughts (Essays), 1976; Music Sounded Out, 1990; Fingerzeig, 1996; Störendes Lachen während des Jaworts, 1997; One Finger Too Many, 1998; Kleine Teufel, 1999; Ausgerechnet Ich, 2000; Alfred Brendel on Music: collected essays, 2001; The Veil of Order: Alfred Brendel in conversation with Martin Meyer, 2002; Spiegelbild und schwarzer Spuk (poems), 2003; Cursing Bagels (poems), 2004; Complete Poems, 2005; Friedrich Hebbel, Weltgericht mit Pausen, 2008; Nach dem Schlussakkord, 2010; Playing the Human Game, 2010; A Pianist's A–Z, 2013; Spielgewohnheiten (essays), 2014; essays on music in: HiFi Stereophonie, Music and Musicians, Phono, Fono Forum, Österreichische Musikzeitschrift, Gramophone, Die Zeit, New York Rev. of Books, Frankfurter Allgemeine, Neue Zürcher Zeitung, etc. *Recreations:* literature, art galleries, architecture, unintentional humour, "kitsch". *Address:* Ingpen & Williams, 7 St George's Court, 131 Putney Bridge Road, SW15 2PA. *T:* (020) 8874 3222.

BRENIKOV, Prof. Paul, FRTPI; Professor and Head of Department of Town and Country Planning, University of Newcastle upon Tyne, 1964–86, now Professor Emeritus; *b* 13 July 1921; *o s* of Pavel Brenikov and Joyce Mildred Jackson, Liverpool; *m* 1943, Margaret (*d* 1994), *e d* of Albert McLevy, Burnley, Lancs; two *s* one *d*. *Educ:* St Peter's Sch., York; Liverpool Coll.; Univ. of Liverpool (BA (Hons Geog.), MA, DipCD); Univ. of Sunderland (BA Fine Art 2006). War service with RNAS, 1941–46. Sen. Planning Officer, Lancs CC, 1950–55; Lectr, Dept of Civic Design, Univ. of Liverpool, 1955–64; Planning Corresp., Architect's Jl, 1957–63; Environmental Planning Consultant: in UK, for former Bootle CB, 1957–64; Govt of Ireland, 1963–67; overseas, for UN; Chile, 1960–61; E Africa, 1964; OECD; Turkey, 1968. Royal Town Planning Institute: Mem. Council, 1967–78; Chm., Northern Br., 1973–74. Member: Subject Cttee of UGC, 1975–86; DoE Local Plans Inspector's Panel, 1985–. FRSA 1979 (Chm., NE Region, RSA, and Council Mem., 1997–2000). *Publications:* contrib. Social Aspects of a Town Development Plan, 1951; contrib. Land Use in an Urban Environment, 1961; (jtly) The Dublin Region: preliminary and final reports, 1965 and 1967; other technical pubns in architectural, geographical, planning and sociological jls. *Recreations:* drawing, painting, listening to music, walking, reading. *Address:* 46 Mitchell Avenue, Jesmond, Newcastle upon Tyne NE2 3LA. *T:* (0191) 281 2773.

BRENNAN, family name of **Baron Brennan**.

BRENNAN, Baron *cr* 2000 (Life Peer), of Bibury in the co. of Gloucestershire; **Daniel Joseph Brennan;** QC 1985; a Recorder of the Crown Court, since 1982; a Deputy High Court Judge, since 1994; *b* 19 March 1942; *s* of late Daniel Brennan and Mary Brennan; *m* 1968, Pilar, *d* of late Luis Sanchez Hernandez; four *s*. *Educ:* St Bede's Grammar Sch., Bradford; Victoria University of Manchester (LLB Hons). President, University Union, 1964–65. Called to the Bar: Gray's Inn, 1967 (Bencher, 1993); King's Inns, Dublin, 1990; NI, 2001. Mem., Criminal Injuries Compensation Bd, 1989–97; Ind. Assessor to MoD and MoJ (formerly to Home Sec.) on miscarriages of justice, 2001–11. Chm., Gen. Council of the Bar, 1999 (Vice Chm., 1998). President: Catholic Union of GB, 2001–; Canning House, 2008–13 (Vice Pres., 2002–07). Patron, UK Consortium for Street Children, 2003–. Chm., Caux Round Table, 2005–10. FRSA 2000. Hon. LLD: Nottingham Trent, 1999; Manchester, 2000; Bradford, 2007; Nat. Inst. for Penal Scis, Mexico, 2008. Delegate for GB and Ireland, Sacred Military Constantinian Order of St George, 2006–10. Cross of St Raimond de Penafort (Spain), 2000; Order of Bernardo O'Higgins (Chile), 2005; Knight Commander of St Gregory (Vatican), 2008; Grand Cross of Order of Isabel la Católica (Spain), 2009. *Publications:* (gen. ed) Bullen and Leake, Precedents of Pleading, 14th edn 2001 to 16th edn 2012. *Address:* Matrix Chambers, Gray's Inn, WC1R 5LN. *T:* (020) 7404 3447, *Fax:* (020) 7404 3448. *Club:* Garrick.

BRENNAN, Anthony John Edward, CB 1981; Deputy Secretary, Northern Ireland Office, 1982–87; *b* 24 Jan. 1927; 2nd *s* of late Edward Joseph Brennan and Mabel Brennan (*née* West); *m* 1958, Pauline Margery (*d* 2008), *d* of late Percy Clegg Lees and Mildred (*née* Middleton); two *s* one *d*. *Educ:* St Joseph's; London Sch. of Economics (Leverhulme Schol., BSc Econ 1946). Served Army, RA, RAEC, 1946–49; Asst Principal, Home Office, 1949; Private Sec. to Parly Under-Sec. of State, 1953–54; Principal, 1954; Principal Private Sec. to Home Sec., 1963; Asst Sec., 1963; Asst Under Sec. of State, Criminal Dept, 1971–75, Immigration Dept, 1975–77; Dep. Under-Sec. of State, Home Office, 1977–82. Sec., Royal Commn on Penal System, 1964–66; Member: UN Cttee on Crime Prevention and Control, 1979–84 (attended conferences in Helsinki, Lagos and Budapest); UK Negotiating Team, Anglo Irish Agreement, 1985. *Recreations:* bridge, athletics and dramatic clubs (Sutton and Cheam Harriers), sixty three roles on the amateur stage (Past Chm., Civil Service Theatre Guild). *Club:* Athenæum.

BRENNAN, Archibald Orr, (Archie), OBE 1981; designer, weaver, teacher and lecturer, since 1984; *b* 7 Dec. 1931; *s* of James and Jessie Brennan; *m* 1956, Elizabeth Hewitt Carmichael (marr. diss.); three *d*. *Educ:* Boroughmuir Sch., Edinburgh; Edinburgh College of Art (DA). Training as tapestry weaver/student, 1947–62; Lectr, Edinburgh College of Art, 1962–78; Dir, Edin. Tapestry Co., 1962–77; co-ordinator/designer of all embellishment, new Nat. Parlt Bldg, PNG, 1978–84; Artist in residence, 1977, established production dept, 1978–84, Nat. Arts Sch., PNG. Pres., Soc. of Scottish Artists, 1977–78; Chm., British Craft Centre, 1977–78; travelling lectr, UK, USA, Canada, Australia, PNG, 1962–. Fellow, ANU, 1974–75. *Publications:* articles in various jls.

BRENNAN, Denis, CVO 2012; Head, Honours and Appointments Secretariat (formerly Ceremonial Officer), Cabinet Office, 2005–11; *b* 4 Nov. 1951; *s* of Michael and Mary Brennan; *m* 1975, Ursula Mary Brennan (*see* Dame Ursula Brennan). *Educ:* Gonville and Caius Coll., Cambridge (BA Philos. 1973). Ministry of Defence, 1973–94: Private Sec. to Parly Sec., RAF, 1977–78; policy posts incl. secondment to Cabinet Office, 1978–84; Private Sec. to Sec. of State, 1984–86; Head: Air Staff Secretariat, 1987–90; Housing Task Force, 1990–94; Cabinet Office: Hd, Infrastructure, Defence and Overseas Secretariat, 1994–2002; on loan to DEFRA, 2003–04. *Club:* Reform.

BRENNAN, Denis Anthony James; a District Judge (Magistrates' Courts), since 2011; *b* Hammersmith, 27 May 1959; *s* of Jeremiah and Kathleen Brennan; *m* 1995 (marr. diss. 2005); two *s*. *Educ:* Cardinal Vaughan Grammar Sch.; King's Coll., London (LLB Hons 1980). Babington Browne & Co.: articled clerk, 1982–84; admitted solicitor, 1984; asst solicitor, 1984–87; Geo. J. Dowse & Co.: asst solicitor, 1987–90; Salaried Partner, 1990–92; Equity Partner, 1992–2008; Associate Solicitor, Sonn, Macmillan Walker, 2008–11; a Dep. Dist Judge (Magistrates' Courts), 2003–11. *Recreations:* tennis, badminton, reading, spraffing, cinema, listening to The Pogues, The Lurkers and Tom Waits, going to Ireland. *Address:* c/o Hendon Magistrates' Court, The Court House, The Hyde, Hendon, NW9 7BY.

BRENNAN, Hon. Sir (Francis) Gerard, AC 1988; KBE 1981; GBS 2013; Non-Permanent Judge, Court of Final Appeal of Hong Kong, 2000–12; Chancellor, University of Technology, Sydney, 1998–2004; *b* 22 May 1928; *s* of Hon. Mr Justice (Frank Tenison) Brennan and Mrs Gertrude Brennan; *m* 1953, Dr Patricia (*née* O'Hara); three *s* four *d*. *Educ:* Christian Brothers Coll., Rockhampton, Qld; Downlands Coll., Toowoomba, Qld; Univ. of Qld (BA, LLB). Called to the Queensland Bar, 1951; QC (Australia) 1965. Judge, Aust. Indust. Court, and Additional Judge of Supreme Court of ACT, 1976–81; Judge, Fed. Court of Australia, 1977–81; Justice of the High Court, 1981–95; Chief Justice of Australia, 1995–98; Foundn Scientia Prof. of Law, Univ. of NSW, 1998–99; external Judge, Supreme Court, Republic of Fiji, 1999–2000. President: Admin. Appeals Tribunal, 1976–79; Admin. Review Council, 1976–79; Bar Assoc. of Qld, 1974–76; Aust. Bar Assoc., 1975–76; National Union of Aust. Univ. Students, 1949. Member: Exec. Law Council of Australia, 1974–76; Aust. Law Reform Commn, 1975–77. Hon. LLD: TCD, 1988; Queensland, 1996; ANU, 1996; Melbourne, 1998; UTS, 1998; NSW, 2005; Hon. DLitt Central Queensland, 1996; DUniv: Griffith, 1996; UTS, 2005. *Address:* (office) Suite 3003, Piccadilly Tower, 133 Castlereagh Street, Sydney, NSW 2000, Australia. *T:* (2) 92618704, *Fax:* (2) 92618113. *Club:* Australian (Sydney).

BRENNAN, Kevin Denis; MP (Lab) Cardiff West, since 2001; *b* 16 Oct. 1959; *s* of Michael John Brennan and Beryl Marie Brennan (*née* Evans); *m* 1988, Amy Lynn Wack; one *d*. *Educ:* St Alban's RC Comprehensive Sch., Pontypool; Pembroke Coll., Oxford (BA); UC, Cardiff (PGCE); Univ. of Glamorgan (MSc). Volunteer organiser/news ed., Cwmbran Community Press, 1982–84; Hd, Econs and Business Studies, Radyr Comprehensive Sch., 1985–94; Res. Officer for Rhodri Morgan, MP, 1995–2000; Special Advr to First Minister, Nat. Assembly for Wales, 2000. An Asst Govt Whip, 2005–06; a Lord Comr of HM Treasury (Govt Whip), 2006–07; Parly Under-Sec. of State, DCSF, 2007–08; Parly Sec. and Minister for the Third Sector, Cabinet Office, 2008–09; Minister for E Midlands, 2008–10; Minister of State, BIS and DCSF, 2009–10. *Recreations:* Rugby (watching now), music (Mem., parly rock gp MP4). *Address:* House of Commons, SW1A 0AA; 33–35 Cathedral Road, Riverside, Cardiff CF11 9HB. *Club:* Canton Labour (Cardiff).

BRENNAN, Dame Maureen, DBE 2005; Executive Headteacher: Barr Beacon School, Walsall and Etone College, Nuneaton, since 2014; Mirus Academy, Walsall, since 2015; *b* 26 March 1954; *d* of Joseph and Elizabeth Eddy; *m* 1989, Denis Brennan; one *s*. *Educ:* St Agnes' RC Grammar Sch. for Girls; Newman Coll., Birmingham (BEd). Teacher, St Chad's RC Comprehensive Sch., Birmingham, 1976–80; Hd of Dept, Ladywood Sch., 1980–85; Staff Develt Tutor, Equal Opportunities Co-ordinator, Birmingham Adv. Service, 1985–90; Dep. Hd, Great Barr Sch., 1990–2000; Principal, Hillcrest Sch. and Community Coll., Dudley, 2000–07; Headteacher, Barr Beacon School (formerly Language Coll.), 2007–14; Exec. Headteacher, Barr Beacon Language Coll. and Sneyd Community Sch., 2010–11. Dir, Matrix Academy Trust, 2013–. Nat. Leader of Educn, 2015. Fellow, Worcester Univ., 2012. *Address:* Barr Beacon School, Old Hall Lane, Aldridge, W Midlands WS9 0RF. *T:* (0121) 366 6600. *E:* mbrennan@barrbeaconschool.co.uk.

BRENNAN, Nicola Jayne Maria Louise; *see* Thorp, N. J. M. L.

BRENNAN, Sarah; Chief Executive, YoungMinds Trust, since 2008 (Interim Chief Executive, 2007–08); *b* London, 31 March 1958; *d* of James and Christine Brennan; partner, Sophie Arnold. *Educ:* Univ. of York (BA Hons Philosophy/Sociol. 1980); London Sch. of Econs and Pol Sci. (MSc Voluntary Sector Orgn 1994); Richmond Coll. (Dip. Counselling 1990). Youth worker, 1982–89; Student Counsellor, Roehampton Art Coll., 1989–91; Develt Manager, St Giles Trust, 1991–94; Dir Services, Centrepoint, 1994–2001; CEO, Motiv 8, 2001–06. *Recreations:* mountain trekking, good wines (WSET Level 3 qualif.), skiing, cinema, day skipper. *Address:* Tythe Barn, Greenways, Ovingdean, E Sussex BN2 7BA. *T:* 07813 876268. *E:* sarah.brennan@youngminds.org.uk.

BRENNAN, (Stephen) Patrick C.; *see* Cracroft-Brennan.

BRENNAN, Timothy Roger; QC 2001; a Recorder, since 2000; a Deputy High Court Judge, since 2008; *b* 11 April 1958. *Educ:* Olchfa Sch., Swansea; Balliol Coll., Oxford (BCL, MA). Called to the Bar, Gray's Inn, 1981 (Atkin Schol. 1981; Bencher, 2006); Addnl Jun. Counsel to Inland Revenue (Common Law), 1991–97, Jun. Counsel, 1997–2001; Asst Recorder, 1997–2000; a Judge of the Employment Appeal Tribunal, 2002–04. Elected Hd of Chambers, 2013–. Mem., Gen. Council of the Bar, 1987, 1988 (Mem., Conduct Cttee, 1989, 1995–98 and 2005; Mem., Professional Practice Cttee, 2010–13; Vice-Chm., 2014); Vice-Chm., Complaints Cttee, Bar Standards Bd, 2006–09. *Publications:* contribs to various tech. legal pubns. *Address:* Devereux Chambers, Queen Elizabeth Building, Temple, EC4Y 9BS. *T:* (020) 7353 7534.

BRENNAN, Dame Ursula (Mary), DCB 2013; Permanent Secretary, Ministry of Justice, 2012–15; Clerk of the Crown in Chancery, 2012–15; *b* 28 Oct. 1952; *d* of Philip and Mary Burns; *m* 1975, Denis Brennan, *qv*. *Educ:* Univ. of Kent at Canterbury (BA Hons English and Amer. Lit). ILEA, 1973–75; Department of Health and Social Security, later of Social Security, 1975–2001; Head, Disability Benefits Policy, 1990–93; Dir, IT Services Agency, 1993–95; Dir, Change Management, Benefits Agency, 1995–97; Gp Dir, Working Age

Services, 1997–2001; Gp Dir, Working Age and Children Strategy, DWP, 2001–04; Dir Gen., Natural Resources and Rural Affairs, DEFRA, 2004–05; Chief Exec., Office for Criminal Justice Reform, 2006–08; Dir Gen., Corporate Performance, MoJ, 2008; Second Perm. Under-Sec. of State, 2008–10, Perm. Under-Sec. of State, 2010–12, MoD.

BRENNER, Sydney, CH 1987; DPhil; FRCP; FRS 1965; Distinguished Research Professor, Salk Institute, La Jolla, California, since 2001; Member of Scientific Staff, MRC, 1957–92; Fellow of King's College, Cambridge, since 1959; *b* Germiston, South Africa, 13 Jan. 1927; *s* of Morris Brenner and Lena (*née* Blacher); *m* 1952, May Woolf Balkind (*d* 2010); one *s* two *d* (and one step *s*). *Educ:* Germiston High School; University of the Witwatersrand, S Africa; Oxford University (Hon. Fellow, Exeter Coll., 1985). MSc 1947, MB, BCh 1951, Univ. of the Witwatersrand; DPhil Oxon, 1954; FRCP 1979; Hon. FRCPath 1990. Director: MRC Lab. of Molecular Biol., Cambridge, 1979–86; MRC Molecular Genetics Unit, Cambridge, 1986–92; Mem., Scripps Res. Inst., La Jolla, 1992–94. Pres. and Dir of Res., Molecular Scis Inst., Berkeley, Calif, 1996–2001. Mem., MRC, 1978–82, 1986–90. Hon. Prof. of Genetic Medicine, Cambridge Univ., 1989–97. Carter-Wallace Lectr, Princeton, 1966, 1971; Gifford Lectr, Glasgow, 1978–79; Dunham Lectr, Harvard, 1984; Croonian Lectr, Royal Soc., 1986. External Scientific Mem., Max-Planck Soc., 1988; Mem., Academia Europaea, 1989; Foreign Hon. Member, American Academy of Arts and Sciences, 1965; Foreign Associate: Nat. Acad. of Sciences, USA, 1977; Royal Soc. of S Africa, 1983; Académie des Sciences, Paris, 1992; Mem., Deutsche Akademie der Naturforscher, Leopoldina, 1975 (Gregor Mendel Medal, 1970); Internat. Mem. (formerly Foreign Mem.), Amer. Philosophical Soc., 1979; Foreign Member: Real Academia de Ciencias, Spain, 1985; Correspondant Scientifique Emérite, Institut National de la Santé et de la Recherche Médicale, Paris, 1991; Hon. Member: Chinese Soc. of Genetics, 1989; Assoc. of Physicians of GB and Ireland, 1991; Alpha Omega Alpha Honor Med. Soc., 1994; German Soc. Cell Biol., 1999. Fellow, Amer. Acad. of Microbiol., 1996. Hon. FRSE 1979. Hon. FIASc 1989; Hon. Fellow, UCL, 2005. Hon. DSc: Dublin, 1967; Witwatersrand, 1972; Chicago, 1976; London, 1982; Leicester, 1983; Oxford, 1985; Rockefeller, 1996; Columbia, 1997; La Trobe, 1999; Harvard, 2002; Yale, 2003; BC, 2004; Hon. LLD: Glasgow, 1981; Cambridge, 2001; Hon. DLitt Nat. Univ. of Singapore, 1995; Dr rer. nat. *hc* Jena, 1998; Hon. Dr Oporto, 2003. Warren Triennial Prize, 1968; William Bate Hardy Prize, Cambridge Philosophical Soc., 1969; (jtly) Lasker Award for Basic Medical Research, 1971; Royal Medal, Royal Soc., 1974; (jtly) Prix Charles Leopold Mayer, French Acad. of Science, 1975; Gairdner Foundn Annual Award, 1978; Krebs Medal, FEBS, 1980; CIBA Medal, Biochem. Soc., 1981; Feldberg Foundn Prize, 1983; Neil Hamilton Fairley Medal, RCP, 1985; Rosenstiel Award, Brandeis Univ., 1986; Prix Louis Jeantet de Médecine, Switzerland, 1987; Genetics Soc. of America Medal, 1987; Harvey Prize, Technion-Israel Inst. of Technol., 1987; Hughlings Jackson Medal, RSocMed, 1987; Waterford Bio-Medical Sci. Award, Res. Inst. of Scripps Clinic, USA, 1988; Kyoto Prize, Inamori Foundn, 1990; Gairdner Foundn Internat. Award, Canada, 1991; Copley Medal, Royal Soc., 1991; King Faisal Internat. Prize for Science, King Faisal Foundn, Saudi Arabia, 1992; Bristol-Myers Squibb Award for Dist. Achievement in Neurosci. Res., NY, 1992; Albert Lasker Award for Special Achievement, 2000; Novartis Drew Award, 2001; (jtly) Nobel Prize for Physiology or Medicine, 2002; Dist. Service Award, Miami Nature Biotechnol., 2002; March of Dimes Prize, 2002; Dan David Prize, 2002; Clinical Sci. Prize, UCL, 2003; Scientist of the Year, ARCS Foundn, Calif, 2004; Rocovich Gold Medal, 2004; Phillip Tobias Lect. Medal, 2004; (jtly) Nat. Sci. Award, Singapore, 2004. Holds various foreign orders and decorations. *Publications:* papers in scientific journals. *Recreation:* rumination. *Address:* King's College, Cambridge CB2 1ST.

BRENT, Prof. Leslie Baruch, FRSB; Professor Emeritus, University of London, since 1990; *b* Köslin, Germany, 5 July 1925; *s* of Charlotte and Arthur Baruch; arrived UK in Kindertransport, 1938; *m* 1st, 1954, Joanne Elisabeth Manley (marr. diss. 1991); one *s* two *d*; 2nd, 1991, Carol Pamela Martin. *Educ:* Bunce Court Sch., Kent; Birmingham Central Technical Coll.; Univ. of Birmingham; UCL. BSc Birmingham, PhD London. FRSB (FIBiol 1964). Laboratory technician, 1941–43; Army service, 1943–47, Captain; Lectr, Dept of Zoology, UCL, 1954–62; Rockefeller Res. Fellow, Calif Inst. of Technology, 1956–57; Res. scientist, Nat. Inst. for Med. Res., 1962–65; Prof. of Zoology, Univ. of Southampton, 1965–69; Prof. of Immunology, St Mary's Hosp. Med. Sch., London, 1969–90. European Editor, Transplantation, 1963–68; Gen. Sec., British Transplantation Soc., 1971–75; Pres., The Transplantation Society, 1976–78; Chairman: Wessex Br., Inst. of Biol., 1966–68; Organising Cttee, 9th Internat. Congress of The Transplantation Soc., 1978–82; Fellowships Cttee, Inst. of Biol., 1982–85; Art Cttee, St Mary's Hosp. Med. Sch., 1988–92. Pres., Guild of Undergrads, Birmingham Univ., 1950–51. Chairman: Haringey Community Relations Council, 1979–80; Haringey SDP, 1981–83. Governor: Creighton Sch., 1974–79; Yerbury Sch., 1999–2006; Mem., Islington Schs Ind. Appeals Panel, 2001–06. Trustee, British Scholarship Trust for Former Yugoslavian Territories, 1997–2014. Mem., Eur. Acad. for Scis and Arts (Salzburg), 2002. Hon. MRCP 1986; Hon. Mem., Koszalin Regl Chamber of Physicians (Poland), 2005. Hon. Member: British Transplantation Soc., 1988; Eur. Soc. for Organ Transplantation, 2011; hon. mem. of several foreign scientific socs. FZS 2007. Vice-Chancellor's Prize, Birmingham Univ., 1951; Scientific Medal, Zool Soc., 1963; Peter Medawar Medal and Prize, Internat. Transplantation Soc., 1994. Played hockey for UAU and Staffs, 1949–51. Co-editor, Immunology Letters, 1983–90. *Publications:* (ed jtly) Organ Transplantation: current clinical and immunological concepts, 1989; History of Transplantation Immunology, 1997; (ed jtly) Verstörte Kindheiten. Das Jüdische Waisenhaus in Pankow als Ort der Zuflucht, Geborgenheit und Vertreibung, 2008; Sunday's Child?: a memoir, 2009 (trans. German); articles in scientific and med. jls on transplantation immunology, and obituaries and book reviews. *Recreations:* music, fell-walking, novels, politics. *Address:* 30 Hugo Road, Tufnell Park, N19 5EU.

BRENT, Michael Leon; QC 1983; a Recorder, 1990–2000; a Deputy High Court Judge, 1994–2000; *b* 8 June 1936; *m* 1965, Rosalind Keller; two *d*. *Educ:* Manchester Grammar Sch.; Manchester Univ. (LLB Hons). Called to the Bar, Gray's Inn, 1961; practised on: Northern Circuit, 1961–67 (Circuit Junior, 1964); Midland and Oxford Circuit, 1967–2000; Hd of Chambers, 1988–97. Mem. Bd, Criminal Injuries Compensation Appeals Panel, 1999–2002. Pres., St John's Wood Soc., 2009–. *Address:* 9 Gough Square, EC4A 3DG.

BRENT, Prof. Richard Peirce, PhD, DSc; Emeritus Professor, Mathematical Sciences Institute and Research School of Computer Science, Australian National University, since 2011; *b* 20 April 1946; *s* of Oscar and Nancy Brent; *m* 1st, 1969, Erin O'Connor (*d* 2005); two *s*; 2nd, 2007, Judy-anne Osborn. *Educ:* Melbourne Grammar Sch.; Monash Univ. (BSc 1968; DSc 1981); Stanford Univ. (PhD 1971). FAA 1982; FIEEE 1991. IBM Res., Yorktown Heights, NY, 1971–72; Australian National University: Res. Fellow, 1972–73; Fellow, 1973–76; Sen. Fellow, 1976–78; Foundation Prof. of Computer Science, 1978–98; Prof. of Computing Sci., Univ. of Oxford, and Fellow of St Hugh's Coll., Oxford, 1998–2005; Fedn Fellow, Mathematical Scis Inst., 2005–10, Distinguished Prof., 2010–11, ANU. Visiting Professor: Stanford Univ., 1974–75; Univ. of Calif at Berkeley, 1977–78; Harvard Univ., 1997. Fellow, ACM, 1994. Aust. Math. Soc. Medal, 1984; Hannan Medal, Aust. Acad. of Sci., 2005. *Publications:* Algorithms for Minimization without Derivatives, 1973, repr. 2002; Computational Complexity and the Analysis of Algorithms, 1980; (with P. Zimmermann) Modern Computer Arithmetic, 2010. *Recreations:* music, chess, bridge. *Address:* Mathematical Sciences Institute, Australian National University, ACT 0200, Australia.

BRENTFORD, 4th Viscount *cr* 1929, of Newick; **Crispin William Joynson-Hicks;** Bt of Holmbury, 1919; Bt of Newick, 1956; Partner, Taylor Joynson Garrett (formerly Joynson-Hicks), 1961–95; *b* 7 April 1933; *s* of 3rd Viscount Brentford and Phyllis (*d* 1979), *o d* of lat Major Herbert Allfrey, Tetbury, Glos; *S* father, 1983; *m* 1964, Gillian Evelyn Schluter (*se* Viscountess Brentford); one *s* three *d*. *Educ:* Eton; New College, Oxford. Admitted solicito 1960. Master, Girdlers' Co., 1983–84. *Heir: s* Hon. Paul William Joynson-Hicks [*b* 18 Apr 1971; *m* 2006, Catharine, *d* of Richard James Kay Muir, *qv*; two *s* (one *d* decd)]. *Address:* Birchfield, Church Road, Sundridge, Kent TN14 6DQ. *T:* (01959) 565846.

BRENTFORD, Viscountess; Gillian Evelyn Joynson-Hicks, OBE 1996; FCA; Thi Church Estates Commissioner, 1999–2005; *b* 22 Nov. 1942; *d* of Gerald Edward Schlute OBE; *m* 1964, Crispin William Joynson-Hicks (*see* Viscount Brentford); one *s* three *d*. *Edu* West Heath Sch. FCA 1965. Director: Edward Schluter & Co. (London) Ltd, 1971–88; M A. F. Europe, 1990–97. Mem., General Synod of C of E, 1990–2005; a Church Com 1991–98 (Mem., Bd of Govs, 1993–98); Chm., House of Laity, Chichester dio., 1991–9 Mem., Crown Appts Commn, 1995–2002. Pres., CMS, 1998–2007. Chm., Café Afric Internat., 2006–12. High Sheriff, E Sussex, 1998–99. *Recreations:* family, gardens, trave *Address:* 5 Birchfield, Church Road, Sundridge, Kent TN14 6DQ.

BRENTON, Sir Anthony Russell, KCMG 2007 (CMG 2001); HM Diplomatic Servic retired; Extraordinary Fellow, Wolfson College, Cambridge, since 2009; Senior Fellow Department of Politics and International Studies, University of Cambridge, since 2011; *b* Jan. 1950; *s* of Ivan Bernard Brenton and Jean Sylvia (*née* Rostgard); *m* 1981, Susan Ma Penrose; one *s* two *d*. *Educ:* Queens' Coll. Cambridge (BA); Open Univ. (MPhil). Joined H Diplomatic Service, 1975; Cairo, 1978–81; European Communities Dept, FCO, 1981–8 with UK Perm. Repn to EC, 1985–86; Dep. Chef de Cabinet, EC, 1986–89; Counsello 1989; Head: UN Dept, FCO, 1989–90; Envmt, Sci. and Energy Dept, FCO, 1990–9 Fellow, Centre for Internat. Affairs, Harvard Univ., 1992–93; Counsellor, Moscow, 1994–9 Dir, FCO, 1998–2001; Minister, Washington, 2001–04; Ambassador to Russia, 2004–0 Dir, Russo-British Chamber of Commerce, 2008–; Advr, Lloyd's Insce Mkt, 2008–; Mem Adv. Bd, EU/Russia Centre, 2010–. Chm., Leys and St Faith's Foundn, 2010–. Hon. Fellow Strategy and Security Inst., Exeter Univ., 2013–. *Publications:* The Greening of Machiavell 1994; press and mag. articles on Russia. *Recreations:* history, Russia. *Address:* Wolfson Colleg Cambridge CB3 9BB.

BRENTON, Howard; playwright; *b* 13 Dec. 1942; *s* of Donald Henry Brenton and Ro Lilian (*née* Lewis); *m* 1970, Jane Fry; two *s*. *Educ:* Chichester High Sch. for Boys; Catharine's Coll., Cambridge (BA Hons English). Hon. DLit: North London; Westminste 2002; Portsmouth, 2008. *Full-length stage plays:* Revenge, 1969; Hitler Dances, and Measu for Measure (after Shakespeare), 1972; Magnificence, 1973; The Churchill Play, 197 Government Property, 1975; Weapons of Happiness, 1976 (Evening Standard Award); Epso Downs, 1977; Sore Throats, 1979; The Romans in Britain, 1980; Thirteenth Night, 198 The Genius, 1983; Bloody Poetry, 1984; Greenland, 1988; H. I. D. (Hess is Dead), 198 Berlin Bertie, 1992; Kit's Play, 2000; Bacchae/Backup, 2001; Paul, 2005; In Extremis, 200 Never So Good, 2008; Anne Boleyn, 2010; The Ragged Trousered Philanthropists (stag adaption), 2010; 55 Days, 2012; Dances of Death (adaptation), 2013; #aiww: The Arrest c Ai Weiwei, 2013; Drawing the Line, 2013; Doctor Scroggy's War, 2014; *one-act stage play* Gum and Goo, Heads, The Education of Skinny Spew, and Christie in Love, 1969; Wesle 1970; Scott of the Antarctic, and A Sky-blue Life, 1971; How Beautiful with Badges, 197 Mug, 1973; The Thing (for children), 1982; *collaborations:* (with six others) Lay-By, 197 (with six others) England's Ireland, 1971; (with David Hare) Brassneck, 1973; (with Trev Griffiths, David Hare and Ken Campbell), Deeds, 1978; (with Tony Howard) A Short Sha Shock, 1980; (with Tunde Ikoli) Sleeping Policemen, 1983; (with David Hare) Pravda, 198 (London Standard Award); Playing Away (opera), 1994 (score by Benedict Mason); *with Tar Ali:* Iranian Nights, 1989; Moscow Gold, 1990; Ugly Rumours, 1998; *with Tariq Ali and An de la Tour:* Collateral Damage, 1999; Snogging Ken, 2000; *television plays:* Lushly, 197 Brassneck (adaptation of stage play), 1974; The Saliva Milkshake, 1975 (also perf. theatre); Th Paradise Run, 1976; Desert of Lies, 1984; *television series:* Dead Head, 1986; (with Dav Wolstencroft and Simon Mirren) Spooks, 2002–03 (BAFTA award for Best TV Drama series *radio play:* Nasser's Eden, 1998; *translations:* Bertolt Brecht, The Life of Galileo, 1980; Geo Buchner, Danton's Death, 1982, 2010; Bertolt Brecht, Conversations in Exile, 1982; Goeth Faust, 1995. *Publications:* Diving for Pearls (novel), 1989; Hot Irons: diaries, essays, journalis 1995; many plays published. *Recreation:* painting. *Address:* c/o Casarotto Ramsay Lt Waverley House, 7–12 Noel Street, W1F 8GQ. *T:* (020) 7287 4450.

BRENTON, Jonathan Andrew, PhD; HM Diplomatic Service; Minister Counsell (Prosperity), Moscow, since 2015; *b* Kampala, Uganda, 24 Dec. 1965; *s* of Prof. Dav Brenton and Anne Brenton; *m* 2001, Sayana Sarbaa; one *s* one *d*. *Educ:* Bristol Univ. (M English Lit.); Boston Univ. (MA English Lit.); PhD Cantab 1998. Entered FCO, 1994; As Desk Officer, EU Dept Internal, 1994–95; Russian lang. trng, 1995–96; Second Se (Commercial), 1996–98, Hd, Econ. Sect., 1998–2000, Moscow; Hd of Sect., EU De External, 2000–02; German lang. trng, 2002–03; Press Sec., Berlin, 2003–06; Dep. Hd, Afric Dept Equatorial, FCO, 2006–08; Hd, Jt Mgt Office, Brussels, 2008–10; Ambassador t Belgium, 2010–14; Hd, Campaigns and Engagement Dept, FCO, 2014–15. *Recreatio* reading. *Address:* c/o Foreign and Commonwealth Office, King Charles Street, SW1A 2A *E:* jonathan.brenton@fco.gov.uk.

BRENTON, Timothy Deane; QC 1998; *b* 4 Nov. 1957; *s* of late Comdr R. W. Brento RN and of P. C. D. Brenton; *m* 1981, Annabel Louisa Robson; one *s* one *d*. *Educ:* King Sch., Rochester; BRNC, Dartmouth; Bristol Univ. (LLB 1st cl. Hons 1979). RN, 1975–7 Lectr in Law, King's Coll. London, 1980; called to the Bar, Middle Temple, 1981; in practic at the Bar, 1981–. Mem., Editl Bd, International Maritime Law, 1994–2001. Hon. Couns and Trustee, Seafarers UK (formerly King George's Fund for Sailors), 2000–09. *Recreation* golf, country pursuits, ski-ing, music. *Address:* 7 King's Bench Walk, Inner Temple, EC4 7DS. *T:* (020) 7910 8300.

BRENTWOOD, Bishop of, (RC), since 2014; **Rt Rev. Alan Williams;** *b* Oldham, 1 March 1951. *Educ:* Durham Univ.; Univ. of Hull (MEd); London Univ. (PhD Psychol. Univ. of Cambridge (LTh); Allen Hall Seminary. Final vows, Soc. of Mary (Marist Fathers 1981, ordained priest, 1983; Parish Priest, St Lawrence of Canterbury, Sidcup; Superio Marist Fathers in Eng., 2000–08; Dir, Nat. Shrine of Our Lady at Walsingham. Catholi Chaplain, Sheffield Hallam Univ. *Address:* Cathedral House, Ingrave Road, Brentwood, Ess CM15 8AT.

BRERETON, Donald, CB 2001; Chairman, Carers UK, since 2005; *b* 18 July 1945; *s* Clarence Vivian and Alice Gwendolin Brereton; *m* 1969, Mary Frances Turley; one *s* two *Educ:* Plymouth Coll.; Univ. of Newcastle upon Tyne (BA Hons Pol. and Soc. Admin). VS Malaysia, 1963–64. Asst Principal, Min. of Health, 1968; Asst Private Sec. to Sec. of State f Social Services, 1971; Private Sec. to Perm. Sec., DHSS, 1972; Prin., Health Servic Planning, 1973; Private Sec. to Sec. of State for Social Services, 1979–82; Asst Sec., DHS Policy Strategy Unit, 1982–83; Sec. to Housing Benefit Rev. Team, 1984; Asst Sec., Housi Benefit, 1985–89; Under Sec., Head of Prime Minister's Efficiency Unit, 1989–93; Und Sec., Social Security Policy Gp, DSS, 1993–2000; Dir, Disability, DSS, then Gp Di Disability and Carers, DWP, 2000–03. Dir, 2004–09, Chm. Pension Trustees, 2010 Motability. Member: Standing Commn on Carers, 2008–; NHS Nat. Quality Bd, 2009 *Recreations:* tennis, holidays, books, gardening, bridge, theatre. *Address:* Carers UK, 20 Gre Dover Street, SE1 4LX.

BRESLAND, (David) Allan; Member (DemU) West Tyrone, Northern Ireland Assembly, 2007–11; *b* 16 Aug. 1945; *s* of Hugh and May Bresland; *m* 1966, Mary Elizabeth Martin; four *d. Educ:* Ballylaw Primary Sch. Lorry driver: R. J. Hemphill, 1967–76; Water Service, 1976–2001. UDR (pt-time), 1970–85. Mem. (DemU), Strabane DC, 1993–. Contested (DemU) W Tyrone, NI Assembly, 2011. *Recreation:* watching and following cricket. *Address:* 41 Millhaven, Sion Mills, Co. Tyrone BT82 9FG. *T:* (028) 8165 8579, *Fax:* (028) 8165 9177. *E:* a.bresland@btconnect.com.

BRESLIN, Theresa; writer; former librarian; *b* Scotland; *d* of Thomas Green and Sarah Green; *m* Tom Breslin; one *s* three *d. Educ:* St Ninian's High Sch., Kirkintilloch; Aston Univ., Birmingham. ALA, then MCILIP. Former mobile librarian, community librarian and Principal Asst, Liby Youth Services, E Dunbartonshire Council. Former Mem., Public Lending Right Adv. Cttee. Manager, Scottish Writers' Proj.; Founder, W of Scotland Children's Book Gp; former Pres., Strathkelvin and Allander Writers' Gp; former Chm., Scottish Youth Librarians Forum; Member: Fedn of Children's Book Gps; IBBY; Cttee, Soc. of Authors (Scotland); Scottish Children's Writers' Gp; Youth Strategy; Focus Gp, Nat. Year of Reading. Former Dir, Scottish Book Trust. Hon. Mem., Scottish Liby Assoc., 2000. Civic Award, Strathkelvin DC. *Publications: novels:* Simon's Challenge, 1988 (Fidler Award, Young Book Trust, 1988; Best of the Decade Award, Scottish Book Trust, 1992); Different Directions, 1989; A Time to Reap, 1991; New School Blues, 1992; Bullies at School, 1993; Kezzie, 1993; Whispers in the Graveyard, 1994 (Carnegie Medal, 1995); Alien Force, 1995; Missing, 1995; A Homecoming for Kezzie, 1995; Name Games, 1996; Death or Glory Boys, 1996 (Sheffield Book Award, 1997); Blair the Winner!, 1997; Across the Roman Wall, 1997; Body Parts, 1997; The Dream Master, 1999; Starship Rescue, 1999; Blair Makes a Splash, 1999; Duncan of Carrick, 2000; Dream Master: Nightmare!, 2000; Remembrance, 2002 (Best Book for Young Adults, Amer. Liby Assoc., 2003); (ed jtly) My Mum's a Punk, 2002; Dream Master: Gladiator, 2003; Saskia's Journey, 2004; Prisoner in Alcatraz, 2004; Dream Master: Arabian Nights, 2004; Divided City, 2005 (Catalyst Book Award, N Lanarkshire Council, 2005, RED Book Award, Falkirk Council, 2008); Mutant, 2005; The Medici Seal, 2006; Cold Spell, 2007; Midsummer Magic, 2007; Trick or Treat?, 2007; Alligator, 2008; The Nostradamus Prophecy, 2008; Prisoners of the Inquisition, 2010; Ghost Soldier, 2014; *plays:* Alligator: the play, 2009; Whispers in the Graveyard: the play, 2009; *non-fiction:* Power Pack: the active guide to using libraries; contrib. short stories in collections; contribs to professional jls on children's literacy and literature. *Recreations:* reading, walking, exploring ancient standing stones, burial grounds and graveyards, old children's books, theatre, film. *W:* www.theresabreslin.com.

BRETHERTON, James Russell; Secretary, 1989–2003, and Director of Corporate Services, 1998–2003, United Kingdom Atomic Energy Authority; *b* 28 March 1943; *y s* of Russell Frederick Bretherton, CB and Jocelyn Nina Mathews; *m* 1968, Harriet Grace Drew, *d* of Sir Arthur Charles Walter Drew, KCB; two *s. Educ:* King's Sch., Canterbury; Wadham Coll., Oxford (MA History). Voluntary Service as Asst Dist Officer, Nigeria, 1965–66; Asst Principal, Min. of Fuel and Power, 1966–70; Principal, Min. of Technol., 1970–76; Principal Private Sec. to Sec. of State for Energy, 1976–78; Head of Oil Industry Div., Internat. Energy Agency, Paris, 1980–82; Asst Sec., Dept of Energy, 1983–86; United Kingdom Atomic Energy Authority: Principal Finance and Programmes Officer, 1986–89; Commercial and Planning Dir, 1990–94; Dir, Property Mgt and Services, 1994–98. *Recreations:* gardening, walking, bassoon playing (St Giles Orch.), bridge. *Address:* Highview, 15 Hid's Copse Road, Oxford OX2 9JJ. *T:* (01865) 863388.
See also P. C. Drew.

BRETON, Guy, CM 2014; MD; FRCPC; Rector, University of Montreal, since 2010; *b* Saint-Hyacinthe, Quebec, 1 April 1950; *s* of Gérard Breton and Jeannette Morin; *m* 1974, Andrée Despins; one *d. Educ:* Univ. of Sherbrooke (MD 1974); Coll. des Médecins du Québec (Cert. specialist in diagnostic radiol. 1978); Royal Coll. of Canada (Cert. specialist in diagnostic radiol. 1978); Amer. Coll. of Radiol. (Cert. specialist in diagnostic radiol. 1978). University of Montreal: Associate Clinical Prof., 1979–94, Prof. of Radiology, 1994–, Chm., 1996–2003, Dept of Radiol., Radio-oncology and Nuclear Medicine, Faculty of Medicine; Exec. Vice Dean, Faculty of Medicine, 2003–06; Exec. Vice-Rector, 2006–10; University of Montreal Hospital Centre: Hd, Radiol. Dept, 1997–2000; Special Advr to Chm. of Bd and to Exec. Dir, 2008; Vice-Pres., Planning—Health and Services, Teaching and Res., Implantation Soc. for Univ. of Montreal Hosp. Centre, 2001–03. Hd, Radiol. Dept, Saint-Luc Hosp., 1983–97; Pres. and CEO, Radiologie Varad, 1983–97. President: Quebec Assoc. of Radiologists, 1987–97 (Sec., 1979–87); Canadian Heads of Academic Radiol. of Canada, 1998–2000. Ambassador, Univ. of Sherbrooke, 2010. Hon. Dr: Shanghai Jiao Tong Univ., 2013; Univ. des Technologies de Compiègne, 2013. Albert-Jutras Prize, 2009, Personality of the Year, 2011, Société Canadienne Française de Radiologie; Palmes Académiques, 2013. *Publications:* (contrib.) Tomodensitométrie Pelvienne, 1988; (contrib. and ed jtly) Guide d'utilisation en radiologie diagnostique, 1997; contrib. Jl de l'Assoc. canadienne des Radiologistes. *Recreations:* family, golf, walking, music. *Address:* University of Montreal, Pavillon Roger-Gaudry, H-401, PO Box 6128, Downtown Branch, Montreal, QC H3C 3J7, Canada. *T:* (514) 3436991. *E:* guy.breton@umontreal.ca.

BRETSCHER, Barbara Mary Frances, (Mrs M. S. Bretscher); *see* Pearse, B. M. F.

BRETSCHER, Mark Steven, PhD; FRS 1985; Visitor, Division of Cell Biology, Medical Research Council Laboratory of Molecular Biology, Cambridge, 2005–12 (Member of Scientific Staff, 1965–2005; Head of Division, 1984–95); *b* 8 Jan. 1940; *s* of late Egon Bretscher, CBE and Hanni (*née* Greminger); *m* 1978, Barbara Mary Frances Pearse, *qv*; one *s* one *d. Educ:* Abingdon Sch., Berks; Gonville and Caius Coll., Cambridge (MA, PhD). Res. Fellow, Gonville and Caius Coll., Cambridge, 1964–70. Vis. Professor: Harvard Univ., 1975; Stanford Univ., 1984. Friedrich Miescher Prize, Swiss Biochemical Soc., 1979. *Publications:* papers in scientific jls on protein biosynthesis, membrane structure and cell locomotion. *Recreation:* gardening. *Address:* Ram Cottage, Commercial End, Swaffham Bulbeck, Cambridge CB25 0ND. *T:* (01223) 811276. *E:* msb@mrc-lmb.cam.ac.uk.

BRETT, family name of **Viscount Esher**.

BRETT, Kieran James; Founder and Director, Improving Care Ltd, since 2011; *b* Co. Durham, 4 July 1968; *s* of James Brett and Joan Brett (*née* Kieran); partner, Sally-Marie Bamford. *Educ:* Harris Manchester Coll., Oxford (BA Hons PPE); Univ. of Nottingham (MA Social Policy and Politics). Various roles in local govt, 1986–99; Audit Commn, 1999–2002; Prime Minister's Delivery Unit, Cabinet Office, 2002–05; Special Advr on Home Affairs to the Prime Minister, 2005–07; Special Advr to Sec. of State for Health, 2009–10. Dir, 16.00 Hours Ltd, 2013–. Trustee, Demos, 2013–. *Recreations:* idling, very dry vodka martini (with a lemon twist), changing the world. *Address:* 252A Dacre Park, Blackheath, SE13 5DD. *T:* 07976 297670. *E:* kjbrett1@gmail.com. *Club:* Newcastle United Football.

BRETT, Michael John Lee; freelance financial journalist, part-time lecturer and writer, since 1982; *b* 23 May 1939; *s* of late John Brett and Margaret Brett (*née* Lee). *Educ:* King's Coll. Sch., Wimbledon; Wadham Coll., Oxford (BA Modern Langs). Investors Review, 1962–64; Fire Protection Assoc., 1964–68; Investors Chronicle, 1968–82: Dep. Editor, 1973–77; Editor, 1977–82. Past Director: Throgmorton Publications; Financial Times Business Publishing Div. *Publications:* Finance for Business: private sector finance; (contrib.) Valuation and Investment Appraisal; How to Read the Financial Pages; Property and Money, 1990; How to Figure Out Company Accounts, 2003. *Recreations:* travelling, reading.
See also S. A. L. Brett.

BRETT, Natalie Ann; Head, London College of Communication and Pro-Vice-Chancellor, University of the Arts, London, since 2013; *b* Sheffield, 3 July 1961; *d* of Kenneth and Hazel Tomlin; *m* 2000, Terrence Brett. *Educ:* The Poly., Wolverhampton (BA Hons Graphic Design 1983). University of the Arts, London: Course Dir, Foundn Art and Design, 2003–06, Dean, 2006–08, Chelsea Coll. of Art and Design; Dean, Camberwell Coll. of Arts, 2008–13. *Recreations:* school governor, global UTC family, collecting, travelling, fishing. *Address:* London College of Communication, Elephant and Castle, SE1 6SB. *T:* (020) 7514 6673. *E:* n.brett@lcc.arts.ac.uk.

BRETT, Richard John; General Manager, Age UK Torbay, since 2011; Consultant, Aston Group UK, since 2002 (Director, 2000–01; Joint Managing Director, 2001–02); *b* 23 Oct. 1947; *s* of Henry William Brett and Dorothy Ada Brett; *m* 1st, 1972, Alison Elizabeth Lambert (marr. diss. 1991); one *d*; 2nd, 1991, Maria Antoinette Brown. *Educ:* Univ. of Bradford (MSc). FCA; Associate, Inst. of Taxation. Leonard C. Bye, Chartered Accountants, Middlesbrough, 1964; ICI Petro-chemicals, 1971; Finance Director: Chloride Shires, 1976; Chloride Automotive Batteries, 1979; Westpark, 1981; Thorn EMI Datatech, 1985–88; Gp Dir, Finance and Mgt Services, CAA, 1988–96; Man. Dir, Solution Partners Ltd, 1996–2000. Finance Manager, Age UK (formerly Age Concern) Torbay, 2005. Trustee: Homeyards Botanical Gardens; Pavilions Teignmouth. *Recreation:* music.

BRETT, Simon Anthony Lee; writer; *b* 28 Oct. 1945; *s* of late Alan John Brett and Margaret Agnes Brett (*née* Lee); *m* 1971, Lucy Victoria McLaren; two *s* one *d. Educ:* Dulwich College; Wadham College, Oxford (BA Hons). Department store Father Christmas, 1967; BBC Radio Producer, 1968–77; LWT Producer, 1977–79. Chm., Adv. Cttee, PLR, 2003–. Chm., Soc. of Authors, 1995–97; Pres., Detection Club, 2001–. Radio and television scripts, incl. After Henry, No Commitments, Smelling of Roses. *Publications: Charles Paris crime novels:* Cast, In Order of Disappearance, 1975; So Much Blood, 1976; Star Trap, 1977; An Amateur Corpse, 1978; A Comedian Dies, 1979; The Dead Side of the Mike, 1980; Situation Tragedy, 1981; Murder Unprompted, 1982; Murder in the Title, 1983; Not Dead, Only Resting, 1984; Dead Giveaway, 1985; What Bloody Man Is That?, 1987; A Series of Murders, 1989; Corporate Bodies, 1991; A Reconstructed Corpse, 1993; Sicken And So Die, 1995; Dead Room Farce, 1997; A Decent Interval, 2013; The Cinderella Killer, 2014; *Mrs Pargeter crime novels:* A Nice Class of Corpse, 1986; Mrs, Presumed Dead, 1988; Mrs Pargeter's Package, 1990; Mrs Pargeter's Pound of Flesh, 1992; Mrs Pargeter's Plot, 1996; Mrs Pargeter's Point of Honour, 1998; *other crime novels:* A Shock to the System, 1984; Dead Romantic, 1985; The Three Detectives and the Missing Superstar, 1986; The Three Detectives and the Knight-in-Armour, 1987; The Christmas Crimes at Puzzel Manor, 1991; Singled Out, 1995; The Body on the Beach, 2000; Death on the Downs, 2001; The Torso in the Town, 2002; Murder in the Museum, 2003; The Hanging in the Hotel, 2004; The Witness at the Wedding, 2005; The Stabbing in the Stables, 2006; Death Under the Dryer, 2007; Blood at the Bookies, 2008; The Poisoning in the Pub, 2009; Blotto, Twinks and the Ex-King's Daughter, 2009; The Shooting in the Shop, 2010; Blotto, Twinks and the Dead Dowager Duchess, 2010; Bones under the Beach Hut, 2011; Blotto, Twinks and the Rodents of the Riviera, 2011; Guns in the Gallery, 2011; Blotto, Twinks and the Bootlegger's Moll, 2012; The Corpse in the Court, 2012; Blotto, Twinks and the Riddle of the Sphinx, 2013; The Strangling on the Stage, 2013; *crime short stories:* A Box of Tricks, 1985; Crime Writers and Other Animals, 1998; *humorous books:* The Child-Owner's Handbook, 1983; Molesworth Rites Again, 1983; Bad Form, 1984; People-Spotting, 1985; The Wastepaper Basket Archive, 1986; How to Stay Topp, 1987; After Henry, 1987; The Booker Book, 1989; How to be a Little Sod, 1992; Look Who's Walking, 1994; Not Another Little Sod!, 1997; The Penultimate Chance Saloon, 2006; On Second Thoughts, 2006; *anthologies:* The Faber Book of Useful Verse, 1981; (with Frank Muir) The Book of Comedy Sketches, 1982; Take a Spare Truss, 1983; The Faber Book of Parodies, 1984; The Faber Book of Diaries, 1987; *stage play:* Silhouette, 1998. *Recreations:* writing, reading, Real tennis, unreal fantasies. *Address:* Frith House, Burpham, Arundel, West Sussex BN18 9RR. *T:* (01903) 882257. *Clubs:* Garrick, Groucho.
See also M. J. L. Brett.

BRETT, Simon Baliol, RE 1991 (ARE 1986); wood engraver, printmaker and illustrator; writer on wood engraving; *b* 27 May 1943; *s* of late Antony Baliol Brett and Bay Helen (*née* Brownell); *m* 1974, Juliet Shirley-Smith (*née* Wood); one *d*, and three step *s* one step *d. Educ:* Ampleforth Coll.; St Martin's Sch. of Art (NDD 1964). Teacher, Marlborough Coll. Art Sch., 1971–89; publisher, under own Paulinus Print imprint, 1981–88. Editl Advr, Printmaking Today, 1994–. Society of Wood Engravers: Mem., 1984–; Chm., 1986–92; Treas., 1990–2002. Presentation print commnd by Medical Household for Golden Wedding of the Queen and Duke of Edinburgh, 1997. Retrospective exhibns incl. Bankside Gall., Holburne Mus., 2013. Exhibitions curated: Wood Engraving Then and Now, 1987; Out of the Wood, 1991; Wood Engraving Here and Now, 1995. *Publications:* Engravers, 1987; Engravers Two, 1992; Mr Derrick Harris, 1999; An Engraver's Globe, 2002; Wood Engraving - How to Do it, 1994, rev. edn 2010; Simon Brett—An Engraver's Progress, 2013; *books illustrated include:* The Animals of St Gregory (Francis Williams/V&A/NBL Illustration Award), 1981; To the Cross, 1984; Shakespeare's Sonnets, 1989; The Reader's Digest Illustrated Bible, 1990; Clarissa, 1991; Jane Eyre, 1991; The Confessions of Saint Augustine, 1993; Amelia, 1995; Shakespeare, The Classical Plays, 1997; (also picture ed.) The Folio Golden Treasury, 1997; Middlemarch, 1999; The Poetry of John Keats, 2001; The Meditations of Marcus Aurelius, 2002; Legends of the Ring, 2004; The Gypsies, 2006; Legends of the Grail, 2007; Shelley, 2008; Pericles, Prince of Tyre, 2010. *Address:* 12 Blowhorn Street, Marlborough, Wilts SN8 1BT. *T:* (01672) 512905. *E:* simon@simonbrett-woodengraver.co.uk.

BRETT, Timothy Edward William; Member (Lib Dem), Fife Unitary Council, since 2003 (Leader, Lib Dem Group, since 2012); *b* 28 March 1949; *s* of Reuben Brett and Edna Brett (*née* Waterman); *m* 1972, Barbara Jane Turnbull; two *s* one *d* (and one *s* decd). *Educ:* Gravesend GS for Boys; Bristol Univ. (BSc Hons). CIHM; FCIPD 2005; FFPH 2007. VSO Teacher, Min. of Educn, Sierra Leone, 1971–73; Nat. Admin. Trainee, Leeds RBH, later Yorks RHA, 1973–75; Sen. Admin. Asst (Planning & Personnel), Leeds AHA, 1975–76; Business Manager, Nixon Meml Hosp., Methodist Church-Overseas Div., Segbwema, Sierra Leone, 1976–78; Community Services Adminr, Humberside AHA, 1978; Dep. Adminr, Derbyshire Royal Infirmary, 1979–80; Unit Adminr, Plymouth Gen. Hosp., 1981–85; Unit Adminr, 1985–87, Unit Gen. Manager, 1987–93, Dundee Gen. Hosps Unit; Chief Exec., Dundee Teaching Hosps NHS Trust, 1993–98; Gen. Manager, then Chief Exec., Tayside Health Board, 1998–2001; Dir, Health Protection Scotland, 2002–07. Chm., Social Work and Health Cttee, Fife Council, 2007–12. Contested (Lib Dem) Fife NE, 2015. *Recreations:* hill-walking, swimming, theatre, church activities. *Address:* Woodend Cottage, Hazelton Walls, Cupar, Fife KY15 4QL. *T:* (01382) 330629.

BRETT-HOLT, Alexis Fayrer; Legal Adviser, Health and Safety Executive, 2004–10; *b* 7 March 1950; *d* of late Raymond Arthur Brett-Holt and Jacqueline Fayrer Brett-Holt (*née* Fayrer Hosken); *m* 1980, (John) Gareth Roscoe, *qv*; one *s* one *d. Educ:* Wimbledon High Sch.; St Anne's Coll., Oxford (BA). Called to the Bar, Lincoln's Inn, 1973, Bencher, 2007; Department of the Environment: Legal Asst, 1974–78; Sen. Legal Asst, 1978–85; Asst Solicitor, 1985–89; Assistant Solicitor: DoH, 1989–93; DoE, 1993–97; Dir, Legal Services C, 1997–2001, Legal Services B, 2001–04, DTI. Pres., Assoc. of First Div. Civil Servants, 1987–89. *Club:* CWIL.

BRETT-SMITH, Adam de la Falaise Brett; Managing Director, Corney & Barrow Ltd, since 1988; *b* Olney, Maryland, USA, 4 June 1956; *s* of Captain Richard Brett-Smith and (Patricia) Karen Brett-Smith (later Lady Beeley). *Educ:* Dragon Sch., Oxford; Westminster

Sch.; St Edmund Hall, Oxford (MA Hons English Lang. and Lit.). Corney & Barrow Ltd, 1981–. Mem. Council, Royal Warrant Holders' Assoc., 1996– (Pres., 2001–02). Chm., Queen Elizabeth Scholarship Trust, 2003–05. Clerk of the Prince of Wales's and Duchess of Cornwall's Cellars, Royal Household, 2003–. *Recreations:* motorcycling, shooting, opera, ballet. *Address:* c/o Corney & Barrow, 1 Thomas More Street, E1W 1YZ. *T:* (020) 7265 2400, *Fax:* (020) 7265 2444. *E:* adam.brett-smith@corneyandbarrow.com. *Clubs:* Brooks's, Groucho, Pitt.

BRETTEN, George Rex; QC 1980; barrister-at-law; *b* 21 Feb. 1942; *s* of Horace Victor Bretten and Kathleen Edna Betty Bretten; *m* 1965, Maureen Gillian Crowhurst; one *d. Educ:* King Edward VII Sch., King's Lynn; Sidney Sussex Coll., Cambridge (MA, LLM). Lectr, Nottingham Univ., 1964–68; Asst Director, Inst. of Law Research and Reform, Alberta, Canada, 1968–70; called to the Bar, Lincoln's Inn, 1965, a Bencher 1989; in practice, 1971–2013. *Publications:* Special Reasons, 1977. *Recreations:* gardening, walking, tennis. *Address:* Sundial House, Weston Road, Edith Weston, Rutland LE15 8HQ. *T:* (01780) 729282. *Club:* Athenæum.

BREW, David Allan; Head of Fisheries (formerly Head of Sea Fisheries), Marine Scotland, 2009–11; *b* 19 Feb. 1953; *s* of Kenneth Frederick Cecil Brew and Iris May (*née* Sharpe). *Educ:* Kettering Grammar Sch.; Heriot-Watt Univ. (BA 1st Cl. Hons 1974; Pres., Students' Assoc., 1974–75); Univ. of Strathclyde (MSc 1976); European Univ. Inst., Florence. Scottish Office, 1979–81; Adminr, Directorate-Gen. V, EC, Brussels, 1981–84; Scottish Office: Principal, Glasgow, 1984–88, Edinburgh, 1988–90; Head: Electricity Privatisation Div., 1990–91; Eur. Funds and Co-ordination Div., 1991–95; Sea Fisheries Div., 1995–98; Devolution Team, Constitution Secretariat, Cabinet Office, 1998–2000; Chief Exec., ICAS, 2000–03; Hd, Cultural Policy Div., Scottish Exec., 2004–06; Hd, Rural Communities Div., Scottish Exec., then Scottish Govt, 2006–09. Mem. Bd, MG Alba, 2012–; Public Mem., Network Rail, 2012–. Member: Court, Heriot-Watt Univ., 1985–91, 2000–06; Bd, Robert Gordon Univ., 2012–. *Publications:* (contrib.) Changing Patterns of Relations between the National Parliaments and the European Parliament, 1979; (contrib.) European Electoral Systems Handbook, 1979; (contrib.) The European Parliament: towards a uniform procedure for direct elections, 1981. *Recreations:* languages, music, film, gastronomy. *Address:* 1 Dundas Street, Edinburgh EH3 6QG. *T:* (0131) 556 4692.

BREW, Richard Maddock, CBE 1982; DL; Chairman, Budget Boilers Ltd, 1984–93; *b* 13 Dec. 1930; *s* of late Leslie Maddock Brew and Phyllis Evelyn Huntsman; *m* 1953, Judith Anne, *d* of late P. E. Thompson Hancock, FRCP; two *s* two *d. Educ:* Rugby Sch.; Magdalene Coll., Cambridge (BA). Called to the Bar, Inner Temple, 1955. After practising for short time at the Bar, joined family business, Brew Brothers Ltd, SW7, 1955, and remained until takeover, 1972. Chm., Monks Dormitory Ltd, 1979–93; Regl Dir, Lloyds Bank, 1988–91. Mem., NE Thames RHA, 1982–90 (Vice-Chm., 1982–86); Chm., Tower Hamlets DHA, 1990–93. Farms in Essex. Member: Royal Borough of Kensington Council, 1959–65; Royal Borough of Kensington and Chelsea Council, 1964–70; Greater London Council: Mem., 1968–86; Alderman, 1968–73; Vice-Chm., Strategic Planning Cttee, 1969–71; Chm., Covent Garden Jt Development Cttee, 1970–71 and Environmental Planning Cttee, 1971–73; Mem. for Chingford, 1973–86; Dep. Leader of Council and Leader, Policy and Resources Cttee, 1977–81; Dep. Leader, Cons. Party and Opposition Spokesman on Finance, 1981–82; Leader of the Opposition, 1982–83. Mem., Nat. Theatre Bd, 1982–86. Mem., Pony Club Council, 1975–93. High Sheriff, Greater London, 1988–89. DL Greater London, 1989. *Recreations:* hunting, gardening. *Address:* Holm Close, Kilton, Somerset TA5 1ST. *T:* (01278) 741293. *Clubs:* Carlton, MCC.

BREWER, Sir David (William), Kt 2007; CMG 1999; CVO 2015; JP; Lord-Lieutenant of Greater London, 2008–15; Chair of Council, St Paul's Cathedral, since 2015; Vice-President, GB-China Centre, since 2004 (Chairman, 1997–2004); Lord Mayor of London, 2005–06; *b* 28 May 1940; *s* of Dr H. F. Brewer and Elizabeth Brewer (*née* Nickell-Lean); *m* 1985, Tessa Suzanne Mary Jordá (OBE 2015); two *d. Educ:* St Paul's Sch.; Univ. of Grenoble. FCII 1966. Joined Sedgwick Group, 1959: Rep., Japan, 1976–78; Director: Sedgwick Far East Ltd, 1982–99 (Chm., 1993–97); Develt Cos, 1982–98; Sedgwick Internat. Risk Mgt Inc., 1990–99; Chairman: Sedgwick Insce and Risk Mgt Consultants (China) Ltd, 1993–97; Sedgwick Japan Ltd, 1994–97. Dir, Sumitomo Marine & Fire Insce Co. (Europe) Ltd, 1985–98; non-executive Director: Tullett Prebon SITICO (China) Ltd, 2007–; Nat. Bank of Kuwait Internat. Ltd, 2008–; Senior Adviser: Travelex, 2012–14; DealGlobe Ltd, 2014–. UK Business Ambassador, 2010–12. Mem. Bd and Hon. Treas., 1991–2007, Chm., 2007–13, China-Britain Business Council; Chm., Financial Services Cttee, TheCityUK (formerly International Financial Services, London)/China-Britain Business Council, 1993–2013; Chief Advr, Assoc. of Chinese Financial Professionals in UK, 2013–. Pres., City of London Br., IoD, 2008– (Chm., 1999–2008; Life Fellow, 2010); Pres., Insce Inst. of London, 2006–07 (Vice-Pres., 2005–06). Mem., Adv. Council, LSO, 1999–. Pres., City of London Br., RNLI, 2007– (Chm., 1997–2007); Vice-Pres., City of London Sector, BRCS, 1986–. Gov. and Trustee, Sons and Friends of the Clergy, 1993–2015 (Treas., 2008–09; Sen. Treas., 2010–13). Trustee, Daiwa Anglo-Japanese Foundn, 2008–12; Dir, Guildhall Sch. Trust, 1999–. Alderman, City of London, Ward of Bassishaw, 1996–2009 (Mem. Ct of Common Council, 1992–96); Sheriff, City of London, 2002–03; HM Comr of Lieutenancy, City of London, 2005–09; Liveryman: Merchant Taylors' Co., 1968– (Mem., Ct of Assts, 1985–; Master, 2001–02); Mem., Ct of Assts, Blacksmiths' Co., 2007– (Hon. Mem., 2001–07; Prime Warden, 2009–10); Hon. Liveryman: Security Professionals' Co., 2008 (Hon. Freeman, 2003–08); Insurers' Co., 2010. Pres., London Cornish Assoc., 2005–13. JP City of London, 1979. Hon. Bencher, Gray's Inn, 2004–. Hon. FCSI 2006. Hon. DPhil London Metropolitan, 2005; Hon. DSc City, 2006; Hon. LLD Exeter, 2008; Hon. DSc (Econs) London, 2008; Hon. DLaws Nottingham, 2013. Magnolia Gold Award, Mayor of Shanghai, 2006; Order of the Rising Sun (Japan), 2006. *Recreations:* music (especially opera and choral music), golf, mechanical gardening, chocolate, paronomasia. *Address:* 16 Cowley Street, SW1P 3LZ. *T:* (020) 7222 5481. *E:* david.brewer@dwbrewer.com; Orchard Cottage, Hellandbridge, Bodmin, Cornwall PL30 4QR. *T:* (01208) 841268. *Clubs:* Garrick, MCC; St Enodoc Golf; New Zealand Golf.

BREWER, Prof. John, PhD; Professor of Applied Sport Science, and Head, School of Sport, Health and Applied Science, St Mary's University, since 2014; *b* Plymouth, 30 Dec. 1961; *s* of Peter and Marguerite Brewer; *m* 1988, Caroline Rule; two *d. Educ:* Knowles Hill Sch.; Loughborough Univ. (BSc, MPhil); Univ. of Bedfordshire (PhD). Head: Human Performance, FA, 1988–93; Lilleshall Human Performance Centre, 1993–2004; Dir, Sports Sci., GlaxoSmithKline, 2004–09; Prof. of Sport and Dir of Sport, Univ. of Bedfordshire, 2009–14. Mem. Bd, UK Anti-Doping, 2009–. Chair: British Handball Assoc., 2008–12; British Ski and Snowboard, 2013–. Mem. Bd, British Univs and Colls Sport, 2011–15. *Publications:* London 2012 Training Guide: Athletics - Track Events, 2010. *Recreations:* running, ski-ing, hiking. *Address:* School of Sport, Health and Applied Science, St Mary's University, Waldegrave Road, Twickenham TW1 4SX. *E:* john.brewer@stmarys.ac.uk.

BREWER, Dame Nicola (Mary), (Dame Nicola Gillham), DCMG 2011 (CMG 2002); PhD; Vice-Provost (International), University College London, since 2014; *b* 14 Nov. 1957; *d* of Trevor James Brewer and late Mary Margaret Eleanor Brewer (*née* Jones); *m* 1991, Geoffrey Charles Gillham, *qv*; one *s* one *d. Educ:* Univ. of Leeds (BA 1980; PhD 1988). Entered FCO, 1983: Second Sec., Mexico City, 1984–87; First Secretary: FCO, 1987–91; (Econ.), Paris, 1991–94; Counsellor: FCO, 1995–98; New Delhi, 1998–2001; Dir, Global Issues, FCO, 2001–02; Dir Gen., Regl Progs, DFID, 2002–04 (on secondment); Dir Gen., Europe, FCO, 2004–07; Chief Exec., Equality and Human Rights Commn, 2007–09; High Comr, S Africa, 2009–13. Mem., Adv. Panel on Judicial Diversity, MoJ, 2009–10. Trustee, Sentebale, 2014–. Hon. Bencher, Middle Temple, 2011. Hon. LLD Leeds, 2009. *Recreations:* reading novels, walking, riding. *Address:* c/o University College London, Gower Street, WC1E 6BT.

BREWER, Richard John, FSA; Research Keeper of Roman Archaeology, Amgueddfa Cymru - National Museum Wales, 2010–13, now Honorary Research Fellow; *b* 23 Oct. 1954; *s* of Kenneth Arthur Brewer and Constance Brewer (*née* Crooks). *Educ:* Birchgrove Primary Sch., Cardiff; Cathays High Sch., Cardiff; Inst. of Archaeol., Univ. of London (BA Hons Archaeol. 1976); City & Guilds (Dip. in Health and Social Care (Level 3) 2013). National Museum of Wales: Res. Asst, 1978–85; Asst Keeper, Roman Archaeol., 1985–96; Keeper of Archaeol. & Numismatics, 1996–2010. Res. Fellow, Sch. of Hist. and Archaeol., Cardiff Univ., 2005–. Chm., Ancient Monuments Adv. Bd for Wales, 2005–10 (Mem., 1997–2010). Mem. Council, 2004–14, and Ed., Britannia, 2009–14, Soc. for Promotion of Roman Studies. Chm., Adv. Cttee, Young Archaeologists' Club, 2002–10. Chm., Diocesan Adv. Cttee, Llandaff, 2011–. FSA 1986. *Publications:* Corpus of Sculpture of the Roman World: Great Britain, Wales, 1986; Caerwent Roman Town, 1993, 3rd edn 2006; Roman Fortresses and Their Legions, 2000; Caerleon and the Roman Army, 2000; The Second Augustan Legion and the Roman Military Machine, 2002; The Romans in Gwent, 2004. *Recreations:* ultra distance and marathon running, crime fiction, travel, Association Football (Cardiff City), tap dancing. *Address:* Department of Archaeology & Numismatics, Amgueddfa Cymru - National Museum Wales, Cathays Park, Cardiff CF10 3NP. *T:* (029) 2057 3247. *E:* richard.brewer@museumwales.ac.uk.

BREWERTON, Prof. Andrew John; Principal, Plymouth Art College, since 2010; Honorary Professor of Fine Art, Shanghai University, since 2000; Chairman, Plymouth Arts Centre, since 2010; *b* 8 Feb. 1958; *s* of Peter John Thomas Brewerton and Jean Patricia Brewerton (*née* Cameron); *m* 1983, Jan Beaver; two *d. Educ:* Wolverhampton Grammar Sch.; Sidney Sussex Coll., Cambridge (R. E. Hentsch Schol.; BA Hons English, MA). Lettore in English, Univ. dell' Aquila, Italy, 1980–82; Glasshouse, Ops, and Prodn Manager, Stuart Crystal, 1984–89; Head of Design and Develt, Dartington Crystal, 1989–94; University of Wolverhampton: Principal Lectr and Hd of Glass, Sch. of Art and Design, 1994–96; Dean, Art and Design, and Prof. of Glass, 1996–2004; Principal, Dartington Coll. of Arts, 2004–08; Director: Plymouth Sch. of Creative Arts Trust, 2012– (Chair, 2012–); GuildHE, 2012– (Vice-Chair, 2013–). Exec. Mem., Council for Higher Educn in Art and Design, 2001–06; Mem., Strategic Adv. Cttee (Business and Community), HEFCE, 2005–08; Bd Mem., Higher Educn Stats Agency, 2006–08; Vice-Chair, Prime Minister's Initiative Higher Educn Adv. Gp, 2006–08. Mem. Council and SW Regl Chm., Arts Council England, 2007–09. Chair, Jury Panel, British Glass Biennale Exhibn, 2004. Chair, Foundn for Higher Educn in Art & Design, 2005– (Trustee, 1999–); Trustee, New Art Gall., Walsall, 1997–2004. *Publications: poetry:* Sirius, 1995; Cade l'uliva, 2003; Raag Leaves for Paresh Chakraborty, 2008; Via, 2010; Glass Tantra: the Art of Loretta H Yang, 2012; contrib. numerous jl articles and catalogue essays on contemporary art. *Recreation:* fresh air. *T:* 07977 462370. *E:* a.j.brewerton@btinternet.com.

BREWIN, Prof. Christopher Ray, PhD; FBA 2012; FBPsS; Professor of Clinical Psychology, University College London, since 1999; Consultant Clinical Psychologist, Camden and Islington NHS Foundation Trust, since 1999; *b* London, 16 Oct. 1953; *s* of Denis and Kathleen Mary Brewin; *m* 1989, Bernice Andrews; one step *s* one step *d. Educ:* Merchant Taylors Sch.; St John's Coll., Oxford (BA; MSc); Sheffield Univ. (PhD 1981). CPsychol; FBPsS 1988. Lectr in Psychol., Leeds Univ., 1980–83; non-clin. scientist, MRC Social Psychiatry Unit, London, 1983–92; Prof. of Psychol., RHUL, 1992–99. Hon. Civilian Consultant Advr in Clin. Psychol. to AMS, 2010–. Trustee, Centre for Study of Emotion and Law, 2007–. FAcSS (AcSS 2001). *Publications:* Cognitive Foundations of Clinical Psychology, 1988; Post-traumatic Stress Disorder: malady or myth?, 2003. *Recreations:* duplicate bridge, tennis, wine. *Address:* Research Department of Clinical Educational and Health Psychology, University College London, Gower Street, WC1E 6BT.

BREWSTER, (Elsie) Yvonne, OBE 1993; Artistic Director, Talawa Theatre Co., 1986–2003; *b* 7 Oct. 1938; *d* of Claude Noel Clarke and Kathleen Vanessa Clarke; *m* 1st, 1961, John Roger Francis Jones (marr. diss. 1965); 2nd, 1971, Starr Edmund Francis Home Brewster; one *s. Educ:* Rose Bruford Coll. of Speech and Drama (Dip.; Fellow, 2004); LRAM. Stage, TV and radio actress, 1960–; theatre, film, TV and radio director, 1965–. Drama Officer, Arts Council of GB, 1982–84. Mem., London Arts Bd, 1993–99; Trustee, Theatres Trust, 1992–; Patron, Rose Bruford Coll., 1994–. Non-executive Director, Riverside Mental Health NHS Trust, 1994–99; Kensington, Chelsea, Westminster and Brent NHS Trust, 1999–2001. Juror, Commonwealth Writers' Prize, 2005. Fellow: Rose Bruford Coll., 2004; Central Sch. of Speech and Drama, 2005. FRSA 1992. DUniv Open, 2002. *Publications:* Black Plays, Vol. 1, 1987, Vol. 2, 1989, Vol. 3, 1995; The Undertaker's Daughter (autobiog.), 2004; (ed) For The Reckord: a collection of plays by Barry Reckord, 2010; (ed) Mixed Company: three early Jamaican plays, 2012. *Recreations:* reading, London. *Address:* 41 Dyne Road, NW6 7XG. *T:* (020) 7328 9306.

BREWSTER, Richard Philip; Executive Director, National Center on Nonprofit Enterprise, Alexandria, USA, since 2003; *b* 25 May 1952; *s* of Peter and Patricia Brewster; *m* 1975, Lindy Udale; three *s* one *d. Educ:* Leeds Grammar Sch.; Trinity Coll., Oxford (BA Hons). ICI, 1976–86: Sales Rep., 1976–79; Product Manager, 1979–81; Purchasing Manager, 1981–83; Marketing Manager, 1983–86; Nat. Appeals Manager, Oxfam, 1986–89; Dir of Mkting, Spastics Soc., then Scope, 1989–95; Chief Exec., Scope, 1995–2003. *Recreations:* arts, watching sport. *Address:* 10717 Oldfield Drive, Reston, VA 20191, USA.

BREWSTER, Yvonne; *see* Brewster, E. Y.

BREYER, Stephen Gerald; Associate Justice, Supreme Court of the United States, since 1994; *b* 15 Aug. 1938; *s* of Irving Breyer and Anne (*née* Roberts); *m* 1967, Joanna Hare; one *s* two *d. Educ:* Stanford Univ. (AM 1959); Magdalen Coll., Oxford (Marshall Schol.; BA 1st Cl. Hons PPE 1961; Hon Fellow 1995); Harvard Law Sch. (LLB 1964). Law Clerk, US Supreme Court, 1964–65; Special Asst to Asst Attorney Gen., US Dept of Justice, 1965–67; Harvard University: Asst Prof. of Law, 1967–70; Prof. of Law, Harvard Law Sch., 1970–80; Lectr, 1981–; Prof., Kennedy Sch. of Govt, 1977–80; Asst Special Prosecutor, Watergate Special Prosecution Force, 1973; US Court of Appeals for First Circuit: Circuit Judge, 1980–94; Chief Judge, 1990–94. US Senate Judiciary Committee: Special Counsel, Admin. Practices Subcttee, 1974–75; Chief Counsel, 1979–80; Mem., US Sentencing Commn, 1985–89. Vis. Lectr, Coll. of Law, Sydney, Aust., 1975; Vis. Prof., Univ. of Rome, 1993. Fellow: Amer. Acad. of Arts and Scis; Amer. Bar Foundn. *Publications:* (with P. MacAvoy) The Federal Power Commission and the Regulation of Energy, 1974; (with R. Stewart) Administrative Law and Regulatory Policy, 1979, 3rd edn 1992; Regulation and its Reform, 1982; Breaking the Vicious Circle: toward effective risk regulation, 1993; contrib. chapters in books; numerous articles in law jls and reviews. *Address:* Supreme Court Building, One First Street NE, Washington, DC 20543–0001, USA. *T:* (202) 4793000.

BRIAULT, Clive Bramwell; Managing Director, Risk and Regulation Consulting Ltd, since 2008; *b* 19 Sept. 1957. *Educ:* Merton Coll., Oxford (BA PPE 1978); Nuffield Coll., Oxford (MPhil Econs 1980). Bank of England, 1980–98; FSA, 1998–2008, Man. Dir, Retail Markets, 2004–08.

BRICE, (Ann) Nuala, OBE 2011; PhD; a Judge of the Upper Tribunal and of the Tax Chamber of the First Tier Tribunal, 2009 (Special Commissioner of Taxes, 1999–2009 (Deputy Special Commissioner, 1992–99)); Chairman, VAT and Duties Tribunals (formerly VAT Tribunals), 1999–2009 (part-time Chairman, 1992–99)); Chairman: Financial Services and Markets Tribunal, 2001–09; Pensions Regulator Tribunal, 2005–09; Claims Management Services Tribunal, 2007–09; *d* of William Connor and Rosaleen Gertrude Connor; *m* 1963, Geoffrey James Barrington Groves Brice, QC (*d* 1999); one *s*. *Educ:* Loreto Convent, Manchester; University Coll. London. LLB (Hons), LLM 1976, PhD 1982, London. Admitted Solicitor of the Supreme Court, 1963 (Stephen Heelis Gold Medal and John Peacock Conveyancing Prize, 1963). The Law Society: Asst Solicitor, 1963; Asst Sec., 1964; Sen. Asst Sec., 1973; Deptl Sec., 1982; Asst Sec.-Gen., 1987–92. Sec., Revenue Law Cttee, 1972–82. Vis. Associate Prof. of Law, Tulane Univ., 1990–99; Vis. Prof. of Law, Univ. of Natal, 1999. MRI 1965. Hon. FIIT 2010. *Recreations:* reading, music, gardening.

BRICKELL, Christopher David, CBE 1991; VMH 1976; Director General, Royal Horticultural Society, 1985–93; *b* 29 June 1932; *s* of Bertram Tom Brickell and Kathleen Alice Brickell; *m* 1963, Jeanette Scargill Flecknoe; two *d*. *Educ:* Queen's College, Taunton; Reading Univ. (BSc Horticulture). Joined Royal Horticultural Society Garden, Wisley, 1958: Asst Botanist, 1958; Botanist, 1960; Sen. Scientific Officer, 1964; Dep. Dir, 1968; Dir, 1969–85. Chm., Internat. Commn for the Nomenclature of Cultivated Plants, 1980–. Pres., Internat. Soc. for Horticl Sci., 1998–2002. George Robert White Medal of Honor, Mass Hort. Soc., 1988; Inst. of Horticulture Award, 1997; Life Time Achievement Award, Garden Media Guild, 2014. *Publications:* Daphne: the genus in cultivation, 1976; Pruning, 1979, reissued as Pruning and Training, 2011; The Vanishing Garden, 1986; An English Florilegium, 1987; (ed and contrib.) The Gardener's Encyclopaedia of Plants and Flowers, 1989, 5th edn 2010; (ed and contrib.) The RHS Encyclopaedia of Gardening, 1992, 4th edn 2012; Garden Plants, 1995; (ed and contrib.) The RHS A-Z of Garden Plants, 1996, 4th edn 2016; botanical papers in Flora Europaea, European Garden Flora, and Flora of Turkey; horticultural and botanical papers in RHS Jl, The New Plantsman and Alpine Garden Soc. Bulletin. *Recreation:* gardening. *Address:* The Camber, The Street, Nutbourne, Pulborough, West Sussex RH20 2HE.

BRIDEN, Prof. James Christopher, PhD, DSc; FGS; Professor of Environmental Studies and Director of the Environmental Change Institute, University of Oxford, 1997–2003, now Professor Emeritus; Fellow, Linacre College, Oxford, 1997–2003, now Fellow Emeritus; *b* 30 Dec. 1938; *s* of late Henry Charles Briden and Gladys Elizabeth (*née* Jefkins); *m* 1968, Caroline Mary (*née* Gillmore); one *s* one *d*. *Educ:* Royal Grammar Sch., High Wycombe; St Catherine's Coll., Oxford (MA); ANU (PhD 1965; DSc 1994). FGS 1962; CGeol 1990. Research Fellow: Univ. of Rhodesia, 1965–66; Univ. of Oxford, 1966–67; Univ. of Birmingham, 1967–68; University of Leeds: Lectr, 1968–73; Reader, 1973–75; Prof. of Geophysics, 1975–86; Head, Dept of Earth Sciences, 1976–79 and 1982–85; Dir of Earth Scis, NERC, 1986–94; Vis. Prof. (NERC Res. Prof.), Univ. of Oxford, 1994–96. Canadian Commonwealth Fellow and Vis. Prof., Univ. of Western Ontario, 1979–80; Hon. Prof., Leeds Univ., 1986–94. Mem., NERC, 1981–86; Chairman: Jt Assoc. for Geophysics, 1981–84 (Chm., Founding Cttee, 1978–79); Exec. Cttee, Ocean Drilling Prog., 1994–96; Member: Science and Engrg (formerly Science) Cttee, British Council, 1990–96; Governing Council, Internat. Seismol Centre, 1978–83; Council: Eur. Geophysical Soc., 1976–84; RAS, 1978–79 (FRAS 1962); Geol Soc., 1992–95. Fellow, Amer. Geophysical Union, 1994. Murchison Medal, Geol Soc., 1984. Editor, Earth and Planetary Science Letters, 1971–97; Ed.-in-chief, Envmtl Sci. and Policy, 2001–10. *Publications:* (with A. G. Smith) Mesozoic and Cenozoic Palaeocontinental World Maps, 1977; (with A. G. Smith and A. M. Hurley) Phanerozoic Palaeocontinental World Maps, 1981; over 90 papers on palaeomagnetism, palaeoclimates, tectonics and aspects of geophysics. *Recreations:* music- and theatre-going, gentle walking, bad golf, mild gardening. *Address:* Stoneleigh House, 1 Paternoster Court, Cassington Road, Yarnton, Oxon OX5 1QB.

BRIDEN, Timothy John; Vicar-General, Province of Canterbury, since 2005; *b* 29 Oct. 1951; *s* of Thomas Dan Briden, MA, DPA and Joan Briden (*née* Garratt); *m* 1989, Susanne. *Educ:* Ipswich Sch.; Downing Coll., Cambridge (BA 1974, MA 1978; LLB 1975). Called to the Bar, Inner Temple, 1976; Chancellor: Dio. Bath and Wells, 1993–; Dio. Truro, 1998–; Dep. Chancellor, Dio. Bristol, 2004–. Mem., Legal Adv. Commn, Gen. Synod of C of E, 1986–. Chm., Ecclesiastical Judges Assoc., 2008– (Sec., 1997–2008). Pres., Old Ipswichian Club, 2010. Ed., Macmorran's Handbook for Church Wardens and Parochial Church Councillors, 1989–. *Publications:* (ed) Moore's Introduction to English Canon Law, 4th edn 2013. *Address:* Lamb Chambers, Elm Court, Temple, EC4Y 7AS. *T:* (020) 7797 8300, *Fax:* (020) 7797 8308.

BRIDGE, Beverley Jane; *see* Glover, B. J.

BRIDGE, Dame Jill; *see* Macleod Clark, Dame J.

BRIDGE, John Neville, PhD; Chairman: Endeavour-SCH plc, 2001–11; Agricultural and Horticultural Development Board (formerly Levy Board (UK)), 2006–11; *b* 18 Sept. 1942; *s* of Tom and Eunice Bridge; *m* 1966, Rosalind Forrester; one *s* one *d*. *Educ:* Lancaster Royal Grammar Sch.; Durham Univ. (BA Geog. 1964; PhD Econs 1974); Indiana Univ. (MA Econs 1965). Lectr in Econs and Fellow, Centre for Middle Eastern and Islamic Studies, 1966–74; Hd of Industrial Develt, N of England Develt Council, 1975–84; Chief Executive: Yorks and Humberside Develt Agency, 1984–88; Northern Develt Co., 1988–98; Chm., One Northeast, 1998–2003. Consultant, PricewaterhouseCoopers, 2004–07. Non-executive Director: Tanfield Gp (formerly Comeleon) plc, 2001–12; Kenmore (UK) Ltd, 2001–05; Watson Burton LLP, 2004–06. Member: Bd, English Partnerships, 2000–03; Urban Sounding Bd, 2001–03; Bd, UK Trade and Investment, 2001–03; Treas. Adv. Council, Partnerships UK, 2001–03; Rural Climate Change Forum, 2008–11. Chairman: Northern Sights, 1996–2012; Council, Durham Cathedral, 2001–11; NE Seedcorn Fund, 2001–04; Alnwick Garden Trust, 2003–10; Yorks and NE Reg., Nat. Trust, 2003–12; Land Restoration Trust, 2004–10; Calvert Trust Kielder, 2004–09; Spirit of Enterprise Trust, 2004–09; Durham Local Educn Partnership, 2010–; Bradford Local Educn Partnership, 2011–13; Integrated Bradford SPV1 Ltd, 2011–13; Integrated Bradford SPV2 Ltd, 2011–13; S Tyneside and Gateshead Local Educn Partnership, 2013–; Mem. Bd, Community Ventures, 2014–. Consultant, Northumbrian Leisure, 2007–. Res. Fellow, Smith Inst., 2009–; Mem., Food Res. Partnership, 2009–11. Visiting Professor: Newcastle Business Sch., 1996–; Durham Univ. Business Sch., 1998–. Member: Adv. Bd, Durham Business Sch., 2003–08; Hatfield Coll. Council and Trust, 2006–. Hon. Fellow, Univ. of Sunderland, 1993. Hon. DCL: Durham, 2005; Northumbria, 2005. *Recreations:* walking, gardening, travel. *Address:* 3 Chains Drive, Corbridge, Northumberland NE45 5BP. *T:* (01434) 634740. *E:* john@bridgedev.co.uk. *Club:* Reform.

BRIDGE, Keith James, CBE 1997; consultant; *b* 21 Aug. 1929; *s* of late James Henry Bridge and Lilian Elizabeth (*née* Nichols); *m* 1960, Thelma Ruby (*née* Hubble); three *d* (and one *s* decd). *Educ:* Sir George Monoux Grammar Sch., Walthamstow; Corpus Christi Coll., Oxford (MA); Univ. of Hull (BTh 2001). CIPFA 1959; CCMI (CBIM 1978). Local govt service, 1953; Dep. City Treasurer, York, 1965; Borough Treas., Bolton, 1967; City Treas., Manchester, 1971; County Treasurer, Greater Manchester Council, 1973; Chief Exec., Humberside CC, 1978–83. Mem., W Yorks Residuary Body, 1985–91. Financial Adviser to Assoc. of Metrop. Authorities, 1971–78; Mem. Council, 1972–84, Pres., 1982–83, Chartered Inst. of Public Finance and Accountancy; Pres., Soc. of Metropolitan Treasurers, 1977–78. Member: Audit Commn for Local Authorities in Eng. and Wales, 1983–86; Exec. Council, Business in the Community, 1982–84; Bd, Public Finance Foundn, 1984–90; Educn Transfer Council (formerly Educn Assets Bd), 1988–2000 (Chm., 1996–2000); Football Licensing Authy, 1990–96. Dir, Phillips & Drew, 1987–89. Chm., York Diocesan Pastoral Cttee, 1989–94. Governor: Univ. of Lincolnshire and Humberside (formerly Humberside Poly.), 1989–98; E Yorks Coll., 2000–01. Hon. LLD Lincs and Humberside, 1999. Freeman, City of London, 1986. *Publications:* papers in professional jls. *Recreations:* gardening, literature, music. *Address:* 1 Fairlawn, Molescroft, Beverley, E Yorks HU17 7DD. *T:* (01482) 887652.

BRIDGE, Prof. Michael Greenhalgh, FBA 2013; Cassel Professor of Commercial Law, London School of Economics, since 2009 (Professor of Law, 2007–09); Professor of Law, National University of Singapore, since 2013; *b* 3 Nov. 1947; *s* of Louis and Sarah Bridge; *m* 1971, Rowena Austin; one *s* one *d*. *Educ:* LSE (LLB 1969; LLM 1970). Called to the Bar, Middle Temple, 1975, Bencher, 2014; Associate Prof., 1977–86, Prof. of Law, 1987–88, McGill Univ., Montreal; Hind Prof. of Commercial Law, Univ. of Nottingham, 1988–2000; Prof. of Commercial Law, UCL, 2001–07. *Publications:* Sales and Sales Financing in Canada, 1981; Sale of Goods, 1988, 3rd edn as The Sale of Goods, 2014; (jtly) The Companies Act 1989, 1989; Personal Property Law, 1993, 3rd edn 2002; The International Sale of Goods, 1999, 3rd edn 2013; (with R. Stevens) Cross-Border Security and Insolvency, 2001; (jtly) International Sale of Goods in the Conflict of Laws, 2005; (jtly) Personal Property Security, 2007, new edn as The Law of Security and Title-Based Financing, 2012; (gen. ed.) Benjamin's Sale of Goods, 8th edn 2010, 9th edn 2014; (jtly) The Law of Personal Property, 2013. *Recreations:* travel, wine, music (opera, orchestral, chamber), art. *Address:* Department of Law, London School of Economics, Houghton Street, WC2A 2AE. *T:* (020) 7955 6255, *Fax:* (020) 7955 7366. *E:* m.g.bridge@lse.ac.uk.

BRIDGE, Stuart Nigel; His Honour Judge Bridge; a Circuit Judge, since 2012; *b* 12 Aug. 1958; *s* of Albert and Nora Bridge; *m* 1st, 1982, Anabelle Jane Baker (marr. diss. 2001); one *s* one *d*; 2nd, 2003, Prof. Beverley Jane Glover, *qv*; one *s* one *d*. *Educ:* Lawnswood Sch., Leeds; Queens' Coll., Cambridge (BA 1980, MA 1984). Called to the Bar, Middle Temple, 1981, Bencher, 2009; Recorder, 2004–12; Lecturer in Law: Univ. of Leeds, 1985–89; Univ. of Cambridge, 1990–2012; Fellow, Queens' Coll., Cambridge, 1990–2012, now Life Fellow; a Law Comr, 2001–08; Vis. Prof., Cornell Law Sch., 1994. *Publications:* Residential Leases, 1994; Assured Tenancies, 1999; (ed) Theobald on Wills, 16th edn 2001; (jtly) Megarry and Wade's Law of Real Property, 7th edn 2008, 8th edn 2012; (jtly) Snell's Equity, 33rd edn 2014. *Recreations:* walking, football, music, literature, gardening, family and other animals. *Address:* Luton Crown Court, 7 George Street, Luton, Beds LU1 2AA.

BRIDGE, Timothy John Walter; DL; Chairman, Greene King plc, since 2005; *b* 1 Feb. 1949; *s* of late Walter John Blencowe Bridge and Susan Mary Bridge (*née* Rushbrooke). *Educ:* Twyford Sch.; Repton Sch.; Univ. of Exeter (BA). Joined Greene King plc, 1970: Dir, 1977–; Man. Dir, 1990–94; Chief Exec., 1994–2005. Non-executive Director: Weatherbys Ltd (formerly Weatherbys Ventures Ltd), 2006–10; William Ransom & Son plc, 2006–10; Chm., Didlington Fisheries Ltd, 2007–. Pres., Gentlemen of Suffolk CC, 1996–. DL Suffolk, 2004. *Recreations:* fishing, shooting, racing. *Address:* Priory Farm, Shudy Camps, Cambs CB21 4RE.

BRIDGEMAN, family name of **Earl of Bradford** and **Viscount Bridgeman**.

BRIDGEMAN, 3rd Viscount *cr* 1929, of Leigh; **Robin John Orlando Bridgeman,** CA; *b* 5 Dec. 1930; *s* of Hon. Geoffrey John Orlando Bridgeman, MC, FRCS (*d* 1974) (2nd *s* of 1st Viscount) and Mary Meriel Gertrude Bridgeman (*d* 1974), *d* of Rt Hon. Sir George John Talbot; *S* uncle, 1982; *m* 1966, (Victoria) Harriet Lucy Turton (*see* V. H. L. Bridgeman); three *s* (and one *s* decd). *Educ:* Eton. CA 1958. 2nd Lieut, Rifle Bde, 1950–51. Partner: Fenn & Crosthwaite, 1973; Henderson Crosthwaite & Co., 1975–86; Director: Nestor-BNA plc, 1988–94; Guinness Mahon & Co. Ltd, 1988–90; Chm., Asset Management Investment Co. plc, 1994–2001. Opposition Whip, H of L, 1999–2010; elected Mem., H of L, 1999. Dir, Bridgeman Art Library Ltd, 1972–; Chm., Friends of Lambeth Palace Liby, 1992–2008. Chairman: Hosp. of St John and St Elizabeth, 1999–2007; CORESS, 2006–12; Special Trustee, Hammersmith Hosp., 1986–99; Treasurer, Florence Nightingale Aid in Sickness Trust, 1995–2006. Trustee, Music at Winchester, 1995–2006. Gov., Reed's Sch., 1994–2002 (Chm.; Jt Life Pres., 2002). Mem. Court, New England Co., 1986– (Treas., 1996–2007). *Recreations:* music, gardening, shooting. *Heir:* *s* Hon. Luke Robinson Orlando Bridgeman [*b* 1 May 1971; *m* 1996, Victoria Rose, *y d* of late Henry Frost; two *s* one *d*]. *Address:* 19 Chepstow Road, W2 5BP. *T:* (020) 7727 5400; Watley House, Sparsholt, Winchester SO21 2LU. *T:* (01962) 776297. *Clubs:* Beefsteak, MCC; Pitt.

BRIDGEMAN, John Stuart, CBE 2001; TD 1995; DL; Chairman, Recovery Career Services, since 2014; *b* 5 Oct. 1944; *s* of late James Alfred George Bridgeman, Master Mariner, and Edith Celia (*née* Watkins); *m* 1967, Lindy Jane Fillmore; three *d*. *Educ:* Whitchurch Sch., Cardiff; University Coll., Swansea (BSc) (Hon. Fellow, Univ. of Wales, Swansea, 1997); McGill Univ., Montreal. Alcan Inds, 1966–69; Aluminium Co. of Canada, 1969–70; Alcan Australia, 1970; Commercial Dir, Alcan UK, 1977–80; Vice-Pres. (Europe), Alcan Basic Raw Materials, 1978–82; Dir, Saguenay Shipping, 1979–82; Divl Man. Dir, Alcan Aluminium (UK) Ltd, 1981–82; Managing Director: Extrusion Div., Brit. Alcan Aluminium plc, 1983–87; Brit. Alcan Enterprises, 1987–91; Chm., Luxfer Hldgs, 1988–91; Dir, Corporate Planning, Alcan Aluminium Ltd, Montreal, 1992–93; Man. Dir, British Alcan Aluminium plc, 1993–95; Dir-Gen. of Fair Trading, 1995–2000; Chm., GPC Europe, 2000–01; Dir, Regulatory Impact Unit, Cardew & Co., 2001–03. Chm., HRA, 2005–07 (Chm., Regulatory Cttee, 2006–07); Regulatory Dir, 2008–12, Pension Fund Trustee, 2009–, British Horseracing Authy; Member: British Airways NE Consumer Council, 1978–86; Monopolies and Mergers Commn, 1990–95; Adv. Council, Consumer Policy Inst., 2000–04; Canal and River Trust (formerly British Waterways): Mem. Bd, 2006–12, Vice Chm., 2009–12; Pension Trustee, 2007–14; Chm., Fair Trading Cttee, 2007–12; Chm., Audit Cttee, 2007–14; Mem., Ombudsman Cttee, 2007–; Chm., Wales Adv. Gp, 2008–12; Trustee, 2011–14. Ind. Appeals Comr, Direct Marketing Authy, 2007– (Chm., 2000–06); Ind. Complaints Adjudicator, Assoc. for Television On-Demand, 2007–11. Vis. Prof. of Mgt, Keele Univ., 1992–2011; Vis. Prof., Univ. of Surrey, 2004–07. Ind. Consultant in corporate governance, competition policy and consumer affairs, 2000–. Vice-President: Aluminium Fedn, 1995; Trading Standards Inst., 2001–. Chairman: N Oxon Business Gp, 1984–92; Enterprise Cherwell Ltd, 1985–91; Oxfordshire Economic Partnership, 2000–06; Dir, Heart of England TEC, 1989–2002 (Chm., 2000–02). Chm., Audit and Standards Cttee, Warwicks CC, 2000–. Chm., Regulatory Cttee, Jockey Club, 2005–06. Commnd TA and Reserve Forces, 1978; QOY, 1981–84; Maj. REME (V), 1985–94; Staff Coll., 1986; SO2 Employer Support SE Dist, 1994–95. Hon. Col, 5 (QOOH) Sqdn, 39 (Skinners), later 31 (City of London) Signal Regt (V), 1996–2009; Hon. Col, Queen's Own Oxfordshire Hussars, 1996–. Mem., TAVRA Oxon and E Wessex, 1985–2000. Member: Defence Science Adv. Council, 1991–94; Nat. Employer Liaison Cttee for Reserve Forces, 1992–2002 (Chm., 1998–2002); SE RFCA, 2001–11. Member: UK-Canada Colloquium, 1993– (Treas., 2005); UK-Canada Chamber of Commerce, 1993–2007 (Vice-Pres., 1995–96; Pres., 1997–98); Canada Club, 1994–. Gov., N Oxon Coll., 1985–99 (Chm., 1989; Vice Chm., 1997–99). Trustee: Oxfordshire Community Foundn, 1995–2002; Oxford Orch. da Camera, 1996–2001; Foundn for Canadian Studies, 1996–2010 (Vice-Chm., 2005–06; Chm., 2007–10); Oxfordshire Yeomanry Trust, 1997–; Soldiers of Oxfordshire Trust, 2010–; Chm., Oxfordshire Yeomanry Assoc., 2008–. Chm. Trustees, Banbury Sunshine Centre, 2002–. Pres., Oxfordshire Gliding Club, 1998–2009. CCMI; FInstD, FRGS, FRSA. Master, Turners' Co., 2014–15 (Liveryman, 2000; Court Asst, 2004–12). DL Oxon, 1989; High Sheriff, Oxon, 1995–96.

Hon. Dr Sheffield Hallam, 1996. US Aluminium Assoc. Prize, 1988. *Recreations:* military history, inland waterways, equestrian sports, gardening, family history, ski-ing, shooting. *Clubs:* Reform, MCC; Glamorgan County Cricket.

BRIDGEMAN, Mrs June, CB 1990; Deputy Chair, Equal Opportunities Commission, 1991–94; *b* 26 June 1932; *d* of Gordon and Elsie Forbes; *m* 1958, (John) Michael Bridgeman, CB (*d* 2013); one *s* four *d*. *Educ:* variously, England and Scotland; Westfield Coll., London Univ. (BA; Fellow, QMW, 1993–2001). Asst Principal, BoT, 1954; subseq. served in DEA, NBPI, Min. of Housing and Local Govt, DoE; Under Secretary: DoE 1974–76; Central Policy Review Staff, Cabinet Office, 1976–79; Dept of Transport, 1979–90. Mem., BSE Inquiry, 1998–2000. Mem., Central Bd of Finance, C of E, 1979–83; Bishops Selector for ACCM, 1974–89. Member of Council: PSI, 1984–90; NCOPF, 1994–2001; GDST (formerly GPDST), 1995–2002. Vice-Pres., Fawcett Soc., 1994–. Trustee, Rees Jeffreys Road Fund, 1992–2008. FRSA 1991. *Recreations:* assisting and representing local voluntary organisations, local history and heritage research projects and publications. *Address:* Bridge House, Culverden Park Road, Tunbridge Wells TN4 9QX. *T:* (01892) 525578.

BRIDGEMAN, (Victoria) Harriet Lucy, (Viscountess Bridgeman), CBE 2014; Founder and Chairman: Bridgeman Art Library, since 1972; Artists' Collecting Society, since 2006; *b* Low Middleton Hall, Co. Durham, 30 March 1942; *d* of Ralph Meredyth Turton and Mary Turton; *m* 1966, Robin John Orlando Bridgeman (*see* Viscount Bridgeman); three *s* (and one *s* decd). *Educ:* private educn with governess; Darlington High Sch., Co. Durham; St Mary's Sch., Wantage; Trinity Coll., Dublin (MA). Exec. Ed., The Master, 1966–68; Ed., Discovering Antiques, 1968–70. Founder Mem., British Assoc. of Picture Libraries and Agencies; Mem., British Copyright Council, 2010–. Trustee, British Sporting Art Trust, 2005–; Mem., Art Cttee, Imperial Healthcare Trust. FRSA. Eur. Women of Year Award (Arts Section), 1997; Internat. Business Women of Year, 2005; Alumni Award, TCD, 2010. *Publications:* with Elizabeth Drury: The Encyclopedia of Victoriana, 1975; Society Scandals, 1977; Needlework: an illustrated history, 1978; Guide to Gardens of Britain and Europe, 1979; Visiting the Gardens of Europe, 1979; The Last Word, 1982. *Recreations:* reading, family, travelling. *Address:* 19 Chepstow Road, W2 5BP. *T:* (home) (020) 7727 5400, (work) (020) 7727 4065. *E:* harriet@bridgemanimages.com. *Club:* Chelsea Arts.

BRIDGEN, Andrew; MP (C) North West Leicestershire, since 2010; *b* Burton upon Trent, Staffs, 28 Oct. 1964; *s* of Alan and Ann Bridgen; *m* 2000, Jacqueline Cremin (marr. diss. 2014); two *s*. *Educ:* Pingle Sch., Swadlincote; Nottingham Univ. (BSc Biol Scis 1986). Officer trng, RM, 1987–88; Officer, Staffords (TA), 1989–91. Non-exec. Chm., AB Produce plc, 2010–14 (Man. Dir, 1988–2010). Business Mem., E Midlands Regl Assembly, 1999–2000. Mem., Regulatory Reform Select Cttee, 2010–15. *Address:* House of Commons, SW1A 0AA.

BRIDGER, Very Rev. Dr Francis William; Rector, St Mary's, Broughty Ferry, since 2012; Dean of Brechin, since 2013; *b* 27 May 1951; *s* of Harry Edward George Bridger and Harriet Rose Bridger; *m* 1st, 1975, Renee Winifred (*d* 2003); one *s* two *d*; 2nd, 2004, Helen Foster. *Educ:* Pembroke Coll., Oxford (BA 1973; MA 1978); Trinity Coll., Bristol; Bristol Univ. (PhD 1981). Ordained deacon, 1978, priest, 1979; Asst Curate, St Jude, Mildmay Park and St Paul, Canonbury, 1978–82; Lectr and Tutor, St John's Coll., Nottingham, 1982–90; Vicar, St Mark, Woodthorpe, 1990–99; Principal, Trinity Theol Coll., Bristol, 1999–2005; Exec. Dir, Center for Anglican Communion Studies, 2006–12, Prof. of Anglican Studies, 2006–, Fuller Theol Seminary, Calif; Principal, E Midlands Ministry Trng Course, 2009–12. Vis. Prof. of Pastoral Care and Counselling, 1999–2005, of Practical Theol., 2005–06, Fuller Theol Seminary, Calif. Member: Gen. Synod of C of E, 1998–2005; Gen. Synod of Scottish Episcopal Church, 2013–. Theol Advr to Archbishop of Burundi, 2007–10. *Publications:* (ed and contrib.) The Cross and the Bomb, 1983; Videos, Permissiveness and the Law, 1984; Children Finding Faith, 1988, 2nd edn 2000 (trans. French and German 1995); Counselling in Context, 1995, 3rd edn 2005; Celebrating the Family, 1995; Why Can't I have Faith?, 1998; The Diana Phenomenon, 1998; Christian Counselling and the Challenge of Postmodernism, 1999; A Charmed Life: the spirituality of Potterworld, 2001; Opening Windows into Heaven, 2001; 23 Days: a story of love, death and God, 2004; (ed and contrib.) Conversations at the Edges of Things, 2012; contrib. to Tyndale Bull., Anvil, Theology, Jl of Christian Educn, Church Times. *Recreations:* politics, current affairs, media. *Address:* St Mary's Scottish Episcopal Church, Queen Street, Broughty Ferry, Dundee DD5 1AJ.

BRIDGER, Rev. Canon Gordon Frederick; Principal, Oak Hill Theological College, 1987–96; *b* 5 Feb. 1932; *s* of late Dr John Dell Bridger and Hilda Bridger; *m* 1962, Elizabeth Doris Bewes; three *d*. *Educ:* Christ's Hospital, Horsham; Selwyn Coll., Cambridge (MA Hons Theology); Ridley Hall, Cambridge. Curate, Islington Parish Church, 1956–59; Curate, Holy Sepulchre Church, Cambridge, 1959–62; Vicar, St Mary, North End, Fulham, 1962–69; Chaplain, St Thomas's Episcopal Church, Edinburgh, 1969–76; Rector, Holy Trinity Church, Heigham, Norwich, 1976–87; RD Norwich (South), 1981–86; Exam. Chaplain to Bishop of Norwich, 1981–86; Hon. Canon, Norwich Cathedral, 1984–87, now Hon. Canon Emeritus. Dir, Open Theol Coll., 1993–97; Mem. Court, Middlesex Univ., 1996–2000. Trustee, Jerusalem Trust, 1998–2006. Fellow, 1996–98, Associate Fellow, 1999–, Coll. of Preachers. Hon. MA Middlesex, 1996. *Publications:* The Man from Outside, 1969, rev. edn 1978; A Day that Changed the World, 1975; A Bible Study Commentary (I Corinthians—Galatians), 1985; The Message of Obadiah, Nahum and Zephaniah, 2010; reviews in The Churchman, Anvil and other Christian papers and magazines. *Recreations:* music, sport, reading. *Address:* The Elms, 4 Common Lane, Sheringham, Norfolk NR26 8PL.

BRIDGER, Timothy Peter M.; *see* Moore-Bridger.

BRIDGES, family name of **Baron Bridges** and **Baron Bridges of Headley**.

BRIDGES, 2nd Baron *cr* 1957; **Thomas Edward Bridges,** GCMG 1988 (KCMG 1983; CMG 1975); HM Diplomatic Service, retired; *b* 27 Nov. 1927; *s* of 1st Baron Bridges, KG, PC, GCB, GCVO, MC, FRS, and late Hon. Katharine Dianthe, *d* of 2nd Baron Farrer; *S* father, 1969; *m* 1953, Rachel Mary (*d* 2005), *y d* of late Sir Henry Bunbury, KCB; two *s* one *d*. *Educ:* Eton; New Coll., Oxford. Entered Foreign Service, 1951; served in Bonn, Berlin, Rio de Janeiro and at FO (Asst Private Sec. to Foreign Secretary, 1963–66); Head of Chancery, Athens, 1966–68; Counsellor, Moscow, 1969–71; Private Sec. (Overseas Affairs) to Prime Minister, 1972–74; RCDS 1975; Minister (Commercial), Washington, 1976–79; Dep. Under Sec. of State, FCO, 1979–82; Ambassador to Italy, 1983–87. Mem., Select Cttee on Eur. Communities, H of L, 1988–92 and 1994–98; elected Mem., H of L, 1999. Dir, Consolidated Gold Fields, 1988–89. Ind. Bd Mem., Securities and Futures Authority (formerly Securities Assoc.), 1989–97. Chairman: UK Nat. Cttee for UNICEF, 1989–97; British-Italian Soc., 1991–97. Mem., E Anglian Regl Cttee, NT, 1988–97. Trustee, Rayne Foundn, 1995–2010. *Heir:* *s* Hon. Mark Thomas Bridges, *qv*. *Address:* The Old Rectory, Berwick St John, Shaftesbury, Dorset SP7 0EY.

See also Baron Bridges of Headley.

BRIDGES OF HEADLEY, Baron *cr* 2015 (Life Peer), of Headley Heath in the County of Surrey; **James George Robert Bridges,** MBE 1997; Parliamentary Secretary, Cabinet Office, since 2015; *b* Wimbledon, 15 July 1970; *s* of late Hon. Robert Oliver Bridges, *s* of 1st Baron Bridges, and of (Rosamund) Theresa Bridges; *m* 2007, Alice Mary Hickman; one *s* two *d* (incl. twin *s* and *d*). *Educ:* Eton Coll.; Exeter Coll., Oxford (Stapledon Schol.; MA 1st cl. Hist.); Fels Center of Govt, Univ. of Pennsylvania (Thouron Schol.). Cons. Res. Dept, 1992–93; Asst Pol Sec. to Prime Minister, 1994–97; Dir of Communications, British Digital Broadcasting, 1997–98; leader writer, The Times, 1998–2000; Consultant, Quiller Consultants, 2000–04; Chm., Cons. Res. Dept, 2004–05; Campaign Dir, Cons. Part 2006–07; Consultant, Quiller Consultants, 2007–09; Campaign Co-ordinator, Cons. Part 2010; Chief Exec., Quiller Consultants, 2010–13; Sen. Advr to Gp Exec. Chm., Santande 2014–15. Mem. Bd, Centre for Policy Studies, 2007–. Trustee, Foundation Years Trus 2014–. *Recreations:* family, walking, history. *Clubs:* Beefsteak, White's.

See also Baron Bridges.

BRIDGES, Alastair; Director of Finance and Performance, Department for Environmer Food and Rural Affairs, since 2014; *b* London, 1964; *s* of Roy Charles Bridges and J Margaret Bridges; *m* 1997, Melanie Knight; one *s* one *d*. *Educ:* Aberdeen Grammar Sch Univ. of Edinburgh (MA); London Sch. of Econs and Pol Sci. (MSc). CPFA 2010. H Treasury, 1988–2001: various posts incl. Hd, Health Team, 1999–2001; Cabinet Offic 1995–97 (on secondment); Sen. Manager, Corporate Finance, KPMG, Moscow, 1997–9 Home Office, 2001–14: various posts incl. Dir of Finance, Crime and Policing, 2005–09; Di Finance and Corporate Services, HM Passport Office, 2009–14. Hon. Treas., Brook Your People, 2012–. *Recreations:* music, sailing. *Address:* Department for Environment, Food ar Rural Affairs, Nobel House, 17 Smith Square, SW1P 3JR.

BRIDGES, Andrew Michael, CBE 2007; independent advisor on making probation wor since 2014; Associate, G4S Care and Justice, 2011–14; *b* Bath, 2 June 1951; *s* of Michael ar Peggy Bridges; partner, Lesley Corina; two *s*. *Educ:* City of Bath Boys' Sch.; Univ. of Yo (BA Hist. 1972); Univ. of Leicester (DipSW 1975); Bristol Poly. (MA 1984); Univ. of Ba (MPhil 1991). Probation Officer, Wilts, 1975–83; Sen. Probation Officer, Gwent, 1983–8 Asst Chief Probation Officer, 1989–98, Chief Probation Officer, 1998–2001, Berks; H Inspector of Probation, 2001–03; HM Dep. Chief Inspector of Probation, 2003–04; H Chief Inspector of Probation, 2004–11. Res. Fellow (pt-time), Univ. of Oxford, 1996. Chm Interdeptl Nat. Offender Employment Forum, 1998–2001. *Publications:* Increasing th Employability of Offenders: an inquiry into Probation Service effectiveness, 1998. *Recreation* early morning running (slowly), travelling to sometimes unusual destinations, occasional continuing to enjoy the Grateful Dead, persistently using a Reading FC season ticket sinc 1995. *W:* ambridges2.webspace.virginmedia.com.

BRIDGES, Prof. James Wilfrid; Professor of Toxicology and Environmental Healt University of Surrey, 1979–2003, Professor Emeritus, since 2004; *b* 9 Aug. 1938; *s* of Wilfr Edward Seymour Bridges and Mary Winifred Cameron; *m* Olga Vorozhbitova. *Edu* Bromley Grammar Sch.; Queen Elizabeth Coll., London Univ.; St Mary's Hosp. Med. Sch London Univ. (BSc, DSc, PhD). Lectr, St Mary's Hosp. Med. Sch., 1962–68; University Surrey: Senior Lectr then Reader, Dept of Biochemistry, 1968–78; Res. Dir, Robens Inst. Industrial and Envmtl Health and Safety, 1978–95; Dean, Faculty of Science, 1988–92; H European Inst. of Health and Med. Scis, 1995–2000; Dean for Internat. Strategy, 2000–0 Visiting Professor: Univ. of Texas at Dallas, 1973, 1979; Univ. of Rochester, NY, 197 Mexico City, 1991; Sen. Scientist, Nat. Inst. of Envmtl Health Scis, N Carolina, 1976. Chm British Toxicology Soc., 1980–81; First Pres., Fedn of European Toxicology Socs, 1985–8 Member: Vet. Products Cttee, 1982–96; HSE WATCH Cttee, 1982–2005; EC Scientif Cttee on Animal Nutrition, 1991–97; EU Scientific Steering Cttee (Public Health 1997–2004; EU Mirror Gp, 2006–; DG SANCO Scientific Cttee Co-ordination G 2004–13; Expert, DG Res., 2008–; mem. of various EFSA working gps, 2004–; form Member: Novel and Irradiated Foods Cttee; Med. Aspects of Water Quality Cttee; Ad Cttee on Toxic Substances; Chairman: Vet. Residues Cttee, 2001–04; EU Harmonisation Risk Assessment Working Party, 1998–2004; EU Scientific Cttee on Emerging and New Identified Health Risks, 2004–13; IDEA project supervisory gp, 2013–; President: E Scientific Adv. Cttee on Toxicology, Ecotoxicology and the Envmt, 1997–2004; E Scientific Cttee on Emerging and Newly Identified Health Risks, 2004–. Founder, Eur. Dru Metabolism Workshops. Foreign Mem., Spanish Royal Acad. of Veterinary Scis. Ho Member: Soc. of Occupnl Med.; British Toxicol. Soc.; Hon. Fellow, Eur. Soc. of Toxic Hon. DSc Baptist Univ. of Hong Kong. *Publications:* (ed jtly) Progress in Drug Metabolism 10 vols, 1976–88; (with Dr Olga Bridges) Losing Hope: the environment and health in Russi 1996; over 400 research papers and reviews in scientific jls. *Recreations:* theatre going, vario sports. *Address:* Liddington Lodge, Liddington Hall Drive, Guildford GU3 3AE.

BRIDGES, Hon. Mark Thomas, CVO 2012; Private Solicitor to the Queen, since 2002; 25 July 1954; *er s* and *heir* of Baron Bridges, *qv*; *m* 1978, Angela Margaret, *er d* of late Joh Leigh Collinson; one *s* three *d*. *Educ:* Eton Coll.; Corpus Christi Coll., Cambridge (Chor Exhibition). Partner, Farrer & Co., 1985–; Solicitor, Duchy of Lancaster affairs, 1998–201 Mem. Council, RSCM, 1989–97; Treas., Bach Choir, 1992–97; Chm., Music in Count Churches, 2006–; Trustee: UCL Hospitals Charity, 1992–2010; Leeds Castle Foundn, 2007 Chm. Govs, Hanford Sch., 2004–13; Governor: Purcell Sch., 2000–12 (Fellow, 2012 Sherborne Sch. for Girls, 2001–11. Academician, Internat. Acad. of Estate and Trust Law 2005. Mem., Court of Assistants, Goldsmiths' Co., 2006–. *Publications:* (ed) Internation Succession Laws, 2001. *Recreations:* music, sailing. *Address:* Farrer & Co., 66 Lincoln's In Fields, WC2A 3LH. *T:* (020) 3375 7000, *Fax:* (020) 7242 9899. *E:* mark.bridges(farrer.co.uk. *Clubs:* Brooks's, House of Lords Yacht, Noblemen and Gentlemen's Catch.

BRIDGES, Dame Mary (Patricia), DBE 1981; *b* 6 June 1930; *d* of Austin Edward and Le Mabel Fawkes; *m* 1951, Bertram Marsdin Bridges; (one step *s* decd one step *d* decd). Chm Honiton Div. Cons. Assoc., 1968–71; Pres., Western Provincial Area, Nat. Union of Con and Unionist Assocs, 1987–. Women's Section of Royal British Legion: Pres., Exmouth Br 1965–; Chm., Devon County Women's Section, 1979–91; County Vice Pres., 1991; Count Pres., 1997–2010; SW Area Rep. to Central Cttee, 1985–89; Nat. Vice-Chm., 1989–92; Na Chm., 1992–95; Nat. Life Vice-Pres., 1999; Mem. House Cttee, Dunkirk Meml Hous 1994–99. Mem., SW Electricity Consultative Council, 1982–90 (Chm., Devon Ctte 1986–90). Former Mem., Exe Vale HMC; Pres., Exmouth Council of Voluntary Servic (Founder Chm., 1975). Member: Exec., Resthaven, Exmouth, 1970–2001 (Chm., League Friends, 1971–90); Devon FPC, 1985–91; President: Exmouth Br., Royal British Legio Women's Section, 1965–2012; Exmouth and Budleigh Salterton Br., CRUSE, 1980–8 Exmouth Campaign Cttee, Cancer Research, 1981– (Chm., 1975–81); Founder Pres Exmouth Br., British Heart Foundn, 1984–2004. Mem., Exmouth Cttee, LEPRA, 1962–8 (Hon. Sec., 1964–87); Dir, Home Care Trust, 1988–90; Co-optative Trustee, Exmou Welfare Trust, 1979–2005; Co-founder, and Trustee, Exmouth and Lympstone Hospiscar 1986– (Pres., 1994–2004); founder Trustee, Exmouth Adventure Trust for Girls, 1987–9 (Patron, 1990–); Exec. Mem., St Loye's Coll. Foundn for Trng the Disabled for Commerc and Industry, 1988–2001; Governor, Rolle Coll., Exmouth, 1982–88. Hon. Life Membe Retford Cricket Club, 1951; Exmouth Cricket Club, 1997 (Hon. Vice-Pres., 1981; Pres 1992–2001). *Recreations:* cricket, reading. *Address:* Walton House, 3 Fairfield Close, Exmout Devon EX8 2BN. *T:* (01395) 265317.

BRIDGES, Stephen John, LVO 1998; HM Diplomatic Service; Consul General, Chicag since 2013; *b* 19 June 1960; *s* of Gordon Alfred Richard Bridges and Audrey Middleton; 1990, Kyung Mi. *Educ:* Devonport High Sch.; London Univ. (International Relations); Uni of Leeds (MA East Asian Studies 2010). Joined FCO, 1980; Third Sec., Luanda, 1984–8 Third, later Second, Sec., Seoul, 1987–91; Second, later First, Sec., UN and SE Asia Dep FCO, 1991–96; First Sec., and Head, Political Section, Kuala Lumpur, 1996–200 Ambassador to Cambodia, 2000–05; Dep. High Comr, Dhaka, Bangladesh, 2005–07; Ma Dir, Greater Mekong Resources Co. Ltd, 2008–11; Corporate Advr, Elemental Energ Technologies Ltd, 2009–11; Hd of Workforce, Appts and Services, HR Directorate, FCC 2011–13. Dir, BSW Energy PTE Ltd, 2009–11. Patron, Soi Dog Foundn (UK). *Recreation* sports, food and wine, Coco and Montague – the dogs. *Address:* c/o Foreign and Commonwealth Office, King Charles Street, SW1A 2AH.

BRIDGEWATER, Emma, CBE 2013; pottery designer; Chairman, Emma Bridgewater Ltd; *b* Cambridge, 23 Dec. 1960; *d* of Adrian Bridgewater and Charlotte Stroud; *m* 1987, Matthew Rice; one *s* three *d. Educ:* Oxford High Sch.; Bedford Coll., London Univ. (BA Hons English Lit.). Started Emma Bridgewater Ltd, 1984. *Address:* Emma Bridgewater Ltd, 739 Fulham Road, SW6 5UL.

BRIDGEWATER, Peter, PhD; FLS; non-executive Chair, Joint Nature Conservation Committee, 2007–14; *b* Bristol, 31 Dec. 1945; *s* of Denis Henry Bridgewater and late Winifred May Bridgewater; one *d. Educ:* Univ. of Durham (BSc 1st Cl. Hons; PhD). Consultant, Forestry Canada, 1969, 1970; Lectr in Botany, Monash Univ., 1970–75; Lectr in Plant Biol., 1976–77, Sen. Lectr in Envmtl Sci., 1977–82, Murdoch Univ.; Dir, Aust. Bureau of Flora and Fauna, 1982–88; First Asst Sec., Aust. Dept of Arts, Sport, the Envmt, Tourism and Territories, 1988–89; Chief Scientist, UK Nature Conservancy Council, 1989–90; Chief Exec., Aust. Nature Conservation Agency, incl. Dir, Nat. Parks and Wildlife Service, 1990–97; Chief Sci. Advr, Envmt Australia, incl. Supervising Scientist, Alligator Rivers Reg., 1997–99; Sec., Man and the Biosphere Prog. and Dir, Div. of Ecol Scis, UNESCO, Paris, 1999–2003; Sec. Gen., Ramsar Convention, Gland, 2003–07. Visiting Professor: Beijing Forestry Univ., 2008–; United Nations Univ., Tokyo, 2010–. Chairman: Standing Cttee Convention on Migratory Species, 1994–97; Internat. Whaling Commn, 1995–97 (Vice Chm., 1992–94); Inter-govt Coordinating Council, Man and Biosphere Prog., UNESCO, 1995–98; 6th meeting, Conf. of Parties for Convention on Wetlands, 1996; Wkg Gp for Starlight Initiative, 2006–; Eur. Platform for Biodiversity Res. Strategy consultation on Biodiversity, 2009; Pew Whales Commn, 2009; Member: Aust. Nat. Commn for UNESCO, 1993–99; Ind. World Commn on the Oceans, 1995–98; Parks and Wildlife Commn, Northern Territory, 1997–99; Commn on Genetic Diversity, 1998–2000; Sci. and Technol. Adv. Panel to Global Envmt Facility, 1998–2000; Bd, Millennium Ecosystem Assessment, 2000–05; Total Petroleum Bd, Fondation pour biodiversité et la mer, 2002–09; Internat. Steering Cttee, Internat. Mechanism for Scientific Expertise or Biodiversity, 2005–08; Internat. Model Forest Prog. Adv. Council, 2007–. Trustee, Parks Forum, 2003–. Member: Screening Cttee, Cosmos Prize, Japan, 2003–04; Jury, Ramon Margalef Prize for Envmtl Scis, Govt of Catalonia, 2005–08; judging panel, St Andrews Prize, 2010–. FLS 2000. Hon. Dr Res. Mgt New England, 1997. *Publications:* over 230 academic papers on sustainable develt, envmtl governance, biodiversity. *Recreations:* cooking, gardening. *Address:* 2 The Wharfside, Station Place, Peel, Isle of Man IM5 1AT. *T:* 07624 221224. *E:* peter@global-garden.net. *Clubs:* Lansdowne; University House (Canberra).

BRIDGWATER, Prof. John, FREng, FIChemE; Shell Professor of Chemical Engineering, Cambridge University, 1993–2004, now Professor Emeritus; Professorial Fellow, 1993–2004 and Senior Tutor, 2004, St Catharine's College, Cambridge; *b* 10 Jan. 1938; *s* of Eric and Mary Bridgwater; *m* 1962, Diane Louise Tucker; one *s* one *d. Educ:* Solihull Sch.; St Catharine's Coll., Cambridge (Major Scholar; MA, PhD, ScD); Princeton Univ. (MSE). FREng (FEng 1987). Chemical Engineer, Courtaulds, 1961–64; University of Cambridge: Demonstrator in Chem. Engrg, 1964–69; Univ. Lectr in Chem. Engrg and Fellow, St Catharine's Coll., 1969–71; Esso Res. Fellow in Chem. Engrg, Hertford Coll., Oxford, 1971–73; Univ. Lectr in Engrg Sci., Univ. of Oxford and Lubbock Fellow in Engrg, Balliol Coll., 1973–80; University of Birmingham: Prof., 1980–93; Head, Sch. of Chem. Engrg, 1983–89; Dean, Faculty of Engrg, 1989–92; Gp Leader in Inter-Disciplinary Res. Centre in Materials for High Performance Applications, 1989–93; Hd, Dept of Chemical Engrg, Cambridge Univ., 1993–98. Dir, Tunkhu Abdul Rahman Fund, St Catharine's College, Cambridge, 2004–06. Vis. Associate Prof., Univ. of British Columbia, 1970–71; Vis. Prof., Univ. of Calif at Berkeley, 1992–93; Erskine Vis. Fellow, Univ. of Canterbury, NZ, 2002; Vis. Fellow, Univ. of NSW, 2004–. Mem., Engrg Bd, SERC, 1986–89; Chm., Process Engrg Cttee, SERC, 1986–89. Pres., IChemE, 1997–98 (Vice-Pres., 1995–97). Chm., Editl Bd, Chem. Engrg Science, 1996–2003 (Exec. Editor, 1983–96). *Publications:* (with J. J. Benbow) Paste Flow and Extrusion, 1993; papers on chem. and process engineering in professional jls. *Address:* St Catharine's College, Cambridge CB2 1RL.

BRIDPORT, 4th Viscount, *cr* 1868; **Alexander Nelson Hood;** Baron Bridport, 1794; 7th Duke of Bronte in Sicily (*cr* 1799); Managing Partner, Bridport & Cie SA, since 1991; *b* 17 March 1948; *s* of 3rd Viscount Bridport and Sheila Jeanne Agatha (*d* 1996), *d* of Johann van Meurs; *S* father, 1969; *m* 1st, 1972, Linda Jacqueline Paravicini (marr. diss.), *d* of Lt-Col and Mrs V. R. Paravicini; one *s*; 2nd, 1979, Mrs Nina Rindt-Martyn (marr. diss. 1999); one *s. Educ:* Eton; Sorbonne. *Heir: s* Hon. Peregrine Alexander Nelson Hood [*b* 30 Aug. 1974; *m* 2013, Serena, *e d* of Shahrokh Nikkhah]. *Address:* 1 Place Longemalle, 1204 Geneva, Switzerland. *T:* (22) 8177000, *Fax:* (22) 8177050. *Club:* Brooks's.

BRIDSON, Prof. Martin Robert, PhD; Whitehead Professor of Pure Mathematics, University of Oxford, since 2007; Fellow, Magdalen College, Oxford, since 2007; *b* Douglas, I of M, 22 Oct. 1964; *s* of late Gerald Patrick Bridson and Lilian Mary Bridson (*née* Stuart); *m* 1995, Julie Ann Lynch; two *s* one *d. Educ:* Douglas High Sch., I of M; Hertford Coll., Oxford (BA 1986); Cornell Univ. (MS 1988; PhD 1991). Instructor, 1991–92, Asst Prof., 1992–96, Princeton Univ.; CUF Lectr, 1994–96, Reader, 1996–99, Prof. of Topology, 1999–2001, Univ. of Oxford; Tutorial Fellow, Pembroke Coll., Oxford, 1994–2001; Prof. of Pure Maths, Imperial Coll. London, 2001–06. Advanced Fellow, 1997–2002, Sen. Fellow, 2007–12, EPSRC. Visiting Professor: Univ. de Genève, 1992–93 and 2006–07; Ecole Poly. Fédérale de Lausanne, 2007. Forder Lectr, NZ, 2005. Mem. Council, LMS, 1999–2006 (Vice Pres., 2004–06). Whitehead Prize, LMS, 1999; Wolfson Award, Royal Soc., 2006. Ed. of various mathematical jls. *Publications:* (with A. Haefliger) Metric Spaces of Non-positive Curvature, 1999; (ed with S. M. Salamon) Invitations to Geometry and Topology, 2002; (ed jtly) Geometric and Cohomological Methods in Group Theory, 2009; (with D. Groves) The Quadratic Isoperimetric Inequality for Mapping Tori of Free-group Automorphisms, 2010; contrib. articles to learned jls. *Recreations:* family life, poetry, ball games. *Address:* Mathematical Institute, University of Oxford, Andrew Wiles Building, Radcliffe Observatory Quarter, Woodstock Road, Oxford OX2 6GG.

BRIEGEL, (Geoffrey) Michael (Olver); Deputy Master of the Court of Protection, 1977–83; *b* 13 July 1923; *s* of late Roy C. Briegel, TD, and Veria Lindsey Briegel; *m* 1947, Barbara Mary Richardson; three *s* one *d. Educ:* Highgate Sch. Served War, RAF, 1942–46 (514 Sqdn Bomber Command). Called to Bar, Lincoln's Inn, 1950; Public Trustee Office, 1954; Clerk of the Lists, Queen's Bench Div., and Legal Sec. to Lord Chief Justice of England, 1963; Dep. Circuit Administrator, South Eastern Circuit, 1971. Legacy Officer, Inst. of Cancer Res., Royal Cancer Hosp., 1983–97; Legacy Consultant, Cancer Res. UK (formerly Imperial Cancer Res. Fund), 1998–2011. *Recreations:* theatre, cinema, music, all sports. *Clubs:* Royal Air Force; Middlesex County Cricket; Armadillos Cricket.

BRIERLEY, David, CBE 1986; Hon. Associate Artist, Royal Shakespeare Company, since 2004; *b* 26 July 1936; *s* of Ernest William Brierley and Jessie Brierley; *m* 1962, Ann Fosbrooke Potter; two *s. Educ:* Romiley County Primary Sch.; Stockport GS; Clare Coll., Cambridge (Exhibnr; Cert Ed 1959; MA; Pres., 1958–59, Trustee, 1969–, CU Amateur Dramatic Club). Teacher: Perse Sch., Cambridge, 1958–59; King Edward VI Sch., Macclesfield, 1959–61; Royal Shakespeare Company: Asst Stage Manager, and Stage Manager, Royal Shakespeare Theatre, 1961–63; Gen. Stage Manager, 1963–66; Asst to Dir, 1966–68; Gen. Manager, Sec. to Govs and Dir, various associated cos, 1968–96; Adv. Dir, 1996–2004. Member: Council of Mgt, Royal Theatrical Support (formerly Royal Shakespeare Theatre) Trust, 1982–; Trustees and Guardians, Shakespeare's Birthplace, 1984–96. Director: West End Theatre Managers Ltd, 1975–96; Theatre Royal, Plymouth, 1997–; Gov., Clwyd Theatr Cymru, 1997–. Chairman: Grant Aided Theatres Standing Cttee, Soc. of London Theatre, 1975–96; Theatres Nat. Cttee, 1986–96; Mem., Theatres Trust, 1996–2002; Adv. Bd Actors Centre, 1996–. Mem. and chm. of panels and cttees, Arts Council of GB, 1975–94; Arts Council England (formerly Arts Council of England): Member: Drama Adv. Panel, 1994–96; Capital Adv. Panel, 1996–2006; Council, 1997–2002; Audit Cttee, 1998–; Chm., Stabilisation Adv. Panel, 1996–2006; Chairman: Drama and Dance Adv. Cttee, British Council, 1997–2006; South West Arts, 1997–98. Trustee, Hall for Cornwall Trust, 1999–2008 (Chm., 2003–06). Member: Cambridge Univ. Careers Service Syndicate, 1980–88; Council, Warwick Univ., 1984–91; Gov., Stratford-upon-Avon Coll., 1971–96. Hon. DLitt Warwick, 1996. Special Award, 10th Internat. Congress, Internat. Soc. for the Performing Arts, 1996. *Recreation:* reading. *Address:* Headland, 8 Pear Tree Close, Chipping Camden, Glos GL55 6DB. *T:* (01386) 840361.

BRIERLEY, Sir Ronald (Alfred), Kt 1988; Chairman, Guinness Peat Group plc (formerly GPG plc), 1990–2010 (non-executive Director, since 2010); *b* Wellington, 2 Aug. 1937; *s* of J. R. Brierley. *Educ:* Wellington Coll. Editor, New Zealand Stocks and Shares, 1957–63; Chairman: Brierley Investments Ltd, 1961–89 (Founder, 1961; Founder Pres. 1989–); Industrial Equity Ltd, 1966–89; Chm., Bank of New Zealand, 1987–88 (Dir, 1985–88; Dep. Chm., 1986). *Address:* Guinness Peat Group plc, 10 Margaret Street, W1W 8RL. *Clubs:* American National, City Tattersall's (NSW).

BRIGGS, family name of **Baron Briggs**.

BRIGGS, Baron *cr* 1976 (Life Peer), of Lewes, E Sussex; **Asa Briggs,** MA, BSc (Econ); FBA 1980; Provost, Worcester College, Oxford, 1976–91; Chancellor, Open University, 1978–94; *b* 7 May 1921; *o s* of William Walker Briggs and Jane Briggs, Keighley, Yorks; *m* 1955, Susan Anne Banwell, *o d* of late Donald I. Banwell, Keevil, Wiltshire; two *s* two *d. Educ:* Keighley Grammar School; Sidney Sussex College, Cambridge (1st cl. History Tripos, Pts I and II, 1940, 1941; Hon. Fellow, 1968); 1st cl. BSc (Econ.), Lond., 1941. Gerstenberg studentship in Economics, London, 1941. Served in Intelligence Corps, Bletchley Park, 1942–45. Fellow of Worcester College, Oxford, 1945–55; Reader in Recent Social and Economic History, Oxford, 1950–55; Member, Institute for Advanced Study, Princeton, USA, 1953–54; Faculty Fellow of Nuffield College, Oxford, 1953–55; Professor of Modern History, Leeds Univ., 1955–61; University of Sussex: Professor of History, 1961–76; Dean, School of Social Studies, 1961–65; Pro Vice-Chancellor, 1961–67; Vice-Chancellor, 1967–76. Chm. Bd of Governors, Inst. of Develt Studies, 1967–76. Visiting Professor: ANU, 1960; Chicago Univ., 1966, 1972; Sen. Gannett Fellow, Columbia Univ., 1988, 1996; Dist. Sen. Kluge Prof., Liby of Congress, Washington, 2005. Lectures: Gregynog, Univ. of Wales, 1981; Ford, Oxford Univ., 1991; Ellen McArthur, Cambridge Univ., 1992. Dep. Pres., WEA, 1954–58, Pres., 1958–67. Mem., UGC, 1959–67; Chm., Cttee on Nursing, 1970–72 (Cmnd 5115, 1972). Trustee: Glyndebourne Arts Trust, 1966–91; Internat. Broadcasting Inst., 1968–87 (Hon. Trustee, 1991–); (Chm.) Heritage Educn Gp, 1976–86; Civic Trust, 1976–86; Chairman: Standing Conf. for Study of Local History, 1969–76; Council, European Inst. of Education, 1975–90; Commonwealth of Learning, 1988–93 (Hon. Dist. Fellow, 2003); Govs and Trustees, Brighton Pavilion, 1975–2008; Adv. Bd for Redundant Churches, 1983–89; Eurydice Consultative Gp, 1996–2001; Vice-Chm. of Council, UN Univ., 1974–80; Governor, British Film Institute, 1970–77; President: Social History Soc., 1976–; Victorian Soc., 1983–; The Ephemera Soc., 1984–; Brontë Soc., 1989–96; British Assoc. for Local History, 1984–86; Assoc. of Research Associations, 1986–88; Vice-Pres., Historical Assoc., 1986–. Mem., Ct of Governors, Administrative Staff Coll., 1971–91. Mem., Amer. Acad. of Arts and Sciences, 1970. Hon. FRCP 2005; Hon. Fellow: Worcester Coll., Oxford, 1969; St Catharine's Coll., Cambridge, 1977. Hon. DLitt: East Anglia, 1966; Strathclyde, 1973; Leeds, 1974; Cincinnati, 1977; Liverpool, 1977; Open Univ., 1979; Birmingham, 1989; Teesside, 1993; Hon. DSc Florida Presbyterian, 1966; Hon. LLD: York, Canada, 1968; New England, 1972; Sussex, 1976; Bradford, 1978; Rochester, NY, 1980; Ball State, 1985; E Asia, 1987; George Washington, 1988; Southampton, 1995; Tulane, 1996; London, 2001. Marconi Medal for Communications History, 1975; Médaille de Vermeil de la Formation, Fondation de l'Académie d'Architecture, 1979; Snow Medal, Royal Coll. of Anaesthetists, 1991; Wolfson History Prize, 2000; Historian Life Award, Historical Assoc., 2010; Lifetime Achievement Award, Archives and Records Assoc., 2012; Pepys Medal, Ephemera Soc., 2012. *Publications:* Patterns of Peace-making (with D. Thomson and E. Meyer), 1945; History of Birmingham (1865–1938), 1952; Victorian People, 1954; Friends of the People, 1956; The Age of Improvement, 1959, rev. edn 2000; (ed) Chartist Studies, 1959; (ed with John Saville) Essays in Labour History, Vol. I, 1960, Vol. II, 1971, Vol. III, 1977; (ed) They Saw it Happen, 1897–1940, 1961; A Study of the Work of Seebohm Rowntree, 1871–1954, 1961; History of Broadcasting in the United Kingdom: vol. I, The Birth of Broadcasting, 1961; vol. II, The Golden Age of Wireless, 1965; vol. III, The War of Words, 1970; vol. IV, Sound and Vision, 1979; vol. V, Competition 1955–1974, 1995; Victorian Cities, 1963, 2nd edn 1996; William Cobbett, 1967; How They Lived, 1700–1815, 1969; (ed) The Nineteenth Century, 1970; (ed with Susan Briggs) Cap and Bell, 1973; (ed) Essays in the History of Publishing, 1974; Iron Bridge to Crystal Palace: impact and images of the Industrial Revolution, 1979; Governing the BBC, 1979; The Power of Steam, 1982; Marx in London, 1982, 2nd edn (with John Callow), 2007; A Social History of England, 1983, 3rd edn 1999; Toynbee Hall, 1984; Collected Essays, 2 vols, 1985, vol. III 1991; The BBC: the first fifty years, 1985; (with Joanna Spicer) The Franchise Affair, 1986; Victorian Things, 1988, 2nd edn 1996; Haut Brion, 1994; The Channel Islands, Occupation and Liberation 1940–1945, 1995; (ed jtly) Fins de Siècle: how centuries end 1400–2000, 1996; (with Patricia Clavin) Modern Europe 1789–1989, 1997, 2nd edn, 1789–2003, 2003; Chartism, 1998; Go To It!: working for victory on the Home Front 1939–1945, 2000; Michael Young; social entrepreneur, 2001, 2nd edn 2005; (with Peter Burke) A Social History of the Media from Gutenberg to the Internet, 2002, 3rd edn 2009; A History of the Royal College of Physicians of London, vol. 4, 2005; A History of Longman and their Books, 1724–1990, 2008; Secret Days: codebreaking in Bletchley Park, 2011; Special Relationships, People and Places, 2012; Loose Ends and Extras, 2014. *Recreations:* memories of travel and of great lunches and dinners, travelling. *Address:* The Caprons, Keere Street, Lewes, Sussex BN7 1TY.

BRIGGS, Andrew; *see* Briggs, G. A. D.

BRIGGS, David John, FRCO; freelance composer and concert organist, since 2002; Artist-in-Residence, St James Cathedral, Toronto, since 2012; *b* 1 Nov. 1962; *s* of late J. R. Briggs and of J. A. Briggs (*née* Jones); *m* 1st, 1986, Elisabeth Anne Baker; two *d*; 2nd, 2004, Madge Nimocks. *Educ:* Solihull Sch. (Music Schol.); King's Coll., Cambridge (Organ Schol.; John Stewart of Rannoch Schol. in Sacred Music; MA 1987). FRCO 1980; ARCM 1986. Studied with Jean Langlais in Paris, 1984–86; Asst Organist, Hereford Cathedral, 1985–88; Organist: Truro Cathedral, 1989–94; Gloucester Cathedral, 1994–2002. Vis. Tutor in Improvisation, RNCM, 1995–; Vis. Prof. of Improvisation, RAM, 2001–. Festival Conductor, Gloucester Three Choirs Fest., 1995, 1998, 2001. Recital tours, Australia, NZ, S Africa, Russia, Finland, Sweden, France, Belgium, Luxembourg, Germany, Italy, Ireland, Canada and USA. Has made numerous recordings. FRSA 1993. 5 prizes and Silver Medal, Co. of Musicians. *Publications: compositions:* Truro Eucharist, 1990; The Music Mountain, 1991; Te Deum Laudamus, 1998; Creation, 2000; Messe pour Notre-Dame, 2002; Magnificat and Nunc Dimittis, 2004; Symphony Missa pro Defunctis, 2004; Four Concert Etudes, 2005; Toccata

Labyrinth, 2006; Cross of Nails, 2009; Hommage à Marcel Dupré, 2009; The Sounding Sea, 2010; *transcriptions:* Cochereau, Improvisations on Alouette, gentille Alouette, 1993; Cantem toto la Gloria, 1997; Suite de Danses improvisées, 1998; Improvisations sur Venez, Divin Messie, 1998; Triptique Symphonique, 1998; for organ: Mahler, Symphony No 5 and No 6; Schubert, Symphony No 8; Tchaikovsky, Symphony No 4; Elgar, Symphony No 1; Ravel, Daphnis et Chloe. *Recreation:* training for private pilot's licence.

BRIGGS, Prof. Derek Ernest Gilmor, PhD; FRS 1999; G. Evelyn Hutchinson Professor of Geology and Geophysics, since 2010 (Professor of Geology and Geophysics, since 2003), Curator in Charge of Invertebrate Paleontology, Peabody Museum, Yale University, since 2003; *b* 10 Jan. 1950; *s* of John Gilmor Briggs and Olive Evelyn Briggs (*née* Scanlon); *m* 1972, Jennifer Olive Kershaw; three *s*. *Educ:* Sandford Park Sch., Dublin; Trinity Coll., Dublin (Foundn Scholar; BA Geology); Sidney Sussex Coll., Cambridge (MA, PhD). Res. Fellow, Cambridge, 1974–77; Goldsmiths' College, London University: Department of Geology: Lectr, 1977; Sen. Lectr, 1980; Principal Lectr and Dep. Dean of Sci. and Maths, 1982–85; Department of Earth Sciences, Bristol University: Lectr, 1985; Reader, 1988; Prof. of Palaeontol., 1994–2002; Head of Dept, 1997–2001; Asst Dir, Biogeochemistry Res. Centre, 1990–97; Dir, Yale Inst. for Biospheric Studies, 2004–07; Frederick William Beinecke Prof. of Geology and Geophysics, 2006–10, Dir, Yale Peabody Mus. of Nat. History, 2009–14, Yale Univ. Res. Associate, Royal Ontario Mus., Toronto, 1983–; Vis. Scientist, Field Mus. of Nat. History, Chicago, 1983; Dist. Vis. Scholar, Univ. of Adelaide, 1994; Vis. Prof., Univ. of Chicago and Field Mus. of Nat. History, Chicago, 2001–02. Lectures: Benedum, Univ. of W Virginia, 1994; Case Meml, Michigan Univ., 2004; Darwin, Duquesne Univ., 2006; Walther Arndt Meml, Berlin, 2008; Bownocker, Ohio State Univ., 2009; Clara Jones Langston, Univ. of Texas, Austin, 2013. Editor, Palaeontology and Special Papers in Palaeontology, 1982–86. President: Palaeontol Assoc., 2002–04; Paleontol Soc., 2006–08. Hon. MRIA 2003. Hon. DSc TCD, 2010. Lyell Medal, Geol Soc., 2000; Boyle Medal, Royal Dublin Soc./Irish Times, 2001; Premio Capo d'Orlando, Italy, 2000; Humboldt Res. Award, Alexander von Humboldt Foundn, 2008. *Publications:* (ed with K. C. Allen) Evolution and the Fossil Record, 1989; (ed with P. R. Crowther) Palaeobiology: a synthesis, 1990; (ed with P. A. Allison) Taphonomy: releasing the data locked in the fossil record, 1991; (jtly) The Fossils of the Burgess Shale, 1994; The Fossils of the Hunsrück Slate, 1998; (ed with P. R. Crowther) Palaeobiology II, 2001; (jtly) Evolution, 2007; Visions of a Vanished World, 2012; contribs to learned jls. *Recreations:* the outdoors, natural history, golf. *Address:* Department of Geology and Geophysics, Yale University, PO Box 208109, New Haven, CT 06520–8109, USA. *T:* (203) 4328590; Flat 4, 65 Pembroke Road, Clifton, Bristol BS8 3DW.

BRIGGS, Prof. (George) Andrew (Davidson), PhD; FInstP; Professor of Nanomaterials, University of Oxford, and Fellow, St Anne's College, Oxford, since 2002; *b* 3 June 1950; *s* of John Davidson Briggs and Catherine Mary Briggs (*née* Lormer); *m* 1981, Diana Margaret Ashley Johnson; two *d*. *Educ:* King's Coll. Sch., Cambridge; Leys Sch., Cambridge; St Catherine's Coll., Oxford (Clothworkers' Schol.; BA, MA); Queens' Coll., Cambridge (PhD 1977); Ridley Hall, Cambridge. FInstP 2004. Physics and RE, House Tutor, Canford Sch., 1971–73; Res. Asst, Engrg Dept, Univ. of Cambridge, 1979; University of Oxford: Res. Fellow, Dept of Metallurgy, 1980–82; Lectr in Physics, 1981–93, Res. Associate, 1982–84, St Catherine's Coll.; Royal Soc. Res. Fellow in Physical Scis, 1983–84; Lectr in Metallurgy and Sci. of Materials, 1984–96; Fellow, Wolfson Coll., 1984–96, now Emeritus; Reader in Materials, 1996–99; Prof. of Materials, 1999–2002. Dir, Quantum Inf. Processing Interdisciplinary Res. Collaboration, and Professorial Res. Fellow, EPSRC, 2002–09. Founding Dir and Vice-Chm., OxLoc Ltd, 2000–08. Vis. Faculty, Center for Quantized Electronic Structures, Univ. of Calif, Santa Barbara, 1990, 1993; Prof. invité, Ecole polytechnique fédérale de Lausanne, 1992–2002; Vis. Scientist, Hewlett-Packard Labs, Palo Alto, 1997–98; Vis. Prof., Univ. of NSW, 2002; Guest Prof., State Key Lab., Wuhan Univ. of Technol., 2005–. Member, Editorial Board: Sci. and Christian Belief, 2001–; Current Opinion in Solid State and Materials Sci., 2002–09; Nanotechnology, 2005–06; Jl of Physics D: Applied Physics, 2009–12. Member: Sci. and Engrg Fellowships Cttee, Royal Commn for the Exhibn of 1891, 2006–; Peer Rev. Coll., EPSRC, 2006–; Internat. Soc. for Sci. and Religion, 2013–. Dir, Oxford Toppan Centre, 1996–2006; Member: Bd of Mgt, Ian Ramsey Centre, 2001–; Internat. Bd of Advrs, John Templeton Foundn, 2007–09, 2011–13; Engrg Panel, Newton Internat. Fellowships, 2008–. MAE 2012. Hon. Fellow, Royal Microscopical Soc. (Chm. Materials Section, Council, 1986–91; Hon. Treas., 1989–91). Liveryman, Clothworkers' Co., 2005–. Holliday Prize, Inst. of Metals, 1986; (jtly) Metrology for World Class Manufg Award, 1999. *Publications:* An Introduction to Scanning Acoustic Microscopy, 1985; Acoustic Microscopy, 1992, 2nd edn 2010; (ed) The Science of New Materials, 1992; (ed) Advances in Acoustic Microscopy 1, 1995, 2, 1996; The Penultimate Curiosity, 2015; numerous contribs to learned jls. *Recreations:* Christian theology, opera, ski-ing, sailing, flying. *Address:* 5 Northmoor Road, Oxford OX2 6UW. *T:* (01865) 273725, *Fax:* (01865) 273730. *E:* andrew.briggs@materials.ox.ac.uk.

BRIGGS, Very Rev. George Peter N.; *see* Nairn-Briggs.

BRIGGS, Isabel Diana, (Mrs Michael Briggs); *see* Colegate, I. D.

BRIGGS, Martin Paul; Chief Executive, East Midlands Development Agency, 1999–2004; *b* 17 April 1948; *s* of late Maurice William John Briggs and Beryl Edna Briggs; *m* 1999, Angela Byrne; three *s* one *d* and two step *s* one step *d*. *Educ:* Forest Sch., Snaresbrook; Univ. of E Anglia (BA Hons Social Studies). Department of Trade and Industry: Res. Officer and other res. posts, 1970–82; Hd, Location/Inward Investment, E Midlands, 1982–87; Dir, Industry, W Midlands, 1987–91; Director: English Unit, Investment in Britain Bureau, 1991–93; Trade and Industry, Govt Office for E Midlands, 1994–98; Business Links, DTI, 1998–99. Special Prof., Nottingham Univ. *Recreations:* recorded music, tastes catholic, travel, philosophy/theology, family pursuits.

BRIGGS, Dr (Michael) Peter, OBE 2010; educational consultant, since 2009; Pro Vice-Chancellor, Roehampton University (formerly Pro-Rector, University of Surrey Roehampton), 2002–07, Special Adviser to Vice-Chancellor, 2007–09; Principal, Southlands College, 2002–09; *b* 3 Dec. 1944; *s* of late Hewieson Briggs and of Doris (*née* Habberley); *m* 1969, Jennifer Elizabeth Watts; one *s* one *d*. *Educ:* Abbeydale Boys' Grammar Sch., Sheffield; Univ. of Sussex (BSc, DPhil). Jun. Res. Fellow in Theoretical Chem., Univ. of Sheffield, 1969–71; Res. Assistant, Dept of Architecture, Univ. of Bristol, 1971–73; Deputation Sec., Methodist Church Overseas Div., 1973–77; Area Sec. (Herts and Essex), Christian Aid, BCC, 1977–80; British Association for the Advancement of Science: Educn Manager, 1980–86; Public Affairs Man., 1986–88; Dep. Sec., 1988–90; Exec. Sec., then Chief Exec., 1990–2002; Hon. Fellow, 2002. Chairman: Management Cttee, Methodist Church Div. of Social Responsibility, 1983–86; Methodist Youth World Affairs Management Cttee, 1984–92; Mem. Bd, Internat. Assoc. of Methodist Schs, Colls and Univs, 2008–11. Trustee: Central Foundn Schs of London, 2009–; Wesley House, Cambridge, 2011–; Dulwich Estate, 2013–. Master, Educators' Co., 2011–12. FRSA 1990. Hon. DSc Leicester, 2002. *Recreation:* walking. *Address:* 42 The Lawns, Pinner HA5 4BL.

BRIGGS, Rt Hon. Sir Michael Townley Featherstone, Kt 2006; PC 2013; **Rt Hon. Lord Justice Briggs;** a Lord Justice of Appeal, since 2013; Deputy Head of Civil Justice, from Jan. 2016; *b* 23 Dec. 1954; *s* of Capt. James William Featherstone Briggs, RN and late Barbara Nadine Briggs (*née* Pelham Groom); *m* 1981, Beverly Ann Rogers; three *s* one *d*. *Educ:* Charterhouse; Magdalen Coll., Oxford (BA History). Called to the Bar, Lincoln's Inn, 1978, Bencher, 2001; Jun. Counsel to Crown Chancery, 1990–94; QC 1994; Attorney Gen., Duchy of Lancaster, 2001–06; a Judge of the High Ct of Justice, Chancery Div., 2006–13 Vice Chancellor, County Palatine of Lancaster, 2011–13. *Recreations:* sailing, singing (solo and choral), cooking, classic cars, garden railways. *Address:* Royal Courts of Justice, Strand, WC2A 2LL. *Clubs:* Bar Yacht; British Classic Yacht; Royal Yacht Squadron.

BRIGGS, Patrick David, MA; Principal, Kolej Tuanku Ja'afar, Malaysia, 1997–2005; *b* 24 Aug. 1940; *s* of late Denis Patrick Briggs and of Nancy Sylvester (*née* Jackson); *m* 1968, Alicia Dorothy O'Donnell; two *s* one *d*. *Educ:* Pocklington Sch.; Christ's Coll., Cambridge (MA) Bedford Sch., 1965–87 (Sen. Housemaster, 1983–87); Head Master, William Hulme's GS 1987–97. Rugby Blue, Cambridge, 1962; England Rugby triallist, 1968 and 1969; Mem Barbarians, 1968–69; RFU staff coach, 1973–95; England Under-23 Rugby coach, 1975–80 Team Manager, England Students Rugby, 1988–95. *Publications:* The Parents' Guide to Independent Schools, 1979. *Recreations:* cricket, Rugby, golf, fell walking, poetry, theatre canal-boating. *Address:* 1A Gresham Road, Cambridge CB1 2EP. *T:* (01223) 309405. *Clubs* East India, Devonshire, Sports and Public Schools, XL; Hawks (Cambridge); Quidnuncs Cheshire County Cricket, Lancashire County Cricket; Royal Selangor (Kuala Lumpur).

BRIGGS, Peter; *see* Briggs, M. P.

BRIGGS, Raymond Redvers, DFA; FCSD; FRSL; freelance illustrator, since 1957; author since 1961; *b* 18 Jan. 1934; *s* of late Ernest Redvers Briggs and Ethel Bowyer; *m* 1963, Jean Taprell Clark (*d* 1973). *Educ:* Rutlish Sch., Merton; Wimbledon School of Art; Slade School of Fine Art. NDD; DFA London. Part-time Lecturer in Illustration, Faculty of Art, Brighton Polytechnic, 1961–87. FRSL 2005. *Publications:* The Strange House, 1961; Midnight Adventure, 1961; Ring-A-Ring O'Roses, 1962; Sledges to the Rescue, 1963; The White Land, 1963; Fee Fi Fo Fum, 1964; The Mother Goose Treasury, 1966 (Kate Greenaway Medal, 1966); Jim and the Beanstalk, 1970; The Fairy Tale Treasury, 1972; Father Christmas 1973 (Kate Greenaway Medal, 1973); Father Christmas Goes On Holiday, 1975; Fungus The Bogeyman, 1977 (adapted for BBC TV, 2004); The Snowman, 1978 (animated film, 1982) Gentleman Jim, 1980 (play, Nottingham Playhouse, 1985); When the Wind Blows, 1982 (play, BBC Radio and Whitehall Th., 1983; text publd 1983; cassette 1984; animated film 1987); Fungus the Bogeyman Plop-Up Book, 1982; The Tin-Pot Foreign General and the Old Iron Woman, 1984; The Snowman Pop-Up, 1986; Unlucky Wally, 1987; Unlucky Wally Twenty Years On, 1989; The Man, 1992; The Bear, 1994; Ethel & Ernest, 1998; UG Boy Genius of the Stone Age, 2001; Blooming Books, 2003; The Puddleman, 2004 *Recreations:* gardening, reading, walking, second-hand bookshops. *Address:* Weston, Underhill Lane, Westmeston, Hassocks, Sussex BN6 8XG.

BRIGGS, Robin, FBA 2009; FRHistS; FRSL; Senior Research Fellow, All Souls College Oxford, 1978–2009, now Emeritus Fellow; *b* Braintree, Essex, 26 May 1942; *s* of Donald Frederick Briggs and Kathleen Ann Briggs; *m* 1st, 1969, Julia Ruth Ballam (marr. diss. 1989) two *s*; 2nd, 1989, Daphne Elizabeth Mariner Nash. *Educ:* Felsted Sch.; Balliol Coll., Oxford (BA 1st Cl. Modern Hist. 1964). Fellow by Exam., 1964–71, Jun. Res. Fellow, 1971–78, All Souls Coll., Oxford; Jun. Proctor, 1972–73, Special Lectr in Modern Hist., 1976–2009, Univ of Oxford. Visiting Professor: Univ. of Paris IV, Sorbonne, 1981; Coll. de France, Paris, 1995 FRHistS 1969; FRSL 2002. *Publications:* The Scientific Revolution of the Seventeenth Century, 1969; Early Modern France, 1560–1715, 1977, 2nd edn 1998; Communities of Belief, 1989; Witches and Neighbours, 1996, 2nd edn 2002 (trans. German, Dutch and Chinese); The Witches of Lorraine, 2007; contrib. articles to learned jls. *Recreations:* painting, music (listening), golf, woodwork. *Address:* All Souls College, High Street, Oxford OX1 4AL *T:* (01865) 279379, *Fax:* (01865) 279299. *E:* robin.briggs@all-souls.ox.ac.uk.

BRIGGS, Thomas David, MBE 2009; Lord-Lieutenant of Cheshire, since 2010; *b* Huddersfield, 25 Aug. 1946; *s* of Thomas and Winnifred Briggs; *m* 1984, Michelle; one *d* *Educ:* Charterhouse Sch.; St Andrews Univ. (LLB 1st Cl. Hons 1969); Wharton Sch., Univ of Pennsylvania (MBA 1972). Called to the Bar, Lincoln's Inn, 1970; Man. Dir, Hanson Transport Gp, 1973–74; with Hepworth Ceramics Gp, latterly Man. Dir, Hepworth Plastics Ltd, 1976–79; Managing Director: Dawsons Music Ltd, 1979–; Maxilin Ltd, 2002–. Chm Council, Cheshire, Order of St John, 2002–10. High Sheriff of Cheshire, 2006–07. Hon. MA Chester, 2009. KStJ 2011. *Recreations:* tennis, ski-ing. *Address:* Dukenfield Hall, Mobberley Knutsford, Cheshire WA16 7PT. *Clubs:* Army and Navy, Royal Automobile; St James (Manchester).

BRIGHOUSE, Sir Timothy Robert Peter, Kt 2009; Chief Adviser for London Schools Department for Education and Skills, 2003–07; *b* 15 Jan. 1940; *s* of Denison Brighouse and Mary Howard Brighouse; *m* 1st, 1962, Mary Elizabeth Demers (marr. diss. 1988); one *s* one *d*; 2nd, 1989, Elizabeth Ann (formerly Kearney). *Educ:* St Catherine's College, Oxford (MA Modern History); DipEd. Head of History Dept, Cavendish Grammar Sch., Buxton 1962–64; Dep. Head and Warden, Chepstow Comm. Coll., 1964–66; Asst Educn Officer Monmouthshire Educn Dept, 1966–69; Sen. Asst Educn Officer, Bucks Educn Dept 1969–74; Under-Sec., Educn, ACC, 1974–76; Dep. Educn Officer, ILEA, 1976–78; Chief Educn Officer, Oxon, 1978–89; Prof. of Educn and Hd of Dept, Keele Univ., 1989–93; Chief Educn Officer, Birmingham CC, 1993–2002. Jt Vice-Chm., Standards Task Force, 1997–99 Visiting Professor: Keele Univ., 1993–2002; London Univ. Inst. of Educn, 2002; Hon. Prof. Birmingham Univ., 1996. Non-exec. Dir, RM Education plc, 2005–11. Hon. DEd (CNAA Oxford Poly., 1989; Hon. PhD UCE, 1996; Hon. DLitt: Exeter, 1996; Birmingham, 1999 Sheffield Hallam, 2001; Hon. MA Open Univ., 1997; Hon. EdD UWE, 2002; Hon. Dr Greenwich, 2003; Middlesex 2004; Wolverhampton, 2006; Sunderland, 2007. *Publications* Revolution in Education and Training (jt editor and author), 1986; Managing the National Curriculum (jt editor and author), 1990; What Makes a Good School, 1991; Successful Schooling, 1991; (jtly) How to Improve Your School, 1999. *Recreations:* gardening, politics golf. *Address:* Institute of Education, 20 Bedford Way, WC1H 0AL; Willowbank, Old Road Headington, Oxford OX3 8TA. *T:* (01865) 766995.

BRIGHT, Andrew John; QC 2000; **His Honour Judge Bright;** a Circuit Judge, since 2007; Resident Judge, St Albans Crown Court, since 2010; *b* 12 April 1951; *e s* of late J. H Bright and of Freda Bright (*née* Cotton); *m* 1976, Sally Elizabeth Carter; three *s* one *d*. *Educ* Wells Cathedral Sch.; University Coll. London (LLB Hons). Called to the Bar, Middle Temple, 1973; in practice at the Bar in field of criminal law, S Eastern Circuit, 1975–2007 Recorder, 2000–07. Co-opted Mem. Cttee, Criminal Bar Assoc., 1993–95; Chm., Herts and Beds Bar Mess, 2003–07. *Recreations:* river and canal boating, fishing, music, singing in a male voice choir. *Address:* St Albans Crown Court, Bricket Road, St Albans, Herts AL1 3JW.

BRIGHT, Colin Charles; HM Diplomatic Service, retired; Counsellor, Foreign and Commonwealth Office, 2006; *b* 2 Jan. 1948; *s* of William Charles John Bright and Doris (*née* Sutton); *m* 1st, 1978, Helen-Anne Michie; 2nd, 1990, Jane Elizabeth Gurney Pease, *d* of Sir (Joseph) Gurney Pease, 5th Bt, *qv*; one *s* one *d* (and one *d* decd). *Educ:* Christ's Hospital; St Andrews Univ. (MA Hons 1971). FCO, 1975–77; Bonn, 1977–79; FCO, 1979–83; seconded to Cabinet Office, 1983–85; British Trade Develt Office, NY, 1985–88; Dep. Head of Mission, Berne, 1989–93; Consul Gen., Frankfurt, 1993–97; Hd of Commonwealth Co-ordination Dept, FCO, 1998–2002; Counsellor, FCO, 2002–03; Consul Gen., Lyon 2004–06.

BRIGHT, Sir Graham (Frank James), Kt 1994; Police and Crime Commissioner (C) for Cambridgeshire, since 2012; *b* 2 April 1942; *s* of late Robert Frank Bright and Agnes Mary (*née* Graham); *m* 1972, Valerie, *d* of late E. H. Woolliams; one *s*. *Educ:* Hassenbrook County Sch.; Thurrock Technical Coll. Marketing Exec., Pauls & White Ltd, 1958–70; Man. Dir

1970–2012, Chm., 1977–2012, Dietary Foods Ltd. Dir, Internat. Sweeteners Assoc., 1997– (Chm., 2002–09); Dir, Mother Nature Ltd, 2012–. Contested (C): Thurrock, 1970 and Feb. 1974; Dartford, Oct. 1974. MP (C) Luton East, 1979–83, Luton South, 1983–97; contested (C) Luton South, 1997; contested (C) Eastern Region, EP elecns, 1999. PPS to Ministers of State, Home Office, 1984–87, DoE, 1988–89, to Paymaster Gen., 1989–90, to Prime Minister, 1990–94. Mem. Select Cttee on House of Commons Services, 1982–84. Jt Sec. to Parly Aviation Gp, 1984–90; Chm., Cons. Backbench Smaller Businesses Cttee, 1983–84, 1987–88 (Vice-Chm., 1980–83; Sec., 1979–80); Vice-Chairman: Cons. Backbench Food and Drink Sub-Cttee, 1983 (Sec., 1983–85); Backbench Aviation Cttee, 1987–88; former Sec., Space Sub-Cttee; Introduced Private Member's Bills: Video Recordings Act, 1984; Entertainment (Increased Penalties) Act, 1990. Trustee, Parly Pension Fund, 2008–; Chm., Former MPs Assoc., 2010–15. Member: Thurrock Bor. Council, 1966–79; Essex CC, 1967–70. Chm., Eastern Area CPC, 1977–79; Mem., Nat. CPC, 1980–97; Vice Chm., YC Org., 1970–72; Pres., Eastern Area YCs, 1981–98; Conservative Party: a Vice-Chm., 1994–97; Chm., Eastern Reg., 2006–. Vice-Chm., Small Business Bureau, 1980–89, and 1991–97 (Dir, 1989–91). Chm., 2008–13, Trustee, 2010–, Hassenbrook Acad. *Publications:* pamphlets on airports, small businesses, education. *Recreations:* golf, gardening. *Address:* Cambridgeshire Police and Crime Commissioner, South Cambridgeshire Hall, Cambourne Business Park, Cambourne, Cambs CB23 6EA. *Club:* Carlton.

BRIGHT, Jonathan Steven Noel; Chief Executive, Oxfordshire Rural Community Council, since 2014; *b* Gloucester, 26 Dec. 1951; *s* of Stanley and Suzanne Bright; *m* 1990, Suzanne Lingard; two *s* one *d*. *Educ:* Hardye's Grammar Sch.; Magdalene Coll., Cambridge (BA Social and Pol Sci. 1974); Leicester Univ. (PGCE). Dir, Safe Neighbourhood Unit, NACRO, 1981–90; Dir of Ops, Crime Concern, 1990–97; Deputy Director: Social Exclusion Unit, Cabinet Office, 1997–2000; Neighbourhood Renewal Unit, ODPM, 2001–06; Dir of Policy, Birmingham CC, 2006–07; Regl Dir, Govt Office for the SW, 2008–11; Dir of Homelessness, Support, Climate Change and Bldg Regulations, DCLG, 2011–14. Harkness Fellow, Univ. of Michigan, 1990–91. Fellow, Australian Inst. Criminol., 1996. FRSA. *Publications:* Crime Prevention in the United States: a British perspective, 1993; Turning the Tide: crime, prevention and neighbourhoods, 1997. *Recreations:* wild swimming, cycling, mountain-walking, architecture. *Address:* Oxfordshire Rural Community Council, Jericho Barns, Worton, Witney, Oxon OX29 4SZ. *T:* (01865) 733233. *E:* jon.bright@oxonrcc.org.uk.

BRIGHT, Robert Graham; QC 2007; barrister; *b* 22 Aug. 1964; *s* of John and Elizabeth Bright; *m* Susan; three *d*. *Educ:* St Paul's Sch.; St John's Coll., Oxford (BA Juris., BCL). Called to the Bar, Gray's Inn, 1987. *Recreation:* horticulture. *Address:* 7 King's Bench Walk, Temple, EC4Y 7DS.

BRIGHT, Roger Martin Francis, CB 2009; Second Commissioner and Chief Executive, The Crown Estate, 2001–11; *b* 2 May 1951. *Educ:* Christ's Hosp.; Trinity Hall, Cambridge (BA 1973). Joined DoE, 1973; posts held include: Hd, Envmtl Policy Co-ordination Div.; Hd, Housing Policy Studies Div.; Hd, Local Govt Review Div.; Principal Private Sec. to Sec. of State for the Envmt, 1989–90; Dir of Information, 1990; Dep. Chief Exec., Housing Corp., 1991–95; Dir of Ops and Finance, 1995–97, Chief Exec., 1998, PIA; Hd of Investment Business Dept (PIA firms), FSA, 1998–99; Dir of Finance and Admin, 1999–2001, a Comr, 2000–11, Crown Estate. Mem., Royal Parks' Bd, 2012–. Non-executive Director: London First, 2008–; Heritage of London Trust, 2008–. Chm., Adv. Bd, Curtin & Co., 2012–. Member: Governing Council, City Univ., 2008– (Dep. Pro-Chancellor, 2012–); Council, RCVS, Univ. of London, 2013–.

BRIGHTMAN, Dr David Kenneth, CBiol, FRSB; FRAgS; sole trader, Brightman Farms, since 2010 (Partner, 1982–2010); *b* 12 Aug. 1954; *s* of late Brian George Brightman and Dorothy Brightman; partner, Gillian Theresa Bolton; two *s*. *Educ:* Univ. of Reading; Univ. of Newcastle upon Tyne (BSc Hons (Agric.) 1977); Univ. of Nottingham (PhD 1983). CBiol, FRSB (FIBiol 2005); ARAgS 2005, FRAgS 2011. Lectr in Crop Prodn, Brooksby Coll., 1980–82. Dir and Co. Sec., Arable Crop Storage Ltd, 1995–2012; Co. Sec., Arable Crop Services Ltd, 1995–2010. Mem. Council, BBSRC, 2003–09 (Mem., Audit Bd, 2009–12). Ministry of Agriculture, Fisheries and Food, later Department for Environment, Food and Rural Affairs: Chm., MAFF/ADAS Drayton Experimental Husbandry Farm Adv. Cttee, 1990–92; Member: Pesticides Forum, 1995–98; Sustainable Arable LINK Prog. Mgt Cttee, 1997–2003; Sub-gp on Biodiversity, Adv. Cttee on Releases to the Envmt, 1999–2001; Agricl Forum, 2008–. Mem., NFU Pesticides Wkg Gp, 1991–2003 (Chm., 1993–2003). Dir, Rothamsted Res. Assoc., 1990–2005 (Chm., 2001–03); Dir and Trustee, Rothamsted Res. Ltd, 2005–13 (Mem., Audit Cttee, 2013); Dir and Mem., Audit Cttee, Centaur Producers Ltd and Centaur Grain Marketing Ltd, 2006–09; Technol. Strategy Bd Assessor, Agri-Tech Catalyst Fund, 2013–; Mem. Res. and Knowledge Transfer Cttee, HGCA, 2014–. Former Dir, Mid-Tak/CMR Ltd Machinery Rings. Formerly Chairman: Warks Farm Mgt Assoc.; Southam Agricl Discussion Club; Chm., Fenny Compton NFU, 1988–90; mem., various cttees, panels and wkg gps. *Publications:* Dietary Nitrogen Requirements of Entire Male Cattle, 1983; conf. papers in Animal Prodn and for BCPC annual conf., and articles in farming press. *Recreations:* playing golf, watching sport, watching people.

BRIGHTON, Wing Comdr Peter, BSc; CEng, FIET, FRAeS; *b* 26 March 1933; *s* of late Henry Charles Brighton and Ivy Irene Brighton (*née* Crane); *m* 1959, Anne Maureen Lewis Jones (*d* 2007); one *d* (one *s* decd). *Educ:* Wisbech Grammar Sch.; Reading Univ. (BSc); RAF Technical Coll. and Staff Coll. CEng 1966; FIET (FIEE 1980); FRAeS 1981. Pilot, Engr and Attaché, RAF, 1955–71. Man. Dir, Rockwell-Collins UK, 1974–77; Regional Man. Dir, Plessey Co., 1977–78; Man. Dir, Cossor Electronics Ltd, 1978–85; British Aerospace PLC: Divl Man. Dir, 1985–87; Co. Dir of Operations, 1988; Dir Gen., EEF, 1989–91. Chm., Princess Alexandra Hosp. NHS Trust, 1996–97. Pres., Electronic Engineering Assoc., 1984–85. Mem. Ct, Cranfield Inst. of Technology, 1989–92. CCMI (CBIM 1984). Liveryman, Coachmakers and Coach Harness Makers Co., 1989; Freeman of City of London, 1989. *Publications:* articles on aviation topics in learned jls. *Recreations:* music, theatre, crosswords, wining and dining with friends. *Address:* 18 Riverside Wharf, Riverside, Bishop's Stortford CM23 3GN. *T:* (01279) 757440. *Club:* Royal Air Force.

BRIGHTON AND LEWES, Archdeacon of; *see* Lloyd Williams, Ven. M. C.

BRIGHTY, (Anthony) David, CMG 1984; CVO 1985; HM Diplomatic Service, retired; Ambassador to Spain, and concurrently (non-resident) to Andorra, 1994–98; *b* 7 Feb. 1939; *s* of C. P. J. Brighty and Winifred Brighty; *m* 1963, Diana Porteous (marr. diss. 1979; she *d* 1993); two *s* two *d*; *m* 1997, Susan Olivier. *Educ:* Northgate Grammar Sch., Ipswich; Clare Coll., Cambridge (BA). Entered FO, 1961; Brussels, 1962–63; Havana, 1964–66; FO, 1967–69, resigned; joined S. G. Warburg & Co., 1969; reinstated in FCO, 1971; Saigon, 1973–74; UK Mission to UN, NY, 1975–78; RCDS, 1979; Head of Personnel Operations Dept, FCO, 1980–83; Counsellor, Lisbon, 1983–86; Dir, Cabinet of Sec.-Gen. of NATO, 1986–87; Resident Chm., CSSB, 1988; Ambassador to Cuba, 1989–91; Ambassador to Czech and Slovak Fed. Republic, later to Czech Republic and (non-resident) to Slovakia, 1991–94. Non-executive Director: EFG Private Bank Ltd, 1999–2005; Henderson EuroMicro Investment Trust, 2000–04. Chairman: Co-ordinating (formerly Consultative) Cttee on Remuneration (NATO, OECD, etc), 1999–2006; Anglo Spanish Cultural Foundn (Cañada Blanch) (formerly Cañada Blanch Foundn (UK)), 2006–. Robin Humphreys Fellow, Inst. for Latin Amer. Studies, London Univ., 2003. Chairman: Anglo-Spanish Soc., 2001–07; Friends of British Liby, 2004–07. Comendador, Order Infante Dom Henrique (Portugal), 1985. *Address:* 15 Provost Road, NW3 4ST.

BRIGNALL, Rt Rev. Peter Malcolm; *see* Wrexham, Bishop of, (RC).

BRIGSTOCKE, Dr Hugh Nicholas Andrew; freelance writer and art historian; *b* 7 May 1943; *s* of late Rev. Canon George Edward Brigstocke and Mollie (*née* Sandford); *m* 1969, Anthea Elizabeth White; one *s* one *d*. *Educ:* Marlborough Coll., Wilts; Magdalene Coll., Cambridge (MA Modern Hist.); Univ. of Edinburgh (PhD Art Hist. 1976). Curator, Italian, Spanish and French Paintings, National Gall. of Scotland, Edinburgh, 1968–83; Editor-in-Chief, 1983–87, Consulting Ed., 1987–89, Hon. Consulting Ed., 1989–96, Grove Dictionary of Art; Old Master Paintings, Sotheby's, London, 1989–95: Dir, 1990–95; Hd of Dept, 1993–94; Sen. Expert, 1994–95; Ed. (freelance), Oxford Companion to Western Art, 1995–2001. Paul Mellon Fellow, British Sch. at Rome, 2001. Ed., Walpole Soc., 2000–12. *Publications:* A Critical Catalogue of the Italian and Spanish Paintings, National Gallery of Scotland, 1978, 2nd edn 1993; William Buchanan and the 19th Century Art Trade: 100 letters to his agents in London and Italy, 1982; (ed) Oxford Companion to Western Art, 2001; (jtly) John Flaxman and William Young Ottley in Italy, 2010; British Travellers in Spain 1766–1849, 2015; *exhibition catalogues:* (jtly) Poussin Bacchanals and Sacraments, 1981; A Loan Exhibition of Poussin Drawings from British Collections, 1990; (jtly) Masterpieces from Yorkshire Houses: Yorkshire families at home and abroad 1700–1850, 1994; (jtly) Italian Paintings from Burghley House, 1995; (jtly) En Torno a Velázquez, 1999; (jtly) A Poet in Paradise: Lord Lindsay and Christian Art, 2000; Procaccini in America, 2002; contrib. articles to various jls incl. Burlington Mag., Apollo, Walpole Soc., British Art Jl, Revue de l'Art, Paragone, Revue du Louvre, Jahrbuch der Berliner Mus., Münchner Jahrbuch, etc. *Recreations:* opera, theatre, wine, horse-racing. *Address:* 118 Micklegate, York YO1 6JX. *T:* (01904) 626013. *E:* hugh.brigstocke@zen.co.uk.

See also Adm. Sir J. R. Brigstocke.

BRIGSTOCKE, Adm. Sir John (Richard), KCB 1997; DL; Judicial Appointments and Conduct Ombudsman, since 2006; *b* 30 July 1945; *s* of late Rev. Canon George Edward Brigstocke and Molly Brigstocke (*née* Sandford); *m* 1979, Heather, *d* of late Dennis and Muriel Day (*née* Glossop); one *s* (and one *s* decd). *Educ:* Marlborough Coll.; BRNC, Dartmouth; RNC Greenwich; RCDS. Joined RN, 1962; trng, 1962–66; HMS Caprice, 1966–69; HMY Britannia, 1969; HMS Whitby, 1969–70; i/c HMS Upton, 1970–71; long gunnery course, HMS Excellent, 1971–72; HMS Minerva, 1972–74; RNSC Greenwich, 1974; Staff, BRNC Dartmouth, 1974–76; First Lieut, HMS Ariadne, 1976–78; i/c HMS Bacchante, 1978–79; Directorate of Naval Plans, MoD, 1980–81 and 1982–84; Comdr Sea Trng, Portland, 1981–82; i/c HMS York and Capt. (D) 3rd Destroyer Sqn, 1986–87; Capt., BRNC Dartmouth, 1987–88; i/c HMS Ark Royal, 1989–90; FO, 2nd Flotilla, 1991–92; Comdr, UK Task Gp, 1992–93; ACNS and Mem. Admiralty Bd, 1993–95; Adm. Pres., RNC, Greenwich, 1994–95; Flag Officer, Surface Flotilla, 1995–97; Second Sea Lord, Mem. Admiralty Bd, C-in-C Naval Home Comd, and Flag ADC to the Queen, 1997–2000. Chief Exec., St Andrew's Gp of Hosps (med. charity), 2000–04; Director: Ind. Healthcare Assoc., 2000–03; Three Shires Hosp. Ltd, 2000–04; Chm., NHS E Midlands (E Midlands Strategic HA), 2006–10. Trustee, Nuffield Trust for the Forces of the Crown, 2003–. Vice Pres., Northants Sea Cadet Unit (TS Laforey), 2003–. Chm. Council, Univ. of Buckingham, 2005–08 (Mem., 2004–05). Younger Brother, Trinity House, 1981. Freeman, City of London, 1995. DL Northants, 2010. DUniv Buckingham 2009. *Address:* c/o Naval Secretary, Sir Henry Leach Building, Whale Island, Portsmouth PO2 8BY.

See also H. N. A. Brigstocke.

BRIGSTOCKE, Timothy David Alexander, MBE 2008; FRSB; Managing Partner, Tim Brigstocke Associates, since 1993; Executive Director, Cattle Health Certification Standards, since 2001; Policy Director, Royal Association of British Dairy Farmers, since 2007; *b* Guildford, 2 Sept. 1951; *s* of Alexander Julian Brigstocke, DL and late Diana Mavis Brigstocke (*née* Eversheđ); *m* 1977, Celia Comber; three *d*. *Educ:* Wellington Coll.; Bicton Coll. of Agric. (Advanced Nat. Cert. in Agric. 1975); Seale-Hayne Coll. (Dip. Farm Mgt 1976); Open Univ. (BA 1980); Univ. of Aston, Birmingham (MPhil 1984). CBiol 1983; FRSB (FIBiol 2008); CEnv 2008; Professional Agriculturist, 2011. Chief Agricl Advr, BOCM Pauls (formerly Silcock) Ltd, 1984–93; Inst. Business Manager, Inst. of Grassland and Envmtl Res., 1993–96; Chief Exec., Holstein Friesian Soc./Holstein UK & Ireland, 1996–99; Executive Chairman: Royal Assoc. of British Dairy Farmers, 2000–07; Rare Breeds Survival Trust, 2008–11. Vis. Fellow, RAU (formerly RAC), Cirencester, 2002– (Dairy Crest Fellowship, 2005). Non-executive Director: Cogent Breeding Ltd, 2003–11; Grosvenor Farms Ltd, 2003–06; Lantra, 2007– (Dep. Chm., 2014–). Member: Pre-Movement Testing Gp, 2004–06, Adv. Gp on Responsibility and Cost Sharing for Animal Health, 2009–10, Nat. Steering Cttee for Farm Animal Genetic Resources, 2003–06, DEFRA; England Implementation Gp, UK Govt's Animal Health and Welfare Strategy, 2005–09; Adv. Cttee on Animal Feedstuffs, Food Standards Agency, 2005–14; RSPCA/Freedom Foods Cattle Health and Welfare Gp, 2005–; Sustainable Agric. Strategy Panel, BBSRC, 2008–11; Veterinary Residues Cttee, Veterinary Medicines Directorate, 2009–15; Chairman: GB Cattle Health and Welfare Gp, 2010–; Nat. Equine Forum, 2013–; Farm Animal Genetic Resources Cttee, DEFRA, 2014–. Director: Soc. of Dairy Technol. Ltd, 2001–14; Soc. for the Envmt, 2006–. Vice Pres., Sci. Policy, Inst. of Biol., 2006–09. Chair, Coll. of Elected Mems, Soc. of Biol., later Royal Soc. of Biol., 2010–. Chm., Adv. Bd, Sch. of Agric., RAC, Cirencester, 2008–. FIAgrM 1992; FRAgS 1996. Harvard Agri-Business Seminar, 1998. Trustee: Inst. of Agricl Mgt, 1999– (Chm., 2010–14); Harper Adams UC Develt Trust Ltd, 2006–; Chm., Bd of Trustees, John Bradburne Meml Soc., 2003–. Princess Royal Award, Royal Assoc. of British Dairy Farmers, 2007. *Publications:* (with P. N. Wilson) Improved Feeding of Cattle and Sheep, 1982; contrib. papers to scientific and tech. jls. *Recreations:* sport, gardening, reading, modern jazz, modern railways. *Address:* Brick House, Risbury, Leominster, Herefordshire HR6 0NQ. *T:* (01568) 760632. *E:* timbrigstocke@hotmail.com. *Clubs:* Farmers, MCC.

BRIKHO, Samir Yacoub; Chief Executive, Amec Foster Wheeler (formerly AMEC) plc, since 2006; *b* 3 May 1958; *s* of Jacob and Victoria Brikho; two *s*. *Educ:* Royal Inst. of Technols, Stockholm (MSc Thermal Technol.); INSEAD (Young Managers Prog.); Stamford Univ. (Sen. Exec. Prog. 2000). Sen. Vice Pres., ABB, 1993–95; Sen. Vice Pres. and Man. Dir, ABB Kraftwerke, 1995–99; CEO, ABB Alstom Kraftwerke, 1999–2001; Sen. Vice Pres., Internat. Business and Chief Internat. Ops Officer, Alstom Power, 2000–03; Chief Exec., ABB Lummus Global, Switzerland, 2003–05; Mem. Exec. Bd, ABB, Hd, Power Systems Div. and Chm., ABB Lummus Global, 2005–06. Chm., UK Energy Excellence, 2008–10; Co-Chm., UK-UAE CEO Forum, 2011–; Member: Internat. Adv. Bd, SOAS, 2007–; Adv. Bd, Stena Offshore, 2011–; Adv. Bd, Asia House, 2012–; Bd, SEB, 2012–; Dir, UK Japan 21st Century Gp, 2007–; Co-chair, UK-Korea Global CEO Forum, 2013–. Chm., Disaster Resource Partnership Steering Bd, WEF, 2010–; Mem., UK Nat. Cttee, World Petroleum Congress, 2010–. Founder, Palestine Internat. Business Forum, 2005. UK Business Ambassador, 2010–. Chm., Step Change Foundn UK, 2011–. FREng 2013. *Recreations:* sports, music, dance. *Address:* Amec Foster Wheeler plc, Old Change House, 128 Queen Victoria Street, EC4V 4BJ. *T:* (020) 7429 7509, *Fax:* (020) 7429 7551. *E:* samir.brikho@amecfw.com. *Clubs:* Arts, Royal Automobile; Wentworth Golf.

BRILL, Elaine; *see* Bedell, E.

BRILL, Patrick, RA 2014; artist, as Bob and Roberta Smith; *b* London, 3 Feb. 1963; *s* of Fredrick Brill and Deirdre Brill (*née* Borlase); *m* 1990, Jessica Voorsanger; one *s* one *d*. *Educ:*

Wandsworth Comp. Sch.; Univ. of Reading (BA 1st Cl. Fine Art); British Sch. at Rome (Schol.); Goldsmiths Coll. (MA Fine Arts 1993). Harkness Fellow, Cooper Union Sch. of Arts and Scis, NY, 1988–90. Group exhibitions include: Altermodern, 2009, Rude Britannia, 2010, Tate Britain; solo exhibitions include: The Gotham Golem, Pierogi Gall., NY, 2011; I should be in Charge, Hales Gall., London, 2011; The Aldwincle Golem, The Salisbury Golem, All Saints, Aldwincle, 2011. Poster design for 2012 Olympics. Trustee, Tate, 2009–13. Patron, Nat. Soc. for Educn in Art and Design, 2012–. Contested (Ind) (as Bob Smith) Surrey Heath, 2015. Hon. Fellow, Univ. of Creative Arts, Bournemouth, 2011. *Publications:* as Bob and Roberta Smith: Make Your Own Damn Art, 2005; Art U Need, 2008; I Should be in Charge (monograph), 2011. *Recreation:* work all the time - no days off! *Address:* 49 Rhodesia Road, Leytonstone, E11 4DF. *E:* bobsmith.lcca@ntlworld.com.

BRIMACOMBE, Prof. John Stuart, FRSE, FRSC, FRSB; Roscoe Professor of Chemistry, University of Dundee, 1969–2002; *b* Falmouth, Cornwall, 18 Aug. 1935; *s* of Stanley Poole Brimacombe and Lillian May Kathleen Brimacombe (*née* Candy); *m* 1959, Eileen (*née* Gibson); four *d*. *Educ:* Falmouth Grammar Sch.; Birmingham Univ. (DSc); DSc Dundee Univ. FRSC 1966; FRSB (FIBiol 2000). Lectr in Chemistry, Birmingham Univ., 1961–69. FRSE 1973. Meldola Medallist, 1964, Haworth Lect. and Medal, 2007, RSC. *Publications:* (co-author) Mucopolysaccharides, 1964; numerous papers, reviews, etc., in: Jl Chem. Soc., Carbohydrate Research, etc. *Recreations:* sport, swimming. *Address:* 29 Dalhousie Road, Barnhill, Dundee DD5 2SP. *T:* (01382) 779214.

BRIMELOW, Alison Jane, CBE 2005; President, European Patent Office, 2007–10 (President-elect, and Vice-Chair of Administrative Council, 2004–07); *b* 6 June 1949. HM Diplomatic Service, 1973–76; DTI, 1976–2003; Comptroller Gen. and Chief Exec., Patent Office, 1999–2003. Associate Fellow, Green Templeton Coll. (formerly Templeton Coll.), Oxford, 2005–13; Chm., Intellectual Property Inst., QMUL, 2011–13. Chair: Hartlebury Castle Preservation Trust, 2010–13 (Vice Pres., 2013–); CREATe Prog. Adv. Council, 2014–; Trustee, Nicholas John Trust, 2010. Gov., Bromsgrove Sch., 2010–13. Mem. Council, Worcester Cath., 2011–. Hon. LLD Wolverhampton, 2007; Hon. DSc Aston, 2015. Bundesverdienstkreuz (Germany), 2011. *Club:* Athenæum.

BRIMELOW, (Janine) Kirsty; QC 2011; *b* Preston, 5 Aug. 1969; *d* of Ron Brimelow and Jean Brimelow (*née* Stockley). *Educ:* Univ. of Birmingham (LLB Hons 1990). Called to the Bar, Gray's Inn, 1991, Bencher, 2015; in practice as a barrister, specialising in criminal, internat. and human rights law. Bar Council: spokesperson, 1998–2008; Member: Bar Public Affairs Gp, 2000–07; Central London Bar Mess Cttee, 2004–07; Bar Conf. Organising Bd, 2006–08; Bar Human Rights Committee: Mem., 2007–11; Vice-Chm., 2007–12; Chm., 2012–; Rep. for Bar Human Rights Cttee on Euro-Med. Human Rights Network, 2005–10; Member: Pro Bono Bar Caribbean Cttee, 2005–08; Child Rights Unit, 2009–12. Member: Cttee, Criminal Bar Assoc., 2004–10; Attorney Gen. Pro Bono Cttee, 2012–. Member: Opinion Leader Res. Panel, 2005–08; Populus Res. Panel, 2006–08; The Times Law Panel, 2007–09. *Recreations:* martial arts, mountain climbing, ski-ing, theatre, music passion. *Address:* Doughty Street Chambers, 54 Doughty Street, WC1N 2LS. *T:* (020) 7404 1313. *E:* k.brimelow@doughtystreet.co.uk.

BRIMS, Lt Gen. Robin Vaughan, CB 2007; CBE 1999 (OBE 1991; MBE 1986); DSO 2003; DL; consultant on military matters and education, since 2010; Rector, University of Kurdistan Hawler, Iraq, 2008–09; *b* 27 June 1951; *s* of late David Vaughan Brims and of Eve Georgina Mary Brims. *Educ:* Winchester Coll. Commissioned LI, 1970; sc 1982–83; CO 3rd Bn LI, 1989–91; Comdr, 24 Airmobile Bde, 1995–96; COS, NI, 1997–98; Dir, Army Resources and Plans, 1999; Comdr, Multinat. Div. (South West), 2000; GOC 1 (UK) Armoured Div., 2000–03; Dep. Chief of Jt Ops, MoD, 2003–05; Dep. Commanding Gen., Multinational Force, Iraq, 2005 (on detachment); Comdr, Field Army, Land Comd, 2005–07. Col, Light Infantry, 2001–06; Col Comdt, Light Div., 2005–07; Dep. Col Comdt, AGC, 2001–06. Hon. Colonel: Northumbrian Univs OTC, 2008–13; 72 Engr Regt (Vols), 2008–14. President: Army Cricket, 2003–05; Army Football Assoc., 2005–07. Chm., N of England, 2010–, Chm., Council, 2011–, RFCA. Patron, Finchale Trng Coll., 2012–. Trustee: Dickon Trust, 1994–2014; Ski 2 Freedom, 2008–14; Oswin Project, 2012–; Director: Norcare, 2010–14; Thirteen Care and Support, 2014–. Chm., Northumbria Historic Churches Trust, 2011–. DL Tyne and Wear, 2009. Officer, Legion of Merit (USA), 2006. *Recreation:* sport. *Address:* c/o RHQ The Rifles, Peninsula Barracks, Romsey Road, Winchester, Hants SO23 8TS.

BRIMSON-LEWIS, Stephen John; freelance theatre designer, since 1985; Associate Artist, since 2013, and Director of Design, since 2014, Royal Shakespeare Company; *b* 15 Feb. 1963; *s* of David and Doris Lewis; adopted stage name Brimson-Lewis. *Educ:* Central Sch. of Art and Design (BA Hons). Designer of productions: for RNT, incl. Les Parents Terribles (Olivier Award for Best Set Design), 1995, A Little Night Music, 1996; for RSC, 1999–, incl. A Midsummer Night's Dream, 2005, Antony and Cleopatra, 2006, Richard II, 2013, Henry IV, 2014, Death of a Salesman, Volpone, Henry V, 2015; Design for Living (Olivier Award for Best Set Design), Donmar Warehouse, 1995; Dirty Dancing, Aldwych and world tour, 2006; Waiting for Godot, Haymarket, 2009; Ghosts, Duchess, 2010; Master Builder, Minerva Th., Chichester, 2010; An Ideal Husband, Vaudeville, 2010; Flare Path, The Lion in Winter, The Tempest, Haymarket, 2011; La Bohème, WNO, 2012; Heartbreak House, Chichester, 2012; Waiting for Godot, No Man's Land, Broadway, 2013; Relative Values, Th. Royal, Bath, 2013, transf. Harold Pinter Th., 2014; also for maj. internat. opera and ballet cos. *Address:* c/o Clare Vidal-Hall, 57 Carthew Road, W6 0DU. *T:* (020) 8741 7647. *E:* cvh@clarevidalhall.com.

BRINCKMAN, Sir Theodore (George Roderick), 6th Bt *cr* 1831; retired antiquarian bookseller; *b* 20 March 1932; *s* of Col. Sir Roderick Napoleon Brinckman, 5th Bt, DSO, MC, and Margaret Wilson Southam; *S* father, 1985; *m* 1st, 1958, Helen Mary Anne Cook (marr. diss. 1983), *d* of Arnold Cook; two *s* one *d*; 2nd, 1983, Hon. Sheira Murray (marr. diss. 2001), formerly wife of Christopher Murray, and *d* of Baron Harvington, AE, PC; 3rd, 2001, Margaret Kindersley, formerly wife of Gay Kindersley, and *d* of Hugh Wakefield. *Educ:* Trinity College School, Port Hope, Ontario; Millfield; Christ Church, Oxford; Trinity Coll., Toronto (BA). *Heir: s* Theodore Jonathan Brinckman, *b* 19 Feb. 1960. *Address:* West Lodge, Aboyne Castle, Aberdeenshire AB34 5JP. *T:* (01339) 887598.

BRIND, (Arthur) Henry, CMG 1973; HM Diplomatic Service, retired; *b* 4 July 1927; *o s* of late T. H. Brind and late N. W. B. Brind; *m* 1954, Barbara Harrison (*d* 2012); one *s* one *d*. *Educ:* Barry; St John's Coll., Cambridge. HM Forces, 1947–49. Colonial Administrative Service: Gold Coast/Ghana, 1950–60; Regional Sec., Trans-Volta Togoland, 1959. HM Diplomatic Service, 1960–87: Acting High Comr, Uganda, 1972–73; High Comr, Mauritius, 1974–77; Ambassador to Somali Democratic Republic, 1977–80; Vis. Research Fellow, RIIA, 1981–82; High Comr, Malaŵi, 1983–87. Grand Comdr, Order of Lion of Malaŵi, 1985. *Publications:* Lying Abroad (memoirs), 1999. *Recreations:* walking, swimming, books. *Address:* 20 Grove Terrace, NW5 1PH. *T:* (020) 7267 1190. *Club:* Reform.

BRINDED, Malcolm Arthur, CBE 2002; FREng; Member of the Board, 2003–12, and Executive Director, Upstream International, 2009–12, Royal Dutch/Shell plc; *b* 18 March 1953; *s* of Cliff and Gwen Brinded; *m* 1975, Carola Telford; three *s*. *Educ:* Churchill Coll., Cambridge (MA Engrg). Shell Internat., The Hague, 1974–75; Project Engr, Brunei Shell Petroleum, 1975–80; Facilities Engr, Shell UK Exploration and Prodn, 1980–82; on secondment to Dept of Energy as Policy Advr, 1982–84; Nederlands Aardolie MIJ, 1984–86; Shell Gp, 1987–88; Business Unit Dir, Petroleum Develt, Shell Oman, 1988–92; Shell UK Exploration and Prodn, 1993–2001 (Man. Dir, 1998–2001); Country Chm., Shell UK Ltd, 1999–2002; Dir, Planning, HSE and External Affairs, Shell Internat., 2001–02; Gp Man. Dir, 2002–03, Vice Chm., Cttee of Man. Dirs, 2003, Royal Dutch/Shell Gp of Cos; CEO, Shell Gas & Power, 2003; Exec. Dir, Shell Exploration and Prodn, 2004–09. Non-executive Director: Network Rail, 2010–; CH2M Hill, 2010–12; BHP Billiton, 2014–. FICE; FREng 2002. Hon. FIMechE 2003. Alec Buchanan Smith Award for contrib. to Scottish oil and gas industry, 2001. *Recreations:* music, mountain biking, Rugby.

BRINDLE, Ian; Deputy Chairman, Financial Reporting Review Panel, 2001–08; *b* 17 Aug. 1943; *s* of John Brindle and Mabel Brindle (*née* Walsh); *m* 1967, Frances Elisabeth Moseby; two *s* one *d*. *Educ:* Blundell's School; Manchester Univ. (BA Econ). FCA 1969. Price Waterhouse: articled in London, 1965; Toronto, 1971; admitted to partnership, 1976; Mem., Supervisory Cttee, 1988–98; Dir, Audit and Business Advisory Services, 1990–91; Mem., UK Exec., 1990–98; Sen. Partner, 1991–98; company merged with Coopers & Lybrand, 1998; UK Chm., PricewaterhouseCoopers, 1998–2001. Sen. Ind. Dir, Elementis plc, 2008– (non-exec. Dir, 2005–08; Chm., 2013–14). Member: Auditing Practices Cttee, CCAB, 1986–9[illegible] (Chm., 1990); Accounting Standards Bd, 1993–2001 (Mem. Urgent Issues Task Force, 1991–93); Council, ICAEW, 1994–97; Financial Reporting Council, 1995–2008. Auditor, Duchy of Cornwall, 1993–. *Recreations:* tennis, golf. *Address:* Milestones, Packhorse Road, Bessels Green, Sevenoaks, Kent TN13 2QP.

BRINDLE, Jane; *see* Cox, Josephine.

BRINDLE, Prof. Kevin Michael, DPhil; FMedSci; Professor of Biomedical Magnetic Resonance, University of Cambridge, since 2005; Senior Group Leader, Cancer Research UK Cambridge Institute, since 2006; *b* Oxford, 27 Aug. 1955; *s* of late Cecil Brindle and of Anne Spencer Brindle (*née* Kilbee, now Hale); *m* 1985, Alexandra Mary Fulton. *Educ:* Gosford Hill Comprehensive Sch., Kidlington, Oxford; Oriel Coll., Oxford (BA; MA; DPhil 1982); Royal Society 1983 University Research Fellow: Dept of Biochem., Univ. of Oxford, 1986–90; Dept of Biochem. and Molecular Biol., Univ. of Manchester, 1990–91; Lectr, Univ. of Manchester, 1991–93; Lectr, 1993–2001, Reader, 2001–05, Univ. of Cambridge. FMedSci 2012. *Publications:* contribs to peer-reviewed jls. *Recreations:* cycling, gardening. *Address:* Department of Biochemistry, University of Cambridge, Tennis Court Road, Cambridge CB2 1GA. *T:* (01223) 333674; Cancer Research UK Cambridge Institute, Li Ka Shing Centre, Robinson Way, Cambridge CB2 0RE. *T:* (01223) 769647. *E:* kmb1001@cam.ac.uk.

BRINDLE, Michael John; QC 1992; a Recorder, since 2000; a Deputy High Court Judge, since 2001; *b* 23 June 1952; *s* of John Arthur Brindle and Muriel Jones; *m* 1st, 1988, Heather Mary (*née* Pearce) (marr. diss. 2005); one *s* two *d*; 2nd, 2007, Alison Jane (*née* Slann). *Educ:* Westminster Sch.; New Coll., Oxford (Ella Stephens Schol. in Classics; 1st Cl. Hons Mods 1972; 1st Cl. Jurisprudence, 1974; MA). Called to the Bar, Lincoln's Inn, 1975 (Hardwicke Scholar), Bencher, 2002. Chairman: Commercial Bar Assoc., 2001–02 (Treas., 1999–2001); Bar Educn and Trng Cttee, 2003–05; Bar Council Internat. Cttee, 2008–09. Member, Financial Reporting Review Panel, 1998–2007; Financial Markets Law Cttee, 2004. Chm., Adv. Council, Public Concern at Work, 2001– (Chm. Trustees, 1997–2001). *Recreations:* classical music, travel, bridge. *Address:* Fountain Court, Temple, EC4Y 9DH.

BRINDLE, Dr Michael John, CBE 1998; FRCP, FRCR, FRCPC, FRCPE, FRCSE; Consultant Radiologist, The Queen Elizabeth Hospital, King's Lynn, 1972–98; President, Royal College of Radiologists, 1995–98; *b* 18 Nov. 1934; *s* of Dr W. S. Brindle and P. M. Brindle; *m* 1960, Muriel Eileen Hayward (*d* 2012); one *s* two *d* (and one *s* decd); *m* 201[illegible] Diana Sarah Fox. *Educ:* Liverpool Univ. (MB ChB 1958; MD 1967; MRad 1971). FRCPC 1972; FRCR 1989; FRCP 1998; FRCPE 1999; FRCSE 1999. Surgeon Lieut, RN, 1959–6[illegible]; Consultant, Royal Alexandra Hosp., Edmonton, Alberta, 1966–72. Treas., RCR, 1990–9[illegible]; LRPS 2007. Hon. FRCGP 1998; Hon. FFSEM 2009. *Recreations:* bird-watching, photography.

BRINDLEY, Very Rev. David Charles; Dean of Portsmouth, since 2002; *b* 11 June 195[illegible]; *m* 1975, Gillian Griffin; one *s* two *d*. *Educ:* Wednesfield Grammar Sch.; King's Coll., London (BD, AKC 1975; MTh 1976; MPhil 1980). VSO, Lebanon, 1971–72. Ordained deacon, 1976, priest, 1977; Curate, Epping, 1976–79; Lectr, Coll. of St Paul and St Mary, Cheltenham, 1979–82; Vicar, Quorn, and Dir of Clergy Trng, dio. Leicester, 1982–86; Principal, W of England Ministerial Trng Course, 1987–94; Team Rector, Warwick, 1994–2002. *Publications:* Stepping Aside, 1993; Story, Song and Law, 1996; Richard Beauchamp: medieval England's greatest knight, 2001; *for children:* (with Gillian Brindley) Moses, 1985; Joseph, 1985. *Recreations:* folk music, modern literature, theatre, ballroom and Latin dancing. *Address:* The Deanery, Pembroke Road, Portsmouth PO1 2NS. *T:* (home) (023) 9282 4400, (office) (023) 9234 7605, *Fax:* (023) 9229 5480. *E:* david.brindley@portsmouthcathedral.org.uk. *Clubs:* Athenæum, Royal Naval.

BRINDLEY, Prof. Giles Skey, MA, MD; FRS 1965; FRCP; Professor of Physiology in the University of London at the Institute of Psychiatry, 1968–91, now Emeritus; *b* 30 April 192[illegible]; *s* of late Arthur James Benet Skey and Dr Margaret Beatrice Marion Skey (*née* Dewhurst), late Brindley; *m* 1st, 1959, Lucy Dunk Bennell (marr. diss.); 2nd, 1964, Dr Hilary Richards; one *s* one *d*. *Educ:* Leyton County High School; Downing College, Cambridge (Hon. Fellow 1969); London Hospital Medical College. Various jun. clin. and res. posts, 1950–54; Russian lang. abstractor, British Abstracts of Medical Sciences, 1953–56; successively Demonstrator, Lectr and Reader in Physiology, Univ. of Cambridge, 1954–68; Fellow: King's Coll., Cambridge, 1959–62; Trinity Coll., Cambridge, 1963–68. Hon. Dir, MRC Neurological Prostheses Unit, 1968–92; Hon. Consultant Physician, Maudsley Hosp., 1971–92. Chm. of Editorial Board, Journal of Physiology, 1964–66 (Mem., 1959–64). Visiting Prof., Univ. of California, Berkeley, 1968. Hon. FRCS 1988; Hon. FRCSE 2000. Liebrecht-Franceschetti Prize, German Ophthalmological Soc., 1971; Feldberg Prize, Feldberg Foundn, 1974; St Peter's Medal, British Assoc. of Urological Surgeons, 1987. *Publications:* Physiology of the Retina and Visual Pathway, 1960, 2nd edn 1970; papers in scientific, musicological and medical journals. *Recreations:* designing, making and playing various musical instruments (inventor of the logical bassoon), composing chamber music, songs and short orchestral pieces; formerly cross-country and track running (silver medallist, 2000m steeplechase and 800m (men over 65), World Veterans' Track and Field Championships, Finland, 1991). *Address:* 10 Ferndene Road, SE24 0AA. *T:* (020) 7274 2598.

BRINDLEY, John Frederick, CB 1996; Circuit Administrator, South Eastern Circuit, 1995–97; *b* 25 Sept. 1937; *s* of Harold and Eva Brindley; *m* 1960, Judith Ann Sherratt; one *d*. *Educ:* Leek Grammar Sch. Lord Chancellor's Department: Court Business Officer, Midland and Oxford Circuit, 1971; HQ Personnel Officer, 1976; Courts Administrator, Exeter Group, 1981; Head, Civil Business Div. HQ, 1987; Court Service Management Gp, 1988; Court Service Business Gp, 1991. Chm., CSSB, 1998–2004. *Publications:* Court in the Act, 200[illegible]; Music for a While, 2014. *Recreations:* hockey, cricket, amateur theatricals, choral and solo singing. *Address:* Sidmouth, Devon. *Club:* Athenæum.

BRINDLEY, Kate Victoria; Director, Arnolfini, since 2014; *b* Sheffield, 27 May 1970; *d* of Roger and Carol Manning. *Educ:* Silverdale Sch., Sheffield; Univ. of Leeds (BA Jt Hons Hist. of Art and Religious Studies); Univ. of Manchester (Dip. Mus and Gall. Studies). AMA 199[illegible]. Curatorial asst, Mead Gall., Warwick Univ., 1992–96; Exhibns Officer, Leamington Spa Art Gall., 1994–98; Art and Exhibns Officer, Rugby Art Gall. and Mus., 1998–2000; freelance curator and consultant, 2000–02; Hd of Arts and Mus., Wolverhampton CC, 2002–05; Dir of Mus, Galleries & Archives, Bristol CC, 2005–09; Dir, Middlesbrough Inst. of Modern Art

2009–14. Advr, Visual Art, Arts Council England, W Midlands, 1996–2002. Lead, SW Hub for Mus, 2005–09. Arts Advr, Paul Hamlyn Foundn, 2008– (Chair, Mus & Galls Special Initiative, 2010–). Trustee: Craftspace Touring, 2002–05; AV Fest. NE, 2010–14 (Vice Chair, 2011–14). *Recreations:* shopping, drinking lattes and wine, watching movies, seeking the sun, horse riding. *Address:* Arnolfini, 16 Narrow Quay, Bristol BS1 4QA. *E:* kate.brindley@arnolfini.org.uk.

BRINDLEY, Dame Lynne (Janie), DBE 2008; Master, Pembroke College, Oxford, since 2013; *b* 2 July 1950; *d* of Ivan Blowers and Janie Blowers (*née* Williams); adopted *d* of Ronald Williams and Elaine Williams (*née* Chapman), 1958; *m* 1972, Timothy Stuart Brindley. *Educ:* Truro High Sch.; Univ. of Reading (BA 1971); UCL (MA 1975; Hon. Fellow, 2002). FIInfSc 1990; FCLIP (FLA 1990). Head of Mktg and of Chief Exec.'s Office, British Library, 1979–85; Dir of Library and Information Services, and Pro-Vice Chancellor, Aston Univ., 1985–90; Principal Consultant, KPMG, 1990–92; Librarian and Dir of Information Services, LSE, 1992–97; Librarian and Pro-Vice Chancellor, Univ. of Leeds, 1997–2000; Chief Exec., British Library, 2000–12. Visiting Professor: Knowledge Mgt, Univ. of Leeds, 2000–09; City Univ., 2002–. Member: Lord Chancellor's Adv. Cttee on Public Records, 1992–98; Jt Inf. Systems Cttee, HEFCs, 1992–98 (Chair, Electronic Libraries Prog., 1993–98); Review of Higher Educn Libraries, HEFCs, 1992–93; Internat. Cttee on Social Sci. Inf., UNESCO, 1992–97; Res. Resources Bd, 1994–2001, Communications and Inf. Cttee, 2004–, ESRC; Liby and Inf. Commn, DCMS, 1999–2000; Stanford Univ. Adv. Council for Libraries and Inf. Resources, 1999–; AHRC, 2008–14; Strategic Adv. Bd for Intellectual Property, 2008–10; Bd, Ofcom, 2011–; Arts Panel, Wolfson Trust, 2012–. Trustee, Thackray Med. Mus., Leeds, 1999–2001. FRSA 1993. CCMI 2004. Freeman, City of London, 1989; Liveryman, Goldsmiths' Co., 1993– (Mem., Court of Assts, 2006–). Honorary Fellow: Univ. of Wales, Aberystwyth, 2007; LSE, 2008; Hon. FBA 2015. Hon. DLitt: Nottingham Trent, 2001; Oxford, Leicester, London Guildhall, 2002; Reading, Sheffield, 2004; Aston, 2008; Loughborough, Manchester, 2011; TCD, 2012; Hon. DSc: City, 2005; Leeds, 2006; DUniv Open, 2006; Hon. DArts de Montfort, 2011; Hon. DLit London, 2012; Hon. DLaws Durham, 2013. *Publications:* numerous articles on electronic libraries and information mgt. *Recreations:* classical music, theatre, modern art, hill walking. *Address:* Pembroke College, Oxford OX1 1DW. *Club:* Reform.

BRINE, Stephen Charles; MP (C) Winchester, since 2010; *b* 28 Jan. 1974; *s* of Clive Charles Brine and late Gloria Elizabeth Brine; *m* 2003, Susie Toulson; one *s* one *d*. *Educ:* Bohunt Comprehensive Sch.; Highbury Coll., Portsmouth; Liverpool Hope UC (BA Hist. Liverpool Univ. 1997). Journalist: BBC Radio Surrey; BBC Southern Counties Radio; WGN Radio, Chicago; work in consultancy firm specialising in customer care; former Dir, Azalea Gp. Area Campaign Dir, Hants and IoW, Cons. Party, 2001–05. *Address:* House of Commons, SW1A 0AA.

BRINK, Prof. Christoffel Hendrik, PhD, DPhil; Vice-Chancellor, Newcastle University, since 2007; *b* Upington, CP, S Africa, 31 Jan. 1951; *s* of Petrus Johannes Brink and Hester Brink; *m* 1981, Tobea du Preez; one *s* two *d*. *Educ:* Upington Primary and Secondary Sch., SA; Rand Afrikaans Univ., Johannesburg (BSc Maths and Computer Sci. 1972; DPhil 1992); Rhodes Univ. (BSc Hons Maths 1973; MSc Maths 1974; MA Phil. 1975); PhD Algebraic Logic Cambridge 1978. Mil. trng, Army Gymnasium Heidelberg, 1969 (2nd Lt). Lectr in Maths, 1979–80, Sen. Lectr, 1980–86, Univ. of Stellenbosch; Associate Prof. of Maths, Univ. of Cape Town, 1987–92; Sen. Res. Fellow, ANU, 1988–90; University of Cape Town: Hd, Dept of Maths, 1991–94; Prof. of Maths, 1993–99; Hd, Dept of Maths and Applied Maths, 1995–99; Dir, Lab. for Formal Aspects and Complexity in Computer Sci., 1994–99; Coordinator of Strategic Planning, 1997; Pro Vice-Chancellor (Res.) and Prof. of Maths, Univ. of Wollongong, NSW, 1999–2001; Vice-Chancellor and Rector, Stellenbosch Univ., 2002–07. Member, Board: Russell Gp, 2007–; N8, 2007–; Equality Challenge Unit, 2008–13; QAA, 2009–13; NE Local Enterprise Partnership, 2011–13; UUK, 2012–15. Founder Mem., Acad. of Sci. of SA, 1995; FRSSAf 1995. Hon. Col, Mil. Acad. of SA, 2004. *Publications:* (jtly) Wiskunde vir Wetenskapstudente (Mathematics for Science Students), 1983; (ed jtly) Relational Methods in Computer Science, 1997; (with I. M. Rewitzky) A Paradigm for Program Semantics: power structures and duality, 2001; No Lesser Place: the taaldebat at Stellenbosch, 2006. *Address:* Newcastle University, King's Gate, Newcastle upon Tyne NE1 7RU. *T:* (0191) 208 6064, *Fax:* (0191) 208 6828. *E:* chris.brink@ncl.ac.uk.

BRINK, Prof. David Maurice, DPhil; FRS 1981; Professor of History of Physics, University of Trento, Italy, 1993–98; *b* 20 July 1930; *s* of Maurice Ossian Brink and Victoria May Finlayson; *m* 1958, Verena Wehrli; one *s* two *d*. *Educ:* Friends' Sch., Hobart; Univ. of Tasmania (BSc); Univ. of Oxford (DPhil). Rhodes Scholar, 1951–54; Rutherford Scholar, 1954–58; Lectr, 1954–58, Fellow and Tutor, 1958–93, Balliol Coll., Oxford; Univ. Lectr, 1958–89, H. J. G. Moseley Reader in Physics, 1989–93, Oxford Univ., retd. Instructor, MIT, 1956–57. Foreign Mem., Royal Soc. of Scis of Uppsala, 1992. Rutherford Medal and Prize, Inst. of Physics, 1982; Lise Meitner Prize for Nuclear Physics, Eur. Physical Soc., 2006. *Publications:* Angular Momentum, 1962, 3rd edn 1993; Nuclear Forces, 1965; Semi-classical Methods in Nucleus-Nucleus Scattering, 1985; (with R. Broglia) Nuclear Superfluidity, 2004. *Recreations:* birdwatching, walking. *Address:* 34 Minster Road, Oxford OX4 1LY. *T:* (01865) 246127.

BRINKLEY, Robert Edward, CMG 2006; HM Diplomatic Service, retired; international affairs consultant, since 2011; *b* 21 Jan. 1954; *s* of Thomas Edward Brinkley and Sheila Doris Brinkley (*née* Gearing); *m* 1982, (Frances) Mary Webster (*née* Edwards); three *s*. *Educ:* Stonyhurst Coll.; Corpus Christi Coll., Oxford (MA). Entered HM Diplomatic Service, 1977: FCO, 1977–78; Mem., UK Delegn to Comprehensive Test Ban Negotiations, Geneva, 1978; Second Sec., Moscow, 1979–82; First Secretary: FCO, 1982–88; Bonn, 1988–92; FCO, 1992–95; Counsellor and Head, Fundamental Expenditure Rev. Unit, FCO, 1995–96; Political Counsellor, Moscow, 1996–99; Head, FCO/Home Office Jt Entry Clearance Unit, 2000–02; Ambassador to Ukraine, 2002–06; High Comr to Pakistan, 2006–09; Business Develt Manager, Associated British Foods plc (on secondment), 2010–11. Vis. Fellow, 2012–, Senator, 2013–, Ukrainian Catholic Univ. Mem., RIIA, 2012–. Trustee: Karachi Educn Initiative (UK), 2010–11; BEARR Trust, 2011– (Chm., 2012–); Keston Inst., 2014–. *Recreations:* walking, swimming, reading, music (violin). *Club:* Athenæum.

BRINLEY JONES, Robert; *see* Jones, Dr R. B.

BRINSDEN, Peter Robert, FRCOG; Consultant Medical Director, Bourn Hall Clinic, Cambridge, 2005–10 and since 2013 (Consultant Gynaecologist and Medical Director, 1989–2005); Medical Director, Clane Fertility Unit, County Kildare, since 1995; Group Medical Director, Bourn Hall International, 2010–13; *b* 2 Sept. 1940; *s* of Dudley and Geraldine Brinsden; *m* 1967, Gillian Susan Heather; two *s*. *Educ:* Rugby Sch.; King's Coll. London; St George's Hosp., London (MB BS 1966). MRCS 1966; LRCP 1966; FRCOG 1989. House officer appts, 1967; Medical Officer, Royal Navy, 1966–82: appointments: HMS Glamorgan, 1967–68; RN Hosps, Haslar, Plymouth, Malta and Gibraltar, 1968–78; civilian hosps, Southampton and Portsmouth, 1972–74; Surgeon Comdr, 1976; Consultant Obstetrician and Gynaecologist, RN Hosps, Portsmouth and Plymouth, 1978–82; retd 1982; Consultant: King Fahd Hosp., Riyadh, 1982–84; Bourn Hall and Wellington Hosp., 1985–89. Affiliated Lectr, Univ. of Cambridge Clinical Sch., Addenbrooke's Hosp., 1992–2007. Vis. Prof. in Gynaecology and Fertility, Capital Medical Univ., Beijing, 2001–; Hon. Prof., Peking Union Medical Coll., Beijing, 2003–; Guest Prof., Southern Medical Univ., Guangzhou, 2008–. Inspector, HFEA, 1997–2010. Pres., British Fertility Soc., 2009–12; Trustee: British Fertility Soc. Educnl Trust, 2014–; Abbeyfield Tavistock Soc., 2014–. Gov., Newton Primary Sch., Cambs, 1998–2001. *Publications:* (ed) A Textbook of In-Vitro Fertilization and Assisted Reproduction, 1992, 3rd edn 2005; (ed jtly) A Manual of Intrauterine Insemination and Ovulation Induction, 2010; contrib. numerous medical articles and book chapters on infertility and assisted reproduction. *Recreations:* sailing, sub-aqua diving, computing, photography. *Address:* Mapledurham, 116b Whitchurch Road, Tavistock, Devon PL19 9BQ. *E:* peter@brinsden.net.

BRINSMEAD, Christopher David, CBE 2015; independent adviser; Adviser on Life Sciences to Prime Minister, Department of Health, and Department of Business, Innovation and Skills, since 2010; *b* Rochford, Essex, 27 March 1959; *s* of Peter Brinsmead and Anne Brinsmead; *m* 1980, Lisa Hemeter; two *d*. *Educ:* Wells Cathedral Sch.; Nottingham Univ. (BSc 1980); Manchester Business Sch. (MSc 1985). Various commercial roles, ICI, later Zeneca, 1980–97, Regl Vice-Pres. Asia, 1997–99; Vice Pres., Product Strategy, AstraZeneca, 1999–2001; Pres., AstraZeneca UK, 2001–08; Pres., 2002–08, Chm., 2008–10, AstraZeneca Pharma UK; Chairman: Proteus Digital Health Europe (formerly Proteus Biomedical Europe), 2011–; Diagnostic Capital Ltd, 2011–; Proveca Ltd, 2013–. Non-executive Director: Domino Printing Sciences, 2008–; Datapharm, 2008–10; United Drug plc, 2010–; Wesleyan Assce Soc., 2010–; Kinapse Ltd, 2010–; Cambian Gp plc, 2014–. Chm., Life Scis Bd, 2008–. Pres., ABPI, 2008–10. Mem. Council, Imperial Coll. London, 2013–. *Recreations:* golf, sailing, walking, running, ski-ing. *Club:* Royal Automobile.

BRINTON, Baroness *cr* 2011 (Life Peer), of Kenardington in the County of Kent; **Sarah Virginia, (Sal), Brinton;** Executive Director, Association of Universities in the East of England, 2006–11; *b* Paddington, 1 April 1955; *e d* of late Timothy Denis Brinton and of Jane-Mari Brinton (now Shearing); *m* 1983, Tim Whittaker; two *s* one *d*. *Educ:* Churchill Coll., Cambridge (BA 1984; MA 1992). BBC: Prodn Sec., Radio 3, 1974–76, Radio Drama, 1976–77; Floor Manager, London and Glasgow, 1977–81; Manager: New Cambridge Research Ltd (venture capital), 1984–87; Cambridge Venture Mgt Ltd, 1987–91; Dir, Cambridge Venture Capital Ltd, 1987–91; Bursar: Lucy Cavendish Coll., Cambridge, 1992–97; Selwyn Coll., Cambridge, 1997–2002. Chm., Learning and Skills Council, Cambs, 2000–06; Mem. Bd, E of England Develt Agency, 1999–2004 (Dep. Chm., 2002–04). Mem. (Lib Dem), Cambs CC, 1993–2004 (Leader, Lib Dem Gp, 1997–2004). Contested (Lib Dem): Cambs SE, 1997, 2001; Watford, 2005, 2010. Liberal Democrat Party: Mem., Federal Policy Cttee, 2004–08 and 2010– (Vice Chm., 2006–08); Pres., 2015–; Vice Chair, Federal Conference Cttee; Chair, Diversity Engagement Gp. Dir and Trustee, Christian Blind Mission UK Ltd, 2003–14; Trustee, University for Industry Charitable Trust, 2003–. *Address:* House of Lords, SW1A 0PW.

BRINTON, Helen Rosemary; *see* Clark, H. R.

BRISBANE, Archbishop of, and Metropolitan of the Province of Queensland, since 2002; **Most Rev. Dr Phillip John Aspinall;** Primate of Australia, 2005–14; *b* 17 Dec. 1959; *m* 1982, Christa Schmitt; two *s*. *Educ:* Univ. of Tasmania (BSc 1980); Brisbane Coll. of Advanced Educn (Grad. DipRE 1985); Ecumenical Inst., Geneva (Cert. 1987); Trinity Coll., Melbourne Coll. of Divinity (BD (Hons) 1988); Monash Univ. (PhD 1989); Deakin Univ. (MBA 1998). Field Officer, C of E Boys' Soc., 1980; Diocesan Youth and Educn Officer, 1981–84; Dep. Warden, Christ Coll., Dio. Tasmania, 1983–84; Dir, Parish Educn, St Stephen's, Mt Waverley, Dio. Melbourne, 1985–88; ordained deacon, 1988, priest, 1989; Asst Curate, St Mark-on-the-Hill, 1988–89; Asst Priest, Brighton, 1989–91; Priest in charge, Bridgewater-Gagebrook, 1991–94; Dir, Anglicare, Tasmania, 1994–98; Acting Archdeacon of Clarence, 1997; Archdeacon for Church and Society, Dio. Tasmania, 1997–98; Asst Bp, Dio. Adelaide, 1998–2002. Member: Standing Cttee, Primates' Meeting of the Anglican Communion, 2007–10; (ex-officio) ACC, 2007–10. *Address:* Bishopsbourne, GPO Box 421, Brisbane, Qld 4001, Australia.

BRISBANE, Archbishop of, (RC), since 2012; **Most Rev. Mark Benedict Coleridge;** *b* 25 Sept. 1948; *s* of Bernard Coleridge. *Educ:* Rostrevor Coll., Adelaide; St Kevin's Coll., Melbourne; Melbourne Univ. (BA 1980); Corpus Christ Coll., Melbourne; Pontifical Biblical Inst., Rome (LSS 1984; DSS 1991). Ordained priest, 1974; Asst Priest, E Doncaster, Ashburton, Pascoe Vale, Melbourne, 1975–80; Catholic Theological College, Melbourne: Lectr in Biblical Studies, 1985–88 and 1991–97; Master, 1995–97; Official, First Section, Secretariat of State, Vatican, 1998–2002; Aux. Bishop of Melbourne, 2002–06; Archbishop of Canberra and Goulburn, (RC), 2006–12. Member: Pontifical Council for Culture, 2004; Bishops' Commission: for Liturgy, 2006, for Doctrine and Morals, 2006. Chairman: Roman Missal Editl Commn, 2004–; Internat. Commn for the Preparation of an English-language Lectionary, 2005–. *Publications:* The Birth of the Lukan Narrative, 1993; Words from the Wound: selected addresses, letters and homilies of Archbishop Mark Coleridge, 2014. *Address:* GPO Box 282, Brisbane, Qld 4001, Australia.

BRISBANE, Assistant Bishops of; *see* Holland, Rt Rev. Dr J. C.; Venables, Rt Rev. C. D.

BRISBY, John Constant Shannon McBurney; QC 1996; a Deputy High Court Judge, since 2004; *b* 8 May 1956; *s* of late Michael Douglas James McBurney Brisby and Liliana Daneva-Hadjikaltcheva Drenska; *m* 1985, Claire Alexandra Anne, *d* of Sir Donald Arthur Logan, KCMG. *Educ:* Westminster Sch.; Christ Church, Oxford (Schol.; MA). 2nd Lieut, 5th Royal Inniskilling Dragoon Guards, 1974. Called to the Bar, Lincoln's Inn, 1978 (Mansfield Schol.; Bencher, 2005); in practice as barrister, 1980–. Member, Executive Council: Friends of Bulgaria, 1991– (Chm., 2010–); British-Bulgarian Legal Assoc., 1991–2001. *Publications:* (contrib.) Butterworth's Company Law Precedents, 4th edn; Konstantin Hadjikaltchoff 1856–1940, 2006. *Recreations:* hunting, shooting, ski-ing, tennis, music, reading, art and architecture. *Address:* 4 Stone Buildings, Lincoln's Inn, WC2A 3XT. *T:* (020) 7242 5524. *Club:* Travellers.

BRISCO, Sir Campbell Howard, 9th Bt *cr* 1982, of Crofton Place, Cumberland; livestock farmer and manager; *b* 11 Dec. 1944; *s* of Gilfred Rimington Brisco (*d* 1981) and Constance Freda Brisco (*d* 1980), 2nd *d* of Charles John Polson, Masterton, NZ; *S* cousin, 1995, but his name does not appear on the Official Roll of the Baronetage; *m* 1969, Kaye Janette, *d* of Ewan William McFadzien; two *s* one *d*. *Educ:* Southland Boys' High Sch. *Recreation:* sport. *Heir: s* Kent Rimington Brisco [*b* 24 Sept. 1972; *m* 2003, Shannon, *d* of Wayne Leahy]. *Address:* 134 Park Street, Winton, Southland 9720, New Zealand. *T:* (3) 2369068.

BRISCOE, Sir Brian (Anthony), Kt 2002; Chairman, Garden City Developments CIC Ltd, since 2013; *b* 29 July 1945; *s* of Anthony Brown Briscoe and Lily Briscoe; *m* 1969, Sheila Mary Cheyne; three *s*. *Educ:* Newcastle Royal Grammar Sch.; St Catharine's Coll., Cambridge (MA); Trent Poly. (DipTP). MRTPI, MRICS. Asst Planner, Derbyshire CC, 1967–71; Section Head, Herefordshire CC, 1971–74; Asst Chief Planner, W Yorks CC, 1974–79; Dep. County Planning Officer, Herts CC, 1979–88; County Planning Officer, Kent CC, 1988–90; Chief Executive: Herts CC, 1990–96; LGA, 1996–2006. Chm., Task Gp on Gypsies and Travellers, DCLG, 2006–. Board Member: Visit England, 2007–11; Land Data, 2007–; High Speed Two Ltd, 2009–14 (Chm., 2010–12). Chair for Reading, 2007–08, for Cambs, 2008–09, Ind. Transport Commn. Trustee, TCPA, 2006–. Hon. DLaws Herts, 2004. FRSA; CCMI. *Publications:* contribs to planning and property jls; chapter in English Structure Planning, 1982. *Recreations:* family, golf, Newcastle United FC. *Address:* Temple House, 257 Boxley Road, Maidstone, Kent ME14 2AS.

BRISCOE, Constance; a part-time Recorder, 1996; barrister; author, since 2003; *b* London, 18 May 1957; *d* of George and Carmen Briscoe; one *s* one *d*. *Educ:* Sacred Heart Sch., Camberwell; Univ. of Newcastle upon Tyne (LLB Hons Law); Council of Legal Educn (Bar Finals). Called to the Bar, Inner Temple, 1983. Hon. DLaws Wolverhampton, 2011. *Publications:* Ugly, 2006; Beyond Ugly, 2008; The Accused (novel), 2011. *Recreations:* gardening, reading, Billie Holliday, writing, running. *E:* constance.briscoe@googlemail.com.

BRISCOE, Sir John Geoffrey James, 6th Bt *cr* 1910, of Bourn Hall, Bourn, Cambridge; *b* (posthumously) 4 Nov. 1994; *o s* of Sir (John) James Briscoe, 5th Bt and of Felicity Mary (now Mrs Christopher Edward Whitley), *e d* of David Melville Watkinson; *S* father, 1994. *Heir: uncle:* Edward Home Briscoe [*b* 27 March 1955; *m* 1st, 1979, Anne Lister (marr. diss. 1989); one *s* one *d*; 2nd, 1994, Sandy Elizabeth King (*née* Lloyd)].

BRISCOE, John Hubert Daly, LVO 1997; FRCGP; Apothecary to HM Household, Windsor, and to HM the Queen Mother's Household at Royal Lodge, 1986–97; Master, Worshipful Society of Apothecaries of London, 2000–01; *b* 19 March 1933; only *s* of late Dr Arnold Daly Briscoe and Doris Winifred Briscoe (*née* Nicholson); *m* 1958, Janet Anne Earlam; one *s* three *d* (and one *d* decd). *Educ:* St Andrew's Sch., Eastbourne; Winchester Coll.; St John's Coll., Cambridge (MA); St Thomas's Hosp. (MB BChir); DObstRCOG 1959; MRCGP 1968, FRCGP 2006. MO, Overseas CS, Basutoland, 1959–62; Asst in gen. practice, Aldeburgh, 1963–65; Principal in gen. practice, Eton, 1965–97; Medical Officer: Eton Coll., 1965–97; St George's Sch., Windsor Castle, 1976–97. Fellow, MOs of Schs Assoc., 2002 (Pres., 1989–91). FRSocMed 1995–2012. Hon. MO, Guards' Polo Club, 1966–83. Hon. Mem., Windsor and Dist Med. Soc., 1999. Hon. Auditor, Eur. Union of Sch. and Univ. Health and Medicine, 1981–89. Lay Steward, St George's Chapel, Windsor Castle, 1999. Bridgemaster, Baldwin's Bridge Trust, Eton, 1988–89 and 2002–03. Pres., Omar Khayyam Club, 2005. Hon. Licentiate, Apothecaries' Hall, Dublin, 2001. *Publications:* contrib. papers on influenza vaccination and adolescent medicine. *Recreations:* growing vegetables, pictures. *Address:* Wistaria House, 54/56 Kings Road, Windsor, Berks SL4 2AH. *T:* (01753) 855321. *Club:* Athenæum.

BRISE, Sir Timothy Edward R.; *see* Ruggles-Brise.

BRISON, Ven. William Stanley; Team Rector, Pendleton, Manchester, 1994–98; permission to officiate, diocese of Manchester, since 1999; *b* 20 Nov. 1929; *s* of William P. Brison and Marion A. Wilber; *m* 1951, Marguerite, (Peggy), Adelia Nettleton; two *s* two *d*. *Educ:* Alfred Univ., New York (BS Eng); Berkeley Divinity School, New Haven, Conn (STM, MDiv). United States Marine Corps, Captain (Reserve), 1951–53. Engineer, Norton Co., Worcester, Mass, 1953–54. Vicar, then Rector, Christ Episcopal Church, Bethany, Conn, 1957–69; Archdeacon of New Haven, Conn, 1967–69; Rector, Emmanuel Episcopal Church, Stamford, Conn, 1969–72; Vicar, Christ Church, Davyhulme, Manchester, 1972–81; Rector, All Saints', Newton Heath, Manchester, 1981–85; Area Dean of North Manchester, 1981–85; Archdeacon of Bolton, 1985–92, then Archdeacon Emeritus; CMS Missionary, Nigeria, 1992–94; Lectr, St Francis of Assisi Theol Coll., Zaria, 1992–94. Chairman: Bury Christian Aid, 2002–; Goshen and Blackford Bridge Tenants' and Residents' Assoc., 2003–. *Publications:* (with Peggy Brison) A Tale of Two Visits to Chechnya, 2005; Judas, Beloved Disciple, 2013. *Recreations:* squash, grandchildren. *Address:* 2 Scott Avenue, Bury, Lancs BL9 9RS. *T:* (0161) 764 3998.

BRISTER, William Arthur Francis, CB 1984; Deputy Director General of Prison Service, 1982–85; *b* 10 Feb. 1925; *s* of Arthur John Brister and Velda Mirandoli; *m* 1949, Mary Speakman (*d* 2012); one *s* one *d* (and one *s* decd). *Educ:* Douai Sch.; Brasenose Coll., Oxford (MA 1949). Asst Governor Cl. II, HM Borstal, Lowdham Grange, 1949–52; Asst Principal, Imperial Trng Sch., Wakefield, 1952–55; Asst Governor II, HM Prison, Parkhurst, 1955–57; Dep. Governor, HM Prison: Camp Hill, 1957–60; Manchester, 1960–62; Governor, HM Borstal: Morton Hall, 1962–67; Dover, 1967–69; Governor II, Prison Dept HQ, 1969–71; Governor, HM Remand Centre, Ashford, 1971–73; Governor I, Prison Dept HQ, 1973–75, Asst Controller, 1975–79; Chief Inspector of the Prison Service, 1979–81; HM Dep. Chief Inspector of Prisons, 1981–82. Mem., Parole Board, 1986–89. Nuffield Travelling Fellow, Canada and Mexico, 1966–67. *Recreations:* shooting, music, Venetian history. *Club:* English-Speaking Union.

BRISTOL, 8th Marquess of, *cr* 1826; **Frederick William Augustus Hervey;** Baron Hervey of Ickworth, 1703; Earl of Bristol, 1714; Earl Jermyn of Horningsheath, 1826; Hereditary High Steward of the Liberty of St Edmund; *b* 19 Oct. 1979; *s* of 6th Marquess of Bristol and of his 3rd wife, Yvonne Marie, *d* of Anthony Sutton; *S* half-brother, 1999. *Educ:* Eton Coll.; Edinburgh Univ. (BCom). Director: Bristol & Stone Real Estate Investment Co., 2004–09; Bristol Estates Ltd (formerly Bristol Settled Estates Ltd), 2010–. Trustee, Gen. Hervey's Charitable Trust, 1999–; Trustee and Chm., Ickworth Church Conservation Trust, 2006–. Patron: Gwrych Castle Preservation Trust, 2002–; Athenaeum, Bury St Edmunds, 2006–; Friends of W Suffolk Hosp., 2013–. *Recreations:* emerging markets, reading, travel. *Address:* Bristol Estates Ltd, 2 Eaton Gate, SW1W 9BJ. *E:* fb@bristolestates.co.uk. *Clubs:* Turf, White's.

BRISTOL, Bishop of, since 2003; **Rt Rev. Michael Arthur Hill;** *b* 17 April 1949; *s* of Arthur and Hilda Hill; *m* 1972, Anthea Jean Hill (*née* Longridge); one *s* four *d*. *Educ:* N Cheshire Coll. of FE (Dip. in Business Studies); Brasted Place Coll.; Ridley Hall, Cambridge (GOE); Fitzwilliam Coll., Cambridge (Postgrad. Cert. in Theology). Junior Exec. in printing industry, 1968–72. Mem., Scargill House Community, 1972–73; ordained deacon, 1977, priest, 1978; Curate: St Mary Magdalene, Addiscombe, Croydon, 1977–80; St Paul, Slough, 1980–83; Priest in charge, 1983–90, Rector, 1990–92, St Leonard, Chesham Bois; RD, Amersham, 1990–92; Archdeacon of Berkshire, 1992–98; Area Bishop of Buckingham, 1998–2003. Entered H of L, 2009. *Publications:* Reaching the Unchurched, 1992; Lifelines, 1997. *Recreations:* playing guitar, listening to music, cricket, soccer, Rugby League and Union, reading. *Address:* 58a High Street, Winterbourne, Bristol BS36 1JQ.

BRISTOL, Dean of; *see* Hoyle, Very Rev. D. M.

BRISTOL, Archdeacon of; *no new appointment at time of going to press.*

BRISTOW, Dr Laurence Stanley Charles, CMG 2015; HM Diplomatic Service; Director, National Security, Foreign and Commonwealth Office, 2012–15; *b* 23 Nov. 1963; *s* of Stanley and Hilary Bristow; *m* 1988, Fiona MacCallum; two *s*. *Educ:* Colchester Royal Grammar Sch.; Trinity Coll., Cambridge (BA 1986; PhD 1991); Open Univ. (MBA 2001). Entered FCO, 1990; Second Sec., Bucharest, 1992–95; First Secretary: FCO, 1995–99; Ankara, 1999–2002; NATO Defence Coll., Rome, 2002–03; FCO, 2003; Ambassador to Azerbaijan, 2004–07; Dep. Hd of Mission, Moscow, 2007–10; Dir, Eastern Europe and Central Asia, FCO, 2010–12. *Address:* c/o Foreign and Commonwealth Office, King Charles Street, SW1A 2AH.

BRITNELL, Mark Douglas; Partner and Head of Healthcare, Europe, KPMG, since 2009; *b* 5 Jan. 1966; *s* of late Robert Britnell and of Veronica Britnell, now Leigh; *m* 2005, Stephanie Joy; one *d*. *Educ:* Univ. of Warwick (BA Hons 1988). NHS Mgt Trng Scheme, 1989–92; Gen. Manager, St Mary's Hosp., London, 1992–95; Exec. Dir, Central Middlesex Hosp., London, 1995–98; Chief Executive: Univ. Hosp. Birmingham NHS, then NHS Foundn, Trust, 1998–2006; NHS S Central Strategic HA, 2006–07; Dir Gen., Commissioning, System Mgt and Commercial Directorate, DoH, 2007–09. Non-exec. Dir, Dr Foster Ltd, 2004–07. Sen. Associate, King's Fund, 2004–. Hon. Sen. Fellow, Univ. of Birmingham, 2006–. *Recreations:* sport, current affairs, family. *Address:* KPMG, 1 Canada Square, Canary Whar E14 5AG. *Club:* Reform.

BRITTAIN, Barbara Jane; *see* Moorhouse, B. J.

BRITTAIN, Clive Edward; racehorse trainer, 1972–2015; *b* 15 Dec. 1933; *s* of Edward Joh Brittain and Priscilla Rosalind (*née* Winzer); *m* 1957, Maureen Helen Robinson. *Educ:* Caln Secondary Mod. Sch. Winning horses trained include: Julio Mariner, St Leger, 1978; Pebbles 1000 Guineas, 1984; Eclipse, Dubai Champion and Breeders Cup Turf, 1985; Jupiter Islan Japan Cup, Tokyo, 1986; Mystiko, 2000 Guineas, 1991; Terimon, Juddmonte Internat. 1991; User Friendly, Oaks, Irish Oaks, Yorkshire Oaks, St Leger, 1992; Sayyedati, 100 Guineas, and Jacque le Marois, 1993, Sussex Stakes, 1995; Luso, Hong Kong Vase, 1996 an 1997; Crimplene, Irish 1000 Guineas, 2000; Var, Prix de l'Abbaye, Longchamp, 200 Warrsan, Coronation Cup, 2003 and 2004, and Grosser Prix von Baden, 2004 and 2005 Rajeem, UAE Equestrian and Racing Fedn Falmouth Stakes, 2006; Hibaayeb, Meon Valle Stud Fillies' Mile, 2009; Rizeena, Moyglare Stud Stakes, 2013. *Recreation:* shooting. *Address* Carlburg, 49 Bury Road, Newmarket, Suffolk CB8 7BY. *T:* (01638) 664347. *Club:* Jocke Club Rooms (Newmarket).

BRITTAIN, Louise Mary; Partner, Wilkins Kennedy, since 2013; *b* London, 19 June 196 *d* of Michael Brittain and Deborah Balding-Brittain; one *s* one *d*. *Educ:* Wycombe High Sch. Portsmouth Poly. (BSc Hons Math. Scis); Coll. of St Paul and St Mary (PGCE). License Insolvency Practitioner 1999; Law of Property Act Receiver; Nat. Coll. of Ireland (Cer Personal Insolvency Practice 2014). Deloitte Haskins & Sells, subseq. Coopers & Lybran Deloitte, then Coopers & Lybrand, 1989–96; Baker Tilly LLP, 1996–2009: Partner, 2001–0 Hd, Special Investigations, 2003–09; Partner and Hd, Contentious Insolvency, Deloitte LLP 2009–13. Non-exec. Dir, Insolvency Service Steering Bd, 2006–10. Mem., Nat. Cttee Assoc. of Business Recovery Professionals, 2009–. *Publications:* contrib. Recovery mag. o Assoc. of Business Recovery Professionals, Accountancy Age. *Recreations:* ski-ing, running swimming, opera, ballet, classical music, violin, art, family. *Address:* Wilkins Kennedy, Bridg House, SE1 9QR. *T:* (020) 7403 1877. *E:* Louise.Brittain@wilkinskennedy.com. *Club* Searcys.

BRITTAIN, Paul Delery; Head, Corporate Finance, Norfolk County Council, 2007–13; Ruislip, Middx, 12 Sept. 1953; *s* of Reginald William and Corinne Dorothy Brittain; partner Julia Weaver; two *s* one *d*. *Educ:* St George's Coll., Weybridge; Exeter Univ. (BA Combine Hons Hist. and Politics 1975). CIPFA 1980. Local government finance roles: Southend BC 1976–82; S Yorks CC, 1982–86; Sheffield CC, 1986; Lincs CC, 1986–2000; HBS Busines Services Ltd, 2000–02; Hd, Financial Mgt, Norfolk CC, 2003–07. *Recreations:* walking travelling, tennis, gardening, the outdoors, sailing. *Address:* 2 Ford Bank, Great Easton, Marke Harborough LE16 8SL. *T:* (01536) 772504. *E:* paulbrittain905@btinternet.com.

BRITTAN OF SPENNITHORNE, Lady; Diana Brittan, DBE 2004 (CBE 1995) Chairman: The Connection at St Martin's, since 2005 (Trustee, since 2005); Independen Age, since 2009; *b* 14 Oct. 1940; *d* of Leslie Howell Clemetson and Elizabeth Agne Clemetson (*née* Leonard); *m* 1st, 1965, Dr Richard Peterson (marr. diss. 1979); two *d*; 2nd 1980, Leon Brittan (Baron Brittan of Spennithorne, PC, QC) (*d* 2015). *Educ:* Westonbirt Sch. Tetbury. Man. Editor, Eibis Internat., London, 1977–88. Deputy Chairman: HFEA 1990–97; EOC, 1994–96 (Comr, 1989–94); Mem., Lord Chancellor's Adv. Cttee on Leg Educn and Conduct, 1997–99. Chairman: Rathbone Training, 1991–2002; Nat. Lotter Charities Bd, later Community Fund, 1999–2004; Nat. Family Mediation, 2001–07; Trustee Action on Addiction, 1993–98; Runnymede Trust, 1995–2006 (Chm., 1998–99); Ope Univ. Foundn, 1996–2000; Multiple Birth Foundn, 1998–2001; Carnegie UK Trust, 2009– Chm., Carnegie Commn for Rural Community Devélt, 2006–07 (Vice-Chm., 2004–06) President: Townswomen's Guild, 1996–; Nat. Assoc. of Connexions Partnerships, 2005–08 Mem., Bd of Mgt, British Sch. of Brussels, 1989–99. JP City of London, 1984–2010 Distinguished Associate, Darwin Coll., Cambridge, 1998. *Recreations:* botany, travel, cinema cards, walking.

BRITTAN, Sir Samuel, Kt 1993; columnist, Financial Times, 1966–2014 (Assistant Edito 1978–95); *b* 29 Dec. 1933; *s* of late Joseph Brittan, MD, and Rebecca Brittan (*née* Lipetz) *Educ:* Kilburn Grammar Sch.; Jesus Coll., Cambridge (Hon. Fellow, 1988). 1st Class i Economics, 1955; MA Cantab. Various posts in Financial Times, 1955–61; Economics Editor Observer, 1961–64; Adviser, DEA, 1965. Fellow, Nuffield Coll., Oxford, 1973–74, Vis Fellow, 1974–82; Vis. Prof. of Economics, Chicago Law Sch., 1978; Hon. Prof. of Politics Warwick Univ., 1987–92. Mem., Peacock Cttee on Financing the BBC, 1985–86. Pres. David Hume Soc., 1996–99. Hon. DLitt Heriot-Watt, 1985; DU Essex, 1994. Financia Journalist of the Year Award 1971; George Orwell Prize (for political journalism), 1980 Ludwig Erhard Prize (for economic writing), 1988. Chevalier de la Légion d'Honneur, 1993 *Publications:* The Treasury under the Tories, 1964, rev. edn, Steering the Economy, 1969 1971; Left or Right: The Bogus Dilemma, 1968; The Price of Economic Freedom, 197 Capitalism and the Permissive Society, 1973, rev. edn as A Restatement of Economi Liberalism, 1988; Is There an Economic Consensus?, 1973; (with P. Lilley) The Delusion o Incomes Policy, 1977; The Economic Consequences of Democracy, 1977; How to End th Monetarist Controversy, 1981; The Role and Limits of Government, 1983; Capitalism wit a Human Face, 1995; Essays: Moral, Political and Economic, 1998; Against the Flow, 2005 articles in various jls. *E:* samuel@gmail.com. *W:* www.samuelbrittan.co.uk.

BRITTEN, Alan Edward Marsh, CBE 2003; Chairman, English Tourism Council 1999–2003; Board Member, British Tourist Authority, 1997–2003; *b* 26 Feb. 1938; *s* c Robert Harry Marsh Britten and Helen Marjorie (*née* Goldson); *m* 1967, Judith Clar Akerman; two *d*. *Educ:* Radley; Emmanuel Coll., Cambridge (MA English); Williams Coll. Mass (American Studies). Mobil Oil Co.: joined 1961; marketing and planning, UK, USA Italy; Chief Exec., Mobil Cos in E Africa, 1975–77, Denmark, 1980–81, Portugal, 1982–84 Benelux, 1984–86; Managing Dir, Mobil Oil Co., 1987–89; Manager, Internat. Planning Mobil Oil Corp., 1989–90; Vice-President: Mobil Europe, 1991–97; Country Management 1993–97; non-exec. Dir, Mobil Oil Co. Ltd, 1997–2001. Dir, Europia, 1994–97. Member Council for Aldeburgh Foundn, 1989–99; Liaison (formerly Develt) Cttee, Britten-Pear Foundn, 2006–; Pres., Friends of Aldeburgh Prodns, 2000–. Member: Council, Roy Warrant Holders' Assoc. (Pres., 1997–98); Adv. Board, Ten Days at Princeton; Counci UEA, 1996–2005 (Vice-Chm., 2003–05); Chm., Tourism Quality Review, 2003–08. Chm. Royal Warrant Holders Assoc. Charity Fund, 2012–; Trustee: Queen Elizabeth Scholarshi Trust, 1997–2003 (Chm., 1999–2003); Leeds Castle Foundn, 2005–; Integrated Neurologica Services, 2006– (Vice-Chm. 2008–); Transglobe Expedition Trust, 2006–. Chm., Leed Castle Enterprises, 2010–. Governor: Trinity Laban (formerly Trinity Coll. of Music) 2001–10 (Chm., Audit Cttee, 2005–10; Hon. Fellow, 2010); Trinity Coll., London, 2004– Hon. DCL UEA, 2010. *Recreations:* music, travel, gardening, letter writing. *Clubs:* Garrick Noblemen and Gentlemen's Catch; Aldeburgh Golf.

BRITTIN, Matthew John; Vice President, Northern and Central Europe, since 2011, an President, Europe, Middle East and Africa, since 2014, Google; *b* Walton-on-Thames, 1 Dec 1968; *s* of Sid and Shirley Brittin; *m* 1995, Kate Betts; two *s*. *Educ:* Hampton Sch.; Robinso Coll., Cambridge (BA 1989); London Business Sch. (MBA Dist. 1997). Chartered Surveyor Connell Wilson, 1989–95; Consultant, McKinsey & Co. Inc., 1997–2004; Commercial Di and Digital Dir, Trinity Mirror, 2004–06; Country Dir, 2007–09, Man. Dir, 2009–11, Googl UK and Ireland. Non-exec. Dir, J. Sainsbury plc, 2011–. Trustee: Media Trust, 2010– Climate Gp, 2010–. Chm., Cambridge Univ. Boat Club, 1990–95. Steward, Henley Roya

Regatta, 2014–. *Recreations:* formerly international rowing and sailing, now keeping up with climbing, cycling and swimming sons. *Address:* Google, 76 Buckingham Palace Road, SW1W 9TQ.

BRITTON, Alison Claire, OBE 1990; ceramic artist, writer and curator, since 1973; tutor, since 1984, Senior Tutor, since 1998, and Research Coordinator, since 2005, Royal College of Art; *b* 4 May 1948; *d* of Prof. James Nimmo Britton and Jessie Muriel Britton (*née* Robertson); two *d. Educ:* N London Collegiate Sch.; Leeds Coll. of Art; Central Sch. of Art and Design (DipAD); Royal Coll. of Art (MA 1973). FRCA 1990. Solo exhibitions: Crafts Council, 1979; Miharudo Gall., Tokyo, 1985; Contemp. Applied Arts, 1987, 1990; Craft Centre Gall., Sydney, 1988; Marianne Heller Galerie, Sandhausen, Germany, 1995; Australian tour, 1996; Barrett Marsden Gall., later Marsden Woo Gall., London, 1998, 2000, 2003, 2005, 2007, 2009, 2012, 2014; Crafts Study Centre, Univ. of Creative Arts, Farnham, 2012; retrospective exhibn (tour), 1990–91. Guest artist, Shigaraki Cultural Ceramic Park, Japan, 2010. Work in internat. public and private collections. Co-curator, The Raw and the Cooked, MOMA, Oxford and tour, 1993. Trustee, Crafts Study Centre, Univ. of Creative Arts, Farnham, 2006– (Chair, 2015–). Hon. MA, Univ. Coll. for the Creative Arts, 2007; Hon. Fellow, Univ. of the Arts, London, 2008. *Publications:* Seeing Things: collected writing on art, craft and design, 2013. *Recreations:* film, walking. *Address:* c/o Marsden Woo Gallery, 23 Charlotte Road, Shoreditch, EC2A 3PB. *T:* (020) 7336 6396.

See also C. M. Britton.

BRITTON, Andrew James Christie; Chairman, Finance Committee, Archbishops' Council, 2007–13; *b* 1 Dec. 1940; *s* of late Prof. Karl William Britton and Sheila Margaret Christie; *m* 1963, Pamela Anne, *d* of His Honour Edward Sutcliffe, QC; three *d. Educ:* Royal Grammar Sch., Newcastle upon Tyne; Oriel Coll., Oxford (BA); LSE (MSc). Joined HM Treasury as Cadet Economist, 1966; Econ. Asst, 1968; Econ. Adviser, 1970; Senior Economic Adviser: DHSS, 1973; HM Treasury, 1975; London Business Sch., 1978–79; Under Sec., HM Treasury, 1980–82; Dir, NIESR, 1982–95. Mem., Treasury Panel of Ind. Forecasters, 1993–95. Vis. Prof., Univ. of Bath, 1998–2001. Licensed Reader, Dio. of Southwark, 1986–; Lay Canon, Southwark Cathedral, 2004–. Mem., Bd of Finance, Dio. of Southwark, 1998–2007 (Vice Chm., 1999–2000; Chm., 2000–07). Exec. Sec., Churches' Enquiry into Unemployment and the Future of Work, 1995–97. *Publications:* (ed) Employment, Output and Inflation, 1983; The Trade Cycle in Britain, 1986; (ed) Policymaking with Macroeconomic Models, 1989; Macroeconomic Policy in Britain 1974–87, 1991; Monetary Regimes of the Twentieth Century, 2001; (jtly) Economic Theory and Christian Belief, 2003. *Address:* 2 Shabden Park, High Road, Chipstead, Surrey CR5 3SF.

BRITTON, Prof. Celia Margaret, PhD; FBA 2000; Professor of French, University College London, 2003–11, now Emeritus; *b* 20 March 1946; *d* of Prof. James Nimmo Britton and Jessie Muriel Britton. *Educ:* New Hall, Cambridge (MA Mod. and Medieval Langs 1969; Postgrad. Dip. Linguistics 1970); Univ. of Essex (PhD Literary Stylistics 1973. Temp. Lectr in French, KCL, 1972–74; Lectr in French Studies, Univ. of Reading, 1974–91; Carnegie Prof. of French, Univ. of Aberdeen, 1991–2002. Chair, RAE French Panel, 2001. Pres., Soc. for French Studies, 1996–98. Chevalier, Ordre des Palmes Académiques (France), 2003. *Publications:* Claude Simon: writing the visible, 1987; The Nouveau Roman: fiction, theory and politics, 1992; Edouard Glissant and Postcolonial Theory, 1999; Race and the Unconscious, 2002; The Sense of Community in French Caribbean Fiction, 2008; Language and Literary Form in French Caribbean Writing, 2014; numerous articles on French and Francophone literature and film. *Recreations:* travel, cinema, cookery, photography.

See also A. C. Britton.

BRITTON, Prof. John Richard, CBE 2013; MD; FRCP, FFPH; Professor of Epidemiology, University of Nottingham, since 2000; Hon. Consultant in Respiratory Medicine, Nottingham City Hospital, since 1990; *b* Saltburn-by-Sea, Yorks, 24 Jan. 1955; *s* of Douglas and Dorothy Britton; *m* 1980, Ros Hill; two *s* two *d* (and one *d* decd). *Educ:* Watford Grammar Sch.; Guy's Hosp. Med. Sch., Univ. of London (BSc Pharmacol. 1975; MB BS 1978; MD 1987; MSc Epidemiol. 1988). MRCP 1981, FRCP 1994; FFPH 2003. Jun. Hse Officer, then SHO, Guy's and London Chest Hosp., 1978–82; Med. Registrar, Royal S Hants Hosp., then Basingstoke Gen. Hosp., 1982–84; Res. Fellow, then Lectr, City Hosp., Nottingham, 1984–90; Sen. Lectr in Respiratory Medicine, 1990–98, Prof. of Respiratory Medicine, 1998–2000, Univ. of Nottingham. *Publications:* (ed) ABC of smoking cessation, 2004; contrib. papers to learned jls; editor of reports on smoking prevention. *Recreations:* time with family, golf, watching Nottingham Forest, cycling. *Address:* Division of Epidemiology and Public Health, University of Nottingham Clinical Sciences Building, City Hospital, Nottingham NG5 1PB. *T:* (0115) 823 1708. *E:* j.britton@virgin.net.

BRITTON, John William; independent consultant, since 1993; *b* 13 Dec. 1936; *s* of John Ferguson and Dinah Britton; *m* 1961, Maisie Rubython; one *s* one *d. Educ:* Bedlington Grammar Sch.; Bristol Univ. (BScEng 1st Cl. Hons). Royal Aircraft Establishment, Bedford, 1959–83: Hd, Flight Res. Div., 1978–80; Chief Supt and Hd, Flight Systems Bedford Dept, 1981–83; RCDS 1984; Dir, Avionic Equipment and Systems, MoD PE, 1985–86; Science and Technology Assessment Office, Cabinet Office, 1987; Dir Gen. Aircraft 3, MoD PE, 1987–90; Asst Chief Scientific Advr (Projects), MoD, 1990–92, retd. *Recreations:* wine, painting, motor racing (watching), gardening (especially dahlias and fuchsias). *Address:* 6 The Drive, Sharnbrook, Bedford MK44 1HU.

BRITTON, Mark Gordon, MD; FRCP; Consultant Physician in respiratory medicine, Ashford and St Peter's Hospitals NHS Trust (formerly St Peter's Hospital, Chertsey), 1983–2011; *b* 23 Nov. 1946; *s* of late Capt. Gordon Berry Cowley Britton, CBE and Vera Britton (*née* Hyman); *m* 1972, Gillian Vaughan Davies; three *s. Educ:* Ipswich Sch.; Med. Coll. of St Bartholomew's Hosp., London; London Univ. (MB BS 1970, MSc 1981, MD 1982). DIH 1981; FRCP 1990. Surg. Lt Comdr, RNR, 1970–90. Hon. Consultant, King Edward VII's Hosp., London, 1980–2014; Hon. Consultant and Sen. Lectr, St George's Hosp., London, 1983–2011; Med. Dir, St Peter's Hosp. NHS Trust, 1994–97; Hon. Sen. Lectr, Imperial Coll., London, 2001–11. Vis. Prof., Faculty of Health and Med. Scis (formerly Faculty of Medicine), 2006–12, Chm., Adv. Council, Postgraduate Med. Sch., 2008–11. Univ. of Surrey. Member: Med. Reference Panel (Coal Bd), DTI, 2000–11; Industrial Injuries Adv. Council, 2003–13. Chm., Bd of Trustees, 1999–2005, Mem. Council, 2005–08, Vice Pres., 2006–, British Lung Foundn. Trustee: Nat. Confidential Enquiry into Patient Outcome and Death, 2005–13; Whiteley Homes Trust, 2012–. Freeman, City of London, 1983; Mem., Soc. of Apothecaries, 1979–. Master, Fountain Club, 2010. *Publications:* contrib. various chapters and papers in learned jls on mgt and treatment of asthma, chronic obstructive airways disease and asbestos related diseases. *Recreations:* Rugby football, golf, sailing, gardening, British stamps, Pembrokeshire cottage. *Address:* Woodham House, 92 Ashley Road, Walton-on-Thames, Surrey KT12 1HP. *T:* (01932) 225472, 07850 428748. *E:* markbritton@btinternet.com. *Clubs:* Burhill Golf; Newport Links Golf.

BRITTON, Sir Paul (John James), Kt 2010; CB 2001; CVO 2014; Head, Economic and Domestic Affairs Secretariat, 2001–09, and Director General, Domestic Policy and Strategy Group, 2006–09, Cabinet Office; Appointments Secretary to the Prime Minister for senior ecclesiastical appointments, 2008–14; *b* 17 April 1949; *s* of Leonard Britton and Maureen Britton (*née* Vowles); *m* 1972, Pauline Bruce; one *s* one *d. Educ:* Clifton Coll.; Magdalene Coll., Cambridge (BA 1971; MA 1974). Department of the Environment: Admin. trainee, 1971–75; Private Sec. to Second Perm. Sec., 1975–77; Principal, 1977; Dept of Transport, 1979–81; DoE, 1981–97: Private Sec. to Minister for Housing and Construction, 1983–84; Asst Sec., 1984; Grade 4, 1991; Dir of Local Govt Finance Policy, 1991–96; Under Sec., 1992; Dir, Envmt Protection Strategy, 1996–97; Dep. Hd, Constitution Secretariat, 1997–98, Dep. Head, Econ. and Domestic Affairs Secretariat, 1998–2001, Cabinet Office; Dir, Town and Country Planning, DTLR, 2001. Member: Crown Nominations Commn, 2008–14; Exec. Cttee, Better Govt Initiative, 2009–. Trustee: Nat. Assoc. for Mental Health, 2010– (Vice Chm., 2013–); Friends of Friendless Churches, 2012–; Nat. Churches Trust, 2015–; Chm., Trustees, Coll. of St Barnabas, Lingfield, 2012–. Gov., Clifton Coll., 2012–. *Recreations:* architectural history, photography, topography. *Address:* 54 Dry Hill Park Road, Tonbridge, Kent TN10 3BX. *T:* (01732) 365794.

BRITZ, Lewis; Executive Councillor, Electrical, Electronic, Telecommunication & Plumbing Union, 1984–95; Member, Industrial Tribunals, 1990–2003; *b* 7 Jan. 1933; *s* of Alfred and Hetty Britz; *m* 1960, Hadassah Rosenberg; four *d. Educ:* Hackney Downs Grammar Sch.; Acton Technical Coll. (OND Elec. Engrg); Nottingham Univ. (BSc (Hons) Engrg); Birkbeck Coll., London Univ. (BA Hons Eng 2002). Head of Research, 1967–71, Nat. Officer, 1971–83, EETPU. Director: LEB, 1977–87; British Internat. Helicopters, 1987–92; Esca Services, 1990–; Chm., Blue Sky Pensions Co. (formerly JIB Pension Scheme Trustee Co. Ltd), 1997–. Mem., Monopolies and Mergers Commn, 1986–92. Sat in Restrictive Practices Court, 1989. *Recreation:* philately. *Address:* 30 Braemar Gardens, West Wickham, Kent BR4 0JW. *T:* (020) 8777 5986.

BRIXWORTH, Bishop Suffragan of, since 2011; **Rt Rev. John Edward Holbrook;** *b* 14 June 1962; *s* of Edward George Holbrook and Ann Holbrook; *m* 1985, Elizabeth Mighall; one *s* one *d. Educ:* Bristol Cathedral Sch.; St Peter's Coll., Oxford (BA 1983; MA 1987); Ridley Hall, Cambridge. Ordained deacon, 1986, priest, 1987; Assistant Curate: St Mary's, Barnes, 1986–89; St Mary's, Bletchley, 1989–93; Vicar, St Mary's, Adderbury, 1993–2002; Rural Dean, Deddington, 2000–02; Rector, Wimborne Minster, 2002–11; Priest-in-charge: St Mary and St Cuthberga and All Saints, Witchampton, 2002–11; St Wolfrida, Horton, 2006–11; Rural Dean, Wimborne, 2004–11. Chaplain, South and East Dorset PCT, 2002–11; Canon and Preb., Salisbury Cathedral, 2006–11; Canon, Peterborough Cathedral, 2011–. *Address:* Orchard Acre, 11 North Street, Mears Ashby, Northampton NN6 0DW. *T:* (01604) 812328. *E:* bishop.brixworth@peterborough-diocese.org.uk.

BROAD, Rev. Canon Hugh Duncan; Permission to officiate: Diocese of Europe, since 2013; Diocese of Gloucester, since 2013; Priest-in-charge, Costa Almeria and Costa Calida, Spain, 2003–13; Area Dean, Gibraltar, 2008–13; *b* 28 Oct. 1937; *s* of Horace Edward Broad and Lucy Broad; *m* 1988, Jacqueline Lissaman; two *d. Educ:* Shropshire Inst. of Agriculture; Bernard Gilpin Soc., Durham Univ.; Lichfield Theol Coll.; Hereford Coll. of Education. Curate, Holy Trinity, Hereford, 1967–72; Asst Master, Bishop of Hereford's Bluecoat Sch., 1972–74; Curate, St Peter and St Paul, Fareham, 1974–76; Vicar, All Saints with St Barnabas, Hereford, 1976–90; Rector, Matson, 1990–97; Vicar, St George, Gloucester and St Margaret, Whaddon, 1997–2003. Chaplain: Victoria Eye Hosp., Hereford, 1976–90; Selwyn Sch., Gloucester, 1990–97. Member: Gen. Synod, C of E, 1995–2003; Crown Appts Commn, 1997–2003. Hon. Canon: Gloucester Cathedral, 2002–03, now Emeritus; Gibraltar Cathedral, 2013. *Recreations:* theatre, music, cricket. *Address:* 44 Vensfield Road, Quedgeley, Gloucester GL2 4FX. *T:* (01452) 541078. *E:* hugh.broad@yahoo.co.uk.

BROADBENT, Adam Humphrey Charles; Chairman, Emap plc, 2001–06; *b* 21 June 1936; *s* of Harold and Celia Broadbent; *m* 1963, Sara Peregrine (*née* Meredith); four *s. Educ:* Stonyhurst Coll.; Magdalen Coll., Oxford (MA); London Sch. of Economics (MSc Econ); Queen Mary, Univ. of London (MA 2008). 2nd Lieut, 1st RTR, 1957–59. Bank of London and South America, 1960–63; COI, 1963–66; NIESR, 1966–68; Schroders plc, 1968–96: Dir, J. Henry Schroder Wagg & Co. Ltd, 1984–96; Dir, 1990–96; Group Managing Director: Corporate Finance, 1990–96; Investment Banking, 1994–96; Chm., Arcadia Gp plc, 1998–2002. Director: Carclo, 1997–2003; REL Consultancy Gp, 1997–2005; Capital One Bank (Europe), 2000–10. Chm., Dover Harbour Bd, 1996–2000. Gov., NIESR, 2002–. Dir, Acad. of Ancient Music, 2003–12. *Clubs:* Brooks's, Boodle's.

See also B. R. H. Broadbent.

BROADBENT, Sir Andrew George, 5th Bt *cr* 1893, of Brook Street, co. London and Longwood, co. Yorkshire; *b* 26 Jan. 1963; *s* of Sqn Ldr Sir George Broadbent, AFC, RAF, 4th Bt and Valerie Anne, *o d* of Cecil Frank Ward; *S* father, 1992, but his name does not appear on the Official Roll of the Baronetage. *Educ:* Oakley Hall Prep. Sch., Cirencester; Monkton Combe Sch.; RMA, Sandhurst. Capt., PWO Regt Yorks, 1984; retd 1994. *Recreations:* music, reading, walking, following sport. *Heir: uncle* Robert John Dendy Broadbent, *b* 4 Nov. 1938.

BROADBENT, Benjamin Robert Hamond, PhD; a Deputy Governor, Bank of England, since 2014 (Member, Monetary Policy Committee, 2011–14); *b* Morston, Norfolk, 1 Feb. 1965; *s* of Adam Humphrey Charles Broadbent, *qv*; one *s. Educ:* St Paul's Sch., London; Ecole Normale Superieure de la Musique, Paris (Dip. Performance); Trinity Hall, Cambridge (BA 1988); Harvard Univ. (PhD 1997). Econ. Advr, HM Treasury, 1988–91, 1993–96; Asst Prof., Columbia Univ., 1997–2000; Sen. Economist, Goldman Sachs, 2000–11. *Recreations:* piano, violin. *Address:* Bank of England, Threadneedle Street, EC2R 8AH. *E:* ben.broadbent@bankofengland.co.uk.

BROADBENT, Christopher Joseph St George B.; *see* Bowers-Broadbent.

BROADBENT, James, (Jim); actor, since 1972; *b* Lincoln, 24 May 1949; *s* of late Roy Broadbent and Dee (*née* Findlay); *m* 1987, Anastasia Lewis; two step *s. Educ:* Leighton Park Sch., Reading; Hammersmith Coll. of Art; LAMDA. Joined Nat. Theatre of Brent, 1983, appeared in: The Messiah, 1983; (jt writer) The Complete Guide to Sex, 1984; (jt writer) The Greatest Story Ever Told, 1987; Founder Member, Science Fiction Theatre of Liverpool: Illuminatus!, 1976; The Warp, 1978; *other theatre* includes: Hampstead Theatre: Ecstasy, 1979; Goose Pimples, 1980; Royal Shakespeare Co.: Our Friends in the North, Clay, 1981; National Theatre: The Government Inspector, 1984; A Place with the Pigs, 1988; The Pillowman, 2003; Theatre of Blood, 2005; Royal Court: Kafka's Dick, 1986; The Recruiting Officer, Our Country's Good, 1988; Old Vic: A Flea in Her Ear, 1989; Donmar: Habeas Corpus, 1996; *films* include: The Time Bandits, 1981; Brazil, 1985; The Good Father, 1986; Life is Sweet, Enchanted April, 1991; A Sense of History (also writer), The Crying Game, 1992; Widow's Peak, 1993; Princess Caraboo, Bullets over Broadway, Wide Eyed and Legless, 1994; Richard III, 1995; The Borrowers, 1997; The Avengers, Little Voice, 1998; Topsy-Turvy, 1999 (Best Actor, Venice Film Fest., Evening Standard British Film Awards, London Film Critics' Circle, 2001); Bridget Jones's Diary, Moulin Rouge, 2001 (Best Supporting Actor, Nat. Bd of Review, LA Film Critics Assoc., 2001, BAFTA, 2002); Iris, 2002 (Best Supporting Actor, Nat. Bd of Review, LA Film Critics Assoc., 2001, Golden Globe, Acad. Award, 2002); Gangs of New York, Nicholas Nickleby, Bright Young Things, 2003; Around the World in 80 Days, Bridget Jones: The Edge of Reason, Vera Drake, 2004; Vanity Fair, The Chronicles of Narnia: The Lion the Witch and the Wardrobe, 2005; Art School Confidential, 2006; And When Did You Last See Your Father?, Hot Fuzz, Inkheart, 2007; The Young Victoria, The Damned United, Harry Potter and the Half-Blood Prince, 2009; Another Year, 2010; Harry Potter and the Deathly Hallows, Pt 2, 2011; The Iron Lady, 2012; Cloud Atlas, Filth, Le Weekend, Closed Circuit, 2013; Paddington, Get Santa, 2014; *television series* include: Victoria Wood as Seen on TV; Blackadder; Only Fools and Horses; Gone to the Dogs; Gone to Seed; The Peter Principle; The Gathering Storm, 2002; The Street, 2006, 2007 (Emmy Award, 2007); Longford, 2006 (Best Actor, BAFTA, 2007; Golden Globe Award, 2008); Any Human Heart, 2010; The Great Train Robbery, 2013; War and

Peace, 2015. *Recreations:* walking, cooking, golf, wood carving, cinema, reading. *Address:* c/o Independent Talent Group Ltd, 40 Whitfield Street, W1T 2RH. *T:* (020) 7636 6565. *Club:* Two Brydges.

BROADBENT, (John) Michael; wine writer; Senior Consultant, Christie's Wine Department, since 1993; *b* 2 May 1927; *s* of late John Fred Broadbent and Hilary Louise Broadbent; *m* 1954, Daphne Joste (*d* 2015); one *s* one *d. Educ:* Rishworth Sch., Yorks; Bartlett Sch. of Architecture, UCL (Cert. in Architecture 1952). Commissioned RA, 1945–48 (Nat. Service). Trainee, Laytons Wine Merchants, 1952–53; Saccone & Speed, 1953–55; John Harvey & Sons, Bristol, 1955–66 (Dir, 1963); Head, Wine Dept, Christie's, 1966–92. Chm., Christie's S Kensington, 1978–79; Director: Christie Manson & Woods, 1967–99; Christie's Fine Art Ltd, 1998–2001; Christie's Internat. (UK) Ltd, 2001–07. Wine Trade Art Society: Founder Mem., 1954; Chm., 1972–2006; Institute of Masters of Wine: MW 1960; Mem. Council, 1966–78; Chm., 1971–72. Distillers' Company: Liveryman, 1964–80; Mem. Council, 1981–90; Master, 1990–91; Vintners' Company: Freeman *hc*, 2001; Liveryman, 2005–. International Wine and Food Society: Life Mem.; Mem. Council, 1969–92; Internat. Pres., 1985–92; Gold Medal, 1989; Confrérie des Chevaliers du Tastevin: Mem., 1973; Officier-Commandeur, 1993; Grand Officier, 2006; Chm., Wine and Spirit Benevolent Soc., 1991–92. Hon. Pres., Wine and Spirit Educn Trust, 2007–09. Numerous awards from wine socs and other instns. Chevalier, l'Ordre National du Mérite, 1979; La Médaille de la Ville de Paris, Echelon Vermeil, 1989; Wine Spectator Annual Lifetime Achievement Award, 1991; Man of the Year, Decanter magazine, 1993; Glenfiddich Wine Writer of the Year, 2001. *Publications:* Wine Tasting, 1st edn 1968 (numerous foreign edns); The Great Vintage Wine Book, 1980 (foreign edns); Pocket Guide to Wine Tasting, 1988; The Great Vintage Wine Book II, 1991; Pocket Guide to Wine Vintages, 1992; The Bordeaux Atlas, 1997; Vintage Wine, 2003 (also German edn; four top internat. awards); Wine Tasting, 2003; Wine Vintages, 2003; Michael Broadbent's Pocket Vintage Wine Companion, 2007; lead monthly contributor to Decanter, 1978–2014. *Recreations:* piano, painting. *Address:* 87/88 Rosebank, Holyport Road, SW6 6LJ. *T:* (020) 3632 9412. *Clubs:* Brooks's, Saintsbury.

See also E. L. Arbuthnot.

BROADBENT, Miles Anthony Le Messurier; Chairman, The Miles Partnership, 1996–2007; *b* 1936; *m* 1980, Robin Anne Beveridge (*d* 2011); two *s* two *d. Educ:* Shrewsbury Sch.; Magdalene Coll., Cambridge Univ. (MA); Harvard Business Sch. (MBA). Non-exec. Dir, Roux Waterside Inn Ltd, 1972–. Chm., Magdalene Coll. Assoc., 2004–14; Trustee, Nat. Playing Fields Assoc., 2008–14. *Recreations:* tennis, golf. *Address:* Brackendene, Golf Club Road, St George's Hill, Weybridge, Surrey KT13 0NJ. *T:* (01932) 844159. *Clubs:* St George's Hill Tennis; St George's Hill Golf, Royal Cape Golf (Cape Town).

BROADBENT, Rt Rev. Peter Alan; *see* Willesden, Area Bishop of.

BROADBENT, Sir Richard (John), KCB 2003; Chairman, Tesco plc, 2011–15; *b* 22 April 1953; *s* of John Barclay Broadbent and Faith Joan Laurie Broadbent (*née* Fisher); *m* 2007, Jill (née McLoughlin). *Educ:* Queen Mary Coll., Univ. of London (BSc); Univ. of Manchester (MA). HM Treasury, 1975–86; Harkness Fellow, Stanford Business Sch., 1983–84; Schroders plc, 1986–99: Head, European Corporate Finance, 1995–99; Gp Man. Dir, Corporate Finance, and Mem., Gp Exec. Cttee, 1998–99; Chm., HM Customs and Excise, 2000–03; Barclays plc: Dir, 2003–11; Sen. Ind. Dir, 2005–11; Dep. Chm., 2010–11; Chm., Arriva plc, 2004–10. Trustee, Relate, 2011–14. Partner, Centre for Compassionate Communication, 2009–. MCSI (MSI 1995).

BROADBENT, Simon Hope; Visiting Fellow, National Institute of Economic and Social Research, 1994–2013; *b* 4 June 1942; *s* of late Edmund Urquhart Broadbent, CBE and Doris Hope; *m* 1966, Margaret Ann Taylor; two *s* one *d. Educ:* University College School; Hatfield College, Durham (BA); Magdalen College, Oxford (BPhil). Malawi Civil Service, 1964; FCO, 1971; UK Treasury and Supply delegn, Washington, 1974; seconded to Bank of England, 1977; Joint Head, Economists Dept, FCO, 1978; Centre for Econ. Policy Res., and Graduate Inst. of Internat. Studies, Geneva, 1984. Hd of Econ. Advrs, later Chief Econ. Advr, FCO, 1984–93. Chm., Friends of Malawi Assoc., 2008–; Trustee, Anglo-German Foundn, 1994–2010. *Recreation:* boating. *Address:* Manor House, Dorchester-on-Thames, Oxon OX10 7HZ. *T:* (01865) 340101.

BROADBRIDGE, family name of **Baron Broadbridge**.

BROADBRIDGE, 4th Baron *cr* 1945, of Brighton, co. Sussex; **Martin Hugh Broadbridge;** Bt 1937; *b* 29 Nov. 1929; *s* of Hon. Hugh Broadbridge and Marjorie Broadbridge; *S* cousin, 2000; *m* 1st, 1954, Norma Sheffield (marr. diss. 1967); one *s* one *d*; 2nd, 1968, Elizabeth Trotman (*d* 2007). *Educ:* St George's Coll., Weybridge; Univ. of Birmingham (BSc 1954). Dist Officer, Northern Nigeria, HMOCS, 1954–63; Dir and Manager, specialist road surface treatments co., 1963–92; consultant, 1992–95. *Recreations:* game fishing, natural history. *Heir: s* Air Vice-Marshal the Hon. Richard John Martin Broadbridge, *qv*. *Address:* 23A Westfield Road, Barton-on-Humber, North Lincolnshire DN18 5AA. *T:* (01652) 632895.

BROADBRIDGE, Air Vice-Marshal the Hon. Richard John Martin, QHS 2009; FRAeS; FRCGP; Director Healthcare Delivery and Training, Defence Medical Services, since 2014; *b* Jos, Nigeria, 20 Jan. 1959; *s* and heir of 4th Baron Broadbridge, *qv*; *m* 1980, Jacqueline Roberts; one *s* one *d. Educ:* Moseley Sch.; Middlesex Hosp. Med. Sch. (MB BS 1982); Univ. of Bath Sch. of Mgt (MBA). FRAeS 2003; FRCGP 2014. ACOS Health, HQ Air Comd, 2009–11; Hd of Healthcare, Defence Med. Services, 2011–13; Hd, Strategy and Integration, Defence Primary Healthcare, 2013–14. FCMI 2006. *Recreations:* golf, woodturning, cycling, windsurfing. *Address:* The Long Barn, Alstone, Tewkesbury, Glos GL20 8JD.

BROADFOOT, Prof. Patricia Mary, CBE 2006; DSc, PhD; Professor of Education, University of Bristol, 2010–14, now Emerita; *b* 13 July 1949; *d* of late Norman John Cole, VRD, sometime MP and Margaret Grace Cole (*née* Potter); *m* 1971, John Ledingham Broadfoot (marr. diss. 1977); *m* 1980, David Charles Rockey, *yr s* of Prof. Kenneth Rockey; two *s* one *d. Educ:* Queen Elizabeth's Girls' Grammar Sch., Barnet; Leeds Univ. (BA 1970); Edinburgh Univ. (MEd 1977); Open Univ. (PhD 1984); PGCE London 1971; DSc Univ. of Bristol 2000. Teacher, Wolmer's Boys' Sch., Jamaica, 1971–73; Researcher, Scottish Council for Res. in Educn, 1973–77; Lectr and Sen. Lectr, Westhill Coll., Birmingham, 1977–81; University of Bristol: Lectr, 1981–90; Reader, 1990–91; Prof. of Educn, 1991–2006; Hd, Sch. of Educn, 1993–97; Dean of Social Scis, 1999–2002; Pro-Vice-Chancellor, 2002–05, Sen. Pro-Vice-Chancellor, 2005–06; Vice-Chancellor, Univ. of Gloucestershire, 2006–10. Visiting Scholar: Macquarie Univ., Aust., 1987; Univ. of Western Sydney, 1992; Vis. Prof., Univ. of Winchester, 2010–13. Member: Conseil Scientifique de l'Institut Nat. de Recherche Pedagogique, 1998–99; Council, ESRC, 2001–06 (Mem., Res. Grants Bd, 1998–99; Chair, Internat. Cttee, 2002–03; Chair, Research Resources Bd, 2003–06; Chm., Gov. Bd, UK Household Longitudinal Study, 2007–15); UUK/SCOP Burgess Steering Gp, 2005–10; Quality Assessment Learning and Teaching Cttee, HEFCE, 2005–10; DEFRA and DECC Social Sci. Expert Panel, 2012–; Chairman: Teaching and Learning Special Interest Gp, HERDA-SW, 2004–06; Pro-Vice-Chancellors Gp, Worldwide University Network, 2004–06; Universities South West (SW Region Assoc. of Univs), 2009–10; Co-Chm., Russell Gp Pro-Vice-Chancellors Gp, 2004–06; Chair: Adv. Bd, What Works, Paul Hamlyn Foundn/HEFCE nat. project, 2008–; Pearson/Edexcel Expert Panel on Educnl Assessment, 2011–. Director: HEA, 2007–09; UCEA, 2007–10; Mem. Bd, UUK, 2008–10. Comr, Marmot Review on Health Inequalities, 2009–10. Member: Res. Adv. Bd, ETS, Princeton, USA, 2006–08; Adv. Bd, Cabot Inst. for Study of Envmtl Change, Bristol Univ., 2010–; Chair, Bd of Dirs, ViTaL Partnerships Professional Services Ltd, 2011–. President: British Educnl Res. Assoc., 1987–88; British Assoc. for Internat. and Comparative Educn, 1997–98. Trustee: St Monica Trust, 2005–09; Lloyds (formerly Lloyds TSB) Foundn, 2011– (Vice Chair, 2012–). Mem. Coll. of Fellows, Internat. Bureau of Educn, Geneva, 1999–2004. Founding Mem., Assessment Reform Gp, 1989–2003; FAcSS (Founding AcSS 1999) (Mem. Commn on Social Scis, 2001–03). Mem., Gloucestershire First, 2006–09. Mem., Adv. Panel, Leverhulme Trust, 2013–. Governor: Gloucestershire Coll., 2006–09; RAU (formerly RAC Cirencester, 2010–; Univ. of St Mark and St John Plymouth, 2014–; Mem. Council, Dean Close Sch., 2007–11. Patron, Cheltenham Art Gall. and Mus., 2009–12. Mem., Gloucester Diocesan Synod, 2012–; Chair, Gloucester Diocesan Internat. Partnerships Gp, 2011–. Hon. Canon, Gloucester Cath., 2007–12, now Emeritus. Mem. Court, Hon. Co. of Gloucestershire, 2009–11. Hon. DLitt Bristol, 2010. Editor: Comparative Education, 1993–2004; Assessment in Education, 1994–2002. *Publications:* Assessment, Schools and Society, 1979; (with J. D. Nisbet) The Impact of Research on Education, 1981; (with H. D. Black) Keeping Track of Teaching, 1982; (ed) Selection, Certification and Control, 1984; (ed) Profiles and Records of Achievement, 1986; Introducing Profiling, 1987; (with M. Osborn) Perceptions of Teaching, 1993; (jtly) The Changing English Primary School, 1994; Education, Assessment and Society, 1996; (ed jtly) Learning from Comparing, 1999; (jtly) Promoting Quality in Learning, 2000; (jtly) What Teachers Do, 2000; (jtly) Assessment: what's in it for schools?, 2002; (jtly) A World of Difference, 2003; An Introduction to Assessment, 2007. *Recreations:* gardening, horse-riding, swimming, walking. *Club:* Athenæum.

BROADHURST, Rt Rev. Mgr John Charles; Bishop Suffragan of Fulham, 1996–2010; *b* 20 July 1942; *s* of late Charles Harold Broadhurst and of Dorothy Sylvia (*née* Prince); *m* 1965, Judith Margaret Randell; two *s* two *d. Educ:* Owen's Sch., Islington; King's Coll., London (AKC 1965); St Boniface Coll., Warminster; STh Lambeth, 1982. Ordained deacon, 1966, priest, 1967; Asst Curate, St Michael-at-Bowes, 1966–70; Priest-in-charge, 1970–75, Vicar, 1975–85, St Augustine, Wembley Park; Team Rector, Wood Green, 1985–96. Area Dean, Brent, 1982–85; E Haringey, 1985–91; ordained RC priest, 2012; Prelate of Honour, 2012. Member: Gen. Synod of C of E, 1972–96 (Mem., Standing Cttee, 1988–96); ACC, 1991–96. Chm., Forward in Faith, 1992–2012; Vice-Chm., Church Union, 1997–2012. Hon. DD Nashotah House, Wisconsin, 2003. *Publications:* (ed and contrib.) Quo Vaditis, 1996; numerous contribs to jls. *Recreations:* gardening, history, travel. *Address:* 19 Spencelayh Close, Wellingborough NN8 4UU.

BROADHURST, Norman Neill, FCA, FCT; Chairman, Chloride Group plc, 2001–10; *b* 19 Sept. 1941; *s* of Samuel Herbert and Ruth Broadhurst; *m* 1964, Kathleen Muriel Joyce; two *d. Educ:* Cheadle Hulme Sch. FCA 1975; FCT 1995. Divl Manager, Finance and Admin, China Light Power Co. Ltd, Hong Kong, 1981–86; Finance Dir, United Engineering Steel Ltd, Sheffield, 1986–90; Finance Dir, VSEL plc, Barrow, 1990–94; Finance Dir, Railtrack plc, 1994–2000. Chairman: Freightliner Ltd, 2001–08; Cattles plc, 2006–09 (non-exec. Dir 2000–09; Dep. Chm., 2006); non-executive Director: Old Mutual, 1999–2008; United Utilities, 1999–2008; Taylor Woodrow, 2000–03; Tomkins, 2000–06. *Recreation:* golf. *Address:* Hobroyd, Pennybridge, Ulverston, Cumbria LA12 7TD. *T:* (01229) 861226. *E:* norman.hobroyd@btinternet.com. *Club:* Ulverston Golf.

BROADHURST, Robin Shedden, CVO 2010; CBE 2003; FRICS; non-executive Chairman, Grainger plc, since 2007 (Director, since 2004); *b* Cambridge, 7 June 1946; *s* of late Alan Broadhurst and Joan Broadhurst; *m* 1972, Penelope Alison Usher; three *s* one *d. Educ:* Felsted Sch.; Coll. of Estate Management. Jones Lang Wootton, later Jones Lang LaSalle, chartered surveyor, 1969–2004; Partner, 1973–2004; Eur. Chm., 1999–2004. Trustee and non-exec. Dir, Grosvenor, 2000–11; non-executive Director: SableKnight, 2001– (Chm., 2006–); Invista Real Estate Investment plc, 2006–09; Partner, Chelsfield Partners, 2006–. Senior Adviser: Credit Suisse, 2004–10; Resolution plc, 2010–; Consultant: Sir Robert McAlpine, 1999–; Fishmongers' Co., 2004–13. Chm., Property Advisory Gp, 1997–2002 (Mem., 1990–2002). Mem., Prince's Council, Duchy of Cornwall, 1999–2010. Trustee: Orchid Cancer Appeal, 1999–2013 (Chm., 2005–13); LandAid, 2008– (Chm., 2008–); CBF Funds Trustee Ltd (CCLA), 1999–2014 (Chm., 2006–14); Gerald Palmer Eling Trust, 2000–; SSAFA, 2006–13; King Edward VII Hosp., 2006– (Chm., 2013–); Royal Marsden Cancer Charity, 2010–; Englefield Estate, 2011–; Handel House Trust, 2012–; Member: Develt Bd, Royal Opera House, 1991–2000; Council, RNLI, 2006–; non-exec. Dir, British Liby, 2004–11. Gov., Rugby Sch., 1996–2006. Liveryman: Chartered Surveyors' Co., 1977– (Master, 1997–98); Drapers' Co., 2004–; Fishmongers' Co., 2014–. *Recreations:* theatre, opera, Rugby, sailing, ski-ing, family life. *Address:* 21 Addison Avenue, W11 4QS. *T:* (020) 760[illegible] 1143. *Clubs:* Honourable Artillery Company, Royal Thames Yacht.

BROADIE, Prof. Sarah Jean, PhD; FBA 2003; FRSE; Professor of Philosophy, University of St Andrews, since 2001; *b* 3 Nov. 1941; *d* of Prof. John Conrad Waterlow, CMG, FRS; *m* 1984, Frederick Broadie. *Educ:* Somerville Coll., Oxford (BA, BPhil); Univ. of Edinburgh (PhD 1978). Lectr in Philosophy, Univ. of Edinburgh, 1967–84; Professor of Philosophy: Univ. of Texas, Austin, 1984–86; Yale Univ., 1987–91; Rutgers Univ., 1991–93; Princeton Univ., 1993–2001. Vice-Pres., British Acad., 2006–08. MAE 2006. FRSE 2002; Fellow, Amer. Acad. of Arts and Scis, 1991. *Publications:* Nature, Change and Agency, 1982; Passage and Possibility, 1982; Ethics with Aristotle, 1991; (with C. Rowe) Aristotle: the Nicomachean ethics, 2002; Nature and Divinity in Plato's Timaeus, 2012; numerous articles on Ancient Greek philosophy. *Recreation:* playing under the auspices of all nine muses. *Address:* Philosophy Departments, University of St Andrews, Edgecliffe, The Scores, St Andrews KY16 9AL. *T:* (01334) 462486, *Fax:* (01334) 462485. *E:* sjb15@st-andrews.ac.uk.

BROADLEY, Ian R.; *see* Rank-Broadley.

BROADLEY, John Kenneth Elliott, CMG 1988; HM Diplomatic Service, retired; Ambassador to the Holy See, 1988–91; *b* 10 June 1936; *s* of late Kenneth Broadley and late Rosamund Venn (*née* Elliott); *m* 1961, Jane Alice Rachel (*née* Gee); one *s* two *d. Educ:* Winchester Coll.; Balliol Coll., Oxford (Exhibnr, MA). Served Army, 1st RHA, 1954–56. Entered HM Diplomatic Service, 1960; Washington, 1963–65; La Paz, 1965–68; FCO, 1968–73; UK Mission to UN, Geneva, 1973–76; Counsellor, Amman, 1976–79; FCO, 1979–84; Dep. Governor, Gibraltar, 1984–88. Trustee: SAT-7 (UK) Trust, 1999–2009 (Chm., 2003–09); Concordis Internat., 2003–; Zimbabwe A Nat. Emergency (ZANE), 2012–. Reader, St Saviour and St Nicholas, Brockenhurst, 1998–. Chm. of Govs, Ballard Sch., 1998–2002. *Recreations:* golf, tennis. *Address:* The Thatched Cottage, Tile Barn Lane, Brockenhurst, Hants SO42 7UE.

BROCK, Deidre Leanne; MP (SNP) Edinburgh North and Leith, since 2015; *b* Western Australia; partner, Dougie; two *d. Educ:* John Curtin Univ. (BA English); WA Acad. of Performing Arts. Manager, office of Rob Gibson, MSP. Mem. (SNP) Edinburgh CC, 2007–15; Depute Lord Provost of Edinburgh, until 2015. Member, Board: Edinburgh Internat. Fest. Council; Centre for the Moving Image; Creative Edinburgh. *Address:* House of Commons, SW1A 0AA.

BROCK, George Laurence; Professor of Journalism, City University, since 2009 (Head of Journalism, 2009–14); *b* 7 Nov. 1951; *s* of late Michael George Brock, CBE; *m* 1978, Katharine Sandeman (*see* K. Brock); two *s. Educ:* Winchester Coll.; Corpus Christi Coll., Oxford (MA). Reporter: Yorks Evening Press, 1973–76; The Observer, 1976–81; The Times: feature writer and ed., 1981–84; Opinion Page Ed., 1984–87; Foreign Ed., 1987–90; Bureau Chief, Brussels, 1991–95; Eur. Ed., 1995–97; Managing Ed., 1997–2004; Saturday

Ed., 2004–08; Internat. Ed., 2008–09. Mem., Defence, Press and Broadcasting Adv. Cttee, 1998–2004. World Editors Forum: Bd Mem., 2001–14; Pres., 2004–08. Mem., British Exec., Internat. Press Inst., 2000– (Chm., 2011–15; Mem. Bd, 2011–15). Trustee: Nat. Acad. of Writing, 2008–; Bureau of Investigative Journalism, 2010–; Internat. News Safety Inst. (UK), 2011–13 (Mem., Adv. Bd, 2013–). Gov., Ditchley Foundn, 2003–12 (Mem., Prog. Cttee, 1995–2003). Mem. Council, Gresham Coll., 2012–. Mem., Editl Bd, The Conversation UK, 2013–. Judge, Olivier Th. Awards, 2004. FRSA 2004. *Publications:* (jtly) Siege: six days at the Iranian Embassy, 1980; (with N. Wapshott) Thatcher, 1983; Out of Print: newspapers, journalism and the business of news in the digital age, 2013. *Recreations:* theatre, cities, walking, music. *Address:* Department of Journalism, City University, Northampton Square, EC1V 0HB. *T:* (020) 7040 3241.

BROCK, Katharine, (Kay), LVO 2002; DL; Chief of Staff to the Archbishop of Canterbury, since 2013 (Secretary for Public Affairs, 2012–13); *b* 23 May 1953; *d* of George Roland Stewart Sandeman and Helen Stewart Sandeman (*née* McLaren); *m* 1978, George Laurence Brock, *qv*; two *s*. *Educ:* Sherborne Sch. for Girls; Somerville Coll., Oxford (BA Hons 1975); London Business Sch. (MBA 1988). MAFF, 1975–85 (Private Sec. to Perm. Sec., 1980–81); consultant in internat. trade, 1985–88; Spicers Consulting Gp, 1988–89; Dir, PDN Ltd, 1990–91; Ext. Relns Directorate, EC, 1992–95; Advr to UK Knowhow Fund and EBRD, 1995–99; Asst Private Sec. to the Queen, 1999–2002; Private Sec. and COS (formerly Private Sec.) to the Lord Mayor of London, 2004–09; Dir, Ashridge Strategic Mgt Centre, 2010. Mem., Ind. Monitoring Bd, Wandsworth Prison, 2003–04. Pres., Somerville Coll. alumni, 2004–08. Chm., Dance United, 2008–12. Trustee, Acad. of Ancient Music, 2009–13; Mem., Adv. Council, LSO, 2009–. Gov., Sherborne Girls, 2011–. Liveryman, Founders' Co., 2005–; Freeman, Merchant Taylors' Co., 2009–. DL Gtr London, 2009. *Recreations:* music, Italy, cycling. *Address:* Lambeth Palace, SE1 7JU. *Club:* Farmers.

BROCK, Dr Sebastian Paul, FBA 1977; Reader in Syriac Studies, University of Oxford, 1990–2003, now Emeritus; Fellow of Wolfson College, Oxford, 1974–2003, now Emeritus; *b* 24 Feb. 1938; *m* 1966, Helen M. C. (*née* Hughes). *Educ:* Eton College; Trinity Coll., Cambridge (BA 1962, MA 1965); MA and DPhil Oxon 1966. Asst Lectr, 1964–66, Lectr, 1966–67, Dept of Theology, Univ. of Birmingham; Fellow, Selwyn Coll., Cambridge, 1967–72; Lectr, Hebrew and Aramaic, Univ. of Cambridge, 1967–74; Lectr in Aramaic and Syriac, Univ. of Oxford, 1974–90. Corresp. Mem., Syriac Section, Iraqi Acad., 1979. Editor, JSS, 1987–90. Hon. Dr: Pontificio Istituto Orientale, Rome, 1992; St Ephrem Ecumenical Res. Inst., Mahatma Gandhi Univ. of Kottayam, India, 2004; Univ. Saint Esprit, Kaslik, Lebanon, 2004; Hon. DLitt Birmingham, 1998. Leverhulme Medal for Humanities and Social Scis, British Acad., 2009. *Publications:* Pseudepigrapha Veteris Testamenti Graece II; Testamentum Iobi, 1967; The Syriac Version of the Pseudo-Nonnos Mythological Scholia, 1971; (with C. T. Fritsch and S. Jellicoe) A Classified Bibliography of the Septuagint, 1973; The Harp of the Spirit: Poems of St Ephrem, 1975, 3rd edn 2013; The Holy Spirit in Syrian Baptismal Tradition, 1979, 2nd edn 2008; Sughyotho Mgabyotho, 1982; Syriac Perspectives on Late Antiquity, 1984; Turgome d'Mor Ya'qub da-Srug, 1984; The Luminous Eye: the spiritual world vision of St Ephrem, 1985, 2nd edn 1992; (with S. A. Harvey) Holy Women of the Syrian Orient, 1987; Vetus Testamentum Syriace III. 1: Liber Isaiae, 1987; The Syriac Fathers on Prayer and the Spiritual Life, 1987; Malpanuto d-abohoto suryoye d-'al ṣluto, 1988; St Ephrem: Hymns on Paradise, 1990; Studies in Syriac Christianity, 1992; Luqoṭo d-Mimre, 1993; Bride of Light: hymns on Mary from the Syriac churches, 1994; Isaac of Nineveh: the second part, ch. IV–XLI, 1995; Catalogue of Syriac Fragments (New finds) in the Library of the Monastery of St Catherine, Mount Sinai, 1995; The Recensions of the Septuaginta Version of I Samuel, 1996; A Brief Outline of Syriac Literature, 1997, 2nd edn 2009; From Ephrem to Romanos: interactions between Syriac and Greek in late antiquity, 1999; (with D. G. K. Taylor and W. Witakowski) The Hidden Pearl: the Syrian Orthodox Church and its Ancient Aramaic Heritage (3 vols), 2001; (with G Kiraz) Ephrem the Syrian: select poems, 2006; Fire from Heaven: studies in Syriac theology and liturgy, 2006; The Bible in the Syriac Tradition, 2006; An Introduction to Syriac Studies, 2006; (ed with A. Butts, G. A. Kiraz and L. van Rompay) The Gorgias Encyclopedic Dictionary of the Syriac Heritage, 2011; Mary and Joseph, and other Dialogue Poems, 2011; Treasurehouse of Mysteries: explorations of the Sacred Text through poetry in the Syriac tradition, 2012; (with L. van Rompay) Catalogue of the Syriac Manuscripts and Fragments in the Library of Deir al-Surian (Egypt), 2014; contrib. Jl of Semitic Studies, JTS, Le Muséon, Oriens Christianus, Orientalia Christiana Periodica, Parole de l'Orient, Revue des études arméniennes. *Address:* Wolfson College, Oxford OX2 6UD; Oriental Institute, Pusey Lane, Oxford OX1 2LE.

BROCK, Timothy Hugh C.; *see* Clutton-Brock.

BROCKES, Prof. Jeremy Patrick, PhD; FRS 1994; MRC Research Professor, Institute for Structural and Molecular Biology (formerly Department of Biochemistry and Molecular Biology), University College London, since 1997; Member, Ludwig Institute for Cancer Research, 1991–97; *b* 29 Feb. 1948; *s* of Bernard A. Brockes and Edna (*née* Heaney). *Educ:* Winchester Coll.; St John's Coll., Cambridge (BA 1969); Edinburgh Univ. (PhD 1972). Muscular Dystrophy Assoc. of America Postdoctoral Fellow, Dept of Neurobiology, Harvard Med. Sch., 1972–75; Research Fellow, MRC Neuroimmunology Project, UCL, 1975–78; Asst, then Associate, Prof., Div. of Biology, CIT, 1978–83; Staff Mem., MRC Biophysics Unit, KCL, 1983–88; scientific staff, Ludwig Inst. for Cancer Res., UCL/Middlesex Hosp. Br., 1988–97; Prof. of Cell Biology, UCL, 1991–97. Mem. Scientific Adv. Bd, Cambridge Neuroscience Inc., 1987–2000. Brooks Lectr, Harvard Med. Sch., 1997. MAE 1989. Scientific Medal: Zool Soc. of London, 1986; Biol Council, 1990; Newcomb Cleveland Prize, AAAS, 2008. *Publications:* Neuroimmunology, 1982; papers in scientific jls. *Recreation:* soprano saxophone. *Address:* Institute for Structural and Molecular Biology, University College London, Gower Street, WC1E 6BT. *T:* (020) 7679 4483.

BROCKET, 3rd Baron *cr* 1933; **Charles Ronald George Nall-Cain;** Bt 1921; *b* 12 Feb. 1952; *s* of Hon. Ronald Charles Manus Nall-Cain (*d* 1961), and of Elizabeth Mary (who *m* 2nd, 1964, Colin John Richard Trotter), *d* of R. J. Stallard; *S* grandfather, 1967; *m* 1st, 1982, Isabell Maria Lorenzo (marr. diss. 1994), *o d* of Gustavo Lorenzo, New York; two *s* one *d*; 2nd, 2006, Harriet Victoria, *d* of James Warren; two *d*. *Educ:* Eton. 14/20 Hussars, 1970–75 (Lieut). Pres., Herts Chamber of Commerce and Industry, 1992; Chm., Business Link Hertfordshire, 1994. Chm., Trust for Information and Prevention (drug prevention initiatives), 1993. Chm., British Motor Centenary Trust; Dir, De Havilland Museum Trust; Patron, Guild of Guide Lectrs, 1992. *Publications:* Call Me Charlie (autobiog.), 2004. *Heir: s* Hon. Alexander Christopher Charles Nall-Cain, *b* 30 Sept. 1984. *E:* pa@lordbrocket.com.

BROCKLEBANK, Sir Aubrey (Thomas), 6th Bt *cr* 1885; ACA; director of various companies; *b* 29 Jan. 1952; *s* of Sir John Montague Brocklebank, 5th Bt, TD, and Pamela Sue, *d* of late William Harold Pierce, OBE; *S* father, 1974; *m* 1st, 1979, Dr Anna-Marie Dunnet (marr. diss. 1989); two *s*; 2nd, 1997, Hazel Catherine, *yr d* of Brian Roden; one *s*. *Educ:* Eton; University Coll., Durham (BSc Psychology). With Guinness Mahon & Co., 1981–86; Director: Venture Founders, 1986–90; Dartington & Co., 1990–92; Manager, Avon Enterprise Fund, 1990–97. *Recreations:* deep sea tadpole wrestling, shooting, motor racing. *Heir: s* Aubrey William Thomas Brocklebank, *b* 15 Dec. 1980. *Club:* Brooks's.

BROCKLEBANK, Edward; freelance journalist and broadcaster, since 2011; *b* 24 Sept. 1942; *s* of Fred Brocklebank and Nancy Mitchell Ainslie Brocklebank; *m* 1st, 1965, Lesley Beverley Davidson (marr. diss. 1978); two *s*; 2nd, 2011, Frances Isabel Finlay. *Educ:* Madras Coll.; St Andrews. Trainee journalist, D. C. Thomson, Dundee, newspaper publishers, 1960–63; freelance journalist, Fleet St, 1963–65; press officer, Scottish TV, Glasgow, 1965–70; Grampian TV, Aberdeen: reporter, 1970–76; Head: News and Current Affairs, 1977–85; Documentaries and Features, 1985–95; Man. Dir, Greyfriars Prodns, St Andrews, 1995–2001. MSP (C) Mid Scotland and Fife, 2003–11. *Recreations:* ornithology, oil painting, walking, Rugby football. *Club:* Royal & Ancient Golf (St Andrews).

BROCKLEBANK-FOWLER, Christopher; certified management consultant; *b* 13 Jan. 1934; 2nd *s* of Sidney Straton Brocklebank Fowler, MA, LLB Cantab and Iris (*née* Beechey); *m* 1st, 1957, Joan Nowland (marr. diss. 1975; she *d* 2006); two *s*; 2nd, 1975, Mrs Mary Berry (marr. diss. 1986); 3rd, 1996, Mrs Dorothea Rycroft (marr. diss. 2000). *Educ:* Perse Sch., Cambridge; DipAgr Agricl Corresp. Coll., Oxford, 1952. Farm pupil on farms in Suffolk, Cambridgeshire and Norfolk, 1950–55. National service (submarines), Sub-Lt, RNVR, 1952–54. Farm Manager, Kenya, 1955–57; Lever Bros Ltd (Unilever Cos Management Trainee), 1957–59; advertising and marketing consultant, 1959–79; Chm., Overseas Trade and Develt Agency Ltd, 1979–83; Man. Dir, Cambridge Corporate Consultants Ltd, 1985–87. Mem. Bow Group, 1961–81 (Chm., 1968–69; Dir, Bow Publications, 1968–71). Mem. London Conciliation Cttee, 1966–67; Vice-Chm. Information Panel, Nat. Cttee for Commonwealth Immigrants, 1966–67; Mem. Exec. Cttee, Africa Bureau, 1970–74; Chm., SOS Children's Villages, 1978–84. MP King's Lynn, 1970–74, Norfolk North West, 1974–83 (C, 1970–81, SDP, 1981–83); Chm., Conservative Parly Sub-Cttee on Horticulture, 1972–74; Vice-Chairman: Cons. Parly Cttee on Agriculture, 1974–75; Cons. Parly Foreign and Commonwealth Affairs Cttee, 1979 (Jt Sec., 1974–75, 1976–77); Cons. Parly Trade Cttee, 1979–80; SDP Agriculture Policy Cttee, 1982–83; Chairman: UN Parly Gp, 1979–83 (Jt Sec., 1971–78); Cons. Parly Overseas Develt Sub-Cttee, 1979–81; SDP Third World Policy Cttee, 1981–87; Member: Select Cttee for Overseas Develt, 1973–79; Select Cttee on Foreign Affairs, 1979–81; SDP Nat. Steering Cttee, 1981–82; SDP Nat. Cttee, 1982; SDP Parly spokesman on Agriculture, 1981–82, on Overseas Develt, 1981–83, on Foreign Affairs, 1982–83. Contested: (C) West Ham (North), 1964; (SDP) 1983, (SDP/Alliance) 1987, Norfolk North West; (Lib. Dem.) Norfolk South, 1992. Mem., Labour Party, 1996–. Vice Chm., Centre for World Develt Educn, 1980–83; Governor, Inst. of Develt Studies, 1978–81. Vice Pres., Inst. of Mgt Consultancy, 1999. Fellow, De Montfort Univ., 1992. Hon. Fellow IDS. *Publications:* pamphlets and articles on race relations, African affairs, overseas development. *Recreations:* painting, fishing, shooting, swimming.

BROCKLESBY, Prof. David William, CMG 1991; FRCVS; Professor of Tropical Animal Health and Director of Centre for Tropical Veterinary Medicine, Royal (Dick) School of Veterinary Studies, University of Edinburgh, 1978–90, now Emeritus; *b* 12 Feb. 1929; *s* of late David Layton Brocklesby, AFC, and Katherine Jessie (*née* Mudd); *m* 1957, Jennifer Mary Hubble, MB, BS (*d* 2012); one *s* three *d*. *Educ:* Terrington Hall Sch.; Sedbergh Sch.; Royal Vet. Coll., Univ. of London; London Sch. of Hygiene and Tropical Med. MRCVS 1954; FRCVS (by election) 1984; MRCPath 1964, FRCPath 1982; DVetMed Zürich 1965. Nat. Service, 4th Queen's Own Hussars (RAC), 1947–49. Vet. Res. Officer (Protozoologist), E Afr. Vet. Res. Org., Muguga, Kenya, 1955–66; Hd of Animal Health Res. Dept, Fisons Pest Control, 1966–67; joined ARC Inst. for Res. on Animal Diseases, Compton, as Parasitologist, 1967; Hd of Parasitology Dept, IRAD, 1969–78. Member: Senatus Academicus, Univ. of Edinburgh, 1978–90; Governing Body, Animal Virus Res. Inst., Pirbright, 1979–86; Bd, Edinburgh Centre of Rural Economy, 1981–88; Council, RCVS, 1985–89. Mem. Editorial Board: Research in Veterinary Science, 1970–88; Tropical Animal Health and Production, 1978–90; British Vet. Jl, 1982–90. *Publications:* papers in sci. jls and chapters in review books, mainly on tropical and veterinary protozoa. *Recreations:* formerly squash and golf, now TV and The Times.

BROCKLISS, Prof. Laurence William Beaumont, PhD; Professor of Early Modern French History, University of Oxford, since 2002; Tutor and Fellow in Modern History, Magdalen College, Oxford, since 1984; *b* 20 March 1950; *s* of Henry Richard Brockliss and Rosemary Brockliss (*née* Beaumont); *m* 1974, Alison Jane Gordon; one *s* two *d*. *Educ:* Dulwich Coll.; Gonville and Caius Coll., Cambridge (BA 1971; PhD 1976). Lectr in Hist., Univ. of Hull, 1974–84; CUF Lectr in Mod. Hist., 1984–97, Reader, 1997–2002, Univ. of Oxford. Sarton Prof. in Hist. of Scis, Univ. of Ghent, 1996–97 (Sarton Medal, 1996); Jean Leclerc Prof. of Sociol., Univ. of Louvain-la-Neuve, 2000–01. Ed., Hist. of Univs, 1988–93. *Publications:* French Higher Education in the Seventeenth and Eighteenth Centuries, 1987; (ed with J. Bergin) Richelieu and His Age, 1992; (with C. Jones) The Medical World of Early Modern France, 1997; (ed with D. Eastwood) A Union of Multiple Identities: the British Isles *c* 1750–*c* 1850, 1997; (ed with Sir John Elliott) The World of the Favourite, 1999; Calvet's Web: enlightenment and the republic of letters in eighteenth-century France, 2002; (jtly) Nelson's Surgeon: William Beatty, naval medicine, and the Battle of Trafalgar, 2005; (jtly) Advancing with the Army: medicine, the professions, and social mobility in the British Isles 1790–1850, 2006; (ed) Magdalen College, Oxford: a history, 2008; (ed with H. Montgomery) Childhood and Violence in the Western Tradition, 2010; (ed with Nicola Sheldon) Mass Education and the Limits of State-Building, c. 1870–1920, 2012. *Recreations:* walking, gardening, camping. *Address:* 85 Whitecross, Wootton, Abingdon, Oxon OX13 6BS. *T:* (01235) 529214. *E:* laurence.brockliss@magd.ox.ac.uk.

BRODIE, Rt Hon. Lord; Philip Hope Brodie; PC 2013; a Senator of the College of Justice in Scotland, since 2002; *b* 14 July 1950; *s* of Very Rev. Peter Philip Brodie and Constance Lindsay Hope; *m* 1983, Carol Dora McLeish; two *s* one *d*. *Educ:* Dollar Academy; Edinburgh Univ. (LLB Hons); Univ. of Virginia (LLM). Admitted Faculty of Advocates, 1976; QC (Scot.) 1987; called to the Bar, Lincoln's Inn, 1991–2012, Bencher, 2013; Standing Junior Counsel, MoD (Scotland) PE, and HSE, 1983–87; Advocate-Depute, 1997–99. Mem., Mental Welfare Commn for Scotland, 1985–96. Part-time Chairman: Industrial Tribunals, 1987–91; Medical Appeal Tribunals, 1991–96; Employment Tribunals, 2002; Chm., Judicial Studies Cttee, 2006–12. Chm., Cockburn Assoc., 2008–. Chancellor's Assessor, Edinburgh Napier Univ., 2013–. *Recreations:* fencing, walking, reading. *Address:* 2 Cobden Crescent, Edinburgh EH9 2BG; Court of Session, Parliament House, Parliament Square, Edinburgh EH1 1RQ.

BRODIE, Sir Benjamin David Ross, 5th Bt *cr* 1834; *b* 29 May 1925; *s* of Sir Benjamin Collins Brodie, 4th Bt, MC, and Mary Charlotte (*d* 1940), *e d* of R. E. Palmer, Ballyheigue, Co. Kerry; *S* father, 1971, but his name does not appear on the Official Roll of the Baronetage; *m*; one *s* one *d*. *Educ:* Eton. Formerly Royal Corps of Signals. *Heir: s* Alan Ross Brodie [*b* 7 July 1960; *m* 1993, Jutta Maria Herrmann].

BRODIE, Charles Gilchrist, (Chic); Member (SNP) Scotland South, Scottish Parliament, since 2011; *b* Dundee, 8 May 1944; *s* of Charles and Eileen Brodie; partner, Mary Ann Mann; one *s* two *d*. *Educ:* Morgan Acad., Dundee; St Andrew's Univ. (BSc). Grad. trainee, IBM (UK) Ltd, 1966–67; N. C. R. (Manufg) Ltd, 1967–76; Logistics Manager, Sidlaw Industries Ltd, 1976–79; Business Manager, Europe Digital Equipment Manufg Ltd, 1979–83; Wang UK Ltd, 1983–88; Financial Dir, Tandem Computers, 1988–94; Gen. Manager, Twinsoft Europe, 1994–99; Chm. and CEO, Sionet Internat. Ltd, 1999–2002; owner/Dir, Caledonian Strategy (Scotland) Ltd, 2001–10. *Recreations:* golf, reading autobiographies. *Address:* 23 Maybole Road, Ayr KA7 2PZ. *T:* (01292) 294603. *E:* cbrodie@calstrat.freeserve.co.uk.

BRODIE of Lethen, Ewen John, CVO 2015; Lord-Lieutenant of Nairnshire, since 1999; *b* 16 Dec. 1942; *s* of Major David J. Brodie of Lethen, OBE and Diana, *d* of Maj. Gen. Sir John Davidson, KCMG, CB, DSO; *m* 1967, Mariota, *yr d* of Lt-Col Ronald Steuart-Menzies of Culdares; three *d*. *Educ:* Harrow. Lieut, Grenadier Guards, 1961–64; IBM (UK) Ltd, 1965–74;

estate mgt, 1975–. Dir, John Gordon & Son, 1992–2011. Vice Chm., Timber Growers Scotland, 1979–82; Chm., Findhorn Dist Salmon Fishing Bd, 2001–07. Mem., N Scotland Regl Adv. Cttee, Forestry Commn, 1977–89. DL Nairn, 1980. *Recreation:* countryside sports. *Address:* Dunearn Farm, Glenferness, Nairn IV12 5UR. *T:* (01309) 651249. *Club:* New (Edinburgh).

BRODIE, Huw David; Director of Culture and Sport, Welsh Government, 2013–15; *b* 20 July 1958; *s* of John Handel James Brodie and June Brodie; *m* 1985, Benita Humphries (*d* 2003); one *s*; *m* 2006, Anna Wigley. *Educ:* Trinity Coll., Cambridge (MA Hist.). Joined Dept of Employment, 1980; MSC and Trng Agency, 1983–90; Head of Policy Analysis Br., Trng Agency, 1987; TEC Policy Team, 1988; Asst Dir, Trng Agency, Wales, 1990–92; joined Welsh Office, 1992: Trng, Educn and Enterprise Dept, 1992–94; Head of Industrial and Trng Policy Div., Industry and Trng Dept, 1994–97; Agriculture Dept, 1997–99; Dir, Agric. Dept, Nat. Assembly for Wales, 1999–2003; Welsh Assembly Government, later Welsh Government: Dir, Strategy and Communications, subseq. Strategy, Equality and Communications, 2003–07; Dir for Rural Affairs and for Heritage, 2007–09; Dir of Policy Integration, 2010–11; Dir of Strategic Planning and Equality, 2011–13. *Recreations:* history, archaeology, hill walking.

BRODIE, Judith Anne; charity leader; leadership consultant, Leadership for Social Change, since 2013; *b* England; *d* of Hilary and Morris Brodie; *m* 2014, William Mumford. *Educ:* Newlands Sch., Maidenhead; University Coll. of N Wales, Bangor (BA Jt Hons Accounting and Maths 1981); Univ. of Southampton (MSc Social Stats 1984); Univ. of Portsmouth Business Sch. (MBA Dist. 1995). Accounting trainee, Ellerman City Liners, 1981–82; Jun. Res. Fellow, Dept of Accounting and Mgt Sci., Univ. of Southampton, 1984–85; Res. Officer, then Sen. Res. Officer, Social Services Dept, Hants CC, 1985–90; Sen. Strategy and Res. Officer, Southampton CC, 1990; Planning Co-ordinator, Social Services Dept, Hants CC, 1991–95; Mgt Consultant, C. A. G. Consultants, 1995; Policy and Communications Manager, Age Concern London, 1995–98; Hd, Cancer Support Service, Cancerbackup, 1998–2003; Chief Exec., Impetus Trust, 2003–06; Dir, VSO UK, 2006–10; Global Funding and Brand Dir, VSO, 2010–11; Chief Exec., Arthritis Care, 2012. Mem. (Lab), Lambeth LBC, 1998–2002 (Lead Mem. for Social Services and Health, 1998–2002). Vice-Chair, 2003–07, Trustee, 2003–09, Turning Point. Non-executive Director: S-E London SHA, 2002–06 (Chair, Audit Cttee, 2002–06); Royal Nat. Orthopaedic Hosp., 2011–13. Mem., Programme Bd, 2012–, Chair, Expert Adv. Cttee, 2014–, NHS Summary Care Record Programme. Trustee, Royal Nat. Orthopaedic Hosp. Charity, 2011–13. Mem., London and SE Bd, CMI, 2013–. CMgr, FCMI 2013. *Recreations:* theatre, cinema, current affairs, swimming, art, eating out.

BRODIE, Philip Hope; *see* Brodie, Rt Hon. Lord.

BRODIE, Robert, CB 1990; Solicitor to the Secretary of State for Scotland, 1987–98; *b* 9 April 1938; *s* of Robert Brodie, MBE and Helen Ford Bayne Grieve; *m* 1970, Jean Margaret McDonald; two *s* two *d*. *Educ:* Morgan Acad., Dundee; St Andrews Univ. (MA 1959, LLB 1962). Admitted Solicitor, 1962. Office of Solicitor to the Sec. of State for Scotland: Legal Asst, 1965; Sen. Legal Asst, 1970; Asst Solicitor, 1975; Dep. Dir, Scottish Courts Admin, 1975–82; Dep. Solicitor to Sec. of State for Scotland, 1984–87. Temporary Sheriff, 1999; part-time Sheriff, 2000–08; part-time Chm., Employment Tribunals (Scotland), 2000–03. Chm., Scottish Assoc. of CABx, 1999–2004. *Recreations:* music, hill-walking. *Address:* 8 York Road, Edinburgh EH5 3EH. *T:* (0131) 552 2028.

BRODIE, Stanley Eric; QC 1975; a Recorder of the Crown Court, 1975–89; *b* 2 July 1930; *s* of late Abraham Brodie, MB, BS and Cissie Rachel Brodie; *m* 1956, Gillian Rosemary Joseph; two *d*; *m* 1973, Elizabeth Gloster (*see* Hon. Dame E. Gloster) (marr. diss. 2005); one *s* one *d*. *Educ:* Bradford Grammar Sch.; Balliol Coll., Oxford (MA). Pres., Oxford Univ. Law Soc., 1952. Called to Bar: Inner Temple, 1954 (Bencher, 1984, Reader, 1999, Treas., 2000); Belize, 1973; BVI, 2009; Mem. NE Circuit, 1954; Lectr in Law, Univ. of Southampton, 1954–55. Mem., Bar Council, 1987–89. Mem., River Doon Fishery Bd, 1990–. *Publications:* (jtly) Inner Temple Millennium Lectures, 2002; The Cost to Justice: government policy and the magistrates' courts, 2011. *Recreations:* opera, boating, winter sports, fishing. *Address:* Balgreen Lodge, Hollybush, Ayrshire KA6 7EB. *T:* (01292) 560546; 9 King's Bench Walk, Temple, EC4Y 7DX. *T:* (020) 7353 3428. *Clubs:* Athenæum, Flyfishers', Beefsteak.

BRODRICK, family name of **Viscount Midleton**.

BRODRICK, Dawn Margaret, CB 2015; Director for People, Capability and Change, Department for Communities and Local Government, since 2012; *b* Woking, Surrey, 17 June 1964; *d* of Desmond and Margaret Ellis. *Educ:* Winston Churchill Secondary Sch.; Kingston Business Sch. (MA Human Resource Mgt). Hd, Organisational Develt, Jobcentre Plus, 2003–06; Dir for Leadership and Learning, DWP, 2006–09; HR Dir, Personal Tax, HMRC, 2009–12. *Recreations:* Member of Chobham Golf Course, Guide Leader of 1st Bisley Guide Company. *Address:* Department for Communities and Local Government, 2 Marsham Street, SW1P 4DF. *T:* 0303 444 1878. *E:* dawn.brodrick@communities.gsi.gov.uk.

BRODRICK, His Honour Michael John Lee; a Senior Circuit Judge, 2002–08 (a Circuit Judge, 1987–2008); Resident Judge, Winchester Combined Court, 1999–2008; *b* 12 Oct. 1941; *s* of His Honour Norman John Lee Brodrick, QC and late Ruth, *d* of Sir Stanley Unwin, KCMG; *m* 1969, Valerie Lois Stroud; one *s* one *d*. *Educ:* Charterhouse; Merton Coll., Oxford (2nd Jurisp.). Called to the Bar, Lincoln's Inn, 1965, Bencher, 2000; Western Circuit; a Recorder, 1981–87; Liaison Judge to SE Hants Magistrates, 1989–93, to IoW Magistrates, 1989–94, to NE and NW Hants Magistrates, 1999–2007; Hon. Recorder of Winchester, 2005–09. Pres., Transport Tribunal, 2012– (Judicial Mem., 1986–2012); a Judge of the Upper Tribunal and Principal Judge for Traffic Comr and Transport Appeals, 2009–. Member: Senate of Inns of Court and Bar, 1979, served 1979–82; Wine Cttee, Western Circuit, 1982–86; Cttee, Council of Circuit Judges, 1990–2003 (Pres., 2003). Mem., Lord Chancellor's Adv. Cttee for the Appointment of Magistrates, for Portsmouth, 1990–93, for SE Hants, 1993–2000. Chm., Area Judicial Forum for Hants, 2004–08. Counsellor to Dean and Chapter, Winchester Cathedral, 1993–. *Recreation:* gardening.

BRODY, Neville, RDI 2011; graphic designer and typographer; Founder and Director, Research Studios (formerly Neville Brody Studio), since 1990; Principal, Brody Associates, since 2013; Dean, School of Communication, Royal College of Art, since 2011; *b* London. *Educ:* Hornsey Sch. of Art; London Coll. of Printing. Designer: Rocking Russian, 1979–80; Stiff Records, 1980–81; Art Director: Fetish Records; The Face mag., 1981–86; Arena mag., 1986–90; Partner, FontShop, 1990–2000; Co-Ed., FUSE, 1991–. Pres., D&AD, 2012–13. Exhibitions include: V&A, 1988; Rocket Gall., Tokyo, 2009. Hon. Fellow, Univ. of the Arts, 2010. *Relevant publication:* The Graphic Language of Neville Brody, by Jon Wozencroft, vol. 1, 1988, vol. 2, 1994. *Address:* Research Studios, 94 Islington High Street, N1 8EG.

BRODY, William Ralph, PhD, MD; FIEEE; President, Salk Institute for Biological Studies, California, since 2009; *b* 4 Jan. 1944; *m* Wendyce H.; one *s* one *d*. *Educ:* Massachusetts Inst. of Technol. (BS Electrical Engrg 1965; MS 1966); Stanford Univ. Sch. of Medicine (MD 1970); Stanford Univ. (PhD Electrical Engrg 1972). Dip. Amer. Bd Radiol., 1977. Stanford University School of Medicine: Fellow, Dept of Cardiovascular Surgery, 1970–71; Intern, Dept of Surgery, 1971–72; Resident, Dept of Cardiovascular Surgery, 1972–73; Clin. Associate, Nat. Heart, Lung and Blood Inst., Bethesda, Md, 1973–75; Resident, Dept of Radiol., Univ. of Calif, San Francisco, 1975–77; Stanford University School of Medicine: Dir, Res. Labs, Div. of Diagnostic Radiol., 1977–84; Associate Prof. of Radiol., 1977–82; Dir, Advance Imaging Techniques Lab., 1978–84; Prof. of Radiol., 1982–86 (on leave of absence, 1984–86); Radiologist-in-Chief, Johns Hopkins Hosp., 1987–94; Johns Hopkins University School of Medicine: Martin Donner Prof. and Dir, Dept of Radiol., 1987–94; secondary apptt in biomed. engrg and jt appt in electrical and computer engrg, 1987–94; Prof. of Radiol., Univ. of Minn, 1994–96; Pres., Johns Hopkins Univ., 1996–2009. Founder, Resonex Inc., 1983: Consultant, 1983–84; Pres., 1984–86; Pres. and CEO, 1986–87; Chm., 1987–89. Mem., Inst. of Medicine, NAS. Founding Fellow, Amer. Inst. Med. and Biol Engrg; Fellow: Amer. Coll. Cardiol.; Amer. Coll. Radiol.; Council on Cardiovascular Radiol., Amer. Heart Assoc.; Internat. Soc. Magnetic Resonance in Medicine. *Publications:* (ed) Digital Radiography: proceedings of the Stanford Conference on digital radiography, 1981; Digital Radiography, 1984; (ed with G. S. Johnston) Computer Applications to Assist Radiology, 1992; contrib. numerous book chapters and to conf. proceedings and tech. reports; contrib. numerous articles to jls, incl. Radiol., Jl Thoracic Cardiovascular Surgery, Med. Phys., IEEE Trans Biomed. Engrg, Investigative Radiol., Amer. Jl Radiol. *Address:* Salk Institute for Biological Studies, 10010 N Torrey Pines Road, La Jolla, CA 92037, USA.

BROERS, family name of **Baron Broers**.

BROERS, Baron *cr* 2004 (Life Peer), of Cambridge in the County of Cambridgeshire; **Alec Nigel Broers,** Kt 1998; PhD, ScD; FRS 1986; FREng; FIET; FInstP; President, Royal Academy of Engineering, 2001–06; Professor of Electrical Engineering, Cambridge University, 1984–96, now Emeritus; Vice-Chancellor, Cambridge University, 1996–2003, now Emeritus; Fellow, Churchill College, Cambridge, since 1990 (Master, 1990–96); *b* 17 Sept. 1938; *s* of late Alec William Broers and of Constance Amy (*née* Cox); *m* 1964, Mary Therese Phelan; two *s*. *Educ:* Geelong Grammar School; Melbourne Univ. (BSc Physics 1958, Electronics 1959); Gonville and Caius College, Cambridge (BA Mech Scis 1962; PhD Mech Scis 1966; ScD 1991; Hon. Fellow, 1996). FIET (FIEE 1984); FREng (FEng 1985); FInstP 1991. IBM Thomas Watson Research Center: Research Staff Mem., 1965–67; Manager, Electron Beam Technology, 1967–72; Manager, Photon and Electron Optics, 1972–80; IBM Fellow, 1977; IBM East Fishkill Laboratory: Manager, Lithography Systems and Technology Tools, 1981–82; Manager, Semiconductor Lithography and Process Develt, 1982–83; Manager, Advanced Develt, 1983–84; Mem., Corporate Tech. Cttee, IBM Corporate HQ, 1984; Cambridge University: Hd of Electrical Div., 1984–92, and of Dept of Engrg, 1992–96; Fellow, Trinity Coll., 1985–90 (Hon. Fellow, 1999). Louis Matheson Prof., Monash Univ., 2010–. BBC Reith Lectures, 2005. Non-exec. Dir, Vodafone (then Vodafone AirTouch, subseq. reverted to Vodafone) plc, 1998–2007. Mem., EPSRC, 1994–2000. Chairman: H of L Sci. and Technol. Select Cttee, 2004–07; Judging Panel, Queen Elizabeth Prize for Engrg, 2012–. Chairman: Bd of Dirs, Plastic Logic Ltd, 2004–06 (Dir, 2006–07); Bd of Dirs, Diamond Light Source, 2008–14; Bio Nano Consulting, 2010–. Trustee: BM, 2004–12; Needham Res. Inst., 2009–. Mem. Council, Univ. of Melbourne; Trustee, American Univ of Sharjah, 1997–. Mem. Council, Royal Acad. of Engineering, 1993–96. Foreign Associate, Nat. Acad. of Engrg, USA, 1994; Mem., Amer. Philosophical Soc., 2001; Foreign Mem., Chinese Acad. Engrg, 2006. DL Cambs, 2000. Hon. Fellow: Univ. of Wales, Cardiff, 2001; St Edmund's Coll., Cambridge, 2003; FIC 2004. Hon. FIEE 1996; Hon. FTSE 2002; Hon. FIMechE 2004; Hon. FMedSci 2004. Hon. DEng: Glasgow, 1996; Trinity Coll., Dublin, 2005; Sheffield, 2007; Durham, 2007; Tufts, 2007; Hon. DSc: Warwick, 1997; UMIST, 2002; Hon. LLD: Melbourne, 2000; Cambridge, 2004; Hon. DTech Greenwich, 2000; DUniv: Anglia Polytech. Univ., 2000; Sheffield Hallam, 2008; Hon. PhD Peking, 2002; Hon. DLaws Monash, 2009. Prize for Industrial Applications of Physics, Amer. Inst. of Physics, 1982; Cledo Brunetti Award, IEEE, 1985; Prince Philip Medal, Royal Acad. Engrg, 2001. *Publications:* The Triumph of Technology (Reith Lectures), 2005; patents and papers on electron microscopy, electron beam lithography, integrated circuit fabrication and nanotechnology. *Recreations:* music, sailing, ski-ing. *Address:* House of Lords, SW1A 0PW.

BROGAN, Prof. (Denis) Hugh (Vercingetorix); R. A. Butler Professor of History, University of Essex, 1992–98, Research Professor, 1999–2014, now Professor Emeritus; *b* 20 March 1936; *s* of Prof. Sir Denis Brogan, FBA and late Olwen Brogan (*née* Kendall). *Educ:* St Faith's Sch., Cambridge; Repton Sch.; St John's Coll., Cambridge (BA Hist. 1959; MA 1964). Staff mem., The Economist, 1960–63; Harkness Fellow, 1962–64; Fellow, St John's Coll., Cambridge, 1963–74; Lectr, then Reader, Dept of Hist., Univ. of Essex, 1974–92. DUniv Essex, 2007. *Publications:* Tocqueville, 1973; The Times Reports The American Civil War, 1975; The Life of Arthur Ransome, 1984; The Longman History of the United States of America, 1985, repr. as The Penguin History of the United States of America, 1990; Mowgli's Sons: Kipling and Baden-Powell's Scouts, 1987; (with Anne P. Kerr) Correspondance et Conversations d'Alexis de Tocqueville et Nassau William Senior, 1991; Kennedy, 1996; (ed) Signalling from Mars: the letters of Arthur Ransome, 1997; Alexis de Tocqueville: a biography, 2006; (with William Dunlop) A Shoal of Sprats, 2011. *Recreation:* collecting English epitaphs. *Address:* Department of History, University of Essex, Colchester, Essex CO4 3SQ. *T:* (01206) 872312. *Club:* Reform.

BROGAN, Melanie Henrietta; *see* Dawes, M. H.

BROKE; *see* Willoughby de Broke.

BROKE, Col (George) Robin (Straton), LVO 1977; Director, Association of Leading Visitor Attractions, 1996–2011; Equerry-in-Waiting to the Queen, 1974–77; *b* 31 March 1946; *s* of Maj.-Gen. Robert Straton Broke, CB, OBE, MC; *m* 1978, Patricia Thornhill Shann, *d* of Thomas Thornhill Shann; one *s*. *Educ:* Eton. Commissioned into Royal Artillery 1965; CO 3 RHA, 1987–89. Mem., HM Bodyguard, Hon. Corps of Gentlemen-at-Arms 1997–. Mem. Bd of Management, King Edward VII's Hosp., London, 1994–96. Trustee Hedley Foundn, 1998–. Gov., Queen Elizabeth Hosp., Kings Lynn, 2010–. *Recreation* country pursuits. *Address:* St Mary's Lodge, Bircham, King's Lynn, Norfolk PE31 6QR. *T:* (01485) 578402. *Clubs:* Cavalry and Guards, Queen's.

BROKENSHIRE, Rt Hon. James (Peter); PC 2015; MP (C) Old Bexley and Sidcup, since 2010 (Hornchurch, 2005–10); Minister of State (Minister for Immigration), Home Office since 2014; *b* 8 Jan. 1968; *m* 1999, Cathrine Anne Mamelok; one *s* two *d*. *Educ:* Davenant Foundn Grammar Sch.; Cambridge Centre for Sixth Form Studies; Univ. of Exeter (LLB) Solicitor with Jones Day Gouldens, 1991–2005. Opposition front bench spokesman on home affairs, 2006–10. Parly Under-Sec. of State, Home Office, 2010–14. *Address:* House of Commons, SW1A 0AA.

BROMHEAD, (Sir) John Desmond Gonville, (6th Bt *cr* 1806); *S* father, 1981, but does not use title. *Heir: cousin* John Edmund de Gonville Bromhead [*b* 10 Oct. 1939; *m* 1965, Jane Frances, *e d* of Harry Vernon Brotherton, Moreton-in-Marsh, Glos; one *s* one *d*].

BROMILOW, Richard Bruce Davies; His Honour Judge Bromilow; a Circuit Judge since 2005; *b* 6 May 1954; *s* of late Comdr Frank Bromilow and of Joyce Bromilow (*née* Davies); *m* 1985, Alison Nina Whitaker Bell; one *s* one *d*. *Educ:* Aldwickbury Sch. Harpenden; Bedford Sch.; Southampton Univ. (LLB); Inns of Court Sch. of Law. Called to the Bar, Gray's Inn, 1977; in practice as barrister, St John's Chambers, Bristol, 1985–2005 Asst Recorder, 1998–2000; Recorder, 2000–05. *Recreations:* bridge, cricket, cycling, golf classical music and opera. *Address:* The Shire Hall, Taunton TA1 4DY. *Clubs:* Bristol and Clifton Golf; Burnham and Berrow Golf.

BROMLEY AND BEXLEY, Archdeacon of; *see* Wright, Ven. P.

BROMLEY, Sir Michael (Roger), KBE 1998; Director, Steamships Trading Co. Ltd, 1986–96 and since 2000; *b* 19 July 1948; *s* of Harry and Joan Margaret Bromley; *m* 1st, 1972, Thierrine Brands (marr. diss. 1976); one *d*; 2nd, 1982, Peta Lynette Baynes (marr. diss. 1998); one *s* three *d*. *Educ:* Kikori Bush Sch., PNG, by corresp.; Mount Hagen Park Sch., PNG; Southport Sch., Qld, Australia. Collins & Leahy: Merchandise Operator, then Night Security, then truck driver, 1966–73; Man. Dir, 1982–98; Chm. and CEO, Collins & Leahy Pty Ltd, 1998–2000; Gen. Manager, Bromley & Manton, 1973–82. Chm., Waratah Resources Ltd, 2012–13; Former Chm., Air Niugini. *Recreations:* polocrosse, flying (pilot), scuba diving, sailing. *Club:* Goroka Polocrosse.

BROMLEY, Sir Rupert Charles, 10th Bt *cr* 1757; *b* 2 April 1936; *s* of Major Sir Rupert Howe Bromley, MC, 9th Bt, and Dorothy Vera (*d* 1982), *d* of late Sir Walford Selby, KCMG, CB, CVO; *S* father, 1966; *m* 1962, Priscilla Hazel, *d* of late Maj. Howard Bourne, HAC; three *s*. *Educ:* Michaelhouse, Natal; Rhodes Univ.; Christ Church, Oxford. Called to the Bar, Inner Temple, 1959. OSC 2012. *Recreations:* equestrian, wetlands. *Heir:* *s* Charles Howard Bromley [*b* 31 July 1963; *m* 1998, Marie, *d* of W. J. Taylor; one *s* one *d*]. *Address:* The Old Manse, Glencairn, Simon's Town, 7975, South Africa.

BROMLEY-DAVENPORT, John; QC 2002; a Recorder of the Crown Court, since 1989; actor, speaker and writer; *b* 13 March 1947; *s* of Togo and Elizabeth Bromley-Davenport; *m* 1971, Judy Francis; one *s* two *d*. *Educ:* Eton Coll.; LAMDA; College of Law. Called to the Bar, Gray's Inn, 1972; Attorney Gen., Northern Circuit, 2007–. *Publications:* Sober in the Morning (anthology of drink and drinking), 2004, 2015; Space Has No Frontier: the biography of Bernard Lovell, 2013; contrib. articles to The Times, Daily Telegraph, Daily Mail, Carmarthen Jl, Country Life. *Recreations:* acting, cricket, shooting, fishing, golf, wine and food. *E:* brommersqc@btinternet.com. *Clubs:* Pratt's, White's; Tarporley Hunt; Delamere Forest Golf, Royal Liverpool Golf.

BROMLEY-DAVENPORT, Sir William (Arthur), KCVO 2010; landowner; chartered accountant; Lord-Lieutenant of Cheshire, 1990–2010; *b* 7 March 1935; *o s* of Lt-Col Sir Walter Bromley-Davenport, TD, DL and Lenette, *d* of Joseph Y. Jeanes, Philadelphia; *m* 1962, Elizabeth Watts, Oldwick, NJ; one *s* one *d*. *Educ:* Eton; Cornell Univ., NY. Mem. ICA, 1966. National Service, 2nd Batt. Grenadier Guards, 1953–54; Hon. Col 3rd (Vol.) Batt. 22nd (Cheshire) Regt, 1985. Owns land in UK and Norway. Mem. Cttee Cheshire Br., CLA, 1962 (past Chm.). Pres., Cheshire Scout Council, 1990– (Chm., 1981–90). Chm. of Govs, King's Sch., Macclesfield, 1986–2005. JP 1975, DL 1982, High Sheriff 1983–84, Cheshire. Hon. DLitt Chester, 2006. *Address:* Capesthorne Hall, Macclesfield SK11 9JY; Fiva, Aandalsnes, Norway.

BROMLEY-DERRY, Kim Daniel; Chief Executive, London Borough of Newham, since 2010; *b* London, 22 Feb. 1961; *s* of Daniel Bromley-Derry and Joan Bromley-Derry; *m* 1990, Deborah; two *d*. *Educ:* Anglia Poly. (CSS Social Care 1986); Anglia Business Sch., Cambridge (DMS Mgt 2004; MBA 2006). Residential social worker, Cambs CC, 1982–86; team leader, then Asst Resource Centre Manager, Beds CC, 1986–89; Resource Centre Manager, 1989–91, Policy and Service Develt Manager, 1991–92, Cambs CC; Gp Manager, Beds CC, 1992–94; Ops Manager, Cities in Schs (UK), 1994–96; Area Manager, then County Manager, Lincs CC, 1996–2000; Service Dir, Children and Families, Leicester CC, 2000–05; Executive Director, Children and Young People: S Tyneside Council, 2005–07; London Bor. of Newham, 2007–10. Mem., Social Work Taskforce, DoH/DCSF, 2009. Chairman: Children's Inter-Agency Gp, 2008–10; Nat. Advisory on Family Intervention, 2010–12; Mem., Adoption Leadership Bd, 2014–. Pres., Assoc. of Dirs of Children's Services, 2009–10. *Recreations:* family, football, cricket. *Address:* London Borough of Newham, 1000 Dockside Road, E16 2QU. *T:* (020) 3373 3506. *E:* kim.bromley-derry@newham.gov.uk.

BROMLEY-MARTIN, Michael Granville; QC 2002; a Recorder of the Crown Court, since 2003; *b* 27 April 1955; *s* of late Captain David Eliot Bromley-Martin, RN, and Angela Felicity Bromley-Martin (*née* Hampden-Ross); *m* 1983, Anna Frances Birley; one *s* two *d*. *Educ:* Eton; Southampton Univ. (BSc Civil Eng). Called to the Bar, Gray's Inn, 1979. Inspector, DTI, 1989, 1990. *Recreations:* sailing, shooting, fishing, arts. *Address:* 3 Raymond Buildings, Gray's Inn, WC1R 5BH. *T:* (020) 7400 6400, *Fax:* (020) 7400 6464. *E:* chambers@3raymondbuildings.com. *Clubs:* Garrick, Royal Ocean Racing; Itchenor Sailing.

BROMPTON, Michael John; QC 2003; a Recorder, since 2006; *b* 6 Sept. 1950; *s* of late Harry and Lena Brompton; *m* 1st, 1983, Sally Elizabeth Mary O'Brien (marr. diss. 1997); two *d*; 2nd, 2003, Clare Elizabeth Gilbert. *Educ:* Stowe Sch., Buckingham; Univ. of Sussex (BA Hons Hist.); Coll. of Law, London. Called to the Bar, Middle Temple, 1973; in practice, specialising in law of crime, fraud, money-laundering and confiscation of assets; Jt Head of Chambers, 2009–. Standing Counsel to HM Customs and Excise (Crime), S Eastern Circuit, 1994–2003. *Recreations:* theatre, cricket and Rugby (spectating), modern history, walking. *Address:* 5 Paper Buildings, Temple, EC4Y 7HB. *T:* (020) 7583 6117, *Fax:* (020) 7353 0075.

BROMWICH, Prof. Michael; CIMA Professor of Accounting and Financial Management, London School of Economics and Political Science, 1985–2006, now Emeritus; *b* 29 Jan. 1941; *s* of William James Bromwich and Margery (*née* Townley); *m* 1972, Christine Margaret Elizabeth Whitehead (OBE 1991). *Educ:* Wentworth High Sch., Southend; London School of Economics (BScEcon 1965); FCMA. Ford Motor Co., 1958–62 and 1965–66; Lectr, LSE, 1966–70; Professor: UWIST, 1971–77; Univ. of Reading, 1977–85. Mem. Council, ICMA, 1980–85; Vice Pres., ICMA, later CIMA, 1985–87, Pres., CIMA, 1987–88. Accounting Advr, OFT, 2001–. Mem., Accounting Standards Cttee, 1981–84; Additional Mem., Monopolies and Mergers Commn, 1992–2000; Research Grants Bd, ESRC, 1992–96. Hon. Treas., Disability Alliance, 2007–11; Foundn Trustee and Hon. Treas., Disability Rights UK, 2012–. Hon. DEcon Lund Univ., Sweden, 1993. *Publications:* Economics of Capital Budgeting, 1976; Economics of Accounting Standard Setting, 1985; (jtly) Management Accounting: evolution not revolution, 1989; (jtly) Housing Association Accounting, 1990; Financial Reporting, Information and Capital Markets, 1992; Management Accounting: pathways to progress, 1994; Accounting for Overheads: critique and reforms, 1997; (jtly) Following the Money: the Enron failure and the state of corporate disclosure, 2003; (jtly) Worldwide Financial Reporting: the development and future of accounting standards, 2006; (jtly) Management Accounting: retrospect and prospect, 2009; co-ed others, incl. Essays in British Accounting Research; many articles. *Recreation:* working and eating in restaurants. *Address:* 14 Thornhill Road, N1 1HW. *T:* (020) 7607 9323.

BRON, Prof. Anthony John, FRCS, FCOphth, FMedSci; Head, Nuffield Laboratory of Ophthalmology, 1973–2003, and Clinical Professor of Ophthalmology, 1989–2003, University of Oxford, now Professor Emeritus; Fellow of Linacre College, Oxford, 1975–2003; Professor of Experimental Ophthalmology, Vision and Eye Research Unit, Anglia Ruskin University, since 2013; *b* 3 Feb. 1936; *s* of late Sydney and Fagah Bron; *m* 1st, 1961, Sandra Ruth Shoot (*d* 1976); one *s* one *d* (and one *s* decd); 2nd, 1981, Diana S. Shortt; one step *s* three step *d*. *Educ:* London Univ. (BSc 1957; MB BS 1961); Guy's Hosp. (DO 1964). LRCP 1960; MRCS 1960, FRCS 1968; FCOphth 1989. Guy's Hosp., 1961–63; Clin. Fellow in Ophthalmol., Wilmer Inst., Johns Hopkins Univ., 1964–65; Res. Assistant, Inst. of Ophthalmol., 1965; Moorfields Eye Hospital: Chief Clin. Assistant, 1965; Resident Surg. Officer, 1965–68; Lectr, 1968–70; Sen. Lectr and Hon. Consultant, 1970–73; Margaret Ogilvie's Reader in Ophthalmol., Oxford Univ., 1973–2003; Hon. Consultant, Oxford Eye Hosp., 1989–. Pres., Ophthalmic Section, RSM, 1986; Vice Pres., Jt Eur. Res. Meetings in Ophthalmol. and Vision, 1994–95; Chm., Assoc. for Eye Res., 1993–95; Chm. Cornea Sect., 1998–2002, Pres., 2002–03, Eur. Assoc. for Vision and Eye Res. Mem., Soc. of Scholars, Johns Hopkins Univ., 1991; Chm. and Co-organiser, Internat. Dry Eye Workshop, 2007; Consultant, Internat. Workshop on Meibomian Gland Dysfunction, 2011; Mem., Workshop on Contact Lens Discomfort, 2013. ARVO Gold Fellow 2010. Founder FMedSci 1998. Hon. MA Oxon, 1973. *Publications:* (contrib.) The Inborn Errors of Metabolism, 1974; The Unquiet Eye, 1983, 2nd edn 1987; (jtly) Lens Disorders, 1996; (ed and contrib.) Wolff's Anatomy of the Eye and Orbit, 1997; (jtly) Lecture Notes in Ophthalmology, 11th edn 2011; papers on the cornea, tears and crystalline lens. *Recreations:* drawing, photography, musing on Life. *Address:* Nuffield Laboratory of Ophthalmology, 6th Floor, John Radcliffe Hospital, Headly Way, Oxford OX3 9DU. *T:* 07768 807735. *E:* anthony.bron@eye.ox.ac.uk. *Club:* Athenæum.

See also E. Bron.

BRON, Eleanor; actress and writer; *d* of late Sydney and Fagah Bron. *Educ:* North London Collegiate Sch., Canons, Edgware; Newnham Coll., Cambridge (BA Hons Mod. Langs). De La Rue Co., 1961. Director: Actors Centre, 1982–93; Soho Theatre Co., 1993–2000. Appearances include: revue, Establishment Nightclub, Soho, 1962, and New York, 1963; Not so much a Programme, More a Way of Life, BBC TV, 1964; several TV series written with John Fortune, and TV series: Making Faces, written by Michael Frayn, 1976; Pinkerton's Progress, 1983; Absolutely Fabulous, 1992; Fat Friends, 2002; Casualty 1909, 2009; Foyle's War, 2010; Midsomer Murders, 2011; Life in Squares, 2015; *TV plays and films include:* Nina, 1978; My Dear Palestrina, 1980; A Month in the Country, 1985; Quartermaine's Terms, 1987; Changing Step, 1989; The Hour of the Lynx, 1990; The Blue Boy, 1994; Vanity Fair, 1998; Gypsy Girl, Randall & Hopkirk (Deceased), 2001; Ted and Alice, 2002. *Stage roles include:* Jennifer Dubedat, The Doctor's Dilemma, 1966; Jean Brodie, The Prime of Miss Jean Brodie, 1967, 1984; title role, Hedda Gabler, 1969; Portia, The Merchant of Venice, 1975; Amanda, Private Lives, 1976; Elena, Uncle Vanya, 1977; Charlotte, The Cherry Orchard, 1978; Margaret, A Family, 1978; On Her Own, 1980; Goody Biddy Bean; The Amusing Spectacle of Cinderella and her Naughty, Naughty Sisters, 1980; Betrayal, 1981; Heartbreak House, 1981; Duet for One, 1982; The Duchess of Malfi, 1985; The Real Inspector Hound, and The Critic (double bill), 1985; Jocasta and Ismene, Oedipus and Oedipus at Colonus, 1987; Infidelities, 1987; The Madwoman of Chaillot, 1988; The Chalk Garden, 1989; The Miser, and The White Devil, 1991; opera, Die Glückliche Hand, Nederlandse Oper, Amsterdam, 1991; Desdemona—if you had only spoken! (one-woman show), 1992; Gertrude, Hamlet, 1993; Agnes, A Delicate Balance, 1996; A Perfect Ganesh, 1996; Doña Rosita: the Spinster, 1997; Be My Baby, 1998; Making Noise Quietly, 1999; Tuppence to Cross the Mersey, 2005; The Clean House, 2006, tour, 2008; In Extremis, 2007; All about my Mother, 2008; The Late Middle Classes, 2010. *Films include:* Help!; Alfie; Two for the Road; Bedazzled; Women in Love; The National Health; The Day that Christ Died, 1980; Turtle Diary, 1985; Little Dorrit, 1987; The Attic, 1988; Deadly Advice, 1994; Black Beauty, A Little Princess, 1995; The House of Mirth, 2000; The Heart of Me, 2001; Love's Brother, 2003; Wimbledon, 2004; Streetdance, 2010; Hyde Park on Hudson, 2012. *Radio:* The Archers, BBC Radio 4, 2014–. Author: song-cycle with John Dankworth, 1973; verses for Saint-Saens' Carnival of the Animals, 1975 (recorded). *Publications:* Is Your Marriage Really Necessary (with John Fortune), 1972; (contrib.) My Cambridge, 1976; (contrib.) More Words, 1977; Life and Other Punctures, 1978; The Pillow Book of Eleanor Bron, 1985; (trans.) Desdemona—if you had only spoken!, by Christine Brückner, 1992; Double Take, 1996; (ed jtly) Cedric Price: retriever, 2005; Martini Days, 2012, The Fight for the Tripod, 2013; Goldilocks and the Forebears, 2014. *Address:* c/o Rebecca Blond Associates, 69A King's Road, SW3 4NX.

See also A. J. Bron.

BRONNERT, Deborah Jane, CMG 2012; HM Diplomatic Service; Chief Operating Officer, Foreign and Commonwealth Office, since 2014; *b* Stockport, 31 Jan. 1967; *d* of Rev. Preb. Dr David Bronnert and Beryl Bronnert; *m* 2006, Alfonso Torrents; one *s*. *Educ:* Featherstone High Sch., Southall; Univ. of Bristol (BSc Hons Maths); University Coll. London (MA Pol Econ. of Russia and E Europe). DoE, 1989–91; Second Sec., Envmt, UK Repn to EC, Brussels, 1991–93; DoE, then FCO, 1993–95; Mem. of Cabinet, EC, Brussels, 1995–99; Dep. Hd, S Eur. Dept, FCO, 1999–2001; Econ. and Trade Counsellor, Moscow, 2002–05; Hd, Future of Europe Gp, then Hd, Europe Delivery Gp, FCO, 2006–08; Jt Dir, Global and Economic Issues, FCO, 2008–11; Dir, Prosperity, FCO, 2011; Ambassador to Zimbabwe, 2011–14. Mem. Bd, Merlin, 2010–13. *Publications:* Making Government Policy: the G8 and G20 in 2010; (contrib.) The New Economic Diplomacy: decision-making and negotiation in international economic relations, 3rd edn, 2011. *Recreations:* travel, running, hill walking, politics. *Address:* Foreign and Commonwealth Office, King Charles Street, SW1A 2AH.

BRONS, Andrew Henry William; Member for Yorkshire and Humber, European Parliament, 2009–14 (BNP, 2009–13; British Democratic, 2013–14); *b* Hackney, London, 17 June 1947; *s* of Ronald Brons and Alice Elizabeth Brons (*née* Spenner); *m* 1969, Susan Firth (marr. diss. 1985); two *d*. *Educ:* Harrogate Grammar Sch.; Univ. of York (BA Politics). Lectr, Harrogate Coll. of Further Educn, later Harrogate Coll., 1970–2005. Contested (BNP) Keighley, 2010. *Recreations:* dogs, horse riding, family history, clay pigeon shooting.

BROODBANK, Prof. Cyprian, PhD; FBA 2015; John Disney Professor of Archaeology and Director, McDonald Institute for Archaeological Research, University of Cambridge, since 2014; Fellow, Gonville and Caius College, Cambridge, since 2014; *b* London, 26 Dec. 1964; *s* of Denis Arthur Broodbank and Hanna Broodbank (*née* Altmann); *m* 2006, Dr Lindsay Close Spencer; one *s* one *d*. *Educ:* Westminster Sch.; Christ Church, Oxford (BA Mod. Hist. 1986); Univ. of Bristol (MA Aegean and Anatolian Prehist. 1987); King's Coll. and Girton Coll., Cambridge (PhD Classics 1996). J. A. Pye Jun. Res. Fellow, University Coll., Oxford, 1991–93; Institute of Archaeology, University College London: Lectr, 1993–2001; Sen. Lectr, 2001–09; Reader, 2009–10; Prof. of Mediterranean Archaeol., 2010–14. Vis. Fellow, All Souls, Oxford, 2005. Samuel H. Kress Fellow, 2007; British Acad. Mid-Career Fellowship, 2012. FSA 2007. Runciman Prize, Anglo-Hellenic League and Bank of Greece, 2001; James R. Wiseman Prize, Archaeol Inst. of Amer., 2002. *Publications:* An Island Archaeology of the Early Cyclades, 2000 (trans. Greek 2008); The Making of the Middle Sea, 2013 (Wolfson History Prize, 2014). *Recreations:* travel, parenthood, art, cooking, Cornwall and Mediterranean, natural history, dogs. *Address:* McDonald Institute for Archaeological Research, Downing Street, Cambridge CB2 3ER. *T:* (01223) 333538.

BROOK, Anthony Donald, FCA; Chairman, Ocean Radio Group Ltd, 1994–2000; *b* 24 Sept. 1936; *s* of Donald Charles Brook and Doris Ellen (*née* Emmett); *m* 1st, 1965, Ann Mary Reeves (*d* 2000); two *d*; 2nd, 2005, Jean Curtis. *Educ:* Eastbourne Coll. FCA 1970 (ACA 1960). Joined Associated Television Ltd, 1966; Financial Controller, ATV Network Ltd, 1969; Dir of External Finance, IBA, 1974; Finance Dir/Gen. Man., ITC Entertainment Ltd, 1978; Dep. Man. Dir, Television South plc, 1981; Man. Dir (Television), TVS Entertainment, 1984–89, Man. Dir Broadcasting, 1989–91; Man. Dir, TVS Television Ltd, 1986–89; Dep. Chm. and Man. Dir, TVS Entertainment plc, 1991–93; Chairman: SelecTV, 1993–95; Advanced Media Gp plc, 1994–95; Southern Screen Commn, 1996–99. *Recreations:* sailing, travel, golf. *Address:* 9 High Street, Rowledge, Farnham GU10 4BS. *Clubs:* Royal Southern Yacht (Hamble, Hants); Tamesis (Teddington, Middx).

BROOK, Prof. Charles Groves Darville, MD; FRCP, FRCPCH; JP; Professor of Paediatric Endocrinology, University College London, 1989–2000, now Emeritus; Consultant Paediatrician, Middlesex Hospital, 1974–2000, and Gt Ormond Street Hospital, 1994–2000, now Hon. Consulting Paediatric Endocrinologist; Director, London Centre for Paediatric

Endocrinology, 1994–2000; *b* 15 Jan. 1940; *s* of Air Vice-Marshal William Arthur Darville Brook, CB, CBE, and Marjorie Jean Brook (*née* Grant, later Hamilton); *m* 1963, Hon. Catherine Mary Hawke, *d* of 9th Baron Hawke; two *d*. *Educ:* Rugby Sch.; Magdalene Coll., Cambridge (MA); St Thomas's Hosp. Med. Sch. (MD 1964). FRCP 1979; FRCPCH 1997. Resident posts at St Thomas' and Gt Ormond St Hosps, 1964–74; Res. Fellow, Kinderspital, Zurich, 1972; University College London: Sen. Lectr in Paediatric Endocrinology, 1983–89; Academic Dir of Endocrinology, 1997–2000. Fellow, UCL Hosps, 2000. Vice Pres., 2004–06, Trustee, 2006–, St Margaret's Somerset Hospice. Member: Pitcombe Parish Council, 2001–07 (Chm., 2003–07); Pitcombe PCC, 2002–11, 2013– (Sec., 2003–05; Church Warden, 2007–11, 2013–). JP Avon and Som, 2002–10. Andrea Prader Prize, European Soc. for Paediatric Endocrinology, 2000. *Publications:* Practical Paediatric Endocrinology, 1978; Clinical Paediatric Endocrinology, 1981, 6th edn as Brook's Clinical Pediatric Endocrinology, 2009; Essential Endocrinology, 1982, 4th edn 2001 (trans. French, Polish, Greek); Growth Assessment in Childhood and Adolescence, 1982; All About Adolescence, 1985; Current Concepts in Paediatric Endocrinology, 1987; The Practice of Medicine in Adolescence, 1993; A Guide to the Practice of Paediatric Endocrinology, 1993; Handbook of Clinical Pediatric Endocrinology, 2008 (trans. Russian), 2nd edn 2012; numerous papers on endocrinology in med. jls. *Recreations:* gardening, DIY. *Address:* Hadspen Farm, Castle Cary, Som BA7 7LX. *T:* (01963) 351492. *E:* c.brook@ucl.ac.uk.

See also Air Vice-Marshal D. C. G. Brook.

BROOK, Air Vice-Marshal David Conway Grant, CB 1990; CBE 1983; *b* 23 Dec. 1935; *s* of late Air Vice-Marshal William Arthur Darville Brook, CB, CBE and Jean Brook (later Jean Hamilton); *m* 1961, Jessica (*née* Lubbock); one *s* one *d*. *Educ:* Marlborough Coll.; RAF Coll. Pilot, Nos 263, 1 (Fighter) and 14 Sqdns, 1957–62 (Hunter aircraft; fighter combat leader); ADC to AOC-in-C Near East Air Force, 1962–64; CO No 1 (Fighter) Sqdn, 1964–66 (Hunter Mk 9); RN Staff Course, 1967 (psc); RAF Adviser to Dir Land/Air Warfare (MoD Army), 1968–69; Wing Comdr Offensive Support, Jt Warfare Estab., 1970–72; CO No 20 (Army Cooperation) Sqdn, 1974–76 (Harrier); Station Comdr, RAF Wittering, 1976–78 (Harrier); RCDS, 1979 (rcds); Principal Staff Officer to Chief of Defence Staff, 1980–82; SASO, HQ RAF Germany, 1982–85; Air Officer Scotland and NI, 1986–89. Civil Emergencies Advr, Home Office, 1989–93. Mem., Lord Chancellor's Panel of Ind. (Highway) Inspectors, 1994–2003. Mem., Chipping Camden Town Council, 1992–94; Chm., Broad Campden Village Hall Cttee, 1993–2006. *Publications:* contrib. to Brasseys Annual. *Recreations:* golf, music, walking. *Address:* Darby's Cottage, Back Ends, Chipping Campden, Glos GL55 6AU. *Club:* Royal Air Force.

See also Prof. C. G. D. Brook.

BROOK, (Gerald) Robert, CBE 1981; Chief Executive, 1977–86, and Chairman, 1985–86, National Bus Company (Deputy Chairman, 1978–85); *b* 19 Dec. 1928; *s* of Charles Pollard Brook and Doris Brook (*née* Senior); *m* 1957, Joan Marjorie Oldfield; two *s* one *d*. *Educ:* King James' Grammar Sch., Knaresborough. FCIS, FCIT. Served Duke of Wellington's Regt, 1947–49. Appointments in bus companies, from 1950; Company Secretary: Cumberland Motor Services Ltd, 1960; Thames Valley Traction Co. Ltd, 1963; General Manager: North Western Road Car Co. Ltd, 1968; Midland Red Omnibus Co. Ltd, 1972; Regional Director, National Bus Company, 1974; Chm., Fleetsoftware Ltd, 1998–2007. Pres., CIT, 1987–88. *Publications:* papers for professional instns and learned socs. *Recreation:* reading military history. *Address:* Pleinmont, 24 Hookstone Drive, Harrogate, N Yorks HG2 8PP. *Club:* Army and Navy.

BROOK, Air Vice-Marshal John Michael, CB 1993; FRCGP; Director General, Royal Air Force Medical Services, 1991–94, retired; *b* 26 May 1934; *s* of late Norman Brook and Nellie Brook (*née* Burns); *m* 1959, Edna Kilburn; one *s* three *d*. *Educ:* Mirfield Grammar Sch.; Leeds Univ. (MB ChB 1957). MRCGP 1972, FRCGP 1992; Dip AvMed RCP 1974; MFOM 1981. Commissioned 1959; served Laarbruch, Stafford, Muharraq, Watton, Linton-on-Ouse, MoD; SMO, RAF Finningley, 1974–76; MoD, 1976; SMO RAF Brize Norton, 1978–81; OC RAF Av. Med. Trng Centre, 1981–83; RAF Exchange Officer, USAF HQ Systems Command, 1983–86; OC Defence Services Med. Rehabilitation Unit, 1986–87; OC Central Med. Estabt, 1987–89; Dep. Principal MO, HQ Strike Comd, 1989–91; Dep. Surgeon Gen., Health Services, 1991–93. QHS 1991–94. OStJ 1981. *Recreations:* all music, travel, walking. *Address:* 2 Vicarage Fields, Hemingford Grey, Cambs PE28 9BY. *Club:* Royal Air Force.

BROOK, Peter Stephen Paul, CH 1998; CBE 1965; producer; Co-Director, The Royal Shakespeare Theatre; *b* 21 March 1925; 2nd *s* of Simon and Ida Brook; *m* 1951, Natasha Parry (*d* 2015), stage and film star; one *s* one *d*. *Educ:* Westminster; Gresham's; Magdalen College, Oxford (MA; Hon. Fellow, 1991). Productions include: The Tragedy of Dr Faustus, 1942; The Infernal Machine, 1945; Birmingham Repertory Theatre: Man and Superman, King John, The Lady from the Sea, 1945–46; Stratford: Romeo and Juliet, Love's Labour's Lost, 1947; London: Vicious Circle, Men Without Shadows, Respectable Prostitute, The Brothers Karamazov, 1946; Director of Productions, Royal Opera House, Covent Garden, 1947–50: Boris Godunov, La Bohème, 1948; Marriage of Figaro, The Olympians, Salome, 1949. Dark of the Moon, 1949; Ring Round the Moon, 1950; Measure for Measure, Stratford, 1950, Paris, 1978; The Little Hut, 1950; The Winter's Tale, 1951; Venice Preserved, 1953; The Little Hut, New York, Faust, Metropolitan Opera House, 1953; The Dark is Light Enough; Both Ends Meet, 1954; House of Flowers, New York, 1954; The Lark, 1955; Titus Andronicus, Stratford, 1955; Hamlet, London, Moscow, 1955, Paris 2000, London, 2001; The Power and the Glory, 1956; Family Reunion, 1956; The Tempest, Stratford, 1957; Cat on a Hot Tin Roof, Paris, 1957; View from the Bridge, Paris, 1958; Irma la Douce, London, 1958; The Fighting Cock, New York, 1959; Le Balcon, Paris, 1960; The Visit, Royalty, 1960; King Lear, Stratford, Aldwych and Moscow, 1962; The Physicists, Aldwych, 1963; Sergeant Musgrave's Dance, Paris, 1963; The Persecution and Assassination of Marat..., Aldwych, 1964 (New York, 1966); The Investigation, Aldwych, 1965; US, Aldwych, 1966; Oedipus, National Theatre, 1968; A Midsummer Night's Dream, Stratford, 1970, NY, 1971; Timon of Athens, Paris, 1974 (Grand Prix Dominique, 1975; Brigadier Prize, 1975); The Ik, Paris, 1975, London, 1976; Ubu Roi, Paris, 1977; Antony and Cleopatra, Stratford, 1978, Aldwych, 1979; Ubu, Young Vic, 1978; Conference of the Birds, France, Australia, NY, 1980; The Cherry Orchard, Paris, 1981, NY, 1988; La tragédie Carmen, Paris, 1981, NY, 1983 (Emmy Award, and Prix Italia, 1984); The Mahabharata, Avignon and Paris, 1985, Glasgow, 1988, televised, 1989 (Internat. Emmy Award 1990); Woza Albert, Paris, 1988; Carmen, Glasgow, 1989; The Tempest, Glasgow and Paris, 1990; Impressions de Pelléas, Paris, 1992; L'Homme Qui, Paris, 1993, The Man Who, Nat. Theatre, 1994, New York, 1995; Qui Est Là, Paris, 1995; Oh les Beaux Jours, Lausanne, Paris, Moscow, Tbilisi, 1995, London, 1997; Don Giovanni, Aix, 1998; Je Suis un Phenomène, Paris, 1998; Le Costume, Paris, 1999, Young Vic, 2001; The Tragedy of Hamlet, Paris, 2000, Young Vic, 2001; La Tragédie d'Hamlet, Paris, 2002; Far Away, Paris, 2002; La Mort de Krishna, Paris and tour, 2002; Ta Main dans la Mienne, Paris and tour, 2003; Tierno Bokar, Paris and NY, 2004; Le Grand Inquisiteur, Paris, 2005, world tour and (as The Grand Inquisitor) Barbican Pit, 2006; Fragments, Paris, 2006, Young Vic, 2007, internat. tour (in French and English), 2008; Sizwe Banzi, internat. tour, 2007; Warum Warum, world tour (in German), 2008; Love is my Sin, internat. tour, 2009; 11 and 12, Paris and Barbican, internat. tour, 2009; Une Flute Enchantée (opera), world tour, 2010; The Suit, Paris, 2012, internat. tour, 2013, world tour, 2014; The Valley of Astonishment, Young Vic and world tour, 2014; work with Internat. Centre of Theatre Research, Paris, Iran, W Africa, and USA, 1971, Sahara, Niger and Nigeria, 1972–73. *Directed films:* The Beggar's Opera, 1952; Moderato Cantabile, 1960; Lord of the Flies, 1962; The Marat/Sade, 1967; Tell Me Lies, 1968; King Lear, 1969; Meetings with Remarkable Men, 1979; The Tragedy of Carmen, 1983; (TV film) The Tragedy of Hamlet, 2001. Hon DLitt: Birmingham; Strathclyde, 1990; Oxford, 1994; Hon. DDra Acad. of Performing Arts, Hong Kong; Dr *hc*: Adam Mickiewicz Univ., Poznan, Poland; New Sorbonne Paris 3; Laurea *hc*, Letters/Th. and Performing Arts, Rome. SWET award, for outstanding contribn by UK theatre artist to US theatre season, 1983. Freiherr von Stein Foundn Shakespeare Award 1973; Medaille Vermeil de la Ville de Paris, 2011. Commandeur de l'Ordre des Arts et des Lettres; Officer of the Legion of Honour (France), 1995. *Publications:* The Empty Space, 1968; The Shifting Point (autobiog.), 1988; Le Diable c'est l'Ennui, 1991; There Are No Secrets, 1993; Threads of Time: a memoir, 1998; Evoking Shakespeare, 1999; Between Two Silences, 1999; Climate de Confiance, 2007; With Grotowski, 2009; The Quality of Mercy, 2013. *Recreations:* painting, piano playing. *Address:* Centre International de Recherche Théâtrale, 37 bis Boulevard de la Chapelle, 75010 Paris, France.

BROOK, Richard; Chief Executive, Orchard Vale Trust, since 2013; *b* 22 Nov. 1956; *s* of Ralph Brook and Doris May Brook; *m* 1979, Sheena Ward; two *d*. *Educ:* Keele Univ. (BSc Hons Biol. 1978); University Coll., Cardiff (CQSW and Dip. Social Work 1981); Essex Univ. (MA Social Service Planning 1992). Asst Dir, Thames Reach Housing Assoc., 1991–94; Dir of Care, Heritage Care, 1994–96; Dir of Care and Community Services, Shaftesbury Soc., 1996–99; Chief Executive: Christian Alliance Housing Assoc., 1999–2001; Mind (Nat. Assoc. for Mental Health), 2001–06; Chief Exec., Public Guardianship Office and Public Guardian designate, 2006–07; Chief Exec. and Public Guardian, Office of the Public Guardian, 2007–08; Chief Executive: Sense, 2008–10; Crossroads Care, Bucks and Milton Keynes, 2011–13. *Recreations:* computing, home restoration, walking.

BROOK, Sir Richard (John), Kt 2002; OBE 1988; ScD; FREng; Chairman, ERA Foundation, 2012–15 (non-executive Director and Board Member, 2002–11); Professor of Materials Science, Oxford University, 1995–2003, now Professor Emeritus; Professorial Fellow, St Cross College, Oxford, 1991–2003, now Hon. Fellow; *b* 12 March 1938; *s* of Frank Brook and Emily Sarah (*née* Lytle); *m* 1961, Elizabeth Christine Aldred; one *s* one *d*. *Educ.* Univ. of Leeds (BSc Ceramics); MIT (ScD Ceramics). FREng (FEng 1998). Res. Asst, MIT, 1962–66; Asst Prof. of Materials Science, Univ. of S California, 1966–70; Gp Leader, AERE, 1970–74; Prof. and Head of Dept of Ceramics, Univ. of Leeds, 1974–88; Scientific Mem., Max Planck Soc. and Dir, Max Planck Inst. Metallforschung, Stuttgart, 1988–91; Cookson Prof. of Materials Sci., 1991–95, and Head, Dept of Materials, 1992–94, Oxford Univ.; Chief Exec., EPSRC, 1994–2001; Dir, Leverhulme Trust, 2001–11. Chairman, Materials Cttee, 1985–88, Materials Commn, 1992–94, SERC; Ext. Mem., Res. Cttee, British Gas, 1989–98; Mem., ESTA, 1994–98; Chm., EU Res. Orgns Hds of Res. Councils, 1997–99. Non-exec. Dir and Bd Mem., Carbon Trust, 2002–11. Mem., Royal Commn for Exhibn of 1851, 2009–. Mem., Res. Cttee, BM, 2012–. Mem., Curatorium, Körber Award, 1995–2003. Editor, Jl of European Ceramic Soc., 1989–2010. Pres., British Ceramic Soc., 1984–86; Vice-Pres., Inst. of Materials, 1993–95; Fellow, Inst. of Ceramics, 1978 (Pres., 1984–86); Dist. Life Fellow, American Ceramic Soc., 1995; Mem. d'Honneur, Soc. Française Métallurgie Matériaux, 1995–. Mem. Senate, Max Planck Soc., 1999–2011. Hon. Prof., Univ. of Stuttgart, 1990–. Mellor Meml Lectr, Swansea, 1989; Stuijts Meml Lectr, Maastricht, 1989. Mem., Deutsche Akad. der Naturforscher Leopoldina, 2002. Hon. FRAM, 2008; Hon. FBA 2011. Dr *hc:* Aveiro, 1995; Limoges, 2003; Hon. DSc: Bradford, 1996; Loughborough, 2000; Brunel, Nottingham Trent, 2001; Strathclyde, 2002. *Publications:* papers in publications of Inst. of Materials, Amer. Ceramic Soc., European Ceramic Soc. *Recreation:* Europe. *Address:* Department of Materials, University of Oxford, Parks Road, Oxford OX1 3PH.

BROOK, Robert; *see* Brook, G. R.

BROOK, (Rowland) Stuart; JP; Managing Director, Community and Social Services, States of Jersey, 2010–12; *b* 17 Nov. 1949; *s* of Geoffrey Brook and Eileen Brook; *m* 1971, Susan Heward; three *s* one *d*. *Educ:* Warwick Univ. (BSc; MBA); Hull Univ. (CQSW; DipASS); Bradford Univ. (MA). Probation Officer, Humberside Probation Service, 1973–77; Humberside County Council: Sen. Social Worker, 1977–81; Area Manager, 1981–84; Principal Officer, Dyfed CC, 1984–87; Asst Dir (Ops), Rotherham MBC, 1987–89; Asst Dir, Bradford MBC, 1989–92; Dep. Dir, 1992–94, Dir, 1995–2005, Notts CC Social Services Dept; Dir of Consulting, Tribal Consulting, 2006–07; Dir, Family Care, Notts, 2007–10; Chm., Man. Bd, Notts Community Health, 2008–10. Non-exec. Dir, Notts County NHS PCT, 2007–09. Chm., Nat. Homecare Council, 2003–05. JP Notts 2007. *Recreations:* family, athletics, garden, music. *Address:* Orchard Barn, Bradmore Lane, Plumtree, Notts NG12 5EW.

BROOK, Prof. Timothy James, PhD; FRSC; Republic of China Chair, Department of History, University of British Columbia, since 2010 (Professor, since 2004); *b* 6 Jan. 1951; *s* of John and Barbara Brook; *m* 1989, Fay Sims; two *s* two *d*. *Educ:* Univ. of Toronto (BA 1973); Harvard Univ. (AM 1977; PhD 1984). Mactaggart Fellow, Dept of Hist., Univ. of Alberta, 1984–86; Professor: Dept of Hist., Univ. of Toronto, 1986–97, 1999–2004; Dept of Hist., Stanford Univ., 1997–99; Principal, St John's Coll., UBC, 2004–09; Shaw Prof. of Chinese, Univ. of Oxford, 2007–09. Getty Foundn Sen. Scholar, 2013–14. Guggenheim Meml Fellowship, 2006; FRSC 2013. Hon. DLitt Warwick, 2010. François-Xavier Garneau Medal, 2005, Wallace K. Ferguson Prize, 2009, Canadian Histl Assoc.; Mark Lynton Prize in History, Columbia Sch. of Journalism and Neiman Foundn, Harvard Univ., 2009; Prix Auguste Pavie, Acad. des Scis d'Outre-mer, 2010. *Publications:* Geographical Sources of Ming-Qing History, 1988, 2nd edn 2002; The Asiatic Mode of Production, 1989; Quelling the People: the military suppression of the Beijing democracy movement, 1992; Praying for Power: Buddhism and the formation of gentry society in Late-Ming China, 1993; (with Hy Van Luong) Culture and Economy: the shaping of capitalism in Eastern Asia, 1997; (with B. Michael Frolic) Civil Society in China, 1997; The Confusions of Pleasure: commerce and culture in Ming China, 1998; Documents on the Rape of Nanking, 1999; (with Gregory Blue) China and Historical Capitalism: genealogies of Sinological knowledge, 1999; (with Andre Schmid) Nation Work: Asian elites and national identities, 2000; (with Bob Tadashi Wakabayashi) Opium Regimes: China, Britain, and Japan, 2000; The Chinese State in Ming Society, 2005; Collaboration: Japanese agents and Chinese elites in wartime China, 2005; (with Jérôme Bourgon and Gregory Blue) Death by a Thousand Cuts, 2008; Vermeer's Hat: the seventeenth century and the dawn of the global world, 2008; The Troubled Empire: China in the Yuan and Ming dynasties, 2010; Mr Selden's Map of China: the spice trade, a lost chart and the South China Sea, 2014. *Recreations:* music, travel, poetry, sailing. *Address:* Department of History, University of British Columbia, 1873 East Mall, Vancouver, BC V6T 1Z1, Canada.

BROOK-PARTRIDGE, Bernard; *b* Croydon, 1927; *o s* of late Leslie Brook-Partridge and late Gladys Vere Burchell (*née* Brooks), Sanderstead; *m* 1st, 1951, Enid Elizabeth Hatfield (marr. diss. 1965); one *d* (and one *d* decd); 2nd, 1967, Carol Devonald, *o d* of late Arnold Devonald Francis Lewis and late Patricia (*née* Thomas), Gower, S Wales; two *s*. *Educ:* Selsdon County Grammar Sch.; Cambridgeshire Tech. Coll.; Cambridge Univ.; London Univ.; Gray's Inn. Military Service, 1945–48. Studies, 1948–50. Cashier/Accountant, Dominion Rubber Co. Ltd, 1950–51; Asst Export Manager, British & General Tube Co. Ltd, 1951–52; Asst Sec., Assoc. of Internat. Accountants, 1952–59; Sec.-Gen., Institute of Linguists, 1959–62; various teaching posts, Federal Republic of Germany, 1962–66; Special Asst to Man. Dir, M. G. Scott Ltd, 1966–68; business consultancy work on own account, incl. various dirships with several client cos, 1968–72 and 1990–; Partner, Carsons, Brook-Partridge & Co. (Planning Consultants), 1972–2004. Chairman: Brompton Troika Ltd, 1985–; Daldorch

Estates Ltd, 1995–98; Dep. Chm., World Trade Centre Ltd, 1997–2002; Director: Edmund Nuttall Ltd, 1986–92; Kyle Stewart, 1989–92; Paramount Hill Ltd, 2003–12 (Chm., 2008–12). Local Govt and Pol Advisor to Transmanche-Link UK, 1988 and 1989. Contested (C) St Pancras North, LCC, 1958; Mem. (C) St Pancras Metropolitan Borough Council, 1959–62. Prospective Parly Cand. (C), Shoreditch and Finsbury, 1960–62; contested (C) Nottingham Central, 1970. Greater London Council: Mem. for Havering, 1967–73, for Havering (Romford), 1973–85; Chm., 1980–81; Chairman: Planning and Transportation (NE) Area Bd, 1967–71; Town Develt Cttee, 1971–73; Arts Cttee, 1977–78; Public Services and Safety Cttee, 1978–79; Opposition spokesman: for Arts and Recreation, 1973–77; for Police Matters, 1983–85; Member: Exec. Cttee, Greater London Arts Assoc., 1973–78; Council and Exec., Greater London and SE Council for Sport and Recreation, 1977–78; GLC Leaders' Cttee with special responsibility for Law and Order and Police Liaison matters, 1977–79; Dep. Leader, Recreation and Community Services Policy Cttee, 1977–79. Vice-Pres., SPCK, 1993– (Gov. and Trustee, 1976–93); Member: BBC Radio London Adv. Council, 1974–79; Gen. Council, Poetry Soc., 1977–86 (Treas., 1982–84); Board Member: Peterborough Develt Corp., 1972–88 (Chm., Queensgate Management Services); London Festival Ballet (and Trustee), 1977–79; Young Vic Theatre Ltd, 1977–88 (Chm., 1983–87); London Orchestral Concert Bd Ltd, 1977–78; ENO, 1977–78; London Contemp. Dance Trust, 1979–84; Governor and Trustee, Sadler's Wells Foundn, 1977–79; Chairman: London Music Hall Trust, 1983–96; London Symphony Chorus Develt Cttee, 1981–88; Samuel Lewis Housing Trust, 1985–92 (Trustee, 1976–94); Council, Royal Philharmonic Soc., 1991–99 (Chm., 1991–95); Exec. Cttee, Henley Soc., 1994–2004, 2009–; Old Sessions House Charitable Trust, 2004–09; Pres., British Sch. of Osteopathy Appeal Fund, 1980–84. President: City of London Rifle League, 1980–2004; Gtr London Horse Show, 1982–85; Gtr London (County Hall), subseq. GLA City Hall, Br., Royal British Legion, 1988–2006. An active Freemason, 1973–; Dep. Chm., Central London Masonic Centre Ltd, 2000–09. FCIS (Mem. Council, 1981–97, Treas., 1984, Vice-Pres. 1985, Pres., 1986); MCMI. Hon. FIET. Hon. PhD Columbia Pacific, 1982. Order of Gorkha Dakshina Bahu (2nd cl.), Nepal, 1981. *Publications:* Europe—Power and Responsibility: Direct Elections to the European Parliament (with David Baker), 1972; numerous contribs to learned jls and periodicals on linguistics and translation, the use of language, political science and contemporary politics. *Recreations:* conversation, opera, classical music and being difficult. *Address:* 28 Elizabeth Road, Henley-on-Thames, Oxfordshire RG9 1RG. *T:* (01491) 412080. *E:* bernard@brook-partridge.freeserve.co.uk. *Club:* Athenæum.

BROOK SMITH, Philip Andrew; QC 2002; a Recorder, since 2006; *b* 6 March 1957; *s* of Alan and Beryl Smith; adopted surname Brook Smith, 1981; *m* 1981, Charlotte Brook; two *s* one *d*. *Educ:* London Sch. of Econs (BSc 1st Cl. Hons Maths; MSc Maths Dist.). Called to the Bar, Middle Temple, 1982; in practice at the Bar, specialising in commercial law, 1983–. *Address:* (chambers) Fountain Court, Temple, EC4Y 9DH. *T:* (020) 7583 3335, *Fax:* (020) 7353 0329. *E:* pbs@fountaincourt.co.uk.

BROOKE, family name of **Viscounts Alanbrooke** and **Brookeborough,** and **Baron Brooke of Sutton Mandeville**.

BROOKE, Lord; Charles Fulke Chester Greville; *b* 27 July 1982; *s* and *heir* of Earl of Warwick, *qv*. *Educ:* Eton; Univ. of S Calif; University Coll. London.

BROOKE OF ALVERTHORPE, Baron *cr* 1997 (Life Peer), of Alverthorpe in the co. of West Yorkshire; **Clive Brooke;** Joint General Secretary, Public Services Tax and Commerce Union, 1996–98; *b* 21 June 1942; *s* of Mary Brooke (*née* Colbeck) and John Brooke; *m* 1967, Lorna Hopkin Roberts. *Educ:* Thornes House School, Wakefield. Asst Sec., 1964–82, Dep. Gen. Sec., 1982–88, Gen. Sec., 1988–95, Inland Revenue Staff Fedn. Trade Union Congress: Member: Gen. Council, 1989–96; Exec. Cttee, 1993–96. Govt Partnership Dir, NATS Ltd, 2001–06; Sen. Strategic Advr, Accenture UK plc, 1997–2010; Advr, Liverpool Victoria Friendly Soc., 2002–08. Member: Council of Civil Service Unions, 1982–97 (Chm., Major Policy Cttee, 1996–97); H of C Speaker's Commn on Citizenship, 1988; Exec. Cttee, Involvement and Participation Assoc., 1991–97; Council, Inst. for Manpower Studies, 1994–2001; Pensions Compensation Bd, 1996–2006. Member: H of L EU Select Cttee, 1999–2002, and Chm., Sub-Cttee B (Energy, Industry and Transport), 1998–2002; Jt Cttee on H of L Reform, 2002–03; H of L EU Select Cttee D (Agriculture, Environment and Fisheries), 2007–10; H of L Select Cttee on Crossrail Bill, 2008; H of L EU Select Cttee B (Internal Market, Energy and Transport), 2010–. Mem., Labour Party. Mem., Churches Enquiry on Employment and Future of Work, 1995–96. Trustee: Duke of Edinburgh Study Conf., 1993–2010 (Mem., Canada Conf., 1980); Community Services Volunteers, 1989–; IPPR, 1997–; Action on Addiction, 2002–13. Jt Patron, Neighbourhood Initiatives Foundn, 1999–2007; Patron: European Assoc. for the Treatment of Addiction (UK), 2001–; Fedn of Drug and Alcohol Professionals, 2002–; Sparrow Schs Foundn, 2005–; Kenward Trust, 2006–; Everyman Project, 2010–; British Liver Trust, 2013–. *Recreations:* painting, reading, watching soccer and Rugby League, walking my cairn terriers. *Address:* House of Lords, SW1A 0PW. *T:* (020) 7219 0478.

BROOKE OF SUTTON MANDEVILLE, Baron *cr* 2001 (Life Peer), of Sutton Mandeville in the County of Wiltshire; **Peter Leonard Brooke,** CH 1992; PC 1988; *b* 3 March 1934; *s* of Lord Brooke of Cumnor, PC, CH and Lady Brooke of Ystradfellte, DBE; *m* 1st, 1964, Joan Margaret Smith (*d* 1985); three *s* (and one *s* decd); 2nd, 1991, Lindsay Allinson. *Educ:* Marlborough; Balliol College, Oxford (MA); Harvard Business School (MBA). Vice-Pres., Nat. Union of Students, 1955–56; Chm., Nat. Conf., Student Christian Movement, 1956; Pres., Oxford Union, 1957; Commonwealth Fund Fellow, 1957–59. Research Assistant, IMEDE, Lausanne, 1960–61; Spencer Stuart & Associates, Management Consultants, 1961–79 (Director of parent company, 1965–79, Chairman, 1974–79); worked in NY and Brussels, 1969–73. Dir, Hambros plc, 1997–98. Mem., Camden Borough Council, 1968–69. Chm., St Pancras N Cons. Assoc., 1976–77. Contested (C) Bedwellty, Oct. 1974; MP (C) City of London and Westminster South, Feb. 1977–1997, Cities of London and Westminster, 1997–2001. An Asst Govt Whip, 1979–81; a Lord Comr of HM Treasury, 1981–83; Parly Under Sec. of State, DES, 1983–85; Minister of State, HM Treasury, 1985–87; Paymaster Gen., HM Treasury, 1987–89; Chm., Conservative Party, 1987–89; Secretary of State: for NI, 1989–92; for Nat. Heritage, 1992–94. Chm., H of C Select Cttee on NI, 1997–2001. Mem., British Irish Parly Body, 1997–2007. Chm., Assoc. of Cons. Peers, 2004–06. Chm., Building Socs Ombudsman Council, 1996–2001. President: IAPS, 1980–83; British Antique Dealers Assoc., 1995–2005; British Art Market Fedn, 1996–2014; Friends of Wilts Churches, 2009–14; Patron, Wilts Heritage Mus., Devizes, 2012–. Mem. Council, Marlborough Coll., 1977–83, 1992–95; Lay Mem., Univ. of London Council, 1994–2006 (Dep. Chm., 2001–02; Chm. and Pro-Chancellor, 2002–06). Chm., Churches Conservation Trust, 1995–98. Trustee: Wordsworth Trust, 1974–2001; Cusichaca Project, 1978–98; Conf. on Trng in Archtl Conservation, 1994–97 (Pres., 1997–). Pres., St Andrew's Youth Club, 1998–2006. Founding Master, Guild of Art Scholars, Dealers and Collectors, 2006. FSA 1998. Sen. Fellow, RCA, 1987; Presentation Fellow, KCL, 1989; Hon. Fellow: QMW, 1996; Univ. of Wales, Lampeter, 2008. Hon. DLitt: Westminster, 1999; London Guildhall, 2001; Hon. LLD London, 2006. *Recreations:* churches, conservation, cricket, visual arts. *Address:* c/o House of Lords, SW1A 0PW. *Clubs:* Beefsteak, Brooks's, Grillions, MCC, I Zingari.

See also D. R. V. Brooke, Rt Hon. Sir H. Brooke.

BROOKE, Sir Alistair Weston, 4th Bt *cr* 1919, of Almondbury; *b* 12 Sept. 1947; *s* of Major Sir John Weston Brooke, 3rd Bt, TD, and Rosemary (*d* 1979), *d* of late Percy Nevill, Birling House, West Malling, Kent; *S* father, 1983; *m* 1982, Susan Mary, *d* of Barry Charles Roger Griffiths, MRCVS, Church House, Norton, Powys; one *d*. *Educ:* Repton; Royal Agricultural Coll., Cirencester. *Recreations:* shooting, farming, racehorse training. *Heir: b* Charles Weston Brooke [*b* 27 Jan. 1951; *m* 1984, Tanya Elizabeth, *d* of Antony Thelwell Maurice; one *s* two *d*].

BROOKE, Rt Hon. Dame Annette (Lesley), DBE 2015 (OBE 2013); PC 2014; *b* 7 June 1947; *m* Mike Brooke; two *d*. *Educ:* Romford Tech. Sch.; LSE (BSc Econ); Hughes Hall, Cambridge (Cert Ed). Teacher of econs and social scis in schs and colls in Reading, Aylesbury and Poole; Hd of Econs, Talbot Heath Sch., Bournemouth, 1984–94; Tutor, Open Univ., 1971–91. Partner, Broadstone Minerals. Poole Borough Council: Mem. (Lib Dem), 1986–2003; Chairman: Planning Cttee, 1991–96; Educn Cttee, 1996–2000; Dep. Gp Leader, 1995–97, 1998–2000; Mayor, 1997–98. MP (Lib Dem) Mid Dorset and N Poole, 2001–15. Lib Dem spokesman on children, 2004–10. Mem., Panel of Chairs, 2010–15. Chm., Lib Dem Parly Party, 2013–15.

BROOKE, Sir Christopher; *see* Brooke, Sir R. C.

BROOKE, Prof. Christopher Nugent Lawrence, CBE 1995; MA; LittD; FSA; FRHistS; FBA 1970; Dixie Professor of Ecclesiastical History, University of Cambridge, 1977–94, now Dixie Professor Emeritus; Fellow, Gonville and Caius College, Cambridge, 1949–56 and since 1977 (Life Fellow, 1994); *b* 23 June 1927; *y s* of late Professor Zachary Nugent Brooke and Rosa Grace Brooke; *m* 1951, Rosalind Beckford (*d* 2014), *d* of Dr and Mrs L. H. S. Clark; two *s* (and one *s* decd). *Educ:* Winchester College (Scholar); Gonville and Caius College, Cambridge (Major Scholar). BA 1948; MA 1952; LittD 1973. Army service in RAEC, Temp. Captain 1949. Cambridge University: College Lecturer in History, 1953–56; Praelector Rhetoricus, 1955–56; Asst Lectr in History, 1953–54; Lectr, 1954–56; Prof. of Mediæval History, University of Liverpool, 1956–67; Prof. of History, Westfield Coll., Univ. of London, 1967–77. Member: Royal Commn on Historical Monuments (England), 1977–83; Reviewing Cttee on Export of Works of Art, 1979–82. Vice-Pres., Soc. of Antiquaries, 1975–79, Pres., 1981–84. Corresp. Fellow, Medieval Acad. of America, 1981; Corresponding Member: Monumenta Germaniae Historica, 1988; Bavarian Acad. of Scis, 1997. DUniv York, 1984. Lord Mayor's Midsummer Prize, City of London, 1981. *Publications:* The Dullness of the Past, 1957; From Alfred to Henry III, 1961; The Saxon and Norman Kings, 1963, 3rd edn 2001; Europe in the Central Middle Ages, 1964, 3rd edn 2000; Time the Archsatirist, 1968; The Twelfth Century Renaissance, 1970; Structure of Medieval Society, 1971; Medieval Church and Society (sel. papers), 1971; (with W. Swaan) The Monastic World, 1974, new edn as The Age of the Cloister, 2004, as The Rise and Fall of the Medieval Monastery, 2006; (with G. Keir) London, 800–1216, 1975; Marriage in Christian History, 1977; (with R. B. Brooke) Popular Religion in the Middle Ages, 1000–1300, 1984; A History of Gonville and Caius College, 1985; The Church and the Welsh Border, 1986; (with J. R. L. Highfield and W. Swaan) Oxford and Cambridge, 1988; The Medieval Idea of Marriage, 1989; (jtly) David Knowles Remembered, 1991; A History of the University of Cambridge, vol. IV, 1870–1990, 1993, (jtly) vol. II, 1546–1750, 2004; Jane Austen: illusion and reality, 1999; (with R. B. Brooke) Churches and Churchmen in Medieval Europe (selected papers), 1999; (jtly) A History of Emmanuel College, Cambridge, 1999; part Editor: The Book of William Morton, 1954; The Letters of John of Salisbury, vol. I, 1955, vol. II, 1979; Carte Nativorum, 1960; (with A. Morey) Gilbert Foliot and his letters, 1965 and (ed jtly) The Letters and Charters of Gilbert Foliot, 1967; (with D. Knowles and V. London) Heads of Religious Houses, England and Wales 940–1216, 1972, 2nd edn 2001; (with D. Whitelock and M. Brett) Councils and Synods, vol. I, 1981; (with Sir Roger Mynors) Walter Map, De Nugis Curialium (revision of M. R. James edn), 1983; (with M. Brett and M. Winterbottom) Hugh the Chanter, History of the Church of York (revision of C. Johnson edn), 1990; (with D. Knowles) The Monastic Constitutions of Lanfranc, 2002; (jtly) English Episcopal Acta, vol. 33, Worcester 1062–1185, 2007, vol. 34, Worcester 1186–1218, 2008; (with D. Greenway and J. Denton) J. Le Neve, Fasti Ecclesiae Anglicanae 1066–1300, vol. 11, Coventry and Lichfield, 2012; contributed to: A History of St Paul's Cathedral, 1957; A History of York Minster, 1977; A Portrait of Gonville and Caius College, 2008; general editor: Oxford (formerly Nelson's) Medieval Texts, 1959–87; A History of the University of Cambridge, 4 vols 1988–2004; Nelson's History of England, etc.; articles and reviews in English Historical Review, Cambridge Historical Journal, Studies in Church History, Bulletin of Inst. of Historical Research, Downside Review, Traditio, Bulletin of John Rylands Library, Jl of Soc. of Archivists, etc. *Address:* Gonville and Caius College, Cambridge CB2 1TA.

BROOKE, Daniel Roderick Villaret; Chief Marketing and Communications Officer, Channel 4 Television Corporation, since 2010; *b* Hammersmith, 1 June 1967; *s* of Baron Brooke of Sutton Mandeville, *qv*; *m* 2004, Juliet Soskice; two *s*. *Educ:* Marlborough Coll.; Newcastle Poly. (BA Hons Graphic Design 1989); Univ. of Stirling (MBA 1990). Dir of Mktg, Paramount Comedy Channel, 1996–98; Head of Marketing and Development: Film4, 1998–2000; Digital Channels, Channel 4, 2000–01; Gen. Manager, E4, 2001–03; Managing Director: Digital Channels, Channel 4, 2003–05; Discovery Networks UK, 2005–09; Rare Day Prodns, 2009–10. Trustee: Mass Extinction Monitoring Observatory; Camden Arts Centre. *Address:* c/o Channel 4, 124 Horseferry Road, SW1P 2TX. *T:* (020) 7306 8579. *E:* dabrooke@channel4.co.uk.

BROOKE, Sir Francis (George Windham), 4th Bt *cr* 1903; Director, Troy Asset Management Ltd, since 2004; *b* 15 Oct. 1963; *s* of Sir George Cecil Francis Brooke, 3rd Bt, MBE, and of Lady Melissa Brooke, *er d* of 6th Earl of Dunraven and Mount-Earl, CB, CBE, MC; *S* father, 1982; *m* 1989, Hon. Katharine Elizabeth, *o d* of Baron Hussey of North Bradley and of Lady Susan Hussey, *qv*; one *s* two *d*. *Educ:* Eton; Edinburgh University (MA Hons). CFA (AIIMR 1993). Investment Analyst, Kleinwort Benson Securities, 1986–88; Fund Manager, 1989–94, Dir, 1994–97, Foreign & Colonial Mgt Ltd; Dir, Mercury Asset Mgt, subseq., Merrill Lynch Investment Managers, 1997–2004. Trustee, Ascot Authy, 2011–. *Heir: s* George Francis Geoffrey Brooke, *b* 10 Sept. 1991. *Address:* Flat 8, 34 Elm Park Gardens, SW10 9NZ; Glenbevan, Croom, Co. Limerick, Ireland. *Clubs:* Turf, White's, Pratt's, Jockey; Royal St George's (Sandwich); Swinley Forest.

BROOKE, Prof. George John, PhD; DD; Rylands Professor of Biblical Criticism and Exegesis, University of Manchester, since 1998; *b* 27 April 1952; *s* of Comdr Henry John Allen Brooke, MBE, DSC, and Lesley Mary Brooke (*née* Noble); *m* 1976, (Rosemary) Jane Peacocke; two *s* one *d*. *Educ:* Wellington Coll.; St Peter's Coll., Oxford (BA 1973; MA 1978; DD 2010); St John's Coll., Cambridge (PGCE 1974); Claremont Graduate Sch., Claremont, Calif (PhD 1978). Fulbright Scholar, 1974–77; Jun. Fellow, Oxford Univ. Centre for Postgrad. Hebrew Studies, 1977–78; Lectr in New Testament Studies, 1978–84, Vice-Principal, 1982–84, Salisbury and Wells Theol Coll.; University of Manchester: Lectr in Intertestamental Lit., 1984–94, Sen. Lectr, 1994–97; Prof. of Biblical Studies, 1997–98. Res. Scholar, Ecumenical Inst., Tantur, 1983; Sen. Res. Fellow, Annenberg Inst., Philadelphia, 1992; Guest Professor: Univ. of Aarhus, 2007; Univ. of Yale, 2015. President: British Assoc. of Jewish Studies, 1999; SOTS, 2012. Founding Editor, Dead Sea Discoveries, 1994–; Editor: Jl of Semitic Studies, 1991–; SOTS Book List, 2000–06; Studies on the Texts of the Desert of Judah, 2013–. *Publications:* Exegesis at Qumran: 4QFlorilegium in its Jewish context, 1985; The Allegro Qumran Collection, 1996; (jtly) The Complete World of the Dead Sea Scrolls, 2002, 2nd edn 2011; Qumran and the Jewish Jesus, 2005; The Dead Sea Scrolls and the New Testament: essays in mutual illumination, 2005; Reading the Dead Sea Scrolls: essays in method, 2013; edited: Temple Scroll Studies, 1989; Women in the Biblical Tradition, 1992; New Qumran Texts and Studies, 1994; The Birth of Jesus, 2000; Jewish Ways of Reading the Bible, 2000; edited jointly: Septuagint, Scrolls and Cognate Writings, 1992; Ugarit and the

Bible, 1994; Narrativity in Biblical and Related Texts, 2000; Copper Scroll Studies, 2002; Studia Semitica, 2005; Ancient and Modern Scriptural Historiography, 2007; The Significance of Sinai, 2008; The Mermaid and the Partridge, 2011; The Scrolls and Biblical Traditions, 2012. *Recreations:* cooking, hill walking. *Address:* Department of Religions and Theology, Samuel Alexander Building, University of Manchester, Oxford Road, Manchester M13 9PL. *T:* (0161) 275 3609, *Fax:* (0161) 306 1241. *E:* george.brooke@manchester.ac.uk.

BROOKE, Rt Hon. Sir Henry, Kt 1988; CMG 2012; PC 1996; a Lord Justice of Appeal, 1996–2006; Vice-President, Court of Appeal (Civil Division), 2003–06; *b* 19 July 1936; *s* of Lord Brooke of Cumnor, PC, CH and Lady Brooke of Ystradfellte, DBE; *m* 1966, Bridget Mary Kalaugher; three *s* one *d*. *Educ:* Marlborough College; Balliol Coll., Oxford. MA (1st Cl. Classical Hon. Mods, 1st Cl. Lit. Hum.; Hon. Fellow, 2014). Called to the Bar, Inner Temple, 1963, Bencher, 1987; Junior Counsel to the Crown, Common Law, 1978–81; QC 1981; a Recorder, 1983–88; a Judge of the High Court, QBD, 1988–96; Judge i/c modernisation, 2001–04. Chm., Law Commn, 1993–95; Counsel to the Inquiry, Sizewell 'B' Nuclear Reactor Inquiry, 1983–85; DTI Inspector, House of Fraser Hldgs plc, 1987–88. Mem., Bar Council, 1987–88 (Chairman: Professional Standards Cttee, 1987–88; Race Relations Cttee, 1989–91); Chairman: Computer Cttee, Senate of the Inns of Court and the Bar, 1985–86; London Common Law and Commercial Bar Assoc., 1988 (Vice-Chm., 1986–87); Ethnic Minority Adv. Cttee, Judicial Studies Bd, 1991–94; Council, Centre for Crime and Justice Studies (formerly Inst. for Study and Treatment of Delinquency), 1997–2001; Civil Mediation Council, 2007–12; Exec. Vice-Pres., Commonwealth Magistrates' and Judges' Assoc., 2006–09. Member: Information Technology and the Courts Cttee, 1986–87, 1990–96; Judicial Studies Bd, 1992–94; Courts and Tribunals Modernisation Prog. Bd, 2001–04. President: Soc. for Computers and Law, 1992–2001; Slynn Foundn (formerly Lord Slynn of Hadley Eur. Law Foundn), 1999–2015. Chairman of Trustees: British and Irish Legal Inf. Inst., 2001–11; Prisoners of Conscience Appeal Fund, 2009–. Fellow, Wordsworth Trust, 2002– (Trustee, 1995–2001). *Publications:* Institute Cargo Clauses (Air), 1986; (contrib.) Halsbury's Laws of England, 4th edn, and to legal jls. *Address:* c/o Fountain Court Chambers, Temple, EC4Y 9DH. *Club:* Brooks's.

See also Baron Brooke of Sutton Mandeville.

BROOKE, Ian Richard, CB 2002; various posts with Ministry of Defence, 1971–2003; *b* 14 Aug. 1946; *s* of Richard Leslie Frederick Brooke and Betty Margaret (*née* Holliday); *m* 1970, Rachel Grace Wade; two *s*. *Educ:* St Clement Danes Grammar Sch.; Southampton Univ. (BSc(Eng)). FCO, 1967–71. Mem., St Albans Diocesan Synod, 2000–03; Churchwarden, 2003–07. *Recreations:* genealogy, walking, visiting cathedrals.

BROOKE, Prof. John Hedley, PhD; Andreas Idreos Professor of Science and Religion, and Director, Ian Ramsey Centre, Oxford University, 1999–2006; Fellow of Harris Manchester College, Oxford, 1999–2006, now Fellow Emeritus; *b* 20 May 1944; *s* of Hedley Joseph Brooke and Margaret Brooke (*née* Brown); *m* 1972, Janice Marian Heffer. *Educ:* Fitzwilliam Coll., Cambridge (MA; PhD 1969). Res. Fellow, Fitzwilliam Coll., Cambridge, 1967–68; Tutorial Fellow, Univ. of Sussex, 1968–69; Lancaster University: Lectr, 1969–80; Sen. Lectr, 1980–91; Reader in History of Science, 1991–92; Prof. of History of Science, 1992–99. Co-ordinator, ESF Network on Sci. and Human Values, 2000–04; Co-Dir, Templeton Project on Sci. and Religion in Schs, 2002–06. Vis. Prof., Leeds Univ., 2013–. (Jtly) Gifford Lectr, Glasgow Univ., 1995–96; Alister Hardy Meml Lectr, Oxford Univ., 2000; Dist. Lectr, Amer. Hist. of Sci. Soc., 2001; Select Preacher, Oxford Univ., 2001; Darwin Fest. Lectr, Cambridge Univ., 2009; Boyle Lectr, St Mary-le-Bow, 2010. Foundn Fellow, Inst. for Advanced Studies, Durham Univ., 2007. President: Historical Section, BAAS, 1996–97; British Soc. for History of Science, 1996–98; Science and Religion Forum, 2006–; Foundn Mem. and Mem. Exec. Cttee, Internat. Soc. for Sci. and Religion, 2001–08 (Pres., 2008–11); Corresp. Mem., 1993, Effective Mem., 2013, Internat. Acad. of History of Science. Ed., British Jl for the History of Science, 1989–93. *Publications:* Science and Religion: some historical perspectives, 1991, 2014; Thinking about Matter: studies in the history of chemical philosophy, 1995; (jtly) Reconstructing Nature: the engagement of science and religion, 1998; (ed jtly) Science in Theistic Contexts, 2001; (ed jtly) Heterodoxy in Early Modern Science and Religion, 2005; (ed jtly) Religious Values and the Rise of Science in Europe, 2005; (ed jtly) Science and Religion around the World, 2011; many articles on history of chemistry and history of natural theology. *Recreations:* music (opera), foreign travel, chess, walking, rhododendrons. *Address:* c/o Harris Manchester College, Oxford OX1 3TD. *T:* (01865) 271006.

BROOKE, John Stephen P.; *see* Pitt-Brooke.

BROOKE, Sir (Richard) Christopher, 12th Bt *cr* 1662, of Norton Priory, Cheshire; *b* London, 10 July 1966; *er s* of Sir Richard Christopher David Brooke, 11th Bt and of Carola Marion (*née* Erskine-Hill, now Countess Cowley); *S* father, 2012; *m* 2002, Sarah Montague; three *d*, and one *d* from previous marriage. *Educ:* Eton Coll.; Edinburgh Univ. (MA Hons). Man. Dir, Hillbrooke Hotels Ltd, 2006–. *Recreations:* ski-ing, shooting, fishing, gardening. *Heir: b* Edward Marcus Brooke [*b* 24 March 1970; *m* 1995, Catherine Janet Corbett; one *s* one *d*]. *Address:* 16 St Peter's Square, W6 9AJ. *T:* 07770 268359. *E:* christoph@hillbrooke.co.uk. *Club:* Boodles.

BROOKE, Sir Rodney (George), Kt 2007; CBE 1996; DL; Chairman: Quality Assurance Agency for Higher Education, 2009–14; West Yorkshire Playhouse, since 2011; *b* 22 Oct. 1939; *s* of George Sidney Brooke and Amy Brooke; *m* 1967, Dr Clare Margaret Cox; one *s* one *d*. *Educ:* Queen Elizabeth's Grammar Sch., Wakefield. Admitted solicitor (hons), 1962. Rochdale County Bor. Council, 1962–63; Leicester CC, 1963–65; Stockport County Bor. Council, 1965–73; West Yorkshire Metropolitan County Council: Dir of Admin, 1973–81; Chief Exec. and Clerk, 1981–84; Clerk to W Yorks Lieutenancy, 1981–84; Chief Exec., Westminster City Council, 1984–89; Clerk to Gtr London Lieutenancy, 1987–89; Sec., AMA, 1990–97. Chm., Bradford HA, 1989–90; Director: Riverside Health Trust, 2000–02; Westminster PCT, 2002–06. Secretary: Yorks and Humberside Tourist Board, 1974–84; Yorks and Humberside Develt Assoc., 1974–84; Hon. Sec., London Boroughs Assoc., 1984–90; Dir, Foundn for IT in Local Govt, 1988–92; Chairman: Electricity Consumers' Cttee (Yorks), 1997–2000; National Electricity Consumers Council, 1999–2000; General Social Care Council, 2002–08. Associate: Local Govt Mgt Bd, 1997–2000; Politics Internat., 1998–2000. Member: Action London, 1988–90; Exec., SOLACE, 1981–84, 1987–89; CS Final Selection Bd, 1991–2000; Ethics Standards Bd for Accountants, 2001–03; Nat. Inf. Governance Bd for Health Records, 2007–13; GMC, 2009. Chm., Durham Univ. Centre for Public Management Res., 1994–97; Vis. Res. Fellow, RIPA, 1989–92; Vis. Fellow, Nuffield Inst. for Health Studies, Leeds Univ., 1989–96; Sen. Vis. Res. Fellow, Sch. of Public Policy, Birmingham Univ., 1997–. Dir, Dolphin Square Trust, 1987–2011 (Chm., 2002–11); Mem. Bd, Capacitybuilders, 2008–11; Chm., London NE, Royal Jubilee and Prince's Trusts, 1984–91. Trustee: Community Develt Foundn, 1996–2000; Dolphin Square Charitable Foundn, 2005–11; Internet Watch Foundn, 2007–13; RNID, 2008–14. Associate, Ernst & Young, 1989–90. Editl Advr, Longman Gp, 1989–90. Mem. Council, Tavistock Inst., 2006–12. Gov., Pimlico Sch., 2000–07 (Chm., 2003–05). Hon. Fellow, Inst. of Govt Studies, Birmingham Univ. FRSA. Freeman, City of London, 1993. DL Greater London, 1989. National Order of Merit (France), 1984; Nat. Order of Aztec Eagle (Mexico), 1985; Medal of Merit (Qatar), 1985; Order of Merit (Germany), 1986; Legion of Merit (Senegal), 1988. *Publications:* Managing the Enabling Authority, 1989; The Environmental Role of Local Government, 1990; (jtly) City Futures in Britain and Canada, 1990; (jtly) The Public Service Manager's Handbook, 1992; (jtly) Strengthening Local Government in the 1990s, 1997; (jtly) Ethics in Public Service for the New Millennium, 2000; The Consumers-Eye View of Utilities, 2000; The Councillor: victim or vulgarian, 2005; articles on local govt and social care. *Recreations:* ski-ing, opera, Byzantium, theatre. *Address:* Stubham Lodge, Clifford Road, Middleton, Ilkley, West Yorks LS29 0AX. *T:* (01943) 601869; 706 Grenville House, Dolphin Square, SW1V 3LR. *T:* (020) 7798 8086. *Clubs:* Athenæum, Ski Club of Great Britain.

BROOKE, Sarah Anne Louise; *see* Montague, S. A. L.

BROOKE-BALL, Patricia Ann; *see* Hitchcock, P. A.

BROOKEBOROUGH, 3rd Viscount *cr* 1952, of Colebrooke; **Alan Henry Brooke,** Bt 1822; farmer; a Personal Lord in Waiting to the Queen, since 1997; Lord-Lieutenant of Co. Fermanagh, Northern Ireland, since 2012; *b* 30 June 1952; *s* of 2nd Viscount Brookeborough, PC and Rosemary Hilda (*née* Chichester); *S* father, 1987; *m* 1980, Janet Elizabeth, *d* of J. P. Cooke, Doagh, Ballyclare. *Educ:* Harrow; Millfield. Commissioned 17th/21st Lancers, 1971; transferred 4th (County Fermanagh) Bn, UDR, 1977; Company Commander, 1981–83; Royal Irish Regt (Co. Comdr, 1988–93); Lt-Col, 1993, transf. to RARO. Now farms and runs an estate with a shooting/fishing tourist enterprise. Member: EEC Agricl Sub-Cttee, H of L, 1988–92, 1993–97; EC Select Cttee and Sub-Cttee B (energy, industry and transport), H of L, 1998–2002; Sub-Cttee D, H of L, 2006–; elected Mem., H of L, 1999. Non-exec. Director: Green Park Unit Hosp. Trust, 1993–2001; Basel International (Jersey), 2000–13 (Chm., 1996–2000). Mem., NI Policing Bd, 2001–06. Hon. Col, 4th/5th Bn, Royal Irish Rangers, 1997–2008. Pres., ABF Soldiers' Charity (formerly ABF), NI, 1995–. DL 1987, High Sheriff 1995, Co. Fermanagh. *Recreations:* shooting, fishing. *Heir: b* Hon. Christopher Arthur Brooke [*b* 16 May 1954; *m* 1990, Amanda Hodges; four *s* one *d*]. *Address:* Colebrooke Park, Brookeborough, Co. Fermanagh, N Ireland BT94 4DW. *T:* (01365) 531402. *Club:* Cavalry and Guards.

BROOKER, Alan Bernard; JP, DL; FCA; Chairman: Kode International, 1988–98; E. T. Heron & Co., 1991–96; *b* 24 Aug. 1931; *s* of late Bernard John Brooker and of Gwendoline Ada (*née* Launchbury); *m* 1957, Diana (*née* Coles); one *s* two *d*. *Educ:* Chigwell School, Essex. FCA 1954. Served 2nd RHA (2nd Lieut), 1954–56. Articled, Cole, Dickin & Hills, Chartered Accountants, 1949–54, qualified 1954; Manager, Cole, Dickin & Hills, 1956–58; Accountant, Independent Dairies, 1958–59; Asst Accountant, Exchange Telegraph Co., 1959–64; Dir, 1964–87, Chm. and Chief Exec., 1980–87, Extel Group. Chm., Serif Cowells, then Serif, 1990–93; Vice-Chairman: Provident Financial, 1983–94; James Martin Associates, 1987–89; non-executive Director: Pauls plc, 1984–85; Aukett Associates, 1988–2002; Plysu, 1988–99; PNA Holdings, 1988–89; Addison Worldwide, 1990–94; Eastern Counties Newspapers (formerly East Anglian Daily Times), 1990–96; ACAL plc, 1996–2002. Member: Council, CBI London Region, 1980–83; Companies Cttee, CBI, 1979–83; Council, CPU, 1975–88. Appeal Chm., Newspaper Press Fund, 1985–86. Governor: Chigwell School, 1968–2006 (Chm., 1978–99); Felixstowe Coll., 1986–94. Essex Pres., RBL, 2002–05. Freeman, City of London; Liveryman, Stationers' and Newspapermakers' Co. (Court Asst, 1985–2007; Master, 1995–96). Churchwarden, St Bride's, Fleet Street, 1986–2002. JP Essex 1972 (Chm. of Bench, Epping and Ongar, 1995–99); DL Essex 1982. FRSA 1980. *Recreations:* cricket, golf. *Address:* Silkwater, East Hill, Evershot, Dorset DT2 0LB. *Clubs:* East India, MCC; Royal Worlington and Newmarket Golf.

BROOKER, David; Director of Sport, Department for Culture, Media and Sport, 2011–14; *b* Epping, Essex, 12 July 1952; *s* of Victor Richard Joseph Brooker and Betty Brooker (*née* Pearson); *m* 1976, Jacqueline Pine; two *s* one *d*. *Educ:* Magee Univ. Coll.; Univ. of Ulster (BA Hons English 1974). Northern Ireland Office, 1975–84: Private Sec. to Minister of State, 1979–81, to Perm. Under-Sec., 1982–83; Police Dept, Home Office, 1984–87; Northern Ireland Office: Security Directorate, 1987–90; Pol Directorate, 1991–2000; rcds 1996; Hd, HR, 2001–02; Principal Private Sec. to Sec. of State for NI, 2003–04; Dir of Communications, 2005–08; Dir of Legacy, Govt Olympic Exec., DCMS, 2008–12. Mem., Appts Cttee, CSSC Sports and Leisure, 2014–. Trustee, HighGround, 2015– (Chm., 2015–). *Recreations:* cricket, golf, tennis. *Address:* c/o HighGround, 95 Horseferry Road, SW1P 2DX. *Clubs:* MCC, Buckinghamshire County Cricket.

BROOKER, Mervyn Edward William; Headmaster, Bolton School Boys' Division, 2003–08; Education Advisor, King Edward Foundation, 2007–14; *b* 24 March 1954; *s* of Derek and Hazel Brooker; *m* 1976, Brigid Mary O'Rorke; two *d*. *Educ:* Lancaster Royal Grammar Sch.; Burnley Grammar Sch.; Jesus Coll., Cambridge (BA Hons Geography 1975; PGCE 1976; cricket blue, 1976). Teacher (Geography and Games): County High Sch., Saffron Walden, 1976–80; Royal Grammar Sch., Worcester, 1980–88; Highfields Sch., Wolverhampton, 1988–91; King Edward VI Camp Hill Sch. for Boys: Teacher, 1992–2002; Dep. Headmaster, 1992–95; Headmaster, 1995–2002. Gov., Wolverhampton GS, 2013–. Played cricket for: Combined Univs CC, 1976; Cambs CCC, 1976–80 (county cap, 1978); Staffs CCC, 1982–86; Birmingham Cricket League XI, 1984; Midlands Clubs Cricket Conf., 1986–90; Hereford and Worcester Cricket Assoc., 1981–86; Staffs Club Cricket League XI, 1994. *Recreations:* cricket, sport in general, hill walking, foreign travel. *Clubs:* Old Wulfrunians Cricket (Wolverhampton); Tything Tramps (Worcester).

BROOKES, James Robert; ICT consultant, since 1998; non-executive Chairman, HomeWorkBase Ltd, 2005–14; non-executive Director, RMS Ltd, 2007–14; *b* 2 Sept. 1941; *s* of James Brookes and Hettie Brookes (*née* Colley); *m* 1964, Patricia Gaskell (*d* 2011); three *d*. *Educ:* Manchester Grammar Sch.; Corpus Christi Coll., Oxford (MA Maths). FBCS; CEng 1990; Eur Ing, 1991. Various posts as systems and applications programmer in develt, tech. support and sales; Northern Branch Manager, Univs and Nat. Research Region, Ferranti/Internat. Computers, 1962–67; Computer Services Manager, Queen's Univ. Belfast, 1967–69; Operations Manager, Univ. of Manchester Regional Computer Centre, 1969–75; Director: SW Univs Regional Computer Centre, 1975–87; Bath Univ. Computer Service, 1983–87; Inf. Services Orgn, Portsmouth Univ., 1992–95; Head of Information Systems, Avon and Somerset Constabulary, 1995–98. Co-founder and non-exec. Chm., Praxis Systems, 1983; Chief Exec., 1986–91, Consultant, 1991–92, BCS; non-executive Director: The Knowledge Gp, 1998–2002; Smart South West, 1999–2004; Consultant, SOCITM, 1998–. Vis. Prof., Business Sch., Strathclyde Univ., 1991–98. Mem. Council, PITCOM, 1989–2011 (Prog. Exec., 1997–2000); Mem., PICTFOR, 2011–; Hon. Sec., Council of European Professional Information Socs, 1991–93. Trustee, Young Electronic Designer Awards, 1994–2005. FRSA 1988. Freeman, City of London, 1989; Liveryman, Information Technologists' Co. (Mem., 1988). *Recreations:* sailing, fell-walking, cycling, bridge, reading, theatre. *Address:* 29 High Street, Marshfield, Chippenham, Wilts SN14 8LR. *T:* (home) (01225) 891294. *E:* jr.brookes@btinternet.com. *Club:* Oxford and Cambridge.

BROOKES, John Andrew, MBE 2004; landscape designer; *b* 11 Oct. 1933; *s* of Edward Percy Brookes and Margaret Alexandra Brookes. *Educ:* Durham; University Coll. London (Dip. Landscape). Asst to Brenda Colvin, 1957, to Dame Sylvia Crowe, 1958–61; private practice, 1964–; Director: Inchbald Sch. of Garden Design, 1970–78; Inchbald Sch. of Interior Design, Tehran, 1978–80; founded Clock House Sch. of Garden Design, Sussex, 1980; gardening corresp., Evening Standard, 1988–89; Principal Lectr, Kew Sch. of Garden Design, 1990–93. Chm., Soc. of Garden Designers, 1997–2000. Design workshops and lectures, UK and overseas; design and construction of gardens, and consultancies, UK, Europe, Japan, USA. Founder, John Brookes Award, Soc. of Garden Designers, 2012. DU Essex, 2006. Hon. Fellow, Kew Guild, 2008. Lifetime Achievement Award, Garden Media Guild, 2011. *Publications:* Room Outside, 1969; Gardens for Small Spaces, 1970; Garden Design and Layout, 1970; Living in the Garden, 1971; Financial Times Book of Garden Design, 1975; Improve Your Lot, 1977; The Small Garden, 1977; The Garden Book, 1984; A Place in the

Country, 1984; The Indoor Garden Book, 1986; Gardens of Paradise, 1987; The Country Garden, 1987; The New Small Garden Book, 1989; Garden Design, 1991, 2nd edn 2001; Planting the Country Way, 1994; Garden Design Workbook, 1994; Home and Garden Style, 1996; The New Garden, 1998; Garden Masterclass, 2002. *Recreations:* reading, pottering, entertaining. *Address:* Clock House, Denmans, Fontwell, near Arundel, West Sussex BN18 0SU. *T:* (01243) 542808, *Fax:* (01243) 544064. *E:* denmans@denmans-garden.co.uk.

BROOKES, Michael John Patrick; General Secretary, National Association of Head Teachers, 2005–10; Director, Mick Brookes Leadership Associates, since 2010; *b* 12 May 1948; *s* of Percival John Brookes and Joan Brookes; *m* 2000, Karen Jane Mann; one *s*. *Educ:* King Alfred's Coll., Winchester (Cert Ed); Open Univ. (BA); Nottingham Univ. (MEd). Teacher: Kanes Hill First Sch., Southampton, 1969–70; Liss Jun. Sch., Hants, 1971–74; Dep. Hd, Gosberton Primary Sch., Lincs, 1975–78; Head: Gosberton Clough & Risegate Sch., Lincs, 1978–85; Sherwood Jun. Sch., Notts, 1985–2005. Chm. Govs, Bolton Primary Sch., 2013–. *Recreations:* walking, motorcycling, music. *Address:* 10 Milton Court, Ravenshead, Notts NG15 9BD.

BROOKES, Nicholas Kelvin, FCA; Chairman, De La Rue plc, 2004–12 (non-executive Director, 1997–2012); *b* 19 May 1947; *s* of Stanley Brookes and Jean (*née* Wigley); *m* 1968, Maria Rosa Crespo; two *s* one *d*. *Educ:* Harrow Sch. FCA 1971. Articles for ACA, Hart Bros Reddall & Co., London, 1965–69; joined Texas Instruments, 1975; Man. Dir, Canada, 1980–85; Man. Dir, Europe, 1985–92; Vice-Pres., Texas Instruments Inc. and Pres., Materials and Controls Gp, 1992–95; Chief Exec., Bowthorpe, then Spirent, plc, 1995–2004. Non-executive Director: Corp. Financiera ALBA SA, Spain, 1999–; Axel-Johnson Inc., Sweden, 2005–. Non-exec. Dir, Inst. of Directors, 2007–. FInstD. *Recreations:* tennis, badminton, opera. *Club:* Reform.

BROOKES, Peter C.; *see* Cannon-Brookes.

BROOKES, Peter Derek, RDI 2002; Political Cartoonist, The Times, since 1993; *b* 28 Sept. 1943; *s* of George Henry Brookes and Joan Elizabeth Brookes; *m* 1971, Angela Harrison; two *s*. *Educ:* Heversham Grammar Sch., Westmorland; RAF Coll., Cranwell (BA London Ext.); Central School of Art and Design (BA). Freelance illustrator, 1969–; Cover Artist, The Spectator, 1986–98, 2005–; stamp designs for Royal Mail, 1995, 1999 and 2003; contributor to: The Times, Sunday Times, Radio Times, New Statesman, The Listener, Spectator, TLS and Glyndebourne Fest. Opera Books. Illustration Tutor: Central Sch. of Art and Design, 1977–79; RCA, 1979–89. Mem., AGI, 1988–. FRSA 2000. Political Cartoonist of the Year, Cartoon Art Trust Awards, 1996, 1998, 2006, 2010 and 2013; Cartoonist of Year, British Press Awards, 2002, 2007, 2009, 2010, 2011 and 2013; Cartoonist of the Year, What the Papers Say Awards, 2005; Cartoonist of the Year, Political Cartoon Soc., 2006, 2009, 2010 and 2014. *Publications:* Nature Notes, 1997; Nature Notes: the new collection, 1999; Nature Notes III, 2001; Peter Brookes of The Times, 2002; Nature Notes IV, 2004; The Best of Times, 2009; Hard Times, 2011; Sign of the Times, 2013; Testing Times, 2015. *Recreations:* music, QPR, arguing. *Address:* 30 Vanbrugh Hill, Blackheath, SE3 7UF. *T:* (020) 8858 9022.

BROOKING, Barry Alfred, MBE 1972; Chief Executive, British Psychological Society, 2000–04; *b* 2 Feb. 1944; *s* of Alfred Brooking and Winifred Joan Brooking; *m* 1978, Julia Irene McBride (marr. diss. 1993). *Educ:* Milford Haven GS; Sir Joseph Williamson's Math. Sch., Rochester; Birkbeck Coll., London Univ. (BA 1976, MA 1980). ACP. Royal Navy, 1965–81: BRNC Dartmouth, 1965; HMS Pembroke, 1966–67; HMS Diamond, 1968–69; CTC RM, Lympstone, 1969; 41 Cdo RM, 1969–70; 40 Cdo RM, 1970–72; HMS Raleigh, 1972–75; RN Sch. of Educnl and Trng Technol., 1976–78; ARE, 1978–81. Business Adminr, Med. Protection Soc., 1981–91; Regl Dir, St John Ambulance, 1992–95; Chief Exec., Parkinson's Disease Soc., 1995–99. Member: Surrey Magistrates' Soc., 1985–2000; Surrey Magistrates' Courts Cttee, 1993–95; Surrey Probation Cttee, 1993–95; Plymouth District Magistrates' Assoc., 2014–; Dep. Chm., North and East PSD, Surrey, 1995–97. Pres., Brooking Soc., 2004–14 (Mem., 1980–; Chm., 1993–2004). JP Surrey, 1985–2000, Leics, 2001–04, S and W Devon (formerly Plymouth and Dist), 2004–14. Business Develt Award, Surrey TEC, 1994. *Publications:* Naval Mathematics Self-Tuition Text, 1966; Naval English Self-Tuition Text, 1966; Naval Mathematics Programmed-Learning Text, 1967; Royal Navy CCTV Production Techniques Handbook, 1977; (contrib.) Educational Technology in a Changing World: aspects of educational technology Vol. XII, 1978; ARE reports, booklets, articles in jls. *Recreations:* travel, theatre, cinema, music, history, sport. *Address:* 9 Hawkmoor Parke, Bovey Tracey, Devon TQ13 9NL.

BROOKING, Sir Trevor (David), Kt 2004; CBE 1999 (MBE 1981); football broadcaster, since 1984; Director of Football Development, Football Association, 2004–14; *b* 2 Oct. 1948; *s* of Henry and Margaret Brooking; *m* 1970, Hilkka Helina Helakorpi; one *s* one *d*. *Educ:* Ilford County High Sch. Professional footballer with West Ham United, 1965–84: played 642 games; scored 111 goals; FA Cup winner, 1975, *v* Fulham, 1980, *v* Arsenal (scoring only goal); won Football League Div. 2, 1980–81; 47 appearances for England, 1974–82. Chm., Eastern Council for Sport and Recreation, 1986–95; Sports Council, then English Sports Council, subseq. Sport England: Mem., 1989–2002; Vice-Chm., 1994–96; Chm., 1998–2002. *Publications:* Trevor Brooking (autobiog.), 1981; Trevor Brooking's 100 Great British Footballers, 1988; My Life in Football, 2014. *Recreations:* golf, tennis.

BROOKMAN, family name of **Baron Brookman**.

BROOKMAN, Baron *cr* 1998 (Life Peer), of Ebbw Vale in the co. of Gwent; **David Keith Brookman;** General Secretary, Iron and Steel Trades Confederation, 1993–99; *b* 3 Jan. 1937; *s* of George Henry Brookman, MM and Blodwin Brookman (*née* Nash); *m* 1958, Patricia Worthington; three *d*. *Educ:* Nantyglo Grammar Sch., Gwent. Nat. Service, RAF, 1955–57. Steel worker, Richard Thomas & Baldwin, Ebbw Vale, 1953–55 and 1957–73; Iron & Steel Trades Confederation: Organiser, 1973–85; Asst Gen. Sec., 1985–93. Trades Union Congress: Member: Educn Adv. Cttee for Wales, 1976–82; Steel Cttee, 1985–90; Gen. Council, 1992–99. Member: Brit. Steel Jt Accident Prevention Adv. Cttee, 1985–93; Brit. Steel Adv. Cttee on Educn and Trng, 1986–93; Nat. Steel Co-ordinating Cttee, 1991–99 (Chm., 1993–99); Consultative Cttee, ECSC, 1993–2002; Operatives' Secretary: Jt Ind. Council for Slag Ind., 1985–93; Brit. Steel Long Products portfolio of cos Jt Standing Cttee, 1993–98; Brit. Steel Strip Trade Bd, 1993–98; Mem. Bd, UK Steel Enterprise (formerly Brit. Steel (Ind.) Ltd), 1993–; Jt Sec., European Works Council, British Steel, 1996–98. Member Executive Council: European Metalworkers' Fedn, 1985–95 (Mem., Steel Cttee, 1994–99); CSEU, 1989–93; International Metalworkers' Federation: Hon. Sec., Brit. Section, 1993–99; Pres., Iron and Steel and Non-Ferrous Metals Dept, 1993–99. Labour Party: Member: Exec. Cttee, Wales, 1982–85; Nat. Constitutional Cttee, 1987–91; NEC, 1991–92. Trustee, Julian Melchett Trust, 1985–95. Gov., Gwent Coll. of HE, 1980–84. *Recreations:* cricket, Rugby, reading, golf.

BROOKNER, Dr Anita, CBE 1990; Reader, Courtauld Institute of Art, 1977–88; *b* 16 July 1928; *oc* of Newson and Maude Brookner. *Educ:* James Allen's Girls' Sch.; King's Coll., Univ. of London (FKC 1990); Courtauld Inst.; Paris. Vis. Lectr, Univ. of Reading, 1959–64; Slade Professor, Univ. of Cambridge, 1967–68; Lectr, Courtauld Inst. of Art, 1964. Fellow, New Hall, Cambridge. *Publications:* Watteau, 1968; The Genius of the Future, 1971; Greuze: the rise and fall of an Eighteenth Century Phenomenon, 1972; Jacques-Louis David, 1980; (ed) The Stories of Edith Wharton, Vol. 1, 1988, Vol. 2, 1989; Soundings, 1997; Romanticism and its Discontents, 2000; *novels:* A Start in Life, 1981; Providence, 1982; Look at Me, 1983; Hotel du Lac, 1984 (Booker McConnell Prize; filmed for TV, 1986); Family and Friends, 1985; A Misalliance, 1986; A Friend from England, 1987; Latecomers, 1988; Lewis Percy, 1989; Brief Lives, 1990; A Closed Eye, 1991; Fraud, 1992; A Family Romance, 1993; A Private View, 1994; Incidents in the Rue Laugier, 1995; Altered States, 1996; Visitors, 1997; Falling Slowly, 1998; Undue Influence, 1999; The Bay of Angels, 2001; The Next Big Thing, 2002; The Rules of Engagement, 2003; Leaving Home, 2005; Strangers, 2009; articles in Burlington Magazine, etc. *Address:* 68 (6) Elm Park Gardens, SW10 9PB. *T:* (020) 7352 6894.

BROOKS, family name of **Barons Brooks of Tremorfa and Crawshaw**.

BROOKS OF TREMORFA, Baron *cr* 1979 (Life Peer), of Tremorfa in the County of South Glamorgan; **John Edward Brooks;** DL; *b* 12 April 1927; *s* of Edward George Brooks and Rachel Brooks (*née* White); *m* 1948 (marr. diss. 1956); one *s* one *d*; *m* 1958, Margaret Pringle; two *s*. *Educ:* elementary schools; Coleg Harlech. Secretary, Cardiff South East Labour Party, 1966–84; Member, South Glamorgan CC, 1973–93 (Leader, 1973–77, 1986–92; Chm., 1981–82). Contested (Lab) Barry, Feb. and Oct. 1974; Parliamentary Agent to Rt Hon. James Callaghan, MP, Gen. Elections, 1970, 1979. Chm., Labour Party, Wales, 1978–79. Opposition defence spokesman, 1980–81. British Boxing Board of Control: Steward, 1986; Vice Chm., 1999–2000; Chm., 2000–04; Pres., 2004. Chm., Welsh Sports Hall of Fame, 1988–. DL S Glam, 1994. *Recreations:* reading, most sports. *Address:* 40 Kennerleigh Road, Rumney, Cardiff, S Glam CF3 4BJ.

BROOKS, Alan; Director, Horace Clarkson plc, 1993–2001; *b* 30 Dec. 1935; *s* of Charles and Annie Brooks; *m* 1959, Marie Curtis; one *s* two *d*. *Educ:* Leeds Univ. (BSc 1st Cl. Mining Engineering; 1st Cl. Cert. of Competency, Mines and Quarries). CEng. Asst Mine Manager, Winsford Salt Mine, ICI, 1961–66; British Gypsum: Dep. Mines Agent, 1966–71; Dir, Midland Region, 1971–74; Production Dir, 1974–77; Dep. Man. Dir, 1977–85; Man. Dir, 1985–88; Chm., 1988; Gp Man. Dir, Gypsum Products, BPB Industries, subseq. BPB Gypsum Industries, 1988–93; Chm., Anglo United plc, 1993–98. Chairman: Westroc Industries, Canada, 1988; Inveryeso, Spain, 1991; Dir, Falkland Is Hldgs, 1998–2000. *Recreation:* fell walking.

BROOKS, Barry Philip Stewart, CEng, FIET; FIMarEST; Director, Wychcote Ltd, 2003–06 and since 2008; President, Institution of Engineering and Technology, 2013–14 (Deputy President, 2011–13); *b* Salisbury, Southern Rhodesia, 1 Nov. 1948; *s* of Peter and Kathleen Brooks; *m* 1971, Linda Seaman; three *s*. *Educ:* Chichester High Sch. for Boys; Imperial Coll. London (BSc(Eng) 1971); Royal Naval Coll., Greenwich (postgrad. Dip. Nuclear Reactor Technol. 1973). CEng 2003; FIET 2003; FIMarEST 2003. Served RN, 1968–2002: Nuclear Engr, HMS Courageous, 1974–77; Admiralty Underwater Weapons Estabt, 1977–79; Submarine Tactics and Weapons Gp, 1979–82; Weapons Engr Officer, HMS Spartan, 1982–84; ARE, 1985–87; MoD and FO Submarines, 1987–92; Cabinet Office, 1992–94; MoD, 1994–96; Ship Support Agency, 1996–98; Defence Logistics Orgn, 1998–2002; retired in rank of Cdre. Sen. Consultant, IBM, 2002–03; Dir, Consulting Services, Hitachi Consulting Ltd, 2006–08. Professional Engr Registration and Fellowship Assessor and interviewer, IET, 2003–. Co-ordinator, Hawley Engrg Innovation for a Better Envmt Award, Engrs' Co., 2008–. Vice Pres., IEE, then IET, 2005–09. Pres., City and Guilds Coll. Assoc., 2005–06. FInstLM 2010; FCGI 2003. Liveryman, Engrs' Co., 2004– (Mem., Ct of Assts, 2007–). *Recreations:* family, walking, international travel, public speaker, Livery Company, mentoring. *Address:* 26 Late Broads, Winsley, Bradford-on-Avon, Wilts BA15 2NW. *T:* (01225) 722714. *E:* bpsbrooks@gmail.com.

BROOKS, Prof. David James, MD, DSc; FRCP, FMedSci; Hartnett Professor of Neurology, Faculty of Medicine, Imperial College, London University at Hammersmith Hospital, since 1993 (Head, Centre for Neuroscience, 2010–11; Deputy Head, Division of Brain Sciences, 2011–14); Hon. Consultant, Hammersmith Hospital, since 1993; Professor of Neurology, Institute of Clinical Medicine, Aarhus University, since 2012; *b* 4 Dec. 1949; *s* of late Prof. James Leslie Brooks and Doris Margaret Adeline Brooks (*née* Welply); *m* 1987, Prof. Gillian Patricia Rowlands; two *s*. *Educ:* Newcastle Royal Grammar Sch.; Christ Church and Wolfson Coll., Oxford (BA 1st Cl. Hons Chem. 1972); University Coll. London (MB BS 1979, MD 1986; DSc Medicine 1998). MRCP 1982, FRCP 1993. Hon. Sen. Lectr, Inst. of Psychiatry, London, 1993; Hammersmith Hospital: Hd, Neurol. Gp, MRC Clinical Scis Centre, 1993–2010; Clinical Dir, Hammersmith Imanet (formerly Imaging Res. Solutions Ltd), 2001–. Sen. Neurologist, 2003–13, Hd of Neurol., 2007–13, Medical Diagnostics, GE Healthcare. Chm., Scientific Issues Cttee, Movt Disorder Soc., 1998–2002; Member: Wellcome Trust Neurosci. Panel, 2000–03; Med. Adv. Panel, UK Huntington's Disease Assoc., 1996–98; Med. Adv. Bd, 1997–2000, Neuroscis Bd, 2004–06, MRC; Scientific Adv. Bd, Alzheimer UK, 2014–. UK Parkinson's Disease Association: Mem., Res. Adv. Panel, 1995–2001 (Chm., 1996–97); Trustee, Council of Mgt, 1996–99 (Chm., 1997–98). Member: Internat. Adv. Panel, Michael J. Fox Foundn for Parkinson's Disease Res., 2002–06; Adv. Bd, Eur. Soc. for Clinical Neuropharmacol., 2000–; Internat. Adv. Bd for German Parkinson Network, 2001–05; Internat. Adv. Bd for German Dementia Network, 2006–08. Patron, Alzheimer's Soc., 2006–. FMedSci 2001. *Publications:* contrib. numerous peer-reviewed pubns to learned jls; h index 97. *Recreations:* golf, music, supporting Arsenal FC. *Address:* Neurology Imaging Unit, 1st Floor, B Block, Hammersmith Hospital, Du Cane Road, W12 0NN. *T:* (020) 8383 3172, *Fax:* (020) 8383 1783. *E:* david.brooks@imperial.ac.uk, dbrooks@clin.au.dk. *Clubs:* Athenæum; West Middlesex Golf.

BROOKS, Edwin, PhD; FAIM, FCIM; Deputy Principal, Charles Sturt University, 1988–89; *b* Barry, Glamorgan, 1 Dec. 1929; *s* of Edwin Brooks and Agnes Elizabeth (*née* Campbell); *m* 1956, Winifred Hazel Soundie; four *s* two *d*. *Educ:* Barry Grammar Sch.; St John's Coll., Cambridge; PhD Cantab 1958. National Service, Singapore, 1948–49. MP (Lab) Bebington, 1966–70. Univ. of Liverpool: Lectr, Dept of Geography, 1954–66 and 1970–72; Sen. Lectr, 1972–77; Dean, College Studies, 1975–77; Riverina College of Advanced Education, later Riverina-Murray Institute of Higher Education, then Charles Sturt University: Dean of Business and Liberal Studies, 1977–82; Dean of Commerce, 1982–88; Dir, Albury-Wodonga Campus, 1982; Dean Emeritus, 1990. Wagga Wagga Base Hospital: Dir, 1989–96; Dep. Chm., 1989–93; Chm., 1995–96; Riverina Dist Health Service: Dir and Dep. Chm., 1994–96; Treas., 1995–96. Councillor, Birkenhead, 1958–67. Mem., Courses Cttee, Higher Educn Bd of NSW, 1978–82; Dir, Australian Business Educn Council, 1986–89. Pres., Wagga Wagga Chamber of Commerce, 1988–90. FAIM 1983; FCIM 1989; ACIS 1995. *Publications:* This Crowded Kingdom, 1973; (ed) Tribes of the Amazon Basin in Brazil, 1973. *Recreations:* gardening, listening to music, computing. *Address:* Inchnadamph, 4 Gregadoo Road, Wagga Wagga, NSW 2650, Australia. *T:* (2) 69226798.

BROOKS, James Wallace; Owner and Director, Jim Brooks Consulting Ltd, since 2010; *b* 15 Sept. 1952; *s* of Leslie Duncan Brooks and Elizabeth June Brooks; *m* 1999, Kim Campbell; one *d*. *Educ:* Bolton Sch.; Univ. of Nottingham (BA); Liverpool Poly. CIPFA 1977. Dep. Dir of Finance, Bolton MBC, 1985–89; City Treasurer, Manchester CC, 1989–93; Chief Executive: Poole BC, 1993–2002; Kingston upon Hull CC, 2002–03; Exec. Dir, Sector Treasury Ltd, 2004–10. Ind. Mem. Bd, Dept of Envmt, NI, 2011–. *Recreations:* family, music, classic Mercedes sports car.

BROOKS, Prof. John Stuart, PhD, DSc; FInstP; Vice-Chancellor, Manchester Metropolitan University, 2005–15; *b* 8 March 1949; *s* of Ernest and Maude Brooks; *m* 1971, Jill Everil (*née* Pusey); two *s*. *Educ:* Cheshunt Grammar Sch.; Sheffield Univ. (BSc; PhD 1973; DSc 1998). CPhys, FInstP 1985; CEng 1992. Lectr, Sheffield City Poly., 1973–84; Head of Applied Physics Dept, 1984–90; Dir, Materials Res. Inst., 1990–92; Asst Principal, Sheffield

Hallam Univ., 1992–98; Vice-Chancellor, Univ. of Wolverhampton, 1998–2005. *Publications:* 75 papers on materials and spectroscopy in learned jls. *Recreations:* travel, walking, music, bridge.

BROOKS, Louise Méarie; *see* Taylor, L. M.

BROOKS, Mel; producer, writer, director, actor; *b* Brooklyn, 28 June 1926; *m* Florence Baum; two *s* one *d*; *m* 1964, Anne Bancroft (*d* 2005); one *s*. TV script writer for series: Your Show of Shows, 1950–54; Caesar's Hour, 1954–57; (co-created) Get Smart, 1965. Films: (cartoon) The Critic (Academy Award), 1964; writer and director: The Producers (Academy Award), 1968 (adapted for stage, NY, 2001 (3 Tony Awards), Th. Royal, London, 2004 (Critics' Circle Award, Olivier Award, 2005)); Young Frankenstein, 1974; writer, director and actor: The Twelve Chairs, 1970; Blazing Saddles, 1974; Silent Movie, 1976; writer, director, actor and producer: High Anxiety, 1977; History of the World Part 1, 1981; Spaceballs, 1987; Life Stinks, 1991; Robin Hood: Men in Tights, 1993; Dracula: Dead and Loving It, 1995; actor, producer: To Be Or Not To Be, 1983. Film productions include: The Elephant Man, 1980; The Fly; Frances; My Favorite Year; 84 Charing Cross Road. Several album recordings. Kennedy Center Honor, 2009. BFI Fellowship, 2015. *Address:* c/o The Culver Studios, 9336 W Washington Boulevard, Culver City, CA 90232–2600, USA.

BROOKS, Michael James; Deputy Chair, MRC Technology, since 2014 (Director, since 2006); *b* Edgware, Middx, 16 July 1946; *s* of late James Brooks and Doreen Brooks (*née* Cornwall); *m* 1973, Susan Elizabeth Dickens; two *d*. *Educ:* Harrow Weald Grammar Sch.; Bushey Grammar Sch.; Portsmouth Coll. of Technol. (Dip. Business Studies 1967); London Sch. of Econs and Pol Sci. (MSc Accounting and Finance 1987). Internal Auditor, BP, 1967–70; Mgt Accountant, ICL, 1970–72; Chief Accountant, Santa Fe Drilling Co., Saudi Arabia and Australia, 1972–77; Consultant, Coopers & Lybrand, 1977–79; Royal Dutch Shell Group: Financial Reporting Manager, Shell UK, 1980–81; Budget Controller, Shell UK Expro, 1981–84; Accounting Res., Shell Internat., and Sec., Oil Industry Accounting Cttee, 1984–87; Hd of Financial Forecasts and Appraisals, Shell Internat., 1987–89; Hd of Finance, Shell Gas, 1989–92; Treas., Nigeria LNG, 1992–96; Sen. Finance Rep., M&A Team, Shell Chemicals, 1996–99; Finance Dir, Trinity Energy Ltd, 2001–04. Non-exec. Dir, DVLA, 2009–; Chair, Audit Cttee, DVA NI, 2010–. Non-exec. Dir and Dep. Chair, NW Surrey NHS Clin. Commng Gp, 2012–. Mem., Gp Audit Cttee, DfT, 2010–. Mem., MRC, 2005–09; Trustee, Med. Res. Foundn, 2006–12. Gov., Univ. of Portsmouth, 2005–14; Mem., Adv. Bd, Portsmouth Business Sch., 2007–. FCMA; FCCA; FInstD; FRSA. *Publications:* contrib. numerous articles to professional accounting jls. *Recreations:* watching and talking about cricket, listening to classical music and Blondie, wine, food, theatre, reading, walking. *Address:* 10 St Omer Road, Guildford, Surrey GU1 2DB. *T:* (01483) 560800. *E:* mikebrooks@gatehouse10.demon.co.uk. *Clubs:* MCC, Naval; Middlesex County Cricket, Surrey County Cricket.

BROOKS, Peter Malcolm; President and Chief Operating Officer, Genting UK plc, since 2011 (Executive Deputy Chairman, 2007–11); *b* 12 Feb. 1947; *s* of Roger Morrison Brooks and Phyllis Fuller Brooks (*née* Hopkinson); *m* 1987, Patricia Margaret Garrett; one *s*; and one *s* by a previous marriage. *Educ:* Marlborough Coll.; Southampton Univ. (LLB). Solicitor, Macfarlanes, 1970–84 (Partner, 1977–84); Clifford Chance: Partner, 1984–96; Hd of Corporate Practice, 1992–96; General Counsel, Deutsche Morgan Grenfell, 1997–99; Chm., Enodis plc, 2000–08. *Recreations:* opera, theatre, travel, cricket, rackets. *Address:* c/o Genting UK plc, 31 Curzon Street, W1J 7TW. *Club:* Brooks's.

BROOKS, Rebekah; Chief Executive, News UK, since 2015; *b* 27 May 1968; *d* of late Robert Wade and of Deborah Wade; *m* 2002, Ross Kemp (marr. diss. 2009); *m* 2009, Charles Brooks; one *d*. *Educ:* Appleton Hall, Cheshire; Sorbonne, Paris. Features Editor, then Associate Editor, subseq. Dep. Editor, News of the World, 1989–98; Dep. Ed., The Sun, 1998–2000; Editor: News of the World, 2000–03; The Sun, 2003–09; Chief Exec., News Internat., 2009–11. Founder Mem. and Pres., Women in Journalism.

BROOKS, Richard John; Arts Editor, Sunday Times, since 1999; *b* 5 Feb. 1946; *s* of late Peter John Brooks and Joan Brooks; *m* 1978, Jane Mannion; two *d*. *Educ:* University College Sch.; Bristol Univ. (BA). Reporter, Bristol Evening Post, 1968–71; Journalist: BBC Radio, 1972–79; Economist, 1979–80; Sunday Times, 1980–85; Media and Culture Editor, Observer, 1986–99. *Recreations:* playing golf and tennis, supporting Arsenal, watching films. *Address:* Sunday Times, 1 London Bridge Street, SE1 9GF. *T:* (020) 7782 5735.

BROOKS, Robert; Chairman, Bonhams, since 2000; *b* 1 Oct. 1956; *s* of late William Frederick Brooks and of Joan Patricia (*née* Marshall); *m* 1981, Evelyn Rachel Durnford; two *s* one *d*. *Educ:* St Benedict's Sch., Ealing. Joined Christie's South Kensington Ltd, 1975, Dir, 1984–87; Dir, Christie Manson and Woods Ltd, 1987–89; established Brooks (Auctioneers) Ltd, 1989; acquired W. & F. C. Bonham and Sons Ltd, 2000. FIA (Gp N Internat. Special Car Series) European Touring Car Champion, 1999. *Recreations:* motor racing, golf, cricket. *Address:* Bonhams, 101 New Bond Street, W1S 1SR. *T:* (020) 7468 8220. *Club:* British Racing Drivers' (Chm., 2007–11).

BROOKS, Simon Jeremy, CB 2006; Honorary Vice-President, European Investment Bank, since 2013 (Vice-President, 2006–12); *b* 1 Aug. 1954; *s* of Stanley William Brooks and Jane Brooks; *m* 1990, Caroline Turk; one *s* one *d*. *Educ:* Queen's Coll., Oxford (BA PPE 1975); Nuffield Coll., Oxford (BPhil Econs 1977). NIESR, 1978–85; HM Treasury, 1985–2006: Econ. Advr, 1985–92; Head: Econ. Analysis 2 Div., 1992–94; Regl and Country Analysis/World Econ. Issues Teams, 1994–98; EU Finance Team, 1998–2000; Dir of Macroeconomics, 2000–06. *Address:* 13 Woodhurst Lane, Oxted RH8 9HN.

BROOKS, Stuart Armitage, CMG 2001; OBE 1991; HM Diplomatic Service; Counsellor, Foreign and Commonwealth Office, 1997–2001; *b* 15 May 1948; *s* of Frank and Audrey Brooks; *m* 1975, Mary-Margaret Elliott; two *d*. *Educ:* Churchill Coll., Cambridge (MA). Entered FCO, 1970: Vice-Consul, Rio de Janeiro, 1972–74; Second Sec., on secondment to Home CS, 1974–75; Second, later First, Sec., Lisbon, 1975–78; First Secretary: FCO, 1978; Moscow, 1979–82; FCO, 1982–87; Stockholm, 1987–91; FCO, 1991–93; Counsellor, Vienna, 1993–97. *Recreations:* music, horticulture. *Address:* c/o Foreign and Commonwealth Office, King Charles Street, SW1A 2AH.

BROOKS, Timothy Stephen; Chief Executive Officer, BMJ Group, since 2012; *b* Kingston, Jamaica, 30 Sept. 1957; *s* of Michael and Mavis Brooks; *m* 1997, Catherine Ann Jenkins; one *s* one *d*. *Educ:* St John's Coll., Cambridge (BA Hons English Lang. and Lit. 1979). Reporter: McGraw-Hill, 1979–80; Haymarket Publishing, 1981–84; Founder and Ed., Media Week Ltd, 1984–90; Hd, Corporate Planning, Emap plc, 1991–95; Director: Emap Business Communications, 1996–99; Emap Digital, 1999–2000; IPC Media Ltd, 2000–06; Man. Dir, Guardian News & Media Ltd, 2006–11; Principal, 2Riders Consulting, 2011–12; Exec. Fellow, Dept of Strategy and Entrepreneurship, London Business Sch., 2011–12. Director: Guardian Media Gp, 2006–11; Audit Bureau of Circulations Ltd, 2010–11, 2012–13; Chairman: Knowledge Engineers, 2011–; NLA Media Access Ltd, 2014–. Chm., NPA, 2008–10. Member: Digital Adv. Gp, Cabinet Office, 2012–; Adv. Council, British Liby, 2014–. Chm. Trustees, Open-City, 2011–14. *Recreations:* reading, running, Arsenal Football Club. *E:* tbrooks@bmj.com.

BROOKS-WARD, Simon Howe, CVO 2012 (LVO 2002); OBE 2005; TD 2005; Chairman and Chief Executive, HPower Group, since 1990; *b* London, 30 Sept. 1963; *s* of Raymond Shirley Brooks-Ward and Denise Howe Brooks-Ward; *m* 2010, Annabel Jane Nash; one *s* two *d* and one step *s* one step *d*. *Educ:* Heath Mt Prep. Sch.; Haileybury. Account Manager: Quentin Bell Orgn, 1984–88; Interaction, 1988–90; Director: Pavarotti Internat. Horse Show, 1992–2002; London Internat. Horse Show, Olympia, 1992–; Royal Windsor Horse Show, 1995–; Diamond Jubilee Pageant, 2012. Lt Col, CO, Royal Yeomanry, 2002–05; Brig. Army Reserve; Asst Divl Comdr, 3 (UK) Div., 2012–15; Dep. Dir, Army Reserve Strategy, Army HQ, 2015–. Trustee, World Horse Welfare, 2010–. *Recreations:* hunting, shooting, sailing, ski-ing. *Address:* HPower Group, Stable House, St Albans Street, Windsor, Berks SL4 1UT. *T:* (01753) 847900, *Fax:* (01753) 847901. *E:* simonbw@hpower.co.uk. *Clubs:* Cavalry & Guards, Ivy; St Mawes Sailing.

BROOKSBANK, Sir (Edward) Nicholas, 3rd Bt *cr* 1919; with Christie's, 1974–97; *b* 4 Oct. 1944; *s* of Sir Edward William Brooksbank, 2nd Bt, TD, and of Ann, 2nd *d* of Col T. Clitherow; *S* father, 1983; *m* 1970, Emma, *d* of Rt Hon. Baron Holderness, PC; one *s* one *d*. *Educ:* Eton. Royal Dragoons, 1963–69; Blues and Royals, 1969–73; Adjutant, 1971–73. *Heir:* *s* (Florian) Tom (Charles) Brooksbank, *b* 9 Aug. 1982. *Address:* Menethorpe Hall, Malton, North Yorks YO17 9QX.

BROOM, Ven. Andrew Clifford; Archdeacon of East Riding, since 2014; *b* Norwich, 1965; *m* Tina; two *c*. *Educ:* Keele Univ. (BSocSc 1986); Trinity Coll., Bristol (BA 1992). Youth worker; ordained deacon, 1992, priest, 1993; Assistant Curate: All Saints, Wellington, 1992–96; St Thomas the Martyr, Brampton, 1996–2000; Vicar, St John, Walton, 2000–09; Dir of Mission and Ministry, Dio. of Derby, 2009–14; Hon. Canon, Derby Cathedral, 2011–14. *Address:* c/o Diocesan House, Aviator Court, Clifton Moor, York YO30 4WJ.

BROOM, Prof. Donald Maurice; Colleen Macleod Professor of Animal Welfare, University of Cambridge, 1986–2009, now Emeritus; Fellow, St Catharine's College, Cambridge, 1987–2009, now Emeritus (President, 2001–04); *b* 14 July 1942; *s* of late Donald Edward Broom and Mavis Edith Rose Broom; *m* 1971, Sally Elizabeth Mary Riordan; three *s*. *Educ:* Whitgift Sch.; St Catharine's Coll., Cambridge (MA, PhD, ScD). Lectr, 1967, Sen. Lectr, 1979, Reader, 1982, Dept of Pure and Applied Zoology, Univ. of Reading. Vis. Asst Prof., Univ. of California, Berkeley, 1969; Vis. Lectr, Univ. of W Indies, Trinidad, 1972; Vis. Scientist, CSIRO Div. of Animal Prodn, Perth, WA, 1983. Mem., EEC Farm Animal Welfare Expert Gp, 1981–89; Chm., EU Scientific Veterinary Cttee on Animal Welfare, 1990–97; Vice-Chairman: EU Scientific Cttee on Animal Health and Animal Welfare, 1997–2003; Eur. Food Safety Authy Scientific Panel on Animal Health and Welfare, 2003–09 (Mem., 2009–12); Scientific Advr, Council of Europe Standing Cttee of Eur. Convention for Protection of Animals kept for Farming Purposes, 1987–2000; EU Rep., Quadripartite Wkg Gp on Humane Trapping Standards, 1995–96; Mem., EU Delegn to WTO on EC prohibiting seal products, 2013. Hon. Res. Associate, BBSRC Inst. of Grassland and Envmtl Res. (formerly AFRC Inst. for Grassland and Animal Production), 1985–. Member: Council, Assoc. for Study of Animal Behaviour, 1971–83 (Hon. Treas., 1971–80); Internat. Ethological Cttee, 1976–79; Council, Soc. for Vet. Ethology, 1981–89 (Vice-Pres., 1986–87, 1989–91; Pres., 1987–89); Animal Welfare Cttee, Zool Soc., 1986–95; NERC Special Cttee on Seals, 1986–96; Farm Animal Welfare Council, MAFF, 1991–99; BSI Panel on ISO Animal (Mammal) Traps, 1993–98; Animal Procedures Cttee, Home Office, 1998–2006; Fellowship and Grant Selection Panels, Nat. Centre for Replacement, Refinement and Reduction of Animals in Res., MRC, 2012–14; REF Vet., Agricl and Food Panel, HEFCE, 2013–14. Chm., Gp on Land Transport, World Orgn for Animal Health, 2003–06. Trustee, Farm Animal Care Trust, 1986–2009 (Chm., 1999–2009). Hon. Coll. Fellow, Myerscough Coll., Univ. of Central Lancs, 1999; Hon. Prof., Univ. Salvador, Buenos Aires, 2004; Hon. Fellow, Internat. Soc. for Applied Ethol., 2009. Hon. Socio Corrispondenti, Accad. Peloritana dei Pericolanti Messina, 2005. Vice-Pres., Old Whitgiftian Assoc., 2000–; Vice-Pres., 2004–05, Pres., 2005–06, St Catharine's Soc. FZS 1986. Hon. DSc De Montfort, 2000; Hon. Dr, Norwegian Univ. of Life Scis, 2005; Hon. Dip. of Recognition, Univ. Nacional Autónoma de México, 2010. George Fleming Prize, British Vet. Jl, 1990; British Soc. of Animal Sci./RSPCA Award for Innovative Develts in Animal Welfare, 2000; Eurogroup Medal, 2001; Michael Kay Award, RSPCA, 2007; Sir Patrick Moore Award, RSPCA, 2014. *Publications:* Birds and their Behaviour, 1977 (trans. French, Portuguese); Biology of Behaviour, 1981; (ed jtly) The Encyclopaedia of Domestic Animals, 1986; (ed) Farmed Animals, 1986 (trans. Japanese, Italian); (with A. F. Fraser) Farm Animal Behaviour and Welfare, 1990; (with K. G. Johnson) Stress and Animal Welfare, 1993; (ed) Coping with Challenge: welfare in animals including humans, 2001; The Evolution of Morality and Religion, 2003; (with A. F. Fraser) Domestic Animal Behaviour and Welfare, 2007, 5th edn 2015 (trans. Portuguese, Chinese); Sentience and Animal Welfare, 2014; over 400 papers in behaviour, psychol, zool, ornithol, agricl and vet. jls. *Recreations:* squash, water-polo, modern pentathlon, ornithology. *Address:* Department of Veterinary Medicine, University of Cambridge, Madingley Road, Cambridge CB3 0ES. *T:* (01223) 337697. *E:* dmb16@cam.ac.uk. *Club:* Hawks (Cambridge).

BROOM, Peter David; HM Diplomatic Service; Deputy Director, UK Trade & Investment, Riyadh, since 2010; *b* 7 Aug. 1953; *s* of Albert Leslie Broom and Annie Myfannwy Broom; *m* 1976, Vivienne Louise Pyatt; five *d*. *Educ:* Hillside Sch., Finchley. Entered FCO, 1970; Attaché: Oslo, 1974–77; Jedda, 1977–79; Islamabad, 1979–81; FCO, 1981–84; Mbabane, 1984–87; New Delhi, 1987–89; Second Sec., FCO, 1989–91; Consul (Commercial), Brisbane, 1991–97; Consul and Dep. High Comr, Yaoundé, 1997–2000; Consul Gen., Cape Town, 2000–02; Dep. Consul Gen., San Francisco, 2003–07; Consular Directorate, FCO, 2007–10. *Recreations:* sport, history. *Address:* c/o Foreign and Commonwealth Office, King Charles Street, SW1A 2AH; 7 Sunny Hill, Waldringfield, Suffolk IP12 4QS.

BROOMAN, Thomas Sebastian, CBE 2008; Music Advisor, Creative Youth Network (formerly Kingswood Foundation), since 2010 (Trustee, since 2011; Associate Artist for Music, 2011–12); *b* Bristol, 1 April 1954; *s* of Frederick Spencer Brooman and Beatrice Lily Brooman; *m* 2004, Amanda Emily Budd; three *s*. *Educ:* Bristol Grammar Sch.; Exeter Coll., Oxford (BA Hons Eng. Lang. and Lit.). Editor, Bristol Recorder, 1979–81; Artistic Dir, WOMAD Festival, 1982–2008; Trustee and Dir, WOMAD Foundn, 1984–2008; Dir, Real World Records, 1988–2008. Mentor, South West Music Sch., 2009–; Artistic Advr, Dartington Hall, 2009–; Music Programmer, Salisbury Arts Centre, 2012–. *Recreations:* music, drumming, film and cinema, fictional writing, travel, photography. *Address:* 82 Charlton Road, Kingswood, Bristol BS15 1HF. *T:* (0117) 909 5820. *E:* thomas@heavenlyplanet.com.

BROOME, Adam Edward; Director, Adam Broome Ltd, since 2014; *b* Cheltenham, 11 Nov. 1968; *s* of Alan John Broome and Boleslawa Anna Broome; *m* Caron Lindsey Reeves; two *s*. *Educ:* Howard Sch., Rainham, Kent; Bristol Univ. (BSc Maths); Univ. of W of England. CIPFA. Avon County Council: trainee and accountant, 1990–95; Mgt Accountant, 1995–96; Hd, Local Mgt of Schs, Bristol CC, 1995–96; Stoke-on-Trent City Council: Hd, Educn Finance, 1997–98; Asst Dir, 1998–2002; Associate Dir, Audit Commn, 2002–04; Plymouth City Council: Director: for Corporate Resources, 2004–09; for Corporate Support, 2009–11; for Corporate Services, 2012–13. Non-exec. Dir, Royal Cornwall Hosps NHS Trust, 2014–Sept. 2016. *Recreations:* family, friends, walking, cinema, Bristol Rovers, Polish history and language, allotment.

BROOME, David McPherson, CBE 1995 (OBE 1970); farmer; British professional show jumper; *b* Cardiff, 1 March 1940; *s* of Fred and Amelia Broome, Chepstow, Gwent; *m* 1976, Elizabeth, *d* of K. W. Fletcher, Thirsk, N Yorkshire; three *s*. *Educ:* Monmouth Grammar Sch. for Boys. European Show Jumping Champion (3 times); World Show Jumping Champion, La Baule, 1970; Olympic Medallist (Bronze) twice, 1960, 1968; King George V Gold Cup 6 times (a record, in 1990). Mounts include: Sunsalve, Aachen, 1961; Mr Softee, Rotterdam,

1967, and Hickstead, 1969; Beethoven, La Baule, France, 1970, as (1st British) World Champion; Sportsman and Philco, Cardiff, 1974; Professional Champion of the World. *Publications:* Jump-Off, 1971; (with S. Hadley) Horsemanship, 1983. *Recreation:* shooting. *Address:* Mount Ballan Manor, Port Skewett, Caldicot, Monmouthshire, Wales NP26 5XP.

BROOME, Prof. John, PhD; FBA 2000; FRSE; White's Professor of Moral Philosophy, University of Oxford, 2000–14, now Emeritus; Fellow, Corpus Christi College, Oxford, 2000–14, now Emeritus; *b* 17 May 1947; *s* of Richard and Tamsin Broome; *m* 1970, Ann Rowland; one *s* one *d*. *Educ:* Trinity Hall, Cambridge (BA); Bedford Coll., Univ. of London (MA); Massachusetts Inst. Technol. (PhD 1972). Lectr in Econs, Birkbeck Coll., London Univ., 1972–78; Reader in Econs, 1979–92, Prof. of Econs and Philosophy, 1992–95, Univ. of Bristol; Prof. of Philosophy, Univ. of St Andrews, 1996–2000. Visiting posts: Univ. of Va, 1975; All Souls Coll., Oxford, 1982–83; ANU, 1986, 1993, 2001, 2007, Adjunct Prof., 2008–; Princeton Univ., 1987–89; Univ. of Washington, 1988; Univ. of BC, 1993–94; Swedish Collegium for Advanced Study, Uppsala, 1997–98, 2004, 2008, 2011, 2014; Univ. of Canterbury, NZ, 2005; Stanford Univ., 2015. Ed., Economics and Philosophy, 1994–99. Mem., Royal Swedish Acad. of Scis, 2007; Hon. Foreign Mem., American Acad. of Arts and Scis, 2014. FRSE 1999. Hon Dr Lund, 2013. *Publications:* The Microeconomics of Capitalism, 1983; Weighing Goods, 1991; Counting the Cost of Global Warming, 1992; Ethics Out of Economics, 1999; Weighing Lives, 2004; Climate Matters, 2012; Rationality Through Reasoning, 2013. *Recreation:* sailing. *Address:* Corpus Christi College, Oxford OX1 4JF.

BROOME, John Lawson, CBE 1987; Founder and Chairman, Alton Towers Theme Park, since 1980 (Chief Executive, 1980–90); *b* 2 Aug. 1943; *s* of late Albert Henry and Mary Elizabeth Broome; *m* 1972, Jane Myott Bagshaw; one *s* two *d*. *Educ:* Rossall School. School master, 1960–65; Dir, JLB Investment Property Group, 1961–, and numerous other companies; Chm. and Chief Exec., Adventure World Theme Park, 1997–99; Chairman: London Launch Ltd, 2000–09; Launch Hldgs, 2005–09. Member: ETB and BTA, 1982–92; Internat. Assoc. of Amusement Parks and Attractions, USA, 1986–89 (Chm., Internat. Cttee; Chm., Internat. Council, 1986–89). Vice-Pres., Ironbridge Gorge Museum Trust. Governor, Staffordshire Univ. (formerly N Staffs Poly.), 1984–95. Vis. Prof., Sunderland Univ., 1996–. *Recreations:* ski-ing, travelling, antiques, old paintings, objets d'art, fine gardens, restoration of historic properties.

BROOMFIELD, Alexander Bryan; property investor; Chairman, Aberdeen Royal Hospitals NHS Trust, 1992–96; *b* 13 Jan. 1937; *s* of late William P. Broomfield, OBE and Eliza M. Broomfield; *m* 1960, Morag Carruthers. *Educ:* Aberdeen Grammar Sch. 26 years with Town & County Motor Garage Ltd; Man. Dir, retired 1992. Member: Grampian Health Bd, 1990–92; Bd, Scottish SHA, 1980–88; Council, Aberdeen Chamber of Commerce, to 1995 (Pres., 1978–79); Vice-Chm., Aberdeen Airport Consultative Cttee, 1990–2015; Chm., Aurora Private Equity Ltd, 2009–11. *Recreations:* walking, fishing, golf. *Address:* 5 Carnegie Gardens, Aberdeen AB15 4AW. *Clubs:* Royal Northern and University (Aberdeen); Royal Aberdeen Golf.

BROOMFIELD, Sir Nigel (Hugh Robert Allen), KCMG 1993 (CMG 1986); HM Diplomatic Service, retired; Chairman, Leonard Cheshire Disability (formerly Leonard Cheshire), 2005–09; *b* 19 March 1937; *s* of Col Arthur Allen Broomfield and Ruth Sheilagh Broomfield; *m* 1963, Valerie Fenton; two *s*. *Educ:* Haileybury Coll.; Trinity Coll., Cambridge (BA (Hons) English Lit.). Commnd 17/21 Lancers, 1959, retired as Major, 1968. Joined FCO as First Sec., 1969; First Secretary: British Embassy, Bonn, 1970–72; British Embassy, Moscow, 1972–74; European Communities Dept, London, 1975–77; RCDS, 1978; Political Advr and Head of Chancery, British Mil. Govt, Berlin, 1979–81; Head of Eastern European and Soviet Dept, 1981–83, and Head of Soviet Dept, 1983–85, FCO; Dep. High Comr and Minister, New Delhi, 1985–88; Ambassador to GDR, 1988–90; Dep. Under Sec. of State (Defence), FCO, 1990–92; Ambassador to Germany, 1993–97. Dir, Ditchley Foundn, 1999–2004. Chairman: Yatra (Jersey) Ltd, 2006–12; Jersey Energy Trust, 2009–; Cambridge Quantum Computing Ltd, 2014–; non-exec. Dir, Lancaster Mgt (Jersey) Ltd, 2009–14. Advr, Smiths Detection, 2007–11. Captain, Cambridge Squash Rackets and Real Tennis, 1957–58; British Amateur Squash Champion, 1958–59 (played for England, 1957–60). *Recreations:* tennis, golf, reading, music. *Address:* Huntington House, Rue du Clos Fallu, Trinity, Jersey JE3 5BG. *Clubs:* Royal Automobile, MCC, All England Lawn Tennis; Hawks (Cambridge).

BROOMHEAD, Steven John; Professor of Entrepreneurial Education and Chief Director of Institutional Advancement, Liverpool Hope University, since 2011, on leave of absence as Chief Executive, Warrington Borough Council, since 2012; *b* 15 Jan. 1956; *s* of Brian and Hazel Broomhead; *m* 1990, Linda Whelan; one *d*. *Educ:* W Glam Inst. of HE (BEd (Hons) Wales); Univ. of Leicester (MA); UC Swansea (CertEd). Lectr in Social Sciences, W Bridgford Coll., Nottingham, 1979; Sen. Lectr, Arnold and Carlton Coll., Nottingham, 1981; Vice-Principal, Skelmersdale Coll., Lancashire, 1986; Principal: Peterlee Coll., 1990–94; Warrington Collegiate Inst., 1994–97; Chief Executive: Warrington BC (Unitary), 1997–2003; NW Develt Agency, 2003–10. Chm., NW Chamber of Commerce, 2002–; Board Member: Basic Skills Agency, 1996–2002; Learning and Skills Develt Agency, 2001–; Lancs Enterprise Partnership, 2011–; Central and W Lancs Chamber of Commerce, 2011–; Mem., Nat. Skills Alliance, 2003–; Policy Advr to DfES, 2000–03. Chairman: Connexions, Chester and Warrington, 2001–; Recycling Lives Ltd (Lancs), 2011–; 3AAAs Training and Develt Co., 2010–. Mem. NW Regl Exec., Prince's Trust, 2001–. Advr, E Lancs Rlwy, 2012. Governor: Univ. of Central Lancs, 2005–; Skelmersdale Coll. (Chm., 2006). CCMI; FCGI; FRSA. Patron, Campaign for Learning, 2001. *Recreations:* railway history, walking, Notts County FC, Warrington RL FC (Chm., 2010–). *Address:* Principal's Lodge, 32 Blackhurst Avenue, Hutton, Preston PR4 4BG. *E:* broomhs@hope.ac.uk.

BROPHY, Michael John Mary, CBE 2014; *b* 24 June 1937; *s* of Gerald and Mary Brophy; *m* 1962, Sarah Rowe; three *s* one *d*. *Educ:* Ampleforth Coll.; Royal Naval Coll., Dartmouth. Entered Royal Navy, 1955; Exec. Br; Fleet Air Arm pilot; Air Warfare Instructor; gunnery specialist; retired as Lt-Comdr, 1966. Associate Dir, J. Walter Thompson, 1967–74; Appeals Dir, Spastics Soc., 1974–82; Chief Exec., CAF, 1982–2002. Dir, European Foundn Centre, 1989–98 (Chm., 1994–95); Chm., Euro Citizens Action Service, 1996–2002. Trustee: The London (formerly Capital) Community Foundn, 2006–13 (Chm., 2010–13); Charity Employees Benevolent Fund, 2007–12; Chm., United Trusts, 2006–08. Fellow, Inst. of Fundraising, 1990; CBIM 1989–94; FRSA. Hon. DBA Greenwich, 2010. *Publications:* Citizen Power, 2005. *Address:* 8 Oldlands Hall, Herons' Ghyll, Uckfield, E Sussex TN22 3DA. *E:* thebrophys@btinternet.com.

BROSNAN, Pierce, Hon. OBE 2003; actor; *b* Navan, Co. Meath, 16 May 1953; *s* of Tom Brosnan and May Smith; *m* 1977, Cassandra Harris (*d* 1991); one *s*, and one step *s* (one step *d* decd); *m* 2001, Keely Shaye Smith; two *s*. *Educ:* Drama Centre, London. Asst stage manager, Theatre Royal, York; *stage* appearances include: Red Devil Battery Sign; Filumena; Wait Until Dark; *television* includes: The Manions of America series, 1981; Remington Steele series (title rôle), 1982–87; Nancy Astor, 1984; Noble House 1988; Around the World in 80 Days, 1989; Robinson Crusoe, 1996; Bag of Bones, 2012; *films* include: Nomads, 1986; The Fourth Protocol, 1987; The Deceivers, 1988; Mr Johnson, 1991; Lawnmower Man, 1992; Mrs Doubtfire, 1993; Love Affair, 1994; The Mirror has Two Faces, Mars Attacks!, 1996; Dante's Peak, 1997; The Nephew, 1998 (also prod); The Thomas Crown Affair, 1999 (also prod); Grey Owl, 2000; The Taylor of Panama, 2001; Evelyn, 2003; Laws of Attraction, After the Sunset, 2004; The Matador, 2006; Seraphim Falls, 2007; Mamma Mia!, Married Life, 2008; Percy Jackson & the Olympians: The Lightning Thief, Remember Me, The Ghost, The Greatest, 2010; Love Is All You Need, 2013; Love Punch, A Long Way Down, 2014; rôle of James Bond in: GoldenEye, 1995; Tomorrow Never Dies, 1997; The World is Not Enough, 1999; Die Another Day, 2002. *Address:* c/o Guttman Associates, 118 South Beverly Drive, Suite 201, Beverly Hills, CA 90212, USA.

BROTHERSTON, Leslie William, (Lez); freelance production designer, since 1984; Associate Artist, New Adventures; *b* 6 Oct. 1961; *s* of L. Brotherston and Irene Richardson. *Educ:* Prescot Grammar Sch., Prescot, Liverpool; Central Sch. of Art and Design (BA Hons Th. Design 1984). First design for Letter to Brezhnev (film); work with Northern Ballet Theatre includes: The Brontes, Strange Meeting, Romeo and Juliet; Giselle, 1997; Dracula, 1997; The Hunchback of Notre Dame, 1998; Carmen (Barclays Th. Award for Outstanding Achievement in Dance, TMA Award), 1999; A Christmas Carol, 2001; designs for *dance* include: for Adventures in Motion Pictures: Highland Fling, 1994; Swan Lake, Piccadilly, 1995, transf. NY (Tony Award for Best Costume Design, Drama Desk Awards for Best Costume Design and Best Set Design, Outer Critics Award for Outstanding Costume Design, 1999); Cinderella, Piccadilly, 1997 (Olivier Award for Outstanding Achievement in Dance, 1998); The Car Man, 2000; Greymatter, Rambert; for Scottish Ballet: Just Scratchin' the Surface, Nightlife, 1999; The Nutcracker, 2014; 6 Faces, K-Ballet, Japan; Bounce, Eur. tour, 2000; Play Without Words, NT, 2002; for Adam Cooper Co.: Les Liaisons Dangereuses (also Co-Dir and writer), Japan, then Sadler's Wells, 2005; for New Adventures: Edward Scissorhands, Sadler's Wells, 2005; Dorian Gray, Edinburgh Fest. and UK tour, 2008; Sleeping Beauty, Sadler's Wells, 2012 (Best Costume Design, Los Angeles Drama Critics Circle Award, 2013); Lord of the Flies, Theatre Royal, Glasgow and UK tour, 2014; *theatre* includes: Jane Eyre, tour; Greenwich: Prisoner of Zenda, 1992; The Sisters Rosensweig, 1994, transf. Old Vic; Handling Bach, 1995; The Last Romantics, Northanger Abbey, 1996; David Copperfield, 1997; Neville's Island, Apollo, 1994; Rosencrantz and Guildenstern are Dead, RNT, 1995; Alarms and Excursions, Gielgud, 1998; Spend, Spend, Spend, Piccadilly, 1999; A Midsummer Night's Dream, Albery, 2000; French and Saunders Live, UK tour, 2000; Little Foxes, Donmar Warehouse, 2001; Victoria Wood - At It Again, Royal Albert Hall, 2001; Bedroom Farce, Aldwych, 2002; Royal Exchange, Manchester: A Woman of No Importance, 2000; Sex, Chips and Rock 'n' Roll, Design for Living, 2002; Volpone, 2004; The Vortex, 2007; Much Ado About Nothing, RSC, 2006; Women Beware Women, NT, 2010; French and Saunders—Still Alive, UK tour, 2008; Under the Blue Sky, Duke of York's 2008; Duet for One, Almeida 2009, transf. Vaudeville; Dancing at Lughnasa, 2009, The Real Thing, 2010, Old Vic; Really Old Like 45, NT, 2010; Measure for Measure, 2010, My City, 2011, Almeida; The Umbrellas of Cherbourg, Gielgud, 2011; The Day We Sang, Manchester Internat. Fest., 2011; Hedda Gabler, Old Vic, 2012; Long Day's Journey into Night, Apollo, 2012; Hysteria, Hampstead Th., 2013; The Duck House, Vaudeville, 2013; The Empress, RSC, 2013; Dawn French: 30 Million Minutes tour, 2014; Seminar, Hampstead Th., 2014; Pride and Prejudice, Crucible, 2015; *opera* includes prodns for Opera Zuid, Hong Kong Arts Fest., Opera North, Glyndebourne Touring Opera, Teatro Bellini, Royal Danish Opera, Opera NI, Buxton Fest., Scottish Opera, WNO; *musicals* include: Side by Side by Sondheim, Greenwich, 1997; Cabaret, Sheffield Crucible; Maria Friedman by Special Arrangement, Donmar Warehouse; My One and Only, Piccadilly, 2002; Brighton Rock, Almeida, 2004; Acorn Antiques, Haymarket, 2005; The Far Pavilions, Shaftesbury, 2005; Sister Act, London Palladium, 2009; Oh What a Lovely War, Th. Royal Stratford East, 2014. Critics Circle Award for Outstanding Achievement in Dance. *Address:* c/o Tracey Elliston, Judy Daish Associates, 2 St Charles Place, W10 6EG. *T:* (020) 8964 8811. *Club:* Soho House.

BROTHERTON, Ven. (John) Michael; Archdeacon of Chichester and Canon Residentiary of Chichester Cathedral, 1991–2002; *b* 7 Dec. 1935; *s* of late Clifford and Minnie Brotherton; *m* 1963, Daphne Margaret Yvonne, *d* of Sir Geoffrey Meade, KBE, CMG, CVO; three *s* one *d*. *Educ:* St John's Coll., Cambridge (MA); Cuddesdon Coll., Oxford; Univ. of London Inst. of Educn (PGCE). Ordained: deacon, 1961; priest, 1962; Asst Curate, St Nicolas, Chiswick, 1961–64; Chaplain, Trinity Coll., Port of Spain, Trinidad, 1965–69; Rector of St Michael's, Diego Martin, Trinidad, 1969–75; Vicar, St Mary and St John, Oxford, and Chaplain, St Hilda's Coll., Oxford, 1976–81; Rural Dean of Cowley, 1978–81; Vicar, St Mary, Portsea, 1981–91. Mem., Legal Adv. Commn, C of E, 1996–2001. Hon. Canon, St Michael's Cathedral, Kobe, Japan, 1986. Proctor in Convocation, 1995–2002. *Recreations:* travel, reading. *Address:* Flat 2, 23 Gledhow Gardens, SW5 0AZ. *T:* (020) 7373 5147. *E:* jmbrotherton@yahoo.co.uk.

BROTHERTON, Michael Lewis; Michael Brotherton Associates, Parliamentary Consultants, 1986–2012; *b* 26 May 1931; *s* of late John Basil Brotherton and Maud Brotherton; *m* 1968, Julia, *d* of Austin Gerald Comyn King and Katherine Elizabeth King, Bath; three *s* one *d*. *Educ:* Prior Park; RNC Dartmouth. Served RN, 1949–64: qual. Observer 1955; Cyprus, 1957 (despatches); Lt-Comdr 1964, retd. Times Newspapers, 1967–74. Chm., Beckenham Conservative Political Cttee, 1967–68; contested (C) Deptford, 1970; MP (C) Louth, Oct. 1974–1983. Pres., Hyde Park Tories, 1975. Mem., Select Cttee on violence in the family, 1975–76. Chm., Friends, 1995–99, Chm., Library Cttee, 1997–99, Boston Parish Church. *Recreations:* cricket, cooking, gardening, talking. *Address:* Ava Cottage, 46 The Butts, Chippenham, Wilts SN15 3JS. *T:* (01249) 651783. *Clubs:* Conservative Working Men's, Louth; Castaways; Cleethorpes Conservative; Immingham Conservative.

BROTHWOOD, Rev. John, MRCP, FRCPsych, FFOM; Hon. Curate, St Barnabas, Dulwich, 1991–99; *b* 23 Feb. 1931; *s* of late Wilfred Cyril Vernon Brothwood and Emma Bailey; *m* 1957, Dr Margaret Stirling Meyer (*d* 2008); one *d* (one *s* decd). *Educ:* Marlborough Coll.; Peterhouse, Cambridge (Schol.); Middlesex Hosp. MB BChir (Cantab) 1955; MRCP 1960, DPM (London) 1964, FFCM 1972, FRCPsych 1976, FFOM 1988. Various posts in clinical medicine, 1955–64; joined DHSS (then Min. of Health) as MO, 1964; SPMO and Under Secretary, DHSS, 1975–78; CMO, Esso Petroleum (UK) and Esso, subseq. Exxon, Chemicals, 1979–90. Lay Reader, Parish of St Barnabas, Dulwich, 1982–91; Southwark Ordination Course, 1988–91; deacon, 1991; priest, 1992. Mem. Council, Missions to Seamen, 1994–2001. *Publications:* various. *Recreation:* diverse. *Address:* 98 Woodwarde Road, SE22 8UT. *T:* (020) 8693 8273.

BROUCHER, David Stuart; HM Diplomatic Service, retired; consultant adviser on foreign relations, since 2005; *b* 5 Oct. 1944; *s* of late Clifford Broucher and Betty Broucher (*née* Jordan); *m* 1971, Marion Monika Blackwell (marr. diss. 2014); one *s*. *Educ:* Manchester Grammar School; Trinity Hall, Cambridge (MA Modern Languages). Foreign Office, 1966; British Military Govt, Berlin, 1968; Cabinet Office, 1972; Prague, 1975; FCO, 1978; UK Perm. Rep. to EC, 1983; Counsellor, Jakarta, 1985–89; Economic Counsellor, Bonn, 1989–93; Counsellor, FCO, 1994; Asst Under Sec. of State, FCO, 1995–97; Ambassador to Czech Republic, 1997–2001; UK Perm. Rep. to Conf. on Disarmament, Geneva (with personal rank of Ambassador), 2001–04. Advr to Pres. of Romania on EU accession, 2005; Advr on EU enlargement to Birmingham Univ., 2006–08. Vice Chm., FCO Assoc., 2009–. Vis. Fellow, Southampton Univ., 2006–11. *Recreations:* music, golf, sailing. *E:* dbroucher@btinternet.com.

BROUGH, Dr Colin, FRCPE; FFCM; Chief Administrative Medical Officer, Lothian Health Board, 1980–88; *b* 4 Jan. 1932; *s* of Peter Brough and Elizabeth C. C. Chalmers; *m* 1957, Maureen Jennings; four *s* one *d*. *Educ:* Bell Baxter Sch., Cupar; Univ. of Edinburgh (MB ChB 1956). DPH 1965; DIH 1965; FFCM 1978; MRCPE 1981; FRCPE 1982. House Officer, Leicester General Hosp. and Royal Infirmary of Edinburgh, 1956–57; Surg.-Lieut, Royal Navy, 1957–60; General Practitioner, Leith and Fife, 1960–64; Dep. Medical Supt, Royal Inf. of Edinburgh, 1965–67; ASMO, PASMO, Dep. SAMO, South-Eastern Regional

Hosp. Board, Scotland, 1967–74; Community Medicine Specialist, Lothian Health Board, 1974–80. *Recreations:* golf, shooting, fishing, first aid. *Address:* The Saughs, Gullane, East Lothian EH31 2AL. *T:* (01620) 842179.

BROUGH, Jonathan; Head, Hurlingham School, since 2010; *b* Bedford, 2 Feb. 1971; *s* of George Ernest Brough and Amy Elizabeth Brough; civil partnership 2006, Harry Small. *Educ:* Walmsley House Sch.; Bedford Sch.; Colyton Grammar Sch.; Homerton Coll., Cambridge (BEd Hons 1994); Nat. Coll. for Sch. Leadership (NPQH 2002). Head of English: York House Sch., Rickmansworth, 1994–96; Cumnor Hse Sch., Croydon, 1996–99; Dep. Hd (Dir of Studies), Bute Hse Prep. Sch. for Girls, Hammersmith, 1999–2004; Hd, Prep. Dept, City of London Sch. for Girls, 2004–10. Team Inspector, ISI, 2006–. Gov., Fairley Hse Sch., Pimlico, 2006–. FCollT 2013. *Recreations:* believing a book in the hand is worth two on the shelf, getting lost in hidden corners of London, New York and San Francisco, hexadecimal sudoku puzzles, enjoying fine wine, good food and good company. *Address:* Hurlingham School, 122 Putney Bridge Road, Putney, SW15 2NQ. *T:* (020) 8874 7186, *Fax:* (020) 8875 0372. *E:* jonathan.brough@hurlinghamschool.co.uk.

BROUGHAM, family name of **Baron Brougham and Vaux**.

BROUGHAM AND VAUX, 5th Baron *cr* 1860; **Michael John Brougham,** CBE 1995; *b* 2 Aug. 1938; *s* of 4th Baron and Jean (*d* 1992), *d* of late Brig.-Gen. G. B. S. Follett, DSO, MVO; *S* father, 1967; *m* 1st, 1963, Olivia Susan (marr. diss. 1968; she *d* 1986), *d* of Rear-Admiral Gordon Thomas Seccombe Gray, CB, DSC; one *d*; 2nd, 1969, Catherine Gulliver (marr. diss. 1981), *d* of late W. Gulliver; one *s*. *Educ:* Lycée Jaccard, Lausanne; Millfield School. Dep. Chm. of Cttees, H of L, 1992–; a Dep. Speaker, H of L, 1995–; elected Mem., H of L, 1999; Member: Select Cttee on H of L Officers, 1997–99, on Hybrid Instruments, 1999–2001; Statutory Instruments Jt Cttee, 2001–07; Information Cttee, 2006–08; Catering Cttee, 2008–12; Admin and Works Cttee, 2010–14; Vice-Chm., Assoc. of Cons. Peers, 1998–2002, 2003–07. President: RoSPA, 1986–89; Safety Gps UK (formerly Nat. Health and Safety Gps Council), 1994–. Chm., Tax Payers Soc., 1989–91. Chm., European Secure Vehicle Alliance, 1992–. *Heir: s* Hon. Charles William Brougham [*b* 9 Nov. 1971; *m* 2010, Nicola, *y d* of David Moore; one *s* one *d*]. *Address:* 11 Westminster Gardens, Marsham Street, SW1P 4JA.

BROUGHAM, Christopher John; QC 1988; *b* 11 Jan. 1947; *s* of late Lt-Comdr Patrick Brougham and of Elizabeth Anne (*née* Vestey); *m* 1974; one *s* three *d*. *Educ:* Radley Coll.; Worcester Coll., Oxford (BA Hons). Called to the Bar, Inner Temple, 1969, Bencher, 2007; Dep. High Court Bankruptcy Registrar, 1984. Dep. Churchwarden, Christ Church, Kensington, 1980–95. *Publications:* (contrib.) Encyclopedia of Financial Provision in Family Matters, 1998–; (jtly) Muir Hunter on Personal Insolvency, 2000–; (contrib.) Jackson's Matrimonial Finance and Taxation, 2008; (contrib.) Jackson's Matrimonial Finance, 2012. *Recreations:* music, crossword puzzles. *Address:* 3–4 South Square, Gray's Inn, WC1R 5HP. *T:* (020) 7696 9900.

BROUGHER, Kerry; Director, Academy of Motion Picture Arts and Sciences Museum, Los Angeles, since 2014; *b* 25 Sept. 1952; *s* of Russell Brougher and Margaret Brougher (*née* Smith); *m* 1987, Nora Halpern; two *d*. *Educ:* Univ. of Calif at Irvine (BA 1974); UCLA (MA 1978). Museum of Contemporary Art, Los Angeles: Asst Curator, 1982–87; Associate Curator, 1987–93; Curator, 1993–97; Dir, MOMA, Oxford, 1997–2000; Hirshhorn Museum and Sculpture Garden: Dep. Dir and Chief Curator, 2001–14; Dir of Art and Progs, 2001–07; Acting Dir, 2007–09 and 2013–14. Co-Artistic Dir, Gwangju Biennale, Korea, 2004. Visitor, Ashmolean Mus., Univ. of Oxford, 1998–; Vis. Fellow, Nuffield Coll., Oxford, 1999–. Mem. Bd of Advrs, Filmforum, Los Angeles, 1994–. FRSA 2000. *Publications:* The Image of Abstraction, 1988; The Beatrice and Philip Gersh Collection, 1989; Wolfgang Laib, 1992; Robert Irwin, 1993; Hiroshi Sugimoto, 1993; Hall of Mirrors: art and film since 1945, 1996; Jeff Wall, 1997; Gustav Metzger, 1998; Notorious: Alfred Hitchcock and contemporary art, 1999; Ed Ruscha, 2000; Enclosed and Enchanted, 2000; Open City: street photographs since 1950, 2001; Visual Music, 2005; Hiroshi Sugimoto, 2005; The Cinema Effect: illusion, reality and the moving image, 2008; Yves Klein: with the void, full powers, 2010. *Address:* Academy of Motion Picture Arts and Sciences Museum, 8949 Wilshire Boulevard, Beverly Hills, CA 902011, USA.

BROUGHTON, family name of **Baron Fairhaven**.

BROUGHTON, Sir David (Delves), 13th Bt *cr* 1660, of Broughton, Staffordshire; *b* 7 May 1942; *s* of Lt-Comdr P. J. D. Broughton, RN, *gggs* of Rev. Sir Henry Delves Broughton, 8th Bt, and of his 1st wife, Nancy Rosemary, *yr d* of J. E. Paterson; *S* kinsman, 1993, but his name does not appear on the Official Roll of the Baronetage; *m* 1969, Diane, *d* of R. L. Nicol. *Heir: half b* Geoffrey Delves Broughton [*b* 1962; *m* 1986, Karen Louise Wright; two *s* two *d*]. *Address:* 31 Mayfield Court, Sandy, Beds SG19 1NF.

BROUGHTON, Sir Martin (Faulkner), Kt 2011; FCA; Deputy Chairman, International Airlines Group, since 2010; Chairman and Managing Partner, Sports Investment Partners LLP, since 2010; *b* 15 April 1947; *m* 1974, Jocelyn Mary Rodgers; one *s* one *d*. *Educ:* Westminster City Grammar Sch. FCA 1969. Career in BAT Group: British-American Tobacco Co.: travelling auditor, 1971–74; Head Office, 1974–80; Souza Cruz, Brazil, 1980–85; Eagle Star, 1985–88 and (Chm.) 1992–93; Chm., Wiggins Teape Gp, 1989–90; Finance Dir, 1988–92; Man. Dir, Financial Services, 1992–98; Gp Chief Exec. and Dep. Chm., BAT Industries, 1993–98; Chm., 1998–2004. Chm., British Airways, 2004–14 (non-exec. Dir, 2000–14); non-exec. Dir, Whitbread, 1993–2000. Ind. Dir, 1999–2007, Chm., 2004–07, British Horseracing Bd; Chm., Liverpool FC, 2010. Member: Takeover Panel, 1996–99; Financial Reporting Council, 1998–2004. Co-Chm., TransAtlantic Business Dialogue, 2006–08. Pres., CBI, 2007–09. *Recreations:* theatre, golf, horseracing, football. *Address:* International Airlines Group, 2 World Business Centre Heathrow, Newall Road, London Heathrow Airport, Hounslow TW6 2SF. *Club:* Tandridge Golf.

BROUGHTON, Dr Peter, FREng; Consultant, NIRAS Fraenkel (formerly Peter Fraenkel Maritime, then Peter Fraenkel and Partners), since 2003; Director, Marine Engineering Energy Solutions Ltd, since 2013; *b* 1944; *s* of late Thomas Frederick Broughton and Mary Theodosia Broughton; *m* 1968, Jan Mary, *d* of late Ronald George Silveston and Molly Silveston; two *s*. *Educ:* Rowlinson Technical Sch., Sheffield; Manchester Univ. (BSc 1966; PhD 1970). FICE; FIStructE; FIMarEST; FRINA; FREng (FEng 1996). Engrg Surveyor, Lloyd's Register of Shipping, 1971–74; Partner, Campbell Reith and Partners, 1974–75; Sen. Structural Engr, Burmah Oil Development, 1975–76; Supervising Structural Engr, BNOC, 1977–79; Phillips Petroleum Co., 1979–2003: Sen Structl Engr, 1979–82, Civil Engrg Supervisor, 1982–86, UK; Project Engr and Co. Rep., Ekofisk Protective Barrier Project, Norway, 1986–90; Engrg and Procurement Manager, Judy/Joanne Develt Project, UK, 1990–94; Project Manager: for Substructures, Ekofisk II Develt Project, Norway, 1994–98; Maureen Platform Re-Float and Decommng Project, UK, 1998–2003. Vis. Prof., Dept of Civil Engrg, ICSTM, 1991–2005; Royal Acad. of Engrg Vis. Prof., Oxford Univ., 2004–07. Stanley Grey Award, IMarE, 1992; George Stephenson Medal, 1993, Bill Curtin Medal, 1997, Overseas Premium, 1998, David Hislop Award, 1999, Contribution to Institution Activity Award, 2002, ICE. *Publications:* The Analysis of Cable and Catenary Structures, 1994; numerous technical papers on offshore structures. *Recreations:* walking, fishing, swimming. *Address:* NIRAS Fraenkel, Consulting Engineers, South House, South Street, Dorking RH4 2JZ.

BROUN, Sir Wayne (Hercules), 14th Bt *cr* 1686 (NS) of Colstoun, Haddingtonshire; 30th Chief of the Clan Broun/Brown; Chief Executive Officer: Australian Asian Pacific Services Pty Ltd, since 2002; New Vision Media, since 2015; Chairman, BrounBrown.com, since 2011; *b* Inverell, NSW, Australia, 23 Jan. 1952; *s* of Hulance Haddington Broun and Joy Maude Broun (*née* Stack); *S* uncle, 2007; *m* 1st, 1976 (marr. diss. 1998); one *s* one *d*; 2nd, 2001, Caroline Mary Lavender; one *d*. *Educ:* Sydney Grammar Sch.; Wagga Agricl Coll Queen's Commn (Army), OTU; Lieut, Royal Australian Regt, 1973. Dist Mgr, G. M. Holden, 1976; Man. Dir, Lorimar Telepictures, 1985; Man. Dir and Vice Pres., Warner Bros Internat. Television, Australia/NZ Asia Pacific, 1990; Chairman: Warner Bros Australia, 1991; Movie Network, 1999. Nat. Service Medal, 2004; Australian Defence Medal, 2006. *Recreations:* sport, reading, travel. *Heir: s* Richard Haddington Broun, *b* 3 May 1984. *Address:* 112 Narrabeen Park Parade, Warriewood Beach, NSW 2102, Australia. *T:* (2) 99974175. *E:* aapswayne@bigpond.com. *Clubs:* Royal Automobile of Australia (Sydney); RSL (Pittwater); Royal Motor Yacht (Broken Bay); Bayview Golf; Millbrook Golf (NZ).

BROUSSE, Olivier, Chevalier, Ordre du Mérite (France), 2005; Chief Executive Officer, John Laing plc, since 2014; *b* Paris, 28 Feb. 1965; *s* of J. P. Brousse and M. C. Brousse (*née* Chambon); *m* 1991, Isabelle Leven; two *s* one *d*. *Educ:* École Polytechnique, France; École Nationale Ponts et Chaussées, France. Commercial Dir, Unic Systèmes, 1990–94; COS, Compagnie Générale des Eaux, 1994–98; Man. Dir, Connex UK, 1998–2003; Chief Executive Officer: Veolia Transportation, USA, 2004–07; Saur, Paris, 2008–14. *Recreations:* golf, photography. *Address:* 83–85 Onslow Gardens, SW7 3BU. *T:* 07500 553449. *E:* olivier.brousse@me.com. *Clubs:* St Cloud Golf, Polo (Paris).

BROWN; *see* Malloch-Brown, family name of Baron Malloch-Brown.

BROWN, family name of **Baron Brown of Eaton-under-Heywood**.

BROWN OF EATON-UNDER-HEYWOOD, Baron *cr* 2004 (Life Peer), of Eaton-under-Heywood in the county of Shropshire; **Simon Denis Brown,** Kt 1984; PC 1992; a Justice of the Supreme Court of the United Kingdom, 2009–12 (a Lord of Appeal in Ordinary, 2004–09); *b* 9 April 1937; *s* of late Denis Baer Brown and Edna Elizabeth (*née* Abrahams); *m* 1963, Jennifer Buddicom; two *s* one *d*. *Educ:* Stowe Sch.; Worcester Coll., Oxford (Hon. Fellow, 1993). Commnd 2nd Lt RA, 1955–57. Called to the Bar, Middle Temple, 1961 (Harmsworth Schol.); Master of the Bench, Hon. Soc. of Middle Temple, 1980; a Recorder, 1979–84; First Jun. Treasury Counsel, Common Law, 1979–84; a Judge of the High Court of Justice, QBD, 1984–92; a Lord Justice of Appeal, 1992–2004; Vice-Pres., Court of Appeal (Civil Div.), 2001–03. President: Security Service Tribunal, 1989–2000; Intelligence Services Tribunal, 1995–2000; Intelligence Services Comr, 2000–06. Chm., Sub-Cttee E (Law and Instns), H of L Select Cttee on EU, 2005–07; Chm., Sub-Cttee on Lords' Conduct, H of L Cttee for Privileges and Conduct, 2013–. Visitor: Pembroke Coll., Cambridge, 2010–; St Hugh's Coll., Oxford, 2011–; High Steward, Oxford Univ., 2011–12. *Recreations:* golf, theatre, reading. *Address:* House of Lords, SW1A 0PW. *Clubs:* Garrick; Denham Golf.

BROWN, Alan; MP (SNP) Kilmarnock and Loudoun, since 2015; *b* Newmilns, 12 Aug. 1970; *s* of Eric and Irene Brown; *m* 2007, Cyndi Aukerman; two *s*. *Educ:* Loudoun Acad.; Glasgow Univ. (BEng Hons). Engineer: West of Scotland Water, then Strathclyde Regl Council, later Scottish Water, 1993–2007; Grontmij, 2007–15. Mem. (SNP), E Ayrshire Council, 2007–15. *Address:* House of Commons, SW1A 0AA.

BROWN, Hon. Alan John; Chairman: Apprenticeships Plus, Victoria, since 2000; Work & Training Ltd, Tasmania, since 2004; IntoWork Australia, since 2014; *b* Wonthaggi, Vic, 25 Jan. 1946; *m* 1972, Paula McBurnie; three *s* one *d*. Councillor, Wonthaggi BC, 1970–78, Mayor, 1974–77; MLA (L): Westernport, Vic, 1979–85; Gippsland W, Vic, 1985–96; Victorian Shadow Minister for: Youth, Sport and Recreation, 1982; Aboriginal Affairs and Housing, 1982–85; Correctional Services, 1984–85; Resources, 1985; Tspt, 1985–89; Dep. Leader of Opposition, 1987–89; Leader of Opposition, 1989–91; Shadow Minister for Transport, 1991–92; Minister for Transport, 1992–96; Agent-Gen. for Victoria in UK, 1997–2000. Bd Mem., Traffic Technologies Ltd, 2004– (Chm., 2010–). Chm., Victorian Bushfire Community Adv. Cttee, 2011–. Silver Jubilee Medal, 1977; Centenary Medal, Australia, 2002. *Recreations:* motor cycle riding, vintage cars, farming. *Address:* Bridgewater Park, Wattle Bank, Vic 3995, Australia.

BROWN, Alan John, FCMA; Group Chief Executive Officer, ASCO Group Ltd, since 2014; *b* Belfast, 8 Nov. 1956; *s* of John and Sallie Brown; *m* 1986, Radhika Edwards; two *s* one *d*. *Educ:* Methodist Coll., Belfast; Liverpool Univ. (LLB). FCMA 1994. Called to the Bar, Gray's Inn, 1981. Unilever: various posts in UK, 1980–91; Chief Financial Officer, Birds Eye Wall's, 1991–94; Chief Financial Officer, Foods Europe, 1994–97; Chm., Unilever Taiwan, 1998–2001; Chm., Unilever China, 2001–05; Chief Financial Officer, ICI, 2005–08; CEO, Rentokil-Initial plc, 2008–13. *Recreations:* sports, vintage cars.

BROWN, Alan Thomas, CBE 1978; DL; Chief Executive, Oxfordshire County Council, 1973–88; *b* 18 April 1928; *s* of Thomas Henry Brown and Lucy Lilian (*née* Betts); *m* 1962, Marie Christine East; two *d*. *Educ:* Wyggeston Grammar Sch., Leicester; Sidney Sussex Coll., Cambridge (Wrangler, Maths Tripos 1950, MA 1953). Fellow CIPFA, 1961. Asst, Bor. Treasurer's Dept, Wolverhampton, 1950–56; Asst Sec., IMTA, 1956–58; Dep. Co. Treas., Berks CC, 1958–61; Co. Treas., Cumberland CC, 1961–66; Town Clerk and Chief Exec., Oxford City Council, 1966–73. Member: SE Econ. Planning Council, 1975–79; Audit Commn, 1989–95. DL Oxon 1978. *Recreations:* chess, horticulture, music, reading. *Address:* 4 Malkin Drive, Beaconsfield, Bucks HP9 1JN. *T:* (01494) 677933.

BROWN, Alan Winthrop, CB 1992; Head of Health Policy Division, Health and Safety Executive, 1992–94; *b* 14 March 1934; *s* of James Brown and Evelyn V. Brown (*née* Winthrop); *m* 1959, Rut Berit (*née* Ohlson); two *s* one *d*. *Educ:* Bedford Sch.; Pembroke Coll., Cambridge (BA Hons); Cornell Univ., NY (MSc). Joined Min. of Labour, 1959; Private Sec. to Minister, 1961–62; Principal, 1963; Asst Sec., 1969. Dir of Planning, Employment Service Agency, 1973–74; Under-Sec. and Head of Incomes Div., DoE, 1975; Chief Exec., Employment Service Div., 1976–79, Trng Services Div., 1979–82, MSC; Hd Electricity Div., Dept of Energy, 1983–85; Dir, Personnel and Management Services, Dept of Employment, 1985–89; Dir, Resources and Planning, HSE, 1989–92. Chm., Godalming Trust, 1999–2005. Lay Mem., Waverley Primary Care Gp, 2000–02; Patient Rep., Surrey PCT, 2007–13. *Publications:* papers on occupational psychology and industrial training. *Recreations:* history of art, literature, gardening, croquet, opera. *Address:* 16 Milford House, Portsmouth Road, Milford, Surrey GU8 5HJ.

BROWN, Alastair Nigel, PhD; Sheriff of Tayside, Central and Fife at Dundee, since 2014; *b* Kirkcaldy, 3 May 1955; *s* of Kenneth and Evelyn Jean Brown; *m* 1977, Susan Harrison; two *s* one *d*. *Educ:* Royal Grammar Sch., Newcastle upon Tyne; Univ. of Edinburgh (LLB Hons 1977; PhD 1999). Admitted as solicitor, 1979; in practice as solicitor, 1979–2009; with Balfour + Manson Solicitors, Edinburgh, 1979–81, Procurator Fiscal Service, 1981–2003; Advocate Depute, 2004–09; admitted as Advocate, 2010; in private practice at Scots Bar, 2010–11; All-Scotland Floating Sheriff, 2011–14. Expert Evaluator, Gp of States Against Corruption, Council of Europe, 2000–. *Publications:* Criminal Evidence and Procedure: an introduction, 1996, 3rd edn 2011; Regulation of Investigatory Powers in Scotland, 2003; Proceeds of Crime, 2004; Money Laundering, 2009; Sexual Offences (Scotland) Act 2009, 2009; Bribery Act 2010, 2011. *Recreations:* Church, walking, reading, bluegrass mandolin and guitar, gardening. *Address:* c/o Sheriff Court, 6 West Bell Street, Dundee DD1 9AD.

BROWN, Alexander Douglas G.; *see* Gordon-Brown.

BROWN, Prof. Alice, CBE 2010; PhD; FRSE; Chairman, Scottish Funding Council, since 2013; Scottish Public Services Ombudsman, 2002–09; Professor of Politics, University of Edinburgh, 1997–2008, now Emeritus; *b* 30 Sept. 1946; *d* of Robert Wilson and Alice (*née* Morgan); *m* 1965, Alan James Brown; two *d*. *Educ:* Boroughmuir High Sch., Edinburgh; Stevenson Coll., Edinburgh; Univ. of Edinburgh (MA 1983; PhD 1990). Lectr in Econs, Univ. of Stirling, 1984–85; University of Edinburgh: Lectr, 1985–92; Sen. Lectr in Politics, 1992–97; Hd, Dept of Politics, 1995; Hd, Planning Unit, 1996; Co-Dir, Governance of Scotland Forum, subseq. Inst. of Governance, 1998–2002; Vice-Principal, 1999–2002. Chm., Community Planning Task Force (Scotland), 2001–02; Member: SHEFC, 1998–2002 (Chm., Mergers Cttee, 2001–02); Cttee on Standards in Public Life, 1999–2003; Res. Grants Bd, ESRC; Adv. Gp, EOC, Scotland, 1995–2002; Adv. Bd, CRE, Scotland, 2003–07; Bd, ARB, 2006–09; Council, Admin. Justice and Tribunals Council, 2008–13; Adv. Bd, Inst. for Advanced Studies in the Humanities, Univ. of Edinburgh, 2011–13; Steering Cttee, Scottish Resource Centre, Edinburgh Napier Univ., 2011–13. Gen. Sec., RSE, 2011–13. Founder Member: Engender (women's res. and campaigning gp), 1991–; Scottish Women's Co-ordination Gp, 1992–99; Mem., Strategic Gp on Women and Work, Scottish Govt, 2013–. Bd Mem., Centre for Scottish Public Policy (formerly John Wheatley Centre), 1992–99; Chm., Lay Adv. Gp, RCPE (Mem., 2003–13). Mem., Bd of Govs, Public Policy Inst. for Wales, 2014–. Asst Ed., Scottish Affairs jl, 1992–2002. Fellow: Stevenson Coll., Edinburgh, 2006; Sunningdale Inst., 2008–12. FRSE 2002; FRSA 2007; FAcSS (AcSS 2002); Hon. Mem., CIPFA, 2004; FRCPE 2012. DUniv Stirling, 2004; Hon. DLaws Edinburgh Napier, 2009; Dr *hc* Edinburgh, 2010; Hon. DLitt Glasgow Caledonian, 2012; Hon. DSc (SocSci) QUB, 2014. *Publications:* (co-ed) The Scottish Government Yearbook, 1989–91; The Changing Politics of Gender Equality in Britain, 2002; jointly: A Major Crisis?, 1996; Politics and Society in Scotland, 1996, 1998; Gender Equality in Scotland, 1997; The Scottish Electorate, 1999; New Scotland, New Politics?, 2001. *Address:* Scottish Funding Council, Apex 2, 97 Haymarket Terrace, Edinburgh EH12 5HD. *E:* alajbrown@hotmail.com.

BROWN, Amanda Margaret B.; *see* Barrington Brown.

BROWN, Ven. Andrew; Archdeacon of Man, since 2011; *b* Haslingden, Lancs, 18 Sept. 1955; *s* of Jack Maxwell Brown and Jean Brown; *m* 1982, Jane Rosanne Shakespeare; three *d*. *Educ:* Haslingden Grammar Sch.; St Peter's Coll., Oxford (MA 1982); Ridley Hall, Cambridge. Ordained deacon, 1980, priest, 1981; Asst Curate, Burnley Parish Church, 1980–83; Priest-in-charge, St Francis, Brandlesholme, 1983–86; Vicar: St Peter, Ashton-under-Lyne, 1986–96; St Luke's, Halliwell, 1996–2003; Canon Theologian and Continuing Ministerial Educn Officer, Derby Cathedral, 2003–11. *Publications:* Preaching at Baptisms, 2008. *Recreations:* supporting Burnley FC, reading detective stories, walking, cooking, watching "chick flicks" with my daughters. *Address:* St George's Vicarage, 16 Devonshire Road, Douglas, Isle of Man IM2 3RB. *T:* (01624) 675430. *E:* archdeacon@sodorandman.im.

BROWN, Andrew Charles, FRICS; Secretary to the Church Commissioners, since 2003; *b* 30 Oct. 1957; *s* of Gordon Charles Brown and Joan Finch Trail Brown (*née* Tomlin); *m* 1983, Marion Denise Chamberlain; one *s* one *d*. *Educ:* Ashmole Sch.; South Bank Poly. (BSc Hons). FRICS 1994; Accredited Mediator, CEDR, 2012. Property Negotiator, Healey and Baker, 1981–84; Investment Surveyor, 1984–87, Associate Partner, 1987–91, Partner, 1991–94, St Quintin; Chief Surveyor, Church Commissioners, 1994–2003. Mem. Council, Westminster Property Owners' Assoc., 1997–2003; Member: LionHeart Administration, Investment and Finance Cttee, 2006–14; LionHeart Investment Cttee, 2014–; Dir, William Leech Foundn, William Leech (Investments) Ltd, 2007–; Chair of Trustees: 2:67 Project, 2007–10; CMS Pension Trust, 2013–. Hon. Sec., Christians in Property, 1991–2003; Hon. Sec. and Treas., 1894 Club, 2006–11. *Recreations:* family, local church, golf, sport, Chelsea FC, gardening. *Address:* Church Commissioners, Church House, Great Smith Street, SW1P 3AZ. *T:* (020) 7898 1000. *E:* andrew.brown@churchofengland.org.

BROWN, Dr Andrew Edward, CBE 2013; independent environmental advisor; Chief Executive, English Nature, 2003–06; Deputy Chairman, Environment Agency, 2009–12 (Board Member, 2006–09); *b* 9 May 1954; *s* of James Andrew Brown and Gwyneth Brown (*née* Watkins); *m* 1980, Christina Joyce Binks; two *d*. *Educ:* University Coll., Cardiff (BSc Zool. and Envmtl Studies); Leicester Poly. (PhD Freshwater Ecol.). Res. Officer and Tutor, Sussex Univ., 1980–81; Lectr, Bayero Univ., Kano, Nigeria, 1981–83; Nature Conservancy Council: Asst Regl Officer, Cheshire, 1983–86; Develt Officer, Scotland, 1986–89; Sen. Officer, York, 1989–90; English Nature: Strategic Planner, 1990–94; Corporate Manager, 1994–96; Chief Officer, Jt Nature Conservation Cttee, 1996–98; a Dir, English Nature, 1998–2002. Dir, Eur. Forum for Nature Conservation and Pastoralism, 2012–. Mem., Broads Authority, 1999–2005. Chairman: UK Cttee, IUCN, 2005–07; Policy Cttee, CPRE, 2006–09; Mem. Council, RSPB, 2006–; Trustee, Wildfowl and Wetlands Trust, 2008–. Mem. Council, Linnean Soc., 2007. FRSB (FIBiol 2006); FLS 2007; CBiol 2010. *Publications:* contrib. to books on freshwater ecology; papers in scientific jls. *Recreations:* reading, DIY, walking, travel, ski-ing. *Address:* Sunny Bank Farm, Carperby, Leyburn, N Yorks DL8 4DR. *T:* (01969) 662601.

BROWN, Andrew Edwin, FRCS; FDSRCS, FDSRCPSGlas; Consultant Maxillofacial Surgeon, Queen Victoria Hospital, East Grinstead, 1981–2008, now Hon. Consultant Surgeon; *b* 22 Aug. 1945; *s* of Edwin and Kathleen Brown; *m* 1969, Joan Elizabeth Phillips; one *s* two *d*. *Educ:* Sir Joseph Williamson's Mathematical Sch., Rochester; Guy's Hosp., Univ. of London (BDS Hons 1969; MB BS 1973). LDSRCS 1968, FDSRCS 1975; LRCP, MRCS 1973, FRCS 1986; FDSRCPSGlas 1975. Registrar, Dept of Oral and Maxillofacial Surgery, Eastman Dental Hosp. and Inst. of Dental Surgery, Univ. of London, 1974–76; Sen. Registrar, Dept of Oral and Maxillofacial Surgery, Queen Victoria Hosp., E Grinstead, 1976–81. Hon. Civil Consultant in Oral and Maxillofacial Surgery, RAF, 2000–09. Chm., Specialist Adv. Cttee in Oral and Maxillofacial Surgery, 2003–05. President: Inst. of Maxillofacial Prosthetists and Technologists, 2002–03; BAOMS, 2006–07. *Publications:* (with P. Banks) Fractures of the Facial Skeleton, 2001, 2nd edn (with M. Perry and P. Banks) 2015; chapters in: Operative Maxillofacial Surgery, 1998, 2nd edn 2010; Maxillofacial Surgery, 1999, 2nd edn 2007; papers on facial trauma, reconstruction, etc in learned jls. *Recreations:* art and graphic design, travel, swimming, medical history, reading history and biography. *Address:* Langleys, West Lane, East Grinstead, W Sussex RH19 4HH.

BROWN, Andrew Gibson, CBE 2003; QPM 1997; HM Chief Inspector of Constabulary for Scotland, 2004–07; *b* 11 April 1945; *s* of Alexander Brown and Euphemia Brown; *m* 1988, Fiona McMillan; one *s* one *d*. *Educ:* Kelso High Sch. Police Cadet, 1961; Police Constable, 1964; Detective Chief Supt, 1992; Asst Chief Constable (Crime), Lothian and Borders Police, 1993–98; Chief Constable, Grampian Police, 1998–2004. *Recreations:* spectating Rugby, Prince's Trust, Common Purpose. *Club:* Melrose Rugby Football.

BROWN, Andrew Lawson; QC (Scot.) 2010; *b* Glasgow, 31 May 1966; *s* of late Prof. Al Brown and of Dr Jenny Brown (*née* Tannahill, now Wormald); *m* 1993, Alison Margaret Shiach; one *s* one *d*. *Educ:* Glasgow Acad.; Aberdeen Univ. (LLB Hons). Solicitor, 1989–94; called to the Scottish Bar, 1995; Convenor, Mental Health Tribunal, Scotland, 2005–; ad hoc Advocate Depute, 2006–11, Advocate Depute, 2011–. Gov., The Burn, Goodenough Coll., 2009–. *Publications:* Wheatley's Road Traffic Law in Scotland, 4th edn, 2007, 5th edn 2014. *Recreations:* flying, military history, Orkney. *Address:* Advocates' Library, Parliament House, Edinburgh EH1 1RF. *T:* (0131) 226 5071. *E:* andrew.brown@advocates.org.uk.

BROWN, Andrew William, CBE 2012; Director General, Advertising Association, 1993–2006; *b* 3 March 1946; *s* of Harry Brown and Geraldine (*née* O'Leary); *m* 1977, Shelby Ann Hill. *Educ:* St Edmund's Coll., Ware, Herts. J. Walter Thompson Co. Ltd, 1965–93, Board Dir, 1982–93. Chm., CAM Foundn, 1994–96. Director: Advertising Standards Bd of Finance, 1993–2011; Broadcast Advertising Standards Bd of Finance Ltd, 2004–11; Chairman: Cttee of Advertising Practice, 1999–2011; Broadcast Cttee of Advertising Practice, 2004–11 (Mem., Advertising Adv. Cttee, 2004–06); Mem., ITC Advertising Adv. Cttee, 1999–2003. *Recreations:* cricket, theatre, London, Bodmin Moor. *Clubs:* Reform, MCC; XL.

BROWN, Prof. Archibald Haworth, CMG 2005; FBA 1991; Professor of Politics, University of Oxford, 1989–2005, now Professor Emeritus; Fellow, St Antony's College, Oxford, 1971–2005, now Fellow Emeritus (Sub-Warden, 1995–97); Director, Russian and East European Centre, St Antony's College, 1991–94 and 1999–2001; *b* 10 May 1938; *s* of late Rev. Alexander Douglas Brown and Mary Brown (*née* Yates); *m* 1963, Patricia Susan Cornwell; one *s* one *d*. *Educ:* Annan Acad.; Dumfries Acad.; City of Westminster Coll.; LSE (BSc Econs, 1st Cl. Hons 1962). MA Oxon 1972. Reporter, Annandale Herald and Annandale Observer, 1954–56. National Service, 1956–58. Lectr in Politics, Glasgow Univ., 1964–71; British Council exchange scholar, Moscow Univ., 1967–68; Lectr in Soviet Instns, Univ. of Oxford, 1971–89. Visiting Professor: of Political Science, Yale Univ. and Univ. of Connecticut, 1980; Columbia Univ., NY, 1985; Univ. of Texas, Austin, 1990–91; INSEAD, 1991; Distinguished Vis. Fellow, Kellogg Inst. for Internat. Studies, Univ. of Notre Dame, 1998. Lectures: Henry L. Stimson, Yale Univ., 1980; Lothian European, Edinburgh, 1999; Alexander Dallin Meml, Stanford, 2006; City of Aberdeen Gorbachev, 2007; James Chace Meml, NY, 2010; BEARR Trust, 2014. Member, Council: SSEES, Univ. of London, 1992–98; British Acad., 2014–. Founder AcSS 1999. For. Hon. Mem., Amer. Acad. of Arts and Scis, 2003. Diamond Jubilee Lifetime Achievement Award, Pol Studies Assoc., 2010. *Publications:* Soviet Politics and Political Science, 1974; (ed jtly and contrib.) The Soviet Union since the Fall of Khrushchev, 1975, 2nd edn 1978; (ed jtly and contrib.) Political Culture and Political Change in Communist States, 1977, 2nd edn 1979; (ed jtly and contrib.) Authority, Power and Policy in the USSR: essays dedicated to Leonard Schapiro, 1980; (ed jtly and contrib.) The Cambridge Encyclopedia of Russia and the Soviet Union, 1982; (ed jtly and contrib.) Soviet Policy for the 1980s, 1982; (ed and contrib.) Political Culture and Communist Studies, 1984; (ed and contrib.) Political Leadership in the Soviet Union, 1989; (ed and contrib.) The Soviet Union: a biographical dictionary, 1990; (ed and contrib.) New Thinking in Soviet Politics, 1992; (ed jtly and contrib.) The Cambridge Encyclopedia of Russia and the Former Soviet Union, 1994; The Gorbachev Factor, 1996 (W. J. M. Mackenzie Prize, Pol Studies Assoc., 1998; Alexander Nove Prize, British Assoc. for Slavonic and E Eur. Studies, 1998); (ed jtly and contrib.) The British Study of Politics in the Twentieth Century, 1999; (ed and contrib.) Contemporary Russian Politics: a reader, 2001; (ed jtly and contrib.) Gorbachev, Yeltsin and Putin: political leadership in Russia's transition, 2001; (ed and contrib.) The Demise of Marxism-Leninism in Russia, 2004; Seven Years that Changed the World: Perestroika in perspective, 2007; The Rise and Fall of Communism, 2009 (Alexander Nove Prize, British Assoc. for Slavonic and E Eur. Studies, 2009; W. J. M. Mackenzie Prize, Pol Studies Assoc., 2010); The Myth of the Strong Leader: political leadership in the modern age, 2014; papers in academic jls and symposia; *Festschriften:* Leading Russia - Putin in Perspective: essays in honour of Archie Brown, ed Alex Pravda, 2005; Political Culture and Post-Communism, ed Stephen Whitefield, 2005; Institutions, Ideas and Leadership in Russian Politics, ed Julie Newton and William Tompson, 2010. *Recreations:* novels and political memoirs, opera and ballet, watching football, cricket and tennis. *Address:* St Antony's College, Oxford OX2 6JF.

BROWN, Sir (Austen) Patrick, KCB 1995; Chairman, Oil and Gas Authority, since 2015; *b* 14 April 1940; *m* 1966, Mary (*née* Bulger); one *d*. *Educ:* Royal Grammar School, Newcastle upon Tyne; School of Slavonic and East European Studies, Univ. of London. Carreras Ltd, 1961–69 (Cyprus, 1965–66, Belgium, 1967–68); Management Consultant, Urwick Orr & Partners, UK, France, Portugal, Sweden, 1969–72; DoE, 1972; Asst Sec., Property Services Agency, 1976–80, Dept of Transport, 1980–83; Under Sec., Dept of Transport, 1983–88; Dep. Sec., DoE, 1988–90; Second Perm. Sec., and Chief Exec., PSA, DoE, 1990–91; Perm. Sec., Dept of Transport, 1991–97. Chairman: Go-Ahead Gp, 2002–13 (Dir, 1999–2013); Amey plc, 2004–08; Dep. Chm., Kvaerner Corporate Devlt, 1998–99; Director: Hunting PLC, 1998–2001; Arlington Securities plc, 1999–2004; Northumbrian Water Gp plc, 2003–12; Camelot UK Lotteries plc, 2010–; Chm., Adv. Bd, Alexander Proudfoot Ltd, 2010–12. Chm., Ind. Transport Commn, 1999–2008. Leader, Way Ahead Study into Ex-Service Charities, 2001–02. Trustee, Charities Aid Foundn, 1998–2006; Chm. Trustees, Mobility Choice, 1998–2008. Vis. Prof., later Mem. Court, Newcastle Univ., 1998–2013.

BROWN, Barry; *see* Brown, James B. C.

BROWN, Benjamin Robert; Presenter, BBC News 24, since 2006; *b* 26 May 1960; *s* of late Antony Victor Brown and of Sheila Mary Brown; *m* 1991, Geraldine Anne Ryan; one *s* two *d*. *Educ:* Sutton Valence Sch., Kent; Keble Coll., Oxford (BA Hons PPE); Centre for Journalism Studies, UC, Cardiff. Reporter: Radio Clyde, 1982; Radio City, 1982–85; Independent Radio News, 1985–88; BBC Television News: Corresp., 1988–91; Moscow Corresp., 1991–94; Foreign Affairs Corresp., 1994–98; Special Corresp., 1998–2006. *Publications:* All Necessary Means: inside the Gulf War (with D. Shukman), 1991; Sandstealers (novel), 2009. *Recreations:* reading, cinema, following Liverpool Football Club. *Address:* c/o BBC News 24, BBC News Centre, Broadcasting House, Portland Place, W1A 1AA.

BROWN, Adm. Sir Brian (Thomas), KCB 1989; CBE 1983; Chairman, P-E International plc, 1995–98; Director: Cray Electronics plc, 1991–96; Lorien plc, 1996–2007; *b* 31 Aug. 1934; *s* of late Walter Brown and Gladys (*née* Baddeley); *m* 1959, Veronica, *d* of late Wing Comdr and Mrs J. D. Bird; two *s*. *Educ:* Peter Symonds' School. Joined RN 1952; pilot in 898 and 848 Sqdns, 1959–62; Dep. Supply Officer, HMY Britannia, 1966–68; Supply Officer, HMS Tiger, 1973–75; Secretary: to VCNS, 1975–78; to First Sea Lord, 1979–82; rcds 1983; CO HMS Raleigh, 1984–85; DGNPS, 1986; Dir Gen., Naval Manpower and Trng, 1986–88, and Chief Naval Supply and Secretariat Officer, 1987–88; Chief of Naval Personnel, Second Sea Lord and Admiral Pres., RNC, Greenwich, 1988–91, retired. Chairman: King George's Fund for Sailors, 1993–2003; Exec. Cttee, Nuffield Trust for the Armed Forces of the Crown, 1996–2003; Michael May Young Cricketers Foundn, 1993–2008; President: Victory Services Assoc., 1993–2002; Friends of RN Mus. and HMS Victory, 1993–2003; Portsmouth Services Fly Fishing Assoc., 2005–15; CPRE Hants, 2008–13. Churchwarden, Froxfield with Privett, 1999–2008. CCMI (CBIM 1989); FIPD (FIPM 1990). Hon. DEd CNAA, 1990. Freeman, City of London, 1989; Liveryman, 1991–2012, Freeman, 2012–15, Gardeners' Co. Jt Master, Clinkard Meon Valley Beagles, 2003–09. *Recreations:* cricket, gardening, fishing. *Address:* The Limes, 62B Borough Road, Petersfield, Hants GU32 3LF. *Club:* Army and Navy.

BROWN, Bruce; *see* Brown, John B.

BROWN, Prof. Bruce; Professor of Design, since 1989, and Pro-Vice Chancellor (Research) since 2006, University of Brighton; *b* 14 June 1949; *s* of George and Grace Brown; *m* 1976, Morag Ross; two *d*. *Educ:* Liverpool Coll. of Art (Foundn Cert. 1968); Canterbury Coll. of Art (DipAD 1971); Royal Coll. of Art (MA 1978). Industrial Design Bursary, RSA, 1971. Lectr, RCA, 1978–81; Head, Department of Graphic Design: Norwich Sch. of Art, 1981–84; Brighton Poly., 1984–89; Dean, Faculty of Arts and Architecture, Univ. of Brighton, 1989–2006. Dir, Subject Centre for Art, Design & Media, Higher Educn Acad., York, 1999–.

Ind. design consultant and Art Dir, Crafts mag., Crafts Council, 1978–84; Mem., Point, Art and Design Res. Jl, 1998–2002. Mem., Panel 64 Art and Design, 2001 RAE, 1997–2001; Chairman: Main Panel O, 2008 RAE, 2005–08; Main Panel D (Arts and Humanities) 2014 RAE, 2010–14. Member: CNAA Bd for Art and Design, 1981–94; Bd, PCFC, 1989–92; CNAA Review Gp of Graphic Design Studies in Polys and Colls, 1990; CNAA and BTEC Jt Review Gp, 1990–92; Hong Kong Council for Acad. Accreditation, 1991–; AHRB Postgrad. Panel for Visual Arts, 1998–2000; Bd of Dirs, SE Arts Bd, Arts Council for England, 1998–2000; RSE and British Acad. Jt Review Gp, 1999–2000; Council for Higher Educn in Art and Design Res. Strategy Gp, 1999–2001; Exec. Cttee, UK Council for Grad. Educn, 2001–04; Exec. Cttee, UK Arts and Humanities Data Service, 2001–07; Steering Cttee, AHRB ICT in Arts and Humanities Res. Prog., 2003–08; HEFCE Cttee for allocation of Res. Capability Funding, 2003, 2005; AHRB Selection Cttees for Peer Review Coll., and for Res. Proposals to ICT Methods Network, 2004; Council, UK Higher Educn Acad., 2004–08 (Mem., Res. Strategy Cttee, 2004–07; Mem., Res. Informed Teaching Gp, 2004–07); Jt Inf. Systems Cttee Selection Cttee, Awareness and Training Prog., Arts and Humanities Researchers in UK, 2004; AHRC/HEFCE Res. Metrics Working Gp for RAE, 2006, 2008; QAA Gp for Qualifs Benchmarks for Masters degrees in UK univs, 2007; Qatar Nat. Res. Fund and Undergrad. Res. Experience Prog., 2007–; Steering Cttee, Handbook for Res. in the Arts, Riksbankens Jubileumsfond, Sweden, 2009–; Internat. Panel of Experts, Review of Nat. Provision in Arts and Culture Higher Educn, Portuguese Min. of Sci., Technol. and Higher Educn, 2009; HEFCE Expert Adv. Gp for the Res. Excellence Framework, 2009–; Adv. Bd, AHRC, 2009–; Scientific Cttee for Humanities, Science Europe, 2014–. Specialist Advr, NZ Quals Authy, 1998. Chairman: Res. Grants Panel, Portuguese Foundn for Sci. and Technol., 2010–; Selection Cttee, UK Nat. Teaching Fellowship Scheme (Projects), 2010–12. Mem., Bd of Dirs, Brighton Photographic Biennale, 2001–04. Member, Board of Trustees: Ditchling Mus., 2006–12; Edward Johnston Foundn, 2006–09; Crafts Council, 2014–. FRSA 1973. Hon. FRCA 2004; Hon. Fellow, Kent Inst. of Art & Design, 2005. Sanderson Award and Herbert Read Award, RCA, 1978. Ed., Design Issues, 2006–. *Publications:* Brown's Index to Photocomposition Typography, 1983; Graphic Memory, 2000. *Recreations:* music, travel, food, wine. *Address:* Faculty of Arts and Architecture, University of Brighton, Grand Parade, Brighton, East Sussex BN2 2JY. *E:* b.brown@brighton.ac.uk. *Clubs:* Savile, Chelsea Arts, Double Crown, Wynkyn de Worde Society.

BROWN, Bruce Macdonald, QSO 1998; Life Member, New Zealand Institute of International Affairs, since 2009 (Director, 1993–97; Chairman, Research Committee, 1993–2004; National Vice-President, 2004–09); *b* 24 Jan. 1930; *s* of John Albert Brown and Caroline Dorothea Brown (*née* Jorgensen); *m* 1st, 1953, Edith Irene (*née* Raynor) (*d* 1989); two *s* one *d*; 2nd, 1990, Françoise Rousseau (*d* 1995); 3rd, 2006, Josephine Stening. *Educ:* Victoria University of Wellington (MA Hons). Private Secretary to Prime Minister, 1957–59; Second Sec., Kuala Lumpur, 1960–62; First Sec. (later Counsellor and Dep. Perm. Rep.), New Zealand Mission to UN, New York, 1963–67; Head of Administration, Min. of Foreign Affairs, Wellington, 1967–68; Director, NZ Inst. of International Affairs, 1969–71; NZ Dep. High Commissioner, Canberra, 1972–75; Ambassador to Iran, 1975–78, and Pakistan, 1976–78; Asst Sec., Min. of Foreign Affairs, 1978–81; Dep. High Comr in London, 1981–85; Ambassador to Thailand, Vietnam and Laos, 1985–88, to Burma, 1986–88; High Comr to Canada, also accredited to Barbados, Guyana, Jamaica and Trinidad and Tobago, 1988–92. Sen. Fellow, Centre for Strategic Studies, Victoria University of Wellington, 2003–. *Publications:* The Rise of New Zealand Labour, 1962; (ed) Asia and the Pacific in the 1970s, 1971; (ed) New Zealand in World Affairs, Vol. III, 1972–1990, 1999. *Recreation:* reading.

BROWN, Bruce Neil C.; *see* Carnegie-Brown.

BROWN, Catherine; Chief Executive, Food Standards Agency, since 2012; *b* Oxford, 3 Jan. 1967; *d* of David and Juliet Brown; civil partnership 2006, Lesley Meagher. *Educ:* St Paul's Girls' Sch.; New Hall, Cambridge (BA Hons English 1988). Commercial trainee and manager, Unilever, 1989–94; Dir of Finance, then Dep. Chief Exec., Newham Community NHS Trust, 1994–97; Hosp. Manager and Regl Manager, BUPA Hosps, 1997–2001; Man. Dir, BUPA Wellness, 2001–06; Dir of Change and Prog. Mgt, BUPA Membership, 2006–07; Chief Operating Officer, 2007–08, Chief Exec., 2008–11, Animal Health and Vet. Labs Agency, DEFRA. *Recreations:* gardening, cowardly horse riding. *Address:* Food Standards Agency, Aviation House, 125 Kingsway, WC2B 6NH. *T:* (020) 7276 8200. *E:* chiefexecutive@foodstandards.gsi.gov.uk.

BROWN, Cedric Harold, FREng, FIGEM, FICE; consultant; Chairman, CB Consultants, since 1996; *b* 7 March 1935; *s* of late William Herbert Brown and Constance Dorothy Brown (*née* Frances); *m* 1956, Joan Hendry; one *s* two *d* (and one *d* decd). *Educ:* Sheffield, Rotherham and Derby Colleges of Technology. Pupil Gas Distribution Engineer, E Midlands Gas Bd, 1953–58, Tech. Asst, 1958–59; Engineering Asst, Tunbridge Wells Borough Council, 1959–60; engineering posts, E Midlands Gas Bd, 1960–75 (Chief Engineer, 1973–75); Dir of Engineering, E Midlands Gas, 1975–78; British Gas Corp., subseq. British Gas plc: Asst Dir (Ops) and Dir (Construction), 1978–79; Dir, Morecambe Bay Project, 1980–87; Regl Chm., British Gas W Midlands, 1987–89; Dir, Man. Dir, Exploration and Production, 1989; Man. Dir, Regl Services, 1989–91; Sen. Man. Dir, 1991–92; Chief Exec., 1992–96. Chairman: Business Champions-E Midlands Develt Agency, 2001–04; Lachesis Investment Adv. Cttee, 2002–07. Pres., IGasE, 1996–97. FREng (FEng 1990). Liveryman, Engineers' Co., 1988–. *Publications:* tech. papers to professional bodies. *Recreations:* sport, countryside, places of historic interest.

BROWN, (Cedric Wilfred) George E.; *see* Edmonds-Brown.

BROWN, Charles Dargie, FREng; consulting engineer, retired; Joint Chairman, Mott, Hay & Anderson, later Mott MacDonald, Consulting Engineers, 1980–89; *b* 13 April 1927; *s* of William Henry Brown and Jean Dargie; *m* 1952, Sylvia Margaret Vallis; one *s* one *d*. *Educ:* Harris Acad., Dundee; St Andrews Univ. (BScEng, 1st Cl. Hons.). FICE; FREng (FEng 1981). Joined staff of Mott, Hay & Anderson, 1947; engaged on highways, tunnels and bridge works, incl. Tamar Bridge, Forth Road Bridge, George Street Bridge, Newport, Kingsferry and Queensferry Bridges, 1947–65; Partner and Director, 1965. Principally concerned with planning, design and supervision of major works, 1965–89, incl. Mersey Queensway tunnels and new London Bridge, and projects in Hong Kong (Tsing Ma Bridge), Malaysia (Pahang River Bridges), highway and bridge works in Indonesia and USA; participated in develt of underground rly systems in Melbourne and Singapore. Member, Smeatonian Soc. of Civil Engrs, 1984–. Hon. LLD Dundee, 1982. *Publications:* papers to Instn of Civil Engrs, on Kingsferry Bridge, George St Bridge, London Bridge and Mersey tunnels; also various papers to engrg confs. *Recreations:* golf, gardening, bird watching, reading. *Address:* 31 Heathfield Road, Petersfield, Hants GU31 4DE. *T:* (01730) 267820. *Club:* Royal Automobile.

BROWN, Christina Hambley, (Lady Evans); *see* Brown, Tina.

BROWN, Christopher; Director and Chief Executive, National Society for Prevention of Cruelty to Children, 1989–95; *b* 21 June 1938; *s* of Reginald Frank Greenwood Brown and Margaret Eleanor Brown; *m* 1968, Helen Margaret, *d* of George A. Woolsey and Hilda M. Woolsey; three *s* one *d*. *Educ:* Hertford Grammar Sch.; King's Coll., London (AKC); Heythrop Coll., London (MA 2005). Home Office Cert. in Probation. Ordained deacon, 1963, priest, 1964; Assistant Curate, Diocese of Southwark: St Hilda's, Crofton Park, 1963; St Michael's, Wallington, 1964–67. Probation Officer, Nottingham, 1968–72; Sen. Probation Officer, W Midlands, 1972–74; Asst Dir, Social Services, Solihull, 1974–76; Asst Chief Probation Officer, Hereford and Worcester, 1976–79; Chief Probation Officer: Oxfordshire, 1979–86; Essex, 1986–89. Member: Parole Bd, 1985–87; Trng Cttee, Inst. for Study and Treatment of Delinquency, 1986–89; Professional Adv. Cttee, NSPCC, 1986–89; Chm., Social Issues Cttee, Assoc. of Chief Officers of Probation, 1985–87; Sec. and Founding Trustee, Friends of the Poor in S India, 2008–. Mem., Green Coll., Oxford, 1981–86. Licensed to officiate, Dio. Chelmsford, 1986–. *Publications:* contribs to various jls on social work practice and community issues, 1971–, to Christian/Islamic studies and dialogues, 2005–, and on Christian/Muslim relations, 2008–. *Recreations:* walking, reading, music, conversation, gardening. *Address:* 7 Baronia Croft, Colchester, Essex CO4 9EE. *E:* chribrow@yahoo.co.uk.

BROWN, Lt Gen. Christopher Charles, CBE 1999; Chief Operating Officer, Equilibrium Gulf Ltd, 2014–15; *b* 26 Oct. 1955; *s* of Philip Alexander George Brown and Gladys Maud Brown; *m* 1983, Leigh Margaret Kennedy; two *s*. *Educ:* University Coll. Cardiff (LLB 1977); Peterhouse, Cambridge (MPhil 2007). Battery Comdr, Chestnut Troop, RHA, 1990–91; UN Mil. Observer, Western Sahara, 1991–92; Directing Staff, Staff Coll., 1992–94; CO, 7th Parachute Regt, RHA, 1994–96; ACOS Plans, HQ ARRC, 1996–99; Comdr RA, 1st Armd Div., 1999–2002; Dep. Sen. British Mil. Advr, US Central Comd, 2002; ADC to the Queen, 2002–03; Director: RA, 2002–03; Mil. Ops, MoD, 2003; COS, Allied Comd Europe RRC, 2004–06; COS, NATO Internat. Security and Assistance Force, Afghanistan, 2006–07; GOC NI, 2007–09; Dep. Comdg Gen. Multi Nat. Force Iraq and Sen. British Mil. Rep. (Iraq), 2009; Iraq Compendium Study Team Leader, 2009–10; Sen. Security Advr, Assessment and Evaluation Commn and African Union High-Level Implementation Panel for Sudan, 2011. Dir, Bellerophon Consulting Ltd, 2014–. QCVS 2007. *Recreations:* cross-country ski-ing (Bd Mem., British Biathlon Union, 2006–09), orienteering, mountaineering, fishing, sailing (Cdre, British Kiel Yacht Club, 2004–06). *Clubs:* Royal Artillery Yacht, Royal Lymington Yacht.

BROWN, Christopher David, MA; Headmaster, Norwich School, 1984–2002; *b* 8 July 1944; *s* of E. K. Brown; *m* 1972, Caroline Dunkerley; two *d*. *Educ:* Plymouth College; Fitzwilliam College, Cambridge (MA). Assistant Master: The Leys School, Cambridge, 1967–71; Pangbourne College, 1971–73; Radley College, 1973–84 (Head of English, 1975–84). Chairman: Choir Schs Assoc., 1997–99; HMC, 2001; Dep. Chm., ISC, 2003–06.

BROWN, Christopher Ledwith, OBE 2004; FRGS; Country Director, Vietnam, British Council, 2013–14; *b* 15 March 1953; *s* of Peter and Joanna Brown; *m* 1977, Elizabeth Varrall; one *s* two *d*. *Educ:* Leicester Univ. (BSc Geol.). Served RN, 1974–79; with British Council, 1979–2014: posts in Nigeria, Nepal, Spain and UK, 1979–95; Dir, Peru, 1995–99; Regl Dir, Western and Southern Europe, 1999–2003; Dir, Turkey, 2003–08; Dir Progs, Sub-Saharan Africa, 2008–13. FRGS 1978. *Recreations:* bricklaying, herding penguins.

BROWN, Prof. Christopher Paul Hadley, CBE 2011; PhD; Director, Ashmolean Museum, 1998–2014, now Emeritus; Senior Research Fellow, Worcester College, Oxford, since 2014 (Fellow, 1998–2014); Professor of Netherlandish Art, University of Oxford, since 2013; *b* 15 April 1948; *s* of late Arthur Edgar Brown and of Florence Marjorie Brown; *m* 1975, Sally Madeleine Stockton; one *s* one *d*. *Educ:* Merchant Taylors' Sch.; St Catherine's Coll., Oxford (BA Hons Modern History, Dip. History of Art; Hon. Fellow, 2010); Courtauld Inst. of Art, Univ. of London (PhD). National Gallery: Asst Keeper, 1971, with responsibility for Dutch and Flemish 17th cent. paintings; Dep. Keeper, 1979; Keeper, then Chief Curator, 1989–98. Trustee, Dulwich Picture Gall., 1993–2001. Visiting Professor: Univ. of St Andrews, 1996–2008; Centre for Golden Age Studies, Univ. of Amsterdam, 2002. Lectures: Ferens Fine Art, Univ. of Hull, 1980; Cargill, Univ. of Glasgow, 1987; Jasper Walls, Pierpont Morgan Library, NY, 1991; Visual Arts, QUB, 1999; Allard Pierson, Univ. of Amsterdam, 2010; Alex Gordon, Frick Mus., NY, 2011. Fellow, Netherlands Inst. for Advanced Study, Wassenaar, 1993–94. Member: Consultative Cttee, Burlington Mag., 1994–; Cttee of Mgt, Royal Mus. of Fine Arts, Antwerp, 1997–2009; Trustee, Barber Inst. of Fine Arts, Univ. of Birmingham, 2010–. Hon. DLitt: Birmingham, 2012; St Andrews, 2013. *Publications:* Carel Fabritius, 1981; Van Dyck, 1982; Scenes of Everyday Life: seventeenth-century Dutch genre painting, 1984; Dutch Landscape (catalogue), 1986; The Drawings of Anthony van Dyck, 1991; (jtly) Rembrandt: the master and his workshop (catalogue), 1991; Making and Meaning: Rubens's landscapes, 1996; (jtly) Van Dyck 1599–1641, 1999; National Gallery catalogues, incl. The Dutch School 1600–1900, 1990; The Ashmolean: Britain's First Museum, 2009; contribs to art magazines, UK and overseas. *Address:* Ashmolean Museum, Oxford OX1 2PH. *E:* christopher.brown@ashmus.ox.ac.uk.

BROWN, Colin James; Principal, Experiential Consultancy Ltd, since 2011; General Manager, Lucasfilm Singapore, since 2014; *b* 27 Nov. 1950; *s* of Gordon and Jeanne Brown; *m* 1st, 1972, Marie-Laure Delvaux (marr. diss. 1984); one *d*; 2nd, 1985, Bendicte Marie Granier; two *s*. *Educ:* George Watson's Boys' Coll., Edinburgh; RMA, Sandhurst; Reading Univ. (BA Hons Hist.). Served RWF, 1971–80 (Captain). Alexander Proudfoot, Paris, 1980–81; Rank Xerox, 1981–82; Bell and Howell, 1982–84; Rank Cintel Ltd, 1984–86; Exec. Vice Pres., Rank Cintel Inc., 1986–89; Man. Dir, Molinare, 1989–92; Divl Man. Dir, Eur. Television Networks, 1992–94; Man. Dir, Cinesite Europe Ltd, 1994–2000; CEO, Cinesite Worldwide, 2000–07; British Film Comr, 2007–11. Member: Bd, UK Film Council, 2003–07; Bd, Nat. Film and TV Sch., 2005–; BAFTA 1993. *Recreations:* travelling, sailing, gastronomy. *Address:* 27 Ennismore Avenue, W4 1SE. *T:* (020) 7861 7905. *E:* cjbexperiential@gmail.com, cobrown@lucasfilm.com, colinxyzbrown@gmail.com. *Club:* Soho House.

BROWN, Craig; *see* Brown, J. C.

BROWN, Craig Edward Moncrieff; freelance writer, since 1977; *b* 23 May 1957; *s* of Peter Brown and Jennifer (*née* Bethell); *m* 1987, Frances Welch; one *s* one *d*. *Educ:* Farleigh House; Eton Coll.; Bristol Univ. Drama Dept. Columnist on: Sunday Telegraph, Daily Telegraph, Daily Mail, Private Eye, Independent on Sunday, Guardian (as Wallace Arnold, and Bel Littlejohn); specializing in parody and satire. What the Papers Say Gen. Pleasure Award, 1996. *Publications:* The Marsh-Marlow Letters, 1984; A Year Inside, 1989; The Agreeable World of Wallace Arnold, 1990; Rear Columns, 1992; Welcome to My Worlds!, 1993; Craig Brown's Greatest Hits, 1993; The Hounding of John Thomas, 1994; The Private Eye Book of Craig Brown Parodies, 1995; (ed jtly) Colin Welch, The Odd Thing About the Colonel and Other Pieces, 1997; Hug Me While I Weep (For I Weep For the World): the lonely struggles of Bel Littlejohn, 1998; This is Craig Brown, 2003; Craig Brown's Imaginary Friends, 2005; 1966 and All That, 2005; The Tony Years, 2006; The Lost Diaries, 2010; One on One, 2012. *Recreations:* swimming in the sea, drinking, shopping. *Address:* c/o Private Eye, 6 Carlisle Street, W1D 3BN.

BROWN, Damian Robert; QC 2012; *b* Birkenhead, 30 Jan. 1966; *s* of Terrence and Elizabeth Brown. *Educ:* St Anselm's Coll., Birkenhead; Queen Mary Coll., Univ. of London (BA Law and Politics); Inns of Court Sch. of Law. Called to the Bar, Inner Temple, 1989; in practice as barrister, 1989–, specialising in employment, commercial and sports law and professional regulation and discipline. Lectr (pt-time) in Internat. Labour Law, KCL, 1995–98. Mem., Professional Conduct Cttee, Bar Standards Bd, 2006–11; Chm., Employment Law Bar Assoc., 2011–. *Publications:* contributor: Blackstone's Employment Law Practice, 2012–; Tolley's Employment Law, 2012–; Employment Precedents and Company Policy Documents, 2012–; Terminations of Employment, 2012–. *Recreations:* sport, cooking. *Address:* Littleton Chambers, 3 King's Bench Walk North, EC4Y 7HR. *T:* (020) 7797 8600. *E:* damianbrown@littletonchambers.co.uk. *Clubs:* Milk and Honey; Arsenal Football.

BROWN, David Allen; Chief Executive, Go-Ahead Group, since 2011; *b* Northolt, Middx, 31 Dec. 1960; *s* of Alan and Pamela Brown; *m* 1990, Gretchen Fisher; one *s* one *d. Educ:* Greenford High Sch.; Reading Univ. (BA Hons Geog.); Univ. of London (Dip. Transport). Various posts, then District Manager, London Transport and London Buses Ltd, 1983–88; Gen. Manager, CentreWest, Mgt Employee Buyout, 1988–96; Man. Dir, Berks Bucks Bus Co., 1996–98; London General and London Central: Ops Dir, 1998–99; Man. Dir, 1999–2003; Chief Exec., 2003–06; Main Bd Advr, Go-Ahead Gp, 2003–06; Man. Dir, Surface Transport, TfL, 2006–11. MCILT 1985, FCILT 2009; FCIHT 2009. *Recreations:* trekking, squash, football, family. *Address:* Go-Ahead Group, 1st Floor, 4 Matthew Parker Street, SW1E 9NP. *E:* david.brown@go-ahead.com.

BROWN, Prof. David Anthony, PhD; FRS 1990; FRSB; Research Professor, Department of Neuroscience, Physiology and Pharmacology (formerly Department of Pharmacology), University College London, since 2005; *b* 10 Feb. 1936; *s* of Alfred William and Florence Brown; *m* Susan Hames; two *s* one *d. Educ:* Univ. of London (BSc, BSc, PhD). FRSB (FInstBiol) 1980. University of London: Asst Lectr 1961–65, Lectr 1965–73, Dept of Pharmacology, St Bart's Hosp. Med. Coll.; Dept of Pharmacology, School of Pharmacy: Sen. Lectr, 1973–74; Reader, 1974–77; Professor, 1977–79; Wellcome Professor, 1979–87; Prof. of Pharmacol., Middx Hosp. Med. Sch., then University Coll. and Middx Sch. of Medicine, UCL, 1987–2005 (Hd, Dept of Pharmacol., 1987–2002). Visiting Professor: Univ. of Chicago, 1970; Univ. of Iowa, 1971, 1973; Univ. of Texas, 1979, 1980, 1981; Univ. of Kanazawa, 1987, 1990; Vis. Scientist, Armed Forces Radiobiology Res. Inst., Bethesda, Md, 1976; Fogarty Schol.-in-Residence, NIH, Bethesda, 1985–86. Member: Physiological Soc., 1970–2004 (Hon. Mem., 2004); British Pharmacological Soc., 1965– (Hon. Fellow 2005); Biochemical Soc., 1969–; Academia Europaea, 1990. Dist. Hon. Dr Kanazawa, 1993. *Publications:* contribs to Jl of Physiology, British Jl of Pharmacology, etc. *Recreation:* filling in forms. *Address:* Department of Neuroscience, Physiology and Pharmacology, University College London, Gower Street, WC1E 6BT. *E:* d.a.brown@ucl.ac.uk.

BROWN, Dr David John, CPhys, CSci, CEng, FInstP, FIChemE, FRSC; Chief Executive, Institution of Chemical Engineers, since 2006; *b* 10 March 1956; *s* of Colin and Patricia Brown; *m* 1985, Vivienne Burges; two *s* one *d. Educ:* Aylesbury Grammar Sch.; Queens' Coll., Cambridge (BA Natural Scis 1978; PhD 1982). CPhys 2001; FInstP 2001; CSci 2004; FIChemE 2011; CEng 2011; FRSC 2013. Various posts, ICI PLC, 1983–93; Dir, Warwick Res. Inst., Univ. of Warwick, 1992–97; Arthur D. Little Ltd, 1997–2006 (Dir and Hd, Technol. and Innovation, 2002–06). Dir, Chemistry Innovation Ltd, 2007–. Mem. Bd, W Midlands in Europe, 2006–11 (Chm., 2008–11); Member: Bd, Advantage W Midlands, 2006–12 (Dep. Chm., 2009–12); Bd, Central Technol. Belt, 2006–11; W Midlands Innovation and Technol. Council, 2006–11; Bd, Birmingham Sci. City, 2007–; Bd, Science Council, 2008–12; Bd, EngineeringUK, 2009–12. MInstKT 2009. Non-exec. Dir, Coventry Refugee Centre, 2007–13. Trustee, St Christopher's Fellowship, 2013–. *Publications:* various, on scientific and mgt subjects. *Recreations:* cooking, Church activities, walking. *Address:* Institution of Chemical Engineers, One Portland Place, W1B 1PN. *E:* dbrown@icheme.org; Institution of Chemical Engineers, Davis Building, Railway Terrace, Rugby CV21 3HQ. *T:* (01788) 534411, *Fax:* (01788) 550904.

BROWN, Sir David (Martin), Kt 2001; FREng; Chairman, British Standards Institution, since 2012 (non-executive Director, 2010–12); *b* 14 May 1950; *s* of Alan Brown and Laura Marjorie Brown (*née* Richardson); *m* 1975, Denise Frances Bowers; two *s. Educ:* Portsmouth Poly. (BSc Electrical Engrg). CEng 1980; FIET (FIEE 1985; Hon. FIET 2008); FREng 1999. With Standard Telephones and Cables, 1979–91; joined Motorola, 1991: Director: UK Ops, Cellular Infrastructure, 1991–93; GSM Product Mgt, 1993–95; Sen. Dir, Radio Access, 1995–97; Chm., Motorola Ltd, 1997–2008. Non-executive Director: P&OSN Co., 2002–06; Domino Printing Scis plc, 2008–; TTG Global Gp (formerly Siatel Hldgs Ltd), 2010–; Sen. Ind. Dir, Ceres Power Hldgs plc, 2008–12; Chm., DRS Data & Res. Services plc, 2009– (Dep. Chm., 2008–09). Mem., Industrial Develt Adv. Bd, 1998–2004; Vice Chm., UK Trade and Investment, 2000–04. President: ASE, 1998; Fedn of Electronics Industry, 1999–2000; IEE, 2003–04 (Mem. Council, 1986–90, 1997–2001; Dep. Pres., 2001–03); CQI, 2007–08 (Hon. FCQI 2007). Chairman: Qualifications Cttee, QCA, 1997–2003; Ofcom Spectrum Adv. Bd, 2004–10; Ofcom Spectrum Clearance Finance Cttee, 2009–14. Mem. Council, 2008–11, Mem. Court, 2011–, Cranfield Univ. Vis. Fellow, Kellogg College, Oxford, 2007–. Fellow, St George's House, Windsor Castle, 2008–. CCMI (MBIM 1976). DUniv Surrey, 2004; Hon. DEng Bath, 2004; Hon. DSc Portsmouth, 2005; Hon. DTech Kingston, 2006. Mountbatten Medal, IEE, 2005. *Recreations:* literature, art, theatre. *Address:* Bridleway Cottage, Stanmore, Newbury, Berks RG20 8SR. *Club:* Athenæum.

BROWN, David Rodney H.; *see* Heath-Brown.

BROWN, Rev. Prof. David William, DLitt; FBA 2002; FRSE; Wardlaw Professor of Theology, Aesthetics and Culture, University of St Andrews, 2007–15, now Emeritus; *b* 1 July 1948; *s* of David William Brown and Catherine Smith. *Educ:* Keil Sch., Dumbarton; Edinburgh Univ. (MA 1st cl. Classics 1970; DLitt 2012); Oriel Coll., Oxford (BA 1st cl. Phil. and Theol. 1972); Clare Coll., Cambridge (PhD 1976); Westcott House, Cambridge. Fellow, Chaplain and Tutor in Theol. and Phil., Oriel Coll., Oxford and Univ. Lectr in Theol., 1976–90; Van Mildert Prof. of Divinity, Univ. of Durham and Canon of Durham Cathedral, 1990–2007. Vice-Chm., Doctrine Commn of C of E, 1990–95. FRSE 2012. *Publications:* Choices: ethics and the Christian, 1983; The Divine Trinity, 1985; Continental Philosophy and Modern Theology, 1987; Invitation to Theology, 1989; (ed) Newman: a man for our time, 1990; The Word To Set You Free, 1995; (ed jtly) The Sense of the Sacramental, 1995; (with D. Fuller) Signs of Grace, 1995; (ed jtly) Christ: the Sacramental Word, 1996; Tradition and Imagination: revelation and change, 1999; Discipleship and Imagination: Christian tradition and truth, 2000; God and Enchantment of Place, 2004; Through the Eyes of the Saints, 2005; God and Grace of Body, 2007; God and Mystery in Words, 2008; La tradition kénotique dans la théologie britannique, 2010; Divine Humanity: Kenosis explored and defended, 2011; (contrib.) Theology, Aesthetics, & Culture: responses to the work of David Brown, 2012; (ed) Durham Cathedral: history, fabric and culture, 2014. *Recreations:* dog and cat, art, listening to music. *Address:* Mansfield, 1A Grey Street, Tayport, Fife DD6 9JF. *T:* (01382) 550063; School of Divinity, St Mary's College, St Andrews, Fife KY16 9JU. *T:* (01334) 462850.

BROWN, Hon. Dean Craig, AO 2008; company director, since 2006; Chairman, Hillgrove Resources Ltd, since 2006; *b* Adelaide, 5 Aug. 1943; *m* 1979, Rosslyn Judith Wadey; one *s* one *d. Educ:* Unley High Sch.; Univ. of New England, NSW (BRurSc, MRurSc); Australian Admin. Staff Coll.; S Australian Inst. of Technol. (Fellowship Dip. in Business Admin). Parliament of South Australia: MP (L) Davenport, 1973–85; Shadow Minister for Industrial Affairs, 1975–79; Minister for Industrial Affairs and for Public Works, 1979–82; Shadow Minister, 1982–85, for: Public Works; Transport; Technology; agricl consultant, 1986–92; MP (L) Alexandra, 1992–93, Finniss, 1993–2006; Leader of Opposition, 1992–93; Shadow Minister for Multicultural and Ethnic Affairs, 1992–93; Premier of SA, and Minister for Multicultural and Ethnic Affairs, 1993–96; Minister: for IT, 1995–96; for Industrial Affairs, Aboriginal Affairs, and Inf. and Contract Services, 1996–97; for Human Services, 1997–2002; Dep. Premier of SA, 2001–02; Dep. Leader of the Opposition, 2002–05. Dir, Scantech Ltd, 2007–; Chm., InterMet Resources Ltd, 2008–13. Community Liaison Manager for River Murray, SA Govt, 2006–11; Premier's Special Advr on Drought, SA, 2007–11. A Dir of state and federal govt bds, company bds and community bds; Director: Foodbank SA, 2007–; Mission Australia Bd, 2012–. Chm., Playford Meml Trust, SA Govt, 2011–. Participant, Duke of Edinburgh Commonwealth Industrial Study Conf., 1980. Hon. DSc New England. Centenary Medal (Australia), 2001. *Publications:* contribs to political, technical and scientific jls. *Recreations:* walking, fishing, gardening. *Address:* 11 Leonard Terrace, Torrens Park, SA 5062, Australia.

BROWN, Sir Derrick H.; *see* Holden-Brown.

BROWN, Douglas Allan; Sheriff of South Strathclyde, Dumfries and Galloway at Hamilton, since 2008; *b* 18 June 1951; *s* of Thomas T. Brown and Thelma R. Cheney or Brown; *m* 1978, Elaine Ann Currie; one *s* one *d. Educ:* Glasgow Univ. (LLB Hons). Procurator Fiscal Depute, Dumbarton and Glasgow, 1977–87; Sen. Procurator Fiscal Depute, Edinburgh, 1987–91; Asst Solicitor, Crown Office, 1991–94; Procurator Fiscal, Ayr, 1994–96; Sen. Asst Procurator Fiscal, Glasgow, 1996–99; Regl Procurator Fiscal, S Strathclyde, Dumfries and Galloway, 1999–2002; Area Procurator Fiscal, Lothian and Borders, 2002–04; all-Scotland floating Sheriff, 2004–08. *Recreations:* music, tennis, swimming, gardening. *Address:* Hamilton Sheriff Court, Beckford Street, Hamilton ML3 0BT. *T:* (01698) 282957, *Fax:* (01698) 284403. *E:* sheriffdbrown@scotcourts.gov.uk.

BROWN, Hon. Sir Douglas (Dunlop), Kt 1989; a Judge of the High Court of Justice, Queen's Bench Division, 1996–2005 (Family Division, 1989–96); Judge of Employment Appeal Tribunal, 2001–05; *b* 22 Dec. 1931; *s* of late Robert Dunlop Brown, MICE, and Anne Cameron Brown; *m* 1960, June Margaret Elizabeth McNamara; one *s. Educ:* Ryleys Sch., Alderley Edge; Manchester Grammar Sch.; Manchester Univ. (LLB). Served in RN, 1953–55; Lieut, RNR. Called to Bar, Gray's Inn, 1953; Bencher, 1989; practised Northern Circuit from 1955; Mem. General Council of Bar, 1967–71; Asst Recorder, Salford City QS, 1971; a Recorder of the Crown Court, 1972–80; QC 1976; a Circuit Judge, 1980–88; Family Div. Liaison Judge, Northern Circuit, 1990–95; Presiding Judge, Northern Circuit, 1998–2001. Mem., Parole Bd for England and Wales, 1985–87. *Recreations:* cricket, golf, music. *Address:* c/o Royal Courts of Justice, Strand, WC2A 2LL. *Club:* Wilmslow Golf.

BROWN, Edmund Gerald, Jr, (Jerry Brown); lawyer, writer and politician; Governor of California, since 2011; *b* 7 April 1938; *s* of late Edmund Gerald Brown and of Bernice (*née* Layne); *m* 2005, Anne Gust. *Educ:* Univ. of California at Berkeley (BA 1961); Yale Law School (JD 1964). Admitted to California Bar, 1965; Research Attorney, Calif. Supreme Court, 1964–65; with Tuttle & Taylor, LA, 1966–69; Sec. of State, Calif, 1970–74; Gov. of California, 1975–83; Attorney with Fulbright Jaworski, 1986–91. Democratic Candidate for US Senator from California, 1982; Chm., California Democratic Party, 1989–91; Candidate for Democratic Presidential Nomination, 1992; Mayor of Oakland, Calif, 1999–2006; Attorney Gen. of Calif, 2006–11. Founder and Chm., We the People Legal Foundn, 1992. Trustee, Los Angeles Community Colls, 1969–70. *Address:* State Capitol, Sacramento, CA 95814, USA.

BROWN, Edmund Walter F.; *see* Fitton-Brown.

BROWN, Edward Francis Trevenen; QC 2008; Senior Treasury Counsel, Central Criminal Court, since 2006; a Recorder, since 2000; *b* 17 Jan. 1958; *s* of late Francis Brown, CMG and Ruth Brown; *m* 1989, Victoria Bell; one *s* two *d. Educ:* Eton Coll.; University Coll. at Buckingham (LLB). Caelt Gall., London, 1978–80; Pres., Weighouse Gall., LA, 1979–80. Called to the Bar, Gray's Inn, 1983; Jun. Treasury Counsel, 2001–06. Mem., UN Detention Commn, Kosovo, 2001. *Recreations:* paintings, architecture. *Address:* QEB Hollis Whiteman, 1–2 Laurence Pountney Hill, EC4R 0EU. *T:* (020) 7933 8855, *Fax:* (020) 7929 3732. *E:* edward.brown@qebholliswhiteman.co.uk.

BROWN, Prof. Edwin Thomas, AC 2001; PhD, DSc Eng; FREng; FTSE; FIMMM; Senior Consultant, Golder Associates Pty Ltd, since 2001; Director, Port of Brisbane Corporation, 2005–11; Senior Deputy Vice-Chancellor, University of Queensland, Australia, 1996–2001 (Deputy Vice-Chancellor, 1990–96; Dean of Engineering, 1987–90); *b* 4 Dec. 1938; *s* of George O. and Bessie M. Brown. *Educ:* Castlemaine High Sch.; Univ. of Melbourne (BE 1960, MEngSc 1964); Univ. of Queensland (PhD 1969); Univ. of London (DSc Eng 1985). MICE 1976; MASCE 1965; FIMMM (FIMM 1980); MIEAust 1965, FIEAust 1987, Hon. FIEAust 2014; FTSE (FTS 1990). Engr, State Electricity Commn of Victoria, 1960–64; James Cook Univ. of North Queensland (formerly UC of Townsville): Lectr, 1965–69; Sen. Lectr, 1969–72; Associate Prof. of Civil Engrg, 1972–75; Imperial College, Univ. of London: Reader in Rock Mechanics, 1975–79; Prof. of Rock Mechanics, 1979–87; Dean, RSM, 1983–86; Hd, Dept of Mineral Resources Engrg, 1985–87. Res. Associate, Dept of Civil and Mineral Engrg, Univ. of Minnesota, 1970; Sen. Visitor, Dept of Engrg, Univ. of Cambridge, 1974; Vis. Prof., Dept of Mining and Fuels Engrg, Univ. of Utah, 1979. Dir, Queensland Rail, 2001–05. Editor-in-Chief, Internat. Jl of Rock Mechanics and Mining Sciences, 1975–82. Chm., British Geotechnical Soc., 1982–83; Pres., Internat. Soc. for Rock Mechanics, 1983–87; Mem. Council, AATSE, 1997–98 and 2002–03. Foreign Mem., Royal Acad. (formerly Fellowship) of Engrg, 1989. Instn of Mining and Metallurgy: Consolidated Gold Fields Gold Medal, 1984; Sir Julius Wernher Meml Lecture, 1985; John Jaeger Meml Award, Aust. Geomechanics Soc., 2004; Müller Award, Internat. Soc. for Rock Mechanics, 2007; Rock Mechanics Award, Soc. for Exploration, Mining and Metallurgy, 2010; Douglas Hay Medal, IMMM, 2013. *Publications:* (with E. Hoek) Underground Excavations in Rock, 1980; (ed) Rock Characterization, Testing and Monitoring, 1981; (with B. H. G. Brady) Rock Mechanics for Underground Mining, 1985, 3rd edn 2004; (ed) Analytical and Computational Methods in Engineering Rock Mechanics, 1987; Block Caving Geomechanics, 2003, 2nd edn 2007; papers on rock mechanics in civil engrg and mining jls. *Recreations:* cricket, jazz. *Address:* 5121 Bridgewater Crest, 55 Baildon Street, Kangaroo Point, Qld 4169, Australia. *T:* (7) 38919833. *Club:* Queensland (Brisbane).

BROWN, Elizabeth, (Mrs Ray Brown); *see* Vaughan, E.

BROWN, Prof. Eric Herbert, PhD; Professor of Geography, University College London, 1966–88, Honorary Research Fellow, since 1988; *b* 8 Dec. 1922; *s* of Samuel Brown and Ada Brown, Melton Mowbray, Leics; *m* 1945, Eileen (*née* Reynolds) (*d* 1984), Llanhowell, Dyfed; two *d. Educ:* King Edward VII Grammar Sch., Melton Mowbray; King's Coll., London (BSc 1st Cl. Hons); MSc Wales, PhD London. Served War: RAF Pilot, Coastal Comd, 1941–45. Asst Lectr, then Lectr in Geography, University Coll. of Wales, Aberystwyth, 1947–49; University College London: Lectr, then Reader in Geog., 1950–66; Dean of Students, 1972–75; Alumnus Dir, 1989–91; Mem. Senate, Univ. of London, 1981–86. Vis. Lectr, Indiana Univ., USA, 1953–54; Vis. Prof., Monash Univ., Melbourne, 1971. Mem., NERC, 1981–84. Geographical Adviser, Govt of Argentina, 1965–66, 1992–94; Hon. Mem., Geograph. Soc. of Argentina, 1968. Chairman: British Geomorphol Res. Group, 1971–72; British Nat. Cttee for Geog., 1985–90. Royal Geographical Society: Back Grant, 1961; Hon. Sec., 1977–87; Vice-Pres., 1988–89, Hon. Vice-Pres., 1989; Hon. Fellow, 1989; Pres., Inst. of British Geographers, 1978. Foreign Mem., Polish Acad. of Scis and Letters, 1992. DUniv York, 2002. *Publications:* The Relief and Drainage of Wales, 1961; (with W. R. Mead) The USA and Canada, 1962; (ed) Geography Yesterday and Tomorrow, 1980; contrib. Geog. Jl, Phil. Trans Royal Soc., Proc. Geologists' Assoc., Trans Inst. of British Geographers, and Geography. *Recreations:* watching Rugby football, wine. *Address:* Monterey, 13 Castle Hill, Berkhamsted, Herts HP4 1HE. *T:* (01442) 864077. *Clubs:* Athenæum, Geographical.

BROWN, Captain Eric Melrose, CBE 1970 (OBE 1945; MBE 1944); DSC 1942; AFC 1947; QCVSA 1949; RN; Vice-President, European Helicopter Association, since 1992 (Chief Executive, 1980–92); *b* 21 Jan. 1919; *s* of Robert John Brown and Euphemia (*née*

Melrose); *m* 1942, Evelyn Jean Margaret Macrory (*d* 1998); one *s*. *Educ:* Royal High Sch., Edinburgh; Edinburgh University. MA 1947. Joined Fleet Air Arm as Pilot, 1939; Chief Naval Test Pilot, 1944–49 (RN Boyd Trophy, 1948); Resident British Test Pilot at USN Air Test Center, Patuxent River, 1951–52; CO No 804 Sqdn, 1953–54; Comdr (Air), RN Air Stn, Brawdy, 1954–56; Head of British Naval Air Mission to Germany, 1958–60; Dep. Dir (Air), Gunnery Div., Admty, 1961; Dep. Dir, Naval Air Warfare and Adviser on Aircraft Accidents, Admty, 1962–64; Naval Attaché, Bonn, 1965–67; CO, RN Air Stn, Lossiemouth, 1967–70. Chief Exec., British Helicopter Adv. Bd, 1970–87, Vice-Pres., 1988–. Chm., British Aviation Bicentenary Exec. Cttee, 1984. Hon. FRAeS 2004 (FRAeS 1964; Pres., 1982–83; Chm., RAeS Rotorcraft Sect., 1973–76). Hon. FEng (Pakistan) 1984; Hon. Fellow, Soc. of Experimental Test Pilots, 1984. Hon. PhD Edinburgh, 2007. Liveryman, Hon. Co. of Air Pilots (formerly GAPAN), 1978. British Silver Medal for Practical Achievement in Aeronautics, 1949; Anglo-French Breguet Trophy, 1983; Bronze Medal, Fédération Aéronautique Internationale, 1986; US Carrier Aviation Test Pilot Hall of Honor, 1995; Gold Medal, British Assoc. of Aviation Consultants, 1997; Award of Honour, GAPAN, 2006. *Publications:* Wings on My Sleeve, 1961, 4th edn 2006; (jtly) Aircraft Carriers, 1969, 2nd edn vol. 1, 2006, vol. 2, 2008; Wings of the Luftwaffe, 1977, 5th edn 2010; Wings of the Navy, 1980, 2nd edn 2013; The Helicopter in Civil Operations, 1981; Wings of the Weird and the Wonderful, vol. 1, 1982, vol. 2, 1985, 2nd edn 2010; Duels in the Sky, 1989; Testing for Combat, 1994; Miles M.52—Gateway to Supersonic Flight, 2012; Too Close for Comfort, 2015. *Recreations:* travel, history, bridge. *Address:* Carousel, Herons Close, Copthorne, W Sussex RH10 3HF. *T:* (01342) 712610. *Clubs:* Naval and Military, Royal Air Force, City Livery; Explorers (New York).

BROWN, Sir Ewan, Kt 2014; CBE 1996; FRSE; Chairman, Scottish Financial Enterprise, since 2012; *b* Perth, 23 March 1942; *s* of John Moir Brown and Isobel Brown; *m* 1966, Christine Lindsay; one *s* one *d*. *Educ:* Perth Acad.; Univ. of St Andrews (MA 1963; LLB 1964). CA 1967. Exec. Dir, Noble Grossart, 1971–2003. Non-executive Director: Pict Petroleum, 1973–95; Scottish Business Sch., 1974–80; Scottish Transport Gp, 1983–88; Scottish Develt Finance, 1983–93; Wood Gp, 1983–2006; Stagecoach Gp, 1988–; Scottish Widows Bank, 1994–97; Dunedin Income Growth Investment Trust, 1995–96 (Chm., 1996–2001); Lloyds TSB Gp, 1999–2009; Harrison Lovegrove, 2002–08; Noble Grossart Hldgs, 2003–; Entrepreneurial Scotland, 2014–; Chairman: Scottish Knowledge, 1996–2001; Lloyds TSB Scotland, 1998–2008; Transport Initiatives Edinburgh, 2002–06; Creative Scotland 2009, 2008–10; James Walker (Leith) Ltd, 2012–. Hon. Prof. of Finance, Heriot-Watt Univ., 1988–2010. Dep. Chm., Edinburgh Internat. Fest., 2006–14. Chm., Court, Heriot-Watt Univ., 1996–2002; Sen. Gov., Court, St Andrews Univ., 2006–; Governor: Edinburgh Coll. of Art, 1986–89; George Watson's Coll., 1990–91. Treas., RSE, 2008–12. Member: Council, ICAS, 1988–91; Council, Assembly of C of S, 2003–06. Master, Merchant Co. of City of Edinburgh, 1994–95; Lord Dean of Guild, 1995–97. Trustee, Carnegie Trust for Univs of Scotland, 1996–2006. FRSE 2001; FCIBS 2008. DUniv Heriot-Watt, 2003. *Recreations:* golf, ski-ing, the arts, grandchildren, mah jongg. *Address:* c/o Scottish Financial Enterprise, 24 Melville Street, Edinburgh EH3 7NS. *T:* 07710 390361. *E:* eb80@st-andrews.ac.uk. *Clubs:* New (Edinburgh); Royal and Ancient (St Andrews).

BROWN, Hon. Dr Ewart Frederick; JP; MP (PLP), Bermuda, 1993–2010; Premier and Minister of Tourism and Transport, Bermuda, 2006–10; Leader, Progressive Labour Party, 2006–10; *b* 17 May 1946; *s* of Ewart D. A. Brown and Helene A. Brown; *m* 2003, Wanda Henton; four *s* from previous marr. *Educ:* Howard Univ. (BSc, MD); Univ. of Calif, Los Angeles (MPH). Med. Dir, Vermont-Century Med. Clinic, Calif, 1974–93; Med. Dir, 1993–2006, Pres. and Chm. Bd, 1993–, Bermuda Healthcare Services. Minister of Transport, 1998–2004, of Tourism and Transport, 2004–06; Dep. Premier, 2003–06. *Recreation:* golf.

BROWN, Frank Henry, OBE 1975; HM Diplomatic Service, retired; *b* 6 Sept. 1923; *s* of late Thomas Henry Brown and Ada Katherine Brown (*née* Clifton); *m* 1943, Sheila Desiree (*d* 1997), *d* of late Rev. Canon John Rees and Elsie Rees; one *s* three *d*. *Educ:* LCC Bonneville Road, Clapham; Bec Sch., Tooting Bec. C. & E. Morton Ltd, 1940; Colonial Office, 1940–42; RN, 1942–46; Colonial Office, subseq. Commonwealth Office, then Foreign and Commonwealth Office, 1946–83: St Helena, 1948–50; Gold Coast/Ghana, 1954–57; Financial Sec., New Hebrides, 1971–75; Dep. High Comr, Guyana, 1978–80; Asst Head, Nationality and Treaty Dept, FCO, 1980–83. *Recreations:* Christian service, family solidarity, happy great-great-grandfather, appreciating creation. *Address:* Woodcote Grove House, Woodcote Park, Meadow Hill, Coulsdon, Surrey CR5 2XL. *T:* (020) 8660 0939. *Club:* Civil Service.

BROWN, Gavin Lindberg; Member (C) Lothian, Scottish Parliament, since 2011 (Lothians, 2007–11); *b* 4 June 1975; *s* of William and Jacqueline Brown; *m* 2006, Hilary Fergus; two *s* one *d*. *Educ:* Boundary Jun. Sch., Hong Kong; Fettes Coll.; Univ. of Strathclyde (LLB Hons 1997; DipLP 1998). Trainee solicitor, 1998–2000, solicitor, 2000–02, McGrigor Donald; Man. Dir, Speak With Impact Ltd, 2002–. Shadow spokesman for enterprise, energy and tourism, 2007–11, for finance, 2011–, Scottish Parlt. *Recreation:* tae kwon-do (black belt). *Address:* Scottish Parliament, Edinburgh EH99 1SP. *T:* (0131) 348 6931. *E:* gavin.brown.msp@scottish.parliament.uk.

BROWN, Geoffrey Howard; journalist, The Times; *b* 1 March 1949; *s* of John Howard Brown and Nancy (*née* Fardoe); *m* 1985, Catherine Ann Surowiec. *Educ:* King Henry VIII Grammar Sch., Coventry; Pembroke Coll., Cambridge (BA); Royal Coll. of Art (Sch. of Film and TV, MA). Dep. Film Critic, Financial Times, 1977–81; Film Critic, Radio Times, 1981–89; Dep. Film Critic, 1981–90, Film Critic, 1990–98, Music Critic, 1999–, The Times. *Publications:* Walter Forde, 1977; Launder and Gilliat, 1977; Der Produzent: Michael Balcon und der Englische Film, 1981; (contrib.) Michael Balcon: the pursuit of British cinema, 1984; The Common Touch: the films of John Baxter, 1989; (contrib.) The British Cinema Book, 1997; (contrib.) The Unknown 1930s, 1998; (contrib.) British Cinema of the 90s, 2000; (contrib.) The Cinema of Britain and Ireland, 2005; (Associate Ed.) Directors in British and Irish Cinema: a reference guide, 2006; (ed) Alistair Cooke at the Movies, 2009; (contrib.) Ealing Revisited, 2012. *Recreations:* art exhibits, children's books. *Address:* The Times, 1 London Bridge Street, SE1 9GF. *T:* (020) 7782 5167.

BROWN, Geoffrey Robert C.; *see* Clifton-Brown.

BROWN, Sir George (Francis) Richmond, 5th Bt *cr* 1863, of Richmond Hill; *b* 3 Feb. 1938; *o s* of Sir Charles Frederick Richmond Brown, 4th Bt and of Audrey Baring; *S* father, 1995; *m* 1978, Philippa Willcox; three *s*. *Educ:* Eton. Served Welsh Guards, 1956–70; Extra Equerry to HRH The Duke of Edinburgh, 1961–63; ADC to Governor of Queensland, 1964–66; Adjt, 1st Bn Welsh Guards, 1967–69. *Heir: s* Sam George Richmond Brown, *b* 27 Dec. 1979. *Address:* Mas de Sudre, 81600 Gaillac, France. *T:* 563410132. *Clubs:* Pratt's, Cavalry and Guards.

BROWN, Prof. George William, OBE 1995; FBA 1986; Honorary Professor, Institute of Psychiatry, King's College London, since 2000; *b* 15 Nov. 1930; *s* of late William G. Brown and Lily Jane (*née* Hillier); *m* 1st, 1954, Gillian M. Hole (marr. diss. 1970); one *s* one *d*; 2nd, 1978, Seija T. Sandberg (marr. diss. 1987); one *d*; 3rd, 1990, Elizabeth A. Davies; one *s* one *d*. *Educ:* Kilburn Grammar Sch.; University Coll. London (BA Anthropol. 1954); LSE (PhD 1961). Scientific Staff, DSIR, 1955–56; MRC Social Psychiatry Res. Unit, Inst. of Psychiatry, 1956–67; joined Social Res. Unit, Bedford Coll., London Univ., 1967; Prof. of Sociology, London Univ. and Jt Dir, Social Res. Unit, Bedford Coll., 1973–80; Mem., Ext. Scientific Staff, MRC, 1980–2000; Hon. Prof. of Sociol., RHBNC, London Univ., 1980–2000, now Emeritus Prof. Mem., Inst. Medicine, 2005. Mem., Academia Europaea, 1990. Founder FMedSci 1998. Hon. FRCPsych, 1987. *Publications:* (jtly) Schizophrenia and Social Care, 1966; (with J. K. Wing) Institutionalism and Schizophrenia, 1970; (with T. O. Harris) Social Origins of Depression, 1978; Life Events and Illness, 1989; numerous contribs to jls. *Address:* 1 Redberry Grove, SE26 4DA. *T:* (020) 8699 0120.

BROWN, Prof. Gillian, CBE 1992; Professor of English as an International Language, University of Cambridge, 1988–2004; Fellow of Clare College, Cambridge, 1988–2007, now Emeritus; *b* 23 Jan. 1937; *d* of Geoffrey Rencher Read and Elsie Olive Chapman; *m* 1959, Edward Keith Brown; three *d*. *Educ:* Perse Sch. for Girls; Girton Coll., Cambridge (MA); Univ. of Edinburgh (PhD 1971); LittD Cantab 1997. Lectr, University Coll. of Cape Coast, Ghana, 1962–64; Lectr, 1965–81, Reader, 1981–83, Univ. of Edinburgh; Prof., Univ. of Essex, 1983–88 (Dean of Social Scis, 1985–88); Dir, Res. Centre for English and Applied Linguistics, Univ. of Cambridge, 1988–2004. Mem., ESRC Educn and Human Develt Cttee, 1983–87; Chm., Research Grants Board, ESRC, 1987–90; Member: Kingman Cttee, 1987–88; UGC, subseq. UFC, 1988–91; Council, Philological Soc., 1988–93; British Council English Teaching Adv. Cttee, 1989–94; Cttee of Mgt, British Inst. in Paris, 1990–2004. Curator, Sch. of Advanced Studies, Univ. of London, 1994–2005. Gov., Bell Educnl Trust, 1987–92. Dr *hc* Univ. of Lyon, 1987. Member, Editorial Boards: Jl of Semantics; Jl of Applied Linguistics; Second Language Acquisition Res. *Publications:* Phonological Rules and Dialect Variation, 1972; Listening to Spoken English, 1977; (with George Yule) Discourse Analysis, 1983; Speakers, Listeners and Communication, 1995; articles in learned jls. *Address:* Clare College, Cambridge CB2 1TL.

BROWN, Prof. Godfrey Norman; Director, Institute of Education and Professor of Education, University of Keele, 1967–80, now Emeritus; Director, Betley Court Gallery, 1980–94; *b* 13 July 1926; *s* of Percy Charles and Margaret Elizabeth Brown; *m* 1960, Dr Freda Bowyer; three *s*. *Educ:* Whitgift Sch.; School of Oriental and African Studies, London; Merton Coll., Oxford (MA, DPhil). Army service, RAC and Intelligence Corps, 1944–48. Social Affairs Officer, UN Headquarters, NY, 1953–54; Sen. History Master, Barking Abbey Sch., Essex, 1954–57; Lectr in Educn, University Coll. of Ghana, 1958–61; Sen. Lectr, 1961, Prof., 1963, Univ. of Ibadan, Nigeria. Visiting Prof., Univ. of Rhodesia and Nyasaland, 1963; Chm., Assoc. for Recurrent Educn, 1976–77; Mem., Exec. Cttee and Bd of Dirs, World Council for Curriculum and Instruction, 1974–77. OECD Consultant on teacher education, Portugal, 1980. Vice-Pres., Community Council of Staffs, 1984–. Collector of the Year Award, Art and Antiques, 1981; Newcastle-under-Lyme Civic Award for Conservation, 1990. *Publications:* An Active History of Ghana, 2 vols, 1961 and 1964; Living History, 1967; Apartheid, a Teacher's Guide, 1981; Betley Through the Centuries, 1985; This Old House: a domestic biography, 1987; Betley's Cultural Heritage, 2002; edited: (with J. C. Anene) Africa in the Nineteenth and Twentieth Centuries, 1966; Towards a Learning Community, 1971; (with M. Hiskett) Conflict and Harmony in Education in Tropical Africa, 1975; Eccentric Harmony, 2003; contrib. educnl and cultural jls. *Recreations:* family life, art history, conservation, writing. *Address:* Betley Court, Betley, near Crewe, Cheshire CW3 9BH. *T:* (01270) 820652.

BROWN, Rt Hon. Gordon; *see* Brown, Rt Hon. J. G.

BROWN, Harold, PhD; Counselor, Center for Strategic and International Studies, since 1992; Partner, Warburg Pincus & Co., 1990–2008; *b* 19 Sept. 1927; *s* of A. H. Brown and Gertrude Cohen Brown; *m* 1953, Colene McDowell; two *d*. *Educ:* Columbia Univ. (BA 1945, MA 1946, PhD in Physics 1949). Res. Scientist, Columbia Univ., 1945–50, Lectr in Physics, 1947–48; Lectr in Physics, Stevens Inst. of Technol., 1949–50; Res. Scientist, Radiation Lab., Univ. of Calif, Berkeley, 1951–52; Gp Leader, Radiation Lab., Livermore, 1952–61; Dir, Def. Res. and Engrg, Dept of Def., 1961–65; Sec. of Air Force, 1965–69; Pres., Calif Inst. of Technol., Pasadena, 1969–77; Sec. of Defense, USA, 1977–81; Vis. Prof., 1981–84, Chm., 1984–92, Johns Hopkins Foreign Policy Inst., Sch. of Advanced Internat. Studies. Sen. Sci. Adviser, Conf. on Discontinuance of Nuclear Tests, 1958–59; Delegate, Strategic Arms Limitations Talks, Helsinki, Vienna and Geneva, 1969–77. Member: Polaris Steering Cttee, 1956–58; Air Force Sci. Adv. Bd, 1956–61; (also Consultant) President's Sci. Adv. Cttee, 1958–61. Chm., Commn on Roles and Capabilities, US Intelligence Cttee, 1995–96. Hon. DEng Stevens Inst. of Technol., 1964; Hon. LLD: Long Island Univ., 1966; Gettysburg Coll., 1967; Occidental Coll., 1969; Univ. of Calif, 1969; Hon. ScD: Univ. of Rochester, 1975; Brown Univ., 1977; Univ. of the Pacific, 1978; Univ. of S Carolina, 1979; Franklin and Marshall Coll., 1982; Chung Ang Univ. (Seoul, Korea), 1983. Member: Amer. Phys. Soc., 1946; Nat. Acad. of Engrg, 1967; Amer. Acad. of Arts and Scis, 1969; Nat. Acad. of Scis, 1977. One of Ten Outstanding Young Men of Year, US Jun. Chamber of Commerce, 1961; Columbia Univ. Medal of Excellence, 1963; Air Force Exceptl Civil. Service Award, 1969; Dept of Def. Award for Exceptionally Meritorious Service, 1969; Joseph C. Wilson Award, 1976; Presidential Medal of Freedom, 1981; Enrico Fermi Award, US Dept of Energy, 1993. *Publications:* Thinking About National Security: defense and foreign policy in a dangerous world, 1983; (ed) The Strategic Defense Initiative: shield or snare?, 1987. *Address:* Center for Strategic and International Studies, 161 Rhode Island Avenue, NW, Washington, DC 20036, USA.

BROWN, (Harold) Vivian (Bigley), CB 2004; Business Adviser, Traidlinks, Uganda, since 2013; *b* 20 Aug. 1945; *s* of late Alec Sidney Brown and Joyce Brown (*née* Bigley); *m* 1970, Jean Josephine Bowyer, *yr d* of Sir Eric Bowyer, KCB, KBE and Lady Bowyer; two *s*. *Educ:* Leeds Grammar Sch.; St John's Coll., Oxford (BA); St Cross Coll., Oxford (BPhil Islamic Philosophy). Min. of Technology, 1970; DTI, 1972–74 (Private Sec. to Permanent Sec., 1972–73); FCO, 1975–79 (First Sec. Commercial Jeddah); DTI, 1979–86; Hd of Sci. and Technol. Assessment Office, Cabinet Office, 1986–89; Hd of Competition Policy Div., 1989–91; Hd of Investigations Div., 1991–92, of Deregulation Unit, 1992–94, of Small Firms and Business Link, 1994–96, DTI; Dep. Dir Gen. and Dir, Business Link, DTI, 1996–97; Chief Exec., ECGD, 1997–2004; Advr to Minister of Finance, Bahrain, 2004–06; Micro-credit Advr, Lea Toto Prog., Nairobi, 2007–09. *Publications:* (with S. M. Stern and A. Hourani) Islamic Philosophy and the Classical Tradition, 1972. *Recreations:* playing piano, cycling, cooking.

BROWN, Prof. Harvey Robert, PhD; FBA 2007; Professor of Philosophy of Physics, University of Oxford, since 2006; Fellow of Wolfson College, Oxford, since 1984; *b* 4 April 1950; *s* of Harvey C. Brown and M. Katrine Brown; *m* 1980, Maria Rita Kessler; one *s* one *d*. *Educ:* Univ. of Canterbury, NZ (BSc Hons 1971); Univ. of London (PhD 1978). Asst Prof., Dept of Philos. and Mem., Centro de Lógica, Epistemologia e História da Ciência, São Paulo State Univ. at Campinas, 1978–84; Lectr in Philos. of Physics, 1984–96, Reader in Philos., 1996–2006, Univ. of Oxford. Long-term Visitor, Perimeter Inst. for Theoretical Physics, Waterloo, Ont, 2007–08. Pres., British Soc. for the Philos. of Sci., 2007–09. *Publications:* Albert Einstein. Um simples homem de visão, 1984; Physical Relativity: space-time structure from a dynamical perspective, 2005 (Lakatos Award in the Philosophy of Science (jtly), 2006); numerous contribns to learned jls. *Recreations:* drawing, swimming, motorcycles, cooking, things Brazilian. *Address:* Philosophy Faculty, Radcliffe Humanities, University of Oxford, Woodstock Road, Oxford OX2 6GG. *T:* (01865) 276930, *Fax:* (01865) 276932. *E:* harvey.brown@philosophy.ox.ac.uk.

BROWN, Hazel Christine P.; *see* Parker-Brown.

BROWN, Col Hugh Goundry, TD 1968; FRCS; Vice Lord-Lieutenant, Tyne & Wear, 1993–2002; *b* 25 Feb. 1927; *s* of Charles Frank Brown and Edith Temple Brown (*née*

Smithson); *m* 1961, Ann Mary Crump; one *s* two *d*. *Educ:* Durham Univ. (MB BS 1949). FRCS 1958. Nat. Service, RMO, 1 (Nyasaland) Bn, KAR, 1950–52. TA 1 (N) Gen. Hosp., 1952–73; OC, 201 (N) Gen. Hosp., 1970–73, Hon. Col, 1982–87. Consultant Plastic Surgeon, Royal Victoria Inf., Newcastle upon Tyne and Sen. Lectr in plastic surgery, Univ. of Newcastle upon Tyne, 1968–92. President: Brit. Soc. for Surgery of the Hand, 1985; Brit. Assoc. Plastic Surgeons, 1988; Brit. Assoc. Clinical Anatomists, 1989. QHS 1972. Tyne & Wear: DL 1986; High Sheriff, 1992. *Publications:* contrib. Brit. Jl Plastic Surgery, Hand, Brit. Jl Anaesthesia. *Recreations:* family, fell-walking. *Address:* 12 Lindisfarne Road, Jesmond, Newcastle upon Tyne NE2 2HE. *T:* (0191) 281 4141. *Club:* Northern Counties (Newcastle).

BROWN, Prof. Ian James Morris, PhD; playwright; poet; Professor of Drama, Kingston University, 2010–14, now Emeritus; *b* 28 Feb. 1945; *s* of Bruce Beveridge Brown and Eileen Frances Scott Carnegie; *m* 1st, 1968, Judith Ellen Sidaway (marr. diss. 1997); one *s* one *d*; 2nd, 1997, Nicola Dawn Axford. *Educ:* Dollar Academy; Edinburgh Univ. MA Hons, MLitt, DipEd; Crewe and Alsager Coll. (PhD). Playwright, 1969–; poet, 1978–; Schoolmaster, 1967–69, 1970–71; Lectr in Drama, Dunfermline Coll., 1971–76; British Council: Asst Rep., Scotland, 1976–77; Asst Regional Dir, Istanbul, 1977–78; Crewe and Alsager College: Head of Drama, 1978–79; Head of Performance Arts, 1979–82; Programme Leader, BA Hons Drama Studies, 1982–86; Programme Dir, Alsager Arts Centre, 1980–86; Drama Dir, Arts Council of GB, 1986–94; Queen Margaret College, subseq. Queen Margaret University College, Edinburgh: Reader, 1994–95; Prof. of Drama, 1995–2002; Head, Dept of Drama, 1995–99; Dir, Scottish Centre for Cultural Mgt and Policy, 1996–2002; Dean of Arts, 1999–2002; Proprietor, Ian Brown Consultancy, 2002–10. Vis. Prof. (Hon. Prof. Res. Fellow), Dept of Scottish Lit., Univ. of Glasgow, 2007–; Vis. Prof., Centre for the Study of Media and Culture in Small Nations, Univ. of Glamorgan, 2007–13. Vice-Chair, Standing Cttee of Univ. Drama Depts, 2013–. Chm., Scottish Soc. of Playwrights, 1973–75, 1984–87, 1997–99, 2010–13 (Mem. Council, 1999–2007); convenor, NW Playwrights' Workshop, 1982–85; Member: NW Arts Assoc. Drama panel, 1980–83, General Arts panel, 1983–86; Arts Council of GB Drama panel, 1985–86; British Theatre Institute: Vice-Chm., 1983–85; Chm., 1985–87. Chairman: Dionysia World Fest. of Contemp. Theatre, Chianti, Italy, 1991–94; Highlands and Islands Theatre Network, 2005–09; Dràma Na h-Alba, Scotland's Internat. Theatre Fest. and Forum, 2006–09. Cultural consultant, Rose Th., Kingston, 2011–14. Mem. Council, 2010–, Mem., Exec. Bd, 2011–, Convener, 2014–, Saltire Soc. Pres., Assoc. for Scottish Literary Studies, 2010–. Productions: Antigone, 1969; Mother Earth, 1970; The Bacchae, 1972; Positively the Last Final Farewell Performance (ballet), 1972; Rune (choral work), 1973; Carnegie, 1973; The Knife, 1973; The Fork, 1976; New Reekie, 1977; Mary, 1977; Runners, 1978; Mary Queen and the Loch Tower, 1979; Joker in the Pack, 1983; Beatrice, 1989; (jtly) First Strike, 1990; The Scotch Play, 1991; Bacchai, 1991; Wasting Reality, 1992; Margaret, 2000; A Great Reckonin, 2000; An Act o Love, 2011. FRSA 1991; FHEA 2010. Series Editor: The Edinburgh Companions to Scottish Literature, 2007–13; The Internat. Companions to Scottish Lit., 2013–. *Publications:* (ed) An Anthology of Contemporary Scottish Drama (in Croatian), 1999; (ed) Cultural Tourism: the convergence of culture and tourism at the start of the 21st century (in Russian), 2001; Poems for Joan, 2001; (ed) Journey's Beginning: the Gateway Theatre building and company 1884–1965, 2004; (ed) The Edinburgh History of Scottish Literature, 2007; (ed) Changing Identities – Ancient Roots: the history of West Dunbartonshire from earliest times, 2006; (ed) The Edinburgh Companion to Twentieth-Century Scottish Literature, 2009; (ed) From Tartan to Tartanry: Scottish culture, history and myth, 2010; (ed) The Edinburgh Companion to Scottish Drama, 2011; (ed) Literary Tourism, the Trossachs and Walter Scott, 2012; (with A. Riach) Lion's Milk: Turkish poems by Scottish poets, 2012; Scottish Theatre, Diversity, Language, Continuity, 2013; (ed jtly) Roots and Fruits: Scottish identities, history and contemporary literature, 2014; articles on drama, theatre and arts policy. *Recreations:* theatre, sport, travel, cooking. *Address:* 2/1, 2 Darnley Road, Glasgow G41 4NB.

BROWN, Col James, CVO 1985; RNZAC (retd); *b* 15 Aug. 1925; *y s* of late John Brown and Eveline Bertha (*née* Cooper), Russells Flat, North Canterbury, NZ; *m* 1952, Patricia Sutton; two *d*. *Educ:* Christchurch Boys' High Sch., NZ; Royal Military Coll., Duntroon, Australia (grad 1947). NZ Regular Army, 1947–71: active service, Korea, 1951–52; Comptroller of Household to Gov.-Gen. of NZ, 1961–62; Reg. Comr of Civil Defence, Dept of Internal Affairs, NZ, 1971–77; Official Sec. to Gov.-Gen. of NZ, 1977–85; Gen. Sec., Duke of Edinburgh's Award Scheme in NZ, 1986–94. Col Comdt, RNZAC, 1982–86; Pres., NZ Army Assoc., 1986–94. *Recreations:* fishing, shooting. *Address:* Apt B8, Huntleigh Apartments, 221 Karori Road, Wellington 6012, New Zealand. *Club:* Wellington (Wellington).

BROWN, James Anthony, (Tony), OBE 2013; Chief Minister, Isle of Man, 2006–11; MHK Castletown, 1981–2011 (Speaker, House of Keys, 2001–06); *b* 5 Jan. 1950; *s* of Margaret Brown; *m* 1979, Rachel (*née* Smith); one *s* one *d*. *Educ:* Victoria Road Primary Sch., Castletown; Castle Rushen High Sch., Castletown. Apprentice electrician, 1965–70, electrician, 1970–80, IOM Electricity Bd; self-employed electrician, 1980–81; Proprietor, Tony Brown Electrics, 1981–2010. Mem., Castletown Town Commn, 1976–81 (Chm., 1980–81). Manx Government: Minister: for Health and Social Security, 1986–89; for Local Govt and Envmt, 1989–94; for Tourism and Leisure, 1994–96; for Transport, 1996–2001; Dep. Pres., Tynwald, 2002–06. Pres., Castletown Chamber of Trade and Commerce, 1987–2011; Mem., Castletown Chamber of Commerce, 2014–. Pres., 1984, Pres. and Chm., 1990–, Castletown and Dist Over 60s Club; Vice-President: Castletown Rifle Club, 1994–; Castletown and Dist Br., RBL, 2014–. Chm., Castletown Metropolitan Silver Band, 2014–. Chm. Trustees, Queen Street Mission Trust, 1993–. *Recreations:* photography, history, historic architecture, motorcycle racing (marshal and spectator), heritage. *Address:* 20 Kissack Road, Castletown, Isle of Man IM9 1NW. *T:* (01624) 824393.

BROWN, Dr (James) Barry (Conway), OBE 1978; Subject Assessor, Higher Education Funding Council for England, 1995–97; *b* 3 July 1937; *s* of Frederick Clarence and Alys Brown; *m* 1963, Anne Rosemary Clough (*d* 2007); two *s* one *d*. *Educ:* Cambridge Univ. (BA Nat. Sci 1959; MA 1963); Birmingham Univ. (MSc 1960; PhD 1963). Research Officer, CEGB, Berkeley Nuclear Labs, 1963–67; British Council: Sen. Sci. Officer, Sci. Dept, 1967–69; Sci. Officer, Madrid, 1969–72, Paris, 1972–78; Head, Sci. and Technology Group, 1978–81; Rep. and Cultural Counsellor, Mexico, 1981–85; Dep. Controller (Higher Educn Div.), 1985–89; Dir, EC Liaison Unit (Higher Education), Brussels, 1989–91; Dir, Poland, 1992–94. Treas., St Mary's Church, Purley-on-Thames, 1994–2000. Mem., Pangbourne Choral Soc., 2001–. *Recreations:* music, travel in (and study of) countries of posting, singing, reading. *Address:* 42 Hazel Road, Purley-on-Thames, Reading RG8 8BB. *T:* (0118) 941 7581.

BROWN, (James) Craig, CBE 1999; International Team Manager, 1993–2001, and Technical Director, 1993–2002, Scottish Football Association; *b* 1 July 1940; *s* of Hugh and Margaret Brown; *m* 1964 (separated 1981); two *s* one *d*. *Educ:* Scottish Sch. of Physical Educn (DipPE (Distinction)), Strathclyde Univ. BEd (Hons); BA Open Univ. 1976. Teacher of PE, City of Dundee, Teacher, High Blantyre Primary Sch., Dep. Hd Teacher, Belvidere Primary Sch., Hd Teacher, Burnhead Primary Sch., 1962–69; Lectr in Primary Educn, Craigie Coll. of Educn, 1969–86. Professional footballer: Rangers FC, 1958–60; Dundee FC, 1960–65; Falkirk FC, 1965–67; Asst Manager, Motherwell FC, 1974–77; Manager, Clyde FC, 1977–86; Asst Nat. Coach and Asst Technical Dir, Scottish FA, 1986–93; Manager: Preston North End FC, 2002–04; Motherwell, 2009–10; Aberdeen, 2010–13. Football Consultant: Fulham FC, 2006–07; Derby FC, 2007–08. Non-exec. Dir, Aberdeen FC, 2013–. Patron: Scottish Disability Sport; Sports Chaplaincy (Scottish Football). DUniv Paisley, 1998; Hon. DArts Abertay Dundee, 2000. *Publications:* Craig Brown (autobiog.), 1998, repr. as The Game of My Life, 2001. *Recreations:* golf, reading, travel. *Address:* 36 Queens Crescent, Aberdeen AB15 4BE.

BROWN, Rt Hon. (James) Gordon; PC 1996; Special Envoy for the UN Secretary-General for Global Education, since 2012; *b* 20 Feb. 1951; *s* of late Rev. Dr John Brown and J. Elizabeth Brown; *m* 2000, Sarah Jane Macaulay; two *s* (one *d* decd). *Educ:* Kirkcaldy High Sch.; Edinburgh Univ. MA 1972; PhD 1982. Rector, Edinburgh Univ., 1972–75; Temp. Lectr, Edinburgh Univ., 1976; Lectr, Glasgow Coll. of Technology, 1976–80; Journalist and Current Affairs Editor, Scottish TV, 1980–83. Mem., Unite (formerly TGWU). Chm., Labour Party Scottish Council, 1983–84. Contested (Lab) S Edinburgh, 1979. MP (Lab) Dunfermline E, 1983–2005, Kirkcaldy and Cowdenbeath, 2005–15. Opposition Chief Sec. to the Treasury, 1987–89; Opposition Trade and Industry Sec., 1989–92; Opposition Treasury Sec., 1992–97; Chancellor of the Exchequer, 1997–2007; Prime Minister and First Lord of the Treasury, 2007–10. Leader of the Labour Party, 2007–10. Chm., Global Strategic Infrastructure Initiative, WEF. Distinguished Global Leader in Residence, New York Univ. DUniv Glasgow, 2015. *Publications:* (ed) The Red Paper on Scotland, 1975; (with H. M. Drucker) The Politics of Nationalism and Devolution, 1980; (ed) Scotland: the real divide, 1983; Maxton, 1986; Where There is Greed, 1989; (with J. Naughtie) John Smith: Life and Soul of the Party, 1994; (with T. Wright) Values, Visions and Voices, 1995; Speeches 1997–2006, 2006; Moving Britain Forward: selected speeches 1997–2006, 2006; Courage: eight portraits, 2007; Britain's Ordinary Heroes, 2007; The Change We Choose: speeches 2007–09, 2010; Beyond the Crash: overcoming the first crisis of globalisation, 2010; My Scotland, Our Britain: a future worth sharing, 2014. *Recreations:* reading and writing, football and tennis.

BROWN, Jane; *see* Finnis, J.

BROWN, Janet Marjorie, PhD; FInstP; FRSE; Chief Executive, Scottish Qualifications Authority, since 2007; *b* Sheffield, 31 July 1951. *Educ:* High Storrs Grammar Sch. for Girls, Sheffield; Univ. of Birmingham (BSc; PhD 1979). FInstP 2005. Vis. Asst Prof., Univ. of Illinois, Urbana, 1981–84; Mem. Tech. Staff, Bell Laboratories, AT&T, Murray Hill, 1984–90; Dir, Process Architecture and Characterisation, SEMATECH, Austin, 1990–93; Motorola: Dir, Reliability and Quality Assurance, Austin, 1993–97; Eur. Ops Dir, Smartcard Div., E Kilbride, 1997–98; Dir of Ops, Networking Systems Memories, Austin, 1998–2000; Man. Dir, Scottish Enterprise, Glasgow, 2000–07. FRSE 2008. *Address:* Scottish Qualifications Authority, The Optima Building, 58 Robertson Street, Glasgow G2 8DQ. *T:* 0345 279 1000. *E:* customer@sqa.org.uk.

BROWN, Janice Margaret; Managing Director and Chief Financial Officer, Cairn Energy PLC, 2011–14; President, Institute of Chartered Accountants of Scotland, 2014–15 (Deputy President, 2013–14); *b* Glasgow, 9 June 1955; *d* of Alex and Phyllis Tinto; *m* 1997, Antony Brown; one *s* one *d*. *Educ:* Trinity Acad., Edinburgh; Edinburgh Univ. (MA Hist. 1978); Heriot Watt Univ. (Dip. Accounting 1987). Senior Tax Manager: KPMG, 1987–97; Deloitte & Touche, 1997–98; Cairn Energy plc: Gp Tax Manager, 1998–99; Gp Financial Controller, 1999–2006; Finance Dir, 2006–11. Sen. Ind. Dir, Hansen Transmissions Internat., 2008–11; non-executive Director: Cairn India Ltd, 2006–11; Troy Income & Growth Trust, 2013–; Mem. Bd, Edinburgh Printmakers, 2004–06; non-exec. Chm., Audit Cttee, John Wood Gp plc, 2014–. Member: ICAS, 1990 (Mem. Council, 2009–); Chartered Inst. of Taxation, 1991. Mem. Exec., Pipeline Steering Gp, 30% Club, 2012–; Trustee, Univ. of Edinburgh Develt Trust, 2013–. *Recreations:* arts, reading, theatre, literature, walking, travel.

BROWN, Jayne; *see* Brown, M. J.

BROWN, Jenny; literary agent; Founder and Owner, Jenny Brown Associates, since 2002; *b* Manchester, 13 May 1958; *d* of William Byers and Pauline Brown; *m* 1992, Alexander Richardson; four *s* (and one *s* decd). *Educ:* George Watson's Coll., Edinburgh; Univ. of Aberdeen (MA Hons 1980). Dir, Edinburgh Internat. Book Fest., 1982–91; Co-ordinator, Readiscovery Campaign, 1994–96; Lit. Dir, Scottish Arts Council, 1996–2002. Mem., Press Complaints Commn, 1993–98. Presenter of book progs, Scottish TV, 1989–94. Mem. Bd, Edinburgh Internat. Book Fest., 2004–. Chair, Bloody Scotland Crime Writing Fest., 2012–. Gov., George Watson's Coll., 2000–05. DUniv Open, 2015. *Recreations:* hill walking, theatre, art, family. *Address:* Jenny Brown Associates, 31 Marchmont Road, Edinburgh EH9 1HU. *T:* (0131) 229 5334. *E:* jenny@jennybrownassociates.com.

BROWN, Jerry; *see* Brown, E. G.

BROWN, Joe, CBE 2011 (MBE 1975); freelance guide and climber, and film maker for television and cinema; *b* 26 Sept. 1930; *s* of J. Brown, Longsight, Manchester; *m* 1957, Valerie Gray; two *d*. *Educ:* Stanley Grove, Manchester. Started climbing while working as plumber in Manchester; pioneered new climbs in Wales in early 1950s; gained internat. reputation after climbing West Face of Petit Dru, 1954; climbed Kanchenjunga, 1955; Mustagh Tower, 1956; Mt Communism, USSR, 1962; Trango Tower, 1976; Cotaphxi, 1979; Mt Kenya, 1984; Mt McInley, 1986; other expedns: El Torro, 1970; Bramah 2, 1978; Thalaysagar, 1982; Everest NE Ridge, 1986 and 1988. Climbing Instructor, Whitehall, Derbs, 1961–65; opened climbing equipment shops, Llanberis, 1965, Capel Curig, 1970; Leader of United Newspapers Andean Expedn, 1970; Roraima Expedn, 1973. Hon. Fellow, Manchester Polytechnic, 1970. *Publications:* (autobiog.) The Hard Years, 1967. *Recreations:* mountaineering, ski-ing, fishing. *Address:* Allandale, Llanberis, Gwynedd LL55 4TF. *T:* (01286) 870727. *Clubs:* Alpine (Hon. Mem.), Climbers' (Hon. Mem.); American Alpine (Hon. Mem. 2011).

BROWN, John, CBE 1982; FREng; Part-time Dean of Technology, Brunel University, 1988–91; *b* 17 July 1923; *s* of George Brown and Margaret Ditchburn Brown; *m* 1st, 1947, Maureen Dorothy Moore (*d* 1991); one *d*; 2nd, 1992, Dr Helen Crawford Gladstone. *Educ:* Edinburgh University. Radar Research and Development Estabt, 1944–51; Lectr, Imperial Coll., 1951–54; University Coll., London: Lectr, 1954–56; Reader, 1956–64; Prof., 1964–67; seconded to Indian Inst. of Technology as Prof. of Electrical Engrg, 1962–65; Prof. of Elect. Engineering, Imperial Coll. of Science and Technology, 1967–81 (Head of Dept, 1967–79); Tech. Dir, Marconi Electrical Devices Ltd, 1981–83; Dir, Univ. and Schs Liaison, GEC, 1983–88. Mem., SRC, 1977–81 (Chm., Engrg Bd, 1977–81); Chm., Joint ESRC-SERC Cttee, 1988–91; Member: Engrg Group, Nat. Advisory Bd, 1983–84; Engrg Cttee, CNAA, 1985–87; Accreditation Cttee, CNAA, 1987–89. Pres., IEE, 1979–80 (Vice-Pres., 1975–78; Dep. Pres., 1978–79); Pres., IEEIE, 1981–85 (Treasurer, 1989–99). Treas., Church Monuments Soc., 2000–07. Governor: S Bank Polytechnic, 1985–90; Willesden Coll. of Technology, 1985–86. FREng (FEng 1984). Hon. FIET (Hon. FIEIE 1986). Hon. DLitt Nanyang Technol Univ., Singapore, 1996. *Publications:* Microwave Lenses, 1953; (with H. M. Barlow) Radio Surface Waves, 1962; Telecommunications, 1964; (with R. H. Clarke) Diffraction Theory and Antennas, 1980; papers in Proc. IEE, etc. *Recreation:* gardening. *Address:* 28 Dale Side, Gerrards Cross, Bucks SL9 7JE.

BROWN, (John) Bruce, FRICS; Chairman, Lambert Smith Hampton, 1988–2008; *b* 15 June 1944; *s* of late Bruce Brown and Margaret Mary (*née* Roberts); *m* 1967, Daphne Jane Walker; one *s* two *d*. *Educ:* Acton Park, Wrexham; Grove Park, Wrexham; Coll. of Estate Management, London Univ. (BSc). FRICS 1977. Surveyor, Samuel Walker & Son, 1967–68; Estates Surveyor, Bracknell Develt Corp., 1968–69; Sen. Develt Surveyor, Town & City

Properties, 1969–71; Sen. Partner, Anthony Brown Stewart, 1971–88. *Recreations:* motor-racing, vintage and veteran cars. *Address:* Radmore Farm, Wappenham, Towcester, Northants NN12 8SX.

BROWN, Prof. John Campbell, PhD; DSc; Regius Professor of Astronomy, University of Glasgow, 1996–2010, now Professor Emeritus, Hon. Senior Research Fellow and Leverhulme Emeritus Fellow; Astronomer Royal for Scotland, since 1995; *b* 4 Feb. 1947; *s* of John Brown and Jane Livingston Stewart Brown (*née* Campbell); *m* 1972, Dr Margaret Isobel Logan; one *s* one *d. Educ:* Hartfield Primary; Dumbarton Acad.; Glasgow Univ. (BSc 1st Cl. Hons Physics and Astronomy 1968; PhD 1973; DSc 1984). University of Glasgow: Research Asst, 1968–70; Lectr, 1970–78; Sen. Lectr, 1978–80; Reader, 1980–84; Prof. of Astrophysics, 1984–96. Fellow: Univ. of Tubingen, 1971–72; Univ. of Utrecht, 1973–74; Vis. Fellow, Nat. Center for Atmospheric Res., Colorado, 1977; NASA Associate Prof., Univ. of Md, 1980; Nuffield/NSF Fellow, UCSD and Univ. of Amsterdam, 1984; Brittingham Prof., Univ. of Wisconsin-Madison, 1987; Visiting Fellow, 1999: Univ. of Amsterdam; ETH Zürich; Observatoire de Paris; NASA Goddard SFC; Univ. of Wisconsin-Madison, 2003; Univ. of Alabama-Huntsville; Univ. of Calif, Berkeley, 2006. Hon. Professor: Univ. of Edinburgh, 1996–; Univ. of Aberdeen, 1998–; Guest Res. Fellow, Nat. Center for Atmospheric Res. High Altitude Observatory, Boulder, Colo, 2010, TCD, 2011. Marlar Lectr, Rice Univ., Texas, 2006. Time & Space Project Astronomer, Royal Observatory, Greenwich, 2004–06. Pres., Physics Section, BAAS, 2001. Patron, Scottish Dark Skies Observatory, 2011–14. Trustee, Brisbane Observatory Heritage Trust, 2011–. FRAS 1973 (Vice Pres., 1986–87); FRSE 1984 (Mem. Council, 1997–2000); FInstP 1996; Associate Mem., Brazilian Acad. of Scis, 1988. Kelvin Prize and Medal, Univ. of Glasgow, 1984; Kelvin Medal, Royal Philosophical Soc., Glasgow, 1996; Robinson Lectr and Medal, Armagh Observatory, 1998; Promotion of Physics Award, Inst. of Physics, 2003; Gold Medal, RAS, 2012. *Publications:* (with I. J. D. Craig) Inverse Problems in Astronomy, 1986; (ed with J. T. Schmeltz) The Sun: a laboratory for astrophysics, 1992; around 300 papers in Astrophysical Jl, Astronomy and Astrophysics, Solar Physic, Nature, etc. *Recreations:* oil-painting, lapidary and silvercraft, woodwork, photography, conjuring, reading, cycling, hiking, alto saxophone. *Address:* School of Physics and Astronomy, University of Glasgow, Glasgow G12 8QQ. *T:* (0141) 330 5182; 21 Bradfield Avenue, Glasgow G12 0QH. *T:* (0141) 581 6789, 07976 270904.

BROWN, John Domenic Weare; Chairman: John Brown Enterprises; John Brown Publishing Ltd, 1987–2004 (Managing Director, 1987–99); John Brown Citrus Publishing, 2002–04; Bob Books Ltd, since 2006; Co-proprietor, The Watch House, St Mawes, since 2010; *b* 29 May 1953; *s* of Sir John Gilbert Newton Brown, CBE and Virginia (*née* Braddell); *m* 1987, Claudia Zeff; one *s* one *d. Educ:* Westminster Sch.; London Coll. of Printing. Managing Director: Eel Pie Publishing, 1982; Virgin Books, 1983–87; Founder, John Brown Publishing Ltd (magazine publisher), 1987. Director: John Wisden and Co., 2003–08; Wisden Gp, 2003–08; The Watch House Ltd, 2011–; non-executive Director: Wanderlust Ltd, 2003–13; Oldie Pubns, 2003–; Aurenis, 2007–14; Pippa Small Jewellery, 2011– (Chm., 2013–); Punk Publishing, 2010–; Songlines Magazine, 2013–; non-executive Chairman: Wild Frontiers, 2008–; Camara UK, 2010–. Chm., Portobello Centre, 2006–08 (Dir, 1997–2009). Gov. (formerly non-exec. Dir), Notting Hill Prep. Sch., 2003–11; Trustee, Sch. of Social Entrepreneurs, 2009–. Marcus Morris Award, PPA, 1997. *Recreations:* music (ukulele, a bit of singing but mainly listening), dogs, cars and boats. *Address:* 241a Portobello Road, W11 1LT. *T:* (020) 7243 7402. *Clubs:* Soho House, MCC.

BROWN, (John) Michael, CBE 1986; HM Diplomatic Service, retired; *b* 16 Nov. 1929; *m* 1955, Elizabeth Fitton; one *s* one *d. Educ:* Sch. of Oriental and African Studies, London. MECAS, 1953. Served at: Cairo, 1954–55; Doha, 1956–57; FO, 1957–60; Havana, 1960–62; FO, 1962–64; Jedda, 1965–66; Maseru, 1966–67; Bogotá, 1967–69; FCO, 1969–71; Ankara, 1971–73; Counsellor, Tripoli, 1973–75; FCO, 1976–79; Ambassador to Costa Rica and Nicaragua, 1979–82; Consul-Gen., Geneva, 1983–85. *Address:* 26 Silchester Place, Winchester, Hants SO23 7FT.

BROWN, Dr John Michael, FRS 1996; Lecturer and Tutor in Chemistry, Chemical Research Laboratory, 1974–2008, Leverhulme Emeritus Fellow, 2008–10, Oxford University; Fellow of Wadham College, Oxford, 1974–2007, now Emeritus; *b* 24 Dec. 1939; *s* of John Caulfield Brown and Winefride Brown; *m* 1963, Una Horner; one *s* one *d. Educ:* Manchester Univ. (BSc 1960; PhD 1963). Various postdoctoral appts, 1963–66; Lectr in Chemistry, Warwick Univ., 1966–74. Tilden Lectr, RSC, 1991. Organometallic Prize, RSC, 1993; (jtly) Descartes Prize, EU, 2001; Horst Pracejus Prize, German Chem. Soc., 2005; Robert Robinson Award, RSC, 2013. *Publications:* (jtly) Mechanism in Organic Chemistry, 1971; *c* 305 articles and reviews in UK, US and European jls. *Recreations:* countryside (UK, France and Spain), good writing, grandchildren, Man Utd. *Address:* Chemistry Research Laboratory, Mansfield Road, Oxford OX1 3TA. *T:* (01865) 275642, *Fax:* (01865) 285002. *E:* john.brown@chem.ox.ac.uk.

BROWN, John Michael; Chairman and Chief Executive, William Hill Organisation, 1989–2004; *b* 17 Sept. 1942; *s* of John Lawrence Brown and Iris May Brown; *m* 1st, 1964, Jennifer Kathleen Dixon (*d* 1993); one *d*; 2nd, 2002, Christine Shine. *Educ:* Stratford Grammar Sch., London. Joined William Hill Orgn, 1959. Dir, Brent Walker, 1991–98. Non-exec. Dir, Satellite Inf. Services, 1989–2004. Dep. Chm., Bookmakers' Cttee, 2000. *Recreation:* horse racing. *Address:* Milford Court, Milford Road, South Milford, Leeds LS25 5AD. *T:* (01997) 689703, 07803 233722. *E:* johnbrown@milfordcourt.com.

BROWN, Rev. Prof. Judith Margaret, (Mrs P. J. Diggle), FRHistS; Beit Professor of Commonwealth History, University of Oxford, 1990–2011; Fellow of Balliol College, Oxford, 1990–2011, now Emeritus; *b* India, 9 July 1944; *d* of late Rev. Wilfred George Brown and Joan M. Brown; *m* 1984, Peter James Diggle; one *s. Educ:* Sherborne Sch. for Girls; Girton Coll., Cambridge (BA 1965; PhD 1968; MA 1969); MA, DPhil Oxon 1990. Research Fellow, Official Fellow and Dir of Studies in History, Girton Coll., Cambridge, 1968–71; Lectr, Sen. Lectr, Reader Elect in History, Univ. of Manchester, 1971–90. Mem., Scholars' Council, Liby of Congress, 2000–09. Trustee, Charles Wallace (India) Trust, 1996–2008; Chm. Trustees, Friends of Delhi Brotherhood Soc., 1997–99. Governor: Bath Spa Univ. (formerly UC), 1997–2011; SOAS, London Univ., 1999–2006; Sherborne Sch. for Girls, 2003–13. Ordained deacon, 2009, priest, 2010. MAE 2011. Hon. DSocSc Natal, 2001. *Publications:* Gandhi's Rise to Power: Indian politics 1915–1922, 1972; Gandhi and Civil Disobedience: the Mahatma in Indian politics 1928–1934, 1977; Men and Gods in a Changing World, 1980; Modern India: the origins of an Asian democracy, 1984, 2nd edn 1994; Gandhi: prisoner of hope, 1989, 2nd edn 1998 (trans. Italian 1995); (ed with R. Foot) Migration: the Asian experience, 1994; (ed with M. Prozesky) Gandhi and South Africa: principles and politics, 1996; (ed with R. Foot) Hong Kong's Transitions 1842–1997, 1997; Nehru, 1999; (ed with W. R. Louis) The Oxford History of the British Empire, vol. IV: the twentieth century, 1999; (ed with R. E. Frykenberg) Christians, Cultural Interactions and India's Religious Traditions, 2002; Nehru: a political life, 2003; Global South Asians: introducing the modern diaspora, 2006; (ed) The Essential Writings of Mahatma Gandhi, 2008; Windows into the Past: life histories and the historian of South Africa, 2009; (ed with A. Parel) Cambridge Companion to Gandhi, 2011. *Recreations:* classical music, gardening, walking. *Address:* Balliol College, Oxford OX1 3BJ.

See also P. W. H. Brown.

BROWN, Dame Julia Elizabeth; *see* King, Dame J. E.

BROWN, Julian Francis, RDI 1998; Owner and Creative Director, Studio Brown; *b* 8 Sept. 1955; *s* of Oliver and Barbara Brown; *m* 1986, Louise Mary Aron; two *s* one *d. Educ:* Leicester Poly. (BA Hons Industrial Design 1978); RCA (MDes 1983). Designer: David Carter Associates, 1979–80; Porsche Design, Austria, 1983–86; Partner, Lovegrove & Brown, 1986–90; Owner, StudioBrown, 1990–2011. Guest Professor: Hochschule der Kunste, Berlin, 1991–92; Essen-Duisburg Univ., 2003–04. External Examiner in Industrial Design: RCA, 1997–99; Glasgow Sch. of Art, 1998–2003. *Address:* Flat F, Portland Lofts, Wilson Street, Bristol BS2 9HE.

BROWN, June Marion; *see* Venters, J. M.

BROWN, Karen Veronica; Chair of Trustees, Oxfam Great Britain, since 2011 (Trustee, Oxfam International, since 2011); *b* Crawley, Sussex, 13 July 1952; *d* of John David Jennings and Katharine Veronica Mary Jennings (*née* Pollok); *m* 1st, 1978, Mark Brown (marr. diss. 1998); 2nd, 1999, John Harrison Blake. *Educ:* Bristol Univ. (LLB Hons 1974); Camberwell Coll. of Arts (BA Hons Fine Art, Drawing, 2011). CEDR Mediation 2001. Asst Ed., WIB Publications, 1975–79; Researcher, then producer, Granada TV, 1979–87; Channel 4 Television: Dep. Commng Ed., News and Current Affairs, 1987–91; Commng Ed., Educn, 1992–96; Controller, Factual Progs, 1996–97; Dep. Dir of Progs, 1997–2001; Dir, Television Corp. plc, 2002–06; Learning Champion, Royal Botanical Gdns, Kew, 2006–07. Associate, Prime Minister's Delivery Unit, 2002–09. Chair, ActionAid UK, 2004–09; Vice-Chair, ActionAid Internat., 2009–10; Chair of Trustees, Booktrust, 2014–. Gov., Ravensbourne Coll., 2014–. *Recreations:* theatre, reading, art, walking, canoeing. *E:* kvbrown@oxfam.org.uk, kvbrown@blueyonder.co.uk.

BROWN, Keith James; Member (SNP) Clackmannanshire and Dunblane, Scottish Parliament, since 2011 (Ochil, 2007–11); Cabinet Secretary for Infrastructure, Investment and Cities, since 2014; *b* 20 Dec. 1961; *s* of Atholl Brown and Carole Brown; *m* 1990, Tammy Joyce (separated 2006); two *s* one *d. Educ:* Univ. of Dundee (MA Hons 1988); Univ. of Prince Edward Is. (MA Hons). Royal Marines, 1980–83. Clerk, Edinburgh DC, 1988–90; Admin. Officer, 1990–96, Civic Officer, 1996–2007, Stirling DC, then Stirling Council. Minister for Skills and Lifelong Learning, 2009–10, for Transport and Infrastructure, 2010–11, for Housing and Transport, 2011–12, for Transport and Veteran Affairs, 2012–14, Scottish Parlt. Mem. (SNP), Clackmannanshire Council, 1996–2007. Mem., European Cttee of the Regions, 1999–2006, 2008–. *Recreations:* smoking Cuban cigars, Hibernian FC. *Address:* c/o Scottish Parliament, Edinburgh EH99 1SP. *T:* (constituency office) (01259) 219333. *E:* keith.brown.msp@scottish.parliament.uk.

BROWN, (Laurence Frederick) Mark; His Honour Judge Mark Brown; a Circuit Judge, since 2000; a Senior Circuit Judge and Resident Judge, Preston Crown Court, since 2015; *b* 16 March 1953; *s* of Rt Rev. Ronald Brown, *qv* and late Joyce Brown; *m* 1978, Jane Margaret Boardman; one *s. Educ:* Bolton Sch.; St John's Coll., Univ. of Durham (BA Jt Hons Law/Econs; Adam Smith Prize in Econs). Called to the Bar, Inner Temple, 1975, Bencher, 2009; practised, Northern Circuit, 1976–2000; Asst Recorder, 1993–97, a Recorder, 1997–2000; Asst Boundary Comr, England and Wales, 2000. Ethnic Minority Liaison Judge, Liverpool, 2002–05; Magistrates' Liaison Judge: Knowsley Bench, 2002–11; Wirral Bench, 2012–. Pt-time tutor in Law, Univ. of Liverpool, 1977–82; Lectr and Tutor Judge, Judicial Coll., 2008–. Criminal Justice Strategy Cttee, Merseyside Area, 1997–2000; Parole Bd, 2003–10; Panel for Judicial Appts, 2004–08. *Recreations:* golf, walking. *Address:* Preston Crown Court, Openshaw Place, Ring Way, Preston, Lancs PR1 2LL. *Club:* Royal Liverpool Golf.

BROWN, Prof. Lawrence Michael, ScD; FRS 1982; Professor of Physics, University of Cambridge, 1990–2001, now Emeritus; Founding Fellow, Robinson College, Cambridge, since 1977; *b* 18 March 1936; *s* of Bertson Waterworth Brown and Edith Waghorne; *m* 1965, Susan Drucker; one *s* two *d. Educ:* Univ. of Toronto (BASc); Univ. of Birmingham (PhD); ScD Cantab 1992. Athlone Fellow, Univ. of Birmingham, 1957; W. M. Tapp Research Fellow, Gonville and Caius Coll., Cambridge, 1963; University Demonstrator, Cavendish Laboratory, 1965; Lectr, 1970–83, Reader, 1983–90, Cambridge Univ.; Lectr, Robinson Coll., Cambridge, 1977–90. *Publications:* many papers on dislocation plasticity and on structure and properties of materials and electron microscopy in Acta Metallurgica and Philosophical Magazine. *Address:* 74 Alpha Road, Cambridge CB4 3DG. *T:* (01223) 337336; SMF Group, Cavendish Laboratory, J. J. Thompson Avenue, Cambridge CB3 0HE. *T:* (01223) 337200.

BROWN, Canon Dr Lydia Akrigg, (Mrs Stephen Robbins), MBE 2011; FRCVS; FRSB; Senior Independent Director, since 2008 and Vice Chairman, since 2010, Salisbury NHS Foundation Trust; *b* 28 June 1954; *d* of late Tom Brown and of Barbara Brown (*née* Blackmore); *m* 1st, 1988, John Heckford Seamer (*d* 2007); 2nd, 2011, Ven. Stephen Robbins, *qv. Educ:* Childwall Valley High Sch. for Girls, Liverpool; Univ. of Liverpool (BVSc 1978); Univ. of Stirling (PhD 1983); BA Open 1992; Univ. of Warwick (MBA 2002). MRCVS 1978, FRCVS 1987; CBiol, FRSB (FIBiol 2002). Wellcome Trust res. schol., 1978–81; Technical Manager: Ewos Aquaculture, 1982–83; Willows Francis, 1984–85; Asst Prof., Coll. of Veterinary Medicine, Mississippi State Univ., 1985–87; Man. Dir, Biological Labs (UK) Ltd, 1987–89; Eur. Tech. Manager, then UK Country Manager, Abbott Labs, 1989–2000; Man. Dir, 2000–10, Exec. Dir, 2011, PHARMAQ Ltd (formerly Alpharma Animal Health Ltd). Hon. Lectr, Univs of Liverpool and London. Mem., Medicines Commn, 2000–05. RCVS specialist in fish health and prodn, 1989–94, 2007–. Royal College of Veterinary Surgeons: Mem. Council, 1991–2007; Chm., various cttees; Pres., 1998–99; Mem., Parly and Scientific Cttee, 1998–2003, Ind. Mem., Planning and Resources Cttee, 2010–; Chm., RCVS Trust, 1998–2004; Pres., Veterinary Benevolent Fund, 2006–14; RCVS rep., Fedn of Veterinarians in Europe, 1998–2000. Mem. Council, Univ. Fedn of Animal Welfare, 2005–14 (Dep. Chm., 2010–12; Chm., 2012–14). Founder Trustee, Veterinary Surgeons Health Support Prog., 1999–2014; Trustee, Humane Slaughter Assoc., 2005–14 (Dep. Chm., 2010–12; Chm., 2012–14). Mem., Steering Cttee, Vet Helpline, 1993–98, 2008–14. Pres., Southern Counties Veterinary Assoc., 1994–95. MInstD 2001. Gov., Salisbury Cathedral Sch., 2005–. Lay Canon, 2007–13, Emeritus Lay Canon, 2014, Salisbury Cathedral. Dalrymple Champneys Silver Cup and Medal, British Vet. Assoc., 2014. *Publications:* (ed) Rearing Healthy Fish under Primitive Conditions, 1987; The Aquaculture Market, 1989; (ed) Aquaculture for Veterinarians, 1993; contrib. papers and chapters on surgical techniques, anaesthesia, pharmacology and husbandry related to aquaculture. *Recreations:* travel, scuba diving, photography, walking. *Address:* Mill Leat, W Gomeldon, Salisbury, Wilts SP4 6JY. *T:* (01980) 611438. *E:* drlydiabrown@gmail.com. *Clubs:* Farmers, Royal Society of Medicine.

BROWN, Lyn Carol; MP (Lab) West Ham, since 2005; *b* 13 April 1960; *m* 2008, John Cullen. *Educ:* Univ. of London (BA). Residential Social Worker, Ealing, 1984–85, Newham, 1985–87, Waltham Forest, 1988–2005. Mem. (Lab) Newham BC, 1988–2005. Founder and Chm., London Libraries Develt Agency, 2000–06. Contested (Lab) Wanstead and Woodford, 1992. An Asst Govt Whip, 2009–10; an Opposition Whip, 2010–13; Shadow Fire and Communities Minister, 2013–15. *Address:* House of Commons, SW1A 0AA.

BROWN, Rev. Dr Malcolm Arthur; Director of Mission and Public Affairs, Church of England, since 2007; *b* 17 Sept. 1954; *s* of Arthur Leslie and Gwendolen Mary Brown; *m* 1983, Angela Josephine; one *s*, and one step *s. Educ:* Eltham Coll.; Oriel Coll., Oxford (BA 1976; MA 1982); Westcott House; Univ. of Manchester (PhD 2000). Ordained deacon, 1979, priest, 1980; Asst Curate, Riverhead with Dunton Green, 1979–83; Team Vicar and Industrial Missioner, Southampton City Centre, 1983–90; Exec. Sec., William Temple Foundn,

1990–2000; Principal, E Anglian Ministerial Trng Course, then Eastern Reg. Ministry Course, 2000–07. Honorary Lecturer: Univ. of Manchester, 1993–2000; Univ. of Wales, Bangor, 2000–06; Anglia Ruskin Univ., 2005–; Sen. Associate, Cambridge Theol Fedn, 2007–. Hon. Distinguished Canon, Manchester Cathedral, 2014–; Hon. Canon, Ely Cathedral, 2014–. FHEA 2007; FRSA 2012. *Publications:* After the Market, 2004; (with P. Ballard) The Church and Economic Life, 2006; Tensions in Christian Ethics, 2010; (ed) Anglican Social Theology, 2014; contrib. numerous essays and articles in academic jls. *Recreations:* driving steam trains, metal bashing, rowing. *Address:* Church House, Great Smith Street, SW1P 3NZ. *T:* (020) 7898 1468. *E:* malcolm.brown@churchofengland.org.

BROWN, Prof. Malcolm Watson, PhD; FRS 2004; Professor of Anatomy and Cognitive Neuroscience, University of Bristol, 1998–2010, now Emeritus (Research Director, Faculty of Medicine and Veterinary Sciences, 2003–10); *b* 24 Feb. 1946; *s* of Denis and Vivian Irene Brown; *m* 1974, Geraldine Ruth Hassall; one *s* one *d*. *Educ:* Crewkerne Sch., Som.; St John's Coll., Cambridge (BA 1st Cl. Natural Scis Tripos, Theoretical Physics 1968; MA 1972; PhD 1974). Asst in Res., Dept of Anatomy, Univ. of Cambridge, 1972–74; Res. Fellow, Downing Coll., Cambridge, 1973–74; Department of Anatomy, University of Bristol: Lectr, 1975–91; Sen. Lectr, 1991–94; Reader in Anatomy and Cognitive Neurosci., 1994–98; Dep. Hd, 1996–98; Hd, 1998–2006. Special Res. Fellow, AFRC, 1991–92. Exec. Mem., Mgt Cttee, MRC Centre for Synaptic Plasticity, 1999–2010. Member: Brain Res., subseq. British Neurosci., Assoc., 1970–; Eur. Brain and Behaviour Soc., 1984–2011; Anatomical Soc. of GB and Ireland, 2000–10. *Publications:* (contrib.) A Textbook of Head and Neck Anatomy, 1988; contrib. scientific papers and reviews to learned jls. *Recreations:* foreign travel, local church responsibilities. *Address:* University of Bristol, School of Physiology and Pharmacology, Medical Sciences Building, Bristol BS8 1TD. *T:* (0117) 331 1909, *Fax:* (0117) 331 2288. *E:* M.W.Brown@bris.ac.uk.

BROWN, (Margaret) Jayne, OBE 2004; Director, Jayne Brown Strategic Solutions, since 2013; *b* Oldham, 2 Jan. 1963; *d* of James Seddon and Margaret Seddon; *m* 1992, Kevin Brown; one *d*. *Educ:* Univ. of Manchester (BA Hons Politics and Mod. Hist. 1984); Univ. of Nottingham (MPH 1997). Senior appts, NHS, 1990–2006; Chief Executive: NHS Doncaster, 2006–08; NHS N Yorks and York, 2008–13. *Recreations:* reading, theatre, genealogy, food (eating and cooking).

BROWN, Prof. Margaret Louise, OBE 2015; PhD; FAcSS; Professor of Mathematics Education, King's College, London, 1990–2013, now Emeritus; *b* 30 Sept. 1943; *d* of (Frederick) Harold Seed and Louisa Seed (*née* Shearer); *m* 1970, Hugh Palmer Brown; three *s*. *Educ:* Merchant Taylors' Sch. for Girls, Liverpool; Newnham Coll., Cambridge (BA Math. 1965; MA 1968); Inst. of Education, London Univ. (PGCE 1966); Chelsea Coll., Univ. of London (PhD 1981). Math. Teacher, Cavendish Sch., Hemel Hempstead, 1966–69; Lectr in Math. Educn, 1969–83, Sen. Lectr, 1983–86, Chelsea Coll., Univ. of London; Reader in Math. Educn, 1986–90, Head of Sch. of Educn, 1992–96, KCL; FKC 1996. Member: Nat. Curriculum Math. Wkg Gp, 1987–88; Numeracy Task Force, 1997–98; Adv. Cttee on Maths Educn, 2005–08; Educn Cttee, Royal Soc., 2013–; Chair: Jt Math. Council of UK, 1991–95; Trustees, School Math. Project, 1996–2006; Educn Sub-Panel, RAE 2008, 2004–08; President: Math. Assoc., 1990–91; British Educnl Res. Assoc., 1997–98. FAcSS (AcSS 2000). Hon. EdD Kingston, 2002; Hon. DSc Loughborough, 2010. Kavli Medal, Royal Soc., 2013. *Publications:* (jtly) Statistics and Probability, 1972, 2nd edn 1977; (jtly) Low Attainers in Mathematics 5–16, 1982; (jtly) Children Learning Mathematics, 1984; Graded Assessment in Mathematics, 1992; (jtly) Intuition or Evidence?, 1995; (jtly) Effective Teachers of Numeracy, 1997; (jtly) Primary Mathematics and the Developing Professional, 2004; papers in jls and contribs to books on math. educn. *Recreations:* walking, music. *Address:* (home) 34 Girdwood Road, SW18 5QS. *T:* (020) 8789 4344.

BROWN, (Marion) Patricia; Under-Secretary (Economics), Treasury, 1972–85; *b* 2 Feb. 1927; *d* of late Henry Oswald Brown and Elsie Elizabeth (*née* Thompson). *Educ:* Norwich High Sch. for Girls; Newnham Coll., Cambridge. Central Economic Planning Staff, Cabinet Office, 1947; Treasury, 1948–54; United States Embassy, London, 1956–59; Treasury, 1959–85. Mem. Council, Royal Holloway and Bedford New Coll., London Univ., 1985–98 (Hon. Fellow, 1999). *Recreations:* bird watching, walking.

BROWN, Mark; *see* Brown, L. F. M.

BROWN, Martin; independent consultant on strategic management of public sector organisations, customs and indirect taxation; Member, panel of fiscal experts, International Monetary Fund, since 2008; *b* 26 Jan. 1949; *s* of late Clarence and Anne Brown; *m* 1971, Frances Leithead; two *s*. *Educ:* Bolton Sch.; New Coll., Oxford (MA). Joined Customs and Excise as Admin. Trainee, 1971; Private Sec. to Minister of State and to Financial Sec., HM Treasury, 1974–76; Principal, HM Customs and Excise, 1976; Customs adviser to Barbados Govt, 1984–86; HM Customs and Excise (later HM Revenue and Customs): Asst Sec., 1987; Comr, 1993–2002; Director: Customs, 1993; Central Ops, 1994–96; VAT Policy, 1996–2000; Customs and Tax Practice, 2001–02; Dir, Eurocustoms, Paris (on secondment), 2002–08. *Recreations:* theatre, walking, gardening, pottering. *E:* martin.brown@live.com.

BROWN, Martin; a District Judge (Magistrates' Courts), 2005–15; *b* 31 Aug. 1958; *s* of Raymond Brown and Beryl Brown (*née* Yorath); *m* 1983, Anne Elizabeth Pooley; one *d*. *Educ:* Univ. of Wales, Aberystwyth (LLB 1979). Admitted solicitor, 1982; High Court (Criminal) Advocate, 1994–2005; Actg Stipendiary Magistrate, subseq. Dep. Dist Judge, 1999–2004. Mem., Test Bd, Centre for Professional Legal Studies, 1998–2005 (Duty Solicitor accreditation scheme). *Recreations:* hill-walking, running, bird-watching, Christian.

BROWN, Sir Mervyn, KCMG 1981 (CMG 1975); OBE 1963; HM Diplomatic Service, retired; *b* 24 Sept. 1923; *m* 1949, Elizabeth Gittings (*d* 2013). *Educ:* Ryhope Gram. Sch., Sunderland; St John's Coll., Oxford. Served in RA, 1942–45. Entered HM Foreign Service, 1949; Third Secretary, Buenos Aires, 1950; Second Secretary, UK Mission to UN, New York, 1953; First Secretary, Foreign Office, 1956; Singapore, 1959; Vientiane, 1960; again in Foreign Office, 1963–67; Ambassador to Madagascar, 1967–70; Inspector, FCO, 1970–72; Head of Communications Operations Dept, FCO, 1973–74; Asst Under-Sec. of State (Dir of Communications), 1974; High Comr in Tanzania, 1975–78, and concurrently Ambassador to Madagascar; Minister and Dep. Perm. Representative to UN, 1978; High Comr in Nigeria, 1979–83, and concurrently Ambassador to Benin. Chairman: Visiting Arts Unit of GB, 1983–89; Council, King's Coll., Madrid, 1995–2003; Vice-Pres., Commonwealth Youth Exchange Council, 1984–87. Pres., Britain-Nigeria Assoc., 2000–03; Chm., Anglo-Malagasy Soc., 1986–2008. Associate Mem., Acad. Malgache. Officier, Ordre National (Madagascar). *Publications:* Madagascar Rediscovered, 1978; A History of Madagascar, 1995; War in Shangri-La, 2001. *Recreations:* music, tennis, history, cooking. *Address:* 195 Queen's Gate, SW7 5EU. *Clubs:* Royal Over-Seas League, Hurlingham, All England Lawn Tennis.

BROWN, Michael; *see* Brown, John M.

BROWN, Prof. Michael Alan, CBE 2008; DL; PhD; CPhys, CEng; Vice-Chancellor and Chief Executive, Liverpool John Moores University, 2000–11, now Ambassador Fellow; Chairman: Alder Hey Children's Charity, since 2012; Procure Plus Holdings, since 2014; *b* 19 May 1946; *s* of Reginald Leslie Brown and Barbara Evelyn Brown; *m* 1966, Andrea Kathleen Evans; one *s* one *d*. *Educ:* Bridgend Boys' Tech./Grammar Sch.; Nottingham Univ. (BSc Physics; PhD 1971). Eur Ing 1991; MInstP 1980, FInstP 2003; CPhys 1980; MIEE 1984, FIET (FIEE 2002); CEng 1984. Demonstrator, Nottingham Univ., 1967–71; Royal Soc. Post-doctoral Eur. Fellow, Grenoble, 1971–72; Lectr, then Sen. Lectr, in Physics, Loughborough Univ., 1972–86; Gen. Manager, Loughborough Consultants Ltd, 1986–87; Pro Vice-Chancellor, Leicester Poly., then De Montfort Univ., 1987–2000. Dir, UCAS, 2001–05. Mem., Cttee for S African Trade, DTI, 1995–2001. Eur. Trng Consultant to Intel Corp., 1981–87. Mem. and Dir, De Montfort Expertise Ltd, 1989–2000 (Man. Dir, 1989–96); Mem., Dir and Co. Sec., E Midlands Regl Technol. Network Ltd, 1989–96; Mem. and Dir, E Midlands Regl Mgt Centre Ltd, 1991–92; Man. Dir, Flexible Learning Systems Ltd, 1992–2000; Dir, Higher Educn Subscription Fund Ltd, 1994–2000; Dir, Leicester Promotions Ltd, 1996–2000; Exec. Chm., De Montfort Univ., S Africa, 1998–2000; Member: Internat. Sub-Cttee, 2002–07, Finance Sub-Cttee, 2003–07, UUK; Steering Gp for Jt Masters Progs, European Univs Assoc., 2002–05. Ind. Chm., Forum for a Better Leics, 1995–2000; Vice-Pres., Personal Service Soc., Liverpool, 2000–11; Member: Bd, Liverpool First, 2001–11; Liverpool Capital of Culture Ltd, 2003–07; Mem., Monitoring Cttee, Merseyside Objective One Prog., 2002–09 (Chairman: Strategy Sub-Cttee, 2002–05; Strategy and Monitoring Sub-Cttee, 2005–08; Closure Cttee, 2008–09); Director: Merseyside Partnership Ltd, 2002–10; Liverpool Vision, 2003–08; Liverpool Ventures Ltd, 2004–05; Chairman: Merseyside and Liverpool Theatres Trust Ltd, 2002–; Liverpool Science Park, 2003–11; Liverpool Strategic Innovation and Improvement Gp, 2008–09; Liverpool Democracy Commn, 2008–09. Advr, Thinspace Ltd, 2012–. Vice-Pres., ESU, Merseyside, 2009–. Mem. and Trustee, Africa Now, 1997–2002; Trustee, Rights and Humanities, 2009–10. CCMI (FIMgt 1991); FCIM 2000; FInstD 2009; MCIH 2014. FRSA 1996. Freeman, City of London, 2007; Liveryman, Engineers' Co., 2007–. DL Merseyside, 2005. Mem. Editl Bd, Laboratory Microcomputer, 1988–93. Hon. DLaws Liverpool, 2011. *Publications:* (contrib.) Collaboration between Business and Higher Education, 1990; (contrib.) The Funding of Higher Education, 1993; (contrib.) Preparing Students for Career Employment, 1998; numerous contribs to learned jls and internat. conf. proc. on physics, mktg and higher educn mgt. *Recreations:* cinema, theatre, travel, spending time with my wife. *Address:* Dawstone Croft, Dawstone Road, Heswall, Wirral, Merseyside CH60 0BU. *Clubs:* Institute of Directors; Athenaeum (Liverpool).

BROWN, Michael Russell; journalist; *b* 3 July 1951; *s* of Frederick Alfred Brown and Greta Mary Brown, OBE (*née* Russell). *Educ:* Andrew Cairns Secondary Modern Sch., Sussex; Univ. of York (BA (Hons) Economics and Politics). Graduate Management Trainee, Barclays Bank Ltd, 1972–74; Lecturer and Tutor, Swinton Conservative Coll., 1974–75; part-time Asst to Michael Marshall, MP, 1975–76; Law Student, 1976–77, Member of Middle Temple; Personal Asst to Nicholas Winterton, MP, 1976–79. MP (C) Brigg and Scunthorpe, 1979–83, Brigg and Cleethorpes, 1983–97; contested (C) Cleethorpes, 1997. PPS to Hon. Douglas Hogg, Minister of State, DTI, 1989–90, FCO, 1990–92; PPS to Sir Patrick Mayhew, Sec. of State for NI, 1992–93; an Asst Govt Whip, 1993–94. Mem., Energy Select Cttee, 1986–89; Sec., 1981–87, Vice-Chm., 1987–89, Conservative Parly N Ireland Cttee. Political columnist, The Independent, 1998–. *Recreations:* cricket, walking. *Address:* 78 Lupus Street, SW1V 3EL. *T:* (020) 7630 9045. *Club:* Reform.

BROWN, Prof. Michael Stuart, MD; Regental Professor, University of Texas; Paul J. Thomas Chair in Medicine, Jonsson Center for Molecular Genetics, since 1977, and W. A. Moncrief Distinguished Chair in Cholesterol and Arteriosclerosis Research, since 1989, University of Texas Southwestern Medical School at Dallas; *b* 13 April 1941; *s* of Harvey and Evelyn Brown; *m* 1964, Alice Lapin; two *d*. *Educ:* Univ. of Pennsylvania (AB 1962, MD 1966). Resident in Internal Medicine, Mass. Gen. Hosp., Boston, 1966–68; Research Scientist, NIH, Bethesda, 1968–71; Asst Prof., Univ. of Texas Southwestern Med. Sch. at Dallas, 1971–74; Associate Prof., 1974–76. Member Board of Directors: Regeneron Inc., 1991–; Pfizer Inc., 1996–2012. For. Mem., Royal Soc., 1991. Lounsbery Award, 1979; Albert D. Lasker Award, 1985; (jtly) Nobel Prize in Medicine or Physiology for the discovery of receptors for Low Density Lipoproteins, a fundamental advance in the understanding of cholesterol metabolism, 1985; US Nat. Medal of Science, 1987. *Publications:* numerous papers to learned jls. *Address:* Department of Molecular Genetics, University of Texas Southwestern Medical School, 5323 Harry Hines Boulevard, Dallas, TX 75390–9046, USA.

BROWN, Michael William Tuke, MVO 2002; FRICS; FCILT; Managing Director, London Underground and London Rail, Transport for London, since 2010; *b* Belfast, 14 April 1964; *s* of Dr William Aiken Brown and Margaret Elisabeth Brown (*née* Tuke); *m* 2000, Barbara Elizabeth McKelvey; one *s*. *Educ:* Brackenber House; Campbell Coll.; Queen's Univ., Belfast (BSc (Econ); MBA). Chief Operating Officer, London Underground, 2003–08; Man. Dir, Heathrow Airport, BAA, 2008–10. Mem., British Transport Police Authy, 2004–08. FRSA. *Recreations:* gym, family, friends. *Address:* London Underground, 55 Broadway, SW1H 0BD. *T:* (020) 7027 8499, *Fax:* (020) 7918 4037. *E:* mike.brown@tube.tfl.gov.uk.

BROWN, Moira; *see* Brown, Susanne M.

BROWN, Prof. Morris Jonathan, FRCP; Professor of Clinical Pharmacology, Cambridge University, and Hon. Consultant Physician, Addenbrooke's Hospital, since 1985; Fellow of Gonville and Caius College, and Director of Clinical Studies, Cambridge, since 1989; *b* 18 Jan. 1951; *s* of Arnold and Irene Brown; *m* 1977, Diana Phylactou; three *d*. *Educ:* Harrow; Trinity College, Cambridge (MA, MD); MSc London. FRCP 1987. Lectr, Royal Postgraduate Medical School, 1979–82; Senior Fellow, MRC, 1982–85. Oliver-Sharpey Lectr, RCP, 1992. Chm., Med. Res. Soc., 1991–97; Pres., British Hypertension Soc., 2005–07. FMedSci 1999; FAHA 2002; FBPhS (FBPharmacolS 2012); FBHS 2014. Hospital Doctor of the Year, Elsevier Press, 2003; Lilly Gold Medal, British Pharmacol Soc., 2002; Walter Somerville Medal, British Cardiac Soc., 2006. *Publications:* Advanced Medicine 21, 1985; (jtly) Clinical Pharmacology, 8th edn 1996 to 11th edn 2012; articles on causes and treatment of hypertension, with special interest in rare adrenal tumours. *Recreations:* violin and oboe playing, tennis. *Address:* 104 Grange Road, Cambridge CB3 9AA. *Club:* Athenæum.

BROWN, Nageena; *see* Khalique, N.

BROWN, Dr Nicholas David; Principal, Linacre College, Oxford, since 2010; *b* Brockworth, Glos, 4 Dec. 1962; *s* of Ray and Avril Brown; one *s* three *d*; *m* Roosa Leimu. *Educ:* United World Coll. of Atlantic; Churchill Coll., Cambridge (BA Hons Geog. 1985); Aberdeen Univ. (MSc Ecol.); DPhil Oxon. Lectr, Manchester Univ., 1989–92; Res. Officer, Oxford Forestry Inst., 1992–94; Lectr, Oxford Univ., 1994–2010; Sen. Tutor and Dean, Linacre Coll., Oxford, 2006–10. Commonwealth Scholarship Comr, 2013–. Trustee: Sylva Foundn, 2009–; Tertiary Educn Scholarship Trust for Africa, 2009–. *Publications:* contrib. papers to learned jls on tropical and temperate forest ecol. *Recreations:* viola, sailing, cycling. *Address:* Linacre College, Oxford OX1 3JA. *T:* (01865) 271662. *E:* nick.brown@linacre.ox.ac.uk.

BROWN, Rt Hon. Nicholas (Hugh); PC 1997; MP (Lab) Newcastle upon Tyne East, since 2010 (Newcastle upon Tyne East, 1983–97; Newcastle upon Tyne East and Wallsend, 1997–2010); *b* 13 June 1950; *s* of late R. C. Brown and G. K. Brown (*née* Tester). *Educ:* Swattenden Secondary Modern Sch.; Tunbridge Wells Tech. High Sch.; Manchester Univ. (BA 1971). Trade Union Officer, GMWU Northern Region, 1978–83. Mem., Newcastle upon Tyne City Council, 1980–84. Opposition front-bench spokesman: on legal affairs, 1984–87; on Treasury affairs, 1987–94; on health, 1994–95; Dep. Chief Opposition Whip, 1995–97; Parly Sec. to HM Treasury (Govt Chief Whip), 1997–98 and 2008–10; Minister, Agriculture, Fisheries and Food, 1998–2001; Minister of State (Minister for Work), DWP, 2001–03; Treasurer of HM Household (Dep. Chief Whip), 2007–08; Minister for NE of

England, 2007–10; Shadow Parly Sec. to HM Treasury (Govt Chief Whip), 2010. Freeman, City of Newcastle, 2001. *Address:* House of Commons, SW1A 0AA. *Clubs:* Shieldfield Working Men's, West Walker Social, Newcastle Labour (Newcastle); Lindisfarne (Wallsend).

BROWN, Nicolas Jerome Danton; Director, Neal Street Productions, since 2013; *b* 11 Sept. 1965; *s* of Simon and Rosemary Brown; *m* 1998, Sarah Barker; two *s*. *Educ:* Portswood Primary Sch., Southampton; St John's Sch., Leatherhead; Choate Rosemary Hall, Conn.; Clare Coll., Cambridge (BA Hist. 1987). Trainee, Central TV, 1987–89; Develt Exec., 1989–91, Production Exec., 1991–94, Central Films; freelance producer, 1995–2006; Dir, UK Drama Prodn, BBC, 2006–12. *Television:* producer: Insiders, 1997; London Bridge, 1998; Hope and Glory, 1999; Deceit, 1999; Nicholas Nickleby, 2000; White Teeth, 2001–02; Friends and Crocodiles, 2003; Gideon's Daughter, 2004; Bradford Riots, 2005; executive producer: Capturing Mary, 2008; Joe's Palace, 2008; Isles of Wonder, Happy and Glorious, 2012 (London Olympic Games Opening Ceremony films); *film:* producer, Ladies in Lavender, 2004. *Recreation:* sailing. *Address:* c/o Sara Putt Associates, The Old House, Shepperton Studios, Shepperton, Middx TW17 0QD.

BROWN, Prof. Nigel Leslie, OBE 2014; PhD; FRSE; FRSC, FRSB; Professor of Molecular Microbiology, University of Edinburgh, 2008–12, now Emeritus; President, Society for General Microbiology, 2012–15; *b* 19 Dec. 1948; *s* of Leslie Charles and Beryl Brown; *m* 1971, Gayle Lynnette Blackah; three *d*. *Educ:* Beverley Grammar Sch.; Univ. of Leeds (BSc 1971; PhD 1974). CBiol, FRSB (FIBiol 1989); CChem, FRSC 1990; FRSE 2011. ICI Fellow, MRC Lab. of Molecular Biology, Cambridge, 1974–76; Lectr in Biochemistry, 1976–81, Royal Soc. EPA Cephalosporin Fund Sen. Res. Fellow, 1981–88, Univ. of Bristol; University of Birmingham: Prof. of Molecular Genetics and Microbiol., 1988–2008; Hd, 1994–99, Dep. Hd, 1999–2000, Sch. of Biol Scis; Hd, Sch. of Chemistry, 2003–04; Dir of Sci. and Technol., BBSRC, 2004–08 (Mem., Strategy Bd, 1997–2004); Vice-Principal and Hd, Coll. of Sci. and Engrg, 2008–11, Sen. Vice-Principal, Planning and Res. Policy, 2011–12, Univ. of Edinburgh. Chm., Genome Analysis Centre, 2013–. Member: Res. Careers Initiative, 1997–98; Scottish Sci. Adv. Council, 2010–15; REF sub-panel, 2012–14; Chairman: Deans of Sci. and Engrg in Scotland, 2010–12; Scottish Consortium for Rural Res., 2011–12; NERC Training Adv. Gp, 2014–. Vis. Fellow in Genetics, Univ. of Melbourne, 1987–88; Leverhulme Trust Res. Fellow, 2000–01. Hon. Professor: Univ. of Nottingham, 2011; Univ. of Swansea, 2012; Hon. DSc Edinburgh 2014. Hon. Pres., W Midlands Reg., ASE, 1997–98. Mem. Editl Bd, Molecular Microbiology, 1986–97; Chief Ed., Fedn of Eur. Microbiology Socs Microbiology Reviews, 2000–04. *Publications:* contribs to scientific jls, books and magazines. *Recreations:* travel, house renovation. *Address:* c/o Society for General Microbiology, Charles Darwin House, 12 Roger Street, WC1N 2JU. *E:* nigel.brown@ed.ac.uk.

BROWN, Pamela; *see* Cameron, P.

BROWN, Patricia; *see* Brown, M. P.

BROWN, Patricia Ann; *see* Heywood, P. A.

BROWN, Patricia Ann; Director, Central Futures Ltd, since 2008; *b* Liverpool, 5 Sept. 1957; *d* of Frederick Brown and Jane Brown (*née* Gallagher). *Educ:* Queen Mary High Sch., Liverpool. CAM Cert. Communications; CAM Dip. PR. Publicity officer, GLC, 1985–86; PR Manager, London Res. Centre, 1986–94; Dir of Information, London First Centre, 1994–97; Chief Exec., Central London Partnership, 1998–2008. Dir, Newlyn Art Gall., 2012–. Trustee: Interchange Trust, 1995–2000; London Internat. Fest. of Th., 2001–13; Borough Mkt Trust, 2007–10; Geffrye Mus., 2009–; Chair, London Fest. of Architecture, 2013–. *Publications:* Quality Streets: the economic case for high quality street environments, 2003; Public Space Public Life, 2004; Legible London: a wayfinding study, 2006; Economic Development Strategy for Central London, 2006, 2008; Open Space: a best practice toolkit for art in the public realm, 2007. *Recreations:* art, architecture and design, walking, swimming, Cornwall. *Address:* 26 Alma Grove, SE1 5PY.

BROWN, Sir Patrick; *see* Brown, Sir A. P.

BROWN, Paul Campbell, CBE 2003; Director, Wightlink Ltd, 2012–14 (Project Manager, 2009–11); *b* 6 Nov. 1945; *s* of James Henry Brown and Edna May Brown (*née* Howell); *m* 1970, Sarah Hunter Bailey; two *s*. *Educ:* Portsmouth Grammar Sch.; RMA Sandhurst; Balliol Coll., Oxford (BA Hons). Served Army, as Officer, 1966–74. British Forces Broadcasting Service, 1974–78; Ops Manager, BRMB Radio, 1979–81; Prog. and News Dir, Radio Victory, 1981–84; Hd, Radio Programming, IBA, 1984–90; Dep. Chief Exec., Radio Authy, 1990–95; Chief Exec., Commercial Radio Cos Assoc., 1995–2006; Chm., RadioCentre, 2006–08. Director: Rajar, 1996–2006; Skillset, 2004–08. Chm., UK Digital Radio Forum, 2000–01; Pres., Assoc. of European Radios, 1998–2000; Vice Pres., World DAB Forum, 2000–05. FRA 1996 (Chm. Council, 2001–04); FRSA 2000. *Recreations:* sailing, tennis, walking, reading. *E:* paul@westernparade.co.uk. *Clubs:* Army and Navy; Thorney Island Sailing (Vice Commodore, 2005–07, Commodore, 2007–09); Emsworth Sailing.

BROWN, Paul G.; Executive Director, UK Retail Banking, Lloyds Bank plc, 1991–97, retired; *b* 10 Sept. 1942; *s* of Col E. G. Brown and Alice Brown (*née* Van Weyenberghe); *m* 1969, Jessica Faunce; one *s* two *d*. *Educ:* Belgium, Germany and UK. Management appts with Lloyds Bank plc in Germany, Switzerland, USA and UK, 1960–97. *Recreations:* sailing, ski-ing.

BROWN, Paul Gareth, RDI 2013; theatre designer, since 1984; *b* Vale of Glamorgan, 13 May 1960; *s* of Alan Tertius Brown and Enfys Ann Brown (*née* Jones); partner, Andrew George Cordy. *Educ:* Christ Coll., Brecon; Univ. of St Andrews (MA). Set and costume designs include: *opera:* for Royal Opera, Covent Garden: Mitridate, re di Ponto, 1991; Midsummer Marriage, 1995; I Masnadieri; Falstaff, 1999; Tosca, 2006; Manon Lescaut, 2014; for Glyndebourne Festival: Lulu; Pelleas et Melisande; Turn of the Screw, 2007; The Fairy Queen, 2009; Don Giovanni, 2010; Hippolyte et Aricie, 2013; Padmavatti, Opera Bastille, Paris; Zemire et Azor, Tom Jones, Drottningholms Slottsteater; Tannhauser, San Francisco; Mephistopheles, Amsterdam; L'Incoronazione di Poppea, Bologna; Rigoletto, Teatro Real, Madrid; Don Carlos, Sydney Opera House; Il Trovatore, Moses Und Aron, Lady Macbeth of Mtsensk; Thais, 2008, Metropolitan Opera, NY; Thais, Lyric Opera, Chicago; Katya Kabanova; Lucio Silla, 2005, The Tempest, 2006, The Marriage of Figaro, 2008, Santa Fe Opera; La Traviata; Anna Bolena, 2007, Arena di Verona; The Magic Flute, Bolshoi, Moscow, 2005; Die Zauberflöte, Salzburg Fest., 2005; Elektra, 2007, Frau Ohne Schatten, 2009, War and Peace, 2014, Mariinsky, St Petersburg; Aida, Bregenz Fest., 2009; Die Gezeichneten, Teatro Massimo, Palermo, 2010; Tristan & Isolde, Deutsche Oper, Berlin, 2011; Nabucco, Tokyo, 2013; Guillaume Tell, Rossini Opera Fest., Pesaro, 2013; *ballet:* Giselle, La Scala, Milan; *musicals:* Man of La Mancha, NY; Marguerite; Phantom of the Opera, UK tour, 2012, USA tour, 2013; *theatre:* Coriolanus, Richard II, Naked, King Lear, Platonov, The Tempest, Almeida; The Sea, Th. Royal, Haymarket, 2008; A Month in the Country, Chichester Fest., 2010; *films:* Angels and Insects, 1995; Up at the Villa, 2000. *Address:* Plas Eglwyswen, Crymych, Pembrokeshire SA41 3RU.

BROWN, Sir Peter (Randolph), Kt 1997; Conservative Constituency Agent for Huntingdon, 1985–2009; *b* 30 Aug. 1945; *s* of Stanley Percival Brown and late Dorothy Ida Brown (*née* Bagge); *m* 1983, Antonia Brenda Taylor; one *s* one *d*. *Educ:* Bushey Sch., New Malden, Surrey. With Inland Revenue, 1961–67; Conservative Constituency Agent: London Bor. of Newham, 1967–70; Lambeth, Norwood, 1970–74; Kingston upon Thames, 1974–85; Cons. Eur. Constituency Agent, Cambridge and N Beds, 1987–90. Dir, PRB Consultancy Services Ltd, 2002–09. Mem. (C), Cambs CC, 2005– (Cabinet Mem. for economy, envmt and climate change, 2008–09, for communities, 2009–11). Mem., Cambridge and Peterborough Fire Authy. Qualified Mem., Nat. Soc. of Cons. and Unionist Agents, 1968. Freeman, City of London, 1992. *Recreations:* reading, following international tennis, gardening. *Address:* 39 Hartford Road, Huntingdon, Cambs PE29 3RF.

BROWN, Prof. Peter Robert Lamont, FBA 1971; FRHistS; Rollins Professor of History, 1986–2011, now Emeritus, and Director, Program in Hellenic Studies, 2002–09, Princeton University (Visiting Professor, 1983–86); *b* 26 July 1935; *s* of James Lamont and Sheila Brown, Dublin; *m* 1st, 1959, Friedl Esther (*née* Löw-Beer); two *d*; 2nd, 1980, Patricia Ann Fortini; 3rd, 1989, Elizabeth Gilliam. *Educ:* Aravon Sch., Bray, Co. Wicklow, Ireland; Shrewsbury Sch.; New Coll., Oxford (MA). Harmsworth Senior Scholar, Merton Coll., Oxford and Prize Fellow, All Souls Coll., Oxford, 1956; Junior Research Fellow, 1963, Sen. Res. Fellow 1970–73, All Souls Coll.; Fellow, All Souls Coll., 1956–75; Lectr in Medieval History, Merton Coll. Oxford, 1970–75; Special Lectr in late Roman and early Byzantine History, 1970–73, Reader, 1973–75, Univ. of Oxford; Prof. of History, Royal Holloway Coll. London Univ., 1975–78; Prof. of History and Classics, Univ. of Calif. at Berkeley, 1978–86. Fellow, Amer. Acad. of Arts and Scis, 1978. Hon. DTheol Fribourg, 1975; Hon. DHL Chicago, 1978; S Methodist Univ., 2004; Hon. DLitt: TCD, 1990; Wesleyan Univ., Conn, 1993; Columbia Univ., NY, 2001; Pisa, 2001; Oxford, 2006; St Andrews, 2014; Hon. DLaws Harvard, 2002; Hon. Dr: Cambridge, 2004; Central Eur. Univ., 2005; Notre Dame, 2008; Aristotle Univ., Thessaloniki, 2010; Hon. DH: Yale, 2006; KCL, 2008; Hon. Dr Humane Studies Amherst Coll., 2009; Hon. DPhil Hebrew Univ., Jerusalem, 2010; Hon. DD St Vladimir's Orthodox Seminary, 2013. Kluge Prize for Lifetime Achievement in Study of Humanity, Liby of Congress, 2008; Balzan Prize, 2011; Jacques Barzun Prize, Amer. Philosophical Soc., 2013; Philip Shaff Prize for Church Hist., American Soc. for Church Hist. 2014. *Publications:* Augustine of Hippo: a biography, 1967; The World of Late Antiquity 1971; Religion and Society in the Age of St Augustine, 1971; The Making of Late Antiquity 1978; The Cult of the Saints: its rise and function in Latin Christianity, 1980, reprint 2014; Society and the Holy in Late Antiquity, 1982; The Body and Society: men, women and sexual renunciation in Early Christianity, 1989, rev. edn 2008; Power and Persuasion in Late Antiquity: towards a Christian Empire, 1992; Authority and the Sacred: aspects of the christianization of the Roman world, 1995; The Rise of Western Christendom: triumph and diversity, AD 200–1000, 1996, rev. edn 2013; Poverty and Leadership in the Later Roman Empire, 2002; Through the Eye of a Needle: wealth, the fall of Rome, and the making of Christianity in the West, 340–550 AD, 2012. *Address:* Department of History, 129 Dickinson Hall, Princeton University, Princeton, NJ 08544–1017, USA.

BROWN, Peter Wilfred Henry, CBE 1996; Secretary of the British Academy, 1983–2006; *b* 4 June 1941; *s* of late Rev. Wilfred George Brown and Joan Margaret (*née* Adams); *m* 1968, Kathleen Clarke (marr. diss.); one *d*. *Educ:* Marlborough Coll.; Jesus Coll., Cambridge (Rustat Schol.). Assistant Master in Classics, Birkenhead Sch., 1963–66; Lectr in Classics, Fourah Bay Coll., Univ. of Sierra Leone, 1966–68; Asst Sec., School of Oriental and African Studies Univ. of London, 1968–75; Dep. Sec., British Academy, 1975–83 (Actg Sec., 1976–77). Mem. Council, British Inst. in Eastern Africa, 1983–2013 (Hon. Treas., 2011–13; Hon. Vice Pres., 2014–). Fellow, National Humanities Center, N Carolina, 1978; Hon. Fellow, British Sch. at Rome, 2007. Hon. DLitt: Birmingham, 1995; Sheffield, 2007. Kt Grand Cross, Order of Merit (Poland), 1995. *Recreation:* the enjoyment of books and classical music. *Address:* 34 Victoria Road, NW6 6PX. *Club:* Athenæum.

See also Rev. J. M. Brown.

BROWN, Philip Anthony Russell, CB 1977; Director of Policy, Investment Management Regulatory Organisation, 1985–93; *b* 18 May 1924; *e s* of late Sir William Brown, KCB, KCMG, CBE, and of Elizabeth Mabel (*née* Scott); *m* 1954, Eileen (*d* 1976), *d* of late J Brennan; *m* 1976, Sarah Elizabeth Dean (*see* S. E. Brown). *Educ:* Malvern; King's Coll. Cambridge. Entered Home Civil Service, Board of Trade, 1947; Private Sec. to Perm. Sec. 1949; Principal, 1952; Private Sec. to Minister of State, 1953; Observer, Civil Service Selection Board, 1957; returned to BoT, 1959; Asst Sec., 1963; Head of Overseas Information Co-ordination Office, 1963; BoT, 1964; Under-Sec., 1969; Head of Establishments Div. 1 BoT, later DTI, 1969; Head of Cos Div., DTI, 1971; Dep. Sec., Dept of Trade, 1974–83 Head of External Relations, Lloyd's of London, 1983–85; Dir, NPI, 1985–90. Mem., Disciplinary Cttee, ICA, 1985–96. Mem., London Adv. Bd, Salvation Army, 1982–92. *Publications:* (contrib.) Multinational Approaches: corporate insiders, 1976; Poems from Square Mile, 1992; articles in various jls. *Recreations:* reading, gardening, music. *Address:* Christmas Croft, Hopgarden Lane, Sevenoaks, Kent TN13 1PX. *Club:* Oxford and Cambridge.

BROWN, Rev. Raymond; *see* Brown, Rev. Robert R.

BROWN, Rev. Raymond, PhD; Senior Minister, Victoria Baptist Church, Eastbourne, 1987–93, retired; *b* 3 March 1928; *s* of Frank Stevenson Brown and Florence Mansfield; *m* 1966, Christine Mary Smallman; one *s* one *d*. *Educ:* Spurgeon's Coll., London (BD, MTh); Fitzwilliam Coll., Cambridge (MA, BD, PhD). Minister: Zion Baptist Church, Cambridge, 1956–62; Upton Vale Baptist Church, Torquay, 1964–71; Tutor in Church History Spurgeon's Coll., London, 1971–73, Principal 1973–86. Pres., Evangelical Alliance, 1975–76 Trustee, Dr Daniel Williams's Charity, 1980–2014; Nat. Chaplain, Girls' Brigade, 1986–90. *Publications:* Their Problems and Ours, 1969; Let's Read the Old Testament, 1971; Skilful Hands, 1972; Christ Above All: the message of Hebrews, 1982; Bible Study Commentary: 1 Timothy-James, 1983; The English Baptists of the Eighteenth Century, 1986; The Bible Book by Book, 1987; Be My Disciple, 1992; The Message of Deuteronomy: not by bread alone 1993; Collins Gem Bible Guide, 1993; Four Spiritual Giants, 1997 (US edn as Giants of the Faith, 1997); The Message of Nehemiah: God's servant in a time of change, 1998; The Message of Numbers: journey to the promised land, 2002; Spirituality in Adversity: English nonconformity in a period of repression, 1660–1689, 2012; (ed) The 1662 Diary of Philip Henry (1631–1696), 2014; contribs to: What the Bible Says, 1974; Dictionary of Christian Spirituality, 1983; My Call to Preach, 1986; Encyclopedia of World Faiths, 1987; New Dictionary of Theology, 1988; The Empty Cross, 1989; Dictionary of Evangelical Biography, 1995; Oxford Dictionary of World Religions, 1997; Oxford Dictionary of the Christian Church, 1998; Called to One Hope, 2000; A Protestant Catholic Church of Christ: essays on the history and life of New Road Baptist Church, Oxford, 2003; Challenge to Change. dialogues with a radical Baptist theologian, 2009. *Recreations:* music, walking. *Address:* 200F Perne Road, Cambridge CB1 3NX. *T:* (01223) 700110.

BROWN, Rebecca Jane; Her Honour Judge Brown; a Circuit Judge, since 2012; *b* Singapore, 1966; *d* of William and Pamela Brown. *Educ:* York Univ. (BA Hons 1987); City Univ. (DipLaw 1988); Inns of Court Sch. of Law. Called to the Bar, Inner Temple, 1989; in practice at the Bar, 1989–2012; a Recorder, 2004–12 (Family Courts, 2008–12). *Recreations:* swimming, walking, pilates, cooking, writing, travelling. *Address:* Milton Keynes County Court, 351 Silbury Boulevard, Witan Gate East, Milton Keynes MK9 2DT; Watford County Court, Cassiobury Court, Cassiobury House, 11–19 Station Road, Watford, Herts WD17 1EZ; Aylesbury Crown Court, County Hall, Market Square, Aylesbury, Bucks HP20 1XD.

BROWN, His Honour Richard George; DL; a Circuit Judge, 1992–2013, a Senior Circuit Judge, 2007–13; *b* Durham, 10 April 1945; *m* 1969, Ann Patricia Bridget Wade; one *s* one *d* (and one *s* decd). *Educ:* Bournville Grammar Sch.; Technical Sch., Birmingham; London Sch. of Economics (LLB Hons); Inns of Court Sch. of Law. Insurance clerk, 1961–62; shop assistant, 1962–63; bus conductor, 1963–64; Trainee Radio Officer, Merchant Navy, 1964–65; taxi driver, 1965–66; assistant, school for children with special needs, 1966–67; bus driver, 1967–68. Called to the Bar, Middle Temple, 1972 (Blackstone Entrance Exhibnr). Asst Recorder, 1986–90; a Recorder of the Crown Court, 1990–92. Resident and Liaison Judge, Crown Courts in E Sussex, 1996–2013. Vice Pres., E Sussex Magistrates' Assoc., 1997–2013. Hon. Recorder, Brighton and Hove, 2008–13. Chm., Bd of Govs, Farney Close Sch., 1984–86; Dir, Deepdene Schs Ltd, Hove, 2014–. DL E Sussex, 2004. *Recreations:* watching sport, travel, being with the family and being a grandpa. *Club:* Armadillos Cricket.

BROWN, His Honour Robert; a Circuit Judge, 1988–2011; a Deputy Circuit Judge; *b* 21 June 1943; *s* of Robert and Mary Brown. *Educ:* Arnold Sch., Blackpool; Downing Coll., Cambridge (Exhibnr; BA, LLB). Called to Bar, Inner Temple, 1968 (Major Schol.); a Recorder, 1983–88. Chm., Parole Bd for Life and Imprisonment for Public Protection Prisoners. *Recreation:* golf. *Club:* Royal Lytham St Annes Golf.

BROWN, Robert Edward, CBE 2014; Member (Lib Dem) South Lanarkshire Council, since 2012; *b* 25 Dec. 1947; *s* of Albert Edward Brown and Joan Brown; *m* 1977, Gwen Morris; one *s* one *d*. *Educ:* Gordon Schools, Huntly; Univ. of Aberdeen (LLB 1st Cl. Hons). Legal Apprentice and Asst, Edmonds and Ledingham, Solicitors, Aberdeen, 1969–72; Procurator Fiscal, Dumbarton, 1972–74; Asst, 1974–75, Partner, 1975–99, Consultant, 1999–2004, Ross Harper and Murphy, Solicitors, Glasgow. Dep. Minister for Educn and Young People, Scottish Exec., 2005–07. Scottish Parliament: Mem. (Lib Dem) Glasgow, 1999–2011; Lib Dem spokesman on communities and housing, 1999–2003, on education, 2003–05, on justice and civil liberties, 2008–11; Convenor, Educn and Young People Cttee, 2003–05; Business Manager, Lib Dem Gp, 2007–08. Convenor, Scottish Lib Dem Policy Cttee, 2002–07. *Recreations:* history, science fiction. *Address:* 90b Blairbeth Road, Burnside, Rutherglen, Glasgow G73 4JA.

BROWN, Robert Alan; His Honour Judge Robert Alan Brown; a Circuit Judge, since 2008; *b* 29 Sept. 1956; *s* of late Norman Brown and Elizabeth Ruby Brown (*née* Watkins); *m* 1979, Frances Mary Warren; one *s*. *Educ:* Northgate Grammar Sch., Ipswich; Queen Mary Coll., Univ. of London (LLB Hons 1978). Called to the Bar, Inner Temple, 1979; in practice as barrister, Leicester, 1980–97, Nottingham, 1997–2008; Recorder, 2001–08. Treasury Counsel for Civil (Provincial), 1992–97. Midland Circuit: Educn and Trng Officer, 2004–08; Rep. on Trng for the Bar Cttee, Bar Council, 2005–06. *Recreations:* ski-ing, golf, vegetable gardening, supporting The Tractor Boys. *Address:* Midland Circuit Secretariat, The Priory Courts, 33 Bull Street, Birmingham B4 6DW.

BROWN, Robert Glencairn; Director (formerly Deputy Chief Officer), Housing Corporation, 1986–91; *b* 19 July 1930; *s* of William and Marion Brown (*née* Cockburn); *m* 1957, Florence May Stalker; two *s*. *Educ:* Hillhead High Sch., Glasgow. Commnd, RCS, 1949–51. Forestry Commn, 1947–68; seconded to CS Pay Res. Unit, 1963–64 and to Min. of Land and Natural Resources, 1964–68; Min. of Housing and Local Govt, later DoE, 1968–71; seconded to Nat. Whitley Council, Staff Side, 1969; Asst Dir, Countryside Commn, 1971–77; Department of the Environment: Asst Sec., 1977–83; Under Sec., 1983–86. Chm., W Middx Centre, Nat. Trust, 1989–93. *Recreations:* walking, reading. *Address:* 35 The Forresters, Winslow Close, Pinner, Middx HA5 2QX. *T:* (020) 8866 1057. *Club:* Pinner Hill Golf.

BROWN, Robert Iain Cameron; Chief Executive Officer, Aon ARS EMEA, since 2012; *b* Auckland, 8 Jan. 1966; *s* of Fredrick John Brown and Jessie Denise Yvonne Brown; *m* 1994, Julia Adler; one *s* one *d*. *Educ:* Felsted, Essex. Chief Multiline Underwriting Officer, Winterthur Internat., Switzerland, 1998–99; Regl Broking Dir, Winterthur Internat., Hong Kong, 1999–2001; Aon, 2001–: CEO, Aon Corporate and Affinity; Bd Dir, Aon Ltd, 2009–; Mem., Global Exec. Cttee, Aon Risk Services, 2009–14; CEO, Aon Ltd, 2009–12. Director: SLE Worldwide Ltd, 2008–; Supercover Ltd, 2009–11; Centurion Safety Products Ltd, 2009–. Dir, BIBA, 2009–. MInstD. Liveryman, Tobacco Pipe Makers' and Tobacco Blenders' Co. (Freeman, 2006). *Recreations:* golf, Rugby. *Address:* Aon UK Ltd, 8 Devonshire Square, EC2M 4PL. *Clubs:* Mosimann's; Gosfield Lake Golf.

BROWN, Rev. (Robert) Raymond; Methodist Minister, responsible for lay training and development, Melton Mowbray, 1994–99; *b* 24 March 1936; *s* of Robert Brown and Elsie (*née* Dudson); *m* 1959, Barbara (*née* Johnson); three *s* (one *d* decd). *Educ:* Stockport Sch.; Univ. of Leeds (BA Hons Philosophy); Univ. of Manchester (BD Hons Theology). Ordained Methodist minister, 1959; Minister: Luton Industrial Coll. and Mission, 1959–64; Heald Green and Handforth, 1964–67; commnd RAF Chaplain, 1967; Vice Principal, RAF Chaplains' Sch., 1978–83; Comd Chaplain, RAF Germany, 1983–87; Asst Prin. Chaplain, 1987–90, Prin. Chaplain, 1990–94, Ch of Scotland and Free Churches, RAF. QHC 1990–94. *Recreations:* music and drama (amateur singer and actor), writing for pleasure; fund-raising for crèche, Sally's Place, set up in remote rural S Africa, in memory of daughter, to look after and feed pre-school children and vulnerable youngsters, managed by World Vision. *Address:* 1 Hazlebadge Close, Poynton, Stockport, Cheshire SK12 1HD. *T:* (01625) 879699. *E:* ray.brown980@ntlworld.com. *Club:* Royal Air Force.

BROWN, Prof. Roger John, PhD; Professor of Higher Education Policy, Liverpool Hope University, 2007–13, now Emeritus; *b* 26 June 1947; *s* of John Richard Brown and Beatrice Anne (*née* Clamp); *m* 1st, 1971, Mary Elizabeth George (*see* M. E. Francis) (marr. diss. 1991); 2nd, 1992, Josephine Ann Titcomb. *Educ:* St Olave's Grammar Sch., Bermondsey; Queens' Coll., Cambridge (Haynes Exhibnr in History; MA); Inst. of Educn, Univ. of London (PhD). Admin. Officer, ILEA, 1969–75; Sec., William Tyndale Schs' Inquiry, 1975–76; Principal, Dept Industry, Dept Trade, Cabinet Office, OFT, DTI, 1976–84; Assistant Secretary: DoE, 1984–86; DTI, 1986–90; Sec., PCFC, 1990–91; Chief Exec., Cttee of Dirs of Polytechnics, 1991–93; Chief Exec., HEQC, 1993–97; Principal, Southampton Inst., 1998–2005; Prof. of Higher Educn Policy, Southampton Inst., subseq. Southampton Solent Univ., 2004–07; Vice-Chancellor, Southampton Solent Univ., 2005–07. Visiting Professor: Univ. of London Inst. of Educn, 1996–98; Middx Univ., 1997–99; Goldsmiths' Coll., 1997–99; Univ. of Surrey Roehampton (formerly Roehampton Inst.), 1997–; Univ. of East London, 2000–; City Univ., 2001–; Univ. of Southampton, 2006–; Edinburgh Napier Univ. (formerly Napier Univ., Edinburgh), 2007–; Open Univ., 2009–; Univ. of W London (formerly Thames Valley Univ.), 2009– (Gov., 2010–). Vis. Fellow, Oxford Centre for Higher Educn Policy Studies, 2007–; Hon. Vis. Fellow, Inst. for Policy Studies in Educn, London Metropolitan Univ., 2007–. Vice-Chm., Standing Conf. of Principals, 1999–2003; Vice-Pres., SRHE, 2007–. Chm., Barton Peveril Coll., Eastleigh, 2009–. Hon. Fellow, AUA, 2010. DUniv: Southampton Solent, 2007; Southampton, 2007; Hon. DLitt W London, 2014. Lifetime Achievement Award, Times Higher Educn, 2013. *Publications:* Educational Policy Making: an analysis, 1983; The Post-Dearing Quality Agenda, 1998; Quality Assurance in Higher Education: the UK experience since 1992, 2004; Higher Education and the Market, 2010; Everything for Sale?: the marketisation of UK higher education, 2013; contribs to educnl jls. *Recreations:* opera, cinema, jazz, collecting books about music. *Address:* 9 Blenheim Avenue, Southampton SO17 1DW.

BROWN, Rt Rev. Ronald; Bishop Suffragan of Birkenhead, 1974–92; Hon. Assistant Bishop of Liverpool, 1992–2003; *b* 7 Aug. 1926; *s* of Fred and Ellen Brown; *m* 1951, Joyce Hymers (*d* 1987); one *s* one *d*. *Educ:* Kirkham Grammar Sch.; Durham Univ. (BA, DipTh). Vicar of Whittle-le-Woods, 1956; Vicar of St Thomas, Halliwell, Bolton, 1961; Rector and Rural Dean of Ashton-under-Lyne, 1970. *Publications:* Bishop's Brew, 1989; Good Lord, 1992; Bishop's Broth, 2000. *Recreation:* hammer and spade activities. *Address:* 16 Andrew Crescent, Queen's Park, Chester CH4 7BQ. *T:* (01244) 629955.

See also L. F. M. Brown.

BROWN, Rosemary Jean, (Rosie); *see* Atkins, R. J.

BROWN, Roswyn Ann H.; *see* Hakesley-Brown.

BROWN, Roy Drysdale, CEng, FIMechE, FIET; Chairman, GKN plc, 2004–12 (Director, 1996–2012); *b* 4 Dec. 1946; *s* of late William Andrew Brown and Isabelle Drysdale (*née* Davidson); *m* 1978, Carol Wallace; two *s*. *Educ:* Tonbridge Sch.; UCL (GEC Schol.; BSc Mech. Eng); Harvard Business Sch. (MBA). CEng, FIMechE 1983; FIET (FIEE 1990). Commercial Gen. Manager, Vosper Thorneycroft Ltd, 1972–74; Unilever plc, 1974–2001: various financial, mktg and tech. posts, 1974–82; Chairman: Pamol Plantations Sdn Bhd, Malaysia, 1982–86; PBI Cambridge Ltd, 1987–88; Tech. Dir, Birds Eye Walls Ltd, 1988–90; Chm., Lever Bros Ltd, 1991–92; Regional Director: Africa, ME, Central and Eastern Europe, 1992–96; Foods and Beverages Europe, 1996–2001; Dir, Unilever plc and NV, 1992–2001; retd, 2001. Non-executive Director: Brambles Industries Ltd & plc, 2001–06; BUPA, 2001–07; Lloyds Franchise Bd, 2003–08; Alliance & Leicester plc, 2007–10 (Vice-Chm., 2007–08); Abbey National plc, 2008–10; Santander UK plc, 2010–. Gov., and Chm Develt Gp and Foundn, Tonbridge Sch., 2007–12. *Recreations:* military history, wild life photography, classical music, opera, woodworking. *Address:* Santander UK plc, 2 Triton Square, Regent's Place, NW1 3AN. *Clubs:* Royal Automobile; Leander (Henley).

BROWN, Russell Leslie; *b* 17 Sept. 1951; *s* of Howard Russell Brown and Muriel Brown (*née* Anderson); *m* 1973, Christine Margaret Calvert; two *d*. *Educ:* Annan Acad. With ICI, 1974–97, Plant Operative, 1992–97. Member: Dumfries and Galloway Regl Council, 1986–96 (Chm., Public Protection Cttee, 1990–94); Annandale and Eskdale DC, 1988–96; Dumfries and Galloway UA, 1995–97. MP (Lab) Dumfries, 1997–2005, Dumfries and Galloway, 2005–15; contested (Lab) same seat, 2015. PPS to Sec. of State for Scotland, 2005–10; Shadow Defence Minister, 2010–15. *Recreations:* walking, football. *Address:* 46 Northfield Park, Annan DG12 5EZ. *T:* (01461) 205365.

BROWN, Prof. Sara Ann, (Sally), OBE 2002; PhD; FRSE; Professor of Education, 1990–2001, now Emeritus, and Deputy Principal, 1996–2001, University of Stirling; *b* 15 Dec. 1935; *d* of Fred Compigné-Cook and Gwendoline Cook (*née* Barrett); *m* 1959, Charles Victor Brown (*d* 1991); two *s*. *Educ:* Bromley High Sch.; University College London (BSc Hons 1957); Smith Coll., Mass (MA 1958); Jordanhill Coll., Glasgow (Teaching Cert. 1966); Univ. of Stirling (PhD 1975). Lectr in Physics, Univ. of Ife and Nigerian Coll. of Tech., 1960–64; Principal Teacher of Science, Helensburgh, 1964–70; Sen. Res. Fellow, Univ. of Stirling, 1970–80; Consultant and Adviser, Scottish Educn Dept, 1980–84; Dir, Scottish Council for Res. in Educn, 1986–90 (Fellow, 1992). Chair: Univs' Assoc. for Continuing Educn (Scotland), 2000–02; Educn Panel, 2001 RAE; Teacher Support Scotland Forum, 2002–10 (Vice Chair, Trustees, 2002–10); Scottish Arts Council Educn Forum, 2003–04; Educn Cttee, RSE, 2011– (Vice Convener, 2009–11); Learned Socs' Gp on Scottish Sci. Educn, 2012–; Professional Adv. Gp on computer sci. in Scottish educn, 2012–; Vice-Chair, ESRC Teaching and Learning Res. prog., 1998–2005. Chair Adv. Bd, Leirsinn Gaelic res. centre, 2000–03; Member: Academic Council, UHI Millennium Inst., 2001–09; Vision Cttee, Royal Soc., 2011–14. Trustee, RSE Scotland Foundn, 2013–. Chair, Alcohol Commn, SLP, 2010. Gov., Queen Margaret Univ. (formerly Queen Margaret UC), Edinburgh, 1999–2008 (Vice Chm., 2005–08). FRSA 1989; FRSE 1996; FEIS 1997; AcSS 2000. Hon. Fellow UHI Millennium Inst., 2005. DUniv: Stirling, 2002; Open, 2004; Queen Margaret, 2009; Hon. DEd Edinburgh, 2003. *Publications:* What Do They Know?, 1980; Making Sense of Teaching, 1993; Special Needs Policy in the 1990s, 1994; numerous academic works. *Recreations:* theatre, music, opera, current affairs. *Address:* 30A Chalton Road, Bridge of Allan, Stirling FK9 4EF. *T:* (01786) 833671. *E:* s.a.brown@stir.ac.uk.

BROWN, Sarah Elizabeth, OBE 2004; Member, General Pharmaceutical Council, since 2010; *b* 30 Dec. 1943; *d* of Sir Maurice Dean, KCB, KCMG and Anne (*née* Gibson); *m* 1976, Philip Anthony Russell Brown, *qv*. *Educ:* St Paul's Girls' Sch.; Newnham Coll., Cambridge (BA Nat. Sci.). Joined BoT as Asst Principal, 1965; Private Sec. to Second Perm. Sec., 1968; Principal, 1970; DTI, 1971–96: Asst Sec., 1978; Sec. to Crown Agents Tribunal, 1978–82; Personnel Management Div., 1982–84; Head of Financial Services Bill team, 1984–86; Under Sec., 1986; Head of Companies Div., 1986–91; Head of Enterprise Initiative Div., 1991–93, and Small Firms Div., 1992–93; Head of Small Firms and Business Link Div., 1993–94; Head of Companies Div., 1994–96; Dir, Company Law, 1996. Comr, Friendly Socs Commn, 1997–2001; Mem., Competition (formerly Monopolies and Mergers) Commn, 1998–2007. Dir, Remploy Ltd, 1997–2000; Mem. Bd, Look Ahead Housing Assoc., 1996–2008; Associate Mem., Kensington & Chelsea and Westminster HA, 1996–99; non-executive Director: Kent and Sussex Weald NHS Trust, 1999–2000; Financial Services Compensation Scheme, 2000–07; SW Kent Primary Care Trust, 2001–06; Accountancy and Actuarial Discipline (formerly Accountants Investigation and Discipline) Bd Ltd, 2001–10; Revenue and Customs Prosecutions Office, 2005–09. Member: Civil Service Appeals Bd, 1998–2004; Disciplinary Panel, Taxation Discipline Bd, 2010–; Lay Mem., Bar Standards Bd, 2006–11 (Special Advr, 2012–15); Mem., Investigations Cttee, RPSGB, 2007–09. Chair, Audit Cttee, Parkinson's UK, 2007–14. Trustee, Horder Centre, 2007–. Gov. Dunton Green Primary Sch., 2014–. *Recreations:* travel, theatre, gardening. *Address:* 32 Cumberland Street, SW1V 4LX.

BROWN, Sarah Elizabeth; writer and broadcaster; Flexible Learning Co-ordinator, Christ's School, Richmond, since 2004; *b* 13 Sept. 1952; *d* of Lewis William Brown, OBE and Gweneth Elizabeth Brown (*née* Richards); *m* 1989, Paul Malcolm Street; two *s*. *Educ:* Brighton and Hove High Sch.; I. M. Marsh Coll., Liverpool (Cert Ed Dance and Drama 1973); London Sch. of Contemporary Dance. TV and theatre work, 1976–78; restaurateur and wholefood shop proprietor, 1978–88; Presenter, Vegetarian Kitchen (series), BBC TV, 1983; vegetarian cookery writer and broadcaster, 1984–. Mem. steering gp, Focus on Food, RSA/Waitrose, 1998–2003. Mem., Guild of Food Writers, 1986–2006. Manager, England Over 35s Orienteering Team, 1998–. Egon Ronay Cellnet Award, 1987; Glenfiddich Special Award for Writing, 1988. *Publications:* Vegetarian Kitchen, 1984; Sarah Brown's Vegetarian Cookbook, 1984; Sarah Brown's Healthy Living Cookbook, 1986; Sarah Brown's Vegetarian Microwave Cookbook, 1987; Sarah Brown's New Vegetarian Kitchen, 1987; Sarah Brown's Quick and Easy Vegetarian Cookery, 1989; Secret England, 1989; Outdoor London, 1991; Sarah Brown's Healthy Pregnancy, 1992; Sarah Brown's Fresh Vegetarian Cookery, 1995; No Fuss Vegetarian Cooking, 1998; The Complete Vegetarian Cookbook, 2002; Sarah Brown's World Vegetarian Cookbook, 2004; Parents and Carers Guide to Options 14–16, 2008. *Recreations:* orienteering, listening to TMS, playing German board games.

BROWN, Rev. Scott James, CBE 2014; Chaplain of the Fleet (formerly Chaplain of the Fleet and Director General), Naval Chaplaincy Service, 2010–14; *b* Bellshill, Lanarkshire, 16 May 1968; *s* of James Brown and Margaret Brown (*née* Bryson); civil partnership 2006, Colin A Fleming. *Educ:* Hamilton Grammar Sch.; Bell Coll. of Technol.; Univ. of Aberdeen (BD 1992). Ordained C of S, 1993; Chaplain, 1993–2007, Principal Chaplain, 2007–10, RN. QHC 2007–14. *Recreations:* travel, interior design, good wine. *Address:* Braeside, 5 Main Street, Drymen, Glasgow G63 0BP. *T:* (01360) 660989, 07824805888. *E:* scott16568@gmail.com.

BROWN, Simon Staley; QC 1995; **His Honour Judge Simon Brown;** an Additional High Court Judge, Senior Circuit Judge and a Specialist Mercantile Judge, Midland Circuit, since 2006; *b* 23 Aug. 1952; *s* of late Peter Brown and Celia Rosamond Brown; *m* 1981, Kathleen Margaret Wain, PhD (Kathy Brown, garden owner, writer and designer); one *s* one *d. Educ:* Harrow Sch.; Queens' Coll., Cambridge (MA). Called to the Bar, Inner Temple, 1976 (Bencher and former Master of the Garden). A Recorder, 2000. Asst Boundary Comr, 2000–05. Mem., Bar Assocs of Professional Negligence, Technology and Construction, London Common and Commercial Law. Formerly: Chm. of Govs, Bedford Sch.; Trustee, The Bedford Charity (The Harpur Trust). *Recreation:* gardening. *Address:* Birmingham Civil Justice Centre, 33 Bull Street, Birmingham B4 6DS. *T:* (Clerk) (0121) 681 3035. *E:* birmingham.mercantile@hmcourts-service.gsi.gov.uk.

BROWN, Rt Hon. Sir Stephen, GBE 1999; Kt 1975; PC 1983; a Lord Justice of Appeal, 1983–88; President of the Family Division, 1988–99; *b* 3 Oct. 1924; *s* of Wilfrid Brown and Nora Elizabeth Brown, Longdon Green, Staffordshire; *m* 1951, Patricia Ann, *d* of Richard Good, Tenbury Wells, Worcs; two *s* (twins) three *d. Educ:* Malvern College; Queens' College, Cambridge (Hon. Fellow, 1984). Served RNVR (Lieut), 1943–46. Barrister, Inner Temple, 1949; Bencher, 1974; Treas., 1994. Dep. Chairman, Staffs QS, 1963–71; Recorder of West Bromwich, 1965–71; QC 1966; a Recorder, and Honorary Recorder of West Bromwich, 1972–75; a Judge of the High Court, Family Div., 1975–77, QBD, 1977–83; Presiding Judge, Midland and Oxford Circuit, 1977–81. Member: Parole Board, England and Wales, 1967–71; Butler Cttee on mentally abnormal offenders, 1972–75; Adv. Council on Penal System, 1977; Chm., Adv. Cttee on Conscientious Objectors, 1971–75. Chm. Council, Malvern Coll., 1976–94; President: Edgbaston High Sch., 1989–2014; Malvernian Soc., 1998–. Hon. FRCPsych 2000. Hon. LLD: Birmingham, 1985; Leicester, 1997; UWE, 2000. *Recreation:* sailing. *Address:* 78 Hamilton Avenue, Harborne, Birmingham B17 8AR. *Club:* Garrick.

BROWN, Stephen David Macleod, PhD; FMedSci; FRS 2015; Director, Medical Research Council Mammalian Genetics Unit, since 1998; *b* Dumfries, 3 May 1955; *s* of David Brown and Pamela Brown; *m* 2009, Dr Heena Lad; one *s* one *d*; two *d* by a previous marriage. *Educ:* Belfast Royal Acad.; St Catharine's Coll., Cambridge (BA 1977; PhD 1981). EMBO Res. Fellow, 1981; Lectr, St Mary's Hosp. Med. Sch., 1982–92; Reader, 1992–94, Prof. of Genetics, 1994–98, Imperial Coll. London. Mem., Nuffield Council for Bioethics, 2009–12; Chm., Steering Cttee, Internat. Mouse Phenotyping Consortium, 2010–. Member, Scientific Advisory Board: Mouse Genome Database, Jackson Lab., 2002–05; Wellcome Trust Trypanotolerance Prog., 2003–08; Centre Integratif de Genomique, Lausanne, 2009–; Helmholtz Centrum, Munich, 2009–; Institut Clinique Souris, Strasbourg, 2013–; GENCODE proj., 2014–; Mem., Adv. Council, Nat. BioResource Centre, Japan, 2003–. FMedSci 2001; Mem., EMBO, 2005. Editor: Mammalian Genome, 1997–; Current Protocols in Mouse Biology, 2010–. *Publications:* res. papers in biol., genetics and molecular genetics in jls incl. Nature and Nature Genetics. *Recreations:* wine, reading, cooking. *Address:* MRC Mammalian Genetics Unit, MRC Harwell, Oxon OX11 0RD. *T:* (01235) 841053. *E:* s.brown@har.mrc.ac.uk.

BROWN, Sir Stephen (David Reid), KCVO 1999; HM Diplomatic Service, retired; advisor to Vermilion Partners, since 2006; Co-Chairman, The Ambassador Partnership (formerly ADRg Ambassadors), since 2010; *b* 26 Dec. 1945; *s* of Albert Senior Brown and Edna Brown; *m* 1966, Pamela Denise Gaunt; one *s* one *d. Educ:* Leeds Grammar Sch.; RMA Sandhurst; Univ. of Sussex (BA Hons). Served HM Forces, RA, 1966–76; FCO, 1976–77; 1st Sec., Nicosia, 1977–80; 1st Sec. (Commercial), Paris, 1980–85; FCO, 1985–89; DTI, 1989; Consul-Gen., Melbourne, 1989–94; Commercial Counsellor and Dir of Trade Promotion, Peking, 1994–97; Ambassador, Republic of Korea, 1997–2000; High Comr, Singapore, 2001–02; Chief Exec. (Permanent Sec.), British Trade Internat., then UK Trade & Investment, 2002–05. *Recreations:* reading, ski-ing, motor sport.

BROWN, Stuart Christopher; QC 1991; a Recorder, since 1992; a Deputy High Court Judge, since 1994; *b* 4 Sept. 1950; *s* of late Geoffrey Howard Brown and Olive Baum; *m* 1973, Imogen Lucas; two *d. Educ:* Acklam High Sch., Middlesbrough; Worcester Coll., Oxford (BA, BCL). Called to the Bar, Inner Temple, 1974, Bencher, 1998. Practises on NE Circuit (Leader, 2009–11). Pres., later Judge, Mental Health Rev. Tribunal, 2000–. *Recreations:* family, theatre, walking. *Address:* The Gatehouse, Copgrove, Harrogate HG3 3SZ; Park Lane Plowden, 19 Westgate, Leeds LS1 2RD.

BROWN, Susan Mary; *see* Spindler, S. M.

BROWN, Prof. (Susanne) Moira, OBE 2007; PhD; FRCPath; FRSE; Director, Crusade Laboratories Ltd, Glasgow, 2000–11 (Chief Scientist, 2000–08); *b* 21 March 1946; *d* of Edmund and Elizabeth Mitchell; *m* 1970, Alasdair MacDougall Brown. *Educ:* Queen's Univ., Belfast (BSc 1968); Univ. of Glasgow (PhD 1971). FRCPath 1997. Sen. Scientist, MRC Virology Unit, Glasgow, 1972–95; Prof. of Neurovirology, Univ. of Glasgow, 1995–2004, Prof. Emeritus, 2004. Chm., Med. Res. Scotland (formerly Scottish Hosp. Endowments Res. Trust), 2001–09. FRSE 1999 (Convener, Cell and Molecular Biol Fellowships Cttee, 2001–06). *Publications:* Methods in Molecular Medicine: herpes simplex virus, 1998. *Recreations:* walking, travel, reading, Christian faith, Scottish painters, beagles. *Address:* Kilure, The Steading, Croy Cunningham, Killearn G63 9QY. *T:* (01360) 551715, *Fax:* (01360) 551716. *E:* s.m.brown@btconnect.com. *Club:* Athenæum.

BROWN, Rt Rev. Dr Thomas John; Bishop of Wellington (NZ), 1998–2012; *b* 16 Aug. 1943; *s* of Ernest Robert Brown and Abby Brown; *m* 1965, Dwyllis Lyon; one *s* two *d. Educ:* Otago Univ.; St John's Theol Coll., Auckland (LTh, STh); Graduate Theol Union, Berkeley, Univ. of California (DMin). Curate: St Matthew, Christchurch, NZ, 1972–74; St James the Greater, Leicester, UK, 1974–76; Vicar: Upper Clutha, 1976–79, St John, Roslyn, 1979–85, Dio. Dunedin, NZ; St James, Lower Hutt, Dio. Wellington, 1985–91; Archdeacon of Belmont, 1987–91; Asst Bishop and Vicar General, Diocese of Wellington, 1991–98. *Publications:* Ministry At The Door, 1981; Learning From Liturgy, 1984; (contrib.) Growing in Newness of Life, 1993; (contrib.) Designer Genes, 2000; (contrib.) Gene Technology in New Zealand: scientific issues and implications, 2000. *Recreations:* golf, fly-fishing, reading, swimming. *Address:* c/o PO Box 12 046, Wellington 6144, New Zealand.

BROWN, Timothy Andrew; Managing Director, TAB Business Solutions Ltd, since 2011; *b* Yorkshire, 27 Sept. 1959; *s* of Ronald Sydney Brown and Marjorie Brown; *m* 1981, Susan Frances Waters; two *s* one *d. Educ:* Cheshunt Sch.; Southampton Univ. (BSc Hons Pol. and Internat. Studies). Asst Auditor, later Sen. Auditor, Nat. Audit Office, 1981–86; KPMG, latterly Principal Consultant, 1986–94; with Royal Mail, 1994–2005: Commercial Dir, 1999–2001; Business and Commercial Strategy Dir, 2001–02; Sales and Mktg Dir, Parcelforce, 2003–05; Sales and Mktg Dir, DHL Express (UK), 2006–07; CEO, Postal Services Commn, 2008–11. Non-exec. Dir, Jersey Post, 2011–. *Recreations:* horse riding, antiques.

BROWN, Timothy Charles; Fellow, since 1979, and Director of Music, 1979–2010, Clare College, Cambridge; Artistic Director, Zürcher Sing-Akademie, since 2011; *b* 9 Dec. 1946; *s* of Roland Frederick John Brown and Ruth Margery Brown (*née* Dawe). *Educ:* Westminster Abbey Choir Sch.; Dean Close Sch., Cheltenham; King's Coll., Cambridge (alto choral schol.; MA); Westminster Coll., Oxford (DipEd). Music Master, Hinchingbrooke Sch., Huntingdon, 1969–72; Dir of Music, Oundle Sch., 1972–79. Mem., Scholars' Vocal Ensemble, 1969–72. Director: Choir of Clare Coll., Cambridge, 1979–2010; Cambridge Univ. Chamber Choir, 1986–2000; English Voices, 1995–; Vis. Dir of Chapel Music, Robinson Coll., Cambridge, 2010–15. *Publications:* (ed) William Walton: shorter choral works, 1999; Choral Works with Orchestra, 2009. *Recreations:* foreign travel, gardens and gardening, walking. *Address:* c/o Clare College, Cambridge CB2 1TL. *T:* (01223) 353088.

BROWN, Timothy William Trelawny T.; *see* Tatton-Brown.

BROWN, Tina, (Christina Hambley Brown), (Lady Evans), CBE 2000; writer and journalist; founder and Chief Executive Officer, Tina Brown Live Media; *b* 21 Nov. 1953; *d* of late Bettina Iris Mary Kohr Brown and George Hambley Brown; *m* 1981, Sir Harold Matthew Evans, *qv*; one *s* one *d. Educ:* Univ. of Oxford (MA). Columnist for Punch, 1978; Editor, Tatler, 1979–83; Editor in Chief, Vanity Fair Magazine, 1984–92; Editor, The New Yorker, 1992–98; Chm. and Editor in Chief, Talk magazine, 1998–2002; Partner and Chm., Talk Media, 1998–2002; founder and Ed.-in-Chief, The Daily Beast, 2008–13; Ed.-in-Chief, Newsweek Global (formerly Newsweek), 2010–13. Columnist: The Times, 2002; Washington Post, 2003–. Catherine Pakenham Prize, Most Promising Female Journalist (Sunday Times), 1973; Young Journalist of the Year, 1978. *Plays:* Under the Bamboo Tree (Sunday Times Drama Award), 1973; Happy Yellow, 1977. *Publications:* Loose Talk, 1979; Life as a Party, 1983; The Diana Chronicles, 2007.

BROWN, Tom C.; *see* Cross Brown, T.

BROWN, Tony; *see* Brown, J. A.

BROWN, Prof. Valerie Kathleen, PhD; agro-ecology science consultant, since 2005; Director, Centre for Agri-Environmental Research, and Research Professor in Agro-Ecology, University of Reading, 2000–04; *b* 11 May 1944; *d* of Reginald Brown and Kathleen (*née* Southerton); *m* 1970, Dr Clive Wall. *Educ:* Imperial Coll., London Univ. (BSc Zoology 1966, ARCS 1966; PhD Entomology 1969; DIC 1969). Lectr, Royal Holloway Coll., London Univ., 1969–74; Imperial College of Science, Technology and Medicine: Lectr, 1975–84; Sen. Lectr, 1984–89; Reader, 1989–94; CAB International: Dir, Internat. Inst. of Entomology, 1994–98; Dir, CABI Bioscience: Environment, 1998–2000. Member: Council, NERC, 2002–04; Sci. Adv. Gp, 2002–03, Res. and Priorities Bd, 2003–04, DEFRA; Nat. Scis Adv. Gp, English Nature, 2002–06; Panel, Govt on the Wildlife Network in England, 2009–; Panel, Govt Rev., Making Space for Nature, 2009–11; Council, Nat. Trust, 2013–; Special Advr, Grasslands, DEFRA, 2000–09; Ind. Sci. Advr, DEFRA/Natural England Envmtl Stewardship Res. Prog., 2009–11. Member: Bd, Internat. Assoc. for Ecology, 1997–2006; Nat. Cttee, Internat. Geosphere-Biosphere Prog., 2001–04; Council, RSPB, 2005–09; Chair: Nat. Moth Recording Scheme Steering Gp, 2006–11; Delivery Cttee, Som Wildlife Trust, 2012–. *Publications:* Grasshoppers, 1983, 2nd edn 1992; (ed) Insect Life History Strategies, 1983; Multitrophic Interactions, 1997; (ed) Herbivores between Plants and Predators, 1999; over 200 scientific pubns. *Recreations:* bird watching, cultivation of alpine plants, wine tasting. *Address:* Woodpeckers, Stawley, Wellington, Som TA21 0HN. *T:* and *Fax:* (01823) 672063. *E:* valeriebrown@letour.fsnet.co.uk.

BROWN, Vivian; *see* Brown, H. V. B.

BROWN, Prof. William Arthur, CBE 2002; Montague Burton Professor of Industrial Relations, 1985–2012, now Emeritus Professor, and Head, School of Humanities and Social Sciences, 2009–12, University of Cambridge; Master, Darwin College, Cambridge, 2000–12, now Emeritus Master; *b* 22 April 1945; *s* of late Prof. Arthur Joseph Brown, CBE, FBA and Joan H. M. (*née* Taylor); *m* 1993, Kim Hewitt (marr. diss. 2013); two step *d. Educ:* Leeds Grammar Sch.; Wadham Coll., Oxford (BA Hons). Economic Asst, NBPI, 1966–68; Res. Associate, Univ. of Warwick, 1968–70; SSRC's Industrial Relations Research Unit, University of Warwick: Res. Fellow, 1970–79; Dep. Dir, 1979–81; Dir, 1981–85; University of Cambridge: Fellow, Wolfson Coll., 1985–2000; Chairman: Faculty of Econs and Politics, 1992–96; Sch. of Humanities and Soc. Scis, 1993–96; Bd of Graduate Studies, 2000–08; Faculty of Social and Political Sci., 2003–08; Colleges' Cttee, 2005–07 (Sec., 2003–05). Ind. Chm., Nat. Fire Brigades Disputes Cttee, 1998–. Member: ACAS Panel of Arbitrators, 1985–; Low Pay Commn, 1997–2007; Council, ACAS, 1998–2004. *Publications:* Piecework Bargaining, 1973; The Changing Contours of British Industrial Relations, 1981; The Individualisation of Employment Contracts in Britain, 1999; The Evolution of the Modern Workplace, 2009; articles in industrial relations jls, etc. *Recreations:* walking, gardening. *Address:* Darwin College, Cambridge CB3 9EU.

BROWN, Sir William Brian P.; *see* Pigott-Brown.

BROWN, William Charles Langdon, CBE 1992 (OBE 1982); Deputy Group Chief Executive and Deputy Chairman, Standard Chartered PLC, 1988–91 (Director, 1987–94); Deputy Chairman, Standard Chartered Bank, 1989–91; *b* 9 Sept. 1931; *s* of Charles Leonard Brown and Kathleen May Tizzard; *m* 1959, Nachiko Sagawa; one *s* two *d. Educ:* John Ruskin Sch., Croydon; Ashbourne Grammar Sch., Derbyshire. Joined Westminster Bank, 1947; transf. to Standard Chartered Bank (formerly Chartered Bank of India, Australia and China, the predecessor of Chartered Bank), 1954; Standard Chartered Bank: Tokyo, 1954–59; Bangkok, 1959–62; Hong Kong, 1962–69; Man., Singapore, 1969–72; Country Man., Bangkok, 1972–75; Area Gen. Man., Hong Kong, 1975–87. Various additional positions in Hong Kong, 1975–87, include: MLC Hong Kong; Chm., Hong Kong Export Credit Insce Corp. Adv. Bd; Mem. Council, Hong Kong Trade Develt Council; Chm., Hong Kong Assoc. of Banks; Director: Mass Railway Corp.; Wing Lung Bank Ltd. Director: Hong Kong Investment Trust, 1991–96; Kexim Bank (UK) Ltd, 1992–2002; Arbuthnot Latham & Co. Ltd, 1993–99; Chm., Atlantis Japan Growth Fund Ltd, 1996–2002. Treas., Royal Commonwealth Soc. and Commonwealth Trust, 1991–96. FCIB 1984; FInstD 1988. Hon. DSSc Chinese Univ. of Hong Kong, 1987. *Recreations:* mountain walking, snow ski-ing, yoga, philately, photography, calligraphy, classical music. *Address:* Appleshaw, 11 Central Avenue, Findon Valley, Worthing, Sussex BN14 0DS. *T:* (01903) 873175; Penthouse B, 15 Portman Square, W1H 6LJ. *T:* (020) 7487 5741, *Fax:* (020) 7486 3005. *Clubs:* Oriental; Hong Kong, Shek-O, Ladies Recreation (Hong Kong).

BROWN, Yasmin A.; *see* Alibhai-Brown.

BROWNBILL, David John; QC 2008; *b* 26 Sept. 1951; *s* of late Joseph Brownbill and Veronica Brownbill; *m* 1974, Carol Ann Allen; two *d. Educ:* Univ. of Nottingham (LLB). Admitted solicitor, 1980; called to the Bar: Gray's Inn, 1989; Lincoln's Inn, 2007; E Caribbean Supreme Court, 2005. Editor: Jl of Internat. Trust and Corporate Planning; International Trust Laws. *Address:* (chambers) XXIV Old Buildings, Lincoln's Inn, WC2A 3UP. *T:* (020) 7691 2424, *Fax:* (020) 7405 1360.

BROWNBILL, Timothy Patrick; HM Diplomatic Service; Deputy Director, Security, Foreign and Commonwealth Office, since 2014; *b* 6 Feb. 1960; *s* of George and Helen Brownbill. *Educ:* Sandbach Sch. MIL. Entered HM Diplomatic Service, 1979; Commercial Attaché, Lagos, 1982–86; Vice Consul, Madrid, 1986–90; Dep. Hd of Mission, Vilnius, 1992–94; Commercial Sec., Havana, 1996–98; Internat. Trade Dir, Trade Partners UK, 2000–02; Ambassador to Nicaragua, 2002–04; Dir for Trade Promotion, subseq. Dep. Hd of Mission, Düsseldorf, 2004–08; Hd of Mission, Ho Chi Minh City, Vietnam, 2008–11; Gp Leader for Communications and Asset Mgt, Estates Directorate, FCO, 2012–14. *Recreations:* music, literature, sports, film, languages (French, Spanish, German and some Lithuanian, Vietnamese and Arabic). *Address:* Foreign and Commonwealth Office, King Charles Street, SW1A 2AH.

BROWNE, family name of **Marquess of Sligo**, and **Barons Kilmaine** and **Oranmore and Browne**.

BROWNE OF BELMONT, Baron *cr* 2006 (Life Peer), of Belmont in the County of Antrim; **Wallace Hamilton Browne;** Member (DemU) Belfast East, Northern Ireland Assembly, 2007–11; *b* 29 Oct. 1947; *s* of Gerald and Phyllis Hamilton Browne. *Educ:* Campbell Coll., Belfast; QUB (BSc (Hons) Zoology 1970). Biology teacher, Raney Endowed Sch., Magherafelt, 1970–2000. Mem. (DemU), Belfast City Council, 1985–2011; Lord Mayor of Belfast, 2005–06. Trustee, Somme Assoc., NI. High Sheriff, Belfast, 2002. *Address:* House of Lords, SW1A 0PW.

BROWNE OF LADYTON, Baron *cr* 2010 (Life Peer), of Ladyton in Ayrshire and Arran; **Desmond Henry Browne;** PC 2005; *b* 22 March 1952; *s* of Peter and Maureen Browne. *Educ:* St Michael's Acad., Kilwinning; Univ. of Glasgow. Apprentice Solicitor, Jas Campbell & Co., 1974–76; Solicitor, 1976; Asst Solicitor, 1976–80, Partner, 1980–85, Ross Harper & Murphy; Partner, McCluskey Browne, 1985–92; admitted, Faculty of Advocates, 1993. Contested (Lab) Argyll and Bute, 1992. MP (Lab) Kilmarnock and Loudoun, 1997–2010. Parly Under-Sec. of State, NI Office, 2001–03; Minister of State: (Minister for Work), DWP, 2003–04; Home Office, 2004–05; Chief Sec. to HM Treasury, 2005–06; Secretary of State: for Defence, 2006–08; for Scotland, 2007–08; Special Envoy for Sri Lanka, 2009–10. *Recreations:* football, reading.

BROWNE OF MADINGLEY, Baron *cr* 2001 (Life Peer), of Cambridge in the County of Cambridgeshire; **Edmund John Phillip Browne,** Kt 1998; FRS 2006; FREng, FIMMM, FInstPet; FInstP; Chairman, L1 Energy, since 2015 (non-executive Director, since 2013); *b* 20 Feb. 1948; *s* of late Edmund John Browne and Paula (*née* Wesz). *Educ:* King's Sch., Ely; St John's Coll., Cambridge (MA Hons; Hon. Fellow, 1997); Stanford Grad. Sch. of Business (MS Business). FIMMM (FIMM 1987); FREng (FEng 1993); FInstPet 1992; FInstP 1992. Joined British Petroleum Co., 1966; Gp Treasurer and Chief Exec., BP Finance Internat., 1984–86; Executive Vice-President and Chief Financial Officer: Standard Oil Co., 1986–87; BP America, 1987–89; Chief Exec. Officer, Standard Oil Prodn Co., 1987–89; Man. Dir and CEO, BP Exploration Co., 1989–95; Man. Dir, 1991–2007, and Gp Chief Exec., 1995–2007, British Petroleum Co. plc, subseq. BP Amoco, later BP plc; Partner, Riverstone Hldgs LLC, 2007–15. Chairman, Advisory Board: Apax Partners, 2007; Stanhope Capital, 2009–; Mubadala Oil and Gas, 2009–; Chm., Huawei Technologies (UK), 2015–; non-executive Director: SmithKline Beecham, 1995–99; Intel Corp., 1997–2006; Goldman Sachs, 1999–2007; Foster + Partners, 2007; Cuadrilla Resources, 2010–15 (Chm., 2011–15); Fairfield Energy, 2012–; Pattern Energy, 2013–; Riverstone Energy Ltd, 2013–15; Mem. Supervisory Bd, DaimlerChrysler AG, 1998–2001; Mem., Climate Change Adv. Bd, Deutsche Bank, 2007–; Chm., Global Energy Adv. Bd, Accenture, 2007–. Govt Lead non-exec. Bd Mem., 2010–15. Chm., Ind. Review of Higher Educn Funding and Student Finance, 2010 (report published 2010). Trustee: BM, 1995–2005; Cicely Saunders Foundn, 2001; Tate Gall., 2007– (Chm., 2009–); Chm., Trustees, Queen Elizabeth II Prize for Engrg, 2011–. President: BAAS, 2006–07; RAEng, 2006–11. Chm., Adv. Bd, Stanford Grad. Sch. of Business, 1995–97, now Chm. Emeritus; Mem. Governing Body, London Business Sch., 1996–2000; Chairman: Adv. Bd, Judge Business Sch., Cambridge (Judge Inst. of Mgt Studies), 2002–10; Internat. Adv. Bd, Blavatnik Sch. of Govt, Oxford Univ., 2011–; Donmar Warehouse, 2015–. Hon. Trustee, Chicago SO; Hon. Counsellor, Conference Bd Inc. CCMI (CIMgt 1993). Hon. FIChemE; Hon. FIMechE 2001; Hon. FRSC 2002; Hon. FGS 1999; Foreign Fellow, Amer. Acad. Arts and Scis, 2003. Hon. degrees from Heriot-Watt, Robert Gordon, Dundee, Warwick, Hull, Cranfield, Sheffield Hallam, Buckingham, Belfast, Surrey, Imperial Coll. London, Aston, Leuven, Notre Dame, Thunderbird, Colorado Sch. of Mines, Medeleyev and Arizona State. Prince Philip Medal, Royal Acad. of Engrg, 1999; Ernest C. Arbuckle Award, Stanford Univ., 2001; Gold Medal, Inst. of Mgt, 2001. *Publications:* Beyond Business, 2010; Seven Elements that Changed the World, 2013; The Glass Closet, 2014; Connect: how companies succeed by engaging radically with society, 2015. *Recreations:* opera, photography, books, pre-Columbian art, 18th century Venetian books and works on paper. *Address:* L1 Energy, Devonshire House, 1 Mayfair Place, W1J 8AJ. *Clubs:* Garrick, Savile.

BROWNE, Anthony Edward Tudor; author and illustrator of children's books, since 1976; Children's Laureate, 2009–11; *b* 11 Sept. 1946; *s* of Jack and Doris Browne; *m* 1980, Jane Franklin; one *s* one *d*. *Educ:* Whitcliffe Mount GS, Cleckheaton; Leeds Coll. of Art (BA 1967). Medical Artist, Manchester Royal Infirmary, 1969–71; designer of greetings cards, Gordon Fraser Gall., 1972–86. Hon. DEd: Kingston, 2005; Canterbury Christ Church, 2013. Silver Medal, US Soc. of Illustrators, 1994; Hans Christian Andersen Award, 2000. *Publications: author and illustrator:* Through the Magic Mirror, 1976; Walk in the Park, 1977; Bear Hunt, 1979; Bear Goes to Town, 1982; Gorilla, 1983 (Kurt Maschler Award, 1983; Kate Greenaway Medal, 1984; Boston Globe Horn Book Award, 1986; Netherlands Silver Pencil Award, 1989); Willy the Wimp, 1984; Piggybook, 1985; Willy the Champ, 1985; I Like Books, 1988; The Tunnel, 1989 (Netherlands Silver Pencil Award, 1990); Changes, 1990; Willy and Hugh, 1991; Zoo, 1992 (Kate Greenaway Medal, 1992); Big Baby, 1993; Willy the Wizard, 1995; Look What I've Got!, 1996; Things I Like, 1997; Willy the Dreamer, 1997; Voices in the Park, 1998 (Kurt Maschler Award, 1998); Willy's Pictures, 1999; My Dad, 2000; The Shape Game, 2003; Into the Forest, 2004; My Mum, 2005; Silly Billy, 2006; My Brother, 2007; Little Beauty, 2008; Me and You, 2010; Play the Shape Game, 2010; Bear's Magic Pencil, 2010; (with Joe Browne) Playing the Shape Game: a life in picture books with the Children's Laureate, 2011; How Do You Feel?, 2011; One Gorilla: a counting book, 2012; What If…?, 2013; Willy's Stories, 2014; (with Hanne Bartholin) Frida and Bear, 2015; *illustrator:* Hansel and Gretel (adapted from trans. by Eleanor Quarrie), 1981; Annalena McAfee, The Visitors Who Came to Stay, 1984; Sally Grindley, Knock, Knock!, Who's There?, 1985; Annalena McAfee, Kirsty Knows Best, 1987; Lewis Carroll, Alice's Adventures in Wonderland, 1988 (Kurt Maschler Award, 1988); Gwen Strauss, Trail of Stones (poems), 1990; Gwen Strauss, The Night Shimmy, 1991; Janni Howker, The Topiary Garden, 1993; King Kong (from story by Edgar Wallace and Merian C. Cooper), 1994; Ian McEwan, The Daydreamer, 1994; Animal Fair (traditional), 2002. *Recreations:* walking, travelling, watching cricket and Rugby, looking at art, being with my (grown-up) children, reading, cinema. *Address:* c/o Walker Books Ltd, 87 Vauxhall Walk, SE11 5HJ. *T:* (020) 7793 0909.

BROWNE, Anthony Howe; Chief Executive, British Bankers' Association, since 2012; *b* Cambridge, 19 Jan. 1967; *s* of Patrick and Gerd Browne; *m* 2003, Paula Higgins; one *s* one *d*. *Educ:* Trinity Hall, Cambridge (BA Hons Maths 1988). Ed., Ford Communications Network, 1991–93; BBC: researcher, Money Prog., 1993–94; broadcast journalist, Business Breakfast, 1994–95; Business Reporter, Radio, 1995–97; Econs corresp., TV and Radio, 1997–98; The Observer: Econs corresp., 1998; Dep. Business Ed., 1999; Health Ed., 1999–2002; The Times: Envmt Ed., 2002–03; Brussels corresp., 2003–06; Chief Political corresp., 2006–07; Dir, Policy Exchange, 2007–08; Policy Dir, London Mayor's Office, 2008–11; Manifesto Dir, Mayor of London's Re-election Campaign, 2011–12; Hd, Govt Relns for Europe, Middle East and Africa, Morgan Stanley, 2012. *Publications:* The Euro: should Britain join?, 2001; Do we Need Mass Immigration?, 2002. *Recreations:* walking, running, climbing, eating, drinking, helping caterpillars turn into butterflies. *Address:* British Bankers' Association, Pinners Hall, 105–108 Old Broad Street, EC2N 1EX.

BROWNE, Anthony Percy Scott; Chairman, British Art Market Federation, since 1996; *b* 8 Jan. 1949; *s* of late Percy Browne and Pamela Browne (*née* Exham); *m* 1976, Annabel Louise Hankinson; three *d*. *Educ:* Eton Coll.; Christ Church, Oxford (MA Modern Hist.). Dir, Christie's, 1978–96; Sen. Consultant, Christie's Internat., 1996–. Member: Cultural Industries Export Adv. Gp, 1998–2001; Ministerial Adv. Panel on Illicit Trade, 1999–2003; Adv. Panel, Goodison Review, 2003 (report, Securing the Best for our Museums). Member: Bd, Eur. Fine Art Foundn, 1999–; Council, Amer. Mus. in Britain, 2011–. Hon. Associate, Soc. of Fine Art Auctioneers, 2005. Vice Chm., Art Fortnight London, 2004–05. Trustee, Raise from the Ruins, 1978–80. *Publications:* (contrib.) Who Owns the Past?, 2005; (contrib.) Fine Art and High Finance, 2010. *Recreations:* fishing, gardening. *Address:* British Art Market Federation, 10 Bury Street, SW1Y 6AA. *T:* (020) 7389 2148. *Clubs:* Turf, Pratt's, Grillion's.

BROWNE, Benjamin James; QC 1996; a Recorder, since 2000; *b* 25 April 1954; *s* of late Percy Basil Browne and Jenefer Mary Browne; *m* 1987, Juliet Mary Heywood; one *s* one *d*. *Educ:* Eton Coll.; Christ Church, Oxford (MA). Called to the Bar, Inner Temple, 1976; Hd of Chambers, 2 Temple Gdns, 2005–. An Asst Recorder, 1998–2000. *Recreations:* country pursuits, gardening. *Address:* 2 Temple Gardens, Temple, EC4Y 9AY. *T:* (020) 7822 1200. *Club:* Boodle's.

BROWNE, Dr (Brendan) Mark; Director of Finance, Strategic Planning and Social Change Directorate, Office of the First Minister and Deputy First Minister, Northern Ireland, since 2015 (Director of Resources, Regeneration, International Relations and Institutional Review Directorate, 2013–15); *b* Belfast, 17 Aug. 1958; *s* of Brendan and Marie Browne; *m* 1984, Maureen Patricia Caldwell; two *s* one *d*. *Educ:* St Patrick's Coll., Knock, Belfast; Queen's Univ. Belfast (BA Hons Econ. and Social Hist. 1980; PhD Econ. and Social Hist. 1989). Statistician, Dept of Finance and Personnel, NI, 1985–91; Department of Education, Northern Ireland: Head: Stats and Res., 1991–96; Sch. Policy, 1996–99; Sch. Funding and Admin, 1999–2002; Post-Primary Rev. Team, 2002–03; Finance Dir and Hd, Strategic Planning, 2003–06; Prog. Dir, Educn and Skills Authy Implementation Team, 2006–09; Dep. Sec., Policy, Dept of Agriculture and Rural Develt, NI, 2009–13. *Recreations:* soccer (coaching and watching) (University Blue), golf, walking, gardening, cycling, reading, foreign travel. *Address:* Office of the First Minister and Deputy First Minister, Castle Buildings, Belfast BT4 3SR.

BROWNE, Carolyn; HM Diplomatic Service; Ambassador to Kazakhstan, since 2013; *b* 19 Oct. 1958; *d* of late Brig. C. C. Ll. Browne and Margaret Browne (*née* Howard). *Educ:* Godolphin Sch.; S Wilts Grammar Sch., Salisbury; Bristol Univ. (BSc Hons Microbiol.); Linacre Coll., Oxford (DPhil Bacterial Genetics 1985). Joined HM Diplomatic Service, 1985; Second, later First, Sec., Moscow, 1988–91; FCO, 1991–93; UKMIS to UN, NY, 1993–97; FCO, 1997–99; Hd, Human Rights Policy Dept, FCO, 1999–2002; Counsellor (External Relns), UK Perm. Repn to EU, Brussels, 2002–05; FCO, 2005–07; Ambassador to Azerbaijan, 2007–11. *Address:* c/o Foreign and Commonwealth Office, King Charles Street, SW1A 2AH.

BROWNE, Colin; *see* Browne, J. C. C.

BROWNE, Most Rev. Denis George; *see* Hamilton (NZ), Bishop of, (RC).

BROWNE, Desmond John Michael; QC 1990; Recorder, 1994–2008; *b* 5 April 1947; *s* of Sir Denis John Browne, KCVO, FRCS and of Lady Moyra Browne, *qv*; *m* 1973, Jennifer Mary Wilmore; two *d*. *Educ:* Eton College; New College, Oxford (Scholar). Called to the Bar, Gray's Inn, 1969, Bencher, 1999 (Vice-Treas., 2014, Treas., 2015). Asst Recorder, 1991–94. Chm., Bar Council, 2009 (Vice-Chm. 2008). Hon. Mem., Australian Bar Assoc., 2009. *Recreations:* Australiana, Venice, Sussex Downs. *Address:* 5 Gray's Inn Square, Gray's Inn, WC1R 5AH. *T:* (020) 7242 2902. *Clubs:* Brooks's, Beefsteak.

BROWNE, Prof. (Elizabeth) Janet, (Janet Bell), PhD; FLS; Aramont Professor of the History of Science, Harvard University, since 2006; *b* 30 March 1950; *d* of Douglas Maurice Bell and Elizabeth Mary Bell (*née* Edelsten); *m* 1972, Nicholas Browne; two *d*. *Educ:* Trinity Coll., Dublin (BA Hons 1972); Imperial Coll., London (MSc 1973; PhD 1978). Antiquarian bookseller, 1973–75; Wellcome Inst. for Hist. of Medicine, 1979–83 and 1993–2006, Lectr, then Reader, 1993–2002; Prof. in Hist. of Biology, Wellcome Trust Centre for Hist. of Medicine at UCL, 2002–06. Associate Ed., Correspondence of Charles Darwin, 1983–91. Vis. Sen. Res. Fellow, King's Coll., Cambridge, 1996–97. Member: Blue Plaque Panel, English Heritage, 1999–2006; Liby Cttee, Royal Soc., 2001–05. Pres., British Soc. for Hist. of Sci., 2002–04; Mem., Acad. Internat. d'histoire des Scis, 2005. FLS 2003; Corresp. FBA 2010. Hon. DSc TCD, 2009. Ed., British Jl for Hist. of Sci., 1993–99. Founders' Medal, Soc. for Hist. of Natural Hist., 2003. *Publications:* The Secular Ark: studies in the history of biogeography, 1983; (jtly) Dictionary of the History of Science, 1981; Charles Darwin: voyaging, 1995; Charles Darwin: the power of place, 2002 (winner, Biog. Section, Nat. Book Critics Circle, 2002; W. H. Heinemann Award, RSL, 2003; James Tait Black Prize (Biog.), 2004; Pfizer Prize, Hist. of Sci. Soc., 2004); Darwin's Origin of Species: a biography, 2006. *Recreation:* gardening. *Address:* Science Center 371, Department of the History of Science, Harvard University, 1 Oxford Street, Cambridge, MA 02138, USA.

BROWNE, Gillian Brenda B.; *see* Babington-Browne.

BROWNE, Graham David; Associate, National College for School Leadership; Education Consultant, Brown and Grey Ltd; *b* 6 July 1953; *s* of Edwin and Pamela Browne; *m* 1977, Janet Manning; two *d*. *Educ:* Coll. of St Mark and St John, Plymouth (BEd Geog., Educn, Geol.). Teacher, Prendergast Sch., Catford, 1975–80; with Murdo Maclean & Sons Ltd, Stornoway, 1980–84; Hd of Year, Barnwell Sch., Stevenage, 1984–88; Sen. Teacher, John Bunyan Upper Sch., Bedford, 1988–91; Dep. Hd, Beaumont Sch., St Albans, 1991–95; Principal, Estover Community Coll., Plymouth, 1995–2009; Exec. Principal, Estover Fedn, later Tor Bridge Partnership, Plymouth, 2009. Regl Leader, Nat. Coll. Sch. Leadership, 2006–07; Associate Headteacher, Specialist Schs and Academies Trust; Chairman: Plymouth Assoc. of Secondary Headteachers, 2005–06; Wise Adv. Gp, Plymouth CC, 2007. Advr, Letts Publishers, 1986–87. Teacher of Year Award, SW Reg., Leadership, 2002. *Recreations:* building, orchards, soccer (West Ham United supporter), travel, writing, film, music, member of Chagford Gospel Church.

BROWNE, Very Rev. Dr Herman Beseah; Dean, Trinity Cathedral, Episcopal Church of Liberia, since 2010; *b* 11 March 1965; *s* of George D. Browne and Clavender Railey Browne; *m* 2008, Tokon Lisa Chea; two *d*, and one *s* decd by a previous marriage. *Educ:* Cuttington UC, Liberia (BA Theol.); King's Coll., London (BD; AKC); Heythrop Coll., London (DPhil 1994). Ordained priest, 1987; Co-ordinator of Studies, Simon of Cyrene Theol Inst., London, 1994–96; Archbp's Asst Sec. for Anglican Communion and Ecumenical Affairs, 1996–2001; Archbishop of Canterbury's Sec. for Anglican Communion Affairs, 2001–05; Hd of Theology Dept, Cuttington Univ. Graduate Sch., Liberia, 2005–08; Vice-Pres. for Academic Affairs, African Methodist Episcopal Univ., Liberia, 2008–10. Canon of Canterbury Cathedral, 2001–05, now Emeritus. Chm., Liberian Community Orgn, UK, 1995–96. *Publications:* Theological Anthropology: a dialectic study of the African and Liberian traditions, 1996, 2nd edn 1998; (ed with G. Griffith-Dickson) Passion for Critique: essays in honour of F. J. Laishley, 1997. *Recreations:* photography, table tennis, movies, music... and often upsetting those I love most. *Address:* Trinity Cathedral, PO Box 10–0277, 1000 Monrovia 10, Liberia. *T:* 77040595, 6912417. *E:* herman_gblayon@yahoo.com.

BROWNE, (James) Nicholas; QC 1995; **His Honour Judge Nicholas Browne;** a Circuit Judge, since 2006; *b* 25 April 1947; *o s* of late James Christopher Browne, MC and Winifred Browne (*née* Pirie); *m* 1981, Angelica Elizabeth Mitchell, a Circuit Judge (*d* 2006); two *d*. *Educ:* Cheltenham Coll.; Liverpool Univ. (LLB 1969). Called to the Bar, Inner Temple, 1971

(Duke of Edinburgh Entrance Schol.); Bencher 2002; Midland (formerly Midland and Oxford) Circuit, 1971–2006; Asst Recorder, 1990–93; a Recorder, 1993–2006. Mem., Bar Council, 1992–94 (Mem., Professional Conduct Cttee, 1993–94). Chairman, Code of Practice Appeal Board: Prescription Medicines Code of Practice Authy, 2000–05; Assoc. of British Pharmaceutical Industry, 2000–05. *Recreations:* cricket, squash, theatre, spending time with family and friends. *Address:* Wood Green Crown Court, Lordship Lane, N22 5LF. *T:* (020) 8826 4100. *Clubs:* MCC, Garrick; Cumberland Lawn Tennis.

BROWNE, Janet; *see* Browne, E. J.

BROWNE, Jeremy Richard; Special Representative to Europe, City of London, since 2015; *b* 17 May 1970; *s* of Sir Nicholas Walker Browne, KBE, CMG and of Diana (*née* Aldwinckle); *m* 2004, Charlotte (*née* Callen) (marr. diss. 2008); partner, Rachel Binks; one *d. Educ:* Univ. of Nottingham (BA 1992). Dewe Rogerson Ltd, 1994–96; Dir of Press and Broadcasting, Lib Dem Party, 1997–2000; Edelman Communications Worldwide, 2000–02; Associate Dir, Reputation Inc., 2003–04. MP (Lib Dem) Taunton, 2005–10, Taunton Deane, 2010–15. Lib Dem spokesman on foreign affairs, 2005–06; Lib Dem dep. spokesman on home affairs, 2006–07; Lib Dem Shadow Chief Sec. to Treasury, 2007–10; Minister of State: FCO, 2010–12; Home Office, 2012–13. Member: Home Affairs Select Cttee, 2005–08; Political and Constitutional Affairs Select Cttee, 2013–14. Contested (Lib Dem) Enfield Southgate, 1997. Mem. Adv. Bd, Reform, 2005–. Internat. Advr and Hon. Prof. of Politics, Univ. of Nottingham, 2015–. *Publications:* Race Plan, 2014; Why Vote Liberal Democrat, 2014. *Recreations:* Somerset CCC, Queens Park Rangers, American politics, travel, 20th century art.

BROWNE, John Anthony; a District Judge (Magistrates' Courts) (formerly Stipendiary Magistrate), S Yorkshire, 1992–2013; *b* 25 Aug. 1948; *s* of George Henry Browne and Margaret Browne (now Wheeler); *m* 1971, Dr Jill Lesley Atfield; one *s* three *d. Educ:* St Peter's de la Salle, Bournemouth; Sheffield Univ. (LLB Hons). Admitted solicitor, 1975; in private practice with Elliot Mather Smith, Chesterfield and Mansfield, 1975–92. *Recreations:* tennis, hill-walking, ski-ing, running (slowly), reading, supporting Sheffield Wednesday. *Address:* c/o The Magistrates' Court, Castle Street, Sheffield S3 8LU.

BROWNE, (John) Colin (Clarke); Founder and Chief Executive Officer, Colin Browne Strategic Communications Ltd, since 2010; Chairman, Voice of the Listener and Viewer, since 2012; Partner, The Maitland Consultancy, 2000–09; *b* 25 Oct. 1945; *s* of late Ernest Browne, JP and Isobel Sarah Browne (*née* McVitie); *m* 1984, Karen Lascelles Barr; one *s. Educ:* Wallace High Sch., Lisburn, Co. Antrim; Trinity Coll., Dublin (BA). Post Office, then British Telecommunications, 1969–94: Dir, Chairman's Office, 1980–85; Chief Exec., Broadband Services, 1985–86; Dir, Corporate Relations, 1986–94; Dir of Corporate Affairs, BBC, 1994–2000. Non-exec. Dir, Centre for Effective Dispute Resolution, 2012–. Member: HDA (formerly HEA), 1996–2003; Spongiform Encephalopathy Cttee, 2003–04; Govt Communications Review Gp, 2003; Communications Consumer Panel, 2008–12. Trustee: BBC Children in Need, 1994–2000; One World Broadcasting Trust, 1997–2003; Inst. of Internat. Communications, 1998–2000; Edinburgh Unesco City of Literature, 2009–14. FCIPR. *Recreations:* sport, music, reading.

BROWNE, John Ernest Douglas Delavalette; Senior Investment Strategist, Euro-Pacific Capital (New York), since 2008; Op-ed Columnist, Pittsburgh Tribune Review, since 2008; Visiting Fellow, Heritage Foundation, Washington DC, since 2008; *b* Hampshire, 17 Oct. 1938; *s* of late Col Ernest Coigny Delavalette Browne, OBE, and Victoria Mary Eugene (*née* Douglas); *m* 1st, 1965, Elizabeth Jeannette Marguerite Garthwaite (marr. diss.); 2nd, 1986, Elaine Margaret Schmid Boylen (marr. diss. 2003). *Educ:* Malvern; RMA Sandhurst; Cranfield Inst. of Technology (MSc); Harvard Business Sch. (MBA). Served Grenadier Guards, British Guiana (Battalion Pilot), Cyprus, BAOR, 1959–67; Captain 1963; TA, Grenadier Guards (Volunteers), 1981–91, Major 1985. Associate, Morgan Stanley & Co., New York, 1969–72; Pember & Boyle, 1972–74; Dir, ME Ops, Eur. Banking Co., 1974–78; Man. Dir, Falcon Finance Mgt Ltd, 1978–95; Vice Pres., Investments, Salomon Smith Barney, subseq. Smith Barney Inc., 1995–2004. Editor, Financial Intelligence Report, Newswax Media Inc., 2006–08. Director: Worms Investments, 1981–83; Scansat (Broadcasting) Ltd, 1988–93; Internat. Bd, World Times (Boston), 1988–2001; Tijari Finance Ltd, 1989–92; Adviser: Barclays Bank Ltd, 1978–84; Trustees Household Div., 1979–83. Director: Churchill Private Clinic, 1980–91; Drug Free America, 1998–2003; Greater Palm Beach Symphony, 1998–2003; World Affairs Council, Palm Beaches, 2003–09. Councillor (C), Westminster Council, 1974–78. MP (C) Winchester, 1979–92; introduced: Trades Description Act (Amendment) Bill, 1988; Protection of Animals (Amendment) Act, 1988; Protection of Privacy Bill, 1989; Armed Forces (Liability for Injury) Bill, 1991. Member: H of C Treasury Select Cttee, 1982–87; Social Services Select Cttee, 1991–92; Secretary: Conservative Finance Cttee, 1982–84; Conservative Defence Cttee, 1982–83; Chairman: Conservative Smaller Business Cttee, 1987–90 (Sec., 1984–87); Lords and Commons Anglo-Swiss Soc., 1979–92 (Treas., 1984–87; Sec., 1987–92); UK deleg. to N Atlantic Assembly, 1986–92 (rapporteur on human rights, 1989–92). Contested: (Ind C) Winchester, 1992; (Ind Against a Federal Europe) Hampshire South and Wight, EP election, 1994; (UK Ind): Falmouth and Camborne, 2001; NE, EP election, 2004; N Devon, 2005. Mem., NFU, 1980–90. Mem., Winchester Preservation Trust, 1980–90; Patron, Winchester Cadets Assoc., 1980–90; Trustee, Winnall Community Assoc., 1981–94; President: Winchester Gp for Disabled People, 1982–92; Hursley Cricket Club, 1985–90. Mem. Court, Univ. of Southampton, 1979–90; Governor, Malvern Coll., 1982–. Liveryman, Goldsmiths' Co., 1982–. OStJ 1979 (Mem., Chapter Gen., 1985–90). Interests include: economics, gold and internat. monetary affairs, defence, broadcasting. *Publications:* Tarantula: an Anglo American Special Forces hunt for bin Laden, 2003; Grenadier Grins, 2006; Hidden Account of the Romanovs, 2013; various articles on finance, gold (A New European Currency—The Karl, ₭), defence, Middle East, Soviet leadership. *Recreations:* golf, riding, sailing, shooting, ski-ing. *E:* johnbrowne@post.harvard.edu. *Clubs:* Boodle's, Turf, Special Forces; Fishers Island Yacht (New York); Palm Beach Yacht.

BROWNE, Air Vice-Marshal John Philip Ravenscroft, CBE 1985; *b* 27 April 1937; *s* of late Charles Harold Browne and Lorna Browne (*née* Bailey); *m* 1962, Gillian Dorothy Smith; two *s. Educ:* Brockenhurst County High Sch.; Southampton Univ. (BSc(Eng)). CEng, FICE. Commissioned Airfield Construction Branch, RAF, 1958; appts in NEAF and UK, 1959–66; transf. to Engineer Branch, 1966; RAF Coll., Cranwell, 1966–67; aircraft engineering appts, RAF Valley and MoD, 1967–71; RAF Staff Coll., 1972; OC Engrg Wing, RAF Valley, 1973–75; staff appts, MoD and HQ RAF Germany, 1975–82; MoD (PE), 1982–89: Asst Dir, Harrier Projects, 1982–85, Dir, Electronics Radar Airborne, 1985–86, Dir, Airborne Early Warning, 1986–89; Dir Gen. Support Services (RAF), MoD, 1989–92; RAF retd, 1992; Dir Engrg, 1992–95, Dir Systems, 1995–96, NATS, CAA. Pres., RAF Airfield Construction Officers' Assoc., 1991–. Trustee, Bletchley Park Trust, 1999–2009. FCMI. *Publications:* (with M. T. Thurbon) Electronic Warfare, 1998. *Recreations:* reading, writing, aviation, military history, photography, music. *Club:* Royal Air Force.

BROWNE, Mark; *see* Browne, B. M.

BROWNE, Lady Moyra (Blanche Madeleine), DBE 1977 (OBE 1962); Governor, 1987–99, Vice President, since 1999, Research into Ageing (formerly British Foundation for Age Research) (National Chairman, Support Groups, 1987–93); *b* 2 March 1918; *d* of 9th Earl of Bessborough, PC, GCMG; *m* 1945, Sir Denis John Browne, KCVO, FRCS (*d* 1967); one *s* one *d. Educ:* privately. Enrolled Nurse (General) (State Enrolled Nurse, 1946). Dep. Supt-in-Chief, 1964, Supt-in-Chief, 1970–83, St John Amb. Bde. Vice-Chm. Central Council, Victoria League, 1961–65; Vice-Pres., Royal Coll. of Nursing, 1970–85. Hon. Mem., British Assoc. of Paediatric Surgeons, 1990. GCStJ 1984 (Mem., Chapter Gen., subseq. Chapter Priory of England and Islands, 1983–). *Recreations:* music, fishing, travel.

See also D. J. M. Browne.

BROWNE, Nicholas; *see* Browne, J. N.

BROWNE, Robert W.; *see* Woodthorpe Browne.

BROWNE, Robert William M.; *see* Moxon Browne.

BROWNE, Simon Peter Buchanan; QC 2011; *b* Birkenhead, 5 Nov. 1959; *s* of late John Browne and of Marcelle Browne; *m* 1991, Amanda Jane Gillett; two *d. Educ:* King Edward VI Sch., Southampton; Univ. of East Anglia (LLB Hons 1981); Inns of Court Sch. of Law (Dist.). Called to the Bar, Middle Temple, 1982; in practice as a barrister, specialising in catastrophic injuries, solicitors' costs and sports law; Barrister Assessor in High Court, 2007–. Chm., Bar Tribunals and Adjudication Service, 2013–; Member: Bar Council and Law Soc. Jt Tribunal, 2013–; Civil Justice Council, 2013–. Chairman: Topsy Ojo Testimonial Cttee, 2013–14; Earlham Hall Develt Cttee, 2013–. *Recreations:* mountains (incl. ski-ing and crofting in Scotland), tennis (playing and spectating), Rugby, cocker spaniels. *Address:* Temple Garden Chambers, 1 Harcourt Buildings, Temple, EC4Y 9DA. *T:* (020) 7583 1315. *Clubs:* Reform, Hurlingham; London Irish Rugby Football.

BROWNE-CAVE, Sir John Robert Charles C.; *see* Cave-Browne-Cave.

BROWNE-WILKINSON, family name of **Baron Browne-Wilkinson**.

BROWNE-WILKINSON, Baron *cr* 1991 (Life Peer), of Camden, in the London Borough of Camden; **Nicolas Christopher Henry Browne-Wilkinson,** Kt 1977; PC 1983; a Lord of Appeal in Ordinary, 1991–2000; Senior Law Lord, 1999–2000; *b* 30 March 1930; *s* of late Canon A. R. Browne-Wilkinson and Molly Browne-Wilkinson; *m* 1st, 1955, Ursula de Lacy Bacon (*d* 1987); three *s* two *d*; 2nd, 1990, Mrs Hilary Tuckwell. *Educ:* Lancing; Magdalen Coll., Oxford (BA; Hon. Fellow, 1993). Called to Bar, Lincoln's Inn, 1953 (Bencher, 1977), QC 1972. Junior Counsel: to Registrar of Restrictive Trading Agreements, 1964–66; to Attorney-General in Charity Matters, 1966–72; in bankruptcy, to Dept of Trade and Industry, 1966–72; a Judge of the Courts of Appeal of Jersey and Guernsey, 1976–77; a Judge of the High Court, Chancery Div., 1977–83; a Lord Justice of Appeal, 1983–85; Vice-Chancellor of the Supreme Court, 1985–91. Pres., Employment Appeal Tribunal, 1981–83. Pres., Senate of the Inns of Court and the Bar, 1984–86. Hon. Fellow, St Edmund Hall, Oxford, 1987. *Recreation:* gardening. *Address:* House of Lords, SW1A 0PW.

See also S. Browne-Wilkinson.

BROWNE-WILKINSON, Simon; QC 1998; barrister; *b* 18 Aug. 1957; *s* of Baron Browne-Wilkinson, *qv*; *m* 1988, Megan Tresidder (*d* 2001); one *s* one *d. Educ:* City of London Sch.; Magdalen Coll., Oxford (BA Jurisprudence 1979). Called to the Bar, Lincoln's Inn, 1981, Bencher, 2008; in practice at the Bar, 1981–. *Recreation:* sailing. *Address:* Fountain Court, Temple, EC4Y 9DH. *T:* (020) 7583 3335.

BROWNING, family name of **Baroness Browning**.

BROWNING, Baroness *cr* 2010 (Life Peer), of Whimple in the County of Devon; **Angela Frances Browning;** *b* 4 Dec. 1946; *d* of late Thomas Pearson and Linda Pearson (later Chamberlain); *m* 1968, David Browning; two *s. Educ:* Westwood Girls' Grammar Sch.; Reading Coll. of Technol.; Bournemouth Coll. of Technol. FInstSMM. Management Consultant. MP (C) Tiverton, 1992–97, Tiverton and Honiton, 1997–2010; Dep. Chm., Cons. Party, 2006–10. Parly Sec., MAFF, 1994–97; Opposition spokesman: on educn and disability, 1997–98; on trade and industry, 1999–2000; Shadow Leader, H of C, 2000–01. Minister of State for Crime Prevention and Anti-social Behaviour Reduction, Home Office, 2011. Mem., Electoral Commn, 2010–11; Chair, Adv. Cttee on Business Appts, 2015–. Vice Pres., InstSMM, 1997–2011. Mem. and Vice Pres., Nat. Autistic Soc.; Nat. Vice Pres., Alzheimer's Disease Soc., 1997–. *Recreations:* theatre, opera. *Address:* House of Lords, SW1A 0PW.

BROWNING, Most Rev. Edmond Lee; Presiding Bishop of the Episcopal Church in the United States, 1986–97; *b* 11 March 1929; *s* of Edmond Lucian Browning and Cora Mae Lee; *m* 1953, Patricia A. Sparks; four *s* one *d. Educ:* Univ. of the South (BA 1952); School of Theology, Sewanee, Tenn (BD 1954). Curate, Good Shepherd, Corpus Christi, Texas, 1954–56; Rector, Redeemer, Eagle Pass, Texas, 1956–59; Rector, All Souls, Okinawa, 1959–63; Japanese Lang. School, Kobe, Japan, 1963–65; Rector, St Matthews, Okinawa, 1965–67; Archdeacon of Episcopal Church, Okinawa, 1965–67; first Bishop of Okinawa, 1967–71; Bishop of American Convocation, 1971–73; Executive for National and World Mission, on Presiding Bishop's Staff, United States Episcopal Church, 1974–76; Bishop of Hawaii, 1976–85. Chm., Standing Commn on World Mission, 1979–82. Member: Exec Council, Episcopal Church, 1982–85; Anglican Consultative Council, 1982–91. Hon. DD: Univ. of the South, Sewanee, Tenn, 1970; Gen. Theol Seminary, 1986; Church Divinity Sch of the Pacific, 1987; Seabury Western Seminary, 1987; Hon. DHL: Chaminade Univ., Honolulu, 1985; St Paul's Coll., Lawrenceville, Va, 1987. *Publications:* Essay on World Mission, 1977. *Address:* 5164 Imai Road, Hood River, OR 97031–9442, USA. *T:* (212) 9225322.

BROWNING, Rt Rev. George Victor; Convenor, Anglican Communion Environment Network, 2005–11; Bishop of Canberra and Goulburn, 1993–2008; *b* 28 Sept. 1942; *s* of John and Barbara Browning; *m* 1965, Margaret Rowland; three *s. Educ:* Ardingly Coll.; Lewes County Grammar Sch., Sussex; St John's Coll., Morpeth, NSW (ThL 1st cl. Hons 1965); Charles Sturt Univ. (BTh Hons 2011; PhD 2015). Curate: Inverell, 1966–68; Armidale, 1968–69; Vicar, Warialda, 1969–73; Vice Warden and Lectr in Old Testament Studies and Pastoral Theol., St John's Coll., Morpeth, 1973–75 (Acting Warden, 1974); Rector of Singleton, Rural Dean and Archdeacon of the Upper Hunter, 1976–84; Rector of Woy Woy and Archdeacon of the Central Coast, 1984–85; Bishop of the Northern Reg., Brisbane, 1985–92; Principal, St Francis' Theol Coll., 1988–92; Bishop of the Coastal Reg., and Asst Bishop, dio. of Brisbane, 1992–93; Priest-in-charge, Wriggle Valley, Salisbury, 2008–09. President: Australia Palestine Advocacy Network, 2013–; Christians for an Ethical Soc., 2014–. Hon. DLitt Charles Sturt Univ., 2007. *Recreations:* reading, beekeeping, landcare. *Address:* 24 Henry Place, Long Beach, NSW 2536, Australia. *T:* (2) 4472 7470.

BROWNING, Helen Mary, OBE 1998; DL; farmer and business woman; Chairman, Eastbrook Farms Organic Meat, since 1997; Director, Soil Association, since 2011; *b* 22 Nov. 1961; *d* of Robert Roland Browning and late Sheila Mary Browning (*née* Harris); *m* 1989, Henry George Stoye (separated); one *d. Educ:* Harper Adams Agricl Coll. (BSc Agricl Technol.). Chairman: British Organic Farmers, 1991–97; Soil Assoc., 1997–2001 (Dir, Food and Farming, 2004–09); Dir of External Affairs, NT, 2010–11. Member: MLC, 1998–2008; Agric. and Envmt Biotechnol. Commn, 1998–2005; Policy Commn on Future of Food and Farming, 2001–02; Chairman: Food Ethics Council, 2000–; Animal Health and Welfare England Implementation Gp, 2005–09. Member: Steering Cttee, Food Chain Centre, 2002–05; Bd, Organic Milk Suppliers Co-op., 2002–11. MInstD 2000. DL Wilts, 2015. *Recreations:* sport, especially squash, walking, food, reading, travel. *Address:* Eastbrook Farm, Bishopstone, Swindon, Wilts SN6 8PW. *T:* (01793) 792042, *Fax:* (01793) 791239. *Club:* Farmers.

BROWNING, Ian Andrew; DL; Chief Executive, Wiltshire County Council, 1984–96; Clerk to the Wiltshire Police Authority, 1976–2002; *b* 28 Aug. 1941; *m* 1967, Ann Carter; two *s*. *Educ:* Liverpool Univ. (BA Hons Pol Theory and Instns). Solicitor. Swindon BC, 1964–70; WR, Yorks, 1970–73; S Yorks CC, 1973–76; Wilts CC, 1976–96. DL Wilts, 1996. *Recreations:* golf, travel, ornithology. *Address:* 10 The Picquet, Bratton, Westbury, Wiltshire BA13 4RU.

BROWNING, Prof. Keith Anthony, PhD; FRS 1978; FRMetS; Director, Joint Centre for Mesoscale Meteorology, 1992–2003, and Professor in Department of Meteorology, 1995–2003, now Professor Emeritus, University of Reading; *b* 31 July 1938; *s* of late Sqdn Ldr James Anthony Browning and Amy Hilda (*née* Greenwood); *m* 1962, Ann Muriel (*née* Baish), BSc, MSc; one *s* two *d*. *Educ:* Commonweal Grammar Sch., Swindon, Wilts; Imperial Coll. of Science and Technology, Univ. of London. BSc, ARCS, PhD, DIC. FRMetS 1962 (Hon. FRMetS 2006); CMet 1994–2015. Research atmospheric physicist, Air Force Cambridge Research Laboratories, Mass, USA, 1962–66; in charge of Meteorological Office Radar Research Lab., RSRE, Malvern, 1966–85; Dep. Dir (Phys. Res.), 1985–89, Dir of Res., 1989–91, Met. Office, Bracknell; Principal Research Fellow, 1966–69; Principal Scientific Officer, 1969–72; Sen. Principal Scientific Officer, 1972–79; Dep. Chief Scientific Officer, 1979–89; Chief Scientific Officer, 1989–91. Director: NERC Univs Weather Res. Network, 2000–03; NERC Univs Facility for Atmospheric Measurements, 2001–03. Ch. Scientist, Nat. Hail Res. Experiment, USA, 1974–75. Visiting Professor: Dept of Meteorology, Reading Univ., 1988–94; Leeds Univ., 2006–. World Climate Research Programme: Member: British Nat. Cttee, 1988–89; Scientific Steering Gp, Global Energy and Water Cycle Expmt, 1988–96 (Chm., Cloud System Sci. Study, 1992–96); WMO/ICSU Jt Scientific Cttee, 1990–94; World Weather Research Programme: Mem., WMO Interim Sci. Steering Cttee, 1996–98; Mem., Sci. Steering Cttee, 1998–2005. Royal Meteorological Society: Mem. Council, 1971–74, 1979–81, 1987–91 and 1994–99 (Vice-Pres., 1979–81, 1987–88 and 1990–91; Pres., 1988–90); Mem., Accreditation Bd, 1993–99; Chm., 1994–99; Member: Editing Cttee, Qly Jl RMetS, 1975–78; Inter-Union Commn on Radio Meteorology, 1975–78; Internat. Commn on Cloud Physics, 1976–84; British Nat. Cttee for Physics, 1979–84; British Nat. Cttee for Geodesy and Geophysics, 1983–89 (Chm., Met. and Atmos. Phys. Sub-Cttee, 1985–89, Vice-Chm., 1979–84); NERC, 1984–87; British Nat. Cttee for Space Res., 1986–89 (Remote Sensing Sub-Cttee, 1986–89); Royal Soc. Interdisciplinary Sci. Cttee for Space Res., 1990–91. MAE, 1989; For. Associate, US Nat. Acad. of Engrg, 1992. UK Nat. Correspondent, Internat. Assoc. of Meteorology and Atmospheric Physics, 1991–94. L. F. Richardson Prize, 1968, Buchan Prize, 1972, William Gaskell Meml Medal, 1982, Symons Gold Medal, 2001, RMetS; L. G. Groves Meml Prize for Meteorology, Met. Office, 1969; Meisinger Award, 1974, Jule Charney Award, 1985, Carl-Gustaf Rossby Research Medal, 2003, Amer. Met. Soc. (Fellow of the Society, 1975; Hon. Mem., 2010); Charles Chree Medal and Prize, Inst. of Physics, 1981. *Publications:* (ed) Nowcasting, 1982; (ed jtly) Global Energy and Water Cycles, 1999; over 200 meteorological papers in learned jls, mainly in Britain and USA. *Recreations:* photography, home and garden, walking, piano.

BROWNING, Prof. Martin James, PhD; FBA 2008; Professor of Economics, University of Oxford, since 2006; Fellow, Nuffield College, Oxford, since 2006; *b* Loughborough, 27 Aug. 1946; *s* of George and Daisy Browning; *m* 1969, Lisbeth Hammer; two *s* one *d*. *Educ:* London School of Econs (MSc 1979); Tilburg Univ. (PhD 1993). Lectr, Bristol Univ., 1979–84; Prof. of Econs, McMaster Univ., 1984–97; Prof. of Econs, 1997–2006, Dir, Centre for Applied Microeconometrics, 2001–08, Univ. of Copenhagen. Fellow, Econometric Soc., 1996. John Rae Prize, Canadian Econs Assoc., 1996. *Publications:* (jtly) Economics of the Family, 2014; over 60 articles. *Address:* 35 The Stream Edge, Oxford OX1 1HT. *E:* martin.browning@economics.ox.ac.uk.

BROWNING, Philip Harold Roger; a District Judge (Magistrates' Courts), Norfolk, 2004–11; *b* 25 Aug. 1946; *s* of late Harold and Barbara Browning; *m* 1972, Linda; two *s*. *Educ:* Hele's Sch., Exeter; Surbiton County Grammar Sch.; Windsor Grammar Sch.; Coll. of Law. Articled T. W. Stuchbery & Son, Windsor and Maidenhead, 1964–69; admitted solicitor, 1969; Asst Solicitor, Baily, Williams & Lucas, Saffron Walden, 1969–71; Prosecuting Solicitor, Devon, 1972–81; Clerk to Justices: Axminster, Exmouth, Honiton and Wonford, 1981–85; Norwich, 1985–94; a Stipendiary Magistrate, subseq. Dist Judge (Magistrates' Courts), Shropshire, 1994–2000; a District Judge (Magistrates' Courts): West Mercia, 2000–03; Wolverhampton, 2003–04. Course Dir, continuation trng for Dist Judges (Magistrates' Courts), Judicial Studies Bd, 1997–2004. *Recreations:* books, music. *Address:* 46A Forton Road, Newport, Shropshire TF10 7JR. *T:* (01952) 876306.

BROWNING, Rev. Canon Wilfrid Robert Francis; Canon Residentiary of Christ Church Cathedral, Oxford, 1965–87, Hon. Canon since 1987; *b* 29 May 1918; *s* of Charles Robert and Mabel Elizabeth Browning; *m* 1948, Elizabeth Beeston (*d* 2009); two *s* two *d*. *Educ:* Westminster School; Christ Church, Oxford (Squire Scholar); Cuddesdon Coll., Oxford (Hon. Fellow, 2011). MA, BD Oxon. Deacon 1941, priest 1942, dio. of Peterborough; on staff of St Deiniol's Library, Hawarden, 1946–48; Vicar of St Richard's, Hove, 1948–51; Rector of Great Haseley, 1951–59; Lectr, Cuddesdon Coll., Oxford, 1951–59 and 1965–70; Canon Residentiary of Blackburn Cath. and Warden of Whalley Abbey, Lancs, 1959–65; Director of Ordinands and Post-Ordination Trng (Oxford dio.), 1965–85; Dir of Trng for Non-Stipendiary Ordinands and Clergy, 1972–88; Tutor, Westminster Coll., Oxford, 1993–99. Examining Chaplain: Blackburn, 1960–70; Manchester, 1970–78; Oxford, 1965–89. Member of General Synod, 1973–85; Select Preacher, Oxford Univ., 1972, 1981. Cross of St Augustine, 2008. *Publications:* Commentary on St Luke's Gospel, 1960, 6th edn 1981; Meet the New Testament, 1964; ed, The Anglican Synthesis, 1965; Handbook of the Ministry, 1985; A Dictionary of the Bible, 1996, 3rd edn 2009. *Address:* The College of St Barnabas, Blackberry Lane, Lingfield RH7 6NJ. *T:* (01342) 872853.

BROWNJOHN, Alan Charles; poet, novelist and critic; *b* 28 July 1931; *s* of Charles Henry Brownjohn and Dorothy Brownjohn (*née* Mulligan); *m* 1st, 1960, (Kathleen) Shirley Toulson (marr. diss. 1969); one *s*, and one step *s* one step *d*; 2nd, 1972, Sandra Lesley Willingham (marr. diss. 2005). *Educ:* Brockley County Sch.; Merton Coll., Oxford (BA Hons Mod. Hist. 1953; MA 1961). Asst Master, Beckenham and Penge Boys' Grammar Sch., 1958–65; Lectr, then Sen. Lectr, Battersea Coll. of Educn, subseq. S Bank Poly., 1965–79. Visiting Lecturer: in Poetry, Polytechnic of North London, 1981–83; in Creative Writing, Univ. of N London, then London Metropolitan Univ., 2000–03. Poetry Critic: New Statesman, 1968–74; Encounter, 1978–82; Sunday Times, 1990–2013. Special Award, Writers' Guild Bks Cttee, 2007. *Publications: poetry:* The Railings, 1961; The Lions' Mouths, 1967; Sandgrains on a Tray, 1969; Warrior's Career, 1972; A Song of Good Life, 1975; A Night in the Gazebo, 1980; Collected Poems, 1983, 3rd edn 2006; The Old Flea-Pit, 1987; The Observation Car, 1990; In the Cruel Arcade, 1994; The Cat Without E-Mail, 2001; The Men Around Her Bed, 2004; Ludbrooke, And Others, 2010; The Saner Places: selected poems, 2011; A Bottle, 2015; *novels:* The Way You Tell Them, 1990 (Authors' Club prize, 1991); The Long Shadows, 1997; A Funny Old Year, 2001; Windows on the Moon, 2009; *translations:* Goethe, Torquato Tasso (with Sandra Brownjohn), 1986; Corneille, Horace, 1995. *Recreations:* walking, listening to music, left-wing censoriousness. *Address:* 2 Belsize Park, NW3 4ET. *T:* (020) 7794 2479.

BROWNLEE, Derek Scott; Director, Scotland, Commercial and Private Banking, Royal Bank of Scotland, since 2014 (Head of Research and Briefing, 2011–13; Director, Corporate Banking Division, 2013–14); *b* 10 Aug. 1974; *s* of David Melville Brownlee and Jean Chisholm Brownlee. *Educ:* Selkirk High Sch.; Univ. of Aberdeen (LLB 1st Cl. Hons). CA 1999. Ernst & Young: Accountant, 1996–99; Consultant, 1999–2001; Sen. Consultant, 2001–02; Hd, Taxation and Pensions Policy, Inst. Dirs, 2002–04; Manager, Deloitte, 2004–05. Contested (C) Tweeddale, Ettrick and Lauderdale, Scottish Parlt, 2003, 2007; MSP (C) S of Scotland, June 2005–2011; contested (C) E Lothian, Scottish Parlt, 2011. Scottish Parliament: Member: Finance Cttee, 2005–11; Scottish Commn for Public Audit, 2007–11. Mem. Adv. Bd, Reform Scotland, 2011–. *Club:* Selkirk Conservative.

BROWNLEE, Prof. George Gow, PhD; FMedSci; FRS 1987; E. P. Abraham Professor of Chemical Pathology, Sir William Dunn School of Pathology, University of Oxford, 1980–2008; Fellow of Lincoln College, Oxford, since 1980; *b* 13 Jan. 1942; *s* of late Prof. George Brownlee; *m* 1966, Margaret Susan Kemp; one *d* (one *s* decd). *Educ:* Dulwich College; Emmanuel Coll., Cambridge (MA, PhD). Scientific staff of MRC at Laboratory of Molecular Biology, Cambridge, 1966–80. Fellow, Emmanuel Coll., Cambridge, 1967–71. Founder FMedSci 1998. Colworth Medal, 1977, Wellcome Trust Award, 1985, Biochemical Soc.; Owren Medal (Norway), 1987; Haemophilia Medal (France), 1988. *Publications:* Determination of Sequences in RNA (Vol. 3, Part I of Laboratory Techniques in Biochemistry and Molecular Biology), 1972; Fred Sanger - Double Nobel Laureate: a biography, 2014; scientific papers in Jl of Molecular Biology, Nature, Cell, Nucleic Acids Research, etc. *Recreations:* gardening, cricket.

BROWNLIE, Albert Dempster; Vice-Chancellor, University of Canterbury, Christchurch, New Zealand, 1977–98; *b* 3 Sept. 1932; *s* of Albert Newman and Netia Brownlie; *m* 1955, Noelene Eunice (*née* Meyer) (*d* 2012); two *d*. *Educ:* Univ. of Auckland, NZ (MCom). Economist, NZ Treasury, 1954–55. Lecturer, Sen. Lectr, Associate Prof. in Economics, Univ. of Auckland, 1956–64; Prof. and Head of Dept of Economics, Univ. of Canterbury, Christchurch, 1965–77. Chairman: Monetary and Economic Council, 1972–78; Australia-NZ Foundn, 1979–83; UGC Cttee to Review NZ Univ. Educn, 1980–82; NZ Vice-Chancellors' Cttee, 1983–84, 1993; Member: Commonwealth Experts Group on New Internat. Economic Order, 1975–77; Commonwealth Experts Gp on Econ. Growth, 1980; Wage Hearing Tribunal, 1976. Silver Jubilee Medal, 1977. *Publications:* articles in learned jls. *Address:* St Nicolas Hospital, 7 Kirkwood Avenue, Ilam, Christchurch 8041, New Zealand. *T:* (3) 3484090.

BROWNLOW, 7th Baron *cr* 1776; **Edward John Peregrine Cust;** Bt 1677; Chairman and Managing Director of Harris & Dixon (Underwriting Agencies) Ltd, 1976–82; *b* 25 March 1936; *o s* of 6th Baron Brownlow and Katherine Hariet (*d* 1952), 2nd *d* of Sir David Alexander Kinloch, 11th Bt, CB, MVO; *S* father, 1978; *m* 1964, Shirlie Edith, 2nd *d* of late John Yeomans, The Manor Farm, Hill Croome, Upton-on-Severn, Worcs; one *s*. *Educ:* Eton. Member of Lloyd's, 1961–88, and 1993–96; Director: Hand-in-Hand Fire and Life Insurance Soc. (branch office of Commercial Union Assurance Co. Ltd), 1962–82; Ermitage International Ltd, 1988–99; Vice Chm., Ermitage Global Wealth Mgt Jersey Ltd, 2007–08. High Sheriff of Lincolnshire, 1978–79. CStJ 1999 (Chm. Council, Jersey, 1996–2005). *Heir: s* Hon. Peregrine Edward Quintin Cust [*b* 9 July 1974; *m* 2010, Vanessa Monica Threapleton-Horrocks]. *Address:* La Maison des Prés, St Peter, Jersey JE3 7EL. *Club:* White's.

BROWNLOW, Air Vice-Marshal Bertrand, (John), CB 1982; OBE 1967; AFC 1962; FRAeS; aviation consultant, since 1997; *b* 13 Jan. 1929; *s* of Robert John Brownlow and Helen Louise Brownlow; *m* 1958, Kathleen Shannon; one *s* one *d* (and one *s* decd). *Educ:* Beaufort Lodge Sch. Joined RAF, 1947; 12 and 101 Sqdns, ADC to AOC 1 Gp, 103 Sqdn, 213 Sqdn, Empire Test Pilots' Sch., OC Structures and Mech. Eng Flt RAE Farnborough, RAF Staff Coll., Air Min. Op. Requirements, 1949–64; Wing Comdr Ops, RAF Lyneham, 1964–66; Jt Services Staff Coll., 1966–67; DS RAF Staff Coll., 1967–68; Def. and Air Attaché, Stockholm, 1969–71; CO Experimental Flying, RAE Farnborough, 1971–73; Asst Comdt, Office and Flying Trng, RAF Coll., Cranwell, 1973–74; Dir of Flying (R&D), MoD, 1974–77; Comdt, A&AEE, 1977–80; Comdt, RAF Coll., Cranwell, 1980–82; Dir Gen., Trng, RAF, 1982–83, retired 1984. Exec. Dir, Marshall of Cambridge (Engineering), subseq. Dir, Marshall Aerospace, 1987–94. Mem., CAA, 1994–96. Gov., Papworth Hosp. NHS Foundn Trust, 2004–08. FRAeS 1981. Silver Medal, Royal Aero Club, 1983, for servs to RAF gliding; Sword of Honour, GAPAN, 2000. *Recreations:* squash, tennis, golf, gliding (Gold C with two diamonds). *Address:* Woodside, Abbotsley Road, Croxton, St Neots PE19 6SZ. *T:* (01480) 880663. *E:* john.brownlow1@btinternet.com. *Club:* Royal Air Force.

BROWNLOW, Air Vice-Marshal John; *see* Brownlow, Air Vice-Marshal B.

BROWNLOW, Kevin; author; film director; *b* 2 June 1938; *s* of Thomas and Niña Brownlow; *m* 1969, Virginia Keane; one *d*. *Educ:* University College School. Entered documentaries, 1955; became film editor, 1958, and edited many documentaries; with Andrew Mollo dir. feature films: It Happened Here, 1964; Winstanley, 1975; dir. Charm of Dynamite, 1967, about Abel Gance, and restored his classic film Napoleon (first shown London, Nov. 1980, NY, Jan. 1981). Directed TV documentaries: Universal Horror, 1998; Lon Chaney: a thousand faces, 2000; Cecil B. DeMille: American Epic, 2003; with David Gill: Hollywood, 1980; Thames Silents, 1981–90 (incl. The Big Parade); Channel Four Silents, 1991–99 (incl. Sunrise); Unknown Chaplin, 1983; Buster Keaton: a Hard Act to Follow, 1987; Harold Lloyd—The Third Genius, 1990; D. W. Griffith, Father of Film, 1993; Cinema Europe—The Other Hollywood, 1995; with Michael Kloft: The Tramp and the Dictator, 2002; with Christopher Bird: Buster Keaton—So Funny It Hurt, 2004; Garbo, 2005; I'm King Kong!—The Exploits of Merian C. Cooper, 2005; prod., British Cinema—Personal View, 1986. Hon. Academy Award, 2011. *Publications:* The Parade's Gone By…, 1968; How it Happened Here, 1968; The War, the West and the Wilderness, 1978; Hollywood: the Pioneers, 1979; Napoleon: Abel Gance's classic film, 1983, 2nd edn 2004; Behind The Mask of Innocence, 1991; David Lean: a biography, 1996, 2nd edn 2008; Mary Pickford Rediscovered, 1999; The Search for Charlie Chaplin, 2010; (ed) The Screen of Change, by Peter Hopkinson, 2007; Winstanley, Warts and All, 2009; many articles on film history. *Recreation:* motion pictures. *E:* kevin@photoplay.co.uk.

BROWNRIGG, Sir Nicholas (Gawen), 5th Bt *cr* 1816; *b* 22 Dec. 1932; *s* of late Gawen Egremont Brownrigg and Baroness Lucia von Borosini, *o d* of Baron Victor von Borosini, California; *S* grandfather, 1939; *m* 1959, Linda Louise Lovelace (marr. diss. 1965), Beverly Hills, California; one *s* one *d*; *m* 1971, Valerie Ann, *d* of Julian A. Arden, Livonia, Michigan, USA. *Educ:* Midland Sch.; Stanford Univ. *Heir: s* Michael Gawen Brownrigg [*b* 11 Oct. 1961; *m* 1990, Margaret Dillon, *d* of Dr Clay Burchell; three *s* one *d*]. *Address:* PO Box 1847, Fort Bragg, CA 95437, USA.

BROWNSWORD, Andrew Douglas, CBE 2014; DL; Chairman and Chief Executive, Andrew Brownsword Group, since 1993; Chairman: Bath Priory Group Ltd, since 1992; Paxton & Whitfield Ltd, since 2002; Andrew Brownsword Hotels Ltd; *s* of Douglas and Eileen Brownsword; *m* 1983, Christina Brenchley; two *d*. *Educ:* Harvey Grammar Sch., Folkestone. Formed A. Brownsword and Co., wholesale distributors of greetings cards and stationery, 1971; formed the Andrew Brownsword Collection Ltd, 1975; acquired Gordon Fraser Gallery, 1989; greetings cards business acquired by Hallmark Cards, 1994. Chairman: Bath Rugby plc, 1996–2011; Snow & Rock Ltd, 2004–11. DL Somerset, 2015. *Recreations:* shooting, sailing, ski-ing, hill-walking. *Address:* 4 Queen Square, Bath BA1 2HA.

BROWNSWORD, Prof. Roger; Professor of Law (part-time), King's College London, since 2010; Professor of Law (part-time), Bournemouth University, since 2014; Chair, UK Biobank Ethics and Governance Council, 2011–15; *b* Bangor, N Wales, 22 June 1946; *s* of Henry Walley Brownsword and Barbara Kathleen Brownsword; *m* 1971, Susan Elizabeth Marsh; two *s. Educ:* Friars Sch., Bangor; London Sch. of Econs and Pol Sci. (LLB 1st Cl. 1968). University of Sheffield: Asst Lectr in Law, 1968–71; Lectr in Law, 1971–80; Sen. Lectr in Law, 1980–88; Reader in Law, 1988–90; Prof. of Law, 1990–2003; Hd, Law Dept, 1999–2002; Hon. Prof., 2003–; Prof. of Law, 2003–10 and Dir, Centre for Technol., Ethics and Law in Society, 2005–10, KCL. Mem., Nuffield Council on Bioethics, 2004–10. *Publications:* (with D. Beyleveld) Law as a Moral Judgement, 1986; (with J. N. Adams) Understanding Contract Law, 1992, 4th edn 2006; (with J. N. Adams) Understanding Law, 1992, 4th edn 2006; (with D. Beyleveld) Mice, Morality and Patents, 1993; (ed jtly) Welfarism in Contract Law, 1994; (with J. N. Adams) Key Issues in Contract, 1995; (ed jtly) Law and Human Genetics: regulating a revolution, 1998; (ed jtly) Good Faith in Contract: concept and context, 1999; Contract Law: themes for the twenty-first century, 2000, 2nd edn 2006; (with D. Beyleveld) Human Dignity in Bioethics and Bio-Law, 2001; Human Rights, 2004; (with D. Beyleveld) Consent in the Law, 2007; Rights, Regulation and the Technological Revolution, 2008; (ed with K. Yeung) Regulating Technologies: legal futures, regulatory frames and technological fixes, 2008; Smith and Thomas: a casebook on contract, 12th edn, 2009, 13th edn 2015; (ed jtly) The Foundations of European Private Law, 2011; (with M. Goodwin) Law and the Technologies of the Twenty-First Century, 2012; (ed jtly) Cambridge Handbook of Human Dignity, 2014; (ed jtly) Oxford Handbook on Law, Regulation and Technology, 2016. *Recreations:* exploring the South-West coastline, jazz guitar and piano, Manchester City Football Club. *Address:* 6 Welbeck Close, Dronfield Woodhouse, Dronfield, Derbys S18 8ZT. *T:* (01246) 410460; Flat 2, Eversleigh, 48 West Cliff Road, Bournemouth BH4 8BB. *T:* (01202) 757455. *E:* roger.brownsword@kcl.ac.uk.

BROWSE, Sir Norman (Leslie), Kt 1994; MD; FRCS, FRCP; President of the States of Alderney, 2002–11; Professor of Surgery and Senior Consultant Surgeon, St Thomas's Hospital Medical School, 1981–96, now Professor Emeritus; Consulting Surgeon, St Thomas' Hospital, since 1996; President, Royal College of Surgeons, 1992–95; *b* 1 Dec. 1931; *s* of Reginald and Margaret Browse; *m* 1957, Dr Jeanne Menage; one *s* one *d*. *Educ:* St Bartholomew's Hosp. Med. Coll. (MB BS 1955); Bristol Univ. (MD 1961). FRCS 1959; FRCP 1993. Capt. RAMC, Cyprus, 1957–59 (GSM 1958). Lectr in Surgery, Westminster Hosp., 1962–64; Harkness Fellow, Res. Associate, Mayo Clinic, Rochester, Minn, 1964–65; St Thomas's Hospital Medical School: Reader in Surgery, 1965–72; Prof. of Vascular Surgery, 1972–81. Hon. Consultant (Vascular Surgery) to: Army, 1980–96; RAF, 1982–96. President: European Soc. for Cardiovascular Surgery, 1982–84; Assoc. of Profs of Surgery, 1985–87; Surgical Res. Soc., 1990–92; Venous Forum, RSM, 1989–91; Vascular Surgical Soc. of GB and Ireland, 1991–92; Mem. Council, RCS, 1986–95 (Mem., Ct of Patrons, 1996–); Co-Chm., Senate of Surgery, 1993–95; Chm., Jt Consultants Cttee, 1994–98. Chairman: British Atherosclerosis Soc., 1988–91; Lord Brock Meml Trust, 1994–2001; Alderney Maritime Trust, 2003–11; Vice-Chm., British Vascular Foundn, 1997–2002. Trustee, Restoration of Appearance and Function Trust, 1996–2001; Patron: INPUT Trust, 1999–2004; HOPE, Wessex Med. Trust, 2002–11. Gov., Amer. Coll. of Surgeons, 1997–2002. Mem. Council, Marlborough Coll., 1990–2001. Sims Travelling Prof., 1990; Lectures: Arris & Gale, 1966, Vicary, 2000, RCS; Marjory Budd, Bristol, 1982; Pierce Golding, London, Leriche, Madrid, 1986; Abraham Colles (also Medal), 1990, Kinmonth (also Medal), 1991, Dublin; Bernstein, La Jolla, 1996; James Mousley, Winchester, 1997; John Clewes, Ann Arbor, Charles Robb, Washington, 1998; Ratschow (also Medal), Mainz, 2007. FKC 2000. Hon. FRCPSGlas 1993; Hon. FSACM 1993; Hon. FRACS 1994; Hon. FDS RCS 1994; Hon. FRCEM (Hon. FFAEM 1994); Hon. FRSCI 1995; Hon. FACS 1995; Hon. FRCSE 1996. Hon. Member: Amer. Surgical Vascular Soc., 1987; Australian Vascular Soc., 1987; Amer. Vascular Biol. Soc., 1988; Amer. Venous Forum, 1991; Soc. for Clin. Vascular Surg., USA, 1993. Distinguished Alumnus, Mayo Clinic, 1993; Hon. Academician, Acad. of Athens, 1995. Hon. Freeman, Barbers' Co., 1997. *Publications:* Physiology and Pathology of Bed Rest, 1964; Symptoms and Signs of Surgical Disease, 1978, 5th edn 2015; Reducing Operations for Lymphoedema, 1986; Diseases of the Veins, 1988, 2nd edn 1999; Diseases of the Lymphatics, 2003; Investigation and Management of Surgical Disease, 2010; papers on all aspects of vascular disease. *Recreations:* marine art, mediaeval history, sailing. *Address:* Corbet House, Butes Lane, Alderney, Channel Islands GY9 3UW. *T:* (01481) 823716. *Club:* East India.

BRUCE; *see* Hovell-Thurlow-Cumming-Bruce.

BRUCE, family name of **Earl of Elgin**, **Baron Aberdare,** and **Lord Balfour of Burleigh**.

BRUCE, Lord; Charles Edward Bruce; DL; board director, not-for-profit sector; *b* 19 Oct. 1961; *s* and *heir* of 11th Earl of Elgin, *qv*; *m* 1st, 1990, Amanda (marr. diss. 2000), *yr d* of James Movius; two *s* one *d*; 2nd, 2001, Dr Alice Enders; one *s*. *Educ:* Eton College; Univ. of St Andrews (MA Hons); Univ. of Dundee (MSc). A Page of Honour to HM the Queen Mother, 1975–77. Dep. Chm., Assoc. for Protection of Rural Scotland, 1998–2001; former Dir, Ashra Gp Ltd (Envmtl Consultants); Director: Scottish Lime Centre Trust, 1994–; Environmental Trust for Scotland, 1996–. Mem., Internat. Adv. Council, Internat. Academic Forum, 2010–. Trustee, Historic Scotland Foundn, 2001–; Chm. Patrons, Nat. Galls of Scotland, 2006–11; Patron, Scottish Centre of Tagore Studies, Edinburgh Napier Univ., 2011–; Chm., Kolkata Scottish Heritage Trust, 2008–. Dir, Canadian Friends of Scotland Foundn, 2006–; Hon. Pres., St Andrew Soc. (formerly Hon. Vice Pres.), 2007–12; Hon. Patron, Japan Soc. of Scotland, 2008–; Hon. Keeper, Keepers of the Quaich, 2009; Pres., Dunfermline United Burns Club, 2011 (Chm., 2005–10). Mem., Queen's Bodyguard for Scotland, Royal Co. of Archers, 2003. DL Fife, 1997. Hon. Major, 31 Combat Engr Regt (The Elgins), Canadian Forces, 2007; Officer, 78th Fraser Highlanders, Fort St Helen Garrison, Montreal. FSAScot. Paolozzi Gold Medal, Nat. Galls of Scotland, 2012. *Heir: s* Hon. James Andrew Charles Robert Bruce, Master of Bruce, *b* 16 Nov. 1991. *Address:* The Abbey House, Culross, Fife KY12 8JB. *T:* (01383) 880333, *Fax:* (01383) 881218.

BRUCE, Hon. Adam Robert; WS; Marchmont Herald of Arms, since 2012; *b* Edinburgh, 18 Jan. 1968; *s* of 11th Earl of Elgin, *qv*; *m* 2003, Maria Sofia, *yr d* of Angelo Granito Pignatelli di Belmonte, 13th Principe di Belmonte; two *s*. *Educ:* Glenalmond Coll.; Balliol Coll., Oxford (BA (Hons) 1989; MA 1994; Pres., Oxford Union, 1989); Univ. of Edinburgh (LLB 1992). Admitted: Solicitor, 1993; WS, 2001; solicitor in private practice, 1993–98; Dir, Public Policy, McGrigors, 1998–2006; CEO, Airtricity UK Ltd, 2006–08; Global Hd of Corporate Affairs, Mainstream Renewable Power, 2008–. Chairman: British Wind Energy Assoc., subseq. RenewableUK, 2007–10; Offshore Wind Prog. Bd, 2012–; Seastar Offshore Wind Industrial Alliance, 2014–; Vice-Pres., European Wind Energy Assoc., 2012–14. Mem., Arbuthnott Commn, 2004–06. Mem., Maths, Phys and Life Scis Develt Bd, Univ. of Oxford, 2010–. Trustee: Policy Inst., 2006–08; St Andrew's Trust for Scots Heraldry, 2007–; Mitsubishi UFJ Trust Oxford Foundn, 2014–. Finlaggan Pursuivant, 2006–08; Unicorn Pursuivant, 2008–12. Mem., Queen's Bodyguard for Scotland, Royal Co. of Archers, 2006–. FRSA; FSA (Scot) 2014. OStJ 2014. *Address:* Mainstream Renewable Power, Arena House, Arena Road, Sandyford, Dublin 18, Ireland. *Clubs:* Pratt's; New (Edinburgh).

See also Lord Bruce.

BRUCE, Prof. Alistair Cameron, PhD; Professor of Decision and Risk Analysis, University of Nottingham, since 1999; Dean, Nottingham University Business School, since 2015; *b* 21 May 1955; *s* of Ian Paterson Bruce and Margaret Muriel Bruce; *m* 1989, Gillian Amy Tinker; one *s* two *d*. *Educ:* Univ. of St Andrews (MA Hons Econs 1977); Heriot-Watt Univ. (PhD Econs 1982). Lectr, Heriot-Watt Univ., 1980–81; University of Nottingham: Lectr, 1981–94; Sen. Lectr, 1994–99; Dir, 2003–07, Dir of Research, 2008–10 and 2011–14, Dep. Dean, 2010–15, Nottingham Univ. Business Sch. *Publications:* Decisions: risk and reward (with J. E. V. Johnson), 2008; articles in learned jls in areas of econs, mgt, finance, organisational behaviour, decision making, psychology and business history. *Recreations:* horseracing, football (especially supporting Derby County FC), visiting pubs, gardening, cooking, wine, railway history. *Address:* Nottingham University Business School, Jubilee Campus, Nottingham NG8 1BB. *T:* (0115) 846 6614. *E:* alistair.bruce@nottingham.ac.uk.

BRUCE, Christopher, CBE 1998; dancer, choreographer, opera producer; Artistic Director, Rambert Dance Company, 1994–2002; Associate Choreographer, Houston Ballet, since 1997 (Resident Choreographer, 1989–97); *b* Leicester, 3 Oct. 1945; *m* Marian Bruce; two *s* one *d*. *Educ:* Ballet Rambert Sch. Joined Ballet Rambert Company, 1963; leading dancer with co. when re-formed as modern dance co., 1966; Associate Dir, 1975–79; Associate Choreographer, 1979–87; Associate Choreographer, London Fest. Ballet, later English Nat. Ballet, 1986–91. Leading roles include: Pierrot Lunaire, The Tempest (Tetley); L'Apres-Midi d'un Faune (Nijinsky); Cruel Garden (also choreographed with Lindsay Kemp); choreographed: for Ballet Rambert: George Frideric (1st work), 1969; For These Who Die as Cattle, 1971; There Was a Time, 1972; Weekend, 1974; Ancient Voices of Children, 1975; Black Angels, 1976; Cruel Garden, 1977; Night with Waning Moon, 1979; Dancing Day, 1981; Ghost Dances, 1981; Berlin Requiem, 1982; Concertino, 1983; Intimate Pages, 1984; Sergeant Early's Dream, 1984; Ceremonies, 1986; Crossing, 1994; Meeting Point, 1995; Quicksilver, 1996; Stream, 1997; Four Scenes, 1998; God's Plenty, 1999; Grinning in Your Face, 2001; A Steel Garden, 2005; Hush, 2009 (Best Choreography Award, Critics' Circle, 2010); for London Festival Ballet, later English National Ballet: Land, 1985; The World Again, 1986; The Dream is Over, 1987; Swansong, 1987; Symphony in Three Movements, 1989; for Tanz Forum, Cologne: Wings, 1970; Cantata, 1981; for Nederlands Dans Theater: Village Songs, 1981; Curses and Blessings, 1983; Moonshine, 1993; for Houston Ballet: Gautama Buddha, 1989; Journey, 1990; Nature Dances, 1992; Hush, 2005; for Geneva: Rooster, 1991 (restaged for London Contemporary Dance Theatre, 1992); Kingdom, 1993; for London Contemporary Dance Theatre, Waiting, 1993; for Royal Ballet, Three Songs, Two Voices, 2005; for Ballet Central: Shift, 2007; Für Alina, 2011; for Ballet Mainz, Dance at the Crossroads, 2007; for Ballet Kiel, Ten Poems, 2009; for Nat. Dance Co. Wales, Dream, 2012; for Phoenix Dance Th., Shadows, 2014; works for Batsheva Dance Co., Munich Opera Ballet, Gulbenkian Ballet Co., Australian Dance Theatre, Royal Danish Ballet, Royal Swedish Ballet. Kent Opera: choreographed and produced: Monteverdi's Il Ballo delle Ingrate, 1980; Combattimento di Tancredi e Clorinda, 1981; chor. John Blow's Venus and Adonis, 1980; co-prod Handel's Agrippina, 1982. Choreographed Mutiny (musical), Piccadilly, 1985. TV productions: Ancient Voices of Children, BBC, 1977; Cruel Garden, BBC, 1981–82; Ghost Dances, Channel 4, 1982, Danmark Radio, 1990; Requiem, Danish-German co-prodn, 1982; Silence is the end of our Song, Danish TV, 1984. Hon. Vis. Prof., Exeter Univ., 2009. Hon. Life Mem., Amnesty Internat., 2002. Hon. DArt De Montfort, 2000; Hon. DLitt Exeter, 2001. Evening Standard's inaugural Dance Award, 1974; Internat. Theatre Inst. Award, 1993; Evening Standard Ballet Award for outstanding artistic achievement, 1996; de Valois Award, Critics' Circle Nat. Dance Awards, 2003. *Address:* c/o Rambert Dance Co., 99 Upper Ground, SE1 9PP; Houston Ballet, 602 Preston, Houston, TX 77002, USA.

BRUCE, Fiona; Presenter: BBC Television News, since 1999; Antiques Roadshow, since 2008; *b* 25 April 1964; *d* of John and Rosemary Bruce; *m* 1995, Nigel; one *s* one *d*. *Educ:* Hertford Coll., Oxford (MA French/Italian). Joined BBC, 1989: researcher, Panorama, 1989–91; reporter: Breakfast News, 1991–92; First Sight, 1992–93; Public Eye, 1993–95; Newsnight, 1995–98; Presenter: Antiques Show, 1998–2000; Six O'Clock News, 1999; Ten O'Clock News, 1999–; Crimewatch UK, 2000–08; Real Story, 2003–07; Call My Bluff, 2003–; Fake or Fortune?, 2011; The Queen's Palaces, 2011; Hive Minds, 2015. *Recreation:* playing with my children. *Address:* c/o BBC News, Broadcasting House, Portland Place, W1A 1AA.

BRUCE, Fiona Claire; MP (C) Congleton, since 2010; *b* Wick, 26 March 1957; *d* of Allan Stewart Riley and late Greta Riley (*née* Scott); *m* 1990, Richard John Bruce; two *s*. *Educ:* Burnley High Sch.; Howell's Sch., Llandaff; Manchester Univ. (LLB); Chester Law Coll. (LLB). Admitted solicitor, 1981; Founder and Sen. Partner, Fiona Bruce & Co. LLP, 1988–. Mem. (C) Warrington BC, 2004–10 (Exec. Mem. for Value for Money and Finance, 2006–09). Contested (C) Warrington S, 2005. Mem., Internat. Develt Select Cttee, 2012–; Vice Chm., All Party Parly Dying Well Gp, 2012–15; Chairman: All Party Parly ProLife Gp, 2013–; All Party Parly Gp Supporting Couple Relationships, 2014–; All Party Parly Gp on Alcohol Harm, 2015–; Cons. Party Human Rights Commn, 2015–; Co-Chm., All Party Gp on N Korea, 2013– (Vice Chm., 2012–13). Mem. Bd, Lawyers' Christian Fellowship, 1996–2004; Pres., Warrington Law Soc., 2009. *Publications:* (contrib.) There is Such a Thing as Society, 2002. *Recreations:* family, countryside. *Address:* House of Commons, SW1A 0AA.

BRUCE, Sir (Francis) Michael Ian; *see* Bruce, Sir M. I.

BRUCE, George John Done, PPRP (RP 1959); painter of portraits, landscapes, still life, flowers; *b* 28 March 1930; *s* of 11th Lord Balfour of Burleigh, Brucefield, Clackmannan, Scotland and Violet Dorothy, *d* of Richard Henry Done, Tarporley, Cheshire; *b* of 12th Lord Balfour of Burleigh, *qv*. *Educ:* Byam Shaw Sch. of Drawing and Painting; by his portrait sitters. Pres., Royal Soc. of Portrait Painters, 1991–94 (Hon. Sec., 1970–84; Vice-Pres., 1984–89). *Recreations:* ski-ing, windsurfing. *Address:* 6 Pembroke Walk, W8 6PQ. *T:* (020) 7937 1493. *Club:* Athenæum.

BRUCE, Rt Rev. George Lindsey Russell; Bishop of Ontario, 2002–11; *b* 20 June 1942; *s* of late Harold George Bruce and Helen Florence (*née* Wade); *m* 1965, Theodora Youmatoff; three *s* two *d*. *Educ:* Coll. Militaire Royal de St Jean; Royal Military Coll., Kingston (BA Hons 1964); Canadian Land Forces Command and Staff Coll., Kingston (psc 1970); Montreal Diocesan Coll. (LTh, Dip. Min. 1987; Hon. DD, 2003). Served in staff appts, Canadian Army, 1959–86; retd with rank of Colonel. Ordained deacon, 1987, priest, 1987; Diocese of Ottawa: Asst Curate, St Matthew's, Ottawa, 1987–90; Rector: Parish of Winchester, 1990–96; St James, Perth, 1996–2000; Dean of Ontario, Rector of Kingston, and Incumbent, St George's Cathedral, Ontario, 2000–02. Regional Dean: Stormont, 1994–96; Lanark, 1998–2000. Regtl Chaplain to Gov. Gen.'s Foot Guards (Militia), 1988–97. *Recreations:* golf, coaching soccer. *Address:* 855 Gainsborough Place, Kingston, ON K7P 1E1, Canada.

BRUCE, Sir Hamish; *see* Bruce-Clifton, Sir H. H. P.

BRUCE, Ian Cameron; Chairman, Ian Bruce Associates Ltd, management consultancy and property co., since 1975; *b* 14 March 1947; *s* of Henry Bruce and Ellen Flora Bruce (*née* Bingham); *m* 1969, Hazel Bruce (*née* Roberts); one *s* three *d*. *Educ:* Chelmsford Tech. High Sch.; Bradford Univ.; Mid-Essex Tech. Coll. Mem., Inst. of Management Services. Student apprentice, Marconi, 1965–67; Work Study Engineer: Marconi, 1967–69; Pye Unicam, 1969–70; Haverhill Meat Products, 1970–71; Factory Manager and Work Study Manager, BEPI (Pye), 1971–74; Factory Manager, Sinclair Electronics, 1974–75; Chm. and Founder, gp of employment agencies and management consultants, 1975–. Contested (C) Burnley, 1983; MP (C) Dorset South, 1987–2001; contested (C): same seat, 2001. PPS to Social Security Ministers, 1992–94. Member, Select Committee: on Employment, 1990–92; on Science and Technol., 1995–97; on Information, 1997–2001; Vice-Chm., PITCOM, 1997–2001; Jt Chm., All Party Street Children Gp, 1992–2001; Vice Chairman: Cons. Employment Cttee, 1992; Cons. Social Security Cttee, 1995–97 (Sec., 1991–92); Cons. Educn and Employment Cttee, 1995–2001; Cons. Trade and Industry Cttee, 1999–2001; Pres., Cons. Technol. Forum, 1999–2001. Jt Chm., British Cayman Island Gp, 1995–2001; Vice Chm., British-Nepal Gp, 1993–2001; Secretary: British-Finnish Gp, 1995–2001; British-Romanian Gp, 1995–2001; Chm., European Informatics Market, 1993–2002. Parly

Consultant to Telecommunication Managers Assoc., 1989–2001, to Trevor Gilbert Associates, 1993–2002, to Fedn of Recruitment and Employment Services, 1996–97. Contested (C) Yorks W, 1984, Yorks, 2004, Eur. Parlt. ICT Consultant, Engrg Manufg Trng Authy, 2001–05; Employment Expert Witness, TGA, 2001–04. Mem., Weymouth and Portland BC, 2006–07, 2012– (Mem. for Tourism and Arts, 2012–). FCMA 2001. Foster parent, 1974–77 and 2006–08. Knight, First Class, Order of Lion of Finland, 2001. *Publications:* numerous articles in press and magazines, both technical and political. *Recreations:* swimming, scuba diving, snorkelling, writing, wind surfing, sailing, camping, walking, RYA Day Skipper, politics. *Address:* 14 Preston Road, Weymouth, Dorset DT3 6PZ. *T:* (01305) 833320. *E:* iancbruce@tiscali.co.uk.

BRUCE, Ian Waugh, CBE 2004; Vice-President, Royal National Institute of Blind People, since 2003 (Director-General, 1983–2003); Founder Director, 1991–2010, Visiting Professor, since 1991 and President, since 2010, Centre for Charity Effectiveness, Sir John Cass Business School, City University London (formerly VOLPROF, the Centre for Voluntary Sector and Not-for-Profit Management, City University Business School); *b* 21 April 1945; *s* of Thomas Waugh Bruce and Una (*née* Eagle); *m* 1971, Anthea Christine, (Tina), *d* of Dr P. R. Rowland, FRSC; one *s* one *d. Educ:* King Edward VI Sch., Southampton; Central High Sch., Arizona; Univ. of Birmingham (BSocSc Hons 1968). Apprentice Chem. Engr, Courtaulds, 1964–65; Marketing Trainee, then Manager, Unilever, 1968–70; Appeals and PR Officer, then Asst Dir, Age Concern England, 1970–74; Dir, The Volunteer Centre UK, 1975–81; Controller of Secretariat, then Asst Chief Exec., Bor. of Hammersmith and Fulham, 1981–83. Chm., Coventry Internat. Centre, 1964; spokesman, Artists Now, 1973–77. Consultant, UN Div. of Social Affairs, 1970–72; Mem., Prime Minister's Gp on Voluntary Action, 1978–79; Founding Sec., Volonteurope, Brussels, 1979–81; Adviser, BBC Community Progs Unit, 1979–81. Member: Art Panel, Art Film Cttee and New Activities Cttee, Arts Council of GB, 1967–71; National Good Neighbour Campaign, 1977–79; Exec. Cttee, 1978–81, 1990–94, Adv. Council, 1998–, NCVO; Council, Retired Executives Action Clearing House, 1978–83; Adv. Council, Centre for Policy on Ageing, 1979–83; Educn Adv. Council, IBA, 1981–83; Disability Alliance Steering Cttee, 1985–93; Exec. Cttee, Age Concern England, 1986–92, 2002–04; Nat. Adv. Council on Employment of People with Disabilities, 1987–98; DHSS Cttee on Inter-Agency Collaboration on Visual Handicap, 1987–88; Bd, Central London TEC, 1990–97 (Dep. Chm., 1996–97); Council for Charitable Support, 1994–2005; Bd, Focus TEC, 1997–99; Founding Co-Chair, Disability Benefits Consortium, 1988–2001; Chair: Nat. Adv. Cttee, Johns Hopkins Univ. Comparative Non Profit Study, 1996–99; Res. Cttee, Nat. Giving Campaign, 2001–04; Internat. Bd, Internat. Soc. for Low Vision Res., 2002–05; Centre Dirs' Gp, Internat. Soc. of Third Sector Res., 2008–10; Sec., World Nonprofit Academic Centres' Council, 2008–10; Advr, Soweto Kliptown Youth Project, 2007–; Co-founder and Sen. Advr, KnowHow NonProfit, 2009–. Pres., City Centre for Charity Effectiveness Trust, 2009–; Vice Pres., Internat. Council of Voluntarism, Civil Soc. and Social Economy Researcher Assocs, 2012–; founder Chair, Charities' Gp, CIM, 2013–. Patron, Nat. Fedn of the Blind, 2007–. FCIM 2012; CCMI (CIMgt 1991); FRSA 1991. Hon. DSocSc Birmingham, 1995. Sir Raymond Priestley Expeditionary Award, Univ. of Birmingham, 1968; UK Charity Lifetime Achievement Award, 2001 and 2003. *Publications:* Public Relations and the Social Services, 1972; (jtly) Patronage of the Creative Artist, 1974; Blind and Partially Sighted Adults in Britain, 1991; Meeting Need: successful charity marketing, 1994, 4th edn 2011; The Art of Raising Money, 2010; papers on vision impairment, voluntary and community work, older people, contemporary art, management and marketing. *Recreations:* the arts, the countryside. *Address:* Ormond House Cottage, Ormond Road, Richmond, Surrey TW10 6TH. *Club:* ICA.

BRUCE, Karen; choreographer and director; *b* 25 March 1963; *d* of George and Elizabeth Bruce. *Educ:* Betty Laine Theatre Arts. *Theatre:* assistant director: Annie, Crucible, Sheffield; Hello Dolly!, My One and Only, Palladium; Dir and Associate Choreographer, Fame, Cambridge Th. and tour, 1996–2007, Aldwych, 2006; Associate Dir and Choreographer, Saturday Night Fever, Palladium, UK and world tour, 1998–99, NY, 1999–2000; Choreographer: Chorus Line, 2003, Sweet Charity, 2004, Crucible, Sheffield; Pacific Overtures, Donmar Warehouse, 2004 (Olivier Award for Best Choreography); Annie Get Your Gun, tour, 2005; Brighton Rock, Almeida, 2005; Far Pavilions, Shaftesbury, 2005; Doctor Dolittle, UK tour, 2007; Never Forget, Savoy, 2008; Director and Choreographer: Footloose, Novello and tour, 2006; Love Me Tender, UK tour, 2015; Dir, Midnight Tango, Phoenix and UK tour, 2013; Dir and Co-choreographer, Dance 'Til Dawn, Aldwych, 2014; has also choreographed for TV, incl. Strictly Come Dancing; choreographer, opening ceremony for Commonwealth Games, Manchester, 2002. *Address:* 2 Lavell Street, N16 9LS. *T:* (020) 7249 9180.

BRUCE, Rt Hon. Sir Malcolm (Gray), Kt 2012; PC 2006; *b* 17 Nov. 1944; *s* of David Stewart Bruce and Kathleen Elmslie (*née* Delf); *m* 1st, 1969, Veronica Jane Wilson (marr. diss. 1992); one *s* one *d*; 2nd, 1998, Rosemary Vetterlein; one *s* two *d. Educ:* Wrekin Coll., Shropshire; St Andrews Univ. (MA 1966); Strathclyde Univ. (MSc 1970). Liverpool Daily Post, 1966–67; Buyer, Boots Pure Drug Co., 1967–68; A. Goldberg & Son, 1968–69; Res. Information Officer, NE Scotland Develt Authority, 1971–75; Marketing Dir, Noroil Publishing House (UK), 1975–81; Jt Editor/Publisher/Dir, Aberdeen Petroleum Publishing, 1981–84. Called to the Bar, Gray's Inn, 1995. MP Gordon, 1983–2015 (L 1983–88, Lib Dem, 1988–2015). Dep. Chm., Scottish Liberal Party, 1975–84 (Energy Spokesman, 1975–83); Liberal Parly Spokesman on Scottish Affairs, 1983–85, on Energy, 1985–87, on Trade and Industry, 1987–88; Alliance Parly Spokesman on Employment, 1987; Lib Dem Spokesman on Natural Resources (energy and conservation), 1988–90, on Trade and Industry, 1992–94, 2003–05, on Treasury affairs, 1994–99; Chm., Parly Lib Dems, 1999–2001; Lib Dem Spokesman on envmt, food and rural affairs, 2001–02. Member: Select Cttee on Trade and Industry, 1992–94, Treasury, 1994–98; Standards and Privileges Cttee, 1999–2001; EP rapporteur on recognition of sign languages, 2001–05, on political prisoners in Azerbaijan, 2003–05; Chair, Select Cttee on Internat. Develt, 2005–15. Leader, Scottish Liberal Democrats, 1988–92; Dep. Leader, Liberal Democrats, 2014–15. Mem. Bd, Britain in Europe, 2004–05. Rector of Dundee Univ., 1986–89. Vice-Pres., Nat. Deaf Children's Soc., 1990– (Pres., Grampian Br., 1985–); Trustee, RNID, 2004–10. *Publications:* A New Life for the Country: a rural development programme for West Aberdeenshire, 1978; Putting Energy to Work, 1981; (with others) A New Deal for Rural Scotland, 1983; (with Paddy Ashdown) Growth from the Grassroots, 1985; (with Ray Michie) Toward a Federal UK, 1997. *Recreations:* theatre, music, travel, fresh Scottish air. *Address:* Grove Cottage, Grove Lane, Torphins AB31 4GW. *E:* mandrbruce@btinternet.com.

[Created a Baron (Life Peer) 2015 but title not yet gazetted at time of going to press.]

BRUCE, Sir Michael Ian, 12th Bt *cr* 1628; partner, Gossard-Bruce Co., since 1953; President, Newport Sailing Club Inc. and Academy of Sail, Newport Beach, 1978–2000; *b* 3 April 1926; *s* of Sir Michael William Selby Bruce, 11th Bt and Doreen Dalziel, *d* of late W. F. Greenwell; *S* father 1957; holds dual UK and US citizenship; has discontinued first forename, Francis; *m* 1st, 1947, Barbara Stevens (marr. diss., 1957), *d* of Frank J. Lynch; two *s*; 2nd, 1961, Frances Keegan (marr. diss., 1963); 3rd, 1966, Marilyn Ann (marr. diss., 1975), *d* of Carter Mulally; 4th, Patricia Gail (marr. diss. 1991), *d* of Frederich Root; 5th, 1994, Alessandra Conforto, MD. *Educ:* Forman School, Litchfield, Conn; Pomfret, Conn. Served United States Marine Corps, 1943–46 (Letter of Commendation); S Pacific area two years, Bismarck Archipelago, Bougainville, Philippines. Master Mariner's Ticket, 1968; Pres., American Maritime Co., 1981–2000. Mem., US Naval Inst. *Recreations:* sailing, spear-fishing. *Heir: s* Michael Ian Richard Bruce, now Ross [*b* 10 Dec. 1950; *m* 2005, Sandra Salemi; one adopted *s*]. *Clubs:* Rockaway Hunt; Lawrence Beach; Balboa Bay (Newport Beach).

BRUCE, Michael Stewart Rae; *see* Marnoch, Rt Hon. Lord.

BRUCE, Prof. Peter George, PhD; FRS 2007; FRSE; FRSC; Wolfson Professor of Materials, University of Oxford, since 2014; Fellow, St Edmund Hall, Oxford, since 2014; *b* 2 Oct. 1956; *s* of George H. Bruce and Gladys I. Bruce; *m* 1982, Margaret Duncan; one *s* one *d. Educ:* Aberdeen Grammar Sch.; Univ. of Aberdeen (BSc 1978; PhD 1982). FRSC 1994; FRSE 1995. Postdoctoral Res. Fellow, Univ. of Oxford, 1982–85; Lectr, Heriot-Watt Univ., 1985–91; University of St Andrews: Reader, 1991–95; Founder and Dir, Centre for Advanced Materials, 1994–97; Prof. of Chemistry, 1995–2007; Hd, Sch. of Chemistry, 1997–2002; Wardlaw Prof. of Chemistry, 2007–13. RSE Res. Fellow, 1989–90; Royal Soc. Pickering Res. Fellow, 1990–95; Leverhulme Res. Fellow, 1995–98. Tilden Lect., RSC, 2009. Award for Achievements in Materials Chem., 1999, Beilby Medal, 2003, Interdisciplinary Award, 2003, John Jeyes Lect. and Medal, 2004, Solid State Chem. Award, 2005, Barker Medal, 2014, RSC; Wolfson Merit Award, Royal Soc., 2001; Gunning Victoria Jubilee Prize Lect., RSE, 2004; Battery Div. Res. Award, 2008, Carl Wagner Award, 2011, Electrochem. Soc.; Arfvedson-Schlenk Award, German Chem. Soc., 2011; Galileo Galilei Medal, 2012; Internat. Medal for Materials Sci. and Technol., Materials Res. Soc. of India, 2015. *Publications:* Solid State Electrochemistry, 1994; articles in Nature, Science, Jl of ACS, Angewandte Chemie. *Recreations:* thinking, dining, music, running. *Address:* Department of Materials, University of Oxford, Parks Road, Oxford OX1 3PH.

BRUCE, Maj. Gen. Robert Bernard, DSO 2013; deployed from Permanent Joint Headquarters, since 2014; *b* Lisburn, 21 Jan. 1965; *s* of John and Edith Bruce; *m* 1995, Lorna McIntyre; one *s* one *d. Educ:* Aberdeen Univ. (MA); Cranfield Univ. (MA); Open Univ. (MBA). Commnd Royal Scots, 1987; Commanding Officer: Royal Scots, 2006; Royal Scots Borderers, 2006–08; Comdr, 4th Mechanized Bde, 2011–13. *Recreations:* fly-fishing, golf, military history. *Address:* c/o Army Personnel Centre, Kentigern House, 65 Brown Street, Glasgow G2 8EX. *T:* (0141) 224 3010. *E:* APC-CMGenStaff-No1Bd-SO2@mod.uk. *Clubs:* Caledonian; Royal Scots (Edinburgh).

BRUCE, Prof. Steve, PhD; FBA 2003; FRSE; Professor of Sociology, University of Aberdeen, since 1991 (Head, School of Social Science, 2002); *b* 1 April 1954; *s* of George Bruce and Maria (*née* Ivanova-Savova); *m* 1988, Elizabeth Struthers Duff; one *s* two *d. Educ:* Queen Victoria Sch., Dunblane; Univ. of Stirling (BA 1976; PhD 1980). Queen's University, Belfast: Lectr in Sociol., 1978–87; Reader in Sociol., 1987–89; Prof. of Sociol. and Hd, Dept of Sociol., 1989–91. FRSE 2005. *Publications:* No Pope of Rome: militant Protestantism in modern Scotland, 1985; God Save Ulster!: the religion and politics of Paisleyism, 1986; The Rise and Fall of the New Christian Right: Protestant politics in America, 1988; A House Divided: Protestantism, schism and secularization, 1990; Pray TV: televangelism in America, 1990; The Red Hand: loyalist paramilitaries in Northern Ireland, 1992; The Edge of the Union: the Ulster Loyalist political vision, 1994; Religion in Modern Britain, 1995; Religion in the Modern World: from cathedrals to cults, 1996; Conservative, Protestant Politics, 1998; Sociology: a very short introduction, 1999; Choice and Religion: a critique of rational choice theory, 1999; Fundamentalism, 2001; God is Dead: secularization in the West, 2002; Politics and Religion, 2003; (with Steven Yearley) A Dictionary of Sociology, 2004; (jtly) Sectarianism in Scotland, 2004; Paisley, 2007; Secularization: in defence of an unfashionable theory, 2011. *Recreation:* shooting. *Address:* School of Social Science, University of Aberdeen, Aberdeen AB24 3QY. *T:* (01224) 272729, *Fax:* (01224) 273442.

BRUCE, Dame Victoria Geraldine, DBE 2015 (OBE 1997); PhD; CPsychol, FBPsS; FRSE; FBA 1999; Professor of Psychology, Newcastle University, since 2015 (Head, School of Psychology, 2008–15); *b* 4 Jan. 1953; *d* of late Charles Frederick Bruce and of Geraldine Cordelia Diane (*née* Giffard). *Educ:* Newcastle upon Tyne Church High Sch.; Newnham Coll., Cambridge (BA Nat. Scis 1974; MA, PhD Psychol. 1978). CPsychol, FBPsS 1989. University of Nottingham: Lectr, 1978–88; Reader, 1988–90; Prof. of Psychology, 1990–92; Prof. of Psychology, 1992–2002, Dep. Principal (Res.), 1995–2001, Stirling Univ.; Vice Principal and Hd, Coll. of Humanities and Social Sci., Univ. of Edinburgh, 2002–08. Member: Neuroscis Bd, MRC, 1989–92; ESRC, 1992–96 (Chm., Res. Progs Bd, 1992–); SHEFC, 1995–2001 (Chm., Res. Policy Adv. Cttee, 1988–2001); Chairman: Psychology Panel, RAE, 1996, 2001, HEFCE; Main Panel K, 2008 RAE, HEFCE. President: Eur. Soc. for Cognitive Psychology, 1996–98; BPsS, 2001–02; EPsS, 2010–12. Editor, British Jl of Psychology, 1995–2000. FRSE 1996. Hon. Fellow: Cardiff Univ., 2005; Edinburgh Coll. of Art, 2008. Hon. DSc: London, 2002; St Andrews, 2006; York, 2010. *Publications:* (with P. R. Green) Visual Perception: physiology, psychology and ecology, 1985, 4th edn (with P. R. Green and M. Georgeson) 2003; Recognising Faces, 1988; (with G. W. Humphreys) Visual Cognition: computational, experimental and neuropsychological perspectives, 1989; (ed) Face Recognition (special edn of European Jl of Cognitive Psychology), 1991; (ed jtly) Processing the Facial Image, 1992; (ed with A. M. Burton) Processing Images of Faces, 1992; (ed with G. W. Humphreys) Object and Face Recognition (special issue of Visual Cognition), 1994; (with I. Roth) Perception and Representation: current issues, 2nd edn 1995; (ed) Unsolved Mysteries of the Mind: tutorial essays in cognition, 1996; (with A. Young) In the Eye of the Beholder: the science of face perception, 1998; (with A. Young) Face Perception, 2011; numerous articles in learned jls and edited books. *Recreations:* dogs, walking, games. *Address:* School of Psychology, Newcastle University, Ridley Building, Newcastle upon Tyne NE1 7RU. *T:* (0191) 222 6579.

BRUCE-CLIFTON, Sir (Hervey) Hamish (Peter), 8th Bt *cr* 1804, of Downhill, Londonderry; *b* 20 Nov. 1986; *s* of Sir Hervey James Hugh Bruce-Clifton, 7th Bt and of Charlotte Sara Jane, *e d* of Jack Temple Gore; *S* father, 2010. *Educ:* Harrow Sch.; Univ. of Northumbria (BSc Hons Estate Mgt). *Recreations:* tennis, golf, polo. *Heir: half b* Louis William Sinclair Bruce, *b* 3 Aug. 1993.

BRUCE-GARDNER, Sir Robert (Henry), 3rd Bt *cr* 1945, of Frilford, Berks; Director, Department of Conservation and Technology, Courtauld Institute, 1990–2000; *b* 10 June 1943; *s* of Sir Douglas Bruce-Gardner, 2nd Bt and of his 1st wife, Monica Flumerfelt (*née* Jefferson; decd); *S* father, 1997; *m* 1979, Veronica Ann Hand Oxborrow; two *s. Educ:* Uppingham; Reading Univ. (BA Fine Art); Courtauld Inst., Univ. of London (Dip.). Asst Lectr, Dept of History of Art, Univ. of Manchester, 1968; Courtauld Institute: Asst to Hd, 1970–76, Lectr, 1976–90, Dept of Technol.; Fellow, 2000. *Publications:* catalogue contrib., Metropolitan Mus., NY; contrib. The Conservator. *Recreation:* Himalayan travel. *Heir: s* Edmund Thomas Peter Bruce-Gardner, *b* 28 Jan. 1982. *Address:* 121 Brackenbury Road, W6 0BQ. *T:* (020) 8932 4627. *Club:* Travellers.

BRUCE LOCKHART, Logie, MA; Headmaster of Gresham's School, Holt, 1955–82; *b* 12 Oct. 1921; *s* of late John Harold Bruce Lockhart; *m* 1944, Josephine Agnew (*d* 2009); two *s* two *d* (and one *d* decd). *Educ:* Sedbergh School; St John's College, Cambridge (Schol. and Choral Studentship). RMC Sandhurst, 1941; served War of 1939–45; 9th Sherwood Foresters, 1942; 2nd Household Cavalry (Life Guards), 1944–45. Larmor Award, 1947; Asst Master, Tonbridge School, 1947–55. Sponsor, Nat. Council for Educnl Standards. *Publications:* The Pleasures of Fishing, 1981; Stuff and Nonsense, 1996; Now and Then, This and That, 2014. *Recreations:* fishing, writing, music, natural history, games; Blue for Rugby football, 1945, 1946, Scottish International, 1948, 1950, 1953; squash for Cambridge, 1946. *Address:* Mead Barn, New Road, Blakeney, Norfolk NR25 7PA. *T:* (01263) 740588.

BRUDENELL-BRUCE, family name of **Marquess of Ailesbury**.

BRUINVELS, Canon Peter Nigel Edward; Principal, Peter Bruinvels Associates, media management and public affairs consultants, founded 1986; Managing Director, Bruinvels News & Media, since 1992; news broadcaster, political commentator and freelance journalist; *b* 30 March 1950; *er s* of late Stanley and Ninette Maud Bruinvels; *m* 1980, Alison Margaret, *o d* of Major David Gilmore Bacon, RA retd; two *d*. *Educ:* St John's Sch., Leatherhead; London Univ. (LLB Hons); Council of Legal Educn. Co. Sec., BPC Publishing, 1978–81; Sec./Lawyer, Amari PLC, 1981–82; Management Consultant and company director, 1982–. Chm., Dorking CPC, 1979–83; Mem., Cons. Nat. Union Exec., 1976–81. MP (C) Leicester E, 1983–87; contested (C): Leicester E, 1987; The Wrekin, 1997. Jt Chm., British Parly Lighting Gp; Vice-Chairman: Cons. Backbench Cttee on Urban Affairs and New Towns, 1984–87; Cons. Backbench Cttee on Education, 1985–87; Sec., Anglo-Netherlands Parly Gp, 1983–87; Chm., British-Malta Parly Gp, 1984–87; Member: Cons. Backbench Cttee on Home Affairs, 1983–87; Cons. Backbench Cttee on NI, 1983–87; Life Mem., British-Amer. Parly Gp, 1983. Promoter, Crossbows Act, 1987. Campaign Co-ordinator, Eastbourne, gen. election, 1992. Pres., Dorking Conservatives, 1995– (Chm., 1992–95). Director: Aalco Nottingham Ltd, 1983–88; Radio Mercury and Allied Radio, 1994–97. Special Advr, DTI Deregulation Task Force on Pharmaceuticals and Chemicals, 1993. Ind. Lay Chm., NHS Complaints Procedure, 1999–2006; Member: Social Security Appeals Tribunal, 1994–99; Child Support Appeals Tribunal, 1995–99. Non-exec. Dir, E Elmbridge and Mid Surrey PCT, 2002–07. Mem., Surrey LEA, 1997–2007 (Admissions Adjudicator). Inspector, 1994–2009, Sen. Inspector, 2009–, Denominational Ch Schs, OFSTED; Mem., Dearing Implementation Gp for Ch Schs, 2001–. Church Comr, 1992– (Member: Pastoral and Houses Cttee, 1993– (Dep. Chm., 2015–); Bd of Govs, 1998–; Mgt Adv. Cttee, 1999–2009; Assets Cttee, 2014–; Dep. Chm., Nominations and Governance Cttee, 2009–12); Dir, Church Army, 1999–2004 (Chm., Remuneration Cttee, 1999–2004); Member: Guildford Dio. Synod, 1974– (Vice-Pres., 2003–13; Chm., House of Laity, 2003–13); Gen. Synod, 1985– (Mem., 1991–96 and 2000–, Dep. Chm., 2011–, Legislative Cttee); Guildford Diocesan Bd of Educn, 1994– (Chm., 2005–08; Dep. Chm., 2008–); Gen. Synod Bd of Educn, 1996–2006; Clergy Discipline (Doctrine) Gp, 1999–; Guildford Crown Nominations Commn, 2003–; Lay Canon, 2002–, Mem. Coll. of Canons, 2002–, Mem. Council, 2006–, Guildford Cathedral; Dir, Guildford Diocesan Educn Trust, 2012–. Mem., Cathedrals Fabric Commn for England, 2006–. Mem., SE England Veterans Adv. and Pensions Cttee (formerly War Pensions Cttee), 2003– (Dep. Chm., 2013–); Chm., Surrey Jt Services' Charities Cttee, 2004–; Hon. Sec., Surrey Military Appeals Cttee (formerly Surrey County Appeals Cttee), 2002–; Liaison Advr, Surrey Civilian-Military Partnership Bd, 2013–; Project Officer, Guildford Nat. Armed Forces Day, 2015; Member: Surrey Assembly, 2010–13; Surrey Standing Adv. Council for Religious Educn, 2013–. Mem., Jersey Wildlife Preservation Trust. Chm., Surrey Schs Orgn Cttee, 2000–07. Governor: York St John Univ. (formerly Ripon and York St John, then UC of York St John), 1999–2007; Whitelands Coll., Roehampton Univ., 2007– (Chm. of Govs, 2009–12); Mem. Council, Roehampton Univ., 2009–12; Mem. Ct, Univ. of Sussex, 2000–08. County Field Officer, Surrey, 2002–12, County Manager, Sussex, 2011–12, RBL. Regl Fundraiser - SE, ABF The Soldiers' Charity, 2013–. MCIPR (MIPR 1981); FRSA 1986; FCIM 1998 (Hon. MCIM 1987; Pres., Norwest Midlands, 1997–98); MCIJ (MJI 1988); Fellow, Industry and Parliament Trust. Granted Freedom, City of London, 1980. *Publications:* Zoning in on Enterprise, 1982; Light up the Roads, 1984; Sharing in Britain's Success—a Study in Widening Share Ownership, Through Privatisation, 1987; Investing in Enterprise—a Comprehensive Guide to Inner City Regeneration and Urban Renewal, 1989. *Recreations:* political campaigning, the media, Church of England. *Address:* 14 High Meadow Close, Dorking, Surrey RH4 2LG. *T:* (01306) 887082, (office) 887680, (mobile) 07721 411688. *Clubs:* Carlton, Inner Temple, Corporation of Church House.

BRUMBY, Hon. John Mansfield; Chairman, Motor Trades Association of Australia Superannuation Fund Pty Ltd, since 2011; Professorial Fellow (formerly Vice Chancellor's Professorial Fellow), University of Melbourne and Monash University, since 2011; *b* Melbourne, 21 April 1953; *s* of late Malcolm Mansfield Brumby and of Alison Jessie Brumby; *m* 1985, Rosemary McKenzie; one *s* two *d*. *Educ:* Melbourne Grammar Sch.; Univ. of Melbourne (BCom 1974); State Coll. of Victoria (DipEd 1975). Secondary sch. teacher, 1976–80; Union Organiser, Victorian Teachers' Union, 1981–83. Consultant to finance and banking industry, 1990; COS to Federal Minister for Tourism and Resources, 1991–92. MHR (ALP) Bendigo, 1983–90; Chm., Parly Standing Cttee on Employment, Educn and Trng, 1986–90. MLA (ALP) Broadmeadows, Vic, 1993–2010; Shadow Minister for Arts and Ethnic Affairs, 1993–94; Shadow Treas., 1994–96; Shadow Minister: for Agric. and Rural Affairs, 1996–99; for Racing, 1996–99; for Multicultural and Ethnic Affairs, 1997–99; for Primary Industries, 1999; for State and Regl Develt, 1999; of Finance, 1999; Leader of the Opposition, Victoria, 1993–99; Minister: for Finance, and Asst Treas., 1999–2000; for State and Regl Develt, 1999–2006; for Regl and Rural Develt, 2006–07; for Innovation, 2002–07; Treas. of Victoria, 2000–07; Premier of Victoria, and Minister for Veterans' Affairs and for Multicultural Affairs, 2007–10. Director: Huawei Technologies (Aust.) Pty Ltd, 2011–; Citywide Service Solutions Pty Ltd, 2012–. Chairman: Centre for Workplace Leadership, 2013–; Olivia Newton-John Cancer Res. Inst., 2014–; Director: US Studies Centre, 2013–; Fred Hollows Foundn, 2013–. Centenary Medal, 2001. *Publications:* Bendigo Almanac and Tourist Guide, 1981; Restoring Democracy, 1999. *Recreations:* tennis, Australian football, Australian film.

BRUMMELL, David, CB 2005; Legal Secretary to the Law Officers, 2000–04; *b* 18 Dec. 1947; *s* of late Ernest Brummell and Florence Elizabeth Brummell (*née* Martin). *Educ:* Nottingham High Sch.; Queens' Coll., Cambridge (MA Law 1973); Inst. of Linguistics (Dips in French, German and Spanish). Articled clerk, 1971–73, Asst Solicitor, 1973–75, Simmons & Simmons, Solicitors, London; Legal Adviser: Devon CC, 1975–77; W Sussex CC, 1977–79; Legal Asst, then Sen. Legal Asst, OFT, 1979–84; Treasury Solicitor's Department: Sen. Legal Asst, 1984–86, Grade 6, 1986, Central Adv. Div.; Grade 5, 1986–89; Litigation Div., 1989–2000, Head, 1995–2000. *Recreations:* tennis, walking, music, languages, poetry. *Address:* 14A The Gateways, Park Lane, Richmond, Surrey TW9 2RB. *T:* (020) 8948 1247. *Clubs:* Athenæum; Thames Hare and Hounds.

BRUMMELL, Paul; HM Diplomatic Service; Ambassador to Romania, since 2014; *b* 28 Aug. 1965; *s* of late Robert George and June Brummell; *m* 2012, Adriana Mitsue Ivama; one *s*. *Educ:* St Albans Sch.; St Catharine's Coll., Cambridge (BA Hons Geog.). Joined HM Diplomatic Service, 1987; Third, later Second, Sec., Islamabad, 1989–92; FCO, 1993–94; First Sec., Rome, 1995–2000; Dep. Hd, Eastern Dept, FCO, 2000–01; Ambassador: to Turkmenistan, 2002–05; to Kazakhstan and (non-resident) to Kyrgyz Republic, 2005–09; High Comr to Barbados and (non-resident) to Antigua and Barbuda, Commonwealth of Dominica, Grenada, St Kitts and Nevis, St Lucia, and St Vincent and Grenadines, 2009–13, and concurrently Perm. Rep. to the Orgn of Eastern Caribbean States and Plenipotentiary Rep. to the Caribbean Community, 2010–13, and Consul-Gen. to the Dutch Caribbean, 2011–13. *Publications:* Turkmenistan—The Bradt Travel Guide, 2005; Kazakhstan—The Bradt Travel Guide, 2008. *Recreations:* travel writing, glam rock. *Address:* c/o Foreign and Commonwealth Office, King Charles Street, SW1A 2AH.

BRUMMER, Alexander; City Editor, Daily Mail, since 2000; *b* 25 May 1949; *s* of Michael Brummer and Hilda (*née* Lyons); *m* 1975, Patricia Lyndsey Magrill; two *s* one *d*. *Educ:* Univ. of Southampton (BSc Econ. Politics); Univ. of Bradford Mgt Centre (MSc Business Admin). The Guardian: Financial Corresp., 1973–79; Washington Ed., 1979–89; Foreign Ed., 1989–90; Financial Ed., 1990–99; Associate Ed., 1998–99; Consultant Ed., Mail on Sunday 1999. Vice-Pres., Bd of Deputies of British Jews, 2012–. DUniv Bradford, 2014. Award include: Financial Journalist of Year, British Press Awards, 1999; Best City Journalist, Medi Awards, 2000; Wincott Award for Sen. Financial Journalist of Year, 2001; Newspape Journalist of Year, 2002, Columnist of the Year, 2007, Lifetime Achievement, 2010 Workworld Media Awards; Business Journalist of Year, World Leadership Forum, 2006 Business Journalist of the Year, London Press Club, 2009; Financial Journalist of the Year City of London Corp., 2013. *Publications:* Hanson: a biography, 1994; Weinstock: the life and times, 1999; The Crunch, 2008; The Great Pensions Robbery, 2010; Britain for Sale, 2012 Bad Banks: greed, incompetence and the next global crisis, 2014. *Recreations:* reading antiques, football. *Address:* Daily Mail, City Office, Northcliffe House, 2 Derry Street, W8 5TT. *T:* (020) 7938 6906. *E:* alex.brummer@dailymail.co.uk.

BRUNA, Dick; graphic designer; writer and illustrator of children's books; *b* 23 Aug. 1927; of A. W. Bruna and J. C. C. Erdbrink; *m* 1953, Irene de Jongh; two *s* one *d*. *Educ:* Primary Sch. and Gymnasium, Utrecht, Holland; autodidact. Designer of book jackets, 1945–, and o posters, 1947– (many prizes); writer and illustrator of children's books, 1953– (1st book, The Apple); also designer of postage stamps, murals, greeting cards and picture postcards. Best-known character in children's books is Miffy; permanent collection of over 7000 artworks housed at dick bruna huis, Utrecht; other works in Rijksmus., Amsterdam; exhibns in Netherlands, Japan, UK and Belgium. Member: Netherlands Graphic Designers; Authors League of America Inc.; PEN Internat.; Alliance Graphique Internat. *Publications:* 120 picture books, 32 of which are about Miffy; Miffy storybooks trans. into over 50 languages, with ove 85 million copies sold. *Address:* 3 Jeruzalemstraat, 3512 KW, Utrecht, Netherlands. *T:* (30) 2316042. *Club:* Art Directors (Netherlands).

BRUNDIN, Clark Lannerdahl, PhD; Founding Peter Moores Director, School o Management Studies, University of Oxford, 1992–96; President, Templeton College Oxford, 1992–96; *b* 21 March 1931; *s* of late Ernest Walfrid Brundin and Elinor Brundin (*née* Clark); *m* 1959, Judith Anne (*née* Maloney); two *s* two *d*. *Educ:* Whittier High Sch., California California Inst. of Technology; Univ. of California, Berkeley (BSc, PhD); MA Oxford Electronics Petty Officer, US Navy, 1951–55. Associate in Mech. Engrg, UC Berkeley 1956–57; Demonstr, Dept of Engrg Science, Univ. of Oxford, 1957–58; Res. Engr, Inst. o Engrg Res., UC Berkeley, 1959–63; Univ. Lectr, Dept of Engrg Sci., Univ. of Oxford 1963–85, Vice-Chm., Gen. Bd of the Faculties, 1984–85; Jesus College, Oxford: Fellow and Tutor in Engrg, 1964–85; Sen. Tutor, 1974–77; Estates Bursar, 1978–84; Hon. Fellow, 1985 Vice Chancellor, Univ. of Warwick, 1985–92. Vis. Prof., Univ. of Calif Santa Barbara, 1978 Vis. Schol., Center for Studies in Higher Educn, UC Berkeley, 1997–. Member: Engrg Bd CNAA, 1976–82; CICHE, British Council, 1987–96; Adv. Bd, Oxford Centre for Higher Educn Studies, 2000–. Director: Cokethorpe Sch. Educnl Trust, 1983–96; Heritage Projects (Oxford) Ltd, 1985–97; Blackwell Science Ltd, 1990–98; Finsbury Growth Trust plc 1995–2000; CAF America, 1997–2000 (Pres., 1998–2000); Chm., Anchor Housing Assoc. 1985–91 (Bd Mem., 1985–94). Mem. (Lib Dem) Oxford City Council, 2004–12. Governor: Oxford Poly., 1979–84; Magdalen College Sch., 1987–99; Coventry Sch. Foundn, 1991–99 Chancellor, Oxonia Univ. Network, 2014–. Freeman, City of Oxford, 2012. Hon. Fellow Green Templeton Coll., Oxford, 2010. Hon. LLD Warwick, 2005. *Publications:* articles on rarefied gas dynamics and higher education. *Recreations:* sailing, mending old machinery, music of all sorts. *Address:* 28 Observatory Street, Oxford OX2 6EW.

BRUNDLE, Martin John; racing driver; presenter and commentator, Formula One, Sky Sports F1, since 2012; *b* 1 June 1959; *s* of late Alfred Edward John Brundle and of Alma Brundle; *m* 1981, Elizabeth Mary Anthony; one *s* one *d*. *Educ:* King Edward VII Grammar Sch., King's Lynn; Norfolk Coll. of Arts and Technol. Formula One racing driver, 1984–96 (158 Grands Prix): World Sportscar Champion, 1988; winner: Daytona 24 hours, 1988; Le Mans 24 hours, 1990. Presenter and commentator: Formula One, ITV, 1997–2008 (Best Sports Prog., BAFTA, 2006, 2007, 2008, 2010); Formula One, BBC, 2009–11. Chm., British Racing Drivers' Club, 2000–03. Grovewood Award, 1982; Segrave Trophy, 1988; RTS Sports Award, 1998, 1999, 2005 and 2006. DCL UEA, 2007. *Publications:* Working the Wheel, 2004; The Martin Brundle Scrapbook, 2013. *Recreations:* helicopter flying, motor biking. *E:* office@mb-f1.com. *Club:* British Racing Drivers' (Silverstone).

BRUNDTLAND, Gro Harlem, MD; Prime Minister of Norway, Feb.–Oct. 1981, 1986–89 and 1990–96; United Nations Special Envoy for Climate Change, 2007–10; Director General World Health Organisation, 1998–2003; *b* 20 April 1939; *d* of Gudmund and Inga Harlem; *m* 1960, Arne Olav Brundtland; two *s* one *d* (and one *s* decd). *Educ:* Oslo and Harvard Univs MPH. MO, Directorate of Health, 1966–68; Asst Med. Dir, Oslo Bd of Health, 1968–74 Minister of Environment, 1974–79; MP (Lab) Oslo, 1977–96; Dep. Leader, Labour Party 1975–81; Dep. Leader, Labour Parly Gp, 1979–81, Leader, 1981–92. Member: Ind. (Palme) Commn on Disarmament and Security Issues, 1979–82; Internat. Commn on Nuclear Non-Proliferation and Disarmament, 2008–10; UN Sec. Gen.'s High Level Panel on Global Sustainability, 2010–12; Chm., UN World Commn on Envmt and Develt, 1983–87 Member: Bd, UN Foundn, 2003–; The Elders, 2007– (Dep. Chm.). Vice-Pres., Socialist Internat. Hon. DCL Oxon, 2001. Third World Prize; Indira Gandhi Prize; Blue Planet Prize *Publications:* articles on preventive medicine, school health and growth studies, internat. issues *Recreation:* cross-country ski-ing. *Address:* 241 Route de Bellet, 06200 Nice, France.

BRUNEI, HM Sultan of; *see* Negara Brunei Darussalam.

BRUNER, Jerome Seymour, MA, PhD; University Professor, New York University, since 1998 (Research Professor of Psychology, 1987–98; Adjunct Professor of Law, 1991–98) Fellow, New York Institute for the Humanities; *b* New York, 1 Oct. 1915; *s* of Herman and Rose Bruner; *m* 1st, 1940, Katherine Frost (marr. diss. 1956); one *s* one *d*; 2nd, 1960, Blanche Marshall McLane (marr. diss. 1984); 3rd, 1987, Carol Fleisher Feldman (*d* 2006). *Educ:* Duke Univ. (AB 1937); Harvard Univ. (AM 1939, PhD 1941). US Intelligence, 1941; Assoc. Dir Office Public Opinion Research, Princeton, 1942–44; govt public opinion surveys on war problems, 1942–43; political intelligence, France, 1943; Harvard University: research 1945–72; Prof. of Psychology, 1952–72; Dir, Centre for Cognitive Studies, 1961–72; Watts Prof. of Psychology, Univ. of Oxford, 1972–80; G. H. Mead Univ. Prof., New Sch. for Social Res., NY, 1980–88. Lectr, Salzburg Seminar, 1952; Bacon Prof., Univ. of Aix-en-Provence 1965. Editor, Public Opinion Quarterly, 1943–44; Syndic, Harvard Univ. Press, 1962–74 Member: Inst. Advanced Study, 1951; White House Panel on Educnl Research and Devel Guggenheim Fellow, Cambridge Univ., 1955; Fellow: Amer. Psychol Assoc. (Pres., 1964–65 Distinguished Scientific Contrib. award, 1962); Amer. Acad. Arts and Sciences; Swiss Psycho Soc. (hon.); Soc. Psychol Study Social Issues (past Pres.); Amer. Assoc. Univ. Profs; Puerto Rican Acad. Arts and Sciences (hon.); Corresp. FBA 2003. Hon. DHL Lesley Coll., 1964 Hon. DSc: Northwestern Univ., 1965; Sheffield, 1970; Bristol, 1975; Hon. MA, Oxford 1972; Hon. DSocSci, Yale, 1975; Hon. LLD: Temple Univ., 1965; Univ. of Cincinnati 1966; Univ. of New Brunswick, 1969; Hon. DLitt: North Michigan Univ., 1969; Duke Univ., 1969; Dr *hc:* Sorbonne, 1974; Leuven, 1976; Ghent, 1977; Madrid, 1987; Free Univ. Berlin, 1988; Columbia, 1988; Stirling, 1990; Rome, 1992; Harvard, Bologna, Geneva, 1996 Salerno, Crete, 2002. Internat. Balzan Prize, Fondazione Balzan, 1987. *Publications:* Mandate from the People, 1944; (with Krech) Perception and Personality: A Symposium, 1950; (with Goodnow and Austin) A Study of Thinking, 1956; (with Smith and White) Opinions and Personality, 1956; (with Bresson, Morf and Piaget) Logique et Perception, 1958; The Process of Education, 1960; On Knowing: Essays for the Left Hand, 1962; (jtly) Studies in Cognitive

Growth, 1966; Toward a Theory of Instruction, 1966; Processes of Cognitive Growth: Infancy, Vol III, 1968; The Relevance of Education, 1971; (ed Anglin) Beyond the Information Given: selected papers of Jerome S. Bruner, 1973; (with Connolly) The Growth of Competence, 1974; (with Jolly and Sylva) Play: its role in evolution and development, 1976; Under Five in Britain, 1980; Communication as Language, 1982; In Search of Mind: essays in autobiography, 1983; Child's Talk, 1983; Actual Minds, Possible Worlds, 1986; Acts of Meaning, 1990; The Culture of Education, 1996; (with A. G. Amsterdam) Minding the Law, 2000; Making Stories, 2002; contribs technical and professional jls. *Recreation:* sailing. *Address:* 200 Mercer Street, New York, NY 10012, USA. *Clubs:* Royal Cruising; Century (New York); Cruising Club of America.

BRÜNJES, Dr Henry Otto; Chairman, Premier Medical Group, since 2007; Group Medical Director, Capita, since 2010; *b* Norwich, 15 Oct. 1954; *s* of late Henry Otto Brünjes and Ellen Jane Brünjes (*née* McColl); *m* 1980, Jacqueline Mary Storey; three *s* one *d*. *Educ:* Bedford Modern Sch.; St Thomas' Hosp. Med. Sch. (BSc Anatomy 1977); Guy's Hosp. Med. Sch. (MB BS 1980). DRCOG 1982. Jun. hosp. posts, Guy's Hosp. and Royal Sussex County Hosp., 1980–85; GP and Partner, then Sen. Partner, Rottingdean, Sussex, 1985–95; CEO, Premier Med. Gp, 1995–2006. Chairman: Rapid Trauma Assessment, 2000–06; Personal Injury Forum, BUPA, 2004–07; Newmans Clinics, 2011–. Non-executive Director: Good Care Gp, 2011–; Equity Syndicate Mgt Ltd, 2013–. Pres., Sussex Medico-Chirurgical Soc., 2007. FRSocMed 1995; Fellow and Gov., Expert Witness Inst., 2002–; Fellow, Woodard Corp., 2004–; Vice-Pres., Coll. of Medicine, 2009–. Member: Bd, ENO, 2010– (Chm., 2015–); Council, Southwark Cathedral Develt Trust, 2012–; Lancing Develt Council, 2009–. Gov., Bedford Modern Sch., 2004–07; Chm., Mowden Sch., 2004–08; Chm., Lancing Coll., 2009–. *Recreations:* golf, soccer, piano, public speaking. *Address:* Folkington Manor, Folkington, E Sussex BN26 5SD; Flat 37, Peninsula Heights, 93 Albert Embankment, SE1 7TY. *Clubs:* Garrick, Reform; Rye Golf, Royal St George's Golf; Valderrama Golf (Sotogrande, Spain).

BRUNNER, Adrian John Nelson; QC 1994; *b* 18 June 1946; *s* of late Comdr Hugh Brunner, DSC, RN and Elizabeth Brunner; *m* 1970, Christine Anne Hughes; one *s* four *d*. *Educ:* Ampleforth Coll.; BRNC; Coll. of Law. Served RN, 1963–66. Called to the Bar, Inner Temple, 1968 (Major Schol., 1967), Bencher, 2006. Recorder, 1990–2010. *Recreations:* yachting, travel. *Address:* Furneaux Pelham Hall, Buntingford, Herts SG9 0LB; Holborn Head Farm, Scrabster, Caithness KW14 7UW. *Clubs:* Royal Yacht Squadron, Bar Yacht.

See also C. J. Brunner.

BRUNNER, Catherine Jane; QC 2015; a Recorder, since 2012; *b* Paddington, 5 Aug. 1972; *d* of Adrian John Nelson Brunner, *qv*; *m* 2004, Robin Pargeter; two *d*. *Educ:* St Paul's Girls' Sch.; Edinburgh Univ. (MA Hons Psychol. 1994); City Univ. (DipLaw 1995); Inns of Court Sch. of Law. Called to the Bar, Inner Temple, 1997; in practice as barrister, 1997–. Judge (pt-time) of Upper Tribunal (Admin. Appeals Chamber), 2014–. *Recreations:* painting, travelling. *Address:* Albion Chambers, Broad Street, Bristol BS1 1DR. *T:* (0117) 927 2144.

BRUNNER, Sir Hugo (Laurence Joseph), KCVO 2008; JP; Lord-Lieutenant of Oxfordshire, 1996–2008; *b* 17 Aug. 1935; *s* of Sir Felix Brunner, 3rd Bt and late Dorothea Elizabeth (*née* Irving); *m* 1967, Mary Rose Pollen; five *s* one *d*. *Educ:* Eton; Trinity Coll., Oxford (MA Hons; Hon. Fellow, 1994). With OUP, 1958–65 (First Rep., Hong Kong, 1960–62); Sales Dir, Chatto & Windus, publishers, 1966–76; Dep. Gen. Publisher, OUP, 1977–79; Man. Dir, then Chm., Chatto & Windus, 1979–85. Director: Caithness Glass Ltd, 1966–96 (Chm., 1984–91); Brunner Investment Trust PLC, 1987–99; SCM Press Ltd, 1991–97. Contested (L) Torquay, 1964 and 1966. Chm., Oxford DAC for Care of Churches, 1985–98. Governor: St Edward's Sch., Oxford, 1991–2005; Ripon Coll. Cuddesdon, 1992–2005. Dep. Steward, Univ. of Oxford, 2001–11. Pres., Oxford Civic Soc., 2010–. High Sheriff, 1988–89, DL 1993, JP 1996, Oxon. Mem., Order of St Frideswide, 2006. Hon. LLD Oxford Brookes, 1999. *Recreations:* hill-walking, church visiting, study of animal-powered engines. *Address:* 26 Norham Road, Oxford OX2 6SF. *T:* and *Fax:* (01865) 316431. *Clubs:* Reform, Chelsea Arts.

BRUNNER, Sir John Henry Kilian, 4th Bt *cr* 1895; *b* 1 June 1927; *s* of Sir Felix John Morgan Brunner, 3rd Bt, and Dorothea Elizabeth, OBE, *d* of Henry Brodribb Irving; *S* father, 1982, but his name does not appear on the Official Roll of the Baronetage; *m* 1955, Jasmine Cecily, *d* of late John Wardrop Moore; two *s* one *d*. *Educ:* Eton; Trinity Coll., Oxford (BA 1950). Served as Lieut RA. On staff, PEP, 1950–53; Talks producer, 1953; Economic Adviser, Treasury, 1958–61; Asst Manager, Observer, 1961. *Heir: s* Nicholas Felix Minturn Brunner, *b* 16 Jan. 1960.

BRUNNING, His Honour David Wilfrid; a mediator, since 2009; a Circuit Judge, 1988–2008; a Deputy High Court Judge, Queen's Bench Division and Family Divisions, 1995–2008; *b* 10 April 1943; *s* of Wilfred and Marion Brunning; *m* 1967, Deirdre Ann Shotton; three *s*. *Educ:* Burton upon Trent Grammar Sch.; Worcester Coll., Oxford (BA (Modern History) 1965; DPA 1966). Called to the Bar, Middle Temple, 1969; Midland and Oxford Circuit, 1970–88; Assigned Judge, Designated Family Judge and Designated Civil Judge, Nottingham; Judge of the Technology and Construction Court at Nottingham, 1995–2004; Designated Family Judge, Leicester County Court, 2004–08. Judge, Mental Health Rev. Tribunal, 1998–. Mem. Council, Leicester Univ., 2003–11. *Recreations:* campanology, walking, wine, military history. *Address:* St Philips Chambers, 55 Temple Row, Birmingham B2 5LS.

BRUNO, Franklin Roy, (Frank), MBE 1990; professional boxer, 1982–96; after dinner speaker and mental health campaigner; *b* 16 Nov. 1961; *s* of late Robert Bruno and of Lynette Bruno (*née* Campbell); *m* 1990, Laura Frances Mooney (marr. diss. 2001); one *s* two *d*; one *d* by Yvonne Clydesdale. *Educ:* Oak Hall Sch., Sussex. Amateur boxer, Sir Philip Game Amateur Boxing Club, 1977–80: 21 contests, 20 victories; London ABA and Nat. ABA Heavyweight Champion, 1980; professional career, 1982–96: 45 contests, 40 victories; European Champion, 1985–86; WBC World Heavyweight Champion, 1995. Pantomime appearances: Aladdin, Dominion, 1989, Nottingham, 1990, Wycombe, 2003; Robin Hood, Bristol, 1991; Jack and the Beanstalk, Bradford, 1996; Goldilocks, Birmingham, 1997, Southampton, 1999, Wolverhampton, 2001; UK theatre tour with Ricky Hatton, 2004–06. Sports Personality of Year, Stars Orgn for Spastics, 1989, 1990. *Publications:* Know What I Mean?, 1987; Eye of the Tiger, 1992; From Zero to Hero, 1996; Frank: fighting back, 2005. *Recreations:* swimming, training, driving, eating, shopping for good clothes. *E:* frank@frankbruno.co.uk.

BRUNSDEN, Prof. Denys, OBE 2004; PhD; Professor of Geography, Department of Geography, King's College, University of London, 1983–96, now Emeritus; *b* 14 March 1936; *s* of Francis Stephen Brunsden and Mabel Florence (*née* Martin); *m* 1961, Elizabeth Mary Philippa (*née* Wright); one *s* one *d*. *Educ:* Torquay Grammar Sch. for Boys; King's Coll., Univ. of London (BSc Hons Geography; PhD 1963; FKC 1998). King's College, London: Tutorial Student, 1959–60; Asst Lectr, 1960–63; Lectr, 1963–75; Reader, 1975–83. Vis. Lectr, 1964–65, Erskine Fellow, 1988, Univ. of Canterbury, NZ; Vis. Associate Prof., Louisiana State Univ., 1971; Visiting Professor: Univ. of Durham, 1996–2002; Bournemouth Univ., 1999–2005. Founder Consultant, Geomorphological Services Ltd, 1972. Chairman: British Geomorphol Res. Gp, 1985–86; Wkg Pty for Collaboration in Internat. Geomorphology, 1985–; President: Geographical Assoc., 1986–87 (Hon. Mem., 1996); Internat. Assoc. of Geomorphologists, 1989–93 (Sen. Past Pres., 1993–97; Hon. Fellow 1997); Vice-Pres., RGS, 1984–87; Hon. Mem., Polish Assoc. of Geomorphologists, 1993. Member: St George's House Consultation, 1989; Nat. Curriculum Wkg Party for Physical Educn, 1990–92. Mem. Steering Cttee, successful bid for World Heritage Site status for Dorset and E Devon Coast, 1993–; Chm., Dorset Coast Forum, 1995–2005; Trustee, Jurassic Coast Trust, 2005–. Hon. DSc: Plymouth, 2000; Bournemouth, 2002. Gill Meml Award, RGS (for contribs to study of mass movement and fieldwork), 1977; Republic of China Award Lectr, 1988–89; Assoc. of American Geographers Honours, 1991; Linton Award, British Geomorphol Res. Gp, 1993; William Smith Medal, 2000, R. H. Worth Prize, 2010, Geol Soc. of London; Glossop Lect. and Medal, Geol Soc., 2001. *Publications:* Dartmoor, 1968; Slopes, Forms and Process, 1970; (with J. C. Doornkamp) The Unquiet Landscape, 1971 (USA 1976, Australia 1976, Germany 1977); (with J. B. Thornes) Geomorphology and Time, 1977; (with C. Embleton and D. K. C. Jones) Geomorphology: present problems, future prospects, 1978; (with J. C. Doornkamp and D. K. C. Jones) The Geology, Geomorphology and Pedology of Bahrain, 1980; (with R. U. Cooke, J. C. Doornkamp and D. K. C. Jones) The Urban Geomorphology of Drylands, 1982; (with D. B. Prior) Slope Instability, 1984; (with R. Gardner, A. S. Goudie and D. K. C. Jones) Landshapes, 1989; Natural Disasters, 1990; (with A. S. Goudie) The Environment of the British Isles: an Atlas, 1995; (with R. Dikau) Landslide Recognition, 1996; (jtly) The History of the Study of Landforms, vol. 4, 2008. *Recreations:* making walking sticks and shepherd's-crooks, painting, reading thrillers, enjoying dinner parties and fine wine, talking, travelling to exotic places. *Address:* Department of Geography, King's College London, Strand, WC2R 2LS. *Club:* Geographical.

BRUNSDON, Norman Keith, AM 2000; Chairman and Senior Partner, Price Waterhouse, Australia, 1982–86; *b* 11 Jan. 1930; *s* of late G. A. Brunsdon; *m* 1953, Ruth, *d* of late W. Legg; one *s* one *d*. *Educ:* Wagga Wagga High Sch., NSW. FCA. Price Waterhouse, Australia: joined, 1951; Partner, 1963; Mem. Policy Cttee (Bd), 1970–86; Partner-in-Charge, Sydney, 1975–81; Mem., World Firm Policy Cttee (Bd) and Council of Firms, 1979–86; Agent Gen. for NSW in London, 1989–91. Dir, Arthur Yates & Co. Ltd, 1993–2001. Chm., Aust. Govt's Taxation Adv. Cttee, 1979–83; Trustee, Econ. Develt of Aust. Cttee, 1977–86. Vice-Pres., Thai-Aust. Chamber of Commerce & Industry, 1982–85; Member: Pacific Basin Econ. Council, 1982–86; Aust. Japan Business Co-op. Cttee, 1982–86. Member: Standing Cttee, C of E Dio. Sydney, 1969–74; C of E Children's Homes Cttee, 1974–84 (Treasurer, 1969–75; Acting Chm., 1972–73); Chairman: Anglican Retirement Villages, dio. Sydney, 1991–98; Anglican Foundn for Aged Care, 1993–2001. Governor, King's Sch., Parramatta, 1977–86; Trustee, Bark Endeavour Foundn Pty Ltd, 1992–2001. Hon. Mem., Cook Soc. Freeman, City of London, 1989. *Recreations:* music, opera, theatre, reading. *Address:* PO Box 675, Northbridge, NSW 1560, Australia. *T:* (2) 99295947, 0419580641. *Clubs:* Australian (Sydney); Royal Sydney Yacht Squadron.

BRUNSKILL, Ronald William, OBE 1990; MA, PhD; FSA; lecturer and author; Professor, Centre for Conservation Studies, School of Architecture (formerly School of the Built Environment), De Montfort University, 1995–2001; *b* 3 Jan. 1929; *s* of William Brunskill and Elizabeth Hannah Brunskill; *m* 1960, Miriam Allsopp; two *d*. *Educ:* Bury High Sch.; Univ. of Manchester (BA Hons Arch. 1951, MA 1952, PhD 1963). Registered Architect and ARIBA, 1951; FSA 1975. National Service, 2nd Lieut RE, 1953–55. Studio Asst in Arch., Univ. of Manchester, 1951–53; Architectural Asst, LCC, 1955; Asst in Arch., Univ. of Manchester, 1955–56; Commonwealth Fund Fellow (arch. and town planning), MIT, 1956–57; Architect to Williams Deacon's Bank, 1957–60; Manchester University: Lectr, 1960–73; Sen. Lectr, 1973–84; Reader in Architecture, 1984–89; Hon. Fellow, Sch. of Architecture, 1989–95; Architect in private practice, 1960–66; Partner, Carter, Brunskill & Associates, chartered architects, 1966–69, Consultant, 1969–73. Vis. Prof., Univ. of Florida, Gainesville, 1969–70; Hon. Vis. Prof., De Montfort Univ., 1994–95. President: Vernacular Arch. Gp, 1974–77; Cumberland and Westmorland Antiquarian and Archaeol Soc., 1990–93 (Vice-Pres., 1975–90); Friends of Friendless Churches, 1999–2009 (Chm., 1990–98); Ancient Monuments Soc., 2004–09 (Hon. Architect, 1983–88; Vice-Chm., 1988–90; Chm., 1990–2000; Vice-Pres., 2000–04); Vice-Pres., Weald and Downland Museum Trust, 1980–; Chm., Urban Parks Adv. Panel, Heritage Lottery Fund, 1995–99; Member: Historic Bldgs Council for England, 1978–84; Royal Commn on Ancient and Historical Monuments of Wales, 1983–97 (Vice Chm., 1993–97); Historic Buildings and Monuments Commn (English Heritage), 1989–95 (Member: Historic Buildings Adv. Cttee, 1984–95 (Chm., 1989–95); Ancient Monuments Adv. Cttee, 1984–90; Chm., Cathedrals and Churches Adv. Cttee, 1989–95); Cathedrals Adv. Commn for England, 1981–91; Cathedrals Fabric Commn for England, 1991–96; Manchester DAC for Care of Churches, 1973–79 and 1987–93; Manchester Cathedral Fabric Cttee, 1987–96; Blackburn Cathedral Fabric Cttee, 1989–96 (Chm.); Chester Cathedral Fabric Cttee, 1989–94 and 2004–09; Council, Soc. for Folk Life Studies, 1969–72 and 1980–83. Trustee, British Historic Buildings Trust, 1985–92. Hon. DArt De Montfort, 2001. Neale Bursar, RIBA, 1962; President's Award, Manchester Soc. of Architects, 1977; Henry Glessie Award, Vernacular Architecture Forum of USA and Canada, 2009. *Publications:* Illustrated Handbook of Vernacular Architecture, 1971, 3rd edn (enlarged) 1987; Vernacular Architecture of the Lake Counties, 1974; (with Alec Clifton-Taylor) English Brickwork, 1977; Traditional Buildings of Britain, 1981, 3rd edn (enlarged) 2004; Houses (in series, Collins Archaeology), 1982; Traditional Farm Buildings of Britain, 1982, 2nd edn (enlarged) 1987; Timber Building in Britain, 1985, 2nd edn (enlarged) 1994; Brick Building in Britain, 1990; Houses and Cottages of Britain, 1997; Traditional Farm Buildings and their Conservation, 1999; Vernacular Architecture: an illustrated handbook, 2000; Traditional Buildings of Cumbria, 2002; Brick and Clay Buildings of Britain, 2009; articles and reviews in archaeol and architectural jls. *Recreation:* enjoying the countryside. *Address:* 8 Overhill Road, Wilmslow SK9 2BE. *T:* (01625) 522099.

BRUNSON, Michael John, OBE 2000; broadcaster and journalist; Political Editor, ITN, 1986–2000; *b* 12 Aug. 1940; *s* of Geoffrey Brunson and Ethel (*née* Mills); *m* 1965, Susan Margaret Brown; two *s*. *Educ:* Bedford Sch.; Queen's Coll., Oxford (BA Theol. 1963; MA). VSO, Sierra Leone, 1963–64; BBC General Trainee, 1964–65; Reporter, BBC SE Radio News, 1965–66; Asst Producer, BBC TV Current Affairs, 1966–68; Independent Television News: Reporter, 1968–72; Washington Corresp., 1972–77; Reporter, 1977–80; Diplomatic Editor, 1980–86; Campaign Reporter with Mrs Thatcher, 1979 and 1983 Gen. Elections. Chairman: Parly Lobby Journalists, 1994; Parly Press Gall., 1999. Member: Govt Adv. Gp on Citizenship Educn, 1997–98; Preparation for Adult Life Gp, QCA, 1998; Adult Learning Cttee, Learning and Skills Council, 2001–03. Trustee, Citizenship Foundn, 2000–06. Chm., Norfolk br., Oxford Univ. Soc. (formerly Oxford Soc.), 2007–. Mem. Council, Friends of Norwich Cathedral, 2008–14. Vice Pres., Livability, 2013–. Columnist: The House Mag. (H of C), 1989–90, 1997–99; Saga Magazine, 2000–05. Hon. LittD UEA, 2003. RTS News Event Award, 1994; RTS Judges' Award for lifetime achievement, 2000. *Publications:* A Ringside Seat (autobiog.), 2000. *Recreations:* choral singing, gardening, Norwich City FC. *Address:* c/o Knight Ayton Management, 35 Great James Street, WC1N 3HB. *T:* (020) 7831 4400. *Clubs:* Oxford and Cambridge; Norfolk (Norwich).

BRUNT, Rev. Prof. Peter William, CVO 2001; OBE 1994; MD, FRCP, FRCPE; Physician to the Queen in Scotland, 1983–2001; Consultant Physician and Gastroenterologist, Grampian Health Board, Aberdeen, 1970–2001; Clinical Professor of Medicine, University of Aberdeen, 1996–2001; Non-Stipendiary Minister, diocese of Aberdeen, Scottish Episcopal Church, since 1996; *b* 18 Jan. 1936; *s* of late Harry Brunt and Florence J. J. Airey; *m* 1961, Dr Anne Lewis, *d* of Rev. R. H. Lewis; three *d*. *Educ:* Manchester Grammar Sch.; Cheadle Hulme Sch.; King George V Sch.; Univ. of Liverpool (MB, ChB 1959; MD 1967). FRCP 1976; FRCPE 1981. Gen. Med. training, Liverpool Royal Infirmary and Liverpool Hosps, 1959–64; Research Fellow, Johns Hopkins Univ. Sch. of Medicine, Baltimore, USA,

1965–67; Lectr in Medicine, Edinburgh Univ., 1967–68; Senior Registrar, Gastrointestinal Unit, Western Gen. Hosp., Edinburgh, 1968–69; Clin. Sen. Lectr in Medicine, Aberdeen Univ., 1970–96. Hon. Lectr in Medicine, Royal Free Hosp. Sch. of Medicine, Univ. of London, 1969–70. Medical Dir, Scottish Adv. Cttee on Distinction Awards, 2000–05; Chairman: Med. Council on Alcohol, 2004–; Alcohol Focus Scotland, 2005–. Mem., Assoc. of Physicians of GB and Ireland (Pres., 1995–96); Jt Vice-Pres., RCPE, 2005–08. Ordained deacon, 1996, priest, 1997, Scottish Episcopal Church. Hon. FRCSE 2009. *Publications:* (with M. Losowsky and A. E. Read) Diseases of the Liver and Biliary System, 1984; (with P. F. Jones and N. A. G. Mowat) Gastroenterology, 1984. *Recreations:* mountaineering, music, operatics. *Address:* Flat 4, 1 Hillpark Rise, Blackhall, Edinburgh EH4 7BB. *T:* (0131) 312 6687; The Knotts, Watermillock, Penrith, Cumbria CA11 0JP. *T:* (017684) 86394. *E:* peterbrunt123@ btinternet.com.

BRUNTISFIELD, 3rd Baron *cr* 1942, of Boroughmuir; **Michael John Victor Warrender;** Bt 1715; *b* 9 Jan. 1949; *s* of 2nd Baron Bruntisfield and Anne Moireen, 2nd *d* of Sir Walter Campbell, KCIE; *S* father, 2007; *m* 1978, Baroness Walburga von Twickel; one *s*. *Educ:* Downside; RMA Sandhurst; Durham Univ. (BA 1972). Major, Irish Guards, 1967–86. Director: Robert Fleming Investment Mgt, 1986–2001; Jardine Fleming Investment Mgt, 1986–2001; JP Morgan Asset Mgt, 2000–01; Atlas Capital, 2001–06; Concordia Advisors, 2006–13; Mariner Investment Gp, 2013–14; CIM Investment Mgt, 2014–. *Heir: s* Hon. John Michael Patrick Caspar Warrender, *b* 1 June 1996.

BRUNTON, Sir Gordon (Charles), Kt 1985; Chairman: Communications and General Consultants, since 1985; Stock Productions Ltd, since 1999; Galahad Gold plc, 2003–07; *b* 27 Dec. 1921; *s* of late Charles Arthur Brunton and late Hylda Pritchard; *m* 1st, 1946, Nadine Lucile Paula Sohr (marr. diss. 1965); one *s* two *d* (and one *s* decd); 2nd, 1966, Gillian Agnes Kirk; one *s* one *d*. *Educ:* Cranleigh Sch.; London Sch. of Economics. Commnd into RA, 1942; served Indian Army, Far East; Mil. Govt, Germany, 1946. Joined Tothill Press, 1947; Exec. Dir, Tothill, 1956; Man. Dir, Tower Press Gp of Cos, 1958; Exec. Dir, Odhams Press, 1961; joined Thomson Organisation, 1961; Man. Dir, Thomson Publications, 1961; Dir, Thomson Organisation, 1963; Chm., Thomson Travel, 1965–68; Man. Dir and Chief Exec., Internat. Thomson Orgn plc (formerly Thomson British Hldgs) and The Thomson Orgn Ltd, 1968–84; Pres., Internat. Thomson Orgn Ltd, 1978–84. Director: Times Newspapers Ltd, 1967–81; Sotheby Parke Bernet Group, 1978–83 (Chm., 1982–83, Chm. Emeritus, Sotheby's Holding Inc., 1983); Cable and Wireless plc, 1981–91; Yattendon Investment Trust, 1985–2001; Chairman: Bemrose Corp., 1978–91; Martin Currie Pacific Trust, 1985–92; Community Industry, 1985–92; Euram Consulting, 1985–92; Cavendish Shops, 1985–93; The Racing Post plc, 1985–97; Mercury Communications, 1986–90; Cavendish Retail, 1987–94; Ingersoll Publications, 1988–91; Wharfedale, then Verity Gp, 1991–97; Green Field Leisure Gp Ltd, 1992–2011; PhoneLink, then Telme.com, 1993–2001. President: Periodical Publishers Assoc., 1972–74, 1981–83; Nat. Advertising Benevolent Soc., 1973–75 (Trustee, 1980–); History of Advertising Trust, 1981–84; CPU, 1991–94; Chm., EDC for Civil Engrg, 1978–84; Member: Printing and Publishing Ind. Trng Bd, 1974–78; Supervisory Bd, CBI Special Programmes Unit, 1980–84; Business in the Community Council, 1981–84; Chm., Independent Adoption Service, 1986–. Mem., South Bank Bd, Arts Council, 1985–92. Governor: LSE, 1971–95 (Fellow, 1978); Ashridge Management Coll., 1983–86; Ct of Governors, Henley—The Management Coll., 1983–85; Mem. Council, Templeton College (formerly Oxford Centre for Management Studies), 1976–95; Mem., Finance Cttee, OUP, 1985–91. *Recreations:* books, breeding horses. *Address:* (office) North Munstead, North Munstead Lane, Godalming, Surrey GU8 4AX. *T:* (01483) 424181, *Fax:* (01483) 426043. *Club:* Garrick.

BRUNTON, Sir James (Lauder), 4th Bt *cr* 1908, of Stratford Place, St Marylebone; MD; FRCPC; Professor of Medicine, and former Head of Division of Infectious Diseases, Department of Medicine, University of Toronto; *b* 24 Sept. 1947; *s* of Sir (Edward Francis) Lauder Brunton, 3rd Bt, physician, and of Marjorie, *o d* of David Sclater Lewis, MSc, MD, CM, FRCPC; *S* father, 2007, but his name does not appear on the Official Roll of the Baronetage; *m* 1st, 1967, Susan Elizabeth (marr. diss. 1983), *o d* of Charles Hons; one *s* one *d*; 2nd, 1984, Beverly Anne Freedman; one *s*. *Educ:* Bishop's Coll. Sch., Montreal; McGill Univ. (BSc 1968); MD. *Heir: s* Douglas Lauder Brunton [*b* 1968; m 2004, Susan Jennifer Leat].

BRUNTON, Rear Adm. Steven Buchanan, CBE 2014; Director and owner, Adjuvo Associates Ltd; *b* Portsmouth, 26 Sept. 1959; *s* of Thomas Brunton and June Brunton; *m* 1984, Andrea Stacey; two *s*. *Educ:* Portsmouth Northern Grammar Sch.; Mayfield Sch.; RNEC Manadon (BSc, MSc); Internat. Project Mgt Assoc. (Certified Projects Dir 2011). CEng 1990; FIET 2004. Joined RN 1978; Dep. Weapons Engr Officer, HMS Sceptre, 1984–85, HMS Courageous, 1985–87; Weapon Engrg Officer, HMS Superb, 1990–92; Submarine Sea Trng Staff, 1992–94; Project Manager, Defence Information Infrastructure, 2002–05; Team Leader: Crypto and Secure Systems Integrated Project, 2005–06; Sustaining Surface Combatant Capability, 2006–07; Head: Capability (Above Water), 2007–10; Destroyers Project Team, 2010–11; Capital Ships, 2011–12; Dir Ship Acquisition, Defence Equipment and Support, 2012–14. MCGI 1990. FCMI 2014. *Recreations:* golf, genealogy, gardening.

BRUTON, Jane; *see* Bruton, V. J.

BRUTON, John (Gerard); company director; President, International Financial Services Centre, since 2010; European Union Ambassador to Washington, 2004–09; *b* 18 May 1947; *s* of Matthew Joseph Bruton and Doris Bruton (*née* Delany); *m* 1981, Finola Gill; one *s* three *d*. *Educ:* St Dominic's Coll., Dublin; Clongowes Wood Coll., Co. Kildare; University Coll., Dublin (BA, BL). King's Inns, Dublin; called to the Bar, 1972. National Secretary, Fine Gael Youth Group, 1966–69. TD (Fine Gael), Meath, 1969–2004. Mem., Dáil Committee of Procedure and Privileges, 1969–73, 1982; Fine Gael Spokesman on Agriculture, 1972–73; Parliamentary Secretary: to Minister for Education, 1973–77; to Minister for Industry and Commerce, 1975–77; Fine Gael Spokesman: on Agriculture, 1977–81; on Finance, Jan.–June 1981; Minister: for Finance, 1981–82, for Industry and Energy, 1982–83, for Industry, Trade, Commerce and Tourism, 1983–86, for Finance, 1986–87; Fine Gael Spokesman on Industry and Commerce, 1987–89, on education, 1989; Leader of the House, 1982–86; Taoiseach (Prime Minister of Ireland), 1994–97; Leader of the Opposition, 1997–2001. Dep. Leader, 1987–90, Leader, 1990–2001, Fine Gael. Pres., EEC Industry, Research and Internal Market Councils, July–Dec. 1984. Member: Parly Assembly, Council of Europe, 1989–90; British-Irish Parly Body, 1993–94; Parly Assembly, WEU, 1997–98; Præsidium, Convention on the Future of Europe, 2002–04. Chm., European Sustainable Materials Platform, 2012–14. Member: Bd, Centre for European Policy Studies, 2010–; Academic Council, Martens Centre, 2012–; Bd, Co-operation Ireland, 2012–. Vice President: Christian Democrat Internat., 1998–2001; EPP, 1999–2005. Director: Ingersoll Rand, 2010–; Montpelier Reinsce, 2010–. Dist. Fellow, Centre for Internat. Relns, Johns Hopkins Univ., 2010–; Vis., Fellow, Eur. Inst., LSE, 2010–12. Hon. DLaw: Memorial Univ., Newfoundland, 2002; NUI, 2005; Missouri, 2009. Schumann Medal, 1998. Comdr, Grand Cross of the Royal Order of Polar Star (Sweden), 2008. *Recreation:* reading history. *W:* www.johnbruton.com.

BRUTON, (Victoria) Jane; Deputy Editor and Director of Lifestyle, Daily Telegraph, since 2015; *b* Billinge, Wigan, 21 March 1968; *d* of Roger and Glynis Bruton; *m* 1996, Johnathan Paul Whitehead; two *s*. *Educ:* Byrchall High Sch., Ashton-in-Makerfield; Winstanley Coll., Wigan; Nottingham Univ. (BA 1st Cl. Hons English); City Univ. (Postgrad. Dip. Periodical Journalism). Sub-Editor, Chat, 1991–92; Features Editor, then Dep. Editor, Wedding and Home, 1993–96; Associate Editor, Prima, 1997; Editor: LivingEtc, 1998–2001; Eve, 2001–04; Editor-in-Chief, Grazia, 2005–15. Founder Mem., 1993–, and Truste 1997–2014, Trees for Cities (formerly Trees for London). *Recreations:* running, charity wor *Address:* Daily Telegraph, 111 Buckingham Palace Road, SW1W 0DT. *T:* (020) 7931 2000

BRUZZI, Prof. Stella, (Mrs Mick Conefrey), PhD; FBA 2013; Professor of Film an Television Studies, University of Warwick, since 2006; *b* Florence, Italy, 28 Jan. 1962; *d* o Dr Stefano Bruzzi and late Zara Bruzzi; *m* 1993, Mick Conefrey; one *s* one *d*. *Educ:* St Paul Girls' Sch., London; Univ. of Manchester (BA 1st Cl. Hons English and Drama); Univ. o Bristol (PhD 1993). Lectr, Drama Dept, Manchester Univ., 1992–93; Royal Hollowa University of London: Lectr, 1993–2000; Sen. Lectr, 2000–02; Reader, 2002–03; Prof. o Film, 2003–06; Chair, Faculty of Arts, Univ. of Warwick, 2008–11. Leverhulme Maj. Re Fellow, 2011–13; Plumer Vis. Res. Fellow, St Anne's Coll., Oxford, 2011–12; Vis. Prof Univ. of Chile, 2012. *Publications:* Undressing Cinema: clothing and identity in the movie 1997; New Documentary, 2000, rev. edn 2006 (Chinese edn 2013); (ed with Pamela Churc Gibson) Fashion Cultures: theories, explorations and analysis, 2000; Bringing Up Dadd fatherhood and masculinity in post-war Hollywood, 2005; Seven Up, 2007; Men's Cinem masculinity and mise-en-scene in Hollywood, 2013; (ed with Pamela Church Gibson Fashion Cultures Revisited, 2013. *Recreations:* going to cinema and theatre, readin swimming, being with family and friends. *Address:* Department of Film and Television Studie University of Warwick, Coventry CV4 7HS. *T:* (home) (01865) 553251. *E:* s.bruzzi@ warwick.ac.uk.

BRYAN, Gerald Jackson, CMG 1964; CVO 1966; OBE 1960; MC 1941; Member, Lo Chancellor's Panel of Independent Inquiry Inspectors, 1982–91; *b* 2 April 1921; *yr s* of lat George Bryan, OBE, LLD, and Ruby Evelyn (*née* Jackson), Belfast; *m* 1947, Georgiar Wendy Cockburn, OStJ, Hon. Belonger, BVI (*d* 2014), *d* of late William Barraud an Winnifred Hull; one *s* two *d*. *Educ:* Wrekin Coll.; RMA, Woolwich; New Coll., Oxfo Regular Commn, RE, 1940; served Middle East with No 11 (Scottish) Commando, 194 retd 1944, Capt. (temp. Maj.). Apptd Colonial Service, 1944; Asst District Comr, Swazilan 1944; Asst Colonial Sec., Barbados, 1950; Estabt Sec., Mauritius, 1954; Administrator, Bri Virgin Is, 1959; Administrator of St Lucia, 1962–67, retired; Govt Sec. and Head of Isle o Man Civil Service, 1967–69; General Manager: Londonderry Develt Commn, NI, 1969–7 Bracknell Develt Corp., 1973–82. Director: Lovaux Engrg Co. Ltd, 1982–88; MDSL Estat Ltd, 1988–2001. Sec. Gen., Assoc. of Contact Lens Manufacturers, 1983–88. Mem. (C), Ber CC, 1983–85. Treasurer, 1979–99, Vice-Chm., 1999–2002, Gordon Foundn; Gov Gordon's Sch. (formerly Gordon Boys' Home), Woking, 1979–2002. Chm., St John Counc for Berks, 1981–88. KStJ 1985, Mem., Chapter Gen., 1987–96. Hon. Belonger, BVI, 200 *Publications:* Be of Good Cheer, 2008. *Club:* Leander.

BRYAN, Katharine Ann; Chief Executive, Northern Ireland Water (formerly Water Servic Northern Ireland), 2004–08; *b* 25 Nov. 1952; *d* of John and Dorothy Ludlow; *m* 197 Michael Bryan; two *d*. *Educ:* Univ. of Durham (BSc Jt Hons Botany and Geog.); Univ. o Aston in Birmingham (MSc Biol. of Water Mgt). National Rivers Authority: Manager, Re Fisheries, Conservation and Recreation, Severn-Trent Reg., 1988–92; Regl Gen. Manag (SW), 1992–95; Regl Dir (SW), Envmt Agency, 1995–2000; Chief Exec., N of Scotlan Water Authy, 2000–02; Chm., Jt Nature Conservation Cttee, 2002–03; Chief Exec Northern Ireland Water (formerly Water Service, NI), 2004–08. Comr, Infrastructu Planning Commn, 2010–11; Non-exec. Dir, Defence Infrastructure Orgn (formerly Defenc Estates), 2009–11. Mem. Bd, and Chm., Remuneration Cttee, Audit Scotland, 2011–14.

BRYAN, Kenneth John; Chairman, Southampton University Hospitals NHS Trus 1996–2001; *b* 22 July 1939; *s* of late Patrick Joseph Bryan and Elsie May Bryan; *m* 1st, 196 (marr. diss. 1999); one *d*; 2nd, 2007, Gillian Silvester. *Educ:* De La Salle Coll.; Farnboroug GS. Insurance Broker, Lloyds, 1957–59; Major, British Army, 1959–78; Sen. Mgt Cons KPMG, 1978–79; Hongkong and Shanghai Banking Corporation: Financial Controlle Hong Kong office, 1979–86; Sen. Manager, Banking Services, 1986–88; Hd of Gp Finance 1988–93; Chief Financial Officer, Midland Bank, 1993–96; Dir Gen., Southampton an Fareham Chamber of Commerce and Industry, 2001–04. Chm. Trustees, Hampshire Autisti Soc., 2001–02 (Trustee, 1996–2002). Gov., Barton Peverill Coll., 1998–2002. Mem Pangbourne Parish Council, 2007–08. *Recreations:* golf, fly fishing, vegetable growing. *Clu* Army and Navy.

BRYAN, Margaret, CMG 1988; HM Diplomatic Service, retired; Ambassador to Panam 1986–89; *b* 26 Sept. 1929; *d* of James Grant and Dorothy Rebecca Galloway; *m* 1952, Pete Bernard Bryan (marr. diss. 1981). *Educ:* Cathedral Sch., Shanghai; Croydon High Sch.; Girto Coll., Cambridge (MA Modern Languages). Second, later First, Secretary, FCO, 1962–8 Head of Chancery and Consul, Kinshasa, 1980–83; Counsellor, Havana, 1983–86. Chm Blockley Cooperative Assoc. *Recreations:* theatre, travel, opera. *Club:* Royal Over-Se League.

BRYAN, Robert Patrick, OBE 1980; Police Adviser to Foreign and Commonwealth Offic and Inspector General of Dependent Territories Police, 1980–85, retired; security consultan *b* 29 June 1926; *s* of Maurice Bryan and Elizabeth (*née* Waite); *m* 1948, Hazel Audrey (*n* Braine) (*d* 1990); three *s*. *Educ:* Plaistow Secondary Sch.; Wanstead County High Sch. India Army (Mahratta LI), 1944–47. Bank of Nova Scotia, 1948–49; Metropolitan Polic Constable, 1950; seconded Security Service, 1967–68; Dep. Asst Commissioner, 1977, retire 1980. National Police College: Intermediate Comd Course, 1965; Sen. Comd Course, 196 occasional lecturer. RCDS 1974. Non-exec. Dir, Control Risks Internat. Ltd, 1986–8 Corporate Security Advr, Unilever, 1986–99; Chm., Los Zapateros (cobblers), 1998–9 Chm., Food Distribn Security Assoc., 1988–99. Gov., Corps of Commissionaires, 1993–9 Gov., Hampton Sch., 1978–97. *Publications:* contribs to police and related pubns, particular on community relations and juvenile delinquency. *Address:* 28 Bolton Gardens, Teddingto Middx TW11 9AY.

BRYAN, Simon James; QC 2006; **Hon. Chief Justice Bryan;** a Recorder, since 2009; Deputy High Court Judge, since 2013; Chief Justice of Falkland Islands, South Georgia an South Sandwich Islands, British Antarctic Territory and British Indian Ocean Territory, sinc 2015; *b* 23 Nov. 1965; *s* of late James Bryan and Dorothy Bryan; *m* 1989, Katharine Hilto one *s* one *d*. *Educ:* Arnold Sch.; Magdalene Coll., Cambridge (Schol.; Maxwell Prize, Georg Long Prize; BA Double 1st Law Tripos 1987). Council of Legal Educn Studentship, 198 called to the Bar, Lincoln's Inn, 1988 (Denning Schol.), Bencher, 2013; Supervisor in Law Magdalene Coll., Cambridge, 1988–89; in practice as a barrister specialising in commerci law, 1989–. CEDR Accredited Mediator, 2006; MCIArb 2007. Mem., Herts Communit Foundn Develt Council, 2011–. Mem. Court, Univ. of Hertfordshire, 2011–15. Freema City of London, 2002; Liveryman, Co. of Gardeners, 2002–. *Publications:* (Asst Ed. an contrib.) Encyclopedia of International Commercial Litigation (annually), 2008–. *Recreation* winter sports, travel, gardening, dogs. *Address:* Essex Court Chambers, 24 Lincoln's Inn Field WC2A 3EG. *T:* (020) 7813 8000, *Fax:* (020) 7813 8080. *E:* sjbryan@essexcourt.com. *Club* Travellers, Alpine (Associate).

BRYANT, Christopher John; MP (Lab) Rhondda, since 2001; *b* 11 Jan. 1962; *s* of Re Bryant and Anne Gracie Bryant (*née* Goodwin). *Educ:* Cheltenham Coll.; Mansfield Coll Oxford (MA); Ripon Coll., Cuddesdon (MA, DipTh). Ordained deacon, 1986, priest, 198 Asst Curate, All Saints, High Wycombe, 1986–89; Youth Chaplain, Dio. Peterboroug 1989–91; Organiser, Holborn & St Pancras Lab. Party, 1991–93; Local Govt Develt Office Lab. Party, 1993–94. London Manager, Common Purpose, 1994–96; freelance write 1996–98; Hd, Eur. Affairs, BBC, 1998–2000. Dep. Leader, H of C, 2008–09; Parly Under

Sec. of State (Minister for Europe and Latin America), FCO, 2009–10; Shadow Minister for Immigration, 2011–13, for Welfare Reform, 2013–14, for Culture, Media and Sport, 2014–15; Shadow Sec. of State for Culture, Media and Sport, 2015; Shadow Leader, H of C, 2015–. *Publications:* (ed) Reclaiming the Ground, 1993; (ed) John Smith: an appreciation, 1995; Possible Dreams, 1996; Stafford Cripps: the first modern Chancellor, 1997; Glenda Jackson: the biography, 1998; Parliament: the biography, 2 vols, 2014. *Recreations:* theatre, modern art, Spain. *Address:* House of Commons, SW1A 0AA. *T:* (020) 7219 8315. *E:* bryantc@parliament.uk. *Club:* Ferndale Rugby Football (Vice-Pres.) (Rhondda).

BRYANT, David John, CBE 1980 (MBE 1969); international bowler, 1958–92; *b* 27 Oct. 1931; *s* of Reginald Samuel Harold Bryant and Evelyn Claire (*née* Weaver); *m* 1960, Ruth Georgina (*née* Roberts); two *d. Educ:* Weston Grammar Sch.; St Paul's Coll., Cheltenham; Redland Coll., Bristol (teacher training colls). National Service, RAF, 1950–52; teacher trng, 1953–55; schoolmaster, 1955–71; company director, sports business, 1971–78; Dir, Drakelite Ltd (Internat. Bowls Consultant), 1978–97. Hon. Pres., English Bowling Assocs (formerly Assoc.) Charity Trust, 2002–. World Singles Champion, 1966, 1980 and 1988; World Indoor Singles Champion, 1979, 1980 and 1981; World Indoor Pairs Champion, 1986, 1987, 1989, 1990, 1991 and 1992; Kodak Masters International Singles Champion, 1978, 1979 and 1982; Gateway International Masters Singles Champion, 1984, 1985, 1986, 1987; Woolwich International Singles Champion, 1988, 1989; World Triples Champion, 1980; Commonwealth Games Gold Medallist: Singles: 1962, 1970, 1974 and 1978; Fours: 1962. Numerous national and British Isles titles, both indoor and outdoor. England Indoor Team Captain, 1993, 1994. *Publications:* Bryant on Bowls, 1966; Bowl with Bryant, 1984; Bryant on Bowls, 1985; The Game of Bowls, 1990; Bowl to Win, 1994. *Recreations:* angling, gardening. *Address:* 47 Esmond Grove, Clevedon, Somerset BS21 7HP. *Clubs:* Clevedon Bowling, Clevedon Conservative, Clevedon Promenade Bowling.

BRYANT, His Honour David Michael Arton; a Circuit Judge, Teeside Combined Court Centre, 1989–2007; Designated Family Judge, 1995–2007; *b* 27 Jan. 1942; *s* of Lt-Col and Mrs A. D. Bryant; *m* 1969, Diana Caroline, *d* of Brig. and Mrs W. C. W. Sloan; two *s* one *d. Educ:* Wellington Coll.; Oriel Coll., Oxford (Open Scholar; MA). Called to the Bar, Inner Temple, 1964; practised North Eastern Circuit, 1965–89. Recorder, 1985–89. Mem., Parole Bd, 2007–. *Recreations:* gardening, shooting, tennis, Byzantine history. *Address:* Park Cottage, Sleningford Park, North Stainley, Ripon, N Yorks HG4 3JA. *Club:* Carlton.

BRYANT, Air Vice-Marshal Derek Thomas, CB 1987; OBE 1974; Air Officer Commanding, Headquarters Command and Staff Training and Commandant, Royal Air Force Staff College, 1987–89, retired; *b* 1 Nov. 1933; *s* of Thomas Bryant and Mary (*née* Thurley); *m* 1956, Patricia Dodge (*d* 2014); one *s* one *d. Educ:* Latymer Upper Grammar Sch., Hammersmith. Fighter pilot, 1953; Qualified Flying Instructor, 1957; Sqdn Comdr, 1968–74; OC RAF Coningsby, 1976–78; SASO HQ 38 Gp, 1982–84; Dep. Comdr, RAF Germany, 1984–87; various courses and staff appts. *Recreations:* gardening, golf. *Address:* The Old Stables, Lower Swell, Fivehead, Taunton, Somerset TA3 6PH. *Club:* Royal Air Force.

BRYANT, Prof. Greyham Frank, PhD; FREng, FIET; FIMA; Professor of Control, Imperial College, London University, 1982–98, now Professor Emeritus and Senior Research Fellow; *b* 3 June 1931; *s* of Ernest Noel Bryant and Florence Ivy (*née* Russell); *m* 1955, Iris Sybil Jardine; two *s. Educ:* Reading Univ.; Imperial Coll. (PhD). FIMA 1973; FIET (FIEE 1987); FREng (FEng 1988). Sen. Scientific Officer, Iron and Steel Res., London, 1959–64; Imperial College: Res. Fellow, 1964–67; Reader in Industrial Control, 1975–82. Chm., Broner Consultants, 1979–88; Director: Greycon Consultants, 1985–2000; Circulation Research, 1989–2008. *Publications:* Automation of Tandem Mills (jtly), 1973; (with L. F. Yeung) Multivariable Control and System Design Techniques, 1996; papers on design of management control schemes, multivariable control and modelling, in learned jls. *Recreations:* music, oil painting. *Address:* 18 Wimborne Avenue, Norwood Green, Middlesex UB2 4HB. *T:* (020) 8574 5648.

BRYANT, John Martin, FREng, FIMMM; Joint Chief Executive, Corus Group plc, 1999–2000; *b* 28 Sept. 1943; *s* of William George Bryant and Doris Bryant; *m* 1965, Andrea Irene Emmons; two *s* one *d. Educ:* West Monmouth Sch.; St Catharine's Coll., Cambridge (BA Nat. Sci. 1965; MA). CEng 1993; FIMMM (FIM 1993). Trainee, Steel Co. of Wales, 1965; British Steel, 1967–99: Production/Technical Mgt, Port Talbot works, 1967–78; Works Manager, Hot Rolled Products, Port Talbot, 1978–87; Project Manager, Hot Strip Mill Develt, 1982–87; Works Manager, Cold Rolled Products, Shotton, 1987–88; Dir, Coated Products, 1988–90; Dir, Tinplate, 1990–92; Man. Dir, Strip Products, 1992–96; Exec. Dir, 1996–99; Chief Exec., 1999. Director: ASW plc, 1993–95; Bank of Wales plc, 1996–2001; Welsh Water plc, 2001–14; Glas Cymru Ltd, 2001–14; Costain Gp plc, 2002–13; Chm., Actoris Property, 2009–13. Mem., Occupational Health Adv. Cttee, 1988–94. Trustee, Ogmore Centre, 2003–08. FREng 2000. Hon. DSc Wales, 2000. *Recreations:* Rugby, cricket, theatre, opera, family. *Address:* Broadway Farm, 24 Rogers Lane, Laleston, Bridgend CF32 0LA.

BRYANT, John William; journalist, author and broadcaster; Editor-in-Chief, The Daily Telegraph and The Sunday Telegraph, 2005–06; *b* 25 April 1944; *s* of late James Douglas John Bryant and Mollie Bryant; *m* 1968, Carol Leffman; two *s. Educ:* Sexey's Sch., Bruton; Queen's Coll., Oxford (BA Hons 1966). Edinburgh Evening News, 1967–70; Daily Mail, 1971–86, Exec. Editor, 1980–86; The Times: Man. Editor, 1986–88; Dep. Editor, 1988–90; Editor: Sunday Correspondent, 1990; The European, 1991; Dep. Editor, The Times, 1991–2000; Consultant Editor, Daily Mail, 2000–05. Chm., Evening Standard Editl Cttee, 2009–12. Chm., Press Assoc. Trust, 2008–. Chm. Trustees, London Marathon, 2010– (Vice Chm., 2007–10). *Publications:* Jogging, 1979; 3:59.4: The Quest to Break the Four Minute Mile, 2004; The London Marathon, 2005; The Marathon Makers, 2008; Aubrey's Official Register of London Marathon Runners, 2010; Chris Brasher: the man who made the London Marathon, 2012. *Recreations:* athletics, cross-country and road running, singing (scrumpy'n western). *Address:* 18 Wonford Close, Coombe Lane, Kingston-upon-Thames, Surrey KT2 7XA. *Clubs:* Garrick; Vincent's (Oxford); Thames Hare and Hounds (Pres., 2010–).

BRYANT, Judith Marie, (Mrs H. M. Hodkinson), RGN; retired; Fellow, King's Fund College, 1990–94 (part-time Fellow, 1986–90); *b* 31 Dec. 1942; *d* of Frederic John Bryant and Joan Marion; *m* 1986, Prof. Henry Malcolm Hodkinson, *qv. Educ:* City of London Sch. for Girls; The London Hosp. (RGN 1964); Brunel Univ. (MPhil 1983). Ward Sister, UCH, 1965–69; Nursing Officer, subseq. Sen. Nursing Officer, Northwick Park Hosp., Harrow, 1969–75; Divl Nursing Officer, Harrow, 1975–78; Dist Nursing Officer, Enfield, 1978–82, Victoria, 1982–85; Chief Nursing Officer and Dir of Quality Assurance, Riverside HA, 1985–86; Regl Nursing Officer, NE Thames RHA, 1986–90. Florence Nightingale Meml Scholar, USA and Canada, 1970. Adviser, DHSS Res. Liaison Cttee for the Elderly, 1977–83; Member: SW Herts DHA, 1981–86; NHS Training Authority, Nurses and Midwives Staff Training Cttee, 1986–89; 1930 Fund for Dist Nurses, 1985–2004; Cttee, Nurseline, 1996–2000. Mem., Criminal Injuries Compensation Tribunal (formerly Appeals Panel), 1999–2012. *Publications:* (with H. M. Hodkinson) Sherratt? A Natural Family of Staffordshire Figures, 1991. *Recreations:* opera, gardening. *Address:* 8 Chiswick Square, Burlington Lane, W4 2QG.

BRYANT, Julius John Victor, FSA; Keeper of Word & Image, Victoria & Albert Museum, since 2005; *b* 17 Dec. 1957; *s* of late Robert Bryant and of Dena Bryant (*née* Bond); *m* 1984, Barbara Ann Coffey; one *s. Educ:* St Albans Sch.; University College London; Courtauld Inst. of Art. Paintings Cataloguer, Sotheby's, 1980–81; Mus. Asst, V&A Mus., 1982–83; Asst Curator, 1983–88, Curator, 1989–90, Iveagh Bequest, Kenwood; English Heritage: Hd of Museums Div. and Dir of London Historic Properties, 1990–95; Dir of Museums and Collections, 1995–2002; Chief Curator, 2003–05. Visiting Fellow: Yale Center for British Art, 1985, 2009; Huntington Liby and Art Gall., Calif, 1992; British Council Res. Scholar, Leningrad, 1989; Sen. Res. Fellow, Bard Graduate Center, NY, 2013–. Guest Curator, Sir John Soane's Mus., 2002–05. Member: London Museums Consultative Cttee, 1989–99; Exec. Council, Area Museums Service for SE England, 1992–95; Art Museum Directors' Conf. (formerly Conf. of Nat. and Regl Mus. Dirs), 1998–2005; Hampstead Heath Mgt Cttee, 1990–95; Council, Furniture History Soc., 1998–2000; Mgt Cttee, AHRC (formerly AHRB) Centre for Study of the Domestic Interior, 2002–05; Anglo Sikh Heritage Trail Adv. Gp, 2003–; Adv. Council, Paul Mellon Centre for Studies in British Art, Yale Univ., 2004–09; Apsley House Adv. Panel, 2004–09; Strawberry Hill Conservation Steering Cttee, 2008–11; Houses of Parlt Curator's Office Steering Gp, 2010–; Dep. Chm., Cttee for Historic House Museums, ICOM, 2002–08 (Mem., 1999–); Expert Advr on architectural designs, Adv. Council on Export of Works of Art and Objects of Cultural Interest, 2005–; Pres., Internat. Adv. Cttee of Keepers of Public Collections of Graphic Art, 2012–14 (Mem., 2006–). Pres., Hampstead Heath DFAS, 1989–. Trustee: Chevening House and Estate, 2011–; William Morris Gall. and Brangwyn Gift, 2013–. FSA 1999. Editor, Collections Review, 1997–2003. *Publications:* Marble Hill: the design and use of a Palladian estate, 1986; Finest Prospects, 1986; The Victoria and Albert Museum Guide, 1986; Marble Hill House, 1988; Mrs Howard: a woman of reason, 1988; (jtly) The Landscape of Kenwood, 1990; The Iveagh Bequest, Kenwood, 1990; Robert Adam, 1992; London's Country House Collections, 1993; (jtly) The Trojan War: sculptures by Anthony Caro, 1994, 3rd edn 1998; Turner: painting the nation, 1996; Marble Hill, 2002; The Wernher Collection, 2002; (ed) Decorative Arts from the Wernher Collection, 2002; Catalogue of Paintings in the Iveagh Bequest, Kenwood, 2003; Anthony Caro: a life in sculpture, 2004; Thomas Banks (1735–1805): Britain's first modern sculptor, 2005; Apsley House: the Wellington Collection, 2005; The English Grand Tour, 2005; The Complete Works of Barry Martin, 2007; Anthony Caro: the figurative and narrative sculptures, 2009; (ed) Art and Design for All: the Victoria and Albert Museum, 2011; (jtly) Caro: close up, 2012; (jtly) Gainsborough, Rembrandt, Van Dyck: the treasures of Kenwood, 2012; Alec Cobbe: designs for historic interiors, 2013; (contrib.) William Kent: designing Georgian Britain, 2013; Magnificent Marble Statues: British sculpture in The Mansion House, 2013; (jtly) Word and Image: art, books and design from the National Art Library, 2015; contribs to Oxford DNB, Grove Dictionary of Art; exhibn catalogues; articles in jls. *Recreations:* running around Hampstead Heath, family life. *Address:* Victoria & Albert Museum, Knightsbridge, SW7 2RL.

BRYANT, Keith; QC 2013; *b* Minster, Kent, 23 June 1965; *s* of Keith Furnival and Margaret Edith Bryant; *m* 1994, Kate Morrogh-Bernard; one *s* two *d. Educ:* King's Sch., Rochester; Clare Coll., Cambridge (BA Hons Natural Scis 1986; MA); King's Coll., Cambridge (Dip. Comp. Sci.). Called to the Bar, Middle Temple, 1991; in practice as barrister, specialising in pensions and employment law, 1991–; fee-paid Employment Judge, 2005–. *Recreations:* singing, cooking (and eating), ski-ing, walking. *Address:* Outer Temple Chambers, 222 Strand, WC2R 1BA. *T:* (020) 7353 6381. *E:* keith.bryantqc@outertemple.com.

BRYANT, Laurence Charles; Director Weapons, Defence Equipment and Support, Ministry of Defence, since 2012; *b* Bath, 4 Oct. 1957; *s* of Philip and Hilary Bryant; *m* 1983, Jean Young; two *s. Educ:* Ralph Allen Sch., Bath; Chippenham Tech. Coll. (HND Electrical Engrg 1988); Cranfield Univ. (MSc 1995). MIET 2004; MAPM 2006; Registered Project Professional 2010. Technician, RN Store Depot, Copenacre, 1978–85; Test Engr, Towed Array Sonar, RN Supply and Transport Service, Colerne, 1985–89; Engrg Consultant, Copenacre Reprovisioning Study Team, 1989–91; Quality Manager, RN Armament Depot, Beith, 1991–95; Project Manager: Seawolf, Procurement Exec., Portsmouth, 1996–99; Naval Systems, Matra BAe Dynamics, Stevenage, 2000–02; Defence Procurement Agency: Dep. Team Leader Ground Based Air Defence, Bristol, 2002–04; Team Leader Flight Simulation, Bristol, 2004–06; Hd, UK Mil. Flying Trng System, Bristol, 2006–09, Dep. Dir Combat Air, Bristol, 2009–12, Defence Equipment and Support. *Recreations:* sailing, gardening, pianist. *E:* lapley.cottage@gmail.com.

BRYANT, Rt Rev. Mark Watts; *see* Jarrow, Bishop Suffragan of.

BRYANT, Martin Warwick; Director, Wesleyan Assurance Society, since 2011; *b* 30 June 1952; *s* of Douglas and Marjorie Bryant; *m* 1979, Hilary Mary Southall; one *s* two *d. Educ:* Christ Church, Oxford (MA Hist. and Econs 1975); Univ. of Leeds (MA Econs 1978); Cranfield Sch. of Mgt (MBA 1983). Planning Manager, BOC Gp, 1983–87; Dir of Corporate Develt, Charles Barker plc, 1987–89; Dir of Corporate Develt, Boots Co. plc, 1989–95; Man. Dir, Boots Opticians Ltd, 1995–97; Ops Dir, Boots The Chemists, 1997–2000; Man. Dir, Boots Retail Internat., 2000; Dir of Business Develt, Boots Co. plc, 2000–02; Chief Operating Officer, BP Retail (UK), 2002–04; Dir of Strategy, Home Office, 2004–06; Chief Exec., Shareholder Executive, 2006–07. Non-executive Director: Fire Service Coll., 2008–13; E Midlands Develt Agency, 2009–12; Buying Solutions, 2009–12; non-exec. Advr, Polbita s.p.a., 2007–13. Trustee, Vision Aid Overseas, 2009–; Gov., Nuffield Health, 2013–. *Recreations:* golf, ski-ing, vintage motor cars. *Address:* Upton Grange, Upton, Newark, Notts NG23 5SY. *T:* (01636) 812901. *E:* martinwbryant@aol.com.

BRYANT, Prof. Peter Elwood, FRS 1991; Watts Professor of Psychology, Oxford University, 1980–2004; Fellow of Wolfson College, Oxford, 1980–2004, now Emeritus; *b* 24 June 1937; *s* of Michael Bryant; *m* (marr. diss.); one *s* two *d*; *m* 1995, Prof. Terezinha Nunes, *qv. Educ:* Blundell's Sch.; Clare College, Cambridge (BA 1963; MA 1967); London Univ. (PhD). University Lecturer in Human Experimental Psychology, Oxford, 1967–80; Fellow, St John's Coll., Oxford, 1967–80. Vis. Prof., Oxford Brookes Univ. Editor: British Jl of Developmental Psychol., 1982–88; Cognitive Development, 2000–06. President's award, BPsS, 1984; Dist. Scientific Contribn Award, Soc. for Scientific Study of Reading, 1999. *Publications:* Perception and Understanding in Young Children, 1974; (with L. Bradley) Children's Reading Problems, 1985; (with U. Goswami) Phonological Skills and Learning to Read, 1990; with T. Nunes: Children Doing Mathematics, 1996; Learning & Teaching Mathematics: an international perspective, 1997; Improving Literacy Through Teaching Morphemes, 2006; Children's Reading and Spelling: beyond the first steps, 2009. *Address:* Wolfson College, Oxford OX2 6UD.

BRYANT, Peter George Francis; Under Secretary, Department of Trade and Industry, 1989–92; *b* 10 May 1932; *s* of late George Bryant, CBE and Margaret Bryant; *m* 1961, Jean (*née* Morriss); one *s* one *d. Educ:* Sutton Valence Sch.; Birkbeck Coll., London Univ. (BA). Min. of Supply, 1953–55; BoT, 1955–69; 1st Sec. (Commercial), Vienna (on secondment), 1970–72; Dir of British Trade Drive in S Germany, 1973; Department of Trade (later Department of Trade and Industry), 1974–85; seconded to HM Diplomatic Service as Consul-Gen., Düsseldorf, 1985–88, and Dir-Gen. of Trade and Investment Promotion, FRG, 1988.

BRYANT, Air Chief Marshal Sir Simon, KCB 2011; CBE 2005; Vice President (Oman), BAE Systems, since 2013; *b* 20 June 1956; *s* of Robert Francis and Audrey Ethel Ashby Bryant; *m* 1984, Helen Burns; one *s* one *d. Educ:* Stamford Sch.; Nottingham Univ. (BA Hons Geog. 1977); King's Coll. London (MA Defence Studies 1993); Cranfield Univ. (DSc 2012). CDir 2010; FCIPD 2010; FRAeS 2012; FRIN 2012. Joined RAF, 1974; served with Fighter Sqdns Nos 19, 56 and 23, 1979–89, and VF-101 USN, 1984–87; RAF Personnel Mgt Centre, 1989–91; RAF Staff Coll., 1992; MoD, 1992–95; OC No 43 (Fighter) Sqdn, 1996–99;

Personal Staff Officer to Dep. Comdr, SHAPE, 1999–2001; Sen. British Officer Oman, 2002; AO Scotland and CO, RAF Leuchars, 2003–05; Dir, Jt Capability, 2005–06; COS Personnel and Air Sec., 2006–09; Dep. C-in-C (Personnel) and Air Mem. for Personnel, HQ Air Comd, 2009–10; C-in-C Air Comd and Air ADC to the Queen, 2010–12. Mil. Advr Combat Air, BAE Systems, 2012–13. *Recreations:* Real tennis, squash, golf, ski-ing, diving, trekking.

BRYANT-HERON, Mark Nicholas; QC 2014; a Recorder, since 2005; *b* London, 29 Nov. 1961; *s* of Thomas Michael Edward Bryant and Janet Bryant-Heron; *m* 1989, Elizabeth Pratt; one *s* twin *d*. *Educ:* Netherhall Sch., Cambridge; Clare Coll., Cambridge (BA Law 1984). Called to the Bar, Middle Temple, 1986; in practice as barrister, 1988–, specialising in criminal law, particularly corporate fraud and business crime, bribery and corruption, money laundering and asset forfeiture, revenue and accountancy fraud. *Recreations:* music, cycling, ski-ing, good wine and good company. *Address:* 9–12 Bell Yard, WC2A 2JR. *T:* (020) 7400 1800. *E:* m.bryantheron@912by.com.

BRYARS, Donald Leonard; Commissioner of Customs and Excise, 1978–84 and Director, Personnel, 1979–84, retired; *b* 31 March 1929; *s* of late Leonard and Marie Bryars; *m* 1953, Joan (*née* Yealand); one *d*. *Educ:* Goole Grammar Sch.; Leeds Univ. Joined Customs and Excise as Executive Officer, 1953, Principal, 1964, Asst Sec., 1971; on loan to Cabinet Office, 1976–78; Director, General Customs, 1978–79. Dir (non-exec.), The Customs Annuity Benevolent Fund Inc., 1986–2004. Trustee, Milton's Cottage Trust, 1993–2002. *Address:* 15 Cedars Walk, Chorleywood, Rickmansworth, Herts WD3 5GD. *T:* (01923) 446752. *Club:* Civil Service (Chm., 1981–85).

BRYARS, (Richard) Gavin; composer; *b* 16 Jan. 1943; *s* of Walter Joseph Bryars and Miriam Eleanor Bryars (*née* Hopley); *m* 1st, 1971, Angela Margaret Bigley (marr. diss. 1993); two *d*; 2nd, 1999, Anna Tchernakova; one *s* one *d*. *Educ:* Goole Grammar Sch.; Sheffield Univ. (BA Hons Philosophy). Freelance bassist, 1963–66; Mem. trio, Joseph Holbrooke (improvising), 1964–66, 1998–2005; Lecturer: Northampton Tech. Coll. and Sch. of Art, 1966–67; Portsmouth Coll. of Art, 1969–70; Sen. Lectr, Leicester Poly., 1970–85; Prof. of Music, Leicester Poly., later De Montfort Univ., 1985–96 (part-time, 1994–96). Visiting Professor: Univ. of Victoria, BC, 1999–2001; Univ. of Hertfordshire, 1999–2004; Associate Res. Fellow, Dartington Coll. of Arts, 2005–08. Founder and Dir, Gavin Bryars Ensemble, 1979–. Mem., Collège de Pataphysique, France, 1974– (Pres., sous-commn des Cliques Claques, 1984–; Regent, 2002–). *Compositions* include: The Sinking of the Titanic, 1969; Jesus' Blood Never Failed Me Yet, 1971; Out of Zaleski's Gazebo, 1977; My First Homage, 1978; The Cross Channel Ferry, 1979; The Vespertine Park, The English Mail-Coach, 1980; Les Fiançailles, Allegrasco, 1983; On Photography, Effarene, 1984; String quartet No 1, 1985; Pico's Flight, Sub Rosa, 1986; By the Vaar, The Old Tower of Löbenicht, 1987; Invention of Tradition, Glorious Hill, Doctor Ox's Experiment (Epilogue), 1988; Incipit Vita Nova, 1989; Cadman Requiem, 1989, revd 1996; Alaric I or II, 1989; After the Requiem, String Quartet No 2, 1990; The Black River, The Green Ray, 1991; The White Lodge, 1991; (with Juan Munoz) A Man in a Room Gambling, Die Letzen Tage, 1992; The War in Heaven, The North Shore, 1993; Three Elegies for Nine Clarinets, One Last Bar Then Joe Can Sing, The East Coast, 1994; The South Downs, In Nomine (after Purcell), After Handel's Vesper, Cello Concerto, 1995; The Adnan Songbook, 1996; The Island Chapel, And so ended Kant's travelling in this world, 1997; String Quartet no 3, 1998; First Book of Madrigals, 1998–99; The Porazzi Fragment, 1999; Violin Concerto, 2000; Second Book of Madrigals, 2002; Double Bass Concerto, 2002; Laude Cortonese, vols I, II and III, 2002–09; Third Book of Madrigals, 2003–04; New York (concerto for percussion quintet and orch.), 2004; Lachrymae (viol consort), 2004; From Egil's Saga, 2004; Eight Irish Madrigals, 2004; Creamer Etudes, 2005; Nine Irish Madrigals, 2006; Silva Caledonia, 2006; The Paper Nautilus, 2006; Nothing Like the Sun, 2007; The Church Closest to the Sea, 2007; Sonnets from Scotland, 2008; Ian in the Broch, 2008; Anail De, 2008; Trondur i Gotu, 2008; A Family Likeness, 2008; Laude 35–38, 2008–09; Lauda: the flower of friendship, 2009; Piano Concerto, 2009; The Apotheosis of St Brendan, 2009; Four Songs from the North, 2009; Four Villa I Tatti Madrigals, 2009; Piano Concerto (The Solway Canal), 2010; Ramble on Cortona, 2010; It Never Rains, 2010; Two Love Songs, 2010; Morrison Songbook, 2010; Fifth Book of Madrigals (I Tatti), 2011; Lauda 40–42, 2011–12; Four Battiferri Madrigals, 2011; Underworlds and Overworlds (installation, Leeds), 2012; Four Children's Songs from the Overworld, 2012; Psalm 141, 2012; Song of the Open Road, 2012; The Beckett Songbook, 2012–14; Psalm 141, 2012; Three Choral Pieces from the Faroe Islands, 2012; Through the Halls, 2012; Dancing with Pannonica, 2012; The Open Road, 2012; The Voice of St Columba, 2012; The Fifth Century, 2014; Sixth Book of Madrigals, 2015; De Profundis Aquarum, 2015; *opera:* Medea, for Opéra de Lyon, 1982, revd 1984, 1995; Doctor Ox's Experiment, for ENO, 1998; G, for Staatstheater Mainz, 2002; Marilyn Forever, Victoria BC, 2013; *ballet*: Four Elements, 1990; Wonderlawn, 1994; 2, 1995; BIPED, 2000; Writings on Water, 2002; Amjad, 2007; The Third Light, Reverence, 2010; Dido-Orfeo, 2011; Pneuma, Bordeaux, 2014; Four Seasons, Sao Paolo, 2014; 11th Floor, Cullberg, 2014; Peer Gynt, Bielefeld, 2014; Laude, Munich 2014; *theatre*: To Define Happiness, Tallinn, 2007; *film music*: Last Summer, 2000; Sea and Stars, 2002; Season of Mists, 2008; Our Chekhov, 2010; Proezd Serova, 2013; *radio:* (with Blake Morrison) The Pythagorean Comma, BBC Radio 3, 2012. Has made recordings. Hon. Fellow, Bath Spa Univ., 2008. Hon. DArts Plymouth, 2006. *Recreations:* supporting, from a distance, Yorkshire CCC and Queens Park Rangers FC; dalmatians. *Address:* c/o Schott Music, 48 Great Marlborough Street, W1F 7BB. *T:* (020) 7534 0750. *W:* www.gavinbryars.com.

BRYCE, Gordon, RSA 1993 (ARSA 1976); RSW 1976; painter; Head of Fine Art, Gray's School of Art, Aberdeen, 1986–95; *b* 30 June 1943; *s* of George and Annie Bryce; *m* 1st, 1966, Margaret Lothian (marr. diss. 1976); two *s*; 2nd, 1984, Hilary Duthie; one *s* two *d*. *Educ:* Edinburgh Acad.; George Watson's Coll., Edinburgh; Edinburgh Coll. of Art. Dip. in Art. Exhibited widely in UK, Europe and USA, 1965–, esp. Scottish Gall., Edinburgh and Thackeray Gall., London; 50 one-man exhibns of painting, UK and overseas; paintings in public and private collections, UK, Europe, USA, Canada. *Recreation:* fly fishing. *Address:* Sylva Cottage, 2 Culter House Road, Milltimber, Aberdeen AB13 0EN. *T:* (01224) 733274.

BRYCE, Ian James G.; *see* Graham-Bryce.

BRYCE, Hon. Dame Quentin Alice Louise, AD 2014 (AC 2003; AO 1988); CVO 2011; Governor-General of Australia, 2008–14; *b* 23 Dec. 1942; *d* of Norman Walter Strachan and Edwina Naida Strachan (*née* Wetzel); *m* 1964, Michael John Strachan Bryce, AM, AE; three *s* two *d*. *Educ:* Moreton Bay Coll., Queensland; Univ. of Queensland (BA 1962; LLB 1965). Admitted to Qld Bar, 1965; Lectr and Tutor, Law Sch., Univ. of Qld, 1968–82; Dir, Women's Inf. Service Qld, Dept of PM and Cabinet, 1984–87; Qld Dir, Human Rights and Equal Opportunity Commn, 1987; Fed. Sex Discrimination Comr, 1988–93; Chm. and CEO, Nat. Childcare Accreditation Council, 1993–96; Principal and CEO, The Women's Coll., Univ. of Sydney, 1997–2003; Governor of Qld, 2003–08. US State Dept Visitor, 1978; Mem., Aust. Delegn to UN Human Rights Commn, Geneva, 1989–92. Nat. Pres., Assoc. for Welfare of Children in Hosp., 1978–81; Vice Pres., Qld Council for Civil Liberties, 1979–80; Pres., Women's Cricket Australia, 1999–2003; Director: Aust. Children's TV Foundn Bd, 1982–92; YWCA, Sydney, 1997–2000; Bradman Foundn, 2002–03; Convener, Nat. Women's Adv. Council, 1982–83 (Mem., 1978–81); Chairman: Jessie Street Nat. Women's Liby, 1996–98; Nat. Breast Cancer Centre Adv. Network, 1996–2003; Member: Internat. Yr for Disabled Persons Legal Cttee, Qld, 1981; Family Planning Council, Qld, 1981–92; Nat. Cttee on Discrimination in Employment and Occupation, 1982–86; Bd, Schizophrenia Foundn Aust., 1987–90; Bd, Abused Child Trust, Qld, 1988–89; Bd, Mindcare Mental Health Foundn, 1990–95; Nat. Alternative Dispute Resolution Adv. Council, 1995–97; Bd, Plan Internat., 1996–2003; Sydney IVF Ethics Cttee, 2000–03. Presiding Mem., Bd of Mgt, Dip. of Policing Practice, NSW, 1998–2001. Mem. Council, Central Qld Univ., 1999–2001. Patron, Nat. Alliance of Girls' Schs, 2001–. Hon. LLD: Macquarie, 1998; Qld, 2006; Sydney, 2010; Melbourne, 2012; Hon. DLitt: Charles Sturt, 2002; Western Sydney, 2012; DUniv Griffith, 2003; Qld Univ. of Technol., 2004; James Cook, 2008. *Address:* GPO Box 2434, Brisbane, Qld 4001, Australia.

BRYDEN, David John, PhD; FSA; Property Manager, Felbrigg Hall and Sheringham Park, National Trust, 1997–2001; *b* 23 Nov. 1943; *s* of George Bryden and Marion (*née* Bellingham); *m* 1964, Helen Margaret Willison; two *s*. *Educ:* Univ. of Leicester (BScEng); Linacre Coll., Oxford (Dip. in Hist. and Philos. of Sci.); Gonville and Caius Coll., Cambridge (MA 1973); St Edmund's Coll., Cambridge (PhD 1993). FSA 1993. Asst Keeper II, Royal Scottish Mus., 1966–70; Curator, Whipple Mus. of Hist. of Sci., Univ. of Cambridge, 1970–78; Fellow and Steward, St Edmund's House, 1977–78; Asst Keeper I, Science Mus. Library, 1979–87; Academic Administrator, Gresham Coll., 1987–88; Keeper, Dept of Sci., Technol. and Working Life, Nat. Museums of Scotland, 1988–96. Medal Lectr, Scientific Instrument Soc., 1998; Somerville Meml Lectr, British Sundial Soc., 2010. Pershore Abbey Flagmaster, 2011–. *Publications:* Scottish Scientific Instrument Makers 1600–1900, 1972; Napier's Bones: a history and instruction manual, 1992; (jtly) A Classified Bibliography on the history of scientific instruments, 1997; articles on early scientific instruments, history of science and technology, printing history and bibliography, numismatics. *Address:* 11 Pensham Hill, Pershore, Worcs WR10 3HA.

BRYDEN, Prof. Harry Leonard, PhD; FRS 2005; Professor of Physical Oceanography, University of Southampton, since 2000; *b* 9 July 1946; *s* of Harry L. and Ruth F. Bryden; *m* 1988, Mary E. Woodgate-Jones; four *s*. *Educ:* Dartmouth Coll. (AB Maths 1968); Massachusetts Inst. of Technol. and Woods Hole Oceanographic Instn (PhD Oceanography 1975). Postdoctoral Res. Associate, Oregon State Univ., 1975–77; Woods Hole Oceanographic Institution: Asst Scientist, 1977–80; Associate Scientist, 1980–88; Sen. Scientist, 1988–92; Physical Oceanographer: Inst. of Oceanographic Scis, Surrey, 1993–95; Southampton Oceanography Centre, 1995–2000. Vis. Fellow, Wolfson Coll., Oxford Univ., 1988–89. Henry Stommel Res. Medal, American Meteorol Soc., 2003; Prince Albert I Medal, IAPSO, 2009; Fridtjof Nansen Medal, Eur. Geoscis Union, 2013; Challenger Medal, Challenger Soc. for Marine Science, 2014. *Publications:* numerous refereed scientific pubns on role of the ocean in climate, ocean heat and freshwater transports, exchange between Atlantic and Mediterranean through the Strait of Gibraltar. *Recreation:* walking in the country. *Address:* Ocean and Earth Science, University of Southampton, Empress Dock, Southampton SO14 3ZH. *T:* (023) 8059 6437, *Fax:* (023) 8059 6400.

BRYDEN, William Campbell Rough, (Bill Bryden), CBE 1993; director and writer; Head of Drama Television, BBC Scotland, 1984–93; *b* 12 April 1942; *s* of late George Bryden and of Catherine Bryden; *m* 1st, 1971, Hon. Deborah Morris (marr. diss.), *d* of 3rd Baron Killanin, MBE, TD; one *s* one *d*; 2nd, 2008, Angela Douglas. *Educ:* Hillend Public Sch.; Greenock High Sch. Documentary writer, Scottish Television, 1963–64; Assistant Director, Belgrade Theatre, Coventry, 1965–67; Royal Court Th., London, 1967–69; Associate Director: Royal Lyceum Th., Edinburgh, 1971–74; National Th., subseq. RNT, 1975–85; Dir, Cottesloe Theatre (Nat. Theatre), 1978–80. Director: *opera:* Parsifal, 1988, The Cunning Little Vixen, 1990, 2003, Royal Opera House, Covent Garden; The Silver Tassie, Coliseum, 2000; *stage:* Bernstein's Mass, GSMD, 1987; A Life in the Theatre, Haymarket, 1989; The Ship, Harland and Wolff Shipyard, Glasgow, 1990; Cops, Greenwich, 1991; A Month in the Country, Albery, 1994; The Big Picnic, Harland and Wolff Shipyard, Glasgow (also writer), 1994 (televised 1996); Son of Man, RSC, 1995; Uncle Vanya, Chichester, 1996; Three Sisters, Birmingham, 1998; The Good Hope, NT, 2001; The Creeper, Playhouse, 2006; Small Craft Warnings, Arcola, 2008. *Television:* Exec. Producer: Tutti Frutti, by John Byrne, 1987 (Best Series, BAFTA awards); The Play on 1 (series), 1989; Dir, The Shawl, by David Mamet, 1989. *Radio:* includes, 2000–: HMS Ulysses, Daisy Miller, The Plutocrat, Charge of the Light Brigade, The Last Tycoon. Member Board, Scottish Television, 1979–85. Dir of the Year, Laurence Olivier Awards, 1985, Best Dir, Brit. Th. Assoc. and Drama Magazine Awards, 1986, and Evening Standard Best Dir Award, 1985 (for The Mysteries, NT, 1985). Hon. FGSM; Hon. Fellow: Rose Bruford Coll.; Queen Margaret Coll., Edinburgh. DUniv Stirling 1991. *Publications:* (with Nobby Clark) Bryden & Clark: lives in the theatre, 2014; *plays:* Willie Rough, 1972; Benny Lynch, 1974; Old Movies, 1977; *screenplay:* The Long Riders, 1980; *films:* (writer and director) Ill Fares The Land, 1982; The Holy City (for TV), 1985; Aria, 1987. *Recreation:* music.

BRYDIE, Isobel Gunning, MBE 1997; Lord-Lieutenant for West Lothian, since 2002; *b* 2 Sept. 1942; *d* of Thomas and Sarah Hardie; *m* 1965, John Lawrie Brydie; one *s* one *d* (and one *s* decd). *Educ:* Broxburn High Sch. Mem. Bd, Livingston Develt Corp., 1982–96; Mem. Bd, 1996, Chm., 1997–99, W Lothian NHS Trust. *Recreations:* walking, curling, equestrian. *Address:* Limekilns, 29 Main Street, East Calder, West Lothian EH53 0ES. *T:* (01506) 880800. *Club:* Edinburgh Ladies Curling.

BRYDON, Donald Hood, CBE 2004 (OBE 1993); Chairman: Medical Research Council, since 2012; Sage Group, since 2012 (non-executive Director, since 2012); Chance to Shine Foundation, since 2014; LifeSight Ltd, since 2015; London Stock Exchange, since 2015; *b* 25 May 1945; *s* of late James Hood Brydon and Mary Duncanson (*née* Young); *m* 1st, 1971, Joan Victoria (marr. diss. 1995); one *s* one *d*; 2nd, 1996, Corrine Susan Jane Green. *Educ:* George Watson's Coll., Edinburgh; Univ. of Edinburgh (BSc). Econs Dept, Univ. of Edinburgh, 1967–70; British Airways Pension Fund, 1970–77; Barclays Investment Manager's Office, 1977–81; Dep. Man. Dir, Barclays Investment Mgt Ltd, 1981–86; BZW Investment Management Ltd: Dir, 1986–88; Man. Dir, 1988–91; BZW Asset Management Ltd: Chm. and Chief Exec., 1991–94; non-exec. Chm., 1994–95; Barclays de Zoete Wedd: Dep. Chief Exec., 1994–96; Acting Chief Exec., 1996; AXA Investment Managers SA: Chief Exec., 1997–2002; Chm., 1997–2006. Chairman: London Metal Exchange, 2003–10; Smiths Group plc, 2004–13; Taylor Nelson Sofres plc, 2006–08; AXA Framlington, 2006–08; Royal Mail, 2009–15. Director: London Stock Exchange, 1991–98; Edinburgh Inca Investment Trust, 1996–2001; Allied Domecq, 1997–2005; Amersham (formerly Nycomed Amersham), 1997–2004 (Chm., 2003–04); Edinburgh UK Tracker Trust, 1997–2006; AXA UK (formerly Sun Life and Provincial Hldgs), 1997–2007; AXA Investment Managers SA, 2006–12. Chairman: Financial Services Practitioner Panel, 2001–04; Code Cttee, Panel on Takeovers and Mergers, 2002–06. Pres., Eur. Asset Mgt Assoc., 1999–2001. Dep. Pres., Inst. for Financial Services, 2005–06; Chm., *ifs* Sch. of Finance, 2006–09. Chairman: Eur. Children's Trust, 1999–2001; EveryChild, 2003–08; David Rattray Meml Trust (UK), 2007–10. *Publications:* (jtly) Economics of Technical Information Services, 1972; (jtly) Pension Fund Investment, 1988. *Recreations:* golf, Reading FC. *Clubs:* Caledonian; Golf House (Elie); Highgate Golf.

BRYDON, Robert, MBE 2013; actor and writer; *b* Swansea, 3 May 1965; *s* of Howard Jones and Joy Brydon Jones; *né* Robert Brydon Jones; surname changed to Brydon by deed poll 2006; *m* 1st; one *s* two *d*; 2nd, 2006, Claire Holland; two *s*. *Educ:* St John's Sch., Porthcawl; Dumbarton House Sch., Swansea; Porthcawl Comp. Sch.; Royal Welsh Coll. of Music and Drama (Hon. Fellow, 2004). Radio and TV presenter, BBC Wales, 1986–92. *Television:* actor and writer: Marion and Geoff, 2000–03; Human Remains, 2000; Director's Commentary, 2004; The Keith Barret Show, 2004–05; Rob Brydon's Annually Retentive, 2006–07; Rob Brydon's Identity Crisis, 2008; The Trip, 2010; The Rob Brydon Show, 2010–12; The Gue

List, 2014; actor: The Way We Live Now, 2001; Cruise of the Gods, 2002; Little Britain, 2005; Kenneth Tynan, In Praise of Hardcore, 2005; Supernova, 2005–06; Gavin and Stacey, 2007–09; Heroes & Villains: Napoleon, 2007; The Gruffalo, 2009; The Trip (series), 2010; The Best of Men, 2012; Room on the Broom (voice), 2012; Gangsta Granny, 2013; The Trip to Italy (series), 2014; presenter: Would I Lie to You?, 2009–; Neil Diamond: One Night Only (Sunday Night at the Palladium), 2014; *radio*: I'm Sorry I Haven't a Clue, 2006–; *films:* First Knight, 1995; Lock, Stock and Two Smoking Barrels, 1998; 24 Hour Party People, 2002; MirrorMask, 2005; A Cock and Bull Story, 2005; stand-up show, Rob Brydon, UK tour, 2009; *theatre*: The Painkiller, Lyric, Belfast, 2011; A Chorus of Disapproval, Harold Pinter Th., 2012; Future Conditional, Old Vic, 2015; *recording:* Islands in the Stream, with Ruth Jones and Sir Tom Jones for Comic Relief, 2009. *Publications:* Making Divorce Work (as Keith Barret), 2004; Small Man in a Book (autobiog.), 2011. *Recreations:* playing the guitar badly, Apple gadgets, country walks, drinking milk and eating biscuits, thinking about Sydney. *Address:* c/o United Agents, 12–26 Lexington Street, W1F 0LE. *E:* mvincent@unitedagents.co.uk.

BRYER, Prof. Anthony Applemore Mornington, OBE 2009; FSA 1972; Professor of Byzantine Studies, University of Birmingham, 1980–99, now Emeritus; Senior Research Fellow, King's College London, since 1996; *b* 31 Oct. 1937; *e s* of late Group Captain Gerald Mornington Bryer, OBE and of Joan Evelyn (*née* Grigsby); *m* 1st, 1961, Elizabeth Lipscomb (*d* 1995); three *d*; 2nd, 1998, Jennifer Ann Banks, widow. *Educ:* Canford Sch.; Sorbonne Univ.; Balliol Coll., Oxford (Scholar; BA, MA; DPhil 1967); Athens Univ. Nat. Service, RAF (Adjutant), 1956–58. University of Birmingham: Research Fellow, 1964–65, Lectr, 1965–73, Sen. Lectr, 1973–76, in Medieval History; Reader in Byzantine Studies, 1976–79; Dir of Byzantine Studies, 1969–76; Dir, Centre for Byzantine, Ottoman and Modern Greek Studies, 1976–94; Public Orator, 1991–98. Fellow, Inst. for Advanced Res. in Humanities, Univ. of Birmingham, 1999–. Visiting Fellow: Dumbarton Oaks, Harvard, 1971–; Merton Coll., Oxford, 1985. Founder and Dir, annual British Byzantine Symposia, 1966–; Chm., British Nat. Cttee, Internat. Byzantine Assoc., 1989–95 (Sec., 1976–89); former Vice-Pres., Nat. Trust for Greece; Pres., British Inst. of Archaeology, Ankara, 2002–07; Consultant to Cyprus Govt on res. in humanities, 1988–89; field trips to Trebizond and Pontos, 1959–; Hellenic Cruise lectr, 1967–97; British Council specialist lectr, Greece, Turkey, Latvia, Albania and Australia; Loeb Lectr, Harvard, 1979; Vis. Byzantinist, Medieval Acad. of America, 1987; Wiles Lectr, QUB, 1990; Runciman Lectr, KCL, 1997. Convenor, Internat. Congress of Byzantine Studies, 2006. Chm., Runciman Award, 1999. Co-founder, Byzantine and Modern Greek Studies, 1975–. *Publications:* Byzantium and the Ancient East, 1970; Iconoclasm, 1977; The Empire of Trebizond and the Pontos, 1980; (with David Winfield) The Byzantine Monuments and Topography of the Pontos, 2 vols, 1985; (with Heath Lowry) Continuity and Change in late Byzantine and Early Ottoman Society, 1986; Peoples and Settlement in Anatolia and the Caucasus 800–1900, 1988; The Sweet Land of Cyprus, 1993; Mount Athos, 1996; The Post-Byzantine Monuments of the Pontos, 2002; articles in learned jls. *Recreation:* cricket in Albania. *Address:* 33 Crosbie Road, Harborne, Birmingham B17 9BG. *T:* (0121) 427 1207. *Clubs:* Buckland (Birmingham); Lochaline Social (Morvern); Black Sea (Trabzon).

BRYER, Dr David Ronald William, CMG 1996; Director, Oxfam, 1992–2001; Chairman, Oxfam International, 2003–07; *b* 15 March 1944; *s* of Ronald Bryer and Betty Bryer (*née* Rawlinson); *m* 1980, Margaret Isabel, *e d* of Sir Eric Bowyer, KCB, KBE and Elizabeth (*née* Nicholls); one *s* one *d*. *Educ:* King's Sch., Worcester; Worcester Coll., Oxford (MA, DPhil); Manchester Univ. (Dip. Teaching English Overseas). Teaching and research, Lebanon and Britain, 1964–65, 1967–74 and 1979–81; Asst Keeper, Ashmolean Museum, 1972–74; Oxfam, 1975–2001: Field Dir, Middle East, 1975–79; Co-ordinator, Africa, 1981–84; Overseas Dir, 1984–91; Sen. Advr, Henry Dunant Centre for Humanitarian Dialogue 2001–03. Vis. Fellow, British Acad., 1972. Chm., Steering Cttee for Humanitarian Response, Geneva, 1995–97; Mem., Sen. Adv. Bd, DFID Humanitarian Emergency Response Rev., 2010–11. Chairman: Eurostep, 1993–94; British Overseas Aid Gp, 1998–2000; Home-Start Internat., 2008–11. Mem., UN High Level Panel on financing for develt, 2001. Member: Council, VSO, 1992–2008; Wilton Park Academic Council, 1999–2008; Court, Oxford Brookes Univ., 1999–2003. Lay Canon and Mem. Chapter, Worcester Cathedral, 2013–. Board Member: Save the Children UK, 2002–10; Oxfam America, 2003–07; WWF-UK, 2009–14. Chm., Malvern Hills DFAS, 2012–15. *Publications:* The Origins of the Druze Religion, in Der Islam, 1975; articles on humanitarian and development issues. *Recreations:* family and friends, travel, esp. Eastern Mediterranean, walking. *Address:* Bracken Lodge, Eaton Road, Malvern Wells, Worcs WR14 4PE.

BRYER, Ven. Paul Donald; Archdeacon of Dorking, since 2014; *b* Worthing, 21 June 1958; *s* of Maurice Bryer and Janine Bryer; *m* 1985, Fiona Mary Linnell; two *s* one *d*. *Educ:* Worthing Boy's High Sch.; Bishop Otter Coll., Chichester (BEd Sussex Univ. 1980); St John's Coll., Nottingham (DipTh 1990); Nottingham Univ. (MA 1996). Teacher: Midhurst Grammar Sch., 1980–82; Therfield Sch., Leatherhead, 1982–88; ordained deacon, 1990, priest, 1991; Curate, St Stephen, Tonbridge, 1990–94; Team Vicar, St Paul, Camberley, 1994–99; Vicar, St Mary, Camberley, 1999–2001; Locum Priest, St John, Trentham, Dio. of Wellington, NZ, 2000; Vicar, St Paul, Dorking, 2001–14; Rural Dean, Dorking, 2009–14. Hon. Canon, Guildford Cathedral, 2014–. *Recreations:* squash, long distance walks, mountain biking, running, sea kayaking, theatre, contemporary art, Southampton FC. *Address:* The Old Cricketers, Portsmouth Road, Ripley, Surrey GU23 6ER. *T:* (01483) 479300, *Fax:* (01483) 790333. *E:* paul.bryer@cofeguildford.org.uk. *W:* www.twitter.com/paulbdorking.

BRYN, Kare; Secretary-General, European Free Trade Association, 2006–12; *b* 12 March 1944; *m*; four *c*. *Educ:* Norwegian Sch. of Econs and Business Admin. Joined Norwegian Foreign Service, 1969; served in London, Belgrade, Oslo, Geneva, 1971–84; Hd of Div., 1984, Asst Dir Gen., 1985–89, Multilateral Econ. Co-operation; Dir Gen., Dept for Natural Resources and Envmtl Affairs, 1989–99; Ambassador: to WTO and EFTA, Geneva, 1999–2003; to Netherlands, 2003–06. Comdr, Order of St Olav (Norway), 1998. *Address:* c/o European Free Trade Association, 9–11 rue de Varembé, 1211 Geneva 20, Switzerland.

BUBB, Sir Stephen (John Limrick), Kt 2011; JP; Chief Executive, Association of Chief Executives of Voluntary Organisations, since 2000; Secretary General, Euclid, European Third Sector Leaders Network, since 2006; *b* 5 Nov. 1952; *s* of John William Edward Bubb and Diana Rosemary Bubb (*née* Willatts); civil partnership 2006, William Anthony Vetters. *Educ:* Gillingham Grammar Sch.; Christ Church, Oxford (MA PPE 1975). FCIPD 2004. Economist, NEDO, 1975–76; Res. Officer, TGWU, 1976–80; Negotiations Officer, NUT, 1980–87; Hd, Pay Negotiations for Local Govt, AMA, 1987–95; Founding Dir, Nat. Lottery Charities Bd, 1995–2000. Chairman: Adventure Capital Fund, 2006–; Social Investment Business (formerly Future Builders England), 2008–. Pt-time tutor, Open Univ., 1982–87. Founder Dir, Metropolitan Authorities Recruitment Agency, 1990–95. Mem. (Lab), Lambeth Council, 1982–86 (Chief Whip). Mem., W Lambeth HA, 1982–89; non-exec. Mem., Lambeth, Lewisham and Southwark HA, 1998–2002. Ind. Assessor for Govt Appts, 1999–2010; Public Appointment Assessor, 2012–. Member: Tyson Task Force on Non-exec. Dir Appts, 2002; Honours Cttee, Cabinet Office, 2005–; Civil Soc. Cttee, Commonwealth Foundn, 2008–12; Dir, Big Society Trust, 2011–14. Chm., Strategy Cttee, Govs of Guy's and St Thomas' Trust, 2004–07. Founding Mem., Pakistan Develt Network, 2006–07. Youth Court Magistrate for Inner London, 1980–2000. Founder Chair, Lambeth Landmark, 1982–88. Chm., City of Oxford Orch., 1993–95. Mem., Court, Southbank Univ., 2012–. Trustee, Helen and Douglas House Hospice, 2014–. JP 1980. FRSA 1998. *Publications:* People are Key?, 2003; And Why Not?: tapping the talent of not-for-profit chief executives, 2004; Only Connect: a leader's guide to networking, 2005; Choice and Voice: Third Sector role in service delivery, 2006; Public Matters, 2007; Castles in the Air, 2007; At Tipping Point, 2009; The Big Society: moving from romanticism to reality, 2010; Rediscovering Charity: defining our role with the state, 2010. *Recreations:* genealogy, travel, fine art and fine wine, the Anglican church, making a difference. *Address:* 4 Lyham Close, SW2 5QE. *E:* stephen.bubb@acevo.org.uk. *Clubs:* Oxford and Cambridge, New Cavendish.

BUCCLEUCH, 10th Duke of, *cr* 1663, **AND QUEENSBERRY,** 12th Duke of, *cr* 1684; **Richard Walter John Montagu Douglas Scott,** KBE 2000; DL; FRSE, FRSGS; Baron Scott of Buccleuch, 1606; Earl of Buccleuch, Baron Scott of Whitchester and Eskdaill, 1619; Earl of Doncaster and Baron Tynedale (Eng.), 1662; Earl of Dalkeith, 1663; Marquis of Dumfriesshire, Earl of Drumlanrig and Sanquhar, Viscount of Nith, Torthorwold and Ross, Baron Douglas, 1684; *b* 14 Feb. 1954; *e s* of 9th Duke of Buccleuch, KT, VRD and Jane (*née* McNeill); *S* father, 2007; *m* 1981, Lady Elizabeth Kerr (*see* Duchess of Buccleuch); two *s* two *d*. *Educ:* Eton; Christ Church, Oxford. Dir, Border Television, 1989–90, 2000. Member: Nature Conservancy Council, 1989–91; Scottish Natural Heritage, 1992–95 (Chm., SW Reg., 1992–95); ITC, 1991–98 (Dep. Chm., 1996–98); Millennium Commn, 1994–2003. Trustee: Nat. Heritage Meml Fund, 2000–05; Royal Collection Trust, 2011–; President: RSGS, 1999–2005; NT for Scotland, 2002–12; Royal Scottish Agricultural Benevolent Inst., 2007–; Royal Blind and Scottish Nat. Inst. for War Blinded, 2007–. Mem. Council, Winston Churchill Meml Trust, 1993–2005. Dist Councillor, Nithsdale, 1984–90. DL Nithsdale and Annandale and Eskdale, 1987, Roxburgh, Ettrick and Lauderdale, 2011. Hon. Col, 52nd Lowland 6th Bn, Royal Regt of Scotland, 2010. FRSGS 2006; FRSE 2007. Hon. Fellow, UHI, 2002. *Heir: s* Earl of Dalkeith, *qv*. *Address:* Dabton, Thornhill, Dumfriesshire DG3 5AR. *T:* (01848) 330467.

BUCCLEUCH, Duchess of; Elizabeth Marian Frances Montagu Douglas Scott; *b* 8 June 1954; *y d* of 12th Marquess of Lothian, KCVO and of Antonella (*née* Newland), OBE; *m* 1981, Earl of Dalkeith (*see* Duke of Buccleuch and Queensberry); two *s* two *d*. *Educ:* London Sch. of Economics (BSc 1975). Radio journalist, BBC R4, 1977–81. Chairman: Scottish Ballet, 1990–95; Heritage Educn Trust, 1999. Mem. Council, National Trust, 2000. Trustee: Nat. Museums of Scotland, 1991–99; British Mus., 1999. Chm. Council of Mgt, Arts Educnl Schs, London, 1999–2003. *Recreations:* reading, theatre, music, gardening. *Address:* 24 Lansdowne Road, W11 3LL. *T:* (020) 7727 6573, *Fax:* (020) 7229 7279.

See also Earl of Dalkeith.

BUCHAN, family name of **Baron Tweedsmuir**.

BUCHAN, 17th Earl of, *cr* 1469; **Malcolm Harry Erskine;** Lord Auchterhouse, 1469; Lord Cardross, 1610; Baron Erskine, 1806; *b* 4 July 1930; *s* of 16th Earl of Buchan and Christina, Dowager Countess of Buchan (*d* 1994), *d* of late Hugh Woolner and adopted *d* of late Lloyd Baxendale; *S* father, 1984; *m* 1957, Hilary Diana Cecil, *d* of late Sir Ivan McLannahan Power, 2nd Bt; two *s* two *d*. *Educ:* Eton. JP Westminster, 1972–2000. *Heir: s* Lord Cardross, *qv*. *Address:* 6 Richmond Hill, Bath BA1 5QT. *Club:* Carlton.

BUCHAN, Prof. Alastair Mitchell, DSc; FRCP, FRCPC, FRCPE, FMedSci; Professor in Stroke Medicine, since 2009, Dean of Medicine and Head, Medical Sciences Division, since 2008, Director, Acute Vascular Imaging Centre (formerly Unit), since 2006, and Hon. Consultant Neurologist, since 2004, University of Oxford; Professorial Fellow of Corpus Christi College, Oxford, since 2009; Senior Investigator, National Institute for Health Research, since 2008; *b* 16 Oct. 1955; *s* of Prof. Alan Robson Buchan and Dorothy Mitchell; *m* 1999, Angelika S. Kaiser; two *d*. *Educ:* Repton Sch.; Sidney Sussex Coll., Cambridge (BA 1977; MA 1981); University Coll., Oxford (BM BCh 1980; MA 2008; DSc 2008). FRCPC 1986; FRCPE 1997; FRCP 2001. Radcliffe Travelling Fellow, UC, Oxford, 1983–85; MRC Centennial Fellow, Cornell Univ., NY, 1985–88; Asst Prof. of Neurol., Univ. of Western Ontario, 1988–91; Associate Prof. of Medicine and Anatomy, Univ. of Ottawa, 1991–95; Prof. of Neurol. and Heart and Stroke Foundn Prof. of Stroke Res., Univ. of Calgary, 1995–2004; Professor of Clinical Geratol., Oxford Univ., 2004–09. R&D Chair, Canadian Stroke Consortium, 1993–06; Director: Canadian Stroke Network, 1999–2004; UK Stroke Network, 2005–08. Member: Stroke Strategy Cttee, DoH, 2006–; Stroke Bd, Charité Hosp., Berlin, 2008–. Dir, Oxford Univ. Hosps NHS Trust Strategic Partnership Bd, 2008– (formerly Strategic Partnership Bd and NHS Trust, John Radcliffe Hosp.). Member: American Acad. of Neurol., 1983–; Canadian Neurol Assoc., 1986–; Internat. Soc. of Cerebral Flow and Metabolism, 1987–; Internat. Stroke Soc., 1988; Soc. for Neurosci., 1988–; Assoc. of British Neurologists, 2000–; American Neurol Assoc., 2002–; Stroke Soc. of Australia, 2005–. Nuffield Med. Trustee, 2008–. Mem. Council, Oxford Univ., 2008–. Gov., Repton Sch., Derbys, 2005–. FMedSci 2007. Hon. Fellow, Green Coll., Oxford, 2004. Hon. LLD Calgary, 2009. *Publications:* Maturation Phenomenon of Cerebral Ischaemic Injury, 2003; contrib. Lancet, New England Jl of Medicine, Nature, Nature Medicine, Jl of Cerebral Blood Flow and Metabolism, Stroke, Jl of Neurosci., Annals of Neurol., Trends in Pharmacol Scis. *Recreations:* archaeology, antiquities, art and world history. *Address:* Medical Sciences Division, University of Oxford, John Radcliffe Hospital, Headington, Oxford OX3 9DU. *T:* (01865) 220346, *Fax:* (01865) 221354. *E:* alastair.buchan@medsci.ox.ac.uk; Ashtree House, Waterperry Road, Worminghall, Bucks HP18 9JN. *Clubs:* Athenæum; Osler House (Oxford).

BUCHAN, Dennis Thorne, RSA 1991 (ARSA 1975); painter; *b* 25 April 1937; *s* of David S. Buchan and Mary Buchan (*née* Clark); *m* 1965, Elizabeth Watson (marr. diss. 1977); one *s* one *d*. *Educ:* Arbroath High Sch.; Dundee Coll. of Art; Patrick Allan Fraser Coll., Arbroath; Dundee Coll. of Art (DA 1958). Nat. Service, RAEC, 1960–62. Lectr in Drawing and Painting, Duncan of Jordanstone Coll. of Art, 1965–94. Mem., SSA, 1961–74. *Solo exhibitions:* Douglas and Foulis Gall., 1965; Saltire Soc., Edinburgh Fest., 1974; Compass Gall., 1975, 2006, A Span of Shores, 1994; Traquair House, Peebles, 1996; Pentacle Business Centre, Glasgow, 2002; The Meffan, Forfar, 2005; *group exhibitions* include: Six Coastal Artists, Demarco Gall., Edinburgh, 1965; Seven Painters in Dundee, Scottish Nat. Gall. of Modern Art, and tour, 1972; Compass Contribution, Tramway, Glasgow, 1990; Scottish Contemporary Painting, Flowers East, London, 1993; Five Scottish Artists, Centre d'Art en l'Ile, Geneva, 1994; Brechin Arts Fest., 2008; Scottish Painters, Kinblethmont House, Arbroath, 2009; work in private and public collections throughout UK and USA. Keith Prize, 1962, Latimer, 1973, William McCauley Award, 1988, Gillies Bequest, 1991, Royal Scottish Acad. *Recreation:* non specific. *Address:* 2 Manor Gardens, Carnoustie, Angus DD7 6HY.

BUCHAN, Hon. Ursula Margaret Bridget, (Hon. Mrs Wide); author; *b* 25 June 1953; twin *d* of 3rd Baron Tweedsmuir and Barbara (*née* Ensor); *m* 1979, Charles Thomas Wide, *qv*; one *s* one *d*. *Educ:* Littlemore Grammar Sch.; Oxford High Sch. for Girls; New Hall, Cambridge (MA); Royal Botanic Gardens, Kew (Dip. Hort.). Freelance journalist, 1980–2011; gardening columnist: Spectator, 1984–2011; Observer, 1987–93; Sunday Telegraph, 1993–97; Independent, 1998–2003; Daily Telegraph, 2004–11. Gardening author and lectr, 1986–. JP 2004–14. *Publications:* An Anthology of Garden Writing, 1986; The Pleasures of Gardening, 1987; (with Nigel Colborn) The Classic Horticulturist, 1987; Foliage Plants, 1988, 2nd edn 1993; The Village Show, 1990; Wall Plants and Climbers, 1992; (with David Stevens) The Garden Book, 1994; Gardening for Pleasure, 1996; Plants for All Seasons, 1999, 2nd edn 2004; Good in a Bed: garden writings from The Spectator, 2001; Better Against a Wall, 2003; The English Garden, 2006; Garden People, 2007; Back to the Garden, 2009; A Green and Pleasant Land: how England's gardeners fought the Second World War,

2013; (ed) The Garden Anthology, 2014. *Recreations:* gardening, fell walking, watching Rugby Union and cricket, choral singing. *Address:* c/o Felicity Bryan Literary Agency, 2a North Parade Avenue, Oxford OX2 6LX.

BUCHAN-HEPBURN, Sir (John) Alastair (Trant Kidd), 7th Bt *cr* 1815, of Smeaton Hepburn, Haddingtonshire; *b* 27 June 1931; *s* of John Trant Buchan-Hepburn (*d* 1953), *g g s* of 2nd Bt, and Edith Margaret Mitchell (*née* Robb) (*d* 1980); *S* cousin, 1992; *m* 1957, Georgina Elizabeth, *d* of late Oswald Morris Turner, MC; one *s* three *d*. *Educ:* Charterhouse; St Andrews Univ.; RMA, Sandhurst. 1st King's Dragoon Guards, 1952–57; Captain, 1954; ADC to GOC-in-C, Malaya, 1954–57. Arthur Guinness & Son Co. Ltd, 1959–86; Director: Broughton Brewery Ltd, 1987–95; Broughton Ales Ltd, 1995–2001; Chairman: Valentine Marketing Ltd, 2002–03; Valentine Holdings Ltd, 2002–03. Mem. Cttee, St Andrews Br., RBL. Life Mem., St Andrews Preservation Trust, 1984–; Mem., Baronets' Trust, 1992–; UK Rep., European Commn of the Nobility. Trustee, Dundee Industrial Heritage Trust, 1999–2006. Vice-Pres., Maritime Volunteer Service, 2001–07. Member: Regtl Assoc., 1st Queen's Dragoon Guards, 1958–; Vestry, All Saints Scottish Episcopal Ch, St Andrews, 2002–06. Mem., Royal Stuart Soc., 2005. Mem., St Andrews Loches Alliance—La Nouvelle Alliance, 2005–. Mem., Kate Kennedy Club, 1950–, After Many Days Club, 2002–, St Andrews Univ. Member: St Andrews Shoot, 1990–2005; Logiealmond Shoot, 2004–07. Chief Marshal: Dunhill Championship, St Andrews, 1999–2005; Open Championship, St Andrews, 2000 and 2006. Leader, European and Scottish campaign for repatriation from Denmark to Scotland for Christian burial of remains of James Hepburn, 4th Earl of Bothwell and 3rd husband of Mary, Queen of Scots, 2000–. *Publications:* trans. from French, Lord James, by Catherine Hermary Vieille, 2010 (also trans. film and TV script). *Recreations:* golf, fishing, shooting, tennis, badminton, travel in Europe (especially France), USA and other parts of the world, antiquities, Buchan and Hepburn genealogical history. *Heir: s* (John) Christopher (Alastair) Buchan-Hepburn [*b* 9 March 1963; *m* 1990, Andrea Unwin]. *Address:* Chagford, 60 Argyle Street, St Andrews, Fife KY16 9BU. *T:* and *Fax:* (01334) 472161, *T:* 07939 139545. *E:* alastairbh@gmail.com. *Clubs:* New, Royal Scots (Edinburgh); Royal and Ancient Golf (St Andrews).

BUCHANAN, Alistair George, CBE 2009; FCA; Chair and Partner, KPMG, since 2013; *b* 22 Dec. 1961; *s* of late Colin Buchanan and of Isobel Buchanan; *m* 1988, Linda Pollock; one *s* two *d*. *Educ:* Malvern Coll.; Durham Univ. (BA Hons). FCA 1986. Chartered Accountant, KPMG, 1983–87; Head: UK Utilities Res., Smith New Court, 1987–94; UK, European and Global Res. Div., BZW, 1994–97; USA Utilities Res., Salomon Smith Barney, NY, 1997–2000; European Res., London, Donaldson, Lufkin & Jenrette (DLJ), 2000–01; ABN AMRO, 2001–03; Chief Exec., Ofgem, 2003–13. Non-exec. Dir, Scottish Water, 2008–09. Mem. Council and Chair, Remuneration Cttee, Durham Univ., 2010–. *Recreations:* season ticket holder Harlequins, classical music, all sports.

BUCHANAN, Sir Andrew (George), 5th Bt *cr* 1878; KCVO 2011; farmer; Lord-Lieutenant and Keeper of the Rolls for Nottinghamshire, 1991–2012; *b* 21 July 1937; *s* of Major Sir Charles Buchanan, 4th Bt, and Barbara Helen (*d* 1986), *o d* of late Lt-Col Rt Hon. Sir George Stanley, PC, GCSI, GCIE; *S* father, 1984; *m* 1966, Belinda Jane Virginia (*née* Maclean), JP, DL, *widow* of Gresham Neilus Vaughan; one *s* one *d*, and one step *s* one step *d*. *Educ:* Eton; Trinity Coll., Cambridge; Wye Coll., Univ. of London. Nat. Service, 2nd Lieut, Coldstream Guards, 1956–58. Chartered Surveyor with Smith-Woolley & Co., 1965–70. Chm., Bd of Visitors, HM Prison Ranby, 1983 (Vice-Chm. 1982). Commanded A Squadron (SRY), 3rd Bn Worcs and Sherwood Foresters (TA), 1971–74; Hon. Col, B Sqn (SRY), Queen's Own Yeo., 1989–94; Hon. Col, Notts ACF, 2001–07. Pres., E Midlands Reserve Forces and Cadets Assoc., 1999–. High Sheriff, Notts, 1976–77; DL Notts, 1985. KStJ 1991. *Recreations:* ski-ing, walking, forestry. *Heir: s* George Charles Mellish Buchanan [*b* 27 Jan. 1975; *m* 2002, Katharine, *d* of late Tom Price]. *Address:* Hodsock Priory Farm, Blyth, Worksop, Notts S81 0TY. *T:* (01909) 591227. *E:* andrew.buchanan@hodsock.com. *Club:* Boodle's.

BUCHANAN, Prof. Ann Hermione, MBE 2012; PhD; FAcSS; Professor of Social Work, 2003, now Emeritus, and Senior Research Associate, Department of Social Policy and Intervention, since 2008, University of Oxford; Fellow of St Hilda's College, Oxford, since 1994; *b* Winchester, 1941; *d* of late Raymond Alexander Baring and Margaret Fleetwood (*née* Campbell-Preston, later Countess of Malmesbury); *m* 1964, Alistair John Buchanan; three *d*. *Educ:* Univ. of London (Dip Soc. Studies (Dist.) 1968); Univ. of Bath (Dip Applied Soc. Studies 1980); Univ. of Southampton (PhD 1990). Research Assistant: to Henry Kempe, NSPCC, 1969–71; Burderop Hosp., Wilts, 1973–79; Psychiatric Social Worker Child Guidance, 1980–89; Lecturer: Bracknell Coll., 1989–91; Univ. of Southampton, 1991–94; University of Oxford: Lectr, 1994–2000; Reader, 2000–03; Dir, Centre for Res. into Parenting and Children, 1996. Vis. Prof., Univ. of St Petersburg, 1996. Member: ESRC, 2008– (Chm., Cttee for updating Framework for Res. Ethics, 2009; Chm., Evaluation Cttee, 2010–); Council, Acad. of Social Scis, 2010–. Trustee: Baring Foundn, 2000–12; Family Action, 2000–08; Oxfordshire Community Foundn, 2008–; Grandparent Plus, 2013–. FAcSS (AcSS 2009). Hon. MA Oxon 1994; Hon. LLD Bath, 2013. *Publications:* Child Maltreatment: facts, fallacies and interventions, 1996; (ed with B. L. Hudson) Parenting, Schooling and Children's Behaviour, 1998; (with B. L. Hudson) Promoting Children's Emotional Well-being, 2000; (jtly) Families in Conflict: perspectives of children and parents on the Family Court Welfare Service, 2001; What Works for Troubled Children, 1999, rev. edn (with Charlotte Ritchie) 2004; (ed) Major Themes in Health and Social Welfare, 4 vols, 2008; (ed with A. Rotkirch) No Time for Children? Fertility Rates and Population Decline, 2013; over 70 articles on child well-being, grand-parenting, fathering, impact of divorce on children, children at risk of social exclusion, child abuse and children in care. *Recreations:* family, flowers, travel. *Address:* 11 London Place, Oxford OX4 1BD. *T:* (01865) 424576. *E:* ann.buchanan@spi.ox.ac.uk.

See also Sir J. F. Baring.

BUCHANAN, Rt Rev. Colin Ogilvie; Area Bishop of Woolwich, 1996–2004; an Hon. Assistant Bishop: Diocese of Bradford, 2004–14; Diocese of West Yorkshire and The Dales, since 2014; *b* 9 Aug. 1934; *s* of late Prof. Robert Ogilvie Buchanan and of Kathleen Mary (*née* Parnell); *m* 1963; two *d*. *Educ:* Whitgift Sch., S Croydon; Lincoln Coll., Oxford (BA, 2nd Cl. Lit. Hum., MA). Theological training at Tyndale Hall, Bristol, 1959–61; deacon, 1961; priest, 1962; Curate, Cheadle, Cheshire, 1961–64; joined staff of London Coll. of Divinity (now St John's Coll., Nottingham), 1964; posts held: Librarian, 1964–69; Registrar, 1969–74; Director of Studies, 1974–75; Vice-Principal, 1975–78; Principal, 1979–85; Hon. Canon of Southwell Minster, 1982–85; Bishop Suffragan of Aston, 1985–89; Hon. Asst Bishop, dio. of Rochester, 1989–96; Vicar, St Mark's, Gillingham, Kent, 1991–96. Member: Church of England Liturgical Commn, 1964–86; Doctrinal Commn, 1986–91; House of Clergy, 1970–85, House of Bishops, 1990–2004, General Synod of C of E; Assembly of British Council of Churches, 1971–80; Steering Cttee, CCBI, 1990–92; Council for Christian Unity, 1991–2001; Steering Gp, Internat. Anglican Liturgical Consultations, 1995–2001. Mem., Lambeth Conf., 1988, 1998 (Mem., Chaplaincy Team, 1998). Chm., Millennium Dome Chaplaincy Gp, 1999–2000. Pres., Movt for Reform of Infant Baptism, 1988–. Vice-Pres., 1987–2005, Pres., 2005–12, Electoral Reform Soc. Grove Books: Proprietor, 1970–85; Hon. Manager, 1985–93; Editorial Consultant, 1993–. DD Lambeth, 1993. *Publications:* (ed) Modern Anglican Liturgies 1958–1968, 1968; (ed) Further Anglican Liturgies 1968–1975, 1975; (jtly) Growing into Union, 1970; (ed jtly) Anglican Worship Today, 1980; (ed) Latest Anglican Liturgies 1976–1984, 1985; (jtly) Reforming Infant Baptism, 1990; Open to Others, 1992; Infant Baptism and the Gospel, 1993; Cut the Connection, 1994; Is the Church of England Biblical?, 1998; (ed) Michael Vasey—Liturgist and Friend, 1999; (ed) The Savoy Conference Revisited, 2002; Historical Dictionary of Anglicanism, 2006 (reissued as The A to Z of Anglicanism, 2009); Taking the Long View, 2006; (jtly) A History of the International Anglican Liturgical Consultations, 2007; (ed) Justin Martyr on Baptism and Eucharist, 2007; An Evangelical among the Anglican Liturgists, 2009; The Hampton Court Conference and the 1604 Book of Common Prayer, 2009; editor: Grove Booklets on Ministry and Worship, 1972–2002; Grove Liturgical Studies, 1975–86; Alcuin/GROW Joint Liturgical Studies, 1987– (regular author in these series); News of Liturgy, 1975–2003; (ed) Anglican Eucharistic Liturgies 1985–2010, 2011; St John's College Nottingham: from Northwood to Nottingham—a history of 50 years 1963–2013, 2013; contrib. learned jls. *Recreations:* interested in electoral reform, sport, etc.

BUCHANAN, Prof. David Alan, PhD; Professor of Organizational Behaviour, School of Management, Cranfield University, 2005–13, now Emeritus; *b* 26 July 1949; *s* of David Stewart and Harriet Buchanan; *m* 1974, Lesley Fiddes Fulton; one *s* one *d*. *Educ:* Heriot-Watt Univ. (BA Hons); Univ. of Edinburgh (PhD). Personnel Asst, Lothian Regl Council, Edinburgh, 1976–77; Lecturer in Organizational Behaviour: Napier Poly., Edinburgh, 1977–79; Univ. of Glasgow, 1979–86, Sen. Lectr, 1986–89; Prof. of Human Resource Management, Loughborough Univ. of Technology, 1989–95; Dir, Loughborough Univ. Business Sch., 1992–95; Prof. of Organizational Behaviour, Leicester Business Sch., De Montfort Univ., 1995–2005. Vis. Prof. of Organizational Behaviour, Nottingham Business Sch., Nottingham Trent Univ., 2014–. FCIPD; FRSA; FBAM. *Publications:* The Development of Job Design Theories and Techniques, 1979; (with A. A. Huczynski) Organizational Behaviour: an introductory text, 1985, Student Workbook, 1994, Instructor's Manual, 1994, 8th edn 2013; (ed jtly) The New Management Challenge: information systems for improved performance, 1988; (with J. McCalman) High Performance Work Systems: the digital experience, 1989; (with R. Badham) Power, Politics, and Organizational Change, 1999, 2nd edn 2008; (ed jtly) The Sustainability and Spread of Organizational Change, 2007; (with A. Bryman) The Sage Handbook of Organizational Research Methods, 2009; with D. Boddy: Organizations in the Computer Age: technological imperatives and strategic choice, 1983; Managing New Technology, 1986; The Technical Change Audit: action for results, 1987; Take the Lead: interpersonal skills for project managers, 1992; The Expertise of the Change Agent: public performance and backstage activity, 1992; numerous contribs to learned jls. *Recreations:* music, reading, photography, diving, fitness, three grandchildren. *Address:* 1 Ascott Gardens, West Bridgford, Nottingham NG2 7TH.

BUCHANAN, Sir Gordon Kelly McNicol L.; *see* Leith-Buchanan.

BUCHANAN, Isobel Wilson, (Mrs Jonathan King); soprano; *b* 15 March 1954; *d* of Stewart and Mary Buchanan; *m* 1980, Jonathan Stephen Geoffrey King (otherwise Jonathan Hyde, actor); two *d*. *Educ:* Cumbernauld High Sch.; Royal Scottish Academy of Music and Drama (DRSAMD 1974). Australian Opera principal singer, 1975–78; freelance singer, 1978–; British debut, Glyndebourne, 1978; Vienna Staatsoper debut, 1978; American debut, Santa Fé, 1979; Chicago, 1979; New York, 1979; German debut, Cologne, 1979; French debut, Aix-en-Provence, 1981; ENO debut, 1985; Paris Opera debut, 1986. Performances also with Scottish Opera, Covent Garden, Munich Radio, Belgium, Norway, etc. Various operatic recordings, notably with Solti, Carlos Kleiber and Bonynge. *Recreations:* reading, cooking, walking. *E:* isobel@totalfiasco.co.uk.

BUCHANAN, Prof. Robert Angus, OBE 1993; PhD; FSA; FRHistS; Founder and Director, Centre for the History of Technology, Science and Society, 1964–95, Professor of the History of Technology, 1990–95, University of Bath, now Emeritus Professor; Director, National Cataloguing Unit for the Archives of Contemporary Scientists, 1987–95; *b* 5 June 1930; *s* of Roy Graham Buchanan and Bertha (*née* Davis); *m* 1955, Brenda June Wade; two *s*. *Educ:* High Storrs Grammar Sch. for Boys, Sheffield; St Catharine's Coll., Cambridge (MA, PhD). FRHistS 1978; FSA 1990. Educn Officer to Royal Foundn of St Katharine, Stepney, 1956–60 (Co-opted Mem., LCC Educn Cttee, 1958–60); Asst Lectr, Dept of Gen. Studies, Bristol Coll. of Science and Technol. (now Univ. of Bath), 1960; Lectr, 1961, Sen. Lectr, 1966, Head of Humanities Gp, Sch. of Humanities and Social Scis, 1970–95, Reader in Hist. of Technol., 1981–90, Univ. of Bath. Vis. Lectr, Univ. of Delaware, USA, 1969; Vis. Fellow, ANU, Canberra, 1981; Vis. Lectr, Huazhong (Central China) Univ. of Science and Tech., Wuhan, People's Repub. of China, 1983; Jubilee Chair in History of Technol., Chalmers Univ., Göteborg, Sweden, Autumn term, 1984. Royal Comr, Royal Commn on Historical Monuments (England), 1979–93; Sec., Res. Cttee on Indust. Archaeology, Council for British Archaeology, 1972–79; President: (Founding), Bristol Indust. Archaeology Soc., 1967–70; Assoc. for Indust. Archaeology, 1974–77 (Hon. Pres., 2004–10); Newcomen Soc. for History of Engrg and Technol., 1981–83; Internat. Cttee for History of Technol., 1993–97 (Sec.-Gen., 1981–93); Vice Pres., Soc. of Antiquaries, 1995–99; Chm., Water Space Amenity Commn's Working Party on Indust. Archaeology, 1982–83; Member: Properties Cttee, National Trust, 1974–2002; Technol Preservation Awards Cttee, Science Museum, 1973–81. FRSA 1993–99. Hon. Fellow, Science Mus., 1992. Hon. DSc (Engrg) Chalmers Univ., Göteborg, Sweden, 1986. Leonardo da Vinci Medal, Soc. for Hist. of Technol., 198[illegible]. *Publications:* Technology and Social Progress, 1965; (with Neil Cossons) Industrial Archaeology of the Bristol Region, 1969; Industrial Archaeology in Britain, 1972, 2nd edn 1982; (with George Watkins) Industrial Archaeology of the Stationary Steam Engine, 1976; History and Industrial Civilization, 1979; (with C. A. Buchanan) Industrial Archaeology of Central Southern England, 1980; (with Michael Williams) Brunel's Bristol, 1982; The Engineers: a history of the engineering profession in Britain, 1989; The Power of the Machine, 1992; Brunel: the life and times of I. K. Brunel, 2002; (ed and contrib.) Landscape with Technology: essays in honour of L. T. C. Rolt, 2011. *Recreations:* Cambridge Judo half blue, 1955; rambling, travelling, exploring. *Address:* 13 Hensley Road, Bath BA2 2DR. *T:* (01225) 311508.

BUCHANAN, Robin William Turnbull, FCA; Chairman, PageGroup (formerly Michael Page International), since 2011; *b* 2 April 1952; *s* of Iain Buchanan and Gillian Pamela Buchanan (*née* Hughes-Hallett); *m* 1986, Diana Tei Tanaka; one *s* one *d*. *Educ:* Harvard Business Sch. (MBA, Baker Scholar). Mann Judd Landau, subseq. Deloitte & Touche, 1970–77; American Express Internat. Banking Corp., 1979–82; Bain & Company Inc, 1982–: Bain Capital, 1982–84; Man. Partner, London, 1990–96; Sen. Partner, London, 1996–2007; Sen. Advr, 2007–. Dean, then Pres., London Business Sch., 2007–09. Non-executive Director: Liberty Internat. plc, 1997–2008; Shire plc (formerly Shire Pharmaceuticals Gp plc), 2003–08; Schroders, 2010–; LyondellBasell NV, 2011–; Trees for Life, 2014–. Mem., Highland Soc. of London. Fellow, Salzburg Seminar. Mem., Northern Meeting. FRSA. Liveryman, Co. of Ironmongers. *Recreations:* farming, forestry, shooting, collecting old children's books. *Club:* Pilgrims.

BUCHANAN-DUNLOP, Col Robert Daubeny, (Robin), CBE 1987 (OBE 1982); Clerk, Goldsmiths' Company, 1988–2004; *b* 11 Aug. 1939; *o s* of late Col Robert Arthur Buchanan-Dunlop of Drumhead, OBE, The Cameronians (Scottish Rifles) and Patricia Buchanan-Dunlop (*née* Upton); *m* 1972, Nicola Jane Goodhart; two *s*. *Educ:* Loretto Sch. William Thomson & Co., Managers Ben Line, 1958–59. National Service, The Cameronians (Scottish Rifles), 1959–61; Regular Commission, 1961; transf. to Scots Guards; served Kenya, Aden, Sharjah, Germany, NI (despatches); Staff Coll., 1971; HQ 1 Div., 1973–75; Armed Forces Staff Coll., USA, 1978; Directing Staff, Canadian Land Forces Staff Coll., 1978–79; CO 8th (Co. Tyrone) Bn, UDR, 1979–81; COS 52 Lowland Bde, 1982–84; COS N[illegible] 1984–86; Dep. Dir, UK C-in-C Cttees, 1987; retired. Mem., Queen's Body Guard for

Scotland (Royal Company of Archers), 1987–. Chm., Lead Body, Jewellery and Allied Industries, 1994–98. Mem., British Hallmarking Council, 1988–2004. Member: Council, Goldsmiths' Coll., 1989–2004; Governing Body: Imperial Coll., 1989–2001; London Guildhall Univ., 1997–2002. Hon. MA London Guildhall, 1994. *Publications:* Ham: the story of a Wiltshire village, 2011. *Recreations:* walking, gardening, visual arts. *Address:* Ham Green Cottage, Ham, Marlborough, Wilts SN8 3QR. *T:* (01488) 668846. *Club:* Army and Navy.

BUCHANAN-JARDINE, Sir John (Christopher Rupert), 5th Bt *cr* 1885, of Castle Milk, co. Dumfries; *b* 20 March 1952; *o s* of Sir Rupert Buchanan-Jardine, 4th Bt, MC and of Jane Fiona, *d* of Sir Charles Edmondstone, 6th Bt; *S* father, 2010; *m* 1975, Pandora Lavinia, *d* of Peter Murray Lee; one *s* five *d*. *Educ:* Harrow; RAC Cirencester. *Heir: s* James Rupert Buchanan-Jardine, *b* 28 July 1994.

BUCK, Emma Louise L.; *see* Lewell-Buck, E. L.

BUCK, John Stephen; HM Diplomatic Service, retired; Founding Partner, Ambassador Partnership (formerly ADRgAmbassadors), since 2010; *b* 10 Oct. 1953; *s* of Frederick George Buck and Amelia Ellen Buck (*née* Stevens); *m* 1980, Jean Claire Webb; one *s* one *d*. *Educ:* East Ham GS; York Univ. (BA History 1975); Wolfson Coll., Oxford (MSc Applied Social Studies, 1979; CQSW 1979). Middlesex Probation Service, 1975–77; social worker, Oxfordshire Social Services, 1979–80; joined HM Diplomatic Service, 1980; Second Sec., Sofia, 1982–84; First Sec., FCO, 1984–88; Head of Chancery, Lisbon, 1988–92; FCO, 1992–94; Counsellor, on loan to Cabinet Office, Prin. Private Sec. to Chancellor of the Duchy of Lancaster, 1994–96; Counsellor and Dep. High Comr, Republic of Cyprus, 1996–2000; Head, Public Diplomacy, FCO, 2000–03; Head, Govt Information and Commns Centre, 10 Downing Street/FCO, 2003; Dir, Iraq, FCO, 2003–04; Ambassador to Portugal, 2004–07. Gp Dir, Govt and Public Affairs, BG Gp plc, 2007–09. Chm. Trustees, Musequality, 2013–. *Recreations:* music, books, swimming, cycling, travel. *E:* john.buck@ambassadorllp.com.

BUCK, Karen Patricia; MP (Lab) Westminster North, since 2010 (Regent's Park and Kensington North, 1997–2010); *b* 30 Aug. 1958; partner, Barrie Taylor; one *s*. *Educ:* Chelmsford High Sch.; LSE (BSc, MSc, MA). R&D worker, Outset, 1979–83; London Borough of Hackney: Specialist Officer, Developing Services and Employment for Disabled People, 1983–86; Public Health Officer, 1986–87; Lab. Party Policy Directorate (Health), 1987–92; Co-ordinator, Lab. Party Campaign Strategy, 1992–96. Parly Under-Sec. of State, DfT, 2005–06; PPS to Leader of the Opposition, 2013–. Member: Social Security Select Cttee, 1997–2001; Work and Pensions Select Cttee, 2001–05; Home Affairs Select Cttee, 2006–09. Chm., London Gp of Labour MPs, 1998–2005. *Address:* House of Commons, SW1A 0AA.

BUCK, Prof. Kenneth William, PhD, DSc; Professor of Plant and Fungal Virology, and Head, Microbiology and Plant Pathology Section, then Plant and Microbial Sciences Section, 1986–2005, and Director of Research, Department of Biological Sciences, 2001–05, Imperial College of Science, Technology and Medicine, University of London; *b* 16 Feb. 1938; *s* of William Buck and Nellie Sebra (*née* Turner); *m* 1961, Gwendoline Maureen Patterson; three *d*. *Educ:* Univ. of Birmingham (BSc 1st Cl. Hons 1959; PhD 1962; DSc 1983). Res. Fellow, Univ. of Birmingham, 1962–65; Imperial College, University of London: Lectr, Dept of Biochem., 1965–81; Reader, Dept of Biol., 1981–86; Chairman: Sub-Bd of Examrs in Microbiol., 1981–98; Bd of Examrs in Biol., 2000–05; Panel of Vis. Examrs in Microbiol., London Univ., 1988–96. Sec., Cttee on Non-Specific Immunity, MRC, 1968–71; Member: Plants and Envmt Res. Grants Bd, AFRC, 1992–94; Plant and Microbial Scis Cttee, BBSRC, 1994–97. International Committee on Taxonomy of Viruses: Mem., Exec. Cttee, 1981–93; Mem., 1975–2005, Chm., 1981–87, Fungal Virus Sub-cttee; Sec., 1984–90; Vice-Pres., 1990–93; Mem., Plant Virus Sub-cttee, 1999–2005; Chm., Narnaviridae Study Gp, 2000–05. Chm. of workshops on fungal virol. and plant virus replication, Internat. Congress of Virology, triennially, 1981–93, 1999, 2002, 2005; Mem., Internat. Adv. Cttee, XII Internat. Congress of Virology, Paris, 2002, XIII, San Francisco, 2005. Mem., Soc. for Gen. Microbiol., 1975–2005. Editor, Jl of Gen. Virology, 1991–96 (Mem., Editl Bd, 1985–90, 1997–2001); Mem., Editl Bd, Virology, 1998–2005. *Publications:* (ed) Fungal Virology, 1986; over 200 papers in scientific jls and books. *Recreations:* genealogy, South West coast path walking.

BUCK, Linda B., PhD; Member, Division of Basic Sciences, Fred Hutchinson Cancer Research Center, since 2002; Affiliate Professor of Physiology and Biophysics, University of Washington, since 2003; *b* 29 Jan. 1947. *Educ:* Univ. of Washington (BS 1975); Univ. of Texas (PhD 1980). Associate, Howard Hughes Med. Inst., Columbia Univ., 1984–91; Asst Prof., 1991–96, Associate Prof., 1996–2001, Prof., 2001–02, Dept of Neurobiol., Harvard Med. Sch.; Asst Investigator, 1994–97, Associate Investigator, 1997–2000, Investigator, 2001–, Howard Hughes Med. Inst. Dir, International Flavors & Fragrances Inc., 2007–. Foreign Mem., Royal Soc., 2015. (Jtly) Nobel Prize in Physiology or Medicine, 2004. *Publications:* articles in learned jls. *Address:* Division of Basic Sciences, Fred Hutchinson Cancer Research Center, 1100 Fairview Avenue North, PO Box 19024, Seattle, WA 98109–1024, USA.

BUCK, Prof. Margaret Ann, OBE 2008; artist, designer; arts and design consultant; *b* 23 Nov. 1948; *d* of late William Ewart Buck and Winifred Annie Buck; *m* 1985, David Martin Burrows; one *s* one *d* (twins). *Educ:* Pate's Grammar Sch. for Girls, Cheltenham; Gloucestershire Coll. of Art and Design (DipAD Fine Art); Royal Coll. of Art (MA Furniture Design). Head of Dept, then Dep. Head of Sch., Central Sch. of Art and Design, 1982–86; Dep. Head of Sch., Camberwell Sch. of Arts and Crafts, 1987–89; London Institute, then University of the Arts, London: Head, Camberwell Coll. of Arts, 1989–91; Asst Rector, 1989–2006; Head of Coll., Central St Martins Coll. of Art & Design, 1991–2006; Mem., Conferments Panel, 1995–2006; Emeritus Prof., 2007; exhibitions: Proj. Dir and Curator, Theatre Design and Interpretation, 1986; Proj. Dir, A Century in the Making, 1999; conceived and designed, The Innovation Centre: Arts, Communication, Fashion, Design, Central St Martins Coll. of Art & Design, 2003. Represented by Updown Gall., Ramsgate. Lectr, Wimbledon Sch. of Art, 1978–82; lectr at internat. confs incl. Saga Internat. Design Conf., Japan, 1993 and Handwerkskammer für München, 1994; various appts as vis. lectr and ext. examr. Advr on strategic develt of arts and design to Ruler of Sharjah and to Coll. of Fine Arts and Design, Univ. of Sharjah, UAE, 2006–10; ext. consultant, Univ. for the Creative Arts, 2013–. Exhibitor, Design of the Times exhibn, RCA, 1996. Director: Develts at London Inst., later London Artscom, Ltd, 1989–2006; Cochrane Th. Co., 1990–2006; Design Lab Ltd, 1999–2006; Connecting Creativity, 2006–11. Chair: London and SE, Nat. Standing Conf. for Foundn Educn in Art and Design, 1981–87; Nat. Council for Foundn Educn in Art and Design, 1987–92. Trustee: Arts Foundn, 1998–2012; V&A Mus., 2000–06 (Mem. Collections Cttee, 2000–06, Remuneration Cttee, 2004–06, Theatre Mus.). Mem. English Lang. Council, ESU, 2003– (Chm., Pres.'s Award for Innovation Design and Excellence in the Use of New Freestanding Technologies in the Teaching and Learning of English, 2003–). Ext. Mem., Profs' and Readers' Conferments Panel, Liverpool John Moores Univ., 2004. Member: Internat. Adv. Cttee, Fashion Fringe, 2004–06; Internat. Adv. Gp, Shanghai Inst. of Visual Arts, Univ. of Fudan, China, 2005–07 (Hon. Prof., 2007). Governor, GSMD, 2000–09. Hon. Associate, Altagamma Internat. Hon. Council, Italy, 2005. Sanderson Art in Industry Award, 1976, Radford Design Award, 1977, Furniture Makers' Co. *E:* mbuck@connectingcreativity.co.uk. *Club:* Chelsea Arts.

BUCK, Prof. Martin, PhD; FRS 2009; FRSB; Professor of Molecular Microbiology, Imperial College London, since 1999; *b* London, 16 Oct. 1955; *s* of Geoffrey Edward Buck and Alice Eva Buck (*née* Alexander); *m* 1996, Madeleine Henrietta Moore; two *s*. *Educ:* Bedford Coll., London (BSc Biochem. 1977); MRC-Nat. Inst. for Med. Res. (PhD Biochem. 1980). Postdoctoral Fellow, Univ. of Calif, Berkeley, 1980–83; Higher Scientific Officer, 1983–89, Sen. Scientific Officer, 1989–91, Grade 7, 1991–94, AFRC-BBSRC Nitrogen Fixation Lab., Univ. of Sussex; Imperial College London: Sen. Lectr, 1994–96; Reader, 1996–99; Hd, Dept of Biol Scis, 2001–04. Fellow, Amer. Acad. Microbiol., 2006; FRSB (FSB 2010). *Publications:* contrib. articles to jls on mechanisms governing bacterial gene expression. *Address:* Department of Life Sciences, SAF Building, Imperial College London, SW7 2AZ. *T:* (020) 7594 5442. *E:* m.buck@imperial.ac.uk.

BUCK, Simon John Langdale; JP; Chief Executive, British Air Transport Association, 2010–14; *b* Otley, W Yorks, 13 Dec. 1957; *s* of Michael Bernard Langdale Buck and Brenda Buck; civil partnership 2006, *m* 2014, Andrew Mark Honour. *Educ:* Leeds Grammar Sch.; Leeds Poly. (BA 1981). MCILT 1997; MCIPR 2010. Civil servant, Dept of Transport, 1983–95; Hd, Industry Affairs, Air 2000 Ltd, 1995–2002; Gp Hd, Industry Affairs, First Choice Holidays plc, 2002–06; Principal Manager, PR, AQA, 2006–10. JP N Sussex, 2000. *Publications:* various articles on aviation issues. *Recreations:* travel, classic motor cars (Member, Rolls-Royce Enthusiasts and Jaguar Enthusiasts Clubs), company of good friends.

BUCKBY, Anthony Jonathan, MBE 1996; Director, Greece, British Council, since 2011; *b* Birmingham, 1 Sept. 1951; *s* of Gordon Buckby and Muriel Buckby (*née* Darby); *m* 1996, Giuliana Salvagno. *Educ:* King's Sch., Worcester; Univ. of Nottingham (BA Hons English Lang. and Lit.); Univ. of Essex (MA Applied Linguistics). Academic Advr, 1982–86, Sch. Dir, 1986–90, British Inst. of Florence; British Council: Director: Bologna, 1990–96; Lang. Services, Italy, Rome, 1996–2000; Deputy Director: Italy, 2000–04; English Lang., London, 2004–07; Dir, Bulgaria, 2007–11. *Address:* British Council, 17 Kolonaki Square, 10673 Athens, Greece. *E:* tony.buckby@britishcouncil.gr.

BUCKELS, Prof. John Anthony Charles, CBE 2002; MD; FRCS; Professor of Hepatobiliary and Transplant Surgery, University of Birmingham, since 2005; Consultant Hepatobiliary and Liver Transplant Surgeon, Queen Elizabeth Hospital, Birmingham, 1986–2011, now Honorary Consultant Surgeon; *b* 4 Jan. 1949; *s* of Noel and Loretta Buckels; *m* 1975, Carol Ann Francis; one *s* four *d*. *Educ:* Birmingham Univ. (MB ChB 1972; MD 1986). FRCS 1977. Raine Vis. Prof., Univ. of Western Australia, 1998; Margery Budd Prof., Univ. of Bristol, 2000; Penman Vis. Prof., Univ. of Cape Town, 2007; Mary Weston Vis. Prof., Univ. of KwaZulu Natal, Durban, 2012. *Publications:* numerous contribs on general surgery and transplantation topics to scientific jls. *Recreations:* French home, fishing, sailing. *Address:* 87 Reddings Road, Moseley, Birmingham B13 8LP. *T:* (0121) 449 3310.

BUCKERIDGE, Frances Mary Theresa; *see* Hughes, F. M. T.

BUCKHURST, Lord; William Herbrand Thomas Sackville; with Quilter Cheviot Investment Management (formerly Cheviot Asset Management), since 2006; *b* 13 June 1979; *s* and *heir* of Earl De La Warr, *qv*; *m* 2010, Countess Xenia, *y d* of Count and Countess Tolstoy-Miloslavsky; one *s*. *Educ:* Eton; Newcastle Univ. *Recreations:* racing, shooting, cricket, football. *Heir: s* Hon. William Lionel Robert Sackville, *b* 24 Jan. 2014. *Address:* Buckhurst Park, Withyham, E Sussex TN7 4BL.

BUCKINGHAM, Area Bishop of, since 2003; **Rt Rev. Alan Thomas Lawrence Wilson,** DPhil; *b* 27 March 1955; *s* of Alan Thomas Wilson and Anna Maria Magdalena Wilson; *m* 1984, Lucy Catherine Janet (*née* Richards); two *s* three *d*. *Educ:* Sevenoaks Sch.; St John's Coll., Cambridge (BA 1977, MA 1981); Balliol Coll., Oxford (DPhil 1989); Wycliffe Hall, Oxford. Ordained deacon, 1979, priest, 1980; Hon. Curate, 1979–81, Curate, 1981–82, Eynsham; Priest i/c, St John's, Caversham, and Asst Curate, Caversham and Mapledurham, 1982–89; Vicar, St John's, Caversham, 1989–92; Rector, Sandhurst, 1992–2003. Anglican Substitute Chaplain, HMP Reading, 1990–92; Area Dean, Sonning, 1998–2003; Hon. Canon, Christ Church, Oxford, 2002–03. Chair: Oxford Diocesan Bd of Educn, 2010–; Art Beyond Belief, 2010–; Chair of Trustees, Christians Aware, 2011–; Co-founding Trustee, Oxford Nandyal Educn Foundn, 2012–. Visitor, Piper's Corner Sch., 2004–; Mem. Council, Wycombe Abbey Sch., 2008–; Gov., Cressex Community Sch., 2008–. Vis. Prof., Univ. of Buckingham, 2009–. *Recreations:* modern history, art and design, photography, singing, running, France. *Address:* Sheridan, Grimms Hill, Great Missenden, Bucks HP16 9BG. *T:* (01494) 862173, *Fax:* (01494) 890508. *E:* bishopbucks@oxford.anglican.org.

BUCKINGHAM, Archdeacon of; *see* Gorham, Ven. K. M.

BUCKINGHAM, Amyand David, CBE 1997; FRS 1975; FAA; Professor of Chemistry, University of Cambridge, 1969–97; Fellow of Pembroke College, Cambridge, 1970–97 (Hon. Fellow, 2005); *b* 28 Jan. 1930; 2nd *s* of late Reginald Joslin Buckingham and late Florence Grace Buckingham (formerly Elliot); *m* 1965, Jillian Bowles; one *s* two *d*. *Educ:* Barker Coll., Hornsby, NSW; Univ. of Sydney; Corpus Christi Coll., Cambridge (Shell Postgraduate Schol.). Univ. Medal 1952, MSc 1953, Sydney; PhD 1956, ScD 1985, Cantab. 1851 Exhibn Sen. Studentship, Oxford Univ., 1955–57; Lectr and subseq. Student and Tutor, Christ Church, Oxford, 1955–65; Univ. Lectr in Inorganic Chem. Lab., Oxford, 1958–65; Prof. of Theoretical Chem., Univ. of Bristol, 1965–69. Vis. Lectr, Harvard, 1961; Visiting Professor: Princeton, 1965; Univ. of California (Los Angeles), 1975; Univ. of Illinois, 1976; Univ. of Wisconsin, 1978; ANU, 1996; Vis. Fellow, ANU, 1979 and 1982; Vis. Erskine Fellow, Univ. of Canterbury, NZ, 1990. FRACI 1961 (Masson Meml Schol. 1952; Rennie Meml Medal, 1958); FRSC (formerly FCS) (Harrison Meml Prize, 1959; Tilden Lectr, 1964; Theoretical Chemistry and Spectroscopy Prize, 1970; Faraday Medal and Lectr, 1998; Mem., Faraday Div. (Pres., 1987–89; Mem. Council, 1965–67, 1975–83, 1987–99)); FInstP (Harrie Massey Medal and Prize, 1995); Fellow: Optical Soc. of America (C. H. Townes Medal, 2001); Amer. Phys. Soc.; Mem., Amer. Chem. Soc.; For. Associate, Nat. Acad. Scis, USA, 1992; Foreign Member: Amer. Acad. of Arts and Scis, 1992; Royal Swedish Acad. Scis, 1996; FAA (Corresp. Mem., 2008). Editor: Molecular Physics, 1968–72; Chemical Physics Letters, 1978–99; Internat. Reviews in Physical Chemistry, 1981–89. Member: Chemistry Cttee, SRC, 1967–70; Adv. Council, Royal Mil. Coll. of Science, Shrivenham, 1973–87; Council, Royal Soc., 1999–2001. Senior Treasurer: Oxford Univ. Cricket Club, 1959–64; Cambridge Univ. Cricket Club, 1977–90 (Pres., 1990–2009). Trustee, Henry Fund, 1977–2006. Hon. Dr: Univ. de Nancy I, 1979; Sydney, 1993; Antwerp, 2004. Hughes Medal, Royal Soc., 1996; Ahmed Zewail Prize in Molecular Scis, Elsevier/Chem. Physics Letters, 2007. *Publications:* The Laws and Applications of Thermodynamics, 1964; Organic Liquids, 1978; Principles of Molecular Recognition, 1993; papers in scientific jls. *Recreations:* walking, woodwork, cricket, travel. *Address:* Crossways, 23 The Avenue, Newmarket CB8 9AA.

BUCKINGHAM, David Anthony, AM 2015; Vice-President Marketing, Communications and Student Recruitment, since 2012, and Principal Advisor (formerly Senior Co-ordinator), Office of the Vice-Chancellor, since 2009, Monash University; *b* 30 March 1946; *s* of Donald Buckingham and Joyce (*née* Craven); *m* 2001, Kiren Mason; one *s* three *d*. *Educ:* Australian National Univ. (BEc 1st Cl. Hons). Aust. Foreign Service, 1972–83; Advr to Prime Minister, Bob Hawke, 1983–86; Dir, Internat. Educn, 1986–89; First Asst Sec., Aviation Div., Aust. Dept of Transport, 1989–92; Dep. Sec., Aust. Dept of Envmt, 1992–94; Exec. Dir, Minerals Council of Australia, 1994–96; Chief Exec., Business Council of Australia, 1996–2001; CEO,

Turnbull Porter Novelli, 2001; Man. Dir, Stratpol Consultants, 2002–04; Agent Gen. for Victoria, Australia, in London, 2004–09; Chm., Linking Melbourne Authy, 2009–12. *Recreations:* fishing, walking. *Club:* Sandringham Anglers' (Melbourne).

BUCKINGHAM, Ven. Hugh Fletcher; Archdeacon of the East Riding, 1988–98, now Archdeacon Emeritus; *b* 13 Sept. 1932; *s* of Rev. Christopher Leigh Buckingham and Gladys Margaret Buckingham; *m* 1967, Alison Mary Cock; one *s* one *d*. *Educ:* Lancing College; Hertford Coll., Oxford (MA Hons). Curate: St Thomas', Halliwell, Bolton, 1957–60; St Silas', Sheffield, 1960–65; Vicar of Hindolveston and Guestwick, dio. Norwich, 1965–70; Rector of Fakenham, 1970–88. Hon. Canon of Norwich Cathedral, 1985–88. *Publications:* How To Be A Christian In Trying Circumstances, 1985; Feeling Good, 1989; Happy Ever After, 2000. *Recreations:* pottery, gardening. *Address:* Orchard Cottage, Rectory Corner, Brandsby, York YO61 4RJ.

BUCKINGHAM, Prof. Julia Clare, (Mrs S. J. Smith), PhD, DSc; FCGI; Vice-Chancellor and President, Brunel University London, since 2012; *b* 18 Oct. 1950; *d* of Jack William Harry Buckingham and Barbara Joan Buckingham; *m* 1974, Simon James Smith. *Educ:* St Mary's Sch., Calne; Univ. of Sheffield (BSc Zool. 1971); Royal Free Hosp. Sch. of Medicine, Univ. of London (PhD Pharmacol. 1974; DSc Neuroendocrine Pharmacol. 1987). Res. Fellow, 1974–80, Sen. Lectr in Pharmacol., 1980–87, Royal Free Hosp. Sch. of Medicine, London; Prof. of Pharmacol., Charing Cross and Westminster Med. Sch., 1987–97 (Pre-clinical Dean, 1992–97); Imperial College London: Prof. of Pharmacology, 1997–2012; Head, Dept of Neuroendocrinology, 1997–2003; Dean for Non-clinical Medicine, 2000–03; Hd, Div. of Neurosci. and Mental Health, 2003–07; Pro-Rector (Educn), 2007–10, (Educn and Academic Affairs), 2010–12. Dir, Imperial College Health Partners, 2014–. Mem., Council, Sch. of Pharmacy, London Univ., 2000–05. Pres., British Pharmacol Soc., 2004–05 (Fellow, 2004); Pres., Soc. for Endocrinol., 2011–12 (Treas., 1996–2001; Gen. Sec., 2005–09; Chm., 2009–12); Mem. Council, Bioscis Fedn, 2008–09; Mem. Council and Trustee, Soc. of Biol., later Royal Soc. of Biol., 2009–. Trustee and Chm., Sci. and Educn Cttee, Royal Instn of GB, 2011–; Chm., Science Community Representing Educn, 2013–; Mem. Bd, Universities UK, 2014–. Dir, Bioscientifica, 1996–2012 (Chm., 2001–05). Ed., Jl of Neuroendocrinology, 2004–08. Governor: King's Coll. Sch., Wimbledon, 1991–94; St Mary's Sch., Calne, 2003–. FRSA 1987; FCGI 2009; FRSB (FSB 2009). Hon. FBPhS (Hon. FBPharmacolS 2015). Hon. DSc Sheffield, 2012. *Publications:* Stress, Stress Hormones and the Immune System, 1997; contribs to endocrinol. and pharmacol. jls. *Recreations:* music, ski-ing, sailing. *Address:* Brunel University London, Kingston Lane, Uxbridge, Middx UB8 3PH. *T:* (01895) 274000. *E:* julia.buckingham@brunel.ac.uk. *Clubs:* Athenæum; Riverside.

BUCKINGHAM, Kathleen Rosemary Bernadette; Her Honour Judge Buckingham; a Circuit Judge, since 2009; *b* Stoke-on-Trent, 16 June 1958; *d* of late James Donnellan and Mary Donnellan; *m* 1981, William Buckingham; two *d*. *Educ:* St Dominic's High Sch., Stoke-on-Trent; Leeds Univ. (BA Hons; PhD Linguistics); City Univ. (Dip. Law). Called to the Bar, Middle Temple, 1986; in practice as barrister, North Eastern Circuit, 1986–2009; a Recorder, 2002–09. *Address:* Great Grimsby Combined Court Centre, Town Hall Square, Grimsby, Lincs DN31 1XH.

BUCKINGHAMSHIRE, 10th Earl of, *cr* 1746; **George Miles Hobart-Hampden;** Bt 1611; Baron Hobart 1728; Partner, Watson Wyatt LLP (formerly Watson Wyatt Partners), consulting actuaries, 1995–2004; *b* 15 Dec. 1944; *s* of Cyril Langel Hobart-Hampden (*d* 1972) (*ggs* of 6th Earl), and Margaret Moncrieff Hilborne Hobart-Hampden (*née* Jolliffe) (*d* 1985); *S* cousin, 1983; *m* 2nd, 1975, Alison Wightman, JP, DL (*née* Forrest); two step *s*. *Educ:* Clifton College; Exeter Univ. (BA Hons History); Birkbeck Coll. and Inst. of Commonwealth Studies, Univ. of London (MA Area Studies). Asst Archivist, Hudson Bay Co., 1968–70; with Noble Lowndes and Partners Ltd, 1970–81; Dir, Scottish Pension Trustees Ltd, 1979–81, resigned; Director: Antony Gibbs Pension Services Ltd, 1981–86; Wardley Investment Services (UK) Ltd, 1986–91; Wardley Investment Services International Ltd (Man. Dir, 1988–91), and of various subsidiaries of Wardley; Gota Global Selection, 1988–95; Korea Asia Fund, 1990–91; Wyatt Co. (UK) Ltd, 1991–95; Russian Pension Trust Co. Ltd, 1994–2001; Associate, 2004, Dir, 2005–14, BESTrustees plc. House of Lords, 1984–99: Member: Sub-Cttee C, 1985–90, Sub-Cttee A, 1990–93, H of L Select Cttee on European Affairs; H of L Sub-Cttee on Staffing of Community Instns, 1987–88. Pres., Buckingham Cons. Constituency Assoc., 1989–2013. President: John Hampden Soc., 1993–; Friends of the Vale of Aylesbury, 1994–2010; Downend Police Community Boxing Club, 2003–. Dir, Britain-Australia Soc., 2004–11 (Dep. Chm., 2006–08; Chm., 2008–10; Dep. Chm., 2010–11); Chairman: Cook Soc., 2007; Aylesbury Vale Community Trust, 2009–13. Mem. Council, Buckinghamshire New Univ. (formerly Buckinghamshire Chilterns UC), 2001–09 (Hon. Fellow, 2009). Gov., Clifton Coll., Bristol, 1991–; Pres., Old Cliftonian Soc., 2000–03. Patron, Chiltern MS Centre, 2005–. FInstD 1983. Affiliate, Inst. of Actuaries, 2001. Patron: Hobart Town (1804) First Settlers Assoc., 1984–; Sleep Apnoea Trust, 1997. Goodwill Ambassador, City of Hobart, Tasmania, 2009. Liveryman, Glovers' Co., 2007; Freeman: City of Geneva, USA, 1987; Glasgow, 1991. *Recreations:* fishing, Real tennis, Rugby football, trekking. *Heir: kinsman* Sir John Vere Hobart, Bt, *qv*. *Address:* The Old Rectory, Church Lane, Edgcott, near Aylesbury, Bucks HP18 0TU. *T:* (01296) 770357. *Clubs:* Royal Over-Seas League; Leamington Tennis, Hatfield Tennis (Dir, 2001–06), Bristol and Bath Tennis, Radley Tennis, Hobart Tennis.

BUCKLAND, David John; artist, designer and film-maker; Creator and Director, Cape Farewell project, since 2000; *b* London, 15 June 1949; *s* of Dennis and Valerie Buckland; partner, Susan, (Siobhan), Davies, *qv*; one *s* one *d*. *Educ:* Hardye's Sch., Dorchester; London Coll. of Communication, Univ. of the Arts. Works exhibited in galleries in London, Paris and NY; works in collections including: NPG; Centre Georges Pompidou, Paris; Metropolitan Mus., NY; Getty Collection, LA; one-man show of digitally mastered portraits of performers, NPG, 1999; work shown and toured worldwide in UN Exhibn for World Envmt Day; video work, Arctic, Millennium Park, Chicago, 2007; *films* include: Dwell Time, 1996; Art in a Changing Climate; Burning Ice, 2010. Cape Farewell project: exhibn, Art & Climate Change, Natural Hist. Mus., 2006, Kampnagel, Hamburg, 2007, Fundación Canal, Madrid, Mirakain, Tokyo, 2008; TV film, Art from the Arctic, 2006. Curator: EARTH for Royal Acad., 2009; Shift Festival, South Bank, 2010. Designer of stage sets and costumes for Royal Ballet, Rambert Dance Co., Second Stride, Compagnie Cré-Ange, Siobhan Davies Dance Co. *Publications:* (with G. Ehrlich) Arctic Heart: a poem cycle, 1992; (jtly) Burning Ice: art and climate change, 2006. *Recreations:* sailing in the High Arctic, cultural activity, love of theatre and dance, keen hill/mountain walker. *E:* davidbuckland@capefarewell.com.

BUCKLAND, Nicholas Brian, OBE 2009; Eur Ing; Chair: Glider Yachts, since 2014; CSW Group, since 2015; Peninsula Community Health Community Interest Company, since 2015; *b* Windsor, 21 Feb. 1951; *s* of William Walter and Eileen Doris Buckland; *m* 1986, Deborah Gaynor Lewis Jeffreys; one *s*. *Educ:* Univ. of Bath (BSc Math. Studies 1973). CEng 1991; CITP 1996; CMgr 2010; Eur Ing 2003. Researcher, BISRA, 1977–80; Support Manager: ICL, 1977–80; Data General, 1980–82; Business Develt Manager, Prime Computer, 1982–87; Sales Manager, Convex, 1987–94; Business Develt Manager, Silicon Graphics, 1994–96. Chair: Tamar Sci. Park, 2006–10; Doctor Communications Solutions, 2008–10; Centre for Modelling and Simulation, 2010–14; Mem. Bd and Dep. Chm., SW RDA, 2001–11; Member, Board: Technol. Strategy Bd, 2004–11; Cornwall Enterprise, 2004–08; Plymouth City Develt Co., 2008–10. Plymouth University: Mem., Bd of Govs, 2002–12 and 2015– (Chm., 2009–12); Pro Chancellor, 2012–. Chm., Engrg Develt Trust, 2012–; Trustee: Plymouth Th. Royal, 2010–; Karst, 2015–. Governor: Shebbear Coll., 2010–; Slough and Eton Business Acad., 2012–. Mem., Governance Community, Nat. Trust, 2012–. MInst 1997; MRI 2002. FRSA 2003; FBCS 2003; FIMA 2006; FCMI 2007. Hon. DTec Plymouth, 2013. *Recreations:* gardening, cricket, Rugby, theatre, music, farming. *Addres* Ditchen Farm, Boyton, Launceston, Cornwall PL15 9RN. *T:* 07768 682683. *E:* buckland01@aol.com. *Clubs:* Farmers; Bude Rugby.

BUCKLAND, Robert James; QC 2014; MP (C) South Swindon, since 2010; Solicitor General, since 2014; *b* Llanelli, 22 Sept. 1968; *s* of Roger Buckland and Barbara Buckland; 1997, Sian Reed; one *s* one *d* (twins). *Educ:* St Michael's Sch., Bryn; Durham Univ. (BA Hons Law 1990). Called to the Bar, Inner Temple, 1991, Bencher, 2015; in practice as a barrister 1992–; a Recorder, 2009–. Mem. (C) Dyfed CC, 1993–96. Contested (C): Islwyn, Feb. 199 Preseli Pembrokeshire, 1997; S Swindon, 2005. Member: Justice Select Cttee, 2010–13 an 2014; Cttee on Standards, 2012–14; Cttee on Privileges, 2012–14; Jt Cttee on Human Right 2013–15; Chairman: Autism All Party Parly Gp, 2011–14; Cons. Party Human Righ Commn, 2011–14; Vice Pres., Tory Reform Gp, 2010–; Jt Sec., 1922 Cttee, 2012–14; Chm Exec. Cttee, Soc. of Cons. Lawyers, 2013–14. Mem., Funding Review Panel for Wales, Leg Services Commn, 2000–09. Gov., Ridgeway Sch., Wroughton, 2005–09; Co-ordinato Swindon Special Educnl Needs Network, 2006–. *Recreations:* music, food, wine, trying t keep up with my family, political and military history, churches, cathedrals, towers, domes an temples. *Address:* House of Commons, SW1A 0AA. *T:* (020) 7219 7168. *E:* robert.buckland.mp@parliament.uk. *Clubs:* Carlton; Llanelli Conservative, Swindo Conservative; Crawshays Welsh Rugby Football.

BUCKLAND, Sir Ross, Kt 1997; Chief Executive and Director, Unigate plc, 1990–2001; 19 Dec. 1942; *s* of William Arthur Haverfield Buckland and Elizabeth Buckland; *m* 196 Patricia Ann Bubb; two *s*. *Educ:* Sydney Boys' High Sch. Various positions in cos engaged i banking, engrg and food ind., 1958–66; Dir, Finance and Admin, Elizabeth Arden Pty Lt 1966–73; Kellogg (Australia) Pty Ltd, 1973–77, Man. Dir, 1978; Pres. and Chief Exec Kellogg Salada Canada Inc., 1979–80; Chm., Kellogg Co. of GB Ltd and Dir, European O and Vice-Pres., Kellogg Co., USA, 1981–90. Director: RJB Mining, 1997–99; Allie Domecq, 1998–2004; Nat. Australia Bank Europe, 1999–2002; Mayne Gp Ltd, 2001–0 Goodman Fielder Ltd, 2001–03; Clayton Utz, 2002–08. FCPA; FCIS; FIGD. *Recreatio* walking. *Address:* GPO Box 511, Sydney, NSW 2001, Australia. *Clubs:* Stadium Australi Royal Sydney Golf (Sydney).

BUCKLAND, Dame Yvonne Helen Elaine, (Dame Yve), DBE 2003; Chair, Roy Orthopaedic Hospital, Birmingham, since 2014; *b* 29 Nov. 1956; *d* of late George Robe Jones and Margaret Ann Jones (*née* O'Hanlon); *m* 1999, Stephen Freer; two *d*. *Educ:* Our Lad of Mercy Grammar Sch., Wolverhampton; Leeds Univ. (BA Hons 1977); Univ. of Liverpo (DipArch 1978); Univ. of Central Lancashire (DMS 1984). FFPH (FFPHM 2001). Archivis 1979–83, Dep. County Archivist, 1983–85, Cheshire CC; Team Leader, Mgt Effectivene Unit, 1985–88, Asst Dir, Social Services, 1988–92, Birmingham CC; Dep. Chief Exec Nottingham CC, 1992–99; Chm., Health Educn Authy for England, 1999–2000; Chai HDA, 2000–05; NHS Inst. for Innovation and Improvement, 2005–11. Non-exec. Dir, Warwicks Primary Care Trust, 2003–05. Dir, Health Partnership, Warwick Business Sch 2003–05. Chm., Consumer Council for Water, 2005–15. Fellow, Warwick Inst. of Govt an Public Mgt, 2001. FRSA 2002. *Recreations:* gardening, bell ringing. *Address:* Roy Orthopaedic Hospital NHS Foundation Trust, Northfield, Birmingham B31 2AP.

BUCKLE, Alan Arthur; independent adviser; *b* 19 May 1959; partner, Adèle; three *s*. *Edu* Durham Univ. (BA). ACA 1986. A Sen. Partner and Chief Exec., KPMG Advisory, 2008–1 Dep. Chm. and CEO, KPMG International, 2011–13. Mem., Bd of Trustees, Britis Council, 2005–12 (Dep. Chm.). *Recreations:* family, small mountains, running, reading and th usual things. *Address:* KPMG, 15 Canada Square, E14 5GL.

BUCKLE, Simon James, CMG 2007; DPhil; FInstP; Head of Climate Change, Biodiversit and Water Division, Organisation for Economic Co-operation and Development, since 201 *b* 29 Feb. 1960; *s* of Roy Thomas Buckle and Muriel May Buckle; *m* 1990, Dr Rajeshre Bhatt; one *d*. *Educ:* Univ. of Bristol (BSc 1st Cl. Jt Hons Physics and Philosophy 1982); Univ of Sussex (DPhil Theoretical Physics 1985); Univ. of London (MSc Financial Econs 1999 Res. Asst, Dept of Physics, Imperial Coll., London, 1985–86; joined HM Diplomatic Servic 1986; Far East Dept, FCO, 1986–88; MoD, 1988–91; Head of Iran Section, Middle Ea Dept, FCO, 1992–94; First Sec., Dublin, 1994–97; Political Counsellor and Consul Gen Seoul, 1997–98; Bank of England, 1998–2002, Sen. Manager (Res.), Market Infrastructur Div., 2001–02; Hd, Res. Analysts, FCO, 2003–04; Political Counsellor, Baghdad, 2004–0 Dep. Hd of Mission, Kabul, 2005–06; Counsellor, Global Issues, Paris, 2006–07; Policy Di Grantham Inst. for Climate Change, 2007–14, Pro Rector for Internat. Affairs, 2011–1 Imperial Coll. London. *Recreations:* hill walking, music. *Address:* Organisation for Economi Co-operation and Development, 2 rue André Pascal, 75775 Paris Cedex 16, France.

BUCKLE, Most Rev. Terrence Owen; Bishop of Yukon, 1995–2010, now Bisho Emeritus; Metropolitan of British Columbia and Yukon, 2005–09; Archbishop of Yukor 2005–10; Founder and Leader, Street Hope Whitehorse; *b* 24 Aug. 1940; *m* 1963, Moyr Blanche Cooke; two *s* two *d*. *Educ:* Church Army Training Coll., Canada; Wycliffe Coll Toronto. Commnd as Church Army Evangelist, 1962; Parish Assistant, St Philip's, Etobicok Ont, 1962–64; Dir of Inner Parish, Little Trinity, Toronto, 1964–66; Church Arm Incumbent: Ch of the Resurrection, Holman, 1966–70; St George's Anglican Missior Cambridge Bay, 1970–72; Incumbent, St David's Anglican Mission, Fort Simpson, 1972–7 ordained deacon, May 1973, priest, Nov. 1973; Priest i/c, Ch of the Ascension, Inuvik, an Regl Dean, Lower Mackenzie, 1975–82; Archdeacon of Liard, dio. of Yukon, 1982–8 Rector: St Mary Magdalene, Fort Nelson, 1982–88; Holy Trinity, Yellowknife, 1988–9 Co-Founder and Evangelist, New Life Evangelism Ministries, 1984–94; Bishop Suffragar dio. of the Arctic, 1993–95. Hon. Canon, St Jude's Cathedral, Iqaluit, 1978. *Recreations:* out of-door activities, canoeing, camping, hiking.

BUCKLER, Very Rev. Philip John Warr; Dean of Lincoln, 2007–Jan. 2016; *b* 26 Apr 1949; *s* of Ernest and Cynthia Buckler; *m* 1977, Linda Marjorie; one *d*. *Educ:* Highgate Sch St Peter's Coll., Oxford (BA, MA); Cuddesdon Theol Coll. Ordained deacon, 1972, pries 1973; Asst Curate, St Peter's, Bushey Heath, 1972–75; Chaplain, Trinity Coll., Cambridge 1975–81; Sacrist and Minor Canon, St Paul's Cathedral, 1981–86; Vicar of Hampstea 1987–99; Area Dean of N Camden, 1993–98; Canon Residentiary, 1999–2007, Treas 2000–07, St Paul's Cathedral. Chaplain, Actors' Church Union, 1983–92; Hon. Chaplair Scriveners' Co., 1984–2007; Merchant Taylors' Co., 1986–87; Spectacle Makers' Co 2000–01; Mem. Court, Corp. of Sons of Clergy, 1996–2004. DUniv Bishop Grossetest 2015. *Recreations:* cricket, walking, gardening. *Address:* (until Jan. 2016) The Deanery, 1 Minster Yard, Lincoln LN2 1PJ. *T:* (01522) 561611. *E:* dean@lincolncathedral.com; (fron Feb. 2016) Green Acre, Whelp Street, Preston St Mary, Suffolk CO10 9NL. *Club* Athenæum, MCC.

BUCKLES, Nicholas Peter; Chief Executive, G4S (formerly Group 4 Securicor), 2005–1 *b* 1 Feb. 1961; *s* of Ronald Peter Buckles and Sylvia Mary Buckles; *m* 1988, Loraine Salte one *s* two *d*. *Educ:* Coventry Univ. (BA Hons Business Studies). Dowty Engrg Gp, 1979–8 Business Analyst, Avon Cosmetics, 1983–85; joined Securicor, 1985: Project Accountan 1985–88; Commercial Manager, 1988–91; Dir, Securicor Cash Services, 1991–93; Dep. Ma Dir, Securicor Guarding, 1993–96; Man. Dir, Securicor Cash Services, 1996–98; Chi Executive: Securicor Europe, 1998–99; Security Div., 1999–2002; Securicor, 2002–0 *Recreations:* soccer, tennis, walking.

UCKLEY, family name of **Baron Wrenbury**.

UCKLEY, Edgar Vincent, CB 1999; PhD; independent defence and security consultant, since 2014; *b* 17 Nov. 1946; *s* of Michael Joseph Buckley and Mary Buckley; *m* 1972, Frances Jacqueline Cheetham; two *s* three *d*. *Educ:* St Ignatius Coll., London; North-Western Poly., London (BA Hons 1967); Birkbeck Coll., London (PhD 1974). Teacher, Redbridge, 1970–73; joined MoD, 1973; Administration Trainee, 1974–76; Private Sec. to Vice Chief of Air Staff, 1976–78; Principal, 1978–79; Assistant Director: Strategic Systems Finance, 1980–84; Nuclear Policy, 1984–85; Head of Resources and Programmes (Navy), 1985–89; rcds, 1990; Efficiency Study, Cabinet Office, 1991 (on secondment); Head of Defence Arms Control Unit, 1991–92; Defence Counsellor, UK Delegn to NATO, 1992–96 (on secondment); Asst Under-Sec. of State (Home and Overseas), 1996–99; Asst Sec. Gen. for Defence Planning and Operations, NATO, 1999–2003; Sen. Vice-Pres., European Marketing and Sales, 2003–11, Sen. Consultant, 2011–13, Thales. *Recreations:* running, swimming, reading, home maintenance. *Address:* 5 Vanbrugh Terrace, SE3 7AP.

UCKLEY, Sir George (William), Kt 2011; PhD; Chairman, Arle Capital LLP, since 2012; *b* 1947. *Educ:* Huddersfield Poly. (BSc Electrical and Electronic Engrg 1972); Huddersfield Poly. and Univ. of Southampton (PhD Engrg 1976). General Motors; GEC; Man. Dir, Central Services Div., British Railways, 1989–93; Emerson Electric Co., 1993–97: Chief Technol. Officer; President: Electric Motors Div.; Automotive and Precision Motors Div.; Brunswick Corporation, 1997–2005: Pres., Mercury Marine, 1997; Chm. and CEO, 2000–05; Chm., Pres. and CEO, 3M, 2005–12. Non-executive Chairman: Expro, 2012–; Ownership Capital, 2013–; Smiths Gp, 2013–; non-executive Director: Archer Daniels Midland Co., 2006–; Stanley Black & Decker, 2010–; PepsiCo, 2012–; Hitachi, 2012–; Technogym, 2012–; Mem. Adv. Bd, Deutsche Bank; Sen. Advr, Rothschild America, 2012–. Hon. DSc: Huddersfield, 2003; Southampton, 2012. *Address:* Arle Capital Partners Ltd, 12 Charles II Street, SW1Y 4QU.

UCKLEY, James; Chief Executive, Baltic Exchange, 1992–2004; *b* 5 April 1944; *s* of late Harold Buckley and of Mabel Buckley; *m* 1972, Valerie Elizabeth Powles; one *d*. *Educ:* Sheffield City Grammar Sch.; Imperial College of Science and Technology (BSc, ARCS). RAF Operational Res., 1965. Principal Scientific Officer, 1971; Asst Sec., CSD; Private Secretary: to Lord Privy Seal, Lord Peart, 1979; to Lord President of Council, Lord Soames, 1979; to Chancellor of Duchy of Lancaster, Baroness Young, 1981; Sec., Civil Service Coll., 1982; Chief Exec., BVA, 1985–87; Dep. Dir Gen., GCBS, 1987–91. *Recreations:* photography, tennis. *Address:* 1 Aldenholme, Weybridge, Surrey KT13 0JF.

UCKLEY, Martin Howard; Chairman, Multichem Ltd, 2009–14 (non-executive Director, 2008–14); non-executive Director, Yorwaste Ltd, since 2009; *b* 10 Aug. 1945; *s* of Charles and Elma Buckley; *m* 1972, Kay Lesley Rowson; one *s* one *d*. FCA 1969. Man. Dir, packaging subsid., Rexam plc, 1976–79; CEO, NY and Philadelphia Box Plants, LINPAC Containers Internat. Ltd, 1979–85; Waddington plc: Divl Chief Exec., 1985–90; Man. Dir, 1990–92; Chief Exec., 1992–2000. Chm., Leeds Teaching Hospitals NHS Trust, 2003–09. Non-exec. Dir, Magnadata Internat. Ltd, 2002–04. *Recreations:* walking, clay-pigeon shooting. *T:* 07836 292633.

UCKLEY, Sir Michael (Sydney), Kt 2002; Parliamentary Commissioner for Administration, and Health Service Commissioner for England, Scotland and Wales, 1997–2002; Scottish Parliamentary Commissioner for Administration and Welsh Administration Ombudsman, 1999–2002; *b* 20 June 1939; *s* of Sydney Dowsett Buckley and Grace Bew Buckley; *m* 1st, 1972, Shirley Stordy (*d* 1991); one *s* one *d*; 2nd, 1992, Judith Cartmell (*née* Cobb); two step *s* one step *d*. *Educ:* Eltham College; Christ Church, Oxford (MA; Cert. of Stats). Asst Principal, Treasury, 1962; Asst Private Sec. to Chancellor of Exchequer, 1965–66; Principal: Treasury, 1966–68 and 1971–74; CSD, 1968–71; Assistant Secretary: Treasury, 1974–77 and 1980–82; DoI, 1977–80; Under Secretary: Cabinet Office, 1982–85; Dept of Energy, 1985–91; Chm., Dartford and Gravesham NHS Trust, 1995–96. Member: CS Appeal Bd, 1991–96; GMC, 2003–08. *Recreations:* photography, listening to music, reading. *Address:* 1 Manor Court, Bearsted, Maidstone, Kent ME14 4BZ.

UCKLEY, Prof. Peter Jennings, OBE 2012; PhD; FBA 2014; Professor of International Business, University of Leeds, since 1995; *b* Ashton-under-Lyne, 11 July 1949; *s* of Robert and Florence Buckley; *m* 1978, Ann Patricia Kelland; one *s* one *d*. *Educ:* Ashton-under-Lyne Grammar Sch.; Univ. of York (BA Hons Social Scis 1970); Univ. of E Anglia (MA Develt Econs 1971); Univ. of Lancaster (PhD Econs 1975). Esmée Fairbairn res. asst, Univ. of Reading, 1973–74; University of Bradford: Lectr in Internat. Business, 1974–80; Sen. Lectr in Internat. Business, 1980–84; Prof. of Managerial Econs, 1984–95. Cheung Kong Schol. Chair Prof., Univ. of Internat. Business and Econs, Beijing, 2010–. Dr *hc* Uppsala, 2010; Hon. DSc Lappeenranta, Finland, 2012. Series Ed., New Horizons in Internat. Business, 1992–. *Publications:* (jtly) The Future of the Multinational Enterprise, 1976 (trans. Japanese, 1993; Korean, 1995), 25th anniv. edn, 2002 (trans. Chinese, 2005); (jtly) Going International, 1978, 2nd edn as Foreign Direct Investment by Smaller UK Firms, 1988; (jtly) European Direct Investments in the USA before World War I, 1982; (jtly) Direct Investment in the UK by Smaller European Firms, 1983; (jtly) The Industrial Relations Practices of Foreign-Owned Firms in British Manufacturing Industry, 1985; (jtly) The Economic Theory of the Multinational Enterprise, 1985; (jtly) Die Multinationalen Unternehmen und der Arbeitsmarkt, 1986; (jtly) North-South Direct Investment in the European Communities, 1987; The Theory of the Multinational Enterprise, 1987; (ed jtly) Handbook of International Trade, 1988; The Multinational Enterprise: theory and applications, 1989; (ed) International Investment, 1990; (jtly) The Management of International Tourism, 1991, 2nd edn 1995; (jtly) International Aspects of UK Economic Activities, 1991; (ed jtly) Multinational Enterprises in Less Developed Countries, 1991; (jtly) Servicing International Markets, 1992; (jtly) International Business Studies: an overview, 1992 (trans. Japanese, 1994); Studies in International Business, 1992; (ed) New Directions in International Business, 1992; (ed jtly) Multinational Enterprises in the World Economy, 1992; (ed jtly) The Internationalisation of the Firm, 1993, 2nd edn 1999; (ed jtly) The Economics of Change in East and Central Europe and its Impact on International Business, 1994; (ed) Cooperative Forms of TNC Activity, 1994; (jtly) Canada–UK: bilateral trade and investment relations, 1995; Foreign Direct Investment and Multinational Enterprises, 1995; (ed jtly) Firms, Organizations and Contracts, 1996; (ed jtly) Multinational Firms and International Relocation, 1997; (ed jtly) Technology Transfer by Small and Medium Sized Enterprises, 1997; International Business: economics and anthropology, theory and method, 1998; International Strategic Management and Government Policy, 1998; (ed jtly) Globalization and Regionalization, 1998; (ed jtly) The Strategy and Organisation of International Business, 1998; (ed jtly) The Global Challenge for Multinational Enterprises, 1999; Multinational Firms, Cooperation and Competition in the World Economy, 2000; (ed jtly) International Mergers and Acquisitions, 2002; The Changing Global Context of International Business, 2003; (ed) International Business, 2003; (jtly) Strategic Business Alliances, 2004; The Challenge of International Business, 2004; (ed) What is International Business?, 2004 (trans. Chinese, 2009); The Multinational Enterprise and the Globalization of Knowledge, 2006; Foreign Direct Investment, China and the World Economy, 2009; (jtly) The Multinational Enterprise Revisited: the essential Buckley and Casson, 2010; Business History and International Business History, 2011; (ed) Globalization and the Global Factory, 2011; Innovations in International Business, 2012; The Multinational Enterprise and the Emergence of the Global Factory, 2014. *Recreations:* cricket, cartography, football, history, theatre, walking, complaining about the Church of England. *Address:* Leeds University Business School, Maurice Keyworth Building, Leeds, W Yorks LS2 9JT. *T:* (0113) 343 4646, *Fax:* (0113) 343 4754. *E:* pjb@lubs.leeds.ac.uk.

BUCKLEY, Lt-Comdr Sir (Peter) Richard, KCVO 1982 (CVO 1973; MVO 1968); *b* 31 Jan. 1928; 2nd *s* of late Alfred Buckley and Mrs E. G. Buckley, Crowthorne, Berks; *m* 1958, Theresa Mary Neve; two *s* one *d*. *Educ:* Wellington Coll. Cadet, RN, 1945. Served in HM Ships: Mauritius, Ulster, Contest, Defender, and BRNC, Dartmouth. Specialised in TA/S. Invalided from RN (Lt-Comdr), 1961. Private Sec. to the Duke and Duchess of Kent, 1961–89; Extra Equerry to the Duke of Kent, 1989–. Director: Vickers Internat., 1981–89; Malcolm McIntyre Consultancy, 1989–92. Governor: Wellington Coll., 1989–98; Eagle House Sch., 1989–98 (Chm. of Govs, 1992–98). FRGS 1999. *Recreations:* fishing, sailing, bee keeping. *Address:* Coppins Cottages, Iver, Bucks SL0 0AT. *T:* (01753) 653004. *Clubs:* Army and Navy; All England Lawn Tennis and Croquet.

BUCKLEY, Hon. Sir Roger (John), Kt 1989; a Judge of the High Court of Justice, Queen's Bench Division, 1989–2004; *b* 26 April 1939; *s* of Harold and Marjorie Buckley; *m* 1965, Margaret Gillian, *d* of Robert and Joan Cowan; one *s* one *d*. *Educ:* Mill Hill Sch.; Manchester Univ. (LLB (Hons)). Called to the Bar, Middle Temple, 1962 (Harmsworth Schol.); Bencher, Middle Temple, 1987; QC 1979; a Recorder, 1986–89; a Judge of the Employment Appeal Tribunal, 1994–2004; Pres., Restrictive Practices Court, 1994–2001. Member: Judicial Panel, City Disputes Panel, 2005–; Investment Adv. Panel, Woodsford Litigation Funding Ltd, 2011–. Chm., British Horseracing Authy Disciplinary Appeal Bd (formerly Jockey Club Appeal Bd), 2005–. Mem. Bd, Painshill Park Trust Ltd, 2007– (Trustee, 2005–). *Recreations:* golf, theatre, breeding and racing thoroughbreds. *Address:* Brick Court Chambers, 2–8 Essex Street, WC2R 3LD. *Club:* Old Millhillians.

BUCKMAN, Dr Laurence, FRCGP; Chairman, General Practitioners Committee, British Medical Association, 2007–13 (Deputy Chairman, 2004–07); General Practitioner, Temple Fortune Health Centre, London, since 1993; *b* London, 19 March 1954; *s* of Allan Buckman and Toni Buckman; *m* 1978, Elise Sider; two *s*. *Educ:* University College Sch.; University Coll. Hosp. Med. Sch. (MB BS 1977). FRCGP 2001. Jun. Hosp. posts, UCH, Hertford Co. Hosp., Edgware Gen., St Bartholomew's Hosp., Royal Marsden Hosp., 1977–81; Med. Registrar, Mount Vernon Hosp., 1981–83; GP, Borehamwood, Herts, 1983–93. Tutor, Gen. Practice, UCL Med. Sch., 1985–. *Publications:* contrib. articles on medicine and med. politics. *Recreations:* photography, music, travel, model railways. *Address:* 21 Southover, Woodside Park, N12 7JG. *T:* (020) 8446 4667.

BUCKMASTER, family name of **Viscount Buckmaster**.

BUCKMASTER, 4th Viscount *cr* 1933, of Cheddington, Buckinghamshire; **Adrian Charles Buckmaster;** Baron 1915; Chief Executive Officer and Director, Avecia Holdings plc, since 2006; *s* of Hon. Colin John Buckmaster and of May Buckmaster (*née* Gibbon); *S* uncle, 2007; *m* 1975, Dr Elizabeth Mary Mark; one *s* two *d*. *Educ:* Charterhouse; Clare Coll., Cambridge (BA 1970; MA 1974). *Heir:* *s* Hon. Andrew Nicholas Buckmaster [*b* 1980; *m* 2014, Dr Helen R. Murray].

BUCKNALL, Lt Gen. Sir James (Jeffrey Corfield), KCB 2013; CBE 2004 (MBE 1994); Chief Executive, Weybourne Partners LLP, since 2013; *b* 29 Nov. 1958; *s* of Captain Robin Bucknall and Diana Bucknall, MBE; *m* 1986, Tessa Jane Freemantle (*née* Barrett); two *s*. *Educ:* Winchester Coll. Joined Army, 1977; commnd Coldstream Guards, 1978; served with 2nd Bn in GB, Germany, NI and Cyprus; Staff Coll., 1990; co. comd NI, 1991 (despatches, 1992); on staff, HQ NI, 1992–96; CO, 1st Bn, Germany and England, 1996–98; COS, 1st (UK) Armd Div., Bosnia and Germany, 1998–2001; HCSC 2001; Comdr, 39 Inf. Bde, Belfast, 2001–03; Dir, Counter Terrorism and UK Ops, MoD, 2004–06; served with HQ Multi-National Force Iraq, Baghdad, 2006; COS, ARRC, Afghanistan, then Germany, 2006–09; Asst Chief of Gen. Staff, 2009–10; Dep. Comdr, ISAF Afghanistan, 2010–11; Comdr Allied Rapid Reaction Corps, 2011–13. Sen. Associate Fellow, RUSI, 2013–. Col, Coldstream Guards, 2009–. QCVS 2011. Officer, Legion of Merit (USA), 2009. *Recreations:* shooting, fishing, cricket, military history, long suffering supporter of Newcastle United. *Clubs:* Pratt's, MCC, Cavalry and Guards.

BUCKNELL, Bruce James; HM Diplomatic Service; Ambassador to Belarus, 2012–15; *b* Reading, 15 April 1962; *s* of John and Mary Bucknell; *m* 1993, Henrietta Dorrington-Ward; two *s*. *Educ:* Taunton Sch.; Durham Univ. (BA Hons Modern Hist. 1984). Entered FCO, 1985; Third Sec., Chancery, Amman, 1988–91; on secondment to EBRD, 1992; Desk Officer, Africa Dept (Equatorial), FCO, 1992–93; Policy Co-ordinator, Africa Comd, FCO, 1993–94; Italian lang. trng, 1994–95; Consul (Press and Public Affairs), Milan, 1995–99; Desk Officer, NATO Section, Security Policy Dept, FCO, 1999–2001; Hd, Central Europe Section, Central and NW Europe Dept (later EU Internal), FCO, 2001–03; Spanish lang. trng, 2003; First Sec., Madrid, 2003–07; Deputy Head: Sudan Unit, FCO/DFID, 2007–09; Estates and Security Directorate, 2009–12. *Recreations:* family, culture, sport, countryside. *Address:* c/o Foreign and Commonwealth Office, King Charles Street, SW1A 2AH. *E:* bruce.bucknell@fco.gov.uk.

BUCKNILL, Thomas Michael, RD 1983; FRCS; Consultant Orthopaedic Surgeon, St Bartholomew's Hospital, since 1977 and Royal London Hospital, since 1995; *b* 11 Jan. 1942; *m* 1st, 1968, Rachael Offer (marr. diss. 1998); one *s* three *d*; 2nd, 1999, Annie Marshall. *Educ:* Douai Sch.; St Bartholomew's Hosp. Med. Coll., London (MB BS 1964). FRCS 1970. House Surgeon, 1965–66, Anatomy Demonstrator, 1966–67, St Bartholomew's Hosp.; Surgical Registrar, St Stephen's Hosp., Chelsea, 1968–70; Registrar, Royal Nat. Orthopaedic Hosp., Stanmore, 1970–76; Clin. Fellow, Harvard Med. Sch., 1976; Cons. Orthopaedic Surgeon, King Edward VII Hosp., London, 1981–. MO, RNR London Div., 1967–93; Surgeon Comdr, RNR, 1987–93, retd; PMO, Royal Marines Reserve, London, 1988–91. FRSocMed 1995. *Publications:* (contrib.) Textbook of General Surgery, 1980. *Recreations:* sailing, golf. *Clubs:* Naval; Moor Park Golf, Royal Southampton Yacht.

BUCKWELL, Prof. Allan Edgar; Senior Research Fellow, Institute for European Environmental Policy, since 2012; *b* 10 April 1947; *s* of George Alfred Donald Buckwell and Jessie Ethel Buckwell (*née* Neave); *m* 1967, Susan Margaret Hopwood (marr. diss. 1990); two *s*; *m* 1997, Dr Elizabeth Gay Mitchell. *Educ:* Wye Coll., Univ. of London (BSc Agric.); Manchester Univ. (MA Econ.). Research Associate, Agricl Adjustment Unit, Newcastle Univ., 1970–73; Lectr in Agricl Economics, Newcastle Univ., 1973–84; Prof. of Agricl Econs, Wye Coll., Univ. of London, 1984–99; Policy Dir, Country Land and Business Assoc., 2000–11. Kellogg Res. Fellow, Univ. of Wisconsin, Madison, 1974–75; Vis. Prof., Cornell Univ., 1983. Auxiliare, DG VI, EC, 1995–96. *Publications:* (jtly) The Cost of the Common Agricultural Policy, 1982; Chinese Grain Economy and Policy, 1989; Privatisation of Agriculture in New Market Economies: lessons from Bulgaria, 1994; articles in Jl Agricl Economics. *Recreations:* walking, gardening, cycling. *Address:* 51 Joy Lane, Whitstable, Kent CT5 4DE. *T:* (01227) 265684. *E:* allan.buckwell@gmail.com.

BUCZACKI, Dr Stefan Tadeusz; biologist; broadcaster, author, expert witness, public speaker and consultant, since 1984; *b* 16 Oct. 1945; *o s* of Tadeusz Buczacki and Madeleine Mary Cato Buczacki (*née* Fry); *m* 1970, Beverley Ann Charman; two *s*. *Educ:* Ecclesbourne Sch., Duffield; Univ. of Southampton (BSc 1st cl. Hons Botany, 1968); Linacre Coll., Oxford (DPhil 1971). FCIHort (FIHort 1986); CBiol, FRSB; ARPS; FLS. Research Biologist, Nat. Vegetable Res. Station, 1971–84; Partner, Stefan Buczacki Associates, landscape and garden design, 2001–12. Gardening Correspondent: The Guardian, 1986–95; Sunday Mirror,

1993–96; Manchester Evening News, 1997–2009; Weekly Columnist: Amateur Gardening 1974–97; Garden News 1997–. *Radio:* Gardeners' Question Time, 1982–94; Classic Gardening Forum, 1994–97; The Gardening Quiz (originator and writer), 1988–93; *television:* Gardeners' Direct Line, 1983–85; That's Gardening, 1989–90, 1992; Bazaar, 1989–93; Gardeners' World, 1990–91; Chelsea Flower Show, 1990–91; Good Morning, 1992–96; Stefan Buczacki's Gardening Britain, 1996; At Home, 1997–98; Stefan's Garden Roadshow, 1998–2000; Open House, 1998–2002; Learn to Garden with Stefan Buczacki, 1999; Stefan's Ultimate Gardens, 2001; Gardens of Kent, 2009; guest appearances on progs incl. Christmas University Challenge, 2013. President: W Midlands ASE, 1996–97; British Mycological Soc., 1999–2000 (Vice-Pres., 1994, Press Officer, 2002–08; Mem. Council, 2009–); Mem. Council, Gardeners' Royal Benevolent Soc., 1990–98. Trustee: Brogdale Horticultural Trust, 1990–95; Hestercombe Gardens Trust, 1996–2006 (Chm., Estates Cttee, 2003–06); North of England Zool Soc./Chester Zoo, 2009–. Chm., Pershore Forward, 2007–. Patron: Parrs Wood Rural Trust, 1990–; Dawlish Gardens Trust, 1990–; Warwick Castle Gdns Trust, 1992–; Friends of Hestercombe Gardens, 1994–2006; Nat. Amateur Gardening Show, 1996–98; Southport Flower Show, 1997–. Hon. Prof., Biol Scis (formerly Plant Pathology), Liverpool John Moores Univ., 1994–. Honorary Fellow: CABI Bioscience, 2003; Warwicks Coll., 2007. Benefactors' Medal, British Mycological Soc., 1996; Veitch Gold Meml Medal, RHS, 2010; Lifetime Achievement Award, Garden Media Guild, 2013. DUniv Derby, 2002. *Publications:* (jtly) Collins Guide to the Pests, Diseases and Disorders of Garden Plants, 1981 (shorter Guide, 1983), 4th edn 2014; Gem Guide to Mushrooms and Toadstools, 1982; (ed) Zoosporic Plant Pathogens, 1983; Beat Garden Pests and Diseases, 1985; Gardeners' Questions Answered, 1985; (jtly) Three Men in a Garden, 1986; Ground Rules for Gardeners, 1986; Beginners Guide to Gardening, 1988; Creating a Victorian Flower Garden, 1988; Garden Warfare, 1988; New Generation Guide to the Fungi of Britain and Europe, 1989; A Garden for all Seasons, 1990; Understanding Your Garden, 1990; The Essential Gardener, 1991; Dr Stefan Buczacki's Gardening Hints, 1992; Mushrooms and Toadstools of Britain and Europe, 1992; The Plant Care Manual, 1992; (ed) The Gardener's Handbook, 1993; The Budget Gardening Year, 1993; Best Climbers, 1994; Best Foliage Shrubs, 1994; Best Shade Plants, 1994; Best Soft Fruit, 1994; (jtly) Classic FM Garden Planner, 1995; Best Water Plants, 1995; Best Herbs, 1995; Best Geraniums, 1998; Best Roses, 1996; Best Container Plants, 1996; Stefan Buczacki's Gardening Britain, 1996; Best Garden Doctor, 1997; Best Summer Flowering Shrubs, 1997; Best Winter Plants, 1997; Best Clematis, 1998; Best Pruning, 1998; Stefan Buczacki's Gardening Dictionary, 1998; Stefan Buczacki's Plant Dictionary, 1998; Best Fuchsias, 1999; Best Evergreens, 1999; First Time Gardener, 2000; Best Water Gardens, 2000; Best Kitchen Herbs, 2000; Essential Garden Answers, 2000; Best Ground Cover, 2000; Best Rock Garden Plants, 2000; Plant Problems: prevention and treatment, 2000; Hamlyn Encyclopaedia of Gardening, 2002; Fauna Britannica, 2002; The Commonsense Gardener, 2004; (jtly) Young Gardener, 2006; Garden Natural History, 2007; Collins Wildlife Gardener, 2007; Churchill and Chartwell: the untold story of Churchill's houses and gardens, 2007; National Trust Chartwell Guide, 2010; Collins Fungi Guide, 2012; The Herb Bible, 2015; My Darling Mr Asquith: the life and times of Venetia Stanley, 2016; contrib. chapters in books and to Oxford DNB; articles in magazines and newspapers; numerous scientific papers in professional jls. *Recreations:* own garden, photography, riding, fishing, natural history, book collecting, theatre, kippers, Derbyshire porcelain, fine music, travelling and then returning to appreciate the British countryside. *Address:* Prospect House, Clifford Chambers, Stratford-upon-Avon, Warks CV37 8HX. *T:* (01789) 298106. *W:* www.stefanbuczacki.co.uk. *Club:* Garrick.

BUD, Dr Robert Franklin; Research Keeper, Science Museum, since 2014 (Keeper of Science and Medicine, 2011–14); *b* 21 April 1952; *s* of Martin Bud and Hanna Bud (*née* Loebl); *m* 1979, Lisa Frierman; one *s*. *Educ:* University Coll. Sch.; Univ. of Manchester (BSc 1st Cl. Liberal Studies in Sci. 1973); Univ. of Pennsylvania (PhD 1980). Science Museum: Asst Keeper, Industrial Chem., 1978–85; Dep. Keeper, Dept of Physical Scis, 1985–89; Hd, Collections Services, 1989–91; Hd, Life and Envmtl Scis, 1991–94; Manager, Life and Commns Technols, and Res. (Collections), subseq. Information and Res., then Electronic Access, 1994–2007; Principal Curator of Medicine, 2002–11. Associate Sen. Res. Fellow, Centre for Evaluation of Public Policy and Practice, Brunel Univ., 1990–95; Adjunct Prof., Univ. of Va, 1993; Associated Scholar, Dept of History and Philosophy of Sci., Univ. of Cambridge, 2002–; Honorary Senior Research Fellow: Dept Sci. and Technol. Studies, UCL, 2003–; Dept History, Classics and Archaeology, Birkbeck Coll., London, 2003–12; Hon. Professorial Fellow, Dept History, QMUL, 2008–13; AHRC Science in Culture Res. Fellow, 2011–12; Sarton Prof. of History of Sci., Univ. of Ghent, 2012–13; AHRC Leadership Fellow, 2014–Feb. 2016. Associate Editor, Outlook on Sci. Policy, 1989–91; Member Editorial Board: Brit. Jl for Hist. of Sci., 1982–2005; History and Technol., 1993–2009; New Genetics and Society, 1999–; Mem., Editl Adv. Bd, Oxford Companion to the History of Science, 1998–. Member of Council: Brit. Soc. for Hist. of Sci., 1985–88; Soc. for Hist. of Technol., 1996–98; Mem. Steering Cttee, Hist. of Twentieth Century Medicine Gp, Wellcome Trust, 1998–. Trustee, RN Submarine Mus., 1994–99. FWAAS 1989; FRHistS 1999. (Jtly) Bunge Prize, Hans Jenemann Stiftung, 1998. *Publications:* (with G. K. Roberts) Science versus Practice: chemistry in Victorian Britain, 1984; (jtly) Chemistry in America 1876–1976: historical indicators, 1984; The Uses of Life: a history of biotechnology, 1993 (trans. German 1995); edited jointly: Invisible Connections: instruments, institutions and science, 1992; Guide to the History of Technology in Europe, 1992, 3rd edn 1996; Instruments of Science: an historical encyclopedia, 1998; Manifesting Medicine: bodies and machines, 1999; Cold War, Hot Science: applied research in British defence laboratories 1945–1990, 1999; (jtly) Inventing the Modern World: technology since 1750, 2000; Penicillin: triumph and tragedy, 2007; articles in learned jls. *Recreations:* family life, walking, second-hand bookshops. *Address:* Science Museum, Exhibition Road, SW7 2DD. *T:* (020) 7942 4200. *E:* robert.bud@sciencemuseum.ac.uk.

BUDD, Sir Alan (Peter), GBE 2013; Kt 1997; *b* 16 Nov. 1937; *s* of late Ernest and Elsie Budd; *m* 1964, Susan (*née* Millott); three *s*. *Educ:* Oundle Sch. (Grocers' Co. Schol.); London School of Economics (Leverhulme Schol.; BScEcon); Churchill Coll., Cambridge (PhD). Lectr, Southampton Univ., 1966–69; Ford Foundn Vis. Prof., Carnegie-Mellon Univ., Pittsburgh, 1969–70; Sen. Economic Advr, HM Treasury, 1970–74; Williams & Glyn's Sen. Res. Fellow, London Business Sch., 1974–78; High Level Cons., OECD, 1976–77; Special Advr, Treasury and CS Cttee, 1979–81; Dir, Centre for Economic Forecasting, 1980–88, Prof. of Econs, 1981–91, Fellow, 1997, London Business Sch.; Gp Economic Advr, Barclays Bank, 1988–91; Chief Economic Advr to HM Treasury, and Head of Govt Economic Service, 1991–97; Mem., Monetary Policy Cttee, Bank of England, 1997–99; Sen. Advr, Credit Suisse, 1999–2012. Provost, The Queen's Coll., Oxford, 1999–2008; Chm., Office for Budget Responsibility, 2010. Reserve Bank of Aust. Vis. Prof., Univ. of New South Wales, 1983. Member: Securities and Investments Board, 1987–88; ABRC, 1991; Chairman: Gambling Rev. Body, 2000–01; Tax Law Review Cttee, 2006–12. Member: Council, Inst. for Fiscal Studies, 1988–91, 2004–; Council, REconS, 1988–93. Chairman: British Performing Arts Medicine Trust, 1998–2005; Schola Cantorum of Oxford, 2002–08. Governor: LSE, 1994–2002; NIESR, 1998–. Econs columnist, The Independent, 1991. Hon. Fellow, Queen's Coll., Oxford, 2008. Hon. DSc Salford, 2009. *Publications:* The Politics of Economic Planning, 1978; articles in professional jls. *Recreations:* music, gardening. *Club:* Reform.

BUDD, Sir Colin (Richard), KCMG 2002 (CMG 1991); HM Diplomatic Service, retired; Ambassador to the Netherlands, 2001–05; *b* 31 Aug. 1945; *s* of Bernard Wilfred Budd, QC and Margaret Alison Budd, MBE (*née* Burgin); *m* 1971, Agnes Smit; one *s* one *d*. *Edu* Kingswood Sch., Bath; Pembroke Coll., Cambridge. Entered HM Diplomatic Service, 196 CO, 1967–68; Asst Private Sec. to Minister without Portfolio, 1968–69; Warsaw, 1969–7 Islamabad, 1972–75; FCO, 1976–80; The Hague, 1980–84; Asst Private Sec. to Sec. of Sta for Foreign and Commonwealth Affairs, 1984–87; European Secretariat, Cabinet Offic 1987–88; Counsellor (Political), Bonn, 1989–92; Chef de Cabinet to Sir Leon Brittan, Vic Pres. of EC, 1993–96; Dep. Sec., Cabinet Office (on secondment), 1996–97; Dep. Unde Sec. of State, FCO, 1997–2001. Member: Commn for Racial Equality, 2006–07; Q Selection Panel, 2009–13; Prime Minister's Adv. Cttee on Business Appts, 2010–. *Recreation* running, mountains, music (Mozart, chansons, Don McLean). *E:* acbudd@hotmail.com.

BUDD, Rt Rev. Mgr Hugh Christopher; Bishop of Plymouth, (RC), 1986–2014, no Emeritus; *b* 27 May 1937; *s* of John Alfred and Phyllis Mary Budd. *Educ:* St Mary's Prima School, Hornchurch, Essex; Salesian Coll., Chertsey, Surrey; Cotton Coll., North Staff English Coll., Rome. PhL; STD. Ordained Priest, 1962; post-ordination studies, 1963–6 Tutor, English Coll., Rome, 1965–71; Lectr at Newman Coll., Birmingham and part-tim Asst Priest, Northfield, Birmingham, 1971–76; Head of Training, Catholic Marriage Adviso Council, National HQ, London, 1976–79; Rector, St John's Seminary, Wonersh, Surre 1979–85; Administrator, Brentwood Cathedral, Essex, Nov. 1985–Jan. 1986. *Recreation* walking, cricket (watching), music (listening). *Address:* The Presbytery, Silver Street, Lym Regis, Dorset DT7 3HS.

BUDD, Prof. Malcolm John, PhD; FBA 1995; Grote Professor of Philosophy of Mind an Logic, University College London, 1998–2001, now Emeritus; *b* 23 Dec. 1941; *s* of Edwar Charles Budd and Hilare (*née* Campbell). *Educ:* Latymer Upper Sch.; Jesus Coll., Cambridg (BA 1964; MA 1967; PhD 1968). William Stone Research Fellow, Peterhouse, Cambridg 1966–70; University College London: Lectr in Philosophy, 1970–87; Reader, 1987–90; Pro of Philosophy, 1990–98. Pres., British Soc. of Aesthetics, 2004–13. Editor, Aristotelian Soc 1989–94. Hon. Fellow, Peterhouse, Cambridge, 2011. *Publications:* Music and the Emotion 1985; Wittgenstein's Philosophy of Psychology, 1989; Values of Art, 1995; The Aesthet Appreciation of Nature, 2002; Aesthetic Essays, 2008. *Address:* 12 Hardwick Stree Cambridge CB3 9JA.

BUDENBERG, Robin Francis, CBE 2015; London Chairman, Centerview Partners, sinc 2014; *b* 8 May 1959; *m* 1989, Jacqueline; two *s* two *d*. *Educ:* Rugby Sch.; Exeter Univ. Pric Waterhouse, 1980–84; with S. G. Warburg, subseq. SBC Warburg, then Warburg Dillo Read, then UBS Warburg, later UBS Investment Bank, 1984–2009; CEO, 2009–12, Chm 2012–13, UK Financial Investments.

BUDGE, Keith Joseph; Headmaster, Bedales Schools, since 2001; *b* 24 May 1957; *s* William and Megan Budge; *m* 1983, Caroline Ann Gent; two *s* one *d*. *Educ:* Rossall Sch University Coll., Oxford (MA Hons English; PGCE). Asst Master, Eastbourne Coll 1980–84; Marlborough College: Asst Master, 1984–88 and 1989–91; Housemaster, Cotto Hse, 1991–95; Instructor in English, Stevenson Sch., Pebble Beach, CA, 1988–8 Headmaster, Loretto Sch., 1995–2000. *Recreations:* hill-walking, trout-fishing, gadget theatre. *Address:* Bedales Schools, Petersfield, Hants GU32 2DG.

BUDGEN, Keith Graham, CBE 2012; Chair and Panel Member, Judicial Appointmen Commission, since 2012; Regional Director, South East, HM Courts Service, 2006–11; *b* 1 Oct. 1950; *s* of Victor Charles Budgen and Norma Budgen (*née* Day); *m* 1980, Penelope An Lane; one *s* two *d*. *Educ:* Claygate Primary Sch.; Waynflete Sch., Esher. Lord Chancellor Department, then Department for Constitutional Affairs, later MoJ, 1967–2011: Grou Manager: Newcastle upon Tyne Gp of Courts, 1990–98; London Gp of Crown Court 1998–2002; Dir, Criminal Justice Improvement, 2002–06. Asst Comr, Boundary Commn fo England, 2011–12. *Recreations:* renovating houses, gardening, walking, socialising.

BUDGETT, Richard Gordon McBride, OBE 2003; Medical and Scientific Directo International Olympic Committee, since 2012; *b* 20 March 1959; *s* of Robert and Fio Budgett; *m* 1987, Sue Moore; one *s* two *d*. *Educ:* Radley Coll.; Selwyn Coll., Cambridge (B 1980, MA 1984); Middlesex Hosp., London (MB BS 1983); London Hosp. (Dip. Spor Medicine 1989); DCH RCP 1986; DRCOG 1987. MRCGP 1988; FISM 2001; FFSEM 2003. Won Gold Medal for rowing (coxed fours), Los Angeles Olympic Games, 198 Principal in General Practice, Acton, 1989–2004; CMO, Olympic Medical Centr 1989–2009; Dir of Med. Services, British Olympic Assoc., 1994–2008; Sports Physicia English Inst. of Sport, 2003–12; Chief Med. Officer, LOCOG, 2007–12. MO, Governin Body, British Bobsleigh Assoc., 1989–2007; Dr, Bobsleigh Team, Olympic Winter Game 1992, 1994; CMO, British Team at Olympic Games, 1996, 1998, 2000, 2002, 2004, 200 Mem., IOC Med. Commn at Olympic Games, 2008, 2010. Chm., British Assoc. of Spor Exercise Medicine, 2008–11; Mem., List Cttee, World Anti-Doping Agency, 2005– (Chm 2011–12); Bd Mem., then Chm., Nat. Sports Medicine Inst., 1994–2000; Examine Intercollegiate Academic Bd of Sports and Exercise Medicine, 2000. Hon. FRCP 201 *Publications:* articles on sports and exercise medicine in med. jls, mainly on 'Unexplaine Underperformance Syndrome'. *Recreations:* sailing, ski-ing and ski-touring, cycling, rowin good food, traditional board games. *Address:* International Olympic Committee, Château d Vidy, PO Box 356, 1001 Lausanne, Switzerland.

BUEHRLEN, Veronique Eira; QC 2010; *b* Watford, Dec. 1965; *m* 1998, Timothy Micha Wormington; one *s* one *d*. *Educ:* Ashford Sch. for Girls; St Andrews Univ. (MA 1st Cl. Ho French and Internat. Relns); City Univ. (CPE Dist.). Called to the Bar, Middle Temple, 199 in practice at the Bar, 1991–, specialising in commercial law. *Address:* Keating Chambers, 1 Essex Street, WC2R 3AA. *T:* (020) 7544 2600.

BUENFELD, Prof. Nicholas Robert, PhD; CEng, FREng, FICE, FIStructE; Professor Concrete Structures, since 2000 and Head, Department of Civil and Environment Engineering, since 2011, Imperial College London; *b* Kent, 4 Oct. 1956; *s* of Robert Willia Buenfeld and Patricia Dorothy Buenfeld (*née* Hart); *m* 1996, Michèle Smith; two *s*. *Edu* Dulwich Coll.; Univ. of Leeds (BSc Hons Civil Engrg 1978); Imperial Coll. London (MSc DIC 1981; PhD 1984). CEng 1984; MICE 1984, FICE 2011; FREng 2011; FIStructE 201 Graduate Engr, Mott, Hay and Anderson, 1978–80; Imperial College London: Res. Ass 1981–84; SERC Res. Fellow, 1984–87; Lectr, 1987–98; Reader in Concrete Structure 1998–2000. Consultant to William J. Marshall & Partners, Mott MacDonald, Arup, Ame Bouygues, London Underground, Hong Kong Govt, Sri Lanka Govt. *Publications:* 180 pape in learned jls and internat. confs. *Recreations:* sport, restoration of old buildings. *Addres* Department of Civil and Environmental Engineering, Imperial College London, SW7 2A *E:* n.buenfeld@imperial.ac.uk. *Clubs:* Alleyn; Chiswick Riverside.

BUENO, Antonio de Padua Jose Maria; QC 1989; a Recorder, since 1989; *b* 28 June 194 *s* of late Antonio and Teresita Bueno; *m* 1966, Christine Mary Lees; three *d*. *Educ:* Downsid School; Salamanca Univ. Called to the Bar: Middle Temple, 1964, Bencher, 1998; NSW Ireland and Gibraltar. An Asst Recorder, 1984–89. *Publications:* (ed jtly) Banking sectio Atkin's Encyclopaedia of Court Forms, 2nd edn 1976; (Asst Editor, 24th edn 1979 and 25t edn 1983, Jt Editor, 26th edn 1988) Byles on Bills of Exchange; (Asst Editor) Paget's Law o Banking, 9th edn 1982. *Recreations:* fishing, shooting. *Address:* Hammoon House, Hammoo Sturminster Newton, Dorset DT10 2DB. *T:* (01258) 861704; Equity House, Blackbrook Par Avenue, Taunton, Somerset TA1 2PX. *T:* 0845 083 3000. *E:* christinebueno@aol.com *Clubs:* Athenaeum, MCC; Kildare Street (Dublin).

UERK, Michael Duncan; journalist and broadcaster, television; *b* 18 Feb. 1946; *s* of Betty Mary Buerk and Gordon Charles Buerk; *m* 1968, Christine Lilley; two *s*. *Educ:* Solihull School. Thomson Newspapers, Cardiff, 1967–69; reporter, Daily Mail, 1969–70; producer, BBC radio, 1970–71; reporter: HTV (West), 1971–72; BBC TV (South), 1972–73; BBC TV London, 1973–76; correspondent, BBC TV: industrial, 1976–77; energy, 1977–79; Scotland, 1979–81; special corresp. and newscaster, 1981–83; Southern Africa, 1983–87; presenter, BBC TV News, 1988–2002; Chm., The Moral Maze, R4, 1991–. Hon. MA Bath, 1991; Hon. LLD Bristol, 1994; Hon. DSc Aston, 2000; DUniv Surrey, 2013. RTS TV Journalist of the Year and RTS News Award, 1984; UN Hunger Award, 1984; numerous other awards, UK and overseas, 1984, 1985; BAFTA News Award, 1985; James Cameron Meml Award, 1988; Science Writer of the Year Award, 1989; Mungo Park Award, RSGS, 1994; Jephcott Medal, Royal Soc. of Medicine, 2013. *Publications:* The Road Taken (autobiog.), 2004. *Recreations:* travel, oenophily, sailing. *Address:* c/o Knight Ayton Management, 35 Great James Street, WC1N 3HB. *Clubs:* Reform, Garrick.

UFFINI, Moira Elizabeth; playwright and screenwriter; *b* Middlewich, Cheshire, 29 May 1965; *d* of John Buffini and Susan Buffini (*née* Clay); *m* 1995, Martin Biltcliffe; one *s* one *d*. *Educ:* Leftwich High Sch.; St Mary's Coll., Rhos-on-Sea; Goldsmiths Coll., Univ. of London (BA Hons Eng. and Drama; Hon. Fellow 2012); Welsh Coll. of Music and Drama (Dip. Acting). *Plays* include: Jordan (with Anna Reynolds), 1992; Blavatsky's Tower, 1997; Gabriel, 1998; Silence, 1999; Loveplay, 2001; Dinner, 2002; A Vampire Story, 2008; Dying For It, 2008; Welcome to Thebes, 2010; Handbagged, 2013; (with Damon Albarn) wonder.land, 2015. *Screenplays* include: Tamara Drewe, 2010; Jane Eyre, 2011; Byzantium, 2013. FRSL 2014. *Publications:* Dinner, 2002; Plays 1, 2006; Dying For It, 2007; Marianne Dreams, 2007; Welcome to Thebes, 2010; (jtly) Greenland, 2011; Handbagged, 2013; Plays 2, 2015; (jtly) wonder.land, 2015. *Recreations:* theatre, cinema, walking, family. *Address:* c/o St John Donald, United Agents, 12–26 Lexington Street, W1F 0LE. *E:* sdonald@unitedagents.co.uk.

UFORD, William Holmes; staff writer, The New Yorker, 2006–11 (Literary and Fiction Editor, 1995–2002); *b* 6 Oct. 1954; *s* of late William H. Buford and of Helen Shiel; *m* 1991, Alicja Kobiernicka (marr. diss. 2000); *m* 2002, Jessica Green; twin *s*. *Educ:* Univ. of California, Berkeley (BA); King's College, Cambridge (MA). Editor, Granta, 1979–95; former Chm., Granta Publications Ltd. *Publications:* (as Bill Buford): Among the Thugs, 1991; (ed) The Best of Granta Travel, 1991; (ed) The Best of Granta Reportage, 1993; (ed) The Granta Book of the Family, 1995; Heat, 2006; (contrib.) Daniel: my French cuisine, by Daniel Boulud, 2013.

UFTON, John Andreas; Member (UK Ind) Wales, European Parliament, 2009–14; *b* Llanidloes, 31 Aug. 1962; *s* of Cecil and Trudy Bufton; *m* 2013, Denise Robinson; one *s*. Manager, residential care home, Powys CC. Member (Ind): Rhayader Town Council, 1987–99 (Mayor, Rhayader, 1995–99); Powys UA, 1995–99. *Recreations:* Rugby, running, sports, walking, reading.

UHARI, Alhaji Haroun Madani; media relations and public affairs consultant; High Commissioner for Sierra Leone in London, and Ambassador for Sierra Leone to Sweden, Denmark, Norway, Spain, Portugal, Greece, India and Tunisia, 1995–96; *b* 23 Aug. 1945; *s* of Alhaji Mohammed Buhari and Haja Fatmatta M'balu (*née* Tejan-Sie); *m* 1st, 1975, Haja Sakinatu Onikeh Adams; three *s*; 2nd, 1990, Máriam Zainab Koroma; one *s* one *d*. *Educ:* St Helena Secondary Sch., Freetown; Islamic Missions Inst. at Al-Azhar Univ., Cairo; El Nasr Boys' Coll., Cairo; Univ. of Alexandria, Egypt (BA Hons 1970); Inst. of Social Studies, Univ. of Alexandria; SW London Coll.; Internat. Inst. for Journalism, W Berlin; Diplomatic Acad., Univ. of Westminster (MA 1997). Ministry of Information and Broadcasting, Sierra Leone: Inf. Officer, 1971–78; Sen. Inf. Officer, 1978–82 (Press. Sec., Office of Pres., 1981–82); Asst Controller/Principal Inf. Officer, 1982–90; Editor-in-Chief, Sierra Leone News Agency, 1986–87; Controller, Govt Inf. Services, 1990–91; Asst Dir of Inf., 1991–92 (Press Sec., Office of Pres., 1987–92); High Comr to Gambia and Ambassador to Senegal, Mauritania and Morocco, 1992–95. Founder Mem., Sierra Leone Assoc. of Journalists, 1971 (Chm., Interim Exec., 1992–93). Member: Sierra Leone Rent Assessment Cttee (Freetown E), 1987–93; Bd of Govs, Sierra Leone Muslim Congress Secondary Sch., 1987–93. Sec.-Gen., Sierra Leone Islamic Foundn, 1982–85; Exec. Sec. Federation of Sierra Leone Muslim Orgns, 1987. Governor: Commonwealth Foundn, 1995–96; Commonwealth Inst., 1995–96. Vice-Pres., Royal Over-Seas League, 1996–. *Publications:* articles on literary, political, social and religious issues for Sierra Leone and internat. press. *Recreations:* football, reading, travelling. *E:* HarounBuhari@hotmail.com.

UITER, Prof. Willem Hendrik, CBE 2000; PhD; FBA 1998; Chief Economist, Citigroup, New York City, since 2013 (Chief Economist, London, 2010–13); *b* 26 Sept. 1949; *s* of Harm Geert Buiter and Hendrien Buiter, *née* van Schooten; *m* 1st, 1973, Jean Archer (marr. diss. 1998); one *s* one *d*; 2nd, 1998, Prof. Anne C. Sibert. *Educ:* Cambridge Univ. (BA 1971); Yale Univ. (PhD 1975). Asst Prof., Princeton Univ., 1975–76; Lectr, LSE, 1976–77; Asst Prof., Princeton Univ., 1977–79; Prof. of Economics, Univ. of Bristol, 1980–82; Cassel Prof. of Economics, LSE, Univ. of London, 1982–85; Prof. of Econs, 1985–90, Juan T. Trippe Prof. of Internat. Econs, 1990–94, Yale Univ.; Prof. of Internat. Macroecons, and Fellow of Trinity Coll., Cambridge Univ., 1994–2000; Chief Economist, EBRD, 2000–05; Prof. of Eur. Political Economy, 2005–09, Prof. of Political Economy, 2009–11, LSE. Adjunct Sen. Res. Scholar, Sch. of Internat. and Public Affairs, Columbia Univ., NY, 2014–. Consultant: IMF, 1979–80; World Bank, 1986–; Inter-American Develt Bank, 1992–; EBRD, 1994–2000; Specialist Advr, House of Commons Select Cttee on the Treasury and CS, 1980–84; Advr, Netherlands Min. of Educn and Science, 1985–86; External Mem., Monetary Policy Cttee, Bank of England, 1997–2000; Chm., Netherlands Council of Econ. Advrs, 2005–07; Mem., Council of Economists, Conference Bd, 2015–. Adjunct Sen. Fellow, Council on Foreign Relations, New York, 2014–. Mem. Council, Royal Economic Soc., 1997–. Blogs for FT.com. Associate Editor, Econ. Jl, 1980–84. Hon. Dr Amsterdam, 2012. *Publications:* Temporary and Long Run Equilibrium, 1979; Budgetary Policy, International and Intertemporal Trade in the Global Economy, 1989; Macroeconomic Theory and Stabilization Policy, 1989; Principles of Budgetary and Financial Policy, 1990; International Macroeconomics, 1990; (jtly) Financial Markets and European Monetary Co-operation: the lessons of the 1992–93 ERM crisis, 1998; articles in learned jls. *Recreations:* science fiction and fantasy novels, tennis, poetry, music, hiking. *Address:* Flat 1104 Mizzen Mast House, Mast Quay, SE18 5NP.

ULFIELD, Prof. Grahame, CBE 2001; PhD; FRSE; FRSB; Vice-Principal, Head of College of Science and Engineering, and Professor of Animal Genetics, University of Edinburgh, 2002–08, now Emeritus Professor of Genetics and Senior Honorary Professorial Fellow; consultant on genetics and biotechnology; *b* 12 June 1941; *s* of Frederick Bulfield and Madge (*née* Jones). *Educ:* King's Sch., Macclesfield; Univ. of Leeds (BSc 1964); Univ. of Edinburgh (Dip. Animal Genetics 1965; PhD 1968). FRSE 1992; FRSB (FIBiol 1995). Fulbright Fellow and NIH Postdoctoral Fellow, Dept of Genetics, Univ. of Calif., Berkeley, 1968–70; SRC Resettlement Fellow, 1970–71, Res. Associate, 1971–76, Inst. of Animal Genetics, Univ. of Edinburgh; Lectr and Convenor of Med. Genetics, Dept of Genetics, Med. Sch. and Sch. of Biol Scis, Univ. of Leicester, 1976–81; Hd, Genetics Gp, AFRC Poultry Res. Centre, Roslin, 1981–86; Hd, Gene Expression Gp, 1986–88, and Hd of Station and Associate Dir, 1988–93, Edinburgh Res. Station of Inst. of Animal Physiology and Genetic Res., Roslin; Dir and Chief Exec., Roslin Inst., BBSRC, 1993–2002. Hon. Fellow, 1981–90, Hon. Prof., 1990–2002, Div. of Biol Scis, Univ. of Edinburgh. Member: Animal Procedures Cttee, Home Office, 1998–2006; Res. Policy Cttee, SHEFC, 2002–05; Res. and Knowledge Transfer Cttee, SFC, 2005–06; Bd, SRUC (formerly Scottish Agricl Coll.), 2007–. Member, Enterprise Fellowship Committee: Scottish Enterprise/RSE, 2001–13; BBSRC/RSE, 2007– (Chm., 2010–). Hon. FRASE 1999. Hon. DSc: Edinburgh, 2000; Abertay, 2002. *Publications:* res. papers, reviews and book chapters on biochemical and molecular genetics. *Recreations:* fell-walking, cricket, genetic genealogy. *Address:* Peter Wilson Building, College of Science and Engineering, University of Edinburgh, The King's Buildings, West Mains Road, Edinburgh EH9 3JY. *T:* (0131) 535 4063. *E:* Grahame.Bulfield@ed.ac.uk.

BULFIELD, Peter William, CA; Deputy Chairman, Yamaichi Bank (UK) PLC, 1991–94 (Managing Director and Chief Executive, 1988–91); *b* 14 June 1930; *s* of Wilfred Bulfield and Doris (*née* Bedford); *m* 1958, Pamela June Beckett; two *d*. *Educ:* Beaumont Coll., Old Windsor. Peat Marwick Mitchell & Co., 1947–59; J. Henry Schroder Wagg & Co., 1959–86, Dir, 1967–86; Director: Schroder Finance, 1966–73; Schroder Darling Hldgs, Sydney, 1973–80; Vice-Chm., Mitsubishi Trust & Banking Corporation (Europe) SA, 1973–84; Jt Dep. Chm., Schroder Internat., 1977–86; Dep. Chm., Crown Agents for Oversea Govts and Admin, 1982–85 (Mem., 1978–85); Director: Yamaichi Internat. PLC, 1986–87; London Italian Bank, 1989–91. Member: Overseas Projects Board, 1983–86; Overseas Promotions Cttee, BIEC, 1984–86; Export Guarantees Adv. Council, 1985–88. Mem., Finance Cttee, CAFOD, 1994–2002; Hon. Treas., W Sussex Assoc. for the Blind, 1998–99. KSG 2001. *Recreations:* sailing, music, painting. *Address:* Snow Goose Cottage, Sandy Lane, East Ashling, W Sussex PO18 9AT. *T:* and *Fax:* (01243) 575298. *Club:* Royal Thames Yacht.

BULFORD, Anne Judith; *see* Weyman, A. J.

BULKELEY, Sir Richard Thomas W.; *see* Williams-Bulkeley.

BULL, Christopher John; book dealer and bodger; Director of Corporate Services, Government Equalities Office, 2007–11; *b* 26 July 1954; *s* of George William and Kathleen Bull; *m* 1983, Alison Jane Hughes; two *d*. *Educ:* UCW, Aberystwyth (BA). CPFA 1983. With Nat. Audit Office, 1977–97; Inspector, Benefit Fraud Inspectorate, DSS, 1997–99; Dir, Benefit Fraud Inspectorate, DSS, subseq. DWP, 1999–2007. Ind. Mem., Audit Cttee, CRE, 2006–07. FRSA 2000. *Recreations:* books, wood, beer.

BULL, David Neill, CBE 2015; Executive Director, UNICEF UK, since 1999; *b* 21 June 1951; *s* of Denis Albert and Doreen Lilian Bull; *m* 1978, Claire Grenger; one *d*. *Educ:* Sussex Univ. (BA Econ); Bath Univ. (MSc Develt Studies). Public Affairs Unit Officer, Oxfam, 1979–84; Dir, Environment Liaison Centre, Nairobi, 1984–87; Gen. Sec., World University Service (UK), 1987–90; Dir, Amnesty Internat. (UK Sect.), 1990–99. Trustee: Refugee Council, 1987–90; Pesticides Trust, 1987–99; Mem., Exec. Cttee, ACENVO, 1994–98. Hon LLD Bath, 2009. *Publications:* A Growing Problem: pesticides and the Third World Poor, 1982; The Poverty of Diplomacy: Kampuchea and the outside world, 1983. *Recreations:* walking, reading, esp. science fiction, family history, photography. *Address:* UNICEF UK, 30a Great Sutton Street, EC1V 0DU. *T:* (020) 7490 2388.

BULL, Deborah Clare, CBE 1999; Director, Cultural Partnerships, King's College London, since 2012; *b* 22 March 1963; *d* of Rev. Michael John Bull and Doreen Audrey Franklin (*née* Plumb). *Educ:* Royal Ballet Sch. Joined Royal Ballet, 1981; Principal Dancer, 1992–2001; Nutrition Teacher, Royal Ballet Sch., 1996–99; Dir, Artists' Develt Initiative, 1999–2001, first Artistic Dir, then Creative Dir of ROH2, later Creative Dir, 2002–12, Royal Opera House. Has danced a wide range of work, incl. leading rôles in: Swan Lake; Sleeping Beauty; Don Quixote; particularly noted for modern rôles, incl. Steptext, and Symbiont(s) (Time Out Outstanding Achievement Award); appeared in Diamonds of World Ballet Gala, Kremlin Palace, Moscow, 1996. Member: Arts Council, 1998–2004 (Mem., Dance Panel, 1996–98; Annual Lecture, 1996); AHRC, 2012–. Governor: S Bank Centre, 1997–2003; BBC, 2003–06. Columnist, The Telegraph, 1999–2002; contributing editor, Harpers & Queen, 2000–01. Wrote and presented: *television:* Dance Ballerina Dance, 1998; Travels with my Tutu, 2000; The Dancer's Body, 2002; Saved for the Nation, 2006; Dancing for Russia, 2014; Bolshoi Unseen, 2014; *radio:* Leaving Barons Court, 1999; Breaking the Law, 2001; Law in Order, 2002; Hothouse Kids, 2009; After I Was Gorgeous, 2011; Something Understood—Steps in Time, 2011; Deborah Bull's Dance Nation, 2012; Dance for your Life, 2012; Classic FM Goes to the Ballet, 2014; regular appearances on Saturday Review, BBC Radio 4. DUniv: Derby, 1998; Sheffield, 2001; Open, 2005; Kent, 2010. Prix de Lausanne, 1980. *Publications:* The Vitality Plan, 1998; Dancing Away, 1998; (jtly) Faber Guide to Classical Ballets, 2004; The Everyday Dancer, 2011; articles in jls and newspapers. *Recreations:* reading, writing, dancing, neurology, psychology, nutrition, people. *Address:* King's College London, Somerset House East Wing, Strand, WC2R 2LS.

BULL, Sir George (Jeffrey), Kt 1998; Group Chief Executive, 1993–95, Chairman, 1995–97, Grand Metropolitan PLC; Joint Chairman, Diageo plc, 1997–98 (non-executive Director, 1998–2000); *b* 16 July 1936; *s* of late Michael Herbert Perkins Bull and Hon. Noreen Madeleine Bull (*née* Hennessy), *d* of 1st Baron Windlesham, OBE; *m* 1960, Jane Fleur Thérèse, *d* of late Patrick Freeland; four *s* one *d*. *Educ:* Ampleforth Coll. Lt Coldstream Guards, 1954–57, served Germany and UK. Dorland Advertising Ltd, 1957; Twiss Browning & Hallowes wine merchants, 1958; Man. Dir, Gilbey Vintners, 1970; International Distillers & Vintners Ltd: Man. Dir, IDV UK Ltd, 1973; Man. Dir, IDV Europe Ltd, 1977; Dep. Man. Dir, 1982–84; Chief Exec., 1984–92; Chm., 1988–92; Dir, Grand Metropolitan Ltd, 1985; Chief Exec., Grand Metropolitan Drinks Sector, 1987; Chm. and Chief Exec., Grand Metropolitan Food Sector, 1992–95. Non-executive Director: United Newspapers, 1993–98; BNP Paribas Ltd, 2000–04; Maersk Co. Ltd, 2001–06; Chm., J Sainsbury PLC, 1998–2004. Dir, BOTB, 1990–95; founding Dir, Marketing Council, 1995–2000. Mem., Adv. Bd, Marakon Associates, 2002–06. Chm., Wine and Spirit Assoc. of GB, 1975–76; Vice-Pres., CIM, 1994 (Hon. FCIM, 1995); Member: Presidents' Cttee, CBI, 1993–96; Adv. Bd, British Amer. Chamber of Commerce, 1994–98. Dir, US Adv. Educ. Foundn, 1994–98; President: Advertising Assoc., 1996–2000; Wine and Spirit Benevolent Soc., 2000–01; Vice Pres., Mencap, 2000–. Chm., Old Codgers Assoc., 2006–. Confrater, Ampleforth Abbey, 2005–; Dir/Sec., Chapel Annunciation, Furneux Pelham, 2010–14. Patron, Anchor House Project, 2010–. Hon. Fellow, Marketing Soc., 1997. Hon. Pres., Perkins Bull Collection, 2008–. Grand Master, Keepers of the Quaich, 1995–96 (Patron, 1996–2005). Freeman, City of London, 1995. Liveryman, Distillers' Co., 1995–. Chevalier, Légion d'Honneur (France), 1994; Chevalier du Tastevin, 2005. *Recreations:* golf, shooting, photography. *Address:* The Old Vicarage, Arkesden, Saffron Walden, Essex CB11 4HB. *T:* (01799) 550445. *Clubs:* Cavalry and Guards, Pilgrims; Royal Worlington and Newmarket Golf (Suffolk) (Mem. Council, 2008–11).

BULL, Gregory; QC 2003; a Recorder, since 2000; Advocate, Public Defender Service, since 2014; *b* 14 Aug. 1953; *s* of Mansel and Joyce Bull; *m* 1983, Helen Ruth Bookes Parsons (marr. diss. 2011); one *s* one *d*. *Educ:* Mardy House Church in Wales Secondary Sch.; Aberdare Boys' Grammar Sch.; Univ. of Birmingham (LLB Hons). Called to the Bar, Inner Temple, 1976; in practice, specialising in crime, fraud and common law; Asst Recorder, 1995–2000. Leader, Wales and Chester Circuit, 2010–13 (Treas., 2007–10). Member: Bar Council, 2007–13; Criminal Bar Assoc., 2007–. *Recreations:* Rugby Union, walking, politics, music, theatre. *Address:* Public Defender Service, Legal Aid Agency, 102 Petty France, SW1H 9AJ.

BULL, John; *see* Bull, R. J.

BULL, His Honour John Michael; QC 1983; DL; a Circuit Judge, 1991–2006; a Deputy Circuit Judge, 2006–08; *b* 31 Jan. 1934; *s* of John Godfrey Bull and Eleanor Bull (*née* Nicholson); *m* 1959, Sonia Maureen, *d* of Frank Edward Woodcock; one *s* three *d*. *Educ:*

Norwich Sch. (State Schol.); Corpus Christi Coll., Cambridge (Parker Exhibnr in Modern History; BA 1958; LLM 1959; MA 1963). Called to the Bar, Gray's Inn, 1960; Dep. Circuit Judge, 1972; Standing Counsel to the Board of Inland Revenue, Western Circuit, 1972–83; a Recorder, 1980–91; Resident Judge, Crown Court at Guildford, 1992–2000. Judge, Employment Appeal Tribunal, 1993–2000. Hon. Recorder of Guildford, 1998–2010. Hon. Vis. Prof., Surrey Univ., 1999–2005. DL Surrey, 1996. DUniv Surrey, 2010.

BULL, Michelle; *see* Harrison, Michelle.

BULL, Nicholas James Douglas; Chairman, De Vere Group, since 2012; Senior Independent Director, Fidelity China Special Situations plc, since 2010; *b* London, 17 April 1952; *s* of late Dr James William Douglas Bull, CBE, FRCP and Edith Bull (*née* Burch Schiff, then Schiff Burch); *m* 1989, Katusha Ostroumoff; one *s*. *Educ:* Eton Coll.; Univ. of Exeter (BSc Chem. 1973). ACA 1976, FCA 1981. Articled Clerk, 1973–76, Audit Sen., 1976–77, Spicer & Pegler; Corporate Finance, Morgan Grenfell & Co. Ltd, 1977–86; Hd of Corporate Finance, 1986, Chief Exec., 1987–88, Morgan Grenfell Australia, Sydney; Corporate Finance Dir, Morgan Grenfell & Co. Ltd, London, 1989–92; Regl Dir, Morgan Grenfell Asia, Singapore, 1993; Regl Dir, Deutsche Morgan Grenfell Asia, Hong Kong, 1994–95; Man. Dir, M&A, Deutsche Bank, London, 1996–99; Man. Dir and Hd of Consumer Sector M&A, Société Générale, 2000–02; Man. Dir and Hd of Global Clients for UK, ABN AMRO, 2002–08; Chm., Smith's Corporate Adv. Ltd, 2009–10. Chm., Adv. Bd, Westhouse Securities, 2011–. Mem. Council, Univ. of Exeter, 2009– (Chm., Fundraising Campaign Bd, 2007–11). Associate Gov., Greig City Acad., 2013–. Trustee: Design Mus., 1988–93 and 2012–; Conran Foundn, 1996–. Liveryman, Tallow Chandlers' Co., 1990–. Chm., Thames Traditional Rowing Assoc., 2005–15. *Recreations:* rowing, propagating philanthropy. *Address:* 19 Spencer Park, SW18 2SZ. *T:* 07900 473513. *E:* nicholasbull@ymail.com. *Clubs:* Leander (Henley-on-Thames); Huntercombe Golf; St Moritz Toboganning; Vail Mountain.

BULL, Prof. (Roger) John, CBE 2002; Deputy Chairman, Universities Superannuation Scheme Ltd, 2006–14 (Director/Trustee, 2004–14); *b* 31 March 1940; *s* of William Leonard Bull and Margery Bull (*née* Slade); *m* 1964, Margaret Evelyn Clifton; one *s* one *d*. *Educ:* Churcher's Coll.; LSE (BSc Econ). FCCA. Research Fellow, DES/ICA, 1967–68; Principal Lectr in Accounting, Nottingham Poly., 1968–72; Head, Sch. of Accounting and Applied Econs, Leeds Poly., 1972–85; Dep. Dir (Academic), Plymouth Poly., 1986–89; Dir and Chief Exec., Poly. SW, Plymouth, 1989–92; Vice-Chancellor and Chief Exec., Univ. of Plymouth, 1992–2002. Chm., Devon and Cornwall LSC, 2002–08. Chm., Open Learning Foundn, 1994–97; Dir, HEQC, 1994–97; Hon. Treas., UUK (formerly CVCP), 1994–2002. Non-exec. Dir/Trustee, UK eUniversities Worldwide Ltd, 2001–04; Chm., Plymouth Hospitals NHS Trust, 2002–10 (non-exec. Dir, 1993–2002). Dir, Plymouth Chamber of Commerce, 1994–97. Member: Council, CNAA, 1981–87; Council for Industry and Higher Educn, 1993–2002. Chm., Dartington Coll. of Arts, 2003–08 (Gov., 1996–2003). *Publications:* Accounting in Business, 1969, 6th edn 1990; articles on accounting and educnl mgt. *Recreations:* music, walking.

BULL, Sir Simeon (George), 4th Bt *cr* 1922, of Hammersmith; former Senior Partner in legal firm of Bull & Bull, now retired; *b* 1 Aug. 1934; *s* of Sir George Bull, 3rd Bt and of Gabrielle, *d* of late Bramwell Jackson, MC; *S* father, 1986; *m* 1961, Annick Elizabeth Renée Geneviève (*d* 2000), *d* of late Louis Bresson and Mme Bresson, Chandai, France; one *s* two *d*. *Educ:* Eton; Innsbruck; Paris. Admitted solicitor, 1959. *Heir: s* Stephen Louis Bull [*b* 5 April 1966; *m* 1994, Maria Brampton; two *s* (twins) three *d*]. *Address:* Gipau, 82110 Cazes Mondenard, Tarn et Garonne, France. *T:* (5) 63943150. *Club:* Royal Thames Yacht.

BULL, Prof. Stephen John, PhD; CEng; FIMMM; FInstP; FREng; Cookson Group Chair of Materials Engineering, since 2008, and Director of Research, since 2012, School of Chemical Engineering and Advanced Materials, Newcastle University (Head of School, 2005–10); *b* Carshalton, Surrey, 12 Aug. 1963; *s* of Ronald John and Jean Margaret Bull; *m* 1989, Catherine Ruth Le Sueur; one *s* three *d*. *Educ:* Wallington High Sch. for Boys; St Catharine's Coll., Cambridge (BA 1984; MA 1988; PhD 1988). FIMMM 1997; FInstP 2007; CEng 2012; FREng 2014. Harwell Laboratory: HSO, Coatings and Interface Technol. Gp, 1988–90; Section Manager: Advanced Physical Vapour Deposited Coatings and Coatings Design Section, 1991; PVD and Ion Assisted Coatings Section, 1991–93; PVD Coatings and Interfaces Section, 1993–96; Newcastle University: Reader in Surface Technol., 1996–2002; Prof. of Surface Engrg, 2002–07; RAEng/Leverhulme Trust Sen. Res. Fellow, 2010–11. *Publications:* contrib. articles to learned jls and conf. proceedings. *Recreations:* music, science fiction reading and writing. *Address:* School of Chemical Engineering and Advanced Materials, Newcastle University, Bedson Building, Newcastle-upon-Tyne NE1 7RU. *T:* (0191) 208 7913. *E:* steve.bull@ncl.ac.uk.

BULL, Tony Raymond, FRCS; Consultant Surgeon, 1965–2000, now Honorary Consultant Surgeon: Charing Cross Hospital; Royal National Throat Nose and Ear Hospital; King Edward VII's Hospital for Officers; *b* 21 Dec. 1934; *m* 1958, Jill Rosemary Beresford Cook; one *s* two *d*. *Educ:* Monkton Combe School; London Hosp. (MB BS 1958). FRCS 1962. President: Eur. Acad. of Facial Plastic Surgery, 1989–96; Section of Otology, RSocMed, 1993–94; Internat. Fedn of Facial Plastic Surgeons, 1997. Yearsley Lectr, 1982, Semon Lectr, 2000, RSocMed. Sir William Wilde Medal, Irish Otolaryngol Soc., 1993. Founding Editor, Facial Plastic Surgery (Quarterly Monographs), 1983. *Publications:* Atlas of Ear, Nose and Throat Diagnosis, 1974, 3rd edn 1995; Recent Advances in Otolaryngology, 1978; Plastic Reconstruction in the Head and Neck, 1986; Diagnostic Picture Test, Ear, Nose and Throat, 1990. *Recreations:* tennis, golf. *Address:* 107 Harley Street, W1G 6AL. *T:* (020) 7935 3171; 25 Pembroke Gardens Close, W8 6HR. *T:* (020) 7602 4362. *Clubs:* Savile, MCC, Hurlingham, Queen's.

BULLARD, Felicity; *see* Lawrence, F.

BULLARD, Gary Bruce; Chairman, New Model Identity, since 2013; *b* Chislehurst, Kent, 3 April 1957; *s* of late Cyril Charles Bullard and of Margaret Irene Elizabeth Bullard; *m* 1983, Elaine May Sullivan. *Educ:* St Olave's and St Saviour's Grammar Sch.; Exeter Univ. (BSc Combined Hons). Gen. Manager, Global Solutions, IBM Corp., 1978–2004; Pres., BT Global Services, BT plc, 2004–08; Chief Executive Officer: Catquin, 2007–11; Logica UK, 2011–12. Non-executive Director: Chloride plc, 2006–10; Rotork plc, 2010–; Smart Cube, 2013–14. MInstD 2010. *Address:* Old Palace Place, The Green, Richmond, Surrey TW9 1NQ. *T:* 07802 246270. *E:* gary.bullard@btopenworld.com. *Club:* Morton's.

BULLER; *see* Manningham-Buller.

BULLER; *see* Manningham-Buller, family name of Viscount Dilhorne.

BULLER; *see* Yarde-Buller, family name of Baron Churston.

BULLER, Prof. Arthur John, ERD 1969; FRCP; Emeritus Professor of Physiology, University of Bristol, since 1982; *b* 16 Oct. 1923; *s* of Thomas Alfred Buller, MBE, and Edith May Buller (*née* Wager); *m* 1946, Helena Joan (*née* Pearson) (*d* 2007); one *s* one *d* (and one *d* decd). *Educ:* Duke of York's Royal Military Sch., Dover; St Thomas's Hosp. Med. Sch. (MB, BS; BSc); PhD Bristol 1992; BA Open Univ., 1996. FRCP 1976; FRSB (FIBiol 1978); FRSA 1979. Kitchener Scholar, 1941–45; Lectr in Physiology, St Thomas' Hosp., 1946–49. Major, RAMC (Specialist in Physiology; Jt Sec., Military Personnel Research Cttee), 1949–53. Lectr in Medicine, St Thomas' Hosp., 1953–57. Royal Society Commonwealth Fellow, Canberra, Aust., 1958–59. Reader in Physiology, King's Coll., London, 1961–65; Gresham Prof. of Physic, 1963–65; Prof. of Physiology, Univ. of Bristol, 1965–82, Dean, Fac. of Medicin 1976–78, on secondment as Chief Scientist, DHSS, 1978–81. Res. Develt Dir, subseq. Dir c Res. and Support Services, Muscular Dystrophy Gp of GB, 1982–90. Hon. Consultant i Clinical Physiology, Bristol Dist Hosp. (T), 1970–82. Vis. Scholar, UCLA, 1966; Visitin Prof., Monash Univ., Aust., 1972. Lectures: Long Fox Meml, Bristol, 1978; Milroy, RCP 1983; Haig Gudenian Meml, Muscular Dystrophy Gp, 1993. Member: Bd of Governors Bristol Royal Infirmary, 1968–74; Avon Health Authority (T), 1974–78; MRC, 1975–81 BBC, IBA Central Appeals Adv. Cttee, 1983–88; Neurosciences and Mental Health Bd MRC, 1973–77 (Chm., 1975–77); Chm., DHSS Working Party on Clinical Accountability Service Planning and Evaluation, 1981–86; Trustee, Health Promotion Res. Trust, 1983–9 External Scientific Advisor, Rayne Inst., St Thomas' Hosp., 1979–85. *Publications:* contribs t books and various jls on normal and disordered physiology. *Recreation:* clarets an conversation. *Address:* Flat 13, Turnpike Court, Hett Close, Ardingly, West Sussex RH1 6GQ. *T:* (01444) 891873.

BULLER, Emma Katherine; *see* Himsworth, E. K.

BULLIMORE, His Honour John Wallace MacGregor; a Circuit Judge, 1991–2010; *b* Dec. 1945; *s* of late James Wallace Bullimore and Phyllis Violet Emily Bullimore (*née* Brandt *m* 1975, Rev. Christine Elizabeth Kinch; two *s* (one *d* decd). *Educ:* Queen Elizabeth Gramma School, Wakefield; Univ. of Bristol (LLB). Called to the Bar, Inner Temple, 1968 Chancellor, Diocese of Derby, 1980–, of Blackburn, 1990–. Mem., Gen. Synod of th Church of England, 1970–2010.

BULLIVANT, Lucy Georgina; author, critic, curator, guest lecturer and consultant; London, 4 Nov. 1958; *d* of Dargan Bullivant and Patricia Bullivant. *Educ:* Leeds Univ. (BA Hons Art Hist. 1980); Royal Coll. of Art (MA Cultural Hist. 1984); London Metropolita Univ. (PhD 2015). Consultant to: Eastern Arts Assoc., RA, Vitra Design Mus., Mila Triennale, ICA, Archis, 1984–; British Council, AD/Wiley, MACBA Barcelona, Yorkshir Forward, FRAC Orléans, V&A, 1990–. Guest lecturer for IAAC Barcelona and othe architectural colls. Member: Quality Review Panel, London Develt Corp., 2012–; Scientifi Cttee, Institut pour la Ville en Mouvement, PSA Peugeot Citroen, Paris, 2012– Correspondent to Domus, The Plan, Indesign, Volume. Mem., AA. Hon. FRIBA 201C *Publications:* Kid size: the material world of childhood, 1997; (ed) Home Front: nev developments in housing, 2003; (ed) 4dspace: interactive architecture, 2004; Anglo Files: UI architecture's rising generation, 2005; Responsive Environments: art, architecture and desigr 2006; (ed) 4dsocial: interactive design environments, 2007; New Arcadians: emerging UI architects, 2012; Masterplanning Futures, 2012 (Book of the Year, Urban Design Grou Awards, 2014); (with Thomas Ermacora) Recoded City: co-creating urban futures, 2015 *Recreations:* travelling, walking, running, photography, cinema. *Address:* 131a Bedford Cou Mansions, Adeline Place, WC1B 3AH. *T:* (020) 7323 4629. *E:* office@lucybullivant.net.

BULLMORE, Prof. Edward Thomas, PhD; FMedSci, FRCPsych, FRCP; Professor c Psychiatry, since 1999, and Head, Department of Psychiatry, since 2014, University c Cambridge; Hon. Consultant Psychiatrist, Addenbrooke's Hospital, Cambridge, since 1999 *b* 27 Sept. 1960; *s* of (John) Jeremy David Bullmore, *qv* and Pamela Audrey Bullmore (*né* Green); *m* 1992, Mary Pitt, *d* of late Arthur Pitt and of Elizabeth Pitt; three *s*. *Edu* Westminster Sch.; Christ Church, Oxford (BA); St Bartholomew's Hosp. Med. Coll. (M BS); PhD London 1997. MRCP 1989; MRCPsych 1992, FRCPsych 2009; FRCP 2010 Lectr in Medicine, Univ. of Hong Kong, 1987–88; SHO in Psychiatry, St George's Hosp. London, 1989–90; Registrar in Psychiatry, Bethlem Royal and Maudsley Hosps, 1990–93 Wellcome Trust Res. Trng Fellow, 1993–96; Advanced Res. Trng Fellow, 1996–99; Hor Consultant Psychiatrist, Maudsley Hosp., London, 1996–99; Clinical Dir, MRC/Wellcom Trust Behavioural and Clin. Neuroscis Inst., Cambridge, 2005–; Fellow, Wolfson Coll Cambridge, 2002–10; Vice-Pres., Exptl Medicine, GlaxoSmithKline, 2005– (Hd, Clin. Unit Cambridge, 2005–13); Dir, R&D, Cambs and Peterborough NHS Foundn Trust, 2011–; Co Chair, Cambridge Neuroscience, 2013–; Chm., Cambridge Health Imaging, Cambridg Univ. Health Partners, 2015–. NIHR Sen. Investigator, 2014–. Vis. Prof., Inst. of Psychiatry KCL, 2000–. Mem., MRC Neuroscis and Mental Health Bd, 2002–06. FMedSci 2008 *Publications:* papers on anatomical and functional brain imaging methods and applications t psychiatry and neuroscience. *Recreations:* running, birding. *Address:* Department of Psychiatry University of Cambridge, Herchel Smith Building for Brain and Mind Sciences, Cambridg Biomedical Campus, Cambridge CB2 0SZ. *T:* (01223) 336582.

BULLMORE, (John) Jeremy David, CBE 1985; Chairman, J. Walter Thompson Co. Ltd 1976–87; Director: The Guardian Media Group (formerly The Guardian and Mancheste Evening News plc), 1988–2001; WPP Group plc, 1988–2004 (Member, Advisory Board since 2005); *b* 21 Nov. 1929; *s* of Francis Edward Bullmore and Adeline Gabrielle Bullmor (*née* Roscow); *m* 1958, Pamela Audrey Green; two *s* one *d*. *Educ:* Harrow; Christ Church Oxford. Military service, 1949–50. Joined J. Walter Thompson Co. Ltd, 1954: Dir, 1964 Dep. Chm., 1975; Dir, J. Walter Thompson Co. (USA), 1980–87. Mem., Nat. Cttee fc Electoral Reform, 1978–. Chm., Advertising Assoc., 1981–87; President: Nat. Advertisin Benevolent Soc., 1999–2001; Market Res. Soc., 2004–09. Mackintosh Medal, Advertisin Assoc., 2011. *Publications:* Behind the Scenes in Advertising, 1991, 3rd edn 2003; Another Ba Day at the Office?, 2001; Ask Jeremy, 2004; Apples, Insights and Mad Inventors, 2006 *Address:* 17/20 Embankment Gardens, SW3 4LW. *T:* (020) 7351 2197.

See also E. T. Bullmore.

BULLOCK, Hugh Jonathan Watson, FRICS, FRTPI; Partner, since 1989, and Chairmar since 2015, Gerald Eve LLP, Chartered Surveyors (Senior Partner, 2008–15); *b* Brussels, 2 Dec. 1957; *er s* of late (Edward) Anthony (Watson) Bullock and of Jenifer Myrtle Bullock, *d* of Sir Richmond Palmer, KCMG; *m* 1980, Gabriella Zofia Stanley, *yr d* of late Major Iva William Stanley Moss, MC and Countess Zofia Tarnowska Moss; three *d*. *Educ:* Eton Coll Univ. of St Andrews; London South Bank Univ. (BSc 1st Cl. Hons 1985; Rubens Meml Priz 1985). ARICS 1986, FRICS 1992; MRTPI 1996, FRTPI 2006. Joined Gerald Eve LLP Chartered Surveyors as grad. trainee, 1985. Vis. Lectr, Univ. of Reading, 2004–. Adv Westminster Property Assoc., 1990–. Mem., Mayor of London's West End Comm 2005–06. Chm., Planning and Develt Adv. Gp, London First, 2009–. Member: Monitorin and Investigation Cttee, RICS, 1996–98; London Regl Council, CBI, 1997–2001 Cambridge Land Economy Adv. Bd, Univ. of Cambridge, 2013–. Mem., Bd of Trustees LAMDA, 2006–; Trustee, Patrick Leigh Fermor Soc., 2015–. FRSA 1999. (Jtly) Londo Planning Award for Best Private Sector Planning Orgn, 2004. *Publications:* Commercia Viability in Planning, 1993; A Positive Approach to Town and Country Planning, 2007 Economic Realities of Taxing Development, 2009; Localism and Growth, 2011; Localisr and Planning, 2012. *Recreations:* theatre, walking dogs, selected history, sports, travel. *Address* Gerald Eve LLP, 72 Welbeck Street, W1G 0AY. *T:* (020) 7333 6302. *E:* hbullock@ geraldeve.com. *Clubs:* Boodle's, Royal Air Force, Surveyors' Association.

BULLOCK, John; Director, Retirement Security Ltd, 2002–05; Joint Senior Partner an Deputy Chairman, Coopers & Lybrand Deloitte, later Coopers & Lybrand, 1989–92; *b* 12 Jul 1933; *s* of Robert and Doris Bullock; *m* 1960, Ruth Jennifer (*née* Bullock); two *s* (and one decd). *Educ:* Latymer Upper School. FCA; FCMA; FIMC. Smallfield Fitzhugh Tillet & Co 1949–56 and 1958–61; RAF Commission, 1956–58; Robson Morrow, 1961, Partne 1965–70; Robson Morrow merged with Deloitte Haskins & Sells; Partner in charge, Deloitt Haskins & Sells Management Consultants, 1971–79; Deloitte Haskins & Sells: Managin Partner, 1979–85; Dep. Senior Partner, 1984–85; Sen. Partner, 1985–90; Vice Chm., Deloitt

Haskins & Sells Internat., 1985–89; Chairman: Deloitte Europe, 1985–89; Coopers & Lybrand Europe, 1989–92. Director: Brightreasons, 1993–96; Nuclear Electric, 1993–98; Kingfisher, 1993–2002; British Energy, 1995–99; More Gp, 1997–98. Mem., UKAEA, 1981–93. Mem., Co. of Chartered Accountants' of England and Wales, 1989–. Chm. Govs, Latymer Upper Sch., 2001–05. *Recreations:* walking, opera, ballet. *Address:* Grove House, 15 Clarendon Road, Sevenoaks, Kent TN13 1EU.

BULLOCK, Hon. Matthew Peter Dominic; Master, St Edmund's College, Cambridge, since 2014; *b* 9 Sept. 1949; *s* of Baron Bullock, FBA and Hilda Yates Bullock; *m* 1970, Anna-Lena Margareta Hansson; one *s* two *d*. *Educ:* Magdalen College Sch., Oxford; Peterhouse, Cambridge (BA Hist. 1970); Harvard Business Sch. (AMP 1991). CBI, 1970–74; Barclays Bank plc, 1974–98: Corporate Finance Dir, 1983–86; Regl Dir, Yorkshire, 1986–91; Dir, Risk Mgt, 1991–93; Man. Dir, BZW/Barclays Capital, 1993–98; Gp Chief Exec., Norwich and Peterborough Bldg Soc., 1999–2011. Chm., Automation Partnership Gp plc, 1999–2012. Member: Cabinet Adv. Cttee on Application of R&D, 1983–88; Econ. Policy Cttee, EEF, 1991–97; Industrial Adv. Bd, DTI, 1993–99; Financial Services Practitioner Panel, 2001–07. Chm., Building Socs Assoc., 2006–07. University of Cambridge: Chm. Adv. Bd, Centre for Business Res., 1994–2013; Mem., Audit Cttee, 2002–10; Mem. Adv. Bd, 1985–2002, Chm., Chinese Big Business Prog., 1999–2001, Judge Inst. of Mgt Studies. Non-exec. Dir, Cambridge Univ. Hosp. Trust, 2010–13 (Chm., Audit Cttee, 2011–13). Chairman: Internat. House Trust Ltd, 2011–14; Pathology Partnership (formerly Transforming Pathology Partnership), 2013–. Dir, Cambridge Ahead Ltd, 2013–. Trustee, Cambridge Past, Present and Future, 2011–. Governor: Imperial Coll., London, 1981–86; Leeds Univ., 1986–91. *Publications:* Academic Enterprise, Industrial Innovation and the Development of High Technology Financing in the USA, 1981. *Recreations:* walking, gardening, music, opera. *Address:* Easby House, High Street, Great Chesterford, Essex CB10 1PL. *E:* mpdbullock@btinternet.com; St Edmund's College, Cambridge CB3 0BN. *Club:* Oxford and Cambridge.

BULLOCK, Ven. Sarah Ruth; Archdeacon of York, since 2013; *b* Manchester, 17 March 1964; *d* of Gerald Wheale and Jean Wheale; *m* 1992, Peter Bullock; one *s*. *Educ:* Fallowfield C of E High Sch.; Univ. of Surrey (BA Hons English 1986); Univ. of Manchester (Dip. Community Work); Univ. of Durham (BA Hons Theol. 1993; Postgrad. CTh 2012). Teacher, Cheadle Hulme Sch., 1986–90; Asst Diocesan Youth Officer, 1986–90; ordained deacon, 1993, priest, 1994; Asst Curate, St Paul, Kersal Moor and St Andrew, Carr Clough, 1993–98; Rector, St Edmund, Whalley Range and St James' with St Clement, Moss Side, 1998–2013; Area Dean of Hulme, 2012–13. Chair, Discipleship and Ministry Trng Cttee, Dio. of Manchester, 2005–13; Bishops Advr for Women's Ministry, 2009–13; Borough Dean, City and Borough of Manchester, 2010–13; Proctor in Convocation, Gen. Synod, 2010–13 and 2014. Hon. Canon, Manchester Cath., 2007–. Chaplain to Lord Mayor of Manchester, 2002–03. *Publications:* (contrib.) Everybody Welcome, 2009. *Recreations:* family, reading, travel, cooking, walking, ski-ing, theatre. *Address:* 1 New Lane, Huntington, York YO32 9NU. *T:* (01904) 758241.

BULLOCK, Sir Stephen Michael, Kt 2007; Executive Mayor, London Borough of Lewisham, since 2002; *b* 26 June 1953; *s* of late Fred George Bullock and Florence (*née* Gott); *m* 1992, Kristyne Margaret Hibbert. *Educ:* Sir William Turner's Sch., Redcar; Leeds Univ. (BA Hons); Goldsmiths' Coll. (PGCE). Greater London Council: Admin. Officer, 1977–79; Dep. Hd, Labour Gp Office, 1979–83; Asst Dir, Public Relns, 1983–86; Chief Officer, Greenwich CHC, 1986–90. Dir, 1993–97, Chm., 1997–2002, Univ. Hosp. Lewisham NHS Trust. London Borough of Lewisham: Councillor (Lab), 1982–98, 2001–02; Leader of Council, 1988–93. Chm., ALA, 1992–93; Dep. Chm., AMA, 1992–94; Hd, Labour Gp Office, LGA, 1997–2002. Board Member: London Pension Fund Authy, 1989–98; London First, 1993–96; Independent Housing Ombudsman Ltd, 1997–2001; Chairman: Deptford City Challenge Ltd, 1992–93; London Connects, 2004–09; Vice-Chm., Local Govt Management Bd, 1994–95 (Chm., 1992–93); Dep. Chm., LGA, 2013–; Dir, Civic Skills Consultancy, 1994–95; Prin. Consultant, Capita Gp, 1995–97. Mem., Commn for Local Democracy, 1994–96. Trustee, Horniman Mus. and Gdns, 1999–2010. *Publications:* (contrib.) A Transatlantic Policy Exchange, 1993; (with R. Hambleton) Revitalising Local Democracy: the leadership options, 1996. *Recreations:* folk music, watching Middlesbrough FC lose, seeking the "Moon under Water". *Address:* Garden Flat, 9 Tyson Road, Forest Hill, SE23 3AA. *T:* (020) 8291 5030. *E:* steve.bullock@lewisham.gov.uk.

BULLOCK, Susan Margaret, CBE 2014; FRAM; soprano; *b* 9 Dec. 1958; *d* of late John Robert Bullock and Mair Bullock (*née* Jones); *m* 1st, 1983, Lawrence Archer Wallington (marr. diss. 2008); 2nd, 2009, Richard Berkeley-Steele. *Educ:* Cheadle Hulme Sch.; Royal Northern Coll. of Music Jun. Sch.; Royal Holloway Coll., Univ. of London (BMus Hons; Hon. Fellow, 2004); Royal Acad. of Music (LRAM; FRAM 1997); Nat. Opera Studio. Mem., Glyndebourne Fest. Opera Chorus, 1983–84; Principal Soprano, ENO, 1985–89; freelance internat. soprano, 1989–; *rôles* include: Madama Butterfly (title rôle) with ENO, Houston Grand Opera, Oper der Stadt, Bonn, New Israeli Opera, Portland Opera, USA, NYC Opera and Teatro Colon, Buenos Aires; Jenůfa (title rôle) with ENO, New Israeli Opera, Glyndebourne and Spoleto Fest., USA; Magda Sorel in The Consul with Teatro Colon, Buenos Aires and Spoleto Fest., Italy; Isolde, in Tristan and Isolde, with Opera North, Bochum Symphony, ENO, Rouen, Oper Frankfurt and Verona; Brünnhilde, in Der Ring des Nibelungen, Tokyo, Perth Fest., Aust., Budapest, Lisbon, Royal Opera, Oper Frankfurt and Vienna State Opera; Elektra (title rôle), with Oper Frankfurt, La Monnaie, Brussels, Royal Opera, Metropolitan Opera, La Scala, Milan, and Washington Opera; Marie, in Wozzeck, Royal Opera; La Fanciulla del West, Edinburgh Fest.; Makropulos Case, Frankfurt; Gloriana (title rôle), Royal Opera; Miss Wingrave, in Owen Wingrave, Aldeburgh Fest.; Mrs Lovett, in Sweeney Todd, Houston Grand Opera; appears with all major British orchestras and also in Europe, N and S America and Australia. Frequent broadcasts; recitals at Wigmore Hall, Edinburgh Fest. and abroad with Malcolm Martineau; soloist in BBC Last Night of the Proms, 2011; has made recordings. Hon. MusD Manchester, 2014. Singers Award, Royal Philharmonic Soc., 2008. *Recreations:* playing the piano, cooking, theatre, jazz. *Address:* c/o HarrisonParrott Ltd, 5–6 Albion Court, Albion Place, W6 0QT.

BULLOUGH, Dr Ronald, FRS 1985; consultant in UK and USA; Chief Scientist, UK Atomic Energy Authority, 1988–93, and Director for Corporate Research, Harwell, 1990–93; *b* 6 April 1931; *s* of Ronald Bullough and Edna Bullough (*née* Morrow); *m* 1954, Ruth Corbett; four *s*. *Educ:* Univ. of Sheffield. BSc, PhD, DSc. FIMMM (FIM 1964); FInstP 1962. Res. Scientist, AEI Fundamental Res. Lab., Aldermaston Court, Aldermaston, 1956–63; Theoretical Physicist and Group Leader, Harwell Res. Lab., Didcot, Berks, 1963–84; Hd, Materials Develt Div., Harwell, 1984–88; Dir for Underlying Res., Harwell, 1988–90. Visiting Professor: Univ. of Illinois, USA, 1964, 1973, 1979; Univ. of Wisconsin, USA, 1978; Rensselaer Polytechnical Inst., USA, 1968; UCL, 1994–; Univ. of Liverpool, 1994–; Visiting Scientist: Nat. Bureau of Standards, USA, 1965; Oak Ridge Nat. Lab., USA, 1969, 1979; Comisión Nacional de Energía Atómica, Buenos Aires, Argentina, 1977. For. Associate, NAE (USA), 2011. Hon. Citizen of Tennessee, 1967. *Publications:* articles in learned jls such as Proc. Roy. Soc., Phil. Mag., Jl of Nucl. Materials etc., on defect properties in crystalline solids, particularly in relation to the irradiation and mechanical response of materials. *Recreations:* golf, walking, reading, music. *Address:* 4 Long Meadow, Manor Road, Goring-on-Thames, Reading, Berkshire RG8 9EG. *T:* (01491) 873266.

BULMER, Derek John; freelance consultant, hotel and catering industry; Editor, Great Britain and Ireland Michelin Guide, 1996–2010; *b* Hampstead, 24 March 1950; *s* of George Henry Bulmer and Barbara Joan Bulmer (*née* Gray); *m* 1979, Lynn Barton; one *s* one *d*. *Educ:* Christ Church, N Finchley; Westminster Hotel Sch. (HND). Trust Houses Forte, 1977–92; Asst Manager, White Horse Inn, Hertingfordbury, 1992–94; Dep. Manager, Randolph Hotel, Oxford, 1994–96; Personnel Manager, Brown's Hotel, Mayfair, 1996–97; Michelin Guide: Hotel and Restaurant Insp., 1977–90; Dep. Ed., GB and Ireland, 1990–96; Editor: Main Cities of Europe, 1998–2010; Eating Out in Pubs, 2005–10. Dir, Martini Consulting, 2010–. *Recreations:* wine, musical theatre, photography. *E:* derekbulmer@gmail.com.

BULMER, (James) Esmond; Director, H. P. Bulmer Holdings plc, 1962–2003 (Deputy Chairman, 1980; Chairman, 1982–2000); *b* 19 May 1935; *e s* of late Edward Bulmer and Margaret Rye; *m* 1st, 1959, Morella Kearton; three *s* one *d*; 2nd, 1990, Susan Elizabeth Bower (*née* Murray). *Educ:* Rugby; King's Coll., Cambridge (BA); and abroad. Commissioned Scots Guards, 1954. Dir (non-exec.), Wales and W Midlands Regional Bd, National Westminster Bank PLC, 1982–92. Chm., Hereford DHA, 1987–94. MP (C): Kidderminster, Feb. 1974–1983; Wyre Forest, 1983–87. PPS to Minister of State, Home Office, 1979–81. Mem. Council, CBI, 1998–2002. Mem. Exec. Cttee, Nat. Trust, 1977–87. *Recreations:* gardening, fishing. *Clubs:* Boodle's, Beefsteak.

BULMER, Dr Michael George, FRS 1997; Professor, Department of Biological Sciences, Rutgers University, 1991–95; *b* 10 May 1931; *s* of Dr Ernest and Dr Eileen Mary Bulmer; *m* 1966, Sylvia Ann House (*d* 2011). *Educ:* Rugby Sch.; Merton Coll., Oxford (MA, DPhil 1957; DSc 1985). Lectr in Med. Stats, Univ. of Manchester, 1957–59; Lectr in Biomaths, 1959–91, Fellow of Wolfson Coll., 1965–91, now Emeritus, Univ. of Oxford. *Publications:* Principles of Statistics, 1965; The Biology of Twinning in Man, 1970; The Mathematical Theory of Quantitative Genetics, 1980; Theoretical Evolutionary Ecology, 1994; Francis Galton: pioneer of heredity and biometry, 2003; articles in scientific jls on biometry and evolutionary biology. *Recreation:* walking.

BULMER, Prof. Simon John, PhD; Professor of European Politics, University of Sheffield, since 2007; *b* 29 June 1954; *s* of late Dawson Vivian Bulmer and of Kathleen Amy Bulmer; *m* 1986, Helen Margaret Donaldson. *Educ:* Univ. of Loughborough (BA Hons Eur. Studies 1975); Univ. of Hull (MA Eur. Politics 1976); London Sch. of Economics (PhD 1982). Lecturer: in Govt, Heriot-Watt Univ., 1979–83; in Eur. Studies, UMIST, 1983–89; Sen. Lectr, then Reader, in Govt, 1989–94, Prof. of Govt, 1995–2007, Univ. of Manchester. Vis. Prof., Coll. of Europe, Bruges, 1994–99. Mem., Trng and Develt Bd, ESRC, 2005–10. FAcSS (AcSS 2001). *Publications:* The Domestic Structure of European Community Policy-Making in West Germany, 1986; (jtly) The European Council, 1987; (jtly) The Federal Republic of Germany and the European Community, 1987; (ed) The Changing Agenda of West German Public Policy, 1989; (ed jtly) The United Kingdom and EC Membership Evaluated, 1992; (ed jtly) Economic and Political Integration in Europe, 1994; (jtly) The Governance of the Single European Market, 1998; (jtly) Germany's European Diplomacy, 2000; (jtly) British Devolution and European Policy-Making, 2002; (ed jtly) The Member States of the European Union, 2005, 2nd edn 2013; (jtly) Policy Transfer in European Union Governance, 2007; (jtly) The Europeanisation of Whitehall, 2009; (ed jtly) Rethinking Germany and Europe, 2010; (jtly) Politics in the European Union, 2011, 4th edn 2015; contrib. numerous jl articles. *Recreations:* travel, jazz, current affairs, walking. *Address:* Department of Politics, University of Sheffield, Elmfield, Northumberland Road, Sheffield S10 2TU. *T:* (0114) 222 1706, *Fax:* (0114) 222 1717. *E:* S.Bulmer@sheffield.ac.uk.

BULMER-THOMAS, Prof. Victor Gerald, CMG 2007; OBE 1998; DPhil; Director, Royal Institute of International Affairs (Chatham House), 2001–06; Emeritus Professor, London University, since 1998; *b* 23 March 1948; *s* of late Ivor Bulmer-Thomas, CBE and of Margaret Joan Bulmer-Thomas; *m* 1970, Barbara Ann Swasey; two *s* one *d*. *Educ:* Westminster Sch.; New Coll., Oxford (MA); St Antony's Coll., Oxford (DPhil). Research Fellow, Fraser of Allander Inst., Strathclyde Univ., 1975–78; Queen Mary, subseq. Queen Mary and Westfield, College, London University: Lectr in Econs, 1978–87; Reader in Econs of Latin America, 1987–90; Prof. of Econs, 1990–98; Institute of Latin American Studies, London University: Dir, 1992–98; Sen. Res. Fellow, 1998–2001; Hon. Res. Fellow, 2001–04; Hon. Res. Fellow, Inst. for the Study of the Americas, 2004–; Hon. Prof., UCL, 2012–. Associate Fellow, Chatham House, 2007–. Vis. Prof., Florida Internat. Univ., Miami, 2007–10. Director: Schroders Emerging Countries Fund, 1996–2003; Deutsche Latin American Companies Trust, 2004; New India Investment Trust, 2004–; Caribbean Foundn, 2008–10; J. P. Morgan Brazil Investment Trust, 2010–. Dir, UK-Japan 21st Century Gp, 2001–03. Editor, Jl of Latin American Studies, 1986–97. Comdr, Order of San Carlos (Colombia), 1998; Comdr, Order of Southern Cross (Brazil), 1998. *Publications:* Input-Output Analysis for Developing Countries, 1982; The Political Economy of Central America since 1920, 1987; Studies in the Economics of Central America, 1988; (ed) Britain and Latin America, 1989; (jtly) Central American Integration, 1992; (ed jtly) Mexico and the North American Free Trade Agreement: Who Will Benefit?, 1994; The Economic History of Latin America since Independence, 1994, 2nd edn 2003; (jtly) Growth and Development in Brazil: Cardoso's *real* challenge, 1995; (ed) The New Economic Model in Latin America and its Impact on Income Distribution and Poverty, 1996; (jtly) Rebuilding the State: Mexico after Salinas, 1996; (ed) Thirty Years of Latin American Studies in the United Kingdom, 1997; (jtly) US-Latin American Relations: the new agenda, 1999; (ed) Regional Integration in Latin America and the Caribbean: the political economy of open regionalism, 2001; (ed jtly) The Cambridge Economic History of Latin America, 2 vols, 2006, 3rd edn 2014; The Economic History of the Caribbean since the Napoleonic Wars, 2012; (jtly) The Economic History of Belize: from 17th century to post-independence, 2012. *Recreations:* tennis, hill-walking, canoeing, music (viola), underwater photography. *Club:* Athenæum.

BUMBRY, Grace; opera singer and concert singer; founder, Grace Bumbry Vocal and Opera Academy; *b* St Louis, Mo, 4 Jan. 1937. *Educ:* Boston Univ.; Northwestern Univ.; Music Academy of the West (under Lotte Lehmann). Début: Paris Opera, 1960; Bayreuth Fest., 1961; Chicago Lyric Opera, 1962; Royal Opera, Covent Gdn, London, 1963; San Francisco Opera, 1963; Vienna State Opera, 1964; Salzburg Festival, 1964; Metropolitan Opera, 1965; La Scala, 1964; has also appeared in all major opera houses in Europe, S America and USA. Has made numerous recordings. Film, Carmen, 1968. Hon. Dr of Humanities, St Louis Univ., 1968; Hon. doctorates: Rust Coll., Holly Spring, Miss; Rockhurst Coll., Kansas City; Univ. of Missouri at St Louis. Richard Wagner Medal, 1963; Kammersänger, Austria; Kennedy Center Honor, 2009. Commandeur de l'Ordre des Arts et des Lettres (France). *Recreations:* psychology, entertaining.

BUNBURY; *see* McClintock-Bunbury, family name of Baron Rathdonnell.

BUNBURY, Bishop of, since 2010; **Rt Rev. Allan Ewing;** *b* Hemel Hempstead, 3 Nov. 1951; *s* of William and Patricia Ewing; *m* 1972, Tricia Fowler; two *s*. *Educ:* Hemel Hempstead Grammar Sch.; Australian Coll. of Theology (BTh). ACA 1975, FCA 1980; ordained priest, Australia, 1988; Asst Priest, Canberra, 1988–89; Rector: Holbrook, NSW, 1989–93; Batemans Bay, NSW, 1993–96; St John's, Canberra, 1996–2004; Archdeacon of N Canberra, 1996–2004; Asst Bishop, Canberra and Goulburn, 2004–09. *Address:* PO Box 15, Bunbury, WA 6231, Australia. *T:* (8) 97212100. *E:* bishop@bunbury.org.au.

BUNBURY, Sir Michael; *see* Bunbury, Sir R. D. M. R.

BUNBURY, Sir Michael (William), 13th Bt *cr* 1681, of Stanney Hall, Cheshire; KCVO 2005; DL; company director, landowner and farmer; Consultant, Smith & Williamson, since 1997 (Partner, 1974–97; Chairman, 1986–93); *b* 29 Dec. 1946; *s* of Sir John William Napier Bunbury, 12th Bt, and of Pamela, *er d* of late Thomas Alexander Sutton; *S* father, 1985; *m*

1976, Caroline Anne, *d* of late Col A. D. S. Mangnall, OBE; two *s* one *d*. *Educ:* Eton; Trinity College, Cambridge (MA). Buckmaster & Moore, 1968–74. Chairman: Fleming High Income Investment Trust plc, 1996–97 (Dir, 1995–97); HarbourVest Global Private Equity Ltd, 2007–; BH Global Ltd, 2013–; Director: JP Morgan Claverhouse Investment Trust plc, 1996–2015 (Chm., 2005–15); Foreign & Colonial Investment Trust plc, 1998–2012; Invesco Perpetual Select Trust plc, 2008–. Mem. Council, Duchy of Lancaster, 1993–2005 (Dep. Chm., 1995–2000, Chm., 2000–05). Mem. Exec. Cttee, CLA, 1992–97 and 1999–2004 (Chm., Taxation Cttee, 1999–2003; Chm. Cttee, Suffolk Br., 1995–97); Pres., Suffolk Agricl Assoc., 2000–02. Trustee, Calthorpe Edgbaston Estate, 1991–2013. DL 2004, High Sheriff, 2006–07, Suffolk. *Heir: s* Henry Michael Napier Bunbury, *b* 4 March 1980. *Address:* Naunton Hall, Rendlesham, Woodbridge, Suffolk IP12 2RD. *T:* (01394) 460235. *Club:* Boodle's.

BUNBURY, Lt-Comdr Sir (Richard David) Michael (Richardson-), 5th Bt, *cr* 1787; RN; *b* 27 Oct. 1927; *er s* of Richard Richardson-Bunbury (*d* 1951) and Florence Margaret Gordon (*d* 1993), *d* of late Col Roger Gordon Thomson, CMG, DSO, late RA; *S* kinsman 1953; *m* 1961, Jane Louise, *d* of late Col Alfred William Pulverman, IA; one *s* (and one *s* decd). *Educ:* Royal Naval College, Dartmouth. Midshipman (S), 1945; Sub-Lieut (S), 1947; Lieut (S), 1948; Lieut-Comdr, 1956; retd 1967. Dir, Sandy Laird Ltd, 1988–96. Pres., HMS Sussex Assoc., 1991–2002. *Publications:* A Short History of Crowcombe, 1999. *Heir: s* Thomas William Richardson-Bunbury [*b* 4 Aug. 1965; *m* 2001, Sallie Ann Lofts; two *s* two *d*]. *Address:* Upper House, Crowcombe, Taunton, Somerset TA4 4AG. *T:* (01984) 618223.

BUNCE, Rev. Dr Michael John, FSAScot; Permission to officiate, Diocese of Norfolk, since 2014; Chaplain, Santa Margarita, Menorca, 2000–12; *b* 5 Dec. 1949; *s* of Harold Christopher and Kathleen June Bunce; *m* 1973, Frances Sutherland; one *s* one *d*. *Educ:* St Andrews Univ. (MTh); Westcott House and Trinity Hall, Cambridge; Greenwich Univ. (PhD). Glazing clerk, Middleton Glass Merchant, 1965–69; Personnel Labour Controller, Bird's Eye Unilever, 1969–75. Ordained deacon, 1980, priest, 1981; Curate, 1980–83, Hosp. Chaplain and Team Vicar, 1983–85, Grantham Parish Church; Rector, St Andrew's, Brechin with St Drostan's, Tarfside and St Peter's, Auchmithie (Angus), 1985–92; Provost, St Paul's Cathedral, Dundee, 1992–97. FRSA. *Recreations:* tennis, ski-ing, art, antiques. *Club:* Edinburgh Angus.

BUNCH, Dr Christopher, FRCP, FRCPE; Consultant Physician, Oxford Radcliffe Hospitals NHS Trust, since 1994 (Medical Director, 1994–2001; Caldicott Guardian, since 1998); *b* 25 Feb. 1947; *s* of Douglas Campbell Bunch and Barbara Bunch (*née* Hall); *m* 1977, Kathleen Josie Andrew; two *d*. *Educ:* King's School, Worcester; Birmingham Univ. (MB ChB 1969). FRCP 1984; FRCPE 1988. University of Oxford: Clinical Lectr in Medicine, 1975–81; Clinical Reader in Medicine, 1981–94; Professorial Fellow, Wolfson Coll., Oxford, 1981–94, Fellow Emeritus 1994–. Dir, British Assoc. of Medical Managers, 1995–2005 (Chm., 2001–04). Secondary Care Consultant Mem., Governing Body, Nene CCG, 2012–. Goulstonian Lectr, RCP, 1985. Mem. Council, RCP, 1999–2002. *Publications:* (ed) Horizons in Medicine I, 1989; contrib. various scientific and medical articles in haematology, especially control of erythropoiesis. *Recreations:* cooking (and eating) Mediterranean, Middle Eastern and SE Asian food, music, photography, computer science and programming. *Address:* Bayswater Farm House, Headington, Oxford OX3 8BY. *T:* (office) (01865) 221343.

BUNCLE, Thomas Archibald; Managing Director, Yellow Railroad Ltd, since 2000; *b* 25 June 1953; *s* of Thomas Edgar Buncle and Helen Elizabeth Buncle; *m* 1979, Janet Michelle Louise Farmer; two *s*. *Educ:* Trinity Coll., Glenalmond; Exeter Univ. (BA Sociology and Law 1975); Sheffield Univ. (MA Criminology 1978). Various posts, incl. Law Tutor, Sheffield Univ., and tour guide, Amer. Leadership Study Gps and Voyages Sans Frontières, 1975–77; British Tourist Authority: graduate trainee, 1978–79; Asst Internat. Advertising Manager, 1979–80; Asst Manager, Western USA, 1981–84; Manager, Norway, 1984–86; Regl Dir, SE Asia, 1986–91; Scottish Tourist Board: Internat. Mktg Dir, 1991–96; Chief Exec., 1996–2000. Dir, Edinburgh Festival Council, 1997–2000; Board Member: Scotland the Brand, 1996–2000; Cairngorm Partnership, 1997–2000; Member: Exec. Council, Scottish Council for Develt and Industry, 1998–2000; Risk Monitoring and Audit Cttee, Scottish Prison Service, 2004–14. Fellow: Tourism Soc.; Tourism Mgt Inst.; Member: Sustainable Tourism Certification Alliance Africa; Experts' Cttee, World Tourism Cities Forum, China. *Recreations:* windsurfing, sailing, scuba diving, Rugby, hill walking, cycling, photography.

BUNDRED, Stephen; Strategic Advisor, Deloitte LLP, 2010–15; *b* 12 Dec. 1952; *s* of George Bundred, CBE, JP, DL and Theresa Bundred (*née* Hynes); *m* 1976, Kathleen McVeigh; one *s*. *Educ:* St Catherine's Coll., Oxford (BA PPE); Birkbeck Coll., London (MSc Econs); Liverpool Poly. (CPFA). Res. Asst to Eric Varley, MP, 1973–74; Special Advr to Sec. of State for Energy, 1974–75; Hd, Res. Dept, NUM, 1975–83; Principal Technical Accountant, Hackney LBC, 1983–87; Chief Accountant, Lewisham LBC, 1987–88; Financial Sec., Birkbeck Coll., Univ. of London, 1988–90; Dep. Dir of Finance, Hackney LBC, 1990–92; Dir of Finance and Dep. Chief Exec., 1992–95, Chief Finance Officer, 1995–99, Chief Exec., 1995–2003, Camden LBC; Clerk, N London Waste Authy, 1995–2003; Exec. Dir, Improvement and Develt Agency, 2003; Chief Exec., Audit Commn, 2003–10; Chm., Monitor, Ind. Regulator of NHS Foundn Trusts, 2010–11. Chm., Higher Educn Regulation Rev. Gp, 2006–08; Member: TEC Assessors Cttee, 1998–99; Rethinking Construction Local Govt Task Force, DETR, 1999–2003; Bd, HEFCE, 1999–2005 (Chm., Audit Cttee, 2002–05); London Central Learning and Skills Council, 2001–03; Putting the Frontline First Taskforce, DCLG, 2010; Bd, Office for Nuclear Regulation, 2011– (Chm., Audit Cttee, 2011–); Higher Educn Commn, 2013–. Member (Lab): Islington LBC, 1975–78; GLC, 1981–86; ILEA, 1981–90. Mem. Council, 1999–2008, Dep. Pro Chancellor, 2006–08, City Univ. Freeman, City of London, 2001. FRSA. Hon. DSc City, 2006. *Publications:* (contrib.) Policing the Riots, 1982; (contrib.) Reinventing Government Again, 2004; (contrib.) Public Services Inspection in the UK, 2008; (contrib.) Opportunities in an Age of Austerity, 2009; contribs to jls. *Address:* 3 Colebrooke Row, Islington, N1 8DB. *T:* (020) 7278 7742.

BUNDY, Prof. Alan Richard, CBE 2012; PhD; FRS 2012; FREng; FRSE; Professor of Automated Reasoning, University of Edinburgh, since 1990 (Head of Division of Informatics, 1998–2001); *b* 18 May 1947; *s* of Stanley Alfred Bundy and Joan Margaret Bundy; *m* 1967, D. Josephine A. Maule; one *d*. *Educ:* Univ. of Leicester (BSc 1st Cl. Maths 1968; PhD Mathematic Logic 1971). Teaching Asst, Dept of Maths, Univ. of Leicester, 1970–71; University of Edinburgh: Res. Fellow, Metamathematics Unit, 1971–74; Department of Artificial Intelligence: Lectr, 1974–84; Reader, 1984–87; Professorial Fellow, 1987–90. Vice Pres. and Trustee, BCS, 2010–12. FAAAI 1990; FRSE 1996; FBCS 2002; FIET (FIEE 2005); FREng 2008; Fellow: Soc. for Study of Artificial Intelligence and Simulation of Behaviour, 1997; Eur. Co-ordinating Cttee for Artificial Intelligence, 1999. Donald E. Walter Dist. Service Award, 2003, Res. Excellence Award, 2007, Internat. Jt Conf. on Artificial Intelligence; Herbrand Award, Internat. Conf. on Automated Deduction, 2007. *Publications:* Artificial Intelligence: an introductory course, 1978; The Computer Modelling of Mathematical Reasoning, 1983, 2nd edn 1986; The Benefits and Risks of Knowledge Based Systems, 1989; Eco-logic: logic based approaches to ecological modelling, 1991; Catalogue of Artificial Intelligence Techniques, 1984, 4th edn 1996. *Recreation:* valley walking. *Address:* School of Informatics, University of Edinburgh, Informatics Forum, 10 Crichton Street, Edinburgh EH8 9AB.

BUNDY, Prof. Colin James, DPhil; Principal, Green Templeton College, Oxford, 2008–10 (Hon. Fellow, 2010); *b* 4 Oct. 1944; *s* of Guy Stanhope Bundy and Winifred Constance Bundy (*née* Tooke); *m* 1st, 1969, Carol Ann Neilson (marr. diss. 1993); one *s* one *d*; 2nd, 2001, Evelyn Jeannette Bertelsen. *Educ:* Graeme Coll., Grahamstown; Univ. of Natal (BA); Univ. of Witwatersrand (BA Hons); Merton Coll., Oxford (Rhodes Schol., 1968); MPhil 1970, DPhil 1976, Oxon. Beit Sen. Res. Scholar, St Antony's Coll., Oxford, 1971–73. Lectr and Sen. Lectr in Hist., Manchester Poly., 1973–78; Res. Fellow, Queen Elizabeth House, Oxford, 1979–80; Tutor in Hist., Dept for External Studies, Oxford Univ., 1980–84; Prof. of Hist., Univ. of Cape Town, 1985–86; Prof. of Hist., concurrently Univs of Cape Town and Western Cape, 1987–90; University of Western Cape: Prof. of Hist., 1991–95; Dir, Inst. of Histl Res., 1992–94; Actg Vice-Rector, 1994–95; Vice-Rector (Academic), 1995–97; Vice-Chancellor and Principal, Univ. of Witwatersrand, Johannesburg, 1998–2001; Dir and Principal, SOAS, 2001–06, and Dep. Vice-Chancellor, 2003–06, Univ. of London; Warden, Green Coll., Oxford, 2006–08. Chm., South African Nat. Commn for UNESCO. Mem. Council, Robben Island Mus., 1997–2001. Hon. Fellow, Kellogg Coll., Oxford, 1998. Hon. DLitt: Manchester Metropolitan, 1999; Univ. of Western Cape, 2005. *Publications:* The Rise and Fall of a South African Peasantry, 1979, 2nd edn 1988; (jtly) Hidden Struggles in Rural South Africa, 1988; (contrib.) Encyclopedia Britannica, other books, and periodicals. *Recreations:* hiking, cricket, chess, music.

BUNEMAN, Prof. (Oscar) Peter, MBE 2013; PhD; FRS 2009; FRSE; Professor of Database Systems, University of Edinburgh, since 2002. *Educ:* Gonville and Caius Coll., Cambridge (BA Maths 1965); Univ. of Warwick (PhD 1970). Res. Associate, then Lectr, Sch. of Artificial Intelligence, Univ. of Edinburgh, 1969–74; University of Pennsylvania: Asst Prof. of Computer Sci., Moore Sch., and Asst Prof. of Decision Scis, Wharton Sch., 1975–81; Associate Prof. of Computer Sci., 1981–89; Grad. Chm., Dept of Computer and Inf. Sci., 1981–87; Prof. of Computer Sci., 1990–2001; Adjunct Prof. of Computer Sci., 2002–; Res. Dir, Digital Curation Centre, Edinburgh, 2004–. FRSE 2004. *Publications:* (contrib.) Theoretical Aspects of Object-oriented Programming, 1994; (contrib.) Bioinformatics, 1998; (contrib.) Semantics of Databases, 1998; (jtly) Data on the Web: from relations to semi-structured data and XML, 1999; contribs to conf. proceedings and to jls incl. Internat. Jl on Digital Libraries, Jl Computer and System Scis, Theoretical Computer Sci. *Address:* Laboratory for Foundations of Computer Science, School of Informatics, University of Edinburgh, 10 Crichton Street, Edinburgh EH8 9AB.

BUNGEY, Michael; Chairman and Chief Executive Officer, Bates Worldwide (formerly BSB Worldwide), 1994–2003; Chief Executive Officer, Cordiant Communications Group, 1997–2003; *b* 18 Jan. 1940; *s* of William Frederick George and Irene Edith Bungey; *m* 1976, Darleen Penelope Cecilia Brooks (marr. diss.); one *s* two *d*. *Educ:* St Clement Danes Grammar Sch.; LSE (BSc Econ). Marketing with Nestlé, 1961–65; Associate Dir, Crawfords Advertising, 1965–68; Account Dir, S. H. Benson Advertising, 1969–71; Chm., Michael Bungey & Partners, 1972–84; Dep. Chm., Dorland Advertising, 1984; Chm., Bates Dorland Advertising Ltd, 1987–96; Chairman and Chief Executive Officer: DFS Dorland, 1987; Bates Dorland, 1988; Bates Europe, 1989; Pres. and Chief Operating Officer, BSB Worldwide, 1993–94; Chairman: Bates Americas' Reg., 1993; Bates USA, 1993; Kingstreet Media Gp, 2004–05. Dir, Cordiant plc (formerly Saatchi & Saatchi), 1995. *Club:* Hurlingham.

BUNKER, Prof. Christopher Barry, MD; FRCP; Consultant Dermatologist, University College London Hospitals NHS Foundation Trust, since 2010; *b* Aylesbury, Bucks, 22 Nov. 1956; *s* of Sqn Leader Nigel Vincent Delahuntey Bunker, MBE and Joy Bunker (*née* Bolsover); *m* 1991, Dr Anna Kurowska; two *d*. *Educ:* Wycliffe Coll. (Scholar.); St Catharine's Coll., Cambridge (Kitchener Scholar.; BA 1978; MD 1992); Westminster Med. Sch. (MB BS 1981). MRCP 1995, FRCP 1996. Sir Jules Thorn Res. Fellow, UCL, 1988–90; Consultant Dermatologist: Charing Cross Hosp., 1992–2003; Chelsea and Westminster (formerly Westminster) Hosp., 1992–; Royal Marsden Hosp., 1997–2010. Honorary Professor: Imperial Coll. London, 2005–; UCL, 2010–. President: St John's Hosp. Dermatol Soc., 2006–07; W London Medico-Chirurgical Soc., 2007–08; Chelsea Clin. Soc., 2010–11; British Assoc. of Dermatologists, 2012–14; Dermatol. Section, RSocMed, 2015–July 2016. Sir Walter Langdon-Down Prize, Univ. of Cambridge, 1992; Bristol Cup, British Assoc. of Dermatologists, 1998. *Publications:* Male Genital Dermatology, 2004; chapters in textbooks and contrib. over 300 pubns. *Recreations:* literature, music, opera, drama, stalking. *Address:* King Edward VII Hospital, Beaumont Street, W1G 6AA. *T:* (020) 7794 5943. *E:* c.bunker@ucl.ac.uk. *Club:* Garrick.

BUNKER, Very Rev. Michael; fundraising consultant, since 2006; Dean of Peterborough 1992–2006, now Dean Emeritus; *b* 22 July 1937; *s* of Murray Bunker and Nora Bunker; *m* 1957, Mary Helena Poulten; four *s*. *Educ:* Acton Technical Coll. and Brunel Coll., Acton (ONC and HNC in Engineering); Oak Hill Theol Coll. Work Study Engr, Napiers of Acton London, 1956–60. Ordained deacon, 1963, priest, 1964; Assistant Curate: St James' Church Alperton, Middlesex, 1963–66; Parish Church of St Helen, Merseyside, 1966–70; Incumbent St Matthew's Church, Muswell Hill, London, 1970–78; St James with St Matthew, Muswell Hill, 1978–92. Prebendary of St Paul's Cathedral, 1990. Chm., Habitat for Humanity GB 2000–02. Trustee, Nat. Kidney Res. Fund, 1999–2002. *Publications:* The Church on the Hill 1988; Peterborough Cathedral 2001–2006: from devastation to restoration, 2007. *Recreations:* flyfishing, walking. *Address:* 21 Black Pot Lane, Oundle, Peterborough PE8 4AT. *T:* (01832) 273032, 07887 854917. *E:* deanbunker@btinternet.com.

BUNTING, Martin Brian, FCA; *b* 28 Feb. 1934; *s* of late Brian and Renee Bunting; *m* 1959, Veronica Mary Cope; two *s* one *d*. *Educ:* Rugby School. 2nd Lieut, 8th Kings Royal Irish Hussars, 1952–54. Deloitte, 1954–60; joined Courage Ltd, 1961, Man. Dir, 1972, Dep. Chm., 1974–84; Dir, Imperial Group plc, 1975–84; Chief Executive, Clifford Foods PLC 1990–93. Non-executive Director: George Gale & Co. Ltd, 1984–2004; Longman Cartermill Ltd, 1985–90; Norcros plc, 1986–93; Shepherd Neame Ltd, 1986–2004; NAAFI, 1993–98 Hobson plc, 1994–96; Chairman: Inn Business Gp plc, 1996–97; Select Catalogues Ltd 1996–98; Bluebird Toys plc, 1996–98 (Dir, 1991–98). Member, Monopolies and Merger Commission, 1982–88. Chm. Trustees and Gov., Lord Wandsworth Coll., 2000–04. *Address:* The Long House, 41 High Street, Odiham, Basingstoke, Hants RG29 1LF. *T:* (01256) 703585, *Fax:* (01256) 703562.

See also Duke of Fife.

BUNTING, Prof. Rebecca Mary; Vice-Chancellor and Chief Executive, Buckinghamshire New University, since 2015; *b* Lytham St Annes, 27 Sept. 1955; *d* of Henry Bunting and Roma Bunting; partner, Dr Peter Weston. *Educ:* Fleetwood Grammar Sch.; Girton Coll. Cambridge (BA 1977); Inst. of Educn, Univ. of London (MA; PGCE). ATCL 1973, LTCL 1974. Roehampton Institute of Higher Education, London, later University of Surrey Roehampton: Sen. Lectr, 1985–87; Hd, English Educn, 1987–89; Dir, Inner London Lang Proj., 1989–92; Principal Lectr, 1992–95; Associate Dean of Educn, 1995–98; Dean of Educn Anglia Polytechnic Univ., 1998–2002; Pro-Rector, University Coll. Northampton, 2002–04 Pro Vice-Chancellor, 2004–07, Dep. Vice-Chancellor, 2007–15, Univ. of Portsmouth FHEA 2004; FRSA. *Publications:* Teaching about Language in the Primary Years, 1998, 2nd edn 2001. *Address:* Buckinghamshire New University, Queen Alexandra Road, High Wycombe, Bucks HP11 2JZ. *T:* (01494) 522141. *E:* rebecca.bunting@bucks.ac.uk.

BUNYAN, Dr Peter John; Chief Scientific Adviser to Ministry of Agriculture, Fisheries and Food, 1990–95; *b* London, 13 Jan. 1936; *o s* of Charles and Jenny Bunyan; *m* 1961, June Rose Child; two *s*. *Educ:* Raynes Park County Grammar Sch.; University Coll., Durham Univ (BSc, DSc); King's Coll., Univ. of London (PhD). FRSC; CChem; FRSB; FIFST. Research at KCL, 1960–62, at UCL, 1962–63; Ministry of Agriculture, Fisheries and Food: Sen Scientific Officer, Infestation Control Lab., 1963–69; PSO, Pest Infestation Control Lab 1969–73, Head of Pest Control Chemistry Dept, 1973–80; Head of Food Science Div

1980–84; Head of Agricl Sci. Service, ADAS, 1984–87; Dir of R & D Service, ADAS, 1987–90; Dir Gen., ADAS and Regl Orgn, 1990–91. Member: AFRC, 1990–94; BBSRC, 1994–95; NERC, 1991–95; Chm., British Crop Protection Council, 1998–2002. Special Advr to Vice-Chancellor, Surrey Univ., 1996–2008. Hon. Sec., Inst. of Biol., 1996–2001. Vis. Prof., Sch. of Agriculture, De Montfort Univ., 1996–2001. Gov., Portsmouth Univ., 2010–. Hon. DSc De Montfort, 2001; DUniv Surrey, 2009. *Publications:* numerous scientific papers in wide variety of scientific jls. *Recreations:* gardening, walking. *Address:* Flushings Meadow, 16A Lavant Road, Chichester, W Sussex PO19 5RG. *T:* (01243) 527542.

BUNYARD, Sir Robert (Sidney), Kt 1991; CBE 1986; QPM 1980; DL; Commandant, Police Staff College, Bramshill and HM Inspector of Constabulary, 1988–93; *b* 20 May 1930; *s* of Albert Percy Bunyard and Nellie Maria Bunyard; *m* 1948, Ruth Martin; two *d. Educ:* Queen Elizabeth Grammar Sch., Faversham; Regent Street Polytechnic Management Sch. (Dip. in Mgt Studies). BA (Hons) Open Univ. MIPD; CCMI. Metropolitan Police, 1952; Asst Chief Constable, Leics, 1972; rcds, 1977; Dep. Chief Constable, 1977, Chief Constable, 1978–87, Essex Police. Man. Editor, Police Jl, 1981–88. Member: Royal Commn on Criminal Justice, 1991–93; Parole Bd, 1994–98. Chm., Essex Reg., Royal Assoc. in Aid of Deaf People, 1994–95; Dir, Addaction, 1998–2001. Pres., Essex Youth Orch. Assoc., 2001–09; Patron, InterAct, 2006–10 (Trustee, 2003–06). DL Essex, 1997. *Publications:* Police: organization and command, 1978; Police Management Handbook, 1979; (contrib.) Police Leadership in the Twenty-first Century, 2003; contrib. Record Collector, 1999–. *Recreations:* music, opera. *Address:* Bellmans, Mounthill Avenue, Springfield, Essex CM2 6DB.

BURBIDGE, Eileen, MBE 2015; Partner, Passion Capital, since 2011; *b* Illinois, 16 June 1971; *d* of Robert Tso and Rae C. Tso; three *s* one *d. Educ:* Univ. of Illinois at Urbana-Champaign (BSc Computer Sci. 1993). Product Mktg, Apple Computer, 1995–96; Mkt Develt, Sun Microsystems, 1996–99; Dir Account Mgt, Palmsource, 2002–04; Product Develt Dir, Skype, 2004–05; Products Dir, Yahoo! Europe, 2005–07; Investment Dir, Ambient Sound Investments, 2007–11; Co-Founder and Dir, White Bear Yard, 2009–. Chair, Tech City UK, 2015–. Special Envoy for FinTech, HM Treasury, 2015–; Mem., Prime Minister's Business Adv. Gp, 2015–. *Address:* Passion Capital, 2nd Floor, White Bear Yard, 144A Clerkenwell Road, EC1R 5DF. *T:* (020) 7833 3373. *E:* eileenburbidge@yahoo.com.

BURBIDGE, (Eleanor) Margaret, (Mrs Geoffrey Burbidge), FRS 1964; Professor of Astronomy, 1964–90, University Professor, 1984–90, now Emeritus, and Research Professor, Department of Physics, since 1990, University of California at San Diego; *d* of late Stanley John Peachey, Lectr in Chemistry and Research Chemist, and of Marjorie Peachey; *m* 1948, Prof. Geoffrey Burbidge, FRS (*d* 2010); one *d. Educ:* Francis Holland Sch., London; University Coll., London (BSc); Univ. of London Observatory (PhD). Asst Director, 1948–50, Actg Director, 1950–51, Univ. of London Observatory; fellowship from IAU, held at Yerkes Observatory, Univ. of Chicago, 1951–53; Research Fellow, California Inst. of Technology, 1955–57; Shirley Farr Fellow, later Associate Prof., Yerkes Observatory, Univ. of Chicago, 1957–62; Research Astronomer, 1962–64, Dir, Center for Astrophysics and Space Scis, 1979–88, Univ. of California at San Diego; Dir, Royal Greenwich Observatory, 1972–73. Abby Rockefeller Mauzé Vis. Prof., MIT, 1968. Chief scientist, Faint Object Spectrograph team, Hubble Space Telescope, 1990–96. Member: American Acad. of Arts and Scis, 1969; US Nat. Acad. of Scis, 1978; Nat. Acad. of Scis Cttee on Science and Public Policy, 1979–81; Pres., Amer. Astronomical Soc., 1976–78; Chairwoman Bd of Dirs, Amer. Assoc. for Advancement of Science, 1983 (Pres., 1982); Mem., Amer. Philosophical Soc., 1980. Fellow University Coll., London, 1967; Hon. Fellow: Girton Coll., Cambridge, 1970; Lucy Cavendish Collegiate Soc., Cambridge, 1971. Hon. DSc: Smith Coll., Massachusetts, USA, 1963; Sussex, 1970; Bristol, 1972; Leicester, 1972; City, 1974; Michigan, 1978; Massachusetts, 1978; Williams Coll., 1979; State Univ. of NY at Stony Brook, 1984; Rensselaer Poly. Inst., 1986; Notre Dame Univ., 1986; Chicago, 1991. Catherine Wolfe Bruce Medal, Astronomical Soc. of the Pacific, 1982; Nat. Medal of Science (awarded by President of USA), 1984; Sesquicentennial Medal, Mt Holyoke Coll., 1987; Einstein Medal, World Cultural Council, 1988; Gold Medal, RAS, 2005. *Publications:* Quasi-Stellar Objects (with Geoffrey Burbidge), 1967 (also USA, 1967); contribs to learned jls (mostly USA), Handbuch der Physik, etc. *Address:* Center for Astrophysics and Space Sciences, 0424, University of California, San Diego, La Jolla, CA 92093, USA. *T:* (858) 5344477.

BURBIDGE, James Michael; QC 2003; **His Honour Judge Burbidge;** a Circuit Judge, since 2011; *b* 16 June 1957; *s* of George John Burbidge and late Margaret Elizabeth Burbidge; *m* 1998, Denise McCabe; one *d. Educ:* Brockley Co. Grammar Sch.; Leicester Univ. (LLB Hons). Called to the Bar, Lincoln's Inn, 1979, Bencher, 2009; specialist in criminal law; Asst Recorder, 1998–2000; Recorder, 2000–11. *Recreations:* ski-ing, golf, travel, theatre. *Address:* Birmingham Crown Court, Queen Elizabeth II Law Courts, 1 Newton Street, Birmingham B4 7NA.

BURBIDGE, Margaret, (Mrs Geoffrey Burbidge); *see* Burbidge, E. M.

BURBIDGE, Sir Peter Dudley, 6th Bt *cr* 1916, of Littleton Park, co. Middlesex; *b* 20 June 1942; *s* of Sir Herbert Dudley Burbidge, 5th Bt and Ruby Bly Burbidge (*née* Taylor); *S* father, 2001; *m* 1967, Peggy Marilyn Anderson; one *s* one *d. Educ:* Sir Winston Churchill Sch., Vancouver. *Heir: s* John Peter Burbidge [*b* 1 April 1975; *m* 2000, Jackie Davies].

BURBRIDGE, Very Rev. (John) Paul, MA Oxon and Cantab; FSA; Dean of Norwich, 1983–95, now Emeritus; *b* 21 May 1932; *e s* of late John Henry Gray Burbridge and Dorothy Vera Burbridge; *m* 1956, Olive Denise Grenfell; four *d. Educ:* King's Sch., Canterbury; King's Coll., Cambridge; New Coll., Oxford; Wells Theol Coll. Nat. Service Commn in RA, 1957. Jun. Curate, 1959, Sen. Curate, 1961, Eastbourne Parish Church; Vicar Choral of York Minster, 1962–66; Chamberlain, 1962–76; Canon Residentiary, 1966–76; Succentor Canonicorum, 1966; Precentor, 1969–76; Archdeacon of Richmond and Canon Residentiary of Ripon Cathedral, 1976–83; Canon Emeritus, 1998. *Recreations:* organ playing, historical research. *Address:* The Clachan Bothy, Newtonairds, Dumfries, Scotland DG2 0JL. *T:* (01387) 820403.

See also S. N. Burbridge.

BURBRIDGE, Stephen Nigel, CB 1992; MA; Secretary, Monopolies and Mergers Commission, 1986–93; *b* 18 July 1934; *s* of late John Henry Gray Burbridge and late Dorothy Vera (*née* Pratt). *Educ:* King's Sch., Canterbury; Christ Church, Oxford. National Service, 2 Lieut, RA, 1953–55. Asst Principal, Bd of Trade, 1958–62; Trade Commissioner, Karachi, 1963–65; 1st Secretary (Economic), Rawalpindi, 1965–67; Principal, BoT, 1967–71; CS Selection Bd, 1971; Department of Trade and Industry: Asst Sec., 1971–80; Under Sec., 1980–86. *Publications:* The Days of Our Age, 2007. *Recreation:* books. *Address:* Chesil Cottage, Brede Hill, Brede, near Rye, E Sussex TN31 6HH. *Club:* Rye Golf.

See also Very Rev. J. P. Burbridge.

BURCH, Monica; Senior Partner, Addleshaw Goddard LLP, since 2010; a Recorder (Civil), since 2010; *b* York, 14 Feb. 1966; *d* of Fraser Burch and Katia Burch (*née* Hajicristofis); *m* 1994, Paul Lister; one *s* two *d. Educ:* Queen's Sch., Rheindahlen; Pembroke Coll., Oxford (BA Juris.); Nottingham Law Sch. (LLM); Guildford Coll. of Law (Law Soc. Finals). Litigation Partner: Theodore Goddard, 1999–2003; Addleshaw Goddard, 2003–10. Non-exec. Dir, Channel 4 Corp., 2010–. Dir, Prime (charity), 2012–. *Recreations:* family, theatre, museums, reading, watching Channel 4. *Address:* Addleshaw Goddard LLP, 60 Chiswell Street, EC1A 4AG. *T:* (020) 7788 5155. *E:* monica.burch@addleshawgoddard.com.

BURCHELL, Andrew; Associate Hospital Manager, South West London and St George's Mental Health Trust, 2011; Chairman, Sutton Citizens Advice Bureaux, since 2010; *b* 26 March 1955; *s* of Joseph Fredrick Bertram Burchell and Myrtle Miriam Burchell; *m* 1974, Susan Margaret Hewing; one *s* one *d. Educ:* London School of Economics and Political Science (BSc (Econ) 1976; MSc 1980). Economist, DHSS, 1976–84; Economic Advr, National Audit Office, 1984–85; Economic Advr, 1985–89, Sen. Economic Advr, 1989–90, Dept of Health; Department of Transport, later Department of the Environment, Transport and the Regions: Sen. Economic Advr, Railways, 1990–96; Director: Strategy and Analysis, 1996; Transport Strategy, 1997; Envmt Protection Strategy, 1998–2001; Department for Environment, Food and Rural Affairs: Dir, Envmt Protection Strategy, 2001; Finance Dir, 2001–05; Chief Operating Officer and Dir Gen., Service Transformation Gp, 2005–08; Business Consultant, Appeals Decision Maker, DfT, 2008–14. Ind. Mem., Sutton and Merton Community Services Bd, 2009–11. *Publications:* articles on health economics. *Recreations:* golf, playing the guitar, spectating football, reading.

BURCHILL, Julie; columnist and author; *b* 3 July 1959; *d* of Thomas William Burchill and Bette Doreen Burchill (*née* Thomas). *Educ:* Brislington Comprehensive Sch., Bristol. Columnist: New Musical Express, 1976–80; The Face, 1980–84; Sunday Times, 1984–86; Mail on Sunday, 1986–98; The Guardian, 1998–2003; The Times, 2004–06. *Publications:* The Boy Looked at Johnny, 1979; Love It or Shove It, 1985; Girls on Film, 1986; Damaged Gods, 1986; Ambition, 1989; Sex and Sensibility, 1992; No Exit, 1993; I Knew I Was Right (autobiog.), 1998; Diana, 1998; Married Alive, 1999; The Guardian Columns 1998–2000, 2001; Burchill on Beckham, 2001; Sugar Rush, 2004; Sweet, 2007; (with Daniel Raven) Made in Brighton, 2007; (with C. Newkey-Burden) Not In My Name, 2008; Unchosen: the memoirs of a philo-Semite, 2014. *Recreations:* sex and shopping. *Club:* Sussex Arts (Brighton).

BURD, Michael; Joint Head of Employment and Incentives, Lewis Silkin LLP, since 1994; *b* New York City, 7 Feb. 1958; *s* of Donald and Shane Gale Burd; *m* 1984, Jacqueline Margaret Thomas; three *d. Educ:* Columbia Univ. (BA 1980); Clare Coll., Cambridge (MPhil 1982). Admitted as solicitor, 1986; Lewis Silkin LLP: articled clerk, 1984–86; Associate, 1986–88; Partner, 1988–. Pres., City of London Law Soc., 1995–96. Mem. Cttee, London Solicitors' Litigation Assoc., 1997–. *Recreations:* hiking, fine food, wines. *Address:* Lewis Silkin LLP, 5 Chancery Lane, Clifford's Inn, EC4A 1BL. *T:* (020) 7074 8176, *Fax:* (020) 7864 1722. *E:* michael.burd@lewissilkin.com.

BURDEKIN, Prof. Frederick Michael, OBE 2008; FREng; FRS 1993; Professor of Civil and Structural Engineering, University of Manchester Institute of Science and Technology, 1977–2002, now Professor Emeritus, University of Manchester; *b* 5 Feb. 1938; *s* of Leslie and Gwendoline Burdekin; *m* 1965, Jennifer Meadley; two *s. Educ:* King's School, Chester; Trinity Hall, Cambridge (MA, PhD). MSc Manchester. FICE, FIMechE, FIStructE, FInstNDT; FREng (FEng 1987). Welding Inst., 1961–68; Associate, Sandberg, Consulting Engineers, 1968–77. Vice-Principal External Affairs, UMIST, 1983–85. Chm., Manchester Science Park Ltd, 1988–95. Mem., Engrg Council, 1990–93. President: Manchester Assoc. of Engrs, 2003–05; Welding Inst., 2004–06 (Hon. FWeldI). Brooker Medal, Welding Inst., 1996; James Alfred Ewing Medal, ICE, 1997; Gold Medal, IStructE, 1998. *Publications:* numerous papers on fracture, fatigue and welded structures. *Recreations:* music, sport, countryside. *Address:* 27 Springbank, Bollington, Macclesfield, Cheshire SK10 5LQ.

BURDEN, family name of **Baron Burden**.

BURDEN, 4th Baron *cr* 1950, of Hazlebarrow, Derby; **Fraser William Elsworth Burden;** *b* 6 Nov. 1964; *s* of 2nd Baron Burden and of Audrey Elsworth, *d* of Maj. W. E. Sykes; *S* brother, 2000; *m* 1991, June Ellen (marr. diss. 2006), *d* of James Canham. *Heir: b* Hon. Ian Stuart Burden, *b* 24 Oct. 1967.

BURDEN, Sir Anthony (Thomas), Kt 2002; QPM 1995; Chief Constable, South Wales Police, 1996–2003; *b* 28 Jan. 1950; *s* of late Thomas Edward Burden and Nora Burden (*née* Dowding); *m* 1971, Beryl Myra Hill; one *s* two *d. Educ:* St Thomas Sch., Salisbury; BSc Hons. Joined Wilts Constabulary, 1969 (Detective Chief Superintendent, 1988–89); Asst Chief Constable, then Dep. Chief Constable, W Mercia Constabulary, 1989–93; Chief Constable, Gwent Constabulary, 1994–96. Member: Morris Inquiry, 2004; Rosemary Nelson Public Inquiry, 2005–11. Advr, Police Assistance Mission of EU in Albania, 2005–07. Deputy Chairman: Reliance Secure Task Mgt, 2005–11; Reliance Security Services Ltd, 2005–10. Pres., ACPO, 2000–01. Life Vice-Pres., Police Sport UK, 2004. Trustee, British Police Symphony Orch., 1994–2010. CCMI 2002. DUniv Glamorgan, 2004. SBStJ 1998. *Recreations:* cycling, walking, gardening.

BURDEN, Maj.-Gen. David Leslie, CB 1996; CVO 2009; CBE 1988; Chapter Clerk and Receiver General, Westminster Abbey, 1999–2008; *b* 14 July 1943; *s* of late Jack Leslie Burden and Elizabeth Mary Burden (*née* Attkins); *m* 1974, Susan Stuart Watson; two *d. Educ:* Portsmouth Grammar School. FCILT. Commissioned RASC 1964, RAOC 1965. Served England, Berlin, W Germany, NI, Cyprus and Hong Kong; NDC, 1981; Chief, Personnel and Logistics, UN Force in Cyprus, 1981–83; CO, 1 Ordnance Bn, 1983–85; ACOS, British Forces, Hong Kong, 1985–87; RCDS, 1988; ACOS, BAOR, 1989–91; Dir-Gen., Resettlement, MoD, 1991–92; Dir-Gen., Logistic Support (Army), 1992–95; Dir Gen., Army Manning and Recruiting, 1995; Dir Gen., Army Personnel Centre, 1996–97; Mil. Sec., and Chief Exec. of Army Personnel Centre, 1997–99. Chm., Right from the Start, 2008–. Chm., Hong Kong Locally Enlisted Personnel Trust, 2011–; Director: Armed Forces Common Investment Fund, 2009–; LGS Matrix, 2009–. Gov., Sutton Valence Sch., 2008–; Trustee, Army Museums Ogilby Trust, 2006–. Freeman, City of London, 1993. *Recreations:* cricket, walking, narrowboating, travelling. *Address:* c/o Barclays Bank, 54 Highgate High Street, N6 5JD. *Clubs:* Army and Navy, MCC; Highgate Taverners (Pres., 2002–), Fadeaways.

BURDEN, Prof. Michael John, PhD; Professor of Opera Studies, University of Oxford, since 2010; Fellow in Music and Pictures and Chattels Fellow, since 1995, and Dean, since 2001, New College, Oxford; *b* Adelaide, SA, 14 March 1960; *s* of Robert Michael Burden and Margaret Anne Burden (*née* Leahy). *Educ:* Pulteney Grammar Sch., Adelaide; Univ. of Adelaide (BA 1980; BA Hons 1981; MA 1987); Univ. of Edinburgh (PhD 1991); MA Oxon 1995. University of Oxford: Stipendiary Lectr in Music, New Coll., 1989–95; Lectr in Opera Studies, 1995–2000; Reader in Music, 2002–10. Founder and Dir, New Chamber Opera, 1990–. Mem., various cttees, Arts Council of England, 1994–2001. Mem. Council, Royal Musical Assoc., 1999–2001. Pres., British Soc. for 18th Century Studies, 2010–13. Judge, Duff Cooper Prize, 2003–08. Visitor, Ashmolean Mus., Oxford, 2008–15. Trustee, Répertoire Internat. des Sources Musicales, UK, 2007–. *Publications:* Lost Adelaide: a photographic record, 1983, repr. 2002; Garrick, Arne and the Masque of Alfred, 1994; (ed) The Purcell Companion, 1995; Purcell Remembered, 1995; (ed) Performing the Music of Henry Purcell, 1996; (ed) A Woman Scorn'd: the myth of Dido, Queen of Carthage, 1998; (ed) Purcell's Operas: the complete texts, 2001; (ed with J. Thorp) Le Ballet de la Nuit, 2010; Regina Mingotti: diva and impresario at the King's Theatre, London, 2013; *editions of music:* Benedetto Marcello, Il pianto e il riso delle quattro stagioni, 2002; Henry Purcell, The Fairy-Queen, 2009; William Walton, The Bear, 2010; contribs to Music Rev., Early Music, Music and Letters, Royal Musical Assoc. Res. Chronicle, Studies in Music, Th. Notebook, Cambridge Companion to Th., Eighteenth-Century Music, Cambridge Companion to Eighteenth-Century Opera, Cambridge Hist. of Eighteenth-Century Music, Music in Art, Revue *LISA*/LISA, Jl for Eighteenth-Century Studies, Cambridge Opera Jl, Eighteenth

Century Shakespeare. *Recreations:* art, architecture, reading detective fiction. *Address:* New College, Oxford OX1 3BN. *T:* (01865) 279555, 07786 061613. *E:* michael.burden@new.ox.ac.uk.

BURDEN, Richard Haines; MP (Lab) Birmingham Northfield, since 1992; *b* 1 Sept. 1954; *s* of late Kenneth Rodney Burden and Pauline Langan Burden (*née* Ronnan). *Educ:* Wallasey Technical Grammar Sch.; Bramhall Comprehensive Sch.; St John's Coll. of Further Educn, Manchester; York Univ. (BA Politics); Warwick Univ. (MA Indust. Relns). Pres., York Univ. Students' Union, 1976–77. Br. Organiser, 1979–81, Dist Officer, 1979–92, NALGO; whilst working for NALGO led Midlands campaign against water privatisation. Founder and Sec., Joint Action for Water Services, 1985–90. Contested (Lab) Meriden, 1987. PPS to Minister of State: MAFF, 1997–99; DSS, 1999–2001; Shadow Minister for Transport, 2013–15. Member: Trade and Industry Select Cttee, 2001–05; Internat. Develt Select Cttee, 2005–13; Cttee on Arms Exports, 2005–; Parly Advr to Sports Minister on Motor Sports, 2002–10. Secretary: All Party Parly Water Gp, 1994–97; PLP Trade and Industry Cttee, 1996–97 (Vice-Chm., 1995–96); Chm., Birmingham Gp of Labour MPs, 2001–11 (Sec., 1997–2001); Chairman: All Party Parly Gp on Electoral Reform, 1997–2011; All Party Parly Motor Gp, 1998–; Britain-Palestine All Party Parly Gp, 2001–; Jordan All Party Parly Gp, 2010–13; W Midlands Regl Select Cttee, 2009–10. Chm., Labour Campaign for Electoral Reform, 1996–98 (Vice-Chm., 1998–99). Mem., Austin Br., RBL. *Publications:* Tap Dancing: water, the environment and privatisation, 1988; contribs to Tribune, Chartist and other jls. *Recreations:* motor racing, cinema, reading, food. *Address:* House of Commons, SW1A 0AA. *T:* (020) 7219 2318, (0121) 477 7746. *W:* www.richardburden.com. *Clubs:* Austin Sports and Social, Kingshurst Labour, 750 Motor.

BURDEN, Roger Francis, FCIB; Director, Football Association, since 2001 (Acting Chairman, 2010–11); *b* 3 June 1946; *s* of Henry A. Burden and Rose K. Burden, SRN; *m* 1970, Julie Hopkins; two *s*. *Educ:* Cheltenham Tech. High Sch. MBCS 1975; FCIB 1983. Cheltenham & Gloucester Building Society, later Cheltenham & Gloucester plc: various appts, 1969–97; Man. Dir, 1997–2003; Chm., 2003–04. Dir, Yorkshire Building Soc., 2010–13. Chm., Council of Mortgage Lenders, 2001–02. Mem. Council, FA, 1995–; Chm., Glos FA, 2002–. Hon. PhD Glos, 2003. *Address:* Football Association, Wembley Stadium, PO Box 1966, London, SW1P 9EQ.

BURDETT, Prof. Richard Michael; Professor of Urban Studies and Director, LSE Cities, London School of Economics and Political Science, since 2010; *b* 27 Jan. 1956; *s* of Winston Burdett and Giorgina Nathan Burdett; *m* 1986, Mika Hadidian; one *s* one *d*. *Educ:* Bristol Univ. (BSc Hons Architecture); Bartlett Sch. of Architecture, University Coll. London (DipArch, MSc). Director: 9H Gall., London, 1985–90; Architecture Foundn, London, 1991–95; Dir, Cities Prog., 1995–2005, Centennial Prof. in Architecture and Urbanism, 2005–10, LSE. Global Dist. Prof., NY Univ., 2010–; Vis. Prof., Graduate Sch. of Design, Harvard Univ., 2014. Architectural Advr to Mayor of London, 2004–06; Chief Advr on Architecture and Urbanism for London 2012 Olympic Games, Olympic Delivery Authy, 2006–10; Chief Advr on Architecture, City of Genoa, 2009. Member: Mayor of London's Promote London Council, 2009–10; Mayor of London's Smart London Bd, 2013–; Ind. Airports Commn for UK Govt, 2012–. Dir, Internat. Architecture Exhibn, Venice Biennale, 2006. Mem. Council, RCA. Trustee, Somerset House. *Publications:* (ed) Richard Rogers Partnership, 1994; (ed) Cities, Architecture and Society, 2006; (ed jtly) The Endless City, 2008; (ed jtly) Living in the Endless City, 2011; (ed jtly) Transforming Urban Economies, 2013; regular contribs to Domus, Casabella, Rassegna. *Recreations:* cities, food, culture, skiing. *Address:* 53 Camden Square, NW1 9XE. *T:* (020) 7267 1942. *E:* r.burdett@lse.ac.uk.

BURDETT, Sir Savile (Aylmer), 11th Bt *cr* 1665; Managing Director, Rapaway Energy Ltd, 1977–99; retired; *b* 24 Sept. 1931; *s* of Sir Aylmer Burdett, 10th Bt; *S* father, 1943; *m* 1962, June E. C. Rutherford; one *s* one *d*. *Educ:* Wellington Coll.; Imperial Coll., London. *Heir: s* Crispin Peter Burdett, *b* 8 Feb. 1967. *Address:* 2 Knapp Cottages, Gore Lane, Kilmington, Axminster, Devon EX13 7NU. *T:* (01297) 34200. *E:* savile@savileburdett.plus.com.

BURDETT-COUTTS, William Walter; Artistic Director: Assembly Theatre, Edinburgh, since 1981; Riverside Studios, London, since 1993; Brighton Comedy Festival, since 2002; *b* 17 Feb. 1955; *m* 1999, Fiona Jane Keaney; one *s* two *d*. *Educ:* Radley Coll.; Rhodes Univ., SA (BA Hons Drama 1978); Univ. of Essex (MA Drama 1980). Artistic Dir, Mayfest, Glasgow, 1981–90; Hd of Arts, Granada Television, 1989–93; Chief Executive: Assembly Film and Television, 1993–2006; Assembly Media Gp, 2000–12; Chm., Kiss 102 and Kiss 105, 1993–97; Chm., Riverside TV Studios, 2002–. *Address:* Riverside Studios, 65 Aspenlea Road, W6 8LH. *T:* (020) 8237 1000, *Fax:* (020) 8237 1001. *E:* wbc@riversidestudios.co.uk. *Club:* Soho House.

BURDUS, (Julia) Ann, (Mrs D. L. Parker), CBE 2003; non-executive Director, Next, 1993–2004; *b* 4 Sept. 1933; *d* of Gladstone Beaty and Julia W. C. Booth; *m* 1st, 1956, William Burdus (marr. diss. 1961); 2nd, 1981, Ian B. Robertson (*d* 1996); 3rd, 2005, David L. Parker. *Educ:* Durham Univ. (BA Psychology). Clinical psychologist, 1956–60; Res. Exec., Ogilvy, Benson & Mather, 1961–67; Res. Dir, McCann Erickson, 1971–75, Vice Chm., 1975–77; Senior Vice-Pres., McCann Internat., 1977–79; Chm., McCann & Co., 1979–81; Director: Strategic Planning and Development, Interpublic, 1981–83; Audits of Great Britain Ltd, 1983–86; AGB Research, 1986–89; Dir of Communications and Marketing, Olympia & York, Canary Wharf, 1989–92. Non-executive Director: Dawson Internat., 1992–98; Argyll Gp, later Safeway, 1993–99; Prudential plc, 1996–2003. Chairman: Advertising Assoc., 1980–81; EDC for Distributive Trades, 1983–87. Jt Dep. Chm. and Mem., Health Educn Authority, 1987–90; Member: Sen. (formerly Top) Salaries Rev. Bd, 1991–94; Adv. Council on Business and the Envmt, 1993–96; part-time Mem., CAA, 1993–97. Member: Cttee, Automobile Assoc., 1995–99; Council, Inst. of Dirs, 1995–2002. *Recreations:* dog walking, gardening.

BURFORD, Earl of, (known as **Charles Beauclerk**); **Charles Francis Topham de Vere Beauclerk;** *b* 22 Feb. 1965; *s* and *heir* of Duke of St Albans, *qv*; *m* 1994, Louise Anne (marr. diss. 2001), *e d* of Col Malcolm Vernon Robey; one *s*. *Educ:* Sherborne; Hertford Coll., Oxford. Vice-Pres., Royal Stuart Soc., 1989–. Trustee, Stringer Lawrence Meml Trust, 1993–. Freeman, City of London, 1986; Liveryman, Drapers' Co., 1990. *Publications:* Visions, 1998; In Defence of Hereditary Peers, 1999; Nell Gwyn: a biography, 2005; Shakespeare's Lost Kingdom, 2010; Piano Man: a life of John Ogdon, 2014. *Heir: s* Lord Vere of Hanworth, (known as James Beauclerk), *qv*. *E:* c.beauclerk446@btinternet.com.

BURG, Gisela Elisabeth, Hon. CBE 1987 (for services to exports); Managing Director, GEB Enterprises Ltd, since 1995; *b* 12 Oct. 1939; *d* of Friedrich and Gerda Schlüsselburg. *Educ:* Gymnasium Philippinum, Weilburg, Germany; Ladies Coll., Wetzlar, Germany; Polytechnic of Central London. Founded Expotus Ltd, 1968, Man. Dir, 1968–96. Vice-Pres., Fedn of British Audio, 1979–85 (Chm., 1976); Member: NEDO, 1979–84 (Mem. Electronic Sector Working Party); BOTB, 1982–89. Non-exec. Dir, Royal Mint, 1993–2001. CIEx 1992. The Times/Veuve Clicquot Business Woman of the Year, 1981. *Recreations:* golf, horseracing. *Address:* 82 Kensington Heights, 91-95 Campden Hill Road, W8 7BD. *T:* (020) 7727 8884. *Clubs:* Hampstead Golf; Erinvale Golf (Somerset West, S Africa); Jockey (S Africa).

BURGE, Richard David Arthur; Chief Executive, Wilton Park, since 2009; *b* 5 April 1958; *s* of Col Arthur Burge and Elsie (*née* Kimberley); *m* 1980, Karen Jayne Bush; one *s* one *d*. *Educ:* Adams Grammar Sch., Newport; Univ. of Durham (BSc Hons Zoology 1980). Biology Master and Asst Housemaster, King Edward's Sch., Witley, 1980–83; Commonwealth Res. Schol., Dept of Zoology, Univ. of Peradeniya, Sri Lanka, 1983–86; British Council: Asst Dir, Nigeria, 1986–90; Projects Dir, Develt and Trng, 1990–93; Hd, Africa and ME Devel, 1993–95; Dir Gen., Zoological Soc. of London, 1995–99; Chief Exec., Countryside Alliance, 1999–2003; Partner, Kimberley Burge Associates, then Dir, Kimberley Burge Ltd, later Dir, Beyond Carbon, 2003–09. Dir, Urban and Rural Catalyst Ltd, 2003–06; Dir of Strategy, African Parks Foundn, 2003–06. Dep. Chm., Rural Regeneration Unit, 2003–05; Member Board: Countryside Agency, 2005–06; Commn for Rural Communities, 2006–09. Member Exec. Cttee, ACEVO, 1997–2001; Council, Shropshire and W Midlands Agricl Soc, 1997–2003; Bd, Assoc. of Chief Execs, 2012–. Non-exec. Dir, Property Merchant Gp, 2008–09. Lay Mem. Council, Durham Univ., 2011– (Chm. Council, Hatfield Coll., 2012–; Chm., Ethics Cttee, 2014–); Comr, Commonwealth Scholarship Commn, 2012–; Mem. Bd, FCO Diplomatic Acad., 2014–. Chm. Trustees, Get Hooked on Fishing, 2002–06; Trustee, Television Trust for the Envmt, 1996–99; Iwokrama Rainforest Project, Guyana, 2002–06; Game Conservancy Trust, 2004–08; Gunmakers' Charitable Trust, 2010–14. Internat. Expert, Internat. Congress on Game and Conservation, 2004–09. Vice Chm. Govs, Bridewell Royal Hosp., 2010–14 (Gov., 2008–14). FRSA 2003. Liveryman, Gunmakers' Co., 2001. *Recreations:* theatre, gardening, fishing, shooting, woodcut printing. *Address:* Wilton Park, Wiston House, Steyning, W Sussex BN44 3DZ.

BURGE, Prof. Ronald Edgar, CPhys; FInstP; Wheatstone Professor of Physics, King's College, London, 1989–2000; Director, Leverhulme Trust Grant to Cavendish Laboratory, University of Cambridge, 1994–98; *b* 3 Oct. 1932; *s* of John Henry Burge and Edith Beatrice Burge (*née* Thompson); *m* 1953, Janet Mary (*née* Pitts); two *s*. *Educ:* Canton High Sch., Cardiff; King's Coll. London (BSc, PhD; FKC 1989); DSc London 1975. FInstP 1963. King's College London: Asst Lectr in Physics, 1954–58; Lectr in Physics, 1958–62; Reader in Biophysics, 1962–63; Prof. and Head of Dept of Physics, Queen Elizabeth Coll., Univ. of London, 1963–84; Prof. of Physics, 1984–89, Head of Dept of Physics, 1984–92, Vice Principal, 1988–92, KCL. Vis. Fellow, 1992, Life Mem., 1993, Clare Hall, Cambridge; Vis. Prof. of Physics, Cavendish Lab., Univ. of Cambridge, 1994–2012. Nanyang Prof. of Elect. Engrg, Nanyang Technol Univ., Singapore, 2000–01. Member: Swinnerton-Dyer Cttee concerning Academic Governance of Univ. of London, 1979–82; Computer Bd for Univs and Res. Councils (responsible for computer develt in univs in Scotland and, latterly, SW England), 1978–82. MRI 1988. Rodman Medal, RPS, 1993. *Publications:* papers in sci. jls on structure of proteins, membranes and bacterial cell walls, and on theory of scattering (electrons, x-rays and radar) and develts in electron microscopy and x-ray microscopy. *Recreations:* gardening, music.

BURGEN, Sir Arnold (Stanley Vincent), Kt 1976; FRCP 1969; FRS 1964; Master of Darwin College, Cambridge, 1982–89 (Hon. Fellow, 1989); Deputy Vice-Chancellor, Cambridge University, 1985–89; *b* 20 March 1922; *s* of late Peter Burgen and Elizabeth Wolfers; *m* 1st, 1946, Judith Browne (*d* 1993); two *s* one *d*; 2nd, 1993, Dr Olga Kennard, *qv*. *Educ:* Christ's Coll., Finchley; student, Middlesex Hospital Med. Sch., 1939–45; MB BS 1945, MD 1950. Ho. Phys., Middlesex Hospital, 1945; Demonstrator, 1945–48, Asst Lectr, 1948–49, in Pharmacology, Middlesex Hospital Med. Sch. Prof. of Physiology, McGill Univ., Montreal, 1949–62; Dep. Dir, Univ. Clinic, Montreal Gen. Hospital, 1957–62; Sheild Prof. of Pharmacology, Univ. of Cambridge, 1962–71; Fellow of Downing Coll., Cambridge, 1962–71, Hon. Fellow 1972; Dir, Nat. Inst. for Med. Res., 1971–82. Medical Research Council: Member, 1969–71, 1973–77; Hon. Dir, Molecular Pharmacology Unit, 1967–72. Chm., Tropical Medicine Res. Bd, 1977–81; Assessor, 1985–86. Pres., Internat. Union of Pharmacology, 1972–75; Member: Council, Royal Soc., 1972–73, 1980–86 (Vice Pres., 1980–86; Foreign Sec., 1981–86); Nat. Biol. Standards Bd, 1975–78; Med. Cttee, British Council, 1973–77; Gen. Cttee, ICSU, 1982–88; Exec. Cttee, Eur. Science Foundn, 1985–90; Bureau, European Science and Technol. Assembly, 1994–; Chm., Adv. Cttee on Irradiated and Novel Foods, 1982–87. Dir, Amersham Internat., 1985–92. Sustaining Corresp., NAS. NAE/Inst. of Medicine Cttee on Human Rights. Trustee, CIBA Foundn, 1985–. Editor, European Review, 1993–2007. Pres., Academia Europaea, 1988–94. Founder FMedSci 1998. Académico Correspondiente, Royal Acad. of Spain, 1983; Mem., Deutsche Akad. der Naturforscher Leopoldina, 1984; For. Associate, US Nat. Acad. of Scis, 1985; For. Mem., Ukraine Acad. of Scis. Hon. Fellow, Wolfson Coll., Oxford, 1990. Hon. FRCP (C); Hon. Mem., Amer. Assoc. of Physicians; Academician of Finland, 1990. Hon. DSc: Leeds, 1973; McGill, 1973; Liverpool, 1989; Hon. MD: Utrecht, 1983; Zürich, 1983; DUniv Surrey, 1983. Gold Medal, British Pharmacol Soc., 1999. *Publications:* (ed with J. F. Mitchell) Gaddum's Pharmacology, 6th rev. edn, 1968; (ed with E. A. Barnard) Receptor Subunits and Complexes, 1992; (ed) Goals and Purposes of Higher Education in the 21st Century, 1996; (ed with K. Härnqvist) Growing up with Science, 1997; papers in Journals of Physiology and Pharmacology. *Address:* Keelson, 8a Hills Avenue, Cambridge CB1 7XA. *E:* asvb@cam.ac.uk.

BURGESS, Hon. Anna Elizabeth; *see* Burke, Hon. A. E.

BURGESS, Anthony Reginald Frank, (Tony), CVO 1983; consultant on Third World development; HM Diplomatic Service, retired; *b* 27 Jan. 1932; *s* of Beatrice Burgess; *m* 1960, Carlyn Shawyer; one *s*. *Educ:* Ealing Grammar Sch.; University College London (BScEcon); National Service, 1953–55; TA, 16 Airborne Div., 1955–57. Journalism, 1955–62; European Community Civil Service, 1962–65; HM Diplomatic Service, 1966–89: 1st Sec., European Economic Organisations Dept, FCO, 1966–67; 1st Sec. (Political), Dhaka, 1967–69; 1st Sec., SE Asia Dept, FCO, 1970–72; 1st Sec. (Economic), Ottawa, 1972–76; Head of Chancery and HM Consul, Bogota, 1976–79; 1st Sec., Rhodesia Dept, FCO, 1979–80; Asst Head of Information Dept, FCO, 1980–82; Dep. High Comr, Dhaka, 1982–86; Counsellor and Head of Chancery, 1986–88, Chargé d'Affaires, 1988–89, Havana. *Publications:* (jtly) The Common Market and the Treaty of Rome Explained, 1967. *Recreations:* travel, photography, shooting. *Address:* 16 Langford Green, Champion Hill, SE5 8BX. *Club:* Brooks's.

BURGESS, Averil, OBE 1994; Chairman, Independent Schools Inspectorate, Independent Schools Council (formerly Accreditation Review and Consultancy Service, Independent Schools Joint Council), 1993–2000; *b* 8 July 1938; *d* of David and Dorothy Evans (*née* Owen); *m* 1959, Clifford Burgess (marr. diss. 1973). *Educ:* Ashby-de-la-Zouch Girls' Grammar Sch.; Queen Mary Coll., Univ. of London. BA Hons History. Assistant Mistress: Langleybury Secondary Modern Sch., 1959–60; Ensham Sch., 1960–62; Hatfield Sch., 1963–65; Fulham County Sch., 1965–69; Wimbledon High Sch., GPDST, 1969–74 (Head of History and Second Mistress); Headmistress, South Hampstead High School, GPDST, 1975–93. Chm., Camden and Islington FHSA, 1993–96. Chm., Policy Gp, ISJC, 1990–97; Member: Council for Accreditation of Teacher Educn, 1990–93; Nat. Commn on Educn, 1991–93. Ind. Public Appts Assessor (formerly Adv. Panel on Public Appointments), DCMS, 1997–2013; Lay Mem., Professional Conduct Cttee, Bar Council, 1996–2005; Ind. Mem., Appts Cttee, Bar Standards Bd, 2005–. Pres., GSA, 1988–89. Governor: Central Sch. of Speech and Drama, 1981–95; Mus. of London, 1994–2000; Alpha Plus Gp, 2011–. *Recreations:* many, including Wales, Welsh, watercolours, birdwatching and good meals. *Address:* 123 North Hill, Highgate, N6 4DP.

BURGESS, Rev. Preb. David John, FSA; Guild Vicar of St Lawrence Jewry Next Guildhall, The Church of the City of London Corporation (formerly Corporation of London), 1987–2008; a Chaplain to the Queen, 1987–2009; Prebendary of St Paul's Cathedral, 2002–08; *b* 4 Aug. 1939; *e s* of Albert Burgess and Mary Burgess (*née* Kelsey); *m* 1976, Dr Kathleen Louise, *d* of Philip Lindsay Costeloe; one *s* one *d*. *Educ:* King's School, Peterborough; Trinity Hall, Cambridge; Cuddesdon Theological Coll. FSA 1992. Orthodox

Studentship, Halki, Istanbul, 1963–64. Curate, All Saints, Maidstone, 1965; Assistant Chaplain, University Coll., Oxford, 1966; Fellow, 1969; Chaplain, 1970; Domestic Bursar, 1971; Canon of St George's Chapel, Windsor, 1978–87. Hon. Fellow, Inst. of Clerks of Works, 1978; Churchill Hon. Fellow, Westminster Coll., Fulton, Miss, 1989. *Publications:* articles and reviews. *Recreations:* opera, art, cooking. *Address:* 62 Orbel Street, SW11 3NZ. *T:* (020) 7585 1572. *Club:* Athenæum.

BURGESS, (David) Patrick (Henry), OBE 2015 (MBE 2002); DL; Chairman, Intu Properties (formerly Liberty International, then Capital Shopping Centres Group) plc, since 2008; *b* Cheam, 31 Oct. 1944; *s* of David Clement Burgess and Dr Ethne Nanette Moira Barnwall Burgess (*née* Ryan); *m* 1st, 1969, Kathryn Mary Ralphs (marr. diss. 1982; she later *m* Sir William Frederick Cotton, CBE); two *s* one *d*; 2nd, 1994, Margaret Ann Mosey. *Educ:* Beaumont Coll.; Gonville and Caius Coll., Cambridge (BA 1967). Admitted solicitor, 1972; Gouldens, solicitors: Partner, 1974; Hd, Corporate Dept, 1982–95; Sen. Partner, 1996–2003. Non-exec. Dir, Standard Bank London plc, 2000–. Chairman: Thrombosis Res. Inst., 2000–; Bulldog Trust, 2009–12; trustee of various charities. Chm., Sussex, St John Ambulance, 2006–12. Chancellor: Lieutenancy of England and Wales, Order of the Holy Sepulchre, 2008–14; Most Venerable Order of Hospital of St John of Jerusalem, 2014–. Master, Feltmakers' Co., 2003–04. High Sheriff, 2013–14, DL 2014, W Sussex. GCStJ 2014 (CStJ 2009). *Recreations:* walking, shooting, sailing, music, history, poetry, divinity, painting, opera. *Address:* Shopwyke Hall, near Chichester. *Clubs:* Boodle's, Royal Thames Yacht, Leander.

BURGESS, Dilys Averil; *see* Burgess, A.

BURGESS, Geoffrey Kelsen; Chief Executive and Clerk, Cornwall County Council, 1982–93 (Deputy Clerk, 1969–82); *b* 4 June 1935; *s* of Monty and Edith Burgess; *m* 1959, Brenda (*née* Martin); three *s*. *Educ:* Central Foundn Boys' Grammar Sch.; London Sch. of Econs and Pol Science (LLB). Admitted solicitor, 1959. Articled with Simon, Haynes, Barlas & Cassels, London, 1956–59; Assistant Solicitor: East Ham CBC, 1960–62; Worcs CC, 1962–63; Northumberland CC, 1963–65; Asst Clerk, Berks CC, 1965–69; Clerk: Cornwall Magistrates' Courts Cttee, 1982–93; Cornwall Sea Fisheries Cttee, 1982–93; Devon and Cornwall Police Authy, 1988–93; Secretary: Adv. Cttee on appt of Magistrates in Cornwall, 1982–93; Cornwall Probation Cttee, 1982–93. Chairman: Jeffrey Kelson Foundn, 1994–2000; Promoting Effective Parenting, 1999–2005; Cornwall Bd for Young Enterprise, 1999–2006. Humanist Rep., Cornwall Standing Adv. Council for Religious Educn, 2010–14. *Recreations:* music, walking, creative writing, discussing philosophy.

BURGESS, Graham; non-executive Chair, Torus Housing Group, since 2015; *b* Liverpool, 1952; *s* of William and Patricia Burgess; *m* 1997, Jan; two *d*. *Educ:* Ellergreen High Sch.; C. F. Mott Coll. of Educn; Liverpool Poly. Social worker, Walton and Kirkdale, and Vauxhall, Liverpool CC; NALGO: Nat. Exec. Co-ordinator; Chm., NW and N Wales Reg.; full time work in Liverpool br.; sen. social worker, Garston and Speke, Liverpool CC; Blackburn with Darwen Council: Exec. Dir Regeneration and Technical, and Dep. Chief Exec., 1997–2006; Chief Exec., 2006–12; Chief Exec., Wirral MBC, 2012–14. *Recreation:* watching Everton Football Club/Team.

BURGESS, Rear-Adm. John, CB 1987; LVO 1975; CEng; Director, Rolls-Royce and Associates, since 1987; *b* 13 July 1929; *s* of Albert Burgess and Winifred (*née* Evans); *m* 1952, Avis (*née* Morgan); two *d*. *Educ:* RN Engineering College; Advanced Engineering RN College, Greenwich; nuclear courses, RN College. HM Ships Aisne, Maidstone, Theseus, Implacable, Cumberland, Caprice; Lectr in Thermodynamics, RNEC, 1962–65; HMS Victorious; nuclear reactor design and manufacture at Rolls Royce, 1968–70; Naval Staff, Washington, DC, 1970–72; Royal Yacht Britannia, 1972–75; Head, Forward Design Group, Ship Dept, 1975–77; Naval Asst to Controller of the Navy, 1977–79; in Command, HMS Defiance, 1979–81; in Command, HMS Sultan, 1981–83; Man. Dir, HM Dockyard, Rosyth, 1984–87. Occasional involvement with urban develt and waterfront management cttees. *Publications:* papers to professional bodies. *Recreations:* golf, sailing. *Club:* Cawsand Bay Sailing (Pres., 1999–).

BURGESS, Ven. John Edward; Archdeacon of Bath, 1975–95, now Emeritus; *b* 9 Dec. 1930; *s* of Herbert and Dorothy May Burgess; *m* 1958, Jonquil Marion Bailey; one *s* one *d*. *Educ:* Surbiton County Gram. Sch.; London Univ. (St John's Hall). BD (2nd Cl.), ALCD (1st Cl.). Shell Chemicals Ltd, 1947–53. Asst Curate, St Mary Magdalen, Bermondsey, 1957–60; Asst Curate, St Mary, Southampton, 1960–62; Vicar of Dunston with Coppenhall, Staffs, 1962–67; Chaplain, Staffordshire Coll. of Technology, 1963–67; Vicar of Keynsham with Queen Charlton and Burnett, Somerset, 1967–75; Rural Dean of Keynsham, 1971–74. Mem. Council, Univ. of Bath, 1990–2005 (Chm., Buildings Cttee, 1992–2002; Life Mem., Court, 2005); Vice-Chm. Trustees, Partis Coll., Bath, 2005–10 (Chm., 1996–2005). Chancellor's Medal, Univ. of Bath, 2003. *Recreation:* history of railways. *Address:* 12 Berryfield Road, Bradford-on-Avon, Wilts BA15 1SX. *T:* (01225) 868905.

BURGESS, John Edward Ramsay; His Honour Judge Burgess; a Circuit Judge, since 2002; Resident Judge, Derby Combined Court, since 2008; *b* 11 March 1956; *s* of Gen. Sir Edward Arthur Burgess, KCB, OBE and Jean Angelique Leslie Burgess (*née* Henderson); *m* 1st, 1980, Juliet Davina Alford (now Bowmaker) (marr. diss. 2000); one *s* one *d*; 2nd, 2001, Cherry Anna Searle; one *d*. *Educ:* St Edward's Sch., Oxford; Exeter Univ. (LLB). Called to the Bar, Middle Temple, 1978; in practice as barrister, 1978–2002; Asst Recorder, 1995–2000; Recorder, 2000–02; Judge Advocate (pt-time), 2001–07. Hon. Recorder of Derby, 2009. *Recreations:* rowing, walking, going to the seaside. *Address:* Midland Circuit Secretariat, The Priory Courts, 33 Bull Street, Birmingham B4 6DW.

BURGESS, Sir (Joseph) Stuart, Kt 1994; CBE 1984; PhD; FRSC; Vice-President, Asthma UK (formerly National Asthma Campaign), since 2007 (Vice-Chairman, 2000–07); Chairman, Finsbury Worldwide Pharmaceutical Trust plc, 1995–2004; *b* 20 March 1929; *s* of late Joseph and Emma Burgess (*née* Wollerton); *m* 1955, Valerie Ann Street; one *s* one *d*. *Educ:* Barnsley Holgate Grammar School; University College London (1st Class Hons BSc Chem., PhD; Fellow, 1994). Amersham International plc (formerly The Radiochemical Centre), 1953–89: Chief Exec., 1979–89; Pres., Amersham Corp. USA, 1975–77; Advr, Immuno Internat. AG, 1990–96; Chm., Immuno UK, 1992–96; Dir, 1992–2003, Chm., 1998–2003, Haemonetics Corp.; Dir, Anagen plc, 1993–96. Chairman: Oxford RHA, 1990–94; Anglia and Oxford RHA, subseq. Anglia and Oxford Reg., NHS Exec., DoH, 1994–97; Mem., NHS Policy Board, 1994–97. Dir, American Chamber of Commerce (UK), 1988–90. Member: Innovation Adv. Bd, DTI, 1988–93; ACOST Med. Res. and Health Cttee, 1991–92; Chm., CBI Res. and Manufacturing Cttee, 1990–93; Mem., CBI Nat. Manufacturing Council, 1991–92. CCMI (CBIM 1986; Mem., 1996–2001, Chm., 1998–2001, Bd of Companions). *Recreations:* family, friends, music, travel. *Address:* 3 Abbotswood, Gregories Road, Beaconsfield, Bucks HP9 1HQ. *T:* (01494) 730142.

BURGESS, Keith, OBE 2004; PhD; Crown Representative, Cabinet Office, since 2014; *b* 1 Sept. 1946; *s* of Bert Burgess and Mary Burgess; *m* 1970, Patricia Mitchell; two *d*. *Educ:* Lewis Sch. for Boys, Pengam; Univ. of Bristol (BSc 1967; PhD 1971). Joined Arthur Andersen & Co., 1971: Partner, 1980–2000; Managing Partner, Andersen Consulting, UK and Ireland, 1989–94; Global Managing Partner: Practice Competency, 1994–97; Business Process Mgt & Enterprises, 1997–99; Sen. Partner, Andersen Consulting UK, 2000; Exec. Chm., QA plc, 2000–06. Chm., EMEA, BearingPoint, 2006–08. Vice-Chm., Public Services Productivity Panel, HM Treasury, 2000–06. Non-exec. Dir, MORI, 2003–05. Pres., Mgt Consultancies Assoc., 1994–95. Chm., Corporate Action for the Homeless, 1993–96. Patron, Univ. of Bristol Campaign for Resource, 1991–2001. Guild of Management Consultants, later Co. of Management Consultants: Mem., 1994–; Master, 1998–99; Warden, 2010–12. Hon. LLD Bristol, 2000. *Publications:* (jtly) Foundations of Business Systems, 1989, 2nd edn 1992. *Recreation:* getting out and about and relearning what I once knew. *Address:* Hengrove, The Chivery, Tring, Herts HP23 6LE.

BURGESS, Margaret; Member (SNP) Cunninghame South, Scottish Parliament, since 2011; Minister for Welfare and Housing, since 2012; *b* Ayrshire. Manager, East Ayrshire CAB, 1987–2011; former Mem. Bd, Citizens Advice Scotland. *Address:* Scottish Parliament, Edinburgh EH99 1SP.

BURGESS, Melvin; author (children and young adults); *b* 25 April 1954; *s* of Chris Burgess and Helen Burgess; *m* 1998, Judith Ligyett; one *s* one *d*, and one step *s*. *Publications:* The Cry of the Wolf, 1990; Burning Issy, 1992; An Angel for May, 1992; The Baby and Fly Pie, 1993; Loving April, 1995; The Earth Giant, 1995; Tiger, Tiger, 1996; Junk, 1996 (Carnegie Medal, 1996; Guardian Fiction Prize, 1997); Kite, 1997; The Copper Treasure, 1998; Bloodtide, 1999 (jt winner, Lancashire County Library Children's Book of the Year, 2001); Old Bag, 1999; The Ghost Behind the Wall, 2000; The Birdman, 2000; Billy Elliot, 2001; Lady, 2001; Doing It, 2003; Robbers on the Road, 2003; Bloodsong, 2005; Sara's Face, 2006; Nicholas Dane, 2009; Kill All Enemies, 2011; The Hit, 2013. *Recreations:* walking, cooking. *Address:* c/o Andersen Press Ltd, 20 Vauxhall Bridge Road, SW1V 2SA.

BURGESS, Patrick; *see* Burgess, D. P. H.

BURGESS, Prof. Sir Robert George, Kt 2010; DL; PhD; Vice-Chancellor, University of Leicester, 1999–2014; *b* 23 April 1947; *s* of George Burgess and Olive (*née* Andrews); *m* 1974, Hilary Margaret Mary Joyce. *Educ:* Univ. of Durham (Teachers' Cert. 1968; BA 1971); Univ. of Warwick (PhD 1981). University of Warwick: Lectr in Sociol., 1974–84; Sen. Lectr in Sociol., 1984–88; Chair of Dept of Sociol., 1985–88; Dir, Centre for Educnl Develt, Appraisal and Res., 1987–99; Prof. of Sociology, 1988–99; Chair, Faculty of Social Studies, 1988–91; Founding Chair, Graduate Sch., 1991–95; Sen. Pro-Vice-Chancellor, 1995–99. Founding Chair, UK Council for Graduate Educn, 1994–99. Economic and Social Research Council: Member: Res. Resources Bd, 1991–96; Council, 1996–2000; Chair, Trng Bd, 1997–2000 (Mem., 1989–93); Jt Equality Steering Gp, 2001–03. Chm., E Midlands Univs Assoc., 2001–04; Higher Education Funding Council for England: Chm., Quality Assessment Cttee, 2001–03; Member: Res. Libraries Strategy Gp, 2001–02; Quality Assurance Learning and Teaching, 2003–07; Chairman: ESRC/Funding Councils Teaching and Learning Res. Prog., 2003–09; Bd, UCAS, 2005–11 (Mem. Bd, 2001–05); Res. Information Network, 2005–11; Scoping Gp, 2003–04, Steering Gp, 2004–07, Implementation Gp, 2008–, UUK/GuildHE Measuring and Recording Student Achievement (Burgess Gp); Bd, Greenwich Sch. of Mgt, 2015–. Mem., British Liby Bd, 2003–10. President: British Sociological Assoc., 1989–91; Assoc. for Teaching of Social Scis, 1991–99; Soc. for Res. into HE, 2013–. Chm., Higher Educn Acad., 2007– (Bd Mem., 2003–07); Trustee and Chm., Bd, NatCen Social Research, 2012–. FAcSS (AcSS 2000); Life Fellow, Bishop Grosseteste Univ., 2015. DL Leics, 2010. Hon. DLitt Staffordshire, 1998; DUniv Northampton, 2007; Hon EdD De Montfort, 2013; Hon. LLD Leicester, 2015. Lifetime Contribution to Midlands Business Award, 2012; E Midlands Chamber Outstanding Contribn to Business Award, 2015. *Publications:* Experiencing Comprehensive Education, 1983; In the Field, 1984; Education, Schools and Schooling, 1985; Sociology, Education and Schools, 1986; (jtly) Implementing In-Service Education, 1993; Research Methods, 1993; (with J. Wood) Reflections of the University of Leicester, 2010; ed. of 24 books; numerous contribs to social sci. jls. *Recreations:* walking, listening to music, some gardening. *Address:* Feldon House, Lower Brailes, Banbury, Oxfordshire OX15 5HS.

BURGESS, Sally Anne; classical singer, vocal teacher and opera director; *b* 9 Oct. 1953; *d* of Edna Rushton (formerly Burgess; *née* Sharman) and Douglas Burgess; *m* 1988, Neal Scott Thornton; one *s*. *Educ:* Royal College of Music (ARCM; FRCM 2011). Joined ENO 1977; for *ENO* rôles incl., as a soprano: Zerlina, Cherubino, Pamina, Mimi, Micaela; as a mezzo: Composer (Ariadne), Sextus (Julius Caesar), Charlotte (Werther), Carmen, Fennimore (Fennimore and Gerda), 1990; Judith (Duke Bluebeard's Castle), 1991; Octavian (Rosenkavalier), 1994; Mrs Begbick (Mahagonny), 1995; Herodias (Salome), 1996; Dulcinée (Don Quixote), 1996; Amelia (Twice Through the Heart), 1997; Baba the Turk (Rake's Progress), Polinesso (Ariodante), 2002; Mistress Quickly (Sir John in Love), 2006; *Opera North:* Amneris (Aida), Dido (Trojans), Julie (Showboat), 1989–90; Orfeo (Glück), 1990; Laura (La Gioconda), 1993; Azucena (Trovatore), 1994; Eboli (Don Carlos), 1998; Margaretha (Genoveva), 2000; Judith (Duke Bluebeard's Castle), 2005; Kabanicha (Katya Kabanova), 2007; *Royal Opera, Covent Garden:* Siebel (Faust), Maddalena (Rigoletto), 1989; *Scottish Opera:* Fricka (Die Walküre), Amneris (Aida), 1991; Mistress Quickly (Sir John in Love), 2008; Mistress Quickly (Falstaff), 2008; *New York Metropolitan:* Carmen, 1995; Queen Isabella (The Voyage), 1996; title rôle (Merry Widow), 2003; *Glyndebourne:* Smeraldina (Love for Three Oranges); Witch (Hansel), tour, 2008; *Welsh National Opera:* Ottavia (Coronation of Poppea), 1998 (also televised); Herodias (Salome), 2009; Mother Marie (The Carmelites), Kabanicha (Katya Kabanova), Munich, 1999; Fricka (Das Rheingold), 1999, (Die Walküre), 2000, Geneva; Polinesso (Ariodante), Houston, 2002; Fortunata (Satyricon), Nancy, Ghent, Antwerp, 2004; Marta/Pantalis (Mefistofele), Netherlands Opera, 2004; Amneris, Strasbourg, Wiesbaden, Lausanne and Nancy; Carmen, Munich, Oregon, Zürich, Berlin, Paris and NZ; Delilah, Nantes; Bernstein on Broadway (tour), 2007; Sally Burgess' Women (one-woman show), Lyric Th., Hammersmith, 1997; numerous concert appearances; concert tour, NZ, 2005; as opera director: Così fan Tutte, English Chamber Opera, London, 2009 and Buxton, 2010, Dubrovnik Summer Fest., 2013; Sonya's Story Thornton/Chekhov, Riverside Studios, Tête à Tête Opera Fest., 2010; Il Trovatore, Dorset Opera, 2012; also dir reduced opera prodns for GSMD: The Magic Flute, 2011, Il Coronazione di Poppea, 2012, Albert Herring, 2013, The Marriage of Figaro, 2014; opera scenes for RCM, 2014; numerous recordings, incl. Liverpool Oratorio, and jazz. Teaching: at RCM, 2002–, and privately, 2005–; annual summer masterclasses for Les Azuriales Opera Fest. Young Artists Prog., 2008–; masterclasses for: London Gates Educn Gp, Moscow, 2010; Amazwi Omzansi Africa, Durban, 2013; Les Azuriales Opera Fest., 2013. *Recreations:* family, cooking, walking, reading, singing jazz, theatre. *Address:* AOR Management, 6910 Roosevelt Way NE PMB 221, Seattle, WA 98115, USA. *E:* aormanagementuk@gmail.com.

BURGESS, Prof. Simon Mark, DPhil; Professor of Economics, since 1998, Director, Centre for Market and Public Organisation, 2004–15, and Director, Centre for Understanding Behaviour Change, 2010–14, University of Bristol; *b* Macclesfield, Cheshire, 11 April 1960; *s* of Norman and Jean Burgess; *m* 1982, Amy Barham; one *s* one *d*. *Educ:* Christ's Coll., Cambridge (BA Econs 1982); St Antony's Coll., Oxford (MPhil Econs; DPhil Econs 1987). Res. Dean, Faculty of Social Sci., Univ. of Bristol, 2000–03. *Publications:* contribs to learned jls incl. Econ. Jl, Jl Labor Econs, Jl Public Econs, Jl Applied Econometrics. *Recreations:* landscape photography, hiking. *Address:* Centre for Market and Public Organisation, University of Bristol, 2 Priory Road, Bristol BS8 1TX. *E:* simon.burgess@bristol.ac.uk.

BURGESS, Sir Stuart; *see* Burgess, Sir J. S.

BURGESS, Rev. Stuart John, CBE 2009; Chairman, Commission for Rural Communities, 2006–13, and Government's Rural Advocate, 2004–13 (Chairman, Countryside Agency, 2004–06); President, Methodist Conference, 1999–2000; Chairman, Hanover Housing Association, since 2014; *b* 18 March 1940; *s* of Frederick John Burgess and Winifred May (*née* Gowan); *m* 1965, Elisabeth Maud Fowler; two *d*. *Educ:* Moseley Grammar Sch., Birmingham;

Univ. of London (BD ext.); Univ. of Nottingham (MEd; MTh). Minister: Headingley Methodist Church, 1965–68; Nottingham W Circuit, and Chaplain, Univ. of Nottingham, 1968–81; Birmingham SW Circuit, and Chaplain, Univ. of Birmingham, 1981–89; Chm., York and Hull Methodist Dist, 1989–2004. Mem., Ethical Cttee, DWP, 2004–. Chm., Patient Liaison Gp, BMA, 2004–07; Mem., Patient Liaison Gp, RCAnaes, 2014–. Mem. Bd, Passenger Focus, 2013–. Hon. Fellow, UC of York St John, 2003. Hon. MA 1989, DUniv 2006, Birmingham; Hon. DD Hull, 2001; DD Lambeth, 2003; Hon. DPh Gloucestershire, 2008. *Publications:* Seeds of Joy, 1985; Spiritual Journey of John Wesley, 1988; Stations of the Cross, 1991; Making Connections, 1998; Coming of Age: challenges and opportunities for the 21st century, 1999. *Recreations:* music, tennis. *Address:* The Wesley, 83–101 Euston Street, NW1 2EZ. *T:* 07900 608249.

BURGESS, Tony; *see* Burgess, A. R. F.

BURGH, 8th Baron *cr* 1529 (called out of abeyance, 1916); **Alexander Gregory Disney Leith;** *b* 16 March 1958; *er s* of 7th Baron Burgh and Anita Lorna Burgh (*née* Eldridge); *S* father, 2001; *m* 1st, 1984, Catherine Mary (marr. diss. 1999), *d* of David Parkes; two *s* one *d*; 2nd, 1999, Emma Jane, *d* of Martin Burdick; one *s* one *d*. Formerly with St James's Place Wealth Management, now with Newhaven Trust Co., Guernsey. Patron, Lord Thomas Burgh Retinue. *Heir: s* Hon. Alexander James Strachan Leith, *b* 11 Oct. 1986. *Address:* Les Reviers, Steam Mill Lane, St Martins, Guernsey GY4 6NJ. *E:* alex@alexburgh.co.uk.

BURGHLEY, Lord; Anthony John Cecil; *b* 9 Aug. 1970; *s* and *heir* of Marquess of Exeter, *qv*; *m* 1996, Holly Stewart; one *d*. *Educ:* Eton; Oxford Univ.

BURGON, Colin; *b* 22 April 1948; *s* of Thomas and Winifred Burgon; *m* (marr. diss.); one *d*; partner, Kathryn Stainburn. *Educ:* St Michael's Coll., Leeds; Carnegie Coll., Leeds; Huddersfield Poly. Former teacher of History, Foxwood High Sch., Leeds; Policy Advr, Wakefield CC, 1987–95. Contested (Lab) Elmet, 1987, 1992. MP (Lab) Elmet, 1997–2010.

BURGON, Richard; MP (Lab) Leeds East, since 2015; *b* Leeds. *Educ:* Cardinal Heenan RC High Sch.; Univ. of Cambridge. Admitted as solicitor, 2006; trade union lawyer, Thompsons Solicitors, Leeds. *Address:* House of Commons, SW1A 0AA.

BURGOYNE, Rear-Adm. (Robert) Michael, CB 1982; *b* 20 March 1927; *s* of Robert and Elizabeth Burgoyne; *m* 1951, Margaret (Hilda) McCook; one *s* one *d*. *Educ:* Bradfield College; Magdalene College, Cambridge. Joined RN 1945; CO HMS Cleopatra, 1967–68; Captain 2nd Frigate Sqdn and CO HMS Undaunted, 1972–73; Dir, Maritime Tactical Sch., 1974–75; CO HMS Antrim, 1975–77; Comdr, British Navy Staff, Washington and UK Rep. to SACLANT, 1977–80; Senior Naval Member, Directing Staff, RCDS, 1980–82. Dir, RIN, 1983–92 (Hon. FRIN 2001). Dep. Stn Manager (Ops), Nat. Coastwatch Instn, Portland Bill, 2010–. Vice-Pres., Sea Safety Gp (UK), 1992–96. Chm., W Dorset Dist Scout Council, 1995–97. Hon. Treas., Friends of SSAFA, W Dorset, 2002–06.

BURK, Prof. Kathleen Mildred, DPhil; Professor of Modern and Contemporary History, University College London, 1995–2011, now Emerita; *d* of Wayne Eliot Burk and Martha Ann Burk (*née* Ankney); *m* 1980, Dr Michael Jewess; one *d*. *Educ:* Sanger Union High Sch., California; Univ. of California, Berkeley (BA 1969); St Hugh's Coll., Oxford (MA, DPhil 1977); Dip. in Wine and Spirits, WSET, 2002. Tutorial Asst in Mod. Hist., Univ. of Dundee, 1976–77; Rhodes Res. Fellow for N America and Caribbean, St Hugh's Coll., Oxford, 1977–80; Lectr in Hist. and Politics, Imperial Coll., London, 1980–90; University College London: Lectr in Hist., 1990–93; Reader in Mod. and Contemp. Hist., 1993–95. Visiting Professor: Kyung Hee Univ., Seoul, Korea, 1986; Univ. of Trondheim, 1994; Univ. of Tübingen, 1999; Univ. of Oslo, 2004; Univ. of Oslo and Nobel Inst., 2009; Vis. Fellow, All Souls Coll., Oxford, 1998. Gresham Prof. of Rhetoric, 2003–06. Alec Cairncross Lecture, 1994; Commonwealth Fund Lecture in American Hist., 2005; Crabtree Oration, 2006. Wine correspondent, Prospect magazine, 2002–05. Chm., Historians' Press, 1983–99; Founding Co-Editor, Contemporary European History, 1989–2001. FRHistS 1989 (Mem. Council, 1994–97; Hon. Treas., 1997–2001). Foreign Member: Royal Norwegian Soc. for Scis and Letters, 2002; Norwegian Acad. of Scis and Letters, 2009. Judge, Internat. Wine and Spirits Comp., 2005–. Henry Adams Prize, Soc. for History in the Federal Govt, 2009. *Publications:* (ed and contrib.) War and the State: the transformation of British Government 1914–1919, 1982; Long Wittenham 1800–1920, 1984; Britain, America and the Sinews of War 1914–1918, 1985; The First Privatisation: the politicians, the city and the denationalisation of steel, 1988; Morgan Grenfell 1838–1988: the biography of a merchant bank, 1989; (with Alec Cairncross) Goodbye, Great Britain: the 1976 IMF crisis, 1992; (with Manfred Pohl) The Deutsche Bank in London 1873–1998, 1998; (ed with Melvyn Stokes) The United States and the Western Alliance since 1945, 1999; Troublemaker: the life and history of A. J. P. Taylor, 2000; (ed) The British Isles since 1945, 2003; Old World, New World: the story of Britain and America, 2007; (with Michael Bywater) Is This Bottle Corked? The Secret Life of Wine, 2008; articles in Histl Jl, Econ. Hist. Rev., Internat. Hist. Rev., World of Fine Wine, etc. *Recreations:* collecting antiquarian history books, playing early music, wine. *Address:* The Long Barn, Townsend, Harwell, Oxon OX11 0DX. *T:* (01235) 835637. *E:* kmbnorway@tiscali.co.uk. *Club:* Academy.

BURKE, Hon. Anna Elizabeth; MLA (ALP) Chisholm, Victoria, Australia, since 1998; Speaker, Australian House of Representatives, 2012–13 (Deputy Speaker, 2008–10 and 2011–12); *b* Melbourne, 1 Jan. 1966; *d* of Bernard and Joan Burke; *m* 1994, Stephen Burgess; one *s* one *d*. *Educ:* Presentation Coll., Windsor (HSC 1983); Monash Univ. (BA Hons); Melbourne Univ. (MCom Hons). Industrial Officer: Victoria Roads Corp., 1988–93; Victoria Inst. of Technol., 1993–94; Nat. Industrial Officer, Finance Sector Union, 1994–98. Member: Fabian Soc.; Amnesty Internat. Associate Mem., RSL Oakleigh. *Recreations:* time with family, reading. *Address:* Level 1, 207 Blackburn Road, Syndal, Vic 3149, Australia. *E:* anna.burke.mp@aph.gov.au. *Clubs:* Box Hill Lions, Mont Albert and Surrey Hills Rotary, Box Hill Hawks (Vic).

BURKE, Hon. Brian Thomas; Australian Ambassador to Republic of Ireland and to the Holy See, 1988–91; *b* 25 Feb. 1947; *s* of late Thomas Burke (Federal ALP Member for Perth, 1942–55), and Madelaine Burke; *m* 1965, Susanne May Nevill; four *s* two *d*. *Educ:* Brigidine Convent; Marist Brothers' Coll.; Univ. of Western Australia. FAMI. Former journalist. MLA (Lab) Balga, WA, 1973–88; Opposition Shadow Minister, 1976–81; Leader of the Opposition, 1981–83; Premier and Treasurer of WA, 1983–88. AC 1988. *Recreations:* reading, swimming, fishing. *Address:* PO Box 668, Scarborough, WA 6922, Australia.

BURKE, David Thomas, (Tom), CBE 1997; Founding Director, since 2003, and Chairman, since 2012, E3G; Environmental Policy Adviser, Rio Tinto plc, since 1997; *b* 5 Jan. 1947; *s* of J. V. Burke, DSM, and Mary (*née* Bradley). *Educ:* St Boniface's, Plymouth; Liverpool Univ. (BA (Hons) Philosophy). Great George's Community Arts Project, 1969–70; Lecturer: West Cheshire Coll., 1970–71; Old Swan Technical Coll., 1971–73; Friends of the Earth: Local Groups Co-ordinator, 1973–75; Executive Director, 1975–79; Dir of Special Projects, 1979–80; Vice-Chm., 1980–81; Dir, The Green Alliance, 1982–91; Special Advr to Sec. of State for the Envmt, 1991–97; Envmtl Policy Advr, BP Amoco, 1997–2001; Advr, Central Policy Gp, Cabinet Office, 2003–04; Sen. Advr to Special Representative on Climate Change, 2006–12. Press Officer, European Environment Bureau, 1979–87; Sec., Ecological Studies Inst., 1987–92. Member: Bd of Dirs, Earth Resources Research, 1975–87; Waste Management Adv. Council, 1976–81; Packaging Council, 1978–82; Exec. Cttee, NCVO, 1984–89; UK Nat. Cttee, European Year of the Environment, 1986–88; Exec. Cttee, European Environment Bureau, 1987–91; Council, English Nature, 1999–2006; Londo Sustainable Develt Commn, 2002–06. Chm., Rev. of Envmtl Governance in NI, 2006–0 Contested (SDP): Brighton Kemptown, 1983; Surbiton, 1987. Vis. Fellow, Cranfiel 1991–94; Vis. Prof., Imperial Coll., 1997–; Sen. Associate, Cambridge Inst. for Sustainabili Leadership, 2012–. Hon. Vis. Fellow, Manchester Business Sch., 1984; Hon. Prof., Faculty Laws, UCL, 2003–. FRSA 1988 (Mem. Council, 1990–92); FEI 2009. Royal Humar Society Testimonials: on Vellum, 1966; on Parchment, 1968; Global 500 Laureate, UNE 1993. *Publications:* Europe: environment, 1981; (jtly) Pressure Groups in the Global Systen 1982; (jtly) Ecology 2000, 1984; (jtly) The Green Capitalists, 1987; (jtly) Green Pages, 198 (jtly) The Fragile City, 2014. *Recreations:* photography, birdwatching. *Address:* Studio 2, Clin Wharf Studios, Clink Street, SE1 9DG. *T:* (020) 7357 9146. *Club:* Reform.

BURKE, Prof. Derek Clissold, CBE 1994; DL; Vice-Chancellor, University of East Angli 1987–95; *b* 13 Feb. 1930; *s* of late Harold Burke and Ivy Ruby (*née* Clissold); *m* 1955, Ma Elizabeth Dukeshire (*d* 2014), New York; one *s* two *d* (and one *d* decd). *Educ:* Univ. Birmingham (BSc, PhD, Chemistry). Res. Fellow, Yale Univ., 1953–55; Scientist, Nat. Ins for Med. Res., London, 1955–60; Lectr and Sen. Lectr, Dept of Biochemistry, Univ. Aberdeen, 1960–69; Prof. of Biol Scis, 1969–82, Pro-Vice-Chancellor, 1971–73, Univ. Warwick; Vice-Pres. and Scientific Dir, Allelix Inc., Toronto, 1982–86. Specialist Advr, H C Select Cttee on Sci. and Technol., 1995–2001. Member: MRC Cell Bd, 1976–7 Scientific Cttee, Cancer Res. Campaign, 1979–82 and of CRC Council, 1987–97; Eu Molecular Biol Orgn, 1980–; Adv. Cttee on Genetic Modification, HSE, 1987–95; Steerin Gp, Technol. Foresight Initiative, OST, 1993–95; Sci. and Engrg Base Bd, 1994–97, Techno Interaction Bd, 1994–97, BBSRC; EU Eur. Life Scis Gp, 2000–04; EU-US Biotechnc Consultative Forum, 2000–01. Chm., Adv. Cttee on Novel Foods and Processes, Dept Health and MAFF, 1989–97. Chm. Council, Paterson Inst. for Cancer Res., 1992–97; Di Babraham Inst., Cambridge, 1995–99; Mem. Governing Body, BBSRC Inst. of Food Res 1995–2002 (Mem. Adv. Bd, AFRC Inst. of Food Res., 1989–95); Member: Societal Issu Panel, EPSRC, 2005–08; Bioscience for Society Strategy Panel, BBSRC, 2008–10. Chm Genome Research Ltd, 1997–98. Mem., Archbishops' Med. Ethics Adv. Gp, 1995–200 Pres., Soc. for Gen. Microbiology, 1987–90; Hon. Pres., British Nutrition Foundn, 2008–1 Hon. Mem., Soc. for Gen. Microbiol., 2001. Editor and Editor in Chief, Journal of Gener Virology, 1976–87. Chm., Norwich Soc., 2011–12. Trustee: Norfolk and Norwich Fest 1988–98; Wingfield Arts, 1995–98. Hon. Fellow, St Edmund's Coll., Cambridge, 1997– Hon. FIBiol 2001. Hon. LLD Aberdeen 1982; Hon. ScD UEA, 1995. DL Norfolk, 199 *Publications:* Creation and Evolution (ed and contrib.), 1985; (with R. Gill) Strategic Churc Leadership, 1996; (ed and contrib.) Cybernauts Awake!, 1999; numerous sci. papers o interferon and animal viruses. *Recreations:* music, walking. *Address:* 12 Cringleford Chas Norwich, Norfolk NR4 7RS; Sea Green Cottage, Walberswick, Suffolk IP18 6TU.

BURKE, Ian; *see* Burke, M. I.

BURKE, Sir James (Stanley Gilbert), 9th Bt *cr* 1797 (Ire.), of Marble Hill, Galway; *b* 1 Ju 1956; *s* of Sir Thomas Stanley Burke, 8th Bt and Susanne Margaretha (*d* 1983), *er d* of Ott Salvisberg, Thun, Switzerland; *S* father, 1989; *m* 1980, Laura, *d* of Domingo Branzuela; on *s* one *d*. *Heir: s* Martin James Burke, *b* 22 July 1980. *Address:* Bleierstrasse 14, 8942 Oberrieder Switzerland.

BURKE, His Honour Jeffrey Peter; QC 1984; a Circuit Judge, 2002–13; *b* 15 Dec. 194 *s* of Samuel and Gertrude Burke; *m*; two *s* one *d*; *m* 1994, Joanna Mary Heal; one *s* one *Educ:* Shrewsbury Sch.; Brasenose Coll., Oxford (BA 1963). Called to the Bar, Inner Templ 1964, Bencher, 1997. A Recorder, 1983–2002. Legal Mem., Mental Health Revie Tribunal, 1994–2014; Judge, Employment Appeal Tribunal, 2000–09, 2012–13; Legal Mem Parole Bd, 2009–. Trustee, Aplastic Anaemia Trust. *Recreations:* sport, wine, choral singin charity triathlons, learning theory of music. *Clubs:* De Todeni (Flamstead); Economicals AFC Flamstead Cricket.

BURKE, Joanna Margaret, CMG 2013; Director, Portugal, British Council, since 2013; *b* May 1960; *d* of James Brian Burke and Margaret Ann Burke; *m* 1987, Eliseo Mayora Martinez; one *s* one *d*. *Educ:* Beijing Langs Inst.; Tübingen Univ.; Leeds Univ. (BA Chines and German 1982). British Council: Asst Dir, China, 1990–95; Dep. Dir, Argentin 1995–99; Dir, Shanghai, 1999–2003; Regl Dir, Americas and Australasia, 2003–04; Di Japan, 2005–07; Regl Dir, China, 2007–13. *Recreations:* Beijing history, book collectin travel, music, gardens. *Address:* British Council, Rua Luis Fernandes 1–3, Lisbon 1249–06 Portugal. *T:* 213214542. *E:* joanna.burke@pt.britishcouncil.org.

BURKE, His Honour John Kenneth; QC 1985; a Circuit Judge, 1995–2005; *b* 4 Aug. 193 *s* of Kenneth Burke and Madeline Burke; *m* 1962, Margaret Anne (*née* Scattergood); three *Educ:* Stockport Grammar Sch. Served Cheshire Regt, 1958–60; TA Parachute Reg 1962–67. Called to the Bar, Middle Temple, 1965, Bencher, 1992. A Recorder, 1980–9 *Recreation:* painting and drawing.

BURKE, Kathy; actress and director; *b* 13 June 1964. *Educ:* Anna Scher Drama Sch. *Film* Scrubbers, Forever Young, 1983; Sacred Hearts, 1985; Sid and Nancy, 1986; Straight to Hel Walker, Eat the Rich, 1987; Work Experience, 1989; Amongst Barbarians, 1990; Sin Bir 1994; Hello, Hello, Hello, 1995; Nil by Mouth, 1997; Dancing at Lughnasa, Elizabeth, 199 This Year's Love, 1999; Kevin and Perry Go Large, Love, Honour and Obey, 2000; Th Martins, 2001; Once Upon a Time in the Midlands, Anita and Me, 2002; Tinker, Tailo Soldier, Spy, 2011. *Television:* Past Caring, 1985; Two of Us, 1987; Harry Enfield's Televisio Programme (series), 1990; Mr Wroe's Virgins, 1993; Harry Enfield and Chums (series), 199 Common as Muck (series), 1994–97; Life's a Bitch, 1995; After Miss Julie, 1995; The Histor of Tom Jones, a Foundling, 1997; Ted & Ralph, 1998; Gimme, Gimme, Gimme (series; als script editor), 1999–2001; Shooting Gallery, 1999; Harry Enfield Presents Kevin's Guide t Being a Teenager, 1999; Harry Enfield Presents Wayne and Waynetta's Guide to Wedde Bliss, 2001; dir, Horne and Corden, 2009. Writer: play, Mr Thomas; film, The End, 199 writer and dir, TV series: Renegade TV Gets Dazed, 1998; Walking and Talking, 201 Director: Out in the Open, 2001, Born Bad, 2003, Love Me Tonight, 2004, Hampstead Th Kosher Harry, Royal Court, 2002; Betty, Vaudeville, 2002; The Quare Fellow (tour), 200 Blue/Orange, Crucible, Sheffield, 2005; The God of Hell, Donmar Warehouse, 200 Smaller, Lyric, 2006; Once a Catholic, Tricycle, 2013. *Address:* c/o Hatton McEwan Penfor 3 Chocolate Studios, 7 Shepherdess Place, N1 7LJ.

BURKE, Hon. Sir Kerry; *see* Burke, Hon. Sir T. K.

BURKE, (Michael) Ian; Chairman, Rank Group plc, since 2011 (Chief Executive, 2006–14 *b* 21 June 1956; *s* of Ronald and Rosemary Burke; *m* 1979, Jane McGuinness; one *s* one *Educ:* Imperial Coll., London (BSc Maths); London Business Sch. (MSc Business Admin ACMA 1981. With Lever Bros, 1978–81; finance and planning, Esso UK, 1981–86; G Planning Manager, Gateway Corp., 1986–90; Bass plc: Commercial Dir, Bass Leisure 1990–92; Man. Dir, Gala Clubs, 1992–95; Exec. Vice Pres. and Man. Dir, Holiday In Worldwide, Europe, ME and Africa, 1995–98; Chief Executive: Thistle Hotels pl 1998–2003; Health Club Hldgs, 2003–06. Dir, London Tourist Bd, 1998–2003; Bd Mem BTA, 2000–03. *Recreations:* fell-walking, cycling. *Address:* Rank Group plc, Statesman House Stafferton Way, Maidenhead SL6 1AY.

BURKE, Peter; *see* Burke, U. P.

BURKE, Prof. Philip George, CBE 1993; FRS 1978; MRIA 1974; Professor of Mathematical Physics, Queen's University of Belfast, 1967–98, now Emeritus; *b* 18 Oct. 1932; *s* of Henry Burke and Frances Mary Burke (*née* Sprague); *m* 1959, Valerie Mona Martin; four *d*. *Educ:* Wanstead County High Sch.; Univ. Coll. of SW of England, Exeter (BSc London (ext.) 1953, 1st cl. Hons Physics); University Coll. London (PhD 1956, Fellow 1986). Granville Studentship, London Univ., 1953; Res. Fellow, UCL, 1956–57; Lectr, Univ. of London Computer Unit, 1957–59; Res. Associate, Alvarez Bubble Chamber Gp and Theory Gp, Lawrence Berkeley Lab., Calif, 1959–62; Res. Fellow, then Principal Scientific Officer, later SPSO, Theoretical Physics Div., AERE, Harwell, 1962–67; Queen's University of Belfast: Head, Dept of Applied Maths and Theoretical Physics, 1974–77; Chm., Sch. of Physics and Math. Scis, 1985–86; Dir, Sch. of Maths and Physics, 1988–90. Science, subseq. Science and Engineering, Research Council: Mem., Physics Cttee, 1967–71; Chm., Synchrotron Radiation Panel, 1969–71; Mem., Atlas Comp. Cttee, 1973–76; Hd, Div. of Theory and Computational Sci., Daresbury Lab. (jt with QUB), 1977–82; Chm., Science Bd Computer Cttee, 1976–77 and 1984–86; Chm., Scientific Computing Adv. Panel, 1989–94; Mem., 1989–94; Chairman: Internat. Conf. on Physics of Electronic and Atomic Collisions, 1973–75; Computational Physics Gp, Eur. Physical Soc., 1976–78; Atomic, Molecular and Optical Physics Div., Inst. of Physics, 1987–90; Allocations and Resources Panel, Jt Res. Councils Supercomputer Cttee, 1988–90; Supercomputing Management Cttee, 1991–94; Inter-Council High Performance Computing Mgt Cttee, 1996–98; Member: ABRC Supercomputing Sub-cttee, 1991–94; Nuclear Res. Adv. Council, MoD, 1997–2009. Mem., Council, Royal Soc., 1990–92. Co-ordinator, EU Human Capital and Mobility Network of nine EU labs and three E European labs, 1993–96. Dir, 1969–2000, Hon. Dir, 2001–, Computer Physics Communications Internat. Program Library. Series Editor: Plenum Series on Physics of Atoms and Molecules (with H. Kleinpoppen), 1974–2004; Springer Series in Atomic, Optical and Plasma Physics, 2005–. Hon. Editor, Computer Physics Communications, 1986– (founding and principal editor, 1969–79). Hon. DSc: Exeter, 1981; QUB, 1999. Guthrie Medal and Prize, 1994, Sir David Bates Prize, 2000, Inst. of Physics; Will Allis Prize, APS, 2012. *Publications:* eight books; many research papers in learned journals. *Recreations:* walking, books, music. *Address:* School of Physics and Applied Mathematics, David Bates Building, Queen's University of Belfast, Belfast BT7 1NN; (home) Brook House, Norley Lane, Crowton, Northwich, Cheshire CW8 2RR. *T:* (01928) 788301.

BURKE, Richard; President, Canon Foundation in Europe, 1988–98; *b* 29 March 1932; *s* of David Burke and Elisabeth Burke; *m* 1961, Mary Freeley; two *s* three *d* (and one *s* decd). *Educ:* University Coll., Dublin (MA). Called to the Bar, King's Inns. Mem., Dublin Co. Council, 1967–73 (Chm., 1972–73); Mem. Dail Eireann, for South County Dublin, 1969–77, for Dublin West, 1981–82; Fine Gael Chief Whip and spokesman on Posts and Telegraphs, 1969–73; Minister for Education, 1973–76. Commission of the European Communities: Member with special responsibility for Transport, Taxation, Consumer Protection, Relations with European Parlt, Research, Educ. and Sci., 1977–81, for Greenland, Greek Memorandum, Personnel and Admin, Jt Interpretation and Conf. Service, Statistical Office and Office of Publications, 1982–85; Vice Pres., 1984–85. Associate Fellow, Center for Internat. Affairs, Harvard Univ., 1980–81. Member: Conseil d'Administration, FIDEPS, UNESCO, 1990–98; Develt Council, HEC, Paris, 1990–96. Mem., Academia Scientiarum et Artium Europaea, Salzburg, 1996. Chieftain, Burke Clan, 1990, Hon. Life Pres., 1992. President: Harvard Club of Ireland, 2005–08; Arts for Peace Foundn, 2006–. FRSA. Pro Merito Europa Medal, 1980. Grand Croix, Leopold II (Belgium), 1981; Grand Croix, Phoenix (Greece), 1983. *Recreations:* music, golf, travel. *Address:* 13 Iris Grove, Mount Merrion, Co. Dublin, Ireland. *T:* (1) 2109830.

BURKE, Simon Paul, FCA; Chairman, Light Cinema Group, since 2014; *b* 25 Aug. 1958; *s* of Vincent Paul Burke and Beryl Mary Burke (*née* Cregan). *Educ:* St Mary's Coll., Dublin. FCA 1980. Man. Dir, Virgin Retail, 1988–94; Chief Executive: Virgin Our Price, 1994–96; Virgin Entertainment Gp, 1996–99; Chairman: Hamleys plc, 1999–2003; Superquinn Ltd, 2005–10; Majestic Wine plc, 2005–10; Hobbycraft Ltd, 2010–14; Mitchells and Butlers plc, 2011 (Dep. Chm., 2010–11); Eagle Eye Solutions, 2011–; Bathstore.com, 2012–14. Dir, W H Smith plc, 1995–96; non-exec. Dir, Co-operative Gp, 2014–. Non-exec. Mem., Exec. Bd, BBC, 2011–. Trustee, Nat. Gall., 2003–11; Chm., Nat. Gall. Co. Ltd, 2004–11. *Recreations:* 17th century Dutch art, mediaeval history, flying (private pilot), astronomy, travel. *E:* 1.simonburke@gmail.com.

BURKE, Hon. Sir (Thomas) Kerry, Kt 1990; Member, 1998–2009, and Chairman, 2004–10, Canterbury Regional Council, Christchurch; *b* 24 March 1942; *m* 1st, 1968, Jennifer Shiel (marr. diss. 1984); two *s*; 2nd, 1984, Helen Paske (*d* 1989); one *s*; 3rd, 1997, Fahimeh Rastar; one step *s* two step *d*. *Educ:* Linwood High Sch.; Univ. of Canterbury (BA); Christchurch Teachers' Coll. (Dip. Teaching). General labourer, Auckland, 1965–66; factory deleg., Auckland Labourers' Union; teacher: Rangiora High Sch., 1967–72; Greymouth High Sch., 1975–78; lang. and immigration consultant, Vienna, Austria, 1991–98. Chm., Rangiora Post-Primary Teachers' Assoc., 1969–71. MP (Lab) Rangiora, NZ, 1972–75, West Coast, 1978–90; Minister of Regional Devlt, and of Employment and Immigration, 1984–87; Speaker, NZ House of Reps, 1987–90. *Recreations:* ski-ing, swimming. *Address:* 44 Naseby Street, Merivale, Christchurch 8014, New Zealand.

BURKE, Tom; *see* Burke, D. T.

BURKE, Tracey Mary; Strategy Director, Department for Economy, Science and Transport, Welsh Government, since 2012; *b* Cardiff; *d* of John F. and June M. Burke. *Educ:* Our Lady's Convent Sch.; Cardiff High Sch.; Sheffield Univ. (BA Hons Psychol. 1985); Trinity Coll., Dublin (MBA 1993). Policy Evaluator, Dept of Enterprise and Employment, Irish Govt, 1993–97; Hd of Chm.'s Office, 1997–2000, Eur. Structural Funds Dir, 2000–01, WDA; PM's Strategy Unit, Cabinet Office, 2001–02; Planning Dir, 2002–05, Exec. Dir, Strategy Develt, 2005–06, WDA; Welsh Assembly Government, later Welsh Government: Dir, Strategy and Review, Dept for Enterprise, Innovation and Networks, 2006–08; Acting Dir, Policy Strategy and Corporate Services, Economy and Transport, 2008–09; Dir, Econ. Renewal Prog., 2009–10, Actg Dir, Strategy and Ops, 2010–12, Welsh Govt. *Recreations:* spending time with my family and friends, passionate supporter of Welsh Rugby team and Cardiff City and Sunderland Football Clubs. *Address:* Welsh Government, Cathays Park, Cardiff CF10 3NQ.

BURKE, Trevor Michael; QC 2001; *b* 16 Oct. 1958; *s* of Michael George Burke and Philomena Burke. *Educ:* Handsworth Grammar Sch.; South Bank Univ., (BA Hons Law). Called to the Bar, Middle Temple, 1981. *Recreation:* golf. *Address:* Three Raymond Buildings, Gray's Inn, WC1R 5BH. *Club:* Brocket Hall Golf.

BURKE, Prof. (Ulick) Peter, FBA 1994; Professor of Cultural History, 1996–2004, now Emeritus, and Fellow of Emmanuel College, since 1979, University of Cambridge; *b* 16 Aug. 1937; *s* of John Burke and Jennie Burke (*née* Colin); *m* 1st, 1972, Susan Patricia Dell (marr. diss. 1983); 2nd, 1989, Maria Lúcia Garcia Pallares. *Educ:* St John's Coll., Oxford (Hon. Fellow, 2009); St Antony's Coll., Oxford (MA). Asst Lectr, then Lectr in History, subseq. Reader in Intellectual History, Sussex Univ., 1962–78; Reader in Cultural History, Univ. of Cambridge, 1988–96. *Publications:* The Renaissance Sense of the Past, 1969; Culture and Society in Renaissance Italy, 1972, 3rd edn 1986; Venice and Amsterdam: a study of Seventeenth Century elites, 1974, 2nd edn 1994; Popular Culture in Early Modern Europe, 1978, 2nd edn 1994; Sociology and History, 1980; Montaigne, 1981; Vico, 1985; Historical Anthropology in Early Modern Italy: essays on perception and communication, 1987; The Renaissance, 1987; The French Historical Revolution: the Annales School 1929–89, 1990; The Fabrication of Louis XIV, 1992, 2nd edn 1994; History and Social Theory, 1992; Antwerp, a Metropolis in Europe, 1993; The Art of Conversation, 1993; The Fortunes of the Courtier, 1995; Varieties of Cultural History, 1997; The European Renaissance, 1998; A Social History of Knowledge, 2000; Eyewitnessing, 2001; (jtly) A Social History of the Media, 2002; What is Cultural History?, 2004; Languages and Communities in Early Modern Europe, 2004; (with M. L. Pallares-Burke) Social Theory in the Tropics, 2008; Cultural Hybridity, 2009; A Social History of Knowledge, Vol. II: from the Encyclopédie to Wikipedia, 2011. *Recreation:* travel. *Address:* Emmanuel College, Cambridge CB2 3AP. *T:* (01223) 334272. *Club:* Paineras de Morumbi (São Paulo).

BURKE-GAFFNEY, John Campion; Director-General, The British Red Cross Society, 1985–90; *b* 27 Feb. 1932; *s* of late Dr Henry Joseph O'Donnell Burke-Gaffney, OBE and Constance May (*née* Bishop); *m* 1956, Margaret Mary Jennifer (*née* Stacpoole); two *s* two *d*. *Educ:* Douai School. Called to the Bar, Gray's Inn, 1956. Served: RAC, 1950–52; E Riding of Yorks Imperial Yeomanry (Wenlock's Horse), 1952–56. Shell-Mex and BP Ltd, 1956–75; Shell UK Ltd, 1976–77; Man. Dir, Shell and BP Zambia Ltd, 1977–81; Gp Public Affairs, Shell Internat. Petroleum Co. Ltd, 1981–85. *Address:* c/o Coutts & Co., 440 Strand, WC2R 0QS.

BURKILL, Guy Alexander; QC 2002; *b* 5 March 1957; *s* of Arthur and Helen Burkill; *m* 1984, Lorely Claire Owen; two *s*. *Educ:* Winchester Coll.; Corpus Christi Coll., Cambridge (MA Engrg (Electrical option) 1st Cl. Hons). Called to the Bar, Middle Temple, 1981; in practice at Patent and Intellectual Property Bar, 1981–. *Publications:* (ed jtly) Terrell on the Law of Patents, 15th edn 2000, 17th edn 2011. *Recreations:* violin (performs with London Phoenix Orchestra), programming, trying to mend things. *Address:* 3 New Square, Lincoln's Inn, WC2A 3RS. *T:* (020) 7405 1111, *Fax:* (020) 7405 7800. *E:* clerks@3newsquare.co.uk.

BURLAND, James Alan, RIBA; Principal Partner, Burland TM, architects, since 2000; Architect, Terrell Associates, since 2014; Consultant, Terrell Group, since 2014; freelance architectural consultant; *b* 25 Sept. 1954; *s* of late James Glyn Burland and Elizabeth Beresford Thompson. *Educ:* King Henry VIII Sch., Coventry; Bath Univ. (BSc 1978; BArch 1980); Acad. of Contemporary Music, Guildford. RIBA 1983. Joined Arup Associates, 1978, Dir and Principal, 1994–2000; projects include: Stockley Park, Heathrow, 1983–2000; Eton Coll. Labs, 1984; Bedford High Sch. Sen. Sch., 1984–85; (with Philip Cox Architects, Sydney) Sydney Olympics 2000 Stadium Studies, 1985–90; City of Manchester Stadium, 1992–2000; Plantation Place, Fenchurch Street, London, 1993–2000; Johannesburg Athletics Stadium, 1993–94; new coll., Durham Univ., 1994–2000; Crystal Palace Sports Complex, 1998; BP Solar Showcase G8 Summit, Arup campus building, Birmingham, 1998; private commn, design for Body Shop, including Bath and Brighton, 1982; Burland TM projects include: Ealing Studios, 2000–; Bermondsey Market, 2000–; Spitalfields Refuge and Convent restoration, 2000–; Falcon Wharf apartments, 2000–03; Harlequins RFC, 2002–; Pinewood and Shepperton Studios, 2003–; Billiardrome, 2003–; Portable Olympic Stadium studies, 2003–; Bristol Arena Quarter, 2005–; Fieldgate St, student housing, 2006; Edward Jenner Unit, Gloucester Royal Hosp., 2008; Stirling Billiardrome, 2010; private house in Arun, 2011; domestic projects on Lake Como, 2012–; stadium projects in Europe and UK, 2012–. Bovis/Architects' Jl RA Summer Exhibn Grand Award, 1998. *Recreations:* music, art, architecture, cycling. *T:* 07968 162128. *E:* jb@burlandtm.com, jb@jamesburland.com. *W:* www.burlandtm.com. *Club:* London Road (Cyclosports).

BURLAND, Prof. John Boscawen, CBE 2005; FRS 1997; FREng; Professor of Soil Mechanics, Imperial College (formerly Imperial College of Science and Technology), University of London, 1980–2001, now Emeritus; *b* 4 March 1936; *s* of John Whitmore Burland and Margaret Irene Burland (*née* Boscawen); *m* 1963, Gillian Margaret, *d* of J. K. Miller; two *s* one *d*. *Educ:* Parktown Boys' High Sch., Johannesburg; Univ. of the Witwatersrand (BSc Eng, MSc Eng, DSc Eng); Univ. of Cambridge (PhD). FICE, Hon. FICE 2014; FIStructE; FREng (FEng 1981). Res. Asst, Univ. of the Witwatersrand, 1960; Engineer, Ove Arup and Partners, London, 1961–63; Res. Student, Cambridge Univ., 63–66; Building Research Station: SSO and PSO, 1966–72; Head of Geotechnics Div., 1972–79; Asst Dir and Head of Materials and Structures Dept, 1979–80. Visiting Prof., Dept of Civil Engineering, Univ. of Strathclyde, 1973–82. Member: Adv. Panel to Sec. of State for Environment on Black Country Limestone, 1983–95; Italian Prime Minister's Commn for stabilising the Leaning Tower of Pisa, 1990–2001. Mem. Council, CIRIA, 1987–95 (Vice Pres., 1995–98); Official Visitor, BRE, 1990–97. Trustee, BRE Trust, 2001–13 (Chm., Res. Cttee, 2001–13). Advr, Ove Arup Foundn, 2003–. Chm., Steering Gp, Centre for Smart Infrastructure and Construction, Univ. of Cambridge, 2011–. Chm., Wheathampstead Churches Together, 1990–97. FIC 2004. Hon. Fellow: Emmanuel Coll., Cambridge, 2004; Cardiff Univ., 2005. Royal Academy of Engineering: Mem. Council, 1994–97; Public Promotion of Engrg Medal, 2006; Institution of Structural Engineers: Mem. of Council, 1979–82; Murray Buxton Silver Medal, 1977; Oscar Faber Bronze Medal, 1979; Gold Medal, 1998; named in Special Award to DoE for Underground Car Park at Palace of Westminster, 1975; Oscar Faber Diploma, 1982; Murray Buxton Diploma, 2002; Sir Arnold Walters Medal, 2006; Murray Buxton Medal, 2007; Institution of Civil Engineers: Vice Pres., 2003–05; Telford Premium, 1972, 1985, 1987; Coopers Hill War Meml Medal, 1985; Baker Medal, 1986; Kelvin Medal, for outstanding contribn to engrg, 1989; Gold Medal, 2001; Brit. Geotechnical Soc. Prize, 1968, 1971, 1974 and 1986; Kevin Nash Gold Medal, Internat. Soc. of Soil Mechanics and Foundn Engrs, 1994; H. Bolton Seed Medal, ASCE, 1996; Gold Medal, World Fedn of Engrg Orgns, 1997; Lord Lloyd of Kilgerran Prize, Foundn for Sci. and Technol., 2002; Dickinson Meml Medal, Newcomen Soc., 2007; Geotechnical Res. Medal, ICE, 2013. Hon. Mem., Japanese Geotechnical Soc., 2005. Hon. DEng: Heriot-Watt, 1994; Glasgow, 2001; Hon. DSc: Nottingham, 1998; Warwick, 2003; Herts, 2011; Hon. DSc (Eng) Witwatersrand, 2007. Commendatore: Nostro Real Ordine di Francesco 1 (Italy), 2001; Ordine della Stella di Solidarietà Italiana, 2003. *Publications:* numerous papers on soil mechanics and civil engineering. *Recreations:* sailing, golf, painting.

BURLEIGH, Prof. Michael Christopher Bennet, PhD; FRHistS; Research Professor, University of Buckingham, since 2011; *b* 3 April 1955; *s* of late Wing Comdr B. G. S. Bennet Burleigh and C. Burleigh; *m* 1990, Linden Mary Brownbridge. *Educ:* University Coll. London (BA 1st Cl. Hons 1977); Bedford Coll., London (PhD 1982). FRHistS 1988. Weston Jun. Res. Fellow, New Coll., Oxford, 1984–87; British Acad. Post-doctoral Fellow, QMC, 1987–88; London School of Economics and Political Science: Lectr, 1988–93; Reader in Internat. Hist., 1993–95; Dist. Res. Prof. in Modern European Hist., Cardiff Univ., 1995–2001; William R. Kenan Jr Prof. of Hist., Washington & Lee Univ., 2001–02. Raoul Wallenberg Vis. Prof. of Human Rights, Rutgers Univ., 1999–2000; Kratter Vis. Prof. of Hist., Stanford Univ., 2003; Dist. Vis. Fellow, Hoover Instn, Stanford Univ., 2006–10. Cardinal Basil Hume Meml Lectr, Heythrop Coll., 2002; Fisher Lect., Cambridge Univ., 2007; Basil Liddell Hart Meml Lect., KCL, 2010. Mem., Academic Adv. Council, Inst. für Zeitgeschichte, Munich, 2004–12. Member, Advisory Board: Standpoint mag., 2009–; New Culture Forum, 2009–; Mem., First World War Centenary Adv. Gp, 2012–. Ed., Totalitarian Movements and Political Religions, 2000–05; Contrib. Ed., Literary Review, 2010–. Writer and presenter, Dark Enlightenment, TV prog., 2006. Award for Archival Achievement, BFI, 1991; Bronze Medal, NY Film and TV Fest., 1994; Master of his Time, Premio Nonino, 2012. *Publications:* Prussian Society and the German Order, 1984; Germany Turns Eastwards, 1988; The Racial State: Germany 1933–45, 1991 (trans. Italian, Japanese, Czech); Death and Deliverance: euthanasia in Germany, 1994 (trans. German); (ed) Confronting the Nazi Past, 1996 (trans. Hungarian); Ethics and Extermination: reflections on Nazi genocide, 1997; The

Third Reich: a new history, 2000 (Samuel Johnson Prize, 2001) (trans. Dutch, Estonian, German, Italian, Finnish, French, Spanish, Czech, Hebrew, Polish, Chinese); Earthly Powers: religion and politics in Europe from the French Revolution to the Great War, 2005 (trans. German, Italian, Spanish, Dutch, French, Polish); Sacred Causes: religion and politics from the European dictators to Al-Qaeda, 2006 (trans. Dutch, German, Italian, Spanish, French); Blood and Rage: a cultural history of terrorism, 2008 (trans. Dutch, Danish, German, Italian, Spanish, French); Moral Combat: a history of World War II, 2010 (trans. Spanish); Small Wars, Far Away Places: the genesis of the modern world 1945–65, 2013 (trans. Italian, Spanish). *Recreations:* gardening, sea fishing. *Address:* c/o Wylie Agency Ltd, 17 Bedford Square, WC1B 3JA. *Club:* Travellers.

BURLEY, Aidan; *b* Auckland, NZ, 22 Jan. 1979; *s* of Geoff Burley and Lois Burley; *m* 2014, Jodie Jones. *Educ:* King Edward's Sch., Edgbaston; St John's Coll., Oxford. Researcher for Philip Hammond, MP; Mgt Consultant, Mouchel. Mem. (C) Hammersmith and Fulham LBC, 2006–10. MP (C) Cannock Chase, 2010–15. *Recreations:* Rugby, tennis, cooking.

BURLEY, George Elder; Manager, Crystal Palace Football Club, 2010–11; *b* Cumnock, Ayrshire, 3 June 1956; *s* of William and Sarah Burley; *m* 1978, Jill Askew; two *s* one *d*. *Educ:* Cumnock Acad. Professional footballer: Ipswich Town, 1973–85 (winner, FA Cup, 1978, EUFA Cup, 1981); Sunderland, 1985–88; Gillingham, 1988–89; Motherwell, 1989–91 and 1993–94; (and Manager) Ayr Utd, 1991–93; Falkirk, 1993; (and Manager) Colchester Utd, 1994; 11 caps for Scotland, 1979–82; Manager: Ipswich Town, 1995–2002; Derby Co., 2003–05; Heart of Midlothian, 2005; Southampton, 2005–08; Scottish Nat. Football Coach, 2008–09. *Recreations:* golf, tennis.

BURLEY, Helen; *see* Boaden, H.

BURLEY, Prof. Jeffery, CBE 1991; PhD; Professor of Forestry, 1996–2002, Director, Oxford Forestry Institute, 1985–2002, Oxford University; Professorial Fellow, Green College, Oxford, 1981–2002, now Emeritus Fellow (Vice-Warden, 1997–2002; Development Fellow, 2003–07); *b* 16 Oct. 1936; *s* of Jack Burley and Eliza Burley (*née* Creese); *m* 1961, Jean Shirley (*née* Palmer); two *s*. *Educ:* Portsmouth Grammar Sch.; New College, Oxford (BA 1961); Yale (MF 1962; PhD 1965). Lieut, Royal Signals, 1954–57. O i/c and Unesco Expert, Forest Genetics Res. Lab., ARC of Central Africa, 1965–69; Sen. Res. Officer, Commonwealth Forestry Inst., Oxford, 1969–76; Lectr, 1976–83, Head of Dept of Forestry, 1983–85, Oxford Univ. Pres., Internat. Union of Forestry Res. Orgns, 1996–2000; Chairman: Tropical Forest Resource Gp, 1994–2006; Marcus Wallenberg Prize Selection Cttee, Stockholm, 1998–2006; Commonwealth Forestry Assoc., 2002–05. Chm. Bd, C-Questor Ltd, 2005–09. Mem. Bd, Marcus Wallenberg Foundn, 2006–. Patron, Speedwell and WellBeing Trust, 2000–. Internat. Fellow, Royal Swedish Acad. of Agriculture and Forestry, 1998; Hon. FICFor, 2003; Hon. Fellow, Soc. of Amer. Foresters, 2003. Hon. DSc CATIE, Costa Rica, 2008. *Publications:* (ed jtly) Multipurpose tree germplasm, 1984; (ed jtly) Increasing productivity of multipurpose species, 1985; (Ed. in Chief) Elsevier Encyclopedia of Forest Sciences, 2004; many book chapters resulting from conference papers; many contribs to periodicals and learned jls on forestry, agroforestry and forest tree breeding. *Recreations:* beekeeping, gardening, piano and church organ, Wantage Male Voice Choir. *Address:* Green Templeton College, Woodstock Road, Oxford OX2 6HG. *T:* (01865) 274770.

BURLEY, Jessica Jane; Chief Executive Officer, m/SIX Communications Ltd (formerly MCHI), since 2010; *b* Lympstone, Devon, 24 Jan. 1966; *d* of Anthony Douglas Wiseman and Jean Shirley Darby (*neé* Evernden); *m* 1994, Mark David Burley. *Educ:* Bristol Poly. (BA Hons Eng. Lit. and Theatre Arts); CAM Cert. Communications Studies. Nat. Accounts Supervisor, Bristol United Press, 1987–90; Sales Exec., Mirror Extra South West, Mirror Gp Newspapers, 1990; Dep. Ad Manager, NME and Melody Maker, IPC Magazines, 1990–92; Advertising Manager, This Week, Daily Express, Express Newspapers, 1992–95; Advertising Director: Company Magazine, 1995, Cosmopolitan Magazine, 1995–96, Nat. Magazine Co.; Publishing Dir, Gruner+Jahr, 1997–99; Gp Publishing Dir, Financial Times Business, 1999–2000; Exec. Gp Publishing Dir, Future Publishing, 2000–01; Gp Publishing Dir, National Magazines Co., 2001–04; Chief Operating Officer, ACP-NatMag Co., 2004–06; Man. Dir, National Magazines Co., 2006–10. Non-executive Director: Jacques Vert plc, 2009–11; Talk Talk Telecom Gp plc, 2010; UK Mail plc, 2012–; Quarto Publishing Gp plc, 2014–. Exec. Mem., WACL, 2008–; Mem., Eur. Professional Women's Network, 2011–. Trustee, Get Connected, 2013. *Recreations:* golf, music, art.

BURLEY, Kay Elizabeth; presenter, Sky News, since 1988; *b* Wigan, 17 Dec. 1960; *d* of Frank and Kathleen McGurrin; *m* 1st, 1980, Steve Burley; 2nd, 1992, Steve Kutner; one *s*. *Educ:* Beech Hill Primary Sch., Wigan; Whitley High Sch., Wigan; Nat. Council for Trng of Journalists Coll., Preston. Reporter, Evening Post and Chronicle, Wigan, 1978–83; freelance TV and radio journalist in NW, 1984; news producer, Tyne Tees TV, 1985; reporter and presenter, TV-am, 1985–88. *Publications:* Blooming Pregnant: the real facts about having a baby (jtly), 1993; First Ladies, 2011; Betrayal, 2012. *Recreations:* sports, theatre, family, friends, animal care. *Address:* Sky News, Unit 1, Centaurs Business Park, Osterley TW7 5QD. *T:* (020) 7032 2113. *E:* Kay.Burley@BSkyB.com.

BURLEY, Lindsay Elizabeth, CBE 2011; FRCPE, FRCGP; Chairman: NHS Education for Scotland, since 2010 (non-executive Director, 2002–10); Scottish Association for Mental Health, since 2009; *b* Blackpool, 2 Oct. 1950; *d* of William and Elizabeth Lamont; *m* 1972, Robin Burley. *Educ:* Edinburgh Univ. (MB ChB 1973). FRCPE 1985; FRCGP 1995. Sen. Lectr, Univ. of Edinburgh, 1982–87, Hon. Sen. Lectr, 1991–2013. Consultant Physician, 1982–91, Dir of Planning and Develt, 1991–95, Lothian Health Bd; Chief Exec., Borders Health Bd, 1995–2003; Chm., Nat. Waiting Times Centre Bd for Scotland, 2003–10. Mem., SFC, 2006–13. Partner, Eskhill & Co., 2003–. *Recreations:* gardening, ski-ing, piano playing. *Address:* Eskhill & Co., Eskhill House, 15 Inveresk Village, Musselburgh EH21 7TD. *T:* (0131) 271 4000, 07831 605858. *E:* lindsay@eskhill.com.

BURLEY, Maj. Gen. Shaun Alex, CB 2013; MBE 1995; Military Secretary, 2013–15; *b* Shipston on Stour, 4 March 1962; *s* of George Burley and Maisie Burley; *m* 1983, Jayne Young; one *s* one *d*. *Educ:* King Edward VI Sch., Stratford on Avon; RMA Sandhurst. Joined Army, 1981; CO 35 Engr Regt, 1999–2002; Dep. Asst COS Orgn, HQ Land Forces, 2004–05; Commander: 8 Force Engr Bde, 2006–07; Operational Support Gp, Land Warfare Centre, 2008–09; Dir, Advanced Comd and Staff Course, JSCSC, 2010–11; GOC Theatre Troops, 2011–13. Hon. Col, Engr and Logistic Staff Corps, 2011–15; Col Comdt, RE, 2011–. Hon. Life Vice Pres., Army Rugby Union, 2014 (Chm., 2011–14). *Recreations:* sport (Pres., Corps Rugby, 2005–), military history, music, cinema, running, family, travel. *Address:* c/o Army Personnel Centre, Kentigern House, 65 Brown Street, Glasgow G2 8EX.

BURLIN, Prof. Terence Eric; Rector, University of Westminster (formerly Polytechnic of Central London), 1984–95, Professor Emeritus, 1996; *b* 24 Sept. 1931; *s* of Eric Jonas Burlin and Winifred Kate (*née* Thomas); *m* 1957, Plessey Pamela Carpenter; one *s* one *d*. *Educ:* Acton County School; University of Southampton (BSc); Univ. of London (DSc, PhD, BSc). CPhys, FInstP 1969; FIBiotech 1992. Physicist, Mount Vernon Hosp. and Radium Inst., 1953–57; Sen. Physicist, Hammersmith Hosp., 1957–62; Principal Physicist, St John's Hosp. for Diseases of the Skin, 1960–90; Polytechnic of Central London: Sen. Lectr, 1962; Reader, 1969; Pro-Director, 1971; Sen. Pro-Rector, 1982–84; Acting Rector, 1982. British Cttee on Radiation Units and Measurements: Mem., 1966–74 and 1979–95; Vice-Chm., 1983–84; Chm., 1984–95; Member: Council, Inst. for Study of Drug Dependence, 1974–86; various Boards, CNAA; Cttee on Practical Determination of Dose Equivalent, Internat. Commn on Radiation Units and Measurements (Chm.), 1979–87; Adv. Council on Adult and Continuing Educn, DES, 1980–83; Cttee on Effects of Ionising Radiation, Physics and Dosimetry Sub-Cttee, MRC, 1983–86; Science Bd, SERC, 1986–89. Mem. Council, BTEC, 1984–86. Member: Council, Westminster Chamber of Commerce, 1994–95; Employment Affairs Cttee, 1994–95, Commercial Educn Trust, 1996–2002, London Chamber of Commerce and Industry. Trustee: Regent St Poly. Trust, 1983–2008; Quintin Hogg Trust, 1983–2008; Quintin Hogg Meml Fund, 1983–2008. Mem. Bd, Bournemouth Univ., 1996–2002. Hon. FCP 1990. Hon. DSc Westminster, 1996. *Publications:* chapters in Radiation Dosimetry, 1968, 2nd edn 1972; papers on radiation dosimetry, radiological protection, biomechanical properties of skin, radiobiology. *Recreations:* music, swimming. *Club:* Athenæum.

BURLINGTON, Earl of; William Cavendish; photographer; *b* 6 June 1969; *s* and *heir* of Duke of Devonshire, *qv*; *m* 2007, Laura Ann Montagu, *d* of Richard Roundell; one *s* two *d*. *Heir:* *s* Lord Cavendish, *qv*. *Address:* c/o Chatsworth, Bakewell, Derbyshire DE45 1PP.

BURMAN, Roger Stephen, CBE 1991; DL; Chairman, since 1976, and Managing Director since 1973, Teledictor; *b* 3 April 1940; *s* of Sir Stephen France Burman, CBE and Lady (Joan Margaret) Burman; *m* 1964, Felicity Jane Crook; four *s*. *Educ:* Oundle Sch.; Univ. of Birmingham (BSc Hon.). Burman & Sons, 1961–72 (Dir, 1965–72); Teledictor, 1972–; Chairman: Nat. Exhibn Centre, 1989–2005 (Dir, 1984–2005); Performances Birmingham Ltd (formerly Symphony Hall (Birmingham) Ltd), 1991–2014; Director: Black Country Devel Corp., 1992–98; Chrysalis Radio (Midlands), 2001–04; Baugh & Weedon Ltd, 2004–08. Gen. Tax Comr, 1973–2009. Member: British Hallmarking Council, 1980–2006 (Chm. 1989–97); BOTB, 1990–94 and 1996–99; Council, ICC, 1990–2006; Pres., Birmingham Chamber of Commerce, 1984–85; Chm., Assoc. of British Chambers of Commerce 1988–90. Guardian, 1965–2010, Chm., 2000–06, Birmingham Assay Office. University of Birmingham: Life Governor, 1983–; Pro-Chancellor, 1994–2001. Liveryman, Goldsmiths Co., 1993–. DL 1991, High Sheriff 1999, W Midlands. Hon. LLD Birmingham, 1994. *Recreation:* golf. *Address:* Astwood Hill House, Astwood Lane, Astwood Bank, Redditch, Worcs B96 6PT. *T:* (01522) 893951.

BURN, Adrian; *see* Burn, B. A. F.

BURN, Angus Maitland P.; *see* Pelham Burn.

BURN, (Bryan) Adrian (Falconer); *b* 23 May 1945; *s* of Peter and Ruth Burn; *m* 1968, Jeanette Carol; one *s* three *d*. *Educ:* Abingdon Sch. FCA. Whinney Murray, 1963–72; joined Binder Hamlyn, 1972; seconded to DTI, 1975–77; Partner, 1977, Managing Partner 1988–94, Binder Hamlyn; Partner, Arthur Andersen, 1994–99. Non-executive Chairman Atlas Gp Hldgs, 1999–2002; Search Holdings Ltd, 2000–06; non-executive Director: Sinclair Stevenson Ltd, 1990–92; Brent Internat. plc, 1994–99; GE Capital Bank Ltd, 1999–2009; Pinewood Shepperton Plc, 2000–11; Wolff Olins Ltd, 1999–2001; Strutt and Parker 1999–2006; Richards Butler, 1999–2006; Smart and Cook Hldgs Ltd, 2004–07; Acertec plc 2006–09; GE Money Home Lending Ltd, 2007–. Mem., Financial Adjudication Panel Second Severn Crossing, 1991–98. Trustee and Hon. Treas., NSPCC, 1999–2008; Trustee Royal British Legion, 2009–. Chm. Govs, Abingdon Sch., 2013–. *Address:* 13 Woodthorpe Road, Putney, SW15 6UQ. *T:* (020) 8788 6383. *E:* email@adrianburn.com. *Club:* Roehampton.

BURN, Colin Richard; His Honour Judge Colin Burn; a Circuit Judge, since 2010; Senior Judge, Sovereign Base Areas Court Cyprus, since 2012; *b* Newcastle upon Tyne, 2 Sept. 1962; *s* of John Burn and Margaret Burn (*née* Smithson); *m* 1994, Susan, *d* of His Honour (Anthony) Nigel Fricker, *qv*; three *s* one *d*. *Educ:* Durham Johnston Sch.; University Coll London (LLB Hons). Called to the Bar, Middle Temple, 1985; pupil barrister, 1985–86; Commnd Officer, Army Legal Corps, 1986–90; Bde Legal Officer, 3 Cdo Bde, RM, 1990; in practice as a barrister, 32/30 Park Sq., Leeds, 1990–2001; Dep. Judge Advocate 1995–2001; Asst Judge Advocate Gen., 2001–10; Recorder, 2003–10; Magistrate, Standing Civilian Court (British Forces Germany), 2004–07. Judicial Mem., Parole Bd, 2010–13; Captain, RMP (TA), 1994–95. *Recreations:* trying to keep fit, food and wine, military history, playing guitar, planning and experiencing travel. *Address:* Bradford Crown Court, Exchange Square, Bradford BD1 1JA. *Club:* Army and Navy.

BURN, Sir John, Kt 2010; MD; FRCP, FRCPE, FRCOG, FRCPCH, FMedSci; Professor of Clinical Genetics, since 1991, and Head, Institute of Human Genetics, 2005–10, University of Newcastle upon Tyne; *b* 6 Feb. 1952; *s* of Harry and Margaret Burn; *m* 1972, Linda M Wilson; one *s* one *d*. *Educ:* Barnard Castle Grammar Sch.; Newcastle upon Tyne Univ (BMedSci 1973; MB BS 1976; MD 1990). FRCP 1989; FRCPCH 1996; FRCOG 1998; FRCPE 2001. Professional trng in medicine and paediatrics, Royal Victoria Infirmary Newcastle Gen. Hosp., Freeman Hosp., Newcastle, 1976–80; Sen. Registrar, Hosp. for Sick Children, Gt Ormond St, and Clinical Scientific Officer, MRC Genetics Unit, Inst. of Child Health, 1980–84; Consultant Clinical Geneticist, Royal Victoria Infirmary, Newcastle upon Tyne, 1984–91. Lead Clinician, NHS North East, 2009–13. Mem., Human Genetics Commn, 1989–2005; Chm., Innovation Cttee, UK Human Genomics Strategy Gp, 2010–12; Chm., Genetics Speciality Gp, 2008–, Sen. Investigator, 2011–, Nat. Inst. of Health Res; Chm., British Soc. for Genetic Medicine (formerly Human Genetics), 2011–13. CMO QuantuMDx Ltd. FMedSci 2000. *Publications:* over 350 peer-reviewed contribs in field of clinical genetics with particular interest in birth defects and hereditary cancers. *Recreations:* playing the drums, running, reading, golf. *Address:* 18 Sanderson Road, Jesmond, Newcastle upon Tyne NE2 2DS. *T:* (0191) 241 8611. *E:* john.burn@ncl.ac.uk.

BURN, His Honour Lindsay Stuart; a Circuit Judge, 2003–14; *b* 29 Aug. 1948; *m* 1975, Hon. Anne-Catherine, *d* of Baron Wilberforce, CMG, OBE, PC; one *s* two *d*. *Educ* Newcastle upon Tyne Univ. (LLB Hons). Called to the Bar, Middle Temple, 1972; barrister 1972–2003; Asst Recorder, 1995–99, Recorder, 1999–2003; Standing Counsel to DTI, SE Circuit, 1995–2003. *Recreations:* photography, historical novels.

BURN, Rear Adm. Richard Hardy, CB 1992; AFC 1969; Director General Aircraft (Navy), Ministry of Defence, 1990–92; *b* 26 May 1938; *s* of Margaret (*née* Hardy) and Douglas Burn; *m* 1967, Judith Sanderson (*née* Tigg); one *s* one *d*, and one step *s* one step *d*. *Educ* Berkhamsted; BRNC Dartmouth; RNEC Manadon. MIMechE. HMS Broadsword 1958; fighter pilot, 890 Naval Air Sqdn, HMS Ark Royal, 1961–62; test flying work (incl. 3 year exchange, US Navy), NDC Latimer, to 1975; develt of Sea Harrier, MoD (PE), 1975–78; Ops Officer, A&AEE, 1978–79; Air Eng. Officer, RNAS Yeovilton, 1980; Asst Dir Eng. (N) MoD, 1981–84; RCDS 1985; Dir, Aircraft Maint. and Repair, MoD (N), 1986–87; Dir Helicopter Projects, MoD (PE), and ADC, 1988–90. Chm., Thomas Heatherley Educn Trust, 2003–09. Mem., Soc. of Experimental Test Pilots. FRAeS 1984. Commendation, US Navy, 1974; Médaille d'Honneur, Soc. d'Encouragement au Progrès, 1989. *Recreations:* golf painting, sculpture.

BURNAND, Aisling Maria, MBE 2007; Director, DNA Coaching, 2013; Chief Executive Association of Medical Research Charities, since 2014; *b* London, 22 Dec. 1964; *d* of Paul Mullen and Maureen Mullen; *m* 1997, William Burnand; two *s*. *Educ:* Coll. for Distributive Trades, London (HND Business Studies 1985). Advertising Exec., Haymarket Publishing 1986; Press and PR Asst, British Safety Council, 1986–87; Public Relns Officer, Rhône-Poulenc Ltd, 1987–89; Internat. Media Relns Manager, Rhône-Poulenc SA, 1989–94

Business Gp Dir, Rowland Co., 1994–97; sabbatical, NY, 1997–98; Bioindustry Association: Public Affairs Dir, 1998–2001; Dep. Chief Exec., 2001–03; Chief Exec., 2003–09; Exec. Dir, Policy and Public Affairs, CRUK, 2009–11. Trustee, Campaign for Sci. and Engrg. Gov., St Joan of Arc Sch., 2008–. *Recreations:* theatre, ballet, opera, cinema, walking, family, art, school governor (primary). *T:* 07775 516760. *E:* a.wburnand@virginmedia.com.

BURNE, Dr Yvonne Ann, OBE 2008; JP; educational consultant; Head, City of London School for Girls, 1995–2007; *b* 29 Aug. 1947; *d* of Archibald Ford and Florence Louise Ford (*née* Knott); *m* 1968, Anthony Richard Burne; one *s* one *d*. *Educ:* Redland High Sch. for Girls, Bristol; Westfield Coll., Univ. of London (BA Hons; PhD). School teacher: Harrow Co. Grammar Sch. for Girls, 1971–74; Lowlands Sixth Form Coll., 1974–77; Hd, Mod. Langs and Careers Guidance, Northwood Coll., 1984–87; Headmistress, St Helen's Sch. for Girls, Northwood, 1987–95. Editor: Educnl Challenges Inc. (VA, USA), 1978–82; Mary Glasgow Pubns, 1983–84; Heinemann Educnl Books, 1984. Mem., Hillingdon FHSA, 1990–96. Lead Education Consultant: Thewlis Graham Associates, 2011–13; RSAcademics, 2013–. Governor: Berkhamsted Sch., 2005–; Brighton Univ., 2006–; Haberdashers' Aske's Boys' and Girls' Schs, 2011–. Patron, Tomorrow's Achievers (Trustee, 2007–); Trustee, 9/11 Project, 2010–. Master, Educators' Co., 2009–10. FRSA 1991. JP City of London, 2007. *Publications:* Tomorrow's News, 1979; The Circus Comes to Town, 1979; articles and children's stories. *Recreations:* theatre, entertaining friends, walking.

BURNELL, Dame (Susan) Jocelyn B.; *see* Bell Burnell.

BURNELL-NUGENT, Adm. Sir James (Michael), KCB 2004; CBE 1999; Commander-in-Chief Fleet, and NATO Maritime Component Commander Northwood, 2005–07; Vice-Admiral of the United Kingdom, 2005–07; company director, since 2008; *b* 20 Nov. 1949; *s* of late Comdr Anthony Frank Burnell-Nugent, DSC, RN and Gian Burnell-Nugent; *m* 1973, Henrietta Mary, (DL, MA, MB, BChir), *d* of Rt Rev. R. W. Woods, KCMG, KCVO; three *s* one *d*. *Educ:* Stowe; Corpus Christi Coll., Cambridge (MA Hons; Hon. Fellow, 2006). Joined RN, 1971; BRNC Dartmouth (Queen's Gold Medal); Submarines, 1973–86; Max Horton Prize, 1974; CO HMS Olympus, 1979–80; CO HMS Conqueror, 1984–86; Comdr, 1985; Captain, 1990; Captain, F2 and CO HMS Brilliant, (Bosnia), 1992–93; Cdre, 1994; on secondment to HM Treasury, 1996; Dep. FO Surface Flotilla, 1997; CO HMS Invincible, (Gulf, Kosovo), 1997–99; Rear Adm., 1999; ACNS, MoD, 1999–2001; Mem., Admiralty Bd, 1999–2001 and 2003–07; Dep. Coalition Maritime Comdr, (Op. Enduring Freedom, Afghanistan), 2001–02; Comdr UK Maritime Forces, and Comdr Anti Submarine Warfare Striking Force, 2001–02; Second Sea Lord and C-in-C Naval Home Comd, Mem. of Admiralty Bd, and Flag ADC to the Queen, 2003–05. Dir, Orchard Leadership Ltd, 2008–; Dep. Chm., Plymouth Marine Lab., 2012– (Trustee and Dir, 2008–; Chm., Develt Council, 2009–14). Internat. Advr, Shell Shipping, 2008–; Sen. Advr, Evercore Partners, 2008–; Special Advr, Oil Cos Internat. Marine Forum, 2008–; Strategic Advr and Chm., Adv. Bd, Risk Internat. 2012–; Leadership Develt Advr, Newton Europe, 2012–. Chm., Aerospace, Defence and Maritime (formerly Industry and Govt) Practice, Regester Larkin, 2013–. Non-exec. Dir, QinetiQ Gp plc, 2010– (Chm., Corporate Social Responsibility and Security Cttees, 2014–); Advr, Dabble Towelling Ltd, 2014–; Strategic Advr, Sonardyne, 2014–. Dir, St George's House, Windsor Castle, 2014–. Sen. Fellow, One Earth Future Foundn, 2012–. Pres., HMS Ganges Assoc., 2009–; Mem. Fundraising Cttee, Sea Cadet TS Royalist, 2013–. Trustee, Annual Nat. Service for Seafarers, 2014–. Ambassador for RN Submarine Mus., 2012–. Gov., Stowe, 2008–. Comp. Inst. of Leadership and Mgt, 2006. Freeman, City of London, 1999. High Sheriff, Devon, 2015–May 2016. Younger Brother, Trinity House, 2004. *Publications:* pamphlets incl. Leadership in the Office, Keeping an Eye on the Cost of Government; numerous articles in Naval Review and RUSI Jl. *Recreation:* living in the country. *Address:* c/o Naval Secretary, Leach Building, Whale Island, Portsmouth, Hants PO2 8BY. *Club:* Cychod Trefdraeth.

BURNER, (Edward) Alan; HM Diplomatic Service, retired; Ambassador to Senegal and, concurrently, to Guinea Bissau, Cape Verde and Mali, 2000–04; *b* 26 Sept. 1944; *s* of late Douglas Keith Burner and of Mary Burner; *m* 1969, Jane Georgine Du Port; one *s* two *d*. *Educ:* Uppingham Sch., Rutland; Emmanuel Coll., Cambridge (MA Hons Mod. Langs). Volunteer, Nigeria, VSO, 1966–67; joined HM Diplomatic Service, 1967: Sofia, 1970–72; Bonn, 1972–74; Bridgetown, 1974–78; N America Dept, FCO, 1979; Asst Private Sec. to Minister for Overseas Devlt, 1979–82; Dep. Head of Recruitment, FCO, 1982–84; Dep. Hd of Mission, Sofia, 1984–87; on loan to ODA, 1987–90; Hd, Med. Welfare Unit, FCO, 1990–92; Commercial Counsellor, then Dep. Hd of Mission, Lagos, 1992–95; Consul-Gen., Munich, 1995–99. *Recreations:* tennis, walking. *Address:* 12 Hillside Road, Sevenoaks, Kent TN13 3XJ. *T:* (01732) 453885.

BURNET, George Wardlaw, LVO 1981; JP; Lord-Lieutenant of Midlothian, 1992–2002; *b* 26 Dec. 1927; *s* of late Sheriff John Rudolph Wardlaw Burnet, KC and Lucy Margaret Ord Burnet (*née* Wallace); *m* 1951, Jane Elena Moncrieff, *d* of late Malcolm Moncrieff Stuart, CIE, OBE; two *s* one *d*. *Educ:* Edinburgh Acad.; Lincoln Coll., Oxford (BA); Edinburgh Univ. (LLB). Served Black Watch (RHR) TA, retired as Captain, 1957. WS 1954; Partner, Murray Beith and Murray, 1956–90. County Councillor, Midlothian, 1967–76. Church of Scotland: Elder, 1961–; Convener, Gen. Finance Cttee, 1980–83. Secretary: Scottish Building Contract Cttee, 1962–87; RIAS, 1964–87. Chairman: Life Assoc. of Scotland, 1985–93; Caledonian Res. Foundn, 1989–99. Captain, Royal Company of Archers, Queen's Body Guard for Scotland, 2004–. Hon. FRIAS 1980. DL 1975, JP 1991, Midlothian. KStJ. *Recreations:* country pursuits, architecture, gardening. *Address:* Rose Court, Inveresk, Midlothian EH21 7TD. *T:* (0131) 665 2689. *Club:* New (Edinburgh).

BURNETT, family name of **Baron Burnett**.

BURNETT, Baron *cr* 2006 (Life Peer), of Whitchurch in the County of Devon; **John Patrick Aubone Burnett;** Consultant, Stephens & Scown, since 2005; *b* 19 Sept. 1945; *s* of late Lt-Col Aubone Burnett, OBE and Joan (*née* Bolt); *m* 1971, Elizabeth Sherwood, *d* of Sir Arthur de la Mare, KCMG, KCVO; two *s* two *d*. *Educ:* Ampleforth Coll., Yorks; Britannia RNC, Dartmouth; Coll. of Law, London. Served RM, 1964–70: Troop Comdr, 42 Commando RM, Borneo, 1965–66; Troop Comdr and Co. 2nd in command, 40 Commando RM, FE and ME, 1967–69. Farmer, 1976–98. Admitted Solicitor, 1975; Partner, then Sen. Partner, Burd Pearse, Okehampton, 1976–97. Mem., Law Soc. Revenue Law Cttee, 1984–96. Contested (Lib Dem) Devon West and Torridge, 1987. MP (Lib Dem) Devon West and Torridge, 1997–2005. Lib Dem spokesman on legal affairs, 1997–2002; Lib Dem Shadow Attorney Gen., 2002–05. Mem. Council, Devon Cattle Breeders' Soc., 1985–97 (winner Nat. Herd competition, 1989). *Address:* Stephens & Scown, Curzon House, Southernhay West, Exeter EX1 1RS.

BURNETT, of Leys, Baronetcy of (unclaimed); *see under* Ramsay, Sir Alexander William Burnett, 7th Bt.

BURNETT, Prof. Alan Kenneth, MBE 2008; MD; FRCPGlas, FRCPE, FRCP, FRCPath, FMedSci; Professor of Haematology, Cardiff University (formerly University of Wales College of Medicine), 1992–2014; *b* 27 May 1946; *s* of George Binnie Burnett and Janet Maloch Burnett (*née* Henderson); *m* 1971, Alison Forrester Liddell; two *s*. *Educ:* Glasgow Acad.; Univ. of Glasgow (ChB; MD Hons 1988). FRCPGlas 1984; FRCPath 1986; FRCPE 1988; FRCP 1993. Res. Fellow, Univ. of Chicago, 1975–76; Consultant Haematologist, Glasgow Royal Infirmary, 1979–92; Clin. Dir of Service, University Hosp. of Wales, 1992–2007. Visiting Professor: Univ. of Miami, 1994; Northwestern Univ., Chicago, 1999; Univ. of Kuwait, 2000. Chairman: MRC Adult Leukaemia Wkg Party, 1990–; Nat. Cancer Res. Network Gp for Haematol Oncology, 2002–07; Mem., Med. Advisory Panel, Leukaemia Res. Fund, 1989–93. Pres., British Soc. of Haematol., 1998–99. FMedSci 2000. Ham Wasserman Award, Amer. Soc. of Hematology, 2012. *Publications:* contrib. more than 300 papers to medical literature predominantly on treatment and biol. of leukaemia. *Recreations:* golf, DIY. *Address:* Ty Mawr, Blackwaterfoot, Isle of Arran KA27 8EU.

BURNETT, Dr Andrew Michael, CBE 2012; FBA 2003; FSA; Deputy Director, British Museum, 2003–13; *b* 23 May 1952; *s* of Sir John (Harrison) Burnett and of E. Margaret Burnett, *er d* of Rev. Dr E. W. Bishop; *m* 1978, Susan Jennifer Allix; two *d*. *Educ:* Fettes Coll., Edinburgh; Balliol Coll., Oxford (BA, MA); Inst. of Archaeology, Univ. of London (PhD). Department of Coins and Medals, British Museum: Res. Assistant, 1974–79; Asst Keeper, 1979–90; Dep. Keeper, 1990–92; Keeper, 1992–2003. Secretary: RNS, 1983–90 (Vice-Pres., 1999–2004; Hon. Vice-Pres., 2009; Pres., 2013–); Internat. Numismatic Commn, 1992–97 (Pres., 1997–2003). Pres., Roman Soc., 2008–12, Vice-Pres., 2012–. Trustee, Royal Armouries, 2014–. Hon. Prof., Inst. of Archaeology, UCL, 2013–. Chm., Adv. Cttee, Inst. of Classical Studies, Univ. of London, 2014–. Corresponding Member: Amer. Numismatic Soc., 1982; German Archaeol. Inst., 2001. FSA 1982. Norwegian Numismatic Soc. Medal, 1991; Silver Medal, RNS, 1993; Prix Allier de Hauteroche, Acad. des Inscriptions et Belles-Lettres, 1999; Meshorer Prize, Israel Mus., 2002; Jeton de Vermeil, Soc. Française de Numismatique, 2004; Huntington Medal, Amer. Numismatic Soc., 2008. *Publications:* Coinage in the Roman World, 1987; Interpreting the Past: Coins, 1991; Roman Provincial Coinage, Vol. 1, 1992, Vol. 2, 1999, Vol. 3, 2015; Behind the Scenes at the British Museum, 2001; contrib. Numismatic Chronicle, Schweizerische Numismatisches Rundschau, Quaderni Ticinesi, Jl Roman Studies, Britannia, etc. *Address:* 19 Almorah Road, N1 3ER.

BURNETT, Sir Charles (David), 4th Bt *cr* 1913, of Selborne House, in the Borough of Croydon; *b* 18 May 1951; *er s* of Sir David Humphery Burnett, 3rd Bt, MBE, TD and Geraldine Elizabeth Mortimer, *d* of Sir Godfrey Fisher, KCMG; *S* father, 2002; *m* 1st, 1989, Victoria Joan Simpson (marr. diss. 1997); one *d*; 2nd, 1998, Kay Rosemary Naylor; one *d*. *Educ:* Harrow; Lincoln Coll., Oxford. *Heir:* *b* John Godfrey Burnett, *b* 29 March 1954.

BURNETT, Charles John; Ross Herald, 1988–2010, Ross Herald Extraordinary, since 2011 (Dingwall Pursuivant, 1983); *b* 6 Nov. 1940; *s* of Charles Alexander Urquhart Burnett and Agnes Watt; *m* 1967, Aileen Elizabeth McIntyre; two *s* one *d*. *Educ:* Fraserburgh Academy; Gray's Sch. of Art, Aberdeen (DA); Aberdeen Coll. of Education (Teaching Cert.); MLitt Edinburgh 1992. AMA. House of Fraser, 1963–64; COI, 1964–68; Asst Dir, Letchworth Mus., 1968–71; Head of Design, Nat. Mus. of Antiquities of Scotland, 1971–85; Curator of Fine Art, Scottish United Services Mus., Edinburgh Castle, 1985–96; Chamberlain, Duff House Country Gall., Banff, 1997–2004. Heraldic Adviser: Girl Guide Assoc. in Scotland, 1978–2010; NADFAS Church Recorders, Scotland, 2000–; Chm., Banff Preservation and Heritage Soc., 2002–10. Vice-Patron, Geneal. Soc. of Queensland, 1986–2010; Vice-Pres., Soc. of Antiquaries of Scotland, 1992–95; Trustee, St Andrews Fund for Scots Heraldry, 2001–; Pres., Heraldry Soc. of Scotland, 2003–15. Pres., Internat. Congress of Geneal and Heraldic Scis, St Andrews, 2006. Trustee, Bield Retirement Housing Trust, 1992–96. Chm., Pitsligo Castle Trust, 2010–14. Hon. Pres., Moray Burial Ground Res. Gp, 2012–. Convenor, Companions of the Order of Malta, 1991–94. KStJ 1991; Librarian, Priory of Order of St John in Scotland, 1987–99. Hon. Citizen, Oklahoma, 1989. Kt, Order of SS Maurice and Lazarus, 1999; Kt, Order of Francis I, 2002. *Publications:* Scotland's Heraldic Heritage, 1997; The Order of St John in Scotland, 1997; Thistle Stall Plates, 2001; numerous articles on Scottish heraldry. *Recreations:* reading, visiting places of historical interest. *Address:* Seaview House, Portsoy, Banffshire AB45 2RS. *T:* (01261) 843378.

BURNETT, Prof. Charles Stuart Freeman, PhD; FBA 1998; Professor of the History of Islamic Influences in Europe, since 1999, and Co-director, Centre for the History of Arabic Studies in Europe, since 2012, Warburg Institute, University of London; *b* 26 Sept. 1951; *m* 1st, 1985, Mitsuru Kamachi (marr. diss. 1991); 2nd, 1995, Tamae Nakamura; two *s*. *Educ:* Manchester Grammar Sch.; St John's Coll., Cambridge (BA 1972; PhD 1976). LGSM 1980. Jun. Res. Fellow, St John's Coll., Cambridge, 1975–79; Sen. Res. Fellow, 1979–82, Lectr, 1985–99, Warburg Inst., Univ. of London; Leverhulme Res. Fellow, Dept of History, Univ. of Sheffield, 1982–84, 1985; Mem., Inst. for Advanced Study, Princeton, 1984–85. Dist. Vis. Prof., Univ. of Calif, Berkeley, 2003; Vis. Prof., Univ. of Munich, 2009. Brauer Fellow, Univ. of Chicago, 2008. Corresp. Fellow, Medieval Acad. of America. Mem., Internat. Acad. of History of Science. *Publications:* (with Masahiro Takenaka) Jesuit Plays on Japan and English Recusancy, 1995; Magic and Divination in the Middle Ages: texts and techniques in the Islamic and Christian worlds, 1996; The Introduction of Arabic Learning into England, 1997; Arabic into Latin in the Middle Ages: the translators and their intellectual and social context, 2009; Numerals and Arithmetic in the Middle Ages, 2010; several edns of Latin and Arabic texts; over 100 articles in learned jls. *Recreations:* playing music (viola, piano, viola da gamba, shakuhachi), hill walking, religious activities (Iona community, Japanese Buddhist and Shinto traditions). *Address:* Warburg Institute, Woburn Square, WC1H 0AB. *T:* (020) 7862 8920.

BURNETT, Rt Hon. Sir Ian Duncan, Kt 2008; PC 2014; **Rt Hon. Lord Justice Burnett;** a Lord Justice of Appeal, since 2014; *b* 28 Feb. 1958; *yr s* of late David John Burnett and Maureen Burnett (*née* O'Brien); *m* 1991, Caroline Ruth Monks; one *s* one *d*. *Educ:* St John's Coll., Southsea; Pembroke Coll., Oxford (MA; Hon. Fellow, 2008). Called to the Bar, Middle Temple, 1980, Bencher, 2001; in practice as barrister, Temple Gdn Chambers, 1982–2008 (Hd of Chambers, 2003–08); Jun. Crown Counsel, Common Law, 1992–98; QC 1998; Asst Recorder, 1998–2000; Recorder, 2000–08; a Dep. High Court Judge, 2008; a Judge of the High Court of Justice, QBD, 2008–14; Presiding Judge, Western Circuit, 2011–14. Dep. Chm., Security Vetting Appeals Panel, 2009–14. *Recreations:* history, music, silver, wine. *Address:* Royal Courts of Justice, Strand, WC2A 2LL.

BURNETT, Sir Keith, Kt 2013; CBE 2004; DPhil; FRS 2001; FInstP; Vice-Chancellor, University of Sheffield, since 2007; *b* 30 Sept. 1953; *s* of Royston Ifor Burnett and Jean Marion Burnett; *m* 1975, Elizabeth Anne Mustoe; one *s* one *d*. *Educ:* Brynteg Comprehensive Sch.; Jesus Coll., Oxford (BA 1975; DPhil 1979; Hon. Fellow, 2007). FInstP 1996. Asst Prof., Univ. of Colorado, 1980–84; Fellow, Jt Inst. for Lab. Astrophysics, Colorado Univ. and Nat. Inst. of Standards and Technol., 1981–84; Lectr in Physics, Imperial Coll., London, 1984–88; Oxford University: Lectr in Physics, 1988–96; Prof., 1996–2007; Hd of Atomic and Laser Physics, 1999–2002; Chm. of Physics, 2002–05; Hd of Math., Physical and Life Scis Div., 2005–07; Fellow, St John's Coll., Oxford, 1988–2007, now Hon. Fellow. Non-exec. Dir, UKAEA, 2010–. Member: EPSRC, 1999–2004; CCLRC, 2005–07; STFC, 2007–11; Council for Sci. and Technol., 2011–14; Bd, HEFCE, 2015–. Chair, UCEA, 2009–11. Fellow: APS, 1996; Optical Soc. of America, 1996. Wolfson Merit Award, Royal Soc., 2003. *Publications:* articles in learned jls, incl. Physical Review, Jl Physics B. *Recreations:* reading, music, Chinese. *Address:* University of Sheffield, Firth Court, Western Bank, Sheffield S10 2TN.

BURNETT, Sir Walter (John), Kt 1988; President, Royal National Agricultural and Industrial Association of Queensland, 1983–97; *b* 15 Jan. 1921; *s* of William Henry and Minna Anna Burnett; *m* 1945, Mabel Nestor Dalton (*d* 1991); two *d*; *m* 1996, Judith Lucy Masel. *Educ:* Maleny Primary School; Church of England Grammar School; Pharmacy College, Queensland. Conducted own pharmacy business in Maleny for 32 years. Dir, Sunshine Coast Hosps Bd, 1958. Past Chm., Maleny Br., Qld Ambulance Transport Bde; Vice Patron, Schizophrenia Fellowship of S Qld, 1987. Mem., Electoral Re-distribution Commn, Brisbane

City Council, 1984–85. Grand Master, United Grand Lodge of Qld, 1983–86. Past Pres., Maroochy Dist Bowls Assoc. *Recreation:* lawn bowls. *Address:* 62 Zillman Road, Clayfield, Qld 4011, Australia. *T:* (7) 32686529.

BURNEY, Sir Nigel (Dennistoun), 4th Bt *cr* 1921, of Preston House, Preston Candover, Southampton; *b* 6 Sept. 1959; *er s* of Sir Cecil Burney, 3rd Bt and Hazel Marguerite de Hamel (*née* Coleman); *S* father, 2002; *m* 1992, Lucy Brooks; two *s* two *d*. *Educ:* Eton; Trinity Coll., Cambridge. *Recreations:* tennis, music, ski-ing. *Heir: s* Max Dennistoun Burney, *b* 15 Sept. 1994. *E:* nigel@nigelburney.com. *Clubs:* White's, Annabel's.

BURNHAM, 7th Baron *cr* 1903, of Hall Barn, Beaconsfield, Bucks; **Harry Frederick Alan Lawson;** Bt 1892; Chief Executive Officer, Ashcourt Rowan Asset Management, since 2013; *b* 22 Feb. 1968; *s* of 6th Baron Burnham and of Lady Burnham (*née* Hilary Margaret Hunter); *S* father, 2005. *Educ:* Summer Fields Sch., Oxford; Eton Coll. Associated Newspapers, 1988–95; Williams de Broë plc, 1996–2000; Dir, Investment Mgt, Brewin Dolphin Securities Ltd, 2000–13. Liveryman, Gunmakers' Co. *Recreations:* shooting, horse and dog racing, tobogganing, oenology, golf. *Heir:* none. *Address:* Woodlands Farm, Beaconsfield, Bucks HP9 2SF. *Clubs:* Turf, Pratt's, City Livery; St Moritz Tobogganing; Burnham Beeches Golf.

BURNHAM, Rt Rev. Mgr Andrew; Bishop Suffragan of Ebbsfleet, 2000–10; Provincial Episcopal Visitor, Province of Canterbury, 2000–10; *b* 19 March 1948; *s* of David Burnham and Eileen Burnham (*née* Franks); *m* 1984, Cathy Ross; one *s* one *d*. *Educ:* New Coll., Oxford (BA 1969, 1971; MA 1973); Westminster Coll., Oxford (CertEd 1972); St Stephen's House, Oxford. ARCO(CHM). Ordained deacon, 1983, priest, 1984; Hon. Curate, Clifton, Southwell Dio., 1983–85; Curate, Beeston, 1985–87; Vicar, Carrington, 1987–94; Vice-Principal, St Stephen's House, Oxford, 1995–2000. Assistant Bishop: Dio. of Bath and Wells, 2001–10; Dio. of Oxford, 2001–10; Dio. of Exeter, 2001–10; Dio. of Lichfield, 2001–10; Dio. of Worcester, 2008–10. Ordained RC deacon and priest, 2011; Prelate of Honour, 2011. *Publications:* A Manual of Anglo-Catholic Devotion, 2000, pocket edn, 2004; Heaven and Earth in Little Space: the re-enchantment of liturgy, 2010; Customary of Our Lady of Walsingham, 2012. *Recreations:* liturgy, music. *Address:* St Mary's Catholic Church, St Mary's Road, East Hendred, Wantage OX12 8LF. *E:* andrew.burnham@ordinariate.org.uk.

BURNHAM, Rt Hon. Andrew (Murray); PC 2007; MP (Lab) Leigh, since 2001; *b* Liverpool, 7 Jan. 1970; *s* of Kenneth Roy Burnham and Eileen Mary (*née* Murray); *m* 2000, Marie-France van Heel; one *s* two *d*. *Educ:* St Aelred's RC High Sch., Merseyside; Fitzwilliam Coll., Cambridge (MA Hons Eng.). Researcher to Tessa Jowell, MP, and Labour Health Team, 1994–97; Parly Officer, NHS Confedn, 1997; Advr to Football Task Force, 1997–98; Special Advr to Rt Hon. Chris Smith, MP, DCMS, 1998–2001. PPS to Sec. of State for Home Dept, 2003–05; Parly Under-Sec. of State, Home Office, 2005–06; Minister of State, DoH, 2006–07; Chief Sec. to HM Treasury, 2007–08; Sec. of State for Culture, Media and Sport, 2008–09, for Health, 2009–10; Shadow Sec. of State for Health, 2010, for Educn and Election Coordinator, 2010–11, for Health, 2011–15; Shadow Home Sec., 2015–. Mem., Health Select Cttee, 2001–03. Chm., Supporters Direct, 2002–05. *Recreations:* football (Everton FC), Rugby league (Leigh RLC), cricket. *Address:* House of Commons, SW1A 0AA. *T:* (020) 7219 8250; (constituency office) 10 Market Street, Leigh WN7 1DS. *T:* (01942) 682353. *Clubs:* Lowton, Hindley, Wigan Road and Leigh Labour; Leigh Catholic.

BURNHAM, Rev. Anthony Gerald; Moderator, Free Churches Group (formerly Free Churches' Council), and a President, Churches Together in England, 1999–2003; *b* 2 March 1936; *s* of Selwyn and Sarah Burnham; *m* 1961, Valerie Florence Cleaver; one *s* two *d*. *Educ:* Silcoates Sch.; Manchester Univ. (BA Admin); Northern Coll., Manchester. Minister: Brownhill Congregational Church, Blackburn, 1961–66; Poulton-le-Fylde and Hambleton Congregational Churches, 1966–69; Lectr, Northern Coll., Manchester, 1969–77; Minister, SW Manchester United Reformed Churches, 1973–81; Moderator, NW Synod, URC, 1981–92; Gen. Sec., URC, 1992–2001. Chm. of Corps, Council for World Mission, 1995–99. Religious broadcasting for radio and TV. *Publications:* In The Quietness, 1981; Say One For Me, 1990. *Recreations:* theatre, jazz. *Address:* 30 Sandhurst Road, Didsbury, Manchester M20 5LR.

BURNHAM, Eleanor; Member (Lib Dem) Wales North, National Assembly for Wales, March 2001–2011; *b* 17 April 1951; one *s* one *d*. *Educ:* Radbrook Coll., Shrewsbury; Yale Coll., Wrexham; Manchester Metropolitan Univ. (BSc). Worked in social services, healthcare and arts mgt; teacher; lectr in complementary therapy and complementary health practitioner. Formerly Mem., Mental Health Tribunal. National Assembly for Wales: Lib Dem spokesman for post 16 educn, 2001, for envmt, planning and transport, 2001–03, for culture, sport and Welsh lang., 2003–11, for children and young people, 2007–11; Lib Dem Shadow Minister for culture, communities and equality, 2007–11; Older Persons' Champion, 2007–11. Contested: (Lib Dem) Alyn and Deeside, 1997; (Lib Dem) Delyn, 1999, Clwyd W, 2003, Wales N, 2011, Nat. Assembly for Wales. JP Wrexham, 1992–2001.

BURNINGHAM, John Mackintosh; free-lance author-designer; *b* 27 April 1936; *s* of Charles Burningham and Jessie Mackintosh; *m* 1964, Helen Gillian Oxenbury, *qv*; one *s* two *d*. *Educ:* Summerhill School, Leiston, Suffolk; Central School of Art, Holborn, 1956–59 (Diploma). Now free-lance: illustration, poster design, exhibition, animated film puppets, and writing for children. Wall friezes: Birdland, Lionland, Storyland, 1966; Jungleland, Wonderland, 1968; Around the World, 1972. Retrospective exhibn, An Illustrated Journey, Fleming Collection, 2011. *Publications:* Borka, 1963 (Kate Greenaway Medal, 1963); John Burningham's ABC, 1964; Trubloff, 1964; Humbert, 1965; Cannonball Simp, 1966 (filmed, 1967); Harquin, 1967; The Extraordinary Tug-of-War, 1968; Seasons, 1969; Mr Gumpy's Outing, 1970 (Kate Greenaway Medal, 1971); Around the World in Eighty Days, 1972; Mr Gumpy's Motor Car, 1973; "Little Books" series: The Baby, The Rabbit, The School, The Snow, 1974; The Blanket, The Cupboard, The Dog, The Friend, 1975; The Adventures of Humbert, Simp and Harquin, 1976; Come Away from the Water, Shirley, 1977; Time to Get Out of the Bath, Shirley, 1978; Would You Rather, 1978; The Shopping Basket, 1980; Avocado Baby, 1982; John Burningham's Number Play Series, 1983; First Words/Granpa, 1984 (filmed, 1989); Play and Learn Books: abc, 123, Opposites, Colours, 1985; Where's Julius, 1986; John Patrick Norman McHennessy—the Boy who is Always Late, 1987; Rhymetime: A Good Job, The Car Ride, 1988, Animal Chatter, A Grand Band, 1989; Oi! Get off our Train, 1989; Aldo, 1991; England, 1992; Harvey Slumfenburger's Christmas Present, 1993 (jt winner, W. H. Smith Award, 1994); Courtney, 1994; Cloudland, 1996; France, 1998; Whadayamean, 1999; Husherbye, 2000; The Magic Bed, 2003; It's a Secret, 2009; John Burningham (memoir), 2009; Picnic, 2013; The Way to the Zoo, 2014; *illustrated:* Chitty Chitty Bang Bang, 1964; The Wind in the Willows, 1983; (also compiled): The Time of Your Life, 2002; When We Were Young, 2004. *Address:* c/o Jonathan Cape Ltd, 20 Vauxhall Bridge Road, SW1V 2FA.

BURNLEY, Bishop Suffragan of, since 2015; **Rt Rev. Philip John North;** *b* London, 2 Dec. 1966; *s* of John and Christine North. *Educ:* Latymer Sch., Edmonton; Univ. of York (BA Hons Hist. 1988); St Stephen's House, Oxford (MA Theol. 2001). Ordained deacon, 1992, priest, 1993; Asst Curate, St Mary and St Peter, Sunderland, 1992–96; Vicar, Holy Trinity, Hartlepool, 1996–2002; Area Dean of Hartlepool, 2000–02; Priest Administrator, Shrine of Our Lady of Walsingham, 2002–08; Team Rector, Parish of Old St Pancras, 2008–15. *Publications:* Sacred Space, 2007. *Recreations:* fell walking, road cycling. *Address:* Dean House, 449 Padiham Road, Burnley BB12 6TE. *T:* (01282) 479300. *E:* bishop.burnley@blackburn.anglican.org.

BURNLEY, Elizabeth, (Liz), CBE 2010; *b* 14 March 1959; *d* of Joan and Jack Noden; *m* 2000, Roger Burnley. *Educ:* Univ. of Nottingham (BSc Hons Psychol.; MSc Occupational Psychol.); Open Univ. (MBA 2009). Human Resources Manager: British Rail Engrg Ltd, 1982–87; RFS Engrg Ltd, 1987–93; occupational psychologist: Barnes Kavelle Ltd, 1994–98; Boots Co. plc, 1998–2001; HR Manager, Huntsman, 2001–07; Chief Guide, Girlguiding UK, 2006–10. Programme Dir, Common Purpose, 2007–. Non-exec. Dir, NHS, 2010–. Lay Mem., Fitness to Practise Cttee, Gen. Pharmaceutical Council, 2011–; Chair of panels, Conduct and Competence Cttee, NMC, 2013–. Trustee, RVS (formerly WRVS), 2011–. DL S Yorks, 2011–14. *Recreations:* girlguiding, hill-walking, interesting textile crafts.

BURNS, family name of **Baron Burns**.

BURNS, Baron *cr* 1998 (Life Peer), of Pitshanger in the London Borough of Ealing; **Terence Burns,** GCB 1995; Kt 1983; Chairman, Channel 4 Television, 2010–Jan. 2016; *b* 13 March 1944; *s* of Patrick Owen and Doris Burns; *m* 1969, Anne Elizabeth Powell; one *s* two *d*. *Educ:* Houghton-le-Spring Grammar Sch.; Univ. of Manchester (BAEcon Hons). London Business School: research posts, 1965–70; Lecturer in Economics, 1970–74; Sen. Lectr in Economics, 1974–79; Prof. of Economics, 1979; Director, LBS Centre for Economic Forecasting, 1976–79, Fellow, 1989; Chief Econ. Advr to the Treasury and Hd of Govt Econ. Service, 1980–91; Perm. Sec., HM Treasury, 1991–98. Member, HM Treasury Academic Panel, 1976–79. Chm., Financial Services and Mkts Jt Cttee, 1999; non-exec. Mem., Office for Budget Responsibility, 2011–. Chm., Cttee of Inquiry into Hunting with Dogs, 2000; Chairman: Nat. Lottery Commn, 2000–01 Commn on Freedom of Information, 2015–. Chairman: Abbey (formerly Abbey National) plc, 2002–10; Santander UK plc, 2010–15; Dep. Chm. and Chm.-designate, 2005–06, Chm., 2006–08, Marks & Spencer; non-executive Director: Legal & General Group plc, 1999–2001; Pearson plc, 1999–2010; British Land Co. plc, 2000–05; Glas Cymru Cyfyngedig, 2000–10; Banco Santander Central Hispano SA, 2004–13. Pres., NIESR, 2003–11. Pres., Soc. of Business Economists, 1999–2012 (Vice-Pres., 1985–99); Vice-Pres., REconS, 1992–. CCMI (CIMgt 1992). Bd Mem., Manchester Business Sch., 1992–98. Dir, Queens Park Rangers FC, 1996–2000. Vice-Pres., Royal Acad. of Music, 1998–2014 (former Chm. Governing Body). Trustee, Monteverdi Choir and Orch., 1998–2001 (Chm. Trustees, 2001–07); Chm., Mid-Wales Music Trust (formerly Cambrian Music Trust), 2010–. Hon. degrees: Manchester Univ.; Sunderland Univ.; Durham Univ.; Sheffield Univ.; Cardiff Univ.; Cardiff Metropolitan Univ. *Publications:* various articles in economic jls. *Recreations:* music, golf. *Club:* Reform.

BURNS, Alison Sarah; Global Client Services Director, New York, JWT, since 2009; *b* 26 April 1963; *d* of Roy Butler and Judith Cornwell; *m* 1996, Anthony John Burns; one *d*. *Educ:* Univ. of York (BA Hons 1984). Account Management: Fletcher Shelton Delaney, 1984–86; Boase Massimi Pollitt, 1986–89; Bartle Bogle Hegarty, 1989–92; Young and Rubicam, 1992–93; Global Vice Pres., Mktg, PepsiCo, 1993–96; CEO, Kendall Tarrant, 1996–98; Pres., Fallon McElligott, 1998–2003; CEO, JWT London, 2006–09. *Recreations:* sport, interior design, travel, good food and wine. *Address:* JWT, 466 Lexington Avenue, New York, NY 10017–3176, USA. *E:* alison.burns@jwt.com.

BURNS, Prof. Alistair Stanyer, CBE 2015; MD; FRCP, FRCPsych; Professor of Old Age Psychiatry, and Hon. Consultant Psychiatrist, University of Manchester, since 1992; National Clinical Director for Dementia, since 2010; *b* 4 July 1958; *s* of Richard and Janet Burns; *m* 1986, Alison Wise; two *d*. *Educ:* Hutchesons' Boys' Grammar Sch., Glasgow; Univ. of Glasgow (MB ChB 1980; MD Hons 1991; DHMSA 1984; MPhil London 1990). FRCPGlas 1993; FRCPsych 1996. Registrar in Psychiatry, Maudsley Hosp., 1983–86; Institute of Psychiatry, London: res. worker/Sen. Registrar, 1986–91; Sen. Lectr, 1991–92. *Publications:* Alzheimer's Disease, 1992; Ageing and Dementia, 1993; Dementia, 1994, 2nd edn 2001; Rating Scales in Old Age Psychiatry, 2000; Alzheimer's Disease Explained, 2005; Severe Dementia, 2005; Geriatric Medicine for Old Age Psychiatrists, 2005; Standards of Care in Dementia, 2005; over 300 contribs to med. and scientific jls. *Recreations:* estate management, walking, cars, writing. *Address:* University of Manchester, Core Technology Facility, 46 Grafton Street, Manchester M13 9NT. *T:* (0161) 306 7942. *E:* Alistair.Burns@manchester.ac.uk.

BURNS, Sir Andrew; *see* Burns, Sir R. A.

BURNS, Andrew Philip; QC 2015; a Recorder, since 2009; *b* Bromsgrove, 8 April 1971; *s* of Christopher Burns and Lynne Burns; *m* 1995, Ruth Farries; two *s*. *Educ:* Dover Grammar Sch. for Boys; Downing Coll., Cambridge (BA Law 1992; MA). Called to the Bar, Middle Temple, 1993; in practice as barrister, specialising in commercial and employment law; Advocate, DIFC Courts, Dubai, 2011–. Mem., Professional Conduct Cttee, Bar Standards Bd, 2007–13. Churchwarden, St Andrew's, Oxshott, 2006–10. *Publications:* (with Colin Edelman) The Law of Reinsurance, 2005, 2nd edn 2013; Discrimination Law, 2012; (with Sir David Bean) Injunctions, 11th edn 2012. *Recreations:* Scout leader, water sports, music, opera, Doctor Who, Scotch malt whisky. *Address:* Devereux Chambers, Queen Elizabeth Building, Temple, EC4Y 9BS. *T:* (020) 7353 7534. *E:* burns@devchambers.co.uk.

BURNS, Conor; MP (C) Bournemouth West, since 2010; *b* Belfast, 24 Sept. 1972; *s* of Thomas Burns and Kathleen Burns (*née* Kennedy). *Educ:* St Columba's Coll., St Albans; Southampton Univ. (BA Hons Modern Hist. and Politics 1994). Co. Sec., De Havilland Global Knowledge Distribution plc, 1998–2003; Regl Sales Manager, Zurich Advice Network, 2003–04; self-employed, 2004–08; Associate Dir, PLMR, 2008–10. Mem. (C) Southampton CC, 1999–2002. Contested (C) Eastleigh, 2001, 2005. PPS to Minister of State in NI Office, 2010–11, to Sec. of State for NI, 2011–12. Member: Educn Select Cttee, 2010; Culture, Media and Sport Select Cttee, 2012–15. *Recreations:* swimming, cooking, watching snooker, collecting political biography. *Address:* House of Commons, SW1A 0AA. *T:* (020) 7219 2071. *E:* conor.burns.mp@parliament.uk, cb@conorburns.com. *Clubs:* Southern Parishes Conservative (Life Mem.) (Southampton); Westbourne Conservative, Kinson Conservative (Bournemouth).

BURNS, Elizabeth Kerr, CMG 2005; OBE 1995; President and Chief Executive, International Association for Volunteer Effort, 2001–07; *b* 6 Jan. 1939; *d* of Thomas Thomson and Morag Thomson (*née* Cunningham); *m* 1964, William Burns (*d* 2000); two *s* one *d*. *Educ:* Edinburgh Univ. (MA Hons; DipEd); Moray House Coll. (Cert. Chapter V). Teacher of modern langs, 1962–67; Develt Officer, SCVO, 1981–83; Dir, Volunteer Develt Scotland, 1983–2001. Active in Scottish Playgps' Assoc., 1970–81 (Nat. Chair, 1978–80; Pres., 1986–90). Mem., Govt Strategy Gps, 1994–95, 1999–2000 and 2000–01. Chair, Historic Envmt Adv. Council for Scotland, 2003–09. Board Member: Scottish Community Educn Council, 1998–2000; Learning & Teaching Scotland, 2000–02. Pres., Eur. Volunteer Centre, 1998–2000. Member: UN Dept of Public Information liaison cttee for voluntary sector, 2007–10; High-level Adv. Gp for UN Report on volunteering in the world, 2011. *Publications:* contrib. papers to specialist and res. jls in field of volunteering. *Recreations:* reading, reading, reading.

BURNS, Gerard, MBE 1988; Pro-Chancellor, 2001–10, and Chairman of Council, 2002–10, University of Ulster; *b* 15 Nov. 1934; *s* of Bernard and Sarah Ellen Burns; *m* 1962, Moyra Connolly; three *s* two *d*. *Educ:* St Mary's Christian Brothers Grammar Sch.; Queen's Univ. Belfast. Divl Inspector, Trading Standards, NI, 1954–68; Lectr in Business Studies, Armagh Coll. of Further and Higher Educn, 1968–76; Chief Exec., Fermanagh DC, 1976–96; Assembly Ombudsman for NI and Comr for Complaints, 1995–2000. Chm., Review Body on Post Primary Educn, NI, 2000–02. Dir, Irish Times Ltd, 1997–2007; Gov., Irish Times

Trust Ltd, 1997–2007. Member: EOC, NI, 1979–85; Historic Bldgs Council, 1988–91; Regl Council, Nat. Trust, 1989–94; Solicitors' Disciplinary Tribunal, NI, 1989–2009; Local Govt Staff Commn, 1990–95; Standing Adv. Commn on Human Rights, 1996–2000; NI Cttee, Heritage Lottery Fund, 2009–. Mem., NI Tourist Bd, 1992–96. Chm., Ind. Appts Commn, Irish FA, 2008–11. Dir, Fermanagh Training Ltd, 1990–2010. Chm., Soc. of Local Authority Chief Execs (NI), 1990–92. Chairman: Fermanagh Univ. Foundn, 1998–2005; Fermanagh-Univ. Partnership Bd, 2001–05. Mem., Clogher and Kilmore Diocesan Cttee for Catholic Maintained Schools, 1987–95. Trustee, Spirit of Enniskillen Trust, 1988–2002 (Vice-Pres., 2002–12); Chm., Enniskillen Civic Trust, 1988–. Patron: Marie Curie Nursing Gp, Co. Fermanagh, 1998–2007; Fermanagh Co. Museum, 1999–. DUniv QUB, 1996; Hon. LLD Ulster, 2009. *Recreations:* walking, swimming, the arts.

BURNS, Sir Henry James Gerard, Kt 2011; FRCS, FRCP, FFPH; Professor of Global Public Health, University of Strathclyde, since 2014; *b* 25 Jan. 1951; *s* of Henry Burns and Mary (*née* Boyle); *m* 1983, Agnes Capaldi; two *s* four *d*. *Educ:* St Aloysius Coll., Glasgow; Glasgow Univ. (MB, ChB). FRCS 1979; MPH 1990; MFPHM 1993, FFPH (FFPHM 2005); FRCP 2000. Glasgow University: Lectr in Surgery, 1975–83; Sen. Lectr, 1983–89; Dir of Public Health, Gtr Glasgow Health, then NHS, Bd, 1994–2005; CMO, Scottish Govt (formerly Exec.) Health Directorate, 2005–14. Mem., MRC, 2007–09. *Recreations:* cycling, running.

BURNS, Ian Morgan, CB 1990; Director-General, Policy (formerly Director of Policy), Lord Chancellor's Department, 1995–99; *b* 3 June 1939; *s* of late Donald George Burns and Margaret Brenda Burns; *m* 1965, Susan Rebecca (*née* Wheeler); two *d*. *Educ:* Bootham, York. LLB, LLM London. HM Forces, 1957–59. Examiner, Estate Duty Office, 1960; Asst Principal, 1965, Principal, 1969, Home Office; Principal, 1972, Asst Sec., 1974, NI Office; Asst Sec., Home Office, 1977; Under Sec., NI Office, 1979–84; Under Sec. (Finance), 1985, and Gen. Manager, Disablement Services, 1986, DHSS; Deputy Under Secretary of State: NI Office, 1987–90; Police Dept, Home Office, 1990–95. FRSA 1993. *Recreations:* travelling, theatre, garden. *Club:* Athenæum.

BURNS, James Andrew; Senior Partner, Clyde & Co. LLP, since 2013; *b* Merton, London, 5 Oct. 1967; *s* of Michael Lowrie Burns and Mary Susan Burns (*née* Miller); *m* 2009, Catherine Bly; two *s* one *d*. *Educ:* Beverley Boys Sch., Surrey; Kent Univ. (BA Hons Law). Admitted as solicitor, 1992. With Clyde & Co., 1989–; trainee solicitor, 1989; Partner, 1998–. Freeman, City of London, 2014. *Recreations:* all types of sport, theatre. *Address:* Clyde & Co. LLP, St Botolph Building, 138 Houndsditch, EC3A 7AR. *T:* (020) 7876 5000, *Fax:* (020) 7876 5111. *E:* james.burns@clydeco.com.

BURNS, Julian Delisle; company director; a founder and Director, All3Media, 2003–14 (Chief Operating Officer, 2003–11); *b* 18 Sept. 1949; *s* of Benedict Delisle Burns, FRS and of Angela Hughesdon (*née* Ricardo); *m* 1976, Cheryl Ann Matthews; one *s* one *d*. *Educ:* Betteshanger Prep. Sch., Kent; Haberdashers' Aske's Sch., Elstree. Manager, Mendel's Garage, Hampstead, 1968–71; musician, various musical groups, 1972–75; Granada Television Ltd, 1976–2004: Prodn Manager, Regl Progs, 1976–80; Manager, Prog. Services, 1980–86; Hd, Business Affairs, 1986–90; Dir, Business and Legal Affairs, 1990–94; Jt Man. Dir, 1994–96; Jt Man. Dir, Granada Production, 1996–2000; Man. Dir, Ops, Granada plc, 2000–02. Dir, Royal Exchange Theatre, Manchester, 1995–2003. Member: Adv. Cttee on Film Finance, DNH, 1996–2001; Adv. Cttee on TV Production, DCMS, 1999–2001; Bd, 2002 Commonwealth Games, 1998–2002; Bd, Liverpool FC, 1999–2007. Trustee: Camden CAB, 2013–; Burgh Hse, 2013–; Hofesh Shechter Co., 2014–; Sadlers Wells, 2014–. *Recreations:* walking, reading, music, television, art, the Lake District.

BURNS, Kevin Francis Xavier, CMG 1984; HM Diplomatic Service, retired; *b* 18 Dec. 1930; *s* of late Frank Burns and Winifred Burns (*née* O'Neill); *m* 1st, 1963, Nan Pinto (*d* 1984); one *s* two *d*; 2nd, 1992, Elizabeth Hassell. *Educ:* Finchley Grammar Sch.; Trinity Coll., Cambridge (BA 1953). CRO, 1956–58; Asst Private Sec. to Sec. of State, 1958; 2nd Sec., 1959, 1st Sec., 1960–63, Colombo; CRO/FO, 1963–67; 1st Sec., Head of Chancery and Consul, Montevideo, 1967–70; FCO, 1970–73; Counsellor, UK Mission, Geneva, 1973–79; RCDS, 1979; Head of SE Asian Dept, FCO, 1980–83; High Comr, Ghana, and Ambassador, Togo, 1983–86; High Comr, Barbados and Eastern Caribbean States, 1986–90; Personnel Assessor, FCO, 1991–99. *Address:* 11 Wentworth Hall, The Ridgeway, NW7 1RJ.

BURNS, Linda Hamilton, (Lady Burns); *see* Urquhart, L. H.

BURNS, Margaret, CBE 2003; Chair, NHS Health Scotland, since 2007; *b* Glasgow, 30 Dec. 1956; *d* of Jim and Jean Burns; *m* 1985, Dr John S. Callender; two *s* one *d*. *Educ:* Kilsyth Acad.; Glasgow Univ. (LLB Hons 1977). Legal Adv. Officer, Scottish Consumer Council, 1981–86; Scottish Affairs Consultant, Consumers' Assoc., 1987–91; Teaching Fellow (pt-time), Law Faculty, Univ. of Aberdeen, 1988–2008. Chair, Partnership for Health and Safety in Scotland, 2005–07; Member: HSC, 1998–2007 (Chair, Rail Industry Adv. Cttee, 2001–05); Cttee on Radioactive Waste Mgt, 2007–12. Non-exec. Mem., NHS Grampian Health Bd, 2003–09. Mem., Scottish Cttee, Council on Tribunals, 1992–98. Chair: PTA, Ferryhill Primary Sch., 1995–99; Sch. Bd, Harlaw Acad., 2004–09. Trustee, Inst. of Occupational Medicine, 2011–. *Recreations:* family, walking, reading, cooking, looking at art. *Address:* NHS Health Scotland, Meridien Court, 5 Cadogan Street, Glasgow G2 6QE. *T:* (0141) 414 2726. *E:* healthscotlandchair@nhs.net. *Club:* Capelrigg Climbing.

BURNS, Richard Ronald James; company director; Partner, Baillie Gifford & Co., 1977–2006; *b* Gourock, 5 May 1946; *s* of Ronald and Mary Burns; *m* 1st, 1974, Catriona Douglas Walker (marr. diss. 1994); two *s* one *d*; 2nd, 1994, Catherine Ogilvie Bryson; one *d*. *Educ:* Dundee High Sch.; Craigflower Prep. Sch.; Trinity Coll., Glenalmond; Merton Coll., Oxford (BA Mod. Hist. 1967); Univ. of Edinburgh (LLB 1969). WS 1972. Apprentice and Asst Solicitor, W. & J. Burness, 1969–73; Baillie Gifford & Co., 1973–2006. Chm., Mid Wynd International Investment Trust plc, 2012– (Dir, 1981–); Director: EP Global Opportunities Trust plc, 2003–14; Bankers Investment Trust plc, 2006–15; JPMorgan Indian Investment Trust plc, 2006–; Standard Life Equity Income Trust plc, 2006–. Trustee: Donaldson Trust, 1999–2013; Nat. Galls of Scotland, 2007–13. Mem. Court, Univ. of Dundee, 2006–14. *Recreations:* reading, foreign travel, golf. *Address:* 31 Saxe Coburg Place, Edinburgh EH3 5BP. *T:* (0131) 332 5819. *Clubs:* New (Edinburgh); Royal and Ancient Golf (St Andrews).

BURNS, Sir (Robert) Andrew, KCMG 1997 (CMG 1992); HM Diplomatic Service, retired; Director: J. P. Morgan Chinese Investment Trust, since 2003; Aberdeen Japan (formerly Aberdeen All Asia) Investment Trust, since 2008; Chairman, Bar Standards Board, since 2015; *b* 21 July 1943; *e s* of late Robert Burns, CB, CMG and Mary Burns (*née* Goodland); *m* 1973, Sarah Cadogan, JP; two *s* and one step *d*. *Educ:* Highgate Sch.; Trinity Coll., Cambridge. BA (Classics), MA. Entered Diplomatic Service, 1965; UK Mission to UN, NY, 1965; FO 1966; Sch. of Oriental and African Studies, 1966–67; Univ. of Delhi, 1967; served New Delhi, FCO, and UK Delegation to CSCE, 1967–76; First Secretary and Head of Chancery, Bucharest, 1976–78; Private Sec. to Perm. Under Sec. and Head of Diplomatic Service, FCO, 1979–82; Fellow, Center for Internat. Affairs, Harvard Univ., 1982–83; Counsellor (Information), Washington, and Head of British Information Services, NY, 1983–86; Head of S Asian Dept, FCO, 1986–88; Head of News Dept, FCO, 1988–90; Asst Under-Sec. of State (Asia), FCO, 1990–92; Ambassador to Israel, 1992–95; Dep. Under Sec. of State, FCO, 1995–97; Consul-Gen., Hong Kong and Macau, 1997–2000; High Comr to Canada, 2000–03. Internat. Gov., BBC, 2005–06. UK Envoy for post-Holocaust Issues, 2010–15. Chairman: Exec. Cttee, Anglo-Israel Assoc., 2004–05, 2008–11; Internat. Holocaust Remembrance Alliance, 2014–15. Chm., Adv. Council, British Expertise (formerly British Consultants and Construction Bureau), 2006–09; Member: British N Amer. Cttee, 2004–13; British N Amer. Res. Assoc., 2004–13. Chm. Council, Royal Holloway, Univ. of London, 2004–11 (Mem., 2003–11); Vice-Chm., 2007–08, Chm., 2008–11, Cttee of University Chairs; Chm., Trinity in the Arts and Media Assoc., 2009–14; Trustee: UK Foundn, Univ. of BC, 2004–11; Foundn for Canadian Studies, 2008–14; Mem., Bd of Govs, GSMD, 2010–. President: Canada UK Colloquia, 2004–11; China Assoc., 2008–14; Mem., HK Soc. Cttee, 2008–11. Chm., Hestercombe Gardens Trust, 2004–; Chm., Internat. Polar Foundn UK, 2006–. FRSA 1997; Fellow, Portland Trust, 2004. *Publications:* Diplomacy, War and Parliamentary Democracy, 1985. *Recreations:* choral singing, theatre, Exmoor. *Address:* Walland Farm, Wheddon Cross, Minehead, Somerset TA24 7EE. *Clubs:* Garrick, Royal Automobile, Royal Over-Seas League; Hong Kong.

BURNS, Sandra Pauline, CB 1989; Parliamentary Counsel, 1980–91, retired; *b* 19 June 1938; *d* of John Burns and Edith Maud Burns. *Educ:* Manchester Central High Sch.; Somerville Coll., Oxford (BCL, MA). Called to the Bar, Middle Temple, 1964. *Recreation:* painting. *Address:* 9 Lark Hill, Oxford OX2 7DR.

BURNS, Rt Hon. Sir Simon (Hugh McGuigan), Kt 2015; PC 2011; MP (C) Chelmsford, 1987–97 and since 2010 (Chelmsford West, 1997–2010); *b* 6 Sept. 1952; *s* of late Brian Stanley Burns, MC, and of Shelagh Mary Nash; *m* 1982, Emma Mary Clifford (marr. diss. 2000); one *s* one *d*. *Educ:* Christ the King Sch., Accra, Ghana; Stamford Sch.; Worcester Coll., Oxford (BA Hons Modern History). Political Adviser to Rt Hon. Sally Oppenheim, 1975–81; Dir, What to Buy Ltd, 1981–83; Policy Exec., Inst. of Dirs, 1983–87. PPS to Minister of State: Dept of Employment, 1989–90; Dept of Educn, 1990–92; DTI, 1992–93; PPS to Minister of Agric., Fisheries and Food, 1993–94; an Asst Govt Whip, 1994–95; a Lord Comr of HM Treasury (Govt Whip), 1995–96; Parly Under-Sec. of State, DoH, 1996–97; Opposition spokesman on: social security, 1997–98; envmt, housing and planning, 1998–99; health, 2001–05; an Opposition Whip, 2005–10; Minister of State: DoH, 2010–12; DfT, 2012–13. Mem., Health Select Cttee, 1999–2005. Treas., 1922 Cttee, 1999–2001 (Mem. Exec., 1999). *Recreations:* American politics, reading, swimming, travelling. *Address:* House of Commons, SW1A 0AA. *T:* (020) 7219 3000. *Clubs:* Essex, Chelmsford Conservative (Patron).

BURNS, Thomas; Member (SDLP) South Antrim, Northern Ireland Assembly, 2003–11; *b* Antrim, 19 Aug. 1960; *m* Therese; three *s*. *Educ:* trained as electrical engr. Mem. (SDLP), Antrim and Newtownabbey (formerly Antrim) BC, 1997–. Founder Mem., Crumlin Credit Union; Dir, Antrim Dist CAB. Governor: Rathenraw Integrated Primary Sch.; St Joseph's Primary Sch.; Crumlin High Sch. Specialist interest in dyslexia and autism support gps. Contested (SDLP) S Antrim, NI Assembly, 2011. *Recreations:* supporter of recycling and environmental issues, sport (supporter of St James', Aldergrove), committed to GAA youth initiatives and campaigner for development of recreational facilities in South Antrim.

BURNS, Rt Rev. Thomas Matthew; *see* Menevia, Bishop of, (RC).

BURNS, Prof. Thomas Patrick, CBE 2006; MD, DSc; FRCPsych; Professor of Social Psychiatry, University of Oxford, 2003–14, now Emeritus; Fellow, Kellogg College, Oxford, 2003–14, now Emeritus; *b* 20 Sept. 1946; *s* of Reginald Burns and Jane Burns (*née* Cassidy); *m* 1976, Eva Burns-Lundgren; two *d*. *Educ:* Churchfields Comprehensive Sch., West Bromwich; Selwyn Coll., Cambridge (MA 1968, MB BChir 1971); Guy's Hosp., London; MD Cambridge 1984; DSc London 2002. FRCPsych 1984. Consultant Psychiatrist: University Hosp., Uppsala, 1980–83; St George's Hosp., London, 1983–93; Prof. of Community Psychiatry, St George's Hosp. Med. Sch., 1984–2003. Chm. Social Psych. Section, RCPsych, 1988–92. *Publications:* Assertive Outreach in Mental Health, 2002; Community Psychiatric Mental Health Teams: a guide to current practices, 2004; Psychiatry: a very short introduction, 2006; Our Necessary Shadow: the nature and meaning of psychiatry, 2013; scientific articles on mental health care, anorexia nervosa in men, etc. *Recreations:* theatre, walking, armchair socialism. *Address:* Department of Psychiatry, University of Oxford, Warneford Hospital, Oxford OX3 7JX. *T:* (01865) 226474. *E:* tom.burns@psych.ox.ac.uk. *Club:* Athenæum.

BURNS, William Joseph, DPhil; President, Carnegie Endowment for International Peace, since 2015; Deputy Secretary of State, United States Department of State, 2011–14; *b* 11 April 1956; *s* of William F. and Margaret C. Burns; *m* 1984, Lisa A. Carty; two *d*. *Educ:* LaSalle Univ. (BA Hist. 1978); St John's Coll., Oxford (MPhil 1980; DPhil 1981 Internat. Relns). Special Asst to the President and Sen. Dir for Near East and S Asian Affairs, Nat. Security Council Staff, 1986–89; Actg Dir and Principal Dep. Dir for State Dept's Policy Planning Staff, 1989–93; Minister Counselor for Pol Affairs, Moscow, 1994–95; Exec. Sec. of the State Dept and Special Asst to the Sec. of State, 1996–98; Ambassador to Jordan, 1998–2001; Asst Sec. of State for Near Eastern Affairs, 2001–05; Ambassador to Russia, 2005–08; Under Sec. for Political Affairs, US Dept of State, 2008–11. Three hon. degrees. Three Presidential Dist. Service Awards. *Publications:* Economic Aid and American Policy Toward Egypt 1955–1981, 1985. *Recreation:* sports. *Address:* Carnegie Endowment for International Peace, 1779 Massachusetts Avenue NW, Washington, DC 20036–2103, USA.

BURNSIDE, David Wilson Boyd; Chairman, New Century Media Ltd, since 2007; *b* 24 Aug. 1951; *s* of Jack and Betty Burnside; *m* 1999, Fiona Rennie; one *d*; and one *d* by a previous marriage. *Educ:* Coleraine Academical Instn; Queen's Univ. Belfast (BA). Teacher, 1973–74; Press Officer, Vanguard Unionist Party, 1974–76; PR Dir, Inst. of Dirs, 1979–84; Public Affairs Dir, British Airways, 1984–93. Chairman: DBA Ltd, 1993–; New Century Hldgs Ltd, 1995–. MP (UU) South Antrim, 2001–05; contested (UU) same seat, 2005. Mem., (UU) South Antrim, NI Assembly, 2003–09. *Recreations:* fishing, shooting, motorcycling. *Address:* The Hill, Secon, Ballymoney, Co Antrim BT53 6QB. *Clubs:* Carlton; Portballintrae Boat; Coleraine and District Motor.

BURNSIDE, John, FRSL; writer; *b* 19 March 1955; *m* 1996, Sarah Dunsby; two *s*. Prof. in Creative Writing, Univ. of St Andrews (Reader, 1999). FRSL 1998. *Publications: poetry:* The Hoop, 1988; Common Knowledge, 1991; Feast Days, 1992; The Myth of the Twin, 1994; Swimming in the Flood, 1995; (jtly) Penguin Modern Poets 9, 1996; A Normal Skin, 1997; The Asylum Dance, 2000 (Whitbread Poetry Award, 2000); The Light Trap, 2002; (ed with M. Riordan) Wild Reckoning (anthology), 2004; The Good Neighbour, 2005; Selected Poems, 2006; Gift Songs, 2007; The Hunt in the Forest, 2009; Black Cat Bone, 2011 (Forward Poetry Prize, 2011; T. S. Eliot Prize, 2011); All One Breath 2014; *fiction:* The Dumb House, 1997; The Mercy Boys, 1999; Burning Elvis, 2000; The Locust Room, 2001; Living Nowhere, 2003; The Devil's Footprints, 2007; Glister, 2008; A Summer of Drowning, 2011; Something Like Happy (short stories), 2013; *memoirs:* A Lie About My Father: a memoir, 2006; Waking Up in Toytown, 2010; I Put a Spell on You, 2014. *Address:* c/o Jonathan Cape, Random House, 20 Vauxhall Bridge Road, SW1V 2SA.

BURNSIDE, Stella Maris, OBE 2003; Vice Lord-Lieutenant of County Londonderry, since 2015; *b* Ballynahinch, Co. Down, 22 Aug. 1949; *d* of Robert John Leahy and Elizabeth Leahy (*née* Baird); *m* 1977, Samuel John Burnside, MBE, PhD; one *s* two *d*. *Educ:* St Mary's High Sch., Downpatrick; Belfast City Hosp. (SRN 1970; RMN 1973); Magee Coll. (Nurse Tutors Dip. 1976); Univ. of Ulster (BPhil Hons 1987). Nursing, clinical teaching and nurse tutor, 1970–80; Asst Dir, Nurse Educn, Magee Coll., 1980; Unit Gen. Manager, Foyle Community Unit, 1989; Chief Executive: Altnagelvin Hosps Trust, 1996; Regulation and Quality Improvement Authy, 2004–07. Vis. Prof., Univ. of Ulster, 2006–11. Member: BBC

Broadcasting Council NI, 1994–97; NHS Health Technol. Assessment Panel, 1997–2000; Equality Commn for NI, 2008–15; Independent Monitoring Bd for NI, 2013–16. Mem. Cttee, Baby Friendly Initiative, UNICEF, 2000–04. Lay Mem., Disciplinary Cttee, Bar Council for NI, 2003–15. Mem., Soroptomist Internat., Londonderry. DL Co. Londonderry, 2002. Medal for Strengthening the Combat Community, Russian Fedn, 2006. *Recreations:* travel (incl. visiting cathedrals), exploring Antrim, Donegal and Londonderry coast, music as much as possible, family and being a grandparent. *E:* stellaleahy@aol.com.

BURNSTOCK, Prof. Geoffrey, FRS 1986; FAA 1971; Professor of Anatomy, University of London, 1975–2004, now Professor Emeritus; Professor and President, Autonomic Neuroscience Centre, UCL Medical School (formerly Royal Free and University College Medical School), since 2004, and Convener, Centre for Neuroscience, since 1979, University College London; *b* 10 May 1929; *s* of James Burnstock and Nancy Green; *m* 1957, Nomi Hirschfeld; three *d*. *Educ:* King's Coll., London; Melbourne Univ. BSc 1953, PhD 1957 London; DSc Melbourne 1971. National Inst. for Medical Res., Mill Hill, 1956–57; Dept of Pharmacology, Oxford Univ., 1957–59; Rockefeller Travelling Fellowship, Univ. of Ill, 1959; University of Melbourne: Sen. Lectr, 1959–62, Reader, 1962–64, Dept of Zoology; Prof. of Zoology and Chm. of Dept, 1964–75; Associate Dean (Biological Sciences), 1969–72; Prof. Emeritus, 1993; Head, Dept of Anatomy and Embryology, then Anatomy and Developmental Biology, UCL, 1975–97, Fellow, UCL, 1996; Prof. and Dir, Autonomic Neurosci. Inst., Royal Free Med. Sch., 1997–2004. Vis. Prof., Dept of Pharmacology, Univ. of Calif, LA, 1970; Hon. Professorial Res. Fellow, Mental Health Res. Inst. of Vic, Australia, 2006. Numerous named lectures, 1976–, including: J. Z. Young, Oxford, 1999; G. W. Harris Prize, Physiol Soc., 1998; Prof. M. Rocha e Silva Award, Caxambu, Brazil, 1999; Horace Davenport Dist., Amer. Physiol. Soc., 2001; Stevenson Meml, London, Ont, 2003. Chm., Scientific Adv. Bd, Eisai London Ltd, 1990–. Editor-in-Chief: Autonomic Neuroscience: Basic & Clinical, 1985–; Purinergic Signalling, 2004–; mem. editl bd of over 20 jls. Vice-Pres., Anatomical Soc. of GB and Ireland, 1990. Member: Academia Europaea, 1992; Russian Soc. of Neuropathology, 1993; Corresp. Academician, Real Acad. Nacional de Farmacia, Spain, 2003. Hon. Member: Physiol Soc., 2003; Pharmacol Soc., 2004; Hungarian Soc. of Exptl and Clin. Pharmacol., 2006; Australian Physiol Soc., 2008. Founder FMedSci 1998. Hon. MRCP 1987, Hon. FRCP 2000; Hon. FRCS 1999. Hon. MSc Melbourne 1962; Dr *hc:* Antwerp, 2002; J. W. Goethe, Frankfurt, 2007. Silver Medal, Royal Soc. of Victoria, 1970; Special Award, NIH Conf., Bethesda, USA, 1989; Royal Gold Medal, Royal Soc., 2000; Janssen Award in Gastroenterol., 2000; Copernicus Gold Medal, Univ. Degli Studi di Ferrara, 2009; Award for Outstanding Contribn to British Neurosci., British Neurosci. Assoc., 2009; Gaddum Meml Award, British Pharmacol Soc., 2010. *Publications:* (with M. Costa) Adrenergic Neurons: their Organisation, Function and Development in the Peripheral Nervous System, 1975; (with Y. Uehara and G. R. Campbell) An Atlas of the Fine Structure of Muscle and its Innervation, 1976; (ed) Purinergic Receptors, 1981; (ed with G. Vrbová and R. O'Brien) Somatic and Autonomic Nerve-Muscle Interactions, 1983; (ed with S. G. Griffith) Nonadrenergic Innervation of Blood Vessels, 1988; (ed with S. Bloom) Peptides: a target for new drug development, 1991; series editor, The Autonomic Nervous System, vols 1–15, 1992–2003; (ed jtly) Nitric Oxide in Health and Disease, 1997; (ed jtly) Cardiovascular Biology of Purines, 1998; papers on smooth muscle and autonomic nervous system, incl. purinergic signalling in health and disease in sci. jls. *Recreations:* tennis, wood sculpture. *Address:* Autonomic Neuroscience Centre, UCL Medical School, University College London, Royal Free Campus, Rowland Hill Street, NW3 2PF.

BURNTON, Rt Hon. Sir Stanley (Jeffrey), Kt 2000; PC 2008; a Lord Justice of Appeal, 2008–12; *b* 25 Oct. 1942; *s* of Harry and Fay Burnton; *m* 1971, Gwenyth Frances Castle; one *s* two *d*. *Educ:* Hackney Downs Grammar Sch.; St Edmund Hall, Oxford (MA; Hon. Fellow, 2008). Called to the Bar, Middle Temple, 1965, Bencher, 1991 (Treas., 2010); QC 1982; a Recorder, 1994–2000; a Judge of the High Court of Justice, QBD, 2000–08. Arbitrator, 2012–. Chm., British and Irish Legal Information Inst., 2011–; Trustee: British Inst. Internat. and Comparative Law, 2011–; Slynn Foundn, 2014–. Vis. Prof., QMUL, 2012–. Mem. Council, University Coll. Sch., 2013–. *Recreations:* classical music, theatre, reading, travel. *Address:* One Essex Court, Temple, EC4Y 9AR.

BURNYEAT, Myles Fredric, CBE 2007; FBA 1984; Senior Research Fellow in Philosophy, All Souls College, Oxford, 1996–2006, now Emeritus Fellow; *b* 1 Jan. 1939; *s* of Peter James Anthony Burnyeat and Cynthia Cherry Warburg; *m* 1st, 1971, Jane Elizabeth Buckley (marr. diss. 1982); one *s* one *d*; 2nd, 1984, Ruth Sophia Padel (marr. diss. 2000); one *d*; 3rd, 2002, Heda Segvic (*d* 2003); partner, Margaret Hilda Bent, *qv*. *Educ:* Bryanston Sch.; King's Coll., Cambridge (BA). Qualified as Russian Interpreter (Civil Service Commn, 2nd Class), 1959. Assistant Lecturer in Philosophy 1964, Lecturer in Philosophy 1965, University Coll. London; Cambridge University: Lectr in Classics, 1978–84; Laurence Prof. of Ancient Philosophy, 1984–96; Fellow, 1978–96, Lectr in Philosophy, 1978–84, Hon. Fellow, 2006, Robinson Coll. For. Hon. Mem., Amer. Acad. of Arts and Scis, 1992. *Publications:* The Theaetetus of Plato, 1990; A Map of Metaphysics Zeta, 2001; Aristotle's Divine Intellect, 2008; co-editor: Philosophy As It Is, 1979; Doubt and Dogmatism, 1980; Science and Speculation, 1982; The Original Sceptics, 1997; (ed) The Skeptical Tradition, 1983; Explorations in Ancient and Modern Philosophy, 2 vols, 2012; contribs to classical and philosophical jls. *Recreation:* travel. *Address:* All Souls College, Oxford OX1 4AL.

BURR, His Honour Michael Rodney; a Circuit Judge, 1992–2008; a Deputy Circuit Judge, since 2008; *b* 31 Aug. 1941; *s* of Frank Edward Burr and Aileen Maud Burr; *m* 1963, Rhoda Rule; four *s* one *d*. *Educ:* Brecon County Grammar Sch.; King Edward VI Sch., Chelmsford; Coll. of Law. Solicitor, 1964. Asst Solicitor, Hilliard & Ward, Chelmsford, 1964–69; Sen. Partner, Peter Williams & Co., Swansea, 1972–92; Recorder, 1988. Sec., Incorp. Law Soc. of Swansea and Dist, 1980–83; Law Society: non-Council Member: Professional Purposes Cttee, 1985–86; Adjudication Cttee, 1986–89. Mem., Parole Bd, 2008–. *Recreations:* flying, travel.

BURR, Timothy John, CB 2008; Comptroller and Auditor General, National Audit Office, 2008–09 (Deputy Comptroller and Auditor General, 2000–08); *b* 31 March 1950; *s* of Eric Cyril Burr and Myrtle Burr (*née* Waters); *m* 1975, Gillian Heather Croot; two *s*. *Educ:* Dulwich Coll. Entered HM Treasury, 1968; Cabinet Office, 1984; Asst Sec., HM Treasury, 1985; Under-Sec., Cabinet Office, 1990; Treasury Officer of Accounts, 1993–94; Asst Auditor Gen., Nat. Audit Office, 1994–2000.

BURRELL, Sir Charles Raymond, 10th Bt *cr* 1774, of Valentine House, Essex; *b* 27 Aug. 1962; *s* of Sir (John) Raymond Burrell, 9th Bt, and of Rowena Frances, *d* of late M. H. Pearce; *S* father, 2008; *m* 1993, Isabella Elizabeth Nancy, adopted *d* of M. L. Tree; one *s* one *d*. *Educ:* Millfield; Royal Agricultural Coll., Cirencester. *Heir: s* Edward Lambert Burrell, *b* 10 Oct. 1996. *Address:* Knepp Castle, West Grinstead, Horsham, W Sussex RH13 8LJ.

BURRELL, Diana Elizabeth Jane; composer; Artistic Director, Spitalfields Festival, 2006–09; AHRC Creative Arts Fellow, Royal Academy of Music, since 2006; *b* 25 Oct. 1948; *d* of Bernard Burrell and Audrey (*née* Coleman); *m* 1971, Richard Fallas; one *s* one *d*. *Educ:* Norwich High Sch.; Girton Coll., Cambridge Univ. (BA Hons Music). Music teacher, Sutton High Sch., 1971–75; freelance viola player and teacher, 1978–90; pianist, Holy Trinity Ch, Mile End, 1985–2006; part-time Lectr in Composition and 20th Century Studies, Goldsmiths' Coll., London, 1989–93; Composer-in-residence, Pimlico Sch., London, 1990–91; Living Composer, Eastern Orchestral Bd, 1993–95; Composer-in-Association, City of London Sinfonia, 1994–96; Composition Prof., GSMD, 1999–2006. Recordings of own works (Classic CD Award, 1998, for Viola Concerto and other works). Hon. FTCL 1997. *Compositions* include: The Albatross (opera), 1987; commissions: Landscape, 1988; Resurrection, 1992; Dunkelhvide Månestråler, 1996; Clarinet Concerto (for Northern Sinfonia), 1996; Symphonies of Flocks, Herds and Shoals (for BBC SO), 1997; Concerto for Violin with Singer and 3 Ensembles, 2009; The Hours, 2011; Blaze (for tenThing), 2013. *Recreations:* birdwatching, walking, gardening. *Address:* c/o United Music Publishers, 33 Lea Road, Waltham Abbey, Essex EN9 1ES.

BURRELL, (Francis) Gary; QC 1996; **His Honour Judge Burrell;** a Circuit Judge, since 2009; *b* 7 Aug. 1953; *s* of Francis Ivan George Burrell and Louisa Shane Burrell; *m* 1979, Heather Young; three *s*. *Educ:* Belfast Boys' Model Sch.; Univ. of Exeter (LLB). Called to the Bar, Inner Temple, 1977, Bencher, 2002; Asst Recorder, 1992–96; Recorder, 1996–2009; Dep. High Court Judge, 2001–10. Mem., Bar Council, 1995–2010. Pres., S Yorks Medico-Legal Soc., 1991–92; NE Circuit Rep., Personal Injury Bar Assoc., 1995–97. *Recreations:* sailing, fly fishing. *Address:* Southampton Combined Court Centre, London Road, Southampton SO15 2XQ.

BURRELL, Mark William; DL; Director, Pearson plc, 1977–97; *b* 9 April 1937; *s* of Sir Walter Burrell, 8th Bt, CBE, TD and Hon. Anne Judith, OBE, *o d* of 3rd Baron Denman, PC, GCMG, KCVO; *m* 1966, Margot Rosemary Pearce; two *s* one *d*. *Educ:* Eton; Pembroke Coll., Cambridge (BA 1st Cl. Hons Engrg). With Sir Alexander Gibb & Partners, 1959, then Vickers, 1960–61; joined Pearson plc, 1963; Whitehall Petroleum: Dir, 1964–88; Chm., 1987–88; joined Lazard Brothers, 1970; Dir, 1974; Man. Dir, 1984–86; non-exec. Dir, 1986–97; Director: BSB Holdings, 1987–99; BSkyB Group plc, 1991–94; Dir, then Chm., Royal Doulton plc, 1993–98; Chm., Millbank Financial Services Ltd, 1986–; non-executive Director: RM plc, 1997–2001; Conafex SA, 1999–2008 (Chm.); Dir, then Chm., Merlin Communications Internat., 1997–2001. Mem. Ct, Sussex Univ. Gov., Northbrook Coll. Sussex, 2004–08. High Sheriff, 2002–03, DL, 2004, W Sussex. *Recreations:* hunting, polo, tennis, golf, ski-ing. *Address:* Bakers House, Bakers Lane, Shipley, W Sussex RH13 8GJ. *Clubs:* White's, Boodle's.

BURRELL, Michael Peter; Deputy High Court Judge, Hong Kong, since 2010; Judicial Commissioner, Brunei Darussalam Court of Appeal, since 2013; *b* 18 July 1948; *s* of Peter Burrell and Gwynneth Burrell; *m* 1975, Anne Hughes; two *d*, and one step *s*. *Educ:* Birkenhead Sch.; Magdalene Coll., Cambridge (MA). Called to the Bar, Inner Temple, 1971; in practice on Northern Circuit, 1972–86 (Junior, 1973); Hong Kong: Perm. Magistrate, 1986–90; Dist Judge, 1991–95; Judge, Ct of First Instance of High Ct (formerly Judge, Supreme Ct), 1995–2009. Mem., Hong Kong Judicial Studies Bd, 1992–95; Chm., Hong Kong Insider Dealing Tribunal, 1996–98; Mem., HK Internat. Arbitration Centre, 2009–; Mem. Panel, Kuala Lumpur Arbitration Centre, 2010–. Fellow, HK Inst. of Arbitrators, 2009–. Hon. Fellow, HK Inst. of Surveyors, 2004. *Recreations:* sport, reading, walking. *Address:* c/o High Court, Queensway, Hong Kong; Brathay, Mill Lane, Willaston, S Wirral CH64 1RG. *Clubs:* Artists' (Liverpool); Royal Liverpool Golf (Hoylake); Oxton Cricket (Wirral); Hong Kong, Hong Kong Cricket (Hong Kong).

BURRETT, (Frederick) Gordon, CB 1974; Deputy Secretary, Civil Service Department, 1972–81; *b* 31 Oct. 1921; *s* of Frederick Burrett and Marion Knowles; *m* 1943, Joan Giddins; one *s* two *d*. *Educ:* Emanuel Sch.; St Catharine's Coll., Cambridge. Served in Royal Engrs, N Africa, Italy, Yugoslavia, Greece, 1942–45 (despatches). HM Foreign, subseq. Diplomatic Service, 1946; 3rd Sec., Budapest, 1946–49; FO, 1949–51; Vice-Consul, New York, 1951–54; FO, 1954–57; 1st Sec., Rome, 1957–60; transf. to HM Treasury, 1960; Private Sec. to Chief Sec., Treasury, 1963–64; Asst Secretary: HM Treasury, 1964; Cabinet Office, 1967–68; Secretary: Kindersley Review Body on Doctors' and Dentists' Remuneration; Plowden Cttee on Pay of Higher Civil Service, 1967–68; Civil Service Dept, 1968, Under-Sec. 1969. Mem., Civil Service Pay Res. Unit Bd, 1978–81; conducted govt scrutiny of V&A and Sci. Museums, 1982; Adviser to Govt of Oman on CS reorganisation, 1984; led govt review of policies and operations of Commonwealth Inst., 1986; leader of review team to examine responsibilities and grading of dirs of nat. museums and galls, 1987; conducted review of sen. posts of Arts Council and BFI, 1987–88; Chm., Cttee of Inquiry into CS Pay, Hong Kong, 1988–89. Chairman: Redundant Churches Fund, later Churches Conservation Trust, 1982–95; Wagner Soc., 1984–88. FSA 1985. Cross of St Augustine, 1995. *Publications:* article on the watercolours of John Massey Wright (1777–1866) in vol. 54 of the Old Water-Colour Society's Club Annual. *Recreations:* music, walking, reading.

BURRIDGE, Rev. Prof. Richard Alan; Dean, since 1994, and Professor of Biblical Interpretation, since 2008, King's College London; Canon Theologian and Sarum Canon, Salisbury Cathedral, since 2013; *b* 11 June 1955; *s* of Alan Burridge and Iris Joyce (*née* Coates); *m* 1979, Susan Morgan (marr. diss. 2009); two *d*; *m* 2014, Megan Warner. *Educ:* University Coll., Oxford (Exhibnr; BA Lit.Hum. 1st Cl. Hons, MA 1981); Univ. of Nottingham (PGCE 1978; Postgrad. DTh 1983; PhD 1989); St John's Coll., Nottingham. Classics Master and House Tutor, Sevenoaks Sch., 1978–82; ordained deacon 1985, priest 1986; Curate, St Peter and St Paul, Bromley, Kent, 1985–87; Lazenby Chaplain, Univ. of Exeter and part-time Lectr, Depts of Theol. and of Classics and Ancient Hist., 1987–94; Dir of NT Studies, Dept of Theol. and Religious Studies, KCL, 2007–14 (FKC 2002). Mem., Gen. Synod of C of E, 1994–. Mem., Ethical Investment Adv. Gp, C of E, 2008– (Dep. Chair, 2010–). Member Council of Mgt, St John's Coll., Nottingham, 1986–99; Council of Ref., Monarch Pubns, Tunbridge Wells, 1992–2000. Mem., Academic Bd (formerly Bd of Studies), N Thames Ministerial Trng Course, 1994–; Ext. Examr, SW Ministerial Trng Course, 1995–99. Commissary, Bp of the High Veld, CPSA, 1997–2009. Member: SNTS, 1995–; Soc. for Study of Theol., 1995–; Soc. of Biblical Lit., 1996–. Expert Advr (Faith Zone, Greenwich Dome), Nat. Millennium Experience Co., 1998–2000. Chaplain to Hendon Golf Club, 2004–. Trustee: Christian Evidence Soc., 1994– (Chm., 2001–); Foundn of St Catherine, Cumberland Lodge, 1998–2008. (Jtly) Ratzinger Prize for Theology, Joseph Ratzinger Benedict XVI Foundn, 2013. *Publications:* Sex Therapy: some ethical considerations, 1985; What are the Gospels?: a comparison with Graeco-Roman biography, 1992, 2nd edn 2004; Four Gospels, One Jesus?: a symbolic reading, 1994 (also Korean edn, 2000), 2nd edn 2005 (also US and Australian edns), Classic edn 2013; John (People's Bible Commentary), 1998, Lambeth Conference edn 2008 (also US edn, 2007); Faith Odyssey: a journey through Lent, 2000; (ed jtly) The Lectionary Commentary, 2002; Faith Odyssey: a journey through life, 2003 (also Norwegian edn, 2003); (jtly) Jesus Now and Then, 2004; Imitating Jesus: an inclusive approach to New Testament ethics, 2007; *contributor to:* A Dictionary of Biblical Interpretation, 1990; The New Dictionary of Christian Ethics and Pastoral Theology, 1995; A Handbook of Classical Rhetoric in the Hellenistic Period 330 BC–AD 400, 1997; The Gospels for all Christians: rethinking the gospel audiences, 1998; Where Shall We Find God?, 1998; The Lion Handbook to the Bible, 1999; Christology, Community and Controversy, 2000; Dictionary of New Testament Background, 2000; The Story of Christian Spirituality, 2001; Exploring and Proclaiming the Apostles' Creed, 2004; The Dictionary for Theological Interpretation of Scripture, 2005; The Written Gospel, 2005; The Person of Christ, 2005; The Oxford Handbook of Biblical Studies, 2006; The Fourfold Gospel Commentary, 2006; Tutu As I Know Him: on a personal note, 2006; The Dictionary of Biblical Criticism and Interpretation, 2007; John, Jesus and History, vol. 2, 2009; Moral Language in the New Testament, 2010; The Dictionary of Scripture and Ethics, 2011; Jesus, Matthew's Gospel and Early Christianity, 2011; Reading Acts Today, 2011; articles in Theology, Church Times, St John the Evangelist Mag., C of E Newspaper, THES, Wholeness, Dialogue, The Times, Sewanee Theological Review. *Recreations:* being with my family, ski-ing, golf, cycling playing guitar and bass. *Address:* Dean's Office, King's College London, Strand, WC2R 2LS. *T:* (020) 7848 2333/2063. *E:* dean@kcl.ac.uk.

BURRILL, Timothy; Managing Director: Burrill Productions, 1966–2014; Cranbury Productions Ltd, since 2014; Chairman, Film Asset Developments Plc, 1987–94; *b* 8 June 1931; *yr s* of L. Peckover Burrill, OBE and Marjorie S. Burrill; *m* 1st, 1959, Philippa (marr. diss. 1966), *o d* of Maurice and Margot Hare; one *d*; 2nd, 1968, Santa (marr. diss. 1993), *e d* of John and Betty Raymond; one *s* two *d*. *Educ:* Eton Coll.; Sorbonne Univ. Served Grenadier Guards, 1949–52: commnd 1950; served 2nd Bn, 1950–52. Jun. management, Cayzer Irvine & Co., 1952–56; entered film industry, 1956; joined Brookfield Prodns, 1965; Dir, World Film Services, 1967–69; first Prodn Administrator, National Film and TV Sch., 1972; Man. Dir, Allied Stars (resp. for Chariots of Fire), 1979–80; Director: Artistry Ltd, 1982–87 (resp. for Superman and Supergirl films); Pathé (formerly Chargeurs) Productions Ltd, 1994–99; Pathé Pictures, 1994–99; Consultant: National Film Develt Fund, 1980–81; Really Useful Group, 1989–90; Script Factory, 1998–; Knight Dragon, 2014–. UK Rep., Eurimages, 1994–96. Chairman: BAFTA, 1981–83 (Vice-Chm., 1979–81); First Film Foundn, 1989–98; Producer Mem., Cinematograph Films Council, 1980–85; Member: Gen. Council, ACTT, 1975–76; Exec. Council, British Film and Television Producers Assoc., 1981–89; Exec. Council, The Producers Assoc., 1989–91; Exec. Council, Producers' Alliance for Cinema and Television, 1991–2001 (Vice-Chm., 1993–94); Sir Peter Middleton's Adv. Cttee of Film Finance, 1996–97; Dir, British Film Commn, 1998–2000. Chm., Impact Campaign, 1994–95. Governor: National Film and Television Sch., 1981–92; National Theatre, 1982–88. Films include Tess, The Fourth Protocol, The Pirates of Penzance, The Pianist, Oliver Twist, La Vie en Rose, The Ghost, etc. *Recreation:* theatre. *Address:* 19 Cranbury Road, SW6 2NS. *T:* (020) 7736 8673, *Fax:* (020) 7731 3921. *E:* timothy@timothyburrill.co.uk.

BURRINGTON, Ernest; Deputy Publisher, 1993–95, Vice President, 1995, Globe Communications, USA; Director, 1985–92, Chairman, 1991–92, Mirror Group Newspapers; *b* 13 Dec. 1926; *s* of late Harold Burrington and of Laura Burrington; *m* 1950, Nancy Crossley; one *s* one *d*. Reporter, Oldham Chronicle, 1941–43; Army service, 1944–47; reporter and sub-editor, Oldham Chronicle, 1947–49; sub-editor, Bristol Evening World, 1950; Daily Herald: sub-editor, Manchester, 1950, night editor, 1955; London night editor, 1957; IPC Sun: night editor, 1964; Asst Editor, 1965; Asst Editor and night editor, News International Sun, 1969; dep. night editor, Daily Mirror, 1970; Dep. Editor, 1971, Associate Editor, 1972, Sunday People; Editor, The People, 1985–88 and 1989–90; Dep. Chm. and Asst Publisher, 1988–91, Man. Dir, 1989–91, Mirror Gp Newspapers; Chm., Syndication Internat., 1989–92; Dep. Chm., Mirror Publishing Co., 1989–91; Director: Mirror Group Magazine and Newsday Ltd, 1989–92; Legionstyle Ltd, 1991–92; Mirror Colour Print Ltd, 1991–92; (non-exec.) Sunday Correspondent, 1990; The European, 1990–91; IQ Newsgraphics, 1990–92; Sygma Picture Agency, Paris, 1990–91; Marketing Consultant, 1996–97, Pres., 1996–98, Atlantic Media; Head of Marketing, Harveys plc, 1998–2000. Member: Council, NPA, 1988–92; IPI (Mem., British Exec., 1988–92); Foreign Press Assoc.; Trustee, Internat. Centre for Child Studies, 1986–90. Life Mem., NUJ, 1996. *Recreations:* travel, bridge, Manchester United FC (Hon. Red Devil, 1985). *Address:* South Hall, Dene Park, Shipbourne Road, near Tonbridge TN11 9NS. *T:* (01732) 368517.

BURROUGHES, Dr Jeremy Henley, FRS 2012; FREng, FIET, FInstP; Chief Technology Officer, Cambridge Display Technology, since 2001; *b* Aug. 1960. With Toshiba, UK and Japan, 1991–97; Cambridge Display Technology Ltd: Co-founder, 1992; Tech. Dir, 1997–2000; Product Business Unit Dir, 2000–01. Dir, Opsys Ltd, 2004–11. Vis. Prof. of Physics, Imperial Coll. London. FREng 2009. *Address:* Cambridge Display Technology Ltd, Unit 12, Cardinal Park, Cardinal Way, Godmanchester, Cambs PE29 2XG.

BURROW, Prof. John Anthony, FBA 1986; Winterstoke Professor of English, University of Bristol, 1976–98, now Emeritus; *b* 3 Aug. 1932; *s* of William and Ada Burrow; *m* 1956, Diana Wynne Jones (*d* 2011); three *s*. *Educ:* Buckhurst Hill County High Sch., Essex; Christ Church, Oxford (BA, MA). Asst Lectr, King's Coll., London, 1955–57; Lectr in English, Christ Church, 1957–61, and Brasenose Coll., 1957–59, Oxford; Fellow in English, Jesus Coll., Oxford, 1961–75; Dean of Faculty of Arts, Univ. of Bristol, 1990–93. Vis. Prof., Yale Univ., 1968–69. Hon. Dir, EETS, 1983–2006. *Publications:* A Reading of Sir Gawain and the Green Knight, 1965; Geoffrey Chaucer (critical anthology), 1969; Ricardian Poetry, 1971; (ed) English Verse 1300–1500, 1977; Medieval Writers and their Work, 1982, 2nd edn 2008; Essays on Medieval Literature, 1984; The Ages of Man, 1986; (with Thorlac Turville-Petre) A Book of Middle English, 1992; Langland's Fictions, 1993; Thomas Hoccleve, 1994; (ed) Hoccleve's Complaint and Dialogue, 1999; The Gawain-Poet, 2001; Gestures and Looks in Medieval Narrative, 2002; The Poetry of Praise, 2008; English Poets in the Late Middle Ages, 2012; articles and reviews in learned jls. *Recreation:* music. *Address:* 9 The Polygon, Clifton, Bristol BS8 4PW. *T:* (0117) 9277845.

BURROW, John Halcrow, CBE 1993 (OBE 1987); QPM 1998; DL; Chief Constable of Essex Police, 1988–98; *b* 1935; *s* of John and Florence Burrow; *m* 1958, Ruth (*née* Taylor); two *s* one *d*. *Educ:* Ulverston Grammar School; University College London (LLB Hons). Lieut, 3rd Kenya Bn, King's African Rifles, 1953–55. Metropolitan Police, 1958–77; Asst/Dep. Chief Constable, Merseyside Police, 1977–88; RCDS, 1979. Pres., ACPO, 1992–93; Chairman: Technical and Res. Cttee, ACPO, 1990–92; ACPO No 5 (SE) Region Cttee, 1991–98; Shotley Training Centre Cttee, 1990–92. Chairman: St John Ambulance, Essex, 2004–10 (Co. Comdr, 1999–2004); Essex Br., SSAFA, 2001–. DL Essex, 1998. *Recreations:* travelling, gardening. *Address:* Acorns, Church End, Shalford, Braintree, Essex CM7 5HA. *T:* (01371) 850577.

BURROWES, David John Barrington; MP (C) Enfield Southgate, since 2005; *b* 12 June 1969; *m* 1996, Janet; four *s* two *d* (of whom one *s* one *d* are twins). *Educ:* Highgate Sch.; Univ. of Exeter (LLB 1991). Asst Solicitor, 1995–2005, Consultant, 2005–, Shepherd Harris and Co., Enfield. Mem. (C), Enfield BC, 1994–2006 (Cabinet Mem. for voluntary and community develt, 2003–04). Parliamentary Private Secretary: to Minister for Cabinet Office and Minister for Policy, 2010; to Minister for Policy, 2010–12; to Sec. of State for Envmt, Food and Rural Affairs, 2012–14. Contested (C) Edmonton, 2001. *Publications:* (jtly) Moral Basis of Conservatism, 1995; Such a Thing as Society: Maggie's children and volunteering, 2006. *Recreations:* sports, particularly football and cricket. *Address:* (office) 1c Chaseville Parade, Chaseville Park Road, Winchmore Hill, N21 1PG. *T:* (020) 8360 0234. *E:* david@davidburrowes.com; House of Commons, SW1A 0AA. *T:* (020) 7219 8144.

BURROWES, Norma Elizabeth; opera and concert singer; teacher of classical voice and Baroque studies, York University, Toronto; *d* of Henry and Caroline Burrowes; *m* 1st, 1969, Steuart Bedford, *qv* (marr. diss.); 2nd, 1987, Emile Belcourt; one *s* one *d*. *Educ:* Sullivan Upper Sch., Holywood, Co. Down; Queen's Univ., Belfast (BA); Royal Academy of Music (FRAM 1992). Operas include: Zerlina in Don Giovanni, Glyndebourne Touring Opera (début); Blöndchen in Die Entführung aus dem Serail, Salzburg Festival, and again Blöndchen, Paris Opera, 1976 (début); Fiakermili, Royal Opera House (début), also Oscar, Despina, Nanetta, Woodbird; Entführung aus dem Serail, Ballo in Maschera, Der Rosenkavalier, Metropolitan, NY; Daughter of the Regiment, Midsummer Night's Dream, Elisir d'Amore, Canada; Così Fan Tutte, Romeo and Juliet, France; Marriage of Figaro, Germany; Gianni Schicchi, Switzerland; Marriage of Figaro, La Scala. Television operas include: Nanetta in Falstaff; Susanna in Marriage of Figaro and Lauretta in Gianni Schicchi. Has sung regularly with major opera companies, giving concerts and recitals, GB and abroad; many recordings. Hon. DMus Queen's Univ. Belfast, 1979. *Recreations:* swimming, gardening, needlework.

BURROWS, Prof. Andrew Stephen, FBA 2007; Professor of the Law of England, and Senior Research Fellow, All Souls College, University of Oxford, since 2010; a Deputy High Court Judge, since 2007; a Recorder, since 2000; *b* 17 April 1957; *s* of William George Burrows and Dora Burrows; *m* 1982, Rachel Jane Gent; three *s* one *d*. *Educ:* Prescot Grammar Sch.; Brasenose Coll., Oxford (Schol.; Martin Wronker Prize 1978; MA; BCL); Harvard Law Sch. (LLM). Called to the Bar, Middle Temple, 1985 (Hon. Bencher, 2000); Mem., Fountain Court Chambers, Temple. Lectr in Law, Merton Coll., Oxford, 1979–80; Harkness Fellow, Harvard Law Sch., 1980–81; Lectr in Law, Univ. of Manchester, 1981–86; Fellow and CUF Lectr in Law, 1986–94, Hon. Res. Fellow, 1994–, LMH, Oxford; Prof. of English Law, UCL, 1994–99; Law Comr for England and Wales, 1994–99; Norton Rose Prof. of Commercial and Financial Law, Univ. of Oxford, 1999–2010; Fellow, 1999–2010, Hon. Fellow, 2010–, St Hugh's Coll., Oxford. Chair, Video Appeals Cttee, 2011–. Hon. QC 2003. DCL 2014. Jt winner, Prize for Outstanding Legal Scholarship, SPTL, 1993. *Publications:* Remedies for Torts and Breach of Contract, 1987, 3rd edn 2004; (ed jtly) Clerk and Lindsell on Torts, 16th edn 1989 to 21st edn 2014; Essays on the Law of Restitution (ed Burrows), 1991; The Law of Restitution, 1993, 3rd edn 2011; (ed jtly) Chitty on Contracts, 28th edn 1999 to 31st edn 2012; (ed jtly) Scrutton on Charterparties, 20th edn 1996, 21st edn 2008; (jtly) Cases and Materials on the Law of Restitution, 1997, 2nd edn 2007; Understanding the Law of Obligations, 1998; (jtly) English Private Law, 2000, (Gen. Ed.) 3rd edn 2013; (ed jtly) Commercial Remedies, 2003; (ed jtly) Mapping the Law, 2006; (ed jtly) Contract Terms, 2007; A Casebook on Contract, 2007, 4th edn 2013; (ed jtly) Contract Formation and Parties, 2010; (ed jtly) Anson's Law of Contract, 29th edn, 2010; A Restatement of the English Law of Unjust Enrichment, 2012; numerous articles in legal jls. *Recreations:* sport (esp. football), mountain walking. *Address:* All Souls College, Oxford OX1 4AL.

BURROWS, Christopher Parker; Director, Orbis Business Intelligence Ltd, since 2009; *b* 12 Sept. 1958; *s* of John Brian and Margaret Katherine Burrows; *m* 1st, 1988, Betty Burrows (*née* Cordi) (marr. diss. 2008); one *s* two *d*; 2nd, 2010, Claire Jane Rothwell; one *s* one *d*. *Educ:* Cleethorpes Grammar Sch.; Liverpool Univ. Entered FCO, 1980; Third Sec., East Berlin, 1982–85; Third, later Second, Sec., Bonn, 1987–89; First Sec. (External), Athens, 1993–96; First Sec., later Counsellor, Brussels, 1998–2002; Counsellor: FCO, 2002–05; New Delhi, 2005–06; FCO, 2006–09. *Recreations:* jazz piano, gardening, football. *Address:* (office) Berkeley Square House, Berkeley Square, W1J 6BD.

BURROWS, Clive, CEng; FREng, FIET, FIMechE, FCILT, FIRSE; Group Engineering Director, FirstGroup plc, since 2008; *b* 1 Aug. 1958; *s* of Gordon and Barbara Burrows; *m* 1999, Norma Silvia de Anda Marquez. *Educ:* Univ. of Bath (BSc Hons Electrical and Electronic Engrg). CEng 1992, FREng 2004; MIEE 1992, FIET (FIEE 2002); FIMechE 2002. Intercity Route Fleet Manager, BR, 1989–91; Depot Manager, N Pole Internat., and Project Engr, Eurostar UK, 1991–93; Man. Dir, Transportation Consultants Internat., 1993–98; Gp Rail Engrg Dir, First Gp plc, 1998–2005; Dir, Technical and Professional, DfT, 2005–08. Hon. Prof. of Railway Engrg, Univ. of Nottingham, 2011–. MInstD 1999. *Publications:* contrib. learned jls. *Recreations:* keen student of all matters relating to travel, transport and technology, collector and restorer of historic vehicles and artifacts. *Address:* FirstGroup, Milford House, 1 Milford Street, Swindon SN1 1HL. *E:* Clive.Burrows@firstgroup.com.

BURROWS, Fred, CMG 1981; PhD; international law consultant, since 1990; *b* 10 Aug. 1925; *s* of late Charles Burrows; *m* 1955, (Jennifer) Winsome Munt; two *s*. *Educ:* Altrincham Grammar Sch.; Trinity Hall, Cambridge (MA). PhD Cantab, 1988. Served in RAF, 1944–47. Called to Bar, Gray's Inn, 1950; Asst Legal Adviser, Foreign Office, 1956–65; Legal Adviser, British Embassy, Bonn, 1965–67; returned to FO, 1967; Legal Counsellor, FCO, 1968–77; Counsellor (Legal Adviser), Office of UK Perm. Rep. to European Communities, 1977–80; Legal Counsellor, FCO, 1980–85; Law Officer (Special Duties), then (International Law), Hong Kong, 1985–90. JP Hong Kong, 1986–90. *Publications:* Free Movement in European Community Law, 1985. *Recreations:* sailing, trombone. *Address:* c/o Foreign and Commonwealth Office, SW1A 2AH.

BURROWS, (George) Richard (William); Chairman, British American Tobacco plc, since 2009; *b* 16 Jan. 1946; *m* 1970, Sherril Dix; one *s* three *d*. *Educ:* Wesley College, Dublin; Rathmines College of Commerce. FICA. Articled Stokes Bros & Pim, 1963–70; Asst to Man. Dir, Edward Dillon & Co., 1970; Man. Dir, Old Bushmills Distillery Co., 1972; Gen. Manager, Irish Distillers, 1976; Man. Dir, 1978, Chief Exec., 1991–2000, Chm., 1991–2007, Irish Distillers Group; Dir Gen., 2000–05, Bd Dir, 2004–08, Pernod Ricard. Non-executive Director: Rentokil Initial plc, 2008–; Carlsberg, 2009–; VoiceSage Global Hldgs Ltd, 2011–. Gov., Bank of Ireland, 2005–09. *Recreation:* sailing. *Address:* British American Tobacco plc, Globe House, 4 Temple Place, WC2R 2PG.

BURROWS, Prof. Malcolm, FRS 1985; Professor of Zoology, University of Cambridge, 1996–2010, now Emeritus; Fellow of Wolfson College, Cambridge, 1991–2010; *b* 28 May 1943; *s* of William Roy Burrows and Jean Jones Burrows; *m* 1966, Christine Joan Ellis; one *s* one *d*. *Educ:* Cambridge Univ. (MA; ScD 1983); St Andrews Univ. (PhD 1967). Reader in Neurobiology, 1983–86, Prof. of Neurosci., 1986–96, Univ. of Cambridge. Vis. Prof., Konstanz Univ., 1987; Cornelius Wiersma Vis. Prof., CIT, 1991; Distinguished Vis. Prof., Univ. of California, Davis, 1992. Pres., Internat. Soc. for Neuroethology, 1998–2001. MAE 1992. Mem., Bayerische Akad. der Wissenschaften, 1996. Scientific Medal, 1980, Frink Medal, 2005, Zoological Soc.; Alexander von Humboldt award, 1993. *Publications:* The Neurobiology of an Insect Brain, 1996.

BURROWS, Margaret Ann; *see* Buck, M. A.

BURROWS, Rt Rev. Michael Andrew James; *see* Cashel, Ferns and Ossory, Bishop of.

BURROWS, Michael Peter; QC 2008; a Recorder, since 2000; *b* Birmingham, 26 June 1957; *s* of Peter and Margaret Burrows; *m* 1990, Gail Burbridge; three *d*. *Educ:* Tudor Grange Grammar Sch., Solihull; Solihull Sixth Form Coll.; Queens' Coll., Cambridge (BA 1978). Called to the Bar, Inner Temple, 1979; in practice at the Bar, specialising in criminal law, 1979–; Asst Recorder, 1997–2000. *Recreations:* walking in the Lake District, holidays in Scotland, theatre and music. *Address:* 5 Fountain Court, Steelhouse Lane, Birmingham B4 6DR.

BURROWS, Rt Rev. Peter; *see* Doncaster, Bishop Suffragan of.

BURROWS, Richard; *see* Burrows, G. R. W.

BURSELL, His Honour Rev. Canon Rupert David Hingston; QC 1986; a Senior Circuit Judge, 2003–08 (a Circuit Judge, 1988–2008); a Deputy High Court Judge, 2009–11; *b* 10 Nov. 1942; *s* of Henry and Cicely Mary Bursell; *m* 1967, Joanna Ruth Gibb; two *s* one *d*. *Educ:* St John's School, Leatherhead; Univ. of Exeter (LLB); St Edmund Hall, Oxford (MA, DPhil). Called to the Bar, Lincoln's Inn, 1968; Sir Thomas More Bursary and Hubert Greenland Studentship, Lincoln's Inn, 1969; a Recorder, 1985–88; an Official Referee, 1992–98; a nominated Judge of the Technology and Construction Court, 1998–2008; Designated Civil Judge, 1999–2008. Chancellor, Vicar-General and Official Principal, Diocese of Durham, 1989–; Chancellor, Dio. of Bath and Wells, 1992–93; Chancellor, VG and Official Principal, Dio. of St Albans, 1992–2002; Dep. Chancellor, Dio. of York, 1994–2007; Chancellor, VG and Official Principal, Dio. of Oxford, 2002–13. Member: Legal Adv. Commn, Gen. Synod, 1990– (Chm., 2007–); Provincial Panels for Canterbury and York, Clergy Discipline Measure, 2006–. Deacon, 1968; Priest, 1969; Hon. Curate: St

Marylebone, 1968–69; St Mary the Virgin, Almondsbury, 1969–71; St Francis, Bedminster, 1971–83; Christ Church, and St Stephen, Bristol, 1983–88; St Andrew, Cheddar, 1993–2011; Gen. Licence to officiate, Oxford dio., 2011–; permission to officiate, Bath & Wells dio., 2011–14. Hon. Canon: St Albans Cathedral, 1996–2002; Cathedral Ch of Christ, Oxford, 2011–. Archbp of Canterbury's visitation commissary to Dio. of Chichester, 2012–13. Hon. Chaplain, 3rd (Vol.) Military Intelligence Bn, 1996–2001. *Publications:* (contrib.) Atkin's Court Forms, 1972, 2nd edn 1985; (contrib.) Halsbury's Laws of England, 1975, 2011; (jtly) Crown Court Practice, 1978; (contrib.) Principles of Dermatitis Litigation, 1985; Liturgy, Order and the Law, 1996; articles in legal jls. *Recreations:* Church music, military history, archaeology of Greece, Turkey and Holy Land, silversmithing. *Address:* Pear Tree Cottage, Hatchet Leys Lane, Thornborough, Bucks MK18 2BU. *Club:* MCC.

BURSLEM, Dame Alexandra Vivien, (Dame Sandra), DBE 2004 (OBE 1993); DL; Vice-Chancellor, Manchester Metropolitan University, 1997–2005; *b* Shanghai, China, 6 May 1940; *d* of Stanley Morris Thornley, CA and Myrra Thornley (*née* Kimberley); *m* 1st, 1960 (marr. diss. 1971); two *s*; 2nd, 1977, Richard Waywell Burslem, MD, FRCOG (*d* 2001); one *d*. *Educ:* Arnold High Sch. for Girls, Blackpool; Manchester Univ. (BA 1st Cl. Hons Politics and Modern Hist. 1971); Manchester Business Sch. (DipBA 1986). Manchester Polytechnic, later Manchester Metropolitan University: Lectr, 1973, Sen. Lectr, 1975–80 and Principal Lectr, 1980–82, Dept of Social Sci., 1973–82; Hd, Dept of Applied Community Studies, 1982–86; Dean, Faculty of Community Studies and Educn, 1986–88; Academic Dir, 1988–92; Dep. Vice-Chancellor, 1992–97. Vice-Chm., Manchester FPC, 1974–89. Chm., BBC Regl Adv. Council, 1983–92. A Civil Service Comr, 2005–10. Member: Council, FEFC, 2000–01; Nat. Learning and Skills Council, 2000–06 (Dep. Chm., 2004–06); Gen. Teaching Council, 2000–02; Council, ACU, 2001–05; HEFCW, 2008–; Bd, Ofqual, 2010–13 (Dep. Chm., 2010–). Chairman: British Council Education-UK Partnership, 2005–11; Educn Honours Cttee, 2005–11. Mem. Bd, Anchor Trust, 1995–97; Chm., Manchester and Cheshire Anchor Trust, 1995–97. Member, Board: RNCM, 2006–14; Cumbria Univ., 2008–11. Gov., Eccles Coll., 1996–98; Feoffee, Chetham's Sch. of Music, 2001– (Chm., Sch. Govs, 2005–). Mem., Manchester Literary and Philosophical Soc., 1988–. FRSA 1989. JP Inner Manchester, 1981; DL 2004, High Sheriff 2006–07, Greater Manchester. Hon. RNCM 2004. Hon. Fellow, St Martin's UC, 2007. Hon. LLD Manchester, 2001; Hon. DLitt: UMIST, 2004; Salford, 2005; Manchester Metropolitan, 2006; Hon. DEd Leeds Metropolitan, 2006. *Recreations:* opera, theatre, reading, travel. *Address:* 17 Bexton Lane, Knutsford, Cheshire WA16 9BW. *T:* (01565) 631200.

BURSTEIN, Joan, CBE 2006; Hon. Chairman, Browns fashion stores, since 2015 (Owner, 1970–2015); *b* 21 Feb. 1926; *d* of Ashley Jotner and Mary Jotner; *m* 1946, Sidney Burstein (*d* 2010); one *s* one *d*. *Educ:* Henrietta Barnett Sch. Owner: Neatawear fashion stores, 1955–67; Feathers boutique, High St Kensington, 1968–70. Hon. Dr Univ. of the Arts, 2007. V&A Award for Outstanding Achievement in Fashion, 2000. *Recreations:* theatre, gardening, travel. *Address:* Browns, 23–27 South Molton Street, W1K 5RD. *T:* (020) 7514 0000, *Fax:* (020) 7408 1281.

BURSTOW, Rt Hon. Paul (Kenneth); PC 2012; *b* 13 May 1962; *s* of Brian Seymour Burstow and Sheila Burstow; *m* 1995, Mary Everdell Kemm; one *s* two *d*. *Educ:* Poly. of South Bank (BA Hons Business Studies). Buying asst, Allied Shoe Repairs, 1985–86; print sales, Kallkwik Printers, 1986–87; research asst (part time), London Borough of Hounslow, 1987–89; Association of Social Democrat, then Liberal Democrat Councillors: Organising Sec. (part time), 1987–89; Councillors Officer, 1989–92; Campaigns Officer, 1992–96; Actg Political Sec., 1996–97. Council, London Borough of Sutton: Mem., 1986–2002; Chm., Envmtl Service Cttee, 1988–91 and 1993–96; Dep. Leader, 1994–97. Contested (Lib Dem) Sutton and Cheam, 1992. MP (Lib Dem) Sutton and Cheam, 1997–2015; contested (Lib Dem) same seat, 2015. Lib Dem Local Govt Team Leader, 1997–99; Lib Dem spokesman on: older people, 1999–2003; health, 2003–05; Lib Dem Chief Whip, 2006–10; Minister of State, DoH, 2010–12. Member: Select Cttee on Health, 2003–04, 2005–06; Modernisation Select Cttee, 2006–08; Finance and Service Cttee, 2006–10; Public Accounts Cttee, 2008–10. *Recreations:* walking, cooking, gym work. *Club:* National Liberal.

BURT, Prof. Alastair David, MD; FRCPath, FRCP, FRCPA; FRSB; Executive Dean of Medicine, Faculty of Health Sciences, University of Adelaide, since 2014; *b* Dunfermline, 9 March 1957; *s* of George Hoggan Burt and Iris Helen Forrest Burt; *m* 1980, Alison Carol Tweedlie; one *s* one *d*. *Educ:* Hawkhill Prim. Sch., Dundee; Hummersknott Grammar Sch., Darlington; Eastwood High Sch., Newton Mearns; Univ. of Glasgow (BSc 1st Cl. Hons 1979; MB ChB with Commendation 1981; MD Hons and Bellahouston Medal 1991). MRCPath 1988, FRCPath 1997; FRSB (FIBiol 1996); FRCP 2009; FRCPA 2014. Jun. House Officer in Medicine and Surgery, Western Infirmary, Glasgow and Glasgow Royal Infirmary, 1981–82; Registrar, then Sen. Registrar in Pathol., Western Infirmary, Glasgow, 1982–89; Peel Trust Travelling Res. Officer, Free Univ. of Brussels, 1985–86; Newcastle University: Sen. Lectr in Pathol., 1989–95; Personal Prof. in Hepatopathol., 1995–98; Prof. of Pathol., 1998–2012; Hd, Sch. of Clin. and Lab. Scis, 2002–05; Dean, Clin. Medicine, 2005–12; Dean of Medicine, Univ. of Adelaide, 2013–14. Hon. Clin. Histopathologist, 1989–2012, Head of Service, Cellular Pathol., 2000–05, Newcastle upon Tyne Hosps NHS Foundn Trust. Hon. Treas. and Trustee, Pathological Soc., 2002–12. Editor-in-Chief: Liver, 1998–2002; Histopathol., 2012–; Member, Editorial Board: Clinical Science, 2002–; Medical Electron Microscopy, 2002–; Jl of Pathology, 2004–; Hepatology, 2006–11; World Jl of Gastroenterology, 2007–; World Jl of Hepatology, 2009–. *Publications:* (ed jtly) Pathology of the Liver, 3rd edn, 1994, 4th edn, 2002; (Ed.-in-Chief) MacSween's Pathology of the Liver, 5th edn, 2006, 6th edn, 2011; (ed jtly) Muir's Textbook of Pathology, 14th edn, 2007; articles in scientific jls on mechanisms and patterns of liver injury, incl. fatty liver disease, fibrosis and autoimmune disease. *Recreations:* chamber music, walking, Asian cookery, foreign travel. *Address:* Faculty of Health Sciences, University of Adelaide, Level 2, Barr Smith South, Frome Road, SA 5005, Australia. *T:* (8) 82224445. *E:* alastair.burt@adelaide.edu.au. *Club:* Athenæum.

BURT, Rt Hon. Alistair (James Hendrie); PC 2013; MP (C) North East Bedfordshire, since 2001; Minister of State, Department of Health, since 2015; *b* 25 May 1955; *s* of James Hendrie Burt, med. practitioner and Mina Christie Robertson; *m* 1983, Eve Alexandra Twite; one *s* one *d*. *Educ:* Bury Grammar Sch.; St John's Coll., Oxford (BA Hons Jurisprudence 1977). Pres., OU Law Soc., Michaelmas term, 1976. Articled Slater Heelis & Co., Manchester, 1978–80; solicitor, Watts, Vallance & Vallance, 1980–92; Consultant, Teeman, Levine and Co. (Solicitors), Leeds, 1992. Councillor, Archway Ward, London Bor. of Haringey, 1982–84. MP (C) Bury North, 1983–97; contested (C) same seat, 1997. Parliamentary Private Secretary: to Sec. of State for the Environment, 1985–86; to Sec. of State for Educn and Science, 1986–89; to Chancellor of Duchy of Lancaster and Chm. of Cons. Party, 1989–90; Parly Under-Sec. of State, DSS, 1992–95; Minister of State (Minister for Disabled People), DSS, 1995–97; Opposition frontbench spokesman on Higher and Further Educn, 2001–02; PPS to Leader of the Opposition, 2002–05; Shadow Minister for Communities and Regeneration, 2005–08; Dep. Chm., Cons. Party, 2007–10; Asst Opposition Chief Whip, 2008–10; Parly Under-Sec. of State, FCO, 2010–13. Vice-Chm., 1985–88, Vice Pres., 2003–, Tory Reform Gp. Secretary: NW Cons. MPs Group, 1984–88; Parly Christian Fellowship, 1984–97 (Chm., 2003–06). Consultant, Whitehead Mann plc, 1997–2001. Chm., Enterprise Forum, 1998–2002. *Recreations:* reading left-wing publications, sport, modern art, marathon running, gardening. *Address:* c/o House of Commons, SW1A 0AA. *W:* www.alistair-burt.co.uk.

BURT, Charles Anthony J.; *see* Johnstone-Burt.

BURT, Gerald Raymond, OBE 1984; BEM (mil.) 1947; FCILT; Chief Secretary, British Railways Board, 1976–84; *b* 15 Feb. 1926; *s* of Reginald George Burt and Lilian May Burt; *m* 1948, Edna Ivy Elizabeth Sizeland (*d* 2008); two *s*. *Educ:* Latymer Upper Sch. FCILT (FCIT 1971). Joined GWR as Booking Clerk, 1942: RE (Movement Control), 1944–47; BR Management Trainee, 1951–54; Gen. Staff, British Transport Commn, 1956–59; Divl Planning Officer, Bristol, 1959–62; Planning Officer, LMR, 1962–64; Divl Man., St Pancras, 1965; Traffic Man., Freightliners, 1967–70; Principal Corporate Planning Officer, British Railways Bd, 1970–76. Member: Council, Chartered Inst. of Transport, 1967–70, 1981–84; British Transport Police Cttee, 1984–88. Governor, British Transport Staff Coll., 1976–82; Trustee, 1984–99, Vice Pres., 2000–, Rly Benevolent Instn. FRSA 1983. Scouting Medal of Merit, 1978. *Publications:* One Railwayman's Life (autobiog.), 2010. *Recreations:* gardening, the countryside. *Address:* 16 Ravens Court, Castle Village, Berkhamsted, Herts HP4 2GX. *T:* (01442) 871725.

BURT, Katherine Victoria; Chief Operating Officer, Greenhouse, since 2014; *b* Roydon, Essex, 7 Nov. 1965; *d* of Jeremy Burt and Victoria Burt (*née* Masefield). *Educ:* Haileybury Coll.; Corpus Christi Coll., Cambridge (BA Hons 1987). Commercial Dir, ReActions Ltd, 1987–91; USA Today, 1992–94; Commercial Dir, BBC Worldwide, 1994–98; Head: Fundraising, Variety Club, 1998–2002; Commercial Develt, Prince's Trust, 2002–09; Vice Pres., Global Develt, Right to Play, 2009–12; CEO, British Rowing, 2012–14. *Recreations:* diving, swimming.

BURT, Lorely Jane; *b* 10 Sept. 1954; *d* of Raymond Claude Baker and Hazel June Baker (*née* Abbiss); *m* 1992, Richard George Burt; one *d*, and one step *s*. *Educ:* University Coll., Swansea (BSc Hons Econ.); Open Univ. (MBA). Asst Gov., HM Prison Service; personnel and trng mgt and consultancy; Man. Dir, trng co.; Director: mktg co.; financial services co.; business consultant. MP (Lib Dem) Solihull, 2005–15; contested (Lib Dem) same seat, 2015. PPS to Chief Sec. to the Treasury, 2013–15; an Asst Govt Whip, 2014–15. Govt Champion for Women in Enterprise, 2014–15. Lib Dem spokesperson for NI, 2015, for business, innovation and skills, 2015–. Mem. (Lib Dem) Dudley MBC, 1998–2003. *Recreations:* keeping fit, metal sculpture, socialising with friends. *Address:* House of Lords, SW1A 0PW.

[Created a Baroness (Life Peer) 2015 but title not yet gazetted at time of going to press.]

BURT, Sir Peter (Alexander), Kt 2003; FRSE; Chairman, Promethean Investments LLP, since 2005; *b* 6 March 1944; *s* of Robert W. Burt and May H. Rodger; *m* 1971, Alison Mackintosh Turner; three *s*. *Educ:* Merchiston Castle Sch., Edinburgh; Univ. of St Andrews (MA); Univ. of Pennsylvania (MBA). FCIBS. Hewlett Packard Co., Palo Alto, 1968–70; CSL, Edinburgh, 1970–74; Edward Bates & Sons Ltd, Edinburgh, 1974; Bank of Scotland: Internat. Div., 1975–88; Asst Gen. Manager, 1979–84; Divisional Gen. Manager, 1984–85; Jt Gen. Manager, 1985–88; Treas. and Chief Gen. Manager, 1988–96; Chief Exec., 1996–2001; Gov., 2001–03; Dep. Chm., HBOS plc, 2001–03. Chairman: Gleacher Shacklock Ltd, 2003–08; ITV plc, 2004–07; Promethean plc, 2005–14. Director: Shell Transport and Trading Co., 2002–04; Royal Dutch Shell, 2004–06; TEMIT plc, 2005–14. Chm., Adv. Bd, Business Bank, 2013. Chairman: Local Govt Finance Review Cttee, 2004–06; Internat. Centre for Math. Scis, 2008–15. Mem., High Constables and Guard of Honour of Holyroodhouse, Edinburgh. FRSE 2002. Hon. LLD St Andrews, 2001. *Recreations:* golf, ski-ing, gardening, reading. *Clubs:* New (Edinburgh); Hon. Co. of Edinburgh Golfers; Royal & Ancient; Gullane Golf; Pine Valley Golf; Loch Lomond Golf.

BURT, Prof. Timothy Peter, PhD, DSc; Master of Hatfield College and Professor of Geography, Durham University, since 1996; *b* Mells, Som, 23 Dec. 1951; *s* of Donald Sydney Burt and Evelean Gertrude Burt (*née* Twynham); *m* 1973, Elizabeth Anne Sapsford; one *s* one *d*. *Educ:* Sexey's Sch., Bruton, Som; St John's Coll., Cambridge (BA Geog. 1st cl. 1973); Carleton Univ., Ottawa (MA 1974); Bristol Univ. (PhD 1978; DSc 1999). Sen. Lectr, Huddersfield Poly., 1977–84; Lectr in Geog., Oxford Univ. and Fellow, Keble Coll., Oxford, 1984–96. Vis. Prof., Oregon State Univ., 2010. Field Studies Council: Trustee, 1982–; Chm., 1996–2014; Pres., 2014–. Fellow: Amer. Geophysical Union, 2012; British Soc. Geomorphol., 2014. *Publications:* Catchment Experiments in Fluvial Geomorphology, 1984; Hydrological Forecasting, 1985; Computer Simulation in Physical Geography, 1987; Process Studies in Hillslope Hydrology, 1990; Nitrate, 1993; Buffer Zones, 1997; (ed) History of the Study of Landforms, vol. 4, 2008; Sediment Cascades, 2010; numerous contribs scientific papers and book chapters. *Recreations:* walking, sport, music, grandchildren, Field Studies Council. *Address:* Hatfield College, North Bailey, Durham DH1 3RQ. *T:* (0191) 334 2601, *Fax:* (0191) 334 3101. *E:* t.p.burt@durham.ac.uk.

BURTENSHAW, Alistair John; Director, Charleston Trust, since 2013; *b* Westminster, 11 Nov. 1969; *s* of George Neville Burtenshaw and Christine Mary Burtenshaw (*née* Menzies); *m* 1998, Francisca Beloso-Garcia; one *d*. *Educ:* Hove Park Upper Sch.; Univ. of Hertfordshire (BA Hons Business Studies 1993). Dip. CIM 1994, MCIM; Dip. Mkt Res. Soc. 1993, AMRS. Sales exec., Centaur Communications plc, 1994–96; Reed Exhibitions Ltd: Sales Exec., 1996–98, Sales Manager, 1998–2000, Internat. Direct Mktg Fair; Exhibn Manager, 2000–01, Exhibn Dir, 2001–05, Gp Exhibn Dir, 2005–12, London Book Fair; Director: Books and Publishing Worldwide, 2011–12; Publishing Connections Ltd, 2012–. Chairman: Trustees, Booktrust, 2012–13 (Trustee, 2006–08; Dep. Chair, 2008–12); Arvon Foundn, 2014–. Pres. of Honour, Paris Cook Book Fair, 2013. Trustee, Book Trade Benevolent Soc., 2002–08. Member: Exec. Cttee, English Pen, 2002–04; The Book Soc. (formerly Soc. of Bookmen), 2005–. FRSA. *Recreations:* family, reading, current affairs, international relations, opera, running, ski-ing, encouraging literacy, the arts, foreign travel, Spanish and Italian languages. *Address:* Charleston Trust, Firle, Lewes, E Sussex BN8 6LL. *T:* (01323) 811626. *E:* a.burtenshaw@charleston.org.uk. *Club:* Academicians' Room.

See also Dr H. J. Caldwell.

BURTON, 4th Baron *cr* 1897; **Evan Michael Ronald Baillie;** *b* 19 March 1949; *s* of 3rd Baron Burton and Elizabeth Ursula Forster Baillie (*née* Wise); *S* father, 2013; *m* 1st, 1970, Lucinda Anne Law (marr. diss. 1984); two *s* one *d*; 2nd, 1998, June Gordon. *Educ:* Harrow; RAC Cirencester. *Heir:* *s* Hon. James Evan Baillie [*b* 3 Dec. 1975; *m* 2011, Katie Elizabeth Wright; two *s*].

BURTON, Air Vice-Marshal Andrew John, OBE 1991 (MBE 1986); FCIS, Chartered FCIPD; Bursar and Clerk to the Governors, Sevenoaks School, since 2003; *b* 11 Nov. 1950; *s* of Walter Joseph Burton and Phyllis Jane Burton (*née* Flear); *m* 1977, Sheila Hanson; two *s*. *Educ:* Llanelli Boys' Grammar Sch.; Univ. of Wales Inst. of Sci. and Technol. (BScEcon 1972). FCIS 1993 (ACIS 1982); Chartered FCIPD 2003 (FCIPD 2000). Commnd RAF, 1972; Sqn Leader, 1980; Wing Comdr, 1986; Defence Staff, British Embassy, Washington, 1988–90; Gp Capt., 1991; Station Comdr, RAF Uxbridge, 1994–95; Air Cdre, 1996; Dir of Personnel (RAF), 1995–98; Air Vice-Marshal, 1998; AOA and AOC Directly Administered Units, HQ Strike Comd, 1998–2001, PTC, 2001–03. *Recreations:* golf, sport, theatre. *Address:* Sevenoaks School, Sevenoaks, Kent TN13 1HU. *T:* (01732) 455133. *Club:* Royal Air Force.

BURTON, Anthony Charles, CBE 2012; solicitor; a Senior Partner, Simons Muirhead and Burton, since 1976; a Recorder, since 1999; *b* Folkestone, 12 July 1947; *s* of late Dr Peter John Charles Burton and Violet Marie Aurelie Burton (*née* Branson); *m* 1996, Leonie Mellinger; one *s* two *d*. *Educ:* Beaumont Coll.; Coll. of Law, London. Admitted solicitor, 1972. Mem. Council, Justice, 1990–. Chm., Royal Court Th., 2005–. *Recreations:* theatre, reading, family, cricket, Rugby. *Address:* 41a Montague Road, Richmond, Surrey TW10 6QJ. *T:* (020) 3206 2713, *Fax:* (020) 3206 2800. *E:* anthony.burton@smab.co.uk. *Clubs:* Groucho, Chelsea Arts.

BURTON, (Anthony) David, CBE 1992; business consultant, since 1998; *b* 2 April 1937; *s* of Leslie Mitchell Burton and Marion Burton (*née* Marsh); *m* 1964, Valerie (*née* Swire); one *s* two *d*. *Educ:* Arnold Sch., Blackpool. FCIB; FCT. Bank of America National Trust and Savings Assoc., 1966–72; S. G. Warburg & Co. Ltd, 1972–92 (Dir, 1977–92). Dir, LIFFE, 1981–94 (Chm., 1988–92). Chairman: Marshalls Finance Ltd, 1989–98; The 181 Fund Ltd (formerly Ludgate 181 plc, then Ludgate 181 (Jersey) Ltd), 1999–; Ashley House plc, 2004–07; Ashley House Medical Properties plc (formerly Ashley House Properties Ltd), 2004–07; Ludgate Investments Ltd, 2004–10; Beechwood House Finance Ltd, 2004–11; Dir, Car Crash Line Gp plc, 2003–05. *Publications:* Antique Sealed Bottles 1640–1900 and the families who owned them, 2015. *Recreations:* antique glass, German pottery, music, opera, historical and genealogical research.

BURTON, Anthony George Graham; author and broadcaster, since 1968; *b* 24 Dec. 1934; *s* of Donald Graham Burton and Irene Burton; *m* 1959, Pip Sharman; two *s* one *d*. *Educ:* King James's Grammar Sch., Knaresborough; Leeds Univ. National Service, RAF, 1955–57. Research chemist, 1958–60; publishing, 1960–68. *Publications:* A Programmed Guide to Office Warfare, 1969; The Jones Report, 1970; The Canal Builders, 1972, 4th edn 2005; Canals in Colour, 1974; Remains of a Revolution, 1975, 2nd edn 2001; Josiah Wedgwood, 1976; (jtly) Canal, 1976; The Miners, 1976; Back Door Britain, 1977; Industrial Archaeological Sites of Britain, 1977; (jtly) The Green Bag Travellers, 1978; The Past At Work, 1980; The Rainhill Story, 1980; The Past Afloat, 1982; The Changing River, 1982; The Shell Book of Curious Britain, 1982; The National Trust Guide to Our Industrial Past, 1983; The Waterways of Britain, 1983; The Rise and Fall of King Cotton, 1984; (ed jtly) Canals: a new look, 1984; Walking the Line, 1985; Wilderness Britain, 1985; (jtly) Britain's Light Railways, 1985; The Shell Book of Undiscovered Britain and Ireland, 1986; (jtly) Landscape Detective, 1986; Britain Revisited, 1986; Opening Time, 1987; Steaming Through Britain, 1987; Walking Through History, 1988; Walk the South Downs, 1988; The Great Days of the Canals, 1989; Cityscapes, 1990; Astonishing Britain, 1990; Slow Roads, 1991; The Railway Builders, 1992; Canal Mania, 1993; (jtly) The Grand Union Canal Walk, 1993; The Railway Empire, 1994; The Rise and Fall of British Shipbuilding, 1994; The Cotswold Way, 1995, new edn 2007; The Dales Way, 1995; The West Highland Way, 1996; The Southern Upland Way, 1997; William Cobbett: Englishman, 1997; The Caledonian Canal, 1998; The Wye Valley Walk, 1998; Best Foot Forward, 1998; The Cumbria Way, 1999; The Wessex Ridgeway, 1999; Thomas Telford, 1999; Weekend Walks Dartmoor and Exmoor, 2000; Weekend Walks the Yorkshire Dales, 2000; Traction Engines, 2000; Richard Trevithick, 2000; Weekend Walks The Peak District, 2001; The Orient Express, 2001; The Anatomy of Canals: the early years, 2001; The Daily Telegraph Guide to Britain's Working Past, 2002; Hadrian's Wall Path, 2003; The Daily Telegraph Guide to Britain's Maritime Past, 2003; The Anatomy of Canals: decline and renewal, 2003; On the Rails, 2004; The Ridgeway, 2005; Tracing your Shipbuilding Ancestors, 2010; Canal 250, 2011; History's Most Dangerous Jobs: The Navvies, 2012; The Miners, 2013; Life on the Farm, 2013; Life in the Mine, 2013; Life in the Mill, 2013; Life on the Railway, 2013; Life on the Canal, 2013; Matthew Boulton, 2013; Mary Rose Museum, 2014; *novels:* The Reluctant Musketeer, 1973; The Master Idol, 1975; The Navigators, 1976; A Place to Stand, 1977. *Recreations:* walking and travelling in search of steam engines and good beer; cinema. *Address:* c/o Sara Menguc, Literary Agent, 58 Thorkhill Road, Thames Ditton, Surrey KT7 0UG. *T:* (020) 8398 7992. *W:* www.anthonyburton.co.uk.

BURTON, Rt Rev. Anthony John; Rector, Church of the Incarnation, Dallas, Texas, since 2008; *b* 11 Aug. 1959; *s* of Peter and Rachel Burton; *m* 1989, Anna Kristine Erickson; one *s* one *d*. *Educ:* Trinity Coll., Toronto Univ. (BA (Hons) 1982); King's Coll., Dalhousie Univ.; Wycliffe Hall, Oxford (BA, MA). Ordained deacon, 1987, priest, 1988; Curate, St John the Baptist, N Sydney, Nova Scotia, 1987–88; Rector, Trinity Church, Sydney Mines, 1988–91; Rector and Canon Residentiary, Cathedral Church of St Alban the Martyr, Saskatchewan, 1991–93; Dean of Saskatchewan, 1991–94; Bishop of Saskatchewan, 1993–2008. Anglican-Roman Catholic Bps' Dialogue, Canada, 1994–97, 2000–02, Co-Chm., 2007–08. Chancellor, James Settee Coll., 1995–2008. Member, Board: Scholarly Engagement with Anglican Doctrine, USA, 2003–04; Living Ch Foundn, 2010–13. Chair, Council of the North, 2004–07; Chairman: Bd, Elliott Hse of Studies, 2010–; Bd of Visitors, Ralston Coll., Savannah, Ga, 2013–. Vice-Chm., Prayer Book Soc. of Canada, 1999–2008. Episcopal Visitor, S American Missionary Soc., Canada, 2002–08. Hon. DD King's Coll., Halifax, 1994. *Publications:* (contrib.) Anglican Essentials: reclaiming faith in the Anglican Church of Canada, 1995; contrib. to Machray Rev., Liturgy Canada, Anglican Digest, Living Ch. *Recreations:* walking, fighting ignominiously in last ditches. *Address:* Church of the Incarnation, 3966 McKinney Avenue, Dallas, TX 75204, USA.

BURTON, Anthony Philip; Senior Research Fellow in Museology and Museum History, Research Department, Victoria and Albert Museum, 1997–2002; Chairman of Trustees, Charles Dickens Museum, London, 2003–05; *b* 25 Oct. 1942; *s* of late Frank Burton and Lottie Burton (*née* Lax); *m* 1985, Carol Deborah Baker. *Educ:* King's Sch., Macclesfield; Wadham Coll., Oxford (BLitt, MA). Res. Asst, Dept of English, Birkbeck Coll., Univ. of London, 1965–68; Victoria and Albert Museum: Asst Keeper, Nat. Art Liby, 1968–79; Asst Keeper, Directorate, 1979–81; Hd, Bethnal Green Mus. of Childhood, 1981–97. Trustee, Hoxton Hall, 2007–13. *Publications:* (with S. Haskins) European Art in the Victoria and Albert Museum, 1983; Children's Pleasures: books, toys and games from the Bethnal Green Museum of Childhood, 1996; Vision & Accident: the story of the Victoria and Albert Museum, 1999; (with E. Bonython) The Great Exhibitor: the life and work of Henry Cole, 2003; articles on liby and mus. subjects. *Recreations:* cultural pursuits, reading crime fiction. *Address:* 20 Lockside, Marple, Stockport SK6 6BN. *T:* (0161) 258 9077, 07847 144901.

BURTON, Caroline Oldcorn; *see* Reid, C. O.

BURTON, David; *see* Burton, A. D.

BURTON, David Harold; Managing Director, West Anglia Great Northern Railway, 1996–99; *b* 28 Jan. 1947; *s* of George and Helen Burton; *m* (marr. diss.); one *s*; *m* 2006, Julia Ramsay; one step *s* two step *d*. *Educ:* Bridlington Sch.; Leeds Univ. (BA (Hons) Geography). British Rail: Network Man., S Central Network SE, 1986; Dep. Gen. Man., Southern Region, 1988; Gen. Man., Anglia Region, 1989–91; Gp Dir North, Network SouthEast, 1991–92; Director: Express Parcels, BR Parcels, 1992–93; Restructuring, Network SouthEast, 1993–94; Dir, Product Quality, and Dep. Man. Dir (S & E), BRB, 1994–96. Transport mgt consultant, 1999–2005. Mem. Bd, Passenger Focus, 2005–12. Non-exec. Dir, Norfolk, Suffolk and Cambs Strategic HA, 2002–06; Gov., Papworth Hosp. Foundn Trust, 2004–06. *Recreations:* spectator sport, golf, reading.

BURTON, Lt-Gen. Sir Edmund Fortescue Gerard, KBE 1999 (OBE); DL; FIET, FBCS; Chairman, Information Assurance Advisory Council, since 2007; *b* 20 Oct. 1943. *Educ:* Trinity Hall, Cambridge (BA 1968; MA 1972). Commissioned RA, 1963; Brig., 1987; Mil. Attaché, Washington, 1990; Maj.-Gen., 1991; Comdt, RMCS, 1991–94; ACDS, Operational Requirements (Land), 1994–97; DCDS (Systems), 1997–99; retd 2000. Vis. Prof., Cranfield Univ., 2000–. Jt Chm., Telecommunications Ind. Security Adv. Council, 2004–11. Exec. Chm., Police Information Technol. Orgn, 2001–03. Pres., Trustworthy Software Initiative, 2013–. Chm., Philip Barker Charity, 1997–. Chm. Council, Chester Cathedral, 2008–14. Hon. Col, OTC (Cambridge), 1996–2003; Col Comdt, RA, 1998–2004; Hon. Regtl Col, 26 Regt RA, 1999–2006. Hon. DSc Cranfield, 2009. DL Cheshire, 2013.

BURTON, Frances Rosemary; an Upper Tribunal Judge (Administrative Appeals Chamber), 2009–11; Co-Director, International Centre for Family Law, Policy and Practice, since 2013; *b* Bury St Edmunds, 19 June 1941; *d* of late Major Richard Francis Heveningham Pughe, DFC, ERD and Pamela Margaret Pughe (*née* Coates); *m* 1st, 1963, Robert Scott Alexander (Baron Alexander of Weedon, QC) (marr. diss. 1973; he *d* 2005); two *s* one *d*; 2nd, 1975, David Michael Burton (*d* 2000); two *d*. *Educ:* St Anne's Coll., Oxford; Univ. of London (LLB); Univ. of Leicester (LLM); Open Univ. (MA). Called to the Bar, Middle Temple, 1970 (Harmsworth Major Entrance Exhibnr); in practice as a barrister, 1972–75, 1989–2012; mediator, 2000–; Family Arbitrator, MCIArb, 2013–. Vis. Lectr, City of London Poly., 1989–93; Vis. Lectr, 1989–93, Sen. Lectr in Law, 1993–2001, London Guildhall Univ.; Lectr, Coll. of Law, London and Birmingham, 2001–02; Principal Lectr, UWE, 2002–08; Dir, BVC Open Learning, 2002–08; Vis. Lectr, 2009, Research Fellow, 2010–13, London Metropolitan Univ.; Associate Lectr, Bucks New Univ., 2012–; Visiting Lecturer: Middlesex Univ., 2013–15; Aston Univ., 2014–15. BVC Course Dir, 1992–93, Consultant, Mem. and Hon. Sec., Academic Adv. Bd, 1993–2000, BPP Law Sch. Co-Dir, Centre for Family Law and Practice, London Metropolitan Univ., 2009–13. Lawyer Chm., Residential Property Tribunal Service, 1996–2011; Chm., Transport Tribunal, 2002–09. Co-Dir, Internat. Centre for Family Law, Policy and Practice, 2013–. *Publications:* Family Law for Law Society Final Examination, 1988, 2nd edn 1990; Bar Final General Paper II Textbook, 1990; (jtly) Criminal Procedure, 1993, 3rd edn 1996; Family Law, 1996; Guide to the Family Law Act 1996, 1996; Teaching Family Law, 1999; Family Law Textbook, 2003; Family Law, 2012, 2nd edn 2015; Core Statutes in Family Law, 10th edn 2015. *Recreations:* opera, history, archaeology. *Address:* 10 Old Square, Lincoln's Inn, WC2A 3SU. *T:* 07775 655088. *E:* frb@frburton.com. *Club:* Oxford and Cambridge.

BURTON, Dr Frank Patrick; QC 1998; a Recorder, since 2000; a Deputy High Court Judge, since 2010; *b* 19 June 1950; *s* of Ronald Burton and late Ita Burton; *m* 1983, Caroline Oldcorn Reid, *qv*; two *s* one *d*. *Educ:* Salesian Coll., Farnborough; Univ. of Kent at Canterbury (BA 1st Cl. Hons 1971); London School of Economics and Political Science (PhD 1974). Lecturer in Social Science: Brunel Univ., 1976–79; City Univ., 1979–82; called to the Bar, Gray's Inn, 1982, Bencher, 2004; in practice at the Bar, 1982–. Chairman: Law Reform Cttee, Bar Council, 2003–05; Personal Injury Bar Assoc., 2004–06 (Vice Chm., 2002–04). Motor Insurers' Bureau Arbitrator, 2001–. *Publications:* Medical Negligence Case Law, 1990, 2nd edn 1995; Personal Injury Limitation Law, 1994, 3rd edn 2013. *Recreations:* sport, reading, Suffolk. *Address:* 12 King's Bench Walk, Temple, EC4Y 7EL.

BURTON, Prof. Graham James, MD, DSc; FMedSci; Mary Marshall and Arthur Walton Professor of the Physiology of Reproduction, since 2013, and Director, Centre for Trophoblast Research, since 2007, University of Cambridge; Fellow, St John's College, Cambridge, since 1982; *b* Cambridge, 27 Jan. 1953; *s* of William and Pamela Burton; *m* 1979, Hilary Jordison; one *s* four *d*. *Educ:* Colchester Royal Grammar Sch.; Christ's Coll., Cambridge (BA Med. Sci. 1974; MD 1984); Magdalen Coll., Oxford (BM BCh 1977; DSc 2005). University of Cambridge: Lectr, 1982–2001; Reader in Human Reproduction, 2001–04; Prof. of Reproductive Biol., 2004–13. Eur. Ed., Placenta, 2008–. FMedSci 2011. *Publications:* Comparative Placentation, 2008; The Human Placenta and Developmental Programming, 2010; Pathology of the Human Placenta, 6th edn 2012; contrib. book chapters; contrib. papers to scientific jls. *Recreations:* walking, family. *Address:* Department of Physiology, Development and Neuroscience, University of Cambridge, Downing Street, Cambridge CB2 3EG. *T:* (01223) 333856, *Fax:* (01223) 333840. *E:* gjb2@cam.ac.uk.

BURTON, Sir Graham (Stuart), KCMG 1999 (CMG 1987); HM Diplomatic Service, retired; High Commissioner, Nigeria, also concurrently Ambassador (non-resident) to the Republic of Benin, 1997–2001; *b* 8 April 1941; *s* of late Cyril Stanley Richard Burton and of Jessie Blythe Burton; *m* 1965, Julia Margaret Lappin; one *s* one *d*. *Educ:* Sir William Borlase's Sch., Marlow. Foreign Office, 1961; Abu Dhabi, 1964; Middle East Centre for Arabic Studies, 1967; Kuwait, 1969; FCO, 1972; Tunis, 1975; UK Mission to United Nations, 1978; Counsellor, Tripoli, 1981; Head, Security Co-ordination Dept, FCO, 1984; Consul General, San Francisco, 1987; Ambassador: UAE, 1990; Indonesia, 1994. Director: Magadi Soda Co., Kenya, 2001–08; Gulf of Guinea Energy, 2006–09; Advr, Control Risks Gp, 2001–12. Dir, W African Business Assoc., 2003–11. Trustee: Royal Commonwealth Soc. for the Blind, 2005–09; Chalker Foundn, 2006–. *Recreations:* golf, watching cricket, baseball and most other sports; opera. *Clubs:* MCC; Wildcat Run Golf and Country (Estero).

BURTON, Humphrey McGuire, CBE 2000; writer and broadcaster; *b* 25 March 1931; *s* of Harry (Philip) and Kathleen Burton; *m* 1st, 1957, Gretel (*née* Davis); one *s* one *d*; 2nd, 1970, Christina (*née* Hellstedt); one *s* one *d*. *Educ:* Long Dene Sch., Chiddingstone; Judd Sch., Tonbridge; Fitzwilliam House, Cambridge (BA; Hon. Fellow, Fitzwilliam Coll., 1997; MA 2008). BBC Radio, 1955–58; BBC TV, 1958–67: Editor, Monitor, 1962; Exec. Producer, Music Programmes, 1963; Head of Music and Arts Programmes, 1965–67, productions inc. Workshop, Master Class, In Rehearsal, Britten at 50, Conversations with Glenn Gould; London Weekend TV: Head of Drama, Arts and Music, 1967–69; Editor/Introducer, Aquarius, 1970–75, programmes incl. Mahler Festival, Verdi Requiem, Trouble in Tahiti, The Great Gondola Race, Anatomy of a Record, etc.; Head of Music and Arts, BBC TV, 1975–81; Presenter: Omnibus, 1976–78, 1984–85 (Producer, West Side Story documentary, 1985; RAI Prize, Prix Italia, BAFTA Robert Flaherty Best Documentary Award, 1985); In Performance, 1978–82; Young Musician of the Year, biennially 1978–94; Producer/Director: TV Proms with Giulini and Solti, 1981, and with others, 1982–95; Walton 80th Birthday Concert (Previn); Verdi Requiem (Abbado), and Call me Kiri (Te Kanawa), 1982; Candide, Scottish Opera, Glasgow, 1988 and Barbican (conducted by Leonard Bernstein), 1989; Covent Garden opera relays, incl. Die Fledermaus (Joan Sutherland farewell), 1990; Artistic Dir, 1988–90, Artistic Advr, 1990–93, Barbican Centre. Other productions include: 5 Glyndebourne operas, adapted and produced, Southern TV, 1972–74; The Beach at Falesa, World Première, Harlech TV, 1974; Channel 4 operas include: Eugene Onegin, 1994; Ermione, 1995; Lulu, 1996; The Damnation of Faust, Manon Lescaut, 1997; Rodelinda, Hansel and Gretel, 1998; Pelléas et Mélisande, Flight, 1999; BBC2 opera, Falstaff, 1999; BBC4 drama, Vincent in Brixton, 2002; UN Day Concert with Pablo Casals, 1971, and subseq. UN days, 1972–92; Berlioz' Requiem, at Les Invalides, 1975, The Return of Ulysses, at Aix-en-Provence, 2002, French TV; many free-lance prodns in Austria, Czechoslovakia, Germany, Hungary, Italy, Israel, Poland, Russia and USA, including: Mahler, Brahms, Schumann and Beethoven Cycles with Bernstein and Vienna Philharmonic; concerts with von Karajan and Berlin and Vienna Philharmonic, Giulini and LA Philharmonic, Mehta and NY Philharmonic, Maazel and Bayerisches Rundfunk Orch., Solti and Chicago SO; world première, Epitaph, by Charles Mingus, NY, 1989; Director: Boris Godunov, Kirov, 1990; War and Peace, Kirov, 1991; Mozart Requiem, Vienna Bicentennial 1991; Producer: Leonard Bernstein's 70th Birthday Gala Season, Tanglewood, 1988; Bernstein Meml Concert, Carnegie Hall, 1990; Guest Dir, 1983 Hollywood Bowl Summer Music Fest.; conducting début, Verdi Requiem, Philharmonia Orch., RAH, 2001 (raised £75,000 for Prostate Research); host, Matinée Musicales, Aldeburgh cinema, 2004–; devised and conducted Schubert season, Snape Maltings and Jubilee Hall, Aldeburgh, 2011; video curator, Aldeburgh Fest., 2013–; *radio:* writer/presenter of series, incl. Life of Leonard Bernstein, Menuhin-Master Musician, William Walton: the romantic loner, Classic FM, Artist in Focus, etc., BBC. Columnist: Classic FM Magazine, 1995–98; BBC Music Magazine, 1998–99. Cruise ship lectr, 2000–. Chairman: EBU Music Experts Gp, 1976–82; EBU TV Music Working Party, 1982–86; Mem., New Music Sub-Cttee, Arts Council, 1981–83; Advr, Manchester Olympic Fest., 1990; Administrator, Royal Philharmonic Soc.'s Music Awards, 1989–91. Hon. Professorial Fellow, University Coll., Cardiff, 1983–87. Hon. FCSD 1990. Desmond Davis Award, SFTA, 1966; Royal TV Soc. Silver Medal, 1971; Emmy, 1971 for 'Beethoven's Birthday' (CBS TV); Peabody Award, 1972; SFTA Best Specialised Series, 1974; Christopher Award, 1979; Emmy, 1988, for 'Celebrating Gershwin' (PBS/BBC TV). Chevalier de l'Ordre des Arts et des Lettres, 1975. *Publications:* Leonard Bernstein, 1994 (trans. German, Chinese and Japanese; ASCAP book award, 1995); Menuhin: a life, 2000 (trans. German); (jtly) William Walton: the romantic loner, 2002. *Recreations:* music-making, travel. *Address:* 13 Linden Road, Aldeburgh, Suffolk IP15 5JQ.

BURTON, Ian Richard; Founder and Senior Partner, BCL Burton Copeland, London, since 1991; *b* Manchester, 25 March 1947; *s* of Jack Burton and Faie Glaisher; *m* 1973, Sarah Ruth Ashbrook; one *s* one *d*. *Educ:* Whittingehame Coll., Brighton. Admitted solicitor, 1971; Partner: Nigel Copeland Glickman, 1971–75; Gardner Burton, 1975–82; Founder and Sen. Partner, Burton Copeland, Manchester, 1982–2001. *Recreations:* family, opera, contemporary art. *Address:* BCL Burton Copeland, 51 Lincoln's Inn Fields, WC2A 3LZ. *T:* (020) 7430 2277, *Fax:* (020) 7430 1101. *E:* ianburton@bcl.com. *Club:* Royal Automobile.

BURTON, Iris Grace, (Mrs Joe Lucas); Editor-in-Chief: Woman's Realm, 1991–99; Woman's Weekly, 1992–99; Eva, 1994–97; Chat, 1997–99; *d* of late Arthur Burton and Alice Burton; *m* 2012, Joe Lucas; one *s* one *d*. *Educ:* Roan Girls' Grammar Sch., Greenwich; City of London Coll. Local newspaper, SE London Mercury, until 1966; Writer, then Features Editor, Woman's Own, 1966–78; Asst Editor, TV Times, 1978–80; Editor, Woman's Own, 1980–86; Editor-in-Chief: Prima magazine, 1986–87; Best magazine, 1987–88; Editorial Dir, G+J of the UK publications, 1988–91; Launch Ed., Now mag., 1996. Mem., Press Complaints Commn, 1993–99. *Address:* 13 Wheathill Road, SE20 7XQ.

BURTON, Jane; Headteacher, Wallington High School for Girls, since 2012; *b* London, 25 Aug. 1965; *d* of Victor Shore and Jean Kritz; *m* 2002, Christopher Burton; one *s*. *Educ:* Marshalls Park Sch.; Univ. of Salford (BSc Econs 1986); Univ. of Kingston (PGCE 2000). Commercial mgt, Marks and Spencer plc and Stirling Gp plc, 1986–99; teacher, Wilsons Sch., 2000–10 (Asst Hd); Dep. Hd, Nonsuch High Sch. for Girls, 2010–12. *Recreations:* family, reading. *Address:* Wallington High School for Girls, Woodcote Road, Wallington, Surrey SM6 0PH. *T:* (020) 8647 2380.

BURTON, Prof. John Lloyd, MD; FRCP; Professor of Dermatology, University of Bristol, 1992–98; *b* 29 Aug. 1938; *s* of Lloyd Burton and Dorothy Mary Burton (*née* Pacey); *m* 1964, Patricia Anne Crankshaw, DRCOG, FRCPath; one *s* two *d*. *Educ:* Heanor Grammar Sch., Derbys; Manchester Univ. (BSc; MD 1971). FRCP 1978. Trng posts in hosps in Manchester, London, Edinburgh and Newcastle upon Tyne, 1964–73; Consultant Dermatologist, Bristol Royal Infirmary, 1973–98. Numerous guest lectures, including: Dowling Oration, 1980, Deville, 1995, RSM; Parkes-Weber, RCP, 1988; Long-Fox, Bristol Univ., 1994. Advr in Dermatol. to CMO, DoH, 1988–94. Examr, RCP, 1987–92. Chm., Dermatol. Cttee, RCP, 1993–95; President: Dermatol. Sect., RSocMed, 1994–95; Brit. Assoc. Dermatologists, 1995–96. Editor, Brit. Jl Dermatol., 1981–85. *Publications:* Aids to Postgraduate Medicine, 1970, 6th edn 1994; Aids to Undergraduate Medicine, 1973, 6th edn 1997; Essentials of Dermatology, 1979, 3rd edn 1990; (ed jtly) Textbook of Dermatology (4 Vols), 4th edn 1986 to 6th edn 1998; 600 Miseries: the 17th century womb, 2005; Why Man Made Gods and Dogs: the evolution of religion, 2010; Birds of the Franschhoek Valley: a guide for the novice, 2012; Cases of a 17th Century Physician, 2015; numerous chapters and scientific papers. *Recreations:* painting, book-binding. *Address:* Eastfield House, East Street, North Perrott, Somerset TA18 7SW. *T:* (01460) 75156.

BURTON, John Malcolm; QC 2010; Advocate, Public Defender Service, since 2014; *b* Blackpool, 29 July 1957; *s* of Malcolm Burton and Ruby Burton; *m* 1st, 1986, Karen Falkingham (*d* 1992); two *s*; 2nd, 2006, Katherine Lissanevitch. *Educ:* Culcheth High Sch.; Queen Mary Coll., London (LLB Hons 1978). Called to the Bar, Inner Temple, 1979; in practice as a barrister, 1979–, specialising in serious crime, fraud, terrorism and murder. *Publications:* articles in law jls and Index on Censorship. *Recreations:* reading, drawing, painting, writing, ski-ing, travel. *Address:* Public Defender Service Advocacy Unit, 102 Petty France, SW1H 9AJ.

BURTON, John Michael, MBE 2013; RIBA; Partner, Purcell LLP (formerly Purcell Miller Tritton), Architects, since 1978; Surveyor to the Fabric, Canterbury Cathedral, 1990–2014; Surveyor of the Fabric of Westminster Abbey, 1999–2012; *b* 21 May 1945; *s* of Gerald Victor Burton and Kathleen Blodwen (*née* Harper); *m* 1971, Sally Bason; one *s* one *d*. *Educ:* Duston Secondary Mod. Sch., Northampton; Northampton Coll. of Further Educn; Oxford Sch. of Architecture (DipArch). RIBA 1972; IHBC 1998; AABC 1999. Asst to Surveyor to Ely Cathedral, 1971–73; Parish Architect to numerous churches in E Anglia incl. Long Melford and Thaxted, 1973–; Commissioned Architect to English Heritage, 1983–2002; Architect to NT, Melford Hall, Lavenham Guildhall and Flatford Mill, 1973–96; work on restoration of Colchester Castle, 1984–90; Architect, American Ambassador's Residence, London, 1998–; Conservation Advr to Crown Urban Estate, 2003–. Chm., Cathedral Architects' Assoc., 1997–99. Member: Cathedrals Fabric Commn for England, 1996–2006; Redundant Churches Cttee, Church Comrs, 1999–2002; Places of Worship Panel, 2000–03, Historic Built Envmt Adv. Cttee, 2000–03, English Heritage; Chm., Redundant Churches Uses Cttee, Chelmsford, 1990–. Mem., DAC for Chelmsford, 1977–, St Edmundsbury and Ipswich, 1986–98. Mem. Council, Nat. Trust, 2007–. Vice Chm., Georgian Gp, 2014– (Chm., Awards Cttee, 2014). Dir, Mercury Theatre, Colchester, 1999–2003. Mem., Colchester Trinity Rotary Club; Pres., Surveyors' Club, 2012–13. Stone Awards Judge, Stone Fedn of GB, 1995 and 1997 (Chm. of Judges, 1999–). Freeman, City of London, 1996; Master, Masons' Co., 2013–14 (Liveryman, 1996–2005; Court Asst, 2005–); Liveryman, Carpenters' Co., 2007–. *Recreations:* cycling, ski-ing, woodwork. *Address:* Purcell LLP, 25 Bermondsey Square, Tower Bridge Road, SE1 3UN. *T:* (020) 7397 7171. *E:* john.burton@purcelluk.com.

BURTON, Hon. Mark; *see* Burton, R. M.

BURTON, Rt Rev. Dr Mark Gregory; Dean of Melbourne, 2009–12; *b* Sydney, 18 May 1956; *s* of late Kenneth Burton and of Patricia Burton; *m* 1st, 1975, Annette Gill (marr. diss. 2013); three *d*; 2nd, 2014, Rena Sofroniou. *Educ:* Ridley Coll., Melbourne (BTh 1988); Australian Coll. of Theology (ThD 2001). Tutor, Ridley Coll., Melbourne, 1989–97; ordained deacon, 1990, priest, 1990; Asst Curate, Werribee, 1990–91; Priest-in-charge, St James', Glen Iris, 1991–97; Examining Chaplain, Dio. of Melbourne, 1996–2000; Chaplain to Archbishop of Melbourne, and Dir of Ordinands, 1997–2000; Archbishop's Chaplain and Aide, 2000; Chaplain: RAN, 2001; HMAS Cerberus West Port, 2002; HMAS Melbourne, 2003; HMAS Kanimbla/HMAS Adelaide, 2004–05; HMAS Creswell, 2006; Asst Bishop, Dio. of Perth, WA, 2006–09. Australian Service Medal, 1983; Australian Active Service Medal, 2003; Iraq Campaign Medal, 2003; Humanitarian Overseas Service Medal, 2004; Australian Defence Medal, 2005. *Recreations:* sailing, scuba diving, motorcycling, archery.

BURTON, Hon. Sir Michael (John), Kt 1998; **Hon. Mr Justice Burton;** a Judge of the High Court of Justice, Queen's Bench Division, since 1998; Judge of the Employment Appeal Tribunal, since 1999 (President, 2002–05); *b* 12 Nov. 1946; *s* of late Henry Burton, QC, and Hilda Burton; *m* 1972, Corinne Ruth (*d* 1992), *d* of late Dr Jack Cowan, MC, and Dorothy Cowan; four *d*. *Educ:* Eton Coll. (KS, Captain of the School; Fellow, 2004); Balliol Coll., Oxford (MA). President, Balliol JCR, 1967; First President, Oxford Univ. SRC, 1968. Called to Bar, Gray's Inn, 1970, Bencher, 1993 (Vice-Treas., 2011; Treas., 2012); Law Lectr, Balliol Coll., Oxford, 1972–74; QC 1984; Head of Chambers, 1991–98; a Recorder, 1989–98. Chm., Central Arbitration Cttee, 2000–; President: Interception of Communications Tribunal, 2000; Investigatory Powers Tribunal, 2013– (Vice Pres., 2000–13). Contested: (Lab) RBK&C (local elections), 1971; (Lab) Stratford upon Avon, Feb. 1974; (SDP) Putney, GLC, 1981. Hon. Fellow, Goldsmiths Coll., London, 1998. *Publications:* (contrib.) Bullen & Leake & Jacob's Precedents of Pleadings, 13th edn 1990; (ed) Civil Appeals, 2002, 2nd edn 2013. *Recreations:* amateur theatricals, lyric writing, singing, grandchildren. *Address:* Royal Courts of Justice, Strand, WC2A 2LL.

BURTON, Sir Michael (St Edmund), KCVO 1992 (CVO 1979); CMG 1987; HM Diplomatic Service, retired; independent consultant and lecturer; *b* 18 Oct. 1937; *s* of late Brig. G. W. S. Burton, DSO (and two Bars), and Barbara Burton (*née* Kemmis Betty); *m* 1967, Henrietta Jindra Hones; one *s* one *d* (and one *d* decd). *Educ:* Bedford Sch.; Magdalen Coll., Oxford (William Doncaster Scholar; BA Hons; MA). 2nd Lt, Rifle Brigade, 1955–57. Foreign Office, 1960; lang. trng, Middle East Centre for Arabic Studies, Lebanon, 1960–62; Asst Political Agent, Dubai, Trucial States, 1962–64; Private Sec. to Minister of State, FO, 1964–67; Second (later First) Sec. (Information), Khartoum, 1967–69; First Sec. (Inf.), Paris, 1969–72; Asst, Science and Technology Dept, FCO, 1972–75; First Sec. and Head of Chancery, Amman, 1975–77; Counsellor, Kuwait, 1977–79; Head of Maritime, Aviation and Environment Dept, FCO, 1979–81; Head of S Asian Dept, FCO, 1981–84; on secondment to BP as Head of Policy Rev. Unit, 1984–85; Berlin: Minister, 1985–92; Dep. Comdt, BMG, 1985–90; Head of Embassy Office, 1990–92; Asst Under-Sec. of State (ME and N Africa), FCO, 1993; Ambassador to Czech Republic, 1994–97. Chairman: Eur.-Atlantic Gp, 2001–02 (Pres., 2002–05); British Czech and Slovak Assoc., 2001–14 (Pres., 2014–); Clovelly Lectures, 2011–; Mem. Council, RSAA, 2001–06, 2007–13. Hon. Pres., Hinduja Foundn, 2003–. Order of Merit, Berlin, 1992. *Recreations:* tennis, travel, wine, allotment. *Address:* 6 Napier Court, Ranelagh Gardens, SW6 3UT. *Clubs:* Oxford and Cambridge, Hurlingham (Chm., 2004–07), Pilgrims; Vincent's (Oxford).

BURTON, Neil Henry, FSA; Director, Architectural History Practice, since 2001; *b* 23 June 1947; *s* of Angus Robert Burton and Joan Burton (*née* Grant); *m* 1989, Susie Barson (marr. diss. 2014); one *s* one *d*. *Educ:* Christ's Hosp. Sch., Horsham; Pembroke Coll., Oxford (BA Hons Modern Hist.); Edinburgh Univ. (Dip. Hist. of Art). Historian, Historic Bldgs Div., GLC, 1973–88; Inspector of Historic Bldgs, English Heritage, 1988–94; Sec., Georgian Gp, 1994–2001. Dir, Architects Accredited in Building Conservation, 2000–06; Jt Dir, Attingham Study Week, 2003–07. Trustee, Historic Chapels Trust, 1995–. IHBC 1998; FSA 1998. *Publications:* Historic Houses Handbook, 1981, 3rd edn 1984; Life in the Georgian City, 1990; Behind the Facade: London town house plans 1660–1840, 2006; contrib. articles to Architectural Rev., Country Life, etc. *Recreation:* walking. *Address:* 18 Gower Mews, WC1E 6HP. *T:* and *Fax:* (020) 7636 9935. *E:* neil.burton@architecturalhistory.co.uk.

BURTON, Hon. (Richard) Mark; MP (Lab) Taupo, 1996–2008 (Tongariro, 1993–96); Deputy Leader of the House, 1999–2008, and Minister of Justice and of Local Government, 2005–08, New Zealand; Minister in Charge of Treaty of Waitangi Negotiations and Responsible for the Law Commission, 2005–08; *b* 16 Jan. 1956; *m* 1977, Carol Botherway; two *s* one *d*. *Educ:* Waikato Univ. (Cert. Contg Educn); Massey Univ. (Cert. Social Service Supervision); NZ Council of Recreation and Sport (Dip.). Residential Social Worker, Dept of Social Welfare, 1976–78; Community Recreation Advr, Palmerston North City Corp., 1978–82; Community Educn Organiser, Central Plateau Rural Educn Activities Prog., 1982–93. Lab. Party spokesman for adult and community educn, 1994–99; Sen. Labour Party Whip, 1996–99; Minister: of Internal Affairs and of Veterans' Affairs, 1999–2002; of State Owned Enterprises, 1999–2004; of Defence and of Tourism, 1999–2005. Various posts with NZ Assoc. for Community and Contg Educn, 1983–93; Member: Bd of Studies, Contg Educn, Waikato Univ., 1985–86; Bd, NZ Career Devolt and Transition Educn Service, 1990–92. NZ Medal, 1990. *Address:* c/o Parliament Buildings, Wellington, New Zealand.

BURTON, Richard St John Vladimir, CBE 1996; RIBA; RWA; Partner, 1961–85, Director, 1985–2003, Ahrends Burton & Koralek; *b* 3 Nov. 1933; *s* of Percy Basil Harmsworth Burton and Vera (*née* Poliakoff); *m* 1956, Mireille, *d* of Joseph Dernbach-Mayen; three *s* one *d*. *Educ:* Bryanston; AA Sch. of Architecture (AA Dip Hons 1956). RIBA 1957; RWA 1985. Founding Partner, Ahrends Burton & Koralek, 1961. Principal works: TCD Library and Arts Bldg, 1967 and 1979; Chalvedon and Northlands Housing, Basildon, 1968 and 1980; Templeton Coll., Oxford, 1969–2007; Nebenzahl House, 1972; extension, Keble Coll., Oxford, 1976; W. H. Smith Head Office Marketing, Swindon, 1985; Burton House, 1987, 1993; Hooke Park Coll., 1990; John Lewis, Kingston-on-Thames, 1991; St Mary's Isle of Wight Low Energy Hosp., 1991; Docklands Light Railway extension, 1993; British Embassy, Moscow, 2000. Convenor, RIBA Energy Gp, 1976–81; Chairman: Arts Council Percent for Art Steering Gp, 1989; RIBA Steering Gp on Educn, 1991; Arts Council Adv. Gp on Architecture, 1994–98; Building a 20/20 Vision for Future Healthcare Environments, Jt Report of Nuffield Foundn, RIBA Futures Gp and Med. Architectural Res. Unit, South Bank Univ., 2000–01. Design Advr, NHS Estates, 2003–06. FRSA 1960. *Publications:* Ahrends Burton and Koralek, 1991; (jtly) Collaborations: the architecture of ABK, 2002; Ahrends Burton and Koralek: twentieth century architects, 2012; Champéry aujourd'hui: les gens, 2014; contribs to learned jls on matters relating to architecture, specifically art and architecture, energy conservation and health and design and its benefits. *Recreations:* drawing, writing.

BURTON, Tim; film director and producer; *b* Burbank, Calif, 25 Aug. 1958; *s* of late Bill Burton and of Jean Burton; *m* 1989, Lena Gieseke; one *s* one *d* with Helena Bonham Carter, *qv*. *Educ:* Calif Inst. of the Arts. Formerly apprentice animator, Walt Disney Studios (projects incl. The Fox and the Hound, 1981; The Black Cauldron, 1985). Animator and dir, Vincent (short film), 1982; *films include: director:* Hansel and Gretel (TV), 1982; Aladdin (TV), 1984; Frankenweenie (short), 1984; Pee-wee's Big Adventure, 1985; Beetlejuice, 1988; Batman, 1989; Sleepy Hollow, 2000; Planet of the Apes, 2001; Big Fish, 2004; Charlie and the Chocolate Factory, 2005; Sweeney Todd: The Demon Barber of Fleet Street, 2008; Dark Shadows, 2012; *director and producer:* Edward Scissorhands, 1991; Batman Returns, 1992; Ed Wood, 1994; Mars Attacks!, 1997; Corpse Bride, 2005; Alice in Wonderland, 2010; Frankenweenie, 2012; Big Eyes, 2014; *producer:* The Nightmare Before Christmas, 1993; Cabin Boy, 1994; Batman Forever, 1996; James and the Giant Peach, 1996; Nine, 2009; Abraham Lincoln: Vampire Hunter, 2012. Chm. Jury, Cannes Film Fest., 2010. Fellow, BFI, 2012. Chevalier des Arts et des Lettres (France), 2010. *Publications:* My Art and Films, 1993; The Melancholy Death of Oyster Boy and Other Stories, 1997. *Address:* c/o William Morris Endeavor Entertainment, 9601 Wilshire Boulevard, Beverly Hills, CA 90210, USA.

BURTON-CHADWICK, Sir Joshua (Kenneth), 3rd Bt *cr* 1935, of Bidston; Trainer, The International Academy of Human Relations; *b* 1 Feb. 1954; *s* of Sir Robert Burton-Chadwick, (Sir Peter), 2nd Bt, and of Beryl Joan, *d* of Stanley Frederick J. Brailsford; *S* father, 1983. *Heir:* none.

BURTON-JONES, Ven. Simon David; Archdeacon of Rochester and Canon Residentiary of Rochester Cathedral, since 2010; *b* Fleetwood, Lancs, 23 Dec. 1962; *s* of Harry and Dorothy Jones; *m* 1989, Julia Burton; one *s* one *d*. *Educ:* Fleetwood High Sch.; Emmanuel Coll., Cambridge (BA 1984; MA 1988); St John's Coll., Nottingham (BTh 1992; MA 1993).

Res. Manager, Jubilee Centre, Cambridge, 1987–90; ordained deacon, 1993, priest, 1994; Vicar, St Mary's Church, Bromley, 1998–2005; Rector, St Nicholas Church, Chislehurst, 2005–10. *Recreations:* eating food with my family round the table, cricket, film, foreign fiction, the day of rest. *Address:* The Archdeaconry, Kings Orchard, Rochester ME1 1TG. *T:* (01634) 813533. *E:* simonburtonjones@btinternet.com.

BURTON-PAGE, Piers John; writer, lecturer, critic and broadcaster; *b* 25 July 1947; *s* of John Garrard Burton-Page and Audrey Ruth Burton-Page (*née* Marley); *m* 1976, Patricia Margaret Cornish; two *s. Educ:* Harrow Sch.; Wadham Coll., Oxford (MA); Univ. of Sussex (MA in Russian Studies). Joined BBC, 1971: studio manager, 1971–75; announcer and newsreader, Radio 4, 1975–77; Producer, Gramophone Dept, 1977–83; External Services Music Organiser, 1983–85; Radio 3: Presentation Editor, 1985–90; presenter/producer, 1990–97; Exec. Producer, 1998–2002. Acting Editor, Opera, 1997. (Jtly) Ohio State Award, for series The Elements of Music, 1984. *Publications:* Philharmonic Concerto: the life and music of Sir Malcolm Arnold, 1994; The Allegri at 50: a quartet in 5 movements, 2004; contrib. articles and reviews on musical subjects. *Recreations:* cricket, theatre, travel, languages, cosmology, the open air. *Club:* Bushmen.

BURTON-RACE, John William; Chef Patron, New Angel, Notting Hill, since 2014; *b* 1 May 1957; *s* of Keith Burton and Shirley Burton, later Race; *m* (marr. diss. 2008); one *s* one *d*; *m* 2010, Suzi Ward; one *s. Educ:* St Mary's Coll., Bitterne; American Sch., Bangkok. Apprentice, Wessex Hotel, Winchester, 1973–75; Commis, Quaglino's Hotel Meurice, London, 1975–76; First Commis, Chewton Glen Hotel, 1976–78; Chef, Olivers, Midhurst, 1978–79; Chef tournant, La Sorbonne, Oxford, 1979–82; Pvte Chef, MacKenzie-Hill Property Develt Internat., 1982–83; Sous Chef, Les Quat' Saisons, Oxford, 1983–84; Head Chef and Manager, Le Petit Blanc, Oxford, 1984–86 (1 Michelin star, 1984–86); Chef-Proprietor, L'Ortolan, Berks, 1986–2000 (1 Michelin star, 1987–90, 2 Michelin stars, 1991–96, 1999); 1st Cl. and Concorde, BA, 1994, 1995, 1996; Chef, John Burton-Race at Landmark Hotel, London, 2000–02 (2 Michelin stars, 2001); in France, 2002–03; Co-owner, 2004, and Chef, The New Angel, Dartmouth, 2004–10 (1 Michelin star, 2005–10); opened New Angel Cookery Sch., 2005; co-owner, New Angel Rooms, 2005; consultant, YTL Gp, Malaysia, 2010; Consultant Exec. Chef, Sanctum on the Green, Berks, 2010–11; Guest Chef, My Dining Room, Fulham, 2011. Brand Ambassador and Exec. Develt Chef, Kerrygold and Pilgrim's Choice, Adam's Foods, 2011–. Television series include: Master Chefs of Europe, 1988; Great British Chefs, 1989; Great European Chefs, 1990; French Leave, 2003; Return of the Chef, 2005; Britain's Best Dish, 2007–11; Best Dish: The Chefs, 2011, 2012; Put Your Menu Where Your Mouth Is, 2013. Many gastronomic awards, incl. Chef of the Year, Caterer and Hotelkeeper Awards, 1996. *Publications:* Recipes from an English Master Chef, 1994; French Leave, 2003; French Leave: a wonderful year of escape and discovery, 2004; Coming Home, 2005; First Crack Your Egg, 2007; Flavour First, 2008; (jtly) Cooking for Beginners, 2008. *Recreations:* Porsche cars, fishing, antiques, horse riding. *Address:* Unitas, JBR Management, 3rd Floor, 197–199 City Road, EC1V 1JN.

BURY, Viscount; Augustus Sergei Darius Keppel; *b* 8 Feb. 2003; *s* and *heir* of Earl of Albemarle, *qv*.

BURY, (Anne) Carolyn; *see* Hayman, Anne C.

BURY, Lindsay Claude Neils; Chairman, Electric & General Investment Trust (formerly Henderson Electric & Investment Trust), 2001–12 (Director, 1995–2012); *b* 13 Feb. 1939; *s* of Frank James Lindsay Bury and Diana Mary Lewis; *m* 1968, Sarah Ann Ingall; one *s* one *d. Educ:* Eton; Trinity College, Cambridge (BA History). J. Henry Schroder Wagg, 1960–66; Singer & Friedlander, 1966–73; Dunbar & Co., 1973–83. Director: ACT (formerly Apricot Computers), 1968–95 (Chm., 1972–89); Portals Holdings, 1973–95; Christie Group, 1989–94; Roxboro Gp, 1993–2001; Sage Gp, 1995–2006; Chairman: Unicorn Internat., 1995–97; S Staffs Gp (formerly S Staffs Waterworks Co.), 1992–2004 (Dir, 1981–2004); Bango plc, 2000–11; Service Power Technologies plc, 2007–14 (non-exec. Dir, 1997–). Trustee, City of Birmingham Touring Opera, 1989–92. Chm. of Govs, Moor Park Sch., 1982–90; Trustee: Millichope Foundn, 1984–; Brazilian Atlantic Rainforest Trust, 2004– (Chm., 2013–); Pres., Fauna and Flora Internat., 2002–12 (Chm., 1994–2002; Chm., Global Canopy Prog., 2008–). High Sheriff, Shropshire, 1998. *Recreations:* music, country pursuits. *Address:* The Old Rectory, Tugford, Craven Arms, Shropshire SY7 9HS. *T:* (01584) 841234; Ruantallain Lodge, Island of Jura, Scotland. *Clubs:* Turf, Pratt's, MCC.

BURY, Very Rev. Nicholas Ayles Stillingfleet; Dean of Gloucester, 1997–2010; *b* 8 Jan. 1943; *s* of Major John J. S. Bury, MC, RA and Joan A. M. Bury; *m* 1973, Jennifer Anne Newbold; two *s* one *d. Educ:* King's Sch., Canterbury; Queens' Coll., Cambridge (MA 1969); MA Oxon 1971; DipEd Oxon; Cuddesdon Theol Coll. Ordained deacon, 1968, priest, 1969; Asst Curate, Our Lady & St Nicholas, Liverpool, 1968–71; Chaplain, Christ Church, Oxford, 1971–75; Vicar: St Mary's, Shephall, Stevenage, Herts, 1975–84; St Peter in Thanet, Broadstairs, 1984–97. Hon. Fellow, Univ. of Gloucester, 2003. *Recreations:* golf, water-colour painting. *Address:* 122 The Homend, Ledbury, Glos HR8 1BZ. *E:* n.bury95@btinternet.com.

BUSBY, George Benedict Joseph Pascal, CMG 2015; OBE 1996; HM Diplomatic Service; Counsellor, Foreign and Commonwealth Office, since 2004; *b* 18 April 1960; *s* of Christopher Raymond Busby and Anne Margaret Busby; *m* 1988, Helen Frances Hurll; one *s* three *d. Educ:* Sch. of Slavonic Studies, London Univ. (BA Hons); St Antony's Coll., Oxford (Diploma). Joined Diplomatic Service, 1987; Second Sec., FCO, 1987; Second, then First Sec., Bonn, 1989–91; First Secretary: FCO, 1991–92; Belgrade, 1992–96; First Sec., then Counsellor, FCO, 1996–2000; Counsellor, Vienna, 2000–04. *Address:* c/o Foreign and Commonwealth Office, King Charles Street, SW1A 2AH.

BUSBY, Prof. Stephen John Williams, DPhil; FRS 2005; Professor of Biochemistry, since 1995, and Head, School of Biosciences, since 2012, University of Birmingham; *b* 5 March 1951; *s* of Peter Busby and Joan Busby (*née* Williams); *m* 1980, (Elizabeth) Jane Cooper; two *s* one *d. Educ:* Moseley Hall Co. Grammar Sch., Cheadle; Sidney Sussex Coll., Cambridge (BA 1972); Merton and St John's Colls, Oxford (DPhil 1975). Postdoctoral scientist, 1975–78, on Scientific Staff, 1979–83, Inst Pasteur, Paris; University of Birmingham: Lectr, 1983–88; Sen. Lectr, 1988–90; Reader, 1990–95; Dean of Sci., then Dean of Life and Health Sci., 2000–04. Vis. Scientist, NIH, Bethesda, USA, 1979–80. Chair, Biochem. Soc., 2014–. *Publications:* contrib. numerous res. papers to learned jls. *Recreations:* family, travel, food, walking, doing nothing! *Address:* School of Biosciences, University of Birmingham, Edgbaston, Birmingham B15 2TT. *T:* (0121) 414 5439. *E:* s.j.w.busby@bham.ac.uk.

BUSCH, Constantinus Albertus Maria; Member, Supervisory Board, Parcom Ventures BV, 1995–2008; *b* 17 Aug. 1937; *m* 1963, Ingrid (*née* Haaksma); two *s* two *d. Educ:* in The Netherlands; Amsterdam Univ. (Economics degree). 1st Lieut, Dutch Army, 1962–64; Corporate Finance Dept, NV Philips Eindhoven, 1964–66; Manager, Philips Internat. Finance, Luxembourg, 1966–70; Naarden International NV: Treasurer, 1970–72; Dir of Finance and Mem. Bd of Management, 1973–80; Financial Dir, Philips Electronics UK, 1981–85; Corporate Finance Dir, NV Philips Eindhoven, 1985–87; UK Vice-Chm. and Financial Dir, Philips Electronics, 1988; Chm. and Man. Dir, Philips Electronics and Associated Industries, 1989–90; Corporate Finance Dir, Philips Internat. BV, 1991–92; Mem. Bd of Dirs, Verenigde Nederlandse Uitgeversbedryven BV, 1993–97. *Recreations:* music, particularly clarinet; tennis, golf. *Address:* Dirck van Hornelaan 23, Waalre 5581 CZ, Netherlands.

BUSCH, Rolf Trygve; Comdr, Order of St Olav; Hon. GCVO 1988; Norwegian Ambassador to the Court of St James's, 1982–88; *b* 15 Nov. 1920; *s* of Aksel Busch and Alette (*née* Tunby); *m* 1950, Solveig Helle; one *s. Educ:* Oslo Univ. (degree in Law); National Defence Coll. Dep. Judge, 1946–47; entered Norwegian Foreign Service, 1947; Min. of For. Affairs, 1947–50; Sec., Cairo, 1950–52; Vice-Consul, New York, 1952–54; Min. of For. Affairs, 1954–56; National Def. Coll., 1956–57; First Sec., Norwegian Delegn to NATO, Paris, 1957–60; Min. of For. Affairs, 1960–65; Counsellor and Dep. Perm. Rep., Norwegian Delegn to NATO, Paris and Brussels, 1965–70; Dir-Gen., Min. of For. Affairs, 1970–71; Perm. Rep. to N Atlantic Council, 1971–77; Ambassador to Fed. Republic of Germany, 1977–82. Officer, Order of the Nile, Egypt; Comdr with Star, Order of the Falcon, Iceland; Grand Cross, Order of Merit, Fed. Republic of Germany. *Address:* 2 Hafrsfjords Gt, 0273 Oslo 2, Norway. *T:* 22431791.

BUSCOMBE, family name of **Baroness Buscombe**.

BUSCOMBE, Baroness *cr* 1998 (Life Peer), of Goring in the co. of Oxfordshire; **Peta Jane Buscombe;** Chairman, Press Complaints Commission, 2009–11; *b* 12 March 1954; *m* 1980, Philip John Buscombe; twin *s* one *d. Educ:* Hinchley Wood Sch.; Rosebery Grammar Sch., Epsom; Inns of Ct Sch. of Law. Called to the Bar, Inner Temple, 1977. Legal Advr, Dairy Trade Fedn, 1979–80; lawyer, Barclays Bank International, NY, then Hd Office Lawyer and Inspector, Barclays Bank plc, UK, 1980–84; Asst Sec., Inst. of Practitioners in Advertising, 1984–87. Mem. (C) S Oxfordshire DC, 1995–99. Opposition front bench spokesman, H of L, on trade and industry, social security and legal affairs, 1999–2001, on Cabinet Office affairs, 2000, on home and legal affairs, 2001–06, on culture, media and sport, 2002–05; Shadow Minister for Educn and Skills, 2005–06. Vice Chm., All Party Gp for Mgt Consultants, 2001–; Member: British-American All Party Gp, 1998–; All Party Gp for Corporate Social Responsibility, 2001–, for Intellectual Property, 2004–, for Corporate Governance, 2004–; H of L Select Cttee on Inquiries Act 2005, 2012–14; Mem., Jt Cttee on Human Rights, 2014–; Vice Pres., All Party Parly Gp for Sexual Equality, 2004–08. Mem., UK Delegn to Parly Assembly, Council of Europe, 2013–. Vice Chm. resp. for Develt, Cons. Party, 1997–99; Founder, Cons. Network and Cons. Cultural Unit; President: Slough Cons. Assoc., 1997–; S Oxfordshire Cons. Patrons, 2008–11; S Oxfordshire Cons. Assoc., 2015– (Vice Chm., 1995–98). Contested (C) Slough, 1997. Mem. Adv. Bd, Gow and Partners, 2003–05. Chief Exec. and Dir-Gen., Advertising Assoc., 2007–09; Dir, Advertising Standards Bd of Finance, 2007–09. Non-executive Director: Affinity Water plc (formerly Three Valleys plc, later Veolia Water Central plc), 2006–; Local World Ltd, 2013–. Chm., Goring and Streatley Amenity Assoc., 1995–98; Mem., Assoc. of Rural Businesses in Oxfordshire, 1994–2002. Vice Pres., Debating Soc., 2005–. Vice Chair, Globe UK, 2007–10; Member: RSA Risk Commn, 2006–10; Council for Child Internet Safety, 2008–. Chm., Adv. Bd, Samaritans, 2011–. Trustee and Gov., Langley Hall Primary Acad., 2015–. Patron: Foundn for Internat. Commercial Arbitration and Alternative Dispute Resolution, 1999–; Inns of Ct Sch. of Law Cons. Assoc.; PALS, 2000–; Westminster Media Forum, 2002–; Robert Bowman Gall. Trust, 2004–08; Westminster eForum, 2005–; Westminster Educn Forum, 2005–; Founder Patron, Inst. of Paralegals, 2005–; Vice Patron, Abbeyfield House Appeal, 1998–2002; Ambassador, Guide Assoc., 2002–. Vice Pres., Henley Soc.; Mem., Chiltern Soc. FRSA 2004. *Recreations:* theatre, opera, shooting, riding, fishing. *Address:* House of Lords, SW1A 0PW.

BUSE, Diana Anjoli; *see* Garnham, D. A.

BUSH, Prof. Andrew, MD; FRCP, FRCPCH; Professor of Paediatrics, and Head, Paediatrics Section, Imperial College London, since 2013 (Professor of Paediatric Respirology, 2002–13); Consultant Paediatric Chest Physician, Royal Brompton and Harefield Foundation Trust, since 1991; *b* London, 24 April 1954; *s* of Geoffrey Bush and Julie Kathleen Bush; *m* 1975, Susan Joan Crucefix; three *s* one *d. Educ:* University College Sch., London; Corpus Christi Coll., Cambridge (BA 1st Cl. Hons 1975; MD 1987); University College Hosp., London (MB BS Hons Surgery 1978). MRCP 1980, FRCP 1996; MRCPCH 1996, FRCPCH 1997. House Physician, Stafford Gen. Infirmary, 1978–79; House Surgeon, UCH, 1979; Med. SHO, Taunton Hosp., 1979–80, Brompton Hosp., 1981; Renal Registrar, St Mary's Hosp., 1981–82; Registrar, St Charles' Hosp., 1982–83; Res. Fellow, Brompton Hosp., 1983–88; SHO, Neonatal Paediatrics, UCH, 1988; Paediatric Registrar, Hillingdon Hosp., 1988–89, Brompton Hosp., 1989–90; Sen. Paediatric Registrar, RPMS Hammersmith Hosp., 1990–91; Consultant Paediatric Chest Physician, Royal Brompton Hosp., 1991–; Academic Dir of Paediatrics, Nat. Heart and Lung Inst., Imperial Coll. London, 1999–. FHEA 2007; FERS. *Publications:* (ed jtly) Growing up with Lung Disease: the lung in transition to adult life (monograph), 2002; Progress in Respiratory Research, vol. 34, Cystic Fibrosis in the 21st Century, 2005; Kendig's Disorders of the Respiratory Tract in Children, 7th edn 2006, 8th edn as Kendig's and Chernick's Disorders of the Respiratory Tract in Children (ed jtly), 2012; Cystic Fibrosis, 3rd edn 2007; Paediatric Respiratory Disease: airways and infection, 2010; Paediatric Respiratory Disease: parenchymal diseases, 2010; co-author of papers, chapters and articles. *Recreations:* reading, listening to music, walking, ball games, the evasion of domestic responsibilities. *Address:* Department of Paediatric Respiratory Medicine, Royal Brompton and Harefield NHS Foundation Trust, Sydney Street, SW3 6NP. *T:* (020) 7351 8232, *Fax:* (020) 7351 8377. *E:* a.bush@imperial.ac.uk.

BUSH, Charles Martin Peter, MA; Headmaster, Oundle School, 2005–15; *b* 28 June 1952; *s* of late Dr John Peter Bush and Edith Mary (*née* Farnsworth); *m* 1977, Rosalind Mary Nevin; three *s. Educ:* Melbourne C of E Grammar Sch.; Univ. of Melbourne; Trinity Coll., Oxford (MA). Aylesbury Grammar Sch., 1975–78, Hd of Pure Maths, 1977–78; Hd of Maths, Abingdon Sch., 1978–82; Marlborough College, 1982–93: Hd of Maths, 1982–89; Housemaster, B1 House, 1988–93; Headmaster, Eastbourne Coll., 1993–2005. *Publications:* (co-author in SMP Team) Revised Advanced Mathematics (Book 1), 1988. *Recreations:* golf, cricket, mathematics, fell walking. *Address:* 8 Conway House, 6 Ormonde Gate, SW3 4EU. *Clubs:* East India, MCC; Melbourne Cricket.

BUSH, Geoffrey Hubert, CB 1998; DL; Deputy Chairman, Board of Inland Revenue, 1998–99, retired; *b* 5 April 1942; *s* of late Sidney Arthur Bush and Dorothy Elizabeth Bush; *m* 1965, Sylvia Mary Squibb; one *s* one *d. Educ:* Cotham Grammar Sch., Bristol. Tax Officer, 1959; Inspector of Taxes, 1968; Dist Inspector of Taxes, 1973; Principal Inspector of Taxes, 1981; Board of Inland Revenue: Under Sec., 1988–94; Dir Gen., 1994–98. Adviser: Office of Govt Commerce, 2000–08; Bank of England, 2003–08; DFE, 2006–10; BIS, 2011–13; Mem. Bd, CAFCASS, 2012–15. Trustee: Devon Co. Agricl Assoc., 2001–; Exeter Univ. Foundn, 2006–; Hospiscare Exeter, 2012–; WESC Foundn, 2012– (Vice Chm., 2014–). Chm. Council, Exeter Cathedral, 2008–. DL Devon, 2008. CStJ 2007 (Chm. Council, Devon, 2001–08). *Recreations:* travel, golf. *Address:* (home) Exmouth, Devon. *Clubs:* Exeter Golf and Country (Devon) (Vice Chm., 2007–09; Chm., 2009–12); Knowle Lawn Tennis (Bristol).

BUSH, George Herbert Walker, Hon. GCB 1993; President of the United States of America, 1989–93; UN Special Envoy for South Asia Earthquake, 2005; *b* Milton, Mass, 12 June 1924; *s* of late Prescott Sheldon Bush and Dorothy (*née* Walker); *m* 1945, Barbara, *d* of Marvin Pierce, NY; four *s* one *d. Educ:* Phillips Acad., Andover, Mass; Yale Univ. (BA Econs 1948). Served War, USNR, Lieut, pilot (DFC, three Air Medals). Co-founder and Dir, Zapata Petroleum Corp., 1953–59; Founder, Zapata Offshore Co., Houston, 1954, Pres., 1956–64, Chm. Bd, 1964–66. Chm., Republican Party, Harris Co., Texas, 1963–64; Delegate, Republican Nat. Convention, 1964, 1968; Republican cand. US Senator from Texas, 1964, 1970; Mem., 90th and 91st Congresses, 7th District of Texas, 1967–71; US

Perm. Rep. to UN, 1971–73; Chm., Republican Party Nat. Cttee, 1973–74; Chief, US Liaison Office, Peking, 1974–75; Dir, US Central Intelligence Agency, 1976–77; Vice-President of the USA, 1981–89. Cand. for Republican Presidential nomination, 1980. Hon. degrees from many colleges and univs. *Publications:* (with Victor Gold) Looking Forward: an autobiography, 1988; (with Gen. Brent Scowcroft) A World Transformed, 1998; All the Best: my life in letters and other writings, 2000. *Recreations:* tennis, jogging, golf, boating, fishing. *Address:* Suite 900, 10000 Memorial Drive, Houston, TX 77024, USA.

See also G. W. Bush.

BUSH, George Walker; President of the United States of America, 2001–09; *b* 6 July 1946; *e s* of George Herbert Walker Bush, *qv*; *m* 1977, Laura Welch; twin *d. Educ:* Phillips Acad., Andover; Yale Univ. (BA History 1968); Harvard Business Sch. (MBA 1975). F-102 Pilot, Texas Air Nat. Guard. Founded Bush Exploration, 1975; merged with Spectrum 7 Energy Corp., 1984 (Pres.), subseq. Harken Energy Corp., 1986 (Consultant); advr and speechwriter to father during Presidential campaign, 1986–88; Governor of Texas, 1995–2000. Republican. Part-owner, Texas Rangers baseball team, 1989–98. *Publications:* A Charge to Keep, 1999; Decision Points, 2010; 41: a portrait of my father, 2014. *Address:* c/o The White House, Washington, DC 20500, USA.

BUSH, Dr Harry John, CB 2000; Senior Regulatory Advisor, KPMG, since 2011; *b* 26 Aug. 1953; *s* of Harold Leslie Bush and Bridget Bush (*née* Gorman). *Educ:* Quintin Grammar Sch.; Quintin Kynaston Sch.; Merton Coll., Oxford (BA Mod. Hist. and Econs 1974); DPhil Oxon 1980. Nuffield College, Oxford: Student, 1974–77; Prize Res. Fellow, 1977–79; Jun. Dean, 1978–79; HM Treasury, 1979–2003: Private Sec. to Minister of State, 1981–82; Principal, 1982; Dep. Press Sec., 1987–89; Asst Sec., 1989; Head of Privatisation, 1993–97; Dep. Dir, then Dir, and Hd of Enterprise and Growth Unit, 1997–2003; Gp Dir, Econ. Regulation, CAA, 2003–10. Chm., OECD Privatisation Network, 1996–98; Dir, EIB, 2002–03; Member: Performance Review Commn, Eurocontrol, 2005–09; Commn for Integrated Transport, 2007–10. Non-executive Director: University Coll. Hosps NHS Trust, 2012– (Vice-Chm., 2013–); Airline Group Ltd, 2014–; NATS Hldgs Ltd, 2014–. FRAeS 2007. *Recreations:* political biography, travel, food, wine, moderate exercise.

BUSH, Janet Elizabeth; Senior Editor, McKinsey Global Institute, since 2006; *b* Lytham St Annes, 2 June 1960; *d* of Arthur and Mary Bush; partner, Nick de Cent; one *d. Educ:* Berkhamsted Sch. for Girls; Somerville Coll., Oxford (BA Eng. Lang. and Lit., MA); Centre for Journalism Studies, Cardiff (Reuters schol., postgrad. degree in journalism). Frankfurt Correspondent, 1983–84, Econs writer, 1984–86, Reuters; Dep. Econs Correspondent, 1986–87, NY Correspondent, 1987–90, Financial Times; Presenter, economic documentaries, Money Prog., BBC, 1990–92; Econs Correspondent, 1992–96, Economics Editor, 1997–99, The Times; Director: New Europe, 1999–2003; The No Campaign, 2000–03; Advocacy International Ltd, 2004–05. Harold Wincott Young Financial Journalist of the Year, 1987. *Publications:* (ed) The Real World Economic Outlook, 2003; Consumer Empowerment and Competitiveness, 2004. *Recreations:* salsa, watching television, family life, enjoying the countryside, seeing the world. *Address:* Blackacre, Colyton, Devon EX24 6SF. *T:* (01404) 871672. *E:* janet@janet-bush.com.

BUSH, John Barnard, CVO 2012; OBE 2004; JP; farmer; Lord-Lieutenant of Wiltshire, 2004–12; *b* 5 Feb. 1937; *s* of Barnard Bush and Elizabeth (*née* Weeks); *m* 1961, Pamela Bagwell; one *s* one *d. Educ:* Monkton Combe Sch.; Balliol Coll., Oxford (MA). Chairman: WMF Ltd, 1995–99; Countrywide Farmers plc, 1999–2004. Member: Agricl Land Tribunal, 1975–85; Dairy Produce Quota Tribunal, 1984–86. Mem. Council, RASE, 1980–92. Co. Chm., Wilts Br., NFU, 1977–78. Chm., Bristol Avon Flood Defences Cttee, 1981–2000. Chm., Wilts Magistrates' Courts Cttee, 2001–05. Patron: Wilts and Swindon Community Foundn, 2004–; Prospect Hospice, Swindon, 2004–; Mediation Plus (N Wilts), 2004–; Carers Support W Wilts, 2004–; Wilts Ind. Living Centre, 2004–; Anglo-Polish Soc., 2004–12; Relate, N Wilts, 2004–; Wilts Br., Royal Soc. St George, 2004–12; Wilts Archaeol and Natural Hist. Soc., 2010–; Vice-Patron, Friends of Erlestoke Prison, 2012–. President: Wilts Council, Order of St John, 2004–12; ABF Wilts, 2004–12; CPRE, Wilts, 2004–12; Salisbury Br., ESU, 2004–12. JP NW Wilts, 1980; High Sheriff, 1997–98, DL 1998, Wilts. Gov., Lackham Coll., 1986–98. KStJ 2010 (CStJ 2005). *Address:* Fullingbridge Farm, Heywood, Westbury, Wilts BA13 4NB. *T:* and *Fax:* (01373) 824609. *E:* johnbush@btconnect.com. *Club:* Farmers.

BUSH, Very Rev. Roger Charles; Dean of Truro, since 2012; *b* 22 Nov. 1956; *s* of Harvey John Bush and Edith May Rose Bush (*née* Spurgeon); *m* 1984, Lois Mary (*née* Nichols); one *s* one *d. Educ:* King's Coll., London (BA Hons 1978); Univ. of Leeds (BA 1985). Ordained deacon, 1986, priest, 1987; Curate, Newbold with Dunstan, Chesterfield, 1986–90; Team Vicar, Parish of the Resurrection, Leicester, 1990–94; Rector, Redruth with Lanner and Treleigh, Cornwall, 1994–2004; RD, Carnmarth North, 1996–2003; Hon. Canon, 2003–04, Residentiary Canon, 2004–06, Truro Cathedral; Archdeacon of Cornwall, 2006–12. *Recreations:* reading history, theology and fiction, music - anything classical (sings tenor in St Mary's Singers, Truro), walking, collecting maps, watching Humphrey Bogart films. *Address:* Westwood House, Tremorvah Crescent, Truro TR1 1NL. *T:* (01872) 225630, (office) (01872) 276782. *E:* dean@trurocathedral.org.uk.

BUSH, Prof. Ronald Lee, PhD; Drue Heinz Professor of American Literature, University of Oxford, 1997–2013, now Emeritus; Fellow, St John's College, Oxford, 1997–2013, now Emeritus Research Fellow; Senior Research Fellow, Institute for English Studies, University of London, since 2013; *b* 16 June 1946; *s* of Raymond J. Bush and Esther Schneyer Bush; *m* 1969, Marilyn Wolin; one *s. Educ:* Univ. of Pennsylvania (BA 1968); Pembroke Coll., Cambridge (BA 1970); Princeton Univ. (PhD 1974). Asst Prof., later Associate Prof. of English, Harvard Univ., 1974–82; Associate Prof., later Prof. of Literature, CIT, 1982–97. NEH Fellow, 1977–78, 1992–93; Vis. Fellow, Exeter Coll., Oxford, 1994–95; Fellow, Amer. Civilization Prog., Harvard, 2004; Vis. Scholar, Amer. Acad. in Rome, 2014. *Publications:* The Genesis of Ezra Pound's Cantos, 1976; T. S. Eliot: a study of character and style, 1984; (ed) T. S. Eliot: the modernist in history, 1991; (ed) Prehistories of the Future: the primitivist project and the culture of modernism, 1995; American Voice/American Voices, 1999; (ed) Claiming the Stones/Naming the Bones: cultural property and the negotiation of national and ethnic identity, 2002. *Recreation:* tennis. *Address:* St John's College, Oxford OX1 3JP. *T:* (01865) 277300.

BUSH, William; Director of Public Policy and Communications, The Premier League (formerly Football Association Premier League), since 2005; *b* 2 Oct. 1951; *s* of Douglas Stewart Murray Bush and Dorothy Yvonne Anna Bush; *m* 1973, Susan Holmes (marr. diss.); one *s. Educ:* Bedford Coll. (BA); London Sch. of Econs (MSc Econ). Head: Leader's Office, GLC, 1981–86; of Ext. Relns, ILEA, 1986–89; of Political Res., 1990–97, of Res., 1997–99, BBC News; of Res. and Inf., No 10 Downing St, 1999–2001; Special Advr, DCMS, 2001–05. *Address:* The Premier League, 30 Gloucester Place, W1U 8PL. *T:* (020) 7864 9149; 43 Huntingdon Street, N1 1BP. *E:* williambush1@hotmail.com. *Club:* London Erratics Cricket.

BUSHELL, (Rosalind) Morag; *see* Ellis, Rosalind M.

BUSHILL-MATTHEWS, Philip Rodway; Member (C) West Midlands, European Parliament, 1999–2009; *b* 15 Jan. 1943; *s* of William Bushill-Matthews, MBE and Phyllis Bushill-Matthews, OBE; *m* 1967, Angela Loveday Bingham; one *s* two *d. Educ:* Malvern Coll.; University Coll., Oxford (MA); Harvard Business Sch. (AMP 1987). Joined Birds Eye Foods Ltd, 1965; seconded to Thomas Lipton Inc., USA, 1976; Nat. Accounts Dir, Birds Eye Sales Ltd, 1977–80; Man. Dir, Iglo industrias de gelados, Lisbon, 1980–81; Sales Dir, then Sales and Distribution Dir, Birds Eye Wall's Ltd, 1981–88; Managing Director: Craigmillar Ltd, 1988–91 (also Dir, Van den Bergh & Jurgens Ltd); Red Mill Snack Foods Ltd, 1991–99; Red Mill Co., BV, Netherlands, 1993–99. Leader, Cons. MEPs, 2008 (Dep. Leader, 2007–08). Non-exec. Dir, Coventry and Warwickshire NHS Partnership Trust, 2011–14 (Vice-Chm., 2012–14). FInstD 1994. *Publications:* The Gravy Train, 2003; Who Rules Britannia?, 2005. *Recreations:* bridge, the theatre, archaeology, enjoying the countryside. *E:* bushillm@outlook.com.

BUSK, Glennis; *see* Haworth, S. G.

BUSK, Maj.-Gen. Leslie Francis Harry, CB 1990; Director General, British Heart Foundation, 1990–2003; *b* 12 Sept. 1937; *s* of late Lt-Col Charles William Francis Busk and Alice (*née* van Bergen); *m* 1st, 1960, Jennifer Helen Ring (*d* 1992); three *s*; 2nd, 1993, Sheila Glennis McElwain (*see* S. G. Haworth). *Educ:* Wellington Coll.; RMA, Sandhurst; RMCS, Shrivenham (BSc (Eng) London Univ.). Commnd RE, 1957; served in UK, NI, BAOR, India and Singapore; Defence Services Staff Coll., India, 1969; OC 25 Field Sqn, 1971–73; Instr, Staff Coll., Camberley, 1975–77; CO 35 Engr Regt, 1977–79; C of S 2nd Armoured Div., 1979–81; Bde Comd 11 Engr Bde, 1981–83; RCDS, 1984; DMO, MoD, 1985–86; Army Pilots Course, 1986–87; Dir, AAC, 1987–89, retd. Hon. Col, RE Volunteers (Sponsored Units), 1986–91; Col Comdt, RE, 1990–95. Chairman: AMRC, 1991–95, 1999–2002; Eur. Heart Network, 1998–2002. DUniv Glasgow, 2003. *Recreations:* golf, tennis. *Address:* Bushwood, Witheridge Hill Bottom, Highmoor, Henley on Thames, Oxon RG9 5PE. *Club:* Boodle's.

BUSQUIN, Philippe; Member (Soc.), European Parliament, 2004–09; *b* 6 Jan. 1941; *m. Educ:* Univ. Libre de Bruxelles (Licence in Phys. Scis 1962; Cand. in Philosophy 1971; post-grad. in Envmt 1976). Asst in Physics, Faculty of Medicine, Univ. Libre de Bruxelles, 1962–77; Prof., Teachers' Coll., Nivelles, 1962–77; Pres., Bd of Dirs, IRE, 1978–80. Deputy: Province of Hainaut, 1977–78; Chamber of Reps, Belgium, 1978–95; Senator, Belgium, 1995–99; Minister of Educn, 1980; Minister for the Interior, 1981; Walloon Minister for Budget and for Energy, 1982–85; Walloon Minister for Economy, 1988; Minister of Social Affairs, 1988–92; Hon. Minister, 1992. Mem., EC, 1999–2004. Mayor of Seneffe, 1995–99. Mem., Community Exec., 1980–81. Pres., Socialist Party, Belgium, 1992–99; Vice-President: Internat. Socialists, 1992–99; European Socialist Party, 1995–97. Chm., Nat. Geographic Inst., Belgium, 2004–.

BUSS, Barbara Ann, (Mrs Lewis Boxall); freelance journalist, 1976–92; Editor-in-Chief, Woman magazine, 1974–75; Consultant, IPC Magazines Ltd, 1975–76; *b* 14 Aug. 1932; *d* of late Cecil Edward Buss and Victoria Lilian (*née* Vickers); *m* 1966, Lewis Albert Boxall (*d* 1983); no *c. Educ:* Lady Margaret Sch., London. Sec., Conservative Central Office, 1949–52; Sec./journalist, Good Taste magazine, 1952–56; Journalist: Woman and Beauty, 1956–57; Woman, 1957–59; Asst Editor, Woman's Illustrated, 1959–60; Editor, Woman's Illustrated, 1960–61; Journalist, Daily Herald, 1961; Associate Editor, Woman's Realm, 1961–62; Editor: Woman's Realm, 1962–64; Woman, 1964–74. *Recreations:* reading, theatre, cinema. *Address:* 1 Arlington Avenue, N1 7BE. *T:* (020) 7226 3265.

BUSSELL, Darcey Andrea, CBE 2006 (OBE 1995); Principal Ballerina, 1989–2006, Principal Guest Artist, 2006–07, Royal Ballet; *b* 27 April 1969; *d* of Philip Michael Bussell and Andrea Pemberton (*née* Williams); *m* 1997, Angus Forbes; two *d. Educ:* Arts Educnl Sch.; Royal Ballet Sch. Joined Sadler's Wells Royal Ballet (later Birmingham Royal Ballet), 1987; joined Royal Ballet, 1988: soloist, 1988; first soloist, 1989. *Leading rôles in:* Giselle; Swan Lake; Sleeping Beauty; La Bayadère (also with Kirov and Australian Ballet, 1998); Laurentia pas de six; Song of the Earth; Requiem; Galanteries; Spirit of Fugue; Pursuit; first Royal Ballet perf. of Balanchine's Rubies; Cinderella; Enigma Variations; Nutcracker; MacMillan's Elite Syncopations; Raymonda; Monotones; Symphony in C; first Royal Ballet perf. of Balanchine's Stravinsky Violin Concerto; Agon; Bloodlines; Les Biches; Tchaikovsky pas de deux; Beyond Bach; first perf. of William Forsythe's In the middle, somewhat elevated; Romeo and Juliet; Gong; Sylvia; The Four Temperaments; Kiss; Theme and Variations; *rôles created:* Princess Rose in Prince of the Pagodas, Royal Opera House, 1989; pas de deux (Farewell to Dreams) for HM Queen Mother's 90th Birthday Tribute, Palladium and Royal Opera House, 1990; Masha in Winter Dreams, 1991; Mr Worldly Wise, 1995; Dances With Death, 1996; Pavane pour une infante défunte, 1996; Amores, 1997; Towards Poetry, 1999; Lento, 1999; There Where She Loves, 2000; Dance Variations, 2000; Tryst, 2002; Tryst à Grande Vitesse, 2005. Touring song and dance show, Viva La Diva, 2007–08. Pres., Royal Acad. of Dance, 2012–; Member, Board: Sydney Dance Co., 2008– (Patron); Margot Fonteyn Foundn. Pres., Fundraising Appeal, Birmingham Royal Ballet. Patron: Internat. Dance Teachers Association; Ceccetti UK; Ceccetti Australia; Dance Teachers' Benevolent Fund UK; Du Boisson Dance Foundn; New English Ballet Th.; Sight for All; Borne; Henry Spink Foundn; Ambassador, Giving Prog., NZ Sch. of Dance. Prix de Lausanne, 1986; Variety Club of GB Award for most promising newcomer, 1990; Dancer of Year Award, Dance and Dancers Mag., 1990; Evening Standard Award for dance, 1990. *Publications:* The Young Dancer, 1994; (with Judith Mackrell) Life in Dance (autobiog.), 1998; Pilates For Life, 2005; Dance Body Workout, 2007; Darcey Bussell: A Life in Pictures, 2012. *Recreations:* art and painting, reading, swimming. *Address:* c/o TCB Group, 24 Kimberley Court, Kimberley Road, Queens Park, NW6 7SL.

BUSSON, André-Arpad Pascal Cyril, (Arpad Busson); Chairman, Gottex Group, since 2014 (Founder and Chairman, EIM, 1992–2014); *b* Boulogne-Billancourt, 27 Jan. 1963; *s* of Pascal Cyril Busson and Florence Harcourt-Smith; two *s. Educ:* Institut Le Rosey. Founder and Chm., Absolute Return for Kids (ARK), 2002–09. *Recreations:* ski-ing, shooting. *Address:* Gottex Group, 5 Savile Row, W1S 3PD. *Clubs:* White's, Travellers; Corviglia Ski; MBC.

BUSTANI, José Mauricio; Ambassador of Brazil to France, since 2008, and to Monaco, since 2011; *b* 5 June 1945; *s* of Mauricio José Bustani and Guajá de Figueiredo Bustani; *m* 1971, Janine-Monique Lazaro; two *s* one *d. Educ:* Pontifícia Universidade Católica, Rio de Janeiro (LLB 1967); Brazilian Diplomatic Acad., Rio Branco Inst. Joined Brazilian Foreign Service, 1965; postings include: Moscow, 1970–73; Vienna, 1973–77; UN, NY, 1977–84; Montevideo, 1984–87; Montreal, 1987–92; Dir-Gen., Dept for Internat. Orgns, 1993–97; has held rank of Ambassador, 1995–; Dir-Gen., Orgn for Prohibition of Chem. Weapons, 1997–2002; Ambassador to the Court of St James's, 2003–08. Delegate to international negotiations including: 3rd UN Conf. on Law of the Sea, 1974–82; UN Gen. Assembly, 1977–83, 1993–96; 1st and 2nd Special Sessions of UN Gen. Assembly (Disarmament Affairs), 1978 and 1982; Montreal Protocol on Substances that Deplete the Ozone Layer (Leader), 1989–92; Multilateral Fund for Implementation of Montreal Protocol, 1990–91; 13th and 15th Sessions of Prep. Commn for Orgn for Prohibition of Chem. Weapons (Leader), 1996–97. *Recreation:* classical music. *Address:* Embassy of Brazil, 34 Cours Albert 1er, 75008 Paris, France. *T:* (1) 45616304, *Fax:* (1) 42890345. *E:* ambassadeur@bresil.org.

BUTCHER, Anthony John; QC 1977; a Recorder, 1985–97; *b* 6 April 1934; *s* of late F. W. Butcher and O. M. Butcher (*née* Ansell); *m* 1959, Maureen Workman (*d* 1982); one *s* two *d. Educ:* Cranleigh Sch.; Sidney Sussex Coll., Cambridge (MA, LLB). Called to the Bar, Gray's Inn, 1957, Bencher, 1986; in practice at English Bar, 1957–97. Mem., Bar Council, 1989–91, and 1993–97; Chm., Official Referees Bar Assoc., 1986–92. *Recreation:* enjoying the arts and acquiring useless information. *Address:* Anthony Cottage, Polecat Valley, Hindhead, Surrey

GU26 6BE. *T:* (01428) 609053; 1 Atkin Building, Gray's Inn, WC1R 5AT. *T:* (020) 7404 0102. *Clubs:* Garrick, Beefsteak.
See also C. J. Butcher.

BUTCHER, Christopher John; QC 2001; a Recorder, since 2009; a Deputy High Court Judge, since 2013; *b* 14 Aug. 1962; *o s* of Anthony John Butcher, *qv*; *m* 1992, Fiona, *y d* of late Prof. Maxwell Gaskin, DFC; one *s* one *d*. *Educ:* Charterhouse (Sen. Schol.); Magdalen Coll., Oxford (Demy; Gibbs Prize in Mod. Hist. 1982; BA 1st Cl. Hons Mod. Hist.; MA); City Univ. (Dip. Law); King's Coll., London (Dip. EC Law). Fellow, All Souls Coll., Oxford, 1983–98, 2005–07 (Jun. Dean, 1988–90 and 1992–98); Eldon Law Schol., Univ. of Oxford, 1987; called to the Bar, Gray's Inn, 1986 (Bacon Schol., Atkin Schol.; Bencher, 2005). Gov., Berkhamsted Collegiate Sch., 1995–2009. FRSA 2002. *Publications:* contrib. to various legal pubns. *Recreations:* history, literature, travel, the arts. *Address:* 7 King's Bench Walk, Temple, EC4Y 7DS. *T:* (020) 7583 0404.

BUTCHER, Peter Roderick; HM Diplomatic Service; Ambassador to Turkmenistan, 2005–10; *b* 6 Aug. 1947. *Educ:* Univ. of Bath. Entered FCO, 1974; Second Sec., Peru, 1979–83; Madrid, 1983; Second Sec., Bombay, 1983–87; First Sec., FCO, 1987–90; Dep. High Comr, Lesotho, 1990–93; St Vincent and the Grenadines, 1994; First Sec., FCO, 1994–96; Dep. Gov., Port Stanley, 1996; on secondment to DFID, 1997–99; Dep. Hd of Mission, Mozambique, 2000–03.

BUTCHER, Richard James; Under Secretary (Legal), Department of Health and Social Security, 1983–87, retired; *b* 5 Dec. 1926; *s* of late James Butcher, MBE and Kathleen Butcher; *m* 1954, Sheila Joan Windridge; one *s* two *d*. *Educ:* City of London Sch.; Peterhouse, Cambridge (BA 1948, MA 1961). Called to the Bar, Lincoln's Inn, 1950. Served Educn Br., RAF, 1948–50 (Flying Officer). Entered Legal Civil Service as Legal Asst, 1951; Sen. Legal Asst, 1960; Asst Solicitor, 1971. *Recreations:* gardening, reading. *Address:* Brooklands, 165 Caxton End, Bourn, Cambs CB23 2ST. *T:* (01954) 715825.

BUTCHERS, Ven. Dr Mark Andrew; Archdeacon of Barnstaple, since 2015; *b* 1959. *Educ:* Trinity Coll., Cambridge (BA 1981); Chichester Theol Coll. (BTh 1987); King's Coll. London (MTh 1990; PhD 2006). Ordained deacon, 1987, priest, 1988; Curate: St Luke, Chelsea, 1987–90; St Peter and St Paul, Mitcham, 1990–93; Rector, St Peter, North Tawton, Bondleigh and Sampford Courtenay with Honeychurch, 1993–99; Chaplain and Fellow, Keble Coll., Oxford, 1999–2005; Curate, 2005–07, Priest-in-charge, 2007–10, Vicar, 2010–15, St Peter, Wolvercote, Oxford; Area Dean, Oxford, 2012–15. *Address:* Stage Cross, Sanders Lane, Bishops Tawton, Barnstaple EX32 0BE.

BUTE, 7th Marquess of, *cr* 1796; **John Colum Crichton-Stuart, (John C. Bute);** Viscount Ayr, 1622; Bt (NS), 1627; Earl of Dumfries, Lord Crichton of Sanquhar and Cumnock, 1633; Earl of Bute, Viscount Kingarth, Lord Mountstuart, Cumrae and Inchmarnock, 1703; Baron Mountstuart, 1761, Baron Cardiff, 1776; Earl of Windsor, Viscount Mountjoy, 1796; Hereditary Sheriff of Bute; Hereditary Keeper of Rothesay Castle; *b* 26 April 1958; *s* of 6th Marquess of Bute, KBE and of his 1st wife, Nicola (*née* Weld-Forester); *S* father, 1993; *m* 1st, 1984, Carolyn E. R. M. (marr. diss. 1993), *d* of late Bryson Waddell; one *s* two *d*; 2nd, 1999, Serena Solitaire Wendell; one *d*. Motor racing career (as Johnny Dumfries), 1980–92: British Formula Three Champion, 1984; FIA European Formula Three Championship runner-up, 1984 (15 wins); Formula One Ferrari test driver, 1985; JPS Team Lotus Formula One Driver, FIA Formula One World Championship, 1986; FIA World Sports Prototype Championship: 1 win, 1987; Team Silk Cut Jaguar Driver, 1988 (Jt Winner, 24 hr Le Mans sports car race, estd new outright lap record); Team Toyota GB Driver, 1989, 1990; test driver for Benetton Formula One and other Sports Prototype teams, 1990–92. *Heir: s* Earl of Dumfries, *qv*.

BUTLER, family name of **Earl of Carrick, Viscount Mountgarret,** and **Barons Butler of Brockwell** and **Dunboyne**.

BUTLER OF BROCKWELL, Baron *cr* 1998 (Life Peer), of Herne Hill in the London Borough of Lambeth; **Frederick Edward Robin Butler,** KG 2003; GCB 1992 (KCB 1988); CVO 1986; PC 2004; Master, University College, Oxford, 1998–2008; Secretary of the Cabinet and Head of the Home Civil Service, 1988–98; *b* 3 Jan. 1938; *s* of late Bernard and Nora Butler; *m* 1962, Gillian Lois Galley; one *s* two *d*. *Educ:* Harrow Sch.; University Coll., Oxford (BA Lit. Hum., 1961). Joined HM Treasury, 1961; Private Sec. to Financial Sec. to Treasury, 1964–65; Sec., Budget Cttee, 1965–69; seconded to Cabinet Office as Mem., Central Policy Rev. Staff, 1971–72; Private Secretary: to Rt Hon. Edward Heath, 1972–74; to Rt Hon. Harold Wilson, 1974–75; returned to HM Treasury as Asst Sec. i/c Gen. Expenditure Intell. Div., 1975; Under Sec., Gen. Expenditure Policy Gp, 1977–80; Prin. Establishments Officer, 1980–82; Principal Private Sec. to Prime Minister, 1982–85; Second Perm. Sec., Public Expenditure, HM Treasury, 1985–87. Mem., Royal Commn on H of L reform, 1999; Chm., Review of Intelligence on Weapons of Mass Destruction, 2004. Non-executive Director: HSBC Hldgs, 1998–2008; ICI plc, 1998–2008. Ind. Chm., Kings Health Partners, 2009–14. Governor, Harrow Sch., 1975–91 (Chm. of Govs, 1988–91); Chm. Govs, Dulwich Coll., 1997–2003. *Recreation:* competitive games. *Address:* House of Lords, SW1A 0PW. *Clubs:* Athenæum, Brooks's, Beefsteak, Royal Anglo-Belgian, MCC, Oxford and Cambridge.

BUTLER, Alison Sarah; *see* Burns, A. S.

BUTLER, Arthur William, ERD 1964; consultant on parliamentary relations; Secretary, Parliamentary & Scientific Committee, 1979–95, Hon. Life Member 1996; *b* 20 Jan. 1929; *s* of late F. Butler and E. Butler; *m* 1958, Evelyn Mary Luetchford; one *d*. *Educ:* Wanstead High Sch.; LSE (BSc (Econ)). Universities' Prize Essayist, RAS, 1950. Nat. Service, India Cadet Co., Queen's Royal Regt, RAOC, 1946–48, 2nd Lt; Lt, AER, RAOC, 1953, Capt., 1957–64. Trainee, Kemsley Newspapers Graduate Trng Course, Middlesbrough Evening Gazette, 1951–55; Political Correspondent, News Chronicle, 1956–60; Political Ed., Reynolds News, 1960–62; Political Correspondent, Daily Express, 1963–69; Political Ed., Daily Sketch, 1969–71; Man. Dir, Partnerplan Public Affairs, 1971–74; Dir, Public Affairs Div., John Addey Associates, 1974–77; Vice-Chm., Charles Barker Watney & Powell, 1988–89 (Jt Man. Dir, 1978–87). Dir, CSM Parly Consultants Ltd, 1995–2012. Secretary: Roads Campaign Council, 1974–86; All-Party Roads Study Gp, 1974–86; Founder Secretary: Parly All-Party Motor Industry Gp, 1978–90; Parly IT Cttee, 1981–84; Associate Parly Gp on Meningitis, 1999–2001. Consultant on Parly Relns, McAvoy Wreford Bayley, 1989–92, GCI London, 1992–93. Media Advr, Archer Inquiry into NHS contaminated blood, 2007–09. Patron, Art Fund. Jt Managing Editor, Science in Parliament, 1989–98; Editor, Free Romanian (English edn), 1985–95. Freeman, City of London, 1976; Liveryman, Co. of Tobacco Pipe Makers, 1977. Governor, Shelley Sch., Kennington, 1999–2003. *Publications:* (with Alfred Morris, MP) No Feet to Drag, 1972; (with C. Powell) The First Forty Years: a history of the Parliamentary & Scientific Committee, 1980; (with D. Smith) Lobbying in the British Parliament, 1986; People, Politics and Pressure Groups, 2010; Jinx of Fleet Street, 2012; Memoirs of a Jazz-Age Babe, 2013; articles in newspapers and various pubns. *Recreations:* travel, collecting books and militaria, gardening. *Address:* 30 Chester Way, Kennington, SE11 4UR. *T:* (020) 7587 5170.

BUTLER, Mrs Audrey Maude Beman, MA; Headmistress, Queenswood (GSA), Hatfield, Herts, 1981–96; *b* 31 May 1936; *d* of Robert Beman Minchin and Vivien Florence Fraser Scott; *m* 1959, Anthony Michael Butler (marr. diss. 1981); two *d*. *Educ:* Queenswood, Hatfield; St Andrews Univ., Scotland (1st Cl. MA Hons, Geography and Polit. Economy; Scottish Univs Medal, RSGS, 1957–58; Double Blue (tennis, hockey)). Asst Geography Teacher, Queenswood, 1958–59; part-time teacher, Raines Foundn Sch. for Girls, Stepney, 1959–61; Head of Geography, S Michael's, Burton Park, 1970–73, VI Form Tutor/ Geography asst, 1974–78; first House Mistress of Manor House, Lancing Coll., 1978–81. Chm., Boarding Schs Assoc., 1989–91 (Hon. Life Mem., 1996); Mem. Exec. Cttee, GSA, 1987–90 (Hon. Life Mem., GSA, 1996). Governor: Duncombe Sch., 1982–97; Tockington Manor Sch., 1984–97 (Chm., 1995–97); Aldenham Sch., 1987–2001; Maltman's Green Sch., 1988–98; St Mary's, Ascot, 1995–2002; St Leonard's, Mayfield, 1999–2004. Trustee, Bloxham Project, 1999–2003 (Vice-Chm., 1992–99). Dir, British Tennis Foundn, 1997–2007. Vice-Pres., Herts LTA, 1986–. Freeman, City of London, 1997. *Recreations:* golf (Sussex County Colours, 1970), travel, music. *Address:* Chandlers Cottage, Lodsworth Common, Petworth, W Sussex GU28 9DT. *T:* (01798) 861750.

BUTLER, Basil Richard Ryland, CBE 1997 (OBE 1976); FREng; FIMMM; Chairman, KS Biomedix plc, 1995–2001; Director, Murphy Oil Corp., Arkansas, 1991–2002; *b* 1 March 1930; *s* of Hugh Montagu Butler and Annie Isabel (*née* Wiltshire); *m* 1954, Lilian Joyce Haswell; one *s* two *d*. *Educ:* Denstone Coll., Staffs; St John's Coll., Cambridge (MA). Reservoir Engr, Trinidad Leaseholds Ltd, 1954; Petroleum Engr to Chief Petroleum Engr and Supt Prodn Planning Div., Kuwait Oil Co., 1958–68; transf. to BP, Operations Man., Colombia, 1968; Ops Man., BP Alaska Inc., Anchorage, 1970; seconded to Kuwait Oil Co. as Gen. Man. Ops, 1972; Manager: Ninian Develts, BP Petroleum Development Co. Ltd, London, 1975; Sullom Voe Terminal, Shetland Is, 1976; BP Petroleum Development Ltd: Gen. Man., Exploration and Prodn, Aberdeen, 1978; Chief Exec., London, 1980; Dir, BP Internat. Ltd; Chm., BP Exploration Co. Ltd, 1986–89 (Man. Dir and Chief Exec., 1986); Man. Dir, British Petroleum Co. plc, 1986–91; Dir, BP Solar Internat., 1991–98 (Chm., 1991–95). Chairman: Devonport Management, 1992–94; Brown and Root Ltd, 1993–98 (Dir, 1991–98). Chm., Eur. Council of Applied Scis and Engrg, 1992–97. Mem., Cttee for ME Trade, 1985–93. Pres., Inst. of Petroleum, 1990–92; Mem. Council, Royal Acad. of Engrg, 1994–2002 (Hon. Sec. for Internat. Affairs, 1995–98; Sen. Vice Pres., 1996–99). FInstPet 1965; Hon. FIChemE 1991. Liveryman, Shipwrights' Co., 1988. Cdre, Royal Western Yacht Club, 2004–08. *Recreations:* sailing, music. *Address:* Royal Academy of Engineering, SW1Y 5DG.

BUTLER, Brian; Managing Director, Lines2take Ltd, since 2010; *b* 3 May 1949; *s* of Joseph and Alice Eileen Butler; *m* 1978, Margaret Ruth Anne Macdonald (marr. diss. 1990). *Educ:* Hunslet Carr Primary Sch., Leeds; Cockburn High Sch., Leeds; Univ. of Birmingham (BA). Journalist, Westminster Press, 1971–75; Central Office of Information: Information Officer, Newcastle upon Tyne, 1975–79; Sen. Information Officer, Birmingham, 1979–86; Sen. Information Officer, then Grade 7, DoH, 1986–88; Media and Govt Relns Manager, Lloyds Bank, 1988–94; Co-ordinator, Deregulation Task Forces, DTI, 1993–94; Head of Information Services, Benefits Agency, 1994–96; Head of News, 1996–98, Dir of Communication, 1998–2002, Home Office; Dir, Counter-Terrorism Communications, Cabinet Office, 2002–03; Dir of Communications, BMA, 2003–10. Pres., Westminster Players, 2001. Chm., The Spokesmen Gp, 2006. FRSA 2000. *Publications:* (ed jtly and contrib.) Oxford Dictionary of Finance, 1993; (ed jtly and contrib.) Oxford Dictionary of Finance and Banking, 1997. *Recreations:* acting, writing, singing, directing, the USA, the works of Stephen Sondheim. *E:* info@lines2take.co.uk. *Club:* Meanwood Working Men's (Leeds) (Life Mem.).

BUTLER, Christine Margaret; *b* 14 Dec. 1943; *d* of late Cecil and Gertrude Smith; *m* 1964, Robert Patrick Butler; three *s*. *Educ:* Middlesex Univ. (BA Hons). MP (Lab) Castle Point, 1997–2001; contested (Lab) same seat, 2001. Mem., Envmt, Transport and Regl Affairs Select Cttee, 1997–2001. *Recreations:* walking, music, art.

BUTLER, (Christopher) David, CB 1995; Director, Department for National Savings, 1991–95 (Deputy Director, 1989–91); *b* 27 May 1942; *s* of Major B. D. Butler, MC (killed in action, 1944) and H. W. Butler (*née* Briggs); *m* 1967, Helen Christine, *d* of J. J. Cornwell and G. Cornwell (*née* Veysey); two *d*. *Educ:* Christ's Hospital; Jesus College, Oxford (BA); St Mary's Twickenham (TESOL Cert. 2006). Joined HM Treasury, 1964; Asst Private Sec. to Chancellor of Exchequer, 1967–69; Sec., Cttee to Review Nat. Savings (Page Cttee), 1970–72; Head of public expenditure divs, HM Treasury, 1978–82; Head of corporate planning div., Central Computer and Telecoms Agency, 1982–85; HM Treasury: Under-Sec., 1985–89; Head of running costs, manpower and superannuation group, 1985–86; Principal Estabt and Finance Officer, 1987–89. Chief Exec., The Princess Royal Trust for Carers, 1996–99; Res. Manager, 1999–2001, Claims Process Manager, 2001–05, Internat. Commn on Holocaust Era Insurance Claims. Governor, Sadler's Wells Foundn, 1989–94; Dir, Sadler's Wells Trust Ltd, 1989–95; Trustee, Royal Ballet Benevolent Fund, 2009–; Mem., Finance and Gen. Purposes Cttee, Birkbeck Coll., London, 2009–12. Sec., Wimbledon Soc., 2006–14. (Pt-time) Teacher of English as foreign lang., 2005–12. *Recreations:* ballet, opera, reading, family interests. *Club:* Civil Service (Chm., 1994–96).

BUTLER, Christopher John; Director, Butler Kelly Ltd, since 1998; *b* 12 Aug. 1950; *s* of late Dr John Lynn Butler and Eileen Patricia Butler; *m* 1989, Jacqueline Clair, *d* of Mr and Mrs R. O. F. Harper, Glos; one *s*. *Educ:* Emmanuel Coll., Cambridge (MA). Market Research Consultant, 1975–77; Cons. Res. Dept, 1977–80; Political Office, 10 Downing Street, 1980–83; Special Advr, Sec. of State for Wales, 1983–85; Market Res. Consultant, 1985–86; Special Advr, Minister for the Arts, and of the Civil Service, 1986–87; Consultant in Public Policy, Public Policy Unit, 1992–95; Dir, Grandfield Public Affairs, 1995–97. MP (C) Warrington South, 1987–92; contested (C) Warrington South, 1992; contested (C) Wales, Eur. Parly elecns, 1999. Mem., Select Cttee on Employment, 1990–92. Vice Chm., All Party Leasehold Reform Gp, 1989–92; Secretary: All Party Drugs Misuse Cttee, 1989–92; All Party Penal Affairs Cttee, 1990–92. Mem., Exec. Cttee, CPA, 1991–92. *Recreations:* writing, deltiology, book collecting. *Address:* Longwall House, Seven Mile Lane, Borough Green, Kent TN15 8QY.

BUTLER, Dr Colin Gasking, OBE 1970; FRS 1970; retired as Head of Entomology Department, Rothamsted Experimental Station, Harpenden, 1972–76 (Head of Bee Department, 1943–72); *b* 26 Oct. 1913; *s* of Rev. Walter Gasking Butler and Phyllis Pearce; *m* 1937, Jean March Innes; one *s* one *d*. *Educ:* Monkton Combe Sch., Bath; Queens' Coll., Cambridge. MA 1937, PhD 1938, Cantab. Min. of Agric. and Fisheries Research Schol., Cambridge, 1935–37; Supt Cambridge Univ. Entomological Field Stn, 1937–39; Asst Entomologist, Rothamsted Exper. Stn, 1939–43. Hon. Treas., Royal Entomological Soc., 1961–69, Pres., 1971–72, Hon. FRES, 1984; Pres., Internat. Union for Study of Social Insects, 1969–73; Mem., NT Regional Cttee for Devon and Cornwall, 1982–89. FRPS 1957; FRSB. Hon. Fellow, British Beekeepers' Assoc., 1983. Silver Medal, RSA, 1945. *Publications:* The Honeybee: an introduction to her sense physiology and behaviour, 1949; The World of the Honeybee, 1954; (with J. B. Free) Bumblebees, 1959; scientific papers. *Recreations:* nature photography, fishing. *Address:* Hope Residential and Nursing Home, Brooklands Avenue, Cambridge CB2 8BQ. *T:* (01223) 359087.

BUTLER, Cortina Maxine Ann Cotterell; Director, Literature, British Council, since 2013; *b* London, 21 April 1958; *d* of Reg Butler and Rosemary Young Butler; one *d*. *Educ:* Berkhamsted Sch. for Girls; Somerville Coll., Oxford (MA Psychol. and Philosophy 1980). Reader's Digest Association Ltd: Asst Ed., 1981–85; Project Ed., 1985–87; Sen. Ed., Conran Octopus, 1987–90; Publisher, Charles Letts, 1990–93; London Office Manager, Dumont Buchverlag, 1993–94; Reader's Digest Association Ltd: Series Ed., 1994–96; Editl Dir, Books,

1996–2005; Reader's Digest Association Inc.: Internat. Ed., 2005–07; Vice Pres. Global Ed.-in-Chief, Books and Home Entertainment, 2007–11; Man. Dir, BookBrunch, 2012–13. Non-exec. Dir, DACS, 2013–. Gov., Dallington Sch., 2008–. *Publications:* (with R. Anness) Cupcakes for Kids, 2014. *Recreations:* reading, country walking, theatre, opera, art exhibitions. *Address:* British Council, 10 Spring Gardens, SW1A 2BN. *T:* (020) 7389 4385. *E:* cortina.butler@britishcouncil.org.

BUTLER, Creon Adrian John Cotterell; HM Diplomatic Service; Director, European and Global Issues Secretariat, Cabinet Office, since 2012; *b* 1960; *m* 1991, Wendy Joanne Niffikeer; one *s* one *d*. *Educ:* LSE (BSc, MSc). Bank of England, 1984–99: posts incl. Hd, Monetary Instruments and Markets Div.; Foreign and Commonwealth Office: Chief Economist, 1999–2006; Dir, Econ. Policy, 2004–06; Minister and Dep. High Comr, New Delhi, 2006–09; Sen. Advr, Internat. and Finance Directorate, subseq. Internat. and EU Gp, HM Treasury, 2009–12. *Address:* European and Global Issues Secretariat, Cabinet Office, Room 421, 70 Whitehall, SW1A 2AS.

BUTLER, David; *see* Butler, C. D.

BUTLER, David; Director, Butler Lasher Ltd, since 2013; *b* 1 Feb. 1936; *s* of James Charles Butler and Ethel Violet (*née* Newell); *m* 1st, 1956, Catherine Anita Harry (marr. diss. 1974); one *s* two *d*; 2nd, 1975, Frances Mary McMahon; one *d*. *Educ:* Mill Hill Sch.; Keble Coll., Oxford (BA Lit. Hum.). Management Trainee, Herts CC, 1960–64; Computer Manager, NW Metropolitan Hosp. Bd, 1964–65; Management Consultant, Urwick Gp, 1965–72; Dir, Diebold Europe, 1972–76; Chm., Butler Cox plc and Butler Cox Foundn, 1977–92; Sen. Advr, Computer Scis Corp., 1994–2004; Chief Executive Officer: Triple IC Ltd, 2007–13; Butler Basford and Lord Ltd, 2012–13. Dir, Istel, 1983–92; Investment Advr, United Bank of Kuwait, 1985–92. Chairman: Executive Learning Alliance Ltd, 2003–05; Global Business Partnership Alliance, 2006. Mem., Fraud Trials Cttee, 1984–85; Vice Pres., BCS, 1981–83. *Publications:* The Convergence of Technologies, 1977; Britain and the Information Society, 1981; A Director's Guide to Information Technology, 1982; Trends in Information Technology, 1984; Information Technology and Realpolitik, 1986; The Men who Mastered Time (novel), 1986; Senior Management IT Education, 1987; Measuring Progress in IT, 1995; The Outsource Revolution, 2010; IT Outsourcing: the end of business as usual?, 2010; Lord of the Lightning (novel), 2011; numerous press articles. *Recreations:* cricket, Rugby, ancient history. *Address:* 12 Laurel Road, SW13 0EE. *T:* (020) 8876 1810.

BUTLER, Sir David (Edgeworth), Kt 2011; CBE 1991; FBA 1994; Fellow of Nuffield College, Oxford, since 1954; *b* 17 Oct. 1924; *yr s* of late Professor Harold Edgeworth Butler and Margaret, *d* of Prof. A. F. Pollard; *m* 1962, Marilyn Speers Evans (Prof. Marilyn Speers Butler, FBA) (*d* 2014); two *s* (and one *s* decd). *Educ:* St Paul's; New Coll., Oxford (MA, DPhil). J. E. Procter Visiting Fellow, Princeton Univ., 1947–48; Student, Nuffield Coll., 1949–51; Research Fellow, 1951–54; Dean and Senior Tutor, 1956–64. Served as Personal Assistant to HM Ambassador in Washington, 1955–56. Co-editor, Electoral Studies, 1982–92. Chm., Hansard Soc., 1993–2001. DUniv Paris, 1978; Hon. DSSc QUB, 1985; Dr *hc* Essex, 1993; Hon. Dr: Plymouth, 1994; Teesside, 1999. OAM 2002. *Publications:* The British General Election of 1951, 1952; The Electoral System in Britain 1918–51, 1953; The British General Election of 1955, 1955; The Study of Political Behaviour, 1958; (ed) Elections Abroad, 1959; (with R. Rose) The British General Election of 1959, 1960; (with J. Freeman) British Political Facts, 1900–1960, 1963; (with A. King) The British General Election of 1964, 1965; The British General Election of 1966, 1966; (with D. Stokes) Political Change in Britain, 1969; (with M. Pinto-Duschinsky) The British General Election of 1970, 1971; The Canberra Model, 1973; (with D. Kavanagh) The British General Election of February 1974, 1974; (with D. Kavanagh) The British General Election of October 1974, 1975; (with U. Kitzinger) The 1975 Referendum, 1976; (ed) Coalitions in British Politics, 1978; (ed with A. H. Halsey) Policy and Politics, 1978; (with A. Ranney), Referendums, 1978; (with A. Sloman) British Political Facts 1900–79, 1980; (with D. Kavanagh) The British General Election of 1979, 1980; (with D. Marquand) European Elections and British Politics, 1981; (with A. Ranney) Democracy at the Polls, 1981; (with V. Bogdanor) Democracy and Elections, 1983; Governing without a Majority, 1983; (with D. Kavanagh) The British General Election of 1983, 1984; A Compendium of Indian Elections, 1984; (with P. Jowett) Party Strategies in Britain, 1985; (with G. Butler) British Political Facts 1900–85, 1986; (with D. Kavanagh) The British General Election of 1987, 1988; British Elections since 1945, 1989; (with P. Roy) India Decides, 1989, 3rd edn as India Decides 1952–1991, 1995; (with A. Low) Sovereigns and Surrogates, 1991; (with B. Cain) Congressional Redistricting, 1991; (with D. Kavanagh) The British General Election 1992, 1992; (with A. Ranney) Electioneering, 1992; Failure in British Government, 1994; (with G. Butler) British Political Facts 1900–94, 1994; (with D. Kavanagh) The British General Election of 1997, 1997; (with M. Westlake) British Politics and European Elections 1994, 1999; (jtly) Law and Politics, 1999; (with G. Butler) British Political Facts 1900–2000, 2000; (with D. Kavanagh) The British General Election of 2001, 2001; (with M. Westlake) British Politics and European Elections 2004, 2005; (with D. Kavanagh) The British General Election of 2005, 2005. *Address:* Nuffield College, Oxford OX1 1NF. *T:* (01865) 278500.

BUTLER, Dawn; MP (Lab) Brent Central, since 2015; training and development executive, since 2010; bespoke training designer and developer, since 2010; *b* 3 Nov. 1969; *d* of Milo and Ambrozene Butler. *Educ:* Tom Hood Sch.; Waltham Forest Coll. Associate CIPD 1993. Systems analyst, Johnson Matthey, 1989–92; Exec. Officer, Employment Service, 1993–97; Union Officer and Race Audit Co-ordinator, GMB, 1997–2005. Voluntary work, incl. at African Caribbean Centre; mentor; fund-raising co-ordinator. MP (Lab) Brent South, 2005–10; contested (Lab) Brent Central, 2010. PPS to Minister of State, Dept of Health, 2005–06; an Asst Govt Whip, 2008–10; Minister for Young Citizens and Youth Engagement, Cabinet Office, 2009–10. Chm., All Party Parly Gp on Youth Affairs, 2006–10. Political commentator, leadership mentor, and consultant on diversity and policy. Founder: Bernie's List, 2008–; Labour Friends of the Caribbean, 2009–. Patron: W Indian Self Effort, Brent; Mathematics, Brent; Black Women's Mental Health Project, Brent; Hindu Forum Britain; City Mission Community Project; Sister Circle; Sickle Cell Soc.; Betterdays Cancer Care; London Young Labour. *Recreations:* salsa, mentoring. *Address:* House of Commons, SW1A 0AA. *E:* dawn@dawnbutler.org.uk.

BUTLER, Eamonn Francis, PhD; Director, Adam Smith Institute, since 1978; *b* 1952; *s* of Richard Henry Bland Butler and Janet Provan Butler; *m* 1986, Christine Anna Pieroni; two *s*. *Educ:* Univ. of Aberdeen; Univ. of St Andrews (MA 1973, MA Hons 1974; PhD 1978). Research Associate, US House of Representatives, 1976–77; Asst Prof. of Philosophy, Hillsdale Coll., Michigan, 1977–78. Editor, The Broker, 1979–87. Sec., Mont Pelerin Soc., 2012–. Hon. DLitt Heriot-Watt, 2012. *Publications:* Hayek: his contribution to the social and economic thought of our time, 1983; Milton Friedman: a guide to his economic thought, 1985; Ludwig von Mises: fountainhead of the modern microeconomics revolution, 1989; Adam Smith: a primer, 2007; The Best Book on the Market, 2008; The Rotten State of Britain, 2009; The Alternative Manifesto, 2010; Austrian Economics: a primer, 2010; Ludwig von Mises: a primer, 2010; Milton Friedman: a guide to the work and influence of the free-market, libertarian economist, 2011; Public Choice: a primer, 2012; The Condensed Wealth of Nations, 2012; Friedrich Hayek: the ideas and influence of the libertarian economist, 2012; Foundations of a Free Society, 2013; The Economics of Success, 2014; Classical Liberalism: a primer, 2015; (with R. L. Schuettinger) Forty Centuries of Wage and Price Controls, 1979; with M. Pirie: Test Your IQ, 1983; Boost Your IQ, 1990; The Sherlock Holmes IQ Book, 1995; IQ Puzzlers, 1995; contrib. articles to various newspapers and jls. *Recreations:* archaeology, antiquarian books and prints. *Address:* The Adam Smith Institute, 23 Great Smith Street, SW1P 3DJ. *E:* eamonn.butler@adamsmith.org.

BUTLER, Edward Thomas; broadcaster, journalist and writer; *b* Newport, S Wales, 8 May 1957; *s* of Kenneth Butler and Margaret Butler; *m* 2009, Susan Roberts; three *s* three *d*. *Educ:* Monmouth Sch.; Fitzwilliam Coll., Cambridge (BA 1979). Rugby player, 1980–84 (Captain, Wales Rugby, 1983); writer and commentator, BBC, 1984, Sports Dept, 1985–; Rugby correspondent, Observer, 1991–. *Publications:* The Tangled Mane, 2001; The Greatest Welsh XV, 2011; The Head of Gonzo Davies, 2014. *Recreation:* mountain walking. *Address:* Great Llyfos Farm, Cross Ash, Monmouthshire NP7 8PT. *E:* edbutler100@btinternet.com.

BUTLER, Elizabeth Jane, (Mrs Ian Jones); Chairman, Lewisham and Greenwich NHS Trust (formerly Lewisham Healthcare NHS Trust), since 2010; *b* Southsea, Hants, 1 June 1961; *d* of Derek and Kathleen Butler; *m* 1988, Ian Jones; two *s* one *d*. *Educ:* Univ. of Exeter (BSc Hons Maths 1982). ACA 1986, FCA 2009. Audit Sen., Dearden Farrow, 1982–86; Manager, Price Waterhouse, 1986–92. Non-exec. Dir, 1995–2000, Chm., 2000–05, Queen Mary's Sidcup NHS Trust; Chm., Bromley PCT, 2005–10. Chair, Audit Committee: RCN, 2004–12; Electoral Commn, 2008–14; RCVS, 2012–; Member: Audit Cttee, Local Govt Boundary Commn for England, 2010–; Audit and Risk Cttee, GMC, 2013–. Mem., Gp Bd, Hyde Housing Assoc., 1998–2012. Trustee and Treas., Dee Beechinor Trust, 2002–14; Treas., 5th Beckenham S Scout Gp, 2002–. Chair of Govs, St Mary's RC Primary Sch., Beckenham, 2005–. Mem., Univ. of Exeter Alumnae. *Recreations:* family, travel. *Address:* Chairman's Office, University Hospital Lewisham, Lewisham High Street, SE13 6LH. *T:* (020) 8333 3000. *E:* lizbutler1@nhs.net.

BUTLER, Georgina Susan; HM Diplomatic Service, retired; Ambassador to Costa Rica and Nicaragua, 2002–06; *b* 30 Nov. 1945; *d* of Alfred Norman Butler, LDS RCS and Joan Mary Butler (*née* Harrington); *m* 1st, 1970, Stephen John Leadbetter Wright (marr. diss. 2000); one *s* one *d*; 2nd, 2003 (marr. diss. 2009). *Educ:* University Coll. London (LLB 1968; Fellow 2003). British Embassy, Paris, 1969–70; Southern European Dept, FCO, 1971–75; UN Secretariat, NY, 1975–77; Directorate Gen. Develt, EC, Brussels, 1982–84; Deputy Head, Information Dept, FCO, 1985–87; Latin American Dept, FCO, 1999–2001. British Consul, Tangier, 2007–09. Election Observer: Nicaragua, 2006; Venezuela, 2006; Azerbaijan, 2008; Algeria, 2012. Clerk, Fletchers' Co., 2010–12. Chair: Foreign Affairs and Defence Gp, Cons. Policy Forum, 2012–14; S Richmond Ward, Cons. Party, 2015–. Chair, Anglo-Central American Soc., 2015–. Chm., Denys Holland Scholarship Fund, UCL, 2010–; Pres., Crabtree Foundn, UCL, 2015. Contested (C) SW and Gibraltar Reg., EP, 2014. *Recreations:* travel, riding, watersports. *Address:* 49 Sheen Road, Richmond, Surrey TW9 1AJ.

BUTLER, Sir James; *see* Butler, Sir P. J.

BUTLER, (James) Pearse; Director of Clinical Engagement, Computer Sciences Corporation, since 2007; Chairman, University Hospitals of Morecambe Bay NHS Foundation Trust, since 2014; *b* 27 Jan. 1957; *s* of James and Nancy Butler; *m* 1979, Deborah Veronica Downing (*d* 2013); one *s* one *d*. *Educ:* St Mary's Coll., Crosby; Keble Coll., Oxford (BA). Community Worker, Liverpool CVS, 1979–80; Hosp. Admin, S Birmingham HA, 1980–83; Dep. Adminr, then Adminr, Bolton Gen. Hosp., 1983–85; Mgt Consultant, HAY MSL Mgt Consultants, 1985–86; Gen. Manager, Obst. and Gyn. Service, Liverpool HA, 1986–88; Dist Gen. Manager, Chester HA, 1988–89; Chief Executive: Royal Liverpool Children's NHS Trust, 1990–93; Wirral HA, 1993–97; Wigan and Leigh NHS Trust, 1997–99; Royal Liverpool and Broadgreen Univ. Hosps NHS Trust, 1999–2002; Cumbria and Lancashire Strategic HA, 2002–06; Interim Chief Exec., E of England Strategic HA, 2006. *Recreations:* family, Everton FC, golf. *Address:* Computer Sciences Corporation, Royal Pavilion, Wellesley Road, Aldershot, Hants GU11 1PZ. *Clubs:* West Lancashire Golf; Campion Lawn Tennis.

BUTLER, James Walter, MBE 2009; RA 1972 (ARA 1964); RWA; FRBS; *b* 25 July 1931; *m* (marr. diss.); one *d*; *m* 1975, Angela, *d* of Col Roger Berry, Johannesburg, South Africa; four *d*. *Educ:* Maidstone Grammar Sch.; Maidstone Coll. of Art; St Martin's Sch. of Art; Royal Coll. of Art. National Diploma in Sculpture, 1950. Worked as Architectural Carver, 1950–53, 1955–60. Tutor, Sculpture and Drawing, City and Guilds of London Art School, 1960–75. Major commissions include: *portrait statues:* Pres. Kenyatta, Nairobi, 1973; Sir John Moore, Sir John Moore Barracks, Winchester, 1987; John Wilkes, New Fetter Lane, 1988, Wilkes Univ. USA, 1995; Thomas Cook, Leicester, 1994; Billy Wright, 1996, Stan Cullis, 2003, Molineux Stadium, Wolverhampton; James Brindley, Coventry Canal Basin, 1998; Duncan Edwards, Dudley, 1999; Jack Walker, Blackburn Rovers FC, 2001; Isambard Kingdom Brunel, for Felix Dennis, 2009; HM Queen Elizabeth II, Runnymede, 2015; *portrait busts:* Sir Nicholas Bacon, St Albans Sch., 1994; Sir Frank Whittle, 1995, R. J. Mitchell, 2001, Roy Chadwick, 2003, RAF Club; Robert Beldam, Corpus Christi Coll., Cambridge, 2000; Queen Mother, Butchers' Co., Butchers' Hall, London, 2008; Prof. Michael Farthing, St George's, Univ. of London, 2009; Dr Thomas (Tommy) Flowers, MBE, Adastral Park, BT, 2013; *memorial statues:* Richard III, Leicester, 1980; Field Marshal Earl Alexander of Tunis, Wellington Barracks, London, 1985; Reg Harris, Manchester, 1994; *other:* Monument to Freedom Fighters of Zambia, Lusaka, 1974; The Burton Cooper, Burton-on-Trent, 1977; Dolphin Fountain, Dolphin Square, London, 1988; Skipping girl, Harrow, 1988; The Leicester Seamstress, Leicester, 1990; James Henry Greathead, Cornhill, 1994; The Stratford Jester, Stratford-upon-Avon, 1995; D-day Memorial for Green Howards, Crépon, Normandy, 1996; Seagull Sculpture, Anchorpoint, Singapore, 1997; Memorial to Fleet Air Arm, Victoria Embankment Gdns, London, 2000; Great Seal of the Realm, 2001; 50p piece commemorating 50th anniv. of first sub 4 min. mile, 2004; crown piece commemorating 200th anniv. of death of Lord Nelson, 2005; Memorial to Men of 167th Alabama Inf. Regt, Rainbow Div., Fère-en-Tardenois, 2011. Silver Medal, RBS, 1988. *Recreation:* interested in astronomy. *Address:* Valley Farm, Radway, Warwick CV35 0UJ. *T:* (01926) 641938. *Club:* Arts.

BUTLER, John Michael, CPFA, FCCA; consultant, since 2005; Director of Finance and Information Technology, East Riding of Yorkshire Council, 1995–2005; *b* 12 Sept. 1943; *s* of late Reginald Butler and Kathleen (*née* Garside); *m* 1964, Daphne Ann Head (*d* 1999); two *s*. *Educ:* Beckenham and Penge Grammar Sch. CPFA 1966; IRRV 1974; FCCA 1980. Audit Asst, Beckenham BC, 1960–61; Accountancy Assistant: Sevenoaks UDC, 1961–63; Caterham UDC, 1963–64; Sen. Accountant, Dorking UDC, 1964–66; Asst Treas., Esher UDC, 1966–70; Asst Borough Treas., Greenwich LBC, 1970–74; Chief Finance Officer, Lambeth LBC, 1974–79; City Treas., Swansea CC, 1979–95. National President: IRRV, 1989–90; Soc. of Dist Council Treasurers, 1992–93; CIPFA, 2007–08 (Mem. Council, 1994–2009). Treasurer: Welsh Orienteering Assoc., 2006–12; Welsh Soc. of Hull and E Yorks (formerly Welsh Soc. of Kingston upon Hull), 2007–; Age Concern E Yorks, 2007–; Humber Bridge Bd, 2011–; Humberside and Lincs Orienteers, 2011–; Yorks and Humberside Orienteering Assoc., 2014–. FCMI (FBIM 1969). *Recreations:* orienteering, ski-ing. *Address:* 33 Hambling Drive, Molescroft, Beverley HU17 9GD. *T:* (01482) 870312. *E:* john@the-butlers.co.uk. *Clubs:* Swansea Bay Orienteering, Beverley Athletic; York Cross Country Ski.

BUTLER, Jonathan Charles; His Honour Judge Jonathan Butler; a Circuit Judge, since 2014; *b* Oxford, 28 May 1959; *s* of Philip and Margaret Butler; *m* 1998, Julie; one *s* two *d*. *Educ:* Univ. of Leicester (BA Hons; MA); Univ. of Manchester (MEd). Teacher and Lectr, British Council, Manchester Univ., Liverpool Univ., 1983–92; Lectr, Dept of Clin. Psychol., Univ. of Liverpool, 1992–99. Called to the Bar, Gray's Inn, 1992; in practice as barrister, Liverpool, 1992–2010, Manchester, 2010–14; a Recorder, 2008–14. Fee-paid Judge, Mental

Health Review Tribunal, 2001–. *Publications:* Community Care Law and Local Authority Handbook, 2007, 2nd edn 2012; Mental Health Tribunals: law, practice and procedure, 2008, 2nd edn 2013. *Recreations:* running, target shooting, reading (not at the same time). *Address:* Chester Civil and Family Justice Centre, Trident House, Little St John Street, Chester CH1 1SN.

BUTLER, Prof. Martin Howard, PhD; FBA 2013; Professor of English Renaissance Drama, University of Leeds, since 1998; *b* Peterborough, 31 May 1956; *s* of Roy Alec Butler and Mavis Eileen Butler (*née* Church); *m* 1977, Jane-Amanda Barsby; one *s* one *d*. *Educ:* Deacon's Sch., Peterborough; Trinity Hall, Cambridge (BA 1977; MA 1981; PhD 1981). British Acad. Res. Fellow, 1980–81; Res. Fellow, Trinity Hall, Cambridge, 1981–84; University of Leeds: Lectr, 1984–92; Sen. Lectr, 1992–95; Reader, 1995–98. Fellow, Woodrow Wilson Center, Washington, 1990–91; Leverhulme Res. Fellow, 1994–95. Chatterton Lectr, British Acad., 1995. Contributing Ed., Oxford DNB, 1998. *Publications:* Theatre and Crisis 1632–1642, 1984; Ben Jonson's Volpone, 1987; (ed) The Selected Plays of Ben Jonson, vol. 2, 1989; (ed) Re-Presenting Ben Jonson: text, history, performance, 1999; (ed) W. Shakespeare, Cymbeline, 2004; (ed) W. Shakespeare, The Tempest, 2007; The Stuart Court Masque and Political Culture, 2008; (ed jtly) The Cambridge Edition of the Works of Ben Jonson, 7 vols, 2012. *Recreations:* flute, piano, opera, fell-walking. *Address:* School of English, University of Leeds, Leeds LS2 9JT. *T:* (0113) 343 4766. *E:* m.h.butler@leeds.ac.uk.

BUTLER, Megan Veronica; Executive Director International Banks, Prudential Regulation Authority, Bank of England, since 2014; Director of Supervision - Investment, Wholesale and Specialist, Financial Conduct Authority (on secondment), 2015–Sept. 2016; *b* London, 23 June 1964; *d* of Dr William Butler and Dr Anne Butler (*née* Stow); *m* 1989, Christopher William Hames, *qv*; one *s* one *d*. *Educ:* Withington Girls' Sch., Manchester; Sheffield Univ. (LLB Law). Called to the Bar, Inner Temple, 1987; in practice as barrister specialising in Chancery Law, 1987–89; London Stock Exchange, 1989–2000: legal advr; Exec. Asst to CEO and Chm.; Hd, Capital Mkts; Dep. Hd of Listing; joined Financial Services Authority, 2000: Chief Legal Counsel of Mkts; Head: of Enforcement Law and Policy; of Investment Bank Supervision, 2008–11; Dir, Internat. Banks Div., 2011–12; joined Prudential Regulation Authy, Bank of England, 2012. *Recreations:* running, travelling, cooking. *Address:* (until Sept. 2016) Financial Conduct Authority, 25 The Colonnade, E14 5HS; Bank of England, Threadneedle Street, EC2R 8AH. *E:* enquiries@bankofengland.co.uk.

BUTLER, Michael Howard, OBE, FCA; Finance Director, British Coal (formerly National Coal Board), 1985–93, Member of the Board, 1986–93; *b* 13 Feb. 1936; *s* of Howard Butler and Constance Gertrude Butler; *m* 1961, Christine Elizabeth Killer; two *s* one *d*. *Educ:* Nottingham High School. Articled pupil, H. G. Ellis Kennewell & Co., Nottingham, 1952–58; Stewarts & Lloyds Gp, 1960–62; National Coal Board: various posts, NCB HQ, W Midlands Div. and NE Area, 1962–68; Chief Accountant, Coal Products Div., 1968; Dep. Treas., NCB HQ, 1970; Treas. and Dep. Dir Gen. of Finance, 1978; Dir Gen. of Finance, 1981; Chm., British Fuels Co., 1992–93. Director: British Coal Enterprises, 1988–96; Edinburgh Fund Managers, 1993–95; Chairman: CIN Management Ltd, 1993–96; British Investment Trust, 1993–97. Trustee, Mineworkers Pension Fund (formerly British Coal Pension Funds), 1981–2000 (Chm., 1995–2000). *Recreations:* gardening, listening to music, playing tennis. *Address:* Banstead Down, Chorleywood Road, Rickmansworth, Herts WD3 4EH. *T:* (01923) 778001.

BUTLER, Nicholas Jones; Visiting Professor and founding Chairman, The Policy Institute, King's College London, since 2010; *b* Amersham, Bucks, 22 Nov. 1954; *s* of Frank Butler and Jessie Butler (*née* Ridge); *m* 1987, Dr Rosaleen Hughes; one *d* (and one *s* decd). *Educ:* Blackpool Grammar Sch.; Trinity Coll., Cambridge (BA Hons 1977). Economic posts with BP, 1977–92; Hd of Internat. Govt Affairs, BP Exploration, 1992–95; Gp Policy Advr, 1995–2002, Gp Vice Pres. for Strategy and Policy Develt, 2002–07, BP; Chm., Cambridge Centre for Energy Studies, 2007–09; Sen. Policy Advr to Prime Minister, 2009–10. Mem., Adv. Bd, Centre for Eur. Reform, 1995– (Chm., 1995–2008); Advr, Cavendish Lab., Univ. of Cambridge, 2009–; Mem., President's Internat. Adv. Bd, Yale Univ., 2006–13. Vice Pres., Hay Fest., 2005–. Hon. Treas., Fabian Soc., 1982–2013 (Chm., 1987). Trustee, Asia Hse, 2009–. Editor, FT energy blog, 2012–. *Publications:* The IMF, Time for Reform, 1982; (ed) The Economic Consequences of Mrs Thatcher, by Baron Kaldor, 1983; The International Grain Market, 1985; (with R. Lambert) European Universities: renaissance or decay, 2006; (contrib.) Trinity: a portrait, 2011. *Recreations:* reading, music. *Address:* King's College, Strand, WC2R 2LS. *E:* Nick.Butler@kcl.ac.uk. *Clubs:* Athenæum, Travellers.

BUTLER, Norman John Terence, (Terry), CBE 1993; Adviser in Public Services and Social Care, since 2005; Director of Social Services, Hampshire, 1988–2005; *b* 18 Feb. 1946; *s* of Arthur Reginald Butler and Lucy Mary Butler; *m*; one *s* two *d*. *Educ:* Peveril Bilateral Sch., Nottingham; Trent Polytechnic, Nottingham (Cert. in Social Work); Nat. Inst. of Social Work, London; Brunel Univ. (MA Public and Social Admin). Mental Welfare Officer, Nottingham, 1965–71; Sen. Social Worker, Nottingham, 1971–73; Area Man., Haringey, 1974–81; Asst Dir of Social Services, Royal Bor. of Kingston upon Thames, 1981–83; Dep. Dir of Social Services, E Sussex, 1983–88. Non-exec. Dir, NHS S of England (formerly NHS S Central Strategic HA), 2006–13. Member: Firth Cttee, examining public expenditure on residential care, 1987; Algebra Gp, 1992–93; Inf. Tribunal (formerly Data Protection Tribunals Bd), 1996–2010; Standing Gp for Service Delivery and Orgn, NHS R & D Directorate, 1997–99; Co-Leader, Community Care Support Force, providing practical support to local and health authorities in implementation of NHS and Community Care Act, 1992–93; Mem. Adv. Bd for Restricted Patients, 1995–2001; Advr, Clinical Speciality (Social Care), to Nat. Patient Safety Agency, 2003–07; Ind. Member: Gen. Social Care Council, 2005–12; Nat. Clinical Audit Adv. Gp, 2008–11. Patron, Relatives and Residents Assoc., 2007–12 (Vice-Pres., 1995–2007). Hon. Treas., 1997–2003, Co-Chm., Mental Health Cttee, 2003–05, Assoc. of Dirs of Social Services. *Publications:* articles in various jls, incl. Social Work Today, Insight and Community Care. *Recreations:* travel, tennis, swimming, golf, Notts County supporter. *Address:* Edgar House, 17 Lansdowne Avenue, St Cross, Winchester, Hants SO23 9TU.

BUTLER, Patricia Josephine; *see* Ferguson, P. J.

BUTLER, Rt Rev. Paul Roger; *see* Durham, Bishop of.

BUTLER, Pearse; *see* Butler, J. P.

BUTLER, Sir (Percy) James, Kt 2001; CBE 1981; DL; FCA; Deputy Chairman, Camelot PLC, 1995–2002 (Director, 1994–2002); farmer, since 1974; *b* 15 March 1929; *s* of late Percy Ernest Butler and Phyllis Mary Butler (*née* Bartholomew); *m* 1954, Margaret Prudence Copland; one *s* two *d*. *Educ:* Marlborough Coll.; Clare Coll., Cambridge (MA). Joined Peat, Marwick, Mitchell & Co. (later KPMG Peat Marwick), 1952; qualified, 1955; Partner, 1965; Gen. Partner, 1971; Managing Partner, London Reg., 1981–85; Dep. Sen. Partner, 1985–86; Sen. Partner, 1986–93; Mem. of KPMG Exec. Cttee and Council, 1987–93; Chm., KPMG Internat., 1991–93. Director: Mersey Docks and Harbour Co., 1972–90 (Dep. Chm., 1987–90); Tompkins PLC, 1994–95; Wadworth and Co. Ltd, 1994–; Nicholson, Graham & Jones, 1994–2004; Chairman: European Passenger Services Ltd, 1994–96; Union Railways, 1995–96. Mem. (part time), BRB, 1994–95. Business Advr to Treasury and CS Cttee, 1980–82; Member: Cttee on review of Railway Finance, 1982; Cadbury Cttee on Financial Aspects of Corporate Governance, 1990–95. Member: Council, Business in the Community, 1988–90; ICAEW Council, 1992–94; Council, CBIs, 1989–94; Governing Body, City Res. Project, 1991–95; Adv. Council, Prince's Youth Business Trust, 1993–2001; Council, SCF, 1994–2000 (Chm., SCF Private Appeal, 1994–2000). Treasurer, Pilgrims Soc., 1982–97; Trustee, Royal Opera House Trust, 1991–99 (Chm., 1993–95; Vice Chm., 1995–99); Dir, Royal Opera House, 1994–98; Trustee: Winchester Cathedral Trust, 1991– (Chm., Cathedral Appeal, 1991–94); RA, 1997–2005 (Mem., Mgt Cttee, 1997–2009; Mem., Audit Cttee, 1994–2010 (Chm., 1996–2006); Trustee Emeritus, 2009–); Brendoncare Foundn Develt Trust, 1998–2005 (Chm., Brendoncare Foundn Appeal, 1998–2005); Chm. Trustees, Music at Winchester, 1999–2009; Chm., Lord Mayor's Appeal, 2002–03. Mem., Marlborough Coll. Council, 1975–2001 (Chm., 1992–2001). Liveryman: Worshipful Co. of Cutlers, 1965– (Mem. Court, 1985–; Master, 1995–96); Worshipful Co. of Chartered Accountants in England and Wales, 1977–2013. DL Hants, 1994. *Recreations:* bridge, opera, farming. *Club:* Boodle's.

BUTLER, Peter; Chief Executive, Flying Scotsman plc, 2001–09; *b* 10 June 1951; *s* of late Kenneth Jonathan Butler and Barbara Butler; *m* 1973, Peggy Mary, *d* of Richard Nott; three *d*. *Educ:* Adams Grammar Sch., Newport, Shropshire; St Edmund Hall, Oxford (MA English Lit.; PGCE 1974). Admitted Solicitor, 1978; Solicitor, Thames Valley Police, 1978–80; Partner, 1981–92, Consultant, 1992–2000, Linnells, solicitors, Oxford. Nat. Chm., Trainee Solicitors, England and Wales, 1976. Mem. (C) Oxfordshire CC, 1985–89. MP (C) Milton Keynes North East, 1992–97; contested (C) same seat, 1997. PPS to Minister of State, DoH, 1994–95, to Chancellor of Exchequer, 1995–97. Mem., Home Affairs Select Cttee, 1992. Contested (C) W Midlands, Eur. Parlt, 2004. Non-exec. Dir, Continental Trustees Ltd. Non-executive Director: Milton Keynes Chamber of Commerce; Milton Keynes City Orch., 2006–; Milton Keynes Theatre and Gall. Co., 2007–. Sch. Gov., 1985–92. *Recreations:* music, three energetic children, avoiding organised exercise, vintage cars (Alvis 12/50 and Austin 7). *Address:* Castle Farm, Lavendon, Olney, Bucks MK46 4JG. *T:* (01234) 240046. *Club:* Vintage Sports Car.

BUTLER, Philip Andrew; His Honour Judge Philip Butler; a Circuit Judge, since 2009; Designated Civil Judge, Cumbria and Lancashire, since 2011; *b* Manchester, 13 April 1957; *s* of Bernard Hannan Butler and Dorothy Eileen Butler (*née* McCann); *m* 1993, Alison Laura Hayden; one *s* one *d*. *Educ:* St Peter's Grammar Sch., Manchester; Manchester Univ. (LLB 1st Cl. Hons 1978; LLM 1980); Inns of Court Sch. of Law. Called to the Bar, Middle Temple, 1979; in practice as barrister, Northern Circuit, 1979–2009; Asst Recorder, 1998–2000; Recorder, 2000–09. Legal Assessor, GMC, 2002–07; Legal Chm., Fitness to Practise Cttee, Council for Registration of Forensic Practitioners, 2004–08. Mem., 1000 Club, Shakespeare's Globe Th. KCSHS 2012 (KCHS 2006; KHS 1999). *Recreations:* mediaeval history and architecture, reading (detective fiction), theatre, travel, family outings. *Address:* Preston Combined Law Courts, Openshaw Place, Ring Way, Preston, Lancs PR1 2LL.

BUTLER, Sir (Reginald) Richard (Michael), 4th Bt *cr* 1922, of Old Park, Devizes; *b* 3 Oct. 1953; *e s* of Sir (Reginald) Michael (Thomas) Butler, 3rd Bt, QC (Ont) and of Marja McLean; *S* father, 2012; *m* 1st, 1982, Dale Karen Piner (marr. diss. 1998); three *s*; 2nd, 1999, Penelope Joy Lipsack. *Heir: e s* Reginald Paul Butler, *b* 26 June 1988. *Address:* 935 Richmond Road, Victoria, BC V8S 3Z4, Canada.

BUTLER, Sir Richard (Pierce), 13th Bt *cr* 1628 (Ire.), of Cloughgrenan, Co. Carlow; *b* 22 July 1940; *s* of Col Sir Thomas Pierce Butler, 12th Bt, CVO, DSO, OBE and Rosemary Liège Woodgate Davidson-Houston (*d* 1997); *S* father, 1994; *m* 1965, Diana, *yr d* of Col S. J. Borg; three *s* one *d*. *Educ:* Eton; NY Univ. MBA. FCA 1963. Partner, Charles Wakeling & Co., 1964–66; Director: The First Boston Corp. (NY), 1967–78; PaineWebber Inc. (NY), 1978–88 (Management Council, 1985–88); PaineWebber International Bank, 1986–89; Emesco Industrial Equity Co. SA, 1987–2005; The Transportation Gp Ltd, 1989–94; RP&C Internat. (formerly Rauscher Pierce & Clark) Inc., 1992–2000. Mem. Council, Pestalozzi Children's Village Trust, 1983–2009 (Chm., 1985–94); Founder, PestalozziWorld (Pestalozzi Overseas Children's Trust), 1995. *Heir: s* Thomas Pierce [*b* 9 Oct. 1966; *m* 1993, Lucinda Pamela Murphy; two *s* two *d*].

BUTLER, Rosemary Jane; Director of Statistics, Department of Health, 1991–98; *b* 15 July 1946; *d* of Samuel Laight Medlar and Rosemary Peggy Medlar; *m* 1971, Anthony David Butler. *Educ:* Maynard School, Exeter; LSE (BSc Econ). Central Statistical Office, 1967–73; Unit for Manpower Studies, 1973–77; Dept of Employment, 1977–80; Statistician and Chief Statistician, MoD, 1980–85; Chief Statistician, HM Treasury, 1985–89; Asst Sec., DSS, 1989–91. FRSA 1993. *Recreations:* theatre, music, birdwatching.

BUTLER, Dame Rosemary (Janet Mair), DBE 2014; Member (Lab) Newport West, since 1999, and Presiding Officer, since 2011, National Assembly for Wales; *b* 21 Jan. 1943; *d* of late Godfrey McGrath and Gwyneth Jones. *Educ:* St Julian's High Sch., Newport. Qualified chiropodist, 1962; in practice, 1962–75. Dir, Tourism S and W Wales, 1993–99. Mem. (Lab) Newport BC, subseq. CBC, 1973–99 (Chm., Leisure Services, 1983–97); Mayor of Newport, 1989–90. National Assembly for Wales: Sec. for Educn and Children, 1999–2000; Chm., Culture, Sport and Welsh Lang. Cttee, 2004–07; Dep. Presiding Officer, 2007–11. Member: Sports Council for Wales, 1993–99; Museums and Galls Commn, 1996–2000; Broadcasting Council for Wales, 1997–99; Eur. Cttee of the Regions, 2002–07. Founder and Chair: Newport Internat. Comp. for Young Pianists, 1979–; Newport-Kutaisi (Republic of Georgia) Twinning Assoc., 1989–99; Chm., Bd, Nat. Industrial and Maritime Mus., Swansea, 2002–. Hon. Fellow: Univ. of S Wales (formerly Univ. of Wales, Newport), 2012; Cardiff Metropolitan Univ., 2012. Hon. Dr S Wales, 2013. Hon. Citizen, Kutaisi, Republic of Georgia, 1997. *Recreations:* museums, galleries, the arts, foreign travel. *Address:* National Assembly for Wales, Cardiff Bay, Cardiff CF99 1NA. *T:* 0300 200 7104; (constituency office) 72 Caerau Road, Newport NP20 4HJ. *T:* (01633) 222523.

BUTLER, Air Vice Marshal Stuart Denham; Military Advisor to BAE Systems Military Air and Information (Defence Information Training and Services), since 2013; *b* 15 Jan. 1956; *s* of Ralph and Melody Butler; *m* 1984, Linda Dorothy Ritchie (marr. diss. 2012); two *d*; partner, Mrs Jane Russell. *Educ:* Lafford Sch., Billinghay, Lincs. Joined RAF, 1974; Nimrod pilot, 1979–84; Jet Provost flying instructor; Nimrod Sqdn Comdr; Stn Comdr, Kinloss; Dep. Dir, Underwater Battlespace, MoD; AO, Intelligence, Surveillance, Target Acquisition and Reconnaissance, HQ Strike Comd; Dir, Equipt Capability (ISTAR), MoD, 2005–06; Capability Manager (Inf. Superiority), 2006–08, and Air Mem. for Equipment Capability, 2007–08, MoD. Sen. Advr, Defence and Security, BAE Systems, 2009–10. FInstD 2014 (Dip. IoD). *Recreations:* fanatical golfer, civil pleasure flying, DIY. *Address:* 3 Silverdale Avenue, Oxshott, Leatherhead, Surrey KT22 0JX. *T:* (01372) 843130. *E:* pilotstu@btinternet.com. *Clubs:* Royal Air Force; South Kyme Golf (Lincs), Bramley Golf.

BUTLER, Terry; *see* Butler, N. J. T.

BUTLER, Rt Rev. Thomas Frederick; Bishop of Southwark, 1998–2010; Assistant Bishop, Diocese of Leeds, since 2014; *b* 5 March 1940; *s* of Thomas John Butler and Elsie Butler (*née* Bainbridge); *m* 1964, Barbara Joan Clark; one *s* one *d*. *Educ:* Univ. of Leeds (BSc 1st Cl. Hons, MSc, PhD). CEng. College of the Resurrection, Mirfield, 1962–64; Curate: St Augustine's, Wisbech, 1964–66; St Saviour's, Folkestone, 1966–68; Lecturer and Chaplain, Univ. of Zambia, 1968–73; Acting Dean of Holy Cross Cathedral, Lusaka, Zambia, 1973; Chaplain to Univ. of Kent at Canterbury, 1973–80; Archdeacon of Northolt, 1980–85; Area Bishop of Willesden, 1985–91; Bishop of Leicester, 1991–98; Asst Bishop, Dio. of Wakefield, 2010–14; Acting Area Bishop of Bradford, 2014. Chairman: Bd of Mission, Gen. Synod of C of E, 1995–2001; C of E Bd for Social Responsibility, 2001–02; Vice-Chm., Council for Mission and Public Affairs, 2002–. Six Preacher, Canterbury Cathedral, 1979–84. Took seat in H of L, 2007. FKC 2008. Hon. LLD: Leicester, 1995; De Montfort, 1998; Hon. DSc Loughborough, 1997; Hon. DD Kent, 2005; Hon. DLit South Bank, 2005. *Publications:* (with B. J. Butler) Just Mission, 1993; (with B. J. Butler) Just Spirituality in a World of Faiths, 1996; Religion and Public Life, 2011. *Recreations:* reading, mountain walking.

BUTLER, Vincent Frederick, RSA 1977; RGI 1989; figurative sculptor; works in bronze; *b* Manchester, 27 Oct. 1933; *m* 1961, Camilla Luisa Meazza; two *s*. *Educ:* Edinburgh Coll. of Art; Acad. of Fine Art, Milan; Paisley Art Inst. (Dip. 2008). Regular exhibitor at major exhibitions in Scotland; works held in RA, Scot. NPG, Royal Scot. Acad. and several private galleries in Edinburgh, Glasgow and London, incl. Open Eye Gall., Edinburgh and GERBER Gall., Glasgow. Prof. of Sculpture, Univ. of Northern Nigeria, 1960–63. Mem., Paisley Art Inst., 2008. *Publications:* Casting for Sculptors, 1997. *Address:* 17 Deanpark Crescent, Edinburgh EH4 1PH. *T:* (0131) 332 5884. *E:* vincent.butler@talktalk.net.

BUTLER, Prof. William Elliott; John Edward Fowler Distinguished Professor of Law and International Affairs (formerly of Law), Pennsylvania State University, since 2005; Professorial Research Associate, School of Oriental and African Studies, University of London, since 2006; Professor of Comparative Law in the University of London, 1976–2005, now Emeritus; Director, Vinogradoff Institute (formerly Centre for the Study of Socialist Legal Systems), University College London, later at Pennsylvania State University, since 1982; *b* 20 Oct. 1939; *s* of late William Elliott Butler and Maxine Swan Elmberg; *m* 1st, 1961, Darlene Mae Johnson (*d* 1989); two *s*; 2nd, 1991, Maryann Elizabeth Gashi. *Educ:* The American Univ. (BA); Harvard Law School (JD); Acad. Law Sch., Russian Acad. of Scis (LLM); The Johns Hopkins Univ. (MA, PhD); London Univ. (LLD). FSA 1989. Res. Asst, Washington Centre of Foreign Policy Res., Sch. of Advanced Internat. Studies, The Johns Hopkins Univ., 1966–68; Res. Associate in Law, and Associate, Russian Res. Centre, Harvard Univ., 1968–70; University of London: Reader in Comparative Law, 1970–76; Mem. Council, SSEES, 1973–93 (Vice-Chm., 1983–88); Dean of Faculty of Laws, UCL, 1977–79; Vice Dean, 1986–88, Dean, 1988–90, Faculty of Laws, London Univ.; Mem., Cttee of Management, Inst. of Advanced Legal Studies, 1985–88. M. M. Speransky Prof. of Internat. and Comparative Law, 1993–2004, Dean, Faculty of Law, 1993–98, Moscow Higher Sch. of Social and Econ. Scis. Visiting Scholar: Faculty of Law, Moscow State Univ., 1972, 1980; Inst. of State and Law, USSR Acad. of Scis, 1976, 1981, 1983, 1984, 1988; Mongolian State Univ., 1979; Harvard Law Sch., 1982; Visiting Professor: NY Univ. Law Sch., 1978; Ritsumeikan Univ., 1985; Harvard Law Sch., 1986–87; Washington and Lee Univ. Law Sch., 2005; Lectr, Hague Acad. of Internat. Law, 1985; Professorial Lectr in Internat. Law, Sch. of Adv. Internat. Studies, Johns Hopkins Univ., 2009. Associé, Internat. Acad. of Comparative Law, 1982–; Member, Bar: Dist of Columbia; US Supreme Court; Union of Jurists, 1990; Member: Russian Ct of Internat. Commercial Arbitration, 1995–; Kazakhstan Ct of Internat. Commercial Arbitration, 2012–. Chm., Civil Rights in Russia Adv. Panel, Univ. of London, 1983–87; Co-ordinator, UCL-USSR Acad. of Sciences Protocol on Co-operation, 1981–2005; Special Counsel, Commn on Econ. Reform, USSR Council of Ministers, 1989–91; Of Counsel, Clifford Chance, London, Moscow and Almaty, 1992–94; Partner: White & Case, 1994–96; PricewaterhouseCoopers, 1997–2001; Sen. Partner, Phoenix Law Associates, Moscow, 2002–12. Member: EC Joint Task Force on Law Reform in CIS, 1992–93; Working Gp on Commercial Law, Govt of Russian Fedn, 1992; Advr, State Property Fund, Rep. of Kyrgyzstan, 1992; Advr on Corporate Law Reform, Russian Min. of Econ. Develt and Trade, 2004–; Consultant, World Bank, 1992–. Mem., Secretariat, Internat. Assoc. of Mongolists (Ulan Bator), 1987–92; Hon. Member: All-Union Soc. of Bibliophiles, USSR, 1989; Soviet Assoc. of Maritime Law, 1990. Mem., Court of Governors, City of London Polytechnic, 1985–89. Sec., The Bookplate Soc., 1978–86 (Foreign Sec., 1988–94); Exec. Sec., Féd. Internat. des Sociétés d'Amateurs d'Ex-Libris, 1986– (Vice-Pres., 1984–86); Exec. Comr, Russian Assoc. of Maritime Law, 2008–. Academician: Internat. Acad. of the Book and Art of the Book, Russia, 1992; Russian Acad. of Natural Scis (Russian Encyclopedia Section), 1992; Nat. Acad. of Scis of Ukraine, 1992; Russian Acad. of Legal Scis, 1999; Nat. Acad. of Legal Scis of Ukraine, 2013. Mem., Amer. Law Inst., 2009. Trustee, Hakluyt Soc., 2004–. Editor, Year Book on Socialist Legal Systems, 1985–90; Co-editor: The Bookplate Jl, 1989–91 (Editor, 1983–86); Jl of Comparative Law, 2008– (Mem., Editl Bd, 2006–); Editor: Bookplate Internat., 1994–; Sudebnik, 1996–2009; Russian Law: Theory and Practice, 2004–09; E European and Russian Yearbook of Internat. and Comparative Law, 2007–; Mem., editorial bds of learned jls, incl. Marine Policy, 1988–2004, European Business Law Rev., 1990–2004, Internat. Law, 2002–; Mem., Acad. Bd, Pravo Ukrainy (Law of Ukraine), 2011–; Member, Senior Editorial Board: Law of Ukraine (Kyiv), 2011–; Comparative Legal Studies (Kyiv), 2011; Kutafin Univ. Law Rev. (Moscow), 2014–; editor of looseleaf services and microfiche projects. FRSA 1986. Hon. LLD Kyiv Univ. of Law, 2012. *Publications:* more than 800 books, articles, translations, and reviews, including: The Soviet Union and the Law of the Sea, 1971; Russian Law, 1977; (with others) The Soviet Legal System, 3rd and 4th edns, 1977–84; A Source Book on Socialist International Organizations, 1978; Northeast Arctic Passage, 1978; International Law in Comparative Perspective, 1980; Basic Documents on Soviet Legal System, 1983, 3rd edn 1992; Chinese Soviet Republic 1931–1934, 1983; Soviet Law, 1983, 2nd edn 1988; Comparative Law and Legal System, 1985; The Law of the Sea and International Shipping, 1985; The Golden Era of American Bookplate Design, 1986; Justice and Comparative Law, 1987; International Law and the International System, 1987; The Non-Use of Force and International Law, 1989; Perestroika and International Law, 1990; The History of International Law in Russia 1647–1917, 1990; (with D. J. Butler) Modern British Bookplates, 1990; Sherlockian Bookplates, 1992; The Butler Commentaries: USSR Law on Ownership, 1991; USSR Fundamental Principles on Investment Activity, 1991; Foreign Investment Legislation in the Republic of the Former Soviet Union, 1993; (with M. E. Gashi-Butler) Doing Business in Russia, 1994; Russian-English Legal Dictionary, 1995, 2nd edn 2001; Russian Law, 1999, 3rd edn 2009; Tadzhikistan Legal Texts, 1999; Uzbekistan Legal Texts, 1999; American Bookplates, 2000; The Law of Treaties in Russia and Other Countries of the Commonwealth of Independent States, 2002; Russian Company and Commercial Law, 2003; Civil Code of the Russian Federation, 2003; Russian Foreign Relations and Investment Law, 2006; Russian Legal Biography, 2007; Russia and the Law of Nations in Historical Perspective, 2009; Peter Stephen Du Ponceau: legal bibliophile, 2010; Russian Criminal Law and Procedure, 2011; The Russian Legal Practitioner, 2011; Russian Law and Legal Institutions, 2014; Russian Inheritance Law, 2014; Russian Family Law, 2015; International and Comparative Law: a personal bibliography, 2015; *translations of:* G. I. Tunkin, Theory of International Law, 1974, 2nd edn 2003; A. Kuznetsov, The Journey, 1984; Kazakhstan Civil Code, 1995, 2008; Uzbekistan Civil Code, 1998, 2007; Russian Civil Legislation, 1999; Foreign Investment Law in the Commonwealth of Independent States, 2002; A. Saidov, Comparative Law, 2003; A. A. Kovalev, Contemporary Issues of the Law of the Sea, 2004; A. N. Vylegzhain and V. K. Zilanov, Spitzbergen, 2007; V. Kuznetsov and B. Tuzmukhamedov, International Law: a Russian introduction, 2009; A. L. Kolodkin, *et al*, The World Ocean: international legal regime, 2010; *festschrift*: The Best in the West: liber amicorum for Professor William Butler, ed N. Erpyleva and M. E. Gashi-Butler, 2014. *Recreations:* book collecting, bookplate collecting. *Address:* 155 Mount Rock Road, Newville, PA 17241–8916, USA. *T:* (717) 7767359. *Clubs:* Cosmos (Washington, DC); Grolier (New York); National Union of Bibliophiles (Moscow).

BUTLER, William Gerard; Chairman, Cordia (Services) LLP, 2012; *b* 30 March 1956; *s* of William Muir Butler and Mary Butler (*née* Watters); *m* 1988, Patricia Josephine Ferguson, *qv*. *Educ:* St Mungo's Acad., Glasgow; Univ. of Stirling (BA Hons); Notre Dame Coll. of Educn (PGCE 1980). Teacher of English: Greenock High Sch., 1980–83; Port Glasgow High Sch., 1983–85; Castlehead High Sch., 1984–85; John Street Secondary Sch., 1985–86; Stonelaw High Sch., 1986–2000. Member (Lab) Glasgow CC, 1987–2001, 2012– (Convener: Property Services, 1995–98, Policy Formulation, 1998–99; Health and Social Care Policy Develt Cttee, 2012; Vice-Convener, Policy and Resources, 1998–2000). Sec., Glasgow City Labour Gp, 1998–2000. Mem. (Lab) Glasgow Anniesland, Scottish Parlt, Nov. 2000–2011; contested (Lab) same seat, 2011. *Recreations:* reading, theatre, film, visiting Italy, following Partick Thistle FC.

BUTLER, William Gibson; third sector leadership and management professional (consultancy and interim management), since 2010; *b* 11 May 1953; *s* of late William Gibson Butler and Anna Elizabeth Butler; *m* 1975, Jennifer Anne (*née* Dickson); two *d*. *Educ:* Ulster Poly. (CQSW 1975); Open Univ. (BA 1984; MBA 1993). Sen. Social Worker (community work), Eastern Health and Social Services Bd, 1979–86; Principal Community Services Develt Officer, Milton Keynes Develt Corp., 1986–92; Regl Dir, 1992–98, Ops Dir, 1998–2001, Nat. Schizophrenia Fellowship; Chief Exec., Arthritis Care, 2001–04; Chief Operating Officer, Addaction, 2005–10. Chm., Substance Misuse Skills Consortium, 2010–12. FRSA. *Recreation:* going to meetings. *E:* william.butler@ellisgibson.co.uk.

BUTLER-ADAMS, William David, OBE 2015; Managing Director, Brompton Bicycle Ltd, since 2008; *b* London, 11 May 1974; *s* of David Bernard Butler-Adams and Rosalie Annette Butler-Adams; *m* 2004, Sarah Georgina MacIntyre; three *d*. *Educ:* Aysgarth Sch., N Yorks; Rugby Sch.; Univ. of Newcastle upon Tyne (MEng and Spanish (1st cl.) 1997). MIMechE 1993, FIMechE 2014; CEng 2001. Proj. Manager, ICI, 1997–2000; Plant Manager, Dupont, 2000–02; Brompton Bicycle Ltd: Proj. Manager, 2002–05; Engrg Dir, 2005–08. Mem., UK Commn for Employment and Skills, 2013–. Trustee, Educn and Employers Taskforce, 2010–; Mem. Bd, London Regl Council, EEF. FRGS 2013. Liveryman, Vintners' Co., 2010. *Recreations:* flying (Private Pilot Licence), ski-ing, climbing, wine, gardening, the environment; led nine-week expedition up Amazon, 1995 (filmed for documentary by Channel 4) and expedition to summit of Aconcagua (raised over £130,000 for charity), 2000; travelled extensively through South America, Europe, Africa and Asia. *Address:* Brompton Bicycle Ltd, Kew Bridge Distribution Centre, Lionel Road South, Brentford TW8 9QR.

BUTLER-BOWDON, Humphrey Anthony Erdeswick, (Humphrey Ocean), RA 2004; painter; *b* 22 June 1951; *s* of late Capt. Maurice Erdeswick Butler-Bowdon, OBE, RN, and Anne (*née* Darlington); *m* 1982, Miranda Argyle; two *d*. *Educ:* Ampleforth; Tunbridge Wells Art Sch.; Brighton Coll. of Art; Canterbury Coll. of Art. Bass player, Kilburn and the Highroads, 1971–73. Prof. of Perspective, Royal Acad. Schs, 2012–. Mem., Artistic Records Cttee, Imperial War Mus., 1985–98. Work includes: The First of England, Nat. Maritime Mus., 1999; *portrait commissions* for National Portrait Gallery: Randy Lerner; Tony Benn; William Whitelaw; A. J. Ayer; Philip Larkin; Paul McCartney; *one-man exhibitions:* Nat. Portrait Gall., 1984; Ferens Art Gall., Hull, 1986; Double-Portrait, Tate Gall., Liverpool, 1992; urbasuburba, Whitworth Art Gall., Manchester, 1997; The Painter's Eye, Nat. Portrait Gall., 1999; how's my driving, Dulwich Picture Gall., 2003; Perfectly Ordinary, Sidney Cooper Gall., Canterbury Christ Church Univ., 2009; Here and There, Jesus Coll., Cambridge, 2011; A handbook of modern life, Nat. Portrait Gall., 2012–13; *group exhibitions* include: Das Automobil in der Kunst, Haus der Kunst, Munich, 1986; Royal Treasures, Queen's Gall., Buckingham Palace, 2002; Works Printed by Maurice Payne, Pace Prints, NY, 2011; Ship to Shore, John Hansard Gall., Univ. Southampton, 2014; *work in collections:* Ferens Art Gall., Hull; Imperial War Mus.; Christ Church, Oxford; Nat. Maritime Mus.; NPG; Royal Liby, Windsor Castle; Royal Opera House, Covent Gdn; Scottish NPG; Southwark Collection; Wellcome Trust; Wolverhampton Art Gall.; British Council; Whitworth Art Gall., Manchester; Goldsmiths Coll., Univ. of London; Port Authy, Bruges-Zeebrugge; V&A; Pallant Hse Gall., Chichester. Hon. Fellow, Kent Inst. of Art and Design, 2002. Hon. Dr, Canterbury Christ Ch, 2012. Imperial Tobacco Portrait Award, 1982; Wellcome Trust Sci-Art Award, 1998. *Publications:* The Ocean View, 1982; (with S. Nugent) Big Mouth: the Amazon speaks, 1990; Zeebrugge, 2001; A handbook of modern life, 2012. *Recreation:* carrying binoculars. *Address:* 22 Marmora Road, SE22 0RX. *T:* (020) 8693 8387, *T:* (studio) (020) 8761 7400. *W:* www.humphreyocean.com.

BUTLER-SLOSS, family name of **Baroness Butler-Sloss.**

BUTLER-SLOSS, Baroness *cr* 2006 (Life Peer), of Marsh Green in the County of Devon; **Ann Elizabeth Oldfield Butler-Sloss,** GBE 2005 (DBE 1979); PC 1988; President of the Family Division, 1999–2005; *b* 10 Aug. 1933; *d* of Sir Cecil Havers, QC and Enid Snelling; *m* 1958, Joseph William Alexander Butler-Sloss, *qv*; two *s* one *d*. *Educ:* Wycombe Abbey Sch. Called to Bar, Inner Temple, Feb. 1955, Bencher, 1979, Treasurer, 1998; practice at Bar, 1955–70; Registrar, Principal Registry of Probate, later Family, Division, 1970–79; a Judge of the High Court, Family Div., 1979–88; a Lord Justice of Appeal, 1988–99. Chairman: Cleveland Child Abuse Inquiry, 1987–88; Security Commn, 1993–2005; Adv. Council, St Paul's Cathedral, 2001–09; Commn on Appointment of Archbishop of Canterbury, 2002. Contested (C), Lambeth, Vauxhall, 1959. Mem., Judicial Studies Bd, 1985–89; Pres., Commonwealth and England Bar Assoc., 2000–07. Pres., Honiton Agricultural Show, 1985–86; Chancellor, Univ. of West of England, 1993–2010; Visitor, St Hilda's Coll., Oxford, 2000–. Gov., Merchant Taylors' Sch., Moor Park, 2006–13. Gov., Coram, 2005–; Pres., Grandparents' Assoc., 2008–. Freedom, City of London; Hon. Mem., Merchant Taylors' Co. Hon. Mem., American Law Inst., 1990. Hon. Fellow: St Hilda's Coll., Oxford, 1988; Sarum Coll., 2004; Fellow, KCL, 1991. FRSocMed 1992, Hon. FRSocMed 1997; Hon. FRCP 1992; Hon. FRCPsych 1993; Hon. FRCPCH 1996 (Hon. Mem., BPA, 1988). Hon. LLD: Hull, 1988; Keele, Bristol, 1991; Exeter, Brunel, 1992; Manchester, 1995; Cantab, Greenwich, 2000; Liverpool, E Anglia, 2001; London, Ulster, 2004; Buckingham, 2006; Hon. DLitt Loughborough, 1992; DUniv: Central England, 1994; Bath, 2004; Open, 2005; UWE, 2009; Wolverhampton, 2010. *Publications:* Joint Editor: Phipson on Evidence (10th edn); Corpe on Road Haulage (2nd edn); a former Editor, Supreme Court Practice, 1976 and 1979. *Clubs:* Lansdowne, Royal Society of Medicine.

BUTLER-SLOSS, Joseph William Alexander; Chairman, 1992 Delimitation Commission, Botswana, 1992–93; *b* 16 Nov. 1926; 2nd and *o* surv. *s* of late Francis Alexander Sloss and Alice Mary Frances Violet Sloss (*née* Patchell); *m* 1958, Ann Elizabeth Oldfield Havers (*see* Baroness Butler-Sloss); two *s* one *d*. *Educ:* Bangor Grammar Sch., Co. Down; Hertford Coll., Oxford. Ordinary Seaman, RN, 1944; Midshipman 1945, Sub-Lieut 1946, RNVR. MA (Jurisprudence) Hertford Coll., Oxford, 1951. Called to Bar, Gray's Inn, 1952; joined Western Circuit, 1954; joined Inner Temple; a Recorder, 1972–84; a Judge of High Court, Kenya, 1984–90. Joint Master, East Devon Foxhounds, 1970–76. Hon. Editor, The Irish Genealogist, 1993–2001. *Recreations:* racing, the violin. *Address:* Higher Marsh Farm, Marsh Green, Rockbeare, Exeter EX5 2EX. *Club:* Carlton.

BUTLER-WHEELHOUSE, Keith Oliver; Chief Executive, Smiths Group (formerly Smiths Industries), 1996–2008; *b* 29 March 1946; *s* of late Kenneth Butler-Wheelhouse and May (*née* Page); *m* 1973, Pamela Anne Bosworth Smith; two *s*. *Educ:* Queen Mary's, Walsall; Grey Sch. and Technicon, Port Elizabeth; Witwatersrand Univ. (BCom); Cape Town Univ. Grad. Sch. Mfg, Product Develt, Finance and Mktg Depts, Ford Motor Co., 1965–85; General Motors, 1985–86, led mgt buy-out of GMSA to form Delta, 1987–92; Pres., Saab Automobile, Sweden, 1992–96. Non-executive Director: Atlas Copco, 1993–96; J. Sainsbury plc, 1999–2004; Plastics Capital plc, 2011–. Chairman: Niu Solutions, 2009–11; Chamberlin,

2012–. Citizen of Year, Port Elizabeth, 1987. *Recreations:* golf, tennis, surfing. *Clubs:* Moor Park Golf, Royal and Ancient, Sunningdale Golf, Queen's Tennis; Humewood Golf, St Francis Golf, Fancourt Golf, Johannesburg Country (S Africa).

BUTLIN, Martin Richard Fletcher, CBE 1990; FBA 1984; Keeper of Historic British Collection, Tate Gallery, 1967–89; *b* 7 June 1929; *s* of late Kenneth Rupert Butlin and Helen Mary (*née* Fletcher), MBE, JP; *m* 1969, Frances Caroline Chodzko. *Educ:* Rendcomb Coll.; Trinity Coll., Cambridge (MA); Courtauld Inst. of Art, London Univ. (BA). DLit London 1984. Asst Keeper, Tate Gall., 1955–67. *Publications:* A Catalogue of the Works of William Blake in the Tate Gallery, 1957, 3rd edn 1990; Samuel Palmer's Sketchbook of 1824, 1962, 2nd edn as Samuel Palmer: the sketchbook of 1824, 2005; Turner Watercolours, 1962; (with Sir John Rothenstein) Turner, 1964; (with Mary Chamot and Dennis Farr) Tate Gallery Catalogues: The Modern British Paintings, Drawings and Sculpture, 1964; The Later Works of J. M. W. Turner, 1965; William Blake, 1966; The Blake-Varley Sketchbook of 1819, 1969; (with E. Joll) The Paintings of J. M. W. Turner, 1977, 2nd edn 1984 (jtly, Mitchell Prize for the History of Art, 1978); The Paintings and Drawings of William Blake, 1981; Aspects of British Painting 1550–1800, from the Collection of the Sarah Campbell Blaffer Foundation, 1988; (with Mollie Luther and Ian Warrell) Turner at Petworth, 1989; (with Ted Gott and Irena Zdanowicz) William Blake in the Collection of the National Gallery of Victoria, 1989; (ed with E. Joll and L. Herrmann) The Oxford Companion to J. M. W. Turner, 2001; (with Morton D. Paley) William Blake's Watercolour Inventions in illustration of The Grave by Robert Blair, 2009; selected paintings and prepared catalogues for following exhibitions: (with Andrew Wilton and John Gage) Turner 1775–1851, 1974; William Blake, 1978; (with Gert Schiff) William Blake, Tokyo, 1990; articles and reviews in Burlington Mag., Connoisseur, Master Drawings, Blake Qly, Blake Studies, Turner Studies. *Recreations:* music, travel. *Address:* 74c Eccleston Square, SW1V 1PJ.

BUTLIN, Prof. Robin Alan, OBE 2004; DLitt; Professor of Historical Geography, University of Leeds, 2000–03, now Emeritus Professor of Geography (Leverhulme Emeritus Research Fellow, 2003–05; Visiting Research Fellow, School of Geography, since 2009); *b* 31 May 1938; *s* of late Rowland Henry Butlin and Mona Butlin; *m* 1961, Norma Coroneo; two *s* one *d.* *Educ:* Liverpool Univ. (BA, MA); DLitt Loughborough, 1987. Demonstrator, University Coll. of N Staffordshire, 1961–62; Lectr in Geography, UC Dublin, 1962–71; Queen Mary College, University of London: Lectr in Geography, 1971; Sen. Lectr, 1975; Reader in Historical Geography, 1977–79; Loughborough University: Prof. of Geography, 1979–95; Hd of Dept, 1979–91; Dean, Sch. of Human and Environmental Studies, 1983–86; Principal, and Prof. of Historical Geography, UC of Ripon and York St John, 1995–98. Vis. Associate Prof. of Geography, Univ. of Nebraska, 1969–70; Vis. Professorial Fellow and Leverhulme Res. Fellow, Wolfson Coll., Cambridge, 1986–87; Vis. Prof., Leeds Univ., 1998–2000. Gov., St Peter's Sch., York, 2002–10. FRGS 1972 (Vice-Pres., RGS/IBG, 1995–98); CGeog 2002. Victoria Medal, RGS, 1999. *Publications:* (ed with A. R. H. Baker) Studies of Field Systems in the British Isles, 1973; (ed) The Development of the Irish Town, 1977; (ed with R. A. Dodgshon) An Historical Geography of England and Wales, 1978, 2nd edn 1990; (ed with H. S. A. Fox) Change in the Countryside: essays on rural England 1500–1900, 1979; The Transformation of Rural England c. 1580–1800, 1982; Historical Geography: through the gates of space and time, 1993; (ed jtly) Geography and Imperialism 1820–1940, 1995; (ed with N. Roberts) Ecological Relations in Historical Times, 1995; (ed with R. A. Dodgshon) Historical Geography of Europe, 1999; (ed with I. S. Black) Place, Culture and Identity, 2001; (ed) Historical Atlas of North Yorkshire, 2003; Geographies of Empire: European empires and colonies *c* 1880–1960, 2009; The Historical Geography Research Group: a history, 2013; The Origins and Development of Geography at the University of Leeds *c* 1874–2014, 2015. *Recreations:* music, walking, reading, collecting wood engravings. *Address:* 15 Lawnway, Stockton Lane, York YO31 1JD. *T:* (01904) 416544.

BUTROS, Prof. Albert Jamil; Istiqlal Order First Class, Jordan, 1987; Professor of English, University of Jordan, 1967–79 and 1985–2004, now Emeritus; *b* 25 March 1934; *s* of Jamil Issa and Virginie Antoine (Albina); *m* 1962, Ida Maria Albina; four *d.* *Educ:* Univ. of London (BA Hons English 1958); Univ. of Exeter (BA *ad eundem* 1958); Columbia Univ. (PhD English 1963). Teacher, Amman, 1950–55; Instructor in English, Teacher's Coll., Amman, 1958–60; Lectr, Hunter Coll., City Univ., NY, 1961; Instructor, Miami Univ., Oxford, Ohio, 1962–63; University of Jordan: Asst Prof., English, 1963–65; Associate Prof., 1965–67; Acting Chm., Dept of English, 1964–67; Chm., Dept of English, 1967–73, 1974–76; Dean, Research and Graduate Studies, 1973–76; Ambassador to UK, 1987–91, and (non-res.) to Ireland, 1988–91, and to Iceland, 1990–91. Special Advr to HRH Crown Prince Hassan of Jordan, 1984–85. Dir Gen./Pres., Royal Sci. Soc., Amman, 1976–84. Vis. Prof., Ohio Wesleyan Univ., 1971–72; Sen. Res. Fellow, Internat. Develt Res. Centre, Canada, 1983–84. Rapporteur, Cttee on Jordan Incentive State Prize in Translation, 2001; Member: Cttee on Selection for Shoman Foundn Prize for Young Arab Scholars in Humanities and Social Scis, 2002; Cttee on Selection of Outstanding Researchers in Jordan, 2004. Member: World Affairs Council, Amman, 1978–91; Arab Thought Forum, 1981–95. Gov., Internat. Develt Res. Centre, Canada, 1986–98; Mem., Bd of Trustees, Philadelphia Univ., Amman, 1995–2009. Mem., Adv. Bd, Jordanian Jl of Modern Langs and Lit., 2006–. Fellow, World Acad. of Art and Sci., 1986. KStJ 1991. Order of Merit, Italy, 1983. *Publications:* Tales of the Caliphs, 1965; Leaders of Arab Thought, 1969; The Translatability of Chaucer into Arabic: a test case, 1997; The English Language and Non-Native Writers of Fiction, 2004; (in Arabic) Geoffrey Chaucer: introduction and selected translations, 2009; translations include: (in English) Suleiman Mousa's T. E. Lawrence: an Arab view, 1966; (in Arabic) Glanville Downey's Antioch in the Age of Theodosius the Great, 1968; articles. *Recreations:* reading, writing, translation, art, world affairs, application of science and technology to development. *Address:* PO Box 309, Amman 11941, Jordan.

BUTT, Amanda Jane; *see* Finlay, A. J.

BUTT, Geoffrey Frank; Principal Assistant Solicitor, Inland Revenue, 1993–96; *b* 5 May 1943; *s* of late Frank Thomas Woodman Butt and Dorothy Rosamond Butt; *m* 1972, Lee Anne Davey; two *s* one *d.* *Educ:* Royal Masonic Sch., Bushey; Univ. of Reading (BA). Solicitor 1970. Joined Solicitor's Office, HM Customs and Excise as Legal Asst, 1971; Sen. Legal Asst, 1974; Asst Solicitor, 1982; Prin. Asst Solicitor, 1986–93. *Recreations:* family life, classical music, literature and art, gardening. *Address:* 14 Richmond Close, Wellswood, Torquay, Devon TQ1 2PW.

BUTT, Prof. John Anthony, OBE 2013; PhD; FBA 2006; FRSE; Gardiner Professor of Music, University of Glasgow, since 2001; *b* 17 Nov. 1960; *s* of late Wilfred Roger Butt and of Patricia Doreen Butt; *m* 1989, Sally Ann Cantlay; four *s* one *d.* *Educ:* Solihull Sch.; King's Coll., Cambridge (BA 1982; MPhil 1984; PhD 1987). FRCO(CHM); ADCM. Temp. Lectr, Univ. of Aberdeen, 1986–87; Res. Fellow, Magdalene Coll., Cambridge, 1987–89; Prof. of Music and Univ. Organist, Univ. of Calif, Berkeley, 1989–97; Lectr in Music and Fellow, King's Coll., Univ. of Cambridge, 1997–2001. Conductor of several recordings with Dunedin Consort, including: Bach, St John Passion and Brandenburg Concertos, 2013; Mozart Requiem, 2014 (Gramophone Classical Music Award for Choral Music, 2014). Mem., AHRC, 2010–14. FRSE 2003. *Publications:* Bach Interpretation, 1990; Bach Mass in B Minor, 1991; Music Education and the Art of Performance in the German Baroque, 1994; (ed) Cambridge Companion to Bach, 1997; Playing with History, 2002; (ed) Cambridge History of 17th Century Music, 2005; Bach's Dialogue with Modernity: perspectives on the passions, 2010. *Recreations:* reading, hill-walking. *Address:* Upper Culverden, 2 West Lennox Drive, Helensburgh G84 9AD. *T:* (01436) 673942.

BUTT, Loren Oliver Wallington; independent consulting engineer, since 1987; *b* London, 24 March 1936; *s* of Roderick Butt and Cynthia Butt (*née* Cooper-Smith); *m* 1959, Jennifer Margaret Perham; two *s.* *Educ:* Clifton Coll., Bristol; University Coll. London (BSc Eng 1959). CEng, MIMechE 1967. Associate, D. W. Thomson & Co., Vancouver, BC, 1967; Exec. Engr, G. N. Haden and Sons Ltd, 1968–70; Design Engr, 1970–72, Associate, 1972–80, Foster Associates; Dir, Foster Associates Ltd, 1980–87. Hon. FRIBA 2009. *Recreations:* architectural and engineering history, walking, playing guitar, playing petanque. *Address:* 22 Croft Road, Wallingford, Oxon OX10 0HT. *T:* (01491) 200316. *E:* loren.butt@virginmedia.com.

BUTT, Michael Acton, OBE 2011; Chairman, AXIS Capital Holdings Ltd, Bermuda, since 2002; *b* Thruxton, 25 May 1942; *s* of Leslie Acton Kingsford Butt and Mina Gascoigne Butt; *m* 1st, 1964, Diana Lorraine Brook; two *s*; 2nd, 1986, Zoé Benson. *Educ:* Rugby; Magdalen Coll., Oxford (MA History); INSEAD, France (MBA 1967). Bland Welch Gp, 1964; Dir, Bland Payne Holdings, 1970; Chm., Sedgwick Ltd, 1983–87; Dep. Chm., Sedgwick Gp plc, 1985–87; Chm. and Chief Exec., Eagle Star Hldgs, 1987–91; Dir, BAT, 1987–91; Pres. and CEO, Mid Ocean Ltd, 1993–98; Dir, XL Capital Ltd, 1998–2002. Director: Marceau Investissements, Paris, 1987–94; Phoenix International (Bermuda), 1992–97; INA, 1994–97; Bank of N. T. Butterfield & Son Ltd, 1996–2002. Board Mem., Internat. Adv. Council, INSEAD, 1982–2010. *Recreations:* travel, tennis, opera, reading, family, the European movement. *Address:* Leamington House, 50 Harrington Sound Road, Hamilton Parish CR 04, Bermuda. *T:* (441) 2931378, *Fax:* (441) 2938511. *Clubs:* Royal Bermuda Yacht, Mid Ocean, Coral Beach (Bermuda).

BUTT, Richard Bevan; Chief Executive, Rural Development Commission, 1989–98; *b* 27 Feb. 1943; *s* of late Roger William Bevan and Jean Mary (*née* Carter); *m* 1975, Amanda Jane Finlay, *qv*; two *s.* *Educ:* Magdalen Coll., Oxford (BA Hist.); Lancaster Univ. (MA Regional Econs). Asst Principal, Min. of Housing, 1965–68; Sen. Res. Associate, Birmingham Univ., 1969–72; Consultant, 1972; HM Treasury: Principal, 1973–78; Asst Sec., 1978–86; seconded as Financial Counsellor, UK Perm. Repn to EC, 1981–84; Head of Conservation, English Heritage, 1986–89. Specialist Advr to Agriculture Select Cttee, 1998–99. Trustee: Action for Market Towns, 1998–2003; Churches Conservation Trust, 1999–2008 (Dep. Chm., 2006–08); TCPA, 2004–08 (Mem., Policy Council, 1998–2008). *Recreations:* ceramics, architecture, gardening, travel. *Address:* 35 Gloucester Circus, SE10 8RY.

BUTT, Simon John; HM Diplomatic Service, retired; Ambassador to Lithuania, 2008–11; *b* 5 April 1958; *s* of William Hedley Butt and Joan Marion Newton Butt. *Educ:* New Coll., Oxford (BA 1st Cl. Hons PPE 1979; MA). Entered FCO, 1979; E Europe and Soviet Dept, FCO, 1979–80; lang. trng, 1980–82; Third Sec., Moscow, 1982–84; Second Secretary: Rangoon, 1984–86; Soviet Dept, FCO, 1986–88; ministerial speechwriter, 1988–90; First Sec., UK Perm. Representation to EC, 1990–94; Dep. Hd, Eastern Dept, FCO, 1994–97; Counsellor and Dep. Hd of Mission, Kiev, 1997–2000; Hd, Eastern Dept, FCO, 2001–04; Dep. High Comr, Islamabad, Pakistan, 2005–08. *Recreations:* travel, the company of friends, history, including a harmless obsession with Napoleon on St Helena. *E:* sjbutt295@yahoo.co.uk.

BUTTER, His Honour Neil (McLaren), CBE 2001; QC 1976; a Circuit Judge, 1982–2001; a Judge of Central London County Court, 1994–2001; Designated Civil Judge, London County Court Group, 1998–2001; Senior Circuit Judge, 1998–2001; *b* 10 May 1933; *y s* of late Andrew Butter, MA, MD and late Ena Butter, MB, ChB; *m* 1974, Claire Marianne Miskin, LLM (*d* 2011). *Educ:* The Leys Sch.; Queens' Coll., Cambridge (MA). Called to Bar, Inner Temple, 1955, Bencher, 1994; an Asst and Dep. Recorder of Bournemouth, 1971; Recorder of the Crown Court, 1972–82; a Judge of Bow County Court, 1986–94; occasional Judge of Employment Appeal Tribunal, 1995–98. Member: Senate of the Inns of Court and the Bar, 1976–79; County Court Rule Cttee, 1993–99; Clinical Disputes Forum, 1997–2001; Chm., Court Mediation Scheme Cttee, 1996–2001. Inspector, for Dept of Trade, Ozalid Gp Hldgs Ltd, 1977–79. A Legal Assessor to GMC and GDC, 1979–82; Mem., Mental Health Review Tribunal, 1983–92. Chm., London County Court Assoc. of Circuit Judges, 1998–2001. Trustee, Kingdon-Ward Speech Therapy Trust, 1980–87. *Publications: collections of short stories*: Doctor George, 2007; Burning Desire, 2010; Below the Window, 2014. *Recreations:* dining out with friends, browsing through Who's Who. *Club:* Royal Over-Seas League.

BUTTER, Peter Joseph Michael, CB 1992; Deputy Managing Director, Property Services Agency, Building Management, Department of the Environment, 1992, retired; *b* 9 Dec. 1932; *s* of Joseph Butter and Kathleen (*née* Woodward); *m* 1956, Pamela Frances Roberts; three *s.* *Educ:* Brighton, Hove and Sussex Grammar School. Served Royal Signals, 1951–53. BR, 1953–67; Principal, Min. of Transport, 1967–73; Private Sec. to Minister of Transport, 1973; joined PSA, 1974: Hd, Defence Secretariat (Navy), 1974–79; Asst Dir, Estate Surveying Services, 1979–84; Dir, SE Region, 1984–88; Dir, Home Regional Services, 1988–90; Dir of Ops, PSA, Bldg Management, DoE, 1990–91. Chm., Sussex Cricket League, 2010 (Sec., 1999–2007; Vice Pres., 2008–). *Recreations:* cricket administration, listening to music, exploring Britain. *Address:* 6 Scarletts Close, Uckfield, E Sussex TN22 2BA. *Club:* Sussex CC.

BUTTERFIELD, Hon. Sir (Alexander) Neil (Logie), Kt 1995; a Judge of the High Court of Justice, Queen's Bench Division, 1995–2012. *Educ:* Sidney Sussex Coll., Cambridge (BA 1964). Called to the Bar, Inner Temple, 1965; a Recorder, 1978–95; QC 1985. Leader, 1992–95, Presiding Judge, 1997–2000, Western Circuit. Member: Parole Bd, 2003– (Vice Chm., 2005–); Bd, Ind. Parly Standards Authy, 2013–. *Address:* c/o Royal Courts of Justice, Strand, WC2A 2LL. *Club:* Athenæum.

BUTTERFIELD, Ven. David John; Archdeacon for Generous Giving and Stewardship, and Residentiary Canon, York Minster, since 2014; *b* 1 Jan. 1952; *s* of John Alfred Butterfield and Agnes Butterfield (*née* Winn); *m* 1977, Irene Mary Abel; two *s.* *Educ:* Belle Vue Boys' Grammar Sch., Bradford; Royal Holloway Coll., London Univ. (BMus 1973); Nottingham Univ. (DipTh 1975); St John's Theol Coll., Nottingham. Ordained deacon, 1977, priest, 1978; Curate, Christ Church, Southport, 1977–81; Minister, St Thomas, Aldridge, 1981–91; Vicar, St Michael's, Lilleshall, St John's, Muxton, and St Mary's, Sheriffhales, 1991–2007; Rural Dean, Edgmond and Shifnal, 1997–2006; Archdeacon of East Riding, 2007–14. Mem., Crown Appts Commn, 2003. Mem., Gen. Synod, C of E, 1990–2005 (Chair, House of Clergy, Dio. of Lichfield, 2003–06). *Publications:* Getting Going, 1987. *Recreations:* piano, organ, walking, swimming, reading, making marmalade. *Address:* 2A Minster Court, York YO1 7JJ. *T:* (01904) 557278. *E:* archdeacondavid@yorkminster.org.

BUTTERFIELD, Jeremy Nicholas, PhD; FBA 1996; Senior Research Fellow, Trinity College, Cambridge, since 2006; *b* 23 Dec. 1954; *s* of Baron Butterfield, OBE, DM, FRCP and of Isabel-Ann Foster Butterfield (*née* Kennedy); *m* 1st, 1978, Sally Damon Snell (marr. diss. 2007); one *s* one *d*; 2nd, 2008, Mari Hirano. *Educ:* Trinity Coll., Cambridge (BA 1976; PhD 1984). Cambridge University: Asst Lectr in Philosophy, 1981–85; Lectr, 1985–97; Reader in Philosophy, 1997; Fellow of Jesus Coll., 1981–97; Sen. Res. Fellow, All Souls Coll., Oxford, 1998–2006. Visiting Professor: Princeton Univ., 1989, 2004; Univ. of Pittsburgh, 2008; Univ. of Sydney, 2009. *Publications:* edited: Language, Mind and Logic, 1986; (with G. Belot and M. Hogarth) Spacetime, 1996; (with C. Pagonis) From Physics to Philosophy, 1999; The Arguments of Time, 1999; (with T. Placek) Non-Locality and Modality, 2002; (with H. Halvorson) Quantum Entanglements: selected papers of Rob

Clifton, 2004; (with J. Earman) The Handbook of Philosophy of Physics, 2 vols, 2006; articles in learned jls. *Recreation:* the Muppets. *Address:* Trinity College, Cambridge CB2 1TQ. *T:* (01223) 338400.

BUTTERFIELD, John Arthur; QC 2014; a Recorder, since 2009; *b* Keighley, W Yorks, 27 Feb. 1972; *s* of James and Muriel Butterfield; *m* 2001, Elizabeth Dolan; one *s* two *d*. *Educ:* Beckfoot Grammar Sch.; Univ. of Liverpool (LLB 1st Cl. Hons; Pres., Legal Soc., 1992–93); Inns of Court Sch. of Law. Called to the Bar, Lincoln's Inn, 1995; in practice as barrister, specialising in crime, 1995–. *Recreations:* songwriting, recording in home music studio, cinema. *Address:* 5 Fountain Court, Steelhouse Lane, Birmingham B4 6DR. *T:* 0845 210 5555, *Fax:* (0121) 606 1501. *E:* jab@no5.com.

BUTTERFIELD, Leslie Paul, CBE 2007; brand strategy consultant; Chief Strategy Officer, Interbrand Group, since 2008; *b* Reading, 31 Aug. 1952; *s* of Leslie John and Ruth Butterfield; *m* 1988, Judy Tombleson (marr. diss. 2012); partner, Penny Harris; one *s* one *d*. *Educ:* North East London Poly. (BA 1st Cl. Hons Business Studies 1974); Lancaster Univ. (MA Mktg 1975). Account Planner, BMP/DDB, 1975–80; Planning Dir, AMV/BBDO, 1980–87; Planning Dir and Chm., Butterfield Day Devito Hockney, subseq. Partners BDDH, 1987–2001; CEO, Butterfield 8, 2001–03; Partner, Ingram, 2003–07; CEO, ButterfieldPartners, 2007–08. *Publications:* Excellence in Advertising, 1997, 2nd edn 1999; Understanding the Financial Value of Brands, 1998; Advalue, 2003; Enduring Passion: the story of the Mercedes-Benz brand, 2005. *Recreations:* cars, ski-ing, railway archaeology, my children Alexa and Cerian. *Address:* The Moat House, Smewins Road, White Waltham, Berks SL6 3SR. *T:* (0118) 932 1894, (mobile) 07885 678581.

BUTTERFIELD, Hon. Sir Neil; *see* Butterfield, Hon. Sir A. N. L.

BUTTERFIELD, Stewart David; Managing Director, Broadcasting, Granada plc (formerly Granada UK Broadcasting), 1997–2002; *b* 10 Sept. 1947; *s* of Bernard and Moray Butterfield. *Educ:* Mount St Mary's Coll., Spinkhill, Derbys; London Sch. of Econs (BSc Econ). McCann-Erickson, 1973–91, European Media Dir, 1989–91; Dir of Advertising Sales and Mktg, Channel Four, 1991–97. Trustee, VSO, 2002–08.

BUTTERFILL, Sir John (Valentine), Kt 2004; *b* 14 Feb. 1941; *s* of George Thomas Butterfill and Elsie Amelia (*née* Watts); *m* 1965, Pamela Ross-Symons; one *s* three *d*. *Educ:* Caterham Sch.; Coll. of Estate Management. FRICS 1974. Valuer, Jones, Lang, Wootton, 1961–64; Sen. Exec., Hammerson Gp, 1964–69; Dir, Audley Properties Ltd (Bovis Gp), 1969–71; Man. Dir, St Paul's Securities Gp, 1971–76; Sen. Partner, Curchod & Co., 1977–91, Consultant, 1992–. Chm., Conservation Investments, 1978–2002; Director: Micro Business Systems, 1977–79; John Lelliott Developments, 1984–88; ISLEF Building and Construction, 1984–91; Pavilion Services Gp, 1992–94; Delphi Gp, 1996–99. Pres., European Property Associates, 1979–2003. MP (C) Bournemouth West, 1983–2010. Parliamentary Private Secretary: to Sec. of State for Energy, 1988–89; to Sec. of State for Transport, 1989–90; to Minister of State for NI, 1991–92. Member: Trade and Industry Select Cttee, 1992–2001; Select Cttee on Unopposed Bills, 1995–2010. Vice-Chairman: Backbench Tourism Cttee, 1986–88; Backbench Finance Cttee, 1992–2000; Sec., Backbench Trade and Industry Cttee, 1987–88, and 1991; Chm., Backbench European Affairs Cttee, 1995–97. Member: Parly Ct of Referees, 1995–2010; Speaker's Panel of Chairmen, 1996–2010. Chm., All Party Parly Gp on Occupational Pensions, 1992–2010; Vice-Chairman: All Party Parly Gp on Bldg Socs and Financial Mutual Instns, 1997–2010 (Sec., 1996); All Party Parly Gp on ELT, 2008–10; Jt Sec., All Party Parly Gp on Insurance and Financial Services, 1997–2010. Chm., Parly Members' Fund, 1997–2002; Trustee, 1997–2010, Chm. of Trustees, 2001–10, Parly Contributory Pension Fund. 1922 Committee: Sec., 1996–97; Vice Chm., 1997–2001, 2005–06; Treas., 2001–05. Vice Pres., Cons. Gp for Europe, 1992–95 (Chm., 1989–92); Vice-Chm., Parly Gp, Cons. Friends of Israel, 1995–2010. Mem., Council of Management, PDSA, 1990–; Chm. of Trustees, PDSA Pension Fund, 2002–07. *Publications:* occasional contribs to property, insurance and financial publications. *Recreations:* ski-ing, tennis, bridge, music.

BUTTERSS, Rt Rev. Robert Leopold; Bishop of the Eastern Region (Assistant Bishop of the Diocese of Melbourne), 1985–94; *b* 17 Jan. 1931; *s* of A. L. Butterss; *m* 1956, Margaret (*née* Hayman) (*d* 2009); two *s* one *d*. *Educ:* Haileybury; Brighton and Ridley Coll., Melbourne. Ordained: deacon, 1955; priest, 1956; Curate, St Andrew's, Brighton, 1955–56; Vicar, Holy Trinity, Lara, 1956–60; Priest in charge, Popondetta, PNG, 1960–64; Vicar: Holy Trinity, Pascoe Vale, 1964–66; St Stephen's, Mt Waverley, 1970–76; Canon, St Peter and St Paul's Cathedral, PNG, 1976–83; Dean, St John's Cathedral, Brisbane, 1983–85. Chm., Australian Bd of Missions, Sydney, 1976–83 (Victorian Sec., 1966–70). *Recreation:* music.

BUTTERWORTH, Anthony; *see* Butterworth, C. A.

BUTTERWORTH, Anthony Edward, PhD; FRS 1994; MRC External Scientific Staff, 1979–95, retired; *b* 8 July 1945; *s* of late Edward Alexander Butterworth and Sylvia (*née* Hardy); *m* 1st, 1972, Margot Lois Hudson (marr. diss. 1999); one *s* one *d*; 2nd, 2001, Elizabeth Lucy Corbett; one *s* one *d*. *Educ:* Harrow Sch.; Trinity Hall, Cambridge (BA); St Mary's Hosp. Med. Sch., London (MB, BChir); Clare Coll., Cambridge (PhD). Wellcome Trust Research Fellow: Nairobi, Kenya, 1973–77; Harvard Med. Sch., Boston, 1977–79; University of Cambridge: Associate Lectr, 1980–89; Hon. Reader, 1989–93; Hon. Prof. of Med. Parasitology, 1993–95. Hon. Professor: LSHTM, 2001–; Coll. of Medicine, Univ. of Malawi, 2009–13. Hon. Scientific Dir, Biomedical Res. and Trng Inst., Harare, 2001–06. Frederick Murgatroyd Prize, RCP, 1979; Bernhard Nocht Medal, 1987; King Faisal Internat. Prize in Medicine, 1990; Chalmers Medal, RSTM&H, 1990. *Publications:* papers and book chapters on immunology and parasitology.

BUTTERWORTH, Prof. Brian Lewis, PhD; FBA 2002; CPsychol, FBPsS; Professor of Cognitive Neuropsychology, University College London, 1992–2009, now Emeritus; *b* 3 Jan. 1944; *s* of Henry Lewis Butterworth and Cicely Rebecca (*née* Haringman); partner, Diana Margaret Laurillard; two *d*. *Educ:* Quintin Sch., London; Merton Coll., Oxford (BA); Univ. of Sussex (MA); PhD London 1972. CPsychol 1990; FBPsS 1990. Jun. Res. Fellow, MRC Speech and Communication Unit, Edinburgh, 1971–72; Lectr in Psychol., Dept of Exptl Psychol., Univ. of Cambridge, 1972–80; Lectr in Psychol., 1980–86, Reader, 1986–92, Dept of Psychol., UCL. Hon. and pt-time posts at Univ. of Tennessee, MIT, Univ. of Padova, Univ. of Trieste, Max Planck Inst. for Psycholinguistics, Nijmegen; Sen. Vis. Res. Fellow, 2000–03, Professorial Fellow, 2003–, Melbourne Univ.; Hon. Prof., Dalian Univ., China, 2007–09; Res. Consultant, Ospedale San Camillo, Venice, 2011–; Adjunct Prof., Nat. Cheng Chi Univ., Taiwan, 2012–. Chair, Centre for Educnl Neurosci., UCL, Inst. of Educn and Birkbeck, Univ. of London, 2008–09. Ed.-in-Chief, Linguistics, 1978–83; Co-founding Ed., Lang. and Cognitive Processes, 1983–; Founding Ed., Mathematical Cognition, 1983–2000. Co-ordinator, Mathematics and the Brain, 1999–2003, Numeracy and Brain Develt, 2004–08, Eur. Network. (Jtly) Babble to Babel (installation in Millennium Dome), 2000; (jtly) The Brain Unravelled (exhibn, Slade Res. Centre, UCL), 2009. *Publications:* (ed) Language Production, Vol. 1 1980, Vol. 2 1983; (ed jtly) Explanations for Language Universals, 1983; The Mathematical Brain, 1999; (ed) Mathematical Cognition, 2000; Dyscalculia Screener, 2003 (British Educn & Teaching with Technology Award for educnl software, 2004); (with Dorian Yeo) Dyscalculia Guidance, 2004; (ed jtly) Educational Neuroscience, 2013; contrib. numerous acad. papers on speech production, aphasia, gestures, dyslexia, mathematical cognition and dyscalculia. *Recreations:* family holidays, rock art, archaeology and anthropology of numbers. *Address:* Institute of Cognitive Neuroscience, University College London, 17 Queen Square, WC1N 3AR. *T:* (020) 7679 1150, *Fax:* (020) 7813 2835. *E:* b.butterworth@ucl.ac.uk.

BUTTERWORTH, Prof. (Charles) Anthony, CBE 1996; PhD; FRCN; FMedSci; Joint Director, Centre for Clinical and Academic Workforce Innovation, University of Lincoln, 2005–08, now Emeritus Professor of Health Care Workforce Innovation; Chair, Foundation for Nursing Studies, since 2011; *b* 14 March 1947; *s* of Norman Butterworth and Anne Alison Butterworth; *m* 1971, Jacqueline; one *s* one *d*. *Educ:* Univ. of Aston, Birmingham (MSc; PhD 1986); Storthes Hall Hosp., Huddersfield (RMN); Manchester Royal Infirmary (RGN); Univ. of Manchester (RNT). Clinical nurse, Yorks and Gtr Manchester, 1968–75; Lectr, then Sen. Lectr, 1975–80, Principal Lectr and Hd of Nursing, 1980–86, Manchester Poly; University of Manchester: Prof. of Community Nursing, Queen's Nursing Inst., 1987–2001; Pro-Vice-Chancellor, 1999–2001; Vis. Prof., 2001–; Chief Exec., Trent NHS Workforce Develt Confedn, 2001–05; Dir, Res. Unit, Univ. of Lincoln, 2005–09; Chair: Acad. of Nursing, Midwifery and Health Visiting Res., 2007–11; NHS Inst. for Innovation and Improvement, 2011–13 (non-exec. Dir, 2005–11). FRCN 1996; Founder FMedSci 1998; FQNI 2008. Hon. FRCPsych 1999. FRSA 1996. Trustee: Dementia UK, 2008–; RCN Foundn, 2010–. *Publications:* Community Psychiatric Nursing, 1980; Caring for the Mentally Ill in the Community, 1981; Clinical Supervision and Mentorship in Nursing, 1992, 2nd edn 1999. *Recreations:* gardening, football, walking. *E:* tbutterworth@lincoln.ac.uk.

BUTTERWORTH, Nicholas John; writer and illustrator of children's books, since 1980; *b* 24 May 1946; *s* of George and Nancy Butterworth; *m* 1975, Annette Fancourt; one *s* one *d*. *Educ:* Royal Liberty Grammar Sch., Romford. Left sch., aged 16; compositor and typographic designer, Printing Dept, NCH, Harpenden, 1962–65; graphic designer: Frank Overton Associates, 1965–67; with Crosby Fletcher Forbes, for Cunard Line, Southampton, then freelance, 1967–68; formed Baxter Butterworth Cope, 1968; worked in various graphic partnerships, 1968–80, incl. partnership with Mick Inkpen in graphics, illustration and writing; started writing for children, 1981 and went solo, 1988. Founding Partner, Snapper Prodns Ltd, 2008–; Dir, Q Pootle 5 Ltd, 2011–; Exec. Prod. and Prodn Designer, Q Pootle 5 (children's animated TV series, 52 episodes; Christmas special, Pootle All the Way!), 2011–. Presenter, Rub-a-dub-tub (children's prog.), TV AM, 1982–83. *Publications:* books include: B B Blacksheep and Company, 1981; (with Mick Inkpen) The Nativity Play, 1985; (with Mick Inkpen) Just Like Jasper, 1989; One Snowy Night, 1989; Amanda's Butterfly, 1991; After the Storm, 1992; (with Mick Inkpen) Jasper's Beanstalk, 1992; Making Faces, 1993; The Rescue Party, 1993; The Secret Path, 1994; All Together Now, 1995; A Year in Percy's Park, 1995; (illus.) Jake, 1995; The Hedgehog's Balloon, 1996; The Treasure Hunt, 1996; THUD!, 1997; Four Feathers in Percy's Park, 1998; Jingle Bells, 1998; Percy's Bumpy Ride, 1999; Q Pootle 5, 2000; Everyone's Friend Percy, 2001; Albert Le Blanc, 2002; Q Pootle 5 In Space!, 2003; The Whisperer, 2004; Tiger!, 2006; Tiger in the Snow, 2006; Albert Le Blanc to the Rescue, 2007; Trixie the Witch's Cat, 2009. *Recreations:* ski-ing, squash, tennis, pottering in the shed, gardening, woodworking, travel, music - listening - and playing piano badly! *Address:* Snapper Productions Ltd, 1 Belmont House, 23 New Street, Henley-on-Thames, Oxon RG9 2BP.

BUTTLE, Eileen, CBE 1995; PhD; FRSB; Member, Scientific Committee, European Environment Agency, 1994–2002; *b* 19 Oct. 1937; *d* of late George Ernest Linford and Mary Stewart Linford; *m* 1970, Hugh Langley Buttle. *Educ:* Harrow Weald County Grammar Sch.; Univ. of Southampton (BSc (Hons); PhD). FRSB (FIBiol 1990). Post-doctoral Res. Fellow, Univ. of Southampton, 1963–65; Research Scientist: Nat. Inst. of Res. in Dairying, 1965–71; Cattle Breeding Centre, MAFF, 1971–76; Policy Administrator, MAFF, 1976–89; Sec., NERC, 1989–94; Dir, World Humanity Action Trust, 1994–97. Dir, Shell Transport and Trading Co. plc, 1998–2005. Trustee: Buckland Foundn, 1994–2002; Horniman Mus. of Gdns, 1994–98; Onyx Envmtl Trust, 1997–2002; Earthwatch Europe, 1997–2003. Mem., 1999–2006, Dep. Chm., 2002–06, Council, ICSTM; Gov., Macaulay Inst., 2001–05. *Recreations:* golf, fly fishing. *Club:* Farmers.

BUTTON, Jenson Alexander Lyons, MBE 2010; Formula 1 racing driver; *b* Frome, 19 Jan. 1980; *s* of late John Button and of Simone Lyons; *m* 2014, Jessica Michibata. *Educ:* Frome Community Coll. Kart racing: winner: British Super Prix, 1989; British Cadet Championship, 1991; British Open Kart series, 1992, 1993; Eur. Super A Championship, 1997; Ayrton Senna Meml Cup, 1997; car racing: winner, British Formula Ford Championship (with Haywood Racing), 1998; Formula 3, with Promatecme team, 1999; Formula One Grand Prix début, 2000; Williams team, 2000; Benetton team, 2001; Renault team, 2002; BAR team, 2003–05; Honda Racing team, 2006–08; Brawn team, 2009 (World Champion); McLaren Honda (formerly Vodafone McLaren Mercedes, later McLaren Mercedes), 2010–; Grand Prix winner: Hungarian, 2006; Australian, Malaysian, Bahrain, Spanish, Monaco, Turkish, 2009; Australian, Chinese, 2010; Canadian, Hungarian, Japanese, 2011; Australian, Belgian, Brazilian, 2012. McLaren Autosport Young Driver Award, 1998. *Address:* c/o Jenson Button Ltd, Paragon House, Ann's Place, St Peter Port, Guernsey GY1 2NU.

BUTTRESS, Donald Reeve, LVO 1997; OBE 2008; FSA; architect; Partner, Buttress Fuller Alsop Williams, Manchester, 1974–2007; Surveyor of the Fabric of Westminster Abbey, 1988–99, now Surveyor Emeritus; *b* 27 April 1932; *s* of Edward Crossley Buttress and Evelyn Edna Reeve-Whaley; *m* 1956, Elsa Mary Bardsley; two *s* three *d*. *Educ:* Stockport Sch.; Univ. of Manchester (MA, DipArch). ARIBA. Flying Officer, RAF, 1958–61. Lectr, Manchester Univ., 1964–78; Vis. Prof. and Fulbright Travelling Scholar, Univ. of Florida, 1967–68. Architect to: Bangor and Sheffield Cathedrals, 1978–88; Leeds (RC) Cathedral, 1983–95; Llandaff Cathedral, 1986–97; Surveyor to the Fabric, Chichester Cathedral, 1984–2007. Principal works: Stockport SS Community Centre, 1973; extn, St Matthew, Hayfield, 1978; St George's Chapel, Sheffield Cathedral, 1981; rebldg, St Matthew, Westminster, 1982; repair of spire, All Souls, Halifax, 1984; repair of nave, choir, North and South transepts and West front, Chichester Cath., 1985–2003; reconstruction, Tonbridge Sch. Chapel, 1992–95; restoration of West front and Henry VII Chapel, Westminster Abbey, 1989–95; design of national Memorial to King George VI and Queen Elizabeth, the Queen Mother, 2009. Member: Cathedrals and Churches Adv. Cttee (formerly Churches Sub-Cttee, English Heritage), 1988–94; Council for the Care of Churches, 1976–86, 1991–96; Council, Royal Archaeological Inst., 1991–94; Chester DAC, 1970–88; St Albans DAC, 1998–2010. President: Ecclesiol Soc., 1995–2010 (Vice Pres., 1992–95); Surveyors' Club, 1994–95; ASCHB, 2006–07; Baconian Club, 2006–07. Gov., Sutton's Hosp. in Charterhouse, 2001–12. Master, Art Workers' Guild, 2000 (Brother, 1989). Mem., Editl Bd, Church Building magazine, 1982–. DLitt Lambeth, 2001. *Publications:* Manchester Buildings, 1967; Gawthorpe Hall (NT guide), 1971; articles in learned jls. *Recreations:* ecclesiology, 18th Century furniture, stained glass, heraldry. *Address:* 95 Fishpool Street, St Albans AL3 4RU. *T:* (01727) 810753. *Club:* Royal Air Force.

BUTTREY, Prof. Theodore Vern, PhD; FSA; Keeper, Department of Coins, Fitzwilliam Museum, Cambridge, 1988–91, Keeper Emeritus, 1991–2011, now Honorary Keeper of Ancient Coins; *b* 29 Dec. 1929; *s* of Theodore Vern Buttrey and Ruth Jeanette Scoutt; *m* 1st, 1954, Marisa Macina (marr. diss. 1967); three *s* one *d*; 2nd, 1967, Ann Elizabeth Johnston (*d* 2010). *Educ:* Phillips Exeter Acad.; Princeton Univ. (BA 1950; PhD 1953). Instr, 1954–58, Asst Prof., 1958–64, Yale Univ.; University of Michigan: Associate Professor, 1964–67; Prof. of Greek and Latin, 1967–85; Prof. Emeritus, 1985–; Chm., Dept of Classical Studies, 1968–71, 1983–84; Dir, Kelsey Mus. of Archaeology, 1969–71. Member: Clare Hall, Cambridge, 1971–; Faculty of Classics, Cambridge Univ., 1975–. Pres., RNS, 1989–94; Sec.,

UK Numismatic Trust, 1994–98. Corresp. Mem., Royal Danish Acad. of Scis and Letters, 1995. Medal, RNS, 1985; Medal, Amer. Numismatic Soc., 1996; Wolfgang-Hahn Medal, Inst. für Numismatik, Univ. of Vienna, 2011. *Publications:* (jtly) Greek, Roman and Islamic Coins from Sardis, 1981; (jtly) Morgantina Studies: the coins, 1989; numerous publications in ancient and modern numismatics. *Recreations:* Ernest Bramah, P. G. Wodehouse, travel. *Address:* 6 de Freville Avenue, Cambridge CB4 1HR. *T:* (01223) 351156. *E:* tvb1@cam.ac.uk.

BUXTON; *see* Noel-Buxton, family name of Baron Noel-Buxton.

BUXTON, Adrian Clarence, CMG 1978; HM Diplomatic Service, retired; Ambassador to Bolivia, 1977–81, and to Ecuador, 1981–85; *b* 12 June 1925; *s* of Clarence Buxton and Dorothy (*née* Lintott); *m* 1st, 1958, Leonora Mary Cherkas (*d* 1984); three *s*; 2nd, 1985, June Samson. *Educ:* Christ's Hosp., Horsham; Trinity Coll., Cambridge (Exhibnr). RNVR, 1944–46; FO, 1947; Bangkok, 1948–52; FO, 1952–53; Khartoum, 1953–55; Bonn, 1955–58; Bogota, 1958–62; FO, 1962–64; Saigon, 1964–67; Havana, 1967–69; Geneva, 1969–73; sabbatical, Univ. of Surrey, 1973–74; FCO, 1974–77. *Recreations:* golf, choral singing. *Address:* 89 Glenferness Avenue, Bournemouth BH3 7ES.

BUXTON, Andrew Robert Fowell, CMG 2003; *b* 5 April 1939; *m* 1965, Jane Margery Grant (*d* 2015); two *d*. *Educ:* Winchester Coll.; Pembroke Coll., Oxford. Joined Barclays Bank, 1963; Man. Dir, 1988–92; Chief Exec., 1992–93; Chm., 1993–99. Director: Capitaland Ltd, Singapore, 2003–07; Development Bank of Singapore, 2006–11. Mem. Court, Bank of England, 1997–2001. Pres., British Bankers' Assoc., 1997–2002. *Club:* Royal Automobile.

BUXTON, Sir Crispin Charles Gerard, 8th Bt *cr* 1840, of Belfield, Dorset; *b* 29 March 1958; *s* of Gerard St John Roden Buxton and Judith Averil Buxton (*née* Campbell); *S* uncle 2014, but his name does not yet appear on the Official Roll of the Baronetage; *m* 2006, Diana Nafula; one *s* [Milo Akizacare Crispin Buxton, *b* 28 Dec. 2005]. *Heir: kinsman* Jonathan Buxton [*b* 27 Feb. 1950; *m* 1st, 1975, Susan Elizabeth Lloyd (marr. diss. 1984); one *s* one *d*; 2nd, 1990, Susan Elizabeth Williamson (marr. diss. 2001); 3rd, 2006, Jennifer Jean O'Reilly (*née* Barnard)].

BUXTON, David Colleton; Director of Campaigns and Communications, British Deaf Association (Chief Executive Officer, 2011); *b* Chiswick, 10 Sept. 1964; *s* of Robert Buxton and Helen Buxton; *m* 2000, Bronwynne Pringle; one *s*. *Educ:* Thames Valley Univ. (HNC Engrg Services); South Bank Univ. (HNC Building Studies; DipM; CertM); Open Univ. (MBA). Asst Dir and Dir of Fundraising and Mktg, Breakthrough Deaf-Hearing Integration, 1996–2001; Sen. Strategic Commng Manager for Disabilities and HIV/AIDS, Hammersmith and Fulham LBC, 2001–06; Regl Ops Manager, Adult Services, Scope, 2006–11. Member (Lib Dem): Southwark LBC, 1990–94; Epsom and Ewell BC, 2007–11. Contested (Lib Dem): Lewisham E, 1997, 2001; Lewisham and Greenwich, London Assembly, GLA, 2000. Co-Founder, Liberal Democrats Disability Assoc., 1991–; Co-op. Trustee, Greater London Action on Disability, 1994–96; Trustee: UK Council on Deafness, 1997–2000; Christian Deaf Link UK, 2002–08 (Chm., 2005–08); Hon. Treas., BDA, 2003–08. Chm., Pumphouse Educnl and Mus. Trust, Rotherhithe, 1991–96. Vice Chm., Peckham Park Primary Sch., 1993–96. Editor, Go!, Sign mag., 1989–2010. *Recreations:* specialist stamp collection (Tristan Da Cunha), politics and law reading, golf, historical visits. *Address:* 4 Norris Close, Epsom, Surrey KT19 8BF. *E:* buxtondc@aol.com.

BUXTON, Prof. Neil Keith; Vice-Chancellor, University of Hertfordshire, 1992–2003; *b* 2 May 1940; *s* of William F. A. Buxton and Janet A. Buxton; *m* 1962, Margaret G. Buxton (*née* Miller); two *s* one *d*. *Educ:* Aberdeen Univ. (MA Hons Political Econs); PhD Heriot-Watt. Asst Lectr, Dept of Political Econ., Aberdeen Univ., 1962–64; Lectr, Dept of Econ., Univ. of Hull, 1964–69; Lectr and Sen. Lectr, 1969–78, Prof., 1979–83, Heriot-Watt Univ.; Depute Dir, Glasgow Coll. of Technology, 1983–87; Dir, Hatfield Poly., 1987–92. Vis. Prof. in Econs and Public Admin, Lewis and Clark Coll., Oregon, 1982. Dir, Herts TEC, 1989–2001; Member: Board: Herts Business Centre (Businesslink), 1993; Herts Learning and Skills Council, 2001; Herts Prosperity Forum, 1998. Hon. DLaws Herts, 2009. *Publications:* (with T. L. Johnston and D. Mair) Structure and Growth of the Scottish Economy, 1971; (with D. I. Mackay) British Employment Statistics, 1977; Economic Development of the British Coal Industry, 1978; (ed) British Industry Between the Wars, 1979; articles in professional jls. *Recreations:* sport, bridge, overseas travel, pipe smoking. *Address:* 74 Marbuk Avenue, Port Macquarie, NSW 2444, Australia.

BUXTON, Rt Hon. Sir Richard (Joseph), Kt 1994; PC 1997; a Lord Justice of Appeal, 1997–2008; *b* 13 July 1938; *o s* of late Bernard Buxton, DSO, chartered mechanical engineer, and Sybil (*née* Hurley), formerly of Burton-upon-Trent; *m* 1987, Mary Tyerman, JP, *y d* of late Donald Tyerman, CBE and Margaret Tyerman. *Educ:* Brighton Coll. (Schol.); Exeter Coll., Oxford (Schol.; First Cl. Final Hon. Sch. of Jurisprudence 1961, First Cl. BCL 1962; Vinerian Schol. 1962; MA; Hon. Fellow, 1998). FCIArb 1992. Lectr, Christ Church, 1962–63; Lectr 1963–64, Fellow and Tutor 1964–73, Sub-Rector 1966–71, Exeter Coll., Oxford. Called to the Bar, Inner Temple, 1969; Bencher, 1992; in practice, 1972–88; QC 1983; a Recorder, 1987–93; a Law Comr, 1989–93; a Judge of the High Court, QBD, 1994–97; a Judge, Restrictive Practices Court, 1994–97. Second Lieut RAOC, 1957–58. Councillor, Oxford CC, 1966–69. Chm. of Governors, Penton I and JM Sch., London N1, 1986–91. Hon. LLD Nottingham, 2000. Médaille de la Ville de Paris (échelon argent), 1999. *Publications:* Local Government, 1970, 2nd edn 1973; articles in legal periodicals. *Recreation:* baseball. *Address:* c/o Royal Courts of Justice, Strand, WC2A 2LL.

BUXTON, Richard Moberly; Partner, Richard Buxton Environmental & Public Law, solicitors, since 1990; *b* Butleigh, Somerset, 30 June 1953; *s* of Robert James Buxton and Lilla Mary Alyson Buxton (*née* Pumphrey); *m* 1979, Julia Grace Elcock; two *s* one *d*. *Educ:* Harrow Sch.; Trinity Coll., Cambridge (BA 1974); Sch. of Forestry, Yale Univ. (MES 1986). Trained as solicitor, Farrer & Co., 1976–78; admitted solicitor, 1978; Sinclair Roche & Temperley, solicitors, 1978–81; Japan Line, Tokyo, 1981–84; DPA Gp, consultants, Halifax, NS, 1986–89; Mills & Reeve, solicitors, Cambridge, 1989–90. *Recreations:* sea-kayaking, hill walking, exercising labrador. *Address:* Richard Buxton Environmental & Public Law, 19B Victoria Street, Cambridge CB1 1JP. *T:* (01223) 328933, *Fax:* (01223) 570990. *E:* richard@richardbuxton.co.uk.

BUXTON, Richard William; Director, Europa-Institut, Reutlingen, since 2013; *b* 11 Oct. 1956; *s* of Rev. William, (Paddy), and Pamela Buxton; *m* 1993, Christiane Regine Topf; two *s*. *Educ:* Downing Coll., Cambridge (MA); Univ. of Westminster (MBA); Open Univ. (MSc Psychology). Coopers & Lybrand, 1989–91; Asst Dir (Housing and Social Services), Bexley BC, 1991–93; Dir, Local Govt Consultancy, Capita plc, 1993–95; Dir of Housing, City of Westminster, 1995–98; Dir of Ops, Legal Services Commn, 1998–2001; Chief Exec., Nat. Lottery Charities Bd, then Community Fund, 2001–04; Hd, Econ. Develt, City of Reutlingen, Germany, 2005–06; Business Redesign Dir, Essex CC, 2006–08; Prog. Dir, leading merger of Age Concern and Help the Aged, 2008–09; Interim Chief Exec., 4ps, then Local Partnerships, 2009; Interim Ops Dir, Refugee Council, 2010–11; Partnership Prog. Manager, Darlington, Hartlepool and Redcar, and Cleveland Bor. Councils, 2012. Mem., ESRC Res. Grants Bd, 2002. Associate Lectr, Open Univ., 2005–. Trustee, Langley House Trust, 1996–2003. FRSA 2007. *Recreations:* my two children, running, World of Warcraft. *Address:* Europa-Institut, Unter den Linden 15, 72762 Reutlingen, Germany.

BUXTON, Ronald Carlile, MA Cantab; *b* 20 Aug. 1923; *s* of Murray Barclay Buxton and Janet Mary Muriel Carlile; *m* 1959, Phyllida Dorothy Roden Buxton; two *s* two *d*. *Educ:* Eton; Trinity Coll., Cambridge. Chartered Structural Engineer (FIStructE). Director of H. Young & Co., London and associated companies. MP (C) Leyton, Jan. 1965–1966. *Recreations:* travel, music, riding. *Address:* The Garden Cottage, Kimberley Hall, Wymondham, Norfolk NR18 0RT; 67 Ashley Gardens, SW1P 1QG. *Club:* Carlton.

BUZAN, Anthony Peter; Founder, Buzan World/Think Buzan, 1971; *b* London, 2 June 1942; *s* of Gordon Frank Buzan and Jean Mary Buzan (*née* Burn). *Educ:* Whitstable Sch. for Boys, Kent; Simon Langton Grammar Sch. for Boys, Canterbury; Kitsilano High Sch., Vancouver; Univ. of British Columbia (BA Hons Arts with Sci. 1964). Inventor, Mind Map, 1960–74; feature journalist, Univ. of BC student newspaper, 1961–62; first job, removing manure on chicken farm, 1964; Lectr in Psychol., English and Creative Thinking, Simon Fraser Univ., 1964–66 (Inaugural Pres., Student Council, 1965–66); Special Assignment Teacher, ILEA, 1966–70; Co-founder, Salatticum Poets, 1967; Ed., MENSA Internat. Jl, 1969–71; ed. and writer, Haymarket Publishing and Daily Telegraph Travel, 1970–74; global lecturing and writing, 1974–2010. Advisor: to govts, incl. Australia, Bahrain, China, Britain, Jamaica, Liechtenstein, Malaysia, Mexico, Scotland, Singapore and S Africa, 1974–2010; to companies, incl. Apple Computers, BBC, Disney, IBM, Intelnecom, Microsoft, Stabilo, Telefonica and Kuwaiti Oil Co., 1974–2010. Member, Coaching Team, GB Olympics rowing squad: Seoul, 1988; Barcelona, 1992; Sydney, 2000; mental toughness coach, Marlow Rowing Club, 1990–2010. Initiated Super Class, teaching 2,000 Soweto sch. students, Soweto 2000, 1981; extended Super Class concept, teaching 9,000 sch. children at Royal Albert Hall, 2005. Founder: World Speed Reading Championships, 1984; Brain Trust charity, 1989; with Raymond Keene: originator, then co-founder, World Memory Championships, 1991; co-founder: World Mind Mapping and Creativity Championships, 1995; Fest. of the Mind, 1995; co-creator, with Prince Philip of Liechtenstein, Renaissance Acad., 1995, Dean, Renaissance Acad., Mexico, 2013; developed and launched new taxonomy, after Bloome's, for reading and learning, 2009. *Television:* Use Your Head (series), 1973–74; The Enchanted Loom (documentary), 1974; Happy Dictionary for China TV, 2005. Thinker-in-Residence, Wellington Coll., 2009–10. Vis. Prof., Stenden Univ. of Applied Sci., 2010; Vis. Lectr, LSE, 2009–10. Founding Mem., Inaugural Internat. Bd of Advrs, Univ. Putra, Malaysia, 2009–. Member: Soc. of Authors; Poetry Soc. MInstD 1990; Mem., MENSA, 1962–. Friend, Henley Fest. Roving Ambassador, Help the Aged, 2008–09. Hon. Fellow, Acad. for Leadership in Higher Educn, Malaysia, 2009. Freeman: City of London, 1984; Guild of Educators, 2009. Eagle Catcher Award, Electronic Data Systems, 1991; Pres. of Mexico's Special Recognition Award, 2005; Lifetime Achievement Award, Amer. Creativity Assoc., 2008; BrandLaureate Signature Award, 2012; Lifetime Achievement Award, Further Training Sector, Germany, 2013. *Publications:* over 120 books include: Spore One (collected poems), 1971; The Speed Reading Book, 1971, 9th edn 2010; Use Your Head, 1974, 7th edn 2010; Use Your Memory, 1986, 7th edn 2010; Master Your Memory, 1988, 7th edn 2010; (with Prof. B. Buzan) The Mind Map Book, 1993, 5th edn 2010; (with R. Keene) Buzan's Book of Genius, 1994; (with R. Keene) Buzan's Book of Mental World Records, 1997, 2nd edn 2005; Head First, 2000; The Power of Intelligence, 5 vols, 2001–03; Brain Child, 2003; Mind Map for Kids, 3 vols, 2003–05, 2nd edns 2007–08; The Ultimate Book of Mind Maps, 2005; Embracing Change, 2005, 2nd edn 2006; Requiem for Ted (Hughes) (poetry), 2007; Concordia (poetry), 2007; Age-Proof Your Brain, 2007; The Study Skills Handbook, 2007; Collins Language Revolution Beginners/Beginners Plus (Spanish, Italian, French), 2008–09; Mind Maps for Business, 2010; The Most Important Graph in the World, 2012; Brain Training for Kids, 2013; Modern Mind Mapping for Smarter Thinking, 2013; *relevant publication*: The Official Biography of Tony Buzan, 2013. *Recreations:* mind sports, especially chess and Go, rowing, swimming, aikido, astronomy, animal behaviour, breeding three-spined sticklebacks, proving that *semper solutio* (there is always a solution) is always correct!, philanthropy, art, music, literature, writing and teaching poetry. *Address:* Harleyford Manor Estate, Henley Road, Marlow-on-Thames, Bucks SL7 2DX. *T:* (01628) 488895. *E:* tony.buzan@buzanworld.com. *W:* www.thinkbuzan.com, www.tonybuzan.com. *Clubs:* Royal Automobile, Home House; Leander, Phyllis Court (Henley-on-Thames); Marlow Rowing.

See also B. Buzan.

BUZAN, Prof. Barry, PhD; FBA 1998; Montague Burton Professor of International Relations, London School of Economics, 2008–11, now Professor Emeritus; *b* 28 April 1946; *s* of Gordon Frank Buzan and Jean Mary Buzan (*née* Burn); *m* 1973, Deborah Skinner. *Educ:* Univ. of British Columbia (BA Hons 1968); London Sch. of Econs (PhD 1973). Res. Fellow, Inst. of Internat. Relns, Univ. of BC, 1973–75; University of Warwick: Lectr, 1976–83, Sen. Lectr, 1983–88, Reader, 1988–90, Dept of Internat. Studies; Prof., Dept of Politics and Internat. Studies, 1990–95; Res. Prof. of Internat. Studies, Univ. of Westminster, 1995–2002; Prof. of Internat. Relns, LSE, 2002–08. Vis. Prof., Internat. Univ. of Japan, 1993; Olof Palme Vis. Prof., Sweden, 1997–98; Hon. Prof., Univ. of Copenhagen, 2002–. Dir, project on European security, Copenhagen Peace Res. Inst., 1988–2002. Chm., British Internat. Studies Assoc., 1988–90; Internat. Vice-Pres., Internat. Studies Assoc., 1993–94. Ed., European Jl of Internat. Relns, 2004–07 (Member: Internat. Adv. Bd, 1994–99; Editl Cttee, 2008–). AcSS 2001. Francis Deak Prize, Amer. Jl of Internat. Law, 1982. *Publications:* Seabed Politics, 1976; (ed with R. J. Barry Jones) Change and the Study of International Relations: the evaded dimension, 1981; People, States and Fear: the national security problem in international relations, 1983, 2nd edn as An Agenda for International Security Studies in the Post-Cold War Era, 1991, 2007; (jtly) South Asian Insecurity and the Great Powers, 1986; An Introduction to Strategic Studies: military technology and international relations, 1987; (ed) The International Politics of Deterrence, 1987; (jtly) The European Security Order Recast: scenarios for the post-cold war era, 1990; (jtly) The Logic of Anarchy: neorealism to structural realism, 1993; (jtly) Identity, Migration and the New Security Agenda in Europe, 1993; (with T. Buzan) The Mind Map Book, 1993; (jtly) Security: a new framework for analysis, 1998; (with G. Segal) Anticipating the Future: twenty millennia of human progress, 1998; (with E. Herring) The Arms Dynamic in World Politics, 1998; (with R. Little) International Systems in World History: remaking the study of international relations, 2000; (with Ole Wæver) Regions and Powers, 2003; From International to World Society?, 2004; The United States and the Great Powers: world politics in the twenty-first century, 2004; (with L. Hansen) The Evolution of International Security Studies, 2009; (ed) International Society and the Middle East, 2009; (ed) Non-Western International Relations Theory: perspectives on and beyond Asia, 2010; An Introduction to the English School of International Relations, 2014; (ed) Contesting International Society in East Asia, 2014; (with G. Lawson) The Global Transformation: history, modernity and the making of international relations, 2015. *Recreations:* chess, travel, gardening. *Address:* Garden Flat, 17 Lambolle Road, NW3 4HS. *T:* (020) 7433 1431.

See also A. P. Buzan.

BUZEK, Jerzy Karol; Member (European People's Party Group), European Parliament, since 2004 (President, 2009–12); *b* 3 July 1940; *s* of Paweł Buzek and Bronisława Szczuka; *m* 1974, Ludgarda; one *d*. *Educ:* Silesian Poly.; Dr Tech. Scis, Polish Acad. of Scis. Chemical Engineering Institute, Polish Academy of Sciences: scientific res.; Dir for Scientific Affairs, 1963–97; Lecturer: Silesian Technical Univ., 1975–80; Technical Univ., Opole, 1993–97; Researcher and Pro-Rector, 2002, Vice Rector, 2002–04, Polonia Univ., Częstochowa. Prime Minister of Poland, 1997–2001. Chm., Cttee of European Integration, 1998; Vice Pres., European Energy Forum, 2004–. Chm., Cttee on Industry, Res. and Energy, EP. Mem., Solidarity, 1980–97: Chm., 1st, 4th, 5th and 6th Nat. Congress; Chm., Econ. Sub-

Cttee, Election Cttee. Dr *hc*: Seoul, 1999; Dortmund, 2000; Isparta 2006. Golden Cross of Commitment (Poland), 1989. *Publications*: books, patents, numerous sci. articles, papers and speeches. *Recreations*: poetry, theatre, horse riding, tennis, sailing, canoeing. *Address*: European Parliament, Bâtiment Paul-Henri Spaak, 08B046, 60 rue Wiertz, 1047 Brussels, Belgium. *E*: jerzy.buzek@europarl.europa.eu.

BUZZARD, Sir Anthony (Farquhar), 3rd Bt *cr* 1929; Lecturer in Theology, Atlanta Bible (formerly Oregon Bible) College, since 1982; *b* 28 June 1935; *s* of Rear-Admiral Sir Anthony Wass Buzzard, 2nd Bt, CB, DSO, OBE, and Margaret Elfreda (*d* 1989), *d* of Sir Arthur Knapp, KCIE, CSI, CBE; *S* father, 1972; *m* 1970, Barbara Jean Arnold, Mendon, Michigan, USA; three *d*. *Educ*: Charterhouse; Christ Church, Oxford (MA 1960); MA Th Bethany Theol Seminary, 1990. ARCM. Peripatetic Music Teacher for Surrey County Council, 1966–68; Lectr in French and Hebrew, Ambassador Coll., Bricket Wood, Herts, 1969–74; teacher of mod. langs, American Sch. in London, 1974–81. Founded Restoration Fellowship, 1981. Hon. PhD Theol. Paul Bible Seminary, LA, 2009. *Publications*: Who is Jesus?: a plea for a return to Jesus as Messiah, 1980; What Happens when we Die?, 1986; The Coming Kingdom of the Messiah: a Solution to the Riddle of the New Testament, 1988; The Doctrine of the Trinity: Christianity's Self-Inflicted Wound, 1994; Our Fathers who Aren't in Heaven: the forgotten Christianity of Jesus the Jew, 1995; The Law, the Sabbath and New Covenant Christianity, 2005; The Amazing Aims and Claims of Jesus: what you didn't learn in Church, 2006; Jesus was Not a Trinitarian: a call for a return to the creed of Jesus, 2007; One God, the Father, One Man Messiah: translation of the New Testament with commentary, 2015; articles on eschatology and Christology in various jls. *Recreations*: oboe, classical music. *Heir*: *b* Timothy Macdonnell Buzzard [*b* 28 Jan. 1939; *m* 1970, Jennifer Mary, *d* of late Peter Patching; one *s* one *d*]. *Address*: (home) 175 West Lake Drive, Fayetteville, GA 30214, USA. *T*: (770) 9641571; (office) PO Box 2950, McDonough, GA 30253, USA. *T*: (404) 3620052.

BYAM SHAW, Jane Elizabeth; *see* Scott, J. E.

BYAM SHAW, Matthew James; theatre producer; Co-Founder and Partner, Playful Productions LLP, since 2010; *b* Sussex, 8 April 1963; *s* of Nicholas Glencairn Byam Shaw, *qv*; partner, Melanie Thaw, *d* of Sheila Hancock, *qv*; two *s* one *d*. *Educ*: Cumnor House Sch., Danehill; Westminster Sch.; Bristol Univ. (BA Drama); RADA. Actor, 1987–98; producer, 2000–; West End productions include: In Flame, 2000; Humble Boy, 2002; Pretending To Be Me, 2003; Don Carlos, 2005; The Anniversary, 2005; A Voyage Round My Father, 2006; See How They Run, 2006; Frost/Nixon, 2006, transf. NY, 2007; Mary Stuart, 2006, transf. NY, 2009; Boeing-Boeing, 2007, transf. NY, 2008; Whipping It Up, 2007; A Midsummer Night's Dream, Roundhouse, 2007; Spring Awakening; Legally Blonde, 2010; Krapp's Last Tape, 2010; Flare Path, 2011; The King's Speech, 2012; Hay Fever, 2012; The Audience, 2013 and 2015, NY 2015; The Weir, 2014; American Buffalo, 2015; Chichester Festival Theatre: Enron, 2009, transf. Royal Court, 2009, Noel Coward, 2010, NY, 2010; Yes, Prime Minister, 2010, transf. Gielgud, 2010; Sweeney Todd, 2011, transf. Adelphi, 2012; South Downs, The Browning Version, 2011, transf. Harold Pinter, 2012; other productions include: Red, NY, 2010; Wolf Hall, Bring up the Bodies, Swan Th., Stratford, 2014, transf. Aldwych, 2014, NY 2015; films include: Frost/Nixon, 2009; exec. prod., TV series, The Crown (based on The Audience), 2015. Trustee: Bush Th., 1998–; Crucible Th., 2001–; Mem. Council, RADA, 2013–. *Address*: c/o Playful Productions LLP, 41–44 Great Queen Street, WC2B 5AD. *T*: (020) 7811 4600. *E*: annie@playfuluk.com.

BYAM SHAW, Nicholas Glencairn; Deputy Chairman, Macmillan Ltd, 1998–99 (Chairman, 1990–97); *b* 28 March 1934; *s* of Lieut. Comdr David Byam Shaw, RN, OBE (killed in action, 19 Dec. 1941) and Clarita Pamela Clarke; *m* 1st, 1956, Joan Elliott; two *s* one *d*; 2nd, 1974, Suzanne Filer (*née* Rastello); 3rd, 1987, Constance Wilson (*née* Clarke). *Educ*: Royal Naval Coll., Dartmouth. Commnd RN, 1955 (Lieut). Joined William Collins Sons & Co. Ltd, Glasgow, as salesman, 1956; Sales Manager, 1960; Macmillan and Co., subseq. Macmillan Publishers Ltd: Sales Manager, 1964; Sales Dir, 1965; Dep. Man. Dir, 1967; Man. Dir, 1969–90. Director: St Martins Press, 1980–99 (Dep. Chm., 1997–99); Pan Books, 1983–99 (Chm., 1986–99); Gruppe Georg von Holtzbrinck, Stuttgart, 1996–99. *Recreations*: gardening, travel. *Address*: 9 Kensington Park Gardens, W11 3HB. *T*: (020) 7221 4547.

See also M. J. Byam Shaw.

BYATT, Antonia; *see* Byatt, H. A.

BYATT, Dame Antonia (Susan), (Dame Antonia Duffy), DBE 1999 (CBE 1990); FRSL 1983; writer; *b* 24 Aug. 1936; *d* of His Honour John Frederick Drabble, QC and late Kathleen Marie Bloor; *m* 1st, 1959, Ian Charles Rayner Byatt (*see* Sir I. C. R. Byatt) (marr. diss. 1969); one *d* (one *s* decd); 2nd, 1969, Peter John Duffy; two *d*. *Educ*: Sheffield High Sch.; The Mount Sch., York; Newnham Coll., Cambridge (BA Hons; Hon. Fellow 1999); Bryn Mawr Coll., Pa, USA; Somerville Coll., Oxford (Hon. Fellow). Extra-Mural Lectr, Univ. of London, 1962–71; Lectr in Literature, Central Sch. of Art and Design, 1965–69; Lectr in English, 1972–81, Sen. Lectr, 1981–83, UCL (Hon. Fellow, 2004). Associate of Newnham Coll., Cambridge, 1977–82. Member: Social Effects of Television Adv. Gp, BBC, 1974–77; Bd of Communications and Cultural Studies, CNAA, 1978–84; Bd of Creative and Performing Arts, CNAA, 1985–87; Kingman Cttee on English Language, 1987–88; Management Cttee, Soc. of Authors, 1984–88 (Dep. Chm., 1986; Chm., 1986–88); Bd, British Council, 1993–98 (Mem., Literature Adv. Panel, 1990–98). Mem. Cttee, London Liby, 1989–92. Broadcaster, reviewer; judge of literary prizes (Hawthornden, Booker, David Higham, Betty Trask). Fellow, Sunday Times Oxford Lit. Fest., 2010. FRSL. Hon. Fellow: London Inst., 2000; RA, 2009. Hon. DLitt: Bradford, 1987; Durham, 1991; Nottingham, 1992; Liverpool, 1993; Portsmouth, 1994; London, 1995; Sheffield, 2000; Kent, 2004; Oxford, 2007; Winchester, 2007; St Andrews, 2012; Hon. LittD Cambridge, 1999; DUniv York, 1991; Hon. Dr Leiden, 2010. Premio Malaparte, Capri, 1995; Shakespeare Prize, Hamburg, 2002. Chevalier de l'Ordre des Arts et des Lettres (France), 2003. *Publications*: Shadow of the Sun, 1964; Degrees of Freedom, 1965 (reprinted as Degrees of Freedom: the early novels of Iris Murdoch, 1994); The Game, 1967; Wordsworth and Coleridge in their Time, 1970 (reprinted as Unruly Times: Wordsworth and Coleridge in their Time, 1989); Iris Murdoch, 1976; The Virgin in the Garden, 1978; (ed) George Eliot, The Mill on the Floss, 1979; Still Life, 1985 (PEN/ Macmillan Silver Pen of Fiction, 1986); Sugar and Other Stories, 1987; (ed) George Eliot: selected essays, 1989; Possession: a romance, 1990 (Booker Prize, 1990; Irish Times/Aer Lingus Internat. Fiction Prize, 1990; Eurasian section of Best Book in Commonwealth Prize, 1991) (filmed 2002); (ed) Robert Browning's Dramatic Monologues, 1990; Passions of the Mind (essays), 1991; Angels and Insects (novellae), 1992 (filmed, 1996); The Matisse Stories (short stories), 1993; The Djinn in the Nightingale's Eye: five fairy stories, 1994 (Mythopoeic Fantasy Award for Adult Lit., 1998); (jtly) Imagining Characters, 1995; (ed jtly) New Writing 4, 1995; Babel Tower, 1996; (ed jtly) New Writing 6, 1997; (ed) The Oxford Book of English Short Stories, 1998; Elementals: stories of fire and ice (short stories), 1998; The Biographer's Tale, 2000; On Histories and Stories (essays), 2000; Portraits in Fiction, 2001; (jtly) The Bird Hand Book, 2001; A Whistling Woman (novel), 2002; Little Black Book of Stories, 2003; (ed jtly) Memory: an anthology, 2008; The Children's Book (novel), 2009 (Blue Metropolis Internat. Literary Grand Prix, Montreal, 2009; James Tait Black Meml Prize, 2010); The Shadow of the Sun, 2009; Ragnarok: the end of the gods, 2011. *Address*: c/o Rogers, Coleridge & White Ltd, 20 Powis Mews, W11 1JN.

See also H. A. Byatt.

BYATT, Deirdre Anne, (Lady Byatt); *see* Kelly, D. A.

BYATT, (Helen) Antonia; Director, Literature and South East, Arts Council England, since 2007; *b* 13 April 1960; *d* of Sir Ian Charles Rayner Byatt, *qv* and Dame Antonia Susan Byatt, *qv*; partner, Sampson Patrick Lincoln Collyns; one *s* two *d*. *Educ*: Mayfield Comprehensive Sch.; Putney High Sch.; Selwyn Coll., Cambridge (BA Hons). Gen. Sec., Fawcett Soc., 1987–88; Literature Officer, Arts Council of England, 1988–93; Hd of Literature, South Bank Centre, 1993–2000; Dir, The Women's Liby, London Metropolitan Univ., 2000–07. Mem., Children's Laureate Cttee, 2001. Member of Board: Bishopsgate Inst., 2004–; New Buckinghamshire Univ., 2009–. Gov., Dog Kennel Hill Primary Sch., 2004–10. *Publications*: (ed) The Chatto Book of Love Stories, 1993. *Recreations*: my family, swimming, walking. *Address*: Arts Council England, 21 Bloomsbury Street, WC1B 3HF.

BYATT, Sir Ian (Charles Rayner), Kt 2000; Chairman, Water Industry Commission for Scotland, 2005–11; Senior Associate, Frontier Economics, since 2001; Director General of Water Services, 1989–2000; *b* 11 March 1932; *s* of Charles Rayner Byatt and Enid Marjorie Annie Byatt (*née* Howat); *m* 1st, 1959, A. S. Byatt (*see* Dame A. S. Byatt) (marr. diss. 1969); one *d* (one *s* decd); 2nd, 1997, Prof. Deirdre Anne Kelly, *qv*; two step *s*. *Educ*: Kirkham Grammar Sch.; Oxford University; Harvard Univ. Commonwealth Fund Fellow, Harvard, 1957–58; Lectr in Economics, Durham Univ., 1958–62; Economic Consultant, HM Treasury, 1962–64; Lectr in Economics, LSE, 1964–67; Sen. Economic Adviser, Dept of Educn and Science, 1967–69; Dir of Econs and Stats, Min. of Housing and Local Govt, 1969–70; Dir Economics, DoE, 1970–72; Under Sec., 1972–78, Dep. Chief Econ. Advr, 1978–89, HM Treasury. Chm., Economic Policy Cttee of the European Communities, 1982–85 (Mem., 1978–89); Member: Central Council of Educn (England), 1965–66; Economics Cttee, CNAA, 1968–70; Urban Motorways Cttee, 1970; Cttee on Water Services: Econ. and Financial Objectives, 1970–73; ESRC, 1983–89; Public Services Productivity Panel, HM Treasury, 2000–02; Chief Sec.'s Adv. Panel on Better Public Services, 2002–06; Adv. Panel, Water Industry Comr for Scotland, 2002–04; Panel of Experts on Water Reforms in NI, 2003–06. Chm., Taskforce to Review Local Govt Procurement in England, 2000–01. Chm., Adv. Cttee to HM Treasury on Accounting for Econ. Costs and Changing Prices, 1986; Member: Bd, Public Finance Foundn, 1984–89; Bd of Mgt, Internat. Inst. of Public Finance, 1987–90, 2000–06; Council of Mgt, NIESR, 1996–2002; Council, Regulatory Policy Inst., 2001–07; non-exec. Mem., Public Interest Cttee, Baker Tilly UK Audit LLP, 2014–. Member: Council, REconS, 1983–92 (Mem. Exec. Cttee, 1987–89); Governing Body, Birkbeck Coll., 1997–2005 (Chm., F and GP Cttee, 2001–05; Fellow, 2005); Bd of Advisors, St Edmund Hall, 1998–2003; Internat. Adv. Cttee, Public Utilities Res. Centre, Univ. of Florida, 2001–; Bd, Acad. of Youth, 2001–05; Mem., Council, 2003–, Chm., Finance Cttee, Chapter, 2012–14, Birmingham Cathedral; Chm. Trustees, David Hume Inst., 2008–11. Hon. Prof., Birmingham Univ., 2003–. President: Econs and Business Educn Assoc., 1998–2001; Human City Inst., 1999–2002; Vice-Pres., Strategic Planning Soc., 1993–; Co-Sec.-Gen., Foundn for Internat. Studies in Social Security, 2000–02. Treas., 1988–2002, Patron, 2006–, Holy Cross Centre Trust. Chm., Friends of Birmingham Cathedral, 1999–2015. FCIWEM 1995; FCIPS 2005. CCMI (CIMgt 1993). Hon. Fellow, St Edmund Hall, 2007. DUniv: Brunel, 1994; Central England, 2000; Hon. DSc: Aston, 2005; Birmingham, 2007. *Publications*: The British Electrical Industry 1875–1914, 1979; Delivering Better Services for Citizens, 2001; (with Sir Michael Lyons) Role of External Review in Improving Performance, 2001; articles on economics in books and learned jls; official reports. *Recreations*: painting, family life. *Address*: Frontier Economics, 71 High Holborn, WC1V 6DA. *T*: (020) 7031 7000; 34 Frederick Road, Birmingham B15 1JN. *T*: (0121) 689 7946; 17 Thanet Street, WC1H 9QL. *T*: (020) 7388 3888. *E*: ianbyatt@blueyonder.co.uk. *Club*: Oxford and Cambridge.

See also H. A. Byatt.

BYATT, Ronald Archer Campbell, (Robin), CMG 1980; HM Diplomatic Service, retired; High Commissioner in New Zealand and concurrently to Western Samoa, and Governor (non-resident), Pitcairn Islands, 1987–90; *b* 14 Nov. 1930; *s* of late Sir Horace Byatt, GCMG and late Olga Margaret Campbell, MBE; *m* 1954, Ann Brereton Sharpe, *d* of C. B. Sharpe; one *s* one *d*. *Educ*: Gordonstoun; New Coll., Oxford; King's Coll., Cambridge. Served in RNVR, 1949–50. Colonial Admin. Service, Nyasaland, 1955–58; joined HM Foreign (now Diplomatic) Service, 1959; FO, 1959; Havana, 1961; FO, 1963; UK Mission to UN, NY, 1966; Kampala, 1970; Head of Rhodesia Dept, FCO, 1972–75; Vis. Fellow, Glasgow Univ., 1975–76; Counsellor and Head of Chancery, UK Mission to UN, NY, 1977–79; Asst Under Sec. of State, FCO, 1979–80; High Comr in Zimbabwe, 1980–83; Mem., Directing Staff, RCDS, 1983–84; Ambassador to Morocco, 1985–87. CSSB Panel Chm., 1992–95. Founder Mem., UK Antarctic Heritage Trust, 1992–2001; Mem., HGTAC, 1993–98 (Chm., Envmt Sub-Cttee, 1993–98). Trustee, Beit Trust, 1987–2011. Alaouite Order, 1st cl. (Morocco), 1987. *Recreations*: sailing, gardening, watching and painting birds. *Address*: Drim-na-Vullin, Lochgilphead, Argyll PA31 8LE. *Club*: Oxford and Cambridge.

BYCROFT, Prof. Barrie (Walsham), PhD; CChem, FRSC; Professor of Pharmaceutical Chemistry, University of Nottingham, 1979–2003, Emeritus Professor, 2004 (Head, Department of Pharmaceutical Sciences and School of Pharmacy, 1985–89 and 1995–2000); *b* 26 Jan. 1939; *s* of Henry Thomas Bycroft and Cissie Bycroft; *m* 1962, Jean Skinner (separated); one *s* one *d*. *Educ*: Univ. of Nottingham (BSc Chem.; PhD 1963). CChem 1982; FRSC 1982. NATO Fellow, Univ. of Zurich, 1963–65; University of Nottingham: Lectr, then Reader, Dept of Chemistry, 1965–79; Pro-Vice Chancellor (Research), 1990–94; Dean, Grad. Sch., 1994–96. Vis. Prof., Med. Sch., Federal Univ., Rio de Janeiro, 1973. Mem., Food Adv. Cttee, MAFF, 1988–92. Non-exec. Mem., Nottingham HA, 1990–94. Biotechnology and Biological Sciences Research Council: Mem., Sci. and Engrg Bd, 1993–96; Chm., Postgrad. Trng Award Panel, 1994–2000. Vice-Chm., UK Council for Grad. Educn, 1993–96. Hon. MRPharmS 1990. *Publications*: numerous contribs to learned jls. *Recreations*: tennis, golf, good food and wine, travel. *Address*: 14 The Cloisters, Beeston, Nottingham NG9 2FR. *T*: (0115) 925 9415.

BYE, Christopher Harwood; freelance writer and music critic; Editor, Yorkshire Evening Post, 1987–98; Director, Yorkshire Post Newspapers Ltd, 1987–98; *b* 6 Feb. 1952; *s* of John Harwood Bye and Joan Alice (*née* Cushing). *Educ*: Tadcaster Grammar Sch.; Univ. of Leeds (Cert. Creative Writing 2008). News Editor, Yorkshire Post, 1980–82; Editor, Yorkshire Post Colour Magazine, 1981–83; Dep. Editor, Yorkshire Post, 1982–87. Mem., British Music Soc. British Press award for investigative journalism, 1986. *Recreations*: classical music, antiques, wine, food, travel, walking, sport.

BYE, Ruby; *see* Wax, R.

BYERS, His Honour the Hon. Charles William; a Circuit Judge, 1999–2014; *b* 24 March 1949; *o s* of Baron Byers, PC, OBE and Joan Elizabeth Byers (*née* Oliver); *m* 1972, Suzan Mary Stone (marr. diss. 1995); two *s*; *m* 2002, Mary Louise Elizabeth Ilett. *Educ*: Westminster Sch.; Christ Church, Oxford. Called to the Bar, Gray's Inn, 1973; Recorder, 1993–99; Resident Judge, Woolwich Crown Court, 2007–12. Dep. Chm., Gray's Inn Continuing Education Cttee, 1997–98; Mem., Adv. Panel, Coll. of Law, 1996–. Gov., Hurstpierpoint Coll., 1993–2003. *Recreations*: gardening, agriculture, sport, aquatics, acquiring practical skills. *Club*: National Liberal.

BYERS, Philippa Tansy Kemp; *see* Saunders, P. T. K.

BYERS, Rt Hon. Stephen (John); PC 1998; *b* Wolverhampton, 13 April 1953; *s* of late Robert Byers. *Educ*: Chester City Grammar Sch.; Chester Coll. of Further Educn; Liverpool Polytechnic (LLB). Sen. Lectr in Law, Newcastle Polytechnic, 1977–92. Mem. (Lab) North

Tyneside MBC, 1980–92 (Dep. Leader, 1985–92; Chm. Educn Cttee, 1982–85). Contested (Lab) Hexham, 1983. MP (Lab) Wallsend, 1992–97, North Tyneside, 1997–2010. An Opposition Whip, 1994–95; frontbench spokesman on educn and employment, 1995–97; Minister of State, DfEE, 1997–98; Chief Sec. to HM Treasury, 1998; Sec. of State for Trade and Industry, 1998–2001; Sec. of State for Transport, Local Govt and the Regions, 2001–02. Mem., Select Cttee on Home Affairs, 1994. Chm., PLP Home Affairs Cttee, 1992–94. Leader, Council of Local Educn Authorities, 1990–92; Chairman: Nat. Employers' Orgn for Teachers, 1990–92; Educn Cttee, AMA, 1990–92; Mem., BTEC, 1985–89. FRSA 1991.

BYFORD, family name of **Baroness Byford**.

BYFORD, Baroness *cr* 1996 (Life Peer), of Rothley in the county of Leicestershire; **Hazel Byford,** DBE 1994; DL; *b* 14 Jan. 1941; *d* of Sir Cyril Osborne, MP and Lady Osborne; *m* 1962, C. Barrie Byford, CBE (*d* 2013); one *d* (one *s* decd). *Educ:* St Leonard's Sch., St Andrews; Moulton Agricl Coll., Northampton. WRVS Leics, 1961–93, County Organiser, 1972–76. House of Lords: an Opposition Whip, 1997–98; Opposition spokesman: on agriculture and rural affairs, 1998–2001; on envmt, 1998–2003; on food, farming and rural affairs, 2001–07. Chm., Nat. Cttee, Conservative Women, 1990–93; Vice Pres., 1993–96, Pres., 1996–97, Nat. Union of Cons. and Unionist Assocs. Member: Transport Users' Consultative Cttee, 1989–94; Rail Users' Consultative Cttee, 1994–95. President: Nat. Farm Attractions Network, 2002–09; Concordia, 2004–09; Guild of Agricl Journalists, 2004–07; Young Leics (formerly Leics Clubs for Young People), 2005–; LEAF, 2006–; Royal Assoc. of British Dairy Farmers, 2007–10; Royal Smithfield Club, 2010. Patron: Village Retail Services Assoc., 1998–2004; Inst. of Agricl Secs and Adminrs, 2000; Rural Stress Inf. Network, 2001–06; Women's Food and Farming Union, 2007–. Mem., Ct, Univ. of Leicester, 2002–08; Pres., St Leonard's Sch., St Andrews, 2003–14. Hon. Canon, Leicester Cathedral, 2003–. Associate Mem., RASE, 2003. DL Leics, 2010. Master, Farmers' Co., 2013–14. *Recreations:* golf, bridge, reading. *Club:* Farmers.

BYFORD, Sir Lawrence, Kt 1984; CBE 1979; QPM 1973; DL; HM Chief Inspector of Constabulary, 1983–87; *b* 10 Aug. 1925; *s* of George Byford and Monica Irene Byford; *m* 1950, Muriel Campbell Massey; two *s* one *d*. *Educ:* Univ. of Leeds (LLB Hons). Served Royal Signals Special Commns Unit, 1944–45: in France, Belgium and Germany, SHAEF and on secondment to G2 Sect., US Army. Barrister-at-Law. Joined W Riding Police, 1947; served on Directing Staff of Wakefield Detective Sch., 1959–62, and Police Staff Coll., Bramshill, 1964–66; Divl Comdr, Huddersfield, 1966–68; Asst Chief Constable of Lincs, 1968, Dep. Chief Constable 1970, Chief Constable, 1973–77; HM Inspector of Constabulary for: SE Region, 1977–78; NE Region, 1978–82. Lecture tour of univs, USA and Canada, 1976; Headed: British Police Mission to Turkey, 1978–79; official review into Yorkshire Ripper case, 1981. DL: Lincs, 1987; N Yorks, 1998. Hon. LLD Leeds, 1987. *Recreations:* cricket, Pennine walking and travel. *Clubs:* Royal Over-Seas League (Chm., 1989–92, Vice-Pres., 1992–), MCC; Yorks County Cricket (Hon. Life Mem.; Chm., 1991–98; Pres., 1991–2000).
See also M. J. Byford.

BYFORD, Mark Julian; author; Deputy Director-General, BBC, and Head of BBC Journalism, 2004–11; *b* 13 June 1958; *s* of Sir Lawrence Byford, *qv*; *m* 1980, Hilary Bleiker; two *s* three *d*. *Educ:* Lincoln Sch.; Univ. of Leeds (LLB 1979). BBC Television: Look North, Leeds, 1979–82; producer, South Today and Inquiry, Southampton, 1982–87; editor, Points West, Bristol, 1987–88; Home Editor, BBC News and Current Affairs, 1988–89; Head of Centre, Leeds, 1989–90; Asst Controller, 1991, Controller, 1991–94, Dep. Man. Dir, 1995–96, Dir, 1996–98, BBC Regl Broadcasting; Director: BBC World Service, 1998–2001; BBC World Service and Global News, 2002–04. Director: BARB, 1993–96; Radio Joint Audience Research Ltd, 1993–96. Trustee: BBC Children in Need Appeal, 1993–96; RNLI, 2011–. Gov., Univ. of Winchester, 2014–. Fellow, Radio Acad., 2000. DUniv Winchester, 2006; Hon. LLD Leeds, 2008; Hon. DLitt Lincoln, 2010. *Publications:* A Name On A Wall, 2013. *Recreations:* family, rock music, football, cricket, travel, the seaside, cathedrals, fell-walking, swimming. *Address:* Bolberry House, 1 Clifton Hill, Winchester, Hants SO22 5BL.

BYLES, Daniel Alan, FRGS; *b* Hastings, 24 June 1974; *s* of Alan Byles and Janice Byles (now Meek); *m* 2007, Prashanthi Reddy. *Educ:* Warwick Sch.; Univ. of Leeds (BA Jt Hons Econs and Mgt Studies 1996); Nottingham Trent Univ. (MA Creative Writing 2007). Served Army, 1996–2005; Royal Army Medical Corps: Dressing Station Comdr, 19 Airmobile Field Ambulance, 1997–99; Regtl Signals Officer, 24 Armd Field Ambulance, 2000; Adjt, 2000–01, Ops Officer, 2002, 3 Close Support Medical Regt; SO2 Medical Manning, Defence Med. Service Dept, MoD, 2002–04; SO2 Med. Ops and Plans, HQ Multinat. Task Force (N), Banja Luka, Bosnia, 2004–05. MP (C) N Warwickshire, 2010–15. Member, Select Committee: on Energy and Climate Change, 2010–15; on Sci. and Technol., 2014–15; Chairman: All-Party Envmt Gp, 2012–15; All-Party Parly Gp for Unconventional Oil and Gas, 2013–15; All-Party Parly Gp for Smart Cities, 2014–15. *Recreations:* writing, reading, sub-aqua, expeditions, sailing.

BYLES, Timothy John, CBE 2006; Chief Executive, Cornerstone Ltd, since 2011; *b* 7 Dec. 1958; *s* of Charles Humphrey Gilbert Byles and Pamela Beatrice Byles; *m* 1985, Shirley Elizabeth Rowland; three *s*. *Educ:* Univ. of Kent (BA Hons); Mid Kent Coll. of Further Educn (DMS London). British Gas, 1980–84: mgt trainee; Marketing Dept; Corporate Planning; English Tourist Board, 1984–88: Manager, Mgt Services, 1984–85; Asst Dir of Develt, 1985–88; Dir of Economic Develt, Kent CC, 1988–96; Chief Executive: Norfolk CC, 1996–2006; Partnerships for Schools, 2006–11. *Recreations:* music, swimming, church.

BYNG, family name of **Earl of Strafford,** and of **Viscount Torrington**.

BYNG, Hon. James Edmund; Publisher, since 1994, and Managing Director, since 2006, Canongate Books Ltd; *b* 27 June 1969; *s* of 8th Earl of Strafford, *qv*; *m* 1st, 1994, Whitney Osborn McVeigh (marr. diss. 2004); one *s* one *d*; 2nd, 2005, Elizabeth Sheinkman. *Educ:* Winchester Coll.; Edinburgh Univ. (BA). FRSA. *Recreations:* cooking, deejaying, reading, tennis. *Address:* Canongate Books Ltd, 14 High Street, Edinburgh EH1 1TE. *T:* (0131) 524 9345, *Fax:* (0131) 557 5211. *E:* jamie@canongate.co.uk. *Clubs:* Black's, Groucho, Union.
See also Viscount Enfield.

BYNUM, Prof. William Frederick, MD; PhD; FRCP, FRCPE; Professor of History of Medicine, University College London, 1992–2003, now Professor Emeritus; *b* 20 May 1943; *s* of Raymond Tapley Bynum and Mary Catherine Adamson Bynum; *m* 1st, 1966, Annetta Boyett (marr. diss.); one *s*; 2nd, 2000, Dr Helen Joy Power. *Educ:* Swarthmore Coll. (BA 1964); Yale Univ. (MD 1969); King's Coll., Cambridge (PhD 1974). FRCP 1996; FRCPE 2000. Lectr, 1973–85, Reader, 1985–92, UCL; Hd, Jt Wellcome Inst./UCL Unit for Hist. of Medicine, 1973–96. Visiting Professor: Univ. of Minnesota, 1975; Union Coll., 1977; Johns Hopkins Univ., 1990, 1996. Co-Ed., Medical Hist., 1980–2002. *Publications:* Dictionary of the History of Science, 1981 (trans. Italian, Spanish and Chinese); Science and the Practice of Medicine in the Nineteenth Century, 1994 (trans. Chinese); Companion Encyclopedia of the History of Medicine, 2 vols, 1993; The Beast in the Mosquito: the correspondence of Ronald Ross and Patrick Manson, 1998; (ed with Roy Porter) Oxford Dictionary of Scientific Quotations, 2005; (ed with Helen Bynum) Dictionary of Medical Biography, 5 vols, 2007; The History of Medicine: a very short introduction, 2008 (trans. German); (ed) Charles Darwin, On the Origin of Species, 2009; (ed with Linda Kalof) A Cultural History of the Human Body, 6 vols, 2010; (ed with Helen Bynum) Great Discoveries in Medicine, 2011; A Little History of Science (trans. 10 langs), 2012; (with Helen Bynum) Remarkable Plants that Shape our World (trans. 2 langs), 2014. *Recreations:* theatre, gardening, duck-keeping. *Address:* The Courtyard, London Road, Shadingfield, Suffolk NR34 8DF. *T:* (01502) 575410. *Club:* MCC.

BYRAM-WIGFIELD, Timothy, FRCO; Director of Music, All Saints, Margaret Street, London, since 2013; *b* 15 Sept. 1963; *s* of David and Morwen Byram-Wigfield. *Educ:* Oundle Sch. (Music Schol.); Royal Coll. of Music; Christ Church, Oxford (Organ Schol.; BA Hons). FRCO 1986. Chorister, King's Coll., Cambridge, 1972–76; Sub-organist, Winchester Cathedral, 1985–91; Master of the Music, St Mary's Episcopal Cathedral, Edinburgh, 1991–99; Director of Music: Jesus Coll., Cambridge, 1999–2003; St George's Chapel, Windsor, 2004–13. Has made numerous recordings. *Recreations:* cooking, gardening, keep fit (swimming, gym, running), reading. *Address:* All Saints, 7 Margaret Street, W1W 8JG.

BYRNE, Colin; Chief Executive Officer, Weber Shandwick, UK and Europe, the Middle East and Africa (formerly UK and Europe), since 2008; *b* 25 Feb. 1957; *s* of late Anthony Byrne and of Catherine Byrne; *m*; four *s* one *d*. *Educ:* Kingston Polytech. (BA Hons English). Press Officer, Automobile Assoc., 1981–83; Press and Campaigns Office, NUS, 1983–86; Press Officer, 1986–88, Chief Press Officer, 1988–92, Labour Party; Communications Dir, Prince of Wales Business Leaders Forum, 1992–95; PR Manager, NFU, 1995; Associate Public Affairs Dir, 1995–96, Dir, 1996–97, Shandwick Consultants; Man. Dir, Public Affairs, Shandwick, 1997–2000; Jt CEO, 2001–03, CEO, 2003–08, Weber Shandwick UK and Ireland. *Recreations:* art, music, cooking, literature. *Address:* Weber Shandwick, No 2 Water House Square, 140 Holborn, EC1N 2AE. *E:* cbyrne@webershandwick.com.

BYRNE, Colin David; Assistant Commissioner, Boundary Commission for England, 2011–13; *b* 11 June 1957; *s* of Liam and Theresa Byrne; *m* 1986, Dr Mary Morrison; four *d*. *Educ:* Univ. of Edinburgh (BSc Hons Envmtl Chem.); Univ. of Pennsylvania. SO, MAFF, 1979–85; Department of the Environment, 1985–91: SSO, 1985–87; Nat. Expert, EC, 1988–91; Grade 6, DETR, 1991–97; Hd of Div., HSE, 1997–2000; Dir for Hampshire and IoW, Govt Office for South East, 2000–06; Dir, Town and Country Planning, 2006–07, Home Information Pack Implementation, 2007, DCLG; Regl Dir, Govt Office for SE, 2008–11. Dir, Retirement Lease Housing Assoc. Gov., Guildford Coll. Gp, 2012–. Trustee, Guildford CAB, 2013–. *Recreations:* walking, gardening, opera.

BYRNE, David; Senior Counsel, 1985; *b* 26 April 1947; *m* 1972, Geraldine Fortune; two *s* one *d*. *Educ:* University Coll. Dublin (BA; Hon. LLD). FCIArb 1998. Called to the Bar, King's Inns, Dublin, 1970; called to Inner Bar, 1985; Attorney General, Ireland, 1997–99; Mem., EC, 1999–2004. Special Envoy, WHO, 2004–05. Chm., Nat. Treasury Mgt Agency Adv. Cttee, 2008–12. Adjunct Prof. of Law, UCD, 2005–06. Chancellor, Dublin City Univ., 2006–11, now Emeritus. Non-exec. Dir, Kingspan Gp, 2005–14; Sen. Ind. Dir and Dep. Chm., DCC plc, 2009–. Chm., Nat. Concert Hall, Dublin, 2006–11. Mem. Council, RCPI, 2013–. Hon. FRCPI 2000; Hon. FRCP. *Address:* (office) Park Lodge Mews, 36A Booterstown Avenue, Blackrock, Co. Dublin, Ireland.

BYRNE, Dorothy; Head of News and Current Affairs, Channel 4 Television, since 2004; *d* of Charles and Agnes Byrne; one *d*. *Educ:* Manchester Univ. (BA Hons Philosophy); Sheffield Univ. (Dip. Business). Producer, World in Action, 1987–94; Ed., The Big Story, 1996–98; Commng Ed., Current Affairs, Channel 4 TV, 1998–2003. Vis. Prof., Sch. of Journalism, Lincoln Univ., 2005–. *Recreation:* being angry. *Address:* Channel 4 Television, 124 Horseferry Road, SW1P 2TX. *T:* (020) 7306 8664, *Fax:* (020) 7306 8359. *E:* dbyrne@channel4.co.uk.

BYRNE, Prof. Edward, AC 2014 (AO 2006); MD, DSc; FRACP, FRCPE, FRCP; FTSE; President and Principal, King's College London, since 2014; *b* 15 Feb. 1952; *s* of Henry Byrne and Marion Byrne (*née* Davis); *m* 1975, Melissa Elisabeth Youl; three *s* one *d*. *Educ:* Univ. of Tasmania (MB BS 1st Cl. Hons 1974; MD 1982); Univ. of Melbourne (DSc 1995); Univ. of Queensland (MBA 2005). FRACP 1980; FRCPE 1998; FRCP 2008; FTSE 2012. Hd of Neurol., St Vincent's Hosp., Melbourne, 1983–2000; University of Melbourne: Prof. of Neurol., 1992–2000; Prof. of Exptl Neurol. and Dir, Centre for Neurosci., 2000–03; Dean, Faculty of Medicine, Nursing and Health Scis, Monash Univ., 2003–07; Exec. Dean, Faculty of Biomed. Scis, Hd, Royal Free and University Coll. Med. Sch., later UCL Med. Sch., and Vice Provost, Health, UCL, 2007–09; Vice-Chancellor and Pres., Monash Univ., 2009–14. Ed., Internal Medicine Jl, 1999–2005. *Publications:* over 200 articles on neuromuscular and metabolic disorders. *Recreation:* fly fishing. *Address:* King's College London, Strand, WC2R 2LS. *Clubs:* Athenæum; Melbourne.

BYRNE, John Anthony; freelance teacher, lecturer, writer, examiner, 1979–97 and since 2005; Founding Director of Ballet and Dance, Sydney Church of England Co-educational Grammar School (Redlands), 1997–2005; *b* Sydney, Australia, 14 Dec. 1945; *s* of late Reginald Thomas Byrne and Mary Ida (*née* Sinclair). *Educ:* Scully-Borovansky Ballet Sch. and Australian Acad. of Ballet, Sydney; Univ. of Sydney (BA); Polytechnic of Central London (Dip. Arts Admin 1977); Royal Acad. of Dancing (ARAD; Dip. PDTC 1979). Professional dancer with various companies in ballet, opera-ballet and musicals, Australia, NZ, Germany, UK and Hong Kong, 1970–76; teaching classical ballet in Australia, 1979–90; Royal Academy of Dance (formerly Dancing): Internat. Vocational Examr, 1987–2015; Tutor, Sydney and London HQ, 1990–91; Artistic Dir and Chm., Bd of Examrs, London, 1991–93. FRAD 2002. *Publications:* (jtly) Body Basics, 1992; Advanced Classical syllabus for boys, 1992; choreographic and syllabus contribs to Higher Grades and Vocational Syllabi of Royal Acad. of Dance; contrib. articles on dance criticism, etc to Dance Australia Mag., 1981–90. *Recreations:* walking, reading, gardens, playing the piano (studies in Pianoforte, Australian Music Exams Bd, 2009–).

BYRNE, Rev. Canon John Victor; Chaplain to the Queen, since 2003; *b* 14 Nov. 1947; *s* of Frederick Albert Victor Byrne and Joan Blumer Byrne (*née* Robin); *m* 1970, Gillian Waveney Bannard-Smith; one *s* two *d*. *Educ:* John Lyon Sch., Harrow; St John's Coll., Nottingham (LTh 1973). FCA 1979. Chartered Accountant, Nevill, Hovey, Gardner & Co., London, 1965–70; ordained deacon, 1973, priest, 1974; Curate: St Mark's, Gillingham, 1973–76; St Luke's, Cranham Park, 1976–80; Vicar: St Mary's, Balderstone, Rochdale, 1980–87; St Jude's, Southsea, 1987–2006; All Saints, Branksome Park, 2006–12; Priest-in-charge, St Peter's, Southsea, 1995–2003. Hon. Canon, Portsmouth Cathedral, 1997–2006, now Canon Emeritus; Rural Dean of Portsmouth, 2001–06. Portsmouth Diocesan Stewardship Advr, 1994–97; Archbishops' Pastoral Advr, 1999–2010. *Recreations:* photography, reading, walking, arts, music. *Address:* 4 St Georges Terrace, Southwick Road, Denmead PO7 6FR.

BYRNE, Lavinia; writer; *b* 10 March 1947; *d* of Basil James Byrne and (Edith Marion) Josephe Byrne. *Educ:* St Mary's Convent, Shaftesbury; Queen Mary College, London (BA Modern Langs); Hughes Hall, Cambridge (PGCE). Entered Inst. of Blessed Virgin Mary, 1964, resigned 2000; Tutor, Westcott House, Cambridge, 1997–2003. Associate Sec., CCBI, 1990–95. Co-Editor, The Way, 1985–90; internet columnist, The Tablet, 1999–2006; reporter, The Wells Jl, 2002–04. Hon. DD Birmingham, 1997. *Publications:* Women Before God, 1988; Sharing the Vision, 1989; (ed) The Hidden Tradition, 1990; (ed) The Hidden Journey, 1992; (ed) The Hidden Voice, 1994; Woman at the Altar, 1995; A Time to Receive, 1997; (ed) The Daily Service, 1997; The Dome of Heaven, 1999; The Journey is My Home, 2000; (ed) Pause for Thought, 2002; (ed) More Pause for Thought, 2004; Original Prayer: themes from the Christian tradition, 2008. *Recreations:* computers, cookery, travel. *Address:* Garden Flat, 6 Cleveland Place West, Bath BA1 5DG.

BYRNE, Rt Hon. Liam (Dominic); PC 2008; MP (Lab) Birmingham, Hodge Hill, since July 2004; *b* 2 Oct. 1970; *s* of Dermot and Ruth Byrne; *m* 1998, Sarah; two *s* one *d*. *Educ:* Manchester Univ. (BA Hons); Harvard Business Sch. (Fulbright Schol.; MBA). Leader, Manchester Univ. Students' Union, 1992–93; Sen. Business Analyst, Strategic Services, Andersen Consulting, 1993–96; Advr on Reinventing Govt, then Dir, Business Liaison, Office of the Leader of the Labour Party, 1996–97; Exec., N. M. Rothschild & Sons Ltd, 1997–99; Co-Founder, EGS Gp Ltd, 2000–04. Associate Fellow, Social Market Foundn, 2001–05. Parly Under-Sec. of State, DoH, 2005–06; Minister of State, Home Office, 2006–08; Minister for the W Midlands, 2007–08; Chancellor of the Duchy of Lancaster and Minister for the Cabinet Office, 2008–09; Chief Sec. to the Treasury, 2009–10; Shadow Chief Sec. to the Treasury, 2010; Shadow Minister for the Cabinet Office, 2010–11; Shadow Sec. of State for Work and Pensions, 2011–13; Shadow Minister for Univs, Sci. and Skills, 2013–15. *Publications:* Local Government Transformed, 1996; Information Age Government, 1998; Cities of Enterprise: new strategies for full employment, 2002; Britain in 2020, 2003; Reinventing Government Again, 2004; Turning to Face the East; how Britain can prosper in the Asian century, 2013; contribs to Parly Affairs and Progress mag. *Recreation:* spending time with family. *Address:* House of Commons, SW1A 0AA. *T:* (020) 7219 3000.

BYRNE, Michael David; His Honour Judge Byrne; a Circuit Judge, since 2002; *b* 7 Dec. 1945; *s* of Gerard Robert Byrne and Margaret Doreen Byrne; *m* 1985, Felicity Jane Davies. *Educ:* St Edward's Coll., Liverpool; Liverpool Univ. (BA, LLB). Called to the Bar, Gray's Inn, 1971; in practice on Northern Circuit, 1971–2002; Asst Recorder, 1989–92; Recorder, 1992–2002. Mem., Lancs and Cumbria Courts Bd, 2007–11. Chm., Managers Adv. Cttee, Ashworth Special Hosp., 1989–98 (non-exec. Dir, 1996–97); Vice-Chm., Ashworth SHA 1997–98. Legal Mem., Restricted Patients Panel, Mental Health Review Tribunal, 2006–. Gov., St Edward's Coll., Liverpool, 1993–2005 (Chm. Govs, 1995–2004). FRSA 2006. KHS 2006; KCHS 2012. *Recreations:* music, literature, theatre, travel. *Address:* Preston Law Courts, Openshaw Place, The Ring Way, Preston PR1 2LL.

BYRNE, Rev. Father Paul Laurence, OMI; OBE 1976; Oblate Mission Fundraiser, since 2010; *b* 8 Aug. 1932; *s* of late John Byrne and Lavinia Byrne. *Educ:* Synge Street Christian Brothers' Sch. and Belcamp Coll., Dublin; University Coll., Dublin (BA, Hons Phil.); Oblate Coll., Piltown. Ordained, 1958. Teacher, Belcamp Coll., 1959–65; Dean of Belcamp Coll., 1961–65; Dir, Irish Centre, Birmingham, 1965–68; Dir, Catholic Housing Aid Soc. (Birmingham) and Family Housing Assoc., Birmingham, 1965–69; Nat. Dir, Catholic Housing Aid Soc., and Dir, Family Housing Assoc., London, 1969–70; Dir, SHAC (a housing aid centre), 1969–76; Sec. Gen., Conf. of Major Religious Superiors of Ire., 1980–87; Provincial Superior, Anglo-Irish Prov. of Missionary OMI, 1988–94; Dir, Irish Episcopal Commn for Emigrants, 1995–2004 (Bd Mem., 2004–); Oblate Mission Procurator, 2004–10. Bd Mem., Threshold Centre; Servite Houses; Housing Corp., 1974–77. Pres., St Stephen's Green Trust, 2005– (Chm., 1994–2005); Chm., Bd of Govs, Belcamp Coll., 2004–09. Trustee, London Irish Centre, 2002–14. Hon. Mem., Inst. of Housing, 1972. *Recreations:* golf, theatre-going. *Address:* House of Retreat, Tyrconnell Road, Inchicore, Dublin 8, Ireland. *E:* procureomi@eircom.net. *Club:* Foxrock Golf.

BYRNE, Richard John Thomas; Regional Employment Judge, South East, since 2015 (East Anglia, 2012–15); *b* Dorking, Surrey, 19 Jan. 1955; *s* of Thomas John and Hilda Margaret Byrne; *m* 1984, Katharine Helen Wilson; one *s*. *Educ:* St Mary's Coll., Southampton; Coll. of Law, Guildford. FRGS 1990. Admitted Solicitor, 1978; Assistant Solicitor: Paris Smith & Randall, Southampton, 1978–80; Warner Goodman & Streat, Southampton, 1980; Reeves and Haynes, Oxford, 1981–82; Asst Solicitor, 1983–85, Partner, Commercial Litigation, 1985–2003, Lester Aldridge, Bournemouth; Fee-paid Chm., Industrial Tribunals, Southampton, 1994–2003; Salaried Chm., Industrial Tribunals, subseq. Employment Judge, Reading, 2003–12. Pres., Council of Employment Judges, 2009–10. Former Hon. Sec., RGS; Sec. and Treas., Geographical Club, 2006–12. Mem., James Caird Soc. *Recreations:* travel, cycling, playing golf (badly), theatre, absorbing the history of polar exploration, watching motor racing and looking at classic cars. *Address:* Employment Tribunals, Radius House, 51 Clarendon Road, Watford, Herts WD17 1HU. *T:* (01923) 281750, *Fax:* (01923) 281781. *E:* gtored@icloud.com. *Clubs:* Geographical; Goodwood Road Racing.

BYRNE, Rt Rev. Robert John, CO; an Auxiliary Bishop of Birmingham, (RC), and Titular Bishop of Cuncacestre, since 2014; *b* 22 Sept. 1956; *s* of Sidney and Monica Byrne (*née* Rigby). *Educ:* St Bede's Coll., Manchester; King's Coll. London (BD; AKC); Pontifical Univ. of St Thomas Aquinas, Rome. Entered Birmingham Oratory, 1980; Chaplain, St Philip's Coll., Edgbaston, 1984–88; ordained priest, 1985; Parish Priest, St Aloysius, Oxford, 1990–99; Founder, 1990, Provost, 1993–2011, Oxford Oratory; Nat. Ecumenical Officer and Sec., Dept of Dialogue and Unity, Bishops' Conf. of Eng. and Wales, 2012–14. Sec., Perm. Deputation, Internat. Fedn of the Congregations of the Oratory, 2000–11. Trustee and Gov., Oratory Sch., 1996–. Prison Chaplain, 1988–2013. Mem., Clockmakers' Co., 2008–. *Recreations:* history, opera, travel. *Address:* Oscott College, Chester Road, Sutton Coldfield, W Midlands B73 5AA. *T:* (0121) 3215130. *E:* bishop.robert@rc-birmingham.org. *Club:* Athenæum.

BYRNE, Rosemary; Member for Scotland South, Scottish Parliament, 2003–07 (Scot Socialist, 2003–06, Solidarity, 2006–07); Co-Convenor, Solidarity (Scotland), 2006. A principal teacher, Ardrossan Acad. Sec., Irvine and N Ayrshire Trades Union Council. Scot Socialist spokesman for educn and young people, Scottish Parlt, 2003–07. Contested (Scot Socialist) Cunninghame South, 2001.

BYRNE, Simon; Chief Constable, Cheshire Police Service, since 2014; *b* Epsom, Surrey, 29 April 1963; *s* of Thomas Byrne and Nola Byrne; *m* 1990, Susan Elaine Kerfoot; two *c* (and one *d* decd). *Educ:* Neston Co. Comp. Sch.; Univ. of Manchester (MA Dist. Police Mgt). Joined Metropolitan Police Service, 1982; Merseyside Police, 1985–2002; BCU Comdr, Knowsley, 2002–06; Asst Chief Constable, Merseyside Police, 2006–09; Dep. Chief Constable, Greater Manchester Police, 2009–11; Asst Comr, Metropolitan Police Service, 2011–14. Police Long Service and Good Conduct Medal, 2005. *Recreations:* cycling, tennis, ski-ing, building model railways. *Address:* Cheshire Constabulary Headquarters, Clemonds Hey, Oakmere Road, Winsford CW7 2UA.

BYRNE, Terence Niall; HM Diplomatic Service, retired; Clerk/Adviser, House of Commons European Scrutiny Committee, 2002; *b* 28 April 1942; *e s* of late Denis Patrick Byrne and Kathleen Byrne (*née* Carley); *m* 1st, 1966, Andrea Dennison (marr. diss. 1977); one *s* one *d*; 2nd, 1981, Susan Haddow Neill; two *d*. *Educ:* Finchley Catholic Grammar Sch.; Open Univ. (BA Hons). Min. of Housing and Local Govt, 1964–68; Prime Minister's Office, 1968–70; MAFF, 1971–78 (Private Sec. to Parly Sec., MAFF, 1974–75); First Sec. (Agriculture), The Hague, 1978–82; Commonwealth Co-ordination Dept, FCO, 1982–84; Asst Head, UN Dept, FCO, 1984–85; Head of Chancery and Consul, Quito, 1986–89; Counsellor and Dep. High Comr, Lusaka, 1990–93; Dir of Trade Promotion, Canberra, 1993–94; Dep. High Comr, Kuala Lumpur, 1994–98; Consul-Gen. and Dir of Trade Promotion, Auckland, 1999–2002. *Recreations:* gardening, history, cinema. *Address:* (office) 14 Tothill Street, SW1H 9NB.

BYRNE, Terrance Dennis, CB 2003; a Commissioner, 1999–2004, and Director General, Law Enforcement, 2002–04, HM Customs and Excise; *b* 26 Nov. 1944; *s* of Thomas Edward Byrne and Sybil Elizabeth Byrne; *m* 1966, Pamela Ashley; one *s* one *d*. *Educ:* Downham Market Grammar Sch., Norfolk. Joined Civil Service, 1962; HM Customs and Excise 1964–2004: specialist investigator, 1971–84; Mgt Consultant, 1984–88; Dep. Chie Investigation Officer, 1988–91; Head, Customs Enforcement Policy, 1991–99; Dir, Fraud and Intelligence, then Law Enforcement, 1999–2000. *Recreations:* horticulture, sport (mainly golf) reading.

BYRNE, Timothy Russell, FCA; Partner, Management Alliance LLP, since 2004; Director Ginger Recruitment Services Ltd, since 2014; *b* 16 March 1959; *s* of late Russell Vincent Byrne and of Barbara Ann Byrne; *m* 1986, Caroline Margaret Lander; three *d*. *Educ:* Stanney High Sch. FCA 1994. With Lowndes McLintock, 1980–84; Accountancy Tuition Centre 1984–85; Granada TV Div., 1985–92; Airtours plc, subseq. Mytravel Group, 1993–2002 Group Financial Controller, 1993–97; Group Finance Dir, 1997–99; Group Chief Exec. 1999–2002; Chairman: Everything4Travel Ltd, 2004–14; Andrew Sumners Associates Ltd 2005–11; Chief Financial Officer, CN Creative Ltd, 2011–12. *Recreations:* country pursuits Prince's Trust Mentor. *T:* 07785 234293.

BYROM, Peter Craig, OBE 1987; self-employed textile consultant, 1985–2010; *b* 4 Dec 1927; *s* of Robert Hunter Byrom, Master Cotton Spinner and Winifred Agnes Byrom (*née* Goodwin); *m* 1st, 1952, Norma Frances Mawdesley Harris (marr. diss. 1984); three *s* three *d* 2nd, 1984, Gillian Elizabeth Hoyte. *Educ:* Virginia Episcopal Sch., Lynchburg, USA; St Edward's Sch., Oxford; Univ. of Liverpool, Sch. of Architecture; Salford Royal Tech. Coll. Admin. Staff Coll., Henley; Open Univ. (BA). CText; FTI 1986. RNVR, 1945–48. Ass Gen. Manager, Robert Byrom (Stalybridge), cotton spinners, 1951–59; Merchandising Manager, British Nylon Spinners, 1959–64; Marketing Manager and Adv. and Promotion Manager, ICI Fibres, 1964–71; Dir, Deryck Healey Internat., 1972–74; Man. Dir, Dartington Hall Tweeds, 1975–85. Non-exec. Dir, Parry Murray & Co. Ltd, 1992–2010. Lay Inspector of Schs, OFSTED, 1993–98. Consultant to: ODA, Nepal, 1980; Intermediate Tech. Gp India, 1986; Chm., British Colour Council, 1971–73; Mem., Textile and Fashion Bd, CNAA 1974–77; Chm. Council, RCA, 1981–86 (Mem., 1973–86; Sen. Fellow, 1983); Mem Council, Textile Inst., 1986–96 (Service Medal, 1992); External Assessor, Manchester Metropolitan Univ., 1992–95. Governor: Dartington Coll. of Arts, 1979–89; Loughborough Coll. of Art and Design, 1993–98 (Vice-Chm., Govs, 1996–98). FRSA 1970 (Mem. Council 1987–93; Mem. Design Bd, 1986–91; Chm., Textiles, Young Designers into Industry 1985–90). Hon. Treas., Woodland PCC, 1995–2011. *Publications:* Textiles: product design and marketing, 1987; (foreword) Fancy Yarns: their manufacture and application, 2002 contrib. to Young Designers into the Textile Industry. *Recreations:* walking, swimming theatre, music, books. *Address:* 29 The Priory, Abbotskerswell, Newton Abbot, Devon TQ12 5PP. *T:* (01626) 335359.

See also Bishop Suffragan of Shrewsbury.

BYRON, family name of **Baron Byron**.

BYRON, 13th Baron *cr* 1643, of Rochdale, Co. Lancaster; **Robert James Byron;** Partner Holman Fenwick & Willan, 1984, now Consultant; *b* 5 April 1950; *o* surv. *s* of 12th Baron Byron, DSO and Dorigen Margaret (*d* 1985), *o d* of Percival Kennedy Esdaile; *S* father, 1989 *m* 1979, Robyn Margaret, *d* of John McLean, Hamilton, NZ; one *s* three *d*. *Educ:* Wellington Coll.; Trinity Coll., Cambridge (MA). Called to the Bar, Inner Temple, 1974; admitted solicitor, 1978. *Heir:* *s* Hon. Charles Richard Gordon Byron, *b* 28 July 1990.

BYRON, Rt Hon. Sir (Charles Michael) Dennis, Kt 2000; PC 2005; President, Caribbean Court of Justice, since 2011; *b* 4 July 1943; *s* of late Vincent Fitzgerald Byron, MBE and Pearl Eulalie Byron (*nee* O'Loughlin); *m* 1st, 1966, Monika Botfeldt (marr. diss.); four *s*; 2nd, 2006 Norma Theobalds-Willie. *Educ:* Fitzwilliam Coll., Cambridge (MA, LLB 1966). Called to the Bar, Inner Temple, 1965, Bencher, 2003; barrister-at-law, W Indies (Leeward Is), 1966–82 Eastern Caribbean Supreme Court: High Ct Judge, 1982–90; Justice of Appeal, 1990–96 Actg Chief Justice, 1996–99; Chief Justice, 1999–2008 (on leave of absence, 2004–08); Judge 2004–11, Pres., 2007–11, Internat. Criminal Tribunal for Rwanda. Pres., Commonwealth Judicial Educn Inst., 1999–. *Recreations:* tennis, golf, reading. *Address:* Caribbean Court of Justice, 134 Henry Street, PO Box 1768, Port of Spain, Trinidad and Tobago.

BYRON, Prof. Tanya, PsyD; consultant clinical psychologist, broadcaster, journalist, author and government adviser; Consultant in Child and Adolescent Mental Health, Hertfordshire Partnership NHS Trust, since 1998; *b* Barnet, 6 April 1967; *d* of John and Elfie Sichel; *m* 1990 Bruce Byron; one *s* one *d*. *Educ:* North London Collegiate Sch. for Girls; Univ. of York (BSc Hons Psychol. 1989); University Coll. London (MSc Clin. Psychol. 1992); Univ. of Surrey (PsyD 1995). Clinical Psychologist, UCH and Middlesex Hosp., 1992–96; Consultant Clinical Psychologist, Herts PCT Adolescent Unit, 1996–2002. BBC TV: Expert Presenter series incl. Little Angels, 2003–05, House of Tiny Tearaways, 2005–07, Am I Normal?, 2008 co-writer (with Jennifer Saunders), The Life and Times of Vivienne Vyle, 2007. Columnist The Times (weekly), 2005–; Good Housekeeping mag., 2009–. Led ind. govt review on Children and New Technol. (Byron Review), 2007–08. Prof. in the Public Understanding of Sci. and Chancellor, Edge Hill Univ., 2008–; Guest Prof., Shandong Normal Univ., China 2011. Pres., Cyber Mentors, 2009–; Patron, Relate. FRSA. DUniv: York, 2009; Open, 2010 *Publications:* Little Angels (jtly), 2005; The House of Tiny Tearaways, 2005; Your Child Your Way, 2007; Your Toddler Month By Month, 2008; The Skeleton Cupboard (autobiog.) 2014. *Recreations:* cinema, theatre, creative arts, creative writing, walking, piano, dancing having a laugh en famille. *Address:* c/o Sophie Laurimore, Factual Management, 105 Tanners Hill, SE8 4QD. *E:* sl@factualmanagement.com. *W:* www.professortanyabyron.com.

BYRT, His Honour (Henry) John; QC 1976; a Circuit Judge, 1983–99; *b* 5 March 1929; *s* of Dorothy Muriel Byrt and Albert Henry Byrt, CBE; *m* 1957, Eve Hermione Bartlett; one *s* two *d*. *Educ:* Charterhouse; Merton Coll., Oxford (BA, MA). Called to the Bar, Middle Temple, 1953; called within the Bar, 1976; a Recorder of the Crown Court, 1976–83. First Pres., Social Security Appeal Tribunals and Medical Appeal Tribunals, 1983–90: Dep. Chm. Employment Appeal Tribunal, 1992–99. Judge, Mayors and City of London Court, 1990–99 (Sen. Judge, 1994–99). Working Men's College, London: teacher, 1952–87; Vice-Principal 1978–82; Principal, 1982–87; Mem. Council, Queen's Coll., London, 1982–99. Trustee Cotswold Community Trust, 2003–11. Patron, Jedidiah Foundn, 2005–. Freeman, City of London, 1999. *Recreations:* building, gardening, travel, music. *Address:* 46 Skyline House Dickens Yard, Longfield Avenue, Ealing, W5 2BJ. *T:* (020) 3665 7791. *Clubs:* Guildhall Alderman's, Leander.

BYWATER, Air Cdre David Llewellyn, FRAeS; aviation consultant; Commandant Aeroplane and Armament Experimental Establishment, Boscombe Down, 1988–92; *b* 16 July 1937; *s* of Stanley and Gertrude Bywater; *m* 1960, Shelagh May Gowling; one *s* one *d*. *Educ:* Liverpool Inst. High Sch.; RAF Coll., Cranwell. No XV Sqdn, 1958–63; Empire Test Pilots Sch., 1964; Test Pilot, A&AEE, Boscombe Down, 1965–68; RAF Staff Coll., 1969; HQ RAF Germany, 1970–73; Wing Comdr Flying, RAE Farnborough, 1974–78; MoD Operational Requirements, 1979–81; Gp Captain, Superintendent of Flying, A&AEE, 1982–85; Gp Dir, RAF Staff Coll., Bracknell, 1985–88; Dir, Airport and Flight Ops, Marshall Aerospace, 1993–2002. Director: RAF Charitable Trust Enterprises, 2002–; Royal Internat. Air Tattoo, 2005– (Vice-Pres., 1992); British Light Aircraft Centre, 2006–; Aircraft Owners and Pilots Assoc., 2006– (Vice Pres., 2004–); Mem., Air League, 1994–. Hon. Mem., Airport Operators' Assoc., 2006. Liveryman, Hon. Co. of Air Pilots (formerly GAPAN), 2006. *Recreations* sailing, ski-ing. *Club:* Royal Air Force.

C

CABALLÉ, Montserrat; Cross of Lazo de Dama of Order of Isabel the Catholic, Spain; opera and concert singer; *b* Barcelona, 12 April 1933; *d* of Carlos and Ana Caballé; *m* 1964, Bernabé Marti, tenor; one *s* one *d*. *Educ:* Conservatorio del Liceo, Barcelona. Continued to study singing under Mme Eugenia Kemeny. Carnegie Hall début as Lucrezia Borgia, 1965; London début in this role, with the London Opera Society, at the Royal Festival Hall, 1968. Has sung at Covent Garden, Glyndebourne, La Scala, Vienna, Metropolitan Opera, San Francisco and most major opera venues. Major roles include Maria Stuarda, Luisa Miller, Queen Elizabeth in Roberto Devereux, Imogene in Il Pirata, Violetta in La Traviata, Marguerite in Faust, Desdemona in Otello, Norma, Tosca, Turandot, Leonora in La Forza del Destino, Semiramide, Salome, Il Viaggio a Reims, Tristan und Isolde, and also those of contemporary opera. Over 120 roles sung and recorded. Numerous hon. degrees, awards and medals.

CABLE, Dr the Rt Hon. Sir (John) Vincent, Kt 2015; PC 2010; *b* 9 May 1943; *s* of John Leonard Cable and Edith Cable; *m* 1st, 1968, Olympia Rebelo (*d* 2001); two *s* one *d*; 2nd, 2004, Rachel Wenban Smith. *Educ:* Fitzwilliam Coll., Cambridge (BA Hons; Pres., Cambridge Union); Glasgow Univ. (PhD). Finance Officer, Kenya Treasury, 1966–68; Lectr in Econs, Univ. of Glasgow, 1968–74; First Sec., FCO, 1974–76; Dep. Dir, ODI, 1976–83; Special Advr (Dir), Econs, Commonwealth Secretariat, 1983–90; Gp Planning Dept, Shell, 1990–93; Hd of Economic Prog., Chatham House, 1993–95; Chief Economist, Shell, 1995–97. Advr to Chm., World Commn on Envmt and Develt, UN, 1975–77; Special Advr to Sec. of State for Trade, 1979. Mem (Lab), Glasgow CC, 1971–74. Contested: (Lab) Glasgow, Hillhead, 1970; (SDP/L Alliance) York, 1983, 1987; (Lib Dem) Twickenham, 1992. MP (Lib Dem) Twickenham, 1997–2015; contested (Lib Dem) same seat, 2015. Lib Dem spokesman on Trade and Industry, 1999–2003, on the economy, 2003–10; Dep. Leader, 2006–10, Acting Leader, 2007, Lib Dems; Sec. of State for Business, Innovation and Skills, 2010–15. Mem., Treasury Select Cttee, 1998–99. Vis. Fellow, Nuffield Coll., Oxford. *Publications:* Protectionism and Industrial Decline, 1983; (with B. Persaud) Foreign Investment and Development, 1985; Global Super Highways, 1994; The New Giants: China and India, 1994; The World's New Fissures, 1994; Globalisation and Global Governance, 2000; Public Services: reform with a purpose, 2005; Multiple Identities, 2005; The Storm, 2009; Free Radical (memoir), 2009; Tackling the Fiscal Crisis, 2009; After the Storm, 2015. *Recreations:* walking, cycling, dancing. *Address:* 102 Whitton Road, Twickenham TW1 1BS. *T:* (020) 8892 3212.

See also S. C. W. Kenny.

CABLE, Margaret Ann, (Mrs J. R. W. Fletcher), FRCM; Professor of Singing, Royal College of Music, 1964–2006; *b* 3 June 1942; *d* of Sidney Frank Cable and Gladys Alfreda Cable (*née* Roberts); *m* 1967, John Richard William Fletcher; one *s* one *d*. *Educ:* Sawston Village Coll., Cambs; Royal Coll. of Music (Foundn Schol. and Exhibnr). FRCM 1985. Concert singer, 1963–2000; sang at major festivals incl. Lucerne, Edinburgh, Utrecht, Aldeburgh, Three Choirs and Henry Wood Promenade Concerts; roles at Kent Opera, 1974–80, include: Dorabella, in Così fan tutte; Marcellina, in Le nozze di Figaro; Mrs Grose, in The Turn of the Screw. Has made numerous recordings. Gov., Royal Soc. of Musicians, 2011–. Warden, Solo Performers' Section, ISM, 1985–86. *Recreations:* walking, theatre. *Address:* 79 Haven Lane, Ealing, W5 2HZ. *T:* (020) 3605 6455.

CABLE, Rt Hon. Sir Vincent; *see* Cable, Rt Hon. Sir J. V.

CABLE-ALEXANDER, Lt-Col Sir Patrick (Desmond William), 8th Bt *cr* 1809, of the City of Dublin; Chief Executive (formerly Chief Executive (Administration)), Institute of Optometry, 1999–2006 and 2007–08; *b* 19 April 1936; *s* of Sir Desmond William Lionel Cable-Alexander, 7th Bt and of Mary Jane, *d* of James O'Brien, Enniskillen; *S* father, 1988, but his name does not appear on the Official Roll of the Baronetage; *m* 1st, 1961, Diana Frances Rogers (marr. diss. 1976); two *d*; 2nd, 1976, Jane Mary Weekes (*née* Lewis); one *s*. *Educ:* Downside School; RMA Sandhurst; Army Staff Coll., 1966–67; National Defence Coll., 1975–76. Commnd 3rd Carabiniers (POWDG), 1956; Lt-Col Royal Scots Dragoon Guards, 1976; comd Duke of Lancaster's Own Yeomanry, 1978–80; Chief of Staff, HQ North West District, 1980–83; retd, 1984. Sec. to the Council and Bursar, Lancing Coll., 1984–98. Trustee, Friends of Sussex Hospices, 2013– (Chm., W Sussex Fundraising Cttee, 2014–). *Recreations:* art, cooking, theatre, fly fishing, city breaks. *Heir: s* Fergus William Antony Cable-Alexander [*b* 19 June 1981; *m* 2011, Claire Whiteside; two *s*]. *Address:* 15 Cambridge Road, Worthing, West Sussex BN11 1XD.

CABORN, Rt Hon. Richard (George); PC 1999; *b* 6 Oct. 1943; *s* of late George and of Mary Caborn; *m* 1966, Margaret Caborn; one *s* one *d*. *Educ:* Hurlfield Comprehensive Sch.; Granville Coll. of Further Educn; Sheffield Polytechnic. Engrg apprentice, 1959–64; Convenor of Shop Stewards, Firth Brown Ltd, 1967–79. Mem. (Lab) Sheffield, European Parlt, 1979–84. MP (Lab) Sheffield, Central, 1983–2010. Minister of State: (Minister for the Regions, Regeneration and Planning), DETR, 1997–99; (Minister for Trade) DTI, 1999–2001; (Minister for Sport), 2001–07, (Minister for Tourism), 2003–05, DCMS; PM's Ambassador for the World Cup 2018, 2007–09. Chm., Select Cttee on Trade and Industry, 1992–95. President: ABA of England, 2008–; YHA, 2008–; UK Sch. Games, 2008–; Trustee, Football Foundn, 2008–. Strategic Advr to Advanced Manufg Res. Centre, Univ. of Sheffield, 2010–; Advr to Nat. Centre for Sport and Exercise Medicine, 2012–. Hon. Fellow, Faculty of Sport and Exercise Medicine, 2007. Hon. Dr Sport Sci. Leeds Metropolitan, 2007; Hon Dr Sheffield Hallam, 2012; Hon. DLitt Sheffield, 2013. *Recreations:* golf, running. *Address:* 29 Quarry Vale Road, Sheffield S12 3EB. *T:* (0114) 239 3802. *Club:* Carlton Working Men's (Sheffield).

CABRERA, Pablo; Director, Diplomatic Academy, Ministry of Foreign Affairs Chile, 2010–14; *b* Santiago, 18 Jan. 1948; *m* 1973, Cecilia Pérez Waulker; two *s* one *d*. *Educ:* Catholic Univ. of Chile (Lic. Juridical and Social Scis). Lawyer; entered Foreign Service, Chile, 1970: Consul, 1974, Second Sec., 1975–76, La Paz; Second Sec., Carácas, 1977–78; Consul Gen., Toronto, 1981–82; Chargé d'Affaires, Bucharest, 1983–85; Counsellor and Minister Counsellor, London, 1987–91; Minister Counsellor, Madrid, concurrent with Greece, 1991–93; Dep. Head, 1993, Head, 1994, Special Policy Dept, Min. of Foreign Affairs, Santiago; Under-Sec. of State for Navy, MoD, Santiago, 1995–99; Ambassador of Chile: to UK and Ireland, 1999–2000; to Russian Fedn, 2000–04, and concurrently to the Ukraine, 2001–04; to China, 2004–06; Ambassador to the Holy See, 2006–10. Formerly Head, Chilean Delegns to internat. confs. Vis. Prof., Nat. Acad. for Political and Strategic Studies, 1993. Mem., Internat. Law Soc. of Chile, 1963–. Mem., Christian Democratic Party, 1963–. Official, 1980, and Great Cross, 1995, Order of Rio Branco (Brazil); Great Cross, Order of Civil Merit (Spain), 1996; Comdr First Cl., Polar Star Royal Order (Sweden), 1996. *Recreations:* golf, tennis, football. *Club:* Los Leones Golf (Santiago).

CACKETTE, Paul Henry; Deputy Solicitor to Scottish Government, since 2009; *b* Edinburgh, 26 March 1960; *s* of George and Erica Cackette; *m* 1987, Helen Elizabeth Thomson; one *s* two *d*. *Educ:* Univ. of Edinburgh (LLB Hons 1982); Univ. of Glasgow (DipLP 1983). Trainee solicitor, Edinburgh DC, 1983–85; Solicitor, Kirkcaldy DC, 1985–88; Govt Legal Service, 1988–; Divl Solicitor (Rural Affairs), 2000–03; Hd, Civil Justice and Internat. Div., Justice Directorate, Scottish Govt, 2003–08; Legal Sec. to Lord Advocate, 2008–09. *Recreations:* athletics, literature. *Address:* Scottish Government Legal Directorate, Room GB-01, Victoria Quay, Edinburgh EH6 6QQ. *T:* (0131) 244 0959, *Fax:* (0131) 244 7417. *E:* paul.cackette@scotland.gsi.gov.uk.

CADBURY, Sir Dominic; *see* Cadbury, Sir N. D.

CADBURY, Sir (Nicholas) Dominic, Kt 1997; Chairman: The Wellcome Trust, 2000–06 (a Governor, 1999–2006); Cadbury Schweppes plc, 1993–2000 (Chief Executive, 1984–93); *b* 12 May 1940; *s* of late Laurence John Cadbury, OBE and Joyce Cadbury, OBE; *m* 1972, Cecilia Sarah Symes; three *d*. *Educ:* Eton Coll.; Trinity Coll., Cambridge; Stanford Univ. (MBA). Chairman: Economist Gp, 1994–2003 (Dir, 1990–2003); Transense Technologies plc, 2000–03; Dep. Chm., Guinness PLC, 1994–97; Jt Dep. Chm., EMI Gp plc, 1999–2004 (Bd Mem., 1998–2004). Director: Misys plc, 2000–09 (Chm., 2005–09); New Star Asset Mgt, 2005–07. Mem., President's Cttee, 1989–94 and 1998–2000, Chm., Educn and Trng Affairs Cttee, 1993–97, CBI; Dep. Chm., Qualifications and Curriculum Authority, 1997–2000; Sen. Advr, FSA, 2010–13; Member: Royal Mint Adv. Cttee, 1986–94; Stanford Adv. Council, 1989–95; Food Assoc., 1989–2000; NACETT, 1993–95; Marketing Council, 1997–2000; Council of Mgt, NIESR, 1998–2000. Pres., Food and Drink Fedn, 1998–99. Chancellor, Univ. of Birmingham, 2002–13. Vice Pres., Edgbaston High Sch. for Girls, Birmingham, 1987–; Gov., Tudor Hall Sch., 1993–96. Fellow, Eton Coll., 1996–2010. CCMI (CBIM 1984); FCIM (Pres., 1996–97). *Recreations:* golf, shooting.

CADBURY, Nigel Robin; District Judge (Magistrates' Courts), West Mercia, since 2011; *b* 6 July 1956; *s* of late Robin Norman Cadbury, JP, and of Rosemary Jayne Cadbury; *m* 1982, Julie Ann Dean; two *s* one *d*. *Educ:* Rugby Sch.; Kent Univ. (BA Law 1978). Called to the Bar, Middle Temple, 1979; in practice at the Bar, 1979–97; Mem., Midland and Oxford Circuit, 1979–97; Stipendiary Magistrate, Leeds, 1997–2000; District Judge (Magistrates' Courts): Birmingham, 2000–05; Solihull and Sutton Coldfield, 2005–11. Mem., Criminal Bar Assoc., 1990–97. Trustee: Edward Cadbury Charitable Trust, 1991–; Bournville Village Trust, 2011–. *Recreations:* golf, ski-ing, gardening. *Address:* Worcester Magistrates' Court, Castle Street, Worcester WR1 3QZ. *T:* (01905) 743200. *Clubs:* Blackwell Golf, Royal Cinque Ports Deal Golf, St Enedoc Golf.

CADBURY, Ruth; MP (Lab) Brentford and Isleworth, since 2015; *m* Nick; two *s*. *Educ:* Mount Sch., York; Bourneville FE Coll.; Univ. of Salford (BSc Hons 1981). Planning Advr, Planning Aid for London, 1989–96; Policy Planner, Richmond upon Thames LBC, 1996–2001; freelance consultant, 2006–10. Mem. (Lab), Hounslow LBC, 1986–94 and 1998– (Dep. Leader, 2010–12; Cabinet Mem., 2010–13). Trustee, Barrow Cadbury Trust. *Address:* House of Commons, SW1A 0AA.

CADDICK, His Honour David William; a Circuit Judge, 2004–14; *b* 24 Dec. 1945; *s* of late William Caddick and Phyllis Caddick (*née* Brown, later Medhurst); *m* 1971, Susan Anne Wyton; two *s* two *d*. *Educ:* Simon Langton Grammar Sch., Canterbury; St John's Coll., Durham (BA 1967). Articled to D. L. Gulland, Solicitor, 1967–70; admitted solicitor, 1970; Partner, Gulland & Gulland, Solicitors, Maidstone, 1971–87; Dep. County Court Registrar, 1983–87; Registrar, then Dist Judge, 1987–2004; Nominated Dist Care Judge, Medway Care Centre, 1991–2004; a Recorder, Crown Court, 1998–2004. Chm. SE Circuit, Dist Judges' Assoc., 1995–98. *Recreations:* gardening, walking, all things connected with France.

CADELL of Grange, William Archibald, RIBA; FRIAS; *b* 9 March 1933; *s* of late Col Henry Moubray Cadell of Grange, OBE, RE and Christina Rose Cadell (*née* Nimmo); *m* 1960, Mary-Jean Carmichael; three *s*. *Educ:* Merchiston Castle Sch.; Trinity Coll., Cambridge (BA 1956; MA); Regent St Poly., London (DipArch). RIBA 1961. Founded William A. Cadell Architects, 1968, retired, 1995; manager, Grange Estate, 1971–2000. Chm., Drum Housing Develt, 1991–2009. Comr, Royal Fine Art Commn for Scotland, 1992–2000; Trustee, Architectural Heritage Fund, 1997–2007. DL 1982–2000, Vice Lord-Lieutenant, 2000–01, West Lothian. *Recreations:* gardening, forestry, the Arts. *Address:* Swordie Mains, Linlithgow, West Lothian EH49 7RQ. *T:* (01506) 842946.

CADMAN, family name of **Baron Cadman**.

CADMAN, 3rd Baron *cr* 1937, of Silverdale; **John Anthony Cadman;** farmer, 1964–85; *b* 3 July 1938; *s* of 2nd Baron Cadman and Marjorie Elizabeth Bunnis; *S* father, 1966; *m* 1975, Janet Hayes; two *s*. *Educ:* Harrow; Selwyn Coll., Cambridge; Royal Agricultural Coll., Cirencester. *Heir: s* Hon. Nicholas Anthony James Cadman, *b* 18 Nov. 1977. *Address:* 8 The Crescent, Whittlebury, Towcester, Northants NN12 8XP. *T:* (01327) 856898. *E:* lord.cadman@gmail.com.

CADMAN, Deborah Ann, OBE 2006; Chief Executive, Suffolk County Council, since 2012; *b* Birmingham, 11 Feb. 1963; *d* of Ronald and Pamela Cadman; *m* 2001, Geoffrey John Rivers; one *s* one *d*. *Educ:* Sir Wilfrid Martineau Sch., Birmingham; Loughborough Univ. (BSc Hons); Birmingham Univ. (MSocSc Urban and Regl Econs); Teesside Univ. (MA Mgt Practice). London Borough of Newnham, 1984–87; community develt voluntary orgn, Birmingham, 1987–89; econ. develt officer, Birmingham CC, 1989–96; Redcar and Cleveland BC, 1996–98; DETR, 1998–99; Audit Commn, 1999–2001; Chief Executive: St Edmundsbury BC, 2001–08; East of England Develt Agency, 2008–12. Vis. Fellow, Sch. of

Business, Leadership and Enterprise, 2011–, Mem. Bd, 2011–, Univ. Campus Suffolk. Chm., Birmingham Univ. Policy Commn, 2011. Member: Bd, New Local Govt Network, 2013–; Social Integration Commn, 2014–. Trustee, Suffolk Foundn. FRSA. *Recreations:* theatre, ceramics, reading, good food and wine. *Address:* Suffolk County Council, Endeavour House, 8 Russell Road, Ipswich IP1 2BX. *T:* (01473) 264002. *E:* Deborah.Cadman@suffolk.gov.uk.

CADMAN, Mark Robert; Executive Vice President and Managing Director, BBDO North America, since 2013; *b* Farnborough, 30 Dec. 1963; *s* of Colin and Jan Cadman; *m* 1998, Ayesha; two *d. Educ:* King's Sch., Canterbury; Queen Mary Coll., Univ. of London (LLB Hons). Managing Director: Lowe London, 2002–04; J. Walter Thomson, 2005; CEO, Euro RSCG London, 2006–08; Chief Exec., Publicis Seattle, 2010–13. *Recreations:* tennis, golf, running. *Club:* Harbour.

CADOGAN, family name of **Earl Cadogan**.

CADOGAN, 8th Earl *cr* 1800; **Charles Gerald John Cadogan,** KBE 2012; DL; Baron Cadogan 1718; Viscount Chelsea 1800; Baron Oakley 1831; *b* 24 March 1937; *o s* of 7th Earl Cadogan, MC and his 1st wife, Hon. Primrose Lilian Yarde-Buller (*d* 1970), *yr d* of 3rd Baron Churston; *S* father, 1997; *m* 1st, 1963, Lady Philippa Wallop (*d* 1984), *d* of 9th Earl of Portsmouth; two *s* one *d*; 2nd, 1989, Jennifer Jane Greig Rae (marr. diss. 1994), *d* of J. E. K. Rae and Mrs S. Z. de Ferranti; 3rd, 1994, Dorothy Ann Shipsey, MVO, *yr d* of late Dr W. E. Shipsey. *Educ:* Eton. Chairman: Leukaemia and Lymphoma Research (formerly Leukaemia Research Fund), 1985–2012; London Playing Fields Foundn, 2001–. Life Fellow, Coll. of Advocates, St Paul's Cath., 2012; Mem., Ct of Patrons, RCS, 2012–. Freeman, City of London, 1979; Liveryman, Hon. Co. of Air Pilots (formerly GAPAN); Hon. Freeman, Apothecaries' Soc., 2012–. DL Greater London, 1996. *Heir: s* Viscount Chelsea, *qv*. *Clubs:* White's, Royal Automobile.

CADOGAN, Prof. Sir John (Ivan George), Kt 1991; CBE 1985; PhD, DSc London; FRS 1976; FRSE, FLSW; CChem, FRSC; first Director General, Research Councils, 1994–98; first President, Learned Society of Wales, 2010–14; *b* Pembrey, Carmarthenshire, 8 Oct. 1930; *er s* of late Alfred Cadogan and Dilys Cadogan, MBE; *m* 1st, 1955, Margaret Jeanne (*née* Evans) (*d* 1992); one *s* (one *d* decd); 2nd, 1997, Elizabeth Purnell; one step *s* one step *d. Educ:* Grammar Sch., Swansea; King's Coll., London (State Scholar, 1948; 1st cl. Hons Chem. 1951; Pres., Chem. Soc., 1951–52; soccer colours, 1952). King's Scout. Research at KCL, 1951–54. Civil Service Research Fellow, 1954–56; Lectr in Chemistry, King's Coll., London, 1956–63; Purdie Prof. of Chemistry and Head of Dept, St Salvator's Coll., Univ. of St Andrews, 1963–69; Forbes Prof. of Organic Chemistry, Edinburgh Univ., 1969–79; Chief Scientist, BP Res. Centre, 1979–81; Dir of Res., BP, 1981–92. Chm., BP Vencap, 1988–92; Director: BP Gas International, 1983–87; BP Ventures, 1981–90 (Chief Exec., 1988–90); BP Chemicals, 1983–92; BP Venezuela, 1985–92; BP Solar International, 1988–92 (Chm., 1988–90); Chairman: Kaldair Internat., 1988–90; DNA Res. Innovations Ltd, 1999–2004, acquired by Invitrogen Corp.; Dir, Fusion Antibodies Ltd, 2001– (Chm., 2005–10). Advr to EC Comr for Sci., R&D, 1993–94. Mem., Royal Commn on Criminal Justice, 1991–93. Chairman: Defence Sci. Adv. Council, 1985–91; Nuclear Weapons Safety Cttee, 1992–98; Nuclear Powered Warships Safety Cttee, 1992–98; Defence Nuclear Safety Cttee, 1998–2000. Member: Chemistry Cttee, SRC, 1967–71 (Chm. 1972–75); Council, SERC, 1981–85 (Chm., Science Bd, 1981–85; Mem., Science Bd, SRC, 1972–75); ACORD, Dept of Energy, 1987–89; HEFCW, 1992–95 (Chm., Res. Gp, 1992–94); HEFCE, 1994–98; Hong Kong Technol. Review Bd, 1992–95; Commn on New Policy, Irish Council for Sci. and Technol., 2002–03; Sci. Policy Advr, Sci. Foundn Ireland, 2000–05. Member: Council, Chem. Soc., 1966–69, 1973–76; Council, RIC, 1979–80; Chem. Soc.-RIC Unification Cttee, 1975–80; Council, RSC, 1980–85, 1989–92 (Pres. RSC, 1982–84); Council of Management, Macaulay Inst. for Soil Res., Aberdeen, 1969–79; Council, St George's Sch. for Girls, 1974–79; Council, RSE, 1975–80 (Vice-Pres., 1978–80); Council, Royal Soc., 1989–91, 1993–95 (Mem., Royal Soc. Sci. Inquiry, 1990–92); COPUS, 1994–97; Conseil d'Admin, Fondation de la Maison de la Chemie, 1994–2012; Vice-Pres., Royal Instn, 1986–87 (Mem. Council, 1984–87). Chm., Develt Bd, Cardiff Univ. Sch. of Medicine, 2008–; Member: Bd of Trustees, Royal Observatory Trust, Edinburgh, 1979–86; Adv. Bd, RCDS, 1989–2001; Adv. Bd, Eur. Business Management Sch., UC Swansea, 1990–95; Adv. Council, RMCS, 1992–2002; Res. Cttee, Univ. of Newcastle upon Tyne, 1992–94; Ind. Adv. Cttee, Univ. of Durham, 1992–94; Trustee: Overseas Students Trust, UC Swansea, 1989–2000; RSE Scotland Foundn, 1998–2001. Governor: Jt Res. Centre, EC, 1994–2000; Salters' Inst. of Industrial Chem., 1999–2015. Pres., Chem. Sect., BAAS, 1981. Chemistry Advr, Carnegie Trust Univ. of Scotland, 1985–. Pres., Techniquest, 1997–99. Professorial Fellow, Univ. Coll. of Swansea, Univ. of Wales, then Univ. of Wales, Swansea, later Swansea Univ., 1979–2009; Vis. Prof. of Chemistry, Imperial Coll., London Univ., 1979–2002. Fellow: KCL, 1976 (Mem. Council, 1980–94; Vice-Chm., 1990–94); UC, Swansea, 1992; Cardiff Univ., 1998; Swansea Inst. of Higher Educn, 2004; FIC 1992. Hon. FREng (Hon. FEng 1992); Hon. FRSC 1999. Lectures: Tilden, Chem. Soc., 1971; first RSE Schs Christmas, 1980; David Martin Royal Soc. BAYS, 1981; Humphry Davy, Royal Instn, 1982; Holroyd Meml, Soc. Chem. Ind., 1984; Salters' Co., Royal Instn, 1984; Philips, Royal Soc., 1985; Pedler, RSC, 1986; Dalton, RSC, 1989; BGS Dist., 1995; Irvine Meml, St Andrews, 1995; Salters' Millennium, 2000; William Menelaus Meml, 2013. Freeman, City of London; Liveryman, Salters' Co., 1993. Hon. DSc: St Andrews, 1983; Wales, 1984; Edinburgh, 1986; Aberdeen, 1991; Durham, 1992; Leicester, 1992; London, 1992; Sunderland, 1994; Cranfield, 1995; Glamorgan, 1996; Nottingham, 1999; Nottingham Trent, 1999; DUniv Stirling, 1984; Hon. Dr l'Université Aix-Marseille, 1984. Samuel Smiles Prize, KCL, 1950; Millar Thomson Medallist, KCL, 1951; Meldola Medallist, Soc. of Maccabaeans and Royal Inst. of Chemistry, 1959; Corday-Morgan Medallist, Chem. Soc., 1965; SCI Medal, 2001; Lord Lewis Prize, RSC, 2010; Royal Medal, RSE, 2013; Menelaus Medal, Learned Soc. of Wales and S Wales Inst. of Engrs Educnl Trust, 2014. *Publications:* Principles of Free Radical Chemistry, 1971; Organophosphorus Reagents in Organic Synthesis, 1979; about 330 scientific papers, mainly in Jl RSC, and patents; contrib. policy papers to www.learnedsocietywales.org.uk. *Recreations:* being in France, music, gardening (preferably watching his wife at work), supporting Rugby football (Vice-Pres., Crawshay's Welsh RFC, London Welsh RFC; Patron, Swansea RFCC). *Address:* Learned Society of Wales, The University Registry, King Edward VII Avenue, Cathays Park, Cardiff CF10 3NS. *T:* (029) 2037 6951. *E:* john@cadogan27.freeserve.co.uk. *Clubs:* Athenæum; Cardiff and County; Bristol Channel Yacht.

CADWALLADER, James Richard, CMG 2007; Counsellor, Foreign and Commonwealth Office, 2001–08; *b* 1953; *s* of George Cadwallader and Kathleen Cadwallader; *m* 1975, Deborah Jane; two *s* one *d. Educ:* Ludlow Grammar Sch.; Keble Coll., Oxford (BA Engrg Sci., MA). FIET. Royal Corps of Signals, 1973–82; joined FCO, 1982. *Recreations:* hill walking, golf, technology and people. *E:* jcadwallader@iee.org. *Clubs:* Army and Navy, Victory Services.

CÆSAR, Rev. Canon Anthony Douglass, CVO 1991 (LVO 1987); an Extra Chaplain to the Queen, since 1991; *b* 3 April 1924; *s* of Harold Douglass and Winifred Kathleen Cæsar. *Educ:* Cranleigh School; Magdalene Coll., Cambridge; St Stephen's House, Oxford. MA, MusB, FRCO. Served War with RAF, 1943–46. Assistant Music Master, Eton Coll., 1948–51; Precentor, Radley Coll., 1952–59; Asst Curate, St Mary Abbots, Kensington, 1961–65; Asst Sec., ACCM, 1965–70; Chaplain, Royal School of Church Music, 1965–70; Deputy Priest-in-Ordinary to the Queen, 1967–68, Priest-in-Ordinary, 1968–70; Resident Priest, St Stephen's Church, Bournemouth, 1970–73; Precentor and Sacrist, Winchester Cathedral, 1974–79; Sub-Dean of HM Chapels Royal, Dep. Clerk of the Closet, Sub-Almoner and Domestic Chaplain to the Queen, 1979–91; Hon. Canon of Wincheste Cathedral, 1975–76 and 1979–91, Residentiary Canon, 1976–79, Canon Emeritus, 1991–. Chaplain, St Cross Hosp., Winchester, 1991–93. Hon. FGCM 2007. *Publications:* (jt ed.) Th New English Hymnal, 1986; part songs, church music. *Recreation:* other people. *Address:* 2 Capel Court, The Burgage, Prestbury, Cheltenham, Glos GL52 3EL. *T:* (01242) 577541.

CAFFARI, Denise, (Dee), MBE 2007; professional sailor; Managing Director, Dee Caffar Ltd, since 2006; *b* 23 Jan. 1973; *d* of late Peter Caffari and of Barbara Caffari; partner, Harry Spedding. *Educ:* St Clement Danes Sch., Chorleywood; Leeds Metropolitan Univ. (BA Hon Sport Sci. 1994; PGCE Sec. Educn 1995). PE teacher, secondary sch.; Manager, Sports Coll First woman to sail single-handed non-stop around the world in both directions (west arounc the world against the prevailing winds and currents, 2005–06 and eastwards, 2008–09) monohull speed record, Round Britain and Ireland Race, 2009; first woman to sail non-stop around the world three times on completion of the Barcelona World Race, 2011. Mem., Inst of Navigation. Hon. Comdr, RNR, 2011. Hon. Dr Sport Sci. Leeds Metropolitan, 2006 Patron: St Mary's Jun. Sailing Club, 2007–; Gosport and Fareham Inshore Rescue Service 2011–. Ambassador for tri-service initiative, Toe in the Water. *Publications:* Against the Flow 2007. *Recreations:* outdoor activities, fitness, travel, reading, theatre. *Address:* Dee Caffari Ltd 4 Talisman Business Centre, Duncan Road, Park Gate, Southampton, Hants SO31 7GA *Club:* Royal Southampton Yacht.

CAGE, Nicolas; actor, director and producer; *b* Nicholas Kim Coppola, 7 Jan. 1964; *s* of Prof August Coppola and Joy Vogelsang; one *s* by Kristina Fulton; *m* 1st, 1995, Patricia Arquette (marr. diss. 2001); 2nd, 2002, Lisa Marie Presley (marr. diss. 2004); 3rd, 2004, Alice Kim; one *s. Educ:* Beverly Hills High Sch. Co-owner, Saturn Films, prodn co. *Films include:* Valley Girl Rumble Fish, 1983; The Cotton Club, Racing with the Moon, Birdy, 1984; Peggy Sue Go Married, 1986; Raising Arizona, Moonstruck, 1987; Vampire's Kiss, 1989; Wild at Heart 1990; Honeymoon in Vegas, 1992; It Could Happen to You, 1994; Leaving Las Vegas, 1995 (Golden Globe and Acad. Awards for Best Actor, 1996); The Rock, 1996; Con Air, Face/Off, 1997; City of Angels, Snake Eyes, 1998; 8mm, 1999; Bringing Out the Dead, Gone in 60 Seconds, The Family Man, 2000; Captain Corelli's Mandolin, 2001; (also dir and prod.) Sonny, Windtalkers, Adaptation, 2002; Matchstick Men, 2003; National Treasure, 2004; (also prod.) Lord of War, 2005; The Weather Man, World Trade Center, The Wicker Man, 2006 Ghost Rider, Next, 2007; National Treasure: Book of Secrets, Bangkok Dangerous, 2008 Kick-Ass, Bad Lieutenant, The Sorcerer's Apprentice, 2010; Trespass, Justice, 2011; The Frozen Ground, 2013; Joe, Tokarev, 2014; Dying of the Light, 2015; producer: Shadow o the Vampire, 2000; The Life of David Gale, 2003; The Dresden Files (TV series), 2007 *Address:* c/o Creative Artists Agency, 2000 Avenue of the Stars, Los Angeles, CA 90067, USA Saturn Films, Suite 911, 9000 Sunset Boulevard, Los Angeles, CA 90069, USA.

CAGIATI, Dr Andrea, Grand Cross, Italian Order of Merit, 1979; Hon. GCVO Ambassador, retired 1988; *b* Rome, 11 July 1922; *m* 1968, Sigrid von Morgen; one *s* one *d* *Educ:* University of Siena (Dr of Law). Entered Foreign Service, 1948. Served: Secretary Paris, 1950; Principal Private Sec. to Minister of State, 1951; Vice-Consul-General, New York, 1953; Prin. Private Sec. to Minister of State and subsequently Dept of Political Affairs 1955; Counsellor, Athens, 1957; Counsellor, Mexico City, 1960; Delegate, Disarmament Cttee, Geneva, March–Dec. 1962; Italian Delegation, UN, June 1962; Head, NATO Dept Dec. 1962; Minister-Counsellor, Madrid, 1966; Ambassador, Bogotá, 1968; Inst. for Diplomatic Studies, 1971; Diplomatic Adviser to Prime Minister, 1972; Ambassador, Vienna 1973; Ambassador, Court of St James's, 1980; Ambassador to the Holy See and to the Order of Malta, 1985. Vice Chm., 1989–94, Dir, 1987–94, Alitalia. President: Circolo di Stud Diplomatici, 1989–98 (now Hon. Pres.); Centro Conciliazione Internazionale, 1989–97 Fondazione Cagiati von Morgen, 1990–; Eurodéfence (Italia), 1994–99 (now Hon. Pres.) Fondazione Assistenza Sanitaria Melitense, 1995–; Vice-Pres., Fondazione De Gasperi 1993–2003. Hon. GCVO during State Visit to Italy of HM The Queen, Oct. 1980; KM 1953; Grand Cross: Order of Merit, Austria, 1980; Order of Merit, Malta, 1987; Order of Pius IX, Holy See, 1988. *Publications:* La Diplomazia dalle origini al XVII secolo, 1944; Verso quale avvenire?, 1958; I Sentieri della Vita, ricordi di un diplomatico, 1990; Scritti di Politica Estera 5 vols 1991–2008; Verso l'Unità Europea, 2008; Alleanza Atlantica, 2009; articles in quarterlies on foreign and defence affairs. *Recreations:* sculpture, golf, shooting. *Address:* Largo Olgiata, 15 (49D)–00123 Rome, Italy. *T:* (6) 30888135. *E:* a.cagiati@libero.it.

CAHILL, Frances Rebecca; *see* Gibb, F. R.

CAHILL, Jeremy; *see* Cahill, P. J.

CAHILL, Kevin James Patrick, CBE 2007; Chief Executive, Comic Relief, since 1997 (Deputy Director, 1993–97); *b* 4 March 1952; *s* of James and Jean Cahill; *m* 1975, Shân Jones (marr. diss. 1982); one *s* one *d*; partner, Becky Webb; one *s. Educ:* Manchester Univ. (BA Hons English and Drama); PGCE Liberal Studies; RSA Dip. TEFL. Head of Educn, Nat. Theatre, later Royal Nat. Theatre, 1982–91; Dir of Educn, 1991–92, of Communications, 1992–93, Comic Relief. Patron, Nxt Theatre Co., 1999. Chm., Gate Theatre, 1988–2008. Member: Council, Drama Centre, 1989–92; Bd, Young Vic Theatre, 1993–2001; Adv Cttee, Active Community Unit, 2000–03. Chair, Trinity Coll. London, 1998–2002. Trustee Internat. Broadcasting Trust, 1993–2002; Pres. Bd, America Gives Back (formerly Charity Projects Entertainment Fund), 2007–; Mem. Bd, Malaria No More UK, 2008–12. Chancellor, Nottingham Trent Univ., 2014–. Hon. DLitt Nottingham Trent, 2008 *Recreations:* football (Manchester United supporter), France, food. *Address:* Comic Relief, 89 Albert Embankment, SE1 7TP. *Clubs:* Groucho, Soho House.

CAHILL, (Paul) Jeremy; QC 2002; *b* 28 Jan. 1952; *s* of late Timothy Cahill and Mary (*née* O'Mahony); two *d*; *m* 2011, Bettina Lugge. *Educ:* Ratcliffe Coll., Leicester; Liverpool Univ. (LLB). Called to the Bar, Middle Temple, 1975 (Blackstone Schol.); in practice, 1976–, specialising in planning and environmental law. *Recreations:* conversation, theatre, golf, West Cork, wine, travel, music, reading. *Address:* No. 5 Chambers, Fountain Court, Steelhouse Lane, Birmingham B4 6DR. *T:* (0121) 606 0500. *E:* jc@no5.com. *Clubs:* Royal Automobile Copt Heath Golf.

CAHILL, Sally Elizabeth Mary; QC 2003; **Her Honour Judge Cahill;** a Circuit Judge, since 2004; *b* 12 Nov. 1955; *m* 1981, Patrick Cahill (*d* 2003); two *s* one *d. Educ:* Harrogate Ladies' Coll.; Leeds Univ. (LLB (Hons)). Called to the Bar, Gray's Inn, 1978; an Asst Recorder, 1997–2000; a Recorder, 2000–04. Chm. Leeds Reg., Family Law Bar Assoc., 1994–2004. Special Trustee, Leeds NHS Trust, 2001–09. Gov., Richmond House Sch., 1994–2004. *Recreations:* sailing, ski-ing, golf. *Address:* Leeds Combined Court Centre, 1 Oxford Row, Leeds LS1 3BG.

CAHILL, Teresa Mary; opera and concert singer; *b* 30 July 1944; *d* of Florence and Henry Cahill; *m* 1st, 1971, John Anthony Kiernander (marr. diss. 1978); 2nd, 2005, Robert Louis Alfred Saxton, *qv*. *Educ:* Notre Dame High Sch., Southwark; Guildhall School of Music and Drama; London Opera Centre (LRAM Singing, AGSM Piano). Glyndebourne début, 1969; Covent Garden début, 1970; La Scala Milan, 1976, Philadelphia Opera, 1981, specialising in Mozart, Strauss and Elgar; concerts: all London orchestras; Boston Symphony Orch., Chicago Symphony Orch., Rotterdam Philharmonic Orch., West Deutscher Rundfunk, Warsaw Philharmonic, RAI Turin, Frankfurt Radio Orch.; Promenade concerts; Festivals: Vienna, 1983; Berlin, 1987; Bath, 2000; BBC radio and TV; recordings, incl. Mozart, Strauss, Elgar and Mahler, for all major companies; master classes: Dartington Fest., 1984, 1986; Oxford Univ., 1995–; s'Hertogenbosch Vocal Concours, 1998 (Mem. Internat. Jury), 2000; Peabody

Inst., Baltimore, 1999; Bowdoin Coll., Maine, 2004; recitals and concerts throughout Europe, USA, Far East. Prof., Trinity Coll. of Music, 1992–. Artistic Advr, Nat. Mozart Competition, 1994–2002. Mem. Jury, Kathleen Ferrier Comp., 1988; Adjudicator, 1988–, Music Advr, 2000–, Live Music Now; Adjudicator: Young Concert Artists' Trust, 1989–; annual music comp., Royal Over-Seas League, 1985–89, 1992, 1995, 2000. Gov., Royal Soc. of Musicians, 2000–. Silver Medal, Worshipful Co. of Musicians, 1966; John Christie Award 1970. *Recreations:* cinema, theatre, travel, reading, collecting things, sales from car boots to Sotheby's, photography. *Address:* 65 Leyland Road, SE12 8DW. *W:* www.teresacahill.net. *Club:* Royal Over-Seas League (Hon. Mem.).

CAHN, Sir Albert Jonas, 2nd Bt *cr* 1934; marital, sexual and hypno therapist; *b* 27 June 1924; *s* of Sir Julien Cahn, 1st Bt, and Phyllis Muriel, *d* of A. Wolfe, Bournemouth; *S* father, 1944; *m* 1948, Malka (*d* 2001), *d* of late R. Bluestone; two *s* two *d*. *Educ:* Headmaster's House, Harrow. Dir, Elm Therapy Centre, New Malden, 1983–93. *Recreations:* cricket, horse riding, photography. *Heir:* *s* Julien Michael Cahn [*b* 15 Jan. 1951; *m* 1987, Marilynne Janelle, *d* of Frank Owen Blyth; one *s* one *d*].

CAHN, Sir Andrew (Thomas), KCMG 2009 (CMG 2001); Vice-Chairman, Nomura International plc, since 2011; Chief Executive, UK Trade and Investment, 2006–11; *b* 1 April 1951; *s* of Prof. Robert Wolfgang Cahn, FRS and of Pat (*née* Hanson); *m* 1976, Virginia Zachry Beardshaw, *qv*; two *s* one *d*. *Educ:* Bedales Sch.; Trinity Coll., Cambridge (BA 1st Cl. Hons). MAFF, 1973–77; FCO, 1977–78; Private Sec. to Perm Sec., MAFF, 1978–79; 1st Sec., Office of UK Perm. Repn to EC, FCO, 1982–84, Cabinet of Vice Pres., CEC, 1984–88; Asst Sec., MAFF, 1988–92; Principal Private Secretary to: Chancellor of Duchy of Lancaster, 1992–94; Minister of Agriculture, 1994–95; Dep. Head, European Secretariat, Cabinet Office, 1995–97; Chef de Cabinet to Rt Hon. Neil Kinnock, EC, Brussels, 1997–2000; Dir, Govt and Industry Affairs, British Airways plc, 2000–06; Acting Perm. Sec., BERR, March–May 2009; Mem., Capability Rev. of HM Treasury, 2008–09. Non-executive Director: Cadbury Ltd, 1990–92; Deutsche BA, 2002–04; Huawei Technologies (UK), 2015– (Chm. Audit and Risk Cttee, 2015–; Chm. UK Adv. Bd, 2011–14). Member, Board: Internat. Financial Services Ltd, 2006–08; City (UK), 2011– (Dep. Chm., 2013–; Chm., Internat. Trade and Investment Gp, 2013–); General Dynamics (UK), 2012–; Financial Services, Trade and Investment Board, 2013–15; Start Up Loans Co., 2013–14. Member: Governing Bd, 2008–, Exec. Cttee, 2009–, Inst. for Govt; Adv. Council, Univ. of the Arts, London, 2012–; Assoc. Mem., BUPA, 2012–. Member: Adv. Council to the Duke of York, 2006–11; Adv. Cttee, British Amer. Business Council, 2007–11; Internat. Bd, SOAS, 2010–11; Franchise Bd, Lloyd's of London, 2011–; Internat. Regulatory Strategy Gp, Corp. of London, 2011–; Internat. Adv. Bd, Asia House, 2011–; Bd, Japan Soc., 2011–14; Adv. Bd, Business for a New Europe, 2011–. Sen. Responsible Officer, UK Participation in Shanghai Expo 2010, 2010. Gov., Bedales Sch., 1993–98. Chm., WWF (UK), 2014–; Trustee: Gatsby Charitable Foundn, 1996–; Royal Botanic Gardens, Kew, 2002–08 (Chm., Audit Cttee, 2004–08); Arvon Foundn, 2011–15. FRSA 1979. *Recreations:* family, reading, long distance walks, golf, tending an allotment. *Address:* Nomura International, One Angel Lane, EC4R 3AB. *E:* andrew.cahn@nomura.com. *Clubs:* Royal Automobile; Hampstead Golf; St Cyr (Poitiers).

CAHN, Virginia Zachry; *see* Beardshaw, V. Z.

CAIE, Andrew John Forbes; HM Diplomatic Service, retired; Senior Adviser (Brunei), QinetiQ Ltd UK, since 2011; *b* 25 July 1947; *s* of Norman Forbes Caie and Joan Margaret Caie (*née* Wise); *m* 1976, Kathie-Anne Williams; one *s* one *d*. *Educ:* St Dunstan's Coll., Catford; Sidney Sussex Coll., Cambridge (MA). Joined FCO, 1969; Manila, 1976–80; FCO, 1980–84; Dep. Head of Mission, Bogotá, 1984–88; FCO, 1988–93; Dep. High Comr, Islamabad, 1993–96; FCO Resident Chair, CSSB, 1996–97; FCO, 1997–98; Ambassador to Guatemala, 1998–2001; High Comr, Brunei, 2002–05. Exec. Sen. Advr, SE Asia, CfBT Educn Trust, 2006–08; Executive Director: CfBT Educn Malaysia, 2007–08; Study Tracks Gp Sdn Bhd Malaysia, 2009–11; Dir, HR Develt and Assessment, L,S&A Sdn Bhd, Brunei Darussalam, 2010–14. *E:* ac@qinetiq.co.

CAIE, Prof. Graham Douglas, CBE 2015; PhD; FRSE; FEA; Professor of English Language, 1990–2012, and Clerk of Senate and Vice-Principal, 2008–12, University of Glasgow, now Professor Emeritus and Professorial Research Fellow, since 2012; a Vice President, Royal Society of Edinburgh, since 2012; *b* Aberdeen, 3 Feb. 1945; *s* of William and Adeline Caie; *m* 1972, Ann Pringle Abbott; one *s* one *d*. *Educ:* Aberdeen Grammar Sch.; Aberdeen Univ. (MA Hons English); McMaster Univ. (MA, PhD 1973). Amanuensis and Lektor, English Dept, 1972–90, Chm., Medieval Centre, 1984–88, Univ. of Copenhagen; University of Glasgow: Hd, Dept of English Lang., 1992–96; Hd of Sch., 1994–98; Associate Dean (Res.), Arts Faculty, 2005–08. Lead Assessor, Teaching Quality Assessment (Scotland), 1996–98. Member, Panel: RAE (English) 2001 and 2008; AHRC, 2005–08. Dep. Chm., Bd of Trustees, 1998–2014, Mem. Governance Cttee, 2014–, Nat. Liby of Scotland. Chairman: Christie's Jt Educn Bd, 2002–; Jt Liaison Bd, Glasgow Sch. of Art and Glasgow Univ., 2008–12, Scottish Agric. Coll. and Glasgow Univ., 2008–12. Senate Assessor, Court, Univ. of Glasgow, 1998–2003; Mem. Court, Queen Margaret Univ., 2014–; Mem. Bd, All European Acads, 2014–. Chairman: Swedish Res. Council Linnaeus Res. Grants, 2007–08; Evaluation Panel, English Studies in Denmark, 1998–99; Assessment of Res. in Mod. Langs, Univs of Helsinki, Oulu and Tampere, (periodically) 2000–10. Vice-Pres., Scottish Text Soc., 1998–; Mem. Council, Dictionary of Older Scottish Tongue, 1990–2000. Member: Erasmus Consultative Gp, British Council, 2011–; Bd, Glasgow Student Villages, 2008–12; Univ. of Glasgow Trust, 2008–12; Faculty of Advocates Abbotsford Collection Trust, 2011–; Internat. Cttee, 2008–, Foundn, 2010–, RSE. Hon. Sec., Eur. Soc. for Study of English, 1998–2002. Founding FEA 2000; FRSE 2004; Fellow, Japan Soc. of Medieval English, 2012. FRSA 1997. Hon. Fellow, Glasgow Univ. Liby, 2012. *Publications:* The Judgement Day Theme in Old English Poetry, 1976; Bibliography of Junius XI Manuscript, 1979; The Old English "Judgement Day II": a critical edition, 2000; (ed jtly) The Power of Words, 2007; (ed jtly) Medieval Texts in Context, 2008; contrib. articles on medieval lang., lit., manuscript studies. *Recreations:* reading, travel. *Address:* Senate Office, University of Glasgow, Glasgow G12 8QQ. *T:* (0141) 943 1192.

CAIGER-SMITH, Frances Mary; *see* Morris, F. M.

CAILLARD, Air Vice-Marshal (Hugh) Anthony, CB 1981; retired 1982; Director General, Britain-Australia Society, and Hon. Secretary, Cook Society, 1982–89; *b* 16 April 1927; *s* of late Col Felix Caillard, MC and Bar (mentioned in despatches), and Mrs Monica Y. Caillard; *m* 1957, Margaret-Ann Crawford, Holbrook, NSW, Australia; four *s*. *Educ:* Downside; Oriel Coll., Oxford. Joined RAF 1945; flying trng, 1946; Cranwell, 1947–49; served, 1949–65: 13 Sqdn, Egypt; ADC to C-in-C MEAF, and to AOC-in-C Tech. Trng Comd; 101 Sqdn, Binbrook; RAAF No 2 Sqdn; 49 Sqdn (Sqdn Ldr) and 90 Sqdn; RN Staff Coll.; HQ Bomber Comd (Wg Comdr); OC 39 Sqdn, Malta, 1965–67; Jt Services Staff Coll., 1967; Planning Staffs, MoD, 1967–70; Asst Air Attaché, Washington (Gp Captain), 1970–73; OC Marham, 1974–75; Def. Intell. Staff (Air Cdre), 1975–79; Dep. Chief of Staff, Ops and Intelligence, HQ Allied Air Forces, Central Europe, 1979–82. Specialist Air Advr, H of C Defence Cttee, 1985–92. Chairman: Ex Forces Fellowship Centre, 1987–93; Ex Services Mental Welfare Soc., 1990–93; Member: Grants and Appeals Cttee, RAF Benevolent Fund, 1987–93; Britain-Australia Bicentennial Cttee, 1984–88; Council, British Atlantic Cttee, 1988–92; Lord Mayor of Sydney's Sister City Cttee, 1994–2011; Trustee, Australian Arts Foundn, 1985–89. *Address:* 58 Hilltop Road, Clareville, NSW 2107, Australia. *Club:* Royal Air Force.

CAIN; *see* Nall-Cain, family name of Baron Brocket.

CAIN, James Crookall, FCA; Speaker, House of Keys, Isle of Man, 1991–96; Deputy President of Tynwald, 1992–96; *b* Douglas, IOM, 19 March 1927; *s* of James Mylchreest Cain, OBE, JP, formerly MHK and Jean (*née* Crookall); *m* 1959, Muriel Duckworth; two *d*. *Educ:* King William's Coll., IOM. Nat. Service, 1945–48, SSC, E Lancs, 1946. Qualified as Chartered Accountant with W. H. Walker & Co. (Liverpool), 1953; returned to Douglas office, 1954; Partner, 1959–71; Pannell Kerr Forster, 1971–86: Sen. IOM Partner, 1974; retd 1986. Mem., House of Keys, 1986–96; Member: Treasury, 1986–88; Dept of Highways Posts & Properties, 1989; Minister for Health and Social Security, 1989–91. Pres., Hospice Care, 1990 (Chm., 1983–89). *Recreations:* walking, reading. *Address:* Maughold, Alexander Drive, Douglas, Isle of Man IM2 3QX. *T:* (01624) 675068.

CAIN, Hon. John; MLA (Lab) for Bundoora, 1976–92; Premier of Victoria, 1982–90; Professorial Associate, School of Social and Political Science (formerly Department of Political Science), University of Melbourne, since 1991; *b* 26 April 1931; *s* of late Hon. John Cain; *m* 1955, Nancye Williams; two *s* one *d*. *Educ:* Melbourne Univ. (LLB). Practised as barrister and solicitor. Mem., Law Reform Commn, 1975–77. Pres., Law Inst. of Victoria, 1972–73 (Treasurer, 1969–70; Chm. of Council, 1971–72); Mem. Exec., Law Council of Australia, 1973–76. Vice-Chm., Vic Br., Australian Labor Party, 1973–75; Mem., Parly Labor Exec., 1977–90; Leader, State Labor Party, 1981–90; Leader of Opposition, 1981–82; Minister: for Fed. Affairs, 1982; for Women's Affairs, 1982–90; Attorney-General of Vic, 1982–83. Commonwealth Observer, S African elecns, Apr. 1994. Member: Academic Adv. Bd, Faculty of Business and Law, Deakin Univ., 2004–; Liby Bd of Victoria, 2005–12 (Pres., 2006–12). Chm., Learning Adv. Bd, Hume Global Village, 2004–14. Trustee, LUCRF Community Partnership Trust, 2010–. Trustee, Melbourne Cricket Ground, 1982–98, 1999–2013; Member: Nat. Tennis Centre (Flinders Park), 1990–94; Melbourne and Olympic Parks Trust, 2005–13. Pres., Grad. Union, Melbourne Univ., 2005–11. *Publications:* John Cain's Years: power, parties and politics, 1994; On with the Show, 1998; (with John Hewitt) Off Course: from public place to marketplace at Melbourne University, 2004. *Address:* 9 Magnolia Road, Ivanhoe, Vic 3079, Australia.

CAIN, Steven Anthony; Chief Executive Officer Supermarkets, Metcash Ltd, since 2015; *b* 30 Sept. 1964; *s* of Peter and Patricia Cain; *m* 1993; two *s* one *d*. *Educ:* Imperial Coll., London (MEng Chem. Engrg); Harvard; London Business Sch. Consultant, Bain & Co., 1987–89; Gp Develt Manager, Kingfisher plc, 1989–92; Asda plc: Mktg Controller, 1992–94; Grocery Trading Dir, 1994–95; Store Develt Dir, 1995–97; Mktg Dir, 1997–99; Chief Exec., Carlton Communications, 1999–2000; Co-Founder and Dir, GoinGreen, 2002–12; Gp Man. Dir, Coles Myer Ltd, 2003–05; Dir, Pacific Equity Partners, 2005–11; non-executive Director: Godfreys, 2006–; ARW, 2007–; Borders (Australia), 2008. Mem., Young Global Leaders, World Econ. Forum, 2005. *Recreations:* golf, tennis, soccer. *Clubs:* Groucho; National Golf, Kooyong Tennis.

CAIN, His Honour Thomas William, CBE 2003; QC 1989; HM First Deemster and Clerk of the Rolls, Isle of Man, 1998–2003; *b* 1 June 1935; *s* of late James Arthur Cain and Mary Edith Cunningham Cain (*née* Lamb); *m* 1961, Felicity Jane, *d* of late Rev. Arthur Stephen Gregory; two *s* one *d*. *Educ:* King's College Choir Sch., Cambridge; Marlborough Coll.; Worcester Coll., Oxford (BA 1958, MA 1961). National Service, 2nd Lieut RAC, 1953–55. Called to the Bar, Gray's Inn, 1959; Advocate, Manx Bar, 1961. Attorney-General, Isle of Man, 1980–93; Second Deemster, 1993–98. Pres., I of M Law Soc., 1985–89. Convener, first meeting of Law Officers, Small Commonwealth Jurisdictions, I of M, 1983. Hon. Fellow, Soc. for Advanced Legal Studies, 2000. Tynwald Medal of Honour, I of M, 2011; Reih Bleeaney Vanannan, Culture Vannin, 2015. *Recreations:* sailing, Manx Wildlife Trust (Chm., 1973–2010; Christopher Cadbury Medal, 2010). *Address:* Ivie Cottage, Kirk Michael, Isle of Man IM6 1AU. *T:* (01624) 878266.

CAINE, Sir Michael, Kt 2000; CBE 1992; actor; *b* Old Kent Road, London, 14 March 1933; (Maurice Joseph Micklewhite); *s* of late Maurice and of Ellen Frances Marie Micklewhite; *m* 1st, 1955, Patricia Haines (marr. diss.); one *d*; 2nd, 1973, Shakira Baksh; one *d*. *Educ:* Wilson's Grammar Sch., Peckham. Began acting in youth club drama gp. Served in Army, Berlin and Korea, 1951–53. Asst Stage Manager, Westminster Rep., Horsham, Sx, 1953; actor, Lowestoft Rep., 1953–55; Theatre Workshop, London, 1955; numerous TV appearances (over 100 plays), 1957–63; *play:* Next Time I'll Sing for You, Arts, 1963; *films:* A Hill in Korea, 1956; How to Murder a Rich Uncle, 1958; Zulu, 1964; The Ipcress File, 1965; Alfie, The Wrong Box, Gambit, 1966; Hurry Sundown, Woman Times Seven, Deadfall, 1967; The Magus, Battle of Britain, Play Dirty, 1968; The Italian Job, 1969; Too Late the Hero, 1970; The Last Valley, Get Carter, 1971; Zee & Co., Kidnapped, Pulp, 1972; Sleuth, 1973; The Black Windmill, Marseilles Contract, The Wilby Conspiracy, 1974; Fat Chance, The Romantic Englishwoman, The Man who would be King, Harry and Walter Go to New York, 1975; The Eagle has Landed, A Bridge Too Far, Silver Bears, 1976; The Swarm, 1977; California Suite, 1978; Ashanti, Beyond the Poseidon Adventure, The Island, Dressed to Kill, 1979; Escape to Victory, 1980; Death Trap, 1981; Jigsaw Man, Educating Rita, The Honorary Consul, 1982; Blame it on Rio, 1984; Water, The Holcroft Covenant, 1985; Hannah and Her Sisters (Academy Award), Half Moon Street, Mona Lisa, 1986; The Fourth Protocol, The Whistle Blower, Surrender, Jaws The Revenge, 1987; Without a Clue, Dirty Rotten Scoundrels, 1989; A Shock to the System, Bullseye, Mr Destiny, 1990; Noises Off, Blue Ice, The Muppet Christmas Carol, 1992; On Deadly Ground, 1993; Bullet to Beijing, 1994; Mandela and de Klerk, 1996; Blood & Wine, Curtain Call, Shadowrun, 1997; The Debtors, 1998; Little Voice, 1999; The Cider House Rules (Academy Award), Quills, Last Orders, Quick Sands, 2000; Miss Congeniality, Shiner, 2001; Last Orders, The Quiet American, Austin Powers in Goldmember, 2002; The Actors, Secondhand Lions, The Statement, 2003; Around the Bend, Batman Begins, Bewitched, 2005; The Weather Man, Children of Men, The Prestige, 2006; Sleuth, 2007; The Dark Knight, Flawless, 2008; Is Anybody There?, Harry Brown, 2009; Inception, 2010; Journey 2: Mysterious Island, 2011; The Dark Knight Rises, 2012; Now You See Me, 2013; Mr Morgan's Last Love, Interstellar, 2014; Kingsman: the Secret Service, 2015; *films for TV:* Jack The Ripper, 1988; Jekyll and Hyde, 1989; World War II: When Lions Roared, 1994. Fellow, BAFTA, 2000. Comdr, Ordre des Arts et des Lettres (France), 2011. *Publications:* Not Many People Know That, 1985; Not Many People Know This Either, 1986; Moving Picture Show, 1988; Acting in Film, 1990; What's It All About (autobiog.), 1992; The Elephant to Hollywood: the autobiography, 2010. *Recreations:* cinema, theatre, travel, gardening. *Address:* 42 M&P Ltd, First Floor, 8 Flitcroft Street, WC2H 8DL.

CAINES, Eric, CB 1993; DPhil; Professor of Health Service Management, Nottingham University, 1993–96; *b* 27 Feb. 1936; *s* of Ernest and Doris Caines; *m* 1st, 1958 (marr. diss. 1984); three *s*; 2nd, 1984, Karen Higgs; two *s*. *Educ:* Rothwell Grammar School, Wakefield; Leeds Univ. (LLB Hons); Oxford Univ. (MA, MSt; DPhil 2011); Dip. Hist. Art, London Univ., 1984; King's Coll. London (MRes 2014). Short Service Commission, RAEC, 1958–61. NCB, 1961–65; BBC, 1965–66; as Principal, Min. of Health, Management Side Sec., General Whitley Council, 1966–70; Sec., NHS Reorganisation Management Arrangements Study, 1970–73; Assistant Sec., DHSS, 1973–77; IMF/World Bank, Washington, 1977–79; Under Sec., DHSS, 1979, Dir, Regl Organisation, 1981–84; Dir,

Personnel and Finance, Prison Dept, Home Office, 1984–87; Dir, Operational Strategy, DHSS, then DSS, 1987–90; Dir of Personnel, NHS, DoH, 1990–93. Mem., Sheehy Inquiry into Police Responsibilities and Rewards. Director: Trebor Ltd, 1985–90; Premier Prisons, 1994–98. *Recreation:* history and family. *Club:* Athenæum.

CAINES, Sir John, KCB 1991 (CB 1983); Permanent Secretary, Department for Education (formerly of Education and Science), 1989–93; *b* 13 Jan. 1933; *s* of late John Swinburne Caines and Ethel May Stenlake; *m* 1963, Mary Large (*d* 2008); one *s* two *d*. *Educ:* Sherborne Prep. Sch.; Westminster Sch.; Christ Church, Oxford (MA). Asst Principal, Min. of Supply, 1957; Asst Private Sec., Min. of Aviation, 1960–61; Principal, Min. of Aviation, 1961–64; Civil Air Attaché in Middle East, 1964–66; Manchester Business Sch., 1967; Asst Sec., BoT, 1968; Sec., Commn on Third London Airport, 1968–71; Asst Sec., DTI, 1971–72; Principal Private Sec. to Sec. of State for Trade and Industry, 1972–74; Under-Sec., Dept of Trade, 1974–77; Sec., 1977–80, Mem. and Dep. Chief Exec., 1979–80, NEB; Dep. Sec., Dept of Trade, and Chief Exec., BOTB, 1980–82; Dep. Sec., Central Policy Review Staff, Cabinet Office, 1983; Dep. Sec., DTI, 1983–87; Permanent Sec., ODA, FCO, 1987–89. Director: Investors Compensation Scheme, 1993–2001 (Dep. Chm., 1997–2001); Norsk Hydro (UK) Ltd, 1994–2000; Medical Defence Union, 1998–2004; Chm., European Capital, 1995–2000. Mem., Gibraltar Financial Services Commn, 1995–2002. Ind. Reviewer for ASA, 1999–2009. Member of Council: Southampton Univ., 1993–2000; Open Univ., 1993–2001 (Chm., Audit Cttee, 1993–2001). Chm., Dr Busby's Trustees, Westminster Sch., 2002–12. DUniv Open, 1993. *Address:* Flat A32 Parliament View Apartments, 1 Albert Embankment, SE1 7XH.

CAINES, Michael Andrew, MBE 2006; Head Chef: Gidleigh Park, since 1994; Bath Priory, since 2008; Director and Operational Partner, Andrew Brownsword Hotels Ltd (ABode Hotels), since 2003; *b* Exeter, 3 Jan. 1969; *s* of Peter and Mary Caines; *m* Zoe Szypillo; one *s* two *d*. *Educ:* Exeter Catering Coll. (Student of Year 1987). Chef: Grosvenor Hse Hotel, Park Lane, 1987–89; Le Manoir aux Quat'Saisons, 1989–92; work in France, 1992–94; founded Michael Caines Restaurants, 2000; opened Michael Caines at Royal Clarence, Exeter, 2000, at Bristol Marriott Royal Hotel, 2003. Hon. LLD St Loyes Sch. of Health Scis, 2004. Chef of Year, Independent, 1994; 2nd Michelin Star for Gidleigh Park, 1999; Chef of Year, Cateys Awards, 2002; AA Chefs Chef of Year, 2007. *Address:* Gidleigh Park, Chagford, Devon TQ13 8HH. *T:* (01392) 223625.

CAIO, Francesco; Chief Executive, Poste Italiane, since 2014; *b* 23 Aug. 1957; *m* 1986, Meryl Wakefield; two *s*. *Educ:* Politecnico of Milan (Master Computer Sci. 1980); Insead, France (Luca Braito Schol.; MBNA 1985). Product Manager, Telecom Systems, Olivetti SpA, 1982–84; McKinsey & Co., London, 1986–91; Olivetti SpA, 1991; founder and CEO, Omnitel Pronto Italia SpA, 1993–96; CEO, Olivetti SpA, Ivrea, 1996; CEO, Merloni Elettrodomestici SpA, 1997–2000; founder and CEO, Netscalibur Co., 2000–03; CEO, Cable and Wireless plc, 2003–06; Vice-Chm., Europe, 2006–08, Chm., European Adv. Bd, 2007–08, Lehman Brothers; Vice-Chm., Investment Banking, Europe, Nomura, 2008–11; Chief Exec., Avio Gp, SpA, 2011–13. Non-executive Director: Invensys plc, 2009–13; Indesit Co. SpA, 2010–; Il Sole 24 Ore SpA, 2010–11. *Recreations:* photography, Inter Milan FC, family. *Address:* Poste Italiane, Viale Europa 190, 00144 Rome, Italy.

CAIRD, Most Rev. Donald Arthur Richard; Archbishop of Dublin and Primate of Ireland, 1985–96; *b* Dublin, 11 Dec. 1925; *s* of George Robert Caird and Emily Florence Dreaper, Dublin; *m* 1963, Nancy Ballantyne, *d* of Prof. William Sharpe, MD, and Gwendolyn Hind, New York, USA; one *s* two *d*. *Educ:* Wesley Coll., Dublin, 1935–44; Trinity Coll., Dublin Univ., 1944–50. Sen. Exhibn, TCD, 1946; elected Schol. of the House, TCD, 1948; 1st cl. Moderatorship in Mental and Moral Science, 1949; Prizeman in Hebrew and Irish Language, 1946 and 1947; Lilian Mary Luce Memorial Prize for Philosophy, 1947; BA 1949; MA and BD 1955; HDipEd 1959. Curate Asst, St Mark's. Dundela, Belfast, 1950–53; Chaplain and Asst Master, Portora Royal Sch., Enniskillen, 1953–57; Lectr in Philosophy, University Coll. of St David's, Lampeter, 1957; Rector, Rathmichael Parish, Shankill, Co. Dublin, 1960–69; Asst Master, St Columba's Coll., Rathfarnham, Co. Dublin, 1960–67; Dept Lectr in Philosophy, Trinity Coll., Dublin, 1962–63; Lectr in the Philosophy of Religion, Church of Ireland Theol Coll., Dublin, 1964–70; Dean of Ossory, 1969–70; Bishop of Limerick, Ardfert and Aghadoe, 1970–76; Bishop of Meath and Kildare, 1976–85. Fellow of St Columba's Coll., Dublin, 1971. Vis. Prof., Gen. Theol Seminary of ECUSA, 1997. Mem., Bord na Gaeilge, 1974; Hon. Life Mem., Royal Dublin Soc., 1996. Hon. DD TCD, 1988; Hon. LLD: NCEA, 1993; NUI, 1995; Hon. PhD Pontifical Univ., St Patrick's Coll., Maynooth, 2002. *Publications:* The Predicament of Natural Theology since the Criticism of Kant, in Directions, 1970 (Dublin); *relevant publication:* Donald Caird: Church of Ireland Bishop, Gaelic Churchman, by Aonghus Dwane, 2014. *Recreations:* swimming, tennis, walking. *Address:* 3 Crofton Avenue, Dun Laoghaire, Co. Dublin, Ireland.

CAIRD, Prof. George, FRAM; oboist, since 1970; Artistic Director, Codarts Classical Music, Rotterdam, since 2011; *b* 30 Aug. 1950; *s* of late Rev. Dr George Bradford Caird, FBA, and Viola Mary Caird (*née* Newport); *m* 1st, 1974, Sarah Dorothy Verney (marr. diss. 1999); three *s* one *d*; 2nd, 2001, Jane Amanda Salmon; one *d*. *Educ:* Magdalen Coll. Sch., Oxford; Royal Acad. of Music (LRAM 1972; FRAM 1989); Peterhouse, Cambridge (MA). ARCM 1972; FRCM 1999. Hd, Woodwind and Orchestral Studies, RAM, 1987–93; Prof. and Principal, Birmingham Conservatoire, 1993–2010, now Emeritus Prof., Birmingham Sch. of Acting, 2006–08, UCE, later Birmingham City Univ. Orchestral musician, notably with Acad. of St Martin-in-the-Fields, 1983–93; chamber musician, notably with Albion Ensemble, Caird Oboe Quartet. Has made recordings. Sec., Fedn of British Conservatoires, 1998–2003; Sec.-Gen., Assoc. of Eur. Conservatoires, 2004–10. Chairman: Music Educn Council, 2001–04; Nat. Assoc. of Youth Orchestras, 2005–10. Mem. Regl Cttee, Arts Council W Midlands, 2002–04. President: ISM, 2004–05; Barbirolli Internat. Oboe Fest. and Competition, 2008–; Chm., ARD Internat. Munich Flute Competition, 2010, Wind Quintet Competition, 2014; Music Advr, Wingate Foundn, 2010–11; Chm., Music Panel, Sir James Caird Travelling Scholarship Trust, 2013–. Second Vice-Pres., Internat. Double Reed Soc., 2006–09 (Dir, Conference, Birmingham, 2009). Trustee: Symphony Hall Birmingham, 1998–2011; G. B. Caird Meml Trust, 2002–; Youth Music, 2004–11; Countess of Munster Musical Trust, 2007–; Chm., Schubert Ensemble Trust, 2015–. Bd Mem., Culture W Midlands (formerly W Midlands Life), 2003–09. Director: New Generation Arts Fest., Birmingham, 2005–10; Boulez in Birmingham Fest., 2008; Internat. Double Reed Soc. Conf., 2009. President: Royal Acad. Music Club, 2007–08; Birmingham Conservatoire Assoc., 2012–. FRSA 1994. FRCM 1999; FRNCM 2004; Hon. FLCM 1999; Hon. FBC 2010. *Publications:* contrib. articles to music and music educn jls. *Recreations:* reading, theatre, languages, travel, fell-walking. *Address:* 77 Oxford Road, Moseley, Birmingham B13 9SG. *W:* www.georgecaird.co.uk.

See also J. N. Caird.

CAIRD, John Newport; director, writer and producer of plays, opera and musical theatre; Hon. Associate Director, Royal Shakespeare Company, since 1990; Principal Guest Director, Royal Dramatic Theatre, Stockholm, since 2009; *b* 22 Sept. 1948; *s* of late Rev. George Bradford Caird, DPhil, DD, FBA and Viola Mary Newport, MA; *m* 1st, 1972, Helen Frances Brammer (marr. diss. 1982); 2nd, 1982, Ann Dorszynski (marr. diss. 1990); two *s* one *d*; 3rd, 1990, Frances Ruffelle (marr. diss. 1997); one *s* one *d*; 4th, 1998, Maoko Imai; one *s* two *d*. *Educ:* Selwyn House Sch., Montreal; Magdalen Coll. Sch., Oxford; Bristol Old Vic Theatre Sch. Associate Dir, Contact Theatre, Manchester, 1974–76; directed, Contact: Games, After Liverpool, Krapp's Last Tape, Look Back in Anger, Downright Hooligan, Twelfth Night; Jt founder and Dir, Circle of Muses, touring music theatre troupe, 1976; Director: Regina v. Stephens, Avon Touring Th. Co.; Last Resort, Sidewalk Th. Co., 1976; Resident Dir 1977–82, Associate Dir, 1983–90, RSC; directed, RSC: Dance of Death, 1977; Savage Amusement, Look Out, Here Comes Trouble, (co-dir, with Howard Davies) The Adventures of Awful Knawful, 1978; Caucasian Chalk Circle, 1979; (co-dir, with Trevor Nunn) Nicholas Nickleby, London, New York and Los Angeles, 1980, 1982, 1986 (SWET Award, 1980, Tony Award, 1982, for Best Dir; televised, 1981, Emmy Award, 1983); Naked Robots, Twin Rivals, 1981; Our Friends in the North, 1982; Peter Pan (adapted and co-dir with Trevor Nunn), 1982–84; Twelfth Night, Romeo and Juliet, 1983; The Merchant of Venice, Red Star, 1984; Philistines, 1985; Les Misérables (adapted and co-dir with Trevor Nunn), London, 1985 and worldwide, 1985– (Tony Award for Best Dir, 1987); Every Man in his Humour, Misalliance, 1986; A Question of Geography, The New Inn, 1987; As You Like It, A Midsummer Night's Dream, 1989; Columbus and the Discovery of Japan, Antony and Cleopatra, 1992; directed, RNT: Trelawny of the 'Wells', 1993; The Seagull, 1994; Stanley, 1996, NY, 1997 (Outer Critics Circle Award for Best Dir); Peter Pan, 1997; Money, Candide (a new version with music by Leonard Bernstein), 1999 (Olivier Award, 2000); Hamlet, 2000 (world tour, 2001); Humble Boy, 2001, transf. Gielgud, 2002, NY, 2003, UK tour, 2003; Chain Play, 2001. Director: Song and Dance, London, 1982; As You Like It, Stockholm, 1984 (also for TV, 1985); Zaïdé by Mozart, Battignano, 1991; Life Sentences, NY, 1993; The Millionairess (UK tour), 1995; Murder in the Red Barn, Tiller-Clowes Marionettes, Theatre Mus., 1999; Midsummer Night's Dream, 2000, Twelfth Night, 2002, Stockholm; What the Night is For, 2002, Rattle of a Simple Man, 2004, Comedy Th.; Becket, Th. Royal, Haymarket, The Screams of Kitty Genovese, NY, 2004; Macbeth, Almeida, 2005; Don Carlos, WNO, 2005; The Beggar's Opera, Tokyo and Osaka, 2006–08 (televised 2006); Dödsdansen, Stockholm, 2007 (televised 2007); A Midsummer Night's Dream, Tokyo, 2007, 2009; Don Carlos, Canadian Opera Co., Toronto, 2007; Aida, WNO, 2008; Private Lives, Tokyo, 2008; Merry Wives of Windsor, Stockholm, 2009; Tosca, Houston Grand Opera, 2010, LA, 2013, Chicago, 2015; Candide, Tokyo, 2010; The Tempest (Stormen), Stockholm, 2010; Romeo and Juliet, Stockholm, 2011; Don Giovanni, WNO, 2011; Don Carlos, La Bohème, Houston Grand Opera, 2012; La Bohème, Canadian Opera Co., 2013, San Francisco Opera, 2014; Parsifal, Chicago Lyric Opera, 2013; Gertrud, Stockholm, 2014; Twelfth Night, Tokyo, 2015; McQueen, St James Th., 2015. Devised and directed: Intimate Letters (a series of concerts for actors and string quartet); At Home in the World (charity concert), Tohoku and Tokyo, 2014; staged: WWF Religion and Interfaith Ceremony, Assisi, 1986; WWF Sacred Gifts for a Living Planet Ceremony, Bakhtapur, Nepal, 2000; wrote and directed: The Kingdom of the Spirit, London, 1986; Siegfried & Roy at the Mirage, Las Vegas, 1989; Children of Eden, a musical drama (with music and lyrics by Stephen Schwartz), London, 1991, and worldwide, 1991–; The Beggar's Opera (a new version with music by Ilona Sekacz), RSC and worldwide, 1992–; Jane Eyre, a musical drama (music by Paul Gordon), Canada and USA, 1995–, Tokyo, 2009, 2012; Daddy Long Legs, a musical romance (music by Paul Gordon), 2004, Ventura, Palo Alto, Cincinnati and N American tour, 2009–12 (LA Ovation Award, 2011), Tokyo, 2012, 2014, transf. St James Th., 2012; Twin Spirits, Royal Opera Hse Gala, 2005, New Victory Th., NY, Windsor Castle, Salisbury Cath., Cortona Fest., and worldwide (televised 2008); Kinshu (with Kiyomi Fujii), Tokyo, 2007 (Japan Maj. Theatres Award, 2008), 2009; wrote: Brief Encounter, opera (with music by André Previn), 2007 (première, Houston Grand Opera, 2009); Little Miss Scrooge (with Paul Gordon and Sam Caird), Ventura, 2012; adapted and dir., Henry IV (BBC TV), 1995. Produced: (with Holly Kendrick) Fortnight of New Writing and Directing, Caird Co., Highgate, 2001; Observe the Sons of Ulster Marching Towards the Somme, Playing Soldiers, Pleasance Th., 2002; Disintegration, Arcola Th., 2002; New British Plays, Jerwood Space, 2002; Northern Lights, Soho Th., 2002; Robin Hood, NT, 2002; Five Corners, Jerwood Centre, 2003; Theatre Café, Arcola Th., 2004; Arab-Israeli Cookbook, Gate Th., 2004; Cancer Time, Theatre 503, New Directions, Th. Royal, Haymarket, 2004. Recordings: Beggar's Opera; Children of Eden; Les Miserables; Jane Eyre; Candide; Daddy Long Legs; Brief Encounter. Trustee: G. B. Caird Meml Trust, 1990–; Friends of Highgate Cemetery Trust Ltd, 1999–; Angus Lindsay Trust, 2000–; Mustardseed Trust (formerly Georgeville Trust), 2001–. Internat. Advr, Ashinaga Ikueikai, 2012–. Hon. FRWCMD. Hon. Fellow, Mansfield Coll., Oxford, 2000. Hon. DLitt UEA, 2006. *Publications:* (with Trevor Nunn) Peter Pan, by J. M. Barrie (new versions), 1993, 1998; (with Stephen Schwartz) Children of Eden, 1996; The Beggar's Opera (new version, with Ilona Sekacz), 1999; Candide (new version, with music by Leonard Bernstein), 2003; (with Paul Gordon) Jane Eyre, 2003; Theatre Craft: a director's practical companion from A–Z, 2010; (with André Previn) Brief Encounter, 2011. *Recreations:* music, birds, mountains. *Address:* Church House, 10 South Grove, Highgate, N6 6BS.

See also G. Caird.

CAIRNCROSS, Dame Frances (Anne), (Dame Frances McRae), DBE 2015 (CBE 2004); Rector, Exeter College, University of Oxford, 2004–14; Chairman, Economic and Social Research Council, 2001–07; *b* 30 Aug. 1944; *d* of Sir Alexander Kirkland Cairncross, KCMG, FBA and late Mary Frances (*née* Glynn); *m* 1971, Hamish McRae, *qv*; two *d*. *Educ:* Laurel Bank Sch., Glasgow; St Anne's Coll., Oxford (MA History; Hon. Fellow 1993); Brown Univ., Rhode Island (MAEcon). On Staff of: The Times, 1967–69; The Banker, 1969; The Observer, 1970–73; Economics Correspondent, 1973–81, Women's Page Editor, 1981–84, The Guardian; The Economist: Britain Ed., 1984–89; Envmt Ed., 1989–94; Media Ed., 1994–97; Public Policy Ed., 1997–98; Mgt Ed., 1999–2004. Member: SSRC Economics Cttee, 1972–76; Newspaper Panel, Monopolies Commn, 1973–80; Council, Royal Economic Soc., 1980–85; Council, PSI, 1987–90; Cttee of Inquiry into Proposals to Amend the Shops Act, 1983–84; Inquiry into British Housing, 1984–85; School Teachers Review Body, 1991–94; Council, Inst. for Fiscal Studies, 1995–2001, 2007– (Chm., Exec. Cttee, 2008–); Scottish Council of Econ. Advrs, 2007–11; Adv. Bd, Foundn for Effective Governance, Ukraine, 2007–13. Director: Prolific Gp plc, 1988–89; Alliance & Leicester Gp plc (formerly Alliance & Leicester Building Soc.), 1990–2004; Stramongate Ltd, 2005–11. Pres., BAAS, 2005–06 (Hon. Fellow, 2006). Gov., NIESR, 1995–2001. Vis. Fellow, Nuffield Coll., Oxford, 2001–04. Hon. Treas., Nat. Council for One Parent Families, 1980–83; Trustee, Kennedy Memorial Trust, 1974–90; Chm., Develt Trust, Natural History Mus., 2015–. Chm. Court, Heriot-Watt Univ., 2015–. High Sheriff, Greater London, 2004–05. Founding Fellow, Inst. of Contemporary Scotland, 2000; FRSE 2003. Hon. Fellow: St Peter's Coll., Oxford, 2003; Cardiff Univ., 2004. Hon. Life FRSA, 2006. Hon. DLitt: Glasgow, 2001; Loughborough, 2003; Hon. DSc: Birmingham, 2002; City, 2003; Bristol, 2004; TCD, 2005; Hon. DPhil London Metropolitan, 2004; Hon. DBA Kingston, 2005; DUniv York, 2011. European Women of Achievement Award, 2002 (Awards Pres., 2007–09). *Publications:* Capital City (with Hamish McRae), 1971; The Second Great Crash (with Hamish McRae), 1973; The Guardian Guide to the Economy, 1981; Changing Perceptions of Economic Policy, 1981; The Second Guardian Guide to the Economy, 1983; Guide to the Economy, 1987; Costing the Earth, 1991; Green, Inc., 1995; The Death of Distance, 1997; The Company of the Future, 2002. *Recreation:* home life. *Address:* 6 Canonbury Lane, N1 2AP.

CAIRNS, family name of **Earl Cairns**.

CAIRNS, 6th Earl *cr* 1878; **Simon Dallas Cairns,** CVO 2000; CBE 1992; Baron Cairns 1867; Viscount Garmoyle 1878; Chairman, Charities Aid Foundation, 2003–10; *b* 27 May 1939; *er s* of 5th Earl Cairns, GCVO, CB and Barbara Jeanne Harrison, *y d* of Sydney H. Burgess; *S* father, 1989; *m* 1964, Amanda Mary, *d* of late Major E. F. Heathcoat Amory, and Mrs Roderick Heathcoat Amory; three *s*. *Educ:* Eton; Trinity Coll., Cambridge. Man. Dir, 1981–84, a Vice-Chm., 1984–86, Mercury Securities plc; S. G. Warburg & Co.: Man. Dir,

1979–85; Dir, 1985–95; a Vice-Chm., 1985–87; Jt Chm., 1987–91; Chief Exec. and Dep. Chm., 1991–95; Chairman: Commonwealth Develt Corp., subseq. CDC Gp plc, 1995–2004, subseq. Actis, 2004–05; BAT Industries, 1996–98 (Dir, 1990–98); Allied Zurich, 1998–2000; Vice-Chairman: Zurich Financial Services, 1998–2000; Zurich Allied AG, 1998–2000; Dep. Chm., 2004–07, Chm., 2007–10, Zain Africa (formerly Celtel Internat.) BV; Dir, Fresnillo plc, 2008–14. Receiver-General, Duchy of Cornwall, 1990–2000. Mem., City Capital Markets Cttee, 1989–94. Chairman: VSO, 1981–92; ODI, 1995–2002; Commonwealth Business Council, 1997–2002 (Chm. Emeritus, 2003); Look Ahead Housing and Care, 2003–05. Curator, Oxford Univ. Chest, 1995–2000. Trustee, The Diana Princess of Wales Meml Fund, 1998–2006; Dir, M. Ibrahim Foundn, 2007–; founding Dir, Africa's Voices Foundn, 2014–. *Heir: s* Viscount Garmoyle, *qv*. *Address:* 39 Arundel Gardens, W11 2LW. *Club:* Turf.

CAIRNS, (Agnes Lawrie Addie) Shonaig; *see* Macpherson, A. L. A. S.

CAIRNS, Alun Hugh; MP (C) Vale of Glamorgan, since 2010; Parliamentary Under-Secretary of State, Wales Office, since 2014; a Lord Commissioner of HM Treasury (Government Whip), since 2014; *b* 30 July 1970; *s* of Hewitt and Margaret Cairns; *m* 1996, Emma Elizabeth Turner; one *s*. *Educ:* Ysgol Gyfun Ddwyieithog Ystalyfera; MBA Wales 2001. Joined Lloyds Bank Gp, 1989; Business Develt Consultant, 1992–98, Field Manager, 1998–99, Lloyds TSB (formerly Lloyds Bank). Mem. (C) S Wales W, Nat. Assembly for Wales, 1999–2011; econ. spokesman, 1997–2007; educn spokesman, 2007–08. Contested (C): Gower, 1997; Vale of Glamorgan, 2005. Joined Conservative Party, 1987. *Address:* House of Commons, SW1A 0AA.

CAIRNS, Andrew Ruaraidh A.; *see* Adams-Cairns.

CAIRNS, David Adam; Music Critic, Sunday Times, 1985–92; *b* 8 June 1926; *s* of Sir Hugh William Bell Cairns, KBE, FRCS and Barbara Cairns, *d* of A. L. Smith, sometime Master of Balliol; *m* 1959, Rosemary, *d* of Aubrey and Hilary Goodwin; three *s*. *Educ:* Trinity Coll., Oxford (1st Cl. Mod. History). Nat. Service, Intell. Corps, 1949–50. Co-Founder, Chelsea Opera Gp, 1950; Jane Eliza Procter Fellow, Princeton, 1950–51; Liby Clerk, H of C, 1951–53; TES, 1955–58; Music Critic, Evening Standard, and Spectator, 1958–62; Arts Editor, Spectator, 1961–62; Asst Music Critic, Financial Times, 1962–67; Music Critic, New Statesman, 1967–70; Classical Programme Co-ordinator, Philips Records, 1968–73; freelance music critic, 1973–85; founder and conductor, Thorington Players, 1983. Dist. Vis. Prof., Univ. of California, Davis, 1985; Vis. Scholar, Getty Center for History of Art and Humanities, 1992; Vis. Res. Fellow, Merton Coll., Oxford, 1993. FRSL 2001. Hon. RAM 2000. Hon. DLitt Southampton, 2001. CBE 1997; Commandeur de l'Ordre des Arts et des Lettres, 2013 (Chevalier, 1975; Officier, 1991). *Publications:* The Memoirs of Hector Berlioz (ed and trans.), 1969, 5th edn 2002; Responses: musical essays and reviews, 1973; Berlioz, vol. 1, The Making of an Artist 1803–1832, 1989 (Yorkshire Post Prize; Royal Phil. Soc. Award; Derek Allen Meml Prize, British Acad.; ASCAP Deems Taylor Award, 2001), vol. 2, Servitude and Greatness 1832–1869, 1999 (Whitbread Award for Biography, Royal Phil. Soc. Award, 1999; Samuel Johnson Non-fiction Prize, 2000; Prix de l'Académie Charles Croz, 2003); Mozart and His Operas, 2006; (jtly) English National Opera Guides: The Magic Flute, 1980; Falstaff, 1982. *Recreations:* conducting, Shakespeare, France and the French, cricket. *Address:* 49 Amerland Road, SW18 1QA. *T:* (020) 8870 4931.

CAIRNS, David Seldon; HM Diplomatic Service; Ambassador to Sweden and Director, Nordic Baltic Region, since 2015; *b* Suffern, NY, 17 April 1969; *s* of Dr Robert Lacock Cairns and Vivienne Cairns; *m* 1996, Sharon Anouk Aeberhard; one *s* one *d*. *Educ:* Oundle Sch.; Pembroke Coll., Oxford (MA Oriental Studies 1992). With Nomura Internat., 1992–93; entered FCO, 1993; Desk Officer, Security Policy Dept, FCO, 1993–95; Second Sec., Commercial, Tokyo, 1995–99; Hd, Public Diplomacy, Europe Comd, FCO, 1999–2000; Private Sec. to Ministers for Africa and N Americas, FCO, 2000–02; Hd, WTO Section, Geneva, 2002–06; Dir, Trade and Investment, Tokyo, 2006–10; Dir, Estates and Security, Corporate Services, FCO, 2010–15. Vice-Chm., Japan Soc., 2010–15. Mem., Coton Parish Council, 2010–15. *Recreations:* sport (almost all of them), travel (almost everywhere). *Address:* The Tower House, 5 St Catharine's Hall, Coton, Cambridge CB23 7GU. *T:* (01954) 212481. *E:* David.Cairns@fco.gov.uk. *Club:* Oxford and Cambridge.

CAIRNS, Hugh John Forster, DM; FRS 1974; Professor of Microbiology, Harvard School of Public Health, 1980–91; *b* 21 Nov. 1922; *er s* of Prof. Sir Hugh Cairns, KBE, DM; *m* 1948, Elspeth Mary Foster; two *s* one *d*. *Educ:* Balliol Coll., Oxford Univ. (BA 1943; BM, BCh 1946; DM 1952). Surg. Registrar, Radcliffe Infirmary, Oxford, 1945; Med. Intern, Postgrad. Med. Sch., London, 1946; Paediatric Intern, Royal Victoria Infirmary, Newcastle, 1947; Chem. Pathologist, Radcliffe Infirmary, 1947–49; Virologist, Hall Inst., Melbourne, Aust., 1950–51; Virus Research Inst., Entebbe, Uganda, 1952–54; Research Fellow, then Reader, Aust. Nat. Univ., Canberra, 1955–63; Rockefeller Research Fellow, California Inst. of Technology, 1957; Nat. Insts of Health Fellow, Cold Spring Harbor, NY, 1960–61; Dir, Cold Spring Harbor Lab. of Quantitative Biology, 1963–68; Prof of Biology (Hon.), State Univ. of New York, Stony Brook, 1968–73, Amer. Cancer Soc. Prof. 1968–73; Head of Imperial Cancer Research Fund Mill Hill Laboratories, 1973–80. MacArthur Fellow, 1982. *Address:* 1A Staverton Road, Flat 2 Newlands Court, Oxford OX2 6XH. *T:* (01865) 516927. *E:* j.cairns500@gmail.com.

CAIRNS, Very Rev. John Ballantyne, KCVO 2013; a Chaplain to the Queen, 1997–2013, an Extra Chaplain, since 2013; Dean: Chapel Royal in Scotland, 2005–13; Order of St John Scotland, since 2011; *b* 15 March 1942; *s* of William Cairns and Isobel Margaret (*née* Thom); *m* 1968, Elizabeth Emma Bradley; three *s*. *Educ:* Sutton Valence Sch., Kent; Bristol Univ. (LLB); Edinburgh Univ. (LTh). Messrs Richards, Butler & Co., Solicitors, 1964–68; E Lothian CC, 1968–69; Asst Minister, St Giles, Elgin, 1973–75; ordained, 1974; Minister: Langholm, Ewes and Westerkirk, 1975–85, also linked with Canonbie, 1981–85; Riverside, Dumbarton, 1985–2001; Aberlady and Gullane, 2001–09; Locum Minister, St Columba's Church, London, 2010–12. Moderator, Presbytery of Dumbarton, 1993–94. General Assembly of the Church of Scotland: Convener: Cttee on Maintenance of the Ministry and Bd of Ministry and Mission, 1984–88; Cttee on Chaplains to HM Forces, 1993–98; Chm., Judicial Commn, 1993–98; Chaplain to the Moderator, 1995–96; Moderator, 1999–2000; Chaplain to Lord High Comr (HRH the Duke of York), 2007. Gen. Trustee, Church of Scotland, 1996–. Chaplain, Queen's Body Guard for Scotland, Royal Co. of Archers, 2007–. Pres., Friends of St Andrew's, Jerusalem, 2005–11. Chm. Govs, Compass Sch., Haddington, 2008–15. Hon. DD Aberdeen, 2003; Hon. LLD Bristol, 2004. *Publications:* Keeping Fit for Ministry, 1988; articles in various theol jls. *Recreations:* golf, gardening, Robert Burns. *Address:* Bell House, Roxburghe Park, Dunbar, East Lothian EH42 1LR. *T:* (01368) 862501. *Club:* New (Edinburgh).

CAIRNS, Patricia Rose Marie R.; *see* Roberts Cairns.

CAIRNS, Richard James; Head Master, Brighton College, since 2006; *b* Nairobi, 2 July 1966; *s* of Brian and Christina Cairns. *Educ:* Oratory Sch., Reading; Lady Margaret Hall, Oxford (BA 1st cl. Hons Mod. Hist.; MA). Asst Master, Oratory Sch., Reading, 1989–91; Asst Master, 1991–92, Hd of Hist., 1992–99, Daniel Stewart's and Melville Coll., Edinburgh; Usher, Magdalen College Sch., Oxford, 1999–2005. Dir, Brighton College International Schools Ltd, 2008–. Governor: King's College Sch., Wimbledon, 2009–; Kingsford Community Sch., Beckton, 2009–; Windlesham House Sch., 2009–; London Acad. of Excellence, 2012–; Brighton Coll. Abu Dhabi, 2012–; Brighton Coll. Al Ain, 2013–. FRSA. *Recreations:* medieval history, cinema, African wildlife, politics. *Address:* Headmaster's House, Brighton College, Eastern Road, Brighton BN2 0AL. *T:* (01273) 704339. *E:* headmaster@brightoncollege.net. *Clubs:* East India, Lansdowne.

CAIRNS, Robert; Chairman, East of Scotland Water, 1998–2002; *b* 16 July 1947; *s* of William and Mary Cairns; *m* 1st, 1972, Pauline Reidy (marr. diss. 1995); two *s*; 2nd, 2003, Jean Margaret Smith (*née* Dow). *Educ:* Morgan Acad., Dundee; Univ. of Edinburgh (MA Hons); Moray House Coll. (DipEd). Asst Ed., Scottish Nat. Dictionary, 1969–74; teacher, James Gillespie's High Sch., 1975–96. Mem. (Lab), Edinburgh CC, 1974–2007 (Convener, Planning Cttee, 1986; Exec. Mem. for Envmt and Streets, 2003–07). Contested (Lab) N Edinburgh, Nov. 1973, Feb. 1974. *Recreations:* walking, photography, genealogy. *Address:* Eastergate Cottage, Harrietfield, Logiealmond, Perthshire PH1 3TD.

CAITHNESS, 20th Earl of, *cr* 1455; **Malcolm Ian Sinclair,** PC 1990; FRICS; Lord Berriedale, 1455; Bt 1631; consultant and trustee to various companies and trusts, since 1994; Chief Executive, Clan Sinclair Trust, since 1999; *b* 3 Nov. 1948; *s* of 19th Earl of Caithness, CVO, CBE, DSO, DL, JP; *S* father, 1965; *m* 1st, 1975, Diana Caroline (*d* 1994), *d* of Major Richard Coke, DSO, MC, DL; one *s* one *d*; 2nd, 2004, Leila Jenkins (marr. diss. 2007). *Educ:* Marlborough; Royal Agricl Coll., Cirencester. Savills, land and estate agents, 1972–78; Brown and Mumford, 1978–80; property developer and other small businesses, 1980–84. A Lord in Waiting (Govt Whip), 1984–85; parly spokesman on health and social security, 1984–85, on Scotland, 1984–86; Parly Under-Sec. of State, Dept of Transport, 1985–86; Minister of State: Home Office, 1986–88; DoE, 1988–89; Paymaster Gen. and Minister of State, HM Treasury, 1989–90; Minister of State: FCO, 1990–92; Dept of Transport, 1992–94; elected Mem., H of L, 1999. Dir, 1995–98, Consultant, 1998–2006, Victoria Soames, Residential Property Consultants; Consultant, Rickett-Tinne, 2006–. Trustee, Queen Elizabeth Castle of May Trust, 1996–. *Heir: s* Lord Berriedale, *qv*. *Address:* c/o House of Lords, SW1A 0PW.

CALATRAVA-VALLS, Dr Santiago; architect; *b* Valencia, 28 July 1951; *m* 1976, Robertina Calatrava-Maragoni; three *s*. *Educ:* art sch., Valencia; Escuela Técnica Superior de Arquitectura de Valencia; Swiss Fed. Inst. of Technol., Zürich (studies in civil engrg; Dr Tech. Sci.). Asst, Inst. for Bldg Statics and Construction and for Aerodynamics and Light Weight Constructions, Zürich, 1979–81; Founder: architectural and civil engrg practice, Zürich, 1981; architectural practice, Paris, 1989, and Valencia, 1991. Major projects include: Stadelhofen Rly Stn, Zürich, 1983–90; Lucerne Stn Hall, 1983–89; BCE Place, Toronto, 1987–92; Alamillo Bridge and La Cartuja Viaduct, Seville, 1987–92; Lusitania Bridge, Merida, 1988–91; Montjuic Communication Tower, Barcelona, 1989–92; Lyon Airport Rly Stn, 1989–94; Campo Volantin Footbridge, Bilbao, 1990–97; Alameda Bridge and underground stn, Valencia, 1991–95; Kuwait Pavilion, Expo '92, Seville, 1991–92; Auditorio de Tenerife, 1991–2003; Oriente Rly Stn, Lisbon, 1993–98; Sondica Airport, Bilbao, 2000; Milwaukee Art Mus. expansion, 2001; Olympic Sports Complex, Athens, 2004; Zürich Univ. Law Faculty, 2004; Turning Torso Tower, Malmö, 2005; Petah-Tikva Footbridge, Tel Aviv, 2006; Reggio Emilia Ponti, 2007; Puente de L'Assut d'Or, Valencia, 2008; Quarto Ponte sul Canal Grande, Venice, 2008; Palau de las Arts, Valencia, 2008; Light Rail Train Bridge, Jerusalem, 2008; Liège Guillemins TGV Railway Station, 2009; Samuel Beckett Bridge, Dublin, 2009; New York City Ballet, 2010; World Trade Center Transportation Hub, NY, 2015. Exhibitions of work include: Mus. of Architecture, Basel, 1987; Design Mus., Zürich, 1991; Mus. of Modern Art, NY, 1993; retrospective, RIBA, London, 1992; Deutsches Mus., Munich, 1993; Valencia, Lübeck and Copenhagen, 1993; Florence, 2000. Member: Union of Swiss Architects, 1987; Internat. Acad. of Architecture, 1987; European Acad., 1992. Hon. FRIBA 1993. Hon. Mem., Union of German Architects, 1989. Hon. doctorates include Dr *hc*: Valencia, 1993; Seville, 1994. Numerous international prizes and awards including: Internat. Assoc. for Bridge and Structural Engrg Award, 1988; Gold Medal, IStructE, 1992. *Address:* Parkring 11, 8002 Zürich, Switzerland. *T:* (1) 204500, *Fax:* (1) 2045001.

CALDAS, Prof. Carlos Manuel Simao da Silva, MD; FRCP, FRCPath, FACP, FMedSci; Professor of Cancer Medicine (formerly Clinical Oncology), University of Cambridge, since 2002; Hon. Consultant, Addenbrooke's Hospital, Cambridge, since 1996, Director, Cambridge Breast Cancer Research Unit, since 2008; *b* 27 June 1960; *s* of Carlos da Silva Caldas and Isilda de Jesus Catarino Simão; *m* 1988, Maria Isabel Rebelo de Andrade e Sousa; one *s* one *d*. *Educ:* Univ. of Lisbon (MD 1984). FACP 1999; FRCP 2002; FRCPath 2008. Jun. House Officer, 1985–86, SHO, 1986–88, Santa Maria Univ. Hosp., Lisbon; Resident in Internal Medicine, Univ. of Texas Southwestern Med. Center, Dallas, 1988–91; Fellow in Med. Oncology, Johns Hopkins Univ. and Med. Instns, Baltimore, 1991–94; Sen. Res. Fellow, Chester Beatty Lab., Inst. of Cancer Res., London, 1994–96. FMedSci 2004; Fellow, Eur. Acad. of Cancer Scis, 2010. Dr *hc* Porto, 2014. Officer, Order of St James of the Sword (Portugal), 2009. *Publications:* articles in New England Jl of Medicine, Nature, Nature Genetics, Cell, Cancer Res., Oncogene, Science Translational Medicine, EMBO Molecular Medicine. *Recreations:* supporter of Benfica (the team of Eusebio), lover of Santa Cruz beach, Portugal. *Address:* Functional Breast Cancer Genomics Laboratory, Cancer Research UK Cambridge Research Institute and Department of Oncology, University of Cambridge, Li Ka Shing Centre, Robinson Way, Cambridge CB2 0RE. *T:* (01223) 769648, *Fax:* (01223) 769510. *E:* cc234@cam.ac.uk.

CALDECOTE, 3rd Viscount *cr* 1939, of Bristol, co. Gloucester; **Piers James Hampden Inskip;** Chairman, Tangent Communications, 2005–12; *b* 20 May 1947; *o s* of 2nd Viscount Caldecote, KBE, DSC and Jean Hamilla, *d* of Rear-Adm. H. D. Hamilton; *S* father, 1999; *m* 1st, 1970, Susan Bridget (*née* Mellen); 2nd, 1984, Kristine Elizabeth, *d* of Harvey Holbrooke-Jackson; one *s*. *Educ:* Eton; Magdalene Coll., Cambridge. Gp Exec., Carlton Communications, 1989–2004. *Heir: s* Hon. Thomas James Inskip, *b* 22 March 1985. *Address:* 18 Langside Avenue, SW15 5QT.

CALDECOTT, Andrew Hilary; QC 1994; *b* 22 June 1952; *s* of Andrew Caldecott, CBE and Zita (*née* Belloc); *m* 1977, Rosamond Ashton Shuttleworth; two *s* two *d*. *Educ:* Eton Coll.; New Coll., Oxford (BA Hons Mod. Hist.). Called to the Bar, Inner Temple, 1975, Bencher, 2004. Specialist Advr to Jt Parly Select Cttee on Defamation Bill, 2011. Play: Higher than Babel, Bridewell Theatre, 1999. *Address:* 1 Brick Court, Temple, EC4Y 9BY. *T:* (020) 7353 8845.

CALDECOTT, Benjamin, FRAS, FRGS; Programme Director, Smith School of Enterprise and the Environment, University of Oxford, since 2013 (Visiting Fellow, 2012–13); *b* London, 30 June 1985; *s* of Dr Julian Caldecott and Hong Caldecott (*née* Tan). *Educ:* Sch. of Oriental and African Studies, Univ. of London (BSc Hons Econs); Selwyn Coll., Cambridge (MPhil Chinese Studies and Econs). FRAS 2005; FRGS 2006. Res. Dir, Envmt and Energy, Policy Exchange, 2008–09; Hd of Policy, Climate Change Capital Gp Ltd, 2009–13; Dep. Dir (on secondment), Strategy Directorate, DECC, 2010–11; Hd of Govt Adv., Bloomberg New Energy Finance, 2013–14. Vis. Schol., Peking Univ., 2007. Member, Senior Common Room: Brasenose Coll., Oxford, 2012–14; Oriel Coll., Oxford, 2014–. Sherpa, Green Investment Bank Commn, 2010; Academic Visitor, Bank of England, 2015–. Trustee, Green Alliance, 2010–. Member: Adv. Bd, Carbon Tracker Initiative, 2011–; Socially Responsible Investment Review Cttee, Univ. of Oxford, 2014–. Advr, Prince's Charities' Internat. Sustainability Unit, 2014–. Sir Peter Holmes Meml Award, RSAA, 2005. *Recreations:* travel, scuba diving, opera, fine wine, good company. *Address:* Smith School of Enterprise and the Environment, University of Oxford, South Parks Road, Oxford OX1 3QY. *E:* ben.caldecott@cantab.net. *Club:* Travellers (Mem., Election Cttee, 2008–14).

CALDER, Prof. Andrew Alexander, MD; FRCSE, FRCPGlas, FRCPE, FRCOG; Professor of Obstetrics and Gynaecology, 1987–2009, now Emeritus, and Assistant Principal for Reproductive Health, since 2009, University of Edinburgh; Hon. Consultant Obstetrician and Gynaecologist, 1987–2009, and Scientific Director, Jennifer Brown Research Laboratory, 2004–12, Queen's Medical Research Institute, Royal Infirmary of Edinburgh; *b* 17 Jan. 1945; *s* of Rev. Alastair Scott Calder and Aileen Calder (*née* Alexander); *m* 1972, Valerie Anne Dugard; one *s* two *d*. *Educ:* Glasgow Acad.; Glasgow Univ. Med. Sch. (MB ChB 1968; MD 1978). FRCOG 1984; FRCPGlas 1987; FRCPE 1993; FRCSE 1994. Res. Fellow, Nuffield Dept of Obstetrics and Gynaecology, Univ. of Oxford, 1972–75; Lectr, then Sen. Lectr in Obstetrics and Gynaecology, Univ. of Glasgow, 1975–86; University of Edinburgh: Vice Dean of Medicine, 1998–2003; Hd, Div. of Reproductive and Develtl Scis, 1999–2009; Dir of Quality Assce, Coll. of Medicine and Vet. Medicine, 2003–09; Scientific Dir, Tommy's Centre for Maternal and Fetal Health, Queen's Med. Res. Inst., Royal Infirmary of Edinburgh, 2007–09. Chm., Acad. of Royal Colls and Faculties in Scotland, 2001–04. British Exchange Prof., UCLA, 1992; Vis. Prof., Univ. of Pretoria, 2005; Hon. Prof., Sch. of Medicine, Univ. of St Andrews, 2012–. Chairman: Tenovus Scotland, 2011–; Scotland's Churches Trust, 2015–. Hon. FCOG(SA) 2005. *Publications:* (with W. Dunlop) High Risk Pregnancy, 1992; (with J. O. Drife) Prostaglandins and the Uterus, 1992; (jtly) Munro Kerr's Operative Obstetrics, 11th (centenary) edn 2007, 12th edn, 2013; numerous scientific papers in Lancet, British Jl of Obstetrics and Gynaecology, Human Reproduction, etc. *Recreations:* music (especially organ), golf, curling, medical history. *Address:* Simpson Centre for Reproductive Health, Royal Infirmary, 51 Little France Crescent, Edinburgh EH16 4SA. *T:* (0131) 242 2700, *Fax:* (0131) 242 2686. *E:* a.a.calder@ed.ac.uk. *Clubs:* New (Edinburgh); Honourable Company of Edinburgh Golfers (Muirfield).

CALDER, Elisabeth Nicole; Director, Full Circle Editions, since 2009; *b* 20 Jan. 1938; *d* of Florence Mary Baber and Ivor George Baber; *m* 1st, 1958, Richard Henry Calder (marr. diss. 1972); one *d* one *s*; 2nd, 2000, Louis Baum. *Educ:* Broadfields, Edgware; Palmerston North Girls' High Sch., NZ; Canterbury Univ., NZ (BA 1958). Reader, Metro-Goldwyn-Mayer story dept, 1969–70; Publicity Manager, Victor Gollancz, 1971–74; Editorial Director: Victor Gollancz, 1975–78; Jonathan Cape, 1979–86; Publisher (formerly Publishing Dir), Bloomsbury Publishing, 1986–2009. Chair, Royal Ct Th., 2000–03. Mem. Bd, Folio Prize, 2013–. Founder Dir, Groucho Club, 1985–95; Co-founder and Pres., Internat. Fest. of Literature, Parati, Brazil, 2003; Founder Dir, Flipside Fest., 2013–; Trustee, Wonderful Beast Th. Co., 2012–. DUniv University Campus Suffolk, 2012. Order of Merit for Culture (Brazil), 2004; Nat. Order of the Southern Cross, 2004. *Recreations:* reading, theatre, music - esp. Brazilian, thinking about gardening, junking.

CALDER, Dr Ian Maddison, TD 1973; FRCPath; FFOM; Medical Director, Medico-Legal Centre, London, since 2005; *s* of late Walter James Calder, MIMechE, and Alice (*née* Maddison); *m* 1964, Dorothy Joan Hubbard, MBE, RGN; one *s* one *d*. *Educ:* Norwich Sch.; Univ. of St Andrews (MB ChB 1962; State Scholar); Univ. of Dundee (MD 1977; DSc 1992). MRCPath 1981, FRCPath 1996; FFOM 1990; FCPath (HK) 1993; MRCP 1996. Served RA, 1955 (2nd Lieut); Hon. Col, 254 Field Ambulance, RAMC (V), 1991–; Mem., E Anglia TAVRA Cttee, 1990. Lectr in Forensic Medicine, St George's Hosp. Med. Sch., Univ. of London, 1972–76; Lectr, London Hosp. Med. Coll., 1976–81, then Hon. Lectr; Lectr in Forensic Science, Anglia Ruskin Univ., Cambridge, 2005. Visiting Fellow: St Edmund's Coll., Cambridge, 1978; Wellcome Inst. of Comparative Neurology, Univ. of Cambridge, 1978–; Travelling Scholar, UCLA, 1976; Advr to Nat. Undersea Res. Centre, Univ. of N Carolina. Ext. Examr, Univ. of Hong Kong, 1985–90; Advr to Labour Dept, Hong Kong, 1991–94; Consultant advr on occupational medicine, MoD, 1994–2000; Advr to E and N Herts NHS Trust, 2000–04. Member: MoD Ethical Cttee, 1983–; DoH Dangerous Pathogens Working Party; E Anglia MoD Pension Adv. Cttee for Veterans; Council, Order of St John, Cambs. Mem., Physicians for Human Rights. *Publications:* chapters in textbooks of pathology and occupational medicine; papers on diving and hyperbaric medicine research. *Recreations:* sailing, boat-building, antique furniture and cabinet making, rowing, church music, industrial archaeology. *Address:* Thorpe, Huntingdon Road, Girton, Cambridge CB3 0LG. *T:* (01223) 277220. *Club:* Athenæum.

CALDER, John Mackenzie; Managing Director, John Calder (Publishers) Ltd, 1950–91; Director, Calder Publications Ltd, 1991–2008 (Managing Director, 1991–2008); President, Riverrun Press Inc., New York, since 1978; *b* 25 Jan. 1927; *e s* of James Calder, Ardargie, Forgandenny, Perthshire, and Lucienne Wilson, Montreal, Canada; *m* 1st, 1949, Mary Ann Simmonds; one *d*; 2nd, 1960, Bettina Jonic (marr. diss. 1975); one *d*; 3rd, 2011, Sheila Gillian Colvin. *Educ:* Gilling Castle, Yorks; Bishop's College Sch., Canada; McGill Univ.; Sir George Williams Coll.; Zürich Univ. Studied political economy; subseq. worked in Calders Ltd (timber co.), Director; founded John Calder (Publishers) Ltd, 1949; Man. Dir, Calder & Boyars, 1964–75; Chm., Calder Educnl Trust, 1975–; estab. Calder Bookshop, 2000. Organiser of literary confs for Edinburgh Festival, 1962 and 1963, and Harrogate Festival, 1969. Founded Ledlanet Nights, 1963, in Kinross-shire (music and opera festival, closed 1974). Active in fields related to the arts and on many cttees; Co-founder, Defence of Literature and the Arts Society; Chm., Fedn of Scottish Theatres, 1972–74; Administrator and Founder Mem., Godot Co., 2003. Contested (L): Kinross and W Perthshire, 1970; Hamilton, Oct. 1974; (European Parlt) Mid Scotland and Fife, 1979. FRSA 1974. Dr *hc* Edinburgh, 2002; Hon. DLitt Napier, 2008. Chevalier des Arts et des Lettres (France), 1975; Chevalier, 1983, Officier, 1997, de l'Ordre nationale de mérite (France). *Publications:* (ed) A Samuel Beckett Reader, 1967; (ed) Beckett at 60, 1967; (ed) William Burroughs Reader, 1982; (ed) New Samuel Beckett Reader, 1983; (ed) Henry Miller Reader, 1985; (ed) The Nouveau Roman Reader, 1986; (ed) As No Other Dare Fail: for Samuel Beckett on his 80th birthday, 1986; The Philosophy of Samuel Beckett, 1997; Pursuit (autobiog.), 2001; The Theology of Samuel Beckett, 2013; The Garden of Eros, 2013; *poetry:* What's Wrong, What's Right, 1999; Solo, 2008; Being, Seeing, Feeling, Healing, Meaning, 2011; (ed) Gambit International Drama Review, etc.; obituaries and reviews for newspapers; articles in many jls. *Recreations:* writing (several plays, stories; criticism, etc; translations); weekly blog for ONE magazine, music, art (pen paintings called shapes), theatre, opera, reading, chess, lecturing, conversation; travelling, promoting good causes, fond of good food and wine. *Address:* 9 Rue de Romainville, 93100 Montreuil, France. *T:* (1) 49887512. *Clubs:* Caledonian; Scottish Arts (Edinburgh).

CALDER, Julian Richard; Director of Statistical Support Services (formerly Survey and Statistical Services) Group, Office for National Statistics, 1996–2000; *b* 6 Dec. 1941; *s* of Donald Alexander and Ivy O'Nora Calder; *m* 1965, Avril Tucker; two *s*. *Educ:* Dulwich College; Brasenose College, Oxford; Birkbeck College, London. Statistician, 1973, Chief Statistician, 1978, Central Statistical Office; Chief Statistician, 1981, Dir of Stats, 1985–94, Board of Inland Revenue; Hd of Div., Govt Statistical Service and Gen. Div., Central Statistical Office, 1994–96. *Recreations:* cycling, listening to music.

CALDER, Prof. Muffy, OBE 2011; PhD; FRSE; FREng, FIEE, FBCS; Professor of Computer Science, since 1998, and Vice Principal and Head, College of Science and Engineering, since 2014, University of Glasgow; *b* Shawinigan, Québec, 21 May 1958; *d* of Carmen van Thomas and Lois van Thomas (*née* Hallen); *m* 1998, David Calder. *Educ:* Univ. of Stirling (BSc); Univ. of St Andrews (PhD 1987). FRSE 2000; FIEE 2002; FBCS 2002; FREng 2013. British Ship Res. Assoc., 1977; with Burroughs Computers; Dept of Computer Sci., Univ. of Edinburgh, 1983–84; Dept of Computing Sci. and Maths, Univ. of Stirling, 1984–87; University of Glasgow, 1988–: Hd, Computing Sci., 2004–07; Dean of Res., Coll. of Sci. and Engrg, 2010–12; Chief Scientific Advr for Scotland, 2012–14. BT Res. Fellow BT Labs, Martlesham, 1992–; Vis. Scientist, Systems Res. Center, Digital Equipt Corp., Calif 1994–. Chair, UK Computing Res. Cttee, 2009–11. *Publications:* contribs to scientific jls *Recreations:* running, string quartet (violin). *Address:* School of Computing Science, Sir Alwyn Williams Building, Lilybank Gardens, University of Glasgow, Glasgow G12 8RZ. *E:* muffy.calder@glasgow.ac.uk. *Club:* Westerlands Cross Country.

CALDER, Simon Peter Ritchie; Senior Travel Editor, The Independent, since 2007; *b* Crawley, 25 Dec. 1955; *s* of late Nigel David Ritchie Calder; *m* 1997, Charlotte Hindle; two *d*. *Educ:* Univ. of Warwick (BSc Maths). Studio Manager, BBC Radio, 1979–94; Travel Editor, The Independent, 1994–2007; presenter: BBC TV, 1996–2011; LBC Radio, 2008–. *Publications:* No Frills: the truth behind the low-cost revolution in the skies, 2002, 3rd edn 2006. *Recreations:* walking, swimming, cycling. *Address:* The Independent, Northcliffe House, 2 Derry Street, W8 5HF. *T:* (020) 3615 2185. *W:* www.simoncalder.com.

CALDERWOOD, (Andrew) Bruce; Director of Mental Health and Disability, Department of Health, 2009–13; *b* 14 March 1954; *s* of Bob and Betty Calderwood; *m* 1989, Vivienne Bennett; two *s* one *d*. *Educ:* York Univ. (BA Hons Philosophy and English). Chocolate packer, Rowntrees, 1978–79; computer programmer, CCTA, 1979–81; Policy Advr, DHSS 1981–92; Policy Manager, DSS, 1993–95; Advr, Premier's Dept, Victoria, 1995–96; Business Architect, DSS, 1997–2002; Dir, Older People, 2003–04, Dir, Disability and Carers Directorate, 2004–09, Dir, Office for Disability Issues, 2005–09, DWP. *Recreations:* my allotment, hill walking, cooking, malt whisky, films.

CALDERWOOD, Catherine Jane, FRCOG; Consultant Obstetrician and Gynaecologist NHS Lothian, since 2006; Chief Medical Officer, Scottish Government, since 2015 (Deputy Chief Medical Officer, 2014–15); *b* Belfast, 26 Dec. 1968; *d* of James and Lesley Calderwood one *s* two *d*. *Educ:* Methodist Coll., Belfast; Newnham Coll., Cambridge (BA 1990); Glasgow Univ. (MB ChB 1993). FRCOG 2015. Trainee in Obstetrics and Gynaecology, SE Scotland 2001–06; trainee in maternal medicine, St Thomas' Hosp., 2003–04; SMO, Scottish Govt 2010–14; Nat. Clin. Dir, Maternity and Women's Health, NHS England, 2013–15. Hon. FRCPE 2012. *Recreations:* laughter, family, friends, golf, running, climbing hills. *Address:* Scottish Government Health Department, St Andrews House, Regent Road, Edinburgh EH1 3DG. *E:* psicmo@scotland.gsi.gov.uk.

CALDICOTT, Dame Fiona, DBE 1996; FRCP, FRCPsych; Principal, Somerville College, Oxford, 1996–2010; a Pro-Vice-Chancellor, Oxford University, 2001–10 (Pro-Vice-Chancellor (Personnel and Equal Opportunities), 2005–09); *b* 12 Jan. 1941; *d* of Joseph Maurice Soesan and Elizabeth Jane (*née* Ransley); *m* 1965, Robert Gordon Woodruff Caldicott; one *d* (one *s* decd). *Educ:* City of London Sch. for Girls; St Hilda's Coll., Oxford (MA, BM, BCh; Hon. Fellow 1996). DPM; FRCPsych 1985; FRCP 1995; FRCPI 1996; FRCGP 1996. House Surgeon and Physician, Coventry Hosps, 1966–67; General Practice, Family Planning and Child Welfare, 1968–70; training in Psychiatry, Walsgrave Hosp., Coventry and Central Hosp., Warwick, 1970–76; Sen. Registrar in Psychiatry, W Midlands Regl Trng Scheme, 1977–79; Consultant Psychiatrist, Univ. of Warwick, 1979–85; Consultant Psychotherapist, Uffculme Clinic, Birmingham, 1979–96; Sen. Clinical Lectr in Psychotherapy, Univ. of Birmingham, 1982–96; Unit General Manager, Mental Health, Central Birmingham, 1989–91; Clin. Dir, Adult Psychiatric and Psychotherapy Service, Mental Health Unit, S Birmingham, 1991–94; Med. Dir, S Birmingham Mental Health NHS Trust, 1994–96 (Hon. Consultant Psychiatrist, 1996–2012). Non-executive Director: Coventry Building Soc., 1997–2001; Oxford Univ. Hosps (formerly Oxford Radcliffe Hosps) NHS Trust, 2002– (Chm., 2009–). Chairman: Cttee to Review Patient-Identifiable Information, reported 1997; Cttee to Review Confidentiality and Sharing of Health and Social Care Information, 2012–13; Nat. Information Governance Bd, 2011–13; Mem., Sec. of State's Standing Adv. Cttee, on Med. Workforce (formerly Manpower) Planning, 1991–2000; Mem., Broadcasting Standards Commn (formerly Council), 1996–2001. Pres., Section for Psychiatry, 1995–99 (Sec., 1991–95), Sec., European Bd of Psychiatry, 1992–96, Union of European Med. Specialists; Member: Council: BMA, 1996–2000 (Chm., Bd of Med. Educn, 1996–2000); RSocMed, 1996–99; Acad. Med. Sci., 1998–2001; GMC, 1999–2003; UN Univ., 2011–; Mem., Hebdomadal Council, 1998–2000, Council, 2000–09, Oxford Univ.; Lay Mem. Council, Warwick Univ., 2011–. Sub-Dean 1987–90, Dean 1990–93, Pres., 1993–96, RCPsych; Chm., Acad. of Med. Royal Colls, 1995–96. Pres., British Assoc. of Counselling, 2000–06. Consultant Advr to Commissioning Bd for High Security Psychiatric Care, 1996–2000. Chm., Ind. Inquiry Panel into Umar Farouk Mutallab's time at UCL, 2009–10. Trustee: Zito Trust, 1994–2009; Bethlem Art and History Collections Trust, 1995–99; Nuffield Trust, 1998–2008. Patron: Oxford Healthy Living Centre, 1996–2005; Family Nurturing Network, Oxford, 1997–2009; Hon. Pres., Guild of Health Writers, 1996–99. Founder FMedSci 1998; Fellow, Acad. of Medicine, Singapore, 1994; Mem., Czech Psychiatric Soc., 1994. Hon. DSc Warwick, 1997; Hon. MD Birmingham, 1997. Chevalier du Tastevin, 1991. *Publications:* contrib. Discussing Doctors' Careers (ed Isobel Allen), 1988; papers in Bull. RCPsych, Current Opinion in Psychiatry, Postgraduate Psychiatry. *Recreations:* family, friends, reading, wine. *Address:* 27 High Street, Warwick CV34 4AX. *Club:* Royal Society of Medicine.

CALDICOTT, Gillian Anne; Director of Operations for India, British Council; *b* 14 July 1954; *d* of Ronald Frederick Caldicott and Grace Anne Caldicott; partner, Jan Alexander Kingsley; one *s*. *Educ:* University Coll., Cardiff (BA Lit. and Lang. 1975); Dip. Teaching English to Adults; Nottingham Trent Univ. (Cert. Teaching in Further Educn); Univ. of Reading (MA Applied Linguistics 1985); Open Univ. (MBA 1992). Teaching posts in UK, Spain and Syria, 1976–86; British Council: Dep. Teaching Centre Manager, Thessaloniki, Greece, 1986–89; Teaching Centre Manager, Kuwait, 1989–90; Product Develt Manager, Central Mgt of Direct Teaching, 1990–93; Hd, Press and PR, 1993–95; Dir, Milan, 1995–98; Dep. Dir and Dir, English Lang. Services, Hong Kong, 1998–2002; Dep. Dir, Egypt, 2002–04; Project Manager, Regionalisation, 2004–05; Regl Dir (Europe and Latin America), English and Exams, 2005–07; Dir, Business Develt (English), 2007–08; Dir, Portugal, 2008–13. *Recreations:* scuba diving, archaeology, literature, travelling. *Address:* British Council Division, British High Commission, 17 Kasturba Gandhi Marg, New Delhi 110 001, India.

CALDWELL, Dr David Hepburn; Keeper, Department of Scotland and Europe, 2004–12, and Department of Archaeology, 2011–12, National Museums Scotland; *b* 15 Dec. 1951; *s* of Alexander Caldwell and Dorothy (*née* Hepburn); *m* 1975, Margaret McGovern; one *s* two *d*. *Educ:* Ardrossan Acad.; Edinburgh Univ. (MA; PhD 1982). Curator, Nat. Mus. of Antiquities of Scotland, 1973–85; Asst Keeper, Scottish Medieval Collections, 1985–2001, Keeper, Hist. and Applied Art Dept, 2001–04, Nat. Mus of Scotland. Dir, Fife Cultural Trust, 2012–. Pres., Soc. of Antiquaries of Scotland, 2014–; Vice-Pres., Soc. for Post Medieval Archaeology, 2014–. *Publications:* The Scottish Armoury, 1979; Scottish Weapons and Fortifications, 1981; Scotland's Wars and Warriors, 1999; An Historical Guide to Islay, Jura and Colonsay, 2001; Islay: the land of the Lordship, 2008; The Lewis Chessmen Unmasked, 2010; The Lewis Chessmen: new perspectives, 2014. *Recreations:* travel, table tennis, sewing.

CALDWELL, Sir Edward (George), KCB 2002 (CB 1990); Parliamentary Counsel, Law Commission, 2002–06; *b* 21 Aug. 1941; *s* of Arthur Francis Caldwell and Olive Caldwell (*née* Riddle); *m* 1st, 1965, Bronwen Crockett (marr. diss.); two *d*; 2nd, 1992, Dr Helen Janet Beynon (*see* H. J. Caldwell); two step *d*. *Educ:* St Andrew's, Singapore; Clifton College; Worcester College, Oxford. Law Commission, 1967–69, 1975–77, 1986–88; joined Office of Parly Counsel, 1969: Parly Counsel, 1981–99; First Parly Counsel, 1999–2002. Hon. QC

2002; Hon. Bencher, Inner Temple, 2005. Patron, Human Rights Lawyers' Assoc. Mem. Cttee, Clarity. *Address:* The Old School, School Lane, Chilson, Chipping Norton, Oxon OX7 3HT.

CALDWELL, Dr Helen Janet, (Lady Caldwell), CB 2007; Parliamentary Counsel, 2002–08; *b* 13 Sept. 1952; *d* of George Neville Burtenshaw and Margaret Deforel Burtenshaw (*née* Rose); *m* 1st, 1975, Gareth Wyn Beynon (marr. diss.); two *d*; 2nd, 1992, Sir Edward George Caldwell, *qv*; two step *d*. *Educ:* Dunottar Sch., Reigate; Reigate Co. Sch. for Girls; Girton Coll., Cambridge (Exhibnr; MA); Wolfson Coll., Oxford (DPhil). Called to the Bar, Lincoln's Inn, 1975 (Hardwick Schol.); Lectr in Law, Univ. of Reading, 1979–87; joined Parliamentary Counsel Office, 1987; at Law Commn, 1996–99; Head of Drafting Team: Tax Law Rewrite Project, 1999–2001; Law Commn, 2001–02. *Publications:* contrib. articles to Law Qly Rev., Modern Law Rev., Criminal Law Rev., etc.

See also A. J. Burtenshaw.

CALDWELL, Prof. John, PhD, DSc; CBiol, FRSB; Chairman, Health Education Thames Valley, since 2014; *b* 4 April 1947; *s* of Reginald and Marian Caldwell; *m* 1969, Jill Gregory; two *s*. *Educ:* Chelsea Coll., Univ. of London (BPharm 1969); St Mary's Hosp. Med. Sch. (PhD Biochem. 1972); DSc Pharmacol. London, 1987. CBiol, FRSB (FIBiol 1992). St Mary's Hospital Medical School: Lecturer: in Biochem., 1972–74; in Biochem. Pharmacol., 1974–78; Sen. Lectr, 1978–82; Reader in Drug Metabolism, 1982–88; Prof. of Biochem. Toxicol., 1988–2002; Hd, Dept of Pharmacol. and Toxicol., 1992–97; Dean, ICSM at St Mary's, 1995–97; Hd, Div. of Biomed. Scis, 1997–2002, Hd, Undergrad. Medicine, 2000–02, Imperial Coll. London; Dean, Faculty of Medicine, 2002–08, Pro-Vice-Chancellor, 2007–12, Exec. Pro-Vice-Chancellor, Faculty of Health and Life Scis, 2008–10, Univ. of Liverpool. Fondation Herbette Vis. Prof., Univ. of Lausanne, 1986; Sterling-Winthrop Dist. Prof., Univ. of Michigan Med. Center, 1995. Dir and Co-founder, Amedis Pharmaceuticals Ltd, 2000–02; Chm., MorEx Develt Partners LLP, 2008–; non-executive Director: Eden Biopharma Gp Ltd, 2004–10; ULive plc, 2008–12. Chm., Mid-Staffs NHS Foundn Trust, 2012–14; Dir, Liverpool Sci. Park, 2008–11. Non-executive Director: St Mary's Hosp. NHS Trust, 1995–98; Cheshire and Merseyside Strategic HA, 2003–06; NW Strategic HA, 2006–11. Chm., Scientific Cttee, NW Cancer Res., Fund, 2003–09. Pres., Internat. Soc. for Study of Xenobiotics, 1994–95 (Hon. Mem., 2001). Hon. MRCP 1998; Hon. Mem., Canadian Soc. for Pharmaceutical Scis, 2002. Founder and Ed., Chirality, 1989– (Best New Jl in Sci., Technol. and Medicine Award, Assoc. Amer. Publishers, 1991). *Publications:* (ed) Amphetamines and Related Stimulants: chemical, biological, clinical and sociological aspects, 1980; *edited jointly:* Metabolic Basis of Detoxication, 1982; Sulfate Metabolism and Sulfate Conjugation, 1982; Biological Basis of Detoxication, 1983; Foreign Compound Metabolism, 1984; Microsomes and Drug Oxidations, 1985; Xenobiotic Conjugation Chemistry, 1986; Metabolism of Xenobiotics, 1988; Intermediary Xenobiotic Metabolism in Animals, 1989; Biochemistry and Redox Reactions, 1994; Organic Stereochemistry: guiding principles and biomedicinal relevance, 2014; contribs on drug metabolism. *Recreations:* weekends in good hotels, some aspects of the Church of England, Venice. *Address:* Faculty of Health and Life Sciences, University of Liverpool, Liverpool L69 7ZX. *T:* (0151) 795 0422. *E:* jcc@liv.ac.uk. *Club:* Athenæum.

CALDWELL, Prof. John Anthony, DPhil; Titular Professor of Music, University of Oxford, 1999–2005; Senior Research Fellow, Jesus College, Oxford, 1999–2005, now Emeritus Fellow; *b* 6 July 1938; *s* of George Wilfrid Caldwell and Susannah Marion Caldwell (*née* Haywood); *m* 1967, Janet Susan Kellar; one *s* one *d*. *Educ:* Birkenhead Sch.; Keble Coll., Oxford (BA 1960; BMus 1961; MA 1964; DPhil 1965). FRCO 1957. Asst Lectr in Music, Bristol Univ., 1963–66; Oxford University: Lectr in Music, 1966–96, Reader in Music, 1996–99; Keble College: Lectr in Music, 1966–67; Res. Fellow, 1967–75; Official Fellow, 1975–92; Emeritus Fellow, 2012; Lecturer in Music: Balliol Coll., 1966–2005; Jesus Coll., 1970–2005; Lincoln Coll., 1972–2005. General Editor: Corpus of Early Keyboard Music, 1982–; Early English Church Music, 1995–2007; Co-editor, Plainsong and Medieval Music, 1992–96; Mem., Editl Bd and Trustee, Music and Letters, 1995– (Chm., 2005–). Organist: St Luke's, Tranmere, Birkenhead, 1955–57; St Giles', Oxford (also Choirmaster), 1966–67; SS Philip and James, Oxford, 1968–77; SS Gregory and Augustine, Oxford, 1995–. MAE 2012. Hon. Fellow, Acad. St Cecilia, 2007. *Compositions:* Divertimento for orch., 1999; dramatic trilogy Paschale Mysterium (opera): Good Friday, prod 1998; The Word, prod 2001; Pascha Nostrum, prod 2002; The Story of Orpheus (opera), prod 2004; La Corona for soprano, chorus and strings, 2005; Seven Words from the Cross, 2008; songs, motets, organ and chamber music. *Publications:* (ed) Early Tudor Organ Music I, 1966; English Keyboard Music before the Nineteenth Century, 1973; Medieval Music, 1978, rev. trans. as La música medieval, 1984; Editing Early Music, 1985, 2nd edn 1996; The Oxford History of English Music, Vol. i 1991, Vol. ii 1999; (ed) Tudor Keyboard Music, 1995; (ed) The Mulliner Book, 2011. *Recreation:* visiting churches and archaeological sites. *Address:* Jesus College, Oxford OX1 3DW. *T:* (home) (01865) 310956.

CALDWELL, Prof. John Bernard, OBE 1979; PhD; FREng, FRINA; Emeritus Professor of Naval Architecture, University of Newcastle upon Tyne, since 1991; *b* 26 Sept. 1926; *s* of John Revie Caldwell and Doris (*née* Bolland); *m* 1955, Jean Muriel Frances Duddridge; two *s*. *Educ:* Bootham Sch., York; Liverpool Univ. (BEng); Bristol Univ. (PhD). CEng; FRINA 1963; FREng (FEng 1976). Res. Fellow, Civil Engrg, Bristol Univ., 1953; Sen. Scientific Officer 1955, Principal Sci. Off. 1958, Royal Naval Scientific Service; Asst Prof. of Applied Mechanics, RNC Greenwich, 1960–66; Newcastle upon Tyne University: Prof. of Naval Architecture, 1966–91; Hd of Dept of Naval Architecture, 1966–83; Hd, Sch. of Marine Technol., 1975–80, 1986–88; Dean of Faculty of Engrg, 1983–86. Director: Nat. Maritime Inst. Ltd, 1983–85; Marine Design Consultants Ltd, 1985–89; Newcastle Technology Centre, 1985–90; Northern Engrg Centre, 1989–92. Vis. Prof. of Naval Arch., MIT, 1962–63. President: N-E Coast Instn of Engrs and Shipbuilders, 1976–78; RINA, 1984–87 (Vice-Pres., 1977–84). Mem., Engineering Council, 1988–94 (Chm., Bd for Engrs' Registration, 1990–92). FRSA 1982. Hon. DSc Gdansk Tech. Univ., 1985. Froude Medal, RINA, 1984; David W. Taylor Medal, SNAME, 1987. *Publications:* numerous papers on research and educn in naval arch. *Address:* Barkbooth, Winster, Windermere, Cumbria LA23 3NZ. *T:* (01539) 568222.

CALDWELL, Marion Allan; QC (Scot.) 2000; *d* of late Henry Caldwell and of Elizabeth Caldwell. *Educ:* Eastbank Acad., Glasgow; Aberdeen Univ. (LLB Hons); European Univ. Inst., Florence; Glasgow Univ. (DipLP). Journalist, 1970–77; trainee Solicitor, 1983–84; Solicitor, 1984–85; admitted to Faculty of Advocates, 1986; called to the Bar, Inner Temple, 1991; Standing Jun. Counsel to Accountant of Court and Accountant in Bankruptcy, Scotland, 1991–2000. Legal Chm., 2001–13, Pres., 2013–, Pensions Appeal Tribunals for Scotland; Dep. Judge, Upper Tribunal, 2014–. *Recreations:* swimming, ski-ing, walking, social tennis, reading. *Address:* Advocates Library, Parliament House, Edinburgh EH1 1RF. *T:* (0131) 226 5071.

CALDWELL, Sandra Mary, CB 2008; JP; Director, Field Operations, 2004–09, and Deputy Chief Executive, 2008–09, Health and Safety Executive; *b* 20 June 1948; *m*. *Educ:* Imperial Coll., Univ. of London (BSc, MSc; dip. occupational health and safety). Joined HSE, 1976; Regl Dir, London and SE, HSC and Chief Inspector of Construction, HSE, 1998–99; Director: Health, then Health and Safety, 2000–03; Policy, 2003–04. Trustee: Victim Support, 2009–; St Albans CAB, 2009–. JP W Herts, 2003.

CALEDON, 7th Earl of, *cr* 1800; **Nicholas James Alexander,** KCVO 2015; Baron Caledon, 1790; Viscount Caledon, 1797; Lord Lieutenant of County Armagh, since 1989; *b* 6 May 1955; *s* of 6th Earl of Caledon, and Baroness Anne (*d* 1963), *d* of late Baron Nicolai de Graevenitz; *S* father, 1980; *m* 1st, 1979, Wendy (marr. diss. 1985), *d* of Spiro Coumantaros and Mrs Suzanne Dayton; 2nd, 1989, Henrietta (marr. diss. 2000), *d* of John Newman, Compton Chamberlayne, Wilts; one *s* one *d*; *m* 2008, Mrs Amanda Cayzer (*née* Squire). *Educ:* Sandroyd School; Gordonstoun School (Round-Square House). *Recreations:* ski-ing, tennis, swimming, photography, travel. *Heir:* *s* Viscount Alexander, *qv*. *Address:* Caledon Castle, Caledon, Co. Tyrone, Northern Ireland BT68 4UA. *T:* (028) 3756 8232.

CALEGARI, Prof. Danny Cornelius, PhD; Professor of Mathematics, University of Chicago, since 2012; *b* Melbourne, Australia, 24 May 1972; *s* of Giacomo Peter Calegari and Cornelia Calegari (*née* Van-Veldhuisen); *m* 1995, Therese Elizabeth Walsh; one *s* two *d*. *Educ:* Univ. of Melbourne (BA Hons 1994); Univ. of Calif, Berkeley (PhD Maths 2000). Benjamin Peirce Asst Prof., Harvard Univ., 2000–02; California Institute of Technology: Asst Prof., 2002; Associate Prof., 2003–06; Prof., 2006–07; Richard Merkin Prof., 2007–12; Prof. of Pure Maths, Univ. of Cambridge, 2011–12. Namboodiri Lectr, Univ. of Chicago, 2012. Clay Res. Award, Clay Maths Inst., 2009. *Publications:* Foliations and the Geometry of 3-Manifolds, 2007. *Recreations:* jogging, walking, used books, spanking. *Address:* c/o Department of Mathematics, 5734 S University Avenue, Chicago, IL 60637, USA. *E:* dannyc@math.uchicago.edu.

CALHOUN, Prof. Craig Jackson, DPhil; FBA 2015; Director, London School of Economics and Political Science, since 2012; *b* Illinois, 16 June 1952; *m* 1980, Pamela DeLargy; one *s* one *d*. *Educ:* Univ. of Southern Calif (BA Anthropol. 1972); Columbia Univ. (MA Anthropol. 1974); Manchester Univ. (MA Social Anthropol. 1975); St Antony's Coll., Oxford (DPhil Mod. Social and Econ. Hist./Sociol. 1980). Univ. of North Carolina, Chapel Hill, 1977–96, Prof. of Sociol. and History, 1989–96; Prof., New York Univ., 1996–2012, Univ. Prof., 2004–12; Prof. of Sociol., Columbia Univ. 2006–07. Vis. Lectr, Univ. of Oslo, 1991; Prof. (pt-time), Humboldt Univ., 2010–; Hon. Prof., Maison des Scis de l'Homme, 2011–; Dist. Affiliated Prof., Tech. Univ. of Munich, 2012–. *Publications:* (ed jtly) The Anthropological Study of Education, 1976; The Question of Class Struggle, 1982; (jtly) Sociology, 1989; (ed) Habermas and the Public Sphere, 1992; (ed jtly) Bourdieu: critical perspectives, 1993; Neither Gods Nor Emperors, 1994; (ed) Social Theory and the Politics of Identity, 1994; Critical Social Theory: culture, history and the challenge of difference, 1995; Nationalism, 1997; (ed jtly) Hannah Arendt and the Meaning of Politics, 1997; (ed) Dictionary of Social Sciences, 2002; (ed jtly) The Classical Social Theory Reader, 2002, 3rd edn 2011; (ed jtly) The Contemporary Social Theory Reader, 2002, 3rd edn 2011; (ed jtly) Understanding September 11, 2002; (ed jtly) The Sage Handbook of Sociology, 2005; (ed jtly) Lessons of Empire?, 2006; (ed) Sociology in America: a history, 2007; (ed jtly) Practicing Culture, 2007; Nations Matter: citizenship, solidarity and the cosmopolitan dream, 2007; (ed jtly) Varieties of Secularism, 2010; (ed) Robert K. Merton: sociology of science, sociology as science, 2010; (ed jtly) Knowledge Matters, 2011; (ed jtly) Business as Usual: the roots of the global financial crisis, 2011; (ed jtly) The Deepening Crisis: governance challenges after neoliberalism, 2011; (ed jtly) Aftermath: a new global economic order?, 2011; (ed jtly) Rethinking Secularism, 2011; The Roots of Radicalism: tradition, the public sphere and early 19th century social movements, 2012; (ed jtly) Habermas and Religion, 2013; (jtly) Does Capitalism Have a Future?, 2013. *Recreations:* jazz, reading. *Address:* London School of Economics and Political Science, Houghton Street, WC2A 2AE. *T:* (020) 7955 7007. *E:* directorsoffice@lse.ac.uk.

CALIGARI, Prof. Peter Douglas Savaria, PhD, DSc; CBiol, FRSB; Titular Professor, Instituto de Ciencias Biológicas (formerly Biología Vegetal y Biotecnología), Universidad de Talca, Chile, since 2002 (Director, 2004–09); Professor of Agricultural Botany, University of Reading, 1986–2006 (on leave of absence, 2002–06) (Head of Department, 1987–98); *b* 10 Nov. 1949; *s* of late Kenneth Vane Savaria Caligari, DFM, RAF, and of Mary Annetta (*née* Rock); *m* 1st, 1973 (marr. diss. 2004); two *d*; 2nd, 2007, Andrea Veronica Moreno Gonzalez; two step *d*. *Educ:* Hereford Cathedral Sch.; Univ. of Birmingham (BSc Biol Sci., 1971; PhD Genetics, 1974; DSc Genetics, 1989). CBiol 1997; FRSB (FIBiol 1997). Res. Asst, 1971–74, Res. Fellow, 1974–81, Dept of Genetics, Univ. of Birmingham; SSO, 1981–84, PSO, 1984–86, Scottish Crop Res. Inst. Managing Director: BioHybrids International Ltd, 1996–; BioMarkers Ltd, 1997–2003. Director: Genberries Ltd, 2008–; Ghana Sumatra Ltd, 2008–12 (Chm., 2008–12); Sumatra Bioscience Pte Ltd, 2008–12; Sustainable Plant Nutrition Ltd, 2011–14; BioHybrids Technologies Limitada (Chile), 2011–; BioHybrids Genetics Ltd, 2011–; BioProperties Private Ltd, 2012–13; Ardent Bioscience Private Ltd, 2012–13; BioSing Private Ltd (Singapore), 2013–; Verdant Bioscience Private Ltd (Singapore), 2013–; PT Timbang Deli Indonesia, 2014–; Chm., NG-Seeds SA (Chile), 2013–. Member: Exec. Cttee, XVIIth Internat. Congress of Genetics, 1991–93; Governing Body, Plant Science Research Ltd, 1991–94; Governing Council, John Innes Centre, 1994–99; European Council, Volcani Centre, 1999–2002; Bd, Internat. Lupin Assoc., 1999–; Comité de Expertos, Beca Presidente de la República, Chile, 2006–07; Academia Chilena de Ciencias Agronómicas, 2013–; Internat. Soc. for Horticultural Sci., 2014–; Chm., Sci. Prog., Triennial EUCARPIA Congress, 1999–2001. Vice Pres., Inst. of Biology, 1999–2002 (Chm., Sci. Policy Bd, 1999–2002). FRSA 1990. Editor, Heredity, 1987–90 (Jun. Editor, 1985–87). *Publications:* (contrib.) The Potato Crop, 1991; (contrib.) Applications of Synthetic Seeds to Crop Improvement, 1992; (jtly) Selection Methods in Plant Breeding, 1995, 2nd edn 2008; (ed jtly) Compositae: biology and utilization, 1996; (contrib.) Lupins: production and utilization, 1998; (ed jtly) Cashew and Coconuts: trees for life, 1998; (jtly) Introduction to Plant Breeding, 2008; (jtly) Plant Breeding, 2014; scientific papers and reports on genetics, plant breeding and biotechnology (*c* 450 papers, *c* 80 reports). *Address:* Instituto de Ciencias Biológicas, Universidad de Talca, 2 Norte 685, Talca, Chile. *T:* (71) 2201523, *Fax:* (71) 2200276. *E:* pcaligari@utalca.cl.

CALLADINE, Prof. Christopher Reuben, ScD; FRS 1984; FREng; Professor of Structural Mechanics, University of Cambridge, 1986–2002, now Emeritus; Fellow of Peterhouse, 1960–2002, now Emeritus; *b* 19 Jan. 1935; *s* of Reuben and Mabel Calladine (*née* Boam); *m* 1964, Mary R. H. Webb; two *s* one *d*. *Educ:* Nottingham High Sch.; Peterhouse, Cambridge; Massachusetts Inst. of Technology. Development engineer, English Electric Co., 1958; Demonstrator in Engrg, Univ. of Cambridge, 1960, Lectr, 1963; Reader, 1978. Vis. Research Associate, Brown Univ., 1963; Vis. Prof., Stanford Univ., 1969–70. Mem. Council, Royal Soc., 2000–02. Trustee, EMF Biol. Res. Trust, 2005– (Chm., 2007–). FREng (FEng 1994). Hon. DEng Univ. of Technol., Malaysia, 2002. James Alfred Ewing Medal, ICE, 1998. *Publications:* Engineering Plasticity, 1969; Theory of Shell Structures, 1983; (with H. R. Drew) Understanding DNA, 1992, 3rd edn 2004; papers in engrg and biological jls. *Recreations:* music, architecture, mending toys. *Address:* 25 Almoners Avenue, Cambridge CB1 8NZ. *T:* (01223) 246742.

CALLAGHAN, Rev. Brendan Alphonsus, SJ; Director of Novices, North-Western European Provinces of Society of Jesus, since 2014; *b* 29 July 1948; *s* of Dr Kathleen Callaghan (*née* Kavanagh) and Dr Alphonsus Callaghan. *Educ:* Stonyhurst; Heythrop, Oxon; Campion Hall, Oxford (MA 1977); Univ. of Glasgow (MPhil 1976); Heythrop Coll., Univ. of London (MTh 1979). Joined Society of Jesus, 1967; Clinical Psychologist, Glasgow, 1974–76; Middx Hosp., 1976–79; ordained priest, 1978; curate, St Aloysius, Glasgow, 1979–80; Heythrop College, University of London: Lectr, 1980–2007, Sen. Lectr, 2007–08, in Psychol.; Principal, 1985–97; Acting Principal, 1998–99; Dir, Academic Standards Cttee, 2005–08; Dir of Academic Develt, 2007–08; Fellow, 2009; Lectr in Psychol., Allen Hall, Chelsea, 1981–87. Superior: Brixton Jesuit Community, 1993–94; Merrivale Jesuit Community, KwaZulu-Natal, 1998; Wimbledon Jesuit Community, 1998–2005; Clapham Jesuit Community, 2007–08; Master of Campion Hall, Oxford, 2008–13. Formation Asst to British Jesuit Provincial, 2001–07. University of London: Chm., Bd of Examrs, Theol and Religious Studies, 1987–89; Schools Examn Bd, 1987–97; Collegiate Council and Senate, 1989–94; Council, 1994–97; Institute of Medical Ethics: Hon. Asst/Associate Dir, 1976–89; Governing Body, 1989–2002; Gen. Sec., 1999–2002. Visiting Lecturer: St Joseph's Theol Inst., KwaZulu-Natal, 1987 and 1997–98; (in Med. Ethics), Imperial Coll., London, 1990–; KCL, 1991–94; Vis. Prof., Fordham Univ., NY, 1990; Vis. Scholar, Weston Sch. of Theol., Cambridge, Mass, 1992. Member: Conf. of Seminary Rectors, 1987–97; Cttee of Catholic Principals, 1985–97; Ethics Cttee, St Thomas' Hosp., 1990–2002; Higher Educn Cttee, RC Bps Conf. of England and Wales, 1986–97; Academic Bd, 1982–97, Governing Body, 1982–97 and 2012–, Heythrop Coll.; Academic Adv. Cttee, Jews' Coll., 1993–97. Chm. Govs, Digby Stuart Coll., 1998–2002, Mem. Council, 1998–2002, Univ. of Surrey Roehampton (formerly Roehampton Inst.); Member, Advisory Boards: Campion Hall, Oxford, 1985–95; Syon House, Angmering, 1985–97; Centre for the Study of Communication and Culture (Chm.), 1990–; Inst. of St Anselm, Westgate (Chm.), 1991–98. Vice Pres., Catholic Students Trust Appeal. Consultant Psychologist to Marriage Care (formerly Catholic Marriage Adv. Council), 1981–, and to religious congregations and orders. Hon. FCP 1996. Broadcaster, BBC and World Service radio, Channel Four. Member, Editorial Board: Law and Justice, 1986–; Jl of Contemp. Religion, 1994–97; Mental Health, Religion and Culture, 1997–. *Publications:* Life Before Birth (with K. Boyd and E. Shotter), 1986; articles, reviews and verse in Br. Jl Psych., Jl Med. Ethics, Heythrop Jl, The Way and magazines. *Recreations:* photography, long distance walking, poetry. *Address:* Manresa House, 10 Albert Road, Hambone, Birmingham B17 0AN. *T:* (0121) 427 2628.

CALLAGHAN, James; *b* 28 Jan. 1927. Lectr, Manchester Coll., 1959–74. Metropolitan Borough Councillor, 1971–74. MP (Lab) Middleton and Prestwich, Feb. 1974–1983, Heywood and Middleton, 1983–97. *Recreations:* sport, art. *Address:* 17 Towncroft Avenue, Middleton, Manchester M24 5DA.

CALLAGHAN, Sir William (Henry), Kt 2007; JP; Chair, Marine Management Organisation, since 2011; *b* 19 May 1948; *s* of Henry William Callaghan and Constance Callaghan; *m* 1st, 1977, Frances Sproat (marr. diss. 1981); 2nd, 2001, Pauline Ortiz (*d* 2002); one *s*; 3rd, 2007, Dr Josephine Glover (marr. diss. 2013). *Educ:* St John's Coll., Oxford (BA PPE); Univ. of Kent at Canterbury (MA Econs). Trades Union Congress: Asst, 1971–74, Asst Sec., 1974–77, Head, 1978–93, Econ. Dept; Head, Econ. and Social Affairs, and Chief Economist, 1994–99; Chairman: HSC, 1999–2007; Legal Services Commn, 2008–13. Member: Low Pay Commn, 1997–2000; Res. Priorities Bd, ESRC, 1994–99; Ind. Mem., Rev. of HE Finance and Pay Data for Univ. Employers and Trade Unions, 2007–08; Chair, Rev. of Regulatory Framework for Animal Pathogens, 2007. Member Board: BITC, 1991–99; Basic Skills Agency, 1996–99; DTI Innovation Gp, 2002–04; DTI Fair Markets Bd, 2004–07. Chair: British Occupational Health Res. Foundn, 2007–; Nat. Examination Bd for Occupational Safety and Health, 2011–. JP Surrey, 2005. Vis. Fellow, Nuffield Coll., Oxford, 1999–2007. *Publications:* numerous TUC pubns on econ. and social affairs. *Recreations:* sailing, cycling, walking, listening to music.

CALLAN, Hilary Margaret West; Director, Royal Anthropological Institute of Great Britain and Ireland, 2000–10, now Director Emerita; *b* 27 Oct. 1942; *d* of late John Sydney Flashman and Marion Louise Flashman (*née* Thornton) (Silver Laurel Leaf Emblem and King's Commendation for Brave Conduct in Civil Defence, 1941); *m* 1965, Ivan Roy Callan (marr. diss. 1987); one *d*. *Educ:* Marsden Sch., NZ; St Paul's Girls' Sch.; Somerville Coll., Oxford (MA, MLitt, Dip. Social Anthropol.). Sen. Res. Associate, Birmingham Univ., 1968–70; Asst Prof., American Univ. of Beirut, Lebanon, 1971–75; Lecturer: Univ. of Kent at Canterbury, 1977–80; Trent Univ., Canada, 1981–84 (Harry Frank Guggenheim Res. Award, 1982–84); Oxford Poly., 1987–88; Brunel Univ., 1988–89; Asst Dir, UKCOSA: Council for Internat. Educn, 1989–93; Exec. Dir, Eur. Assoc. for Internat. Educn, 1993–2000 (Hon. Life Mem., 2000). Mem. Bd of Trustees, Gemini Action Internat., 2005–12; Trustee, Mass Observation Archive, 2012–. Mem., Common Room, St Cross Coll., Oxford, 2010–. Contested (SDP/Lib Alliance) Scarborough, 1987. Patron's Medal, Royal Anthropol Inst., 2011. Ed.-in-Chief, Wiley-Blackwell Internat. Encyclopedia of Anthropology, 2010–. *Publications:* Ethology and Society: towards an anthropological view, 1970; (ed jtly) The Incorporated Wife, 1984; (ed) International Education: towards a critical perspective, 2000; (contrib.) Engagements with Learning and Teaching in Higher Education: a view from anthropology, 2006; (contrib.) Identity and Networks, 2007; (contrib.) Professional Identities, 2007; (ed jtly) Early Human Kinship: from sex to social reproduction, 2008; (contrib.) Pathways to Anthropology, 2010; (ed jtly) Introductory Readings in Anthropology, 2012; numerous articles in books and jls in anthropology and internat. educn. *Recreations:* reading, music, family and friends. *Address:* c/o St Cross College, St Giles, Oxford OX1 3LZ.

CALLAN, Sir Ivan, KCVO 1998; CMG 1990; HM Diplomatic Service, retired; Ambassador to Oman, 1999–2002; *b* 6 April 1942; *s* of Roy Ivan Callan and (Gladys) May Callan (*née* Coombe); *m* 1st, 1965, Hilary Flashman; one *d*; 2nd, 1987, Mary Catherine Helena Williams; two step *s* one step *d*. *Educ:* Reading Sch.; University Coll., Oxford. BA, Dip. Soc. Anthrop., BLitt, MA. Entered FCO, 1969; Middle East Centre for Arab Studies, 1970–71; Second, later First Sec., Beirut, 1971–75; FCO, 1975–80; First Sec. and Head of Chancery, Ottawa, 1980–83; Counsellor, Hd of Chancery and Consul-General, Baghdad, 1983–87; Consul-General, Jerusalem, 1987–90; Counsellor, FCO, 1991–94; High Comr, Brunei, 1994–98. Gt Commander, Orthodox Knights of the Holy Sepulchre, 1988. *Recreations:* fine arts, painting, craftsmanship, fly fishing. *Clubs:* Reform; Kildorrery Gun; Kildorrery Trout Anglers.

CALLAN, Maj.-Gen. Michael, CB 1979; President, and Chairman of Board of Trustees, Royal Army Ordnance Corps Charitable Trust, 1993–96; *b* 27 Nov. 1925; *s* of Major John Callan and Elsie Dorothy Callan (*née* Fordham); *m* 1948, Marie Evelyn Farthing; two *s*. *Educ:* Farnborough Grammar Sch., Hants. rcds, jssc, psc. Enlisted Hampshire Regt, 1943; commnd 1st (KGV's Own) Gurkha Rifles (The Malaun Regt), 1944; resigned commn, 1947; re-enlisted, 1948; re-commnd, RAOC, 1949; overseas service: India, Burma, French Indo China, Netherlands East Indies, 1944–47; Kenya, 1950–53; Malaya/Singapore, 1958–61; USA, 1966–68; Hong Kong, 1970–71; Comdr, Rhine Area, BAOR, 1975–76; Dir Gen., Ordnance Services, 1976–80. Col Comdt, RAOC, 1981–89; Hon. Col, SW London ACF, 1982–89. Registrar, Corporation of the Sons of the Clergy, 1982–83; consultant in defence logistics and admin, 1984–89. *Recreations:* DIY, gardening. *Address:* c/o Royal Bank of Scotland, Drummonds Branch, 49 Charing Cross, SW1A 2DX.

CALLANAN, family name of **Baron Callanan**.

CALLANAN, Baron *cr* 2014 (Life Peer), of Low Fell in the County of Tyne and Wear; **Martin John Callanan;** Member (C) North East Region, England, European Parliament, 1999–2014; *b* 8 Aug. 1961; *s* of John and Ada Callanan; *m* 1997, Jayne Burton; one *s*. *Educ:* Newcastle Poly. (BSc Electrical and Electronic Engrg). Project Engr, Scottish & Newcastle Breweries, 1986–99. European Parliament: Leader, UK Conservatives, 2010–14; Chm., Eur. Conservatives and Reformists Gp, 2011–14. Contested (C) NE Reg., EP, 2014. *Recreations:* squash, football.

CALLANDER, Lt Col Richard, OBE 2008; TD 1986; landowner, farmer; Secretary, Queen's Body Guard for Scotland, Royal Company of Archers, since 2007; Vice Lord-Lieutenant of Midlothian, since 2014; *b* London, 2 April 1950; *s* of Major John Davi Callander, MC and Mary Crompton-Roberts; *m* 1973, Lady Mary Douglas, *d* of Earl o Morton, *qv*; one *s* two *d*. *Educ:* Eton; Royal Agricultural Coll., Cirencester. FRICS Chartered Surveyor in private practice, 1968–91; Hd Factor, NT for Scotland, 1991–95 QOY, 1972–2012; Commanded City of Edinburgh Univs OTC, 1992–94; Full-Tim Reserve Service: operational tour, Bosnia and Herzegovina, 1996; staff appt, MoD, London 2000; Project Dir, Armed Forces Meml, 2001–08. Chm., Scottish Veterans' Garden Cit Assoc., 2011–. DL Midlothian, 2011. *Recreations:* longbow archery, gardening, country sports travelling, ski-ing. *Address:* Saughland House, Pathhead, Midlothian EH37 5XP. *Club:* Nev (Edinburgh).

CALLAWAY, Anthony Leonard; a District Judge (Magistrates' Courts), since 2002; *b* 1 Oct. 1953; *s* of Leonard Cecil Callaway, CEng, MICE and Daphne Noreen Callaway (*né* Ibbett); *m* 2000, Heather Jean Foot, FIDM; one step *s* one step *d*. *Educ:* St Lawrence Coll KCL (BA Hons Pol Sci.; MA War Studies; MSc with Dist. War and Psychiatric Medicine MPhil Psychol Medicine Res.). Called to the Bar, Middle Temple, 1978; in practice, S Easter Circuit, 1978–2002; Actg Dep. Dist Judge, formerly Metropolitan Stipendiary Magistrate 1997–2002; Designated Dist Judge, Croydon Magistrates' Court, 2007–09. Member: IISS 2003–; RIIA, 2011–. *Recreations:* sailing, ski-ing, reading (military history). *Address:* Steeple Mill Lane, Steep, Hants GU32 2DJ. *Clubs:* Royal Automobile, Royal Thames Yacht, Ba Yacht; Royal Solent Yacht (Yarmouth).

CALLBECK, Hon. Catherine Sophia; Senator, Senate of Canada, 1997–2014; wit Callbeck's Ltd, family business, 1968–74, 1978–88 and since 1996; *b* 25 July 1939; *d* of Ralp Callbeck and Ruth Callbeck (*née* Campbell), Central Bedeque, PEI. *Educ:* Mt Allison Univ (BComm 1960); Dalhousie Univ. (BEd 1963); Syracuse Univ. Prince Edward Island: ML (L) Fourth Dist, 1974–78; Minister of Health and Social Services, Minister responsible fo Disabled and Minister responsible for Non-Status Indians, 1974–78; MP (L) Malpeque 1988–93; Official Opposition Critic for Consumer and Corporate Affairs, Energy, Mines an Resources and Financial Instns, 1988–93; former Associate Critic for Privatization an Regulatory Affairs; MLA (L) First Dist of Queens, and Premier of PEI, 1993–96; Membe Senate Standing Committees: on Internal Economy, Budgets and Admin; on Social Affair Sci. and Technol.; on Banking, Trade and Commerce; on Transport and Communication on Nat. Finance; on Agriculture and Forestry; Vice-Chm., Task Force on Wome Entrepreneurs, 2002–03. Former Mem., Higher Educn Commn, Maritime Provinces. Leade Liberal Party of PEI, 1993–96; Vice-Chm., Nat. Liberal Caucus, 2005–07. Member: Na Adv. Council of Family Resource Progs Canada; Child Alliance Adv. Cttee, PEI, 1998– Former Vice-Pres., Canada-Cuba Interparly Gp. Hon. Mem. Bd, Glaucoma Res. Soc. o Canada, 1998–. Hon. LLD Mt Allison, 1996. *Address:* Box 3947, Central Bedeque, PE C0 1G0, Canada. *T:* (902) 8872988. *E:* catherine.callbeck@bellaliant.net.

CALLENDER, Margaret; *see* Burns, M.

CALLER, Maxwell Marshall, CBE 2005; Chair, Local Government Boundary Commissio for England, since 2010 (Chair, Boundary Committee for England, 2007–10); Interventio Commissioner, London Borough of Tower Hamlets, since 2014; *b* 9 Feb. 1951; *s* of Abraha Leon Caller and Cynthia Rachel Caller; *m* 1972, Linda Ann Wohlberg; three *s* one *d*. *Educ* Newport High Sch.; University Coll. London (BSc Hons Engrg). CEng, MICE; CDipAF GLC, 1972–74; Thames Water Authority, 1974–75; London Boroughs of: Hammersmith 1975–78; Newham, 1978–81; Merton, 1981–85 (Asst Dir of Development); Barne Controller of Engrg Services, 1985–87; Dir of Technical Services, 1987–89; Chief Exec. 1989–2000; Man. Dir, subseq. Chief Exec., London Bor. of Hackney, 2000–04; Interi Chief Exec., London Bor. of Haringey, 2005–06. Mem., Electoral Commn, 2007–14 Interim Chair, Local Govt Boundary Commn for Wales, 2011–12. Technical Advr, N London Waste Authy, 1985–87; Adviser, Highways Cttee 1987–89, Public Works Ctte 1990–97, AMA. Founder Mem., 1990, and Vice Chm., Steering Cttee, 1990–2000, Barne Crime Reduction Partnership; Director: Enfield Enterprise Agency, 1994–99; N Londo TEC, 1995–2000; Prospects Careers Services Ltd, 1999–2000; The Learning Trust, 2002–04 Bernie Grant Centre Ltd, 2005–06; Chm., Barfield Group Ltd, 1995–98. Trustee, Barnet Wa Memorials Initiative, 1994–2000. Mem., Adv. Council, Norwood, 2006–. Freeman, City o London, 1991. DUniv Middlesex, 2000. *Recreation:* watching Welsh Rugby Union. *Addres* Local Government Boundary Commission for England, Layden House, 76–86 Turnmi Street, EC1M 5LG. *E:* max.caller@lgbce.org.uk.

CALLICOTT, Richard Kenneth, OBE 2012; Founder, 2004, and Chief Executive Office since 2013, Reddenhill Consulting (Managing Director, 2004–13); *b* 18 Sept. 1946; *s* o Ernest Victor Callicott and Joan Alfreda Callicott (*née* Furley); *m* 1st, 1972, Diane Lesley Kid (marr. diss. 1984); two *s*; 2nd, 1985, Jacqueline Steele (marr. diss. 1995); one *s*; 3rd, 2003 Maroline Lasebikan. *Educ:* Colston's Sch., Bristol; City of Birmingham Coll. of Educn (Ce Ed); Univ. of Birmingham (BPhil Ed). Teacher, jun. schs, Smethwick and Warley, 1968–74 Warden, Churchbridge Teachers' Centre, 1974–80; Community Educn and Recreatio Officer, Birmingham CC, 1980–83; Vice Principal, Central Inst., Birmingham, 1983–85 Area Manager, Recreation and Community, Birmingham CC, 1985; Co-ordinator Birmingham's Olympic Bid, 1985–86; Develt Manager, Sport and Leisure, Birmingham CC 1988–89; Dir of Sport, NEC Gp, 1989–99, and Hd of Sport, City of Birmingham, 1996–99 Chief Exec., UKSport, 1999–2004. Director: Saga Radio, 2001–; SBM (Sports) Ltd, 2007– Dir, British Paralympic Assoc., 2005–; Member: Leisure Infrastructure Adv. Gp, UK Trade & Investment, 2003–; Nat. Olympic Cttee, 2006–. President: British Volleyball Fedn, 2005–14 Commonwealth Volleyball Fedns, 2010–; Trustee, World Professional Billiards and Snooke Assoc. Benevolent Fund, 2008–12; Hon. Pres., Volleyball England, 2013–; Hon. Vice Pres GB Wheelchair Basketball Assoc., 2012. *Recreations:* golf, cycling, reading, gardening, theatre insatiable appetite for sport. *Address:* Reddenhill Consulting, Stourbridge Road, Wombourne S Staffs WV4 5NF.

CALLIL, Carmen Thérèse; Founder, 1972, and Chairman, 1972–95, Virago Press; writer critic; *b* 15 July 1938; *d* of Frederick Alfred Louis Callil and Lorraine Clare Allen. *Educ:* Sta of the Sea Convent, Gardenvale, Melbourne; Loreto Convent, Mandeville Hall, Melbourne Melbourne Univ. (BA). Buyer's Asst, Marks & Spencer, 1963–65; Editorial Assistan Hutchinson Publishing Co., 1965–66; B. T. Batsford, 1966–67; Publicity Manager, Panthe Books, later also of Granada Publishing, 1967–70; André Deutsch, 1971–72; publicity for In newspaper, 1972; founded Carmen Callil Ltd, book publicity co., 1972; founded Virago Press 1972, incorp. as co., 1973, Man. Dir, 1972–82. Man. Dir, Chatto & Windus: The Hogart Press, 1983–93; Publisher-at-Large, Random House UK, 1993–94; Ed.-at-Large, Knop NY, 1993–94. Mem. Bd, Channel 4, 1985–91. FRSA. Hon. LittD: Sheffield, 1994; Oxfor Brookes, 1995; DUniv: York, 1995; Open, 1997. *Publications:* (ed with Craig Raine) Nev Writing 7, 1998; (with Colm Tóibín) The Modern Library: the 200 best novels in Englan since 1950, 1999; Bad Faith: a forgotten history of family and fatherland, 2006. *Recreations* friends, reading, animals, television, sport, politics, films, gardening, France.

CALLINAN, Hon. Ian David Francis, AC 2003; Judge (*ad hoc*), International Court o Justice, since 2013; Judge of the High Court of Australia, 1998–2007; *b* 1 Sept. 1937; *s* o William Peter Callinan and Lilian Rose Callinan; *m* 1960, Wendy Mary Ruth Hamon; one one *d*. *Educ:* Univ. of Queensland (LLB). Admitted solicitor, 1960, called to the Bar, 1965 Qld; QC (Aust.) 1978. Hon. Dir, Barr Chambers Ltd, 1974–91. Chm., Qld Barrister Bd 1987–88; Hon. President: Qld Bar Assoc., 1984–87; Australian Bar Assoc., 1984–85. Vis Prof. of Law, Newcastle Univ., 1993; Adjunct Prof. of Law, Univ. of Queensland, 2009–

Chm., Australian Defence Force Acad., 2000–. Chm., Qld Totalizator Agency Bd, 1985–90; Director: QCT Ltd, 1988–97; Santos Ltd, 1996–97; ABC, 1997. Chm. Trustees, Qld Art Gallery, 1997–98; Dir, Nat. Gall. of Australia, 2007–. Hon. Fellow, Inst. of Arbitrators and Mediators Australia, 2008. *Publications: plays:* Brazilian Blue, 1995; The Cellophane Ceiling, 1996; The Acquisition, 2000; A Hero's Funeral; *novels:* The Lawyer and the Libertine, 1997; The Coroner's Conscience, 1999; The Missing Masterpiece, 2001; Appointment at Amalfi, 2003; After the Monsoon, 2005; The Russian Master, 2009; Betrayals, 2011; Dislocation, 2012; The Only Case, 2014; contrib. short stories to various anthologies. *Recreations:* history of Australian art, reading, tennis, cricket, Rugby. *Clubs:* Queensland, Tattersall's (Brisbane).

CALLMAN, His Honour Sir Clive (Vernon), Kt 2012; a Circuit Judge, 1973–2000, assigned to South-Eastern Circuit; a Deputy Circuit Judge, 2000–02; a Deputy High Court Judge, 1976–2000; *b* 21 June 1927; *o s* of Felix Callman, DMD, LDS, RCS and Edith Callman, Walton-on-Thames, Surrey; *m* 1967, Judith Helen Hines, BA, DipSocStuds (Adelaide), *o d* of Gus Hines, OBE, JP, and Hilde Hines, St George's, Adelaide, S Aust.; one *s* one *d*. *Educ:* Ottershaw Coll.; St George's Coll., Weybridge; LSE, Univ. of London (BSc(Econ), Commercial Law); Univ. of Notre Dame (Mediator Dip. 2000). Called to the Bar, Middle Temple, 1951; Blackstone Pupillage Prizeman, 1951; practised as Barrister, London and Norwich, 1952–73 (Head of London chambers, 1963), South-Eastern Circuit; Hon. Mem., Central Criminal Court Bar Mess; Dep. Circuit Judge in Civil and Criminal Jurisdiction, 1971–73; Mediator, Ct of Appeal, 2004–. Legal Assessor: GMC, 2000–04; GDC, 2000–04. Dir, Woburn Press, Publishers, 1971–73; dir of finance cos, 1961–73; non-executive Director: Frank Cass & Co. Ltd, 2000–03; Vallentine Mitchell & Co. Ltd, 2000–. University of London: Fac. Mem., Standing Cttee of Convocation, 1954–79; Senator, 1978–94; Mem. Careers Adv. Bd, 1979–92; Mem., Commerce Degree Bureau Cttee, 1980; Mem., Adv. Cttee for Magistrates' Courses, 1979; Mem., Univ. Governing Council, 1994–2001; Vice-Pres., Graduates' Soc.; Governor: Birkbeck Coll., 1982–2000 (Fellow, 2000); LSE, 1990–2008 (Gov. Emeritus, 2008); Hebrew Univ. of Jerusalem, 1992–; Mem. Court, City Univ., 1991–2001. Mem. Exec. Cttee, Soc. of Labour Lawyers, 1958; Chm., St Marylebone Constituency Labour Party, 1960–62. Mem. Council, Anglo-Jewish Assoc., 1956–; Trustee, Jewish Studies Foundn, 2004–. Editor, Clare Market Review, 1947; Member Editorial Board: Professional Negligence, 1985–95; Jl of Child Law, 1989–95; Child and Family Law Qly, 1995–2002. *Recreations:* reading, travelling, the arts. *Address:* 11 Constable Close, NW11 6UA. *T:* (020) 8458 3010. *Clubs:* Garrick, Bar Yacht.

CALLOW, Maj. Gen. Christopher George, CB 2001; OBE 1984; Chief Executive, Defence Secondary Care Agency, 1998–2000; *b* 12 July 1941; *s* of George Alexander Callow and Barbara Callow (*née* Tannahill); *m* 1967, Elizabeth Anne Macmillan Hynd; one *s* two *d*. *Educ:* Duke of York Sch., Nairobi; Univ. of Edinburgh (MB ChB 1966); DPhysMed 1971; MSc London 1984. MFCM 1987, FFPH (FFPHM 1996). RMO, 1st Bn, Green Howards, 1968–69; Army Staff Coll., 1976; Dep. Asst Dir Gen. AMS, MoD, 1977–79; CO, Armd Field Amb., 1979–83; Col, Med. Ops & Plans, MoD, 1985–88; Comdr Med., 1 Armd Div., 1988–90; Chief, Med. Plans & Policy, SHAPE, 1990–93; Comdr Med., BAOR, subseq. UKSC (Germany), 1993–96; Dir Gen., Defence Med. Trng, 1996–99. QHP 1995–2000. Consultant in Army Occupnl and Public Health Medicine, 1987–2000. OStJ 1995. *Publications:* articles on noise-induced hearing loss. *Recreations:* golf, music, travel, computing.

CALLOW, Prof. James Arthur, PhD; Mason Professor of Botany, University of Birmingham, 1983–2012, now Emeritus; *b* 17 Jan. 1945; *s* of James and Olive Callow; *m* 1968, Dr Maureen Elizabeth Wood; one *s*. *Educ:* Barrow-in-Furness Grammar Sch. for Boys; Univ. of Sheffield (BSc 1st cl. Hons Botany 1966; PhD 1969). Lectr in Botany, Univ. of Leeds, 1969–83. *Publications:* numerous, including books, professional academic jl articles. *Recreations:* golf, gardening, antiques, photography, travel. *Address:* School of Biosciences, University of Birmingham, Birmingham B15 2TT. *T:* (0121) 414 5559.

CALLOW, Simon Phillip Hugh, CBE 1999; actor, director, writer; *b* 15 June 1949; *s* of Neil Callow and Yvonne Mary Callow. *Educ:* London Oratory Grammar Sch.; Queen's Univ. Belfast; Drama Centre. London productions include: Schippel, 1975; A Mad World My Masters, 1977; Arturo Ui, Mary Barnes, 1978; As You Like It, Amadeus, NT, 1979; The Beastly Beatitudes of Balthazar B, Total Eclipse, Restoration, 1981; The Relapse, 1983; On the Spot, 1984; Kiss of the Spider Woman, 1985; Faust I and II, Lyric, Hammersmith, 1988; Single Spies (double bill: A Question of Attribution (also dir); An Englishman Abroad), NT, 1988, Queen's, 1989; The Destiny of Me (also dir), Leicester Haymarket, 1994; The Alchemist, RNT, 1996; The Importance of Being Oscar, Savoy, 1997; In Defence of Fairies, Criterion, 1997; Chimes at Midnight, Chichester, 1998; The Mystery of Charles Dickens, Comedy, transf. Albery, 2000; Chicago, Albery, NY, Australia, 2002; Through the Leaves, Southwark, transf. Duchess, 2003; The Holy Terror, Duke of York's, 2004; The Woman in White, Palace, 2005; Aladdin, Richmond, 2005; Present Laughter, tour, 2006; Merry Wives: the Musical, RSC, 2006; Equus, tour, 2008; There Love Reigns, Stratford Ontario, 2008; A Festival Dickens, Edinburgh, 2008; Waiting for Godot, tour and Th. Royal Haymarket, 2009; Dr Marigold and Mr Chops, Riverside Studios, 2009, transf. Duke of York's, 2010, and UK tour; Shakespeare - the man from Stratford, UK Tour, 2010, (as Being Shakespeare) Trafalgar Studios, 2011, transf. Brooklyn Acad. of Music, Broadway Th. Chicago, 2012, Harold Pinter, 2014; Twelfth Night, NT, 2011; Tuesdays at Tescos, Edinburgh, 2011; A Christmas Carol, Arts Th., 2011 and 2012; The Mystery of Charles Dickens, Playhouse, 2012; The Man Jesus, Lyric, Belfast, 2013, UK tour, 2014; Inside Wagner's Head, Linbury Studio Th., 2013; Chin-Chin, tour, 2013; *directed:* Loving Reno, Bush, 1984; The Passport, 1985, Nicolson Fights, Croydon, 1986, Offstage; Amadeus, Theatr Clwyd, 1986; The Infernal Machine, 1986; Cosi fan Tutte, Switzerland, 1987; Jacques and his Master, LA, 1987; Shirley Valentine, Vaudeville, 1988, NY, 1989; Die Fledermaus, Theatre Royal, Glasgow, 1988, 1989; Stevie Wants to Play the Blues, LA Theater Center, 1990; Carmen Jones, Old Vic, 1991; Ballad of the Sad Café (film), 1991; Shades, 1992; My Fair Lady, 1992; Les Enfants du Paradis, Barbican, 1996; Stephen Oliver Trilogy, 1996; Calisto, NY, 1996; Il Turco in Italia, Broomhill Opera, 1997; HRH, Playhouse, 1997; The Consul, Holland Park, 1999; The Pajama Game, Victoria Palace, 1999; Jus' Like That!, Garrick, 2003; Le Roi Malgré Lui, Grange Park, 2003; The Magic Flute, Opera Holland Park, 2008; A Christmas Carol (opera), Houston Grand Opera (world premiere), 2014. *Films:* Amadeus, 1983; A Room with a View, The Good Father, 1986; Maurice, 1987; Manifesto, 1988; Mr & Mrs Bridge, Postcards from the Edge, Crucifer of Blood, 1991; Soft Top, Hard Shoulder, Don't Look Away (also dir), 1993; Four Weddings and a Funeral, 1994; Jefferson in Paris, 1995; Ace Ventura: when Nature calls, James and the Giant Peach, 1996; The Scarlet Tunic, 1998; Bedrooms and Hallways, Shakespeare in Love, 1999; Thunderpants, No Man's Land, George and the Dragon, 2002; Angels in America, Bright Young Things, 2003; Merci Docteur Rey, Phantom of the Opera, 2004; Bob the Butler, Ragtale, 2005; Surveillance, 2006; Chemical Wedding, 2008; No Ordinary Trifle, Acts of Godfrey, 2010. *Television series:* Chance in a Million, 1983, 1985–86; David Copperfield, 1986; *other television includes:* Cariani and the Courtesans, 1987; Charles Laughton (documentary), 1987; Old Flames, 1989; Revolutionary Witness, 1989; Femme Fatale, 1993; The Purcell Film, 1995; An Audience with Charles Dickens, 1996; The Woman in White, 1997; A Christmas Dickens, 1997; The Mystery of Charles Dickens, 2002; Galileo's Daughter, 2003; Marple: The Body in the Library, 2004; Dr Who, Rome, 2005; Midsomer Murders, Roman Mysteries, 2006; Lewis, 2009; (and writer) Orson Welles Over Europe (documentary), 2009; Space Age, 2014. *Publications:* Being an Actor, 1984, rev. edn 2004, trans. French as Dans la Peau d'un Acteur, 2006; A Difficult Actor: Charles Laughton, 1987; trans. Jacques et son Maître, by Kundera, 1986; Acting in Restoration Comedy, 1990; Shooting the Actor, 1990, rev. edn 2004; Orson Welles: The Road to Xanadu, 1995; Snowdon on Stage: with a personal view of the British theatre 1954–1996, 1997; The National, 1997; Love is Where it Falls, 1999; Shakespeare On Love, 2000; Oscar Wilde and his Circle, 2000; The Night of the Hunter, 2001; Dickens' Christmas, 2003; Actors on Shakespeare series: Henry IV Part One, 2002; Henry IV Part Two, 2003; Orson Welles: Hello Americans, 2006; Classical Destinations, 1, 2007, 2, 2008; My Life in Pieces (autobiog.), 2010; Charles Dickens and the Great Theatre of the World, 2012; Orson Welles: One-Man Band, 2015. *Address:* c/o Brebners, 130 Shaftesbury Avenue, W1D 5AR.

CALLOWAY, Carol Elspeth Goodeve; *see* Brayne, C. E. G.

CALLUM, Ian Stuart, RDI 2007; Director of Design, Jaguar Cars, since 1999; *b* 30 July 1954; *s* of late Stuart Callum and Sheila Callum; *m* 1977, Lesley Anne Watson; two *s*. *Educ:* Glasgow Sch. of Art (BA Product Design 1977); Royal Coll. of Art (MA Automotive Design 1979). Designer, Ford Motor Co., 1979–90, Manager, Ghia design studio, Turin, 1988–90; Manager, TWR Design, 1990–99. Hon. FRIBA 2006. Hon. DHL Acad. of Art, San Francisco, 2000; Hon. DDes De Montfort, 2002; Hon. DArts Abertay, 2006; DUniv: Birmingham City, 2012; Glasgow, 2012. Jim Clark Meml Award, Assoc. of Scottish Motoring Writers, 1995, 2006; Minerva Medal, CSD, 2014. *Recreations:* painting, designing, building hot rods, cycling. *T:* (024) 7656 4200, *Fax:* (024) 7620 6177. *E:* icallum@jaguar.com.

CALLWAY, Eric Willi; HM Diplomatic Service, retired; Consul General, Frankfurt, 1997–2001; *b* 30 Jan. 1942; *s* of Edward and Auguste Callway; *m* 1st, 1965, Gudrun Viktoria Granström (*d* 2001); two *s*; 2nd, 2008, Barbara Anne Kleiner. Joined HM Foreign, later Diplomatic, Service, 1960: FO, 1960–61; CRO, 1961–63; New Delhi, 1963–66; Georgetown, Guyana, 1966–70; Second Sec., FCO, 1970–72; RAF Staff Coll., Bracknell, 1972; UK Mission, Geneva, 1973–77; First Secretary: FCO, 1977–79; on loan to MoD, 1979–80; FCO, 1980–81; (Commercial), E Berlin, 1981–84; (Labour), 1984–86, then (Commercial), Stockholm, 1986–88; on loan to ODA, 1988; FCO, 1989–94; Counsellor, and Dep. High Comr, Karachi, 1994–97. Vice Chm., Pakistan Soc., 2001–04. *Address:* 76 York Mansions, Prince of Wales Drive, SW11 4BW. *T:* (020) 7720 3994. *E:* ericcallway@gmail.com. *Club:* Hurlingham.

CALMAN, Sir Kenneth (Charles), KCB 1996; DL; MD; FRCP, FRCS; FRSE; Chairman, National Trust for Scotland, 2010–15; Chancellor, University of Glasgow, since 2006; Deputy Chairman, British Library, since 2011; *b* 25 Dec. 1941; *s* of Arthur McIntosh Calman and Grace Douglas Don; *m* 1967, Ann Wilkie; one *s* two *d*. *Educ:* Allan Glen's Sch., Glasgow; Univ. of Glasgow (BSc, MD, PhD). FRCSGlas 1971; FRCP 1985, FRCPE 1989; FRCGP 1989; FFPH (FFCM 1989); FRSE 1979. Hall Fellow in Surgery, Western Infirmary, Glasgow, 1968; Lectr in Surgery, Univ. of Glasgow, 1969; MRC Clinical Res. Fellow, Inst. of Cancer Res., London, 1972; University of Glasgow: Prof. of Clinical Oncology, 1974; Dean of Postgrad. Medicine and Prof. of Postgrad. Med. Educn, 1984–88; Chief Medical Officer: Scottish Office Home and Health Dept, 1989–91; DES, later DFE, then DFEE, based at DoH, 1991–98; Vice-Chancellor and Warden, Univ. of Durham, 1998–2007. Chm., Nat. Cancer Res. Inst., 2008–11. Mem., Statistics Commn, 2000–08; Chm., Commn on Scottish Devolution, 2008–09. Pres., BMA, 2008–09. Lectures include: Honeyman Gillespie, Edinburgh Royal Infirmary, first annual Douglas, Liverpool Univ., Neil Wates Meml, RSocMed, Stanley Melville Meml, ICE, Wade, Keele Univ., 1993; Sir William Weipers Meml, Glasgow Univ., 1994; Frank Lowe, Liverpool Univ., 1995; Calman Muir Meml, RCPE, Brough, Paisley Univ., 1996; Dow Meml, Dundee Univ., 1997; Harben, RIPHH, 1998; Finlayson, RCPSGlas, Meriel, Academic Vet. Soc., first Hastings, Oxford, 1999; Henry Cohen, Hebrew Univ., Jerusalem, 2000. DL Durham, 2000–07, Glasgow, 2009. Hon. FRCR 1990; Hon. FRCSE 1991; Hon. FRCPath 1992; Hon. FFPM 1992; Hon. FFOM 1993; Hon. FRCS 1995; Hon. FRCOG 1996; Hon. FRCSI 1997; Hon. FRSocMed 1997; Founder FMedSci 1998; Hon. FRCOphth 1999; Hon. Fellow, Inst. of Cancer Res., 1999; Hon. FRIAS 2015. DUniv: Stirling, 1992; Open, 1996; Paisley, 1997; Hon. DSc: Strathclyde, 1993; Westminster, 1995; Glasgow Caledonian, 1995; Glasgow, 1996; Brighton, 2000; Hon. MD: Nottingham, 1994; Newcastle, 1995; Birmingham, 1996; Hon. LLD Aberdeen, 2005. Medals include: Sir Thomas and Lady Dixon, Belfast, 1994; Francis Bissett Hawkins, RCP, 1995; Crookshanks, RCR, 1995; Alexander Hutchison, RSocMed, 1995; Gold, Macmillan Cancer Relief, 1996; Heberden (also Orator), British Soc. of Rheumatol., 1996; Silver, RCSI, 1997; Allwyn Smith, FPHM, 1998; Bradlaw, RCS Dental Faculty, 1999; Thomas Graham, Royal Philosophical Soc., Glasgow, 1999. *Publications:* Basic Skills for Clinical Housemen, 1971, 2nd edn 1983; Basic Principles of Cancer Chemotherapy, 1982; Invasion, 1984; Healthy Respect, 1987, 2nd edn 1994; The Potential for Health, 1998; Risk Communication and the Public Health, 1999, 2nd edn 2009; Storytelling, Humour and Learning in Medicine, 2001; Medical Education: past, present and future, 2006; A Doctor's Line, 2014. *Recreations:* gardening, golf, collecting cartoons, Scottish literature. *Address:* University of Glasgow, Glasgow G12 8QQ.

CALNE, Sir Roy (Yorke), Kt 1986; MA, MS; FRCS; FRS 1974; Professor of Surgery, University of Cambridge, 1965–98, now Emeritus; Fellow of Trinity Hall, Cambridge, 1965–98, now Emeritus; Visiting Professor, National University of Singapore, 1998 (Yeoh Ghim Seng Professor of Surgery, 1998–2006); *b* 30 Dec. 1930; *s* of Joseph Robert and Eileen Calne; *m* 1956, Patricia Doreen Whelan; two *s* four *d*. *Educ:* Lancing Coll.; Guy's Hosp. Med. Sch. MB, BS London with Hons (Distinction in Medicine), 1953. House Appts, Guy's Hosp., 1953–54; RAMC, 1954–56 (RMO to KEO 2nd Gurkhas); Deptl Anatomy Demonstrator, Oxford Univ., 1957–58; SHO Nuffield Orthopædic Centre, Oxford, 1958; Surg. Registrar, Royal Free Hosp., 1958–60; Harkness Fellow in Surgery, Peter Bent Brigham Hosp., Harvard Med. Sch., 1960–61; Lectr in Surgery, St Mary's Hosp., London, 1961–62; Sen. Lectr and Cons. Surg., Westminster Hosp., 1962–65; Hon. Consulting Surgeon, Addenbrooke's Hosp., Cambridge, 1965–98. Royal Coll. of Surgeons: Hallet Prize, 1957; Jacksonian Prize, 1961; Hunterian Prof., 1962; Cecil Joll Prize, 1966; Mem. Ct of Examiners, 1970–76; Mem. Council, 1981–90; Vice-Pres., 1986–89; Hunterian Orator, 1989. Founder FMedSci 1998. Fellow Assoc. of Surgeons of GB; Mem. Surgical Research Soc.; Pres., European Soc. for Organ Transplantation, 1983–84; Corresp. Fellow, Amer. Surgical Assoc., 1972, Hon. Fellow 1981; Hon. FRCP 1989; Hon. FRCS Thailand, 1992; Hon. FRCSE 1993. Hon. MD: Oslo, 1986; Athens, 1990; Hanover, 1991; QUB, 1994; Karachi, 1994; Hon. DSc Edinburgh, 2001. Prix de la Société Internationale de Chirurgie, 1969; Faltin Medal, Finnish Surgical Soc., 1977; Lister Medal, 1984; Fothergill Gold Medal, Med. Soc. of London, 1989; Cameron Prize, Edinburgh Univ., 1990; Ellison-Cliffe Medal, 1990; Ernst Jung Preis, 1992; Medawar Prize, Transplantation Soc., 1992; Medal of Helsinki Univ., 1993; Gold Medal, Catalan Transplantation Soc., 1996; King Faisal Internat. Prize for Medicine, 2001; Prince Mahidal Internat. Award for Medicine, 2002; Hamdan Award for Med. Res. Excellence, Dubai, 2008; Maharshi Sushruta Prize, Ahmedabad, 2009; ASTS-Roche Pioneer Award, Amer. Soc. of Transplant Surgeons, 2009; (jtly) Lasker~DeBakey Clinical Medical Res. Award, Lasker Foundn, 2012. Grand Officer, Order of Merit (Republic of Italy), 2000; Encomienda con Placa, Orden Civil de Sanidad (Spain) 2008. *Publications:* Renal Transplantations, 1963, 2nd edn 1967; (with H. Ellis) Lecture Notes in Surgery, 1965, 12th edn 2010; A Gift of Life, 1970; (ed and contrib.) Clinical Organ Transplantation, 1971; (ed and contrib.) Immunological Aspects of Transplantation Surgery, 1973; (ed and contrib.) Liver Transplantation, 1983; (ed and contrib.) Transplantation Immunology, 1984; Surgical Anatomy of the Abdomen in the Living Subject, 1988; (ed) Operative Surgery, 1992; Too Many People, 1994; Art Surgery and Transplantation, 1996; The Ultimate Gift, 1998; (ed jtly) Scepticism: hero and villain, 2013; The Ratchet of Science: curiosity killed the cat, 2014; papers on tissue transplantation and general surgery; sections in several surgical text-books. *Recreations:* tennis, squash, painting, sculpture (art exhibitions at Barbican, Rotterdam, Basle, 1991; New Orleans, 1992; Toronto, Cambridge, Edinburgh, 1993; Rio de Janeiro, Kyoto, 1994; Karachi, 1998; Shalini Ganendra Fine Art, Malaysia, 1998, 2003, 2008, 2011; Trinity Hall, Cambridge, 2001; Churchill Coll., Cambridge, 2003; London, 2011). *Address:* 22 Barrow Road, Cambridge CB2 8AS. *T:* (01223) 359831.

CALOW, Prof. Peter, OBE 2000; PhD, DSc; CBiol, FRSB; FLS; Professor of Zoology, University of Sheffield, 1984–2004, now Emeritus; Adjunct Professor, University of Roskilde, Denmark, since 2004; Research Professor, University of Nebraska-Lincoln, since 2011; *b* 23 May 1947; *s* of late Harry Calow and Norah K. Calow; *m* 1st, 1971, Lesley Jane Chapman (marr. diss. 1991); one *s* one *d*; 2nd, 2010, Valery E. Forbes. *Educ:* William Rhodes Sch., Chesterfield; Univ. of Leeds (BSc; PhD 1972; DSc 1984). CBiol, FRSB (FIBiol 1985); FLS 1987. Lectr, then Reader, Univ. of Glasgow, 1972–84; Warden, Wolfson Hall of Residence, 1975–84. Dir, Envmt Assessment Inst., Denmark, 2004–06. Founding Editor (with J. Grace), Functional Ecology, 1986–98; Editor, Integrated Environmental Management, 1991–95. Chairman: UK Govt Adv. Cttee on Hazardous Substances, 1991–2000; Jt Govt/Business Task Force on Application of Risk Benefit Analysis to Chemical Controls, 1993–95; Member: NE Regl Envmtl Adv. Cttee, Envmt Agency, 1996–2000; Adv. Cttee on Pesticides, 1997–2002 (Chm., Envmtl Panel, 1999–2002); Expert Panel, Res. Inst. for Fragrance Materials, 1999–; External Sci. Adv. Panel, European Chemical Industry Long-range Res. Initiative, 1999–2004 (Chm., 2003–04); Scientific Cttee on Toxicity, Ecotoxicity and Envmt, EC, 2000–04; Scientific Cttee, European Centre for Ecotoxicology and Toxicology of Chemicals, 2001–11; Scientific Cttee on Health and Envmtl Risks, EU, 2004–11 (Vice-Chm. (Envmt), 2009–11); UK Chemicals Stakeholder Forum, DEFRA, 2010. Vice-Pres., European Soc. of Evolutionary Biol., 1988–89; Pres., Soc. of Envmtl Toxicol. and Chemistry (UK), 1990–91, (Europe) 1991–92. Mem., Bd of Trustees, Health and Envmtl Scis Inst., 1996–2002; Member Council: Freshwater Biol Assoc., 1988–92 and 1995–99; Univ. of Buckingham, 1997–2002 (Chm., Acad. Adv. Council, 1999–2002). FRSA 1992–2014. *Publications:* Biological Machines, 1976; Life Cycles, 1979; Invertebrate Biology, 1981; Evolutionary Principles, 1983; (with R. Sibly) Physiological Ecology of Animals, 1986; (with R. S. K. Barnes and P. J. W. Olive) The Invertebrates: a new synthesis, 1988, 3rd edn 2001; (ed) Handbook of Ecotoxicology, vol. 1 1993, vol. 2 1994; Controlling Environmental Risks from Chemicals, 1997; Handbook of Environmental Risk Assessment and Management, 1998; (Ed.-in-Chief) The Encyclopedia of Ecology & Environmental Management, 1998; numerous contribs to learned jls. *Recreations:* reading, writing, running. *Address:* School of Biological Sciences, University of Nebraska-Lincoln, 348 Manter Hall, Lincoln, NE 68588–0118, USA.

CALTHORPE; *see* Anstruther-Gough-Calthorpe.

CALVER, Rev. Canon Gillian Margaret; Chaplain to the Queen, since 2008; permission to officiate, Diocese of Canterbury, since 2012; *b* Dulwich, 12 Jan. 1947; *d* of Eric Burnett and Hilda Burnett; *m* 1971 (marr. diss. 1999); one *s* two *d*. *Educ:* Queen Elizabeth Coll., London (BSc Hons 1968); Canterbury Sch. of Ministry; Univ. of Kent (Cert. in Counselling Studies 2001). VSO, Zambia, 1968–69; Lectr in Nutrition, Thanet Technical Coll., Broadstairs, 1969–71; Science Teacher, Channel High Sch., Folkestone, 1971–74, 1986–89; child rearing, 1974–81; Sci. Teacher and Year Hd, Pent Valley Sch., Folkestone, 1989–95; ordained deacon, 1992, priest, 1994; Priest-in-charge, Alkham Capel and Hougham, and Chaplain, Dover Coll., 1995–2002; Rector, All Saints, Staplehurst, 2002–11; Area Dean of Weald, 2006–10. Hon. Canon, Canterbury Cathedral, 2008–11, now Canon Emeritus. *Recreations:* walking, foreign travel, cooking and sharing meals with family and friends. *Address:* 6 Grand Court, Grand Parade, Littlestone, Kent TN28 8NT. *E:* gill.calver@btinternet.com.

CALVER, Marie-Eleni Eliza; *see* Demetriou, M.-E. E.

CALVER, Neil Richard; QC 2006; a Recorder, since 2009; *b* 4 Sept. 1963; *s* of Richard George and Joyce Elizabeth Calver; *m* 2009, Marie-Eleni Eliza Demetriou, *qv*; one *s* one *d*, and one *d* by a previous marriage. *Educ:* York Rd Co. Primary Sch., Kent; Dartford Grammar Sch.; Christ's Coll., Cambridge (BA 1st Cl. Hons Law 1986). Called to the Bar, Gray's Inn, 1987; in practice, 1987–, specialising in commercial and European law. *Recreations:* my children, Charlton Athletic FC, occasional climbing of mountains, opera. *Address:* Brick Court Chambers, 7–8 Essex Street, WC2R 3LD. *T:* (020) 7520 7895, *Fax:* (020) 7520 4137. *E:* calver@brickcourt.co.uk. *Club:* Ivy.

CALVERLEY, 3rd Baron *cr* 1945; **Charles Rodney Muff;** *b* 2 Oct. 1946; *s* of 2nd Baron Calverley and of Mary, *d* of Arthur Farrar, Halifax; *S* father, 1971; *m* 1972, Barbara Ann (marr. diss. 2000), *d* of Jonathan Brown, Kelbrook, near Colne; two *s*; *m* 2008, Jenifer, *d* of late Leslie Green, Brighouse, W Yorks. *Educ:* Fulneck School for Boys. Police Officer, City of Bradford Police, 1963–74, W Yorks Police, 1974–97 (RUC secondment, 1979–80). *Heir:* *s* Hon. Jonathan Edward Brown (surname changed from Muff by Deed Poll), *b* 16 April 1975. *Address:* 35 South Sea Road, Quinns Rocks, Perth, WA 6030, Australia. *T:* (8) 64013298.

CALVERLEY, Prof. Peter Martin Anthony, DSc; FRCP, FRCPE, FMedSci; Professor of Medicine (Pulmonary Rehabilitation), University of Liverpool, 1995–2010, now Emeritus; *b* 27 Nov. 1949; *s* of Peter Calverley and Jennifer (*née* Taylor); *m* 1973, Margaret Tatam; four *s*. *Educ:* Univ. of Edinburgh (MB ChB; DSc 2012). FRCP 1990; FRCPE 1990. Jun. physician posts in Edinburgh and Leicester, 1973–76; MRC Clinical Fellow, 1976–79, Sen. Registrar, 1979–85, Dept of Medicine, Royal Infirmary, Edinburgh; Consultant Physician, Aintree NHS Trust, Liverpool (later Aintree Univ. Hosps NHS Foundn Trust), 1988–95 (Hon. Consultant Physician, 1995–). Chm., Respiratory Disorders Specialty Gp, NIHR, 2009–15. Travelling Fellow, Meakin-Christie Labs, McGill Univ., Montreal, 1982–83. Pres., British Thoracic Soc., 2005. FMedSci 2011; FERS 2014. *Publications:* (ed jtly) Chronic Obstructive Pulmonary Disease, 1994; papers on pathophysiology and treatment of chronic obstructive pulmonary disease and sleep-related breathing disorders. *Recreations:* sailing, ski-ing, travel, family. *Address:* University Hospital Aintree, Aintree University Hospitals NHS Foundation Trust, Longmoor Lane, Liverpool L9 7AL. *T:* (0151) 529 5886. *Club:* Artists (Liverpool).

CALVERT, Prof. (Alan) Hilary, MD; FRCP, FMedSci; Director, Cancer Drug Discovery and Development, UCL Cancer Institute, 2009–14, Head, Department of Oncology, 2010–14, and Professor of Cancer Therapeutics, 2011–14, now Emeritus, University College London; *b* 18 Feb. 1947; *s* of Norman Geoffrey Calvert and Mary Christine Calvert (*née* Whitehead); *m* 1969, Drusilla Dean; three *d*. *Educ:* Birkenhead Sch.; Peterhouse, Cambridge (BA Med. Sci. and Maths 1969; MB BChir 1972; MD 1981); University Coll. Hosp., London (Clinical Studies); Chelsea Coll., London (MSc Biochem. 1978). MRCP 1975, FRCP 1988; Accreditation Med. Oncol., RCP 1987. Clinical Res. Fellow, Royal Marsden Hosp., 1975–77; Institute of Cancer Research, London: Lectr in Clinical Pharmacol., 1977–80; Sen. Lectr, 1980–85; Reader, 1985–89; University of Newcastle upon Tyne: Prof. of Med. Oncol., 1989–2009; Dir, Cancer Res. Unit, 1989–2003; Clinical Dir, subseq. Dir of Clinical and Translational Res., Northern Inst. for Cancer Res., 2003–09. Hon. Consultant: in Medicine, Royal Marsden Hosp., 1980–89; in Med. Oncol., Northern Centre for Cancer Treatment, Newcastle upon Tyne, 1989–2009; UCH London, 2009–. Vis. Prof., Dept of Maths and Statistics, Newcastle Univ., 2010–13. Mem., Gene Therapy Adv. Cttee, 2006–12; Chm., New Agents Cttee, CRUK, 2009–13; Mem., Internat. Scientific Adv. Bd, Associazione Italiana per la Ricerca sul Cancro, 2012–16. FMedSci 2002. Pfizer Award for Innovative Sci., 2005; Lifetime Achievement Award: British Oncol Assoc., 2009; Eur. Soc. of Med. Oncol., 2010; (jtly) Translational Res. Prize, CRUK, 2010. *Publications:* (ed jtly) Handbook of Anticancer Drug Development, 2003; contribs on cancer research, esp. cancer therapy, incl. develt of platinum drugs, antifolates and inhibitors of poly (ADP-ribose) polymerase; also contribs on application of mathematical methods to cancer treatment. *Recreations:* ski-ing, hill-walking, classical music, opera, hi-fi circuit design and development, olive oil production, computer programming of MACREX indexing software (with Drusilla). *Address:* UCL Cancer Institute, Paul O'Gorman Building, 72 Huntley Street, WC1E 6BT. *T:* (020) 7679 0744. *E:* hilary.calvert@cancer.ucl.ac.uk.

CALVERT, Denis; *see* Calvert, L. V. D.

CALVERT, Hilary; *see* Calvert, A. H.

CALVERT, John Raymond; Chairman, Worcestershire Partnership Mental Health NHS Trust, 1999–2007; *b* 14 June 1937; *s* of Matthew and Eva Mary Calvert; *m* 1962, Elspeth Sarah Naish; one *s* one *d*. *Educ:* Bootham, York; Manchester Univ. (BA Econs). FIPD (FIPM 1986). Cadbury Schweppes Ltd, 1961–70; Delta Metals Ltd, 1970–73; Pilkington Bros Ltd, 1973–84: Personnel Dir, Triplex Safety Glass Ltd, 1973–80; Dir, Chance Bros Ltd, 1973–80; Gp Employee Relations Manager, 1980–84; Dir, Industrial Relations, ITCA, 1984–88; Gp Personnel Dir, Yorkshire Tyne Tees TV Hldgs plc, 1988–93; Man. Dir, 1993–97, Dep. Chm., 1996–97, Tyne Tees TV. Director: Northern Sinfonia, 1993–; Newcastle Initiative, 1994–. Council Member: Industrial Soc., 1994–; NE Chamber of Commerce, 1995–. Chm., Newcastle Educn Business Partnership, 1995–. Trustee, Cleveland Community Foundn, 1995–. Gov., Newcastle Coll., 1994–. Chm., Feckenham Community Shop, 2009–13. FRSA 1989. *Recreations:* church organist and choirmaster, fell walking, tennis. *Address:* Strands, Droitwich Road, Feckenham, near Redditch, Worcs B96 6RT. *T:* (01527) 821607.

CALVERT, Kate; musician and poet; *b* Lewisham, London, 22 Dec. 1985. *Educ:* BRIT Sch. for Performing Arts and Technol.; Goldsmiths, Univ. of London (Eng. Lit.). *Publications:* as Kate Tempest: Brand New Ancients, 2013; Wasted (play), 2013; Hold Your Own, 2014; Hopelessly Devoted (play), 2014.

CALVERT, Lorne Albert; Principal, St Andrew's College, University of Saskatchewan, since 2009; *b* Moose Jaw, Sask, 24 Dec. 1952; *s* of Albert Calvert and Beulah Awilda (*née* Phillips); *m* 1975, Betty Anne Sluzalo; one *s* one *d*. *Educ:* Univ. of Regina (BA 1973); Univ. of Saskatchewan (BD 1976). Ordained minister, United Ch of Canada, 1976; Minister, Gravelbourg United Ch, 1976–79; Zion United Ch, Moose Jaw, 1979–86. MLA (NDP) Moose Jaw South, 1986–91, Moose Jaw Wakamow, 1991–2001, Saskatoon Riversdale, 2001–09; Associate Minister of Health, and Minister resp. for Wakamow Valley Authy, 1992–95; Minister resp. for SaskPower and SaskEnergy, 1992–93; Minister: of Health, 1995; of Social Services, 1995–98 (also resp. for Seniors and Public Service Commn); Minister resp. for Disabilities Issues, 1997–98; Premier, and Pres., Exec. Council, 2001–07; Leader of the Opposition, 2007–09. Dep. Chm., Crown Corporations Cttee, 1991–92; Mem., Standing Cttee on the Envmt, 1991–92. Leader, NDP, 2001–09. *Address:* St Andrew's College, 112 College Drive, Saskatoon, SK S7N 0W3, Canada.

CALVERT, (Louis Victor) Denis, CB 1985; Comptroller and Auditor General for Northern Ireland, 1980–89, retired; *b* 20 April 1924; *s* of Louis Victor Calvert, Belfast and Gertrude Cherry Hobson, Belfast; *m* 1949, Vivien Millicent Lawson; two *s* one *d*. *Educ:* Belfast Royal Academy; Queen's Univ., Belfast (BScEcon); Admin. Staff Coll., Henley-on-Thames. Served with RAF, 1943–47, navigator (F/O). Northern Ireland Civil Service, 1947–80: Min. of Agriculture, 1947–56; Dep. Principal 1951; Principal, Min. of Finance, 1956–63; Min. of Health and Local Govt, 1963–65; Asst Sec. 1964; Min. of Development, 1965–73; Sen. Asst Sec. 1970; Dep. Sec. 1971; Min. of Housing, Local Govt and Planning, 1973–76; DoE for NI, 1976–80. Mem. Bd, Internat. Fund for Ireland, 1989–92. *Recreations:* gardening, golf, reading.

CALVERT, Margaret Vivienne, RDI 2011; (independent) graphic designer and typographer, since 2001; *b* Durban, SA, 12 May 1936; *d* of Stanley Gordon Calvert and Jessie Margaret Calvert (*née* Tassie). *Educ:* Hatfield Primary Sch., Pretoria; Pretoria High Sch. for Girls; St Paul's Sch. for Girls, London; Chelsea Sch. of Art. Asst Designer to Jock Kinneir, 1957–66; Partner, Kinneir Calvert & Associates, 1966–72; Dir, Kinneir Calvert Tuhill, 1972–79; Hd, Graphic Design, RCA, 1987–91 (Sen. Fellow, 2001). Pt-time Lectr in Graphic Design and Typography, RCA, 1966–2001. Mem., Alliance Graphique Internat., 1977–. Hon. Fellow, Univ. of Arts, London, 2004. Hon. DLitt Brighton, 2006. *Publications:* (contrib.) AGI: graphic design since 1950, 2007. *Recreations:* cinema, reading, walking, table-tennis.

CALVERT, Michael, OBE 1998; Chief Executive, Royal Agricultural Society of England, 2000–05; *b* 1950; *s* of Noel and Nancy Calvert; *m*; three *s*. *Educ:* Edinburgh Univ. (BSc Hons 1972). Tech. Rep., ICI, 1972–74; Partner, Northwold Agricl Services, 1974–80; General Manager: Farmplan Pty, 1980–81; Sentry Farm Mgt, 1981–85; CWS Farms Gp, 1985–2000. Bd Mem., Rothamsted Exptl Stn, 2000–03. Mem., Council, BBSRC, 1998–2003; Chm., LINK Sustainable Livestock Prodn Prog., 1996–2004.

CALVERT, Rev. Canon Peter Noel; House for Duty Team Vicar, Cartmel Peninsula Team Ministry, 2012–15; Chaplain to the Queen, 1998–2011; *b* 20 Dec. 1941; *s* of Harry and Beatrice Annie Calvert; *m* 1980, Stella Christine Horrocks; two *s* one *d*. *Educ:* Queen Elizabeth GS, Wakefield; Arnold Sch., Blackpool; Christ's Coll., Cambridge (BA 1963; MA 1967). Ordained deacon, 1966, priest, 1967; Curate, Brighouse, 1966–71; Vicar, Heptonstall, 1971–82; Vicar of Todmorden, W Yorks, 1982–2007; Priest-in-charge, Cross Stone, 1983–93; Rural Dean, Calder Valley, 1984–2006; House for Duty Priest-in-charge, Leven Valley Benefice, 2007–11; Hon. Canon, Wakefield Cathedral, 1992–2007, now Canon Emeritus. *Recreations:* photography, philately, walking, interest in transport. *Address:* 26 Stonemere Avenue, Todmorden OL14 5RW. *T:* (01706) 817166.

CALVERT-SMITH, Sir David, Kt 2002; Chairman, Parole Board of England and Wales, since 2012; a Judge of the Courts of Appeal of Jersey and Guernsey, since 2012; *b* 6 April 1945; *s* of late Arthur and Stella Calvert-Smith; *m* 1971, Marianthe Phoca; one *s* one *d*. *Educ:* Eton; King's Coll., Cambridge (MA). Called to the Bar, Middle Temple, 1969, Bencher, 1994; Recorder, 1986–98; Jun. Treasury Counsel, 1986; Sen. Treasury Counsel, 1991; First Sen. Treasury Counsel, 1995; QC 1997; Dir of Public Prosecutions, 1998–2003; a Judge of the High Court of Justice, QBD, 2004–12; a Presiding Judge, SE Circuit, 2006–10. Mem., CRE, 2004–06. Vice-Chm., 1997–98, Chm., 1998, Criminal Bar Assoc.; Mem., Criminal Cttee, Judicial Studies Bd, 1997–98. *Recreations:* music, sports. *Address:* Parole Board of England and Wales, 52 Queen Anne's Gate, SW1H 9AG.

CALVET, Jacques; President, Peugeot SA, 1984–97; Referendary Councillor, Cour des Comptes (Audit Office), since 1963; *b* 19 Sept. 1931; *s* of Prof. Louis Calvet and Yvonne Calvet (*née* Olmières); *m* 1956, Françoise Rondot; two *s* one *d*. *Educ:* Lycée Janson-de-Sailly; Law Faculty, Paris (Licencié en droit; Dipl. Inst. d'Etudes Politiques; Dipl. d'Etudes Supérieures d'Economie Politique et des Sciences Economiques). Trainee, l'Ecole Nationale d'Administration, 1955–57; Audit Office, 1957–59; Office of Sec. of State for Finance, 1959–62, of Minister of Finance, 1962–66; Dep. Dir, 1964, Head of Dept, 1967, Central Finance Admin; Head of Finance Dept, Paris Préfecture, 1967–69; Asst Dir, later Dir, Office of Minister of Economy and Finance, 1969–74; Dir in Ministry of Finance, 1973; Asst Dir Gen., 1974, Dir Gen., 1976, Pres., 1979–82, Banque Nationale de Paris; Vice-Prés. du Conseil d'Administration, 1984, Prés., 1990, Automobiles Peugeot; Président du Conseil d'Administration: Automobiles Citroën, 1983–97; Publicité Française, 1991–97. Vice Prés. Conseil de surveillance, Galeries Lafayette; Prés., Comité de surveillance, Bazar de l'hôtel de Ville; Administrateur: Icade Foncière des Pimonts; Cottin Frères; Société Foncière Lyonnaise

Consulting Advr, Banque de France. Commandeur, Légion d'Honneur, 1996; Officier: Ordre Nat. du Mérite, 1970; Ordre Nat. du Mérite Agricole, 1970; Chevalier des Palmes académiques, 1964; Grande Ufficiale, Ordine al Merito della Repubblica Italiana, 1995. *Address:* 31 avenue Victor Hugo, 75116 Paris, France.

CALVIN, Michael; columnist, Independent on Sunday, since 2012; owner, Integr8Communications, since 2007; *b* 3 Aug. 1957; *s* of Charles Calvin and Margaret Calvin (*née* Platts); *m* 1977, Lynn Goss; three *s* one *d*. *Educ:* Watford Grammar Sch. Reporter: Watford Observer, 1975–77; Hayters Sports Agency, 1977–79; writer and broadcaster, Thames TV, 1983–84; Chief Sports Writer, Westminster Press, 1979–83; Feature Writer, 1984–86, Chief Sports Writer, 1986–96, Daily Telegraph; Sen. Sports Writer, The Times, 1997–98; Chief Sports Feature Writer, Mail on Sunday, 1998–2002; Dep. Dir, English Inst. of Sport, 2002–07; Chief Sports Writer, Sunday Mirror, 2008–11. Segrave Trophy for Outstanding Achievement, 1990; Sports Journalist of the Year, English Sports Council, 1992; Sports Reporter of the Year, British Press Awards, 1992, 1999; Award for Services to Yachting Journalism, RYA, 1993; led winning team for coverage of disabled sport, British Sports Assoc. for Disabled, 1994, 1995, 1996. *Publications:* Captaincy, 1977; Only Wind and Water, 1998; Family: life, death and football, 2010; Life's a Pitch, 2012; The Nowhere Men, 2013 (The Times Sports Book of the Year, 2014); (with G. Thomas) Proud, 2014. *Recreation:* long distance sailing. *Clubs:* Royal Ocean Racing; Cape Horners.

CALVOCORESSI, Richard Edward Ion, CBE 2008; Director, Henry Moore Foundation, since 2007; *b* 5 May 1951; *s* of late Ion Melville Calvocoressi and of Katherine (*née* Kennedy); *m* 1976, Francesca Temple Roberts; one *s* two *d*. *Educ:* Eton; Brooke House, Market Harborough; Magdalen Coll., Oxford (Exhibnr; BA (Hons) English Lang. and Lit.); Courtauld Inst. of Art (MA Hist. of Art, 19th and 20th centuries). Research Assistant: Scottish Nat. Gall. of Modern Art, Edinburgh, 1977–79; Modern Collection, Tate Gall., 1979–82; Asst Keeper, Tate Gall., 1982–87; Keeper, then Dir, Scottish Nat. Gall. of Modern Art, 1987–2007. Art Advr, Chelmsford Mus., 1980–86; Member: Cttee, British Council, Scotland, 1989–98; Visual Arts Adv. Cttee, British Council, 1991–2006 (Chm., 1999–2006); Visual Arts Cttee, Scottish Arts Council, 1993–95; Reviewing Cttee on Export of Works of Art, 2012–. Dir, Grimsthorpe and Drummond Castle Trust, 1993–. Governor, Glasgow Sch. of Art, 1988–91; Expert Mem., Comité Magritte, 2001–; Mem., Francis Bacon catalogue raisonné Cttee, 2006–. Trustee: Edward James Foundn, 2007–10; Art Fund, 2008–. *Publications:* Magritte, 1979, rev. edn 1984; Lee Miller: portraits from a life, 2002; Lucian Freud on Paper, 2008; numerous exhibn catalogues, reviews and articles. *Address:* 20 Warriston Crescent, Edinburgh EH3 5LB.

CAMBRIDGE, Archdeacon of; *see* Hughes, Ven. A. J.

CAMBRIDGE, Alan John; HM Diplomatic Service, retired; *b* 1 July 1925; *s* of Thomas David Cambridge and Winifred Elizabeth (*née* Jarrett); *m* 1947, Thelma Elliot; three *s* one *d*. *Educ:* Beckenham Grammar Sch. Served War, FAA and RAFVR, 1943–47 (Air Gunner, Bomber Comd). War Pensions Office and MPNI, 1948–55; entered CRO, 1955; Chief Clerk: Madras, 1956–58; Kuala Lumpur, 1959–62; 2nd Sec., Salisbury, Fedn of Rhodesia and Nyasaland, 1962–65; 1st Sec. (Political), Freetown, 1965–66; UN Dept, FCO, 1966–68; 1st Sec., Prague, 1969; 1st Sec. (Consular/Aid), Suva, 1970–72; HM Consul, Milan, 1972–74; Asst Head of Inf. Dept, FCO, 1974–78; 1st Sec., Ankara, 1978–81; Asst Head, 1981–82, Head and Counsellor, 1983–85, Migration and Visa Dept, FCO; Assessor, FCO, 1985–90. *Recreations:* photography, swimming. *Address:* 9 The Ferns, Carlton Road, Tunbridge Wells TN1 2JT. *T:* (01892) 531223. *Club:* Civil Service.

CAMBRIDGE, Sydney John Guy, CMG 1979; CVO 1979; HM Diplomatic Service, retired; *b* 5 Nov. 1928; *o s* of late Jack and Mona Cambridge; unmarried. *Educ:* Marlborough; King's Coll., Cambridge. Entered HM Diplomatic Service, Sept. 1952; Oriental Sec., British Embassy, Jedda, 1953–56; Foreign Office, 1956–60; First Sec., UK Delegn to United Nations, at New York, 1960–64; Head of Chancery, British Embassy, Djakarta, 1964–66; FO, 1966–70; Counsellor, British Embassy, Rome, 1970–73; Head of Financial Relations Dept, FCO, 1973–75; Counsellor, British High Commn, Nicosia, 1975–77; Ambassador: to Kuwait, 1977–82; to Morocco, 1982–84. *Address:* Saint Peter's House, Filkins, Lechlade, Glos GL7 3JQ.

CAMDEN, 6th Marquess *cr* 1812; **David George Edward Henry Pratt;** Baron Camden, 1765; Earl Camden, Viscount Bayham, 1786; Earl of Brecknock, 1812; *b* 13 Aug. 1930; *o s* of 5th Marquess Camden and Marjorie, Countess of Brecknock, DBE (*d* 1989); *S* father, 1983; *m* 1961, Virginia Ann (marr. diss. 1984), *o d* of late F. H. H. Finlaison, Arklow Cottage, Windsor, Berks; one *s* one *d* (and one *s* decd). *Educ:* Eton. Late Lieutenant, Scots Guards. Dir, Clive Discount Co. Ltd, 1958–69. *Heir: s* Earl of Brecknock, *qv*. *Address:* Wherwell House, Andover, Hants SP11 7JP. *T:* (01264) 860020.

CAMDESSUS, Michel Jean, Hon. CBE 2007; Managing Director, International Monetary Fund, 1987–2000; *b* 1 May 1933; *s* of Alfred Camdessus and Madeleine Camdessus (*née* Cassembon); *m* 1957, Brigitte d'Arcy; two *s* four *d*. *Educ:* Inst. of Political Studies, Paris; Diploma, Nat. Sch. of Administration. Administrateur Civil, French Treasury, 1960; Financial Attaché, Permt French Delegn to European Communities, 1966–68; Asst Dir, Treasury, 1971, Dep. Dir, 1974, Dir, 1982; Dep. Governor, Bank of France, Aug. 1984, Governor, Nov. 1984. Chm., Paris Club, 1978–84. Grand Officier de la Légion d'Honneur; Chevalier de l'Ordre National du Mérite; Croix de la valeur militaire. *Address:* 27 rue de Valois, 75001 Paris, France.

CAMERON, family name of **Barons Cameron of Dillington** and **Cameron of Lochbroom**.

CAMERON OF DILLINGTON, Baron *cr* 2004 (Life Peer), of Dillington in the County of Somerset; **Ewen James Hanning Cameron,** Kt 2003; DL; FRICS; Owner and Manager, Dillington Estate, Somerset, since 1971; *b* 24 Nov. 1949; *s* of Maj. Allan John Cameron and Elizabeth Cameron (*née* Vaughan-Lee); *m* 1975, Caroline Anne Ripley; three *s* one *d*. *Educ:* Harrow Sch.; Christ Church, Oxford (MA). FRICS 1992; FRAgS 1995. Founding Chm., Orchard Media Ltd, 1989–99; Chairman: Lets Go Travel Ltd, 1998–2006; Airports Direct Travel Ltd, 2006–. Mem., Minister of Agriculture's CAP rev. gp, 1995; Govt's Rural Advocate, 2000–04. Jt Chm., All Party Parly Gp for Agric., Food and Develt, 2009–; Chm., Strategy Adv. Bd, Global Food Security Prog., 2011–. Dir, Village Retail Services Assoc. for Village Shops, 1992–2000. Nat. Pres., CLA, 1995–97. Mem., UK Round Table for Sustainable Develt, 1997–2000. Chairman: Countryside Agency, 1999–2004; Charities' Property Assoc., 2005–; Dir, Lawes Agricl Trust (Rothamsted), 2005–; Pres., British Guild of Agricl Journalists (formerly Agricl Guild of Journalists), 2010–15. Pres., Somerset Young Farmers, 1990–91; Mem., Mgt Bd, Nat. Fedn of Young Farmers, 1998–2000. Chm., Somerset Strategic Partnership, 2004–10. Dir, Royal Bath and West Soc., 2005–15 (Pres., 2006–07). Crossbencher, H of L. FRSA 1996. High Sheriff, 1986–87, DL 1989, Somerset. Hon. Fellow, RAU, 2013. Hon. LLD Exeter, 2004. *Recreations:* golf, shooting, windsurfing. *Address:* Dillington Farms, Ilminster, Som TA19 9EG.

CAMERON OF LOCHBROOM, Baron *cr* 1984 (Life Peer), of Lochbroom in the District of Ross and Cromarty; **Kenneth John Cameron;** PC 1984; a Senator of the College of Justice in Scotland, 1989–2003; *b* 11 June 1931; *s* of Hon. Lord Cameron, KT, DSC; *m* 1964, Jean Pamela Murray; two *d*. *Educ:* The Edinburgh Academy; Corpus Christi Coll., Oxford (MA 1955; Hon. Fellow, 1989); Edinburgh Univ. (LLB). Served RN, 1950–52; commissioned RNVR, 1951 (Lt). Admitted Faculty of Advocates, 1958; QC (Scot.) 1972; Standing Junior to Dept of Transport, 1964–71; to DoE, 1971–72; Chairman of Industrial Tribunals in Scotland, 1966–81; Advocate Depute, 1981–84; Lord Advocate, 1984–89. Chm. of Pensions Appeal Tribunal (Scotland), 1975, Pres. 1976–84. Chairman: Cttee for Investigation in Scotland of Agricultural Marketing Schemes, 1980–84; Scottish Civic Trust, 1989–95; Edinburgh New Town Conservation Cttee, 1991–94; Royal Fine Art Commn for Scotland, 1995–2005. Pres., Scottish Council for Voluntary Orgns, 1989–2001. Hon. Bencher, Lincoln's Inn, 1984. FRSE 1990. Hon. FRIAS 1994. *Recreations:* fishing, music. *Address:* Stoneyhill House, Musselburgh EH21 6RP. *T:* (0131) 665 1081. *Club:* New (Edinburgh).

CAMERON, Prof. Alan Douglas Edward, FBA 1975; Anthon Professor of Latin Language and Literature, Columbia University, New York, 1977–2008, now Emeritus; *b* 13 March 1938; *er s* of A. D. Cameron, Egham; *m* 1st, 1962, Averil Sutton (*see* Dame A. M. Cameron) (marr. diss. 1980); one *s* one *d*; 2nd, 1987, Charlotte Innes (marr. diss. 1992); 3rd, 1998, Carla Asher. *Educ:* St Paul's Sch. (Schol.); New Coll., Oxford (Schol.). Craven Scholar 1958; 1st cl. Hon. Mods 1959; De Paravicini Scholar 1960; Chancellor's Prize for Latin Prose 1960; 1st cl. Lit. Hum. 1961; N. H. Baynes Prize 1967; John Conington Prize 1968. Asst Master, Brunswick Sch., Haywards Heath, 1956–57; Asst Lectr, then Lectr, in Humanity, Glasgow Univ., 1961–64; Lectr in Latin, 1964–71, Reader, 1971–72, Bedford Coll., London; Prof. of Latin, King's Coll., London, 1972–77. Visiting Professor: Columbia Univ., NY, 1967–68; UCLA, 1989; Visiting Fellow: Humanities Research Centre, ANU, 1985; Inst. for Advanced Study, Princeton, 1990; Guggenheim Fellow, 1986. Fellow: Amer. Acad. of Arts and Sciences, 1979; Amer. Philosophical Soc., 1992. Charles J. Goodwin Award, Amer. Philol Assoc., 1996; Lionel Trilling Award, Columbia Univ., 2005; Kenyon Medal, British Acad., 2013. *Publications:* Claudian: Poetry and Propaganda at the Court of Honorius, 1970; (contrib.) Prosopography of the Later Roman Empire, ed Jones, Morris and Martindale, i, 1971, ii, 1980; Porphyrius the Charioteer, 1973; Bread and Circuses, 1974; Circus Factions, 1976; Literature and Society in the Early Byzantine World, 1985; (jtly) The Consuls of the Later Roman Empire, 1985; (with J. Long) Barbarians and Politics at the Court of Arcadius, 1993; The Greek Anthology: from Meleager to Planudes, 1993; Callimachus and his Critics, 1995; Greek Mythography in the Roman World, 2004; The Last Pagans of Rome, 2011; Wandering Poets and Other Essays in Later Greek Poetry and Philosophy, 2015; articles and reviews in learned jls. *Recreation:* the cinema. *Address:* 450 Riverside Drive, New York, NY 10027, USA.

CAMERON, Alan John, AO 2011 (AM 1997); Chairman and Director, Property Exchange Australia Ltd (formerly National e-Conveyancing Development Ltd), since 2010; *b* 9 Feb. 1948; *s* of John and Norma Cameron; *m* 1971, Susan Patricia Sanders; two *s*. *Educ:* Sydney Univ. (BA, LLB, LLM). Principal Solicitor, NSW Aboriginal Legal Service, 1973–75; Lectr in Law, Univ. of N Sumatra, 1975–77; Dawson Waldron, Solicitors, later Blake Dawson Waldron: Partner, 1979–91; Man. Partner, 1982–85, 1989–91; Commonwealth Ombudsman (Australia), 1991–92; Chairman: Australian Securities & Investments Commn, 1993–2000; NSW Growth Centres Commn, 2005–08; ASX Compliance Pty Ltd (formerly ASX Market Supervision Pty Ltd), 2008–; Hastings Funds Mgt Ltd, 2009–; ASX Corporate Governance Council, 2011–; Chm. and Dir, Reliance Rail Gp, 2007–10. Mem., Judicial Commn of NSW, 2001–09. Dir, Westpac Funds Management Ltd, 2006–10. Dep. Chancellor, Univ. of Sydney, 2007–14. *Recreations:* tennis, walking, reading. *Address:* 32 Hart Street, Balmain, NSW 2041, Australia.

CAMERON, Alexander, CBE 2000; Chairman, Parole Board for Scotland, 2006–13; *b* 29 April 1950; *s* of Æneas and Ruby Cameron; *m* 1975, Linda J. T. Dobbie; two *s*. *Educ:* Duncanrig Sen. Secondary Sch.; Univ. of Strathclyde (BA); Univ. of Aberdeen (Cert. Applied Social Studies; CQSW 1973). Social worker, Clackmannan Co., 1973–75; Principal Officer, 1975–81, Asst Dir of Social Work, 1981–87, Central Reg.; Dir of Social Work, Borders Reg., 1987–95; Exec. Dir of Social Work, S Lanarks, 1995–2006. Vis. Prof., Strathclyde Univ., 1997–. Chair: Inst. for Res. and Innovation in Social Services (formerly Scottish Inst. for Excellence in Social Work Educn), 2003–; Scottish Inst. for Residential Child Care, 1996–2007. Non-exec. Dir, State Hosps Bd for Scotland, 2005–13. Chm., Exec. Governance Gp, Centre for Youth and Criminal Justice, Univ. of Strathclyde, 2013–; Member: Bd, SACRO, 2013– (Chm., 2014–); Panel, Ind. Jersey Care Inquiry, 2014–. Dir, Care Visions, 2006–; Trustee, Lloyds TSB Foundn for Scotland, 2009–; Chm., Fred Edwards Trust, 2010–. Pres., Assoc. of Dirs of Social Work, 1996–97. Mem. Bd, Capability Scotland, 2012. Fellow, British Amer. Project, 1988. *Recreations:* reading, architecture and design, cooking, dining out, travel, especially to USA. *T:* 07792 229964. *E:* cameronsathome@btinternet.com.

CAMERON, Alexander Allan; QC 2003; *b* 27 Aug. 1963; *s* of late Ian Donald Cameron and of Mary Fleur Cameron; *m* 1990, Sarah Louise Fearnley-Whittingstall; one *s* one *d*. *Educ:* Eton Coll.; Bristol Univ. (LLB Hons). Called to the Bar, Inner Temple, 1986; in practice, specialising in law of crime, incl. commercial crime, extradition and licensing. *Recreation:* various. *Address:* 3 Raymond Buildings, Gray's Inn, WC1R 5BH. *T:* (020) 7400 6400. *E:* clerks@3rblaw.com. *Clubs:* White's, Queen's, MCC.

See also Rt Hon. D. W. D. Cameron.

CAMERON, Rt Rev. Andrew Bruce; Bishop of Aberdeen and Orkney, 1992–2006 and Primus of the Episcopal Church in Scotland, 2000–06; *b* 2 May 1941; *s* of Andrew and Helen Cameron; *m* 1974, Elaine Gingles; two *s*. *Educ:* Eastwood Secondary Sch., Glasgow; Edinburgh Theol Coll.; Edinburgh Univ. (Cert. in Past. Studies); Urban Theology Unit, Sheffield (Dip. in Theology and Mission). Ordained deacon 1964, priest 1965; Assistant Curate: St Michael and All Angels, Helensburgh, 1964–67; Holy Cross, Edinburgh, 1967–70; Diocesan and Provincial Youth Chaplain and Chaplain, St Mary's Cathedral, Edinburgh, 1970–75; Rector, St Mary's, Dalmahoy and Anglican Chaplain, Heriot-Watt Univ., 1975–82; Churches Develt Officer in Livingston Ecumenical Parish, 1982–88; Rector, St John's, Perth and Convenor of Provincial Mission Bd, 1988–92. Resident Scholar, Bruton Parish Church, Williamsburg, Va, 2006–07. Interim Warden, Scottish Churches House, 2008. *Recreations:* golf, swimming, walking, gardening, singing, listening to music, theatre, reading. *Address:* 2 Newbigging Grange, Coupar Angus, Perthshire PH13 9GA. *T:* (01821) 650482. *E:* bruce2541@gmail.com.

See also Rt Rev. D. M. Cameron.

CAMERON, Dame Averil (Millicent), DBE 2006 (CBE 1999); MA, PhD, DLitt; FBA 1981; FSA 1982; historian; Warden, Keble College, 1994–2010, Professor of Late Antique and Byzantine History, 1998–2010, Pro-Vice-Chancellor, 2001–10, University of Oxford; *b* 8 Feb. 1940; *d* of T. R. Sutton, Leek, Staffs; *m* 1962, Alan Douglas Edward Cameron, *qv* (marr. diss. 1980); one *s* one *d*. *Educ:* Westwood Hall Girls' High Sch., Leek, Staffs; Somerville Coll., Oxford (Passmore Edwards Schol. 1960; Rosa Hovey Schol. 1962; MA); Univ. of Glasgow; University Coll. London (PhD; FKC 1987); Univ. of Oxford (DLitt 2008). King's College London: Asst Lectr, 1965; Lectr, 1968; Reader in Ancient History, 1970; Prof. of Ancient History, 1978–89; Head of Dept of Classics, 1984–89; Prof. of Late Antique and Byzantine Studies, and Dir, Centre for Hellenic Studies, 1989–94. Visiting Professor: Columbia Univ., 1967–68; Collège de France, 1987; Sather Prof., Univ. of Calif. at Berkeley, 1985–86; Vis. Member, Inst. of Advanced Study, Princeton, 1977–78; Summer Fellow, Dumbarton Oaks Center for Byzantine Studies, 1981; British Acad. Wolfson Res. Reader in Hist., 1990–92. Chm., British Nat. Byzantine Cttee, 1983–89; President: Roman Soc., 1995–98 (Vice-Pres., 1983–95, 1999–); Council for British Res. in the Levant, 2004–; Ecclesiastical History Soc., 2005–06; Fédn Internat. des Assocs d'Etudes Classiques, 2009–14

(Vice-Pres., 2005–09). Mem., British Acad. Council, 1983–86. Chm., Cathedrals Fabric Commn for England, 1999–2005 (Vice-Chm., 1999). Editor, Jl of Roman Studies, 1985–90. Corresp. mem., Akad. der Wiss. zu Göttingen, phil.-hist. Klasse, 2006; Corresp. Fellow, Centre for Byzantine Res., Aristotelian Univ., Thessaloniki, 2014. Hon. DLitt: Warwick, 1996; St Andrews, 1997; QUB, 2000; Aberdeen, 2003; London, 2005; DTheol Lund, 2001. *Publications:* Procopius, 1967; Agathias, 1970; Corippus: In laudem Iustini minoris, 1976; Change and Continuity in Sixth-Century Byzantium, 1981; (ed jtly) Images of Women in Antiquity, 1983, 2nd edn 1993; (ed jtly) Constantinople in the Eighth Century: the Parastaseis Syntomoi Chronikai, 1984; Procopius and the Sixth Century, 1985; (ed) History as Text: the writing of ancient history, 1989; Christianity and the Rhetoric of Empire, 1991; (ed jtly) The Byzantine and Early Islamic Near East, vol. I: Problems in the Literary Source Material, 1992, vol. II: Land Use and Settlement Patterns, 1994, vol. III: States, Resources and Armies, 1995; The Later Roman Empire, 1993; The Mediterranean World in Late Antiquity, AD 395–600, 1993, AD 395–700, 2nd edn 2011; Changing Cultures in Early Byzantium, 1996; (ed with P. D. Garnsey) Cambridge Ancient History, vol. XIII, 1998; (ed with S. G. Hall) Eusebius, Life of Constantine, 1999; (ed jtly) Cambridge Ancient History, vol. XIV, 2001; (ed) Fifty Years of Prosopography, 2003; (ed jtly) Cambridge Ancient History, vol. XII, 2005; The Byzantines, 2006; (ed with R. Hoyland) Doctrine and Debate in the East Christian World, 300–1500, 2011; (ed) Late Antiquity on the Eve of Islam, 2013; Byzantine Matters, 2014; Dialoguing in Late Antiquity, 2014; numerous articles in learned jls. *Address:* Keble College, Oxford OX1 3PG.

CAMERON, Barbara Alexander; Her Honour Judge Cameron; a Circuit Judge, since 2007; *b* Totteridge, 3 June 1950; *d* of Thomas and Paula Alexander Cameron; *m* 1983; two *d*. *Educ:* Queen's Coll., Harley St; Lucy Cavendish Coll., Cambridge (BA Hons Law 1980). Dental nurse; ran dental practices in Herts and Harley St, 1967–77. Called to the Bar, Lincoln's Inn, 1979; Mem., Inner Temple, 1983. Lectr in Law, City of London Poly., 1980–82; barrister, Henderson Chambers, Temple, 1982–2007; Recorder, 1999–2007; Dep. Dist Judge, 1999–2007. Family and Divorce Mediator, 1998–2007. Legal Assessor: to NMC, 1993–2007; to GDC, GMC and Gen. Chiropractic Council, 2004–07. Member: Appeals Cttee, Legal Services Commn, 1993–2007; Bar Disciplinary Tribunal, 1997–2007. Member: Family Law Bar Assoc., 1983–; Professional Negligence Bar Assoc., 1990–2008 (Mem., Exec. Cttee, 1993–95); Personal Injuries Bar Assoc., 1995–2008; Assoc. of Women Lawyers, 2003–08; Assoc. of Regulatory and Disciplinary Lawyers, 2004–08. Panel Mem., Barristers' Complaints Adv. Service, 1997–2007. *Recreations:* family and country life, opera, cooking, walking. *Address:* Medway County Court, Anchorage House, 47–67 High Street, Chatham, Kent ME4 4DW. *T:* (01634) 810720.

CAMERON, Colin Neil; freelance television producer; *b* 30 March 1950; *s* of late Hector MacDonald Cameron and Frances (*née* Majury); *m* 1978, Christine Welsh Main; two *s*. *Educ:* Glasgow Acad.; Duke of York, Nairobi; Poly. of Central London (Dip. Communication Studies). Journalist, BBC Scotland, 1973–76; BBC TV: Film Dir, That's Life, 1976–77; Producer/Dir, Everyman and Heart of the Matter, 1977–85; Editor, Features and Documentaries, BBC North, 1985–88; Hd, Documentary Features, BBC TV, 1988–91; BBC Scotland: Hd of TV, 1991–96; Hd of Production, 1996–2000; Hd of Network Progs, 2000–01; Controller, Network Develt, BBC Nations and Regions, 2001–04; Man. Dir, Lion TV Scotland, 2004–07. Trustee, The Research Centre, 1998–2008 (Chm., 2004–07); non-exec. Dir, Distance Lab, 2008–10; Mem., Advertising Adv. Cttee, 2009–. Hon. Prof., Film and Media Studies, Univ. of Stirling, 2006–. Member: RTS, 1984–2010; BAFTA, 1984–. Community Councillor, Balfron, 2014–. Life Mem., John Muir Trust, 2006–. UNA Media Peace Prize, 1984. *Address:* 2 The Old Manse, Station Road, Balfron G63 0SX.

CAMERON, Rt Hon. David William Donald; PC 2005; MP (C) Witney, since 2001; Prime Minister and First Lord of the Treasury, since 2010; Leader of the Conservative Party, since 2005; *b* 9 Oct. 1966; *s* of late Ian Donald Cameron and of Mary Fleur Cameron; *m* 1996, Samantha Gwendoline, *e d* of Sir Reginald Sheffield, Bt, *qv*; one *s* two *d* (and one *s* decd). *Educ:* Eton Coll.; Brasenose Coll., Oxford (BA 1st Cl. Hons PPE; Hon. Fellow, 2006). Cons. Res. Dept, 1988–92; Special Adviser: HM Treasury, 1992–93; Home Office, 1993–94; Hd, Corporate Affairs, Carlton Communications plc, 1994–2001. Shadow Sec. of State for Educn and Skills, 2005; Leader of the Opposition, 2005–10. Mem., Select Cttee on Home Affairs, 2001–05. Dep. Chm., Cons. Party, 2003–04. *Publications:* (with Dylan Jones) Cameron on Cameron: conversations with Dylan Jones, 2008. *Recreations:* tennis, cooking. *Address:* 10 Downing Street, SW1A 2AA. *T:* (020) 7930 4433.

See also A. A. Cameron.

CAMERON, Rt Rev. Donald; *see* Cameron, Rt Rev. E. D.

CAMERON, Donald Allan, MBE 2014; RDI 2004; FRAeS; Managing Director, Cameron Balloons Ltd, since 1970; *b* 16 July 1939; *s* of late David Stuart Cameron and Madge Kaye Cameron; *m* 1st, 1969, Dorothy Anne Golding (marr. diss. 1980); one *s* one *d*; 2nd, 1980, Margaret Louise Tobin; six *s* one *d*. *Educ:* Allan Glen's Sch.; Glasgow Univ. (BSc); Cornell Univ. (MS). FRAeS 2010. Chm., Bristol Balloon Fiestas Ltd, 1992–. British Delegate to FAI (Ballooning), 1987–2002 and 2010–. Mem. Bd, Children's Hospice SW, 2003–08. Mem., Bath Royal Literary and Scientific Instn, 2002– (Convenor, 2004–; Trustee, 2006–). Treas., 2011–14, Chm., 2014–, N Somerset Conservative Assoc. Hon. Pres., 2494 Sqdn ATC, 2003–10. Hon. Pres., City of Bristol Pipes & Drums, 2001–. Patron, IMechE, 2003–. Mem., Portishead (formerly Portishead and North Weston) Town Council, 2007– (Chm., 2014–15). Hon. Freeman, City of Bristol, 2007. Hon. MA Bristol, 1980; Hon. DEng Glasgow, 2000; Hon. DBA UWE, 2001. *Publications:* Ballooning Handbook, 1981; Purpose of Life, 2001. *Recreations:* ballooning, sailing, natural history. *Address:* c/o Cameron Balloons Ltd, St John Street, Bristol BS3 4NH. *T:* (0117) 963 7216, *Fax:* (0117) 966 1168. *E:* dcameron@cameronballoons.co.uk. *Clubs:* Royal Aero (Mem. Council, 1990–), British Balloon and Airship (Mem. Cttee, 1972–).

CAMERON of Lochiel, Donald Angus; 27th Chief of the Clan Cameron; Lord-Lieutenant of Inverness, since 2002; *b* 2 Aug. 1946; *s* of Col Sir Donald Hamish Cameron of Lochiel, KT, CVO, TD, 26th Chief of the Clan Cameron and Margaret (*née* Gathorne-Hardy); *S* father as 27th Chief, 2004; *m* 1974, Lady Cecil Kerr, OBE, *d* of 12th Marquess of Lothian, KCVO; one *s* three *d*. *Educ:* Harrow; Christ Church, Oxford (MA). FCA. Dir, J. Henry Schroder Wagg, subseq. J. Henry Schroder & Co., 1984–99. 2nd Lieutenant, Queen's Own Cameron Highlanders (TA), 1966–68. Pres., Highland Soc. of London, 1994–97. JP Highland, 2002–07. *Address:* Achnacarry, Spean Bridge, Inverness-shire PH34 4EJ. *T:* (01397) 712708.

CAMERON, Donald William; President, Maritime Steel and Foundries Ltd, 2002; *b* 20 May 1946; *m* 1969, Rosemary Simpson; one *s* two *d*. *Educ:* East Pictou Rural High Sch.; Nova Scotia Agricl Coll.; McGill Univ. (BSc). Dairy farmer; MLA (PC) Pictou East, 1974–93; Minister of: Recreation, 1978–79; Fisheries, 1978–80; Industry, Trade and Technology, 1988–91; Leader, Nova Scotia Progressive Cons. Party, 1991; Premier of Nova Scotia, 1991–93; Canadian Consul Gen. to New England, 1993–97. *Recreations:* ski-ing, boating, hockey, tennis. *Address:* RR #1, New Glasgow, NS B2H 5C4, Canada.

CAMERON, Rt Rev. Douglas Maclean; Bishop of Argyll and The Isles, 1993–2003; *b* 23 March 1935; *s* of Andrew McIntyre Cameron and Helen Adam McKechnie; *m* 1969, Anne Patricia Purnell; two *d*. *Educ:* Eastwood Grammar Sch., Clarkston, Glasgow; Theol Coll., Edinburgh; Univ. of the South, Sewanee, Tennessee, USA. Bank of Scotland, 1951–59; RAF, 1953–55. Ordained: deacon, 1962; priest, 1963; curate, Christ Church, Falkirk, 1962–65; Anglican Church in Papua New Guinea: Mission Priest, 1966–67; priest in charge, Movi 1967–72; Rector, St Francis, Goroka, 1972–74; Archdeacon of New Guinea Mainland 1972–74; Priest in charge, St Fillan's, Edinburgh, 1974, Rector, 1978–88; Rector: St Hilda's Edinburgh, 1977–88; St Mary's, Dalkeith and St Leonard's, Lasswade, 1988–93; Canon, S Mary's Cathedral, Edinburgh and Synod Clerk, 1990–91; Dean of Edinburgh, 1991–92 *Recreations:* walking, travelling, cooking, grandchildren. *Address:* 23 Craigs Way, Rumford Falkirk FK2 0EU. *T:* (01324) 714137.

See also Rt Rev. A. B. Cameron.

CAMERON, Elizabeth; Member, Glasgow City Council, since 1992; Lord Provost an Lord-Lieutenant of Glasgow, 2003–07; *o d* of John and Elizabeth Gregory; *m* Dunca Cameron; one step *d*. *Educ:* Glasgow Univ. (MA Hons English Lang. and Lit.). Lectr, Furthe and Adult Educn. Glasgow City Council: Deputy Convener: Women's Cttee, 1993–95; Art and Culture, 1995–98; Convener, Culture and Leisure Services, 1998–2003. Vice Chm. Glasgow City Mktg Bureau, 2007–; Chm., Culture and Sport Glasgow. Member: Scottis Arts Council, 2002–06; Bd of Trustees, Nat. Galls of Scotland, 2002–06; Board: Scottis Ensemble (Chm.); Arches Th.; Glasgow Film Th. (Chm., 2008–); Scottish Internat. Pian Comp. (Chm., 2009–); Nat. Youth Choir Scotland; Royal Scottish Nat. Orch. Chorus Trust Pres., Culture Commn Confedn of Cities of Atlantic Arc; Vice Chm., Les Rencontres Assoc of European Cultural Cities. Patron, Glasgow Celtic Soc. Vis. Prof., Glasgow Caledonia Univ., 2007–. DUniv: Glasgow, 2006; Caledonian, 2006; Strathclyde, 2006. Officier, Ordr des Arts et des Lettres (France). *Recreations:* music, choral singing, languages (French an Italian), reading, theatre. *Address:* Glasgow City Council, City Chambers, Glasgow G2 1DU.

CAMERON, Rt Rev. (Ewen) Donald; Assistant Bishop, Diocese of Sydney, 1975–93; *b* Nov. 1926; *s* of Ewen Cameron, Balranald, NSW, and Dulce M. Cameron, Sydney, NSW *m* 1952, Joan R., *d* of T. Wilkins, Mosman, NSW; one *s* two *d*. *Educ:* Sydney C of E Gramma Sch., N Sydney; Moore Theological Coll., Sydney. CA; BD (London); ThSchol (Aust. Col of Theol.). Public Accountancy, 1945–57. Lectr, Moore Theological Coll., 1960–63; Rector St Stephen's, Bellevue Hill, 1963–65; Federal Secretary, CMS of Aust., 1965–72; Archdeaco of Cumberland with Sydney, 1972–75; Bishop of North Sydney, 1983–90; Registrar, dio. o Sydney, 1990–93. Mem., ARCIC, 1983–90. *Address:* Unit 1, Gowrie Village, 10 Edwar Street, Gordon, NSW 2072, Australia. *T:* (2) 94992493.

CAMERON, Francis (Ernest), MA, DipEth (Oxon); FRCO(CHM), ARAM; independen scholar, pagan priest, thinker, writer, speaker; Choirmaster and Organist, City Church of S Michael at the North Gate, Oxford, 1988–94; *b* London, 5 Dec. 1927; *er s* of Ernest and Dori Cameron; *m* 1952, Barbara Minns; three *d*. *Educ:* Mercers' Sch.; Caerphilly Boys' Secondar Sch.; Royal Acad. of Music; University Coll., Oxford; Univ. of Sydney. Henry Richard Prizewinner, RAM, 1946. Organist, St Peter's, Fulham, 1943; Pianist, Canadian Legion 1944; Organist, St Luke's, Holloway, 1945; Sub-organist, St Peter's, Eaton Square, 1945 Organist, St James-the-Less, Westminster, 1946; commissioned RASC, 1948; Organ Scholar University Coll., Oxford, 1950; Organist: St Anne's, Highgate, 1952; St Barnabas', Pimlico 1953; St Mark's, Marylebone Road, 1957–58; Choirmaster, St Aloysius, Somers Town, 1959 Master of Music, Westminster Cathedral, 1959; Visiting Organist, Church of St Thomas c Canterbury, Rainham, Kent, 1961; Organist and Choirmaster, Church of Our Lady of th Assumption and St Gregory, Warwick Street, W1, 1962–68. Travel for UNESCO, 1952–55 Dep. Dir of Music, LCC (subsequently GLC), 1954–68; Asst-Dir of Music, Emanuel Sch. 1954; Music Master, Central Foundation Boys' Grammar Sch., 1956; Prof. of Organ an Composition, RAM, 1959–68; *locum tenens* Dir of Music, St Felix Sch., Southwold, 1963 an 1964; Asst Dir, 1968, Chm. of Musicology, 1974–79, NSW State Conservatorium of Music Organist, Church of St Mary the Virgin, Iffley, 1980–88; Sen. Lectr, Musical Studies, Oxfor Poly., 1982–86; Demonstrator: Oxford Univ. Computing Services, 1988–96; computing Univ. of Oxford Dept for Continuing Educn, 1994–96, 2000–04; computer programmin tutor, Oxford Centre for Adult Learning, 1992–96. Inaugural Conductor, Witan Operati Soc., 1957–58; Conductor: "I Cantici", 1961–65; Francis Cameron Chorale, 1965–68 Singers of David, 1973–76; British Adjudicator, Fedn of Canadian Music Festivals, 1965 Examr Associated Bd of Royal Schools of Music, 1965–68; Dep. Chm., NSW Adv. Bd, Aust Music Exams Bd, 1969–74. Field Officer, Deep Creek Aboriginal Monuments res. an recording prog., 1973; Mem., Lancefield Archaeol Expedn, 1975. President: "Open Score" 1946–68; Musicol Soc. of Aust., 1971–75 (jt leader, ethnomusicol expedn to New Hebrides 1971–72); Sydney Univ. Anthropol Soc., 1974–75; Phoenix Photographic Circle, 1977–79 Conservatorium Professional Staff Assoc., 1978–79; Vice-Pres., Aust. Chapter, ISCM 1970–77; Ed., INFO, European Seminar in Ethnomusicology, 1986–90. Beethove Commemorative Medal, Fed. Repub. of Germany, 1970. *Publications:* editor (with Joh Steele) Musica Britannica vol. xiv (The Keyboard Music of John Bull, part I), 1960; Ol Palace Yard, 1963; Eight dances from Benjamin Cosyn's Second Virginal Book, 1964; I Sin of a Maiden, 1966; John Bull, ausgewählte Werke, 1967; I Believe, 1969; incidental music fo film The Voyage of the New Endeavour, 1970; songs and incidental music for Congreve' Love for Love, 1972; Alleluia, 1990; contributor to: Church Music; Composer; Th Conductor; Liturgy; Musical Times; Australian Jl of Music Education; Studies in Music Music in Tertiary Educn; Con Brio; Musicology IV; Aust. Nat. Hist.; Nation Review Quanta; ICTM (UK) Bulletin; Eur. Studies in Ethnomusicol.; Pagan Dawn; Pagan Times Pentacle; Druids Voice; The Cauldron. *Address:* 12 Norreys Avenue, Oxford OX1 4SS. *T* (01865) 240058.

CAMERON, Rt Rev. Gregory Kenneth; *see* St Asaph, Bishop of.

CAMERON, Sir (Hugh) Roy (Graham), Kt 1999; QPM 1994; HM Chief Inspector c Constabulary, Scotland, 2002–04; *b* 14 April 1947; *s* of Angus and May Cameron; *m* 1969 Margaret Scott; two *s*. *Educ:* Bearsden Acad.; Univ. of Strathclyde (BA 1976; MPhil 1992) Cadet, Dunbartonshire Constabulary, 1964–66; Constable, 1966, Asst Chief Constable 1990–94, Strathclyde Police; Chief Constable: Dumfries and Galloway Constabulary 1994–96; Lothian and Borders Police, 1996–2002. DL East Lothian, 2004–08. *Recreations* golf, music, cinema, reading.

CAMERON, Prof. Iain Thomas, MD; Professor of Obstetrics and Gynaecology, since 1999 and Dean, Faculty of Medicine, since 2010, University of Southampton (Head, School o Medicine, 2004–10); *b* 21 Feb. 1956; *s* of late James David Cameron and Stella (*née* Turner) *m* 1st, 1983 (marr. diss.); two *d*; 2nd, 1992, Heidi Wade; one *s* one *d*. *Educ:* Hutton Gramma Sch.; Univ. of Edinburgh (BSc Med. Sci. 1977; MB ChB 1980; MD 1988); MA Cantab 1992 MRCOG 1986, FRCOG 1999; MRACOG 1987; ILTM 2002; FRCPEd 2011; FRSB (FSI 2011). House Officer and Sen. House Officer, Western Infirmary, Glasgow, Royal Infirmary Edinburgh and Simpson Meml Maternity Pavilion, Edinburgh, 1980–82; University o Edinburgh: Research Fellow, Dept of Obstetrics and Gynaecology, 1982–84; Lectr an Registrar, 1984–86; Monash University: Clinical Res. Fellow, 1986–88; Lectr, 1987–88; Sen Registrar, Royal Women's Hosp., Melbourne, 1988–89; University of Cambridge: Lectr 1989–92; Sen. Registrar, 1989–91; Consultant, 1991–92; Regius Prof. of Obstetrics an Gynaecology, Glasgow Univ., 1993–99; Mem., HFEA, 2001–06. Chm., Blair Bell Res. Soc. 1999–2002, Chm., Meetings Cttee, and Convenor, Postgrad. Meetings, 2000–03, Chm., J Wellbeing of Women Res. Adv. Cttee, 2004–08, Mem., Academic Cttee, 2006–15, RCOG Specialist Advr, Menorrhagia, NICE, 2000; Member: Pharmaceuticals Panel, 2001–04 Expert Adv. Network, 2004–10, Dean for Trng's Adv. Panel, 2010–13, NIHR Healt Technol. Assessment Prog.; Scientific and Ethical Rev. Gp, Special Prog. in Huma Reproduction, WHO, 2003–14; MRC Coll. of Experts, 2005–09; Exec. Cttee, Med. Sch Council (formerly Council of Hds of Med. Schs), 2006– (Dep. Chm., 2012–13; Chm.

2013–July 2016); Clin. Academic Staff Adv. Gp, UCEA, 2008–14; UK Clin. Res. Collaboration Bd, 2008–; UK Res. Integrity Office Adv. Bd, 2009–13; NIHR Adv. Bd, 2013–July 2016; Health Educn England Medical Adv. Gp, 2013–July 2016. Non-exec. Dir, University Hosp. Southampton NHS Foundn Trust, 2011–. Ed.-in-Chief, Reproductive Medicine Rev., 1999–2002. *Publications:* articles and other contribs on menstrual disorders, endometrium, and reproductive medicine. *Recreation:* solo piping. *Address:* Level B (801), South Academic Block, Southampton General Hospital, Tremona Road, Southampton SO16 6YD. *Club:* Athenæum.

CAMERON, Ian Alexander; Sheriff of Grampian, Highland and Islands at Elgin, 2001–08; *b* 5 Nov. 1938; *s* of late James Cameron and Isabella Cameron; *m* 1968, Dr Margaret Anne Innes; one *s*. *Educ:* Elgin Acad.; Edinburgh Univ. (MA); Aberdeen Univ. (LLB with dist.). Qualified as solicitor, 1961; Partner, Stewart & McIsaac, Solicitors, Elgin, 1962–87; Sheriff: of Lothian and Borders at Edinburgh, 1987–93; of Grampian, Highland and Is at Wick, Dornoch and Stornoway, 1993–2001. *Recreations:* travel, railway history. *Address:* Braemoray, Elgin, Moray IV30 4NJ. *T:* (01343) 542731; 19/4 Damside, Dean Village, Edinburgh EH4 3BB.

CAMERON, Prof. Ian Rennell, CBE 1999; DM; FRCP, FMedSci; Vice-Chancellor, University of Wales College of Medicine, 1994–2001; Chairman, Enfis Ltd, 2001–07; *b* 20 May 1936; *s* of James and Frances Mary Cameron; *m* 1st, 1964, Jayne Bustard (marr. diss.); one *s* one *d*; 2nd, 1980, Jennifer, *d* of Stewart and Josephine Cowin. *Educ:* Westminster Sch.; Corpus Christi Coll., Oxford (BA 1958 1st Cl. Hons Animal Physiol.; MA 1961; DM 1969; Hon. Fellow, 2000); St Thomas's Hosp. Med. Sch. (BM BCh 1961). FRCP 1976. Jun. med. appts, St Thomas' Hosp., 1961–64; Res. Asst, Dept of Physiol., UCL, 1966–68; Lectr 1967, Sen. Lectr 1969, Reader 1975, St Thomas's Hosp. Med. Sch.; Prof. of Medicine, UMDS of Guy's and St Thomas' Hosps, 1979–94 (Dean, St Thomas', 1986–89; Principal, UMDS, 1989–92, Hon. Fellow, 1997); Hon. Consultant Physician, St Thomas' Hosp., 1970–94. NIH Postdoctoral Fellowship at Cedars-Sinai Med. Center, LA, and Asst Prof., Dept of Physiol., UCLA, 1968–69. Mem., Medway HA, 1981–86; non-exec. Dir, Bro Taf HA, 1996–99; Dir, R&D, SE Thames RHA, 1993–94. Examiner, Univ. of London Final MB, 1980–94; Mem. Senate, Univ. of London, 1989–92. Member: Med. Res. Soc., 1966–; Physiol Soc., 1974–; Assoc. of Physicians of GB and Ire., 1979–; Council, RCP, 1992–95; GMC, 1994–2001 (Treas., 1997–2001); Univs UK (formerly CVCP), 1994–2001; Commn for Health Improvement, 1999–2004. Chm., UK Centre for Advancement of Inter-professional Educn, 1998–99. Mem. Council, KCL, 1993–99. Hon. FKC 1998; Hon. Fellow, Cardiff Univ., 2002; Founder FMedSci 1998. Hon. LLD Wales, 2001; Hon. DSc Glamorgan, 2001; Hon. PhD: Kobe Gakuin Univ., Tokyo Women's Medical Univ., 2001. *Publications:* Respiratory Disorders (with N. T. Bateman), 1983; papers in various med. and physiol jls. *Recreation:* collecting (and selling) paintings. *Club:* Athenæum.

CAMERON, Ivor Gill S.; *see* Smith-Cameron.

CAMERON, James; *see* Cameron, J. J. O'G.

CAMERON, John Alastair; *see* Abernethy, Rt Hon. Lord.

CAMERON, John Bell, CBE 1982; Chairman, World Meats Group, International Federation of Agricultural Producers, since 1984; Director, Argent Energy, since 2010; *b* 14 June 1939; *s* of John and Margaret Cameron; *m* 1964, Margaret (*née* Clapperton). *Educ:* Dollar Academy. AIAgrE; FRAgS. Studied agriculture in various countries, Scandinavia, S America and Europe, 1956–61; farmed in Scotland, 1961–64. National Farmers' Union of Scotland: Mem. National Council, 1964; Vice-Pres., 1976; Pres., 1979–84 (first long-term Pres.). Mem., Agricultural Praesidium of EEC, 1979–89; Chairman: EEC Adv. Cttee for Sheep Meat, 1982–89; UK Sheep Consultative Cttee, 1986–87; Scottish Beef Council, 1997–2000; Standards Cttee, Quality Meat Scotland, 2005–. President: British Hereford Cattle Soc., 2003–05; Scottish Beef Cattle Assoc., 2005–; Scottish Nat. Sheep Assoc., 2005–. Chm., BR (Scotland) and Scottish Mem., BRB, 1988–93; Dir, SW Trains and Island Line, 1996–2007. Chm. Governors, Dollar Acad., 1984–. Hon. DTech Napier, 1998. Winner: George Headley Award to the UK Sheep Industry, 1986; Sir William Young Award to the Scottish Livestock Industry, 1986; NFU Scotland Ambassador Award, 2013. *Recreations:* flying, shooting, travelling. *Address:* Balbuthie Farm, By Leven, Fife, Scotland KY9 1EX. *T:* (01333) 730210.

CAMERON, Prof. John Robinson; Regius Professor of Logic, University of Aberdeen, 1979–2001; *b* 24 June 1936; *s* of Rev. George Gordon Cameron and Mary Levering (*née* Robinson); *m* 1st, 1959, Mary Elizabeth Ranson (*d* 1984); one *s* two *d*; 2nd, 1987, Barbara Elizabeth Blair. *Educ:* Dundee High Sch.; Univ. of St Andrews (MA 1st Cl. Hons Maths, BPhil Philosophy); Univ. of Calif, Berkeley; Cornell Univ. Harkness Fellow, Berkeley and Cornell, USA, 1959–61; University of Dundee (formerly Queen's College): Asst in Phil., 1962–63; Lectr in Phil., 1963–73; Sen. Lectr in Phil., 1973–78. FRSA 2002. *Publications:* articles in phil jls. *Recreation:* bricolage. *Address:* 70 Cornhill Road, Aberdeen AB25 2EH. *T:* (01224) 486700.

CAMERON, John Taylor; *see* Coulsfield, Rt Hon. Lord.

CAMERON, (Jonathan) James (O'Grady); international lawyer, policy adviser and entrepreneur; Founder, and Chairman, since 2012, Climate Change Capital, specialist investment group (Vice-Chairman, 2003–12); *b* 28 Oct. 1961; *s* of late John O'Grady Cameron and Valerie Cameron (*née* Bromley); *m* 1988, Juliet Mary May, *qv*; three *d*. *Educ:* Windlesham House Sch., Sussex; Stowe Sch., Bucks; Univ. of Western Australia; University Coll. London (LLB); Queens' Coll., Cambridge (LLM 1st Cl.). Called to the Bar, Inner Temple, 1987; Res. Associate, Centre for Internat. Law, Cambridge, 1986–87; Dir of Studies in Law, Clare Hall, Cambridge, 1986–89; Lecturer in Law: KCL, 1989–92; SOAS, 1992–98; Prof., Coll. of Europe, Bruges, 1994–2002; Counsel, Baker & McKenzie, 1997–2003. Founder Director: Centre for Internat. Envmtl Law, 1989–99; Foundn for Internat. Envmtl Law and Devlt (negotiated UN framework for Convention on Climate Change, 1992 and Kyoto Protocol, 1997 on behalf of Alliance of Small Island States). Visiting Professor: Australian Centre for Envmtl Law, Univ. of Sydney, 1996; Yale Center for Envmtl Law & Policy, 2005–. Chm., Carbon Disclosure Project, 2002–; Treas., Renewable Energy and Energy Efficiency Partnership, 2004–10; Member, Advisory Board: Centre Forum, 2007–; Policy Exchange, 2009–; Member: World Econ. Forum Global Agenda Council on Climate Change, 2008–; Adv. Devlt Bd, Oxfam, 2009–; Prime Minister's Business Adv. Gp, 2010–12; Adv. Council, Infrastructure UK, HM Treasury, 2013–. Trustee, Climate Gp, 2006–11. Mem., GE Ecomagination Adv. Bd, 2006–. Chm., ODI, 2012–. FRSA. *Publications:* (with M. Sheridan) EC Legal Systems: an introductory guide, 1992; (with M. Sheridan) EFTA Legal Systems, 1993; (with D. Gerardin) Trade and Environment: the search for balance, 1994; (with T. O'Riordan) Interpreting the Precautionary Principle, 1994; Improving Compliance with International Environmental Law, 1995; (with K. Campbell) Dispute Resolution in the WTO, 1998; (jtly) Trade and Environment: law and policy introduction, cases and materials, 2000; (jtly) Re-Interpreting the Precautionary Principle, 2001; articles in legal jls. *Recreations:* sport, music, journeys, clothes, conversation, family. *Clubs:* George, Berkshire Golf.

CAMERON, Juliet Mary; *see* May, J. M.

CAMERON, Lewis; Sheriff of South Strathclyde, Dumfries and Galloway at Hamilton, 1994–2002; part-time Sheriff, 2002–05; *b* 12 Aug. 1935; *s* of James Aloysius Cameron and Marie Isobel McKenzie; *m* 1962, Sheila Colette Gallacher; two *s* two *d*. *Educ:* Blairs Coll., Aberdeen; St Sulpice, Paris; Glasgow Univ. (MA, LLB). Admitted Solicitor, 1962. RAF (Nat. Service), 1954–56. Chm., Social Security Appeal Tribunals, 1983–88; Mem., Legal Aid Central Cttee, 1970–80; Legal Aid Sec., Airdrie, 1978–87; Dean, Airdrie Soc. of Solicitors, 1984–85; Tutor, Strathclyde Univ., 1981–88; Sheriff of S Strathclyde, Dumfries and Galloway at Dumfries, 1988–94. Treas., Monklands Victim Support Scheme, 1983–88; Chairman: Dumfries and Galloway Family Conciliation Service, 1988–92; Dumfries and Galloway Scottish Assoc. for Study of Delinquency, 1989–92. Mem., Scotland Cttee, Nat. Children's Homes, 1991–94; Chm., Phew (Parental Help Evenings/Weekends, Mentally Handicapped), 1994–2000. Trustee, Oscar Marzaroli Trust, 1990–93. *Publications:* occasional articles and journalism. *Recreations:* cinema, theatre, tennis, travel. *Club:* Glasgow Art.

CAMERON, Dr Lisa; MP (SNP) East Kilbride, Strathaven and Lesmahagow, since 2015; *b* Glasgow, 8 April 1972; *d* of Campbell McCulloch and Sandra Cameron; *m* 2009, Mark Hersham; two *d*. *Educ:* Univ. of Strathclyde (BA Hons); Univ. of Stirling (MSc Psychol. and Health); Univ. of Glasgow (DClinPsy). NHS Greater Glasgow, 1999–2001; Clin. Psychologist, NHS Lanarks, 2001–04; Consultant Clin. Psychologist, State Hosp., 2004–06; Consultant Forensic and Clin. Psychologist, NHS Greater Glasgow and Clyde, 2006–15. Accredited Risk Assessor, Risk Mgt Authy Scotland, 2012–15. *Recreations:* gym, swimming, travel. *Address:* House of Commons, Room 510, 1 Parliament Street, Westminster, SW1A 0AA. *E:* lisa.cameron.mp@parliament.uk. *Club:* Rotary (Lanark).

CAMERON, Neil St Clair; QC 2009; a Recorder, since 2002; a Deputy High Court Judge, since 2013; *b* Cuckfield, Sussex, 11 July 1959; *s* of Donald Cameron and Jill Cameron; *m* 1987, Phoebe, *d* of late (Cecil) James (Olaf) Moorhouse and Elizabeth Moorhouse; one *s* two *d*. *Educ:* Eton Coll.; Durham Univ. (BA Hons; Pres., Durham Union Soc.). Short Service Ltd Commn, 14th/20th King's Hussars, 2nd Lieut, 1978. Called to the Bar, Gray's Inn, 1982; barrister specialising in town and country planning. Mem. (C), Lambeth LBC, 1986–90. Contested (C) Worsley, 1992. *Recreations:* ski-ing, country. *Address:* Landmark Chambers, 180 Fleet Street, EC4A 2HG. *Clubs:* Cavalry and Guards; Southampton Football.

CAMERON, Pamela; Member (DemU) South Antrim, Northern Ireland Assembly, since 2011; *b* Belfast, 30 Dec. 1971. *Educ:* Glengormley High Sch. Mem. (DemU), Antrim BC, 2005–13 (Mayor, 2010–11). *Address:* Northern Ireland Assembly, Parliament Buildings, Stormont, Belfast BT4 3XX. *T:* (028) 9034 2234. *E:* pam.cameron@mla.niassembly.gov.uk.

CAMERON, Sir Roy; *see* Cameron, Sir H. R. G.

CAMERON, Sheila Morag Clark, (Mrs G. C. Ryan), CBE 2004; QC 1983; Dean, Arches Court of Canterbury and Auditor, Chancery Court of York, 2001–09; *b* 22 March 1934; *d* of Sir James Clark Cameron, CBE, TD, and Lady (Irene M.) Cameron; *m* 1960, Gerard Charles Ryan, *qv*; two *s*. *Educ:* Commonweal Lodge Sch., Purley; St Hugh's Coll., Oxford (MA); Cardiff Univ. (LLM Canon Law 2008). Called to the Bar, Middle Temple, 1957, Harmsworth Law Scholar, 1958, Bencher, 1988; Part-time Lectr in Law, Southampton Univ., 1960–64; part-time Tutor, Council of Legal Educn, 1966–71; a Recorder, 1985–99. Mem., Bar Council, 1967–70. Comr, Boundary Commn for England, 1989–96 (Asst Comr, 1981–89). Official Principal, Archdeaconry of Hampstead, 1968–86; Chancellor: Dio. of Chelmsford, 1969–2001; Dio. of London, 1992–2001; Vicar-Gen., Province of Canterbury, 1983–2005. Chairman: Archbishops' Group on the Episcopate, 1986–90; Ecclesiastical Judges Assoc., 1997–2004; Member: Legal Adv. Commn, Gen. Synod of C of E, 1975–; Gen. Synod Marriage Commn, 1975–78; Council on Tribunals, 1986–90. Pres., Ecclesiastical Law Soc., 2010–. Mem. Council, Wycombe Abbey Sch., 1972–86. DCL Lambeth, 2002. *Address:* Bayleaves, Bepton, Midhurst, W Sussex GU29 9RB.

CAMERON, Stuart Gordon, MC 1943; Chairman and Chief Executive, Gallaher Ltd, 1980–89; *b* 8 Jan. 1924; *s* of late James Cameron and Dora Sylvia (*née* Godsell); *m* 1946, Joyce Alice, *d* of Roland Ashley Wood; three *s* one *d*. *Educ:* Chigwell School, Essex. Served War, 2nd Gurkha Rifles, 1942–46 (MC). Managing Dir, 1976–78, Dep. Chm., 1978–80, Gallaher Ltd. Director: American Brands Inc., 1980–89; Royal Mint, 1989–94; Saatchi & Saatchi Ltd, 1990–94. *Club:* Royal Thames Yacht.

CAMERON, Susan Ruth; Headmistress, North Foreland Lodge, 1996–2002; *b* Edinburgh; *e d* of late James Norval Cameron and Ruth Scott Doig (*née* Nicolson). *Educ:* Wycombe Abbey Sch.; Westfield Coll., London (Exhibnr; BA Hons; Pres., Students' Union). VSO, Oguta, Eastern Nigeria; Housemistress, Godstowe Sch., High Wycombe; teacher, Housemistress, then Dep. Head, Woodford House, Hawkes Bay, NZ; Housemistress: Queenswood Sch., 1977–78; Sherborne Sch. for Girls, 1978–84; Headmistress: Cobham Hall, 1985–89; Downe House, 1989–96. Governor: Queen Margaret's Sch., York, 1986–95; Farlington Sch., Horsham, 1987–95; Repton Sch., 1995–2002; Gordonstoun Schs, 2000–02; Maynard Sch., Exeter, 2003–08; Bearwood Coll., 2004–; Marchant-Holliday Sch., 2005–. Vice-Pres., Seniors' Assoc., Wycombe Abbey Sch., 2004– (Pres., 1996–2004); Sec., Sherborne Abbey Fest. Cttee, 2004–. *Recreations:* music, sport (mostly non-active now), travel, language, creative thinking. *Address:* 5 Minterne House, Minterne Magna, Dorchester, Dorset DT2 7AX. *T:* (01300) 341616.

CAMERON, Thomas Anthony, (Tony), CB 2007; Chief Executive, Scottish Prison Service, 1999–2007; *b* 3 Feb. 1947; *o s* of late Thomas Alexander and Olive Cameron; *m* 1970, Elizabeth Christine Sutherland; two *s*. *Educ:* Stranraer High Sch. Dept of Agric. and Fisheries for Scotland, Scottish Office, 1966–72; Private Secretary: to Dep. Under Sec. of State, 1972; to Perm. Under Sec. of State, 1973–74; Department of Agriculture and Fisheries for Scotland: HEO(D), 1974–77; Principal, 1977–82; Asst Sec., 1982–87; Scottish Office Finance Div., 1987–92; Under Sec., 1992; Head of Food and Agric., Scottish Office, 1992–99. Mem., Duke of Edinburgh's Sixth Commonwealth Study Conf., Australia, 1986. Pres., Internat. Corrections and Prisons Assoc., 2003–11. Chm., Turning Point Scotland, 2011–. *Recreations:* reading, mountaineering. *Address:* 18 St Ninians Terrace, Edinburgh EH10 5NL.

CAMERON-RAMSAY-FAIRFAX-LUCY; *see* Fairfax-Lucy.

CAMLEY, Mark; Executive Director, Park Operations and Venues, London Legacy Development Corporation, since 2013 (Director, Park Operations, 2012–13); *b* 11 June 1964; *s* of Martin and Frances Camley; *m* 2002, Camilla Rosier; two *d*. *Educ:* Lornshill Acad., Alloa; Univ. of Edinburgh (MA). Exec. Officer, Cabinet Office, 1986–88; Asst Statistician, CSO, 1988–90; Lord Chancellor's Department: Statistician, 1990–97; Hd, Estates Policy, 1997–98; Private Sec. to Perm. Sec., 1998–99; Dir, Crown Court, 1999–2001; Customer Service Dir, 2001–03; Dir, Supreme Court, 2003–05; Chief Exec., Royal Parks, 2005–12. Chairman of Governors: Norwood Sch., 2005–07; Royal Docks Sch., 2007–12. Hon. Crown Estate Paving Comr, 2005–12. Member: Places Bd, Poplar Housing and Regeneration Community Assoc., 2009–14; Social Enterprise Cttee, Bromley-by-Bow Centre, 2009–12 (Dir, 2011–14); Dir, Royal Docks Co-op. Learning Partnership, 2010–12; Trustee, GreenSpaces, 2012–13. Mem. Council, London Garden Soc., 2011–; Chm., Parks Alliance, 2013–. *Publications:* contributor: Economic Trends, 1986; Social Trends and Regional Trends, 1988; Judicial Statistics, annually 1990–97; contribs to New Law Jl. *Recreations:* sport, nature, culture, art. *Address:* London Legacy Development Corporation, Level 10, 1 Stratford Place, Montfichet Road, E20 1EJ. *T:* (020) 3288 1857. *E:* markcamley@londonlegacy.co.uk.

CAMM, Prof. A(lan) John, MD; FRCP, FRCPGlas, FRCPE, FMedSci; FACC, FAHA, FESC; QHP; Professor of Cardiology, Imperial College London, since 2012; St George's, University of London (formerly St George's Hospital Medical School): Prudential Professor of Clinical Cardiology (British Heart Foundation), 1986–2012, now Emeritus; Chairman:

Department of Medicine, 1991–94; Department of Cardiological Sciences, 1986–2002; Division of Cardiac and Vascular Sciences, 2002–10; *b* 11 Jan. 1947; *s* of John Donald and Joan Camm; *m* 1987, Joy-Maria Frappell (LVO 2015); one *s* one *d*. *Educ:* Guy's Hosp. Med. Sch., London Univ. (BSc 1968; MB BS 1971; MD 1981). LRCP, MRCS 1971; FACC 1981; FRCP 1984; FESC 1988; FRCPE 2003; FRCPGlas (*ad eundem*) 2011. Guy's Hospital: House Surgeon, 1971; House Physician, 1971–72; Jun. Registrar, 1972; Jun. Lectr in Medicine, 1972–73; Registrar in Cardiology, 1973–74; Clin. Fellow in Cardiology, Univ. of Vermont, USA, 1974–75; St Bartholomew's Hospital: British Heart Foundn Res. Registrar, 1975–76, Sen. Registrar 1977–79; Wellcome Sen. Lectr and Hon. Consultant Cardiologist, 1979–83; Sir Ronald Bodley Scott Prof. of Cardiovascular Medicine, 1983–86. Convener of Medicine, London Univ., 1994–. Editor in Chief: Europace Jl, 2007–; Clinical Cardiology Jl, 2011–. Dir, Eur. Soc. of Cardiol. Res. Foundn, 2008. Member, Council: RCP, 1994–97; British Cardiac Soc., 1997–98 (Pres. elect, 1998–2001, Pres., 2001–03); Eur. Heart Rhythm Assoc., 2007–; Pres., Arrhythmia Alliance, 2005–. QHP 1992–. FCGC 1997; FAHA 2000; FMedSci 2005; FHRS 2006. Trustee: N American Soc. of Pacing and Electrophysiology, 1998–2001 (Dist. Teacher, 2001); Amer. Coll. of Cardiology, 2007–12; Drug Safety Res. Unit, 2009–; Founder Trustee, Atrial Fibrillation Assoc., 2008–. Hon. Internat. Mem., Japanese Circulation Soc., 2006; Hon. Fellow, Hong Kong Coll. of Cardiology, 2006. Freeman, City of London, 1984. Gold Medal, European Soc. of Cardiology, 2006; Berzelius Medal, Swedish Soc. of Cardiology, 2006; Cardiostim Medal, Cardiostim, 2006; Mackenzie Medal, British Cardiovascular Soc., 2008; Libin Prize for Cardiovascular Res. Excellence, Calgary Heart Inst., 2011. CStJ 1990. *Publications:* First Aid, Step by Step, 1978; Pacing for Tachycardia Control, 1983; Heart Disease in the Elderly, 1984, 2nd edn 1994; Clinical Electrophysiology of the Heart, 1987; Heart Disease in Old Age, 1988, 2nd edn 1990; Clinical Aspects of Cardiac Arrhythmias, 1988; Diseases of the Heart, 1989, 2nd edn 1996; Geriatric Cardiology, 1994; Heart Rate Variability, 1998; Evidence Based Cardiology, 1998, 3rd edn 2010; Atrial Fibrillation, 2000, Hungarian edn 2002; Drug-induced Long QT Syndrome, 2002; Cardiovascular Risk Associated with Schizophrenia and its Treatment, 2003; Acquired Long QT Syndrome, 2004; Clinical Electrophysiological Disorders of the Heart, 2004, 2nd edn 2011; Dynamic Electrocardiography, 2004; European Society of Cardiology Textbook, 2005, 2nd edn 2009; Comprehensive Electrocardiology, 2nd edn, 2011; approx. 1,400 papers in major jls and over 300 chapters in med. textbooks. *Recreations:* collector of prints, watercolours and other antiques, model railway enthusiast. *Address:* St George's, University of London, Cranmer Terrace, Tooting, SW17 0RE. *Clubs:* Oriental, Royal Society of Medicine.

CAMM, Gillian Elizabeth; DL; NHS Regional Appointments Commissioner for South West, 2001–03; *b* 31 Dec. 1959; *d* of Sir Robert Shields; *m* 1987, Ian Sutcliffe Camm; one *s* one *d*. *Educ:* Birkenhead High Sch. for Girls; Univ. of Liverpool (BSc Hons Psychol.). Personnel Officer, Perkins Diesel Engines, 1981–84; Personnel Manager, Internat. Computers Ltd, 1984–87; Partner, Hay Mgt Consultants, 1987–94; Gen. Manager, Human Resources, 1994–97, Business Transformation Dir, 1997–2001, Clerical Medical Investments Gp. Non-executive Director: Supervisory Bd, Immigration and Nationality Directorate, Home Office, 2002; Wessex Water, 2011–; Capsticks, 2012–. Non-exec. Dir, 2002–, Sen. Ind. Dir, 2006–10, Rok plc. Mem., GMC, 2003. Chairman: Bd of Govs, UWE, 2009–; Council, Wycliffe Coll., 2009–. Vice-Pres., Quartet Community Foundn (formerly Gtr Bristol Foundn), 2010–; Mem. Council, St Monica Trust, 2003–12. Mem., Hon. Glos Soc., 2009–. DL Glos 2010. *Recreations:* ski-ing, reading. *E:* gillian.camm1@gmail.com.

CAMOYS, 7th Baron *cr* 1264 (called out of abeyance, 1839); **Ralph Thomas Campion George Sherman Stonor,** GCVO 1998; PC 1997; DL; Lord Chamberlain of HM Household and Chancellor of Royal Victorian Order, 1998–2000; a Permanent Lord in Waiting to the Queen, since 2000; *b* 16 April 1940; *s* of 6th Baron Camoys and Mary Jeanne (*d* 1987), *d* of late Captain Herbert Marmaduke Joseph Stourton, OBE; *S* father, 1976; *m* 1966, Elisabeth Mary Hyde, *d* of Sir William Stephen Hyde Parker, 11th Bt; one *s* three *d*. *Educ:* Eton Coll.; Balliol Coll., Oxford (MA). Chm., Jacksons of Piccadilly, 1968–85; Gen. Manager and Director, National Provincial and Rothschild (London) Ltd, 1968; Man. Director, Rothschild Intercontinental Bank Ltd, 1969; Chief Exec. Officer and Man. Dir, 1975–77, Chm., 1977–78, Amex Bank Ltd; Man. Dir, 1978–84, Exec. Vice-Chm., 1984–86, Barclays Merchant Bank; Chief Exec., 1986–88, Dep. Chm., 1987–98, Barclays de Zoete Wedd (BZW); Dep. Chm., Sotheby's, 1993–97. Director: Barclays Bank Internat. Ltd, 1980–84; Barclays Bank PLC, 1984–94; Mercantile Credit Co. Ltd, 1980–84; National Provident Instn, 1982–93; Administrative Staff Coll., 1989–2000; 3i Group, 1991–2002; Perpetual, 1994–2000. A Lord in Waiting, 1992–97. Member: House of Lords EEC Select Cttee, 1979–81; Historic Bldgs and Monuments Commn for England, 1985–87; Royal Commn on Historical MSS, 1987–94. Pres., Mail Users' Assoc., 1977–84. Consultor, Extraordinary Section of Administration of Patrimony of Holy See, 1991–2006. Chm., Tablet Trust, 2009–. Mem. Court of Assistants, Fishmongers' Co., 1980– (Prime Warden, 1992–93). DL Oxfordshire, 1993. Hon. DLitt Sheffield, 2001. Order of Gorkha Dakshina Bahu, 1st class (Nepal), 1981. GCSG 2006. *Recreations:* the arts, family. *Heir:* *s* Hon. (Ralph) William (Robert Thomas) Stonor [*b* 10 Sept. 1974; *m* 2004, Lady Ailsa Mackay, *d* of Earl of Inchcape, *qv*; two *s*]. *Address:* Stonor Park, Henley-on-Thames, Oxon RG9 6HF. *Clubs:* Boodle's; Leander (Henley-on-Thames).

See also Earl of Stair.

CAMP, Anthony John, MBE 1999; Director, Society of Genealogists, 1979–97; *b* 27 Nov. 1937; *s* of late Henry Victor Camp and Alice Emma Camp (*née* Doidge); *m* 1976, Deborah Mary (marr. diss. 1978), *d* of D. J. Jeavons; one *s*. *Educ:* Alleyne's Sch., Stevenage; University College London (BA Hons). Society of Genealogists: Res. Assistant, 1957; Librarian, 1959; Dir of Res., 1962; Hon. Fellow, 1982. Association of Genealogists and Researchers in Archives (formerly Association of Genealogists and Record Agents): Mem. Council, 1968–75; Chm., 1973–75; Vice-Pres., 1980–2011; Fellow, 2011; Member, Council: British Record Soc., 1967–71, 1983–2005; British Records Assoc. (Record Preservation Sect.), 1980–83, 1985–88; English Genealogical Congress, 1975–90 (Pres., 1991–92); Friends of Public Record Office, 1988–94; Marc Fitch Fund, 1991–2003; Fedn of Family History Socs, 1992–98 (Pres., 1998–2000); Pres., Herts Family and Population Hist. Soc., 1982–. Lecturer: yearly Nat. Geneal. Soc. Confs, USA, 1981–; Australasian Congress, Canberra, 1986; Sesquicentennial Conf., Auckland, 1990; First Irish Genealogical Congress, 1991. Fellow, Utah Geneal. Assoc., 1989. Freeman, City of London, 1984. Award of Merit, Nat. Geneal. Soc., USA, 1984. *Publications:* (with P. Spufford) Genealogists Handbook, 1961; Wills and their Whereabouts, 1963; Tracing Your Ancestors, 1964; Index to Wills proved in the Prerogative Court of Canterbury 1750–1800, 6 vols, 1976–92; Everyone has Roots, 1978; (contrib.) My Ancestor series, 1987–; (contrib.) The Records of the Nation, 1990; Royal Mistresses and Bastards: fact and fiction 1714–1936, 2007; articles to Family Tree and other jls. *Recreation:* genealogy. *Address:* 19 Tudor Rose Court, 35 Fann Street, EC2Y 8DY. *T:* (020) 7374 6836.

CAMP, Jeffery Bruce, RA 1984 (ARA 1974); artist; Lecturer, Slade School of Fine Art, 1963–88; *b* 1923. *Educ:* Edinburgh Coll. of Art. DA (Edin.). One-man exhibitions include: Galerie de Seine, 1958; Beaux Arts Gallery, 1959, 1961, 1963; New Art Centre, 1968; S London Art Gall., 1973 (retrospective); Serpentine Gall., 1978; Bradford City Art Gallery, 1979; Browse & Darby, 1984, 1993, 1997, 2001; Aldeburgh Fest., 1986; Nigel Greenwood Gall., 1986, 1990, 1993; Royal Acad., 1988 (retrospective); Flowers East, 1999; Art Space Gall., 2002, 2005, 2007, 2010; other exhibitions include: Hayward Annual, 1974, 1982, 1985; Serpentine Gall., 1974, 1987; Narrative Painting, ICA and Arts Council tour, 1979; British Council touring exhibns to China and Edinburgh, 1982, to India, 1985, to Kuala Lumpur, 1988; Chantrey Bicentenary, Tate Gall., 1981; The Hardwon Image, Tate Gall., 1984; group exhibn, Twining Gall., NY, 1985; Peter Moores exhibn, Liverpool, 1986; Athena Art Awards, 1987; represented in public collections including Arts Council, British Council, Tate Gall. and Royal Acad. *Publications:* Draw, 1981; Paint, 1996; Almanac, 2010. *Address:* 27 Stirling Road, SW9 9EF; c/o Art Space Gallery, Michael Richardson Contemporary Art, 84 St Peter's Street, N1 8JS.

CAMPBELL; *see* Methuen-Campbell, family name of Baron Methuen.

CAMPBELL, family name of **Duke of Argyll,** of **Earl Cawdor,** and of **Barons Colgrain** and **Stratheden.**

CAMPBELL OF LOUGHBOROUGH, Baroness *cr* 2008 (Life Peer), of Loughborough in the County of Leicestershire; **Susan Catherine Campbell,** CBE 2003 (MBE 1991); Chairman: UK Sport, 2003–13; Youth Sport Trust, since 2005 (Chief Executive, 1995–2005); *b* 10 Oct. 1948. *Educ:* Long Eaton Grammar Sch.; Bedford Coll. of Physical Educn; Univ. of Leicester (Adv. DipEd; MEd). Teacher of Physical Educn, Whalley Range High Sch., Manchester, 1970–72; Dep. Dir of Physical Educn, Univ. of Leicester, 1972–76; Lectr, Dept of Physical Educn and Sports Sci., Univ. of Loughborough, 1976–80; Regl Officer, E Midlands, Sports Council, 1980–84; Dep. Chief Exec., 1984, Chief Exec., 1985–95, Nat. Coaching Foundn. Advr, DCMS and DFES, 2000–03.

CAMPBELL OF SURBITON, Baroness *cr* 2007 (Life Peer), of Surbiton in the London Borough of Kingston upon Thames; **Jane Susan Campbell,** DBE 2006 (MBE 2000); Member, House of Lords Appointments Commission, 2008–14; *b* 19 April 1959; *d* of Ronald James Campbell and Jessie Mary Campbell; *m* Roger Symes. *Educ:* Hatfield Poly. (BA Hons Humanities (Hist. Major) 1979); Sussex Univ. (MA Political Hist. 1982). Admin. Officer to REMAP, RADAR, 1983–84; Equal Opportunities Liaison Officer, GLC, 1984–86; Disability Training Develt Officer, London Boroughs Jt Disability Cttee, 1986–87; Prin. Disability Advr, Hounslow Council, 1987–88; Dir of Training, London Boroughs Disability Resource Team, 1988–94; freelance consultant, 1994–96; Co-Dir, Nat. Centre for Independent Living, 1996–2001; Exec. Chair, Social Care Inst. for Excellence, 2001–05. Comr, Disability Rights Commn, 2000–07. Chair: British Council of Disabled People, 1991–95; Right to Control Adv. Gp (formerly Right to Control Individual Budgets Wkg Gp), 2008–12, Independent Living Scrutiny Gp, 2009–11, Office for Disability Issues, DWP; Member: Commn for Equality and Human Rights, 2006–09; Standing Commn on Carers, DoH, 2008–09. Mem., H of L Jt Cttee on Human Rights, 2010–12. Voluntary Sector Rep., Kingston LA Social Services Cttee, 1990–96; Trustee, Disability Awareness in Action, 1991–2003; Gov., NISW, 1995–2001; Patron, Just Fair, 2014–. Hon. LLD Bristol, 2002; DUniv: Sheffield Hallam, 2002; Birmingham, 2009. Lifetime Achievement Award, Liberty Human Rights Awards, 2012. Mem., Editl Bd, British Jl of Social Work, 2007–11. *Publications:* Good Guide to Disability Training, 1990; (with Mike Oliver) Disability Politics, 1996; (jtly) Direct Routes to Independence, 1999; (jtly) Disabled People and the Right to Life, 2008. *Recreations:* gardening, theatre, travel. *Address:* 116A Princes Avenue, Surbiton, Surrey KT6 7JW.

CAMPBELL, Aileen Elizabeth; Member (SNP) Clydesdale, Scottish Parliament, since 2011 (Scotland South, 2007–11); Minister for Children and Young People, since 2011; *b* 18 May 1980; *d* of Peter Campbell and Ann Campbell (*née* Webster); *m* 2009, Fraser White; two *s*. *Educ:* Collace Primary Sch.; Perth Acad.; Univ. of Glasgow (MA Hons Econ. and Soc. Hist. with Pols). Editor, Keystone (construction mag.), 2004–05; Editl Asst, Scottish Standard, 2005; Parly Asst to Nicola Sturgeon, MSP, 2005–06; Parly Researcher to Shona Robison, MSP, and Stewart Hosie, MP, 2006–07. Minister for Local Govt and Planning, Scottish Parlt, 2011. *Recreations:* music, cinema, reading, football (St Johnstone FC). *Address:* Scottish Parliament, Holyrood, Edinburgh EH99 1SP. *T:* (0131) 348 6707, *Fax:* (0131) 348 6709. *E:* aileen.campbell.msp@scottish.parliament.uk.

CAMPBELL, Rt Hon. Alan; PC 2014; MP (Lab) Tynemouth, since 1997; *b* 8 July 1957; *s* of Albert Campbell and Marian Campbell (*née* Hewitt); *m* 1991, Jayne Lamont; one *s* one *d*. *Educ:* Univ. of Lancaster (BA Hons); Univ. of Leeds (PGCE); Newcastle Poly. (MA). Teacher: Whitley Bay High Sch., 1980–89; Hirst High Sch., Ashington, 1989–97. An Asst Govt Whip, 2005–06; a Lord Comr of HM Treasury (Govt Whip), 2006–08; Parly Under-Sec. of State, Home Office, 2008–10; Dep. Opposition Chief Whip, 2010–. *Address:* House of Commons, SW1A 0AA; (office) 99 Howard Street, North Shields NE30 1NA.

CAMPBELL, Alan Dermont; Managing Partner, Dundas & Wilson CS LLP, 2006–12; *b* 17 Sept. 1960; *s* of late Dermont Campbell and Doreen Catherine Campbell (*née* McCreath, later Morton); *m* 1986, Jane Porteous; two *d*. *Educ:* Fettes Coll.; Edinburgh Univ. (LLB Hons; DipLP). Joined Dundas & Wilson, Solicitors, 1984, Partner, 1992. *Recreations:* golf, ski-ing, walking, cooking. *Clubs:* Golf House (Elie); Gullane Golf.

CAMPBELL, Alan Grant, CBE 2002; Member, Accounts Commission for Scotland, since 2011; Chief Executive, Aberdeenshire Council, 1995–2008; *b* 4 Dec. 1946; *s* of late Archie and Catherine Campbell; *m* 1974, Susan Marion Black; one *s* two *d*. *Educ:* Aberdeen GS; Aberdeen Univ. (LLB 1968). Admitted Solicitor, Scotland, 1970; legal appts, Aberdeen CC, 1968–75; Grampian Regional Council: Asst Dir, 1975–79, Depute Dir, 1979–84, Dir, 1984–91, of Law and Admin; Chief Exec., 1991–95. Chm., SOLACE (Scotland), 1997–99. Chm., Inquiry into Future Fisheries Mgt for Scottish Govt, 2009–10; Mem., Cttee of Inquiry into professional conditions of service for teachers, 2000. Hon. LLD Aberdeen, 2005. *Recreations:* competitive cycling and following the Tour de France, gardening, photography, the enjoyment of wine. *Address:* 72 Hamilton Place, Aberdeen AB15 5BA.

CAMPBELL, Alastair John; freelance speaker, consultant and writer; *b* 25 May 1957; *s* of late Donald Campbell and of Elizabeth (*née* Caldwell); partner, Fiona Millar, *qv*; two *s* one *d*. *Educ:* City of Leicester Boys Sch.; Gonville and Caius Coll., Cambridge (MA). Trainee reporter, Tavistock Times and Sunday Independent, 1980–82; freelance reporter, London, 1982–83; reporter, Daily Mirror, 1982–85; news editor, Sunday Today, 1985–86; reporter, Daily Mirror, 1986; Sunday Mirror: Political Corresp., 1986–87; Political Editor, 1987–89; Columnist, 1989–91; Daily Mirror: Political Editor, 1989–93; Columnist, 1991–93; Asst Editor and Columnist, Today, 1993–95; Press Sec. to Leader of Opposition, 1994–97; Prime Minister's official spokesman, 1997–2001; Dir of Communications and Strategy, Prime Minister's Office, 2001–03; Strategy and Commns Consultant, British and Irish Lions Tour to NZ, 2005; Dir, Election Communications, Labour Party, 2005; Advr to Labour Party, General Election, 2010; Member, Advisory Board: Portland, 2011–; Univ. Coll. of Football Business, Burnley, 2011–; Strategic Adviser: Albanian Socialist Party, 2011–; Albanian govt, 2013–; Chief Interviewer, GQ mag., UK, 2014–. Humanitas Vis. Prof. of Media, Cambridge Univ., 2013. Chm., Fundraising, Leukaemia and Lymphoma Res. (formerly Leukaemia Res. Fund), 2004–; Ambassador: Time to Change campaign, 2008–; Alcohol Concern, 2013–; Mind Champion of the Year, 2009. Hon. Life Mem., Law Soc., UCD, 2014. Freelance writer, The Times and elsewhere, 2003–. *Publications:* The Blair Years, 2007; (with Bill Hagerty) The Alastair Campbell Diaries: Volume One: prelude to power 1994–1997, 2010, Volume Two: power and the people 1997–99, 2011, Volume Three: power and responsibility 1999–2001, 2011, Volume Four: the burden of power 2001–03, 2012; The Happy Depressive, 2012; The Irish Diaries, 2013; Winners and How They Succeed, 2015; *novels:* All in the Mind, 2008; Maya, 2010; My Name is…, 2013. *Recreations:* running, triathlon, bagpipes, Burnley Football Club.

CAMPBELL, Alastair Peter; *see* Bracadale, Rt Hon. Lord.

CAMPBELL, Prof. Alastair Vincent; Chen Su Lan Centennial Professor of Medical Ethics, and Director, Centre for Biomedical Ethics, National University of Singapore, since 2006; *b* 16 April 1938; *s* of William Lee Campbell and Jean Graham Dow; *m* 1st, 1959, Paula Barker (marr. diss.); one *s* four *d*; 2nd, 1979, Sally Barbara Forbes; two *s*. *Educ:* Hamilton Acad.; Univ. of Edinburgh (MA, BD); San Francisco Theol Seminary (ThD). Ordained Minister, Church of Scotland, 1963. Associate Chaplain, Univ. of Edinburgh, 1964–69; Lectr in Ethics, RCN, Scotland, 1966–72; University of Edinburgh: Lectr and Sen. Lectr, Dept of Christian Ethics and Practical Theology, 1969–90; Head of Dept, 1987–90; Associate Dean, Faculty of Divinity, 1978–81; Prof. of Biomedical Ethics, Otago Med. Sch., and Dir, Bioethics Res. Centre, Dunedin, Univ. of Otago, NZ, 1990–96; Prof. of Ethics in Medicine, Univ. of Bristol, 1996–2003, now Emeritus. Fellow: Hastings Center, NY, 2002; Ethox Centre, Univ. of Oxford, 2012. Foundn Editor, Jl of Medical Ethics, 1975–80. Corresp. FRSE, 2011. Milligan Soc. Medallion, 1980; H. K. Beecher Award, Hastings Center, NY, 1999. *Publications:* Moral Dilemmas in Medicine, 1972; Medicine, Health and Justice, 1978; Rediscovering Pastoral Care, 1981; (with R. Higgs) In That Case, 1982; Moderated Love, 1984; Paid to Care?, 1985; The Gospel of Anger, 1986; The Dictionary of Pastoral Care, 1987; (with G. R. Gillett and D. G. Jones) Practical Medical Ethics, 1992, 4th edn, as Medical Ethics, 2005; Health as Liberation, 1995; The Body in Bioethics, 2009; Bioethics: the basics, 2013; articles in learned jls. *Recreations:* music, cross country ski-ing, hill walking. *Address:* Yong Loo Lin School of Medicine, National University of Singapore, Centre for Biomedical Ethics, Blk MD 11, # 02–01, Clinical Research Centre, 10 Medical Drive, Singapore 117597.

CAMPBELL, Hon. Alexander Bradshaw, OC 2013; OPEI 2013; PC (Canada) 1967; Premier of Prince Edward Island, 1966–78; Judge, Supreme Court of Prince Edward Island, 1978–94; *b* 1 Dec. 1933; *s* of Dr Thane A. Campbell and late Cecilia B. Campbell; *m* 1961, Marilyn Gilmour; two *s* one *d*. *Educ:* Dalhousie Univ. (BA, LLB). Called to Bar of Prince Edward Island, 1959; practised law with Campbell & Campbell, Summerside, PEI, 1959–66; QC (PEI) 1966. MLA, Prince Edward Island, 1965–78; Leader of Liberal Party, Dec. 1966–78; served (while Premier) as Attorney-Gen., 1966–69, Minister of Development, 1969–72, Minister of Agriculture, 1972–74, and Minister of Justice, 1974–78. Dir, Inst. of Man and Resources, 1976–80. Pres., Summerside YMCA, 1981–91; Founder Pres., Summerside Area Historical Soc., 1983; Founder Chm., PEI Council, Duke of Edinburgh Awards (Canada), 1984. Mem., Wyatt Foundn, 1993–2006. Mem., Heedless Hoarsemen Men's Chorus, Largo, Fla, 1996– (Manager, 2004–09). Chm., PEI Day Cttee, Fla, 2000–. Elder of Trinity United Church, Summerside. Sigma Chi Fraternity. Hon. LLD: McGill 1967; PEI, 1978. *Recreations:* golf, boating, gardening. *Address:* Stanley Bridge, Kensington, RR #6, PE C0B 1M0, Canada. *T:* (902) 8862081. *Club:* Y's Men's (Summerside).

CAMPBELL, Sir Alexander Thomas C.; *see* Cockburn-Campbell.

CAMPBELL, Andrew Bruce; His Honour Judge Andrew Campbell; a Circuit Judge, since 2004; *b* 20 Feb. 1949; *s* of Keith Bruce Campbell and Betty Joan Campbell; *m* 1977, Felicity Jane (*née* Owen); two *d*. *Educ:* Harrow Sch.; Brasenose Coll., Oxford (MA Jurisprudence). Called to the Bar, Inner Temple, 1972; Asst Recorder, 1998–2000, Recorder, 2000–04. *Recreations:* long distance walking, theatre. *Address:* Kingston upon Thames Crown Court, 6–8 Penrhyn Road, Kingston upon Thames, Surrey KT1 2BB. *T:* (020) 8240 2500, *Fax:* (020) 8240 2675.

CAMPBELL, Andrew Neville; QC 1994; a Recorder, 1989–2014; *b* 17 June 1949; *s* of Archibald Campbell, CMG and of Peggie Campbell (*née* Hussey); *m* 1980, Rebecca Thornton; two *s* one *d*. *Educ:* Berkhamsted Sch.; New Coll., Oxford (BA Hons Jurisprudence). Called to the Bar, Middle Temple, 1972, Bencher, 2005. *Recreations:* fishing, shooting, cricket, squash, ski-ing, walking. *Clubs:* Vincent's (Oxford); Harrogate Cricket (Pres.).

CAMPBELL, Andrew Simon, CB 2013; Director General, Finance and Corporate Services, Department for Communities and Local Government, since 2013; *b* 30 Sept. 1957; *s* of Brian Andrew Humphrey Campbell and Rita Audrey Campbell; *m* 1982, Jacqueline Fraser Craik; two *s* one *d*. *Educ:* St Andrews Univ. (MA); University Coll. London (MPhil). Joined Dept of Transport, 1983; DoE, 1988–96; seconded to EC, Brussels, 1990–93; Sec., Econ. and Domestic Secretariat, Cabinet Office, 1996–98; Area Dir, Kent, Govt Office for SE, 1998–2001; Private Secretary to Secretary of State: for Transport, Local Govt and the Regions, 2001–02; for Transport and Sec. of State for Scotland, 2002–03; Dir, Regl Co-ordination Unit, ODPM, subseq. DCLG, 2003–06; Dir, Local Strategic Partnerships and Performance, later Local Govt Policy and Performance, DCLG, 2006–11; Dir, Strategy and Progs, later Strategy and Performance, DCLG, 2011–13; Acting Director General: for Local Govt and Regeneration, 2010; for Neighbourhoods, 2011–12; Exec. Dir for Civil Service Reform, Cabinet Office (on secondment), 2012. *Recreations:* tennis, golf, football, reading novels, listening to nearly all types of music. *Address:* (office) 4th Floor, 2 Marsham Street, SW1P 4DF. *Clubs:* Southampton FC; West Surrey Golf.

CAMPBELL, Angus; *see* Campbell, I. A.

CAMPBELL, Anne; Chairman, Parkside Federation Academies, Cambridge, since 2012; *b* 6 April 1940; *d* of late Frank Lucas and Susan (*née* Chadwick); *m* 1963, Archibald MacRobert Campbell; one *s* two *d*. *Educ:* Newnham Coll., Cambridge (Maths Tripos Pt II, 1962; MA 1965). CStat (FSS 1985). Sen. Lectr in Statistics, Cambs Coll. of Arts and Technol., 1970–83; Head of Stats and Data Processing, Nat. Inst. of Agricl Botany, Cambridge, 1983–92. MP (Lab) Cambridge, 1992–2005; contested (Lab) same seat, 2005. PPS to Minister for E-commerce and Small Businesses, 1999–2001, to Sec. of State for Trade and Industry, 2001–03. Mem., Cambs CC, 1985–89. Chm., Cambs and Peterborough NHS Foundn Trust, 2005–12. FRSA 1992. *Publications:* Calculation for Commercial Students, 1972. *Recreations:* tennis, ski-ing, gardening, mountain walking. *Address:* 20 St Barnabas Road, Cambridge CB1 2BY.

CAMPBELL, Rt Hon. Sir Anthony; *see* Campbell, Rt Hon. Sir W. A.

CAMPBELL, Prof. Anthony Keith, PhD; Professor, School of Pharmacy and Pharmaceutical Sciences (formerly Welsh School of Pharmacy), Cardiff University, 2010–14, Honorary Professor, since 2014; *b* 30 April 1945; *s* of Harold Keith Campbell and Jennet Mary Seth Campbell; *m* 1985, Dr Stephanie Beatrix Matthews; one *s* two *d*, and two *s* by previous marriage. *Educ:* City of London Sch.; Pembroke Coll., Cambridge (Exhibnr; Foundn Schol.; MA 1st cl. Natural Sci. 1967; PhD 1971). Lectr, 1970–78, Sen. Lectr, 1978–83, Welsh Nat. Sch. of Medicine; Reader, 1983–91, Prof. in Med. Biochem., 1991–2010, Univ. of Wales Coll. of Medicine, later Cardiff University. Founder, 1993, and Dir, Cardiff, 1993–2000, Pembs, 2000–, Darwin Centre. FLS 1995; FRSA 1995. Mem. Council, Linnean Soc., 2014–. Founder, Internat. Soc. for Bioluminescence and Chemiluminescence, 1994; Foreign Mem., Royal Soc. of Scis, Uppsala, 2001. FLSW 2013. Inspire Wales Award for Sci. and Technol., 2011. *Publications:* Intracellular Calcium: its universal role as regulator, 1983; Chemiluminescence: principles and applications in biology and medicine, 1988; Rubicon: the fifth dimension of biology, 1994; (with S. B. Matthews) Lactose Intolerance and the MATHS Syndrome, 2001; Tony's Lactose-free Cookbook: the science of lactose intolerance and how to live without lactose, 2005; Hands on Darwin: Charles Darwin in the 21st century, 2011; Intracellular Calcium, 2015; 7 patents; contrib. numerous scientific pubns, and papers to Nature, Proc. of NAS, Lancet, Postgrad. Med. Jl, Jl of Molecular Biol. *Recreations:* music (singing/conducting), bridge, cooking, natural history. *Address:* School of Pharmacy and Pharmaceutical Sciences, Cardiff University, Redwood Building, King Edward VII Drive, Cardiff CF10 3NB. *E:* campbellak@cf.ac.uk.

CAMPBELL, Arthur McLure, CBE 1990; Principal Clerk of Session and Justiciary, Scotland, 1982–89, retired; *b* 15 Aug. 1932; *s* of late Hector Brownlie Campbell, MBE (Mil.), AIPA and Catherine Smylie (*née* Renwick). *Educ:* Queen's Park Sch., Glasgow; Open Univ. (BA Hons 2001; BSc Hons 2008; MA (Dist.) 2012). Deptl Legal Qual., Scottish Court Service, 1956. National Service, FAA, 1950–52. Admiralty Supplies Directorate, 1953–54; entered Scottish Court Service, 1954; Sheriff Clerk Depute, Kilmarnock, 1957–60; Sheriff Clerk of Orkney, 1961–65; seconded HM Treasury (O & M), 1965–69; Principal Sheriff Clerk Depute, Glasgow, 1969; Sheriff Clerk, Airdrie, 1969–72; Principal, Scottish Court Service Staff Trng Centre, 1973–74; Asst Sheriff Clerk of Glasgow and Strathkelvin, 1974–81. Clerk of Cttees, H of L (temp.), 1991. Secretary: Lord Chancellor's Cttee on Re-sealing of Probates and Confirmations, 1967–68; Scottish Office Cttee on Money Transfer Services, 1968–69; Chm., Simplified Divorce (Scotland) Implementation Gp, 1981–82 (Scottish Consumer Council's Consumer Champion Award, 1983); Mem., Review Body on Use of Judicial Time in Superior Courts in Scotland, 1985–86. Chm., Sheriff Clerks' Assoc., 1971–72. *Recreation:* opsimathy. *Address:* 1 West Hill, Lord Street West, Southport PR8 2BJ; Carrer Mestre Nicolau 8, 07181 Palma Nova-Calvia, Mallorca. *Clubs:* National Liberal, Civil Service.

CAMPBELL, Rt Hon. Avril Phaedra; *see* Campbell, Rt Hon. Kim.

CAMPBELL, Bridget; Director, Environment and Forestry, Scottish Government, since 2015; *b* 9 March 1959; *d* of Allan Walter Campbell and Margaret Campbell (*née* Brettell). *Educ:* St Anne's Coll., Oxford (BA Hons Lit. Hum.). Various posts in Depts of Envmt and Transport, dealing with housing, local govt and internat. envmtl policy, 1982–96; Cycle Internat. course, l'Ecole Nat. d'Admin, Paris, 1989–90; Head, Housing Policy and Home Ownership Div., DoE, 1996–98; Scottish Executive: Head: Envmt Protection Unit, 1998–99; Cabinet Secretariat, 2000–01; Dir, Public Service Delivery, 2002–03; Hd, Police and Community Safety Gp, Scottish Exec., later Scottish Govt, Justice Dept, then Dir, Police and Community Safety, Scottish Govt, 2005–09; Scottish Government: Dir, Criminal Justice, then Justice, 2009–14; Dir, Readiness, 2014. *Address:* Scottish Government, St Andrew's House, Edinburgh EH1 3DG. *T:* (0131) 244 4891. *E:* bridget.campbell@scotland.gsi.gov.uk.

CAMPBELL, Bruce; *see* Campbell, W. B.

CAMPBELL, Prof. Bruce Mortimer Stanley, PhD; FBA 2009; FRHistS; Professor of Medieval Economic History, Department of Economic and Social History, 1995–2003, School of Geography, Archaeology and Palaeoecology, 2003–14, Queen's University Belfast, now Emeritus Professor; *b* Rickmansworth, 11 June 1949; *s* of Reginald Arthur Mortimer and Mary Campbell. *Educ:* Liverpool Univ. (BA 1st Cl. 1970); Darwin Coll., Cambridge (PhD 1975). FRHistS 2001. Lectr in Geog., 1973–89, Reader in Econ. Hist., 1992–95, QUB (on secondment to Dept of Econ. and Social Hist., 1989–2003). Fellow, Wissenschaftskolleg zu Berlin, 2010–11. Ellen McArthur Lectr, Cambridge Univ., 2013. MRIA 1997. FAcSS (AcSS 2003); MAE 2013. *Publications:* (ed with M. Overton) Land, Labour and Livestock: historical studies in European agricultural productivity, 1991; (ed) Before the Black Death: studies in the 'crisis' of the early fourteenth century, 1991; (jtly) A Medieval Capital and its Grain Supply: agrarian production and its distribution in the London region *c.* 1300, 1993; (ed with R. H. Britnell) A Commercialising Economy: England 1086–*c.* 1300, 1995; English Seigniorial Agriculture 1250–1450, 2000; (with K. Bartley) England on the Eve of the Black Death: an atlas of lay lordship, land and wealth, 1300–49, 2006; The Medieval Antecedents of English Agricultural Progress, 2007; Field Systems and Farming Systems in Late Medieval England, 2008; Land and People in Late Medieval England, 2009; (jtly) British Economic Growth 1270–1870, 2015; contrib. chapters to books and articles to Agricl Hist. Rev., Continuity and Change, Econ. Hist. Rev., Explorations in Econ. Hist., Jl Econ. Hist. (Arthur H. Cole Prize, Econ. Hist. Assoc. 1984), Jl Histl Geog., Past and Present, Trans IBG, Trans Geographical Inf. System. *Recreations:* attending live performances of classical music and opera, looking at architecture of all periods, Newfoundland dogs. *Address:* School of Geography, Archaeology and Palaeoecology, Queen's University Belfast, Belfast BT7 1NN. *Fax:* (028) 9097 3212. *E:* b.m.campbell@qub.ac.uk.

CAMPBELL, Camilla Anne MacNeill; Joint Founder and Director, Noho Film and Television, since 2012; *b* Rinteln, W Germany, 1 Dec. 1971; *d* of Alasdair Campbell and Carol Campbell; *m* 2005, Julian Kingsland; two *s*. *Educ:* Roedean Sch.; Newnham Coll., Cambridge (BA Hons Classics 1993). Editorial Assistant: AP Watt, 1994–96; Whitehall Films, 1996–99; Development Executive: Granada Television, 1999–2001; Tiger Aspect Prodns, 2001–04; Channel 4, 2004–09; Head of Drama, Channel 4, 2009–11. *Recreation:* sons Hal and Brock. *Address:* Noho Film and Television, Third Floor, 59 Charlotte Street, W1T 4PE.

CAMPBELL, Cheryl Anne; actress. *Educ:* London Acad. of Music and Dramatic Art (Rodney Millington Award). Acted at Glasgow Citizens Theatr, Watford Rep., Birmingham Rep., King's Head, National Theatre and Theatre Clwyd; Blanche Dubois in A Streetcar Named Desire (Best Actress, Regl Theatre Awards); Nora in A Doll's House (SWET Award, 1983, for best actress of 1982 in a revival), RSC; title rôle in Miss Julie, Lyric, Hammersmith, and Duke of York's, 1983; title rôle in Daughter-in-Law, Hampstead, 1985; The Sneeze, Aldwych, 1988; Betrayal, Almeida, 1991; The Changeling, RSC, 1992; Misha's Party, Macbeth, RSC, 1993; The Strip, Royal Court, 1995; Some Sunny Day, Hampstead, 1996; The Last Yankee, Mercury Th., Colchester, 1996; The Seagull, Donmar, 1997; What the Butler Saw, Sheffield Crucible, 1997; Passion Play, Donmar, 2000; Noises Off, Piccadilly and tour, 2003. *Television* serials and series include: Pennies from Heaven, 1978; Testament of Youth (Best Actress Award, BAFTA, and British Broadcasting Press Guild Award, 1979); Malice Aforethought; Centrepoint; The Secret Agent, 1992; The Way We Live Now, 2001; William and Mary, 2003, 2004, 2005; Fantabulosa, 2006; Spooks, 2006; Peep Show, 2007; Poirot, 2008. *Films* include: Chariots of Fire, 1981; Greystoke, 1983; The Shooting Party, 1985. *Address:* c/o Amanda Howard Associates, 74 Clerkenwell Road, EC1M 5QA. *T:* (020) 7250 1760.

CAMPBELL, Christopher James, CBE 1993; Chairman, British Shipbuilders, 1989–2002; *b* 2 Jan. 1936; *s* of David Heggie Campbell and Nettie Phyllis (*née* Burgess). *Educ:* Epsom College. FCA. Served RAPC, 1959–61. Debenhams and subsidiaries, 1966–86, incl. Man. Dir, Hardy Amies, 1978–79; former Director: Debenhams dept stores; Harvey Nichols; Lotus; Debenhams Finance; Debenhams (M & S). Mem., and chief negotiator, 1986–88, non-exec. Mem., 1988–91, National Bus Co.; Finance Dir, Nat. Rivers Authy Adv. Cttee, 1988–89; Director: Harrods Bank Ltd, 1991–2000; Crown Timber plc, 1996–2000; Riverside Mental Health NHS Trust, 1993–96; Mem., BRB, 1994–97 (Vice-Chm., 1994–96). Mem. Council, Specialist Schs and Academies Trust (formerly Technology Colls, then Specialist Schs, Trust), 2001–07. Gov., United World Coll. of the Atlantic, 1993–2002. Trustee: Cobbe collection of ancient keyboard instruments, 1998–2007; British Youth Opera, 2003–10. Chm., Lucy Crowe Fan Club, 2006–. Captain Paymaster, HAC Inf. Bn, 1960–63. *Recreations:* politics, opera, entertaining, visual arts. *Address:* 19 Morpeth Mansions, Morpeth Terrace, SW1P 1ER. *T:* (020) 7630 7527. *Club:* Garrick.

CAMPBELL, Christopher John; HM Diplomatic Service; Ambassador to the Dominican Republic, since 2015; *b* London, 12 April 1963; *s* of John and Kathleen Campbell; *m* 1989, Sharon Isabel Hale (*see* S. I. Campbell). *Educ:* Wimbledon Coll.; Open Univ. (Professional Cert. and Dip. Mgt). Entered FCO, 1982; N America Dept, FCO, 1982–84; Sec. of State's Office, FCO, 1984–85; Accountant, Khartoum, 1985–88; Third Secretary: (Immigration),

Dhaka, 1988–92; (Mgt), Jakarta, 1992–96; Desk Officer, Polar Regns Section, FCO, 1996–98; Second Secretary: (Commercial), Caracas, 1999–2003; Ext. Relns Policy, UK Delegn NATO, Brussels, 2003–07; Strategy Manager, Internat. Mil. Capacity Bldg, 2008–09, Hd of Peacekeeping, 2009–11, Conflict Gp, FCO; non-resident Ambassador to Nicaragua, 2011–15. *Recreations:* playing golf and tennis, scuba diving, watching Rugby, cooking. *Address:* c/o Foreign and Commonwealth Office, King Charles Street, SW1A 2AH. *E:* chris.campbell@fco.gov.uk.

CAMPBELL, Colin Donald Norman; Master of the Senior Court Costs Office (formerly Supreme Court Taxing, later Costs, Office), 1996–2015; *b* 26 Nov. 1952; *s* of late Maj. Gregory Campbell, TD and Myra Campbell (*née* Robertson); *m* 1985, Jacqueline Merete Mollett; one *s* one *d*. *Educ:* Oundle; Univ. of London (BA). Admitted as solicitor, 1983; Partner, Brown Cooper Solicitors and Privy Council Agents, 1987–96; Dep. Taxing Master, 1993–96; Dep. Dist Judge, Midland Circuit, 2001–. *Recreations:* Rugby Union, ski-ing, fly-fishing. *Address:* The Old Vicarage, Syleham, near Eye, Suffolk IP21 4LN. *T:* (01379) 668306. *Club:* MCC.

CAMPBELL, Colin MacIver; Member (SNP) Scotland West, Scottish Parliament, 1999–2003; *b* 31 Aug. 1938; *s* of Archibald James Campbell, MB ChB, DPH, and Christina Ellen Campbell (*née* MacIver); *m* 1963, Evelyn Jean Marcella George; three *s* (and one *s* decd). *Educ:* Paisley Grammar Sch.; Glasgow Univ. (MA Hons); Jordanhill Coll. of Educn. Teacher: Hillhead High Sch., 1961–63; Paisley GS, 1963–67; Principal Teacher, Greenock Acad., 1967–73; Depute Head, Merksworth High Sch., 1973–77; Head, Westwood Secondary Sch., 1977–89; Tutor, Sen. Studies Inst., Strathclyde Univ., 1995–98. Mem., Renfrewshire Council, 1995–99. Nat. Sec., SNP, 1997–99 (Defence Spokesperson, 1995–2003). Chair, Kilbarchan Pipe Band, 2006–11. Mem., Lowland Reserve Forces and Cadets Assoc., 1999–2004. *Publications:* (jtly) Can't Shoot a Man with a Cold: Lt E. Alan Mackintosh, MC, 1893–1917, Poet of the Highland Division, 2004; Engine of Destruction: the 51st (Highland) Division in the Great War, 2013. *Recreation:* military history of the Great War. *Address:* Braeside, Shuttle Street, Kilbarchan, Renfrewshire PA10 2PR.

CAMPBELL, Colin Malcolm; *see* Malcolm, Rt Hon. Lord.

CAMPBELL, Sir Colin (Murray), Kt 1994; DL; Vice-Chancellor, University of Nottingham, 1988–2008; Professor Emeritus, Queen's University, Belfast; First Commissioner for Judicial Appointments, 2001–06; *b* 26 Dec. 1944; *s* of late Donald Campbell and Isobel Campbell; divorced; one *s* one *d*. *Educ:* Robert Gordon's Coll., Aberdeen; Univ. of Aberdeen (LLB 1st Cl. Hons). Lecturer: Faculty of Law, Univ. of Dundee, 1967–69; Dept of Public Law, Univ. of Edinburgh, 1969–73; Prof. of Jurisprudence, 1974–88, Dean of Faculty of Law, 1977–80, Pro-Vice-Chancellor, 1983–87, QUB. Member: Council, Soc. for Computers and Law, 1973–88; Standing Adv. Commn on Human Rights, 1977–80; Legal Aid Adv. Cttee, NI, 1978–82; Mental Health Legislation Rev. Cttee, NI, 1978–82; UGC, 1987–88; Nottingham Develt Enterprise, 1988–91; UFC Scottish Cttee, 1989–93; HEFCE, 1992–97; Inquiry into Police Responsibilities and Rewards, 1992–93; Trent RHA, 1992–96. Chairman: QUBIS Ltd, 1983–88; Zeton Ltd, 1990; Ind. Adv. Gp on Consumers Protection in NI, 1984; NI Economic Council, 1987–94 (Mem., 1985–94); Lace Market Develt Co., 1989–97; Human Fertilisation and Embryology Authy, 1990–94; Med. Workforce Standing Adv. Cttee, 1991–2001; Food Adv. Cttee, 1994–2001; Human Genetics Adv. Commn, 1996–99. Non-exec. Dir, Swiss Re GB, 1999–2005. DL Notts, 1996. *Publications:* (ed jtly) Law and Society, 1979; (ed) Do We Need a Bill of Rights?, 1980; (ed) Data Processing and the Law, 1984; numerous articles in books and jls. *Recreations:* sport, walking, music, reading.

CAMPBELL, Darren Andrew, MBE 2005; international athlete; *b* 12 Sept. 1973; *s* of Marva Campbell; *m* 2004, Clair Jacobs; two *s* one *d*. Athletic achievements include: Gold medals, 100m, 200m and 4 x 100m relay, Eur. Jun. Championships, 1991; Gold medal, 4 x 100m relay, Silver medals, 100m and 200m, World Jun. Championships, 1992; winner, 100m, National Championships, 1998; European Championships: Gold medals, 100m and 4 x 100m relay, 1998; Gold medal, 4 x 100m relay, 2002; World Championships: Bronze medal, 4 x 100m relay, 1997; Silver medal, 4 x 100m relay, 1999; Silver medal, 4 x 100m relay and Bronze medal, 100m, 2003; Commonwealth Games: Gold medal, 4 x 100m relay, Malaysia, 1998; Bronze medal, 200m, Gold medal, 4 x 100m relay, Manchester, 2002; Olympic Games: Silver medal, 200m, Sydney, 2000; Gold medal, 4 x 100m relay, Athens, 2004. *Recreation:* football. *Address:* c/o Nuff Respect, No 1 Constable's Boatyard, 15 Thames Street, Hampton, Middx TW12 2EW. *Club:* Sale Harriers.

CAMPBELL, David; Director, Sports and Entertainment (UK) Ltd, since 2012; Chief Executive, Wagamama, since 2013; *b* 4 Sept. 1959; *s* of Archibald and Jean Campbell; *m* 1995, Tracey; three *s* (incl. twin *s*) one *d*. *Educ:* Kelvinside Acad., Glasgow; Reed's Sch., Cobham; Washington Univ., St Louis (MBA, AB Media). Mktg, General Mills, 1981–92; Mktg Manager, Pepsi-Cola, 1982–86; various posts, Virgin Gp, 1986–90; Chief Executive Officer: Virgin TV (Europe), 1990–92; Virgin Radio, 1992–96; Virgin Media, 1997; Ginger Media Gp, 1997–2000; Vice Chm., Ministry of Sound, 2001–02; CEO, Visit London, 2003–05; CEO, AEG Europe and The O2, 2005–11; Main Bd Dir, Formula One (Delta Topco), 2011–12. *Recreations:* music, travel, family. *E:* david.campbell@sportsnet.com. *Clubs:* Soho House, Marketing Gp of GB.

CAMPBELL, David Ian; HM Diplomatic Service; High Commissioner to Brunei, since 2013; *b* 9 July 1958; *s* of Ian Flett Campbell and Irene Joyce Campbell (*née* Cook). *Educ:* St Nicholas Grammar Sch., Northwood; Univ. of Bristol (LLB Hons 1980). Joined FCO, 1981; served: Budapest, 1984–85; Georgetown, 1985–87; FCO, 1987–89; First Sec., UK Mission to UN, Geneva, 1989–93; Dep. Hd of Mission, Belgrade, 1994; Dep. Hd, then Hd, Human Rights Policy Dept, FCO, 1995–99; Dep. Hd of Mission, Manila, 2000–03; Deputy High Commissioner: Singapore, 2003–07; Canberra, 2008; Dir, British Trade and Cultural Office, Taiwan, 2009–13. *Recreations:* books, theatre, travel. *Address:* c/o Foreign and Commonwealth Office, King Charles Street, SW1A 2AH.

CAMPBELL, David Ross, CBE 2000; Chairman, NHS National Services Scotland, 2004–08; *b* 27 Sept. 1943; *s* of William Pancost Clyde Campbell and Davidina (*née* Ross); *m* 1968, Moira Bagley Donald. *Educ:* Whitehill Sch.; James Watt Meml Coll. Radio Officer, MN, 1961–67; Sales Exec., Remington Rand, 1967–69; various posts, Glasgow Herald & Evening Times, 1969–75; Man. Dir, Scottish & Universal Newspapers, 1975–79; Exec. Dir, Scottish & Universal Investments, 1978–83; Dir, Clyde Cablevision Hldgs Ltd, 1983–87; Chm. and Chief Exec., West Independent Newspapers Ltd, 1984–94. Chairman: Saltire Hldgs Ltd, 1990–93; Clansman Leisure Ltd, 1990–93; Dep. Chm., Enterprise Ayrshire, 1991–2000. Scotland Bd Mem., New Opportunities Fund, 1998–2004, Big Lottery Fund, 2004–06; Chm., Health Educn Bd for Scotland, 1995–2001. Dir, Wise Gp, 2009–. Public Mem., Network Rail, 2009–. Member: PPITB, 1976–78; Press Council, 1988–90. Pres., Glasgow Chamber of Commerce, 1988–90. Also holds various other public and private sector chm. and dir positions. FInstD 1980. Scottish Free Enterprise Award, Aims of Industry, 1990. *Recreations:* golf, theatre, travel, reading. *Address:* Summerlea, Summerlea Road, Seamill, W Kilbride KA23 9HP. *Club:* Western (Glasgow).

CAMPBELL, Duncan; Director of Communications, Scottish Natural Heritage, 1992–95; *b* 23 Sept. 1935; *s* of late Duncan Campbell, sometime Manager, Chartered Bank of India and Australasia, and Mary Beryl Campbell; *m* 1959, Morny Key (*d* 2012); two *s*. *Educ:* Merchiston Castle Sch., Edinburgh; Edinburgh Univ.; Newcastle upon Tyne Univ. Nat. service, RHA, 1954–56. Forestry Commission: Forest Manager, 1960–73; Landscape Architect, 1973–8[illegible] Head of Design and Recreation Br., 1980–85; Head of Environment Br., 1985–88; Di[illegible] Countryside Commission for Scotland, 1988–92. Director: Edinburgh & Lothians Greenspac[illegible] Trust Ltd, 1997–2007; Colinton Community Conservation Trust Ltd, 2000–; Mavisban[illegible] Trust Ltd, 2002–; Chm., Colinton Amenity Assoc., 2002–05. Member Council: Scottis[illegible] Council for Nat. Parks, 1997–2007; Edinburgh Civic Trust, 2003–12, 2013–. Civi[illegible] Champion, Scottish Civic Trust, 2013. *Publications:* articles in Landscape Design, Jl of RAS[illegible] Landscape Design Trust. *Recreations:* landscape appreciation, fishing. *Address:* 62 Bonal[illegible] Wester, Edinburgh EH13 0RQ.

CAMPBELL, Prof. Eleanor Elizabeth Bryce, PhD; FRS 2010; FRSE; FRSC, FInst[illegible] Professor of Chemistry, Edinburgh University, since 2013 (Professor of Physical Chemistr[illegible] 2007–13); *b* Rothesay, Isle of Bute, 13 April 1960; *d* of William and Isobel Cowan; *m* 1s[illegible] 1984, Iain Campbell (marr. diss. 1991); 2nd, 2003, Prof. Mats Jonson. *Educ:* Rothesay Acad[illegible] Edinburgh Univ. (BSc; PhD 1985); Freiburg Univ. (Dr rer. nat. habil. 1991). FRSC 200[illegible] FInstP 2008. Asst Prof., Freiburg Univ., 1988–93; Dept Hd, Max Born Inst., Berlin, 1993–9[illegible] Prof. of Atomic and Molecular Physics, Gothenburg Univ., 1998–2007. FRSE 200[illegible] *Publications:* Fullerene Collision Reactions, 2003. *Address:* School of Chemistry, Edinburg[illegible] University, Edinburgh EH9 3JJ. *T:* (0131) 650 4729. *E:* eleanor.campbell@ed.ac.uk.

CAMPBELL, Francis Martin; HM Diplomatic Service; Vice Chancellor, St Mary[illegible] University, Twickenham, since 2014; *b* 20 April 1970; *s* of Daniel Joseph Campbell and Brig[illegible] Mary Campbell (*née* Cosgrove). *Educ:* Queen's Univ., Belfast (BA 1992); Katholiek[illegible] Universiteit, Leuven (MA 1995); Univ. of Pennsylvania (MA). Joined HM Diplomat[illegible] Service, 1997; FCO, 1997; EC Delegn to the UN, NY, 1997–98; FCO, 1998–99; Polic[illegible] Advr, 1999–2001, Private Sec., 2001–03, to the Prime Minister; First Sec. (External), Rom[illegible] 2003–05; Sen. Dir of Policy, Amnesty Internat., 2005; Ambassador to the Holy See, 2005–11[illegible] Dep. High Comr and Dir, Trade and Investment, Pakistan, 2011–13; Hd, Policy Unit, FC[illegible] 2013–14. Hon. Fellow, St Edmund's Coll., Cambridge, 2014. DUniv QUB, 2009; Ho[illegible] PhD: Catholic Univ. of Steubenville, 2010; Fordham, NY, 2010. President's Medal, Catholi[illegible] Univ. of America, 2009. *Publications:* (contrib.) Federalism Doomed, 2001. *Recreation*[illegible] reading, walking, travelling. *Address:* St Mary's University, Waldegrave Road, Strawberr[illegible] Hill, Twickenham TW1 4SX. *T:* (020) 8240 4000.

CAMPBELL, Gordon Muir; High Commissioner for Canada in the United Kingdom, sinc[illegible] 2011; *b* 12 Jan. 1948; *s* of Charles Gordon Campbell and Margaret Janet Campbell (*née* Muir[illegible] *m* 1970, Nancy Jean Chipperfield; two *s*. *Educ:* Dartmouth Coll., New Hampshire; Simo[illegible] Fraser Univ. (MBA). Secondary sch. teacher, and basketball and track coach, Yola, Nigeri[illegible] with Can. Univ. Students Overseas orgn, 1970–72; asst to Mayor of Vancouver, 1972–7[illegible] Marathon Realty, 1976–81 (Gen. Manager); Founder, Citycore Develt Corp., 1981. Mem[illegible] Vancouver CC, 1984–86, Mayor, 1986–93. MLA (L) Vancouver-Quilchene, 1994–9[illegible] Vancouver-Point Grey, 1996–2011; Premier, British Columbia, Canada, 2001–11. Leade[illegible] Liberal Party of BC, 1993–2011. *Publications:* (for children) Tuaq: The Only One, 199[illegible] *Address:* Canadian High Commission, Canada House, Trafalgar Square, SW1Y 5BJ.

CAMPBELL, Prof. Gordon Roy, DPhil, DLitt; FBA 2011; Professor of Renaissanc[illegible] Studies, University of Leicester, since 1994; *b* Carshalton, Surrey, 29 Nov. 1944; *s* of Cliffo[illegible] Earl Campbell and Diamond Davina Campbell (*née* Lecky); *m* 1966, Mary Elisabeth Freelan[illegible] two *s* one *d*. *Educ:* state schs in Canada; Univ. of Waterloo (BA 1967); Queen's Univ., Canad[illegible] (MA 1969); Univ. of York (DPhil 1973; DLitt 1998). Lectr in English, Univ. of Aarhu[illegible] 1973–74; Lectr in English Lit., Univ. of Liverpool, 1974–79; University of Leicester: Lectr i[illegible] English, 1979–87; Reader in Renaissance Lit., 1987–94; Internat. Relns Advr, 1983–201[illegible] Public Orator, 2004–; Chm., 1993–95, Pres., 1995–97, English Assoc.; Chm., Soc. f[illegible] Renaissance Studies, 1998–2001. Founder Chairman: UK-Saudi Interest Gp, 2002–1[illegible] British Univs Iraq Consortium, 2004–06. Patron, Milton's Cottage Trust, 2005–. Founde[illegible] Ed., Renaissance Studies, 1987–96; Ed., The Year's Work in English Studies, 1991–93; Seri[illegible] Ed., Essays and Studies, 1996–2001; Gen. Ed., Review of English Studies, 1997–2009; Jt Ge[illegible] Ed., The Complete Works of John Milton, 11 vols, 2008–; Mem., ten editl bds. FRHist[illegible] 1988; FRGS 1998; FRAS 2006; FSA 2008; FLS 2012. Hon. FEA 2015. Dr *hc* Buchares[illegible] 1999. *Publications:* (ed) John Milton: the complete poems, 1980; (ed) The Renaissanc[illegible] 1550–1660, 1989; (ed) John Milton, Complete English Poems, Of Education, Areopagitic[illegible] 1990; (ed) Ben Jonson: The Alchemist and other plays, 1995; (ed) John Milton: selecte[illegible] poems, 1996; (ed) Milton: a biography, by W. R. Parker, 2 vols, 1996; (ed) Andrew Marvel[illegible] selected poems, 1997; A Milton Chronology, 1997; The Oxford Dictionary of th[illegible] Renaissance, 2003; Renaissance Art and Architecture, 2004; (ed and contrib.) Grov[illegible] Encyclopedia of Decorative Arts, 2 vols, 2006; (jtly) Milton and the Manuscript of 'D[illegible] Doctrina Christiana', 2007; John Milton, 2007; (ed) Grove Encyclopedia of Classical Art an[illegible] Architecture, 2 vols, 2007; (jtly) John Milton: life, work and thought, 2008; (ed) John Milto[illegible] Paradise Lost and Paradise Regained, 2009; (ed) Grove Encyclopedia of Norther[illegible] Renaissance Art, 3 vols, 2009; Bible: the story of the King James Version 1611–2011, 201[illegible] (ed) The Holy Bible: quatercentenary edition, 2010; The Hermit in the Garden: fro[illegible] Imperial Rome to ornamental gnome, 2013. *Recreations:* travel, theatre, art, classical musi[illegible] Italian opera, walking. *Address:* School of English, University of Leicester LE1 7RH. *E:* leb[illegible] le.ac.uk.

CAMPBELL, Gregor Bruce Loudoun; Secretary-General, Institute of Actuaries, and Chi[illegible] Executive (Joint Affairs), Faculty of Actuaries and Institute of Actuaries, 1997–2002; *b* 22 Apr[illegible] 1942; *s* of Donald and Alison Campbell; *m* 1966, Suzanne Elizabeth Austin; one *s* two *d*. *Edu*[illegible] Glasgow Acad.; London Univ. (BScEng). Corps of Royal Engineers, 1962–92; retd as Brig[illegible] Dep. Sec., Inst. of Actuaries, 1993–97. *Recreations:* family, travel, gardening, motor cycles.

CAMPBELL, Gregory Lloyd; MP (DemU) Londonderry East, since 2001; Memb[illegible] (DemU) East Londonderry, Northern Ireland Assembly, since 1998; *b* 15 Feb. 1953; [illegible] Frances; one *s* three *d*. *Educ:* Ebrington Primary Sch.; Londonderry Tech. Coll.; Magee Col[illegible] Civil Servant, 1972–82 and 1986–94; businessman, 1994–. Mem. (DemU) Londonderry C[illegible] 1981–. Mem. (DemU), NI Assembly, 1982–86; Mem., NI Forum for Political Dialogu[illegible] 1996–98. Minister for Regl Develt, 2000–01, for Culture, Arts and Leisure, 2008–09, N[illegible] Contested (DemU): Foyle, 1992; E Londonderry, 1997. *Publications:* Discrimination: th[illegible] truth, 1987; Discrimination: where now?, 1993; Ulster's Verdict on the Joint Declaratio[illegible] 1994; Working Toward 2000, 1998. *Recreations:* soccer, music, reading. *Address:* (office) 2[illegible] Bushmills Road, Coleraine, Co. Londonderry, Northern Ireland BT52 2BP; 6–8 Catherin[illegible] Street, Limavady BT49 9DB.

CAMPBELL, Guy McGregor; Chairman, Baltic Exchange, 2014–July 2016; Gener[illegible] Manager (Atlantic), China Navigation Co. Pte Ltd, since 2013; *b* Walthamstow, 17 July 196[illegible] *s* of late Peter Campbell and of Monica Campbell; *m* 1991, Virginia Julie; two *s* one *d*. *Edu*[illegible] Herne Bay Secondary Sch. FICS; MCIArb. Shipbroker, JE Hyde & Co., 1990–97; charterin[illegible] manager, later Dir, Ocean Freight, Koch Carbon LLC, 1997–2007; Man. Dir, Dry Carg[illegible] Chartering, H. Clarksons & Co., 2007–13. Chm., Freight Mkt Users Inf. Gp, 2005, Bd Di[illegible] 2009–, Baltic Exchange. *Recreations:* rowing (winner, Thames Challenge Cup, Henley Roy[illegible] Regatta, 1992), cycling. *Address:* c/o Baltic Exchange, St Mary Axe, EC3A 8BN. *T:* (02[illegible] 7283 9300; Swire Bulk, China Navigation Co. Pte Ltd, Swire House, 59 Buckingham Gat[illegible] SW1E 6AJ. *T:* (020) 7963 9485.

CAMPBELL, Dr Henrietta, CB 2000; FRCP, FRCPGlas, FFPH; Chief Medical Officer f[illegible] Northern Ireland, 1995–2006; *b* 2 Nov. 1948; *d* of Thomas James Hanna and Jean Hanna; [illegible] 1972, William McBride Campbell; one *s* two *d*. *Educ:* Queen's Univ., Belfast (MD 1998[illegible]

FFPH (FFPHM 1996); FRCP 1997; FRCPGlas 2000. GP, NI, 1974–79; civilian medical practitioner, BAOR, 1979–83; SMO, 1983–90, Dep. CMO, 1990–95, Dept of Health and Social Services, NI. Mem., UK Electoral Commn, 2007–11; Mem. Bd, Food Standards Agency, 2010– (Chair, NI Food Adv. Cttee, 2010–); Mem., Commn overseeing pay, pensions and expenses of Members of NI Assembly, 2011–. Trustee, Oxfam Ireland, 2006– (Chm., Bd of Trustees, 2014–). *Recreations:* gardening, water-colour painting, hill-walking. *Address:* 1A The Rookery, Killinchy, Co. Down, Northern Ireland BT23 6SY. *T:* (028) 9754 2800.

CAMPBELL, Hugh Hall; QC (Scot.) 1983; FCIArb; *b* 18 Feb. 1944; *s* of William Wright Campbell and Marianne Doris Stuart Hutchison or Campbell; *m* 1969, Eleanor Jane Hare; three *s*. *Educ:* Glasgow Acad.; Trinity Coll., Glenalmond (Alexander Cross Scholar); Exeter Coll., Oxford (Open Scholar in Classics; BA Hons, MA); Edinburgh Univ. (LLB Hons). FCIArb 1986. Called to the Scottish Bar, 1969; Standing Jun. Counsel to Admiralty, 1976. Hon. Citizen, Antigua and Barbuda, 2010. *Recreations:* carnival, wine, music. *Address:* 12 Ainslie Place, Edinburgh EH3 6AS. *T:* (0131) 225 2067. *Club:* Hon. Company of Edinburgh Golfers.

CAMPBELL, (Ian) Angus; farmer, since 1980; Lord-Lieutenant for Dorset, since 2014; *b* London, 4 Sept. 1949; *s* of late Lt Col Duncan Lorne Campbell, MBE, MC and Christine Marion Campbell (*née* Phillipps); *m* 1977, Carola Claire Schulte; two *d*. *Educ:* Shebbear Coll., N Devon; Poole Tech. Coll.; RMA, Sandhurst; Army Sch. of Flying. Herd Tester, Auckland Herd Improvement Assoc., NZ, 1970–72. Served AAC, Officer and helicopter pilot, 658 Sqdn, 1975–79: W Germany; Aviation Flight, UN Peacekeeping Force in Cyprus; emergency tours, S Armagh and Belfast (AAC Commendation); Suffield Battle Gp Trng, Canada; Second i/c, 16 Flight AAC, Cyprus; TA 662 Sqdn AAC, 1979–81. Mem. (C) Dorset CC, 1989–93 and 2001–13 (Vice Chm., Educn Cttee, 1992–93; Dep. Leader, with portfolio resp. for Educn, then Roads, Transport and Regl Strategy, 2002–06; Leader, 2006–13); Mem. (C) N Dorset DC, 1999–2011 (Leader, 1999–2003). Chm., Strategic Leaders Bd for SW and SW Councils, 2008–13. Chm., Dorset Olympic Bd (sailing events), 2006–12. Chm., 1998–2001 and 2002–03, Pres., 2004–13, N Dorset Cons. Assoc. Chm., Lord Chancellor's Adv. Cttee on JPs for Dorset/Custos Rotolorum, 2014–. President: Dorset Co. Priory Gp of St John, 2014–; Dorset Br., Army Benevolent Fund, 2014–; Dorset SSAFA, 2014–; Dorset Army Cadet League, 2014–; Dorset Historic Chs Trust, 2014–; Dorset Youth Assoc., 2014–; Jt Pres., Somerset and Dorset Marine Soc. and Sea Cadets, 2014–; Patron: Dorset Child and Family Counselling Trust, 2014–; Dorset Community Action, 2014–; Dorset Community Foundn, 2014–; Dorset Co. Arts in Hosp., 2014–; Somerset and Dorset Air Ambulance, 2014–; Friends of Salisbury Cath., 2014–; Dorset SafeWise, 2014–; Wessex Br., Western Front Assoc., 2014–. *Recreations:* game shooting, fly-fishing, writing. *Address:* Lieutenancy Office, County Hall, Colliton Park, Dorchester, Dorset DT1 1XJ; Preston Hill Farm, Iwerne Minster, Blandford, Dorset DT11 8NL. *T:* (01747) 811219. *E:* prestonhil@aol.com.

CAMPBELL, His Honour Ian Burns, CMG 2003; a Circuit Judge, 1984–2003; Deputy High Representative for Legal Affairs, and Head, Legal Affairs Department, Office of High Representative, Sarajevo, 2000–03 (on secondment from Lord Chancellor's Department); *b* 7 July 1938; *s* of late James Campbell and Laura Campbell; *m* 1967, Mary Elisabeth Poole, BArch, MCD Liverpool; two *s* one *d*. *Educ:* Tiffin Boys' Sch.; Cambridge Univ. (MA, LLM, PhD); Diplôme d'Etudes Supérieures de Droit Comparé, Strasbourg, 1964. Called to the Bar, Middle Temple, 1966. French Govt Scholar, Univ. of Paris, 1961–62; Asst Lectr in Law, Liverpool Univ., 1962–64, Lectr 1964–69; a Recorder, 1981–84; Liaison Judge, N and S Sefton Benches, 1988–2000; seconded to Legal Dept, Office of High Rep., Sarajevo, 1999–2000. Mem., Franco-British Judicial Co-operation Cttee, 1996–2000. Hon. Mem., Albanian Nat. Judicial Conf., 1999–2000. A Dep. Chm. Adv. Bd, CARDS Regl Project 2003, for estabt of an indep., reliable and functioning judiciary in Western Balkans, 2006–07. Hon. Vis. Prof., Sch. of Law, Liverpool Univ., 1995–2006, 2009–12, 2014–. Chm., Adv. Bd, Liverpool Univ. Law Sch., 2008–13. Member, Editorial Board: Liverpool Law Review, 1996–2005; Judicial Studies Bd Jl, 1996–2000. Hon. LLD Liverpool, 2005. *Publications:* (contrib.) Legal Visions of the New Europe, 1993; contrib. legal jls. *Recreations:* journeying, Gaelic studies.

CAMPBELL, Ian H.; *see* Hay-Campbell.

CAMPBELL, Sir Ian (Tofts), Kt 1988; CBE 1984; VRD 1961; JP; Director, Conservative Board of Finance, 1978–90; Director of Finance and Administration, Scottish Conservative Party, 1988–90; *b* 3 Feb. 1923; *o s* of John Walter Campbell and Mary Hardie Campbell (*née* Scott); *m* 1961, Marion Kirkhope Paterson (*née* Shiel) (*d* 2010); one *d*. *Educ:* Daniel Stewart's College, Edinburgh. FInstD 1964. RN 1942–46, RNR 1946–65 (Comdr). Man. Dir, MacGregor Wallcoverings, 1966–78. Chm., Select Assured Properties, Glasgow, 1989–96; Dep. Chm., Heath (Scotland) Ltd, 1988–95 (Dir, 1987–96; consultant, 1996–2000); Director: Travel System, 1987–89; Hermiston Securities, 1990–. Mem., Transport Users' Cons. Cttee for Scotland, 1981–87. Councillor, City of Edinburgh District Council, 1984–88. JP Edinburgh, 1987. Freeman, City of Glasgow, 1992. OStJ 1987. KLJ 1984. *Recreations:* golf, water colour painting, vintage cars. *Address:* Merleton, 10 Boswall Road, Edinburgh EH5 3RH. *T:* (0131) 552 4825. *Club:* New (Edinburgh).

CAMPBELL of Succoth, Sir Ilay (Mark), 7th Bt *cr* 1808, of Succoth, Dunbartonshire; *b* 29 May 1927; *o s* of Sir George Ilay Campbell, 6th Bt; *S* father, 1967; *m* 1961, Margaret Minette Rohais, *o d* of J. Alasdair Anderson; two *d*. *Educ:* Eton; Christ Church, Oxford. BA 1952; MA 1970. Chm., Christie's Scotland, 1978–96. Dir, High Craigton Farming Co. Member: Historic Buildings Council for Scotland, 1989–98; Gardens Cttee, Nat. Trust for Scotland, 1994–2001. Pres., Assoc. for Protection of Rural Scotland, 1978–90. Mem., C of S Cttee for Artistic Matters, 1984–91 (Convener, 1987–91); Convener, Church Bldgs Renewal Trust, Glasgow, 1995–98. Hon. Vice Pres., Scotland's Gardens Scheme, 1960–; Trustee, Crarae Gardens Charitable Trust, 1978–2002. *Publications:* (with Brian North Lee) Scottish Bookplates, 2006. *Recreations:* heraldry, collecting heraldic bookplates. *Heir:* none. *Address:* Crarae Lodge, Inveraray, Argyll PA32 8YA. *T:* (01546) 886274, *Fax:* (01546) 886262. *Club:* Turf.

CAMPBELL, James, FBA 1984; FSA 1971; Professor of Medieval History, University of Oxford, 1996–2002; Fellow of Worcester College, Oxford, since 1957; *b* 26 Jan. 1935; *m* 2006, Bärbel Brodt. *Educ:* Mill Road Mixed Infants, Clowne, Derbyshire and other primary schools; Lowestoft Grammar School; Magdalen College (Exhibitioner; BA 1955, MA). Oxford University: Junior Research Fellow, Merton College, 1956–57; Tutorial Fellow, 1957, Fellow Librarian, 1977–2002, Sen. Tutor, 1989–93, Worcester College; Lectr in Modern History, 1958–90; Reader in Medieval History, 1990–96; Senior Proctor, 1973–74. Visiting Professor: Univ. of South Carolina, 1969; Univ. of Rochester, 1986–87. Creighton Lectr, Univ. of London, 1995; Ford's Lectr, Univ. of Oxford, 1996. Hon. DLitt UEA, 2006. *Publications:* Norwich, 1975; (ed) The Anglo-Saxons, 1982; Essays in Anglo-Saxon History, 1986; The Anglo-Saxon State, 2000; articles in learned jls. *Recreation:* topography. *Address:* Worcester College, Oxford OX1 2HB; 9 The Willows, Newland Mill, Witney, Oxon OX28 3HN. *T:* (01993) 706019. *E:* b.brodt@gmx.net.

CAMPBELL, James Alastair G.; *see* Graham-Campbell.

CAMPBELL, Sir James (Alexander Moffat Bain), 9th Bt *cr* 1667, of Aberuchill, Perthshire; farmer; insurance broker, Lycetts Insurance Brokers, since 2007; *b* 23 Sept. 1956; *er s* of Sir Colin Campbell, 8th Bt and of Mary Campbell (*née* Bain); *S* father, 1997; *m* 1993, Carola Jane Denman; one *s* two *d*. *Educ:* Stowe. Scots Guards (Capt.), 1975–83. Motorcycle despatch rider, 1984; insurance broker: Bain Dawes Ltd, Bain Clarkson plc, Bain Hogg plc, Aon Corp., 1984–97; R. K. Harrison Ltd, 1997–2001; indep. insurance consultant, 2001–07. *Recreations:* shooting, trees, gardening. *Heir:* *s* Colin George Denman Bain Campbell, *b* 1 Oct. 1999. *Address:* Kilbryde Castle, Dunblane, Perthshire FK15 9NF. *T:* (01786) 824897.

CAMPBELL, James MacRae, CBE 2012; Director (formerly Head) of Energy Development (formerly Licensing and Consents, later Energy Resources and Development) Unit, Energy Markets and Infrastructure (formerly Energy) Group, Department of Energy and Climate Change (formerly Department of Trade and Industry, then Department for Business, Enterprise and Regulatory Reform), 2003–12; *b* 17 June 1952; *s* of late Alistair Campbell and Flora MacKay Campbell (*née* MacRae); *m* 1975, Catherine Russell; one *s* one *d*. *Educ:* Strathclyde Univ. (BSc Hons (Physics) 1974). MInstP 1975; CPhys 1987. Res. Scientist, NEL, 1974–79; Offshore Supplies Office: Res. and Develt Assessor, 1979–82; Industrial Liaison, 1982–91; Asst Dir, and Hd UK Continental Shelf Develts, 1991–94; Asst Dir, Oil and Gas Projects and Supplies Office, 1994–96; Director: Industry and Downstream Exports, British Trade Internat., 1996–2000; Oil and Gas Envmt and Decommissioning, DTI, 2000–02. Mem. Bd, Aberdeen Foyer, 2012–. Hon. FEI 2010. FRSA 2000. *Recreations:* hill walking, reading, running, cinema, photography.

CAMPBELL, Jim; *see* Campbell, R. J.

CAMPBELL, Prof. John Joseph, DPhil; Willis S. and Marion Slusser Professor of Philosophy, University of California at Berkeley, since 2004; *b* 2 Nov. 1956; *s* of Roderick Campbell and Catriona (*née* MacKinnon); *m* 1st, 1978, Patricia Carrol (marr. diss. 1986); 2nd, 2002, Allison Harvey (marr. diss. 2007). *Educ:* Univ. of Stirling (BA); Univ. of Calgary (MA); Wolfson Coll., Oxford (BPhil, DPhil 1986). University of Oxford: Res. Lectr, Christ Church, 1983–86; Fellow and Tutor in Philosophy, New Coll., 1986–2001; British Acad. Res. Reader, 1995–97; Reader in Philosophy, 1997–2001; Wilde Prof. of Mental Philosophy, 2001–04; Fellow, Corpus Christi Coll., 2001–04. Visiting posts at: UCLA, 1988; Univ. of Cambridge, 1990–91; ANU, 1991–92; Cornell Univ., 1998. *Publications:* Past, Space and Self, 1994; Reference and Consciousness, 2002; (with Quassim Cassam) Berkeley's Puzzle, 2014. *Recreations:* gardening, country pubs. *Address:* University of California, Department of Philosophy, Berkeley, CA 94720–2390, USA.

CAMPBELL, His Honour (John) Quentin; a Circuit Judge, 1996–2008; *b* 5 March 1939; *s* of late John McKnight Campbell, OBE, MC, and late Katharine Margaret Campbell; *m* 1st, Penelope Jane Redman (marr. diss. 1976); three *s* one *d*; 2nd, 1977, Ann Rosemary Beeching, DL, a Circuit Judge; one *s* one *d*. *Educ:* Loretto Sch., Musselburgh, Scotland; Wadham Coll., Oxford (MA). Admitted as solicitor, 1965; private practice, Linnell & Murphy, Oxford (Partner, 1968–80); Metropolitan Stipendiary Magistrate, 1981–96; Asst Recorder, 1983–89; a Recorder, 1989–96. A Pres., Mental Health Review Tribunals, 1996–2008; Mem., Parole Bd, 2000–07. Mem., Student Appeal Panel, Univ. of Oxford, 2009–. Chairman, Bd of Governors, Bessels Leigh Sch., near Oxford, 1979–96. *Recreations:* opera, music, travel. *Clubs:* Travellers; Frewen (Oxford).

CAMPBELL, Juliet Jeanne d'Auvergne, CMG 1988; HM Diplomatic Service, retired; Mistress of Girton College, Cambridge, 1992–98, now Life Fellow; *b* 23 May 1935; *d* of Maj.-Gen. Wilfred d'Auvergne Collings, CB, CBE and of Nancy Draper Bishop; *m* 1983, Prof. Alexander Elmslie Campbell (*d* 2002). *Educ:* a variety of schools; Lady Margaret Hall, Oxford (BA; Hon. Fellow, 1992). Joined Foreign Office 1957; Common Market Delegation, Brussels, 1961–63; FO, 1963–64; Second, later First Secretary, Bangkok, 1964–66; News Dept, FO, 1967–70; Head of Chancery, The Hague, 1970–74; European Integration Dept, FCO, 1974–77; Counsellor (Inf.), Paris, 1977–80; RCDS, 1981; Counsellor, Jakarta, 1982–83; Head of Training Dept, FCO, 1984–87; Ambassador to Luxembourg, 1988–91. Member: Cambridge Univ. Council of Senate (later Council), 1993–97; Wilton Park Academic Council, 1993–2000. Dep. Vice-Chancellor, Cambridge Univ., 1993–98. Mem. Council, RSAA, 2008–14. Trustee: Changing Faces, 1992–2006; Cambridge European Trust, 1994–98; Kurt Hahn Trust, 1995–98; Cambridge Overseas Trust, 1995–98; Henry Fellowships, 1997–2005. Governor: Queen's Coll., Harley St, 1992–2002; Marlborough Coll., 1999–2007. *Address:* 3 Belbroughton Road, Oxford OX2 6UZ. *Club:* Oxford and Cambridge.

CAMPBELL, Air Vice-Marshal Kenneth Archibald, CB 1989; consulting engineer; Air Officer Maintenance, RAF Support Command, 1987–89; *b* 3 May 1936; *s* of John McLean and Christina Campbell; *m* 1959, Isobel Love Millar (*d* 2005); two *d*. *Educ:* George Heriot's Sch.; Glasgow Univ. (BSc); College of Aeronautics, Cranfield (MSc). Various engrg appts, RAF, 1959–90; Air Officer, Wales, 1977–79; Dir, Engrg Policy (RAF), 1981–83; AO, Engrg and Supply, RAF Germany, 1983–85; DG Personal Services (RAF), 1985–87. *Recreation:* golf.

CAMPBELL, Kenneth Ewen; Director, Campbell Brown PR, since 2014; *b* 20 Nov. 1967; *s* of Ewen and Christine Campbell; *m* 2012, Helen Jane Beckett. *Educ:* Caol Primary Sch., Caol; Lochaber High Sch., Fort William; Univ. of Aberdeen (MA Hons Politics and Econs). Trainee manager, Marks & Spencer, Perth, 1989–90; journalist: Press and Jl, Aberdeen, 1990–92; Evening News, Edinburgh, 1992–94; Chief Sub-Ed., Daily Mail, Glasgow, 1994–97; Night Ed., Daily Express, Glasgow, 1997–99; Deputy Editor: Metro, London, 1999–2000; Daily Mail, Glasgow, 2000–01; Ed., Metro (UK), London, 2001–14. Dir, London Press Club, 2014–. Freeman, Co. of Stationers and Newspaper Makers, 2007. *Recreations:* motor racing, whisky, photography. *E:* kennyc@hotmail.co.uk.

CAMPBELL, Rt Hon. Kim; PC (Canada) 1989; CC 2008; OBC 2012; QC (BC) 1990; international speaker and consultant, since 2007; Founding Principal, Peter Lougheed Leadership College, University of Alberta, since 2014; *b* 10 March 1947; *m* 1997, Hershey Felder. *Educ:* Univ. of British Columbia (BA 1969; LLB 1983); LSE (Hon. Fellow, 1994). Called to the Bar of BC, 1984, Ont, 1990. Lectr in Pol Sci., Univ. of BC, 1975–78; Lectr in Pol Sci. and Hist., Vancouver Community Coll., 1978–81; Articled student, 1983–84, Associate, Gen. Litigation, 1984–85, Ladner Downs Vancouver; Exec. Dir, Office of Premier of BC, 1985–86; MLA Vancouver Point Grey, 1986–88; MP (PC) Vancouver Centre, 1988–93; Minister of State, Indian Affairs and Northern Develt, 1989–90; Minister of Justice and Attorney Gen., 1990–93; Minister of Nat. Defence and Minister of Veterans' Affairs, 1993; Prime Minister of Canada, 1993; Canadian Consul-Gen., LA, 1996–2000. Club of Madrid: Founding Mem., 2001; Interim Pres., 2002–03; Vice Pres., 2003–04; Sec. Gen., 2004–06; Mem. Bd, 2007–11. Lectr, John F. Kennedy Sch. of Govt, Harvard Univ., 2003–04 (Vis. Prof. of Practice, 2001–04). Chair Emerita, Council of Women World Leaders, 2003 (Chair, 1999–2003); Pres., Internat. Women's Forum, 2003–05; Chair, Internat. Steering Cttee, World Movt for Democracy, 2008–. Trustee, Vancouver School Bd, 1980–84. Hon. LLD: Law Soc. of Upper Canada, 1991; Brock Univ., 1998; UBC, 2000; Mt Holyoke Coll., 2004; Chatham Coll., 2005; Alberta, 2010; Trent, 2011; Simon Fraser, 2014; Hon. DPS Northeastern, 1999; Hon. LHD Arizona State, 2005. *Publications:* Time and Chance: the political memoirs of Canada's first woman prime minister, 1996, 3rd edn 2008. *W:* www.kimcampbell.com, www.bitesizechunks.org.

CAMPBELL, Sir Lachlan (Philip Kemeys), 6th Bt *cr* 1815; book illustrator and author, since 2007; *b* 9 Oct. 1958; *e s* of Col Sir Guy Campbell, 5th Bt, OBE, MC and Lizbeth Webb, *d* of late Frederick Holton; *S* father, 1993; *m* 1986, Harriet Jane Sarah, *o d* of F. E. J. Girling; two *s* one *d*. *Educ:* Temple Grove; Eton; RMA Sandhurst. The Royal Greenjackets (Capt.); served NI. *Recreations:* golf, Rugby, cricket, painting, drawing. *Heir:* *s* Archibald Edward

FitzGerald Campbell, *b* 13 June 1990. *Address:* The Dairy House, Hanford, Blandford Forum, Dorset DT11 8HH. *Clubs:* Royal Greenjackets, MCC; London Scottish Golf and Rugby; Rushmore Golf; Eton Rambler Cricket.

CAMPBELL, Mark; Partner, Finance Practice, since 1991 and Head, Bank Client Coverage, since 2014, Clifford Chance LLP; *b* Liverpool, 23 June 1960; *s* of George and Thelma Campbell; *m* 1994, Susan Gaye Carter; four *s* three *d. Educ:* St Wilfrid's High Sch., Litherland; Oriel Coll., Oxford (MA Juris. 1978); Coll. of Law, Guildford. Admitted solicitor, 1984; with Clifford Chance LLP, 1982–: Managing Partner, London Finance Practice, 1998–2002; Hd, Global Finance Practice, 2002–14; Mem., Mgt Cttee, 2002–14. Mem., Finance Law Cttee, City of London Solicitors' Co., 1996–2011. Member: Bd, Tower Hamlets Educn Business Partnership, 2011–; MLF Adv. Bd, Univ. of Oxford, 2011–; MCL Practitioners Adv. Bd, Univ. of Cambridge, 2012–. Chm. Govs, Shapla Sch., 2008–. *Publications:* (jtly) Syndicated Lending: Documentation and Practice, 1993, 6th edn 2013. *Recreations:* music, novels, football, golf. *Address:* c/o Clifford Chance LLP, Canary Wharf, E14 5JJ.

CAMPBELL, Melfort Andrew, OBE 2003; Chairman, Imes Group Ltd, since 2009 (Founder and Chief Executive Officer, 1997–2009); *b* Budleigh Salterton, 6 June 1956; *s* of Lt Col Robert Campbell and Norma Campbell; *m* 1983, Hon. Lucy Jane, *d* of Baron Nickson, *qv*; three *d. Educ:* Ampleforth Coll. Founder and Owner, Water Weights, 1984–. Chairman: CBI Scotland, 2005–07; Tax Reform Commn, 2005–06; Mem. Bd, Scottish Enterprise, 2013–; Co Chair, Innovation Scotland Forum, 2014–. Director: Dreamstore, 2005–; Lord Stafford Awards, 2007–. Chm., Bd of Govs, Robert Gordon Univ., 2008–10. FRSA. Hon. DBA Robert Gordon, 2006. *Recreations:* fishing, travel, family, classic cars. *Address:* (office) Old School, Maryculter, Aberdeen AB12 5GN. *T:* (01224) 533533. *Club:* MCC.

CAMPBELL, Rt Hon. Sir Menzies; *see* Campbell, Rt Hon. Sir W. M.

CAMPBELL, Prof. Michael, OBE 2004; Director, Policy and Research, UK Commission for Employment and Skills, 2008–11; independent labour market and skills expert, since 2011; *b* 31 Dec. 1948; *s* of Patrick Campbell and Phyllis Campbell (*née* Conn); partner, Prof. Janie Percy-Smith; two *d. Educ:* St Anselm's Grammar Sch., Birkenhead; Univ. of Sheffield (BA 1970); Univ. of Lancaster (MA 1972); Univ. of Leeds (MA 1985). Leeds Polytechnic, subseq. Leeds Metropolitan University: Lectr, Sen. Lectr, then Principal Lectr in Econs, 1972–90; Prof. of Policy Studies and Founding Dir, Policy Res. Inst., 1990–2002; Dir, Strategy and Res., Sector Skills Develt Agency, 2002–08. Expert: EC, 1989–; OECD, 1996–. British Council Dist. Vis. Fellow, Japan, 1993; Visiting Professor: Univ. of Hiroshima, 1993; Univ. of Durham, 2006–. *Publications:* Capitalism in the UK, 1981; Capitalism and Public Policy in the UK, 1985; Controversy in Applied Economics, 1989; Local Economic Policy, 1990; Local Labour Markets, 1992; Learn to Succeed: the case for a skills revolution, 2002; Skills and Economic Performance, 2006; over 100 professional and tech. papers, book chapters and pubd reports on unemployment, skills and econ. performance. *Recreations:* cricket, Blackpool Football Club, travel. *E:* ProfMikeC@aol.com.

CAMPBELL, Rt Rev. Michael Gregory; *see* Lancaster, Bishop of, (RC).

CAMPBELL, Niall Gordon; Under Secretary, Civil and Criminal Law Group, Scottish Executive Justice (formerly Scottish Office Home) Department, 1997–2001; *b* 9 Nov. 1941; *s* of Ian M. Campbell and Jean G. Sanderson; *m* 1975, Alison Margaret Rigg; three *s. Educ:* Edinburgh Academy; Merton College, Oxford (BA). Entered Scottish Office, 1964; Asst Sec., 1978; posts in Scottish Educn and Scottish Develt Depts; Under Sec., Social Work Services Gp, SHHD, then Scottish Office Home Dept, 1989–97. Mem., Parole Bd for Scotland, 2003–09. Chairman: Scottish Assoc. for Study of Offending, 2001–06; SACRO, 2002–07. Mem. Council, 2006–11, Treas., 2008–11, British Trust for Ornithol. *Address:* 15 Warriston Crescent, Edinburgh EH3 5LA. *T:* (0131) 556 2895.

CAMPBELL, Nicholas Charles Wilson; QC 2000; *b* 8 May 1954; *s* of late Wilson Campbell and Pearl Campbell (*née* Ackrill); *m* 1987, Hon. Nicole Montagu. *Educ:* King's Sch., Canterbury; Trinity Coll., Cambridge (BA). Called to the Bar, Inner Temple, 1978. *Address:* KBW Chambers, The Engine House, 1 Foundry Square, The Round Foundry, Leeds LS11 5DL.

CAMPBELL, Oliver Edward Wilhelm; QC 2014; *b* Edinburgh, 20 July 1970; *s* of Edward Campbell and Ellen Campbell; *m* 2006, Annabel Walker; two *d. Educ:* Edinburgh Acad.; St Hugh's Coll., Oxford (BA 1991). Called to the Bar, Middle Temple, 1992; in practice as a barrister, specialising in commercial and regulatory law, Henderson Chambers, 1992–. Mem., Examinations Bd, Bar Standards Bd, 2011–; Chief Examr, Civil Litigation, Bar Professional Trng Course, 2015. Trustee, Lambeth Law Centre, 2010–. Pres., Oxford Union, 1990. *Recreations:* cricket, football. *Address:* Henderson Chambers, 2 Harcourt Buildings, Temple, EC4Y 9DB. *T:* (020) 7583 9020. *Club:* MCC.

CAMPBELL, Sir Philip Henry Montgomery, Kt 2015; PhD; Editor-in-Chief: Nature, since 1995; Nature Publications, since 1995; *b* 19 April 1951; *s* of Hugh and Mary Montgomery Campbell; *m* 1st, 1980, Judie Yelton (*d* 1992); two *s*; 2nd, 2014, Charis Mary Thompson. *Educ:* Shrewsbury Sch.; Bristol Univ. (BSc Aeronautical Engrg 1972); Queen Mary Coll., Univ. of London (MSc Astrophysics 1974; Hon. Fellow 2009); Leicester Univ. (PhD Ionospheric Physics 1978). FRAS 1979; FInstP 1995. Res., Leicester Univ., 1977–79; Asst Editor, 1979–82, Physical Scis Editor, 1982–88, Nature; Founding Editor, Physics World, 1988–95. Dir, Nature Publishing Gp, 1997–. Broadcasts on BBC. Trustee: Cancer Res. UK, 2003–12; MQ: transforming mental health, 2012– (Chm., 2015–). Associate, Clare Hall, Cambridge, 2008–13 (Life Mem., 2013). Hon. Prof., Peking Union Med. Coll., 2009. Hon. DSc: Leicester, 1999; Bristol, 2008. *Publications:* papers and articles in learned jls, magazines and newspapers. *Recreations:* music, art galleries. *Address:* Nature, 4 Crinan Street, N1 9XW. *T:* (020) 7833 4000.

CAMPBELL, Quentin; *see* Campbell, His Honour J. Q.

CAMPBELL, Prof. Robert James, (Jim); Professor of Education, University of Warwick, 1992–2007, now Emeritus; *b* 19 Dec. 1938; *s* of William Campbell and Elsie Campbell (*née* O'Connor); *m* 1st, 1964, Jennifer Rhodes (marr. diss. 1970); 2nd, 1972, Sarah Miranda Frankland (marr. diss. 2006); two *d*; 3rd, 2007, Wendy Robinson. *Educ:* Hull Univ. (BA Upper 2nd Cl. Classics 1959; PGCE 1960); Bradford Univ. (MSc Educnl Res. 1971). Teacher: Westgate Primary Sch., Newcastle upon Tyne, 1959; Nettleswell Comprehensive Sch., Harlow, 1960–62; Mkt Res. Officer, Mkt Res. Associates, London, 1962–63; Teacher, Latton Bush Comprehensive Sch., Harlow, 1963–64; Lectr, W Suffolk Coll. of Further Educn, Bury St Edmunds, 1964–67; Res. Student, Univ. of Bradford, 1967–68; Res. Officer, Curriculum Res. Unit, Inst. of Educn, Univ. of London, 1968–70; Lectr, Coventry Coll. of Educn, 1970–78; University of Warwick: Lectr, 1978–86; Sen. Lectr, 1986–89; Reader, 1989–92; Dir, Inst. of Educn, 1996–2001; Dir of Res., Nat. Acad. for Gifted and Talented Youth, Univ. of Warwick, 2004–07. Vis. Prof., Univ. of Plymouth, 2009–11. FRSA 1998. Phi Delta Kappa, 1974. *Publications:* Developing the Primary School Curriculum, 1985; Humanities in the Primary School, 1989; Breadth and Balance in the Primary School Curriculum, 1991; Primary Teachers at Work, 1994; Secondary Teachers at Work, 1994; The Meaning of Infant Teachers' Work, 1994; Curriculum Reform at Key Stage 1: teacher commitment and policy failure, 1994; Assessing Teacher Effectiveness, 2004; Effective Teaching in Gifted Education, 2010; Families, Education and Giftedness, 2012; contrib. numerous articles to jls. *Recreations:* wine, whisky, jazz. *Address:* Institute of Education, University of Warwick, Coventry CV4 7AL. *T:* (024) 7652 3850.

CAMPBELL, Sir Robin Auchinbreck, 15th Bt *cr* 1628 (NS); *b* 7 June 1922; *s* of Sir Louis Hamilton Campbell, 14th Bt and Margaret Elizabeth Patricia (*d* 1985), *d* of late Patrick Campbell; *S* father, 1970; *m* 1st, 1948, Rosemary, (Sally) (*d* 1978), *d* of Ashley Dean, Christchurch, NZ; one *s* two *d*; 2nd, 1978, Mrs Elizabeth Gunston (*d* 2005), *d* of Sir Arthur Colegate, Bembridge, IoW. Formerly Lieut (A) RNVR. *Heir: s* Louis Auchinbreck Campbell [*b* 17 Jan. 1953; *m* 1976, Fiona Mary St Clair, *d* of Gordon King; two *d*]. *Address:* 287A Waikawa Road, Picton, New Zealand.

CAMPBELL, Sir Roderick (Duncan Hamilton), 9th Bt *cr* 1831, of Barcaldine and Glenure, Argyllshire; Managing Partner, Barcaldine holdings, since 2003; *b* 24 Feb. 1961; *s* of Sir Niall Campbell, 8th Bt and Norma Joyce Campbell (*née* Wiggin); *S* father, 2003; *m* 1989, Jean Caroline (*née* Bicknell); three *d. Educ:* Chiswick. Vardon plc, 1988–99; Nat. Trust for Scotland, 1999–2004; Historic Scotland, 2013. *Recreations:* talking to my wife, household maintenance, following sport, family history. *Heir: b* Angus Charles Dundas Campbell, *b* 27 Oct. 1967. *Address:* 47/1 East London Street, Edinburgh EH7 4BW; Lossit, Benderloch, Oban PA37 1QS. *E:* rdhcampbell@btconnect.com. *Clubs:* West Bromwich Albion; Argyllshire Gathering.

CAMPBELL, Ronald, (Ronnie); MP (Lab) Blyth Valley, since 1987; *b* 14 Aug. 1943; *m* 1967, Deirdre (*née* McHale); five *s* one *d. Educ:* Ridley High Sch., Blyth. Miner, 1958–86. Member: Blyth Borough Council, 1969–74; Blyth Valley Council, 1974–88 (Chm., Environmental Health Cttee; Vice-Chm., Housing Cttee). Mem., NUM. *Address:* 82 Middleton Street, Blyth, Northumberland NE24 2LX; House of Commons, SW1A 0AA.

CAMPBELL, Sharon Isabel; HM Diplomatic Service; non-resident Ambassador to Haiti, since 2015; *b* 12 Feb. 1962; *née* Hale; *m* 1989, Christopher John Campbell, *qv*. Entered FCO, 1983; Trade Relns and Exports Dept, 1983–84, Minister of State's Office, 1984–85, FCO; Third Sec., Warsaw, 1985; Desk Officer, Finance Dept, FCO, 1986–88; Third Sec. (Mgt), Dhaka, 1988–92; Vice Consul, Jakarta, 1992–95; Asst Private Sec. to Minister of State, FCO, 1996–99; Sen. Mgt Officer and Consul, Cararcas, 2000–03; Deputy Head: Jt Mgt Office, Brussels, 2003–07; Consular Resources Gp, FCO, 2008–11; Ambassador to Costa Rica, 2011–15. *Address:* c/o Foreign and Commonwealth Office, King Charles Street, SW1A 2AH.

CAMPBELL, Sir Simon (Fraser), Kt 2015; CBE 2006; PhD; FRS 1999; FRSC; FMedSci; Senior Vice-President, Worldwide Discovery and Medicinals R&D Europe, Pfizer Central Research, 1996–98; Director and Board Member, Pfizer Ltd, 1996–98, retired; *b* 27 March 1941; *s* of William Fraser Campbell and Ellen Mary Campbell; *m* 1966, Jill Lewis; two *s. Educ:* Birmingham Univ. (BSc 1st Cl. Hons 1962; PhD 1965). FRSC 1985. Postdoctoral Fellow: Univ. Tecnica Santa Maria, Valparaiso, 1966–67; Stanford Univ., Calif, 1968–70; Vis. Prof., Univ. do São Paulo, 1970–72; joined Pfizer Central Research, Sandwich, 1972: staff chemist, 1972–78; Manager, 1978–83, Dir, 1983–92, Discovery Chemistry; Gp Dir, 1992–93, Vice-Pres., 1993–96, Medicinals Discovery. Visiting Professor: Birkbeck Coll., Univ. of London, 1987–90; Univ. of Leeds, 1996–99. Chm., WHO Expert Scientific Adv. Cttee for Malaria, 1999–2003; Member: BP Technology Council, 1999–2004; Expert Scientific Adv. Cttee, Medicines for Malaria Venture, 2009–; Council, Royal Soc., 2011–13. Pres., RSC, 2004–06 (Chm., Strategy Cttee, 2001–02). FMedSci 2003. Jt-Ed., Current Opinion in Drug Discovery and Develt, 1998–2004. Member: Acad. Adv. Bd, Dept of Chem., Bristol Univ., 1998–2001; Council, Univ. of Kent, 1999–2007. Award for Medicinal Chem., RSC, 1989; E. B. Hershberg Award, ACS, 1997; Achievement Award, Industrial Res. Inst. (US), 1997; Individual Achievement Award, CIA, 2006; Galen Medal, Soc. of Apothecaries, 2007; Sir James Black Award for Contribns to Drug Discovery, British Pharmacol Soc., 2012. *Publications:* contribs to learned jls; patents. *Recreations:* gardening, travel, wine, active sports player.

CAMPBELL, Dr Thomas Patrick, FSA; Director and Chief Executive Officer, Metropolitan Museum of Art, New York, since 2009; *b* Singapore, 12 July 1962; *m* Phoebe Anne; one *s* one *d. Educ:* New Coll., Oxford (BA 1984); Dip. Christie's Fine and Decorative Arts Course, 1985; Courtauld Inst. of Art, Univ. of London (MA 1984; PhD 1999). Creator, Franses Tapestry Archive, 1987–94; Metropolitan Museum of Art: Supervising Curator, Antonio Ratti Textile Center, 1995–2008; Asst Curator, 1995–97, Associate Curator, 1997–2003, Curator, 2003–08, Dept of Eur. Sculpture and Decorative Arts. *Publications:* Tapestry in the Renaissance: art and magnificence, 2002; The Art of Majesty: Henry VIII's tapestry collection, 2007; Tapestry in the Baroque: threads of splendor, 2008. *Address:* Metropolitan Museum of Art, 1000 Fifth Avenue, New York, NY 10028–0198, USA. *T:* (212) 5703902, *Fax:* (212) 6502102.

CAMPBELL, Rt Hon. Sir (Walter) Menzies, CH 2013; Kt 2004; CBE 1987; PC 1999; QC (Scot.) 1982; Leader, Liberal Democrats, 2006–07 (Deputy Leader, 2003–06); *b* 22 May 1941; *s* of George Alexander Campbell and Elizabeth Jean Adam Phillips; *m* 1970, Elspeth Mary Urquhart or Grant-Suttie, *d* of Maj.-Gen. R. E. Urquhart, CB, DSO. *Educ:* Hillhead High School, Glasgow; Glasgow Univ. (MA 1962, LLB 1965; President of the Union, 1964–65); Stanford Univ., Calif. Advocate, Scottish Bar, 1968; Advocate Depute, 1977–80; Standing Jun. Counsel to the Army, 1980–82. Member: Clayson Cttee on licensing reform, 1971; Legal Aid Central Cttee, 1983–87; Scottish Legal Aid Bd, 1987; Broadcasting Council for Scotland, 1984–87. Part-time Chairman: VAT Tribunal, 1984–87; Medical Appeal Tribunal, 1985–87. Chm., Scottish Liberal Party, 1975–77; contested (L): Greenock and Port Glasgow, Feb. 1974 and Oct. 1974; E Fife, 1979; NE Fife, 1983. MP NE Fife, 1987–2015 (L 1987–88, Lib Dem, 1988–2015). Lib. spokesman on arts, broadcasting and sport, 1987–88; Lib Dem spokesman on arts, broadcasting and sport, 1988, on sport and defence, 1988–94, on foreign affairs and defence, 1994–97, chief spokesman on foreign affairs, 1997–2006, on Europe, 1997–2001, on defence, 1997–2001; Mem., Jt Cabinet Cttee on Constitutional Reform, 1997–2001. Member: Select Cttee on Members Interests, 1987–90; Select Cttee on Trade and Industry, 1990–92; Defence Select Cttee, 1992–99; Intelligence and Security Cttee, 2008–15; Foreign Affairs Cttee, 2008–15. Member: UK Delegn to N Atlantic Assembly, 1989–2015 (Leader, 2010–15); UK Delegn to Parly Assembly, OSCE, 1992–97 and 1999–2006. Mem. Bd, British Council, 1998–2002; Gov., Ditchley Foundn, 1999–; Chancellor, Univ. of St Andrews, 2006–. Chm., Royal Lyceum Theatre Co., Edinburgh, 1984–87. Member: UK Sports Council, 1965–68; Scottish Sports Council, 1971–81. Governor, Scottish Sports Aid Foundn, 1981–90; Trustee: Scottish Internat. Educn Trust, 1984–2012; London Marathon, 1997–2000; Mem., London 2012 Olympic Bd, 2010–12. AAA 220 Yards Champion, 1964 and 1967; UK 100 Metres Record Holder, 1967–74; competed at Olympic Games, 1964 and Commonwealth Games, 1966; Captain, UK Athletics Team, 1965 and 1966. *Publications:* Menzies Campbell: my autobiography, 2008. *Recreations:* all sports, reading, music, theatre. *Clubs:* Reform, National Liberal.

See also Sir J. Grant-Suttie, Bt.

[Created a Baron (Life Peer) 2015 but title not yet gazetted at time of going to press.]

CAMPBELL, Rt Hon. Sir (William) Anthony, Kt 1988; PC 1999; a Lord Justice of Appeal, Supreme Court of Northern Ireland, 1998–2008; a Judge of the Court of Appeal, Cayman Islands, 2010–14; *b* 30 Oct. 1936; *s* of late H. E. Campbell and of Marion Wheeler; *m* 1960 Gail, *e d* of F. M. McKibbin; three *d. Educ:* Campbell Coll., Belfast; Queens' Coll., Cambridge. Called to the Bar, Gray's Inn, 1960, Hon. Bencher, 1995; called to the Bar of NI, 1960 (Bencher, 1983; Chm., Exec. Council, 1985–87). Jun. Counsel to Attorney-Gen. for NI, 1971–74; QC (NI) 1974; Senior Crown Counsel in NI, 1984–88; Judge of the High Ct of Justice, NI, 1988–98. Chairman: Council of Legal Educn in NI, 1994–2008; Judicial

Studies Bd, NI, 1995–2008. Governor, Campbell Coll., 1976–98 (Chm., 1984–86). Hon. Fellow, Amer. Bar Foundn, 1997. *Recreations:* sailing, hill walking. *Clubs:* New (Edinburgh); Royal Ulster Yacht.

:AMPBELL, Prof. (William) Bruce, FRCP, FRCS; Consultant in Vascular and General Surgery, Royal Devon and Exeter Hospital, since 1986; Chairman, Interventional Procedures Advisory Committee, since 2002 and Medical Technologies Advisory Committee, since 2010, National Institute for Health and Care (formerly Clinical) Excellence; *b* London, 3 Dec. 1950; *s* of Dr William Campbell and Jill Campbell; *m* 2008, Janet Elizabeth Birch; one *s* one *d* from former marriage. *Educ:* Sherborne Sch.; Medical Coll. of St Bartholomew's Hosp., Univ. of London (MB BS Hons 1974; MS 1984). FRCS 1978; FRCP 1996. Registrar, 1979–81, Res. Fellow, 1981–83, Bristol Royal Infirmary; Clin. Lectr in Surgery, Univ. of Oxford, 1983–86. Chm., Therapeutic Procedures Panel, NIHR Health Technol. Assessment Prog., 2000–08. Hon. Professor: Univ. of Exeter, 2000–02; Peninsula Med. Sch., Univs of Exeter and Plymouth, 2003–. Hon. Sec., Vascular Soc. of GB and Ireland, 1998–2002. *Publications:* Complications in Arterial Surgery, 1996; Understanding Varicose Veins, 2000; contrib. surgical and med. jls. *Recreations:* gardening, enjoying our home, walking, military history. *Address:* Royal Devon and Exeter Hospital, Exeter EX2 5DW. *T:* (01392) 410433, *Fax:* (01392) 421889.

:AMPBELL BANNERMAN, David; Member for Eastern, European Parliament, since 2009 (UK Ind, 2009–11, C, since 2011); *b* Bombay, 28 May 1960; *s* of Henry Campbell Bannerman and Elizabeth Monica Scott Bannerman. *Educ:* Univ. of Edinburgh (MA Hons Econs and Politics); Wharton Business Sch., Univ. of Pennsylvania (Exchange Schol.). Exec. Dir, Vantagepoint Communications, 1987–; Special Advr to Sec. of State for NI, 1996–97; Communications Dir, Assoc. of Train Operating Cos, 1997–99; Hd of Communications, United News and Media, 2000; Public Affairs Dir, 2005. Chm., 2005–06, Dep. Leader and Hd of Policy, 2006–10, UKIP. Contested (UK Ind) S Suffolk, 2010. FInstD. *Recreations:* film screenplay writing, heritage associations, country walks. *Address:* 19 Allison Road, W3 6JF. *E:* dcbdcbuk@yahoo.co.uk.

:AMPBELL DAVIS, Trevor Fraser; Chief Executive, Oxford Radcliffe Hospitals NHS Trust, 2003–09; Lead, World Economic Forum, Department of Health, 2009–11; *b* 16 July 1950; *o s* of Rev. Thomas Campbell Davis and Elizabeth Mary Evelyn, (Maeve), Davis (*née* Fraser); *m* 1978, Anne Eperon; partner, 1991, Dr Gwenda Elizabeth Porter; one *d*. *Educ:* Methodist Coll., Belfast; UMIST (BSc 1971). Accountant, Coopers and Lybrand, 1971–76; Financial Controller, Howard & Wyndham Gp, 1976–77; Financial Dir, W. H. Allen & Co. Ltd, 1977–80; Dir of Finance and Admin, McGraw-Hill Book Co. (UK) Ltd, 1980–84; Man. Dir, McGraw-Hill Internat. Trng Systems Ltd, 1984–87; Trustee, McGraw-Hill UK Pensions Schemes, 1980–87; Man. Dir, 1987–98, Chm., 1998, European Communications Gp Ltd. Director: The Not So Silly Trng Co. Ltd, 1992–; Training Media and Copyright Assoc., 1992–2001; Future Health Network Ltd, 2002–. Chairman: Parkside NHS Trust, 1992–98; St Mary's Hosp. NHS Trust, Paddington, 1998–2000; Chief Exec., Whittington Hosp. NHS Trust, 2000–03. Member: London NHS Communications Gp, 1994–96; London Ambulance Service Communications Task Force, 1995–96; Consultant Workforce Review Gp, London, 2001–02; DoH Day Surgery Review Gp, 2001–02; Dr Foster Ethics Cttee, 2001–; Council, UCL Clin. Res. Network, 2001–03; Steering Gp, HFEA, 2002–03. Treasurer: MCB Assoc. in London, 1990– (Pres., 2002–04); Assoc. of UK Univ. Hosps, 2004–. Trustee, NHS Confedn, 2001 (Vice-Chm., 2001–03; Chm., Acute Services Policy Adv. Cttee, 1998–2000, 2001). Special Trustee, St Mary's Hosp., Paddington, 1998–2000. Chm., British Amateur Radio Teledata Gp, 1978–83. Member Court: Middx Univ., 2000–03; Oxford Brookes Univ., 2004. AIEE 1975; FInstD 1980; FIAA 1983; FCIM 1985; FRSA 1998. *Publications:* articles in jls on leadership, change mgt and communications. *Recreations:* helping organisations to change, opera, alpine sports, scuba diving, managing collections. *Club:* Downhill Only (Wengen).

:AMPBELL-GRAY, family name of **Lord Gray**.

:AMPBELL-JOHNSTON, Very Rev. Michael Alexander Ninian, SJ; Assistant Priest, Jesuit Church of the Immaculate Conception, since 2010; *b* 27 Sept. 1931; *s* of Ninian Campbell-Johnston and Marguerite Antoinette Shakespear. *Educ:* Beaumont College; Séminaire Les Fontaines, France (Lic. Phil); LSE (BSc Econs, DipEd); Col. Max. Christi Regis, Mexico (STL). Dir, Guyana Inst. for Social Research and Action, 1967–75; Dir, Social Secretariat, Jesuit Generalate, Rome, 1975–84; Regional Co-ordinator, Jesuit Refugee Service for Mexico and Central America, El Salvador, 1984–87; Provincial, British Province, SJ, 1987–93; Dir, Servicio Jesuita para el Desarrollo, San Salvador, 1994–2002; Parish Priest, St Francis of Assisi, Barbados, 2002–10. Editor: Gisra; Promotio Justitiae. *Recreations:* reading, motorbike riding. *Address:* 114 Mount Street, W1K 3AH. *T:* (020) 7529 4814. *E:* mancjsj@gmail.com.

:AMPBELL-JOHNSTON, Rachel, PhD; Chief Art Critic, The Times, since 2002; *b* 4 Oct. 1963; *d* of Christopher Campbell-Johnston and Mary Campbell-Johnston (*née* Symington); *m* 2007, William Nickerson (marr. diss. 2014); one adopted *d*. *Educ:* Convent of the Sacred Heart, Woldingham; Univ. of Edinburgh (MA 1st Cl. Hons Eng. Lit.; PhD Eng. Lit. 1991). The Times: Dep. Lit. Editor, 1995–97; Obituary Writer, 1997–99; Leader Writer, 1999–2002; Poetry Critic, 1998–. FRSA. *Publications:* Mysterious Wisdom: the life and work of Samuel Palmer, 2011; The Child's Elephant, 2013. *Recreations:* wildlife, wandering about. *Address:* The Times, 1 London Bridge Street, SE1 9GF. *T:* (020) 7782 5000. *E:* rachel.johnston@thetimes.co.uk.

:AMPBELL-ORDE, Sir John (Alexander); *see* Orde, Sir J. A. C.

:AMPBELL-PRESTON, Dame Frances (Olivia), DCVO 1990 (CVO 1977); Woman of the Bedchamber to HM Queen Elizabeth the Queen Mother, 1965–2002; *b* 2 Sept. 1918; *d* of Lt-Col Arthur Grenfell and Hilda Margaret Grenfell (*née* Lyttelton); *m* 1938, Lt-Col George Patrick Campbell-Preston (*d* 1960), The Black Watch; two *s* two *d*. *Educ:* St Paul's Girls' Sch. WRNS, 1941–43. Mem., Argyll CC, 1960–64; Chm., Children's Panel, Argyle and Argyll and Bute, 1970–80. *Publications:* The Rich Spoils of Time (autobiog.) (with Hugo Vickers), 2006; Grandmother's Steps (reminiscences), 2010. *Address:* 93 Whitelands House, Cheltenham Terrace, SW3 4RA.

See also R. G. Campbell-Preston.

:AMPBELL-PRESTON, Robert Grenfell; Vice Lord-Lieutenant for Argyll and Bute, 2011–15; *b* 8 Jan. 1948; *s* of late Lt-Col George Patrick Campbell-Preston and of Dame Frances (Olivia) Campbell-Preston, *qv*; *m* 1971, Rosalind Mary; one *s* one *d* (and one *d* decd). *Educ:* Eton Coll. Owner and Chm., Inverawe Smokehouses, Taynuilt. Trustee: Argyll and Bute Trust; St Conan's Kirk; Dunstaffnage Estate; Laura Campbell-Preston Charitable Trust. *Recreations:* golfing, gardening, walking, farming. *Address:* Inverawe House, Taynuilt, Argyll PA35 1HU. *T:* (01866) 822542, (office) (01866) 822777. *E:* robertcp@inverawe.co.uk.

:AMPBELL-SAVOURS, family name of **Baron Campbell-Savours**.

:AMPBELL-SAVOURS, Baron *cr* 2001 (Life Peer), of Allerdale in the County of Cumbria; **Dale Norman Campbell-Savours;** *b* 23 Aug. 1943; *s* of late John Lawrence and of Cynthia Lorraine Campbell-Savours; *m* 1970, Gudrun Kristin Runolfsdottir; two *s* (and one *s* decd). *Educ:* Keswick Sch.; Sorbonne, Paris. Technical and Export agent, 1964–69; Dir, manufacturing co., 1969–77. Member, Ramsbottom UDC, 1972–73. Mem., UNISON (formerly COHSE), 1970–. Contested (Lab): Darwen Division of Lancashire, Feb. 1974, Oct. 1974; Workington, Nov. 1976. MP (Lab) Workington, 1979–2001. Opposition front bench spokesman on overseas develt, 1990–92, on agric., 1992–94. Member: Public Accounts Cttee, 1979–90; Select Committees: on Members Interests, 1983–91; on Procedure, 1984–90; on Agric., 1994–97; Intelligence and Security Cttee, 1997–2001; Standards and Privileges Cttee, 1996–2001. *Publications:* The Case for the Supplementary Vote (pamphlet), 1990; research into case for the University of the Lakes, 1996. *Address:* House of Lords, SW1A 0PW.

CAMPBELL-TIECH, Andrew; QC 2003; a Recorder, since 2000; *b* 5 Aug. 1955; *s* of Dr Paul Campbell-Tiech and Maureen (*née* Windsor, who *m* 1973, 3rd Baron Ponsonby of Shulbrede); *m* 1992, Sarah Rosemary Ann Lewis; one *d*. *Educ:* Highgate Sch.; College of Law. Called to the Bar, Inner Temple, 1978. *Recreations:* piano, violin, paying bills. *Address:* Drystone Chambers, 35 Bedford Row, WC1R 4JH. *T:* (020) 7404 1881, *Fax:* (020) 7404 1991.

CAMPBELL-WHITE, Martin Andrew, MBE 2014; Joint Chief Executive, Askonas Holt Ltd, 1999–2013, now Consultant; *b* 11 July 1943; *s* of late John Vernon Campbell-White and Hilda Doris (*née* Ash); *m* 1969, Dr Margaret Mary Miles; three *s*. *Educ:* Dean Close Sch., Cheltenham; St John's Coll., Oxford; Univ. of Strasbourg. Thomas Skinner & Co. Ltd (Publishers), 1964–66; Ibbs & Tillett Ltd (Concert Agents), 1966–72, Dir, 1969–72; Harold Holt Ltd (Concert Agents), subseq. Askonas Holt Ltd, 1972–: Dir, 1973–; Dep. Chm., 1989–92; Chief Exec., 1992–99. Consultant, Opera Comique, Paris. Chm., Brit. Assoc. of Concert Agents, 1978–81. Council Mem., London Sinfonietta, 1973–86; Dir, Chamber Orchestra of Europe, 1983–93; Mem. Bd, Première Ensemble, 1991–. Asst Dir, Fest. of German Arts, 1987; Founding Dir, Japan Fest. 1991, 1991. Trustee: Abbado Trust for Young Musicians, 1987–2006; Salzburg Fest. Trust, 1996–2000; Exec. Trustee, Help Musicians UK (formerly Musicians Benevolent Fund), 2006–. Mem. Bd, Riverside Studios, 1988–2000. FRSA 1980. Hon. Mem., Royal Philharmonic Soc., 2014. Hon. DArts City, 2010. Sebetia Ter Prize for Culture, Naples, 1999. *Recreations:* golf, watching cricket, classical music, travel, bird watching. *Address:* c/o Askonas Holt Ltd, Lincoln House, 300 High Holborn, WC1V 7JH. *T:* (020) 7400 1700, *Fax:* (020) 7400 1799. *Club:* MCC.

CAMPDEN, Viscount; Henry Robert Anthony Noel; *b* 1 July 1977; *s* and *heir* of Earl of Gainsborough, *qv*; *m* 2005, Zara, *yr d* of Geoffrey van Cutsem; two *s* one *d*. *Heir: s* Hon. Edward Noel, *b* 30 April 2007. *Address:* Exton Park, Oakham, Rutland LE15 8AN.

CAMPION, Charles Robert; restaurant critic, since 1992; food writer and broadcaster, since 1994; *b* Leamington Spa, 17 Oct. 1951; *s* of Geoffrey Campion and Meriel Campion; *m* 1986, Sylvia Murray; one *s* one *d*. *Educ:* Blundell's Sch., Tiverton; Watford Art Sch. Advertising copy writer, 1970–88; hotel proprietor and chef, Cold Springs House, Buxton, 1988–92. Glenfiddich Restaurant Writer of the Year, 1997. *Publications:* (with Theodore Kyriakou) The Livebait Cookbook, 1998; (with Theodore Kyriakou) Real Greek Food, 2000; (with Theodore Kyriakou) The Real Greek at Home, 2004; Fifty Recipes to Stake Your Life On, 2004; Food from Fire, 2006; Charles Campion's London Restaurant Guide, 2009; Eat Up!, 2010. *Recreations:* cider making, fly fishing, pickles and preserves, bread making. *T:* 07721 340071. *E:* charles@charlescampion.com. *W:* www.charlescampion.com. *Club:* Worcester Rugby Football.

CAMPION, Peter James, DPhil; FInstP; physicist; *b* 7 April 1926; *s* of Frank Wallace Campion and Gertrude Alice (*née* Lambert); *m* 1st, 1950, Beryl Grace Stanton (*d* 1995), *e d* of John and Grace Stanton; one *s* one *d* (and one *s* decd); 2nd, 1997, Rev. Patricia Adele Houseman (*née* O'Brien); three step *d*. *Educ:* Westcliff High Sch., Essex; Exeter Coll., Oxford (MA, DPhil). FInstP 1964. RNVR, 1943. Nuffield Res. Fellow, Oxford, 1954; Chalk River Proj., Atomic Energy of Canada Ltd, 1955; National Physical Lab., Teddington, 1960–86: Supt, Div. of Radiation Science, 1964; Supt, Div. of Mech. and Optical Metrology, 1974; Dep. Dir, 1976. Mem., Comité Consultatif pour les Etalons de Mesure des Rayonnements Ionisants, 1963–79; Chm., Sect. II, reconstituted Comité Consultatif, Mesure des radionucléides, 1970–79; Mem., NACCB, 1984–86. Editor, Internat. Jl of Applied Radiation and Isotopes, 1968–71. *Publications:* A Code of Practice for the Detailed Statement of Accuracy (with A. Williams and J. E. Burns), 1973; A Campion Saga, 2000; Some Campion Wives, 2003; technical and rev. papers in learned jls on neutron capture gamma rays, measurement of radioactivity, and on metrology generally. *Recreations:* watercolour painting, genealogy.

CAMPLING, Very Rev. Christopher Russell; Dean of Ripon, 1984–95; *b* 4 July 1925; *s* of Canon William Charles Campling; *m* 1953, Juliet Marian Hughes; one *s* two *d*. *Educ:* Lancing Coll.; St Edmund Hall, Oxford (MA; Hons Theol. cl. 2); Cuddesdon Theol Coll. RNVR, 1943–47. Deacon 1951, priest 1952; Curate of Basingstoke, 1951–55; Minor Canon of Ely Cathedral and Chaplain of King's School, Ely, 1955–60; Chaplain of Lancing Coll., 1960–67; Vicar of Pershore with Pinvin and Wick and Birlingham, 1968–76; RD of Pershore, 1970–76; Archdeacon of Dudley and Director of Religious Education, Diocese of Worcester, 1976–84. Mem., General Synod of Church of England, 1970–92; Chm., House of Clergy, Diocese of Worcester, 1981–84; Chm., Council for the Care of Churches, 1988–94. Lectr, Leeds Parish Church, 1988–. *Publications:* The Way, The Truth and The Life: Vol. 1, The Love of God in Action, 1964; Vol. 2, The People of God in Action, 1964; Vol. 3, The Word of God in Action, 1965; Vol. 4, God's Plan in Action, 1965; also two teachers' volumes; Words of Worship, 1969; The Fourth Lesson, Vol. 1 1973, Vol. 2 1974; The Food of Love, 1997; I Was Glad (memoirs), 2005; Sonnets of Faith, 2010. *Recreations:* music, drama, golf. *Address:* Pebble Ridge, Aglaia Road, Worthing, West Sussex BN11 5SW. *Club:* Naval.

CAMPOS, Prof. Christophe Lucien, OBE 1994; Director, British Institute in Paris, 1978–2003; *b* 27 April 1938; *s* of Lucien Antoine Campos and Margaret Lilian (*née* Dunn); *m* 1977, Lucy Elizabeth Mitchell; one *s* two *d*; two *d* by former marriage. *Educ:* Lycée Lamoricière, Oran; Lycée Français de Londres; Lycée Henri IV, Paris; Gonville and Caius Coll., Cambridge. LèsL (Paris), PhD (Cantab). Lector in French, Gonville and Caius Coll., 1959; Lecturer in French: Univ. of Maryland, 1963; Univ. of Sussex, 1964; Lectr in English, Univ. i Oslo, 1969; Prof. of French, University Coll., Dublin, 1974. Gen. Editor, Franco-British Studies, 1988–2004; author and webmaster, http://fleurusalgerie.fr, 2012–. Chevalier de l'Ordre des Arts et des Lettres (France), 1988. *Publications:* The View of France, 1964; L'Enseignement de la civilisation française, 1988; contribs to Th. Qly, TLS, Univs Qly, Franco-British Studies, Bulletin d'histoire et d'archéologie du Ried nord. *Recreations:* bees, football, gastronomy, environment. *Address:* La Hocherie, 86230 Sossay, France.

CAMPRUBI, Catherine Jane; *see* Royle, C. J.

CAMRE, Henning Niels Juel; Knight, Order of the Dannebrog, 2005; Executive Director, European Think Tank on Film and Film Policy, since 2007 (Founding President, 2006); *b* 15 Nov. 1938; *s* of Sigfred N. J. Camre and Carna (*née* Petersen); *m* 1st, 1967, Merete Friis (marr. diss.); one *d*; 2nd, 1978, Janne Giese (marr. diss.); one *d* and one adopted *d*; 3rd, 2005, Regitze Oppenhejm. *Educ:* Univ. of Copenhagen; Nat. Film Sch. of Denmark (Dip. in Cinematography). Dir of Photography (feature and documentary film), 1968–88; Director: Nat. Film Sch. of Denmark, 1975–92; Nat. Film and TV Sch., UK, 1992–98; Chief Exec., Danish Film Inst., 1998–2007. Adjunct Prof., Copenhagen Business Sch., 2005. Chairman: Nordic Film Council, 1979–89; Danish State Film Studio, 1989–92; European Film Coll., 2014–; Centre International de Liaison des Ecoles de Cinéma et de Télévision: Mem., Exec. Council, 1980–86; Chm., Programme for Developing Countries, 1982–2002; Vice-Pres., 1986–2002; Hon. Mem., 2002. Chairman: Cultural Area, Danish Nat. UNESCO Commn, 1999–2010; Screen Inst. Beirut, 2009–; Member, Board: Norwegian Film Inst.,

2009–12; Greek Film Centre, 2011–. Chevalier de l'Ordre des Arts et des Lettres (France), 1990; Gloria Artis Medal (Poland), 2005. *Publications:* Bridging the Gap, 1982; Film and Television Training in Indonesia, 1985; Asia-Pacific Film and Television Schools, 1991. *Recreation:* cycling. *Address:* Callisensvej 25, 2900 Hellerup, Denmark; European Think Tank on Film and Film Policy, Filmbyen 22, 2650 Hvidovre, Denmark. *E:* henning.camre@filmthinktank.org.

CAMROSE, 4th Viscount *cr* 1941, of Hackwood Park, Southampton; **Adrian Michael Berry;** Bt 1921; Baron 1929; *b* 15 June 1937; *er s* of Baron Hartwell (Life Peer), MBE, TD (who disclaimed his hereditary peerages for life, 1995); *S* father, 2001; *m* 1967, Marina Beatrice, *d* of Cyrus Sulzberger; one *s* one *d*. *Educ:* Eton; Christ Church, Oxford. Science Corresp., Daily Telegraph, 1977–96; Consulting Editor (Science), Daily Telegraph, 1996–. *Publications:* The Next Ten Thousand Years, 1974; The Iron Sun, 1977; From Apes to Astronauts, 1980; High Skies and Yellow Rain, 1983; The Super-Intelligent Machine, 1983; Koyama's Diamond, 1984; Ice With Your Evolution, 1986; Labyrinth of Lies, 1986; Harrap's Book of Scientific Anecdotes, 1989; (ed) Eureka!: The Book of Scientific Anecdotes, 1993; The Next 500 Years, 1995; Galileo and the Dolphins, 1996; The Giant Leap, 1999. *Heir: s* Hon. Jonathan William Berry [*b* 26 Feb. 1970; *m* 1996, Aurélie E. C. Molin; two *s* two *d*]. *Address:* Apt 3, 81 Holland Park, W11 3RZ.

See also N. W. Berry.

CANAVAN, Dennis Andrew; Member (Ind) Falkirk West, Scottish Parliament, 1999–2007; *b* 8 Aug. 1942; *s* of late Thomas and Agnes Canavan; one *s* one *d* (and three *s* decd). *Educ:* St Columba's High Sch., Cowdenbeath; Edinburgh Univ. (BSc Hons, DipEd). Head of Maths Dept, St Modan's High Sch., Stirling, 1970–74; Asst Head, Holy Rood High Sch., Edinburgh, 1974. District Councillor, 1973–74; Leader of Labour Gp, Stirling District Council, 1974; Member: Stirling Dist Educn Sub-cttee, 1973–74; Stirlingshire Youth Employment Adv. Cttee, 1972–74. Sec., W Stirlingshire Constituency Labour Party, 1972–74; Labour Party Agent, Feb. 1974; Treasurer, Scottish Parly Lab. Gp, 1976–79, Vice-Chm., 1979–80, Chm., 1980–81. MP (Lab 1974–99, Ind. 1999–2000) W Stirlingshire, Oct. 1974–1983, Falkirk W, 1983–2000. Member: H of C Select Cttee on For. Affairs, 1982–97, on Internat. Develt, 1997–99; Chair: PLP NI Cttee, 1989–97; Parly Br., EIS, 1983–2000; Vice-Chm., All-Party Hospice Gp, 1992–2000; Founder and Convener, All-Party Parly Scottish Sports Gp, 1987–99; Mem., British-Irish Inter-Parly Body, 1992–2000. Scottish Parliament: Mem., European and External Relns Cttee, 1999–2007; Founder and Convener, Sports Gp, 1999–2007. Columnist, The Herald, 1999–2000. Ramblers Scotland: Pres., 2007–09; Convener, 2009–12; Vice-Pres., 2012–. Chm., YesScotland, 2012–14. Mem., Bd of Trustees, Scottish Mining Mus., 2007–. Chm., Parent Council, St Mary's Sch., Bannockburn, 2009–14; Chair, Falkirk Football Community Foundn, 2010–. Hon. Pres., Rivers Forth and Teith Anglers Assoc., 2008–. Patron: William Simpson's Home, Plean, 2007–14; Falkirk and Dist Assoc. for Mental Health, 2008–; Driving Force, Bonnybridge, 2009–; Falkirk Forum, Crossroads Caring Scotland, 2010–; Wiston Lodge Charity, 2012–. Mem., Panel of Judges, Dennis Canavan Scholarship, 2008–. DUniv Stirling, 2008; LLD Strathclyde, 2008. *Publications:* Let the People Decide (autobiog.), 2009; contribs to various jls on educn and politics. *Recreations:* hill walking, swimming, reading, football (Scottish Univs football internationalist, 1966–67 and 1967–68; Hon. Pres., Milton Amateurs FC). *Address:* Ardsonas, Sauchieburn, Bannockburn, Stirlingshire FK7 9PZ. *T:* (01786) 812581. *E:* canavan897@btinternet.com.

CANAVAN, Sheelagh Mary, (Sandy); Her Honour Judge Canavan; a Circuit Judge, since 2014; *b* London, 8 Aug. 1964; *d* of Brendan and Margaret Canavan; *m* 2006, Kalai Sivanadian. *Educ:* Our Lady's Convent High Sch., Hackney; King's Coll. London (LLB Hons); Inns of Court Sch. of Law. Called to the Bar, Lincoln's Inn, 1987; in practice as barrister, specialising in criminal law, 1987–2014; a Recorder, 2010–14. *Recreations:* gardening, theatre, jam making, travelling, school governor (primary), singing in a choir, retail therapy. *Address:* Snaresbrook Crown Court, 75 Hollybush Hill, E11 1QW. *T:* (020) 8530 0000.

CANAVAN, Vincent Joseph; Sheriff of North Strathclyde at Greenock, 2001–11; *b* 13 Dec. 1946; *s* of James Canavan and Catherine Ludivine Brogan; *m* 1973, Mary Allison; three *s* three *d*. *Educ:* St Aloysius Coll., Glasgow; Univ. of Glasgow (LLB Hons 1968). Qualified as Solicitor, 1970; passed Advocate, 1980. Sheriff of S Strathclyde, Dumfries and Galloway at Hamilton, 1987–2001. Member: Victim Support (Scotland) Hamilton Court Project Working Party, 1990–94; Strathclyde Regl Council Cons. Cttee on Social Work in criminal justice system, 1991–96; Council, Sheriffs' Assoc., 1997–2000; Working Party on law of foreshore, 2000. Chm., Lanarks Br., Scottish Assoc. for Study of Delinquency, 1992–95 (Vice-Chm., 1991–92). *Recreations:* reading history, Italian cuisine, visiting art exhibitions. *Club:* Glasgow Art.

CANBERRA AND GOULBURN, Archbishop of, (RC), since 2013; **Most Rev. Christopher Charles Prowse;** *b* E Melbourne, 14 Nov. 1953; *s* of Francis Joseph Prowse and Marian Lois Prowse (*née* Atkinson). *Educ:* Monash Univ. (BA 1978); Melbourne Coll. of Divinity (BTh 1979); Gregorian Univ., Rome (LTh; STL 1987); Lateran Univ., Rome (STD 1995). Vicar General, Archdiocese of Melbourne, 2001–03; Auxiliary Bishop of Melbourne, 2003–09; Bishop of Sale, 2009–13. Mem., Pontifical Council for Inter-religious Dialogue, Vatican, 2009–; Chm., Australian Catholic Bishops Commn for Ecumenism and Inter-religious Relations, 2012–; Consultor, Commn for religious relations with the Jews, 2014–. *Recreations:* walking, bicycle riding, swimming. *Address:* GPO Box 89, Canberra, ACT 2601, Australia. *T:* (2) 62019811, *Fax:* (2) 62480287. *E:* archbishop@cg.catholic.org.au.

CANDELAS, Prof. Philip, DPhil; FRS 2010; Rouse Ball Professor of Mathematics, University of Oxford, and Fellow of Wadham College, Oxford, since 1999; *b* 24 Oct. 1951; *m* Xenia de la Ossa. *Educ:* Christ's Coll., Cambridge (BA 1973); Wadham Coll., Oxford (DPhil 1977). Jun. Res. Fellow, Balliol Coll., Oxford, 1975–76; Res. Asst, 1976–77, Asst Prof., 1977–82, Associate Prof., 1982–89, Prof., 1989–99, Dept of Physics, Univ. of Texas, Austin. *Publications:* papers in learned jls. *Address:* Wadham College, Oxford OX1 3PN.

CANDLIN, Prof. Christopher Noel; Senior Research Professor in Linguistics, Macquarie University, Sydney, part-time 2002–06, full-time, 2006, now Emeritus; *b* 31 March 1940; *s* of late Edwin Frank Candlin, OBE and of Nora Candlin (*née* Letts); *m* 1964, Sally (*née* Carter); one *s* three *d*. *Educ:* Jesus Coll., Oxford (MA); Univ. of London (PGCE); Yale Univ. (MPhil). Research Associate, Univ. of Leeds, 1967–68; University of Lancaster: Lectr, 1968, later Sen. Lectr; Prof. of Linguistics and Modern English Language, 1981–87; Macquarie University, Sydney: Prof. and Chm., Linguistics Dept, 1987–98; Exec. Dir, Nat. Centre for Eng. Lang. Teaching and Res., 1988–98; Dir, Centre for Lang. in Social Life, 1993–98; Adjunct Prof. of Linguistics, 1998; Chair Prof. of Applied Linguistics and Dir, Centre for English Lang. Educn and Communication Res., City Univ. of Hong Kong, 1998–2002; Prof. of Applied Linguistics (pt-time), Open Univ., 2002–05. Visiting Professor: Univ. of Giessen, 1975; East-West Centre, Honolulu, 1978; Ontario Inst. for Studies in Educn, Toronto, 1983; Univ. of Hawaii at Manoa, 1984; Univ. of Melbourne, 1985; Jyväskylä Univ., Finland, 1993; Univ. of Wales, Cardiff, 1995 (Hon. Prof., 1995); Adjunct Prof., Univ. of Technol., Sydney, 1998. General Editor: Applied Linguistics and Language Study; Language in Social Life; Language Teacher Educn Scheme; Language Teaching Methodology Series; Applied Linguistics in Action; Advances in Applied Linguistics. Pres., Internat. Assoc. of Applied Linguistics, 1996–2002. FRSA. Hon. PhD Jyväskylä, 1996. *Publications:* Challenges, 1978; The Communicative Teaching of English, 1981; Computers in English Language Teaching and Research, 1985; Language Learning Tasks, 1986; Language, Learning and Community, 1989; English at Work, vol. 1, 1991, vol. 2, 1992; (ed jtly) Australian Learners' Dictionary, 1997; Writing: texts, processes and practices, 1999. *Recreations:* theatre, concerts, sailing, cooking. *Address:* Department of Linguistics, Macquarie University, Sydney, NSW 2109, Australia.

CANDLISH, Thomas Tait, FREng; Managing Director, George Wimpey PLC, 1978–85 (Director, 1973–85); *b* 26 Nov. 1926; *s* of John Candlish and Elizabeth (*née* Tait); *m* 1964, Mary Trinkwon; two *s*. *Educ:* Perth Acad.; Glasgow Univ. (BSc Eng). FICE 1971; FREng (FEng 1980). Served RE, 1946–49 (commnd). Student Engr, George Wimpey & Co. Ltd, 1944–46; rejoined Wimpey, 1951; served in: Borneo, 1951–54; Papua New Guinea, 1955–57; Arabian Gulf area, 1958–62; W Africa, 1962–65; Director: Wimpey Internat. 1973–85 (Chm., 1979–85); Wimpey ME & C, 1973–85; Wimpey Marine Ltd, 1975–85 (Chm., 1979–85); Brown & Root-Wimpey Highlands Fabricators, 1974–89 (Chm. 1981–86); British Smelter Constructions Ltd, 1977–83 (Chm., 1977–83); Hill Samuel Developments, 1978–85; A & P Appledore Holdings, 1979–85; Brown & Root (UK) Ltd 1985–89; OGC Internat., 1993–97; Chairman: Howard Humphreys Gp Ltd, 1987–89; Historic Cars Ltd, 1989–97. Chm., Export Gp for Constructional Industries, 1983–85; Member: EDC for Civil Engrg, 1979–82; British Overseas Trade Bd, 1984–87. *Recreations:* motor sport, golf. *Address:* 42 Denton Road, Ilkley, W Yorks LS29 0AA. *Clubs:* Royal Automobile; Denham Golf.

CANDY, Elizabeth Mary; Head Mistress, The Lady Eleanor Holles School, Hampton, 1981–2004; *b* 12 Oct. 1942; *d* of late Donald Glen Candy and Phyllis Mary Candy (*née* Denbury). *Educ:* Merrywood Grammar Sch., Bristol; Westfield Coll., London (BSc 1965). Chemistry Mistress then Jt Head of Science, Bromley High Sch., 1965–71; Head of Science then Second Mistress, Putney High Sch., 1971–81. Mem. Council, Royal Holloway, London Univ., 1995–2003. FRSA 1994. Gov., Old Vicarage Sch., Richmond, 2005–. Dame Chevalier, Ordre des Coteaux de Champagne, 1998. *Recreations:* opera, reading, France and French wine, photography, cycling, tennis, golf. *Address:* Miranda Cottage, 5 St John's Road, East Molesey, Surrey KT8 9JH. *T:* (020) 8941 3066. *Club:* Cripplegate Ward.

CANDY, Lorraine Ann; Editor, Elle, since 2004; *b* 8 July 1968; *d* of A. R. Butler and V. S. Butler; *m* 2000, C. James Candy; one *s* three *d*. *Educ:* Liskeard Comprehensive Sch., Cornwall. Feature writer, Daily Mirror, 1990–93; Woman's Editor: Sun, 1993; Today, 1993–95; Associate Ed., Marie Claire mag., 1995–97; Dep. Ed., Times Saturday Mag., 1997–98; Ed., B mag., 1998–99; Features Ed., The Times, 1999–2000; Ed., Cosmopolitan, 2000–04. *Recreations:* riding, shopping. *Address:* Elle, Hearst UK, 72 Broadwick Street, W1F 9EP.

CANDY, Stuart Graham C.; *see* Cull-Candy.

CANE, Anthony Richard Godwin; Senior Partner, Strutt & Parker, 2003–09; *b* 4 Oct. 1948; *s* of late Dr C. S. Cane, VRD, FRCP and Rachel Cane; *m* 1975, Susan Mary Mortimer; two *s*. *Educ:* Eton Coll.; RAC, Cirencester. FRICS 1986. With Strutt & Parker, 1973–2009; Partner, 1987. Dir, 2006–, Chm., 2008–, Epsom Downs Racecourse. Trustee, Childwick Trust, 2000–; Dir, Leverhulme Family Trusts. *Recreations:* racing, shooting, Chelsea Football Club. *Club:* Jockey.

CANHAM, Paul George, LVO 1991; JP; Official Secretary to Governor-General of New Zealand, 1985–90; *b* 25 Oct. 1933; *s* of George Ernest Canham and Ella Mary (*née* Mackenzie); *m* 1964, Diane Alderton; one *s* one *d*. *Educ:* Timaru Boys' High Sch.; Victoria Univ. of Wellington (BA, MA Hons History). Teacher: Pomfret Sch., Conn., 1957; Matamata Coll., NZ, 1960; Hauraki Plains Coll., 1967; Heretaunga Coll., 1969; Dep. Prin. Hutt Valley High Sch., 1973; Prin., Wanganui High Sch., 1979. Dist Manager, Baucau Timor Leste, UN Population Fund Nat. Census, 2004. JP Hawkes Bay, 1991. *Publications:* The Return (novel), 1999; Ben and the Stag, 2012; The Final Redemption, 2013; No Way Back, 2014. *Recreation:* bridge. *Address:* 10 Waimea Way, Poraiti, Napier 4112, New Zealand. *T:* (6) 8438877. *E:* panddcanham@gmail.com.

CANN, Anthony; *see* Cann, J. W. A.

CANN, Charles Richard, CB 1996; Deputy Secretary, Ministry of Agriculture, Fisheries and Food, 1991–96; *b* 3 Feb. 1937; *s* of late Charles Alfred Cann and Grace Elizabeth Cann; *m* 1979, Denise Ann Margaret Love; two *s*. *Educ:* Merchant Taylors' Sch., Northwood, Middx; St John's Coll., Cambridge (MA). Asst Principal, MAFF, 1960, Principal 1965; Cabinet Office, 1969–71; Asst Sec., MAFF, 1971; Under Sec., 1981; Fisheries Sec., MAFF, 1987–91. Mem. Policy Cttee, CPRE, 1996–2002.

CANN, (John William) Anthony; Partner, 1978–2006, Senior Partner, 2001–06, Linklaters; *b* 21 July 1947; *s* of late Dr John Cann and Enid Grace Cann (*née* Long); *m* 1973, Anne Clausen; two *s* one *d*. *Educ:* Shrewsbury Sch.; Southampton Univ. (LLB Law 1969); Coll. of Law/Law Soc. (Hons). With Linklaters, 1970–2006: articled clerk, 1970–72; Associate Solicitor, 1972–78; NY Office, 1975–82; Hd of Corporate Dept, 1995–2000. Director: Connect (formerly Smiths News PLC), 2006–; Panmure Gordon & Co. plc, 2007–; Social Investment Business (formerly Futurebuilders England Fund Management) Ltd, 2008–. Chm. Changing Faces, 2007–09; Trustee, Adventure Capital Fund, 2006–. Governor, Haberdashers' Aske's Fedn, 2007–11; Haberdashers' Adams' Fedn, 2011– (Chm., 2013–); Liveryman, Haberdashers' Co., 2012 (Ct of Assts, 2013). *Publications:* Mergers and Acquisitions Handbook Part D, 1986; European Mergers and Acquisitions (United Kingdom), 1991. *Recreations:* photography, travel, ski-ing, sailing. *Address:* Langrick, 1. Murray Road, SW19 4PD. *T:* (020) 8946 6731. *E:* anthony.cann@yahoo.com. *Clubs:* Athenæum, MCC.

CANN, Prof. Johnson Robin, ScD; FRS 1995; Professor of Earth Sciences, University of Leeds, 1989–2003, Senior Fellow, since 2003; *b* 18 Oct. 1937; *er s* of Johnson Ralph Cann and (Ethel) Mary (*née* Northmore); *m* 1st, 1963, Janet Hamson (*d* 1994); two *s*; 2nd, 2001, Helen Dunham. *Educ:* St Albans Sch.; St John's Coll., Cambridge (MA, PhD, ScD). Research Fellow, St John's Coll., 1962–66; post-doctoral work in Depts of Mineralogy and Petrology and Geodesy and Geophysics, Cambridge, 1962–66; Dept of Mineralogy, British Museum (Natural History), 1966–68; Lectr, then Reader, School of Environmental Sciences, Univ. of East Anglia, 1968–77; J. B. Simpson Prof. of Geology, Univ. of Newcastle upon Tyne, 1977–89; current research in oceanic detachment faults, hot springs of mid-ocean ridges, seafloor volcanoes, creation of oceanic crust, origin of dykes and sills. Member, then Chm., ocean crust panel, 1975–78, UK rep. on planning cttee, 1978–84, Jt Oceanographic Instns for Deep Earth Sampling; co-chief scientist on Glomar Challenger, 1976 and 1979; Adjunct Scientist, Woods Hole Oceanographic Instn, 1987–; Chief Scientist, British Mid-Ocean Ridge Initiative, 1992–2001. Chm., UK Ocean Drilling Program Grants Cttee, 1987–90; Mem., UGC physical sciences sub-cttee, 1982–88. Murchison Medal, Geol Soc. of London, 1990. *Publications:* papers in jls of earth science and archaeology. *Address:* School of Earth and Environment, University of Leeds, Leeds LS2 9JT. *T:* (01931) 712429. *E:* j.r.cann@leeds.ac.uk.

CANN, Mark James Alexander; Chief Executive Officer, British Forces Foundation, since 2000; *b* Holywood, 28 Nov. 1965; *s* of John and Penny Cann; *m* 1999, Emma Francis; two *s* one *d*. *Educ:* Repton Sch.; Loughborough Univ. (BA Hons Pols and Econ. Hist.); RMA Sandhurst. Served Army, Queen's Royal Lancers, 1988–99. Dir, CU2 Ltd, 1999–. Chm., First Defence, 2011– (Dir, 2001–11). Director: Armed Forces Charities Adv. Co., 2009–; Global Forces Entertainment, 2014–; Adminr, Erach and Roshan Sadri Foundn, 2007–; Trustee, Wilts Bobby Van Trust, 2009–. Trustee, Combined Services Polo Assoc., 2012–

(Dir, 1997–2012); Mem. Council, Hurlingham Polo Assoc., 1997–. *Recreations:* all sport (especially polo, ski-ing and tennis), enthusiastic but awful golfer, supporting Arsenal, collecting first edition political autobiographies, early 20th century novels and portrait photographs. *Address:* British Forces Foundation, 10A High Street, Pewsey, Wilts SN9 5AQ. *T:* (01672) 564911, *Fax:* (01672) 562101. *E:* info@bff.org.uk. *Clubs:* Cavalry and Guards, Royal Automobile.

CANN, Paul Lewis; Chief Executive, Age UK Oxfordshire (formerly Age Concern Oxfordshire), since 2009; *b* 29 Aug. 1953; *s* of John Samuel Jones Cann and Eileen Dorothy Jean (*née* Daymond John); *m* 1981, Phillippa Terese Cook; one *s* one *d*. *Educ:* Tiffin Sch.; King's Coll., Cambridge (BA Hons 1975; MA 1979); Westminster Coll., Oxford (Cert Ed 1976). Schoolmaster: Christchurch Cathedral Sch., 1976–78; Abingdon Sch., 1978–81; Civil Service, 1981–88: Asst Private Secretary to: Lord Privy Seal, 1982–83; Minister for Arts, 1983–84; Principal, Cabinet Office, 1985–88; Sen. Consultant, Hay Mgt Consultants, 1988–90; Hd of Personnel, Newspaper Publishing plc, 1990–92; Exec. Dir, British Dyslexia Assoc., 1992–97; Chief Exec., Nat. Autistic Soc., 1997–2000; Dir, Policy, Res. and Internat. Dept, Help the Aged, 2000–09. Chm., Social Inclusion Adv. Gp, 2010–. Vis. Fellow, Inst. of Ageing, Oxford Univ., 2004–07; Associate Fellow, Internat. Longevity Centre, 2009–. Trustee: Contact a Family, 2001–06; Oxford Lieder, 2006–; Age and Employment Network, 2006–. Corporate Mem., Inst. Personnel and Devlt, 1986. Medal for outstanding contribn to older people, British Geriatrics Soc., 2008. *Publications:* (ed jtly) Unequal Ageing, 2009. *Recreations:* singing, drinking wine, enjoying Hook Norton. *Address:* 7 Bell Hill, Hook Norton, Oxon OX15 5NG. *T:* (01608) 737282.

CANNADINE, Prof. Sir David (Nicholas), Kt 2009; DPhil, LittD; FRHistS; FBA 1999; FSA; FRSL; Dodge Professor of History, Princeton University, since 2011 (Whitney J. Oates Senior Research Scholar, Humanities Council, 2008–11); Editor, Oxford Dictionary of National Biography, since 2014; *b* 7 Sept. 1950; *s* of Sydney Douglas Cannadine and Dorothy Mary Cannadine (*née* Hughes); *m* 1982, Linda Jane Colley, *qv*; one *d* decd. *Educ:* King Edward's Five Ways Sch., Birmingham; Clare Coll., Cambridge (schol.; BA 1st cl. Hons 1972; MA 1975; LittD 1993; Hon. Fellow, 2012); Princeton Univ. (Jane Eliza Procter Vis. Fellow); St John's Coll., Oxford (Sen. Schol.; DPhil 1975; Hon. Fellow, 2015). FRHistS 1981; FSA 2005. Cambridge University: Res. Fellow, St John's Coll., 1975–77; Asst Lectr, 1976–80, Lectr, 1980–88, in Hist.; Christ's College: Fellow, 1977–88 (Hon. Fellow, 2005); Dir of Studies in Hist., 1977–83; Tutor, 1979–81; Prof. of History, 1988–92, Moore Collegiate Prof. of History, 1992–98, Columbia Univ.; Prof. of History and Dir, 1998–2003, Queen Elizabeth the Queen Mother Prof. of British History, 2003–08, Hon. Fellow, 2005, Inst. of Historical Res., Sch. of Advanced Study, Univ. of London. Dist. Sen. Fellow, Sch. of Advanced Study, 2008, Hon. Prof., 2008, Univ. of London. Vis. Mem., 1980–81, Dir's Visitor, 2011, Inst. for Advanced Study, Princeton; Visiting Professor: Birkbeck Coll., London Univ., 1995–97; Univ. of Oxford, 2014–; Vis. Scholar, Pembroke Coll., Cambridge, 1997; Visiting Fellow: Whitney Humanities Center, Yale Univ., 1995–98; Humanities Council, Princeton Univ., 2003–05; ANU, 2005; Nat. Humanities Center, N Carolina, 2006; Adjunct Prof., ANU, 2006–; Fletcher Jones Foundn Dist. Fellow, Huntington Liby, 2010; Vis. Prof., Stern Business Sch., New York Univ., 2013–14. Lectures: Motitz, Kalamazoo, 1992; Leonard Hastings Schoff, Columbia Univ., 1993; Hayes Robinson, RHC, 1994; Raleigh, British Acad., 1997; Charles Edmonson, Baylor Univ., 1997; George Orwell Meml, Sheffield Univ., 1997; Curtis, Univ. of Central Lancs, 1998; Earl, Keele, 1999; Beall-Russell, Baylor Univ., 1999; Esmée Fairbairn, Lancaster Univ., 1999; London Liby, 2001; Carnochan, Stanford Univ., 2001; Throckmorton, Lewis and Clark Coll., 2001; Burrows, Univ. of Essex, 2002; Rothschild Archive, 2002; Linbury, Nat. Gall., 2002; Golden Jubilee, Univ. of Newcastle, 2002; Dickinson, Newcomen Soc., 2003; T. S. Eliot, Washington Univ., St Louis, 2003; Roy Jenkins Meml, RSL, 2004; Thorpe, Princeton Univ., 2004; PSCP, Getty Res. Inst., 2006; Ramsay Murray, Selwyn Coll., Cambridge, 2006; History of Parlt, 2006; University, Carnegie-Mellon, 2006; George Macaulay Trevelyan, Cambridge Univ., 2007; John Hayes Meml, NPG, 2007; Eaton, Boston Athenaeum 2008; Fulbright, BL, 2009; Linbury, Dulwich Picture Gall., 2010; Eugene Meyer, Bard Coll., 2011; Crosby Kemper, Westminster Coll., Fulton, Mo, 2012; Jon Sigurdsson, Univ. of Iceland, 2012; Gladstone, Gladstone's Liby, 2012; Haaga, Huntington Liby, San Marino, Calif, 2012; Creighton, Univ. of Toronto, 2013; Fred Freeman, Univ. of Liverpool, 2013; Robb, Univ. of Auckland, 2015; Wolfson Anniversary, Univ. of Glasgow, 2015. Fellow: Berkeley Coll., Yale Univ., 1985–; ACLS, 1990–91; J. P. Morgan Liby, NY, 1992–98. Regular broadcaster on wireless and television; presenter: A Point of View, BBC Radio 4, 2005–; Churchill's Other Lives, BBC Radio 4, 2011. Member: Eastern Regl Cttee, Nat. Trust, 2001–10; Cttee of Mgt, Centre for Res. in the Arts, Social Scis and Humanities, Univ. of Cambridge, 2001–03; Archives Task Force, 2002–04; Royal Mint Adv. Cttee, 2004–14; Rev. of 30 Year Rule, 2007–09; Adv. Cttee, Center for Hist. of Collecting in America, Frick Collection, NY, 2009–; Bank Note Character Adv. Cttee, Bank of England, 2015–; Historical Consultant, Cabinet War Rooms, 2002–04; Historical Advr, Ian Fleming Centenary Exhibn, Imperial War Mus., 2007–08; Comr, English Heritage, 2001–09 (Chm., Blue Plaques Panel, 2006–13). Vice-President: British Records Soc., 1998–; RHistS, 1998–2002; Victorian Soc., 2009–; Worcs Histl Soc., 2011– (Pres., 1999–2010). Mem. Adv. Council, PRO, then Nat. Archives, 1999–2004; London University: Member Advisory Council: Warburg Inst. (formerly Adv. Bd), 1998–2003; Inst. of US Studies, 1999–2003; Inst. of English Studies, 2000–03; Inst. of Latin Amer. Studies, 2000–03; Inst. for Study of the Americas, 2004–08. Trustee: Kennedy Meml Trust, 2000–10 (Vice-Chm., 2005–10); Nat. Portrait Gall., 2000–12 (Vice-Chm., 2003–05; Chm., 2005–12; Trustee, Portrait Trust, 2012–); British Empire and Commonwealth Mus., 2003–13; Rothschild Archive Trust, 2005–; Wolfson Foundn, 2010– (Chm., Arts Panel, 2010–); Gladstone Library, 2011–; Gordon Brown Archives Trust, 2011–; Liby of Birmingham Trust, 2011–; RA Trust, 2013–; Historic Royal Palaces, 2015–; Vice Chm., Fabric Cttee, Westminster Abbey, 2010–; Dir, Royal Oak Foundn, NY, 2011–. Pres., Friends of Imperial War Mus., 2012–; Chm., Churchill 2015, 2013–15. Patron: Attingham Trust, 2006–; Friends of Birmingham Archives and Heritage, 2009–. Gov., Ipswich Sch., 1982–88. General Editor: Studies in Modern Hist., 1979–2002; Penguin Hist. of Britain, 1989–; Penguin Hist. of Europe, 1991–; Historical Res., 1998–2003; Reviews in History, 1998–2003; History Compass, 2000–03; Member, Editorial Board: Urban Hist. Yearbook, 1979–83; Past and Present, 1983– (Vice Chm., 2000–); Midland Hist., 1985–88; Twentieth Century British Hist., 1990–2007; Rural Hist., 1995–; Prospect, 1995–; Library Hist., 1998–; England's Landscape, 2000–06; History of Parliament, 2004–. MAE 2010. FRSA 1998; FRSL 1999. Hon. FHA 2011 (Hon. Vice Pres., 2013); Hon. Churchill Fellow, Westminster Coll., Fulton, Mo, 2012. Hon. DLitt: UEA, 2001; South Bank, 2001; Birmingham, 2002; Worcester, 2011. T. S. Ashton Prize, Econ. Hist. Soc., 1977; Silver Jubilee Prize, Agricl Hist. Soc., 1977; Dean's Dist. Award in the Humanities, Columbia Univ., 1996; Dickinson Medal, Newcomen Soc., 2003; Tercentenary Medal, Soc. of Antiquaries, 2008; Minerva Medal, Royal Philosophical Soc. of Glasgow, 2012; Norton Medlicott Medal, Histl Assoc., 2013. *Publications:* Lords and Landlords: the aristocracy and the towns 1774–1967, 1980; (ed and contrib.) Patricians, Power and Politics in Nineteenth-Century Towns, 1982; (ed jtly and contrib.) H. J. Dyos, Exploring the Urban Past, 1982; (ed jtly and contrib.) Rituals of Royalty: power and ceremonial in traditional societies, 1987; The Pleasures of the Past, 1989; (ed and contrib.) Winston Churchill's Famous Speeches, 1989; (ed jtly and contrib.) The First Modern Society: essays in English history in honour of Lawrence Stone, 1989; The Decline and Fall of the British Aristocracy (Lionel Trilling Prize), 1990; G. M. Trevelyan: a life in history, 1992; Aspects of Aristocracy: grandeur and decline in modern Britain, 1994; (ed jtly and contrib.) History and Biography: essays in honour of Derek Beales, 1996; Class in Britain, 1998; History in Our Time, 1998; Ornamentalism: how the British saw their Empire, 2001; In Churchill's Shadow: confronting the past in modern Britain, 2002; (ed and contrib.) What is History Now?, 2002; (ed and contrib.) History and the Media, 2004; (ed and contrib.) Admiral Lord Nelson: his context and legacy, 2005; (ed and contrib.) Trafalgar in History: a battle and its afterlife, 2006; Mellon: an American life, 2006; The National Portrait Gallery: a brief outline history, 2007; (ed and contrib.) Empire, the Sea and Global History: Britain's maritime world 1763–1833, 2007; (ed jtly and contrib.) History and Philanthropy: past, present, future, 2008; Making History Now and Then: discoveries, controversies and explorations, 2008; (jtly) Review of the 30 Year Rule, 2009; (jtly) The Right Kind of History, 2011; The Undivided Past: humanity beyond our differences, 2013; George V: the unexpected king, 2014; Heroic Chancellor: Winston Churchill and the University of Bristol, 1929–1965, 2015; numerous contribs to other books and learned jls. *Recreations:* life, laughter. *Address:* Department of History, Dickinson Hall, Princeton University, NJ 08544, USA. *E:* david.cannadine@sas.ac.uk. *Clubs:* Athenæum, Brooks's; Norfolk (Norwich); Century (NY).

CANNAN, (John) David (Qualtrough); Speaker, House of Keys, Isle of Man, 2000–01; MHK (Ind) Michael, 1982–2011; *b* 24 Aug. 1936; *s* of Rev. Canon Charles Alfred Cannan and Mary Eleanor Cannan (*née* Qualtrough); *m* 1966, Patricia Mary, *d* of Bernard and Jean Roberts, Taranaki, NZ; three *s* one *d*. *Educ:* King William's Coll., IOM. Martin's Bank, IOM, 1953–54; Nat. Service, RA, 1954–56; tea and rubber industries, Ceylon, 1956–61, Malaya, 1961–67; business interests, Berks, 1967–79. Mem. (C), Bradfield DC, 1970–74; returned to IOM, 1980; Minister for Treasury, 1986–89; Chm., Financial Supervision Commn, 1987–89; Vice-Chm., Public Accounts Commn, 1997–2000. *Recreations:* gardening, bee-keeping, Manx history. *Address:* White Gables, Curragh Road, Ballaugh, Isle of Man IM7 5BG. *T:* and *Fax:* (01624) 897926. *E:* whitegables@manx.net.

CANNELL, Prof. Robert Quirk; Director, Virginia Agricultural Experiment Station and Associate Dean for Research, Virginia Polytechnic Institute and State University, 1994–99, now Emeritus; *b* 20 March 1937; *s* of William Watterson Cannell and Norah Isabel Corjeag; *m* 1962, Edwina Anne Thornborough; two *s*. *Educ:* King's Coll., Newcastle upon Tyne; Univ. of Durham (BSc, PhD). FRSB (FIBiol 1986). Shell Chemical Co., London, 1959; School of Agriculture, Univ. of Newcastle upon Tyne, 1961; Dept of Agronomy and Plant Genetics, Univ. of Minnesota, 1968–69; Letcombe Lab., AFRC, Oxon, 1970; Dir, Welsh Plant Breeding Station, Aberystwyth, 1984–87; Head of Crop and Soil Envmtl Scis Dept, Virginia Polytech. Inst. and State Univ., 1987–94. *Publications:* papers in agricultural science jls. *Address:* Berk, Peel Road, Kirk Michael, Isle of Man IM6 1AP. *T:* (01624) 878039. *E:* robertcannell@manx.net.

CANNELL, Sheila Elizabeth; Director, Library Services, 2003–12, and Deputy Head, Information Services, 2007–12, University of Edinburgh; *b* 2 Oct. 1951; *d* of late Prof. Ernest and Sadie Best; *m* 1981, Peter Malcolm Cannell; one *s*. *Educ:* Univ. of Edinburgh (MA Hons); Univ. of Sheffield (MA Librarianship). Asst Librarian, Univ. of Glasgow, 1975–85; Medical Librarian, 1985–98, Dep. Librarian, 1998–2003, Univ. of Edinburgh. Project Dir, Enhancing Res. Infrastructure in Scotland, 2009–12. Member: Mgt Cttee, Scottish Liby and Inf. Council, 1994–97 and 2004–09; Res. Libraries UK (formerly Consortium of Univ. and Res. Libraries Bd), 2007–12 (Treas., 2009–12); Steering Gp, Scottish Higher Educn Digital Liby, 2007–12; Steering Gp, Designing Libraries, 2008–11; Council, Edinburgh City of Literature, 2013–; Chair: Wkg Gp on Space, SCONUL, 2006–11; Scottish Confedn of Univ. and Res. Libraries, 2007–09; Jt Chm., Bd, Scottish Digital Liby Consortium, 1999–2012. Dir, My Edinburgh Life Ltd, 2014–. Researcher, Scottish Love in Action, 2013–. Trustee, Edinburgh City of Literature, 2005–13. FRSA 2007. *Recreations:* gardening, music, family life. *E:* sheila.cannell@googlemail.com.

CANNING, family name of **Baron Garvagh**.

CANNING, Hugh Donaldson; Music Critic, The Sunday Times, since 1989; *b* 28 May 1954; *s* of David Donaldson Canning and Olga Mary Canning (*née* Simms). *Educ:* Oakham Sch.; Pembroke Coll., Oxford (BA). Freelance music critic, 1979–87; Music Critic: London Daily News, 1987; The Guardian, 1987–89; Opera Critic, The Listener. Critic of Year Award, Brit. Press Awards, 1994. *Recreations:* music, theatre, tennis, food, gossip. *Address:* c/o The Sunday Times, 1 London Bridge Street, SE1 9GF.

CANNING, Iain; film producer; Co-Founder, Producer and Managing Director, See-Saw Films Ltd, since 2008; *b* Bristol, 23 July 1979; *s* of John Canning and Alexis King (*née* Wilson). *Educ:* Univ. of Cardiff (BA Journalism, Film and Broadcasting). Devlt and Logistics Co-ordinator, South West Film Commn, 1999–2000; Renaissance Films: Devlt and Mktg Manager, 2000–01; Devlt and Acquisitions Exec., 2001–03; Hd, Devlt, Acquisitions and Prodn, 2003–05; Hd, Sales and Acquisitions, Becker International and Dendy Films, 2005–08. *Address:* See-Saw Films Ltd, 2nd Floor, 74 Rivington Street, EC2A 3AY. *T:* (020) 3301 6268. *E:* info@see-saw-films.com.

CANNING, Mark, CMG 2009; HM Diplomatic Service, retired; Ambassador to Indonesia (and concurrently to Association of South East Nations and to East Timor), 2011–14; *b* 15 Dec. 1954; *s* of late John Canning, OBE and of Paula Canning; *m* 2004, Cecilia Kenny; one *d*. *Educ:* Downside Sch.; University Coll. London (BA (Hons)); MBA 2003. First Sec., FCO, 1988–93; First Sec. (Commercial), Jakarta, 1993–97; First Sec., FCO, 1997–2001; Counsellor, FCO, 2001; Dep. High Comr, Kuala Lumpur, 2001–05; Ambassador to Burma, 2005–09; Ambassador to Zimbabwe, 2009–11. *Recreations:* cooking, reading, hiking, fishing. *Address:* 50 Belgrave Square North, Rathmines, Dublin 6, Ireland. *E:* aldwickpartners@gmail.com.

CANNON, Jane Elizabeth, MBE 2003; Executive in Residence, Amadeus Capital Partners Ltd, since 2013; *b* UK, 15 Nov. 1964; *d* of Edgar David Cannon and Barbara Mary Cannon; *m* 2000, Ian Gould; twin *d*. *Educ:* Herts and Essex High Sch.; University Coll. London (BSc Engrg); Open Univ. (MBA Technol. Mgt). FIET. Tech. Dir, Cannon Electronics and Automation Ltd, 1988–99; Hd, BT Internat., BT plc, 1999–2004; Gp Dir, Strategy and Planning, 2004–06, Man. Dir, Security Solutions, 2006–08, QinetiQ; Gp Man. Dir, UK Inf. Systems and Global Services, Lockheed Martin, 2008–10; Partner, Advisory, Ernst & Young, 2010–13. *Recreations:* horse riding, guitar playing, scuba diving, spending time with family. *Address:* Cambridge. *T:* 07860 810485. *E:* janecannon@theiet.org.

CANNON, Mark Rennison Norris; QC 2008; *b* 9 June 1961; *s* of late Brian Norris Cannon and Ann Buckham Cannon (*née* Williams). *Educ:* St Dunstan's Coll., London; Lincoln Coll., Oxford (BA Mod. Hist. 1983); Robinson Coll., Cambridge (Pt 1B Law Tripos 1984). Called to the Bar, Middle Temple, 1985, Bencher, 2012; in practice as a barrister, 1986–. *Publications:* (ed) Jackson & Powell on Professional Liability, 3rd edn 1992, 7th edn 2012; (with B. McGurk) Professional Indemnity Insurance, 2010. *Recreations:* ski-ing, history, wine, Italy. *Address:* 95 Portland Road, W11 4LN; Brinshope House, Wigmore, Leominster, Herefordshire HR6 9UR; 4 New Square, Lincoln's Inn, WC2A 3RJ. *Clubs:* Buck's, Oxford and Cambridge.

CANNON, Nicholas, OBE 2002; HM Diplomatic Service; Ambassador to Republic of Albania, since 2012; *b* 29 May 1958; *m* 1982, Alice Cheung; two *s*. Entered FCO, 1988; Desk Officer, Econ. Relns Dept, 1988, Hong Kong Dept, 1989, FCO; Third, later Second Sec., Paris, 1990–92; Desk Officer, EC Dept (Ext.), FCO, 1992–93; Turkish lang. trng, 1993–94; Second Sec. (Pol/Commercial), Nicosia, 1994–97; Hd, Gibraltar Sect., Southern Eur. Dept, FCO, 1997–2000; First Sec. and Hd, Pol Sect., Islamabad, 2000–02; Asst Private Sec., Prime Minister's Office (on secondment), 2003–04; Iraq Directorate, FCO, 2004; Dep. Hd, Africa

Dept (Southern), FCO, 2004–07; Ambassador, then High Comr, Republic of Rwanda, 2008–11. *Address:* c/o Foreign and Commonwealth Office, King Charles Street, SW1A 2AH.

CANNON, Prof. Paul Stephen, OBE 2014; PhD; FREng; CEng; Professor of Radio Science and Systems, University of Birmingham, since 2013; *b* Enfield, Middx, 28 Oct. 1953; *s* of late John James Peter Cannon and Betty Cannon (*née* Carter); *m* 1976, Vivian Avis Goodwin; one *s* one *d. Educ:* Edmonton County Grammar Sch.; Univ. of Southampton (BSc 1975; MSc 1976; PhD 1981). CEng 1993; FREng 2003. Res. Asst, Space Radio Physics Gp, Southampton Univ., 1978–79; Sen. Communications Engr, Marconi Space Systems, 1979–81; HSO, 1981–83, SSO, 1983–86, PSO, 1986–89, Royal Aerospace (formerly Aircraft) Establishment; Vis. Scientist, Center for Atmospheric Res., Univ. of Mass, Lowell, 1989–90; Fellow, DERA, 1993–2002; Qinetiq: Tech. Dir, Communications Dept, 2000–04; Sen. Fellow, 2002–13; Chief Scientist, Communications Div., 2004–08; Univ. Partnership Dir, 2004–05; Dir, Poynting Inst., Univ. of Birmingham, 2011–13. Prof. of Communications and Atmospheric Scis (pt-time), Univ. of Bath, 1998–2011. Mem., DSAC, 2014–. Pres., URSI, 2014–. Editor, Radio Sci. Jl, 2009–14. *Publications:* articles in learned jls. *Recreations:* photography, travelling, American presidential history. *Address:* School of Electronic, Electrical and Systems Engineering, University of Birmingham, Edgbaston, Birmingham B15 2TT. *T:* (0121) 414 4323, 07990 564772. *E:* p.cannon@bham.ac.uk.

CANNON, Richard, RIBA, FRIAS; RSA 2007; Consultant, Elder & Cannon Architects, since 2009 (Partner, 1980–2006; Director, 2006–09); *b* 18 Nov. 1943; *s* of Richard Cannon and Clara Cannon (*née* Benassi); *m* 1971, Angela Boyle; two *s* one *d. Educ:* Duncan of Jordanstone Coll. of Art. RIBA 1974; FRIAS 1986. Work on schs prog., Lanark Co. Architects, 1970–80. Major projects include: Ingram Sq. Develt, Glasgow, 1991 (Civic Trust Scotland Award); St Aloysius Jun. Sch., Glasgow, 1999 (RIBA and Glasgow Inst. of Archts Awards); Homes for the Future, Glasgow, 2000 (awards from RIBA, Glasgow Inst. of Archts, Civic Trust, Saltire Soc.; Regeneration of Scotland Supreme Award); Clavius Maths, Science and Technology Building, 2004 (Best Scottish Building Award, RIAS; awards from RIBA and Glasgow Inst. of Archts); Castlemilk Stables Block, Glasgow, 2008 (Best Scottish Building Award, RIAS). Gold Medal for Architecture, Royal Scottish Acad., 1991; (jtly) Lifetime Achievement Award for Architecture, Scottish Design Awards, 2010. *Publications:* contribs to numerous architectural jls and books. *Recreation:* travel in Italy. *Address:* Elder & Cannon, 40 Berkeley Street, Glasgow G3 7DW. *T:* (0141) 204 1833, *Fax:* (0141) 204 1844. *E:* d.cannon@elder-cannon.co.uk.

CANNON, Richard Walter, CEng, FIET; Joint Managing Director, 1977–83, Managing Director, 1983, Cable and Wireless plc; retired; *b* 7 Dec. 1923; *s* of Richard William Cannon and Lily Harriet Cannon (*née* Fewins); *m* 1949, Dorothy (formerly Jarvis); two *d. Educ:* Eltham Coll. Joined Cable and Wireless Ltd, 1941; Exec. Dir, 1973. Director: Batelco (Bahrain), 1981–90; Teletswana (Botswana), 1984–86. *Publications:* several telecommunications papers for IEE and IERE.

CANNON, Stephen Robert, FRCS; Honorary Consultant Orthopaedic Surgeon, Royal National Orthopaedic Hospital, Stanmore, since 1988; Vice President, Royal College of Surgeons of England, since 2014; *b* Sheffield, 8 Feb. 1950; *s* of Arthur Cannon and Adeline Cannon; *m* 1975, Doreen Catherine Clancy; one *s* two *d. Educ:* Frith Park Grammar Sch., Sheffield; Trinity Coll., Cambridge (BA 1971; MB BChir 1974); Middlesex Hosp. Med. Sch.; Univ. of Liverpool (MChOrth 1985). FRCS 1979. Sen. Orthopaedic Registrar, Middx Hosp., 1983–88; Consultant Orthopaedic Surgeon, Edgware Gen. Hosp., 1988–96. Orthopaedic Advr to FA, 1991–2005. President: British Orthopaedic Assoc., 2008–09; Eur. Fedn of Nat. Assocs of Orthopaedics and Traumatol., 2014–15. Mem. Council, RCS, 2008–. Chm., Skeletal Cancer Action Trust, 2002–; Trustee, Newman Foundn, 2012–. *Publications:* (contrib.) Oxford Textbook of Oncology, 1995, 2nd edn 2002; (contrib.) Oxford Textbook of Orthopaedics and Traumatology, 2002; (section ed) European Surgical Orthopaedics and Traumatology, 2014; contrib. chapters on orthopaedic oncol. in many textbooks; over 120 articles on knee pathol. and orthopaedic oncol. *Recreations:* golf, tennis, National Hunt racing, theatre. *Address:* St Giles Lodge, Amersham Road, Chalfont St Giles, Bucks HP8 4RZ. *T:* (01494) 872440, *Fax:* (01494) 872242. *E:* cannon.frcs@gmail.com. *Club:* Stephen's Green Hibernian (Dublin).

CANNON, Prof. Thomas; Professor of Strategic Development, and Special Adviser to the Vice Chancellor, University of Liverpool, since 2009; Chief Executive, Ideopolis International Ltd, since 2004; *b* 20 Nov. 1945; *s* of Albert and Bridget Cannon; *m* 1971, Frances Cannon (*née* Constable); one *s* one *d. Educ:* St Francis Xavier's Grammar Sch., Liverpool; Borough Polytechnic. BSc (Hons) Sociology (London Univ. external degree). Res. Associate, Warwick Univ., 1969–71; Lectr, Middlesex Poly., 1971–72; Products Man., Imperial Gp, 1972–74; Lectr, Durham Univ., 1975–81; Prof., Univ. of Stirling, 1981–89; Dir, 1989–92, Vis. Prof., 1992–95, Manchester Business Sch.; Associate Rector, Hajioannion Univ., Cyprus, 1993–94. Visiting Professor: Kingston Univ., 1993–; Bradford Univ., 1997–2004; Middlesex Univ., 1997–; Mercers' Sch. Meml Prof. of Commerce, Gresham Coll., 1996–2000. Chief Exec., MDE Services, 1982; Director: Stirling Gp, 1993–99; HIT Ltd, 2006–09; Chief Executive: Mgt Charter Initiative, 1995–2001; Respect London Ltd, 2001–06. Member: ESRC; Industry, Environment and Economy R&D Gp, 1990–92; Jt Cttee, ESRC/SERC, 1990–94; Business Links Gp, 1993–94; Chairman: Jt Working Party, Scottish Examinations Bd, 1988–90; Rail Users Consultative Cttee for NW, 1996–97; Dep. Chm., Management Develt to the Millennium, Inst. of Management, 1992–95. Member: Quality Standard Cttee, NCVO, 1997–99; BBC Educn Council, 1998–2000. Trustee: CAPITB Trust, 2000–; ITB Pension Trust, 2004–. FCGI; FRSA. Man. Editor, New Academy Rev., 2001. *Publications:* Advertising Research, 1972; Distribution Research, 1973; Advertising: the economic implications, 1974; Basic Marketing, 1976, 6th edn 1998; How to Win Profitable Business, 1983; How to Win Business Overseas, 1984; Enterprise, 1991; The World of Business, 1991; Women as Entrepreneurs, 1992; Corporate Responsibility, 1993; (ed jtly) The Times Good University Guide, 1994; How to Get Ahead in Business, 1994; The Guinness Book of Business Records, 1996; Welcome to the Revolution, 1998; The Good Sales Manager's Guide; The Ultimate Book of Business Breakthroughs, 2000; Football Finance After the Revolution, 2005; papers in learned jls. *Recreations:* soccer, supporting Everton FC, walking, writing. *Address:* 13 Old Broadway, Manchester M20 3DH. *T:* (0161) 434 2989.

CANNON-BROOKES, Peter, PhD; FMA, FIIC; international museum consultant; *b* 23 Aug. 1938; *s* of late Victor Montgomery Cannon Brookes and Nancy Margaret (*née* Markham Carter); *m* 1966, Caroline Aylmer, *d* of John Aylmer Christie-Miller; one *s* one *d. Educ:* Bryanston; Trinity Hall, Cambridge (MA); Courtauld Inst. of Art, Univ. of London (PhD). FMA 1975. Gooden and Fox Ltd, London, 1963–64; Keeper, Dept of Art, City Museums and Art Gall., Birmingham, 1965–78; Sessional Teacher in History of Art, Courtauld Inst. of Art, London, 1966–68; Keeper of Dept of Art, Nat. Mus. of Wales, Cardiff, 1978–86; Mus. Services Dir, STIPPLE Database Services, 1986–90. Internat. Council of Museums: Mem. Exec. Bd, UK Cttee, 1973–81; Pres., Internat. Art Exhibns Cttee, 1977–79 (Dir, 1974–80; Sec., 1975–77); Dir, Conservation Cttee, 1975–81 (Vice Pres., 1978–81). Member: Town Twinning Cttee, Birmingham Internat. Council, 1968–78; Birm. Diocesan Synod, 1970–78; Birm. DAC for Care of Churches, 1972–78; Edgbaston Deanery Synod, 1970–78 (Lay Jt Chm., 1975–78); Abingdon Deanery Synod, 2000–06, 2009–; Oxford Dio. Synod, 2003–06; Oxford Dio. Bd of Educn, 2004–06. Member: Society of Authors, 1972–; Chartered Inst. Journalists, 1972–; Art and Design Adv. Panel, Welsh Jt Educn Cttee, 1978–86; Welsh Arts Council, 1979–84 (Member: Art Cttee, 1978–84; Craft Cttee, 1983–87); Projects and Orgns Cttee, Crafts Council, 1985–87. President: Welsh Fedn of Museums and Art Galleries, 1980–82; S Wales Art Soc., 1980–87. Trustee: Welsh Sculpture Trust, 1981–94; Bosnia-Herzegovina Heritage Rescue, 1992–99; Consultant Curator, Tabley House Collection, Manchester Univ., 1988–. Jt Editor, Museum Management and Curatorship, 1981–2003 (Founder Editor, 2003–). Freeman 1969, Liveryman 1974, Worshipful Co. of Goldsmiths. FRSA. JP Birmingham, 1973–78, Cardiff, 1978–82. Prize, Masaryk Acad. of Arts, Prague, 1998. *Publications:* (with H. D. Molesworth) European Sculpture, 1964; (with C. A. Cannon-Brookes) Baroque Churches, 1969; Omar Ramsden, 1973; Lombard Painting, 1974; After Gulbenkian, 1976; The Cornbury Park Bellini, 1977; Michael Ayrton, 1978; Emile Antoine Bourdelle, 1983; Ivor Roberts-Jones, 1983; Czech Sculpture 1800–1938, 1983; Paintings from Tabley, 1989; The Painted Word, 1991; William Redgrave, 1998; The Godolphin Arabian, 2004; Pantaloon, 2011; contrib. Apollo, Art Bull., Arte Veneta, Burlington Mag., Connoisseur, Internat. Jl of Museum Management and Curatorship, and Museums Jl. *Recreations:* photography, growing vegetables, cooking. *Address:* Thrupp Farm, Abingdon, Oxon OX14 3NE. *T:* (01235) 520595. *E:* cannonbrookesassociates@gmail.com. *Club:* Athenæum.

CANTACUZINO, Sherban, CBE 1988; FSA; FRIBA; Secretary, Royal Fine Art Commission, 1979–94; *b* 6 Sept. 1928; *s* of late Georges M. Cantacuzino and Sanda Stirbey; *m* 1954, Anne Mary Trafford; two *d* (one *s* decd). *Educ:* Winchester Coll.; Magdalene Coll. Cambridge (MA). Partner, Steane, Shipman & Cantacuzino, Chartered Architects, 1956–65; private practice, 1965–73; Asst Editor, Architectural Review, 1967–73, Exec. Editor, 1973–79. Sen. Lectr, Dept of Architecture, College of Art, Canterbury, 1967–70. Trustee: Thomas Cubitt Trust, 1978–98; Design Museum, 1981–98; Member: Arts Panel, Arts Council, 1977–80; Steering Cttee, Aga Khan Award for Architecture, 1980–83 (Mem., Master Jury, 1980); Council, RSA, 1980–85; Design Cttee, London Transport, 1981–82; Adv. Panel, Railway Heritage Trust, 1985–2002; Fabric Cttee, Canterbury Cathedral, 1987–2011; Adv. Cttee, Getty Grant Prog., 1993–98; Design Panel, Plymouth Develt Corp., 1994–98; Bd, Landscape Foundn, 1995–2005. Advr, Earth Centre, 1995–. Dir, Taylor Warren Ltd, 1995–2001. Pres., UK Cttee, ICOMOS, 1987–93 (Mem., Exec. Cttee, 1990–99). Chm., Princess Margarita of Roumania Trust, 1995–98; Trustee, Wallingford Arts Park Gallery Trust, 1995–98. FSA 1995. DUniv York, 1996. EU Prize for Cultural Heritage, Europa Nostra Award, 2006. *Publications:* Modern Houses of the World, 1964, 3rd edn 1966; Great Modern Architecture, 1966, 2nd edn 1968; European Domestic Architecture, 1969; New Uses for Old Buildings, 1975; (ed) Architectural Conservation in Europe, 1975; Wells Coates, a monograph, 1978; (with Susan Brandt) Saving Old Buildings, 1980; The Architecture of Howell, Killick, Partridge and Amis, 1981; Charles Correa, 1984; (ed) Architecture in Continuity: building in the Islamic world today, 1985; Re/Architecture: old buildings/New uses, 1989; What makes a good building?: an inquiry by Royal Fine Art Commission, 1994; articles in Architectural Rev. *Recreations:* music, cooking. *Address:* 140 Iffley Road, W6 0PE. *T:* (020) 8748 0415. *Club:* Garrick.

CANTER, Prof. David Victor, PhD; Professor of Psychology and Director, International Research Centre for Investigative Psychology (formerly International Centre for Investigative Psychology), University of Huddersfield, since 2009; *b* 5 Jan. 1944; *s* of late Hyman Victor Canter and Coralie Lilian Canter (*née* Hyam); *m* 1967, Sandra Lorraine Smith; one *s* two *d. Educ:* Liverpool Collegiate Grammar Sch.; Liverpool Univ. (BA Hons 1964; PhD 1969); Univ. of Huddersfield (MA 2015). Research Associate, Liverpool Univ., 1964–65; Strathclyde University: Res. Associate, 1966; Res. Fellow, Building Performance Res. Unit, 1967–70; Lectr, 1971–72; University of Surrey: Lectr, 1972–78; Reader, 1978–83; Prof. of Applied Psychology, 1983–87; Prof. of Psychology, 1987–94; Hd of Dept of Psychology, 1987–91; University of Liverpool: Prof. of Psychology, 1994–2009, now Emeritus; Dir, Centre for Investigative Psychology, 1996–2009. Managing Editor: Jl of Envmtl Psychology, 1981–2001; Jl of Investigative Psychology and Offender Profiling, 2004–; Ed., Jl of Contemporary Social Sci. (formerly Jl of 21st Century Soc.), 2010–. Writer and presenter, TV documentary series Mapping Murder, 2002. CPsychol 1988; FAPA; FRSocMed 2009; FHEA 2012; FAcSS. Mem., Forensic Sci. Soc. Hon. Mem., Japanese Inst. of Architects, 1971. Hon. FBPsS 2008. Hon. Fellow, Psychol Soc. of S Africa, 1998. Freedom, City of Quito, 1983. Life Time Achievement Award, Alliant Univ., Calif, 2011. *Publications:* Architectural Psychology, 1970; Psychology for Architects, 1974; (ed jtly) Psychology and the Built Environment, 1974; Environmental Interaction, 1975; (with P. Stringer) Psychology of Place, 1977; (ed jtly) Designing for Therapeutic Environments, 1979; (ed) Fires and Human Behaviour, 1980, 2nd edn 1990; (ed jtly) Psychology in Practice, 1982; (ed) Facet Theory, 1985; (ed jtly) The Research Interview, 1985; (ed jtly) Environmental Perspectives, 1988; (ed jtly) Environmental Policy, Assessment and Communication, 1988; (ed jtly) New Directions in Environmental Participation, 1988; (ed jtly) Environmental Social Psychology, 1988; (with M. Comber and D. Uzzell) Football in its Place, 1989; (ed jtly) Empirical Approaches to Social Representations, 1992; Criminal Shadows: inside the mind of the serial killer (Golden Dagger Award, Anthony Award), 1994; (jtly) The Faces of Homelessness, 1995; Psychology in Action, 1996; (ed jtly) Criminal Detection and the Psychology of Crime, 1997; (ed jtly) Profiling in Policy and Practice, 1999; Interviewing and Deception, 1999; The Social Psychology of Crime, 2000; Profiling Property Crimes, 2000; Mapping Murder, 2003; (with G. Fairbairn) Becoming an Author, 2006; (with D. Youngs) Geographical Offender Profiling vols 1 and 2, 2008; (with R. Zukauskiene) Psychology and Law, 2008; Criminal Psychology, 2008, 2nd edn 2016; The Faces of Terrorism, 2009; (jtly) Safer Sex in the City, 2009; (with D. Youngs) Investigative Psychology: offender profiling and the analysis of criminal action, 2009; Forensic Psychology: a very short introduction, 2010; Forensic Psychology for Dummies, 2012; (ed jtly) Biologising the Social Sciences, 2014; Social Science Perspectives on Climate Change, 2015; contribs to learned jls, newspapers, radio, TV. *Recreations:* clarinet, musical composition, horticulture. *Address:* Rupert Crew Ltd, 6 Windsor Road, N3 3SS. *T:* (020) 8346 3000.

CANTERBURY, Archbishop of, since 2013; **Most Rev. and Rt Hon. Justin Portal Welby;** PC 2013; *b* 6 Jan. 1956; *s* of late Gavin Welby and of Jane Gillian Welby (*née* Portal, now Lady Williams of Elvel); *m* 1979, Caroline Eaton; two *s* three *d* (and one *d* decd). *Educ:* Eton Coll.; Trinity Coll., Cambridge (BA 1978); St John's Coll., Durham (BA 1991). Manager, Project Finance, Société Nationale Elf Aquitaine, Paris, 1978–83; Treas., Elf UK, 1983–84; Gp Treas., Enterprise Oil plc, 1984–89; ordained deacon, 1992, priest, 1993; Curate, All Saints, Chilvers Coton, Nuneaton, with St Mary the Virgin, Astley, 1992–95; Rector: St James, Southam, 1995–2002; St Michael and All Angels, Ufton, 1996–2002; Coventry Cathedral: Co-Dir of Internat. Ministry and Canon Residentiary, 2002–05; Sub-Dean and Canon for Reconciliation Ministry, 2005–07; Dean of Liverpool, 2007–11; Bishop of Durham, 2011–13. Non-exec. Dir, S Warwicks Gen. Hosps NHS Trust, 1998–2000 (Chm., 2000–02). Mem., Cttee of Reference, F&C Stewardship Funds, 2006– (Chm. 2010–). Mem., ACT, 1983. *Publications:* numerous articles on treasury mgt, finance and ethics and reconciliation. *Recreations:* anything French, sailing. *Address:* Lambeth Palace, SE1 7JU.

CANTERBURY, Dean of; *see* Willis, Very Rev. R. A.

CANTERBURY, Archdeacon of; *see* Watson, Ven. S. A.

CANTLAY, Michael Brian, OBE 2015; Chair: VisitScotland, since 2010 (Deputy Chair, 2001–05); William Glen & Son, since 1982; William Glen Ltd, since 1993; *b* Galashiels, 2 Feb. 1964; *s* of Alan and Daphne Cantlay; *m* 1997, Linda McCombe; one *s* one *d. Educ:* McLaren High Sch., Callander; Strathclyde Univ. (BA 1985; MBA 1989). Pres., William Glen & Son, San Francisco, 1995–; Chair, Cairngorm Scottish Imports, Toronto, 1997–. Non-executive

Director: Highlands & Islands Airports Ltd, 2008– (Mem., Audit Cttee, 2012–); Airport Mgt Services Ltd, 2009–; Dundee Airport Ltd, 2009–. Chair, Forth Valley Enterprise, 1995–2001; Mem. Adv. Bd, Scottish Enterprise, 2000–02. Mem. Bd, VisitBritain, 2010–. Convenor, Loch Lomond and The Trossachs Nat. Park Authy, 2006–11. Chair, Forth Valley Coll., 2005–09. Mem., Callander and Dist Round Table. DUniv Stirling, 2003. *Recreations:* golf, hill running, percussion. *Address:* Callandrade, Callander, Perthshire FK17 8HW. *T:* (01877) 339999. *E:* mike@williamglen.co.uk. *Clubs:* Dun Whinny Golf, Callander Golf.

CANTLE, Edward Francis, CBE 2004; DL; Director, iCoCo Foundation CIC, since 2012; *b* 12 Feb. 1950; *s* of John Victor Cantle and Isabel Ruth Cantle; *m* 1974, Heather Ann Welburn; two *d. Educ:* Shooters Hill Grammar Sch., London; Portsmouth Poly. (BSc Hons); Dip. Housing 1978. FCIH 1986 (Hon. Life Mem., 2005). Housing Advr, 1972–73, Area Improvement Officer, 1973–74, Manchester CC; Asst Chief Housing Officer, 1974–80, Chief Housing Officer, 1980–83, City of Wakefield; Under Sec., AMA, 1983–88; Dir of Housing, Leicester City, 1988–90; Chief Exec., City of Nottingham, 1990–2001. Prof., Inst. of Community Cohesion, Coventry Univ., 2005–12. Associate Dir, Improvement and Develt Agency, subseq. Local Govt Improvement and Develt, 2001–11; Chairman: DETR Local Govt Construction Task Force, 1999–2002; Community Cohesion Ind. Review Team, 2001–04 (reported on racial disturbances in northern towns and cities, 2001; final report, 2004); Integration of New and Renewable Energy in Buildings, Faraday Partnership, 2004–07. Mem. Bd, EA, 2000–08 (Dep. Chm., 2005–08). Chm., Queen's Medical Centre, Nottingham Univ. Hosp. NHS Trust, 2001–06. Chm., Nottingham and Notts Co. Sports Partnership, 2006–12. Chairman: Sustainability First (charity), 1999–; Nottingham Castle Trust, 2012–. Vis. Prof., Business Sch., Nottingham Trent Univ., 2003–; Hon. Prof., Nottingham Univ., 2011–. DL Notts, 2004. Hon. LLD Portsmouth, 2006; DUniv Oxford Brookes, 2006. *Publications:* Community Cohesion: a new framework for race and diversity, 2005, 2nd edn 2008; Interculturalism: the new era of cohesion and diversity, 2012; contrib. AMA studies, incl. Defects in Housing series; contrib. various chapters in academic books; numerous contribs to academic jls and specialist press. *Recreations:* sports, including walking, tennis and golf. *W:* www.tedcantle.co.uk.

CANTOR, Anthony John James; HM Diplomatic Service, retired; Ambassador to Armenia, 2006–08; *b* 1 Feb. 1946; *s* of late John Stanley Frank Cantor and Olive Mary Cantor (*née* McCartney); *m* 1968, Patricia Elizabeth Naughton; one *s* two *d. Educ:* Bournemouth Grammar Sch. Joined Diplomatic Service, 1965; FCO, 1965–68; Rangoon, 1968–71; Japanese lang. trng, Sheffield Univ., 1971–72, Tokyo, 1972–73; Third, then Second, Sec., Tokyo, 1973–76; Accra, 1977–80; Aid Policy Dept, 1980–82, W Indian and Atlantic Dept, 1982–83, FCO; Consul (Commercial), Osaka, 1983–89; Dep. Hd of Mission, Hanoi, 1990–92; Dep. Dir, Invest UK, 1992–94; First Sec., Tokyo, 1994–95; Dep. Consul-Gen., Osaka, 1995–98; EU Dept (Bilateral), FCO, 1999–2000; Dep. Comr-Gen., UK Pavilion, Hanover, 2000; Public Diplomacy Dept, FCO, 2000–01; Ambassador to Paraguay, 2001–05. Mem., Britain-Burma Soc. *Recreations:* travel, languages, World War II in Asia. *Club:* Kobe (Japan).

CANTOR, Prof. Brian, CBE 2013; PhD; FREng; FIMMM; FInstP; Vice-Chancellor, University of Bradford, since 2013; *b* 11 Jan. 1948; *s* of Oliver Horace Cantor and Gertrude Mary Cantor (*née* Thompson); *m* 1st, 1967, Margaret Elaine Pretty (marr. diss. 1979); two *s*; 2nd, 1981, Anne Catherine Sharry (*d* 1993); partner, 1996, Gill Partridge. *Educ:* Manchester Grammar Sch.; Christ's Coll., Cambridge (BA, MA, PhD 1972). CEng 1979, FREng (FEng 1998); FIMMM (FIM 1989); FRMS 1993–2003; FInstP 1999. Res. Fellow, Sch. of Engrg, Sussex Univ., 1972–81; Oxford University: Lectr, 1981–91, Reader in Materials Processing, 1991–95, Head, 1995–2000, Dept of Materials; Cookson Prof. of Materials, 1995–2002; Head, Div. of Math. and Physical Scis, 2000–02; Sen. Res. Fellow, Jesus Coll., 1987–95; Fellow, St Catherine's Coll., 1995–2002; Dir, Oxford Centre for Advanced Materials and Composites, 1990–95; Academic Dir, Begbroke Sci. Park, 1998–2002; Vice-Chancellor, Univ. of York, 2002–13. Industrial Fellow, GE Corporate Labs, Schenectady, NY, 1982. Chm. Bd, Amaethon, 2003–06; Dep. Chm. Bd, Yorkshire Innovation (formerly Yorkshire Science), 2005–10; Member, Board: Isis Innovation, 2000–02; White Rose, 2002–13 (Chm., 2007–11); Worldwide University Network, 2002–13; Yorkshire Univs, 2002– (Dep. Chm., 2011–13); Nat. Sci. Learning Centre, 2003–13 (Chm., 2003–04); York Economic Partnership, 2008–13; Leeds City Region Local Enterprise Partnership, 2011–13; Producer City Bradford, 2013–; Chm. Bd, People and Innovation Bradford, 2013–. Dir, Univ. of York Pensions Trust Fund Ltd, 2002–13 (Chm., 2002–10); Chm., UUK/UCEA Employers Pension Forum, 2010–13. Consultant: Alcan Internat., Banbury Labs, Oxon, 1986–94; Rolls-Royce, 1996–. Mem., World Technol. Network, 2000–. Mem. Council, RAEng, 2009–13 (Vice Pres., 2010–13). Mem. Bd, Without Walls, 2003–13. Hon. Professor: Zhejiang Univ.; Nanjing Univ.; Northeastern Univ., Shenyang, 1996; Nat. Materials Inst., Chinese Acad. of Scis, 2000; India Inst. of Sci., Bangalore, 2013. CCMI 2008. Rosenhaim Medal, 1993, Platinum Medal, 2002, IMMM; Lifetime Achievement Award, York Press, 2011. Editl Advr, Inst. of Physics Press, 1983–2006; Jt Ed., Progress in Materials Science, 1988–. *Publications:* (ed) Rapidly Quenched Metals III, 1978; (ed with P. B. Hirsch) Tribute to J. W. Christian, 1992; (jtly) Stability of Microstructure in Metallic Systems, 1997; (ed jtly) Aerospace Materials, 2001; (ed jtly) Solidification and Casting, 2003; (ed jtly) Metal and Ceramic Matrix Composites, 2004; Novel Nanocrystalline Alloys & Magnetic Nanomaterials, 2005. *Recreations:* mountain walking, playing the guitar, collecting modern art. *Address:* University of Bradford, Richmond Road, Bradford BD7 1DP.

CANTOR, Deborah; *see* Klein, D.

CANTRELL, Prof. Doreen Ann, CBE 2014; FRS 2011; FRSE; FMedSci; Professor of Cellular Immunology, and Head, College of Life Sciences and Vice Principal, since 2011, University of Dundee; Wellcome Trust Principal Research Fellow, since 2012. Formerly Project Leader, Lymphocyte Activation Lab., ICRF. Mem., MRC, 2014–. FMedSci 2000; FRSE 2005. *Publications:* contribs to scientific jls incl. Nature Immunol., Molecular Cell Biol., Jl Immunol., Biochem. Jl, Blood, Eur. Jl Immunol. *Address:* College of Life Sciences, University of Dundee, Dow Street, Dundee DD1 5EH.

CANTRILL, Eilís Veronica; *see* Ferran, E. V.

CANTY, Brian George John, CBE 1993 (OBE 1988); HM Diplomatic Service, retired; Governor of Anguilla, 1989–92; *b* 23 Oct. 1931; *s* of George Robert Canty and Phœbe Charlotte Canty (*née* Cobb); *m* 1954, Maureen Kathleen Kenny; one *s* one *d. Educ:* South West Essex Technical College; external student, London University (Social Studies); RAF Staff College (psc 1970). RN 1950; Air Ministry, 1957; Financial Adviser's Office, Cyprus, 1960; MoD (Air), 1963; FCO, 1971; served Oslo, 1973, Kingston, 1977, Vienna, 1979; FCO, 1984; Dep. Governor, Bermuda, 1986. Director: A. S. Trust Ltd, 1993–2006; St Helena Transhipment Services Ltd, 2002–06. JP Bermuda, 1986. *Publications:* (as Byron Casey) The Holy Loch Affair, 2006; The Lives of Brian (autobiog.), 2011. *Recreations:* travel, writing.

CAPALDI, Nicholas; Chief Executive, Arts Council of Wales, since 2008; *b* Lichfield, 25 July 1961; *s* of Nicholas and Norma Capaldi; *m* 1989, Lucy Marsh; one *s* one *d. Educ:* Chetham's Music Sch., Manchester (ARCM 1978); Royal Coll. of Music, London (Dip. RCM); City Univ., London (Dip. Arts Policy and Mgt). LRAM 1979. Performing pianist, 1982–88; South West Arts: Music Officer, 1988–89; Dir of Performing Arts, 1989–97; Chief Exec., 1997–2001; Chief Exec., Arts Council England SW, 2001–08. Chair, Arts 2000, 1999–2001; Member: Bd, Bristol Cultural Develt Partnership, 1996–2008; Bd, Culture SW, 2004–08. *Recreations:* reading, travel, watching sport (especially Rugby and cricket), blurring lines between work and leisure by taking every opportunity to enjoy arts. *Address:* Arts Council of Wales, Bute Place, Cardiff CF10 5AL. *T:* (029) 2044 1358, *Fax:* (029) 2044 1400. *E:* nick.capaldi@artscouncilofwales.org.uk.

CAPE TOWN, Archbishop of, and Metropolitan of Southern Africa, since 2008; **Most Rev. Dr Thabo Cecil Makgoba;** *b* S Africa, 15 Dec. 1960; *s* of Masilo and Kedibome Makgoba; *m* 1991, Lungi Manona; one *s* one *d. Educ:* St Paul's Coll., Grahamstown (DipTh 1989); Univ. of Witwatersrand (MEd 1993); Univ. of Cape Town (PhD 2009). Asst Priest, St Mary's Cathedral, Johannesburg, 1990–99; Priest-in-charge, St Albans Parish, 1993–99; Lectr, 1993–96, Chaplain, 1994–98, Univ. of Witwatersrand; Dean, Knockando Residence and Sen. Lectr, Witwatersrand Coll. of Educn, 1996–98; Rector and Archdeacon, Sophiatown, 1998–2002; Suffragan Bishop of Grahamstown, 2002–04; Bishop of Grahamstown, 2004–08. Mem., Design Gp, Lambeth Conf., 2008. Patron, Western Cape Religious Forum, 2010–. Chancellor, Univ. of Western Cape, 2012–. Involved with NGOs incl. Hope Africa, Anglican Aids Trust, Tshwaranang, Trevor Huddleston Meml Centre, 1999–; Patron: Africa for Haiti Campaign; Equal Educn and Social Justice Coalition. Patron to several children's homes and orphanages. Visitor to several church schs. Hon. DD Gen. Theol Seminary, Episcopal Ch in NY, 2009. Cross of St Augustine, 2008. *Publications:* Connectedness, 2005; contrib. Jl of Anglican Studies. *Recreations:* reading theology, walking, writing, promoting leadership development. *Address:* 20 Bishopscourt Drive, Cape Town, 7708, South Africa. *E:* archpa@anglicanchurchsa.org.za.

CAPECCHI, Prof. Mario Renato, PhD; Professor of Human Genetics, since 1989 and Distinguished Professor of Human Genetics and Biology, since 1993, University of Utah School of Medicine; Investigator, Howard Hughes Medical Institute, since 1988; *b* Verona, Italy, 6 Oct. 1937; *s* of Luciano Capecchi and Lucy Ramberg; *m* Laurie Fraser; one *d. Educ:* George Sch., Philadelphia; Antioch Coll., Yellow Springs, Ohio (BS Chem. and Physics 1961); Harvard Univ. (PhD Biophysics 1967). Jun. Fellow, Soc. of Fellows, Harvard Univ., 1967–69; Asst Prof., 1969–71, Associate Prof., 1971–73, Harvard Med. Sch.; University of Utah: Prof. of Biol., 1973–; Adjunct Prof. of Oncol Scis, 1982–, Co-Chm., Dept of Human Genetics, 2002–08, Sch. of Medicine. Member: NAS, 1991; Eur. Acad. Scis, 2002. Albert Lasker Award, Lasker Foundn, 2001; Nat. Medal of Sci., USA, 2001; Wolf Prize in Medicine, Wolf Foundn, 2002/03; (jtly) Nobel Prize in Physiol. and Medicine, 2007. *Publications: contributor:* Regulation of Nucleic Acid and Protein Synthesis, 1967; RNA Phages, 1975; Mutations and tRNA Nonsense Suppressors, 1978; (and ed) Molecular Genetics of Early Drosophila and Mouse Development, 1989; Accomplishments in Cancer Research 1994, 1995; Molecular and Cellular Approaches to Neural Development, 1997; Engineering the Human Germline, 2000; contribs to learned jls. *Address:* University of Utah, 15 North 2030 East, Room 5440, Salt Lake City, UT 84112–5331, USA.

CAPELL, family name of **Earl of Essex**.

CAPELLA, Josephine Marie; *see* Durning, J. M.

CAPELLAS, Michael D.; Senior Advisor, Kohlberg Kravis Roberts & Co., since 2010; Chairman, Virtual Computing Environment Co., since 2011 (Chief Executive, 2010–11); *m* Marie; two *c. Educ:* Kent State Univ. (BBA 1976). CPA. Systems analyst and manufg posts, Republic Steel Corp., 1976–81; Schlumberger Ltd, 1981–96: posts included Dir for Inf. Systems; Controller and Treas., Asia Pacific; Chief Financial Officer, Dowell Schlumberger Inc.; Ops Manager, Fairchild Semiconductor Unit; Founder, and Man. Partner, Benchmarking Partners, 1996; Dir of Supply Chain Mgt, SAP America, 1996–97; Sen. Vice-Pres. and Gen. Manager, Oracle Corp., 1997–98; Chief Inf. Officer, 1998–99, Chief Operating Officer, 1999, CEO, 1999–2002, Compaq Computer Corp.; Pres., Hewlett-Packard Co., 2002; CEO, 2002–06, Chm., 2002–04, and Pres., 2004–06, WorldCom, later MCI; Chm. and CEO, First Data, Colorado, 2007–10. Dir, Cisco Systems Inc., 2006–; Sen. Advr, Silver Lake Partners, 2006–.

CAPELLO, Fabio; Manager, Russian National Football Team, since 2012; *b* San Canzian d'Isonzo, Italy, 18 June 1946; *s* of Guerrino and Evelina Capello; *m* Laura; two *c.* Footballer: SPAL, 1964–67 (youth team, 1963–64); Roma, 1967–70; Juventus, 1970–76; AC Milan, 1976–80; Italian Nat. Team, 1972–76 (32 appearances); football pundit, Italian TV; caretaker Manager, AC Milan, 1986–87; coach, Atalanta Bergamasca Calcio, 1987–89; Manager: AC Milan, 1991–96 (winner, UEFA Champions League, 1994); Real Madrid, 1996–97; AC Milan, 1997–98; Roma, 1999–2004; Juventus, 2004–06; Real Madrid, 2006–07; England Football Team, 2008–12. Sports Personality of Year Coach Award, BBC, 2009.

CAPES, Mark Andrew; HM Diplomatic Service; Governor, St Helena, Ascension Island and Tristan da Cunha, since 2011; *b* England, 1954; *m* 1980, Tamara Rossmanith; two *d.* Entered FCO, 1971; UK Repn, Brussels, 1974; Lisbon, 1975; Zaghreb, 1978; FCO 1980; Commercial Attaché, Lagos, 1982–85; Third Sec. (Pol), Vienna, 1986–89; Second Sec., FCO, 1989–91; Dep. Chief Sec., Providenciales, Turks and Caicos Is, 1991–94; First Secretary: (Econ.), Wellington, 1994–99; FCO, 1999; Deputy Governor: Anguilla, 2002–06; Bermuda, 2006–09; CEO, Turks and Caicos Is, 2009–11. *Recreations:* spending time with my daughters, fishing, travel, New Zealand wine. *Address:* Governor's Office, The Castle, Jamestown, St Helena. *E:* capes.ma@gmail.com.

CAPEWELL, Lt Gen. Sir David (Andrew), KCB 2014; OBE 2002; Chief of Joint Operations, 2011–14; *b* Huddersfield, 21 Aug. 1959; *s* of late Dennis Capewell and Greta Capewell (*née* Rhodes); *m* 1981, Deborah Joy Snookes; two *d. Educ:* Holme Valley Grammar Sch.; Canadian Forces Command and Staff Coll. Joined RM, 1979; COS 3 Cdo Bde, 1998–2000; CO 40 Cdo RM, 2000–02; COS UK Jt Force HQ, 2002–04; HCSC 2004; UK CDS Liaison Officer to US Chm. of Jt Chiefs, 2005; ACOS J3 PJHQ, 2005–07; Comdr, 3 Cdo Bde, 2007–08; Dep. Comdr, NATO RRC (Italy), 2008–10; ACDS (Ops), MoD, 2010–11. Pres., RM Rugby League Assoc., 2007–08. RN Hudson Vis. Fellow, Univ. of Oxford, 2015. *Publications:* UK Approach to Amphibious Operations, 1997. *Recreations:* hill-walking, military history, kite surfing.

CAPEWELL, Vasanti Emily Indrani; *see* Selvaratnam, V. E. I.

CAPLAN, Prof. (Ann) Patricia (Bailey), PhD; FRAI; Professor of Social Anthropology, Goldsmiths College, University of London, 1989–2003, now Emeritus; *b* 13 March 1942; *d* of Sylvester Launcelot Bailey and Marjorie Bailey (*née* Parr); *m* 1967, Prof. Lionel Caplan; one *s* one *d. Educ:* Sch. of Oriental and African Studies, Univ. of London (BA Hons African Studies 1963; MA Social Anthropology 1965; PhD 1968). Tutor: Birkbeck Coll., Univ. of London, 1964–65 and 1968–69; Open Univ., 1970–71 and 1974–75; Postdoctoral Fellow, SOAS, 1968–70 and 1974–76; Lectr, then Sen. Lectr, in Anthropology, Goldsmiths Coll., Univ. of London, 1977–89; Dir, Inst. of Commonwealth Studies, Univ. of London, 1998–2000. Chair, Assoc. of Social Anthropologists, 1997–2001. Trustee and Mem. Bd, Action Aid, 2006–09. *Publications:* Priests and Cobblers: social change in a Hindu village in Western Nepal, 1972; Choice and Constraint in a Swahili Community: property, hierarchy and cognatic descent on the East African Coast, 1975; (ed with J. Bujra) Women United, Women Divided: cross cultural perspectives on female solidarity, 1978; Class and Gender in India: women and their organisations in a South Indian city, 1985; (ed) The Cultural Construction of Sexuality, 1987; (ed with F. le Guennec-Coppens) Les Swahili entre Afrique et Arabie, 1992; (ed jtly) Gendered Fields: women, men and ethnography 1993; (ed) Understanding Disputes: the politics of law, 1995; African Voices, African Lives: personal narratives from a Swahili village, 1997; (ed) Food, Health and Identity: approaches from the social sciences, 1997; (ed) Risk Revisited, 2000; (ed) The Ethics of Anthropology, 2003; (ed jtly) Swahili Modernities, 2004; numerous articles in learned jls. *Recreations:* swimming, walking, classical music, gardening. *Address:* Department of Anthropology, Goldsmiths, University of London, SE14 6NW. *T:* (020) 7919 7800, *Fax:* (020) 7919 7813. *E:* p.caplan@gold.ac.uk.

CAPLAN, Jonathan Michael; QC 1991; a Recorder, since 1995; *b* 11 Jan. 1951; *s* of Dr Malcolm Denis Caplan and late Jean Hilary Caplan, JP; *m* 1993, Selena Lennard (*née* Peskin); one *s*, and one step *s* one step *d*. *Educ:* St Paul's Sch.; Downing Coll., Cambridge (MA). MCIArb. Called to Bar, Gray's Inn, 1973, Bencher, 2000; Asst Recorder, 1989–95. Mem., General Council of Bar, 1986–90; Chairman: Bar Council Report on Televising the Courts, 1989; Public Affairs Cttee, Bar Council, 1991–92. Mem., Broadcast and Publishing Standards Tribunal, Dubai, 2003–. Member: BBC Ind. Rev. Panel on documentaries, 1997; Develt Bd, Royal Court Theatre, 1997–2006. Chairman: BAFTA Management Ltd, 2003–; BAFTA Hong Kong Adv. Bd, 2013–. Patron, Wiener Liby, 2006–. Mem. Editl Bd, Jl of Criminal Law, 1988–2005. *Publications:* The Confait Confessions, 1977; (contrib.) Disabling Professions, 1978. *Recreations:* writing, tennis, collecting historical newspapers and manuscripts, Khmer and Thai sculpture, cinema, ballet, books, flat horseracing, ufology. *Address:* 5 Paper Buildings, Temple, EC4Y 7HB. *T:* (020) 7583 6117. *Club:* Queen's.

CAPLAN, Michael Geoffrey; QC 2002; solicitor; Partner, Kingsley Napley LLP, since 1982; a Recorder, since 2000; a Deputy High Court Judge, since 2010; *b* 3 May 1953; *s* of late Alf and Hetty Caplan; *m* 1977, Jane Freedman; one *s* one *d*. *Educ:* Henry Thornton Sch., Clapham; King's Coll., London (LLB Hons, AKC 1974). Qualified solicitor, 1977. An Asst Recorder, 1994–2000. Chm., Solicitors' Assoc. of Higher Court Advocates, 2001–03. A Chm., Police Appeals Tribunal, 2003–. Mem., Sentencing Council, 2013–. Mem., Law Soc., 1977–. *Recreations:* reading, writing, sport. *Address:* Kingsley Napley LLP, Knights Quarter, 14 St John's Lane, EC1M 4AJ. *T:* (020) 7814 1200. *E:* mcaplan@kingsleynapley.co.uk.

CAPLAN, Patricia; *see* Caplan, A. P. B.

CAPLAN, Prof. Richard Dana, PhD; Professor of International Relations, since 2006 and Director, Centre for International Studies, since 2009, University of Oxford; Fellow, Linacre College, Oxford, since 2003; *b* Waterbury, Conn, 31 May 1957; *s* of Leonard Caplan and Hilary Caplan; *m* 2001, Luisa Calè; one *s*. *Educ:* McGill Univ. (BA Hons 1980); King's Coll., Cambridge (MPhil 1996); Univ. of London (PhD 2000). Editor, World Policy Jl, 1986–92; Dep. Dir, Inst. for War and Peace Reporting, 1992–94; Research Fellow: Jesus Coll., Oxford, 1998–2001; Centre for Internat. Studies, Oxford, 2001–03; Lectr in Internat. Relns, Univ. of Reading, 2001–03; Univ. Lectr in Internat. Relns, Univ. of Oxford, 2003–06. Mem., Global Agenda Council on Fragile States, World Economic Forum, 2009–11. Res. Associate, IISS, 1999–2001. Specialist Advr, Select Cttee on Foreign Affairs, 1999–2001. Visiting Professor: Univ. of Konstanz, 2010; Princeton Univ., 2010; Vis. Sen. Res. Fellow, Eur. Univ. Inst., 2007–08. *Publications:* (ed jtly) State of the Union: the Clinton Administration and the nation in profile, 1994; (ed jtly) Europe's New Nationalism: states and minorities in conflict, 1996; A New Trusteeship?: the international administration of war-torn territories, 2002; International Governance of War-torn Territories: rule and reconstruction, 2005; Europe and the Recognition of New States in Yugoslavia, 2005; (ed) Exit Strategies and State Building, 2012. *Recreations:* walking, cooking, film. *Address:* Department of Politics and International Relations, Manor Road, Oxford OX1 3UQ. *T:* (01865) 288563, *Fax:* (01865) 278725.

CAPLEN, Andrew Howard Arthur; Consultant, Heppenstalls, Solicitors, Lymington and New Milton, since 2012; President, Law Society of England and Wales, 2014–15; *b* Awbridge, Hants, 3 July 1958; *s* of Frederick Gordon Caplen and Beryl Maud Caplen (*née* Scurlock); *m* 1995, Rev. Lindsay Andrea Shaw. *Educ:* Barton Peveril Grammar Sch. and Sixth Form Coll., Eastleigh; Univ. of Hull (LLB Hons); Coll. of Law, Guildford. Admitted Solicitor, 1982; NP 1988. Solicitor, Abels, Southampton, 1982–2012. Dep. Vice Pres., 2012–13, Vice Pres., 2013–14, Law Soc. of England and Wales. *Recreations:* long-distance trail walker, Southampton Football Club supporter, committed Christian, married to a Baptist Minister. *Address:* 19 Forrest Close, South Woodham Ferrers, Chelmsford, Essex CM3 5NR. *T:* (01245) 327992. *E:* andrew.caplen@yahoo.co.uk.

CAPLIN, Anthony Lindsay; Chairman, North West London Hospitals NHS Trust, 2008–13; *b* Southport, 13 April 1951; *s* of Maxwell and Vera Caplin; *m* 1985, Angie Littlechild; two *d*. *Educ:* Merchant Taylors' Sch., Liverpool. Former Chairman: Panmure Gordon plc; Durlacher plc; Alternative Networks plc; Dep. Chm., Strand Partners. Comr, Public Works Loan Bd, 2004–14 (Chm., 2013–14). Non-exec. Dir, MRC, 2009–14 (Chm., Audit Cttee, 2009–14). *Recreation:* politics. *T:* 07774 611611.

CAPLIN, Carol Ann; *see* Homden, C. A.

CAPLIN, Ivor Keith; Founder, Ostblut Productions Ltd, 2005; Founder, owner and Managing Director, Ivor Caplin Consultancy Ltd, since 2005; Head of Public Affairs, English UK, 2014–15; *b* 8 Nov. 1958; *s* of late Leonard Caplin and of Alma Caplin (*née* Silver); two *s* one *d*. *Educ:* King Edward's Sch., Witley; Brighton Coll. of Technol. (Nat. Cert. Business Studies 1979). Joined Legal & General Assurance Society, 1978: various mgt posts, 1989–94; Quality Manager, Sales Div., 1994–97. Nat. Sec., ASTMS, 1983–88. Hove Borough Council: Mem. (Lab), 1991–97; Leader, 1995–97; Mem., Brighton and Hove UA, 1996–98. MP (Lab) Hove, 1997–2005. PPS to Leader of H of C, 1998–2001; an Asst Govt Whip, 2001–03; Parly Under-Sec. of State, MoD, 2003–05. Treas., All Party Animal Welfare Gp, 1997–2001; Sec., Parly Lab. Local Govt Gp, 1997–99; Officer, All Party Football Gp, 1998–2001. Chief Exec., Mayfair Capital Management Gp, 2009–11. Vice-Chm., Lab. Friends of Israel, 1997–2005. Trustee, Old Market Trust, Brunswick, Hove, 1997–2003. *Recreations:* supporter Brighton and Hove Albion FC and Sussex CCC, music, reading, film, theatre. *Address:* Sterling House, 20 Station Road, Gerrards Cross, Bucks SL9 8EL. *E:* ivorcaplin@outlook.com.

CAPLIN, Maj. Gen. Nicholas John, CB 2012; FRAeS; Chief Executive, Blind Veterans UK, since 2014; *b* England, 4 Dec. 1958; *s* of John and Daphne Caplin; *m* 1983, Isobel McIntosh; one *s* one *d*. *Educ:* Broadstone Primary Sch.; Poole Grammar Sch.; Univ. of Surrey (BSc Hons Econ); RMA, Sandhurst; Army Staff Coll. CGIA. Commnd AAC, 1980; Infantry Attachment, 1 RGJ, 1981; Army Pilot Trng, 1981–82; Flight Comdr, 1982–85; Adjt, 1985–87; Ind. Flight Comdr, 1988 (Maj.); Army Staff Coll., 1989–90; MoD, 1991–93; Sqdn Comdr (incl. Bosnia), 1993–95; Directing Staff, Army Staff Coll., 1995–97 (Lt Col); CO, 3 Regt, AAC, 1997–2000; Private Office, 2000–01; Comdt, Sch. of Army Aviation, 2001–02 (Col); Dep. Comdr, Jt Helicopter Comd, 2003–05 (Brig.); Comdr, Collective Trng Gp, 2006–07; Kosovo Protection Corps Co-ordinator, 2008–09; GOC UK Support Comd, 2009–12; GOC British Forces Germany, 2012; Sen. Directing Staff (Army), RCDS, 2012–13. Advr, Coode Associates, 2013–. Dir, COBSEO, 2013–. FRAeS 2004. *Recreations:* classical music (especially organ and piano), sailing (dinghy and offshore), enjoying the family and the Hebrides, President of Crossed Swords Pipe Band 2009–12. *Address:* c/o AAC Regimental Office, HQ Director Army Air Corps, Middle Wallop, Stockbridge, Hants SO20 8DY. *Club:* British Kiel Yacht (Cdre, 2009–12).

CAPON, Very Rev. Gerwyn Huw; Vicar, Cathedral of St Peter and St Paul, Llandaff, and Dean of Llandaff, since 2014; *b* 9 April 1965. *Educ:* Liverpool John Moores Univ. (BSc Hons 1992); St Stephen House, Oxford. Chartered Surveyor, 1994; ordained deacon, 2003, priest, 2004; Curate, St Mary, West Derby, Liverpool, 2003–07; Chaplain to the Archbishop of Wales and Dir of Ordinands, 2007–09; Priest-in-charge, Holy Trinity, Bolton-le-Sands, 2009–12; Bishop's Domestic Chaplain, Dio. of Llandaff, 2012–14. *Address:* The Deanery, The Cathedral Green, Cardiff CF5 2YF. *T:* (029) 2056 1545. *E:* thedean@llandaffcathedral.org.uk.

CAPP, Prof. Bernard Stuart, DPhil; FBA 2005; FRHistS; Professor of History, University of Warwick, 1994–2010, now Emeritus; *b* 19 Nov. 1943; *s* of Walter Henry Capp and Marjorie Highwood Capp (*née* Coast); *m* 1966, Elizabeth Seal (marr. diss. 1980); one *s* one *d*. *Educ:* City of Leicester Boys' Sch.; Pembroke Coll., Oxford (Open Exhibnr 1962; BA 1st Cl Hons Hist. 1965; Bryce Res. Student; MA; DPhil 1970). FRHistS 1975. University of Warwick: Asst Lectr in Hist., 1968–70; Lectr, 1970–80; Sen. Lectr, 1980–90; Reader 1990–94; Chair, Hist. Dept, 1992–95. *Publications:* The Fifth Monarchy Men, 1972, reissued 2008; Astrology and the Popular Press: English almanacs 1500–1800, 1979, reissued 2008; Cromwell's Navy: the Fleet and the English Revolution 1648–60, 1989; The World of John Taylor, the Water Poet, 1578–1653, 1994; When Gossips Meet: women, family and neighbourhood in early modern England, 2003; England's Culture Wars: Puritan reformation and its enemies in the Interregnum, 1649–1660, 2012; (contrib. and Associate Ed.) Oxford DNB, 2004; contribs to many ed collections; contrib. to Past and Present, Historical Jl, Seventeenth Century, English Historical Rev., Jl of Religious History. *Address:* Department of History, University of Warwick, Coventry CV4 7AL. *T:* (024) 7652 3410, *Fax:* (024) 7652 3437. *E:* b.s.capp@warwick.ac.uk.

CAPPE, Melvin Samuel, OC 2009; Professor, School of Public Policy and Governance, University of Toronto, since 2009; *b* 3 Dec. 1948; *s* of Dave and Patty Cappe; *m* 1971, Marni Pliskin; one *s* one *d*. *Educ:* Univ. of Toronto (BA); Univ. of Western Ontario (MA). Sen. official, Treasury Bd, Dept of Finance, and Consumer & Corporate Affairs, Canada, 1975–86; Asst Dep. Minister, Consumer & Corporate Affairs, 1986–90; Dep. Sec., Treasury Bd, 1990–94; Deputy Minister: of Envmt, 1994–96; of Human Resources Develt, 1996–99; Clerk of Privy Council, Sec. to Cabinet and Hd, Public Service of Canada, 1999–2002; High Comr of Canada in UK, 2002–06; Pres. and CEO, Inst. for Res. on Public Policy, Montreal, 2006–11. Vice Chm., Canadian Partnership Against Cancer, 2009–; Mem. Bd, Canadian Consortium for Stem Cell Res., 2012–; Chm., Health Res. Foundn, 2014–. Hon. LLD Univ. of Western Ontario, 2006; Toronto, 2008. Queen's Golden Jubilee Medal, 2002; Queen's Diamond Jubilee Medal, 2012. *Recreations:* hiking, travel, family. *E:* mel.cappe@utoronto.ca.

CAPPER, Lynne; *see* Sedgmore, L.

CAPRON, (George) Christopher; independent television producer; Director, Capron Productions, 1987–99; *b* 17 Dec. 1935; *s* of late Lt-Col George Capron and Hon. Mrs (Edith) Christian Capron (*née* Hepburne-Scott); *m* 1958, Edna Naomi Goldrei; one *s* one *d*. *Educ:* Wellington Coll.; Trinity Hall, Cambridge (MA). Served Army, 12th Royal Lancers (Prince of Wales's), 1954–56. British Broadcasting Corporation: radio producer, 1963–67; television producer, 1967–76; Editor, Tonight, 1976–77; Editor, Panorama, 1977–79; Asst Head 1979–81, Head, 1981–85, TV Current Affairs Programmes; Head of Parly Broadcasting 1985–87. FRTS 1996. *Recreations:* tennis, golf. *Address:* Old Rectory, Church Lane, Stoke Doyle, Peterborough PE8 5TH. *Club:* MCC.

CAPSTICK, Charles William, CB 1992; CMG 1972; Deputy Secretary, Food Safety Directorate, Ministry of Agriculture, Fisheries and Food, 1989–94; *b* 18 Dec. 1934; *s* of late William Capstick and Janet Frankland; *m* 1962, Joyce Alma Dodsworth; two *s*. *Educ:* King's Coll., Univ. of Durham (BSc (Hons)); Univ. of Kentucky, USA (MS). Ministry of Agriculture, Fisheries and Food: Asst Agricl Economist, 1961; Principal Agricl Economist 1966; Senior Principal Agricl Economist, 1968; Sen. Econ. Advr and Head, Milk and Milk Products Div., 1976; Under Sec., 1977, Dir of Econs and Statistics, 1977. Chm., Salix Estates Ltd, 2002–. Pres., Agricultural Economics Soc., 1983. Pres., Old Clitheronians Assoc., 2001. *Recreations:* gardening, golf. *Address:* 6 The Hazels, Wilpshire, Blackburn, Lancs BB1 9HZ.

CAPSTICK, Martin Harold; Director, High Speed Rail Policy, Funding and Legislation, Department of Transport, since 2013; *b* Keighley, 19 Sept. 1965; *s* of John Harold Capstick and Marjorie Capstick (*née* Mitchell); *m* 1988, Wendy Bristow; one *s* one *d*. *Educ:* Ermysted's Grammar Sch., Skipton; Univ. of Exeter (BA Hons Modern Langs (French and German)). Joined Dept of Transport, 1988: Private Sec. to Minister for Roads and Traffic, 1990–92; Team Leader: Public Transport London, 1992–95; Railways Directorate, 1995; Econ. and Domestic Secretariat, Cabinet Office, 1995–98; Water Supply and Regulation, 1998–2000; Private Sec. to Perm. Sec., 2000–02, DETR; Hd, Europe Wildlife Div., DEFRA, 2002–04; Department for Transport: Hd, Aviation Envmtl Div., 2005–09; Dir, Strategic Roads and Nat. Networks, 2009–10; Dir, High Speed Rail, Smart Ticketing and Safe Transport of Dangerous Goods, 2011–13. Gov., All Saints Sch., Didcot, 2004–13. *Recreations:* walking, running, cycling. *Address:* Department for Transport, Great Minster House, 33 Horseferry Road, SW1P 4DR. *E:* martin.capstick@dft.gsi.gov.uk.

CARBERRY, Kay, CBE 2007; Assistant General Secretary, Trades Union Congress, since 2003; *b* 19 Oct. 1950; *d* of Sean and Sheila Carberry; one *s* by Peter Ashby. *Educ:* Royal Naval Sch., Malta; Sussex Univ. (BA Hons English); QTS. Secondary sch. teacher, 1972–75; Researcher, NUT, 1975–78; Trades Union Congress: Policy Officer, 1978–84; Sen. Policy Officer, 1984–88; Head, Equal Rights Dept, 1988–2003. Member: Women's Nat. Commn, 1987–92; EOC, 1999–2007; Equality and Human Rights Commn (formerly Commn for Equality and Human Rights), 2006–12; Low Pay Commn, 2012–. Member: Nat. Adv. Body for Public Sector Higher Educn, 1984–87; Adv. Cttee for Women's Employment, Dept of Employment, 1987–90; Race Relations Employment Adv. Gp, Dept of Employment, then DfEE, 1990–96; Ministerial Adv. Cttee on Work-Life Balance Employment, DfEE, 2000–02; Ministerial Adv. Gp on Age, DTI, 2001–03; Work and Parents Taskforce, DTI, 2001; Steering Gp on Illegal Working, Home Office, 2003–06; Pensions Adv. Gp, DWP, 2003–04; Women and Work Commn, DTI, 2004–06. Gov., Pensions Policy Inst., 2009–. Trustee, Gingerbread (formerly NCOPF), 1990–2010; People's History Mus., 2003–; Work Foundn, 2005–10. Mem., Franco-British Council, 2004–09. *Address:* Trades Union Congress, Congress House, Great Russell Street, WC1B 3LS. *T:* (020) 7467 1266.

CARBERY, 12th Baron *cr* 1715 (Ire.); **Michael Peter Evans-Freke;** Bt 1768; *b* 11 Oct. 1942; *e s* of 11th Baron Carbery and Joyzelle Mary (*née* Binnie); *S* father, 2012; *m* 1st, 1967, Claudia Janet Elizabeth Gurney (marr. diss. 2007); one *s* three *d*; 2nd, 2008, Dr Wei Li Qiu; one *s*. *Educ:* Downside; Christ Church, Oxford (MA 1969); Strathclyde Univ. (MBA); King's Coll. London (PGCE). *Heir: s* Hon. Dominic Ralfe Cecil Evans-Freke [*b* 29 June 1969; *m* 2003, Marina Whetherly; two *s* one *d*].

CARDELLI, Luca, PhD; FRS 2005; Principal Researcher, Microsoft Research Ltd, since 2006. *Educ:* Univ. of Pisa; Univ. of Edinburgh (PhD 1982). Mem. of technical staff, AT&T Bell Labs, Murray Hill, 1982–85; mem. of res. staff, Digital Equipment Corp., Systems Res. Center, Palo Alto, 1985–97; Researcher, 1997–2000, Asst Dir, 2000–06, Microsoft Res. Ltd; Royal Soc. Research Prof., Univ. of Oxford, 2013–. *Publications:* (with Martin Abadi) A Theory of Objects, 1996. *Address:* Microsoft Research Ltd, 21 Station Road, Cambridge CB1 2FB.

CARDEN, (Sir) Christopher Robert, (5th Bt *cr* 1887, of Molesey, Surrey; but does not use the title); tropical forest management consultant; conservationist; Forestry and Rural Development Consultant, Santa Cruz, Bolivia, since 1991; *b* 24 Nov. 1946; *o s* of Sir Henry Carden, 4th Bt, OBE and of his 1st wife, Jane St Clare Daniell; *S* father, 1993, but his name does not appear on the Official Roll of the Baronetage; *m* 1st, 1972, Sainimere Rokotuibau (marr. diss. 1979), Suva, Fiji; 2nd, 1981, Clarita Eriksen (marr. diss. 1996), Manila, Philippines. *Educ:* Eton; Univ. of Aberdeen (BSc Forestry, 1970). Guide, Internat. Raëlian Movement; Forester, Govt of Papua New Guinea, 1970–74; Manager, Mgt Services Div., Fiji Pine Commn, 1976–79; Sen. Partner, CR Forestry Services, UK, 1980–81; Forest Planning and Trng Manager, Usutu Pulp Co. Ltd, Swaziland, 1982–86; Forestry Lectr, Coll. of Higher Educn, Solomon Islands, 1987–88; Internat. Forestry Consultant, 1989–90. *Address:* Casilla 1341, Santa Cruz, Bolivia.

CARDEN, Sir John (Craven), 8th Bt *cr* 1787, of Templemore, Tipperary; *b* 17 Nov. 1953; *s* of Derrick Charles Carden, CMG and Elizabeth Anne, *d* of late Capt. Alfred Spalding Russell, DSO, RN; *S* cousin, 2008; *m* 1983, Celia Jane Cameron, *d* of late Angus Cameron Howitt; one *s*. *Educ:* Winchester Coll.; Sch. of Oriental and African Studies, London Univ.; Portsmouth Poly. (BA Arch.); Dept of Psychol., Univ. of Surrey. Sch. of Arch., Portsmouth Poly., 1980–82; Carden Publishing Services, 1982–88; Carden Publications Ltd, 1988–92; Fernhurst Books, 1995–98; John Wiley & Sons Ltd, 1999–2001; Tesco Stores Ltd, 2002–. *Recreations:* music of the romantic era, having my head in a book. *Heir:* *s* Patrick John Cameron Carden, *b* 7 March 1988. *Address:* 154 St Pancras, Chichester, W Sussex PO19 7SH. *T:* (01243) 784943.

CARDEN, Kathryn Ann; *see* Bishop, K. A.

CARDEN, Richard John Derek, CB 1998; Directorate-General for Trade, European Commission (on secondment), 2003–05; *b* 12 June 1943; *s* of late John and Hilda Carden; *m* 1971, Pamela Haughton; one *s* one *d*. *Educ:* Merchant Taylors' Sch., Northwood; St John's Coll., Oxford (Craven Scholar, 1964; Derby Scholar, 1966; MA Lit. Hum. 1969; DPhil 1970); Freie Universität, Berlin. Research for Egypt Exploration Soc., 1969–70; entered Civil Service, MAFF, 1970; HM Treasury, 1977–79; MAFF, 1979–93 and 1994–2000: Chief Regional Officer, Midlands and Western Region, 1983–86; Under Sec., European Community and Ext. Trade Policy, 1987–91; Fisheries Sec., 1991–93; Dep. Hd, Eur. Secretariat, Cabinet Office, 1993–94; Dep. Sec., Food Safety Directorate, 1994–96; Hd, Food Safety and Envmt Directorate, 1996–2000; actg Perm. Sec., Feb.–May 2000; Dir-Gen., Trade Policy, subseq. Europe and World Trade, DTI, 2000–03. Dir (non-exec.), Golden Wonder Ltd, 1985–86; Associate, Mega Ace Consultancy (Mumbai and London), 2005–07; Mem. Bd, Centre for Business and Strategic Affairs (Mumbai), 2013–. Vis. Fellow, Internat. Relations Dept, LSE, 2003–05. Member, Council: RSPB, 2003–08; World Pheasant Assoc., 2008– (Chm., 2011–13); Anglo-Hellenic League, 2010–. Fellow, St George's House, Windsor Castle, 2008–. *Publications:* The Papyrus Fragments of Sophocles, 1974; (contrib.) The Oxyrhynchus Papyri, vol. LIV, 1987; (contrib.) The New Economic Diplomacy, 2003; articles on Greek literature. *Address:* Rectory House, Brandon Road, Hilborough, Thetford, Norfolk IP26 5BW. *E:* rcarden2@btinternet.com. *Club:* Travellers.

CARDEW, Anthony John; Founder and Chairman, Cardew Group (formerly Cardew & Co. Ltd), since 1991; *b* 8 Sept. 1949; *s* of late Dr Martin Philip Cardew and Anne Elizabeth Cardew (*née* Foster); *m* 1971, Janice Frances Smallwood; one *s* one *d*. *Educ:* Thornegate; army schools in Kuala Lumpur and Hong Kong; Bishop Wordsworth's Sch.; Marlborough Coll. Journalist, regl newspapers, 1967–70; news reporter, United Press Internat., 1970–71; Financial Corresp., Reuters Economic Services, 1971–74; developed financial communication, investor relns, M&A and crisis mgt, Charles Barker City, 1974–83: Dir, 1976–83; Hd, Financial Public Relns, 1979–83; Dep. Chm., 1983–85, Chm., 1985–91, Grandfield Rork Collins Financial. Trustee, Awareness Foundn, 2009–12. *Recreations:* book collecting, walking, grandchildren, theatre. *Clubs:* Reform (Chm., 2009–12), Athenæum.

CARDIFF, Archbishop of, (RC), since 2011; **Most Rev. George Stack;** *b* 9 May 1946; *s* of Gerald Stack and Elizabeth (*née* McKenzie). *Educ:* St Aloysius Coll., Highgate; St Edmund's Coll., Ware; St Mary's Coll., Strawberry Hill. BEd (Hons). Ordained priest, 1972; Curate, St Joseph's, Hanwell 1972–75; Diocesan Catechetical Office, 1975–77; Curate, St Paul's, Wood Green, 1977–83; Parish Priest, Our Lady Help of Christians, Kentish Town, 1983–90; VG, Archdiocese of Westminster, 1990–93; Administrator, Westminster Cathedral, 1993–2001; Auxiliary Bishop of Westminster (RC), and Titular Bp of Gemellae in Numidia, 2001–11. Hon. Canon Emeritus, St Paul's Cathedral, 2001. Prelate of Honour to HH The Pope, 1993; KCHS 2003. *Address:* Archbishop's House, 41–43 Cathedral Road, Cardiff CF11 9HD. *T:* (029) 2022 0411.

CARDIGAN, Earl of; David Michael James Brudenell-Bruce; Manager, since 1974, owner, and 31st Hereditary Warden, since 1987, Savernake Forest; *b* 12 Nov. 1952; *s* and *heir* of 8th Marquess of Ailesbury, *qv*; *m* 2011, Joanne Powell, Flagstaff, Arizona; one *d*, and one *s* one *d* from a previous marriage. *Educ:* Eton; Rannoch; Royal Agricultural Coll., Cirencester. Sec., Marlborough Conservatives, 1985–; Mem. Exec., Devizes Constituency Cons. Assoc., 1988–. *Heir:* *s* Viscount Savernake, *qv*. *Address:* Savernake Lodge, Savernake Forest, Marlborough, Wilts SN8 3HP.

CARDIN, Pierre; Commandeur de la Légion d'Honneur, 1997; couturier; *b* 2 July 1922. Designer: Paquin, Paris, 1945–46; Dior, Paris, 1946–50; founded own fashion house, 1950. Founder and Dir, Théâtre des Ambassadeurs, now Espace Pierre Cardin complex, 1970–; Chm., Maxim's Restaurant, 1981–. Designed costumes for films, including: Cocteau's La Belle et la Bête, 1946; The Yellow Rolls Royce, 1965. Retrospective exhibition, V&A, 1990. Dé d'Or, 1977, 1979, 1982; Fashion Oscar, 1985; prize of Foundn for Advancement of Garment and Apparel Res., Japan, 1988. Grand Officer, Order of Merit (Italy), 1988. *Address:* (office) 27 avenue Marigny, 75008 Paris, France; 59 rue du Faubourg Saint-Honoré, 75008 Paris, France.

CARDINAL, Martin John; His Honour Judge Cardinal; a Circuit Judge, since 2004; *b* 10 June 1952; *s* of Ralph William Cardinal and Ella Winifred Cardinal; *m* 1977, Janet Dorothy Allnutt; one *s* one *d*. *Educ:* King Edward's Sch., Birmingham; Magdalene Coll., Cambridge (BA 1974); Coll. of Law, Chester. Admitted solicitor, 1977; Partner: Wood Amphlet Wild & Co., 1978–85; Anthony Collins, 1985–94. Legal Chm., Mental Health Rev. Tribunal, 1987–94; Dep. Dist Judge, 1992–94, Dist Judge, 1994–2004; Asst Recorder, 1998–2000, Recorder, 2000–04. Chancellor, Dio. of Birmingham, 2005–12. *Publications:* Matrimonial Costs, 2000, 2nd edn 2007. *Recreations:* gardening, walking, swimming, lay reader. *Address:* Birmingham County Court, 33 Bull Street, Birmingham B4 6DS. *T:* (0121) 681 4441.

CARDOSO E CUNHA, António José Baptista; Commissioner General, EXPO '98, 1993–98; Chairman: PARQUE EXPO '98 SA, 1993–98; TAP Air Portugal, 2003–05; *b* 28 Jan. 1934; *s* of Arnaldo and Maria Beatriz Cardoso e Cunha; *m* 1958, Dea Cardoso e Cunha; four *s*. *Educ:* Instituto Superior Técnico; Lisbon Univ. MSc Chem. Engrg. Professional engineer, Lisbon, 1957–65; Man. Dir/Chief Exec. Officer of private cos, Sa da Bandeira, Angola, 1965–77; in business, director of private cos, Lisbon, 1977–78 and 1982–85. Mem. Portuguese Parlt, 1979–83 and 1985–89; Mem. Portuguese Government: Sec. of State for Foreign Trade, 1978, for Industry, 1979; Minister for Agriculture/Fisheries, 1980–82; Mem., European Commn, 1986–92. Medalha de Honra, Lisbon, 2003. Grã-Cruz: Ordem Infant D. Henrique (Portugal), 1993; Ordem de Cristo (Portugal), 1999; Grand Croix, Leopold II (Belgium), 1980; Gran Cruz, Merito Agricola (Spain), 1981.

CARDOZO, Prof. Linda Dolores, OBE 2014; MD; FRCOG; Professor of Urogynaecology, King's College London School of Medicine (formerly Guy's, King's and St Thomas' School of Medicine, King's College London), since 1994; Consultant Obstetrician and Gynaecologist, King's College Hospital, since 1985; *b* 15 Sept. 1950; *d* of Felix Cardozo and Olga Cardozo (*née* Watts); *m* 1974, Stuart Hutcheson; one *s* two *d*. *Educ:* Liverpool Univ. Med. Sch. (MB ChB 1974; MD 1979). MRCOG 1980, FRCOG 1991. Hse Officer, Liverpool, 1974–75; SHO, Mill Rd Maternity Hosp., Liverpool, 1975–76; Clin. Res. Fellow in Urodynamics, St George's Hosp., London, 1976–78; Registrar, 1979–81, Sen. Registrar, 1981–84, Obstetrics and Gynaecol., KCH. Co-Dir, WHO Internat. Consultation on Incontinence, 2001, 2004, 2008, 2012. Chairman: Continence Foundn UK, 1998–2006; British Menopause Soc., 2001–03; founder Chm., British Soc. of Urogynaecology, 2001–06; President: Assoc. of Chartered Physiotherapists in Women's Health, 1995–2009; Internat. Urogynaecol Assoc., 1998–2000; Sect. of Obstetrics and Gynaecol., RSocMed, 2001–02; Eur. Urogynaecol Assoc., 2011–; Mem. Exec., 2001–, and Chm. Educn Cttee, 2001–07, Internat. Continence Soc.; Internat. Fellows Rep., RCOG, 2010–16. *Publications:* 23 books incl. Update on drugs and the lower urinary tract, 1988; (jtly) Basic Urogynaecology, 1993 (trans. Italian, 1994, Polish, 1995); Urogynaecology: the King's approach, 1997; (jtly) Understanding Female Urinary Incontinence, 1999, 2nd edn 2002; (jtly) Family Doctor Guide to Urinary Incontinence in Women, 1999; (jtly) Urinary Incontinence in Primary Care, 2000; Gynaecological Urology, 2000; (jtly) The Effective Management of Detrusor Instability, 2001; (with D. Staskin) Textbook of Female Urology and Urogynaecology, 2001, 3rd edn 2010; (ed jtly) Incontinence, 2nd edn 2002 to 5th edn 2013; Incontinence in Women, 2002; (jtly) Female Urinary Incontinence, 2004; (ed jtly) Incontinence, 2005; (ed jtly) Clinical Manual of Incontinence in women, 2005; (ed jtly) The Effective Management of Stress Urinary Incontinence, 2006; (jtly) Obstetrics and Gynaecology: an evidence based text, 2nd edn 2010; contrib. over 500 papers and articles in peer review jls and 130 book chapters relating to lower urinary tract problems in women, incl. urinary incontinence, prolapse and reconstructive surgery. *Address:* King's College Hospital, Denmark Hill, SE5 9RS. *T:* (020) 3299 3449, *Fax:* (020) 7346 3449; 8 Devonshire Place, W1G 6HP. *T:* (020) 7935 2357, *Fax:* (020) 7224 2797. *E:* linda@lindacardozo.co.uk. *Club:* Royal Society of Medicine.

CARDOZO, Lydia Helena L.; *see* Lopes Cardozo Kindersley.

CARDROSS, Lord; Henry Thomas Alexander Erskine; glass designer; joint Partner, Cardross Glass, since 2006; *b* 31 May 1960; *s* and *heir* of 17th Earl of Buchan, *qv*; *m* 1987, Charlotte (*d* 2013), *d* of Hon. Matthew Beaumont and Mrs Alexander Maitland; two *s*. *Educ:* Central St Martin's Sch. of Art.

CARDY, Prof. John Lawrence, PhD; FRS 1991; Professor of Physics, University of Oxford, 1996–2014; Senior Research Fellow, All Souls College, Oxford, 1993–2014, now Emeritus Fellow; *b* 19 March 1947; *s* of late George Laurence Cardy and Sarah Cardy; *m* 1985, Mary Ann Gilreath. *Educ:* Downing Coll., Cambridge (BA 1968; PhD 1971). Research Associate: European Orgn for Nuclear Res., Geneva, 1971–73; Daresbury Lab., 1973–74; Res. Associate, 1974–76, Prof. of Physics, 1977–93, Univ. of California, Santa Barbara; Fellow: European Orgn for Nuclear Res., 1976–77; Alfred P. Sloan Foundn, 1978; Guggenheim Foundn, 1986. Paul Dirac Medal, Inst. of Physics, 2000; Lars Onsager Prize, APS, 2004; Boltzmann Medal, IUPAP, 2010; Dirac Medal, Abdus Salam Internat. Centre for Theoretical Physics, 2012. *Publications:* Finite-Size Scaling, 1988; Scaling and Renormalization in Statistical Physics, 1996; Non-Equilibrium Statistical Mechanics and Turbulence, 2008; contrib. to learned jls. *Recreation:* mountaineering. *Address:* All Souls College, Oxford OX1 4AL.

CARDY, Peter John Stubbings; Secretary, Marine Business Network (Gosport Marine Scene), since 2013; *b* 4 April 1947; *s* of Gordon Douglas Stubbings and Eva Stubbings (*née* Walker), assumed name of Cardy, 1987; *m* 1987, Christine Mary Cardy (marr. diss. 2011). *Educ:* University Coll., Durham (BA 1968); Cranfield Inst. of Technol. (MSc 1983). Adult Educn Principal, Cromwell Community Coll., Cambs, 1968–71; Dist Sec., WEA N of Scotland, 1971–77; Dep. Dir, Volunteer Centre, UK, 1977–87; Dir, Motor Neurone Disease Assoc., 1987–94; Chief Executive: Multiple Sclerosis Soc. of GB and NI, 1994–2001; Macmillan Cancer Relief, then Macmillan Cancer Support, 2001–07 (Vice Pres., 2007–); Maritime and Coastguard Agency, 2007–10; Chief Executive Officer: Aquaterra, 2010–11; Sail Training Internat., 2012–13. Chm., Nat. Assoc. of Volunteer Bureaux, 1988–91; Member: Charities Effectiveness Rev. Trust, 1990–93; HTA Pharmaceuticals Panel, 2002–04; Taskforce on Medicines Partnership, 2003–05; NHS Modernisation Bd, 2004; Bd, NCRI, 2003–06 (Chm., Lung Cancer Strategic Planning Gp); Sec.-Gen., Internat. Alliance of MND/ALS Assocs, 1991–94; Chairman: Neurological Alliance, 1998–2001; OST Foresight Healthcare Panel, 1999–2000; Brain and Spine Foundn, 2005–08; Disability Benefits Consortium, 2006; The Health Hotel, 2006; Comr, Medicines Commn, 1998–2003. Non-executive Director: Northampton NHS Community Health Trust, 1993–97; Commonwealth Navigation Ltd, 2013–. Patron, The Cancer Resource Centre, 2007–12. Vis. Fellow, Cass Business Sch., City Univ., 2006–. Dep. Chm., Southampton Solent Univ., 2011–. Writer, Agony, column for Third Sector mgt jl, 2014–. Companion, Nautical Inst., 2009–. Associate Mem., Master Mariners' Co., 2010–. Mem., RYA, 2010–. Charcot Medal, Assoc. British Neurologists and MS Soc., 2001. *Publications:* numerous articles in voluntary sector, medical and nautical jls. *Recreations:* offshore sailing, conversation, travel, drawing. *Address:* 20 Beaufoy House, Regent's Bridge Gardens, SW8 1JP. *Club:* Reform.

CAREW, 7th Baron (UK) *cr* 1838; **Patrick Thomas Conolly-Carew;** Baron Carew (Ire.) 1834; *b* 6 March 1938; *er s* of 6th Baron Carew, CBE and Lady Sylvia Maitland (*d* 1991), *o d* of 15th Earl of Lauderdale; *S* father, 1994; *m* 1962, Celia Mary, *d* of Col Hon. (Charles) Guy Cubitt, CBE, DSO, TD; one *s* three *d*. *Educ:* Harrow Sch.; RMA Sandhurst. RHG (The Blues), 1958–65 (Captain); served UK, Cyprus, Germany. Mem., Irish Olympic Three Day Event Team, Mexico 1968, Munich 1972, Montreal 1976. President: Equestrian Fedn of Ireland, 1979–84; Irish Horse Trials Soc., 1998–; Ground Jury, 3 Day Event, Olympic Games, 1992, 1996. Mem. Bureau, Fédération Equestre Internationale, 1989–97 (Hon. Mem., 1997; Chm., 3 Day Event Cttee, 1989–97). Trustee and Mem. Council, World Horse Welfare (formerly Internat. League for Protection of Horses), 2004–12. Dir, Castletown Foundn, 1995–. Gold Medal for Three Day Eventing, FEI, 1991. *Recreations:* all equestrian sports, cricket, shooting, bridge. *Heir:* *s* Hon. William Patrick Conolly-Carew [*b* 27 March 1973; *m* 2000, Jane Anne, *d* of Joseph Cunningham, Dublin; one *s* three *d*]. *Address:* The Garden House, Donadea, Naas, Co. Kildare, Ireland. *T:* (45) 868204, *Fax:* (45) 861105. *Club:* Kildare Street and University (Dublin).

See also Hon. G. E. I. Maitland-Carew.

CAREW, Hon. Gerald Edward Ian M.; *see* Maitland-Carew.

CAREW, Sir Rivers (Verain), 11th Bt *cr* 1661; journalist; *b* 17 Oct. 1935; *s* of Sir Thomas Palk Carew, 10th Bt, and Phyllis Evelyn (*d* 1976), *oc* of Neville Mayman; *S* father, 1976; *m* 1st, 1968, Susan Babington (marr. diss. 1991), *yr d* of late H. B. Hill, London; one *s* three *d* (and one *s* decd); 2nd, 1992, Siobhán (marr. diss. 2003), 2nd *d* of late C. MacCárthaigh, Cork. *Educ:* St Columba's Coll., Rathfarnham, Co. Dublin; Trinity Coll., Dublin. MA, BAgr (Hort.). Asst Editor, Ireland of the Welcomes (Irish Tourist Bd magazine), 1964–67; Joint Editor, The Dublin Magazine, 1964–69; Irish Television, 1967–87; BBC World Service, 1987–93. *Publications:* (with Timothy Brownlow) Figures out of Mist (verse). *Recreations:* reading, music, reflection. *Heir:* *s* Gerald de Redvers Carew, *b* 24 May 1975. *Address:* Cherry Bounds, 37 Hicks Lane, Girton, Cambridge CB3 0JS.

CAREW POLE, Sir (John) Richard (Walter Reginald), 13th Bt *cr* 1628, of Shute House, Devonshire; OBE 2000; DL; farmer and chartered surveyor; *b* 2 Dec. 1938; *s* of Sir John Gawen Carew Pole, 12th Bt, DSO, TD and Cynthia Mary (*d* 1977), OBE, *o d* of Walter

Burns; *S* father, 1993; *m* 1st, 1966, Hon. Victoria Marion Ann Lever (marr. diss. 1974), *d* of 3rd Viscount Leverhulme, KG, TD; 2nd, 1974, Mary (CVO 2003), *d* of Lt-Col Ronald Dawnay; two *s*. *Educ:* Eton Coll.; Royal Agricultural Coll., Cirencester. MRICS (ARICS 1967). Lieut, Coldstream Guards, 1958–63. Asst Surveyor, Laws & Fiennes, Chartered Surveyors, 1967–72. Director: South West Venture Capital, 1985–87; Eden Project Ltd, 1999–2001; Mem. Regional Bd, West of England, subseq. Portman, Bldg Soc., 1989–91. Chm., Devon and Cornwall Police Authority, 1985–87 (Mem., 1973–89); Member: SW Area Electricity Bd, 1981–90; NT Cttee for Devon and Cornwall, 1979–83. President: Surf Life Saving Assoc. of GB, 1976–86; Royal Cornwall Agricultural Show, 1981; RHS, 2001–06 (Mem. Council, 1999–2006); Trustee: Nat. Heritage Meml Fund, 1991–2000; Countryside Commission, 1991–96; Tate Gall., 1993–2003. Chm., Steering Cttee, Combined Univs in Cornwall, 2000–03. Governor: Seale Hayne Agric. Coll., 1979–89; Plymouth Coll., 1985–96; Mem. Bd, Theatre Royal, Plymouth, 1985–97. Trustee: Eden Trust, 1996–2007; Trusthouse Charitable Foundn, 1999–2009 (Chm., 2002–09); Pilgrim Trust, 2000–08; Royal Acad. of Arts Trust, 2007–. County Councillor, Cornwall, 1973–93 (Chairman: Planning Cttee, 1980–84; Finance Cttee, 1985–89; Property Cttee, 1989–93); High Sheriff of Cornwall, 1979; DL Cornwall, 1988. Liveryman, Fishmongers' Co., 1960 (Mem. Court of Assistants, 1993–; Prime Warden, 2006). *Recreations:* gardening, daydreaming, contemporary art. *Heir:* *s* Tremayne John Carew Pole [*b* 22 Feb. 1974; *m* 2010, Charlotte Watkins; one *d*]. *Address:* Clift Barn, Antony, Torpoint, Cornwall PL11 3AA. *T:* (01752) 814914.

CAREY, family name of **Baron Carey of Clifton**.

CAREY OF CLIFTON, Baron *cr* 2002 (Life Peer), of Clifton in the City and County of Bristol; **Rt Rev. and Rt Hon. George Leonard Carey;** Royal Victorian Chain, 2002; PC 1991; Archbishop of Canterbury, 1991–2002; Chancellor, London School of Theology, 2005–14; *b* 13 Nov. 1935; *s* of George and Ruby Carey; *m* 1960, Eileen Harmsworth Hood, Dagenham, Essex; two *s* two *d*. *Educ:* Bifrons Secondary Modern Sch., Barking; London College of Divinity; King's College, London. BD Hons, MTh; PhD London. National Service, RAF Wireless Operator, 1954–56. Deacon, 1962; Curate, St Mary's, Islington, 1962–66; Lecturer: Oak Hill Coll., Southgate, 1966–70; St John's Coll., Nottingham, 1970–75; Vicar, St Nicholas' Church, Durham, 1975–82; Principal, Trinity Coll., Stoke Hill, Bristol, 1982–87; Hon. Canon, Bristol Cathedral, 1983–87; Bishop of Bath and Wells, 1987–91; Hon. Asst Bp, Swansea and Brecon, 2004–. Chancellor, Univ. of Glos, 2003–10. Freeman: City of Wells, 1990; City of Canterbury, 1992; City of London, 1997. FKC 1994; Fellow, Canterbury Christ Church UC, 1999. Hon. doctorates from UK and USA univs. *Publications:* I Believe in Man, 1975; God Incarnate, 1976; (jtly) The Great Acquittal, 1980; The Church in the Market Place, 1984; The Meeting of the Waters, 1985; The Gate of Glory, 1986, 2nd edn 1992; The Message of the Bible, 1988; The Great God Robbery, 1989; I Believe, 1991; (jtly) Planting New Churches, 1991; Sharing a Vision, 1993; Spiritual Journey, 1994; My Journey, Your Journey, 1996; Canterbury Letters to the Future, 1998; Jesus 2000, 1999; Know the Truth (autobiog.), 2004; (jtly) We Don't Do God: the marginalization of public faith, 2012; contributor to numerous jls. *Recreations:* reading, writing, walking. *Address:* House of Lords, SW1A 0PW.

CAREY, Charles John, CMG 1993; Member, European Communities' Court of Auditors, 1983–92; *b* 11 Nov. 1933; *s* of Richard Mein Carey and Celia Herbert Amy (*née* Conway); *m* 1990, Elizabeth Dale (*née* Slade). *Educ:* Rugby; Balliol Coll., Oxford. Nat. Service, Russian interpreter, 1951–53. HM Treasury: Asst Principal, 1957; Principal, 1962; Asst Sec., 1971; seconded to HM Diplomatic Service as Counsellor (Econs and Finance), Office of UK Perm. Rep. to EEC, Brussels, 1974–77; Under Sec., HM Treasury, 1978–83. Chm., EC Conciliation Body for clearance of European Agricl Guidance and Guarantee Fund accounts, 1994–2001. Mem., CIPFA, 1988. Grand Croix de l'ordre de Merite (Luxembourg), 1992. *Publications:* (contrib.) Encyclopaedia of the European Union, 1998; articles on audit and financial mgt of EC funds in jls in UK, France and Netherlands. *Recreations:* Russian history and culture, Trollope novels. *Club:* Oxford and Cambridge.

CAREY, Prof. Christopher, PhD; FBA 2012; Professor of Greek, University College London, since 2003 (Head of Department of Greek and Latin, 2004–09); Vice-Dean, Faculty of Arts and Humanities, 2005–06); *b* 14 Sept. 1950; *s* of Christopher and Alice Carey; *m* 1969, Pauline Hemmings; two *s* one *d*. *Educ:* Alsop High Sch., Liverpool; Jesus Coll., Cambridge (BA 1972, MA; PhD 1976). Res. Fellow, Jesus Coll., Cambridge, 1974–77; Lectr in Greek, St Andrews Univ., 1977–91; Prof. of Classics, RHUL (formerly RHBNC, Univ. of London), 1991–2003 (Dean of Arts, 1998–2000; acting Vice-Principal, 2001); Acting Dir, Inst. of Classical Studies, London Univ., 2003–04. Visiting Professor: Univ. of Minn, 1987–88; Carleton Coll., Minn, 1988; British Acad./Leverhulme Sen. Res. Fellow, 1996–97, 2009–10. Arts and Humanities Research Board (later Council): Mem., 1998–2002, Chm., 2002–06, Postgrad. Panel (Classics); Member: Postgrad. Cttee, 2002–06; Bd of Mgt, 2002–04; Strategic Adv. Gp, 2004–06; Nominations Cttee, 2005–07. Chairman: Classics, Ancient History, Byzantine and Modern Greek Panel, 2001 RAE; Classical Assoc. Jls Bd, 2009–15; Pres., Soc. for Promotion of Hellenic Studies, 2011–14. Hon. PhD Athens, 2005. *Publications:* A Commentary on Five Odes of Pindar, 1981; (with R. A. Reid) Demosthenes: Selected Private Speeches, 1985; Lysias: Selected Speeches, 1989; Apollodoros Against Neaira: [Demosthenes] 59, 1992; Trials from Classical Athens, 1997, 2nd edn 2011; The Speeches of Aeschines, 2000; Democracy in Classical Athens, 2000, 2nd edn 2001; Lysiae orationes cum fragmentis, 2007; (ed jtly) Reading the Victory Ode, 2012; (ed jtly) Receiving the Komos, 2012; (ed jtly) Marathon: 2,500 years, 2013; (ed jtly) Eros in Ancient Greece, 2013; articles on Greek lyric, epic, drama, oratory and law. *Address:* Department of Greek and Latin, University College London, Gower Street, WC1E 6BT. *T:* (020) 7679 7522.

CAREY, Brig. Conan Jerome; Chief Executive (formerly Director General), The Home Farm Trust, 1988–2001; *b* 8 Aug. 1936; *s* of late Dr James J. Carey and Marion Carey; *m* 1966, Elizabeth Gay Docker, *d* of late Col L. R. Docker, OBE, MC, TD and Cynthia Docker (*née* Washington); one *s* two *d*. *Educ:* Belvedere College, Dublin; RMA Sandhurst; RMCS Shrivenham; Staff Coll., Camberley (psc). FIPD. Enlisted Royal Hampshire Regt, 1954; Commissioned RASC, 1956; qualified aircraft pilot, 1960; seconded Army Air Corps, 1960–65; flying duties Malaya, Brunei, Borneo, Hong Kong, BAOR; transf. to RCT, 1965; Comdr 155 (Wessex) Regt RCT(V), 1976–78; Defence Staff, British Embassy, Washington DC, 1979–82; HQ BAOR, 1982; Dep. Dir-Gen., Transport and Movements, MoD, 1985; Comdr Training Gp, RCT, 1988. FRSA. *Recreations:* golf, walking, cooking, writing. *Clubs:* Army and Navy; Park Golf (Bath).

CAREY, Sir de Vic (Graham), Kt 2002; Bailiff of Guernsey, 1999–2005; a Judge of the Court of Appeal, Guernsey, 2005–12; Commissioner, Royal Court of Jersey, 2006–10 (Judge of the Court of Appeal, 1999–2005); *b* 15 June 1940; *s* of Victor Michael de Vic Carey and Jean Burnett (*née* Bullen); *m* 1968, Bridget Lindsay Smith; two *s* two *d*. *Educ:* Cheam Sch.; Bryanston Sch.; Trinity Hall, Cambridge (BA 1962; MA 1967); Univ. of Caen (Cert. des études juridiques françaises et normandes 1965). Admitted Solicitor, 1965; Advocate, Royal Court of Guernsey, 1966; QC (Guernsey) 1989. People's Dep., States of Guernsey, 1976; Solicitor-Gen. for Guernsey, 1977–82; Attorney-Gen., 1982–92; Receiver-Gen., 1985–92; Dep. Bailiff, 1992–99. Mem., Gen. Synod of C of E, 1982–98; Chm., House of Laity, Winchester Dio. Synod, 1993–97. *Address:* Les Padins, St Saviours, Guernsey GY7 9JJ. *T:* (01481) 264587.

CAREY, Godfrey Mohun Cecil; QC 1991; a Recorder of the Crown Court, since 1986; *b* 31 Oct. 1941; *s* of Dr Godfrey Fraser Carey, LVO and Prudence Loveday (*née* Webb); *m* 1st, 1965, Caroline Jane Riggall (marr. diss. 1975); one *s* one *d* (and one *s* decd); 2nd, 1978, Dorothy May Sturgeon (marr. diss. 1983); one *d*. *Educ:* Highfield, Liphook; Eton. Legal Advr Small Engine Div., Rolls Royce Ltd, 1964–70. Called to the Bar, Inner Temple, 1969, Bencher, 2000; in practice at the Bar, 1971–2009. Legal Mem., Mental Health Review Tribunals, 2000–12. Fellow, NSPCC Full Stop Campaign, 2000–09. *Recreations:* music, tennis, Aztec culture. *Address:* 5 Paper Buildings, EC4Y 7HB. *T:* (020) 7583 6117. *Club:* Boodle's.

CAREY, Jeremy Reynolds; His Honour Judge Carey; DL; a Circuit Judge, since 2004; Resident Judge, Maidstone Crown Court, since 2010; *b* 15 Jan. 1950; *s* of late Edward Carey and Dr Audrey Carey (*née* Coghlan); *m* 1972, Alysoun Marshall; one *s* two *d*. *Educ:* King's Sch., Canterbury; Selwyn Coll., Cambridge (BA 1973). Called to the Bar, Inner Temple, 1974; Asst Recorder, 1998–2000, Recorder, 2000–04; Liaison Judge for Kent Magistracy, 2005–10. Hon. Recorder, Maidstone, 2006–. Lay Assessor to GMC, 2000–04. Mem. Disciplinary Cttee, Bar Council, 2001–04. Member: Inst. of Arbitrators, 2000–04; Parole Bd, 2010–. DL Kent, 2013. *Publications:* (sub-ed) Butterworth's Law of Limitation, 2003. *Recreations:* walking, golf, cricket, wine-tasting. *Address:* Maidstone Combined Court, Barker Road, Maidstone, Kent ME16 8EQ. *Clubs:* Boodle's; Royal St George's Golf (Sandwich); Rye Golf, Band of Brothers Cricket; Lucifer Golfing Society.

CAREY, Prof. John, FBA 1996; FRSL 1982; Merton Professor of English Literature, Oxford University, 1976–2001; Fellow of Merton College, Oxford, 1976–2001, now Emeritus; *b* 5 April 1934; *s* of Charles William Carey and Winifred Ethel Carey (*née* Cook); *m* 1960, Gillian Mary Florence Booth; two *s*. *Educ:* Richmond and East Sheen County Grammar Sch.; St John's Coll., Oxford (MA, DPhil; Hon. Fellow, 1991). 2nd Lieut, East Surrey Regt, 1953–54. Harmsworth Sen. Scholar, Merton Coll., Oxford, 1957–58; Lectr, Christ Church, Oxford, 1958–59; Andrew Bradley Jun. Research Fellow, Balliol, Oxford, 1959–60; Tutorial Fellow, Keble Coll., Oxford, 1960–64; St John's Coll., Oxford, 1964–75. Principal book reviewer, Sunday Times, 1977–. Chairman: Booker Prize Judges, 1982, 2003; Man Booker Internat Prize Judges, 2005; W. H. Smith Prize Judge, 1990–2004; Irish Times Lit. Prize Judge, 1993. Mem. Council, RSL, 1989–95. Hon. Fellow, Balliol Coll., Oxford, 1992. Honored Scholar, Milton Soc. of America, 2013. *Publications:* The Poems of John Milton (ed with Alastair Fowler), 1968, 2nd edn 1997; Milton, 1969; (ed) Andrew Marvell, 1969; (ed) The Private Memoirs and Confessions of a Justified Sinner, by James Hogg, 1969, 2nd edn 1981; The Violent Effigy: a study of Dickens' imagination, 1973, 2nd edn 1991; (trans.) Milton, Christian Doctrine, 1973; Thackeray: Prodigal Genius, 1977; John Donne: Life, Mind and Art, 1981, 2nd edn 1990; (ed) William Golding—the Man and his Books: a tribute on his 75th birthday, 1986; Original Copy: selected journalism and reviews, 1987; (ed) The Faber Book of Reportage, 1987; (ed) Donne, 1990; The Intellectuals and the Masses, 1992; (ed) Saki, Short Stories, 1994; (ed) The Faber Book of Science, 1995; (ed) The Faber Book of Utopias, 1999; Pure Pleasure, 2000; What Good Are the Arts?, 2005; William Golding, the Man Who Wrote Lord of the Flies: a life, 2009 (James Tait Black Meml Prize, 2010); The Unexpected Professor: an Oxford life in books, 2014; articles in Rev. of English Studies, Mod. Lang. Rev. etc. *Recreations:* swimming, gardening, bee-keeping. *Address:* Brasenose Cottage, Lyneham, Oxon OX7 6QL; 57 Stapleton Road, Headington, Oxford OX3 7LX. *T:* (01865) 764304.

CAREY, Dr Nicholas Anthony Dermot; Chairman, Alzheimer's Society, 2001–07; *b* 4 May 1939; *s* of Eustace Dermot Carey and Audrey Mabel Carey (*née* Grenfell); *m* 1964, Helen Margaret Askey; two *s*. *Educ:* Shrewsbury Sch.; Trinity Coll., Dublin (BA, MA); King's Coll. Cambridge (PhD). ICI, 1968–93: Gen. Manager, Chlorine and derivatives, 1980–87; Man Dir, Petrochemicals and Plastics, 1987–92; Planning Manager, Millbank, 1992–93; Dir Gen., City and Guilds of London Inst., 1993–2001. Chm., Llandudno Dwellings Co., 1998–. Governor, Reaseheath Coll., 2001–13. Liveryman: Vintners' Co., 1960–; Tallow Chandlers' Co., 1995–; Guild of Educators, 2001– (Master, 2004–05; Treas., 2008–14). *Recreations:* opera, travel, an occasional game of golf. *E:* nadcarey@aol.com. *Club:* Athenæum.

CAREY, Peter Philip, AO 2012; FRSL; writer; *b* 7 May 1943; *s* of Percival Stanley Carey and Helen Jean Carey; *m* 1st, 1964, Leigh Weetman; 2nd, 1985, Alison Margaret Summers; two *s*; 3rd, 2007, Frances Rachel Coady, *qv*. *Educ:* Geelong Grammar Sch., Vic, Aust. FRSL 1988. Hon. DLitt: Queensland, 1989; Monash, 2000; Hon. DFA New School Univ., NY, 1998. *Publications:* Fat Man in History, 1980; Bliss, 1981; Illywhacker, 1985; Oscar and Lucinda, 1988 (Booker Prize, 1988; filmed, 1998); The Tax Inspector, 1991; The Unusual Life of Tristan Smith, 1994; Collected Stories, 1995; The Big Bazoohley, 1995; Jack Maggs, 1997; True History of the Kelly Gang, 2000 (Commonwealth Writers' Prize, Booker Prize, 2001); 30 Days in Sydney, 2001; My Life as a Fake, 2003; Wrong About Japan, 2004; Theft: a love story, 2006; His Illegal Self, 2008; Parrot and Olivier in America, 2010; The Chemistry of Tears, 2012; Amnesia, 2014. *Recreation:* sleeping. *Address:* c/o Rogers, Coleridge & White, Powis Mews, W11 1JN.

CAREY-ELMS, Marsha Marilyn; *see* Elms, M. M.

CAREY EVANS, David Lloyd, OBE 1984; JP; DL; farmer; *b* 14 Aug. 1925; *s* of Sir Thomas Carey Evans, MC, FRCS and Lady Olwen Carey Evans, DBE; *m* 1959, Annwen Williams; three *s* one *d*. *Educ:* Rottingdean Sch.; Oundle Sch.; Univ. of Wales, Bangor. BSc (Agric.), 1950. Sub-Lieut, RNVR, 1943–46; farming, 1947–; Chm., Welsh Council, NFU, 1976–79; Welsh Representative and Chm., Welsh Panel, CCAHC, 1974; Chm., WAOS. JP Portmadoc, Gwynedd, 1969. DL Gwynedd 1988. *Address:* Eisteddfa, Pentrefelin, Criccieth, Gwynedd LL52 0PT. *T:* (01766) 522104.

CAREY-HUGHES, Richard John; QC 2000; a Recorder, since 2000; *b* 18 Dec. 1948; *s* of John Carey-Hughes and Esme (*née* Klein); *m* 1st, 1972, Elizabeth Blackwood (marr. diss. 1976); one *d*; 2nd, 1987, Sophia Bayne-Powell (marr. diss. 1998); one *s* two *d*. *Educ:* Rugby Sch. Airline pilot with BOAC, then British Airways, 1969–76; called to the Bar, Gray's Inn, 1977, Bencher, 2007; specialist in crime cases. Member, Committee: Criminal Bar Assoc., 1991–98 (Hon. Sec., 1996–98); S Eastern Circuit, 1998–2001. *Recreations:* gardening, cycling, cinema. *Address:* 9 Bedford Row, WC1R 4AZ. *T:* (020) 7489 2727. *Club:* Chelsea Arts.

CARFRAE, Tristram George Allen, RDI 2006; FREng; FTSE; Deputy Chair, Arup Group Ltd, since 2014 (Director, since 2005); Chairman: Arup Design and Technical Executive, 2004–07; Arup Buildings Executive, 2007–14; *b* 1 April 1959; *s* of Lt Col Charles Cecil Allen Carfrae and June Beatrice de Warrenne Carfrae; *m* 1987, Jane Irving Burrows; one *s* one *d*. *Educ:* Dartington Primary Sch., Devon; King Edward VI Comprehensive Sch., Totnes; Clare Coll., Cambridge (BA Mech. Scis Tripos 1981). MIStructE 1989; MIE(Aust) 1992, FIE(Aust) 2010; FTSE 2004; FREng 2011. Structural engr with Arup, in London and Sydney, 1981–; involved in design of: Lloyds of London, 1986; Schlumberger Res. Centre, Cambridge, 1984; Sydney Football Stadium, 1988; San Nicola Stadium, Bari, 1990; Pavilion of the Future, Seville, 1992; Brisbane Convention Exhibn Centre, 1994; Sydney Olympic Velodrome, Tennis Centre and Sports Halls, 2000; Aurora Place, Sydney, 2000; City of Manchester Stadium, 2002; Khalifa Olympic Stadium, Doha, 2005; Northern Stand, Melbourne Cricket Ground, 2006; Beijing Olympic Aquatic Centre, 2008; 1 Shelley Street, Sydney, 2009; Kurilpa Bridge, Brisbane, 2009; Helix Bridge, Singapore, 2009; AAMI Park Stadium, Melbourne, 2010; 111 Eagle Street, Brisbane, 2012; Singapore Sports Hub, 2014. Trustee, Powerhouse Mus. Trust, 2009–11. Arup Fellow, 2002–. FRSA. Australian Professional Engr of Year, Instn of Engrs, Australia, 2001; Milne Medal, British Gp, IABSE, 2006; MacRobert Award, RAEng, 2009; Gold Medal, Instn of Structural Engrs,

2014. *Publications:* contribs to Australian Jl Structural Engrg, The Structural Engr. *Recreations:* sailing, travelling, eating and drinking. *Address:* (office) 13 Fitzroy Street, W1T 4BQ. *E:* tristram.carfrae@arup.com.

CARINE, Rear-Adm. James; Chief of Staff to Commander-in-Chief Naval Home Command, 1989–91; Registrar, Arab Horse Society, 1992–2000; *b* 14 Sept. 1934; *s* of Amos Carine and Kathleen Prudence Carine (*née* Kelly); *m* 1961, (Carolyn) Sally Taylor; three *s* one *d* (and two *s* decd). *Educ:* Victoria Road Sch., Castletown, IoM; King William's Coll., IoM. FCIS 1971. Joined Royal Navy 1951; Captain 1980; Sec., Second Sea Lord, 1979–82; SACLANT HQ, Norfolk, Va, 1982–85; Naval Home Staff, 1985–88; Commodore in Comd, HMS Drake, 1988–89. Pres., RN Assoc. (IOM), 1992–2000. Member: London Campaign Cttee for Multiple Sclerosis, 1993–95; Cttee, Ex-Services Mental Welfare Soc., 1997–2003; Copyright Tribunal, 1999–2009. Chairman: Age Concern Swindon, 2000–05; Wilts NHS Ambulance Service, 2002–06; Royal United Hosp. Bath NHS Trust, 2006–10. Dir, United Services Trust, 1995–2005. Governor, St Antony's-Leweston Sch., 1996–2003. Chartered Secretaries' & Administrators' Co.: Liveryman, 1988; Mem., Court of Assistants, 1989; Jun. Warden, 1995–96; Sen. Warden, 1996–97; Master, 1997–98. KSG. *Publications:* Odyssey of a Castletown Boy, 2012. *Recreation:* horse racing. *Address:* 5 Little Sands, Yatton Keynell, Chippenham, Wilts SN14 7BA.

CARINGTON, family name of **Baron Carrington**.

CARLAW, (David) Jackson; Member (C) Scotland West, Scottish Parliament, since 2007; *b* 12 April 1959; *s* of Ian Alexander Carlaw and Maureen Patricia Carlaw; *m* 1987, Wynne Stewart Martin; two *s*. *Educ:* Glasgow Acad. Man. Dir, Wylies Ltd, 1987–2000; Chm., First Ford (trading name of Eleander Ltd), 2000–02. Nat. Chm., Scottish Young Conservatives, 1984–86; Chm., Eastwood Conservatives, 1988–92; Scottish Conservative and Unionist Party: Vice Chm., 1992–97; Dep. Chm., 1997–98, 2005–06; Mem. Scottish Conservative Exec., 2003–07. Shadow Minister for Public Health, 2007–10, for Transport, Infrastructure and Climate Change, 2010–11, for Health, 2011–, Scottish Govt. Convenor, Forth Crossing Bill Cttee, Scottish Parlt, 2009–10. Mem., Public Petitions Cttee, 2012–. Dep. Leader, Scottish Cons. and Unionist Party, 2011–. Trustee, Glasgow Educnl and Marshall Trust, 2000–14. Gov., Hutchesons' Grammar Sch., 2000–03. *Recreations:* theatre, film, reading, travel, family life. *Address:* Scottish Parliament, Edinburgh EH99 1SP. *T:* (0131) 348 6800. *E:* jackson.carlaw.msp@scottish.parliament.uk.

CARLETON, Air Vice-Marshal Geoffrey Wellesley, CB 1997; Director, Royal Air Force Legal Services, Ministry of Defence, 1992–97; Head of RAF Prosecuting Authority, 1997, retired; *b* 22 Sept. 1935; *s* of Gp Capt. Cyril Wellesley Carleton and Frances Beatrice (*née* Hensman); *m* 1985, Dianne Margaret Creswick; one *s*. *Educ:* Sherborne Sch. Admitted solicitor, 1959; commnd RAF, 1959, Pilot Officer, 1959–61; Asst Solicitor, Herbert Smith & Co., 1961–65; re-joined RAF, 1965 as Flt Lieut; Legal Officer, HQ MEAF, Aden, HQ NEAF, Cyprus, HQ FEAF, Singapore, HQ RAF, Germany, 1965–78; Deputy Director of Legal Services: HQ RAF, Germany, 1978–82 and 1985–88; MoD, 1988–92. Non-exec. Dir, Poole Hospital NHS Trust, 1998–2006; Gov., Poole Hospital NHS Foundn Trust, 2009– (Vice Chm., 2014–). *Publications:* articles in professional and service jls and pubns. *Recreations:* sailing, ski-ing, equitation, opera. *Address:* c/o National Westminster Bank, 5 Old Christchurch Road, Bournemouth BH1 1DU. *Clubs:* Royal Air Force, Royal Ocean Racing.

CARLETON-SMITH, Maj. Gen. Mark Alexander Popham, CBE 2009 (OBE 2003; MBE 1999); Director Strategy, Army Headquarters, since 2015; *b* Bielefeld, W Germany, 9 Feb. 1964; *s* of Maj.-Gen. Sir Michael (Edward) Carleton-Smith, *qv*; *m* 1991, Catherine Mary Nalder; one *s* one *d*. *Educ:* Eton Coll.; Durham Univ. (BA Hons Hist. and Politics); RMA, Sandhurst. Commnd Irish Guards, 1986; psc 1996; COS, 19 Mechanized Bde, 1999–2001; MA to C-in-C Land Forces, 2001–02; CO 22 SAS Regt, 2002–05; Dep. Dir, Policy Planning, MoD, 2005–06; Commander: 16 Air Assault Bde, 2006–08; Helmand Task Force, and British Forces, Afghanistan, 2008; Dir, Army Resources and Plans, MoD, 2008–11; Dir, Special Forces, MoD, 2012–15. Regtl Lt Col, Irish Guards, 2012–. Trustee, Gerry Holdsworth Charitable Trust, 2011–. *Recreations:* travel, hill-walking, history, riding, ski-ing. *Address:* Regimental Headquarters, Irish Guards, Wellington Barracks, Birdcage Walk, SW1E 6HQ. *Clubs:* Pratt's, Pilgrims', Chelsea Arts.

CARLETON-SMITH, Maj.-Gen. Sir Michael (Edward), Kt 1998; CBE 1980 (MBE 1966); *b* 5 May 1931; *s* of late Lt-Col D. L. G. Carleton-Smith and Mrs B. L. C. Carleton-Smith (*née* Popham); *m* 1st, 1963, Helga Katja Stoss (*d* 1993); three *s*; 2nd, 2011, Lady Francis, (Penny), *widow* of Sir Richard Francis, KCMG; two step *s*. *Educ:* Cheltenham Coll. Jun. Sch.; Radley Coll.; RMA, Sandhurst. Graduate: Army Staff Coll.; JSSC; NDC; RCDS. Commissioned into The Rifle Brigade, 1951; Rifle Bde, Germany, 1951–53; active service: Kenya, 1954–55; Malaya, 1957; Exchange PPCLI, Canada, 1958–60; GSO2 General Staff, HQ1(BR) Corps, 1962–63; Rifle Brigade: Cyprus, Hong Kong, active service, Borneo, 1964–66; Sch. of Infantry Staff, 1967–68; Comd Rifle Depot, 1970–72; Directing Staff NDC, 1972–74; Col General Staff, HQ BAOR, 1974–77; Commander Gurkha Field Force, Hong Kong, 1977–79; Dep. Director Army Staff Duties, MoD, 1981; Defence Advr and Head of British Defence Liaison Staff, Canberra, Australia, also Mil. Advr, Canberra, and Wellington, NZ, and Defence Advr, PNG, 1982–85, retd. Dir-Gen., Marie Curie Meml Foundn, then Marie Curie Cancer Care, 1985–96 (Vice-Pres., 2010–); Chm., Marie Curie Trading Co., 1990–95. Chm., Leicester Royal Infirmary NHS Trust, 1998–2000. Vice-Chm., Nat. Council for Hospice and Specialist Palliative Care Services, 1992–96. Chairman: Suzy Lamplugh Trust, 2000–01; Progressive Supra Nuclear Palsy Assoc. (Europe), 2001–07; Patron, Integrated Neurological Services, 2009–. Gov., Royal Star and Garter Home, 1998–2002. Trustee, Britain Australia Soc., 1999–2003. DL Leics, 1992–2011. *Recreations:* travel, current affairs, history. *Address:* Cambridge Villa, Jocelyn Road, Richmond, Surrey TW9 2TJ. *E:* mike@carleton-smith.com.

See also Maj. Gen. M. A. P. Carleton-Smith.

CARLIER, Maj.-Gen. Anthony Neil, CB 1992; OBE 1982; Director, Haig Homes, 1992–2002; *b* 11 Jan. 1937; *s* of Geoffrey Anthony George and Sylvia Maude Carlier; *m* 1974, Daphne Kathleen Humphreys; one *s* one *d*. *Educ:* Highgate Sch.; RMA Sandhurst; RMCS. BSc(Eng) London. Troop Comdr, Cyprus, 1962–64; GSO3, 19 Inf. Bde, Borneo, 1965–66; Instructor, RMA Sandhurst, 1967–70; Staff Course: RMCS Shrivenham, 1971; BRNC Greenwich, 1972; GSO2, Staff of Flag Officer, Carriers and Amphibious Ships, 1973–74; Sqn Comdr, 1975–76; Regtl Comdr, 1977–80; Mil. Asst to Army Bd Mem., 1980–83; Engr Gp Comdr, 1983–85; rcds, 1986; Comdr British Forces, Falkland Is, 1987–88; Chief, Jt Services Liaison Organisation, Bonn, 1989–90; Team Leader, QMG's Logistic Support Review, 1991–92. Col Comdt, RE, 1993–2000. President: Officers' Christian Union, 1992–97; Mission to Mil. Garrisons, 1992–; Chm., UK Appeal Cttee for Christ Church Cathedral, Falkland Is, 1989–2000. Trustee: Cornelius Trust, 1992–2002; Royal Engineer Yacht Club, 1992–13; Leadership and Ethics Centre, Ballycastle, Co. Antrim, 2001–. Gov., Monkton Combe Sch., 1996–2004; Chm., Clare Park Private Retirement Residences, 2007–. *Recreations:* offshore sailing, fishing, gardening, DIY. *Clubs:* Royal Engineer Yacht; International Association of Cape Horners (Faversham).

See also Master of Polwarth.

CARLILE, family name of **Baron Carlile of Berriew**.

CARLILE OF BERRIEW, Baron *cr* 1999 (Life Peer), of Berriew in the County of Powys; **Alexander Charles Carlile,** CBE 2012; QC 1984; a Recorder, 1986–2014; a Deputy High Court Judge, 1998–2014; *b* 12 Feb. 1948; *m* 1st, Frances (marr. diss. 2007), *d* of Michael and Elizabeth Soley; three *d*; 2nd, Alison Frances Josephine Levitt, *qv*. *Educ:* Epsom Coll.; King's Coll., London (LLB; AKC; FKC 2003). Called to the Bar, Gray's Inn, 1970, Bencher, 1992. Hon. Recorder, 1995–2009, Dep. Chief Steward, 2009–, City of Hereford. Contested (L) Flint E, Feb. 1974, 1979. MP (L) 1983–88, (Lib Dem) 1988–97, Montgomery. Chm., Welsh Liberal Party, 1980–82; Leader, Welsh Lib Dems, 1992–97. Chm., Welsh Assembly Review on Safety of Children in the NHS, 2000–02; Ind. Reviewer of Terrorism Legislation, 2002–11. Non-exec. Dir, Wynnstay Group (formerly Wynnstay & Clwyd Farmers) plc, 1998–. Member: Adv. Council on Public Records, 1989–95; GMC, 1989–99; Bar Council, 2012–14; Commn on Freedom of Information, 2015–. Chairman: Competition Appeals Tribunal, 2005–13; Lloyd's Enforcement Bd, 2011–; Chartered Security Professionals Registration Authy, 2011–; London Policing Ethics Panel, 2014–. Pres., Howard League for Penal Reform, 2006–11. Director and Trustee: Nuffield Trust, 1997–2007; White Ensign Assoc. Ltd, 2002–; Trustee, Royal Med. Foundn of Epsom Coll., 2003–. Fellow, Industry and Parlt Trust, 1985. *Recreations:* reading, music, Burnley FC. *Address:* House of Lords, SW1A 0PW.

CARLILE OF BERRIEW, Lady; *see* Levitt, A. F. J.

CARLILE, Trevor Mansfield; Director, Strategy, Health and Safety Executive, since 2010; *b* Portland, Dorset, 23 April 1961; *s* of Owen Carlile and Yvonne Carlile; *m* 1985, Maureen Hutchings; two *s* one *d*. *Educ:* Royal Hospital Sch., Ipswich; Open Univ. (BSc 1st Cl. Hons; MBA). Royal Military Police, 1978–86; Scenes of Crime Officer, Kent Police, 1987–98; Scientific Support Officer, 1998–2000, Hd, Forensic Services, Major Crime Scenes, 2000–04, Metropolitan Police Service; Hd, Cross Govt Identity Strategy, Home Office, 2004–07; Dir, Services Delivery, Criminal Records Bureau, 2007–10. *Recreations:* Rugby, golf, running, gym, reading. *Address:* 4 Roseleigh Road, Sittingbourne, Kent ME10 1RP. *T:* 07814 711544, (01795) 474970. *Club:* Sittingbourne Rugby.

CARLILL, Rear Adm. John Hildred, OBE 1969; DL; Royal Navy, retired 1982; *b* 24 Oct. 1925; *o s* of late Dr and Mrs H. B. Carlill; *m* 1955, (Elizabeth) Ann, *yr d* of late Lt Col and Mrs W. Southern; three *d*. *Educ:* RNC Dartmouth. psc 1961; jssc 1967. Served War 1939–45. Joined RN as Exec. Cadet 1939, transferred to Accountant Branch 1943; HMS Mauritius 1943–45. Comdr 1963, Captain 1972 (Sec. to FO Naval Air Comd, Dir Naval Manning and Training (S), Sec. to Second Sea Lord, Admty Interview Board, Cdre HMS Drake); Rear Admiral 1980; Adm. President, RNC Greenwich, 1980–82. Sec., Engineering Council, 1983–87. Chm., ABTA Appeal Bd, 1996–2010. President: Guildford Br., RN Assoc., 1989–2010; Guildford Sea Cadets, 1998–2007. Freeman, City of London, 1980; Freeman, 1983, Liveryman, 2009, Drapers' Co. DL Surrey, 1994. Chevalier de la Légion d'Honneur (France), 2004. *Address:* 1 Wonersh Court, The Street, Wonersh, Guildford, Surrey GU5 0PG. *T:* (01483) 893077.

CARLING, Philip George; Chairman, Sports Council Wales, 2004–10; Partner, Equus International, since 2010; *b* Carshalton, 25 Nov. 1946; *s* of late George Carling and Alice Carling; *m* 2009, Janet Powell; one step *s* one step *d*, and two *s* two *d* by a previous marriage. *Educ:* Kingston Grammar Sch.; St Catharine's Coll., Cambridge (BA 1969; MA 1972). Schoolmaster, Dulwich Coll., 1971–73; Man. Dir, Lambton Squash Hldgs, 1973–78; Chief Executive: Nottinghamshire CCC, 1978–83; Glamorgan CCC, 1983–90; Chm., Carling Associates, 1990–2004. UK Sport: Mem. Bd, 2004–10; Chm., Remuneration Cttee, 2005–; Member: Audit Cttee, 2006–; Major Events Panel, 2006–. Chair, Nat. Anti-Doping Proj. Bd, 2008–09; Vice Chair, UK Anti-Doping, 2009–. Member: TCCB, 1983–90; UK Sports Cabinet, 2004–10; London 2012 Olympic Legacy Bd, 2009–10. *Recreations:* golf, folk music, cinema, watching cricket and Association Football (cricket and hockey blue, Cambridge). *T:* 07802 200122. *E:* carlingphil@gmail.com. *Club:* Southerndown Golf.

CARLING, William David Charles, OBE 1991; Rugby football commentator, ITV, since 1997; *b* 12 Dec. 1965; *s* of Pamela and Bill Carling; *m* 1999, Lisa Cooke; two *c*. *Educ:* Sedbergh School; Durham Univ. (BA Psych.). Played for Harlequins, 1987–97 and 1999–2000; international career, 1988–97: 1st cap for England, 1988; 72 caps, 59 as Captain; Captain of England, 1988–96 (centre three-quarter); captained: three Grand Slam sides, 1991, 1992, 1995; World Cup final, 1991; Barbarians, in Hong Kong 7's, 1991; England tour, South Africa, 1994; World Cup, South Africa, 1995; Mem., British Lions, NZ tour, 1993. *Publications:* Captain's Diary, 1991; Rugby Skills, 1994; (with R. Heller) The Way to Win, 1995; (with P. Ackford) Will Carling: my autobiography, 1998. *Recreations:* theatre, sketching, golf. *Address:* WCM, 3000 Hillswood Drive, Chertsey, Surrey KT16 0RS. *Clubs:* Special Forces, Groucho; Harlequins, Harbour.

CARLISLE, 13th Earl of, *cr* 1661; **George William Beaumont Howard;** Viscount Howard of Morpeth, Baron Dacre of Gillesland 1661; Lord Ruthven of Freeland 1651; *b* 15 Feb. 1949; *s* of 12th Earl of Carlisle, MC, and Hon. Ela Hilda Aline Beaumont, *o d* of 2nd Viscount Allendale, KG, CB, CBE, MC; *S* father, 1994. *Educ:* Eton Coll.; Balliol Coll., Oxford; Army Staff Coll., Camberley. 9th/12th Royal Lancers, 1967–87; Lieut 1970, Captain 1974, Major 1981. Lectr, Estonian Nat. Defence and Public Service Acad., 1995–96. Sec., British-Estonian All-Party Parly Gp, 1997–99. Contested: (L/Alliance) Easington, 1987; (Lib Dem): Northumbria, European parly elecn, 1989; Leeds West, 1992. Order of Marjamac, 1st class, 1998. *Recreations:* reading, travel, learning Estonian. *Heir:* *b* Hon. Philip Charles Wentworth Howard [*b* 25 March 1963; *m* 1992, Elizabeth Harrison (*née* Moore); one *s* one *d*]. *Clubs:* Beefsteak, Pratt's.

CARLISLE, Bishop of, since 2009; **Rt Rev. James William Scobie Newcome;** DL; Clerk of the Closet to the Queen, since 2014; *b* 24 July 1953; *s* of John Newcome and Jane Newcome (*née* Scobie); *m* 1977, Alison Margaret (*née* Clarke); two *s* two *d*. *Educ:* Marlborough Coll.; Trinity Coll., Oxford (BA Mod. Hist. 1974, MA 1978); Selwyn Coll., Cambridge (BA Theol. 1977, MA 1981); Ridley Hall, Cambridge. Ordained deacon, 1978, priest, 1979; Asst Curate, All Saints, Leavesden, 1978–82; Minister, Bar Hill LEP, 1982–94; Tutor in Pastoral Studies, Ethics and Integrating Theology, Ridley Hall, Cambridge, 1983–88; RD, N Stowe, 1993–94; Residentiary Canon, Chester Cathedral, 1994–2002; Diocesan Dir of Ordinands, 1994–2000, of Ministry, 1996–2002, dio. Chester; Bishop Suffragan of Penrith, 2002–09. Lead Bishop: on Health, 2010–; for URC, 2012–; Chm., Nat. Stewardship Cttee, 2011–. Mem., Soc. for Study of Christian Ethics, 1985–. Pres., St John's Coll., Durham. DL Cumbria, 2013. FRSA. *Publications:* (contrib.) Setting the Church of England Free, 2003; At the End of the Day, 2014; book reviews for Anvil. *Recreations:* film, contemporary novels, cross-country running, furniture restoration. *Address:* Bishop's House, Ambleside Road, Keswick, Cumbria CA12 4DD. *T:* (01768) 773430. *E:* bishop.carlisle@carlislediocese.org.uk. *Club:* Athenæum.

CARLISLE, Dean of; *see* Boyling, Very Rev. M. C.

CARLISLE, Archdeacon of; *see* Roberts, Ven. K. T.

CARLISLE, Hugh Bernard Harwood; QC 1978; *b* 14 March 1937; *s* of late W. H. Carlisle, FRCS (Ed), FRCOG, and Joyce Carlisle; *m* 1964, Veronica Marjorie, *d* of late George Arthur Worth, MBE; one *s* one *d*. *Educ:* Oundle Sch.; Downing Coll., Cambridge. Nat. Service, 2nd Lt, RA. Called to the Bar, Middle Temple, 1961, Bencher, 1985. Jun. Treasury Counsel for Personal Injuries Cases, 1975–78; a Recorder, 1983–2002; a Deputy High Court Judge, 1984–2002. Dept of Trade Inspector: Bryanston Finance Ltd, 1978–87; Milbury plc, 1985–87. Pres., Transport Tribunal, 1997–2009; a Judge of Upper Tribunal, 2009–12.

Member: Criminal Injuries Compensation Bd, 1982–2000; Bar Council, 1989–92 (Chm., Professional Conduct Cttee, 1991–92). *Recreations:* fly fishing, woodworking, croquet. *Address:* Temple Garden Chambers, 1 Harcourt Buildings, Temple, EC4Y 9DA. *T:* (020) 7583 1315. *Clubs:* Garrick, Hurlingham (Chm., 1982–85).

See also A. J. L. Worth.

CARLISLE, Sir James (Beethoven), GCMG 1993; Governor-General of Antigua and Barbuda, 1993–2007; *b* 5 Aug. 1937; *s* of late James Carlisle and of Jestina Jones; *m* 1st, 1963, Umilta Mercer (marr. diss. 1973); one *s* one *d*; 2nd, 1973, Anne Jenkins (marr. diss. 1984); one *d*; 3rd, 1984, Nalda Amelia Meade; one *s* one *d*. *Educ:* Univ. of Dundee (BDS). General Dentistry, 1972–93. Chief Scout of Antigua and Barbuda. Chm., Nat. Parks Authority, 1986–90. Member: BDA; Amer. Acad. of Laser Dentistry; Internat. Assoc. of Laser Dentistry. Hon. FDSRCSE 1995. Hon. LLD Andrews Univ., USA, 1995. Kt Grand Cross, Order of Queen of Sheba (Ethiopia), 1995. KStJ 2001. *Recreation:* gardening. *Address:* PO Box W1644, St John's, Antigua, West Indies.

CARLISLE, Sir (John) Michael, Kt 1985; DL; CEng, FIMechE, FIMarEST; Chairman, Trent Regional Health Authority, 1982–94; *b* 16 Dec. 1929; *s* of John Hugh Carlisle and Lilian Amy (*née* Smith); *m* 1957, Mary Scott Young; one *s* one *d*. *Educ:* King Edward VII Sch., Sheffield; Sheffield Univ. (BEng). Served Royal Navy (Lieut), 1952–54. Production Engr, Lockwood & Carlisle Ltd, 1954–57, Man. Dir, 1958–70, Chm. and Man. Dir, 1970–81; Dir of several overseas subsid. cos; Director: Eric Woodward (Electrical) Ltd, 1965–85; Diesel Marine Internat., 1981–89; Torday & Carlisle, 1981–94. Chairman: N Sheffield Univ. HMC, 1971–74; Sheffield AHA(T), 1974–82; Community Health Sheffield NHS Trust, 1994–99; Scarborough and NE Yorks Healthcare NHS Trust, 2007–12; Healthwatch N Yorks, 2014–; Member: Sheffield HMC, 1969–71; Bd of Governors, United Sheffield Hosps, 1972–74; MRC, 1991–95; NHS Policy Bd, 1993–94; Scarborough, Whitby and Ryedale Patient and Public Involvement Forum, 2003–07. Member Council: Sheffield Chamber of Commerce, 1967–78; Production Engrg Res. Assoc., 1968–73; Chm., Sheffield Productivity Assoc., 1970; Pres., Sheffield Jun. Chamber of Commerce, 1967–68; non-executive Director: Fenchurch Midlands Ltd, 1986–94; Norhomes plc, 1989–97; Welpac plc, 1991–95; Residences at York plc, 1992–97; York Science Park Ltd, 1992–; York Science Park (Innovation) Centre Ltd, 1992–2001; Headrow Northern plc, 1992–97; Headrow Western plc, 1993–97; Xceleron (formerly CBAMS) Ltd, 1997–2005; SE Sheffield Primary Care Gp, 1999–2001. Chm., Sheffield Macmillan Horizons Appeal, 1999–2002; Trustee, Age Concern (Scarborough and Dist.), 2004–09. Governor: Sheffield City Polytechnic, 1979–82 (Hon. Fellow, 1977); Sheffield High Sch., 1977–87; Member: Sheffield Univ. Court, 1968–2005; Sheffield Univ. Careers Adv. Bd, 1974–82; Nottingham Univ. Court, 1982–94; Court, York Univ., 1991– (Mem. Council, 1991–2006; Pro-Chancellor, 1996–2006; Vice-Chm., 2001–06); Bd, Hull-York Med. Sch., 2002–07 (Chm., Fitness to Practise Cttee, 2006–13). CCMI. Freeman, City of London, 1989; Freeman, Co. of Cutlers in Hallamshire. DL S Yorks, 1996. Hon. LLD: Sheffield, 1988; Nottingham, 1992; DUniv York, 1998. *Recreations:* golf, country walking, oil and water colour painting, genealogy, Scottish dancing. *Address:* St Ovin, Lastingham, N Yorks YO62 6TL. *T:* (01751) 417341. *Clubs:* Royal Society of Medicine; Kirkbymoorside Golf.

CARLISLE, John Russell; political and media consultant, 2002–07; *b* 28 Aug. 1942; *s* of Andrew and Edith Carlisle; *m* 1964, Anthea Jane Lindsay May; two *d*. *Educ:* Bedford Sch.; St Lawrence Coll.; Coll. of Estate Management, London. Sidney C. Banks Ltd, Sandy, 1964–78; Consultant: Louis Dreyfus plc, 1982–87; Barry Simmons PR, 1987–97; non-executive Director: Bletchley Motor Gp, 1988–95; Charles Sidney plc, 1995–97; Member: London Corn Exchange, 1987–97; Baltic Exchange, 1991–97; Exec. Dir, Tobacco Manufrs' Assoc., 1997–2001. Chm., Mid Beds Cons. Assoc., 1974–76. MP (C) Luton West, 1979–83, Luton North, 1983–97. Chm., Cons Parly Cttee on Sport, 1981–82, 1983–84, 1985–97; Vice Chm., All-Party Football Cttee, 1987–97; Mem., Commons Select Cttee on Agriculture, 1985–88. Chm., British-S Africa Gp, 1987 (Sec., 1983–87); Treas., Anglo-Gibraltar Gp, 1981–82. Governor, Sports Aid Foundn (Eastern), 1985–96. President: Luton 100 Club; Luton Band; Bedfordshire CCC, 1993–97; Chm., Parliamentary Dinosaurs, 2004–. *Recreations:* sport, music, shooting. *Address:* Apple Tree Cottage, Seal Chart, Sevenoaks, Kent TN15 0ES. *Clubs:* Carlton, MCC.

CARLISLE, Judith Margaret; Head, Oxford High School, since 2011; *b* Leics, 15 Jan. 1959; *d* of Anthony and Joan Carlisle; *m* 1996, David Gough. *Educ:* Convent of the Nativity, Sittingbourne; Univ. of Bristol (BA Hons Drama and English 1979); Drama Studio, London (Dip. Acting 1981); Goldsmiths Coll., Univ. of London (PGCE 1986); Nat. Coll. of Sch. Leadership (NPQH 2004). Actor, Theatre in Education, 1981–85; Teacher of Drama and Media Studies, Trinity Sch., Leamington Spa, 1986–89; Hd of Drama Dept, 1990–94, Academic Team Leader, 1994–98, Whitley Abbey Sch., Coventry; Dep. Head, King Edward VII Sch., King's Lynn, 1998–2004; Headteacher, Dover GS for Girls, 2004–10. *Recreations:* trekking, cycling, cross-country ski-ing, theatre, gardening, owl and hare watching in N Norfolk. *Address:* Oxford High School, Belbroughton Road, Oxford OX2 6XA. *T:* (01865) 559888, *Fax:* (01865) 552343. *E:* oxfordhigh@oxf.gdst.net. *Club:* Lansdowne.

CARLISLE, Sir Kenneth (Melville), Kt 1994; *b* 25 March 1941; *s* of late Kenneth Ralph Malcolm Carlisle, TD and of Hon. Elizabeth Mary McLaren, *d* of 2nd Baron Aberconway; *m* 1986, Carla, *d* of A. W. Heffner, Md, USA; one *s*. *Educ:* Harrow; Magdalen Coll., Oxford (BA History). Called to Bar, Inner Temple, 1965. Brooke Bond Liebig, 1966–74; farming in Suffolk, 1974–. MP (C) Lincoln, 1979–97. PPS to: Minister of State for Energy, 1981–83; Minister of State for Home Office, 1983–84; Sec. of State for NI, 1984–85; Home Secretary, 1985–87; an Asst Govt Whip, 1987–88; a Lord Comr of HM Treasury, 1988–90; Parly Under-Sec. of State, MoD, 1990–92, Dept of Transport, 1992–93. Mem., Public Accts Cttee, 1994–97. Member Council: RSPB, 1985–87; RHS, 1996–2006; Suffolk Wildlife Trust, 2007–14. Trustee, World Land Trust, 2009–. *Recreations:* botany, gardening, history. *Address:* Wyken Hall, Stanton, Bury St Edmunds, Suffolk IP31 2DW. *T:* (01359) 250240.

CARLISLE, Sir Michael; *see* Carlisle, Sir J. M.

CARLOW, Viscount; Charles George Yuill Seymour Dawson-Damer; *b* 6 Oct. 1965; *s* and *heir* of 7th Earl of Portarlington, *qv*; *m* 2002, Clare, *y d* of Rodney Garside; one *s* three *d*. *Educ:* Eton College; Univ. of Edinburgh (MA Hons 1988). A Page of Honour to the Queen, 1979–80. *Heir: s* Hon. Henry, (Harry), Charles Yuill Seymour Dawson-Damer, *b* 13 Nov. 2009. *Address:* 7 Cambridge Avenue, Vaucluse, Sydney, NSW 2030, Australia. *Clubs:* Australian, Royal Sydney Golf (Sydney).

CARLOWAY, Rt Hon. Lord; Colin John MacLean Sutherland; PC 2008; a Senator of the College of Justice in Scotland, since 2000; Lord Justice Clerk and President, Second Division, Court of Session, since 2012; *b* 20 May 1954; *s* of Eric Alexander Cruickshank Sutherland and Mary Macaulay or Sutherland; *m* 1988, Jane Alexander Turnbull; two *s*. *Educ:* Hurst Grange Prep. Sch., Stirling; Edinburgh Acad.; Edinburgh Univ. (LLB Hons). Advocate, 1977; Advocate Depute, 1986–89; QC (Scot.) 1990. Treas., Faculty of Advocates, 1994–2000. *Address:* Supreme Courts, Parliament House, Edinburgh EH1 1RQ. *T:* (0131) 240 6883. *Club:* Scottish Arts (Edinburgh).

CARLSSON, Prof. Arvid, MD; Professor of Pharmacology, University of Gothenburg, 1959–89, now Emeritus; *b* Uppsala, Sweden, 25 Jan. 1923. *Educ:* Univ. of Lund, Sweden (ML; MD 1951). Asst Prof., 1951–56, Associate Prof., 1956–59, Univ. of Lund. Vis. Scientist, Lab. of Chemical Pathol., Nat. Heart Inst., Bethesda, Md, 1955–56. Mem., Scientific Adv. Bd, Acadia Pharmaceuticals, 1999–. (Jtly) Nobel Prize for Physiol. or Medicine, 2000. *Publications:* articles in jls. *Address:* Department of Pharmacology, University of Gothenburg, Medicinaregatan 7, Box 431, 40530 Gothenburg, Sweden.

CARLTON, Viscount; Reed Montagu Stuart Wortley; *b* 5 Feb. 1980; *s* and *heir* of Earl of Wharncliffe, *qv*; *m* 2001, Kim Smith; two *s* one *d*.

CARLTON, Prof. John Stephen, FREng; CEng, CMarEng, FIMechE, FRINA, FIMarEST; Professor of Marine Engineering, City University London, since 2010; President, Institute of Marine Engineering, Science and Technology, 2011–12; *b* 26 Nov. 1946; *s* of Cecil Leonard Carlton and Florence Emily Carlton; *m* 1st, 1975, Jeanette Barham (marr. diss. 2005); one *d* (one *s* decd); 2nd, 2007, Janet Rosemary Gooding; two step *d*. *Educ:* Winchelsea Sch.; Pernovena Sch.; Cannock House Sch.; Bromley Tech. Coll. (IMechE Pts I, II, III); Open Univ. (BA). CEng 1973; FREng 2011. Served RN Scientific Service, 1965–70. Design and Res. engr, Stone Manganese Marine, 1970–75; Lloyd's Register: Tech. Investigation, 1975–84; Deputy Head: Advanced Engrg, 1984–87; Performance Technol., 1987–90; Principal Surveyor and Hd, Propulsion, Performance and Envmtl Engrg, 1990–92; Sen. Principal Surveyor and Hd, Tech. Investigation, 1992–2003; Global Hd, Marine Technol., 2003–10. Dir, Thermo-Fluids Res. Centre, City Univ. London, 2014–. Chairman: internat. res. gps on ship propulsion, propeller backing stresses, 1992–96, cavitation phenomenology I, 1997–2000, and II, 2000–04, cavitation erosion, 2004–07, multi-hull ship performance, 2007–10; RAEng Wkg Gp on Future Ship Powering Options, 2009–13. Mem., Master Mariners' Co. (Mem., Tech. Cttee, 2014–). Hon. DSc City, 2006. Stanley Gray Award, 1990 and 1998, Denny Gold Medal, 1998 and 2008, Inst. of Marine Engrg, Sci. and Technol. Marine Propulsion Lifetime Achievement Award, 2015. *Publications:* Marine Propellers and Propulsion, 1994, 3rd edn 2012; (contrib.) Maritime Engineering Reference Book, 2008; Ship Noise and Vibration, 2015; contrib. 129 technical papers and articles. *Recreations:* sailing, railway history and steam locomotives, bird watching and animal behaviour, watercolour and pastel painting and drawing, music, literature and poetry, theatre. *Address:* School of Engineering and Mathematical Sciences, City University London, Northampton Square, EC1V 0HB. *Club:* Royal Over-Seas League.

CARLUCCIO, Antonio Mario Gaetano, Hon. OBE 2007; Commendatore, Order of Merit (Italy), 1999; restaurateur, cook, broadcaster and author; *b* 19 April 1937; *s* of Giovanni Carluccio and Maria (*née* Trivellone); *m* 1981, Priscilla Marion Conran (marr. diss. 2009). *Educ:* Roland Matura Schule, Vienna. Reporter, Gazzetta del Popolo, and La Stampa, Turin, 1953–54; wine merchant, Germany, 1963–75, England, 1975–81; restaurateur, 1981–89; Proprietor, 1989–2007, The Neal Street Restaurant; Jt Proprietor, Carluccio's Italian Food Shop and Caffe, 1991–2007; Consultant, Carluccio's Caffes, 2008–. *Television:* various appearances, BBC2, 1986–; *series:* Italian Feast, BBC2, 1996; Southern Italian Feast, BBC2, 1998; Two Greedy Italians, BBC2, 2011–12. Hon. Associate, Altagamma Internat. Hon. Council, 2005. Ambassador for Italian Food, Melbourne Food Festival, 2012; Patron, Canberra Truffle Festival, 2014. *Publications:* Invitation to Italian Cooking (Bejam Cookery Book of the Year), 1986; Passion for Mushrooms, 1989; Passion for Pasta, 1993; Italian Feast (Best Cookery Book, Good Food mag.), 1996; Carluccio's Complete Italian Food, 1997; Southern Italian Feast, 1998; The Carluccio Collection, 1999; Antonio Carluccio's Vegetables, 2000; Antonio Carluccio Goes Wild, 2001; The Complete Mushroom Book: the quiet hunt, 2003; Italia, 2005; Antonio Carluccio's Simple Cooking, 2009; Two Greedy Italians, 2011; A Recipe for Life, 2012; The Collection, 2012; Two Greedy Italians Eat Italy, 2012; Pasta, 2014. *Address:* 63 Amerland Road, SW18 1QA.

CARLYLE, Joan Hildred; soprano; *b* 6 April 1931; *d* of late Edgar James and Margaret Mary Carlyle; *m*; two *d*. *Educ:* Howell's Sch., Denbigh, N Wales. Became Principal Lyric Soprano, Royal Opera House, Covent Garden, 1955; Oscar in Ballo in Maschera, 1957–58 season; Sophie in Rosenkavalier, 1958–59; Micaela in Carmen, 1958–59; Nedda in Pagliacci (new Zeffirelli production), Dec. 1959; Mimi in La Bohème, Dec. 1960; Titania in Gielgud production of Britten's Midsummer Night's Dream, London première, Dec. 1961; Pamina in Klemperer production of The Magic Flute, 1962; Countess in Figaro, 1963; Zdenko in Hartman production of Arabella, 1964; Sœur Angelica (new production), 1965; Desdemona in Otello, 1965, 1967; Sophie in Rosenkavalier (new production), 1966; Pamina in Magic Flute (new production), 1966; Arabella in Arabella, 1967; Marschallin in Rosenkavalier, 1968; Jenifer, Midsummer Marriage (new prod.), 1969; Donna Anna, 1970; Reiza, Oberon, 1970; Adrianna Lecouvreur, 1970; Rusalka, for BBC, 1969; Elizabeth in Don Carlos, 1975. Roles sung abroad include: Oscar, Nedda, Mimi, Pamina, Zdenko, Micaela, Desdemona, Donna Anna, Arabella, Elizabeth. Has sung in Buenos Aires, Belgium, Holland, France, Monaco, Naples, Milan, Berlin, Cape Town, Munich. Has made numerous recordings; appeared BBC TV (in film). Teaches at home and gives masterclasses. *Recreations:* gardening, cooking, interior decorating, countryside preservation. *Address:* Laundry Cottage, Hanmer, N Wales SY13 3DQ. *E:* joan.carlyle@BTclick.com. *W:* www.joancarlyle.co.uk.

CARLYLE, Robert, OBE 1990; actor; *b* Glasgow, 14 April 1961; *s* of late Joseph Carlyle and of Elizabeth Carlyle; *m* 1997, Anastasia Shirley; two *s* one *d*. *Educ:* North Kelvinside Secondary Sch.; RSAMD. Founder, Rain Dog Theatre Co., 1990; dir of prodns incl. Wasted, One Flew Over the Cuckoo's Nest, Conquest of the South Pole, Macbeth. *Theatre includes:* Twelfth Night; Dead Dad Dog; Nae Problem; City; No Mean City; Cuttin' a Rug; Othello. *Television includes:* The Part of Valour, 1981; Hamish Macbeth, 1995; Cracker, 1993, 1997, 1999–2001; Safe, 1993; The Advocates; Arena; Byrne on Byrne; Taggart; Looking After Jo Jo, 1998; Hitler: the rise of evil, 2003; Gunpowder, Treason and Plot, 2004; Class of '76, 2005; The Last Enemy, 2008; The Unloved, Zig Zag Love, 2009; Stargate Universe (series), 2009–11; Once Upon a Time, 2011–. *Films include:* Riff Raff, 1990; Silent Scream, 1990; Safe, 1993; Being Human, 1993; Priest, 1994; Go Now, 1995; Trainspotting, 1996; Carla's Song, 1996; Face, 1997; The Full Monty, 1997 (Best Actor, BAFTA, 1998); Ravenous, 1999; Plunkett & Macleane, 1999; The World is Not Enough, 1999; Angela's Ashes, 2000; The Beach, 2000; There's Only One Jimmy Grimble, 2000; To End All Wars, 2000; The 51st State, 2001; Once Upon a Time in the Midlands, 2002; Black and White, 2004; The Mighty Celt, Marilyn Hotchkiss' Ballroom Dancing and Charm School, 2005; Eragon, 2006; Flood, 2007; 28 Weeks Later, 2007; Summer, Stone of Destiny, 2008; I Know You Know, 2010; The Tournament, 2010; The Legend of Barney Thomson (also dir), 2015. Best Actor, Evening Standard Film Awards, 1998; Film Critics' Circle Awards, 1998; Bowmore Whisky, Scottish Screen Awards, 2001; Michael Elliott Awards, 2001; David Puttnam Patrons Award. *Address:* c/o Hamilton Hodell, 20 Golden Square, W1F 9JL.

CARMICHAEL, Ailsa Jane; QC (Scot.) 2008; *b* Paisley, 28 Nov. 1969; *d* of Ian Henry Buist Carmichael and Jean Cowie Carmichael (*née* Davidson); *m* 1997, Paul Barnaby (marr. diss. 2008); one *s* one *d*; *m* 2010, Pino Di Emidio; one *d*. *Educ:* Univ. of Glasgow (LLB Hons, DipLP). Admitted as Advocate, 1993; Standing Jun. Counsel to Home Dept in Scotland, 2000–08; Mem., Mental Health Tribunal Scotland, 2005–; pt-time Sheriff, 2007–; a Dep. Judge, Upper Tribunal (Admin. Appeals Chamber), 2014–. *Publications:* (with D. Auchie) The Scottish Mental Health Tribunal: practice and procedure, 2010. *Recreations:* music, cinema, literature, cooking, travel. *Address:* Parliament House, Edinburgh EH1 1RF. *T:* (0131) 226 5071, *Fax:* (0131) 225 3642. *E:* ailsa.carmichael@ampersandstable.com.

CARMICHAEL, Rt Hon. Alexander Morrison, (Rt Hon. Alistair); PC 2010; MP (Lib Dem) Orkney and Shetland, since 2001; *b* 15 July 1965; *s* of Alexander C. Carmichael and Mina Neil McKay or Carmichael; *m* 1987, Kathryn Jane Eastham; two *s*. *Educ:* Port Ellen Primary Sch.; Islay High Sch.; Aberdeen Univ. (LLB 1992; DipLP 1993). Hotel Manager

Glasgow and Orkney, 1984–89; Procurator Fiscal Depute, Crown Office, Edinburgh and Aberdeen, 1993–96; solicitor in private practice, Aberdeen and Macduff, 1996–2001. Comptroller of HM Household (Dep. Chief Whip), 2010–13; Sec. of State for Scotland, 2013–15. *Recreations:* music, theatre. *Address:* House of Commons, SW1A 0AA. *T:* (020) 7219 8181; The Old Manse, Evie, Orkney KW17 2PH. *T:* (01856) 751343.

CARMICHAEL, Sir David Peter William G. C.; *see* Gibson-Craig-Carmichael.

CARMICHAEL, (Katharine) Jane, (Mrs A. Craxton); Director of Collections, National Museums Scotland, 2003–15; *b* 12 March 1952; *d* of Donald and Margaret Carmichael; *m* 1989, Adrian Craxton; two *d*, and one step *s* two step *d*. *Educ:* St Leonard's, St Andrews; Edinburgh Univ. (MA Modern Hist.). Imperial War Museum, 1974–2003: Keeper, Photographic Archive, 1982–95; Dir of Collections, 1995–2003. Served various cttees of Nat. Museums Dirs Conf., 1995–. FRSA 2000; FSAScot 2011. *Publications:* First World War Photographers, 1989; contrib. various jl articles. *Recreations:* the family, country walking, going to the ballet. *Address:* 7 Otterburn Park, Edinburgh EH14 1JX.

CARMICHAEL, Keith Stanley, CBE 1981; FCA, FRICS; chartered accountant in practice, 1969–81 and since 1990; *b* 5 Oct. 1929; *s* of Stanley and Ruby Dorothy Carmichael; *m* 1958, Cynthia Mary (née Jones); one *s*. *Educ:* Charlton House Sch.; Bristol Grammar Sch.; qualified as Chartered Accountant, 1951; FTII 1961, FCA 1961. FRICS 2010. Partner, Wilson Bigg & Co., 1957–69; Man. Partner, Longcrofts, 1981–90. Director: H. Foulks Lynch & Co. Ltd, 1957–69; Radio Rentals Ltd, 1967–69. Member: Monopolies and Mergers Commn, 1983–92; Soc. of Trust and Estate Practitioners, 1996–. Founder Mem., Soc. of Share and Business Valuers, 1995–. Lloyd's Underwriter, 1976–90. Pres., Hertsmere Cons. Assoc., until 2012. Chm. Bd of Governors, Royal Masonic Sch. for Girls (formerly Rickmansworth Masonic Sch.), 1984–2010, Pres., 2010– (Trustee, RMIG Endowment Trust, 1984–2013). Freeman, City of London, 1960. FInstD. Mem., Editl Bd, Simon's Taxes, 1970–82. CStJ 2001. *Publications:* Spicer and Pegler's Income Tax (ed), 1965; Corporation Tax, 1966; Capital Gains Tax, 1968; Ranking Spicer and Pegler's Executorship Law and Accounts (ed), 1969, 1987; (with P. Wolstenholme) Taxation of Lloyd's Underwriters, 1980, 4th edn 1993. *Recreations:* gardening, reading, golf. *Address:* 117 Newberries Avenue, Radlett, Herts WD7 7EN. *T:* (01923) 855098. *Clubs:* Carlton (Dep. Chm., 1989–95; Trustee, 1999–), MCC, Lord's Taverners.

CARMICHAEL, (William) Neil; MP (C) Stroud, since 2010; *b* Northumberland, 15 April 1961; *m* 1995, Laurence Jagodzinski; one *s* two *d*. *Educ:* St Peter's Sch., York; Nottingham Univ. (BA Politics 1982). Farmer, 1982–2001; land mgt, 2001–; Business Consultant, 2001–10. Vis. Lectr in British Political Hist. and Rural Econs in Europe, Sunderland and De Montfort Univs, 1996–99. Mem. (C) Northumberland CC, 1989–93. Contested (C): Leeds E, 1992; Stroud, 2001, 2005. Member: Educn Select Cttee, 2010– (Chm., 2015–); Envmtl Select Cttee, 2010–15. Chair: All-Party Parly Gp for Educn Leadership and Governance, 2011–; All-Party Parly Gp for Vascular Disease, 2012–; Sec., All-Party Health Gp, 2010–. Chair, Cons. Europe Gp, 2014–. Dir, Modern Europe, 2013–. Chm., Northumbria Daybreak, 1992–99. Chm. Govs, Marling Sch., 2008–09; Governor: Kirkley Hall Coll. of Agric., 1989–93; Stroud Coll., 2001–10 (Vice-Chm., 2007–08). *Address:* House of Commons, SW1A 0AA.

CARNAC, Sir Jonathan James R.; *see* Rivett-Carnac.

CARNALL, Dame Ruth, DBE 2011 (CBE 2004); Managing Partner, Carnall Farrar, consultancy; *b* 26 July 1956; *d* of Alan and Joan Taylor; *m* 1988, Colin Carnall; two *s*. *Educ:* Henley Coll. of Mgt (MBA). ACMA 1980; CPFA (IPFA 1984); IHSM 1988. Various posts in finance, St Thomas' Hosp., 1977–87; Dir of Finance, Hastings HA, 1987–89; Unit Gen. Manager, Hastings Acute Hosps, 1989–90; Dist Gen. Manager, then Chief Exec., Hastings and Rother HA, then NHS Trust, 1990–92; Dir of Perf. Mgt, 1992–93, Actg Regl Gen. Manager, 1993–94, SE Thames RHA; Chief Exec., W Kent HA, 1994–2000; Department of Health: Regl Dir, SE, NHS Exec., 2000–02; Regl Dir of Health and Social Care (S), 2002; Dir, Change Mgt Prog., 2003–04; freelance consultant to Govt depts and NHS, 2004–06; Interim Chief Exec., 2006–07, Chief Exec., 2007–13, Strategic Health Authy for London (NHS London). Non-exec. Dir, Care UK plc, 2004–06. *Recreations:* family, cooking, sport. *Address:* Eversleigh, London Road, Westerham, Kent TN16 1DP. *T:* (01959) 561211, *Fax:* (01959) 563999.

CARNARVON, 8th Earl of, *cr* 1793; **George Reginald Oliver Molyneux Herbert;** Baron Porchester 1780; sole trader, Porchester Farms, since 2002; Partner, Highclere Enterprises LLP, since 2002; *b* 10 Nov. 1956; *er s* of 7th Earl of Carnarvon, KCVO, KBE; *S* father, 2001; *m* 1st, 1989, Jayne (marr. diss. 1997), *d* of K. A. Wilby, Cheshire; one *s* one *d*; 2nd, 1999, Fiona, *e d* of late R. Aitken; one *s*. *Educ:* St John's Coll., Oxford (BA). A Page of Honour to the Queen, 1969–73. Set up Highclere Castle commercial business, 1988. Founder shareholder, Telecom Express, 1992–97; Founder and Dir, Digital People, 1995–98. Chm., Corn Exchange Trust Arts Centre, Newbury, 2007–12; Regl Chm., Thames and Chilterns Area HHA, 2009–; Patron: Greenham Common Trust, Newbury, 1997–; Little Stars Children's Charity, 2006–; Langa Langa Scholarship Fund, Kenya, 2009–. Pres., Southern Counties Show, 2011. *Heir:* *s* Lord Porchester, *qv*. *Address:* The Field House, Highclere Park, Newbury RG20 9RN. *Club:* White's.

CARNE, Dr Stuart John, CBE 1986 (OBE 1977); FRCGP; Senior Partner, Grove Health Centre, 1967–91; *b* 19 June 1926; *s* of late Bernard Carne and Millicent Carne; *m* 1951, Yolande (*née* Cooper); two *s* two *d*. *Educ:* Willesden County Grammar Sch.; Middlesex Hosp. Med. Sch. MB BS; MRCS; LRCP; DCH. House Surgeon, Middlesex Hosp., 1950–51; House Physician, House Surgeon and Casualty Officer, Queen Elizabeth Hosp. for Children, 1951–52; Flight Lieut, Med. Branch, RAF, 1952–54; general practice in London, 1954–99; Sen. Tutor in General Practice, RPMS, 1970–91. DHSS appointments: Chm., Standing Med. Adv. Cttee, 1982–86 (Mem., 1974–86); Member: Central Health Services Council, 1976–79; Children's Cttee, 1978–81; Personal Social Services Council, 1976–80; Chm., Jt Cttee on Contraception, 1983–86 (Mem., 1975–86). Hon. Civil Consultant in Gen. Practice to RAF, 1974–. Royal College of General Practitioners: Mem. Council, 1961–91; Hon. Treasurer, 1964–81; Pres., 1988–91; Royal Society of Medicine: President: Section of General Practice, 1973–74; United Services Sect., 1985–87; Mem. Council, World Orgn of Nat. Colls and Acads of Gen. Practice and Family Medicine, 1970–80 (Pres., 1976–78); Hon. Treas., ASME, 1972–75; Mem. Exec. Council, British Diabetic Assoc., 1981–87. Examr in medicine, Soc. of Apothecaries, 1980–88. Chm., St Mary Abbots Court Ltd, 1981–2004. Hon. MO, 1959–89, Vice-Pres., 1989–96, Queens Park Rangers FC. Hon. Fellow, Royal NZ Coll. of GPs, 1989; Hon. FRCPCH 1996; Hon. Mem., BPA, 1982. *Publications:* Paediatric Care, 1976; (jtly) DHSS Handbook on Contraceptive Practice, 3rd edn 1984, 4th edn 1988; numerous articles in Lancet, BMJ and other jls. *Recreations:* music, theatre, philately. *Address:* 5 St Mary Abbots Court, Warwick Gardens, W14 8RA. *T:* (020) 7602 1970. *E:* stuart@stuartcarne.com.

CARNEGIE, family name of **Duke of Fife**.

CARNEGIE, Sir Roderick (Howard), AC 2003; Kt 1978; FTS; Executive Chairman, Pacific Edge Holdings Pty Ltd, since 1997; *b* 27 Nov. 1932; *s* of late Douglas H. Carnegie and Margaret F. Carnegie, AO; *m* 1959, Carmen (*d* 2008), *d* of W. J. T. Clarke; three *s*. *Educ:* Geelong Church of England Grammar Sch.; Trinity Coll., Univ. of Melbourne (BSc 1954; Hon. Fellow, 1981); New Coll., Oxford Univ. (MA; Dip. Agricl Econs 1957); Harvard Business Sch., Boston (MBA 1959). FTSE (FTS 1985). McKinsey & Co., New York, 1958–70: Principal, 1964–68, Director, 1967–70; Exec. Dir, 1970–72, Man. Dir and Chief Exec., 1972–74, Chm. and Chief Exec., 1974–86, CRA Ltd; Chairman: Hudson Conway Ltd, 1987–2000; GIO Australia Hldgs Ltd, 1992–94; Newcrest Mining Ltd, 1993–98; Adacel Technologies Ltd, 1997–2003; World Competitive Practices Pty Ltd, 1997–2001; Director: ANZ Banking Gp, 1986–90; ANZ Executors & Trustee Co., 1990–92; John Fairfax Holdings, 1992–2004; Lexmark Internat. Inc., USA, 1994–98; Lexmark Internat. Gp Inc., 1994–98; AUSI Ltd, 1994–2002. Member: Internat. Council, J P Morgan & Co., 1986–95; Asia-Pacific Bd, IBM Corp., 1988–89; Internat. Adv. Bd, Internat. Finance Corp., 1991–92; Internat. Adv. Bd, World Bank, 1991–94. Director: Aust. Mining Industry Council, 1974 (a Sen. Vice-Pres., 1985); Macfarlane Burnet Centre for Med. Res., 1997–2000; Member: General Motors Aust. Adv. Council, 1979–2003; Aust.-China Council, 1979–82; Bd, CSIRO, 1986–91; Gp of Thirty, 1985–2001; Chm., Consultative Cttee on Relations with Japan, 1984–87; Chm., WA Energy Rev. Bd, 1992–93; President: German-Aust. Chamber of Industry and Commerce, 1985; Business Council of Aust., 1987–88; Consultant, Aust. Wool Corp., 1989–90; Patron, Australian Centre for Blood Diseases. Chm., Adv. Bd, Salvation Army, 1991–96 (Mem., 1990–91). Hon. DSc Newcastle, 1985; Hon. LLD Monash, 2011. Centenary Medal, Australia, 2003. Comdr's Cross, Order of Merit (Germany), 1991. *Recreation:* reading. *Address:* Pacific Edge Holdings Pty Ltd, PO Box 7458, St Kilda Road, Melbourne, Vic 8004, Australia. *Clubs:* Melbourne (Vic); Australia (Vic and NSW); Harvard (New York).

CARNEGIE-BROWN, Bruce Neil; DL; Chairman: Aon UK Ltd, since 2012; Moneysupermarket.com Group plc, since 2014 (non-executive Director, since 2010); *b* Freetown, Sierra Leone, 27 Dec. 1959; *s* of Neil Colin Carnegie-Brown and June Carola Carnegie-Brown (*née* Tate); *m* 1986, Jane Spaven; three *s* one *d*. *Educ:* Cheltenham Coll.; Exeter Coll., Oxford (Stapeldon Schol.; MA). Bank of America, 1981–85; J. P. Morgan, 1985–2003: Sen. Credit Officer (EMEA), 1995–97, CEO, J. P. Morgan Securities (Asia) Ltd, 1997–2000; Hd, Debt Capital Mkts (Europe and Asia), 2000–03; CEO, Marsh Ltd, 2003–06; Managing Partner, 3i Gp plc, 2007–09; non-executive Director: Close Brothers Gp plc, 2006–14; Jelf Gp plc, 2008–10; Catlin Gp Ltd, 2010–14; Santander UK plc, 2012–; Vice Chm. and lead Ind. Dir, Banco Santander SA, 2015–. Chm., IFS Sch. of Finance, 2010–11. Trustee: Shakespeare's Globe Trust, 2007–; Historic Royal Palaces Trust, 2014–. Freeman, City of London, 1989. DL Greater London, 2015. FCIB 2004. *Recreations:* theatre, golf, skiing, tennis. *Address:* Aon UK Ltd, 8 Devonshire Square, EC2M 4PL. *Clubs:* MCC; Roehampton; Walton Heath Golf.

CARNEGY, family name of **Earl of Northesk**.

CARNELL, Rev. Canon Geoffrey Gordon; Chaplain to the Queen, 1981–88; Non-Residentiary Canon of Peterborough Cathedral, 1965–85, Canon Emeritus since 1985; *b* 5 July 1918; *m* 1945, Mary Elizabeth Boucher Smith (*d* 2008); two *s*. *Educ:* City of Norwich Sch.; St John's Coll., Cambridge (Scholar, 1937; BA 1940; Naden Divinity Student, 1940; Lightfoot Scholar, 1940; MA 1944); Cuddesdon Coll., Oxford. Ordained deacon, Peterborough Cathedral, 1942; priest, 1943. Asst Curate, Abington, Northampton, 1942–49; Chaplain and Lectr in Divinity, St Gabriel's Coll., Camberwell, 1949–53; Rector of Isham with Great and Little Harrowden, Northants, 1953–71; Rector of Boughton, Northampton, 1971–85. Examining Chaplain to Bishop of Peterborough, 1962–86; Dir, Post-Ordination Trng and Ordinands, 1962–86; Peterborough Diocesan Librarian, Ecton House Diocesan Centre, 1967–93. Chaplain: to High Sheriff of Northants, 1972–73; to Mayor of Kettering, 1988–89. Member: Ecclesiastical History Soc., 1979–; Church of England Record Soc., 1992–; Acting Vice-Chm., Northants Record Soc., 1982–89 (Hon. Life Mem., 2012). *Publications:* The Bishops of Peterborough 1541–1991, 1993. *Recreations:* walking, music, art history, local history.

CARNELLEY, Ven. Desmond; Archdeacon of Doncaster, 1985–94, now Archdeacon Emeritus; *b* 28 Nov. 1929; *m* 1st, 1954, Dorothy Frith (*d* 1986); three *s* one *d*; 2nd, 1988, Marjorie Freeman. *Educ:* St John's Coll., York; St Luke's Coll., Exeter; William Temple Coll., Rugby; Ripon Hall, Oxford; BA (Open Univ.); Univ. of Wales, Cardiff (LLM Canon Law, 2002); Cert. Ed. (Leeds); Cert. Rel. Ed. (Exon). Curate of Aston, 1960–63; Priest-in-charge, St Paul, Ecclesfield, 1963–67; Vicar of Balby, Doncaster, 1967–72; Priest-in-charge, Mosborough, 1973; Vicar of Mosborough, 1974–85; RD of Attercliffe, 1979–84; acting Dir of Educn, dio. of Sheffield, 1991–92. *Recreations:* reading, theatre, walking, gardening. *Address:* 11 Fairways, Wickersley, Rotherham S66 1AE. *T:* (01709) 544927.

CARNEY, Mark Joseph, OC 2014; Governor, Bank of England, since 2013; *b* Fort Smith, NWT, 16 March 1965; *s* of Robert and Verlie Carney; *m* 1995, Diana, *d* of Christopher Fox; four *d*. *Educ:* Harvard Univ. (BA Econs 1988); St Peter's Coll., Oxford (MPhil Econs 1993); Nuffield Coll., Oxford (DPhil Econs 1995). With Goldman Sachs, London, Tokyo, NY and Toronto, 1990–2003; Dep. Gov., Bank of Canada, 2003–04; Sen. Associate Dep. Minister of Finance, Canada, 2004–08; Gov., Bank of Canada, 2008–13; Bank of England: Chairman: Monetary Policy Cttee, 2013–; Financial Policy Cttee, 2013–. Chm. Bd, Prudential Regulation Authy, 2013–. Chairman: Cttee on Global Financial Systems, Bank for Internat. Settlements, 2010–12; Financial Stability Bd, 2011–14. Member: Gp of Thirty; Foundn Bd, WEF. Hon. LLD Manitoba, 2013. *Address:* Bank of England, Threadneedle Street, EC2R 8AH.

CARNEY, Michael; Secretary, Water Services Association (formerly Water Authorities Association), 1987–92; *b* 19 Oct. 1937; *s* of Bernard Patrick Carney and Gwyneth (*née* Ellis); *m* 1963, Mary Patricia (*née* Davies) (marr. diss. 2000); two *s* one *d*. *Educ:* University College of North Wales, Bangor (BA). Administrative Officer, NCB, 1962–65; Staff Officer to Dep. Chm., NCB, 1965–68; Electricity Council: Administrative Officer, 1968–71; Asst Sec. (Establishments), 1971–74; Sec., S Western Region, CEGB, 1974–80, Personnel Man., Midlands Region, 1980–82; Personnel Dir, Oxfam, 1982–87. *Publications:* Britain in Pictures: a history and bibliography, 1995; Stoker: the life of Hilda Matheson, OBE, 1888–1940, 1999. *Recreations:* reading, book collecting, music, theatre. *Address:* Apartment 143 Ulysses, 50 Sherborne Street, Birmingham B16 8FN. *T:* (0121) 454 9323. *E:* carney877@btinternet.com.

CARNLEY, Rt Rev. Peter Frederick, AC 2007 (AO 1998); PhD; Archbishop of Perth and Metropolitan of Western Australia, 1981–2005; Primate of Australia, 2000–05; *b* 17 Oct. 1937; *s* of Frederick Carnley and Gweyenneth Lilian Carnley (*née* Read); *m* 1966, Carol Ann Dunstan; one *s* one *d*. *Educ:* St John's Coll., Morpeth, NSW; Australian Coll. of Theol. (ThL 1st Cl., 1962); Univ. of Melbourne (BA, 1st Cl. Hons, 1966); Univ. of Cambridge (PhD 1970). Deacon 1962, priest 1964, Bath; Licence to Officiate, dio. Melbourne, 1963–65; Asst Curate of Parkes, 1966; Licence to Officiate, dio. Ely, 1966–69; Chaplain, Mitchell Coll. of Advanced Education, Bath, 1970–72; Research Fellow, St John's Coll., Cambridge, 1971–72 (Hon. Fellow, 2000); Warden, St John's College, St Lucia, Queensland, 1973–81; Residentiary Canon, St John's Cathedral, Brisbane, 1975–81; Examining Chaplain to Archbishop of Brisbane, 1975–81. Adjunct Prof. of Theol., Murdoch Univ., 2004–; Vis. Prof. of Systematic Theol., Gen. Theol Seminary, NY, 2010–. Co-Chm., ARCIC, 2003–09. Hon. Fellow: Trinity Coll., Univ. of Melbourne, 2000; Emmanuel Coll., Cambridge, 2006. DD *hc* Gen. Theological Seminary, NY, 1984; Hon. DLitt: Newcastle, 2000; W Australia, 2000; Queensland, 2002; DUniv Charles Sturt, 2001; Hon. Dr Sacred Theol. Melbourne Coll. of Divinity, 2004. ChStJ 1982 (Sub Prelate, 1991). *Publications:* The Structure of Resurrection Belief, 1987; The Yellow Wallpaper and Other Sermons, 2001; 'Friendship' in Faithfulness in Fellowship: reflections on homosexuality and the church, 2001; Reflections in Glass: trends and tensions in the Anglican church of Australia, 2004. *Recreations:* gardening, swimming. *Address:* PO Box 221, Nannup, WA 6275, Australia. *Clubs:* Weld (Perth); St John's (Brisbane).

CARNOCK, 5th Baron *cr* 1916, of Carnock; **Adam Nicolson,** FRSL, FSAScot, FSA; Bt (NS) of that Ilk and Lasswade 1629, of Carnock 1637; author; *b* Bransgore, Hants, 12 Sept. 1957; *o s* of Nigel Nicolson, OBE, author, and Philippa Janet, *d* of Sir (Eustace) Gervais Tennyson-d'Eyncourt, 2nd Bt; *S* cousin, 2008; *m* 1st, 1982, Olivia Mary Rokeby Fane (marr. diss. 1992); three *s*; 2nd, 1992, Sarah Clare Raven; two *d*. *Educ:* Eton Coll.; Magdalene Coll., Cambridge (BA 1979; MA 1983). FRSL 2005; FSAScot 2006; FSA 2010. Journalist, Sunday Times, 1985–95; Columnist: Sunday Telegraph, 1995–2000; Daily Telegraph, 2000–06; Presenter: Atlantic Britain (series), C4, 2004; Sissinghurst (series), BBC TV, 2009; When God Spoke English, BBC TV, 2011; The Century that Wrote Itself, BBC TV, 2012; Britain's Whale Hunters, BBC TV, 2014. Director: Toucan Books, 1986–; Sarah Raven's Cutting Garden, 1996–. Trustee, Land Trust, 2008–. *Publications:* The National Trust Book of Long Walks, 1981; Long Walks in France, 1983; Frontiers (Somerset Maugham Award), 1985; (with Nigel Nicolson) Two Roads to Dodge City, 1986; Wetland (PBFA Topography Prize), 1987; Prospects of England, 1990; Restoration: the rebuilding of Windsor Castle, 1997; Regeneration: the story of the Dome, 1999; Perch Hill: a new life, 2000; Mrs Kipling, 2001; Sea Room, 2001; Power and Glory (W. H. Heinemann Prize; US edn as God's Secretaries), 2003; Seamanship, 2004; Men of Honour (US edn as Seize the Fire), 2005; Earls of Paradise (US edn as Quarrel with the King), 2008, rev. edn as Arcadia: the dream of perfection in Renaissance England, 2009; Sissinghurst: an unfinished history, 2008 (Ondaatje Prize, 2009); (with Sir Eric Anderson) About Eton, 2010; The Smell of Summer Grass, 2011; The Gentry, 2011; The Mighty Dead, 2014. *Recreations:* walking, sailing. *Heir: s* Hon. Thomas Nicolson, *b* 5 March 1984. *Address:* Perch Hill Farm, Brightling, Robertsbridge, E Sussex TN32 5HP. *E:* adam@shiantisles.net.

See also J. Nicolson.

CARNWATH OF NOTTING HILL, Rt Hon. Lord; Robert John Anderson Carnwath, Kt 1994; CVO 1995; PC 2002; a Justice of the Supreme Court of the United Kingdom, since 2012; *b* 15 March 1945; *s* of Sir Andrew Carnwath, KCVO; *m* 1974, Bambina D'Adda. *Educ:* Eton; Trinity Coll., Cambridge (MA, LLB; Hon. Fellow 2013). Called to the Bar, Middle Temple, 1968, Bencher 1991; QC 1985. Junior Counsel to Inland Revenue, 1980–85; Attorney Gen. to the Prince of Wales, 1988–94; a Judge of the High Court, Chancery Div., 1994–2002; a Lord Justice of Appeal, 2002–12; Chm., Law Commn, 1999–2002; Sen. Pres. of Tribunals, 2004–12. Jt Founder and Sec. Gen., EU Forum of Judges for Envmt, 2004–05; Mem., UNEP Internat. Adv. Cttee on Envmtl Justice, 2012–. Chairman: Shepherds Bush Housing Assoc., 1988–93; Administrative Law Bar Assoc., 1993–94; Tabernacle Trust, 1996–99. Pres., UK Envmtl Law Assoc., 2006–. Governor, RAM, 1989–2002 (Hon. Fellow 1994). Trustee, 1996–, Chm., 2001–09, Britten-Pears Foundn. *Publications:* Knight's Guide to Homeless Persons Act, 1977; (with Rt Hon. Sir Frederick Corfield) Compulsory Acquisition and Compensation, 1978; Enforcing Planning Control (report commnd for DoE), 1989; various legal texts and reports on envmtl and local govt law. *Recreations:* viola, singing (Bach Choir), tennis, golf, etc. *Address:* Supreme Court of the United Kingdom, Parliament Square, SW1P 3BD.

See also F. A. A. Carnwath.

CARNWATH, Dame Alison (Jane), DBE 2014; Senior Advisor, Evercore Partners, since 2010; Chairman, Land Securities plc, since 2008 (non-executive Director, 2004–08); *b* 18 Jan. 1953; *d* of Kenneth and Lois Tresise; partner, Peter Thomson. *Educ:* Howell's Sch., Denbigh; Univ. of Reading (BA Econ/German 1975). ACA 1979. Peat Marwick Mitchell, later KPMG, 1975–79; J. Henry Schroder Wagg, 1983–93; Phoenix Partnership, 1993–97; Donaldson Lufkin Jenrette, 1997–2000. Chm., Isis Private Equity, 2005–; non-executive Director: Man Group plc, 2001–13; Paccar Inc., 2005–; Barclays plc, 2010–12; Ind. Dir, Zurich Insce Gp, 2011–; Mem. Supervisory Bd, BASF SE, 2014–. Trustee, BL, 2013–. Mem. Adv. Council, St George's Society of New York, 2013–. FRSA. Hon DLaws Reading, 2010. *Recreations:* food and wine, ski-ing, music. *Address:* Evercore Partners, 15 Stanhope Gate, W1K 1LN.

CARNWATH, Francis Anthony Armstrong, CBE 1997; Director, Greenwich Foundation for the Royal Naval College, 1997–2002; *b* 26 May 1940; *s* of Sir Andrew Hunter Carnwath, KCVO, DL and Kathleen Marianne (*née* Armstrong); *m* 1975, Penelope Clare Rose (separated); one *s* one *d* (and one *d* decd). *Educ:* Eton (Oppidan Schol.); Cambridge (BA Econs). With Baring Brothers & Co., 1962–89: postings to S Africa, 1965–66, USA, 1969, France, 1972–73; Chief Exec. and Dir, Pertanian Baring Sanwa Multinational, Malaysia, 1977–79; Dir, 1979–89; Chm., Ravensbourne Registration Services Ltd, 1981–89. Dep. Dir, Tate Gall., 1990–94; Actg Dir, 1995, Advr, 1996–97, Nat. Heritage Meml Fund/Heritage Lottery Fund. English Heritage: Mem., London Adv. Cttee, 1990–99; Chm., Commemorative Plaques Panel, 1995–2002. Trustee and later Dep. Chm., Shelter, 1968–76; Treas., VSO, 1979–84. Chairman: Musgrave Kinley Outsider Trust, 1999–2011; Spitalfields Historic Buildings Trust, 1984–2000; Thames 21, 2003–; Architectural Panel, NT, 2004–12; Trustee: Phillimore Estates, 1983– (Chm., 1992–); Whitechapel Art Gall., 1994–2000 (Dep. Chm., 1996–2000); Royal Armouries, 2000–07; Spitalfields Fest., 2003–10; Yorkshire Sculpture Park, 2003–12 (Chm., 2004–12). Musicians' Co.: Master, 1995–96; Treas., 1993–97; Chm., various cttees, 1993–08. Hon. FTCL 2002; Hon. RCM 2003. *Recreations:* music, the arts, walking. *Address:* 31 Crag Path, Aldeburgh, Suffolk IP15 5BS. *Clubs:* Garrick, Beefsteak.

See also Rt Hon. Lord Carnwath of Notting Hill.

CARNWATH, Robert John Anderson; *see* Carnwath of Notting Hill, Rt Hon. Lord.

CAROE, Oliver Bragg, RIBA; Director: Caroe Architecture Ltd, since 2009; Cambridge Architectural Research Ltd, since 2009; Cathedral Architect, Ripon Cathedral, since 2010; Surveyor to the Fabric, St Paul's Cathedral, since 2012; *b* London, 24 Aug. 1968; *s* of Martin Caroe and Mary Caroe (*née* Roskill); *m* 1998, Carole Mills; two *d*. *Educ:* Winchester Coll.; Trinity Coll., Cambridge (BA; DipArch). RIBA 1995; AABC 2008. Tim Ronalds Architects, 1994–98; Caroe & Partners, 1998–2003 (Associate, 2001–03); Purcell, Miller, Tritton, 2003–09 (Partner, 2006–09). Member: Church Bldg Council, 2000–; Design and Conservation Panel, Cambridge City Council, 2002–; Founder Mem., Shrinking the Footprint Steering Gp, 2002–. Brother, Art Workers' Guild. *Recreations:* sculling, cycling, sailing. *Address:* Caroe Architecture Ltd, Office 5, Unit 8, 23–25 Gwydir Street, Cambridge CB1 2LG. *E:* info@caroe.biz.

CAROL, Sister; *see* Griese, Sister Carol.

CAROLIN, Prof. Peter Burns, CBE 2000; ARIBA; Professor and Head of Department of Architecture, University of Cambridge, 1989–2000, now Professor Emeritus, and Fellow of Corpus Christi College, since 1989; *b* 11 Sept. 1936; *s* of late Joseph Sinclair Carolin and Jean Bell Carolin (*née* Burns); *m* 1964, Anne-Birgit Warning; three *d*. *Educ:* Radley Coll.; Corpus Christi Coll., Cambridge (MA); University Coll. London (MA Architecture). Served RNR, Lieut, 1955–61. Asst to John Voelcker, 1960–63; Architect: with Colin St John Wilson, 1965–70 (Biochemistry Laboratory, Babraham); with Sir John Burnet, Tait and Partners, 1970–71; Associate, 1971–73, and Partner, 1973–80, Colin St John Wilson and Partners (British Library, and Dunbar Cooperage housing, Haringey); Partner, Cambridge Design, 1980–81; Technical Ed., 1981–84, Editor, 1984–89, Architects' Jl. Syndic, Fitzwilliam Mus., Cambridge, 1990–2001; Chairman: Cambridge Futures, 1997–2001; Fitzwilliam Mus. Enterprises, 1998–2001. Chm., Cambridge Design and Conservation Panel, 2006–10; Co-dir, 2030 Vision, Cambridge sub-region, 2011–13. Co-founder, Facilities Newsletter, 1983; Chm. Editl Bd, and Editor, arq (Architectural Res. Qly), 1995–2004. Magazine of Year Award (jtly), 1985; (jtly) numerous publishing awards, 1985–87; (jtly) Award for Innovation in Local Planning, RTPI, 2000; (jtly) Award for Learned Jls, ALPSP/Charlesworth, 2002. *Publications:* articles in professional jls. *Address:* Orchard End, 15E Grange Road, Cambridge CB3 9AS. *T:* (01223) 352723. *E:* pc207@cam.ac.uk.

CARON, Leslie (Claire Margaret); film and stage actress; *b* 1 July 1931; *d* of Claude Caron and Margaret Caron (*née* Petit); *m* 1st, 1951, George Hormel (marr. diss.); 2nd, 1956, Peter Reginald Frederick Hall (marr. diss. 1965); one *s* one *d*; 3rd, 1969, Michael Laughlin (marr. diss.). *Educ:* Convent of the Assumption, Paris. With Ballet des Champs Elysées, 1947–50, Ballet de Paris, 1954. *Films:* American in Paris, 1950; The Man With a Cloak, 1951; Lili, Story of Three Loves, 1953; Glory Alley, The Glass Slipper, 1954; Daddy Long Legs, 1955; Gaby, 1956; Gigi, The Doctor's Dilemma, 1958; The Man Who Understood Women, 1959; The Subterraneans, Austerlitz, 1960; Fanny, 1961; The L-Shaped Room, 1962; Guns of Darkness, 1963; Father Goose, A Very Special Favour, 1964; Les Quatres Vérités, Is Paris Burning?, 1965; Promise Her Anything, 1966; Head of the Family, 1968; Madron, 1970; Chandler, 1971; QB VII; Valentino, Sérail, 1975; L'homme qui aimait les femmes, 1976; Goldengirl, 1978; Tous Vedettes, 1979; The Contract, 1980; Impératif, 1981; The Unapproachable, 1982; La Diagonale du Fou, 1983; Le Génie du Faux, 1984; Le Train de Lenine, 1987; Courage Mountain, Guerriers et Captives, 1988; Master of the Game; Damage, 1992; Funny Bones, Let it be Me, 1994; The Ring, 1995; The Reef, 1996; The Last of the Blonde Bombshells, 1999; Chocolat, 2001; Crime on the Orient Express, 2001; Le Divorce, 2003. *Plays:* Orvet, Paris, 1955; La Sauvage (TV), England; Gigi, (title rôle), New Th., 1956; 13 rue de l'Amour, USA and Australia; Ondine (title rôle), RSC, Aldwych, 1961; Carola (TV), USA; The Rehearsal, UK tour, 1983; On Your Toes, US tour, 1984; One for the Tango, USA tour, 1985; L'Inaccessible, Paris, 1985; George Sand, Greenwich Fest., 1995; Nocturne for Lovers, Chichester, 1997; A Little Night Music, Théâtre du Châtelet, 2010. *Musical:* Grand Hotel, Berlin, 1991. *Television:* Tales of the Unexpected, 1982; Law & Order: Special Victims Unit, 2006. *Publications:* Vengeance (short stories), 1982; Thank Heaven (autobiog.), 2009. *Recreation:* collecting antiques. *Address:* c/o Maureen Vincent, United Agents, 12–26 Lexington Street, W1F 0LE.

CARPANINI, Prof. David Lawrence, RE 1982 (ARE 1979); RWA 1983 (ARWA 1977); RBA 1976; NEAC 1983; RCA 1992; painter and etcher; Professor of Art, University of Wolverhampton School of Education, 1992–2000, retired; *b* Abergwynfi, W Glam, 22 Oct. 1946; *o s* of Lorenzo and Gwenllian Carpanini; *m* 1972, Jane Allen, RWS, RBA, RWA; one *s*. *Educ:* Glanafan Grammar Sch., Port Talbot; Glos Coll. of Art & Design, Cheltenham (DipAD 1968); Royal Coll. of Art (MA 1971); Univ. of Reading (ATC 1972). Dir, Bankside Gall. Ltd, 1995–2003. Royal Society of British Artists: Hon. Treas., 1979–82; Vice-Pres., 1982–88; Mem. Council, 1993–95; Mem. Council, RWA, 1987–90; PRE, 1995–2003. Has exhibited at: RA, RBA, RWA, NEAC, Bankside Gall., Piccadilly Gall., Attic Gall., Agnews, Albany Gall., New Acad. Gall., Tegfryn; numerous one-man exhibitions, 1972–, including: Welsh Arts Council Gall., 1980; Warwick Arts Fest., 1986; Mostyn Gall., 1988; Rhondda Heritage Park, 1989, 1994; Walsall Mus., 1989; Swansea Arts Fest., 1994; Attic Gall., 1998, 2002, 2005, 2008, 2011, 2014; St David's Hall, Cardiff, 1999, 2009; Taliesin Gall., 2000; Oriel Plas Glyn-y-Weddw, Rhondda Heritage Park Gall., Pontardawe Arts Centre, 2010; Leamington Spa Mus. and Art Gall., 2014. Work in collections, including: Nat. Mus. of Wales; Contemporary Art Soc. for Wales: Nat. Liby of Wales; Newport Mus. and Art Gall.; Govt Art Collection, DoE; Fitzwilliam Mus., Cambridge; BNOC; Univ. of Wales; Ashmolean Mus., Oxford. Gov., Fedn of British Artists, 1982–86. De Lazlo Medal, RBA, 1980; Agnews Drawing Prize, NEAC, 1992; Catto Gall. Award, 1993, First Prize, Daler Rowney Award, 1995; Painter-Stainers' Co. Drawing Prize, 2012, RWS Open. Hon. RWS 1996; Hon. RBSA 2002. *Publications:* Vehicles of Pictorial Expression, 1982; numerous articles and illustrations for instructional books and art periodicals. *Recreation:* opera. *Address:* Fernlea, 145 Rugby Road, Milverton, Leamington Spa, Warwicks CV32 6DJ. *T:* (01926) 430658.

CARPENTER; *see* Boyd-Carpenter.

CARPENTER, Prof. Gary Malcolm; composer; Professor of Composition: Royal Northern College of Music, since 2001; Royal Academy of Music, since 2003; *b* Hackney, London, 13 Jan. 1951; *s* of Albert Carpenter and Dorothy Carpenter (*née* Stock); one *s* one *d*. *Educ:* Henry Maynard Jun. Sch., Walthamstow; Sir George Monoux Grammar Sch., Walthamstow; Royal Coll. of Music, London (ARCM 1972). LRAM 1969. Kapellmeister and pianist, Vereinigte Städtische Bühnen, Krefeld/Mönchengladbach, 1974–76; composer-in-residence and pianist, Nederlands Dans Theater, 1976–79; Hd, Music, London Contemporary Dance Sch., 1982–86; composer-in-residence, City of Wakefield, 1987–88; Hd, Music, Liverpool Inst. for Performing Arts, 1994–95. Associate Music Dir, The Wicker Man (film), 1973. Resident musician, King's Head Th. Club, Islington, 1973–74; Musical Associate, Extemporary Dance Th., 1983–85; Co-Dir, The Dance Band, 1985–86. Part-time teacher: Jun. Dept, RCM, 1982–84; GSMD, 1990–94; Welsh Coll. of Music and Drama, 1991–92; Lectr, Bretton Hall Coll. of Higher Educn, 1988–90; examiner: Univ. of Kent, 1984–86; Manchester Metropolitan Univ., 1996–99; Lectr (pt-time), Liverpool Hope University Coll., 1997–99. Vis. Lectr, 2001–03, Teaching Fellow, 2004–05, Liverpool Inst. for Performing Arts; Composition Tutor, Nat. Youth Orch., 2001–08. Member: RAM Club; Old Monovians Assoc. *Compositions include:* Concerto for Orchestra, The Continuing Story (ballet/orch.), 1977; Chorinho Cariñoso (alto sax and piano), Da Capo (6 players), Di Flimmerkiste (11 players), 1985; Goodnight Mister Tom (musical), 1992; Bermuda Suite and Dolphin (quintet), CHI (brass band), Love's Eternity (song cycle), Sonata for Alto Sax and Piano, Sonata for clarinet and Piano, Theatre Fountain (concert band), 1993; Antiques and Curios (wind), Flying God Suite (concert band), Missa Beata Virgine (2 a capella choirs), 1994; Pantomime (13 winds), 1995; The Lamplighter (children's choir), 1996; Sunderland Lasses and Wearmouth Lads (wind band), 1997; SATIE - Variations for Orchestra, 1998; Creepy Crawlies (piano solo), Podgy Tourers (piano solo), 2002; Secret Love Songs (trombone quartet), Time Line (17 trombones), 2003; Dioscuri (2 cellos), Doubles (concerto for oboe, clarinet and wind band), Fred and Ginger (orch.), Go-Slow (guitar quartet), Sonatinas (concerto for alto sax and orch.), Sonatinas (alto sax and piano), Songs of Sadness and Piety, 2010; Bassoon Concerto (bassoon and orch.), Horn Concerto (horn and orch.), 2011; blue (solo flute), 2012; The Food of Love, SET (concerto for tenor saxophone and orch.), Two Hart Crane Songs, 2014; Dadaville, 2015. Hon. RAM 2013. *Publications:* (contrib.) The Quest for 'The Wicker Man', 2006. *Recreations:* travel, cinema, walking, food, hang gliding, theatre, art. *Address:* c/o Royal Academy of Music, Marylebone Road, NW1 5HT. *E:* yrag@garycarpenter.net.

CARPENTER, Leslie Arthur; Chief Executive, 1982–86, Chairman, 1985–87, Reed International PLC; *b* 26 June 1927; *s* of William and Rose Carpenter; *m* 1st, 1952; one *d*; 2nd, 1989, (Elizabeth) Louise Botting, *qv*. *Educ:* Hackney Techn. Coll. Director: Country Life, 1965; George Newnes, 1966; Odhams Press Ltd (Managing), 1968; International Publishing Corp., 1972; Reed International Ltd, 1974; IPC (America) Inc., 1975; Chairman: Reed Hldgs Inc. (formerly Reed Publishing Hldgs Inc.), 1977; Reed Publishing Hldgs Ltd, 1981; Chm. and Chief Exec., IPC Ltd, 1974; Chief Exec., Publishing and Printing, Reed International Ltd, 1979. Dir, Watmoughs (Hldgs) plc, 1988–98. *Recreations:* racing, gardening. *Address:* Gable House, 75 High Street, Broadway, Worcs WR12 7AL.

CARPENTER, Louise, (Mrs L. A. Carpenter); *see* Botting, E. L.

CARPENTER, Michael Alan; Chief Executive Officer, Ally Financial Inc. (formerly GMAC Financial Services), since 2009; *b* 24 March 1947; *s* of Walter and Kathleen Carpenter; *m* 1975, Mary A. Aughton; one *s* one *d*. *Educ:* Univ. of Nottingham (BSc 1968); Harvard Business Sch. (MBA 1973). Business analyst, Mond Div., ICI, Runcorn, 1968–71; Consultant, 1973–78, Vice-Pres., 1978–83, Boston Consulting Gp; joined General Electric Co., 1983: Vice-Pres., Corporate Business Develt and Planning, 1983–86; Exec. Vice-Pres., GE Capital Corp., 1986–89; Chm., Pres. and CEO, Kidder, Peabody Gp Inc., 1989–94; Chm. and CEO, Travelers Life and Annuity Co., and Vice-Chm., Travelers Gp, Inc., 1995–98; CEO, Global Corporate Investment Bank, and Chm. and CEO, Salomon Smith Barney, 1998–2002; Chm. and CEO, Citigroup Alternative Investments, 2002–06; Chm., Southgate Alternative Investments, 2006–09. Hon. LLD Nottingham, 2003. *Address:* Ally Financial Inc., 1177 Avenue of the Americas, New York, NY 10036, USA.

CARPENTER, Michael Charles Lancaster, CB 2014; Speaker's Counsel, House of Commons, since 2008; *b* Bristol, 16 March 1949; *s* of Charles Frederick Lancaster and Margaret Florence Carpenter (*née* Richmond); *m* 1970, Susan Valerie Robinson; one *s* three *d*. *Educ:* Hampton Grammar Sch.; Keble Coll., Oxford BA Juris. 1970; MA 1982). Called to the Bar, Inner Temple, 1971; EC Commission: Adminr, Restrictive Practices and Monopolies, Directorate-Gen. for Competition, 1973–80; Prin. Adminr, Legal Service, 1980–81; Hd, Private and Internat. Law Div., Lord Chancellor's Dept, 1985–88; Dep. Legal Sec. to Law Officers, 1989–92; Hd, Cabinet Office and Central Adv. Div., Treasury Solicitor's Dept, 1993–2000; Counsel for Eur. Legislation, H of C, 2000–08. *Publications:* (with J. A. L. Sterling) Copyright Law in the United Kingdom, 1986; (contrib.) Civil Jurisdiction and Judgements in Europe, 1992. *Recreations:* ancient and modern history, making things work. *Address:* House of Commons, 7 Millbank, SW1P 3JA. *T:* (020) 7219 3776. *E:* carpenterm@parliament.uk.

CARPENTER, Michael Stephen Evans; charity consultant, since 2003; Legal Commissioner, Charity Commission, 1998–2002; *b* 7 Oct. 1942; *s* of Ernest Henry Carpenter and Eugenie Carpenter (*née* Evans); *m* 1968, Gabriel Marie Lucie Brain; one *s* one *d*. *Educ:* Eastbourne Coll.; Bristol Univ. (LLB). Admitted Solicitor, 1967; Slaughter and May, 1967–94 (Partner, 1974–94); Withers, 1994–97 (Partner, 1994–96; Consultant, 1997). Sec., Garfield Weston Foundn, 1997. Dep. Chm., Charity Trustee Network, 2005–10; Trustee, Carpenter Charitable Trust, 1981–. *Recreations:* hill-walking, golf, Scottish islands, the church.

CARR, Alan Michael; Senior Partner, Simmons & Simmons, 1992–96; *b* 1 Sept. 1936; *m* 1963, Dalia Lebhar; two *s* one *d*. *Educ:* Gresham's Sch., Holt; King's Coll., Cambridge (MA). Articled Simmons & Simmons, 1957; admitted solicitor, 1961; Partner, 1966–96. FRGS 1989. *Recreation:* travel among remote people.

CARR, Andrew Jonathan, FRCS, FMedSci; Nuffield Professor of Orthopaedic Surgery and Head, Nuffield Department of Orthopaedics, Rheumatology and Musculoskeletal Science, University of Oxford, since 2001; Fellow, Worcester College, Oxford, since 2001; *b* 18 June 1958; *s* of John Malcolm Carr and Patricia (*née* Hodgson); *m* 1985, Clare Robertson; one *s* three *d*. *Educ:* Bradford Grammar Sch.; Bristol Univ. (MB ChB 1982; ChM 1989). FRCS 1986; FMedSci 2009. House surgeon and physician, 1982–83, anatomy demonstrator, 1983–84, Bristol Univ.; Surgical Lectr, Sheffield Univ., 1984–85; Metabolic Medicine Res. Fellow, Univ. of Oxford, 1985–87; Orthopaedic Registrar and Sen. Registrar, Nuffield Orthopaedic Centre and John Radcliffe Hosp., Oxford, 1988–92; Consultant Orthopaedic Surgeon, Nuffield Orthopaedic Centre, Oxford, 1993–2001. Research Fellow: Seattle, 1992; Melbourne, 1992; Hunterian Prof., RCS, 2000; Visiting Professor: Chinese Univ. of Hong Kong, 2004; Nat. Univ. of Singapore, 2005. Trustee: Arthritis Res. Campaign, 2004–11; Jean Shanks Foundn, 2006–. Assoc. Ed., Jl of Bone and Joint Surgery, 2003–08. Robert Jones Gold Medallist and British Orthopaedic Assoc. Prize Winner, 2000. *Publications:* (jtly) Outcomes in Orthopaedic Surgery, 1993; (jtly) Outcomes in Trauma, 1995; (jtly) Assessment Methodology in Orthopaedic Surgery, 1997; (jtly) Orthopaedics in Primary Care, 1999; (jtly) Classification in Trauma, 1999; (jtly) Oxford Textbook of Orthopaedic Surgery, 2001; contrib. to learned jls etc. on shoulder surgery, genetics and osteoarthritis, patient-reported outcomes of surgery, tissue engrg. *Recreations:* rowing, Real tennis, hill walking, cooking. *Address:* Nuffield Department of Orthopaedics, Rheumatology and Musculoskeletal Sciences, Nuffield Orthopaedic Centre NHS Trust, Oxford OX3 7LD; Worcester College, Oxford OX1 2HB. *Club:* Leander (Henley-on-Thames).

CARR, Annabel; *see* Carr, E. A.

CARR, Anthony Paul; a District Judge (Magistrates' Courts), since 2003; *b* 30 March 1952; *s* of Alexander and June Carr; *m* 1983, Hilary (*née* Taylor); one *s* one *d*. *Educ:* Stockport Grammar Sch.; Selwyn Coll., Cambridge (BA 1974, MA 1975). Called to the Bar, Middle Temple, 1976; Dep. Clerk to Peterborough Justices, 1983–87; Clerk to SW Essex Justices, 1987–2000; Dir, Legal Services, and Clerk to Essex Justices, 2000–03. Mem., Family Procedure Rule Cttee, 2008–. Trustee, Ephraim Hallam Charity. Gov., Stockport GS, 2014–. *Publications:* Criminal Procedure in Magistrates' Courts, 1982; (jtly) The Children Act in Practice, 4th edn 2008; (ed) Stone's Justices Manual, 127th edn 1995 to 147th edn 2015; (ed) Clarke Hall and Morrison on Children, 10th edn 2004. *Recreations:* reading, railways, ancient Greek. *Address:* Manchester Civil Justice Centre, 1 Bridge Street West, Manchester, Lancs M60 9DJ. *T:* (0161) 240 5000.

CARR, Prof. Antony Michael, DPhil; FMedSci; Director, Genome Damage and Stability Centre, University of Sussex, since 2001; *b* Dunfermline, 2 May 1960; *s* of Michael and Olga Carr; *m* 1991, Johanne Milne Murray; one *s* one *d*. *Educ:* Helston Comprehensive Sch.; Univ. of E Anglia (BSc Biol. 1981); Univ. of Sussex (DPhil Biochem. 1987). Postdoctoral Fellow, Univ. of Sussex, 1988–89; Mem., Scientific Staff, MRC Cell Mutation Unit, 1989–2001. Editor: Genes and Genetic Systems, 2002–; Molecular and Cellular Biol., 2007–. Mem., EMBO, 2007. FMedSci 2014. Flemming Award, Soc. of Gen. Microbiol., 1996. *Publications:* contributor: Molecular Biology for Oncologists, 1993; Hormonal Carcinogenesis II, 1996; (with J. M. Murray) Microbial Genome Methods, 1996; (with D. J. F. Griffiths) DNA Damage and Repair, 1998; (jtly) DNA Replication and Human Diseases, 2006; contribs to learned jls incl. Microbiol., Microbiol. Today, MRC News, Jl Molecular Biol., DNA Repair, Science, Biochemie, Gene, EMBO Jl, Jl Virol., Molecular and Cell Biol. *Recreations:* dinghy sailing, reading literature, walking. *Address:* Genome Damage and Stability Centre, School of Life Sciences, University of Sussex, Falmer, Brighton BN1 9RQ. *T:* (01273) 678122, *Fax:* (01273) 678123. *E:* a.m.carr@sussex.ac.uk.

CARR, Very Rev. (Arthur) Wesley, KCVO 2006; PhD; Dean of Westminster, 1997–2006; *b* 26 July 1941; *s* of Arthur and Irene Carr; *m* 1968, Natalie Gill. *Educ:* Dulwich College; Jesus Coll., Oxford (MA); Jesus Coll., Cambridge (MA); Ridley Hall, Cambridge; Univ. of Sheffield (PhD). Curate, Luton Parish Church, 1967–71; Tutor, Ridley Hall, Cambridge, 1970–71, Chaplain 1971–72; Sir Henry Stephenson Fellow, Dept of Biblical Studies, Univ. of Sheffield, 1972–74; Hon. Curate, Ranmoor, 1972–74; Chaplain, Chelmsford Cathedral, 1974–78; Dep. Director, Chelmsford Cathedral Centre for Research and Training, 1974–82; Dir of Training, Diocese of Chelmsford, 1976–82; Canon Residentiary, Chelmsford Cathedral, 1978–87; Dean of Bristol, 1987–97. Mem., Gen. Synod of C of E, 1980–87, 1989–2000. Select Preacher, Univ. of Oxford, 1984–85. Fellow, Westminster Sch., 2009. Hon. Fellow, New Coll., Edinburgh, 1986–94. Hon. DLitt: UWE, 1997; Sheffield, 2003. *Publications:* Angels and Principalities, 1977; The Priestlike Task, 1985; Brief Encounters, 1985; The Pastor as Theologian, 1989; Ministry and the Media, 1990; (with E. R. Shapiro) Lost in Familiar Places, 1991; Manifold Wisdom, 1991; (ed) Say One for Me, 1992; A Handbook of Pastoral Studies, 1997; (ed) The New Dictionary of Pastoral Studies, 2002; articles in Theology, etc. *Recreations:* music, reading, writing, gardening. *Address:* 16 Church Road, Romsey, Hants SO51 8EY. *T:* (01794) 511143.

CARR, Bennet, FRGS; Headmaster, King Edward VI School, Stratford-Upon-Avon, since 2010; *b* Bucks, 7 Dec. 1970; *s* of Francis David and Janet Mary Carr; *m* 2002, Beverley Olga Crass; two *d* (and one *d* decd). *Educ:* Queen Mary Coll., Univ. of London (BA Hons Geog. 1992); Inst. of Educn, Univ. of London (PGCE 1993); Nat. Coll. of Sch. Leadership (NPQH 2009). Teacher, 1993–97, Asst Headmaster, 1997–2002, Bishop's Stortford High Sch.; on sabbatical, travelling, 2000–01; Dep. Headmaster, St Olave's Grammar Sch., 2002–10. Trustee: Shakespeare Birthplace Trust, 2010–; Hampton Lucy Grammar Sch. Foundn, 2010–. FRGS 2010. *Recreations:* Rugby (retired), running, theatre, travel, biographies, family. *Address:* The Old Vicarage, King Edward VI School, Church Street, Stratford-Upon-Avon, Warks CV37 6HB. *T:* (01789) 293351, *Fax:* (01789) 293564. *E:* headspa@kes.net.

CARR, Bruce Conrad; QC 2009; a Recorder, since 1998; *b* Cambridge, 21 June 1960; *s* of William Ian Carr and Kathleen Ann Carr; *m* 2005, Tamara Nikolic; two *s*. *Educ:* London Sch. of Econs (BSc Econ.). Called to the Bar, Inner Temple, 1986. *Recreation:* all things Croatian. *Address:* Devereux Chambers, Queen Elizabeth Building, Temple, EC4Y 9BS. *T:* (020) 7353 7534. *E:* carr@devchambers.co.uk. *Club:* Leeds United Supporters.

CARR, Donald Bryce, OBE 1985; Secretary, Cricket Council and Test and County Cricket Board, 1974–86, retired; *b* 28 Dec. 1926; *s* of John Lillingston Carr and Constance Ruth Carr; *m* 1953, Stella Alice Vaughan Simpkinson; one *s* one *d*. *Educ:* Repton Sch.; Worcester Coll., Oxford (MA). Served Army, 1945–48 (Lieut Royal Berks Regt). Asst Sec., 1953–59, Sec., 1959–62, Derbyshire CCC; Asst Sec., MCC, 1962–74. *Recreations:* golf, following most sports. *Address:* 28 Aldenham Avenue, Radlett, Herts WD7 8HX. *T:* (01923) 855602. *Clubs:* MCC, British Sportsman's, Lord's Taverners; Vincent's, Oxford University Cricket (Oxford).

CARR, (Elizabeth) Annabel; QC 1997; **Her Honour Judge Annabel Carr;** a Circuit Judge, since 2001; Designated Family Judge for South Yorkshire, since 2008; *b* 14 Nov. 1954; *d* of William John Denys Carr and Norah Betty Carr; one *s* one *d*. *Educ:* Queenswood Sch., Hatfield; Sheffield Univ. (LLB Hons 1975). Called to the Bar, Gray's Inn, 1976; in practice at the Bar, 1977–2001; Recorder, 1995–2001. *Recreations:* travelling, family, theatre. *Address:* Sheffield Combined Court Centre, 50 West Bar, Sheffield S3 8PH.

CARR, Hon. Sir Henry (James), Kt 2015; **Hon. Mr Justice Carr;** a Judge of the High Court, Chancery Division, since 2015; *b* 31 March 1958; *s* of Malcolm Carr and Dr Sara Carr; *m* 1988, Jan Dawson; three *s* one *d*. *Educ:* Hertford Coll., Oxford (BA 1st cl. Hons Jurisp.); Univ. of British Columbia (LLM). Called to the Bar, Gray's Inn, 1982, Bencher, 2005; in practice at the Bar, 1982–2015; QC 1998; Dep. Chm., Copyright Tribunal, 2007–15; a Dep. High Ct Judge, Chancery Div., 2007–15. Chm., Council of Experts, Intellectual Property Inst. *Publications:* Computer Software: legal protection in the United Kingdom, 1987, 2nd edn (jtly) 1992. *Recreations:* tennis, swimming, theatre. *Address:* Royal Courts of Justice, Rolls Building, Fetter Lane, EC4A 1NL. *Clubs:* Royal Automobile, Hurlingham, Harbour.

CARR, His Honour Maurice Chapman; a Circuit Judge, 1986–2005; *b* 14 Aug. 1937; *s* of John and Elizabeth Carr; *m* 1959, Caryl Olson; one *s* one *d*. *Educ:* Hookergate Grammar Sch.; LSE (State Scholar; LLB); Harvard Univ. (Fulbright Scholar; Westengaard Fellow; LLM). Lectr in Law, 1960–62, Asst Prof. of Law, 1963–64, Univ. of British Columbia; Lecturer in Law: UCW, 1964–65; Univ. of Newcastle upon Tyne, 1965–69. Called to the Bar, Middle Temple, 1966; Designated Family Judge, 1990–2005. *Recreations:* walking, music.

CARR, Michael; teacher; *b* 31 Jan. 1946; *s* of James and Sheila Mary Carr; *m* 1st (wife *d* 1979); one *s*; 2nd, 1980, Georgina Clare; four *s* two *d*. *Educ:* St Joseph's Coll., Blackpool; Catholic Coll., Preston; Margaret McMillan Coll. of Educn, Bradford (CertEd); Bradford and Ilkley Community Coll. (DPSE). Engrg apprentice, 1962–63; Local Govt Officer, 1964–68; partner in family retail newsagency, 1968–70; Teacher of Geography: Brookside Sec. Sch., Middlesbrough, 1973–74; Stainsby Sch., Middlesbrough, 1974–75; Head of Geog., St Thomas Aquinas RC High Sch., Darwen, Lancs, 1975–82; Head of Gen. Studies, Blackthorn County Sec. Sch. and Blackthorn Wing of Fearns CS Sch., Bacup, 1982–87; Mem., Lancs Educn Cttee Sch. Support Team (Disruptive Behaviour), 1988–91. Mem., Sabden Parish Council, 1976–78, 1979–83; Mem. (C 1979–81, SDP 1981–83), Ribble Valley BC, 1979–83. Joined SDP, 1981; contested (SDP/Lib Alliance) Ribble Valley, 1983, 1987; MP (Lib Dem) Ribble Valley, March 1991–1992; contested (Lib Dem) Ribble Valley, 1992, 1997, 2001. Mem., NAS/UWT (Dist Sec., Rossendale Assoc., 1983–87; Press Officer, Lancs Fedn, 1983–87, 1988–90). *Recreations:* hill walking, cooking, music.

CARR, Michael Douglas; Chief Science Officer, BT, 2007–09; *b* Bletchley, 14 Sept. 1955; *s* of John Joseph Carr and Pamela Mary Carr; *m* 1981, Caroline Jane Daniels; two *d*. *Educ:* Plymouth Poly. (BScEng Hons Communication Engrg 1980). CEng, FIET 2004; FREng 2008. Joined BT as Technician Apprentice Field Engr, 1972; Researcher, Picture Compression, 1980–84, Hd, Video Conference Res. Gp, 1984–89, Gen. Manager, Video Res., 1989–94, BT Labs; Principal Advr, Multimedia, 1994–96; Hd, ICT Strategy Unit, 1996–99; Vice-Pres., Technology and Venturing USA, 1999–2001; Dir, Res. and Venturing, 2001–07. Non-exec. Dir, Ordnance Survey, 2009–. Member: Bd, EPSRC, 2008–11; Technology Strategy Bd, 2011–. Trustee and Vice-Pres., IET, 2010–13. Hon. DTech Plymouth, 2009. *Publications:* articles in jls on video comparison and video transmission. *Recreations:* woodworking, gardening, playing the piano. *E:* mike.d.carr@btinternet.com.

CARR, Peter; His Honour Judge Peter Carr; a Circuit Judge, since 2007; *b* Hamburg, 14 Nov. 1954; *s* of Derek and Anneliese Carr; *m* 1997, Julie Ann Campbell; one *d*. *Educ:* Dr Challoner's Grammar Sch., Amersham; Birmingham Univ. (LLB). Called to the Bar, Inner Temple, 1976; Recorder, 2001–07. *Recreations:* golf, bridge, cooking. *Address:* Birmingham Crown Court, 1 Newton Street, Birmingham B4 7NA. *T:* (0121) 681 3300. *Clubs:* Edgbaston Golf, Warwickshire County Cricket.

CARR, Sir Peter (Derek), Kt 2007; CBE 1989; DL; Chairman, NHS Trust Development Authority, 2012–15; *b* 12 July 1930; *s* of George William Carr and Marjorie (*née* Tailby); *m* 1958, Geraldine Pamela (*née* Ward); one *s* one *d*. *Educ:* Fircroft Coll., Birmingham; Ruskin Coll., Oxford; London Univ. National Service, RAF, 1951–53. Cabinet maker, carpenter and joiner, construction industry, 1944–51 and 1953–56; college, 1956–60; Lectr, Percival Whitley Coll., Halifax, 1960–65; Sen. Lectr in Indust. Relations, Thurrock Coll., and part-time Adviser, NBPI, 1965–69; Director: Commn on Industrial Relations, 1969–74; ACAS, 1974–78; Labour and Economic Attaché, Diplomatic Service, Washington, 1978–83; Regl Dir, Northern Regl Office, Dept of Employment, and Leader, City Action Team, 1983–89; Chm., Co. Durham Develt Co., 1990–2001. Chairman: Northern Screen Commn, 1990–2002; Northern RHA, 1990–94; Occupational Pensions Bd, 1994–97; Newcastle and N Tyne HA, 1998–2002; Northumberland Tyne and Wear Strategic HA, 2002–06; Northern Regl Assembly Health Forum, 2002–06; Northern Adv. Cttee on Clinical Excellence Awards, 2003–09; NE Strategic HA, 2006–11; Commn on Rural Health NE, 2008–11; Nat. Steering Gp on Provider Develt, NHS, 2010–12; Vice Chm., NHS N of England, 2011–12. Chairman: Durham County Waste Mgt Co., 1993–2010; Premier Waste Mgt, 1997–99; Acorn Energy Supplies Ltd, 1998–2000. Vis. Fellow, Durham Univ., 1989–99. Mem. Ct, Univ. of Newcastle, 2006–. DL Durham, 1997; Hon. DSc Sunderland, 2009; Hon. DLaws

Teesside, 2011; Hon. DCL Northumbria, 2012. Director and Editor: study for CIR, Worker Participation and Collective Bargaining in Europe, 1974; study for ACAS, Industrial Relations in National Newspaper Industry, 1976. *Publications:* It Occurred to Me, 2004; Achievement of Efficiency in Healthcare through Continuous Improvement, 2009. *Recreations:* cycling, photography, cooking, furniture-making, American history. *Address:* 4 Corchester Towers, Corbridge, Northumberland NE45 5NP. *T:* (01434) 632841. *E:* petercarr@aol.com.

CARR, Reginald Philip; Director, University Library Services, and Bodley's Librarian, University of Oxford, 1997–2006, now Bodley's Librarian Emeritus; Fellow, Balliol College, Oxford, 1997–2006; *b* 20 Feb. 1946; *s* of Philip Henry Carr and Ida Bayley Carr (*née* Wood); *m* 1968, Elizabeth Whittaker; one *s* three *d. Educ:* Manchester Grammar Sch.; Univ. of Leeds (BA 1968); Univ. of Manchester (MA 1971); MA Cantab 1983; MA Oxon 1997. English lang. teaching asst, Lycée Fontenelle, Rouen, 1966–67; Asst Librarian, John Rylands Univ. Liby, Manchester, 1970–72; Librarian-in-Charge, Sch. of Educn Liby, Univ. of Manchester, 1972–76; Sub-Librarian, Univ. of Surrey, 1976–78; Deputy Librarian: Univ. of Aston, 1978–80; Univ. of Cambridge, 1980–86; University of Leeds: Univ. Librarian and Keeper, Brotherton Collection, 1986–96; Dean, Information Strategy, 1996. Mem., Jt Information Systems Cttee, 1997–2005. Chairman: Standing Conference of Nat. and Univ. Libraries, 1994–96; Res. Libraries Gp Inc., 1999–2003. Hon. Sec., Consortium of Univ. Res. Libraries, 1991–97; Trustee, Chawton House Library, 2006–12. Hon. DLitt Leicester, 2000. Hon. Citizen, Toyota City, 1998. *Publications:* Anarchism in France: the case of Octave Mirbeau, 1977; (jtly) Spirit in the New Testament, 1985; The Mandrake Press, 1985; (jtly) An Introduction to University Library Administration, 1987; (ed) For the Study and Defence of the Holy Scripture, vol. 1, 1987, vol. 2, 2015; The Academic Research Library in a Decade of Change, 2007; Micah Study Guide, 2010; (ed) The Pen of a Ready Writer, 2010; (ed) Testimony Handbook of Bible Principles, 2010; A Goodly Heritage, 2012; contribs to professional and learned jls; contrib. Testimony mag. *Recreations:* Bible study, book collecting, editing and publishing, grandchildren. *Address:* c/o The Bodleian Library, Broad Street, Oxford OX1 3BG.

CARR, Prof. the Hon. Robert John; Senator (ALP) for New South Wales, 2012–13; Federal Minister for Foreign Affairs, 2012–13; Professor of International Relations and Director, Australia-China Relations Institute, University of Technology, Sydney, since 2014; *b* 28 Sept. 1947; *s* of Edward and Phyllis Carr; *m* 1973, Helena. *Educ:* Univ. of NSW (BA Hons). Journalist, ABC Current Affairs Radio, 1969–72; Educn Officer, Labor Council, NSW, 1972–78; journalist, The Bulletin, 1978–83. Government of New South Wales: MP (ALP) Maroubra, 1983–2005; Minister: for Planning and Envmt, 1984–88; for Consumer Affairs, 1986; for Heritage, 1986–88; Leader of the Opposition, 1988–95; Minister: for Ethnic Affairs, 1995–99; for the Arts, 1995–2005; for Citizenship, 1999–2005; Premier of NSW, 1995–2005. Mem., Internat. Climate Change Taskforce, 2004. World Conservation Union Internat. Parks Award, 1998; Fulbright Dist. Fellow Award, 1999. *Publications:* Thoughtlines: reflections of a public man, 2002; What Australia Means to Me, 2003; My Reading Life: adventures in the world of books, 2008; Diary of a Foreign Minister, 2014.

CARR, Rodney Paul, CBE 2010 (OBE 2005); yachtsman; Chairman, UK Sport, since 2013 (Member of Board, since 2005); *b* 10 March 1950; *s* of Capt. George Paul Carr and Alma Carr (*née* Walker); *m* 1971, Lynne Alison Ashwell; one *s* one *d. Educ:* Carlton le Willows Grammar Sch., Nottingham; Univ. of Birmingham (BSc Geology 1972). Chief Sailing Instructor, London Bor. of Haringey, 1972–75; Instructor, 1975–79, Chief Instructor, 1979–81, Nat. Sailing Centre, Cowes, IoW; Mem., winning British Admiral's Cup team, 1981; joined RYA, 1984; Coach, GB Olympic Team: Los Angeles, 1984; Seoul, 1988; Barcelona, 1992; Overall GB Team Manager, Atlanta Olympic Games, 1996; Racing Manager and Performance Dir, RYA, 1997–2000; Dep. Chef de Mission, GB Olympic Team, Sydney, 2000; Chief Exec., RYA, 2000–10. Member, Board: Weymouth and Portland Sailing Acad., 2008–; Outward Bound Trust, 2011–. Trustee: John Merricks Sailing Trust, 1997–; 1851 Trust, 2014–. Hon. MBA Southampton Inst., 2002. *Recreations:* played county level U19 Rugby for Nottinghamshire, keen interest in most sports, current affairs, music, long distance walking. *Address:* UK Sport, 40 Bernard Street, WC1N 1ST. *Clubs:* Hayling Island Sailing, Emsworth Slipper Sailing.

CARR, Sir Roger (Martyn), Kt 2011; Chairman, BAE SYSTEMS, since 2014; Vice Chairman, BBC Trust, since 2015; *b* 22 Dec. 1946; *s* of John and Kathleen Carr; *m* 1973, Stephanie Elizabeth; one *d. Educ:* Nottingham High Sch.; Nottingham Poly. Dir, Williams Hldgs plc, 1988–2000; Chief Exec., Williams plc, 1994–2000; Chm., Chubb plc, 2000–02. Dir, 1994–99, Chm., 1999–2000, Thames Water plc. Chm., Mitchells & Butlers, 2003–08; Sen. non-exec. Dir, 2000–03, Dep. Chm., 2003–08, Chm., 2008–10, Cadbury plc; Sen. non-exec. Dir, Six Continents (formerly Bass) plc, 1996–2003; non-exec. Dir, 2000–14, Chm., 2004–14, Centrica. Dep. Chm., Bank of England, 2011–14 (non-exec. Dir, 2007–14). Pres., CBI, 2011–13 (Mem., Council, 2001–04). Sen. Advr, Kohlberg, Kravis & Roberts & Co. Ltd, 2000–. Member: Industrial Adv. Bd, 2001–04; Prime Minister's Business Adv. Gp, 2011–15. Vis. Fellow, Oxford Univ., 2008–. CCMI (CIMgt 1997); FRSA 1996; FCIS 2013. *Recreations:* theatre, opera, golf. *Address:* BAE SYSTEMS, Stirling Square, 6 Carlton Gardens, SW1Y 5AD. *Clubs:* Brooks's, London Capital; China (Hong Kong).

CARR, Simon Andrew; His Honour Judge Simon Carr; a Circuit Judge, since 2009; *b* Stafford, 9 Aug. 1961; *s* of Brian and Pamela Carr; *m* 1990, Stephanie Farrimond. *Educ:* Perse Sch., Cambridge; Southampton Univ. (LLB). Called to the Bar, Inner Temple, 1984; Recorder, 2003–09. Trustee, Jane Goodall Inst., 1990– (Chm. of Trustees, 2011–). *Recreations:* hockey, sub-aqua diving, travel, animal conservation. *E:* HHJudgeSimonCarr@judiciary.gsi.gov.uk. *Clubs:* Spencer Hockey; Anglesey Aquanauts.

CARR, Hon. Dame Sue (Lascelles), (Hon. Dame Sue Birch), DBE 2013; **Hon. Mrs Justice Carr;** a Judge of the High Court of Justice, Queen's Bench Division, since 2013; Presiding Judge, Midland Circuit, from Jan. 2016; *b* 1 Sept. 1964; *d* of Richard Carr and Edda Harvey (*née* Armbrust); *m* 1993, Alexander Birch; two *s* one *d. Educ:* Trinity Coll., Cambridge (MA Law and Mod. Langs). Called to the Bar, Inner Temple, 1987, Bencher, 2006; QC 2003; a Recorder, 2009–13; Hd of Chambers, 2012–13. Complaints Comr to Internat. Criminal Court, The Hague, 2011–. Chm., Complaints Cttee, 2008–10; Mem., Bar Standards Bd, 2008–10. Mem., Investigatory Powers Tribunal, 2014–. Gov., Wycombe Abbey Sch., 2007–. *Publications:* (ed) Professional Liability Precedents, 2000. *Recreations:* theatre, ski-ing, tennis. *Address:* Royal Courts of Justice, Strand, WC2A 2LL.

CARR, Very Rev. Wesley; *see* Carr, Very Rev. A. W.

CARR, Prof. Wilfred; Professor, School of Education, University of Sheffield, 1994–2009, now Emeritus; *b* 18 March 1943; *s* of Wilfred and Leah Carr; *m* 1976, Marisse Evans; three *d. Educ:* Xaverian Coll., Manchester; Shenstone Coll. of Educn, Worcs (DipEd); Warwick Univ. (BA, MA). History teacher, Oldbury Tech. Sch., Warley, Worcs, 1966–70; Lectr, Sch. of Educn, UCNW, 1974–88; University of Sheffield: Sen. Lectr, Dept of Educnl Studies, 1988–90, Reader 1990–94; Dean, Faculty of Educnl Studies, 1992–94; Head, Dept of Educnl Studies, then Sch. of Educn, 1996–2002 and 2005–06; Dean, Fac. of Soc. Scis, 2003–05. Honorary Professor: Faculty of Educn and Soc. Work, Univ. of Sydney, 2006–; Sch. of Educn, Charles Sturt Univ., NSW, 2008–. Ed., Pedagogy, Culture and Society, 1993–2009. Chm., Philosophy of Educn Soc. of GB, 1996–99, Hon. Vice-Chm., 1999. *Publications:* (with S. Kemmis) Becoming Critical: education knowledge and action research, 1986 (trans. Spanish 1988); For Education: towards critical educational inquiry, 1995 (trans. Spanish 1996, Chinese 1997); (with A. Hartnett) Education and the Struggle for Democracy: the politics of educational ideas, 1996; (ed) The RoutledgeFalmer Reader in Philosophy of Education, 2005. *Recreations:* cookery, reading, walking. *Address:* School of Education, Department of Educational Studies, University of Sheffield, 388 Glossop Road, Sheffield S10 2JA. *T:* (0114) 222 8085. *E:* w.carr@sheffield.ac.uk.

CARR-SMITH, Maj.-Gen. Stephen Robert; speaker on cruise ships, since 2007; Chairman, Moving Office Ltd, since 2009; *b* 3 Dec. 1941; *s* of Charles Carr-Smith and Elizabeth Carr-Smith (*née* Marsh); *m* 1967, Nicole Bould; two *s* one *d. Educ:* Welbeck College; RMA; RMCS; BA Open Univ., 1992. Commissioned Royal Signals, 1962; served in UK, Germany, Aden and Belgium; Mil. Secretariat, 1973–74, Operational Requirements, 1978–79, MoD; CO, 1st Armoured Div. HQ and Signal Regt, 1979–82; Instructor, Army Staff Coll., 1982–84; Comdt, Army Apprentices Coll., Harrogate, 1984–86; Col MGO Secretariat, MoD, 1986–88; Chief CIS Policy Branch, SHAPE, Mons, 1988–91; Dep. Dir Gen., NATO CIS Agency, Brussels, 1992–95; Dir of Special Projects, Defence Systems Ltd, 1995–98; Sen. Mil. Advr, CORDA, BAe and SEMA, 1995–99. Ombudsman for Estate Agents, 1999–2006; Chm., Applied Systems International plc, 1999–2001. Non-exec. Dir, Council for National Land and Property Information Service, later Land Data, 2006–10; Chm., Nat. Assembly for Property Search Standards, 2007–08. Chm., Cancer Res. UK Winchester, 2007–13. Hon. Col, FANY, Princess Royal's Volunteer Corps, 1996–2006 (Vice Pres., 2006–); Col Comdt, RCS, 1996–2002. Pres., Stragglers of Asia CC, 2003–13. *Recreations:* cricket, golf, bridge, military history. *Address:* c/o Cox's & King's, PO Box 1190, 7 Pall Mall, SW1Y 5NA.

CARRAGHER, Anna; Controller, BBC Northern Ireland, 2000–06; Commissioner, Equality Commission, Northern Ireland, since 2009; Electoral Commissioner for Northern Ireland, since 2012; *b* 9 July 1948; *d* of Thomas Carragher and Eileen Carragher; *m* 1974, Alain Le Garsmeur; two *s* one *d. Educ:* St Dominic's High Sch., Belfast; Queen's Univ., Belfast (BA Hons). BBC Radio: studio manager, 1970–73; Producer, Today prog., 1973–81; BBC Television: Producer: Television News progs, 1981–85; Question Time, 1985–89; Any Questions, 1989–92; Editor: Election Call, 1992; European progs, 1992–95; Hd of Programmes, BBC NI, 1995–2000. Dir, NI Film Commn, 1995–2003. Member: Radio Acad., 2000–02; Bd, BITC NI, 2001–06; Bd, Radio Jt Audience Res. Bd Ltd, 2002–06; Human Fertilisation and Embryology Authy, 2006–12; Bd, Arts Council of NI, 2012–. Chm., Grand Opera House Trust, Belfast, 2006–11. Mem. Council, Wildfowl and Wetlands Trust, 2009–. *Recreations:* hill-walking, opera, reading, bird-watching, theatre. *Address:* 24 College Park Avenue, Belfast BT7 1LR.

CARRAHER, Terezinha; *see* Nunes, T.

CARRELL, Prof. Robin Wayne, FRS 2002; FRSNZ 1980; FRCP; Professor of Haematology, University of Cambridge, 1986–2003; Fellow of Trinity College, Cambridge, since 1987; *b* 5 April 1936; *s* of Ruane George Carrell and Constance Gwendoline Carrell (*née* Rowe); *m* 1962, Susan Wyatt Rogers; two *s* two *d. Educ:* Christchurch Boys' High School, NZ; Univ. of Otago (MB ChB 1959); Univ. of Canterbury (BSc 1965); Univ. of Cambridge (MA, PhD 1968, ScD 2002). FRACP 1973; FRCPath 1976; MRCP 1985, FRCP 1990. Mem., MRC Abnormal Haemoglobin Unit, Cambridge, 1965–68; Dir, Clinical Biochemistry, Christchurch Hosp., NZ, 1968–75; Lectr and Consultant in Clinical Biochem. Addenbrooke's Hosp. and Univ. of Cambridge, 1976–78; Prof. of Clinical Biochem. Christchurch Sch. of Clinical Medicine, Univ. of Otago, 1978–86. Founder Dir, Canterbury Scientific Ltd, NZ, 1985–2012. Pres., British Soc. of Thrombosis and Haemostasis, 1999. Mem., Spongiform Encephalopathy Adv. Cttee, 2001–04. Member: Gen. Bd, Univ. of Cambridge, 1989–92; Court, Imperial Coll., London, 1997–2006. Commonwealth Fellow St John's Coll. and Vis. Scientist, MRC Lab. of Molecular Biol., 1985. Founder FMedSci 1998. Hon. FRCPA 2005. Pharmacia Prize for biochem. res., NZ, 1984; Hector Medal Royal Soc., NZ, 1986. *Publications:* articles in sci. jls defining the SERPIN family of proteins that control key functions of cells and blood. *Recreations:* topiary, archaeology. *Address:* 19 Madingley Road, Cambridge CB3 0EG. *T:* (01223) 312970. *Club:* Athenaeum.

CARRERAS, José; tenor; *b* 5 Dec. 1946; *s* of José and Antonia Carreras; *m* (marr. diss. 1992) one *s* one *d*; *m* 2006, Jutta Jäger. Opera début as Gennaro in Lucrezia Borgia, Barcelona, 1970; US début in Madama Butterfly, NY City Opera, 1972; Tosca, NY Met, 1974; Covent Garden début in La Traviata, 1974; Un Ballo In Maschera, La Scala, 1975; after break owing to illness, concerts in Barcelona, 1988, Covent Gdn, 1989; Music Dir, Barcelona Olympics 1992; first UK perf., Stiffelio, Covent Gdn, 1993; has appeared at all major opera houses and festivals in Europe, USA and S America; has made many recordings. *Films:* Don Carlos, 1980; West Side Story (TV), 1985. Pres., José Carreras Internat. Leukaemia Foundn, 1988–. RAM 1990. Personality of the Year, Classical Music Awards, 1994; Lifetime Achievement in Music Award, Classical Brits, 2009. *Address:* c/o FIJC, Muntaner 383, 2°, 08021 Barcelona, Spain.

CARRICK, 11th Earl of, *cr* 1748; **Arion Thomas Piers Hamilton Butler;** Viscount Ikerrin 1629; Baron Butler (UK) 1912; *b* 1 Sept. 1975; *s* of 10th Earl of Carrick and of Philippa Janice Victoria (*née* Craxton); *S* father, 2008; *m* 2006, Yoko Shibao; two *d. Heir: b* Hon. Piers Edmund Theobald Lismalyn Butler, *b* 27 Feb. 1979.

CARRICK, Hon. Sir John (Leslie), AC 2008; KCMG 1982; Senator, Commonwealth Parliament of Australia, 1971–87; *b* 4 Sept. 1918; *s* of late A. J. Carrick and of E. E. Carrick (*née* Terry); *m* 1951, Diana Margaret Hunter; three *d. Educ:* Univ. of Sydney (BEc; Hon. DLitt 1988). Res. Officer, Liberal Party of Aust., NSW Div., 1946–48, Gen. Sec., 1948–71. Minister: for Housing and Construction, 1975; for Urban and Regional Develt, 1975; for Educn, 1975–79; Minister Assisting Prime Minister in Fed. Affairs, 1975–78; Minister for Nat. Develt and Energy, 1979–83; Dep. Leader, 1978, Leader, 1978–83, Govt in the Senate. Vice-Pres., Exec. Council, 1978–82. Chairman: NSW Govt Cttee of Review of Schs, 1988–89; Review of Report Implementation, 1990–95; Gas Council of NSW, 1990–95. Pres., Univ. of Sydney Dermatology Res. Foundn, 1989–2003; Mem. Adv. Bd, Macquarie Univ. Inst. of Early Childhood, 1992–2001 (Chm. Res. Foundn, 2001–08); Chm., Adv. Cttee, GERRIC (Gifted Children), Univ. of NSW, 1998–2007. Carrick Nat. Inst. for Learning and Teaching in Higher Educn, estabd by Commonwealth Govt, 2004. Mem. Exec. Cttee, Foundn for Aged Care, 1989–2001. Mem., Commonwealth Roundtable (Indigenous), 2000–01. Hon. FACE 1994. Hon. DLitt: Macquarie, 2000; Western Sydney, 2006; Hon. DEd NSW, 2006. Centenary Medal, 2000. *Recreations:* swimming, reading. *Address:* 21 Cambridge Apartments, 162E Burwood Road, Concord, NSW 2137, Australia. *Club:* Australian (Sydney).

CARRICK, Mervyn; *see* Carrick, W. M.

CARRICK, Sir Roger (John), KCMG 1995 (CMG 1983); LVO 1972; HM Diplomatic Service, retired; international consultant; author; Member, Advisory Group, The D Group, since 2010 (Deputy Chairman, 1999–2006); Chairman, Lime Finance, since 2010; *b* 13 Oct. 1937; *s* of John H. and Florence M. Carrick; *m* 1962, Hilary Elizabeth Blinman; two *s. Educ.* Isleworth Grammar Sch.; Sch. of Slavonic and East European Studies, London Univ. Served RN, 1956–58. Joined HM Foreign (subseq. Diplomatic) Service, 1956; SSEES, 1961; Sofia 1962; FO, 1965; Paris, 1967; Singapore, 1971; FCO, 1973; Counsellor and Dep. Head Personnel Ops Dept, FCO, 1976; Vis. Fellow, Inst. of Internat. Studies, Univ. of Calif. Berkeley, 1977–78; Counsellor, Washington, 1978–82; Hd, Overseas Estate Dept, FCO, 1982–85; Consul-Gen., Chicago, 1985–88; Asst Under-Sec. of State (Economic), FCO, 1988–90; Ambassador, Republic of Indonesia, 1990–94; High Comr, Australia, 1994–97. Chairman: CMB Ltd, 2001–03; Strategy Internat. Ltd, 2007–10 (non-exec. Dir, 2001–06).

Churchill Fellow (Life), Westminster Coll., Fulton, Missouri, 1987. Member: Britain-Australia Soc., 1998– (Life Mem.; Dep. Chm., 1999; Chm., 1999–2001; Vice-Pres., 2002–; Mem., 2001–09, Chm., 2007–09, Educn Trust; Pres., W Country Branch, 2003–14); Anglo-Indonesian Soc.; Mem., Cook Soc., 1997 (Chm., 2002; Hon. Mem., 2013–). Mem., Bd of Trustees, Chevening Estate, 1998–2003. Jt Founder, WADE. Freeman, City of London, 2002. *Publications:* East-West Technology Transfer in Perspective, 1978; Rolleround Oz, 1998; (contrib.) Symphony of Australia, 2010; Diplomatic Anecdotage, 2012; contrib. to London Papers in Australian Studies; articles in jls. *Recreations:* travel, lecturing, dabbling in carpentry, reading, writing, enjoying music, recalling sailing and avoiding gardening. *Address:* Windhover, Wootton Courtenay, Minehead, Somerset TA24 8RD. *Club:* Royal Over-Seas League (Mem., Central Council, 2009–; Vice-Chm., 2011–; Hon. Mem., 2012–; Chm., Bldgs Sub-Cttee, 2012–).

CARRICK, (William) Mervyn; Member (DemU) Upper Bann, Northern Ireland Assembly, 1998–2003; *b* 13 Feb. 1946; *s* of late William and of Margaret Carrick; *m* 1969, Ruth Cardwell; three *s* one *d*. *Educ:* Portadown Technical Coll. Accountant, 1961–. Mem., NI Forum for Political Dialogue, 1996–98. Mem. (DemU), Craigavon BC, 1990–2001 (Dep. Mayor, 1997–98, Mayor, 1998–99). *Recreation:* gardening. *Address:* 72 Dungannon Road, Portadown, Co. Armagh BT62 1LQ. *T:* (028) 3833 6392.

CARRIE, Anne Marie; Chief Executive: Kensington and Chelsea Education Ltd, since 2013; Children's Services, Cambian Group plc, since 2015; *b* Glasgow, 25 Aug. 1955; *d* of Angus Wilson and Agnes Wilson (*née* Thomson); *m* 1983, Scott Carrie; one *d*. *Educ:* Lochend Secondary Sch., Easterhouse, Glasgow; Royal Scottish Acad. of Music and Drama (Dip. Speech and Drama); Jordanhill Coll. (Secondary Teaching Cert. (merit)). Asst Principal Teacher, Deans Community High Sch., 1979–85; Hd, Guidance and Counselling, Telford Coll., 1985–88; Lothian Region: Regl TVEI Manager, 1988–93; Asst Dir, Secondary Schs, 1993–95; Hd, Educn, E Lothian Council, 1995–2001; Exec. Dir, Educn, N Tyneside Council, 2001–03; Regl Dir, Office of the Dep. Prime Minister, 2003–06; Dep. Chief Exec., Royal Bor. of Kensington and Chelsea, 2006–11; Chief Exec., Barnardo's, 2011–13. Non-executive Director: Scottish Seabird Centre, 1998–2001; Health Educn Bd for Scotland, 1998–2001. Chm., Nat. Educn Cttee, Assoc. of Dirs of Children's Services, 2009–10. Comr, Social Mobility and Child Poverty Commn, 2012–. Gov. and Trustee, Chelsea Acad., 2007–10; Gov., Basildon and Thurrock Univ. Hosp. Trust; Chair of Govs, Holland Park Sch.; Mem. Bd, Nat. Virtual Coll., 2010–. FRSA. *Recreations:* theatre, walking, cycling, fire walking, singing.

CARRIER, Dr John Woolfe; Senior Lecturer in Social Policy, 1974–2005, and Dean of Graduate Studies, 2002–05, London School of Economics and Political Science; Chair, North Middlesex University Hospital NHS Trust, since 2013; *b* 26 Sept. 1938; *s* of Louis Carrier and Rachel Carrier; *m* 1964, Sarah Margaret Dawes; two *s* two *d*. *Educ:* Regent's Park Central Sch.; Chiswick Poly.; London Sch. of Econs (BSc (Soc) 1965; MPhil 1969; PhD 1983); Univ. of Westminster (LLB Hons 1994). Principal Lectr, Goldsmiths' Coll., Univ. of London, 1967–74. Lectures: William Marsden, Royal Free Hosp., 1996; Richard Titmuss Meml, Hebrew Univ. of Jerusalem, 1997. Vis. Prof., Univ. of Greenwich, 2006–07. Mem. (Lab) Camden BC, 1971–78. Mem. and Vice-Chm., Hampstead HA, 1982–91; Vice-Chm., 1991–97, Chm., 1997–2001, Royal Free Hampstead NHS Hosp. Trust; Chairman: Camden PCT, 2001–13; N Middlesex Univ. Hosp. Trust, 2014–. Vice-Chm. and Trustee, Centre for Advancement of Inter-professional Educn, 1990–99; Chair, Cttees in Obstetrics and Gynaecol., Public Health Medicine, and Surgery, London Deanery, 2010–. Trustee: William Ellis and Birkbeck Schs Trust, 1996– (Chm. Trustees, 2005–); British Cardiovascular Soc., 2009–; Mem. Council, Royal Free Hosp. Med. Sch., 1988–98; Trustee, RNTNEH, 1997–99; Special Trustee, Royal Free Hosp., 1999–2008; Mem., London NE Sub-Cttee, Adv. Cttee on Clinical Excellence Awards, 2003–10 (Chm., 2008–10); Mem., 2005–11 (Chm., Educn and Trng Cttee, 2007–11), Special Advr on Legal Educn, 2012–13, Bar Standards Bd. Chairman: Camden Victim Support Scheme, 1978–83; Highgate Cemetery Trust, 1983–97; NE London and City Cluster of PCTs, 2012–13. Trustee, Hackney Youth Orch. Trust, 2002–09. Governor: Gospel Oak Primary Sch., 1972–80 (Chm., 1977–80); Brookfield Primary Sch., 1974–89 (Chm., 1981–87); William Ellis Sch., 1971–96 (Chm., 1987–96); Trustee, NE Thames Foundn Sch., 2012–. JP Highbury, 1983–90. Hon. FRSocMed 1999; Hon. FRCP 2010. Hon. Bencher, Lincoln's Inn, 2011; Chm., Lincoln's Inn Scholarship Cttee, 2013–. Jt Ed., Internat. Jl of Law, Crime and Justice (formerly Internat. Jl Sociol. of Law), 1993–; Member, Editorial Board: Jl Social Policy, 1975–81; Ethnic and Racial Studies, 1990–96. *Publications:* with Ian Kendall: Medical Negligence: complaints and compensation, 1990; (ed) Socialism and the NHS, 1990; Health and the National Health Service, 1998, 2nd edn 2015; (ed jtly) Interprofessional Issues in Community and Primary Health Care, 1995; (ed jtly) Asylum in the Community, 1996; contrib. articles to learned jls. *Recreations:* running, tennis, walking, films, art galleries. *Address:* 37 Dartmouth Park Road, NW5 1SU. *T:* (020) 7267 1376.

CARRINGTON, family name of **Baron Carrington of Fulham**.

CARRINGTON, 6th Baron (Ireland) *cr* 1796, (Great Britain) *cr* 1797; **Peter Alexander Rupert Carington,** KG 1985; GCMG 1988 (KCMG 1958); CH 1983; MC 1945; PC 1959; Baron Carington of Upton (Life Peer), 1999; Chairman, Christies International plc, 1988–93; Director, The Telegraph plc, 1990–2004; Chancellor, Order of the Garter, 1994–2012; *b* 6 June 1919; *s* of 5th Baron and Hon. Sibyl Marion (*d* 1946), *d* of 2nd Viscount Colville; *S* father, 1938; *m* 1942, Iona (*d* 2009), *yr d* of late Sir Francis McClean; one *s* two *d*. *Educ:* Eton Coll.; RMC Sandhurst. Served NW Europe, Major Grenadier Guards. Parly Sec., Min. of Agriculture and Fisheries, 1951–54; Parly Sec., Min. of Defence, Oct. 1954–Nov. 1956; High Comr for the UK in Australia, Nov. 1956–Oct. 1959; First Lord of the Admiralty, 1959–63; Minister without Portfolio and Leader of the House of Lords, 1963–64; Leader of the Opposition, House of Lords, 1964–70 and 1974–79; Secretary of State: for Defence, 1970–74; for Energy, 1974; for For. and Commonwealth Affairs, 1979–82; Minister of Aviation Supply, 1971–74. Chm., Cons. Party Organisation, 1972–74. Chm., GEC, 1983–84; Sec.-Gen., NATO, 1984–88. Chm., EC Conf. on Yugoslavia, 1991–92. Sec. for Foreign Correspondence and Hon. Mem., Royal Acad. of Arts, 1982–; Chm., Bd of Trustees, V&A Museum, 1983–88. Chancellor, Univ. of Reading, 1992–2007. President: The Pilgrims, 1983–2002; VSO, 1993–99. Hon. Bencher, Middle Temple, 1983; Hon. Elder Brother of Trinity House, 1984. Chancellor, Order of St Michael and St George, 1984–94. JP 1948, DL Bucks. Fellow of Eton Coll., 1966–81; Hon. Fellow, St Antony's Coll., Oxford, 1982. Hon. LLD: Cambridge, 1981; Leeds, 1981; Aberdeen, 1985; Nottingham, 1993; Birmingham, 1993; Newcastle, 1998; Hon. Dr Laws: Univ. of Philippines, 1982; Univ. of S Carolina, 1983; Harvard, 1986; Reading, 1989; Sussex, 1989; DUniv: Essex, 1983; Buckingham, 1989; Hon. DSc Cranfield, 1988; Hon. DCL Oxford, 2003. *Publications:* Reflect on Things Past (autobiog.), 1988. *Heir: s* Hon. Rupert Francis John Carington [*b* 2 Dec. 1948; *m* 1989, Daniela, *d* of Mr and Mrs Flavio Diotallevi; one *s* two *d*]. *Address:* The Manor House, Church End, Bledlow, Princes Risborough, Bucks HP27 9PB. *T:* (01844) 273675. *Clubs:* Pratt's, White's.

CARRINGTON OF FULHAM, Baron *cr* 2013 (Life Peer), of Fulham in the London Borough of Hammersmith and Fulham; **Matthew Hadrian Marshall Carrington;** Director, since 2007, and Deputy Chairman, since 2008, Gatehouse Bank PLC; Chief Executive, Retail Motor Industry Federation, 2002–06; *b* 19 Oct. 1947; *s* of late Walter Carrington and Dilys Carrington; *m* 1st, 1975, Mary Lou Darrow (*d* 2008); one *d*; 2nd, 2011, Margaret Ann Milward. *Educ:* London Lycée; Imperial Coll. of Science and Technol., London (BSc Physics); London Business Sch. (MSc). Prodn Foreman, GKN Ltd, 1969–72; banker: with The First National Bank of Chicago, 1974–78; with Saudi Internat. Bank, 1978–87; Chm., Outdoor Advertising Assoc., 1998–2002. MP (C) Fulham, 1987–97; contested (C) Hammersmith and Fulham, 1997, 2001. PPS to Rt Hon. John Patten, MP, 1990–94; an Asst Govt Whip, 1996–97. Mem., Treasury and Civil Service Select Cttee, 1994–96; Chm., Treasury Select Cttee, 1996. London Regl Chm., 2005–08, Chm., London NW Area, 2008–10, Cons. Party. Dir, Arab British Chamber of Commerce, 2011–. *Recreations:* cooking, political history. *Address:* 34 Ladbroke Square, W11 3NB.

CARRINGTON, Maj.-Gen. Colin Edward George, CB 1991; CBE 1983; Commander, Army Security Vetting Unit, 1991–2000; *b* 19 Jan. 1936; *s* of Edgar John Carrington and Ruth Carrington (*née* West); *m* 1967, Joy Bracknell; one *s* one *d*. *Educ:* Royal Liberty Sch.; RMA Sandhurst. FCILT (FCIT 1988). Troop Comdr, BAOR, 1956–59; Air Despatch duties, 1960–64; Instructor, RMA, 1964–68; Sqdn Comdr, BAOR, 1972–74; Directing Staff, Staff Coll., 1975–77; CO 1 Armd Div. Transport Regt, 1977–79; DCOS 1 Armd Div., 1979–82; RCDS 1983; Dir, Manning Policy (Army), 1984–86; Comd Transport 1 (BR) Corps, 1986–88; Dir Gen. Transport and Movements (Army), MoD, 1988–91, retd. President: RASC & RCT Assoc., 1992–; SSAFA (formerly SSAFA/Forces Help) Devon, 2007–. Freeman, City of London, 1988. *Recreations:* gardening, reading.

CARRINGTON, Michael; Chief Executive Officer, The Foundation, since 2014; *b* Camden, Australia, 5 May 1961; *s* of Hubert Carrington Plicha and Elaine (*née* Marshall); *m* 2006, S. Palluel. *Educ:* Parkes High Sch., Parkes, NSW; Ashridge Business Sch.; Said Business Sch., Oxford Univ. (High Perf. Leadership Prog. 2009); London Business Sch. (Corporate Finance, 2010). Radio presenter, 2PK, Australia, 1979–82; communications sailor, RAN, 1982–86; Prodn Manager, Channel 10, Australia, 1986–89; Acquisitions Asst, BBC, 1990–91; Acquisitions Exec., Discovery Channel Europe, 1991–93; Producer, Co-prodns and Acquisitions, BBC, 1993–99; Hd, Television and New Media, Create TV & Film Ltd, 1999–2003; Hd, Children's Animation and Acquisitions, 2004–06, Controller, CBeebies, 2006–10, BBC; Chief Content Officer, Turner Broadcasting, 2010–13; Vice Pres. Creative, HIT Entertainment, 2013–14. Mem., BAFTA. *Address:* Zodiak Kids, Avon House, Avonmore Road, Kensington Village, W14 8TS. *T:* (020) 7013 4455. *Clubs:* Century, Ivy.

CARRINGTON, Nigel Martyn; Vice-Chancellor (formerly Rector), University of the Arts London, since 2008; *b* Amersham, 1 May 1956; *s* of Ron and Vera Carrington; *m* 1988, Elisabeth Buchanan; one *s* two *d*. *Educ:* St John's Coll., Oxford (MA Hons Juris.); Courtauld Inst. of Art, Univ. of London (Grad. Dip. Hist. of Art). Solicitor and Partner, Baker & McKenzie, 1979–2000: Man. Partner, London, 1994–98; Chm., Eur. Regl Council, 1998–2000; Man. Dir, McLaren Gp Ltd, 2000–05 (Dep. Chm., 2005–07). Non-executive Director: University Coll. London Hosps NHS Foundn Trust, 2005–08; Hornby plc, 2007–14. Trustee: Crisis, 2005–11 (Treas., 2005–08); English Concert, 2005– (Chm., 2006–12); Independent Opera, 2006–10; Chm., Jeans for Genes, 2006–08. Chm., Henry Moore Foundn, 2014–. Governor: N London Collegiate Sch., 2008–15; Internat. Students House, 2009–. *Publications:* Acquiring Companies and Businesses in Europe, 1994. *Recreations:* chamber music, swimming, ski-ing, walking in the mountains. *Address:* University of the Arts London, 272 High Holborn, WC1V 7EY. *T:* (020) 7514 6002, *Fax:* (020) 7514 6236. *E:* n.carrington@arts.ac.uk. *Clubs:* Chelsea Arts, Royal Automobile.

CARRINGTON, Ruth; *see* James, M. L.

CARROLL, Cynthia; Chair, Vedanta Resources Holdings Ltd, since 2015; *b* Philadelphia, 13 Nov. 1956; *m* 1988, David Carroll; one *s* three *d*. *Educ:* Skidmore Coll., NY (BS Geol.); Univ. of Kansas (MS Geol.); Harvard Univ. (MBA). FREng 2012. Petroleum geologist, Amoco, 1981–87; Business Devlt Gp, Rolled Products Div., Alcan Inc., 1989–91; Vice-Pres./Gen. Manager, Alcan Foil Products, 1991–96; Man. Dir, Aughinish Alumina Ltd, 1996–98; Pres., Bauxite, Alumina & Speciality Chemicals, 1998–2001, Pres. and CEO, Primary Metal Gp, 2002–06, Alcan Inc.; Chief Exec., Anglo American plc, 2007–13. Non-exec. Dir, BP plc, 2007–. *Recreations:* ski-ing, swimming, tennis, sailing, golf, horseback riding, sewing, family.

CARROLL, Eileen Philomena, (Mrs E. P. Carroll-Mackie); Deputy Chief Executive, Centre for Effective Dispute Resolution, since 1996; *b* 5 Dec. 1953; *d* of late Matthew Francis Carroll and of Mary Philomena Carroll; *m* 1st, Richard Peers-Jones (marr. diss.); one *d*; 2nd, 2001, Karl Joseph Mackie, *qv*. *Educ:* Holy Cross, Gerrards Cross; Univ. of Kent, Canterbury (LLB Hons (Law) 1979). Analyst, British Sulphur Corp., London, 1972–74; admitted as solicitor, 1981; Lawyer/Partner, then Internat. Strategy Partner, Turner Kenneth Brown, 1981–94; Vis. Partner, Thelen Reid Priest, San Francisco, 1988 and 1994; involved in foundn of CEDR, 1990 (Mem., Bd of Trustees, 1990–96); accredited CEDR mediator, 1993. Mem., Litigation Cttee, London Solicitors, 1987–90. Adv. Mem., Conflict Analysis Res. Centre, Univ. of Kent at Canterbury, 2006–; Member: Forum UK, 2006–; Follett Gp, 2006–; Mem. Council, Distinguished Advisors, Straus Inst. for Dispute Resolution, 2007–. Gov., Surbiton High Sch., 2004–. Exec. Coach, Henley Bus. Sch., 2008. Hon. QC 2013. Prize for Excellence in Dispute Resolution, Center for Public Resources Inst. for Dispute Resolution, NY, 1997; European Women of Achievement Award, EUW, 2005. *Publications:* (with Dr Karl Mackie) International Mediation: the art of business diplomacy, 2000, 2nd edn 2006. *Recreations:* spending time with family, ski-ing, photography, travel, the outdoor life. *Address:* Centre for Effective Dispute Resolution, International Dispute Resolution Centre, 70 Fleet Street, EC4Y 1EU.

CARROLL, Most Rev. Francis Patrick; Archbishop of Canberra and Goulburn, (RC), 1983–2006; *b* 9 Sept. 1930; *s* of P. Carroll. *Educ:* Devlin Subsidised Sch., St Brendan's Sch., Ganmain; De La Salle Coll., Marrickville; St Columba's Coll., Springwood; St Patrick's Coll., Manly; Pontifical Urban Univ. De Propaganda Fide. Ordained priest, 1954; Asst Priest, Griffith, NSW, 1955–59; Asst Inspector of Catholic Schs, dio. of Wagga, 1957–61; Asst Priest, Albury, 1959–61; Bishop's Sec., Diocesan Chancellor, Diocesan Dir of Catholic Educn, 1965–67; consecrated Co-Adjutor Bishop, 1967; Bishop of Wagga Wagga, 1968–83. Chm., Nat. Catholic Educn Commn, 1974–78; Mem., Internat. Catechetical Council, Rome, 1974–93; Pres., Australian Catholic Bishops' Conf., 2000–06. Hon. DLitt Charles Sturt Univ., NSW, 1994; DUniv Australian Catholic Univ., 2006. *Publications:* The Development of Episcopal Conferences, 1965. *Address:* PO Box 2396, Wagga Wagga, NSW 2650, Australia.

CARROLL, Prof. John Edward, FREng; Professor of Engineering, University of Cambridge, 1983–2001; Fellow of Queens' College, Cambridge, since 1967; *b* 15 Feb. 1934; *s* of Sydney Wentworth Carroll and May Doris Carroll; *m* 1958, Vera Mary Jordan; three *s*. *Educ:* Oundle Sch.; Queens' Coll., Cambridge (Wrangler; Foundn Schol., 1957). BA 1957; PhD 1961; ScD 1982. FIET; FREng (FEng 1985). Microwave Div., Services Electronic Res. Lab., 1961–67; Cambridge University: Lectr, 1967–76; Reader, 1976–83; Dep. Hd of Engrg Dept, 1986–90; Head of Electrical Div., 1992–99; Chm. Council, Sch. of Technol., 1996–99. Vis. Prof., Queensland Univ., 1982. Editor, IEE Jl of Solid State and Electron Devices, 1976–82. *Publications:* Hot Electron Microwave Generators, 1970; Physical Models of Semiconductor Devices, 1974; Solid State Devices (Inst. of Phys. vol. 57), 1980; Rate Equations in Semiconductor Electronics, 1986; Distributed Feedback Semiconductor Lasers, 1998; contribs on microwaves, semiconductor devices and optical systems to learned jls. *Recreations:* piano, walking, reading thrillers, carpentry. *Address:* Queens' College, Silver Street, Cambridge CB3 9ET. *T:* (01223) 332829. *E:* jec1000@cam.ac.uk.

CARROLL, Jonathan Neil; His Honour Judge Jonathan Carroll; a Circuit Judge, since 2015; *b* Prescot, Lancs, 3 Nov. 1967; *s* of John Carroll and Joan Carroll; *m* 1996, Melanie

Welford; one *s* one *d*. *Educ:* St Edward's Coll., Liverpool; King's Coll., London (BA Hons Hist. 1990; AKC; MA Law in the Modern World 2011); Coll. of Law (DipLaw 1993). Project Officer, British Aerospace, 1990–92; called to the Bar, Gray's Inn, 1994; barrister, 1994–2010; a Dep. Judge Advocate, 2006–15; a Recorder, 2008–15; Internat. Criminal Judge, EU Rule of Law Mission, Kosovo, 2010–14. Commnd officer, Royal Mercian and Lancastrian Yeo., TA, 1990–2000. *Recreations:* shooting, fishing, running, Rugby, gardening. *Address:* Crown Court, Bricket Road, St Albans, Herts AL1 3JW. *T:* (01727) 753220.

CARROLL, Mark Steven; Director of Housing Strategy, Essex County Council, since 2014; *b* 17 June 1962; *s* of late Albert Carroll and of Anne Carroll; *m* 1998, Randhirajpall Kaur Bilan; one *s* one *d*. *Educ:* Leicester Poly. (BA Hons Public Admin 1984); Univ. of Nottingham (MA Soc. Work 1988). Social worker, 1988–90; charity director, 1990–94; mgt consultant, 1994–2002; Home Office: Advr to Permanent Sec., 2002–03; Dir, Race and Cohesion, 2003–06; Department for Communities and Local Government: Dir, Race, Cohesion and Preventing Extremism, 2006–07; short-term projects, 2008–09; Dir, Housing Mgt and Support, 2009–10; Dir, Strategy and Progs, 2010–11; Dir, Big Society and Decentralisation, 2011–13. *Club:* Nottingham Forest Football.

CARROLL, Michael John; His Honour Judge Carroll; a Circuit Judge, since 1996; *b* 26 Dec. 1948; *s* of late Matthew and Gladys Carroll; *m* 1974, Stella Reilly; two *s* two *d* (and one *d* decd). *Educ:* Shebbear Coll., N Devon; City of London Business Sch. (BA Hons); Inns of Court Sch. of Law. Called to the Bar, Gray's Inn, 1973. Factory worker, 1964; shop asst, 1967; fast food chef, 1968; public service vehicle conductor, 1968–72, and driver, 1973; part-time PO counter clerk, 1968–73. Asst Recorder, 1990–94; Recorder, 1994–96. Chairman: Abbeyfield Addiscombe Soc., 2002–07; Croydon Charitable Foundn, 2007–. *Recreations:* reading, antiques, football. *Address:* Maidstone Combined Court Centre, Barker Road, Maidstone ME16 8EQ. *T:* (01622) 202000.

CARROLL, Nancy, (Mrs Jonathan Stone-Fewings); actress; *b* London, 29 Sept. 1973; *d* of Kenneth Carroll and Susie Carroll (*née* Cosgrove, now Perring), and step *d* of Ian Perring; *m* 2003, Jonathan Stone-Fewings; one *s* one *d*. *Educ:* Alleyn's Sch., Dulwich; Instituti di Lorenzo di Medici, Florence; Univ. of Leeds (BA Hons Fine Art); London Acad. of Music and Dramatic Art. *Theatre:* Hamlet, Bristol Old Vic; Royal Shakespeare Company: Winter's Tale, 1998; The Lion, the Witch and the Wardrobe, 1998; Henry IV, Pts 1 and 2, 2000; As You Like It, 2000; Twelfth Night, 2009; National Theatre: The Talking Cure, 2002; The False Servant, 2004; The Voysey Inheritance, 2006; The Man of Mode, 2007; The Enchantment, 2007; After the Dance, 2010 (Natasha Richardson Award, Evening Standard, 2010; Best Actress, Olivier Awards, 2011); Almeida Theatre: Waste, 2008; House of Games, 2010; Midsummer Night's Dream, Sheffield Crucible, 2003; Still Life/Astonished Heart, Liverpool Playhouse, 2004; Mammals, Bush Th., 2005; You Never Can Tell, Garrick Th. and tour, 2005; See How They Run, Duchess, 2006; Arcadia, Duke of York Th., 2009; The Recruiting Officer, Donmar, 2012; The Magistrate, Olivier Th., 2012; The Duck House, Vaudeville, 2013; Closer, Donmar, 2015; *films:* Iris, 2002; *television:* The Gathering Storm, 2002; Cambridge Spies, 2003; In Search of Shakespeare, 2003; Midsomer Murders; The Bill; Dalziel and Pascoe; Words of the Titanic, 2012; Father Brown, 2013–; The Suspicions of Mr Whicher, 2014; *radio* incl. Villette, Fatal Loins, Words and Music, Fine Days in May, The Family Project. *Publications:* (contrib.) Players of Shakespeare. *Recreations:* painter, juggling. *Address:* c/o United Agents, 12–26 Lexington Street, W1F 0LE. *T:* (020) 3214 0800.

CARROLL, Rt Rev. Mgr Philip; Parish Priest, St Paul's, Alnwick, 2011–15; *b* 30 Nov. 1946; *s* of Joseph Carroll and Jean Carroll (*née* Graham). *Educ:* Venerable English College, Rome (PhL, STL). Ordained 1971; Assistant Priest, Our Blessed Lady Immaculate, Washington, 1972–78; Hexham and Newcastle Diocesan Religious Educn Service, 1979–88; Asst Gen. Sec., 1988–91, Gen. Sec., 1992–96, Catholic Bishops' Conf.; Parish Priest, St Bede's Ch, Washington, 1996–2006; VG, then Episcopal Vicar, RC Dio. Hexham and Newcastle, 2001–06; Spiritual Dir, Venerable English Coll., Rome, 2006–11. *Recreations:* cricket, fell walking. *Address:* St Andrew's RC Church, Worswick Street, Newcastle upon Tyne NE1 6UW.

CARROLL, Terence Patrick, (Terry); author, sports journalist, consultant and non-executive director, since 2009; *b* 24 Nov. 1948; *s* of George Daniel Carroll and Betty Doreen Carroll (*née* Holmes); *m* 1st, 1971, Louise Mary (*née* Smith) (marr. diss. 1984); one *s*; 2nd, 1984, Penelope Julia, (Penny) (*née* Berry) (marr. diss. 1994); 3rd, 1994, Heather Carmen (*née* Summers). *Educ:* Gillingham Grammar Sch.; Univ. of Bradford (BSc Business Studies). FCA 1980; FCT 1990 (MCT 1985); FCIB (FCBSI 1986). Auditor and Computer Auditor, Armitage & Norton, 1970–76; Management Accountant, Bradford & Bingley Building Soc., 1976–80; Exec. and Mem. Stock Exchange, Sheppards & Chase, 1980–82; Treasurer, Halifax Building Soc., 1982–85; National & Provincial Building Society: Gen. Manager Finance, 1985–86; Acting Chief Exec., 1986–87; Finance Dir, 1987–90; Treasury Dir, 1990–91; Finance Dir, United Leeds Teaching Hosps NHS Trust, 1991–94; Managing Director: Hollins Consulting, later How To Be Your Best Ltd, 1994–2006; Portland Internat. HR Consultants Ltd, 1996–97; Gp Finance Dir, Eatonfield Gp plc, 2006–07; Hd of Corporate Finance, Broadhead Peel Rhodes, 2008–09. Chief Exec., Hadrian's Wall Heritage Ltd, 2006. Chairman: Bradford Breakthrough Ltd, 1989–91; Central Yorks Inst. of Mgt, 1996–98. Coach and Consultant, Performance Alchemist, 2009–. *Publications:* The Role of the Finance Director, 1997, 3rd edn 2002; Moving Up, 1998; Understanding Swaps in a Day, 1999, new edn 2012; NLP for Traders, 2000, new edn 2012; The Risk Factor, 2001, new edn 2013; Be Your Best with NLP, 2001, new edn 2012; (contrib.) QFinance, 2009, new edn 2012. *Recreations:* golf, bridge, share trading. *Address:* 18 Skipton Road, Ilkley LS29 9EJ. *Clubs:* Ilkley Golf, Ilkley Rugby.

CARROLL-MACKIE, Eileen Philomena; *see* Carroll, E. P.

CARRUTHERS, Sir Ian James, Kt 2003; OBE 1997; Chairman, Portsmouth Hospitals NHS Trust, since 2014; *m*; one *s* one *d*. Dist Gen. Manager, W Dorset HA, 1987; Chief Executive: S and W RHA, until 1996; Dorset HA, then Dorset and Som Strategic HA, 1996–2006; Hants and IoW Strategic HA, 2005–06; on secondment as Transitional Dir, NHS Inst. for Innovation and Improvement, DoH, 2004–05; Actg Dir of Commissioning, then Actg Chief Exec. of NHS, DoH, 2006; Chief Exec., SW Strategic Health Authy (NHS SW), later NHS S of England, 2006–13. Chm., Healthcare UK, 2013–15. Mem., NHS Modernisation Bd, then Nat. Leadership Network. Chancellor, UWE, 2011–.

CARRUTHERS, James Edwin; Assistant Secretary, Royal Hospital Chelsea, 1988–94; *b* 19 March 1928; *er s* of James and Dollie Carruthers; *m* 1955, Phyllis Williams (*d* 1996); one *s*. *Educ:* George Heriot's Sch.; Edinburgh Univ. (MA; Medallist in Scottish Hist.). FSAScot. Lieut, The Queen's Own Cameron Highlanders, 1949–51, and TA, 1951–55. Air Ministry: Asst Principal, 1951; Private Sec. to DCAS, 1955; Asst Private Sec. to Sec. of State for Air, 1956; Principal, 1956; Min. of Aviation, 1960–62; Private Secretary: to Minister of Defence for RAF, 1965–67; to Parly Under Sec. of State for RAF, 1967; Asst Sec., 1967; Chief Officer, Sovereign Base Areas Admin, Cyprus, 1968–71; Dep. Chief of Public Relations, MoD, 1971–72; Private Sec. to Chancellor of Duchy of Lancaster, Cabinet Office, 1973–74; Sec., Organising Cttee for British Aerospace, DoI, 1975–77; Under-Sec., 1977; seconded as Asst to Chm., British Aerospace, 1977–79; Dir Gen., Royal Ordnance Factories (Finance and Procurement), 1980–83; Chm., CSSB, 1983–84; Asst Under Sec. of State, MoD, 1984–88. *Recreations:* painting, travel. *Address:* 11 John's Lee Close, Loughborough, Leics LE11 3LH.

CARRUTHERS-WATT, Miranda Lucy Mary, (Mrs P. Vercoe); Chief Executive, Office of the Police and Crime Commissioner for Lancashire (formerly Lancashire Police Authority), since 2007; *b* 1 Sept. 1961; *d* of late Calverley Vernon Carruthers-Watt and Pauline Mary Carruthers-Watt; *m* 1988, Philip Vercoe; two *s* (one *d* decd). *Educ:* Burnley High Sch. for Girls; Lancaster Univ. (LLB Hons Law 1983); Coll. of Law, Chester; Univ. of Hull (MBA 1998); Law Soc. Dip. in Local Govt Law 1991. Admitted Solicitor, 1987; private practice and local govt, 1986–97; Asst Dir, Rights, Advice and Entitlements, Blackburn with Darwen BC, 1997–2005; Dir, NW Centre of Excellence, 2005–07. FCMI 2009; CMgr 2012. *Recreations:* family, wine, walking, Cubs. *Address:* Office of the Police and Crime Commissioner for Lancashire, PO Box 653, Preston PR2 2WB.

CARSBERG, Sir Bryan (Victor), Kt 1989; Director General of Telecommunications, 1984–92; *b* 3 Jan. 1939; *s* of Alfred Victor Carsberg and Maryllia (*née* Collins); *m* 1960, Margaret Linda Graham; two *d*. *Educ:* Berkhamsted Sch.; London Sch. of Econs and Pol Science (MScEcon; Hon. Fellow, 1990). Chartered Accountant, 1960. Sole practice, chartered accountant, 1962–64; Lectr in Accounting, LSE, 1964–68; Vis. Lectr, Grad. Sch. of Business, Univ. of Chicago, 1968–69; Prof. of Accounting, Univ. of Manchester, 1969–81 (Dean, Faculty of Econ. and Social Studies, 1977–78); Arthur Andersen Prof. of Accounting, LSE, 1981–87; Dir of Res., ICA, 1981–87; Dir Gen. of Fair Trading, 1992–95; Sec.-Gen., Internat. Accounting Standards Cttee, 1995–2001. Visiting Professor: of Business Admin, Univ. of Calif, Berkeley, 1974; of Accounting, LSE, 1988–89. Asst Dir of Res. and Technical Activities, Financial Accounting Standards Bd, USA, 1978–81; Mem., Accounting Standards Bd, 1990–94 (Vice-Chm., 1990–92); Chm., Pensions Compensation Bd, 2001–05. Mem. Council, ICA, 1975–79; Mem. Bd, Radiocommunications Agency, 1990–92. Director: Economists Adv. Gp, 1976–84; Economist Bookshop, 1981–91; Philip Allan (Publishers), 1981–92, 1995–2006; Cable & Wireless Communications, 1997–2000; RM plc, 2002–12; Novae Gp plc (formerly SVB Hldgs plc), 2003–; Inmarsat plc, 2005–; Chm., MLL Telecom Ltd, 1999–2002; Advr on telecoms, KPMG, 2001–06; Mem., Equality of Access Bd, BT Gp plc, 2005–13. Member, Council: Univ. of Surrey, 1990–92; Loughborough Univ., 1999–2011 (Chm., 2001–11). Mem., Royal Swedish Acad. of Engrg Scis, 1994. Hon. FIA 2000; Hon. RICS 2010 (Mem., Governing Council, 2010–13). Hon. MA Econ Manchester, 1973; Hon. ScD UEA, 1992; Hon. DLitt Loughborough, 1994; DUniv Essex, 1995; Hon. LLD Bath, 1996; Hon. DBA Nottingham Trent, 2008. Chartered Accountants Founding Societies Centenary Award, 1988; Sempier Award, IFAC, 2002. *Publications:* An Introduction to Mathematical Programming for Accountants, 1969; (with H. C. Edey) Modern Financial Management, 1969; Analysis for Investment Decisions, 1974; (with E. V. Morgan and M. Parkin) Indexation and Inflation, 1975; Economics of Business Decisions, 1975; (with A. Hope) Investment Decisions under Inflation, 1976; (with A. Hope) Current Issues in Accountancy, 1977, 2nd edn 1984; (with J. Arnold and R. Scapens) Topics in Management Accounting, 1980; (with S. Lumby) The Evaluation of Financial Performance in the Water Industry, 1983; (with M. Page) Current Cost Accounting, 1984; (with M. Page *et al*) Small Company Financial Reporting, 1985. *Recreations:* gardening, theatre, music, opera. *E:* bryan.carsberg@ntlworld.com.

CARSON, Ciaran Gerard; Director, Seamus Heaney Centre for Poetry, Queen's University Belfast, since 2003; *b* 9 Oct. 1948; *s* of William and Mary Carson; *m* 1982, Deirdre Shannon; two *s* one *d*. *Educ:* QUB (BA Hons). Traditional Arts Officer, 1976–94, Literature Officer, 1994–98, Arts Council of NI; freelance writer, 1998–2003. FRSL 2014. *Publications: poetry:* The New Estate, 1976; The Irish for No, 1987; Belfast Confetti, 1989; First Language, 1993; Opera Et Cetera, 1996; The Twelfth of Never, 1998; The Alexandrine Plan, 1998; Breaking News, 2003; *prose:* The Pocket Guide to Irish Traditional Music, 1986; Last Night's Fun, 1996; The Star Factory, 1997; Fishing for Amber, 1999; Shamrock Tea, 2001; *translation:* The Inferno of Dante Alighieri: a new translation, 2002. *Recreation:* playing Irish traditional music. *E:* ciaran.carson@ntlworld.com.

CARSON, Hugh Christopher Kingsford; Headmaster, Malvern College, 1997–2006; *b* 29 Dec. 1945; *s* of late Lt-Col James Kingsford Carson and Elsie Adeline Carson (*née* Cockersell); *m* 1972, Penelope Susan Elizabeth Hollingbury, PhD. *Educ:* Tonbridge Sch.; RMA, Sandhurst; Royal Holloway Coll., London Univ. (BA Mod. Hist., Hist. of Econs and Politics, 1979); Reading Univ. (PGCE). Commnd RTR, 1967–76. Asst Master, then Housemaster, Epsom Coll., 1980–90; Headmaster, Denstone Coll., 1990–96. Chairman: Dovedale Arts Fest., 2010–; Ecton Mine Educnl Trust, 2011–. Master, Skinners' Co., 2010–11. Hon. Col 39 Signal Regt (Vol.), 2011–. Church Warden, St Margaret's, Wetton, 2007–14. *Recreations:* photography, historical research, hill-walking, music. *Address:* Broadview, Old Road, Elham, Canterbury, Kent CT4 6UH.

CARSON, Joan; *see* Carson, M. J.

CARSON, John, CBE 1981; draper; Member (OUP) for Belfast North, Northern Ireland Assembly, 1982–86; *b* 1934. Member, Belfast District Council, (formerly Belfast Corporation), 1971–97; Official Unionist Councillor for Duncairn; Lord Mayor of Belfast, 1980–81, 1985–86. MP (UU) Belfast North, Feb. 1974–1979. Dir, Laganside Corp., 1989; non-exec. Dir, Royal Gp of Hosps & Dental Hosp. HSS Trust, 1992–. Vice-Chm., NI Youth Council, 1985. Mem., Adv. Bd, Salvation Army. High Sheriff, Belfast, 1978. *Address:* 75 Donaghadee Road, Millisle, Co. Down, N Ireland BT22 2BZ.

CARSON, (Margaret) Joan; Member (UU) Fermanagh and South Tyrone, Northern Ireland Assembly, 1998–2003; *b* 29 Jan. 1935; *d* of Charles Patterson and Gladys Patterson (*née* Irvine); *m* 1957, James Carson; two *s* one *d*. *Educ:* Stranmillis Coll., Belfast. Teacher: Enniskillen Model Primary Sch., 1956–62; Granville Primary Sch., 1972–79; Dungannon Primary Sch., 1979–82; Principal, Tamnamore Primary Sch., 1982–88. Mem. (UU), Dungannon DC, 1997–2001. Constituency Sec., Fermanagh and S Tyrone, 1990–, Deleg. to Exec. Cttee, UUP (former Party Officer). *Recreations:* ornithology, painting, reading. *Address:* Drumgold House, 115 Moy Road, Dungannon, Co. Tyrone BT71 7DX. *T:* (028) 8778 4285.

CARSON, Neil Andrew Patrick; Chief Executive Officer, Johnson Matthey plc, 2004–14; *b* 15 April 1957; *s* of Patrick Carson and Sheila Margaret Rose; *m* 1988, Helen Barbara Huppler; two *s* one *d*. *Educ:* Emanuel Sch., Wandsworth; Coventry Univ. (BSc Combined Engrg). Joined Johnson Matthey plc, 1980: various sales and mktg roles, 1980–88; Mktg Dir, USA, 1988–90, Gen. Manager, London, 1990–93, Precious Metals Mktg; Sales and Mktg Dir, 1993–96, Man. Dir, 1996–97, Catalytic Systems Div., Europe; Dir, Catalysts Systems Div., 1997–99; Executive Director: Catalysts Div., 1999–2003; Catalysts and Precious Metals Div., 2003–04. Senior Independent Director: AMEC Foster Wheeler (formerly AMEC) plc, 2010–; Pay Point plc, 2014–; Chm., TT Electronics, 2015–. Jt Chm., Chemistry Growth Partnership, 2013–. *Recreations:* watching Rugby, ski-ing, family.

CARSON, William Hunter Fisher, OBE 1983; jockey, retired 1997; racing pundit, BBC, 1997–2012; *b* 16 Nov. 1942; *s* of Thomas Whelan Carson and Mary Hay; *m* 1963, Carole Jane Sutton (marr. diss. 1979); three *s*; *m* 1982, Elaine Williams. *Educ:* Riverside, Stirling, Scotland. Apprenticed to Captain G. Armstrong, 1957; 1st winner, Pinkers Pond, Catterick, 1962; trans. to Fred Armstrong, 1963–66; First Jockey to Lord Derby, 1967; first classic win, High Top, 1972; Champion Jockey, 1972, 1973, 1978, 1980 and 1983; became First Jockey to W. R. Hern, 1977; also appointed Royal Jockey, riding Dunfermline to the Jubilee Oaks and St Leger wins in the colours of HM the Queen; won the 200th Derby on Troy, trained by W. R. Hern, 1979; the same combination won the 1980 Derby, with Henbit, and the 1980 Oaks, with Bireme; also won King George VI and Queen Elizabeth Stakes, on Troy, 1979, on Ela-Mana-Mou, 1980, on Petoski, 1985, on Nashwan, 1989; 1983 Oaks and St Leger, with Sun

Princess; Ascot Gold Cup, on Little Wolf, 1983; St Leger, on Minster Son, 1988 (only jockey ever to breed and ride a Classic winner); Derby, on Nashwan, 1989; 1,000 Guineas, Oaks and Irish Derby, on Salsabil, 1990; 1,000 Guineas and Oaks, on Shadayid, 1991; Derby, on Erhaab, 1994. During the 1989 season rode 100th Group One winner in England; by 1997 had ridden 3,828 winners including 18 Classics. DUniv Stirling, 1998; Hon. DSc Chester, 2010. *Address:* Minster House, Barnsley, Cirencester, Glos GL7 5DZ.

CARSS-FRISK, Monica Gunnel Constance; QC 2001. *Educ:* University Coll. London (LLB); University Coll., Oxford (BCL). Called to the Bar, Gray's Inn, 1985, Bencher, 2004; in practice at the Bar, 1986–; Jt Hd, Blackstone Chambers, 2012–. Part-time tutor in law, UCL, 1984–87. Mem., HM Treasury Solicitor's Supplementary Common Law Panel, 1997–99; Jun. Counsel to the Crown (A Panel), 1999–2001. *Publications:* contributor: Human Rights Law and Practice, 1999; European Employment Law in the UK, 2001; Halsbury's Laws of England. *Recreation:* literature. *Address:* Blackstone Chambers, Blackstone House, Temple, EC4Y 9BW.

CARSTEN, Prof. Janet, PhD; FBA 2011; FRSE; Professor of Social and Cultural Anthropology, University of Edinburgh; *m* 1994, Prof. Jonathan Robert Spencer, *qv*; one *d*. *Educ:* London Sch. of Econs and Pol Sci. (PhD). Res. Fellow, Univ. of Cambridge; Lectr, Univ. of Manchester. Leverhulme Maj. Res. Fellow, 2007–10. FRSE 2006. *Publications:* (ed with S. Hugh-Jones) About the House: Lévi-Strauss and beyond, 1995; The Heat of the Hearth: the process of kinship in a Malay fishing community, 1997; (ed) Cultures of Relatedness: new approaches to the study of kinship, 2000; After Kinship, 2004; (ed) Ghosts of Memory: essays on remembrance and relatedness, 2007; (ed) Blood Will Out: essays on liquid transfers and flows, 2013; contribs to jls incl. Jl RAI, Annual Rev. Anthropol., Amer. Ethnologist, Anthropol Qly. *Address:* School of Social and Political Science, University of Edinburgh, 5.24 Chrystal Macmillan Building, 15a George Square, Edinburgh EH8 9LD.

CARSTEN, Prof. Oliver Michael John, PhD; Professor of Transport Safety, Institute for Transport Studies, University of Leeds, since 2003; *b* 9 Aug. 1948; *s* of Francis and Ruth Carsten; *m* 1987, Svetlana; one *s* one *d*. *Educ:* Merton Coll., Oxford (BA Modern Hist. 1969); Univ. of Michigan (MA Hist. 1973; PhD Hist. 1981). University of Michigan Transportation Research Institute: Res. Asst, 1977–79; Res. Associate, 1979–85; Asst Res. Scientist, 1985–87; Institute for Transport Studies, University of Leeds: Res. Fellow, 1987–89; Sen. Res. Fellow, 1993–2003. Visiting Professor: Helsinki Univ. of Technol., 1999; Univ. of Valenciennes, 2012–13. Chm., Road Behaviour Wkg Party, Parly Adv. Council for Transport Safety, 1993–. Ed.-in-Chief, Cognition, Technol. & Work, 2014–. *Publications:* contribs to learned jls and books. *Recreations:* walking, cycling, travel. *Fax:* (office) (0113) 343 5334. *E:* o.m.j.carsten@its.leeds.ac.uk.

CARSTENSEN, Laura Martine; Commissioner, Equality and Human Rights Commission, since 2013; *b* Stockport, 11 Nov. 1960; *d* of Gordon McRoberts and Pauline McRoberts; *m* 1995, Peter Andreas Günter Frithjof Carstensen; five *s* one *d*. *Educ:* Withington Girls Sch., Manchester; St Hilda's Coll., Oxford (BA Hons 1st Cl. Eng. Lang. and Lit. 1982; MA). Admitted Solicitor, 1985. Partner, Slaughter and May, 1994–2004. Mem., 2005–14, Dep. Chm., 2010–11, Competition Commn. Mem., Business Oversight Bd, Law Soc., 2012–14. Mem., Co-operation and Competition Panel, NHS Funded Services, 2009–14; non-exec. Dir, Countess of Chester Hosp. NHS Foundn Trust, 2011–13. Non-executive Director: Park Group plc, 2013– (Chm., Audit Cttee, 2013–); Co-operative Bank plc, 2014– (Chm., Values and Ethics, 2014–). Chm. Council, Women's Liby, 2010–12; Gov., London Metropolitan Univ., 2010–12. Trustee, Nat. Mus Liverpool, 2011–. Founder and Dir, Blue Banyan Ltd, 2004–14. *Recreations:* gardening, theatre, detective fiction. *E:* laura@carstensen.co.uk.

CARSWELL, family name of **Baron Carswell**.

CARSWELL, Baron *cr* 2004 (Life Peer), of Killeen in the county of Down; **Robert Douglas Carswell,** Kt 1988; PC 1993; a Lord of Appeal in Ordinary, 2004–09; *b* 28 June 1934; *er s* of late Alan E. Carswell and Nance E. Carswell; *m* 1961, Romayne Winifred Ferris (*see* R. W. Carswell); two *d*. *Educ:* Royal Belfast Academical Instn; Pembroke Coll., Oxford (Schol.; 1st Cl. Honour Mods, 1st Cl. Jurisprudence, MA; Hon. Fellow, 1984); Univ. of Chicago Law Sch. (JD). Called to Bar of N Ireland, 1957 (Bencher, 1979), and to English Bar, Gray's Inn, 1972 (Hon. Bencher, 1993); Counsel to Attorney-General for N Ireland, 1970–71; QC (NI), 1971; Sen. Crown Counsel in NI, 1979–84; Judge of High Court of Justice, NI, 1984–93; Lord Justice of Appeal, Supreme Court of Judicature, NI, 1993–97; Lord Chief Justice of NI, 1997–2004. Chancellor, Dios of Armagh and of Down and Dromore, 1990–97. Chairman: Council of Law Reporting for NI, 1987–97; Law Reform Adv. Cttee for NI, 1989–97. Pres., NI Scout Council, 1993–2014. Pres., Royal Belfast Academical Instn, 2004– (Gov., 1967–2004; Chm. Bd of Govs, 1986–97); Pro-Chancellor and Chm. Council, Univ. of Ulster, 1984–94. Hon. Bencher, King's Inns, Dublin, 1997. Hon. DLitt Ulster, 1994. *Publications:* Trustee Acts (Northern Ireland), 1964; articles in legal periodicals. *Recreations:* golf, hill walking. *Address:* House of Lords, SW1A 0PW. *Club:* Ulster Reform (Belfast).

CARSWELL, Lady, (Romayne Winifred Carswell), CVO 2010; OBE 1988; Lord-Lieutenant, County Borough of Belfast, 2000–09; *d* of late James Ferris, JP and Eileen Ferris, JP, of Greyabbey, Co. Down; *m* 1961, Robert Douglas Carswell (*see* Baron Carswell); two *d*. *Educ:* Victoria Coll., Belfast; Queen's Univ., Belfast (BA, LLB). Asst Principal, NICS, 1959–61; Mem., 1977–83, Dep. Chm., 1983–94, Police Complaints Bd for NI, subseq. Ind. Commn for Police Complaints; Member: Standing Adv. Commn on Human Rights, 1984–86; Industrial Tribunals, 1987–97. Mem., Bd of Govs, Victoria Coll., Belfast, 1979–99 (Dep. Chm., 1995–99). President: Friends of Ulster Mus., 1996–2011; Ulster Soc. for the Protection of the Countryside, 2009–15; Trustee: Ulster Histl Foundn, 1991–2004 (Dep. Chm., 1997–2000); Winston Churchill Meml Trust, 2002–09. Pres., RFCA for NI, 2005–09; Hon. Captain, RNR, 2005–13; Vice-Pres., Belfast Br., RN Assoc., 2010–. DL Belfast, 1997; JP 2000. DStJ 2010 (CStJ 2000). *Recreations:* heritage, conservation. *Address:* c/o Lord Carswell, House of Lords, SW1A 0PW.

CARSWELL, (John) Douglas (Wilson); MP (UK Ind) Clacton, since Oct. 2014 (MP (C) Harwich, 2005–10, Clacton, 2010–Aug. 2014); *b* 3 May 1971; *s* of John Wilson Carswell, OBE, FRCS and Margaret Carswell (*née* Clark); *m* 2008, Clementine Bailey; one *d*. *Educ:* Charterhouse; Univ. of E Anglia (BA Hons 1993); King's Coll. London (MA). Corporate Develt Manager, Orbit Television, Rome, 1997–99; Chief Project Officer, Invesco Continental Europe, 1999–2003. Mem., Cons. Party Policy Unit, 2004–05. Member: Commons Select Cttee on Educn, 2006–10; Public Accounts Cttee, 2009–10. Founder, www.direct-democracy.co.uk, 2006–09. *Publications:* (jtly) Direct Democracy: an agenda for a new model party, 2005; (with Daniel Hannan) The Plan: 12 months to renew Britain, 2008; The End of Politics and the birth of iDemocracy, 2012; pamphlets. *Recreations:* blogs each day at www.TalkCarswell.com, keen swimmer, occasional rider, passionate gardener. *Address:* House of Commons, SW1A 0AA. *E:* douglas@douglascarswell.com. *W:* www.TalkCarswell.com, www.douglascarswell.com.

CARTER; *see* Bonham-Carter and Bonham Carter.

CARTER, family name of **Barons Carter of Barnes** and **Carter of Coles**.

CARTER OF BARNES, Baron *cr* 2008 (Life Peer), of Barnes in the London Borough of Richmond upon Thames; **Stephen Andrew Carter,** CBE 2007; Group Chief Executive, Informa, since 2014 (non executive Director, 2010–13); *b* 12 Feb. 1964; *s* of Robert and Margaret Carter; *m* 1992, Anna Gorman; one *s* one *d*. *Educ:* Aberdeen Univ. (BA Hons Law); Harvard Business Sch. (AMP 1997). Man. Dir and Chief Exec., J. W. Thompson, 1992–2000; Chief Operating Officer and Man. Dir, ntl, UK and Ireland, 2000–02; CEO, OFCOM, 2003–06; Gp Chief Exec., Brunswick Gp LLP, 2007–08; Chief of Strategy and Principal Advr to the Prime Minister, 2008; Parly Under Sec. of State, BIS (formerly BERR) and DCMS, 2008–09; Pres. and Man. Dir, EMEA, and Chief Marketing and Communications Officer, Alcatel-Lucent, 2010–13. Non-executive Director: Travis Perkins plc, 2006–08; Royal Mail Hldgs plc, 2007–08; United Utilities plc, 2014–. Vice Pres., UNICEF, 2005–. Trustee, RSC, 2007–. Gov., Ashridge Business Mgt Sch., 2005–14 (Chm., 2007–14). Hon. LLD Aberdeen, 2010. *Address:* House of Lords, SW1A 0PW.

CARTER OF COLES, Baron *cr* 2004 (Life Peer), of Westmill in the County of Hertfordshire; **Patrick Robert Carter;** Chairman, NHS Procurement and Efficiency Board, since 2014; *b* 9 Feb. 1946; *s* of Robert Carter and Ann Carter (*née* Richards); *m* 1969, Julia Bourne; two *d*. *Educ:* Brentwood Sch.; Hatfield Coll., Univ. of Durham. Hambros Bank, 1967–70; Whitecross Equipment Ltd, 1970–75; Dir, MAI plc, 1975–85; founder and Dir, Westminster Health Care plc, 1985–99. Review Chairman: Commonwealth Games, 2001; Nat. Stadium, 2002; Payroll Services, 2003; Criminal Records, 2003; Offender Services, 2004; Legal Aid, 2005–06; Pathology, 2005–08; Efficient Use of Property Across Public Sector, 2008–09. Chm., Sport England, 2002–06. *Recreations:* reading, opera, walking, ski-ing, gardening. *Address:* House of Lords, SW1A 0PW.

CARTER, Andrew, CMG 1995; HM Diplomatic Service, retired; Warden, St George's House, Windsor Castle, 2003–08; *b* 4 Dec. 1943; *s* of Eric and Margaret Carter; *m* 1st, 1973, Anne Caroline Morgan (marr. diss. 1986); one *d*; 2nd, 1988, Catherine Mary Tyler (marr. diss. 2003); one *s* one *d*; 3rd, 2009, Lynn Marie Marcell Collins. *Educ:* Latymer Upper Sch., Hammersmith; Royal Coll. of Music; Jesus Coll., Cambridge (Scholar 1962; MA). FRCO; LRAM; ARCM. Asst Master, Marlborough Coll., 1965–70. Joined HM Diplomatic Service, 1971; Warsaw, 1972; Geneva, 1975; Bonn, 1975; FCO, 1978; Brussels, 1986; Dep. Gov., Gibraltar, 1990–95; Minister, Moscow, 1995–97; UK Perm. Rep. to Council of Europe, Strasbourg, 1997–2003. *Recreation:* music.

CARTER, Sir Andrew Nicholas, Kt 2014; OBE 2003; Head Teacher, South Farnham School, since 1988; *b* Oswestry, Shropshire, 19 July 1949; *s* of Norman Carter and Alice Carter; *m* 1978, Mary Daniel; one *s* two *d*. *Educ:* Bishop Otter Coll.; Univ. of Sussex (BEd 1977). Teacher, Kempshott Prim. Sch., Basingstoke, 1971–78; Dep. Head, Mayfield Jun. Sch., Farnborough, 1978–83; Head Teacher, Greenfields Jun. Sch., Hartley Wintney, 1983–88. Nat. Sch. Leader, 2009. Ambassador, Investors in People UK, 2004–; Trustee, Helen Arkell Dyslexia Centre, 2010–. *Recreations:* theatre, gardening, antiques, football, reading, shed making. *Address:* South Farnham School, Menin Way, Farnham GU9 8DY. *T:* (01252) 716155. *E:* head@south-farnham.surrey.sch.uk.

CARTER, Bernard Thomas, Hon. RE 1975; full-time artist (painter and etcher), since 1977; *b* 6 April 1920; *s* of Cecil Carter and Ethel Carter (*née* Darby); *m* Eugenie Alexander, artist and writer; one *s*. *Educ:* Haberdashers' Aske's; Goldsmiths' College of Art, London Univ. NDD, ATD. RAF, 1939–46. Art lectr, critic and book reviewer, 1952–68; National Maritime Museum: Asst Keeper (prints and drawings), 1968; Dep. Keeper (Head of Picture Dept), 1970; Keeper (Head of Dept of Pictures and Conservation), 1972–77. One-man exhibns in London: Arthur Jeffress Gall., 1955; Portal Gall., 1963, 1965, 1967, 1969, 1974, 1978, 1979, 1981, 1984, 1987, 1990 and 1993; mixed exhibns: Royal Academy, Arts Council, British Council and galleries in Europe and USA; works in public collections, galleries abroad and British educn authorities, etc. TV and radio include: Thames at Six, Pebble Mill at One, Kaleidoscope, London Radio, etc. *Publications:* Art for Young People (with Eugenie Alexander), 1958. *Recreations:* reading, listening to music, gardening, theatre.

CARTER, Dr Brandon, FRS 1981; Directeur de Recherche (Centre National de la Recherche Scientifique), Observatoire de Paris-Meudon, 1986–2009, now Emeritus; *b* Sydney, Australia, 26 May 1942; *s* of Harold Burnell Carter and Mary (*née* Brandon Jones); *m* 1969, Lucette Defrise; three *d*. *Educ:* George Watson's Coll., Edinburgh; Univ. of St Andrews; Pembroke Coll., Cambridge (MA, PhD 1968, DSc 1976). Res. Student, Dept of Applied Maths and Theoretical Physics, Cambridge, 1964–67; Res. Fellow, Pembroke Coll., Cambridge, 1967–68; Staff Mem., Inst. of Astronomy, Cambridge, 1968–73; Univ. Asst Lectr, 1973–74, Univ. Lectr, 1974–75, Dept of Applied Maths and Theoretical Physics, Cambridge; Maître de Recherche, co-responsable Groupe d'Astrophysique Relativiste (CNRS), Paris-Meudon, 1975–86. *Recreation:* wilderness. *Address:* 19 rue de la Borne au Diable, 92310 Sèvres, France. *T:* (1) 45344677.

CARTER, Carolyn Jayne; *see* Davidson, C. J.

CARTER, David; *see* Carter, Ronald D.

CARTER, Dr David, CVO 1995; HM Diplomatic Service, retired; High Commissioner, Bangladesh, 2000–04; *b* 4 May 1945; *s* of John Carter and Kathleen Carter (*née* Oke); *m* 1968, Susan Victoria Wright; one *s* one *d*. *Educ:* Zambia; Univ. of Wales (BA Jt Hons); Univ. of Durham (PhD 1978). Joined HM Diplomatic Service, 1970; FCO, 1970–71; Accra, 1971–75; FCO, 1975–80; Hd of Chancery, Manila, 1980–83; 1st Sec., S Africa Desk, later Dep. Hd, SE Asia Dept, FCO, 1983–86; Dep. High Comr and Counsellor, Lusaka, 1986–90; Counsellor and Overseas Inspector, FCO, 1990–92; Counsellor and Dep. Hd of Mission, Cape Town/Pretoria, 1992–96; Minister and Dep. Head of Mission, New Delhi, 1996–99. Dep. Dir, Centre for Security and Diplomacy, Birmingham Univ., 2005–06. Bursar, Lucy Cavendish Coll., Cambridge, 2006–10. Advr, Advocates for Internat. Develt, 2010–11. Mem., Royal Soc. for Asian Affairs, 2012–. *Publications:* contrib. jls on Southern Africa. *Recreations:* distant travel, music, reading, walking, manual labour. *E:* dcarter@carter42.com. *Club:* Royal Over-Seas League.

CARTER, Sir David (Craig), Kt 1996; MD; FRCSE, FMedSci, FRSE; Chief Medical Officer, Scottish Executive (formerly Scottish Office) Department of Health, 1996–2000; *b* 1 Sept. 1940; *s* of Horace Ramsay Carter and Mary Florence Carter (*née* Lister); *m* 1967, Ilske Ursula Luth; two *s*. *Educ:* Cockermouth Grammar Sch.; St Andrews Univ. (MB ChB, MD). FRCSE 1967; FRCSGlas 1980; FRCPE 1993; FRCS 1995; FFPH (FFPHM 1998). FRSE 1995. British Empire Cancer Campaign Fellow, 1967; Lecturer in Surgery: Edinburgh Univ., 1969; Makerere Univ., Uganda, 1972; Wellcome Trust Sen. Lectr, Edinburgh Univ., 1974, seconded for 12 months to Center for Ulcer Res. and Educn, LA, 1976; Sen. Lectr in Surgery, Edinburgh Univ., 1974–79; St Mungo Prof. of Surgery, Glasgow Univ., 1979–88; Regius Prof. of Clinical Surgery, Edin. Univ., 1988–96. Hon. Consultant Surgeon, Royal Infirmary, Edin., 1988–96; Hon. Consultant Surgeon and Chm., Scottish Liver Transplantation Unit, 1992–96; Surgeon to the Queen in Scotland, 1993–97. External Examiner at univs incl. London, Oxford, Leeds, Dundee, Newcastle, Hong Kong, Nairobi, Penang and Kuwait. Chairman: Scottish Foundn for Surgery in Nepal, 1988–2010; Scottish Council for Postgrad. Med. Educn, 1990–96; Scientific Adv. Cttee, CRC, 2000–02; BMA Bd of Science, 2002–05; Queen's Nursing Inst., Scotland, 2002–10; Scottish Stem Cell Network, 2003–05; Bd for Academic Med., Scotland, 2005–; Managed Service Network for Neurosurgery in Scotland, 2009–13; Mem. Council, WMA, 2002–05; Dir, Scottish Cancer Foundn, 2000–10; Member: Jt Med. Adv. Cttee, HEFC, 1993–96; Scientific Exec. Bd, Cancer Res. UK, 2002–04. President: Internat. Hepatobiliary-Pancreatic Assoc., 1988–89; Surgical Res. Soc., 1996–97; Assoc. of Surgeons of GB and Ire., 1996–97; BMA, 2001–02; Vice-Pres., RSE, 2000–03. Member: Council, RCSE, 1980–90; James IV Assoc. of Surgeons, 1981–; Internat. Surgical Gp, 1984–2005. Mem., Broadcasting Council, BBC Scotland, 1989–94. Non-exec. Dir,

Lothian Health Bd, 1994–96. Company Sec., British Jl of Surgery Soc., 1991–95; Co-Editor, British Journal of Surgery, 1986–91; General Editor, Operative Surgery, 1983–96. Mem. Court, St Andrews Univ., 1997–2000; Vice-Principal, Edinburgh Univ., 2000–02; Governor: Beatson Inst. for Cancer Res., 1997–2000; The Health Foundn (formerly PPP Healthcare Med. Trust), 2001–08 (Chm., 2002–08). Trustee, CRUK, 2004–07 (Chm. Council, Res. Strategy Gp, 2004–07; Vice Chm. Council, 2005–07). Mem., Amer. Surgical Assoc., 1997; Founder FMedSci 1998. Hon. FACS 1996; Hon. FRCSI 1996; Hon. FRACS 1998; Hon. FRCGP 1999; Hon. FRCPGlas 2003; Hon. FRCP 2005; Hon. Fellow: Deutsche Ges. für Chirurgie, 1994; Coll. of Surgeons of Hong Kong, 2003; Hon. Mem., Soc. of Surgeons of Nepal, 1994; For. Associate Mem., Inst. of Medicine, USA, 1998. Hon. DSc: St Andrews, 1997; Queen Margaret Coll., 1997; Aberdeen, 2000; Hull, 2010; Inst. of Cancer Res., London, 2011; Hon. LLD Dundee, 1997; Hon. MD Edinburgh, 2005. William Leslie Prize in Surgery, Univ. of Edinburgh, 1968; Moynihan Prize in Surgery, Assoc. of Surgeons of GB and Ire., 1973; Gold Medal, RCSE, 2000; G. B. Ong Medal, Hong Kong Univ., 2005; Gold Medal, BMA, 2006; Gold Medal, RSE, 2007. Gorka Dakshi Bahu (Nepal), 1999. *Publications:* Peptic Ulcer, 1983; Principles and Practice of Surgery, 1985; Pancreatitis, 1988; Surgery of the Pancreas, 1993, 2nd edn 1997; numerous contribs to surgical and gastroenterological jls. *Recreations:* music, gardening, philately. *Address:* 19 Buckingham Terrace, Edinburgh EH4 3AD. *T:* (0131) 332 5554. *Club:* New (Edinburgh).

CARTER, Rt Hon. David (Cunningham); MP (Nat.) New Zealand, since 1999 (Selwyn, 1994–96; Banks Peninsula, 1996–99); Speaker, House of Representatives, New Zealand, since 2013; *b* Christchurch, NZ, 3 April 1952; *s* of Maurice Rhodes Carter and Pauline Merle Carter; *m* 1991, Heather Robyn Guest; one *s* three *d*. *Educ:* Loreto Coll., Christchurch; St Bede's Coll., Christchurch; Lincoln Univ. (BAgrSc). Former farmer and business proprietor. Jun. Govt Whip, 1996–98; Associate Minister, for Food Fibre, Biosecurity and Border Control, for Revenue, and for Educn, 1998–99; Minister: for Sen. Citizens, 1998–99; for Biosecurity, 2008–11; of Agriculture and of Forestry, 2008–11; for Econ. Devel, 2011; of Local Govt, 2012–13; for Primary Industries, 2011–13. Pres., Simmental Cattle Breeders Soc. of NZ, 1989–93. *Recreations:* farming (sheep and beef), aviation, fitness. *Address:* Office of the Speaker, Parliament House, Parliament Buildings, Wellington 6160, New Zealand. *T:* 48179321. *E:* David.Carter@parliament.govt.nz.

CARTER, (Edward) Graydon; Editor in Chief, Vanity Fair, since 1992; *b* 14 July 1949; *s* of E. P. Carter and Margaret Ellen Carter; *m* 1st, 1982, Cynthia Williamson (marr. diss. 2003); three *s* one *d*; 2nd, 2005, Anna Scott, *d* of Sir Kenneth Bertram Adam Scott, *qv*; one *d*. *Educ:* Carleton Univ. (incomplete); Univ. of Ottawa (incomplete). Editor, The Canadian Review, 1973–77; Writer, Time, 1978–83; Writer, Life, 1983–86; Founder and Editor, Spy, 1986–91; Editor, New York Observer, 1991–92. Hon. Editor, Harvard Lampoon, 1989. Documentary producer: 9/11, 2002; The Kid Stays in the Picture, 2002; Chicago 10, Surfwise, 2007; Public Speaking, 2010; His Way, 2011. Theatrical producer, I'll Eat You Last: a chat with Sue Mengers, 2013. *Publications:* (ed) Vanity Fair's Hollywood, 2000; (ed) Vanity Fair's Oscar Nights, 2004; What We've Lost, 2004; (ed) Vanity Fair Portraits, 2008; (ed) Vanity Fair's Tales of Hollywood, 2008; (ed) Vanity Fair's Proust Questionnaire, 2009; (ed) The Great Hangover, 2010. *Recreation:* fly fishing. *Address:* (office) 1 World Trade Center, New York, NY 10007, USA. *Clubs:* Brook (New York); Washington (Washington, Connecticut); Mill Reef (Antigua).

CARTER, Elizabeth Angela; *see* Shaw, E. A.

CARTER, Elizabeth Mary; Consultant Editor, Good Food Guide, since 2006; *b* Stockport, 1 July 1960; *d* of James Wilfrid Carter and Betty Carter; *m* 1989, Neil Shilling; one *s* one *d*. *Educ:* Manchester Sch. of Art (BA Hons Graphic Design). Inspector, Egon Ronay's Guides, 1986–90; Ed., AA Restaurant Guide, 1995–2000; Ed.-in-Chief, Les Routiers UK and Ireland Guide, 2001–03. *Publications:* Majorcan Food and Cookery, 1989. *Recreations:* restaurants, cooking, family, cinema, reading, working out, walking. *Address:* Waitrose Good Food Guide, Waite House, Southern Industrial Estate, Bracknell, Berks RG12 8YA. *E:* elizabeth.carter@thegoodfoodguide.co.uk.

CARTER, Maj. Gen. Sir Evelyn John W.; *see* Webb-Carter.

CARTER, His Honour Frederick Brian; QC 1980; a Circuit Judge, 1985–2001; *b* 11 May 1933; *s* of late Arthur and Minnie Carter; *m* 1960, Elizabeth Hughes, JP, *d* of late W. B. Hughes and Mrs B. M. Hughes; one *s* three *d* (and one *s* decd). *Educ:* Stretford Grammar Sch.; King's Coll., London (LLB). Called to Bar, Gray's Inn, 1955, practised Northern Circuit, 1957–85; Prosecuting Counsel for Inland Revenue, Northern Circuit, 1973–80; a Recorder, 1978–85. Acting Deemster, 2001–03. *Recreations:* golf, travel. *Address:* Eccles Pike House, The Cockyard, Manchester Road, Chapel-en-le-Frith, High Peak SK23 9UH. *Clubs:* Big Four (Manchester); Chapel-en-le-Frith Golf.

CARTER, George; *see* Carter, W. G. K.

CARTER, Rev. Graham; *see* Carter, Rev. R. G.

CARTER, Graydon; *see* Carter, E. G.

CARTER, Harold Mark, CB 2015; Deputy Legal Adviser, Home Office, since 2009; *b* Haslemere, 21 Sept. 1958; *s* of Denis Mark and Ursula Mary Carter; *m* 1989, Hilary Jane Pharaoh; one *d*. *Educ:* Reading Univ. (LLB Hons). Legal Advr's Br., Home Office, 1989–2006; FCO, 2006–09. Bencher, Gray's Inn, 2014. *Recreations:* chess, music, running. *Address:* Home Office, 2 Marsham Street, SW1P 4DF. *T:* (020) 7035 1386.

CARTER, Imelda Mary Philomena Bernadette; *see* Staunton, I. M. P. B.

CARTER, James Earl, Jr, (Jimmy); President of the United States of America, 1977–81; *b* Plains, Georgia, USA, 1 Oct. 1924; *s* of late James Earl Carter and Lillian (*née* Gordy); *m* 1946, Rosalynn Smith; three *s* one *d*. *Educ:* Plains High Sch.; Georgia Southwestern Coll.; Georgia Inst. of Technology; US Naval Acad. (BS); Union Coll., Schenectady, NY (post grad.). Served in US Navy submarines and battleships, 1946–53; Ensign (commissioned, 1947); Lieut (JG) 1950, (SG) 1952; retd from US Navy, 1953. Became farmer and warehouseman, 1953, farming peanuts at Plains, Georgia, until 1977. Member: Sumter Co. (Ga) School Bd, 1955–62 (Chm. 1960–62); Americus and Sumter Co. Hosp. Authority, 1956–70; Sumter Co. (Ga) Library Bd, 1961; President: Plains Develt Corp., 1963; Georgia Planning Assoc., 1968; Chm., W Central Georgia Area Planning and Develt Commn, 1964; Dir, Georgia Crop Improvement Assoc., 1957–63 (Pres., 1961). State Chm., March of Dimes, 1968–70; Dist Governor, Lions Club, 1968–69. State Senator (Democrat), Georgia, 1963–67; Governor of Georgia, 1971–75. Chm., Congressional Campaign Cttee, Democratic Nat. Cttee, 1974; Democratic Candidate for the Presidency of the USA, 1976. Founder, Carter Center, Emory Univ., 1982. Mem., Bd of Dirs, Habitat for Humanity, 1984–87; Chairman, Board of Trustees: Carter Center, Inc., 1986–2005; Carter-Menil Human Rights Foundn, 1986–; Global 2000 Inc., 1986–; Chairman: Council of Freely-Elected Heads of Government, 1986–; Council of Internat. Negotiation Network, 1991–. Distinguished Prof., Emory Univ., 1982–. Baptist. Hon. LLD: Morehouse Coll., and Morris Brown Coll., 1972; Notre Dame, 1977; Emory Univ., 1979; Kwansei Gakuim Univ., Japan, and Georgia Southwestern Coll., 1981; New York Law Sch., and Bates Coll., 1985; Centre Coll., and Creighton Univ., 1987; Hon. DE Georgia Inst. Tech., 1979; Hon. PhD: Weizmann Inst. of Science, 1980; Tel Aviv Univ., 1983; Haifa Univ., 1987; Hon. DHL Central; Connecticut State Univ., 1985. Awards include: Gold Medal, Internat. Inst. for Human Rights, 1979; Internat. Mediation Medal, American Arbitration Assoc., 1979; Harry S. Truman Public Service Award, 1981; Ansel Adams Conservation Award, Wilderness Soc., 1982; Distinguished Service Award, Southern Baptist Convention, 1982; Human Rights Award, Internat. League for Human Rights, 1983; Albert Schweitzer Prize for Humanitarianism, 1987; Jefferson Award, Amer. Inst. of Public Service, 1990; Nobel Peace Prize, 2002. *Publications:* Why Not the Best?, 1975; A Government as Good as its People, 1977; Keeping Faith: memoirs of a President, 1982; Negotiation: the alternative to hostility, 1984; The Blood of Abraham, 1985; (with Rosalynn Carter) Everything to Gain: making the most of the rest of your life, 1987; An Outdoor Journal, 1988; Turning Point: a candidate, a state and a nation come of age, 1992; Talking Peace: a vision for the next generation, 1993; Always a Reckoning (poetry), 1995; Living Faith, 1996; Sources of Strength, 1997; The Virtues of Ageing, 1998; An Hour Before Daylight: memoirs of a rural boyhood, 2001; Christmas in Plains, 2001; The Hornet's Nest (novel), 2003; Sharing Good Times, 2004; Our Endangered Values: America's moral crisis, 2005; Palestine: peace not apartheid, 2006; Beyond the White House: waging peace, fighting disease, building hope, 2007; A Remarkable Mother, 2008; We Can Have Peace in the Holy Land, 2009; White House Diary, 2010; Through the Year with Jimmy Carter, 2011; (ed) NIV Lessons from the Life Bible, 2012; A Call to Action: women, religion, violence and power, 2014. *Address:* (office) The Carter Center, One Copenhill, 453 Freedom Parkway, Atlanta, GA 30307, USA.

CARTER, John, RA 2007; sculptor; *b* Hampton Hill, Middx, 3 March 1942; *s* of E. Gordon Carter and Mercia Carter (*née* Edmonds); *m* 1986, Belinda Cadbury. *Educ:* Halliford Sch.; Twickenham Sch. of Art; Kingston Sch. of Art; British Sch. at Rome. Leverhulme Travelling Scholar, 1963. Part time lectr in various art schs, 1965–99, Chelsea Coll. of Art and Design, 1980–99. *Solo exhibitions include:* in London: Redfern Gall., 1968, 1971, 1974, 1977, 2010, 2013; Nicola Jacobs Gall., 1980, 1983, 1987, 1990; Warwick Arts Trust (retrospective), 1983; Knoedler Gall., 1991; Francis Graham Dixon Gall., 1996; Blue Gall., 2004; Between Dimensions, Tennant Gall., Royal Acad. of Arts, 2013–14; Galerie Leonhard, Graz, 2014; in Germany: Galerie Hoffmann, Friedberg, 1990, 2008, 2014–15; Galerie Wack, Kaiserslautern, 1991, 2002, 2007, 2012, 2015; Gudrun Spielvogel, Munich, 1995, 1999, 2008, 2013; Galerie St Johann, Saarbrücken, 1998, 2009; Museum Moderner Kunst Landkreis Cuxhaven, Otterndorf, 1994; also in Austria, Belgium, Netherlands, Sweden, Switzerland, Japan, USA; *group exhibitions include:* Whitechapel Art Gall., 1966; Hayward Gall., London, 1974; British Art Show, 1979, 1984; British Council Collection, Serpentine Gall., London, 1980; Hayward Gall., London, 1981; Galerie Hoffmann, 1986; Wilhelm Hack Mus., Ludwigshafen, 1986; Musée André Malraux, Le Havre, 1988; Galerie New Space, Fulda, 1988; Musée des Beaux-Art, Mons, 1994; Pfalzgalerie Kaiserslautern, 1994; Magyar Képzömüveézeti Foiskola, Budapest, 1996; Mondriaanhuis, Amersfoort, 2000; Musée Matisse, Le Cateau-Cambresis, 2003; Southampton City Art Gall., 2008; Musées de Monbéliard, 2009; Musées de Sens, 2010; work in many public and corporate collections. Arts Council of GB Award, 1977, 1979; Prize, Tolly Cobbold Eastern Arts 3rd Nat. Exhibn, 1981. Peter Stuyvesant Foundn Travel Bursary to the USA, 1966. *Publications:* occasional articles for German gallery publications; *relevant publication:* (monograph) John Carter, by Chris Yetton, 2010. *Recreation:* hill walking in Wales. *Address:* c/o Redfern Gallery, 20 Cork Street, W1S 3HL. *T:* (020) 7734 1732, *Fax:* (020) 7494 2908. *E:* art@redfern-gallery.com; 71a Westbourne Park Road, W2 5QH. *E:* west2studios@waitrose.com. *Clubs:* Chelsea Arts, Arts.

CARTER, Sir John (Gordon Thomas), Kt 1998; FIA; Chief Executive, Commercial Union plc, 1994–98; *b* 28 Dec. 1937; *s* of Gordon Percival Carter and Mary Ann Carter (*née* Edgington); *m* 1961, Margaret Elizabeth Dobson; three *s*. *Educ:* City of Oxford High Sch.; Jesus Coll., Oxford (Lawrence Exhibnr; MA Maths; Hon. Fellow, 1998). FIA 1966. Nat. Service, MEAF, 1956–58. Joined Commercial Union, 1961: Life Manager, 1978–80; Dep. Gen. Manager, 1981–82; Gen. Manager, 1983–86; Dir, 1987–98. Director: Trade Indemnity plc, 1991–95; Credito Italiano Bank, 1994–99; NHBC, 1998–2011 (Chm., 2002–11); Canary Wharf Gp plc, 1999–2004; Mem., UK Bd Cttee, CGU plc, 1998–2000; Chm., Travelers Insce (formerly St Paul Travelers Insce) Co., 2007–; Dep. Chm., Travelers Syndicate Mgt, 2011–. Mem., Council for Industry and Higher Educn, 1993–98. Chairman: Mgt Cttee, Motor Insurers Bureau, 1985–90; Loss Prevention Council, 1991–94; Assoc. of British Insurers, 1995–97; Policyholders Protection Bd, 2000–01. Adviser: HSBC Investment Bank, 1998–2001; Munich Reinsurance Co. Ltd, 1998–2002 and 2004–11. Curator, Univ. Chest, 1998–2000, Mem. Investment Cttee, 2000–07, Oxford Univ.; Gov., London Guildhall Univ., 1998–2002 (Chm. Govs, 1999–2002); Chairman: London Metropolitan Univ., 2002–06; Cttee of Univ. Chairmen, 2004–06. *Recreations:* golf, ski-ing, hill walking, opera, theatre. *Address:* 42 Wolsey Road, Moor Park, Northwood, Middx HA6 2EN. *Club:* Moor Park Golf.

CARTER, Prof. (John) Timothy, PhD; FRCP, FFOM; Professor, Norwegian Centre for Maritime Medicine, University of Bergen, 2010–14, now Emeritus; *b* 12 Feb. 1944; *s* of Reginald John Carter and Linda Mary (*née* Briggs); one *s* two *d*. *Educ:* Dulwich Coll.; Corpus Christi Coll., Cambridge (MB, MA); University Coll. Hosp., London; Birmingham Univ. (PhD 2005). FFOM 1984; FRCP 1987. London Sch. of Hygiene, 1972–74 (MSc). MO, British Petroleum, 1974–78; SMO, BP Chemicals, 1978–83; Health and Safety Executive: Dir of Med. Services, 1983–92, and of Health Policy, 1989–92; Dir of Field Ops Div., 1992–96; Med. Advr, 1996–97; Chief Med. Advr, Maritime and Coastguard Agency (formerly DETR, then DTLR, later DfT), 1999–2014. Member: MRC, 1983–96; Bd, Faculty of Occupnl Medicine, 1982–88 (Vice Dean, 1996–98); Hon. Sec., Occupnl Medicine Section, RSM, 1979–83; President: British Occupnl Hygiene Soc., 1987–88; Internat. Maritime Health Assoc., 2005–07. *Publications:* Merchant Seamen's Health 1860–1960: medicine, technology, shipowners and the state, 2014; articles and books on transport safety and investigation and control of occupnl health hazards and med. history. *Recreations:* history—natural, medical and local.

CARTER, Prof. Joy, PhD; DL; Vice Chancellor, University of Winchester, since 2006; *b* 26 Dec. 1955; *d* of Douglas and Joyce; *m* Dr Martin Carter; four *s*. *Educ:* Univ. of Durham (BSc 1977); Univ. of Lancaster (PhD 1980). CGeol; FGS. Reader in Geochem., Univ. of Reading; Dean of Sci., Univ. of Derby; Pro-Vice-Chancellor (Academic), Univ. of Glamorgan. DL Hants, 2013–. *Publications:* (with T. Jickells) Biogeochemistry of Intertidal Sediments, 1997; (with A. Parker) Environmental Interactions of Clay Minerals, 1998; (with A. Stewart) Thematic Set on Environmental Geochemistry and Health, 2000; over 100 academic papers. *Recreations:* sports, antiques, her dog! *Address:* University of Winchester, Winchester, Hants SO22 4NR. *T:* (01962) 827222, *Fax:* (01962) 879033. *E:* joy.carter@winchester.ac.uk.

CARTER, Lucy Marianne; Chief Executive Officer, Sound Seekers, since 2012; *b* Portsmouth, 2 April 1970; *d* of Robin and Valerie Carter. *Educ:* Gonville and Caius Coll., Cambridge (BA Hons 1992). Teacher of Mathematics, James Allen's Girls' Sch., London, 1992–94; Policy Advr, Asst Pvte Sec. to Perm. Sec., then Pvte Sec. to Perm. Under-Sec., DFE, then DfEE, 1994–2000; mgt consultant, 2000–09; Sen. Governance Advr, 2009–12; Dir of Ops, Griffin Schs Trust, 2012–13. *Recreations:* knitting, studying for ICSA exam, planting lettuce and then watching it bolt. *Address:* 91 Shenley Road, SE5 8NE. *E:* lucymarianne@gmail.com. *Club:* Cavendish.

CARTER, Matthew, RDI 1981; Principal, Carter & Cone Type Inc., Cambridge, Mass, since 1992; *b* London, 1 Oct. 1937; *s* of late Harry Graham Carter, OBE and Ella Mary Carter (*née* Garratt). Punch Cutter, Netherlands, 1956; freelance designer of lettering and type, London, 1957–63; typographical advr, Crosfield Electronics, 1963–65; type designer: Mergenthaler Linotype, NY, 1965–71; Linotype Cos, London, 1971–81; Co-founder, Sen. Vice Pres. and

Dir, Bitstream Inc., 1981–92. Typographical Advr, HMSO, 1980–84; Consultant, Printer Planning Div., IBM, 1980–81. Typefaces designed include: Snell Roundhand, 1966; Olympian, 1970; Galliard, 1978; Bell Centennial, 1978; Bitstream Charter, 1987; Mantinia, 1993; Verdana, and Georgia, 1996; Miller, 1997; Yale, 2004; refinements to Franklin Gothic (for MOMA, NY), 2004. Seven typefaces acquired by MOMA, NY for Architecture and Design collection, 2011. Hon. DFA Art Inst. of Boston, 1992. Middleton Award, Amer. Center for Design, 1995; Chrysler Award for Innovation in Design, 1996; Amer. Inst. of Graphic Arts Medal, 1996; Vadim Award, Moscow Acad. of Graphic Design, 1998; Special Commendation, Prince Philip Designers Prize, CSD, 2004; MacArthur Fellow, 2010; Lifetime Achievement Award, Smithsonian Cooper-Hewitt Nat. Design Mus., 2011. *Address:* 36–A Rice Street, Cambridge, MA 02140, USA.

CARTER, Matthew John; Founder and Director, Message House, since 2013; *b* 22 March 1972; *s* of John Carter and Jill Tasker; *m* 1997, Erica Moffitt; three *s*. *Educ:* Univ. of Sheffield (BA Hons (Social and Pol Studies) 1993); Univ. of York (MA (Pol Philos.) 1994, DPhil (Politics) 1999). Tutor in Politics, Univ. of York, 1994–98; Labour Party: Regl Organiser, N and Yorks, 1998–99; Regl Dir, SW, 1999–2001; Asst Gen. Sec. (Policy and Pol Develt), 2001–03; Gen. Sec., 2004–05; Man. Dir, Penn, Schoen & Berland Associates Inc., 2006–10; Chm., Penn, Schoen & Berland Associates EMEA, 2010–13; Chief Exec., Burson-Marsteller, UK, 2010–13. Mem., Bd of Trustees, Tamasha Th. Co., 2007– (Vice Chm., 2009–). Mem. Bd, People United, 2013–. *Publications:* The People's Party: the history of the Labour Party (with A. W. Wright), 1997; T. H. Green and the Development of Ethical Socialism, 2003. *Recreations:* enjoys hill walking in the Lake District, running, supporting Grimsby Town FC.

CARTER, Gen. Sir Nicholas (Patrick), KCB 2014; CBE 2003 (MBE 1996; OBE 2001); DSO 2011; Chief of the General Staff, since 2014; Aide-de-Camp General to the Queen, since 2014; *b* Nairobi, 11 Feb. 1959; *s* of late Gerald and Elspeth Carter; *m* 1984, Louise Anne Ewart; three *s* one *d*. *Educ:* Winchester Coll.; RMA Sandhurst. Commnd RGJ, 1978; Regtl duty, NI, Cyprus, Germany and GB, 1978–90; Staff Coll., 1991; Co. Comd, 3 RGJ, 1992–93; Mil. Asst CGS, 1994–95; DS Staff Coll., 1996–98; CO, 2 RGJ, 1998–2000; Comdr, 20 Armd Bde, 2004–05; Dir, Army Resources and Plans, 2006–08; GOC 6th (UK) Div., 2009; Comdr, Regl Comd S, ISAF, Afghanistan, 2009–10; Dir Gen. Land Warfare, 2011; Comdr Field Army, 2012; Army 2020 Team Leader, 2012; Dep. Comdr ISAF, Afghanistan and UK Nat. Contingent Comdr, Afghanistan, 2012–13; Comdr Land Forces, 2013–14. Regtl Col, London Rifles, 2007–09; Dep. Col Comdt, AGC, 2011–14; Col Comdt, The Rifles, 2013–. Col, Mil. Ops Gp (Vol.), 2011–. QCVS 1998 and 2004. *Recreations:* golf, cricket, field sports. *Clubs:* Boodles; Berkshire Golf, St Enodoc Golf.

CARTER, Nigel, OBE 2012; Chief Executive, British and International Dental Health Foundation, since 1997; *b* Wolverhampton, 7 Aug. 1952; *s* of Wilfrid and Vera Carter. *Educ:* John Port Sch., Etwall, Derbys; Birmingham Univ. (BDS 1975). LDS 1975. General Dental Practice, Birmingham, 1975–97; Man. Dir, India Hse Trng and Recruitment, 1983–2001. Mem. Bd, Platform for Better Oral Health in Europe, 2013–. Chm., British Dental Health Foundn, 1987–89 (Trustee, 1978–97); Trustee, 2003–, Treas., 2005–, RSPH (formerly RSH). *Recreations:* music, opera, books, travel. *Address:* British Dental Health Foundation, Smile House, 2 East Union Street, Rugby CV22 6AJ. *T:* (01788) 546365. *E:* nigel@dentalhealth.org.

CARTER, Peter; QC 1995; *b* 8 Aug. 1952. *Educ:* University Coll. London (LLB 1973). Called to the Bar, Gray's Inn, 1974, Bencher, 2002. *Publications:* (jtly) Offences of Violence, 1991, supplement 1994. *Recreations:* poetry, cricket, walking. *Address:* 18 Red Lion Court, EC4A 3EB. *T:* (020) 7520 6000.

CARTER, Dr Peter John, OBE 2006; Chief Executive and General Secretary, Royal College of Nursing, since 2007; *s* of Reginald and Mary Carter; *m* Lilian Yap; two *d*. *Educ:* Univ. of Birmingham (MBA 1992; PhD 1998). MCIPD 1986. Psychiatric nurse trng, Hill End Hosp., St Albans, 1971; gen. nurse trng, St Albans City Hosp. and Inst. of Urology, London, 1976; clinical and managerial posts in Herts and Bedfordshire; Chief Exec., Brent, Kensington, Chelsea and Westminster Mental Health Trust, then Central and NW London Mental Health NHS Trust, 1995–2007. Visiting Professor: KCL, 2009–; Anglia Ruskin Univ., 2009–. Mem., Commn on the Future of Nursing and Midwifery, 2009–. Hon. Col 203 Field Hosp. (V), 2011–. Hon. FRCGP 2013. President's Medal, RCPsych, 2011. *Recreations:* Rugby, cricket, scuba diving, cycling, music, literature. *Address:* Royal College of Nursing, 20 Cavendish Square, W1G 0RN.

CARTER, Rev. (Ralph) Graham; Chair, Darlington District of the Methodist Church, 1997–2008; President, Methodist Conference, 2006–07; *b* 11 July 1943; *s* of Thomas Wilfrid Carter and Eva Carter (*née* Williams); *m* 1967, Rosamond Catherine Shaw; one *s* one *d*. *Educ:* Bede Grammar Sch., Sunderland; Queens' Coll., Cambridge (MA); Hartley Victoria Coll., Manchester. Ordained Minister, 1970; served in: Newcastle-upon-Tyne, 1967–71; Cramlington, Northumberland, 1971–74; Birkenhead, 1974–81; Liverpool, 1981–92; Durham, 1992–97. Religious producer, BBC Radio Merseyside, 1987–92. Chm., Trustees, Epworth Old Rectory, 2008–. *Recreations:* bird-watching, walking, model railways, supporting Sunderland FC and Durham CCC, listening to music, enjoying grandparenting, gardening.

CARTER, Raymond John, CBE 1991; Executive, 1980–2003, Director, 1983–2003, Marathon Oil Co.; *b* 17 Sept. 1935; *s* of late John Carter and Nellie Carter (*née* Woodcock); *m* 1959, Jeanette Hills; one *s* two *d*. *Educ:* Mortlake Co. Secondary Sch.; Reading Technical Coll.; Staffordshire Coll. of Technology. National Service, Army, 1953–55. Sperry Gyroscope Co.: Technical Asst, Research and Development Computer Studies, 1956–65. Electrical Engineer, Central Electricity Generating Bd, 1965–70, Mem., CEGB Management, 1979–80. Mem., Gen. Adv. Council, BBC, 1974–76. Mem., Interim Adv. Cttee (Teachers' Pay and Conditions), DES, 1987–91; Dep. Chm., School Teachers' Review Body, 1991–93. Mem. Easthampstead RDC, 1963–68. Contested: Wokingham, Gen. Elecn, 1966; Warwick and Leamington, By-elecn, March 1968; MP (Lab) Birmingham, Northfield, 1970–79; Parly Under-Sec. of State, Northern Ireland Office, 1976–79. Member: Public Accounts Cttee, 1973–74; Parly Science and Technology Cttee, 1974–76; author of Congenital Disabilities (Civil Liability) Act, 1976. Delegate: Council of Europe, 1974–76; WEU, 1974–76. Trustee, BM (Nat. Hist.), 1986–96; Patron, Guild of Handicraft Trust, 1991–. Mem., Develt Cttee, Arvon Foundn, 1991–2001. Gov., Wexham and Heatherwood Hosp. NHS Trust, 2011–14. Co-cataloguer and exhibitor, works of Sir John Betjeman, 1983. *Recreations:* walking, reading, writing. *Address:* 1 Lynwood Chase, Warfield Road, Bracknell, Berkshire RG12 2JT. *T:* (01344) 420237.

CARTER, Richard David; Director, Business Environment, Department for Business, Innovation and Skills, since 2011; *b* 1962; *s* of David and Dorothy Carter; *m* 1997, Ruth. *Educ:* Trinity Coll., Cambridge (BA Natural Scis 1984). MRSC 1987. DTI, 1984–94; Cabinet Office, 1994–95; DTI, 1995–98; Dir of Policy, Charity Commn (on loan from DTI), 1998–2001; with DTI, later BERR, then BIS, 2001–; Dir, Corporate Law and Governance and Dir, Europe, BIS, 2009–11. Non-exec. Bd Mem., Insolvency Service, 2013–. FRSA 2013. *Recreations:* gardening, fossicking in old public records. *Address:* Department for Business, Innovation and Skills, 1 Victoria Street, SW1H 0ET. *T:* (020) 7215 5000. *E:* Richard.Carter@bis.gsi.gov.uk.

CARTER, Prof. Richard Lawrance, CBE 1997; DM, DSc; Professorial Fellow, University of Surrey, 1994–2003; *b* 5 Sept. 1934; *o s* of Thomas Lawrance Carter and Rhoda Edith Carter (*née* Horton). *Educ:* St Lawrence Coll., Ramsgate; Corpus Christi Coll., Oxford (MA 1960; DM 1966); UCH, London (DSc 1978). FRCPath 1978; FRCP 2002. Med. posts, Radcliffe Infirmary, Oxford, Yale Univ., UCH; Reader in Pathology, Inst. of Cancer Research, and Consultant Histopathologist, Royal Marsden Hosp., Sutton, 1985–99. Consultant, Thames Cancer Registry, 1990–2004. Ombudsman, Lancet, 1998–2004. Former chm. or mem. of govt adv. cttees and wkg parties, DoH, DoE, MAFF, MoD; former examr, RCPath, RCS, RCSI; Fellow or Mem., RSocMed, UK Children's Cancer Study Gp. *Publications:* author, jt author or editor of books and papers on lab. and experimental aspects of human cancers, mainly of the head and neck, tumours in children, and human carcinogenesis. *Recreations:* gardening, birds, books, music. *Address:* Pine Cottage, The Street, Hascombe, Surrey GU8 4JN. *Club:* Athenæum.

CARTER, Roland; HM Diplomatic Service, retired; *b* 29 Aug. 1924; *s* of Ralph Carter; *m* 1950, Elisabeth Mary Green; one *s* two *d*. *Educ:* Cockburn High Sch., Leeds; Leeds Univ. Served War of 1939–45: Queen's Royal Regt, 1944; 6th Gurkha Rifles, 1945; Frontier Corps (South Waziristan and Gilgit Scouts), 1946. Seconded to Indian Political Service, as Asst Political Agent, Chilas, Gilgit Agency, 1946–47; Lectr, Zurich Univ. and Finnish Sch. of Economics, 1950–53. Joined Foreign Service, 1953: FO, 1953–54; Third Sec., Moscow, 1955; Germany, 1956–58; Second Sec., Helsinki, 1959 (First Sec., 1962); FO, 1962–67; Kuala Lumpur, 1967–69; Ambassador to People's Republic of Mongolia, 1969–71; seconded to Cabinet Office, 1971–74; Counsellor: Pretoria, 1974–77; FCO, 1977–80, retired. Area Appeals Manager, N and NE England, Nat. Soc. for Cancer Relief, 1981–89. Vis. Fellow, 1990–91, Vis. Sen. Res. Fellow, 1991–92, Inst. for Res. in the Social Scis, York Univ. *Publications:* Näin Puhutaan Englantia (in Finnish; with Erik Erämetsä), 1952. *Recreations:* music, linguistics, Iranian history and culture. *Address:* 4 Feversham Road, Helmsley, N Yorks YO62 5HN.

CARTER, (Ronald) David, CBE 1980; RDI 1975; Founder, DCA Design International Ltd, 1975 (Chairman, 1975–95; Director, 1995–99); Professor of Industrial Design Engineering, Royal College of Art, and Imperial College of Science, Technology and Medicine, 1991–95; *b* 30 Dec. 1927; *s* of H. Miles Carter and Margaret Carter; *m* 1953, Theo (Marjorie Elizabeth), *d* of Rev. L. T. Towers; two *s* two *d*. *Educ:* Wyggeston Sch., Leicester; Central Sch. of Art and Design, London. Served RN, 1946–48. Appts in industry, 1951–60; Principal, David Carter Associates, 1960–75. Visiting Lectr, Birmingham Coll. of Art and Design, 1960–65. Examr, RCA, 1976–79 and 1987–90. Mem., Design Council, 1972–84 (Dep. Chm., 1975–84; Chm., Report on Industrial Design Educn in UK, 1977). Pres., Soc. of Industrial Artists and Designers, 1974–75; Chm., DATEC, 1977–82; Royal Fine Arts Comr, 1986–98. Vice-Chm., Design Mus. (formerly Conran Foundn), 1992– (Chm., 1986–92; Trustee, 1981–95); Moderator, Hong Kong Polytechnic, 1981–86; Mem., Prince of Wales Award for Indust. Innovation, 1981–85. Governor, London Inst., 1988–91. Design Awards, 1961, 1969, 1983; Duke of Edinburgh Prize for Elegant Design, 1967. FCSD (FSIA 1967); Sen. FRCA 1995. FRSA 1975. Hon. DDes: De Montfort, 1993; UCE, 2000. *Recreations:* dry stone walls, boats, County Cork. *Address:* The Old Parsonage, Compton Abdale, near Cheltenham, Glos GL54 4DS. *T:* (01242) 890340. *Club:* Reform.

CARTER, Sir Ronald (Powell), ONZ 2014; KNZM 1998; consulting engineer, 2002–14; *b* Auckland, NZ, 1935; *s* of Eric Powell Carter and Sybil Muriel Carter (*née* Townsend); *m* 1960, Dianne Lewell Oxspring; two *s* one *d*. *Educ:* Auckland Grammar Sch.; Univ. of Auckland (BE 1956; ME 1958). Beca Carter Hollings and Ferner: Founding Partner, 1968; Mem. Bd, 1968–2002; CEO and Chm., 1986–97. Director: Electricity Corp. of NZ, 1992–99; Air New Zealand, 1998–2007; Rural Equities Ltd, 2004–. Chm., CAA NZ, 1992–98. Mem., Royal Commn of Inquiry into Canterbury Earthquake, 2011–12. Pres., Instn of Professional Engrs NZ, 1999. Chair, Selection Panel, Sir Peter Blake Leadership Awards, 2003–13 (Trustee, 2003–09). Hon. DEng Auckland, 2001; Hon. Dr Auckland Univ. Technol., 2013. *Recreations:* sailing, Rugby, developing a seaside garden, watching grandchildren activities. *Clubs:* Northern; Royal New Zealand Yacht Squadron.

CARTER, Sebastian; *see* Carter, T. S.

CARTER, Thomas Henry; HM Diplomatic Service; Ambassador to Guatemala, since 2015; *b* Norwich, 22 Nov. 1953; *s* of Claude and Anne Carter; *m* 1997, Carolyn Jayne Davidson, *qv*; two *s*. *Educ:* Norwich Sch.; Univ. of Kent (BA Hons French and German); Ecole Nat. d'Admin, Paris (Cycle Etranger); Open Univ. (MBA 2010). Entered FCO, 1976; Third Sec., Paris, 1979–82; Third, later Second Sec., Bogotá, 1983–86; UK Mission to UN, NY, 1986; FCO, 1987–90; First Secretary: Paris, 1990; Bonn, 1990–95; FCO, 1995–99; Hd, Political Section, Bangkok, 1999–2003; Jt Dep. Hd of Mission, Bratislava, 2004–08; Jt High Comr to Zambia, 2008–12; FCO, 2012–15. *Recreations:* sailing, ski-ing, cycling, collecting old bicycles and rickshaws. *Address:* c/o Foreign and Commonwealth Office, King Charles Street, SW1A 2AH.

CARTER, (Thomas) Sebastian; designer and printer; Partner, since 1971, and owner, since 1991, Rampant Lions Press; *b* 20 Feb. 1941; *s* of late William Nicholas Carter, OBE and Barbara Ruth Carter (*née* Digby); *m* 1966, Penelope Ann Bowes Kerr; one *s* one *d*. *Educ:* Christ's Hosp.; King's Coll., Cambridge (MA). Designer: John Murray, 1962–63; The Trianon Press, Paris, 1963–65; Ruari McLean Associates, 1965–66; joined Rampant Lions Press, 1966. Mem., Internat. Acad. of the Book and Art of the Book, Russia, 1995. Ed., Parenthesis (jl of Fine Press Bk Assoc.), 2006–. Francis Minns Meml Prize (for Shades by David Piper), NBL, 1971; Laureate Award, Amer. Printing History Assoc., 2013. *Publications:* The Book Becomes, 1984; Twentieth Century Type Designers, 1987, 2nd edn 1995; The Rampant Lions Press: a narrative catalogue, 2013; (jtly) The History of the Monotype Corporation, 2014; contributor: Matrix, 1983–; Oxford Companion to the Book, 2010. *Recreations:* gardening, food, listening to music. *Address:* 14 Magrath Avenue, Cambridge CB4 3AH. *T:* (01223) 363669.

CARTER, Timothy; *see* Carter, J. T.

CARTER, Prof. Timothy, PhD; David G. Frey Distinguished Professor of Music, University of North Carolina, since 2001; *b* 3 July 1954; *s* of Thomas Carter and Thais (*née* Epifantseff); *m* 1995, Annegret Fauser. *Educ:* Univ. of Durham (BA); Univ. of Birmingham (PhD 1980). Lectr in Music, Univ. of Lancaster, 1980–87; Lectr, 1987–92, Reader, 1992–95, Prof. of Music, 1995–2001, RHBNC, Univ. of London. Fellow, Harvard Center for Italian Renaissance Studies, Villa I Tatti, Florence, 1984–85. Ed., Music & Letters, 1992–99. Has made broadcasts. *Publications:* W. A. Mozart: Le Nozze di Figaro, 1987; Jacopo Peri (1561–1633): his life and works, 1989; Music in Late Renaissance and Early Baroque Italy, 1992; Monteverdi's Musical Theatre, 2002; Oklahoma!: the making of an American musical, 2007; articles and essays in Jl Royal Musical Assoc., Early Music Hist., Jl Amer. Musicological Soc. *Address:* Music Department, University of North Carolina, Chapel Hill, NC 27599–3320, USA.

CARTER, (William) George (Key), CBE 1994; DL; FCA; Chairman, Black Country Development Corporation, 1994–98; *b* 29 Jan. 1934; *s* of late William Tom Carter, OBE, JP and Georgina Margaret Carter (*née* Key); *m* 1965, Anne Rosalie Mary Flanagan; one *s* one *d*. *Educ:* Warwick School. FCA 1957. Articled with Loarridge Beaven & Co., 1951–56; joined Price Waterhouse, 1956; Nat. Service, 2nd Lieut, 16/5th Queen's Royal Lancers, 1958–60; returned to Price Waterhouse, 1960: Manager, 1963–66; Partner, London, 1966–82; Dir of Finance, 1966–70; Sen. Partner, W Midlands, 1982–94. Dir, W Midlands Develt Agency, 1989–95 (Chm., 1991–95); Mem., NW Worcs HA, 1994–96. Mem., Pharmacists Rev.

Panel, 1981–97. Member: CBI W Midlands Regl Council, 1988–98; DTI Industry '96 Steering Gp, 1993–97. Pres., Birmingham Chamber of Industry and Commerce, 1993–94; Vice-Chm., Birmingham Mkting Partnership, 1993–95; Non-executive Director: Birmingham Econ. Develt Partnership, 1991–95; Birmingham Children's Hosp. NHS Trust, 1996–2003. Institute of Chartered Accountants: Member: Insce Industry Cttee (Chm., 1974–80); Parly and Law Cttee, 1978–83; Co-Chm., Auditors and Actuaries Cttee, 1975–80; Courses Cttee 1978–81. Member: Birmingham Univ. Business Sch. Adv. Bd, 1989–99; Council, Aston Univ., 1995–98. Pres., ESU, Worcs, 1998–2003. Gov. and Feoffee, Old Swinford Hosp. Sch., 1986–2000. FRSA 1993. DL W Midlands, 1996; High Sheriff, W Midlands, 1998–99. CStJ 1998 (Chm., Council, W Midlands, 1994–2001; Mem., Chapter Gen., 1996–99; Mem., Priory of England Chapter, 1999–2002). *Publications:* (jtly) Institute of Chartered Accountants Guide to Investigations, 1978. *Recreations:* gardening, golf, shooting. *Address:* The Old Rectory, Elmley Lovett, Droitwich, Worcs WR9 0PS. *T:* (01299) 851459. *E:* wgkcarter@btinternet.com. *Club:* Cavalry and Guards.

CARTER-MANNING, Jeremy James; QC 1993; a Recorder, since 1993; *b* 25 Dec. 1947; *s* of Landon and Nancie Carter-Manning; *m* 1970, Bridget Mary Simpson; one *s* one *d*. *Educ:* St Paul's Sch. Solicitor, 1971; called to the Bar, Middle Temple, 1975, Bencher, 2002. Mem., Mental Health Rev. Tribunal, 1998–2003. Dir, Council for Registration of Forensic Practitioners, 1999–2006. *Recreations:* tennis, golf, food and wine. *Address:* Furnival Chambers, 30–32 Furnival Street, EC4A 1JQ. *T:* (020) 7405 3232. *Clubs:* Reform, Ivy; Southampton Football.

CARTER-STEPHENSON, George Anthony; QC 1998; *b* 10 July 1952; *s* of Raymond M. Stephenson and Brenda S. Stephenson; *m* 1974, Christine Maria; one *s* one *d*. *Educ:* Leeds Univ. (LLB Hons). Called to the Bar, Inner Temple, 1975; in practice at the Bar, 1975–. Jt Head of Chambers, 2009–. *Recreations:* motorcycling, theatre, cinema, music. *Address:* 25 Bedford Row, WC1R 4HD. *T:* (020) 7067 1500.

CARTLEDGE, Sir Bryan (George), KCMG 1985 (CMG 1980); Principal of Linacre College, Oxford, 1988–96 (Hon. Fellow, 1996); *b* 10 June 1931; *s* of Eric Montague George Cartledge and Phyllis (*née* Shaw); *m* 1st, 1960, Ruth Hylton Gass (marr. diss. 1994; she *d* 1998), *d* of John Gass; one *s* one *d*; 2nd, 1994, Dr Freda Gladys Newcombe (*d* 2001); 3rd, 2005, Helen Manolatos (*née* Mostra). *Educ:* Hurstpierpoint; St John's Coll., Cambridge (Hon. Fellow, 1985). Queen's Royal Regt, 1950–51. Commonwealth Fund Fellow, Stanford Univ., 1956–57; Research Fellow, St Antony's Coll., Oxford, 1958–59 (Hon. Fellow, 1987). Entered HM Foreign (subseq. Diplomatic) Service, 1960; served in FO, 1960–61; Stockholm, 1961–63; Moscow, 1963–66; DSAO, 1966–68; Tehran, 1968–70; Harvard Univ., 1971–72; Counsellor, Moscow, 1972–75; Head of E European and Soviet Dept, FCO, 1975–77; Private Sec. (Overseas Affairs) to Prime Minister, 1977–79; Ambassador to Hungary, 1980–83; Asst Under-Sec. of State, FCO, 1983–84; Dep. Sec. of the Cabinet, 1984–85; Ambassador to the Soviet Union, 1985–88. Commander's Cross, Order of Merit (Hungary), 2010. Lánchíd Prize (Hungary), 2013. *Publications:* (ed) Monitoring the Environment, 1992; (ed) Energy and the Environment, 1993; (ed) Health and the Environment, 1994; (ed) Population and the Environment, 1995; (ed) Transport and the Environment, 1996; (ed) Mind, Brain and Environment, 1997; The Will to Survive: a history of Hungary, 2006; Makers of the Modern World: Károlyi and Bethlen: Hungary, 2009. *Clubs:* Reform, Hurlingham.

CARTLEDGE, Prof. Paul Anthony, DPhil, PhD; FSA; A. G. Leventis Professor of Greek Culture, University of Cambridge, 2008–14, now Emeritus; Fellow, since 1981, and A. G. Leventis Senior Research Fellow, since 2014, Clare College, Cambridge (President, 2011–14); *b* 24 March 1947; *s* of Marcus Raymond and Margaret Christobel Cartledge; *m* 1976, Judith Portrait; one *d*. *Educ:* St Paul's Sch.; New Coll., Oxford (MA; DPhil 1975); MA TCD 1978; PhD Cantab 1979. FSA 1980. Craven Fellow, Oxford Univ., 1969–70; Harold Salvesen Jun. Fellow, University Coll., Oxford, 1970–72; Lecturer: in Classics, NUU, 1972–73, TCD, 1973–78; in Classical Civilization, Univ. of Warwick, 1978–79; University of Cambridge: Lectr in Classics, 1979–93; Reader in Greek History, 1993–99; Prof. of Greek History, 1999–2008; Chm., Faculty Bd of Classics, 2001–02; actg Master, Clare Coll., Cambridge, Lent term, 2012. Visiting Professor: Centre Louis Gernet, Paris, 1990; Sorbonne, Univ. de Paris VII, 1998–99; Ecole des Hautes Etudes en Sciences Sociales, Paris, 2007–08; Hellenic Parlt Global Dist. Prof., New York Univ., 2006–. Lectures: Lansdowne, Univ. of Victoria, BC, 1989, 1993; Crayenborgh Res. Seminar, Univ. of Leiden, 1999; T. B. L. Webster Meml, Stanford Univ., 1999; M. I. Finley Meml, Syracuse Univ., 2008. Syndic, Fitzwilliam Mus., 2002–. Gov., St Paul's Schs, 1991–2007. FRSA 2007. Hon. Dr Thessaly, 2011. Hon. Citizen, Sparta, Greece, 2004. Gold Cross, Order of Honour (Greece), 2002. *Publications:* Sparta and Lakonia: a regional history 1300–362 BC, 1979, 2nd edn 2002; Agesilaos and the Crisis of Sparta, 1987; (with A. Spawforth) Hellenistic and Roman Sparta: a tale of two cities, 1989, rev. edn 2002; Aristophanes and his Theatre of the Absurd, 1990, rev. edn 1999; (ed jtly) Nomos: essays in Athenian law, politics and society, 1990; (ed and trans.) Religion in the Ancient Greek City, 1992; The Greeks: a portrait of self and others, 1993, 2nd edn 2002; (ed jtly) Hellenistic Constructs: essays in culture, history and historiography, 1997; (ed) The Cambridge Illustrated History of Ancient Greece, 1997, 2nd edn 2002; (with R. Waterfield) Xenophon: Hiero the Tyrant and other treatises, 1997, rev. edn 2005; (ed jtly) Kosmos: essays in order, conflict and community in classical Athens, 1998; Democritus and Atomistic Politics, 1998; The Greeks: crucible of civilization, 2001; Spartan Reflections, 2001; (ed jtly) Money, Labour and Land: approaches to the economies of ancient Greece, 2001; The Spartans: an epic history, 2002, 2nd edn 2003; Alexander the Great: the hunt for a new past, 2004; Thermopylae: the battle that changed the world, 2006; Eine Trilogie über die Demokratie, 2008; Ancient Greek Political Thought in Practice, 2009; Ancient Greece: a history in eleven cities, 2009; Forever Young: why Cambridge has a Professor of Greek Culture, 2009; (ed jtly) Responses to Oliver Stone's Alexander: film, history and cultural studies, 2010; (ed jtly) The Cambridge World History of Slavery, vol. I, 2011; Ancient Greece: a very short introduction, 2011; After Thermopylae: the oath of Plataea and the end of the Graeco-Persian Wars, 2013; (with T. Holland) Herodotus: the Histories, 2013. *Recreations:* ballet, opera, theatre. *Address:* Clare College, Cambridge CB2 1TL. *T:* (01223) 335163, *Fax:* (01223) 333219. *Club:* Athenæum.

CARTLIDGE, James Roger; MP (C) South Suffolk, since 2015; *m* Emily, *d* of Sir (James) Gerald (Douglas) Howarth, *qv*; four *c* (incl. twins). *Educ:* Univ. of Manchester. Researcher for Cons. Party; leader writer, Daily Telegraph; Founder, Share to Buy Ltd, 2004. Mem. (C) Babergh DC, 2013–15. Contested (C) Lewisham Deptford, 2005. *Address:* House of Commons, SW1A 0AA.

CARTTISS, Michael Reginald Harry; Regional Volunteer Organiser, SOS Children's Villages UK, since 1999; *b* Norwich, 11 March 1938; *s* of Reginald Carttiss and Doris Culling. *Educ:* Filby County Primary Sch.; Great Yarmouth Tech. High Sch.; Goldsmiths' Coll., London Univ. (DipEd); LSE (part time, 1961–64). Nat. Service, RAF, 1956–58. Teacher: Orpington, Kent, and Waltham Cross, Herts, 1961–64; Oriel Grammar Sch., 1964–69; Cons. Party Agent, Gt Yarmouth, 1969–82. Norfolk County Council: Mem., 1966–87, 2001– (Dep. Leader, Cons. Gp, 2013–); Vice-Chm., 2006–07; Chm., 2007–08; Vice-Chm., 1972, Chm., 1982–84, Educn Cttee; Mem., Gt Yarmouth BC, 1973–82 (Leader, 1980–82). MP (C) Great Yarmouth, 1983–97; contested (C) same seat, 1997. Chm., Norfolk Museums Service, 1981–85; Comr, Gt Yarmouth Port and Haven Commn, 1982–86. Mem., E Anglian RHA, 1981–85; Chairman: Gt Yarmouth and Waveney CHC, 2001–03; Norfolk Health Scrutiny Cttee, 2005–07; Norfolk Health Overview and Scrutiny Cttee, 2009–. *Recreations:* reading, writing, talking, walking, theatre. *Address:* Melrose, Main Road, Filby, Great Yarmouth, Norfolk NR29 3HN.

CARTWRIGHT, David Edgar, DSc; FRS 1984; Assistant Director, Institute of Oceanographic Sciences, Bidston Observatory, Birkenhead, 1973–86, retired; *b* 21 Oct. 1926; *s* of Edgar A. Cartwright and Lucienne Cartwright (*née* Tartanson); *m* 1952, Anne-Marie Guerin; one *s* two *d* (and one *s* decd). *Educ:* St John's Coll., Cambridge (BA); King's Coll., London (BSc, DSc). Dept of Naval Construction, Admiralty, Bath, 1951–54; Nat. Inst. of Oceanography (later Inst. of Oceanographic Sciences), Wormley, Surrey: Sci. Officer, rising to Individual Merit SPSO, 1954–73; Research Associate, Univ. of California, La Jolla, 1964–65, 1993, 1994; Sen. Res. Associate, NASA-Goddard Space Flight Center, Greenbelt, Md, 1987–89; Consultant, NASA, 1990–92. Vis. Res. Fellow, Nat. Oceanographic Centre, Southampton, 1992–. Fellow: Royal Astronomical Soc., 1975; Amer. Geophysical Union, 1991. Dr (*hc*) Toulouse, 1992. *Publications:* Tides—a Scientific History, 1999; over 80 papers on marine sci. research; reviews, etc, in various learned jls. *Recreations:* music, walking. *Address:* 3 Borough House West, Borough Road, Petersfield, Hants GU32 3LF. *T:* (01730) 267195.

CARTWRIGHT, John Cameron; JP; Deputy Chairman, Police Complaints Authority, 1993–99 (Member, 1992–99); *b* 29 Nov. 1933; *s* of Aubrey John Randolph Cartwright and Ivy Adeline Billie Cartwright; *m* 1959, Iris June Tant (*d* 2014); one *s* one *d*. *Educ:* Woking County Grammar School. Exec. Officer, Home Civil Service, 1952–55; Labour Party Agent, 1955–67; Political Sec., RACS Ltd, 1967–72; Director, RACS Ltd, 1972–74. Leader, Greenwich Borough Council, 1971–74. Mem., Labour Party Nat. Exec. Cttee, 1971–75 and 1976–78. MP Greenwich, Woolwich East, Oct. 1974–1983, Woolwich, 1983–92 (Lab, 1974–81; SDP, 1981–90; Soc. Dem., 1990–92); contested (Soc. Dem.) Woolwich, 1992. PPS to Sec. of State for Education and Science, 1976–77; Chm., Parly Labour Party Defence Group, 1979–81; Mem., Select Cttee on Defence, 1979–82 and 1986–92; SDP party spokesman on environment, 1981–87, on defence and foreign affairs, 1983–87; SDP/Liberal Alliance spokesman on defence, 1987; SDP Parly Whip, 1983–92; Vice Pres., SDP, 1987–88, Pres., 1988–91. Jt Chm., Council for Advancement of Arab British Understanding, 1983–87; Vice-Chm., GB-USSR Assoc., 1983–91. Mem., Calcutt Cttee on Privacy and Related Matters, 1989–90. Non-executive Director: Lambeth, Southwark and Lewisham HA, 1995–2000; Maidstone and Tunbridge Wells NHS Trust, 2000–03. Vice-Pres., Assoc. of Metropolitan Authorities, 1974–. Trustee, Nat. Maritime Museum, 1976–83. Co. Sec., Maidstone Christian Care, 2002–10. JP Inner London, 1970. *Publications:* (jtly) Cruise, Pershing and SS20, 1985. *Recreations:* do-it-yourself, listening to jazz, supporting Lincoln City FC. *Address:* 64 Squires Way, Dartford, Kent DA2 7NW. *T:* (01322) 316152.

CARTWRIGHT, Prof. Nancy Lynn Delaney, (Lady Hampshire), PhD; FBA 1996; Professor of Philosophy, Durham University, since 2012; Professor of Philosophy, University of California at San Diego, since 1997; *b* 24 June 1944; *m* 1985, Sir Stuart Hampshire, FBA (*d* 2004); two *d*. *Educ:* Pittsburgh Univ. (BS Maths 1966); Univ. of Illinois (PhD 1971). Asst Prof. of Philosophy, Univ. of Maryland, 1971–73; Stanford University: Asst Prof., 1973–77; Associate Prof., 1977–83; Prof. of Philosophy, 1983–91; Prof. of Philosophy, Logic and Scientific Method, LSE, 1991–2012. Vis. Lectr, Cambridge Univ., 1974; Visiting Professor: UCLA, 1976; Princeton Univ., 1978; Pittsburgh Univ., 1984; Oslo Univ., 1993, 1994; Univ. of Calif, San Diego, 1995; Old Dominion Fellow, Princeton Univ., 1996. Assoc. Mem., Nuffield Coll., Oxford, 2001–05. President: Hist. of Sci., BAAS, 2001–02; Phil. of Sci. Assoc.; Past Pres., APA (Pacific Div.). Fellow, Amer. Phil Soc.; MacArthur Fellow, MacArthur Foundn, 1993. Mem., Acad. Leopoldina, 1999; Hon. For. Mem., Amer. Acad. of Arts and Sci., 2001. Hon. DLit St Andrews, 2013; Hon. DHL Southern Methodist, 2012. *Publications:* How the Laws of Physics Lie, 1983; Nature's Capacities and their Measurement, 1989; (jtly) Otto Neurath: philosophy between science and politics, 1995; The Dappled World: a study of the boundaries of science, 1999; Measuring Causes: invariance, modularity and the Causal Markov Condition (monograph), 2000; Hunting Causes and Using Them: approaches to philosophy and economics, 2007; Causal Powers: What are they? Why do we need them? What can and cannot be done with them?, 2007; (with J. Hardie) Evidence Based Policy: a practical guide to doing it better, 2012; Evidence: for policy and wheresoever rigor is a must, 2013. *Address:* Department of Philosophy, Durham University, 50 Old Elvet, Durham DH1 3HN. *T:* (0191) 334 6049.

CARTWRIGHT, Lt-Col Robert Guy, LVO 2005; Secretary, Central Chancery of Orders of Knighthood, 1999–2005, and Assistant Comptroller, 1999–2004, Lord Chamberlain's Office; Extra Equerry to the Queen, since 2000; *b* 6 Aug. 1950; *s* of late Major Robin Vivian Cartwright and Loveday Elizabeth Cartwright (*née* Leigh-Pemberton); *m* 1972, Caroline, *d* of late Gilbert Stephenson and Eleanor Stephenson; two *s*. *Educ:* Wellington Coll.; RMA Sandhurst; RMCS Shrivenham; RN Staff Coll. Commissioned Grenadier Guards, 1970; CO, 1st Bn Grenadier Guards, 1990–92; Directing Staff, RN Staff Coll., 1993–94; MoD, 1995–96; retired, 1996. Bursar, Ibstock Place Sch., Roehampton, 2005–. *Recreations:* running, reading, wine. *Address:* 151 Wakehurst Road, SW11 6BW.

CARTWRIGHT, Hon. Dame Silvia (Rose), PCNZM 2001; DBE 1989; QSO 2006; Governor-General of New Zealand, 2001–06; Trial Chamber Judge, Extraordinary Chambers in the Courts of Cambodia, 2006–14; *b* 7 Nov. 1943; *d* of Monteith Poulter and Eileen Jane Poulter, both of Dunedin, NZ; *m* 1969, Peter John Cartwright. *Educ:* Univ. of Otago, NZ (LLB). Partner, Harkness Henry & Co., Barristers and Solicitors, Hamilton, NZ, 1971–81; Dist Court and Family Court Judge, 1981–89; Chief Dist Court Judge, 1989–93; Judge of the High Court, NZ, 1993–2001. Mem., Commn for the Future, 1975–80; conducted Inquiry into: Soc. Sci. Funding in NZ, 1986–87; Treatment of Cervical Cancer at Nat. Women's Hosp., Auckland, NZ, 1987–88. Mem. Cttee, UN Human Rights Convention to eliminate discrimination against women, 1992–2000; Chair, NZ Commission to UNESCO, 2006–08; Advr, UN Human Rights Council Investigation on Sri Lanka, 2014–. Hon. LLD: Otago, 1993; Waikato, 1994; Canterbury, 2004; Ewha, Seoul, 2006.

CARTWRIGHT, Sonia Rosemary Susan, (Mrs C. Cartwright); *see* Proudman, Hon. Dame S. R. S.

CARTWRIGHT, Stacey Lee; Chief Executive, Harvey Nichols Group Ltd, since 2014; *b* Stourbridge, 18 Nov. 1963; *d* of John and Eirwen Gainham; two *s* one *d*. *Educ:* London Sch. of Econs and Pol Sci. (BSc Econ). ACA 1988. With PricewaterhouseCoopers, 1985–88; Granada Gp plc: Hd Office Accountant, 1988–89; Gp Accounting Manager, 1989–91; Gp Financial Controller, 1991–94; Finance Dir, Spring Grove Services, 1994–96; Dir, Corporate Develt, 1996–98; Commercial Dir, Granada Media, 1998–99; Chief Financial Officer, Egg plc, 1999–2003; Exec. Vice Pres. and Chief Financial Officer, Burberry Group plc, 2004–13. Non-exec. Dir, GlaxoSmithKline plc, 2011–. *Recreations:* cycling, tennis, travelling, eating out. *Address:* Harvey Nichols Group Ltd, 361–365 Chiswick High Road, W4 4HS.

CARTY, Hilary; consultant, leadership, organisation development, cultural services and change, since 2011; *b* 26 May 1962; *d* of Solomon Carty and Catherine (*née* Bailey). *Educ:* Leicester Poly. (BA Hons Performing Arts, 1983); Cultural Trng Centre, Jamaica (Cert. in Dance Educn, 1984); Univ. of Westminster (MBA 1994). Advanced Cert. in Coaching and Mentoring, CIPD, 2009; Cert. in Orgn Develt, Nat. Trng Labs Inst. of Applied Scis, Oxford, 2011. Community Arts Officer, Leics Expressive Arts, 1985; Community Arts Develt Officer, The Cave, Birmingham, 1985; Arts Officer (Dance and Mime), E Midlands Arts, 1986–90; Gen. Manager, Adzido Pan African Dance Ensemble, 1990–94; Dir of Dance, Arts Council, 1994–2003; Arts Council England: Dir, Performing Arts, 2003–06; on secondment as Dir, Culture and Educn, London 2012, 2004–06; Dir, London (Arts), 2006; Dir, Cultural

Leadership Prog., 2006–11. Vis. Prof., Kufstein Tirol Univ. of Applied Scis, 2012. Fellow, Goldsmiths, Univ. of London, 2012. Hon. DA De Montfort, 2001; DUniv Middx, 2009; Hon. DLitt Westminster, 2014. *Publications:* Folk Dances of Jamaica, 1988. *Recreations:* theatre, dance, sports, walking.

CARUANA, Hon. Sir Peter (Richard), KCMG 2013; QC (Gibraltar) 1998; MP (GSD) Gibraltar, since 1991; Leader of the Opposition, Gibraltar, 2011–13; *b* 15 Oct. 1956; *s* of John Joseph Caruana and Maria Teresa Caruana (*née* Vasquez); *m* 1982, Cristina Maria Triay; three *s* three *d* (and one *s* decd). *Educ:* Ratcliffe Coll., Leicester; Queen Mary Coll., London Univ. (Hon. Fellow, 1997); Council of Legal Educn, London. Called to the Bar, Inner Temple, 1979, Overseas Bencher, 2011; with law firm Triay & Triay, Gibraltar, 1979–95, Partner specialising in commercial and shipping law, 1990–95. Joined GSD, 1990, Leader, 1991–2013; Leader of the Opposition, Gibraltar, 1992–96; Chief Minister of Gibraltar, 1996–2011. *Recreation:* golf. *Address:* 10/3 Irish Town, Gibraltar.

CARUS, Roderick; QC 1990; a Recorder, since 1990; *b* 4 June 1944; *s* of Anthony and Kathleen Carus; *m* 1972, Hilary Mary (*née* Jones); two *s* two *d*. *Educ:* Wirral GS, Merseyside; University Coll., Oxford (BA Law); Manchester Business Sch. (Postgrad. Diploma in Advanced Business Studies). Called to the Bar, Gray's Inn, 1971. Merchant bank, investments, 1966–70. Asst Recorder, 1987–90. *Recreations:* chess, crosswords, fishing, gardening, sailing. *Address:* Pant Farm, Bwlchtocyn, Pwllheli, Gwynedd LL53 7BY.

CARUSO, Adam; Partner, Caruso St John Architects, since 1990; *b* 8 Feb. 1962; *s* of Irving and Naomi Caruso; *m* 1996, Helen Thomas; one *s*. *Educ:* McGill Univ., Montreal (BSc Arch 1984; BArch 1986). ARB 1990; RIBA 1991. Architectural asst, Florian Beigel, 1986–87; Architect, Arup Associates, 1987–90. Projects include: New Art Gall. and Public Sq., Walsall, 1996; Gagosian Galls, phases 1 and 2, 1999–2001, phase 3, 2004; Barbican concert hall refurbishment, 2001; Stortorget, Kalmar, Sweden, 2003; Bethnal Green Mus. of Childhood, phase 1, 2003, phase 2, 2006; Brick House, London, 2005; Hallfield Sch., London, 2005; West Range Project, Downing Coll., Cambridge, 2006; Tate Britain Masterplan, 2006; Nottingham Contemporary, 2009; Chiswick Café, London, 2009. Taught, Univ. of North London, 1990–98; Professor: Univ. of Bath, 2002–04; ETH Zurich, Switzerland, 2011– (Guest Prof., 2007–09). Guest Prof., Acad. of Architecture, Mendrisio, Switzerland, 1999–2001; Design Critic, Graduate Sch. of Design, Harvard Univ., 2005; Vis. Prof., Cities Prog., LSE, 2006–08. *Publications:* contributor to: New Art Gallery Walsall, 2002; Caruso St John Architects: knitting, weaving, wrapping, pressing, 2002; As Built: Caruso St John Architects, 2005; Almost Everything, 2008; Feeling of Things, 2008. *Address:* Caruso St John Architects, 1 Coate Street, E2 9AG. *T:* (020) 7613 3161, *Fax:* (020) 7729 6188. *E:* acaruso@carusostjohn.com.

CARVEL, John Douglas; journalist; Social Affairs Editor, The Guardian, 2000–09; *b* 26 May 1947; *s* of late Robert Burns Carvel and Florence Annie Carvel (*née* Wilson); marr. diss.; two *s*; partner, Alison Hargreaves. *Educ:* Merchant Taylors' Sch., Northwood; Exeter Coll., Oxford (BA Hons PPE). Reporter, Newcastle Jl, 1969–72; The Guardian, 1973–2009: Business Reporter, 1973–75; News Ed., Financial Guardian, 1975–76; Industrial Corresp., 1976–79; Dep. Features Ed., 1979–81; Local Govt Corresp., 1981–85; Political Corresp., 1985–89; Associate Ed., 1989–2009; Home Affairs Ed., 1989–92; Eur. Affairs Ed., 1992–95; Educn Ed., 1995–2000. Core Mem., NHS Nat. Leadership Council, 2009–11; Member: Quality Inf. Cttee, 2010–13, Inf. Governance Review, 2012–13, DoH; Healthwatch England Nat. Cttee, 2012– (Sen. Ind. Mem., 2014–); Nat. Inf. Governance Cttee, 2013– (Dep. Chm., 2014–); Ind. Inf. Governance Oversight Panel, 2013–. Commendation, British Press Awards, 1984 and 1990; Local Govt Journalist of Year, Local Govt Inf. Services, 1985; Legal Affairs Journalist of Year, Bar Council, 1991; Freedom of Information Award, Campaign for Freedom of Inf., 1995; Medical Journalist of the Year, BMA, 2004. *Publications:* Citizen Ken, 1984, 2nd edn 1986; An Account of the Guardian Case, in Openness and Transparency in the EU, ed V. Deckmyn and I. Thomson, 1998; Turn Again Livingstone, 1999. *Recreations:* golf, gardening. *Address:* The Shutters, Buckhorn Weston, Gillingham, Dorset SP8 5HF.

CARVER, James Bruce; Member (UK Ind) West Midlands, European Parliament, since 2014; *b* Farnborough, Kent, 15 Aug. 1969; *s* of late Joseph Carver and Judith Carver (*née* Dale); *m* 1998, Carmen Harding (*d* 2009). *Educ:* St John Rigby RC Comprehensive Sch., W Wickham; Orpington Coll. of Further Educn. Solicitors' clerk, Speechly Bircham, 1989–91; Proprietor, James Carver Umbrellas, 1991–. Mem., UKIP, 1996–; Chm., Orpington UKIP, 1996–99. Contested (UK Ind): Orpington, 1997; Cheltenham, 2001; Preseli Pembrokeshire, 2005; Stourbridge, 2015; London, EP, 1999. Mem., London Scottish Regtl Assoc., 1992. *Recreations:* my Jack Russell terriers, running, military history, Rugby Union, metal detecting. *Address:* European Parliament, Altiero Spinelli 03F158, 60 Rue Wiertz, 1047 Brussels, Belgium. *T:* 22845744, *Fax:* 22849744. *E:* mep@jamescarver.org; 117 Coventry Street, Kidderminster, Worcs DY6 7ED.

CARVER, Margaret Adela Miriam; Managing Director, Carver Care Group, since 2006; Chairman: RaceTech Ltd, since 2013; Racecourse Association, since 2015; *b* Sutton-upon-Hull, 10 July 1964; *d* of Dr Ivan Hall and Elisabeth Hall; *m* 1992, William Carver; two *d*. *Educ:* Beverley High Sch.; St Edmund Hall, Oxford (MA Biochem. 1986). ARCM 1987. Investment banker (Banking, Equities, Corporate Finance), S. G. Warburg, 1987–91; Gp Corporate Affairs, MAI plc, 1991–95; Man. Dir, Channel Four Racing and Global Broadcasting, 1995–97. Chm., ITN, 2009–14; non-executive Director: Avenir Havas Media SA, 1991–93; Satellite Information Services, 1998–99; SDN Ltd, 2000–05; Link Licensing Ltd, 2001; Sporting Index plc, 2001–03; Channel 5 Television, 2005; RDF Media plc, 2005–09; British Waterways, 2007–11; BBFC, 2009–; Eden Project, 2010–13; Services Sound and Vision Corp., 2013–. Mem., Adv. Council, Rehearsal Orch., 1997–. Trustee, One Voice Europe charity, 2006–13. *Recreations:* music, flute playing, dance, art, architecture, the environment, athletics, horse racing. *Address:* c/o ITN, 200 Gray's Inn Road, WC1X 8XZ.

CARVER, Prof. Martin Oswald Hugh; Professor of Archaeology, University of York, 1986–2008, now Emeritus; *b* 8 July 1941; *s* of John Hobart Carver and Jocelyn Louisa Grace Tweedie; *m* 1st, 1963, Carolyn Rose Haig (marr. diss. 1978); one *s* one *d*; 2nd, 1981, Madeleine Rose Hummler; three *s* one *d*. *Educ:* Ladycross Sch., Seaford; Wellington Coll., Crowthorne; RMA, Sandhurst; Royal Military Coll., Shrivenham (BSc London); Univ. of Durham (Dip. Archaeol). Commnd RTR, 1961; Adjt, 4th RTR, 1969; retd in rank of Captain, 1972. Freelance archaeologist, researching and digging in England, Scotland, France and Italy, 1973–86; Founder Dir, Birmingham Univ. Field Archaeol. Unit, 1978–86; Dir, Centre for Medieval Studies, Univ. of York, 2001–02. Excavation campaigns: Durham, 1974; Shrewsbury, 1975; Stafford, 1975–83; Worcester, 1979–81; Castelseprio, Italy, 1980–82; Sutton Hoo, 1983–91; Achir, Algeria, 1992–93; Portmahomack, Scotland, 1994–2007; Castronovo, Sicily, 2014–. Lectures: Dalrymple, Glasgow, 1990; Univ. of New Mexico, 2003; RSAI, 2004; Merchant Adventurers Public Sci., York, 2005; Harvard Univ., 2006; Russian Acad. of Scis, 2007; Groam House, 2007; Medieval Europe, Paris, 2007; J. M. Kemble, Dublin, 2008; Jarrow, 2008; Internat. Soc. of Anglo-Saxonists, Helsinki 2001, Newfoundland 2009; Haskins, Boston, 2009; Rhind, Edinburgh, 2010; NRA, Dublin, 2011; World Heritage, Osaka, 2012; Pirenne, 2013; Midwest Archaeol. Congress, Ill, 2014. Ed., Antiquity, 2003–12. Presenter/writer, BBC 2 progs on Sutton Hoo, 1985–88. Director: W Midlands Rescue Archaeol. Cttee, 1975–78; Tarbat Discovery Prog., 1994–. Sec., Inst. Field Archaeologists, 1983–88; Chm., Field Archaeol. Specialists (FAS-Heritage Ltd), 1998–; Vice-Pres., Soc. for Medieval Archaeology, 2010–. Dir, Sutton Hoo Res. Trust, 1983–. Corresp. Mem., Deutsches Archaeologisches Institut, 2002. FSA 1981 (Vice Pres., 2001–06); FSAScot 1994, Hon. FSAScot 2011. Open Prize, BAAS, 2004; Best Project, British Archaeol Awards, 2010. *Publications:* (ed) Medieval Worcester, 1980; (ed) Two Town Houses in Medieval Shrewsbury, 1983; Underneath English Towns, 1987; (ed) Prehistory in Lowland Shropshire, 1991; (ed) The Age of Sutton Hoo, 1992; (ed) In Search of Cult, 1993; Arguments in Stone, 1993; Sutton Hoo: burial ground of Kings?, 1998; Surviving in Symbols: a visit to the Pictish nation, 1999; (ed) The Cross Goes North, 2003; Archaeological Value and Evaluation, 2003; Sutton Hoo: a seventh century princely burial ground and its context, 2005; Portmahomack: monastery of the Picts, 2008; (with C. Hills and J. Scheschkewitz) Wasperton: a Roman, British and Anglo-Saxon community in central England, 2009; Archaeological Investigation, 2009; The Birth of a Borough, 2010; (ed jtly) Signals of Belief in Early England, 2010; Making Archaeology Happen, 2011; (ed with Jan Klapste) The Archaeology of Medieval Europe, Twelfth to Sixteenth Century, 2011; (ed jtly) Field Archaeology from Around the World: ideas and approaches, 2015; numerous contribs to archaeol jls and magazines. *Recreation:* playing the flute. *Address:* Ella House, Ellerton, York YO42 4PB. *E:* martin.carver@york.ac.uk.

CARVILL, Patrick, CB 1994; Permanent Secretary, Department of Finance and Personnel, Northern Ireland, 1998–2003; *b* 13 Oct. 1943; *s* of Bernard and Susan Carvill; *m* 1965, Vera Abbott; two *s*. *Educ:* St Mary's Christian Brothers Grammar School, Belfast; Queen's Univ., Belfast (BA Hons). Min. of Fuel and Power, Westminster, 1965; Min. of Development, Stormont, 1967; Min. of Community Relations, 1969; Asst Sec., Dept of Educn, 1975–83; Under-Secretary: Dept of Finance and Personnel, 1983–88; Dept of Econ. Develt, 1988–89; Dept of Finance and Personnel, 1989–90; Perm. Sec., Dept of Educn for NI, 1990–98. Comr, S Eastern Educn and Libraries Bd, 2006–15; Mem. Bd, NI Libraries Authy, 2009–14. Chm., NI Clinical Excellence Awards Cttee. Trustee, Nat. Museums of NI, 2009–13. *Recreations:* reading, hill-walking, diving.

CARWARDINE, Mark; freelance zoologist and environmentalist, since 1986; *b* Luton, 9 March 1959; *s* of David and Betty Carwardine; partner, Debra Taylor. *Educ:* Queen Mary's Coll., Basingstoke; Bedford Coll., London Univ. (BSc Hons Zool. 1979). Conservation Officer, WWF, UK, 1979–86. Consultant, World Conservation Union, Switzerland, 1986–90. Co-founder, wildlife tour cos, Discover the World, Wild Oceans and Ocean Wanderers. Presenter: radio progs incl. Nature, BBC Radio 4, 1997–2003; TV series incl. (with Stephen Fry) Last Chance to See, 2009–10, Museum of Life, 2010; columnist, BBC Wildlife mag., 2004– (Mem., Adv. Bd); Science Writer, UNEP, Kenya. Editl Advr, Good Book Guide; Contributing Ed., Wanderlust mag. Chair, BBC Wildlife Photographer of Year competition, 2005–11. Sen. Consultant, Whale and Dolphin Conservation; Vice-President: Wildfowl & Wetlands Trust; Avon Wildlife Trust; Vice-Pres. and Conservation Advr, David Shepherd Wildlife Foundn; Mem. Council, World Land Trust. Patron: ORCA; Save the Rhino. *Publications:* over 50 books, including: (with J. Craven) Wildlife in the News, 1990; (with D. Adams) Last Chance to See, 1990, 3rd edn 2009; Whales, Dolphins and Porpoises, 1995, 2nd edn 2000; Animal Records, 1995, 4th edn 2013; The Shark Watcher's Handbook, 2002; Shark, 2004; Last Chance to See: following in Douglas Adams' footsteps, 2009; Mark Carwardine's Ultimate Wildlife Experiences, 2011. *Recreations:* family and friends, swimming, photography, Rugby, comedy, reading, astronomy, polar exploration, scuba diving, sleeping in own bed (i.e. not travelling). *Address:* c/o Rachel Ashton, 5 Chesterfield Road, Bristol BS6 5DN. *T:* (0117) 904 8934. *E:* rachel@markcarwardine.com.

CARWARDINE, Prof. Richard John, DPhil; FBA 2006; FRHistS, FLSW; President, Corpus Christi College, Oxford, since 2010; *b* 12 Jan. 1947; *s* of John Francis Carwardine and Beryl Carwardine (*née* Jones); *m* 1975, Dr Linda Margaret Kirk. *Educ:* Monmouth Sch.; Corpus Christi Coll., Oxford (BA 1968, MA 1972); Queen's Coll., Oxford (Ochs-Oakes Sen. Schol.; DPhil 1976; Hon. Fellow 2010). FRHistS 1983. University of Sheffield: Lectr in American Hist., 1971–90; Sen. Lectr, 1990–94; Reader in Hist., 1994; Prof. of Hist., 1994–2002; Dean, Faculty of Arts, 1999–2001; University of Oxford: Rhodes Prof. of Amer. Hist. and Fellow, St Catherine's Coll., 2002–09; Pro Vice Chancellor, 2012–. Vis. Asst Prof., Syracuse Univ., 1974–75; Fulbright-ACLS Res. Fellow, Univ. of NC, Chapel Hill, 1989; Stewart Fellow in Religion, Princeton Univ., 2011; Vis. Fellow, Henry E. Huntington Liby, 2014. Lectures: Birkbeck, Trinity Coll., Cambridge, 2004; Stenton, Univ. of Reading, 2004; Harry Allen, Univ. of London, 2006; Burns, Univ. of Richmond, 2008; Ramsey Murray, Selwyn Coll., Cambridge, 2010; Watson, Sulgrave Manor and BL, 2013; Roger Anstey, Univ. of Kent, 2015. Editl advr, BBC Hist., 2000–; Member, Editorial Board: Jl Ecclesiastical Hist., 1991–; Amer. Nineteenth Century Hist., 2000–. Founding Mem. Council for the Defence of British Univs., 2012. Elected Laureate, Lincoln Acad. of Illinois, 2009. Founding FLSW 2010. Mem., Pilgrims' Soc. of GB, 2009–. Gov., Manchester Grammar Sch., 2010–. Freeman, Haberdashers' Co., 2011. Hon. Fellow, St Catherine's Coll., Oxford, 2009. Arthur Miller Amer. Studies Prize, 1997. *Publications:* Transatlantic Revivalism: popular evangelicalism in Britain and America 1790–1865, 1978; Evangelicals and Politics in Antebellum America, 1993; Lincoln, 2003 (Lincoln Prize, 2004); Lincoln: a life of purpose and power, 2006; The Global Lincoln, 2011; contrib. numerous articles and essays to learned jls, incl. Jl Amer. Hist., Jl Amer. Studies, Church Hist., Jl Ecclesiastical Hist. *Recreations:* acting, theatre-going. *Address:* Corpus Christi College, Merton Street, Oxford OX1 4JF. *T:* (01865) 276740, *Fax:* (01865) 276769.

CARWOOD, Andrew; tenor; conductor; Director of Music, St Paul's Cathedral, since 2007; Artistic Director, The Cardinall's Musick, since 1989; *b* 30 April 1965; *s* of Thomas George Carwood and Daisy Ninnes. *Educ:* John Lyon Sch., Harrow; St John's Coll., Cambridge. Lay Clerk: Christ Ch, Oxford, 1987–90; Westminster Cathedral, 1990–95; Dir of Music, Brompton Oratory, 1995–2000. Director: Edington Fest., 1992–97; Edington Schola Cantorum, 1998–2010; Jt Prin. Guest Conductor, BBC Singers, 2007–10. Has made numerous recordings as singer and as conductor. ARSCM 2005. Hon. Fellow Royal Acad. of St Cecilia, 2003. *Recreations:* theatre, British comedy. *E:* directorofmusic@stpaulscathedral.org.uk.

CARY, family name of **Viscount Falkland.**

CARY, Anthony Joyce, CMG 1997; HM Diplomatic Service, retired; High Commissioner to Canada, 2007–10; *b* 1 July 1951; *s* of Sir Michael Cary, GCB and Isabel Cary; *m* 1975, Clare Elworthy; three *s* one *d*. *Educ:* Eton; Trinity Coll., Oxford (MA English); Stanford Business Sch. (MBA). Joined FCO, 1973: BMG Berlin, 1974–77; Policy Planning Staff, FCO, 1978–80; Harkness Fellow, Stanford Business Sch., 1980–82; EC Dept, FCO, 1982–84; Private Sec. to Minister of State, FCO, 1984–86; Head of Chancery, Kuala Lumpur, 1986–88; on loan to Cabinet of Sir Leon Brittan, EC, Brussels, 1989–92; Head of EU Dept (Internal), FCO, 1993–96; Counsellor, Washington, 1997–99; on loan as Chef de Cabinet to Rt Hon. Christopher Patten, Mem. of EC, 1999–2003; Ambassador, Sweden, 2003–06. Exec. Dir, Queen's-Blyth Worldwide, 2011–13. UK Commonwealth Scholarship Comr, 2011–. Mem. Jury, Cundill Hist. Prize, 2011, 2013, 2015. Hon. Pres., Canada-UK Council (formerly Canada-UK Colloquia), 2011–. *Address:* The Old Vicarage, 97A Knatchbull Road, SE5 9QU.

CARY, Dr Nathaniel Roger Blair, FRCPath; Consultant Forensic Pathologist, Home Office Registered, since 1992; Founder Member, Forensic Pathology Services, since 2001; *b* 13 Nov. 1957; 2nd *s* of Sir Roger Hugh Cary, 2nd Bt; *m* 1st, 1978, Tesney Diane Vera Partington (marr. diss. 1994); two *s* one *d*; 2nd, 1994, Sally Ann Taylor; one *d*. *Educ:* St Paul's Sch., London (Foundn Schol.); Trinity Coll., Oxford (Open Schol.; MA 1982); Charing Cross Hosp. Med. Sch. (MB BS 1981; MD 1992). DMJ 1992; FRCPath 1997. Hse physician and hse surgeon, 1981–82, trainee pathologist, 1982–85, Charing Cross Hosp.; Charing Cross

Trustees Res. Fellow, 1985–86; Lectr in Histopathol., Charing Cross and Westminster Med. Sch., 1986–89; Consultant Cardiac Histopathologist, Papworth Hosp., Cambs, 1989–98; Sen. Lectr in Forensic Medicine, 1998–2001, Dir, Guy's Campus, 1999–2001, GKT. Chm., Specialty Adv. Cttee on Forensic Pathol., RCPath, 2014–. Pres., British Assoc. in Forensic Med., 2010–12. *Publications:* contrib. chapters in books on pathology, and papers to med. scientific literature, mainly relating to heart pathol., incl. transplantation. *Recreations:* walking (uphill), ski-ing (downhill). *Address:* Forensic Pathology Services, Unit 12, The Quadrangle, Grove Technology Park, Wantage, Oxon OX12 9FA. *T:* (01235) 773332. *Club:* Royal Society of Medicine.

CARY, Sir Nicolas (Robert Hugh), 3rd Bt *cr* 1955, of Withington, co. Lancaster; *b* 17 April 1955; *er s* of Sir Roger Hugh Cary, 2nd Bt, and Ann Helen Katharine, *e d* of Hugh Blair Brenan, OBE; *S* father, 2011, but his name does not appear on the Official Roll of the Baronetage; *m* 1st, 1979, Pauline Jean (marr. diss. 1991), *d* of Dr Thomas Ian Boyd; three *s*; 2nd, 1994, Lesley Anne Gilham, one *s* one *d*. *Educ:* St Paul's Sch.; University Coll. London (BA). Technical Partner, Cary Digital LLP, 2008–. *Recreations:* walking, cooking, creative writing. *Heir: s* Alexander Robert Cary, *b* 27 Nov. 1981. *Address:* Westgate, 7 Lansdowne Road, Chesham, Bucks HP5 2BA.

CASADEI, Prof. Barbara, MD; DPhil; FRCP, FMedSci; British Heart Foundation Professor of Cardiovascular Medicine, University of Oxford, since 2013; Fellow, Wolfson College, Oxford, since 2013; Hon. Consultant Cardiologist, John Radcliffe Hospital, Oxford, since 1995; *b* Italy, 6 Nov. 1959; *d* of Urbano Casadei and Adriana Gori; one *d*. *Educ:* Univ. of Pavia, Italy (MD 1984); Pembroke Coll., Oxford (DPhil 1995). FRCP 2001. Joan and Richard Doll Fellow, Green Coll., Oxford, 1991–94; Sen. Fellow, BHF, 2001–12; Reader, 2002–06, Prof. of Cardiovascular Medicine, 2006–12, Univ. of Oxford. Vice Pres. for Scientific Affairs and Res., Eur. Soc. of Cardiol., 2014–Aug. 2016. FMedSci 2013. *Recreations:* Baroque music, snorkelling. *Address:* Division of Cardiovascular Medicine, Radcliffe Department of Medicine, L6, West Wing, John Radcliffe Hospital, Oxford OX3 9DU. *T:* (01865) 234664. *E:* barbara.casadei@cardiov.ox.ac.uk.

CASALE, Roger Mark; Founder and Director, New Europeans Association, since 2013; *m* 1997, Fernanda Miucci; two *d*. *Educ:* King's Coll. Sch., Wimbledon; Hurstpierpoint Coll., Sussex (Scholar); Brasenose Coll., Oxford (BA Hons); Bologna Centre, Johns Hopkins Univ. (MA). Head, trng inst., Germany, 1986–92; Lectr in Politics, Greenwich Univ., 1994–97. MP (Lab) Wimbledon, 1997–2005; contested (Lab) same seat, 2005. PPS, FCO, 2002–05. Mem., Select Cttee on Eur. Legislation, 1997–2002; Chm., All Party British-Italian Gp, 1998–2005; Hon. Sec., PLP Foreign Affairs Cttee, 1999–2002. Chm., The Portofino Dialogues, 2004–08. Hon. Pres., London and SE Direct Aid to Kosovo, 1998–2005. Governor, Wimbledon Sch. of Art, 1999–2004. Comdr, Order of Merit (Italy), 2011. *Recreations:* European history, modern art.

CASALE, Dr Silvia Suzen Giovanna, CMG 2010; independent consultant in criminal justice and human rights, since 1984; *b* Amersham, 15 Feb. 1945; *d* of Tanga Casale and Ida Narduzzo; *m* 1974, Jerrold Katzman; one *d*. *Educ:* Haberdashers' Aske's Sch., Middx; St Hilda's Coll., Oxford (MA Mod. Langs); Univ. of Pennsylvania (MA Internat. Relns); Yale Univ. (MPhil Pol Sci.; PhD Criminol. 1978). Project Res. Dir, Vera Inst. of Justice, NY, 1977–80; Project Dir, Vera Inst. of Justice, London, 1980–83. Mem., Parole Bd England and Wales, 1987–90. UK Mem., Cttee for Prevention of Torture, Council of Europe, 1997–2009 (Pres., 2000–07); Chair, UN Subcttee on Prevention of Torture, 2007–09; Advr to Eur. Nat. Preventive Mechanism Proj., Council of Europe, 2009–12; Mem., Internat. Contact Gp for peace initiative in Basque Country, 2010–. Sentence Rev. Comr (NI), 1998–2012; Leader, Ind. Rev. of IPCC investigation into death of Sean Rigg, 2012–13 (report, 2013); Member: Daniel Morgan Ind. Panel, 2013–; Hillsborough Article 2 Reference Gp., 2013–. Trustee: Prison Advice and Care Trust, 1993–2012; Prison Reform Trust, 1994–2013; Patron, Unlock. Hon. LLD Glasgow, 2013. *Publications:* Fines in Europe, 1981; The Fine Process: the use of fines as a criminal sanction in English Magistrates' Courts, 1983; Minimum Standards for Prison Establishments, 1984; Female Remands in Custody, 1988; Minimum Standards in Prisons: a programme of change, 1989; Women Inside: the experience of women remand prisoners, 1989; Regimes for Remand Prisoners, 1990; London Prisons Community Links: a feasibility study, 1991; (ed with E. Stockdale) Criminal Justice Under Stress, 1992; (ed) HIV and Custody, 1995; contrib. articles to law and internat. jls. *Recreations:* learning languages, gardening, brass rubbing, tea with friends.

CASE, Anthea Fiendley, (Mrs D. C. Case), CBE 2003; Principal Adviser, Arcadia, since 2006; *b* 7 Feb. 1945; *d* of late Thomas Fiendley Stones and Bess Stones (*née* Mackie); *m* 1967, David Charles Case; one *d* (and one *d* decd). *Educ:* Christ's Hospital, Hertford; St Anne's Coll., Oxford (BA). HM Treasury: Asst Principal, 1966–70; Private Sec. to Financial Sec., 1970–71; Principal, 1971–79; Asst Sec., 1980–88; Under Sec., 1988–95 (with Fiscal Policy Gp, 1993–95); Asst Dir, Budget & Public Finances Directorate, 1995; Dir, Nat. Heritage Meml Fund (Heritage Lottery Fund), 1995–2003. Chm., Heritage Link, 2003–09. Member: Bd, Living East (Regl Cultural Consortium), 2003–09; East of England Regl Assembly, 2003–07; NT East of England Regl Adv. Bd (formerly NT East of England Regl Cttee), 2003– (Chm., 2009–); Comr, CABE, 2004–11. Trustee: Lakeland Arts Trust, 2003–; Norwich Heritage and Econ. Regeneration Trust, 2005–; Inst. for Philanthropy, 2007–14; Wende Mus. of the Cold War, LA, 2010–; Norfolk and Norwich Fest. Trust, 2011–. Chm., Coalition for Efficiency, 2010–12. *Address:* Arcadia, 6th Floor, 5 Young Street, W8 5EH. *T:* (020) 7361 4900.

CASE, Christopher John; Group Manager, St Helens District, Merseyside Fire and Rescue, since 2011; *b* St Helens, Lancs, 2 Feb. 1970; *s* of David John and Catherine Case; *m* 2001, Michele Amanda; one *s* three *d*. *Educ:* Cowley High Sch.; Anglia Ruskin Univ. (Postgrad. Dip. Strategic Public Sector Mgt). Merseyside Fire and Rescue Service: Gp Manager, Threat Response, 2005–09; Community Protection Manager, 2009–11; St Helens Dist Manager, 2011–12. Director: Blackpowder Ltd, 2002–; Royal Armouries Trading and Enterprise, 2010–. Vis. Fellow, Glasgow Univ., 2010. Vice Pres., IExpE, 2010. Trustee, Royal Armouries, 2008–. CLJ 2012. *Recreations:* holidays, reading, pyrotechnics and explosives research. *Address:* Royal Armouries, Armouries Way, Leeds LS10 1LT. *T:* (0151) 296 4000. *E:* chris@casent.co.uk.

CASE, Her Honour Janet Ruth; a Circuit Judge, 2001–13; *b* 29 June 1943; *d* of James and Cathleen Simpson; *m* 1965, Jeremy David Michael Case (marr. diss. 1982); one *s* one *d*. *Educ:* Univ. of Durham (LLB 1965). Called to the Bar, Inner Temple, 1975; barrister, Wales and Chester Circuit, 1975–2001; Chm., Med. Appeals Tribunals, 1988–96; an Asst Recorder, 1992–95; a Recorder, 1995–2001; Designated Family Judge for Newport, S Wales, 2001–05. Chm., Mental Health Review Tribunals, 2006–13. Treas., UK Assoc. of Women Judges, 2007–12. *Recreations:* gardening, opera, travel. *Address:* Croeswylan, Morda Road, Oswestry, Shropshire SY11 2AL. *Club:* Lansdowne.

CASE, Richard Ian, CBE 2002; DL; FREng, FRAeS; Chairman, WFEL (formerly William Fairey Engineering Ltd), 2007–12; consultant to aerospace industry, 2005–12; *b* 14 June 1945; *m* 1975, Denise Margaret Mills; one *s* one *d*. *Educ:* Cranfield Inst. of Technology (MSc Aircraft Propulsion). FRAeS 1985; FREng (FEng 1993). Technical Manager, Arab British Helicopters, Egypt, 1978–82; Westland Helicopters Ltd: Chief Designer, 1982–85; Engrg Dir, 1985–88; EH101 Project Dir and Engrg Dir, 1988–92; Man. Dir, 1992–95; Chief Exec., GKN Westland Helicopters Ltd, 1995–2001; Man. Dir, AgustaWestland, 2001–05; Chm., Westland Helicopters, 2001–04. Non-exec. Dir, FKI plc, 2007–08. DL Somerset, 2005. RAeS Gold Medal, 1998. Cavaliere dell 'Ordine al Merito (Italy), 1995. *Recreations:* golf, opera.

CASE, Stephen M.; Chairman and Chief Executive Officer, Revolution LLC, since 2005; *b* Honolulu, 21 Aug. 1958; *s* of Dan and Carol Case; *m* 1st, 1985, Joanne (marr. diss.); three *d*; 2nd, Jean; two *c*. *Educ:* Punahou Sch., Honolulu; Williams Coll., Mass. (BA Pol Sci. 1980). Marketing Dept, Procter & Gamble, 1980–82; Manager, new pizza develt, Pizza Hut Div., PepsiCo, 1982–83; joined Control Video Corp., 1983, as mktg asst; co. renamed Quantum Computer Services, 1985, and became America Online, (AOL), 1991; CEO, 1991–2001, and Chm., 1995–2001, when merged with Time Warner; Chm., Time Warner Inc., 2001–03; Chm., Exclusive Resorts, 2004–07. Founder and Chm., Case Foundation, 1997–. *Address:* Case Foundation, Seventh Floor,1717 Rhode Island Avenue NW, Washington, DC 20036, USA.

CASEBOURNE, Michael Victor, CEng, FICE, FASCE; private consultant; Project Director, BBCJV (Balfour Beatty Carillion) London Overground East London Line, since 2006; *b* 7 Oct. 1945; *s* of Eric Thomas Casebourne and Marjorie May Casebourne (*née* Chapman); *m* 1972, Margaret Dunlop (*d* 2002); one *s* one *d*. *Educ:* Harrow Co. Grammar Sch.; Nottingham Univ. (BSc). CEng 1967; FICE 1984. With Costain Civil Engrg, 1967–73; Trafalgar House Construction, 1973–90 (Dir, 1984–90); Managing Director: Wimpey Engrg & Construction UK, 1990–96; GT Railway Maintenance, 1996–99; Dir, Railtrack, 2001–02. Project Director: Nottingham Tram, 2003–04; ACTJV (Alstom and Carillion) Channel Tunnel Rail Link, 2004–06. Chief Exec. and Sec., ICE, 1999–2001. FASCE. *Recreations:* sailing, motor boating.

CASEBY, Richard David; Director of Communications, Department for Work and Pensions, since 2014; *b* St Annes-on-Sea, 30 July 1960; *s* of late Donald Brown Caseby and Joan Caseby; *m* 1986, Joanna Winter; one *s* two *d*. *Educ:* King Edward VII Sch., Lytham St Annes; Durham Univ. (BA Hons Eng. Lang. and Lit.). Trainee reporter, Westmorland Gazette, 1983–84; reporter: Oxford Mail and Times, 1985–86; Daily Mail, 1986–89; Sunday Times: reporter, 1989; Asst News Ed., 1990; Dep. Focus Ed., 1991; Dep. Foreign Ed., 1992–94; Focus Ed., 1994–96; Man. Ed. (News), 1996–98; Man. Ed., 1998–2011; non-exec. Dir, Times Newspapers Hldgs Ltd, 1998–2010; Man. Ed., The Sun, 2011–13. Co-Founder, Sunday Times Best Companies to Work For, 2000; Founder, Sunday Times Best Green Companies, 2008. *Publications:* The Opium Eating Editor: Thomas de Quincey, 1985. *Recreations:* cycling, sea swimming, 20th century art. *Address:* Department for Work and Pensions, Caxton House, Tothill Street, SW1H 9NA.

CASELLI, Prof. Francesco, PhD; FBA 2010; Norman Sosnow Chair in Economics, London School of Economics and Political Science, since 2012 (Professor of Economics, 2004–12); *b* Trieste, 14 Oct. 1966; *s* of Giovanni Caselli and Maria Teresa Marozzi; *m* 2003, Silvana Tenreyro; two *s*. *Educ:* Univ. of Bologna (Laurea 1991); Harvard Univ. (PhD 1997). Asst Prof. of Econs, Univ. of Chicago, 1997–2000; Associate Prof. of Econs, Harvard Univ., 2000–04. Man. Ed., Rev. of Econ. Studies, 2010–14. *Publications:* contrib. articles to jls incl. Amer. Econ. Rev., Jl Political Econ., Qly Jl Econs.

CASELY-HAYFORD, Augustus, PhD; broadcaster and art historian; *b* London, 25 May 1964; *s* of Victor and Ransolina Casely-Hayford; partner, Sarah Wason; one *d*. *Educ:* Sch. of Oriental and African Studies, Univ. of London (PhD African Hist. 1992). Freelance lectr and arts mgt consultant, 1992–2003; Director: Africa 05, British Mus., 2003–05; Inst. of Internat. Visual Arts, 2006; Exec. Dir, Arts Strategy, Arts Council England, 2007. Presenter, TV programmes: State of the Art, 2009; Lost Kingdoms of Africa, 2009; History of British Art, 2009; Where Is Modern Art Now?, 2009; The Miracle of British Art, 2010; Lost Kingdoms of Africa (series), 2011, 2012; Panellist, Big Art Project, 2009. Mem. Council, Tate Britain, 2007–; Exec. Dir, Zamyn, 2008–; Trustee, NPG, 2008–. *Publications:* (contrib.) Peoples and Empire in Africa, 1992; (contrib.) Tam Tam to Internet, 1998; (contrib.) Cultural Politics in a Global Age, 2008; The Lost Kingdoms of Africa, 2012; catalogues on Mah Rana and Magdalene Odundo; contribs to History Workshop Jl, Jl of Museum Ethnography, Crafts, Internat. Jl of Art and Design Educn, London Mag. *Recreations:* watercolours, photography. *Address:* Zamyn, South Building, Somerset House, WC2R 1LA. *T:* (020) 7845 4681. *E:* augustus@runbox.com.

CASELY-HAYFORD, Margaret Henrietta Augusta, (Mrs G. T. Quarme); Chairman, ActionAid, since 2014; *b* London; *d* of Victor Ward and Rosalina Casely-Hayford; *m* 1986, Giles Thomas Quarme, *qv*; one *d*. *Educ:* Somerville Coll., Oxford (BA Hons Juris. 1982). Called to the Bar, Gray's Inn, 1983; in practice as barrister, 1984–86; admitted as solicitor, 1987; solicitor, 1987–94 and 1996–2006, Partner, 1998–2006, Denton Wilde Sapte; solicitor, Berwin Leighton Paisner, 1994–95; Gen. Counsel, Dir of Legal Services and Co. Sec., John Lewis Partnership plc, 2006–14. Section Ed., Jl Leisure and Retail Property, 1998–2006. Non-executive Director: British Retail Consortium, 2010–14; NHS England, 2012–. Freeman, City of London, 1998. Special Trustee, Gt Ormond St Hosp. Charity, 2000–07. Trustee, Geffrye Mus., 2000–07. *Publications:* Practical Planning: permission and the application, 1995; (contrib.) Sustaining Architecture, 2001; contribs to jls incl. Estates Gazette, Bldg Design, Planning, Leisure and Hospitality Business. *Recreations:* the perpetual combat with nature that is gardening, friends, film, opera, family, an unequal struggle with the 'cello continues.

See also A. Casely-Hayford.

CASEMENT, David John; QC 2008; a Recorder, since 2005; Deputy High Court Judge, Queen's Bench Division and Chancery Division, since 2013; *b* Belfast, 19 Nov. 1969; *s* of late John Casement and of Helena Casement; *m* 1994, Ruth Ann Hadden; two *d*. *Educ:* Methodist Coll., Belfast; St Hugh's Coll., Oxford (MA). Called to the Bar: Middle Temple, 1992 (Astbury Schol.); Ireland, 1996; NI, 2007; in practice as barrister specialising in chancery and commercial litigation. Accredited Mediator 2007. Chairperson's List, Sport Resolutions, 2010–; Legal Chairperson, Nat. Anti-Doping Panel, 2011–. Chm., Northern Circuit Commercial Bar Assoc., 2013–; Jt Chm., British Irish Commercial Bar Assoc., 2013–. Pres. Oxford Univ. Law Soc., 1990. Exec. Bd, Anglo-Irish Encounter, 2000–06. *Address:* Kings Chambers, 36 Young Street, Manchester M3 3FT. *T:* (0161) 832 9082; Serle Court, 6 New Square, Lincoln's Inn, WC2A 3QS. *T:* (020) 7242 6105.

CASEY, Aprampar Apar Jot Kaur, (Joti); *see* Bopa Rai, A. A. J. K.

CASEY, Ben; *see* Casey, R. B.

CASEY, Derek Grant; international consultant; Chairman, World Leisure Organisation, 2004–13, now Emeritus (Executive Member, 2002–13); *b* 19 Feb. 1950; *s* of Andrew Casey and Jean Grant. *Educ:* St Aloysius' Coll., Glasgow; Univ. of Glasgow (MA Hons). Dir of Ops, Scottish Sports Council, 1979–88; GB Sports Council: Dir of Nat. Services, 1988–93; Chief Exec., 1993–96; Chief Exec., English Sports Council, subseq. Sport England, 1997–2001. Chairman: Cttee for Development of Sport, Council of Europe, 1993–95; UK Youth, 2003–10. Bid Dir for Glasgow, 2014 Commonwealth Games, 2006–07; Interim Chief Exec. Glasgow 2014 Commonwealth Games, 2007–08. Pres., Youth Scotland, 2012–. Sen. Fellow, Amer. Leisure Acad., 2008. Hon. Res. Fellow, Univ. of Stirling, 2003–. Hon. DSc Southampton, 1996; DUniv Strathclyde, 2009; DUniv Stirling, 2010. *Publications:* contribs on sport, recreation and physical activity, to jls and periodicals. *Recreations:* walking, theatre, American literature. *Address:* 42/5 Barnton Park Avenue, Edinburgh EH4 6EY.

CASEY, Most Rev. Eamonn, DD; RC Bishop of Galway and Kilmacduagh, 1976–92; Apostolic Administrator of Kilfenora, 1976–92; *b* Firies, Co. Kerry, 23 April 1927; *s* of late John Casey and late Helena (*née* Shanahan). *Educ:* St Munchin's Coll., Limerick; St Patrick's Coll., Maynooth. LPh 1946; BA 1947. Priest, 1951; Curate, St John's Cath., Limerick, 1951–60; Chaplain to Irish in Slough, 1960–63; set up social framework to re-establish people into new environment; started social welfare scheme; set up lodgings bureau and savings scheme; invited by Cardinal Heenan to place Catholic Housing Aid Soc. on national basis; founded Family Housing Assoc., 1964; Dir, British Council of Churches Housing Trust; Trustee, Housing the Homeless Central Fund; Founder-Trustee of Shelter (Chm. 1968); Mem. Council, Nat. Fedn of Housing Socs; Founder Mem., Marian Employment Agency; Founder Trustee, Shelter Housing Aid Soc., 1963–69; Bishop of Kerry, 1969–76. Missionary work, Ecuador, 1992–98. Exec. Chm., Trocaire, 1973–92; Mem. Bd, Siamsa Tire, Nat. Folk Th. of Ireland. Launched Meitheal, 1982; estab. Galway Adult Educn Centre, 1985, Galway Family Guidance Inst., 1986. Chm., Nat. Youth Resource Gp, 1979–86. Member: Commn for Social Welfare, 1971–74; Maynooth Coll. Exec. Council, 1974–84; Episcopal Commn for Univs, 1976–92; Governing Body, University Coll., Galway, 1976–92. *Publications:* (with Adam Ferguson) A Home of Your Own; Housing—A Parish Solution; contribs to journals, etc. *Recreations:* music, theatre, concerts, films when time, conversation, motoring. *Address:* Priest's House, Shanaglish, Gort, Co. Galway, Ireland.

CASEY, Gavin Frank, FCA; Chief Executive, London Stock Exchange, 1996–2000; Chairman: Tragus Hldgs Ltd, 2002–05; Integrated Dental Holdings Ltd, 2006–08; VSA Capital Group plc, since 2012; *b* 18 Oct. 1946; *s* of Frank Frederick Casey and Diana Casey; *m* 1970, Lesley Riding; two *s* one *d*. Chartered Accountant, 1970; Harmood Banner & Co., 1965–70; Coopers & Lybrand, 1970–71; County Bank, later County NatWest, 1972–89; Smith New Court, later Merrill Lynch International, 1989–96; Dep. Chm., Corporate Finance Adv. Bd, PricewaterhouseCoopers, 2001–05. Chm., EDM Gp Ltd, 2004–11; Director: Lawrence plc, 2002–07; VTB Bank Europe plc (formerly Moscow Narodny Bank Ltd), 2005–07; Baronsmead AiM VCT plc, 2006–08; Sen. Advr, Gardant Communications Ltd (formerly The Policy Partnership), 2005–09. Chm. of Treasurers, USPG, 1991–96. *Recreations:* theatre, horse racing. *Clubs:* Turf, City of London.

CASEY, Louise, CB 2008; Director General, Troubled Families Team, Department for Communities and Local Government, since 2011; *b* Redruth, 29 March 1965; *d* of late Martin and Peggy Casey. *Educ:* Oaklands RC Comprehensive Sch., Portsmouth; Goldsmiths' Coll., Univ. of London (BA Hons Hist.). Co-ordinator, St Mungo Assoc., 1988–90; Dir, Homeless Network, 1990–92; Dep. Dir, Shelter, 1992–99; Govt Homelessness Czar, 1999–2003; Nat. Dir, Anti-Social Behaviour Policy, 2003–05; Govt Co-ordinator, Respect, 2005–07; Hd, Cabinet Office review, Engaging Communities in Fight Against Crime, 2008; Dir Gen., Neighbourhood Crime and Justice Gp, Home Office, 2008–10; Comr for Victims and Witnesses, 2010–11. *Recreations:* reading novels, socialising. *Address:* (office) 2 Marsham Street, SW1P 4DF.

CASEY, Michael Bernard; Chairman, Michael Casey & Associates, 1993–2000; *b* 1 Sept. 1928; *s* of late Joseph Bernard Casey, OBE, and Dorothy (*née* Love); *m*; two *s* two *d*. *Educ:* Colwyn Bay Grammar Sch.; LSE (Scholar in Laws, 1952; LLB 1954). RAF, 1947–49. Principal, MAFF, 1961; Office of the Minister for Science, 1963–64; Asst Sec., DEA, 1967; DTI (later Dept of Prices and Consumer Protection), 1970; Under Sec., DoI, 1975–77; a Dep. Chm. and Chief Exec., British Shipbuilders, 1977–80; Chm. and Man. Dir, Mather & Platt, 1980–81; Chm., Sallingbury Casey Ltd, later Rowland Sallingbury Casey, 1982–92. *Recreations:* golf, chess, bridge. *Address:* Old Mill, Llantrithyd, Cowbridge, Glam CF71 7UB. *T:* (01446) 781181. *Club:* Reform.

CASEY, Nigel Philip, MVO 1995; HM Diplomatic Service; Private Secretary to the Prime Minister for Foreign Policy, since 2014; *b* Leamington Spa, 29 May 1969; *s* of late Michael Casey and of Josephine Casey; *m* 2002, Clare Crocker; one *s* one *d*. *Educ:* Blundell's Sch.; Balliol Coll., Oxford (BA Hons Mod. Hist.). Joined FCO, 1991; Vice-Consul, Johannesburg, 1993–95; Private Sec. to Ambassador, Washington, DC, 1996–98; Head: Nuclear and Missile Defence Section, Security Policy Dept, 1999–2000; G8 and OECD Section, Econ. Policy Dept, 2001; Moscow, 2003–06; Hd, Iraq Policy Unit, 2006–07; Political Counsellor, 2007–09, Dep. High Comr, 2007–11, New Delhi; Ambassador to Bosnia and Herzegovina, 2011–14. *Recreations:* tennis, squash, golf, theatre, cinema. *Address:* 10 Downing Street, SW1A 2AA.

CASEY, Dr Raymond, FRS 1970; retired; Senior Principal Scientific Officer (Special Merit), Institute of Geological Sciences, London, 1964–79; *b* 10 Oct. 1917; *s* of Samuel Gardiner Casey and Gladys Violet Helen Casey (*née* Garrett); *m* 1943, Norah Kathleen Pakeman (*d* 1974); two *s*. *Educ:* St Mary's, Folkestone; Univ. of Reading. PhD 1958; DSc 1963. Geological Survey and Museum: Asst 1939; Asst Exper. Officer 1946; Exper. Officer 1949; Sen. Geologist 1957; Principal Geologist 1960. *Publications:* A Monograph of the Ammonoidea of the Lower Greensand, 1960–80; (ed, with P. F. Rawson) The Boreal Lower Cretaceous, 1973; numerous articles on Mesozoic palaeontology and stratigraphy in scientific press. *Recreation:* research into early Russian postal and military history (Past Pres., British Soc. of Russian Philately). *Address:* 38 Reed Avenue, Orpington, Kent BR6 9RX. *T:* (01689) 851728.

CASEY, Prof. Robert Bernard, (Ben); Co-Founder and Executive Creative Director, Chase Creative Consultants Ltd, since 1986; Professor (part-time) of Visual Communication, University of Central Lancashire, since 1999; *b* 19 Oct. 1949; *s* of Thomas and Marie Casey; partner, Fiona Candy. *Educ:* Blackpool Coll. of Art. MCSD 1978. Typographer, Horniblow Cox-Freeman, London, 1969–72; Berkoff Associates, London, 1972–73; Designer: Conways, London, 1973–74; G&H, Manchester, 1974–77; Lecturer: Carlisle Coll. of Art, and Blackburn Coll. of Art, 1977–78; Harris Coll., Preston, 1978–83; Hd, Dept of Design, Lancs Poly., 1983–85; Sen. Lectr, Sch. of Communication Arts, London, 1985–86. Designer, Preston North End's Deepdale Stadium, 1995. Mem., Design Skills Panel, Design Council, 2005–09. External Moderator: Staffs Univ., 1989–92; Manchester Metropolitan Univ., 1990–93 and 2002–05; Bretton Hall Coll., 1998–2001; Univ. of Northumbria, 2006–09; Falmouth Univ., 2013–; Blackpool and Fylde Coll., 2013–. Design and Art Directors Association: Chm., Educn Gp, 1991–95; Mem., Exec. Cttee, 1991–95; Chm., D&AD North, 2006–. *Publications:* How a Graphic Design Consultancy Thinks it Thinks, 1993. *Recreation:* watching Preston North End. *Address:* Woodbine Cottage, Dilworth Bottoms, Longridge, Preston PR3 2ZP. *E:* ben.casey@thechase.co.uk.

CASH, Sir Andrew (John), Kt 2009; OBE 2001; Chief Executive, Sheffield Teaching Hospitals NHS Foundation Trust, since 2004; *b* 14 Oct. 1955; *m* Debora; one *s* one *d*. Joined NHS as grad. mgt trainee; Chief Executive: Northern General Hosp. NHS Trust; Sheffield Teaching Hosps NHS Trust, 2001–04; Dir Gen., Provider Develt, DoH (on secondment), 2006–07. Co-Chair, DoH/MoD Partnership Bd; Chair, NHS Pay Policy Bd, 2011–; Dep. Chair, NHS Confederation, 2014–. Non-exec. Dir, Medilink. Vis. Prof. in Leadership Develt, Univs of York and Sheffield. *Address:* Sheffield Teaching Hospitals NHS Foundation Trust, Royal Hallamshire Hospital, Glossop Road, Sheffield S10 2JF.

CASH, Prof. John David, CBE 1998; PhD; FRCP, FRCPE, FRCPath, FRCSE, FRCPGlas; National Medical and Scientific Director, Scottish National Blood Transfusion Service, 1988–98; *b* 3 April 1936; *s* of John Henry Cash and May Annie Cash (*née* Taylor); *m* 1962, Angela Mary Thomson; one *s* one *d*. *Educ:* Ashville College, Harrogate; Edinburgh Univ. (BSc 1959, MB ChB 1961, PhD 1967). FRCPE 1970; FRCPath 1986; FRCPGlas 1994; FRCSE 1995; FRCP 1997. Regional Transfusion Centre Dir, Edinburgh and SE Scotland, 1974–79; Nat. Med. Dir, Scottish Nat. Blood Transfusion Service, 1979–88. Pres., RCPE, 1994–97 (Vice-Pres., 1992–94); Pres., British Blood Transfusion Soc., 1997–99. Chm., Govt Inquiry into Nat. Blood Authy, 1997–98; Member: Nat. Biol Standards Bd, 1997–2003; Internat. Review Panel, Irish Blood Transfusion Service, 2002. Hon. Prof., Edinburgh Univ., 1986. Governor, Fettes Coll., Edinburgh, 1988–2002. *Publications:* Progress in Transfusion Medicine, 1988. *Recreations:* fishing, gardening. *Address:* 1 Otterburn Park, Edinburgh EH14 1JX.

CASH, Sir William (Nigel Paul), Kt 2014; MP (C) Stone, since 1997 (Stafford, 1984–97); *b* 10 May 1940; *s* of Paul Trevor Cash, MC (killed in action Normandy, July 13, 1944) and Moyra Roberts (*née* Morrison); *m* 1965, Bridget Mary Lee; two *s* one *d*. *Educ:* Stonyhurst Coll.; Lincoln Coll., Oxford (MA History). Qualified as Solicitor, 1967; William Cash & Co. (constitutional and administrative lawyer), 1979–. Shadow Attorney-General, 2001–03; Shadow Sec. of State for Constitutional Affairs, 2003. Chm., European Scrutiny Cttee (formerly Select Cttee on European Legislation), 2010– (Mem., 1985–); Chairman: Cons. Backbench Cttee on European Affairs, 1989–91; All Party Cttee on Uganda (formerly on E Africa), 1988–, on Kenya, 2007–; All Party Gp, Jubilee 2000, 1997–2003; All Party Cttee, Malaysia, 2006–; All Party Cttee, Sanitation and Water, 2007–; Jt Chm., All Party Jazz Gp, 1991–2000; Mem., Jt Cttee on Privileges, 2012–15. Founder, and Chm., European Foundn, 1993–. Vice Pres., Cons. Small Business Bureau, 1986–2000. KStJ. *Publications:* Against a Federal Europe—The Battle for Britain, 1991; Europe: the crunch, 1992; John Bright—Statesman, Orator, Agitator, 2011. *Recreations:* history, cricket, jazz. *Address:* The Tithe Barn, Upton Cressett, near Bridgnorth, Shropshire WV16 6UH. *T:* (01746) 714307. *E:* bcash@me.com. *Clubs:* Garrick, Carlton; Vincent's (Oxford).

CASHEL, FERNS AND OSSORY, Bishop of, since 2006; **Rt Rev. Michael Andrew James Burrows;** *m* Claire; three *s* one *d*. *Educ:* Wesley Coll., Dublin; Trinity Coll. Dublin (MLitt). Ordained, 1987; Curate, Douglas Union with Frankfield, Cork; Dean of Residence, TCD, and Minor Canon, St Patrick's Cathedral, Dublin, 1991–94; Incumbent, Bandon Union, 1994–2002; Canon, Cork and Cloyne Cathedrals, 1996; Dean of Cork and Incumbent, St Fin Barre's Union, 2002–06. *Address:* Diocesan Office, Palace Coach House, Church Lane, Kilkenny, Co. Kilkenny, Republic of Ireland.

CASHMAN, Baron *cr* 2014 (Life Peer), of Limehouse in the London Borough of Tower Hamlets; **Michael Maurice Cashman,** CBE 2013; Member (Lab) West Midlands Region, European Parliament, 1999–2014; *b* 17 Dec. 1950; *s* of John Cashman and Mary Cashman (*née* Clayton); civil partnership 2006, Paul Cottingham (*d* 2014). *Educ:* St Mary's and St Joseph's Primary Sch.; Cardinal Griffin Secondary Modern Sch., London; Gladys Dare's Sch., Surrey; Borlands Tutorial, London. Actor, director and playwright, 1963–99; work includes: actor: *stage:* Oliver, Albery, 1963; Bent, RNT, 1990, transf. Garrick; Noises Off, Mobil Touring Theatre, nat. tour, 1995; Merchant of Venice, and Gypsy, W Yorks Playhouse, 1996; The Tempest, internat. tour, 1997; *television:* Eastenders, 1986–89; director: Kiss of the Spiderwoman, New Victoria Th., Newcastle-under-Lyme, 1998; playwright: Before your very Eyes; Bricks 'n' Mortar. Mem. Council and Hon. Treas., Equity, 1994–98; Mem., Labour Party NEC, 1998–2000 and 2001–12. Labour Party Lesbian Gay Bisexual and Transgender Global Envoy, 2014–. Founding Chm., Stonewall Gp, 1988–96. FRSA 1996. Hon. Dr Staffordshire, 2007. Special Service Award, Amer. Assoc. Physicians for Human Rights and Gay Med. Assoc., 1988; MEP of the Year Award, Justice and Human Rights, 2007, Culture and Educn, 2012, The House Mag.; Lifetime Achievement Award, European Diversity Awards, 2012; Outstanding Achievement Award, PinkNews, 2014; Stonewall Politician of Year, 2014. *Recreations:* travel, writing, photography, theatre. *Address:* House of Lords, SW1P 0PW.

CASHMORE, Prof. Roger John, CMG 2004; DPhil; FRS 1998; FInstP; Principal, Brasenose College, Oxford, 2002–11 (Hon. Fellow, 2011); Chairman, United Kingdom Atomic Energy Authority, since 2010; *b* 22 Aug. 1944; *e s* of C. J. C. and E. M. Cashmore; *m* 1971, Elizabeth Ann, *d* of Rev. S. J. C. Lindsay; one *s*. *Educ:* Dudley Grammar Sch.; St John's Coll., Cambridge (schol.; BA 1965; MA); Balliol Coll., Oxford (DPhil 1969). FInstP 1985. Weir Jun. Res. Fellow, University Coll., Oxford, 1967–69; 1851 Res. Fellow, 1968; Res. Associate, Stanford Linear Accelerator Centre, Calif, 1969–74; Oxford University: Res. Officer, 1974–79; Lectr, Christ Church, 1976–78; Fellow, Balliol Coll., 1979–2002 (Emeritus Fellow, 2003); Sen. Res. Fellow, Merton Coll., 1977–79; Tutor, Balliol Coll., and Univ. Lectr in Physics, 1979–90; Reader in Experimental Physics, 1990–91; Prof. of Experimental Physics, 1991–2003; Chm. of Physics, 1996–98; Res. Dir for Collider Progs, 1999–2003; Dep. Dir Gen., 2002–03, CERN. SERC Sen. Res. Fellow, 1982–87; Vis. Prof., Vrije Univ., Brussels, 1982; Guest Scientist, Fermilab, Chicago, 1986. Chairman: Sci. Cttee, Nat. Lab. of San Grasso, Italy, 2004–10; Nuclear Res. Adv. Council, 2005–; Member: Sci. Adv. Cttee, Nat. Inst. for Nuclear Physics and High Energy Physics, Amsterdam, 2005–11; policy and prog. cttees, CERN, Deutsches Elektronen-Synchrotron, Hamburg, and SERC. Abdus Salam Meml Lect., Islamabad, 2001. Gov., Ludlow Coll., 1995–98. Trustee, Tanner Foundn, 2002–11. MAE 1992. FRSA 1996; Fellow, Eur. Phys. Soc., 2010. Hon. Doctor Jt Inst. for Nuclear Res., Dubna, 2004. C. V. Boys Prize, Inst. of Physics, 1983; Humboldt Res. Award, Alexander Von Humboldt Stiftung, 1995. *Publications:* contrib. Nuclear Physics, Physics Letters, Phys. Rev., Phys. Rev. Letters. *Recreations:* sports, wine.

CASIDA, Prof. John Edward, PhD; Professor of the Graduate School, University of California at Berkeley, since 2008; *b* 22 Dec. 1929; *s* of Lester Earl Casida and Ruth Casida (*née* Barnes); *m* 1956, Katherine Faustine Monson; two *s*. *Educ:* Univ. of Wisconsin (BS 1951; MS 1952; PhD 1954). Served USAF, 1953. University of Wisconsin: Res. Asst, 1951–53; Prof. of Entomology, 1954–63; University of California at Berkeley: Prof. of Entomology and Toxicology, 1964–; Dir, Envmtl Chemistry and Toxicology Lab., 1964–; William Muriece Hoskins Prof. of Chemical and Molecular Entomology, 1996–2008; Faculty Res. Lectr, 1998–2008. Schol.-in-Res., Bellagio Study and Conf. Centre, Rockefeller Foundn, Lake Como, 1978; Sterling B. Hendricks Lectr, US Dept of Agric., and ACS, 1992; Lectr, Third World Acad. of Sci., Univ. of Buenos Aires, 1997 (DUniv 1997). Mem., US Nat. Acad. of Sci., 1991; Foreign Mem., Royal Soc., 1998; Mem., Eur. Acad. of Sci., 2004. Hon. Mem., Pesticide Sci. Soc., Japan, 2005. Wolf Prize in Agriculture, 1993; Founder's Award, Soc. Envmt Toxicology and Chemistry, 1994; Kôrô-sho Prize, Pesticide Sci. Soc., Japan, 1995; Career Achievement Award, Coll. of Natural Resources, Univ. of Calif at Berkeley, 2009; Distinguished Service Award, American Coll. of Toxicology, 2009. *Address:* (office) University of California, Department of Environmental Science Policy Management, Wellman Hall, Berkeley, CA 94720-3112, USA.

CASKEN, Prof. John, DMus; composer; Professor of Music, University of Manchester, 1992–2008, now Emeritus; *b* 15 July 1949. *Educ:* Birmingham Univ. (BMus, MA); DMus Durham, 1992. FRNCM 1996. Polish Govt Scholarship, Warsaw, 1971–72. Lectr, Birmingham Univ., 1973–79; Res. Fellow, Huddersfield Poly., 1980–81; Lectr, Durham Univ., 1981–92. Composer in Association, Northern Sinfonia, 1990–2000; Rockefeller Foundn Residency (Bellagio), 1992. Northern Electric Performing Arts Award, 1990. Hon. DCL Univ. of King's Coll., Halifax, Nova Scotia, 2011; Hon. DMus Birmingham, 2011. *Compositions include: orchestral:* Tableaux des Trois Ages, 1977; Masque, 1982; Orion over Farne, 1984; Maharal Dreaming, 1989; Cello Concerto, 1991; Still Mine (baritone and orch.), 1992 (Prix de Composition Musicale, Prince Pierre de Monaco, 1993); Darting the Skiff, 1993; Violin Concerto, 1995; Sortilège, 1996; Distant Variations (saxophone quartet and wind orch.), 1997; Symphony (Broken Consort), 2004; Rest-ringing (string quartet and orch.), 2005; Farness - three poems of Carol Ann Duffy (soprano, solo viola and chamber orch.), 2006; Concerto for Orchestra, 2007; That Subtle Knot (double concerto for violin and viola), 2013; *ensemble and instrumental:* Amarantos, 1978; Firewhirl (soprano and ensemble), 1980; String Quartet No 1, 1982; Vaganza, 1985; Salamandra, 1986; Piano Quartet, 1990; String Quartet No 2, 1994; Infanta Marina, 1994; Après un silence, 1998; The Haunting Bough (solo piano), 1999; Nearly Distant (saxophone quartet), 2000; Piano Trio, 2002; Blue Medusa (bassoon and piano), 2003; Amethyst Deceiver (solo oboe), 2009; Inevitable Rifts (string quintet), 2009; Winter Reels (mixed ensemble), 2011; Apollinaire's Bird (oboe concerto), 2014; *vocal and choral:* Ia Orana Gauguin, 1978; To Fields We Do Not Know, 1984; Three Choral Pieces, 1990–93; Sharp Thorne, 1992; To the Lovers' Well, 2001; The Dream of the Rood, 2008 (BASCA Award, 2010); Deadly Pleasures (melodrama), 2009; Magnificat and Nunc Dimittis, 2012; *opera:* Golem, 1988 (first Britten Award, 1990; Gramophone Award for best contemp. recording, 1991); God's Liar, 2000; *electronic:* A Belle Pavine, 1980; Piper's Linn, 1984; Soul Catcher, 1988, rev. 2004. *Address:* Holystone Mill, Holystone, Rothbury, Northumberland NE65 7AJ.

CASLEY, Henry Roberts; non-executive Director, Scottish and Southern Energy plc, 1998–2005; *s* of Benjamin Rowe Casley and May Casley; *m* 1960, Sheila Laity; one *s* one *d.* MCIM. Eastern Electricity: Energy Mkting Manager, 1975–78; Supplies Manager, 1978–82; Mkting Dir, 1982–86; Southern Electric plc: Dep. Chm., 1986–89; Man. Dir, 1989–93; Chief Exec., 1993–96; non-exec. Dir, 1996–98. *Recreations:* sport, gardening.

CASPI, Prof. Avshalom, PhD; FBA 2006; Edward M. Arnett Professor of Psychology and Neuroscience, Duke University, since 2008; Professor of Personality Development, Institute of Psychiatry, Psychology and Neuroscience (formerly Institute of Psychiatry), King's College London, since 1997; *b* Jerusalem, 5 May 1960; *m* 1990, Prof. Terrie Edith Moffitt, *qv. Educ:* Univ. of Calif, Santa Cruz (BA 1981); Cornell Univ. (MA 1983; PhD 1986). Asst Prof. of Psychol., Harvard Univ., 1986–89; Asst Prof., 1989–91, Associate Prof., 1991–95, Prof. of Psychol., 1995–2007, Univ. of Wisconsin; Prof., Dept of Psychol. and Neurosci., Duke Univ., 2007–08. Mem. Council, Internat. Soc. for Study of Behavioural Develt, 2000–06. FMedSci 2002. *Publications:* (jtly) Persons in Context; (jtly) Sex Differences in Antisocial Behaviour, 2001; (jtly) Paths to Successful Development, 2002; (jtly) Causes of Conduct Disorder and Juvenile Delinquency, 2003; articles in learned jls. *Address:* Department of Psychology and Neuroscience, Duke University, Grey House, 2020 Main Street, Durham, NC 27708, USA; Social Genetic and Developmental Psychiatry Department, Institute of Psychiatry, Psychology and Neuroscience, King's College London, De Crespigny Park, SE5 8AF.

CASS, Sir Geoffrey (Arthur), Kt 1992; MA; Chairman: Royal Shakespeare Company, 1985–2000; Royal Theatrical Support (formerly Royal Shakespeare Theatre) Trust, since 1983; President, The Tennis Foundation (formerly British Tennis Foundation), since 2007 (Chairman, 2003–07); President, and Chairman of the Council, Lawn Tennis Association, 1997–99; Chief Executive, Cambridge University Press, 1972–92; Fellow of Clare Hall, Cambridge, since 1979; *b* 11 Aug. 1932; *oc* of late Arthur Cass and Jessie Cass (*née* Simpson), Darlington and Oxford; *m* 1957, Olwen Mary, MBE, JP, DL, *oc* of late William Leslie Richards and Edith Louisa Richards, Llanelli and Brecon; four *d. Educ:* Queen Elizabeth Grammar Sch., Darlington (Head of Sch.); Jesus Coll., Nuffield Coll., and Dept of Social and Admin. Studies, Oxford Univ. (BA 1954; MA 1958; Hon. Fellow, Jesus Coll., 1998); MA Cantab, 1972. FInstD 1968; FIWM, FIIM 1979; CCMI (CBIM 1980). Commnd RAFVR, fighter control, 1954; served RAF, 1958–60: Air Min. Directorate of Work Study; Pilot Officer, 1958; Flying Officer, 1960. Consultant: PA Management Consultants Ltd, 1960–65; British Communications Corp., and Controls and Communications Ltd, 1965; Dir, Controls and Communications Ltd, 1966–69; Managing Director, George Allen and Unwin Ltd, 1967–71; Cambridge University Press: Sec., Press Syndicate, 1974–92; Univ. Printer, 1982–83, 1991–92; Consultant, 1992–; Director: Weidenfeld (Publishers) Ltd, 1972–74; Chicago Univ. Press (UK), 1971–86; Mem., Jesus Coll., Cambridge, 1972–. Member: Univ. of Cambridge Cttee of Management of Fenner's (and Exec. Cttee), 1976–; Univ. of Cambridge Careers Service Syndicate (formerly Appts Bd), 1977–2002 (Exec. Cttee, 1982–2002); Governing Syndicate, Fitzwilliam Mus., Cambridge, 1977–78; Chm., Univ. of Cambridge Sports Centre Appeal, 2001–05; Chm. Governors, Perse Sch. for Girls, Cambridge, 1978–88 (Governor, 1977–98); Trustee, Univ. of Cambridge Foundn, 1998–13 (Chm., Audit Cttee, 2006–13); Chm., Univ. of Cambridge ADC Theatre Appeal, 2000–07. Founder Mem. Council, Royal Shakespeare Theatre Trust, 1967–; Gov., 1975–, Dep. Pres. of Govs, 2000–11, RSC (Mem., Council, 1975–2000; Mem., 1976–2000, Chm. 1982–2000, Exec. Cttee, Council); Trustee and Guardian, Shakespeare Birthplace Trust, 1982– (Life Trustee, 1994; Chm., Audit Cttee, 2008–); Founder Mem., Inigo Productions, 1996. Director: Newcastle Theatre Royal Trust, 1984–89; American Friends of the Royal Shakespeare Theatre, 1985–2000; Method & Madness (formerly Cambridge Theatre Co.), 1986–95; Cambridge Arts Th., 1997–98; Theatres Trust, 1991–2000; Marc Sinden Productions, 2001–02; The All England LTC (Wimbledon) Ltd, 1997–2000; The All England Lawn Tennis Ground PLC, 1997–2000. Pres., Macmillan Cancer Support, Cambridgeshire (formerly Macmillan Cancer Relief Cambs and Peterborough Project), 1998–. Cambridgeshire LTA: Mem. Exec., 1974–84; Chm., F and GP Cttee 1982–84; Captain 1974–78; Pres., 1980–82; Hon. Life Vice-Pres., 1982–; The Lawn Tennis Association of GB: Dep. Pres., 1994–96; Member: Council, 1976–; Management Bd, 1985–90, 1993–2000; Nat. Trng and Internat. Match Cttee (Davis Cup, Fedn Cup, Wightman Cup, etc), 1982–90, 1992–93 (Chm., 1985–90); Internat. Events Cttee, 1991–93; Chm., Nat. Ranking Cttee, 1990–99; Wimbledon Championships: Member: Cttee of Management, 1990–2002; Jt Finance Bd, 1989–93; Jt Finance Cttee, 1993–2002 (Chm., 1997–99); British Jun. Championships Cttee of Management, 1983–90 (Chm., 1985–90); Nat. Championships Cttee of Management, 1988–89; Rules and Internat. Cttee, 1980–81; Re-orgn Wkg Party, 1984–85; Chm., Reconstruction Wkg Gp, 1994–99. Tennis singles champion: Durham County, 1951; Cambridgeshire, 1976; Oxford University: tennis Blue, 1953, 1954, 1955 (Sec., 1955); badminton, 1951, 1952 (Captain, 1952); Pres., Cambridge Univ. Lawn Tennis Club, 2007– (Chm., 1977–2007; Hon. Cambridge tennis Blue, 1980); Chm., Cambridge Univ. Cricket and Athletic Club, 2003–; played in Wimbledon Championships, 1954, 1955, 1956, 1959; played in inter-county lawn tennis championships for Durham County, then for Cambridgeshire, 1952–82; represented RAF, 1958–59; Brit. Veterans (over 45) singles champion, Wimbledon, 1978; Mem., Brit. Veterans' Internat. Dubler Cup Team, Barcelona, 1978, Milano Marittima, 1979 (Captain). Patron: Cambridge Rowing Trust, 2001–; Theatre Royal Bury St Edmunds Restoration Appeal Cttee, 2001–08. FRSA 1991. Chevalier, Ordre des Arts et des Lettres (France), 1982. *Recreations:* lawn tennis, theatre. *Address:* Middlefield, Huntingdon Road, Girton, Cambridge CB3 0LH. *Clubs:* Garrick, Institute of Directors, All England Lawn Tennis and Croquet (Hon.), Queen's (Hon.), International Lawn Tennis of GB, The 45 (Hon.), Veterans' Lawn Tennis of GB; Hawks (Hon.) (Cambridge); Cambridge University Lawn Tennis; West Hants Lawn Tennis (Hon.).

CASS, Hilary Dawn, OBE 2015; FRCP, FRCPCH; Paediatric Neurodisability Consultant, Evelina London Children's Hospital, Guy's and St Thomas' NHS Foundation Trust, since 2009; President, Royal College of Paediatrics and Child Health, 2012–15; *b* London, 19 Feb. 1958; *d* of Ralph and Mildred Cass. *Educ:* City of London Sch. for Girls; Royal Free Hosp. Sch. of Medicine (BSc 1979; MB BS 1982). FRCPCH 1992; FRCP 2004. House Physician, Royal Free Hosp., 1982–83; House Surgeon, Northwick Park Hosp., 1983; SHO, Hammersmith Hosp., 1983–84; Whittington Hospital: SHO Gen. Medicine, 1984–85; SHO Gen. Paediatrics, 1985; SHO Obstetrics and Gynaecology, 1985–86; SHO Neonatal Paediatrics, 1986–87; SHO, Harper House Children's Services, UCH, 1986; SHO, Queen Elizabeth Children's Hosp., 1987–88; Community Med. Officer and Hon. Registrar Paediatrics, Islington HA, 1988–89; Rotational Registrar Paediatrics, Newham Gen. Hosp. and London Hosp., 1989–90; Sen. Registrar in Paediatric Disability, UCH, 1990–92; Consultant in Paediatric Disability, Harper House Children's Services, 1992–98; Hon. Consultant, Camden and Islington Community Trust, 1992–2001; Great Ormond Street Hospital: Paediatric Neurodisability Consultant, 1994–2009; Dir, Med. Educn, 1998–2008; Dep. Med. Dir, 2003–08; Hd, London Sch. of Paediatrics, 2007–09. Hon. Sen. Lect, Inst. of Child Health, UCL, 1996–2009. FHEA 2008. Hon. FRCPE 2013. *Publications:* The NHS Experience: the 'Snakes and Ladders' guide for patients and professionals, 2006. *Recreations:* theatre, books, music. *Address:* 31 Tithe Walk, NW7 2PY.

CASS, John, QPM 1979; National Co-ordinator of Regional Crime Squads, 1981–84; Security Consultant; *b* 24 June 1925; *m* 1948, Dilys Margaret Hughes, SRN; three *d. Educ:* Nelson Sch., Wigton, Cumbria; UCW, Lampeter (DipTh 1997; BA Hons (Theol.) 1999). Served no 40 RM Commando, 1944–45. Joined Metropolitan Police, 1946; Comdt, Detective Training Sch., Hendon, 1974; Commander: CID, New Scotland Yard, 1975; Complaints Bureau, 1978; Serious Crime Squads, New Scotland Yard, 1980. UK Rep., Interpol Conf. on crime prediction, Paris, 1976. Student in Criminology, Cambridge Univ., 1966. Adviser, Police Staff Coll., on multi-Force major investigations, 1982–83; Chief Investigator, War Crimes Inquiry, Home Office, 1988–89. Mem., British Acad. of Forensic Scis, 1965. Member: Association of Chief Police Officers; Metropolitan Police Commanders' Assoc.; Internat. Police Assoc. Lay preacher; Asst Lay Chaplain, W Wales Hosp. Mem., Lampeter Soc. Freeman, City of London, 1979. *Recreations:* Lakeland, walking, wild life; and Janet (BA), Anne (BDS), Sarah (LLB), James (MB BS, MRCP), Gwilym (LLB), Bryn (BSc), Elizabeth, Ieuan Jack, Catherine Olivia and Joshua James. *Address:* Bryn Eryl, Peniel, Carmarthenshire SA32 7HT. *T:* (01267) 236948. *Club:* Special Forces.

CASS, Richard Martin; Founding Partner, 1983–2013, Consultant, since 2013, Cass Associates; Chairman and Trustee, Cass Foundation, since 2012; Built Environment Expert, Design Council, since 2012; *b* Princes Risborough, 25 May 1946; *s* of Edward and Hazel Cass; *m* 1977, Judith Claire Snaith; two *s. Educ:* High Wycombe Royal Grammar Sch.; Univ. of Sheffield (BArch; MA). RIBA 1972–2014. Architect: Sheffield CC, 1968–70; Ryder and Yates (Architects & Engrs), 1970–72; Architect and Landscape Architect, Brian Clouston and Partners, 1972–81; Project Manager, Merseyside Develt Corp., 1981–83. Projects include: Silksworth Park, Sunderland, 1978 (Community Architecture Award); Liverpool Internat. Garden Fest., 1984 (Civic Trust Award); Duisburg Nord Landscape Park, 1990; Buckshaw Village, Lancs, 1994 (Planning Achievement Award, RTPI, 2000); Birkenhead Bus Station, 1997 (RIBA, Civic Trust and Structural Steel Awards). Dir, CPL Mgt Ltd, 2013–. Mem., London 2012 Olympic Park Design Rev. Panel, 2007–12; Mem., CABE, 2008–11. Trustee: Heritage Works Bldg Preservation Trust, 2007–; Jewel on the Hill Building Preservation Trust, 2012–. MLI 1975–2014. *Recreations:* music, theatre, opera, art, travel, gardening, sailing, hill walking, reading. *Address:* Osborne House West, Fulwood Park, Liverpool L17 5AD. *T:* 07711 570955. *E:* richard.m.cass@btinternet.com.

CASS, Wilfred, CBE 2006; Co-Founder, Cass Sculpture Foundation, 1992; *b* Berlin, 11 Nov. 1924; *s* of Hans and Edith Cassirer; *m* 1983, Jeannette Futter; one *s* one *d. Educ:* Regent St Poly., London (HND Communication Technol. 1951). With Pye Ltd, Cambridge, 1951–57; Joint Founder (with brother, Eric): and Dep. Chm., Cass Electronics Ltd, 1955–85; Cass McLaren Ltd (Consultancy), 1959; Founder, and Man. Dir, 1965–71, non-exec. Dir, 1971–75, Gunson Sortex Ltd (Queen's Awards to Industry for export achievement and for tech. innovation, 1968); Managing Director: Hadfield Paints Ltd, 1972–75; Buck & Hickman Ltd, 1974–75; Chm. and Man. Dir, Reeves and Sons Ltd, subseq. Reeves Dryad Ltd, 1971–76; set up: Cass Arts & Crafts Ltd, 1976, sold 1985; Image Bank UK, 1979, sold 2001; Chm. and Chief Exec., Moss Bros plc, 1987–91. UK Founder and Chm., Kennedy Foundn, 1976–93. Hon. FRCA 1995. DUniv Open, 2008. *Recreations:* films, reading, photography, travel, art. *Address:* Cass Sculpture Foundation, Goodwood, Chichester, W Sussex PO18 0QP. *T:* (01243) 538449. *E:* wilfred@sculpture.org.uk. *Club:* Kennels (Goodwood).

CASSAM, Prof. Quassim, DPhil; Professor of Philosophy, University of Warwick, since 2009 (Head, Department of Philosophy, 2010–12); *b* 31 Jan. 1961; *s* of Amir and Sultan Cassam; *m* 2010, Dr Deborah Ghate. *Educ:* Keble Coll., Oxford (BA 1st Cl. Hons PPE; BPhil Philosophy; DPhil Philosophy 1985). Fellow and Lectr in Philosophy, Oriel Coll., Oxford, 1985–86; Fellow and Tutor in Philosophy, Wadham Coll., Oxford, 1986–2004; Prof. of Philosophy, UCL, 2005–06; Knightbridge Prof. of Philosophy, Univ. of Cambridge, 2007–08; Fellow, King's Coll., Cambridge, 2007–08. Vis. Associate Prof., Univ. of Calif, Berkeley, 1993; John Evans Dist. Vis. Prof., Northwestern Univ., 2004. Sen. Res. Fellow, Mind, 2012–13. Bechtel Lectr, Harvard Univ., 2000; Lipkind Lectr, Univ. of Chicago, 2010. Pres., Aristotelian Soc., 2010–11. *Publications:* Self and World, 1997; The Possibility of Knowledge, 2007; (with J. Campbell) Berkeley's Puzzle; what does experience teach us?, 2014; Self-knowledge for Humans, 2014. *Recreations:* films, music, food, cricket, Arsenal FC. *Address:* Department of Philosophy, University of Warwick, Coventry CV4 7AL.

CASSANI, Barbara Ann, Hon. CBE 2007; Chairman, Jurys Inns, Dublin, 2008–10; *b* 22 July 1960; *d* of James and Noreen Cassani; *m* 1985, Guy Davis; one *s* one *d. Educ:* Mount Holyoke Coll., USA (BA Hons *magna cum laude* Internat. Relns); Woodrow Wilson Sch. of Public and Internat. Affairs, Princeton Univ. (MPA). Mgt Consultant, Coopers & Lybrand, in Washington and London, 1984–87; various mgt rôles with British Airways in UK and USA, 1987–97; CEO, Go Fly Ltd, 1997–2002; Chm., 2003–04, Vice-Chm., 2004–05, London 2012 Olympic Bid. *Publications:* (with K. Kemp) Go: an airline adventure, 2003. *Recreations:* reading, horse-riding, travel. *E:* bacassani@aol.com.

CASSEL, family name of **Baroness Mallalieu**.

CASSEL, Sir Timothy (Felix Harold), 4th Bt *cr* 1920; QC 1988; *b* 30 April 1942; *s* of Sir Harold Cassel, 3rd Bt, TD, QC; *S* father, 2001; *m* 1st, 1971, Jenifer Puckle (marr. diss. 1976); one *s* one *d*; 2nd, 1979, Ann Mallalieu (marr. diss. 2007) (*see* Baroness Mallalieu); two *d. Educ:* Eton College. Called to the Bar, Lincoln's Inn, 1965, Bencher, 1994; Jun. Prosecuting Counsel at Central Criminal Court, 1978, Sen. Prosecuting Counsel, 1986–88; Asst Boundaries Comr, 1979–85. *Heir: s* Alexander James Felix Cassel, *b* 25 May 1974. *Address:* West Wing, Kirtlington Park, Oxon OX5 3JN. *Clubs:* Garrick, Turf.

CASSELL, Michael Robert; writer; freelance journalist, specialising in energy and renewable energy markets, since 2000; *b* 2 June 1946; *s* of Donald and Joyce Cassell; *m* 1995, Linda Radway. *Educ:* Lode Heath High Sch.; Solihull Coll. Reporter, W Midlands Press, 1964–67; Business Reporter, Birmingham Post, 1967–69; City Reporter, Daily Express, 1969–70; Financial Times, 1970–2000: successively Property, Political, Industry, and Business Correspondent; Ed., Observer column, 1996–2000. *Publications:* One Hundred Years of Co-operation, 1984; Readymixers, 1986; Dig it, Burn it, Sell it!, 1990; Long Lease, 1991. *Recreations:* horse riding, walking, watercolours, writing. *Address:* Barnard Acres, Nazeing EN9 2LZ.

CASSELS, Sir John (Seton), Kt 1988; CB 1978; Chairman, UK SKILLS, 1990–2000; *b* 10 Oct. 1928; *s* of Alastair Macdonald Cassels and Ada White Cassels (*née* Scott); *m* 1956, Mary Whittington (*d* 2008); two *s* two *d. Educ:* Sedbergh Sch., Yorkshire; Trinity Coll., Cambridge (1st cl. Hons, Classics, 1951). Rome Scholar, Classical Archaeology, 1952–54. Entered Ministry of Labour, 1954; Secretary of the Royal Commission on Trade Unions and

Employers' Associations, 1965–68; Under-Sec., NBPI, 1968–71; Managing Directors' Office, Dunlop Holdings Ltd, 1971–72; Chief Exec., Training Services Agency, 1972–75; Dir, Manpower Services Commn, 1975–81; Second Permanent Sec., MPO, 1981–83; Dir Gen., NEDO, 1983–88. Dir, Nat. Commn on Educn, 1991–95. Chm., Ind. Inquiry into the Role and Responsibilities of the Police, 1994–96. Member Council: Inst. of Manpower Studies, subseq. Inst. of Employment Studies, 1982–2009 (Pres., 1989–95; Hon. Life Pres., 2001); Policy Studies Inst., 1983–88; Industrial Soc., 1984–93; Assoc. for Consumer Res., 1989–94; NIESR, 1993–2009. Chm., Internat. Comparisons in Criminal Justice, 1990–95; Mem., Prince's Trust Volunteers Mgt Adv. Bd, 1998–2001; Chairman: Sussex Careers Services, 1995–98; Modern Apprenticeship Adv. Cttee, DfES, 2001; Mem., Apprenticeship Ambassadors Network, 2006–09 (Hon. Apprenticeship Award, 2009). Chm., Richmond Adult and Community Coll., 1996–2001. Dist. Vis. Fellow, 1989, Sen. Fellow, 1990, PSI. FIPD; FRSA. Hon. Dr: Sussex, 1995; Heriot-Watt, 1996; Brunel, 1997; Companion, De Montfort Univ., 1995. Hon. CGIA 1989. *Publications:* Britain's Real Skill Shortage—and what to do about it, 1990. *Club:* Reform.

CASSELS, Prof. John William Scott, MA, PhD; FRS 1963; FRSE 1981; Sadleirian Professor of Pure Mathematics, Cambridge University, 1967–84; Head of Department of Pure Mathematics and Mathematical Statistics, 1969–84; *b* 11 July 1922; *s* of late J. W. Cassels (latterly Dir of Agriculture in Co. Durham) and late Mrs M. S. Cassels (*née* Lobjoit); *m* 1949, Constance Mabel Merritt (*née* Senior) (*d* 2000); one *s* one *d. Educ:* Neville's Cross Council Sch., Durham; George Heriot's Sch., Edinburgh; Edinburgh and Cambridge Univs. MA Edinburgh, 1943; PhD Cantab, 1949. Fellow, Trinity, 1949–; Lecturer, Manchester Univ., 1949; Lecturer, Cambridge Univ., 1950; Reader in Arithmetic, 1963–67. Mem. Council, Royal Society, 1970, 1971 (Sylvester Medal, 1973); Vice Pres., 1974–78, Mem. Exec., 1978–82, Internat. Mathematical Union; Pres., London Mathematical Soc., 1976–78. Dr (*hc*) Lille Univ., 1965; Hon. ScD Edinburgh, 1977. De Morgan Medal, London Mathematical Soc., 1986. *Publications:* An Introduction to Diophantine Approximation, 1957; An Introduction to the Geometry of Numbers, 1959; Rational Quadratic Forms, 1978; Economics for Mathematicians, 1981; Local Fields, 1986; Lectures on Elliptic Curves, 1991; (with E. V. Flynn) Prolegomena to a Middlebrow Arithmetic of Curves of Genus 2, 1996; papers in diverse mathematical journals on arithmetical topics. *Recreations:* arithmetic (higher only), gardening (especially common vegetables). *Address:* 3 Luard Close, Cambridge CB2 8PL. *T:* (01223) 246108.

CASSELS, Adm. Sir Simon (Alastair Cassillis), KCB 1982; CBE 1976; *b* 5 March 1928; *o s* of late Comdr A. G. Cassels, RN, and Clarissa Cassels (*née* Motion); *m* 1962, Jillian Francies Kannreuther; one *s* one *d. Educ:* RNC, Dartmouth. Midshipman 1945; Commanding Officer: HM Ships Vigilant, Roebuck, and Tenby, 1962–63; HMS Eskimo, 1966–67; HMS Fearless, 1972–73; Principal Staff Officer to CDS, 1973–76; CO HMS Tiger, 1976–78; Asst Chief of Naval Staff (Op. Requirements), 1978–80; Flag Officer, Plymouth, Port Adm. Devonport, Comdr Central Sub Area Eastern Atlantic and Comdr Plymouth Sub Area Channel, 1981–82; Second Sea Lord, Chief of Naval Personnel and Adm. Pres., RNC, Greenwich, 1982–86. Dir Gen., TSB Foundn for Eng. and Wales, 1986–90. Younger Brother of Trinity House, 1963. Pres., Regular Forces Employment Assoc., 1990–93 (Chm., 1989). Freeman, City of London, 1983; Liveryman, Shipwrights' Co., 1984. FRGS 1947. *Publications:* Peninsular Portrait 1811–1814, 1963. *Recreations:* appreciation of archaeology, architecture and art, historical research. *Address:* c/o Lloyds Bank, Bishop's Waltham, Southampton SO32 1GS. *Club:* Army and Navy.

CASSEN, Prof. Robert Harvey, OBE 2008; Visiting Professor, London School of Economics, since 1997; Professor of the Economics of Development, Queen Elizabeth House, International Development Centre, University of Oxford, 1986–97, and Professorial Fellow, St Antony's College, 1986–97, now Emeritus; *b* 24 March 1935; *s* of John and Liliane Cassen; *m* 1988, Sun Shuyun. *Educ:* Bedford School; New Coll., Oxford (BA LitHum, MA); Univ. of California, Berkeley; Harvard (PhD Econ). Dept of Economics, LSE, 1961–69; Sen. Economist, ODM, 1966–67; First Sec. (Econ.), New Delhi, 1967–68; Sen. Economist, World Bank, Washington, 1969–72 and 1980–81; Fellow, Inst. of Develt Studies, Sussex Univ., 1972–86; Sen. Res. Fellow, Centre for Population Studies, LSHTM, 1976–77; Dir, Queen Elizabeth House, Internat. Develt Centre, Oxford Univ., 1986–93. Special Adviser, H of C Select Cttee on Overseas Develt, 1973–74; Secretariat, Brandt Commn, 1978–79 and 1981–82; Mem., Bd of Trustees, Population Council, NY, 1978–87; UK Mem., UN Cttee for Develt Planning, 1982–84. *Publications:* India: Population, Economy, Society, 1978; (ed and contrib.) Planning for Growing Populations, 1979; (ed and contrib.) World Development Report, 1981; (ed and contrib.) Rich Country Interests and Third World Development, 1982; (ed) Soviet Interests in the Third World, 1985; Does Aid Work? (report), 1986, 2nd edn 1994; (ed) Poverty in India, 1992; (ed and contrib.) Population and Development: old debates, new conclusions, 1994; (ed) India: the future of economic reform, 1995; (ed and contrib.) 21st Century India: population, economy, human development and the environment, 2004; Tackling Low Educational Achievement (report), 2007; (jtly) Making a Difference in Education: what the evidence says, 2015; contribs to learned jls. *Recreations:* music, walking. *Address:* Centre for Analysis of Social Exclusion, LSE, Houghton Street, WC2A 2AE. *T:* (020) 7955 6679.

CASSERLEY, Dominic James Andrew; Chief Executive, Willis Group, since 2013; *b* Gosport, 23 Dec. 1957; *s* of Christopher and Pamela Casserley; *m* 1986, Nancy Broadbent; two *s* one *d. Educ:* University Coll. Sch., London; Jesus Coll., Cambridge (BA Hons Hist. 1979). Pres., Cambridge Union Soc., 1979. Exec., Investment Mgt, then Mergers & Acquisitions, Morgan Grenfell & Co., 1979–83; McKinsey & Co.: Associate, 1983–87; Principal, 1988–93; Dir, 1993–; Leader: Gtr China Practice, 1994–99; Eur. Banking and Securities Practice, 1999–2003; Man. Partner, UK and Ire., 2003–10; Global Hd, Corporate and Investment Banking, 2010–13. David Rockefeller Fellow, NY, 1991–92. Mem., US Presidential Taskforce on Mkt Mechanisms, 1987. Member: Bd, Manhattan Th. Club, 1991–94; Bd, Donmar Th., London, 2003–11; Bd, Asia House, 2009–13; Chairman: Action on Addiction, 2007–11; Charities Aid Foundn, 2010–; Trustee, National Th., 2011–. Mem. Council, Univ. of Cambridge, 2011–13. *Publications:* Facing up to the Risks: how financial institutions can survive and prosper, 1993, 4th edn 1997; (with G. Gibb) Banking in Asia, the End of Entitlement, 1999. *Recreations:* tennis, travelling. *Address:* Willis Group, 51 Lime Street, EC3M 7DQ. *Clubs:* Reform, MCC, Queen's; University (NY); Field (Greenwich, CT); Links (NY).

CASSIDI, Adm. Sir (Arthur) Desmond, GCB 1983 (KCB 1978); President, Royal Naval Association, 1987–96; Deputy Grand President, British Commonwealth Ex-Services League, 1986–96; *b* 26 Jan. 1925; *s* of late Comdr Robert A. Cassidi, RN and late Clare F. (*née* Alexander); *m* 1st, 1950, Dorothy Sheelagh Marie (*née* Scott) (*d* 1974); one *s* two *d*; 2nd, 1982, Dr Deborah Marion Pollock (*née* Bliss), FRCS. *Educ:* RNC Dartmouth. Qual. Pilot, 1946; CO, 820 Sqdn (Gannet aircraft), 1955; 1st Lieut HMS Protector, 1955–56; psc 1957; CO, HMS Whitby, 1959–61; Fleet Ops Officer Home Fleet, 1962–64; Asst Dir Naval Plans, 1964–67; Captain (D) Portland and CO HMS Undaunted, 1967–68; idc 1969; Dir of Naval Plans, 1970–72; CO, HMS Ark Royal, 1972–73; Flag Officer Carriers and Amphibious Ships, 1974–75; Dir-Gen., Naval Manpower and Training, 1975–77; Flag Officer, Naval Air Command, 1978–79; Chief of Naval Personnel and Second Sea Lord, 1979–82; C-in-C Naval Home Comd, 1982–85; Flag ADC to the Queen, 1982–85. Mem. Adv. Council, Science Museum, 1979–84, Trustee, 1984–92; Pres., FAA Museum, 1985–95. FRSA 1986. *Recreation:* country pursuits.

CASSIDY, Bryan Michael Deece; Founder, Cassidy and Associates International, EU Consultants, 1999; Member, European Economic and Social Committee, 2002–14 (Chairman, Single Market Observatory, 2004–06; Co-Chairman, EU/Turkey Joint Consultative Committee, 2006–08; President, Single Market Production and Consumption section, 2008–14); *s* of late William Francis Deece Cassidy and Kathleen Selina Patricia Cassidy (*née* Geraghty); *m* 1960, Gillian Mary Isobel Bohane; one *s* two *d. Educ:* Ratcliffe College; Sidney Sussex College, Cambridge (MA Law). Commissioned RA, 1955–57 (Malta and Libya); HAC, 1957–62. With Ever Ready, Beecham's and IPC Business Press (Dir, European associates). Mem. Council, CBI, 1981–84. Dir Gen., of a trade assoc., 1981–84. Contested (C) Wandsworth Central, 1966; Mem. GLC (Hendon North), 1977–86 (opposition spokesman on industry and employment, 1983–84). MEP (C), Dorset E and Hampshire W, 1984–94, Dorset and E Devon, 1994–99; contested (C) SW Reg., 1999. Assignments for BESO in Estonia, 2000, Mongolia, 2002. Dir of Studies, Hawksmere Brussels Briefings, 2001–04. Vis. Woodrow Wilson Fellow, American Univs, 2000, 2004. Mem., Adv. Bd, European Performance Inst., Brussels, 1999–2002. *Publications:* Hawksmere European Lobbying Guide, 2000; regular contribs to Industry Europe. *Recreations:* history, theatre, spending time at home in Dorset. *Address:* 11 Esmond Court, Thackeray Street, W8 5HB. *T:* (020) 7937 3558. *E:* bmdcassidy@aol.com.

CASSIDY, His Eminence Cardinal Edward; *see* Cassidy, His Eminence Cardinal I. E.

CASSIDY, Elizabeth Grace; Royal Navy Resources Director, since 2012; *b* 6 July 1951; *er d* of late William Charles Cassidy and Mildred Joan Cassidy (*née* Ross); *m* 1984, Edward Roy Dolby. *Educ:* Girls' Grammar Sch., Prescot, Lancs; Girton Coll., Cambridge (MA); Wye Coll., Univ. of London (MSc). Ministry of Defence: Admin. Trainee, 1978; Private Sec. to Chief of Defence Procurement, 1983; Principal, 1984; Private Sec. to CAS, 1990–93; Asst Sec., Hd, IT Business Systems, then IT Strategy, 1993–95; Advr to Jt Services Comd and Staff Coll. Project, 1995–97; Dir, Finance Policy, 1997–99; Command Sec. to Second Sea Lord and C-in-C Naval Home Command, and Asst Under-Sec. of State (Naval Personnel), 1999–2001; Review of Business Continuity for MoD HQ post-9/11, 2001–02; Comd Sec. to Adjt Gen., 2002–06; Comd Sec., Navy, 2007–12. Mem., Admiralty and Navy Bds, 2012–. Dir, Regular Forces Employment Assoc. Ltd, 2006–. Mem., Royal Patriotic Fund Corp., 2003–06. Chm. Adv. Panel, Greenwich Hosp., 1999–2001 and 2007–; Comr, Royal Hosp. Chelsea, 2002–06. *Recreations:* music, reading, travel, sailing. *Address:* c/o HSBC, 9 Rose Lane, Canterbury, Kent CT1 2JP.

CASSIDY, Rt Rev. George Henry; Bishop of Southwell and Nottingham (formerly Bishop of Southwell), 1999–2009; an Assistant Bishop, Diocese of Bath and Wells and Diocese of Bristol, since 2009; *b* 17 Oct. 1942; *s* of Joseph Abram Cassidy and Ethel McDonald; *m* 1966, Jane Barling Stevens; two *d. Educ:* Belfast High School; Queen's Univ., Belfast (BSc 1965; Cert. Bib. Studies 1968); University Coll. London (MPhil 1967); Oak Hill Theological College. MRTPI 1969. Civil Servant: N Ireland, 1967–68; Govt of Kenya, 1968–70. Curate, Christ Church, Clifton, Bristol, 1972–75; Vicar: St Edyth, Sea Mills, Bristol, 1975–82; St Paul's, Portman Square, W1, 1982–87; Archdeacon of London and Canon Residentiary, St Paul's Cathedral, 1987–99; Sub-Dean, Order of the British Empire, 1996–99. Mem., Cathedrals Fabric Commn for England, 2001–05; Chm., Churches Legislation Adv. (formerly Main) Cttee, 2005–09. Freeman: City of London, 1988; Tylers' & Bricklayers' Co., 1988; Hon. Liveryman, Founders' Co., 1994. Hon. DLitt Heriot-Watt, 2005. Entered House of Lords, 2004. *Recreations:* Rugby football, art, chamber music, walking in the Quantocks. *Address:* Darch House, 17 St Andrews Road, Stogursey, Bridgwater, Som TA5 1TE. *Club:* National (Pres., 2010–).

CASSIDY, His Eminence Cardinal Idris Edward, AC 1990; President, Pontifical Council for Promoting Christian Unity, and Commission for Religious Relations with the Jews, 1989–2001; *b* 5 July 1924; *s* of Harold George Cassidy and Dorothy May Phillips. *Educ:* Parramatta High Sch.; St Columba Seminary, Springwood; St Patrick's Coll., Manly; Lateran Univ., Rome (DCnL 1955); Diploma of Pontifical Eccl. Acad., Rome, 1955. Ordained priest, 1949; Asst Priest, Parish of Yenda, NSW, Australia, 1950–52; Secretary, Apostolic Nunciature, India, 1955–62 and Ireland, 1962–67; El Salvador, 1967–69; Counsellor, Apostolic Nunciature, Argentina, 1969–70; ordained Archbishop, Rome, 1970; Apostolic Pro-Nuncio: to Republic of China, 1970–79; to Bangladesh, 1973–79; to Lesotho, 1979–84, and Apostolic Delegate to Southern Africa; to the Netherlands, 1984–88; Substitute of Vatican Secretariat of State, 1988–89. Cardinal, 1991. Orders from El Salvador, China, Netherlands, Italy, France, Sweden and Germany. *Recreations:* tennis, golf. *Address:* 16 Coachwood Drive, Warabrook, NSW 2304, Australia.

CASSIDY, Michael John, CBE 2004; Chairman: Board of Governors, Museum of London, 2005–13; Homerton University Hospital Foundation Trust, 2006–13; *b* 14 Jan. 1947; *s* of Frank and Vera Cassidy; *m* 1st, 1974, Amanda (marr. diss. 1988); one *s* two *d*; 2nd, 1997, Amelia Simpson; two *d. Educ:* Downing Coll., Cambridge (BA); MBA (with distinction), City Univ. Business Sch., 1985. Qualified Solicitor, 1971; Partner: Maxwell Batley, 1971–2002 (Sen. Partner, 1991–2002); D. J. Freeman, 2002–03; Hammonds, 2003–04. Director: British Land Plc, 1996–2007; UBS Investment Bank (formerly UBS Warburg, then UBS Ltd), 2000–; Crossrail Ltd, 2008–; Haymarket Risk Mgt Ltd, 2012–14; Chairman: Askonas Holt Ltd, 2002–; Hemingway Properties Ltd, 2003–06; Gruppo Norman, 2004–05; Trikona Trinity Capital plc (formerly Trinity Property Co.), 2005–09; Bulgarian Land Development plc, 2005–07; non-exec. Dir, P2P Global Investments plc, 2014–. Chm., Ebbsfleet Urban Develt Corp., 2015–. Corporation of London: Mem., Common Council, 1980–; Chairman: Planning Cttee, 1986–89; Policy and Resources Cttee, 1992–97; Property Investment Bd, 2012–; Chm., Barbican Arts Centre, 2000–03. Pres., London Chamber of Commerce and Industry, 2005–07 (Dep. Pres., 2004–05). Mem. Bd, London Pension Fund Authy, 2007–13. Liveryman, Solicitors' Co. (Master, 2001–02). Hon. Fellow, London Business Sch., 1995; Hon. FRIBA 1995. Hon. LLD South Bank, 1995; Hon. DCL City, 1996. *Publications:* articles on City matters and pension fund investment. *Recreation:* Barbican concerts. *Address:* 202 Cromwell Tower, Barbican, EC2Y 8DD. *T:* (020) 7628 5687. *Club:* London Capital.

CASSIDY, Seamus John; television producer; Director, Happy Endings television production company, since 2001; *b* 20 Nov. 1958; *s* of late Michael Cassidy and of Patricia Cassidy. *Educ:* St Columb's Coll., Derry; Queen's Univ., Belfast (LLB Hons). Researcher, 1982–84; Asst Ed., 1984–87; Sen. Commissioning Ed., Comedy and Entertainment, Channel 4 TV, 1987–97; Sen. Producer, Comedy and Entertainment, Planet 24, 1997–99; Producer, The Panel, Saturday Night with Miriam, Podge and Rodge, Smoke and Mirrors, Buried Alive, all RTE, 2003–09; Executive Producer: The History of the Future, BBC4, 2009; Things That Went Boom in the Bust, RTE, 2009; The Panel, RTE, 2009–11; Dirty Old Towns?, RTE, 2011–12. *Address:* Happy Endings Productions, 3 Carysfort Avenue, Blackrock, Co. Dublin, Eire.

CASSIDY, Dr Sheila Anne; lecturer and psychotherapist; Specialist in Psychosocial Oncology, Plymouth Oncology Centre, 1993–2002; *b* 18 Aug. 1937; *d* of late Air Vice-Marshal John Reginald Cassidy and Barbara Margaret Cassidy. *Educ:* Univ. of Sydney; Somerville Coll., Oxford (BM BCh 1963; MA). Worked in Oxford and Leicester to 1971; went to Chile to work, 1971; arrested for treating wounded revolutionary, 1975; tortured and imprisoned 2 months, released Dec. 1975; lectured on human rights; in monastic religious order, 1978–80; returned to medicine, 1980; Medical Dir, St Luke's Hospice, Plymouth, 1982–93; Palliative Care Physician, Plymouth Gen. Hosp., 1993; lecturer in UK and overseas, preacher, writer, broadcaster. Freedom, City of Plymouth, 1998. Hon. DSc Exeter, 1991; Hon. DLitt CNAA, 1992; Hon. DM Plymouth, 2001. Valiant for Truth Media Award, 1977. *Publications:* Audacity to Believe, 1977; Prayer for Pilgrims, 1979; Sharing the Darkness, 1988; Good Friday People, 1991 (Collins Religious Book Award Special Prize, 1991); Light from the Dark Valley, 1994; The Loneliest Journey, 1995; Made for Laughter, 2006; Confessions of a Lapsed Catholic, 2010; Lent is for Loving, 2012. *Recreations:* writing, sewing, creative pursuits, reading, TV, walking her two Chows.

CASSIDY, Stuart; ballet dancer, ballet teacher and Pilates instructor; Founder Member and Principal, since 1999, and Assistant Director, since 2010, K. Ballet Co.; *b* 26 Sept. 1968; *s* of John and Jacqueline Cassidy; *m* 1993, Nicola Searchfield; two *s*. *Educ:* Royal Ballet Sch. (Hons 1987); RAD PDTDip (Dist.) 2003; Dreas Reyneke Pilates Instructor Course, 2004. Principal, Royal Ballet Co., 1991–99. *Principal rôles with Royal Ballet Company include:* Romeo and Mercutio, in Romeo and Juliet, Albrecht in Giselle, Siegfried in Swan Lake, Solor in La Bayadère, Jean de Brienne in Raymonda, Daphnis in Daphnis and Chloë, Florimund in Sleeping Beauty, Prince in Prince of the Pagodas, Prince in Nutcracker, Prince in Cinderella, Colas in La Fille Mal Gardée, Lescaut in Manon, Basilio in Don Quixote; Thaïs Pas de Deux, Tchaikovsky Pas de Deux. Nora Roche Award, 1986; Prix de Lausanne Prof. Prize, 1987. *Recreations:* golf, gardening, antiques, cars.

CASSON, Prof. Andrew John, FRS 1998; Philip Schuyler Beebe Professor of Mathematics, Yale University, since 2011 (Professor of Mathematics, 2000–11). *Educ:* Trinity Coll., Cambridge (BA 1965). Res. Fellow, 1967–71, Lectr in Maths, 1971–81, Trinity Coll., Cambridge; Professor of Mathematics: Univ. of Texas, Austin, 1981–86; Univ. of Calif, Berkeley, 1986–99; Chair, Dept of Maths, Yale Univ., 2004–07. *Publications:* (with S. A. Bleiler) Automorphisms of Surfaces after Nielsen and Thurston, 1988. *Address:* Department of Mathematics, Yale University, New Haven, CT 06520, USA.

CASSON, Dinah Victoria, (Lady Moses), RDI 2006; FCSD; Co-founder and Director, Casson Mann Ltd, since 1983; *b* 8 Oct. 1946; *d* of Sir Hugh Maxwell Casson, CH, KCVO, RA, RDI and late Margaret MacDonald Casson; *m* 1992, Alan George Moses (*see* Rt Hon. Sir A. G. Moses); one *s* one *d* from previous marriage. *Educ:* Ravensbourne Coll. of Art (BA 1st Cl. Hons). Jun. designer, Conran Design Gp, 1968–70; freelance design practice, 1970–83. Casson Mann design practice has worked on interior, architectural, product devel t, th. and mus. projects in USA, Italy, Russia and UK; major projects include: Grangelato ice cream shop, London, 1984; CSD HQ, London, 1988; The Garden, 1996, Wellcome Wing, 2000, Atmosphere, 2010, Science Mus.; British Galls, 2001, Portrait Miniatures, 2005, Hollywood Costume, 2012–13, V&A Mus.; Churchill Mus., 2005, Camouflage, 2007, For Your Eyes Only, 2008, Extraordinary Heroes, 2010, Imperial War Mus.; Beningbrough Hall, NPG/NT, 2006; Museo Santa Caterina, Treviso, 2007; Time Galls, Royal Observatory, Greenwich, 2007; Topolski Memoir, Waterloo, 2008; Museolobby, Stanislavsky Factory, Moscow, 2008; Great North Mus., Newcastle, 2009; Beaney Inst., Canterbury, 2012. Teacher (pt-time), Kingston Poly. and RCA, 1974–94; Dir of Architecture and Interior Design, RCA, 1993–95. External Examiner: Chelsea Sch. of Art, 1985–92; Manchester Poly., 1989–91; Plymouth Sch. of Architecture, 1990–93; Newcastle Sch. of Architecture, 1994–98; Middx Univ., 1994–97; Bournemouth Univ., 1994–96; N London, 1995–99; Glasgow Sch. of Art, 1999–2003; Cardiff Sch. of Art, 2004–. Member: Design Council, 1978–82; Exec., D&AD, 2006–09; Royal Stamp Adv. Cttee, 2013–. Governor: Middx Poly., 1990–94; Sevenoaks Sch., 2005–09. Trustee: Creative Educn Trust, 2010–; Charleston Trust, 2011–. Master, Faculty of RDI, 2011–14. Hon. FRCA 1995. Hon. DDes UC for Creative Arts, Farnham, 2003. *Publications:* (contrib.) Creating the British Galleries at the V&A, ed C. Wilk and N. Humphrey, 2004; contrib. Blueprint, Architects' Jl, Designers' Jl, Building Design, Eye. *Address:* Casson Mann Ltd, 45 Mitchell Street, EC1V 3QD. *T:* (020) 7324 1964. *E:* dinah.c@cassonmann.co.uk.

CASSON, John David, CMG 2014; HM Diplomatic Service; Ambassador to Egypt, since 2014; *b* Birmingham, 4 June 1971; *s* of Rev. David and Helen Casson; *m* 2000, Kathryn Rachel Clarke. *Educ:* Ashcroft High Sch., Luton; Tiffin Sch., Kingston-upon-Thames; Richmond upon Thames Coll.; Queens' Coll., Cambridge (BA Hons Hist. 1993; MA); Christ's Coll., Cambridge (DipTh 1994). Parly Res. Asst, 1994–95; Res. Asst, Faculty of Divinity, Univ. of Cambridge, 1996–98; joined FCO, 1998; Desk Officer, EU Dept, 1998–99; Second Sec., UK Repn to EU, Brussels, 1999–2000; Private Sec. to Ambassador to USA, 2000–02; First Sec. (Pol), Washington, 2002–05; Sen. Policy Advr, HM Treasury, 2005–07; Arabic lang. trng, 2007; Dep. Hd of Mission, Amman, 2007–09; Hd, Near East and N Africa Dept, FCO, 2009–10; (on secondment) Private Sec. to Prime Minister, 10 Downing St, 2010–14. *Publications:* contrib. articles to jls on religion and politics in Kenyan history. *Recreations:* kayaking, baseball, mountains, plants, poems. *Address:* BFPO 5305 (Cairo), RAF Northolt, Ruislip, Middx HA4 6EP. *T:* (Egypt) 227916120.

CASSON, Prof. Mark Christopher; Professor of Economics, University of Reading, since 1981; *b* 17 Dec. 1945; *s* of Stanley Christopher Casson and Dorothy Nowell Barlow; *m* 1975, Janet Penelope Close; one *d*. *Educ:* Manchester Grammar Sch.; Univ. of Bristol (BA 1st cl. hons 1966); Churchill Coll., Cambridge (graduate student). University of Reading: Lecturer in Economics, 1969; Reader, 1977; Head, Dept of Econs, 1987–94. Visiting Professor: of Internat. Business, Univ. of Leeds, 1995–; of Mgt, Queen Mary, Univ. of London, 2004–; of Mgt, Univ. of York, 2010–13. Mem. Council, REconS, 1985–90. Vice-Pres., 2006–07, Pres., 2007–08, Assoc. of Business Historians. Chm., Business Enterprise Heritage Trust, 2000–. Fellow, Acad. of Internat. Business, 1993; FRSA 1996. Freeman, City of London, 2013. *Publications:* Introduction to Mathematical Economics, 1973; (jtly) The Future of the Multinational Enterprise, 1976; Alternatives to the Multinational Enterprise, 1979; Youth Unemployment, 1979; Unemployment: a disequilibrium approach, 1981; The Entrepreneur: an economic theory, 1982; Economics of Unemployment: an historical perspective, 1983; (ed) The Growth of International Business, 1983; (jtly) The Economic Theory of the Multinational Enterprise: selected papers, 1985; (jtly) Multinationals and World Trade: vertical integration and the division of labour in world industries, 1986; The Firm and the Market: studies in multinational enterprise and the scope of the firm, 1987; Enterprise and Competitiveness: a systems view of international business, 1990; (ed) Entrepreneurship, 1990; (ed) Multinational Corporations, 1990; Economics of Business Culture: game theory, transaction costs and economic performance, 1991; (ed) Global Research Strategy and International Competitiveness, 1991; (ed) International Business and Global Integration, 1992; (ed jtly) Multinational Enterprise in the World Economy: essays in honour of John Dunning, 1992; (ed jtly) Industrial Concentration and Economic Inequality: essays in honour of Peter Hart, 1993; Entrepreneurship and Business Culture, 1995; The Organization of International Business, 1995; (ed) The Theory of the Firm, 1996; Information and Organization: a new perspective on the theory of the firm, 1997; (ed) Culture, Social Norms and Economic Performance, 1997; (ed jtly) Institutions and the Evolution of Modern Business, 1997; (ed jtly) The Economics of Marketing, 1998; (ed jtly) Cultural Factors in Economic Growth, 2000; Economics of International Business, 2000; Enterprise and Leadership, 2000; (ed jtly) Oxford Handbook of Entrepreneurship, 2005; (ed jtly) Economics of Networks, 2008; The World's First Railway System, 2009; The Multinational Enterprise Revisited: the essential Buckley and Casson, 2009; Entrepreneurship: theory, networks, history, 2010; (ed) Markets and Market Institutions: their origin and evolution, 2011; (jtly) The Entrepreneur in History, 2013; (ed jtly) History of Entrepreneurship: innovation and risk-taking 1200–2000, 2013; (ed jtly) Large Databases in Economic History: research methods and case studies, 2013. *Recreations:* collecting old books, studying old railways, visiting old churches, drawing in pastel. *Address:* 6 Wayside Green, Woodcote, Reading RG8 0QJ. *T:* (home) (01491) 681483, (office) (0118) 931 8227.

CASTALDI, Dr Peter; Chief Medical Officer, Scottish Equitable, 2004–10 (Company Medical Officer, 1997–2004); *b* 13 Jan. 1942; *s* of Frank and Sarah Jane Castaldi; *m* 1967, Joan Sherratt; one *s* one *d*. *Educ:* Grammar Sch. for Boys, Neath; Welsh Nat. Sch. of Medicine (MB, BCh 1966). Resident hosp. posts, N Wales, 1966–69; Principal in General Practice, Bangor, Gwynedd, 1969–79; MO 1979–84, SMO 1984–86, DHSS; PMO, DSS, 1986–92. Chief Med. Advr, DSS, and Dir of Med. Services, Benefits Agency, 1992–95. Company Medical Officer: UNUM UK, 1996–99; AEGON UK (formerly Guardian Royal Exchange), Lytham, 1997–2014; UNUM Ltd, 2001–04 (CMO, 1999–2001); Med. Mem., Ind. Tribunal Service, MoJ, 1996–2014. CStJ 1993. *Recreation:* armchair Rugby critic. *Address:* 24 Cavendish Road, Lytham St Annes, Lancs FY8 2PX.

CASTELL, Sir William (Martin), Kt 2000; LVO 2004; FCA; Chairman, Wellcome Trust, 2006–15; *b* 10 April 1947; *s* of William Gummer Castell and Gladys (*née* Doe); *m* 1971, Renice Mendelson; one *s* two *d*. *Educ:* St Dunstan's Sch.; City of London Coll. (BA). ACA 1974, FCA 1980. Various posts in marketing, finance and admin, Wellcome Foundn, 1975–86; Co-founding Dir, Biomedical Res. Centre, Vancouver, 1983; Man. Dir, Wellcome Biotech., 1984–87; Commercial Dir, Wellcome plc, 1987–89; Chief Exec., Amersham Internat., then Nycomed Amersham, subseq. Amersham plc, later Pres. and CEO, GE Healthcare, 1990–2006. Non-executive Director: Marconi (formerly GEC), 1997–2003; BP plc, 2006–12 (Sen. Ind. Dir, 2010–12); a Vice-Chm., 2004–06, External Dir, 2006–11, General Electric; Mem., Adv. Bd, Ondra Partners, 2009–13 (Chm., 2012–13). Chairman: Cttee on Design Bursaries Health and Envmt, RSA, 1986–88; Design Dimension, 1994–99 (Dep. Chm., 1988–94); Regeneration Through Heritage, BITC, 1997–2000; Prince's Trust, 1998–2003. Member: MRC, 2001–04; Royal Commn for the Exhibn of 1851, 2011– (Mem. Bd of Mgt, 2011–; Chm., Finance Cttee, 2012–). Trustee: Natural Hist. Mus., 2004–08; Educn and Employers' Taskforce, 2009–. Mem. Bd, Life Scis Inst., Michigan Univ., 2003–07; non-exec. Dir, Nat. Bureau of Asian Res., 2006–11. Mem. Bd, Chichester Festival Th., 2009– (Chm., 2012–). Hon. Mem., Russian Academia Europaea, 1996. Hon. FMedSci 2004; Hon. Fellow: Green Coll., Oxford, 2005 (Vis. Fellow, 1993–2005); Univ. of Cardiff, 2005; Hon. FKC 2006. Hon. DSSc Brunel, 2004; Hon. DCL Oxford, 2005; Hon. DSc Imperial Coll. London, 2008. *Recreations:* international affairs, theatre, shooting, golf, tennis. *Club:* Athenæum.

CASTLE, Andrew Nicholas; lead commentator, BBC Tennis, since 2003; Presenter, Andrew Castle Breakfast, Smooth Radio, since 2014; *b* Epsom, 15 Nov. 1963; *s* of Frank James Castle and Lyn Castle (later Mathers); *m* 1991, Sophia Runham; two *d*. *Educ:* Millfield Sch.; Richard Hulsh Sch., Taunton; Seminole Jun. Coll., Orlando, Florida; Wichita State Univ., Kansas (BA Mktg and Business 1985). Professional tennis player, 1986–92: Mem., GB Team, Davis Cup and Eur. Cup, 1986–92; Mem., GB Olympic Team, Seoul, 1988, Barcelona, 1992. Presenter: Skysports: tennis, 1992–2000; basketball, 1994–96; golf, 1995–2000; GMTV, 2000–10; LBC Radio, 2013–14. *Publications:* squash, golf, tennis, running, yoga. *Clubs:* All England Lawn Tennis, International Lawn Tennis of GB.

CASTLE, Rt Rev. Dr Brian Colin; Bishop Suffragan of Tonbridge, 2002–15; *b* 7 Sept. 1949; *s* of Ernest and Sarah Castle; *m* 1979, Jane Richmond; one *s* two *d*. *Educ:* UCL (BA (Hons) Classics 1972); Cuddesdon Theol Coll. (MA Theol. Oxford 1980); Birmingham Univ. (PhD Theol. 1989). Social worker, 1972–74; teacher, Lesotho, Southern Africa, 1974. Ordained deacon, 1977, priest, 1978; Assistant Curate: St Nicholas, Sutton, 1977; Limpsfield, Surrey, 1977–81; Priest i/c, Chingola, Chililabombwe and Solwezi, Zambia, 1981–84; Vis. Lectr, Ecumenical Inst., Geneva, 1984–85; Vicar, N Petherton and Northmoor Green, Somerset, 1985–92; Vice-Principal and Dir of Pastoral Studies, Ripon Coll. Cuddesdon, Oxford, 1992–2001. Archbps' Advr in alternative spiritualities and new religious movements, 2005–. *Publications:* Hymns: the making and shaping of a theology for the whole people of God, 1990; Sing a New Song to the Lord, 1994; Unofficial God: voices from beyond the walls, 2004; Reconciling One and All: God's gift to the world, 2008; Reconciliation: the journey of a lifetime, 2014; articles in various theol jls. *Recreations:* fly fishing, cross country ski-ing.

CASTLE, Enid, OBE 1997; JP; Principal, The Cheltenham Ladies' College, 1987–96; *b* 28 Jan. 1936; *d* of Bertram and Alice Castle. *Educ:* Hulme Grammar Sch. for Girls, Oldham; Royal Holloway Coll., Univ. of London. BA Hons History. Colne Valley High Sch., Yorks, 1958–62; Kenya High Sch., Nairobi, 1962–65; Queen's Coll., Nassau, Bahamas, 1965–68; Dep. Head, Roundhill High Sch., Leicester, 1968–72; Headmistress: High Sch. for Girls, Gloucester, 1973–81; Red Maids' Sch., Bristol, 1982–87. Pres., GSA, 1990–91. JP Glos, 1989. *Recreations:* travel, tennis, bridge, music.

CASTLE, John Christopher; *b* 4 Nov. 1944; *s* of George Frederick Castle and Winifred Mary Castle; *m* 1966, Susan Ann Neal; one *s* two *d*. *Educ:* Royal Grammar Sch., Guildford; Pembroke Coll., Cambridge (MA). With BP, 1963–68; Associated Industrial Consultants, 1968–73; Alcan Aluminium UK Ltd: Divl Dir of Industrial Relns, 1973–77; Chief Personnel Officer, 1977–80; Dir of Ops, 1980–82; Man. Dir, Base Internat. Ltd, 1982–86; Man. Dir, Thermalite, 1986–89, Gp Man. Dir, 1989–93, Marley plc; President: Avdel Textron, 1994–97; Textron Europe, 1995–97; Chief Exec., Taylor Woodrow plc, 1997. Non-executive Director: GKR Gp, 1993–99; ER Consultants Ltd, 1998–2000; Gibbs & Dandy plc, 2003–08. Chm. Governing Council, Northampton Univ., 2005–08. *Recreations:* bridge, restoration. *Address:* Farthingstone House, Farthingstone, Towcester, Northants NN12 8HB.

CASTLE, (John) Mark, OBE 2004; Chief Executive Officer, Victim Support, since 2014; *b* Irvine, 15 July 1960; *s* of John Castle and Patricia Castle; *m* 1988, Frances Evans; one *s* two *d*. *Educ:* Irvine Royal Acad.; Royal Mil. Acad. Sandhurst; Army Staff Coll., Camberley. Commnd officer RHF, 1979–99; CO KOSB, 2000–03; Dep. Dir Army Personnel Strategy, 2003–07; Chief of Campaign Plans, Iraq, 2007–08; Comdr Mission Support, Warminster, 2008; Dep. Commanding Central Min. of Interior Transition Team, Iraq, 2008–09. Chief Executive: Assoc. of Police Authorities, 2009–12; Assoc. of Police and Crime Comrs, 2012–14. Mem., Sentencing Council, 2015–. Trustee, Soc. for Protection of Animals Abroad, 2010–15. QCVS 2001. Bronze Star (USA), 2009; Legion of Merit (USA), 2010. *Recreations:* horse riding, ski-ing, gardening, military history, family. *Address:* Victim Support, Hallam House, 56–60 Hallam Street, W1W 6JL. *T:* (020) 7268 0200. *E:* mark.castle@victimsupport.org.uk.

CASTLE, Rt Rev. Merwyn Edwin; Bishop of False Bay, 2006–12; *b* 2 Nov. 1942; *s* of Ernest Edwin and Catherine Castle. *Educ:* Federal Theol Seminary, Alice (DipTh). Ordained deacon, 1969, priest, 1970; Rector, Christ the King, Coronationville, 1977–82; Dean, Johannesburg, 1982–87; Rector: Gambleville, Uitenhage, 1987–90; Matroosfontein, Cape Town, 1990–92; Chaplain, Archbishop of Cape Town, 1992–93; Rector, St Saviour's, Claremont, 1993–94; Bishop Suffragan of Cape Town, 1994–2006, Southern Reg., 1994–98, False Bay Reg., 1998–2006. Chairman: Provincial Liturgical Cttee, 2000–; Anglican AIDS and Healthcare Trust, 2007–; Liaison Bishop, Council for the Religious Life, 2000–; Mem., Provincial Pensions Bd, 2009–. Bishop Protector, African Province, Third Order of St Francis, 2005. *Recreations:* gardening, music, reading.

CASTLE STEWART, 8th Earl *cr* 1800 (Ireland); **Arthur Patrick Avondale Stuart;** Viscount Castle Stewart, 1793; Baron, 1619; Bt (NS) 1628, of Castle Stewart; farming and countryside management; *b* 18 Aug. 1928; 3rd but *e* surv. *s* of 7th Earl Castle Stewart, MC, and Eleanor May (*d* 1992), *er d* of late S. R. Guggenheim, New York; *S* father, 1961; *m* 1st, 1952, Edna Fowler (*d* 2003); one *s* one *d*; 2nd, 2004, Gillian, DL, *d* of Frederick William Savill, Blaby, Leics; three step *d*. *Educ:* Brambletye; Eton; Trinity Coll., Cambridge (BA). Lieut Scots Guards, 1949. Vice-Pres., S. R. Guggenheim Mus., NY, 1967–97; Peggy Guggenheim Museum, Venice: Vice-Pres., Adv. Bd, 1980–2011; Pres., 2011–13; Pres. Emeritus, 2013; Mem., Bd of Trustees, Guggenheim UK Charitable Trust, 2001–13. Trustee, Christian Community in UK, 1973–2003. FCMI. *Recreations:* woodland management, travel, walking, singing. *Heir:* *s* Viscount Stuart, *qv*. *Address:* Stuart Hall, Stewartstown, Co. Tyrone BT71 5AE. *T:* (028) 8773 8208; Willoughby House, Barbican, EC2Y 8BN. *Club:* Carlton.

CASTLEMAINE, 8th Baron *cr* 1812; **Roland Thomas John Handcock,** MBE (mil.) 1981; *b* 22 April 1943; *s* of 7th Baron Castlemaine and Rebecca Ellen (*d* 1978), *o d* of William T. Soady, RN; *S* father, 1973; *m* 1st, 1969, Pauline Anne (marr. diss.), *e d* of John Taylor Bainbridge; 2nd, 1989, Lynne Christine, *e d* of Maj. Justin Michael Gurney, RAEC; one *s*. *Educ:* Campbell Coll., Belfast. psc, ph (cfs). Lt-Col, AAC, retd 1992. *Heir:* *s* Hon. Ronan Michael Edward Handcock, *b* 27 March 1989.

CASTLES, Prof. Stephen, DPhil; Research Professor in Sociology, University of Sydney, since 2009; Research Associate, International Migration Institute, Oxford Martin School (formerly James Martin 21st Century School), University of Oxford, since 2011 (Associate Director and Senior Researcher, 2009–11); *b* Melbourne, 9 Nov. 1944; *s* of Heinz and Fay Castles; *m* 2000, Ellie Vasta. *Educ:* Oxted Co. Grammar Sch.; Univ. of Frankfurt am Main (Vor-Diplom); Univ. of Sussex (MA; DPhil). FASSA 1997. Res. Fellow, Res. Inst. Friedrich Ebert Foundn, Bonn, 1971–72; Lectr, 1972–75, Sen. Lectr, 1975–78, Prof. of Political Econ., 1978–79, Fachhochschule Frankfurt am Main; Co-ordinator, Totterdown Children's Community Workshop, Bristol, 1979–80; Lectr (pt-time) in Sociol., Bristol Poly., 1979–80; Co-ordinator, Design and Media, Foundn for Educn with Prodn, Botswana, 1981; Prof. of Political Econ. and Sociol., Fachhochschule Frankfurt am Main, 1982–86; Director: Centre for Multicultural Studies, Univ. of Wollongong, 1986–96; Centre for Asia Pacific Social Transformation Studies (jt venture of Univs of Wollongong and Newcastle), 1996–2001; University of Oxford: Prof. of Migration and Refugee Studies, 2001–09; Dir, Refugee Studies Centre, 2001–06; Sen. Res. Fellow, Internat. Migration Inst., James Martin 21st Century Sch., 2006–09. Vis. Prof. of Migration Studies, Univ. of Sussex, 1998–2000; Vis. Fellow, Centre d'Etudes et Recherches Internat., Paris, 1995; Visiting Scholar: Cornell Univ., 1988; Eur. Univ. Inst., Florence, 1991–92. Dir Secretariat, UNESCO-MOST Asia Pacific Migration Res. Network, 1995–2000. Chm., UK Home Office Adv. Panel on Country Information, 2003–05. Member: Nat. Population Council, 1987–91; Multicultural and Population Res. Adv. Bd, Australian Bureau of Immigration, 1989–96. *Publications:* (with G. Kosack) Immigrant Workers and Class Structure in Western Europe, 1973 (Italian edn 1976, Spanish edn 1984); (with W. Wüstenberg) The Education of the Future, 1979 (Spanish edn 1982); Here for Good: Western Europe's new ethnic minorities, 1984 (German edn 1987); (jtly) Mistaken Identity: multiculturalism and the demise of nationalism in Australia, 1988, 3rd edn 1992; (with M. Miller) The Age of Migration: international population movements in the modern world, 1993, (with M. Miller and H. de Haas) 5th edn 2014 (Japanese edn 1996, Spanish edn 2004, Turkish and Chinese edns 2008, Korean edn 2013); (jtly) A Shop Full of Dreams: ethnic small businesses in Australia, 1995; (jtly) Immigration and Australia, 1998; (with A. Davidson) Citizenship and Migration: globalization and the politics of belonging, 2000; Ethnicity and Globalization: from migrant worker to transnational citizen, 2000; (jtly) Migration, Citizenship and the European Welfare State: a European dilemma, 2006; *edited jointly:* Australia's Italians, 1992; The Teeth are Smiling… the persistence of racism in multicultural Australia, 1996; Migration in the Asia Pacific, 2003; Migration and Development: perspectives from the South, 2008 (Spanish edn 2007). *Recreations:* swimming, walking, photography, yoga. *Address:* School of Sociology and Social Policy, University of Sydney, NSW 2006, Australia. *T:* (2) 93512641, *Fax:* (2) 90369380. *E:* stephen.castles@sydney.edu.au.

CASTON, Geoffrey Kemp, CBE 1990; Vice-Chancellor, University of the South Pacific, 1983–92; *b* 17 May 1926; *s* of late Reginald and Lilian Caston, West Wickham, Kent; *m* 1st, Sonya Chassell (*d* 2003); two *s* one *d*; 2nd, Dr Judith Roizen, Berkeley, Calif; two step *s* one step *d*. *Educ:* St Dunstan's Coll.; (Major Open Scholar) Peterhouse, Cambridge (MA). First Cl. Pt 1 History; First Cl. Pt II Law (with distinction) and Geo. Long Prize for Jurisprudence, 1950; Harvard Univ. (Master of Public Admin 1951; Frank Knox Fellow, 1950–51). Sub-Lt, RNVR, 1945–47. Colonial Office, 1951–58; UK Mission to UN, New York, 1958–61; Dept of Techn. Co-op., 1961–64; Asst Sec., Dept of Educn and Sci. (Univs and Sci. Branches), 1964–66; Jt Sec., Schools Council, 1966–70; Under-Secretary, UGC, 1970–72; Registrar of Oxford Univ. and Fellow of Merton Coll., Oxford, 1972–79; Sec.-Gen., Cttee of Vice-Chancellors and Principals, 1979–83. Project Manager, GAP, 1993–2001. Sec., Assoc. of First Div. Civil Servants, 1956–58; Adv. to UK Delegn to seven sessions of UN Gen. Assembly, 1953–63; UK Rep. on UN Cttee on Non-Self-Governing Territories, 1958–60; UN Techn. Assistance Cttee, 1962–64; Mem., UN Visiting Mission to Trust Territory of Pacific Islands, 1961; Consultant, Commonwealth Secretariat, 1992–2001. Chm., SE Surrey Assoc. for Advancement of State Educn, 1962–64; UK Delegn to Commonwealth Educn Confs, Ottawa, 1964, Gaborone, 1997. Ford Foundn travel grants for visits to schools and univs in USA, 1964, 1967, 1970. Vis. Associate, Center for Studies in Higher Educn, Univ. of Calif, Berkeley, 1978–2000. Chairman: Planning Cttee, 3rd and 4th Internat. Curriculum Confs, Oxford, 1967, New York, 1968; Ford Foundn Anglo-American Primary Educn Project, 1968–70; Library Adv. Council (England), 1973–78; Nat. Inst. for Careers Educn and Counselling, 1975–83; DES/DHSS Working Gp on Under 5s Res., 1980–82; Commonwealth Scholarship Commn in the UK, 1996–2002; Vice-Chm., Educnl Res. Bd, SSRC, 1973–77; Member: Steering Gp, OECD Workshops on Educnl Innovation, Cambridge 1969, W Germany, 1970, Illinois 1971; Exec. Cttee, Inter-Univ. Council for Higher Educn Overseas, 1977–83; Council, Univ. of Papua New Guinea, 1984–92; Council, ACU, 1987–88; Governor, Centre for Educnl Development Overseas, 1969–70; Dep., Admin. Bd, Internat. Assoc. of Univs, 1990–96. Trustee: Just World Partners, 1993–2005; Exeter CAB, 2004–10. Bank of Hawaii Distinguished Lectr, Univ. of Hawaii, 1992; Dist. Fellow, Flinders Univ. Inst. of Internat. Educn, 1999–. Hon. Fellow, Univ. of Exeter, 2004. Hon. LLD Dundee, 1982; Hon. DLitt Deakin, 1991. Symons Medal, ACU, 2002. *Publications:* The Management of International Co-operation in Universities, 1996; contribs to educnl jls. *Address:* 3 Pennsylvania Park, Exeter EX4 6HB. *T:* (01392) 272986.

CASTRO, Alicia Amalia; Ambassador of Argentina to the Court of St James's, since 2012; Permanent Representative to International Maritime Organization, since 2012; *b* Bahia Blanca, Argentina, 27 July 1949; *d* of Juan Manuel Castro Justo and Alicia Beatriz Altube; one *d*. Cabin Crew, Aerolineas Argentinas, 1970–91; Gen. Sec., Argentine Flight Crew Mems' Assoc., 1991–2000; Founder, Argentine Workers' Union, 1994; Vice Pres., Internat. Transport Workers' Fedn, 2000–06. MP Argentina, 1997–2005; Mem., MERCOSUR Parly Cttee; drafted MERCOSUR Parly Protocol; Vice Pres., Transport Cttee; Spokesperson, Workers' Legislation Cttee; Pres., Friendship Parly Gp with Venezuela; Internat. Parly Rep. for MERCOSUR, UNASUR, World Social Forum, G15 Summit of the Americas (Mar del Plata), 2001–05; Ambassador to Venezuela, 2006–11. Mem., Exec. Bd, Internat. Transport Workers' Fedn, 2002–14. Founder, UK Pro-Dialogue Gp on Malvinas Question, 2012. Order del Libertador (Venezuela), 2007; Order Antonio José de Sucre (1st Cl.) (Venezuela), 2011; Order Francisco de Miranda (1st Cl.) (Venezuela), 2012. *Address:* Argentine Embassy, 49 Belgrave Square, SW1X 8QZ. *T:* (020) 7318 1321, *Fax:* (020) 7318 1305. *E:* aliciacastro@argentine-embassy-uk.org.

CASTRO, Susan Rochford; *see* Bickley, S. R.

CASTRO RUZ, Dr Fidel; Head of State, Cuba, 1976–2008; *b* 13 Aug. 1927; *s* of Angel Castro y Argiz and Lina Ruz de Castro (*née* González); *m* 1948, Mirta Diaz-Balart (marr. diss. 1955); one *s*. *Educ:* Colegio Lassalle; Colegio Dolores; Colegio Belén; Univ. of Havana (Pres., Students' Fedn; Dr Law 1950). Lawyer, Havana, 1950–53; imprisoned, 1953–55; C-in-C, Armed Forces, Cuba, 1959; Prime Minister of Cuba, 1959–76; Head, Nat. Defence Council, 1992–2008. Chm., Agrarian Reform Inst., 1965–2008. First Sec., Partido Comunista (formerly Partido Unido de la Revolución Socialista), 1963–2011. *Publications:* Ten Years of Revolution, 1964; History Will Absolve Me, 1968; Major Speeches, 1968; (jtly) Fidel, 1987; (jtly) How Far We Slaves Have Come, 1991; (jtly) My Life, 2007; Obama and the Empire, 2010; Guantanamo, 2010; The Strategic Victory (memoir), 2012. *Address:* Palacio del Gobierno, Havana, Cuba.

CATCHPOLE, Nancy Mona, OBE 1987; Chairman, Board of Trustees, Bath Royal Literary and Scientific Institution, 2002–06 (a Trustee, since 1997); *b* 6 Aug. 1929; *d* of George William Page and Mona Dorothy Page (*née* Cowin), New Eltham; *m* 1959, Geoffrey David Arthur Catchpole; one *s* one *d*. *Educ:* Haberdashers' Aske's Hatcham Girls' Sch.; Bedford Coll., Univ. of London (BA Hons Hist.). Asst mistress, Gravesend Grammar Sch. for Girls, 1952–56; i/c History, Ipswich High Sch. GPDST, 1956–62; part time lectr in History and General Studies, Bath Tech. Coll., 1977–96. Sec., Bath Assoc. of University Women, 1970–75; Regional Rep. on Exec., BFUW, 1975–77, Vice-Pres., 1977–80, Pres., 1981–84. Women's National Commission: Co-Chairman, 1983–85; Immediate Past Co-Chairman, 1985–86; part-time Sec. with special responsibility for Women's Trng Roadshow prog., 1985–88; Actg Sec., March–Dec. 1988; Consultant for Women's Trng Roadshow prog. to RSA Women's Wkg Gp/Industry Matters, 1989–90; Vice-Chm., RSA Women's Adv. Gp (formerly Women's Working Group for Industry Year 1986), 1985–95; British Federation of Women Graduates Charitable Foundation (formerly Crosby Hall): Gov., 1992–98, 2002–04; Vice-Chm. of Govs, 1992–95, Chm., 1995–98; Chm., Grants Cttee, 1992–95; Archivist, 2012–. Chm., U3A, Bath, 2001–03. Chm., Bath Branch, Historical Assoc., 1993–96 (Sec., 1975–79; Hon. Treas., 2001–04). A Governor, Weston Infants' Sch., Bath, 1975–85 (Chm., 1981–83; Vice-Chm., 1983–86); Member: Managers, Eagle House Community Sch., Somerset CC, 1979–82; Case Cttee, Western Nat. Adoption Soc., 1975–77; Wessex RHA, 1986–90; Avon FHSA Service Cttee, 1990–96; Discipline Cttee, Avon HA, 1997–2003. FRSA 1986. Hon FHA (Jubilee Fellow), 2013. *Recreations:* listening, viewing, talking, writing. *Address:* 66 Leighton Road, Weston, Bath BA1 4NG. *T:* (01225) 423338.

CATCHPOLE, Stuart Paul; QC 2002; international arbitrator, since 2004; *b* 21 July 1964; *s* of Robert James Catchpole and Celia Catchpole; *m* 1995, Rebecca (marr. diss 2013); one *s* two *d*. *Educ:* Univ. of Durham; Inns of Court Sch. of Law. Called to the Bar, Inner Temple, 1987, Bencher, 2008; in practice at the Bar, 1988–. Treasury Supplemental Panel (Common Law), 1992–98; Jun. Counsel to the Crown, 1998–2002; a Recorder, 2004–14; a Dep. High Court Judge, 2010–14; Mem., States of Jersey Complaints Bd, 2013–. Part-time Legal Mem., Proscribed Orgns Appeal Commn, 2001–. *Publications:* (ed) Crown Proceedings, Halsbury's Laws, 4th edn, vol. 12 (1), 1998; (contrib.) Extradition, Halsbury's Laws, 4th edn, vol. 17 (2), 2000. *Recreations:* cinema, theatre, reading, wine, horse riding, sailing. *Address:* 39 Essex Street, WC2R 3AT. *T:* (020) 7832 1111, *Fax:* (020) 7353 3978. *E:* stuart.catchpole@39essex.com. *Club:* Royal Automobile.

CATER, Dr John, CBE 2015; Vice-Chancellor, Edge Hill University (formerly Principal, Edge Hill College of Higher Education), since 1993; *b* Northampton, 3 Feb. 1953; *s* of William Ernest and Frances Brenda Cater; *m* 1981, Sue Lawlor; one *s* one *d*. *Educ:* Univ. of Wales, Lampeter (BA Hons Geog. 1974); Council for Nat. Academic Awards (PhD 1984). Res. Asst, Lectr and Res. Fellow, Liverpool Poly., 1974–79; Edge Hill College of Higher Education: Lectr, Sen. Lectr, then Hd of Dept of Urban Policy and Race Relns, 1979–86; Dep. Dean, 1986–90; Hd, Policy Res. and Develt, 1990–92; Dir of Resources, 1992–93. Chair: Higher Educn NW, 1999–2001; Gtr Merseyside and W Lancs Lifelong Learning Network, 2006–11. Director: Higher Educn Careers Service, 1994–2013; Standing Conf. of Principals, 1994–2004 (Vice-Chm., 1997–2001; Chm., 2001–03); TTA, 1999–2005 (Chairman: Audit Cttee, 2001–03; Accreditation Cttee, 2003–05); Graduate Prospects, 1999–2013; Trng and Develt Agency for Schs, 2005–06 (Chm., Accreditation Cttee, 2005–06). Mem., Adv. Cttee on Degree-Awarding Powers, QAA, 2006–12. Universities UK: Mem., Health and Social Care Cttee, 2004–; Mem., 2007–, Chm., 2014–, Teacher Educn Adv. Gp; Mem., DFE/DoH Social Work Reform Bd, 2010–. Dir, 1994–2013, Chm., 2003–05, Liverpool City of Learning. *Publications:* (with T. P. Jones) Social Geography, 1989; contrib. articles and chapters on residential segregation, black and Asian business, housing and public policy. *Recreations:* most sports (Rugby, cricket, golf, squash), current affairs, reading, travel. *Address:* Edge Hill University, St Helens Road, Ormskirk, Lancs L39 4QP. *T:* (01695) 584234, *Fax:* (01695) 577137.

CATES, Prof. Michael Elmhirst, PhD; FRS 2007; FRSE; Lucasian Professor of Mathematics, University of Cambridge, since 2015; *b* 5 May 1961. *Educ:* Trinity Coll., Cambridge (BA 1982, MA; PhD 1986; Hon. Fellow, 2013). Cavendish Laboratory, Cambridge: Asst Lectr, 1989–92; Univ. Lectr, 1992–95; Prof. of Natural Philosophy, Sch. of Physics, 1995–2015, Royal Soc. Res. Prof., 2007–15, Univ. of Edinburgh. FRSE 2005. *Publications:* articles in learned jls. *Recreations:* hill-walking, painting, music. *Address:* Faculty of Mathematics, Centre for Mathematical Sciences, Wilberforce Road, Cambridge CB3 0WA.

CATESBY, (William) Peter; Chairman, Real Hotel Company (formerly Choice Hotels Europe Group) plc, 2002–09 (non-executive Director, 2001–09); *b* 11 Sept. 1940; *s* of late Robert Cooper Catesby, MBE; *m* 1972, Cynthia Nixon (marr. diss. 2005); two *d*. *Educ:* Ipswich Sch.; Battersea Coll. of Advanced Technol. (ACT). Joined Grosvenor House Ltd, 1962; Hotel Manager, 1964–68; Hotels Trng Manager, Trust House Hotels Ltd, 1968–70; Dist Manager (SE), 1970–72, Asst Regl Dir (S), 1972–73, Trust House Forte Ltd; joined Swallow Hotels, 1973: Gen. Manager, Swallow Hotels Div., Vaux Breweries Ltd, 1973–75; Man. Dir, Swallow Hotels Ltd, 1975–77; Vaux Group plc: Main Bd Dir, 1977–2000; Gp Dep. Chm., 1990–99; Jt Man. Dir, 1992–99; Vaux Gp plc renamed Swallow Gp, 1999; Chm., Swallow Hotels Ltd, 1999–2000; Chief Exec., Swallow Gp plc, 1999–2000. FIH (FHCIMA 1974). Dir, BHA Ltd, 1998–2009 (Chm., Finance Cttee). Hon. Dep. Col, D Rifles Co., 5 Bn RRF (formerly Hon. Col, 7 Bn DLI), 1994–2010. Vice Chm., N of England, RFCA, 1996–2008. DL Co. Durham, 1997–2010. *Address:* The Barn, 90A Netherton Lane, Netherton, W Yorks WF4 4HG.

CATHCART, family name of **Earl Cathcart.**

CATHCART, 7th Earl *cr* 1814; **Charles Alan Andrew Cathcart,** ACA; Lord Cathcart (Scot.) 1447; Viscount Cathcart, Baron Greenock 1807; *b* 30 Nov. 1952; *s* of 6th Earl Cathcart, CB, DSO, MC and Rosemary (*d* 1980), *yr d* of Air Cdre Sir Percy Smyth-Osbourne, CMG, CBE; *S* father, 1999; *m* 1981, Vivien Clare, *o d* of F. D. McInnes Skinner; one *s* one *d*. *Educ:* Eton. Commnd Scots Guards, 1972–75. Whinney Murray, 1976–79; Ernst & Whinney, 1979–83; Gardner Mountain and Capel-Cure Agencies Ltd, 1983–94; Director: Murray Lawrence Members Agencies Ltd, 1995–96; RGA Holdings Ltd, 1996–2011; RGA Capital Ltd, 1996–2011; RGA Reinsurance UK Ltd, 1996–2011; Vivien Greenock Ltd, 2007–; Spring Garden Eggs Ltd, 2011–. Mem. (C) Breckland DC, 1997–2007. Elected Mem., H of L, 2007. Mem., Queen's Bodyguard for Scotland, Royal Co. of Archers. *Recreations:* ski-ing, sailing, country pursuits. *Heir:* *s* Lord Greenock, *qv*. *Address:* Gateley Hall, Norfolk. *Club:* Pratt's.

CATHCART, Samuel; Sheriff of Glasgow and Strathkelvin at Glasgow (formerly Floating Sheriff), since 2000; *b* 5 March 1950; *s* of Samuel Cathcart and Margaret Gordon or Cathcart; *m* 1985, Sandra Fullarton; one *s* one *d*. *Educ:* Dalry High Sch.; Edinburgh Univ. (LLB). Admitted Solicitor, 1974, in practice, 1974–77; Procurator Fiscal Depute, 1977–88; called to the Scottish Bar, 1989; Advocate, 1989–99; Advocate Depute, Crown Office, 1996–99. *Recreations:* sailing, fishing. *Address:* 43 Douglas Street, Largs, Ayrshire KA30 8PT. *T:* (01475) 672478.

CATHERWOOD, Andrea Catherine, (Mrs R. G. Smith); television and radio broadcaster; *b* 27 Nov. 1967; *d* of late Henry Robert Courtney Catherwood and of Adrienne Catherwood; *m* 2002, Richard Gray Smith; three *s* (of whom two are twins). *Educ:* Strathearn Sch., Belfast; Manchester Univ. (LLB Hons). Reporter, Ulster TV, 1991–93; reporter, 1994–96, news anchor, 1996–98, CNBC Asia, in Hong Kong; corresp. and newscaster, ITV News, 1998–2000; evening newscaster, Channel 5 News, 2000–01; Internat. Corresp. and newscaster, ITV News, 2001–06; Presenter: Sunday Edition, 2006–07; Bloomberg Television, 2009–12; BBC Radio 4, 2013–. *Recreations:* sailing, scuba-diving, art and literature, travel, food. *Clubs:* Soho House; Royal North of Ireland Yacht.

CATLIN, John Anthony, CB 2004; Director (Legal Services), Departments of Health and for Work and Pensions (formerly of Social Security), 1996–2007; *b* 25 Nov. 1947; *s* of John Vincent Catlin and Kathleen Glover Catlin (*née* Brand); *m* 1974, Caroline Jane Goodman; one *s* two *d*. *Educ:* Ampleforth Coll., York; Birmingham Univ. (LLB 1969). Solicitor of the Supreme Court, 1972. Articled Clerk, 1970–72, Asst Solicitor, 1972–75, Gregory Rowcliffe & Co.; Legal Asst, 1975–78, Sen. Legal Asst, 1978–84, Treasury Solicitor's Dept; Asst Solicitor, 1984–89, Dep. Solicitor, 1989–96, DoE. *Recreations:* history, music, languages. *E:* jcatlin0@googlemail.com.

CATLIN, Stephen John Oakley; Executive Deputy Chairman, XL Catlin, since 2015 (Chief Executive and Deputy Chairman, Catlin Group Ltd, 1995–2015); *b* Aldershot, 25 June 1954; *s* of Robin John Oakley Catlin and Rita Fortune Catlin; *m* 1975, Helen Margaret Gill; two *d*. ACII 2011. Dep. underwriter, B. L. Evens and Others, 1982–84; Founder and Chief Exec., Catlin Underwriting Agencies Ltd, 1984–95, Chm., 1987–95. Lloyd's Nominated Dir, Equitas Hldgs Ltd, 1996–2002. Chm., Lloyd's Market Assoc., 2000–03; Member: Council, Lloyd's, 2002–04; Lloyd's Franchise Bd, 2003–06. Pres., Insce Inst. of London, 2010–11. Chm., Assoc. Bermuda Insurers and Reinsurers, 2015–. Vis. Fellow, Oxford Univ. Centre for Corporate Reputation, 2008–. Chm., Sick Children's Trust, 1999–2015. Ernst & Young Entrepreneur of the Year, 2011. *Recreations:* fishing, shooting, ski-ing. *Address:* XL Catlin, 20 Gracechurch Street, EC3V 0BG. *T:* (020) 7626 0486, *Fax:* (020) 7623 3667.

CATLING, Christopher Paul; Secretary, Royal Commission on the Ancient and Historical Monuments of Wales, since 2015; *b* Stamford, Lincs, 11 Oct. 1955; *s* of Harry Catling and Elizabeth Catling; *m* 1983, Katharine Owen; one *s* one *d*. *Educ:* Cirencester Comp. Sch.; St Catharine's Coll., Cambridge (BA 1979). FSA 2004; MCIfA (MIfA 2004). PR consultant, 1979–85; independent author and heritage advocate, 1985–2015. Founder Dir, Heritage Alliance, 2002–05; Director: Cotswold Archaeol., 2005–15; Marc Fitch Fund, 2010–. *Publications:* Cirencester: the development and buildings of a Cotswold town, 1975; Eyewitness Travel: Florence and Tuscany, 1990, 20th edn 2015; Eyewitness Travel: Venice and the Veneto, 1992, 20th edn 2014; National Geographic Amsterdam, 2000, 2nd edn 2014; Eyewitness Travel: Madeira, 2005, 10th edn 2013; Practical Archaeology, 2009, 3rd edn 2011. *Recreations:* performing and listening to live music, reading, thinking and arguing, exploring the heritage. *Address:* Royal Commission on the Ancient and Historical Monuments of Wales, Plas Crug, Aberystwyth SY23 1NJ. *T:* (01970) 621201. *E:* christopher.catling@rcahmw.gov.uk.

CATLOW, Prof. (Charles) Richard (Arthur), DPhil; FRS 2004; FRSC, FInstP; Professorial Research Associate, Department of Chemistry, University College London, since 2014 (Professor of Solid State Chemistry and Dean, Mathematics and Physical Sciences Faculty, 2007–14; Head, Department of Chemistry, 2007–08); *b* 24 April 1947; *s* of Rolf M. Catlow and Constance Catlow (*née* Aldred); *m* 1978, Carey Anne Chapman; one *s*; *m* 2000, Nora de Leeuw. *Educ:* Clitheroe Royal Grammar School; St John's College, Oxford (MA, DPhil). FRSC 1990; FInstP 1995. Research Fellow, Oxford Univ., 1973–76; Lectr, Dept of Chemistry, UCL, 1976–85; Prof. of Physical Chemistry, Univ. of Keele, 1985–89; Wolfson Prof. of Natural Philosophy, 1989–2007, Dir, Davy Faraday Lab., 1998–2007, Royal Instn of GB. Member: CCLRC, 2006–07; Council, Royal Soc., 2009–11. Liversidge Lect., RSC, 2009. Medal for Solid State Chem., 1992, Award for Interdisciplinary Science, 1998, RSC. *Publications:* (jtly) Point Defects in Materials, 1988; ed jtly and contrib. to works on computational and materials sciences; 700 papers in learned jls. *Recreations:* reading, music, walking. *Address:* Mathematics and Physical Sciences Faculty, University College London, Gower Street, WC1E 6BT. *E:* c.r.a.catlow@ucl.ac.uk. *Club:* Athenæum.

CATON, Martin Philip; *b* 15 June 1951; *s* of William John Caton and Pauline Joan Caton; *m* 1996, Bethan, *d* of late Hermus Evans and of Menai Evans; two step *d*. *Educ:* Newport Grammar Sch., Essex; Norfolk Sch. of Agriculture; Aberystwyth Coll. of FE (HNC). Scientific Officer, Welsh Plant Breeding Stn, Aberystwyth, 1974–84; Political Researcher, David Morris, MEP, 1984–97. Mem. (Lab) Swansea CC, 1988–97. MP (Lab) Gower, 1997–2015.

CATON, Dr Valerie, (Mrs D. M. Harrison); HM Diplomatic Service, retired; Ambassador to Finland, 2006–10; *b* 12 May 1952; *d* of Robert Caton and Florence Amy Caton (*née* Aspden); *m* 1987, David Mark Harrison; one *s* one *d*. *Educ:* Blackburn High Sch. for Girls; Bristol Univ. (BA, PhD); Grad. Sch. of European Studies, Univ. of Reading (MA). Lectrice, Univ. of Sorbonne, Paris, 1977–78; Tutor in French, Exeter Univ., 1978–80; joined HM Diplomatic Service, 1980: FCO, 1980–82; Second, later First Sec., EC Affairs, Brussels, 1982–84; First Sec. (Chancery), Paris, 1988–92; Dep. Head of Mission, Stockholm, 1993–96; Counsellor (Financial and Economic), Paris, 1997–2001; Sen. Associate Mem., St Antony's Coll., Oxford, 2001–02, 2012–13 (Vis. Fellow, 2012); Head: Envmt Policy Dept, FCO, 2002–04; Climate Change and Energy Gp, FCO, 2004–06. Dir, UK Nordic Baltic Summit, 2010–11; Dir and Trustee, CAMFED Internat., 2013–. Vis. Fellow, Sch. of Politics and Internat. Relations, Univ. of Reading, 2013–. *Publications:* France and the Politics of European Economic and Monetary Union, 2015; various articles in jls on France and EU issues, and on works of French writer, Raymond Queneau. *Recreations:* reading, theatre, collecting humorous books, walking, riding. *Address:* Department of Politics and International Relations, University of Reading, Whiteknights, Reading RG6 6AA.

CATOVSKY, Prof. Daniel, MD, DSc; FRCP, FRCPath, FMedSci; Professor of Haematology, and Head of Department of Haematology and Cytogenetics, Institute of Cancer Research, 1988–2004, now Professor Emeritus; Hon. Consultant, Royal Marsden Hospital, 1988–2004; *b* 19 Sept. 1937; *s* of Felix Catovsky and Ana Kabanchik; *m* 1960, Julia Margaret Polak (Dame Julia Polak, DBE) (*d* 2014); two *s* (one *d* decd). *Educ:* Faculty of Medicine, Buenos Aires Univ. (MD 1961); London Univ. (DSc Med. 1985). FRCPath 1986; FRCP 1990. Royal Postgraduate Medical School: Fellow, 1967–76; Hon. Sen. Lectr in Haematol. and Medicine, 1976–87; Prof. of Haematol Oncology, 1987–88; Consultant, Hammersmith Hosp., 1976–88. Visiting Professor: Mount Sinai Med. Sch., NY, 1981; M. D. Anderson Cancer Center, Univ. of Texas, 2004–05. Ham-Wasserman Lecture (first annual), Amer. Soc. of Hematology, 1984. FMedSci 1999. British Soc. for Haematology Medal, 2000; Binet-Rai Medal, Internat. Workshop on Chronic Lymphocytic Leukaemia, 2005. *Publications:* The Leukemic Cell, 1981, 2nd edn 1991; (with A. Polliack) Chronic Lymphocytic Leukaemia, 1988; (with R. Foa) The Lymphoid Leukaemias, 1990; (ed with A. V. Hoffbrand and E. G. Tuddenham) Postgraduate Haematology, 5th edn 2005, (ed with A. V. Hoffbrand, A. R. Green and E. G. Tuddenham) 6th edn 2010; 840 articles in learned jls. *Recreations:* walking, films, theatre. *Address:* Section of Haemato-Oncology, Institute of Cancer Research, 15 Cotswold Road, Sutton, Surrey SM2 5NG. *T:* (020) 8722 4461.

CATTANACH, Bruce Macintosh, PhD, DSc; FRS 1987; Senior Scientist, MRC, 1970–98; *b* 5 Nov. 1932; *s* of James and Margaretta Cattanach; *m* 1st, 1966, Margaret Bouchier Crewe (*d* 1996); two *d*; 2nd, 1999, Josephine Peters. *Educ:* King's Coll., Univ. of Durham (BSc, 1st Cl. Hons); Inst. of Animal Genetics, Univ. of Edinburgh (PhD, DSc). Scientific Staff, MRC Induced Mutagenesis Unit, Edinburgh, 1959–62, 1964–66; NIH Post Doctoral Res. Fellow, Biology Div., Oak Ridge Nat. Lab., Tenn, USA, 1962–64; Sen. Scientist, City of Hope Med. Centre, Duarte, Calif, 1966–69; Scientific Staff, 1969–86, Hd of Genetics Div., 1987–96, MRC Radiobiology Unit, Chilton, Oxon; Actg Dir, MRC Mammalian Genetics Unit, Harwell, 1996–97. *Publications:* contribs to several learned jls on X-chromosome inactivation, sex determination, mammalian chromosome imprinting, and genetics generally. *Recreations:* squash; breeding, showing and judging pedigree dogs; investigating inherited disease in dogs and devising control schemes for elimination. *Address:* Downs Edge, Reading Road, Harwell, Oxon OX11 0JJ. *T:* (01235) 835410.

CATTERALL, Dr John Ashley, OBE 1995; FIMMM, FInstP; Senior Executive, Engineering Council, 1997–99; *b* 26 May 1928; *s* of John William Catterall and Gladys Violet Catterall; *m* 1960, Jennifer Margaret Bradfield (*d* 2010); two *s*. *Educ:* Imperial Coll. of Science and Technol., London (BSc, PhD, DIC). ARSM; FIMMM (FIM 1964); FInstP 1968; CPhys 1965; CEng 1978. National Physical Lab., 1952–74; Dept of Industry, 1974–81; Head, Energy Technology Div., and Dep. Chief Scientist, Dept of Energy, 1981–83; Sec., SERC, 1983–88; Sec., Inst. of Metals, 1988–91, then Sec. and Chief Exec., Inst. of Materials, 1991–97. Inst. of Metals Rosenhain Medal for Physical Metallurgy, 1970. *Publications:* (with O. Kubaschewski) Thermochemical Data of Alloys, 1956; contrib. Philos. Mag., Jl Inst. of Physics, Jl Inst. of Metals. *Recreation:* reading. *Address:* Hill House, The Doward, Whitchurch, Ross-on-Wye, Herefordshire HR9 6DU. *T:* (01600) 890341.

CATTERALL, John Stewart; Director, C&T Partnerships, since 2012 (Managing Director, 1993–2001, Director, 2002–12, C&T (formerly Conferences and Training Ltd)); *b* 13 Jan. 1939; *s* of John Bernard and Eliza Catterall; *m* 1965, Ann Beryl Hughes; two *s*. *Educ:* Blackpool Tech. Coll. and Sch. of Art. Mem. CIPFA. Posts in local authorities, 1961–70; Management Accountant, Cambridgeshire and Isle of Ely CC, 1970–72, Chief Accountant, 1972–73; Asst County Treasurer, Financial Planning and Accounting, Cambs CC, 1973–76; Dist Treasurer, Southampton and SW Hants DHA, 1976–78, Area Treasurer, 1978–82; Regional Treasurer, NE Thames RHA, 1982–85; Dep. Dir, Finance, NHS Mgt Bd, 1985–89; Head of Health Services, 1985–89, Head of Health Adv. Services, 1989, CIPFA. Chm. and Chief Exec., C International Ltd, 1990–92; Director: Capita PLC, 1992–93; Agenda Planning Res. Ltd, 2001–10. *Publications:* contribs to professional jls. *Recreations:* golf, swimming, reading. *Address:* 18 Lipizzaner Fields, Whiteley, Fareham, Hants PO15 7BH. *T:* 07407 280398.

CATTERSON, Marie Thérèse; Her Honour Judge Catterson; a Circuit Judge, since 2001; *b* 14 Oct. 1948; *e d* of late James Joseph Catterson and Rosemary Catterson; *m* 1984; two *d*. *Educ:* Wyggeston Girls' Grammar Sch., Leicester; University Coll. London (LLB 1970). Called to the Bar, Gray's Inn, 1972; in practice as barrister, S Eastern Circuit, 1972–2001; a Recorder, 1996–2001. *Recreations:* gardening, travel. *Address:* The Crown Court, Bricket Road, St Albans, Herts AL1 3JW.

CATTO, family name of **Baron Catto.**

CATTO, 3rd Baron *cr* 1936, of Cairncatto, co. Aberdeen; **Innes Gordon Catto;** Bt 1921; *b* 7 Aug. 1950; *e s* of 2nd Baron Catto; *S* father, 2001; *m* 2014, Ali Farhan Negyaz. *Educ:* Grenville Coll.; Shuttleworth Agric. Coll. *Heir:* *b* Hon. Alexander Gordon Catto [*b* 22 June 1952; *m* 1981, Elizabeth Scott, twin *d* of Maj. T. P. Boyes; two *s* one *d*].

CATTO, Sir Graeme (Robertson Dawson), Kt 2002; MD; DSc; FRCP, FRCPE, FRCPGlas, FMedSci; FRSE; Professor of Medicine, University of Aberdeen, 2005–09, now Emeritus; *b* 24 April 1945; *s* of William Dawson Catto and Dora Elizabeth (*née* Spiby); *m* 1967, Joan Sievewright; one *s* one *d*. *Educ:* Robert Gordon's Coll., Aberdeen; Univ. of Aberdeen (MB ChB Hons 1969; MD Hons 1975; DSc 1988). FRCPGlas 1982; FRCP 1984; FRCPE 1988; FRSE 1996. House Officer, Aberdeen Royal Infirmary, 1969–70; Res. Fellow, then Lectr, Univ. of Aberdeen, 1970–75; Harkness Fellow, Commonwealth Fund of NY; Fellow in Medicine, Harvard Univ., 1975–77; University of Aberdeen: Sen. Lectr, then Reader, 1977–88; Dean, Faculty of Medicine and Med. Scis, 1992–98; Prof. of Medicine and Therapeutics, 1988–2000; Vice Principal, 1995–2000; Hon. Consultant Physician and Nephrologist, Aberdeen Royal Infirmary, 1977–2000; Pro-Vice Chancellor (Medicine), Univ. of London, 2003–05, Prof. Emeritus; Vice Principal, KCL and Dean, GKT, 2000–05; Hon. Consultant Nephrologist, Guy's and St Thomas' NHS Trust, 2000–05; Hon. Consultant Physician and Nephrologist, NHS Grampian, 2005–09. Vice-Chm., Aberdeen Royal Hosps NHS Trust, 1992–99. Chief Scientist, Scottish Executive (formerly Scottish Office) Health Dept, 1997–2000. Member: GMC, 1994–2009 (Pres., 2002–09; Chm. Educn Cttee, 1999–2002); SHEFC, 1996–2002; Specialist Trng Authority, 1999–2002; Standing Medical Adv. Cttee, 2002–05; Council, Regulation of Healthcare Professionals, 2003–08; Scottish Stem Cell Network, 2006–11 (Chm., 2008–11); Commn on Assisted Dying, 2010–11; Chm., Dignity in Dying, 2012–. Member: Lambeth, Southwark and Lewisham HA, 2000–02; SE London Strategic HA, 2003–05; Qatar Council for Healthcare Practitioners, 2013–. Chm., HE Better Regulation Gp, Universities UK, 2009–12. Pres., ASME, 2009–13; Vice Pres., Acad. of Experts, 2009–. Founder FMedSci 1998 (Treas., 1998–2001); Fellow, Acad. of Med. Educators, 2012. Patron, Med. Council on Alcohol, 2007–. Chairman: Robert Gordon's Coll., Aberdeen, 1995–2005; Lathallan Sch., 2012–; Gov., Qatar Sci. and Technol. Park, 2005–07; Pres., Coll. of Med., 2010–15. Hon. FRCGP 2000; Hon. FRCSE 2002; Hon. FFPM 2008. FRSA 1996. FKC 2005. Hon. LLD Aberdeen, 2002; Hon. DSc: St Andrews, 2003; Robert Gordon's Univ., 2004; Kent, 2007; South Bank, 2008; London, 2009. Hon. MD: Southampton, 2004; Brighton, 2010; Buckingham, 2015. *Publications:* (ed) Clinical Transplantation: current practice and future prospects, 1987; (with D. A. Power) Nephrology, 1988; (ed) Calculus Disease, 1988; (ed) Chronic Renal Failure, 1988; (ed) Haemodialysis, 1988; (ed) Management of Renal Hypertension, 1988; (ed) Pregnancy and Renal Disorders, 1988; (ed) Drugs and the Kidney, 1989; (ed) Glomerulo-nephritis, 1989; Multisystem Diseases, 1989; Transplantation, 1989; (ed) Urinary Tract Infections, 1989; (with A. W. Thomson) Immunology of Renal Transplantation, 1993; contrib. to learned jls on aspects of renal disease. *Recreation:* hills and glens. *Address:* 4 Woodend Avenue, Aberdeen AB15 6YL. *T:* (01224) 310509; Maryfield, Glenbuchat, Aberdeenshire AB36 8TS. *T:* (01975) 641317. *Clubs:* Athenæum; Royal Northern and University (Aberdeen).

CAU, Antoine Emond André; Founding President, Antedman SA, Switzerland, since 2006; *b* 26 Aug. 1947; *s* of Henri and Laure Cau; *m* 1978, Patricia Stamm. *Educ:* Lycée Mignet, Aix-en-Provence; Institut d'Etudes Commerciales de Grenoble (diplôme de direction et de gestion des entreprises; maîtrise de gestion). Hertz: Station Manager, Avignon, 1970–75; station manager posts, 1975–77; District Manager: Nice, 1977; Côte d'Azur, 1978–80; Zone Manager, S of France, 1980–82; Ops Manager, Italy, 1982–84; Corporate Accounts Manager, Hertz Europe, 1984; Ops Manager, France, 1985–90; Vice Pres., Ops, Hertz Europe, 1990; Vice Pres., Hertz Corp., and Pres., Hertz International, 1990–97; Chief Executive: Forte

Hotels, 1998–2001; W Eur. Div., Compass Gp, 2001–05. Chevalier: de l'Ordre National du Mérite (France), 1992; de la Légion d'Honneur (France), 2004. *Recreations:* motorsport, music. *Address:* Antedman, 6 Place des Perrières, 1296 Coppet, Switzerland. *E:* antoine.cau@antedman.ch.

CAUDWELL, John David; Founder, Chairman and Chief Executive, Caudwell Group, 1978–2006; *b* 7 Oct. 1952; *s* of Walter and Beryl Caudwell; partner, Claire Johnson; two *s* three *d*. *Educ:* Berryhill Jun. High Sch.; Stoke-on-Trent Polytech. (HNC Mech. Engrg). With Michelin Tyre Co., 1970–80. Founder and Chm., The Caudwell Charity, later Caudwell Children, 2000–. *Recreations:* charity fundraising, cycling, flying, diving, motorcycling, antiques. *Address:* Caudwell Children, Minton Hollins Building, Shelton Old Road, Stoke-on-Trent, Staffs ST4 7RY. *T:* (0845) 3001348, *Fax:* (01782) 600639. *E:* charity@caudwellchildren.com.

CAULCOTT, Thomas Holt; Chief Executive, Birmingham City Council, 1982–88; *b* 7 June 1927; *s* of late L. W. Caulcott and Doris Caulcott; *m* 1st, 1954, C. Evelyn Lowden (marr. diss. 1987); one *d* (and one *s* decd); 2nd, 1988, Jane Marguerite Allsopp. *Educ:* Solihull Sch.; Emmanuel Coll., Cambridge. Asst Principal, Central Land Bd and War Damage Commn, 1950–53; transferred to HM Treasury, 1953; Private Sec. to Economic Sec. to the Treasury, 1955; Principal, Treasury supply divs, 1956–60; Private Sec. to successive Chancellors of the Exchequer, Sept. 1961–Oct. 1964; Principal Private Sec. to First Sec. of State (DEA), 1964–65; Asst Sec., HM Treasury, 1965–66; Min. of Housing and Local Govt, 1967–69; Civil Service Dept, 1969–70; Under-Sec., Machinery of Govt Gp, 1970–73; Principal Finance Officer, Local Govt Finance Policy, DoE, 1973–76; Sec., AMA, 1976–82. Chm., Royal Shrewsbury Hosps NHS Trust, 1998–2003; non-exec. Dir, Heart of Birmingham PCT, 2006–11. Mem., S Shropshire DC, 1991–95 (Chm., Policy and Resources Cttee, 1993–95). Mem. Cttee of Mgt, Hanover Housing Assoc., 1988–94. Mem. Bd, W Midlands Arts, 1996–97. Harkness Fellowship, Harvard and Brookings Instn, 1960–61; Vis. Fellow, Dept of Land Economy, Univ. of Cambridge, 1984–85; Hon. Fellow: Inst. of Local Govt Studies, Univ. of Birmingham, 1979–; Birmingham City Univ. (formerly Birmingham Polytechnic, later Univ. of Central England), 1990–. *Publications:* Management and the Politics of Power, 1996. *Address:* 12 Dinham, Ludlow, Shropshire SY8 1EJ. *T:* (01584) 875154.

CAULFEILD, family name of **Viscount Charlemont**.

CAULFIELD, Ian George, CBE 2000; DL; Clerk of the Council and Chief Executive, Warwickshire County Council, and Clerk to the Warwickshire Lieutenancy, 1986–2005; *b* 14 Dec. 1942; *s* of William and Elizabeth Caulfield; *m* 1967, Geraldine Mary Hind; three *s*. *Educ:* Liverpool Inst. High Schs for Boys; Univ. of Manchester (BA Hons Geography); Liverpool Poly. (DipTP). Jun. Planning Assistant, Liverpool City, 1964–65; Planning Assistant, Lancs CC, 1965–69; Sen. Planning Officer, Hants CC, 1969–74; Asst Hd, Res. and Intelligence Unit, 1974–76, Prin. Assistant to Chief Exec., 1976–78, Oxford CC; Asst Exec., 1978–83, Dep. Clerk and Asst Chief Exec., 1983–86, Warwicks CC. DL Warwicks, 2005. *Publications:* (jtly) Planning for Change: strategic planning and local government, 1989. *Recreations:* sport, particularly soccer.

CAULFIELD, Rev. James Edward; Principal Roman Catholic Chaplain to the Royal Air Force, since 2012; *b* Downpatrick, NI, 10 May 1961; *s* of William Caulfield and Margaret Mary Caulfield. *Educ:* Mount St Mary's Coll., Spinkhill; Rutland Sixth Form Coll., Oakham; Southfield's Coll. of FE, Leicester (OND Catering); All Hallow's Coll., Dublin (Dip. Philosophy; BD). Assistant Priest: Our Lady and the English Martyrs Church, Cambridge, 1989–92; Lowestoft, 1992–94; Parish Priest, Huntingdon, 1994–97; RAF Chaplain, 1997–. Mem., Standing Cttee, Nat. Conf. of Priests for Eng. and Wales, 2001–06. Provincial Chaplain, Knights St Columba, East Anglia, 1992–97. *Recreations:* photography, hill-walking, reading, exploring history, travel. *Address:* 12 The Oval, Ashby de La Launde, Lincoln LN4 3JE. *E:* cardinal-biggles@hotmail.co.uk. *Club:* Royal Air Force.

CAULFIELD, Maria Colette; MP (C) Lewes, since 2015. Nurse and Research Sister, Royal Marsden Hosp. An owner and shareholder, Lewes FC. Non-exec. Dir, BHT Sussex. Mem. (C) Brighton and Hove CC, 2007–11. Contested (C) Caerphilly, 2010. *Address:* House of Commons, SW1A 0AA.

CAUSTON, Richard John; composer; *b* London, 12 March 1971; *s* of John and Ann Causton; *m* 2005, Jessica Summers; one *s* one *d*. *Educ:* William Ellis Sch.; Univ. of York (BA 1st Cl. Hons 1993; MA 1994); Royal Coll. of Music (Postgrad. ARCM 1995). Fellow Commoner in Creative Arts, Trinity Coll., Cambridge, 2003–05; Composition Tutor, Birmingham Conservatoire, 2006–; Lectr in Composition, Cambridge Univ., 2012–. Work with ensembles incl. City of Birmingham SO, BBC SO, Philharmonia Orch., Orch. of Age of Enlightenment, Sinfonie-Orchester Basel, Rundfunksinfonieorchester Saarbrücken, Halle Orch., EU Youth Orch., London Sinfonietta, Birmingham Contemp. Music Gp and Nash Ensemble. Has made recordings. 1st prize, 3rd Internat. Nuove Sincronie Composition Award, 1996; British Composer Award, BASCA, 2004; Royal Philharmonic Soc. Award, 2006. *Publications:* The Persistence of Memory, 1995; Notturno, 1998, rev. edn 2001; Millennium Scenes, 1999, rev. edn 2001; Seven States of Rain, 2002; Between Two Waves of the Sea, 2004; Phoenix, 2006, rev. edn 2007; La Terra Impareggiabile, 2007; As Kingfishers Catch Fire, 2007, rev. edn 2008; Chamber Symphony, 2009, rev. edn 2010; Twenty-Seven Heavens, 2012; Out of Your Sleep, 2012; Ricercare, 2012; De Profundis, 2014; Night Piece, 2014. *Address:* c/o Music Department, Oxford University Press, Great Clarendon Street, Oxford OX2 6DP. *T:* (01865) 355020/355019, *Fax:* (01865) 355060. *E:* repertoire.promotion.uk@oup.com.

CAUTE, (John) David, MA, DPhil; FRSL, FRHistS; writer; *b* 16 Dec. 1936; *m* 1st, 1961, Catherine Shuckburgh (marr. diss. 1970); two *s*; 2nd, 1973, Martha Bates; two *d*. *Educ:* Edinburgh Academy; Wellington; Wadham Coll., Oxford. Scholar of St Antony's Coll., 1959. Spent a year in the Army in the Gold Coast, 1955–56, and a year at Harvard Univ. on a Henry Fellowship, 1960–61. Fellow of All Souls Coll., Oxford, 1959–65; Visiting Professor, New York Univ. and Columbia Univ., 1966–67; Reader in Social and Political Theory, Brunel Univ., 1967–70. Regents' Lectr, Univ. of Calif., 1974; Vis. Prof., Bristol Univ., 1985. Literary Editor, New Statesman, 1979–80. Co-Chm., Writers' Guild, 1981–82; Chm., Sinclair Fiction Prize, 1984. FRSL 1998. JP Inner London, 1993. *Plays:* Songs for an Autumn Rifle, staged by Oxford Theatre Group at Edinburgh, 1961; The Demonstration, Nottingham Playhouse, 1969; The Fourth World, Royal Court, 1973; Brecht and Company, BBC TV, 1979; BBC Radio: Fallout, 1972; The Zimbabwe Tapes, 1983; Henry and the Dogs, 1986; Sanctions, 1988; Animal Fun Park, 1995. *Publications:* At Fever Pitch (novel), 1959 (Authors' Club Award and John Llewelyn Rhys Prize, 1960); Comrade Jacob (novel), 1961; Communism and the French Intellectuals, 1914–1960, 1964; The Left in Europe Since 1789, 1966; The Decline of the West (novel), 1966; Essential Writings of Karl Marx (ed), 1967; Fanon, 1970; The Confrontation: a trilogy, 1971 (consisting of The Demonstration (play), 1970; The Occupation (novel), 1971; The Illusion: an essay on politics, theatre and the novel, 1971); The Fellow-Travellers, 1973, rev. edn 1988, as The Fellow-Travellers, Intellectual Friends of Communism; Collisions, 1974; Cuba, Yes?, 1974; The Great Fear: the anti-communist purge under Truman and Eisenhower, 1978; Under the Skin: the death of white Rhodesia, 1983; The K-Factor (novel), 1983; The Espionage of the Saints, 1986; News from Nowhere (novel), 1986; Sixty Eight: the year of the barricades, 1988; Veronica or the Two Nations (novel), 1989; The Women's Hour (novel), 1991; Joseph Losey: a revenge on life, 1994; Dr Orwell and Mr Blair (novel), 1994; Fatima's Scarf (novel), 1998; The Dancer Defects: the struggle for cultural supremacy during the cold war, 2003; Marechera and the Colonel, 2009; Politics and the Novel During the Cold War, 2010; Isaac and Isaiah: the covert punishment of a cold war heretic, 2013; *as John Salisbury: novels:* The Baby-Sitters, 1978; Moscow Gold, 1980. *Address:* 41 Westcroft Square, W6 0TA.

CAUTHEN, Stephen Mark; jockey, 1976–93; *b* Covington, Kentucky, 1 May 1960; *e s* of Ronald (Tex) Cauthen and Myra Cauthen; *m* Amy Kathrine Roth Fuss; three *d*. Apprentice jockey, 1976, Churchill Downs, Kentucky; first win, Red Pipe, 1976; raced at Aqueduct and Santa Anita; champion jockey, USA, 1977; won US Triple Crown on Affirmed, 1978; moved to Lambourn, 1979; champion jockey, UK, 1984, 1985, 1987; races won include: with Tap on Wood, 2,000 Guineas, 1979; with Slip Anchor, Derby, 1985; with Oh So Sharp, Oaks, 1,000 Guineas and St Leger, 1985; with Reference Point, Derby, St Leger and King George V and Queen Elizabeth Diamond Stakes, 1987; with Diminuendo, Oaks, 1988; with Michelozzo, St Leger, 1989; with Old Vic, French Derby and Irish Derby, 1989; Champion Stakes 3 times (Cormorant Wood, Indian Skimmer, In the Groove); Grand Prix de St Cloud (Atcatanango, Diamond Shoal); Prix de Diane (Indian Skimmer). *Address:* 167 S Main Street, Walton, KY 41094, USA.

CAUTLEY, (Edward) Paul (Ronald), CMG 2001; OBE 2015; DL; Founder, Helping People Win Ltd, since 2011; *b* 1 March 1940; *s* of Ronald Lockwood Cautley and Ena Lily Medwin; *m* 1966, Sandra Elizabeth Baker; two *d*. *Educ:* Downside Sch. Syndication Manager, Central Press Features, 1958–60; Retail Marketing Manager, ICI Paints, 1960–62; Finance Negotiator, GDM Finance, 1962–64; General Manager, Marling Industries, 1964–66; Account Dir, S. H. Benson, 1966–70; Dir, New Product Development, BRB, 1971–73; Chief Executive and Founder Chairman: Strategy Ltd, 1974–94; The D Group, 1994–2011. HAC, 1958–61; RM Reserve, 1961–68. Hon. Col, RM Reserve, London, 1999–11; Pres., Chatham Royal Marine Cadets, 2000–09; Col Comdt, Royal Marine Cadets, 2011– (Col, 2004–11). Trustee, Marine Soc. and Sea Cadets (formerly Sea Cadet Assoc.), 2001–09. Freeman, City of London, 2008. DL Greater London, 2001. FRGS 1991; life mem., 15 railway preservation socs. *Publications:* The Cautley Chronicle, 1986. *Recreations:* photography (mainly landscapes), 00 gauge model railway owner (pre-1948, Southern Railway). *Address:* 5 Warden Court, Cuckfield, W Sussex RH17 5DN. *E:* paulcautley@gmail.com. *Club:* Honourable Artillery Company.

CAVACO SILVA, Anibal; President of Portugal, since 2006; *b* 15 July 1939; *s* of Teodoro Silva and Maria do Nascimento Cavaco; *m* 1963, Maria Alves; one *s* one *d*. *Educ:* Superior Inst. Econs and Financial Scis, Lisbon; York Univ. (PhD 1973). Teacher of public economics and political economy: Inst. Econ. and Financial Studies, Lisbon, 1966–78; Catholic Univ., Lisbon, 1975–2006 (Prof., 1979–2006); New Univ. of Lisbon, 1978–2001 (Prof., 1979–2001); Res. Fellow, Calouste Gulbenkian Foundn, 1967–77; Dir, Res. and Statistical Dept, Bank of Portugal, 1977–80 and 1981–85; Minister of Finance and Planning, 1980–81; Pres., Council for Nat. Planning, 1981–84; Prime Minister of Portugal, 1985–95. Leader, PSD, 1985–95. Econ. Advr to Bank of Portugal, 1995–2004. Member: Scientific Soc., Catholic Univ. of Portugal; Inst. of Public Finance; Royal Acad. of Moral and Pol Scis of Spain; Club of Madrid on Democratic Transition and Consolidation; Global Leadership Foundn. Hon. Dr: York, 1993; Coruña, Spain, 1996; Goa, India, 2007; Léon, Spain, 2008; Heriot-Watt, Edinburgh, 2009. Joseph Bech Prize, 1991; Freedom Prize, Schmidheiny Foundation, 1995; Carl Bertelsmann Prize, Bertelsmann Foundn, 1995; Mediterranean Award for Instns, Fondazione Mediterraneo, 2009. *Publications:* Budget Policy and Economic Stabilization, 1976; Economic Effects of Public Debt, 1977; The Macroeconomic Policy, 1992; A Decade of Reforms, 1995; Portugal and the Single Currency, 1997; European Monetary Union, 1999; Political Autobiography, 2002; numerous articles on financial mkts, public econs and Portuguese econ. policy. *Address:* Palácio de Belém, 1349–022 Lisbon, Portugal.

CAVADINO, Paul Francis; freelance consultant in criminal justice and penal affairs, since 2010; Chief Executive, Nacro, 2002–09; Member, Parole Board for England and Wales, since 2010; *b* 5 Dec. 1948; *s* of John Joseph and Mary Patricia Cavadino; *m* 1970, Maria Claire Carrack; two *s*. *Educ:* St Michael's Coll., Leeds; Balliol Coll., Oxford (BA Jurisprudence). Univs and Colls Sec., Christian Aid, 1970–72; National Association for the Care and Resettlement of Offenders: NE Regl Orgnr, 1972–75; Sen. Inf. Officer, 1975–82; Sen. Press Officer, 1982–90; Principal Officer (Criminal Justice Policy), 1990–94; Director: of Communications, 1997–99; of Policy and Inf., 1999–2001; of Policy, Race and Resettlement, 2001–02. Chairman: Penal Affairs Consortium, 1989–2001 (full-time, 1994–97); Voluntary Sector Community Engagement Project, 2005–08. Sec., New Approaches to Juvenile Crime, 1978–84; Clerk, Parly All-Party Penal Affairs Gp, 1980–2001; Mem., Reducing Reoffending Third Sector Adv. Gp, MoJ, 2009–11. Advr, Sentencing Council of England and Wales, 2010–15. Trustee: Coalition for Racial Justice (UK), 2010–14; African Prisons Project, 2011– (Vice Chm., 2012–13; Chm., 2013–); User Voice, 2011–. *Publications:* Bail: the law, best practice and the debate, 1993; Introduction to the Criminal Justice Process, 1995, 3rd edn, 2008; Children Who Kill, 1996. *Recreations:* cricket, jazz music, Italian food and drink. *Address:* 136 Onslow Gardens, Wallington, Surrey SM6 9QE. *T:* (020) 8274 2382. *E:* pc003f3813@blueyonder.co.uk.

CAVALIER-SMITH, Prof. Thomas, PhD; FRS 1998; FRSC 1997; Professor of Evolutionary Biology, Department of Zoology, University of Oxford, 2000, now Emeritus; *b* 21 Oct. 1942; *s* of Alan Hailes Spencer Cavalier-Smith and Mary Maude Cavalier-Smith; *m* 1st, 1964, Gillian Glaysher; one *s* one *d*; 2nd, 1991, Ema E-Yung Chao; one *d*. *Educ:* Kenninghall Primary Sch.; Norwich Sch.; Gonville and Caius Coll., Cambridge (MA 1967); King's Coll., London (PhD 1967); Open Univ. (BA). FLS; FRSB. Tutorial Student, King's Coll., London, 1964–67; Guest Investigator, and Damon Runyon Meml Res. Fellow, Rockefeller Univ., NY, 1967–69; Lectr, 1969–82, Reader, 1982–89, in Biophysics, King's Coll., London; Prof. of Botany, Univ. of BC, 1989–99; NERC Professorial Fellow, Dept of Zool., Univ. of Oxford, 1999–2007. Vis. Fellow, Res. Sch. of Biol. Scis, ANU, 1981, 1985–86; Fellow, Canadian Inst. for Advanced Res. (Evolutionary Biol. Prog.), 1988–2007; Vis. Scientist, Univ. of Cape Town, 1995–96. Pres., British Soc. for Protist Biol., 2006–09. FRSA. Internat. Prize for Biol., Japan Soc. for Promotion of Sci., 2004; Linnean Medal for Zool., Linnean Soc. of London, 2007; Frink Medal, Zool Soc. of London, 2008. *Publications:* (ed with J. P. Hudson) Biology, Society and Choice, 1982; (ed) The Evolution of Genome Size, 1985; over 200 scientific articles in jls, contribs to books. *Recreations:* reading, natural history, travel. *Address:* Department of Zoology, University of Oxford, South Parks Road, Oxford OX1 3PS. *T:* (01865) 281065.

CAVALIERO, Roderick; Deputy Director General, British Council, 1981–88 (Assistant Director General, 1977–81); *b* 21 March 1928; *s* of Eric Cavaliero and Valerie (*née* Logan); *m* 1957, Mary McDonnell (*d* 2007); one *s* four *d*. *Educ:* Tonbridge School; Hertford Coll., Oxford. Teaching in Britain, 1950–52; teaching in Malta, 1952–58; British Council Officer, 1958–88 (service in India, Brazil, Italy). Chm., Educnl and Trng Export Cttee, 1979–88; Dir, Open Univ. Educnl Enterprises, 1980–88; Pres., British Educnl Equipment Assoc., 1987–92. Mem., British Section, Franco-British Council, 1981–88. Trustee, Charles Wallace India Trust, 1981–2000. Mem. Council, British Sch. at Rome, 1989–96 (Chm., Management Cttee, 1991–95); Trustee, St George's English Sch., Rome, 1979–96. *Publications:* Olympia and the Angel, 1958; The Last of the Crusaders, 1960; The Independence of Brazil, 1993; Admiral Satan: the life and campaigns of Suffren, 1994; Strangers in the Land: the rise and decline of the British Indian Empire, 2002; Italia Romantica, English Romantics and Italian

Freedom, 2005; Caverns of the Heart, 2007; Ottomania: the Romantics and the Islamic Orient, 2010; Genius, Power and Magic, 2013. *Address:* 10 Lansdowne Road, Tunbridge Wells, Kent TN1 2NJ. *T:* (01892) 533452.

CAVAN, 13th Earl of, *cr* 1647 (Ire.); **Roger Cavan Lambart;** Baron Cavan 1618; Baron Lambart 1618; Viscount Kilcoursie 1647; *b* 1 Sept. 1944; *s* of Frederick Cavan Lambart (*d* 1963) and Audrey May, *d* of Albert Charles Dunham; *S* kinsman, 1988, but has not yet established his right to the Peerage. *Educ:* Wilson's School, Wallington, Surrey.

CAVANAGH, Diana Lesley; Director of Educational Studies (formerly Strategic Director of Education), City of Bradford Metropolitan District Council, 1996–2001; *b* 19 Nov. 1944; *d* of Arthur and Nellie Eggleston; *m* 1973, Michael Cavanagh. *Educ:* Fairfield High Sch.; Westfield Coll., London (BA Hons 1966); Univ. of Liverpool (PGCE 1967); Univ. of Edinburgh (Dip. Applied Linguistics 1973); Sheffield Poly. (MSc 1982); Leeds Univ. (MA 2006). German Teacher, Cumberland, 1967–70; English Teacher, Sulingen Gymnasium, W Germany, 1970–73; Lectr in English Lang./Educn, Univ. of Birmingham, 1973–75; British Council Project Co-ordinator, Medical Coll., Jeddah, 1975–77; Section Hd, ESOL, Abraham Moss Centre, Manchester, 1977–83; Professional Asst, and Dep. Area Educn Officer, Derbyshire, 1983–85; Asst Educn Officer (Reorgn and Curriculum), Rochdale, 1985–89; Chief Asst Exec. Officer (Policy Develt), 1989–91, Mem. Bd, 1992–93, Inst. of Citizenship Studies; Chief Educn Officer, Rochdale MBC, 1991–96. Chair, Assessment and Qualifications Alliance, 2003–07 (Dep. Chair, 1999–2003). Sec., Glossop Guild, 2010–. FRSA 1991. *Publications:* Introducing PET, 1980; Power Relations in the Further Education College, 1983; Staff Development in the Further Education College, 1984. *Recreations:* hill walking, polar travel, reading. *Address:* 4 Cross Cliffe, Glossop, Derbys SK13 8PZ.

CAVANAGH, John Patrick; QC 2001; a Recorder, since 2004; *b* 17 June 1960; *s* of Dr Gerry Cavanagh and Anne Cavanagh (*née* Kennedy); *m* 1989, Suzanne Tolley; one *s* three *d*. *Educ:* Mt Carmel Convent Sch., Stratford-on-Avon; Warwick Sch.; New Coll., Oxford (MA); Clare Coll., Cambridge (LLM); Univ. of Illinois Coll. of Law. Residential social worker, St Philip's Sch., Airdrie, 1979–80; Instructor in Law, Univ. of Illinois Coll. of Law, Urbana-Champaign, 1983–84; part-time Lectr in Law, New Coll., Oxford, 1984–87; called to the Bar, Middle Temple, 1985; in practice at the Bar, 1986–; Jun. Counsel to Crown, B Panel, 1997–2001; Jt Head of Chambers, 11 King's Bench Walk, 2013–. Chm., Employment Law Bar Assoc., 2005–07. Judge, Administrative Tribunal, Bank for Internat. Settlements, 2009–. Pres., Old Warwickian Assoc., 2009; Governor: Warwick Sch., 2009–; Aldwickbury Sch., 2009–. *Publications:* (ed and contrib.) Tolley's Employment Handbook, 9th edn 1985 to 15th edn 2001; (contrib.) Butterworth's Local Government Law, 1998–2006; (ed jtly and contrib.) Harvey on Industrial Relations and Employment Law, annually 2000–04. *Recreations:* family, reading, football (Celtic from afar), tennis, avoiding gardening. *Address:* 11 King's Bench Walk, Temple, EC4Y 7EQ. *T:* (020) 7632 8500.

CAVE, Hon. Sir Charles Anthony H.; *see* Haddon-Cave.

CAVE, Sir John (Charles), 5th Bt *cr* 1896, of Sidbury Manor, Sidbury, co. Devon; farmer and landowner; Vice Lord-Lieutenant of Devon, since 2007; *b* 8 Sept. 1958; *e s* of Sir Charles Cave, 4th Bt and of (Mary) Elizabeth, Lady Cave, *yr d* of late John Francis Gore, CVO, TD; *S* father, 1997; *m* 1984, Carey Diana (*née* Lloyd); two *s* one *d*. *Educ:* Eton; RAC, Cirencester. DL 2001, High Sheriff, 2005, Devon. *Heir: s* George Charles Cave, *b* 8 Sept. 1987. *Address:* Sidbury Manor, Sidmouth, Devon EX10 0QE. *Clubs:* Army and Navy, Farmers, MCC.

CAVE, Prof. Martin Edward, OBE 2009; DPhil; BP Centennial Professor, London School of Economics and Political Science, 2010–11; *b* 13 Dec. 1948; *s* of D. T. and S. M. Cave; *m* 1972, Kathryn Wilson; one *s* two *d*. *Educ:* Balliol Coll., Oxford (BA 1969); Nuffield Coll., Oxford (BPhil 1971; DPhil 1977). Res. Fellow, Birmingham Univ., 1971–74; Brunel University: Lectr, 1974–81; Sen. Lectr, 1981–86; Prof. of Economics, 1986–2001; Vice-Principal, 1996–2001; Prof., and Dir, Centre for Mgt Under Regulation, Warwick Business Sch., Univ. of Warwick, 2001–10. Vis. Prof., Business Sch., Imperial Coll. London, 2011–. Economic Consultant: HM Treasury, 1986–90; OFTEL, subseq., OFCOM, 1990–2006. Mem., 1996–2002, Dep. Chm. and Mem. Council, 2012–14, Competition (formerly Monopolies and Mergers) Commn; Dir, Payments Council, 2007–11; Panel Dep. Chm. and Inquiry Chm., CMA, 2014–. *Publications:* Computers and Economic Planning: the Soviet experience, 1980; (with Paul Hare) Alternative Approaches to Economic Planning, 1981; (jtly) The Use of Performance Indicators in Higher Education, 1988, 3rd edn 1997; (ed jtly) Output and Performance Measurement in Government, 1990; (ed with Saul Estrin) Competition and Competition Policy: a comparative analysis of Central and Eastern Europe, 1993; (ed jtly) Reconstituting the Market: the political economy of microeconomic transformation, 1999; (with Robert Baldwin) Understanding Regulation, 1999, 2nd edn 2011; (ed jtly) Handbook of Telecommunications Economics, vol. 1, 2002, vol. 2, 2005; Every Tenant Matters, 2007; Review of Competition and Innovation in the Water Sector, 2009; (ed jtly) Oxford Handbook of Regulation, 2010; (with W. Webb) Using Spectrum, 2015; contrib. to jls on regulatory economics and other subjects. *Recreations:* tennis, cinema.

CAVE, Prof. Terence Christopher, CBE 2013; FBA 1991; Professor of French Literature, Oxford University, 1989–2001, now Emeritus; Fellow and Tutor in French, St John's College, Oxford, 1972–2001, now Emeritus Research Fellow; *b* 1 Dec. 1938; *s* of Alfred Cyril Cave and Sylvia Norah (*née* Norman); *m* 1965, Helen Elizabeth Robb (marr. diss. 1990); one *s* one *d*; *m* 2013, Kirsti Sellevold. *Educ:* Winchester Coll.; Gonville and Caius Coll., Cambridge (MA; PhD; Hon. Fellow 1997). University of St Andrews: Assistant, 1962–63; Lectr, 1963–65; University of Warwick: Lectr, 1965–70; Sen. Lectr, 1970–72. Dir, Balzan Interdisciplinary Seminar, Res. Centre, St John's Coll., Oxford, 2010–14. Visiting Professor: Cornell Univ., 1967–68; Univ. of California, Santa Barbara, 1976; Univ. of Virginia, Charlottesville, 1979; Univ. of Toronto, 1991; Univ. of Alberta, 1992; Univ. of Paris VII, 1995; UCLA, 1997; RHUL, 2001–04; Visiting Fellow: All Souls Coll., Oxford, 1971; Princeton Univ., 1984; Royal Norwegian Soc. of Scis and Letters, Trondheim, 1991 (Mem., 1993); Hon. Sen. Res. Fellow, Inst. of Romance Studies, Univ. of London, 1990; Hon. Fellow, QMUL, 2010. MAE 1990. Hon. DLit London, 2007. Balzan Prize for Literature since 1500, 2009. Chevalier, l'Ordre Nat. du Mérite (France), 2001. *Publications:* Devotional Poetry in France, 1969; Ronsard the Poet, 1973; The Cornucopian Text: problems of writing in the French Renaissance, 1979; Recognitions: a study in poetics, 1988; (trans.) Madame de Lafayette, The Princesse de Clèves, 1992; (ed) George Eliot, Daniel Deronda, 1995; (ed) George Eliot, Silas Marner, 1996; Pré-histoires: textes troublés au seuil de la modernité, 1999; Pré-histoires II: langues étrangères et troubles économiques, 2001; (with S. Kay and M. Bowie) A Short History of French Literature, 2003; How to Read Montaigne, 2007; (ed) Thomas More's 'Utopia' in Early Modern Europe: paratexts and contexts, 2008; Mignon's Afterlives: crossing cultures from Goethe to the twenty-first century, 2011; Retrospectives: essays in literature, poetics and cultural history, 2009; Thinking with Literature, 2016; articles and essays in learned jls, collective vols, etc. *Recreations:* music, languages. *Address:* St John's College, Oxford OX1 3JP.

CAVE-BROWNE-CAVE, Sir John Robert Charles, 17th Bt *cr* 1641, of Stanford, Northamptonshire; *b* 22 June 1957; *o s* of Sir Robert Cave-Browne-Cave, 16th Bt, and Lois Shirley, *d* of John Chalmers Huggard; *S* father, 2011; *m* 2001, Jennifer Angelica Fong. *Address:* 7701 Barrymore, Delta, BC V4C 4C8, Canada.

CAVELL, His Honour John James; a Circuit Judge, 1994–2012; *b* 1 Oct. 1947; *s* of Eric Essery Cavell and Edith Emma Doreen (*née* Jose); *m* 1977, Philippa Julia Frances (*née* Kelly); one *s* one *d*. *Educ:* King Edward's Sch., Stourbridge; Churchill Coll., Cambridge (MA). Called to the Bar, Middle Temple, 1971. Practising Barrister on Midland and Oxford Circuit, 1971–94; a Recorder, 1991–94. *Recreations:* playing the piano, music generally, walking, bridge, gardening. *Address:* c/o Midland Circuit Secretariat Judicial Team, 6th Floor, Temple Court, 33 Bull Street, Birmingham B4 6DW.

CAVELL, Rt Rev. John Kingsmill; Assistant Bishop, Diocese of Salisbury, 1988–2010; Hon. Canon, Salisbury Cathedral, 1988–2010, now Emeritus; *b* 4 Nov. 1916; *o s* of late William H. G. Cavell and Edith May (*née* Warner), Deal, Kent; *m* 1942, Mary Grossett (*née* Penman) (*d* 1988), Devizes, Wilts; one *d*. *Educ:* Sir Roger Manwood's Sch., Sandwich; Queens' Coll., Cambridge (MA; Ryle Reading Prize); Wycliffe Hall, Oxford. Ordained May 1940; Curate: Christ Church, Folkestone, 1940; Addington Parish Church, Croydon, 1940–44; CMS Area Secretary, dio. Oxford and Peterborough, and CMS Training Officer, 1944–52; Vicar: Christ Church, Cheltenham, 1952–62; St Andrew's, Plymouth, 1962–72; Rural Dean of Plymouth, 1967–72; Prebendary of Exeter Cathedral, 1967–72; Bishop Suffragan of Southampton, 1972–84; Bishop to HM Prisons and Borstals, 1975–85. Hon. Canon, Winchester Cathedral, 1972–84. Proctor in Convocation; Member of General Synod (Mem., Bd for Social Responsibility, 1982–84); Surrogate. Chm., Home Cttee, CMS London; Chm., Sarum Dio. Readers' Bd, 1984–88. Chaplain, Greenbank and Freedom Fields Hosps, Plymouth; Member: Plymouth City Educn Cttee, 1967–72; City Youth Cttee; Plymouth Exec. Council NHS, 1968–72; Chairman: Hants Assoc. for the Deaf, 1972–84; Salisbury Diocesan Assoc. for the Deaf, 1988–91; Pres., Hants Genealogical Soc., 1979–84; Vice-Pres., Soc. of Genealogists. Life Fellow, Pilgrim Soc., Massachusetts, 1974. Patron, Southampton RNLI Bd, 1976–84. Governor: Cheltenham Colls of Educn; King Alfred's College of Educn, 1973–84; Croft House Sch., Shillingstone, 1986–88; Chairman: St Mary's Coll., Cheltenham, Building Cttee, 1957–62; Talbot Heath Sch., Bournemouth, 1975–84; Queensmount Sch., Bournemouth, 1980–84. *Recreations:* historical research, genealogy, philately. *Address:* 143 The Close, Salisbury, Wilts SP1 2EY. *T:* (01722) 334782.

CAVENDER, David John; QC 2010; *b* Erith, Kent, 17 Sept. 1964; *s* of Kenneth and Maureen Cavender; *m* 1995, Naomi Taylor; one *s* three *d*. *Educ:* Glyn Grammar Sch.; King's Coll. London (LLB 1st Cl. Hons; AKC). Served RM Commandos, 1982–86. Trainee Solicitor, Herbert Smith, 1991–93; called to the Bar, Middle Temple, 1993; in practice as barrister, specialising in commercial litigation, 1993–. *Recreations:* ski-ing, tennis, running, music festivals. *Address:* 1 Essex Court, Temple, EC4Y 9AR. *E:* dcavender@oeclaw.co.uk.

CAVENDISH, family name of **Duke of Devonshire** and **Barons Cavendish of Furness, Chesham,** and **Waterpark**.

CAVENDISH, Lord; James William Patrick Cavendish; *b* 12 Dec. 2010; *s* and *heir* of Earl of Burlington, *qv*.

CAVENDISH OF FURNESS, Baron *cr* 1990 (Life Peer), of Cartmel in the County of Cumbria; **Richard Hugh Cavendish;** Chairman, Holker Estate Group of Companies (interests including agricultural and urban property, leisure, mineral extraction, export, construction, national hunt racing and forestry), since 1971; *b* 2 Nov. 1941; *s* of late Richard Edward Osborne Cavendish and of Pamela J. Lloyd Thomas; *m* 1970, Grania Mary Caulfeild; one *s* two *d*. *Educ:* Eton. International banking, 1961–71. Dir, UK Nirex Ltd, 1993–99. A Lord in Waiting (Govt Whip), 1990–92. Member, House of Lords Select Committee: on Croydon Tramlink Bill, 1992–93; on EU Sub-Cttee B, 1999–2003; on EU, 2001–03. Mem., Hist. Buildings and Monuments Commn for England, 1992–98. Chm., Lancs & Cumbria Foundn for Med. Res., 1994–2000. Chm., Morecambe and Lonsdale Conservative Assoc., 1975–78. Chm. Governors, St Anne's Sch., Windermere, 1983–89. Mem., Cumbria CC, 1985–90. High Sheriff 1978, DL 1988, Cumbria. FRSA. *Recreations:* gardening, National Hunt racing, collecting drawings, reading, travel, fly fishing. *Address:* Holker Hall, Cark-in-Cartmel, Cumbria LA11 7PL. *T:* (015395) 58220. *Clubs:* Brooks's, Pratt's, White's, Beefsteak.

CAVENDISH, Camilla Hilary; Head, Policy Unit, No 10 Downing Street, since 2015; *b* London, 20 Aug. 1968; *d* of Richard Cavendish and Jean Mavis Hay; *m* 1999, Huw van Steenis; three *s*. *Educ:* Putney High Sch.; Brasenose Coll., Oxford (BA 1st Cl. Hons PPE 1989); John F. Kennedy Sch. of Govt, Harvard Univ. (Kennedy Meml Trust Schol.; MPA 1991). Business analyst, McKinsey & Co., 1991–93; Dir of Progs, London First, 1993–95; Chief Exec., S Bank Employers Gp, 1995–99; Advr to CEO, Pearson plc, 1999–2002; The Times: leader writer, 2002–13; op-ed columnist, 2004–13; Chief Leader Writer, 2010–13; Associate Ed., 2011–13; Associate Ed. and columnist, Sunday Times, 2013–15. Leader, Cavendish Rev. into Care Assts, 2013 (report pubd, 2013). Non-exec. Dir, Care Quality Commn, 2013–. *Recreations:* reading crime thrillers, playing piano, tennis, architecture. *Address:* 10 Downing Street, SW1A 2AA. *Club:* Soho House.

CAVENDISH, Lady Elizabeth (Georgiana Alice), CVO 1997 (LVO 1976); Extra Lady-in-Waiting to Princess Margaret, 1951–2002; Chairman, Cancer Research Campaign, 1981–96; Member, Press Complaints Commission, 1991–96; *b* 24 April 1926; *d* of 10th Duke of Devonshire, KG, and Lady Mary Cecil, GCVO, CBE (*d* 1988), *d* of 4th Marquess of Salisbury, KG, GCVO. *Educ:* private. Member: Advertising Standards Authority, 1981–91; Marre Cttee on Future of Legal Profession, 1986–89; Lay Mem., Disciplinary Cttee of Gen. Council of the Bar (formerly Senate of Inns of Court's Professional Conduct Cttee of Bar Council and Disciplinary Cttee Tribunal), 1983–. Chm., Bd of Visitors, Wandsworth Prison, 1970–73; Mem. Council, St Christopher's Hospice, Sydenham, 1991–. JP London, 1961; Chairman: N Westminster Magistrates' Court PSD, 1980–83; Inner London Juvenile Courts, 1983–86. *Address:* 19 Radnor Walk, SW3 4BP. *T:* (020) 7352 0774; Moor View, Edensor, Bakewell, Derbyshire DE45 1PH. *T:* (01246) 582204.

CAVENDISH, Mark Simon, MBE 2011; professional cyclist, Etixx (formerly Omega Pharma)-Quick-Step Team, since 2013; *b* Douglas, IOM, 21 May 1985; *s* of David Cavendish and Adele Towns; *m* 2013, Peta Todd; one *d*. *Educ:* Ballkermeen High Sch., IOM. Track cyclist: Gold Medal, Madison, Union Cycliste Internat. World Championships, 2005, 2008; Gold Medal, Men's Scratch, Commonwealth Games, Melbourne, 2006; road cyclist: T-Mobile Team, 2007; Team High Road, 2008; Team Columbia High Road, 2009; Team HTC-Columbia, 2010; HTC High Road, 2011 (winner, Union Cycliste Internat. Road Race World Championships); Team Sky, 2012; winner, British National Road Race Championship, 2013. Winner of 26 Tour de France stages (2008, 2009, 2010, 2011, 2012, 2013, 2015). BBC Sports Personality of Year, 2011. *Publications:* Boy Racer, 2009; At Speed, 2013. *Recreations:* cars, music. *Address:* c/o Simon Bayliff, 5th Floor, 33 Soho Square, W1D 3QU. *T:* (020) 7009 6000. *E:* sbayliff@wmgllc.com. *Club:* Velo Rocacorba (Girona, Spain).

CAVENDISH, Dr Michael William Patrick, (Will), CB 2014; Director General, Innovation, Growth and Technology, Department of Health, since 2014; *b* Windsor, 9 Dec. 1964; *s* of Patrick Cavendish and Pamela Cavendish; *m* 1994, Cavelle Creightney; one *s* one *d*. *Educ:* Magdalen Coll., Oxford (BA Hons PPE 1986; MSc Develt Econs 1987; PhD 1997). Jun. Res. Fellow, St John's Coll., Oxford, 1994–99; Lectr in Envmtl Econs, Imperial Coll., London, 1999–2000; Hd of Policy, Labour Party, 2000–01; Special Adviser: DFES, 2001–02; Prime Minister's Strategy Unit, 2003–05; Dir, Strategy, 2005–07, Dir, Health and Wellbeing, 2008–09, DoH; Dir Gen., Internat. Energy and Climate Change, DECC, 2009–11; Dir Gen., Red Tape Challenge, Efficiency and Reform Gp, then Implementation Gp, Cabinet Office, 2011–14. *Publications:* (jtly) Adjusting Privatization, 1992. *Address:* Department of Health, Richmond House, 79 Whitehall, SW1A 2NS.

CAVENDISH, Ruth; *see* Glucksmann, M. A.

CAVENDISH, Will; *see* Cavendish, M. W. P.

CAWDOR, 7th Earl *cr* 1827; **Colin Robert Vaughan Campbell;** Baron Cawdor, 1796; Viscount Emlyn, 1827; DL; Vice Lord-Lieutenant for the Area of Nairn, since 2013; *b* 30 June 1962; *s* of 6th Earl and of his 1st wife, Cathryn, *d* of Maj.-Gen. Sir Robert Hinde, KBE, CB, DSO; *S* father, 1993; *m* 1994, Lady Isabella Stanhope, *y d* of 11th Earl of Harrington; one *s* three *d*. *Educ:* Eton; St Peter's College, Oxford. Member, James Bridal Meml Soc., London. DL Nairn, 1996. *Heir: s* Viscount Emlyn, *qv*. *Address:* Carnoch, The Streens, Nairn IV12 5RQ.

CAWLEY, family name of **Baron Cawley**.

CAWLEY, 4th Baron *cr* 1918; **John Francis Cawley;** Bt 1906; *b* 28 Sept. 1946; *s* of 3rd Baron Cawley and Rosemary Joan (*née* Marsden); *S* father, 2001; *m* 1979, Regina Sarabia, *d* of late Marqués de Hazas, Madrid; three *s* one *d*. *Educ:* Eton. *Heir: s* Hon. William Robert Harold Cawley, *b* 2 July 1981. *Address:* Castle Ground, Ashton, Leominster, Herefordshire HR6 0DN. *T:* (01584) 711209.

CAWLEY, Prof. Peter, PhD; FRS 2010; CEng, FREng, FIMechE; Professor of Mechanical Engineering, since 1996, and Head of Department, since 2012, Imperial College London; Chairman, Permasense Ltd, since 2009; *b* Sheffield, 25 Nov. 1953; *s* of Bernard and Florence Cawley; partner, Wendy Quill. *Educ:* St Michael's Coll., Leeds; St Ignatius Coll., Enfield; Univ. of Bristol (BSc 1975; PhD 1979). CEng 1985; FIMechE 2001; FREng 2006. Vibration engr, Lucas CAV, 1979–81; Imperial College, London: Lectr, 1981–89; Sen. Lectr, 1989–92; Reader, 1992–96. Dir, Guided Ultrasonics Ltd, 1999–. *Publications:* contrib. papers to jls. *Recreations:* watching football (Sheffield Wednesday) and cricket, walking, theatre, cinema. *Address:* Department of Mecahnical Engineering, Imperial College London, SW7 2AZ. *T:* (020) 7594 7000. *E:* p.cawley@imperial.ac.uk.

CAWLEY, Stephen Ingleby, CVO 2007 (LVO 2003); FCA; Deputy Treasurer to the Queen, 2003–07; *b* 14 March 1947; *s* of Joe Cawley and Madge (*née* Ingleby); *m* 1971, Mariquet Scott; two *s*. *Educ:* Hull Grammar Sch.; Edinburgh Univ. (MA 1970). FCA 1973. Joined KPMG, 1970; Partner, 1984–94; Sen. Partner, Sussex, 1992–94; financial consultancy and Lectr, Univ. of Brighton, 1994–96; Dir of Finance, Property Services and Royal Travel, Royal Household, 1996–2003. *Recreations:* wine, opera, gardening, hill-walking, sports, travelling. *Address:* Robin Post, Firle Road, Seaford, E Sussex BN25 2HJ.

CAWSEY, Ian Arthur; *b* 14 April 1960; *s* of Arthur Henry Cawsey and Edith Morrison Cawsey; *m* 1987, Linda Mary, *d* of Henry and Joy Kirman; one *s* two *d*. *Educ:* Wintringham Sch. Computer operator, 1977–78; computer programmer, 1978–82; systems analyst, 1982–85; IT consultant, 1985–87; PA to Elliot Morley, MP, 1987–97. Member (Lab): Humberside CC, 1989–96; N Lincs Unitary Council, 1995–97 (Leader, 1995–97); Chm., Humberside Police Authy, 1993–97. MP (Lab) Brigg and Goole, 1997–2010; contested (Lab) same seat, 2010. PPS to Leader of House of Lords, 2001–02; an Asst Govt Whip, 2005–07. Chm., All Party Gp on Animal Welfare, 1998–2010.

CAWSON, (Peter) Mark; QC 2001; a Recorder, since 2000; a Deputy High Court Judge, Chancery Division, since 2004; *b* 4 June 1959; *s* of late Frederick Helenus Peter Cawson and Patricia Mary Cawson; *m* 1986, Julia Louise Hoe; two *s* one *d*. *Educ:* Wrekin Coll., Telford; Liverpool Univ. (LLB Hons). Called to the Bar, Lincoln's Inn, 1982, Bencher, 2010; Junior, Northern Circuit, 1987; Asst Recorder, 1998–2000. Chairman: Northern Circuit Commercial Bar Assoc., 2008–13; Northern Chancery Bar Assoc., 2013–. Mem. Council, Church Soc., 2013–. *Recreations:* church affairs, armchair politics, travel, watching sports. *Address:* Exchange Chambers, 201 Deansgate, Manchester M3 3NW. *T:* (0161) 833 2722, *Fax:* (0161) 833 2789. *E:* Cawsonqc@exchangechambers.co.uk. *Club:* Royal Birkdale Golf.

CAWTHRA, David Wilkinson, CBE 1997; FREng; FICE; Principal, Cawthra & Co., 1995–2005; *b* 5 March 1943; *s* of Jack and Dorothy Cawthra; *m* 1967, Maureen Williamson; one *s* one *d*. *Educ:* Heath Grammar Sch., Halifax; Univ. of Birmingham (BSc Hons). Mitchell Construction Co., 1963–73; Tarmac Construction, 1973–78; Balfour Beatty Ltd, 1979–91; Chief Executive: Balfour Beatty, 1988–91; Miller Group, 1992–94. Dir, BICC, 1988–91. Chm., Nat. Rail Contractors' Gp, 1999–2005. Vice-Pres., ICE, 1996–99. FREng (FEng 1990). *Recreations:* family history, second home in rural France, genealogical one name study of Cawthras, medieval history. *Address:* Willow House, Riverside Close, Oundle, Peterborough PE8 4DN.

CAYFORD, Philip John Berkeley; QC 2002; *b* 28 July 1952; *s* of late Berkeley Cayford and Christabel Cayford (*née* Robson); partner, Tanya; one *s*. *Educ:* Marlborough Coll.; University Coll., Cardiff (LLB). Called to the Bar, Middle Temple, 1975, Bencher, 2013; in practice as barrister, 1978–. Mem., Bar Standards Bd Complaints Cttee, 2005–11. Photographer and conservation film maker: producer, African Hunters, 1984; producer/director: The Rhino War, 1987; Ivory Wars, 1989; The Last Show on Earth, 1992; Vicuña, the Golden Fleece, 2009. Dir, Tusk USA, 2008–; Trustee, Tusk Trust, 2003–. FRGS; FZS. Consultant Ed., Family Affairs, Family Law Bar Assoc. *Publications:* (contrib. illus.) The Percy Bass Book of Traditional Decoration, 2005. *Recreations:* country sports, cricket, flying, classic car rallying. *Address:* (chambers) 29 Bedford Row, WC1R 4HE. *E:* pcayford@29br.co.uk. *Clubs:* Garrick, Royal Automobile, Chelsea Arts, Royal Air Force, MCC; Refreshers Cricket (Club Captain, 2009–), I Zingari.

CAYGILL, Hon. David Francis, CNZM 1997; Deputy Chairman of Commissioners, Environment Canterbury Regional Council; *b* 15 Nov. 1948; *s* of Bruce Allott Caygill and Gwyneth Mary Caygill; *m* 1974, Eileen Ellen Boyd; one *s* three *d*. *Educ:* St Albans Primary Sch.; Christchurch Boys' High Sch.; Univ. of Canterbury (BA, LLB). Pres., Univ. of Canterbury Students' Assoc., 1971. Barrister and Solicitor, 1974–78; Partner, Buddle Findlay, 1996–2004. Christchurch City Councillor, 1971–80; MP (Lab) St Albans, NZ, 1978–96; Minister of Trade and Industry, Minister of Nat. Develt, Associate Minister of Finance, 1984–87; Minister of Health, Dep. Minister of Finance, 1987–88; Minister of Finance, 1988–90; Dep. Leader of the Opposition, 1994–96. Dep. Chair, Commerce Commn, 2004–09; Chm., Electricity Commn, NZ, 2007–10. *Recreations:* collecting and listening to classical records, following American politics.

CAYLEY, Andrew Thomas, CMG 2014; QC 2012; Director of Service Prosecutions, since 2013; *b* E Preston, W Sussex, 24 March 1964; *s* of Granville Cayley and Elizabeth Mary Cayley (*née* Cook); *m* 1996, Andrea Maria Matačić; two *s* two *d*. *Educ:* University Coll. London (LLB 1985; LLM 1986); RMA, Sandhurst (Professionally Qualified Officers' Course 1991). Admitted as solicitor, 1989; commnd Army Legal Services (Adjt Gen.'s Corps), 1991; served in Belize, Germany, UK and The Hague; retd as Major, 1998; Prosecuting Counsel and Sen. Prosecuting Counsel, Internat. Criminal Tribunal for Former Yugoslavia, 1995–2005; Sen. Prosecuting Counsel, Internat. Criminal Court, The Hague, 2005–07; called to the Bar, Inner Temple, 2007, Bencher, 2015; Defence Counsel, Special Court for Sierra Leone and Internat. Criminal Tribunal for Former Yugoslavia, 2007–09; Internat. Co-Prosecutor, Extraordinary Chambers in the Courts of Cambodia (Khmer Rouge Tribunal), 2009–13. *Recreations:* reading history, running, fine wine. *Address:* Service Prosecuting Authority, RAF Northolt, West End Road, Ruislip HA4 6NG. *E:* acayley@tgchambers.com. *Clubs:* Reform, East India.

CAYLEY, Sir Digby (William David), 11th Bt *cr* 1661; MA; private tutor in Classics; Head of Classics, Pinewood School, Bourton, 2003–08; *b* 3 June 1944; *s* of Lieut-Comdr W. A. S. Cayley, RN (*d* 1964) (*ggs* of 7th Bt), and Natalie Maud Cayley, BA (*d* 1994); *S* kinsman, 1967; *m* 1st, 1969, Christine Mary Gaunt (marr. diss. 1987); two *d*; 2nd, 1993, Cathryn Mary Russell, MA Cantab; two *s*. *Educ:* Malvern Coll.; Downing Coll., Cambridge (MA). Assistant Classics Master: Portsmouth Grammar Sch., 1968–73; Stonyhurst Coll., 1973–81; dealer in antiques, 1981–89; Assistant Classics Master: Marlborough Coll., 1989–90 and 1994–97; Abingdon Sch., 1990–94; Master i/c Shooting, Marlborough Coll., 1994–2000. *Recreations:* bridge, gardening. *Heir: s* Thomas Theodore William Cayley, *b* 17 Feb. 1997. *Address:* Meadowside, Hyde Lane, Marlborough, Wilts SN8 1JN. *T:* (01672) 513188, 07766 010666. *E:* digbycayley@gmail.com.

CAYLEY, Michael Forde; Director, Personnel and Support Services, Department of Social Security, 1998–2000; *b* 26 Feb. 1950; *s* of late Forde Everard De Wend Cayley and Eileen Lilian Cayley; *m* 1987, Jennifer Athalie Jeffcoate (*née* Lytle). *Educ:* Brighton Coll.; St John's Coll., Oxford (MA English). Admin. Trainee, Inland Revenue, 1971–73; Private Sec. to Chm., Price Commn, 1973–75; Inland Revenue: Principal, 1975; Asst Sec., 1982; Under Sec., 1991; Dir, Financial Instns Div., 1994–98, Company Tax Div., 1995–98. *Publications: poems:* Moorings, 1971; (ed) Selected Poems of Richard Crashaw, 1972; The Spider's Touch, 1973; poems and articles on modern poets in various mags. *Recreations:* piano and organ-playing, art, genealogy. *Address:* 7 The Strand, Hayling Island, Hants PO11 9UB.

CAYTON, William Henry Rymer, (Harry), CBE 2014 (OBE 2001); Chief Executive, Professional Standards Authority for Health and Social Care (formerly Council for Healthcare Regulatory Excellence), since 2007; *b* 27 March 1950; *s* of late Dr Henry Rymer Cayton and Marion Cromie (*née* Young). *Educ:* Bristol Cathedral Sch.; New Univ. of Ulster (BA Hons 1971; Dist. Grad. Award, 2003); Univ. of Durham (Dip. Anth. 1973); Univ. of Newcastle upon Tyne (BPhil 1979). Teacher: King's Sch., Rochester, 1972; Dame Allan's Sch., Newcastle upon Tyne, 1973–76; Northern Counties Sch. for the Deaf, 1976–80; National Deaf Children's Society: Educn Officer, 1980–82; Dir, 1982–91; Exec. Dir, Alzheimer's Disease Soc., subseq. Chief Exec., Alzheimer's Soc., 1991–2003; Nat. Dir, Patients and the Public, DoH, 2003–07. Canadian Commonwealth Fellow, 1983. Chairman: Nat. Information Governance Bd for Health and Social Care, 2008–12; Patient and Public Expert Adv. Gp, Commn on Human Medicines, 2012–; Member: Sec. of State for Health's Adv. Gp on Youth Treatment Service, 1991–96; Central R&D Cttee, NHS, 1999–; NHS Modernisation Bd, 2000–02; Human Genetics Commn Sub-Cttee, 2000–03; Vice Chm., Consumers in NHS Research, 1996–2003. Mem., Press Recognition Regulation Panel, 2014. Chm., Voluntary Council for Handicapped Children, 1986–91. Trustee: Hearing Res. Trust, 1985–2005; Nat. Children's Bureau, 1987–91; Age Concern England, 1992–94; Comic Relief, 2005–. Mem. Bd, Alzheimer Europe, 1998–2003. Pres. and Hon. Life Mem., European Fedn of Deaf Children's Assocs, 1990–91. Frequent broadcasts. FFPH (through distinction) 2007. Alzheimer Europe Award, 2003; Life-Time Achievement Award, RCPsych, 2007. *Publications:* Dementia: Alzheimer's and other dementias, 2002; numerous essays and articles. *Recreations:* art, music, food. *Address:* 24 Barlby Gardens, North Kensington, W10 5LW. *T:* (office) (020) 7389 8030. *Club:* Athenæum.

CAYZER, family name of **Baron Rotherwick**.

CAZALET, Hon. Lady; Camilla Jane; *b* 12 July 1937; *d* of 6th Viscount Gage, KCVO, and Hon. Alexandra Imogen Clare Grenfell (*d* 1969); *m* 1965, Sir Edward Stephen Cazalet, *qv*; two *s* one *d*. *Educ:* Benenden Sch. Dir, Lumley Cazalet, 1967–2001. Trustee, Glyndebourne Arts Trust, 1978–2004; Member: Royal Nat. Theatre Bd, 1991–97; Exec. Cttee, Friends of Covent Garden, 1994–2000; Royal Nat. Theatre Develt Council, 1996–2008; Gov., Royal Ballet, 2000–08. *Recreations:* theatre, music, dance. *Address:* Shaw Farm, Plumpton Green, Lewes, Sussex BN7 3DG. *T:* (01273) 890207.

CAZALET, Sir Edward (Stephen), Kt 1988; DL; a Judge of the High Court of Justice, Family Division, 1988–2000; *b* 26 April 1936; *s* of late Peter Victor Ferdinand Cazalet and Leonora Cazalet (*née* Rowley, then Wodehouse); *m* 1965, Camilla Jane (*née* Gage) (*see* Hon. Lady Cazalet); two *s* one *d*. *Educ:* Eton Coll. (Fellow, 1989–2004); Christ Church, Oxford (MA Jurisprudence). Called to the Bar, Inner Temple, 1960, Bencher, 1985. QC 1980; a Recorder, 1985–88; Family Division Liaison Judge for SE Circuit, 1990–96. Chairman: Horserace Betting Levy Appeal Tribunal, 1977–88; Sussex Assoc. for Rehabilitation of Offenders, 1991–98; CAB, Royal Courts of Justice, 1992–98; British Agencies for Adoption and Fostering, 2000–05; Jockey Club Appeal Bd, 2001–05; Injured Jockeys' Fund, 2002–06 (Trustee, 1987–2006). Chm. Trustees, Charles Douglas-Home Award, 1986–96; Trustee, Winston Churchill Meml Fund, 2004–11. DL E Sussex, 1989. *Recreations:* riding, ball games, chess. *Address:* Shaw Farm, Plumpton Green, Lewes, East Sussex BN7 3DG. *Club:* Garrick.

CAZALET, Sir Peter (Grenville), Kt 1989; Chairman: Seascope Shipping Holdings plc, 2000–01 (Director, 1997–2000); Braemar Seascope Group plc, 2001–02; *b* 26 Feb. 1929; *e s* of Vice-Adm. Sir Peter (Grenville Lyon) Cazalet, KBE, CB, DSO, DSC, and Lady (Elise) Cazalet (*née* Winterbotham); *m* 1957, Jane Jennifer, *yr d* of Charles and Nancy Rew, Guernsey, CI; three *s*. *Educ:* Uppingham Sch., Uppingham, Rutland (schol.); Magdalene Coll., Cambridge (Schol.; MA Hons). General Manager, BP Tanker Co. Ltd, 1968; Regional Co-ordinator, Australasia and Far East, 1970; Pres., BP North America Inc., 1972–75; Director: Standard Oil Co. of Ohio, 1973–75; BP Trading Ltd, 1975–81; Peninsular & Oriental Steam Navigation Co., 1980–99; Man. Dir, 1981–89, Dep. Chm., 1986–89, BP; Chm., BP Oil International, 1981–89. Chm., APV plc, 1989–96; Dep. Chm., GKN, 1989–96; Chm., Hakluyt and Co., 1998–99 (Mem., Hakluyt Foundn, 1997–2000). Director: De La Rue Co., 1983–95; Energy Capital Investment Co. plc, 1994–98; General Maritime Corp., US, 2000–02. Chm., Armed Forces Pay Review Body, 1989–93; Mem., Top Salaries Review Body, 1989–94. Pres., China Britain Trade Gp, 1996–98 (Vice-Pres., 1993–96); a Vice-Pres., ME Assoc., 1982–2011; Hon. Sec., King George's Fund for Sailors, 1989–2000; Gov., Wellcome Trust Ltd, 1992–96 (Trustee, Wellcome Trust, 1989–92); Mem. Council, RIIA, 1995–98; Trustee, Uppingham Sch., 1976–95; Mem., Gen. Cttee, Lloyd's Register of Shipping, 1981–99 (Mem. Bd, 1981–86). CCMI (CBIM 1982). Liveryman: Tallow Chandlers' Co. (Master, 1991–92); Shipwrights' Co. *Recreations:* theatre, fishing. *Address:* c/o 1 St James's Square, SW1Y 4PD. *Club:* Brooks's.

CEARNS, Kathryn; independent consultant, since 2014; *b* Harrogate, Yorks, 30 April 1964; *d* of Michael Verity and Vicki Verity (later Clifford); *m* 1989, Simon Justin Cearns. *Educ:* Leeds Girls' High Sch.; Goldsmiths' Coll., London (BA Hons Eng. Lit. 1995). ACA 1990; FCA 2001; FCCA 2002. Auditor, Ernst and Young, 1987–91; Tech. Author, BPP plc, 1991–98; Project Dir, Accounting Standards Bd, 1998–2000; Consultant Accountant, Herbert Smith Freehills (formerly Herbert Smith) LLP, 2000–14. Chairman: Financial Reporting Cttee, ICAEW, 2008–; Financial Reporting Adv. Bd to HM Treasury, 2010–. *Recreations:* bridge, theatre, opera, ballet, literature, needlework.

CECIL; *see* Gascoyne-Cecil, family name of Marquess of Salisbury.

CECIL, family name of **Marquess of Exeter,** and **Barons Amherst of Hackney** and **Rockley**.

CECIL, Charles Anthony, MBE 2011; Founder and Chief Executive, Revolution Software, since 1990; *b* London, 11 Aug. 1962; *s* of Charles David Cecil and Veronica Mary Cecil (*née* Lawley); *m* 1991, Noirin Carmody; one *s* one *d*. *Educ:* Bedales Sch.; Univ. of Manchester

(BSc/BEng Hons Engrg, Manuf. and Mgt 1985). Dir, Artic Computing, 1981–86; Founder and Man. Dir, Paragon Programming, 1986–87; Develt Dir, US Gold, 1987–88, Activision (UK), 1988–90; Director/Designer, computer game projects including: Broken Sword adventure series, 1996–; Da Vinci Code, Imagine Entertainment/Take 2, 2006; Doctor Who Adventure Games, 2006 (BAFTA Wales Award). Director: Screen Yorkshire, 2004–; BFI, 2013–. Member: BAFTA, 2000; Co. of Merchant Adventurers, York, 2011. *Recreations:* competing in national and international rowing events, travel, history (popular, medieval and biblical). *E:* charlesc@revolution.co.uk.

CECIL, Clementine; Director: SAVE Britain's Heritage, since 2012; SAVE Europe's Heritage, since 2012; *b* London, 22 Oct. 1975; *d* of Hugh and Mirabel Cecil. *Educ:* Cheltenham Ladies' Coll.; Glasgow Univ. (MA Double 1st Jt Hons Russian and Scottish Lit.); Birmingham Univ. (MA Historic Envmt Conservation). Moscow corresp., The Times, 2001–04; freelance journalist, 2001–: World of Interiors, Cornerstone mag. (SPAB), Blueprint, TLS. Moscow Architecture Preservation Society: Co-Founder, 2004; Trustee, 2005–; Chm., 2012–. Member: Internat. Melnikov Hse Cttee, 2007–11; Tbilisi Heritage Gp, 2011–. *Publications:* editor and compiler: Moscow Heritage at Crisis Point (Russian and English), 2007, 2nd edn 2009; Samara: endangered city on the Volga (Russian and English), 2009; St Petersburg Heritage at Risk (Russian and English), 2012. *Recreations:* swimming, drawing, reggae music. *Address:* 6 Basterfield House, Golden Lane Estate, Golden Lane, EC1Y 0TN. *E:* clemcecil@gmail.com.

CECIL, Desmond Hugh, CMG 1995; international political and funding adviser, charity trustee; Expert Chair, AREVA UK, since 2012 (UK Representative, AREVA, then Senior Vice-President, AREVA UK, 2006–12); *b* 19 Oct. 1941; *s* of Dr Rupert Cecil, DFC, and Rosemary Cecil (*née* Luker); *m* 1964, Ruth Elizabeth Sachs; three *s* one *d*. *Educ:* Headington Co. Primary Sch.; Magdalen Coll. Sch., Oxford; Queen's Coll., Oxford (MA); studied violin/viola and oboe with Max Rostal, Berne and Joy Boughton, London. Violinist and oboist in Switzerland; Leader, Neuchâtel Chamber Orchestra, 1965–70; joined HM Diplomatic Service, 1970; Second Sec., FCO, 1970–73; First Secretary: Bonn, 1973–74; FCO, 1974–76; also Press Officer, Mission to UN, Geneva, 1976–80; FCO, 1980–85; Counsellor and Chargé d'Affaires, Vienna, 1985–89; FCO, 1989–92; on secondment with Board of P&O European Ferries, 1992; Under Sec., FCO, 1992–95. Senior Advisor: British Telecom, 1996–97; BNFL, 1996–2006; GEC/Marconi Communications, subseq. Marconi, 1998–2001. Chm., Arena Pal Ltd, 2002–03. Antiquarian book dealer, 1997–. Council Mem., Britain Russia Centre, 1998–2000; Member Board: Germany Project, Panel 2000, 1999–2000; Internat. Mendelssohn Foundn, Leipzig, 2001– (Chm., UK Friends, 2005–). Council Mem., Royal Philharmonic Soc., 1995–2005 (Chm., Sponsorship Cttee, 1998–2005; Hon. Co-Treas., 1999–2005); Dir and Trustee, Jupiter Orch., 1996–2002; Trustee, later Dir, LPO, 2005–; Adviser: Russian Arts Help Charity, Moscow, 2000–05; Nuclear Management Partners Ltd Bd, 2008, 2014–; Mem. Bd, Nuclear Industry Assoc., 2010–; Mem. Adv. Bd, OMFIF, 2013–; Internat. Rep., Gstaad Menuhin Fest. and Acad., 2001–; Mem., Adv. Council, Park Lane Gp, 2015–. Trustee: Voices for Hospices, 2000–04; Norbert Brainin Foundn, Asolo, 2003–09. Mem., Develt Cttee (formerly Appeal Cttee), Queen's Coll., Oxford, 2005–. Member: Mensa, 1968–2005; Sherlock Holmes Soc. of London, 1970–; Kingston Chamber Music Soc., 1990–; British-German Assoc., 2001–05. Liveryman, Musicians' Co., 2015–. Distinguished Friend of Oxford Univ. Award, 2012. *Recreations:* playing music and cricket, downhill ski-ing, chess, antiquarian travel books. *Address:* 38 Palace Road, East Molesey, Surrey KT8 9DL. *T:* (020) 8783 1998. *Clubs:* Athenæum (Chm., Wine Cttee, 1999–2001, Gen. Cttee, 2003–06; Trustee, 2008–), MCC (Eur. Cricket Advr, 1998–2002); Claygate Cricket (Life Vice Pres.).

CECIL, Rear-Adm. Sir (Oswald) Nigel (Amherst), KBE 1979; CB 1978; *b* 11 Nov. 1925; *s* of Comdr the Hon. Henry M. A. Cecil, OBE, RN, and the Hon. Mrs Henry Cecil; *m* 1961, Annette (CStJ 1980), *d* of Maj. Robert Barclay, TD, Bury Hill, near Dorking, Surrey; one *s*. *Educ:* Ludgrove; Royal Naval Coll., Dartmouth. Joined Navy, 1939; served World War II, Russian convoys, Western approaches and English Channel, 1943–45; HMS Swiftsure, British Pacific Fleet, 1945–46; in comd HM MTB 521, 1947–48; Flag Lieut to Admiral, BJSM, Washington, 1950–52; Comdr, 1959; Chief Staff Officer, London Div. RNR, 1959–61; in command: HMS Corunna, 1961–63; HMS Royal Arthur, 1963–66; Captain 1966; Central Staff, MoD, 1966–69; Captain (D) Dartmouth Trng Sqdn and in comd HMS Tenby and HMS Scarborough, 1969–71; Senior British Naval Officer, S Africa, Naval Attaché, Cape Town, and in command HMS Afrikander, as Cdre, 1971–73; Dir, Naval Operational Requirements, 1973–75; Naval ADC to the Queen, 1975; Rear-Adm., 1975; NATO Comdr SE Mediterranean, 1975–77; Comdr British Forces Malta, and Flag Officer Malta, 1975–79; Lieut Gov., Isle of Man, and Pres. of Tynwald, 1980–85. Pres., St John Council, IoM, 1980–85, IoW, 1996–2001; County Pres., IoW, St John Ambulance, 1991–96; Vice Pres., RUKBA (IndependentAge), 1991–2010; Vice Patron, Naval Officers Assoc. of Southern Africa, 1973–. FCMI (FBIM 1980). KStJ 1980 (OStJ 1971). *Address:* The Old Rectory, Shorwell, Isle of Wight PO30 3JL. *Clubs:* Lansdowne, MCC.

CEENEY, Natalie Anna, CBE 2010; Chief Executive, HM Courts and Tribunals Service, since 2015; *b* 22 Aug. 1971; *d* of Anthony and Jacky Ceeney; *m* 2007, Dr Simon David John Chaplin, *qv*. *Educ:* Newnham Coll., Cambridge (MA 1st Cl. Maths/Social and Pol Sci.). NHS Manager: Northwick Park Hosp., 1992–94; Herts Health Agency, 1994–96; Gt Ormond St Hosp., 1996–98; Strategy Consultant, McKinsey, 1998–2001; Dir, Ops and Services, British Liby, 2001–05; Chief Exec., Nat. Archives, Keeper of the Public Records and Historical MSS Comr, 2005–10; Chief Exec. and Chief Ombudsman, Financial Ombudsman Service, 2010–13; Head of Customer Standards, HSBC UK, 2014–15. *Recreations:* cycling, literature, theatre, Rugby union. *Address:* HM Courts and Tribunals Service, 102 Petty France, SW1H 9AJ.

CEFAI, Dame Sally (Anne); *see* Coates, Dame S. A.

CELLAN-JONES, Diane; *see* Coyle, D.

CELLAN-JONES, (Nicholas) Rory; Technology Correspondent, BBC News, since 2007; *b* London, 17 Jan. 1958; *s* of Alan James Gwynne Cellan-Jones and Sylvia Margaret Rich; *m* 1990, Dr Diane Coyle, *qv*; two *s*. *Educ:* Dulwich Coll.; Jesus Coll., Cambridge (BA Mod. and Medieval Langs 1981). BBC: researcher, BBC Leeds, 1981–83; producer, BBC TV News, 1983–86; reporter: Wales Today, 1986–88; BBC TV News, 1988–98; Business Correspondent, BBC TV, 1998–2007. *Publications:* Dot.Bomb, 2001. *Address:* c/o BBC News Centre, Broadcasting House, Portland Place, W1A 1AA.

CERF, Vinton Gray, PhD; Vice-President and Chief Internet Evangelist, Google Inc., since 2005; *b* New Haven, Conn, 23 June 1943; *s* of Vinton Thruston Cerf and Muriel Cerf (*née* Gray); *m* 1966, Sigrid L. Thorstenberg; two *s*. *Educ:* Van Nuys High Sch., Calif; Stanford Univ. (BS 1965); UCLA (MS 1970; PhD 1972). Systems Engr, IBM Corp., 1965–67; Principal Programmer, Computer Sci. Dept, UCLA, 1967–72; Asst Prof. of Elec. Engrg and Computer Sci., Stanford Univ., 1972–76; Prog. Manager, 1976–81, Principal Scientist, 1981–82, Defense Advanced Res. Projects Agency; Vice-Pres. of Engrg, MCI Digital Inf. Services Co., 1982–86; Vice-Pres., Corp. for Nat. Res. Initiatives, 1986–94; Sen. Vice-Pres. for Data Architecture, MCI Telecoms Corp., 1994–95; Senior Vice-President: for Internet Architecture and Engrg, MCI Communications Corp., 1996–98; for Internet Architecture and Technol. Strategy, MCI WorldCom Corp., subseq. MCI, 1998–2005. Mem. Bd, Cttee on Sci. and Engrg Indicators, Nat. Sci. Bd, 2013–. Dist. Vis. Scientist, Jet Propulsion Lab., CIT, 1998–. Internet Society: Founder Mem., 1992; Founder Pres., 1992–95; Chm., 1998–99; Trustee, 1992–2002; Chm., Internet Societal Task Force, 1999–2000. FAAAS, 1990. (Jtly) Queen Elizabeth Prize for Engrg, Royal Acad. of Engrg, 2013. Presidential Medal of Freedom (USA), 2005.

CESARANI, Prof. David, OBE 2006; DPhil; Research Professor of History, Royal Holloway, University of London, since 2004; *b* 13 Nov. 1956; *s* of late Henry Cesarani and Sylvia Cesarani (*née* Packman); *m* 1991, Dawn Waterman; one *s* one *d*. *Educ:* Latymer Upper Sch.; Queens' Coll., Cambridge (BA Hist.); Columbia Univ., NY (MA Jewish Hist.); St Antony's Coll., Oxford (DPhil 1986). Montague Burton Fellow in Modern Jewish Hist., Univ. of Leeds, 1983–86; part-time Lectr, Oxford Centre for Postgrad. Hebrew Studies, 1986–87; Barnett Shine Sen. Res. Fellow and Lectr in Politics, Dept of Political Studies, QMC, 1986–89; Dir of Studies and Educnl Activities, 1989–92, Dir, 1992–95 and 1996–2000, Inst. of Contemporary Hist. and Wiener Liby, London; Adjunct Lectr, Dept of Hebrew and Jewish Studies, UCL, 1990–95; Alliance Family Prof. of Modern Jewish Studies, Dept of Religions and Theol., Univ. of Manchester, 1995–96; Parkes-Wiener Prof. of Twentieth Century European Jewish Hist. and Culture, 1996–2000, Dir, AHRB Parkes Centre for the Study of Jewish/non-Jewish Relations and Prof. of Modern Jewish Hist., 2000–04, Southampton Univ. Trustee, Holocaust Meml Day, 2006–12. *Publications:* (ed) The Making of Modern Anglo-Jewry, 1990; Justice Delayed: how Britain became a refuge for Nazi war criminals, 1992; (ed with T. Kushner) The Internment of Aliens in Twentieth Century Britain, 1993; (ed) The Final Solution: origins and implementation, 1994; The Jewish Chronicle and Anglo-Jewry 1841–1991, 1994; (ed with M. Fulbrook) Citizenship, Nationality and Migration in Europe, 1996; (ed) Genocide and Rescue: the Holocaust in Hungary 1944, 1997; (ed jtly) Belsen in History and Memory, 1997; Arthur Koestler: the homeless mind, 1998; (ed with Paul Levine) Bystanders to the Holocaust: a re-evaluation, 2002; (ed) Port Jews: Jewish communities in cosmopolitan maritime trading centres 1650–1950, 2002; Eichmann: his life and crimes, 2004; (ed) After Eichmann: collective memory and the Holocaust since 1961, 2005; (ed with G. Romain) Jews and Port Cities 1590–1990: commerce, community and cosmopolitanism, 2006; (ed jtly) Place and Displacement in Jewish History, 2009; Major Farran's Hat: murder, scandal and Britain's war against Jewish terrorism 1945–1948, 2009; (with E. Sundquist) After the Holocaust: challenging the myth of silence, 2012. *Recreations:* running, cycling, films, friends and family. *Address:* Department of History, Royal Holloway, University of London, Egham, Surrey TW20 0EX.

CESCAU, Patrick Jean-Pierre; Chevalier, Légion d'Honneur, 2005; Group Chief Executive Officer, Unilever, 2005–08; Chairman, InterContinental Hotels Group, since 2013; *b* Paris, 27 Sept. 1948; *s* of Pierre and Louise Cescau; *m* 1974, Ursula Kadansky; one *s* one *d*. *Educ:* ESSEC Business Sch., Paris (business degree); INSEAD (MBA dist.). Unilever, 1973–2008: consultant, 1973–76, sen. consultant, 1976–77, Unilever France; Commercial Manager, Astra Calve, France, 1977–81; Chief Accountant, Union Deutsche Lebensmittelwerke GmbH, 1981; Germany, 1984; Commercial Mem., Unilever Edible Fats and Dairy Netherlands, 1984; Financial Dir, PT Unilever Indonesia, 1986–89; Nat. Manager, Unilever Portugal, 1989–91; Chm., PT Unilever Indonesia, 1991–95; Pres. and CEO, Van den Bergh Foods, USA, 1995–97; Mem. Bd Dirs, Unilever US, Inc., 1995–96; Pres., Lipton USA, 1997–98; Gp Financial Controller and Dep. Chief Financial Officer, 1998–99; Financial Dir, 1999–2000; Foods Dir, 2001–04; Chm., Unilever plc and Dep. Chm., Unilever NV, 2004–05. Non-executive Director: Pearson plc, 2002–12 (Sen. Ind. Dir, 2010–12); Tesco plc, 2009–15 (Sen. Ind. Dir, 2010–15); Internat. Airlines Gp, 2010–. Conseiller du Commerce Extérieur de la France, Netherlands, 2002–. Chm., Nat. Assoc. of Margarine Manufacturers, USA, 1996–98; Mem. Bd and Exec. Cttee, Tea Council, USA, 1997–98. Trustee, Leverhulme Trust, 2005–09. Chm., St Jude Children Charity, 2009–13. *Recreations:* arts, photography, reading, theatre. *Address:* Intercontinental Hotels Group, Broadwater Park, Denham, Bucks UB9 5HR.

CHADLINGTON, Baron *cr* 1996 (Life Peer), of Dean in the county of Oxfordshire; **Peter Selwyn Gummer;** Chief Executive, 2000–15, Group Senior Advisor, since 2015 Huntsworth plc; *b* 24 Aug. 1942; *s* of late Rev. Canon Selwyn Gummer and Sybille (*née* Mason); *m* 1982, Lucy Rachel, *er d* of A. Ponsonby Dudley-Hill; one *s* three *d*. *Educ:* King's Sch., Rochester, Kent; Selwyn Coll., Cambridge (BA, MA). Portsmouth and Sunderland Newspaper Gp, 1964–65; Viyella International, 1965–66; Hodgkinson & Partners, 1966–67; Industrial & Commercial Finance Corp., 1967–74; Founder, 1974–94, Chm., 1994–98, Shandwick Internat. plc; Internat. Public Relations, 1998–2000. Non-executive Director: CIA Group PLC, 1990–94; Halifax plc (formerly Halifax Building Soc.), 1994–2001 (non-exec. Mem., London Bd, 1990–94); Britax Childcare Hldgs Ltd, 2005–11; Director: Black Box Music Ltd, 1999–2001; Oxford Resources, 1999–2002; Chairman: hotcourses.com, 2000–04; guideforlife.com, 2000–02. Marketing Gp of GB, 1993–95. Chairman: Royal Opera House, Covent Gdn, 1996–97; LAPADA, 2011–. Member: NHS Policy Bd, 1991–95; Arts Council of England (formerly of GB), 1991–96 (Chm., Nat. Lottery Adv. Bd for Arts and Film, 1994–96). Mem., EU Select Sub-Cttee B (Energy, Industry and Transport), H of L, 2000–03. Chm., Action on Addiction, 2000–07; Mem. Bd, Mending Broken Hearts Appeal, British Heart Foundn, 2010–. Chm., Understanding Industry Trust, 1991–96; Trustee, Atlantic Partnership, 1999–; Mem. Bd of Trustees, Amer. Univ., 1999–2001; Mem. Council, Cheltenham Ladies' Coll., 1998–2003. Gov., Ditchley Foundn, 2008–. FRSA. Hon. Fellow, Bournemouth Univ., 1999–. *Publications:* various articles and booklets on public relations and marketing. *Recreations:* opera, Rugby, cricket. *Clubs:* Garrick, White's, Carlton, MCC, Walbrook (Dir, 1999–2004).

See also Baron Deben, Baron Hindlip.

CHADWICK, Charles McKenzie, CBE 1992 (OBE 1984); British Council Director (formerly Representative), Poland, 1989–92; *b* 31 July 1932; *s* of late Trevor McKenzie Chadwick and Marjory Baron; *m* 1st, 1965, Evelyn Ingeborg Ihlenfeldt (marr. diss.); one *s*; 2nd, 1999, Mary Christina Beatrice Teale; one *s*. *Educ:* Charterhouse School; Trinity Coll., Toronto (BA). Army service, 1950–52; HMOCS Provincial Administration, Northern Rhodesia, 1958–64; Lectr, 1964–66, and Head, Administrative Training, 1966–67, Staff Trng Coll., Lusaka; British Council Officer, 1967–92; service in Kenya, Nigeria, Brazil, London; British Election Supervisor, Zimbabwe, 1980; British Council Rep., Canada, 1981–88. Member: Commonwealth Observer Gp, Ghanaian Presidential elections, 1992, Pakistan National elections, 1993, Cameroon Parly elections, 1997; EU observer team, S African election, 1994; FCO Observer, Uganda elections, 1996; OSCE Supervisor, Bosnia elections, 1996. Gov., Hampstead Sch., 1992–2000. *Publications:* It's All Right Now, 2005; A Chance Acquaintance, 2009; Brief An Sally, 2010; Die Frau, die zu viel fühlte, 2013; Josefa, 2014. *Address:* c/o United Agents Ltd, 12–26 Lexington Street, W1F 0LE.

CHADWICK, Derek James, DPhil; CChem, FRSC; Director, Novartis (formerly Ciba) Foundation, 1988–2008; *b* 9 Feb. 1948; *s* of Dennis Edmund and Ida Chadwick; *m* 1980, Susan Reid (*d* 2002); two *s*. *Educ:* St Joseph's Coll., Blackpool; Keble Coll., Oxford (BA, BSc, MA, DPhil). FRSC 1982; MACS 1989. ICI Fellow, Cambridge Univ., 1972–73; Prize Fellow, Magdalen Coll., Oxford, 1973–77; Lectr and Sen. Lectr, Liverpool Univ., 1977–88. Vis. Prof., Univ. of Trondheim, Norway, 1995–2012. Member: Sci. Cttee, Louis Jeantet Foundn, Geneva, 1989–98; Hague Club of European Foundn Dirs, 1989–2008 (Sec., 1993–97); Sci. Adv. Cttee, 1990–96, Exec. Council, 1991–2000 (Vice-Chm., 1994–2000), AMRC; CCLRC, 2002–07. Mem., Soc. of Apothecaries, 1990. Hon. FRCP 2009. *Publications:* chapters in: Aromatic and Heteroaromatic Chemistry, 1979; Comprehensive Heterocyclic Chemistry, 1984; The Research and Academic Users' Guide to the IBM PC, 1988; Pyrroles, Pt 1, 1990; ed many vols in Novartis (formerly Ciba) Foundn symposium series; many papers in chemistry jls, e.g. Jl Chem. Soc., Tetrahedron, Tet. Letters, etc. *Recreations:* music, gardening. *Address:* 4 Bromley Avenue, Bromley, Kent BR1 4BQ. *T:* (020) 8460 3332. *E:* derekchadwick@hotmail.com.

CHADWICK, Fiona Jane; Ballet Administrator, Junior Royal Ballet School, 1996–99; *b* 13 May 1960; *d* of late William Chadwick and of Anne Chadwick; *m* 1st, 1990, Anthony Peter Dowson (marr. diss.); one *d*; 2nd, 1996, Robert Cave; one *s* one *d*. *Educ:* Royal Ballet Sch. Joined Royal Ballet Co., 1978; Soloist, 1981–84; Principal, 1984–96. Leading rôles included: Swan Lake, Romeo and Juliet, Sleeping Beauty, Cinderella, La Fille Mal Gardée, Giselle, Prince of the Pagodas, La Bayadère, Pursuit, Firebird. Patron, London Children's Ballet, 2001–. DLitt Lancaster, 2009.

CHADWICK, Rear Adm. John, CB 2001; Director, Greenwich Hospital, 2003–07; *b* 26 March 1946; *s* of Alec and Elsie Chadwick; *m* 1970, Jacqueline Cosh; two *s*. *Educ:* Cheadle Hulme Sch. CEng 1973; FIET (FIEE 1996). BRNC Dartmouth, 1966; RNC Greenwich (electronic engrg), 1967–69; submarine service, 1970; served in HM Submarines Otter, Ocelot, Spartan, 1970–82; Sqdn Weapon Engr, 3rd Submarine Sqdn, 1984–86; Submarine Weapon System Manager, MoD(PE), 1987–89; Captain 1989; Asst Dir, Operational Requirements, MoD, 1990–93; Dir, Underwater Weapons, MoD(PE), 1993–96; i/c HMS Collingwood, 1996–98; Chief Naval Engr Officer, 1999–2001; FO Trng and Recruiting, 1998–2001. Pres., RN Rugby League, 1997–2001. Chm., RN & RM Charity, 2008–12. *Recreations:* walking, gardening, house renovation.

CHADWICK, Rt Hon. Sir John (Murray), Kt 1991; ED; PC 1997; a Lord Justice of Appeal, 1997–2007; *b* 20 Jan. 1941; *s* of Hector George Chadwick and Margaret Corry Chadwick (*née* Laing); *m* 1975, Diana Mary Blunt; two *d*. *Educ:* Rugby School; Magdalene Coll., Cambridge (MA). Called to the Bar, Inner Temple, 1966 (Bencher, 1986; Treasurer, 2004). Standing Counsel to DTI, 1974–80; QC 1980; Judge of Courts of Appeal of Jersey and Guernsey, 1986–93; a Recorder, 1989–91; Judge of the High Court, Chancery Div., 1991–97; Chancery Supervising Judge, Birmingham, Bristol and Cardiff, 1995–97. Pres., Court of Appeal of Cayman Is, 2008–15. A Lieut Bailiff of Guernsey, 2008–; a Judge, Dubai Internat. Financial Centre Court, 2008–15 (Dep. Chief Justice, 2013–15); Mem., Special Tribunal Related to Dubai World, 2009–. Vice-Pres., Corp. of the Sons of the Clergy, 2004–15. Dir, Utd Services Trust, 2005–14. Visitor, Green Templeton Coll., Oxford, 2010–. *Address:* One Essex Court, Temple, EC4Y 9AR. *Clubs:* Athenæum, Beefsteak; Royal Yacht Squadron (Cowes).

CHADWICK, Sir Joshua Kenneth B.; *see* Burton-Chadwick.

CHADWICK, Peter, PhD, ScD; FRS 1977; Professor of Mathematics, University of East Anglia, 1965–91, now Emeritus; *b* 23 March 1931; *s* of late Jack Chadwick and Marjorie Chadwick (*née* Castle); *m* 1956, Sheila Gladys Salter (*d* 2004), *d* of late Clarence F. and Gladys I. Salter; two *d*. *Educ:* Huddersfield Coll.; Univ. of Manchester (BSc 1952); Pembroke Coll., Cambridge (PhD 1957, ScD 1973). Scientific Officer, then Sen. Scientific Officer, Atomic Weapons Res. Estabt, Aldermaston, 1955–59; Lectr, then Sen. Lectr, in Applied Maths, Univ. of Sheffield, 1959–65; Dean, Sch. of Maths and Physics, 1979–82, Leverhulme Emeritus Fellow, 1991–93, UEA. Vis. Prof., Univ. of Queensland, 1972. Hon. Mem., British Soc. of Rheology, 1991. Hon. DSc Glasgow, 1991. *Publications:* Continuum Mechanics: concise theory and problems, 1976, repr. 1999; numerous papers on theoretical solid mechanics and the mechanics of continua in various learned journals and books. *Address:* Small Croft, 44 Main Street, Cononley, near Keighley, W Yorks BD20 8LS. *T:* (01535) 634773.

CHADWICK, Dr Priscilla; education consultant; Principal, Berkhamsted Collegiate School, 1996–2008; Chair, Dioceses Commission, 2008–10; *b* 7 Nov. 1947; *d* of Prof. Henry Chadwick, KBE, FBA. *Educ:* Oxford High Sch.; Clarendon Sch., N Wales; Girton Coll., Cambridge (BA Theol Tripos 1970); Oxford Univ. (PGCE); London Univ. (MA Curriculum Studies 1983; PhD 1993). Head of Religious Education: St Helen's Sch., Northwood, 1971–73; Putney High Sch., 1973–78; St Bede's C of E/RC Comprehensive, Redhill, 1979–82; Dep. Head, Twyford C of E High Sch., Acton, 1982–85; Headteacher, Bishop Ramsey C of E Sch., Ruislip, 1986–91; Dean, Educnl Devlt, South Bank Univ., 1992–96. Chm., HMC, 2005. Member: English Anglican/RC Cttee, 1981–2006; BBC/ITC Central Religious Adv. Cttee, 1983–93; Youth Crime Cttee, NACRO, 1988–94; Goldsmiths' Coll. Council, 1991–97; Southwark Cathedral Council, 2009–; Council, Nat. Soc., C of E, 2015–. Chairman: Culham St Gabriel's Trust (formerly St Gabriel's Trust), 1987–; School Chaplains and Leaders Assoc. (formerly Bloxham Project), 2011–; Church Sch. of the Future Rev., 2011–12. Chm. Govs, Wren Acad., London, 2008–14; Governor: Westminster Sch., 1997–; Uppingham Sch. (Vice-Chm., 2013–), 2008–. FRSA 1992. Hon. DEd Herts 2006; Hon. DLaws Roehampton 2011. *Publications:* Schools of Reconciliation, 1994; Shifting Alliances: the partnership of Church and State in English education, 1997; (contrib.) Anglican Church School Education, 2013; articles in various educnl jls. *Recreations:* music and the arts, world travel. *Club:* East India.

CHADWICK-JONES, Prof. John Knighton, PhD, DSc(Econ); Research Professor, University of Fribourg, Switzerland, 1993–2002; *b* 26 July 1928; *s* of Thomas Chadwick-Jones and Cecilia Rachel (*née* Thomas); *m* 1965, Araceli Carceller y Bergillos, PhD; two *s* one *d*. *Educ:* Bromsgrove Sch.; St Edmund Hall, Oxford (MA). PhD Wales, 1960; DSc(Econ) Wales, 1981. CPsychol, FBPsS. Scientific Staff, Nat. Inst. of Industrial Psychol., London, 1957–60; Lectr, then Sen. Lectr, in Industrial Psychol., UC, Cardiff, 1960–66; Reader in Social Psychol., Flinders Univ. of South Australia, 1967–68; Dir, Occupational Psychol. Res. Unit, UC, Cardiff, 1968–74; Prof. of Psychology, Saint Mary's Univ., Halifax, Canada, 1974–93, now Emeritus (Mem., Exec. Cttee, Bd of Governors, 1975–78). Canada Soc. Scis and Humanities Res. Council Leave Fellow: Darwin Coll., Cambridge, 1980–81; MRC Unit on Devlt and Integration of Behaviour, Cambridge, 1984–85; Visiting Fellow: Clare Hall, Cambridge, 1982; Wolfson Coll., Cambridge, 1984–85; Wolfson Coll., Oxford, 1988–89; St Edmund's Coll., Cambridge, 1990–91. Dir, Cambridge Canadian Trust (Toronto), 1988–94. Fellow, Amer. Psychol Assoc.; Hon. Fellow, Canadian Psychol Assoc. *Publications:* Automation and Behavior: a social psychological study, 1969; Social Exchange Theory: its structure and influence in social psychology, 1976; (jtly) Brain, Environment and Social Psychology, 1979; Absenteeism in the Canadian Context, 1979; (jtly) Social Psychology of Absenteeism, 1982; Developing a Social Psychology of Monkeys and Apes, 1998; articles in academic jls. *Address:* Clare Hall, Herschel Road, Cambridge CB3 9AL.

CHADWYCK-HEALEY, Sir Charles (Edward), 5th Bt *cr* 1919, of Wyphurst, Cranleigh, Co. Surrey and New Place, Luccombe, Somerset; DL; Chairman, Chadwyck-Healey Ltd, 1973–99; President, Chadwyck-Healey Inc., 1975–99; *b* 13 May 1940; *s* of Sir Charles Arthur Chadwyck-Healey, 4th Bt, OBE, TD, and of Viola, *d* of late Cecil Lubbock; *S* father, 1986; *m* 1967, Angela Mary, *e d* of late John Metson; one *s* two *d*. *Educ:* Eton; Trinity Coll., Oxford (MA; Hon. Fellow, 2006). Member: Marshall Aid Commemoration Commn, 1994–2000; Liby and Inf. Commn, 1995–2000; Lord Chancellor's Adv. Council on Nat. Records and Archives (formerly Public Records), 2001–06. Dir, openDemocracy Ltd, 2001–09. Mem., Ely Cathedral Council, 2001–07. Chm., Cambs Police Shrievalty Trust, 2005–10. Chairman: Beds, Cambs and Northants (formerly Beds, Cambs, Northants and Peterborough) Wildlife Trusts, 2009–13; Vanishing Worlds Foundn, 2010–; Pres., CPRE Cambs, 2008–13. High Sheriff, 2004–05, DL, 2004, Cambs. *Heir: s* Edward Alexander Chadwyck-Healey [*b* 2 June 1972; *m* 1999, Denise Suzanne, (Denny), *e d* of Caroline Osborne; two *d*]. *Address:* 5 Madingley Road, Cambridge CB3 0EE. *T:* (01223) 316766. *Clubs:* Athenæum, Brooks's.

CHAFFEY, Ven. Jonathan Paul Michael, QHC 2012; Director General Chaplaincy Services, Headquarters Air Command and Chaplain-in-Chief and Archdeacon, Royal Air Force, since 2014; *b* London, 1962; *s* of Rev. Michael Chaffey and Shirley Chaffey; *m* 1988, Jane Frances Page, (Rev. Jane Chaffey); three *d*. *Educ:* Worksop Coll.; Univ. of Durham (BA Hons Sociol. 1983; CTh 1987); Nottingham Univ. (MA Theol. 2007). Ordained deacon, 1987, priest, 1988; Curate, St Stephen's Gateacre, Liverpool, 1987–90; RAF Chaplain, 1990–; rcds 2013–14. Hon. Canon, Lincoln Cathedral, 2015–. *Recreations:* historical biographies, several sports, flute, family. *Address:* Chaplaincy Services (RAF), Headquarters Air Command, RAF High Wycombe, Bucks HP14 4UE. *T:* (01494) 493802. *E:* airchapservs-chapinchiefdes@mod.uk. *Club:* Royal Air Force.

CHAHAL, Saimo; Senior Partner, since 1995, and Joint Head of Public Law, since 2012, Bindmans LLP; First-tier Tribunal Judge (Mental Health), since 2004; *b* Punjab, India, 18 July 1958; *d* of Shere and Chanan Chahal; partner, Stephen Pierce; one *s* one *d*. *Educ:* Twickenham Green Primary Sch.; Knellar Girls' Secondary Sch.; Sussex Univ. (BA Hons Sociol.). Legal Advr, Deptford Law Centre, 1984–89; articles with Hornby and Levy Solicitors, 1989–90; admitted as solicitor, 1990; Legal Advr, Wandsworth Law Centre, 1990–92; Housing, Civil and Employment Law Solicitor, HCL Hanne and Co., 1992–94. Legal Aid Lawyer of Year, Mental Health, Legal Aid Practitioners Gp, 2006; Solicitor of Year, Law Soc. Excellence Award, 2008; Public Law and Human Rights Lawyer of Year, Soc. of Asian Lawyers, 2011. Hon. QC 2014. *Recreations:* reading group, film club, walking, art, architect, interior design, gardening. *Address:* Bindmans LLP, 236 Gray's Inn Road, WC1X 8HB. *T:* 07919 307115. *E:* s.chahal@bindmans.com.

CHAILLY, Riccardo; conductor; Kapellmeister, Gewandhaus Orchestra, Leipzig, since 2005; Principal Conductor, La Scala, Milan, since 2015; Music Director, Lucerne Festival Orchestra, from Aug. 2016; *b* 20 Feb. 1953; *s* of late Luciano Chailly and of Anna Maria Chailly; *m* 1987, Gabriella Terragni; two *s*. *Educ:* Conservatory of Music, Perugia; St Cecilia, Rome; Giuseppe Verdi, Milan. Chief Conductor, Berlin Radio Symph. Orch., 1982–89; Principal Conductor and Music Dir, Teatro Comunale, Bologna, 1986–93; Principal Conductor: Royal Concertgebouw Orch., Amsterdam, 1988–2004, now Conductor Emeritus; Orch. Giuseppe Verdi, Milan, 1999–2005, now Conductor Laureate; has conducted world's leading orchestras, including Vienna and Berlin Philharmonic, Chicago Symphony, Philadelphia and Cleveland; has performed in major opera houses, including: La Scala, Milan, Vienna State Opera, Covent Garden, Munich, Metropolitan Opera, NY. Hon. RAM 1996. Numerous recordings. Grand Prix du Disque, Acad. Charles Cros, 1984, 1985, 1987, 1992, and other recording awards. Grande Ufficiale, Italian Republic, 1994. *Address:* c/o Gewandhaus zu Leipzig, Augustusplatz 8, 04109 Leipzig, Germany.

CHAISTY, Paul; QC 2001; a Recorder, since 2000; a Deputy High Court Judge, since 2006; *b* 12 March 1958; *s* of Dora Cranston (*née* Preston); *m* 1987, Margaret Judith Lewis; one *s* one *d*. *Educ:* Parrs Wood High Sch., Manchester; Nottingham Univ. (LLB); Exeter Coll., Oxford (BCL). Called to the Bar, Lincoln's Inn, 1982; in practice as barrister, Manchester, 1982–, London, 2006–, specialising in commercial and Chancery law. *Recreations:* fishing, family, football, friends. *Address:* Kings Chambers, 36 Young Street, Manchester M3 3FT. *T:* (0161) 832 9082; Serle Court, 6 New Square, Lincoln's Inn, WC2A 3QS. *T:* (020) 7242 6105.

CHAKRABARTI, Reeta; journalist; Newsreader and Correspondent, BBC, since 2014; *b* 12 Dec. 1964; *d* of Bidhan Kumar and Ruma Chakrabarti; *m* 1992, Paul Hamilton; two *s* one *d*. *Educ:* King Edward VI High Sch., Birmingham; Internat. Sch., Calcutta; Exeter Coll., Oxford (BA Hons English and French). BBC: current affairs producer, Today, The World at One and PM, Radio 4, 1992–94; reporter, Radio 5 Live Breakfast Prog., 1994–96; Community Affairs Corresp., 1997–99; Political Corresp., 1999–2010; Educn and Social Affairs Corresp., 2010–14. Patron: Naz Project, 2001–; Nat. Mentoring Consortium, 2003–; Pan Intercultural Arts. Hon. Fellow, UEL, 2003. *Recreations:* reading, swimming, tennis, visiting beautiful European cities, enjoying my children! *Address:* c/o W1 NBH 02A, BBC Broadcasting House, Portland Place, W1A 1AA.

CHAKRABARTI, Shami, CBE 2007; Director, Liberty, since 2003; *b* 16 June 1969; *d* of Shyamalendou and Shyamali Chakrabarti; one *s*. *Educ:* London Sch. of Econs and Pol Sci. (LLB). Called to the Bar, Middle Temple, 1994, Bencher, 2006; lawyer, Legal Advr's Br., Home Office, 1996–2001; In-house Counsel, Liberty, 2001–03. Vis. Fellow, Nuffield Coll., Oxford, 2006–. Member: Tate Members Council, 2006–15; Leveson Inquiry, 2011–12. Chancellor: Oxford Brookes Univ., 2008–15; Univ. of Essex, 2014–. Hon. Fellow, Mansfield Coll., Oxford, 2009–. Governor: LSE, 2005–11; BFI, 2006–13. *Publications:* On Liberty, 2014; contribs to Public Law and European Human Rights Law Review, and various newspapers and magazines. *Recreations:* friends, popular cinema, playing with my son. *Address:* Liberty, Liberty House, SW1P 2HR. *T:* (020) 7403 3888, *Fax:* (020) 7607 5354. *E:* info@liberty-human-rights.org.uk.

CHAKRABARTI, Sir Sumantra, KCB 2006; President, European Bank for Reconstruction and Development, since 2012; *b* 12 Jan. 1959; *s* of Hirendranath Chakrabarti and Gayatri Chakrabarti (*née* Rudra); *m* 1983, Mari Sako, *qv*; one *d*. *Educ:* City of London Sch. for Boys; New Coll., Oxford (BA PPE 1981; Hon. Fellow 2004); Sussex Univ. (MA Econ 1984). ODI Fellow and Economist, Govt of Botswana, 1981–83; Sen. Economic Asst and Economic Advr, ODA, 1984–88; Asst to UK Exec. Dir, IMF and World Bank, Washington, 1988–90; Private Sec. to Rt Hon. Lynda Chalker, 1990–92; Assistant Secretary: Aid Policy and Resources Dept, ODA, 1992–96; Envmt, Transport, and Regions Team, Spending Directorate, HM Treasury, 1996–98; Dep. Dir, Budget and Public Finances, HM Treasury, 1998; Dir, Performance and Innovation Unit, 1998–2000, Head, Econ. and Domestic Affairs Secretariat, 2000–01, Cabinet Office; Dir Gen. for Regl Progs, 2001–02, Perm. Sec., 2002–07, DFID; Perm. Sec., MoJ, 2007–12; Clerk of the Crown in Chancery, 2007–12. Hon. Bencher, Middle Temple, 2009. Hon. LLD Sussex, 2004; Hon. DCL E Anglia, 2010; Dr *hc* Bucharest Univ. Econ. Studies, 2013. *Recreations:* Indian history, soul music, football. *Address:* European Bank for Reconstruction and Development, One Exchange Square, EC2A 2JN.

CHALAYAN, Hussein, MBE 2006; RDI 2013; fashion designer; artist; *b* Nicosia, Cyprus, 12 Aug. 1970. *Educ:* Central Saint Martins, London (BA Hons Fashion Design 1993; Hon. Fellow 2011). Founder, own label, 1994; Creative Director: TSE New York, 1998–2000; Asprey, 2001–04; Puma, 2008–10. Exhibitions include: From Fashion and Back, Design Mus., London, 2009, Mus. of Contemporary Art, Tokyo, 2010; 1994–2010, Modern Mus., Istanbul, 2010; Fashion Narratives, Les Arts Décoratifs, Paris, 2011. Designer of the Year, British Fashion Awards, 1999, 2000; Outstanding Lifetime Achievement to Design, FX Internat. Interior Design Awards, London, 2009. *Publications:* Hussein Chalayan, 2005; *relevant publication:* Hussein Chalayan, 2011. *Address:* Block H, Zetland House, 109–123 Clifton Street, EC2A 4LD. *T:* (020) 7613 3914, *Fax:* (020) 7613 3741. *E:* press@chalayan.com.

CHALFIE, Prof. Martin, PhD; William R. Kenan Jr Professor of Biological Sciences, Columbia University, since 2002 (Chair, Department of Biological Sciences, 2007–10); *b* Chicago, 15 Jan. 1947; *s* of Eli and Vivian Chalfie; *m* 1989, Tulle Hazelrigg; one *d*. *Educ:* Harvard Univ. (PhD 1977). Teacher, Hamden Hall County Day Sch., Connecticut, 1970–72; Research Scientist, MRC Laboratory of Molecular Biology, Cambridge, 1977–82; Columbia University: Asst Prof., 1982–89; Associate Prof., 1989–93; Prof., 1994–. (Jtly) Nobel Prize in Chemistry, 2008. *Publications:* contrib. articles in jls. *Address:* Columbia University, Department of Biological Sciences, 1018 Fairchild Center, MC 2446, New York, NY 10027, USA.

CHALFONT, Baron *cr* 1964 (Life Peer); **Alun Arthur Gwynne Jones;** PC 1964; OBE 1961; MC 1957; Chairman: Marlborough Stirling Group, 1994–99; Southern Mining Corp., 1997–99; *b* 5 Dec. 1919; *s* of Arthur Gwynne Jones and Eliza Alice Hardman; *m* 1948, Dr Mona Mitchell, MB ChB (*d* 2008); one *d* decd. *Educ:* West Monmouth Sch. Commissioned into South Wales Borderers (24th Foot), 1940; served in: Burma 1941–44; Malayan campaign 1955–57; Cyprus campaign 1958–59; various staff and intelligence appointments; Staff Coll., Camberley, 1950; Jt Services Staff Coll., 1958; Russian interpreter, 1951; resigned commission, 1961, on appt as Defence Correspondent, The Times; frequent television and sound broadcasts and consultant on foreign affairs to BBC Television, 1961–64; Minister of State, Foreign and Commonwealth Office, 1964–70; UK Permanent Rep. to WEU, 1969–70; Foreign Editor, New Statesman, 1970–71. Dep. Chm., IBA, 1989–90; Chm., Radio Authy, 1991–94. Director: W. S. Atkins International, 1979–83; IBM UK Ltd, 1973–90 (Mem. IBM Europe Adv. Council, 1973–90); Lazard Bros & Co. Ltd, 1983–90; Shandwick plc, 1985–95; Triangle Holdings, 1986–90; Dep. Chm., Television Corp. plc, 1996–2001; Chairman: Industrial Cleaning Papers, 1979–86; Peter Hamilton Security Consultants Ltd, 1984–86; VSEL Consortium, later VSEL, 1987–95; President: Abington Corp. (Consultants) Ltd, 1981–; Nottingham Bldg Soc., 1983–90. Pres., All Party Defence Gp, H of L, 1995– (Chm., 1980–94). President: Hispanic and Luso Brazilian Council, 1975–80; RNID, 1980–87; Llangollen Internat. Music Festival, 1979–90; Freedom in Sport, 1982–88; Chairman: UK Cttee for Free World, 1981–89; Eur. Atlantic Gp, 1983–; Member: Nat. Defence Industries Council, 1992–; IISS; Bd of Governors, Sandle Manor Sch. MRI; MInstD. FRSA. Hon. Fellow UCW Aberystwyth, 1974. Hon. Col, Univ. of Wales OTC, 1991–94. Liveryman, Worshipful Co. of Paviors. Freeman, City of London. *Publications:* The Sword and The Spirit, 1963; The Great Commanders, 1973; Montgomery of Alamein, 1976; (ed) Waterloo: battle of three armies, 1979; Star Wars: suicide or survival, 1985; Defence of the Realm, 1987; By God's Will: a portrait of the Sultan of Brunei, 1989; The Shadow of My Hand (autobiog.), 2000; contribs to The Times, and other national and professional journals. *Recreations:* formerly Rugby football, cricket, lawn tennis; now music and theatre. *Address:* House of Lords, SW1A 0PW. *Clubs:* Garrick, MCC, City Livery.

CHALISE, Dr Suresh Chandra; Ambassador of Nepal to the Court of St James's and to Ireland, 2010–14; *b* Rajbiraj, Nepal, 24 Oct. 1957; *s* of late Ram Nath Chalise and of Chet Kumari Chalise; *m* 1996, Dr Milan Adhikary; two *d*. *Educ:* Banaras Hindu Univ., India (PhD Pol Sociol. 1990); Univ. of Justus Liebig, Giessen, Germany (postdoctoral studies in Develt Sociol. 2005); Asia Pacific Centre for Security Studies, Honolulu (Sen. Exec. Course 2006). Sec. on Internat. Affairs to Rt Hon. K. P. Bhattarai, 1991–96; Sen. Res. Fellow, Inst. of Sociol., Univ. of Justus Liebig, 1996–97; Alexander von Humboldt Foundn Postdoctoral Res. Fellow, Inst. of Political Sci., Univ. of Dortmund, 1998–99; Foreign Relns Advr to Hon. G. P. Koirala, 2003–06; leader of team of Nepalese generals to encourage interaction with Maoist rebels, July 2006; assisted Hd of Nepalese Govt and hd of Maoist rebels in Nepal's Peace Process, Aug. 2006; Advr to Prime Minister of Nepal on Foreign Affairs (with Minister of State status), 2006–07; Ambassador to USA, 2007–08; Policy Advr to former Prime Minister and Pres. of Nepali Congress, Hon. G. P. Koirala, 2008–09. Consultant, US Nat. Democratic Inst., DFID, Friedrich Ebert Foundn, Berlin, UNDP, Nexant/SARI (energy) and WHO. Hon. Citizen, Galveston City, Texas, 1992. Mahendra Vidhya Bhusan (Gold Medal) Grade A (Nepal), 1994. *Publications:* Sociology of the Legislative Elite in a Developing Society, 1995; (jtly) Women in Politics in Nepal: their socioeconomic, health, legal and political constraints, 1996; Coalition Governments and Political Acculturation in Germany, 1997. *Recreations:* light music, movies.

CHALK, Alexander John Gervase; MP (C) Cheltenham, since 2015; *b* 8 Aug. 1976; *s* of Gilbert Chalk and Gillian Miller (*née* Blois); *m* 2011, Sarah Beslee; two *d*. *Educ:* Winchester Coll.; Magdalen Coll., Oxford (BA Mod. Hist. 1998); City Univ. (DipLaw Dist. 2000). Called to the Bar, Middle Temple, 2001; barrister, 6 King's Bench Walk, then 6KBW College Hill, 2001–. Mem. (C), Hammersmith and Fulham Council, 2006–14. *Recreations:* cycling, playing guitar, reading, family. *Address:* House of Commons, SW1A 0AA. *E:* alex.chalk.mp@parliament.uk. *Club:* MCC.

CHALK, Gerald Anthony; a District Judge (Magistrates' Courts), since 2004; *b* 26 Nov. 1950; *s* of William Pickering Chalk and Winifred Chalk (*née* James); one *s*. *Educ:* Univ. of Newcastle upon Tyne (LLB Hons 1973). Admitted as solicitor, 1978; articled to McKenzie Bell & Sons, (Solicitors), Sunderland, later Asst Solicitor, 1975–79; Asst Prosecutor to Prosecuting Solicitors' Dept, Northumbria Police, 1979–83; Asst Solicitor, then Partner, Hawley & Rodgers, (Solicitors), Nottingham, 1983–2001; Partner, Johnson Partnership, (Solicitors), Nottingham, 2001–04. Actg Stipendiary Magistrate, 1999. *Recreations:* sport, history, literature. *Address:* c/o Carlisle Magistrates' Court, Rickergate, Carlisle, Cumbria CA3 8QH. *T:* (01228) 518838.

CHALKE, Rev. Stephen John, MBE 2004; charity founder, educationalist, Baptist minister, author, and television and radio broadcaster; *b* 17 Nov. 1955; *s* of Victor Joseph Chalke and Ada Elizabeth (*née* Wroth); *m* 1980, Cornelia Maria Reeves; two *s* two *d*. *Educ:* Spurgeon's Coll., London (DipTh 1981). Ordained Minister, 1981; Minister, Tonbridge Baptist Ch, 1981–85; Founder, Oasis Trust, 1985–; Exec. Chair (formerly CEO), Oasis Community Learning, 2005–; Founder, Faithworks, 2001–; Sen. Minister, Oasis Church Waterloo (formerly church.co.uk, Waterloo), 2003–; Founder, Stop the Traffik, 2006–; UN GIFT Special Advr, Community Action Against Human Trafficking, 2008–. Dir, Parentalk, 1998–2011. FRSA 1998. Hon. Fellow Sarum Coll., 2005. Templeton UK Award, 1997. Hon. Dr Staffs, 2015. *Publications:* books include: More Than Meets the Eye, 1995, rev. edn 2003; The Parentalk Guide to Your Child and Sex, 2000; He Never Said, 2000; Faithworks, 2001; The Parentalk Guide to Great Days Out, 2001; Faithworks Stories of Hope, 2001; Faithworks Unpacked, 2002; Intimacy and Involvement, 2003; Faithworks 100 Proven Ways for Community Transformation, 2003; (jtly) The Lost Message of Jesus, 2003; Trust: a radical manifesto, 2004; Intelligent Church, 2006; Change Agents, 2007; Stop the Traffik, 2009; (jtly) Apprentice: walking the way of Christ, 2009; Different Eyes: the art of living beautifully, 2010; Being Human: becoming the best version of yourself, 2015. *Recreations:* gym, running, football, Crystal Palace FC. *Address:* The Oasis Centre, 75 Westminster Bridge Road, SE1 7HS. *T:* (020) 7921 4200, *Fax:* (020) 7921 4201. *E:* steve.chalke@oasisuk.org. *Club:* Riverside.

CHALKER OF WALLASEY, Baroness *cr* 1992 (Life Peer), of Leigh-on-Sea in the County of Essex; **Lynda Chalker;** PC 1987; Chairman, Africa Matters Ltd, since 1998; independent consultant on Africa and development to business and governments; company director; *b* 29 April 1942; *d* of late Sidney Henry James Bates and Marjorie Kathleen Randell; *m* 1st, 1967, Eric Robert Chalker (marr. diss. 1973); no *c*; 2nd, 1981, Clive Landa (marr. diss. 2003). *Educ:* Heidelberg Univ.; London Univ.; Central London Polytechnic. Statistician with Research Bureau Ltd (Unilever), 1963–69; Dep. Market Research Manager with Shell Mex & BP Ltd, 1969–72; Chief Exec. of Internat. Div. of Louis Harris International, 1972–74. MP (C) Wallasey, Feb. 1974–1992; Opposition Spokesman on Social Services, 1976–79; Parly Under-Sec. of State, DHSS, 1979–82, Dept of Transport, 1982–83; Minister of State, Dept of Transport, 1983–86; Minister of State, 1986–97, and Minister for Overseas Develt, 1989–97, FCO. Non-executive Director: Freeplay Energy plc, 1997–2006; Capital Shopping Centres plc, 1997–2000; Develt Consultants Internat., 1999–2003; Ashanti Goldfields Co. Ltd, 2000–04; Group 5 (Pty) Ltd, 2001–12; Unilever plc and Unilever NV, 2004–07 (Adv. Dir, 1998–2004); Member, International Advisory Board: Lafarge et Cie, 2004–; Merchant Bridge & Co., 2005–. Member: BBC Gen. Adv. Cttee, 1975–79; RIIA, 1977–. Pres., BESO, 1998–2005 (Chm., 1998–2004); Chm., Medicines for Malaria Venture, 2006–11. Chm. Mgt Bd, LSHTM, 1998–2006. Hon. Col, 156(NW) Transport Regt, RLC(V), 1995–2000. *Publications:* (jtly) Police in Retreat (pamphlet), 1967; (jtly) Unhappy Families (pamphlet), 1971; (jtly) We are Richer than We Think, 1978; Africa: turning the tide, 1989. *Recreations:* music, cooking, theatre, driving. *Address:* House of Lords, SW1A 0PW.

CHALKLEY, Richard; a Judge of the Upper Tribunal (Immigration and Asylum Chamber) (formerly a Vice President, Immigration Appeal Tribunal, later a Senior Immigration Judge, Asylum and Immigration Tribunal), since 2002; *b* 23 March 1949; *s* of late Kenneth Arthur Chalkley and Vera Chalkley; *m* 1st, 1973 (marr. diss. 2007); one *s* one *d*; 2nd, 2011, Caroline Maud, BA, *widow* of Henry Macintosh MacPhee, Scarinish, Isle of Tiree. *Educ:* College of Law. Articled to Ormsby Izzard-Davies, Woburn, 1969; admitted solicitor, 1974; Asst Solicitor, Graham Withers & Co., Solicitors, Shrewsbury, 1974–77; Partner: Bradfield & Howson, Solicitors, Maidstone, 1977–87; Thomson Snell & Passmore, Solicitors, Tunbridge Wells, 1987–99. Pt-time, 1995–99, full-time, 1999–2000, Immigration Adjudicator; pt-time Chm., Immigration Appeal Tribunal, 2000–02; Legal Mem., Special Immigration Appeals Commn, 2005–. Chm., Kent Dental Services Cttee, 1985–95; Dep. Chm., Kent Medical Services Cttee, 1985–94; Member: Kent FPC, 1985–90; Bd, Kent Family Health Services Cttee, 1990–95. Freeman, City of London, 2010. *Publications:* Professional Conduct: a handbook for chartered surveyors, 1990, 2nd edn 1994; contrib. various articles to Chartered Surveyor Weekly. *Recreations:* reading, history, fly fishing, learning about Tiree. *Address:* Upper Tribunal (Immigration and Asylum Chamber), Field House, 15–25 Breams Buildings, EC4A 1DZ. *T:* (020) 7073 4200, *Fax:* (020) 7073 4004. *Clubs:* Bearsted and Thurnham (Bearsted), Savage.

CHALLACOMBE, Prof. Stephen James, PhD; FRCPath; FDSRCS, FDSRCSE; FMedSci; educator and medical researcher; Professor of Oral Medicine, King's College London, since 1988; Director of External Strategy, 2004–11, and Vice Dean, 2005–11, King's College London Dental Institute; Dean for External Affairs, King's College London Health Schools, 2008–11; Consultant in Diagnostic Microbiology, Guy's and St Thomas' NHS Foundation Trust, 1984–2011; *b* London, 5 April 1946; *s* of late Kenneth Vivian Challacombe, Sudbury, Suffolk, and Caryl Graydon (*née* Poore); *m* 1969, Christine Barbara (Tina), *d* of Rt Rev. Francis William Cocks, CB; one *s* one *d*. *Educ:* Culford Sch.; Guy's Hosp. Dental Sch. (BDS 1969); PhD London 1976. LDSRCS 1968; FRCPath 1992; FDSRCSE 1994; FDSRCS 2004. Department of Immunology, Guy's Hospital Medical and Dental Schools: Res. Fellow, 1971–72; Lectr, 1972–76; Sen. Lectr, 1976–85; Reader in Oral Immunol., Univ. of London, 1985–88; King's College London Dental Institute: Sub-dean of Dental Studies, 1983–87; Hd, Dept of Oral Medicine and Pathol., 1986–2003; Postgrad. Sub-dean (Dental), 1992–2002. Sen. Res. Fellow, Dept of Immunol., Mayo Clinic, Rochester, Minn, 1978–79 (Edward C. Kendall Res. Fellow); Vis. Prof., Dept of Oral Biol., UCSF, 1995. Hon. Consultant in Oral Medicine to UK Armed Forces, 1998–2012. President: British Soc. for Oral Medicine, 1995–97; Odontological Section, RSM, 1996–97; Metropolitan Br., BDA, 1999; British Soc. for Dental Res. (British Div. of IADR), 2000–02; Internat. Assoc. Dental Res., 2003–04; Eur. Assoc. Oral Medicine, 2008–10. FKC 2010. FMedSci 1998. Mem., Hunterian Soc. (Pres., 2007–08). Hon. DSc Athens, 2011. Colgate Res. Prize, British Div., 1977, Basic Res. in Oral Sci. Award, 1981, Dist. Scientist Award for Exptl Pathol., 1997, IADR. *Publications: edited jointly:* Food Allergy and Intolerance, 1985, 2nd edn 2002; Practical and Theoretical Aspects of ELISA, 1988; Mucosal Immunology, 1990; Oral AIDS Research, 1997, 3rd edn 2011; Immunology of Oral Diseases, 1998; Oral Health and Disease in AIDS, 2006; The Mouth and AIDS, 2011; contrib. 300 acad. papers on mucosal immunity, oral medicine, immunological, dermatological and microbiol aspects of oral diseases. *Recreations:* golf, tennis, ski-ing, sailing, theatre, formerly Rugby (Pres., Guy's Hosp. RFC, 1991–2001), water polo (Pres., Guy's Hosp. Swimming and Water Polo Club, 1985–98), being a grandfather, dog walking. *Address:* 101 Mycenae Road, Blackheath, SE3 7RX; King's College London Dental Institute, Guy's Hospital, SE1 9RT. *T:* (020) 7188 4373, *Fax:* (020) 7188 1159. *E:* stephen.challacombe@kcl.ac.uk. *Clubs:* Athenæum, Savage, MCC; Nobody's Friends.

CHALLEN, Colin Robert; environmental policy campaigner, since 2010; artist; *b* 12 June 1953; *s* of late Grenfell Stephen William Challen and of Helen Mary Challen (*née* Swift). *Educ:* Hull Univ. (BA Hons Philosophy 1982). Served RAF, 1971–74. Postman, 1974–78; publisher and printer, Hull, 1983–94; Labour Party Organiser, Leeds and W Yorks, 1994–2000. Member (Lab): Hull CC, 1986–94; Scarborough BC, 2011–15 (Leader, Lab Gp, 2014–15). MP (Lab) Morley and Rothwell, 2001–10. Member: Envmtl Audit Select Cttee, 2001–10; Energy and Climate Change Select Cttee, 2009–10; Chairman, All Party Parliamentary Group: on Climate Change, 2005–10; on Intelligent Energy, 2005–10. FRSA 2007. Hon. Fellow, Soc. for Envmt, 2008; Hon. FCIWEM 2009. *Publications:* Price of Power: the secret funding of the Conservative Party, 1998; Too Little, Too Late: the politics of climate change, 2009. *Recreations:* rambling, art, music. *E:* colinchallen@gmail.com.

CHALLEN, David John, CBE 2002; Chairman, EMEA Governance Committee, Citigroup, 2010–14 (Co-Chairman, Schroder Salomon Smith Barney, then Vice-Chairman, European Investment Bank, Citigroup, 2000–10); *b* 11 March 1943; *s* of Sydney Albert Challen and Doris Ellen Challen (*née* Hardy); *m* 1967, Elizabeth McCartney; one *s* one *d*. *Educ:* The High Sch., Dublin; Trinity Coll., Dublin; Harvard Univ. (MBA). With J. Walter Thompson, 1964–72; J. Henry Schroder & Co. Ltd, 1972–2000: Dir, 1979–2000; Hd, Corporate Finance, 1990–94; Vice Chm., 1995–97; Chm., 1997–2000. Non-executive Director: Anglian Water PLC, 1993–2002; Thomson Travel Group plc, 1998–2000; Anglo American plc, 2002–14; Amersham plc, 2003–04; Smiths Group plc, 2004–. Chm., Financial Services Practitioner Panel, 1998–2001; Member: Adv. Cttee on Business and the Envmt, 1991–92; Panel on Takeovers and Mergers, 1993–94, 1999– (Dep. Chm., 2006–); Financial Reporting Council, 1995–2003. Gov., Morley Coll., 1993–99. *Club:* Athenæum.

CHALLEN, Rt Rev. Michael Boyd, AM 1988; Executive Director, Brotherhood of St Laurence, 1991–99; Adjunct Professor of Ethics, Curtin University of Technology, Perth, since 2000; *b* 27 May 1932; *s* of late B. Challen; *m* 1961, Judith, *d* of A. Kelly; two *d*. *Educ:* Mordialloc High School; Frankston High School; Univ. of Melbourne (BSc 1955); Ridley College, Melbourne (ThL 1956). Deacon 1957, priest 1958; Curate of Christ Church, Essendon, 1957–59; Member, Melbourne Dio. Centre, 1959–63; Director, 1963–69; Priest-in-charge, St Luke, Fitzroy, 1959–61; St Alban's, N Melbourne, 1961–65; Flemington, 1965–69; Dir, Anglican Inner-City Ministry, 1969; Dir, Home Mission Dept, Perth, 1971–78; Priest-in-charge, Lockridge with Eden Hill, 1973; Archdeacon, Home Missions, Perth, 1975–78; Asst Bp, dio. of Perth, WA, 1978–91; Exec. Dir, Anglican Health and Welfare Service, Perth, 1977–78. *Address:* Unit 7, 30 Kwong Alley, North Fremantle, WA 6159, Australia. *T:* and *Fax:* (8) 94336784.

CHALLINOR, Robert Michael; His Honour Judge Challinor; a Circuit Judge, since 2004; *b* 10 July 1950; *s* of Henry Clive Challinor and Gladys Violet Challinor (*née* Chapman); *m* 1984, Jill; two *s*. *Educ:* St Peter's Sch., Bournemouth; Trent Polytech. (LLB London 1973). Called to the Bar, Gray's Inn, 1974; Asst Recorder, 1991–97; Recorder, 1997–2004. *Recreations:* art, walking, music, being with my family. *Address:* c/o Wolverhampton Crown Court, Pipers Row, Wolverhampton WV1 3LQ.

CHALLONER, Very Rev. Janet; *see* Henderson, Very Rev. J.

CHALMERS, Sir Iain (Geoffrey), Kt 2000; FRCP, FRCPE, FFPH, FCOG(SA); Editor, James Lind Library, since 2003; Co-ordinator, James Lind Initiative, since 2003; Director, UK

Cochrane Centre, 1992–2002; *b* 3 June 1943; *s* of Hamish and Lois Chalmers; *m* 1972, Jan Skitmore; two *s*. *Educ:* Middlesex Hosp. Med. Sch., London Univ. (MB BS 1966; MSc Social Medicine 1975). MRCS 1966; LRCP 1966; DCH 1973; MRCOG 1973, FRCOG 1985; FFPH (FFPHM 1986); FRCPE 1996; FCOG(SA) 2001; FRCP 2002. House Physician, House Surgeon, Middlesex Hosp.; House Physician, Welsh Nat. Sch. of Medicine; House Surgeon, Raigmore Hosp., Inverness; MO, UNRWA for Palestinian Refugees, Gaza; Registrar, Dept of Obst. and Gynaecol., then MRC Fellow, Dept of Med. Stats, Welsh Nat. Sch. of Medicine, Cardiff; Oxford University: Dir, Nat. Perinatal Epidemiology Unit, 1978–92; Clin. Lectr in Obst. and Gynaecol., 1978–92; Archie Cochrane Res. Fellow, Green Coll., 1992–94; Hon. Consultant in Public Health Medicine, Oxfordshire HA, 1978–2002; Hon. Specialist in Public Health Medicine, Milton Keynes PCT, 2003–13; Hon Mem., Sen. Scientific Staff, MRC Clin. Trials Unit, 2003–; Specialist in Public Health Medicine, Oxford Univ. Hosp. NHS Trust, 2013–. Visiting Professor: Univ. of Liverpool, 1993–; Inst. of Child Health, 1997–2003, Sch. of Public Policy, 1998–2003, UCL; Exeter Univ., 2000–03; Hon. Professor: Cardiff Univ., 2006; Univ. of Edinburgh, 2008. Editor: Oxford Database of Perinatal Trials, 1988–92; Testing Treatments Interactive, 2012–. FMedSci 1999. Hon. FRSocMed 2005; Hon. Fellow, Royal Statistical Soc. 2006. Hon. DSc: Aberdeen, 1999; London, 2004; Plymouth, 2008; Oxford Brookes, 2008; Hon. MD Liverpool, 2001; DUniv York, 2001; Hon. Dr, Free Univ., Amsterdam, 2006. *Publications:* (ed jtly) Effectiveness and Satisfaction in Antenatal Care, 1982; (ed jtly) Effective Care in Pregnancy and Childbirth, 1989; (ed jtly) Systematic Reviews, 1995; (ed jtly) Non-random Reflections on Health Services Research, 1997; (jtly) Testing Treatments, 2006, 2nd edn 2011. *Address:* James Lind Initiative, Summertown Pavilion, Middle Way, Oxford OX2 7LG. *T:* (01865) 518951.

CHALMERS, Prof. James Peter; Regius Professor of Law, University of Glasgow, since 2012; *b* Dundee, 4 Nov. 1976; *s* of John Macdonald Chalmers and Margaret Ann Chalmers (*née* Watt). *Educ:* Inverurie Acad.; Univ. of Aberdeen (LLB Hons 1998; DipLP 2000); Tulane Univ. of Louisiana (LLM 1999). Lectr in Law, 2000–06, Sen. Lectr, 2006–07, Univ. of Aberdeen; Sen. Lectr in Law, Univ. of Edinburgh, 2007–12. Visiting Professor: Univ. of Baltimore, 2001; Univ. of Maryland, 2001; Vis. Jun. Res. Fellow, QMUL, 2007; Vis. Researcher, Uppsala Univ., 2014. Ed., Edinburgh Law Rev., 2011–13. Mem., Criminal Courts Rules Council, 2008–14. Trustee, HIV Scotland, 2010–13. *Publications:* Trusts: cases and materials, 2002; (with F. Leverick) Criminal Defences and Pleas in Bar of Trial, 2006; Legal Responses to HIV and AIDS, 2008; (with M. L. Ross) Walker and Walker: the law of evidence in Scotland, 3rd edn 2009; (ed jtly) Essays in Criminal Law in Honour of Sir Gerald Gordon, 2010; The New Law of Sexual Offences in Scotland, 2011; contrib. articles to learned jls. *Recreations:* Swedish language, cinema. *Address:* School of Law, University of Glasgow, 5–9 Stair Building, Glasgow G12 8QQ. *T:* (0141) 330 5408. *E:* james.chalmers@glasgow.ac.uk.

CHALMERS, Very Rev. John Pearson; Moderator of the General Assembly of the Church of Scotland, 2014–15; a Chaplain in Ordinary to the Queen, since 2013; *b* Bothwell, 5 June 1952; *s* of Isaac Macmillan Chalmers and Mary Ann Pearson; *m* 1976, Elizabeth Barbara Boning; two *s* one *d*. *Educ:* Univ. of Strathclyde; Univ. of Glasgow (BD; CPS). Ordained Minister, 1979; Minister, Renton Trinity, 1979–86; Clerk, Dumbarton Presbytery, 1982–86; Minister, Palmerston Place, Edinburgh, 1986–95; Church of Scotland: Depute Gen. Sec., Bd of Ministry, 1995–2001; Pastoral Advr and Associate Sec., Ministries Council, 2001–10; Principal Clerk to the Gen. Assembly, 2010–. *Recreations:* golf, bee-keeping, reading, gardening. *Address:* Church of Scotland, 121 George Street, Edinburgh EH2 4YN. *T:* (0131) 225 5722. *E:* jchalmers@cofscotland.org.uk. *Club:* Royal Troon Golf.

CHALMERS, Prof. John Philip, AC 1991; FAA, FAAHMS; Professor of Medicine, since 1996, and Senior Director at the George Institute for Global Health (formerly the Institute for International Health, then the George Institute for International Health), since 2000 (Professorial Fellow, 1999–2000), University of Sydney; *b* 12 Jan. 1937; *m* 1977, Dr Alexandra Bune; four *s* one *d*. *Educ:* King's Sch., Parramatta; St Paul's Coll., Univ. of Sydney (BSc, MB BS); Univ. of NSW (PhD). FRCP, FRCPG, FRCPE, FACP, FRACP, FRACMA. Medical appts, Royal Prince Alfred Hosp., to 1968; Research Fellow: Nat. Heart Foundn, Univ. of NSW, 1965–66; MIT, 1969–70; RPMS, 1970–71; University of Sydney: Sen. Lectr, 1971–72; Assoc. Prof. of Medicine, 1973–75; Prof. of Medicine, Flinders Univ., 1975–96. Hon. Physician, Royal Prince Alfred Hosp., 1971–75; Vis MO, Repatriation Gen. Hosp., Concord, 1972–75; Mem., Bd of Management, Flinders Med. Centre, 1977–; Dean, Sch. of Medicine, Flinders Univ., 1991–92; Res. Chm., Royal N Shore Hosp., 1996–2000; Chm., Res. Develt for Faculty of Medicine, Sydney Univ., 2000–02. Royal Australian College of Physicians: Chm., State Cttee for SA, 1982–86; Chm., Bd of Censors, 1984–88; Vice-Pres., 1988–90; Pres., 1990–92; Pres., Internat. Soc. of Hypertension, 1992–94; Chm., Scientific Adv. Bd, Internat. Soc. and Fedn of Cardiology, 1997–; former mem. and chm., numerous sci. adv. cttees and govt med. bodies. FAA 1987; FAAHMS 2015; Hon. FRACS. Hon. MD: Queensland, 1991; NSW, 1994; Flinders, 1999; Sydney, 2007. Wellcome Medal for contrib. to Med. Res., 1981; Volhard Award, Internat. Soc. of Hypertension, for contrib. to Hypertension Res., 1998; Zanchetti Award, Eur. Soc. of Hypertension, 2008; Res. Medal, Nat. Heart Foundn of Australia, 2009. Officer, Order of Merit (France), 2010. Mem., editl bds of learned jls. *Publications:* over 650 articles in medical jls, on pharmacology, physiology, blood pressure, hypertension and other medical research. *Recreations:* cricket, cooking, theatre, travel. *Address:* George Institute for Global Health, University of Sydney, Royal Prince Alfred Campus (C39), PO Box M201, Missenden Road, Sydney, NSW 2050, Australia; 3A Dettmann Avenue, Longueville, NSW 2066, Australia.

CHALMERS, Michael John; Solicitor to the Advocate General for Scotland and Head, Office of the Advocate General, since 2012; *b* Dundee, 20 June 1974; *s* of David Chalmers and Elizabeth Chalmers; *m* 2008, Leigh Davidson; three *s* one *d*. *Educ:* James Gillespie's High Sch.; Univ. of Edinburgh (LLB Hons 1996; DipLP 1997; LLM Dist. Internat. Law and Human Rights 2011). Admitted as solicitor, 1998. Dundas & Wilson CS, 1997–2005; Solicitor, Office of the Advocate Gen., 2005–07; Branch Hd, Litigation, Scottish Govt, 2007–09; Solicitor (Scotland) to HM Revenue and Customs, 2009–11; Hd, Adv. and Legislation Div., Office of the Advocate Gen., 2011–12. *Recreations:* spending time with family, reading, following Dundee United FC, listening to music, attempting to improve a high golf handicap. *Address:* Office of the Advocate General, Victoria Quay, Edinburgh EH6 6QQ. *T:* (0131) 244 1634. *E:* michael.chalmers@advocategeneral.gsi.gov.uk.

CHALMERS, Sir Neil (Robert), Kt 2001; Warden, Wadham College, Oxford, 2004–12; *b* 19 June 1942; *s* of William King and Irene Margaret Chalmers (*née* Pemberton); *m* 1970, Monica Elizabeth Byanjeru (*née* Rusoke); two *d*. *Educ:* King's College Sch., Wimbledon; Magdalen Coll., Oxford (MA); St John's Coll., Cambridge (PhD). Lectr in Zoology, Makerere University Coll., Kampala, 1966–69; Scientific Dir, Nat. Primate Res. Centre, Nairobi, 1969–70; Open University: Lectr, subseq. Sen. Lectr, then Reader in Biology, 1970–85; Dean of Science, 1985–88; Dir, British Mus. (Natural History), then Natural History Mus., 1988–2004. Chm., Nat. Biodiversity Network Trust, 2005–12. President: Marine Biol Assoc. UK, 2002–07; Inst. of Biology, 2004–06. Fellow, Birkbeck Coll., Univ. of London, 2002. Hon. Fellow: King's College Sch., Wimbledon, 2003; Wadham Coll., Oxford, 2013. Hon. DSc Plymouth, 2004. *Publications:* Social Behaviour in Primates, 1979; numerous papers on animal behaviour in Animal Behaviour and other learned jls. *Recreations:* music, golf, astronomy.

CHALMERS, Patrick Edward Bruce; JP; Chairman: Upper Deeside Access Trust, 2003–09; Cairngorms Outdoor Access Trust, 2008–10; *b* Chapel of Garioch, Aberdeenshire, 26 Oct. 1939; *s* of L. E. F. Chalmers, farmer, Lethenty, Inverurie, and Helen Morris Campbell; *m* 1st, 1963, Ailza Catherine Reid (*d* 2004), *d* of late William McGibbon, Advocate in Aberdeen; three *d*; 2nd, 2008, Rosemary Newsome (*née* Larkins). *Educ:* Fettes Coll., Edinburgh; N of Scotland Coll. of Agriculture (NDA); Univ. of Durham (BScA). Joined BBC as radio talks producer, BBC Scotland, 1963; television producer, 1965; sen. producer, Aberdeen, 1970; Head of Television, Scotland, 1979–82; Gen. Man., Co-Productions, London, 1982; Controller, BBC Scotland, 1983–92; Dir, BBC World Service Television, Asia, 1992–93, retd 1994; Dir, Scottish Ensemble, 1995–2002. Director: Hutchvision News Ltd, 1992–93; Grampian Venture Capital Fund, 1996–. President: Edinburgh Television Fest., 1984–92; BAFTA, Scotland, 1990–92. Dir, Scottish Film Production Fund, 1988–91. Mem., Aberdeenshire Council, 1995–99 (Chm., Lib Dem Gp); Convenor, Grampian Police Bd, 1998–99. Chm., Marr Area Cttee, 1996–99. Mem., Grampian Region Children's Panel, 1974–79. FRSA 1990. Bailie of Bennachie, 1975. JP Aberdeenshire, 1996. *Recreations:* skiing, gardening. *Address:* The Bridge House, Bibury, Glos GL7 5NP. *T:* and *Fax:* (01285) 740749. *Clubs:* New (Edinburgh); Royal Northern (Aberdeen); Foreign Correspondents' (Hong Kong); Kandahar Ski.

CHALONER, family name of **Baron Gisborough**.

CHALONER, Prof. William Gilbert, FRS 1976; Hildred Carlile Professor of Botany and Head of School of Life Sciences, Royal Holloway (formerly Royal Holloway and Bedford New College), University of London, 1985–94 (at Bedford College, 1979–85), Emeritus Professor, 1994, Hon. Fellow, 2002, and engaged in research, Department of Earth Sciences (formerly of Geology), since 1994; *b* London, 22 Nov. 1928; *s* of late Ernest J. and L. Chaloner; *m* 1955, Judith Carroll; one *s* two *d*. *Educ:* Kingston Grammar Sch.; Reading Univ. (BSc, PhD). 2nd Lt RA, 1955–56. Lectr and Reader, University Coll., London, 1956–72. Visiting Prof., Pennsylvania State Univ., USA, 1961–62; Prof. of Botany, Univ. of Nigeria, 1965–66; Prof. of Botany, Birkbeck Coll., Univ. of London, 1972–79. Wilmer D. Barrett Prof. of Botany, Univ. of Mass, 1988–91. Vis. Prof., UCL, 1995–2010. Member: Senate, Univ. of London, 1983–91; Bd of Trustees, Royal Botanic Gardens, Kew, 1983–96. Mem., NERC, 1991–94. President: Palaeontological Assoc., 1976–78; Internat. Orgn of Palaeobotany, 1981–87; Linnean Soc., 1985–88; Vice-Pres., Geol Soc. London, 1985–86. Corresponding Mem., Botanical Soc. of Amer., 1987–. Associé Etranger de l'Acad. des Scis, Inst de France, 1989. Linnean Medal (Botany), Linnean Soc., 1991; Lyell Medal, Geol. Soc., 1994; Lapworth Medal, Palaeontol Assoc., 2006. *Publications:* papers in Palaeontology and other scientific jls, dealing with fossil plants. *Recreations:* swimming, painting. *Address:* 26 Warren Avenue, Richmond, Surrey TW10 5DZ. *T:* (020) 8878 2080.

CHALSTREY, Sir (Leonard) John, Kt 1996; MD; FRCS; JP; Lord Mayor of London, 1995–96; Consultant Surgeon, St Bartholomew's Hospital, 1969–96, now Surgeon Emeritus, St Bartholomew's and the Royal London Hospitals; Senior Lecturer, St Bartholomew's Hospital Medical College, University of London, 1969–96; *b* 17 March 1931; *s* of late Leonard Chalstrey and Frances Mary (*née* Lakin); *m* 1958, Aileen Beatrice Bayes; one *s* one *d*. *Educ:* Dudley Grammar Sch., Worcs; Queens' Coll., Cambridge (BA Hons 1954; MA 1958); Med. Coll., St Bartholomew's Hosp. (MB, BChir 1957; MD 1967). MRCS, LRCP 1957; FRCS 1962. Nat. Service, RAEC, 1949–51. Jun. med. and surgical posts, St Bartholomew's Hosp., 1958–59; Lectr in Anatomy, Middx Hosp. Med. Sch., 1959–61; Jun. Surgical Registrar, St Bartholomew's Hosp., 1962; Registrar, then Sen. Surgical Registrar, Royal Free Hosp., 1963–69; Hon. Consultant Surgeon, St Luke's Hosp. for Clergy, 1975–93. Examiner in Surgery: Univ. of London, 1976–95; Univ. of Cambridge, 1989–94. Non-exec. Mem., City and Hackney HA, 1992–93. City University: Mem. Court, 1986–92; Mem. Council, 1992–2001; Chancellor, 1995–96. Maj., 357 Field Surgical Team, RAMC(V), TA, 1991–96; Hon. Col, 256 (City of London) Field Hosp., RAMC(V), 1996–2000; Member: City of London TAVRA, 1992–2000 (Pres., 1995–96); Gtr London TAVRA, 1992–2000. Governor, Corp. of Sons of the Clergy, 1992–. Mem., Court of Common Council, City of London Corp., 1981–84; Alderman (Vintry Ward), City of London, 1984–2001; Sheriff, City of London, 1993–94; HM Lieut, City of London, 1995–2001; JP 1984. Member, Court of Assistants: Soc. of Apothecaries (Sen. Warden, 1992–93 and 1993–94; Master, 1994–95); Barbers' Co. (Master, 1998–99); Member: Parish Clerks' Co., 1993–2007; HAC, 1995– (Hon. Mem., Ct of Assts, 1984–2001). Vice-Pres., City of London Sect., BRCS, 1992–. Trustee, Morden Coll., 1995–2005; Special Trustee: St Bartholomew's Hosp., 1998–2001; Royal London Hosp., 1999–2001; Life Gov., Christ's Hosp., 1996–; Trustee, St Bartholomew's and The Royal London Hosps Charitable Foundn, 2001–08. Pres., Guildhall Historical Assoc., 2000–07. FRSocMed 1965; Fellow, Assoc. of Surgeons of GB and Ireland, 1969; FRSA 1996. Hon. GSM 1996; Hon. FRSPH (Hon. FRSH 1996); Hon. Fellow, QMW, 1996. Hon. DSc City, 1995. KStJ 1995 (Mem., Chapter-Gen., 1994–99); Surgeon-in-Chief, and Chm., Med. Bd, St John Ambulance, 1993–99; Hospitaller, Priory of England, 1999–2002 (Mem., Priory Council and Chapter, 1999–2002). Grand Officier, Ordre National du Merité (France), 1996. *Publications:* (with Coffman and Smith-Laing) Gastro-Intestinal Disorders, 1986; (contrib.) Cancer in the Elderly, 1990; (contrib.) Maingot's Abdominal Operations, 7th edn 1980, 8th edn 1986; The Aldermen of the City of London, 1900–2010, 2011; papers on surgical subjects in Brit. Jl Surgery, Brit. Jl Cancer and Jl RSM; contribs to Jl of Cambridge Univ. Heraldic and Genealogical Soc. *Recreations:* painting in oils, history of City of London. *Address:* Danebury, 113 The Chine, N21 2EG. *T:* (020) 8360 8921. *Clubs:* Oxford and Cambridge, East India, Guildhall, City Pickwick (Pres., 2007–); Honourable Artillery Company Mess.

CHAMBERLAIN, Very Rev. Father George Ford, (Leo), OSB; Parish Priest, St John the Evangelist, Easingwold, York, since 2008; *b* 13 Aug. 1940; *s* of Brig. Noel Joseph Chamberlain, CBE and Sarah (Sally) (*née* Ford). *Educ:* Ampleforth Coll.; University Coll., Oxford (BA 1961; MA 1965). Novitiate, Ampleforth Abbey, 1961, solemn profession, 1965; ordained priest, 1968; Ampleforth College: Housemaster, St Dunstan's House, 1972–92; Sen. History Master, 1973–92; Headmaster, 1992–2003; Master, St Benet's Hall, Oxford, 2004–07. Involved with aid to Church in Central and Eastern Europe under Communism, 1968–90; organised A Time for Change Conf., Ampleforth Coll., 1990. Member: Council of Management, Keston Inst. (formerly Keston Coll.), 1985–2003; Catholic Bishops' Cttee for European Affairs, 1992–2000; HMC, 1993–2003; Catholic Ind. Schs Conf., 1993–2003 (Mem. Cttee, 1994–2000). Gov., St Gregory the Great Sch., Oxford, 2005–07. Titular Cathedral Prior of St Peter, Glos, 2008–. Hon. Fellow, St Benet's Hall, Oxford, 2008. *Address:* St John's Priory, 151a Long Street, Easingwold, York YO61 3JB.

CHAMBERLAIN, Kevin John, CMG 1992; barrister; Deputy Legal Adviser, Foreign and Commonwealth Office, 1990–99; *b* 31 Jan. 1942; *s* of late Arthur James Chamberlain and Gladys Mary (*née* Harris); *m* 1967, Pia Rosita Frauenlob; one *d*. *Educ:* Wimbledon Coll.; King's Coll., London (LLB). Called to the Bar, Inner Temple, 1965. HM Diplomatic Service, 1965–99: Asst Legal Adviser, FCO, 1965–74; Legal Adviser: British Mil. Govt, Berlin, 1974–76; British Embassy, Bonn, 1976–77; Asst Legal Adviser, FCO, 1977–79; Legal Counsellor, FCO, 1979–83; Counsellor (Legal Advr), Office of UK Perm. Rep. to EC, Brussels, 1983–87; Legal Counsellor, FCO, 1987–90. Panel Mediator, Specialist Mediators LLP, 2010–. Mem., NATO Appeals Bd, 2004–13. Legal Advr, Ministerial Adv. Panel on Illicit Trade in Cultural Objects, 2000–04; Consultant to DCMS on applications for immunity for cultural property, 2008–. Chm., Ind. Remuneration Panel, Reigate and Banstead BC, 2001–09. Mem., Cultural Heritage Law Cttee, ILA, 2007–. CEDR Accredited Mediator, 2002. Vis. Sen. Lectr in Laws, KCL, 2006–08. Hon. Sen. Lectr in Laws, UCL, 2004–05. Fellow, Soc. of Advanced Legal Studies, 2001–. *Publications:* War and Cultural Heritage, 2004,

2nd edn 2013; (contrib.) Protecting Cultural Property in Armed Conflict, 2010; (contrib.) Research Handbook on the Law of Cultural Heritage and Trade, 2013. *Recreations:* opera, tennis, antiques, choral singing. *Address:* Fairfield, Warren Drive, Kingswood, Tadworth, Surrey KT20 6PY.

CHAMBERLAIN, Very Rev. Father Leo; *see* Chamberlain, Very Rev. Father G. F.

CHAMBERLAIN, (Leslie) Neville, CBE 1990; Chairman, The Northern Way, 2006–09; Deputy Chairman, British Nuclear Fuels plc, 1995–99 (Chief Executive, 1986–96); *b* 3 Oct. 1939; *s* of Leslie Chamberlain and Doris Anne Chamberlain (*née* Thompson); *m* 1971, Joy Rachel Wellings; one *s* three *d*. *Educ:* King James I Grammar School, Bishop Auckland; King's College, Univ. of Durham (BSc 1961; MSc 1962). FInstP. UKAEA, 1962–71; Urenco Ltd, 1971–77; British Nuclear Fuels: Fuel Production, 1977–81; Enrichment Business Manager, 1981–84; Dir, Enrichment Div., 1984–86. Dir, 1981–2005, Chm., 2002–05, Urenco Ltd; non-executive Director: Dennis Gp plc, 1994–98; Manchester 2002 Ltd, 1999–2002; New East Manchester Ltd, 1999–2002; RBG Resources plc, 2001–02; AMEC Nuclear Ltd, 2005–14; Essar Oil UK Ltd, 2013–14; Chm., Structure Vision Ltd, 2007–. Chm., Nat Council, TEC, 1999–2001; Mem., NACETT, 1999–2001. Mem. Bd, NW Develt Agency, 2001–04. Chairman: British Energy Assoc., 1999–2001; Internat. Nuclear Energy Acad., 2001–04; Manufg Inst., 2002–; Cheshire and Warrington Econ. Alliance, 2005–10; Nat. Centre for Zoonosis Res., 2008–; Cheshire Business Leaders, 2011–; Co-Chm., Trans-Atlantic Nuclear Energy Forum, 2005–10. Trustee, N of England Zool Soc., 2004–13. Mem., Council, Salford Univ., 2000–09. Freeman, Fuellers' Co., 1997– (Master, 2014–15). FInstE; CCMI; FRSA. Hon. FINucE 1994; Hon. Fellow, European Nuclear Soc., 1994. Hon. DSc: Salford, 1989; Chester, 2012. Melchett Lectr and Medal, Inst. of Energy, 1989. *Recreations:* horse racing, swimming, music, endangered animals. *Address:* Oaklands, 2 The Paddock, Hinderton Road, Neston, South Wirral, Cheshire CH64 9PH. *T:* (0151) 353 1980. *Club:* Athenæum.

CHAMBERLAIN, Ven. Malcolm Leslie; Archdeacon of Sheffield and Rotherham, since 2014; *b* Newmarket, 1 Dec. 1969; *s* of Alan Leslie Chamberlain and Marylyn Sandra Chamberlain; *m* 1994, Joanne Eckersley; one *s* one *d*. *Educ:* Univ. of York (BA Hons 1992); Wycliffe Hall, Oxford (BTh 1996); Univ. of Liverpool (MPhil 2011). Ordained deacon, 1996, priest, 1997; Curate: St John's, Pleck and Bescot, Walsall, 1996–99; St Matthew and St James, Mossley Hill, 1999–2002; Associate Chaplain, 1999–2002, Anglican Chaplain, 2002–07, Univ. of Liverpool; Emerging Church Consultant, Dio. of Liverpool, 2002–07; Rector, St Mary's, Wavertree, 2008–13; Area Dean, Toxteth and Wavertree, 2012–13. *Recreations:* family, football, cinema, music. *Address:* 34 Wilson Road, Sheffield S11 8RN; Diocesan Church House, 95–99 Effingham Street, Rotherham S65 1BL. *T:* (01709) 309110. *E:* malcolm.chamberlain@sheffield.anglican.org.

CHAMBERLAIN, Martin Daniel; QC 2013; *b* Edinburgh, 25 Nov. 1973; *s* of David and Maria Chamberlain; *m* 2001, Samantha Broadfoot; one *s* two *d*. *Educ:* Stewart's Melville Coll., Edinburgh; University Coll., Oxford (BA 1994; BCL 1996); City Univ., London (DipLaw 1995); Inns of Court Sch. of Law. Called to the Bar, Middle Temple, 1997; in practice as barrister, specialising in public law and human rights, 1998–. Mem., Attorney Gen.'s Panels of Jun. Counsel to Crown, 2001–13. *Address:* Brick Court Chambers, 7–8 Essex Street, WC2R 3LD. *T:* (020) 7379 3550. *E:* clerks@brickcourt.co.uk.

CHAMBERLAIN, Prof. Mary Christina, FRHistS; Professor of Modern History, Oxford Brookes University, 1995–2009, now Emeritus; *b* 3 Sept. 1947; *d* of Arthur James Chamberlain and Gladys Mary Chamberlain (*née* Harris); *m* 1st, 1971, Carey Harrison (marr. diss. 1977); one *d*; 2nd, 1980, Peter Lane (marr. diss. 1997); two *d*; 3rd, 2002, Prof. Stein Ringen, *qv*. *Educ:* Univ. of Edinburgh (MA Hons); London Sch. of Econs and Pol Sci. (MSc); Royal Holloway, Univ. of London (MA 2010). Researcher, Arms Control and Disarmament Res. Unit, FCO, 1970–71; Lecturer: Norfolk Coll. of Art and Technol., 1973–74; London Coll. of Fashion, 1974–75; Ipswich Civic Coll., 1975–77; Sen. Lectr, London Coll. of Printing (London Inst.), 1977–87; Lectr (pt-time), Univ. of WI (Cave Hill, Barbados), 1988–91; Fellow, Univ. of Essex, 1991–93; Sen. Lectr, Oxford Brookes Univ., 1993–95. Visiting Professor: Univ. of WI, 2004, 2006; NY Univ., 2004. Founding Ed., Studies in Memory and Narrative, 1997–2008. Mem., Adv. Gp, Virago Press, 1976–91. Member: UK Govt Caribbean Adv. Gp, 1998–2002; Panel of Assessors, Big Lottery Fund, 2001–06. Consultant, Barbados Nat. Oral Hist. Project, 1999; Trustee, Nat. Life Story Collection, Nat. Sound Archive, BL, 1991–2004. FRHistS 2002. Mem., Adv. Gp, Raphael Samuel History Centre, 2002–07. *Publications:* Fenwomen, 1975, 3rd edn 2011; Old Wives' Tales, 1981, 2nd edn 2006; (ed) Writing Lives, 1988; Growing Up in Lambeth, 1989; Narratives of Exile and Return, 1997, 2nd edn 2004; (ed with P. Thompson) Narrative and Genre, 1998, 2nd edn 2004; (ed) Caribbean Migration: globalised identities, 1998; (ed with H. Goulbourne) Caribbean Families in Britain and the Atlantic World, 2001; Family Love in the Diaspora: migration and the Anglo-Caribbean experience, 2006; Empire and Nation-building in the Caribbean: Barbados 1937–1966, 2010; The Mighty Jester, 2014; The Dressmaker of Dachau, 2015. *Recreations:* walking, ski-ing, travel, cooking, grandchildren, gardening, cinema. *Address:* c/o Department of History, Philosophy and Religion, Faculty of Humanities and Social Sciences, Oxford Brookes University, Gipsy Lane, Oxford OX3 0BP. *T:* (020) 8940 1101, *Fax:* (01865) 484082. *E:* marychamberlain@blueyonder.co.uk.

CHAMBERLAIN, Michael Aubrey, OBE 2007; FCA; Consultant, KPMG, Leicester, 1994–2004; *b* 16 April 1939; *s* of George Thomas Everard Chamberlain and Doris (*née* Arden). *Educ:* Repton Sch., Derbys. FCA 1963. Sen. Partner, KPMG Peat Marwick, 1974–93. Pres., Inst. of Chartered Accountants in England and Wales, 1993–94 (Vice-Pres., 1991–92; Dep. Pres., 1992–93); Chm., Chartered Accountants Compensation Scheme, 1998–2009. Chairman: Leicester Diocesan Bd of Finance, 1983–98; Corp. of Church House, 2008–14 (Chm. Council, 2009–14); Audit Cttee, Corp. of Sons of Clergy, 2010–; Member: Archbishops' Council, 1999–2007 (Chm. Finance Cttee, 1999–2007); Adv. Bd, RSCM, 2000–. Dir, Allchurches Trust Ltd, 2006–. Mem. Council, Univ. of Leicester, 1996–2008 (Treas., 1999–2008). Lay Canon, 1988–2014, Canon Emeritus, 2015, Mem. Council, 2012–, Leicester Cathedral. Hon. Fellow, Univ. of Leicester, 2009. Hon. LLD Leicester, 1993. *Address:* Willow End, 3 Spinney Nook, Main Street, Tugby, Leics LE7 9EY. *T:* (0116) 259 8064.

CHAMBERLAIN, Rt Rev. Neville; Master, Hugh Sexey's Hospital, Bruton, 2005–12; *b* 24 Oct. 1939; *s* of Albert Victor Chamberlain and Miriam Chamberlain; *m* 1964, Diana Hammill (*d* 2009); three *s* one *d*. *Educ:* Salford Grammar Sch.; Nottingham Univ. (BA Theol.; MA Applied Social Studies; CQSW); Ripon Hall, Oxford (DPSA 1962). Ordained deacon, 1963, priest, 1964; Asst Curate, St Paul's, Birmingham, 1963–64; Priest-in-charge, St Michael's, Birmingham, 1964–69; Rector, Deer Creek Parish, USA, 1967–68; Vicar, St Michael's Anglican/Methodist Church, Birmingham, 1969–72; Probation Officer, Grimsby, 1972–74; Exec. Sec., Lincoln Diocesan Social Responsibility Cttee, 1974–82; Rector, St John the Evangelist, Edinburgh, 1982–97; Bishop of Brechin, 1997–2005. Prebend and Canon, Lincoln Cathedral, 1979–. *Recreations:* golf, cycling, cinema, walking. *Address:* Wessex House, Quaperlake Street, Bruton, Som BA10 0HG.

CHAMBERLAIN, Neville; *see* Chamberlain, L. N.

CHAMBERLAIN, Dr Nira Cyril; Chief Mathematician, LSC Group, since 2014; *b* Birmingham, 17 June 1969; *s* of Sylvester Chamberlain and Esmeralda Chamberlain; two *s*. *Educ:* Coventry Poly. (BSc Maths 1991); Loughborough Univ. (MSc Industrial Mathematical Modelling 1993); Univ. of Portsmouth (PhD Maths 2013). CMath 1998; CSci 2005. Mathematical Simulation Engineer: T and N, 1994–97; EDS, 1998–2001; Mathematical Engr, Advantica, 2002; Modelling Consultant, LSC Gp, 2002–12; Analytics Modeller, RWE npower, 2012–13. Mem. Council, IMA, 2008–14. Mem., Industrial Adv. Bd, Aston Univ. 2014–. Gov., King's Norton Boys' Sch., 2014–. Speaker, Speakers for Schs, 2014–. *Recreations:* cycling, cricket, pool, table football, cinema. *E:* nira.chamberlain@yahoo.com.

CHAMBERLAIN, Paul Arthur; Headmaster, Cheltenham College, 1997–2004; *b* 10 June 1948; *s* of Arthur and Lilian Amy Chamberlain; *m* 1970, Kathleen Eleanor Hopley; one *s* one *d*. *Educ:* Verdin Grammar Sch., Winsford, Cheshire; Univ. of Durham (BSc Hons Zoology 1969; PGCE 1970). Haileybury College: Asst Master, 1970–83; Housemaster, 1983–88. Headmaster, St Bees Sch., Cumbria, 1988–97. *Recreations:* fell walking, fly-fishing, music, photography. *Address:* Drumlins, Lowick Green, Ulverston, Cumbria LA12 8DY. *T:* (01229) 885424.

CHAMBERLAIN, Peter Edwin, FREng; FRINA; Director, Pai Faena Srl, since 2003; *b* 25 July 1939; *s* of late Dr Eric Alfred Charles Chamberlain, OBE, FRSE, and Winifred Louise (Susan) (*née* Bone); *m* 1963 (separated 2010); two *s* one *d*; partner, 2011, Annamaria Tarallo. *Educ:* Royal High Sch.; Edinburgh Univ. (Keasby Schol., BSc); RN Colls Manadon and Greenwich (Naval Architecture). RCNC. Asst Constructor, ship and submarine design, MB and Bath, 1963–68; Constructor: submarine design, Bath, 1968–69; submarine construction Birkenhead, 1969–72; ship structures R&D, Dunfermline, 1972–74; postgrad. programmes in Naval Architecture, UCL, 1974–77; ship design, Bath, 1977–78; Chief Constructor: Hd of Secretariat, Bath, 1978–80; Surface Ship Forward Design, Bath, 1980–82; RCDS 1983; Asst Sec., Hd of Secretariat to Master Gen. of Ordnance, London, 1984–85; Under Sec., Dir Gen Future Material Programmes (Naval), London, 1985–87; Dep. Controller Warship Equipments, MoD, 1987–88; Chief Underwater Systems Exec., MoD, 1988–89; creation of Defence Res. Agency, MoD, 1989–92; Engr Dir, System and Services Div., BAe, 1992–98 Dir, ANZAC WIP Project, BAe Australia, 1999. Director: Timely Solutions Ltd, 2000–06 Xienta, 2001–03. Mem., Internat. Council on Systems Engrg, 1995–. FREng (FEng 1988). FRINA 1988. *Recreations:* visual arts, poetry, music, maintaining a part of rural Italy. *Address:* via San Martino 7, 06057 Monte Castello di Vibio (PG), Italy. *E:* peter@paifaena.com.

CHAMBERLEN, Nicholas Hugh; Chairman, Clive Discount Company, 1977–93; *b* 18 April 1939; *s* of late Rev. Leonard Saunders Chamberlen, MC, and Lillian Margaret (*née* Webley); *m* 1st, 1962, Jane Mary Lindo (*d* 1998); three *s* one *d*; 2nd, 2001, Christine Mary Lacy. *Educ:* Sherborne Sch.; Lincoln Coll., Oxford (BA Hons). Nat. Cash Register Co., 1962–67; Clive Discount Co. Ltd, 1967–93. *Recreations:* shooting, golf, cricket. *Address:* Lampool, Fairwarp, East Sussex TN22 3DS. *Clubs:* Turf; Royal and Ancient Golf (St Andrews).

CHAMBERS, Aidan, FRSL; writer; *b* 27 Dec. 1934; *m* 1968, Nancy Lockwood. Teacher 1957–68; Jt Founder, Thimble Press, 1969, publisher of Signal: Approaches to Children's Books, 1970–2003. Pres., Sch. Library Assoc., 2003–06. Hon. PhD Umeå, 2003; Hon. LLD Gloucestershire, 2008; Hon. DLitt Oxford Brookes, 2011. FRSL 2009. Children's Lit. Assoc award, USA, 1979; Eleanor Farjeon Award, Children's Book Circle, 1982; Hans Andersen Award, Internat. Bd on Books for Young People, 2002; Lifetime Achievement Award for Services to English Educn, Nat. Assoc. for Teaching of English, 2010. *Publications:* The Reluctant Reader, 1969; Introducing Books to Children, 1973; Booktalk, 1985; The Reading Environment, 1991; Tell Me: children, reading and talk, 1993; Reading Talk, 2001; *novels:* Breaktime, 1978; Dance on my Grave, 1982; Now I Know, 1987; The Toll Bridge, 1992; Postcards from No Man's Land, 1999 (Carnegie Medal, LA, 1999; Michael Printz Award, USA, 2003); This Is All: the pillow book of Cordelia Kenn, 2005; Dying to Know You, 2012; Blindside, 2015; *short stories:* The Kissing Game, 2011; *for children:* Seal Secret, 1980; The Present Takers, 1983; *plays for young people:* Johnny Salter, 1966; The Car, 1967; The Chicken Run, 1968; The Dream Cage, 1981; Only Once, 1998; The Toll Bridge, 1998; ed. of anthologies etc. *Address:* Lockwood, Station Road, South Woodchester, Stroud, Glos GL5 5EQ. *W:* www.aidanchambers.co.uk.

CHAMBERS, Prof. Andrew David, PhD; consultant in board practice and in internal auditing; Academic Director, FTMS Global, since 2014; *b* 7 April 1943; *s* of Lewis Harold and Florence Lilian Chambers; *m* 1st, 1969, Mary Elizabeth Ann Kilbey (marr. diss. 1984); two *s*; 2nd, 1987, Celia Barrington (*née* Pruen); two *s* two *d* (incl. twin *s* and *d*), and one step *s*. *Educ:* St Albans Sch.; Hatfield Coll., Univ. of Durham (BA Hons); London South Bank Univ. (PhD 2013). CEng; EurIng; CITP; FCA, FBCS, FCCA, FIIA. Arthur Andersen & Co., 1965–69; Barker & Dobson, 1969–70; United Biscuits, 1970–71; City University Business School: Lectr in Computer Applications in Accountancy, 1971–74; Leverhulme Sen. Res. Fellow in Internal Auditing, 1974–78; Sen. Lectr in Audit and Management Control, 1978–83; Prof. of Internal Auditing, 1983–93, then Emeritus; Administrative Sub-Dean, 1983–86; Acting Dean, 1985–86; Dean, 1986–91; Head of Dept of Business Studies, 1986–89; Warden, Northampton Hall, City Univ., 1983–86 (Dep. Warden, 1972–76); Prof. of Audit and Control, Univ. of Hull, 1994–98; Academic Dir, FTMS, 1999–2001; Prof. of Corporate Governance (formerly of Internal Auditing), London S Bank Univ., 2004–13. Vis. Professor: in Computer Auditing, Univ. of Leuven, Belgium, 1980–81, 1992–93; of Internal Auditing, Birmingham City Univ. (formerly Univ. of Central England), 2006–11. Mem., Mgt Audit LLP (formerly Dir, Mgt Audit Ltd), 1991–2014. Chm., Harlequin IT Services Ltd, 1998–99. Consultant: MacIntyre Hudson, Chartered Accountants, 1987–89; BBHW, Chartered Accountants, 1990–92; Director: Paragon Gp of Cos (formerly Nat. Home Loans Hldgs), 1991–2003 (Chm., Remuneration Cttee, 1992–95, Audit Cttee, 1995–2003); Nat. Mortgage Bank, 1991–92; IIA Inc., 1993–96 (Mem. Internat. Standards Bd, 1992–95, 2008–); Pilgrim Health NHS Trust, 1996–99; FTMS Online, 1999–2002. Mem. Auditing Practices Bd, 2006–09. Specialist Advr, Inquiry into Auditors: Market Concentration and their Role, H of L Economic Affairs Select Cttee, 2010–12. Institute of Internal Auditors-UK: Mem. Council, 1985–86; Mem., Professional Standards and Guidelines Cttee (Chm., 1991–95); Association of Chartered Certified Accountants: Mem., Auditing Cttee, 1994–2011; Chm., Internal Auditing Cttee, 2002–06; Chm., Corporate Governance and Risk Mgt Cttee, 2006–10; Mem., Governance, Risk and Perf. Forum, 2011–. Member: Council, BCS, 1979–82 (Mem., Tech. Bd, 1979–82; Chm., Meetings Cttee, 1980–82); IT Cttee, 1986–91, Internal Audit Cttee, 1998–2003 and 2011–14, Corporate Governance Cttee, 2004–06, ICAEW; Educn, Training and Technol. Transfer Cttee, British Malaysian Soc., 1987–90; MBA Adv. Bd, Ashridge Management Coll., 1986–92; UK Cttee on Internal Audit Guidance for Financial Services, 2012–13; Council, Tavistock Inst., 2004–08 (Chm., Audit Cttee, 2006–08). Director: Council of Univ. Management Schs, 1988–92; Med. Defence Union, 2004–06 (Chm., Audit Cttee, 2004–06); Hon. Auditor, RSAA, 1986–91. External Examr, Dundee Univ., 1998–2002. MInstD 1986; FRSA. Gov., Islington Green Comprehensive Sch., 1989–91. Liveryman, Loriners' Co., 2003–. Member, Editorial Board: Computer Fraud and Security, 1981–87; Managerial Auditing Jl, 1986–94; Asian Acad. of Mgt Jl, 2003–; Gen. Editor, Internat. Jl of Auditing, 1995–2003; Editor: Internal Control, 1997–2005; Corporate Governance, 1998–2004; Fraud, 2000–01. *Publications:* (with O. J. Hanson) Keeping Computers Under Control, 1975; (ed) Internal Auditing: developments and horizons, 1979; Internal Auditing: theory and practice, 1981, 2nd edn (with G. M. Selim and G. Vinten) 1987; Computer Auditing, 1981, 3rd edn (with J. M. Court) 1991; Effective Internal Audits: how to plan and implement, 1992; (with G. Rand) Auditing the IT Environment, 1994; (with G. Rand) Auditing Contracts, 1994; (ed) Internal Auditing, 1996; (with G. Rand) The Operational Auditing Handbook: auditing business processes, 1997, 2nd edn 2010; (with J.

Ridley) Leading Edge Internal Auditing, 1998; Tolley's Corporate Governance Handbook, 2002, 6th edn 2014 as Chambers' Corporate Governance Handbook; Tolley's Internal Auditor's Handbook, 2005, 2nd edn 2009; papers in learned jls. *Recreation:* family. *Address:* Moat Lane, Old Bolingbroke, Spilsby, Lincs PE23 4ES. *T:* (020) 7099 9355. *E:* ac@m-a.myzen.co.uk. *Club:* Reform.

CHAMBERS, Daniel; Joint Company Director, Blink Films (formerly Blink Film and Television) Ltd, since 2007; *b* 13 Sept. 1968; *s* of Michael Earnest Chambers and Florence Ruth Cooper; partner, Rebecca Claire Eisig Cotton. *Educ:* William Ellis Sch.; University Coll. Sch.; Brasenose Coll., Oxford (BA Hons). Journalist, Evening Standard, 1991–92; researcher/asst producer, Panorama, Dispatches and Equinox, 1992–96; Director: Equinox Sun Storm, 1996; Equinox Russian Roulette, 1997; Science Department, Channel 4: Dep. Commng Ed., 1998–99; Editor, 1999–2001: devised Secrets of the Dead; commnd Escape from Colditz, Cannibal, Extinct and Salvage Squad; responsible for Scrapheap Challenge; jtly responsible for Big Brother; Controller of Factual Progs, Channel 5, subseq. Five, 2001–03: devised History Strand Revealed; commnd World War I in Colour, Kings & Queens, Britain's Worst Driver, Fifth Gear; Dir of Programmes, Five, 2003–06; Blink: Exec. Producer of Great Sperm Race, When Boris Met Dave, Ancients Behaving Badly, Chinese Food in Minutes, True Stories, Extraordinary Animals, The Lion Cub from Harrods, Monty Don's Italian Gardens, Classic Car Rescue, Treasures Decoded, My Wild Affair, Rebuilding Noah's Ark, Super Skyscrapers, Mexican Food Made Simple, The Woman Raised by Monkeys, Nazi Titanic: What Destroyed the Hindenberg?, The Missing Evidence, Shut-Ins, Meet the Orangutans. Gov., London Film Sch., 2006–. Trustee, Freud Mus., 2014–. Author of play, Selling Out (first dir. by Alan Ayckbourn, Scarborough, 1992). *Recreations:* cinema, playing the piano. *Address:* Blink Films Ltd, Bankstock Building, 42–44 De Beauvoir Crescent, N1 5SB. *T:* (020) 3150 0777. *Club:* Shoreditch House.

CHAMBERS, Dominic Kern; QC 2008; *b* Solihull, 28 Feb. 1963; *s* of Martin Royston Chambers and Marcia Parsons Chambers; *m* 1992, Georgina Kent, *qv* (marr. diss. 2009); one *s* two *d*. *Educ:* Sandroyd Sch.; Harrow Sch.; King's Coll. London (LLB Hons). Called to the Bar, Gray's Inn, 1987; in practice as barrister, 1988–, specialising in internat. and commercial litigation and arbitration. Freeman, City of London, 1983; Liveryman, 1992, Mem., Ct of Assts, 2009, Co. of Pewterers. *Recreations:* horology, wine, shooting, Brazil rainforest.

CHAMBERS, Ernest George Wilkie; Managing Director, Beattie Communications Group (formerly Beattie Media), 2001–08; *b* 10 May 1947; *s* of Ernest and Ada Chambers; *m* 1971, Jeanette; one *s* one *d*. *Educ:* Harris Acad., Dundee; Dundee Univ. (BSc 1st Cl. Hons Applied Sci. 1969); Strathclyde Univ. (MBA 1987). Graduate civil engr, E of Scotland Water Bd, 1969–73; Asst Engr, Lower Clyde Water Bd, 1973–75; Area Engr (Renfrew), 1975–78; Lower Clyde Division: Divl Ops Engr, 1978–84; Asst Divl Manager, 1984–86; Asst Dir (Ops and Maintenance), 1986–88; Dir of Water, 1988–94; Dir, Water Services, Strathclyde Regl Council, 1994–95; Chief Exec., West of Scotland Water, 1995–2001. *Recreations:* DIY, gardening.

CHAMBERS, Fredrick Rignold H.; *see* Hyde-Chambers.

CHAMBERS, John T.; Executive Chairman, Cisco Systems Inc., since 2015 (President and Chief Executive Officer, 1995–2006; Chairman and Chief Executive, 2006–15); *m* Elaine; two *c*. *Educ:* West Virginia Univ. (BS/BA business; JD); Indiana Univ. (MBA). Formerly posts with IBM (incl. Exec. Vice-Pres.), and Wang Labs (latterly Sen. Vice-Pres. of US Ops); Sen. Vice-Pres. for Worldwide Ops, 1991–94, Exec. Vice-Pres., 1994–95, Cisco Systems Inc. Mem., US President's Adv. Cttee for Trade Policy and Negotiations and Nat. Security Adv. Cttee, 1997–99. *Address:* Cisco Systems Inc., 170 West Tasman Drive, San Jose, CA 95134, USA.

CHAMBERS, Prof. Jonathon Arthur, PhD, DSc; CEng, FREng; FIET, FIEEE; Professor of Signal and Information Processing, Newcastle University, since 2015; *b* Peterborough, 10 March 1960; *s* of Arthur Chambers and Dr Betty Chambers, MBE. *Educ:* Orton Longueville Sch., Peterborough; Peterborough Regl Coll.; HMS Fisgard and HMS Collingwood; Poly. of Central London (BSc 1st Cl. Electrical Engrg 1985); Imperial Coll. London (PhD Signal Processing 1990; DSc 2014). CEng 1994; FIET 2005; FIEEE 2011; FREng 2012. Lectr, Poly. of Central London, 1985–86; res. scientist, Schlumberger Cambridge Res., 1991–93; Lectr, 1994–98, Reader, 1998–2000, Imperial Coll. London; Prof. of Signal Processing, KCL, 2001–04; Professorial Res. Fellow, Cardiff Univ., 2004–07; Prof. of Communications and Signal Processing, Univ. of Loughborough, 2007–14. *Publications:* (jtly) Recurrent Neural Networks for Prediction: learning algorithms, architectures and stability, 2001; (jtly) EEG Signal Processing, 2007. *Recreations:* classical music, cycling, motor vehicles. *Address:* School of Electrical and Electronic Engineering, Merz Building, Newcastle University, Newcastle upon Tyne NE1 7RU. *T:* (0191) 208 5965. *E:* jonathon.chambers@ncl.ac.uk.

CHAMBERS, Michael Laurence; QC 2003; **His Honour Judge Michael Chambers;** a Circuit Judge, since 2011; *b* 3 Dec. 1956; *s* of late Lawrence Chambers, CEng and Maureen Chambers; *m* 1989, Verity Susan Stowell Hunt; one *s* one *d*. *Educ:* Cheltenham Coll.; St Peter's Coll., Oxford (MA). Called to the Bar, Lincoln's Inn, 1980; in practice, Wales and Chester Circuit, 1981–2011; Circuit Jun., 2002. An Asst Recorder, 1997–2000; a Recorder, 2000–11; Standing Counsel to HM Customs and Excise, 2001. Legal Assessor, GMC, 2002–. *Address:* Birmingham Crown Court, 1 Newton Street, Birmingham B4 7NA. *Club:* Chester City.

CHAMBERS, His Honour Nicholas Mordaunt; QC 1985; mediator and arbitrator, since 2012; a Circuit Judge (a Specialist Judge), 1999–2012; Mercantile Judge for Wales and Chester, 1999–2007, for Wales, 2007–12; *b* 25 Feb. 1944; *s* of late Marcus Mordaunt Bertrand Chambers and Lona Margit Chambers (*née* Gross); *m* 1966, Sally Elizabeth, *er d* of T. H. F. (Tony) Banks; two *s* one *d*. *Educ:* King's School, Worcester; Hertford College, Oxford (BA 1965). Called to the Bar, Gray's Inn, 1966, Bencher, 1994; a Recorder, 1987–99; a Dep. High Court Judge, 1994–99. Member: Civil Procedure Rule Cttee, 1997–99; Civil Cttee, Judicial Studies Bd, 2002–08. Chm., Incorporated Council of Law Reporting, 2001–13. *Publications:* (author and illustrator) Missed Moments in Legal History, 2012; Case Handling: an illustrated view from the Bench, 2014. *Recreations:* illustration, sketching, writing. *Address:* Brick Court Chambers, 7–8 Essex Street, WC2R 3LD. *Club:* Garrick.

CHAMBERS, Maj.-Gen. Peter Antony, CB 2002; MBE 1982; Director, McWhirter Foundation, since 2009; *b* 23 April 1947; *s* of Mary Eugenie Chambers and Vincent Gerard Chambers; *m* 1968, Valerie Anne Straker; one *d* (and one *d* decd). *Educ:* De La Salle Grammar Sch.; Liverpool Univ. (BA Hons). Commissioned RAOC, 1969; Staff Coll., 1979 (psc); OC 51 Ordnance Co., 1982–83; CO 1 Ordnance Bn, 1985–88; Col Ordnance 1, 1988–90; Higher Comd and Staff Course, 1990; Comdr Supply, 1st (BR) Corps, 1990–93; Mem., RCDS, 1993; Dir, Logistic Support Policy, 1995–97; Sen. Army Mem., RCDS, 1997–98; DCS, HQ Land Command, 1998–2002. Dir, Hill Homes, 2002–06; Interim CEO, Richmond upon Thames Council for Voluntary Services, 2006–07. Rep. Col Comdt, RLC, 2003–04, 2006–07. Chm., RAOC Assoc., 2005–14 (Pres., Council, 2013–). *Recreations:* walking, voluntary charity work, family. *Address:* RAOC Secretary, RHQ the RLC, Dettingen House, The Princess Royal Barracks, Deepcut, Camberley, Surrey GU16 6RW.

CHAMBERS, Prof. Richard Dickinson, PhD, DSc; FRS 1997; Professor of Chemistry, University of Durham, 1976–2000, now Emeritus; *b* 16 March 1935; *s* of Alfred and Elizabeth Chambers; *m* 1959, Anne Boyd; one *s* (one *d* decd). *Educ:* Stanley Grammar Sch.; Univ. of Durham (BSc; PhD 1959; DSc 1968). Research Fellow, UBC, Vancouver, 1959–60; University of Durham: Lectr, 1960–69; Reader, 1969–76; Head of Dept, 1983–86; Sir Derman Christopherson Res. Fellow, 1988–89. Vis. Lectr and Fulbright Fellow, Case-Western Reserve Univ., Cleveland, Ohio, 1966–67; Tarrant Vis. Prof., Univ. of Florida, Gainesville, 1999. Non-exec. Dir, F2 Chemicals Ltd, 1995–2000. Internat. Award for Creative Work in Fluorine Chemistry, ACS, 1991; Moissan Internat. Prize, 2003. *Publications:* Fluorine in Organic Chemistry, 1973, 2nd edn 2004; contribs to jls on many aspects of organo-fluorine compounds. *Recreations:* opera, golf, soccer. *Address:* 5 Aykley Green, Whitesmocks, Durham DH1 4LN. *T:* (0191) 386 5791. *E:* rd.chambers@btinternet.com.

CHAMBERS, Robert Alexander H.; *see* Hammond-Chambers.

CHAMBERS, Prof. Robert Guy; Professor of Physics, University of Bristol, 1964–90, Emeritus, 1990; *b* 8 Sept. 1924; *s* of A. G. P. Chambers and C. K. Chambers (*née* Dixon); *m* 1st, 1950, Joan Brislee (marr. diss. 1981); one *d*; 2nd, 1988, Susan Eden. *Educ:* King Edward VI Sch., Southampton; Peterhouse, Cambridge. Work on tank armament (Ministry of Supply), 1944–46; Electrical Research Association, 1946–47; Royal Society Mond Laboratory, Cambridge, 1947–57; Stokes Student, Pembroke Coll., 1950–53; PhD 1952; ICI Fellow, 1953–54; NRC Post-doctoral Fellow, Ottawa, 1954–55; University Demonstrator, Cambridge, 1955–57; Bristol University: Sen. Lectr, 1958–61; Reader in Physics, 1961–64; Dean of Science, 1973–76, 1985–88; Pro-Vice-Chancellor, 1978–81. Member: Physics Cttee, 1967–71, Nuclear Physics Bd, 1971–74, Sci. Bd, 1975–78, SRC; Physical Sci. Sub-Cttee, UGC, 1974–81. Institute of Physics: Mem., Publications Cttee, 1969–81 (Chm., 1977–81); Vice-Pres., 1977–81. Chm., Standing Conf. of Physics Profs, 1987–89. Chairman: SLS (Information Systems) Ltd, 1986–89; Track Analysis Systems Ltd, 1986–92. Hon. Fellow, Univ. of Bristol, 1994. Hughes Medal, Royal Soc., 1994. *Publications:* Electrons in Metals and Semiconductors, 1990; various papers in learned journals on the behaviour of metals at low temperatures. *Recreation:* resting. *Address:* 9 Apsley Road, Clifton, Bristol BS8 2SH. *T:* (0117) 973 9833.

CHAMBERS, Prof. Ruth Margaret, OBE 2012; DM; FRCGP; general practitioner; Clinical Associate, since 2011, and Clinical Lead for Telehealth, since 2013, Stoke-on-Trent Clinical Commissioning Group; *b* Gloucester, 13 March 1952; *d* of Ronald Campbell and Hilda Campbell (*née* Probyn); *m* 1977, Christopher Chambers; two *s* one *d*. *Educ:* Altrincham Grammar Sch. for Girls; Nottingham Univ. (BMedSci 1973; BM BS 1975; DM 1995). FRCGP 1992. General Practitioner: Mobberley, 1982–85; Stone, 1985–96; Tunstall, 1997– (now pt-time). Prof. of Primary Care, Staffs Univ., 1996–2005, now Hon. Prof.; Dir, Gen. Practice Educn, W Midlands SHA, 2005–06; Clin. lead for practice develt, NHS Stoke on Trent, 2008–11. Mem., Governing Council, Coll. of Medicine, 2010–11. *Publications:* Clinical Effectiveness Made Easy, 1998, 4th edn (jtly) as Clinical Effectiveness and Clinical Governance Made Easy, 2007; (with M. Davies) What Stress!, 1999; (with M. Davies) What Stress in Primary Care!, 1999; Survival Skills for GPs, 1999; Fertility Problems: a simple guide, 1999; Involving Patients and the Public: how to do it better, 1999, 2nd edn 2003; (jtly) Survival Skills for Nurses, 1999; (jtly) Teaching Made Easy: a manual for health professionals, 1999, 3rd edn 2011 (Korean edn 2008); (jtly) Opportunities and Options in Medical Careers, 2000; (with G. Wakley) Making Clinical Governance Work for You, 2000 (Japanese edn 2004); (jtly) Continuing Professional Development in Primary Care, 2000; (ed with M. Baker) A Guide to General Practice Careers, 2000; (with K. Mohanna) Risk Matters in Healthcare: communicating, explaining and managing risk, 2000; (jtly) Tackling Teenage Pregnancy: sex, culture and needs, 2000; (jtly) Occupational Health Matters in General Practice, 2000; (jtly) Back Pain Matters in Primary Care, 2001; (jtly) Diabetes Matters in Primary Care, 2001; (jtly) Implementing the National Service Framework for Coronary Heart Disease in Primary Care, 2001; (jtly) Clinical Effectiveness and Clinical Governance for Midwives, 2001, 2nd edn 2008; (jtly) Mental Healthcare Matters in Primary Care, 2001; (jtly) Musculoskeletal Matters in Primary Care, 2001; (jtly) Cardiovascular Disease Matters in Primary Care, 2001; (with G. Wakley) Obesity and Overweight Matters in Primary Care, 2001; (with G. Wakley) Sexual Health Matters in Primary Care, 2001; (jtly) Prescription for Learning: techniques, games and activities, 2002; (ed) A Guide to Accredited Professional Development: pathway to revalidation, 2002; (ed) A Guide to the Accredited Professional Development Modules File: evidence of learning, 2002; (jtly) Clinical Governance in General Dental Practice, 2002; (jtly) Beating Stress in the NHS, 2002; (jtly) Appraisal for the Apprehensive, 2002; (jtly) Smoking Cessation Matters in Primary Care, 2002; (jtly) Infertility Matters in Healthcare, 2003; (jtly) Survival Skills for Doctors and their Families, 2003; (jtly) Make Your Healthcare Organisation a Learning Organisation, 2003; (jtly) Improving Sexual Health Advice, 2003; (jtly) Demonstrating Your Competence 1: healthcare teaching, 2004; (jtly) Demonstrating Your Competence 2: women's health, 2004; (jtly) Demonstrating Your Competence 3: cardiovascular and neurological conditions, 2004; (jtly) The Good Appraisal Toolkit for Primary Care, 2004; (jtly) The Good Mentoring Toolkit for Healthcare, 2004; (jtly) Demonstrating your Clinical Competence in Women's Health, 2004; (jtly) Demonstrating your Competence 4: respiratory disease, mental health, diabetes and dermatology, 2004; Beat Back Pain, 2004; (ed with K. Licence) Looking after Children in Primary Care: a companion to the Children's National Service Framework, 2005; (jtly) Demonstrating your Clinical Competence in Cardiovascular and Neurological Conditions, 2005; (jtly) Demonstrating your Competence 5: substance abuse, palliative care, musculoskeletal conditions, prescribing practice, 2005; (with G. Wakley) Chronic Disease Management in Primary Care: quality and outcomes, 2005; (jtly) Demonstrating your Competence in Reproductive Health: a guide for hospital doctors, their trainers and practitioners with a special interest, 2005; (jtly) Demonstrating your Clinical Competence in Respiratory Disease, Diabetes and Dermatology, 2005; (ed) Career Planning for Everyone in the NHS: the toolkit, 2005; (with G. Wakley) Clinical Audit in Primary Care: demonstrating quality and outcomes, 2005; Healthy Heart, 2005; (jtly) Demonstrating your Clinical Competence in Depression, Dementia, Alcoholism, Palliative Care and Osteoporosis, 2005; (jtly) Guiding Doctors in Managing their Careers, 2006; (jtly) Supporting Self Care in Primary Care, 2006; (jtly) How to Succeed in Writing a Book, 2006; (ed) Making an Effective Bid, 2007; (ed jtly) How to Succeed as a Leader, 2007; (jtly) Your Teaching Style, 2007; (jtly) Revalidation: prepare now and get it right, 2008; articles in jls. *Recreations:* theatre, walking, family, especially husband and grandchildren. *Address:* Furlong Medical Practice, Furlong Road, Tunstall ST6 5UD. *T:* (01782) 577388. *E:* ruth.chambers@stoke.nhs.uk.

CHAMBERS, Ruth Marian; *see* Arlow, R. M.

CHAMBERS, Sarah Penelope; independent consultant; Director, Office for Renewable Energy Deployment, Department of Energy and Climate Change, 2011–13; *b* 8 Nov. 1958; *d* of Sir (Stanley) Paul Chambers, KBE, CB, CIE and of Edith Chambers; *m* 1985, Andrew Hearn; three *s*. *Educ:* Channing Sch., N London; Somerville Coll., Oxford (BA Hons PPE). Department of Trade and Industry, 1979–2004: on loan to OFT, 1980–81; on loan to Oftel as Dir, Licensing, 1994–98; Dir, Strategy and Competitiveness Unit, 1999–2001; Dir, Automotive Unit, 2001–04; Chief Exec., Postal Services Commn, 2004–08; Dir, Consumer and Competition Policy, BERR, subseq. BIS, 2008–11. Panel Member: Judicial Appts Commn, 2012–; Bar Standards Bd, 2012–; CAA Consumer Panel, 2012–; Renewable Energy Consumer Code, 2013–; Reporting Panel Mem. and Specialist Panel Mem., CMA (formerly Competition Commn), 2013–. Ind. Dir, UK Payments Council, 2014–. Mem., Adv. Bd, Centre for Competition Policy, UEA, 2009–. Chm. Trustees, Shepherds Bush Families Project, 2013–; Trustee, Zamcog, 2014–. *Recreations:* tennis, running.

CHAMBERS, Stephen Lyon, RA 2005; artist; *b* 20 July 1960; *s* of John Tangye Chambers and Gillian Mure Chambers; *m* 1991, Denise de Cordova; three *s*. *Educ:* Winchester Sch. of Art (Fellow 1986); St Martin's Sch. of Art (BA 1st Cl. Hons 1982); Chelsea Sch. of Art (MA 1983). Rome Schol., 1983–84; Fellow, Downing Coll./Kettle's Yard, Cambridge, 1998–99. Trustee, Bryan Robertson Trust, 2003–. *Solo exhibitions* include: Flowers East Gall., London, 1989, 1992, 1995, 1998, 2000, 2003, 2006; Flowers Graphics, London, 1995, 1997, 2003, 2005; Flowers West, Santa Monica, 1998, 2000; Ikon Gall., Birmingham, 1993; Kettle's Yard, Cambridge, 1998, 1999; Gal. Kemper, Munich, 2000, 2001; Frissiras Mus., Athens, 2002; Gal. Frank Pages, Baden-Baden, 2005, 2015; Kings Place Gall., 2010; RA, 2012; Gall. 10, Milan, 2013; Pera Mus., Istanbul, 2014; *group exhibitions* include: Flowers East Gall.; RCA; Winchester Gall.; Plymouth Arts Centre; Riverside Studios; London Inst.; Flowers, NY; Nigel Greenwood Gall., London; Eagle Gall., London. Set designs for Royal Ballet, 2001. Trustee: Bryan Robertson Trust, 2003–; Arthur Koestler Trust, 2013–. *Publications:* Long Pig, 1994; Four Heads, 1994; Healing Poems for the Great Ape, 1997; (with Marina Warner) Lullaby for an Insomniac Princess, 2006; A Year of Ranting Hopelessly, 2007; The Long Feast, 2010; *relevant publication:* Stephen Chambers (monograph), by Andrew Lambirth, 2008; Stephen Chambers: the big country, by Rod Mengham, 2012. *Recreations:* cryptic crosswords, avoiding listening to speeches, Middle Eastern cooking, growing vegetables, Liverpool Football Club, contemplating revenge. *Address:* c/o Royal Academy of Arts, Burlington House, Piccadilly, W1J 0BD. *E:* stephenlyonchambers@btinternet.com.

CHAMBERS, Stuart John; Chairman: Rexam plc, since 2012; ARM Holdings plc, since 2014; President and Chief Executive, NSG Group (formerly Nippon Sheet Glass Co. Ltd), 2008–09 (Director, 2006–09); Executive Vice President, 2007–08; Chief Executive, Pilkington Group, 2006–07); *b* 25 May 1956; *s* of Reginald and Eileen Chambers; *m* 1984, Nicolette Horrocks; one *s* two *d*. *Educ:* Friends Sch., Great Ayton; UCL (BSc Hons). Shell, 1977–88; Mars Corp., 1988–96; Pilkington: Gp Vice Pres. Marketing, Building Products, 1996–97; Gen. Manager, Pilkington UK Ltd, 1997–98; Man. Dir, Primary Products Europe, 1998–2000; Pres., Building Products Worldwide, 2000–07; Gp Chief Exec., Pilkington plc, 2002–06. Non-executive Director: ABP Hldgs plc, 2002–06 (Chm., Remuneration Cttee, 2005–06); Smiths Gp plc, 2006–12 (Chm., Remuneration Cttee, 2006–12); Tesco plc, 2010–15 (Chm., Remuneration Cttee, 2010–15); Manchester Airport Gp plc, 2010–12; Tesco Personal Finance, 2012–14. Mem., NorthWest Business Leadership Team, 1997–2009 (Chm., 2006–08). *Recreations:* sailing, supporting Rugby Union.

CHAMBERS, Timothy Lachlan, OBE 2009; JP; FRCP; Consultant Physician (general and renal medicine), Bristol Royal Hospital for Children (formerly Royal Hospital for Sick Children, Bristol), 1979–2010; Vice Lord-Lieutenant of the County and City of Bristol, since 2012; *b* 11 Feb. 1946; *né* Seamus Rory Dorrington; *s* of late Mary Teresa Dorrington, Moate, Co. Westmeath, and adopted *s* of late Victor Lachlan Chambers and Elsie Ruth (*née* Reynolds); *m* 1971, (Elizabeth) Joanna Ward, DL, FRCP; one *s* one *d* (and one *d* decd). *Educ:* Wallington County Grammar Sch.; King's College London; King's Coll. Hosp. Med. Sch. (MB BS 1969). FRCP 1983; FRCPE 1985; FRCPI 1995 (Fellow, Faculty of Paediatrics, RCPI, 1989). Jun. med. posts, London and SE England, 1969–73; Tutor in paed. and child health, Univ. of Leeds, 1973–76 (Sen. Registrar in (renal) medicine, St James's Hosp., Leeds, 1974–75); Physician and nephrologist, Derbyshire Children's Hosp. and Nottingham Hosps, 1976–79; Physician (gen. and renal medicine), paediatric depts, Southmead Hosp., Bristol, and Weston-super-Mare Gen. Hosp., 1979–2010; Sen. Clinical Lectr in Child Health, Univ. of Bristol, 1979–2010; Clinical Dean, Southmead Hosp., 1983–90; Mem. Court, Univ. of Bristol, 1994–99; Member: Governing Body, Inst. of Child Health, 1987–97; Bd of Govs, Hosps for Sick Children (London) SHA, 1993–94. Dep. Med. Dir, Southmead Health Services NHS Trust, 1994–96. Consultant in paediatrics to MoD, 1985–2010; Civilian Consultant Advr (Paediatrics) to Medical Dir. Gen. (Navy), 1993–2012. Medicines and Healthcare Products Regulatory Agency (formerly Medicines Control Agency): Member: Cttee on Safety of Medicines, 1999–2005; Expert Adv. Gp on Paediatric Medicines (formerly Paediatric Medicines Working Gp), 2000–05, 2008–12; Adv. Bd on Registration of Homoeopathic Products, 2000–14 (Chm., 2003–14); Alternate UK Delegate, Paediatric Cttee, EMA, 2008–12. Mem., SW Adv. Sub Cttee on Clinical Excellence Awards, 2003–09 (Med. Vice Chm., 2006–09). Royal College of Physicians: Mem. Council, 1990–92; Censor, 1992–94. Regl (SW England) Advr, RCPE, 1996–2001; Mem., BMA 1979–2014 (Chm., Paed. Sub-Cttee, Central Consultants and Specialists Cttee, 1989–94); Associate (perf. assessor), GMC, 1998–2010; Mem., 1976–97, Hon. Asst Sec., 1981–84, Hon. Sec., 1984–89, BPA, subseq. CPCH, then RCPCH; FRSocMed 1977 (a Vice-Pres., 2001–03; Mem. Council, 1995–2003; Pres., Sect. of Paediatrics, 1994–95; Hon. Editor, 1997–2001; Pres., United Services Section, 2001–03); President: Union of Nat. Eur. Paed. Socs and Assocs, 1990–94; Bristol Medico-Chirurgical Soc., 1996–97; Bristol Div., BMA, 1999–2000; SW Paediatric Club, 2004–06; Bristol Medico-Legal Soc., 2007–09. Sometime examr to med. bodies and univs at home and abroad; chm. and mem., other prof. and govtl cttees and adv. bodies in UK and Europe. Member: Philosophical Soc., Oxford; British Assoc. for Paed. Nephrology (Hon. Mem. 2011); Corresp. Mem., Société Française de Pédiatrie, 1994. Mem., Editl Bd, Sri Lanka Jl of Child Health, 2002–. Trustee: St John's Home, Bristol, 1985–93; Royal Med. Benevolent Fund, 1988–2004; Educn and Resources for Improving Childhood Continence, 2006–14 (Acting Chm., 2012–14); Chm., Bristol, NSPCC, 2011–14 (Vice Pres., 2014–). Ambassador: Alabaré Charity, 2010– (Vice Chm., Bristol Ambassadors, 2011–); Girlguiding Bristol and S Glos, 2010–. Gov., Redland High Sch. for Girls, Bristol, 2011– (Chm., 2012–). Commnd Capt., 1984, retired Lt Col, 2010, RAMC(V); Clin. Dir 243 (The Wessex) Field Hosp. (V), 2006–08 (Hon. Mem., Officers' Mess); MO, Lt Col, Somerset Cadet Bn The Rifles (formerly Light Infantry) (ACF), 1999–2012; non-regtl Mem., HAC, 2013–; Chm., Co. and City of Bristol, Wessex RFCA, 2014–; Hon. Mem., Officers' Mess, RM Reserve Bristol, 2013. Eucharistic Minister and Reader, RC Cathedral Church of SS Peter and Paul, Clifton, 1991–; Oblate of Downside, 2010–. Master, Bristol Br., Guild of Catholic Doctors, 2006–08. Freeman, City of London, 1982; Liveryman: Apothecaries' Soc., 1985– (Master, 2011–12; Member: Court of Assts, 2000–); Barbers' Co., 2012–. JP Bristol, 1993; High Sheriff, Co. and City of Bristol, 2009–10; DL 2012. Hon. FSLCPaed 2002; Hon. FRCPCH 2014. CFM 2011. Diamond Jubilee Medal, 2012; Good Samaritan Medal, Pontifical Council for Health Care Workers, 2013. CLJ 2013. *Publications:* Fluid Therapy in Childhood, 1987; contribs to med. and lay jls and collective works. *Recreation:* Verdauungsspaziergänge. *Address:* 4 Clyde Park, Bristol BS6 6RR. *T:* (0117) 974 2814. *Clubs:* Athenæum, MCC (Associate Mem.), Victory Services; Clifton (Bristol); Bristol Savages (Green Feather); Galle Face Hotel (Colombo).

CHAMBERS, Tony; Editor-in-Chief, Wallpaper*, since 2007; *b* Liverpool, 4 Sept. 1963; *s* of Joseph and Anne Chambers; *m* 2012, Georgia Dehn; one *d*. *Educ:* Central St Martin's Coll. of Art and Design (BA 1st Cl. Hons Graphic Design 1987). Art Ed., Sunday Times, 1987–97; Art Dir, GQ, 1997–2002; Creative Dir, Wallpaper*, 2003–07. *Address:* Wallpaper*, Blue Fin Building, 110 Southwark Street, SE1 0SU. *T:* (020) 3148 7755. *E:* contact@wallpaper.com. *Clubs:* Walbrook, Soho House.

CHAMIER, Michael Edward Deschamps, FCA; European Financial Consultant, Molitor Europe, since 2003; Director of Finance, European Parliament, 1983–2002; *b* 4 Feb. 1941; *s* of late Saunders Edward Chamier and Mary Frances (*née* Chapman); *m* 1977, Deborah Mary Unwin; one *s* two *d*. *Educ:* Ampleforth Coll., York. FCA 1975. Sen. Audit Mgr, Arthur Young, Paris, 1965–68; Dep. Dir, Finance and Admin, Reckitt & Coleman, France, 1968–72; Asst Financial Controller for Europe, Squibb Europe, 1972–77; Dep. Dir of Financial Admin, Europe, CABOT Europe, 1977–83. Sec. Gen., Fondation Mérite Européen, 2012–. Silver Medal, European Foundn of Merit, 2006. *Publications:* Property Purchasing in France, 1981. *Recreations:* worldwide travel, opera, Anglo-French theatre and films. *Address:* 1 rue de Limpach, Reckange-sur-Mess, 4980 Luxembourg. *E:* chamier@europe.com.

CHAMP, Andrea Helen; *see* Quinn, A. H.

CHAMPION, Prof. Justin Adrian Ivan, PhD; FRHistS; Professor of History of Early Modern Ideas, Royal Holloway, University of London, since 2003 (Head, Department of History, 2005–10); President, Historical Association, since 2014; *b* 22 Dec. 1960; *s* of late Ivan Champion and Ann (*née* Davies); *m* 2014, Sylvia Carter; one *d*. *Educ:* Churchill Coll. Cambridge (BA 1983; MA 1985; PhD 1989). FRHistS 1995. Lectr in Early Modern Hist., La Sainte Union, Southampton, 1990–92; Lectr, 1992–95, Sen. Lectr, 1995–99, Reader 1999–2003, Royal Holloway, Univ. of London. John Hinkley Chair of British Hist., Johns Hopkins Univ., 2003. FRSA 2005. Hon. FHA 2013. Presenter, television programmes: The Great Plague of London, 1999; Secrets of the Palace, 2002; Kings and Queens, 2003; also regular radio broadcasts for In Our Time and Making History. *Publications:* The Pillars of Priestcraft Shaken, 1992; (ed) Epidemic Disease in London, 1993; London's Dreaded Visitation, 1995; John Toland's Nazarenus, 1999; Republican Learning, 2003; contrib learned jls. *Recreations:* squash, cricket, walking the line, fine cheese. *Address:* Department of History, Royal Holloway, University of London, Egham Hill, Egham TW20 0EX. *T:* (01784) 443749. *Club:* Royal Ascot Cricket.

CHAMPION, Sarah Deborah; MP (Lab) Rotherham, since Nov. 2012; *b* Maldon, Essex, 10 July 1969. *Educ:* Prince William Sch., Oundle; Sheffield Univ. (BA Hons Psychol. 1991). Manager, Rotherham Arts Centre, Rotherham MBC, 1992–94; Arts Officer, Ashfield DC, 1994–96; CEO, Chinese Arts Centre, Manchester, 1996–2008; Chief Exec., Bluebell Wood Children's Hospice, 2008–12. *Publications:* Representing the People, 1999; Made in China, 2001; Vital: international artists of Chinese descent, 2008; (jtly) 21: discussions with artists of Chinese descent in the UK, 2009. *Recreations:* gardening, food, travel, wine, endurance horse riding, pets. *Address:* House of Commons, SW1A 0AA. *T:* (constituency office) (01709) 331035. *E:* sarah.champion.mp@parliament.uk.

CHAN, Cho-chak John, GBS 1999; CBE 1993 (OBE 1985); LVO 1986; JP; Managing Director: Transport International Holdings Ltd (formerly Kowloon Motor Bus Holdings Ltd) 1997–2008 (non-executive Director, 2008–11; Independent non-executive Director and Deputy Chairman, since 2012); Kowloon Motor Bus Co. (1933) Ltd, 1993–2007 (non-executive Director, since 2008); *b* 8 April 1943; *s* of late Kai Kit Chan and Yuk Ying Wong; *m* 1965, Wai-chun Agnes Wong; one *s* one *d*. *Educ:* St Rose of Lima's Sch.; Wah Yan Coll. Kowloon; La Salle Coll., Univ. of Hong Kong (BA (Hons), DMS). Commerce and Industry Dept, 1964; Economic Br., Govt Secretariat, 1970; Private Sec. to Gov., 1973; City Dist Comr (Hong Kong), 1975; Asst Dir of Home Affairs, 1976; Dep. Dir of Trade, 1977; Exec Dir and Gen. Man., Sun Hung Kai Finance Co. Ltd, 1978; Principal Assistant Secretary: for Security, Govt Secretariat, 1980; for CS, 1982; Dep. Dir of Trade, 1983; Dep. Sec. (Gen Duties), 1984; Dir of Inf. Services, 1986; Dep. Chief Sec., 1987; Sec. for Trade and Industry 1989; Sec. for Educn and Manpower, 1991. Non-exec. Dir and Chm., RoadShow Hldgs Ltd 2001–; non-exec. Dir, Long Win Bus Co. Ltd, 2008–; Independent non-executive Director Hang Seng Bank Ltd, 1995–; Guangdong Investments Ltd, 1998–; Swire Properties Ltd 2010–; Fordwell Internat. Hldgs Ltd, 2011–14. Chm. Court, Hong Kong Univ. of Sci. and Technol., 2008–. JP Hong Kong, 1984. CCMI 2006. Hon. Fellow, Univ. of Hong Kong 2000. Hon. DBA Internat. Management Centres, 1997; Hon. DSocSc: Hong Kong Univ. of Sci. and Technol., 2009; Univ. of Hong Kong, 2011; Lingnan, 2012. *Recreations:* swimming music, reading. *Address:* Room A, 7/F Glory Heights, 52 Lyttelton Road, Hong Kong. *T:* 90138883. *Clubs:* Hong Kong Jockey (Chm., 2006–10); Hong Kong (Chm., 2007–08).

CHAN FANG, Anson Maria Elizabeth, (Mrs Anson Chan), GBM 1999; Hon. GCMG 2002; CBE 1992; JP; Member (Hong Kong Island), Legislative Council of Hong Kong 2007–08; *b* 17 Jan. 1940; *d* of Howard Fang and Fang Zhao Ling; *m* 1963, Archibald John Chan Tai-wing, MBE, QPM, CPM; one *s* one *d*. *Educ:* Univ. of Hong Kong (BA Hons) Admin. Officer, Hong Kong Govt, 1962–70; Asst Financial Sec., 1970–72; Asst Sec. for New Territories, 1972–75; Principal Asst Sec. for Social Services, 1975–79; Dep. Dir, 1979–84 Dir, 1984–87, Social Welfare; Sec. for Econ. Services, 1987–93; Sec. for CS, April–Nov 1993; Chief Sec., 1993–97; Chief Sec. for Admin, Govt Secretariat, HKSAR, 1997–2001 Convenor, Hong Kong 2020. JP Hong Kong, 1975. Chevalier, Ordre National de la Légion d'Honneur (France), 2009. *Recreation:* music. *Address:* 10B Park Avenue Tower, 5 Moreton Terrace, Causeway Bay, Hong Kong. *Clubs:* Zonta (Hong Kong East); Hong Kong, Hong Kong Jockey, Hong Kong Country (Hong Kong).

CHAN, Rt Hon. Sir Julius, GCMG 1994; KBE 1980 (CBE 1975); PC 1981; MP (People' Progress), Papua New Guinea, 1968–97 and since 2007; Governor of New Ireland, since 2007; *b* 29 Aug. 1939; *s* of Chin Pak and Tingoris Chan; *m* 1966, Stella Ahmat. *Educ:* Maris Brothers Coll., Ashgrove, Qld; Univ. of Queensland, Australia (Agricl Science). Co-operative Officer, Papua New Guinea Admin, 1960–62; private business, coastal shipping and merchandise, 1963–70. Minister for Finance, 1972–77; Dep. Prime Minister and Minister for Primary Industry, 1977–78; Prime Minister, 1980–82; Minister for Finance and Planning, 1985–86; Dep. Prime Minister, 1985–88; Minister for Trade and Industry, 1986–88; Dep Opposition Leader, 1988–92; Dep. Prime Minister and Minister for Finance and Planning 1992–94; Prime Minister and Minister for Foreign Affairs, 1994–97; Parly Leader, People' Progress Party, 1970–97. Hon. Dr Dankuk, S Korea, 1977; Hon. Dr Technol., Univ. of Technol., PNG, 1983. *Recreations:* swimming, walking, boating. *Address:* Parliament House Waigani, NCD, Papua New Guinea.

CHAN, Dr Margaret F. C., OBE 1997; FFPHM 1997; Director-General, World Health Organization, since 2007; *b* Hong Kong, 1947; *m* David Chan; one *s*. *Educ:* Northcote Coll. of Educn, Hong Kong; Univ. of Western Ontario (BA 1973; MD 1977); National Univ. of Singapore (MSc Public Health 1985); Harvard Business Sch. Hong Kong Department of Health: MO, Maternal and Child Health Services, 1978–85; SMO, Family Health Services 1985–87; PMO, Health Admin, 1987–89; Asst Dir, Personal Health Services, 1989–92; Dep Dir, 1992–94; Dir, 1994–2003; World Health Organization: Dir, Dept for Protection of Human Envmt, 2003–05; Dir, Communicable Diseases Surveillance and Response, and Rep of Dir-Gen. for Pandemic Influenza, 2005; Asst Dir-Gen. for Communicable Diseases 2005–06. Prince Mahidol Award in Public Health (Thailand), 1999. *Address:* World Health Organization, Ave Appia 20, 1211 Geneva 27, Switzerland.

CHAN SEK KEONG, Hon.; Chief Justice, Supreme Court of Singapore, 2006–12; *b* Ipoh Perak, 5 Nov. 1937; *m* 1965, Elisabeth Albyn Eber; three *d*. *Educ:* Univ. of Malaya in Singapore (LLB Hons). Legal Asst, Bannon & Bailey, Fedn of Malaya, 1962–63; Legal Asst 1963–66, Partner, 1966–69, Braddell Bros, Singapore; Partner, Shook Lin & Bok, Singapore and Malaya, 1969–86; Judicial Comr of the Supreme Court, 1986–88; Judge of the Supreme Court, 1988–92; Attorney-Gen. of Singapore, 1992–2006; Sen. Counsel 1996. Mem., Mil Ct of Appeal, Singapore, 1971–86. Pres., Legal Service Commn, 2006–12. Chm., Presidential Council for Minority Rights, 2006–. Pres., Singapore Acad. of Law, 2006–12. Dist. Fellow Nat. Univ. of Singapore, 2013–. Hon. Bencher, Lincoln's Inn, 2008. Hon. LLD Nat. Univ of Singapore, 2010. DSO, Darjah Utama Bakti Cemerlang (Singapore), 1999; Darjah Dato Seri Paduka Mahkota Perak (Malaysia), 1999; Order of Temasek (2nd Class) Darjah Utama Temasek (Singapore), 2008. Internat. Jurists' Award, Internat. Council Jurists, 2009 *Recreation:* reading. *Address:* c/o Supreme Court of Singapore, 1 Supreme Court Lane Singapore 178879.

CHAN, Siu-Oi, Patrick; Hon. Mr Justice Chan; Non-Permanent Judge, Court of Final Appeal, Hong Kong, since 2013 (Permanent Judge, 2000–13); *b* 21 Oct. 1948; *s* of late Chan Chu-Yau and Li Man-Yee; *m* 1990, Lisa Chiang Miu-Chu. *Educ:* Univ. of Hong Kong (LLB 1974; Postgrad. Cert. in Laws, 1975; Hon. Fellow 2003). Barrister in private practice, Hong Kong, 1977–87; Judge of District Court, 1987–91; Dep. Registrar of Supreme Court, 1991–92; Judge, 1992–97, Chief Judge, 1997–2000, High Court of Hong Kong. Hon. Bencher, Inner Temple, 2001. Hon. Fellow, Chinese Univ. of Hong Kong, 2011. Hon. LLD: City Univ. of Hong Kong, 2008; Univ. of Hong Kong, 2011. Grand Bauhinia Medal (Hong Kong), 2013. *Address:* Court of Final Appeal, 1 Battery Path, Central, Hong Kong. *T:* 21230033.

CHAN, Dr Stephen Ming Tak; HM Coroner, Inner North London, 1995–2002; *b* 16 Oct. 1948; *s* of late Kwok Kong Chan and Fun Ching Cheung; *m* 1972, Margaret Ann Small, *y d* of Francis Shadrack Small and Edith May Small. *Educ:* Bishop Hall Jubilee Sch., Hong Kong; RMN 1970; Kent Univ.; Charing Cross Hosp. Med. Sch., Univ. of London (MB, BS 1978; DMJ 1988); Cardiff Law Sch., Univ. of Wales (LLM 1992). Psychiatric nurse, St Augustine's Hosp., near Canterbury, 1967–70; jun. med. posts, Radcliffe Infirmary and John Radcliffe Hosp., Oxford and Charing Cross Hosp., 1979–80; postgrad. medical trng, Hammersmith Hosp., RPMS, Univ. of London, 1980–83; Principal in general practice, Epsom, 1983–86; Forensic Medical Examr, 1984–90, Sen. Forensic Medical Examr, 1990–94, Metropolitan Police; Forensic Medical Consultant in private practice, 1986–94; Asst Dep. Coroner, 1989–93, Dep. Coroner, 1993–94, Southern Dist, Gtr London; Asst Dep. Coroner, City of London, 1990–93. Member: Coroners' Soc. for England & Wales, 1989–2002; Council, Medico-Legal Soc., 1994–2002 (Hon. Treas., 1990–94); British Acad. Forensic Sci., 1988–2002; RSAA, 1992– (Trustee and Mem. Council, 2006–10; Benefactor, 2010–); RIIA, 1993– (Founder Mem. and Donor, Life Membership Legacy Fund, 2005–). Mem., Pugin Soc., 2002–. Patron, NACF, 2000–. *Publications:* Suicide Verdict: the coroner's dilemma, 1992; papers on medico-legal subjects. *Recreations:* Italian opera, Victorian antiques, Chinese history, song writing. *Address:* 1 Foreland Heights, Broadstairs, Kent CT10 3FU. *Clubs:* Lansdowne, Royal Over-Seas League.

CHANCE, Sir (George) Jeremy (ffolliott), 4th Bt *cr* 1900, of Grand Avenue, Hove; retired; *b* 24 Feb. 1926; *s* of Sir Roger James Ferguson Chance, 3rd Bt, MC and Mary Georgina (*d* 1984), *d* of Col William Rowney; *S* father, 1987; *m* 1950, (cousin) Cecilia Mary Elizabeth (*d* 2015), *d* of Sir William Hugh Stobart Chance, CBE; two *s* two *d*. *Educ:* Gordonstoun School; Christ Church, Oxford (MA). Sub-Lieut RNVR, 1944–47. Harry Ferguson Ltd, 1950–53; Massey-Ferguson, 1953–78; Director, Massey-Ferguson (UK) Ltd, 1973–78; farmer, 1978–87. *Recreations:* choral singing, painting. *Heir: s* (John) Sebastian Chance [*b* 2 Oct. 1954; *m* 1977, Victoria Mary, *d* of Denis McClean; two *s* one *d*]. *Address:* Ty'n-y-Berllan, Criccieth, Gwynedd LL52 0AH.

CHANCE, Michael Edward Ferguson, CBE 2009; counter-tenor; *b* Penn, Bucks, 7 March 1955; *s* of John Wybergh Chance and Wendy Muriel (*née* Chance); *m* 1991, Irene, *d* of late Hon. Francis Edward Noel-Baker; one *s* one *d*. *Educ:* St George's Sch., Windsor; Eton Coll.; King's Coll., Cambridge (MA English 1977; Mem., King's Coll. Choir, 1974–77). Stockbroker, Mullens & Co., 1977–80. Founder Mem., The Light Blues, 1977–83; Mem., Monteverdi Choir, 1980–83; solo career, 1983–: operatic débuts: Buxton Fest., 1983; Kent Opera, Opéra de Lyon, Göttingen Handel Fest., 1985; Paris Opera, 1988; Glyndebourne Fest., 1989; ENO, Netherlands Opera, 1991; Covent Garden, Scottish Opera, 1992; Australian Opera, 1993; Buenos Aires, 1996; WNO, 1997; San Francisco Opera, 1998; Maggio Musicale, Florence, 1999; Leipzig Opera, 2000; Munich State Opera, 2003; rôles include: Oberon in A Midsummer Night's Dream; Apollo in Death in Venice; Julius Caesar; Andronico in Tamerlano; Bertarido in Rodelinda; Orfeo in Orfeo ed Euridice; Ottone in Agrippina; Ottone in L'incoronazione di Poppea; Military Governor in A Night at the Chinese Opera; Orpheus in The Second Mrs Kong; concert performances in Europe, USA and Japan. Vis. Prof., RCM, 1996–; Prof., Royal Conservatorium, Den Haag, 2004–; Prof. of Singing, Royal Acad. of Music, 2010–. Numerous recordings of oratorio, opera and recitals. *Recreations:* card games (mainly bridge), golf, squash, cooking, chaotic boating. *Address:* c/o Ingpen & Williams, 7 St George's Court, 131 Putney Bridge Road, SW15 2PA. *T:* (020) 8874 3222, *Fax:* (020) 8877 3113.

CHANCE, Michael Spencer; Executive Counsel, Joint Disciplinary Scheme for Accountants, 1993–97; *b* 14 May 1938; *s* of Florence and Ernest Horace Chance; *m* 1962, Enid Mabel Carter; three *d*. *Educ:* Rossall School. Solicitor. With Challinor & Roberts, Warley, 1962–70; Senior Asst Prosecuting Solicitor, Sussex Police Authy, 1970–72; Office of Director of Public Prosecutions, 1972–86: Asst Dir, 1981–86; Chief Crown Prosecutor, North London, 1986–87; Asst Head of Legal Services, Crown Prosecution Service, 1987; Dep. Dir, Serious Fraud Office, 1987–90; Consultant, Cameron Markby Hewitt, 1991–93. *Address:* 28 Beaufort Place, Cambridge CB5 8AG.

CHANCELLOR, Alexander Surtees, CBE 2012; columnist, The Spectator, since 2012; Editor, The Oldie, since 2014; *b* 4 Jan. 1940; *s* of Sir Christopher Chancellor, CMG and Sylvia Mary, OBE, *e d* of Sir Richard Paget, 2nd Bt and Lady Muriel Finch-Hatton, *d* of 12th Earl of Winchilsea and Nottingham; *m* 1964, Susanna Elisabeth Debenham; two *d*. *Educ:* Eton College; Trinity Hall, Cambridge. Reuters News Agency, 1964–74; ITN, 1974–75; Editor: The Spectator, 1975–84; Time and Tide, 1984–86; Dep. Editor, Sunday Telegraph, 1986; US Editor, The Independent, 1986–88; Editor: The Independent Magazine, 1988–92; The New Yorker's Talk of the Town, 1992–93; columnist, The Times, 1992–93; Associate Ed., Sunday Telegraph, 1994–95; Founding Ed., Sunday Telegraph Mag., 1995; columnist: The Guardian, 1996–2012; Daily Telegraph, 1998–2004. Comr, English Heritage, 1990–92. *Publications:* Some Times in America, 1999. *Address:* Stoke Park, Stoke Bruerne, Towcester, Northamptonshire NN12 7RZ. *T:* (01604) 862329. *Clubs:* Garrick, Chelsea Arts.

CHAND, Ravi Parkash, CBE 2011; QPM 2002; Director, Workforce and Human Resources, HM Revenue and Customs, since 2014; *b* Bedford, 23 Dec. 1969; *s* of late Mehar Chand and of Charan Kaur; *m* 2002, Elizabeth Mary Rose White; two *s* one *d*. FCIPD 2009. With Police Service, 1989–2003, incl. Head of Equality, Bedfordshire Police, 1999–2001; Mgt Consultant, Veredus Exec. Resourcing, 2003–06; estabd small financial services co.; Home Office: Dir, Strategic Diversity Action Team, 2006–07; Dir, Gp Equality and Diversity, 2006–12; Dir, Capability, Talent and Diversity, 2012–14. Mem., Home Sec.'s Stephen Lawrence Steering Gp, 2000–03. Comr, Formal Investigation into Police Service in England and Wales under Race Relns Act, 2004–05. Pres., Nat. Black Police Assoc., 2001–03. Advr on equality issues, nationally and internationally. *Publications:* (jtly) The Police Service in England and Wales, 2005. *Recreations:* golf, travelling, DIY, entertaining my children. *Address:* HM Revenue and Customs, 100 Parliament Street, SW1A 2BQ. *T:* 07917 177693. *E:* ravichand1@virginmedia.com, ravi.chand@hmrc.gsi.gov.uk.

CHANDE, Jayantilal Keshavji, (Andy), Hon. KBE 2003; Chairman, Kioo Ltd, since 1972; *b* 27 Aug. 1929; *s* of Keshavji Jethabhai and Kankuben Chande; *m* 1955, Jayalaxmi Madhvani; three *s*. Chairman: Air Tanzania Corp., 1977–89; Tanzania Harbours Authy, 1987–95; Tanzania Rlys Corp., 1995–2007; Barclays Bank Tanzania Ltd, 2000–08; Dir, Barclays Bank Uganda Ltd, 2001–05; Chm., Alexander Forbes Tanzania Ltd, 2002–. Founder Board Director: East African Railways Corp., 1967–69; East African Harbours Corp., 1967–77; Director: World Business Acad., 1996–2003 (Fellow, 2004); Internat. Inst. for Peace through Tourism, 2002; Chm., Inst. for Envmtl Innovation, 2005–09, now Chm. Emeritus. Chairman: Exec. Cttee, Muhimbili Nat. Hosp., Dar es Salaam, 2001–04; Muhimbili Orthopaedic Inst., Dar es Salaam, 2004–10; Chancellor, Internat. Med. and Tech. Univ., Dar es Salaam, 2003–14. Fellow: Internat. Acad. of Mgt, 1995; World Innovation Foundn, 2002. Chm., Rotary Foundn of UK, 2003–07; Trustee, Rotary Foundn of Rotary Internat., 2003–07; Founder Trustee, Tanzania Soc. for Deaf, 1970–. Hon. Rep., Royal Commonwealth Soc., 1963–2011 (Vice-Pres., 2008–); Chm., Nat. Museums of Tanzania, 1963–84, 1989–92; Vice-Chm., Governing Body, Coll. of Business Educn, 1965–90 (Chm., Bd of Examiners, 1966–2011). Pravasi Bharatiya Samman (India), 2005. *Publications:* Whither Directing Your Course, 1995, 4th edn 2006; A Knight in Africa: journey from Bukene, 2005 (trans. Swahili); Transitions of a Life, 2011. *Recreations:* reading, walking, theatre. *Address:* PO Box 9251, Dar es Salaam, Tanzania. *T:* (22) 2863196, 784780250, *Fax:* (22) 2863822, (22) 736502641. *E:* jkchande@gmail.com, andychande@yahoo.com. *Clubs:* Arts, National Liberal; Upanga Sports, Dar es Salaam Gymkhana (Hon. Mem.) (Dar es Salaam); Cricket of India (Mumbai) (Hon. Mem.).

See also M. J. Chande.

CHANDE, Manish Jayantilal, FRICS; Senior Partner: Mountgrange Investment Management LLP, since 2009; Clearbell Capital LLP, since 2012; *b* 23 Feb. 1956; *s* of Jayantilal Keshavji Chande, *qv*; one *s* one *d*. *Educ:* City Univ. (Dip. Accountancy). ACA 1980. FRICS 2008. Chief Exec. and Finance Dir, Imry Plc, 1985–97; Chief Exec., Trillium plc, then Land Securities Trillium, 1997–2002; Chief Exec. and Co-founder, Mountgrange Capital plc, 2002–09. Non-exec. Chm., Nat. Car Parks Ltd, 2003–05; non-exec. Dir, Mitie plc, 2003–06. Comr, English Heritage, 2004–11. Mem., ICAEW, 1980–. Trustee: Windsor Leadership Trust, 2005–09; London Clinic, 2009–; Canal and River Trust, 2012–. *Address:* Mountgrange Investment Management LLP, 6 Cork Street, W1S 3NX. *T:* (020) 7494 7620, *Fax:* (020) 7494 7626. *E:* manish@mountgrange.com; Clearbell Capital LLP, 2 Harewood Place, W1S 1BX. *E:* manish@clearbell.com. *Clubs:* Lansdowne, Arts.

CHANDLER, Sir Colin (Michael), Kt 1988; FRAeS; Chairman, easyJet plc, 2002–09; *b* 7 Oct. 1939; *s* of Henry John Chandler and Mary Martha (*née* Bowles); *m* 1964, Jennifer Mary Crawford; one *s* one *d*. *Educ:* St Joseph's Acad.; Hatfield Polytechnic. FCMA; FRAeS 1994. Commercial Apprentice, De Havilland Aircraft Co., 1956; Hawker Siddeley Aviation, later British Aerospace, Kingston: Commercial Manager, 1967–72; Exec. Dir, Commercial, 1973–78; Divl Man. Dir, 1978–82; Gp Marketing Dir, 1983–85; Hd of Defence Export Services, MoD, 1985–89; Vickers plc: Man. Dir, 1990–92; Chief Exec., 1992–98; Chm., 1997–2000; Chm., Vickers Defence Systems Ltd, 2000–02. Chairman: TI Automovie Ltd, 2003–07; Automotive Technik Ltd, 2004–08; Clarity Commerce Solutions, 2009–11 (Dep. Chm., 2007–09); Future Film, 2010–. Non-executive Director: Siemens Plessey Electronic Systems, 1990–95; TI Group, subseq. Smiths Group, 1992–2007 (Dep. Chm., 1999–2004); Guardian Royal Exchange, 1995–99; Racal Electronics plc, 1999–2000 (Chm., 2000); Thales plc, 2000–02; Holiday Taxis.com, 2009–. Vice Pres., EEF, 1991; Member: NDIC, 1992–2002; Cttee, DTI Priority Japan Campaign, 1992–2001. Pro-Chancellor, Cranfield Univ., 2001–07. Gov., Reigate GS, 2004– (Vice-Chm., Bd of Govs, 2010–; Chm., Finance and Foundn Cttee, 2008–). Commander, Order of the Lion of Finland, 1982. *Recreations:* playing tennis, reading, gardening, listening to music. *Address:* 11 Coleherne Mews, SW10 9DZ. *Clubs:* Reform, Mark's; Harbour.

CHANDLER, Ven. Ian Nigel; Archdeacon of Plymouth, since 2010; *b* Stockton on Tees, 9 Nov. 1965; *s* of Kenneth Chandler and Marian Chandler. *Educ:* Bishopsgarth Sch., Stockton on Tees; Stockton Sixth Form Coll.; King's Coll. London (BD; AKC 1989); Chichester Theological Coll. Ordained deacon, 1992, priest, 1993; Asst Curate, All Saints, Hove, 1992–96; Domestic Chaplain to Bishop of Chichester, 1996–2000; Vicar, St Richard's, Haywards Heath, 2000–10; Rural Dean, Cuckfield, 2004–06; Proctor in Convocation, 2005–10. *Recreations:* theatre, music, art, travel. *Address:* St Mark's House, 46a Cambridge Road, Ford, Plymouth PL2 1PU. *T:* (01752) 202401. *E:* archdeacon.of.plymouth@exeter.anglican.org. *Club:* Nikæan.

CHANDLER, Very Rev. Michael John; Dean of Ely, 2003–11, now Dean Emeritus; *b* 27 May 1945; *s* of late John Godfrey Chandler and Ena Doris (*née* Holdstock); *m* 1966, Janet Mary (*née* Raines); one *s* one *d*. *Educ:* Brasted Place Coll.; Lincoln Theol Coll.; KCL (PhD 1987); Dip. Theol. London Univ. (ext.) 1975; Dip. Theol. (STh) Lambeth (ext.) 1980. Ordained deacon, 1972, priest, 1973; Curate: St Dunstan's, Canterbury, 1972–75; St John the Baptist, Margate, 1975–78; Vicar of Newington, 1978–88 (with Bobbing and Iwade, 1978–80, with Hartlip and Stockbury, 1980–88); Rector, St Stephen's, Hackington, 1988–95; Canon Res., Canterbury Cathedral, 1995–2003. Rural Dean: Sittingbourne, 1984–88; Canterbury, 1994–95. *Publications:* The Life and Work of John Mason Neale, 1995; The Life and Work of Henry Parry Liddon, 2000; An Introduction to the Oxford Movement, 2003; contrib. Oxford DNB. *Recreations:* walking, birdwatching, reading, sailing, boating about in mud. *Address:* 218 Tankerton Road, Whitstable, Kent CT5 2AT. *T:* (01227) 262937.

CHANDLER, Paul Geoffrey; Chief Executive, Traidcraft, 2001–13; Chairman: Durham Cathedral Council, since 2011 (Member, since 2008); William Leech Foundation, since 2014; *b* 13 Oct. 1961; *s* of late Dr David Geoffrey Chandler and of Gillian Chandler; *m* 1993, Sarah Gillian Munro-Faure; three *d*. *Educ:* Wellington Coll., Berks; St John's Coll., Oxford (Stanhope Histl Essay Prize, 1983; BA Mod. Hist. 1983; MA 1987); Henley Mgt Coll. (MBA 1987). ACIB 1985. Joined Barclays Bank, 1983: Manager, Moorgate Br., 1986–87; on secondment to Church Urban Fund, 1987; Manager, Gp Strategic Planning, 1987–89; Asst Personal Sector Dir, London Western Reg., 1990–92; Gen. Sec., SPCK, 1992–2001 (Vice-Pres., 2001–). Non-executive Director: Engage Mutual Assce, 2012–15; Co-operative Gp, 2015–. Mentor (formerly Tutor), 2005–, Fellow, 2009–, Gov., 2015–, St Chad's Coll., Durham Univ. Member: Council, Overseas Bishoprics Fund, 1992–2001; Bd of Mission, C of E, 1994–2001; Exec. Cttee, Feed the Minds, 1996–2001; Trustee, C of E Pensions Bd, 1998–2001. Trustee, SPCK-USA, 1992–2001; Member: Cttee of Mgt, Assoc. for Promoting Christian Knowledge (Ireland), 1995–2001; Exec. Cttee, Indian SPCK, 1998–2001; Exec. Cttee, European Fair Trade Assoc., 2002– (Pres., 2007–10); Gen. Council, S American Mission Soc., 2002–06; IPPR North, 2005–10; NE Regl Council, CBI, 2008–12. Dir, Cafédirect Guardian Share Co., 2006–11 (Chm., 2007–08); Chair, UK Fair Trade Leaders Forum, 2011–12. Churchwarden: St Stephen's, S Lambeth, 2000–01 (Mem. PCC, 1984–94, 1996–2001); St John's, Neville's Cross, 2013–15 (Mem. PCC, 2007–11 and 2013–); Mem. PCC, St Nicholas, Durham, 2002–05; Lay Canon, Durham Cathedral, 2008–. Gov., St Martin-in-the-Fields High Sch. for Girls, 1992–2001 (Vice-Chm., 1993–2001); Lay Adv. Gov., Chorister Sch., Durham, 2005–. Trustee: All Saints Educnl Trust, 1992–2005; Co. Durham Community Foundn, 2013–; Bible Soc., 2015–. Director: William Leech Foundn, 2001– (Mem., Research (formerly Professorial) Fellowship Mgt Cttee, 2006–14); Shared Interest, 2013–. *Recreations:* time with my family, reading, history, walking on Yorkshire Moors, collecting works of John Buchan, keeping chickens.

CHANDLER, Victor William; Chairman, Victor Chandler International Ltd, since 1996; *b* 18 April 1951; *s* of late Victor and Elizabeth Chandler; *m* 1st (marr. diss. 2010); three *s*; 2nd, 2012, Caroline Villar. *Educ:* Millfield Sch. Chm. and Man. Dir, Victor Chandler Ltd, 1974–96. *Recreation:* equestrian pursuits. *Address:* Leanse Place, 50 Town Range, Gibraltar. *T:* 20041313, *Fax:* 20044066. *E:* victor.chandler@betvictor.com.

CHANDLER, Dame Wendy; *see* Hall, Dame W.

CHANDOS, 3rd Viscount *cr* 1954, of Aldershot; **Thomas Orlando Lyttelton;** Baron Lyttelton of Aldershot (Life Peer) 2000; *b* 12 Feb. 1953; *s* of 2nd Viscount Chandos and of Caroline Mary (who *m* 1985, Hon. David Hervey Erskine), *d* of Rt Hon. Sir Alan Lascelles,

GCB, GCVO, CMG, MC; *S* father, 1980; *m* 1985, Arabella Sarah, *d* of Adrian Bailey and Lady Mary Russell; two *s* one *d*. *Educ:* Eton; Worcester College, Oxford (BA). Banker, 1974–93, Dir, 1985–93, Kleinwort Benson. Opposition spokesman on Treasury matters, 1995–97. Chief Exec., Northbridge Ventures Ltd; Chairman: Lopex plc, 1997–99; Capital & Regional plc, 2000–10; Director: Botts Co. Ltd, 1993–97; Cine-UK Ltd, 1995–2004; Middlesex Hldgs; Global Natural Energy plc, 2000–; Northbridge (UK) Ltd, 2001–11. Chm., Television Corporation, 2004–06. Director: ENO, 1995–2004; Education 2000; Gov., Nat. Film and Television Sch., 1996–2001. Chm. Trustees, Esmée Fairbairn Foundn. *Heir: s* Hon. Oliver Antony Lyttelton, *b* 21 Feb. 1986. *Address:* 149 Gloucester Avenue, NW1 8LA. *T:* (020) 7722 8329.

CHANEY, Prof. Edward Paul de Gruyter, PhD; FSA, FRHistS; Professor of Fine and Decorative Arts, and Chair, History of Collecting Research Centre, Southampton Solent University (formerly Southampton Institute), since 1998; *b* 11 April 1951; *s* of Edward Robert Dell Chaney and Maaike Louise Chaney (*née* de Gruyter); *m* 1973, Lisa Maria Jacka (writes as Lisa Chaney) (marr. diss. 2002); two *d*. *Educ:* Leighton Park Sch., Reading; Ealing Sch. of Art; Reading Univ. (BA Hist. of Art); Warburg Inst. (MPhil 1977; PhD 1982); Eur. Univ. Inst., Florence. Lectr, Univ. of Pisa, 1979–85; Adjunct Asst Prof., Georgetown Univ. in Florence, Villa Le Balze, 1982–83; Associate, Harvard Univ. Center for Italian Renaissance Studies, Villa I Tatti, Florence, 1984–85; Shuffrey Res. Fellow in Architectural Hist., Lincoln Coll., Oxford, 1985–90; Lectr in Hist. of Art (pt-time), Oxford Poly., 1990–91; Historian to London Div., English Heritage, 1991–93; Lectr in Hist. of Art (pt-time), Oxford Brookes Univ., 1993–; Sen. Lectr in Fine Arts Valuation, Southampton Inst., 1996. Res. Fellow, Huntington Liby, San Marino, Calif, 1994; Leverhulme Maj. Res. Fellow, 2010–12; Fernand Braudel Fellow, Eur. Univ. Inst., Florence, 2015. Visiting Prof. of Art History, New College of Humanities, London, 2014–. FSA 1993; FRHistS 2006. Commendatore, Stella della Solidarietà (Italy), 2003. *Publications:* (ed with N. Ritchie) Oxford, China and Italy: writings in honour of Sir Harold Acton, 1984; The Grand Tour and the Great Rebellion: Richard Lassels and "The Voyage of Italy" in the Seventeenth Century, 1985; A Traveller's Companion to Florence, 1986, rev. edn 2002; (ed with P. Mack) England and the Continental Renaissance: essays in honour of J. B. Trapp, 1990; (ed with J. Bold) English Architecture Public and Private: essays for Kerry Downes, 1993; The Evolution of the Grand Tour: Anglo-Italian cultural relations since the Renaissance, 1998, rev. edn 2000; (with G. Worsdale) The Stuart Portrait: status and legacy, 2001; (with C. Clearkin) Richard Eurich (1903–1992): visionary artist, 2003; The Evolution of English Collecting: receptions of Italian art in the Tudor and Stuart periods, 2003; Inigo Jones's 'Roman Sketchbook', 2 vols, 2006; William Rose: tradition and an individual talent, 2009; (with T. Wilks), The Jacobean Grand Tour: Early Stuart travellers in Europe, 2014; contribs to books, jls, newspapers, exhibition catalogues, etc. *Address:* Faculty of the Creative Industries and Society, Southampton Solent University, East Park Terrace, Southampton SO14 0YN. *E:* edward.chaney@solent.ac.uk.

CHANG, Dr Jung; author; *b* Sichuan, China, 25 March 1952; *d* of Shou-yu Chang and De-Hong Xia; *m* 1991, John Arthur George Halliday. *Educ:* Sichuan Univ., China; Univ. of York (PhD Linguistics 1982). Dir of Chinese Studies, External Services, SOAS, 1986–91. Hon. DLit: Buckingham, 1993; Warwick, 1997; Bowdoin Coll., USA, 2005; York, 1997; Open, 1998. *Publications:* Wild Swans: three daughters of China, 1991; (with J. Halliday) Mao: the unknown story, 2005; Empress Dowager Cixi: the concubine who launched modern China, 2013. *Recreations:* ski-ing, snorkelling. *Address:* c/o Aitken Alexander Associates, 291 Gray's Inn Road, WC1X 8EB.

CHANG, Sarah Young Joo; violinist; *b* Philadelphia, 10 Dec. 1980; *d* of Min Soo Chang and Myoung Jun Chang (*née* Lee). *Educ:* Juilliard Sch. of Music, NY. Began violin studies at age of 4; engagements at age of 8 with NY Philharmonic and Philadelphia Orch.; recorded first album at age of 10; has performed with orchestras in Asia, Europe and the Americas, incl. NY Philharmonic, Philadelphia Orch., Berlin Philharmonic, Vienna Philharmonic, Royal Concertgebouw Orch., Amsterdam, LSO, LPO, NHK SO, Tokyo, Hong Kong SO, Washington Nat. SO; recitals incl. performances at Kennedy Center, Washington, Carnegie Hall, NY, Orchestra Hall, Chicago, Symphony Hall, Boston and Barbican Centre, London. Has made numerous recordings. Young Artist of Year, Gramophone mag., 1993; Nan Pa Award, S Korea, 1993; Newcomer of Year, Internat. Classical Music Awards, 1994; Avery Fisher Prize, 1999; Internazionale Accademia Musicale Chigiana Prize, 2005; Young Global Leader, WEF, 2008. *Address:* c/o IMG Artists, The Lightbox, 111 Power Road, W4 5PY. *T:* (020) 7957 5800, *Fax:* (020) 7957 5801. *E:* info@imgartists.com.

CHANG-HIM, Rt Rev. French Kitchener, Hon. OBE 2014; Bishop of the Seychelles, 1979–2004; Archbishop of the Indian Ocean, 1984–95; *m* 1975, Susan Talma; twin *d*. *Educ:* Lichfield Theol Coll.; St Augustine's Coll., Canterbury; Trinity Coll., Univ. of Toronto (LTh 1975); Oxford Centre for Mission Studies (MPhil Univ. of Wales 2010). Deacon, Sheffield, 1962; priest, Seychelles, 1963; Curate of Goole, 1962–63; Rector of Praslin, Seychelles, 1963–66 and 1969–71; Asst Priest, St Leonard's, Norwood, Sheffield, 1967–68; Vicar General, Seychelles, 1972–73; Rector, S Mahé Parish, 1973–74; Archdeacon of Seychelles, 1973–79; Priest-in-charge, St Paul's Cathedral, Mahé, 1977–79; Dean, Province of the Indian Ocean, 1983–84. DD (*hc*) Trinity Coll., Toronto, 1991. *Address:* PO Box 44, Victoria, Mahé, Seychelles. *T:* (+248) 4248151. *E:* bishop@seychelles.net.

CHANNER, Jillian; independent historic building and architectural glass consultant, since 2011; *b* 2 July 1949; *d* of Eric David Kerr, MC and Betty (*née* Knight); *m* 1998, Donal Gilbert O'Connell Channer. *Educ:* Univ. of York (BA Hons 1970, MA 1971). Dept of MSS and Early Printed Books, TCD, 1971–72; Photo-Archives, Courtauld Inst. of Art, Univ. of London, 1973–75; Sec., Corpus Vitrearum Medii Aevii, GB, 1975–84; English Heritage: Inspector, Ancient Monuments and Historic Buildings, 1984–88; Head of SW and W Midlands, Historic Buildings Div., 1988–91; Head of SW Team, 1991–98; Project Dir, 1998–2002; Phoenix Trust, later Prince of Wales's Regeneration Trust: Dir, 2002–07; Heritage Policy Advr, English Partnerships, subseq. Homes and Communities Agency (on secondment), 2007–11. Mem., Stained Glass Adv. Cttee, Council for Care of Churches, 1984–91; Mem., Inst. of Historic Buildings Conservation, 1997–. AABC Register Lay Assessor, 1999– (Mem. Bd, 2009–). Member: Council, British Soc. of Master Glass Painters, 1969–86 (Jt Ed., Jl, 1983–86); British Archaeol Assoc., 1972–85 (Mem. Council, 1981–85); Assoc. for Studies in Conservation of Historic Buildings, 1984– (Mem. Council, 1988–2002); Wells Cathedral Fabric Adv. Cttee, 2007–; Salisbury DAC, 2009–. FRSA 2002; FSA 2003. Hon. Sec. to Trustees, Ely Stained Glass Mus., 1978–84; Trustee: Ancient Monuments Soc., 2002–; Woodchester Mansion Trust, 2007–10; Internat. Monuments Trust, 2012–. Freeman, City of London, 1984; Liveryman, Co. of Glaziers, Painters and Stainers of Glass, 1984–. *Publications:* various contribs to specialist pubns on historic buildings conservation and stained glass. *Recreations:* fly-fishing, gardening, talking. *Address:* The Notch, 50 Tower Hill, Hisomley, Westbury, Wilts BA13 4DA. *T:* (01373) 824895. *E:* jill.channer@gmail.com.

CHANNING, Alastair; *see* Channing, R. A.

CHANNING, Jeffrey Paul; Programme Manager (Solent Enterprise Zone), Solent Local Enterprise Partnership, since 2012; *b* 8 Aug. 1950; *s* of Leonard Herbert Channing and Joy Channing; *m* 1994, Kate Munson. *Educ:* Aylesbury Grammar Sch.; University Coll. London (BSc Geog.). Joined Civil Service as trainee, 1974; Hd of Central Policy, 1989–92, Hd of Urban Develt Corps, 1992–94, DoE; Cabinet Office, 1994–95; Hd of Construction Policy, DoE, 1995–98; Hd of Planning Policy, DETR, 1998–2003; Dir, Thames Gateway, later Thames Gateway, Olympics and Sustainable Bldgs, ODPM, later DCLG, 2003–06; consultant, 2006–09; Develt (formerly Prog.) Manager, Partnership for Urban S Hants, 2009–12; Develt Manager, Solent Local Enterprise Partnership, 2012–. Mem. of Bd, First Wessex Housing Gp Ltd, 2007–. *Recreations:* ceramics, horse-riding. *E:* jchanning1@btinternet.com.

CHANNING, (Raymond) Alastair, FCILT; Managing Director, Associated British Ports, 1995–97; *b* 2 May 1943; *s* of late Geoffrey Channing, FRCS and Kathleen Channing; *m* 1976, Victoria Margaret Nish. *Educ:* Clifton Coll.; Clare Coll., Cambridge (MA; athletics Blue, 1965, and competed for Oxford and Cambridge against various American Univs, 1965). Various posts in Depts of Transport and Envmt, incl. Asst Private Sec. to successive Ministers of Transport; British Transport Docks Board, later Associated British Ports: Sec., 1979–84; Dir, 1984; Dep. Man. Dir, 1991–95; Dir, ABP Hldgs plc, 1992–97. FCILT (FCIT 1994 (Chm., 1996–98)). *Recreation:* music. *Address:* The Old Manor House, Hampnett, Cheltenham, Glos GL54 3NW. *T:* (01451) 860795. *Club:* Reform.

CHANT, Ann; *see* Chant, E. A.

CHANT, Christopher Marc; Executive Director, and Director, Government G-Cloud Programme (formerly Government Cloud and Data Centre Consolidation Programme), Cabinet Office, 2010–12 (Executive Director, Government Digital Service, 2010–11); *b* 3 July 1955; *s* of Frank and Olive Chant; *m* 1977, Beryl; one *s* one *d*. *Educ:* Dane Court Tech. High Sch. Inland Revenue: Ops and Investigation, 1976–99; E Service Delivery Dir, 1999–2002; Hd of Service Delivery, Cabinet Office, 2002–05; Chief Inf. Officer, DEFRA, 2005–08; Govt Chief Inf. Officer for London 2012 Olympics, DCMS, 2008–10. *Recreations:* ski-ing, photography, cooking. *E:* chrischant@mac.com. *W:* www.twitter.com/cantwaitogo.

CHANT, (Elizabeth) Ann, CB 1997; Deputy Director of Charities to TRH the Prince of Wales and the Duchess of Cornwall, 2005–10; *b* 16 Aug. 1945; *d* of late Capt. Harry Charles Chant and Gertrude Chant (*née* Poel). *Educ:* Blackpool Collegiate Sch. for Girls. Nat. Assistance Bd, Lincoln, 1963–66; Min. of Social Security, Lincoln, 1966–70; NHS Whitley Council, DHSS London, 1970–72; DHSS, Lincoln, 1972–74; DHSS Regl Office, Nottingham, 1974–82; Manager, DHSS Sutton-in-Ashfield, 1982–83; DHSS HQ, London, 1983–85; Prin. Private Sec. to Permanent Sec., DHSS, 1985–87; Head: Records Br., DSS, Newcastle upon Tyne, 1987–89; Contribns Unit, 1990–91; Chief Executive: Contributions Agency, DSS, 1991–94; Child Support Agency, DSS, 1994–97; Man. Dir for Corporate Social Responsibility, BITC, 1997–99; Reviews of Public Trust Office and Legal Services Ombudsman's Office for Lord Chancellor's Dept, 1999; a Comr and Dep. Chm., Bd of Inland Revenue, 2000–04; acting Chm., Bd of Inland Revenue, 2004; Dir Gen., HM Revenue and Customs, 2005. Exec. Council Mem., Industrial Soc., 1993–2000. Trustee: Citizens Advice, 2005–07; Garfield-Weston Trust for St Paul's Cathedral, 2012–; Foundn Years Trust, 2012–. Lay Gov., London South Bank (formerly S Bank) Univ., 2001–09. Hon. LLD London South Bank, 2010. *Recreations:* friends, music (especially opera), theatre. *Club:* Athenæum.

CHANTLER, Sir Cyril, Kt 1996; MD; FRCP; Founding Chairman and Honorary Fellow, University College London Partners, since 2014 (Chairman, 2009–14); Children Nationwide Medical Research Fund Professor of Paediatric Nephrology, London University, 1990–2000, Emeritus Professor, since 2001; *b* 12 May 1939; *s* of Fred Chantler and Marjorie Chantler (*née* Clark); *m* 1963, Shireen Saleh; two *s* one *d*. *Educ:* Wrekin Coll.; St Catharine's Coll., Cambridge (BA 1960; MB BChir 1963; MD 1973); Guy's Hosp. Med. Sch. MRC Travelling Fellow, Univ. of California, 1971; Guy's Hospital: Sen. Lectr and Consultant Paediatrician, 1972–80; Prof. of Paediatric Nephrology, 1980–2000; General Manager, 1985–88; Clinical Dean, Principal, 1989–92, 1992–98, UMDS, Guy's and St Thomas' Hosps; Vice Principal, KCL, and Dean, GKT Hosps' Med. and Dental Sch. of KCL, 1998–2000; Pro-Vice-Chancellor, London Univ., 1997–2000. Med. Dir, Well Child, 2001–05. Member: NHS Policy Bd, 1989–95; GMC, 1994–2003 (Chm., Standards Cttee, 1997–2002). Chairman: Sci. Adv. Cttee, Foundn for the Study of Infant Deaths, 1988–90; Council of Heads of UK Med. Schs, 1998–99; Beit Meml Fellowships for Med. Res., 2003–09; Complex Primary Care Practice Prog. Bd, 2014–; Mem. Council, St George's Med. Sch., 2000–03. Chairman: Gt Ormond St Hosp. for Sick Children NHS Trust, 2001–08; King Edward VII Hosp. Fund for London, 2004–10 (Sen. Associate, 2001–04); non-executive Director: Guy's and Lewisham NHS Trust, 1991–92; Guy's and St Thomas' NHS Trust, 1993–97; Lambeth, Southwark, Lewisham HA, 1998–2000; Private Health Information Network, 2015–. Pres., British Assoc. of Medical Managers, 1991–97. Advr, Associate Parly Health Gp, 2005–; Member: Public Sector Adv. Panel, Doctors.net.uk, 2007–14; Adv. Bd, Inst. of Healthcare Optimisation, Boston, USA, 2012–; Co-Chm., SARS Expert Adv. Enquiry, Hosp. Authy of Hong Kong, 2003; Chairman: Clinical Adv. Gp, NHS London, 2007–08; NHS England Quality and Clinical Risk Audit Cttee, 2013–14; Review of Standardised Packing of Tobacco Products, HM Govt, 2014. Trustee: Media Standards Trust; Dunhill Med. Trust, 2001–09; British Kidney Patients Assoc., 2007–10; non-exec. Dir, By the Bridge, 2006–. Mem. Council, Southwark Cathedral, 2000–. Gov., South Bank Univ., 2002–05. Teale Lectr, 1987, Censor, 1989–90, Harveian Orator, 2002, RCP. FKC 1998. Founder FMedSci 1998. Hon. Fellow, Inst. of Child Health. Foreign Associate, Inst. of Medicine, Nat. Acad. of Scis, USA, 1999. Hon. Mem., Amer. Paed. Assoc., 1992. James Spence Medal, RCPCH, 2005; Ira Greifer Award, Internat. Ped. Nephrol. Assoc., 2007. Co-Editor, Pediatric Nephrology Jl, 1986–96. Mem., Editl Bd, Jl Amer. Med. Assoc., 2002–11. Dr *hc* Lille, 1998; Hon. DSc London South Bank, 1999; Hon. DSc(Med): London, 2005; Kent, 2009; UCL, 2012. *Recreations:* golf, opera, reading. *Address:* 22 Benbow House, 24 New Globe Walk, Bankside, SE1 9DS. *T:* (020) 7401 3246. *Club:* Athenæum.

CHAPLIN, Edward Graham Mellish, CMG 2004; OBE 1988; HM Diplomatic Service, retired; Appointments Secretary to the Prime Minister for senior ecclesiastical appointments since 2014; *b* 21 Feb. 1951; *s* of late James and Joan Chaplin; *m* 1983, Nicola Helen Fisher; one *s* two *d*. *Educ:* Queens' Coll., Cambridge (BA 1st Cl. Hons Oriental Studies 1973). Entered FCO, 1973; Muscat, 1975–77; Brussels, 1977–78; Ecole Nat. d'Admin, Paris, 1978–79; on secondment to CSD as Private Sec. to Lord Pres. of the Council and Leader of H of L, 1980–81; FCO, 1981–84; Head of Chancery, Tehran, 1985–87; FCO, 1987–89; on secondment to Price Waterhouse Management Consultants, 1990–92; Dep. Perm. Rep. UKMIS Geneva, 1992–96; Hd, ME Dept, FCO, 1997–99; Ambassador to the Hashemite Kingdom of Jordan, 2000–02; Dir, Middle East and N Africa, FCO, 2002–04; Ambassador to Iraq, 2004–05; Ambassador to Italy, 2006–11. Vis. Fellow, Centre of Internat. Studies, Univ. of Cambridge, 2005–06. Sen. Advr, Good Governance Gp, 2011–. Associate, Darwin Coll., Cambridge, 2011–. Comr, Commonwealth War Graves Commn, 2011–. Trustee: Mowgli Foundn, 2011–; British Inst. for Study of Iraq, 2012–. Gov., Wellington Coll., 2011–. *Recreations:* music, tennis, hill/mountain walking. *E:* egmc51@gmail.com.

CHAPLIN, John Cyril, CBE 1988; FREng; FRAeS; Member, Civil Aviation Authority and Group Director, Safety Regulation (formerly Safety Services), 1983–88; *b* 13 Aug. 1926; *s* of late Ernest Stanley Chaplin and Isabel Chaplin; *m* 1st, 1949, Ruth Marianne Livingstone (*d* 2004); two *s* two *d*; 2nd, 2005, Margaret Bronwen Nelson (*née* Evans), *widow* of William Nelson. *Educ:* Keswick School. Miles Aircraft, 1946; Vickers-Supermarine, 1948; Handley Page, 1950; Somers-Kendall Aircraft, 1952; Heston Aircraft, 1956; Air Registration Board, 1958; Civil Aviation Authority, 1972, Dir-Gen. Airworthiness, 1979. FREng (FEng 1987). *Publications:* papers to RAeS, incl. Concorde airworthiness certification and safety regulation in Jl of Aeronautical Hist. *Recreations:* sailing, photography, travel. *Club:* Cruising Association (Vice-Pres., 1995–98; Pres., 2003–04).

CHAPLIN, Laura Susan; *see* McGillivray, L. S.

CHAPLIN, Sir Malcolm (Hilbery), Kt 1991; CBE 1984; FRICS; Chairman, Hilbery Chaplin, chartered surveyors, Romford and Essex (formerly Senior Partner, Hilbery Chaplin Porter, chartered surveyors, London, W1); *b* 17 Jan. 1934; *s* of Sir George Chaplin, CBE, FRICS and Lady Chaplin, (Doris Evelyn, *née* Lee); *m* 1959, Janet Gaydon; three *s*. *Educ:* Summer Fields, Oxford; Rugby Sch.; Trinity Hall, Cambridge (MA Est. Mgt 1961; Athletics Blue, 440 yds). Former Member: Barking, Havering and Brentwood DHA; Essex AHA. Treasurer: Billericay Cons. Assoc., 1970–73; Brentwood and Ongar Cons. Assoc., 1973–79 (Pres., 1988–92); Eastern Area Cons. Assocs, 1980–88 (Vice Pres., 1988–98); Mem., Nat. Union Exec. and Gen. Purposes Cttees, 1980–98; Chm., Cons. Bd of Finance, 1993 (Dep. Chm., 1988–93); Conservative Party: Mem. Bd of Mgt, 1993–98; Treasurer, 1993–2000; Association Chm., 1994–2011; Trustee, Cons. Agents Superannuation and Benevolent Funds, 1992. Former Governor: Brentwood Sch.; St Martins Schs, Hutton. Trustee, Romford War Meml Old Folks Club and other trusts. Freeman, City of London. Liveryman: Innholders' Co. (Master, 1992–93); Chartered Surveyors' Co. *Recreations:* dairy farming (retired), golf, watching cricket and Rugby. *Address:* c/o 84 Market Place, Romford, Essex RM1 3JE. *Clubs:* Carlton, Oxford and Cambridge, MCC; Hawks (Cambridge); Gentlemen of Essex CC.

CHAPLIN, Dr Simon David John, FDSRCS; Director of Culture and Society, Wellcome Trust, since 2014; *b* Dagenham, 17 March 1969; *s* of David John Chaplin and Diane Elizabeth Chaplin (*née* Lewis); *m* 2007, Natalie Anna Ceeney, *qv*. *Educ:* Hitchin Boys' Sch.; Fitzwilliam Coll., Cambridge (BA Natural Scis 1991; MA 1995); King's Coll. London (PhD Hist. 2009). FDSRCS 2010. Asst Curator, 1992–95, Associate Curator, 1995–98, Science Mus.; Sen. Curator, 1998–2007, Dir, Museums and Special Collections, 2007–10, RCS; Hd, Wellcome Liby, 2010–14. Menzies Campbell Lectr, 2006, Hunterian Orator, 2010, RCS. Hon. Secretary: Soc. for Hist. of Natural Hist., 2005–08; British Soc. for Hist. of Sci., 2010–14. *Publications:* contrib. book chapters and articles to learned jls on hist. of medicine. *Address:* Pearson's Cottage, Frittenden, Kent TN17 2DD.

CHAPMAN, Angela Mary, (Mrs I. M. Chapman); Headmistress, Central Newcastle High School (GDST), 1985–99; *b* 2 Jan. 1940; *d* of Frank Dyson and Mary Rowe; *m* 1959, Ian Michael Chapman; two *s*. *Educ:* Queen Victoria High Sch., Stockton; Univ. of Bristol (BA Hons French); Sorbonne (Dip. de Civilisation Française). Teacher of French, Bede Sch., Sunderland, 1970–80; Dep. Headmistress, Newcastle upon Tyne Church High Sch., 1980–84. *Recreations:* military history, walking, tennis. *Address:* 14 Alpine Way, Sunderland, Tyne and Wear SR3 1TN.

CHAPMAN, Prof. Antony John, PhD; CPsychol, FBPsS; FAcSS; President and Vice-Chancellor (formerly Vice-Chancellor and Principal), Cardiff Metropolitan University (formerly University of Wales Institute, Cardiff), since 1998; Professor, University of Wales, since 1998 (Senior Vice-Chancellor and Chief Executive, 2004–07); *b* 21 April 1947; *s* of Arthur Charles Chapman and Joan Muriel Chapman (*née* Brown); *m* 1985, Dr Siriol David; two *s* two *d*. *Educ:* Milford Haven Grammar Sch.; Bexley Grammar Sch.; Univ. of Leicester (BSc 1968; PhD 1972). FBPsS 1978; CPsychol 1988. University of Wales Institute of Science and Technology, Cardiff: Lectr, 1971–78; Sen. Lectr, 1978–83; University of Leeds: Prof. of Psychol., 1983–98 (on secondment, pt-time, to CVCP Acad. Audit Unit, 1990–94); Dir, Centre for Applied Psychol Studies, 1987–90; Dean of Sci., 1992–94; Pro-Vice-Chancellor, 1994–98; Vis. Prof., 1998–2003. Associate Ed., British Jl Develtl Psychol., 1983–88; Ed.-in-Chief, Current Psychol., 1985–89; Mem., Editl Bd, Jl of Organizational Behavior, 1988–92; Ed., British Jl Psychol., 1989–95; Mem., Editl Cttee, British Jl Educnl Psychol., 1991–95; Senior Editor, book series: Psychol. for Professional Gps, 1981–88; Psychol. in Action, 1985–89; Internat. Liby of Critical Writings in Psychol., 1991–95; Mem. Bd, BPS Communications, 1979–; Founding Co-Dir, Sound Alert Ltd, 1994 (winner, Prince of Wales Award for Innovation, 1997); Member: Council, CBI Wales, 1999–2004, 2006–12, 2013–; Bd, Cardiff Business Technol. Centre, 2000–; Council, Cardiff Chamber of Commerce, 2004–07; Prince's Trust, Wales, 2012–; Adv. Bd, Cardiff Business Council, 2013–. Economic and Social Research Council: Vice-Chm., Trng Bd, 1995–96; Chairman: Res. Recognition Exercise, 1993–96; Policy Rev. Gp, 1994–96; Psychol Subject Panel, 1996–2001. Chairman: Assoc. of UK Heads of Psychol. Depts, 1990–92; UK Deans of Sci. Cttee, 1992–94; Mem., Cttee Eur. Assoc. Deans of Sci., 1993–94; a Vice-Pres., UUK, 2002–04 (Mem. Bd, 2002–06, 2015); Chm., Higher Educn Wales, 2002–04. Member: RAE Psychol. Panel, HEFCE, 1992, 1996; Northern Exams and Assessment Bd, 1994–98; Bd, QAA, 2000–06, 2011– (Chairman: Access Recognition and Licensing Cttee, 2003–06; Cttee for Wales, 2004–06, 2013–); Council for Ind. and Higher Educn, 2002–12; Bd, Univs and Colls Employers' Assoc., 2002–05; Bd, Leadership Foundn for Higher Educn, 2003–07; Council, Parly Univ. Gp (formerly All Party Parly Gp), 2004–; Bd, Univs and Colls Admissions Service, 2007–11; Adv. Bd, London Sch. of Commerce, 2007–11; Bd, Higher Educn Acad., 2009– (Chm., Academic Council, 2009–11); Welsh Leadership Council, Nat. Centre for Univs and Business, 2013–. Chm., Academic Accreditation Cttee, Singapore Assoc. Private Schs and Colls, 2009–12; Advr to Bd of Govs, S Australia Mgt Inst., 2009–12; UUK Internat. Policy Network, 2011–; Governance and Adv. Bd, Arab European Leadership Bd, Assoc. Arab Univs, 2014–. British Psychological Society: Chm., Bd of Examrs, Qualifying Exam, 1986–90; Pres., 1988–89; Chm., Jls Cttee, 1995–98; Hon. Fellow, 1999; President: Psychol. Section, BAAS, 1993–94; Assoc. of Learned Socs for the Social Scis, 1995–98. Vice-Pres., Cardiff Business Club, 2007–. Gov., Bramhope Primary Sch., 1997–98. Fellow, Inst. of Welsh Affairs, 2007–08, 2010–. FAcSS (AcSS 1999); FRSA 1997; FInstD 2015. Liveryman, Livery Co. of Wales, 2014–. Hon. DSc Leicester, 2008. *Publications:* jointly: Humour and Laughter: theory, research and applications, 1976, 2nd edn 1995; It's a Funny Thing, Humour, 1977; Friendship and Social Relationships in Children, 1980, 2nd edn 1995; Models of Man, 1980; Children's Humour, 1980; Road Safety: research and practice, 1981; Pedestrian Accidents, 1982; Psychology and People, 1983; Psychology and Social Problems, 1984; Elements of Applied Psychology, 1984; Psychology and Law, 1984; Noise and Society, 1984; Cognitive Processes in the Perception of Art, 1984; Cognitive Science, Vols I, II and III, 1995; Biographical Dictionary of Psychology, 1997; guest co-ed., collections of papers in various jls; contrib. articles to jls and chapters in books. *Recreations:* family, music, cricket, soccer. *Address:* Hill House, 95 Cyncoed Road, Cardiff CF23 6AE. *T:* (office) (029) 2041 6101, *Fax:* (029) 2041 6910. *E:* ajchapman@cardiffmet.ac.uk. *Clubs:* Athenæum; Cardiff and County (Cardiff).

CHAPMAN, Ben; *see* Chapman, J. K.

CHAPMAN, Charles Cyril Staplee; corporate development consultant; Member for Corporate Development and Finance, UK Atomic Energy Authority, 1988–90; *b* 9 Aug. 1936; *s* of Thomas John Chapman and Gertrude Gosden Chapman; *m* 1963, Lorraine Dorothy Wenborn; two *s*. *Educ:* St Peter's Sch., York; Univ. of Sheffield (BSc Hons). British Petroleum Co., 1958, Manager, Chemicals, Corporate Planning, Minerals, 1962–85; Senior Strategy Advisor, British Telecom, 1986–88. *Recreation:* growing rhododendrons.

CHAPMAN, Maj. Gen. Chip; *see* Chapman, Maj. Gen. Clive.

CHAPMAN, Christine; Member (Lab) Cynon Valley, National Assembly for Wales, since 1999; *b* 7 April 1956; *d* of late John Price and Edith Jean Price; *m* 1981, Dr Michael Chapman; one *s* one *d*. *Educ:* Porth County Girls' Sch.; UCW, Aberystwyth (BA Hons); South Bank Poly. (Dip. Careers Guidance 1989); UWCC (MSc Econ 1992; MPhil 2001); Univ. of Wales Swansea (PGCE 1995). Mid Glamorgan County Council: Community Services Agency, 1979–80; Mid Glamorgan Careers, 1980–93; Educn Business Partnership (on secondment), 1993–94; teaching and consultancy posts, 1995–96; Co-ordinator, Torfaen Educn Business Partnership, 1996–99. Mem. (Lab) Rhondda Cynon Taff Council, 1995–99. Dep. Minister for Educn and Lifelong Learning and for Local Govt, Welsh Assembly Govt, 2005–07. Chair, Petitions Cttee, 2009–11, Children and Young People's Cttee, 2011–, Nat. Assembly for Wales. Nat. Assembly for Wales Rep., Cttee of Regions, 2008–12. *Recreations:* theatre, walking and women's history. *Address:* National Assembly for Wales, Cardiff Bay, Cardiff CF99 1NA. *T:* 0300 200 7164; (constituency office) Bank Chambers, 28a Oxford Street, Mountain Ash, Rhondda Cynon Taff CF45 3EU. *T:* (01443) 478098.

CHAPMAN, Prof. Christopher Hugh; Scientific Consultant, Schlumberger Gould Research (formerly Schlumberger Cambridge Research), since 2005 (Scientific Adviser, 1991–2005); *b* 5 May 1945; *s* of late John Harold Chapman and Margaret Joan Weeks; *m* 1974, Lillian Tarapaski; one *s* one *d*. *Educ:* Latymer Upper School; Christ's College, Cambridge (MA); Dept of Geodesy and Geophysics, Cambridge (PhD). Asst Prof., Univ. of Alberta, 1969–72, Associate Prof., 1973–74; Asst Prof., Univ. of California, Berkeley, 1972–73; University of Toronto: Associate Prof., 1974–80; Prof., 1980–84; Killam Research Fellow, 1981–83; Adjunct Prof., 1984–88; Prof. of Physics, 1988–90; Prof. of Geophysics, Dept of Earth Scis, and Fellow, Christ's Coll., Cambridge, 1984–88. Hon. Prof. of Theoretical Seismology, Univ. of Cambridge, 2005–12; Emeritus Hon. Prof. of Theoretical Seismology, Univ. of Cambridge, 2012–. Green Scholar, Univ. of California, San Diego, 1978–79, 1986. Gold Medal, RAS, 2013. *Publications:* Fundamentals of Seismic Wave Propagation, 2004; research papers in sci. jls. *Recreations:* sailing, photography, woodwork. *Address:* SchlumbergerGould Research, High Cross, Madingley Road, Cambridge CB3 0EL. *T:* (01223) 315576.

CHAPMAN, Clare Fiona Louise; *see* Stanley, C. F. L.

CHAPMAN, Maj. Gen. Clive, (Chip), CB 2012; Senior British Military Advisor, United States Central Command, 2010–12; Consultant, Skarbek Associates, since 2013; *b* Launceston, 27 March 1959; *s* of Peter and Fay Chapman; *m* 1987, Geinor Bolton; one *s* one *d*. *Educ:* Lancaster Univ. (BA Hons 1980); Royal Military Acad. Sandhurst. COS, 5 Airborne Bde, 1992–94; JSSC, 1996–98; SO1 Ops/Trng HQ NI, 1998–99; in command 2nd Bn, Parachute Regt, 1999–2001; Col Mil. Ops 2, MoD, 2001–04; in command 19 Light Bde, 2004–05; COS NI, 2006–07; Hd, Counter Terrorism and UK Ops, 2007–10. Home Office rev. of police discipline, 2014. *Publications:* Notes from a Small Military, 2013. *Recreations:* country walks, football, ski-ing, theatre. *Address:* c/o 16 Oak Ash Green, Wilton, Salisbury, Wilts SP2 0RR. *T:* 07808 520118. *E:* chipchapman@hotmail.co.uk.

CHAPMAN, Sir David (Robert Macgowan), 3rd Bt *cr* 1958, of Cleadon, Co. Durham; DL; Consultant, UBS AG (formerly Laing & Cruickshank Investment Management, then UBS Laing & Cruickshank, later UBS Wealth Management (UK) Ltd), 2002–12; *b* 16 Dec. 1941; *s* of Sir Robert Macgowan Chapman, 2nd Bt, CBE, TD and Barbara May, *d* of Hubert Tonks; *S* father, 1987; *m* 1965, Maria Elizabeth de Gosztonyi-Zsolnay, *o d* of late Dr N. de Mattyasovsky-Zsolnay; one *s* one *d*. *Educ:* Marlborough; McGill Univ., Montreal (BCom). Wise Speke Ltd, then Wise Speke Div., Brewin Dolphin Securities Ltd, stock and share brokers, Newcastle upon Tyne: Partner, 1971–87; Dir, 1987–99; First Vice-Pres. and Sen. Relationship Manager for NE England, Merrill Lynch Internat. Bank, 1999–2002. Chairman: Team General Partner Ltd, 1994–2012; Northern Enterprise General Partner Ltd, 2000–13; Dep. Chm., Adv. Bd, North East Finance Ltd, 2010–; Director: Northern Rock plc (formerly North of England Building Soc. then Northern Rock Building Soc.), 1974–2004 (Chm., Trustees, Northern Rock Pension Schemes, 2004–13); Breathe North Appeal Ltd, 1988–2001; British Lung Foundation Ltd, 1989–95; Gordon Durham & Co. Ltd, 1994–98; High Gosforth Park Ltd, 1999–2004; NE Regl Investment Fund Ltd, 1999–2009; NES General Partner Ltd, 1999–; Zytronic plc, 2000–; Salle Farms Ltd, 2000–15; Guestwick Farms Ltd, 2000–15; NE Regl Investment Fund Two Ltd, 2001–09; Three Ltd, 2002–09; CNE General Partner Ltd, 2001–; Farmstar Polska Sp. z o.o. Co., 2006–; NE Regl Investment Fund Partner Ltd, 2006–09. Chairman: Virgin Money Pension Scheme, 2011–; Virgin Money Ind. Governance Cttee, 2015–. Stock Exchange: Mem. Council, 1979–88; Chairman: Northern Unit, 1988–91; NE Reg. Adv. Gp, 1991–98. MCSI (MSI 1991) (NE Pres., 1993–2008). Mem. Council, CBI, 2001–03; Chm., 2001–03, Dep. Chm., 2003–05, NE Reg., CBI. Chm., Northumbria Coalition Against Crime, 1995–2000. Mem., Greenbury Cttee, 1995. Dir, Shrievalty Assoc. Ltd, 1999–2001. Trustee: Northern Rock Foundn, 2002–; Industrial Trust, 2004–10. Governor: St Aidan's Coll., Durham, 1987–97; UC, Durham, 1998–2000 (Chm., Graduates' Soc., 2001–04); Mem. Council, Univ. of Durham, 1997–2003. Tyne and Wear: High Sheriff, 1993–94; DL 1997. *Heir:* *s* Michael Nicholas Chapman [*b* 21 May 1969; *m* 1998, Eszter, *y d* of Dr Attila Perlényi; two *s*]. *Address:* Pinfold House, 6 West Park Road, Cleadon, Sunderland, Tyne and Wear SR6 7RR.

CHAPMAN, Douglas; MP (SNP) Dunfermline and West Fife, since 2015; *b* Edinburgh, 1955; *m*; two *c*. *Educ:* W Calder High Sch.; Napier Coll. Branch banking, then personnel mgt, TSB Scotland; work for Bruce Crawford, MSP, 1999–2005; Campaign Manager, SNP, 2006–07. Mem. (SNP) Fife Council, 1997–98 and 2007– (Chm., Educn and Children's Services Cttee, 2007–12). Educn spokesman, COSLA, 2012–. Contested (SNP): Dunfermline and W Fife, 2005, Feb. 2006; Kirkcaldy and Cowdenbeath, 2010. *Address:* House of Commons, SW1A 0AA.

CHAPMAN, (Francis) Ian, CBE 1988; Chairman, Radiotrust PLC, 1997–2001; Chairman, 1991–96, Deputy Chairman, 1997–99, Guinness Publishers Ltd; Chairman, Scottish Radio Holdings (formerly Radio Clyde) PLC, 1972–96 (Hon. President, 1996–2001); *b* 26 Oct. 1925; *s* of late Rev. Peter Chapman and Frances Burdett; *m* 1953, Marjory Stewart Swinton; one *s* one *d*. *Educ:* Shawlands Academy, Glasgow; Ommer Sch. of Music, Glasgow. Served RAF, 1943–44; worked in coal mines as part of national service, 1945–47. Joined Wm Collins Sons & Co. Ltd, 1947 as management trainee; Sales Manager, 1955; Gp Sales Dir, 1960; Jt Man. Dir, 1968–76; Dep. Chm., William Collins Hldgs, 1976–81; Chm., William Collins Publishers Ltd, 1979–81; Chm. and Gp Chief Exec., William Collins Hldgs plc, 1981–89. Chairman: Harvill Press Ltd, 1976–89; Hatchards Ltd, 1976–89; Ancient House Bookshop (Ipswich) Ltd, 1976–89; Co-Chm. and Actg Chief Exec., Harper & Row, NY, 1987–89; Chm. and Man. Dir, Chapmans Publishers, 1989–94. Chm., The Listener Publications PLC, 1988–93; Dep. Chm., Orion Publishing Gp, 1993–94; Director: Independent Radio News, 1984–85; Pan Books Ltd, 1962–84 (Chm., 1974–76); Book Tokens Ltd, 1981–94; Stanley Botes Ltd, 1985–89; (non-exec.) Guinness PLC, 1986–91; (non-exec.) United Distillers PLC, 1987–91; Pres.-Dir Gen., Guinness Media SAS, Paris, 1996–99. Publishers' Association: Mem. Council, 1963–76, 1977–82; Vice Pres., 1978–79 and 1981–82; Pres., 1979–81; Trustee, 1993–97. Chm., Nat. Acad. of Writing, 2000–03; Member: Bd, Book Develt Council, 1967–73; Governing Council, Scottish Business in the Community, 1983–98; Dir, Scottish Opera, Theatre Royal Ltd, 1974–79; Trustee, Book Trade Benevolent Soc., 1982–2003. Chm. Council, Strathclyde Univ. Business School, 1985–88. FRSA 1985; CCMI (CBIM 1982). Hon. DLitt Strathclyde, 1990. Scottish Free Enterprise Award, 1985. *Publications:* various articles on publishing in trade jls. *Recreations:* music, golf, reading, grandchildren. *Address:* Kenmore, 46 The Avenue, Cheam, Surrey SM2 7QE. *T:* (020) 8642 1820, *Fax:* (020) 8642 7439. *E:* fichapman25@googlemail.com. *Clubs:* Garrick, MCC; Royal Wimbledon Golf; Walton Heath Golf.

See also I. S. Chapman.

CHAPMAN, His Honour Frank Arthur; a Senior Circuit Judge, 2003–09 (a Circuit Judge, 1992–2009); *b* 28 May 1946; *s* of Dennis Arthur Chapman and Joan Chapman; *m* 1968, Mary Kathleen Jones; one *s* one *d*. *Educ:* Newton-le-Willows Grammar School; University College London (LLB, LLM; Brigid Cotter Prize). Called to the Bar, Gray's Inn, 1968; practice at

Birmingham. Resident Judge, Wolverhampton, 1997–2007; Hon. Recorder, Birmingham, 2007. Practising Anglican. *Recreations:* travel, mountaineering, antiques, theatre, good food, wine and company.

CHAPMAN, Sir Frank (Joseph), Kt 2011; CEng, FIMechE, FREng; Chief Executive, BG Group plc, 2000–12; *b* 17 June 1953; *s* of Frank William Chapman and Clara Minnie Chapman; *m* 1st, 1975, Evelyn Mary Hill (marr. diss. 1995); two *d*; 2nd, 1996, Kari Elin Theodorsen; one *s* one *d*. *Educ:* East Ham Tech. Coll. (OND (Dist.) 1971); Queen Mary Coll., London Univ. (BSc 1st Cl. Hons Mech. Engrg 1974). CEng 1999; FIMechE 1999; FREng 2012. Engr, BP, 1974–78; various engrg and mgt appts, Shell, 1978–96; joined British Gas, 1996; Man. Dir, BG Exploration and Production, 1996–99; Dir, BG Gp (formerly BG) plc, 1997–2012; Pres., BG Internat., 1999–2000. Non-exec. Dir, Rolls-Royce, 2011–. FRSA 2000. CCMI (CIMgt 2001). *Recreations:* yachting, ski-ing, music.

CHAPMAN, Frederick John; Group Treasurer, LucasVarity, 1996–98; *b* 24 June 1939; *s* of late Reginald John Chapman and Elizabeth Chapman; *m* 1964, Paula Brenda Waller; one *s* two *d*. *Educ:* Sutton County Grammar Sch. Joined ECGD, 1958; Principal, 1969; Asst Sec., 1977; Under Sec., 1982; Principal Estabt and Finance Officer, 1985–88; Varity Corporation: Treas. (Europe), 1988–89; Treas. and Vice-Pres., 1990–96. *Recreations:* reading, music. *Address:* 17136 Wrigley Circle, Fort Myers, FL 33908, USA.

CHAPMAN, Sir George (Alan), Kt 1982; FCA; FCIS; Senior Partner, Chapman Upchurch, Chartered Accountants, 1958–2000; *b* 13 April 1927; *s* of late Thomas George Chapman and Winifred Jordan Chapman; *m* 1950, Jacqueline Sidney (*née* Irvine) (*d* 2009); two *s* five *d*. *Educ:* Trentham Sch.; Hutt Valley High Sch.; Victoria University. Fellow, Chartered Inst. of Secretaries, 1969 (Mem., 1948–); Fellow, Inst. of Chartered Accountants of NZ (formerly NZ Soc. of Accountants), 1969 (Mem., 1948–). Joined Chapman Ross & Co., subseq. Chapman Upchurch, 1948. Chairman: Norwich Union General Insurance (formerly Norwich Winterthur) (NZ), 1985–92 (Dir, 1982–92); BNZ Finance, 1979–88 (Dir, 1977–88); Mitel Telecommunications, 1984–91; Pilkington (formerly Pilkington Brothers) (NZ), 1989–94 (Dir, 1982–94); Director: Bank of New Zealand, 1968–86 (Dep. Chm., 1976–86); Maui Developments Ltd, 1979–85; Offshore Mining Co. Ltd, 1979–85; Liquigas Ltd, 1981–85 (Chm., 1982–84); NZ Bd, Norwich Union Life Insurance Soc., 1982–92; Skellerup Industries Ltd, 1982–90 (Dep. Chm., 1984–87); Skellerup Industries, Malaysia, 1986–90; State Insurance Ltd, 1990–99 (Vice Chm., 1992–99); Norwich Union Holdings (NZ) Ltd, 1990–99 (Vice Chm., 1992–99); Vice Chm., Norwich Union Life Insurance (NZ) Ltd, 1993–98. Chairman: NZ Building Industry Authority, 1992–2000; Housing New Zealand Ltd, 1992–95 (Chm. Housing Corp. of NZ and Housing NZ Estabt Bd, April–July 1992). NZ National Party: Member, 1948–; Vice-Pres., 1966–73; Pres., 1973–82. Councillor, Upper Hutt Bor. Council, 1952–53, Deputy Mayor, Upper Hutt, 1953–55; Member: Hutt Valley Drainage Bd, 1953–55; Heretaunga Bd of Governors, 1953–55; Pres., Upper Hutt Chamber of Commerce, 1956–57. MInstD 1970, FInstD 1979. *Publications:* The Years of Lightning, 1980. *Recreations:* golf, reading, tennis. *Address:* 53 Barton Avenue, Heretaunga, Wellington, New Zealand. *T:* (4) 5283512. *Clubs:* Royal Wellington Golf, Wellington Racing (Life Mem.).

CHAPMAN, Graham Andrew; QC 2014; *b* Basildon, 28 Dec. 1975; *s* of Michael Chapman and Sheila Chapman; *m* 2002, Wendy Appleby; one *s* one *d*. *Educ:* Westcliff High Sch. for Boys; Oriel Coll., Oxford (BA Hons 1st Cl. Juris.). Called to the Bar, Inner Temple, 1998, Bencher; in practice as barrister, specialising in commercial litigation and arbitration, 4 New Square, 1999–. Jun. Bench Auditor, Inner Temple, 2015–. *Publications:* (ed) Jackson and Powell on Professional Liability, 5th edn 2002, 6th edn 2007. *Recreations:* family, music, art, theatre, motor sport, cricket, football, golf. *Address:* 4 New Square, Lincoln's Inn, WC2A 3RJ. *T:* (020) 7822 2000. *E:* g.chapman@4newsquare.com.

CHAPMAN, Prof. Hilary Anne, (Mrs Anthony Neil), CBE 2012; Chief Nurse and Chief Operating Officer, Sheffield Teaching Hospitals NHS Foundation Trust, since 2009 (Chief Nurse, since 2013); *b* Sheffield, 16 Aug. 1963; *d* of Alec and Jeanne Margaret Brown; *m* 2010, Anthony Neil. *Educ:* Sheffield Sch. of Nursing (RN 1985); Leeds Metropolitan Univ. (BSc Hons 1992); Sheffield Business Sch. (MBA 1997). Staff Nurse: Cardiothoracic, 1985–86, Intensive Care Areas, 1986–87, Northern Gen. Hosp., Sheffield; Intensive Care Unit, Leicester Royal Infirmary, 1987; Staff Nurse, 1987–89, Sister, 1989–92, Intensive Care Areas, Northern Gen. Hosp., Sheffield; Sen. Nurse Manager, Theatre and Critical Care, Leicester Royal Infirmary, 1992–95; Dep. Chief Nurse, Queen's Med. Centre, Nottingham, 1995–99; Director of Nursing and Midwifery: Kettering Gen. Hosp., 1999–2001; Univ. Hosps Coventry and Warwickshire, 2001–06. Vis. Prof., Faculty of Health and Wellbeing, Sheffield Hallam Univ., 2008–. Hon. DMed Sheffield 2015. *Recreations:* walking, travel, fine cuisine, friends and family. *Address:* Sheffield Teaching Hospitals NHS Foundation Trust, 8 Beechill Road, Sheffield S10 2SB. *T:* (0114) 271 2251, *Fax:* (0114) 271 1762. *E:* hilary.chapman@sth.nhs.uk.

CHAPMAN, Ian; *see* Chapman, F. I.

CHAPMAN, Ian Stewart; Chief Executive and Publisher, Simon and Schuster UK Ltd, since 2013 (formerly Managing Director and Chief Executive Officer, 2000–13); *b* 15 Jan. 1955; *s* of (Francis) Ian Chapman, *qv*; *m* 1978, Maria Samper; one *s* two *d*. *Educ:* Cranleigh Sch., Surrey; Univ. of Durham (BA (French and Spanish) 1980). Bookseller: Hatchards, Oxford St, 1973–74; WH Smith, Paris, 1974–75; trainee: Doubleday and Co. Inc., NY, 1980–81; Berkley Publishers, Putnam Gp, NY, 1981; editl asst, William Morrow Inc. NY, 1981–82; Ed., then Editl Dir, Hodder and Stoughton Ltd, 1983–88; Pan Macmillan: Publishing Dir, 1988–94; Man. Dir, 1994–2000. *Recreations:* golf, walking, ski-ing, gym. *Address:* Benedict House, Staplecross Road, Northiam, E Sussex TN31 6JJ. *T:* (01580) 830222, *Fax:* (01580) 830027; Simon and Schuster UK Ltd, 222 Gray's Inn Road, WC1X 8HB. *T:* (020) 7316 1910, *Fax:* (020) 7316 0331. *E:* ian.chapman@simonandschuster.co.uk. *Clubs:* Garrick, MCC.

CHAPMAN, James Keith, (Ben); *b* 8 July 1940; *s* of John Hartley and Elsie Vera Chapman; *m* 1st (marr. diss); three *d*; 2nd, 1999, Maureen Ann (*née* Byrne), pharmacist; one step *s*. *Educ:* Appleby Grammar Sch., Appleby in Westmorland. Pilot Officer, RAFVR, 1959–61. Min. of Pensions and Nat. Insce, 1958–62; Min. of Aviation/BAA, 1962–67; Rochdale Cttee of Inquiry into Shipping, 1967–70; BoT, 1970–74; First Sec. (Commercial), Dar es Salaam, 1974–78; First Sec. (Econ.), Accra, 1978–81; Asst Sec., DTI, 1981–87; Commercial Counsellor, Peking, 1987–90; Dep. Regl Dir, NW, and Dir, Merseyside, 1991–93, Regl Dir, Northwest, 1993–94, DTI; Dir, Trade and Industry, Govt Office for NW, 1994–95. Founder Consultant, Ben Chapman Associates, 1995–97. MP (Lab) Wirral S, Feb. 1997–2010. PPS to Minister of State, DETR, 1997–99, DTI, 1999–2001, DCMS, 2001–05. Member: Intelligence and Security Cttee, 2005–10; Ecclesiastical Cttee, 2005–10. All-Party Parliamentary Groups: Chairman: China, 1997–2010 (Pres., 2010–); Britain-Turkey, 1998–2001; Soap and Detergents Industry, 1999–2001; Cleaning and Hygiene Products Industry, 2001–10; Vietnam, 2003–10 (Pres., 2010–); Vice-Chair, Turkish Northern Cyprus, 2006–10; Sec., Chile, 2005–10. Mem., Commonwealth Parly Assoc. Exec. Cttee, 2005–10. Fellow, Industry and Parlt Trust, 2006–10. Dir, Wirral Chamber of Commerce, 1995–96; Chm., Adv. Bd, China Gateway-North West, 1996–97; Pres., Wirral Investment Network, 2007–10 (Hon. Vice-Pres., 1997–2007). Exec. Chm., UK-Vietnam Network, 2013–. Member: Adv. Bd, China Britain Law Inst., 2010–; Bd, Univ. of Central Lancs, 2011–12 (Special Internat. Advr, 2011–). Patron; Wirral Fund for Children with Special Needs, 2010–; Dep. Patron, BESO, 2003–05. Trustee, Historic Cheshire Churches Preservation Trust, 2011–. Hon. Ambassador: for Cumbria, 1995–; for Merseyside, 1997–. Fellow, 48 Gp Club (Vice Pres., 2011–). *Recreations:* opera, music, walking, theatre, art appreciation. *Address:* Lawnwood, Wallrake, Lower Heswall, Wirral CH60 8PQ.

CHAPMAN, Jeffrey Paul; QC 2010; *b* London, 23 Aug. 1963; *s* of Cliff and Joyce Chapman; *m* 2000, Annette Caseley; two *d*. *Educ:* Wakeman Sch., Shrewsbury; Univ. of Sussex (BA Hons 1985); Trinity Hall, Cambridge (LLM 1986). Called to the Bar, Middle Temple, 1989; in practice as barrister, 1990–. *Recreations:* playing squash and chess, watching football, scuba diving, being at home with family and friends. *Address:* Fountain Court, Temple, EC4Y 9DH. *T:* (020) 7583 3335. *E:* jpc@fountaincourt.co.uk. *Clubs:* Blacks, West Ham; Shrewsbury Town.

CHAPMAN, Jennifer; MP (Lab) Darlington, since 2010; *b* 25 Sept. 1973; *m* 2014, Nicholas Desmond John Smith, *qv*; two *s* by a previous marriage. *Educ:* Hummersknott Sch., Darlington; Queen Elizabeth Sixth Form Coll., Darlington; Brunel Univ. (BSc Psychol. 1996); Durham Univ. (MA Medieval Archaeol. 2004). Sen. Parly researcher to Alan Milburn, MP, 1997–2005. Mem. (Lab) Darlington BC, 2007–10. *Address:* House of Commons, SW1A 0AA.

CHAPMAN, Rt Rev. John Holland; *see* Ottawa, Bishop of.

CHAPMAN, Prof. John Newton, PhD; FRSE; FIEEE, FInstP; Professor of Physics, 1988–2014, and Vice Principal and Head, College of Science and Engineering, 2010–14, University of Glasgow (Dean of Physical Sciences, 2008–10), now Emeritus Vice Principal; *b* 21 Nov. 1947; *s* of John Avi Chapman and Nora Chapman; *m* 1972, Judith Margaret Brown; one *s* one *d*. *Educ:* St John's Coll., Cambridge (BA 1st Cl. Hons Natural Scis 1969), Fitzwilliam Coll., Cambridge (PhD 1973). Res. Fellow, Fitzwilliam Coll., Cambridge, 1971–74; Lectr, 1974–84, Reader, 1984–88, Univ. of Glasgow. Mem., EPSRC, 2003–08. FRSE. *Recreations:* tennis, hill walking, photography, music. *Address:* Kelvin Building, University of Glasgow, Glasgow G12 8QQ. *T:* (0141) 330 4462, *Fax:* (0141) 330 4464. *E:* john.chapman@glasgow.ac.uk.

CHAPMAN, Jonathan; *see* Chapman, S. J.

CHAPMAN, Ven. Justine Penelope Heathcote A.; *see* Allain Chapman.

CHAPMAN, Keith; Founder, Keith Chapman Productions, since 2012; *b* 12 Dec. 1958; *s* of Roy Kenneth Chapman and Patricia Margaret Chapman (*née* Rose); *m* 1984, Kirsty Jane Asher; three *s*. *Educ:* St Nicholas Comp. Sch., Basildon; Great Yarmouth Art Coll. (Graphics Distn and Coll. Award). Art Dir, Garrat Baulcombe Advertising Agency, 1980–82; Creative Dir, McCarthy Oswin Advertising, 1982–85; Art Dir, Jim Henson Entertainment, 1985–88; Art Dir, Bastable Daley, 1988–95; freelance art dir/illustrator, 1995–2000; Co-Founder and Creative Dir, Chapman Entertainment, 2001–12. Children's television shows: Creator: Bob the Builder, 1999; Fifi and the Flowertots, 2005; Co-Creator, Roary the Racing Car, 2007; Producer: Little Charley Bear, 2011; Raa Raa the Noisy Lion, 2011. Hon. DA Norwich Univ. Coll. of the Arts, 2009. *Recreations:* writing, painting, football, golf. *Address:* Keith Chapman Productions, 90 Point Pleasant, Wandsworth, SW18 1PP. *T:* 07885 765674, (office) 0870 403 0556, *Fax:* 0870 403 0557. *Clubs:* Coombe Hill Golf, Nairn Golf; Bank of England Veterans Football.

CHAPMAN, Mark Fenger, CVO 1979; HM Diplomatic Service, retired; Member, Police Complaints Authority, 1991–95; *b* 12 Sept. 1934; *er s* of late Geoffrey Walter Chapman and Esther Marie Fenger; *m* 1959, Patricia Mary Long; three *s* (and one *s* decd). *Educ:* Cranbrook Sch.; St Catharine's Coll., Cambridge. Entered HM Foreign Service, 1958; served in: Bangkok, 1959–63; FO, 1963–67; Head of Chancery, Maseru, 1967–71; Asst Head of Dept, FCO, 1971–74; Head of Chancery, Vienna, 1975–76; Dep. High Comr and Counsellor (Econ. and Comm.), Lusaka, 1976–79; Diplomatic Service Inspector, 1979–82; Counsellor, The Hague, 1982–86; Ambassador to Iceland, 1986–89. *Club:* Norfolk (Norwich).

CHAPMAN, Mary Madeline, (Mrs A. R. Pears); Chairman, Institute of Customer Service, since 2009; *b* 9 March 1949; *d* of Kenneth F. Chapman, MBE and Agnes G. B Chapman (*née* Thompson); *m* 1st, 1976, Robert Henry Lomas (marr. diss. 1986); 2nd, 1990, Andrew Roger Pears; one *d*. *Educ:* Sutton High Sch.; Univ. of Bristol (BA Hons). Dip CIM 1975; CDir 2005. Mkting Exec., BTA, 1971–76; Mkting Manager, L'OREAL (Golden Ltd), 1976–82; General Manager: Nicholas Labs Ltd, 1982–86; Biotherm, 1986–88; Man. Dir, Helena Rubinstein, 1988–90; Dir, Personnel Ops, L'OREAL (UK), 1990–93; Chief Exec., Investors in People UK, 1993–98; Dir Gen., Inst. of Mgt, later Chief Exec., Chartered Mgt Inst., 1998–2008. Non-exec. Dir, Royal Mint, 2008–14. Member: Nat. Lottery Commn 2008–13; Gambling Commn, 2013–. Mem., Archbps' Council, C of E, 2010–. Mem. Council, Brunel Univ., 2009–. Trustee, Girls' Day Sch. Trust, 2005–14. *Recreations:* walking sailing, theatre, church and community projects.

CHAPMAN, Ven. Michael Robin; Archdeacon of Northampton, 1991–2004; *b* 29 Sept 1939; *s* of Frankland and Kathleen Chapman; *m* 1973, Bernadette Taylor; one *s* one *d*. *Educ:* Lichfield Cathedral Sch.; Ellesmere Coll.; Leeds Univ. (BA 1961); Coll. of the Resurrection Mirfield. Ordained, dio. of Durham, deacon, 1963, priest, 1964; curate, St Columba, Sunderland, 1963–68; Chaplain, RN, 1968–84; Vicar, St John the Evangelist, Farnham 1984–91; Rural Dean of Farnham, 1988–91. *Recreations:* flying light aircraft, music, hill walking. *Address:* Dolphin House, High Street, Caenby, Market Rasen, Lincs LN8 2EE. *T:* (01673) 876190.

CHAPMAN, Nicholas John; Managing Director, The Irish Times Ltd, 1999–2001; *b* 17 June 1947; *s* of Frank and Elizabeth Chapman; *m* 1995, Louise Shaxson; two *d*. *Educ:* Merchant Taylors' Sch.; Clare Coll., Cambridge (MA); Exeter Univ. (MA 2007). With Hodder and Stoughton: Graduate Trainee, 1969; European Sales, 1970; Editor, 1973; Publishing Dir Associated Business Press, 1975; Editor-in-Chief, Futura Paperbacks, 1979; Publishing Director: Macdonald Futura, 1980; Macmillan London, 1983; Head of BBC Books and Educn, 1986–89, Dir, Consumer Products Gp, 1989–94, BBC Enterprises; Man. Dir, BBC Worldwide Publishing, 1994–97; Director: BBC Worldwide Ltd, 1994–97; BBC Americas Inc., 1994–97; Mem., BBC Bd of Management, 1994–96; Man. Dir & Publisher, Orion Military, subseq. Cassell Mil. Publishing, Orion Publishing Gp, 1998–99. Pres., Publishers Assoc., 1994–96. Non-exec. Dir, Dorset Healthcare Univ. NHS Foundn Trust, 2011–14 Chm., Trustee Bd, St Margaret's Hospice, Somerset, 2008–12. Gov., Norwood Sch. 1998–99. *Recreations:* walking, natural history, reading, mountain climbing. *Address:* Ferncroft House, Walton Elm, Marnhull, Dorset DT10 1QG.

CHAPMAN, Nigel Conrad, CMG 2008; Chief Executive, Plan International, since 2009; *b* 14 Dec. 1955; *s* of late Prof. Norman Bellamy Chapman; *m* 1984, Margaret Farrar; two *d*. *Educ:* Hymers Coll., Hull; Magdalene Coll., Cambridge (MA Hons English Lit.). Joined BBC 1977: researcher and producer, BBC News and Current Affairs, incl. Nationwide, Newsnight and Breakfast News, 1979–89; Editor, Public Eye, 1989–92; Head: Regl and Local Progs, SE 1992–94; Broadcasting, Midlands and East, 1994–96; Controller, English Regions, 1996–98 Dir, BBC Online, 1999–2000; Dep. Dir, 2000–04, Dir, 2004–09, BBC World Service Chairman: BBC World Service Trust, 2002–09; Plan UK, 2003–09. Trustee, Shelter UK 2012–. *Recreations:* sport (football and cricket), music, walking, reading. *Address:* 34 Chalfont Road, Oxford OX2 6TH. *T:* (01865) 554757.

CHAPMAN, Patricia Maud; journalist; *b* 3 May 1948; *d* of Arthur and Elizabeth Chapman *m* 1970, David Clark; one *s*. *Educ:* Rochford Secondary Sch., Essex. Tea-girl, sub-ed. and columnist, Boyfriend mag., 1964–67; reporter, Romford Times and Havering Express, then sub-ed., Western Daily Press, Bristol, 1967–71; sub-ed., The Sun, 1971–79; sub-ed., Daily Mirror, 1979–82; Asst Night Ed., 1982–86, Dep. Ed., 1986–88, The Sun; Ed., News of the World, 1988–94. A Founder Mem., Press Complaints Commn, 1991–93 (Chm., Code of Practice Cttee, 1991). *Recreations:* painting, ephemera, cooking and eating! *Address:* c/o News UK, 1 London Bridge Street, SE1 9GF.

CHAPMAN, Rev. Canon Rex Anthony; Residentiary Canon of Carlisle Cathedral, 1978–2004, now Canon Emeritus; Diocesan Director of Education, 1985–2004; Chaplain to the Queen, 1997–2008; *b* 2 Sept. 1938; *s* of Charles Arthur Chapman and Doris Chapman (*née* Eldred); *m* 1964, Margaret Anne (*née* Young); one *s* one *d*. *Educ:* Leeds Grammar Sch.; UCL (BA Classics 1962); St Edmund Hall, Oxford (BA Theol. 1964; MA 1968); Wells Theol Coll.; Univ. of Birmingham (DPS 1967). National Service, RAF, 1957–59 (Chinese linguist). Ordained deacon, 1965, priest, 1966; Asst Curate, St Thomas', Stourbridge, 1965–68; Associate Chaplain, Univ. of Aberdeen, 1968–78; Hon. Canon, St Andrew's Cathedral, Aberdeen, 1976–78; Vice-Dean, Carlisle Cathedral, 1980, 1982, 1984, 1989, 1994, 1998, 2002; Bishop's Advr for Educn, dio. of Carlisle, 1978–85; Bishops' Selector for Ministry in C of E, 1985–2004 (Sen. Selector, 1997–2004); warrant, dio. of Aberdeen and Orkney, 2006–. Chm., Vacancy-in-See Cttee, dio. of Carlisle, 1997–2003; Mem., Crown Appts Commn for See of Carlisle, 1988, 2000. Member: Gen. Synod of C of E, 1985–2000 (Mem., Bd of Educn, 1985–96; Chm., Schs Cttee, 1990–96); Carlisle Diocesan Synod, 1978–2003; Chm., House of Clergy, dio. of Carlisle, 1996–2003. Member: Cumbria Educn Cttee, 1978–98; Cumbria Educn Forum, 1999–2004; Standing Adv. Council for Religious Educn, Cumbria, 1978–2003 (Chm., 1989–2003); Cumbria Learning and Recreation Scrutiny Panel, 2001–04; Standing Cttee, Nat. Soc. for Promoting Religious Educn, 1982–97; Chm. Orgn Cttee, Cumbria Schs, 2001–04 (Vice-Chm., 1999–2001). Governor: Trinity Sch., Carlisle, 1978–2003 (Chm., 1989–2003); Carlisle and Blackburn (formerly Carlisle) Dio. Trng Inst., 1979–2004 (Vice-Chm., 2001–04); St Martin's Coll. (formerly UC of St Martin), Lancaster, 1985–2004; St Chad's Coll., Durham, 1989–94. Trustee, Carlisle Educnl Charity, 1978–2004 (Chm. of Trustees, 1998–99). Chm., Carlisle and Eden Valley Marriage Guidance Council, 1984–87; Mem., Cumbria Cttee, Royal Jubilee and Prince's Trust, 1985–87. *Publications:* A Kind of Praying, 1970; Out of the Whirlwind, 1971; A Glimpse of God, 1973; The Cry of the Spirit, 1974; The Glory of God, 1978; contrib. to A Dictionary of Christian Spirituality, 1983. *Recreation:* variable. *Address:* Myreside Cottage, Finzean, Banchory, Aberdeenshire AB31 6NB. *T:* (01330) 850485. *Club:* Royal Over-Seas League.

See also Ven. M. J. Everitt.

CHAPMAN, Hon. Rhiannon Elizabeth, FCIPD; Managing Director, Plaudit, 1994–2010; *b* 21 Sept. 1946; *d* of 2nd Viscount St Davids and Doreen Guinness Jowett; *m* 1974, Donald Hudson Chapman (marr. diss. 1992); two step *s*. *Educ:* Tormead Sch., Guildford; King's Coll., London Univ. (LLB Hons 1967; AKC). FCIPD (FIPM 1972). Industrial Soc., 1968; LWT, 1968–70; Philips Electronics Industries, 1970–77; CPI Data Peripherals Ltd, 1977–80; Personnel Dir, London Stock Exchange, 1980–90; business consultant, 1990–91; Dir, Industrial Soc., 1991–93; Mem., WDA, 1994–98. Chairman: National Australia CIF Trustee Ltd, 1994–96; Fleming Managed Growth plc, 1999–2002; Visions Consulting, 2004–05; non-executive Director: S. R. Gent plc, 1994–97; Bibby Financial Services, 2002–03. Dir, South West of England Urban Regeneration Fund, 2003–. Member: UFC, 1989–93; Employment Appeal Tribunal, 1991–; Council, PSI, 1993–98; Technical Mem., BUPA, 1997–. External Reviewer of Complaints, TTA, 1998–2004; Advr, People and Skills Agenda, SBAC, 2005–07. CCMI. *Recreations:* yoga, drawing, handcrafts. *Address:* 3 Church Green, Great Wymondley, Hitchin, Herts SG4 7HA. *T:* (01438) 759102.

CHAPMAN, Roger Ralph, CBE 2007; Chairman, GARS Search and Recovery Ltd, since 2015; *b* 29 July 1945; *s* of Ralph Aubrey Hector Chapman and Hilda Bisset Chapman; *m* 1971, Patricia June Nelson Sansom; two *s*. *Educ:* Chesterton Sch., Seaford; Bedford Sch.; BRNC, Dartmouth. Royal Navy Submarines, 1963–71: 2nd i/c conventional submarine (Long (N) Specialist); invalided out due to poor eyesight; submersible pilot and Survey Manager, Vickers Oceanics Ltd, 1971–76 (with co-pilot, rescued from submersible at 1575ft in Atlantic, 1973); Managing Director: Subsea Surveys Ltd, 1976–84 (pioneering robotics in North Sea and worldwide); James Fisher Rumic Ltd (specialising in submarine rescue services for RN, incl. rescue of 7 Russian sailors trapped in submarine in Russian Far East, 2005), 1984–2003; James Fisher Defence Ltd: Vice Chm., 2003–12; Chm., 2012–14; non-exec. Dir, 2014. Fellow, Soc. for Underwater Technol., 1985. Pres., Barrow Br., RNLI, 1998–2003. Founder, with wife, Rumic Foundn Trust (helping young disadvantaged people in Cumbria), 2003. Gov., Chetwynde Sch., Barrow, 2005–09. *Publications:* No Time on Our Side, 1975. *Recreations:* golf, sailing (Clipper Round World Race, 1998–99), rock-climbing, music, Italian food and red wine at lunchtime, laughing and having fun with my family, ski-ing. *Address:* Rumic Foundation Trust, 38½ The Gill, Ulverston, Cumbria LA12 7BP. *T:* (01229) 586426. *E:* chapman_roger@hotmail.com. *Club:* Sloane.

CHAPMAN, Roy de Courcy; Headmaster of Malvern College, 1983–96; *b* 1 Oct. 1936; *s* of Edward Frederic Gilbert Chapman and Aline de Courcy Ireland; *m* 1959, Valerie Rosemary Small; two *s* one *d*. *Educ:* Dollar Academy; St Andrews Univ. (Harkness Schol.: MA 1959); Moray House Coll. of Educn, Edinburgh. Asst Master, Trinity Coll., Glenalmond, 1960–64; Marlborough College: Asst Master, 1964–68; Head of Mod. Langs, 1968–75; OC CCF, 1969–75; Rector of Glasgow Acad., 1975–82. Chairman: Common Entrance Bd, 1988–93; HMC, 1994. *Publications:* Le Français Contemporain, 1971; (with D. Whiting) Le Français Contemporain: passages for translation and comprehension, 1975. *Recreations:* cruising, France, snorkelling. *Address:* 41 North Castle Street, St Andrews, Fife KY16 9BG.

CHAPMAN, Roy John, FCA; Chairman: Royal Mail (formerly Post Office, then Consignia) Pension Fund, 1995–2004; AEA Technology Pension Fund, 1996–2004; Director, Eurotunnel plc, 1995–2004; *b* 30 Nov. 1936; *s* of William George Chapman and Frances Harriet (*née* Yeomans); *m* 1961, Janet Gibbeson Taylor; two *s* one *d*. *Educ:* Kettering Grammar Sch.; St Catharine's Coll., Cambridge (Athletics Blue; MA). Joined Arthur Andersen & Co., Chartered Accountants, 1958; consulting, UK and abroad, incl. France, USA, Algeria, Greece, Turkey, Thailand and Switzerland, 1964–84; admitted to Partnership, 1970; Hd of Financial Services Practice, 1970–84; Man. Partner, London, 1984–89; Sen. Partner, 1989–93; Mem., Internat. Bd, 1988–93. Director: Halifax Bldg Soc., then Halifax plc, 1994–2001; Westminster Forum Ltd, 1989–99. Member: Adv. Council, London Enterprise Agency, 1985–88; Jt Disciplinary Scheme for Accounting Profession, 1994–2011. Mem. Governing Body, SOAS, London, 1990–2000. Council Mem., BITC, 1991–93. London Marathon, 1983 (Save the Children). St Catharine's College, Cambridge: Pres., St Catharine's Coll. Cambridge Soc., 1994–95; Chm., Develt Campaign, 1994–2000; Fellow Commoner, 2006–. Liveryman, Farriers' Co., 1992–. CCMI; FRSA. *Publications:* contribs to professional jls. *Recreations:* walking, reading, travel. *Address:* 9 Chislehurst Road, Bickley, Kent BR1 2NN. *T:* (020) 8467 3749. *Clubs:* Athenæum, Oxford and Cambridge, MCC; Hawks (Cambridge); Chislehurst Golf.

CHAPMAN, Prof. (Stephen) Jonathan, DPhil; FIMA; Professor of Mathematics and its Applications, since 1999, and Director, Oxford Centre for Industrial and Applied Mathematics, since 2008, University of Oxford; Fellow of Mansfield College, Oxford, since 1999; *b* 31 Aug. 1968; *s* of Stephen Cyril Chapman and Pauline Mary Chapman; *m* 1996, Aarti Chand; one *s* one *d*. *Educ:* Merton Coll., Oxford (BA Maths 1989); St Catherine's Coll., Oxford (DPhil Applied Maths 1991). FIMA 2007. Research Fellow: Stanford Univ., Calif, 1992–93; St Catherine's Coll., Oxford, 1993–95; Royal Soc. Res. Fellow, Univ. of Oxford, 1995–99. Richard C. Diprima Prize, 1994, Julian Cole Prize, 2002, SIAM; Whitehead Prize, London Mathematical Society, 1998. *Publications:* papers in learned jls. *Recreations:* music, walking. *Address:* Mathematical Institute, University of Oxford, Andrew Wiles Building, Radcliffe Observatory Quarter, Woodstock Road, Oxford OX2 6GG. *T:* (01865) 270507.

CHAPMAN, Prof. Stephen Kenneth, PhD; FRSC, FRSE; Principal and Vice Chancellor, Heriot Watt University, since 2009; *b* 12 May 1959. *Educ:* Univ. of Newcastle upon Tyne (BSc 1st Cl. Hons Chem. 1980; PhD 1983). FRSC 2005. NATO Postdoctoral Fellow, MIT, 1983–85; University of Edinburgh: Lectr, then Reader, 1985–96; Prof. of Biol Inorganic Chem., 1996–2009; Hd of Chem., 2000–05; Vice Principal for Planning, Resources and Res. Policy, 2006–09. FRSE 2005. *Address:* Heriot Watt University, George Heriot Wing, Riccarton, Edinburgh EH14 4AS.

CHAPMAN, Timothy James Patrick, FREng; Director, Arup, since 2004; *b* Dublin, Ireland, 19 May 1965; *s* of Dr David Chapman and Dr Valerie Chapman; *m* 1989, Dr Marisa Fernandez; three *d*. *Educ:* University Coll. Dublin (BE Civil Engrg 1986); Imperial Coll. London (MSc DIC Soil Mechanics 1987). CEng 1992; FICE 2002. Graduate Engr, 1987, Associate Dir, 2000–04, Arup. FREng 2014. *Publications:* (ed) ICE Manual of Geotechnical Engineering, 2012; ICE and CIRIA reports. *Recreations:* reading, socialising. *Address:* Arup, 13 Fitzroy Street, W1T 4BQ. *T:* (020) 7755 3238. *E:* tim.chapman@arup.com.

CHAPMAN, Gen. Sir Timothy John G.; *see* Granville-Chapman.

CHAPMAN, Tony; film maker and writer; Head of Awards, Royal Institute of British Architects, since 1996; *b* York, 23 Dec. 1950; *s* of James Chapman and Mary Chapman (*née* Alcock); *m* 1979, Jane Bentley (annulled 1992); *m* 2011, Wendy Akers. *Educ:* Pocklington Sch., Yorks; Univ. of Nottingham (BA Hons English). Researcher/writer, BBC TV Comedy, 1979–82: Not the Nine O'Clock News, Q9, Q10 (There's a Lot of it About); researcher/producer, BBC TV Current Affairs and Features, 1982–92: That's Life, Nationwide, 60 Minutes, Friday Report, First Sight, documentaries on early flying, architecture, envmtl and planning issues; Producer, 7 Days, ITV Meridian, 1992–93; Dir, Time Code Prodns, 1992–; Hd of Press, RIBA, 1996–99. Formerly Artistic Dir, Man in the Moon, Chelsea, 1978–82. Mem., Twentieth Century Soc., 2007–. Author of performed plays, incl. Pilate, Essay on Nam, 1926 and All That, Seven Deadly Sins, On the Road, There'll Always be a Brentford. Hon. FRIBA 2011. *Publications:* Architecture 98, 1998; Architecture 99, 1999; Architecture 00, 2000; Architecture 01, 2001; Architecture 02, 2002; Architecture 03, 2003; Architecture 04, 2004; Architecture 2005, 2005; The Stirling Prize: a decade of architecture and innovation, 2006; Architecture 2006, 2006; Architecture 2007, 2007; Architecture 2008, 2008; Architecture 2009, 2009; Architecture 10, 2010; Architecture 11, 2011; Buildings of the Year 2012, 2012. *Recreations:* travel and travel writing, theatre, writing. *Address:* c/o Royal Institute of British Architects, 66 Portland Place, W1B 1AD. *T:* 07921 767139. *E:* tonytimecode@me.com. *Club:* Questors.

CHAPMAN, William Edward, CVO 2008; Private Secretary and Chief of Staff to the Lord Mayor of London, since 2009; *b* 20 March 1952; *s* of late Philip Chapman and Pam Chapman. *Educ:* High Wych Primary Sch.; Bishop's Stortford Coll.; St Peter's Coll., Oxford (MA); Hertford Coll., Oxford (MLitt). Joined DoE (subseq. DETR), 1976; Information Directorate and speech writer for two Secs of State, 1988–91; Private Sec. for Home Affairs, then Parly Affairs, to the Prime Minister, 1991–94; Head: Planning Policies Div., 1994–98; Regeneration Div., 1998–99; Sec. for Appts to the Prime Minister and Ecclesiastical Sec. to the Lord Chancellor, 1999–2008; PM's Advr on Sen. Church and Lord-Lieut Appts, 2008; Dir of Policy, Tony Blair Faith Foundn, 2008–09. Mem., Adv. Council, McDonald Centre for Theology, Ethics and Public Life, 2008–. Trustee: Mitzvah Trust, 1998–2008; S Hackney Parochial Sch. Charity, 1998–2008. Fellow, Sion Coll., 2009–. *Recreations:* books, pictures, music, liming. *Address:* City of London, Guildhall, PO Box 270, EC2P 2EJ.

CHAPPELL, Julie Louise Jo, OBE 2005; Partner, Hawthorn London, since 2014; *b* Poole, 2 April 1978; *d* of John Chappell and Kathryn Chappell; *m* Bradley Porter; two *d*. *Educ:* Brasenose Coll., Oxford (BA PPE). Joined FCO, 1999; Central Africa Desk, Africa Directorate, FCO, 1999–2000; Second Sec., Amman, 2000–03; seconded to Coalition Provisional Authy, Baghdad, 2003; seconded to State Dept, Washington, DC, 2004; Hd, NATO Section, FCO, London, 2005–06; Regl Conflict Advr, Addis Ababa, 2006–09; Ambassador to Guatemala and (non-resident) to Honduras and El Salvador, 2009–12; Hd, Emerging Powers Prog. and GREAT Britain Campaign, FCO, 2012–14. *Recreations:* travel, sports. *E:* jules.chappell@hawthornlondon.com.

CHAPPELOW, Peter Raymond; company chairman; *b* 23 March 1947; *s* of Raymond and Stella Chappelow and step *s* of James Tillett; *m* 1990, Tina Margaret Jones; two *d*. *Educ:* Hanson Grammar Sch., Bradford. Mktg Dir, Grattan, 1969–89; CEO, The Marketing Co., 1989–91; Dir, Racing Green, 1991–96; Man. Dir, Country Holidays, 1992–94; Dir, Thomson Travel Gp, 1994–2001. Chairman: Supreme Imports, 2003–06; M and M Direct, 2004–07; Bounty, 2004–07; School-Safe, 2004–08; Graphic-Inline, 2005–08; Advantage Healthcare, 2005–07; Kingswood, 2006–08; Travelsphere, 2006–12; Hotter, 2007–14; Baker Ross, 2008–10; CVS, 2010–; OKA, 2014; Pure Collection, 2014. Member: Bd, English Tourism Council, 1995–2003; Cabinet Office Honours Cttee (Economy), 2005–13. *Recreations:* squash, tennis, golf, real music. *E:* chappelow@hotmail.com. *Clubs:* Lansdowne; Bradenton Country (Florida); Otley Golf, Ilkley Lawn Tennis and Squash.

CHAPPLE, Field Marshal Sir John, GCB 1988 (KCB 1985); CBE 1980 (MBE 1969); DL; Vice Lord-Lieutenant of Greater London, 1997–2005; *b* 27 May 1931; *s* of C. H. Chapple; *m* 1959, Annabel Hill; one *s* three *d*. *Educ:* Haileybury; Trinity Coll., Cambridge (MA). Joined 2nd KEO Goorkhas, 1954; served Malaya, Hong Kong, Borneo; Staff Coll., 1962; jssc 1969; Commanded 1st Bn 2nd Goorkhas, 1970–72; Directing Staff, Staff Coll., 1972–73; Services Fellow, Fitzwilliam Coll., Cambridge, 1973; Commanded 48 Gurkha Infantry Bde, 1976; Gurkha Field Force, 1977; Principal Staff Officer to Chief of Defence Staff, 1978–79; Comdr, British Forces Hong Kong, and Maj.-Gen., Brigade of Gurkhas, 1980–82; Dir of Military Operations, 1982–84; Dep. Chief of Defence Staff (Progs and Personnel), 1985–87; C-in-C, UKLF, 1987–88; CGS, 1988–92; Gov. and C-in-C, Gibraltar, 1993–95. ADC Gen. to the Queen, 1987–92. Col, 2nd Goorkhas, 1986–94. Hon. Col, Oxford Univ. OTC, 1988–95. Chm., UK Trust for Nature Conservation in Nepal (formerly King Mahendra UK Trust), 1993–; Trustee, King Mahendra Trust, Nepal, 1993–2006. Mem. Council, WWF UK, 1984–99 (Trustee, 1988–93; Amb., 1999– (Chm. of Ambs, 2003–11)). Vice Patron: Army Mus. Ogilby Trust, 1995–; Gurkha Mus., 2003– (Trustee, 1973–2003); Nat. Army Mus., 2003– (Trustee, 1981–2003); President: Indian Mil. Hist. Soc., 1991–; Mil. Hist. Soc., 1992–2013; Soc. for Army Histl Res., 1993–2012; Trekforce, 1998–2006; Stoll Foundn (formerly Sir Oswald Stoll Foundn), 1998–2012; BSES Expeditions, 1999–2009; Cobra (formerly Bilimoria) Foundn, 2005–; Kipling Soc., 2008–11; Friends of Imperial War Mus., 2008–13; Friends of Nat. Army Mus., 2009–; Vice Pres., British Assoc. for Cemeteries in S Asia, 2013–. Pres., Combined Services Polo Assoc., 1991–2006. FZS (Pres., 1992–94), FLS, FRGS, FSA, FRSA. DL Greater London, 1996. KStJ. *Clubs:* Beefsteak, Cavalry and Guards.

CHAPPLE, Keith, FIET; Chairman, Alliance for Electronic Business, 2001–02; *b* 11 Aug. 1935; *s* of Reginald Chapple and Gladys Evelyn (*née* Foster); *m* 1962, Patricia Margaret Aitchison; one *s* two *d*. *Educ:* City of Bath Boys' Sch.; Rugby Coll. of Technol. FIET (FIEE 1984). Engrg Manager, Gen. Precision Systems Ltd, 1961–66; Sales Engr, SGS-Fairchild Ltd, 1966–69; Mktg Manager, SGS-Fairchild SpA (Italy), 1969–70; Sales Manager, Intel Corp. (Belgium), 1970–72; Chm. and Man. Dir, Intel Corp. (UK) Ltd, 1972–2000. President: Fedn of Electronics Industry, 1996–97 (Vice-Pres., 1997–99); Swindon Chamber of Commerce, 1996–98; Chm., EU Cttee, American Chamber of Commerce in Belgium, 1998–2001. Mem., Oxford Isis Br., Rotary Club. MCMI (MIMgt 1976); FRSA 1999. Hon. DTech Loughborough, 1986. *Recreations:* music, family. *Club:* Clarendon (Oxford) (Pres., 2003–04).

CHAPPLE, Air Vice-Marshal Robert, CB 1994; Principal Medical Officer, Royal Air Force Support Command, 1991–94, retired; *b* 2 May 1934; *s* of Kevin Chapple and Florence Elsie (*née* Cann); *m* 1960, Barbara Ann (*née* Webster); one *s* one *d. Educ:* Finchley Catholic Grammar Sch.; St Mary's Hosp. Med. Sch. (MB, BS 1958). MRCS, LRCP 1958; DPH 1973; MFPHM 1978; MFOM 1980. Joined RAF Med. Br., 1960; served in UK, Singapore, Gibraltar, Germany and Cyprus; Officer Commanding: Princess Mary Hosp., Cyprus, 1982–85; Princess Mary's RAF Hosp., Halton, 1987–89; Princess Alexandra Hosp., Wroughton, 1989–91; Commandant, RAF Central Med. Estabt, 1991. QHP, 1992–94. MCMI (MBIM 1974). *Recreations:* golf, watching most sports, archaeology, visiting old churches, matters of general interest. *Address:* Hazel House, Withington, Cheltenham, Glos GL54 4DA.

CHAPPLE, Roger Graham; His Honour Judge Chapple; a Circuit Judge, since 2004, a Senior Circuit Judge, since 2007; Resident Judge, Inner London Crown Court, since 2007; *b* 28 Aug. 1951; *s* of Robert William Chapple and Elsie Mary Chapple (*née* Hubbard). *Educ:* Univ. of Leeds (LLB Hons). Called to the Bar, Gray's Inn, 1974, Bencher, 2009; in practice as a barrister, specialising in common law, 1974–94; Dep. JA, 1994–95; an Asst JAG, 1995–2004; Asst Recorder, 1999–2000, Recorder, 2000–04; Resident Judge, Middlesex Guildhall Crown Court, 2005–07; Sen. Judge, Sovereign Base Areas, Cyprus, 2007–. Hon. Recorder of Southwark, 2012–. *Recreations:* travel, music (particularly opera), combining the two. *Address:* Crown Court at Inner London, Sessions House, Newington Causeway, SE1 6AZ.

CHAREST, Hon. Jean; Partner, McCarthy Tétrault, since 2013; Premier of Quebec, 2003–12; *b* 24 June 1958; *s* of Claude Charest and Rita Charest (*née* Leonard); *m* 1980, Michèle Dionne; one *s* two *d. Educ:* Univ. of Sherbrooke (LLB 1980). Called to the Bar, Quebec, 1981; Lawyer: Legal Aid Office, 1980–81; Beauchemin, Dussault, 1981–84. MP (PC), Sherbrooke, 1984–98; Asst Dep. Speaker, 1984–86; Minister of State for Youth, 1986–90; Dep. Govt Leader; Minister: for Fitness and Amateur Sport, 1988–90; of Envmt, 1991–93; Dep. Prime Minister, 1993; Minister: for Industry, Sci. and Technol., 1993; responsible for Federal Business Develt Bank, 1993. Mem. (Quebec L) for Sherbrooke, Nat. Assembly of Quebec, 1998–2012. Leader: Progressive Conservative Party, 1993–98; Quebec Liberal Party, 1998; Leader of Official Opposition, 1998–2003. *Address:* McCarthy Tétrault, Suite 2500, 1000 De La Gauchetière Street West, Montréal, QC H3B 0A2, Canada.

CHARETTE, Janice Maria; Clerk of the Privy Council and Secretary to the Cabinet, Canada, since 2014; *b* Ottawa, 11 July 1962; *d* of Leo Villeneuve and Wilhelmina Villeneuve Emmerson; *m* 1984, Reginald Charette; one *s* one *d. Educ:* Carleton Univ. (BComm). Officer, Dept of Finance, Canada, 1984–88; Policy Analyst, Office of Privatization and Regulatory Affairs, 1989–91; Sen. Deptl Asst, Office of Minister of Finance, 1989–91; Sen. Policy Advr, Federal-Provincial Relns Office, 1991–92; Sen. Deptl Asst, Office of Minister of Finance, then Exec. Asst to COS, Office of Prime Minister, 1992–93; Coordinator, Base Closures Task Force, then Dir of Ops, Program Review Secretariat, later Exec. Dir, Strategic Projects Unit, Privy Council Office, 1994–96; Principal, Public Sector/Strategy Practice, Ernst & Young, 1996–97; COS, Leader of Progressive Conservative Party of Canada, 1997–98; Dir, Transition Team, Canada Pensions Plan Investment Bd, 1998–99; Sen. Asst Dep. Minister, Policy Sector, Justice, 1999–2000; Privy Council Office: Asst Sec. to Cabinet (Priorities and Planning), 2000–02; Associate Dep. Minister of Health and Dep. Sec. to Cabinet, Plans and Consultations, 2003–04; Deputy Minister: of Citizenship and Immigration Canada, 2004–06; of Human Resources and Skills Develt, 2006–10; of Intergovtl Affairs, 2010–12; Dep. Clerk of Privy Council and Associate Sec. to Cabinet, 2010–13. *Address:* Privy Council Office, 80 Wellington Street, Langevin Building, Ottawa, ON K1A 0A3, Canada. *T:* (613) 9575400. *E:* janice.charette@pco-bcp.gc.ca.

CHARING CROSS, Archdeacon of; *no new appointment at time of going to press.*

CHARKIN, Richard Denis Paul; Executive Director, Bloomsbury Publishing plc, since 2007; *b* 17 June 1949; *s* of Frank Charkin and Mabel Doreen Charkin (*née* Rosen); *m* 1972, Susan Mary Poole; one *s* two *d. Educ:* Haileybury and ISC; Trinity College, Cambridge (MA); Harvard Business Sch. (AMP). Science Editor, Harrap & Co., 1972; Sen. Publishing Manager, Pergamon Press, 1973; Oxford University Press: Medical Editor, 1974; Head of Science and Medicine, 1976; Head of Reference, 1980; Managing Dir, Academic and General, 1984; Octopus Publishing Group (Reed International Books), 1988; Chief Exec., Reed Consumer Books, 1989–94; Exec. Dir, 1988–96 and Chief Exec., 1994–96, Reed Internat. Books; CEO, Current Science Gp, 1996–97; Chief Exec., Macmillan Ltd, 1998–2007. Mem., Bd of Mgt, John Wisden & Son, 1995–2009; non-executive Director: Scoot.com plc, 2000–02; Xrefer Ltd, 2000–04 (Chm., 2003–04); Melbourne University Publishing, 2006–08; Inst. of Physics Publishing, 2009–; Chm., Macmillan India Ltd, 2004–07. Executive Director: Internat. Publishers Assoc., 2011– (Vice Pres., 2013–14; Pres., 2015–); Fedn of European Publishers, 2011–14. Member: Wkg Gp on UK Literary Heritage, 2006–; Adv. Council, Inst. of English Studies, 2008–; Internat. Adv. Bd, Frankfurt Book Fair, 2008–. Vice-Pres., 2004–05, 2006–07, Pres., 2005–06, Publishers Assoc. Vis. Fellow, Green College, Oxford, 1987; Vis. Prof., Univ. of the Arts, London (formerly London Inst.), 2003–. Chm. Trustees, Whitechapel Art Gall., 1997–2000; Chm., Common Purpose UK, 1998–2007; Trustee, Common Purpose Charitable Trust, 2007–; Mem. Strategy Adv. Cttee, BL, 2004–11. *Publications:* Charkin Blog: the archive, 2008; Top Tips for Wannabe CEOs, 2009. *Recreations:* music, cricket, eight grandchildren. *E:* richard.charkin@bloomsbury.com.

CHARLEMONT, 15th Viscount *cr* 1665 (Ire.); **John Dodd Caulfeild;** Baron Caulfeild of Charlemont 1620 (Ire.); *b* 15 May 1966; *o s* of 14th Viscount Charlemont and Judith Ann (*née* Dodd); *S* father, 2001; *m* 1991, Nadea Stella, *d* of Wilson Fortin; two *s. Heir: s* Hon. Shane Andrew Caulfeild, *b* 19 May 1996.

CHARLES, Hon. Sir (Arthur) William (Hessin), Kt 1998; **Hon. Mr Justice Charles;** a Judge of the High Court of Justice, Queen's Bench Division, since 2014 (Family Division, 1998–2014); President, Upper Tribunal (Administrative Appeals Chamber), since 2012; Vice President, Court of Protection, since 2014; *b* 25 March 1948; *s* of late Arthur Attwood Sinclair Charles and May Davies Charles (*née* Westerman); *m* 1974, Lydia Margaret Ainscow; one *s* one *d. Educ:* Malvern College; Christ's College, Cambridge (MA Hons). Called to the Bar, Lincoln's Inn, 1971; Junior Counsel to the Crown (Chancery), 1986; First Junior Counsel to HM Treasury on Chancery Matters, 1989–98. *Recreation:* golf. *Address:* Royal Courts of Justice, Strand, WC2A 2LL. *Clubs:* Hawks (Cambridge); Denham Golf.

CHARLES, Caroline, (Mrs Malcolm Valentine), OBE 2002; fashion designer; Founder, Caroline Charles, 1963; *b* 18 May 1942; *m* 1966, Malcolm Valentine; one *s* one *d. Educ:* Sacred Heart Convent, Woldingham; Swindon Art Sch. *Recreations:* gardening, tennis, theatre, travel. *Address:* 56/57 Beauchamp Place, SW3 1NY. *T:* (020) 7225 3197.

CHARLES, Hampton; *see* Martin, R. P.

CHARLES, James Anthony, ScD; FREng; Reader in Process Metallurgy, University of Cambridge, 1978–90, now Emeritus; Fellow, St John's College, Cambridge, since 1963; *b* 23 Aug. 1926; *s* of John and Winifred Charles; *m* 1st, 1951, Valerie E. King (*d* 2001); one *s* (and one *s* decd); 2nd, 2003, Dr Marcia Edwards. *Educ:* Imperial College of Science and Technology, Royal School of Mines (BScEng, ARSM); MA, ScD Cantab. J. Stone & Co Ltd, 1947–50; British Oxygen Ltd, 1950–60; Dept of Metallurgy and Materials Science, Univ of Cambridge, 1960–90. Vis. Prof., UCL (Inst. of Archaeology), 1991–; Special Prof., Univ of Nottingham, 1993–99. Hon. Keeper of Metalwork, Fitzwilliam Museum, 1996– (Syndic, 1986–96). FREng (FEng 1983); Hon. FIMMM 2002. Sir George Beilby Medal and Prize RIC, Soc. Chem. Ind. and Inst. of Metals, 1965; Sir Robert Hadfield Medal, Metals Soc. 1977; Kroll Medal, Inst. of Metals, 1989; Elegant Work Prize, Inst. of Materials, 1992. *Publications:* Oxygen in Iron and Steel Making, 1956; Selection and Use of Engineering Materials, 1984, 3rd edn 1997; Out of the Fiery Furnace: recollections and meditations of metallurgist, 2000; Light Blue Materials, 2005; One Man's Cambridge, 2006; numerous papers on the science and technology of metals and archaeometallurgy. *Recreations:* philately listening to music, archaeology. *Address:* 2A Buristead Road, Great Shelford, Cambridge CB22 5EJ. *T:* (01223) 843812.

CHARLES, Jonathan James; District Judge (Magistrates' Courts), South Wales, 2003–14; 4 Sept. 1946; *s* of William Robert Charles and Elizabeth Charles; *m* 1970, Linda Ann Llewellyn; two *s* one *d. Educ:* Bridgend Boys' Grammar Sch.; Bristol Poly. Admitted Solicitor 1980; Justices' Clerk: Merthyr Tydfil, 1981–85; Lower Rhymney Valley, 1985–88; Bridgend 1988–97; Consultant Solicitor, Keith Evans & Co., Newport, 1997–2001; District Judge (Magistrates' Courts), Wolverhampton, 2001–03. Sec., Lord Chancellor's Adv. Cttee fo Mid-Glamorgan, 1995–97. *Recreations:* travel, Rugby football, cricket.

CHARLES, Michael Geoffrey A.; *see* Audley-Charles.

CHARLES, Nicola; *see* Perry, J. A.

CHARLES, Sir Robert (James), ONZ 2011; KNZM 1999; CBE 1992 (OBE 1972); go professional, since 1960; *b* 14 March 1936; *s* of Albert Ivor Charles and Phyllis Irene Charles *m* 1962, Verity Joan Aldridge; one *s* one *d. Educ:* Wairarapa Coll. Nat. Bank of NZ, 1954–60 Golf tournament victories include: NZ Open, 1954 (amateur), 1966, 1970, 1973; NZ PGA 1961, 1979, 1980; Swiss Open, 1962, 1974; British Open, 1963; Atlanta Classic, USA, 1967 Canadian Open, 1968; Piccadilly World Match Play, England, 1969; John Player Classic and Dunlop Masters, England, 1972; S African Open, 1973; joined Senior Tour, 1986: 7 victories incl. Sen. British Open, 1989 and 1993. *Publications:* Left Handed Golf, 1965; The Bob Charles Left Handers Golf Book, 1985, 2nd edn 1993; Golf for Seniors, 1994. *Recreations* farming, golf course architecture, tennis, boating. *Address:* Lytham, 456 Burnt Hill Road Oxford 7495, New Zealand. *Club:* Christchurch Golf (New Zealand).

CHARLES, Hon. Sir William; *see* Charles, Hon. Sir A. W. H.

CHARLES-EDWARDS, Prof. Thomas Mowbray, DPhil; FBA 2001; Jesus Professor c Celtic, University of Oxford, 1997–2011, now Emeritus Professor of Celtic; Fellow of Jesu College, Oxford, 1997–2011, now Emeritus; *b* 11 Nov. 1943; *s* of Thomas Charles-Edward and Imelda Charles-Edwards (*née* Bailey); *m* 1975, Davina Gifford Lewis (pen name Giffor Lewis) (*d* 2008); two *s. Educ:* Ampleforth Coll.; Corpus Christi Coll., Oxford (BA, MA DPhil, Dip. Celtic Studies). Scholar, Dublin Inst. for Advanced Studies, 1967–69; P. S. Alle Jun. Res. Fellow in History, 1969–71, Fellow and Tutor in Modern Hist., 1971–96, Corpu Christi Coll., Oxford, Emeritus Fellow, 1997. Hon. MRIA 2006. *Publications:* Bechbreth (with Fergus Kelly), 1983; The Welsh Laws, 1989; Early Irish and Welsh Kinship, 1993; Early Christian Ireland, 2000; (ed) After Rome, 2003; The Chronicle of Ireland, 2006; Wales and the Britons, 350–1064, 2013. *Address:* 32 Harbord Road, Oxford OX2 8LJ. *T:* (01865 556943; Corpus Christi College, Oxford OX1 4JF. *T:* (01865) 616789. *E:* thomas.charles edwards@jesus.ox.ac.uk.

CHARLESWORTH, Anita Rose; Chief Economist, Health Foundation, since 2014; *b* 1 Jan. 1967; *d* of Terry and Jean Bird; *m* 1998, Nick Charlesworth; one *s* three *d. Educ:* PC (BA Hons Social Sci.); Univ. of York (MSc Health Econs). Economist: DoH, 1990–95; HM Treasury, 1995–96; Associate Dir, SmithKline Beecham, 1996–98; Team Leader, Welfare to Work and various public services, 1998–2003, Dir, Public Services, 2003–06, HM Treasury Dir, 2006–08, Dir, Evidence and Analysis Unit, and Chief Analyst, 2008–10, DCMS; Chie Economist, Nuffield Trust, 2010–14. Non-executive Director: Islington PCT, 2007–11; The Whittington, 2011–. Trustee, Tommy's. *Recreations:* spending time with my husband and children, camping, theatre, tennis.

CHARLESWORTH, Prof. Brian, PhD; FRS 1991; FRSE; Senior Honorary Professoria Fellow, Institute of Evolutionary Biology (formerly Institute of Cell, Animal and Populatio Biology), University of Edinburgh, since 2010 (Royal Society Research Professor 1997–2007; Professorial Fellow, 2007–10); *b* 29 April 1945; *s* of Francis Gustave Charleswort and Mary (*née* Ryan); *m* 1967, Deborah Maltby (*see* D. Charlesworth); one *d. Educ:* Queens Coll., Cambridge (BA Natural Scis; PhD Genetics). FRSE 2000. Post-Doctoral Fellow, Univ of Chicago, 1969–71; Lectr in Genetics, Univ. of Liverpool, 1971–74; Lectr, 1974–82 Reader, 1982–84, in Biology, Univ. of Sussex; Prof., 1985–92, Chm., 1986–91, G. W. Beadle Distinguished Service Prof., 1992–97, Dept of Ecology and Evolution, Univ. of Chicago President: Soc. for Study of Evolution, 1999; Genetics Soc., 2006–09; Eur. Soc. for Evolution and Biology, 2011–13. Fellow, Amer. Acad. of Arts and Scis, 1996. Foreign Associate, Nat Acad. of Scis, USA, 2013. Darwin Medal, Royal Soc., 2000; Darwin-Wallace Medal, Linnea Soc., 2010; Thomas Hunt Morgan Medal, Genetics Soc. of America, 2015. *Publications* Evolution in Age-Structured Populations, 1980, 2nd edn 1994; (with Deborah Charlesworth Evolution: a very short introduction, 2003; (with Deborah Charlesworth) Elements o Evolutionary Genetics, 2010; papers in Nature, Science, Genetics, Genetical Res., Evolution Amer. Naturalist, Procs Roy. Soc. *Recreations:* reading, listening to classical music, walking *Address:* Institute of Evolutionary Biology, School of Biological Sciences, University o Edinburgh, West Mains Road, Edinburgh EH9 3FL.

CHARLESWORTH, Prof. Deborah, PhD; FRS 2005; FRSE; Professorial Researc Fellow, Institute of Evolutionary Biology (formerly Institute of Cell, Animal and Populatio Biology), University of Edinburgh, 1997, now Emeritus Professor; *née* Maltby; *m* 1967, Bria Charlesworth, *qv*; one *d. Educ:* Newnham Coll., Cambridge (BA 1965; PhD 1968). FRS 2001. MRC Jun. Res. Fellow, Univ. of Cambridge, 1968–69; Postdoctoral Fellow, Univ. o Chicago, 1969–71; Hon. Res. Fellow, Univ. of Liverpool, 1971–74; temp. Lectr, Univ. o Sussex, 1974–84; Res. Associate, 1984–88, Asst Prof., 1988–92, Prof., 1992–97, Univ. o Chicago. *Publications:* (with Jonathan Silvertown) Introduction to Plant Population Biology 2001; (with Brian Charlesworth) Evolution: a very short introduction, 2003; (with Bria Charlesworth) Elements of Evolutionary Genetics, 2010. *Address:* Institute of Evolutionary Biology, University of Edinburgh, West Mains Road, Edinburgh EH9 3FL.

CHARLESWORTH, His Honour Peter James; a Circuit Judge, 1989–2004; *b* 24 Aug 1944; *s* of late Joseph William Charlesworth and Florence Mary Charlesworth; *m* 1967 Elizabeth Mary Postill (*d* 2010); one *s* one *d. Educ:* Hull Grammar Sch.; Leeds Univ. (LL 1965, LLM 1966). Called to the Bar, Inner Temple, 1966. In practice on North-Easter Circuit, 1966–89; a Recorder, 1982–89. Judicial Mem., Parole Bd, 2005–09. Rugby Footba League: Mem., Adv. Panel, 1994–2004; Sen. Mem., Judiciary Panel, 2004–07; Chairman Disciplinary Cttee, 1998–; Operational Rules Tribunal, 2007–. Mem., Yorks Dales Nat. Par Authy, 2008– (Dep. Chm., 2012–13, Chm., 2013–; Dep. Chm., Planning Cttee, 2009–12) Member: Council, Bodington Hall, Univ. of Leeds, 2001–10; Council of Mgt, Yorkshir Dales Soc., 2005–13. Trustee, Yorks Dales Millennium Trust, 2003– (Chm., 2006–09)

Mem., Bramhope Parish Council, 2006–10. *Recreations:* tennis, reading, Rugby League football (spectating), walking in the Yorkshire dales. *Address:* 6 Briery Close, Ilkley, W Yorks LS29 9DL. *Club:* Skipton Tennis.

CHARLIER, Rear Adm. Simon Boyce, CBE 2013; FRAeS; Senior Defence and Political Advisor, MBDA UK, since 2013; *b* Pembury, Kent, 15 March 1958; *s* of Wing Comdr Dennis Claude Charlier, MC and Mary Pepper Charlier; *m* 1990, Margaret Anna Johns; two *s* one *d. Educ:* Dover Coll. FRAeS 2008. Royal Navy, 1978–: CO HMS Sheraton, 1990–91; Sen. Pilot, 815 Sqdn, 1992–95; CO HMS Northumberland, 1996–98; MoD DN Plans, then MoD NATO and EU Policy Directorate, 1998–2002; CO HMS Cornwall, 2002–04; COS (Aviation and Carriers) to C-in-C Fleet, and Rear Adm. Fleet Air Arm, 2008–10; Dir, Operating Airworthiness, Mil. Aviation Authy, 2010–12. ADC to the Queen, 2006–09. President: RN Equestrian Soc., 2008–; Combined Services Equestrian Assoc., 2011–; RN Winter Sports, 2012–13. *Recreations:* eventing, golf, mountain biking, ski-ing, clarinet. *Address:* Sydling St Nicholas, Dorset. *Club:* Naval and Military.

CHARLTON, Alan, CMG 1996; CVO 2007; HM Diplomatic Service, retired; Ambassador to Brazil, 2008–13; *b* 21 June 1952; *s* of Henry and Eva Charlton; *m* 1974, Judith Angela Carryer; two *s* one *d. Educ:* Nottingham High Sch.; Gonville and Caius Coll., Cambridge (MA); Leicester Univ. (PGCE); Manchester Univ. (BLing). Teacher, Gesamtschule, Gelsenkirchen, Germany, 1975–77; West Africa Dept, FCO, 1978–79; Amman, 1981–84; Near East and North Africa Dept, FCO, 1984–86; BMG Berlin, 1986–90; Dep. Chief, Assessments Staff, Cabinet Office, 1991–93; Head, Eastern Adriatic Unit, FCO, 1993–95; Bosnia Contact Group Rep., 1995–96; Political Counsellor, 1996–98, Dep. Hd of Mission, 1998–99, Bonn; Dep. Hd of Mission, Berlin, 1999–2000; Dir, SE Europe, FCO, 2001; Dir, Personnel, then HR Dir, FCO, 2002–04; Dep. Hd of Mission, Washington, 2004–07, and Ambassador to Orgn of American States, 2006–07. Founder, British-Brazilian Conversa, 2014. Mem., Adv. Bd, Brazil Inst., KCL, 2015–. Robin Humphreys Fellow, Inst. of Latin American Studies, Univ. of London, 2013–; Hon. Prof., Univ. of Nottingham, 2013–. Gov. and Advr, De Montfort Univ., 2013–; Gov., Sherborne Sch., 2013–. FRSA. *Recreations:* history, genealogy, football, cricket.

CHARLTON, Alexander Murray; QC 2008; *b* Herts, 13 March 1958; *s* of Murray Anthony Charlton and Pamela Charlton; *m* 1989, Emma Marie Clezy; one *s* two *d. Educ:* Tonbridge Sch.; St Andrews Univ. (MA Hons English); City Univ. (Dip. Law). Called to the Bar, Middle Temple, 1983. Contributing Ed., Professional Negligence and Liability, 1st edn 2000, updated annually. *Recreations:* sailing, ski-ing, Rugby. *Address:* 4 Pump Court, EC4Y 7AN. *T:* (020) 7842 5555, *Fax:* (020) 7583 2036. *E:* acharlton@4pumpcourt.com.

CHARLTON, Sir Bobby; *see* Charlton, Sir R.

CHARLTON, Celia Anne; *see* Dawson, C. A.

CHARLTON, Prof. Graham, MDS; FDSRCSE; Professor of Conservative Dentistry, University of Edinburgh, 1978–91, now Emeritus Professor (Dean of Dental Studies, 1978–83); *b* 15 Oct. 1928; *s* of Simpson R. Charlton and Georgina (*née* Graham); *m* 1956, Stella Dobson (*d* 2005); two *s* one *d. Educ:* Bedlington Grammar Sch., Northumberland; St John's Coll., York (Teaching Cert.); King's Coll., Univ. of Durham (BDS); Univ. of Bristol (MDS). Teacher, Northumberland, 1948–52; National Service, 1948–50; Dental School, 1952–58; General Dental Practice, Torquay, 1958–64; University of Bristol: Lecturer, 1964–72; Cons. Sen. Lectr, 1972–78; Dental Clinical Dean, 1975–78. *Address:* 17 Northumberland Avenue, Forest Hall, Newcastle upon Tyne NE12 9NR.

CHARLTON, Henry Marshall, DPhil; FRS 1994; Reader in Neuroendocrinology, University of Oxford, 1990–2006, now Emeritus; Fellow of Linacre College, Oxford, 1970–2006, now Emeritus; *b* 10 March 1939; *s* of Joseph Douglass Charlton and Lilian Charlton; *m* 1965, Margaret Jeffrey; one *s* one *d. Educ:* Corpus Christi Coll., Oxford (MA, DPhil). Mem., MRC Neuroendocrinology Unit, Oxford, 1964–68; Lectr, Oxford Univ., 1968–90. Founder FMedSci 1998. *Publications:* contrib. scientific jls. *Recreations:* Real tennis, hill walking, gardening. *Address:* 61 Plantation Road, Oxford OX2 6JE. *T:* (01865) 554248.

CHARLTON, John, (Jack), OBE 1974; DL; Manager, Republic of Ireland Football Team, 1986–95; broadcaster; *b* 8 May 1935; *s* of late Robert and Elizabeth Charlton; *m* 1958, Patricia; two *s* one *d. Educ:* Hirst Park Sch., Ashington. Professional footballer, Leeds United, 1952–73; 35 England caps, 1965–70; Manager: Middlesbrough, 1973–77; Sheffield Wednesday FC, 1977–83; Newcastle United FC, 1984–85. Mem., Sports Council, 1977–82. DL Northumberland, 1997. *Publications:* Jack Charlton's American World Cup Diary, 1994; The Autobiography, 1996. *Recreations:* shooting, fishing, gardening.
See also Sir Robert Charlton.

CHARLTON, John, CBE 2007; JP; Director and Chairman, JCC Consultancy Ltd, 1996–2001; Chairman, University Hospital Birmingham NHS Foundation Trust (formerly NHS Trust), 1998–2006; *b* 11 Oct. 1940; *s* of late F. E. Charlton and Esther (*née* Lakin); *m* 1965, Carol Rosemary Shaw; two *s. Educ:* King Edward's Grammar Sch., Five Ways; Birmingham Univ. (BDS, LDS). DDH, DDPH 1970. Area Dental Officer, Oldbury, 1964–66; Dep. Chief Dental Officer, 1966, Chief Dental Officer, 1966–74, Warley; Area Dental Officer, Sandwell, 1974–82; Sandwell Health Authority: Dist Dental Officer, 1982–92; Consultant in Dental Public Health, 1992–96; Exec. Dir, 1993–96. Mem., Birmingham AHA, 1974–82; Dental Advr, W Midlands RHA, 1977–80; Chm., S Birmingham HA, 1981–91. Chm., Arden Gp Sec., Weoley Ward Lab. Party, 1967–83. Birmingham District Council: Mem. (Lab), Weoley Ward, 1980–82, Bartley Gn Ward, 1982–90; Hon. Alderman, 1990. Dir, British Fluoridation Soc., 1993–. Founder Member: Bournville Village Lessees Assoc.; SW Birmingham Assoc. for Advancement of State Educn; Lunar Soc., 1990. Trustee, University Hosp. Birmingham Charities, 1999–2011. Gov., Birmingham City Univ., 2007–. JP Birmingham, 1992–2000. *Recreations:* racketball, travelling, politics. *Address:* 48 Middle Park Road, Selly Oak, Birmingham B29 4BJ. *T:* (0121) 475 7700.

CHARLTON, Louise; Co-founder, 1987, and Vice Chairman, since 2012, Brunswick Group LLP (Group Senior Partner, 2004–12); *b* Wakefield, 25 May 1960; *d* of John Charlton and Patricia Crawford (*née* Hulme); *m* 1985, Andrew Durant; two *s* one *d. Educ:* Univ. of Reading (BA Hons French). Non-exec. Dir, RPS Gp, 2008–. Dir and Trustee, Natural Hist. Mus., 2006–. *Recreations:* family, fishing, cinema, travel, reading. *Address:* c/o Brunswick Group LLP, 16 Lincoln's Inn Fields, WC2A 3ED. *T:* (020) 7396 7437. *E:* lcharlton@brunswickgroup.com.

CHARLTON, Richard McKenzie, AM 1996; FTS; FInstPet; Chairman, South East Water Ltd, 1995–2002; *b* 20 March 1935; *s* of Richard Rutherford Charlton and Yvonne Gladys Charlton (*née* McKenzie); *m*; two *s* two *d. Educ:* Sydney Univ. (BE Mining 1957; MESc 1959). Joined Shell as trainee petroleum engr, 1959: various posts in The Hague, UK, Nigeria, Kuwait, Trinidad and Brunei, 1959–75; Shell Australia: Gen. Manager, Exploration & Prodn, 1975–76; Exec. Dir, NW Shelf Project, 1976–80; Dir Ops, Shell UK Exploration & Prodn, Aberdeen, 1980–83; Chm., Shell Cos in Malaysia, 1983–86; Hd, Exploration & Prodn Ops & Liaison, The Hague, 1986–91; Chm. and Chief Exec. Officer, Shell Gp of Cos in Australia, 1991–95, retd. Director: Fujitsu Australia Ltd, 1994–97; Coles-Myer Ltd, 1995–2003; Hongkong Bank of Australia, 1996–2001; Chm., Adcorp Australia Ltd, 1999–2005. Chancellor, Univ. of Newcastle, NSW, 1994–2004. Chairman: Art Foundn, Victoria, 1994–97 (Dep. Chm., 1992–94); Hunter Symphony Orch., 1995–97; Australia-Malaysia Soc., 1995–. Chm., Nat. Basketball League, 1997–2000. Mem., Soc. Petroleum Engrs, 1971; FAICD; FInstD; FAIM. *Publications:* papers on petroleum industry. *Recreations:* horse racing, Rugby, snow ski-ing, surfing, tennis. *Clubs:* Melbourne, Australia (Melbourne); Victoria Racing, Moonee Valley Racing.

CHARLTON, Sir Robert, (Sir Bobby), Kt 1994; CBE 1974 (OBE 1969); Director, Manchester United Football Club, since 1984; *b* 11 Oct. 1937; *s* of late Robert and Elizabeth Charlton; *m* 1961, Norma Ball; two *d. Educ:* Bedlington Grammar Sch., Northumberland. Professional Footballer with Manchester United, 1954–73, for whom he played 751 games and scored 245 goals; FA Cup Winners Medal, 1963; FA Championship Medals, 1956–57, 1964–65 and 1966–67; World Cup Winners Medal (International), 1966; European Cup Winners medal, 1968. 100th England cap, 21 April 1970; 106 appearances for England, 1957–73. Manager, Preston North End, 1973–75. Mem., Cttee, FIFA. Hon. Freeman, City of Manchester, 2009. Hon. Fellow, Manchester Polytechnic, 1979. Hon. MA Manchester Univ. Sir Stanley Matthews Award, 2000; Lifetime Achievement Award, BBC Sports Personality of the Year, 2008; Lifetime Achievement Award, Laureus World Sports Awards, 2012. *Publications:* My Soccer Life, 1965; Forward for England, 1967; This Game of Soccer, 1967; Book of European Football, Books 1–4, 1969–72; My Manchester United Years: the autobiography, 2007. *Recreation:* golf.
See also John Charlton.

CHARLTON-WEEDY, Maj. Gen. Michael Anthony, CBE 1997 (OBE 1993); DL; Director, UK Resilience Training, Cabinet Office, since 2010 (Chief Executive, Emergency Planning College, 2003–10); *b* 11 June 1950; *s* of late Kenneth Charlton Weedy and of Valerie (*née* Reed); *m* 1979, Julia Redfern; two *s* one *d. Educ:* Millfield; Sandhurst. Commnd RA, 1971; sc 1982; CO 4th Regt RA, 1990–92 (despatches 1992); rcds 1995; Chief Faction Liaison Officer, Bosnia, 1995–96; Dir, OR (Land CIS), MoD, 1997–2000; Sen. Directing Staff (Army), RCDS, 2001–02; Dep. Adjt Gen., MoD, 2002–03. DL N Yorks, 2010. *Recreation:* country sports. *Address:* c/o HSBC, Kingsbridge, Devon TQ7 1PB.

CHARMLEY, Prof. John Denis, DPhil; FRHistS; Professor of Modern History, since 1998, Director, East Anglian Film Archive, since 2010, Director of Employability, since 2011, Director, Centre of East Anglian Studies, since 2012, Head, Institute for Interdisciplinary Humanities, since 2014, and Associate Dean, Enterprise, since 2005, University of East Anglia (Head, School of Music, 2009–14); *b* 9 Nov. 1955; *s* of John Charmley and Doris Charmley; *m* 1st, 1977, Ann Dorothea Bartlett (marr. diss. 1992); three *s* (incl. twins); 2nd, 1992, Lorraine Fegan (marr. diss. 2003; she *d* 2012); 3rd, 2004, Rachael Heap. *Educ:* Rock Ferry High Sch., Birkenhead; Pembroke Coll., Oxford (BA 1977; MA 1982; DPhil 1982). FRHistS 1987. University of East Anglia: Lectr in English Hist., Sch. of English and American Studies, 1979–92; Sen. Lectr in Hist., Sch. of Hist., 1992–96; Reader in Hist., 1996–98; Hd, Sch. of Hist., 2002–12; Associate Dean, Res., Faculty of Arts and Humanities, 2005–10. Fulbright Prof., Westminster Coll., Fulton, Mo, 1992–93. Chm., Mid-Norfolk Cons. Assoc., 2000–03; Election Agent: Mid Norfolk, 2000–02; S Norfolk, 2005, 2010. Dir, Low Carbon Innovation Fund, 2011–. Pres., Norfolk and Norwich Br., Historical Assoc., 2000–; Vice Chm., Cons. Hist. Gp, 2003–. Dir, Norwich Heritage and Regeneration Trust, 2009–. Editor, History, 2010–. *Publications:* Duff Cooper, 1986; Lord Lloyd and the Decline of the British Empire, 1987; (ed) Descent to Suez: the diaries of Sir Evelyn Shuckburgh, 1987; Chamberlain and the Lost Peace, 1989; Churchill: the end of glory, 1993; Churchill's Grand Alliance, 1995; A History of Conservative Politics 1990–1996, 1996; Splendid Isolation?: Britain and the balance of power 1874–1914, 1999; The Princess and the Politicians, 2005; A History of Conservative Politics since 1830, 2008. *Recreations:* reading, walking, dining out. *Address:* School of History, University of East Anglia, Norwich NR4 7TJ. *T:* (01603) 592790. *Club:* Norfolk (Norwich).

CHARNLEY, Helen; *see* Dunmore, H.

CHARNLEY, Sir (William) John, Kt 1981; CB 1973; MEng, FREng, FRAeS, FRIN; *b* 4 Sept. 1922; *s* of George and Catherine Charnley; *m* 1945, Mary Paden (*d* 2007); one *s* one *d. Educ:* Oulton High Sch., Liverpool; Liverpool Univ. MEng 1945; FREng (FEng 1982); FRIN 1963; FRAeS 1966. Aerodynamics Dept, RAE Farnborough, 1943–55; Supt, Blind Landing Experimental Unit, 1955–61; Imperial Defence Coll., 1962; Head of Instruments and Electrical Engineering Dept, 1963–65, Head of Weapons Dept, 1965–68, RAE Farnborough; Head of Research Planning, Min. of Technol., 1968–69; Dep. Controller, Guided Weapons, Min. of Technology, later MoD (PE), 1969–72; Controller, Guided Weapons and Electronics, MoD (PE), 1972–73; Chief Scientist (RAF), 1973–77, and Dep. Controller, R&D Establishments and Res. C, MoD, 1975–77; Controller, R&D Establishments and Res., MoD, 1977–82. Director: Fairey Holdings Ltd, 1983–86; Winsdale Investments Ltd, 1985–88. Technical Advr, Monopolies and Mergers Commn, 1982; Specialist Advr to House of Lords Select Cttee on Science and Technology, 1986. Chm., Civil Aviation Res. and Devel Programme Bd, 1984–92; Mem., Air Traffic Control Bd, 1985–96. President: Royal Inst. of Navigation, 1987–90; European Orgn for Civil Aviation Equipment, 1993–97. Trustee, Richard Ormonde Shuttleworth Remembrance Trust, 1987–98. Hon. FRAeS 1992. Hon. DEng Liverpool, 1988. Bronze Medal, 1960, Gold Medal, 2001, RIN, Silver Medal, 1973, Gold Medal, 1980, RAeS. *Publications:* papers on subjects in aerodynamics, aircraft all weather operation, aircraft navigation, defence R&D. *Club:* Royal Air Force.

CHARONE, Barbara; Director, MBC PR, since 2000; *b* Chicago, 22 March 1952; *d* of Rose Charone. *Educ:* New Trier High Sch.; Northwestern Univ. (BA Hons). Journalist, Sounds mag., 1974–77, Dep. Ed., until 1977; freelance journalist, Daily Mail, Rolling Stone, Cream, Crawdaddy, 1979–81; with Warner Bros Records, 1981–2000, Dir of Press, until 2000. *Publications:* Life as a Rolling Stone: authorised biography of Keith Richards, 1978 (also German, Japanese and US edns). *Recreations:* tennis, Chelsea Football Club (season ticket holder, since 1980), music, theatre. *Address:* MBC PR, The Wellington Building, 28–32 Wellington Road, NW8 9SP. *T:* (020) 7483 9205. *E:* bc@mbcpr.com. *Clubs:* Groucho, Home House, Ivy.

CHART, Jennifer Ann, CBE 2004; Head Teacher, Portland College (formerly Portland School), Sunderland, 1996–2011; *b* 23 April 1951; *d* of John and Edna Hunt; *m*; one *s* one *d. Educ:* Univ. of Newcastle upon Tyne (Cert Ed SEN; Dip. Adv. Educnl Studies SEN; BPhil). Teacher, 1972–75; class teacher, 1980–89, Dep. Head Teacher, 1989–96, Ashleigh Sch., N Tyneside. Asst Sec., Thompson Hall (Tyneside MENCAP), 1968–72; Chm., N Tyneside Toy Liby, 1977–89. Trustee, Adventure Holidays (for disabled/disadvantaged children in Tyneside), 2001– (Chm. Trustees, 2012–). *Recreations:* outdoor activities, including walking, cycling and golf; needlecraft, painting. *Address:* Lianachan, Scott Street, East Hartford, Northumberland NE23 3AW.

CHARTER, Joseph Stephen; High Commissioner for Grenada to the Court of St James's, 2005–08; *b* 26 Dec. 1943; *s* of late Vivian Charter and Daphne (later Mrs Daphne Johnson); *m* 1968, Aileen Valerie Cox; three *s* one *d. Educ:* Avery Hill Coll., Univ. of London (BEd Hons). Perm. Sec., Min. of Educn, Grenada, 1981; Ambassador, Libya, 1982–84; Permanent Secretary: Min. of Communication and Works, 1996–2001; Min. of Health and Envmt, 2001–04. Vice Pres., Chamber of Commerce, 1992–95; Chairman: Grenada Broadcasting Corp., 1998–2001; Nat. Water and Sewerage Authy, 1999–2002; Hosp. Governance Bd, 2003–05; Nat. Insce Bd, 2003–05. *Recreations:* music, theatre, sport. *Club:* Royal Over-Seas League.

CHARTERIS, family name of **Earl of Wemyss.**

CHARTRES, Rt Rev. and Rt Hon. Richard John Carew; *see* London, Bishop of.

CHASE, Graham Frank; Chairman, Chase and Partners, since 1995; President, Royal Institution of Chartered Surveyors, 2006–07; *b* 5 Jan. 1954; *s* of late Frank Augustus Chase, FSVA and of Joan Lynette Chase (*née* Hibbert); *m* 1980, Fiona Anderson Batley; two *d*. *Educ:* Mill Hill Sch.; Willesden Coll. of Professional Building (DipEstMan 1976). FRICS 1988; FCIArb 1999; FICPD 2005; Chartered Arbitrator 2009. Estates Surveyor, BBC, 1976–79; Estates Manager, Ladbroke Racing Ltd, 1978–79; Clive Lewis and Partners: Shops Surveyor, 1980–84; Partner, 1984–86; Dir, 1986–93; Dir, Colliers Erdman Lewis, 1993–94. Non-exec. Dir, Assura Gp Ltd (formerly Med. Property Investment Fund plc), 2003–10. Royal Institution of Chartered Surveyors: Chairman: Internat. Cttee, 1991–94; Metrication Cttee, 1993–94; Commercial Mkt Panel, 1995–99; Commercial Property Fac., 2000–04; Review Cttee, Code of Practice for Commercial Leases, 2004; Conflicts of Interest Working Gp, Dispute Resolution Service, 2010–11; Wkg Gp on Practice Statement and Guidance Notes for chartered surveyors actg as expert witnesses, RICS, 2012–. Representative: on H of C Select Cttee on future of shopping, 1993; Retail Property, 1996–99; on Modernising Stamp Duty Cttee, HM Treasury, 2003–04; to H of L Select Cttee on property taxation reform, 2004; Member: Code of Measuring Practice, 1993–94; Commercial Property Policy Panel, 1996–99. Royal Institution of Chartered Surveyors: President's Arbitrators Panel, 1998–; President's Ind. Experts Panel, 2000–; Leadership Team, 2004–07; Gen. Council, 1999–2000; Governing Council, 2001–03, 2004–; Nominations Cttee, 2010–; Gen. Practice Divl Pres., 2000; Vice Pres., 2004–05; Sen. Vice Pres., 2005–06; Valuers Registration Scheme Rev. Gp, 2014–15. External Examiner: Northumbria Univ., 2008–12; Kingston Univ., 2009–13. Pres., Assoc. of Town and City Mgt (formerly Assoc. of Town Centre Mgt), 2011– (Chm., 2008–11); Member: Shops Agents Soc., 1980–; Accessible Retail, 1987–; Investment Property Forum, 1995–; British Council of Shopping Centres, 1995– (Mem., Adv. Panel, 2012–); Property Industry Forum, 1996–99, Property Adv. Gp, 1999–2004, DETR; Property Forum, Bank of England, 2000–04; Empty Property Gp, ODPM, 2003–06; Bd, Expert Advisors in Planning Services, 2009–; Bd, Assoc. of British Crime Partnership, 2010–11. Pres., Old Millhillians in Property, 2014–. Jt Chm., Property Mktg Awards. Governor: Woodhouse VI Form Coll., 1996–2000; Mill Hill Sch., 2000–08; Trustee, Alford House Youth Club, Lambeth, 1999–; Trustee, Gov. and Dir of Bd, Coll. of Estate Mgt, 2004– (Chm., Educn and Res. Cttee, 2010–11); Trustee: Maritime Heritage Mus., 2012–; Covent Garden Area Trust, 2014–. Freeman, City of London, 1991; Liveryman, Co. of Chartered Surveyors, 1991– (Master, 2014–15). Mem., Old Millhillians Club, 1972–. Hon. Fellow, South Bank Univ., 2012. *Publications:* Business Tenancy Renewal Handbook, 2006. *Recreations:* Rugby, cricket, hockey, wine, food, disc jockey (as Fat Boy Fat), cycling, reading, sailing, UK history, UK geography, walking, curry. *Address:* 146 Green Dragon Lane, Winchmore Hill, N21 1ET. *T:* (020) 8364 0738; Chase and Partners LLP, Highlight House, 57 Margaret Street, W1W 8SJ. *T:* (020) 7462 1340. *E:* gfc@chaseandpartners.co.uk. *Clubs:* Old Millhillians Rugby Football (player, 1972–97); Saracens; Arsenal Football; Winchmore Hill and Enfield Hockey (player, 1997–2012); Hazelwood Lawn Tennis and Squash.

CHASE, Prof. Howard Allaker, PhD, ScD; FREng, CEng; CSci; CChem, FIChemE; Fellow and Director of Studies in Chemical Engineering, Magdalene College, Cambridge, since 1984; Professor of Biochemical Engineering, University of Cambridge, since 2000; Director of Research and Development, since 2005 and Chairman, 2005–08, Enval Ltd; *b* 17 Nov. 1954; *s* of Peter Howard Chase and Phoebe Farrar Chase (*née* Winn); *m* 1st, 1982, Penelope Jane Lewis (marr. diss. 2003); one *s* one *d*; 2nd, 2003, Dawn Christine Leeder. *Educ:* Westminster Sch., London; Magdalene Coll., Cambridge (Exhibnr; BA 1975, MA 1978); PhD 1979, ScD 2001, Cantab. CChem, MRSC 1987; FIChemE 1998; CEng 1998, FREng 2005; CSci 2005. Hirst Res. Centre, GEC, Wembley, 1971–72; University of Cambridge: Bye Fellow, Magdalene Coll., 1977; Res. Fellow, St John's Coll., 1978; post-doctoral res. asst, Dept of Biochem., 1978–81; Department of Chemical Engineering: Res. Associate, 1982–83; Royal Soc. Res. Fellow, 1983–84; Asst Lectr in Chem. Engrg, 1984–86; Lectr, 1986–96; Reader in Biochem. Engrg, 1996–2000; Hd of Dept, 1998–2006; Hd, Sch. of Technol., 2010–13; Magdalene College: Lectr in Natural Sci., 1984–2000; Tutor for Grad. Students, 1987–93; Sen. Tutor, 1993–96; Tutor, 1996–98. University College London: Vis. Prof., Dept of Chem. and Biochem. Engrg, 1991–92; Hon. Res. Fellow, 1993–. Mem. editl cttees and bds of scientific jls. External Examiner: Dept of Chem. Engrg, Univ. of Bradford, 2001–05; Dept of Chem. Engrg, Univ. of Newcastle upon Tyne, 2003–05; Dept of Biochem. Engrg, UCL, 2007–10; Dept of Chem. Engrg, Univ. of Manchester, 2008–10. Sir George Beilby Medal and Prize, Soc. Chem. Ind., RSC and Inst. Metals, 1993; BOC Envmtl Award, 2001, Donald Medal, 2010, IChemE Awards. *Publications:* contribs to scientific jls specialising in biotechnol., biochem. engrg, microbiol., etc. *Recreations:* food and drink, public transport, hot beaches. *Address:* Department of Chemical Engineering and Biotechnology, University of Cambridge, Pembroke Street, Cambridge CB2 3RA. *T:* (01223) 334781, *Fax:* (01223) 334796. *E:* hac1000@cam.ac.uk.

CHASE, Prof. Mark Wayne, PhD; FRS 2003; Keeper of the Jodrell Laboratory, since 2006, and Distinguished Senior Researcher, since 2014, Royal Botanic Gardens, Kew (Head of Molecular Systematics, 1992–2006); *b* 17 Jan. 1951; *s* of Wayne Marshall Chase and Helen Louise Chase (*née* Andrews). *Educ:* Paw Paw High Sch., Mich; Albion Coll., Albion, Mich. (BA Hons Hist. 1973); Univ. of Michigan, Ann Arbor (MS Biology 1980; PhD Botany 1985). Postdoctoral Res. Fellow, Dept of Biol., 1986–88, Lectr, Botany (Plant Systematics), 1987, Univ. of Mich., Ann Arbor; Asst Prof., 1988–92, Dir, Univ. Herbarium, 1990–92, Univ. of N Carolina, Chapel Hill. *Publications:* (ed jtly) Genera Orchidacearum: vol. 1, Introduction, Apostasioideae, and Cypripedioideae, 1999; vol. 2, Orchidoideae I, 2001; vol. 3, Orchidoideae II and Vanilloideae, 2003; contribs to books and many articles in professional jls. *Recreation:* gardening. *Address:* Jodrell Laboratory, Royal Botanic Gardens, Kew, Richmond, Surrey TW9 3DS.

CHASE, Robert John; HM Diplomatic Service, retired; Secretary General, International Aluminium Institute (formerly International Primary Aluminium Institute), 1997–2008; Adviser to IAI on International Relations, since 2008; *b* 13 March 1943; *s* of late Herbert Chase and of Evelyn Chase; *m* 1966, Gillian Ann Chase (*née* Shelton); one *s* two *d*. *Educ:* Sevenoaks Sch.; St John's Coll., Oxford. MA (Mod. Hist.). Entered HM Diplomatic Service, 1965; Third, later Second Sec., Rangoon, 1966–69; UN Dept, FCO, 1970–72; First Sec. (Press Attaché), Brasilia, 1972–76; Hd Caribbean Section, Mexico and Caribbean Dept, FCO, 1976–80; on secondment as a manager to Imperial Chemical Industries PLC, 1980–82; Asst Hd, S American Dept, FCO, 1982–83; Asst Hd, Maritime, Aviation and Environment Dept, FCO, 1983–84; Counsellor (Commercial), Moscow, 1985–88; Overseas Inspector, FCO, 1988–89; Hd, Resource Mgt Dept, FCO, 1989–92; Consul-Gen., Chicago, 1993–96; Dir Gen. of Trade and Investment, and Consul-Gen., Milan, 1996–97. Chm., Westminster Decorative and Fine Arts Soc., 2012–. *Recreations:* military history, politics, visiting historic sites, swimming. *Address:* Flat 14, St Thomas Wharf, 78 Wapping High Street, E1W 2NB. *T:* (020) 7709 7376. *Club:* Oxford and Cambridge.

CHASE, Rodney Frank, CBE 2000; Chairman, Genel Energy plc (formerly Vallares), 2011–15; *b* 12 May 1943; *s* of late Norman Maxwell Chase, MBE and of Barbara Chase (*née* Marshall). *Educ:* Liverpool Univ. (BA Hons Hist.). Joined British Petroleum, 1964: various posts in marketing, oil trading and shipping distribn, 1964–81; Dir (Exploration and Prodn), BP Australia, 1982–85; Gp Treas., BP, 1986–89; Chief Exec. Officer, BP Exploration (USA), 1989–92; a Man. Dir, BP, 1992–98; Chm. and Chief Exec. Officer, BP America, 1992–94; Dep. Gp Chief Exec., BP, 1998–2003. Dep. Chm. and Sen. non-exec. Dir, Tesco plc, 2004–10 (non-exec. Dir, 2002–10); Chm., Petrofac, 2005–11; non-executive Director, BOC, 1995–2001; Diageo, 1999–2004; Computer Sciences Corp., 2001– (Chm., 2012–); Nalco Co., 2005–11; Tesoro Corp., 2006–; Hess Corp., 2013–; Sen. Advr, Lehman Brothers, 2003–08. Chm., UK Emissions Trading Gp, 1998–2002; Mem., Adv. Cttee on Business and the Envmt, 1993–2000. Mem., Amer. Petroleum Inst., 2000–02. *Recreations:* golf, ski-ing. *E:* rodney@rfchase.com.

CHASE, Roger Robert; Director of Personnel, BBC, 1989–91; *b* 19 Sept. 1928; *s* of Robert Joseph Chase and Lillian Ada (*née* Meredith); *m* 1958, Geraldine Joan Whitlamsmith; three *d*. *Educ:* Gosport Grammar Sch. Served RN, 1947–49. Joined BBC, 1944; Engrg Div., 1944–47 and 1949–67; Television Personnel Dept, 1967–74; Head, Central Services Dept, 1974–76; Controller, Personnel, Television, 1976–82; Dep. Dir of Personnel, 1982–89. Chm., BBC Club, 1979–91. *Recreation:* sailing. *Address:* Vernons, Vernons Road, Chappel, Colchester, Essex CO6 2AQ. *T:* (01206) 240143. *Club:* Royal Naval Sailing Association.

CHATELIER, Trevor Mansel; a District Judge (Magistrates' Courts), Liverpool, 2001–13; Recorder, 2006–13; *b* 5 Oct. 1950; *s* of Dr Mansel Frederick Chatelier and Barbara Winifred Chatelier; *m* 2012, Cornelia Petronella Bax; twin *s* from a previous marriage. *Educ:* Uxbridge Tech. Coll.; Mid-Essex Tech. Coll. (LLB); Coll. of Law. Admitted solicitor, 1974; asst solicitor posts, 1974–79; Solicitor, Messrs Wilson Houlder & Co., Southall, 1979–2001; Act Stipendiary Magistrate, Leeds Magistrates' Court, 1998–2001. Member: YHA; NT; Cruising Assoc.; Westerly Owners Assoc. *Publications:* Criminal Advocacy in the Magistrates' Court, 1981; article in Law Soc. Gazette. *Recreations:* coastal sailing, angling, cycle touring, camping, motor-cycling, classical guitar, languages, good food, good company and going out. *T:* 07801 208955. *E:* smart.alec@sky.com.

CHATER, Dr Anthony Philip John; Editor, Morning Star, 1974–95; parents both shoe factory workers; *m* 1954, Janice (*née* Smith); three *s*. *Educ:* Northampton Grammar Sch. for Boys; Queen Mary Coll., London. BSc (1st cl. hons Chem.) 1951, PhD (Phys. Chem.) 1954. Fellow in Biochem., Ottawa Exper. Farm, 1954–56; studied biochem. at Brussels Univ., 1956–57; Teacher, Northampton Techn. High Sch., 1957–59; Teacher, Blyth Grammar Sch., Norwich, 1959–60; Lectr, subseq. Sen. Lectr in Phys. Chem., Luton Coll. of Technology, 1960–69; Head of Press and Publicity of Communist Party, 1969–74; Nat. Chm. of Communist Party, 1967–69. Contested (Com) Luton, Nov. 1963, 1964, 1966, 1970. Mem. Presidential Cttee, World Peace Council, 1969–74. *Publications:* Race Relations in Britain, 1966; numerous articles. *Recreations:* walking, swimming, music, camping.

CHATER, Prof. Keith Frederick, PhD; FRS 1995; Head, Department of Molecular Microbiology, John Innes Centre, 2001–04, now Emeritus Fellow; *b* 23 April 1944; *s* of Frederick Ernest Chater and Marjorie Inez Chater (*née* Palmer); *m* 1966, Jean Wallbridge; three *s* one *d*. *Educ:* Trinity Sch. of John Whitgift, Croydon; Univ. of Birmingham (BSc 1st Cl. Hons Bacteriol. 1966; PhD Genetics 1969). John Innes Institute, later John Innes Centre: research scientist in Streptomyces genetics, 1969–; Dep. Head, 1989–98, Head, 1998–2001, Dept of Genetics. Fulbright Scholar, Harvard Univ., 1983; Hon. Professor: UEA, 1988–; Chinese Acad. of Scis, Inst. of Microbiology, 1999; Huazhong Agricl Univ., Wuhan, 2000; Univ. of Newcastle upon Tyne, 2006–09. *Publications:* (jtly) Genetic Manipulation of Streptomyces: a laboratory manual, 1985; (ed jtly) Genetics of Bacterial Diversity, 1989; (jtly) Practical Streptomyces Genetics, 2000. *Recreations:* painting, gardening, bird-watching. *Address:* John Innes Centre, Norwich Research Park, Norwich NR4 7UH. *T:* (01603) 450297, *Fax:* (01603) 450045. *E:* keith.chater@jic.ac.uk.

CHATER, Prof. Nicholas John, PhD; FBA 2012; Professor of Behavioural Science, since 2010, and Head, Behavioural Science Group, since 2011, Warwick Business School, University of Warwick; *b* Salisbury, 8 July 1965; *s* of Robert John Chater and Dorothy Chater; partner, Louie Fooks; two *d*. *Educ:* Trinity Coll., Cambridge (BA 1986); Univ. of Edinburgh (PhD 1990). Lecturer in Psychology: UCL, 1989–90; Univ. of Edinburgh, 1990–94; Lectr in Exptl Psychol., Univ. of Oxford, 1994–96; Fellow, Somerville Coll., Oxford, 1994–96; Professor: of Psychol., Univ. of Warwick, 1996–2005; of Cognitive and Decision Scis, UCL, 2005–10. Fellow, Cognitive Sci. Soc., 2011. *Publications:* with Michael Oaksford: Rationality in an Uncertain World, 1998; Rational Models of Cognition, 1998; Bayesian Rationality, 2007; The Probabilistic Mind, 2008; Cognition and Conditionals, 2010; (with Morten Christiansen) Connectionist Psycholinguistics, 2001; (with Susan Hurley) Perspectives on Imitation, 2005; Judgement and Decision Making, 2009. *Recreations:* reading, philosophy. *Address:* Behavioural Science Group, Warwick Business School, University of Warwick, Coventry CV4 7AL. *E:* nick.chater@wbs.ac.uk.

CHATTERJEE, Prof. (Vengalil) Krishna (Kumar), FRCP, FMedSci; Professor of Endocrinology, University of Cambridge, since 1998; Fellow of Churchill College, Cambridge, since 1990; *b* 23 April 1958. *Educ:* Wolfson Coll., Oxford (BA, BM BCh). FRCP 1996. SHO, Hammersmith, Brompton and St Thomas' Hosps, 1983–85; Registrar, Hammersmith Hosp., 1985–87; Res. Fellow, Massachusetts Gen. Hosp., 1987–90; Wellcome Sen. Fellow and Hon. Cons. Physician, Addenbrooke's Hosp., 1994–. NIHR Sen. Investigator, 2009–; Wellcome Trust Sen. Investigator, 2011–. FMedSci 2000. *Recreations:* travel, music. *Address:* Wellcome-MRC Institute of Metabolic Science, University of Cambridge, Metabolic Research Labs, PO Box 289, Addenbrooke's Hospital, Hills Road, Cambridge CB2 0QQ.

CHATTERTON DICKSON, Robert Maurice French; HM Diplomatic Service; Deputy Ambassador to Kabul, since 2013; *b* 1 Feb. 1962; *s* of Capt. W. W. F. Chatterton Dickson, RN and Judith Chatterton Dickson (*née* French); *m* 1995, Teresa Bargielska Albor; two *d* and one step *s* one step *d*. *Educ:* Wellington Coll.; Magdalene Coll., Cambridge (Exhibnr; BA 1984, MA 1988). Investment analyst, subseq. instnl and internat. portfolio manager, Morgan Grenfell Asset Mgt Ltd, 1984–90; entered FCO, 1990; 2nd Sec. (Chancery/Inf.), Manila, 1991–94; First Secretary: FCO, 1994–97; Washington, 1997–2000; FCO, 2000–03; Counsellor, FCO, 2003–04; Ambassador to Republic of Macedonia, 2004–07; Hd of Counter-Terrorism Policy, later Counter Terrorism, Dept, 2007–10; Consul Gen., Chicago, 2010–13. Chm., Diplomatic Service Assoc., 2002–04. *Recreations:* history, recreational running, messing about in boats. *Address:* c/o Foreign and Commonwealth Office, King Charles Street, SW1A 2AH. *Club:* Bosham Sailing (W Sussex).

CHATTO, Beth, OBE 2002; VMH 1988; Creator and Chairman of The Beth Chatto Gardens; *b* 27 June 1923; *d* of William George and Bessie Beatrice Little; *m* 1943, Andrew Edward Chatto (*d* 1999); two *d*. *Educ:* Colchester County High Sch.; Hockerill Training Coll. for Teachers. No formal horticultural educn; parents enthusiastic gardeners; husband's lifelong study of natural associations of plants was original inspiration in use of species plants in more natural groupings, thus introducing ecology into garden design; Sir Cedric Morris' knowledge and generosity with many rare plants from his rich collection at Benton End, Suffolk, became basis for gdns at Elmstead Market; began career demonstrating flower arranging; Beth Chatto Gardens, 1960–, Nursery, 1967–; a keen advocate of organic gardening and diet for over 40 yrs. Founder Mem., Colchester Flower Club (2nd Flower Club in England). Lectures throughout UK; lecture tours and talks: USA, 1983, 1984 and 1986; Holland and Germany, 1987; Australia and Toronto, 1989. DUniv Essex, 1988; Hon. DSc Anglia Ruskin, 2009. Lawrence Meml Medal, RHS, 1988. *Publications:* The Dry Garden, 1978; The Damp Garden, 1982, rev. edn 2005; Plant Portraits, 1985; The Beth Chatto Garden Notebook, 1988; The Green Tapestry, 1989 (also USA); (with Christopher Lloyd) Dear Friend and Gardener: letters exchanged between Beth Chatto and Christopher Lloyd, 1998; The Gravel Garden, 2000; The Woodland Garden, 2002; articles in The Garden, The English Garden, Horticulture

Amer. Jl of Hort., Sunday Telegraph, and Hortus. *Recreations:* family, cooking, entertaining, music, reading—and always creating the garden. *Address:* The Beth Chatto Gardens, Elmstead Market, Colchester, Essex CO7 7DB. *T:* (01206) 822007.

CHATTY, Prof. Dawn, PhD; FBA 2015; Professor of Anthropology and Forced Migration, University of Oxford, 2010–15, now Emeritus; Fellow, St Cross College, Oxford, 2002–15, now Emeritus; *b* New York, 16 Oct. 1947; *d* of Diaeddine Chatty and Eleonora Swanson (*née* Dorfman); *m* 1979, Oliver Nicholas Patrick Mylne; one *s* one *d*. *Educ:* Univ. of Calif, Los Angeles (BA Anthropol.; PhD Anthropol.); Inst. of Social Studies, The Hague (MA Social Develt). Fulbright Prof., Univ. of Damascus, Syria, 1977–79; UNDP Tech. Assistance Expert, Oman, 1979–88; Associate Prof., Sultan Qaboos Univ., Oman, 1988–94; Dulverton Sen. Fellow, Queen Elizabeth House, Univ. of Oxford, 1994–2002; Reader of Anthropol. of Forced Migration, 2002–10, Dir, Refugee Studies Centre, 2011–14, Univ. of Oxford. Chair, Commn on Nomadic Peoples, Internat. Union of Anthropol and Ethnol Scis, 1998–2013. Founder, Dana Declaration on Conservation and Nomadic Peoples, Jordan, 2002. Pres., Syrian Studies Assoc., 2002–05. *Publications:* From Camel to Truck, 1986, 2nd edn 2013; Mobile Pastoralist: development planning in the Sultanate of Oman, 1996; Displacement and Dispossession in the Modern Middle East, 2010. *Recreations:* travel, photography, hill walking. *Address:* Refugee Studies Centre, University of Oxford, Queen Elizabeth House, 3 Mansfield Road, Oxford OX1 3TB. *T:* (01865) 281715, *Fax:* (01865) 281230. *E:* dawn.chatty@qeh.ox.ac.uk.

CHATWANI, Jaswanti; Legal Chairman, Immigration Appeal Tribunal, 2000–03 (Vice President, 1992–2000); *b* 23 Nov. 1933; *d* of Keshavji Ramji Tanna and Shantaben Tanna; *m* 1953, Rajnikant Popatlal Chatwani; one *s* one *d*. *Educ:* Government Sch., Dar-es-Salaam, Tanzania. Called to the Bar, Lincoln's Inn, 1959; attached to Chopra & Chopra, Legal Practice, Mwanza, Tanzania, 1959–60; in private practice, Zanzibar, 1960–65; Sec. and Legal Aid Counsel, Tanganyika Law Soc., 1965–68; in private practice, Dar-es-Salaam, Tanzania, 1968–70; Sen. Immigration Counsellor, UKIAS, 1971–78; Legal Officer, then Sen. Complaints Officer, CRE, 1979–87; part-time Adjudicator, Immigration Appeals, 1980–87, full-time Adjudicator 1987–92. Mem., Judicial Studies Bd, Ethnic Minorities Adv. Cttee, 1991–94. *Recreations:* walking, travel, reading.

CHATWIN, (John) Malcolm, CEng, FIET; Chairman, Warrington Homes, since 2003; *b* 19 July 1945; *s* of John Edward Chatwin and Louie Valerie Chatwin; *m* 1969, Elizabeth Joy West; one *s* two *d*. *Educ:* City of London Sch.; University College London (BSc(Eng) Elect. Eng.). Operations Engr, LEB, 1969–73; Commercial Economist, Seeboard, 1973–77; Pricing Policy Manager, Electricity Council, 1977–79; Dep. Commercial Dir and Commercial Dir, N of Scotland Hydro-Electric Bd, 1980–87; Yorkshire Electricity: Dir, Business Planning, 1987–90; Commercial Dir, 1990–92; Chief Exec., 1992–97. Dir, Electricity Assoc., 1992–97; Chm., Regional Power Generators, 1992–94, 1996–97. Dir, Century Inns, 1995–99. *Recreations:* ski-ing, sailing.

CHAUDHRY, Mahendra Pal; MP, Fiji, 1987, 1992–99 and 2001–06; Prime Minister of Fiji, 1999–2000; Leader of the Opposition, 2004–06; *b* 2 Sept. 1942; *m* Virmati Frank; two *s* one *d*. *Educ:* Tavua Indian Sch.; Shri Vivekananda High Sch. Assistant, Res. Lab., Emperor Gold Mines, 1959–60; Office of the Auditor Gen., 1960–75 (Sen. Auditor, 1973–75); General Secretary: Fiji Public Service Assoc., 1970–99; Nat. Farmers' Union, 1978–. Asst Nat. Sec., 1975–87, Nat. Sec., 1988–92, Fiji TUC. Minister: of Finance, April–May 1987; of Finance, Public Enterprises, Sugar Industry and Information, 1999–2000; of Finance, Nat. Planning, Sugar Industry and Public Utilities (Water and Energy) in Interim Admin, 2007–08. Fiji Labour Party: Founder Mem., 1985; Asst Sec.-Gen., 1985–94; Sec.-Gen. and Parly Leader, 1994–.

CHAUDHURI, Prof. Kirti Narayan, PhD; FBA 1990; External Professor of History, European University Institute, Florence; *b* 8 Sept. 1934; *s* of late Nirad C. Chaudhuri, CBE, FRSL, FRAS; *m* 1961, Surang Chaudhuri; one *s*. *Educ:* privately in India; London Univ. (BA Hons Hist., 1959; PhD 1961). Derby Postgrad. Schol., London Univ., 1959–61; School of Oriental and African Studies, London University: Res. Fellow in Econ. Hist., 1961–63; Lectr in Econ. Hist. of Asia, 1963–74; Reader, 1974–81; Prof. of Econ. Hist. of Asia, 1981–91; Chairman: S Asia Area Studies Centre, 1982–85; History Exam. Bd, 1982–87; Vasco da Gama Prof. of Hist. of European Expansion, European Univ. Inst., Florence, 1991–99; Director: Centre for Comparative Studies, Provence, 1999; Gallery Schifanoia, Mas de San Vitale, 1999. FRHistS 1993; MAE 1994. D. João de Castro Internat. History Prize. Producer, director and scriptwriter: Four Nights in Tunis (audio play), 2007; Twelve Days of Summer in Benito Juarez (audio story), 2008; Jaguar of Chaco (film story), 2010; Dolor de Rosita Valdez (film story), 2010; Night Blooming Flower of the Poison Tree (film story in three parts), 2011; Nostos Algos? Nostalgia? (film story), 2012; Guilt from a Night of the Full Moon (film story), 2013; prod., dir, script and screenplay writer, Downfall and Redemption of Dr John Faustino (film story), 2010; dir and script writer: Dr Johannes von Faust: a kinematic interlace (feature film), 2013; Personal journey to the equinoctial regions of New Continent (narrative film), 2014; Fiesta de Buleria: a day under the Cordillera in the life of a failed revolutionary (feature film), 2014. *Publications:* The English East India Company: the study of an early joint-stock company 1600–1640, 1965; The Economic Development of India under the East India Company 1814–58: a selection of contemporary writings, 1971; The Trading World of Asia and the English East India Company 1660–1760, 1978; Trade and Civilisation in the Indian Ocean: an economic history from the rise of Islam to 1750, 1985; Asia before Europe: the economy and civilisation in the Indian Ocean from the rise of Islam to 1750, 1990; From the Atlantic to the Arabian Sea, 1995; The Dream of the Unicorn in the Year of Geneviève, 1996; A Mediterranean Triptych, 1998; The Landscape of the Corvo, 1998; (ed jtly) Historia Expansão Portuguesa, 5 vols, 1998–99; The Sacrifice, 2000; Venezia, the Vision of the Blind Gladiator, 2000; Interlace, Variations on Ornamental Space, 2001; Polyphony, 2002; Notre Dame sous la Neige, 2002; Sea & Civilisation: a visual archive, 3 vols, 2003; Veneto, 2003; Capri: resurrection of the drowned Aphrodite, 2003; Avignon in July: a midnight and two afternoons in the life of Lady Georgina Saville, 2004; Form in an Arid Land: Sahara and the Maghreb, 2004; Tango in San Telmo, 2005; A Purple Land, 2005; Tree of Blood, 2005; Cleopatra in Tripolitania: an imaginary text in images, 2005; Islam and Space: a transcontinental visual narrative of space and architectonics, 3 vols, 2005; Roman Mediterranean and the Passion of Perpetua, 2006; Forms of Perception: point, straight line, curve, solid, monochrome, and colour, 2006; Garden of the Tuareg, 2006; Bodas de Sangre, 2006; Jaguar of Chaco, 2007; Entre Primavera y Invierno, 2007; Bailarinas del Camba, 2007; Jane and Idle Days in Patagonia, 2007; El Asesino del Rio Grande, 2007; South America 2008: Cinco Tierras, 2009; contribs to Econ. Hist. Rev., Eng. Histl Rev., Jl of European Econ. Hist., Jl of RAS, Modern Asian Studies, TLS. *Recreations:* exploration, making professional feature films, printing and designing limited edition livres d'artistes, collecting 20th century graphic prints, wine tasting and gastronomic cuisine. *E:* gattinara8@hotmail.com. *Club:* Athenæum.

CHAUNY de PORTURAS-HOYLE, Gilbert; Director General, Treaties and other International Agreements, Ministry of Foreign Affairs, Peru, 2011–13; *b* Lima, 8 March 1944; *m* 1971, Carmen Loreto y Laos; two *s* one *d*. *Educ:* UNI (BA Arch 1966); Pontificia Universidad Católica, Peru (BA Arts 1967); Peruvian Diplomatic Acad. (Dip. and Licentiate Internat. Relns 1969). Joined Peruvian Diplomatic Service, 1970: Third Secretary: Under-Secretariat for Political and Diplomatic Affairs, Dept of Europe, Africa, Asia and Oceania, Min. of Foreign Affairs, Lima, 1970–72; Bogotá, 1972–75; Second Sec., Perm. Representation to Internat. Orgns, Geneva, and Consul Gen., Geneva and Vaud, 1975–78; First Secretary: Head: of Ceremonials, Protocol Dept, 1978–79; OAS Dept, Dept for Internat. Orgns and Confs, 1979–80; Counsellor, Hd of Political Dept, Washington, 1980–84; Minister Counsellor: and Consul Gen., Toronto, 1984–86; Asst Dir for America, Min. of Foreign Affairs, 1986–88; Minister, Dir of Aeronautical and Space Affairs, Min. of Foreign Affairs, 1988–89 (Delegate to Internat. Civil Aviation Orgn, Montreal); Minister and Hd of Chancery, London, and Perm. Rep. to IMO, 1989–93 (Chargé d'Affaires, March–June 1989 and March–Nov. 1993); Ambassador: Dir Gen. of Special Pol Affairs, Min. of Foreign Affairs, 1993–95; to Austria, and concurrently to Slovenia, Slovakia and Turkey, 1995–2000; Perm. Rep. of Peru to UN Office, Vienna, UNIDO, IAEA and Comp. Nuclear Test-Ban Treaty Orgn, 1995–2000; Ambassador to UK and to Ireland, 2000–01; Nat. Dir for Frontier Develt, Min. of Foreign Affairs, 2002–03; Under-Sec. for Internat. Cultural Affairs, Min. of Foreign Affairs, 2003–05; Ambassador to Hungary, and concurrently to Croatia and Bosnia-Herzegovina, 2005–07; Ambassador to The Netherlands, Perm. Rep. to OPCW, and Gov. to Common Fund for Commodities, 2007–08; Ambassador to Kingdom of Sweden, and concurrently to Republic of Iceland, 2008–11, and to Kingdoms of Denmark and Norway, 2009–11. President, National Commission: for Antarctic Affairs, 1993–95; for Biol Diversity, 1993–95; for Climatic Changes and Ozone, 1993–95. Member: Peruvian Inst. for Genealogical Res., 1962–; Peruvian Inst. Aerospace Law, 1994–2000. Mem., Confrérie des Chevaliers du Tastevin. Pres., Peruvian Assoc. of Kts of SMO, Malta. Kt 1988, Grand Cross of Merit, 2001, SMO Malta; Kt Comdr with Star, Constantinian Order of St George, 2000. Kt Comdr, Orden de Bogotá (Colombia), 1974; Official: Order of San Carlos (Colombia), 1975; Orden de Isabel la Católica (Spain), 1978; Grand Cross, Orden del Condor de los Andes (Bolivia), 1995; Gold Grand Cross, Honour Badge for Merit (Austria), 2000; Grand Cross, Orden al Mérito por Servicios Distinguidos (Peru), 2005; Grand Cross, Order of Polar Star (Sweden), 2010. *Publications:* contrib. books and periodicals on internat. diplomatic relns, protocol, hist. of art, hist., and genealogy. *Recreations:* art and old map collecting, historical and genealogical research, tennis, bridge. *Address:* Lima Los Cedros 475, San Isidro, Lima 27, Peru. *T:* (1) 4410941, 0990319390, *Fax:* (1) 2214555; Ministerio de Relaciones Exteriores del Peru, Jirón Lampa 545, Lima 1, Peru. *T:* (1) 2042400. *Clubs:* Nacional, Regatas, Lima Golf (Lima); St Johanns (Vienna); Haagsche Club-Plaats Royaal (The Hague); Nya Sällskapet (Stockholm).

CHAUVIRÉ, Yvette; Grand Officier de la Légion d'Honneur, 2010 (Officier, 1974; Commandeur, 1988); Commandeur des Arts et des Lettres, 1975; Grand Croix, Ordre National du Mérite, 1998 (Officier, 1972; Commandeur, 1981; Grand Officier, 1994); prima ballerina assoluta, Paris Opera Ballet, since 1950; *b* Paris, 22 April 1917. *Educ:* Ecole de la Danse de l'Opéra, Paris. Paris Opera Ballet, 1931; first major rôles in David Triomphant and Les Créatures de Prométhée; Danseuse étoile 1941; danced Istar, 1941; Monte Carlo Opera Ballet, 1946–47; returned to Paris Opera Ballet, 1947–49. Has appeared at Covent Garden, London; also danced in the USA, and in cities of Rome, Moscow, Leningrad, Berlin, Buenos Aires, Johannesburg, Milan, etc; official tours: USA 1948; USSR 1958, 1966, 1969; Canada 1967; Australia. Leading rôles in following ballets: Les Mirages, Lac des Cygnes, Sleeping Beauty, Giselle, Roméo et Juliette, Suite en Blanc, Le Cygne (St Saens), La Dame aux Camélias, etc; Giselle, Moscow, 1966 (guest for 125th anniversary celebration); acting rôle, Reine Léda, Amphitryon 38, Paris, 1976–77; La Comtessa de Doris in Raymonda, Paris, 1983. Choreographer: La Péri, Roméo et Juliette, Le Cygne; farewell performances: Paris Opera, Giselle, Nov. 1972, Petrouchka and The Swan, Dec. 1972; Berlin Opera, Giselle, 1973; Artistic and Tech. Adviser, Paris Opera, 1963–72, teacher of dance for style and perfection, 1970–; Acad. Internat. de la Danse, Paris, 1972–76. *Films:* La Mort du Cygne, 1937 (Paris); Carrousel Napolitain, 1953 (Rome); Yvette Chauviré, une étoile pour l'exemple, 1988. *Publications:* Je suis Ballerine. *Recreations:* painting and drawing, collections of swans. *Address:* 21 Place du Commerce, Paris 75015, France.

CHAVEZ, Victor Manuel, CBE 2015; Chief Executive, Thales UK, since 2011; *b* Barrow-in-Furness, 19 Jan. 1963; *s* of Victor Chavez and Janet Chavez; *m* 1992, Fiona Mary Black; two *d*. *Educ:* Barrow Boys' Grammar Sch.; Univ. of York (BSc Hons Phys 1984); Univ. of Surrey (MSc Satellite Engrg and Telecommunications 1993). Systems Engr, GEC Telecommunications, 1984–86; Principal Consultant, Systems Designers Ltd, 1986–92; Business Manager, EDS-Scicon, 1992–99; Business Develt Dir, Thomson-CSF, 1999–2000; Thales UK: Sales and Mktg Dir, 2000–09; Dep. Chief Exec., 2009–11. Pres., techUK, 2013–15; Mem. Bd, Engineering UK, 2014–. *Recreations:* cycling, photography, hiking, travel. *Address:* Thales UK, 4 Carlton Gardens, SW1Y 5AA.

CHAYTOR, Sir Bruce Gordon, 9th Bt *cr* 1831, of Croft, Yorkshire and Witton Castle, Durham; *b* 31 July 1949; *s* of Herbert Gordon Chaytor and Mary Alice Chaytor (*née* Craven); *S* kinsman, Sir George Reginald Chaytor, 8th Bt, 1999, but his name does not appear on the Official Roll of the Baronetage; *m* 1st, 1969, Rosemary Lea Stephen (marr. diss. 1978); one *s* one *d*; 2nd, 2011, Donnalaine Marie Hruby. *Heir:* *s* John Gordon Chaytor, *b* 17 Jan. 1973. *Address:* 2785 Sooke Road, Victoria, BC V9B 1Y8, Canada.

CHAYTOR, David Michael; *b* 3 Aug. 1949; *m*; one *s* two *d*. *Educ:* Bury Grammar Sch.; Royal Holloway Coll., London (BA Hons 1970); Leeds Univ. (PGCE 1976); London Univ. (MPhil 1979). Sen. Staff Tutor, Manchester Coll. of Adult Educn, 1983–90; Hd, Dept of Continuing Educn, Manchester Coll. of Arts and Technology, 1993–97. Mem., Calderdale MBC, 1982–97. Contested (Lab) Calder Valley, 1987, 1992. MP (Lab) Bury North, 1997–2010.

CHAZOT, Georges-Christian; international consultant; *b* 19 March 1939; *s* of late Raymond Chazot, banker and Suzanne Monnet; *m* 1962, Marie-Dominique Tremois, painter; one *s* two *d*. *Educ:* Lycée Gauthier; Lycée Bugeaud Algiers; Ecole Polytechnique, Paris; Univ. of Florida (MSEE 1964); Internat. Marketing Inst., Harvard, 1972. Joined Schlumberger Group, 1962; Electro-Mechanical Research, USA, 1962–65; Schlumberger Instrument and Systems, 1965–76; Alcatel Alsthom, 1977–92; Saft, 1977–88; Chairman and Chief Executive: Saft, 1984–88; Alcatel Business Systems, 1989–92; ADIA France, 1992–93; Gp Man. Dir, Eurotunnel, 1994–2000; Chairman: Prosegur France, 2003–05; Eurotunnel Development Ltd, 2002–04. Mem. Adv. Council, X-PM Transition Partners, 2001–; Mem. Bd, Giat Industries, 2002–10. Dir, Actim, Paris, 1988–92. Treas., Fondn Franco Japonaise Sasakawa, 1990–; Vice-Chm., FM Radio Notre-Dame, 2001–; Dir and former Dir, internat. cos. Mem., Adv. Council, World Economic Forum, Switzerland, 1983–87; Vice-Pres., French Chamber of Commerce in London, 1995–2002. Chm., Hôpital Paris St Joseph Foundn, 2008–. Chevalier, Ordre de St Grégoire Le Grand, 2007; Officier: Ordre National du Mérite (France), 1996; Légion d'honneur, 2014 (Chevalier, 1990). *Recreations:* sailing, ski-ing. *Address:* 24 rue des Réservoirs, Versailles 78000, France. *E:* georgeschazot@orange.fr. *Club:* UNCL (Union Nationale pour la Course au Large) (Paris).

CHEADLE, Rear Adm. Richard Frank, CB 2005; DL; Advisor: WS Atkins, since 2012 (Director, 2006–12); Newton Europe, since 2012 (Director, 2010–12); *b* 27 Jan. 1950; *s* of Marcus and Marion Cheadle; *m* 1972, Sonja Arntzen; one *s* one *d*. *Educ:* Peter Symonds Sch.; RNEC (MSc Marine Engrg). Joined RN, 1968; engrg appts in nuclear submarines, Renown, Dreadnought and Splendid, 1975–85; Dep. Sqn Engr, 1985–87; Hd, In Service Submarine Propulsion Systems, 1987–90; jsdc 1991–92; CSO (Nuclear), Rosyth, 1992–95; Director: Naval Manpower Develt, 1995–97; Nuclear Propulsion, 1997–2000; Comdr, Devonport Naval Base, 2000–02; COS, Second Sea Lord and Chief Naval Engrg Officer, 2003; Controller of the Navy and Dir, Land Maritime, 2003–06. Pres., Devon, RBL. DL Devon, 2008. *Recreations:* painting, golf, repairing broken machinery.

CHECKETTS, Sir David (John), KCVO 1979 (CVO 1969; MVO 1966); Squadron Leader, retired; an Extra Equerry to the Prince of Wales, since 1979; *b* 23 Aug. 1930; 3rd *s* of late Reginald Ernest George Checketts and late Frances Mary Checketts; *m* 1958, Rachel Leila Warren Herrick; one *s* three *d*. Flying Training, Bulawayo, Rhodesia, 1948–50; 14 Sqdn, Germany, 1950–54; Instructor, Fighter Weapons Sch., 1954–57; Air ADC to C-in-C Malta, 1958–59; 3 Sqdn, Germany, 1960–61; Equerry to Duke of Edinburgh, 1961–66, to the Prince of Wales, 1967–70; Private Sec. to the Prince of Wales, 1970–79. *Recreation:* ornithology. *Address:* Forges, Fulford Barnyard, Cullompton, Devon EX15 1TJ. *T:* (01884) 839779.

CHECKETTS, Guy Tresham, CBE 1982; Deputy Chairman and Managing Director, Hawker Siddeley International, 1975–90, retired; *b* 11 May 1927; *s* of John Albert and Norah Maud Checketts; *m* 1957, Valerie Cynthia Stanley; four *s*. *Educ:* Warwick Sch.; Birmingham Univ. (BScEng Hons). British Thompson Houston Co., Rugby, 1948–51; Brush Group, 1951–57; Hawker Siddeley International, 1957–90. Chm., SE Asia Trade Adv. Gp, 1979–83; Mem., BOTB, 1981–84. *Recreation:* sailing. *Club:* Royal Over-Seas League.

CHECKLAND, Sir Michael, Kt 1992; Director-General, BBC, 1987–92; Chairman, Higher Education Funding Council for England, 1997–2001; *b* 13 March 1936; *s* of Leslie and Ivy Florence Checkland; *m* 1st, 1960, Shirley Frances Corbett (marr. diss. 1983); two *s* one *d*; 2nd, 1987, Sue Zetter. *Educ:* King Edward's Grammar Sch., Five Ways, Birmingham; Wadham Coll., Oxford (BA Modern History; Hon. Fellow, 1989). FCMA; CCMI. Accountant: Parkinson Cowan Ltd, 1959–62; Thorn Electronics Ltd, 1962–64; BBC: Senior Cost Accountant, 1964; Head of Central Finance Unit, 1967; Chief Accountant, Central Finance Services, 1969; Chief Accountant, Television, 1971; Controller, Finance, 1976; Controller, Planning and Resource Management, Television, 1977; Director of Resources, Television, 1982; Dep. Dir-Gen., 1985; Director: BBC Enterprises, 1979–92 (Chm., 1986–87); Visnews, 1980–85; Nynex Cable Communications, 1995–97. President: Commonwealth Broadcasting Assoc., 1987–88; Birmingham & Midland Inst., 1994; Vice-President: RTS, 1985–94 (FRTS 1987); EBU, 1991–92; Methodist Conf., 1997; Mem., ITC, 1997–2003. Chairman: NCH, 1991–2001; Brighton Internat. Fest., 1993–2002; CBSO, 1995–2001; Director: Nat. Youth Music Theatre, 1992–2002; Wales Millennium Centre, 2003–09. Chm., Horsham YMCA, 2005–11. Trustee, Reuters, 1994–2009. Governor: Westminster Coll., Oxford, 1993–97; Birkbeck Coll., 1993–97; Brighton Univ., 1996–97 and 2001–07 (Chm., 2002–06); Wesley House, 2002–08. *Recreations:* sport, music, travel. *Address:* Orchard Cottage, Park Lane, Maplehurst, near Horsham, West Sussex RH13 6LL.

CHECKLEY, Prof. Stuart Arthur, FRCPsych; Consultant Psychiatrist, Maudsley Hospital, 1981–2001; Dean, 1989–2001, and Professor of Psychoneuroendocrinology, 1994–2001, now Emeritus, Institute of Psychiatry; *b* 15 Dec. 1945; *s* of Arthur William George Checkley and Hilda Dorothy Checkley; *m* 1970, Marilyn Jane Evans, BA; one *s* one *d*. *Educ:* St Albans Sch.; Brasenose Coll., Oxford (BA, BM BCh). FRCP, FRCPsych. House appts, London Hosp. and St Charles Hosp., 1970–73; Registrar in Psych., London Hosp., 1973–74; Maudsley Hospital: Registrar, 1974–76; Hon. Sen. Registrar, 1977–78; Hon. Consultant, 1980–81; research worker, supported by Wellcome Trust, 1978–81; Mapother Travelling Fellow, USA, 1979; Institute of Psychiatry: Sen. Lectr, 1979–81; Sen. Lectr, Metabolic Unit, 1985–94. Non-exec. Dir, S London and Maudsley NHS Trust, 1999–2001. FKC 2001. *Publications:* (ed) The Management of Depression, 1998; papers on treatment of depression and hormones in relation to depression. *Recreation:* bird watching.

CHEEMA, Parmjit-Kaur, (Bobbie), (Mrs R. P. S. Cheema-Grubb); QC 2013; a Recorder, since 2006; a Deputy High Court Judge, since 2010; Senior Treasury Counsel, since 2011; *b* Derby, 6 Oct. 1966; *d* of Darshan Singh and Harbans Kaur Cheema; *m* 1990, Russell Paul Stephen Grubb; one *s* two *d*. *Educ:* City of Leeds Sch., Leeds; King's Coll. London (LLB Hons; AKC). Called to the Bar, Gray's Inn, 1989; barrister in private practice, specialising in criminal and administrative law, 1989–; Jun. Treasury Counsel, 2006–11. *Recreations:* art, architecture, theatre. *Address:* 2 Hare Court, Temple, EC4Y 7BH. *T:* (020) 7353 5324. *E:* bobbiecheemaqc@2harecourt.com.

CHEESMAN, Dr Clive Edwin Alexander; Richmond Herald of Arms, since 2010; Earl Marshal's Secretary, since 2012; *b* London, 21 Feb. 1968; *s* of Wilfrid Henry Cheesman, architect, and Elizabeth Amelia Cheesman (*née* Hughes), bio-chemist; *m* 2002, Roberta, *d* of Ciro Suzzi Valli, of Chiesanuova, San Marino. *Educ:* Latymer Upper Sch.; Oriel Coll., Oxford (BA 1st Cl. Hons Lit.Hum. 1989; MA 1995); Univ. degli Studi, San Marino (PhD 1993). Called to the Bar, Middle Temple, 1996 (Harmsworth Maj. Exhibnr and Astbury Schol.); British Museum: Special asst, 1990–91, 1994; full-time curator, 1995; pt-time curator, 1995–2000; Rouge Dragon Pursuivant, Coll. of Arms, 1998–2010. Lectr in Roman Hist., Birkbeck Coll., London, 2002–03. Advr, Portable Antiquities Scheme, DCMS, 2006–; Mem., Lord Chancellor's Forum on Histl Manuscripts and Academic Res., 2011–. Trustee: Oriel Coll. Develt Trust, 2006–; Thames Explorer Trust, 2006–. FSA 2011. *Publications:* (with J. H. C. Williams) Rebels, Pretenders and Imposters, 2000; (ed) The Armorial of Haiti, 2007. *Address:* College of Arms, Queen Victoria Street, EC4V 4BT. *T:* (020) 7236 2191, *Fax:* (020) 7248 6448. *E:* richmond@college-of-arms.gov.uk.

CHEESMAN, Colin; Chief Executive, Cheshire County Council, 1998–2002; *b* 8 Nov. 1946; *s* of John Hamilton Cheesman and Elsie Louisa Cheesman; *m* 1969, Judith Mary Tait; one *s* three *d*. *Educ:* Alleyn's Sch., Dulwich; Liverpool Univ. (LLB Hons). Admitted Solicitor, 1971. Portsmouth County BC, 1969–71; Notts CC, 1971–73; joined Cheshire CC, 1973; Group Director: Support Services, 1991–94; Information and Leisure Services, 1994–97. Clerk, Cheshire Lieutenancy and Sec. to Cheshire Adv. Cttee, 1998–2002; Sec. and Solicitor, Cheshire Fire Authy, 1998–2002; Sec., Cheshire Probation Bd, 1998–2002. Mem. Court, Univ. of Liverpool, 1999–2002. Gov., Walton Centre NHS Foundn Trust, 2012–. Hon. Sec., Parkinson's Disease Soc., 2007–. *Recreations:* reading, hill walking, keeping fit, theatre. *Address:* 7 Radnor Drive, Westminster Park, Chester CH4 7PS. *T:* (01244) 678866.

CHEETHAM, Anthony John Valerian; Chairman, Head of Zeus Ltd, since 2012; *b* 12 April 1943; *s* of Sir Nicolas John Alexander Cheetham, KCMG; *m* 1st, 1969, Julia Rollason (marr. diss.); two *s* one *d*; 2nd, 1979, Rosemary de Courcy (marr. diss.); two *d*; 3rd, 1997, Georgina Capel. *Educ:* Eton Coll.; Balliol Coll., Oxford (BA). Editorial Dir, Sphere Books, 1968; Managing Director: Futura Publications, 1973; Macdonald Futura, 1979; Chm., Century Publishing, 1982–85; Man. Dir, Century Hutchinson, 1985; Chm. and Chief Exec., Random Century Gp, 1989–91; Chief Exec., Orion Books, subseq. Orion Publishing Gp Ltd, 1991–2003; Consultant to CEO of Random House UK and Publisher of Knopf, USA, 2004–05; Chm. and Publisher, Quercus Publishing plc, 2005–09; Associate Publisher and Dir, Grove Atlantic Ltd, 2009–11. *Publications:* Richard III, 1972. *Recreations:* gardening, oak trees, forestry, early medieval history. *Address:* 8 Morpeth Mansions, Morpeth Terrace, SW1P 1ER. *T:* (020) 7834 3684.

CHEETHAM, Prof. Anthony Kevin, FRS 1994; FRSC; FIMMM; Goldsmiths' Professor of Materials Science, University of Cambridge, since 2008 (Professor of Materials Science, 2007–08); Fellow, Trinity College, Cambridge, 2007–14; Professor of Solid State Chemistry, Royal Institution, 1986–2007; Emeritus Student, Christ Church, Oxford, since 1991; *b* 16 Nov. 1946; *s* of Norman James Cheetham and Lilian Cheetham; *m* 1984, Janet Clare (*née* Stockwell); one *s* one *d*, and one *d* (one *s* decd) from a previous marriage. *Educ:* Stockport Grammar Sch.; St Catherine's Coll., Oxford (Hon. Scholar); Wadham Coll., Oxford (Sen. Scholar). BA (Chem.) 1968; DPhil 1971. FIMMM 2008. University of Oxford: Cephalosporin Fellow, Lincoln Coll., 1971–74; Lectr in Inorganic Chem., St Hilda's Coll., 1971–85; Lectr in Chemical Crystallography, 1974–90; Tutor in Inorganic Chem., Christ Church, 1974–91; Reader in Inorganic Materials, 1990–91; University of California at San Barbara: Prof. of Materials, 1991–2007; Prof. of Chemistry, 1992–2007; Dir, Materials Re Lab., 1992–2004; Dir, Internat. Center for Materials Res., 2004–07. Visiting Professo Arizona State Univ., 1977; Univ. of California, Berkeley, 1979; Blaise Pascal Internat. Re Prof., Paris, 1997–99; Vis. Foreign Scientist, Amer. Chem. Soc., 1981; Francqui Interna Chair, Brussels, 2001–02; Raman Chair, Indian Acad. Scis, 2011. Humphry Davy Lect Royal Soc., 2003. Mem. Council, 2010–12, Treas. and Vice-Pres., 2012–, Royal So Member: Scientific Council, Institut Laue-Langevin, Grenoble, 1988–90; Scientific Adviso Board: Max-Planck-Institut für Festkörperforschung, Stuttgart, 1999–; Center for Advance Interdisciplinary Res. in Materials Sci., Universidad de Chile, Santiago, 2000–; Materia Creation Trng Prog., Integrative Grad. Educn and Res. Traineeship, UCLA, 2002–06; Na High Magnetic Field Lab., Florida, 2003–07; Dept of Chem., Southampton Univ., 2004–0 African Insts for Sci. and Technol., 2004–; Dept of Chem., UCL, 2006–; Internat. Centre f Materials Sci., Bangalore, 2008–; International Advisory Board: CSIRO Div. Manufacturing and Infrastructure Technol., Australia, 2003–06; Nat. Inst. for Materials Res Tsukuba, Japan, 2006–; King Abdulla Univ. of Sci. and Technol., Saudi Arabia, 2010–. Di Gen. Funds Investment Trust plc, 1984–87; Founder, NGEN Enabling Technologies Fun 2001. Science Adviser: Bd, Unilever, 2000–08; Deutsche Bank Asset Mgt, 2009–. MAE 200 Member: German Nat. Acad. Scis (Leopoldina), 2011; German Acad. of Engrg, 2013; Foreig Member: Indian Nat. Acad. of Scis, 1998; Mongolian Acad. of Scis, 2008; Foreign Fellov Pakistan Acad. of Scis, 1997; Distinguished Fellow, Nehru Center for Advanced Scientif Res., Bangalore, 1999; Associate Fellow, Acad. of Scis for the Developing World (former Third World Acad. of Scis), 1999; Fellow, Amer. Acad. of Arts and Scis, 2014. Dr *hc* Versaill Saint-Quentin-en-Yvelines, 2006; Hon. DSc: St Andrews, 2011; Tumkur, India, 201 Warwick, 2015. Corday-Morgan Medal and Prize, 1982, Solid State Chemistry Award, 198 Structural Chemistry Award, 1996, RSC; Bonner Chemiepreis, Univ. of Bonn, 2001; (jtl Somiya Award, Internat. Union of Materials Res. Socs, 2004; Wolfson Merit Award, Roy Soc., 2007; Advanced Investigator Award, Eur. Res. Council, 2008; Leverhulme Meda Royal Soc., 2008; TWAS Medal Lectr, Acad. of Scis for the Developing World, 2011; Körb Eur. Sci. Award, Trustee Cttee, Körber Foundn, 2011; Platinum Medal, IMMM, 201 Nyholm Prize for Inorganic Chem., RSC, 2012; Chemical Pioneer Award, Amer. Inst. Chemists, 2014; Humboldt Res. Award, 2014. *Publications:* Solid State Chemistry: techniqu (with P. Day), 1986; Solid State Chemistry: compounds (with P. Day), 1992; contribs to sc jls. *Recreations:* international affairs, golf. *Address:* Department of Materials Science an Metallurgy, University of Cambridge, 27 Charles Babbage Road, Cambridge CB3 0FS. (01223) 767061. *E:* akc30@cam.ac.uk; (home) 1695 East Valley Road, Montecito, C 93108, USA. *T:* (805) 5651211.

CHEETHAM, Julia Ann; QC 2015; a Recorder, since 2008; *b* Niagara Falls, Canada, 2 Sept. 1967; *d* of Dr John Cheetham and Pamela Cheetham; *m* 1991, Marc Paul Bernard Albe Willems, *qv*; two *s* one *d*. *Educ:* Wilmslow High Sch.; Nottingham Univ. (LLB Hons). Calle to the Bar, Lincoln's Inn, 1990. *Recreations:* travel, cooking, cycling. *Address:* Deans Cou Chambers, 24 St John's Street, Manchester M3 4DF. *T:* (0161) 214 6000. *Club:* Bareg Cycling.

CHEETHAM, Prof. Juliet, OBE 1995; Member, Mental Health Tribunal for Scotland, sinc 2005; Sessional Inspector, Care Inspectorate, Scotland (formerly Social Work Inspectio Agency), since 2006; *b* 12 Oct. 1939; *d* of Harold Neville Blair and Isabel (*née* Sanders); 1965, Christopher Paul Cheetham; one *s* two *d*. *Educ:* St Andrews Univ. (MA); Oxford Univ (Dip. in Social and Admin. Studies). Qual. social worker. Probation Officer, Inner Londo 1960–65; Lectr in Applied Social Studies, and Fellow of Green Coll., Oxford Univ., 1965–8 Prof. and Dir, Social Work Res. Centre, Stirling Univ., 1986–95, now Prof. Emeritu Contract Res. Co-ordinator, SHEFC, 1996–97; Develt Officer, E Lothian Council, 199 Social Work Comr, Mental Welfare Commn for Scotland, 1998–2005. Member: Cttee Enquiry into Immigration and Youth Service, 1966–68; Cttee of Enquiry into Working Abortion Act, 1971–74; NI Standing Adv. Commn on Human Rights, 1974–77; Centr Council for Educn and Trng in Social Work, 1973–89; Commn for Racial Equality, 1977–8 Social Security Adv. Cttee, 1983–88; CNAA Social Scis Cttee, 1989–91; ESRC Re Resources Bd, 1993–96. Vice-Chm., Social Policy and Social Work Panel, HEFCE Re Assessment Exercise, 1996. *Publications:* Social Work with Immigrants, 1972; Unwante Pregnancy and Counselling, 1977; Social Work and Ethnicity, 1982; Social Work with Blac Children and their Families, 1986; (jtly) Evaluating Social Work Effectiveness, 1992; (jtly) Th Working of Social Work, 1998; contrib. collected papers and prof. jls. *Recreation:* canal boat *Address:* October House, 14 Abbey Close, Abingdon, Oxon OX14 3JD. *T:* (01235) 532132

CHEETHAM, Rt Rev. Richard Ian; *see* Kingston-upon-Thames, Area Bishop of.

CHEFFINGS, (Charles) Nicholas; Global Chair, Hogan Lovells, since 2012; *b* Laceby, 2 Jan. 1960; *s* of Charles Ronald and Eden Eileen Cheffings; *m* 1983, Ann Elizabeth Thies *Educ:* Univ. of Leicester (LLB Hons). Qualified as lawyer, 1983; with NCB, 1983–90; Partne Nabarro Nathanson, 1990–99; Partner and Hd, Real Estate Disputes, Lovell White Durran then Lovells, later Hogan Lovells, 1999–. Member: Law Soc.; Property Litigation Assoc Council, Heart of the City, 2014–. Hon. Mem., ARBRIX, 2012. Hon. MRICS, 201 Trustee, Internat. Sen. Lawyers Project-UK, 2012–. *Publications:* (Gen. Ed.) Sweet Maxwell's Commercial Property Disputes: Law and Practice, 1999; contribs to learned an professional jls. *Recreations:* travelling, photography, watching most sports, theatre, sporad periods of inactivity. *Address:* Hogan Lovells International LLP, Atlantic House, Holbor Viaduct, EC1A 2FG. *T:* (020) 7296 2000, *Fax:* (020) 7296 2001; Hogan Lovells US LL Columbia Square, 555 Thirteenth Street NW, Washington, DC 20004, USA. nicholas.cheffings@hoganlovells.com.

CHEFFINS, Prof. Brian Robert; S. J. Berwin Professor of Corporate Law, and Fellow Trinity Hall, University of Cambridge, since 1998; *b* 21 Jan. 1961; *s* of Ronald Ian Cheffi and Sylvia Joy Cheffins; *m* 1992, Joanna Hilary Thurstans; two *d*. *Educ:* Univ. of Victoria, B (BA, LLB); Trinity Hall, Cambridge (LLM). Faculty of Law, University of British Columbi Vancouver: Asst Prof., 1986–91; Associate Prof., 1991–97; Prof., 1997. Vis. Prof., Harvar Law Sch., 2002; Visiting Fellow: Duke Univ., 2000; (also Lectr) Stanford Law Sch., 200 UBC (Fasken Martineau Vis. Sen. Scholar), 2013; Harvard Business Sch. (Thomas K McCraw Fellowship in US Business History), 2014. John S. Guggenheim Meml Fellow 2002–03; J. M. Keynes Fellow in Financial Econs, Univ. of Cambridge, 2014–. *Publication* Company Law: theory, structure and operation, 1997 (SPTL Prize, 1998); The Trajectory (Corporate Law) Scholarship, 2004; Corporate Ownership and Control: British busine transformed, 2008; (ed) The Modern History of US Corporate Governance, 2011. *Addres* Faculty of Law, University of Cambridge, 10 West Road, Cambridge CB3 9DZ. *T:* (0122 330084. *E:* brc21@cam.ac.uk.

CHELMSFORD, 4th Viscount *cr* 1921, of Chelmsford, co. Essex; **Frederic Corin Pier (Kim), Thesiger;** Baron Chelmsford 1858; *b* 6 March 1962; *o s* of 3rd Viscount Chelmsfor and Clare Rendle, *d* of Dr G. R. Rolston; *S* father, 1999; *m* 2002, Charlotte, *d* of Patric Robin and Madeleine de Gerault de Langalarie; one *s*. *Heir: s* Hon. Frederic Thesiger, *b* 9 Fe 2006. *Address:* 4/4 Hampstead Hill Gardens, NW3 2PL.

CHELMSFORD, Bishop of, since 2010; **Rt Rev. Stephen Geoffrey Cottrell;** *b* 31 Au 1958; *s* of John Geoffrey and Eileen Beatrice Cottrell; *m* 1984, Rebecca Jane Stirling; three *Educ:* Belfairs High Sch. for Boys; Poly. of Central London (BA (Hons) Media Studies, 1979 St Stephen's House, Oxford. Ordained deacon, 1984, priest, 1985; Curate, Christ Ch, Fores

Hill, 1984–88; Priest-in-charge, St Wilfrid's, Chichester, and Asst Dir of Pastoral Studies, Chichester Theol Coll., 1988–93; Diocesan Missioner, Wakefield, 1993–98; Springboard Missioner, 1998–2001; Canon Pastor, Peterborough Cathedral, 2001–04; Area Bishop of Reading, 2004–10. *Publications:* (ed jtly) Follow Me: a programme of Christian nurture for all ages, 1991; Sacrament, Wholeness and Evangelism: a Catholic approach, 1996; (jtly) Emmaus: the way of faith, 1996; Catholic Evangelism, 1998; Praying Through Life: at home, at work and in the family, 1998; Travelling Well: a companion guide to the Christian life, 2000; (jtly) Vital Statistics, 2002; (jtly) Youth Emmaus, 2003; On This Rock: Bible foundations for Christian living, 2003; I Thirst: the cross-the great triumph of love, 2003; From the Abundance of the Heart: Catholic evangelism for all Christians, 2006; Do Nothing to Change Your Life, 2007; Do Nothing Christmas is Coming: an advent calendar with a difference, 2008; The Things He Carried: a journey to the cross, 2008; Hit the Ground Kneeling: seeing leadership differently, 2008; The Things He Said: the story of the first Easter Day, 2009; How to Pray, 2011; The Nail: being part of the Passion, 2011; Christ in the Wilderness: reflecting on the paintings by Stanley Spencer, 2012; Walking Backwards to Christmas, 2014. *Recreations:* reading poetry, cooking, playing the guitar, trying to play the ukulele banjo, lino printing. *Address:* Bishopscourt, Main Road, Margaretting, Ingatestone, Essex CM4 0HD. *T:* (01277) 352001, *Fax:* (01277) 355374.

See also D. J. Cottrell.

CHELMSFORD, Dean of; *see* Henshall, Very Rev. N. J.

CHELMSFORD, Archdeacon of; *see* Lowman, Ven. D. W.

CHELSEA, Viscount; Edward Charles Cadogan; DL; *b* 10 May 1966; *s* and *heir* of 8th Earl Cadogan, *qv*; *m* 1990, Katharina Johanna Ingeborg, *d* of Rear-Adm. D. P. A. Hülsemann; two *s* one *d*. *Educ:* St David's Coll., Llandudno. Joined RAF, 1987; served Germany, UK and Cyprus; Flt Lt. Gulf War Medal with Clasp, 1991. DL Greater London, 2012. *Recreations:* country pursuits, ski-ing, rock climbing, hill walking. *Heir:* *s* Hon. George Edward Charles Diether Cadogan, *b* 24 Sept. 1995. *Club:* Royal Air Force.

CHELTENHAM, Archdeacon of; *see* Springett, Ven. R. W.

CHELTON, Captain Lewis William Leonard, RN; Secretary, Engineering Council, 1987–97; *b* 19 Dec. 1934; *s* of Lewis Walter Chelton and Doris May Chelton (*née* Gamblin); *m* 1957, Daphne Joan Landon; three *s*. *Educ:* Royal Naval College, Dartmouth. Called to the Bar, Inner Temple, 1966. Entered RN as Cadet, 1951; served in ships and shore estabts, home and abroad; Fleet Supply Officer, 1979–81; Captain, 1981; Chief Naval Judge Advocate, 1982–84; retired (voluntarily), 1987. Sec., 1997–2007, Treas., 1997–2015, Hatch Beauchamp and Dist Cons. Assoc.; Dep. Chm., Taunton Constituency Cons. Assoc., 1999–2004. Mem., Exec. Cttee, R. S. Surtees Soc., 1984–. Gov., Bruton Sch. for Girls, 1999–. Mem., Hatch Beauchamp PCC, 1997–. *Recreations:* shooting, gardening, country life. *Address:* Palmers Green House, Hatch Beauchamp, near Taunton, Som TA3 6AE. *T:* (01823) 480221. *Club:* Farmers.

CHEN, Prof. Min, PhD; Professor of Scientific Visualization, University of Oxford, since 2011; Fellow, Pembroke College, Oxford, since 2011; *b* Shanghai, 25 May 1960; *s* of Jun-ning Chen and Feng-yu Kong; *m* 1985, Rona Chen; one *s* one *d*. *Educ:* Fudan Univ. (BSc 1982); Univ. of Wales, Swansea (PhD 1991). University of Wales, Swansea, later Swansea University: Res. Asst, 1987–90; Lectr, 1990–98; Sen. Lectr, 1998–2001; Prof., 2001–11; Dep. Hd, 2009–10, Actg Hd, 2010–11, Dept of Computer Scis. *Publications:* High Performance Computing for Computer Graphics and Visualisation, 1996; Volume Graphics, 2000. *Recreations:* family, reading, gardening, walking. *Address:* Oxford e-Research Centre, University of Oxford, 7 Keble Road, Oxford OX1 3QG. *T:* (01865) 610600, *Fax:* (01865) 610612. *E:* min.chen@oerc.ox.ac.uk.

CHEN, Prof. Sheng, PhD, DSc; FIEEE, FREng; Professor of Intelligent System and Signal Processing, University of Southampton, since 2005; *b* Qianzhou, Fujian, China, 20 Sept. 1957; *s* of Zuoying Chen and Manyun Wang; *m* 1995, Qian Yao; one *s*. *Educ:* China Petroleum Inst. (BEng 1982); City Univ., London (PhD 1986); Southampton Univ. (DSc 2005). FIET 2005; FIEEE 2008; FREng 2014. Sen. Lectr, 1993–96, Reader, 1996–99, Portsmouth Univ.; Reader, Southampton Univ., 1999–2005. ISI highly cited research, 2004. *Publications:* contrib. res. papers to learned jls. *Address:* Electronics and Computer Science, University of Southampton, Highfield, Southampton SO17 1BJ. *T:* (023) 8059 6660, *Fax:* (023) 8059 4508. *E:* sqc@ecs.soton.ac.uk.

CHENERY, Peter James; Chief Executive, The Royal Anniversary Trust, since 2010 (General Manager, 2007–10); *b* 24 Oct. 1946; *s* of late Dudley James Chenery and Brenda Dorothy (*née* Redford); *m* 1979, Alice Blanche Faulder; three *d*. *Educ:* Forest Sch.; Christ Church, Oxford (MA); SOAS, London Univ. (Cert. in Arabic and Islamic Studies). Teacher, Ghana Teaching Service, 1967–70; joined British Council, 1970: Amman, 1971–73; Middle East Dept, 1973–76; Iran, 1976; Riyadh, 1977; Freetown, 1978–80; Jedda, 1981–84; Representative, Sana'a, 1984–88; Munich, 1988–90; Sec. of the Council and Hd of Public Affairs, 1990–97; Director and Cultural Counsellor: Greece, 1997–2000; Canada, 2000–06. Mem. British Cttee and Hon. Treas., UK-Canada Council (formerly UK-Canada Colloquia), 2006–. Associate Mem., St Antony's Coll., Oxford, 2000. FRSA 1996. Freeman, City of London, 2015; Liveryman, Broderers' Co., 2015–. *Publications:* (contrib.) The International Encyclopaedia of Cheese, 2007. *Recreations:* books, amusing conversation, lunch, history, numismatics, light recreational travel in the Mediterranean. *Address:* The Royal Anniversary Trust, Sanctuary Buildings, 20 Great Smith Street, SW1P 3BT. *Clubs:* Travellers; Leander.

CHENEVIX-TRENCH, Jonathan Charles Stewart; Co-founder and Partner, African Century Group, since 2008; *b* 24 March 1961; *s* of Anthony Chenevix-Trench and Elizabeth (*née* Spicer); *m* 1998, Lucy Ward; two *s* two *d*. *Educ:* Eton Coll.; Merton Coll., Oxford (BA Lit.Hum. 1984). Morgan Stanley International, 1984–2007: Vice Pres., Financial Engrg, 1990–92; Exec. Dir, Overall Risk Manager for Eur. Derivative Products, 1992–94; Man. Dir, 1994–99; Hd, Fixed Income in Europe, 1999–2004; Global Hd, Interest Rates and Foreign Exchange, 2000–05; Chm., 2006–07; Chief Operating Officer, Institutional Securities Gp, 2007. Gov., Royal Ballet Sch., 2007–. *Recreations:* reading, outdoor activities, gardening, natural history, ballet. *Clubs:* Pratt's, White's, Traveller's.

CHENEY, Richard Bruce; Vice-President of the United States of America, 2001–09; *b* 30 Jan. 1941; *s* of Richard H. Cheney and Marjorie Dickey Cheney; *m* 1964, Lynne Ann Vincent; two *d*. *Educ:* Casper Elementary Sch.; Natrona County High Sch.; Univ. of Wyoming (BA 1965; MA 1966); Univ. of Wisconsin. Public service, Wyoming, 1965–69; Federal service, 1969–73; Vice-Pres., Bradley Woods, 1973–74; Dep. Asst to Pres. Ford, 1974–75; Asst to Pres. Ford and White House Chief of Staff, 1975–77; Mem. (Republican) for Wyoming House of Representatives, 1978–89; Chm., Repub. Policy Cttee, 1981, Repub. House Conf., 1987; Repub. House Whip, 1988; Sec. of Defense, USA, 1989–93; Mem., Cttees on Interior and Insular Affairs, Intelligence, Iran Arms Deals. Sen. Fellow, Amer. Enterprise Inst., 1993–95. Chm. Bd, and CEO, Halliburton Co., 1995–2000. *Publications:* (with Lynne V. Cheney) Kings of the Hill, 1983; (with Liz Cheney) In My Time: a personal and political memoir, 2011; (with Jonathan Reiner) Heart: an American medical odyssey, 2013. *Address:* c/o American Enterprise Institute, 1150 17th Street NW, Washington, DC 20036, USA.

CHENG, Prof. Kar Keung, PhD; FRCGP, FFPH, FMedSci; Professor of Public Health and Primary Care, University of Birmingham, since 1995; Founding Head, Department of General Practice, Peking University Health Science Center, since 2011; *b* Hong Kong, 20 Aug. 1958; *s* of Yiu Chiu Cheng and Yuk Kung Cheng; *m* 1986, Jane Tam; one *s* one *d* (and one *s* decd). *Educ:* St Paul's Co-educnl Coll., Hong Kong; Univ. of Hong Kong (BSc 1982; MB BS 1984); Hughes Hall, Cambridge (PhD 1994). FRCGP 1991; FFPH 1997. Lectr, Univ. of Hong Kong, 1986–93; Sen. Lectr, Univ. of Birmingham, 1993–95. Guest Prof., Peking Univ. Health Sci. Center, 2011–. FMedSci 2012. *Recreations:* family, listening to classical music, watching football. *Address:* School of Health and Population Sciences, University of Birmingham, Birmingham B15 2TT. *E:* k.k.cheng@bham.ac.uk.

CHÉRIF, Taïeb, PhD; Secretary General, International Civil Aviation Organization, 2003–09; *b* 29 Dec. 1941; *m* 1971, Meryem Elkaouakibi; three *s*. *Educ:* Univ. d'Alger, Algiers (BMaths); École nationale de l'aviation civile, Toulouse (Dip. Aeronautical Engrg); Cranfield Inst. of Technology (MSc Air Transport; PhD Air Transport Econs). Various positions of responsibility, Civil Aviation Authy, Algeria, 1971–92; State Sec. for Higher Educn, Algeria, 1992–94; civil aviation consultant, 1995–97; Rep. of Algeria, Council, ICAO, 1998–2003. *Address:* c/o International Civil Aviation Organization, 999 University Street, Montreal, QC H3C 5H7, Canada.

CHERN, Dr Cyril, RIBA; FCIArb; barrister, architect and arbitrator; *b* Los Angeles, 17 June 1946; *s* of George and Lola Chern. *Educ:* Univ. of S Calif (BArch 1969; JD 1972). CIArb 2000, FCIArb 2000; RIBA 2002. Captain/Ship Master, Merchant Navy, 1976–97. Called to the Bar: Gray's Inn, 1972; Calif, 1972; US Supreme Court, 1975; Partner: Acquaro, Chern, Cooper & Wright, Architects, 1970–73; Chern & Brown, 1973–80; Chern & Culver, 1980–83; Musick, Peeler & Garrett, 1984–86; Judge, *pro tem*, Calif Superior Court, 1986–93; Gen. Counsel and Dir, Maritime Ops, Turner Marine & Shipping, Hong Kong, London, 1993–98; Partner, Clinton, Clinton & Chern, London, 1998–2000; barrister: 5 Pump Court Chambers, 2002–05; Crown Office Chambers, 2006–. Dispute Board Federation: Hon. Sec., 2005–; Chair, Internat. Cttee on Dispute Resolution in Immediate Post-Conflict Countries, 2009–; Fellow, 2002; Mem., 2000, Fellow, 2006, and Mem., Adjudicators' Assessment Panel, 2008–, Fédn Internat. des Ingénieurs-conseils, Geneva. Mem., President's List of Adjudicators, Internat. Mediation Soc., Paris, 1975. Fellow, Centre for Internat. Legal Studies, Austria, 1981. Freeman, City of London, 2002. *Publications:* (jtly) Emden's Construction Law (annually), 2006–; Chern on Dispute Boards, 2007, 3rd edn 2015; International Commercial Mediation, 2008; (contrib.) Atkin's Encyclopaedia of Court Forms in Civil Proceedings, 2008; The Law of Construction Disputes, 2010, 2nd edn 2015; The Commercial Mediator's Handbook, 2014. *Recreations:* sailing, fly fishing. *Address:* Crown Office Chambers, 2 Crown Office Row, Temple, EC4Y 7HJ. *T:* (020) 7797 6166, *Fax:* (020) 7900 6909. *E:* chern@crownofficechambers.com.

CHERNAIK, Judith Sheffield, Hon. OBE 2002; PhD; writer; Founder and Co-Editor, Poems on the Underground, since 1986; *b* 24 Oct. 1934; *d* of Reuben Sheffield and Gertrude Lapidus; *m* 1956, Warren Lewis Chernaik; one *s* two *d*. *Educ:* Cornell Univ. (BA); Yale Univ. (PhD). Instr in English, Columbia Univ., 1963–65; Asst Prof. of English, Tufts Univ., 1965–69 (Scholar, Radcliffe Inst., 1966–68); Lectr, QMW, Univ. of London, 1975–88. Writer: features and documentaries for BBC Radio; The Two Marys (play), perf. in London and Bologna, 1997. Dir, Underground Poems CIC, 2008–. Fellow, Amer. Council of Learned Socs, 1972. *Publications:* The Lyrics of Shelley, 1972; *novels:* Double Fault, 1975; The Daughter, 1979; Leah, 1987; Mab's Daughters, 1991 (US title, Love's Children, 1992; trans Italian, 1997); *poetry anthologies:* (ed jtly) 100 Poems on the Underground, 1991, 10th edn 2001; (ed) Reflecting Families, 1995; (ed jtly) New Poems on the Underground, 2004, new edn 2006; (ed) Carnival of the Animals, 2005; (ed) Best Poems on the Underground, 2009; (ed) Poems on the Underground: a new edition, 2012; reviews and essays in TLS, The Times, New York Times, Guardian, Musical Opinion, PN Review, Musical Times, etc. *Recreations:* piano, chamber music, opera. *Address:* 124 Mansfield Road, NW3 2JB.

CHERRY, Bridget Katherine, OBE 2003; FSA; Editor: Buildings of England, 1983–2002; Buildings of Scotland, Ireland and Wales, 1991–2002; *b* 17 May 1941; *d* of Norman Stayner Marsh, CBE, QC and Christiane Marsh (*née* Christinnecke); *m* 1966, John Cherry, *qv*; one *s* one *d*. *Educ:* Oxford High Sch. for Girls; Lady Margaret Hall, Oxford (BA Modern Hist.); Courtauld Inst. of Art, Univ. of London (Dip. Hist. of Art). FSA 1980. Asst Librarian, Conway Library, Courtauld Inst., 1964–68; Res. Asst to Sir Nikolaus Pevsner, Buildings of England, 1968–83. Mem., Royal Commn on Historical Monuments of England, 1987–94; English Heritage: Comr, 1992–2001; Mem., Adv. Cttee, 2003–09; Mem., London Adv. Cttee, 1985–99; Mem., Historic Built Environment (formerly Buildings) Adv. Cttee, 1986–2003. Mem. Council, London Topographical Soc., 1999–. Trustee: Sir John Soane's Mus., 1994–2015; Historic Royal Palaces, 2003–08; Chair, Heritage of London Trust, 2008–10; Ironbridge Heritage Foundn, 2014–. Hon. FRIBA 1993. *Publications:* reviser or part author, 2nd edns, Buildings of England series, incl. Wiltshire, 1975, Hertfordshire, 1977, London 2: South, 1983, Devon, 1989, London 3: North West, 1991, London 4: North, 1998, London 5: East, 2005; articles and reviews on arch. subjects in learned jls. *Recreations:* walking, gardening. *Address:* Bitterley House, Cleestanton Road, Bitterley, near Ludlow, Shropshire SY8 3HJ.

CHERRY, Joanna Catherine; QC (Scot.) 2009; MP (SNP) Edinburgh South West, since 2015; *b* Edinburgh, 18 March 1966; *d* of Thomas Alastair Cherry and Mary Margaret Cherry (*née* Haslette). *Educ:* Holy Cross Sch., Edinburgh; St Margaret's Convent Sch. for Girls, Edinburgh; Univ. of Edinburgh (LLB Hons 1988; LLM 1989; DipLP 1990). Called to the Bar, 1995; Standing Jun. to Scottish Govt, 2003–09; Advocate Depute, 2008–11. *Recreations:* travel, reading, swimming. *Address:* Advocates Library, Parliament House, Edinburgh EH1 1RF. *T:* (0131) 466 4429, 07710 769081. *E:* joanna.cherry@advocates.org.uk.

CHERRY, John, FSA; Keeper, Department of Medieval and Modern Europe, British Museum, 1998–2002; *b* 5 Aug. 1942; *s* of Edwin Lewis Cherry and Vera Edith Blanche (*née* Bunn); *m* 1966, Bridget Katherine Marsh (*see* B. K. Cherry); one *s* one *d*. *Educ:* Portsmouth Grammar Sch.; Christ Church, Oxford (Open Scholar 1960, MA). British Museum: Asst Keeper, Dept of British and Medieval Antiquities, 1964–69; Asst Keeper, 1969–81, Dep. Keeper, 1981–98, Dept of Medieval and Later Antiquities. Dir, British Archaeological Assoc., 1977–82; Vice Pres., Soc. of Antiquaries of London, 1996–2000 (Sec., 1986–96); Pres., Soc. of Jewellery Historians, 2006–10. Vis. Fellow, All Souls Coll., Oxford, 2003. Mem., Treasure Valuations Cttee, DCMS, 2006–14. Chm., Emery Walker Trust, 2007–14 (Trustee, 1999–); Trustee, York Museums Trust, 2002–07. *Publications:* (jtly) The Ring from Antiquity to the 20th Century, 1981; (ed with I. H. Longworth) Archaeology in Britain since 1945, 1986; Medieval Decorative Art, 1991; Goldsmiths, 1992; The Middleham Jewel and Ring, 1994; (ed) Mythical Beasts, 1995; (ed with M. Caygill) Sir Augustus Wollaston Franks: Collecting and the British Museum, 1997; Medieval Love Poetry, 2005; (jtly) Good Impressions: image and authority in medieval seals, 2008; The Holy Thorn Reliquary, 2010; articles in learned jls on topics of archaeology and collecting.

CHERRY, John Mitchell; QC 1988; a Recorder, 1987–2003; *b* 10 Sept. 1937; *s* of John William and Dorothy Mary Cherry; *m* 1972, Eunice Ann Westmoreland; one *s* two *d* (and one *s* decd). *Educ:* Cheshunt Grammar Sch.; Council of Legal Education. Called to the Bar, Gray's Inn, 1961. Mem., Criminal Injuries Compensation Bd, 1989–2002; Legal Mem., Mental Health Review Tribunals, 2002–07. *Recreations:* cricket, Rugby, food, wine. *Address:* Winterton, Turkey Street, Bulls Cross, Enfield, Middx EN1 4RJ. *T:* (01992) 719018.

CHERRYMAN, John Richard; QC 1982; *b* 7 Dec. 1932; *s* of Albert James and Mabel Cherryman; *m* 1963, Anna Greenleaf Collis; three *s* one *d*. *Educ:* Farnham Grammar Sch.;

London School of Economics (LLB Hons); Harvard Law Sch. Called to Bar, Gray's Inn, 1955, Bencher, 1988. Recorder and Dep. High Ct Judge, 1984–97. *Recreations:* music, theatre, reading, ten grandchildren, restoring old coaching inn on Watling Street. *E:* john@svedberglaw.com.

CHESHAM, 7th Baron *cr* 1858; **Charles Gray Compton Cavendish;** *b* 11 Nov. 1974; *er s* of 6th Baron Chesham and of Suzanne Adrienne (*née* Byrne); *S* father, 2009; *m* 2002, Sarah Elizabeth, *d* of Bruce Dawson; one *s* two *d. Educ:* King's Sch., Parramatta; Durham Univ.; City Univ. *Heir: s* Hon. Oliver Nicholas Bruce Cavendish, *b* 15 Feb. 2007.

CHESHER, Prof. Andrew Douglas, FBA 2001; William Stanley Jevons Professor of Economics and Economic Measurement, University College London, since 2013 (Professor of Economics, 1999–2013); *b* 21 Dec. 1948; *s* of late Douglas George Chesher and of Eileen Jessie Chesher (*née* Arnott); *m* 1st, 1971, Janice Margaret Elizabeth Duffield (marr. diss.); two *s*; 2nd, 2000, Valérie Marie Rose Jeanne Lechene; two *d. Educ:* Whitgift Sch.; Univ. of Birmingham (BSocSc Maths, Econs and Stats). Res. Associate, Acton Soc., 1970–71; Lectr in Econometrics, Univ. of Birmingham, 1972–83; Prof. of Econometrics, 1984–99, Hd, Dept of Econs, 1987–90 and 1996–98, Univ. of Bristol; Dir, Centre for Microdata Methods and Practice, Inst. for Fiscal Studies and Dept of Econs, UCL, 2000–. Vis. Prof., Univ. of Bristol, 2000–10; Res. Fellow, Inst. for Fiscal Studies, 2001–. Mem. Council, ESRC, 2001–05 (Mem., 1996–2000, Vice-Chm., 1997–2000, Res. Resources Bd; Chm., Res. Grants Bd, 2001–05). Mem. Cttee, Nat. Food Survey, 1987–. Mem. Council, REconS, 1998–2004. Governor, NIESR, 2002–. Fellow, Econometric Soc., 1999 (Mem. Council, 2011–). Foreign Hon. Mem., Amer. Economic Assoc., 2011. Associate Editor: Econometrica, 1990–96 and 2000–03; Jl Econometrics, 1995–2003; Econ. Jl, 1997–2000; Jl Royal Statistical Soc., Series A, 1999–2001; Co-Ed., Econometric Soc. Monograph Series, 2001–09. *Publications:* (with R. Harrison) Vehicle Operating Costs in Developing Countries, 1987; contribs to learned jls in econs and stats. *Address:* Glebe Lodge, 289 Hills Road, Cambridge CB2 8RP.

CHESHIRE, Dr (Christopher) Michael, FRCP, FRCGP, FACP; Senior Medical Advisor, Haelo, since 2013; Medical Advisor, Broughton House Nursing Home, since 2012; *b* 18 July 1946; *s* of Gordon Sydney Cheshire and Vera Cheshire; *m* 1970, Jane Mary Cordle; one *s* one *d. Educ:* Manchester Univ. (BSc Hons 1969; MB ChB Hons 1976). DCH 1979; FRCP 1990; FRCGP 2010; FACP 2010. House Officer, Medicine and Surgery, Manchester Royal Infirmary, 1976–77; Senior House Officer: Cardiothoracic Medicine, Wythenshawe, 1977–78; Paediatrics, Univ. Hosp., S Manchester, 1978–79; SHO, Medicine, 1979–80, Consultant Physician, 1983–2010, Manchester Royal Infirmary; Lectr in Geriatric Medicine, Univ. Hosp., S Manchester, 1980–83; Med. Dir, 1993–97, Dir of Educn, 1997–2005, Central Manchester Healthcare NHS Trust; Clinical Dir of Service Redesign, 2005–06, Clinical Head of Intermediate Care, 2006–07, Central Manchester PCT; Med. Dir, NHS N of England (formerly NW SHA), 2009–13; secondary care doctor, Central Manchester Commng Gp, 2012–13; Clinical Leader, Patient and Family Centred Care, King's Fund, 2012–13. Non-exec. Dir, Stockport Foundn Trust, 2013–. Censor, 2006–07, Clin. Vice-Pres., 2007–10, RCP. Chairman: NW, British Geriatrics Soc., 1998–2001; Educn Gp, British Assoc. of Med. Managers, 1998–2001. Patron, METrust, 2011–. *Publications:* contribs on topics of medicine and management. *Recreations:* swimming, reading novels, garden, family. *Address:* Long Ridge, Derwent Lane, Hathersage S32 1AS.

CHESHIRE, Lt Col Colin Charles Chance, OBE 1993; Vice President, International Confederation of Fullbore Rifle Associations, since 2011 (Secretary General, 2003–11); *b* 23 Aug. 1941; *s* of Air Chief Marshal Sir Walter Graemes Cheshire, GBE, KCB and Mary Cheshire (*née* Chance), DL; *m* 1st, 1968, Cherida Evelyn (marr. diss. 1975), *d* of Air Chief Marshal Sir Wallace Hart Kyle, GCB, KCVO, CBE, DSO, DFC; one *s* one *d*; 2nd, 1976, Angela, *d* of D. Fulcher. *Educ:* Worksop Coll. Royal Tank Regiment: served Borneo, Singapore, Malaysia, BAOR, NI, UK; Armour Sch., Bovington Camp, 1968; RMCS, 1972–73; Staff Coll., Camberley, psc† 1974; Bde Major, RAC, HQI (BR) Corps, 1978–80; Lt Col, 1980; GSO1 (W) (Principal Quality Engr) Quality Assurance Directorate, MoD, 1980–81; retd 1981. Sales and Marketing Manager: Vickers Instruments Ltd, 1981–83; Army Systems, Ferranti Computer Systems, 1983–85; Sales and Mktg Dir, Wallop Gp, and Man. Dir, Walloptronics Ltd, 1985–87; Bursar, Oundle Sch., 1987–95; Chief Exec., NRA, 1995–2002. Mem., Exec. Cttee, Independent Schs Bursars Assoc., 1992–95. Chm., GB Target Shooting Fedn, 1994–97; Member: British Rifle Team, 1971–2006 (Captain, 1991, 1992, 1994, 1995, Vice Captain, 1982, 1999); GB Veterans Rifle Team, 2001–15 (Captain, 2014–15); Winner, World Long Range Rifle Team Championships, Palma Match, 1992, 1995. Mem., HAC, 1960–. Mem., Guild of Sports Internationalists, 1998–2002 (Middle Warden, 2001). FCMI (FIMgt 1985). *Publications:* History and Records of the World Long Range Rifle Championships - the Palma Match 1876 to date, 1992. *Recreations:* rifle shooting, golf, Freemasonry. *Address:* 16 Cygnet Way, Staverton, Trowbridge, Wilts BA14 8UU.

See also Sir J. A. Cheshire.

CHESHIRE, Sir Ian (Michael), Kt 2014; Chief Executive, Kingfisher plc, 2008–15; *b* 6 Aug. 1959; *s* of Donald and Pamela Cheshire; *m* 1984, Kate Atherton; two *s* one *d. Educ:* King's Sch., Canterbury; Christ's Coll., Cambridge (Schol.; BA 1st Cl. Hons Law and Econs 1980). Partner, Piper Trust Ltd, 1992–95; Gp Commercial Dir, Sears plc, 1995–98; Kingfisher plc, 1998–2015: Strategy Dir, 1998–2000; Dir, 2000–15; Chief Executive Officer, eKingfisher, 2000–03; Internat. and Develt, 2003–05; Chief Exec., B&Q plc, 2005–08. Chm., Skillsmart Retail, 2004–06; non-executive Director: Bradford & Bingley plc, 2003–08; Whitbread plc, 2011– (Sen. non-exec. Dir, 2013–). Lead non-exec. Dir, DWP, 2011–14; Govt Lead non-exec. Dir, 2015–; Chairman, Advisory Board: Start, 2010–; Cambridge Prog. for Sustainability Leadership, 2011–; Chairman: British Retail Consortium, 2012–14; Prince of Wales Corporate Leaders Gp on Climate Change, 2012–15 (Mem., 2006–). Chm. Trustees, Medicinema (charity), 2003–. Chm., Govs, Ernest Bevin Coll., 2000–08. FRSA 1999; MInstD 1992. Chevalier, Ordre Nat. du Mérite (France), 2012. *Recreations:* reading, arts, music, sailing, ski-ing. *E:* siriancheshire@gmail.co.uk. *Clubs:* Reform, Hurlingham; Bembridge Sailing.

CHESHIRE, Prof. Jennifer Lilian, PhD; FBA 2011; Professor of Linguistics, Queen Mary University of London, since 1996; *b* 26 Feb. 1946; *d* of Sydney Harold Russell and Elsie Millicent Russell; *m* 1970, Paul Charles Cheshire; one *s* one *d. Educ:* London Sch. of Econs (BA Hons 1st cl. French and Linguistics 1971); Univ. of Reading (PhD 1979). Lectr, Univ. of Bath, 1980–83; Lectr, then Sen. Lectr, Birkbeck Coll., London, 1983–91; Prof. of English Linguistics, Univ. of Fribourg, 1991–96. Member: ESRC Bd of Examiners, 1999–2003; ESRC Recognition Exercise, Linguistics, 2001, 2005; Linguistics Panel, 2001 and 2008 RAEs; Mod. Langs Panel, 2014 REF; NZ Peer-based Review Funding Exercise, Humanities and Law Panel, 2003, 2006 and 2012. Ed., Language in Society, 2013–. Gov., Raines Foundn Sch., 1998–2011. *Publications:* Variation in an English Dialect, 1982; English Around the World: sociolinguistic perspectives, 1991; (with P. Trudgill) A Reader in Sociolinguistics, 1998; (with D. Britain) Social Dialectology, 2003; articles in Jl of Sociolinguistics, Language and Educn, Language in Society, Language Variation and Change, Lingua, etc. *Recreations:* mountain walking, cinema. *Address:* Department of Linguistics, School of Languages, Linguistics and Film, Queen Mary University of London, Mile End Road, E1 4NS. *T:* (020) 7882 8923, *Fax:* (020) 8980 5400. *E:* J.L.Cheshire@qmul.ac.uk.

CHESHIRE, Air Chief Marshal Sir John (Anthony), KBE 1995 (CBE 1991; OBE 1982); CB 1994; FRAeS; Lieutenant-Governor and Commander-in-Chief, Jersey, 2001–06; *b* 4 Sept. 1942; *s* of Air Chief Marshal Sir Walter Cheshire, GBE, KCB and Lady Cheshire; *m* 1964, Shirley Ann Stevens; one *s* one *d. Educ:* Ipswich Sch.; Worksop Coll.; RAF Coll. Cranwell. Operational Flying Duties, UK and Singapore, 1964–70; Air Ops Officer, Special Forces, 1971–73; Canadian Forces Staff Coll., 1973–74; Operational Flying Duties, Special Forces, 1975–76; Air Plans, MoD, 1976–79; Commander: Air Wing, Brunei, 1980–82; RAF Lyneham, 1983–85; Plans Br., HQ Strike Command, 1986–87; Defence and Air Attaché Moscow, 1988–90; Dep. Comdt, RAF Staff Coll., 1991–92; ACOS (Policy), SHAPE 1992–94; UK Mil. Rep., HQ NATO, 1995–97; C-in-C, Allied Forces NW Europe 1997–2000. Chm., RAF Charitable Trust, 2009–13. Pres., Royal Internat. Air Tattoo 2009–13. KStJ 2002. *Recreations:* golf, field shooting, writing an historical novel. *Address:* Littl Court, Batcombe, Som BA4 6HF. *Club:* Royal Air Force.

See also C. C. C. Cheshire.

CHESHIRE, Michael; *see* Cheshire, C. M.

CHESSELLS, Sir Arthur David, (Sir Tim), Kt 1993; Chairman of Trustees, British Telecommunications Pension Scheme, 1999–2007; *b* 15 June 1941; *s* of late Brig. Arthur Chessells and Carmel Mary (*née* McGinnis); *m* 1966, Katharine, *d* of Dick and Rache Goodwin; two *s* two *d. Educ:* Stonyhurst Coll. CA 1965. Partner, Arthur Young, 1972–89. Mem., Kent AHA, 1979–82; Vice-Chm., Tunbridge Wells HA, 1982–88; Mem., SE Thames RHA, 1988–90; Chairman: NE Thames RHA, 1990–92; London Implementation Gp 1992–95; Legal Aid Bd, 1995–2000. Non-exec. Mem., NHS Policy Bd, 1992–95. Director: Odgers and Co. Ltd, 1989–95; Price and Pierce Inc., 1993–97; Dixons Gp, 1995–2001; Car UK, 1995–2005; Hermes Pension Mgt, 1999–2007 (Chm., 1999–2004), and other cos. Chm., Nat. Approval Council for Security Systems, 1995–99. Mem. Council, St Christopher's Hospice, 1989–92. Gov., Heythrop Coll., Univ. of London, 2009–13. Trustee: Kent Community Housing Trust, 1990–95; Stonyhurst Charitable Fund, 1980–93; Chatham Historic Dockyard, 1992–97; Charities Aid Foundn, 1998–2005; Chairman, Trustees: Guy's and St Thomas' Charitable Foundn, 1996–2006; Horder Centre for Arthritis, 2000–09, 2012–. *Recreations:* reading, shooting, gardening. *Address:* Coach House Cottage, North Street, Mayfield TN20 6AN. *Club:* Carlton.

See also J. M. Chessells.

CHESSELLS, Prof. Judith Mary, OBE 2004; MD; FRCP, FRCPath; Leukaemia Research Fund Professor of Haematology and Oncology, Institute of Child Health, London University 1988–2002; *b* 30 Dec. 1938; *d* of late Brig. Arthur Edgar Chessells and Carmel Mary Chessell (*née* McGinnis); *m* 1969, Dr Gerald McEnery; one *d. Educ:* Sacred Heart Convent, Brighton London Hosp. Med. Coll., London Univ. (MB BS Hons; MD). Lectr in Haematology, Inst of Child Health, 1972–73; Consultant Haematologist, Hosp. for Sick Children, Great Ormond St, 1973–87, Hon. Consultant, 1988–2002. FRCPCH 1997. *Publications:* contrib. to learned jls. *Recreations:* theatre, literature.

See also Sir A. D. Chessells.

CHESSELLS, Sir Tim; *see* Chessells, Sir A. D.

CHESSHYRE, (David) Hubert (Boothby), CVO 2004 (LVO 1988); FSA; Clarenceux King of Arms, 1997–2010; Secretary, Most Noble Order of the Garter, 1988–2003; Registrar of the College of Arms, 1992–2000; *b* 22 June 1940; *e s* of late Col Hubert Layard Chesshyre and Katharine Anne (*née* Boothby), Canterbury, Kent. *Educ:* King's Sch., Canterbury; Trinity Coll., Cambridge (Choral Clerk; MA); Christ Church, Oxford (DipEd 1967). FSA 1977; FHS 1990. Taught French in England and English in France, at intervals 1962–67; wine merchant (Moët et Chandon and Harvey's of Bristol), 1962–65; Hon. Artillery Co., 1964–65 (fired salute at funeral of Sir Winston Churchill, 1965); Green Staff Officer at Investiture of the Prince of Wales, 1969; Rouge Croix Pursuivant, 1970–78, and on staff of Sir Anthony Wagner, Garter King of Arms, 1971–78; Chester Herald of Arms, 1978–95; Norroy and Ulster King of Arms, 1995–97. Mem., Westminster Abbey Fabric Commn (formerly Architectural Adv. Panel), 1985–2003. Member: Council, Heraldry Soc., 1973–85; Bach Choir, 1979–93; Madrigal Soc., 1980–; London Docklands Singers, 2002–. Hon. Genealogist to Royal Victorian Order, 1987–2010. Lectr, NADFAS, 1982–2002. Lay Clerk, Southwark Cathedral, 1971–2003. Freeman: City of London, 1975; Musicians' Co., 1994 (Liveryman 1995–). *Publications:* (Eng. lang. editor) C. A. von Volborth, Heraldry of the World, 1973; The Identification of Coats of Arms on British Silver, 1978; (with A. J. Robinson) The Green: a history of the heart of Bethnal Green, 1978; (with Adrian Ailes) Heralds of Today, 1986, 2nd edn 2001; (ed with T. Woodcock) Dictionary of British Arms, vol. I, 1992; Garter Banners of the Nineties, 1998; (with P. J. Begent) The Most Noble Order of the Garter, 650 Years, 1999; genealogical and heraldic articles in British Heritage and elsewhere. *Recreations:* singing, gardening, mountain walking, motorcycling. *Address:* 12 Pensioners Court, Charterhouse Square, EC1M 6AN. *T:* (020) 7253 4222.

CHESSUN, Rt Rev. Christopher Thomas James; *see* Southwark, Bishop of.

CHESTER, Bishop of, since 1996; **Rt Rev. Peter Robert Forster;** *b* 16 March 1950; *s* of Thomas and Edna Forster; *m* 1978, Elisabeth Anne Stevenson; two *s* two *d. Educ:* Merton Coll., Oxford (MA 1973); Edinburgh Univ. (BD 1977; PhD 1985); Edinburgh Theol Coll. Ordained deacon, 1980, priest, 1981; Asst Curate, St Matthew and St James, Mossley Hill Liverpool, 1980–82; Senior Tutor, St John's Coll., Durham, 1983–91; Vicar, Beverley Minster and Asst Curate, Routh, 1991–96. Introduced to H of L, 2001. *Recreations:* tennis woodcrafts, family. *Address:* Bishop's House, Abbey Square, Chester CH1 2JD. *T:* (01244) 350864.

CHESTER, Dean of; *see* McPhate, Very Rev. G. F.

CHESTER, Archdeacon of; *see* Gilbertson, Ven. M. R.

CHESTER, Dr Peter Francis, FREng; FInstP; FIET; Chairman, National Wind Power Ltd 1991–95; *b* 8 Feb. 1929; *s* of late Herbert and of Edith Maud Chester (*née* Pullen); *m* 1953 Barbara Ann Collin; one *s* four *d. Educ:* Gunnersbury Grammar Sch.; Queen Mary College London (BSc 1st Physics 1950); PhD London 1953. Post-doctoral Fellow, Nat. Research Council, Ottawa, 1953–54; Adv. Physicist, Westinghouse Res. Labs, Pittsburgh, 1954–60 Head of Solid State Physics Section, CERL, 1960–65; Head of Fundamental Studies Section CERL, 1965–66; Res. Man., Electricity Council Res. Centre, 1966–70; Controller of Scientific Services, CEGB NW Region, 1970–73; Dir, Central Electricity Res. Labs 1973–82; a Dir, Technol. Planning and Res., Div., CEGB, 1982–86; Dir, Environment CEGB, 1986–89; Exec. Dir, Technology and Environment, Nat. Power, 1990–92. Science Research Council: Mem., 1976–80; Mem., Science Bd, 1972–75; Chm., Energy Round Table and Energy Cttee, 1975–80. Mem., ACORD, DTI, 1992–93. Vice-Pres., Inst. of Physics, 1972–76. A Dir, Fulmer Res. Inst., 1976–83. Faraday Lectr, IEE, 1984–85. Robens Coal Science Medal, 1985. *Publications:* original papers in solid state and low temperature physics, reports on energy and the environment, acid rain, clean technology, renewable energy and windpower.

CHESTERFIELD, Archdeacon of; *see* Wilson, Ven. C. L.

CHESTERMAN, Alex; Founder and Chief Executive Officer, Zoopla Property Group plc (formerly Zoopla.co.uk), since 2007; *b* London, 9 Jan. 1970; *s* of John and Carol Chesterman; *m* 2001, Angela; two *s. Educ:* St Paul's Sch.; University Coll. London (BSc Hons Econ). Exec. Vice Pres., Planet Hollywood Internat. Inc., 1991–99; Founder and Chief Executive Officer, Bagelmania plc, 2000–03; Founder, ScreenSelect, subseq. LoveFilm Internat., 2003–07. *Recreations:* art, travel, tennis, ping pong.

CHESTERMAN, Rev. Canon (George) Anthony, PhD; Chaplain to the Queen, 1998–2008; Continuing Ministerial Education Adviser to Bishop of Derby and Residentiary Canon (later Canon Theologian), Derby Cathedral, 1989–2003; *b* 22 Aug. 1938; *s* of late Francis John Chesterman and Frances Annie Chesterman; *m* 1964, Sheila Valerie Wilkinson; one *s* one *d*. *Educ:* Lancaster Royal Grammar Sch.; Univ. of Manchester (BSc); Nottingham Univ. (DipAE 1974; PhD 1989); Coll. of the Resurrection, Mirfield. Ordained deacon, 1964, priest, 1965; Curate, St John the Evangelist, Newbold, Chesterfield, 1964–67; Litchurch Gp Ministry, Derby (youth and adult educn specialist), 1967–70; Rector, All Saints, Mugginton and Kedleston, 1970–89; Diocesan Adult Educn Officer, Derby, 1970–79; Vice-Principal, E Midlands Ministry Trng Course, 1979–88. Mem., Gen. Synod, 1990–95. *Publications:* occasional articles and book reviews. *Recreations:* cooking, gardening, music, the visual arts, golf. *Address:* 7 Hillside, Lesbury, Alnwick, Northumberland NE66 3NR.

CHESTERMAN, Gordon; Director, Careers Service, University of Cambridge, since 2002; Fellow, St Edmund's College, Cambridge, since 2012; *b* 14 March 1957; *s* of Frederick and Marie Chesterman; *m* 1984, Deirdre McCormack; two *s* one *d*. *Educ:* University College Sch., Hampstead; London Coll. of Printing (HND Printing). Graduate trainee, then Personnel Officer, De La Rue Company, 1978–83; Graduate Recruitment Manager, Deloitte Haskins & Sells, 1983–86; Account Manager, Publishing Resources Ltd, Cambridge, 1986–90; self employed, 1990–95; Careers Advr, then Dep. Dir, Careers Service, Univ. of Cambridge, 1995–2002. Member: Steam Boat Assoc.; Ely Choral Soc. *Recreations:* choral singing, historic ship preservation, oil painting, fine letterpress printing. *Address:* Cambridge University Careers Service, Stuart House, Mill Lane, Cambridge CB2 1XE. *T:* (01223) 338288. *E:* gc214@cam.ac.uk. *Club:* Oxford and Cambridge.

CHESTERS, Rt Rev. Alan David, CBE 2007; Bishop of Blackburn, 1989–2003; an Hon. Assistant Bishop: of Chichester, since 2011; of Southwark, 2011–14; of Chester, 2003–10; of St Asaph, 2009–10; *b* 26 Aug. 1937; *s* of Herbert and Catherine Rebecca Chesters; *m* 1975, Jennie Garrett (*d* 2011); one *s*. *Educ:* Elland Grammar Sch., W Yorks; St Chad's Coll., Univ. of Durham (BA Mod. History; Hon. Fellow, 2010); St Catherine's Coll., Oxford (BA Theol., MA); St Stephen's House, Oxford (Hon. Fellow, 2008). Curate of St Anne, Wandsworth, 1962–66; Chaplain and Head of Religious Education, Tiffin School, Kingston-upon-Thames, 1966–72; Director of Education and Rector of Brancepeth, Diocese of Durham, 1972–84; Hon. Canon of Durham Cathedral, 1975–84; Archdeacon of Halifax, 1985–89. A Church Comr, 1982–98 (Mem., Bd of Governors, 1984–89, 1992–98). Mem., General Synod, 1975–2003 (Mem., Standing Cttee, 1985–89, 1990–95); Chm., C of E Bd of Educn, and Council, Nat. Soc., 1999–2003. Mem. Cathedral Chapter, Chester, 2003–10. Member: Countryside Commn, 1995–99; Countryside Agency, 1999–2001; Chm., NW Rural Affairs Forum, 2002–06. Pres., Cheshire Assoc. of Local Councils, 2005–10. Chairman: Govs, St Martin's Coll. of Higher Educn, Lancaster, 1990–2002; Council, St Stephen's House, Oxford, 1995–2003; Mem. Council, Univ. of Chester, 2005–10. House of Lords, 1995–2003. Hon. Fellow: Univ. of Central Lancs, 2001; St Martin's Coll. of HE, 2003; Blackburn Coll., 2004; Myerscough Coll., 2004; Univ. of Cumbria, 2007. DTheol Chester, 2010. *Recreations:* railways, classical music, reading. *Address:* 14 Pegasus Court, Deanery Close, Chichester PO19 1EA.

CHESTERS, Pamela Joy, CBE 2013; Chairman, Central London Community Healthcare NHS Trust, since 2012; *b* 28 April 1956; *d* of late Ian Storrie Beveridge and Kathleen Mary Beveridge; *m* 1991, Alan Chesters. *Educ:* St Andrews Univ. (MA Hons Mediaeval Hist.; Pres., Students' Rep. Council, 1977–78). British Petroleum: various posts in UK and USA, latterly CEO, Duckhams Oils, 1979–98. Chair, Royal Free Hampstead NHS Trust, 2001–09; Advr to Mayor of London on Health and Youth Opportunities, GLA, 2009–12. Contested (C) Bristol W, 2001. Mem. (C) London Borough of Camden, 1990–2000 (Leader of Opposition, 1998–2000). Mem., Nat. Educn Exec., LGA, 1997–2000. Chair, English Churches Housing Gp, 2003–09. Dir, Opera della Luna, 1994–2004. Trustee: Common Purpose, 2005–09; Action for Children (formerly NCH), 2006–12 (Chm., 2007–12); Chair: Anchor Trust, 2013–; Prince's Initiative for Mature Enterprise, 2014. *Recreations:* theatre, travel. *Address:* 62 Redington Road, NW3 7RS. *T:* (020) 7435 4190.

CHESTERTON, David, CB 1999; Chief Executive, UK Sports Council, 1998–99 (on secondment); *b* 30 Nov. 1939; *s* of Raymond and Joyce Chesterton; *m* 1st, 1965, Ursula Morgan; one *s* three *d*; 2nd, 1977, Lindsay Fellows; three step *d*. *Educ:* Reading Sch.; St Catherine's Coll., Oxford (BA). Editorial Assistant: Financial World, 1961–62; Fleet Street Letter, 1962–65; Producer, BBC External Services, 1965–68, Exec. Producer, 1968–74; Northern Ireland Office: Principal, 1974–80; Asst Sec., 1980–85; Under Sec., 1985–92; Hd of Heritage and Tourism Gp, DNH, 1992–96; Head of Sport, Tourism, Millennium and Nat. Lotteries Charities Bd Gp, DNH, then DCMS, 1996–98. *Recreations:* walking, food and drink.

CHESWORTH, Air Vice-Marshal George Arthur, CB 1982; OBE 1972; DFC 1954; JP; Lord-Lieutenant of Moray, 1994–2005; Chairman, Moray, Badenoch and Strathspey Enterprise Co., 1996–2000 (Deputy Chairman, 1991–96); *b* 4 June 1930; *s* of Alfred Matthew Chesworth and Grace Edith Chesworth; *m* 1951, Betty Joan Hopkins; two *d* (one *s* decd). *Educ:* Carshalton and Wimbledon. Joined RAF, 1948; commissioned, 1950; 205 Flying boat Sqdn, FEAF, 1951–53 (DFC 1954); RAF Germany, RAF Kinloss, RAF St Mawgan, 1956–61; RN Staff Coll., 1963; MoD, 1964–67; OC 201 Nimrod Sqdn, 1968–71 (OBE); OC RAF Kinloss, 1972–75; Air Officer in Charge, Central Tactics & Trials Orgn, 1975–77; Director, RAF Quartering, 1977–80; C of S to Air Comdr CTF 317 during Falkland Campaign, Apr.–June 1982 (CB); C of S, HQ 18 Gp, RAF, 1980–84. Chief Exec., Glasgow Garden Fest. (1988), 1985–89; Dir, SEC Ltd, 1989–95. Hon. Col, 76 Engr Regt (Vols), 1992–97. Chm., ATC Council for Scotland and NI, 1989–95; Pres., Highland RFCA (formerly TAVR), 1998–2005 (Vice-Chm. (Air), 1990–98). Develt Dir, Military and Aerospace Mus. (Aldershot) Trust, 1990–91; Trustee, MacRobert Trusts, 1994–2000; Mem. Management Bd, RAF Benevolent Fund Home, Alastrean House, Tarland, Aberdeenshire, 1990– (Chm., 1994–2001). Hon. Air Cdre, No 2622 (Highland) Sqdn, RAuxAF Regt, 2000–08. DL Moray, 1992; JP Moray, 1994. *Address:* Pindlers Croft, Lower Califer, Forres, Moray IV36 2RQ. *T:* (01309) 674136. *Club:* Royal Air Force.

CHETWODE, family name of **Baron Chetwode**.

CHETWODE, 2nd Baron *cr* 1945, of Chetwode; **Philip Chetwode;** Bt, 1700; *b* 26 March 1937; *s* of Capt. Roger Charles George Chetwode (*d* 1940; *o s* of Field Marshal Lord Chetwode, GCB, OM, GCSI, KCMG, DSO) and Hon. Molly Patricia Berry, *d* of 1st Viscount Camrose (she *m* 2nd, 1942, 1st Baron Sherwood, from whom she obtained a divorce, 1948, and *m* 3rd, 1958, Sir Richard Cotterell, 5th Bt, CBE); *S* grandfather, 1950; *m* 1st, 1967, Mrs Susan Dudley Smith (marr. diss. 1979); two *s* one *d*; 2nd, 1990, Mrs Fiona Holt. *Educ:* Eton. Commissioned Royal Horse Guards, 1956–66. *Heir: s* Hon. Roger Chetwode [*b* 29 May 1968; *m* 1998, Miranda, *d* of Comdr Graeme Rowan-Thomson; two *s* one *d*]. *Address:* 134 The Marsh, Bath Road, Hungerford, Berks RG17 0SN. *Club:* White's.

CHETWYN, Robert; *b* 7 Sept. 1933; *s* of Frederick Reuben Suckling and Eleanor Lavinia (*née* Boffee). *Educ:* Rutlish, Merton, SW; Central Sch. of Speech and Drama. First appeared as actor with Dundee Repertory Co., 1952; subseq. in repertory at Hull, Alexandra Theatre, Birmingham, 1954; Birmingham Repertory Theatre, 1954–56; various TV plays, 1956–59; 1st prodn, Five Finger Exercise, Salisbury Playhouse, 1960; Dir of Prodns, Opera Hse, Harrogate, 1961–62; Artistic Dir, Ipswich Arts, 1962–64; Midsummer Night's Dream, transf. Comedy (London), 1964; Resident Dir, Belgrade (Coventry), 1964–66; Assoc. Dir, Mermaid, 1966, The Beaver Coat, three one-act plays by Shaw; There's a Girl in My Soup, Globe, 1966 and Music Box (NY), 1967; A Present for the Past, Edinburgh Fest., 1966; The Flip Side, Apollo, 1967; The Importance of Being Earnest, Haymarket, 1968; The Real Inspector Hound, Criterion, 1968; What the Butler Saw, Queens, 1968; The Country Wife, Chichester Fest., 1968; The Bandwagon, Mermaid, 1968 and Sydney, 1970; Cannibal Crackers, Hampstead, 1969; When We are Married, Strand, 1970; Hamlet, in Rome, Zurich, Vienna, Antwerp, Cologne, then Cambridge (London), 1971; Parents Day, Globe, 1972; Restez Donc Jusqu'au Petit Déjeuner, Belgium, 1973; Who's Who, Fortune, 1973; At the End of the Day, Savoy, 1973; Chez Nous, Globe, 1974; Qui est Qui, Belgium, 1974; The Doctor's Dilemma, Mermaid, 1975; Getting Away with Murder, Comedy, 1976; Private Lives, Melbourne, 1976; It's All Right If I Do It, Mermaid, 1977; A Murder is Announced, Vaudeville, 1977; Arms and The Man, Greenwich, 1978; LUV, Amsterdam, 1978; Brimstone and Treacle, Open Space, 1979; Bent, Royal Court and Criterion, 1979; Pygmalion, National Theatre of Belgium, 1979; Moving, Queen's, 1980; Eastward Ho!, Mermaid, 1981; Beethoven's 10th, Vaudeville, 1983 (also Broadway, New York); Number One, Queen's, 1984; Why Me?, Strand, 1985; Selling The Sizzle, Hampstead, 1988; Independent State, Sydney Opera House, 1995. Has produced and directed for BBC (incl. series Private Shultz, by Jack Pullman, film, That Uncertain Feeling, Born In the Gardens) and ITV (Irish RM first series, Small World, Case of the Late Pig). Trustee, Dirs' Guild of GB, 1984. *Publications:* (jtly) Theatre on Merseyside (Arts Council report), 1973. *Recreations:* tennis, films, gardening. *Address:* 1 Wilton Court, Eccleston Square, SW1V 1PH.

CHETWYND, family name of **Viscount Chetwynd**.

CHETWYND, 11th Viscount *cr* 1717 (Ire.); **Adam Douglas Chetwynd;** Baron Rathdown 1717 (Ire.); *b* 26 Feb. 1969; *er twin s* of 10th Viscount Chetwynd and Celia Grace Chetwynd (*née* Ramsay); *S* father, 2015; *m* 2000, Johanna Marie Karatau; two *s* one *d*. *Heir: s* Hon. Connor Adam Chetwynd, *b* 18 Oct. 2001.

CHETWYND, Sir Peter James Talbot, 10th Bt *cr* 1795, of Brocton Hall, Staffordshire; *b* 21 Sept. 1973; *o s* of Sir Robin John Talbot Chetwynd, 9th Bt and Heather Helen Chetwynd (*née* Lothian); *S* father, 2012, but his name does not appear on the Official Roll of the Baronetage.

CHETWYND-TALBOT, family name of **Earl of Shrewsbury and Waterford**.

CHEWTON, Viscount; Edward Robert Waldegrave; *b* 10 Oct. 1986; *e s* of 13th Earl Waldegrave, *qv*. *Educ:* Eton Coll.; Christ Church, Oxford. *Address:* Chewton House, Chewton Mendip, Radstock, Som BA3 4LL.

CHEYNE, David Watson; Vice Chairman, Europe, Middle East and Africa, Moelis & Company, since 2011; *b* 30 Dec. 1948; *s* of Brig. W. W. Cheyne, DSO, OBE and L. A. Cheyne; *m* 1978, J. Gay Passey; three *s*. *Educ:* Stowe Sch.; Trinity Coll., Cambridge (BA Law 1971; MA). Admitted solicitor, 1974; Linklaters: Asst Solicitor, 1974–80; Partner, 1980–2011; Hd of Corporate, 2000–05; Sen. Partner, 2006–11; Consultant, 2011–. Non-exec. Dir, Blackrock World Mining Trust plc, 2012–. *Recreations:* shooting, fishing, collecting antiques. *Address:* 19 Ladbroke Gardens, W11 2PT. *T:* (020) 7229 0096. *E:* davidcheyne1@hotmail.com.

CHEYNE, Iain Donald, CBE 1995; Member, Professional Oversight Board, Financial Reporting Council, 2009–12; *b* 29 March 1942; *s* of Andres Delporte Gordon Cheyne and Florence Muriel Cheyne; *m* 1st, 1969, Amelia Martinez Arriola (marr. diss. 2008); two *s* one *d*; 2nd, 2011, Susan Souter. *Educ:* Hertford Coll., Oxford (MA English Lit. 1963); Coll. of Law, London; Stanford Univ. (Exec. Prog. 1987); London Business Sch. (Corporate Finance Prog. 1989); London Univ. (MPhil Archaeol. 1994). Articled Clerk, Droogleever and Co., Solicitors, 1964–68; admitted solicitor, 1967; Partner, Alfille and Co., Solicitors, 1968–72; Lloyds Bank, subseq. Lloyds TSB, plc: Legal Advr, 1972–86; General Manager: Corporate Communications, 1986–88; Strategic Planning, 1988–91; Corporate and Instnl Banking, 1991–97; Man. Dir, Internat. Banking, 1997–2000; Dir of Private Affairs to HH the Aga Khan, 2000–05; Dir Gen., Aga Khan Agency for Microfinance, 2005–07. Dir, Habib Bank, Pakistan, 2004–09; Vice-Chm., Habib and Allied Bank, UK, 2004–09; Exec. Dir, R M Walkden and Co. Investment Mgrs, 2011–12. *Recreations:* archaeology, game shooting, vintage car racing. *Address:* Gooselands, Aldbourne Road, Baydon, Marlborough, Wilts SN8 2HZ; 39 Quai D'Anjou, 75004 Paris, France.

CHEYNE, Sir Patrick (John Lister), 4th Bt *cr* 1908, of Leagarth, Fetlar; *b* 2 July 1941; *s* of Sir Joseph Lister Watson Cheyne, 3rd Bt, OBE and Mary Mort Allen; *S* father, 2007; *m* 1968, Helen Louise Trevor (*née* Smith); one *s* three *d*. *Educ:* Lancing Coll. FRICS 1997 (ISVA 1973). Cadet Seaman, British India Steam Navigation Co. Ltd, 1959; Seaman Cadet, RN, 1963; completed Commn as Lt Torpedo Anti-Submarine Officer, 1973. *Recreations:* fell walking, photography, gardening, croquet. *Heir: s* Louis Richard Patrick Lister Cheyne, *b* 25 March 1971. *Address:* Laurel Bank, 34 Stamford Road, Bowdon, Altrincham, Cheshire WA14 2JX. *T:* (0161) 928 0448. *E:* cheynepatrick@btinternet.com.

CHIBNALL, Christopher Antony; writer and producer, since 1999; *b* Watford, 21 March 1970; *s* of Robert and Gill Chibnall; birth mother, Veronica Oxley; *m* 2002, Madeline Joinson; two *s*. *Educ:* Range High Sch., Formby; St Mary's Coll., Strawberry Hill (BA 1st Cl. Hons Drama and English Univ. of Surrey); Sheffield Univ. (MA Theatre and Film). Videotape Librarian, Sky TV, 1991–93; Administrator, Théâtre de Complicité, 1996–99. Writer and producer for television: Born and Bred, 2001–04; Life on Mars, 2005–06; Torchwood, 2006–08; Dr Who (5 episodes), 2007–13; Law & Order UK, 2009; United, 2011; Broadchurch, 2013 (Best Writer Award, BPG, 2014), 2015; The Great Train Robbery, 2013. Writer in Residence, Grip Th., 1998–99; writer on attachment: NT Studio, 1999; Soho Th., 2000–01; writer and producer of plays: Best Daze, Grip Th., 1997; Gaffer, Grip Th., 1999, Southwark Playhouse, 2004; Kiss Me Like You Mean It, Soho Th., 2002; Worst Wedding Ever, Salisbury Playhouse, 2014. Mem., BAFTA, 2014–. *Publications:* Kiss Me Like You Mean It, 2002; Worst Wedding Ever, 2014. *Recreations:* music, cinema, theatre, football, walking, apologising to family for working too much. *Address:* c/o Cathy King, Independent Talent Group Ltd, 40 Whitfield Street, W1T 2RH. *T:* (020) 7636 6565. *E:* hello@imaginary-friends.co.uk.

CHIBWA, Anderson Kaseba; High Commissioner of Zambia to Malaysia, since 2010; *b* 24 March 1950; *s* of Chulu and Sarah Chibwa; *m* 1990, Grace Mwewa Kasese; three *s* three *d*. *Educ:* Univ. of Zambia (BA 1974); Univ. of Miami (MA 1979). Sen. Researcher, Nat. Council for Scientific Res., Zambia, 1974–82; Sen. Lectr, Pan African Inst. for Develt, 1982–99; Project Manager, CARE Internat., Zambia, 1999–2003; High Comr for Zambia in the UK, 2003–09. *Publications:* Population Atlas of Zambia, 1974; Internal Migrations in the Commonwealth of the Bahamas 1970–75, 1980. *Recreations:* reading, meeting people.

CHICHESTER, family name of **Marquess of Donegall**.

CHICHESTER, 9th Earl of, *cr* 1801; **John Nicholas Pelham;** Bt 1611; Baron Pelham of Stanmer, 1762; *b* (posthumously) 14 April 1944; *s* of 8th Earl of Chichester (killed on active service, 1944) and Ursula (*d* 1989) (she *m* 2nd, 1957, Ralph Gunning Henderson; marr. diss. 1971), *o d* of late Walter de Pannwitz, de Hartekamp, Bennebroek, Holland; *S* father, 1944; *m* 1975, Mrs June Marijke Hall; one *d*. *Recreations:* music, flying. *Heir: kinsman* Richard Anthony Henry Pelham [*b* 1 Aug. 1952; *m* 1987, Georgina, *d* of David Gilmour; two *s*]. *Address:* Little Durnford Manor, Salisbury, Wilts SP4 6AH.

CHICHESTER, Bishop of, since 2012; **Rt Rev. Martin Clive Warner,** PhD; *b* 24 Dec. 1958; *s* of John Warner and Anona Warner (now McGeorge). *Educ:* King's Sch., Rochester; Maidstone Grammar Sch.; Durham Univ. (BA 1980, MA 1985; PhD 2003); St Stephen's House, Oxford. Ordained deacon, 1984, priest, 1985; Asst Curate, St Peter, Plymouth, 1984–88; Team Vicar, Parish of the Resurrection, Leicester, 1988–93; Priest Administrator, Shrine of Our Lady of Walsingham, 1993–2002; Associate Vicar, St Andrew, Holborn, 2002–03; Canon Residentiary, St Paul's Cathedral, 2003–10; Bishop Suffragan of Whitby, 2010–12. Master of Guardians, Shrine of Our Lady of Walsingham, 2006–. *Publications:* Walsingham: an ever-circling year, 1996; Say Yes to God, 1999; (ed) The Habit of Holiness, 2004; Known to the Senses, 2005; Between Heaven and Charing Cross, 2009. *Recreations:* medieval and Renaissance art, contemporary architecture, cinema, modern fiction, travel. *Address:* The Palace, Chichester, W Sussex PO19 1PY. *T:* (01243) 782161.

CHICHESTER, Dean of; *see* Waine, Very Rev. S. J.

CHICHESTER, Archdeacon of; *see* McKittrick, Ven. D. H.

CHICHESTER, Giles Bryan; Member (C) South West England and Gibraltar, European Parliament, 2004–14 (Devon and East Plymouth, 1994–99; South West Region, England, 1999–2004); *b* 29 July 1946; *s* of Sir Francis Chichester, KBE and Sheila Mary (*née* Craven); *m* 1979, Virginia Ansell; two *s* one *d*. *Educ:* Westminster Sch.; Christ Church, Oxford (BA Hons Geography; MA). FRGS 1972. Trainee, Univ. of London Press and Hodder & Stoughton, publishers, 1968–69; Francis Chichester Ltd: Production Manager, 1969–71; Co. Sec., 1970–89; Dir, 1971–2013; Man. Dir, 1983–2013; Chm., 1989–2013. Chm., Foreign Affairs Forum, 1987–90. European Parliament: Cons. spokesman: on Research, Technol Develt and Energy Cttee, 1994–99; on Industry, External Trade, Res. and Energy Cttee, 1999–2004; Chm., Industry, Research and Energy Cttee, 2004–07; Leader, Cons. MEPs, 2007–08; Pres., Delegn for Relns with Australia and NZ, 2007–08 and 2008–09; Vice-Pres., 2011–12. Pres., European Energy Forum (formerly Foundn), 2004–14 (Vice Pres., 1995–2004). Mem. Council, Air League, 1995–99. *Publications:* pamphlets on nuclear energy, small business, opportunities for young people in Europe, sustainable energy. *Recreations:* rowing, sailing, vegetarian cooking. *Address:* (office) 9 St James's Place, SW1A 1PE. *T:* (020) 7493 0932; Longridge, West Hill, Ottery St Mary, Devon EX11 1UX. *E:* gbchichester@gmail.com. *Clubs:* Pratt's; London Rowing; Royal Western Yacht (Plymouth); Royal Yacht Squadron (Cowes).

CHICHESTER, Sir James (Henry Edward), 12th Bt *cr* 1641, of Raleigh, Devonshire; founder and Chairman, Chichester Trees and Shrubs Ltd; *b* 15 Oct. 1951; *s* of Sir (Edward) John Chichester, 11th Bt and Hon. Anne, *d* of 2nd Baron Montagu of Beaulieu; *S* father, 2007; *m* 1990, Margaret Anne, *o d* of late Major John Walkelyne Chandos-Pole, Radbourne Hall, Derbys; two *s*. *Educ:* Eton. *Recreations:* dendrology, stalking, shooting, ornithology. *Heir:* *s* Edward John Chandos-Pole Chichester, *b* 27 July 1991. *Address:* (office) The Mill Studio, Beaulieu, Hampshire SO42 7YG. *T:* (01590) 612198, *Fax:* (01590) 612194. *Clubs:* Pratt's, Shikar; Beaulieu River Sailing.

CHICHESTER CLARK, Emma, (Mrs C. R. Wace); freelance illustrator and author, since 1983; *b* 15 Oct. 1955; *d* of Sir Robin Chichester-Clark, *qv*; *m* 2008, C. Rupert Wace. *Educ:* Chelsea Sch. of Art (BA Hons); Royal Coll. of Art (MA Hons). Teacher, 1983–85: foundn students, City & Guilds Sch. of Art; Middx Poly. *Publications: author and illustrator:* Catch that Hat!, 1986; The Story of Horrible Hilda and Henry, 1988; Myrtle, Tertle and Gertle; The Bouncing Dinosaur, 1990; Tea with Aunt Augusta, 1991; Miss Bilberry's New House, 1993; Piper; Little Miss Muffet counts to Ten, 1997; More!, 1998; I Love you, Blue Kangaroo!, 1998; Follow my Leader, 1999; Where are you, Blue Kangaroo?, 2000; It was you, Blue Kangaroo!, 2001; No more kissing!, 2001; I'll show you, Blue Kangaroo!, 2003; Up in Heaven, 2003; No more teasing!, 2004; Just for you, Blue Kangaroo!, 2004; Will and Squill, 2005; Melrose and Croc, 2005; Amazing Mr Zooty!, 2006; Melrose and Croc Find a Smile, 2006; Melrose and Croc Friends for Life, 2006; Happy Birthday to You, Blue Kangaroo!, 2006; Eliza and The Moonchild, 2007; Melrose and Croc By the Sea, 2007; Melrose and Croc Go to Town, 2007; Minty and Tink, 2008; Melrose and Croc: a hero's birthday, 2008; Mummy and Me, 2009; My Baby Sister, 2009; Goldilocks and the Three Bears, 2009; Plum, Rabbit and Me, 2010; Lulu and the best cake ever!, 2012; Come to School Too, Blue Kangaroo!, 2012; Lulu and the Treasure Hunt, 2013; Bears Don't Read!, 2014; Plumdog, 2014; *illustrated books include: Laura Cecil:* Listen to this!, 1987; Stuff and Nonsense, 1989; Boo!, 1990; A Thousand Yards of Sea, 1992; Preposterous Pets, 1994; The Frog Princess, 1994; Noah and the Space Ark, 1998; The Kingfisher Book of Toy Stories, 2000; Cunning Cat Tales, 2001; Wicked Wolf Tales, 2001; *Geraldine McCaughren:* The Orchard Book of Greek Myths, 1992; The Orchard Book of Greek Gods and Goddesses, 1997; The Orchard Book of Roman Myths, 1999; *Adele Geras:* Sleeping Beauty, 2000; Giselle, 2000; Swan Lake, 2000; The Nutcracker, 2000; Primrose Lockwood, Cissy Lavender, 1989; Margaret Ryan, Fat Witch Rides Again, 1990; James Reeves, Ragged Robin, 1990; Pat Thomson, Beware of the Aunts!, 1991; Margaret Mahy, The Queen's Goat, 1991; Roald Dahl, James and the Giant Peach, 1991; Ben Frankel, Tertius and Pliny, 1992; D. J. Enright, The Way of the Cat, 1992; Peter Dickinson, Time and the Clockmice, 1993; Ann Turnbull, Too Tired, 1993; Anne Fine, The Haunting of Pip Parker, 1994; Gina Pollinger, Something Rich and Strange, 1995; Allan Ahlberg, Mrs Vole the Vet, 1996; Sam McBratney, Little Red Riding Hood, 1996; John Yeoman, The Glove Puppet Man, 1997; Jane Falloon, Thumbelina, 1997; Adrian Mitchell, The Adventures of Robin Hood and Marian, 1998; Naomi Lewis, Elf Hill, 1999; Kevin Crossley-Holland, Enchantment, 2001; Rosemary Sutcliff, The Minstrel and the Dragon Pup, 2001; Diana Wynne Jones, Wild Robert, 2001; Oxford First Illustrated Dictionary, 2004; Michael Morpurgo, Aesop's Fables, 2004; Reinhardt Jung, Bambert's Book of Missing Stories, 2008; Michael Morpurgo, Hansel and Gretel, 2008; Michael Morpurgo, The Best of Times, 2009; Lewis Carroll, Alice in Wonderland (abridged), 2009; Oscar Wilde, A Picture of Dorian Grey, 2009; Colin McNaughton, Not Last Night But The Night Before, 2009; Martin Waddell, The Orchard Book of Hans Christian Andersen, 2010; Michael Morpurgo, The Pied Piper of Hamelin, 2011; Nanette Newman, What Will You Be, Grandma?, 2011; Colin McNaughton, Have You Ever Ever Ever?, 2011; Lewis Carroll, Alice Through the Looking Glass 2013; Michael Morpurgo, Pinocchio 2013. *Recreations:* walking, cinema, music, friends. *Address:* c/o Laura Cecil, 17 Alwyne Villas, N1 2HG. *Club:* Chelsea Arts.

CHICHESTER-CLARK, Sir Robert, (Sir Robin), Kt 1974; *b* 10 Jan. 1928; *s* of late Capt. J. L. C. Chichester-Clark, DSO and Bar, DL, MP, and Mrs C. E. Brackenbury; *m* 1st, 1953, Jane Helen Goddard (marr. diss. 1972); one *s* two *d*; 2nd, 1974, Caroline, *d* of late Anthony Bull, CBE; two *s*. *Educ:* Royal Naval Coll.; Magdalene Coll., Cambridge (BA Hons Hist. and Law). Journalist, 1950; Public Relations Officer, Glyndebourne Opera, 1952; Asst to Sales Manager, Oxford Univ. Press, 1953–55. MP (UU) Londonderry City and Co., 1955–Feb. 1974; PPS to Financial Secretary to the Treasury, 1958; Asst Government Whip (unpaid), 1958–60; a Lord Comr of the Treasury, 1960–61; Comptroller of HM Household, 1961–64; Chief Opposition Spokesman on N Ireland, 1964–70, on Public Building and Works and the Arts, 1965–70; Minister of State, Dept of Employment, 1972–74. Mem. Council of Europe and Delegate to WEU, 1959–61. Dir, Instn of Works Managers, 1968–72. Chairman: Restoration of Appearance and Function Trust, 1988–2000; Arvon Develt Cttee, 1995–; Arvon Foundn, 1997–2001 (Jt Pres., 2001–); Trustee: Royal Philharmonic Orchestra Develt Trust, 1993–95; House of Illustration, 2002–08. Hon. FIWM 1972. *Recreations:* fishing, reading. *Club:* Brooks's.

See also E. Chichester Clark, P. Hobhouse, P. A. C. Russell-Cobb.

CHICK, John Stephen; HM Diplomatic Service, retired; educational consultant, 1994–2005; *b* 5 Aug. 1935; *m* 1966, Margarita Alvarez de Sotomayor; one *s* three *d*. *Educ:* St John's Coll. Cambridge (BA 1959); Univ. of Pennsylvania (MA 1960). Entered FO, 1961; Madrid 1963–66; First Sec., Mexico City, 1966–69; FCO, 1969–73; First Sec. and Head of Chancery Rangoon, 1973–76; Head of Chancery, Luxembourg, 1976–78; Commercial Counsellor and Consul-Gen., Buenos Aires, 1978–81; Head of Arms Control Dept, FCO, 1981–83; Head of S Pacific Dept, FCO, 1983–85. Consul-Gen., Geneva, 1985–89. Dir of Internat. Affair Sallingbury Casey Ltd, 1990–91; Associate Dir, Rowland Public Affairs, 1991. *Address:* 2 Ranelagh Avenue, SW13 0BL. *T:* (020) 8876 5916.

CHICKEN, Maj. Gen. Simon Timothy, OBE 2003 (MBE 1996); Senior Directing Sta (Navy), Royal College of Defence Studies, 2011–13; *b* Blyth, Northumberland, 24 July 195 *s* of Joseph Leonard and Isobel Chicken; *m* 1987, Charlotte Kate Davies; two *s*. *Educ:* Kin Edward VI Sch., Morpeth; King's Coll. London (MA Defence Studies). Royal Marine Young Officer Trng, 1977; Regtl Duty, 1978–90; Royal Netherlands Marine Corps (o exchange), 1990–92; RNSC, 1993; Officer Comdg K Co., 42 Commando, 1993–95; Sta Officer, Operational Requirements, 1995–97; Officer Comdg, 539 Assault Sqdn, 1997–200 CO, 45 Commando Gp, 2000–02; British Defence Staff, Washington, 2003–06; COS, Force HQ, 2006–08; ACOS, Perm. Jt HQ, 2008–10. *Recreations:* walking, running, cyclin playing guitar. *Address:* c/o Corps Secretary, Whale Island, Portsmouth PO2 8ER. *T:* (02 9254 7214. *E:* fleet-corpssec@mod.uk. *Clubs:* Royal Automobile, Caledonian.

CHIDDICK, Prof. David Martin, CBE 2010; Chairman, Leicestershire Partnership NH Trust, since 2011; *b* 26 Oct. 1948; *s* of Derek and Jeanette Chiddick; *m* 1973, Jane Elizabet Sills; one *s* two *d*. *Educ:* Poly. of Central London; Cranfield Univ. (MSc). FRICS 197 MRTPI 1979. Sen. Planning Officer, Herts CC, 1977–79; Prof. of Land Econ., 1985–8 Sen. Dean, 1987–89, Dep. Dir, 1989–93, Leicester Poly., then De Montfort Univ.; Pro-Vic Chancellor, De Montfort Univ., 1993–2000; Vice Chancellor, Univ. of Lincoln, 2000–0 now Prof. Emeritus. Chm., NHS E Midlands Strategic HA, 2010–11 (non-exec. Di 2004–10); non-exec. Dir, Leicester Royal Infirmary, 1993–2000. Chm., HEFCE Space Mg Gp. Mem. Council, Lincs Agricl Soc. (Pres., 2010). Founding Ed., Jl of Property Mg 1984–95. Liveryman, Merchant Taylors' Co. FRSA 1992. *Publications:* (ed with A Millington) Land Management: new directions, 1983; Lincoln 2020, 2006. *Recreation* mountain walking, watching Rugby Union, golf, reading, music. *Address:* 64 Dalby Avenue Bushby, Leicester LE7 9RD.

CHIDGEY, family name of **Baron Chidgey**.

CHIDGEY, Baron *cr* 2005 (Life Peer), of Hamble-le-Rice in the county of Hampshire; **Davi William George Chidgey,** CEng, FICE, FCIHT, FIEI; *b* 9 July 1942; *s* of Cyril Cec Chidgey and Winifred Hilda Doris Chidgey (*née* Weston); *m* 1965, April Carolyn Idris-Jone one *s* two *d*. *Educ:* Royal Naval Coll., Portsmouth; Portsmouth Poly. CEng 1971; MCI 1985; FCIHT (FIHT 1990); FIEI 1990; FICE 1993; MConsEI 1993. Mech. and aeronautic engr, Admiralty, 1958–64; Highways and Civil Engr, Hants CC, 1965–72; Brian Colquhou and Partners: Chartered Engr and Project Manager, UK, ME and W Africa, 1973–8 Associate Partner and Man. Dir, Ireland, 1981–88; Associate Partner, Central Souther England, 1988–93; Thorburn Colquhoun: Associate Dir, Southern England and Project Di Engrg Facilities Management, mil. estabts in Hants, 1994–. Mem. Adv. Bd, UK Br Transparency Internat., 2008–. Chm., Internat. Adv. Bd, Commonwealth Policy Studie Unit, 2008–11. Mem. Council, 2007–, Political Coordinator for Aid Effectiveness Progs 2011–, Eur. Parliamentarians for Africa. Contested: (SLD) Hampshire Central, Eur. Parl Dec. 1988 and 1989; (Lib Dem) Eastleigh, 1992. MP (Lib Dem) Eastleigh, June 1994–200 Lib Dem spokesman for: employment, 1994–95; transport, 1995–97; trade and industry 1997–99; for Internat. Develt and Foreign and Commonwealth Affairs (Africa), H of I 2010–; Lib Dem dep. spokesman for defence, 2006–07; Lib Dem delegate to Council c Europe and WEU, 2009–10. Member: Foreign Affairs Cttee, 1999–2005; Chairmen's Pane 2001–05; Jt Cttee on Human Rights, 2003–05; EU Sub Cttee C, Foreign Affairs, Defenc and Develt, H of L, 2006–09; Co-Chm., Lib Dem Parly Party Cttee on Internat. Devel 2010–; Chm., Africa All-Party Parly Gp, 2013–. CRAeS 2004. *Publications:* papers in technica jl, Traffic Engineering and Control. *Recreations:* walking, reading. *Address:* House of Lord SW1A 0PW. *Club:* National Liberal.

CH'IEN, Dr Raymond Kuo Fung, GBS 1999; CBE 1994; JP; Chairman: MTI Corporation Ltd, since 2003; Hang Seng Bank Ltd, since 2007; *b* 26 Jan. 1952; *s* of Jame Ch'ien and Ellen Ma; *m* Whang Hwee Leng; one *s* two *d*. *Educ:* Rockford Coll., Illinois (B. 1973); Univ. of Pennsylvania (PhD Econs 1978). Gp Man. Dir, Lam Soon Hong Kong Gp 1984–97; Chm., China.com Inc., 1999–2013. MEC, Hong Kong, then HKSAR, 1992–200 Trustee, Univ. of Pennsylvania, 2006–. JP Hong Kong, 1993. Young Industrialist Awarc Hong Kong, 1988. *Recreations:* scuba diving, hiking, tennis, Chinese paintings and ceramic *Address:* Suites 28 & 30, 2/F., Casey Building, 38 Lok Ku Road, Hong Kong. *T:* (office 25430887. *Clubs:* Hong Kong, Hong Kong Jockey.

CHIENE, John; *b* 27 Jan. 1937; *s* of John and Muriel Chiene; *m* 1st, 1965, Anne; one *s* on *d*; 2nd, 1986, Carol; one *d*. *Educ:* Rugby; Queens' Coll., Cambridge (BA). Wood Mackenzi joined, 1962; Man. Partner, 1969; Sen. Partner, 1974; Jt Chief Exec., Hill Samuel & Co. Lt (who had merged with Wood Mackenzie), 1987; Chm., County NatWest Securities, on the merger with Wood Mackenzie, 1988–89; Dep. Chm., County NatWest Ltd, 1989–90; Chm Gartmore Capital Strategy Fund, 1996–2002. *Recreations:* golf, opera, ski-ing. *Address:* 7 S Leonard's Terrace, SW3 4QB. *Clubs:* City of London; New (Edinburgh).

CHIGNELL, Anthony Hugh, MBE 2009; FRCS; FRCOphth; Consulting Ophthalmi Surgeon: St Thomas' Hospital, 1973–99; King Edward VII Hospital, 1985–2000; Hospitalle St John of Jerusalem, 2002–08; *b* 14 April 1939; *s* of Thomas Hugh Chignell and Phyllis Un (*née* Green); *m* 1962, Phillippa Price Brayne-Nicholls; one *s* two *d*. *Educ:* Worth Sch Downside Sch.; St Thomas' Hosp. (MB BS 1962). DO 1966; FRCS 1968; FRCOphth 198 (Hon. FRCOphth 2006). Registrar, Moorfields Eye Hosp., 1966–69; Sen. Registrar, Retin Unit, Moorfields Eye Hosp. and St Thomas' Hosp., 1969–73; Teacher in Ophthalmology London Univ., 1980–99. Civilian Consultant in Ophthalmology to Army, 1983–9 Consultant Advr in Ophthalmology to Metropolitan Police, 1988–99. Scientific Advr, Na Eye Inst., 1991–99; International Advisor: Dept of Ophthalmology, Hong Kong Univ 2011–; Lifeline Express Foundn, Hong Kong, 2012–; Rwanda Inst. of Interna Ophthalmology, 2012–. Chm., World Sight Foundn, 2012–. Gov., Royal Nat. Coll. fo Blind, 1987–97; Mem. Council, GDBA, 1989–2002 (Dep. Chm., 2001–02). Mem., Jul Gonin Club, 1972. Trustee: Ridley Eye Foundn (formerly Ridley Foundn), 1988–201 (Chm., 2001–04); Fight for Sight, 1992–95; British Humane Assoc., 2008– (Chm., 2010– Mem. Court, Spectacle Makers' Co., 1988–2010 (Master, 1999–2000). GCStJ 2008 (OS 1987; KStJ 2002). *Publications:* Retinal Detachment Surgery, 1979, 2nd edn 1988; Vitreo Retinal Surgery, 1998; numerous articles related to retinal detachment surgery. *Recreations* fly-fishing, golf, Herefordshire. *Address:* 3 Tedworth Square, SW3 4DU. *Clubs:* MCC; Ne Zealand Golf (Weybridge); Seniors Golfing Soc.

CHIKETA, Stephen Cletus; Ambassador of Zimbabwe to Sweden, since 2010; *b* 16 Sep 1942; *s* of Mangwiro S. Chiketa and Mary Magdalene (*née* Chivero); *m* 1976, Juliet Joalane one *s* two *d*. *Educ:* Univ. of South Africa (BA Hons); Univ. of Basutoland, Botswana an Swaziland (BA, PGCE). Asst Teacher, Swaziland schs, 1967–73; part-time Lectr, Univ. c Botswana, Lesotho and Swaziland, 1972–73; Principal, High School in Lesotho, 1974–8 Under Sec., Min. of Foreign Affairs, 1982; Dep. Perm. Rep., UN, 1982–86; Dep. Sec., Mi of Foreign Affairs, 1986–87; Ambassador to Romania and Bulgaria, 1987–90; High Comr for Zimbabwe in London, 1990–93; Dep. Sec., Ministry of Foreign Affairs, Harare, 1993–95; Ambassador: to Kuwait, Bahrain, Oman, Qatar and UAE, 1995–2002; to Iran, 2002–07; to Australia, 2007–08. *Publications:* history articles in Swaziland weekly newspapers. *Recreations:* photography, tennis, reading, table tennis, cards. *Address:* Embassy of Zimbabwe, PO Box 3253, 103 65 Stockholm, Sweden.

CHILCOT, Rt Hon. Sir John (Anthony), GCB 1998 (KCB 1994; CB 1990); PC 2004; Chairman, B & CE Group, 1999–2013; Chairman, Iraq Inquiry, since 2009; President, Police Foundation, since 2011 (Chairman of Trustees, 2001–11); *b* 22 April 1939; *s* of Henry William Chilcot and Catherine Chilcot (*née* Ashall); *m* 1964, Rosalind Mary Forster. *Educ:* Brighton Coll. (Lyon Scholar); Pembroke Coll., Cambridge (Open Scholar; MA; Hon. Fellow, 1999). Joined Home Office, 1963; Asst Private Sec. to Home Secretary (Rt Hon. Roy Jenkins), 1966; Private Sec. to Head of Civil Service (late Baron Armstrong of Sanderstead), 1971–73; Principal Private Secretary to Home Secretary (Rt Hon. Merlyn Rees; Rt Hon. William Whitelaw), 1978–80; Asst Under-Sec. of State, Dir of Personnel and Finance, Prison Dept, 1980–84; Under-Sec., Cabinet Office (MPO), 1984–86; Asst Under Sec. of State, 1986 (seconded to Schroders, 1986–87), Dep. Under Sec. of State, 1987–90, Home Office; Permanent Under Sec. of State, NI Office, 1990–97. Staff Counsellor: Security and Intelligence Agencies, 1999–2004; Nat. Criminal Intelligence Service, 2002–06. Member: Ind. Commn on the Voting System, 1997–98; Lord Chancellor's Adv. Council on Public Records, 1999–2003; Nat. Archives Council, 2003–04; Review of Intelligence on Weapons of Mass Destruction, 2004; Chairman: Privy Council Cttee on Intercept as Evidence, 2007–09, Adv. Cttee, 2009–. Director: RTZ Pillar, 1986–90; NBW Ltd, 2002–12. Pres., First Div. Pensioners' Gp, 1998–2002. Trustee, The Police Rehabilitation Trust, 2002–. Mem., Awards Council, Royal Anniversary Trust, 2003–. Vice-Pres. and Fellow, Brighton Coll., 2005–. *Recreations:* reading, music and opera, travel. *Address:* c/o Police Foundation, 1st Floor, Park Place, 12 Lawn Lane, SW8 1UD. *Club:* Travellers.

CHILCOTT, Dominick John, CMG 2003; HM Diplomatic Service; Ambassador to Ireland, since 2012; *b* 17 Nov. 1959; *s* of Michael and Rosemary Chilcott; *m* 1983, Jane Elizabeth Bromage; three *s* one *d*. *Educ:* St Joseph's Coll., Ipswich; Greyfriars Hall, Oxford (BA Hons (Philosophy and Theol.) 1982). Midshipman, RN, 1978–79; entered FCO, 1982; Southern African Dept, FCO, 1982–83; Turkish lang. trng, 1984; Third, later Second, Sec., Ankara, 1985–88; First Sec., Central African Dept, then EC Dept (Internal), FCO, 1988–92; Hd, Political Section, Lisbon, 1993–95; Private Sec. to Foreign Sec., 1996–98; Counsellor, Ext. Relns, UK Perm. Repn to EU, Brussels, 1998–2002; Dir, Iraq Policy Unit, 2002–03; Dir, EU Directorate, FCO, 2003–06: High Comr, Sri Lanka, 2006–07; Dep. Hd of Mission, Washington, 2008–11; Middle East and N Africa Directorate, FCO, 2011; Ambassador to Iran, 2011. *Recreations:* reading, walking, watching sport, music, theatre. *Address:* c/o Foreign and Commonwealth Office, King Charles Street, SW1A 2AH. *E:* dominick.chilcott@fco.gov.uk; Glencairn, Murphystown Road, Dublin 18, Ireland.

CHILCOTT, Robert Lionel; tenor; conductor; full-time composer, since 1997; *b* Plymouth, 9 April 1955; *m* 1st, Polly (marr. diss.); one *s* three *d*; 2nd, 2005, Kate Ledger; one *d*. *Educ:* King's Coll., Cambridge (choral scholar; BA 1976). Mem., King's Singers, 1986–97. Principal Guest Conductor, BBC Singers; former Conductor, Royal Coll. of Music Chorus; conductor of choirs worldwide incl. World Youth Choir, RIAS Kammerchor, Orphei Drangar, Jauna Musika, Taipei Chamber Singers and Tower NZ Youth Choir. Composer of choral music, esp. for youth choirs. *Compositions include:* Can you hear me?, 1998; The Making of the Drum, 1999; Jubilate, 1999; Canticles of Light, 2000; A Little Jazz Mass, 2004; Advent Antiphons, 2005; Weather Report, 2006; Missa Cantate, 2006; This Day, 2007; Salisbury Vespers, 2009; Requiem, 2010; On Christmas Night, 2011; Jazz Songs of Innocence, 2011; Nidaros Jazz Mass, 2012; Angry Planet, 2012; St John Passion, 2013. *Address:* c/o Choral Connections, 14 Stevens Close, Prestwood, Great Missenden, Bucks HP16 0SQ. *W:* www.bobchilcott.com.

CHILD, Sir (Coles John) Jeremy, 3rd Bt *cr* 1919; actor; *b* 20 Sept. 1944; *s* of Sir Coles John Child, 2nd Bt, and Sheila (*d* 1964), *e d* of Hugh Mathewson; *S* father, 1971; *m* 1971, Deborah Jane (*née* Snelling) (marr. diss. 1976); one *d*; *m* 1978, Jan (marr. diss. 1986), *y d* of B. Todd, Kingston upon Thames; one *s* one *d*; *m* 1987, Elizabeth, *y d* of Rev. Grenville Morgan, Canterbury, Kent; one *s* one *d*. *Educ:* Eton; Univ. of Poitiers (Dip. in French). Trained at Bristol Old Vic Theatre Sch., 1963–65; Bristol Old Vic, 1965–66; repertory at Windsor, Canterbury and Colchester; Conduct Unbecoming, Queen's, 1970; appeared at Royal Court, Mermaid and Bankside Globe, 1973; Oh Kay, Westminster, 1974; Donkey's Years, Globe, 1977; Hay Fever, Lyric, Hammersmith, 1980; Out of Order, Far and Middle East tour, 1995; Plenty, Albery, 1999; Pride and Prejudice, UK tour, 2000; The Circle, UK tour, 2002; Ying Tong, New Ambassadors, 2005; An English Tragedy, Palace Th., Watford, 2008; Balmoral, UK tour, 2009; Artist Descending a Staircase, Old Red Lion, 2009; *films include:* Privilege, 1967; Oh What a Lovely War!, 1967; The Breaking of Bumbo, 1970; Young Winston, 1971; The Stud, 1976; Quadrophenia, 1978; Sir Henry at Rawlinson's End, 1979; Chanel Solitaire, 1980; High Road to China, 1982; Give my Regards to Broad Street, 1983; Taffin, 1987; A Fish called Wanda, 1989; The Madness of King George, 1994; Regeneration, 1996; Don't Go Breaking My Heart, 1997; Whatever Happened to Harold Smith?, 1999; Lagaan, 2000; Laissez Passer, South Kensington, 2001; Wimbledon, Separate Lies, 2003; Porter, 2010; The Iron Lady, 2011; *television includes:* 'Tis Pity She's a Whore; Diana, Her True Story; Falklands Play, 2002; *series:* Father, Dear Father, Edward and Mrs Simpson, The Jewel in the Crown, Bergerac, The Glittering Prizes, Wings, Fairly Secret Army, Oxbridge Blues, Edge of Darkness, First Among Equals, Game, Set and Match, Lovejoy, Perfect Scoundrels, Gravy Train Goes East, Headhunters, Harnessing Peacocks, Sharpe's Enemy, Frank Stubbs Promotes, A Dance to the Music of Time, Mosley, A Touch of Frost, Love in a Cold Climate, Doc Marten, Midsomer Murders, Judge John Deed, Amnesia, East Enders, Doctors. *Heir: s* Coles John Alexander Child, *b* 10 May 1982. *Club:* Garrick.

CHILD, Denis Marsden, CBE 1987; Director, Eurotunnel plc, 1985–98; *b* 1 Nov. 1926; *s* of late Percival Snowden Child and Alice Child (*née* Jackson); *m* 1973, Patricia Charlton; two *s* one *d* by previous marr. *Educ:* Woodhouse Grove Sch., Bradford. Joined Westminster Bank, Leeds, 1942; RN, 1944–48; rejoined Westminster Bank; National Westminster Bank: Asst Area Manager, Leeds, 1970; Area Manager, Wembley, 1972; Chief Manager, Planning and Marketing, 1975; Head, Management Inf. and Control, 1977; Gen. Manager, Financial Control Div., 1979; Dir, NatWest Bank, 1982–96; Dep. Gp Chief Exec., 1982–87; Dir, Coutts & Co., 1982–97; Chm., Lombard North Central, 1991–96. Chairman: Exec. Cttee, BBA, 1986–87; Council, Assoc. for Payment Clearing Services, 1985–86; Financial Markets Cttee, Fedn Bancaire, EC, 1985–87; Director: Internat. Commodities Clearing House, 1982–86 (Chm., 1990–93); Investors Compensation Scheme Ltd, 1988–92. Bd Mem., CAA, 1986–90. Mem., IBM UK Pensions Trust, 1984–97 (Chm., 1994–97). Member: Accounting Standards Cttee, 1985–90; Securities and Investments Bd, 1986–92. FCIB; FCIS. *Recreations:* golf, gardening. *Address:* Fairways, Park Road, Farnham Royal, Bucks SL2 3BQ. *T:* (01753) 648096. *Club:* Stoke Park Golf.

CHILD, Sir Jeremy; *see* Child, Sir C. J. J.

CHILD, Prof. John, FBA 2006; Professor of Management, University of Plymouth, since 2012; Professor of Commerce, University of Birmingham, 2000–09 and since 2013; *b* 10 Nov. 1940; *s* of late Clifton James Child, OBE and Hilde Child (*née* Hurwitz); *m* 1965, Elizabeth Anne Mitchiner; one *s* one *d*. *Educ:* St John's College, Cambridge (scholar; MA, PhD, ScD). Rolls-Royce, 1965–66; Aston Univ., 1966–68; London Business Sch., 1968–73; Prof. of Organizational Behaviour, Aston Univ., 1973–91 (Dean, Aston Business Sch., 1986–89); Dean and Dir, China-Europe Management Inst., Beijing, 1989–90; Diageo Prof. of Mgt Studies, Univ. of Cambridge, and Fellow of St John's Coll., Cambridge, 1991–2000. Vis. Fellow, Nuffield Coll., Oxford, 1973–78; Visiting Professor: Univ. of Hong Kong, 1998–2000; Lingnan Coll., Sun Yat-Sen Univ., Guangzhou, China, 2012–. Editor-in-Chief, Organization Studies, 1992–96. Hon. Dr: Helsinki Sch. of Econs, 1996; Corvinus, Budapest, 2009; DLit Aston, 2013. *Publications:* British Management Thought, 1969; The Business Enterprise in Modern Industrial Society, 1969; Organization, 1977; (jtly) Lost Managers, 1982; (ed) Reform Policy and the Chinese Enterprise, 1990; (jtly) Reshaping Work, 1990; (jtly) New Technology in European Services, 1990; Management in China, 1994; (jtly) Co-operative Strategy, 1998, 2nd edn 2005; (jtly) The Management of International Acquisitions, 2001; Organization, 2005, 2nd edn 2015; (jtly) Corporate Co-evolution, 2008 (George R. Terry Award, Acad. of Mgt, 2009); (ed) The Evolution of Organizations, 2012; (ed) Knowledge and the Study of Organization and Management, 2013; (jtly) The Dynamics of Corporate Co-evolution, 2013; numerous contribs to learned jls. *Recreations:* sailing, mountain walking, bridge. *Address:* Birmingham Business School, University House, University of Birmingham, Birmingham B15 2TT. *T:* (0121) 414 8322. *E:* j.child@bham.ac.uk. *Club:* Earlswood Sailing.

CHILD, Prof. Mark Sheard, PhD; FRS 1989; Coulson Professor of Theoretical Chemistry, University of Oxford, 1994–2004, and Fellow of University College, Oxford, 1994–2007; *b* 17 Aug. 1937; *s* of George Child and Kathleen (*née* Stevenson); *m* 1964, Daphne Hall; one *s* two *d*. *Educ:* Pocklington Sch., Yorks; Clare Coll., Cambridge (BA, PhD). Vis. Scientist, Berkeley, California, 1962–63; Lectr in Theoretical Chem., Glasgow Univ., 1963–66; Oxford University: Lectr in Theoretical Chem., 1966–89; Aldrichian Praelector in Chemistry, Oxford Univ., 1989–92; Prof. of Chemical Dynamics, 1992–94; Fellow, St Edmund Hall, 1966–94, Emeritus Fellow, 1994–. *Publications:* Molecular Collision Theory, 1974; Semiclassical Methods with Molecular Applications, 1991, 2nd edn 2014; Theory of Molecular Rydberg States, 2011. *Recreations:* gardening, walking, local history. *Address:* 50 Ashley Drive, Swinton, Manchester M27 0AX.

CHILD VILLIERS, family name of **Earl of Jersey**.

CHILDREN, Sally-Ann; *see* Hales, S.-A.

CHILDS, Darren Michael; Chief Executive Officer, UKTV Media (formerly UKTV), since 2010; *b* Doncaster, March 1966; *s* of Alan Childs and Sonia Childs; *m* 2000, Dr Jacqueline; one *s* one *d*. *Educ:* Doncaster Grammar Sch.; Stanford Graduate Sch. of Business (Exec. Prog. in Internat. Mgt). Dir, Business Develt, Star TV, Hong Kong, 1991–98; Sen. Vice Pres., Sony Pictures Television Internat., 1998–2005; Man. Dir, Global Networks, BBC Worldwide, 2005–10. Non-exec. Dir, Antenna Gp Adv. Bd, 2014–. Mem., Angel Investor Network, London Business Sch. Enterprise 100, 2013–. Mem., BAFTA, 2011–. *Recreations:* TV (of course), Rugby, technology, cycling. *Address:* UKTV Media, 10 Hammersmith Grove, W6 7AP. *T:* (020) 3752 7658. *E:* dmc@uktv.co.uk.

CHILDS, David Robert; Managing Partner, Clifford Chance, 2006–14; *b* 28 June 1951; *s* of Robert and Gwenifer Childs; *m* 1993, Julie Meyer; two *s* one *d*. *Educ:* Sheffield Univ. (LLB); University Coll. London (LLM). Admitted solicitor, 1976; Clifford Chance: Partner, 1981–2014; Hd, Global Corporate Practice Area, 2000–05; Chief Operating Officer, 2003–06. Chm., Conduct Cttee, Financial Reporting Council, 2014–. *Recreations:* good restaurants, reading, woodland, travel.

CHILDS, Richard John Nicholas, QPM 1998; Chairman, Lincolnshire West Clinical Commissioning Group, since 2013; Director, Community Safety Consultancy Ltd, since 2003; *b* Plymouth, 20 Sept. 1954; *s* of John Peter Childs and Daphne Rosamond Childs (*née* Whiter); *m* 1984, Caroline Mary Cocks; one *s*, and one step *s* one step *d*. *Educ:* Plymouth Coll.; Open Univ. (BSc Psychol. and Stats 1996). Metropolitan Police, 1973–87; Asst Chief Constable, Sussex Police, 1987–97; Dep. Chief Constable, Crime Prevention Agency, Home Office, 1997–98; Chief Constable, Lincolnshire Police, 1998–2003. Chm., NHS Lincs, 2007–13. Member: Prison Service Pay Review Body, 2006–12; Commn for Rural Communities, 2009–13; GDC Fitness to Practise Panel, 2011–. *Recreations:* railways, book binding, travelling.

CHILDS, Robert Simon; Chairman, Hiscox Ltd, since 2013 (Chief Underwriting Officer, 2001–13); *b* Brentwood, 21 June 1951; *m* 1977, Mary; two *s* one *d*. *Educ:* Bedford Coll., Univ. of London (BA Hons Hist.). Joined Hiscox, 1986; Active Underwriter, Hiscox Lloyd's Syndicate 33, 1993–98; Chm., Hiscox USA, 1998–; CEO, Hiscox Insce Co. (Bermuda) Ltd, 2005–09. Chairman: Lloyd's War, Civil War and Financial Guarantee Sub-Cttee, 2000; Lloyd's Market Assoc., 2003–05; Mem., Council, Lloyd's, 2012–. Non-exec. Dir, HIM Capital Hldgs Ltd, 2009. Chm., Adv. Bd, Mgt Sch., Royal Holloway, Univ. of London, 2004–12. Trustee, Enham, 2010–. Chm., Bermuda Soc., 2010–. *Recreations:* sailing, tennis, golf. *Address:* Hiscox Ltd, 45 Reid Street, Hamilton, HM12, Bermuda. *T:* 2788300. *E:* lauren.kane@hiscox.com. *Club:* Royal Bermuda Yacht.

CHILLINGWORTH, Most Rev. David Robert; *see* St Andrews, Dunkeld and Dunblane, Bishop of.

CHILSTON, 4th Viscount *cr* 1911, of Boughton Malherbe; **Alastair George Akers-Douglas;** Baron Douglas of Baads, 1911; film producer; *b* 5 Sept. 1946; *s* of Ian Stanley Akers-Douglas (*d* 1952) (*g s* of 1st Viscount) and of Phyllis Rosemary (who *m* 2nd, John Anthony Cobham Shaw, MC), *d* of late Arthur David Clere Parsons; *S* cousin, 1982; *m* 1971, Juliet Anne, *d* of Lt-Col Nigel Lovett, Glos Regt; three *s*. *Educ:* Eton College; Madrid Univ. *Recreation:* sailing. *Heir: s* Hon. Oliver Ian Akers-Douglas [*b* 13 Oct. 1973; *m* 2005, Camilla Elizabeth Haldane Edwards; two *s* one *d*]. *Address:* Tichborne Cottage, Tichborne, Alresford, Hants SO24 0NA. *T:* (01962) 734010.

CHILTON, John James; jazz musician and author; *b* 16 July 1932; *s* of Thomas William Chilton and Eileen Florence (*née* Burke); *m* 1963, Teresa McDonald; two *s* one *d*. *Educ:* Yardley Gobion Sch., Northants; Claremont Sch., Kenton, Middx. Nat. Service, RAF, 1950–52. Worked in an advertising agency and for nat. newspaper before becoming professional musician, leading own band, 1958; played in a ship's orchestra, 1960; with Bruce Turner's Jump Band, 1960–63; jt-leader with Wally Fawkes, 1969–72; formed The Feetwarmers, 1972, regular accompanists for George Melly, 1972–2002. Recording, composing and arranging, 1972–. Grammy Award, USA, for best album notes, 1983; ARSC Award, USA, for best researched jazz or blues book, 1992; Jazz Writer of the Year, British Jazz award, 2000. *Publications:* Who's Who of Jazz, 1970, 5th edn 1989; Billie's Blues, 1974, 5th edn 1990; McKinney's Music, 1978; Teach Yourself Jazz, 1979, 2nd edn 1980; A Jazz Nursery, 1980; Stomp Off, Let's Go, 1983; Sidney Bechet: the wizard of jazz, 1987, 2nd edn 1996; The Song of the Hawk, 1990; Let the Good Times Roll, 1992; Who's Who of British Jazz, 1996, 2nd edn 2004; Ride, Red, Ride, 1999; Roy Eldridge: little jazz giant, 2002; Hot Jazz, Warm Feet (autobiog.), 2007; articles on jazz in books and newspapers. *Recreations:* watching cricket, soccer, collecting modern first editions.

CHILVERS, Prof. Clair Evelyn Druce, DSc; Chair, Gloucestershire Hospitals NHS Foundation Trust, since 2011; *b* 8 Feb. 1946; *d* of Air Cdre Stanley Edwin Druce Mills, CB, CBE and Joan Mary Mills (*née* James); *m* 1st, 1965, Antony Stuart Chilvers, MA, MChir, FRCS (marr. diss. 1995); one *s* one *d*; 2nd, 1998, Bill Crampin (marr. diss. 2007). *Educ:* Cheltenham Ladies' Coll.; LSE (BSc Econ); LSHTM (MSc); DSc Nottingham 1995. Scientist,

Inst. of Cancer Res., 1979–90; Prof. of Epidemiology, Med. Sch., 1990–99, now Emeritus, and Dean of Grad. Sch., 1996–99, Nottingham Univ.; Department of Health: Dir of R & D, Trent Region, NHS Exec., 1999–2002; Head of R & D, Directorate of Health and Social Care, Midlands and E of England, 2002–04; Dir, NHS R & D, Mental Health, 2004–06; Research Director: Nat. Inst. for Mental Health, 2004–06; Care Services Improvement Partnership, DoH, 2006–07; Mental Health Act Commission, 2006; Chm., Notts Healthcare NHS Trust, 2007–10. Mem., Royal Commn on Envmtl Pollution, 1994–98. Mem., Cttee on Carcinogenicity of Chemicals in Food, Consumer Products and Envmt, DoH, 1993–2000. Non-executive Director: Nottingham Community Health NHS Trust, 1991–96; Learning and Skills (formerly Further Education) Develt Agency, 1998–2001. Trustee, Lloyds TSB Foundn, 2005–10; Founder Trustee, Mental Health Res. UK, 2008–; Trustee: Centre for Mental Health, 2010–14; Barnwood Trust, 2012–. Member, Council: Nottingham Univ., 1994–99; Cheltenham Coll., 2011–; Chm. Council, Southwell Cathedral, 2000–06. MRSocMed 2011. DL Notts, 2007–10. *Publications:* numerous in learned jls, mainly in field of cancer epidemiology. *Recreations:* opera, classical music, cinema, walking, food and wine.

CHILVERS, Prof. Edwin Roy, PhD; FRCP, FRCPE; FMedSci; Professor of Respiratory Medicine, since 1998, Director, Clinical Academic Training Office, since 2009, and Deputy Head, Department of Medicine, since 2010, University of Cambridge; Fellow of St Edmund's College, Cambridge, since 1999; *b* 17 March 1959; *s* of Derek John Chilvers and Marjorie Grace Chilvers; *m* 1982, Rowena Joy Tyssen; two *s* one *d*. *Educ:* Univ. of Nottingham Med. Sch. (BMedSci 1980; BM BS Hons 1982); PhD London 1991; MA Cantab 2002. MRCP 1985, FRCP 1999; FRCPE 1995. Registrar, Ealing and Hammersmith Hosps, 1985–87; MRC Clinical Trng Fellow, 1987–90; Edinburgh University: Lectr in Respiratory Medicine, 1990–92; Wellcome Trust Sen. Res. Fellow in Clinical Sci., 1992–98; Reader in Medicine, 1997–98. Hon. Consultant Physician: Royal Infirmary, Edinburgh, 1992–98; Addenbrooke's and Papworth Hosps, 1998–. Non-exec. Dir, Papworth Hosp. NHS Trust, 2002–06. FMedSci 2007; FHEA 2007. *Publications:* (ed jtly) Davidson's Principles and Practice of Medicine, 17th edn 1995 to 19th edn 2002; contrib. scientific papers on inflammatory cell biol. and intracellular signalling. *Recreations:* wine, music, spectator sport. *Address:* 4 Mallows Close, Comberton, Cambridge CB23 7GN. *T:* (01223) 331531.

CHINERY, David John; District Judge (Magistrates' Courts), Thames Valley, since 2013; a Recorder, since 2002; *b* 10 Aug. 1950; *s* of Oliver John Chinery and Gladys Alberta Chinery; *m* 1973, Jeannette Elizabeth Owens; two *d*. *Educ:* Alleyne's Sch., Stevenage; Coll. of Law. Justices' Clerk's Asst, Hitchin Magistrates' Court, 1969–75; Asst Clerk to Justices, Northampton Magistrates' Court, 1975–79; admitted solicitor, 1979; Asst Solicitor, 1979–82, Partner, 1982–90, Borneo, Martell & Partners, Northampton; sole practitioner, 1990–98. Deputy Stipendiary Magistrate: Nottingham, 1993–98; Doncaster, 1996–98; Birmingham, 1997–98; Stipendiary Magistrate, later District Judge (Magistrates' Court), W Midlands, 1998–2013. *Recreations:* Rugby Union football, cricket, music, Victorian poetry. *Address:* Westminster Magistrates' Court, 181 Marylebone Road, NW1 5BR.

CHING, Henry, CBE 1982; Secretary General, Caritas-Hong Kong, 1990–91; *b* 2 Nov. 1933; *s* of Henry Ching, OBE and Ruby Irene Ching; *m* 1963, Eileen Frances Peters; two *d*. *Educ:* Diocesan Boys' School, Hong Kong; Hong Kong Univ. (BA Hons); Wadham Coll., Oxford (MA, DipEd). Schoolmaster, 1958–61; Hong Kong Civil Service: various appts, 1961–73; Principal Asst Financial Sec., 1973–76; Dep. Financial Sec., 1976–83; Sec. for Health and Welfare and MLC, Hong Kong, 1983–85, retired. Chief Administrator, Hong Kong Foundn, 1989. Chm., Hong Kong Volunteer and ex-POW Assoc. of NSW, 2006–10. *Recreations:* cricket, rowing. *Address:* 39 Saiala Road, East Killara, NSW 2071, Australia.

CHINKIN, Prof. Christine, PhD; FBA 2009; barrister; Professor of International Law, now Emerita, and Director, Women, Peace and Security Centre, since 2015, London School of Economics and Political Science; William W. Cook Global Law Professor, University of Michigan. *Educ:* Univ. of London (LLB 1971; LLM 1972); Yale Univ. (LLM 1981); Univ. of Sydney (PhD 1990). Mem., Law Faculty, Univ. of Sydney; Prof. and Dean, Faculty of Law, Univ. of Southampton, 1993. Called to the Bar, 2003; Member, Matrix Chambers. Visiting Professor: AHRC, Australian Nat. Univ., 2003; Columbia Univ., 2004; Dir of Studies, Internat. Law Assoc., 2004; Scholar in Residence, Amnesty Internat., 2005. Consultant on human rights and human trafficking, UN Office of High Comr of Human Rights, 2002; Expert Consultant on violence against women, UN Div. for the Advancement of Women, 2005; Mem., Kosovo Human Rights Adv. Panel, 2010–. Cert. of Merit, 2001, Goler T. Butcher Medal (jtly), 2006, Amer. Soc. of Internat. Law. *Publications:* Third Parties in International Law, 1993; (jtly) The Boundaries of International Law: a feminist analysis, 2000 (trans. Japanese, 2004); (contrib.) Halsbury's Laws of Australia, vol. 14, 1994; (jtly) Dispute Resolution in Australia, 2nd edn, 2002; (jtly) The Making of International Law, 2007. *Address:* Department of Law, London School of Economics and Political Science, Houghton Street, WC2A 2AE.

CHINN, Antony Nigel Caton; QC 2003; a Recorder, since 2000; *b* 20 May 1949; *s* of Edward William Chinn and Barbara Ursula Neene Chinn (*née* Tilbury); *m* 1973, Margot Susan Elizabeth Emery; two *s*. *Educ:* Ardingly Coll.; Inns of Court Sch. of Law. Called to the Bar, Middle Temple, 1972; in practice, specialising in criminal law; Asst Recorder, 1996–2000. *Recreations:* motor sport, football, music. *Address:* 9 Bedford Row, WC1R 4AZ. *T:* (020) 7489 2727, *Fax:* (020) 7489 2828. *Club:* Goodwood Road Racing.

CHINN, Susan Avril, (Lady Chinn), CBE 2012; *b* Cobham, 4 April 1943; *d* of late Louis Speelman and of Meryl Speelman; *m* 1965, Sir Trevor Edwin Chinn, *qv*; two *s*. *Educ:* The Warren, Worthing. PR Consultant, 1983–95. Mem. Bd, 2005–15, and Chm., Develt Council, 2003–, RNT. Vice Chm., Royal Marsden Cancer Appeal, 1990–93. Special Trustee, Gt Ormond St Hosp. for Sick Children, 1990–2000; Trustee: Child Psychotherapy Trust, 1993–96; Kids Company, 2009–13; The Silverline, 2012–. JP Inner London, 1980–2009. *Recreations:* theatre, gardening, fly fishing. *E:* susan@chinn.com.

CHINN, Sir Trevor (Edwin), Kt 1990; CVO 1989; Senior Adviser, CVC Capital Partners, since 2002; *b* 24 July 1935; *s* of late Rosser and Susie Chinn; *m* 1965, Susan Avril Speelman (*see* S. A. Chinn); two *s*. *Educ:* Clifton Coll.; King's Coll., Cambridge. Lex Service, subseq. RAC plc: Dir, 1959–2003; Man. Dir, 1968–73; Chief Exec., 1973–96; Chm., 1973–2003; Chm., Kwik-Fit, 2002–05; Chm., AA, 2004–07. Chairman: ITIS, 2000–11; Streetcar Ltd, 2007–11; Tesco Cars, 2010–12; Tusker, 2011–. Vice-Chm., Commn for Integrated Transport, 1999–2004; Chm., Motorists' Forum, 2000–10. Chm., Mayor's Fund for London, 2008–11. Pres., United Jewish Israel Appeal, 1993–; Mem., Exec. Cttee, Jewish Leadership Council, 2006–; Vice Pres., Jewish Assoc. for Business Ethics, 1995–2011; Pres., Norwood Ravenswood, subseq. Norwood, 1996–2006; Vice Chm., Wishing Well Appeal, Gt Ormond St Hosp. for Sick Children, 1985–89. Vice Chm., Hampstead Th., 1990–2004. Trustee, Royal Acad. Trust, 1989–2004 (Dep. Chm., 1996–2004). Trustee, Duke of Edinburgh's Award, 1978–88. Freeman of the City of London. Chief Barker, Variety Club of GB, 1977, 1978. *Recreations:* fishing, theatre, antique glass and maps. *Address:* 14 Basil Street, SW3 1AJ. *T:* (020) 7868 8836. *Clubs:* Garrick, Royal Automobile.

CHINNERY, Prof. Patrick Francis, PhD; FRCP, FRCPath, FMedSci; Professor of Neurology and Head, Department of Clinical Neurosciences, University of Cambridge, since 2015; *b* Leeds, 11 Feb. 1968; *s* of late Brendan Chinnery and of Mary Chinnery; *m* 1991, Rachel Mary Kean; one *s* three *d*. *Educ:* Univ. of Newcastle (BMedSci 1st Cl. Hons 1989; MB BS Hons 1992; PhD 2000); Specialist Training Authy (Cert. of Completion of Higher Specialist Trng Neurol. 2002). MRCP 1995, FRCP 2006; MRCPath 2001, FRCPath 2001. House Physician, Royal Victoria Infirmary, Newcastle upon Tyne, 1992–93; SHC Newcastle Teaching Hosps, 1993–95; University of Newcastle upon Tyne, later Newcastl University: Wellcome Clinical Res. Trng Fellow, 1995–98; Wellcome Advanced Clinica Res. Fellow, 1998–2000; Clinical Lectr in Neurol., 2000–02; Sen. Lectr in Neurogenetics 2002–04; Prof. of Neurogenetics, 2004–15; Dir, Inst. of Human Genetics, then Inst. c Genetic Medicine, 2010–15; Wellcome Trust Sen. Fellow in Clinical Sci., 2003–15; Publi Orator, 2007–13; Specialist Registrar in Neurol., Northern Region, 1997–2002; Newcastl Hospitals NHS Foundation Trust: Hon. Consultant Neurologist, 2002–; Dir, NIHI Biomedical Res. Centre, 2008–. Sen. Investigator, NIHR, 2010. FMedSci 2009; Fellow American Neurol Assoc., 2011. Foulkes Foundn Medal, Acad. of Med. Scis, 2011. Associat Ed., Brain: a Jl of Neurology, 2004–13. *Publications:* over 400 articles in medical and scientifi jls incl. Lancet and Nature Genetics. *Recreations:* fell running, flute. *Address:* MRC Mitochondrial Biology Unit, Wellcome Trust/MRC Building, Cambridge Biomedica Campus, Hills Road, Cambridge CB2 0XY.

CHINUBHAI, Sir Prashant, 4th Bt *cr* 1913, of Shahpur, Ahmedabad, India; *b* 15 Dec. 1955 *o s* of Sir Udayan Chinubhai (formerly Ranchhodlal), 3rd Bt and of Muneera Khodada Fozdar; *S* father, 2006, but his name does not appear on the Official Roll of the Baronetage *m* 1977, Swati Hrishikesh Mehta; three *d*. *Heir: uncle* Kirtidev Chinubhai [*b* 15 March 1932 *m* 1967, Meera Ratilal Nanavati]. *Address:* Chinubhai House, Lal Darwaja, Ahmedaba 380001, India.

CHIPMAN, Dr John Miguel Warwick, CMG 1999; Director General and Chief Executive The International Institute for Strategic Studies, since 1993; Director, IISS-US and IISS-Asia since 2001; *b* 10 Feb. 1957; *s* of Lawrence Carroll Chipman and Maria Isabel (*née* Prados); *m* 1997, Lady Theresa Helen Margaret Manners, *yr d* of 10th Duke of Rutland, CBE; twin *s* *Educ:* Harvard Coll. (BA Hons); London Sch. of Economics (MA Dist.); Balliol Coll., Oxford (MPhil, DPhil). Research Associate: IISS, 1983–84; Atlantic Inst. for Internat. Affairs, Paris 1985–87; The International Institute for Strategic Studies: Asst Dir for Regl Security 1987–90; Dir of Studies, 1990–93. Mem., Internat. Adv. Bd, Reliance Industries Lt (Mumbai), 2006– (Special Advr to Chm.); Mem., Bd of Dirs, Abraaj Capital (Dubai) Founder, Strategic Comments jl, 1995. *Publications:* Vième République et Défense d l'Afrique, 1986; (ed and jt author) NATO's Southern Allies, 1988; French Power in Africa 1989; numerous contribs to edited vols, learned jls and newspapers. *Recreations:* tennis, ski-ing scuba diving, riding, collecting travel books. *Address:* The International Institute for Strategi Studies, Arundel House, 13–15 Arundel Street, Temple Place, WC2R 3DX. *T:* (020 7379 7676. *Clubs:* Brooks's, Beefsteak, Garrick, White's; Harvard (New York).

CHIPPERFIELD, Sir David (Alan), Kt 2010; CBE 2004; RDI 2006; RA 2007; RIBA Principal, David Chipperfield Architects, since 1984; *b* 18 Dec. 1953; *s* of Alan John Chipperfield and Peggy Chipperfield (*née* Singleton); partner, Dr Evelyn Stern; two *s* one *d* and one *s* from previous relationship. *Educ:* Wellington Sch., Somerset; Kingston Poly. Architectural Assoc. (AA Dip). RIBA 1982. Designer, Douglas Stephens & Partners, 1977–78 Architect, Richard Rogers & Partners, 1978–79; Project Architect, Foster Associates 1981–84. Projects include: Toyota Auto, Kyoto, Japan, 1990; Gotoh Museum, Chiba, Japan 1991; Matsumoto Corp. HQ, Okayama, Japan, 1992; Joseph Menswear, London, 1996 River and Rowing Mus., Henley-on-Thames, 1997 (Best Building in England, RFAC Trust BSkyB Bldg of the Year Award, 1999); Ernsting Service Center, Coesfeld-Lette, Germany 1998; Bryant Park Hotel, NY, 2001; Gormley Studio, London, 2003; Private House, NY 2004; Housing Villaverde, Madrid, 2005; Figge Art Mus., Davenport, 2005; Hotel Puert America, Madrid, 2005; Mus. of Modern Lit., Marbach am Neckar, Germany, 2006 (RIBA Stirling Prize, 2007); Des Moines Public Liby, Iowa, 2006; America's Cup Bldg, Valencia 2006; BBC Scotland, Glasgow, 2006; Liangzhu Culture Mus., China, 2007; Empire Riversid Hotel, Hamburg, 2007; Gall. 'Am Kupfergraben 10', Berlin, 2007; Rena Lange HQ, Munich 2007; Ninetree Village, Hangzhou, China, 2008; Kivik Pavilion, Kivik, Sweden, 2008; Neue Museum, Berlin, 2009; City of Justice, Barcelona, 2009; Anchorage Mus. at Rasmuso Center, Alaska, 2009; Mus. Folkwang, Essen, 2010; Kaufhaus Tyrol Dept Store, Innsbruck 2010; Lab. Bldg, Basel, 2010; Rockbund Art Mus., Shanghai, 2010; Turner Contemp Margate, 2011; Hepworth Wakefield, 2011. Founder and Dir, 9H Gall., London. Design Tutor, RCA, 1988–89; Prof. of Architecture, Staatliche Akad. der Bildenden Künste Stuttgart, 1995–2000; Mies van der Rohe Chair, Escuela Técnica, Barcelona, 2001; Visitin Professor: Harvard Univ., 1987–88; Graz Univ., 1992; Naples Univ., 1992; Ecol Polytechnique, Lausanne, 1993–94. Trustee, Architecture Foundn, 1992–97. Awards include Andrea Palladio Prize, 1993; Tessenow Gold Medal, 1999; RIBA Award, 1998, 1999, 2002 2003, 2004, 2007, 2008, 2009, 2010; Tessenow Gold Medal, 1999; Civic Trust Award, 1999 Royal Gold Medal, RIBA, 2011; Praemium Imperiale (Japan), 2013. Order of Meri (Germany), 2009. *Publications:* Theoretical Practice, 1994; *relevant publications:* El Croqui (monograph), 1998, 2001, 2004, 2006, 2010; David Chipperfield, Architectural Work 1990–2002, 2003; David Chipperfield, Idea e Realta, 2005; David Chipperfield 1984–2009 2009; David Chipperfield Architects: form matters, 2009; Neues Museum Berlin, 2009 *Recreations:* reading, drawing, swimming. *Address:* (office) 11 York Road, SE1 7NX. *T:* (020 7620 4800. *Club:* Royal Automobile.

CHIPPERFIELD, Sir Geoffrey (Howes), KCB 1992 (CB 1985); Deputy Chairman 2000–03, and Director, 1993–2003, Pennon Group (formerly South West Water plc); *b* 2 April 1933; *s* of Nelson Chipperfield and Eleanor Chipperfield; *m* 1959, Gillian James; two *s* *Educ:* Cranleigh; New Coll., Oxford. Called to the Bar, Gray's Inn, 1955. Joined Min. c Housing and Local Govt, 1956; Harkness Fellow, Inst. of Govtl Studies, Univ. of Calif Berkeley, 1962–63; Principal Private Sec., Minister of Housing, 1968–70; Sec., Greate London Develt Plan Inquiry, 1970–73; Under Sec., 1976, Dep. Sec., 1982–87, DoE; Dep Sec., Dept of Energy, 1987–89; Perm. Under-Sec. of State, Dept of Energy, 1989–91; Perm Sec. and Chief Exec., PSA Services, 1991–93. Chm., Heliodynamics Ltd, 2000–. Chairman DTI Energy Adv. Panel, 1996–2001; British Cement Assoc., 1996–2001. Pro-Chancellor Univ. of Kent, 1998–2005. Mem. Council, Foundn of Sci. and Technol., 2005–. *Recreations* reading, gardening. *Clubs:* Oxford and Cambridge, Athenæum.

CHIPPINDALE, Christopher Ralph, PhD; Reader in Archaeology, University c Cambridge, at University Museum of Archaeology and Anthropology, 2001–13; *b* 13 Oct 1951; *s* of Keith and Ruth Chippindale; *m* 1976, Anne Lowe (marr. diss. 2008); two *s* two *d* civil partnership 2008, Justice Oleka. *Educ:* Sedbergh School; St John's College, Cambridg (BA Hons); Girton Coll., Cambridge (PhD). MCIfA; FSA. Editor, freelance, Penguin Books Hutchinson Publishing Group, 1974–82; Res. Fellow in Archaeology, 1985–88, Bye-Fellow 1988–91, Girton Coll., Cambridge; Asst Curator, 1988–93, Sen. Asst Curator, 1993–2013 Cambridge Univ. Mus. of Archaeol. Vis. Prof., Univ. of Witwatersrand, 2002–11. Editor Antiquity, 1987–97. *Publications:* Stonehenge Complete, 1983, 4th edn 2012; (ed jtly) Th Pastmasters, 1989; (jtly) Who owns Stonehenge?, 1990; A High Way to Heaven, 1998; (e jtly) The Archaeology of Rock Art, 1999; (ed jtly) Landscapes of European Rock-art, 2002 articles in jls. *Recreations:* gardening, taking things easier, worrying. *Address:* 46 High Street Chesterton, Cambridge CB4 1NG.

CHIPPING, Hilary Jane; Head of Infrastructure, South East Midlands Local Enterpris Partnership, since 2013; *b* 31 Jan. 1955; *d* of late Clarence John Watts and Alice Mary Watts *m* 1975, Richard Frank Chipping; one *s* one *d*. *Educ:* Bletchley Grammar Sch.; Univ. c Manchester (BA (Econ) 1975, MA (Econ) 1977). Joined Civil Service, 1977; Head: Loca Govt Finance Div., 1990–94, Water Services Div., 1994–95, DoE; Local Authy Housing Div., DETR, 1995–2000; Roads Policy Div., DTLR, 2000–01; Dir, Network Strategy

Highways Agency, 2001–07; Dir, mksm Inter-Regional Bd, 2008–11; Consultant, Hilary Chipping Consulting Ltd, 2011–. *Recreations:* walking, cookery.

CHIRAC, Jacques René; Grand Croix de la Légion d'Honneur; Grand Croix de l'Ordre National du Mérite; President of the French Republic, 1995–2007; Member, Constitutional Council of France, since 2007; *b* Paris, 29 Nov. 1932; *s* of François Chirac, company manager and Marie-Louise (*née* Valette); *m* 1956, Bernadette Chodron de Courcel; two *d*. *Educ:* Lycée Carnot and Lycée Louis-le-Grand, Paris; Diploma of Inst. of Polit. Studies, Paris, and of Summer Sch., Harvard Univ., USA. Served Army in Algeria. Ecole Nat. d'Admin, 1957–59; Auditor, Cour des Comptes, 1959; Head Dept: Sec.-Gen. of Govt, 1962; Private Office of Georges Pompidou, 1962–67; Counsellor, Cour des Comptes, 1965; State Secretary: Employment Problems, 1967–68; Economy and Finance, 1968–71; Minister for Parly Relations, 1971–72; Minister for Agriculture and Rural Development, 1972–74; Home Minister, March–May 1974; Prime Minister, 1974–76 and 1986–88. Deputy from Corrèze, elected 1967, 1968, 1973, 1976 (UDR), 1978 (RPR), 1981, 1986, 1988 and 1993; Sec.-Gen., UDR, Dec. 1974–June 1975; Pres., Rassemblement pour la République, 1976–81 and 1982–94. Mayor of Paris, 1977–95. Member from Meymac, Conseil Général of Corrèze, 1968–88, Pres. 1970–79. Mem., European Parlt, 1979–80. Treasurer, Claude Pompidou Foundn (charity for elderly and for handicapped children), 1969–. Founder, Jacques Chirac Foundation for Sustainable Develt and Cultural Dialogue, 2008. Croix de la valeur militaire; Chevalier du Mérite agricole, des Arts et des Lettres, de l'Etoile noire, du Mérite sportif, du Mérite touristique; Médaille de l'Aéronautique. *Publications:* a thesis on development of Port of New Orleans, 1954; Discours pour la France à l'heure du choix, 1978; La lueur de l'espérance: réflexion du soir pour le matin, 1978; Une Nouvelle France, 1994; La France pour Tous, 1995; Chaque pas doit être un but (memoir), 2009. *Address:* Constitutional Council, 2 rue de Montpensier, 75001 Paris, France.

CHISHOLM, family name of **Baroness Chisholm of Owlpen**.

CHISHOLM OF OWLPEN, Baroness *cr* 2014 (Life Peer), of Owlpen in the County of Gloucestershire; **Hon. Caroline Elizabeth Chisholm;** a Baroness in Waiting (Government Whip), since 2015; *b* 23 Dec. 1951; *d* of 1st Baron Egremont, MBE; *m* 1976, Colin Chisholm; two *s* one *d*. Co-Chm., Conservatives Candidates Committee. Trustee, Nat. Osteoporosis Soc.

CHISHOLM, Alex; Chief Executive, Competition and Markets Authority, since 2013; *b* London, 2 Jan. 1968; *s* of late Duncan Chisholm and of Annabelle Chisholm; *m* 1993, Eliza Pakenham; three *s*. *Educ:* Downside Sch., Som; Merton Coll., Oxford (BA Hist.); INSEAD, Fontainebleau (MBA). Civil Servant, DTI and OFT, 1990–97; Sen. Exec., media, technol. and services businesses, 1997–2007; Chm. and Mem., Commn for Communication Regulation, 2007–13. Trustee, Breadline Africa, 2003–. *Recreations:* travel, history, gardening, cycling. *Address:* Competition and Markets Authority, Victoria House, Southampton Row, WC1B 4AD.

CHISHOLM, Catherine Alexandra, (Kitty), (Lady Chisholm); Consultant and coach, since 2007; *b* 19 April 1946; *d* of Gregory Panas and Aleca Panas, Athens; *m* 1969, Sir John Alexander Raymond Chisholm, *qv*; one *s* one *d*. *Educ:* Girton Coll., Cambridge (BA 1969); Open Univ. (BSc 2001); Henley Business Sch. (MSc Coaching and Behavioural Change 2012). Open University: Res. Asst in Classics, 1976–82; Course Co-ordinator in Contg Educn, 1982–83; Adminr, Sci. and Technol. Updating, 1983–89; Business Develt Manager, 1989–91; Dir of Develt, 1991–2002; Dir of Develt, Brunel Univ., 2003–07. Dir, Boardwalk Leadership, 2012–. Member: Bd, British Telecom Acad., 2000–02; Borderless Educn Observatory Bd, 2001–10; Adv. Bd, Vosper Thorneycroft Educn Services, 2003–06; Adv. Bd, JRBH Strategy Mgt, 2007–13; Adv. Bd, Magna Carta Inst., 2010–; Chair, Adv. Bd, RHUL, 2012–. Trustee: CASE Europe, 1995–2001 (Chm., 1998–2001); Reach, 2003–11 (Dep. Chm., 2009–11; Chm., 2011); Nat. Mus. of Sci. and Industry, 2007–15. FRSA 2000. *Publications:* Political and Social Life in the Great Age of Athens, 1978; Rome, the Augustan Age, 1981; (jtly) Neuroscience for Leadership: harnessing the brain gain advantage, 2015; contrib. IEDP Developing Leaders. *Recreations:* pink roses, reading, grandchildren, classic car race photography. *Club:* Reform.

CHISHOLM, Sir John (Alexander Raymond), Kt 1999; FREng; Chairman: Medical Research Council, 2006–12; Nesta, since 2012; Genomics England, since 2013; *b* 27 Aug. 1946; *s* of Ruari Ian Lambert Chisholm and Pamela Harland Chisholm; *m* 1969, Catherine Alexandra (*née* Pana) (*see* C. A. Chisholm); one *s* one *d*. *Educ:* Queens' Coll., Cambridge (BA 1968). CEng 1974, FREng (FEng 1996); FIET (FIEE 1995); FRAeS 1996; FInstP 1999. Vauxhall Motors, 1964–69; Scicon Ltd, 1969–79; Cap Scientific Ltd, 1979–91: Man. Dir, 1981–86; Chm., 1986–91; Chm., Yard Ltd, 1986–91; UK Man. Dir, Sema Group plc, 1988–91; Chief Executive: DRA, subseq. DERA, 1991–2001; QinetiQ plc, 2001–05; Chm., QinetiQ Group plc, 2005–10. Chm., NESTA, 2009–12. Non-executive Director: Expro Internat. plc, 1994–2003; Bespak plc, 1999–2005. Mem., UK Foresight Steering Gp, 1993–2000. President: Electronic and Business Equipment Assoc., 1989–90; IEE, 2005–06; IET, 2006. Mem. Council, Cranfield Univ., 1995–2002. *Recreations:* participative sports, old cars. *Address:* Batchworth Hill House, London Road, Rickmansworth WD3 1JS.

CHISHOLM, John William, CBE 2000; FRCGP; Director, Concordia Health Ltd, since 2006; Adviser, NHS Working in Partnership Programme, since 2005; *b* 29 Dec. 1950; *s* of late William Chisholm and of Olive Chisholm (*née* Tomlinson); *m* 1977, Caroline Mary Colyer (*née* Davis) (marr. diss. 2006); two *d*, and one step *s*; partner, Prof. Ann Marie Sommerville (*née* Pryal). *Educ:* Clifton Coll. Prep. Sch.; Clifton Coll.; Peterhouse, Cambridge (exhibnr; BA 1971, BChir 1974, MB 1975); Westminster Med. Sch. DRCOG 1977; MRCGP 1978, FRCGP 1995. House surgeon, 1974–75, house physician, 1975, Croydon Gen. Hosp.; GP trainee, Reading Vocational Trng Scheme, 1976–79; GP, Twyford, 1979–2004. Member Board: DPP 2000, 2004–; BMJ Pubns Gp, 2002–04. Member: Jt Cttee on Postgrad. Trng for Gen. Practice, 1980–90, 1995–2005; Supervisory Bd, NHS Centre for Coding and Classification, 1990–97; Standing Med. Adv. Cttee, 1998–2005; Partners' Council, NICE, 1998–2001; Expert Patients Task Force, 1999–2000; Patient Care (Empowerment) Modernisation Action Team, 2000; NHS IT Task Force, 2002–04; Primary Care Task Gp, 2003; Nat. Primary Care Develt Team Adv. Bd, 2004–06. Observer, Clinical Standards Adv. Gp, 1993–96. Mem., GMC, 1999–2003 (Mem., Standards Cttee, 1999–2002); British Medical Association: Chm., Junior Members Forum, 1981–82; Mem. Council, 1981–82, 1988–; Member: Finance Cttee, 2002–06, 2007–; Med. Ethics Cttee, 2004– (Dep. Chm., 2007–); Gen. Med. Services Cttee, subseq. GPs Cttee, 1977– (Negotiator, 1990–97; Jt Dep. Chm., 1991–97; Chm., 1997–2004; Chairman: Trainees Subcttee, 1978–80; Jt (with RCGP) Computing Gp, 1984–86; Practice Orgn Subcttee, 1986–90; Nurse Prescribing Wkg Gp, 1988–89); Mem. Council, RCGP, 2005– (Observer, 2004–05). Chairman: Gen. Med. Services Defence Fund, 1997–2001; Gen. Practitioners Defence Fund, 2001–04. Observer, Acad. of Med. Royal Colls, 2002–04. Rep., European Union of GPs (UEMO), 1988–2004. Patron, Men's Health Forum, 2004–. *Publications:* (ed jtly) Micros in Practice: report of an appraisal of GP microcomputer systems, 1986; (ed) Making Sense of the Red Book, 1989, (with N. D. Ellis) 2nd edn 1993, 3rd edn 1997; (ed) Making Sense of the New Contract, 1990; (ed) Making Sense of the Cost Rent Scheme, 1992; articles esp. concerning gen. practice orgn. *Recreations:* reading, art, photography, music (former amateur flautist, singer, conductor). *Address:* 5 Elmers End Road, Anerley, SE20 7ST. *T:* (020) 8778 2550. *E:* john.chisholm@john-chisholm.demon.co.uk, john.chisholm@concordiahealth.co.uk.

CHISHOLM, Kitty; *see* Chisholm, C. A.

CHISHOLM, Malcolm George Richardson; Member (Lab) Edinburgh Northern and Leith, Scottish Parliament, since 2011 (Edinburgh North and Leith, 1999–2011); *b* 7 March 1949; *s* of late George and Olive Chisholm; *m* 1975, Janet Broomfield, writer; two *s* one *d*. *Educ:* George Watson's Coll.; Edinburgh Univ. (MA Hons, Dip Ed). Formerly Teacher of English, Castlebrae High School and Broughton High School. MP (Lab) Edinburgh, Leith, 1992–97, Edinburgh North and Leith, 1997–2001. Parly Under-Sec. of State, Scottish Office, 1997. Scottish Executive: Dep. Minister, 2000–01, Minister, 2001–04, for Health and Community Care; Minister for Communities, 2004–06. *Recreations:* cinema, swimming, literature. *Address:* Scottish Parliament, Edinburgh EH99 1SP. *T:* (0131) 558 8358.

CHISHOLM, Prof. Malcolm Harold, FRS 1990; Distinguished University Professor and Chair, Department of Chemistry, Ohio State University, since 2000; *b* 15 Oct. 1945; *s* of Angus and Gweneth Chisholm; *m* 1st, 1969, Susan Sage (marr. diss.); one *s*; 2nd, 1982, Cynthia Brown; two *s*. *Educ:* London Univ. (BSc 1966; PhD 1969). Sessional Lectr, Univ. of W Ontario, 1970–72; Asst Prof. of Chemistry, Princeton Univ., 1972–78; Indiana University: Associate Prof., 1978–80; Prof., 1980–85; Distinguished Prof. of Chemistry, 1985–99. Guggenheim Fellow, 1985–86. Editor, Polyhedron, 1983–98; Associate Editor: Dalton Trans., 1988–2003; Chemical Communications, 1995–99. FAAAS 1987; FRSE 2005; Fellow: Amer. Acad. Arts and Scis, 2004; German Acad. of Scis Leopoldina, 2005; Amer. Chem. Soc., 2009; MNAS, 2005. Hon. DSc: London, 1980; Western Ontario, 2008. RSC Award for Chem. and Electrochem. of Transition Elements, 1987; Alexander von Humboldt Sen. Scientist Award, 1988; (jtly) ACS Nobel Laureate Signature Award, 1988; ACS Award in Inorganic Chm., 1989; Centenary Medal and Lectr, RSC, 1995; ACS Distinguished Service to Inorganic Chemistry, 1999; Davy Medal, Royal Soc., 1999; Ludwig Mond Medal and Lectr, RSC, 2000; Basolo Medal, Northwestern Univ., Chicago, 2004; Bailar Medal, 2006; Nyholm Prize, RSC, 2010. *Publications:* Reactivity of Metal-Metal Bonds, 1982; Inorganic Chemistry: towards the 21st century, 1983; Early Transition Metal Clusters with π-Donor Ligands, 1995; numerous articles, mostly in chem. jls. *Recreations:* squash, gardening. *Address:* 100 Kenyon Brook Drive, Worthington, OH 43085, USA. *T:* (614) 9850942; 38 Norwich Street, Cambridge CB2 1NE. *T:* (01223) 312824.

CHISHOLM, Prof. Michael Donald Inglis, FBA 2002; Professor of Geography, University of Cambridge, 1976–96, now Emeritus; Professorial Fellow, St Catharine's College, Cambridge, 1976–96; *b* 10 June 1931; *s* of M. S. and A. W. Chisholm; *m* 1st, 1959, Edith Gretchen Emma (*née* Hoof) (marr. diss. 1981); one *s* two *d*; 2nd, 1986, Judith Carola Shackleton (*née* Murray). *Educ:* St Christopher Sch., Letchworth; St Catharine's Coll., Cambridge (MA; ScD 1996). Nat. Service Commn, RE, 1950–51. Deptl Demonstrator, Inst. for Agric. Econs, Oxford, 1954–59; Asst Lectr, then Lectr in Geog., Bedford Coll., London, 1960–64; Vis. Sen. Lectr in Geog., Univ. of Ibadan, 1964–65; Lectr, then Reader in Geog., Univ. of Bristol, 1965–72; Prof. of Economic and Social Geography, Univ. of Bristol, 1972–76. Associate, Economic Associates Ltd, consultants, 1965–77. Geography Editor for Hutchinson Univ. Lib., 1973–82. Mem. SSRC, and Chm. of Cttees for Human Geography and Planning, 1967–72; Member: Local Govt Boundary Commn for England, 1971–78; Rural Develt Commn, 1981–90; English Adv. Cttee on Telecommunications, 1990–92; Local Govt Commn for England, 1992–95. Mem. Council, IBG, 1961 and 1962 (Jun. Vice-Pres., 1977; Sen. Vice-Pres., 1978; Pres. 1979). Conservator of River Cam, 1979–2007 (Chm., 1991–2007); Bd Mem., Cambridge Preservation Soc., 2000–08; Vice-Chm., Cambs ACRE, 2001–02. Hon. Sec., Spalding Gentlemen's Soc., 2013–. Gill Memorial Prize, RGS, 1969. *Publications:* Rural Settlement and Land Use: an essay in location, 1962; Geography and Economics, 1966; (ed jtly) Regional Forecasting, 1971; (ed jtly) Spatial Policy Problems of the British Economy, 1971; Research in Human Geography, 1971; (ed) Resources for Britain's Future, 1972; (jtly) Freight Flows and Spatial Aspects of the British Economy, 1973; (jtly) The Changing Pattern of Employment, 1973; (ed jtly) Studies in Human Geography, 1973; (ed jtly) Processes in Physical and Human Geography: Bristol Essays, 1975; Human Geography: Evolution or Revolution?, 1975; Modern World Development, 1982; Regions in Recession and Resurgence, 1990; (ed jtly) Shared Space: Divided Space, 1990; Britain on the Edge of Europe, 1995; (ed jtly) A Fresh Start for Local Government, 1997; Structural Reform of British Local Government: rhetoric and reality, 2000; (jtly) Botched Business: the damaging process of reorganising local government 2006–2008, 2008; In the Shadow of the Abbey: Crowland, 2013; papers in Farm Economist, Oxford Econ. Papers, Trans Inst. British Geographers, Geography, Geographical Jl, Applied Statistics, Area, Envmt and Planning, Jl of Local Govt Law, Jl of Histl Geography, Proceedings of Cambridge Antiquarian Soc., etc. *Recreations:* gardening, theatre, opera, interior design. *Address:* 5 Clarendon Road, Cambridge CB2 8BH.

CHISHOLM, (Peter) Nicolas, MBE 2011; Headmaster, Yehudi Menuhin School, 1988–2010; *b* 7 Dec. 1949; *s* of David Whitridge Chisholm and Marjorie Chisholm; *m* 1977, Auriol Mary Oakeley. *Educ:* Christ's Hospital, Horsham; St John's Coll., Cambridge (MA). Tenor Lay Vicar, Chichester Cathedral, 1972–76; Asst Master, Prebendal Sch., Chichester, 1972–76; Hurstpierpoint College: Hd Classics, 1976–88; Housemaster, Eagle Hse, 1982–88. Chairman: Sussex Assoc. of Classical Teachers, 1982–88; Trustees, SE Music Schemes, 1996–2009; Nat. Assoc. of Music and Dance Schools, 2001–09. Member: Performing Arts Panel, SE Arts Bd, 1990–96; Music and Dance Scheme Expert Panel, DCSF, 2007–09 (Chm., Excellent! Gala Steering Cttee, 2007–09); Mem., 2008–10, Chm., 2008–10, Sports, Arts, Recreation Cttee, Soc. of Heads of Ind. Schs (Mem., Educn Cttee, 1996–2003). Member: Council, Eur. String Teachers Assoc., 2008–11; Council, ISM, 2011–; Council, Brighton Early Music Fest., 2011–; Trustee, Brighton Philharmonic Soc., 2011– (Chm., 2014–). Pres., Surrey Philharmonic Orch., 2000–01. Governor: Royal Ballet Sch., 1997–2014 (Chm., Academic and Pastoral Cttee, 2000–14); St Paul's Girls' Sch., 2011– (Chm., Educn Cttee, 2013–). Mem., Iford PCC, 1988–. Dir, Iford Village Choir, 2012–. FRSA. Freeman: Co. of Musicians, 2006 (Yeoman, Coordination Cttee, 2010– (Chm., 2013–14); Liveryman, 2012); City of London, 2010. *Publications:* Menuhin's Vision: fifty years of the Yehudi Menuhin School, 2012. *Recreations:* music, classic cars, walking, photography, archaeology, gardening, watercolour painting. *Address:* 2 Iford Manor Cottages, Iford, Lewes, E Sussex BN7 3EP. *T:* (01273) 471733, 07710 179599.

CHISHTI, Rehman; MP (C) Gillingham and Rainham, since 2010; *b* Muzaffarabad, Pakistan, 4 Oct. 1978; *s* of Abdul Rehman Chishti and Zarina Chishti. *Educ:* Fort Luton High Sch. for Boys; Chatham Grammar Sch. for Girls; University of Wales, Aberystwyth (LLB Hons 2000). Called to the Bar, Lincoln's Inn, 2001; in practice as a barrister, Goldsmith Chambers, 2003–09. Special Adviser: to Benazir Bhutto, 1999–2007; to Rt Hon. Francis Maude, MP, 2006–07. Mem., Medway Council, 2003– (Lab, 2003–06, C, 2006–) (Mem. Cabinet, 2007–10). Contested (Lab) Horsham, 2005. *Recreations:* running, cricket, tennis, football, theatre, cinema. *Address:* House of Commons, SW1A 0AA. *T:* (020) 7219 3000. *E:* rehman.chishti.mp@parliament.uk.

CHISLETT, Derek Victor; Warden, Sackville College, 1988–96; *b* 18 April 1929; *s* of Archibald Lynn Chislett and Eva Jessie Chislett (*née* Collins); *m* 1954, Joan Robson; two *d*. *Educ:* Christ's Hospital. Admiralty, 1946–53; HM Forces, 1947–49; Nat. Assistance Board, 1953–66; Min. of Social Security, 1966–68; Department of Health and Social Security, 1968–88: Under Sec., 1983; Controller, Newcastle Central Office, 1983–86; Dir of Finance (Social Security), 1986–88. Mem. Exec. Cttee, Nat. Assoc. of Almshouses, 1989–2001 (Vice-Chm., 1995–2001). Trustee, Motability Tenth Anniversary Trust, 1989–2000. Freeman, City of London, 1998; Mem., Guild of Freemen, City of London, 1999. *Publications:* Sackville

College: a short history and guide, 1995. *Recreations:* opera, listening to the 'cello, growing vegetables. *Address:* Greensands, Mill Lane, Ripe, Lewes, East Sussex BN8 6AX. *T:* (01323) 811525.

CHISNALL, Air Vice-Marshal Steven, CB 2008; Director of Strategy, Southampton University, since 2012; *b* Urmston, Manchester, 12 June 1954; *s* of Eric and Muriel Chisnall; *m* 1980, Elizabeth Ennis; three *s*. *Educ:* Urmston Grammar Sch.; Univ. of Sheffield (BA English 1976; PGCE 1977); St John's Coll., Cambridge (MPhil Internat. Relns 1989). English Teacher, Hinde House, Sheffield, 1977–79; RAF, 1980–2008: tours incl. Germany, 1981–84, NI, 1991–93; Cabinet Office, 1993–95; Dep. Dir, Defence Policy, MoD, 1996–98; Station Comdr, RAF Halton, 1998–99; Liaison Officer, Islamabad, 2002; Sen. Directing Staff (Air), RCDS, 2004–08; Chief Operating Officer, Simulstrat Ltd, 2008–09; Strategic Relns Dir, Xchanging, 2009–11; CEO and Dir, Andrews Outcomes Internat., 2011–12. Vis. Prof. in War Studies, KCL, 2009–. Trustee: Victory Services Club; Officers' Assoc. Patron, RAF Holmpton, 2006–. Chm., RAF Oxford and Cambridge Soc., 2012–. *Recreations:* sport, reading and writing—history, international relations, fiction, jazz. *Address:* Southampton. *Club:* Royal Air Force (Chm., 2005–08).

CHISWELL, Maj. Gen. James Robert, CBE 2011; MC 2001; General Officer Commanding 1st (UK) Armoured Division, 2012–14; *b* Berlin, 29 March 1964; *s* of Maj.-Gen. Peter Irvine Chiswell, *qv*; *m* 2006, Linda Metcalf; one *s*. *Educ:* Allhallows Sch.; King's Coll. London (MA Defence Studies). Commnd Parachute Regt, 1983; CO 2nd Bn, 2004; Comdr, 16 Air Assault Bde, 2009; Hd, Overseas Ops, MoD, 2011–12. *Recreations:* sailing, walking, family.

CHISWELL, Maj.-Gen. Peter Irvine, CB 1985; CBE 1976 (OBE 1972; MBE 1965); Chairman, Buckland Leadership Development Centre, 1996–2006; *b* 19 April 1930; *s* of late Col Henry Thomas Chiswell, OBE (late RAMC) and Gladys Beatrice Chiswell; *m* 1958, Felicity Philippa, *d* of R. F. Martin; two *s*. *Educ:* Allhallows School; RMA Sandhurst. Commissioned Devonshire Regt, 1951; served Kenya Emergency, 1953–55; served Cyprus and Suez; transf. Parachute Regt, 1958; DAAG HQ Berlin Inf. Bde, 1963–65; Brigade Major, 16 Para Bde, 1967–68; GSO1 (DS), Staff Coll., 1968–69; CO 3 PARA, 1969–71; Col GS (Army Training), 1971–74; Comd British Contingent DCOS UN Force Cyprus, 1974–76; Comd, 44 Para Bde, 1976–78; ACOS (Operations), HQ Northern Army Gp, 1978–81; Comd, Land Forces NI, 1982–83; GOC Wales, 1983–85. Gov., Christ Coll., Brecon, 1987–2008. DL Powys, 1989–95. *Recreation:* travel.

See also Maj. Gen. J. R. Chiswell.

CHISWICK, Prof. Malcolm Leon, MD; FRCP, FRCPCH; Hon. Professor of Neonatal Medicine (formerly of Child Health), University of Manchester, since 1992; Director and Governor, Manchester Health Academy, since 2009; *b* 26 July 1940; *s* of Samuel and Polly Chiswick; *m* 1964, Claire Dodds; one *s* one *d*. *Educ:* Univ. of Newcastle upon Tyne (MB BS 1965; MD 1974). DCH 1967; FRCP 1980; FRCPCH 1997. Registrar in Paediatrics: Southampton Children's and General Hosps, 1969–70; St George's Hosp., London, 1970–71; Med. Dir, Central Manchester and Manchester Children's Univ. Hosps NHS Trust, 2002–06. Lead Gov., Central Manchester Univ. Hosps NHS Trust, 2009–13. Consultant Paediatrician, 1975–2006, Hon. Consultant Neonatal Paediatrician, 2006–, St Mary's Hospital for Women and Children, Manchester. Pres., British Assoc. of Perinatal Medicine, 2002–05. Member: Manchester Medico-Legal Soc., 1992–; Manchester Literary and Philosophical Soc., 1999–; Pres., Manchester Med. Soc., 2010–11. Ed., Archives of Diseases in Childhood, 1987–99. Hon. FRCOG 2010. *Publications:* Neonatal Medicine, 1978; The Complete Book of Baby Care, 1978, 2nd edn 1988; Birth Asphyxia and the Brain, 2002; papers in learned jls on disorders of the newborn and birth injury. *Recreations:* Coronation Street, writing. *Address:* Highclere, Parkfield Road, Altrincham, Cheshire WA14 2BT. *E:* malcolm.chiswick@manchester.ac.uk.

CHITTENDEN, Rear Adm. Timothy Clive, CEng, FIMechE, FNucI; Associate, BAE Systems Submarines Solutions, since 2011 (Programme Director, Astute, 2005–07; Safety Assurance Director, 2007–10; Project Management Director, 2011); *b* 25 May 1951; *s* of late Frederick William John Chittenden and Pauline Beryl (*née* Cockle); *m* 1974, Anne Clare Style; three *d*. *Educ:* Chatham House Grammar Sch.; Churchill Coll., Cambridge (MA Engrg Sci.); MSc Marine Engrg RNEC; Royal Naval Coll., Greenwich (Dip. Nuclear Technol.). MINucE 1982; CEng 1988; MIMechE 1988, FIMechE 2001; FNucI (FINucE 2005). Marine Engineer Officer: HMS Warspite, 1982–85; HMS Talent, 1988–90; Asst Dir, Nuclear Safety, MoD (PE), 1990–93; Prodn Manager, Clyde Submarine Base, 1993–94; Captain 1994; Assistant Director: Business and Safety, Chief Strategic Systems Exec., MoD (PE), 1995–97; Swiftsure & Trafalgar Update, Defence Procurement Agency, MoD, 1997–99; Dir, Inservice Submarines, Ship Support Agency, MoD, Naval Support Comd, 1999–2000; Submarine Support Integrated Project Team Leader and Dir, Warship Support Agency, 2000–03; COS (Support) to C-in-C Fleet, 2003–05. Non-exec. Dir, Sellafield Ltd, 2008–. Pres., Nuclear Inst., 2013–15 (Vice Pres., 2012–13). Freeman, Co. of Carmen, 2004–. *Recreations:* sailing and dinghy racing, hill-walking, 0.22 target rifle shooting, reading, listening to music. *Address:* c/o Office of the Managing Director, Sellafield Ltd, Seascale, Cumbria CA20 1PG. *T:* (01946) 775531. *Clubs:* Hawks (Cambridge); Bassenthwaite Sailing.

CHITTICK, Carolyn Julie; *see* Fairbairn, C. J.

CHITTY, Alison Jill, OBE 2004; RDI 2009; theatre designer; *b* 16 Oct. 1948; *d* of late Ernest Hedley Chitty, Prebendary of St Paul's Cathedral and of Irene Joan Waldron. *Educ:* King Alfred School, London; St Martin's School of Art; Central School of Art and Design (Degree in Theatre Design); Arts Council Scholarship. Victoria Theatre, Stoke-on-Trent, 1970–79 (designed over 40 productions; Head of Design 4 years); designer, 1970–, for *theatre: RNT* incl. A Month in the Country, Don Juan, Much Ado About Nothing, The Prince of Homburg, Danton's Death, Major Barbara, Kick for Touch, Tales from Hollywood, Antigone, Martine, Venice Preserv'd, Fool for Love, Neaptide, Antony and Cleopatra, The Tempest, The Winter's Tale, Cymbeline, Cardiff East, Remembrance of Things Past, 2000 (Olivier Award, 2001), Luther, 2001, Scenes from the Big Picture, 2003, Two Thousand Years, 2005, The Voysey Inheritance, 2006 (Best Costume Designer, Olivier Award, 2007), Grief, 2011; *RSC* incl. Tartuffe, Volpone, Breaking the Silence, Romeo and Juliet, Hamlet, 2001; other productions include: Old King Cole (Th. Royal Stratford East); Orpheus Descending (Haymarket); The Rose Tattoo (Playhouse); Uncle Vanya (Hampstead Th.); Measure for Measure, Julius Caesar (Riverside Studios); The Way South (Bush); Carmen Jones, Lennon (Crucible Sheffield); Merchant of Venice, The Master and Margherita, 2004, King Lear, 2005 (Chichester); Days of Wine and Roses (Donmar Warehouse); The Vortex (UK tour and Apollo Th.), 2007–08; Uncle Vanya (Rose Th., Kingston and UK tour), 2008; Ecstasy (Hampstead and West End), 2011; A Provincial Life (Nat. Th. Wales), 2012; for *opera:* Marriage of Figaro (Opera North); New Year (Houston Grand Opera); Bow Down/Down By the Riverside (Southbank); Siege of Calais (Wexford); The Vanishing Bridegroom (St Louis Opera Th.); Gawain (Royal Opera House); Falstaff (Göteborg Music Theatre); Jenufa (Dallas Opera, 1994, 2004; San Francisco Opera, 2000); Billy Budd (Grand Th. Geneva, 1994; Royal Opera House, 1995; Bastille Opera Paris, 1996; Dallas Opera and Houston Grand Opera, 1997–98; Seattle Opera, Tel Aviv Opera, 2000; Washington, 2004; LA Opera, 2014); Khovanshchina (ENO, 1994, 2003); Blond Eckbert (Santa Fe Opera, 1994); Modern Painters (Santa Fe Opera, 1995); Arianna (Royal Opera House, 1995); Mask of Orpheus (Royal Fest. Hall, 1996); Die Meistersinger von Nürnberg (Danish Royal Opera Copenhagen, 1996); Misper (Glyndebourne, 1997); Turandot (Bastille Opera Paris, 1997); The Flying Dutchman (Bordeaux Opera, 1998; Vilnius, 2004; Bergen, 2008); Tristan and Isolde (Seattle Opera 1998; Lyric Opera Chicago, 2000); The Bartered Bride (Royal Opera House at Sadlers Wells 1998); Julius Caesar (Bordeaux Opera, 1999); Otello (Bavarian State Opera, Munich, 1999 2013); Dialogues of the Carmelites (Santa Fe Opera, 1999); Aida (Grand Th. Geneva, 1999) The Last Supper (Staats Oper Berlin and Glyndebourne, 2000); Ion (Aldeburgh Fest. an Almeida Opera, 2000); La Vestale (ENO, 2002); Bacchae (RNT, 2002); Original Si (Crucible Sheffield, 2002); Cavalleria Rusticana, Pagliacci (Royal Albert Hall, 2002); L'Enfan et les Sortilèges (Maastricht, 2003); Cosi Fan Tutti (ENO, 2003); The Io Passion (Aldeburg Fest., Almeida Opera, Bregenz and UK tour, 2004); Tangier Tattoo (Glyndebourne, 2005) Midsummer Marriage (Chicago Lyric Opera, 2005); Carmen (Greek Nat. Opera, 2007); Th Minotaur (Royal Opera House, 2008, 2013); Adrianna's Fall (Cologne, 2008); Hippolyte e Aricie (Reis Opera, Holland, 2009); Semper Dolors, Semper Dowland/The Corrido (Aldeburgh, QEH and Bregenz, 2009); Forza del Destino (Holland Park Opera, 2010) Rigoletto (La Fenice, Venice and Reggio Emelia, 2010; Venice, 2012); Betrothal in Monastery (Toulouse and Paris, 2011; Toulouse, 2015); Madame Butterfly (Oslo, 2012 Nabucco (La Scala, Milan, Royal Opera House, 2013); Parsifal (Royal Opera House, 2013 Pirates of Penzance (ENO), 2015; The Corridor/The Cure (Aldeburgh, Royal Opera Hous Linbury), 2015; Theodora, Théâtre Champs Elysées, Paris, 2015); for *films:* Blue Jean, Aria Life is Sweet, Black Poppies (BBC), Naked, 1993; Secrets & Lies, 1995 (Palme d'Or, 1996) The Turn of the Screw (BBC), 2004. Retrospective exhibition, Alison Chitty Design Proces 1970–2010, NT, 2010. Dir, Motley Theatre Design Sch., 2000– (Co-Dir, 1992–2000) Associate, NT, 2003–; Design Consultant, Rose Th., Kingston, 2007–08. Fellow: Birkbeck Univ. of London, 2011; Univ. of the Arts, London, 2013. DUniv Staffordshire, 2005. Mish Black Medal, CSD, 2007; Young Vic Award, 2008. *Publications:* (contrib.) Theatre in a Coo Climate. *Address:* c/o Rayfield Allied, Southbank House, Black Prince Road, SE1 7SJ. *T* (020) 7589 6243, *Fax:* (020) 7662 1720.

CHITTY, Sir Andrew Edward Willes, 4th Bt *cr* 1924, of The Temple; DPhil; Lecturer i Philosophy, University of Sussex, since 1994; *b* 20 Nov. 1953; *s* of Sir Thomas Willes Chitty 3rd Bt and of Susan Elspeth Chitty, *qv*; *S* father, 2014 , but his name does not yet appear o the Official Roll of the Baronetage. *Educ:* Univ. of Sussex (BA Develtl Psychol.; MA Philos.) Univ. of Oxford (DPhil). Lectr in Philosophy, Birkbeck Coll., Univ. of London and Univ. c Bristol, 1990–94. *Heir: uncle* Michael Willes Chitty [*b* 10 June 1929; *m* 1954, Janet Leonor Messenger; one *s* one *d*].

CHITTY, Dr Anthony; retired; Director of Corporate Engineering, Rolls-Royce Powe Engineering Ltd (formerly Northern Engineering Industries, R-R Industrial Power Group) 1989–93 (Deputy Director, 1988–89); *b* 29 May 1931; *s* of Ashley George Chitty and Dor Ellen Mary Buck; *m* 1956, Audrey Munro; two *s* one *d*. *Educ:* Glyn Grammar Sch., Epsom Sir John Cass Coll. (BSc); Imperial Coll., London. (PhD, DIC). CEng. GEC Res. Labs, 1955 Hd, Creep of Steels Lab., ERA, 1959; GEC Power Gp, 1963; Chief Metallurgis (Applications), C. A. Parsons, 1966; Dir, Advanced Technol. Div., Clarke Chapman-Joh Thompson, 1973; Internat. Res. and Develt, 1978; Gen. Manager, Engrg Products, N. E. I Parsons, 1979; Regional Industrial Adviser, NE Region, DTI, 1984–88. Vis. Prof., Univ. c Aston in Birmingham, 1977–84. Chairman: Bd of Newcastle Technol. Centre, 1988–9 (Dep. Chm., 1985–88); Centre for Adhesive Technol., 1990–93; Member, Board: Newcastl Univ. New Ventures Ltd, 1989–93; Newcastle Polytechnic Products Ltd, 1989–93 *Publications:* research publications in the fields of materials and welding for power generation *Recreations:* hill walking, gardening. *Address:* 2 The Pound, Westcott Street, Westcot Dorking, Surrey RH4 3NU.

CHITTY, Susan Elspeth, (Lady Chitty); author; *b* 18 Aug. 1929; *d* of Rudolph Glosso and Mrs E. A. Hopkinson (writer, as Antonia White); *m* 1951, Sir Thomas Willes Chitty, 3r Bt (*d* 2014); one *s* three *d*. *Educ:* Godolphin Sch., Salisbury; Somerville Coll., Oxford. Mem editorial staff, Vogue, 1952–53; subseq. journalist, reviewer, broadcaster and lecture *Publications: novels:* Diary of a Fashion Model, 1958; White Huntress, 1963; My Life an Horses, 1966; *biographies:* The Woman who wrote Black Beauty: a life of Anna Sewell, 1972 The Beast and the Monk: a life of Charles Kingsley, 1975; Charles Kingsley and North Devon 1976; Gwen John 1876–1939, 1981; Now to My Mother, 1985; That Singular Person Calle Lear, 1988; Playing the Game: a biography of Sir Henry Newbolt, 1997; *non-fiction:* (wit Thomas Hinde) On Next to Nothing, 1976; (with Thomas Hinde) The Great Donkey Walk 1977; The Young Rider, 1979; *edited:* The Intelligent Woman's Guide to Good Taste, 1958 The Puffin Book of Horses, 1975; As Once in May, by Antonia White, 1983; Antonia White Diaries 1926–1957, vol. I, 1991, vol. II, 1992. *Recreations:* riding, travel. *Address:* Bov Cottage, West Hoathly, Sussex RH19 4QF. *T:* (01342) 810269.

See also Sir A. E. W. Chitty, Bt.

CHIVERS, Rev. Canon Christopher Mark; Principal, Westcott House, Cambridge, sinc 2015; *b* Bristol, 16 July 1967; *s* of Rev. Ernest Alfred John Chivers and Margaret-Rose Lilia Chivers; *m* 1998, (Elizabeth) Mary Rumble (*née* Philpott); three *s*. *Educ:* Bristol Cathedral Sch (chorister); Magdalen Coll., Oxford (Academical Clerk; BA Hons Music 1988; MA 1992) Selwyn Coll., Cambridge (BA Hons Theol. and Religious Studies 1996 (Univ. Theol Studie Prize); MA 1999); Westcott House, Cambridge (CTM 1997). Asst Master and Lay Clerk, S Michael's Coll., Tenbury, 1984–85; Dir of Music, New Coll. Sch., Oxford, 1988; Asst to D of Music and Hd of Music, Cheltenham Ladies' Coll., 1989; Lay Chaplain, Housemaster an Choristers' Tutor, King's Coll. Sch., Cambridge, 1989–94; ordained deacon, 1997, pries 1998; Asst Curate, St James' and St John's Churches, Friern Barnet, 1997–99; Cano Precentor, St George's Cathedral, Cape Town, 1999–2001; Minor Canon, 2001–05 Precentor, 2002–05, Priest Vicar, 2012–, Westminster Abbey; Canon Chancellor an Founding Dir of ExChange, Blackburn Cathedral, 2005–10, now Canon Emeritus; Vica John Keble Church, Mill Hill, 2010–15; Asst Priest, St Michael's Church, Mill Hill, 2011–15 Area Dean, W Barnet, 2014–15. Hon. Canon, Dio. of Saldanha Bay, S Africa, 2014–. Truste Kay Mason Foundn, 2002–15; S African Church Develt Trust, 2003–15; USPG, 2005 (Chair of Trustees, 2012–); Anglican Communion Fund, 2012–; Montgomery Trust Lect 2013–. Presenter, Daily Service and Act of Worship, BBC Radio 4, 2006–. *Publication* Echoes of a Rainbow Song, 1999; The Hard Road to Glory, 2001; Rumours of God Amid the Ruins, 2001; The Open Window, 2004; Dear Dom and Greg…, 2007; Jerusalem Haiku 2007; South African Haiku, 2008; Fully Alive, 2010, Faith from the Belly of the Whale, 2012 Telling it Slant: broadcasting faith in a contemporary world, 2013; contrib. The Time Independent, Guardian, Church Times, C of E Newspaper, The Tablet, Cape Times, Cap Argus, Pretoria News, Johannesburg Star, Sunday Independent (S Africa); compositior include antiphons, carols and canticles. *Recreations:* writing poetry, composing choral music lawn tennis, Western Province Rugby, Glos CCC, Blackburn Rovers, African travel. *Addres* Westcott House, Jesus Lane, Cambridge CB5 8BP. *T:* (01223) 741000. *E:* principal@westcott.cam.ac.uk.

CHIVERS, (Tom) David; QC 2002; *b* 17 Nov. 1960; *s* of Tom Alan Chivers and Annelies Chivers (*née* Ungar); *m* 1996, Helen Lorraine Searle; one *s* one *d*. *Educ:* Millfield Sch Downing Coll., Cambridge (BA Hons Law). Called to the Bar, Lincoln's Inn, 1983, Benche 2013. *Publications:* (contrib.) Co-operatives That Work, 1988; (contrib.) Practice an Procedure in the Companies Court, 1997; The Law of Majority Shareholder Power, 2008 *Address:* Erskine Chambers, 33 Chancery Lane, WC2A 1EN. *T:* (020) 7242 5532, *Fax:* (020 7831 0125. *Club:* Athenæum.

CHO, Yoon-Je; Professor of Economics, Graduate School of International Studies, Sogan University, since 1997 (Dean, Graduate School of International Studies, 2009–11); *b* 22 Feb

1952; *s* of Yong-Chan Cho and Kwi-Ju Chung; *m* 1980, Sun-Ae Woo; one *s* two *d*. *Educ:* Seoul Nat. Univ. (BA Econs); Stanford Univ. (MA; PhD Econs 1984). Sen. Economist, World Bank, 1984–88 and 1992–93; Economist, IMF, 1989–92; Vice Pres., Korea Inst. of Public Finance, 1994–95; Sen. Advr to Minister of Finance and Dep. Prime Minister, Republic of Korea, 1995–97; Chief Econ. Advr to Pres. of Republic, 2003–05; Ambassador of Republic of Korea to Court of St James's, 2005–08. Mem., Nat. Econ. Adv. Council, Republic of Korea, 2013–. *Publications:* Lessons of Financial Liberalization from Asia and Latin America, 1987; Industrialization of Korea, 1992; State Governance Structure and Economic Policies in Korea, 2009; contrib. numerous articles to Jl Money, Credit Banking, Jl Develt Econs, World Econ., World Develt, World Bank Econ. Rev., World Bank Res. Observer, etc. *Address:* J720, GSIS, Sogang University, #35, Baebeom-ro (Sinsu-dong), Mapo-gu, Seoul 121–742, Korea. *Club:* Travellers.

CHOLERTON, Dr Simon Derrick; Operations Director, Defence and Security Organisation, UK Trade and Investment, since 2013; *b* Sheffield, 7 Jan. 1968; *s* of Vernon and Brenda Cholerton. *Educ:* Henry Fanshawe Sch., Dronfield; Imperial Coll. London (BSc; ARCS; MBA; DIC); Pembroke Coll., Cambridge (PhD 1994). Joined MoD, 1993; Private Sec. to Under Sec. of State for Defence, 1996–2001; Hd, Middle East Section, 2001–03; Policy Advr, Baghdad, 2003–09; Hd, Equipt Capability Secretariat, 2009–11; COS, Defence Equipment and Support, MoD, 2011–13. LGBT Champion, MoD, 2012. *Recreations:* Radio 4, travel, Charlton Athletic. *Address:* UK Trade and Investment, 1 Victoria Street, SW1H 0ET.

CHOLMELEY, Sir (Hugh John) Frederick (Sebastian), 7th Bt *cr* 1806, of Easton, Lincolnshire; *b* 3 Jan. 1968; *o s* of Sir Montague Cholmeley, 6th Bt and of Juliet Auriol Sally (*née* Nelson); *S* father, 1998; *m* 1993, Ursula Anne, *d* of Hon. Sir H. P. D. Bennett, *qv*; one *s* one *d*. *Educ:* Eton Coll.; RAC Cirencester. MRICS (ARICS 1992). *Recreation:* the countryside. *Heir:* *s* Montague Hugh Peter Cholmeley, *b* 19 May 1997.

CHOLMONDELEY, family name of **Marquess of Cholmondeley,** and of **Baron Delamere**.

CHOLMONDELEY, 7th Marquess of, *cr* 1815; **David George Philip Cholmondeley,** KCVO 2007; Bt 1611; Viscount Cholmondeley (Ire.), 1661; Baron Cholmondeley of Namptwich (Eng.), 1689; Earl of Cholmondeley, Viscount Malpas, 1706; Baron Newborough (Ire.), 1715; Baron Newburgh (Gt Brit.), 1716; Earl of Rocksavage, 1815; Joint Hereditary Lord Great Chamberlain of England (acting for the reign of Queen Elizabeth II); *b* 27 June 1960; *s* of 6th Marquess of Cholmondeley, GCVO, MC and of Lavinia Margaret (DL Cheshire), *d* of late Col John Leslie, DSO, MC; *S* father, 1990; *m* 2009, Rose, *d* of Timothy Hanbury; two *s* (twins). *Heir:* *s* Earl of Rocksavage, *qv*. *Address:* Cholmondeley Castle, Malpas, Cheshire SY14 8AH.

CHOMSKY, Prof. (Avram) Noam, PhD; Institute Professor, Massachusetts Institute of Technology, 1976–2002, now Emeritus (Ferrari P. Ward Professor of Modern Languages and Linguistics, 1966–76); *b* Philadelphia, 7 Dec. 1928; *s* of late William Chomsky and of Elsie Simonofsky; *m* 1st, 1949, Carol Doris Schatz (*d* 2008); one *s* two *d*; 2nd, 2014, Luisa Valeria Galvao-Wasserman. *Educ:* Central High Sch., Philadelphia; Univ. of Pennsylvania (BA 1949; MA 1951; PhD 1955); Society of Fellows, Harvard, 1951–55. Massachusetts Institute of Technology: Asst Prof., 1955–58; Associate Prof., 1958–61; Prof. of Modern Langs, 1961–66. Res. Fellow, Harvard Cognitive Studies Center, 1964–65. Vis. Prof., Columbia Univ., 1957–58; Nat. Sci. Foundn Fellow, Inst. for Advanced Study, Princeton, 1958–59; Linguistics Soc. of America Prof., Univ. of Calif, LA, 1966; Beckman Prof., Univ. of Calif, Berkeley, 1966–67; Vis. Watson Prof., Syracuse Univ., 1982; Lectures: Shearman, UCL, 1969; John Locke, Oxford, 1969; Bertrand Russell Meml, Cambridge 1971; Nehru Meml, New Delhi, 1972; Whidden, McMaster Univ., 1975; Huizinga Meml, Leiden, 1977; Woodbridge, Columbia, 1978; Kant, Stanford, 1979. Member: Nat. Acad. of Scis; Amer. Acad. of Arts and Scis; Linguistic Soc. of America; Amer. Philosophical Assoc.; Bertrand Russell Peace Foundn; Utrecht Soc. of Arts and Scis; Deutsche Akademie der Naturforscher Leopoldina; Corresp. Mem., British Acad., 1974; Hon. Mem., Ges. für Sprachwissenschaft, Germany, 1990. Fellow, Amer. Assoc. for Advancement of Science; William James Fellow, Amer. Psychological Assoc., 1990. Hon. FBPsS; Hon. FRAI 1990. Hon. DLitt: London, 1967; Visva-Bharati, West Bengal, 1980; Cambridge, 1995; Harvard, 2000; Calcutta, 2001; Hon. DHL: Chicago, 1967; Loyola Univ., Chicago, 1970; Swarthmore Coll., 1970; Bard Coll., 1971; Delhi, 1972; Massachusetts, 1973; Pennsylvania, 1985; Maine, 1992; Gettysburg Coll., 1992; Amherst Coll., 1995; Buenos Aires, 1996; Rovira i Virgili, Tarragona, 1998; Guelph, 1999; Columbia, 1999; Connecticut, 1999; Scuola Normale Superiore, Pisa, 1999; Toronto, 2000; Western Ontario, 2000; Free Univ. of Brussels, 2003; Central Conn State, 2003; Athens, 2004; Florence, 2004; Bologna, 2005; Ljubljana, 2005; Santa Domingo Inst. of Technol., 2006; Dr *hc*: Univ. Nacional del Comahue, Argentina, 2002; Univ. Nacional de Colombia, 2002; Univ. of Cyprus, 2006; Univ. de Chile, Santiago, 2006; Univ. de la Frontera, Temuco, 2006. Distinguished Scientific Contribution Award, Amer. Psychological Assoc., 1984; Kyoto Prize in Basic Science, Inamori Foundn, 1988; Orwell Award, Nat. Council of Teachers of English, 1987, 1989; Killian Award, MIT, 1992; Lannan Literary Award, for non-fiction, 1992; Homer Smith Award, New York Univ. Sch. of Medicine, 1994; Loyola Mellon Humanities Award, Loyola Univ., Chicago, 1994; Helmholtz Medal, Berlin-Brandenburgische Akad. Wissenschaften, 1996; Rabindranath Tagore Centenary Award, Asiatic Soc., Calcutta, 2000. *Publications:* Syntactic Structures, 1957; Current Issues in Linguistic Theory, 1964; Aspects of the Theory of Syntax, 1965; Cartesian Linguistics, 1966; Topics in the Theory of Generative Grammar, 1966; Language and Mind, 1968; (with Morris Halle) Sound Pattern of English, 1968; American Power and the New Mandarins, 1969; At War with Asia, 1970; Problems of Knowledge and Freedom, 1971; Studies on Semantics in Generative Grammar, 1972; For Reasons of State, 1973; The Backroom Boys, 1973; Peace in the Middle East?, 1974; (with Edward Herman) Bains de Sang, 1974; Reflections on Language, 1975; The Logical Structure of Linguistic Theory, 1975; Essays on Form and Interpretation, 1977; Human Rights and American Foreign Policy, 1978; Language and Responsibility, 1979; (with Edward Herman) Political Economy of Human Rights, 1979; Rules and Representations, 1980; Radical Priorities, 1981; Lectures on Government and Binding, 1981; Towards a New Cold War, 1982; Some Concepts and Consequences of the Theory of Government and Binding, 1982; Fateful Triangle: the United States, Israel and the Palestinians, 1983; Modular Approaches to the Study of the Mind, 1984; Turning the Tide, 1985; Barriers, 1986; Pirates and Emperors, 1986; Knowledge of Language: its nature, origin and use, 1986; Generative Grammar: its basis, development and prospects, 1987; On Power and Ideology, 1987; Language in a Psychological Setting, 1987; Language and Problems of Knowledge, 1987; The Chomsky Reader, 1987; The Culture of Terrorism, 1988; (with Edward Herman) Manufacturing Consent, 1988; Necessary Illusions, 1989; Deterring Democracy, 1991; Chronicles of Dissent, 1992; Year 501: the conquest continues, 1993; Rethinking Camelot: JFK, the Vietnam war, and US political culture, 1993; Letters from Lexington: reflections on propaganda, 1993; World Orders, Old and New, 1994; The Minimalist Program, 1995; Powers and Prospects, 1996; Class Warfare (interviews), 1996; The Common Good (interviews), 1998; Profit Over People, 1998; The New Military Humanism, 1999; New Horizons in the Study of Language and Mind, 2000; Rogue States, 2000; A New Generation Draws the Line, 2000; 9–11, 2001; Understanding Power, 2002; On Nature and Language, 2002; Hegemony or Survival, 2003; Middle East Illusions, 2003; Imperial Ambitions, 2005; Failed States, 2006; (with Gilbert Achcar) Perilous Power, 2006; What We Say Goes, 2008; Hopes and Prospects, 2010; Occupy, 2012. *Address:* Department of Linguistics and Philosophy, Massachusetts Institute of Technology, 32–D808, 77 Massachusetts Avenue, Cambridge, MA 02139–4307, USA. *T:* (617) 2537819.

CHOPE, Christopher Robert, OBE 1982; MP (C) Christchurch, since 1997; barrister; *b* 19 May 1947; *s* of late His Honour Robert Charles Chope and Pamela Durell; *m* 1987, Christo Hutchinson; one *s* one *d*. *Educ:* St Andrew's Sch., Eastbourne; Marlborough Coll.; St Andrews Univ. (LLB Hons). Called to the Bar, Inner Temple, 1972. Mem., Wandsworth Borough Council, 1974–83; Chm., Housing Cttee, 1978–79; Leader of Council, 1979–83. Consultant, Ernst & Young, 1992–98. MP (C) Southampton, Itchen, 1983–92; contested (C) Southampton, Itchen, 1992. PPS to Minister of State, HM Treasury, 1986; Parly Under-Sec. of State, DoE, 1986–90; Parly Under-Sec. of State (Minister for Roads and Traffic), Dept of Transport, 1990–92; front bench spokesman on trade and industry, 1998–99, on Treasury, 2001–02, on Transport, 2002–05. Jt Sec., Cons. Backbench Environment Cttee, 1983–86; Member: Select Cttee on Procedure, 1984–86, 2005–10; Select Cttee on Trade and Industry, 1999–2001; H of C Admin Cttee, 2006–10; Speaker's Panel of Chairmen, 2005–; Select Cttee on: Constitutional and Political Reform, 2010–15; Standards Cttee, 2013–15; Privileges Cttee, 2013–15; Scottish Affairs, 2015–. Member: Exec., 1922 Cttee, 2005–12 (Jt Sec., 2006–12); Delegn, Council of Europe, 2005– (Vice Chm., Legal Affairs and Human Rights Cttee, 2012–). Chm., Cons. Parly Candidates Assoc., 1995–97. A Vice Chm., Cons. Party, 1997–98. Chm., Cons. Way Forward, 2002–09. Member: HSC, 1993–97; Local Govt Commn for England, 1994–95; Vice-Pres., LGA, 2000. Mem. Exec. Cttee, Soc. of Cons. Lawyers, 1983–86. *Address:* House of Commons, SW1A 0AA. *T:* (020) 7219 5808. *Clubs:* Royal Southampton Yacht; Christchurch Conservative.

CHORLEY, family name of **Baron Chorley**.

CHORLEY, 2nd Baron *cr* 1945, of Kendal; **Roger Richard Edward Chorley,** FCA; Chairman, National Trust, 1991–96; *b* 14 Aug. 1930; *er s* of 1st Baron Chorley, QC, and Katharine Campbell (*d* 1986), *d* of late Edward Hopkinson, DSc; *S* father, 1978; *m* 1964, Ann, *d* of late A. S. Debenham; two *s*. *Educ:* Stowe Sch.; Gonville and Caius Coll., Cambridge (BA). Pres., CU Mountaineering Club. Expedns to Himalayas, 1954 (Rakaposhi), 1957 (Nepal); joined Cooper Brothers & Co. (later Coopers & Lybrand), 1955; New York office, 1959–60; Pakistan (Indus Basin Project), 1961; Partner, 1967–89; seconded to Nat. Bd for Prices and Incomes as accounting adviser, 1965–68; Visiting Prof., Dept of Management Sciences, Imperial Coll. of Science and Technology, Univ. of London, 1979–82. National Trust: Member: Finance Cttee, 1970–90; Exec. Cttee, 1989–96; Council, 1989–98; British Council: Mem. Rev. Cttee, 1979–80; Bd Mem., 1981–99; Dep. Chm., 1990–99. Mem., H of L Select Cttee on Sci. and Technology, 1983, 1987, 1988, 1989, 1993, 1994, 2007, and Select Cttee on Sustainable Develt, 1994–95; elected Mem., H of L, 2001–14. Member: Royal Commn on the Press, 1974–77; Finance Act 1960 Tribunal, 1974–79; Ordnance Survey Rev. Cttee, 1978–79; Nat. Theatre Bd, 1980–91; Top Salaries Review Body, 1981–90; Ordnance Survey Adv. Bd, 1983–85; NERC, 1988–94; Council, City and Guilds of London Inst., 1977–90; Council, RGS, 1984–93 (Pres., 1987–90); Council, RSA, 1987–89; Chm., Cttee into Handling of Geographic Information, 1985–87; Vice Pres., Council for Nat. Parks, 1997–. Hon. Sec., Climbers Club, 1963–67; Mem. Management Cttee, Mount Everest Foundn, 1968–70; Pres., Alpine Club, 1983–85; Hon. Pres., Assoc. for Geographic Inf., 1993–2010. Hon. Fellow, Central Lancs Univ., 1993; Hon. FRICS 1995. Hon. DSc: Reading, 1990; Kingston, 1992; Hon. LLD Lancaster, 1995. *Recreation:* mountains. *Heir:* *s* Hon. Nicholas Rupert Debenham Chorley, *b* 15 July 1966. *Address:* 50 Kensington Place, W8 7PW. *Club:* Alpine.

CHOTE, Robert William; Chairman, Office for Budget Responsibility, since 2010; *b* 24 Jan. 1968; *s* of Morville Vincent William Chote and Mary Isabel Chote (*née* Davis); *m* 1997, Sharon Michele White, *qv*; two *s*. *Educ:* Queens' Coll., Cambridge (MA Econs). Econs corresp. and commentator, The Independent and Independent on Sunday, 1990–94; Econs Ed., FT, 1995–99; Advr and speechwriter to First Dep. Man. Dir, IMF, Washington, 1999–2002; Dir, Inst. for Fiscal Studies, 2002–10. Gov., NIESR, 1997–. Member: Stats Adv. Cttee, ONS, 1998–99; Adv. Bd, UK Centre for Measurement of Govt Activity, ONS, 2006–10; Acad. and Policy Bd, Oxford Inst. for Econ. Policy, 2003–; Finance Cttee, Cambridge Univ., 2009–. *Publications:* (with J. Cremona) Exploring Nature in the Wilds of Europe, 1988; (with J. Cremona) Exploring Nature in North Africa, 1989; (contrib.) Insight Guide to Tunisia, 1990; An Expensive Lunch: the political economy of Britain's new monetary framework, 1997; (ed jtly) IFS Green Budget (annual report), 2003–10. *Address:* Office for Budget Responsibility, 20 Victoria Street, SW1H 0NF. *T:* (020) 7271 2442. *E:* obrenquiries@obr.gsi.gov.uk.

CHOTE, Sharon Michele; *see* White, S. M.

CHOTHIA, Cyrus Homi, PhD; FRS 2000; Member of Scientific Staff, MRC Laboratory of Molecular Biology, Cambridge, 1990–2007, now Emeritus; Senior Research Fellow, Wolfson College, Cambridge, 2003–09, now Emeritus; *b* 19 Feb. 1942; *s* of Homi and Betty Chothia; *m* 1967, Jean Sandham; one *s* one *d*. *Educ:* Alleyn's Sch., London; Univ. of Durham (BSc 1965); Birkbeck Coll., London Univ. (MSc 1967); UCL (PhD 1970). Mem., Scientific Staff, MRC Lab. of Molecular Biology, Cambridge, 1970–73; EMBO Fellow, Dept of Molecular Biochemistry and Biophysics, Yale Univ., and Dept of Chemical Physics, Weizmann Inst. of Science, Israel, 1974; Chargé de Recherche, Service du Biochimie Cellulaire, Institut Pasteur, Paris, 1974–76; Res. Associate, Dept of Chemistry, UCL, 1976–80; Royal Soc. EPA Cephalosporin Fund Sen. Res. Fellow, MRC Lab. of Molecular Biology, Cambridge, and Dept of Chemistry, UCL, 1980–90; Mem., Scientific Staff, Cambridge Centre for Protein Engrg, 1990–93. Mem., EMBO, 1988. *Publications:* papers on molecular biology in scientific jls. *Recreations:* cinema, books, conversation. *Address:* MRC Laboratory of Molecular Biology, Francis Crick Avenue, Cambridge CB2 0QH; 26 Clarendon Street, Cambridge CB1 1JX.

CHOUDHURY, Akhlaq Ur-Rahman; QC 2015; a Recorder, since 2009; *b* Winchester, 1967; *s* of Azizur Rahman Choudhury and Sultana Choudhury; *m* 1993, Safina Rahman; two *s* one *d*. *Educ:* Univ. of Glasgow (BSc Hons 1988); Sch. of Oriental and African Studies, Univ. of London (LLB Hons 1991); Inns of Court Sch. of Law (BVC 1992). Called to the Bar, Inner Temple, 1992; in practice as a barrister, 11 King's Bench Walk, 1992–; Mem., Attorney Gen.'s Panel of Counsel, B Panel, 2000, A Panel, 2013. Gov., W Herts Coll., 1991–. *Publications:* (contrib.) Tolley's Employment Law Handbook, 1996–. *Recreations:* cycling, hiking, music, cinema. *Address:* 11 King's Bench Walk, Temple, EC4Y 7EQ.

CHOUDHURY, Anwar; HM Diplomatic Service; Ambassador to Peru, since 2014; *b* 15 June 1959; *s* of Afruz Bokth Choudhury and Ashrafun Nessa Choudhury; *m* 2001, Momina Laskar; one *s* two *d*. *Educ:* Salford Univ. (BSc Engrg); Durham Univ. (MBA). Principal Design Engr, Siemens and Plessey Radar, 1985–90; Design Engr/Strategist, RAF, 1990–93; Asst Dir, MoD, 1994–99; Dir, Policy, Cabinet Office, 2000–03; Dir, Policy/Strategy, FCO, 2003–04; High Comr, Bangladesh, 2004–08; Dir, Internat. Security and Institutions, FCO, 2008–11; Dir, FCO, 2011–13. Hon. DSc Salford. *Recreations:* cricket, bridge, addicted to Bengali Baul music. *Address:* c/o Foreign and Commonwealth Office, King Charles Street, SW1A 2AH.

CHOUDHURY, Sumit P.; *see* Paul-Choudhury.

CHOW, Sir Chung Kong, Kt 2000; FREng; FIChemE; FHKEng, FCILT; Chairman, Hong Kong Exchanges and Clearing Ltd, since 2012; *b* 9 Sept. 1950. *Educ:* Univ. of Wisconsin (BS Chem. Engrg 1972); Univ. of California (MS Chem. Engrg 1974); Chinese Univ. of Hong

Kong (MBA 1981); Harvard (AMP 1991). CEng; FIChemE 1997; FREng 2001. Res. Engr, Climax Chemical Co., New Mexico, 1974–76; Process Engr, Sybron Asia Ltd, Hong Kong, 1976–77; with BOC Group, 1977–96: Hong Kong Oxygen, Hong Kong and BOC, Australia, 1977–84; Man. Dir, Hong Kong Oxygen, 1984–86; Pres., BOC Japan, 1986–89; Gp Manager, Gases Business Develt, BOC Gp plc, England and USA, 1989–91; Regl Dir, N Pacific, based in Tokyo and Hong Kong, 1991–93; Chief Exec., Gases, 1993–96; joined Main Bd, 1994; Man. Dir, 1994–97; Chief Executive: GKN plc, 1997–2001; Brambles Industries, 2001–03; Mass Transit Railway Corporation, Hong Kong, 2003–11. Non-executive Director: Standard Chartered plc, 1997–2008; Anglo American plc, 2008–; AIA Gp Ltd, 2010–; Chairman: Standard Chartered Bank (Hong Kong) Ltd, 2004–10; Hong Kong Gen. Chamber of Commerce, 2012–. Pres., 1999–2000, Dep. Pres., 2000–01, SBAC. FCGI 2000; FCILT 2004; FHKEng 2005. Hon. FHKIE 2004. Hon. DEng Bath, 2001. *Address:* Hong Kong Exchanges and Clearing Ltd, 12/F One International Finance Centre, 1 Harbour View Street, Central, Hong Kong.

CHOWDHURY, Ajay; Managing Director, BCG Digital Ventures London, since 2015; *b* 29 April 1962; *s* of Micky and Indira Chowdhury; *m* 1995, Liz McDonnell (marr. diss. 2010); two *d*; *m* 2015, Angelina Melwani. *Educ:* Sydenham Coll., Bombay (BCom 1st Cl.); Wharton Sch., Univ. of Penn (MBA); Central Sch. of Speech and Drama; Metropolitan Film Sch. Manager, Bain & Co., 1986–91; Gp Develt Manager, MAI PLC, 1991–92; Develt Dir, MAI Media, 1993–94; Man. Dir, United Interactive, 1994–99; Chief Executive Officer: Lineone, 1999–2000; NBC Internet Europe, 2000; Man. Partner, IDG Ventures Europe, 2000–06; Gen. Partner, Acacia Capital, 2006–07; Chief Executive Officer: ComQi Group (formerly EnQii Hldgs plc), 2007–13; Seatwave, 2013–14. Chm., Shazam Entertainment, 2001–07; Director: Index on Censorship, 1994–2000; Empower Interactive, 2002–06; Lionhead Games, 2004–06. Mem. Council, Arts Council London, 2009–13. Director: MLA (formerly Resource: Council for Mus, Archives and Libraries), 2000–06; British Screen Adv. Council, 2003– (Dep. Chm., 2013–); DCMS, 2013–. Trustee, 24 Hour Museum, 2002–06. Artistic Dir, Rented Space Th. Co., 1988–. *Recreations:* directing plays, theatre, films, music, bridge, diving. *Address:* 30D South Hill Park, NW3 2SB.

CHOWN, John Francis; International Tax Adviser, Chown Dewhurst LLP, since 1992; *b* Hutton Rudby, 12 Dec. 1929; *s* of Walter Redvers and Mary Elizabeth Chown; *m* 1969, Vera Marie Luise Wohl; two *d*. *Educ:* Gordonstoun; Selwyn Coll., Cambridge (Wrenbury Schol.; Adam Smith Prize; BA Econs 1954; Hon. Fellow 1997). Nat. Service, RAF, 1949–51. Mgt trainee, Pye Ltd, 1956–58; Asst to Chm., Robinson Frere, 1958–60; Dir, Maxwell Stamp, 1960–62. Co-Founder and Mem., Exec. Cttee, Inst. for Fiscal Studies, 1969–; Mem., Adv. Bd, OMFIF, 2012–. Member: Cttee, Internat. Tax Specialist Gp; Cttee, Political Econ. Club; Internat. Financial Services, London. Mem., Tax Cttee, IoD, 1972–2002, now Hon. Life Fellow; former Member: Taxation and Tech. Cttee, Assoc. of Corporate Treasurers; London Cttee, Internat. Fiscal Assoc. Mem. Cttee, London Handel Soc.; Hon. Financial Advr, Royal Soc. Musicians. Tax corresp., FT; reviewer of books, TLS. Former Trustee, Handel Opera Gp. *Publications:* (with R. Valentine) International Bond Market in the 1960s, 1968; (ed) International Fund Year Book, 1970; VAT Explained, 1972, 2nd edn 1973; Taxation and Multinational Enterprise, 1974; A Guide to Capital Transfer Tax, 1975; Offshore Financial Centres, 1975, 4th edn, 1981; (with L. Halpern) Taxation of Direct Investment in the United States, 1980; Foreign Exchange Risk: a tax and financial analysis, 1983; Tax Efficient Forex Management, 1986; Tax Efficient Foreign Exchange Management, 1990; A History of Money - from AD 800, 1994; (with K. Desai) The Taxation of Foreign Exchange and Derivatives, 1997; A History of Monetary Unions, 2004; contrib. articles on internat. tax, finance, internat. money and numismatics to jls incl. Central Banking. *Recreations:* music, monetary history, numismatics, walking. *Address:* 7 Acacia Road, NW8 6AB. *T:* (020) 7722 9916. *E:* jchown@chowndewhurst.com. *Club:* Reform.

CHRÉTIEN, Rt Hon. Jean; CC 2007; OM 2009; PC (Canada) 1967; QC (Canada) 1980; Prime Minister of Canada, 1993–2003; Counsel, Dentons Canada LLP, since 2014; *b* 11 Jan. 1934; *s* of Willie Chrétien and Marie Chrétien (*née* Boisvert); *m* 1957, Aline Chaîné; two *s* one *d*. *Educ:* Trois-Rivières; Joliette; Shawinigan; Laval Univ. (BA, LLL). Called to the Bar, and entered Shawinigan law firm of Chrétien, Landry, Deschênes, Trudel and Normand, 1958; Counsel, Lang Michener Lawrence and Shaw, 1986–90; Director: Shawinigan Sen. Chamber of Commerce, 1962; Bar of Trois-Rivières, 1962–63. Government of Canada: MP (L): St Maurice, 1963–86; Beauséjour, New Brunswick, 1990–93; St Maurice, 1993–2003; Parly Sec. to Prime Minister, 1965, and to Minister of Finance, 1966; Minister of State, 1967; Minister of National Revenue, Jan. 1968; Minister of Indian and Northern Affairs, July 1968; Pres., Treasury Bd, 1974; Minister of Industry, Trade and Commerce, 1976; Minister of Finance, 1977–79; Minister of Justice, responsible for constitutional negotiations, Attorney General, Minister of State for Social Develt, 1980–82; Minister of Energy, Mines and Resources, 1982–84; Deputy Prime Minister and External Affairs Minister, 1984; External Affairs Critic for official Opposition, 1984–86; Leader of the Opposition, 1990–93. Elected Leader, Liberal Party of Canada, June 1990. Counsel, Heenan Blaikie, 2004–14. Hon LLD: Wilfred Laurier, 1981; Laurentian, 1982; W Ontario, 1982; York, Ont., 1986; Alberta, 1987; Lakehead, 1988; Ottawa, 1994; Meiji, Tokyo, 1996; Warsaw Sch. of Econs, Michigan State, 1999; Hebrew Univ. of Jerusalem, Meml, St Johns, 2000. *Publications:* Straight from the Heart, 1986; My Years as Prime Minister, 2007. *Recreations:* ski-ing, fishing, golf, reading, classical music. *Address:* Dentons Canada LLP, 99 Bank Street, Suite 142, Ottowa, ON K1P 1H4, Canada.

CHRÉTIEN, Prof. Michel, OC 1986; OQ 1994; MD; FRS 2009; FRSC; Emeritus Senior Scientist, Chronic Disease, Ottawa Hospital Research Institute (formerly Ottawa Health Research Institute); *b* Shawinigan, Quebec, 26 March 1936; *s* of Willie Chrétien and Marie Chrétien (*née* Boisvert); *m* Micheline Ruel; two *d*. *Educ:* Séminaire de Joliette (BA cum laude 1955); Univ. of Montreal (MD cum laude 1960); McGill Univ. (MSc 1962). CSPQ (Endocrinology) 1969; FACP 1971; FRCP&S (Canada) 1973. Clinical Research Institute of Montreal: Dir, Lab. of Molecular Neuroendocrinol., 1967–99; Scientific Dir and CEO, 1984–94; EJLB Foundn Prof., 1994–98; Physician, Dept of Medicine and Endocrine Div., 1967–99, Chief of Endocrinol., 1978–84, Hôtel-Dieu Hosp., Montreal; Prof. of Medicine, Univ. of Montreal, 1975–99, Prof. Emeritus, 2002; Physician, Dept of Endocrinol., Ottawa Hosp., 1998–; Scientific Dir and CEO, Loeb Health Res. Inst., Ottawa Civic Hosp., 1998–2001; Prof., Dept of Medicine, Univ. of Ottawa, 1998–; Ottawa Health Research Institute: Dir, Regl Protein Chemistry Centre and Diseases of Ageing Unit, 2001–06; Sen. Scientist, Hormone, Growth and Develt, 2006. FRSC 1981; Fellow: AAAS, 1996; Molecular Medicine Soc., 1999. Adjunct Prof., Fac. of Medicine, McGill Univ., Montreal, 1970–; Hon. Prof., Chinese Acad. of Med. Scis and Peking Union Med. Coll., 1986. Chevalier, Légion d'Honneur (France), 2004. *Publications:* articles in scientific jls. *Address:* Ottawa Hospital Research Institute, 725 Parkdale Avenue, Ottawa, ON K1Y 4E9, Canada.

CHRIMES, Neil Roy; Head of Programmes, Lord Mayor's Office, City of London, since 2006; *b* 10 June 1954; *er s* of Geoffrey Richard Chrimes and Dorothy Enid Chrimes (*née* Wyatt); *m* 1982, Anne Margery, (Henny), Barnes; one *s* one *d*. *Educ:* Queen Mary's Grammar Sch., Basingstoke; Univ. of Exeter (BA 1975); MIT (SM 1979). Economic Assistant, MAFF, 1975–77; Harkness Fellow, MIT, 1977–79; Sen Economic Assistant, MAFF, 1979–81; HM Diplomatic Service, 1981–2006: Economic Advr, FCO, 1981–87; Economist, Res. Dept, IMF, Washington, 1987–89; Sen. Econ. Advr, FCO, 1989–94; Dep. UK Perm. Rep. and Counsellor (Econ. and Financial), OECD, Paris, 1994–98; Economic Counsellor, Jakarta, 1998; Hd, African Dept (Southern), FCO, 1999–2001; Counsellor (Econ., Sci. and Trade), Ottawa, 2001–06. Trustee, Florence Nightingale Foundn, 2011–. Liveryman, Horners' Co., 1980. FRSA 2006. *Recreations:* travel, wine, music (especially mediaeval), gardening, cricket. *Address:* c/o Mansion House, EC4N 8BH. *Club:* MCC.

CHRIST CHURCH, Dublin, Dean of; *see* Dunne, Very Rev. D. P. M.

CHRIST CHURCH, Oxford, Dean of; *see* Percy, Rev. Canon M. W.

CHRISTCHURCH, Bishop of, since 2008; **Rt Rev. Victoria Matthews;** *b* 1954; *d* of late Beverley Matthews and Pauline Ritchie Matthews. *Educ:* Trinity Coll., Univ. of Toronto (BA (Hons) 1976; ThM 1987); Yale Univ. Divinity Sch. (MDiv 1979). Ordained deacon, 1979, priest, 1980; Asst Curate, St Andrew, Scarborough, 1979–83; Incumbent: Parish of Georgina, York-Simcoe, 1983–87; All Souls, Lansing, York-Scarborough, 1987–94; Suffragan Bishop of Toronto (Bishop of the Credit Valley), 1994–97; Bishop of Edmonton (Alberta), 1997–2007; Bishop-in-residence, Wycliffe Coll., Toronto, 2008. N Amer. Theol Fellow, 1976–79. Mem., Inter-Anglican Standing Commn on Unity Faith and Order, 2008–. *Recreations:* reading, hiking, swimming, travel. *Address:* The Anglican Centre, PO Box 4438, Christchurch 8140, New Zealand.

CHRISTENSEN, Jayne, (Mrs P. L. Christensen); *see* Torvill, J.

CHRISTENSEN, Jens; Commander First Class, Order of the Dannebrog; Hon. GCVO; Ambassador of Denmark to Organization for Economic Co-operation and Development, 1989–91; *b* 30 July 1921; *s* of Christian Christensen and Sophie Dorthea Christensen; *m* 1st, 1950, Tove (*née* Jessen) (*d* 1982); one *s* two *d*; 2nd, 1983, Vibeke Pagh. *Educ:* Copenhagen Univ. (MPolSc 1945). Joined Danish Foreign Service, 1945; Head of Section, Econ Secretariat of Govt, 1947; Sec. to OEEC Delegn in Paris, 1949 and to NATO Delegn, 1952; Hd of Sect., Min. of Foreign Affairs, 1952, Actg Hd of Div., 1954; Chargé d'Affaires *a.i.* and Counsellor of Legation, Vienna, 1957; Asst Hd of Econ.-Polit. Dept, Min. of For. Affairs, 1960; Dep. Under-Sec., 1961; Under-Sec. and Hd of Econ.-Polit. Dept, 1964–71; Hd of Secretariat for Eur. Integration, 1966; Ambassador Extraord. and Plenipotentiary, 1967; State Sec. for Foreign Econ. Affairs, 1971; Ambassador to the Court of St James's, 1977–81; Pres., Danish Oil and Natural Gas Co., 1980–84; Ambassador to Austria, 1984–89. Governor for Denmark, The Asian Development Bank, 1967–73. Chm., Cross Cultures Project Assoc., 1999–2006. Knight Grand Cross: Order of Icelandic Falcon; Order of Northern Star, Sweden; Order of St Olav, Norway; Royal Victorian Order; Austrian Order of Honour. *Address:* Strandvejen 647, 2930 Klampenborg, Denmark.

CHRISTENSEN, Lisa Ellen Buch; Director, Lisa Christensen Consulting Ltd, since 2013; *b* Preston, 11 Sept. 1956; *d* of late Poul Buch Christensen and of Marjorie Christensen (later Hayes); *m* 1992, Jack Prescott (*d* 2009); two *d*. *Educ:* Ackworth Sch.; Shrewsbury High Sch. for Girls; Imberhorne Sch.; Univ. of Kent at Canterbury (BA Hons English and Philosophy 1978). Various admin. posts, Islington Council, 1979–85; Develt Officer, then Dir, Haringey Assoc. for Ind. Living, 1986–89; Wakefield Case Mgt Project, 1989–91; Develt Officer, Carers Project, Yorks RHA, 1991–92; Dir, Community Services, Bradford Community Health NHS Trust, 1992–97; Exec. Dir, Hackney Council, 1997–99; Dir, Social Services Lambeth Council, 1999–2002; Dir, Social Services, 2002–05, Children's Services, 2005–13, Norfolk CC. *Recreations:* cinema, theatre, reading, walking, having dinner with friends. *Address:* The Ramblers, Mill Road, Mattishall, Norfolk NR20 3RH. *T:* (01362) 850646.

CHRISTIAN, Louise; Co-Founder, 1985, Senior Partner, 1985–2010, Senior Consultant, 2010–14, Christian Khan (formerly Christian Fisher), Solicitors; Senior Consultant, Public Law Project, since 2015; *b* Oxford, 22 May 1952; *d* of late John, (Jack) and Maureen Christian. *Educ:* St Anne's Coll., Oxford (BA Hons Hist. 1973). Solicitor: Lovell White & King, 1976–79; Plumstead Law Centre, 1979–81; Legal Advr to Police Cttee, GLC, 1981–84. Chair: Inquest, 1998–2007 (Mem. Bd, 2007–); Liberty, 2007–09; Member Board: Centre for Corporate Accountability, 2002–09; Article 19, 2006–08; Mem., Adv. Bd, Kurdish Human Rights Project, 1997–. Has undertaken human rights missions to ME, Turkey, etc. Hon. Dr Staffs, 2003. Legal Aid Personality of Year Award, Legal Aid Practitioners Gp, 2004; Human Rights Award, Liberty/Law Soc./Justice, 2004. *Publications:* (jtly) Inquests: a practitioner's guide, 2002. *Address:* Public Law Project, 150 Caledonian Road, N1 9RD. *T:* (020) 7843 1260, 07884 363630, *Fax:* (020) 7837 7048. *E:* l.christian@publiclawproject.org.

CHRISTIAN, Prof. Reginald Frank; Professor of Russian, St Andrews University 1966–92, Emeritus Professor 1992; *b* Liverpool, 9 Aug. 1924; *s* of late H. A. Christian and late Jessie Gower (*née* Scott); *m* 1952, Rosalind Iris Napier; one *s* one *d*. *Educ:* Liverpool Inst.; Queen's Coll., Oxford (Open Scholar; MA). Shortened Hon. Mods Class. (Oxon), 1943; 1st cl. hons Russian (Oxon), 1949. RAF, 1943–46; Flying Officer, 1944, flying with Atlantic Ferry Unit and 231 Sqdn. FO, British Embassy, Moscow, 1949–50; Lectr and Head of Russian Dept, Liverpool Univ., 1950–55; Sen. Lectr and Head of Russian Dept, Birmingham Univ., 1956–63; Vis. Prof. of Russian, McGill Univ., Canada, 1961–62; Prof. of Russian, Birmingham Univ., 1963–66; Exchange Lectr, Moscow, 1964–65. Mem. Univ. Ct, 1971–73 and 1981–85, Dean, Fac. of Arts, 1975–78, St Andrews Univ. Pres., British Univs Assoc. of Slavists, 1967–70; Member: Internat. Cttee of Slavists, 1970–75; UGC Atkinson Cttee 1978–81. *Publications:* Korolenko's Siberia, 1954; (with F. M. Borras) Russian Syntax, 1959 2nd rev. edn, 1971; Tolstoy's War and Peace: a study, 1962; (with F. M. Borras) Russian Prose Composition, 1964, 2nd rev. edn, 1974; Tolstoy: a critical introduction, 1969; (ed and trans.) Tolstoy's Letters, 2 vols, 1978; (ed and trans.) Tolstoy's Diaries, 2 vols, 1985, abridged edn Tolstoy's Diaries, 1994; Alexis Aladin: the tragedy of exile, 1999; numerous articles and reviews in Slavonic and E European Review, Slavonic and E European Jl, Mod. Language Review, Survey, Forum, Birmingham Post, Times Lit. Supp., Oxford Slavonic Papers, etc *Address:* 48 Lade Braes, St Andrews KY16 9DA. *T:* (01334) 474407.

CHRISTIANI, Alexander, Dr jur; Ambassador of Austria to the Court of St James's, 2000–05; *b* 31 May 1940; *s* of Dr Alfred Christiani-Kronwald, (Baron von Christiani-Kronwald), and Rose Christiani-Kronwald; *m* 1968, Renate Sedlmayer, PhD; one *s* one *d*. *Educ:* Univ. of Vienna (Dr jur 1964); Diplomatic Acad., Vienna. Federal Ministry for Foreign Affairs, Austria: Political Dept, 1966–69; Asst to Sec.-Gen. for Foreign Affairs, 1969; UN Mission, NY, 1970–75; Alternate Rep. of Austria to Security Council, 1973–74; Dir, Div. i/c of Vienna Internat. Centre, 1976–81; Consul Gen., Austrian Delegn, Berlin, 1981–86; Ambassador to South Africa, 1986–90; Dir, Dept for ME and Africa, 1990–96; Ambassador to the Netherlands, 1996–2000. Mem., Austrian Delegns to UN Gen. Assemblies, 1967–81 Cross, KM. Grand Cross: Order of Oranje-Nassau (Netherlands), 2000; Al-Istiqlal Order (Jordan); Grand Officer, Order of Merit (Syria); Comdr, Order of Oak Crown (Luxembourg); Grand Decoration of Honour in Gold (Austria). *Recreations:* music, travelling, theatre. *Address:* Reithlegasse 9, 1190 Vienna, Austria. *T:* and *Fax:* (1) 3681525. *E:* achristiani@hotmail.com *Clubs:* Rotary, St Johann's (Vienna).

CHRISTIANSON, Rev. Canon Rodney John, (Bill); Vicar, St Michael Paternoster Royal, 2000–09; Secretary General, The Mission to Seafarers, 2001–09; *b* S Africa, 19 March 1947; *s* of late Kenneth Alfred John Christianson and Jessie Winifred Nelson (*née* Kelly). *Educ:* Glenwood High Sch., Durban; Officer Trng Sch., S Africa; St Paul's Theol Coll. Grahamstown (DipTh); Open Univ. Ordained deacon 1972, priest 1973; Curate Pietermaritzburg, SA, 1972–75; Missions to Seamen, subseq. Mission to Seafarers: Asst Chaplain, Gravesend, 1976–81; Sen. Chaplain, Port of London, 1981–82; Port Chaplain Richards Bay, SA, 1982–91; also Parish Priest, St Andrew, Richards Bay and St Aidan Kwambonambi, 1982–91; Trng Chaplain, Hull, 1991–93; Ministry Sec., 1993–2000. Mem.

Archbp of Cape Town's Commn to conduct investigation into work amongst young people in the Church of SA, 1974. Guild Chaplain, St Bride's Ch, London, 1990; Chaplain, Innholders' Co., 2002–14 (Mem., Ct of Assts, 2013–); Liveryman, Tallow Chandlers' Co., 2011. Hon. Chaplain, Shipwrights' Co., 2012. Hon. Canon: Bloemfontein Cathedral, SA, 1993–; Anglican Church of Canada, 2009. Hon. Master Mariner, SA, 1988. Hon. FNI 2009. *Recreations:* painting/art, music, theatre, photography. *Address:* 45 Wimbledon Park Court, Wimbledon Park Road, SW19 6NN.

CHRISTIE, Aidan Patrick; QC 2008; a Recorder, since 2009; *b* Edinburgh, 26 Oct. 1962; *s* of late William James Christie and Maeve Patricia Christie (*née* Gallacher); *m* 1991, Claire Elliott; one *s* one *d*. *Educ:* Edinburgh Acad.; Hertford Coll., Oxford (BA Lit.Hum. 1985); Downing Coll., Cambridge (MA Law 1987). Called to the Bar, Middle Temple, 1988. Mem., Professional Conduct Cttee, Bar Standards Bd, 2011– (Barrister Vice-Chair, 2014–). Panel Deemster, Isle of Man High Court, 2012–. *Recreation:* reading. *Address:* 4 Pump Court, Temple, EC4Y 7AN. *T:* (020) 7842 5555. *E:* achristie@4pumpcourt.com. *Club:* New (Edinburgh).

CHRISTIE, Andrew George; Tri-borough Executive Director of Children's Services, London Borough of Hammersmith and Fulham, Royal Borough of Kensington and Chelsea and City of Westminster, since 2011; *b* Bristol, 10 Oct. 1953; *s* of Michael George Christie and Mary Shirley Christie; *m* 2008, Deborah Jane Hickland; one *s* one *d* and two step *s*. *Educ:* George Watson's Coll., Edinburgh; Manchester Univ. (BA Econs 1974); Sussex Univ. (MSW, CQSW 1979). With MENCAP, 1974–76; trainee social worker, 1977–79, social worker, 1979–83, E Sussex CC; Asst Team Manager, 1984–86, Team Manager, 1986–88, Actg Divl Manager, 1988–89, London Borough of Lewisham; Surrey County Council: Asst Area Dir, W Surrey, 1989–93; Gen. Manager, Children's Services, 1993–96; Actg Jt Hd of Children's Services, 1996–97; Children's Services Manager, 1997–98; London Borough of Hammersmith and Fulham: Asst Dir (Community Services), 1998–2000; Asst Dir (Children's Services), 2000–02; Jt Actg Dir, Social Services, 2002–03; Dir, Hammersmith and Fulham Children's Trust, 2003–06; Dir, Children's Services, 2006–11. *Recreations:* golf, snowboarding, hill walking. *Address:* Kensington Town Hall, Hornton Street, W8 7NX. *T:* (020) 7361 3300.

CHRISTIE, Augustus Jack; Executive Chairman, Glyndebourne Productions Ltd, since 2000 (Director, since 1989); *b* 4 Dec. 1963; *s* of Sir George William Langham Christie, CH; *m* 1993, Imogen Lycett Green (marr. diss. 2006); four *s*; *m* 2009, Danielle de Niese; one *s*. *Educ:* St Aubyns, Rottingdean; Eton Coll.; King's Coll., London (2nd Cl. Hons Zool.). Worked in various theatres, incl. Tricycle, NT, Batignano Opera, Robert Fox Associates, 1987; asst ed. and asst cameraman, Partridge Films, 1989–91; freelance cameraman, 1991–; documentaries include: A Puffin's Tale, Halloween, 1991; A New Fox in Town, 1993; The Lion's Share, Lions, 1994; Hugo's Diary, 1995; Red Monkeys of Zanzibar, 1996; The Battle of the Sexes, The Tale of Two Families, 1998; Buffalo: the African boss, Triumph of Life, 1999. *Recreations:* sport, music, nature. *Address:* Glyndebourne, Lewes, E Sussex BN8 5UU.

CHRISTIE, David; Warden, St Edward's School, Oxford, 1988–2004; *b* 22 Feb. 1942; *s* of William and Jean Christie, Bannockburn; *m* 1969, Elsa Margaret Shearer; one *s* two *d*. *Educ:* Dollar Acad.; Univ. of Strathclyde; Univ. of Glasgow. Lektor, British Centre, Folkuniversity of Sweden, 1965–66; Asst Master, George Watson's Coll., 1966–71; Lectr in Economics, Moray House Coll., Edinburgh, 1971–77; Res. Associate (part-time), Esmée Fairbairn Research Centre, Heriot-Watt Univ., 1972–77; Teacher, European Sch., Luxembourg, 1977–83; pt-time Faculty Mem., Miami Univ. European Center, Luxembourg, 1980–83; Head of Econs, Winchester Coll., 1983–88. Member: Econs and Business Studies Panel, Scottish Cert. of Educn Exam. Bd, 1973–77 (Convenor, 1975–77); Scottish Cttee, IBA, 1973–77; Dep. Chm., HMC Wkg Party on Inspection, 1993–97; Chm., Oxford Conf. in Educn, 1997–2002. Educn Adviser, Haberdashers' Co., 2005–11. Dir, Ecclesiastical Insurance Gp plc, 2001– (Dep. Chm. and Sen. Ind. Dir, 2013–). Mem., Council of Mgt, Hebridean Trust, 1998–2009; Trustee: Allchurches Trust Ltd, 2013–; Friends of Panmure House, 2013–. *Publications:* (contrib.) Curriculum Development in Economics, 1973; (contrib.) Teaching Economics, 1975; (with Prof. A. Scott) Economics in Action, 1976; articles, reviews and entries in jls. *Recreations:* books, golf, hills. *Address:* Sunnybank, Blebo Craigs KY15 5UF. *Club:* Royal & Ancient (St Andrews).

CHRISTIE, Elizabeth Mary, (Mrs Stuart Christie); *see* Steel, Her Honour E. M.

CHRISTIE, Herbert; Director General, European Investment Bank, 1995–99, now Hon. Director General (Director, Research Department, 1983–95); *b* 26 Sept. 1933; *s* of Brig.-Gen. H. W. A. Christie, CB, CMG, and Mary Ann Christie; *m* 1982, Gilberte F. M. V. Desbois; one *s*. *Educ:* Methodist Coll., Belfast; Univ. of St Andrews (MA). Asst Lectr, Univ. of Leeds, 1958–60; Econ. Asst, HM Treasury, 1960–63; First Sec., Washington, DC, 1963–66; Econ. Adviser, J. Henry Schroder Wagg and Co. Ltd, 1966–71, with secondment as Econ. Adviser, NBPI, 1967–71; Sen. Econ. Adviser, Min. of Posts and Telecommunications, 1971–74, and Dept of Prices and Consumer Protection, 1974–76; Econ. Adviser, EEC Commn, Brussels, 1976–78; Under Sec., HM Treasury, 1978–83. Hon. Vis. Prof., Middlesex Univ., 1990–95. Order of European Merit, 2005. *Publications:* contrib. to books and learned jls. *Recreations:* languages, foreign travel. *Address:* 47 Rue J-B Esch, 1473 Luxembourg. *Club:* Reform.

CHRISTIE, Prof. Ian Leslie, FBA 1994; Anniversary Professor of Film and Media History, Birkbeck College, University of London, since 1999; *b* 23 Feb. 1945; *s* of late Robert Christie and Ethel Christie; *m* 1979, Patsy Nightingale; one *s* three *d*. *Educ:* Belfast Royal Acad.; Queen's Univ., Belfast (BA 1966). Lectr in Complementary Studies, Derby Coll. of Art, 1969–73; Sen. Lectr in Art Hist. and Film Studies, Derby Coll. of Higher Educn, 1973–75; British Film Institute: Regl Prog. Advr, then Hd of Programming, 1976–84; Hd of Distribn, 1984–92; Head of Special Projects, 1993–94; Associate Ed., Sight and Sound, 1995–97; Prof. of Film Studies, Univ. of Kent at Canterbury, 1997–99. Vis. Dir, Film Centre, Art Inst. of Chicago, 1985–86; Visiting Professor: Univ. of S Florida, 1989; Palacky Univ., Olomouc, Czech Republic, 2012–15; Dist. Vis. Fellow, European Humanities Res. Centre, 1995–98, Vis. Lectr in Film, and Fellow, Magdalen Coll., 1995–98, Oxford Univ.; Slade Prof. of Fine Art, Cambridge Univ., 2005–06; Founder and Dir, London Screen Study Collection, Birkbeck Coll., 2006–. Dir, Connoisseur Video, 1990–97. Vice-Pres., 1993–2012, Pres., 2012–14, Europa Cinemas. Mem. Exec. Cttee, GB-USSR Assoc., 1983–89. Jt Ed., Film Studies jl, 1999–2009. Co-curator of exhibitions: Eisenstein: his life and art, MOMA, Oxford, and Hayward Gall., 1988; Spellbound: art and film, Hayward Gall., 1996; The Director's Eye, MOMA, Oxford, 1996; Modernism: designing a new world, V&A Mus., 2006; Lights, Camera, London!, London Film Mus., 2012–13; All that Life Can Afford?, London Screen Study Collection archive, Birkbeck, Univ. of London, 2013. Frequent radio and television broadcaster on cinema; consultant on film policy, archiving and programming. *Publications:* Powell, Pressburger and Others, 1978; Arrows of Desire: the films of Michael Powell and Emeric Pressburger, 1985, 2nd edn 1994; (ed) The Life and Death of Col Blimp, 1994; The Last Machine, 1995; (ed) Gilliam on Gilliam, 1999; A Matter of Life and Death, 2000; The Art of Film: John Box and production design, 2009; Audiences, 2012; *edited jointly:* FEKS, Formalism, Futurism, 1978; The Film Factory, 1988, 2nd edn 1994; Eisenstein at 90, 1988; Scorsese on Scorsese, 1989, 3rd edn 2003; Inside the Film Factory, 1991; Eisenstein Rediscovered, 1993; Protazanov and the Continuity of Russian Cinema, 1993; Spellbound: art and film, 1996; Law's Moving Image, 2004; The Cinema of Michael Powell: international perspectives on an English film-maker, 2005; Stories We Tell Ourselves: the cultural impact of film in the UK, 2009; Opening Our Eyes: how film contributes to the culture of the UK, 2011; Audiences: defining and researching screen entertainment reception, 2012; Living Politics, Making Music: the writings of Jan Fairley, 2014. *Recreations:* running, ski-ing, occasional carpentry, stereoscopy, affordable wine, unaffordable opera, new media. *Address:* 131 Mount View Road, N4 4JH. *T:* (020) 8348 3656. *W:* www.ianchristie.org.

CHRISTIE, Very Rev. John Cairns; Church of Scotland Minister; Moderator of the General Assembly of the Church of Scotland, 2010–11; *b* Glasgow, 9 July 1947; *s* of John Cairns Christie and Agnes Christie (*née* Ritchie); *m* 1st, 1972, Elizabeth McDonald McIntosh (*d* 1993); one *d*; 2nd, 1995, Annette Cooke Carnegie Evans (*née* Hamill). *Educ:* Hermitage Sch., Helensburgh; Univ. of Strathclyde (BSc 1971); Jordanhill Coll. of Educn, Glasgow (PGCE 1973); Univ. of Glasgow (BD Hons 1989). CBiol 1976; MRSB (MIBiol 1976). Teacher, Albert Secondary Sch., Glasgow, 1973–78; Principal Teacher of Sci., Tiree High Sch., 1978–84; Warden, Dalneigh Hall of Residence, Inverness Royal Acad., 1984–86; ordained minister, 1990; Minister, Hyndland Parish Ch, Glasgow, 1990–2004; Interim Minister: Cumnock Trinity, 2004–05; Kilmacolm Old, 2005–07; North West Lochaber, 2007–08; Scots Kirk Lausanne and West Kilbride, 2008–09; Greenock Finnart St Paul's, 2009–10; Paisley Oakshaw Trinity, 2011–12; (and Locum) Renfrew North Ch, 2013–14. Convener, Bd of Parish Educn, 2001–05, Safety and Protection of Children, 2001–05, Safeguarding, 2005–10, Theol. of Forgiveness and Proportionality, 2007–09, Church of Scotland. Qualified Mediator, Church Congregations, 2010. *Recreations:* hill-walking, gardening. *Address:* 10 Cumberland Avenue, Helensburgh, Argyll and Bute G84 8QG. *E:* rev.jcc@btinternet.com.

CHRISTIE, Julie (Frances); actress; *b* 14 April 1940; *d* of Frank St John Christie and Rosemary Christie (*née* Ramsden). *Educ:* Convent; Brighton Coll. of Technology; Central Sch. of Speech and Drama. *Films:* Crooks Anonymous, 1962; The Fast Lady, 1962; Billy Liar, 1963; Darling, 1964 (Oscar, NY Film Critics Award, Br. Film Academy Award, etc); Young Cassidy, 1964; Dr Zhivago, 1965 (Donatello Award); Fahrenheit 451, 1966; Far from the Madding Crowd, 1966; Petulia, 1967; In Search of Gregory, 1969; The Go-Between, 1971; McCabe and Mrs Miller, 1972; Don't Look Now, 1973; Shampoo, 1974; Heaven Can Wait, 1978; Memoirs of a Survivor, 1981; The Animals Film, 1982; Return of the Soldier, 1982; Heat and Dust, 1983; The Gold Diggers, 1984; Power, 1987; Miss Mary, 1987; Fools of Fortune, 1990; The Railway Station Man, 1992; Hamlet, 1997; Afterglow, 1998; No Such Thing, 2001; The Phantom of the Louvre, 2001; Troy, Finding Neverland, 2004; The Secret Life of Words, 2005; Away From Her, 2007 (Golden Globe and Screen Actors Guild awards for Best Actress, 2008); Glorious 39, 2009; Red Riding Hood, 2011; The Company You Keep, 2012; *stage:* Old Times, Wyndham's, 1995; Suzanna Andler, Chichester, 1997. Fellow, BAFTA, 1997. Motion Picture Laurel Award, Best Dramatic Actress, 1967; Motion Picture Herald Award, Best Dramatic Actress, 1967.

CHRISTIE, Linford, OBE 1998 (MBE 1990); athlete; athletics coach; Managing Director, Nuff Respect, sports management company; *b* Jamaica, 2 April 1960; *s* of James and late Mabel Christie. *Educ:* Wandsworth Tech. Coll. Competed as a runner over 50 times for Great Britain, 1980–97. *European indoor championships:* Gold medal (200 m), 1986; Gold medal (60 m), 1988 and 1990; *European championships:* Gold medal (100 m), 1986 and 1990; *Commonwealth Games:* Silver medal (100 m), 1986; Gold medal (100 m), 1990 and 1994; *European Cup:* Gold medals (100 and 200 m), 1987; Gold medal (100 m), 1991, 1992 and 1994; Gold medals (100 and 200 m), 1997 (Men's Team Captain); *Olympic Games:* Silver medal (100 m), 1988; Gold medal (100 m), 1992 (British Men's Team Captain); *World indoor championships:* Silver medals (60 and 200 m), 1991; *World Cup:* Silver medal (200 m), 1992; Gold medal (100 m), 1989 and 1992; *World championships:* Gold medal (100 m), 1993; Silver medal (100 m relay), 1993. British and European 100 m record (9.87 seconds), and British 200 m record (20.09 seconds), 1988; British 100 yards record (9.30 seconds), Edinburgh, 1994; European 60 m record (6.47 seconds) and World indoor 200 m record (20.25 seconds), 1995. British Athletics Writers' Assoc., Male Athlete of the Year, 1988 and 1992. Hon. MSc Portsmouth Univ., 1993. *Publications:* Linford Christie (autobiog.), 1989; To Be Honest With You (autobiog.), 1995. *Address:* Nuff Respect, No.1 Constable's Boatyard, 15 Thames Street, Hampton, Middx TW12 2EW. *T:* (020) 8891 4145. *E:* nuff_respect@msn.com. *Club:* Thames Valley Harriers (Pres., 1997).

CHRISTIE, Richard Hamish; QC 2006; a Recorder, since 2009; *b* 17 April 1963; *s* of Martin and Phoebe Christie; *m* 1989, Jane; three *d*. *Educ:* Clifton Coll.; Manchester Univ. (LLB 1984). Called to the Bar, Inner Temple, 1986; Head of Chambers, 2 Pump Court, 2008–14; Jt Head of Chambers, 187 Fleet Street, 2014–. *Recreations:* cinema, Scotland, walking. *Address:* 187 Fleet Street, EC4A 2AT.

CHRISTIE, Sally Ann; *see* Shuttleworth, S. A.

CHRISTIE, Prof. Thomas; Director, The Aga Khan University Examination Board, 2003–14; Professor of Educational Assessment and Evaluation, University of Manchester, 1994–2003, now Professor Emeritus; *b* 12 May 1939; *s* of John Frew Christie and Margaret Watson Christie; *m* 1962, Patricia Ray Bozie; two *s* one *d*. *Educ:* Univ. of Edinburgh (MA, BEd). Res. Associate, 1963–66, Lectr in Educn, 1966–73, Sen. Lectr, 1973–76 and 1978–86, Dept of Educn, Univ. of Manchester; Sen. Lectr in Educnl Res., Dept of Educn, Univ. of Guyana, and Commonwealth Fund for Tech. Co-operation Consultant to Caribbean Exams Council, Barbados, 1976–78; University of Manchester: Dir, Centre for Formative Assessment Studies, Sch. of Educn, 1986–96; Dean, Fac. of Educn and Dir, Sch. of Educn, 1997–2002. Distinguished Prof., Aga Khan Univ., 2013. Hon. DSc National Univ. of Mongolia, 1998. *Publications:* (jtly) Creativity: a selective review of research, 1968, 2nd edn 1971; (with G. M. Forrest) Standards at GCE A Level: 1963 and 1973, 1980; (with G. M. Forrest) Defining Public Examination Standards, 1981; A Guide to Teacher Assessment (3 vols), 1990; (ed with B. Boyle) Issues in Setting Standards: establishing comparabilities, 1996. *Recreations:* reading, crossword puzzles, desert travel. *Address:* 24 Blenheim Road, Moseley, Birmingham B13 9TY. *T:* (0121) 449 7939.

CHRISTIE, William Lincoln; harpsichord player, organist and conductor; Founder and Director, Les Arts Florissants, since 1979; *b* Buffalo, New York State, 19 Dec. 1944; *s* of William Lincoln Christie and Ida Jones Christie; adopted French citizenship. *Educ:* Harvard Coll. (BA 1966); Yale Univ. (MusM 1969). Student of piano and harpsichord in US, 1957–70; Asst in Hist. of Music and Dir, Collegium Musicum, Dartmouth Coll., USA, 1970–71; moved to France, 1971; Collaborator, Soc. de musique d'autrefois, Paris, 1972–75; Visiting Professor: Conservatoires of Paris, Lyon and The Hague, and GSMD, 1977–81; Sommer Akademie für Musik, Innsbrück, 1978–83; Prof., Paris Conservatoire, 1982–95. Musical Dir, Hippolyte et Aricie, L'Opéra de Paris, 1985; regularly conducts orchs in France, Switzerland, UK and USA; Glyndebourne début, Handel's Theodora, 1996. Mem., Vis. Cttee for Music, Harvard Univ., 1993–96; Artist in Residence, Les Arts Florissants, Juilliard Sch. Mem., Acad. des Beaux Arts, 2008. Has made numerous recordings, 1976–, esp. works for harpsichord, and vocal works of 17th and 18th centuries with Les Arts Florissants. Hon. DMus NY at Buffalo, 1997. Prix Georges Pompidou, 2005. Officier des Arts et des Lettres (France); Commandeur de la Légion d'Honneur (France), 2010. *Publications:* Sonate Baroque, 1989; Purcell au Coeur du Baroque, 1995. *Recreations:* gardening, cooking. *Address:* Les Arts Florissants, 46 rue Fortuny, 75017 Paris, France. *T:* (1) 43879888; Le Logis du Bâtiment, 85210 Thiré, France. *W:* www.jardindewilliamchristie.fr.

CHRISTO AND JEANNE-CLAUDE; artist; Christo Javacheff, *b* Gabrovo, Bulgaria, 13 June 1935; *m* Jeanne-Claude de Guillebon (*d* 2009); one *s*. Emigrated to USA 1964. Completed works include: Wrapped Objects, 1958; Stacked Oil Barrels and Dockside

Packages, Cologne Harbour, 1961; Iron Curtain-Wall of Oil Barrels, blocking Rue Visconti, Paris, 1962; Store Fronts, NYC, 1964; Wrapped Kunsthalle, Berne, and Wrapped Fountain and Wrapped Medieval Tower, Spoleto, Italy, 1968; 5,600 Cubicmeter Package, Documenta 4, Kassel, 1968; Wrapped Floor and Stairway, Mus. of Contemporary Art, Chicago, 1969; Wrapped Coast, Little Bay, Sydney, Australia, 1969; Wrapped Monuments, Milan, 1970; Wrapped Floors and Covered Windows and Wrapped Walk Way, Krefeld, Germany, 1971; Valley Curtain, Grand Hogback, Rifle, Colo, 1970–72; The Wall, Wrapped Roman Wall, Via V. Veneto and Villa Borghese, Rome, 1974; Ocean Front, Newport, RI, 1974; Running Fence, Sonoma and Marin Counties, Calif, 1972–76; Wrapped Walk Ways, Kansas City, Mo, 1977–78; Surrounded Islands, Biscayne Bay, Miami, Fla, 1980–83; The Pont Neuf Wrapped, Paris, 1975–85; The Umbrellas, Japan-USA, 1984–91; Wrapped Floors and Stairways and Covered Windows, Mus. Würth, Künzelsau, Germany, 1995; Wrapped Reichstag, Berlin, 1971–95; Wrapped Trees, Switzerland, 1997–98; The Wall - 13,000 Oil Barrels, Gasometer Oberhausen, Germany, 1999; The Gates, Central Pk, NYC, 2005; Big Air Package, Gasometer Oberhausen, Germany, 2013. *Fax:* (212) 9662891. *W:* www.christojeanneclaude.net.

CHRISTOFIAS, Demetris; President, Republic of Cyprus, 2008–13; *b* Kyrenia Dist, Cyprus, 29 Aug. 1946; *s* of late Christofis and of Ana Christofia; *m* 1972, Elsi Chiratou; one *s* two *d. Educ:* Acad. of Social Sci. of Soviet Union (PhD). United Democratic Youth Organisation: Mem., Central Council, 1969–74; Central Organisational Sec., 1974–77; Gen. Sec., 1977–87; Progressive Party of the Working People, Cyprus: Mem., Nicosia-Kyrenia Dist Cttee, 1976–82; Member: Central Cttee, 1982; Central Cttee, Political Bureau, 1987–2009; Secretariat, Central Cttee, 1987–2009; Gen. Sec., Central Cttee, 1988–2009. Mem., 1996–2008, Pres., 2001–08, House of Representatives. Hon. Dr: Macedonia, 2004; Moscow State Inst. of Internat. Relns, 2008; Univ. for Foreigners of Perugia, 2009; Patras, 2010; Nat. and Kapodistrian Univ. of Athens, 2010; European Univ., Cyprus, 2011; Marupol, Ukraine, 2011. *Recreations:* football, lover of nature, theatre and reading, gardening.

CHRISTOPHER, Baron *cr* 1998 (Life Peer), of Leckhampton in the co. of Gloucestershire; **Anthony Martin Grosvenor Christopher,** CBE 1984; Chairman, TU Fund Managers Ltd (formerly Trades Union Unit Trust), since 1983 (Director, 1981–2012; President, since 2012); public and political affairs consultant, since 1989; General Secretary, Inland Revenue Staff Federation, 1976–88; *b* 25 April 1925; *s* of George Russell Christopher and Helen Kathleen Milford Christopher (*née* Rowley); *m* 1962, Adela Joy Thompson. *Educ:* Cheltenham Grammar Sch.; Westminster Coll. of Commerce. Articled Pupil, Agric. Valuers, Gloucester, 1941–44; RAF, 1944–48; Inland Revenue, 1948–57; Asst Sec. 1957–60, Asst Gen. Sec. 1960–74, Jt Gen. Sec. 1975, Inland Revenue Staff Fedn. Member: TUC General Council, 1976–89 (Chm., 1988–89); TUC Economic Cttee, 1977–89; TUC Education Cttee, 1977–85; TUC Educn and Training Cttee, 1985–86; TUC Employment Policy and Orgn Cttees, 1985–89; TUC International Cttee, 1982–89; TUC Finance and General Purposes Cttee, 1983–89; TUC Media Working Group, 1979–89 (Chm., 1985–89); TUC Employment Policy and Orgn Cttee, 1979–85; TUC Social Insurance Cttee, 1986–89; Mems Auditor, ICFTU, 1984–2004. House of Lords: Member, Select Committees: Audit, 2003–06; Consolidation of Bills, 2003–14; Mem., European Cttee on Envmt and Agric., 2000–03, 2005–06. Member: Tax Reform Cttee, 1974–80; Tax Consultative Cttee, 1980–88; Royal Commn on Distribution of Income and Wealth, 1978–79; IBA, 1978–83; Council, Inst. of Manpower Studies, 1984–89; ESRC, 1985–88; GMC, 1989–94. Chm., Tyre Industry EDC, 1983–86; Vice Pres., Building Socs Assoc., 1985–90; Director: Civil Service Building Soc., 1958–87 (Chm., 1978–87); Birmingham Midshires Building Soc., 1987–88; Policy Studies Inst. Council, 1983–91; Member: Bd, Civil Service Housing Assoc., 1958–96 (Vice-Chm., 1988–96); Council, NACRO, 1956–98 (Chm., 1973–98); Home Sec.'s Adv. Council for Probation and After-care, 1967–77; Inner London Probation and After-care Cttee, 1966–79; Audit Commn, 1989–95; Broadcasting Complaints Commn, 1989–97; Council, 1985–90, Assembly, 1990–, SCF; Chm., Alcoholics Recovery Project, 1970–76; Member: Home Sec.'s Working Party on Treatment of Habitual Drunken Offenders, 1969–71; Inquiry into Rover Cowley Works Closure, 1990; Trustee: Commonwealth Trades Union Council Charitable Trust, 1985–89; Inst. for Public Policy Res., 1989–94 (Treas., 1990–94). Vis. Fellow, Univ. of Bath, 1981–; Mem. Council, Royal Holloway and Bedford New Coll., 1985–89. FRSA 1989. *Publications:* (jtly) Policy for Poverty, 1970; (jtly) The Wealth Report, 1979; (jtly) The Wealth Report 2, 1982. *Recreations:* gardening, reading, walking dogs. *Address:* c/o TU Fund Managers Ltd, Congress House, Great Russell Street, WC1B 3LQ. *Club:* Beefsteak.

CHRISTOPHER, Ann, RA 1989 (ARA 1980); FRBS; sculptor; *b* 4 Dec. 1947; *d* of William and Phyllis Christopher; *m* 1969, Kenneth Cook. *Educ:* Harrow School of Art (pre-Diploma); West of England College of Art (DipAD Sculpture). RWA, 1983–2010; FRBS 1992. Represented by Pangolin London. Prizewinner, Daily Telegraph Young Sculptors Competition, 1971; Arts Council grants, 1973–76; Silver Medal for Sculpture of Outstanding Merit, RBS, 1994. *Exhibitions include:* RA Summer Exhibns, 1971–; Oxford Gallery, Oxford, 1973, 1974, 1978; Dorset County Mus. and Art Gall. (retrospective), 1989; Victoria Art Gall., Bath, 1992; Courcoux & Courcoux, 1991, 1999; Sculpture 93, London, 1993; Summer Exhibns, Redfern Gall., 1995, 1996; solo exhibitions: Redfern Gall., 1997; Jubilee Park, Canary Wharf, 2004; The Power of Place, RA, 2008; Pangolin, London, 2010, 2013, 2016; The Lines of Time, RA, 2016. *Work in Collections:* Bristol City Art Gallery; Contemporary Arts Soc.; Chantrey, London; Glynn Vivian Art Gall., Swansea; RWA; British Mus.; Gruss & Co., NY; RA; Corcoran Art Gall., Washington. *Commissions:* 3½m bronze, Tower Bridge Rd, London, 1990; 4½m bronze, Castle Park, Bristol, 1993; 2.3m bronze, Washington, USA, 1994; 4.8m corten steel, Plymouth, 1996; 2.3m bronze, Linklaters & Paines, London, 1997; 3m bronze, Great Barrington, Mass, USA, 1998; 5.5m corten steel, Portmarine, 2001; 2.2m bronze, Cordes, France, 2002; 12 bronzes, Kings Place, London, 2008; medal for British Art Medal Soc., 2004. *Recreation:* cinema.

CHRISTOPHER, Sir (Duncan) Robin (Carmichael), KBE 2000; CMG 1997; HM Diplomatic Service, retired; Projects Director, Global Leadership Foundation, since 2010 (Secretary General, 2007–10); *b* 13 Oct. 1944; *m* 1980, Merril Stevenson; two *d. Educ:* Keble Coll., Oxford (BA); Fletcher Sch., Tufts Univ., USA (MA). FCO, 1970; Second, then First, Sec., New Delhi, 1972; First Sec., FCO, 1976; Dep. Hd of Mission, Lusaka, 1980; FCO, 1983; on secondment to Cabinet Office, 1985; Counsellor: Madrid, 1987; FCO, 1991; Ambassador: to Ethiopia, 1994–97; to Indonesia, 1997–2000; to Argentina, 2000–04. Dir, Rurelec plc, 2005–10. Trustee: The Brooke Hosp., 2005–13; St Matthew's Children's Fund, Ethiopia, 2005–; Prospect Burma, 2005–; Redress, 2005–. *Recreations:* ski-ing, motorcycling, music. *E:* rchristopher2@yahoo.co.uk.

CHRISTOPHER, John Anthony, CB 1983; BSc; FRICS; Chief Valuer, Valuation Office, Inland Revenue, 1981–84, retired; *b* 19 June 1924; *s* of John William and Dorothy Christopher; *m* 1947, Pamela Evelyn Hardy; one *s* one *d* (and one *s* decd). *Educ:* Sir George Monoux Grammar Sch., Walthamstow; BSc Estate Management (London). Chartered Surveyor; LCC Valuation Dept, 1941. Served War, RAF, 1943–47. Joined Valuation Office, 1952; District Valuer and Valuation Officer, Lincoln, 1965; Superintending Valuer, Darlington, 1972; Asst Chief Valuer, 1974; Dep. Chief Valuer, Valuation Office, Inland Revenue, 1978. *Recreation:* golf. *Address:* 40 Svenskaby, Orton Wistow, Peterborough, Cambs PE2 6YZ. *T:* (01733) 238199.

CHRISTOPHER, Sir Robin; *see* Christopher, Sir D. R. C.

CHRISTOPHERS, Richard Henry Tudor, (Harry), CBE 2012; conductor; Founder an Conductor, The Sixteen, since 1979; Artistic Director, Handel and Haydn Society, Bostor since 2008; *b* 26 Dec. 1953; *s* of Richard Henry Christophers and Constance Claverin Christophers (*née* Thorp); *m* 1979, Veronica Mary Hayward; two *s* two *d. Educ:* Canterbur Cathedral Choir Sch.; King's Sch., Canterbury; Magdalen Coll., Oxford (Mods Classics, B Music, MA; Hon. Fellow, 2009). Conducting débuts: BBC Prom. concert, 1990; Salzbur Fest., 1989; Lisbon Opera, 1994; ENO, 2000; freelance conductor: BBC Philharmonic, Cit of London Sinfonia, Acad. of St Martin in the Fields, Hallé, London Symphony, San Francisc Symphony, etc. Principal Guest Conductor, Granada Symphony Orchestra, 2008– Numerous recordings. FRWCMD 2009; FRSCM 2014. Hon. DMus Leicester, 2008. Gran Prix du Disque, 1988; Deutschen Schallplattenkritik, 1992 and 1993; Gramophone Awar 1992; Diapason d'or, 1995 and 1996; Classical Brit Award, 2005; Gramophone Artist of th Year, 2009. *Recreations:* cooking, Arsenal FC. *Address:* The Sixteen, Quadrant House, 10 Flee Street, EC4Y 1AU.

CHRISTOPHERSEN, Henning; Senior Partner, Kreab Gavin Anderson (formerly Kreab) Brussels, since 2002; *b* Copenhagen, 8 Nov. 1939; *m* Jytte Risbjerg Christophersen; one *s* tw *d. Educ:* Copenhagen University (MA Econs, 1965). Head, Economic Div., Danish Fedn c Crafts and Smaller Industries, 1965–70; economics reporter for periodical NB, 1970–71, fo weekly Weekendavisen, 1971–78. MP (L) for Hillerød, 1971–84; Nat. Auditor, 1976–78 Minister for Foreign Affairs, 1978–79; Pres., Liberal Party Parly Gp, 1979–82; Dep. Prim Minister and Minister for Finance, 1982–84; a Vice-Pres., EC (formerly CEC), 1985–95 Mem., parly finance and budget cttee, 1972–76 (Vice-Chm., 1975); Chm., parly foreig affairs cttee, 1979–81; Mem., Nordic Council, 1981–82. Dep. Leader, Danish Liberal Party Venstre, 1972–77; Political spokesman of Liberal MPs, 1973–78; Acting Leader, Liberal Party 1977, Party Leader, 1978–84. Vice-Pres., Fedn of European Liberals and Democrat 1980–84. Man. Dir, Epsilon SPRL, 1995–2001; Sen. Advr to Czech Govt, 1996–99 Chairman: Örestad Develt Co., 1999–2007; Copenhagen Metro Co., 2007–; Vice-Chm Scania Danmark AS, 2000–06. Director: Danish Central Bank, 1979–82; Scancem AB 1998–99; Den Danske Bank, 1995–; Mem. Bd, KS Consult AS, 1999–2002. Member: Danis Council for Eur. Policy, 1995–98; Prime Minister's Adv. Council for Baltic Sea Co operation, Sweden, 1996–2000; European Convention and Presidium, 2002–03; Pres Energy Charter Conf., Brussels, 1998–2006. Mem. Bd, Rockwool Foundn, 1995–. Chm. Eur. Inst. of Public Admin, Maastricht, 1996–. *Publications:* books and articles on political an economic subjects. *Address:* Kreab Gavin Anderson, Avenue de Tervueren 2, 1040 Brussel Belgium.

CHRUSZCZ, Charles Francis; QC 1992; a Recorder, 1990; *b* 19 Nov. 1950; *s* of Janic Francis Chruszcz and Kathleen Whitehurst Chruszcz; *m* 1972, Margaret Olivia Chapmar three *s. Educ:* Queen Mary Coll., London (LLB Hons). Called to the Bar, Middle Templ 1973; Asst Recorder, 1985–90. *Recreations:* reading, music, building renovation, the outdoors.

CHU, Prof. Steven, PhD; William R. Kenan, Jr Professor of Physics and Professor c Molecular and Cellular Physiology, Stanford University, since 2013; *b* 28 Feb. 1948; *s* of J Chin Chu and Ching Chen Li; *m* Dr Jean Fetter; two *s* by a previous marriage. *Educ:* Univ of Rochester (AB Maths 1970, BS Physics 1970); Univ. of Calif, Berkeley (PhD Physic 1976). Postdoctoral Res. Fellow, Univ. of Calif, Berkeley, 1976–78; Mem., Technical Staf Bell Labs, Murray Hill, 1978–83; Hd, Quantum Electronics Res. Dept, AT&T Bell Labs Holmdel, 1983–87; Prof. of Physics and Applied Physics, 1987, Theodore and France Geballe Prof. of Physics and Applied Physics, 1990–2004, Chm., Physics Dept, 1990–93 1999–2001, Stanford Univ.; Prof. of Physics and of Molecular and Cell Biology, Univ. c Calif, Berkeley, 2004–09; Dir, Lawrence Berkeley Nat. Lab., 2004–09; Sec. of Energy, USA 2009–13. Vis. Prof., Collège de France, 1990. Fellow: APS, 1987; Optical Soc. of America 1988; Amer. Acad. Arts and Scis, 1992. Member: NAS, 1993; Academia Sinica, 1994; Amer Philosophical Soc., 1998; Foreign Member: Chinese Acad. Scis, 1998; Korean Acad. Scis an Technol., 1998; Royal Soc., 2014. Internat. FREng 2011. Broida Prize for Lase Spectroscopy, 1987, Schawlow Prize for Laser Sci., 1994, APS; King Faisal Internat. Prize fo Sci., 1993; Meggers Award for Spectroscopy, Optical Soc. of America, 1994; Humboldt Sen Scientist Award, 1995; Science for Art Prize, LVMH, 1995; (jtly) Nobel Prize for Physics 1997. *Recreations:* swimming, cycling, tennis. *Address:* Department of Physics, Stanfor University, Stanford, CA 94305, USA.

CHUA, Nam-Hai, FRS 1988; Andrew W. Mellon Professor and Head of Laboratory of Plan Molecular Biology, Rockefeller University, since 1981; *b* 8 April 1944; *m* 1970, Suat Cho Pearl; two *d. Educ:* Univ. of Singapore (BSc Botany and Biochem.); Harvard Univ. (AM, PhI Biol.). Lectr, Biochem. Dept, Univ. of Singapore, 1969–71; Rockefeller University, Ce Biology Department: Res. Associate, 1971–73; Asst Prof., 1973–77; Associate Prof., 1977–81 Chm., Management Bd, 1995, Scientific Adv. Bd, 1995, Inst. of Molecular Agrobiology, Na Univ. of Singapore. Fellow, Acad. Sinica, Taipei, 1988; Associate Fellow, Third World Acad of Scis, 1988; Hon. Member: Japanese Biochemical Soc., 1992; Japanese Soc. of Plan Physiologists; Foreign Mem., Chinese Acad. of Scis. Nat. Sci. and Technol. Medal, Singapore 1998; Singapore Public Admin Gold Medal, 2002; Internat. Prize in Biol., Japan Soc. fo Promotion of Sci., 2005; Lawrence Bogorad Award for Excellence in Plant Biol. Res., Amer Soc. for Plant Biologists, 2010. *Publications:* Methods in Chloroplast Molecular Biology, 1982 Plant Molecular Biology, 1987; Methods in Arabidopsis Research, 1992; 317 pubns i professional jls. *Recreations:* squash, ski-ing. *Address:* Rockefeller University, 1230 Yor Avenue, New York, NY 10065–6399, USA. *T:* (212) 3278126, *Fax:* (212) 3278327.

CHUAN LEEKPAI; MHR, Trang Province, Thailand, 1969–2007; Leader of th Opposition, 1995–97 and 2001–03; *b* 28 July 1938. *Educ:* Trang Wittaya Sch.; Silpakorn Pre Univ.; Thammasat Univ. (LLB 1962). Barrister-at-Law, Thai Bar, 1964; lawyer. Thailand Dep. Minister of Justice, 1975; Minister to Prime Minister's Office, 1976; Minister: of Justice 1976 and 1980–81; of Commerce, 1981; of Agric. and Co-operatives, 1982–83; of Educn 1983–86; Speaker, House of Reps, 1986–88; Minister of Public Health, 1988–89; Dep. Prim Minister and Minister of Agric. and Co-operatives, 1990–92; Prime Minister, 1992–95; Prim Minister and Minister of Defence, 1997–2001. Chm., Adv. Cttee, Democrat Party. Vis. Lect Forensic Medicine Dept, Faculty of Medicine, Chulalongkorn Univ. Hon. Dr Politica Science: Srinakharinwirot, 1985; Ramkhamhaeng, 1987; Hon. LLD: Philippines, 1993 Vongchavalitkul, 1998; Hon. LitD: (Painting) Silpakorn, 1994; Nat. Univ. of San Marcos Lima, 1999. Kt Grand Cross (First Cl.), 1979, Kt Grand Cordon, 1981, Order of Crow (Thailand); Kt Grand Cross (First Cl.), 1980, Kt Grand Cordon (Special Cl.), 1982, Order o White Elephant (Thailand). *Address:* c/o Democrat Party, 67 Setsiri Road, Samsen NI Phay Thai, Bangkok 10400, Thailand.

CHUBB, family name of **Baron Hayter**.

CHUBB, Anthony Gerald Trelawny, FCA; Chairman, Foseco (formerly Foseco Minsep PLC, 1986–90; *b* 6 April 1928; *s* of Ernest Gerald Trelawny Chubb and Eunice Chubb; *n* 1951, Beryl Joyce (*née* Cross); two *s. Educ:* Wylde Green Coll., Sutton Coldfield. FCA 196 (ACA 1951); ACMA 1956. CBIM 1981. Joined Foundry Services Ltd, 1951; Man. Dir Foseco UK, 1964–69; Dir, Foseco Ltd, 1966; Man. Dir, Foseco International, 1969–78; Dep Gp Man. Dir, 1974–79, Gp Man. Dir, 1979–86, Foseco Minsep PLC; Chm. Electrocomponents PLC, 1986–90 (Dep. Chm., 1983–86; Dir, 1980–90). *Recreations:* gol gardening, reading.

CHUBB, Prof. Ian William, AC 2006 (AO 1999); Chief Scientist of Australia, since 2011 *b* 17 Oct. 1943; *s* of Ian and Lillian Chubb; *m* 1971, Claudette Maes; three *d. Educ:* Chris

Church, Oxford (MSc, DPhil 1975). Heyman's Res. Fellow, Univ. of Ghent, 1969–71; Wellcome Schol., Christ Church, Oxford, 1971–74; Res. Fellow, St John's Coll., Oxford, 1974–77; Lectr, Sen. Lectr, then Associate Prof., Flinders Univ., 1977–85; Dep. Vice-Chancellor, 1986–90, Emeritus Prof., 1990, Univ. of Wollongong; Chair, Commonwealth Higher Educn Council, 1990–95; Dep. Vice-Chancellor, Monash Univ., 1993–95; Vice Chancellor: Flinders Univ., 1995–2000; ANU, 2001–11, now Prof. Emeritus. Chm., Australian Vice-Chancellors' Cttee, 2000–01; Pres., Gp of Eight Univs, 2005–09. Mem. Bd, CSIRO, 2008–11. Hon. DSc Flinders, 2000; DUniv ANU, 2011; Hon. DLitt Charles Darwin Univ., 2011; Hon. LLD Monash, 2012. *Address:* (office) Industry House, 10 Binara Street, Canberra City, ACT 2601, Australia.

CHUNG, Kyung-Wha, Korean Order of Merit; concert violinist; *b* 26 March 1948; *d* of Chun-Chai Chung and Won-Sook (Lee) Chung; *m*; two *s*. *Educ:* Juilliard Sch. of Music, New York. Moved from Korea to New York, 1960; 7 years' study with Ivan Galamian, 1960–67; New York début with New York Philharmonic Orch., 1967; European début with London Symphony Orch., Royal Festival Hall, London, 1970. Mem. Faculty, Juilliard Sch. of Music, NY, 2007–. First prize, Leventritt Internat. Violin Competition, NY, 1967. *Address:* c/o Opus 3 Artists, 470 Park Avenue South, 9th Floor North, New York, NY 10016, USA.

CHUNG, Sir Sze-yuen, GBE 1989 (CBE 1975; OBE 1968); Kt 1978; PhD; FREng; JP; Pro-Chancellor, Hong Kong University of Science and Technology, since 1999 (Founding Chairman, 1988–99); *b* 3 Nov. 1917; *m* 1942, Nancy Cheung (*d* 1977); one *s* two *d*. *Educ:* Hong Kong Univ. (BScEng 1st Cl. Hons, 1941); Sheffield Univ. (PhD 1951). FREng (FEng 1983); FIMechE 1957, Hon. FIMechE 1983; Hon. FHKIE 1976; FIET (FIProdE 1958); CCMI (FBIM 1978). Consulting engr, 1952–56; Gen. Man., Sonca Industries (now Sonca Products), 1956–60, Man. Dir 1960–77, Chm. 1977–88. Director: CLP Hldgs (formerly China Light & Power Co.), 1968–; Sun Hung Kai Properties Ltd, 2001–09. Mem., Hong Kong Legislative Council, 1965–74, Sen. Mem., 1974–78; Mem., Hong Kong Exec. Council, 1972–80, Sen. Mem., 1980–88; Advr to Govt of People's Republic of China on Hong Kong affairs, 1992–96; Mem., Chinese Govt's Preparatory Cttee for establishment of HKSAR, 1996–97; Convenor, HKSAR Exec. Council, 1997–99. Chairman: Standing Commn on CS Salaries and Conditions of Service, 1980–88; Hong Kong Productivity Council, 1974–76; Asian Product. Orgn, 1969–70; Hong Kong Industrial Design Council, 1969–75; Fedn of Hong Kong Industries, 1966–70 (Hon. Life Pres. 1974); Hong Kong Metrication Cttee, 1969–73; Hong Kong-Japan Business Co-operation Cttee, 1983–88; Hong Kong-US Econ. Co-operation Cttee, 1984–88. Founding Chairman: Hong Kong Polytechnic, 1972–86; City Polytechnic of Hong Kong, 1984 (Founding Fellow, 1986); Hong Kong Hosp. Authy, 1991–95 (Chm., Provisional Hosp. Authy, 1988–90). Founding Pres., Hong Kong Acad. of Engrg Scis, 1994–97; Pres., Engrg Soc. of Hong Kong, 1960–61. LLD (*hc*): Chinese Univ. of Hong Kong, 1983; Sheffield, 1985; DSc (*hc*) Hong Kong Univ., 1976; DEng (*hc*) Hong Kong Polytechnic, 1989; DBA (*hc*) City Polytechnic of Hong Kong, 1989. JP Hong Kong, 1964. Man of the Year, Hong Kong Business Today magazine, 1985. Defence Medal, 1948; Silver Jubilee Medal, 1977; Gold Medal, Asian Productivity Orgn, 1980; HKSAR Grand Bauhinia Medal, 1997. Japanese Order of Sacred Treasure (3rd cl.), 1983. *Publications:* Hong Kong's Journey to Reunification (memoirs), 2001; contrib. Proc. IMechE, Jl Iron and Steel Inst., Jl Hong Kong Instn of Engrs, and Jl Engrg Soc. of Hong Kong. *Recreation:* swimming. *Address:* House 25, Bella Vista, Silver Terrace Road, Clear Water Bay, Kowloon, Hong Kong. *T:* 27610281, 27192857, *Fax:* 27607493, 23580689. *Clubs:* Hong Kong, Hong Kong Jockey, Kowloon Cricket, Pacific (Hong Kong).

CHUNN, Louise Frances, (Mrs A. J. Anthony); Founder and Editor, welldoing.org, since 2013; *b* Auckland, NZ, 24 July 1956; *d* of late Jeremiah Alfred Chunn and of Yvonne Chunn; *m* 2001, Andrew John Anthony; one *s* two *d*. *Educ:* Baradene Coll.; Univ. of Auckland (BA Hist. 1977). Reporter, Fashion Weekly, 1982–83; Features Ed., then Dep. Ed., 1983–85, Ed., 1985–86, Just Seventeen; Dep. Ed., Elle, 1986–89; Women's Page Ed., Guardian, 1989–94; Associate, then Features Ed., 1995–98, Dep. Ed., 1998, Vogue; Ed., ES Mag., Evening Standard, 1998–2000; Dep. Ed., 2000–02, Ed., 2002–06, In Style; Editor: Good Housekeeping, 2006–08; Psychologies, 2009–12. *Recreations:* fantasy travel, family, friends, books. *Address:* 4 Dunmore Road, NW6 6TR. *T:* 07817 011806. *E:* louisechunn@btinternet.com.

CHURCH, Ian David, CBE 2002; Editor, Official Report (Hansard), House of Commons, 1989–2002; *b* 18 Oct. 1941; *s* of John Jasper and Violet Kathleen Church; *m* 1964, Christine Stevenson; one *d*. *Educ:* Roan School. Journalist with: Dundee Courier and Advertiser, 1958–64; Press Association, 1964; The Scotsman, 1966; The Times, 1968; joined Hansard, 1972; Dep. Editor, 1988. Sec., Commonwealth Hansard Editors Assoc., 1990–2002 (Pres., 1996–99). Ind. Mem., Standards Cttee, Mid-Sussex DC, 2007–11 (Vice Chm., 2010–11). *Publications:* Hansard Centenary Volume, 2009; The Remains of the Living (fiction), 2013.

CHURCH, John Carver, CMG 1986; CVO 1988; MBE 1970; HM Diplomatic Service, retired; *b* 8 Dec. 1929; *s* of Richard Church, CBE, FRSL, and Catherina Church; *m* 1953, Marie-Geneviève Vallette; two *s* two *d*. *Educ:* Cranbrook Sch., Kent; Ecole Alsacienne, Paris; Christ's Coll., Cambridge (MA 1953). Reuters News Agency, 1953–59; Central Office of Information, 1959–61; Commonwealth Relations Office: Information Officer, Calcutta, 1961–65; Foreign and Commonwealth Office: Second Secretary (Commercial) Rio de Janeiro, 1966–69; First Sec. (Information) Tel Aviv, 1969–74; First Sec., News Dept, FCO, 1974–77; Consul (Commercial) Milan, 1977–78; Consul-General: São Paulo, 1978–81; Naples, 1981–86; Barcelona, 1986–89. *Address:* La Métairie, Le Maine, 24510 Ste Alvère, France.

CHURCH, John George, CBE 1998; DL; FCA; President, Church & Co. plc, since 2002 (Chairman, 1991–2001); *b* 14 May 1936; *s* of Dudley Ross Church and Louise Elizabeth Church; *m* 1965, Rhona Elizabeth Gibson; one *s* one *d*. *Educ:* Stowe Sch. FCA 1959. Mgt Consultant, Annan Impey Morrish, 1961–64; joined Church & Co. plc, 1964: Asst Co. Sec., 1964–67; Co. Sec., 1967–76; Dir, 1968–2001; Man. Dir, 1976–97. Non-executive Director: Babers Ltd, 1972– (Chm., 1996–); James Southall and Co. Ltd, 1985–98 and 2000–06 (Dep. Chm., 2002–06); Start Rite Ltd, 1985–98 and 2000–06; Kingsley Park Properties (formerly St Matthew's Hosp.) Ltd, 1981–2003. President: British Footwear Mfrs Fedn, 1988–89; Boot Trade Benevolent Soc., 1984–85. St Andrew's Group of Hospitals, Northampton: Gov., 1995–; Mem. Bd Mgt, 1999–2010; non-exec. Dir, 2004–10. Member: Ct, Univ. of Northampton (formerly Nene Coll., Northampton, subseq. UC of Northampton), 1994–; Bd of Mgt, Cordwainers' Coll., 1976–2000. Liveryman, Cordwainers' Co., 1958– (Mem. of Ct, 1992–; Master, 1998–99). High Sheriff, Northants, 1993–94; DL Northants, 1997. FRSA 1995. Hon. Fellow, UC of Northampton, 2002. *Recreation:* country pursuits. *Club:* Royal Automobile.

CHURCH, Jonathan, CBE 2015; Founder and Director, Jonathan Church Productions, since 2015; *b* Nottingham, 4 March 1967; *s* of Tony Church and Marielaine Church (*née* Douglas); *m* Yvonne Thompson; four *d*. *Educ:* Frank Weldon Comprehensive Sch., Nottingham; Clarendon Coll. of Further Educn, Nottingham. Asst Dir, 1990–91, Asst Producer, 1992, Nottingham Playhouse; Associate Dir, Derby Playhouse, 1994–95; Artistic Dir, Salisbury Playhouse, 1995–99; Associate Dir, Hampstead Th., 1999–2001; Artistic Dir, Birmingham Rep. Th., 2001–06; Artistic Dir, Chichester Fest. Th., 2006–15. *Director:* The Ballad of Reading Gaol, The Bear, 1988, Crucible Th., Sheffield; Saint Oscar, 1992, Angels Rave On, 1998, Nottingham Playhouse; Derby Playhouse: Frankie & Johnny, Two, 1993; Someone Who'll Watch Over Me, Absurd Person Singular, Importance of Being Earnest, 1994; Oleanna, Derby 100, 1995; Salisbury Playhouse: Comic Cuts, The Rover, The Banished Cavaliers, Oleanna, Educating Rita, The Merchant of Venice, 1996; Time and the Conways, The Rehearsal, The Double Inconstancy, Disappearances, The Cherry Orchard, Racing Demon, 1997; Romeo and Juliet (and nat. tour), The Alchemical Wedding, Top Girls (and Plymouth Th. Royal), 1988; Colombe, Just Between Ourselves, 1999; Birmingham Repertory Theatre: The Crucible, 1995; Private Lives, Closer, 2001; Of Mice and Men, 2001 (and Liverpool, Savoy, 2003, Old Vic, 2004); Peter Pan, Elizabeth Rex, 2002; Murmuring Judges, Absence of War, Racing Demon, 2003; The Witches, transf. Wyndham's Th., 2005; Promises and Lies, 2006; Chichester Festival Theatre: Oleanna/Educating Rita, 1996; Pravda, 2006; (Co-Dir) Nicholas Nickleby Part I and Part II, 2006 and 2007, transf. Gielgud Th., 2007; Hobson's Choice, 2007; The Circle, 2008; The Grapes of Wrath, 2009; The Critic, Master Class, (Co-Dir) The Real Inspector Hound, 2010; Singin' in the Rain, 2011, transf. Palace Th., 2012; The Resistible Rise of Arturo Ui, transf. Duchess, 2013; Amadeus, 2014; Taken at Midnight, 2014, transf. Th. Royal, Haymarket, 2015; Mack & Mabel, 2015; *other productions:* Mirror of the Moon (Man in the Moon), In Lambeth, Ensemble Th., Vienna, 1992 and Lyric Hammersmith, 1993; Magnetic North, W Yorks Playhouse, 1993; The Broken Heart, Lyric Hammersmith, 1994; You Be Ted and I'll be Sylvia, Hampstead Th., 1999; A Busy Day, Bristol Old Vic and Lyric Shaftesbury Ave, 2000; Red Velvet, Hampstead Th., 2000; God and Stephen Hawking, Bath Th. Royal and tour, 2000; The Diary of Anne Frank, tour, 2000; Hobson's Choice, Plymouth Th. Royal and tour, 2002; *co-producer:* Macbeth, Gielgud Th., 2007; The Last Confession, Haymarket Th., 2007; Taking Sides, Collaboration, Duchess Th., 2009; ENRON, Noël Coward Th., 2010; Top Girls, Trafalgar Studios, 2011; Rosencrantz and Guildenstern are Dead, Haymarket Th., 2011; South Downs, The Browning Version, Harold Pinter Th., 2012; Sweeney Todd, Adelphi Th., 2012.

CHURCH, Judith Ann; *b* 19 Sept. 1953; *d* of late Edmund Church and of Helen Church; two *s*. *Educ:* Leeds Univ. (BA Hons Maths and Phil.); Huddersfield Poly. (PGCE Technical); Aston Univ. (Postgrad. Dip. Occupational Health and Safety); Thames Valley Coll. (DMS). Teacher, VSO, 1975–77; Process Research, Mars UK, 1979–80; HM Inspector of Factories, HSE, 1980–86; Nat. Health and Safety Officer, MSF, 1986–94. Contested (Lab) Stevenage, 1992; MP (Lab) Dagenham, June 1994–2001. *Recreation:* keeping fit.

CHURCHHOUSE, Prof. Robert Francis, CBE 1982; PhD; Professor of Computing Mathematics, University of Wales, College of Cardiff (formerly University College, Cardiff), 1971–95; *b* 30 Dec. 1927; *s* of Robert Francis Churchhouse and Agnes Howard; *m* 1954, Julia McCarthy; three *s*. *Educ:* St Bede's Coll., Manchester; Manchester Univ. (BSc 1949); Trinity Hall, Cambridge (PhD 1952). Royal Naval Scientific Service, 1952–63; Head of Programming Gp, Atlas Computer Lab., SRC, 1963–71. Vis. Fellow, St Cross Coll., Oxford, 1972–90. Chm., Computer Bd for Univs and Res. Councils, 1979–82; Mem., Welsh Cttee, UFC, 1989–93. Pres., IMA, 1986–87. Hon. DSc South Bank, 1993. KSG 1988. *Publications:* (ed jtly) Computers in Mathematical Research, 1968; (ed jtly) The Computer in Literary and Linguistic Studies, 1976; Numerical Analysis, 1978; Codes and Ciphers, Julius Caesar, the Enigma and the Internet, 2002; papers in math. and other jls. *Recreations:* cricket, astronomy. *Address:* 15 Holly Grove, Lisvane, Cardiff CF14 0UJ. *T:* (029) 2075 0250.

CHURCHILL; *see* Spencer-Churchill.

CHURCHILL, 3rd Viscount *cr* 1902; **Victor George Spencer,** OBE 2001; Baron Churchill of Wychwood 1815; Managing Director, CCLA Investment Management Ltd, 1988–99; *b* 31 July 1934; *s* of 1st Viscount Churchill, GCVO, and late Christine Sinclair (who *m* 3rd, Sir Lancelot Oliphant, KCMG, CB); *S* half-brother, 1973. *Educ:* Eton; New Coll., Oxford (MA). Lieut, Scots Guards, 1953–55. Morgan Grenfell & Co. Ltd, 1958–74; Investment Manager: Central Bd of Finance, C of E, 1974–99; Charities Official Investments Fund, 1974–95. A Church Comr, 2001–04. Director: Local Authorities' Mutual Investment Fund, 1974–99; Charter Pan-European Trust, 1992–2004; F & C Income and Growth Investment Trust, 1994–2005; Allchurches Trust, 1994–2006; Schroder Split Fund, 1995–2002. Trustee, Royal Foundn of St Katharine, Limehouse, 1979–2011. *Heir:* (to Barony only): *kinsman* Richard Harry Ramsay Spencer [*b* 11 Oct. 1926; *m* 1st, 1958, Antoinette Rose-Marie de Charrière (*d* 1994); two *s*; 2nd, 1999, Cressida Josephine Alice Sykes (*née* Van Halle)]. *Address:* 6 Cumberland Mansions, George Street, W1H 5TE. *T:* (020) 7262 6223.

CHURCHILL, Caryl, (Mrs David Harter); playwright; *b* 3 Sept. 1938; *d* of Robert Churchill and Jan (*née* Brown); *m* 1961, David Harter; three *s*. *Educ:* Trafalgar Sch., Montreal; Lady Margaret Hall, Oxford (BA 1960). Student prodns of early plays, 1958–61; *radio plays:* The Ants, 1962; Lovesick, 1966; Identical Twins, 1968; Abortive, 1971; Not… not… not… not… not enough oxygen, 1971; Schreiber's Nervous Illness, 1972; Henry's Past, 1972; Perfect Happiness, 1973; *television plays:* The Judge's Wife, 1972; Turkish Delight, 1973; The After Dinner Joke, 1978; The Legion Hall Bombing, 1978; Crimes, 1981; (with Ian Spink) Fugue, 1987; *stage plays:* Owners, 1972; Moving Clocks Go Slow, 1975; Objections to Sex and Violence, 1975; Light Shining in Buckinghamshire, 1976; Vinegar Tom, 1976; Traps, 1977; (contrib.) Floorshow, 1977; Cloud Nine, 1979; Three More Sleepless Nights, 1980; Top Girls, 1982; Fen, 1983; Softcops, 1984; (collaborator) Midday Sun, 1984; (with David Lan and Ian Spink) A Mouthful of Birds, 1986; Serious Money, 1987; Ice cream, 1989; Hot Fudge, 1989; Mad Forest, 1990; (with Ian Spink and Orlando Gough) Lives of the Great Poisoners, 1991; The Skriker, 1994; (trans.) Seneca's Thyestes, 1994; Blue Heart, 1997; This is a Chair, 1997, Far Away, 2000; A Number, 2002; Drunk Enough to Say I Love You?, 2006; Love and Information, 2012. *Publications:* Owners, 1973; Light Shining in Buckinghamshire, 1976, new edn 1989; Traps, 1977, new edn 1989; Vinegar Tom, 1978; Cloud Nine, 1979, new edn 1989; Top Girls, 1982; Fen, 1983; Fen and Softcops, 1984; A Mouthful of Birds, 1986; Serious Money, 1987; Plays I, 1985; Plays II, 1988; Objections to Sex and Violence in Plays by Women, vol. 4, 1985; Ice cream, 1989; Mad Forest, 1990; Lives of the Great Poisoners, 1992; The Skriker, 1994; Thyestes, 1994; Blue Heart, 1997; This is a Chair, 1999; Far Away, 2000; A Number, 2002; Drunk Enough to Say I Love You?, 2006; anthologies. *Address:* c/o Casarotto Ramsay Ltd, Waverley House, 7–12 Noel Street, W1F 8GQ. *T:* (020) 7287 4450.

CHURCHILL, Emma Jane; Director, Process Transformation, HM Revenue and Customs, since 2015; *b* Swindon, 3 May 1975; *d* of Lawrence Churchill and Ann Churchill; one *d*. *Educ:* Cheltenham Ladies' Coll.; St John's Coll., Oxford (BA Lit.Hum. 1st Cl. 1996). Policy Advr, DSS, 1996–98; Private Sec. to Sec. of State for Social Security, 1998–99; Operational Policy and Judicial Support Manager, Appeals Service, 1999–2001; Policy Advr to the Prime Minister, 2001–03; Hd, Domestic Violence Unit, 2003–04, Prin. Private Sec. to Sec. of State, 2004–07, Home Office; UK Border Agency: Dir, Immigration Policy, 2008–10; Dir, Asylum, 2010–11; Dir, Strategy and Assurance, 2011–13; Dir, Civil Service, Cabinet Office, 2013–15. *Recreations:* watching England win the Ashes, supporting Liverpool FC, taking daughter Jennifer on fast rollercoasters, eating and drinking with family. *Address:* HM Revenue and Customs, 1st Floor, 100 Parliament Street, SW1A 2HQ. *T:* 0300 055 1177. *E:* emma.churchill@hmrc.gsi.gov.uk.

CHURCHILL, Johanna Peta; MP (C) Bury St Edmunds, since 2015; *m* 1992, Peter Ian Churchill; four *d*. *Educ:* Dame Alice Harper Sch., Bedford; Univ. of Lincoln (BSc); Univ. of Nottingham (MSc). Retail work for regl and global brands, then site develt and building industry; manager of contracting cos, 1994–2015. Mem. (C) Lincs CC, 2013–15. *Address:* House of Commons, SW1A 0AA.

CHURCHILL, Lawrence, CBE 2010; Chairman, Financial Services Compensation Scheme, since 2012; *b* 5 Aug. 1946; *s* of Austin and Kathleen Churchill; *m* 1991, Karen Darcy; twin *d*, and one *s* one *d* from previous marriage. *Educ:* Birkenhead Sch.; St John's Coll., Oxford (MA). Systems Analyst, Proctor & Gamble, 1969–73; Sen. Systems Designer, then Exec. Dir, Hambro Life Assce, 1973–85; Exec. Dir, Allied Dunbar Assce, 1985–91; Chief Exec., NatWest Life, 1991–95; Man. Dir, NatWest Life Investments, 1995–98; Chm., Unum Ltd, 1998–2002; CEO, Zurich Financial Services, 2002–04. Chairman: Pension Protection Fund, 2004–10; NEST Corp., 2010–15; Applegate Marketplace Ltd, 2015–. Senior Independent Director: Good Energy (formerly Monkton) plc, 2004–12; Children's Mutual, 2005–10; BUPA, 2015– (non-exec. Dir, 2009–). Non-executive Director: PIA, 1994–98; ABI, 1995–98; Employers' Forum on Disability, 2000–03; Financial Ombudsman Service, 2002–05. Chm., Raising Standards Quality Mark Scheme, 2000–02; Mem., Bd for Actuarial Standards, 2006–12; Chm., Ind. Governance Cttee, Prudential Assce Co., 2015–; Trustee, Prudential Corporate Trustee Ltd, 2015–. Vice Pres., Employment Opportunities, 2004–; Prince's Initiative for Mature Enterprise: Ambassador, 2009–; Thought Leadership Gp, 2013–; Chm., Commissioning Gp, 2014–. Trustee, RSA, 2000–02; Internat. Longevity Centre - UK, 2007–. Gov., Pension Policy Inst., 2010–. *Publications:* (jtly) A Changing Nation, 1997; (jtly) New Beginnings, 2000; (jtly) The Concept of Value, 2007. *Recreations:* Rugby, theatre, opera, family. *Address:* 4 Lansdown Crescent, Bath BA1 5EX. *E:* lawrence.churchill@thechurchillsonline.com. *Club:* Oxford and Cambridge.

CHURCHILL, Neil Gareth; Director for Patient Experience (Domain 4 Lead), NHS England (formerly NHS National Commissioning Board), since 2013; *b* Carshalton, 6 Sept. 1966; *s* of Ronald and Shirley Churchill; *m* 1996, Anna Barlow; two *d*. *Educ:* Fitzwilliam Coll., Cambridge (BA Hist. 1988); London South Bank Univ. (MBA 2000). Head of Communications: Barnardo's, 1991–96; PSI, 1996–98; Dep. Chief Exec., Crisis, 1998–2001; Ext. Affairs Dir, Age Concern, 2001–07; Chief Exec., Asthma UK, 2007–13. Non-exec. Dir, NHS South of England (formerly NHS SE Coast), 2009–13. Member: Nat. Information Governance Bd, 2011–13; Exec. Bd, Beryl Inst., 2015–. Res. Fellow, Smith Inst., 2010–. Trustee: Cardboard Citizens, 2001–07; Crisis, 2005–08; Prisoners' Advice Service, 2010–14; Students' Union, London S Bank Univ., 2013–; Tavistock Centre for Couple Relationships, 2014–. Member, Editorial Board: Cultural Trends, 2000–10; Research Involvement and Engagement Jl, 2014–. *Publications:* (ed) Advancing Opportunity: older people and social care, 2008; (ed) Health Futures, 2009; (ed) More For Less in Health, 2010; (ed) Prospects for Health and Wellbeing Boards, 2013. *Recreations:* reading, 40s cinema, early medieval art and history, live music and theatre. *Address:* NHS England, Nursing Directorate, Skipton House, 80 London Road, SE1 6LH. *T:* 07876 851854. *E:* neilchurchill@nhs.net. *W:* www.twitter.com/neilgchurchill.

CHURSTON, 5th Baron *cr* 1858; **John Francis Yarde-Buller;** Bt 1790; *b* 29 Dec. 1934; *s* of 4th Baron Churston, VRD and Elizabeth Mary (*d* 1951), *d* of late W. B. du Pre; *S* father, 1991; *m* 1973, Alexandra Joanna, *d* of A. G. Contomichalos; one *s* two *d*. *Educ:* Eton Coll. 2nd Lt RHG, 1954. A Freemason. *Heir: s* Hon. Benjamin Anthony Francis Yarde-Buller [*b* 13 Sept. 1974; *m* 2000, Sophie Frances, *e d* of Brian Duncan]. *Address:* Yowlestone House, Puddington, Tiverton, Devon EX16 8LN. *T:* (01884) 860328. *Clubs:* Buck's, White's.

CIAMPI, Dr Carlo Azeglio; President of the Republic of Italy, 1999–2006, now President Emeritus and Life Senator; *b* Livorno, 9 Dec. 1920; *s* of Pietro and Maria Ciampi; *m* 1946, Franca Pilla; one *s* one *d*. *Educ:* Scuola Normale Superiore, Pisa; Univ. of Pisa (BA, LLB 1946). Served Italian Army, 1941–44 (MC). Joined Bank of Italy, Rome, 1946: work in various branches, 1946–60; Economist and Hd, Res. Dept, 1960–73; Sec.-Gen., 1973–76; Dep. Dir Gen., 1976–78; Dir Gen., 1978; Gov., and Chm., Ufficio Italiano dei Cambi, 1979–93 (Hon. Gov., 1993–); Gov. for Italy, IBRD, IDA, IFC, Washington, and ADB, Manila, 1979–93; Pres., Council of Ministers, Rome, 1993–94; Vice-Pres., BIS, Basle, 1994–96 (Dir, 1979–93); Chm., Competitiveness Adv. Gp, EU, 1995–96; Minister of the Treasury, Budget and Econ. Programming, 1996–99; Chm., Interim Cttee, IMF, Washington, 1998–99. Pres., Venice Internat. Univ., 1996–99. *Publications:* Un Metodo per Governare, 1996; contrib. numerous reports and articles. *Address:* c/o Senato della Repubblica, Via Della Dogana Vecchia 29, 00187 Rome, Italy.

CICCONE, Madonna Louise Veronica, (Madonna); singer and actress; *b* 16 Aug. 1958; *d* of Sylvio, (Tony), Ciccone and late Madonna Ciccone; *m* 1st, 1985, Sean Penn (marr. diss. 1989); one *d* by Carlos Leon; 2nd, 2000, Guy Ritchie (marr. diss. 2008); one *s* and one adopted *s*; one adopted *d*. *Educ:* Adams High Sch.; Univ. of Michigan (dance scholarship); Alvin Alley Studios, NY. Formed Maverick Records Co., 1992; *recordings* include: first hit single, Holiday, 1983; albums: Madonna, 1983; Like a Virgin, 1984; True Blue, 1986; Like a Prayer, 1989; Erotica, 1992; Bedtime Stories, 1994; Ray of Light, 1998; Music, 2000; American Life, 2003; Confessions on a Dance Floor, 2005; I'm Going to Tell You a Secret, 2006; The Confessions Tour, 2007; Hard Candy, 2008; Celebration, 2009; MDNA, 2012; Rebel Heart, 2015. *Films:* A certain Sacrifice, 1979; Vision Quest, 1985; Desperately seeking Susan, 1985; Shanghai Surprise, 1986; Who's that Girl?, 1987; Bloodhounds of Broadway, 1989; Dick Tracy, 1989; Soap-Dish, 1990; Shadows and Fog, 1991; A League of their Own, 1991; In Bed with Madonna, 1991; Truth or Dare, 1991; Body of Evidence, 1992; Snake Eyes, 1994; Dangerous Game, 1994; Blue in the Face, 1995; Girl 6, 1996; Evita (Golden Globe Award for best actress), 1996; Four Rooms, 1996; The Next Best Thing, 2000; Swept Away, 2002; Die Another Day, 2002; dir, Filth and Wisdom, 2008; writer and exec. prod., I Am Because We Are, 2008; dir and co-writer, W. E., 2012; *theatre:* Up For Grabs, Wyndham's, 2002. *Publications:* Sex, 1992; *for children:* The English Roses, 2003; Mr Peabody's Apples, 2003; Yakov and the Seven Thieves, 2004; The Adventures of Abdi, 2004.

CICUTTO, Francis John; Chairman, Chord Capital Pty Ltd, since 2005; *b* 9 Nov. 1950; *s* of Francesco Cicutto and Ultima (*née* Margaritta); *m* 1982, Christine Bates; one *s*. *Educ:* Univ. of NSW. Chief Manager, Central Business Dist, Victoria Nat. Australia Bank Ltd, 1986–88; Exec. Vice Pres., Americas, NAB, USA, 1988–89; NAB Australia: Gen. Manager, Credit Bureau, 1989–92; State Manager, NSW and ACT, 1992–94; Dir and Chief Exec., Clydesdale Bank PLC, 1994–96; Chief Gen. Manager, 1996–99, Man. Dir and CEO, 1999–2004, Nat. Australia Bank Ltd; Chairman: ORIX Australia, 2004–08; Run Corp., 2005–07. Dir, St Vincent Health, 2004–. Dir, Melbourne Business Sch., 1999–. *Recreations:* Rugby, golf, cricket, theatre. *Clubs:* Union, Killara Golf (Sydney); Australian (Melbourne).

CIECHANOVER, Prof. Aaron J., MD, DSc; Professor, since 1992, and Distinguished Research Professor, since 2002, Faculty of Medicine, Technion-Israel Institute of Technology, Haifa, Israel; *b* 1 Oct. 1947; *s* of Yitzhak and Bluma Ciechanover; *m* 1975, Dr Menucha Siletzky; one *s*. *Educ:* Hebrew Univ., Jerusalem (MSc 1970; MD 1974); Technion-Israel Inst. of Technol., Haifa (DSc 1982). Nat. Compulsory Service, Israel Defence Forces, 1974–77: Mil. Physician, Israeli Navy and Unit for R&D, Surgeon-Gen. HQ. Department of Biochemistry, Faculty of Medicine, Technion-Israel Institute of Technology: Res. Fellow, 1977–79; Lectr, 1979–81; Sen. Lectr, 1984–87; Associate Prof., 1987–92; Dir, Rappaport Family Inst. for Res. in Med. Scis, 1993–2000. Vis. Scientist, Inst. for Cancer Res., Fox Chase Cancer Center, Philadelphia, 1978, 1979, 1980, 1981; Postdoctoral Fellow, Dept of Biol., MIT and Whitehead Inst. for Biomed. Res., Cambridge, Mass, 1981–84; Visiting Professor: Dana Farber Cancer Inst. and Harvard Med. Sch., 1985, 1986; Div. of Haematol.-Oncology, Dept of Pediatrics, Children's Hosp., Washington Univ. Sch. of Medicine, St Louis, annually, 1987–99 and 2001; Univ. of Kyoto Sch. of Medicine, 2000; Northwestern Univ. Sch. of Medicine, 2002, 2003; Microbiol. and Tumor Biol. Center, Karolinska Inst., Stockholm, 2003; City Univ. of Osaka Sch. of Medicine, 2003–04, 2005; Rockefeller Univ., NY, 2004; Amer. Cancer Soc. Eleanor Roosevelt Meml Fellow, 1988–89. Mem., EMBO, 1996. Hon. FRSC 2005. Hon. PhD: Tel Aviv, 2002; Ben Gurion, 2004; City Univ. of Osaka, 2005. Holds numerous awards and prizes, including: (jtly) Albert and Mary Lasker Award for Basic Med. Res., 2000; (jtly) Nobel Prize in Chemistry, 2004. *Publications:* contrib. numerous original articles, book chapters and review articles on intracellular proteolysis. *Address:* The Ruth and Bruce Rappaport Faculty of Medicine, Technion-Israel Institute of Technology, Efron Street, PO Box 9649 Bat Galim, Haifa 31096, Israel. *T:* 48295379, *Fax:* 48513922. *E:* c_tzachy@netvision.net.il.

CIMA, Maj. Gen. Keith Harington, CB 2007; CEng; Staff Helmsman, Royal National Lifeboat Institution, Central London, since 2012 (Member, Thames Crew, 2007–12); various executive and non-executive positions in France and UK; *b* 28 May 1951; *s* of late Peter Harington Cima and Ivy Rose Cima; *m* 1985, Susan Diane Rook; three *s* one *d* (and one *d* decd). *Educ:* Brasenose Coll., Oxford (MA); Open Univ. (MBA); RMA Sandhurst; RMCS Shrivenham; RAF Staff Coll. CEng, MIMechE 1992. Grad. trainee, Babcock and Wilcox Ltd, 1973–74. Troop Commander: 1 Trng Regt, RE, 1975–76; 20 Field Sqn, 1977–78; Intelligence Officer, HQ RE, 2nd Div., 1978; Adjt 25 Engr Regt, 1979–80; psc(a)† 1981; SO2 MoD, 1982–83; OC 3 Field Sqn, 1984–85; SO2 RE, HQ UK Mobile Force, 1986–87; SO1 Directing Staff, RMCS, 1988–90; CO 38 Engr Regt, 1991–93; Project Manager, Mines and Demolitions, 1994, Gen. Engrg Equipt, 1995, Procurement Exec.; Col Personnel Br. 7, Mil. Sec., 1995; rcds 1996; Director: Engr Support (Army), 1997–99; Manning (Army), 1999–2000; COS, Adjt Gen., 2001–02; Sen. Army Mem., RCDS, 2002–05; Team Leader, Project Hyperion - the co-location and integration of HQ Land and Adjt Gen., MoD, 2005–06; Resident Gov. and Keeper of the Jewel House, HM Tower of London, 2006–10. Consultant, ES-KO Internat., 2011–; case worker, SSAFA France, 2011–. Non-exec. Dir, Ex-Forces Jobs, 2012–13. Chairman: Cosmissus, 2013–14; Lakeside Resources Ltd, 2014–; Lakeside Energy Ltd, 2015–. FCMI 2004. Pres., Instn of RE, 2007–12. Col Comdt, RE, 2003–; Hon. Col, Royal Monmouthshire RE (Militia), 2006–14 (Chm., Regtl Trust, 2006–14). Freeman: City of London, 2007; Carpenters' Co., 2010; Comr of Lieutenancy for City of London, 2010; Liveryman, Engineers' Co., 2015. *Publications:* Reflections from the Bridge, 1994. *Recreations:* dinghy and offshore sailing, marathons, gardening, philately (GB), DIY, building a $^{1}/_{8}$ scale steam railway. *Address:* c/o RHQ Royal Engineers, Brompton Barracks, Chatham, Kent ME4 4UG.

CIPOLLA, Prof. Roberto, DPhil; FIET; CEng, FREng; Professor of Information Engineering, University of Cambridge, since 2000; Managing Director, Cambridge Research Laboratory, Toshiba Research Europe, since 2007; Fellow, Jesus College, Cambridge, since 1992; Professor of Computer Vision, Royal Academy of Arts, since 2004; *b* Solihull, 3 May 1963; *s* of Salvatore Cipolla and Concetta Criminisi; *m* 2000, Maria Cristina Bordin; one *d*. *Educ:* Queens' Coll., Cambridge (BA Engrg 1984); Univ. of Pennsylvania (MSE 1985); Univ. of Electro-communications, Tokyo (MEng Robotics 1988); Balliol Coll., Oxford (DPhil 1991). FIET 2009; CEng 2010; FREng 2010. Res. Asst, Valley Forge Res. Center, Penn, 1984–85; Vis. Researcher, Electrotech. Lab., Tsukuba, Japan, 1987–88; Lady Wolfson Res. Fellow, St Hugh's Coll., Oxford, 1990–92; Toshiba Fellow, Toshiba R&D Centre, Kawasaki, Japan, 1991–92; Lectr, 1992–97, Reader, 1997–2000, Univ. of Cambridge. *Publications:* Active Visual Inference of Surface Shape, 1995; (ed jtly) Computer Vision: ECCV '96 (2 vols), 1996; (ed jtly) New Geometric Techniques in Computer Vision, 1998; (ed) Computer Vision for Human-Machine Interaction, 1998; (ed jtly) Shape, Contour and Grouping in Computer Vision, 1999; (with P. J. Giblin) Visual Motion of Curves and Surfaces, 2000; (ed jtly) The Mathematics of Surfaces IX, 2000; (ed jtly) Computer Vision: detection, recognition and reconstruction, 2010; contrib. papers to jls on computer vision. *Recreations:* Japanese language and culture, photography, art. *Address:* Department of Engineering, University of Cambridge, Cambridge CB2 1PZ. *T:* (01223) 332849. *E:* cipolla@eng.cam.ac.uk.

CITARELLA, Victor Thomas; social care, children's services and management consultant; Director, CPEA Ltd, since 2001; *b* 8 May 1951; *s* of Thomas and Evelyn R. M. Citarella; *m* 1975, Jacqueline Hopley; three *s* one *d*. *Educ:* Sweyne Grammar Sch., Essex; University Coll., Cardiff (BSc Hons Econs 1973, Cert. Social Work 1978). Residential Child Care Officer, S Glamorgan, 1974–80; Team Manager, Hillingdon Social Services, 1980–82; Day and Residential Care Officer, W Sussex, 1982–85; Area Manager, Bristol, Avon, 1985–88; Dep. Dir of Social Services, 1988–91, Dir of Social Services, 1991–2000, City of Liverpool. Pres., Social Care Assoc., 1992. *Address:* 5 New Acres, Newburgh, Wigan, Lancs WN8 7TU. *T:* (01257) 462698. *E:* vic.citarella@cpea.co.uk.

CIUMEI, Charles Gregg; QC 2014; *b* London, 1 April 1964; *s* of Arminio Ciumei and Elizabeth Whatley (*née* Cusworth); *m* 2007, Anne Schädle; one *s* two *d*. *Educ:* Queen Elizabeth's Comprehensive Sch., Wimborne; Wadham Coll., Oxford (BA Exptl Psychol. 1987); City Univ., London (DipLaw 1990). Scientist, ARE, 1987–89; called to the Bar, Middle Temple, 1991; in practice as barrister, 1991–. *Recreation:* rock climbing. *Address:* Essex Court Chambers, 24 Lincoln's Inn Fields, WC2A 3EG. *T:* (020) 7813 8000. *E:* cciumei@essexcourt.com.

CLACK, Prof. Jennifer Alice, PhD, ScD; FRS 2009; Curator in Vertebrate Palaeontology, since 2005, and Professor, since 2006, University Museum of Zoology, Cambridge; Fellow, Darwin College, Cambridge, since 1997; *b* Manchester, 3 Nov. 1947; *d* of Ernest and Alice Agnew; *m* 1980, Robert Neil Garfield Clack. *Educ:* Bolton Sch. (Girls' Div.); Univ. of Newcastle upon Tyne (PhD 1984); MA 1989, ScD 2000 Cantab; Univ. of Leicester (Grad. Cert. Museum Studies); Museums Dip., Museums Assoc. Display technician, 1971–75, Asst Mus. Educn Officer, 1975–78, Birmingham City Museums and Art Gall.; University Museum of Zoology, Cambridge: Asst Curator, 1981–95; Sen. Asst Curator, 1995–2000; Reader in Vertebrate Palaeontol., 2000–05. FLS 1986. Foreign Hon. Member: Amer. Acad. of Arts and Scis, 2009; Royal Swedish Acad. of Sci., 2014. Hon. DSc: Chicago, 2013; Leicester, 2014. Daniel Giraud Elliot Medal, NAS, 2008; T. Neville George Medal, Glasgow Geol Soc., 2013. *Publications:* Gaining Ground: the origin and evolution of early tetrapods, 2002, 2nd edn 2012; contrib. papers, book chapters and articles. *Recreations:* choral singing, especially chamber choirs and English Church music, gardening, wine, cooking. *Address:* University Museum of Zoology, Cambridge, Downing Street, Cambridge CB2 3EJ. *T:* (01223) 336613, *Fax:* (01223) 336679. *E:* j.a.clack@zoo.cam.ac.uk.

CLAES, Willy; Secretary General, NATO, 1994–95; *b* Hasselt, Belgium, 24 Nov. 1938; *m*; one *s* one *d*. *Educ:* Free Univ., Brussels. Asst Sec., then Provincial Sec., De Voorzorg, 1962–65; Local Councillor, Hasselt, 1964–94; MHR (Socialist), Hasselt, 1968–94; Minister of: Nat. Educn, Flemish Reg., 1972–73; Econ. Affairs, 1973–74 and 1977–79; Deputy Prime Minister and Minister of: Econ. Affairs, 1979–81; Econ. Affairs and Planning and Nat. Educn, 1987; Foreign Affairs, 1992–94. Belgian Socialist Party: Mem., Exec. Cttee, 1965–94; Co-Pres., 1975–77. Pres., Flemish Council Universities-High Schs, 2014. Numerous decorations from Europe, Mexico and Bolivia. *Publications:* Tussen droom en werkelijkheid: bouwstenen voor en ander Europa, 1979; La Chine et l'Europe, 1980; Livre Blanc de l'Energie, 1980; Quatre Années aux Affaires Economiques, 1980; Elementen voor een nieuw energiebeleid, 1980; Belgie … quo vadis?: un conte moderne, 1980; De Derde Weg: beschouwingen over de Wereldcrisis, 1987. *Recreations:* piano music, conducting orchestras. *Address:* Berkenlaan 62, 3500 Hasselt, Belgium.

CLAGUE, Joan; Director of Nursing Services, Marie Curie Memorial Foundation, 1986–90; *b* 17 April 1931; *d* of James Henry Clague and Violet May Clague (*née* Johnson). *Educ:* Malvern Girls' Coll.; Guy's Hosp.; Hampstead Gen. Hosp.; Simpson Meml Maternity Pavilion. Asst Regional Nursing Officer, Oxford Regional Hosp. Bd, 1965–67; Principal, then Chief Nursing Officer, St George's Hosp. Bd of Governors, 1967–73; Area Nursing

Officer, Merton, Sutton and Wandsworth AHA, 1973–81; Regl Nursing Officer, NE Thames RHA, 1981–86. Pres., Assoc. of Nurse Administrators, 1983–85. Trustee, WRVS Trustees Ltd, 1991–96. WHO Fellow, 1969; Smith and Nephew EEC Scholar, 1981. *Recreations:* walking, domestic pursuits. *Address:* 7 Tylney Avenue, SE19 1LN. *T:* (020) 8670 5171.

CLAHSEN, Prof. Harald, PhD; FBA 2008; Alexander von Humboldt Professor of the Psycholinguistics of Multilingualism and Founding Director, Potsdam Research Institute of Multilingualism, University of Potsdam, since 2011; *b* Germany, 2 July 1955. *Educ:* Univ. of Wuppertal (MA 1978; PhD 1981); Univ. of Düsseldorf (Habilitation 1987). Lectr, Univ. of Düsseldorf, 1983–93; Prof., Dept of Lang. and Linguistics, Univ. of Essex, 1993–2011. Gerhard Hess Award, German Sci. Foundn. *Publications:* (ed jtly) Language Development and Language Disorders (series); (contrib.) The Handbook of Clinical Linguistics, 2008; articles in jls. *Address:* Human Sciences Faculty, Universität Potsdam, Karl-Liebk necht-Str. 24–25, 14476 Potsdam, Germany.

CLANCARTY, 9th Earl of, *cr* 1803; **Nicholas Power Richard Le Poer Trench;** Baron Kilconnel 1797; Viscount Dunlo 1801; Baron Trench (UK) 1815; Viscount Clancarty (UK) 1823; Marquess of Heusden (Kingdom of the Netherlands) 1818; *b* 1 May 1952; *o s* of Hon. Power Edward Ford Le Poer Trench (*d* 1975), *y s* of 5th Earl of Clancarty, and Jocelyn Louise Courtney (*d* 1962); *S* uncle, 1995; *m* 2005, Victoria Frances Lambert; one *d. Educ:* Westminster Sch.; Ashford Grammar Sch.; Plymouth Polytech.; Univ. of Colorado; Sheffield Polytech. Elected Mem., H of L, 2010.

CLANCY, Claire Elizabeth; Chief Executive and Clerk, National Assembly for Wales, since 2007; *b* 14 March 1958; *d* of Douglas and Teresa Coates; *m* 1994, Michael John Clancy (*d* 2010). *Educ:* Dartford Grammar Sch. for Girls; Open Univ. (BA 1st Cl. Psychol.). Manpower Services Commn, 1977–88; Dept of Employment, 1988–90; Chief Exec., Powys TEC, 1990–92; Govt Office for SW, 1992–96; Dir of Policy and Planning, Companies House, 1996–97; Dir, Patent Office, 1999–2002; Registrar of Companies and Chief Exec., Companies House, 2002–07. *Recreations:* dressage, walking. *Address:* National Assembly for Wales, Cardiff Bay, Cardiff CF99 1NA. *T:* 0300 200 6230. *E:* claire.clancy@assembly.wales.

CLANCY, Deirdre V., (Mrs M. M. Steer); set and costume designer; portrait painter; *b* 31 March 1943; adopted *d* of Julie M. Clancy; *m* 1975, Michael Maxwell Steer; one *s* two *d. Educ:* Convent of the Sacred Heart, Tunbridge Wells; Birmingham Coll. of Art (NDD 1st Cl. Hons). Arts Council Asst, Lincoln Rep., 1965; House Designer, Royal Court Theatre, 1966–68: productions include costumes for D. H. Lawrence Trilogy, 1966; sets and costumes for: Early Morning, 1967; The Sea, 1973; has designed for RNT, RSC, ENO, Scottish Opera, New Sadlers Wells Opera, Chichester Fest. Theatre; costumes for Oliver, Tivoli, 2007, Napoli, Stanislavski Th., Moscow, 2009; numerous prodns in Europe, N America, Japan and Australia, incl. Marriage of Figaro, LA Opera, 2004; Opéra Lyon: Così fan Tutte, Marriage of Figaro, Don Giovanni, 2007–10; Old Globe, San Diego: King Lear, The Madness of George III, Taming of the Shrew, 2010, Shakespeare Fest. (12 prodns); Amadeus, The Tempest (transf. Th. Royal Bath, 2012), Much Ado About Nothing, 2011; Aarhus: Die Tote Stadt, 2010, Tristan and Isolde, 2012; Die Fledermaus, WNO, 2011. Founder dir, Cherubim Music Trust, 2001–. *Films* include: The Virgin and The Gypsy, 1969; Mrs Brown, 1997 (Best Film Costumes, BAFTA Award, 1998); Tom's Midnight Garden, 1998; *television:* Wives and Daughters, 1999. Has exhibited designs. DUniv UCE, 2003. Green Room Award, Vic, Australia, for Best Costume (opera), 1990 and 1991; Olivier Award for Best Costume Design (for A Month in the Country, Triumph Prodns, and Loves Labours Lost, RSC), 1997, (for All's Well That Ends Well, RSC), 2005. *Publications:* Costume Since 1945, 1996, 2nd edn 2015; Costumes of Colonial America, 2009; Costumes of the 1980s and 90s, 2009; Designing Costume for Stage and Screen, 2014. *Recreations:* infrequent domesticity, family pursuits, more painting. *Address:* 125 Duck Street, Tisbury, Wilts SP3 6LJ. *E:* d@clancy.uk.com.

CLANCY, Richard Francis Stephen; District Judge (Magistrates' Courts), Liverpool, since 2005; *b* 2 Sept. 1948; *s* of Francis Gerrard Clancy and Evaline Margaret Clancy; *m* 1976, Anne Margaret Lawless; one *s* one *d. Educ:* St Ambrose Coll., Altrincham; Coll. of Law, Guildford. Articled to John Arthur Wheeler, OBE, Solicitor, Warrington, 1969–74; admitted solicitor, 1974; prosecuted, W Midlands and Merseyside, 1974–83; in private practice as partner, Ridgway Greenall, Warrington, and E. Rexmakin & Co., Liverpool, 1983–2000; Acting Stipendiary Magistrate for Staffs, 1998–2000; District Judge (Magistrates' Cts), Birmingham, 2001–05. Member: Risley Prison Visitors' Centre Cttee, 1990–2000 (Chm., 1998–2000); Merseyside Criminal Justices Strategy Cttee, 1997–2000; Merseyside Justices' Issues Cttee, 2005–. Mem., Warrington Sports Council (Chm., 1996–99); former Auditor, Warrington Athletic Club. *Recreations:* sport, piano, accordion, history, literature.

CLANFIELD, Viscount; Ashton Robert Gerard Peel; *b* 16 Sept. 1976; *s* and *heir* of 3rd Earl Peel, *qv*; *m* 2004, Matilda Rose Aykroyd; one *s* three *d. Educ:* Ampleforth; Durham Univ. (BA Hons 1999); Univ. of Buckingham (MBA 2004). With Cazenove Fund Management, 2000–02; Dir, Panmure Gordon and Co., 2006–10; Partner, Oriel Securities, 2010–. *Heir: s* Hon. Nicholas Robert William Peel, *b* 4 May 2015.

CLANMORRIS, 8th Baron *cr* 1800 (Ire.); **Simon John Ward Bingham,** MA; FCA; *b* 25 Oct. 1937; *s* of 7th Baron Clanmorris and of Madeleine Mary, *d* of late Clement Ebel; *S* father, 1988; *m* 1971, Gizella Maria, *d* of Sandor Zverkó; one *d. Educ:* Downside; Queens' College, Cambridge (MA). ACA 1965, FCA 1975. Former Finance Dir, PYRECO Ltd. *Heir: cousin* Robert Derek de Burgh Bingham [*b* 29 Oct. 1942; *m* 1969, Victoria Mary, *yr d* of P. A. Pennant-Rea; three *d*]. *Address:* c/o Coutts & Co., 440 Strand, WC2R 0QS.

See also Hon. C. M. T. Bingham.

CLANWILLIAM, 8th Earl of, *cr* 1776 (Ire.); **Patrick James Meade;** Bt 1703 (Ire.); Viscount Clanwilliam, Baron Gillford 1766; Baron Clanwilliam (UK) 1828; Founding Partner, 1995, Chairman, since 1996, Meade Hall (formerly The Policy Partnership, later Gardant Communications); *b* 28 Dec. 1960; *s* of 7th Earl of Clanwilliam and Maxine (*née* Hayden-Scott); *S* father, 2009; *m* 1st, 1989, Serena Emily (marr. diss. 1994), *d* of late Lt-Col B. J. Lockhart; one *d*; 2nd, 1995, Cara de la Peña (marr. diss. 2009); one *s* one *d. Educ:* Eton Coll. 1 Bn, Coldstream Guards, 1979–83. Exec., Hanson plc, 1983–90, attached Home Office as special advr to Home Sec., 1986–88; with Ian Greer & Associates, 1990–93; Man. Dir, Westminster Policy Partnership Ltd, 1993–95; Chairman: Cleveland Bridge UK Ltd, 2001–04; Eurasia Drilling Co. Ltd, 2008–; Director: Polyus Gold, 2006–13; CBM Oil plc, 2007–11; Otkritie OUCP, 2008–09; NMC Health Gp, 2012–; SOMA Oil and Gas, 2013–. Councillor (C) Royal Bor. of Kensington and Chelsea, 1990–98 (Chm., Traffic and Highways Cttee). Mem. Bd of Trustees, British Sch. of Osteopathy, 1997–2000; Trustee, Benevolent Soc. of St Patrick, 1993–. Gov., Knightsbridge Sch., 2006–08. *Recreations:* helicopter flying, prison reform and prison sentencing policy, free fall parachuting, sub-aqua diving, Palladian architecture, golf, fishing, motorbiking. *Heir: s* Lord Gillford, *qv*. *Address:* 1 Meade Mews, SW1P 4EG. *T:* (020) 7976 5555. *E:* cl@nwilliam.co.uk. *Clubs:* White's, Turf, Chatham Dining; Mill Reef (Antigua, WI); New Zealand (Weybridge).

CLAPHAM, Michael; *b* 15 May 1943; *s* of late Thomas Clapham and of Eva Clapham; *m* 1965, Yvonne Hallsworth; one *s* one *d. Educ:* Leeds Polytechnic (BSc); Leeds Univ. (PGCE); Bradford Univ. (MPhil). Miner, 1958–70; Lectr, 1974–77; Dep. Head, Yorks NUM Compensation Dept, 1977–83; Head of Industrial Relations, NUM, 1983–92. MP (Lab) Barnsley West and Penistone, 1992–2010. PPS to Minister of State for Health, 1997. Member: Trade and Industry Cttee, 1992–97, 2003–05; DTI, then BERR Select Cttee, 2004–10; Vice Chm., back-bench Trade and Industry Gp, 1996–97; Chairman, All-Party Group: on Occupational Safety and Health, 1996–10; on Coalfield Communities, 1997–2008; on NATO Parly Assembly, 2000; Jt Chm., All-Party Gp on Fire Safety, 2001–10; Hon. Sec., All-Party Gp on Energy Studies, 1997–10; Chm., Minister's Adv. Panel on Mines Compensation, 1999–2010. Chair, NATO Civil Dimensions and Security, 2004–08. Chairman: Barnsley Community Safety Partnership (formerly Barnsley Crime Prevention Partnership), 1995–2007; Multi Agency Panel, 1999–2007; Construction Skills and Certification Scheme, 2011–. Chm., review of coalfield regeneration, 2010. Trustee, Coalfields Regeneration Trust, 2012–. *Recreations:* reading, walking, gardening.

CLAPHAM, Peter Brian, CB 1996; PhD; CEng, FInstP; Consultant on technology and public administration reform, since 1996; Director, National Physical Laboratory, 1990–95; *b* 3 Nov. 1940; *s* of Wilfred Clapham and Una Frances (*née* Murray); *m* 1965, Jean Margaret (*née* Vigil); two *s. Educ:* Ashville Coll., Harrogate; University Coll. London (BSc, PhD; Fellow, 1996). Research in optics and metrology, NPL, 1960–70; Sec., Adv. Cttee on Res. on Measurements and Standards, 1970–71; res. management and head of marketing, NPL, 1972–81; Res. and Technology Policy, DoI, 1981–82; Supt of Div. of Mech. and Optical Metrology, NPL, 1982–84; Dir 1985, Chief Exec. 1989, Nat. Weights and Measures Lab. Chm., W European Legal Metrology Cooperation, 1989–90; Member: Presidential Council of Internat. Orgn of Legal Metrology, 1985–90; Internat. Cttee of Weights and Measures, 1991–96; British Hallmarking Council, 2001–09. Dir, Bushy Park Water Gardens Trust, 1997–2002. *Publications:* numerous sci. contribs to learned jls. *Recreations:* peregrination, crafts, Catenians.

CLAPP, Captain Michael Cecil, CB 1982; RN retired; *b* 22 Feb. 1932; *s* of Brig. Cecil Douglas Clapp, CBE and Mary Elizabeth Emmeline Palmer Clapp; *m* 1975, Sarah Jane Alexander; one *s* two *d. Educ:* Chafyn Grove Sch., Salisbury; Marlborough College. Joined Royal Navy, 1950 (despatches, 1965); commanded HM Ships Puncheston, Jaguar and Leander, and 801 Sqdn; Commander, Falklands Amphibious Task Gp, 1982. Mem., Stock Exchange, 1987–95. Gov., Kelly Coll., 1985–2010. *Publications:* Amphibious Assault, Falklands, 1996. *Recreations:* sailing, shooting, fishing, country life. *Club:* Royal Cruising.

CLAPP, Susannah, FRSL; Theatre Critic, The Observer, since 1997; *b* 9 Feb. 1949; *d* of Ralph James Clapp and Marion (*née* Heeremans). *Educ:* Ashford Co. Grammar Sch.; Univ. of Bristol (BA Hons). Sub-editor, The Listener, 1970–74; reader and ed., Jonathan Cape, 1974–79; radio critic, Sunday Times, 1978–80; Asst Ed., London Rev. of Books, 1979–92; Theatre Critic: Nightwaves, Radio 3, 1994–2013; New Statesman, 1996–97. FRSL 2013. *Publications:* With Chatwin: portrait of a writer, 1997; A Card from Angela Carter, 2012. *Address:* 37 Granville Square, WC1X 9PD. *T:* (020) 7837 1686.

CLAPPISON, (William) James; *b* 14 Sept. 1956; *m* 1984, Helen Margherita Carter; one *s* three *d. Educ:* St Peter's Sch., York; Queen's Coll., Oxford (Schol.; PPE). Called to the Bar, Gray's Inn, 1981. Contested (C): Barnsley E, 1987; Bootle, May and Nov. 1990. MP (C) Hertsmere, 1992–2015. Parly Under-Sec. of State, DoE, 1995–97; Opposition frontbench spokesman on home affairs, 1997–2001; Shadow Minister for Work, 2001–02; Opposition front bench spokesman, Treasury affairs, 2002; Shadow Minister for Work and Pensions, 2007–10. Mem., Select Cttee on Home Affairs, 2002–15, on European Scrutiny, 2007–15. *Recreations:* bridge, walking. *Club:* Carlton.

CLAPTON, Eric Patrick, CBE 2004 (OBE 1995); singer, guitarist and songwriter; *b* 30 March 1945; *s* of Patricia Clapton; *m* 1979, Patricia Ann Harrison (*née* Boyd) (marr. diss. 1988); (one *s* decd by Lori Del Santo); one *d* by Yvonne Kelly; *m* 2002, Melia McEnery; three *d. Educ:* St Bede's Sch., Surrey; Kingston Coll. of Art. Guitarist with: Roosters, 1963; Yardbirds, 1963–65; John Mayall's Bluesbreakers, 1965–66; Cream, 1966–68; Blind Faith, 1969; Delaney and Bonnie, 1970; Derek and the Dominoes, 1970; solo performer, 1972–. Albums include: (with Yardbirds): Five Live Yardbirds, 1964; For Your Love, 1965; (with Bluesbreakers) Blues Breakers, 1966; (with Cream): Fresh Cream, 1967; Disraeli Gears, 1967; Wheels of Fire, 1968; Goodbye, 1969; (with Blind Faith) Blind Faith, 1969; (with Derek and the Dominoes) Layla and Other Assorted Love Songs, 1970; *solo:* Eric Clapton, 1970; 461 Ocean Boulevard, 1974; There's One in Every Crowd, 1975; E. C. Was Here, 1975; No Reason to Cry, 1976; Slowhand, 1977; Backless, 1978; Just One Night, 1980; Another Ticket, 1981; Money and Cigarettes, 1983; Behind the Sun, 1985; August, 1986; Journeyman, 1989; 24 Nights, 1992; Unplugged, 1992; From the Cradle, 1994; Pilgrim, 1998; Blues, 1999; (with B. B. King) Riding with the King, 2000; Reptile, 2001; One More Car One More Rider, 2002; Me and Mr Johnson, 2004; Sessions for Robert J, 2004; Back Home, 2005; (with J. J. Cale) The Road to Escondido, 2006; Clapton, 2010; Old Sock, 2013; Forever Man, 2015. Co-owner and Design Dir, Cordings of Piccadilly, 2003–. Founder, Crossroads Centre, Antigua, 1997. Numerous awards. *Publications:* Eric Clapton: the autobiography, 2007.

CLARE; *see* Sabben-Clare.

CLARE, John Charles, CBE 2005; non-executive Chairman: JobCentre Plus, 2007–11; Dreams plc, 2008–11; Capital and Regional plc, since 2010; *b* 2 Aug. 1950; *s* of Sidney Charles and Joan Mildred Clare; *m* 1974, Anne Ross; two *s. Educ:* Edinburgh Univ. (BSc Hons Applied Maths). Sales and marketing roles in UK, Switzerland, Denmark, Sweden, Mars Ltd, 1972–82; Business Develt Dir and Marketing Dir, Racing Div., Ladbroke Gp plc, 1982–85; Dixons Group plc: Marketing Dir 1985–86, Man. Dir 1986–88, Dixons Ltd; Gp Dir, 1988–92; Man. Dir, Dixons Stores Gp, 1988–92; Gp Man. Dir, 1992–94; Chief Exec., Dixons Gp, later DSG Internat. plc, 1994–2007. Non-executive Director: Dyson Ltd, 2007–12; JJB Sports plc, 2009–10 (Chm., 2010). *Recreations:* cricket, music, family, Tottenham Hotspur supporter.

CLARE, John Robert; Education Editor, Daily Telegraph, 1988–2006; *b* 19 Aug. 1941; *s* of late John Arnold Clare and Ludmilla Clare (*née* Nossoff); two *s* (one *d* decd) from former marriages. *Educ:* St George's Grammar Sch., Cape Town; Univ. of Cape Town. Reporter: Post, Johannesburg, 1963–64; The Journal, Newcastle upon Tyne, 1965–66; sub-editor, Daily Mirror, 1966–67; sub-editor, then reporter, The Times, 1967–72; reporter, ITN, 1972–73; Dep. Ed., LBC, 1973–74; Labour Corresp., The Observer, 1974–76; Social Services Corresp., Evening Standard, 1976–77; Community Relns Corresp., then Educn Corresp., BBC, 1977–86; Educn Corresp., The Times, 1986–88. Reporter of Year, BPA, 1971. *Publications:* The Daily Telegraph Schools Guide, 1992, 1994, 1998; John Clare's Education Answers, 2001; Captured in Time—Five Centuries of South African Writing, 2010. *Address:* 11 Blackmore's Grove, Teddington, Middx TW11 9AE. *E:* clarejr@msn.com.

See also Rear Adm. R. A. G. Clare.

CLARE, Michael George; DL; Founder, and President, since 2008, Dreams plc (Executive Chairman and Managing Director, 1987–2008); Executive Chairman, Clarenco LLP, since 2008; *b* 8 Feb. 1955; *s* of late Thomas Isaac Clare and Betty Clare (*née* Jeffries); *m* 1979, Carol Ann Ballingall; two *s* two *d. Educ:* Davenies Sch.; High Wycombe Coll. Br. Manager, Williams Furniture, 1976–78; Area Manager: Hardys Furniture, then Queensway, 1978–80; Perrings Furniture, 1980–83; Sales Dir, Deanes Furniture, 1983–85; Proprietor, Sofa Bed Centres, 1985–87. Dir, British Retail Consortium, 2006–. Pres., Furniture Trade Benevolent Assoc., 2006–07; Patron, Retail Trust, 2007–. FInstD 1990. Freeman, City of London, 2001; Liveryman, Co. of Furniture Makers, 2001–. DL Bucks 2011. Chm. of Trustees, Clare Foundn, 2009–. Gov., Bucks Chiltern UC, 2006–08; Patron: Chalfonts Community Coll., 2008–; Clare Business Sch., 2012–. Bucks Ambassador, 2007–. DUniv Buckingham, 2009.

Regl Entrepreneur of Year, Ernst & Young, 2002. *Recreations:* travelling the world, making dreams a reality. *Address:* c/o Clarenco LLP, Clarenco House, Ibstone Road, Stokenchurch HP14 3EF. *T:* (01494) 682000. *E:* mike@clarenco.com.

CLARE, Pauline Ann, CBE 2002; QPM 1996; DL; executive coach, since 2002; Chief Constable of Lancashire, 1995–2002; *b* 26 July 1947; *d* of Kathleen and Thomas Rostron; *m* 1983, Reginald Stuart Clare; two step *d. Educ:* St Mary's Secondary Modern Sch., Leyland, Lancs; Open Univ. (BA Hons). CCMI (CIMgt 1996). Lancashire Constabulary: Police Cadet, 1964; Constable to Inspector, Policewomen's Dept, Juvenile Liaison, 1966; Merseyside Police: Inspector Uniform Patrol and Computer Project Team, 1973; Chief Inspector, Uniform Patrol, Community Services Dept, 1983; Supt, Community Services Dept, Sub Divl and Dep. Divl Comd, Sefton, 1987; Chief Supt, Divl Comd, Sefton, 1991; Asst Chief Constable, Crime and Ops, 1992–94; Dep. Chief Constable, Cheshire Constabulary, 1994–95. Hon. Col, Lancs ACF, 1996–2002. Pres., Lancs Assoc. of Clubs for Young People (formerly Lancs Assoc. of Boys' Clubs), 1995–2002. Comdr, St John Ambulance, Lancs, 2004–07. DL Lancs 1998. FRSA 2002. Hon. Fellow, Univ. of Central Lancashire, 1994. DUniv Open, 1999. Police Long Service and Good Conduct Medal, 1988; Lancashire Woman of the Year, 1993. SSStJ 1985 (Mem. Council, Lancs, 1998–2009). *Recreations:* gardening, horse riding, tapestry, reading novels, entertaining at home. *Address:* Dalton, Wigan, Lancs.

CLARE, Rear Adm. Roy Alexander George, CBE 2007; Director, Auckland War Memorial Museum, New Zealand, since 2011; *b* 30 Sept. 1950; *s* of late John Arnold Clare and Ludmilla Clare (*née* Nossoff); *m* 1st, 1979, Leonie (Mimi) Hutchings (*d* 1979); 2nd, 1981, Sarah Catherine Jane Parkin; one *s* two *d. Educ:* St George's Grammar Sch., Cape Town; BRNC, Dartmouth (Queen's Sword, 1972). Joined Royal Navy, 1966; jun. rating, HMS Ganges and HMS Decoy, 1966–68; Upperyardman Cadet, Dartmouth, 1968; Midshipman, HMS Ashanti, 1970–71; Sub-Lieut, Yacht Adventure, Whitbread Round The World Race, 1973–74; Lieut, HMS Diomede, 1974–75; First Lieut, HMS Bronington (HRH The Prince of Wales), 1975–77; Principal Warfare Officer, HMS Juno, 1978–80; CO, HMS Bronington, 1980–81; Ops Officer, HMS Glamorgan (Lt Comdr), 1982–83; Staff of Flag Officer Sea Trng, 1984–85; rnsc, Greenwich (Comdr), 1985–86; CO, HMS Birmingham, 1987–89; MA to Minister of State for Armed Forces, 1989–91; CO, HMS York and Capt., Third Destroyer Sqdn, 1991–92; rcds, 1993; Asst Dir, Naval Plans and Programmes Div., MoD, 1993–96; CO, HMS Invincible, 1996–97; Commodore, BRNC, 1998–99; Rear-Adm. 1999; Dir Operational Mgt, NATO Regl Comd North, 1999–2000; Dir, Nat. Maritime Mus., 2000–07; Chief Exec., Museums, Libraries and Archives Council, 2007–11. Member, Board: Creative and Cultural Skills, 2005–07; MLA, 2006–07; Qualifications and Curriculum Develt Agency, 2009–11; Chm., Museums Aotearoa, 2015– (Mem. Bd, 2014–). Trustee: Bronington Trust, 1990–99 (Vice Pres., 1999–2002); Naval Review, 1990–11; Britannia Assoc., 2001–04. Chm., Midland Naval Officers' Assoc., 2000–02; Member: Greenwich Forum, 2000–07; Univ. of Greenwich Assembly, 2000–07; RNSA. Freeman: City of London, 2001; Clockmakers' Co., 2004; Shipwrights' Co., 2005– (Liveryman, 2002–05). CCMI, until 2011 (CIMgt 2001); FRSA 2005–08; MInstD 2006–11; FRIN 2006–07. Hon. DLitt Greenwich, 2007. *Publications:* (ed) HMS Bronington: a tribute to one of Britain's last wooden walls, 1996; contrib. to Naval Rev. *Recreations:* family, sailing, walking. *Address:* Auckland War Memorial Museum, The Domain, Private Bag 92018, Auckland 1142, New Zealand. *E:* rclare@aucklandmuseum.com. *Clubs:* Anchorites, Royal Navy of 1765 and 1785, City Naval, Royal Over-Seas League NZ; Royal Yacht Squadron (Naval Mem.); Buckland's Beach Yacht.
See also J. R. Clare.

CLARENDON, 8th Earl of, 2nd *cr* 1776; **George Edward Laurence Villiers;** Baron Hyde 1756; Partner, Knight Frank, since 2006; *b* 12 Feb. 1976; *s* of 7th Earl of Clarendon and Jane Diana, *d* of late E. W. Dawson; *S* father, 2009; *m* 2007, Bryonie, *d* of Maj.-Gen. Anthony de C. L. Leask, *qv*; three *s. Educ:* Milton Abbey Sch.; Royal Agricl Coll. (BSc Hons). MRICS. Liveryman, Fishmongers' Co., 2008. Page of Honour to the Queen, 1987–89. *Heir: s* Lord Hyde, *qv. Address:* c/o Holywell House, Swanmore, Hants SO32 2QE. *Club:* Boodle's.

CLARIDGE, Prof. Michael Frederick; Emeritus Professor of Entomology, Cardiff University; *b* 2 June 1934; *s* of Frederick William Claridge and Eva Alice (*née* Jeffery); *m* 1967, Lindsey Clare Hellings; two *s* one *d. Educ:* Lawrence Sheriff Sch., Rugby; Keble Coll., Oxford (MA, DPhil). Lectr in Zoology 1959–74, Sen. Lectr in Zoology 1974–77, Univ. Coll., Cardiff; Reader in Entomology, 1977–83, Prof. of Entomology, 1983–99, Head of Sch. of Biol., 1989–94, Univ. of Wales, Cardiff. President: Linnean Soc. of London, 1988–91; Systematics Assoc., 1991–94; Royal Entomol Soc., 2000–02 (Hon. Fellow, 2006). Linnean Medal for Zool., Linnean Soc., 2000. *Publications:* Handbook for the Identification of Leafhoppers and Planthoppers of Rice, 1991; chapters in: The Leafhoppers and Planthoppers, 1985; Organization of Communities—Past and Present, 1987; Prospects in Systematics, 1988; The Biodiversity of Micro-organisms and Invertebrates, 1991; Evolutionary Patterns and Processes, 1993; Planthoppers: their ecology and management, 1993; Identification of Pest Organisms, 1994; Species—the Units of Biodiversity, 1997; Insect Sounds and Communication: physiology, behaviour, ecology and evolution, 2006; Contemporary Debate on the Philosophy of Biology, 2009; Insect Biodiversity: science and society, 2009; papers in Biol Jl of Linnean Soc., Ecological Entomology, Amer. Naturalist. *Recreations:* classical music, cricket, natural history. *Address:* School of Biosciences, Cardiff University, Cardiff CF10 3TL. *E:* claridge@cardiff.ac.uk.

CLARK; *see* Chichester Clark and Chichester-Clark.

CLARK; *see* Gordon Clark.

CLARK, family name of **Baron Clark of Windermere**.

CLARK OF CALTON, Baroness *cr* 2005 (Life Peer), of Calton in the City of Edinburgh; **Lynda Margaret Clark;** PC 2013; PhD; a Senator of the College of Justice in Scotland, since 2006; Chairman, Scottish Law Commission, 2012–14; *b* 26 Feb. 1949. *Educ:* St Andrews Univ. (LLB Hons); Edinburgh Univ. (PhD). Lectr, Univ. of Dundee, 1973–76; admitted Advocate, Scots Bar, 1977; QC (Scot.) 1989; called to the English Bar, Inner Temple, 1988, Bencher, 2000. Advocate Gen. for Scotland, 1999–2006. Contested (Lab) Fife North East, 1992. MP (Lab) Edinburgh Pentlands, 1997–2005. Mem. Court, Edinburgh Univ., 1995–97; Chancellor's Assessor, Edinburgh Napier Univ., 2008–13. *Address:* Court of Session, Parliament House, Parliament Square, Edinburgh EH1 1RQ.

CLARK OF WINDERMERE, Baron *cr* 2001 (Life Peer), of Windermere in the County of Cumbria; **David George Clark;** PC 1997; DL; Chairman, Forestry Commission, 2001–09; *b* 19 Oct. 1939; *s* of George and Janet Clark; *m* 1970, Christine Kirkby; one *d. Educ:* Manchester Univ. (BA(Econ), MSc); Sheffield Univ. (PhD 1978). Forester, 1956–57; Laboratory Asst in Textile Mill, 1957–59; Student Teacher, 1959–60; Student, 1960–63; Pres., Univ. of Manchester Union, 1963–64; Trainee Manager in USA, 1964; University Lecturer, 1965–70. Non-executive Director: Homeowners Friendly Soc., 1987–97, 1999–2010; Thales plc, 1999–2011; Carlisle Utd Ltd, 2001–; Sellafield Ltd, 2007–. Contested Manchester (Withington), 1966; MP (Lab) Colne Valley, 1970–Feb. 1974; contested same seat, Oct. 1974; MP (Lab) South Shields, 1979–2001. Opposition spokesman on Agriculture and Food, 1973–74, on Defence, 1980–81, on the Environment, 1981–86; Opposition front bench spokesman on: environmental protection and develt, 1986–87; food, agriculture and rural affairs, 1987–92; defence, disarmament and arms control, 1992–97; Chancellor, Duchy of Lancaster, 1997–98. Mem., Parly Assembly, NATO, 1981–2005 (Leader, UK delegn, 2001–05); Chm., Atlantic Council of UK, 1998–2003. Pres., Open Spaces Soc., 1979–88. Vis. Prof. of Hist. and Politics, Univ. of Huddersfield, 2013–. Hon. Fellow, Univ. of Cumbria, 2009. DL Cumbria, 2007. Freedom, Borough of S Tyneside, 1989. *Publications:* The Industrial Manager, 1966; Colne Valley: Radicalism to Socialism, 1981; Victor Grayson, Labour's Lost Leader, 1985; We Do Not Want The Earth, 1992; The Labour Movement in Westmorland, 2012; Voices from Labour's Past, 2015; various articles on Management and Labour History. *Recreations:* fell-walking, ornithology, watching football, gardening. *Address:* House of Lords, SW1A 0PW.

CLARK, Alan Richard; HM Diplomatic Service, retired; *b* 4 Sept. 1939; *s* of George Edward Clark and Norah Ivy Maria Clark (*née* Hope); *m* 1961, Ann Rosemary (*née* Hosford); (one *s* decd). *Educ:* Chatham House Grammar Sch., Ramsgate. Foreign Office, 1958; HM Forces, 1960–62; FO 1962; served Tehran, 1964–66; Jedda, 1966–68; Second Sec. (Economic), later First Sec., Paris, 1969–71; FCO, 1972–76; Dep. Hd of Mission, Freetown, 1976–80; FCO, 1980–84; secondment (with rank of Counsellor) to Vickers Shipbuilding and Engineering Ltd, 1984–86; Counsellor and Head of Chancery, Bucharest, 1986–89; Consul-Gen., Montreal, 1990–93; Sen. Overseas Inspector, FCO, 1994–96. Vice-Chm., Thanet Community Housing Assoc., 1999–2003. Complaint Convenor, Kent and Medway HA, 2002–05; Perf. Assessor, GMC, 2002–14. Non-exec. Dir, E Kent Univ. Foundn Hosps NHS Trust, 2003–10; Interim Chm., Shepway PCT, 2004–05. Trustee, Michael Yoakley's Charity, 2000– (Chm. of Trustees, 2005–11). *Recreations:* swimming, walking, reading. *Address:* Dane End, 103 Sea Road, Westgate-on-Sea, Kent CT8 8QE.

CLARK, Alistair MacDonald, PhD; QC (Scot.) 2007; *b* Glasgow, 3 Dec. 1955; *s* of John and Matilda Clark; *m* 1980, Jacqueline Wright; one *s* two *d. Educ:* Univ. of Glasgow (LLB); Univ. of Strathclyde (PhD). Lectr, Glasgow Coll. of Technol., 1978; Lectr, Sen. Lectr, then pt-time Lectr and Tutor, Univ. of Strathclyde, 1978–96; Advocate, 1994. *Publications:* Product Liability, 1989; contrib. legal jls. *Recreations:* reading, hill-walking, music, football, golf. *E:* alistair.clark@advocates.org.uk.

CLARK, Andrew George; Chief Music Critic, Financial Times, 1996–2014; *b* 30 Nov. 1952; *s* of George Clark and Georgina Brenda Clark (*née* Gibson); *m* 1987, Alison Gibson; one *s. Educ:* Sedbergh Sch.; Durham Univ. (BA Hons Modern Hist.). Eur. Arts Corresp., Financial Times, 1981–95. Mem., Editl Bd, Opera mag., 1992–. Critic Prize, Cultural Foundn of City of Salzburg, 1998; Special Prize, Anglo-German Foundn, 2000. *Publications:* Il Verdi del Centenario, 2003; Old Millport, 2006; A World Apart: the story of Hebridean shipping, 2010; Pleasures of the Firth: two hundred years of the Clyde steamers, 2012.

CLARK, Antony Roy; Headmaster, Malvern College, since 2008; *b* 7 Nov. 1956; *s* of Roger and Betty Clark; *m* 1981, Dr Brigitte Jennifer Lang; one *s* two *d. Educ:* St Andrew's Coll., S Africa; Rhodes Univ. (BA; HDE); Downing Coll., Cambridge (Douglas Smith Scholar, MA 1981). Teacher, Westerford High Sch., Cape Town, 1984–90; investment business, 1990–91; Headmaster: St Joseph's Marist Coll., Cape Town, 1992–93; St Andrew's Coll., Grahamstown, 1994–2002; Gresham's Sch., Holt, 2002–08. Mem., Old Andrean Club. *Recreations:* cricket, squash, chess, reading, hiking. *Address:* Malvern College, College Road, Malvern, Worcs WR14 3DF. *Clubs:* Quidnuncs; Hawks.

CLARK, Sir Arnold; *see* Clark, Sir J. A.

CLARK, Brian Robert, FRSL 1985; playwright; *b* 3 June 1932; *s* of Leonard and Selina Clark; *m* (marr. diss.); two *s*; *m* 1990, Cherry Potter. *Educ:* Merrywood Grammar Sch., Bristol; Redland Coll. of Educn, Bristol; Central Sch. of Speech and Drama, London; Nottingham Univ. BA Hons English. Teacher, 1955–61, and 1964–66; Staff Tutor in Drama, Univ. of Hull, 1966–70. Since 1971 has written some thirty television plays, incl. Whose Life Is It Anyway? and The Saturday Party; television film, (with Cherry Potter) House Games; also series: Telford's Change; Late Starter. Stage plays: Whose Life Is It Anyway? (SWET award for Best Play, 1977; filmed, 1982); Can You Hear Me At the Back?, 1978; Campions Interview; Post Mortem; Kipling, London and NY, 1985; The Petition, NY and Nat. Theatre, 1986; (with Kathy Levin) Hopping to Byzantium, Germany 1989, Sydney, Aust., 1990; In Pursuit of Eve (also acted), London, 2001. Founded Amber Lane Press, publishing plays and books on the theatre, 1978. *Publications:* Group Theatre, 1971; Whose Life Is It Anyway?, 1978; Can You Hear Me At the Back?, 1979; Post Mortem, 1979; The Petition, 1986; In Pursuit of Eve, 2001. *Address:* c/o Judy Daish Associates, 2 St Charles Place, W10 6EG. *T:* (020) 8964 8811.

CLARK, Brodie; *see* Clark, Robert B.

CLARK, Rt Rev. Bruce Quinton; Bishop of Riverina, 1993–2004; *b* Brisbane, Qld, 22 May 1939; *s* of Quinton Clark; *m* 1965, Elizabeth Shufflebotham. *Educ:* Brisbane Boys' Coll.; St Francis Theol Coll., Brisbane (ThL). Ordained deacon and priest, 1963; Assistant Curate: All Saints, Chermside, 1963–65; St Matthew's, Groveley, 1965–67; Vicar, St Luke's, Miles, 1967–70; Rector: St Matthew's, Gayndah, 1970–76; St Peter's, Gympie, 1976–83; St Paul's, Maryborough, 1983–89; Surfers Paradise Parish, 1989–93. Archdeacon: Wide Bay, Burnett, 1985–89; Moreton, 1989–91; Gold Coast and Hinterland, 1991–93. *Recreations:* restoring furniture, music, photography.

CLARK, Charles Anthony, (Tony), CB 1994; higher education consultant; Director, Student Support, Department for Education and Employment, 1999–2000; *b* 13 June 1940; *s* of late Stephen and Winifred Clark; *m* 1968, Penelope Margaret (*née* Brett); one *s* two *d. Educ:* King's Coll. Sch., Wimbledon; Pembroke Coll., Oxford (MA Nat. Sci.). Pressed Steel Co., 1961; Hilger & Watts Ltd, 1962–65; DES, subseq. DFE, later DFEE, 1965–2000; seconded to UGC, 1971–73; Under Sec., 1982; Hd of Finance Br. and Prin. Finance Officer, 1987–89; Dir (formerly Under Sec.), Higher Educn, 1989–99. Mem., Effingham Parish Council, 2003–. Mem. Council, Surrey Univ., 1999–2006; Gov., Southampton Solent Univ. (formerly Southampton Inst.), 2000–09. Hon. LLD Nottingham Trent, 2000. *Recreations:* gardening, golf, travel, long distance walking. *Address:* The Paddock, Guildford Road, Effingham, Surrey KT24 5QA.

CLARK, Rt Hon. Charles Joseph, (Joe), CC 1995; PC (Canada) 1979; President, Joe Clark & Associates (Principal Partner, 1994); company director; Professor of Practice, Institute for the Study of International Development, McGill University, since 2005; Vice-President, Global Leadership Foundation, since 2010; *b* 5 June 1939; *s* of Charles and Grace Clark; *m* 1973, Maureen Anne McTeer (she retained her maiden name); one *d. Educ:* High River High Sch.; Univ. of Alberta (BA History; MA Polit. Sci.). Journalist, Canadian Press, Calgary Herald, Edmonton Jl, High River Times, 1964–66; Lectr in Political Science, Univ. of Alberta, Edmonton, 1966–67; Exec. Asst to Hon. Robert L. Stanfield, Leader of the Opposition, 1967–70. MP (Progressive C): Rocky Mountain, later Yellowhead, 1972–93; Kings-Hants, 2000; Calgary Centre, 2000–04; Leader of the Opposition, Canada, 1976–79; Prime Minister of Canada, 1979–80; Leader of the Opposition, 1980–83; Sec. of State for External Affairs, 1984–91; Minister for Constitutional Affairs, 1991–93. Leader, Progressive Cons. Party of Canada, 1976–83 and 1998–2002. UN Special Rep. for Cyprus, 1993–95. Pres., Queen's Privy Council for Canada, 1991–93. Hon. LLD: New Brunswick, 1976; Calgary, 1984; Alberta, 1985; King's Coll., Halifax, 1994; Concordia, 1994; St Thomas, Minn, 1999; York, 2009; Carleton, 2010; UBC, 2012; McGill 2015. Alberta Order of Excellence, 1983. *Publications:* How We Lead: Canada in a century of change, 2013. *Recreations:* riding, reading, walking, film going.

CLARK, Prof. Christopher David, PhD; FRGS; Sorby Professor of Geoscience, University of Sheffield, since 2009; *b* Hampton Court, 3 July 1963; *s* of late Robin Cresswell Howes and of Pauline Ruby Howes (*née* Russell, now Clark) and step *s* of Terence Charles Clark; *m* 2000, Margaret Rose Stuckey; one *d*. *Educ:* Otford Primary Sch.; Wildernesse Sch.; University Coll. of Wales, Aberystwyth (BSc 1985); Univ. of Edinburgh (PhD 1990). Mountaineer (made first ascent of Shimshall Whitehorn, Karakorum, 1986). University of Sheffield: Lectr in Remote Sensing, 1990–97; Sen. Lectr, 1998–2002; Reader, 2002–04; Prof., 2004–09. Mem., Editl Adv. Bd, Earth Surface Processes and Landforms, 2008–. Member: Peer Rev. Coll., NERC, 2006–10; Assessment Bd, Res. Council of Norway, 2010–11; Sub-panel C17 - Geog., Envmtl Studies and Archaeol., REF 2014, 2011–14. Mem. Council, Remote Sensing Soc., 1993–96. Mem., Nat. Sheep Assoc. FRGS 2009. *Publications:* (jtly) Remote Sensing Handbook for Tropical Coastal Management, 2000; contrib. articles to learned jls on glacial geomorphol., glaciol. and Quaternary sci., and also on remote sensing of corals, mangroves, snow and archaeol. *Recreations:* mountaineering (regrettably, now armchair), white water kayaking, Landrover trialling, sheep farming. *Address:* Brough Lea Farm, Brough, Hope Valley, Derbys S33 9HG. *T:* (01433) 623646. *E:* c.clark@sheffield.ac.uk. *Clubs:* Alpine; XABA Mountaineering.

CLARK, Christopher Harvey; QC 1989; **His Honour Judge Christopher Harvey Clark;** a Circuit Judge, since 2005; Resident Judge, Truro Combined Court, since 2012; *b* 20 Dec. 1946; *s* of Harvey Frederick Beckford Clark and Winifred Julia Clark; *m* 1st, 1972, Gillian Elizabeth Ann Mullen (marr. diss. 2004); one *s* two *d*; 2nd, 2004, Mrs Wendy Gay Keith. *Educ:* Taunton's Grammar Sch., Southampton; The Queen's Coll., Oxford (BA 1968; MA 1987). Called to the Bar, Gray's Inn, 1969, Bencher, 2000–11; Mem., Western Circuit, 1969–2005; an Asst Recorder, 1982–86; a Recorder, 1986–2005. Head of Pump Court Chambers, 2001–05. Hon. Recorder, City of Truro, 2015–. President: Dorset Magistrates' Assoc., 2007–11; City of Winchester Trust, 2007–11. Chancellor: dio. of Winchester, 1993–; dio. of Portsmouth, 2003–14 (Dep. Chancellor, 1994–2003); Deputy Chancellor: dio. of Chichester, 1995–2006; dio. of Salisbury, 1997–2007. Lay Reader, C of E, 1998–. Pres., Stockbridge Amateur Dramatic Soc., 2007–11 (Chm., 1977–2007). *Recreations:* golf, cricket, gardening, walking, fly-fishing, exploring Cornwall, enjoying his grandchildren's company. *Address:* Truro Combined Court, Edward Street, Truro, Cornwall TR1 2PB. *Club:* Flyfishers'.

CLARK, Sir Christopher Munro, Kt 2015; PhD; FBA 2010; Regius Professor of History, University of Cambridge, since 2014; Fellow and Director of Studies, St Catharine's College, Cambridge, since 2007; *b* Sydney, Australia, 14 March 1960; *m* 1993, Dr Nina Lübbren; two *s*. *Educ:* Sydney Grammar Sch.; Sydney Univ.; Freie Univ., Berlin; Univ. of Cambridge (PhD 1992). Formerly Reader in European History, then Prof. of Modern European History, 2007–14, Univ. of Cambridge. FAHA 2008. Officer's Cross, Order of Merit (Germany), 2011. *Publications:* The Politics of Conversion: missionary protestantism and the Jews in Prussia, 1728–1947, 1995; (contrib.) The Napoleonic Legacy, 2000; Kaiser Wilhelm II: a life in power, 2000; (contrib.) Confessional Conflict in Nineteenth-Century Germany, 2001; (ed with W. Kaiser) Culture Wars: secular-Catholic conflict in nineteenth century Europe, 2004; Iron Kingdom: the rise and downfall of Prussia, 1600–1947, 2006 (Wolfson Hist. Prize, 2007; Deutscher Historikerpreis, 2010); The Sleepwalkers: how Europe went to war in 1914, 2012; contribs to jls incl. Past & Present, Jl Modern Hist., Comparativ, Correspondence. *Address:* St Catharine's College, Trumpington Street, Cambridge CB2 1RL.

CLARK, Christopher Richard Nigel, CBE 2011; Chairman, JSC Severstal, since 2007; *b* 29 Jan. 1942; *s* of late Rev. Vivian George Clark and Aileen Myfanwy Clark (*née* Thompson); *m* 1964, Catherine Ann Mather; two *s* one *d* (and one *s* decd). *Educ:* Marlborough Coll.; Trinity Coll., Cambridge; Brunel Univ. MIMMM (MIM 1967). Johnson Matthey plc, 1962–2004: Mem. Bd, 1990–2004; Chief Operating Officer, 1996–98; Chief Exec., 1998–2004. Chairman: Associated British Ports Holdings Ltd, 2004–11; Urenco Ltd, 2006–11; RusPetro, 2011–13; non-executive Director: Trinity Holdings (Dennis), 1993–98; FKI plc, 2000–06; Rexam plc, 2003–06 (Dep. Chm., 2003–06); Mem., Adv. Bd, Citicorp Venture Capital, 2009–. MInstD 1990; CCMI 2001. Centenary Medal, SCI, 2002. *Recreations:* shooting, golf, opera, ballet, watching Rugby and cricket. *Address:* 30 Marryat Road, SW19 5BD. *T:* (020) 8946 5887. *E:* christopher.clark64@gmail.com. *Clubs:* Travellers; Jesters.

CLARK, Claire Madeleine Ridgway, MBE 2011; patisserie consultant; Owner, Claire Clark Ltd, since 2010; *b* Swindon, 1964; *d* of Rev. David Ridgway Hemsley and Grace Ridgway Hemsley; *m* Stephen Peter Clark (marr. diss.). *Educ:* Waddesdon C of E Secondary Sch.; Aylesbury Coll. of Further Educn (City & Guilds); Thames Valley Univ. (City & Guilds 706/3 pt 1 and pt 2). Commis Chef, Randolph Hotel, Oxford, 1982–84; Commis Pastry Chef: Ritz Hotel, London, 1984–85; Intercontinental Hotel, London, 1985–88; Head Pastry Chef: Sutherlands Restaurant, London, 1988–90; Portman Intercontinental Hotel, London, 1990–93; teaching and compiling pastry progs, Le Cordon Bleu, London, 1993–95; Pastry Consultant, H of C, 1995–97; Head Pastry Chef: Bluebird Restaurant, London, 1995–97; Claridges Hotel, London, 1997–2000; Dir, Claire Clark Ltd, pastry mgt co. and consultancy, 2000–01; Head Pastry Chef: Hilton Metropole Hotel, London, 2001–03; Wolsely, London, 2003–05; French Laundry, Calif, 2005–09; Pastry Consultant, Sandy Lane Hotel, Barbados, 2009–10; pop-up shop, Harvey Nicholls, London, 2010. Examr for Advanced Pastry, City & Guilds, 1995. Master of Culinary Arts (Meilleur Ouvrier de GB 1996). *Publications:* Indulge, 2007; 80 Cakes from Around the World, 2014. *E:* claire@claire-clark.com.

CLARK, Prof. Colin Whitcomb, PhD; FRS 1997; FRSC 1988; Professor of Mathematics, University of British Columbia, 1969–94, Professor Emeritus, since 1994; *b* 18 June 1931; *s* of George Savage Clark and Irene (Stewart) Clark; *m* 1955, Janet Arlene Davidson; one *s* two *d*. *Educ:* Univ. of BC (BA 1953); Univ. of Washington (PhD 1958). Instructor, Univ. of Calif, Berkeley, 1958–60; Asst Prof., then Associate Prof. of Maths, Univ. of BC, 1960–69. Regent's Lectr in Maths, Univ. of Calif, Davis, 1986; Visiting Professor: of Ecology and Systematics, Cornell Univ., 1987; of Ecology and Evolutionary Biol., Princeton Univ., 1997. Hon. DSc Victoria, BC, 2000. *Publications:* Mathematical Bioeconomics, 1976, 3rd edn 2010; Bioeconomic Modelling and Fisheries Management, 1985; (with M. Mangel) Dynamic Modelling in Behavioral Ecology, 1988; (with M. Mangel) Dynamic State Variable Models in Ecology, 2000; The Worldwide Crisis in Fisheries, 2007; Math Overboard! (Basic Math for Adults), Pt 1, 2012, Pt 2, 2013. *Recreations:* natural history, ski-ing, hiking. *Address:* Institute of Applied Mathematics, University of British Columbia, Vancouver, BC V6T 1Z2, Canada. *T:* (604) 2745379.

CLARK, Dr Cynthia Zang Facer; Administrator, National Agricultural Statistics Service, US Department of Agriculture, 2008–14; *b* 1 April 1942; *d* of Joseph Elmer Facer and Flora Burnell Zang Facer (*née* Zang); *m* 1963, Glenn Willet Clark; three *s* three *d*. *Educ:* Mills Coll. (BA Maths 1963); Univ. of Denver (MA Maths 1964); Iowa State Univ. (MS 1974; PhD Stats 1977). Mathematical Statistician, Statistical Res. Div., US Census Bureau, 1977–79; Econ. Statistician, Statistical Policy Office, Office of Mgt and Budget, 1979–83; Asst Div. Chief for Res. and Methodology, Agric. Div., US Census Bureau, 1983–90; Dir, Survey Methods Div., Nat. Agricl Stats Service, US Dept of Agriculture, 1990–96; Associate Dir for Methodology and Standards, Census Bureau, US Dept of Commerce, 1996–2004; Exec. Dir for Methodology, ONS, 2004–07; internat. statistical consultant, 2007–08. Fellow: Amer. Statistical Assoc., 1997; Royal Statistical Soc., 2005. Member: Amer. Assoc. of Public Opinion Res., 1994; (elected) ISI, 1997– (Chair, Cttee on Women in Statistics, 2003–11). Meritorious Presidential Rank Award, 2011; Dist. Alumnae Award, Iowa State Univ., 2014. *Publications:* (ed jtly) Computer Assisted Survey Information Collection, 1998; Training for the Future: addressing tomorrow's survey tasks, 1998; (jtly) Understanding American Agriculture: challenges for the Agricultural Resource Management Survey, 2007; (with F. Nolan) Quality Improvement in the Office for National Statistics, 2007. *Recreations:* genealogy, ice-skating, travel, cultural events, family activities with siblings, 6 children and 16 grandchildren and 4 foster grandchildren. *Address:* 6628 McLean Court, McLean, VA 22101, USA. *T:* (703) 6638746. *E:* czfclark@cox.net.

CLARK, David Beatson, CBE 1986; TD 1966; DL; Chairman, Rotherham District Health Authority, 1993–96 (Member, 1985–96); *b* 5 May 1933; *s* of late Alec Wilson Clark, OBE, JP, DSc(Tech) and Phyllis Mary Clark; *m* 1959, Ann Morgan Mudford; two *s* one *d*. *Educ:* Wrekin College; Keele Univ. (BA Hons Physics and Econs). Beatson Clark: joined 1958; Managing Dir, 1971; Chm. and Managing Dir, 1979; Exec. Chm., 1984–88. Non-executive Director: Royal Bank of Scotland, 1988–91; Yorkshire Electricity Gp, 1990–94 (Mem., Yorkshire Electricity Bd, 1980–90); Rotherham TEC, 1990–92. President: Rotherham Chamber of Commerce, 1975–76; Sheffield Br., BIM, 1983–86; Glass Manufacturers' Fedn, 1982–83; Mem. Council, Univ. of Sheffield, 1984–2000. Liveryman, Glass Sellers' Co., 1967; Freeman, Cutlers' Co. in Hallamshire, 1980. DL S Yorks, 1990; High Sheriff, S Yorks, 1992. Hon. Fellow, Sheffield City Polytechnic, 1988. *Address:* 19 Beech Avenue, Rotherham, South Yorks S65 3HN.

CLARK, Prof. David Millar, CBE 2013; DPhil; FMedSci; FBA 2003; FBPsS; Professor of Experimental Psychology, University of Oxford, since 2011; Fellow, Magdalen College, Oxford, since 2011; *b* 20 Aug. 1954; *s* of Herbert Clark and Doris Alice Millar; *m* 1994, Prof. Anke Ehlers, *qv*; two *s*. *Educ:* Christ's Hosp.; Oxford Univ. (MA Exptl Psychol.; DPhil); London Univ. (MPhil Clinical Psychol.). Lectr, 1983–93, Prof., 1996–2000, Dept of Psychiatry, Univ. of Oxford; Wellcome Principal Res. Fellow, 1993–2000; Fellow, University Coll., Oxford, 1987–2000; Prof. of Psychology, Inst. of Psychiatry, 2000–11, Head, Dept of Psychology, 2000–06, KCL. President: British Assoc. of Behavioural and Cognitive Psychotherapies, 1992–93; Internat. Assoc. of Cognitive Psychotherapy, 1992–95. Nat. Clinical Advr, Government's Increasing Access to Psychological Therapies Initiative, 2008–. FMedSci 1999; FBPsS 2009. Hon. DSc: LSE, 2011; Roehampton, 2013. Dist. Scientist Award for the Application of Psychol., Amer. Psychol Soc., 2010; Lifetime Achievement Award, BPsS, 2014. *Publications:* Cognitive Behaviour Therapy for Psychiatric Problems, 1989; Science and Practice of Cognitive Behaviour Therapy, 1996; (with Richard Layard) Thrive, 2014; contrib. numerous articles on causes and treatment of anxiety disorders to learned jls. *Recreations:* travel, wine, modern art. *Address:* Department of Experimental Psychology, Tinbergen Building, 9 South Parks Road, Oxford OX1 3UD.

CLARK, Prof. (David) Stuart (Thorburn), PhD; FBA 2000; FRHistS; FLSW; Professor of Early Modern History, Swansea University (formerly University of Wales, Swansea), 1998–2008, now Emeritus; *b* 22 Nov. 1942; *m* 1965, Janet Stephanie Gaze; one *s* two *d*. *Educ:* UC Swansea (BA 1964); Trinity Hall, Cambridge (PhD 1971). Lectr, 1967–95, Sen. Lectr, 1995–98, Dept of History, UC Swansea, subseq. Univ. of Wales, Swansea. Fellow: IAS, Princeton, 1988–89; Nat. Humanities Centre, NC, 1999–2000; British Acad. Reader, 1998–2000; Vis. Prof., Univ. of Richmond, Va, 2003; Vis. Fellow, 2004–05, Vis. Prof., 2008–09, Princeton Univ. FRHistS 1985; FLSW 2010. *Publications:* Thinking with Demons: the idea of witchcraft in early modern Europe, 1997; (ed) Annales School: critical assessments in history, 4 vols, 1999; (ed) The Athlone History of Witchcraft and Magic in Europe, 6 vols, 1999–2002; (ed) Languages of Witchcraft: narrative, ideology and meaning in early modern culture, 2001; Vanities of the Eye: vision in early modern European culture, 2007. *Recreations:* music, Arsenal FC. *Address:* 44 Manselfield Road, Murton, Swansea SA3 3AR.

CLARK, His Honour Denis; a Circuit Judge, 1988–2007; *b* 2 Aug. 1943; twin *s* of John and Mary Clark; *m* 1967, Frances Mary (*née* Corcoran); four *d*. *Educ:* St Anne's RC Primary, Rock Ferry, Birkenhead; St Anselm's Coll., Birkenhead; Sheffield Univ. LLB. Called to the Bar, Inner Temple, 1966; practised Northern Circuit, 1966–88; a Recorder, 1984–88. *Recreations:* medieval history, cricket, theatre.

CLARK, Derek Roland; Member (UK Ind) East Midlands, European Parliament, 2004–14; *b* 10 Oct. 1933; *m* 1973, (Rosemary) Jane Purser. *Educ:* Univ. of Bristol (Teaching Cert.); Univ. of Exeter (Dip. Sci.). ACP 1971. Teacher of Sci., Air Balloon Hill Secondary Sch., Bristol, 1954–62; Hd of Sci. Dept, 1962–74, Sen. Master, 1970–74, Cherry Orchard Sch., Northampton; Sen. Hd of House, Lings Upper Sch., Northampton, 1974–85; Teacher of Sci., Falcon Manor Sch., Northants, 1985–93. Chm., Physics Subject Panel, CSE, E Midlands, 1970–76. UK Independence Party: Chm., Northants Br., 1995–2004; Chm., E Midlands Regl Cttee, 1996–2003 and 2008–12; Mem., NEC, 2001–04 and 2006–; Party Sec., 2002–04.

CLARK, Prof. (Edith) Gillian, DPhil; FBA 2012; Professor of Ancient History, University of Bristol, 2000–10, now Emerita; *b* Denbigh, N Wales, 30 Dec. 1946; *d* of late Prof. John Callan James Metford and Edith Metford (*née* Donald); *m* 1972, Stephen R. L. Clark; one *s* two *d*. *Educ:* Clifton High Sch., Bristol; Somerville Coll., Oxford (MA; DPhil 1973). Lectr in Ancient Hist., Univ. of Leicester, 1970–71; Mary Ewart Jun. Res. Fellow, Somerville Coll., Oxford, 1972–74; Lectr in Classics, 1989–95, Sen. Lectr, 1995–2000, Univ. of Liverpool. Part-time posts: Tutor in Moral Philosophy and in NT Studies, Univ. of Glasgow, and in Classical Civilisation, Open Univ. in Scotland, 1980–83; Tutor in Ancient Hist., St Andrews Univ., 1981–82; Tutor, Dept of Greek, 1983–86, Hon. Lectr in Greek and Ancient Hist., 1986–89, Univ. of Liverpool; Lectr in Ecclesiastical Hist., Manchester Univ., 1986–89. Chair, Council of Univ. Classical Depts, 2001–03. Convenor, AHRC Res. Panel 1, 2002–06. Member, Advisory Council: Inst. for Classical Studies, Univ. of London, 2004–09; Inst. for Advanced Studies, Univ. of Durham, 2006–13. Dir, Internat. Conf. on Patristic Studies, Oxford, 2003–; Mem., Internat. Organising Cttee, Fédn Internat. des Assocs d'Etudes Classiques, 2011–14. Mem. Council, Classical Assoc., 1998–2003. Co-editor: Translated Texts for Historians 300–800, 1989–; Oxford Early Christian Studies, 1996–; Member: Editl Cttee, Jl Roman Studies, 2000–11; Editl Adv. Bd, Jl Ecclesiastical Hist., 2009–; Consulting Ed., Jl Late Antiquity, 2009–. *Publications:* Iamblichus: On the Pythagorean Life, 1989; Augustine: Confessions, 1993, rev. edn 2005; Women in Late Antiquity, 1993; Augustine: Confessions 1–4, 1995; Porphyry: On Abstinence from Killing Animals, 2000; Christianity and Roman Society, 2004; Late Antiquity: a very short introduction, 2011; Body and Gender, Soul and Reason in Late Antiquity, 2011; contrib. papers to jls and ed vols; *festschrift:* Being Christian in Late Antiquity: a festschrift for Gillian Clark, ed C. Harrison, C. Humfress and B. Sandwell, 2014. *Recreations:* walking, music, art and architecture. *Address:* 49 Bellevue Crescent, Bristol BS8 4TF. *E:* gillian.clark@bristol.ac.uk.

CLARK, Sir Francis (Drake), 5th Bt *cr* 1886, of Melville Crescent, Edinburgh; *b* 16 July 1924; *yr s* of Sir Thomas Clark, 3rd Bt and Ellen Mercy (*d* 1987), *d* of late Francis Drake; *S* brother, 1991; *m* 1958, Mary (*d* 1994), *yr d* of late John Alban Andrews, MC, FRCS; one *s*. *Educ:* Edinburgh Acad. RN 1943–46. Dir, Clark Travel Service Ltd, London, 1948–80. *Recreations:* tennis, cricket, music, gardening. *Heir:* *s* Edward Drake Clark [*b* 27 April 1966; *m* 2000; three *d*].

CLARK, Frank, CBE 1991; Chair, Care Inspectorate, Scotland, 2011–13; Member: Healthcare Improvement, Scotland, 2011–13; Scottish Social Services Council, 2011–13; *b* 17 Oct. 1946; *m*; two *d*. MHSM 1974; DipHSM 1974. Clerical Trainee, Bd of Mgt for Royal Cornhill and Associated Hosps, 1965–67; Higher Clerical Officer, Kingseat Hosp., 1967–69; Dep. Hosp. Sec., 1969–70, Hosp. Sec., 1970–71, Canniesburn and Schaw Hosps; Dep. Hosp. Sec., Glasgow Royal Infirmary and Sub-Gp, 1971–74; Administrator, Glasgow Royal Infirmary, 1974–77; Greater Glasgow Health Board Eastern District: Asst Dist Administrator,

1977–81; Dist Gen. Administrator, 1981–83; Hamilton and E Kilbride Unit, Lanarkshire Health Board: Dist Administrator, 1983–84; Dir of Admin. Services, June–Sept. 1984; Sec. to Bd, Lanarks Health Bd, 1984–85; General Manager: Lanarks Health Bd, 1985–96; Lothian Health Bd, May–Dec. 1990; Dir, Strathcarron Hospice, 1996–2006. Vis. Prof., Health Fac., Glasgow Caledonian Univ., 1993–; Hon. Prof., Dept of Nursing and Midwifery, Univ. of Stirling, 1997–. Chairman: W of Scotland Health Service Res. Network, 1990–95; Scottish Health Bd Gen. Managers Gp, 1993–95 (Vice Chm., 1995–96); Lanarks Drugs Action Team, 1995–96; Scottish Hospices Forum, 1998–2001; Central Scotland Health Care NHS Trust, Jan.–March 1999; Forth Valley Primary Care Trust, April–Sept. 1999; Ministerial Task Force, NHS Tayside, 2000; Bd, NHS Forth Valley, 2001–02; Scottish Partnership for Palliative Care, 2003–06; Social Care and Social Work Improvement, Scotland, 2010–11; Vice Chm., Scottish Partnership Agency for Palliative and Cancer Care, 1998–2001; Member: Chief Scientist's Health Service Res. Cttee, 1989–93; Scottish Health Service Adv. Council, 1990–93; Scottish Overseas Health Support Policy Bd, 1990–96; Jt Wkg Gp on Purchasing, 1992–96; Scottish Implementation Gp, Jun. Doctors' and Dentists' Hours of Work, 1992–96; Scottish Council for Postgrad. Med. and Dental Educn, 1993–96; Implementation Gp, Scottish Health Services Mgt Centre, 1993–96; Strategy Gp, R&D Strategy for NHS in Scotland, 1994–96; Ind. Hospices Representative Cttee, Help the Hospices, 1998–2001; Convenor, Scottish Commn for the Regulation of Care, 2006–10. Mem. Bd, New Lanarkshire Ltd, 1992–98. Non-exec. Dir, Voluntary Assoc. for Mental Welfare, 1997–2006. Consultant in Corporate Governance, 2013–. Mem. Editl Adv. Bd, Health Bulletin, 1993–96. Pres., Cumbernauld Rotary Club, 2000–01, 2005–06. Paul Harris Fellow, Rotary Internat., 2011. *Address:* 7 Heatherdale Gardens, Head of Muir, Stirlingshire FK6 5JN.

CLARK, Gabrielle Seal; *see* Hinsliff, G. S.

CLARK, Gerald, CBE 1990; Inspector of Companies, Head of Companies Investigation Branches, Department of Trade and Industry, 1984–90; *b* 18 Sept. 1933; *s* of John George and Elizabeth Clark (*née* Shaw); *m* 1958, Elizabeth McDermott (*d* 2014); one *s*. *Educ:* St Cuthbert's Grammar School, Newcastle upon Tyne. Chartered Secretary. National Health Service, Northumberland Exec. Council, 1949–55; National Coal Board, 1955–60; Board of Trade, Official Receiver's Service, 1960–71; Companies Investigation Branch, 1971–79; Official Receiver, High Court of Justice, 1981–83; Principal Examiner, Companies Investigation Branch, 1983–84. Mem., Herts Area Cttee, Sanctuary Housing Assoc., 1990–2001 (Chm., 1992–2000). *Recreations:* music, photography. *Clubs:* Civil Service, Middlesex CC.

CLARK, Gerald Edmondson, CMG 1989; Chairman, International Nuclear Energy Academy, 2013–14 (Secretary, 2000–12); General Secretary, Energy Strategists Consultancy Ltd, 2001–14; Consultant, Pell Frischmann, since 2006; *b* 26 Dec. 1935; *s* of Edward John Clark and Irene Elizabeth Ada Clark (*née* Edmondson); *m* 1967, Mary Rose Organ; two *d*. *Educ:* Johnston Grammar School, Durham; Jt Services Sch. for Linguists; New College, Oxford (MA). FEI (FInstE 1998). HM Diplomatic Service, 1960–93: Foreign Office, 1960; Hong Kong, 1961; Peking, 1962–63; FO, 1964–68; Moscow, 1968–70; FCO, 1970–73; Head of Chancery, Lisbon, 1973–77; Asst Sec., Cabinet Office, 1977–79; seconded to Barclays Bank International, 1979–81; Commercial Counsellor, Peking, 1981–83; FCO, 1984–87; UK Perm. Rep to IAEA, UNIDO, and to UN in Vienna, 1987–92; Sen. DS, RCDS, 1993; Sec. Gen., Uranium Inst., 1994–2000. Patron, New London Orchestra, 1993–2006. Chm., London Gp, Henley Alumni Assoc., 1997–2007. *Publications:* articles and speeches on the civil nuclear fuel cycle and related subjects. *Recreations:* conversation with my wife and friends, gardening, long distance walking. *Address:* Lew Hollow, Beer Hill, Seaton, Devon EX12 2PY. *T:* (01297) 22001. *E:* geraldeclark@aol.com. *Club:* Athenæum.

CLARK, Gillian; *see* Clark, E. G.

CLARK, Hon. Glen David; President, since 2011, and Member, Board of Directors, since 2009, Jim Pattison Group (Executive Vice-President, 2005–11); Premier of British Columbia, 1996–99; *b* 22 Nov. 1957; *m* 1980, Dale Babish; one *s* one *d*. *Educ:* Simon Fraser Univ. (BA Pol Sci. & Canadian Studies); Univ. of BC (MA Community & Regl Planning). MLA (NDP) Vancouver East, 1986–91, Vancouver-Kingsway, 1991–2001. Minister of: Finance and Corporate Relns, 1991–93; Employment and Investment, 1993–96; Leader, NDP, BC, 1996–2001. Pacific NW Manager, 2001, then Vice-Pres., Jim Pattison Sign Gp. Member, Board of Directors: Canfor Corp., 2009–; SunRype Products, 2009–; Westshore Terminals, 2009–. *Recreation:* spending time with family. *Address:* Jim Pattison Group, Suite 1800-1067 West Cordova Street, Vancouver, BC V6C 1C7, Canada.

CLARK, Prof. Gordon Leslie, DSc; FBA 2005; Professor and Director, Smith School of Enterprise and the Environment, University of Oxford, since 2013; Professorial Fellow, St Edmund Hall, Oxford, since 2013; Research Fellow, Institute of Ageing, University of Oxford, since 2001; Sir Louis Matheson Visiting Professor, Faculty of Business and Economics, Monash University, Melbourne, since 2009; *b* 10 Sept. 1950; *s* of Bryan Clark and Florence Lesley Clark (*née* Cowling); *m* 1972, Shirley Anne Spratling; one *s*. *Educ:* Monash Univ. (BEcon, MA); McMaster Univ. (PhD 1978; Dist. Alumni Award, 1998); MA, DSc 2002, Oxon. Asst Prof., Harvard Univ., 1978–83; Associate Prof., Univ. of Chicago, 1983–85; Prof., Carnegie Mellon Univ., 1985–91; Monash University: Prof., 1989–95; Hd of Dept, 1990–93; Associate Dean, 1991–94; Actg Dean, 1993–94; Dir, Inst. of Ethics and Public Policy, 1991–95; University of Oxford: Halford Mackinder Prof. of Geography, 1995–12; Chm., Faculty Bd of Anthropology and Geography, 1999–2001; Professorial Fellow: St Peter's Coll., 1995–2012; Saïd Business Sch., 2000–03; Head, Centre for the Envmt (incl. Sch. of Geog. and the Envmt), 2003–08; Sen. Res. Fellow, Harvard Law Sch., 2005–08. Nat. Research Council Fellow, US Nat. Acad. of Sci., 1981–82; Fellow, Lincoln Land Inst., 1981–82. FASSA 1993. Chancellor's Medal, UCSB, 2000. *Publications:* Interregional Migration, National Policy and Social Justice, 1983; (jtly) State Apparatus, 1984; Judges and the Cities, 1985; (jtly) Regional Dynamics, 1986; Unions and Communities Under Siege, 1989; Pensions and Corporate Restructuring in American Industry, 1993; (ed jtly) Multiculturalism, Difference and Postmodernism, 1993; (ed jtly) Management Ethics, 1995; (ed jtly) Asian Newly Industrialised Economies in the Global Economy, 1996; (ed jtly) Accountability and Corruption: public sector ethics, 1997; Pension Fund Capitalism, 2000; (ed jtly) Oxford Handbook of Economic Geography, 2000; European Pensions & Global Finance, 2003; (ed jtly) Pension Security in the 21st Century, 2003; (jtly) Global Competitiveness and Innovation, 2004; (ed jtly) The Oxford Handbook of Pensions and Retirement Income, 2006; (jtly) The Geography of Finance, 2007; (ed jtly) Managing Financial Risk, 2009; (jtly) Saving for Retirement: intention, context and behaviour, 2012; (jtly) Sovereign Wealth Funds: legitimacy, governance and global power, 2013. *Recreations:* walking, reading, holidays. *Address:* Smith School of Enterprise and the Environment, University of Oxford, Hinshelwood Road, Oxford OX1 3QY. *Club:* Athenæum.

CLARK, Prof. Graeme Milbourne, AC 2004 (AO); PhD; FRS 2004; Laureate Professor Emeritus, since 2006, and Distinguished Researcher, ICT 4 Life Sciences in Electrical and Electronic Engineering, since 2012, University of Melbourne; Otolaryngologist Emeritus, Eye and Ear Hospital, Melbourne; *b* 16 Aug. 1935; *s* of Colin and Dorothy Clark; *m* 1961, Margaret Burtenshaw; one *s* four *d*. *Educ:* Univ. of Sydney (MB BS Hons 1957; MS 1968; PhD 1969). FRCSE 1961; FRCS 1962 (Hon. FRCS 2004); FRACS 1966. University of Melbourne: Foundn Prof. of Otolaryngology and Chm., 1970–2004; Hd and Founder, Cochlear Implant Prog., 1970–2004; Laureate Prof., 1999–2004; Laureate Professorial Fellow, 2004; Founder and Dir, Bionic Ear Inst., Melbourne, 1984–2005, Dir Emeritus, 2006; Hon. Prof., Electrical Engrg; Hd and Founder, Cochlear Implant Clinic, Royal Victoria Eye and Ear Hosp., 1985–2004; Principal Scientist, St Vincent's Hosp., Melbourne, 2006–09; Adjunct Prof., Univ. of Wollongong, 2006–12; Dist. Prof., La Trobe Univ., 2008–12. Leader, Bionics Prog., Aust. Res. Council Centre of Excellence for Electromaterials Sci., 2005–12. Director: Human Communication Res. Centre, Aust. Res. Council, 1988–96; Co-op. Res. Centre for Cochlear Implant, Speech and Hearing Res., Melbourne, 1992–98. Mem., Adv. Council for Children with Impaired Hearing, 1982–; Exec. Mem., Deafness Foundn of Victoria, 1973–91. FAA 1998; FTSE 1998. Hon. FRSocMed 2003. Hon. MD: Medizinische Hochschule, Hannover, 1988; Sydney, 1989; Hon. DSc Wollongong, 2002; Hon. DEng Chung Yuan Christian Univ., Taiwan, 2003; Hon. LLD Monash, 2004; DUniv Zargoza, 2010. Ian Wark Medal, Aust. Acad. of Sci., 2006; Lister Medal, RCS, 2010; Florey Medal, Aust. Inst. of Policy and Sci. and Commonwealth Serum Labs, 2011; Zotterman Medal, Nobel Inst. for Neurophysiol., 2011; Lasker-DeBakey Clinical Med. Res. Award, Lasker Foundn, 2013; Fritz J. and Dolores H. Russ Prize, NAE and Ohio Univ., 2015. Asst Ed., Jl of Otolaryngol Soc. of Aust., 1973–80; Mem., Editl Bd, Cochlear Implants Internat., 2007–. *Publications:* Sounds from Silence, 2000; Cochlear Implants: fundamentals and applications, 2003; 52 book chapters, more than 420 refereed contribs to scientific jls, 1 monograph and 5 edited books and jl supplements. *Recreations:* surfing, science and theology, bush walking. *Address:* Centre for Neural Engineering, Level 1, Building 261, University of Melbourne, 203 Bouverie Street, Carlton, Vic 3053, Australia. *E:* gclark@unimelb.edu.au. *Club:* Melbourne (Melbourne).

CLARK, Gregor Munro, CB 2006; Parliamentary Counsel to the Scottish Law Commission, 1995–2000 and since 2006; *b* 18 April 1946; *s* of late Ian Munro Clark and Norah Isobel Joss; *m* 1st, 1974, Jane Maralyn Palmer (*d* 1999); one *s* two *d*; 2nd, 2000, Alexandra Plumtree (*née* Miller). *Educ:* Queen's Park Senior Secondary Sch., Glasgow; St Andrews Univ. (LLB Hons). Admitted Faculty of Advocates, 1972; entered Lord Advocate's Dept, London, 1974; Asst Parly Draftsman, then Dep. Parly Draftsman, 1974–79; Asst Legal Sec. to Lord Advocate, and Scottish Parly Counsel, 1979–99; Scottish Exec., 1999–2002 and 2004–06; Scottish Parly Counsel (UK), Scotland Office, 2002–04. *Recreations:* piano, opera, Scandinavian languages and literature. *Address:* 18 Rocheid Park, Inverleith, Edinburgh EH4 1RU. *T:* (0131) 315 4634. *Club:* New (Edinburgh).

CLARK, Rt Hon. Greg(ory David); PC 2010; PhD; MP (C) Tunbridge Wells, since 2005; Secretary of State for Communities and Local Government, since 2015; *b* 28 Aug. 1967; *s* of John and Patricia Clark; *m* 1999, Helen Fillingham; one *s* two *d*. *Educ:* St Peter's Comprehensive Sch., S Bank, Middlesbrough; Magdalene Coll., Cambridge (MA Econs); LSE (PhD 1992). Consultant, Boston Consulting Gp, 1991–94; res. and teaching, LSE and Open Univ. Business Sch., 1994–96; Special Advr to Sec. of State for Trade and Industry, 1996–97; Chief Advr, 1997–99, Controller, 1999–2001, Commercial Policy, BBC; Dir of Policy, 2001–03, of Policy and Res., 2003–05, Cons. Party. Shadow Minister: for Charities, Social Enterprise and Volunteering, 2006–08; for Cabinet Office, 2007–08; Shadow Energy and Climate Change Sec., 2008–10; Minister of State: DCLG, 2010–12; BIS, 2011–12; Financial Sec., HM Treasury, 2012–13; Minister of State, Cabinet Office, 2013–15; Minister of State (Minister for Univs and Sci.), BIS, 2014–15. Mem. (C) Westminster CC, 2002–05 (Cabinet Mem., 2003–05). Vis. Fellow, Nuffield Coll., Oxford, 2007–. *Address:* House of Commons, SW1A 0AA.

CLARK, Guy Wyndham Nial Hamilton, FCSI; Lord-Lieutenant, Renfrewshire, since 2007 (Vice Lord-Lieutenant, 2002–07); *b* 28 March 1944; *s* of late Capt. George Hubert Wyndham Clark and Lavinia Mariquita Smith (*née* Shaw Stewart); *m* 1967, Brighid Lovell Greene; two *s* one *d*. *Educ:* Eton Coll.; Mons Officer Cadet Sch. Commnd Coldstream Guards, 1962–67; Investment Manager, Murray Johnstone, 1973–77; Partner, R. C. Greig & Co. (Glasgow), 1977–86; Dir, Greig, Middleton & Co. Ltd, 1986–97; Managing Director: Murray Johnstone Private Investors Ltd, 1997–2001; Aberdeen Private Investors Ltd, 2001–06; Sen. Divl Dir, Bell Lawrie, 2006–08. Mem., Internat. Stock Exchange, 1983; MSI 1992, FCSI (FSI 2005). Mem. Exec. Cttee, Erskine Hosp. for Ex Servicemen, 1981–97. Vice Pres., W Lowland Bn Army Cadet Force League, 2007–; Pres., Lowland Reserve Forces and Cadets Assoc., 2014–. Pres., E Renfrewshire and Inverclyde Br., SSAFA (formerly SSAFA Forces Help) Renfrewshire, 2007–; Patron, Accord Hospice, 2007–; Hon. Patron, Incorporated Glasgow Renfrewshire Soc., 2007–; Hon. Pres., St Columba's Sch., 2008–. Inverclyde: JP 1981–2007; DL 1987–2007. Vice Chm., JP Adv. Cttee for Inverclyde, 1990–2003. *Recreations:* country sports, gardening. *Address:* (home) Braeton House, Inverkip, Renfrewshire PA16 0DU. *T:* (01475) 520619, *Fax:* (01475) 521030. *E:* g.clark282@btinternet.com. *Clubs:* Turf, MCC; Western (Glasgow).

CLARK, Rt Hon. Helen Elizabeth, ONZ 2010; PC 1990; Administrator, United Nations Development Programme, since 2009; Prime Minister of New Zealand, 1999–2008; *b* 26 Feb. 1950; *d* of George and Margaret Clark; *m* 1981, Dr Peter Byard Davis. *Educ:* Epsom Girls' Grammar School; Auckland Univ. (BA 1971; MA Hons 1974). Junior Lectr in Political Studies, Auckland Univ., 1973–75; UGC Post Graduate Scholar, 1976; Lectr, Political Studies Dept, Auckland Univ., 1977–81. MP (Lab): Mount Albert, NZ, 1981–96 and 1999–2009; Owairaka, 1996–99. Minister: of Housing, of Conservation, 1987–89; of Health, of Labour, 1989–90; Dep. Prime Minister, 1989–90; Dep. Leader of the Opposition, 1990–93, Leader, 1993–99; Minister of Arts, Culture and Heritage, 1999–2008; Minister in Charge of Security Intelligence Service and Govt Commns Security Bureau, 1999–2008; Minister for Ministerial Services, 1999–2008. *Recreations:* theatre, opera, ballet, film music, ski-ing, trekking, reading. *Address:* United Nations Development Programme, One United Nations Plaza, New York, NY 10017, USA.

CLARK, Helen Rosemary; writer, since 2005; policy adviser and consultant specialising in climate change and health, since 2007; educational examiner and assessor, since 2010; associate consultant on youth, 2010; Associate Director, Royal Public Affairs, since 2013; *b* 23 Dec. 1954; *d* of George Henry Dyche and Phyllis May Dyche (*née* James); *m* (marr. diss.); two *c*; *m* 2001, Alan Clark. *Educ:* Spondon Park Grammar Sch.; Bristol Univ. (BA Hons Eng Lit. 1976; MA Medieval Lit. 1978; PGCE 1979). English Teacher, 1979–97. Examr, English Lit. and Lang., London, Cambridge, Southern and Northern Exam. Bds, 1985–97. MP (Lab) Peterborough, 1997–2005; contested (Lab) same seat, 2005. *Publications:* contrib. to various political jls, national newspapers, specialist mags and policy documents. *Recreations:* reading novels, political and historical biography, modern films and theatre.

CLARK, Prof. Ian, PhD; FBA 1999; FLSW; Professor of International Relations, University of Queensland, since 2014; *b* 14 March 1949; *m* 1970, Janice (*née* Cochrane); one *s* one *d*. *Educ:* Glasgow Univ. (MA); Australian National Univ. (PhD 1975). Lectr, 1974–81, Sen. Lectr, 1981–84, Univ. of Western Australia; Fellow, Selwyn Coll., Cambridge, 1985–97, Hon. Fellow, 2000; Dep. Dir, Centre of Internat. Studies, Cambridge, 1993–97; University of Wales, Aberystwyth, later Aberystwyth University: Prof. of Internat. Politics, 1998–2008; E. H. Carr Prof., 2008–14. Leverhulme Major Res. Fellow, 2002–04; Vis. Fellow, ANU, 2003; Professorial Fellow, ESRC, 2007–10; Vis. Prof., S. Rajaratnam Sch. of Internat. Studies, Singapore, 2014–. British Academy: Mem. Council, 2001–04; Chair, Political Studies, 2005–08, Posts, 2005–11. Founding FLSW 2010. *Publications:* The Hierarchy of States, 1989; Nuclear Diplomacy and the Special Relationship, 1994; Globalization and Fragmentation: international relations in the twentieth century, 1997; Globalization and International Relations Theory, 1999; The Post-Cold War Order, 2001; Legitimacy in International Society, 2005; International Legitimacy and World Society, 2007; Hegemony in International Society, 2011; The Vulnerable International Society, 2013; Waging War: a new philosophical introduction, 2015. *Recreations:* hill walking, grandfather. *Address:* School of Political Science and International Studies, University of Queensland, St Lucia Campus, Brisbane, Qld 4072, Australia.

CLARK, Ian Robertson, CBE 1979; PhD; former Chairman, Clark & Associates Ltd; *b* 18 Jan. 1939; *s* of Alexander Clark and Annie Dundas Watson; *m* 1961, Jean Scott Waddell Lang; one *s* one *d*. *Educ:* Dalziel High Sch., Motherwell; Univ. of Wales Trinity St David (PhD 2010). FCCA, CPFA. Trained with Glasgow Chartered Accountant; served in local govt, 1962–76, this service culminating in the post of Chief Executive, Shetland Islands Council; full-time Mem., BNOC, from 1976 until privatisation in 1982; Jt Man. Dir, Britoil plc, 1982–85; Chm., Ventures Div., Costain Gp, subseq. Urban Enterprises Ltd, 1987–93; former Chm., C & M (Hydraulics) Ltd. Hon. LLD Glasgow, 1979. *Publications:* Reservoir of Power, 1980; contribs to professional and religious periodicals. *Recreations:* theology, general reading, walking. *Address:* Bellfield House, High Askomil, Campbeltown, Argyll PA28 6EN. *T:* (01586) 553905.

CLARK, Jacqueline; *see* Davies, Jacqueline.

CLARK, James Frame; HM Diplomatic Service, retired; Managing Director, Clear Coaching & Consulting Ltd, since 2007; *b* 12 March 1963; *s* of James F. Clark and Anne Clark (*née* Wilson); partner, Anthony J. Stewart. *Educ:* Edinburgh Univ. (BSc Hons Geog.). Teacher, W Berlin, 1985–87; entered FCO, 1988; Mexico and Central America Dept, 1988–89; Arabic lang. trng, 1989; Cairo, 1990; ME Dept, FCO, 1990–91; UK Rep., Brussels, 1991–93; First Secretary: Econ. Relns Dept, FCO, 1994–95; Press Office, FCO, 1995–97; on loan to German Foreign Min., Bonn, 1997–98; EU, Bonn, 1998–99; Hd, Conf. and Visits Gp, FCO, 1999–2003; Commercial Dir, FCO Services, 2003–04; Ambassador to Luxembourg, 2004–07; Consul Gen., Chicago, 2007–10. Dir, UK Internat. Coach Fedn, 2012–13. *Recreations:* friends, food, fitness, reading, writing, travel.

CLARK, Dame Jill M.; *see* Macleod Clark.

CLARK, Rt Hon. Joe; *see* Clark, Rt Hon. C. J.

CLARK, Sir (John) Arnold, Kt 2004; Chairman and Chief Executive, Arnold Clark Automobiles Ltd; *b* 27 Nov. 1927; *m* Philomena, (Mena); five *s* four *d* (and one *s* decd). Served RAF. Founded Arnold Clark Automobiles Ltd, 1956. Trustee: Kelvingrove Art Gall. and Mus., Glasgow, 2002–; Riverside Mus. Appeal, Glasgow, 2008–. Fellow, Stirling Smith Art Gall. and Mus., 2010. Elder, Church of Scotland. FIMI. DUniv Glasgow, 2005. *Address:* Arnold Clark Automobiles Ltd, 134 Nithsdale Drive, Glasgow G41 2PP. *Clubs:* Glasgow Art, Rotary (Glasgow).

CLARK, John Edward, OBE 1995; Secretary, National Association of Local Councils, 1978–95; *b* 18 Oct. 1932; *s* of Albert Edward Clark and Edith (*née* Brown); *m* 1969, Judith Rosemary Lester; one *s* (one *d* decd). *Educ:* Royal Grammar Sch., Clitheroe; Keble Coll., Oxford (MA, BCL). Called to the Bar, Gray's Inn, 1957; practised at the Bar, 1957–61. Dep. Sec., National Assoc. of Local (formerly Parish) Councils, (part-time) 1959–61, (full-time) 1961–78. Hon. Legal Consultant, Assoc. of Burial Authorities, 1998–2012; Mem., Burial and Cremation Adv. Gp, MoJ, 2005–12. Publicity Asst, Dulwich Fest., annually, 1999–2004. Archivist, All Saints, W Dulwich, 2003–. Mem., Penguin Collectors Soc., 2001–. *Publications:* chapters on local govt, public health, and theatres, in Encyclopaedia of Court Forms, 2nd edn 1964 to 1975. *Recreations:* walking, home wine-making, indoor games, collecting detective fiction, fortifications, rough ecclesiastical carpentry, opera. *Address:* 14 Idmiston Road, West Norwood, SE27 9HG.

CLARK, John Mullin; Director, Mission and Public Affairs, Archbishops' Council, Church of England, 2002–07; *b* 19 April 1946; *s* of James and Margaret Clark; *m* 1975, Jenny Brown; one *s*. *Educ:* St Peter's Coll., Oxford (MA); Inst. of Educn, London Univ. (PGCE 1974); King's Coll., London (MA 1999); Heythrop Coll., Univ. of London (MA Psychol. of Religion 2009). Operation Mobilisation, Iran, 1967–73; Iran Literature Assoc., Tehran, 1976–80; Church Missionary Society: Regl Sec., ME and Pakistan, 1980–86; Communications Sec., 1987–91; Sec., Overseas Bishoprics' Fund, and Partnership Sec., Partnership for World Mission, Bd of Mission, C of E, 1992–2000; Chief Sec. for Mission, Archbishops' Council, C of E, 2000–02. Chairman: Friends of Dio. of Iran, 1994–; United Soc. for Christian Literature, 1996–; Jerusalem and E Mission Trust, 2008–. Anglican Lay Reader, 1974–. *Recreations:* opera, walking, church history, T. E. Lawrence, Iran. *Address:* 32 Weigall Road, Lee, SE12 8HE. *T:* (020) 8852 2741.

CLARK, Sir John S.; *see* Stewart-Clark.

CLARK, Rt Rev. Jonathan; *see* Croydon, Area Bishop of.

CLARK, Prof. Jonathan Charles Douglas, PhD; Hall Distinguished Professor of British History, University of Kansas, since 1995; *b* 28 Feb. 1951; *s* of Ronald James Clark and Dorothy Margaret Clark; *m* 1996, Katherine Redwood Penovich. *Educ:* Downing Coll., Cambridge (BA 1972); Corpus Christi Coll., Cambridge (MA 1976); Peterhouse, Cambridge (PhD 1981). Research Fellow: Peterhouse, Cambridge, 1977–81; Leverhulme Trust, 1983; All Souls Coll., Oxford, 1986–95 (Sen. Res. Fellow, 1995). Vis. Prof., Cttee on Social Thought, Univ. of Chicago, 1993; Dist. Vis. Lectr, Univ. of Manitoba, 1999; Vis. Fellow, Forschungszentrum Europäische Aufklärung, Potsdam, 2000; Visiting Professor: Univ. of Northumbria, 2001–03; Oxford Brookes Univ., 2009–13. Initiated Oxford American Inst. (now Rothermere Amer. Inst.), 1990. Gov., Pusey House, Oxford, 1991–98. *Publications:* The Dynamics of Change, 1982; English Society 1688–1832, 1985, 2nd edn, as English Society 1660–1832, 2000; Revolution and Rebellion, 1986; (ed) The Memoirs and Speeches of James, 2nd Earl Waldegrave, 1988; (ed) Ideas and Politics in Modern Britain, 1990; The Language of Liberty 1660–1832, 1994; Samuel Johnson, 1994; (ed) Edmund Burke, Reflections on the Revolution in France, 2001; (ed jtly) Samuel Johnson in Historical Context, 2002; Our Shadowed Present, 2003; (ed) A World by Itself: a history of the British Isles, 2010; (ed jtly) The Politics of Samuel Johnson, 2012; (ed jtly) The Interpretation of Samuel Johnson, 2012; Restoration to Reform: British history 1660–1832, 2014; articles in learned jls. *Recreation:* more history. *Address:* Department of History, University of Kansas, 1445 Jayhawk Boulevard, Lawrence, KS 66045–7590, USA. *T:* (785) 8643569. *Club:* Beefsteak.

CLARK, Sir Jonathan (George), 5th Bt *cr* 1917, of Dunlambert, City of Belfast; Managing Director, DC Training and Recruitment Solutions, since 2002; *b* 9 Oct. 1947; *o s* of Sir Colin Douglas Clark, 4th Bt and Margaret Coleman Clark (*née* Spinks); *S* father, 1995; *m* 1971, Susan Joy, *d* of Brig. T. I. G. Gray; one *s* two *d*. *Educ:* Eton. Royal Green Jackets, 1966–78. Various appts within private health care industry, 1978–2001. *Recreations:* horse trials, hunting. *Heir:* *s* Simon George Gray Clark [*b* 3 Oct. 1975; *m* 2010 Aoife Sisk]. *Address:* Somerset House, Threapwood, Malpas, Cheshire SY14 7AW. *T:* (01948) 770205.

CLARK, Judy Anne M.; *see* MacArthur Clark.

CLARK, Dame June; *see* Clark, Dame M. J.

CLARK, Kathryn Sloan, (Katy); *b* 3 July 1967. *Educ:* Kyle Acad., Ayr; Univ. of Aberdeen (LLB 1990); Univ. of Edinburgh (DipLP 1991). Admitted solicitor, 1992; in private practice as solicitor, 1992–98; Legal Officer, 1998, Hd of Membership Legal Services, 1999–2005, UNISON. Contested (Lab) Galloway and Upper Nithsdale, 1997. MP (Lab) N Ayrshire and Arran, 2005–15; contested (Lab) same seat, 2015. Member: Scottish Affairs Select Cttee, 2005–10; Procedure Cttee, 2005–10; European Scrutiny Cttee, 2006–10; Envmtl Audit Cttee, 2010–15; Speaker's Panel of Chairmen, 2010–15; BIS Select Cttee, 2010–15; Cttee on Arms Control, 2010–15. Mem., Labour Party, 1985–.

CLARK, Keith; International General Counsel, Morgan Stanley, 2002–09; *b* 25 Oct. 1944; *s* of Douglas William Clark and Evelyn Lucy (*née* Longlands); *m* 2001, Helen Paterson; one *s* one *d* by a previous marriage. *Educ:* Chichester High Sch. for Boys; St Catherine's Coll., Oxford (MA Jurisprudence; BCL). Joined Clifford Chance, 1971; Partner, 1976; Sen. Partner, 1993; Chm., 2000–02. Trustee, Pallant House Gall., Chichester, 2007–. *Publications:* (jtly) Syndicated Lending Practice Documentation, 1993; articles on banking and financial topics. *Recreations:* walking, ballet, theatre, novels.

CLARK, Malcolm, CB 1990; Inspector General, Insolvency Service, Department of Trade and Industry, 1984–89, retired; *b* 13 Feb. 1931; *s* of late Percy Clark and Gladys Helena Clark; *m* 1956, Beryl Patricia Dale; two *s*. *Educ:* Wheelwright Grammar Sch., Dewsbury, Yorks. FCCA 1980. Department of Trade and Industry Insolvency Service: Examiner, 1953–62; Sen. Examiner, 1962–66; Asst Official Receiver, Rochester, 1966–70; Official Receiver, Lytham St Annes, 1970–79; Principal Inspector of Official Receivers, 1979–81; Dep. Inspector Gen., 1981–84. *Recreations:* theatre, gardening, reading. *Address:* 7 Sea Point, Martello Park, Canford Cliffs, Poole BH13 7BA.

CLARK, Dr Malcolm Brian, OBE 2001; Chairman, Grant & Cutler, 2000–11; Director, Queen Elizabeth's Foundation for Disabled People, 1980–2001; *b* 17 May 1934; *s* of Herbert Clark and Doris May Clark (*née* Waples); *m* 1st, 1960, Jennifer Anne Thonger (*d* 1985); one *s* one *d*; 2nd, 1988, Lorna Stephanie Killick (marr. diss. 1995); 3rd, 2009, Helen Patricia Farr. *Educ:* Univ. of Birmingham (BSc Chem. Engrg; PhD 1958). Chemical Engineer: Albright & Wilson, 1958–62; A. Boake Roberts, 1962–66; Marketing Manager, Bush Boake Allen, 1966–68; Albright & Wilson: Res. Manager, 1968–70; Personnel Dir, 1970–72; Personnel and Prodn Dir, 1972–74; Man. Dir, Bush Boake Allen, 1975–80. Mem. Council, Grange Centre, 2001–14. *Recreations:* books, walking, theatre, music, wine. *Address:* The Birches, 13 Cleveland Road, Worcester Park, Surrey KT4 7JQ.

CLARK, Margaret Anita, (Mrs P. D. Walton), CBE 2015 (OBE 1999); Chairman, Plunkett Foundation, since 2013; *b* London, 1947; *d* of Reginald and Maud Clark; *m* 1998, Peter David Walton, *qv*. *Educ:* Trinity Grammar Sch.; Wood Green Sch.; Holborn Coll. of Law, Langs and Commerce. Various appts from Exec. Officer to Dir of Policy, Rural Develt Commn, 1967–99; Countryside Agency: Dir, 1999–2001; Dep. Chief Exec., 2001–06; Actg Chief Exec., 2005; Dep. Chief Exec., Commn for Rural Communities, 2006–07. Mem. Bd, 1998–2008, Chm., 2008–15, Hastoe Housing Assoc. Member: Prince of Wales's Affordable Rural Housing Initiative, 2003–09; Commn for Rural Community Develt and Rural Cttee, Carnegie Commn, 2004–10; Rural Affairs Cttee, BBC, 2007–11; Policy Cttee, CPRE, 2008–14. Chair, Wkg Party on Territorial Policy in Rural Areas, OECD, 2000–07. Trustee, Arkleton Trust, 2001–14. Hon. Fellow, Centre for Rural Economy, Univ. of Newcastle upon Tyne. FRSA. *Recreations:* theatre, opera, ballet, cinema, entertaining friends and family, walking the dog, shopping. *Address:* Tolpuddle, Dorchester, Dorset. *Club:* Army and Navy.

CLARK, Dame (Margaret) June, DBE 1995; FRCN; FLSW; Professor of Community Nursing, University of Wales, Swansea, 1997–2003, now Emeritus; *b* 31 May 1941; *d* of Ernest Harold Hickery and Marion Louise Hickery (*née* Walters); *m* 1966, Roger Michael Geoffrey Clark; one *s* one *d*. *Educ:* Pontywaun Grammar Sch.; University College London (BA Hons Classics 1962); University College Hosp. (SRN 1965); Royal College of Nursing (RHV 1967); Univ. of Reading (MPhil 1972); PhD South Bank Polytechnic 1985. FRCN 1982. Nurse, 1965; health visitor, 1967; clinical nursing appts, combined with teaching and research while bringing up a family; resumed as health visitor, Berks, 1981; Senior Nurse (Research), 1983; Health Authority posts: Special Projects Co-ordinator, Lewisham and N Southwark, 1985–86; Dir, Community Nursing Services, W Lambeth, 1986–88; Chief Nursing Adviser, Harrow, 1988–90; Prof. of Nursing, Middlesex Poly., later Univ., 1990–96. Member: Royal Commn on Long Term Care of the Elderly, 1997–98; Bevan Commn on NHS Wales, 2009–11. Pres., RCN, 1990–94. Council of Europe Fellow, 1981; Churchill Fellow, 1996. Mem., Sigma Theta Tau Internat. the Honor Soc. of Nursing, 1997. Special interests incl. nursing informatics and services for older people. FAAN 2010; FLSW 2012. *Publications:* A Family Visitor, 1973; (with R. Hiller) Community Care, 1975; What Do Health Visitors Do?, 1981; (with S. Parsonage) Infant Feeding and Family Nutrition, 1981; (with J. Henderson) Community Health, 1983; (with M. Baly) District Nursing, 1981; (contrib.) Nursing Practice and Health Care, 5th edn 2008; (contrib.) Policy and Politics in Healthcare, 6th edn 2011; contrib. numerous papers to med. and nursing jls. *Recreations:* travel, gardening, grandchildren, charity organisations (Age Cymru, Gwalia Care and Support, St John Ambulance Brigade), writing my memoirs.

CLARK, Air Vice-Marshal Martin Adrian, CEng, FIET; FRAeS; Technical Director, Military Aviation Authority, since 2012; *b* Hillingdon, 17 Feb. 1961; *s* of David and Frances Clark; *m* 1987, Valerie Hillyard; one *s* one *d*. *Educ:* St George's Sch., Hong Kong; Queen Mary Coll., Univ. of London (BSc (Eng) Electrical and Electronic Engrg 1982); Open Univ. (MBA 1999). CEng 1991; MIET 1991, FIET 2011; FRAeS 2013. Joined RAF, 1979; Jun. Engrg Officer, 55 Sqn, RAF Marham, 1984–85; OC Aircraft Servicing Flight, 1985–87, Aircraft Systems Gp, Nimrod Engrg Develt and Investigation Team, 1987–89, RAF Kinloss; Sen. Engrg Officer, 27 Sqn, RAF Marham, 1989–91; SO to AO Engrg and Supply, HQ Strike Comd, 1991–94; acsc 1994; Harrier Engrg Authy, RAF Wyton, 1994–98; OC Engrg and Supply Wing, RAF Kinloss, 1998–2000; Military Asst 2 to Chief of Defence Logistics, 2000–01, Asst Dir, Prog. Mgt, 2001–05, HQ Defence Logistics Orgn; Gp Capt. Support, HQ 2 Gp, 2005–06; Dep. Team Leader, Nimrod MRA4 Project, Defence Procurement Agency, 2006–07; Head: Air ISTAR Defence Equipment and Support, 2007–11; Tech. Certification, Mil. Aviation Authy, 2011–12. *Recreations:* family, ski-ing, following Bath Rugby, reading historical novels, theatre, ballet, cycling. *Address:* D(Tech) Military Aviation Authority, Juniper 1, #5102, MoD Abbey Wood North, Bristol BS34 8QW. *T:* 0306 798 1729. *E:* martin.clark857@mod.uk. *Club:* Royal Air Force.

CLARK, Martin Charles; Director, Bergen Kunsthall, since 2013; *b* Chelmsford, 15 Jan. 1976; *s* of John and Ann Clark; *m* 2002, Rosie Hill; one *s* one *d*. *Educ:* Sheffield Hallam Univ. (BA Hons Fine Art 1998); Royal Coll. of Art (MA Curating and Commng Art 2001). Record buyer and disc jockey, The Store, Sheffield, 1996–99; Exhibns Curator, and Tutor, Kent Inst. of Art and Design, 2001–05; Curator, Exhibns, Arnolfini, Bristol, 2005–07; Artistic Dir, Tate St Ives, 2007–13. *Recreations:* reading magazines, buying books, collecting records, drinking in pubs, dancing hard. *Address:* Bergen Kunsthall, Rasmus Meyers alle 5, 5015 Bergen, Norway.

CLARK, Maxwell Robert Guthrie Stewart S.; *see* Stafford-Clark.

CLARK, Dr Michael; Executive Chairman, MAT Group, 2002–04 (Director, 1992–2002); *b* 8 Aug. 1935; *s* of late Mervyn Clark and of Sybilla Norma Clark (*née* Winscott); *m* 1958, Valerie Ethel, *d* of C. S. Harbord; one *s* one *d*. *Educ:* King Edward VI Grammar School, East Retford; King's College London (BSc (1st cl. Hons) Chemistry, 1956; FKC 1987); Univ. of Minnesota (Fulbright Scholar, 1956–57); St John's College, Cambridge (PhD 1960). FRSC 1988. Research Scientist, later Factory Manager, ICI, 1960–66; Smith's Industries Ltd, 1966–69; PA International Management Consultants, 1969–73; Marketing Manager, St Regis Paper Co., 1973–78; Dir, Courtenay Stewart International, 1978–81; PA International Management Consultants, 1981–93 (Trustee, 1994–2000). Treasurer, 1975–78, Chm., 1980–83, Cambs Cons. Assoc.; Cons. Eastern Area Exec., 1980–83. Contested (C) Ilkeston,

1979; MP (C) Rochford, 1983–97, Rayleigh, 1997–2001. Chm., Sci. and Technol. Select Cttee, 1997–2001; Member: Select Cttee for Energy, 1983–92 (Chm., 1989–92); Select Cttee on Trade and Industry, 1992–94; Council, Parly IT Cttee, 1984–90; Speaker's Panel of Chairmen, 1997–2001; Chairman: All Party Gp for the Chemical Industry, 1994–97 (Hon. Sec. 1985–90; Vice-Chm., 1990–94); Parly Gp for Energy Studies, 1992–97; Bd, Parly Office of Sci. and Technol., 1993–97; Parly British-Russian Gp, 1994–2001; Parly British-Venezuelan Gp, 1995–2001; Hon. Secretary: Parly and Scientific Cttee, 1985–88; Parly Anglo-Nepalese Soc., 1985–90; Parly Anglo-Malaŵi Gp, 1987–90; Parly Space Cttee, 1989–91; Cons. Backbench Energy Cttee, 1986–87 (Vice-Chm., 1987–90); Mem., 1922 Exec. Cttee, 1997–2001; Chm., IPU, 1990–93 (Mem. Exec., 1987–94). Mem., Adv. Panel, Conservation Foundn, 1995–2000. Mem., Adv. Bd, Fulbright Commn, 1995–2001. Governor, Melbourn Village Coll., 1974–83 (Chm., 1977–80). *Publications:* The History of Rochford Hall, 1990; Clark of the House, 2005. *Recreations:* gadding about, golf, grandchildren. *Address:* 5 Moorgarth, New Road, Ingleton, Carnforth, N Yorks LA6 3PR. *T:* (015242) 41856.

CLARK, Michael Duncan, CBE 2014; choreographer; Artistic Director, Michael Clark Company; Artistic Associate, Barbican, since 2005; *b* 2 June 1962; *s* of late William Clark and Elizabeth Duncan. *Educ:* Kintore Primary Sch.; Rubislaw Acad., Aberdeen; Royal Ballet Sch. Resident choreographer, Riverside Studios, London, 1982; launched the Michael Clark Company, 1984. Key works: New Puritan, 1984; Do You Me? I Did, 1984; not H.air, 1985; Because We Must, 1987; I am curious, Orange, 1988; Mmm…, 1992; "O", 1994; current/SEE, 1998; Oh My Goddess, 2003; I Do, 2007; come, been and gone, 2009; th, 2011; WHO'S ZOO, 2012; The Barrowlands Project, 2012; New Work, 2012; animal/vegetable/mineral, 2013. Hon. DArts Robert Gordon Univ., Aberdeen, 2011. *Address:* Michael Clark Company, Barbican Centre, Silk Street, EC2Y 8DS.

CLARK, Neil Andrew; His Honour Judge Neil Clark; a Circuit Judge, since 2012; *b* Sunderland, 1964; *s* of Andrew Clark and Margaret Rosannia Clark (*née* Rae); *m* 1998, Susan Godley. *Educ:* Bede Sch., Sunderland; Univ. of Leeds (LLB). Called to the Bar, Inner Temple, 1987, Bencher, 2012; in practice as a barrister, 1987–2012; a Recorder, 2005–12; Judge (pt-time), Mental Health Review Tribunals, 2008–12. *Recreations:* sports particularly football (Sunderland AFC), cricket and equestrian, all things related to Scotland, reading. *Club:* Durham County Cricket.

CLARK, Oswald William Hugh, CBE 1978; Assistant Director-General, Greater London Council, 1973–79; *b* 26 Nov. 1917; *s* of late Rev. Hugh M. A. Clark and Mabel Bessie Clark (*née* Dance); *m* 1966, Diana Mary (*née* Hine); one *d*. *Educ:* Rutlish Sch., Merton; Univ. of London (BA; BD Hons); Univ. of Wales (LLM). Local Govt Official, LCC (later GLC), 1937–79. Served War, HM Forces, 1940–46: Major, 2nd Derbyshire Yeo., Eighth Army, Middle East, NW Europe. Member: Church Assembly (later General Synod), 1948–90; Standing and Legislative Cttees, 1950–90; Standing Orders Cttee (Chm.), 1950–90; Crown Appts Commn, 1987–90; Chm., House of Laity, 1979–85 (Vice-Chm., 1970–79); a Church Commissioner, 1958–88 (Mem. Bd of Governors, 1966–68, 1969–73, 1977–88); a Reader, 1951–96. Vice-Pres., Corp. of Church House, 1981–98. Principal, Soc. of the Faith, 1987–92. Parish Clerk, 1992–2008, and Churchwarden, 1990–2000, St Andrew by the Wardrobe. Co. of Parish Clerks, 1986– (Master, 1997–98); Liveryman, Upholders' Co., 1999–. Life Fellow, Guild of Guide Lectrs, 1982. *Recreations:* London's history and development, Goss china, heraldry. *Address:* 5 Seaview Road, Highcliffe, Christchurch, Dorset BH23 5QJ. *T:* (01425) 280823. *Clubs:* Cavalry and Guards, Pratt's.

CLARK, Paul Anthony Mason; a District Judge (Magistrates' Courts) (formerly Metropolitan Stipendiary Magistrate), since 1996; Designated District Judge for West London, 2007–12; a Recorder, since 2003; *b* 19 Aug. 1952; *s* of Thomas James, (Tony), Clark and Winifred Mary Clark (*née* Mason); *m* 1979, Jane Ann; one *s* two *d*. *Educ:* John Leggott GS, Scunthorpe; Jesus Coll., Oxford (MA). Called to the Bar, Middle Temple, 1975 (Astbury Schol.); in practice, 1975–96. Chm., Inner London Youth Courts, 1997–2000. Mem., Council of Dist Judges for England and Wales, 2001–13. Lectr, Gen. Council of the Bar, 1998–2004. Mem. Bd, Internat. Inst. on Special Needs Offenders, 2003–07. Pres., David Isaacs Fund, 2004– (Vice Pres., 1998–2004). Contributing Ed., Archbold Magistrates' Courts Criminal Practice, 2011–. *Recreations:* anything Italian, cricket, painting, gardening, book and ceramics collecting. *Address:* Office of the Senior District Judge, Westminster Magistrates' Court, 181 Marylebone Road, NW1 5BR. *Club:* Oxford and Cambridge.

CLARK, Air Vice-Marshal Paul Derek, CB 1993; CEng, FRAeS; Vice President, Homeland Security, BAE SYSTEMS North America, Arlington, Virginia, 2003–05, retired 2006; *b* 19 March 1939; *s* of John Hayes Clark and Kathleen Clark; *m* 1963, Mary Elizabeth Morgan; two *d*. *Educ:* Orange Hill Grammar Sch.; RAF Henlow Technical Coll.; BA Open Univ., 1985. CEng 1970; FRAeS 1987. Commnd Engr Br., RAF, 1961; RAF Wittering, 1961–63, Topcliffe, 1963, Wittering, 1964–69, Cranwell, 1969–70; RAF Staff Coll., Bracknell, 1971; HQ Logistics Comd, USAF, 1972–74; HQ Strike Comd, 1974–76; Nat. Defence Coll., 1977; OC Engrg Wing, RAF Leuchars, 1977–79; HQ No 1 Gp, RAF Bawtry, 1980–81; Stn Comdr No 30 Maintenance Unit, RAF Sealand, 1981–83; RCDS, 1984; MoD, 1985–86; Directorate Electronics Radar Air, MoD (PE), 1986–87; Dir, European Helicopter 101 Project, MoD (PE), 1987–89; Comdt RAF Signals Engrg Estabt, 1990–91; AO, Engrg and Supply, HQ Strike Comd, 1991–93; retd, 1994; Dir of Mil. Support, Support Div., GEC-Marconi Avionics, 1994–95; RMPA Prog. Dir, GEC-Marconi Aerospace Systems Ltd, 1995–97; Pres. and CEO, GEC-Marconi Avionics Inc., Atlanta, 1997–98; Vice President: GEC Account Dir for Lockheed Martin, 1998–99; C–130 Avionics Modernization Prog., BAE SYSTEMS Aerospace Sector, Austin, Texas, 2000–01; Inf. and Electronics System Integration Sector, BAE SYSTEMS Nashua, New Hampshire, 2001–03. *Recreations:* gardening, volunteer work. *Club:* Royal Air Force.

See also Prof. T. J. H. Clark.

CLARK, Paul Gordon; *b* 29 April 1957; *s* of Gordon Thomas Clark and Sheila Gladys Clark; *m* 1980, Julie Hendrick; one *s* one *d*. *Educ:* Gillingham Grammar Sch.; Keele Univ. (BA Hons 1980; Sec., Students' Union, 1977–78); Univ. of Derby (DMS 1996). Res. Assistant to Pres., then Educn Adminr, AEU, 1980–86; Admin. Asst Sec., then Manager, Nat. Educn Centre, TUC, 1986–97. Mem., Gillingham BC, 1982–90 (Leader, Lab. Gp, 1989–90). Contested (Lab) Gillingham, 1992. MP (Lab) Gillingham, 1997–2010; contested (Lab) Gillingham and Rainham, 2010, 2015. PPS, LCD, 1999–2001, to Minister for Housing and Planning, 2001–02, to Minister for Criminal Justice, 2002–03, to Dep. Prime Minister, 2005–07; an Asst Govt Whip, 2003–05; Parly Under-Sec. of State, DfT, 2008–10. Mem. Bd, Thames Gateway Kent Partnership, 2000. Mem. Bd, Groundwork Medway/Swale, 2001.

CLARK, Peter Charles Lister; His Honour Judge Peter Clark; a Circuit Judge, since 1995; a Senior Circuit Judge, Employment Appeal Tribunal, since 2006; *b* 16 June 1948; *s* of Charles Lister Clark and Mary Isobel Clark; *m* 1973, Josephine Neilson Hogg; one *s* one *d*. *Educ:* Repton Sch.; Southampton Univ. (LLB). Called to the Bar, Gray's Inn, 1970, Bencher, 2012; in practice at the Bar, 1971–95; a Recorder, Midland and Oxford Circuit, 1994–95. *Recreation:* various. *Address:* Devereux Chambers, Queen Elizabeth Building, Temple, EC4Y 9BS. *T:* (020) 7353 7534. *Club:* Reform.

CLARK, Prof. Peter Irving, MD; FRCP; Consultant Medical Oncologist, Clatterbridge Cancer Centre, since 1989; Chair, NHS England Chemotherapy Clinical Reference Group and Cancer Drug Fund, since 2013; *b* Worthing, 1 July 1956; *s* of Denis and Beth Clark; *m* 1985, Cecile Messent; three *s*. *Educ:* Worthing High Sch.; Gonville and Caius Coll., Cambridge (BA 1978); Univ. of London (MB BS 1981; MD 1989). FRCP 1995. Med. Dir, Clatterbridge Cancer Centre, Merseyside, 1993–2000. Chair: Assoc. of Cancer Physicians, 2000–06; Nat. Chemotherapy Adv. Gp, 2004–13; Technol. Appraisal Cttee, NICE, 2009–13. *Publications:* contrib. papers to med. jls. *Recreations:* family, wine, viticulture, walking, jazz, reading, Everton Football Club. *Address:* Clatterbridge Cancer Centre, Wirral, Merseyside CH63 4JY. *T:* (0151) 482 7828, *Fax:* (0151) 482 7675. *E:* peter.clark@clatterbridgecc.nhs.uk.

CLARK, Petula, (Sally Olwen), CBE 1998; singer, actress; *b* 15 Nov. 1932; *d* of Leslie Clark; *m* 1961, Claude Wolff; one *s* two *d*. Own BBC radio series, Pet's Parlour, 1943; early British films include: Medal for the General, 1944; I Know Where I'm Going, 1945; Here Come the Huggetts, 1948; Dance Hall, 1950; White Corridors, 1951; The Card, 1951; Made in Heaven, 1952; The Runaway Bus, 1953; That Woman Opposite, 1957. Began career as singer in France, 1959. Top female vocalist, France, 1962; Bravos du Music Hall award for outstanding woman in show business, France, 1965; Grammy awards for records Downtown and I Know A Place. Numerous concert and television appearances in Europe and USA including her own BBC TV series; world concert tour, 1997; UK tour, 2013. *Films:* Finian's Rainbow, 1968; Goodbye Mr Chips, 1969; Second to the Right and Straight on till Morning, 1982; *musicals:* The Sound of Music, Apollo Victoria, 1981; (also composer and creator) Someone Like You, Strand, 1990; Blood Brothers, NY, 1993, nat. tour, 1994–95; Sunset Boulevard, Adelphi, 1995, 1996, NY, 1998, nat. US tour, 1998–2000. *Address:* c/o Claude Wolff, 15 chemin Rieu, 1208 Geneva, Switzerland.

CLARK, Ramsey; lawyer in private practice, New York City, since 1969; *b* Dallas, Texas, 18 Dec. 1927; *s* of late Thomas Clark, and of Mary Ramsey; *m* 1949, Georgia Welch (*d* 2010), Corpus Christi, Texas; one *s* one *d*. *Educ:* Public Schs, Dallas, Los Angeles, Washington; Univ. of Texas (BA); Univ. of Chicago (MA, JD). US Marine Corps, 1945–46. Engaged private practice of law, Dallas, 1951–61; Asst Attorney Gen., Dept of Justice, 1961–65; Dep. Attorney Gen., 1965–67, Attorney Gen., 1967–69. UN Human Rights Award, 2008. *Address:* 37 West 12th Street, New York, NY 10011–8503, USA.

CLARK, Rebecca Faye; *see* Pow, R. F.

CLARK, Reginald Blythe, FCSI; Chief Executive, Rhino Sport & Leisure, since 2006; *b* 15 March 1958; *s* of Thomas Harold Clark and Catherine Clark; *m* 1983, Judith Anne Brown; one *s* one *d*. *Educ:* Brinkburn Comprehensive Sch., Hartlepool; Christ Church, Oxford (MA). Capital markets career with Yamaichi Securities, Swiss Bank Corp. and J P Morgan, then European Finance Dir, Kobe Steel, Japan, 1988–97; Man. Dir, Loxko Venture Managers Ltd, 1991–2005; Director: London & Oxford Gp, 1993–2011; Darwin Rhodes Gp, 2005–07. Party Treasurer, Liberal Democrats, 2000–05; Contested (Lib Dem), Hartlepool, 1997 and 2010. FIC (FIBC 1999); FCSI (FSI 2005); CMC; FRSA. *Recreations:* reading, Rugby (Oxford Blue 1978, 1979; founder, Kew Occasionals RFC), Japanese culture. *Clubs:* Garrick, National Liberal; Vincent's (Oxford) (Pres., 1979–80).

CLARK, Richard David; Chief Executive, Devon County Council, 1989–96; Clerk to Devon and Cornwall Police Authority, 1993–97 (Associate Clerk, 1989–93); *b* 2 Sept. 1934; *s* of David and Enid Clark; *m* 1958, Pamela Mary (*née* Burgess); two *d*. *Educ:* Luton Boys' Grammar Sch.; Keele Univ. (BA, DipEd); Univ. de Paris, Sorbonne. Teaching, Woodberry Down Comprehensive School, 1957–61; Education Admin, Herts CC, 1961–69; Asst Educn Officer, Lancs CC, 1969–71; Second Dep. County Educn Officer, Hants CC, 1972–76; Chief Educn Officer, Glos CC, 1976–83; County Educn Officer, Hants CC, 1983–88. Dir, Devon and Cornwall TEC, 1989–95. Mem., Adv. Cttee on Supply and Educn of Teachers. Adviser to: Burnham Cttee, 1982–87; Educn Cttee, ACC, 1982–89, 1990–95; Council of Local Educn Authorities, 1983–89. Governor: Plymouth Univ., 1995–2000; Sidmouth Coll., 1995–2000. Fellow Commoner, Churchill Coll., Cambridge, 1983; Vis. Fellow, Southampton Univ., 1986–88; Hon. Fellow, Exeter Univ., 1992–98. FRSA 1977. *Recreations:* books, gardening, wood turning, croquet. *Address:* Glendale House, Rannoch Road, Crowborough, East Sussex TN6 1RB.

CLARK, Richard Jeffrey; Executive Partner, Slaughter and May, since 2013; *b* Yorkshire, 20 Nov. 1959; *s* of late Jeffrey Clark and of Patricia Clark (*née* Halls). *Educ:* Bingley Beckfoot Grammar Sch.; Univ. of Hull (LLB; Lionel Rosen and Sweet & Maxwell Prize). MCIArb 2005; CEDR Accredited Mediator, 2006. Admitted Solicitor, 1984. Slaughter and May, 1982–: Partner, 1991; Hd, Dispute Resolution, 2008–13. Chm., Michael Grandage Co. Ltd, 2012–. Mem., Adv. Council, Tate St Ives, 2004–10. Gov., Falmouth Coll. of Arts, 1996–2004. Ed., Dispute Resolution Rev., 2009–12. *Publications:* contrib. articles to legal jls. *Recreations:* art, jazz, theatre, walking. *Address:* c/o Michael Grandage Company Ltd, Fourth Floor, Gielgud Theatre, Shaftesbury Avenue, SW1D 6AR. *Club:* Two Brydges.

CLARK, (Robert) Brodie, CBE 2010; consultant in security, risk and border operations, since 2012; Director, Clark Advisory Ltd, since 2012; *b* Glasgow, 16 June 1951; *s* of David Clark and Mary Clark; *m* 1976, Jennifer Taylor; one *s* one *d*. *Educ:* Hutchesons' Grammar Sch., Glasgow; Univ. of Glasgow (MA Hons Philos. and Sociol.). HM Prison Service, 1973–2004: Gov., HM Prisons Bedford, 1988–91, Woodhill, 1991–94, and Whitemoor, 1994–97; Hd of Industrial Relations, 1997–99; Dir, High Security Prisons, 1999–2000; Dir, Security, Prisons Bd, 2000–04; Sen. Dir, Immigration and Nationality Directorate, 2004–07; Strategic Dir, Border and Immigration Agency, 2007–08; Hd, Border Force, UK Border Agency, 2008–11. Non-executive Director: Leeds Community Healthcare Trust, 2012–; Compass, 2012–; Associate, JSi. Contrib., Government training experts, Dods. *Recreations:* walking, sport, reading, cooking.

CLARK, Prof. Robin Jon Hawes, CNZM 2004; FRS 1990; Sir William Ramsay Professor of Chemistry, University College London, 1989–2008, now Emeritus; *b* 16 Feb. 1935; *s* of Reginald Hawes Clark, JP, BCom, FCA and Marjorie Alice Clark (*née* Thomas); *m* 1964, Beatrice Rawdin Brown, JP; one *s* one *d*. *Educ:* Christ's Coll., NZ; Canterbury University Coll., Univ. of NZ (BSc 1956; MSc (1st cl. hons) 1958); Univ. of Otago; University Coll. London (British Titan Products Scholar and Fellow; PhD 1961); DSc London 1969. FRSC 1969. University College London: Asst Lectr in Chemistry, 1962; Lectr 1963–71; Reader 1972–81; Prof., 1982–89; Dean of Faculty of Science, 1988–89; Hd, Dept of Chemistry, 1989–99; Mem. Council, 1991–94; Fellow, 1992. Mem., Senate and Academic Council, Univ. of London, 1988–93. Visiting Professor: Columbia, 1965; Padua, 1967; Western Ontario, 1968; Texas A&M, 1978; Bern, 1979; Fribourg, 1979; Auckland, 1981; Odense, 1983; Sydney, 1985; Bordeaux, 1988; Pretoria, 1991; Würzburg, 1996; Indiana, 1998; Thessaloniki, 1999; Lectures: Kresge-Hooker, Wayne State, 1965; Frontiers, Case Western Reserve Univ., Cleveland, 1967; John van Geuns, Amsterdam, 1979; Firth, Sheffield, 1991; Carman, SA Chemical Inst., 1994; Moissan, Paris, 1998; UK-Canada Rutherford, 2000, Bakerian, 2008, Royal Soc.; Leermakers, Wesleyan Univ., 2000; Hassel, Oslo, 2000; Ralph Anderson, Horners' Co., 2003; Denny, Barber-Surgeons' Co., 2009; Rutherford, Canterbury NZ, 2010; Minerva, Scientific Instruments Makers' Co., 2011; Royal Soc. of NZ Dist. Speaker, 2011. Mem. Council, Royal Soc., 1993–94; Royal Society of Chemistry: Mem., Dalton Divl Council, 1985–88, Vice-Pres., 1988–90; Lectures: Tilden, 1983–84; Nyholm, 1989–90; Thomas Graham, 1991; Harry Hallam, 1993, 2000; Liversidge, 2003–04; Sir George Stokes Medal, 2009. Member: SRC Inorganic Chem. Panel, 1977–80; SERC Post-doctoral Fellowships Cttee, 1983; SERC Inorganic Chem. Sub-Cttee, 1993–94; Chairman: XI Internat. Conf. on Raman Spectroscopy, London, 1988; Steering Cttee, Internat. Confs on Raman Spectroscopy, 1990–92 (Mem., 1988–). Mem. Council, Royal Instn of GB, 1996– (Vice-Pres., 1997–; Sec., 1998–2004; Hon. Life Fellow, 2004). Chm., NZ Univs Graduates' Assoc. (UK), 1996–2012. Trustee, Ramsay Meml Fellowships Trust, 1993– (Chm. Adv.

Council, 1989–; Vice-Chm., Trustees, 2007–09); Chm., Univ. of Canterbury Trust, 2004–. Internat. Mem., Amer. Philosophical Soc., 2010. MAE 1990; FRSA 1992. Hon. FRSNZ, 1989. Foreign Fellow, Nat. Acad. of Scis, India, 2007. Hon. DSc Canterbury, 2001. Johannes Marcus Marci Medal, Czech Spectroscopy Soc., 1998; T. K. Sidey Medal, Royal Soc. of NZ, 2001; Lifetime Achievement Award, NZ Soc., London, 2004; Franklin-Lavoisier Prize, Maison de la Chimie, Paris and Chemical Heritage Foundn, Philadelphia, 2008. *Publications:* The Chemistry of Titanium and Vanadium, 1968; (jtly) The Chemistry of Titanium, Zirconium and Hafnium, 1973; (jtly) The Chemistry of Vanadium, Niobium and Tantalum, 1973; (ed jtly) Advances in Spectroscopy, vols 1–26, 1975–98; (ed jtly) Raman Spectroscopy, 1988; (ed) nine monographs on Inorganic Chemistry, 1978–; over 500 contribs to learned jls, in fields of transition metal chem. and spectroscopy. *Recreations:* golf, long distance walking, travel, bridge, music, theatre, wine. *Address:* Christopher Ingold Laboratories, University College London, 20 Gordon Street, WC1H 0AJ. *T:* (020) 7679 7457, *Fax:* (020) 7679 7463; 3a Loom Lane, Radlett, Herts WD7 8AA. *T:* (01923) 857899. *Clubs:* Athenæum, Porters Park Golf (Radlett).

CLARK, Roderick David; Chief Executive, Prisoners' Education Trust, since 2013; *b* 10 May 1961; *s* of Sydney Clark and Mary Anne Clark (*née* Kellas); *m* 1995, Kate Paul; one *d*. *Educ:* Corpus Christi Coll., Oxford (BA Lit.Hum.). Civil Servant, 1984–2012, posts mainly in field of social security; Dir Gen. Strategy, DCA, then MoJ, 2005–08; Principal and Chief Exec., Nat. Sch. of Govt, 2008–12. *Recreations:* cooking, walking, running.

CLARK, Prof. Ronald George, FRCSE, FRCS; Professor of Surgery, 1972–93, now Emeritus, and Pro-Vice-Chancellor, 1988–93, University of Sheffield; Consultant Surgeon: Northern General Hospital, 1966–93; Royal Hallamshire Hospital, 1966–85; *b* 9 Aug. 1928; *s* of late George Clark and of Gladys Clark; *m* 1960, Tamar Welsh Harvie; two *d*. *Educ:* Aberdeen Acad.; Univ. of Aberdeen (MB, ChB); MD Sheffield 1996. FRCSE 1960; FRCS 1980. House appts, Aberdeen Royal Infirmary, 1956–57; Registrar, Western Infirmary, Glasgow, 1958–60; Surgical Res. Fellow, Harvard, USA, 1960–61; Lectr in Surgery, Univ. of Glasgow, 1961–65; Sheffield University: Sen. Lectr in Surgery, 1966–72; Dean, Faculty of Medicine and Dentistry, 1982–85. Examiner, Universities of: Aberdeen, Glasgow, Edinburgh, Liverpool, Newcastle, Leicester, London, Southampton, Malta, Ibadan, Jos. Chm., European Soc. for Parenteral and Enteral Nutrition, 1982–87; Council Mem., Nutrition Soc., 1982–85; Scientific Governor, British Nutrition Foundn, 1982–98; Member: GMC, 1983–93; GDC, 1990–93; Assoc. of Surgeons of GB and Ireland, 1968–; Surgical Res. Soc., 1969–. Mem., Editorial Bd, Scottish Medical Jl, 1962–65; Editor-in-Chief, Clinical Nutrition, 1980–82. *Publications:* contribs to books and jls on surgical topics and metabolic aspects of acute disease. *Recreation:* golf. *Address:* The Gables, Sway Road, Brockenhurst, Hants SO42 7RX. *T:* and *Fax:* (01590) 622883.

CLARK, Ven. Sarah Elizabeth; Archdeacon of Nottingham, since 2014; *b* S Wales, 21 April 1965; *d* of Kenneth Clarke and Shirley Fletcher. *Educ:* Abersychan Grammar Sch.; Loughborough Univ. of Technol. (BA Jt Hons PE, Sports Sci. and Hist. 1986); Keele Univ. (MBA 1994); St John's Coll., Nottingham (MA Theol Studies 1997). Civil Servant, Dept of Employment, 1987–95; ordained deacon, 1998, priest, 1999; Asst Curate, Porchester, Nottingham, 1998–2002; Rector of Carlton-in-Lindrick and Langold with Oldcotes, 2002–09; Area Dean of Worksop, 2006–09; Team Rector, Clifton, Nottingham, 2009–14; Dean of Women's Ministry, Dio. of Southwell and Nottingham, 2011–14. Hon. Canon, Southwell Minster, 2011–. *Recreations:* sport, walking, bird-watching, history. *Address:* 4 Victoria Crescent, Nottingham NG5 4DA. *T:* (01636) 814331. *E:* archd-nottm@southwell.anglican.org.

CLARK, Stuart; *see* Clark, D. S. T.

CLARK, Sir Terence (Joseph), KBE 1990; CMG 1985; CVO 1978; HM Diplomatic Service, retired; Senior Consultant, MEC, 1995–2008; *b* 19 June 1934; *s* of Joseph Clark and Mary Clark; *m* 1960, Lieselotte Rosa Marie Müller; two *s* one *d*. *Educ:* Thomas Parmiter's, London. RAF (attached to Sch. of Slavonic Studies, Cambridge), 1953–55; Pilot Officer, RAFVR, 1955. HM Foreign Service, 1955; ME Centre for Arab Studies, 1956–57; Bahrain, 1957–58; Amman, 1958–60; Casablanca, 1961–62; FO, 1962–65; Asst Pol Agent, Dubai, 1965–68; Belgrade, 1969–71; Hd of Chancery, Muscat, 1972–73; Asst Hd of ME Dept, FCO, 1974–76; Counsellor (Press and Information), Bonn, 1976–79; Chargé d'Affaires, Tripoli, Feb.–March 1981; Counsellor, Belgrade, 1979–82. Dep. Leader, UK Delegn, Conf. on Security and Co-operation in Europe, Madrid, 1982–83; Hd of Information Dept, FCO, 1983–85; Ambassador to Iraq, 1985–89; Ambassador to Oman, 1990–94. Dir, Internat. Crisis Gp Bosnia Project, Sarajevo, 1996. Chm., Anglo-Omani Soc., 1995–2004 (Vice-Pres., 2004–); Mem., Exec. Cttee of Mgt, ME Assoc., 1998–2004. Member: Council, British Sch. of Archaeology in Iraq, later British Inst. for the Study of Iraq, 2003–08; Adv. Bd, Iraq Infrastructure Fund, 2009–; Chm. Trustees, Friends of Basrah Mus., 2010–. Member: RSAA, 1991 (Mem. Council, 2001–07); RIIA, 1995–2007; FRGS 1993. Chm., Saluki Coursing Club, 2000–05; Vice Chm., British Iraqi Friendship Soc., 2008–12. Commander's Cross, Order of Merit (Fed. Republic of Germany), 1978. *Publications:* (jtly) The Saluqi: coursing hound of the East, 1995; (jtly) Oman in Time, 2001; (jtly) Al-Mansur's Book on Hunting, 2001; (jtly) Dogs in Antiquity, 2001; Underground to Overseas: the story of Petroleum Development Oman, 2007; (jtly) British Missions around the Gulf 1575–2005, 2008; Oman's Invisible Energy, 2014; articles on Salukis and coursing in magazines. *Recreations:* Salukis, walking. *Club:* Hurlingham.

CLARK, Sir Timothy (Charles), KBE 2014; President, Emirates Airline, since 2004; *b* Aruba, 22 Nov. 1949; *s* of late Capt. J. F. G. Clark, MBE and of Mrs R. Granville; *m* 1997, Geraldine; one *s* two *d*. *Educ:* Kent Coll., Canterbury; London Univ. (Econs degree 1971). Planner, British Caledonian, 1972–75; Cost Economist, Gulf Air, 1975–85; Emirates Airline, 1985–, various directorships. Founder and Chm., Emirates Airline Foundn. FRAeS. Officier de la Légion d'Honneur (France), 2009. *Recreations:* ski-ing, aeronautical history, maritime history, interior design.

CLARK, Timothy Howard, OBE 2008; Joint Managing Director, ie:music, since 2002; *b* Kitale, Kenya, 20 May 1945; *s* of Rev. Canon Robert Clark and Doris Clark; *m* 1973, Jane Andrea Vincent Johns; three *d*. *Educ:* Prince of Wales Sch., Nairobi. Island Records: Sales Rep., 1968–70; Production Manager, 1970–72; Mktg Dir, 1972–76, Man. Dir, 1976–80; Man. Dir, Telling Editions, 1985–2004. Vice Pres., UNICEF, 2002–. *Recreations:* literature, music, Rugby, swimming. *Address:* 52 Lebanon Park, Twickenham, Middx TW1 3DG. *T:* (020) 8892 2190. *E:* tc@iemusic.co.uk. *Clubs:* Soho House; Lensbury (Teddington); Harlequins Rugby.

CLARK, Prof. Timothy John Hayes, FRCP; Professor of Pulmonary Medicine, Imperial College Faculty of Medicine at the National Heart and Lung Institute, since 1990; *b* 18 Oct. 1935; *s* of John and Kathleen Clark; *m* 1961, Elizabeth Ann Day; two *s* two *d*. *Educ:* Christ's Hospital; Guy's Hospital Medical Sch. BSc 1958; MB BS (Hons) 1961, MD 1967 London. FRCP 1973 (LRCP 1960, MRCP 1962); MRCS 1960. Fellow, Johns Hopkins Hosp., Baltimore USA, 1963; Registrar, Hammersmith Hosp., 1964; Lecturer and Sen. Lectr, Guy's Hospital Med. Sch., 1966; Consultant Physician: Guy's Hosp., 1968–90; Royal Brompton Hosp., 1970–98; Prof. of Thoracic Med., Guy's Hosp. Med. Sch., later UMDS, 1977–89; Dean: Guy's Hosp., 1984–89; UMDS, 1986–89; Pro-Vice-Chancellor for Medicine and Dentistry, Univ. of London, 1987–89; Dean, Nat. Heart and Lung Inst., 1990–97; Pro-Rector (Medicine), 1995–97, (Educnl Qly), 1997–2000, Imperial Coll.; Pro-Rector and Provost, Imperial Coll. at Wye, 2000–01; Pro-Rector (Admission), Imperial Coll., 2001–02. Mem., Council of Governors, UMDS, 1982–89, 1990–95. Specialist Adviser to Social Services Cttee, 1981 and 1985. Special Trustee, Guy's Hosp., 1982–86. Pres., British Thoracic Soc., 1990–91; Chm., Global Initiative for Asthma, 2000–04; Vice-Chairman: Nat. Asthma Campaign, 1993–2000; ICRF, 1997–2002; Trustee and Mem. Council, Stroke Assoc., 2002–11. FKC 1995. *Publications:* (jtly) Asthma, 1977, 4th edn 2000; (ed) Small Airways in Health and Disease, 1979; (jtly) Topical Steroid Treatment of Asthma and Rhinitis, 1980; (ed) Clinical Investigation of Respiratory Disease, 1981; (jtly) Practical Management of Asthma, 1985, 3rd edn 1998; articles in British Medical Jl, Lancet, and other specialist scientific jls. *Recreation:* cricket. *Address:* 8 Lawrence Court, NW7 3QP. *T:* (020) 8959 4411. *Club:* MCC.

See also Air Vice-Marshal P. D. Clark.

CLARK, Timothy Nicholas; Senior Adviser, G3 Group, since 2009; Senior Partner, Slaughter and May, 2001–08; *b* 9 Jan. 1951; *s* of Sir Robert Anthony Clark, DSC and of Andolyn Marjorie Clark (*née* Lewis); *m* 1974, Caroline Moffat; two *s*. *Educ:* Sherborne Sch.; Pembroke Coll., Cambridge (MA Hist.). Admitted solicitor, 1976; with Slaughter and May (Solicitors), 1974–2008, Partner, 1983–2008. Non-executive Director: Big Yellow Gp plc, 2008–; COIF Funds, 2008–13; Mint Partners Ltd, 2008–10. Member: Governing Body, ICC UK, 2003–; Adv. Bd, Uria Menendez, 2008–; Bd of Sen. Advrs, Chatham House, 2008–; Bd of Sen. Advrs, Centre for Eur. Reform, 2011–; Vice Chm., Business for New Europe, 2008–. Member: Develt Cttee, Nat. Gall., 2001–; Bd, RNT, 2008–; Audit Cttee, Wellcome Trust, 2011–. Trustee, Economist Trust, 2009– (Chm., 2010–); Chm., WaterAid UK, 2013–. *Recreations:* flying, football, cricket, theatre. *E:* timnclark@gmail.com. *Club:* Air Squadron (Chm., 2010–).

CLARK, Tony; *see* Clark, C. A.

CLARK, Gen. Wesley Kanne, Hon. KBE 2000; Chairman and Chief Executive Officer, Wesley K. Clark & Associates, since 2003; Supreme Allied Commander, Europe, 1997–2000; Commander-in-Chief, United States European Command, 1997–2000; *m* Gert; one *s*. *Educ:* US Military Acad.; Magdalen Coll., Oxford (Rhodes Schol.; BA 1968). Served in Vietnam (Silver and Bronze Stars); Sen. Military Asst to Gen. Alexander Haig; Head, Nat. Army Trng Centre; Dir of Strategy, Dept of Defense; Mem., American negotiating team, Bosnian peace negotiations, Dayton, Ohio, 1995; Head, US Southern Comd, Panama. Consultant, 2000–01, Man. Dir, Merchant Banking, 2001–03, Stephens Gp Inc. Vice-Chm. and Sen. Advr, James Lee Witt Associates, 2004; Chm., Rodman & Renshaw, 2006; Mem., Adv. Bd, Mutualink, 2009–. Co-Chm., Growth Energy, 2009–; Dir, Juhl Wind Inc., 2009–. Presidential Medal of Freedom (USA), 2000. *Publications:* Waging Modern War, 2001; Winning Modern Wars, 2003; A Time to Lead, 2007. *Address:* Wesley K. Clark & Associates, PO Box 3276, Little Rock, AR 72203, USA. *T:* (501) 2449522, *Fax:* (501) 2442203.

CLARKE, family name of **Barons Clarke of Hampstead** and **Clarke of Stone-cum-Ebony**.

CLARKE OF HAMPSTEAD, Baron *cr* 1998 (Life Peer), of Hampstead in the London Borough of Camden; **Anthony James Clarke,** CBE 1998; *b* 17 April 1932; *s* of Henry Walter and Elizabeth Clarke; *m* 1954, Josephine Ena (*née* Turner); one *s* one *d*. *Educ:* New End Primary Sch., Hampstead; St Dominic's RC Sch., Kentish Town; Ruskin Coll., Oxford (TU educn course, 1954). Nat. Service, Royal Signals, 1950–52; TA and AER, 1952–68. Joined PO as Telegraph Boy at 14; worked as Postman until elected full-time officer, Union of Post Office Workers, 1979; Nat. Editor, The Post, UPW jl, 1979–82; Dep. Gen. Sec., UPW, later CWU, 1982–93. Member: Hampstead Lab Party, 1954–86; St Albans Lab Party, 1986–; Lab Party NEC, 1983–93; Chm., Lab Party, 1992–93. Mem. (Lab) Camden LBC, 1971–78. Contested (Lab) Camden, Hampstead, Feb. and Oct. 1974. Member: Exec. Cttee, Camden Cttee for Community Relns, 1974–81; Camden Council of Social Services, 1978–87. Mem., Labour Friends of Israel, 1972–. Governor, Westminster Foundn for Democracy, 1992–98. Trustee, RAF Mus., 2001–. Trustee, Wells and Campden Charitable Trust; Founder Mem., and Trustee, One World Action (formerly One World), 1984–. KSG 1994. *Recreations:* Arsenal FC, The Archers, reading. *Address:* 83 Orchard Drive, St Albans, Herts AL2 2QH. *T:* (01727) 874276; House of Lords, SW1A 0PW.

CLARKE OF STONE-CUM-EBONY, Baron *cr* 2009 (Life Peer), of Stone-cum-Ebony in the County of Kent; **Anthony Peter Clarke;** Kt 1993; PC 1998; a Justice of the Supreme Court of the United Kingdom (formerly a Lord of Appeal in Ordinary), since 2009; a non-permanent Judge, Court of Final Appeal, Hong Kong, since 2013; *b* 13 May 1943; *s* of late Harry Alston Clarke and Isobel Corsan Clarke (*née* Kay); *m* 1968, Rosemary (*née* Adam); two *s* one *d*. *Educ:* Oakham Sch.; King's Coll., Cambridge (Econs Pt I, Law Pt II; MA). Called to the Bar, Middle Temple, 1965, Bencher, 1987 (Master Treas., 2012); QC 1979; a Recorder, 1985–92; a Judge of the High Court of Justice, QBD, 1993–98; Admiralty Judge, 1993–98; a Lord Justice of Appeal, 1998–2005; Master of the Rolls, 2005–09; Head of Civil Justice, 2005–09. Prime Warden, Shipwrights' Co., 2014–15. *Recreations:* golf, tennis, holidays, bridge. *Address:* Supreme Court of the United Kingdom, Parliament Square, SW1P 3BD.

See also C. A. Clarke.

CLARKE, Rt Hon. Lord; Matthew Gerard Clarke; PC 2008; a Senator of the College of Justice in Scotland, 2000–13 (a Judge of the Inner House of the Court of Session, 2008–13); *s* of Thomas Clarke and Ann (*née* Duddy). *Educ:* Holy Cross High Sch., Hamilton; Univ. of Glasgow (MA; LLB; Francis T. Hunter Scholar; Cunninghame Bursar). Solicitor, 1972. Lectr, Dept of Scots Law, Edinburgh Univ., 1972–78; admitted to Faculty of Advocates, 1978; Standing Junior Counsel to Scottish Home and Health Dept, 1983–89; QC (Scot.) 1989; a Judge of the Courts of Appeal of Jersey and Guernsey, 1995–2000. Member: Consumer Credit Licensing Appeal Tribunal, 1976–2000; Estate Agents Tribunals, 1980–2000; Trademarks Tribunal, 1995–2000; Chm. (part-time), Industrial Tribunals, 1987–2000. Leader, UK Delegn, Council of the Bars and Laws Socs of EC, 1992–96 (Mem., 1989–99). British Council: Mem., Scottish Cttee, 2001–08; Chm., Scottish Law Cttee, 2001–07. Hon. Fellow, Europa Inst., Univ. of Edinburgh, 1995–. *Publications:* (Scottish Editor) Sweet & Maxwell's Encyclopaedia of Consumer Law, 1980; (contrib.) Corporate Law: the European dimension, 1991; (contrib.) Butterworth's EC Legal Systems, 1992; (contrib.) Green's Guide to European Laws in Scotland, 1995; (contrib.) McPhail, Sheriff Court Practice, 1999; (contrib.) A True European: essays for Judge David Edward, 2004; (contrib.) Court of Session Practice, 2005. *Recreations:* cooking, opera, chamber music, the music of Schubert, travel. *Address:* c/o Parliament House, Parliament Square, Edinburgh EH1 1RQ.

CLARKE, Prof. Adrienne Elizabeth, AC 2004 (AO 1991); PhD; FTSE, FAA; Chancellor, La Trobe University, since 2011; Personal Chair in Botany, since 1985, and Laureate Professor, since 1999, University of Melbourne; *b* Melbourne, 6 Jan. 1938; *d* of Valentine Clifford and Alice Louise Petty; *m* (marr. diss.); two *d* one *s*. *Educ:* Ruyton Grammar Sch.; Univ. of Melbourne (PhD). Melbourne University: Reader in Botany, 1981–85; Dir, Plant Cell Biol. Res. Centre, 1982–99; Dep. Head, Sch. of Botany, 1992–2000. Chm., CSIRO, 1991–96; Mem., Sci. Adv. Bd, Friedrich Meischer Inst., 1991. Director: Alcoa of Australia, 1993–96; AMP Ltd, 1994–99; Woolworths Ltd, 1994–2007; WMC Ltd, 1996–2002; WMC Resources Ltd, 2002–05; Fisher & Paykel Healthcare Corp. Ltd, 2002–08; Chief Sci. Advr, 2006–10, Dep. Chm., 2006–10, Hexima Ltd. Lt-Governor, Victoria, 1997–2001. Victoria's first Ambassador for Biotechnology, 2001–02. Member: PM's Supermarket to Asia Cttee, 1996–2002; Innovation Econ. Adv. Bd Vic, 2002–06. Member, Board: Mental Health Res. Inst., 2002–06 (Mem., Cttee for Melbourne, 1994–2003); Inst. for Commercialisation, 2002–04. Pres., Internat. Soc. for Plant Molecular Biology, 1997–98. Foreign Associate, Nat. Acad. of Scis, USA, 1993; Comp., Inst. of Engrs, Australia, 1993; Fellow, Amer. Coll. of Arts and Scis, 1998. Mueller Medal, ANZAAS, 1992; Outstanding Achievers Award, Nat. Aust. Day, 1993; Centenary Medal, 2003. *Publications:* (ed with I. Wilson) Carbohydrate-Protein Recognition, 1988; (with B. A. Stone) Chemistry and Biology of (1–3)-B-glucans, 1992; (jtly) Genetic Control of Self-Incompatibility and Reproductive Development in Flowering Plants, 1994; (jtly) Cell and Developmental Biology of Arabinogalactan-Proteins, 2002; chapters in numerous books; over 140 papers in learned jls. *Recreations:* swimming, bush walking, ski-ing. *Address:* Chancellery, La Trobe University, Bundoora, Vic 3086, Australia. *E:* aeclarke@unimelb.edu.au. *Club:* Lyceum (Melbourne).

CLARKE, Alan, CBE 2011; Chief Executive, One NorthEast Regional Development Agency, 2003–12; *b* 18 Aug. 1953; *s* of late Neville Clarke and Jean Clarke; *m* 1977, Deborah Anne Hayes; one *s* two *d*. *Educ:* Univ. of Lancaster (BA Hons Econs 1974); Univ. of Liverpool (MCD 1977). MRTPI 1980. Policy Officer, South Ribble BC, 1974–75; Planning Asst, S Tyneside Council, 1977–79; Newcastle City Council: Planning Asst, 1979–83; Sen. Econ. Develt Asst, 1983–86; Hd, Econ. Develt, 1986–91; Chief Econ. Develt Officer, 1991–95; Asst Chief Exec., Sunderland CC, 1995–2000; Chief Exec., Northumberland CC, 2000–03. Non-exec. Dir, South Tyneside NHS Foundn Trust, 2012–. *Recreations:* cycling, football, hill-walking. *Address:* 13 Langholm Road, East Boldon, Tyne and Wear NE36 0ED.

CLARKE, Andrew Bertram; QC 1997; *b* 23 Aug. 1956; *s* of Arthur Bertram Clarke and Violet Doris Clarke; *m* 1981, Victoria Clare Thomas; one *s* two *d*. *Educ:* Crewe Grammar Sch.; King's Coll., London (LLB; AKC); Lincoln Coll., Oxford (BCL). Called to the Bar, Middle Temple, 1980; in practice at the Bar, 1981–; Co-Hd, Littleton Chambers, 2006–14. Gov., Goffs Foundn Sch., Cheshunt, 1996–2011; non-exec. Dir, Goffs Acad., 2011–. Chm., Friends of St Mary's Church, Cheshunt, 1994–. *Recreations:* supporter of Crewe Alexandra FC, Gloucestershire CCC; collector of European ceramics and modern prints. *Address:* 38 Albury Ride, Cheshunt, Herts EN8 8XF. *T:* (020) 7797 8600.

CLARKE, Anthony Richard; *b* 6 Sept. 1963; *s* of Walter Arthur Clarke and Joan Ada Iris Clarke; *m* Carole Chalmers; one *s* one *d*. *Educ:* Lings Upper Sch., Northampton. Social Work Trainer, Northamptonshire CC; Disability Trng Officer. MP (Lab) Northampton South, 1997–2005; contested (Lab) same seat, 2005; contested (Ind) same seat, 2010. Mem. (Ind) Northampton BC, 2007–13.

CLARKE, Rt Rev. Barry Bryan; *see* Montreal, Bishop of.

CLARKE, Prof. Barry Goldsmith, PhD; CEng, Eur Ing; FICE; Professor of Civil Engineering Geotechnics, University of Leeds, since 2008; *b* Newcastle upon Tyne, 13 July 1950; *s* of Denis Goldsmith Clarke and Eileen Clarke; *m* 1997, Sandra Elsie Tindale. *Educ:* S Shields Grammar Sch.; Univ. of Newcastle upon Tyne (BSc 1971); Gonville and Caius Coll., Cambridge (PhD 1978). CEng 1988; Eur Ing 1990; FICE 1999. VSO, W Indies, 1971–73. Dir, PM Insitu Techniques, 1977–84; University of Newcastle upon Tyne: Lectr, 1984–98; Prof., 1998–2008; Hd, Civil Engrg, 1998–2002. President: Engrg Profs' Council, 2009–11; ICE, 2012–13. *Publications:* Pressuremeters in Geotechnical Design, 1994; contrib. papers to Geotechnique, ICE Geotech. Engrg, ICE Civil Engrg, ASTM Geotech. Testing, ASCE Geotechnics and Geoenvmtl, Qly Jl Engrg Geol. *Recreations:* walking, gardening. *Address:* Harrogate, N Yorks HG2 9AB. *E:* b.g.clarke@leeds.ac.uk.

CLARKE, Dr Belinda Rosanna; Director, Agri-Tech East, since 2014; *b* Norwich. *Educ:* Norwich High Sch. for Girls; Newnham Coll., Cambridge (BA Hons Natural Scis Tripos 1995; MA 1998); John Innes Centre (PhD 1999). Science Liaison Manager, Norwich Res. Park, 1999; Nuffield Schol., 2001. Internat. Trade Advr (biotech and pharma), UKTI, 2005–07; Life Scis Manager, One Nucleus, 2007–11; Dir, Innovation Ecosystems, Ideaspace, Univ. of Cambridge, 2011–12; Lead Technologist, Bioscis, Innovate UK, 2012–14. Dir, Leatherhead Food Res., 2012–15. Mem., BBSRC, 2015–. Trustee, Royal Norfolk Agricl Assoc., 2014–. *E:* belinda.clarke@agritech-east.co.uk.

CLARKE, Brian; *see* Clarke, J. B.

CLARKE, Brian; artist; *b* 2 July 1953; *s* of late Edward Ord Clarke and of Lilian Clarke (*née* Whitehead); *m* 1972, Elizabeth Cecilia (marr. diss. 1996; remarried 2013), *d* of Rev. John Finch; one *s*. *Educ:* Clarksfield Sch., Oldham; Oldham Sch. of Arts and Crafts (Jr Schol.); Burnley Sch. of Art; North Devon Coll. of Art and Design (Dip. Art and Design). Vis. Prof., Archtl Art, UCL, 1993–. Executor, Estate of Francis Bacon, 1998–. Trustee and Mem. Cttee, Robert Fraser Foundn, 1990–; Trustee: Ely Stained Glass Mus.; Lowe Educnl Charitable Foundn, 2001; Winston Churchill Meml Trust, 2007– (Mem. Council, 1985–); Chm., Architecture Foundn, 2007–13. *Major exhibitions* include: Glass/Light Exhibn, Fest. of City of London, 1979; Der Architektur der Synagogue, Deutsches Architektur Mus., Frankfurt, 1980; New Paintings, Constructions and Prints, RIBA, 1981; Paintings, Robert Fraser Gall., 1983; 1976–86, Seibu Mus. of Art, Tokyo, 1987; Malerei und Farbfenster 1977–88, Hessisches Landesmuseum, 1988; Paintings, Indar Pasricha Gall., New Delhi, 1989; Intimations of Mortality, Galerie Karsten Greve, Köln; Into and Out of Architecture, 1990, New Paintings, 1993, Mayor Gall., London; Architecture and Stained Glass, Sezon Mus. of Art, Tokyo, 1990; Designs on Architecture, Oldham Art Gall., 1993; Paintings and Stained Glass Works in Architecture, 1995, The Glass Wall, 1998, Transillumination, 2003, Tony Shafrazi Gall., NY; Brian Clarke Linda McCartney, Musée Suisse du Vitrail au Château de Romont and German Mus. for Stained Glass, Linnich, 1997–98; 80 Artistes autour du Mondial, Galerie Enrico Navarra, Paris, 1998; Fleurs de Lys, Faggionato Fine Arts, London, 1999; Flowers for New York, Corning Gall., Steuben, NY, 2002; Lamina, Gagosian Gall., London, 2005; Don't Forget the Lamb, Phillips de Pury, NY, 2008; Brian Clarke, Life and Death, Vitromusée Romont, Switzerland, 2011; Brian Clarke Works on Paper 1969–2011; New Paintings, Gemeentemuseum den Haag, Netherlands, 2011; Phillips De Pury at the Saatchi Gall., London, 2011; Brian Clarke Born Oldham 1953, Oldham Gall., 2013; Piper & Clarke. Stained Glass: art or anti-art, Verey Gall. and Eton Coll., 2014; Spitfires and Primroses, Pace London, 2015; *major stained glass works* include: St Gabriel's Ch, Blackburn, 1976; All Saints Ch, Habergham, 1976; Queen's Med. Centre, Nottingham, 1978; Laver's & Barraud Building, London, 1981; Olympus Optical Europa GmbH HQ Building, Hamburg, 1981; King Kahled Internat. Airport, Riyadh, 1982; Buxton Thermal Baths, 1987; Lake Sagami Country Club, Yamanashi, 1988; New Synagogue, Darmstadt, 1988; Victoria Quarter, Leeds, 1989; Cibreo Restaurant, Tokyo, 1990; Glaxo Pharmaceuticals, Uxbridge, 1990; Stansted Airport, 1991; Spindles Shopping Centre, Oldham, 1991–93; España Telefonica, Barcelona, 1991; Number One America Square, London, 1991; 35–38 Chancery Lane, London, 1991; Carmelite, London, 1992; 100 New Bridge St, London, 1992; (with Will Alsop) facade of Hotel de Ville des Bouches-du-Rhone, Marseille, 1992–94; Glass Dune, Hamburg, 1992; EAM Building, Kassel, Germany, 1992–93; New Synagogue, Heidelberg, 1993; Hammersmith Hosp., London, 1993; WH Smith & Sons, Abingdon, 1994; The Grace Building, NY, 1994; Crossrail Paddington, London, 1994; Cliveden Hotel, 1994; Frankfurter Allee Plaza, Berlin, 1994; New Synagogue, Aachen, 1994; Norte Shopping, Rio de Janeiro, 1995; (with Linda McCartney) Rye Hosp., 1995; Valentino Village, Noci, 1996; Center Villa-Lobos (design), São Paulo, 1997; Offenbach Synagogue, 1997; Future Systems Tower NEC, 1997; Praça Norte Clock Tower, 1997; Heidelberg Cathedral, 1997; New Catholic Church, Obersalbach, 1997; Pfizer Pharmaceuticals, NY, 1997, 2001, 2003; Chep Lap Kok Airport, Hong Kong; Chicago Sinai, 1997; Warburg Dillon Read (stained glass cone), Stamford, Conn, 1998; (with Lord Foster) Al Faisaliah Centre, Riyadh, 2000; West Winter Garden (design), Heron Quays, London, 2001; Hotel and Thalassotherapy Centre, Nova Yardinia, Italy, 2002; Ascot Racecourse (stained glass façade), 2003; (with Lord Foster) Pyramid of Peace (stained glass apex), Astana, Kazakhstan, 2006; Linköping Cathedral (stained glass), Sweden, 2010; Papal Nunciature, London (stained glass), 2010; stage designs for Paul McCartney World Tour, 1990; designed: stadia sets for Paul McCartney New World Tour, 1993; stage sets for The Ruins of Time (ballet), Dutch Nat. Ballet, 1993; curator, A Strong Sweet Smell of Incense: a portrait of Robert Fraser, Pace London, 2015. Gov., Capital City Acad., 2001–; Trustee: Lowe Educnl Charitable Foundn, 2001; Architecture Foundn, 2002– (Chm., 2007–); Winston Churchill Meml Trust, 2007. Cttee of Honour, Fondation Vincent van Gogh, Arles, 2001. FRSA 1988. Hon. FRIBA 1993; Hon. DLitt Huddersfield, 2007. Hon. Liveryman, Glaziers' and Master Glass Painters' Co., 2012. Churchill Fellow in architectl art, 1974; special commendation award, Art and Work, Arts Council, 1989; Europa Nostra award, 1990; Special Award for Stained Glass, Leeds Award for Architecture, 1990; special commendation award, Working for Cities, British Gas, 1992; Eur. Shopping Centre Award, 1995; BDA Auszeichnung guter Bauten, Heidelberg, 1996. *Recreations:* reading, hoarding. *W:* www.brianclarke.co.uk.

CLARKE, (Charles) Giles, CBE 2012; DL; President, England and Wales Cricket Board (Chairman, 2007–15; Director, since 2004); *b* Bristol, 29 May 1953; *s* of Charles Nigel Clarke and Stella Rosemary Clarke, *qv*; *m* 1983, Judy Gould; one *s*. *Educ:* Rugby Sch.; Oriel Coll., Oxford (BA Hons Persian with Arabic); Damascus Univ. Chm. and Founder, Majestic Wine Warehouses, 1981–89; Chief Exec. and Co-founder, Pet City plc, 1990–98; Chairman: Fosters Rooms, 1989–2007; Safestore plc, 2001–03; Westleigh Investments, 2002–; Boston Tea Party Ltd, 2006–; Amerisur Resources plc, 2007–; Ironveld plc, 2012–; Kennedy Ventures plc, 2014–; CCI Internat., 2014–. Mem. Council, LSC, 2002–07 (Mem., Adult Learning Cttee, 2002–07). Dir, Internat. Cricket Council, 2007– (Chm., Pakistan Task Team, 2010–; Chm., Finance and Commercial Cttee, 2012–). Chm., Somerset CCC, 2002–08. Mem., Chief Execs Orgn. President: Canynges Soc., 1990; YPO London Chapter, 1997; Dolphin Soc., 2005. Conseil, Commanderie de Bordeaux, 2009–. Master, Soc. of Merchant Venturers, 2010. DL Wilts, 1998–2002, Som, 2004. *Recreations:* Persian poetry, wine, military history, coral reef marine fish, cricket, shooting. *Address:* Lord's Cricket Ground, St John's Wood, NW8 8QN. *T:* (020) 7432 1200, *Fax:* (020) 7286 5583. *E:* giles.clarke@ecb.co.uk. *Clubs:* Army and Navy, MCC; Somerset County Cricket.

CLARKE, Sir (Charles Mansfield) Tobias, 6th Bt *cr* 1831; *b* Santa Barbara, California, 8 Sept. 1939; *e s* of Sir Humphrey Orme Clarke, 5th Bt, and Elisabeth (*d* 1967), *d* of Dr William Albert Cook; *S* father, 1973; *m* 1971, Charlotte (marr. diss. 1979), *e d* of Roderick Walter; *m* 1984, Teresa L. A. de Chair, *d* of late Somerset de Chair; one *s* two *d*. *Educ:* Eton; Christ Church, Oxford (MA); Univ. of Paris; New York Univ. Graduate Business Sch. Bankers Trust Co., NY, 1963–80 (Vice-Pres., 1974–80). Associate Dir, Swiss Bank Corp., London, 1992–94. Underwriting Mem., Lloyds, 1984–; MCSI (MSI 1993). Chm., Standing Council of the Baronetage, 1993–96 (Vice-Chm., 1990–92; Hon. Treas., 1980–92; Vice Pres.); Editor and founder, The Baronets Journal, 1987–99; Chm. Trustees, Baronets Trust, 1996–2002 (Trustee, 1989–); Publisher, The Official Roll of the Baronetage, 1997. Lord of the Manor of Bibury. *Recreations:* accidental happenings, riding, gardening, photography, stimulating conversation; Pres., Bibury Cricket Club. *Heir:* *s* (Charles Somerset) Lawrence Clarke, *b* 12 March 1990. *Clubs:* White's, Boodle's, Beefsteak, Pratt's, Pilgrims, MCC; Jockey (Paris); The Brook, Racquet and Tennis (New York).

CLARKE, Rt Hon. Charles (Rodway); PC 2001; *b* 21 Sept. 1950; *s* of Sir Richard Clarke, KCB, OBE and Brenda Clarke (*née* Skinner); *m* 1984, Carol Marika Pearson; two *s*. *Educ:* Highgate Sch.; King's Coll., Cambridge (BA Hons 1973). Pres., NUS, 1975–77; various admin. posts, 1977–80; Head, Office of Rt Hon. Neil Kinnock, MP, 1981–92; Chief Exec., Quality Public Affairs, 1992–97. Mem. (Lab) Hackney LBC, 1980–86. MP (Lab) Norwich South, 1997–2010; contested (Lab) same seat, 2010. Parly Under-Sec. of State, DfEE, 1998–99; Minister of State, Home Office, 1999–2001; Minister without Portfolio and Chm., Labour Party, 2001–02; Sec. of State for Educn and Skills, 2002–04, for the Home Dept, 2004–06. Mem., Treasury Select Cttee, 1997–98. Visiting Professor: Sch. of Pol, Social and Internat. Studies, UEA, 2010–14; Sch. of Politics and Philosophy, Univ. of Lancaster, 2010–15; Sch. of Econs, UCL, 2012–14. *Recreations:* chess, reading, walking. *E:* pearsonclarke@pavilion.co.uk. *W:* www.charlesclarke.org.

CLARKE, Christopher Alan; Member, 2001–10, a Deputy Chairman, 2004–10, Competition Commission; *b* 14 May 1945; *s* of late Harry Alston Clarke and of Isobel Corsan Clarke (*née* Kay); *m* 1st, 1971, Jessica Pearson (marr. diss. 1976); 2nd, 1978, Charlotte Jenkins; one *s* one *d*. *Educ:* Oakham Sch.; Selwyn Coll., Cambridge (BA Econs 1967, MA); London Business Sch. (MSc/MBA 1972). With Shell Internat. Petroleum Co. Ltd, 1967–73; IDJ Ltd, 1973–74; Man. Dir, Arbuthnot Latham Asia Ltd, 1979–82; Arbuthnot Latham & Co. Ltd, 1974–82 (Dir, 1978–82); Director: Samuel Montagu & Co. Ltd, 1982–96; HSBC Investment Banking, 1996–98. Non-executive Director: Weir Gp, 1999–2008; Omega Underwriting Hldgs, 2005–06; Omega Insurance Hldgs, 2006–10. Mem., Privatisation Project Bd, Cabinet Office, 2005–. Dir, Trustee and Hon. Treas., Classics for All, 2014–. *Recreations:* golf, fishing, reading, wine, theatre, ballet. *Club:* Berkshire Golf.

See also Baron Clarke of Stone-cum-Ebony.

CLARKE, (Christopher) Michael, CBE 2009; FRSE; Director, Scottish National Gallery, since 2001; *b* 29 Aug. 1952; *s* of Patrick Reginald Clarke and Margaret Catherine Clarke (*née* Waugh); *m* 1978, Deborah Clare Cowling; two *s* one *d*. *Educ:* Felsted; Manchester Univ. (BA (Hons) History of Art). FRSE 2008. Art Asst, York City Art Gall., 1973–76; Res. Asst, British Mus., 1976–78; Asst Keeper in Charge of Prints, Whitworth Art Gall., Manchester Univ., 1978–84; Asst Keeper, 1984–87, Keeper, 1987–2000, Nat. Gall. of Scotland. Vis. Fellow: Yale Center for British Art, 1985; Clark Art Inst., 2004. Chevalier, Ordre des Arts et des Lettres (France), 2004. *Publications:* Pollaiuolo to Picasso: Old Master prints in the Whitworth Art Gallery, 1980; The Tempting Prospect: a social history of English watercolours, 1981; (ed with N. Penny) The Arrogant Connoisseur: Richard Payne Knight, 1982; The Draughtsman's Art: Master Drawings in the Whitworth Art Gallery, 1983; Lighting up the Landscape: French Impressionism and its origins, 1986; Corot and the Art of Landscape, 1991; Eyewitness Art: watercolour, 1993; (ed jtly) Corot, Courbet und die Maler von Barbizon, 1996; Oxford Concise Dictionary of Art Terms, 2001; The Playfair Project, 2004; articles, reviews, etc, in Apollo, Art Internat., Burlington Magazine, Museums Jl. *Recreations:* golf, travel, cycling slowly. *Address:* c/o Scottish National Gallery, The Mound, Edinburgh EH2 2EL. *Club:* Royal and Ancient (St Andrews).

CLARKE, Rt Hon. Sir Christopher (Simon Courtenay Stephenson), Kt 2005; PC 2013; **Rt Hon. Lord Justice Christopher Clarke;** a Lord Justice of Appeal, since 2013; *b* 14 March 1947; *s* of late Rev. John Stephenson Clarke and Enid Courtenay Clarke; *m* 1974, Caroline Anne Fletcher; one *s* two *d*. *Educ:* Marlborough College; Gonville and Caius College, Cambridge (MA). Called to the Bar, Middle Temple, 1969, Bencher, 1991; Attorney of Supreme Court of Turks and Caicos Islands, 1975; QC 1984; a Recorder, 1990–2004; a Deputy High Ct Judge, 1993–2004; a Judge of the Cts of Appeal of Jersey and Guernsey, 1998–2004; a Judge of the High Ct of Justice, QBD, 2005–13. Counsel to Bloody Sunday Inquiry, 1998–2004. Councillor, Internat. Bar Assoc., 1988–90; Chm., Commercial Bar Assoc., 1993–95; Mem., Bar Council, 1993–99. FRSA 1995. *Address:* Royal Courts of Justice, Strand, WC2A 2LL. *Clubs:* Brooks's, Hurlingham.

CLARKE, Darren Christopher, OBE 2012; professional golfer, since 1990; *b* 14 Aug. 1968; *m* Heather (*d* 2006); two *s*; *m* 2012, Alison Campbell. Amateur wins include: Spanish, Irish, N of Ireland and S of Ireland Championships, 1990; has played on European Tour, 1991–, PGA Tour, 2005–; wins include: Alfred Dunhill Open, 1993; Benson and Hedges Internat.,

Volvo Masters, 1998; Compass Gp Eur. Open, 1999; Compass Gp English Open, 1999, 2000, 2002; World Golf Championships (WGC) Accenture Match Play, 2000 (first European to win a WGC event); Smurfit Eur. Open, Chunichi Crowns, Japan, 2001; WGC NEC-Invitational, NI Masters, 2003; Mitsui Sumitomo VISA Taiheijo Masters, Japan, 2004, 2005; BMW Asian Open, KLM Open, 2008; Open, Royal St George's, 2011; Member: Alfred Dunhill Cup team, 1994, 1995, 1996, 1997, 1998, 1999; World Cup team, 1994, 1995, 1996; Ryder Cup team, 1997, 1999, 2002, 2004, 2006, 2010, 2012 (a Vice-Captain), 2016 (Captain); Seve Trophy team, 2000, 2002; Royal Trophy team, 2007. Founder, Darren Clarke Foundn, 2002. *Publications:* The Mind Factor, 2005; Darren Clarke: my Ryder Cup story, 2006; An Open Book: my autobiography, 2012. *Recreations:* films, reading, cars, fishing, Liverpool FC. *Address:* c/o ISM Ltd, Cherry Tree Farm, Cherry Tree Lane, Rostherne, Cheshire WA14 3RZ. *T:* (01565) 832100, *Fax:* (01565) 832200. *E:* ism@sportism.net.

CLARKE, Hon. Sir David (Clive), Kt 2003; DL; a Judge of the High Court of Justice, Queen's Bench Division, 2003–10; a Presiding Judge, Northern Circuit, 2006–09; *b* 16 July 1942; *s* of Philip George Clarke and José Margaret Clarke; *m* 1969, Alison Claire, *d* of Rt Rev. Percy James Brazier; two *s* (and one *s* decd). *Educ:* Winchester Coll.; Magdalene Coll., Cambridge (BA 1964, MA 1968). Called to the Bar, Inner Temple, 1965, Bencher, 1992; in practice, Northern Circuit, 1965–93 (Treas., 1988–92); a Recorder, 1981–93; QC 1983; a Circuit Judge, 1993–97; a Sen. Circuit Judge, and Hon. Recorder of Liverpool, 1997–2003; Asst Surveillance Comr, 2010–. Mem., Criminal Justice Consultative Council, 1999–2003. DL Merseyside, 2011. Hon. Fellow, Liverpool John Moores Univ., 2007. Hon. LLD Liverpool, 2004. *Recreations:* walking, sailing, swimming, canals. *Club:* Trearddur Bay Sailing (Anglesey).

CLARKE, Prof. David William, DPhil; FRS 1998; FREng, FIET; Professor of Control Engineering, Oxford University, 1992–2008, now Emeritus; Fellow, New College, Oxford, 1969–2008, now Emeritus; *b* 31 May 1943; *s* of Norman William Clarke and Laura (*née* Dewhurst); *m* 1967, Lynda Ann Weatherhead; two *s*. *Educ:* Balliol Coll., Oxford. MA, DPhil Oxon. FIET (FIEE 1984); FREng (FEng 1989). Oxford University: Astor Res. Fellow, New Coll., 1966–69; Lectr, 1969–86; Reader in Information Engrg, 1986–92; Hd, Dept of Engrg Sci., 1994–99. Former Dir, now Consultant, Invensys UTC for Advanced Instrumentation. Sir Harold Hartley Silver Medal, Inst. of Measurement and Control, 1983; Gold Medal of Achievement (Sen. Award), IEE, 2002. *Publications:* Advances in Model-Based Predictive Control, 1994; papers in learned jls. *Recreations:* gardening, historical ship models, learning C++ for Windows API. *Address:* New College, Oxford OX1 3BN. *T:* (01865) 279507.

CLARKE, Donald Roberts; Finance Director, 3i (formerly Investors in Industry) Group plc, 1988–91; *b* 14 May 1933; *s* of Harold Leslie Clarke and Mary Clarke; *m* 1959, Susan Charlotte Cotton (*d* 2014); one *s* three *d*. *Educ:* Ealing Grammar Sch.; The Queen's Coll., Oxford (MA). Articled Peat Marwick Mitchell & Co., 1957–62; Accountant, The Collingwood Group, 1962–64; Industrial and Commercial Finance Corporation: Investigating Accountant, 1964; Controller, 1964–67; Br. Manager, 1967–68; Co. Sec., 1968–73; Investors in Industry Gp (formerly Finance for Industry): Sec./Treasurer, 1973–76; Asst Gen. Manager, 1976–79; Gen. Manager, Finance, 1979–88. Dir, Consumers' Assoc. Ltd, 1990–92. Member: UGC, 1982–85; Industrial, Commercial and Prof. Liaison Gp, National Adv. Body for Local Authority Higher Educn, 1983–85; Continuing Educn Standing Cttee, Nat. Adv. Body for Local Authority Higher Educn and UGC, 1985–89; Council, Royal Holloway, Univ. of London (formerly RHBNC), 1987–2002 (Hon. Fellow, 2005). Trustee, Hestercombe Gardens Trust, 2001–14 (Patron, 2014). *Publications:* (jtly) 3i: 50 years investing in industry, 1995. *Recreation:* opera. *Club:* Oxford and Cambridge.

CLARKE, Most Rev. E(dwin) Kent, DD; *b* 21 Jan. 1932. *Educ:* Bishop's Univ., Lennoxville (BA 1954, LST 1956); Union Seminary, NY (MRE 1960); Huron Coll., Ontario (DD). Deacon 1956, priest 1957, Ottawa. Curate of All Saints, Westboro, 1956–59; Director of Christian Education, Diocese of Ottawa, 1960–66; Rector of St Lambert, Montreal, 1966–73; Diocesan Sec., Diocese of Niagara, 1973–76; Archdeacon of Niagara, 1973–76; Bishop Suffragan of Niagara, 1976–79; Bishop of Edmonton, 1980; Archbishop of Edmonton and Metropolitan of Rupert's Land, 1986–87. *Address:* 418–400 Bell Street, Pembroke, ON K8A 2K5, Canada.

CLARKE, Elaine Denise; *see* Watson, E. D.

CLARKE, Prof. Eric Fillenz, PhD; FBA 2010; Heather Professor of Music, University of Oxford, since 2007; *b* 31 July 1955; *s* of John Clarke and Marianne (*née* Fillenz); *m* Catherine Ferreira; one *s* one *d*. *Educ:* Univ. of Sussex (BA Music 1977, MA Music 1978); Univ. of Exeter (PhD Psychol. 1984). Lectr, 1981–88, Sen. Lectr, 1988–91, Reader, 1991–93, in Music, City Univ., London; James Rossiter Hoyle Prof. of Music, Univ. of Sheffield, 1993–2007. *Publications:* Empirical Musicology (ed with Nicholas Cook), 2004; Ways of Listening, 2005; (with N. Dibben and S. Pitts) Music and Mind in Everyday Life, 2010; (ed with David Clarke) Music and Consciousness, 2011; contrib. numerous papers to jls of Music Perception, Psychology of Music, Musicae Scientiae, Music Analysis, Popular Music. *Recreations:* cycling, gardening, walking, playing music. *Address:* Music Faculty, University of Oxford, St Aldate's, Oxford OX1 1DB. *T:* (01865) 276125, *Fax:* (01865) 276128. *E:* eric.clarke@music.ox.ac.uk.

CLARKE, Eric Lionel; *b* 9 April 1933; *s* of late Ernest and Annie Clarke; *m* 1955, June Hewat; two *s* one *d*. *Educ:* St Cuthbert's Holy Cross Acad.; W. M. Ramsey Tech. Coll.; Esk Valley Tech. Coll. Coalminer: Roslin Colliery, 1949–51; Lingerwood Colliery, 1951–69; Bilston Glen Colliery, 1969–77; Trade Union Official, 1977–89; Gen. Sec., NUM Scotland; redundant, unemployed, 1989–92. Mem., Midlothian CC and then Lothian Regl Council, 1962–78. MP (Lab) Midlothian, 1992–2001. An Opposition Whip, 1994–97. *Recreations:* fly fishing, gardening, carpentry, football spectator. *Address:* 32 Mortonhall Park Crescent, Edinburgh EH17 8SY. *T:* (0131) 664 8214. *Club:* Danderhall Miners' Welfare.

CLARKE, Frank; Hon. Mr Justice Clarke; a Judge of the Supreme Court of Ireland, since 2012; *b* Dublin, 10 Oct. 1951; *s* of Bernard Clarke and Sheila Clarke (*née* Bailey); *m* 1977, Prof. Jacqueline Hayden; one *s* one *d*. *Educ:* Drimnagh Castle Christian Brothers Sch., Dublin; University Coll. Dublin (BA). Called to the Bar, King's Inns, Dublin, 1973, Bencher, 1994; in practice as barrister, 1973–2004; Sen. Counsel, 1985–2004; a Judge of the High Court, 2004–12. Chair, Referendum Commn on Lisbon Treaty, 2010. Chair, Irish Legal Terms Adv. Cttee, 2014–. Adjunct Professor: TCD, 2012–; University Coll. Cork, 2014–. Judge in Residence, Griffith Coll., Dublin, 2010–. Chairman: Bar Council, 1993–95; Council of King's Inns, 1999–2004. Mem. Council, IBA, 1992–2004 (Co-Chair, Barristers and Advocates, 1998–2002). Pres., Irish Soc. for European Law, 2015–. Hon. Member: Canadian Bar Assoc., 1994; Australian Bar Assoc., 2002. *Recreations:* horse racing, Rugby, music, theatre. *Address:* Supreme Court of Ireland, Four Courts, Dublin 7, Ireland. *T:* (1) 8886500. *Club:* Turf (Dep. Sen. Steward, 2003–05).

CLARKE, Garth Martin; Chief Executive, Transport Research Laboratory, 1997–2001; *b* 1 Feb. 1944; *s* of Peter Oakley Clarke and Ella Audrey (*née* Jenner); *m* 1966, Carol Marian Trimble; three *d*. *Educ:* Duke's Grammar Sch., Alnwick, Northumberland; Liverpool Univ. (BSc Hons). FCIHT (FIHT 1996). Research Physicist, 1966–73, Ops Dir, 1983–87, Plessey Research (Caswell) Ltd; Dir, Commercial Ops, Plessey Res. and Technology Ltd, 1987–89; Business Develt Dir, Business Systems Gp, GPT Ltd, 1990–93; Business Dir, TRL, 1993–97. Chief Exec., Transport Res. Foundn, 1997–2001; Chm., Viridis, 1999–2001. Dir, Parly Adv. Council for Transport Safety, 2001–05. Fellow, Transport Res. Foundn, 1998. CCMI. *Recreations:* birdwatching, water colour painting, photography.

CLARKE, Geoff James; QC (Scot.) 2008; *b* Edinburgh, 3 May 1966; *s* of Owen Clarke, CBE and Elizabeth Clarke; *m* 2002, Kelly Loughran; two *s*. *Educ:* N Berwick High Sch.; Edinburgh Univ. (LLB Hons). Solicitor, 1989–93, Advocate, 1994–2008, specialising in personal injury, valuation for rating, Simpson & Marwick, Edinburgh. *Recreations:* walking, reading, judo. *Address:* Stair Park, North Berwick, E Lothian EH39 4DD. *T:* (01620) 890754, *Fax:* (01620) 890758. *E:* geoff.clarke@compasschambers.com. *Club:* North Berwick Golf.

CLARKE, Giles; *see* Clarke, C. G.

CLARKE, Giles Colin Scott, PhD; museums and heritage consultant; Head, Department of Exhibitions and Education, Natural History Museum, 1994–2001; *b* 9 Jan. 1944; *s* of Colin Richard Clarke and Vera Joan, (Georgie), Clarke (*née* Scott); *m* 1967, Helen Parker (*see* Helen Clarke); one *s*. *Educ:* Sevenoaks Sch.; Keble Coll., Oxford (MA 1970); Birmingham Univ. (PhD 1970). VSO, Gambia, 1963; Mem., Internat. Biological Prog. Bipolar Expeditions, 1967–68; Asst Keeper of Botany, Manchester Mus., 1970–73; Head, Pollen Section, 1973–79, Dep. Head, Dept of Public Services, 1979–94, British Mus. (Natural History), later Natural History Mus. Member: Council, British Bryological Soc., 1971–2001 (Pres., 1998–99; Hon. Mem., 2005); Cttee, Wildlife Photographer of the Year, 1984–2001; Cttee, Trends in Leisure and Entertainment Conf. and Exhibn, 1993–2005 (Chair, 1998). Trustee: Eureka! Children's Mus., 1999–2011; Royal Tunbridge Wells SO, 2010– (Chm., 2013–). Japanese Soc. for Promotion of Sci. Fellow, Nagoya Univ. Mus., 2008. Hon. Mem., Kennel Club, 2008. FLS 1971; FMA 1996; FRSA 1997. *Publications:* numerous papers in prof. jls on botany and museums. *Recreations:* opera, organ music, art galleries, reading, making things. *Address:* Kynance, Clarence Road, Tunbridge Wells, Kent TN1 1HE.

CLARKE, Graham Neil; Chairman, Hamdene Horticultural Publishing Services Ltd, since 2006; *b* 23 July 1956; *s* of late Henry Charles Owen Clarke, RVM and Doris May Clarke; *m* 1980, Denise Carole (*née* Anderson); two *d*. *Educ:* Rutherford Sch., N London; Wisley School of Horticulture (WisCertHort). Staff gardener, Buckingham Palace, 1975–76; Nurseryman, Hyde Park, 1976; Amateur Gardening: Sub-Editor, 1976–79; Chief Sub-Editor, 1979–81; Dep. Editor, 1981–86; Editor, 1986–98; Editor, Home Plus Magazine, 1984–85; IPC gardening titles: Gp Editor, 1993–95; Special Projects Editor, 1995–98; Editor-at-Large, 1998–99; Editor: Exotic & Greenhouse Gardening, 2000–01; Garden Calendar, 2000–01; Develt Ed., 1999–2001, Man. Ed., 2000–02, Guild of Master Craftsman Pubns; Editor: Water Gardening, 1999–2002; Business Matters, 2002–03; Guild News, 2003–04, 2007–14; Horticulture Week, 2004–05; publishing and horticulture consultant, 2002–04 and 2005–; gardening presenter, Ideal World TV, 2012. FLS 1990; FCIHort (FIHort 2011) (AIHort 1991; MIHort 1995). *Publications:* Step by Step Pruning, 1985; Autumn and Winter Colour in the Garden, 1986; Complete Book of Plant Propagation, 1990; The Ultimate House Plant Handbook, 1997; Beginner's Guide to Water Gardening, 2002; Collins Practical Guide: Water Gardening, 2004; Collins Practical Guide: Pruning, 2005; Success with Roses, 2007; Success with Shade-Loving Plants, 2007; Success with Sun-Loving Plants, 2007; Success with Water Gardens, 2007; Success with Water-Saving Gardens, 2007; Success with Acid-Loving Plants, 2008; Success with Alkaline-Loving Plants, 2008; The Organic Gardener's Year, 2008; Coastal Gardening, 2009; Success with Small-Space Gardening, 2009; Success with Alpine Gardening, 2009; The Organic Herb Gardener, 2010; Growing for Food and Colour, 2012; Amateur Gardening Yearbook, 2015. *Recreations:* writing, genealogy, philately, gardening. *Address:* Hamdene Horticultural Publishing Services Ltd, Hamdene House, 127 Magna Road, Bournemouth, Dorset BH11 9NE. *Club:* Royal Horticultural Society Garden (Surrey).

CLARKE, Gregory; Chairman: Football League, since 2010; Redefine International plc, since 2011; UK2, since 2011; Easynet, since 2012; Met Office, since 2012; *b* 27 Oct. 1957; *s* of George and Mary Clarke; *m* 1984, Anne Wilson; four *d*. *Educ:* Gateway Grammar Sch., Leicester; Wolverhampton Poly (BA Hons 1980); City Univ. Business Sch. (MBA 1983). Vice Pres., Global Cellular, Nortel, 1992–95; Chief Exec., Cable & Wireless Mobile, 1995–97; Chief Operating Officer, 1997–99, Chief Exec., 1999–2000, Cable & Wireless Communications plc; Chief Executive Officer: ICO Teledisc, 2000–02; Lend Lease Corp., Sydney, 2002–09; O3b, 2009–10. Chm., Eteach UK Ltd, 2000–02; non-executive Director: Leicester City, 2000–07; BUPA Ltd, 2001–07. *Recreations:* family, football, Leicester City FC, opera, Rugby, reading.

CLARKE, Dr Helen, FSA; Director, Society of Antiquaries, 1990–94; *b* 25 Aug. 1939; *d* of George Parker and Helen (*née* Teare); *m* 1967, Giles Colin Scott Clarke, *qv*; one *s*. *Educ:* Univ. of Birmingham (BA; PhD); Univ. of Lund, Sweden. FSA 1972. Dir of Excavations, King's Lynn, 1963–67; Res. Fellow, Sch. of History, Birmingham Univ., 1965–67; Lecturer in Medieval Archaeology: Glasgow Univ., 1967–69; UCL, 1976–90. Visiting Professor in Medieval Archaeology: Lund Univ., Sweden, 1991; Århus Univ., Denmark, 1992; Kiel Univ., Germany, 1993. Hon. Sen. Lectr, Inst. of Archaeol., UCL, 2000–. Editor and Translator: Royal Swedish Acad. of Letters, History and Antiquities, 1975–2008; Bd of National Antiquities, Sweden (also Consultant), 1990–95; Consultant, English Heritage, 1987–94. Trustee, Council for British Archaeol., 2004–07. Member: Svenska Arkeologiska Samfundet, 1988; Vetenskapssocieteten i Lund, 1988. Hon. Fil Dr Lund, 1991. Silver Medal for services to Swedish archaeol., Royal Swedish Acad. of Letters, History and Antiquities, 2012. *Publications:* Regional Archaeologies: East Anglia, 1971; Excavations in King's Lynn, 1963–1970, 1977; The Archaeology of Medieval England, 1984, 2nd edn 1986; Towns in the Viking Age, 1991, 2nd edn 1995; Sandwich: the 'completest medieval town in England', 2010; Walks Through Historic Sandwich, 2011; Discover Medieval Sandwich: a guide to its history and buildings, 2012. *Recreations:* attending opera, watching cricket, looking at the landscape.

CLARKE, Henry Benwell; Board Member, Rail Estate Consultancy, since 1998; *b* 30 Jan. 1950; *yr s* of late Stephen Lampard Clarke and Elinor Wade Clarke (*née* Benwell); *m* 1973, Verena Angela Lodge; four *s* one *d*. *Educ:* St John's Sch., Leatherhead; South Bank Polytechnic (BSc Estate Management 1972); Imperial College London (MSc Management Science 1977; DIC 1977). ARICS 1973, FRICS 1986; ACIArb 1979. British Rail Property Board: S Region, 1972–78; NW Region, 1978–82; E Region, 1982–85; Regional Estate Surveyor and Manager, Midland Region, 1985–86; Chief Estate Surveyor, HQ, 1986–87; Nat. Develt Manager, 1987–88; Dep. Chief Exec., Crown Estate Comrs, 1988–92, Acting Chief Exec. and Accounting Officer, 1989. Mem., Gen. Council, British Property Fedn, 1989–92. Dir, Henry Clarke Associates, 2004–. Member, Board: People and Places Internat., 1993–2004; Telecom Property Ltd, 1999–2010; Crownmead Properties Ltd, 2001–; Kings Yard Developments, 2003–04; Intelligent Business Space Ltd, 2004–08; The Model Bus Co., 2006–; Jackson Green Ltd (formerly Jackson-Green Partnership), 2006–; Revetment Ltd, 2008–; Aquobex Ltd, 2013–. Mem. Council, Christian Union for Estate Profession, 1983–88; Member, Board: Youth with a Mission (England), 1990–; Mercy Ships (UK), 1995–; Moggerhanger House Preservation Trust, 1997–2005; Railway Children Trust, 2002–; Lindow Ministry Trust Ltd, 2002–; advisor to various Christian trusts. Freeman: City of London, 2008; Plumbers' Co., 2008. *Recreations:* reading, walking, transport, architecture, Church. *Address:* 42 Wordsworth Road, Harpenden, Herts AL5 4AF.

CLARKE, Hilda Mary Maude; Headteacher, Tiffin School, 2009–15; *b* Loughborough, 9 Nov. 1954; *d* of Frederick Clarke and Rosie Clarke (*née* de Taranto). *Educ:* Kelvin Hall Sch., Hull; Sussex Univ. (BA Hons Hist.); Hull Univ. (PGCE); Inst. of Educn, London (NPQH).

Teacher, then Sen. Teacher and Hd of History, Alsager Sch., Cheshire, 1977–92; Dep. Head, Tiffin Girls' Sch., 1992–2000; Headteacher, Langley Grammar Sch., 2000–09. Chm., Berks Assoc. of Secondary Hds, 2007–09. *Recreations:* classical music, sport.

CLARKE, (James) Brian; author and journalist; Fishing Correspondent, The Times, since 1991; *b* 28 May 1938; *s* of Thomas Clarke and Annette Clarke (*née* Vickers); *m* 1968, (Edith Isobel) Anne Farley; three *d. Educ:* St Mary's Grammar Sch., Darlington; Darlington Tech. Coll. Reporter and sub-ed., Northern Echo, Darlington, 1955–59; Dep. Features Ed., Evening Gazette, Middlesbrough, 1959–61; home news sub-ed., Scottish Daily Mail, Edinburgh, 1961–62; home news and Parly sub-ed., The Guardian, 1962–67; Nat. Press Officer, IBM UK, 1967–68; Public Affairs Advr, Nat. Computing Centre, 1968–69; indep. mgt consultant, 1969–74; various corporate communications and envmtl mgt posts, IBM UK, 1974–91 (on secondment to BBC, 1988–90: series producer, In the Name of the Law (television), 1988–89; Consultant, BBC Bd of Mgt, 1989–90); consultant, envmtl progs, IBM UK, 1990–91; Fishing Corresp., Sunday Times, 1975–96. Vice-Pres., Wild Trout Trust, 2009– (Pres., 2004–09). *Publications:* The Pursuit of Stillwater Trout, 1975, 8th edn 2014; (contrib.) The Masters on the Nymph (US), 1976; (contrib.) Stillwater Trout Fisheries, 1976; (contrib.) The Complete Salmon and Trout Fisherman, 1978; (jtly) The Trout and the Fly, 1980, 7th edn 2005; (contrib.) West Country Fly Fishing, 1983; (contrib.) The Fly-Fishers, 1984; (contrib.) The One That Got Away, 1991; (jtly) Flyfishing for Trout (US), 1993; Trout etcetera: selected writings 1982–1996, 1996; (contrib.) Lessons from the Fish, 1996; (contrib.) Trout and Salmon, 1999; (contrib.) Fly-Fishers' Progress, 2000; The Stream (novel), 2000 (Natural World Book Prize, 2000; Authors' Club Best First Novel Award, 2000); (jtly) Understanding Trout Behaviour (US), 2002; (contrib.) The World of Fly-Fishing, 2003; (contrib.) The Literary Non-Fiction Collection, 2005; (contrib.) Richard Walker: a biography, 2007; On Fishing: journalism and essays 1996–2007, 2007. *Recreations:* fishing, walking, photography, sitting still in the countryside watching and listening. *Address:* c/o Watson, Little Ltd, 48–56 Bayham Place, NW1 0EU. *Club:* Flyfishers'.

CLARKE, Jane; author (as Jane Lythell); *d* of Michael David Hilborne-Clarke and Margaret Lythell; one *d* by Howard Austin Trevette. *Educ:* Norwich High Sch. for Girls; University College London (BA Hons English Lang. and Lit. 1975); Slade Sch. of Fine Art. Film Programmer, BFI, 1980–82; Features Prod., TV-am, 1982–88: Ed., Henry Kelly Saturday Show, 1984–85; Features Ed., Good Morning Britain, 1985–87; Ed., After Nine, 1987–88; Independent Prod., Pithers, Clarke and Ferguson, 1988–89 (prod., Children First for Granada TV, 1989); Series Ed., New Living for British Satellite Broadcasting, 1990–91; Controller, Features, West Country TV, 1992–95; Dep. Dir, BFI, 1995–97; Chief Exec., BAFTA, 1998; Foreign and Commonwealth Office: Head: Broadcast and Allied Media, subseq. TV and Radio, Public Diplomacy Dept, 1999–2002; Strategy and Progs, then Strategy and Campaigns, Public Diplomacy Team, 2002–05; Internal Communications, 2005–06; Head of Communications: Sport England, 2006–08; Kent CC, 2008–11. Bd Mem., London Fest. of Literature, 2000–01. *Publications:* (with Diana Simmonds) Move Over Misconceptions: Doris Day reappraised, 1981; as Jane Lythell: The Lie of You, 2014; After the Storm, 2015. *Recreations:* Tottenham Hotspur FC, reading, walking, cricket, astronomy. *E:* clarke.jane22@gmail.com. *W:* www.twitter.com/janelythell, http://chroniclesofchloegreene.blogspot.co.uk.

CLARKE, Prof. Jane, PhD; FRS 2015; FRSC; FMedSci; Professor of Molecular Biophysics, since 2009, and Wellcome Trust Senior Research Fellow, since 2001, University of Cambridge; Fellow, Trinity Hall, Cambridge, since 2010; *b* London, 10 Sept. 1950; *d* of Cyril Morgan and Shirley Morgan (*née* Jenkins); *m* 1973, Christopher Clarke; one *s* one *d. Educ:* Univ. of York (BA 1st Cl. Hons Biochem. 1972); Univ. of Cambridge (PGCE 1973); Georgia Inst. of Technol., Atlanta (MSc Applied Biol. 1990); Univ. of Cambridge (PhD 1993). FRSC 2013; FMedSci 2013. Science teacher in secondary schs, incl. Hd of Sci., Northumberland Park Sch., Tottenham, 1973–86; Postdoctoral Fellow, Centre for Protein Engrg, MRC Centre, Cambridge, 1994–97; Wellcome Trust Career Develt Fellow, 1997–2001, Reader in Molecular Biophysics, 2007–09, Dept of Chemistry, Univ. of Cambridge. Mem., EMBO, 2012. Ed., Current Opinion in Structural Biol., 2001, 2003; Member, Editorial Board: Protein Sci.; Biophysical Jl; Protein Engrg, Design & Selection; Mem., Editl Adv. Bd, Protein Sci. *Publications:* contribs to learned jls incl. Biochem., Structure, Jl Biol Chem., Biophysics Jl, Nature, Proc. NAS, Jl Amer. Chem. Soc., Current Opinion Structural Biol., Jl Molecular Biol. *Address:* Department of Chemistry, University of Cambridge, Lensfield Road, Cambridge CB2 1EW. *T:* (01223) 331697. *E:* janeclarke@ch.cam.ac.uk.

CLARKE, Prof. John, FRS 1986; Professor of Physics, since 1973, and Luis W. Alvarez Memorial Chair for Experimental Physics, since 1994, University of California, Berkeley; *b* 10 Feb. 1942; *s* of Victor Patrick and Ethel May Clarke; *m* 1979, Grethe F. Pedersen; one *d. Educ:* Christ's Coll., Cambridge (BA, MA 1968; Hon. Fellow, 1997); Darwin Coll., Cambridge (PhD 1968; ScD 2003). Postdoctoral Scholar, 1968, Asst Prof., 1969, Associate Prof., 1971–73, Univ. of California, Berkeley. Alfred P. Sloan Foundn Fellow, 1970; Adolph C. and Mary Sprague Miller Inst. for Basic Research into Science Prof., 1975, 1994; John Simon Guggenheim Fellow, 1977; Vis. Fellow, Clare Hall, Cambridge, 1989; By-Fellow, Churchill Coll., Cambridge, 1998; Faculty Res. Lectr, Univ. of California, Berkeley, 2005; 150th Anniv. Vis. Prof., Chalmers Univ. of Technol., Gothenburg, 2009–13; Chair Prof., Nat. Taiwan Normal Univ., Taipei, 2012–. For. Mem., Royal Soc. of Arts and Scis, Sweden, 2007; For. Associate, Nat. Acad. of Scis, USA, 2012. FAAAS 1982; Fellow, Amer. Phys. Soc. 1985; FInstP 1999. Charles Vernon Boys Prize, Inst. of Physics, 1977; Calif. Scientist of the Year, 1987; Fritz London Meml Award for Low Temperature Physics, 1987; Joseph F. Keithley Award, APS, 1998; Comstock Prize for Physics, NAS, 1999; IEEE Council on Superconductivity Award, 2002; Scientific American 50 Award, 2002; Lounasmaa Prize, Finnish Acad. of Arts and Scis, 2004; Hughes Medal, Royal Soc., 2004; Outstanding Performance Award, Lawrence Berkeley Nat. Lab., 2010; Berkeley Citation, Berkeley Univ., 2011. *Publications:* approx. 460 contribs to learned jls. *Address:* Department of Physics, University of California, 366 Le Conte Hall, Berkeley, CA 94720–7300, USA. *T:* (510) 6423069.

CLARKE, John Francis; Chief Executive, Welsh European Funding Office, National Assembly for Wales, 2000–03; *b* 10 June 1947; *s* of Francis William Clarke and Joan Margaret Clarke; *m* 1969, Lynda Mary Hudson; three *s. Educ:* Windermere Grammar Sch.; Manchester Univ. (BA Hons); Harvard Business Sch. (PMD 1984). ACIB. Barclays Bank: Mgt Trainee, 1968–75; Asst Manager, 1975–78; Asst District Manager, 1978–81; Sen. Corporate Manager, 1981–84; Corporate Finance Dir, 1986–91; Regl Dir, 1991–99; Sen. Vice Pres., Barclays USA, 1984–86. Chm., Greater Nottingham TEC, 1997–98; Mem., East Midlands Regl IDB, 1992–97. Chairman: The Stables Theatre, Wavendon, 1977–91; St Donats Arts Centre Ltd, 2006–10. Pres., Llantwit Major Rotary Club, 2002–03 and 2012–13 (Mem., 1999–); Vice-Pres., Cardiff Business Club, 1998–2011. Mem., Audit Cttee, Univ. of Wales Inst., Cardiff, 2006–11; Gov., Llantwit Major Comprehensive Sch., 2005–. Trustee, World at Play, 2011–12. *Recreations:* golf, gardening. *Address:* The Old Vicarage, St Donats, Llantwit Major, Vale of Glamorgan CF61 1ZB. *T:* (01446) 793180. *Club:* Cottrell Park Golf.

CLARKE, Prof. John Innes, OBE 2003; DL; Chairman, NE Regional Awards Committee, National Lottery Charities Board, 1997–2002; *b* 7 Jan. 1929; *s* of late Bernard Griffith Clarke and Edith Louie (*née* Mott); *m* 1955, Dorothy Anne Watkinson (*d* 2008); three *d. Educ:* Bournemouth Sch.; Univ. of Aberdeen (MA 1st cl., PhD); Univ. of Paris (French Govt scholar). FRGS 1963. RAF 1952–54 (Sword of Merit, 1953). Asst Lectr in Geog., Univ. of Aberdeen, 1954–55; Prof. of Geog., Univ. Coll. of Sierra Leone, 1963–65; University of Durham: Lectr in Geog., 1955–63; Reader in Geog., 1965–68; Prof. of Geog., 1968–90, now Emeritus; Acting Principal, Trevelyan Coll., 1979–80; Pro-Vice-Chancellor and Sub-Warden, 1984–90; Leverhulme Emeritus Fellow, 1990–92. Visiting Professor: Univ. of Wisconsin, 1967–68; Cameroon, 1965, 1966, 1967; Clermont-Ferrand, 1974; Cairo, 1982; Shanghai, 1986. Acting Chm., Human Geog. Cttee, SSRC, 1975; RGS rep. on British Nat. Cttee for Geography, 1976–81, 1988–89; Chairman: IGU Commn on Population Geography, 1980–88; Higher Educn Support for Industry in the North, 1987–89; Cttee on Population and Environment, Internat. Union for Scientific Study of Population, 1990–95; Durham, then N Durham DHA, 1990–96. Vice-President: Eugenics Soc., 1981–84; RGS, 1991–95; Co. Durham Foundn, 2008– (Bd Mem., 1995–2008). DL Durham, 1990. FRSA 1990. Silver Medal, RSGS, 1947; Victoria Medal, RGS, 1991. *Publications:* Iranian City of Shiraz, 1963; (jtly) Africa and the Islands, 1964, 4th edn 1977; Population Geography, 1965, 2nd edn 1972; (with B. D. Clark) Kermanshah: an Iranian Provincial City, 1969; Population Geography and the Developing Countries, 1971; (jtly) People in Britain: a census atlas, 1980; The Future of Population, 1997; The Human Dichotomy, 2000; *edited:* Sierra Leone in Maps, 1966, 2nd edn 1969; An Advanced Geography of Africa, 1975; Geography and Population: approaches and applications, 1984; Without Her, 2011; Better or Worse, 2012; War Memories, 2013; Durham Delights, 2014; Jimmy Mulhall's Military Memories, 2014; *co-edited:* Field Studies in Libya, 1960; Populations of the Middle East and North Africa: a geographical approach, 1972; Human Geography in France and Britain, 1976; Régions Géographiques et Régions d'Aménagements, 1978; Change and Development in the Middle East, 1981; Redistribution of Population in Africa, 1982; Population and Development Projects in Africa, 1985; Population and Disaster, 1989; Mountain Population Pressure, 1990; Environment and Population Change, 1994; Population-Environment-Development Interactions, 1995; Population and Environment in Arid Regions, 1997; Arid Land Resources and their Management, 1998; author of many learned articles. *Recreations:* travel, sports (now vicariously), countryside, family history. *Address:* Tower Cottage, The Avenue, Durham DH1 4EB. *T:* (0191) 384 8350.

CLARKE, Very Rev. John Martin; Dean of Wells, since 2004; *b* 20 Feb. 1952; *s* of Roland Ernest Clarke and Edna Lucy Hay; *m* 1985, Constance Elizabeth Cressida Nash; two *s* one *d. Educ:* West Buckland Sch.; Hertford Coll., Oxford (MA); Edinburgh Theol Coll. (BD). Ordained deacon, 1976, priest, 1977; Asst Curate, The Ascension, Kenton, Newcastle, 1976–79; Precentor, St Ninian's Cathedral, Perth, 1979–82; Information Officer and Communications Advr to the Gen. Synod of the Scottish Episcopal Church, 1982–87; Philip Usher Scholarship, Greece, 1987–88; Vicar, St Mary, Battersea, 1989–96; Principal, Ripon Coll., Cuddesdon, 1997–2004; Canon and Preb., Lincoln Cathedral, 2000–04. *Recreations:* walking, reading, music, cricket. *Address:* The Dean's Lodging, 25 The Liberty, Wells, Somerset BA5 2SZ.

CLARKE, Rear-Adm. John Patrick, CB 1996; LVO 1986; MBE 1978; Chief Executive, British Marine Federation, 2001–06; Hydrographer of the Navy and Chief Executive, United Kingdom Hydrographic Office (formerly Hydrographic Agency), 1996–2001; *b* 12 Dec. 1944; *s* of Frank and Christine Clarke; *m* 1st, 1969, Ann Parham (marr. diss. 1997); one *s* two *d*; 2nd, 1998, Mrs Jeffy J. Salt. *Educ:* Epsom Coll.; BRNC. Commanding Officer, HM Ships: Finwhale, 1976; Oberon, 1977; Dreadnought, 1979–80; CO, Submarine CO's Qualifying Course, 1983–84; Exec. Officer, HM Yacht Britannia, 1985–86; Captain: Submarine Sea Training, 1986–89; Seventh Frigate Squadron, 1989–90; Asst Dir, Naval Staff Duties, 1990–92; Dir, Naval Warfare, 1992; Dir, Naval Management, Communications and Inf. Systems, 1993–94; Flag Officer Trng and Recruiting, 1994–96. Adjudicator, Solicitors' Regulation Authy, 2008–13. Younger Brother, Trinity House, 1997. QDR 2007. Hon. Mem., RICS. *Recreations:* golf, sailing. *Club:* Yeovil Golf.

CLARKE, Most Rev. John Robert; Archbishop of Athabasca, 2003–09; Metropolitan of the Ecclesiastical Province of Rupert's Land, 2003–09; *b* 27 July 1938; *s* of Rt Rev. Neville and Alice Clarke; *m* 1964, Nadia Juliann Slusar; one *s* two *d. Educ:* Univ. of W Ontario (BA); Huron Coll., London, Ontario (LTh; DD *jure dignitatis*, 1992). Ordained: deacon, 1963; priest, 1964; Curate, St Michael and All Angels, Toronto, 1964–66; Priest-in-charge, Church of the Apostles, Moosonee, 1966–84; Exec. Archdeacon and Treas., Dio. of Athabasca, 1984–91; Bishop of Athabasca, 1992–2009. *Recreations:* woodworking, travelling, canoeing, gardening. *T:* (home) (780) 6241008.

CLARKE, His Honour Sir Jonathan (Dennis), Kt 1981; a Circuit Judge, 1982–93; *b* 19 Jan. 1930; *e s* of late Dennis Robert Clarke, Master of Supreme Court, and of Caroline Alice (*née* Hill); *m* 1956, Susan Margaret Elizabeth (*née* Ashworth); one *s* three *d. Educ:* Kidstones Sch.; University Coll. London. Admitted Solicitor, 1956; partner in Townsends, solicitors, 1959–82; a Recorder of the Crown Court, 1972–82. Mem. Council, Law Soc., 1964–82, Pres., 1980–81; Sec., Nat. Cttee of Young Solicitors, 1962–64; Member: Matrimonial Causes Rule Cttee, 1967–78; Legal Studies Bd, CNAA, 1968–75; Judicial Studies Bd, 1979–82; Criminal Injuries Compensation Bd, 1993–2004; Criminal Injuries Compensation Appeals Panel, 1996–2004. Governor, College of Law, 1970–90, Chm. of Governors, 1982. *Recreations:* sailing, ski-ing. *Clubs:* Garrick, Farmers; Royal Western Yacht.

CLARKE, Rt Hon. Kenneth Harry; CH 2014; PC 1984; QC 1980; MP (C) Rushcliffe, since 1970; *b* 2 July 1940; *e c* of Kenneth Clarke and Doris (*née* Smith), Nottingham; *m* 1964, Gillian Mary Edwards (*d* 2015); one *s* one *d. Educ:* Nottingham High Sch.; Gonville and Caius Coll., Cambridge (BA, LLB; Hon. Fellow, 1997). Chm., Cambridge Univ. Conservative Assoc., 1961; Pres., Cambridge Union, 1963; Chm., Fedn Conservative Students, 1963. Called to Bar, Gray's Inn 1963, Hon. Bencher, 1989, Bencher, 1998; Mem., Midland Circuit. Research Sec., Birmingham Bow Group, 1965–66. Contested Mansfield, 1964 and 1966. PPS to Solicitor General, 1971–72; an Asst Govt Whip, 1972–74 (Govt Whip for Europe, 1973–74); a Lord Comr, HM Treasury, 1974; Parly Sec., DoT, later Parly Under Sec. of State for Transport, 1979–82; Minister of State (Minister for Health), DHSS, 1982–85; entered Cabinet as Paymaster General and Minister for Employment, 1985–87; Chancellor of Duchy of Lancaster and Minister for Trade and Industry (with addnl responsibility to co-ordinate Govt policy on Inner Cities), 1987–88; Secretary of State: for Health, 1988–90; for Educn and Science, 1990–92; for the Home Dept, 1992–93; Chancellor of the Exchequer, 1993–97; Minister of State (Minister without Portfolio), 2012–14. Mem., Parly delegn to Council of Europe and WEU, 1973–74; Sec., Cons. Parly Health and Social Security Cttee, 1974; Opposition Spokesman on: Social Services, 1974–76; Industry, 1976–79; Shadow Sec. of State for Business (formerly Business, Enterprise and Regulatory Reform), 2009–10; Lord Chancellor and Sec. of State for Justice, 2010–12. Liveryman, Clockmakers' Co., 2001–. Hon. LLD: Nottingham, 1989; Huddersfield, 1993; DUniv Nottingham Trent, 1996. *Publications:* New Hope for the Regions, 1969; pamphlets published by Bow Group, 1964–. *Recreations:* modern jazz music; watching Association Football and cricket, bird-watching. *Address:* House of Commons, SW1A 0AA. *Clubs:* Garrick; Nottinghamshire CC (Pres., 2002–04).

CLARKE, Rt Rev. Kenneth Herbert; Bishop of Kilmore, Elphin and Ardagh, 2001–12; Mission Director, South American Mission Society Ireland, since 2012; *b* 23 May 1949; *s* of Herbert Clarke and Anne Clarke (*née* Gage); *m* 1971, Helen Good; four *d. Educ:* Holywood Primary Sch.; Sullivan Upper Sch., Holywood, Co. Down; TCD (BA 1971; Div. Testimonium 1972). Ordained deacon, 1972, priest, 1973; Curate: Magheralin, 1972–75; Dundonald, 1975–78; served in Chile with S Amer. Mission Soc., 1978–81; Incumbent: Crinken Ch, Dublin, 1982–86; Coleraine Parish, 1986–2001; Archdeacon of Dalriada,

1998–2001. *Publications:* Called to Minister?, 1990; Going for Growth, 2011. *Recreations:* walking, reading, golf. *Address:* SAMS House, 1 Irwin Crescent, Lurgan, Craigavon BT66 7EZ. *T:* (28) 3831 0144. *E:* info@samsukireland.com.

CLARKE, Laurence; *see* Clarke, S. L. H.

CLARKE, Prof. Malcolm Alistair, PhD; Professor of Commercial Contract Law, Cambridge University, 1999–2010, now Emeritus; Fellow, St John's College, Cambridge, since 1970; *b* 1 April 1943; *s* of Kenneth Alfred William Clarke and Marian Florence Clarke (*née* Rich); *m* 1968, Eva Olga Bergman; two *s*. *Educ:* Kingswood Sch., Bath; L'Ecole des Roches, Verneuil-sur-Avre, France; St John's Coll., Cambridge (LLB 1965; MA 1968; PhD 1973). Asst, Institut de Droit Comparé, Paris, 1965–66; Research Fellow, Fitzwilliam Coll., Cambridge, 1966–68; Lectr, Univ. of Singapore, 1968–70; Cambridge University: Asst Lectr in Law, 1970–75; Lectr, 1975–93; Reader in Commercial Contract Law, 1993–99; Dir of Studies, St John's Coll., Cambridge, 1972–92. *Publications:* Aspects of the Hague Rules, 1976; (jtly) Shipbuilding Contracts, 1981, 2nd edn 1992; The International Carriage of Goods by Road: CMR, 1982, 6th edn 2014; The Law of Insurance Contracts, 1989, 6th edn 2009, and bi-annually, 1999–; Policies and Perceptions of Insurance, 1997; Contracts of Carriage by Air, 2002, 2nd edn 2010; (jtly) Butterworths Law of Contract, 2nd edn 2003, 4th edn 2010; Contracts of Carriage by Land and Air, 2004, 2nd edn 2008; Policies and Perceptions of Insurance in the Twenty-First Century, 2005; (ed and contrib.) Principles of European Insurance Contract Law, 2009, 2nd edn 2015; (jtly) Palmer on Bailment, 3rd edn 2009; (jtly) Insurance: the laws of Australia, 2009; (jtly) Contractual Duties: performance, breach, termination and remedies, 2011. *Recreations:* cycling, music, photography, walking. *Address:* St John's College, Cambridge CB2 1TP. *T:* (01223) 338600, *Fax:* (01223) 337720.

CLARKE, Mark Galbraith, FCA; Director General, Finance and Strategy, Department for Business, Enterprise and Regulatory Reform (formerly Department of Trade and Industry), 2006–08; *b* 19 June 1953; *s* of Sir Richard William Barnes Clarke, KCB, OBE and Brenda Clarke; *m* 1982, Dr Alexandra Macleod; one *s* two *d*. *Educ:* Jesus Coll., Oxford (MA PPE). Arthur Andersen & Co., 1975–82; TSB Gp plc, 1982–89; Coopers & Lybrand, then PricewaterhouseCoopers, mgt consultants, 1989–2000; Barclays plc, 2000–03; Abbey National plc, 2003–05; Bank of Ireland, 2005–06. Non-executive Director: British Chambers of Commerce, 2010– (Chm., Audit and Risk Cttee, 2011–); Kent Reliance Provident Soc., 2011–13 (Chm., Audit and Risk Cttee, 2011–13); One Housing Gp, 2013–14 (Chm., Audit and Controls Cttee, 2013–14). Member: Exchequer Funds Audit Cttee, HM Treasury, 2007–10; Members Estimate Audit Cttee and Admin Estimate Audit Cttee, H of C, 2009–13; Finance Cttee, 2009–14, Investment Cttee, 2009–14, Enterprise Ext. Adv. Bd, 2011–, UCL; Risk and Audit Cttee, Jesus Coll., Oxford, 2012–. Gov., Highgate Sch., 2007–.

CLARKE, Martin Gerald, FIA; Government Actuary, since 2014; *b* Urmston, 17 March 1956; *s* of Rev. Roland Clarke and Eva Mary Clarke; two *s* one *d*; *m* 2015, Julia Clare Heaton. *Educ:* Canon Slade Grammar Sch., Bolton; Jesus Coll., Cambridge (BA Maths 1977); Harvard Business Sch. (Gen. Manager Prog. 2003). FIA 1982. Co-operative Insurance Society: Actuary, 1980–85; Mktg Manager, 1985–97; Mktg Dir, 1997–2002; Life & Savings Dir, Co-operative Financial Services, 2002–06; Exec. Dir, Pension Protection Fund, 2006–14. Chm., UK Sustainable Investment and Finance Assoc., 2010–14. Trustee, Lankelly Chase Foundn, 2013–. Mem., Actuaries' Co., 2014. *Publications:* contrib. papers to professional actuarial bodies. *Recreations:* music, art, sport. *Address:* Government Actuary's Department, Finlaison House, 15–17 Furnival Street, EC4A 1AB. *T:* (020) 7211 2620. *E:* martin.clarke@gad.gov.uk. *Club:* Actuaries.

CLARKE, Martin Peter; Publisher and Editor, MailOnline, since 2008; *b* 26 Aug. 1964; *s* of Robert William Clarke and Doris May (*née* Snowden); *m* 1998, Veronica (*née* Gilfedder); one *s*. *Educ:* Gravesend Grammar Sch. for Boys; Bristol Univ. (BA Hons). Daily Mail Executive, 1988–94; News Ed., Daily Mirror, 1995; Editor: Scottish Daily Mail, 1995–97; The Scotsman, 1997–98; Editor-in-Chief: Daily Record and Sunday Mail Ltd, 1998–2000; Ireland on Sunday, 2001–04; Exec. Ed., Mail on Sunday, 2004–05; Associate Ed., The Daily Mail, 2005–08. *Address:* The Daily Mail, Northcliffe House, 2 Derry Street, W8 5TS. *T:* (020) 7938 6000.

CLARKE, Matthew Gerard; *see* Clarke, Rt Hon. Lord.

CLARKE, Michael; *see* Clarke, C. M.

CLARKE, Prof. Michael, CBE 2003; FRCP, FRCPE, FFPH, FMedSci; Professor of Epidemiology, University of Leicester, 1981–2002; Hon. Consultant, Leicestershire Health, 1974–2002; *b* 2 Nov. 1940; *s* of late Leslie Frederick Clarke and Gertrude Mary Clarke (*née* Dring); *m* 1966, Susan Jenkins Thompson (marr. diss. 1994); one *s* one *d*. *Educ:* Middlesex Hosp. Med. Sch., Univ. of London (MB BS 1965). MRCS, LRCP 1965; DPH 1968; MFPHM 1974, FFPH (FFPHM 1979); FRCP 1991; FRCPE 1996. Lectr, St Thomas' Hosp., London, 1968–74; Vis. Scientist, R&D, Nat. Centre for Health Services, 1972–73; Sen. Lectr, Dept of Community Health, Univ. of Leicester, 1974–80. Dir, Trent Inst. for Health Services Res., 1993–2002. Member: MRC Public Health & Health Services Res. Bd, 1990–94; Chair, Strategic Review of the NHS R&D Levy, 1998–2000. Vice Pres., FPHM, 1995–2000. FMedSci 2002. *Publications:* articles on epidemiology and health services res., particularly in relation to reproduction, care of the elderly and urinary incontinence. *Recreations:* cooking, interior design. *Address:* The Stables, Coombs Yard, Welland Rise, Sibbertoft, Northants LE16 9UP.

CLARKE, Prof. Michael; Director General (formerly Director), Royal United Services Institute, since 2007; *b* Wallasey, Cheshire, 29 July 1950; *s* of Leonard George Clarke and Evelyn Clarke (*née* Stanley); *m* 1977, Janet Reynolds. *Educ:* Cardinal Wiseman Secondary Modern Sch.; Churchfields Comprehensive Sch.; University Coll. of Wales, Aberystwyth (BSc (Econ) 1971; MSc (Econ) 1973; Fellow 2012). Lecturer: Dept of Govt, Univ. of Manchester, 1975–79; Dept of Politics, Univ. of Newcastle upon Tyne, 1979–90; King's College London: Dir, Centre for Defence Studies, 1990–2001; Prof. of Defence Studies, 1995–2007; Dir, Internat. Policy Inst., 2001–05; Dir of Res. Develt and Dep. Vice-Principal, 2005–07; Vis. Prof. of Defence Studies, 2007–. FKC 2015. Hon. Prof., Univ. of Exeter, 2012. MInstD 2000. *Publications:* British External Policy-making in the 1990s, 1992; Global Development and Human Security, 2007; contrib. articles to Internat. Affairs, RUSI Jl, Conflict, Security and Develt. *Recreations:* running very slowly, theatre, cricket, sailing. *Address:* Royal United Services Institute, 61 Whitehall, SW1A 2ET. *T:* (020) 7747 2601. *E:* michael.clarke@rusi.org. *Club:* Reform.

CLARKE, Canon Prof. Michael Gilbert, CBE 2000; DL; Professor, School of Public Policy, 1993–2008, now Emeritus, Pro-Vice-Chancellor, 1998–2003, and Vice-Principal, 2003–08, University of Birmingham; *b* 21 May 1944; *s* of Rev. Canon Reginald Gilbert Clarke and Marjorie Kathleen Clarke; *m* 1967, Angela Mary Cook; one *s* two *d*. *Educ:* Queen Elizabeth Grammar Sch., Wakefield; Sussex Univ. (BA 1966; MA 1967). Teaching Assistant, Essex Univ., 1967–69; Lectr and Dir of Studies in Politics, Edinburgh Univ., 1969–75; Asst Dir and Depute Dir, Policy Planning, Lothian Regl Council, 1975–81; Dir, LGTB, 1981–90; Chief Exec., Local Govt Mgt Bd, 1990–93; Head, Sch. of Public Policy, Univ. of Birmingham, 1993–98. Chm., Birmingham Royal Ballet, 2009–. Trustee: Worcs Community Foundn, 2004–; Elgar Foundn, 2008–; Barber Inst., 2008–; Three Choirs Fest., 2014–; Hult Internat. Business Sch., 2015–; Pres., Herefordshire and Worcs Community First, 2005–; Governor: King's Sch., Worcester, 2006–; Univ. of Worcester, 2007; Chm., Univ. of Birmingham Sch., 2012–15. Fellow, Ashridge Coll., 2015–. Mem., Gen. Synod of C of E, 1990–93, 1995–; Dioceses Commission, 2008– (Chm., 2010–); Lay Canon and Mem. Chapter, 2001–10, Canon Emeritus, 2010, Worcester Cathedral. DL Worcs, 2000. Hon. MA Worcester, 2000; Hon. DLitt Aston, 2009; DUniv Birmingham, 2014. *Publications:* Getting the Balance Right, 1990; Choices for Local Government: the 1990s and beyond, 1991; How Others See Us, 1995; Breaking Down the Barriers, 1995; Renewing Public Management, 1996; articles on UK public policy and management issues esp. local govt and central-local relns. *Recreations:* music, reading, grandchildren, gardening. *Address:* Millington House, 15 Lansdowne Crescent, Worcester WR3 8JE. *T:* (01905) 617634. *Club:* Reform.

CLARKE, Maj.-Gen. Michael Hugo Friend; Immigration Appeals Adjudicator, 1993–2004; *b* 22 Sept. 1936; *s* of Patrick Joseph Clarke and Catherine Amy Clarke (*née* Friend); *m* 1962, Gerritje van der Horst; one *s* one *d*. *Educ:* Rutland House Sch.; Allhallows Sch. Called to the Bar, Lincoln's Inn, 1959; enlisted RASC, 1959; commissioned 2nd Lieut RASC, 1960; Captain, Army Legal Services, 1961; served BAOR, Singapore, Nairobi, Hong Kong, Cyprus, N Ireland; HQ Army Legal Aid, 1981; MoD, 1983; Army Legal Aid, BAOR, 1986; Army Legal Group UK, 1987; Brig., Legal HQ BAOR, 1989; Dir, Army Legal Services, 1992–94. Trustee, Inst. of Obs and Gyn., 1995–2003. *Recreations:* gardening, walking, sport.

CLARKE, Michael John, PhD; Chief Executive, Royal Society for the Protection of Birds, since 2010; *b* Dartford, Kent, 2 Jan. 1960; *s* of George Fredrick Albert Clarke and Barbara Patricia Clarke; *m* 1982, Naomi Joan; two *d*. *Educ:* Gravesend Grammar Sch.; Hertford Coll., Oxford (BA Zoology 1981; MA); Southampton Univ. (PhD 1988). Nature Conservancy Council, 1981–88; Royal Society for the Protection of Birds: Conservation Manager, 1988–91, Regl Dir, 1991–98, SE England; Ops Dir, 1998–2010. Member: England Forestry Forum, 2001–06; Ind. Forestry Panel, 2011–12. Mem. Council, Southampton Univ., 1996–99; Dir, N Beds Schs Trust, 2009–10. FRSA. *Publications:* papers on envmtl sci. *Recreations:* birds and wildlife, archaeology, slow food. *Address:* Royal Society for the Protection of Birds, The Lodge, Sandy, Beds SG19 2DL. *T:* (01767) 693258, *Fax:* (01767) 685001. *E:* mike.clarke@rspb.org.uk.

CLARKE, Nicholas Stephen; QC 2006; a Recorder, since 2000; *b* Rochdale, 30 Dec. 1959; *s* of Thomas Clarke and Marjorie Clarke; *m* Barbara Louise. *Educ:* Sheffield Univ. (LLB Hons 1980). Called to the Bar, Middle Temple, 1981; Asst Recorder, 1999–2000. *Recreations:* walking three dogs, growing orchids, playing golf and snooker, Manchester United season ticket holder. *Address:* 9 St John Street, Manchester M3 4DN. *T:* (0161) 955 9000, *Fax:* (0161) 955 9001. *E:* clerks@9stjohnstreet.co.uk.

CLARKE, Nicky, OBE 2007; hair stylist; Co-Founder and Co-Director, Nicky Clarke Salon, Mayfair, and Nicky Clarke Haircare Products; *b* 17 June 1958; *m* 1982, Lesley Anne Gale; one *s* one *d*. Director: Southern Tropics Ltd; Nicky Clarke Products Ltd. Has made numerous TV appearances as expert and spokesperson on matters related to hair. Numerous awards, including: British Hairdresser of Year Award; London Hairdresser of Year Award. *Publications:* Hair Power, 1999; contribs to newspapers and magazines, incl. Vogue, Tatler, Marie Claire and Harpers Bazaar. *Recreations:* ski-ing, water ski-ing, contemporary music. *Address:* 11 Carlos Place, W1K 3AX.

CLARKE, Sir Paul (Robert Virgo), KCVO 2013 (CVO 2009); FRICS; Chief Executive, Clerk of the Council, Keeper of the Records and Surveyor General, Duchy of Lancaster, 2000–13; independent mentor, since 2013; *b* 13 Aug. 1953; *s* of Robert Charles Houghton Clarke and Joan Clarke (*née* Stanton); *m* 1978, Vanessa Carol Pike; two *d*. *Educ:* Abingdon Sch.; W London Coll. FRICS 1988. Valuation Surveyor and Tech. Asst to Exec. Trustee, Grosvenor Estate, 1974–82; Equity Partner, Clarke & Green, Chartered Surveyors, 1982–96; Property Investment Manager, Wellcome Trust, 1996–2000. Property Adv. Mem., Greenwich Hosp. Adv. Panel, 2002–12; Chm., Adv. Panel, CBRE Global Investors (formerly ING) UK Property Income Fund, 2006–14; Vice-Chm., Northbank BID, 2012–13; non-executive Director: Berkshire Investment Capital, 2013–; Rural Estates Bd, Grosvenor Estate, 2014–; Ind. Mem., Knight Frank Investment Mgt Investment Cttee, 2014–. Member: Estates Cttee, Oxford Univ. Endowment Mgt, 2013–. Trustee: Duke of Lancaster Housing Trust, 2008–14; Addington Fund, 2013–; Ind. Trustee, 69 Brook Street Trust, 2014–. Pres., Assoc. of Lancastrians in London, 2014–. *Recreations:* walking, ski-ing, drawing/painting, travel. *E:* prvclarke@gmail.com.

CLARKE, Prof. Peter Frederick, LittD; FBA 1989; Master of Trinity Hall, Cambridge, 2000–04 (Hon. Fellow, 2005); Professor of Modern British History, Cambridge University, 1991–2004; *b* 21 July 1942; *s* of late John William Clarke and Winifred Clarke (*née* Hadfield); *m* 1st, 1969, Dillon Cheetham (marr. diss. 1990); two *d*; 2nd, 1991, Dr Maria Tippett, FRS(Can), British Columbia. *Educ:* Eastbourne Grammar Sch.; St John's Coll., Cambridge (BA 1963; MA 1967; PhD 1967; LittD 1989). FRHistS 1972. Asst Lectr and Lectr in History, 1966–78, Reader in Modern Hist., 1978–80, UCL; Cambridge University: Fellow, St John's Coll., 1980–2000 (Tutor, 1982–87); Lectr in History, 1980–87; Reader in Modern History, 1987–91; Sec., Faculty Bd of Hist., 1985–86. Vis. Prof. of Modern British Hist., Harvard Univ., 1974; Vis. Fellow, Res. Sch. of Social Scis, ANU, 1983; Heath Dist. Vis. Prof., Grinnell Coll., Iowa, 1995; Dir's Visitor, Inst. for Advanced Study, Princeton, 2009. Lectures: Creighton, London Univ., 1998; Ford's, Univ. of Oxford, 2002; Del Grauer Meml, Vancouver Inst., 2008; Frank Turner Meml, Univ. of Texas at Austin, 2011; Kemper, Westminster Coll., Fulton, 2013. Member: Council, RHistS, 1979–83; Adv. Council on Public Records, 1995–2000; Royal Commn on Historical MSS, 2000–03; Adv. Council on Nat. Records and Archives, 2003–05. Chm., S Cambs Area Party, SDP, 1981–82. Jt Review Ed., History, 1967–73; Chm., Editl Bd, Twentieth Century British History, 1988–98. *Publications:* Lancashire and the New Liberalism, 1971, 2nd edn 1993; Liberals and Social Democrats, 1978, 3rd edn 1993; The Keynesian Revolution in the Making, 1988, 2nd edn 1990; A Question of Leadership: from Gladstone to Thatcher, 1991, 2nd edn 1992, new edn, from Gladstone to Blair, 1999; Hope and Glory: Britain 1900–1990, 1996, 2nd edn as Hope and Glory: Britain 1900–2000, 2004; The Keynesian Revolution and its Economic Consequences, 1998; The Cripps Version: the life of Sir Stafford Cripps, 2002; The Last Thousand Days of the British Empire, 2007; Keynes: the twentieth century's most influential economist, 2009; Mr Churchill's Profession: statesman, orator, writer, 2012; articles in learned jls; contribs to TLS, London Rev. of Books, FT, etc. *Recreations:* walking, cooking. *Address:* 3 The Light Building, Brooklands Avenue, Cambridge CB2 8DG; 9919 Gowlland Point Road, Pender Island, BC V0N 2M3, Canada. *Clubs:* Oxford and Cambridge; Union (Victoria, BC).

CLARKE, Peter Henry, FRICS; Member of the Lands Tribunal, part time, 1993–96, full time, 1996–2005; *b* 22 Sept. 1935; *s* of late Henry George Clarke and Winifred Eva Clarke (*née* Sharp); *m* 1964, May Connell; one *d*. *Educ:* Ealing Technical Coll.; Coll. of Estate Management; LLB 1972, MPhil 1993, London. ARICS 1957, FRICS 1973; ACIArb 1976. With G. L. Hearn & Partners, 1952–57, 1959–60; Cubitt Estates, 1960–64; Eldonwall Ltd, 1964–69; Donaldsons, 1969–96 (Partner, 1972–96). *Publications:* (jtly) Land Values, 1965; (jtly) Valuation: Principles into Practice, 1980, 5th edn 2000; The Surveyor in Court, 1985; articles on compensation and rent reviews in various jls. *Recreations:* music, opera, reading, walking, dogs. *Address:* 65 Brittains Lane, Sevenoaks, Kent TN13 2JS. *T:* (01732) 456437.

CLARKE, Peter John Michael, CVO 2001; OBE 2006; QPM 2002; Deputy Assistant Commissioner, Head of Anti-Terrorist Branch and National Co-ordinator of Terrorist Investigations, Metropolitan Police, 2002–08; *b* Epsom, Surrey, 27 July 1955; *s* of Ernest John

Wallace Clarke and Doris Louisa Emma Clarke (*née* Wakeham); *m* 1983, Deborah Ann Bazalgette; two *s* one *d*. *Educ:* Glyn Grammar Sch., Epsom; Univ. of Bristol (LLB Hons 1977); Cabinet Office Top Mgt Prog., 1998. Joined Metropolitan Police, 1977; Inspector, 1984–89; Chief Inspector, 1989–92; Superintendent, 1992–94; Staff Officer to Comr, 1993–94; Divl Comdr, Brixton Div., 1994–96; Comdr, Royalty and Diplomatic Protection Dept, 1997–2000; Dep. Asst Comr, HR, 2001; rcds 2002. Non-executive Director: Knightsbridge Guarding Ltd, 2008–; SOCA, 2009–13; Senior Adviser: Olive Gp, 2008–12; Kellogg, Brown and Root, 2011–. Member: Bd of Trustees, Crimestoppers, 2008–; Nat. Security Forum, 2009–10; Bd, Charity Commn, 2013–. Terrorism and Security Consultant, CBS News, 2008–. Educn Comr, Birmingham, 2014 (Report into allegations concerning Birmingham schs arising from Trojan Horse letter). Fellow, Center for Law and Security, NY Univ., 2008–12; Vis. Prof., Cranfield Univ., 2010–12. Patron, Internat. Centre for the Study of Radicalisation, KCL, 2011–. Pres., Metropolitan and City Police Relief Bd, 1997–2008. Chm., Metropolitan Police Cricket Club, 2002–08. Hon. LLD Bristol, 2008. *Publications:* (contrib.) Investigating Terrorism: current political, legal and psychological issues, 2015. *Recreations:* watching cricket, walking, cycling. *E:* peterjmclarke@aol.com. *Clubs:* Special Forces, MCC.

CLARKE, Peter William; QC 1997; **His Honour Peter William Clarke;** a Circuit Judge, since 2009; *b* 29 May 1950; *s* of His Honour Edward Clarke, QC, and Dorothy May Clarke (*née* Leask); *m* 1978, Victoria Mary, *d* of Michael Francis Gilbert, CBE, TD; one *s* one *d*. *Educ:* Sherborne Sch.; Inns of Court Sch. of Law. Called to the Bar, Lincoln's Inn, 1973, Bencher, 2003; in practice at the Bar, specialising in criminal law, 1974–; Asst Recorder, 1987–91; Recorder, 1991–2009. *Recreations:* losing at tennis to my children, ski-ing, golf, digital photography, enjoying my wife's paintings. *Address:* Blackfriars Crown Court, 1–15 Pocock Street, SE1 0BJ. *Club:* Garrick.

CLARKE, Philip Brian; Head of Comedy, Channel 4, since 2013; *b* Watford, 14 May 1961; *s* of Brian and Hazel Clarke; *m* 1992, Isabel Katharine Lloyd; two *s*. *Educ:* Rickmansworth Sch.; Univ. of Manchester (BA Hons Combined Studies (Mil. and American)). Sub Ed., Hammerville Publishers, 1984; Press Officer, Nat. Army Mus., 1985–86; stand-up comedian, 1986–90; Producer, Light Entertainment, BBC Radio, 1990–97; TV Producer, Absolutely Prodns, 1997–98; TV Producer, 1999–2001, Editor, Comedy, 2001–03, Talkback Prodns; Hd of Comedy, Objective Prodns, 2003–13. Non-exec. Dir, Improbable Th. Co., 2013–. *Recreations:* kickboxing, gardening. *Address:* c/o Channel 4, 124 Horseferry Road, SW1P 2TX. *E:* pclarke@channel4.co.uk. *Club:* Chiswick House.

CLARKE, Rachel Emma; *see* Cusk, R. E.

CLARKE, Rebecca Astley, (Bec Astley Clarke), MBE 2013; Founder and Chairman, Astley Clarke, since 2006; *b* Islington, 3 Feb. 1973; *d* of Dr Charles Clarke and late Dr Ruth Seifert; *m* 2009, Chris Pearson; one *s* one *d*. *Educ:* City of London Sch. for Girls; Edinburgh Univ. (MA Hons Politics and Philosophy). Andersen Consulting, 1996–99; Commercial Dir, iVillage.co.uk, 2000–03; Hd, Non-Retail Strategy, Tesco.com, 2003–05. *Recreations:* cooking, running, Seinfeld. *E:* bec@astleyclarke.com.

CLARKE, Richard Ian; HM Diplomatic Service, retired; Director, Child Soldiers International, since 2012; *b* 7 Sept. 1955; *s* of Sydney Thomas Reginald Clarke and Joan Clarke; *m* 1st, 1978, Anne Elizabeth Menzies (marr. diss. 1993); one *s*; 2nd, 1993, Sheenagh Marie O'Connor; two *s* one *d*. *Educ:* Market Harborough Upper Sch.; Univ. of E Anglia (BSc). Joined FCO, 1977: 3rd, later 2nd, Sec., Caracas, 1978–83; 2nd, later 1st, Sec., FCO, 1983–87; 1st Sec., Washington, 1987–91; Asst Hd, Planning Staff, FCO, 1991–93; Dep. Hd, UN Dept, FCO, 1993–96; Counsellor and Dep. Hd of Mission, Dublin, 1996–98; Hd, Policy Planning Staff, FCO, 1998–2001; High Comr, Tanzania, 2001–03. Mem., Audit Commn, 2004–11. Ian St James Award for short fiction, 1991. *Publications:* (contrib.) Midnight Oil, 1991. *Recreations:* Leicester City, reading, Wars of the Roses, American Civil War, cheese straws, Glam and Punk and R and B, early 20th century art, ethnographic art.

CLARKE, Most Rev. Richard Lionel; *see* Armagh, Archbishop of, and Primate of All Ireland.

CLARKE, Sir Robert (Cyril), Kt 1993; Chairman, Thames Water Plc, 1994–99 (non-executive Director, since 1988); *b* 28 March 1929; *s* of Robert Henry Clarke and Rose Lilian (*née* Bratton); *m* 1952, Evelyn (Lynne) Mary, *d* of Cyrus Harper and Ann Ellen (*née* Jones); three *s* (incl. twin *s*) one *d*. *Educ:* Dulwich Coll.; Pembroke Coll., Oxford (MA Hist.; Hon. Fellow, 1993). Served Royal West Kent Regt, 1947–49. Joined Cadbury Bros, as trainee, 1952; Gen. Manager, John Forrest, 1954; Marketing Dir, Cadbury Confectionery, 1957; Man. Dir, 1962–69, Chm., 1969–71, Cadbury Cakes; Dir, Cadbury Schweppes Foods, 1969–71; Man. Dir, McVitie & Cadbury Cakes, 1971–74; Dir, 1974–95, Chm. and Man. Dir, 1984–95, United Biscuits UK Ltd; Man. Dir, UB Biscuits, 1977–84; Dir, 1984–95, Gp Chief Exec., 1986–90, Chm., 1990–95, United Biscuits (Holdings). Member: Council, Cake and Biscuit Alliance, 1965–83; Council, ISBA, 1977–84; Resources Cttee, Food and Drink Fedn, 1984–86; Bd of Dirs, Grocery Manufrs of America, 1991–95. Gov., World Economic Forum, 1990–. Special Trustee, Gt Ormond St Hosp. for Children NHS Trust, 1991–99 (Chm., Special Trustees, 1994–99; non-exec. Mem., Trust Bd, 1994–99). Fellow, Dulwich Coll., 2003. Hon. Fellow, Inst. of Child Health, 1997. FIGD; CCMI. *Recreations:* reading, walking, renovating old buildings, planting trees.

CLARKE, Rev. Robert Sydney, OBE 2000; Secretary and Director of Training, Hospital Chaplaincies Council, 1994–2000; Chaplain to HM the Queen, 1987–2005; *b* 31 Oct. 1935; *s* of George Sydney and Elizabeth Clarke. *Educ:* St Dunstan's College; King's Coll., Univ. of London (AKC 1964; MA 1965). Chaplain: New Cross Hospital, Wolverhampton, 1970–74; Herrison and West Dorset County Hosp., Dorchester, 1974–79; Westminster Hosp. and Westminster Medical School, Univ. of London, 1979–85; Winchester HA, 1985–94. Sen. Hon. Chaplain, Winchester and Eastleigh NHS Trust, 1994–2000. *Recreations:* breeding and showing dogs, music, travel, DIY. *Address:* c/o 3 Brook Court, Middlebridge Street, Romsey, Hants SO51 8HR. *E:* robertsclarke@tiscali.co.uk. *Club:* Kennel.

CLARKE, Roger Eric; literary translator and editor; Director of Shipping and Ports, Department of the Environment, Transport and the Regions, 1997–99; *b* 13 June 1939; *s* of late Frederick Cuérel Clarke and Hilda Josephine Clarke; *m* 1983, Elizabeth Jane, *d* of late Gordon W. Pingstone and Anne Ellen Pingstone; one *d*. *Educ:* UCS, Hampstead; Corpus Christi Coll., Cambridge (MA). Various posts in Min. of Aviation, BoT and Depts of Trade and Transport, 1961–72 and 1974–85; Air Traffic Rights Advr to Govt of Fiji, 1972–74; Under Sec., Civil Aviation Policy Directorate, 1985–89, Public Transport Directorate, 1989–91, Shipping Policy Directorate, 1991–97, Dept of Transport. Reader, Rochester Dio., C of E, 1976–. *Publications:* The Trawler Gaul: why was no search made for the wreck?, 2000; The Trawler Gaul: the search for bodies of the crew in northern Russia, 2000; (trans.) M. Benoît, Prisoner of God, 2008; (ed) Pushkin: The Queen of Spades and other stories, 2011; Pushkin, The Captain's Daughter and History of Pugachov, 2012; (translations with commentaries): Pushkin, Eugene Onegin, 1999, new trans. and commentary 2011; Pushkin, Boris Godunov, 1999; Pushkin, Ruslan and Lyudmila, 2005, new edn 2009; Pushkin, Eugene Onegin and other works, 2005; Erasmus, Praise of Folly and Pope Julius Barred from Heaven, 2008; Pushkin, Boris Godunov and Little Tragedies, 2010; Pushkin, Love Poems, 2013, new edn 2014; Pushkin, Belkin's Stories and A History of Goryukhino Village, 2014. *Recreations:* family, friends, church, philately, garden, theatre, music, languages, travel. *Address:* 64 Scotts Lane, Shortlands, Bromley, Kent BR2 0LX. *Club:* Reform.

CLARKE, Roger Howard, CBE 2005; PhD; Director, National Radiological Protection Board, 1987–2003; *b* 22 Aug. 1943; *s* of late Harold Pardoe and Laurie Gwyneth Clarke; *m* 1966, Sandra Ann (*née* Buckley); one *s* one *d*. *Educ:* King Edward VI Sch., Stourbridge; Univ. of Birmingham (BSc, MSc); Polytechnic of Central London (PhD). Res. Officer, Berkeley Nuclear Laboratories, CEGB, 1965–77; Hd of Nuclear Power Assessments, NRPB, 1978–83; Bd Sec., 1983–87. Deleg. to UN Sci. Cttee on the Effects of Atomic Radiation, 1979–2004; Chairman: OECD Nuclear Energy Agency Cttee on Radiation Protection and Public Health, 1987–92; Internat. Commn on Radiol Protection, 1993–2005 (Mem., 1989–93; Emeritus Mem., 2005); Mem., Gp of Experts, Article 31, Euratom, 1988–2004. Visiting Professor: Imperial Coll. of Science, Technol. and Medicine, 1993–2002; Univ. of Surrey, 1994–. Lindell Lectr, Swedish Risk Kollegiat, 1999. Hon. FRCR 1994; Hon. FSRP 1995; Hon. FINucE 2002. DUniv Surrey, 2004. G. William Morgan Award, US Health Physics Soc., 1994; Ellison-Cliffe Medal, RSocMed, 1996; Hanns Langendorff Medal, Voreinigung deutscher Strahlenschutzärtze, 2002; Medal, French Nat. Assembly, 2005. *Publications:* Carcinogenesis and Radiation Risk (with W. V. Mayneord), 1975; Evolution of ICRP Recommendations 1977, 1990 and 2007, 2011; numerous papers in sci. and technical literature. *Recreations:* gardening, theatre, travel. *Address:* Corner Cottage, Woolton Hill, Newbury, Berks RG20 9XJ. *T:* (01635) 253957.

CLARKE, Roy, OBE 2002; writer, since 1965; *b* 28 Jan. 1930; *s* of Austin and Alice Clarke; *m* 1953, Enid Kitching; one *s* one *d*. *Educ:* badly during World War II. Soldier, salesman, policeman and teacher until I was able to persuade people I was actually a writer. *Television series:* The Misfit, 1970–72; Last of the Summer Wine, 1972–2010 (31 series); Open All Hours, 1975–82; Potter, 1979–83; Pulaski, 1987; Single Voices, 1990; The World of Eddie Weary, 1990; Keeping Up Appearances, 1990–96; Ain't Misbehaving, 1994; Still Open All Hours, 2013, 2014; *films:* Hawks, 1988; A Foreign Field, 1993; *stage:* Mr Wesley, Lincoln Cathedral, Southwell Minster etc, 2003. Freeman of Doncaster, 1994. Hon. DLitt: Bradford, 1988; Huddersfield, 1997; DUniv Sheffield Hallam, 2001. Best Series Award, Writers' Guild, 1970; Pye TV Award, 1982, Denis Potter Award, 1996, BAFTA; Lifetime Achievement Award, British Comedy Awards, 2010. *Publications:* Summer Wine Chronicles, 1986; The Moonbather, 1987; Summer Wine Country, 1995; (with J. Rice) Hyacinth Bucket's Hectic Social Calendar, 1995. *Recreations:* walking, reading, hiding. *Address:* c/o The Agency, 24 Pottery Lane, Holland Park, W11 4LZ. *T:* (020) 7727 1346.

CLARKE, Sir Rupert (Grant Alexander), 4th Bt *cr* 1882, of Rupertswood, Colony of Victoria; *b* 12 Dec. 1947; *s* of Major Sir Rupert Clarke, 3rd Bt, AM, MBE and Kathleen Clarke (*née* Hay); *S* father, 2005; *m* 1978, Susannah, *d* of Sir Robert Law-Smith, CBE, AFC; one *s* two *d*. *Educ:* Melbourne Univ. (LLB). *Heir:* *s* Rupert Robert William Clarke, *b* 24 June 1981. *Address:* Bolinda Vale, Clarkefield, Vic 3430, Australia.

CLARKE, (Samuel) Laurence (Harrison), CBE 1988; CEng, FIET; Assistant Technical Director, GEC plc, 1981–91; Director: Sira Ltd, 1989–95; Filtronic Ltd, 1989–93; *b* 16 Dec. 1929; *s* of late Samuel Harrison Clarke, CBE; *m* 1952, Ruth Joan Godwin, *yr d* of Oscar Godwin, OBE and Muriel Godwin; one *s* three *d*. *Educ:* Westminster Sch.; Trinity Coll., Cambridge (BA). Technical Dir, GEC-Elliott Automation Ltd, 1970–74; Technical Dir (Automation), GEC-Marconi Electronics Ltd, 1974–81; Director, GEC Computers Ltd, 1971–83. Dep. Dir, 1983–87, Dir, 1987, Alvey Programme, DTI. *Publications:* various papers in learned and technical jls. *Recreations:* tapestry, church kneeler and grave recording, family history. *Address:* Sarum End, Salisbury Road, Southwold, Suffolk IP18 6LG. *T:* (01502) 725116.

CLARKE, Mrs Stella Rosemary, CBE 1997; JP; Chairman, Community Self Build Agency, since 1989; Vice Lord-Lieutenant, County of Bristol, 2004–07; *b* 16 Feb. 1932; *d* of John Herbert and Molly Isabel Bruce King; *m* 1952, Charles Nigel Clarke; four *s* one *d*. *Educ:* Cheltenham Ladies' Coll.; Trinity Coll. Dublin. Long Ashton RDC: Councillor, Chm. Council, Housing and Public Health Cttees, 1955–73; Mem., Woodspring Dist Council, 1973–76; co-opted Mem., Somerset CC, Social Services and Children's Cttee, 1957–73. A Governor, BBC, 1974–81. Purchased and restored Theatre Royal, Bath, with husband, 1974–76. Dir, Fosters Rooms Ltd, 1975–96. Member: Housing Corp., 1988–95; Bristol Develt Corp., 1989–96; Lord Chancellor's Lay Interviewers Panel for Judges, 1994–2001; Nat. Lottery Charities Bd, 1995–99 (Chm., England Cttee, 1997–99). Member, Board: Knightstone Housing Assoc., 1976–2000 (Chm., 1997–2000); At-Bristol (formerly The Exploratory), 2000–09. Pro-Chancellor, Bristol Univ., 1997–2007 (Chm. Council, 1987–97; Hon. Fellow, 2008). JP Bristol, 1968 (Chm., Bench, 1991–95); DL Bristol (formerly Avon), 1986. *Recreations:* family and the variety of life. *Address:* Gatcombe Court, Flax Bourton, Bristol BS48 3QT. *T:* (01275) 393141, *Fax:* (01275) 394274.

See also C. G. Clarke.

CLARKE, His Honour Stephen Patrick; a Circuit Judge, 1995–2013; *b* 23 March 1948; *s* of Leslie Clarke and Anne Mary Clarke; *m* 1974, Margaret Roberta Millar; two *s*. *Educ:* Rostrevor Coll., Adelaide, SA; Univ. of Hull (LLB Hons). Called to the Bar, Inner Temple, 1971; practised as barrister on Wales and Chester Circuit, 1971–95; Circuit Junior, 1988–89; Asst Recorder, 1988–92; Recorder, 1992–95; Liaison Judge: N Powys Magistrates, 2000–07; Chester and Ellesmere Port Magistrates, and Vale Royal Magistrates, 2007–11. Asst Parly Boundary Comr for Wales, 1994–95. Member: Probation Bd, Cheshire, 2001–11; HM Council of Circuit Judges, 2005–09. *Recreations:* rambling, watching cricket, theatre.

CLARKE, Rt Hon. Thomas, CBE 1980; PC 1997; JP; *b* 10 Jan. 1941; *s* of James Clarke and Mary (*née* Gordon). *Educ:* All Saints Primary Sch., Airdrie; Columba High Sch., Coatbridge; Scottish College of Commerce. Started working life as office boy with Glasgow Accountants' firm; Asst Director, Scottish Council for Educational Technology, before going to Parliament. Councillor: (former) Coatbridge Council, 1964; (reorganised) Monklands District Council, 1974; Provost of Monklands, 1975–77, 1977–80, 1980–82. Vice-President, Convention of Scottish Local Authorities, 1976–78, President, 1978–80. MP (Lab) Coatbridge and Airdrie, June 1982–1983, Monklands W, 1983–97, Coatbridge and Chryston, 1997–2005, Coatbridge, Chryston and Bellshill, 2005–15; contested (Lab) same seat, 2015. Opposition front bench spokesman on: Scottish Affairs, 1987; health and social security (personal social services), 1987–90; Scotland, 1992–93; overseas aid, 1993–94; disabled people's rights, 1994–97; Minister of State (Minister for Film and Tourism), Dept of Culture, Media and Sport, 1997–98. Chm., PLP Foreign Affairs Cttee, 1983–86. Author and main sponsor: Disabled Persons (Consultation, Representation and Services) Act, 1986; Internat. Develt (Reporting and Transparency) Act, 2006. Director, award winning amateur film, Give Us a Goal, 1972; former President, British Amateur Cinematographers' Central Council. JP County of Lanark, 1972. *Recreations:* films, reading, walking. *Address:* 37 Blair Road, Coatbridge, Lanarkshire ML5 1JQ. *T:* (01236) 600800.

CLARKE, Timothy; Chief Executive, Mitchells & Butlers plc, 2003–09; *b* 24 March 1957; *s* of David Clarke and Molly Clarke; *m* 1986, Fiona Haigh (*d* 2014); two *s*. *Educ:* Corpus Christi Coll., Oxford (BA 1978, MA). Panmure Gordon & Co., 1979–90; Bass plc, subseq. Six Continents plc, 1990–2003: Chief Exec., Bass Retail, 1995–2000; Chief Exec., 2000–03. Non-executive Director: Associated British Foods plc, 2004– (Sen. Ind. non-exec. Dir, 2007–); Hall & Woodhouse Ltd, 2010–; Timothy Taylor & Co. Ltd, 2010–; Triplepoint VCT 2011 plc, 2011–. Dir, British Beer and Pub Assoc., 1995–2007 (Chm., 2002). Trustee, Drinkaware Trust, 2007–09. Trustee Director: Birmingham Royal Ballet, 2006–14; Elgar Foundn, 2009–. Gov., Schs of King Edward VI in Birmingham Foundn, 2010– (Chm., Ind. Schs Governing Body, 2014–).

CLARKE, Sir Tobias; *see* Clarke, Sir C. M. T.

CLARKE, William Michael; *b* 13 Oct. 1966; *s* of Patrick and Margaret Clarke; *m* 2001, Paula Sloan; one *d*. *Educ:* St Malachy's High Sch., Castlewellan, Co. Down. Mem. (SF), Down DC, 2001– (Chm., 2006–07). Mem. (SF) S Down, NI Assembly, 2003–April 2012. *Recreations:* hill walking, reading, cycling. *Address:* 37 King Street, Newcastle, Co. Down BT33 0HD. *T:* (028) 4377 0185, *Fax:* (028) 4377 1826.

CLARKE-HACKSTON, Fiona; Chief Executive, British Screen Advisory Council, since 2010 (Secretary, 1987–90; Director, 1990–2010); *b* 30 April 1954; *d* of Donald Gordon Hackston and Muriel Lesley Hackston (*née* Glover); *m* 1984, Norman Malcolm Clarke; one *s* one *d*. *Educ:* UC of S Wales and Monmouthshire, Cardiff (BA Hons); Univ. of Southampton (MA 1977). Sec. to Marketing Dir, Grants of St James, 1978–79; Editor, and Head of Book Dept, Truman & Knightley, 1979–81; Personnel Advr, Ernst & Whinney, Middle East, 1981–84; Asst, Film, TV and Video, British Council, 1986. *Recreations:* film, walking, music, family. *Address:* 353 Wimbledon Park Road, SW19 6NS.

CLARKSON, Rt Hon. Adrienne; PC (Can.) 1999; CC 1999 (OC 1992); CMM; CD; co-founder and co-Chair, Institute for Canadian Citizenship, since 2005; Governor General of Canada, 1999–2005; *b* Hong Kong, 10 Feb. 1939; naturalised Canadian citizen; *m* John Ralston Saul, CC, writer. *Educ:* Univ. of Toronto (BA Hons English Lit.; MA 1961); Sorbonne, Univ. of Paris. Agent-Gen. for Ontario, Paris, 1982–87; Pres. and Publisher, McClelland & Stewart, 1987–88; Presenter, Writer and Producer: Take Thirty, Adrienne at Large, The Fifth Estate, CBC TV, 1965–82; Adrienne Clarkson's Summer Festival, 1988–98; Adrienne Clarkson Presents, 1988–98; Exec. Prod. and Presenter, Something Special. Chair, Bd of Trustees, Canadian Mus. of Civilization, Quebec, 1995–99; formerly Pres., Exec. Bd, IMZ, Vienna. Lay Bencher, Law Soc. of Upper Canada, 1999. CBC Massey Lectr, 2014. Sen. Fellow, Massey Coll., 1993. Hon. Fellow: Royal Conservatory of Music, Toronto, 1993; Univ. of Trinity Coll., Toronto, 1996. Hon. LLD: Dalhousie, 1991; Acadia, 1994; PEI, 1996; Victoria, 2000; Laval, 2002; York, Queen's, Western Ontario, Ottawa, Law Soc. of Upper Canada, 2003; Royal Roads, 2011; Hon. DCL Lakehead, 1992; Hon. DLitt: Manitoba, 2001; Bishop's, 2003; Thorneloe, 2011; Dr *hc* Siena, 2002. *Publications:* three novels; Heart Matters (memoirs), 2006; Norman Bethune (biog.), 2009; Room for All of Us, 2011; numerous articles in newspapers and jls.

CLARKSON, Ven. Alan Geoffrey; Archdeacon of Winchester, 1984–99, Archdeacon Emeritus, since 1999; *b* 14 Feb. 1934; *s* of Instructor Captain Geoffrey Archibald Clarkson, OBE, RN and Essie Isabel Bruce Clarkson; *m* 1959, Monica Ruth (*née* Lightburne); two *s* one *d*. *Educ:* Sherborne School; Christ's Coll., Cambridge (BA 1957, MA 1961); Wycliffe Hall, Oxford. Nat. Service Commn, RA, 1952–54. Curate: Penn, Wolverhampton, 1959–60; St Oswald's, Oswestry, 1960–63; Wrington with Redhill, 1963–65; Vicar, Chewton Mendip with Emborough, 1965–74; Vicar of St John Baptist, Glastonbury with Godney, 1974–84; Priest in Charge: West Pennard, 1981–84; Meare, 1981–84; St Benedict, Glastonbury, 1982–84; Vicar of Burley, Ringwood, 1984–99. Proctor in Convocation, 1970–75, 1990–95. Hon. Canon, Winchester Cathedral, 1984–99. *Recreations:* music, gardening, carpentry, wood-turning. *Address:* 4 Harefield Rise, Linton, Cambridge CB21 4LS. *T:* (01223) 892988. *E:* a.clarkson@talktalk.net.
See also P. J. Clarkson.

CLARKSON, Prof. Brian Leonard, DSc; FREng; Principal, University College of Swansea, 1982–94; Vice-Chancellor, University of Wales, 1987–89; *b* 28 July 1930; *s* of L. C. Clarkson; *m* 1953, Margaret Elaine Wilby; three *s* one *d*. *Educ:* Univ. of Leeds (BSc, PhD). FREng (FEng 1986); FRAeS; Hon. FIOA. George Taylor Gold Medal, RAeS, 1963. Dynamics Engineer, de Havilland Aircraft Co., Hatfield, Herts, 1953–57; Southampton University: Sir Alan Cobham Research Fellow, Dept of Aeronautics, 1957–58; Lectr, Dept of Aeronautics and Astronautics, 1958–66; Prof. of Vibration Studies, 1966–82; Dir, Inst. of Sound and Vibration Res., 1967–78; Dean, Faculty of Engrg and Applied Science, 1978–80; Deputy Vice-Chancellor, 1980–82. Sen. Post Doctoral Research Fellow, Nat. Academy of Sciences, USA, 1970–71 (one year's leave of absence from Southampton). Chm., ACU, 1992–93 (Vice-Chm., 1990–92). Sec., Internat. Commn on Acoustics, 1975–81. Pres., Fedn of Acoustical Socs of Europe, 1982–84. Member: SERC, 1984–88; CNAA, 1988–91. Hon. DSc: Leeds, 1984; Southampton, 1987; Universiti Sains Malaysia, 1990; Hon. LLD Wales, 1996. *Publications:* author of sections of three books: Technical Acoustics, vol. 3 (ed Richardson) 1959; Noise and Acoustic Fatigue in Aeronautics (ed Mead and Richards), 1967; Noise and Vibration (ed White and Walker), 1982; (ed) Stochastic Problems in Dynamics, 1977; technical papers on Jet Noise and its effect on Aircraft Structures, Jl of Royal Aeronautical Soc., etc. *Recreations:* walking, gardening, travelling, golf. *Address:* 17 Southgate Road, Southgate, Swansea SA3 2BT.

CLARKSON, His Honour Derek Joshua; QC 1969; a Circuit Judge, 1977–95; Middlesex Liaison Judge, 1985–95; *b* 10 Dec. 1929; *o s* of Albert and Winifred Charlotte Clarkson (*née* James); *m* 1960, Peternella Marie-Luise Ilse Canenbley; one *s* one *d*. *Educ:* Pudsey Grammar Sch.; King's Coll., Univ. of London. LLB (1st cl. Hons) 1950. Called to Bar, Inner Temple, 1951; Nat. Service, RAF, 1952–54 (Flt Lt). In practice as Barrister, 1954–77; Prosecuting Counsel to Post Office on North-Eastern Circuit, 1961–65; Prosecuting Counsel to Inland Revenue on North-Eastern Circuit, 1965–69; Recorder of Rotherham, 1967–71; Recorder of Huddersfield, 1971; a Recorder of the Crown Court, 1972–77. Mem., Gen. Council of the Bar, 1971–73. Inspector of companies for the Department of Trade, 1972–73, 1975–76. Pres., Middlesex Magistrates' Assoc., 1994–95. *Recreations:* theatre-going, talking, book collecting. *Address:* 2 Harlow Oval Court, Harlow Oval, Harrogate HG2 0DT.

CLARKSON, Prof. Geoffrey Peniston Elliott, PhD; Chairman, Circle L Ltd, since 1990; Professor of Business Administration, Trident (formerly Touro) University International, since 2003; *b* 30 May 1934; *s* of George Elliott Clarkson and Alice Helene (*née* Manneberg); *m* 1960, Eleanor M. (*née* Micenko); two *d*. *Educ:* Carnegie Mellon Univ., Pittsburgh, Pa (BSc, MSc, PhD). Asst Prof., Sloan Sch. of Management, MIT, 1961–65, Associate Prof., 1965–67, Vis. Prof., 1975–77. Vis. Ford Foundn Fellow, Carnegie-Mellon Univ., 1965–66; Vis. Prof., LSE, 1966–67; Nat. Westminster Bank Prof. of Business Finance, Manchester Business Sch., Univ. of Manchester, 1967–77; Prof. of Business Admin, 1977–89, and Dean, Coll. of Business Admin, 1977–79, Northeastern Univ., Boston. Dir of and consultant to public and private manufg and financial services cos, 1969–; Chairman: Polymerics Inc., 1983–89; Sealcorp Ltd, 1990–94. MInstD 1973. *Publications:* Portfolio Selection: a simulation of trust investment, USA 1962 (Ford Dissertation Prize, 1961); The Theory of Consumer Demand: a critical appraisal, USA 1963; Managerial Economics, 1968; (with B. J. Elliott) Managing Money and Finance, 1969, 3rd edn 1982; Jihad (novel), 1981; Day Trader (novel), 2000. *Recreations:* fishing, sailing, reading, USA.

CLARKSON, Gerald Dawson, CBE 1990; QFSM 1983; Chief Fire Officer and Chief Executive, London Fire and Civil Defence Authority, 1987–91, retired; Chairman, Dawson Usher International Ltd, 1994–2002; *b* 4 June 1939; *s* of Alexander Dickie Clarkson and Agnes Tierney Price; *m* 1959, Rose Lilian Hodgson; one *s* one *d*. *Educ:* Westminster Technical Coll.; Polytechnic of Central London (BA Hons). FIMS, FCMI, FRSPH. Served Royal Engineers, 1960–61. Joined London Fire Bde, 1961; Dep. Chief Officer, 1983; Reg. Fire Comdr No 5, Greater London Region, 1987–91. Member: Central Fire Bdes Adv. Council, 1987–91; Fire Service Central Examinations Bd, 1987–91; Ind. Mem., Kent Police Authy, 1995–2003; Mem., Kent Police and Crime Panel, 2012–14; Adviser: Nat. Jt Council for Local Authorities Fire Bdes, 1987–91; Assoc. of Metropolitan Authorities, 1987–91; Chairman: Fedn of British Fire Orgns, 1990–91; London Fire Brigade Retired Members Association, 1991–2010 (Pres. Emeritus, 2010); President: London Fire Brigade Widows' and Orphans' Friendly Soc., 1987–91; Commonwealth and Overseas Fire Service Assoc., 1990–2000; Dir, Nat. Fire Protection Assoc., USA, 1990–93. Founder Chm., Firefighters Meml Charitable Trust, 1990–2013 (granted Royal Charter, 2010) (Life Pres., 2014). Mem. (C), Ashford BC, 2006– (Mem., Planning Cttee, 2006–10; Exec. Portfolio Holder for Cultural Services, 2007–10, for Envmtl Services, 2010–11; Dep. Leader, 2011–13; Leader, 2013–). Chairman: Charing Rd Safety and Traffic Mgt Cttee, 2005–10; Charing Playing Fields Managing Trustees, 2007–11 (Vice Chm., 2005–07). Freeman: City of London, 1983; Glasgow, 2004; Founder Mem., Worshipful Co. of Firefighters (formerly Guild of Firefighters, then Co. of Firefighters), 1988– (Founder Master, 1988); Mem., HAC, 2004–. OStJ 1989. Hon. FIFireE 1989. *Recreations:* reading, sailing, fishing, music. *Address:* Charing Lodge, Pett Lane, Charing, Kent TN27 0DL. *Club:* East India.

CLARKSON, Harriet; *see* Green, H.

CLARKSON, Jeremy Charles Robert; journalist and broadcaster, since 1978; *b* 11 April 1960; *m* 1993, Frances Catherine Cain, *d* of Major Robert Henry Cain, VC and Mary Denise Addison; one *s* two *d*. *Educ:* Repton Sch. Rotherham Advertiser, 1978–81; family co., selling Paddington Bears, 1981–84; established Motoring Press Agency, 1984–94; columnist: Performance Car magazine, 1986–93; Top Gear magazine, 1993–; Esquire magazine, 1992–93; Sunday Times, 1993–; The Sun, 1996–; *television:* presenter: Top Gear, 1989–99, and 2002–15; Jeremy Clarkson's Motorworld, 1995, 1996; Extreme Machines, 1998; Robot Wars, 1998; Clarkson, 1998, 1999, 2000; Clarkson's Car Years, 2000; Speed, 2001; Meet the Neighbours, 2002; Great Britons: Brunel, 2003; The Victoria Cross: For Valour, 2003; Inventions That Changed the World, 2004; The Greatest Raid of All Time, 2006; PQ17: An Arctic Convoy Disaster, 2014. *Publications:* Clarkson on Cars, 1996; Clarkson Hot 100, 1997; Planet Dagenham, 1998; Born to be Riled, 1999; Jeremy Clarkson on Ferrari, 2000; The World According to Jeremy Clarkson, 2004; I Know You Got Soul, 2004; And Another Thing: the world according to Clarkson, vol. 2, 2006; Don't Stop Me Now, 2007; For Crying Out Loud!: the world according to Clarkson, vol. 3, 2008; Driven to Distraction, 2009; How Hard Can it Be?: the world according to Clarkson, vol. 4, 2010; Is It Really Too Much To Ask?: the world according to Clarkson, vol. 5, 2013.

CLARKSON, John; *see* Clarkson, P. J.

CLARKSON, Patrick Robert James; QC 1991; a Recorder, since 1996; *b* 1 Aug. 1949; *s* of Commander Robert Anthony Clarkson, LVO, RN and Sheila Clarissa Neale; *m* 1975, Bridget Cecilia Doyne (*d* 2013); two *s* one *d*. *Educ:* Winchester. Called to the Bar, Lincoln's Inn, 1972. *Recreation:* country. *Address:* Landmark Chambers, 180 Fleet Street, EC4A 2HG. *T:* (020) 7430 1221. *Clubs:* Boodle's, MCC.
See also Lord Irwin.

CLARKSON, Dr Peter David, MBE 2010; Executive Secretary, Scientific Committee on Antarctic Research, 1989–2005; Emeritus Associate, Scott Polar Research Institute, since 2005; *b* 19 June 1945; *s* of late Maurice Roland Clarkson and of Jessie Yoxall (*née* Baker); *m* 1974, Rita Margaret Skinner; one *d*. *Educ:* Epsom Coll.; Univ. of Durham (BSc 1967); Univ. of Birmingham (PhD 1977). FGS 1980. Geologist with British Antarctic Survey, 1967–89: wintered in Antarctica, Halley Bay, 1968 and 1969; Base Comdr, 1969; Antarctic field seasons in Shackleton Range (leader 3 times), 1968–78; in S Shetland Is, 1974–75; in Antarctic Peninsula, 1985–86 (leader). UK adviser to PROANTAR, Brazil, 1982. Chm., Trans-Antarctic Assoc., 2006– (Hon. Sec., 1980–93; Grants Sec., 1993–96; Trustee, 1996–). Polar Medal, 1976. *Publications:* (jtly) Natural Wonders of the World: 100 spectacular wonders of the natural world, 1995; Volcanoes, 2000; (jtly) 100 Great Wonders of the World, 2004; (jtly) Science in the Snow: fifty years of international collaboration through the Scientific Committee on Antarctic Research, 2011; articles on Antarctic geology. *Recreations:* walking, woodwork, photography, music, lecturing on Antarctic cruise ships, all matters Antarctic. *Address:* Scott Polar Research Institute, Lensfield Road, Cambridge CB2 1ER. *T:* (01223) 336531; 35 King's Grove, Barton, Cambridge CB23 7AZ. *T:* (01223) 263417. *Club:* Antarctic.

CLARKSON, Prof. (Peter) John, PhD; CEng, FREng; FIET, FIED; Professor of Engineering Design, since 2004, and Director, Cambridge Engineering Design Centre, since 1997, University of Cambridge; Fellow, Trinity Hall, Cambridge, since 1995 (Vice Master, 2009–13); *b* Oswestry, 11 Nov. 1961; *s* of Ven. Alan Geoffrey Clarkson, *qv*; *m* 1988, Mary Susan Joan Moore; two *s* two *d*. *Educ:* Wells Cathedral Sch.; Trinity Hall, Cambridge (BA 1984; MA 1988; PhD 1988). CEng 1990, FREng 2012; FIET 2004; FIED 2011. Student engr, English Electric Valve Co., UK, 1980–84; Consulting Engr, PA Consulting Gp, UK, 1988–95; Lectr in Engrg Design, 1995–2001, Reader in Engrg Design, 2001–04, Univ. of Cambridge. Dr *hc* Katholieke, Leuven, 2012. *Publications:* (with S. Keates) Countering Design Exclusion, 2003; (ed jtly) Inclusive Design, 2003; (jtly) Design for Patient Safety, 2004; (ed with C. Eckert) Design Process Improvement, 2005; (ed jtly) Design for Inclusivity, 2007; (jtly) Inclusive Design Toolkit, 2007; contrib. papers to design jls. *Recreations:* music, cycling, church. *Address:* Department of Engineering, University of Cambridge, Trumpington Street, Cambridge CB2 1PZ. *T:* (01223) 748246. *E:* pjc10@eng.cam.ac.uk.

CLARRICOATS, Prof. Peter John Bell, CBE 1996; FRS 1990; FREng; Professor of Electronic Engineering, Queen Mary and Westfield (formerly Queen Mary) College, University of London, 1968–97, now Emeritus Professor, Queen Mary, University of London (Head of Department, 1979–97); *b* 6 April 1932; *s* of John Clarricoats and Cecilia (*née* Bell); *m* 1st, 1955, Gillian (*née* Hall) (marr. diss. 1962); one *s* one *d*; 2nd, 1968, Phyllis Joan (*née* Lloyd); two *d*, and one step *s* one step *d*. *Educ:* Minchenden Grammar Sch.; Imperial Coll. (BSc (Eng), PhD, DSc (Eng) 1968). FInstP 1964; FIET (FIEE 1967); FIEEE 1967; FCGI 1980; FREng (FEng 1983). Scientific Staff, GEC, 1953–58; Lectr, Queen's Univ. Belfast, 1959–62; Sheffield Univ., 1962–63; Prof. of Electronic Engineering, Univ. of Leeds, 1963–67; Mem., Governing Body, QMC, 1976–79, Dean of Engineering, 1977–80; Fellow, QMW, 1999. Founder Editor, Electronics Letters (IEE Jl), 1964–. Chm., Defence Scientific Adv. Council, MoD, 1997–2000. Chm., British Nat. Cttee for Radio Sci., subseq. UK Panel for URSI, 1985–93; Vice-Pres., URSI, 1993–99. Chairman: 1st Internat. Conf. on Antennas and Propagation, IEE, 1978; European Microwave Conf., 1979; Mil. Microwaves Conf., 1988; Microwaves and RF Conf., 1994. Distinguished Lectr, IEEE, 1987–88. Institution of Electrical Engineers: Vice-Pres., 1989–91; Mem. Council, 1964–67, 1977–80; Chm., Electronics Div., 1978–79; Hon. Fellow, 1993; awards: Premia, Electronics Section, 1960, 1961; Marconi, 1974; Measurement Prize, 1989; J. J. Thomson Medal, 1989; Oliver Lodge, 1992. Hon DSc: Kent, 1993; Aston, 1995. Coopers Hill Meml Prize, IEE, 1964; European Microwave Prize, 1989, Dist. Achievement Medal, 2005, European Microwave Assoc.; Cert. of Appreciation, 1989, Millennium Medal, 2000, Distinguished Achievement Award, 2001, IEEE. *Publications:* Microwave Ferrites, 1960; (with A. D. Olver) Corrugated Horns for Microwave Antennas, 1984; (with A. D. Olver) Microwave Horns and Feeds, 1994; papers on antennas and waveguides. *Recreations:* music, history. *Address:* The Red House, 3 Grange Meadows, Elmswell, Suffolk IP30 9GE. *T:* (01359) 240585.

CLARY, Prof. David Charles, FRS 1997; President, Magdalen College, Oxford, since 2005; Professor of Chemistry, University of Oxford, since 2002; *b* Halesworth, Suffolk, 14 Jan. 1953; *s* of late Cecil Raymond Clary and Mary Mildred Clary; *m* 1975, Heather Ann Vinson; three *s*. *Educ:* Colchester Royal Grammar Sch.; Sussex Univ. (BSc 1974); Corpus Christi Coll., Cambridge (PhD 1977); ScD Cantab 1998. CChem, FRSC 1997; CPhys, FInstP 1997.

IBM World-Trade Postdoctoral Fellow, San Jose, Calif, 1977–78; Postdoctoral Fellow, Manchester Univ., 1978–80; Research Lectr in Chemistry, UMIST, 1980–83; Department of Chemistry, Cambridge University: Demonstrator, 1983–87; Lectr, 1987–93; Reader in Theoretical Chem., 1993–96; Magdalene College, Cambridge: Fellow, 1983–96 (Hon. Fellow, 2005); Dir of Studies in Natural Scis, 1988–96; Sen. Tutor, 1989–93; Fellow Commoner, 1996–2002; Prof. of Chem. and Dir, Centre for Theoretical and Computational Chem., UCL, 1996–2002; Hd, Div. of Mathematical and Physical Scis, Univ. of Oxford, and Fellow, St John's Coll., Oxford, 2002–05. Chief Scientific Advr, FCO, 2009–13. Visiting Fellow: Univ. of Colo, 1987–88; Canterbury Univ., NZ, 1992; Univ. of Sydney, Australia, 1994; Hebrew Univ. of Jerusalem, 1994; Université de Paris Sud, 1995; Miller Vis. Prof., Univ. of Calif at Berkeley, 2001; Vis. Prof., Nat. Univ. of Singapore, 2002; Einstein Prof., Chinese Acad. of Scis, 2014. Lectures: George B. Kistiakowsky, Harvard Univ., 2002; Kenneth Pitzer, Univ. of Calif at Berkeley, 2004; Burton Meml, Imperial Coll., London, 2004; Paul Grandpierre, Columbia Univ., 2004; Thomas Graham, UCL and RSC, 2004; Charles Coulson, Univ. of Georgia, 2009; IBM Hursley, Univ. of Southampton, 2009; Noel Hush, Univ. of Sydney, 2014. Trustee, Henry Fund, 2007–. Mem. Council, Royal Soc., 2003–05; Royal Society of Chemistry: Mem. Council, 1990–93 and 1994–2001, Vice-Pres., 1997–2001, Pres., 2006–09, Faraday Div.; Meldola Medal, 1981; Marlow Medal, Faraday Div., 1986; Corday-Morgan Medal, 1989; Tilden Medal and Lectr, 1998; Chemical Dynamics Prize, 1998; Polanyi Medal, 2004; Liversidge Award, 2010. Fellow: AAAS, 2003; APS, 2003; FRSA 2005; Foreign Hon. Mem., Amer. Acad. of Arts and Scis, 2003. Hon. DSc Sussex, 2011 (50th Anniversary Fellow, 2012). Annual Medal, Internat. Acad. of Quantum Molecular Scis, 1989 (Mem., 1998–). Editor, Chemical Physics Letters, 2000–. *Publications:* papers on chemical physics and theoretical chemistry in learned jls. *Recreations:* family, football, foreign travel. *Address:* Magdalen College, Oxford OX1 4AU. *T:* (01865) 276101.

CLASPER, Michael, CBE 1995; Chairman: Which? Ltd, since 2008; Coats plc, since 2013; Coats Group (formerly Guinness Peat Group) plc, since 2014; *b* 21 April 1953; *s* of Douglas and Hilda Clasper; *m* 1975, Susan Rosemary Shore; two *s* one *d*. *Educ:* Bede Sch., Sunderland; St John's Coll., Cambridge (1st cl. Hons Engineering). British Rail, 1974–78; joined Procter & Gamble 1978, Advertising Dir, 1985–88; Gen. Manager, Procter & Gamble Holland, 1988–91; Man. Dir and Vice-Pres., Procter & Gamble UK, 1991–95; Regl Vice-Pres., Laundry Products, Procter & Gamble Europe, 1995–99; Pres., Global Home Care and New Business Develt, Procter & Gamble, 1999–2001; Dep. Chief Exec., 2001–03, Chief Exec., 2003–06, BAA plc; Operational Man. Dir, Terra Firma, 2007–08; Chm., HM Revenue and Customs, 2008–12. Non-executive Director: ITV plc, 2006–14 (Sen. Ind. Dir, 2010–14); Serco, 2014–; Mem., Investor Bd, EMI, 2007–08. Member: Adv. Council on Business and the Envmt, 1993–99; Mgt Cttee, Business and Envmt Prog., Univ. of Cambridge Prog. for Industry, 2000–07; Nat. Employment Panel, 2006–08; Chair, BITC Marketplace Taskforce, 2005–07. Gov., RSC, 2011–. Pres., Chartered Mgt Inst., 2014–Oct. 2016. *Recreations:* walking, ski-ing, tennis, golf.

CLAUGHTON, John Alan; Chief Master, King Edward's School, Birmingham, since 2006; *b* 17 Sept. 1956; *s* of Ronald Claughton and Patricia Claughton (*née* Dobell); *m* 1993, Alexandra Dyer; three *s*. *Educ:* King Edward's Sch., Birmingham; Merton Coll., Oxford (MA 1st Cl. Lit. Hum.). Professional cricketer, Warwickshire CCC, 1979–80; corp. finance advr, N. M. Rothschild & Sons, 1980–82; schoolmaster: Bradfield Coll., 1982–84; Eton Coll., 1984–2001; Headmaster, Solihull Sch., 2001–05. Chm., Sports Cttee, HMC, 2009–. Governor: Highgate Sch., 2008–; Priory Sch., Birmingham, 2008–; Manchester GS, 2010–. *Recreations:* sport, travel, ballet, reading. *Address:* Vince House, 341 Bristol Road, Edgbaston, Birmingham B5 7SW. *T:* (0121) 472 0652. *E:* jac@kes.org.uk.

CLAXTON STEVENS, Christopher Paul; consultant in antique and contemporary furniture, since 2009; *b* Pinner, 15 May 1952; *s* of Edward Arthur George Stevens and Barbara Joan Stevens (*née* Claxton); *m* 1976, Patricia Mary Payne (marr. diss. 1982); one *s*. *Educ:* Haileybury Coll.; Christ Church, Oxford (MA). With Christie's Auctioneers, 1975–81; Norman Adams Ltd, London, 1981–2009 (Dir, 1986–2009); Course Advr and Lectr, W Dean Coll., W Sussex, 1998–. Chm., Regl Furniture Soc., 1993–2001 (Life Vice-Pres., 2011). Trustee: Chiltern Open Air Mus. of Buildings, 1980–; Geffrye Mus., 1997–2012; Frederick Parker Foundn, 1997–; Art Workers' Guild, 2008–14; Patron, British Antique Furniture Restorers' Assoc., 2009– (Vice-Pres., 2014–). Master: Furniture Makers' Co., 2002; Arts Scholars' Co., 2012. *Publications:* 18th Century English Furniture: the Norman Adams collection, 1983; (jtly) British Furniture 1600–2000, 2005; The Frederick Parker Collection: a selection of chairs, 2006; contrib. articles to magazines, jls and exhibn catalogues. *Recreations:* England, architecture. *Address:* 24 Shandon Road, Clapham, SW4 9HR. *E:* c.claxtonstevens@normanadams.com.

CLAY, Sir Edward, KCMG 2005 (CMG 1994); HM Diplomatic Service, retired; High Commissioner, Kenya, 2001–05; *b* 21 July 1945; *m* 1969, Anne Stroud; three *d*. FO, later FCO, 1968; Nairobi, 1970; Second, later First, Sec., Sofia, 1973; FCO, 1975; First Secretary: Budapest, 1979; FCO, 1982; Counsellor: Nicosia, 1985; FCO, 1989; Ambassador (non-resident) to Rwanda, 1994–95, to Burundi, 1994–96; High Comr to Uganda, 1993–97; Dir, Public Diplomacy and Public Services, FCO, 1997–99; High Comr to Cyprus, 1999–2001. Associate Dir, Centre for Political and Diplomatic Studies, 2007–; Mem., Adv. Bd, Governance and Justice Gp, 2009–. Trustee: Leonard Cheshire Disability, 2005–11; Constant Gardener Trust, 2005–; RODI-UK, 2005–; Kitchen Table Charities Trust, 2008–; Internat. Alert, 2010–; Patron, Excellent Develt, 2006–.

CLAY, John Martin; Deputy Chairman: Hambros plc, 1986–90; Hambros Bank Ltd, 1972–84 (Director, 1961–84); *b* 20 Aug. 1927; *s* of late Sir Henry Clay and Gladys Priestman Clay; *m* 1st, 1952, Susan Jennifer (*d* 1997), *d* of Lt-Gen. Sir Euan Miller, KCB, KBE, DSO, MC; four *s*; 2nd, 2001, Ann Monica (*d* 2005), *widow* of Martin Beale, OBE, JP and *d* of Eric Barnard, CB, CBE, DSO. *Educ:* Eton; Magdalen Coll., Oxford. Chairman: Johnson & Firth Brown Ltd, 1973–93; Hambro Life Assurance Ltd, 1978–84. Dir, Bank of England, 1973–83. Mem., Commonwealth Develt Corp., 1970–88. FCMI (FBIM 1971). *Recreation:* sailing. *Club:* Royal Thames Yacht.

CLAY, Lindsey Anne; Chief Executive Officer, Thinkbox, since 2013; *b* Workington, Cumbria, 28 Nov. 1965; *d* of late Michael John Clay and Patricia Anne Clay (*née* Dunn); *m* 2000, Matthew Richard White; two *d*. *Educ:* St Bees Sch., Cumbria; Jesus Coll., Cambridge (BA Hons 1988). Account manager, Clarke Hooper Consulting, 1988–92; Director: McCann Erickson, 1992–97; J Walter Thompson, 1997–2007; Mktg Dir, 2007–10, Man. Dir, 2010–12, Thinkbox. Member: Steering Cttee, Rank Fellowship, 2007–; Bd, British Arrows (formerly British TV Advertising) Awards, 2008–. Member: WACL, 2005– (Pres., 2015–July 2016); Mktg Gp of GB, 2014–. Fellow, Mktg Soc., 2014. *Recreations:* netball playing for Weston Park, N London Netball League, running, reading, theatre, television. *Address:* Thinkbox TV, Manning House, 22 Carlisle Place, SW1P 1JA. *T:* (020) 7630 2320. *E:* Lindsey.Clay@thinkbox.tv.

CLAY, Sir Richard (Henry), 7th Bt *cr* 1841, of Fulwell Lodge, Middlesex; *b* 2 June 1940; *s* of Sir Henry Felix Clay, 6th Bt, and Phyllis Mary (*d* 1997), *yr d* of late R. H. Paramore, MD, FRCS; *S* father, 1985; *m* 1963, Alison Mary, *d* of late Dr James Gordon Fife; three *s* two *d*. *Educ:* Eton. FCA 1966. *Recreation:* sailing. *Heir:* *s* Charles Richard Clay [*b* 18 Dec. 1965; *m* 2000, Janette Maria, *o d* of Steve Carothers, USA; one *s* one *d*]. *Address:* The Copse, Shiplate Road, Bleadon, N Somerset BS24 0NX.

CLAY, Robert Alan; Member (Lab), City and County of Swansea Council, since 2013; *b* 2 Oct. 1946; *s* of Albert Arthur Clay, OBE and Joyce Doris (*née* Astins); *m* 1980, Uta Christa. *Educ:* Bedford Sch.; Gonville and Caius Coll., Cambridge. Bus driver, Tyne and Wear PTE, 1975–83. Branch Chm., GMBATU, 1977–83. MP (Lab) Sunderland North, 1983–92. Treas., 1983–86, Sec., 1986–87, Campaign Gp of Labour MPs. Chief Exec., Pallion Engrg Ltd, 1992–93; Partner, Roots Music, 1993. *Recreations:* walking, reading.

CLAYDON, David John; Chairman and Chief Executive Officer, D. Claydon Advisers, since 2013; Co-Founder, Macro Advisory Partners LLP; *b* Chipping Sodbury, Glos, 17 Dec. 1970; *s* of Terry John and Joan Elizabeth Claydon; *m* 2000, Tabitha Lockwood Estabrook; two *s* one *d*. *Educ:* Ridings Sch., Winterbourne, Bristol; Univ. of Essex (BA 1st Cl. Govt). ESU Congressional Schol., US House of Reps, Washington, Office of the Majority Leader, 1993–94; Associate, Chem. Banking Corp., New York, NY, 1995–97; Vice Pres., J. P. Morgan, NY, 1997–2000; Man. Dir, Morgan Stanley, London, 2000–08; Econ. Advr to Foreign Sec., FCO, 2008–10; Hd, Macro Strategy, FICC, UBS Securities Co. Ltd, 2010–12. Mem. Bd, Gt Ormond St Hosp. Mem., ESU. Trustee, IPPR. FRSA. *Recreations:* yoga, cycling, charitable work, current affairs, classic cars, relaxing! *Address:* Ashton Hill Farm, Corston, Bath BA2 9EY. *T:* (01225) 872935. *E:* claydon123@btinternet.com.

CLAYDON, Geoffrey Bernard, CB 1990; Member, Legal Directorate, Department of Transport, 1990–95; *b* 14 Sept. 1930; *s* of Bernard Claydon and Edith Mary (*née* Lucas); unmarried. *Educ:* Leeds Modern; King Edward's, Birmingham; Birmingham Univ. (LLB). Articled at Pinsent & Co., Birmingham, 1950; admitted Solicitor, 1954. Legal Asst, 1959, Sen. Legal Asst, 1965, Treasury Solicitor's Dept; Asst Solicitor, DTI, 1973; Asst Treasury Solicitor, 1974; Principal Asst Treasury Solicitor and Legal Advr, Dept of Energy, 1980. Mem., Editorial Bd, Jl of Energy and Natural Resources Law, 1983–90. National Tramway Museum: Sec., 1958–84; Vice-Chm., 1969–99; Vice-Pres., 1998–2005; Pres., 2005–06. Vice-Pres., 1968–2008, Pres., 2008–11, Patron, 2011–, Light Rail Transit Assoc. (formerly Light Railway Transport League) (Chm. of League, 1963–68); Pres., Tramway and Light Railway Soc., 1996–2001 and 2011– (Chm., 1967–93; Vice-Pres., 1993–96); Dir, Heritage Railway Assoc., 2003– (Chairman: Legal and Parly Affairs (formerly Legal Services) Cttee, 2002–; Heritage Tramways Cttee, 2006–). Chm., Consultative Panel for Preservation of British Transport Relics, 1982–; Member: Inst. of Transport Admin, 1972–; Fixed Track Section, Confedn of Passenger Transport, 1996–2014; CIT Working Party on transport legislation, 1996–98. CMILT (MCIT 1997; MILT 1999). *Publications:* (contrib. on tramways) Halsbury's Laws of England, 2000; (ed) British Tramway Accidents, 2006. *Recreations:* rail transport, travel. *Address:* 3 The Park, Duffield, Derbys DE56 4ER. *T:* (01332) 841007. *Club:* Royal Automobile.

CLAYDON, Nick; Senior Partner, Brunswick Group LLP, since 2010 (Partner, 2001–10); *b* London, 24 Feb. 1967; *s* of Ralph and Valerie Claydon; *m* 1st, 2000, Manisha Vadhia (*d* 2007); one *s*; 2nd, 2013, Charlotte Wheeler. *Educ:* Caterham Sch.; Univ. of Leeds (BA Hons Politics). Researcher for Chris Smith, MP, 1990; Editl, The House Mag., 1991; Political Consultant: Advocacy Partnership, 1991–92; Ian Greer Associates, 1992–95; Associate Partner, Brunswick Gp LLP, 1995–98; Hd, Ext. Communications, British Airways, 1998–2001. Member: Corporate Bd, ENO, 2012–; London Develt Bd, Maggie's, 2012–. Trustee, Demos, 2006–. *Address:* Brunswick Group LLP, 16 Lincoln's Inn Fields, WC2A 3ED. *T:* (020) 7404 5959. *E:* nclaydon@brunswickgroup.com. *Club:* Ivy.

CLAYMAN, David, CEng, FIChemE; Managing Director, Esso UK plc, 1986–95; *b* 28 May 1934; *s* of Maurice and Nancy Clayman; *m* 1956, Patricia Moore; two *s*. *Educ:* Purley Grammar Sch.; University College London (BSc Chem. Engrg). Joined Esso Petroleum Co., 1956; Supply Manager, London, 1966–67, Esso Europe Inc., 1970–71; Marketing Div. Dir, 1971–79; Exec. Asst to Chm., Exxon Corp., 1979–80; Dir, Esso Petroleum Co., 1982–83; Pres., Esso Africa Inc., 1983–86; Director: Esso Europe Inc., 1983–86; Esso Exploration and Production UK, 1986–95; Esso Pension Trust, 1986–95; Chm., Mainline Pipeline, 1986–95. Mem., Sen. Salaries Review Body, 1997–2006 (Chm., Judicial Sub-cttee, 2002–06). Council Member: GCBS, 1986–87; Foundn for Management Educn, 1986–95; Pres., UKPIA, 1988–90 and 1992–94 (Vice Pres., 1986–88); Vice-Pres., Oil Industries Club, 1988–95. *Clubs:* Royal Automobile; Burhill Golf.

CLAYSON, Timothy; His Honour Judge Clayson; a Circuit Judge, since 2004; Honorary Recorder of Bolton, since 2012; *b* 19 Aug. 1952; *s* of Victor Clayson and Elsie Clayson (*née* Cryer); *m* 1st, 1976, Anita Morton (marr. diss. 1995); two *s* one *d*; 2nd, 1997, Heidi Svensgaard (marr. diss. 2002); 3rd, 2009, Joanne Lowe. *Educ:* Christ's Hosp.; University Coll. London (LLB 1973). Called to the Bar, Gray's Inn, 1974; a Recorder, 1996–2004; International Judge, UN, Kosovo, 2001–03: Dist Court, Gjilan, 2001, Mitrovica, 2002; Supreme Court, 2003. *Recreations:* sailing, classical music. *Address:* Bolton Crown Court, The Law Courts, Blackhorse Street, Bolton BL1 1SU.

CLAYTON, Rear Adm. Christopher Hugh Trevor; Assistant Director Intelligence, NATO International Military Staff, 2004–07; *b* 21 May 1951; *s* of Arthur Henry Trevor Clayton and Patricia June Norma Clayton; *m* 1997, Deirdre Hannah; one *s* two *d*, and two step *s*. *Educ:* Bishop McKenzie's Sch., Lilongwe, Nyasaland; Wells House, Malvern Wells, Worcs; St John's Sch., Leatherhead. Entered BRNC as naval aviator, 1970; Commanding Officer: HMS Beaver (T22 Frigate), 1993–94; HMS Chatham (T22 Frigate), 1996–97; Commodore Naval Aviation, i/c Naval Air Comd, 2000–02; HCSC 2003; CO, HMS Ocean (Helicopter Carrier), 2003–04; Rear Adm. 2004. Chairman: RN Winter Sports Assoc., 1997–2004, Pres., 2004; Combined Services Winter Sports Assoc., 2003. *Recreations:* squash, golf, winter sports, modern history, carpentry and cabinet making, tending 6 acres. *Address:* c/o Naval Secretary, Fleet Headquarters, Whale Island, Portsmouth PO2 8BY. *Club:* Naval and Military.

CLAYTON, Captain Sir David (Robert), 12th Bt *cr* 1732, of Marden; Shipmaster since 1970; Director, Oceanic Lines (UK) Ltd, since 1989; *b* 12 Dec. 1936; *s* of Sir Arthur Harold Clayton, 11th Bt, DSC, and of Alexandra, Lady Clayton, *d* of late Sergei Andreevsky; *S* father, 1985; *m* 1971, Julia Louise, *d* of late Charles Henry Redfearn; two *s*. *Educ:* HMS Conway. Joined Merchant Service, 1953; promoted to first command as Captain, 1970. *Recreations:* shooting, sailing. *Heir:* *s* Robert Philip Clayton [*b* 8 July 1975; *m* 2004, Rachel Kathleen Hughes; one *s* one *d*]. *Address:* Rock House, Kingswear, Dartmouth, Devon TQ6 0BX. *T:* (01803) 752433. *Club:* Royal Dart Yacht (Kingswear).

CLAYTON, Jeremy Paul; Director, Knowledge and Innovation Strategy and International, Department for Business, Innovation and Skills, since 2014 (Director, Research Base, 2011–14); *b* 3 Feb. 1956; *s* of Giles Conrad Clayton and Anne Margaret Clayton (*née* Crennell); *m* 1990, Mary Lucille Hindmarch. *Educ:* Bedales Sch.; Christ Church, Oxford (MA Physics). Department of Energy, 1978–91: Private Sec. to Norman Lamont, MP, David Mellor, MP, and Rt Hon. Nigel Lawson, MP, 1981–83; Secretariat, Sizewell B Public Inquiry, 1984–87; electricity privatisation, 1989–91; Dir, Building Mgt Privatisation Unit, PSA Services, 1991–94; Department of Trade and Industry: Director: Prog. Finance and Public Expenditure Survey, 1994–97; Radiocommunications Agency Third Generation Mobile Communications Auction Team, 1997–2000; Export Control, 2000–03; Gp Dir, Transdeptl Sci. and Technol., OST, subseq. Office of Sci. and Innovation, 2003–07; Dep. Head, Govt Office for Science, DIUS, later BIS, 2007–11. UK/US Fulbright Comr, 2014–. Member: Glyndebourne Fest. Soc.; Wagner Soc.; Benslow Music Trust; Ramblers Assoc.; London Wildlife Trust; Woodland Trust; RSPB; London Parks and Gardens Trust; Friend: Covent Gdn; Aldeburgh Fest.; Wigmore Hall; RA; Lake Dist. *Recreations:* cello, piano, singing, walking, reading, classical music, theatre and film. *Address:* Department for Business, Innovation and Skills, 1 Victoria Street, SW1H 0ET. *T:* (020) 7215 1227. *E:* jeremy.clayton@bis.gsi.gov.uk.

CLAYTON, John Pilkington, CVO 1986 (LVO 1975); MA, MB, BChir; Apothecary to HM Household at Windsor, 1965–86; Surgeon Apothecary to HM Queen Elizabeth the Queen Mother's Household at the Royal Lodge, Windsor, 1965–86; Senior Medical Officer, Eton College, 1965–86 (MO, 1962–65); *b* 13 Feb. 1921; *s* of late Brig.-Gen. Sir Gilbert Clayton, KCMG, KBE, CB, and Enid, *d* of late F. N. Thorowgood. *Educ:* Wellington Coll.; Gonville and Caius Coll., Cambridge; King's Coll. Hospital. RAFVR, 1947–49; Sqdn Ldr 1949. Senior Resident, Nottingham Children's Hosp., 1950. MO, Black and Decker Ltd, 1955–70; MO, 1953–62, SMO 1962–81, Royal Holloway Coll. *Address:* Knapp House, Market Lavington, near Devizes, Wilts SN10 4DP.

CLAYTON, Margaret Ann; *b* 7 May 1941; *d* of late Percy Thomas Clayton and of Kathleen Clayton (*née* Payne). *Educ:* Christ's Hospital, Hertford; Birkbeck Coll., London (BA, MSc). Entered Home Office, 1960; Executive Officer/Asst Principal, 1960–67; Asst Private Secretary to Home Secretary, 1967–68; Principal, 1968–75 (seconded to Cabinet Office, 1972–73); Asst Sec., 1975–82; Asst Under Sec. of State, 1983–96; Resident Chm., CSSB, 1983; Dir of Services, Prison Service, 1986–90; Police Dept, 1990–93; Personnel Dept, 1994. Dir, Butler Trust, 1996–99; Chm., Mental Health Act Commn, 1999–2002. Chm., Farriers Registration Council, 2001–06. Mem., Lambeth, Southwark and Lewisham HA, 1995–99. Freeman, City of London, 1984; Liveryman, Farriers' Co., 1984–. *Recreations:* gardening, theatre, reading, bell-ringing.

CLAYTON, Michael Aylwin; Editor of Horse and Hound, 1973–96; Editor-in-Chief, IPC country titles, 1994–97; *b* 20 Nov. 1934; *s* of late Aylwin Goff Clayton and Norah (*née* Banfield); *m* 1988, Marilyn Crowhurst (*née* Orrin); one *s* one *d* from a previous marriage. *Educ:* Bournemouth Grammar School. National Service, RAF, 1954–56. Reporter: Lymington Times and New Milton Advertiser, 1951–54; Portsmouth Evening News, 1956–57; London Evening News, 1957–61; reporter/feature writer, New Zealand Herald, 1961; reporter, London Evening Standard, 1961, Dep. News Editor, 1962–64; News Editor, Southern Ind. Television, 1964–65; staff correspondent, BBC TV and radio (incl. Vietnam, Cambodia, India, Pakistan and Middle East), 1965–73; Presenter, Today, BBC Radio 4, 1973–75. Dir, IPC Magazines, 1994–97. Chm., British Soc. of Magazine Editors, 1986. Mem., Press Complaints Commn, 1991–93. Chairman: BHS, 1998–2001; British Horse Industry Confedn, 1999–2004; Trustees, Mus. of Hunting, 2006–. *Publications:* A Hunting We Will Go, 1967; (with Dick Tracey) Hickstead—the First Twelve Years, 1972; (ed) The Complete Book of Showjumping, 1975; (ed) Cross-Country Riding, 1977; The Hunter, 1980; The Golden Thread, 1984; Prince Charles: horseman, 1987; The Chase: a modern guide to foxhunting, 1987; Foxhunting in Paradise, 1993; Endangered Species, 2004; The Glorious Chase, 2005; Peterborough Royal Foxhound Show - a history, 2006; The Duke of Rutland's Hounds, the Belvoir, 2011; (with Alastair Jackson) A Short History of Foxhunting, 2013. *Recreations:* foxhunting, music, bridge.

CLAYTON, Prof. Nicola Susan, PhD; FRS 2010; Professor of Comparative Cognition, University of Cambridge, since 2005; Fellow of Clare College, Cambridge, since 2000; Scientist in Residence, Rambert Dance Company, since 2011 (Scientific Adviser, 2009–11); *b* 22 Nov. 1962; *d* of Colin and Angela Clayton; *m* 2001, Dr Nathan Jon Emery. *Educ:* Pembroke Coll., Oxford (BA Hons Zoology 1984; Domus Scholarship); Univ. of St Andrews (PhD Bird Song 1987). University of California, Davis: Asst Prof., 1995–98; Associate Prof., 1998–2000; Chair, Animal Behavior Grad. Gp, 1999–2000; Full Prof., 2000; University of Cambridge: Univ. Lectr, 2000–02, Reader in Comparative Cognition, 2002–05, Dept of Experimental Psychol.; Co-founder, The Captured Thought, Dept of Psychology; Tutor and Dir of Studies, Clare Coll., Cambridge, 2000–. Member: Cognitive Neurosci. Section, Fac. of 1000 Biology, 2002–; Animal Scis Cttee, 2003–05, 2008–11, Res. Cttee A (Animal Systems, Health and Well Being), 2009–12, BBSRC; Adv. Bd, Culture and Mind Proj., AHRC, 2004–; Dorothy Hodgkin Fellowship Selection Panel B Side, Royal Soc., 2008–10; Ecol. and Evolution Panel, Eur. Res. Cttee FP8, 2008–14. Member: Council, Assoc. for Study of Animal Behaviour, 2009–12; British Neurosci. Assoc. (Mem., Organizing Cttee, 2002–03); Eur. Psychological Soc.; Council, Eur. Brain and Behaviour Soc., 2009–. FRSB (FSB 2010). Internat. Affiliate, Amer. Psychol Assoc.; Fellow, Assoc. for Psychol Scis, 2010. Consulting Editor: Behavioural Neuroscience, 1999–2002; Learning and Behavior, 2007–; Associate Editor: Learning and Motivation, 2000–03; Qly Jl of Experimental Psychology, 2001–04; Animal Behaviour, 2001–04; Mem., Editl Cttee, Biological Reviews, 2003–06; Member, Editorial Board: Public Library of Science One, 2006–; Procs of Royal Soc. B, 2007–. Frank Beach Award, Amer. Psychol Assoc., 2000; Klaus Immelmann Prize in animal behaviour, Bielefeld Univ., 2003; Jean-Marie Delwart Award in Comparative and Evolutionary Neurosci., Belgium Acad. of Scis, 2010; Mid-career Award, Experimental Psychol. Soc., 2012. *Publications:* (jtly) Social Intelligence: from brain to culture, 2007; 256 articles in scientific jls incl. Nature and Science. *Recreations:* dancing, especially Argentine tango and salsa but also jazz and ballet, yoga, bird watching, playing clarinet and saxophone. *Address:* Department of Psychology, University of Cambridge, Downing Street, Cambridge CB2 3EB. *T:* (01223) 333559, *Fax:* (01223) 333564. *E:* nsc22@cam.ac.uk, nickyclayton@rambert.org.uk.

CLAYTON, Richard Anthony; QC 2002; a Recorder, since 2006; *b* 25 May 1954; *s* of Dennis Lloyd and Patricia Estelle Clayton; *m* 1st, 1980, Isabel Glen Japp (marr. diss.); one *s*; 2nd, 1992, Anne Bernadette Burns (marr. diss.); one *s*; 3rd, 2010, Claer Lloyd-Jones. *Educ:* New Coll., Oxford (BA PPE). Called to the Bar, Middle Temple, 1977, Bencher, 2010. South Islington Law Centre, 1980–82; Osler, Hoskin Harcourt, Toronto, 1982–83; in Chambers, 1984–. UK Rep., Venice Commn, 2011–. Associate Fellow, Centre for Public Law, Univ. of Cambridge, 2001–. *Publications:* Practice and Procedure at Industrial Tribunals, 1987; (jtly) Civil Actions Against the Police, 1987, 3rd edn 2004; Judicial Review Procedure, 1993, 2nd edn 1996; Police Actions, 1993, 2nd edn 1996; The Law of Human Rights, 2000, 2nd edn 2009. *Recreations:* theatre, reading, ski-ing. *Address:* 4–5 Gray's Inn Square, WC1R 5AH. *T:* (020) 7404 5252, *Fax:* (020) 7242 7803. *E:* rclayton@4-5.co.uk.

CLAYTON, Prof. Robert Norman, FRS 1981; Professor, Departments of Chemistry and of the Geophysical Sciences, University of Chicago, 1966–2001, now Emeritus; *b* 20 March 1930; *s* of Norman and Gwenda Clayton; *m* 1971, Cathleen Shelburne Clayton; one *d*. *Educ:* Queen's Univ., Canada (BSc, MSc); California Inst. of Technol. (PhD). Res. Fellow, Calif. Inst. of Technol., 1955–56; Asst Prof., Pennsylvania State Univ., 1956–58; University of Chicago: Asst Prof., 1958–62; Associate Prof., 1962–66. *Publications:* over 200 papers in geochemical journals. *Address:* 5201 South Cornell, Chicago, IL 60615, USA. *T:* (773) 6432450; Department of the Geophysical Sciences, University of Chicago, 5734 South Ellis Avenue, Chicago, IL 60637, USA.

CLAYTON, Stanley James; Town Clerk of the City of London, 1974–82; *b* 10 Dec. 1919; *s* of late James John Clayton and late Florence Clayton; *m* 1955, Jean Winifred, *d* of late Frederick Etheridge; one *s* one *d*. *Educ:* Ensham Sch.; King's Coll., London (LLB). Served War of 1939–45, commnd RAF. Admitted Solicitor 1958. City of Westminster, 1938–52; Camberwell, 1952–60; Asst Solicitor, Holborn, 1960–63; Deputy Town Clerk: Greenwich, 1963–65; Islington, 1964–69; City of London, 1969–74. Comdr, Order of Dannebrog (Denmark); holds other foreign orders. *Address:* Fairfield, Purston Lane, High Ackworth, W Yorks WF7 7EQ. *Club:* Royal Air Force.

CLEARY, (Anthony) Shaun; HM Diplomatic Service; High Commissioner to Mozambique, 2010–14; *b* Brigg, 27 Oct. 1965; *s* of Michael Cleary and Marlene Cleary; *m* Kathryn Anne Douglas; two *s* four *d*. *Educ:* Clare Coll., Cambridge (BA 1987; MPhil Internat. Relns 1988; MBA 2009; MSc Finance 2013). Joined HM Diplomatic Service, 1988; S America Dept, FCO, 1989–90; Pol Officer, S Africa, 1990–93; Hd, NATO Team, then Hd, Baltic/Balkans Team, FCO, 1994–97; Energy, Envmt and Budget Counsellor, OECD, Paris, 1998–2002; Dep. Hd, Aviation, Maritime and Energy Dept, FCO, 2003–04; Dep. Consul Gen., Basra, 2004–05; Spending Review Team, then Hd, Capability Review Team, FCO, 2005–07; Financial Planning Dir, E Sussex NHS Trust (on secondment), 2007; Asst Dir of Protocol, FCO, 2008; Dep. Leader, Stabilisation Review Team, Cabinet Office (on secondment), 2008; Actg High Comr, Suva, 2009; Hd, Flu Crisis Unit, Consular Crisis Gp, FCO, 2009. *Publications:* contrib. article in African Affairs. *Recreation:* cooking. *Address:* c/o Foreign and Commonwealth Office, King Charles Street, SW1A 2AH. *E:* shaun.cleary@fco.gov.uk.

CLEARY, Anthony Simon Lissant; His Honour Judge Cleary; a Circuit Judge, since 2006; a Deputy High Court Judge, Family Division, since 2011; *b* 21 Jan. 1946; *s* of Bruce and Patricia Cleary; *m* 1st, 1968, Georgina Clark (marr. diss. 1973); one *s* two *d*; 2nd, 1974, Carmel Briddon; one *s*. *Educ:* Fettes Coll.; Sheffield Univ. (LLB Hons). Account Exec., Benton & Bowles Advertising Agency, 1968–70; admitted solicitor, 1971; Registrar, then Dist Judge, 1986–2006; Asst Recorder, 1989–92, Recorder, 1992–2006. Civil Tutor Judge, 2001–10, IT Liaison Judge, 2003–10, Judicial Studies Bd. Member: Lord Chancellor's Matrimonial Causes Rules Cttee, 1984–86; Lord Chancellor's Children Act Procedure Adv. Gp, 1989–91; Lord Chancellor's Children Act Adv. Cttee, 1991–93; Judicial Liaison Panel, CAFCASS, 2004–06. Chm., Sheffield Family Conciliation Service, 1984–86 (Chm., Steering Cttee); Mem. Cttee, Birmingham Family Mediation Service, 1987–89. Mem., Family Law Cttee, Law Soc., 1984–86. Lecturer in Family Law: for Jordans (publishers of Family Law Jl), Birmingham Law Soc. and FLBA, 1987–2006; for Judicial Studies Bd, 1999–2010. Contributing Ed., Butterworth's County Court Precedents and Pleadings, 1988–93; Gen. Ed., Family Court Practice, annually, 1993–. *Publications:* Nobody Comes, 2014. *Recreations:* music (choral clerk, Coventry Cathedral; Mem., Armonico Consort, 2005–09), rifle shooting, planning, with occasional success, return trips to homeland, NZ.

CLEARY, Prof. Mark Christopher, PhD; Vice Chancellor and Principal, University of Bradford, 2007–13; *b* Birmingham, 27 Dec. 1954; *s* of Michael and Dorothy Cleary; *m* 1980, Marie Frances Brophy; two *s*. *Educ:* Jesus Coll., Cambridge (BA Hons Geog. 1977; PhD 1983). Lectr, Univ. of Exeter, 1980–89; Senior Lecturer: Univ. of Brunei, 1989–92; Univ. of Waikato, NZ, 1992–93; University of Plymouth: Reader, 1995–99; Prof. of Geog., 1999–2003; Dean of Social Sci. and Business, 2003–04; Dep. Vice-Chancellor, 2005–07. *Publications:* Peasants, Politicians and Producers: the organisation of agriculture in France since 1918, 1989, repr. 2006; (with P. Eaton) Borneo: change and development, 1992; (with S. Y. Wong) Oil, Economic Development and Diversification in Brunei Darussalam, 1994; (with P. Eaton) Tradition and Reform: land tenure and rural development in Southeast Asia, 1996; (with Goh Kim Chuan) Environment and Development in the Straits of Malacca, 2000. *Recreations:* cycling, walking.

CLEARY, Shaun; *see* Cleary, A. S.

CLEAVE, Brian Elseley, CB 1995; Solicitor of Inland Revenue, 1990–99; *b* 3 Sept. 1939; *s* of Walter Edward Cleave and Hilda Lillian Cleave (*née* Newman); *m* 1979, Celia Valentine Williams. *Educ:* Eastbourne Coll. (Duke of Devonshire's schol.); Exeter Univ. (LLB 1961); Kansas Univ.; Manchester Univ. Admitted Solicitor, 1966; called to the Bar, Gray's Inn, 1999. Asst Solicitor, Wilkinson Howlett and Durham, 1966–67; Inland Revenue Solicitor's Office, 1967–99: Asst Solicitor, 1978; Prin. Asst Solicitor, 1986. Senior Consultant: EU/Tacis Taxation Reform Project, Moscow, 2000–05; EU/Tacis Assistance to the State Tax Administration, Ukraine Project, 2006–07; Consultant, Govt of Tanzania and Govt of Zanzibar on sharing profits from oil prodn, 2008–09. Hon. QC 1999. FRSA 1995. *Publications:* (contrib.) The Impact of the OECD and UN Model Conventions on Bilateral Tax Treaties, 2012; (contrib.) Tax Rules in Non-Tax Agreements, 2012; case notes and other contribs to tax periodicals incl. British Tax Rev., European Taxation and Bulletin for Internat. Taxation. *Recreations:* theatre, travel, walking.

CLEAVER, Sir Anthony (Brian), Kt 1992; Chairman, Natural Environment Research Council, since 2014; Chairman: SThree plc, 2000–10; Working Links (Employment) Ltd, 2003–09; Novia Financial plc (formerly Novia Financial Holdings Ltd), since 2008; *b* 10 April 1938; *s* of late William Brian Cleaver and Dorothea Early Cleaver (*née* Peeks); *m* 1st, 1962, Mary Teresa Cotter (*d* 1999); one *s* one *d*; 2nd, 2000, Mrs Jennifer Guise Lloyd Graham, widow. *Educ:* Berkhamsted Sch.; Trinity Coll., Oxford (Schol.; MA; Hon. Fellow 1989). FBCS 1976; FRCM 2008. Joined IBM United Kingdom, 1962; IBM World Trade Corp., USA, 1973–74; Dir, DP Div., IBM UK, 1977; Vice-Pres. of Marketing, IBM Europe, Paris, 1981–82; Gen. Man., 1984, Chief Exec., 1986–91, Chm., 1990–94, IBM United Kingdom Holdings Ltd; Chairman: General Cable PLC, 1995–98 (Dir, 1994–98); IX Europe plc, 1999–2007. Chairman: UKAEA, 1993–96; AEA Technology plc, 1996–2001; MRC, 1998–2006; Nuclear Decommissioning Authy, 2004–07; Engrg and Technol. Bd, subseq. EngineeringUK, 2007–10. Chairman: The Strategic Partnership Ltd, 1997–2000; Baxi Partnership, 1999–2000; UK eUnivs Worldwide Ltd, 2001–04; Asia Pacific Advisers (UK Trade & Investment, formerly Trade Partners UK), 2000–03. Director: General Accident plc (formerly General Accident, Fire & Life Assurance Corp.), 1988–98; Smith & Nephew PLC, 1993–2002; Loral Europe Ltd, 1995–96; Cable Corp., 1995–96; Lockheed Martin Tactical Systems UK Ltd, 1996–99; Lockheed Martin UK Ltd, 1999–2006. Dir, Nat. Computing Centre, 1976–80. Member Board: UK Centre for Econ. and Environmental Develt, 1985–98 (Dep. Chm., 1992–98); BITC, 1985–2000 (Chm., Business in the Envmt Target Team, 1988–99; Mem., President's Cttee, 1988–91; Dep. Chm., 1991–2000); RIPA, 1985–90; Mem., Council, ABSA, 1985–97 (Dir, 1991–97); Pres., Involvement and Participation Assoc., 1997–2002. Chairman: Industrial Develt Adv. Bd, DTI, 1993–99; TEC Ind. Assessors Cttee, 1994–98; Council for Excellence in Mgt and Leadership, 2000–02; Member: Nat. Adv. Council for Educn and Trng Targets, 1993–98; Electronics EDC, NEDO, 1986–92; CBI, 1986–97 (Mem., President's Cttee, 1988–92); BOTB, 1988–91; Nat. Trng Task Force, 1989–92; Adv. Council, Centre for Dispute Resolution, 1996–2007; Partnership Korea, 1997–99; PPARC Appointments Cttee, 1996–2000; Cttee on Standards in Public Life, 1997–2003; British Government Panel on Sustainable Develt, 1998–2000; Singapore British Business Council, 1999–2000, 2003–04. Dir, American Chamber of Commerce, 1989–91. Member: HRH Duke of Edinburgh's Seventh Commonwealth Study Conf. Council, 1990–92; Council for Industry and Higher Educn, 1991–94; Carnegie Inquiry into Third Age, 1991–93. Chm., Portsmouth Univ. Business Adv. Bd, 1992–99; Member: Oxford Univ. Adv. Council on Continuing Educn, 1993–99; Oxford Univ. Develt Prog. Adv. Bd, 1999–2005; President's Cttee, Oxford Univ. Appeal, 1988; Appeal Chm., Trinity Coll., Oxford, 1989–98; Chm., RCM, 1999–2007 (Mem. Council, 1998–99; Vice-Pres., 2008–); Member Council: Templeton Coll., Oxford, 1982–93; PSI, 1985–88; Pres., Inst. of Mgt, 1999–2000; Chm. Govs, Birkbeck Coll., 1989–98; Mem., Cttee of Chm. of Univ. Councils, 1992–98; Trustee, Oxford Univ. Higher Studies Fund, 1994–2009. Dep. Chm., ENO, 1998–2000 (Dir, 1988–2000). Pres., Classical Assoc., 1995–96. Pres., Business Commitment to the Envmt, 2000–14. Freeman, City of London, 1987; Co. of Information Technologists, 1985– (Liveryman, 1994); Co. of Musicians, 2003– (Liveryman, 2005; Master, 2013–14). FCGI 2004. Hon. FCIM 1989 (Hon. Vice-Pres., 1991–; Pres., London Br., 1993–2000);

Hon. FCIPS 1996; Hon. FREng 2011. FRSA 1987 (Chm., RSA Inquiry into Tomorrow's Co., 1993–95). Mem. Council, WWF, 1988–92. Patron, Friends of Classics, 1991–. Hon. Fellow: Birkbeck Coll., London, 1999; Univ. of Central Lancashire, 2007. Hon. LLD: Nottingham, 1991; Portsmouth, 1996; Hon. DSc: Cranfield, 1995; Hull, 2002; City, 2002; Hon. DTech London Metropolitan, 2003; DUniv Middx, 2003. UN Envmt Program Global 500 Roll of Honour, 1989. *Recreations:* music, especially opera; sport, especially cricket, golf. *Clubs:* Athenæum, Royal Automobile, MCC, Serpentine Swimmers.

CLEE, Christopher; QC 2009; a Recorder, since 2005; *b* Cardiff, 20 July 1961; *s* of Bernard Clee and Gaye Clee; *m* 1987, Kim Wibberley; two *s* two *d*. *Educ:* Bishop Vaughan Comp. Sch., Swansea; University Coll., Cardiff (LLB Hons); Inns of Court Sch. of Law. Called to the Bar, Gray's Inn, 1983. *Recreations:* football, Rugby, cricket, 1970s new wave music. *Address:* 18 Withy Park, Bishopston, Swansea SA3 3EY. *T:* (01792) 232020. *E:* christopherclee471@hotmail.com.

CLEERE, Henry Forester, OBE 1992; FSA; Director, Council for British Archaeology, 1974–91 (Hon. Vice-President, 1994); World Heritage Co-ordinator, International Council on Monuments and Sites, 1991–2002; *b* 2 Dec. 1926; *s* of late Christopher Henry John Cleere and Frances Eleanor (*née* King); *m* 1st, 1950, Dorothy Percy (marr. diss.); one *s* one *d*; 2nd, 1975, Pamela Joan Vertue; two *d*. *Educ:* Beckenham County Sch.; University Coll. London (BA Hons 1951; Fellow 1992); Univ. of London Inst. of Archaeology (PhD 1981). FSA 1967. Commissioned Royal Artillery, 1946–48. Successively, Production Editor, Asst Sec., Man. Editor, Dep. Sec., Iron and Steel Inst., 1952–71; Industrial Development Officer, UN Industrial Develt Org., Vienna, 1972–73. Archaeol Advr, GLC Historic Buildings Panel, 1979–84; World Heritage Advr, State Admin for Cultural Heritage, People's Republic of China, 2002–05; Sen. Advr, Global Heritage Fund, 2008–. Member: Exec. Cttee, ICOMOS, 1981–90; Duchy of Cornwall Archaeol Adv. Panel, 1983–90; Scientific Cttee, Centro Universitario Europeo per i Beni Culturali, 1985–95; NT Archaeol. Panel, 1990–94. President: Sussex Archaeol Soc., 1987–91 (Vice Pres., 1994); Eur. Forum of Heritage Assocs, 1991–93; Sec., Eur. Assoc. of Archaeologists, 1991–96. Editor, Antiquity, 1992. MIFA 1982, Hon. MIFA 1991; FCMI; Hon. Foreign Mem., Archaeol Inst. of America, 1995. Winston Churchill Fellow, 1979; Hon. Vis. Fellow, Univ. of York, 1988–92; Vis. Res. Fellow, Univ. de Paris I (Sorbonne), 1989; UK Trust Sen. Fellow, Indian Nat. Trust for Art and Cultural Heritage, 1990. Hon. Prof., Inst. of Archaeology, UCL, 1998–. Hon. DLitt Sussex, 1993. European Archaeological Heritage Prize, 2002; Conservation and Mgt Award, Archaeol Inst. of America, 2010; Piero Gazzola Prize, Internat. Council on Monuments and Sites, 2014. *Publications:* Approaches to the Archaeological Heritage, 1984; (with D. W. Crossley) The Iron Industry of the Weald, 1985; Archaeological Heritage Management in the Modern World, 1989; Oxford Archaeological Guide to Southern France, 2001; papers in British and foreign jls on heritage mgt, early ironmaking, Roman fleets, etc. *Recreation:* gardening. *Address:* Acres Rise, Acres Rise, Ticehurst, Wadhurst, East Sussex TN5 7DD. *T:* (01580) 200752. *E:* henry.cleere@btinternet.com.

CLEESE, John Marwood; writer and actor; *b* 27 Oct. 1939; *s* of late Reginald and Muriel Cleese; *m* 1st, 1968, Connie Booth (marr. diss. 1978); one *d*; 2nd, 1981, Barbara Trentham (marr. diss. 1990; she *d* 2013); one *d*; 3rd, 1993, Alyce Faye Eichelberger (marr. diss. 2009); 4th, 2012, Jennifer Wade. *Educ:* Clifton Sports Acad.; Downing College, Cambridge (MA). Founder and former Dir, Video Arts Ltd. Started making jokes professionally, 1963; started on British television, 1966; TV series have included: The Frost Report, At Last the 1948 Show, Monty Python's Flying Circus, Fawlty Towers, The Human Face (documentary). Films include: Interlude, 1968; And Now For Something Completely Different, 1970; The Magic Christian, 1971; Monty Python and the Holy Grail, 1974; Romance with a Double Bass, 1974; Life of Brian, 1978; Privates on Parade, 1982; The Meaning of Life, 1982; Yellowbeard, 1983; Silverado, 1985; Clockwise, 1986; A Fish Called Wanda, 1988; Erik the Viking, 1989; Splitting Heirs, 1993; Mary Shelley's Frankenstein, 1994; Rudyard Kipling's The Jungle Book, 1995; Fierce Creatures, 1997; The Out of Towners, 1998; Isn't She Great, 1998; The World Is Not Enough, 1999; Rat Race, 2002; Die Another Day, 2002; Harry Potter and the Chamber of Secrets, 2002; Scorched, 2005; The Pink Panther 2, 2009. Solo show: The Alimony Tour, UK, 2011. *Live show:* Monty Python Live (Mostly), 02 Arena, 2014. Andrew D. White Prof.-at-Large, Cornell Univ., 1999–. Hon. LLD St Andrews. *Publications:* (with Robin Skynner) Families and How to Survive Them, 1983; The Golden Skits of Wing Commander Muriel Volestrangler FRHS and Bar, 1984; The Complete Fawlty Towers, 1989; (with Robin Skynner) Life and How to Survive It, 1993; (with Brian Bates) The Human Face, 2001; (jtly) The Pythons Autobiography by the Pythons, 2004; So, Anyway… (autobiog.), 2014. *Recreations:* gluttony, sloth. *Address:* c/o David Wilkinson, 115 Hazlebury Road, SW6 2LX.

CLEGG, Prof. John Brian, PhD; FRS 1999; Professor of Molecular Medicine, University of Oxford, 1996–2001, now Emeritus; *b* 9 April 1936; *s* of John Richard and Phyllis Clegg. *Educ:* Arnold Sch., Blackpool; Fitzwilliam House, Cambridge (MA 1963; PhD 1963). Univ. of Washington, Seattle, 1963; Johns Hopkins Univ., 1964–65; MRC Lab. of Molecular Biology, 1965; Department of Medicine, University of Liverpool: Lectr, 1966–68; Sen. Lectr, 1969–74; University of Oxford: Lectr, Dept of Medicine, 1974–79; Reader in Molecular Haematology, 1987–96; Asst Dir, Inst. of Molecular Medicine, 1989–2001; MRC Sen. Scientific Staff, 1979–2001. Hon. MRCP 1986, Hon. FRCP 1999. *Publications:* (with D. J. Weatherall) The Thalassaemia Syndromes, 1965, 4th edn 2001; scientific contribs to learned jls. *Recreations:* gardening, travel in France. *Address:* Institute of Molecular Medicine, John Radcliffe Hospital, Oxford OX3 9DS. *T:* (01865) 222398.

CLEGG, Judith Caroline; Founder and Chief Executive Officer: Takeout (formerly Venturing Unlimited), since 2006; LiveKind, since 2015; Second Chance Tuesday, since 2006; The Glasshouse, since 1998; angel investor, since 1998; *b* Reading, 24 Oct. 1971; *d* of (Geoffrey) Peter (Scott) Clegg and (Caroline) Jane Clegg. *Educ:* Warkworth C of E Primary Sch., Northumberland; Amble Middle Sch.; St Anne's Sch. for Girls, Windermere; Warwick Univ. (BSc 1st Cl. Hons Mgt Sci.). With Arthur Andersen Business Consulting, 1993–97; Operational Develt Manager, Pret, 1997–98; Co-founder and Chief Operating Officer, Moonfruit.com, 1999–2001; Advr, Philip Gould Associates, 2002–04; Associate Dir, Egremont, 2004–06. Non-exec. Dir, Onalytica Ltd. Mem., Adv. Bd, Tech City, 2013–. Founder, Battersea Courage Trust, 1998. *Recreations:* sailing in everything from tiny dinghies to ocean-going yachts (sailed across Pacific Ocean from Tahiti to Auckland), horse-riding, yoga, running, cooking, especially baking cakes, drinking earl grey tea, New York, the ocean, the internet. *Address:* Takeout, Second Home, 68 Hanbury Street, E1 5JL.

CLEGG, Rt Hon. Nicholas (William Peter); PC 2008; MP (Lib Dem) Sheffield, Hallam, since 2005; *b* 7 Jan. 1967; *s* of Nicholas P. Clegg and Hermance Eulalie van den Wall Bake; *m* 2000, Miriam Gonzalez Durantez; three *s*. *Educ:* Westminster Sch.; Robinson Coll., Cambridge (MA Anthropol.); Univ. of Minnesota (post grad. res., Political Theory); Coll. of Europe, Bruges (MA European Studies). Trainee journalist, The Nation mag., NY, 1990; Consultant, GJW Govt Relns, London, 1992–93; Official, Relns with New Independent States, EC, 1994–96; Mem. of Cabinet, Office of Sir Leon Brittan, EC, 1996–99; MEP (Lib Dem) E Midlands, 1999–2004. Lib Dem Home Affairs spokesman, 2006–07; Leader, Liberal Democrats, 2007–15; Dep. Prime Minister and Lord President of the Council, 2010–15. Political Columnist, Guardian Unlimited, 2000–05. Pt-time Lectr, Sheffield Univ., 2004–05. Trustee, NPG, 2012–. David Thomas Prize, Financial Times, 1993. *Recreations:* outdoors, arts. *Address:* (office) 85 Nethergreen Road, Sheffield S11 7EH. *T:* (0114) 230 9002. *Club:* National Liberal.

CLEGG, Peter Alexander, RDI 2010; RIBA; Senior Partner, Feilden Clegg Bradley Studio (formerly Architects), since 1978; *b* 29 Aug. 1950; *s* of Alexander Bradshaw Clegg and Jessi Coverdale Clegg (*née* Phillips); *m* 1975, Elizabeth Derry Watkins; two *s*. *Educ:* Tadcaste Grammar Sch.; Clare Coll., Cambridge (BA 1972, MA); Yale Univ. Sch. of Architectur (MED 1974). Worked for Herbert Newmann Associates, New Haven, Conn, 1974–75 Cambridge Design Architects, 1975–78. Vis. Prof., Bath Univ., 1998–; Sir Arthur Marsha Vis. Prof. of Sustainable Urban Design, Univ. of Cambridge, 2012–13. Major project include: envmtl office, BRE; gall. and visitor facilities, Yorks Sculpture Park; Central Office Nat. Trust, Swindon; Woodland Trust HQ, Grantham; housing, Accordia, Cambridg (RIBA Stirling Prize, 2008); Chelsea Academy; Broadcasting Place, Leeds; Visitor Centre Jodrell Bank, 2011. *Publications:* (with D. Watkins) The Complete Greenhouse Book, 1975 (with D. Watkins) Sunspaces, 1978; (jtly) Feilden Clegg Bradley: the environmenta handbook, 2007; contribs to UK-based architectural jls. *Recreations:* walking, music gardening, work. *Address:* Hill Farm Barn, Cold Ashton, Chippenham, Wilts SN14 8LA Feilden Clegg Bradley Studios, Bath Brewery, Tollbridge Road, Bath BA1 7DE.

CLEGG, His Honour Philip Charles; DL; a Circuit Judge, 1987–2009; a Deputy Circui Judge, 2009–13; *b* 17 Oct. 1942; *s* of Charles and Patricia Clegg; *m* 1st, 1965, Caroline France Peall (marr. diss. 1996); one *s* two *d*; 2nd, 1997, Fiona Cameron. *Educ:* Rossall; Bristol Univ (LLB Hons). Called to the Bar, Middle Temple, 1966; in practice on Northern Circuit; Ass Recorder, 1980–83; Recorder, 1983–87; Resident Judge, Basildon Combined Crown Court 1996–2007; Itinerant Murder Judge, SE Circuit, 2008–09. Mem., Sentencing Adv. Panel 2005–08. Mem., Vintage Austin Trans-Africa Expedn, 1963. Volunteer, Stow Marie Aerodrome, 2013–. Trustee, WW1 Aviation Heritage Trust, 2014. DL Essex, 2009 *Recreations:* sailing, vintage cars, carriage driving.

CLEGG, Richard Ninian Barwick; QC 1979; a Recorder of the Crown Court, 1978–93; *b* 28 June 1938; *o s* of Sir Cuthbert Clegg, TD; *m* 1963, Katherine Veronica, *d* of A. A. H Douglas; two *s* one *d*. *Educ:* Aysgarth; Charterhouse; Trinity Coll., Oxford (MA). Captain o Oxford Pentathlon Team, 1959. Called to Bar, Inner Temple, 1960, Bencher, 1985. Chm. NW section of Bow Group, 1964–66; Vice-Chm., Bow Group, 1965–66; Chm., Winstor Circle, 1965–66; Pres., Heywood and Royton Conservative Assoc., 1965–68. *Publications* (jtly) Bow Group pamphlet, Towards a New North West, 1964; Forged by Fire (memoir) 2009; The Secret Room (poems), 2013; Give Me a Vision (poems); Shadow Across the Moor (poems), 2014. *Recreations:* sport, music, travel. *Address:* Ford Farm, Wootton Courtenay Minehead, Somerset TA24 8RW. *T:* (01643) 841669. *Club:* Lansdowne.

CLEGG, Simon Paul, CBE 2006 (OBE 2001); Chairman, Great Britain Badminton, since 2013; Managing Director, Zeus International Management, since 2014; *b* 11 Aug. 1959; *s* o Peter Vernon Clegg and Patricia Anne Clegg (*née* Long); *m* 1985, Hilary Anne Davis; one one *d*. *Educ:* Stowe Sch. Commnd RA, 1981; OC Battery, 7th Parachute Regt, RHA, 1989 Manager, British Biathlon Team, 1984–85; British Olympic Association: Asst Gen. Sec. 1989–91; Dep. Gen. Sec., 1991–96; Chief Exec., 1997–2009; Olympic Quartermaster Summer and Winter Olympic Games, 1988 (on secondment); Great Britain Team: Dep. Che de Mission, Olympic Games, 1992 and 1996, Olympic Winter Games, 1994; Chef de Mission: Olympic Winter Games, 1998, 2002 and 2006; Olympic Games, 2000, 2004 and 2008; Chief Executive: European Youth Olympic Games, Bath, 1995; Ipswich Towr Football Club, 2009–13 (Dir, Ipswich Town plc, 2009–13). Director: London Olympic Bid 2003–05; LOCOG, 2005–08; Dir and Mem. Exec. Bd, British Olympic Assoc., 2013–; Exec Dir, European Olympic Cttees, European Games, 2013–14; Chief Operating Officer European Games Organising Cttee, Azerbaijan, 2014–15. Trustee, Royal Artillery Charitabl Fund, 2006–. Hon. Dr University Campus Suffolk, 2011. *Clubs:* Leander, Cavalry and Guards.

CLEGG, William; QC 1991; a Recorder, since 1992; *b* 5 Sept. 1949; *s* of Peter Hepworth Clegg and Sheila Clegg; *m* 1st, 1974, Wendy Doreen Chard (marr. diss. 2002); one *s* one *d* 2nd, 2008, Judith Gay Matthews. *Educ:* St Thomas More High School; Bristol Univ. (LLB) Called to the Bar, Gray's Inn, 1972; in practice, SE Circuit. Head of Chambers, 1995–. *Recreations:* squash, cricket. *Address:* 2 Bedford Row, WC1R 4BU. *T:* (020) 7440 8888. *Clubs* Garrick, MCC.

CLEGG-HILL, family name of **Viscount Hill**.

CLEGHORN, Bruce Elliot, CMG 2002; HM Diplomatic Service, retired; High Commissioner, Malaysia, 2001–06; *b* 19 Nov. 1946; *s* of Ivan Robert Cleghorn and Margaret (*née* Kemplen); *m* 1976, Sally Ann Robinson; three *s*. *Educ:* Sutton Valence Sch., Kent; St John's Coll., Cambridge (BA Hons, MA). Commonwealth Fellow, Panjab Univ., 1970–72; Jun. Res. Fellow, Inst. of Commonwealth Studies, Univ. of London, 1972–74; joined HM Diplomatic Service, 1974; Delegn to CSCE, 1974–75; FCO, 1975–76; First Secretary Delegn to NATO, 1976–79; New Delhi, 1980–83; FCO, 1983–87; Counsellor, CSCE Delegn, Vienna, 1987–89; Dep. Hd, UK Delegn to negotiations on conventional arms control, Vienna, 1989–91; Dep. High Comr and Counsellor (Econ. and Commercial), Kuala Lumpur, 1992–94; Head of Non-Proliferation Dept, FCO, 1995–97; Minister and Dep Perm. Rep., UK Delegn to NATO, Brussels, 1997–2001. Staff Performance Assessor, 2007–08, Records Sensitivity Reviewer, 2008–, FCO. Mem., Mgt Cttee, SE Asia Rainforest Res. Prog., Royal Soc., 2006–11. *Publications:* (with V. N. Datta) A Nationalist Muslim and Indian Politics, 1974. *Recreations:* walking, potting, gardening, birdwatching.

CLEIN, Natalie; 'cellist; *b* 25 March 1977; *d* of Peter Clein and Channa Clein (*née* Salomonson). *Educ:* Royal Coll. of Music; Hochschule Vienna (with Heinrich Schiff). BBC Proms début, 1997; has performed as a soloist with all major orchestras in the UK, and as a recitalist in UK, Europe, New York and Tokyo; participates in internat. chamber festivals; has premiered works by Peter Maxwell Davies, Elvis Costello and John Tavener; recordings include Elgar Cello Concerto and Sonatas by Brahms, Schubert and Rachmaninov. Artist in Association, 2005, now Vis. Prof., RCM; Prof., Trinity Laban Conservatoire, 2009–. Young Musician of Year, BBC, 1994; Eurovision Young Musician, 1994; Ingrid zu Zolms Kultur Preis, 2003; Young Artist Brit Award, 2005.

CLELAND, Helen Isabel; Headteacher, Woodford County High School, 1991–2010; *b* 3 July 1950; *d* of John Douglas Cleland and Hilda Malvina Cleland; *m* 1973, Dr Robin Hoult (*d* 2001); one *s* one *d*. *Educ:* King Edward VI High Sch. for Girls, Birmingham; Exeter Univ (BA Hons English); Homerton Coll., Cambridge (PGCE). English Teacher, Dame Alice Owen's Sch., London, 1972–76; English Teacher, 1976–79, Sen. Teacher, 1979–86, Haverstock Sch., London; Dep. Head, Edmonton Sch., Enfield, 1986–91. *Recreations:* reading, theatre, hill walking, horse-riding, travel.

CLELAND, Prof. John Goodhart, CBE 2008; FBA 2003; Professor of Medical Demography, London School of Hygiene and Tropical Medicine, since 1993; *b* 9 March 1942; *s* of late William Paton Cleland; *m* 1st, 1969, Susan Gilbert Harman (marr. diss. 1990); one *s* one *d*; 2nd, 2004, Sandra Carr. *Educ:* Charterhouse Sch.; Selwyn Coll., Cambridge (MA). Res. Officer, LSE, 1966–69; Sociologist, Population Bureau, ODA, 1969–72; Demographer, Med. Dept, Fiji, 1972–74; Demographic Analyst, World Fertility Survey, ISI, 1975–87; Sen. Res. Fellow, LSHTM, 1988–92. Mem., Scientific and Adv. Gp, Dept of Reproductive Health and Res., WHO, 1999–2005; Chm., Population Investigation Cttee, 2003–14. President: British Soc. for Population Studies, 1997–99; Internat. Union for Scientific Study of Population, 2006–09. *Publications:* (with J. Hobcraft) Reproductive Change in Developing Countries: insights from the World Fertility Survey, 1985; (with C.

Scott) The World Fertility Survey: an assessment, 1987; (with A. Hill) The Health Transition: methods and measures, 1991; (jtly) The Determinants of Reproductive Change in Bangladesh, 1994; (with B. Ferry) Sexual Behaviour and AIDS in the Developing World, 1995. *Recreations:* fishing, woodland management. *Address:* The Manor House, Silver Street, Barton St David, Somerset TA11 6DB. *T:* and *Fax:* (01458) 851266. *E:* John.Cleland@lshtm.ac.uk.

CLELAND, Victoria Mary Florence; Chief Cashier and Director of Notes, Bank of England, since 2014; *b* England; *d* of Robert Francis Doxford Cleland and Joan Cleland. *Educ:* Malvern Coll.; Hereford VI Form Coll.; St Hilda's Coll., Oxford (BA PPE 1991); Imperial Coll. Mgt Sch. (MBA). BDO Binder Hamlyn, 1991–92; Bank of England: Analyst, Business Finance Div., 1992–95, Wholesale Markets Supervision Div., 1995–96; Graduate Recruitment Manager, 1996–98; Manager, Domestic Finance Div., 1999–2001, Market Infrastructure Div., 2001–03; Private Sec. to Dep. Gov., 2003–06; Sen. Manager, Payment and Settlement Systems, 2006–08; Dep. Hd, Special Resolution Unit, 2008–10; Hd, Notes Div., 2010–14. *Recreations:* road cycling, hiking, wine tasting, theatre, art history, charity trustee. *Address:* Bank of England, Threadneedle Street, EC2R 8AH. *T:* (020) 7601 4402.

CLELLAND, David Gordon; *b* 27 June 1943; *s* of Archibald and Ellen Clelland; *m* 2004, Brenda; two *d* from former marr. *Educ:* Kelvin Grove Boys' School, Gateshead; Gateshead and Hebburn Technical Colleges. Apprentice electrical fitter, 1959–64; electrical tester, 1964–81. Gateshead Borough Council: Councillor, 1972–86; Recreation Chm., 1976–84; Leader of Council, 1984–86. Nat. Sec., Assoc. of Councillors, 1981–85. MP (Lab) Tyne Bridge, Dec. 1985–2010. An Asst Govt Whip, 1997–2000; a Lord Comr of HM Treasury (Govt Whip), 2000–01. Member: Home Affairs Select Cttee, 1986–88; Energy Select Cttee, 1989–90; OPDM Select Cttee, 2001–05; Transport Select Cttee, 2005–10. Chairman, All Party Group: on non-profit-making Members' Clubs; on Turks and Caicos Is, 2005–10; Chairman: Backbench Envmt Cttee, 1990–97; PLP Regl Govt Gp, 1992–97; PLP Trade Union Gp, 1994–97; Vice-Chm., Northern Gp of Lab MPs (Sec., 1990–98). Parly Advr, Working Men's Club and Institute Union, 2011–. Chm., Trustees Bd, Gateshead Carers Assoc., 2014–. Hon. Alderman, 2004, Hon. Freeman, 2010, Gateshead. *Recreations:* golf, music, reading, playing guitar.

CLEMENT, David James, OBE 2006; Chairman, Systems Network, 1997–2013; *b* 29 Sept. 1930; *s* of James and Constance Clement; *m* 1958, Margaret Stone; two *s* one *d*. *Educ:* Chipping Sodbury Grammar Sch.; Univ. of Bristol (BA). CPFA 1957. Internal Audit Asst, City of Bristol, 1953–56; Accountancy/Audit Asst, 1956–60, Chief Accountancy Asst, 1960–65, City of Worcester; Dep. Chief Finance Officer, Runcorn Develt Corp., 1965–68; Chief Finance Officer, Antrim and Ballymena Develt Commn, 1968–72; Asst Sec., Dept of Finance, NI, 1972–75, Dep. Sec., 1975–80; Under Sec., DoE, NI, 1980–84. Financial consultant, 1985–90; Chm., HELM Corp., 1990–98. Mem., Investigations Cttee, CIPFA, 2001–11. Dir, NI Council for Integrated Educn, 2007–. Chm. Trustees, Ulster Historical Foundn, 2000–08. Hon. Treas., NI Council for Voluntary Action, 2000–05. *Recreations:* lawn tennis, Association football, contract bridge, philately.

CLEMENT, John; Chairman: Culpho Consultants, 1991–2011; Tuddenham Hall Foods, since 1991; *b* 18 May 1932; *s* of Frederick and Alice Eleanor Clement; *m* 1956, Elisabeth Anne (*née* Emery); two *s* one *d*. *Educ:* Bishop's Stortford College. Howards Dairies, Westcliff on Sea, 1949–64; United Dairies London Ltd, 1964–69; Asst Managing Director, Rank Leisure Services Ltd, 1969–73; Chairman, Unigate Foods Div., 1973; Chief Executive, 1976–90, Chm., 1977–91, Unigate Group. Non-executive Chairman: The Littlewoods Organisation, 1982–90; Nat. Car Auctions Ltd, 1995–98; Director: NV Verenigde Bedrijven Nutricia, 1981–92; Eagle Star Holdings plc, 1981–86; Eagle Star Insce Co., 1981–84; Anglo American Insce Co., 1991–94 (Chm., 1993–94); Ransomes plc, 1991–98 (Chm., 1993–98); Dresdner RCM Second Endowment Policy Trust plc (formerly Kleinwort Second Endowment Trust plc), 1993– (Chm., 1998–); Jarvis Hotels Ltd, 1994–2004. Mem., Securities and Investments Bd, 1986–89. Chairman: King's Coll., Cambridge I-IV (business expansion scheme), 1993–98; Govs, Framlingham Coll., 1991–2001 (Gov., 1982–2001). Chairman: Children's Liver Disease Foundn, 1979–95; British Liver Trust, 1992–99. High Sheriff, Suffolk, 2000–01. CCMI (FBIM 1977); FIGD 1979. *Recreations:* shooting, sailing, bridge, Rugby, tennis. *Address:* Tuddenham Hall, Tuddenham, Ipswich, Suffolk IP6 9DD. *T:* (01473) 785099. *Clubs:* Cumberland Lawn Tennis; Royal Harwich Yacht; Royal Danish Yacht.
See also R. Clement.

CLEMENT, Marc; *see* Clement, R. M.

CLEMENT, Richard, (Dick), OBE 2007; freelance writer, director and producer; *b* 5 Sept. 1937; *s* of Frederick and Alice Eleanor Clement; *m* 1st, Jennifer F. Sheppard (marr. diss. 1981); three *s* one *d*; 2nd, 1982, Nancy S. Campbell; one *d*. *Educ:* Bishop's Stortford Coll.; Westminster Sch., Conn, USA. Co-writer (with Ian La Frenais): *television:* The Likely Lads, 1964–66; Whatever Happened to the Likely Lads, 1972–73; Porridge, 1974–76 (stage version, 2009); Thick as Thieves, 1974; Going Straight, 1978; Auf Wiedersehen, Pet, 1983–84, 2002–04; Freddie and Max, 1990; Full Stretch, 1993; The Rotters' Club (adaptation), 2005; Archangel (adaptation), 2005; Spies of Warsaw (adaptation), 2013; *films:* The Jokers, 1967; Otley, 1968; Hannibal Brooks, 1968; Villain, 1971; Porridge, 1979; Water, 1984; Vice Versa, 1987; The Commitments, 1991; Still Crazy, 1998; Honest, 2000; Goal, 2005; Flushed Away, 2006; Across the Universe, 2007; The Bank Job, 2008; Killing Bono, 2011. Director: *films:* Otley, 1968; A Severed Head, 1969; Porridge, 1979; Bullshot, 1983; Water, 1984; co-producer (with Ian La Frenais) Vice Versa, 1987; The Commitments, 1991 (jtly, Evening Standard Peter Sellers Award, 1992); *stage:* Billy, 1974; Anyone for Denis?, 1981. *Recreations:* work, tennis, backgammon; Chelsea FC. *Address:* 9700 Yoakum Drive, Beverly Hills, CA 90210, USA. *Clubs:* Garrick; Mulholland Tennis (LA).
See also John Clement.

CLEMENT, Prof. (Robert) Marc, PhD; CPhys, FIET, FInstP; Professor of Medical Devices and Director of Enterprise and Innovation, Institute of Life Science, Swansea University, since 2012; *b* Llwynhendy, Llanelli, 19 Nov. 1953; *s* of Gerald Edmund Clement and Eira Mary Clement; one *d*. *Educ:* Univ. of Wales, Swansea (BSc 1st cl. Hons Physics 1976; Postgrad. Dip. Ionisation Physics 1977); Univ. of Wales (PhD Laser Physics 1979). CPhys, MInstP 1984; FIET 2002; FInstP 2007. Teacher of Maths and Physics, Ystalyfera Sch., 1980; Royal Soc. Scholarship for Postdoctoral Study, Centre d'Etudes Nucléaire de Saclay, Paris, 1981–82; West Glamorgan Institute of Higher Education: Temp. Lectr, 1982, Lectr I, 1983, Lectr II, 1984, in Maths; transfer to Fac. of Electronic Engrg, 1985; Sen. Lectr in Microelectronics, 1986; Principal Lectr and Hd, Sch. of Electrical Engrg, 1987; Dean, Fac. of Electronic Engrg, 1988; University of Wales, Swansea: Chair of Innovation, Sch. of Engrg, 2000; Sen. Exec. to Vice Chancellor's Office, 2004; Vice-Chancellor and Chief Exec., 2007–11, Pres., 2011–12, Univ. of Wales. Founding FLSW 2010. P. M. Davidson Prize for Theoretical Physics, Univ. of Wales, Swansea, 1976; Business Award, HTV/Western Mail, 1990. *Publications:* books and articles in academic jls. *Recreations:* ski-ing, squash, weight training, choral singing, Sunday school teacher, adjudicator at many National and Urdd Eisteddfodau. *Address:* Institute of Life Science, Swansea University, Singleton Park, Swansea SA2 8PP. *T:* (01792) 295685. *E:* r.m.clement@swansea.ac.uk.

CLEMENT-JONES, family name of **Baron Clement-Jones**.

CLEMENT-JONES, Baron *cr* 1998 (Life Peer), of Clapham in the London Borough of Lambeth; **Timothy Francis Clement-Jones,** CBE 1988; International Business Relations Partner, 2010–11, and London Managing Partner, since 2011, Global Government Relations (formerly Upstream), government and media relations practice of DLA Piper UK LLP (formerly Dibb Lupton Alsop, later DLA Piper Rudnick Gray Carey) (Chairman, 1999–2009); *b* 26 Oct. 1949; *s* of late Maurice Llewelyn Clement-Jones and Margaret Jean Clement-Jones (*née* Hudson); *m* 1st, 1973, Dr Vicky Veronica Yip (*d* 1987); 2nd, 1994, Jean Roberta Whiteside; one *s*. *Educ:* Haileybury; Trinity Coll., Cambridge (Economics Pt I, Law Tripos Pt II; MA). Admitted Solicitor, 1974. Articled Clerk, Coward Chance, 1972–74; Associate, Joynson-Hicks, 1974–76; Corporate Lawyer, Letraset Internat. Ltd, 1976–80; Hd Legal Services, LWT, 1980–83; Legal Dir, Grand Metropolitan Retailing, 1984–86; Gp Co. Sec. and Legal Advr, Woolworth Hldgs, then Kingfisher plc, 1986–95; Dir, Political Context Ltd, 1996–99; Chm., Envmtl Context, later Context Gp Ltd, 1997–2009; Dir, British American Business Inc., 2006–. Lib Dem spokesman on health, H of L, 1998–2004, on culture, media and sport, 2004–10. Mem., Select Cttee on Communications, H of L, 2010–; Vice-Chairman: All-Party Autism Gp, 2003–10; All-Party China Gp, 2005–; All-Party Turkey Gp, 2010–; All-Party UAE Gp, 2010–; All-Party Ovarian Cancer Gp, 2010–. Introduced Tobacco Advertising and Sponsorship Act 2002 and Live Music Act 2012 as private members' bills. Chm., Assoc. of Liberal Lawyers, 1982–86. Chairman: Liberal Party, 1986–88; Lib Dem Finance Cttee, 1991–98; Dir, Lib Dem EP election campaign, 1994; Chm., Lib Dem Mayoral and Assembly campaign, London, 2000, 2004; Federal Treas., Lib Dems, 2005–10. Trustee and Dir, Cancer BACUP, subseq. Cancerbackup (founded by Dr V. V. Clement-Jones), 1986–2008. Chairman: Crime Concern, 1991–95; Lambeth Crime Prevention Trust, 2004–09; Trustee, CentreForum (formerly Centre for Reform), 1998–2009. Chm. Council, Sch. of Pharmacy, Univ. of London, 2008–12; Mem., Adv. Bd, Coll. of Medicine, 2011–; Mem. Council, UCL, 2012–. Pres., Ambitious About Autism (formerly Treehouse, educnl charity for autistic children), 2011– (Chm. Trustees, 2001–08); Trustee, Barbican Centre Trust, 2013–; Mem. Council, Heart of the City, 2013–. Gov., Haileybury, 2001–. FRSA. *Recreations:* reading, eating, talking, theatre and film, travelling, walking. *Address:* 10 Northbourne Road, SW4 7DJ. *T:* (020) 7622 4205. *E:* clementjonest@parliament.uk.

CLEMENTI, Sir David (Cecil), Kt 2004; Chairman, King's Cross Central General Limited Partnership, since 2008; *b* 25 Feb. 1949; *s* of Air Vice-Marshal Cresswell Montagu Clementi, CB, CBE and Susan (*née* Pelham); *m* 1972, Sarah Louise, (Sally), Cowley; one *s* one *d*. *Educ:* Winchester Coll.; Lincoln Coll., Oxford; Harvard Business Sch. (MBA 1975). With Arthur Andersen & Co., 1970–73; qualified as CA 1973; with Kleinwort Benson Ltd, 1975–97: Dir, 1981–97; Man. Dir, KB Securities, 1987–89; Head, Corporate Finance, 1989–94; Chief Exec., 1994–97; Vice Chm., 1997; Dep. Gov., Bank of England, 1997–2002; Chairman: Prudential plc, 2002–08; Virgin Money, 2011–15; World First, 2011–. Non-executive Director: Rio Tinto plc, 2003–10; Foreign & Colonial Investment Trust, 2008–12; Dep. Chm., Ruffer LLP, 2010–. Conducted review of regulation of legal services in England and Wales, 2004. Trustee, Royal Opera House, 2006–14. Warden, Winchester Coll., 2008–14. *Recreations:* sailing, ballet. *Club:* Royal Yacht Squadron.

CLEMENTS, Alan William, CBE 1990; Director, Capital Value Brokers Ltd, 1999–2006; *b* 12 Dec. 1928; *s* of William and Kathleen Clements; *m* 1953, Pearl Dorling (*d* 1993); two *s* one *d*. *Educ:* Culford School, Bury St Edmunds; Magdalen College, Oxford (BA Hons). HM Inspector of Taxes, Inland Revenue, 1952–56; ICI: Asst Treasurer, 1966; Dep. Treasurer, 1971; Treasurer, 1976; Finance Director, 1979–90. Chairman: David S. Smith (Hldgs), 1991–99; Cementone, 1994–97; Non-executive Director: Trafalgar House, 1980–95 (Chm., 1992–93); Cable & Wireless, 1985–91; Guinness Mahon Hldgs, 1988–92; Granada Gp, 1990–94; Mirror Gp (formerly Mirror Gp Newspapers), 1991–99 (Dep. Chm., 1992–99); Brent Walker Gp, 1991–93. Lay Mem., Internat. Stock Exchange, 1984–88. Founder Pres., Assoc. of Corp. Treasurers, 1979–82 (Hon. Fellow). *Publications:* articles on finance in jls. *Recreations:* golf, music, reading.

CLEMENTS, Andrew; *see* Clements, F. A.

CLEMENTS, Andrew Joseph; Music Critic, Guardian, since 1993; *b* 15 Sept. 1950; *s* of Joseph George Clements and Linda Helen Clements; *m* 1977, Kathryn Denise Coltman (marr. diss. 2007); two *d*. *Educ:* Crypt Sch., Gloucester; Emmanuel Coll., Cambridge (BA). Music Critic: New Statesman, 1977–88; Financial Times, 1979–93; Editor, Musical Times, 1987–88. Dir, Holst Foundn, 1992–. *Publications:* Mark-Anthony Turnage, 2000. *Recreation:* birding. *Address:* c/o Guardian, Kings Place, 90 York Way, N1 9AG.

CLEMENTS, Dr (Frederick) Andrew; Director, British Trust for Ornithology, since 2007; *b* Morecambe, Lancs, 25 Oct. 1954; *s* of Frederick George Clements and Clarice Clements (*née* Hartley); *m* 1997, Susannah Burton (marr. diss. 2008); one *s* one *d*. *Educ:* Haberdashers' Aske's Sch.; University Coll. of Wales, Bangor (BSc Hons Zool.); Univ. of Wales (PhD Zool. 1980). Conservation Officer, NCC, 1982–87; Chief Wildlife Inspector, DoE, 1987–91; Manager, 1991–2000, Dir, Protected Areas, 2000–06, English Nature; Dir, Ferrypath Consulting Ltd (own co.), 2006–08. Mem. Bd, Natural England, 2014–. Trustee, Nat. Biodiversity Network, 2013–. Pres., Norfolk and Norwich Naturalists' Soc., 2014–15. Wildlife Tour Leader (pt-time), Himalayas, Ethiopia, Namibia, 1990–2002. *Publications:* (contrib.) AA Field Guide to the Birds of Britain and Europe, 1998; (contrib.) Silent Summer, 2010; contrib. scientific papers to New Scientist, Animal Behaviour, Behaviour, Zeitschrift für Tierpsychologie, Science, Plosone, The Auk. *Recreations:* birding, watching wildlife round the world, rowing on an Ergo, veggie cooking. *Address:* c/o British Trust for Ornithology, The Nunnery, Thetford, Norfolk IP24 2PU. *T:* (01842) 750050, (01842) 750030. *E:* andy.clements@bto.org, andy.clements@ferrypath.co.uk.

CLEMENTS, John Rodney, FCA; Finance Manager, People & Planet Ltd, since 2006; *b* 19 Jan. 1947; *s* of late Peter Larby Clements and of Ethel Blanche Lillian Clements (*née* Steele); *m* 1st, 1969, Janet Sylvia Mallender (marr. diss. 1992); two *d*; 2nd, 1999, Georgina Margaret Eckles (marr. diss. 2005); 3rd, 2012, Caroline Mary Kramer. *Educ:* Univ. of Manchester (BA Hons Mod. Hist. with Econs and Politics 1968). ACA 1973, FCA 1978. Auditor, KPMG Peat Marwick, Accountants, 1968–73; Financial Accountant, Co-operative Bank, 1973–74; Asst to Chief Accountant, Stock Exchange, 1974–79; Dep. Finance Officer, UCL, 1979–85; Dep. Dir of Finance, Univ. of Sheffield, 1985–92; Dir of Finance, Univ. of Leeds, 1992–94; independent consultant, 1994–95; Sec. of the Chest, then Dir of Finance and Sec. of the Chest, Univ. of Oxford, 1995–2004; Fellow, Merton Coll., Oxford, 1995–2004. *Recreations:* history, literature, hill walking, model railways. *Address:* 19 Raleigh Park Road, Oxford OX2 9AZ.

CLEMENTS, Judith M.; Chief Executive, Mental Health Foundation of New Zealand, since 2005; *b* 27 June 1953; *d* of Robert and Margaret Dunn; *m* 1st, 1975, Paul Clements (marr. diss. 1979); 2nd, 1998, Rex Hewitt. *Educ:* Birmingham Univ. (LLB Hons 1974); Brunel Univ. (MA Public and Social Admin 1979). Dip. Inst. Housing 1976. London Borough of Camden: Estate Manager, 1974–76; Sen. Estate Manager, 1976–79; Tenancy Services Officer, 1979–81; Business System Analyst, 1981–82; Asst Dir of Housing, 1982–87; Dep. Chief Housing Officer, Brighton BC, 1987–91; Hd of Management Practice, Local Govt Management Bd, 1991–92; Chief Exec., Mind (Nat. Assoc. of Mental Health), 1992–2001; ind. consultant, 2001–05. Trustee, Mentality, 2001–03; Mem., UK Grants Cttee, Comic Relief, 2003–05. Mem. Bd of Govs, Brighton Univ., 2000–05. FRSA 1999. Hon. DSocSci Brunel, 1997. *Recreations:* reading, especially crime fiction and feminist fiction, yoga. *Address:* Mental Health Foundation of New Zealand, Unit 110, Zone 23, 23 Edwin Street, Mt Eden, Auckland, New Zealand. *T:* (9) 3007010. *E:* judi@mentalhealth.org.nz.

CLEMENTS, Judy, OBE 2000; Adjudicator, HM Revenue and Customs, since 2009; *b* Guyana, 20 Feb. 1958; *d* of Vernon Clements and Annette Clements; *m* (marr. diss.); one *d*. *Educ:* Open Univ. (BA Hons Social Scis); Univ. of Central England (LLB). Police officer, West Midlands Police, 1978–89; Co-ordinator, Safer Cities Crime Prevention Project, Home Office, 1989–94; Race and Equalities Advr to HM Prison Service, 1999–2003 (report, Investigation into Racism, Brixton Prison, 2001); Dir, SE England, 2003–08, Dir, Customer Services and Communications, 2008–09, Ind. Police Complaints Commn. Chm., Diana Princess of Wales NHS Children's Hosp. Trust, Birmingham, 1998–99. Mem., Video Appeals Panel, BBFC, 2011–. Trustee, Turning Point, 2004–08; Vice Chm., Barnardo's, 2011–. *Publications:* various reports; (section ed.) British Jl of Leadership in Public Services. *Recreations:* theatre, walking, cooking, reading, committed Seventh Day Adventist Christian. *Address:* Adjudicator's Office, 8th Floor, Euston Tower, 286 Euston Road, NW1 3US. *T:* 0300 057 1111, (020) 7667 1832.

CLEMENTS, Rev. Keith Winston, PhD; General Secretary, Conference of European Churches, 1997–2005; *b* Sichuan, China, 7 May 1943; *s* of Harry Clements and Alfreda (*née* Yarwood); *m* 1967, Margaret Hirst; two *s*. *Educ:* King Edward VII Sch., Lytham; King's Coll., Cambridge (MA 1969); Regent's Park Coll., Oxford (MA 1972, BD 1980); PhD Bristol 1997. Ordained to Baptist Ministry, 1967; Associate Minister, Mid-Cheshire Fellowship of Baptist Chs, 1967–71; Minister, Downend Baptist Ch, Bristol, 1971–77; Tutor, Bristol Baptist Coll., 1977–90; Sec. for Internat. Affairs, CCBI, 1990–97. Part-time Lectr, Dept of Theol. and Religious Studies, Univ. of Bristol, 1984–90; Select Preacher, Univ. of Cambridge, 1993; Adjunct Lectr, Whitley Coll., Melbourne, 2008–. Hon. Fellow, New Coll., Edinburgh, 1990–99. Ed., Baptist Historical Soc., 1980–85. *Publications:* Faith, 1981; A Patriotism for Today: dialogue with Dietrich Bonhoeffer, 1984; The Theology of Ronald Gregor Smith, 1986; Friedrich Schleiermacher, 1987; Lovers of Discord, 1988; What Freedom?: the persistent challenge of Dietrich Bonhoeffer, 1990; Learning to Speak: the Church's voice in public affairs, 1995; Faith on the Frontier: a life of J. H. Oldham, 1999; The Churches in Europe as Witnesses to Healing, 2003; Bonhoeffer and Britain, 2006; (ed) Dietrich Bonhoeffer Works, Vol. 13 (London 1933–35), 2007; (ed) The Moot Papers: faith, freedom and society 1938–44, 2009; The SPCK Introduction to Bonhoeffer, 2010; Ecumenical Dynamic: living in more than one place at once, 2013; We Will Remember, 2014; Dietrich Bonhoeffer's Ecumenical Quest, 2015; numerous articles in learned jls on theol. and religion. *Recreations:* grandchildren, ornithology, reading, listening to music, walking, choral singing. *Address:* 67 Hillcrest Road, Portishead, N Somerset BS20 8HN. *T:* (01275) 845242.

CLEMENTS, Kirsty Anne; *see* Wark, K. A.

CLEMENTS, Michael Alan; a Judge of the Upper Tribunal (Immigration and Asylum Chamber) (formerly Resident Senior Immigration Judge, Asylum and Immigration Tribunal), since 2007; President, First-tier Tribunal Immigration and Asylum Chamber, since 2011; *b* 25 Nov. 1954; *s* of Philip and Gwendoline Clements; *m* 1978, Carol Mary; three *s*. *Educ:* King Edward VI Sch., Bath. Admitted solicitor, 1983; NP; articled clerk, solicitor, then Partner, Giffin Couch & Archer, Leighton Buzzard, 1979–90; Solicitor, Horwood & James, Aylesbury, 1990–2001; Immigration Adjudicator, 2001–; Sen. Immigration Judge, 2006. Legal Mem., Tribunals Service, 1993–. *Address:* President's Office, Field House, Bream's Buildings, EC4A 1DZ. *T:* (020) 7073 4221.

CLEMENTS, Prof. Ronald Ernest; Samuel Davidson Professor of Old Testament Studies, King's College, University of London, 1983–92, now Professor Emeritus; *b* 27 May 1929; *m* 1955, Valerie Winifred (*née* Suffield); two *d*. *Educ:* Buckhurst Hill County High Sch.; Spurgeon's Coll.; Christ's Coll., Cambridge; Univ. of Sheffield. MA, DD Cantab. Asst Lectr 1960–64, Lectr 1960–67, Univ. of Edinburgh; Lectr, Univ. of Cambridge, 1967–83. Hon. For. Sec., SOTS, 1973–83 (Pres., 1985); Hon. Mem., OTWSA, 1979–. Hon. DLitt Acadia, Nova Scotia, 1982. Burkitt Medal for Biblical Studies, British Acad., 2013. *Publications:* God and Temple, 1965; Prophecy and Covenant, 1965; Old Testament Theology, 1978; Isaiah 1–39, 1979; A Century of Old Testament Study, 1976, 2nd edn 1983; Prayers of the Bible, 1986; Jeremiah, 1988; (ed) The World of Ancient Israel, 1989; Wisdom in Theology, 1993; Old Testament Prophecy: from oracles to canon, 1996; Israel and the Nations, 2011; contrib. Vetus Testamentum, Jl of Semitic Studies. *Recreations:* reading, travel, photography, aeromodelling. *Address:* 8 Brookfield Road, Coton, Cambridge CB23 7PT.

CLEMITS, John Henry, RIBA; Managing Director, PSA Projects Cardiff, 1990–92; *b* 16 Feb. 1934; *s* of late Cyril Thomas Clemits and Minnie Alberta Clemits; *m* 1958, Elizabeth Angela Moon; one *s* one *d*. *Educ:* Sutton High Sch.; Plymouth College of Art; Bucks New Univ. (BA Hons Creative Arts 2010); Open Univ. (BA Hons Humanities with Art Hist. 2012). ARIBA 1962 (Dist. in Thesis). National Service, RAF, 1959–61; Captain, RE (TA), 43 Wessex Div. and Royal Monmouthshire RE (Militia), 1964–69. Plymouth City Architects Dept, 1954–59; Watkins Gray & Partners, Architects, Bristol, 1961–63; SW RHB, 1963–65; Architect, MPBW, Bristol, 1965–69; Sen. Architect, MPBW, Regional HQ, Rheindahlen, Germany, 1969–71; Naval Base Planning Officer, MPBW, Portsmouth, 1971–73; Suptg Architect, PSA, Directorate of Bldg Develt, 1973–75; Suptg Planning Officer, PSA, Rheindahlen, 1975–79; Dir of Works (Army), PSA, Chessington, 1979–85; Dir for Wales, PSA, Central Office for Wales, DoE, 1985–90. Chairman: Cowbridge Choral Soc., 1988–90; Vale of Glamorgan Buildings Preservation Trust, 1994–97; Chm., 1995–2001, Vice-Chm., 2001–, Dewi Sant Housing Assoc. Member: Nat. Council, Welsh Fedn of Housing Assocs, 1996–99; Dio. of Llandaff Parsonage Bd, 2009–14. Chm., S Wales Art Soc., 2005–06 (Prog. Sec., 2002–05). *Recreations:* music, life-long learning, painting, travel. *Address:* The Lodge, Hendrescythan, Creigiau, Cardiff CF15 9NN. *T:* (029) 2089 0559.

CLEMMOW, Jana Eve; *see* Bennett, J. E.

CLEMMOW, Simon Phillip; Founder, CHI & Partners (formerly Clemmow Hornby Inge Ltd), advertising agency, since 2001; *b* Cambridge, 30 June 1956; *s* of late Dr Phillip Charles and Joan Alicia Clemmow; *m* 1987, Elizabeth Danuta Kaminska; one *s* and one step *d*. *Educ:* Univ. of Reading (BA Hons Typography and Graphic Communication). Trainee, Benton & Bowles, 1982; Account Planner, Gold Greenlees Trott, 1983–88; Founder, Simons Palmer Denton Clemmow & Johnson, 1988–97; CEO, TBWA, 1997–2001. *Recreations:* cycling, reading, river boating, keeping fit (swimming and going to gym), restoring an old house in Italy, walking, playing golf, listening to rock music, playing the drums, studying local history, doing the Times crossword, watching Arsenal FC and England cricket team. *Address:* CHI & Partners, 7 Rathbone Street, W1T 1LY. *T:* (020) 7462 8580, *Fax:* (020) 7462 8501. *E:* simon.clemmow@chiandpartners.com. *Clubs:* Union; Brocket Hall Golf.

CLEOBURY, Nicholas Randall, MA; FRCO; conductor; *b* 23 June 1950; *s* of John and Brenda Cleobury; *m* 1978, Heather Kay; one *s* one *d*. *Educ:* King's Sch., Worcester; Worcester Coll., Oxford (MA Hons). Assistant Organist: Chichester Cathedral, 1971–72; Christ Church, Oxford, 1972–76; Chorus Master, Glyndebourne Opera, 1977–79; Asst Director, BBC Singers, 1977–79; Conductor: main BBC, provincial and London orchestras and opera houses, also in Albania, Australia, Austria, Belgium, Canada, Denmark, France, Germany, Holland, Hong Kong, Italy, Lithuania, Macedonia, Norway, Poland, Singapore, Slovenia, S Africa, Spain, Sweden, Switzerland, USA; regular BBC TV appearances; numerous CD recordings. Principal Opera Conductor, Royal Academy of Music, 1981–88; Artistic Director: Aquarius, 1983–92; Cambridge Symphony Soloists, 1990–92; Britten Sinfonia, 1992–2005; Britten in Oxford, 2012–13; Music Dir, Oxford Bach Choir, 1997–; Founder and Artistic Dir, 1997–2006, Principal Conductor, 2006–, Sounds New; Associate Dir, Orchestra of the Swan, 2004–08; Artistic Dir and Principal Conductor, Mid Wales Opera, 2010–; Principal Conductor, John Armitage Meml, 2010–. Principal Guest Conductor, Gävle, Sweden, 1989–91; Guest Conductor, Zürich Opera, 1993–2005. Music Dir, Broomhill Arts, 1990–94; Artistic Director: Cambridge Fest., 1992; Mozart Now, 2004–06; Artistic Advr, Berks Choral Fest., USA, 2002–08. Fellow, Canterbury Christ Church Univ., 2006. Hon. RAM 1985. *Recreations:* cricket, food, reading, theatre, walking, wine. *Address:* c/o Rayfield Allied, Southbank House, Black Prince Road, SE1 7ST. *T:* (020) 3176 5500. *E:* info@rayfieldallied.com. *W:* www.NicholasCleobury.net. *Clubs:* MCC, Lord's Taverners.

See also S. J. Cleobury.

CLEOBURY, Stephen John, CBE 2009; FRCM; FRCO; Fellow, Director of Music and Organist, King's College, Cambridge, since 1982; Organist, Cambridge University, since 1991; *b* 31 Dec. 1948; *s* of John Frank Cleobury and Brenda Julie (*née* Randall); *m*; two *d*; *m* 2004, Emma Sian, *d* of John Ivor Disley, *qv*; two *d*. *Educ:* King's Sch., Worcester; St John's Coll., Cambridge (MA, MusB). FRCO 1968; FRCM 1993. Organist, St Matthew's, Northampton, 1971–74; Sub-Organist, Westminster Abbey, 1974–78; Master of Music, Westminster Cathedral, 1979–82; Conductor, 1983–2009, Chorus Dir, 2009–, Cambridge Univ. Musical Soc. Chief Conductor, 1995–2007, Conductor Laureate, 2007–, BBC Singers. President: IAO, 1985–87; Cathedral Organists' Assoc., 1988–90; RCO, 1990–92 (Hon. Sec., 1981–90); Mem. Council, RSCM, 1982–2000. FRSCM 2008; FRSA. Hon. FGCM 2005. Hon. DMus Anglia Poly., 2001. *Recreation:* reading. *Address:* King's College, Cambridge CB2 1ST. *T:* (01223) 331224.

See also N. R. Cleobury.

CLERK, Sir Robert (Maxwell), 11th Bt *cr* 1679, of Penicuik (NS); OBE 1995; Lord-Lieutenant, Midlothian, since 2013 (Vice Lord-Lieutenant, 2011–13); *b* 3 April 1945; *er s* of Sir John Dutton Clerk, 10th Bt, CBE, VRD and Evelyn Elizabeth Clerk (*née* Robertson); *S* father, 2002; *m* 1970, Felicity Faye Collins; two *s* one *d*. *Educ:* Winchester Coll.; Wye Coll., London Univ. (BScAgric). Partner, Smiths Gore, Chartered Surveyors, 1980–2003. Chm., Atlantic Salmon Trust, 2005–10; Vice-Pres., Assoc. of Salmon Fishery Bds, 1996–2011. Brig., Queen's Body Guard for Scotland (Royal Company of Archers). DL Midlothian, 1995. *Recreations:* bee-keeping, landscape gardening, field sports. *Heir: s* George Napier Clerk, *b* 27 May 1975. *Club:* New (Edinburgh).

CLERKE, Sir Francis Ludlow Longueville, 13th Bt *cr* 1660, of Hitcham, Buckinghamshire; *b* 25 Jan. 1953; *e s* of Sir John Edward Longueville Clerke, 12th Bt, and Mary, *d* of Lt-Col Ivor Reginald Veniss Bond, OBE, MC; *S* father, 2009; *m* 1st, 1982, Vanessa Anne (marr. diss. 2011), *o d* of Charles Cosman Citron and Olga May Citron; one *s* one *d*; 2nd, 2014, Louise, *d* of late Martin Louis Botha. *Educ:* Diocesan Coll., Cape Town; Stellenbosch Univ. (BA); Witwatersrand Univ. (LLB); Cape Town Univ. (LLM). *Heir: s* William Francis Talbot Cary, *b* 17 Jan. 1987. *Address:* 9 Lourens River Estate, Bizweni Avenue, Somerset West, 7130 Cape Town, South Africa.

CLEVELAND, Archdeacon of; *see* Rushton, Ven. S. J.

CLEVELAND, Alexis Jane, CB 2004; *b* 28 Jan. 1954; *d* of late Arthur and Peggy Cleveland. *Educ:* Brighton and Hove High Sch.; Univ. of Salford. Business Develt Dir, IT Services Agency, 1989–93; Benefits Agency, Department of Social Security, subseq. Department for Work and Pensions: Territorial and Jobseekers Allowance Dir, 1993–97; Ops Support Dir, 1997–2000; Chief Exec., 2000–02; Chief Exec., Pension Service, 2002–07; Cabinet Office: Dir Gen., Transformational Govt and Cabinet Office Mgt, 2007–09; Dir Gen., Corporate Services, 2009–11. Non-exec. Advr, HM Treasury, 2011–; non-exec. Chm., Food and Envmt Res. Agency, 2013– (non-exec. Dir, 2011–); Chair, Animal and Plant Health Agency, 2014–. Ind. consultant, 2013–. Lay Mem. Council, 2011–, Chair, UC Council, 2012–, Durham Univ. Trustee and Co. Dir, Barnardo's, 2011–. *Recreations:* travel, walking, opera, theatre, cinema.

CLEVERDON, Dame Julia (Charity), (Dame Julia Garnett), DCVO 2008 (CVO 2003); CBE 1996; Vice President, Business in the Community, since 2008 (Chief Executive, 1992–2008); Special Adviser to Prince of Wales's Charities on responsible business practice, since 2014 (Special Adviser to Prince of Wales's Charities, 2008–13); Chairman, National Literacy Trust, since 2014; *b* 19 April 1950; *d* of late Thomas Douglas James Cleverdon, BBC producer and Elinor Nest Lewis; *m* 1st, 1973, Martin Christopher Ollard (marr. diss. 1978); 2nd, 1985, (William) John (Poulton Maxwell) Garnett, CBE (*d* 1997); two *d*. *Educ:* Newnham Coll., Cambridge (BA Hons History). Communication Adviser, British Leyland and Anglo-American Mining Corp., S Africa, 1972–75; Industrial Society: Head, Eastern and Public Services Dept, 1975–77; Head, Common Purpose Campaign, 1977–79; Dir, Communication and Publicity Div., 1979–81; founded Pepperell Dept for Inner Cities and Educn work, 1981–88; Man. Dir, Develt, BITC, 1988–92. Chair, Teach First, 2006–13 (Vice Patron, 2014–); Business Leader, Nat. Council of Educn Excellence, 2007–09; Mem. Bd, NCVO, 2011–. Chm., Building Stronger Communites Taskforce, 2009 (Report, 2009); jtly led ind. rev. into youth social action, 2012–13 (Report, In the Service of Others: a vision for youth social action by 2020, 2013). Chm., Campaign Bd, Newnham Coll., Cambridge, 2009; Mem. Bd, Teach for All, 2009; Co-Founder and Trustee, Step Up To Serve, 2013–; Patron: Helena Kennedy Bursary Scheme; Volunteer Reading Help. Hon. LLB Warwick, 2003; Hon. DLit Harper Adams, 2008; Hon. Dr: Middlesex, 2009; Central Lancashire, 2010; Aston, 2011; Exeter, 2011. *Publications:* Why Industry Matters, 1978. *Recreations:* children, gardening, collecting pink lustre, entertaining. *Address:* (office) 8 Alwyne Road, Islington, N1 2HH.

CLEVERLY, James Spencer, TD; MP (C) Braintree, since 2015; Member (C) Bexley and Bromley, London Assembly, Greater London Authority, since 2008; *b* Lewisham, 4 Sept. 1969; *s* of James Philip Cleverly and Evelyn Suna Cleverly; *m* 2000, Susannah Janet Temple Sparks; two *s*. *Educ:* Colfe's Sch. for Boys; Thames Valley Univ. (BA Hons Hospitality Mgt). Sales Manager, VNU, 1996–2002; Internat. Advertising Manager, Informa, 2002–04; mobilised service, British Army, 2004; Gp Advertising Manager, Crimson Publishing, 2005–06; Online Commercial Manager, Caspian Publishing, 2006–07; Dir, Point & Fire Media Ltd, 2007–11. Mem. Bd, London Develt Agency, 2008–12; Chairman: London Waste and Recycling Bd, 2010–12; London Fire and Emergency Planning Authy, 2012–15; London Local Resilience Forum, 2012–15. Served Army Reserves (formerly TA), 1989–. *Recreations:* Rugby, triathlon, spending time with my family. *Address:* House of Commons, SW1A 0AA. *T:* (020) 7219 3000. *E:* james.cleverly.mp@parliament.uk; Greater London Authority, City Hall, The Queen's Walk, SE1 2AA. *T:* (020) 7983 6571. *E:* james.cleverly@london.gov.uk. *Club:* Carlton.

CLIBBORN, John Donovan Nelson dalla Rosa, CMG 1997; HM Diplomatic Service, retired; Senior Careers Manager, GPW and Co. Ltd, since 2011; *b* 24 Nov. 1941; *s* of Donovan Harold Clibborn, CMG, and Margaret Mercedes Edwige (*née* Nelson); *m* 1968, Juliet Elizabeth Pagden; one *s* two *d*. *Educ:* Downside Sch., Stratton-on-the-Fosse, Bath; Oriel Coll., Oxford (1st Cl. Hon. Mods and Lit.Hum. BA, MA). Joined HM Diplomatic Service, 1965; FCO, 1965–67; 3rd, subseq. 2nd Sec., Nicosia, 1967–69; FCO, 1970–72; 1st Secretary: Bonn, 1972–75; UK Mission to EC, Brussels, 1975–78; Jt Res. Centre, EEC, 1978–81; FCO, 1981–88; Counsellor, Washington, 1988–91; FCO, 1991–93; Counsellor, Washington, 1994–95; FCO, 1996–2011. Member: Soc. for the Promotion of Roman Studies, 1963–; Soc. for the Promotion of Hellenic Studies, 1964–; Palestine Exploration Fund, 1965–. *Recreations:* classical literature, ancient history. *Club:* Athenæum.

CLIFF, Prof. Andrew David, FBA 1996; FSS; CGeog; Professor of Theoretical Geography, 1997–2010, now Emeritus, and Pro-Vice-Chancellor, 2004–10, University of Cambridge;

Fellow, Christ's College, Cambridge, since 1974; *b* 26 Oct. 1943; *s* of Alfred Cliff and Annabel Cliff (*née* McQuade); *m* 1964, Margaret Blyton; three *s*. *Educ:* King's Coll. London (BA 1964); Northwestern Univ. (MA 1966); Univ. of Bristol (PhD 1969; DSc 1982); MA Cantab 1973. FSS 1968; CGeog 2002. Teaching Asst in Geog., Northwestern Univ., 1964–66; Res. Associate in Geog., 1968–69, Lectr, 1969–72, Bristol Univ.; Lectr in Geog., 1973–91, Reader in Theoretical Geog., 1991–97, Univ. of Cambridge. MAE 2002. *Publications:* jointly: Spatial Autocorrelation, 1973; Elements of Spatial Structure: a quantitative approach, 1975; Locational Analysis in Human Geography, 2nd edn 1977; Locational Models, 1977; Locational Methods, 1977; Spatial Processes: models and applications, 1981; Spatial Diffusion: an historical geography of epidemics in an island community, 1981; Spatial Components in the Transmission of Epidemic Waves through Island Communities: the spread of measles in Fiji and the Pacific, 1985; Spatial Aspects of Influenza Epidemics, 1986; Atlas of Disease Distributions: analytical approaches to epidemiological data, 1988; London International Atlas of AIDS, 1992; Measles: an historical geography of a major human viral disease from global expansion to local retreat 1840–1990, 1993; Deciphering Global Epidemics: analytical approaches to the disease records of world cities 1888–1912, 1998; Island Epidemics, 2000; War and Disease, 2004; World Atlas of Epidemic Diseases, 2004; Poliomyelitis: a world geography - emergence to eradication, 2006; Infectious Diseases: emergence and re-emergence. A geographical analysis, 2009; An Atlas of Epidemic Britain, 2012; The Control of Epidemic Communicable Diseases, 2013. *Recreations:* watching Grimsby Town FC, old roses, theatre. *Address:* Department of Geography, University of Cambridge, Downing Place, Cambridge CB2 3EN. *T:* (01223) 333366.

CLIFF, Anita, OBE 2007; Headteacher, Manor Primary Teaching School, Coseley, since 1999; National Leader of Education, since 2009; *b* Bilston, Wolverhampton, 15 Sept. 1964; *d* of David Moss and Mary Ivy Moss; *m* 1987, David Edward Cliff. *Educ:* Moseley Park Sch., Wolverhampton; Univ. of Birmingham (BEd 1986; MEd Sch. Improvement 1996). Teacher, Lozells Primary Sch., Birmingham, 1986; Dep. Hd, 1998, Actg Hd, 1999, Manor Primary Sch., Coseley. *Recreations:* reading, writing. *Address:* 5 Canalside Close, Penkridge, Stafford ST19 5TX. *T:* (school) (01902) 556460. *E:* acliff@manorprimary.com.

CLIFF, Ian Cameron, OBE 1991; HM Diplomatic Service; Chargé d'Affaires, Croatia, 2015–April 2016; *b* 11 Sept. 1952; *s* of late Gerald Shaw Cliff and Dorothy Cliff; *m* 1988, Caroline Mary Redman; one *s* two *d*. *Educ:* Hampton Grammar Sch.; Magdalen Coll., Oxford (MA Modern Hist.). Asst Master (Hist.), Dr Challoner's GS, Amersham, 1975–79; joined HM Diplomatic Service, 1979: SE Asia Dept, 1979–80; Arabic lang. trng, St Andrews Univ. and Damascus, 1980–82; First Sec., Khartoum, 1982–85; Head, Arabian Peninsula Section, ME Dept, FCO, 1985–87; Perm. Under Sec.'s Dept, FCO, 1987–89; First Sec., UK Mission to UN, NY, 1989–93; Counsellor, on loan to DTI as Dir, Exports to ME, Near East and N Africa, 1993–96; Deputy Hd of Mission, Consul-Gen. and Dir of Trade Promotion, Vienna, 1996–2001; Ambassador to: Bosnia and Herzegovina, 2001–05; Sudan, 2005–07; UK Perm. Rep. to OSCE, Vienna, 2007–11; Ambassador to Kosovo, 2011–15. *Publications:* occasional articles in railway magazines. *Recreations:* railways, philately, music. *Address:* c/o Foreign and Commonwealth Office, King Charles Street, SW1A 2AH.

CLIFFE, Air Vice-Marshal John Alfred, CB 2008; OBE 1994; Managing Director, JacAero Ltd, since 2013; *b* Hyde, Cheshire, 14 June 1953; *s* of Kenneth Cliffe and Mary Vickerman Cliffe (*née* Ellor); *m* 1975, Amanda Penelope Barr. *Educ:* Hyde Co. Grammar Sch. Commnd RAF, 1972; flying trng, 1972–74; Pilot, XI, 19, 23 and 43 Sqdns and Lightning Trng Flight, 1974–88; RNSC, 1988; Personal Staff Officer to AOC 11 Gp, 1989–90; OC XI Sqdn, 1991–94; Air Plans, MoD, 1994–95; Plans, HQ RAF Stike Comd, 1995–97; rcds, 1998; OC RAF Leeming, 1999–2000; Comdr, British Forces, Falkland Is, 2001; Dir, Flying Trng, 2002–03; COS Ops, HQ RAF Strike Comd, 2003–05; Dir Gen., Trng and Educn, MoD, 2005–07. Gen. Manager, Special Mission Business Gp, 2008–11, Dir, Sales and Business Develt, 2011–13, Cobham Aviation Services. *Recreations:* flying, ornithology, hill walking, golf. *Club:* Royal Air Force.

CLIFFORD, family name of **Baron Clifford of Chudleigh**.

CLIFFORD OF CHUDLEIGH, 14th Baron *cr* 1672; **Thomas Hugh Clifford;** Count of The Holy Roman Empire; DL; *b* 17 March 1948; *s* of 13th Baron Clifford of Chudleigh, OBE and Hon. Katharine Vavasseur Fisher, 2nd *d* of 2nd Baron Fisher; *S* father, 1988; *m* 1st, 1980, (Muriel) Suzanne (marr. diss. 1993), *d* of Major Campbell Austin and Mrs Campbell Austin; two *s* one *d*; 2nd, 1994, Clarissa, *er d* of His Honour A. C. Goodall, MC. *Educ:* Downside Abbey. Commnd Coldstream Guards, 1967; stationed British Honduras, 1967–68; Instructor, Guards Depot, 1968–69; Northern Ireland, 1969, 1971, 1972; ADC to Chief of Defence Staff, 1972–73; served with ACE Mobile Force, 1973; Adjutant, Guards Depot, 1974–75. Royal Agricultural College, Cirencester, 1977–79. DL Devon, 1998. *Recreations:* fishing, croquet and crolf. *Heir: s* Hon. Alexander Thomas Hugh Clifford, *b* 24 Sept. 1985. *Address:* Ugbrooke Park, Chudleigh, South Devon TQ13 0AD. *T:* (office) (01626) 852179.

CLIFFORD, Daniel; Chef/Patron, Midsummer House Restaurant, Cambridge, since 1998; *b* Canterbury, Kent, 6 Aug. 1973; *s* of Tony Clifford and Denise (*née* Wynn); *m* Valerie Arnou; five *d*. *Educ:* Canterbury High Sch. Commis chef, Howfield Manor Hotel and Restaurant, Canterbury, 1989–92; first commis chef, Bell Inn, Aston Clinton, 1992; Demi-chef de Partie, Box Tree, Ilkley, 1992–93; Chef de Partie, Millers, Harrogate, 1993; Sous Chef, Provence Restaurant, Hordle, 1993–95; Chef de Partie, Jean Bardet Restaurant, Tours, 1995–96; Sen. Sous Chef, Rascasse, Leeds, 1996–98. Michelin Stars, 2002, 2005. *Address:* Midsummer House Restaurant, Midsummer Common, Cambridge CB4 1HA. *T:* (01223) 369299. *E:* reservations@midsummerhouse.co.uk.

CLIFFORD, Most Rev. Dermot, DD; Archbishop of Cashel and Emly, (RC), 1988–2014; *b* 25 Jan. 1939. *Educ:* St Brendan's Coll., Killarney, Co. Kerry; St Patrick's Coll., Maynooth (BSc 1960); Irish Coll., Rome; Lateran Coll., Rome (STL 1964); NUI (HDipE 1966); LSE (MSc 1974); Loughborough (PhD 1989). Ordained priest, Rome, 1964; Dean of Studies, St Brendan's Coll., Killarney, 1964–72; Diocesan Sec., Kerry, 1974–86; Lectr, Univ. Coll., Cork, 1975–81; Chaplain, St Mary of the Angels Home for Handicapped Children, Beaufort, Co. Kerry, 1976–86; ordained Archbishop, Thurles, 1986; Coadjutor Archbishop of Cashel and Emly, 1986–88; Apostolic Administrator, Cloyne Diocese, 2009–. Chm., Dept of Planning and Communications, Council for R&D of Irish Episcopal Commn, 1991–. Trustee: Mary Immaculate Teachers' Trng Coll., Limerick, 1987–; Bothar, Third World Aid Orgn, 1991–. Patron, Gaelic Athletic Assoc., 1989–. *Publications:* The Social Costs and Rewards of Caring, 1990. *Recreations:* reading, walking, sport. *Address:* Archbishop's House, Thurles, Co. Tipperary, Ireland. *T:* (504) 21512, *Fax:* (504) 22680.

CLIFFORD, Maxwell; Founder and Proprietor, Max Clifford Associates Ltd, press and public relations consultants, 1968–2014; *b* 6 April 1943; *s* of Frank and Lilian Clifford; *m* Elizabeth (*d* 2003); one *d*. Formerly: jun. reporter, Merton and Morden News; Jun. Publicity Officer, EMI Records (promoter of The Beatles); asst to Syd Gillingham (promoter of Tom Jones, Jimi Hendrix, Bee Gees, Cream). Clients of Max Clifford Associates have included: Muhammad Ali, Shane Warne, Simon Cowell, David Copperfield, Diana Ross, O. J. Simpson, Mohamed Al Fayed, Peter Jones (owner, Phones Internat.), Shilpa Shetty, Jade Goody, Rolls Royce Motors. Media advisor/commentator for TV, radio, newspapers on major news stories; public speaker. *Publications:* Max Clifford: Read All About It (autobiog.), 2005.

CLIFFORD, Nigel Richard; Chief Executive, Ordnance Survey, since 2015; *b* 22 June 1959; *s* of Dr John Clifford and Barbara Dorothy Clifford; *m* 1989, Jeanette Floyd; two *s* one *d*. *Educ:* Portsmouth Grammar Sch.; Downing Coll., Cambridge (MA 1983); Strathclyde Univ. (MBA 1994); DipCAM 1986; Dip. Inst. Mkting 1984. British Telecom, 1981–92: Head, Internat. Operator Services, 1987–90; Sen. Strategy Advr, Chm.'s Office, 1990; Head, Business Strategy and Develt, Mobile Communications, 1990–92; Chief Exec., Glasgow Royal Infirmary Univ. NHS Trust, 1992–98; Sen. Vice Pres., Service Delivery, Cable & Wireless Communications, 1998–2000; Chief Executive: Tertio Ltd, 2000–05; Symbian, 2005–10; Micro Focus Internat. plc, 2010–11; Procserve Holdings Ltd, 2012–15; Sen. Vice Pres., Nokia, 2008–10. Founding Dir, Herald Foundn for Women's Health, 1994. FCMI (FIMgt 1995); FRSA 1996; FRGS 2012. *Recreations:* family life, walking, running. *Club:* Morpeth Comrades Social (Morpeth).

CLIFFORD, Sir Roger (Joseph), 7th Bt *cr* 1887; *b* 5 June 1936; *s* of Sir Roger Charles Joseph Gerard Clifford, 6th Bt and Henrietta Millicent Kiver (*d* 1971); *S* father, 1982; *m* 1968, Joanna Theresa, *d* of C. J. Ward, Christchurch, NZ; two *d*. *Educ:* Beaumont College, England. *Recreations:* golf, Rugby football. *Heir: b* Charles Joseph Clifford [*b* 5 June 1936; *m* 1983, Sally Green (marr. diss. 1990)]. *Clubs:* Blenheim (Blenheim, NZ); Christchurch, Christchurch Golf.

CLIFFORD, Stephen Mark; General Director, Evangelical Alliance, since 2009; *b* Bradford, May 1954; *s* of Rev. Albert Clifford and Joyce Clifford; *m* 1976, Ann Mary Alford; one *s* one *d*. *Educ:* Grange Boys Grammar Sch., Bradford; London Bible Sch. (BA Theology 1976). Secondary Sch. Teacher, 1980–85; Team Mem. and Church Leader, Pioneer Network, 1985–2008. Internat. Chair, March for Jesus, 1988–2000; Chair: Soul in the City, 2003–04; Hope 08, 2006–08; Member, Board: Evangelical Alliance; Spring Harvest. Co-founder, Leader and Lecturer: DNA; Equipped to Lead. *Recreations:* ski-ing, diving, tennis, cycling, films, theatre, art - particularly portraits. *Address:* Evangelical Alliance, 176 Copenhagen Street, N1 0ST. *T:* (020) 7520 3850. *E:* S.Clifford@eauk.org.

CLIFFORD, Susan Merlyn, MBE 1994; Founder Director, 1982, Honorary Director, 1983–88, Joint Executive Director, 1988–2012, Common Ground (initiated Apple Day annual festival, 21 October); *b* 16 April 1944; *d* of Bernard Clifford and Hilda Clifford (*née* Moorley). *Educ:* Brincliffe Grammar Sch., Nottingham; Univ. of Hull (BSc Hons); Edinburgh Coll. of Art (DipTP). Work in planning consultancy, Edinburgh, 1966–68; landscape architecture practice, 1968–69; Lectr in Extra-Mural Studies, Edinburgh Univ., 1968–69; Lectr, then Sen. Lectr in Planning and Natural Resource Mgt, PCL, 1970–74; Lectr, Bartlett Sch. of Architecture and Planning, UCL, 1975–90. Friends of the Earth (UK), 1971–82 (Hon. Dir); Founder Trustee, Earth Resources Res., 1972; Hon. Mem., Culture SW (Regl Cultural Consortium), 2000–03; Mem., Design Review Cttee, CABE, 2000–02. Has initiated and toured exhibns, including: The Tree of Life, with S Bank Centre, 1989–90; Out of the Wood, with Crafts Council, 1989–90; Leaves by Andy Goldsworthy, Natural Hist. Mus., 1989; from place to PLACE, Barbican Centre, 1996. *Publications:* (ed jtly) Second Nature, 1984; (ed jtly) Pulp!, 1989; Places: the city and the invisible, 1993; with Angela King: Holding Your Ground: an action guide to local conservation, 1985; The Apple Source Book, 1991, enlarged edn 2007; Celebrating Local Distinctiveness, 1994; A Manifesto for Fields, 1997; Rivers, Rhynes and Running Brooks, 2000; England in Particular: a celebration of the commonplace, the local, the vernacular and the distinctive, 2006; Community Orchards Handbook, 2008, 2nd edn 2011; Journeys Through England in Particular: on foot, 2014; Journeys Through England in Particular: coasting, 2014; edited with Angela King: Trees Be Company: an anthology of tree poetry, 1989, 3rd edn 2001; Local Distinctiveness: place particularity and identity, 1993; from place to PLACE: maps and parish maps, 1996; Field Days: an anthology of poetry about fields, 1998; The River's Voice: an anthology of poetry about rivers, 2000; The Common Ground Book of Orchards, 2000. *Recreation:* looking at the land. *Address:* c/o Common Ground, Lower Dairy, Toller Fratrum, Dorchester, Dorset DT2 0EL. *T:* (01300) 321778.

CLIFFORD, Sir Timothy (Peter Plint), Kt 2002; Director-General, National Galleries of Scotland, 2001–06 (Director, 1984–2000); *b* 26 Jan. 1946; *s* of late Derek Plint Clifford and Anne (*née* Pierson); *m* 1968, Jane Olivia, *yr d* of Sir George Paterson, OBE, QC; one *d*. *Educ:* Sherborne, Dorset; Perugia Univ. (Dip. Italian); Courtauld Inst., Univ. of London (BA Hons, History of Art). Dip. Fine Art, Museums Assoc., 1972; AMA. Asst Keeper, Dept of Paintings, Manchester City Art Galleries, 1968–72, Acting Keeper, 1972; Asst Keeper, Dept of Ceramics, Victoria and Albert Mus., London, 1972–76; Asst Keeper, Dept of Prints and Drawings, British Mus., London, 1976–78; Dir, Manchester City Art Galls, 1978–84. Member: Manchester Diocesan Adv. Cttee for Care of Churches, 1978–84; NACF Cttee (Cheshire and Gtr Manchester Br.), 1978–84; North Western Museum and Art Gall. Service Jt Adv. Panel, 1978–84; Cttee, ICOM (UK), 1980–82; Chm., Internat. Cttee for Museums of Fine Art, ICOM, 1980–83 (Mem., Exec. Cttee, 1983–88); Board Member: Museums and Galleries Commn, 1983–88; British Council, 1987–92 (Fine Arts Adv. Cttee, 1988–92); Founder, Museo di Casteldilago, Umbria, 2012; Founder and Committee Member: Friends of Manchester City Art Galls, 1978–84; Patrons and Associates, Manchester City Art Galls, 1979–; Mem. Exec. Cttee, Scottish Museums Council, 1984–2006; Mem. Adv. Council, Edinburgh Internat. Fest., 2012–; Consultant, Simon C. Dickinson Ltd, London, 2007–. Cttee Mem., Derby Internat. Porcelain Soc., 1983–86; Vice-Pres., Turner Soc., 1984–86, and 1989–; Pres., NADFAS, 1996–2006; Mem., Adv. Cttee, Come and See Scotland's Churches, 1989–90. Member Consultative Committee: Sculpture Jl, 1998–; Gazette des Beaux-Arts, 1999–. Vice-Pres., Frigate Unicorn Preservation Soc., 1987–2003. Trustee: Lake Dist Art Gall. and Mus. Trust, 1989–97; Royal Yacht Britannia, 1998–2011; Hermitage Develt Trust, 1999–2003; Stichting Hermitage aan de Amstel, 1999–2005; Wallace Collection, 2003–11. Patron: Friends of Sherborne House, 1997–; Art and Antiques Fair, Olympia, 2008–10; Attingham Summer Sch. Member: Accademia Italiana delle Arti Applicate, 1988; Ateneo Veneto, Italy, 1997; Opificio delle Pietre Dure, Florence; Comitato Scientifico, Foundn of the Civic Museums of Venice. FRSA; FRSE 2001; FSAScot 1986. Freeman: Goldsmiths' Co., 1989 (Liveryman, 2007–); City of London, 1989. Hon. LLD: St Andrews, 1996; Aberdeen, 2005; Hon. DLitt Glasgow, 2001. Special Award, BIM, 1991. Commendatore: al Ordine della Repubblica Italiana, 1999 (Cavaliere, 1988); Ordine de S Maurizio e Lazzaro, 2000; Grand Ufficiale della Solidarietà Italiana, 2004. *Publications:* (with Derek Clifford) John Crome, 1968; (with Dr Ivan Hall) Heaton Hall, 1972; (with Dr T. Friedmann) The Man at Hyde Park Corner: sculpture by John Cheere, 1974; Vues Pittoresques de Luxembourg … par J. M. W. Turner, (Luxembourg) 1977; Ceramics of Derbyshire 1750–1975 (ed, H. G. Bradley), 1978; J. M. W. Turner, Acquerelli ed incisioni, (Rome) 1980; Turner at Manchester, 1982; (with Ian Gow) The National Gallery of Scotland: an architectural and decorative history, 1988; (jtly) Raphael: the pursuit of perfection, 1994; (with Ian Gow) Duff House, 1995; (with A. Weston-Lewis) Effigies and Ecstasies: Roman Baroque sculpture and design in the age of Bernini, 1998; Designs of Desire: architectural and ornament prints and drawings 1500–1850, 2000; (with Nicholas Barker and Hugh Brigstocke) A Poet in Paradise: Lord Lindsay and Christian Art, 2000; (jtly) The Age of Titian, 2004; Choice: twenty-one years of collecting in Scotland, 2005; (contrib.) Croatia: aspects of Art & Architecture, 2009; contrib. Burlington Magazine, Apollo, etc. *Recreations:* bird watching, entomology. *Address:* Ampthill Park House, Ampthill, Beds MK45 2HF. *Clubs:* Turf, Beefsteak, Garrick, Pratt's; New (Edinburgh).

CLIFT, Richard Dennis, CMG 1984; HM Diplomatic Service, retired; *b* 18 May 1933; *s* of late Dennis Victor Clift and Helen Wilmot Clift (*née* Evans); *m* 1st, 1957, Barbara Mary Travis (marr. diss. 1982); three *d*; 2nd, 1982, Jane Rosamund Barker (*née* Homfray) (*d* 2014). *Educ:* St Edward's Sch., Oxford; Pembroke Coll., Cambridge. BA 1956. FO, 1956–57; Office of

British Chargé d'Affaires, Peking, 1958–60; British Embassy, Berne, 1961–62; UK Delegn to NATO, Paris, 1962–64; FO, 1964–68; Head of Chancery, British High Commn, Kuala Lumpur, 1969–71; FCO, 1971–73; Counsellor (Commercial), Peking, 1974–76; Canadian Nat. Defence Coll., 1976–77; seconded to NI Office, 1977–79; Hd of Hong Kong Dept, FCO, 1979–84; High Comr in Freetown, 1984–86; Political Advr, Hong Kong Govt, 1987–89. Advr and Social Policy Co-ordinator, CAB, Twickenham CAB, 2000–11. Student, London Coll. of Furniture, 1989–91. *Recreations:* sailing, walking. *Address:* 18 Langwood Chase, Teddington, Middx TW11 9PH.

CLIFT, Prof. Roland, CBE 2006 (OBE 1994); FREng, FIChemE; Professor of Environmental Technology and Director, Centre for Environmental Strategy, 1992–2005, Distinguished Professor, 2005–08, Emeritus Professor, 2008, University of Surrey; *b* 19 Nov. 1942; *s* of Leslie William Clift and Ivy Florence Gertrude Clift (*née* Wheeler); *m* 1st, 1968, Rosena Valory (*née* Davison); one *d*; 2nd, 1979, Diana Helen (*née* Manning); one *s* (and one *s* decd). *Educ:* Trinity Coll., Cambridge (BA 1963; MA 1967); PhD McGill 1970. CEng, FIChemE 1984; FREng (FEng 1986). Technical Officer (Chem. Engr), ICI, 1964–67; Lectr, Asst Prof. and Associate Prof., McGill Univ., 1967–75; Lectr, Imperial Coll., London, 1975–76; Lectr, Univ. of Cambridge, 1976–81; Fellow, Trinity Coll., Cambridge, 1976–81 (Praelector, 1980–81); University of Surrey: Prof. of Chem. Engrg, 1981–92; Dir, Centre for Envmtl Strategy, 1992–2005. Visiting Professor: Univ. di Napoli, 1973–74; Chalmers Univ. of Technol., Gothenburg, 1989–; Adjunct Prof., Univ. of British Columbia, 2009–. Editor in Chief, Powder Technology, 1987–95. Director: ClifMar Associates, 1986–2007; Blackrock New Energy Investment Trust (formerly Merrill Lynch New Energy Technologies), 1999–2010. Chairman: Clean Technology Management Cttee, SERC, 1990–94; Engrg Bd, AFRC, 1992–94; Member: UK Ecolabelling Bd, 1992–98; Royal Commn on Envmtl Pollution, 1996–2005; Sci. Adv. Council, DEFRA, 2006–11; specialist advr to H of L on energy efficiency, 2004–05. Exec. Dir, Internat. Soc. for Industrial Ecology, 2011–13 (Pres., 2009–10). Mem., Governing Body, Charterhouse Sch., 1982–91. Hon. Citizen of Augusta, Georgia, 1987. FRSA 1986. Hon. FCIWEM 2001. Sir Frank Whittle Medal, Royal Acad. of Engrg, 2003. *Publications:* (jtly) Bubbles, Drops and Particles, 1978, repr. 2005; (ed jtly) Fluidization, 1985; (jtly) Slurry Transport using Centrifugal Pumps, 1992, 3rd edn 2005; (jtly) Processing of Particulate Solids, 1997; (ed jtly) Sustainable Development in Practice, 2004; (ed jtly) Taking Stock of Industrial Ecology, 2014. *Recreation:* arguing and thinking. *Address:* Centre for Environmental Strategy, University of Surrey, Guildford, Surrey GU2 7XH. *T:* (01483) 689271, *Fax:* (01483) 686671. *Club:* Athenæum.

CLIFTON, Lord; Ivo Donald Stuart Bligh; *b* 17 April 1968; *s* and *heir* of 11th Earl of Darnley, *qv* and Countess of Darnley, *qv*; *m* 1997, Peta, *d* of A. R. Beard; three *s*. *Educ:* Marlborough Coll.; Edinburgh Univ. *Heir:* *s* Hon. Henry Robert Stuart Bligh, *b* 23 April 1999.

CLIFTON, Bishop of, (RC), since 2001; **Rt Rev. Declan Lang;** *b* 15 April 1950; *s* of Francis and Mai Lang. *Educ:* Ryde Sch., IoW; Allen Hall, St Edmund's Coll., Ware; Royal Holloway Coll., Univ. of London (BA Hons). Ordained priest, 1975; Asst Priest, St John's Cathedral, Portsmouth, 1975–79; Sec. to Bishop of Portsmouth, 1979–82; Diocesan Advr for Adult Religious Educn, 1982–90; Parish Priest: Our Lady of the Apostles, Bishop's Waltham, Hants, 1982–86; Sacred Heart, Bournemouth, 1986–90; Administrator, St John's Cathedral, Portsmouth, 1990–96; VG, Dio. Portsmouth and Parish Priest, St Edmund, Abingdon, 1996–2001. *Publications:* (jtly) Parish Project: a resource book for parishes to review mission, 1992. *Recreations:* walking, travel, cinema, theatre. *Address:* St Ambrose, North Road, Leigh Woods, Bristol BS8 3PW. *T:* (0117) 973 3072.

CLIFTON, His Honour Gerald Michael; a Circuit Judge, 1992–2012; *b* 3 July 1947; *s* of Frederick Maurice Clifton and Jane Clifton; *m* 1973, Rosemary Anne Vera Jackson; two *s*. *Educ:* Liverpool Coll. (Schol.); Brasenose Coll., Oxford (Open Classical Schol., MA). Called to the Bar, Middle Temple, 1970, Bencher, 2006; joined Northern Circuit, 1970; Asst Recorder, 1982; Recorder, 1988; Mem., Manx Bar, 1992. Pres., NW Area, Mental Health Review Tribunal (Restricted Cases), 1997–2004; Tutor Judge, Judicial Studies Bd, 2003–12; Liaison Judge for Liverpool Magistrates, 2003–12; Additional Judge, Central Criminal Court, 2003–12; Mem., Parole Bd, 2004–10. Foundn Mem., 1992–, and Vice-Pres., 2001–, Liverpool Coll. *Recreations:* walking, philately, sailing, water colouring, genealogy. *Clubs:* Bar Yacht; Athenæum (Liverpool).

CLIFTON, Sir (Hervey) Hamish (Peter) B.; *see* Bruce-Clifton.

CLIFTON, Richard Francis; Head, UK Delegation, Channel Tunnel Safety Authority, 2003–11; *b* 18 Sept. 1946; *s* of Joseph Walter Clifton and Georgina Clifton (*née* Naughton); *m* 1970, Gloria Christine Hugill; two *d*. *Educ:* Univ. of Warwick (BA Econs 1969; MA Industrial Relns 1970). Policy Advr, Dept of Employment, 1974–86; Health and Safety Executive, 1986–2006: Head of Med. Admin, 1986–90; Head of Finance and Planning, 1990–96; Head of Policy Unit, 1996–2001; Dir, Railway Policy, 2001–03. Chm. Bd, European Agency for Safety and Health at Work, Bilbao, 2000–01. Chm., wkg party on Obstruction of the Railway by Road Vehicles, reported 2002. Mem. (Lib Dem), Sutton LBC, 2010– (Chair, Planning Cttee, 2014–). *Recreations:* Mem., Phoenix Concert Band, Sutton. *Address:* 55 The Ridgway, Sutton, Surrey SM2 5JX. *T:* (020) 8643 5603. *E:* richard.clifton@sutton.gov.uk.

CLIFTON, Rita Ann, CBE 2014; Chairman, BrandCap, since 2013; *b* 30 Jan. 1958; *d* of late Arthur Leonard Clifton and Iris Mona Clifton (*née* Hill); *m* Brian Martin Astley; two *d*. *Educ:* Newnham Coll., Cambridge (MA Hons Classics). Sen. Account Rep., J. Walter Thompson, 1983–86; Strategic Planning Dir, then Vice Chm. and Exec. Planning Dir, Saatchi & Saatchi, 1986–97; CEO, 1997–2001, Chm., 2002–12, Interbrand. Non-exec. Chm., Populus Ltd, 2004–; non-executive Director: Dixons Retail (formerly Dixons Gp, then DSG Internat.) plc, 2003–12; EMAP plc, 2005–08; Bupa, 2010–; Nationwide Bldg Soc., 2012–; ASOS plc, 2014–. Vis. Prof., Henley Business Sch. (formerly Henley Mgt Coll.), 2006–. Mem., Sustainable Develt Commn, 1999–2005. President: WACL, 1997–98; Market Res. Soc., 2010–; Mem., Mktg Gp of GB, 1999–. Mem., Adv. Bd, Judge Inst. of Mgt Studies, Cambridge, 2000–06. Trustee, WWF-UK, 2007–13; Chm., TCV (formerly BTCV), 2011–. Dir, Henley Fest., 2010–. FRSA 1997; Fellow, Mktg Soc., 2004. *Publications:* How to Plan Advertising, 1997; The Future of Brands, 2000; Brands and Branding, 2004, 2nd edn 2009. *Recreations:* dance, environment, fashion, media. *Address:* c/o BrandCap, Northburgh House, 10 Northburgh Street, EC1V 0AT. *T:* (020) 7780 7602.

CLIFTON, Shaw, PhD; General of The Salvation Army, 2006–11; *b* 21 Sept. 1945; *s* of Albert Clifton and Alice Jane Clifton (*née* Shaw); *m* 1967, Helen Ashman (*d* 2011); two *s* one *d*. *Educ:* Latymer Sch., Edmonton; King's Coll., London (LLB Hons, BD 1st Cl. Hons, AKC 1968; Relton Prize for Histl and Biblical Theol.; PhD 1988). Lecturer in Law: Inns of Court Sch. of Law, 1968–70; Univ. of Bristol, 1970–71; commnd and ordained Officer of The Salvation Army, 1973; Salvation Army appointments: Burnt Oak, London, 1973; Mazoe, 1975, Bulawayo, 1978, Rhodesia; Enfield, London, 1979; Legal and Parly Sec., Internat. HQ, London, 1982–89; Bromley, Kent, 1989–92; Divisional Commander: Durham and Tees, 1992–95; Mass, USA, 1995–97; Territorial Commander: Pakistan, 1997–2002; NZ, Fiji and Tonga, 2002–04; UK with Republic of Ireland, 2004–06. Principal Lectr, Samuel Logan Brengle Insts, UK, Pakistan, India, Australia, NZ; Frederick Coutts Meml Lectr, Sydney, 2003. Member: Vis. Faculty, Internat. Coll. for Officers, London, 1982–; Internat. Doctrine Council, 1980–83; Internat. Moral and Social Issues Council, 1983–93. Freeman, City of London, 2007. *Publications:* What Does the Salvationist Say?, 1977; Growing Together, 1984; Strong Doctrine, Strong Mercy, 1985; Never the Same Again, 1997; Who Are These Salvationists?, 1999; New Love - Thinking Aloud About Practical Holiness, 2004; Selected Writings, Vol. 1, 1974–1999, Vol. 2, 2000–2010, 2010; From Her Heart: the preaching and teaching of Helen Clifton, 2012; Something Better: autobiographical essays, 2014. *Recreations:* music, reading, walking, family. *Address:* The Salvation Army, 101 Queen Victoria Street, EC4V 4EH. *T:* (020) 7332 8001. *E:* shaw_clifton@salvationarmy.org.

CLIFTON-BROWN, Geoffrey Robert; MP (C) The Cotswolds, since 2010 (Cirencester and Tewkesbury, 1992–97, Cotswold, 1997–2010); chartered surveyor and farmer; *b* 23 March 1953; *s* of Robert and late Elizabeth Clifton-Brown; *m* 1979, Alexandra Peto-Shepherd (marr. diss. 2004); one *s* one *d*. *Educ:* Tormore Sch., Kent; Eton Coll.; RAC, Cirencester. FRICS 2002. Chm., N Norfolk Cons. Assoc., 1986–91. PPS to Minister of Agric., Fisheries and Food, 1995–97; an Opposition Whip, 1999–2001, 2003, Opposition Asst Chief Whip, 2005; Opposition front bench spokesman on local and devolved govt, 2003–04; Shadow Minister: for Foreign Affairs and Trade, 2005–07; for Internat. Develt and Trade, 2007–10. Member: Envmt Select Cttee, 1992–95; Public Accounts Commn, 1997–99; Public Accounts Cttee, 1997–99. Vice Chm., Euro Atlantic Gp, 1996–. Freeman, City of London, 1981; Liveryman, Farmers' Co., 1984. *Recreations:* fishing, all country pursuits. *Address:* House of Commons, SW1A 0AA. *T:* (020) 7219 3000. *Clubs:* Carlton, Farmers.

CLIMER, Naomi Wendy; President, Institution of Engineering and Technology, 2015–Sept. 2016; *b* London, 18 Dec. 1964; *d* of Benjamin Climer and Wendy Climer; *m* 2008, Carl Schofield; one *d*. *Educ:* Imperial Coll. London (BSc Jt Hons Chem. with Mgt Sci. 1986). Engr, BBC, 1987–90; Proj. Manager, Island Technical, 1990–93; yr travelling, 1993–94; BBC: Manager, Engrg and Ops Trng, BBC World Service, 1994–97; Controller, Technol., BBC News, 1997–2000; Dir, Ops, ITV Digital, 2000–02; Dir, Professional Services, Sony Europe Ltd, 2002–06; Dir, Sony UK Ltd, 2005–10; Vice Pres., Sony Europe Ltd, 2006–12; Pres., Sony Media Cloud Services, 2012–15. Dir, Parliamentary Broadcasting Unit Ltd, 1998–2000. Trustee, IET, 2010–14 (Dep. Pres., 2012–14). FREng 2013. *Recreations:* family, sailing, cycling, motorbiking, theatre, cello, piano. *Address:* Institution of Engineering and Technology, 2 Savoy Place, WC2R 0BL.

CLINCH, David John, (Joe), OBE 1997; Secretary, Open University, 1981–98; *b* 14 Feb. 1937; *s* of Thomas Charles Clinch and Madge Isabel Clinch (*née* Saker); *m* 1963, Hilary Jacques; one *s* one *d*. *Educ:* Nautical Coll., Pangbourne; St Cuthbert's Soc., Univ. of Durham (BA); Indiana Univ. (MBA); Open Univ. (BSc 2009). National Service, Royal Navy (Sub-Lieut), Supply and Secretariat, 1955–57. Administrator, Univ. of Sussex, 1963–69; Deputy Secretary and Registrar, Open University, 1969–81; Registrar Counterpart, Allama Iqbal Open Univ., Pakistan, 1976–77. Consultant: Univ. for Industry, 2000–02; UNESCO, 2003–04; Consultant Higher Education Adviser: Milton Keynes Econ. and Learning Partnership, 2001–10; University Centre Milton Keynes, 2010–13. Member: Conf. of Univ. Administrators, 1973–99; British Fulbright Scholars Assoc., 1978–; Conf. of Registrars and Secs, 1981–98 (Chm., 1990–91); Bd of Govs (formerly Council of Foundn), Internat. Baccalaureate Orgn, 1999–2005 (Treas., 2000–05; Sec., 2003–05; Hon. Life Mem., 2005); Trustee and Secretary: Internat. Baccalaureate Fund Inc., USA, 2004–07; Internat. Baccalaureate Fund, Canada, 2004–07; Internat. Baccalaureate Fund UK, 2006–07. Dir, Nat. Educnl Resources Information Service Trust, 1989–93; Bd Mem., COUNTEC, 2005–11. Trustee, Open Univ. Superannuation Scheme, 1989–97; Hon. Vice Pres., Open Univ. Students Assoc., 2000–05 (Hon. Life Mem., 2005). Mem. Ct, Univ. of Surrey, Roehampton, 2000–04. Dir, Milton Keynes City Orch., 2001–08; Trustee, Milton Keynes City Orch. Foundn, 2010–13. FRSA 1997. DUniv Open, 2000. *Recreations:* music, natural history, reading, walking. *Address:* 39 Tudor Gardens, Stony Stratford, Milton Keynes MK11 1HX. *T:* (01908) 562475.

CLINCH, Stephen David; Chief Inspector of Marine Accidents, Marine Accident Investigation Branch, Department for Transport, since 2010; *b* London, 16 June 1955; *s* of David and Mary Clinch; *m* 1983, Susan Maria Cullen; one *s* one *d*. *Educ:* City of London Poly.; Merchant Navy Coll. (Master Mariner). Deck Officer, P&O Bulk Shipping, 1971–85; Ops Superintendent, P&O Bulk Carriers, 1985–88; Ship Master, P&O Bulk Shipping, 1988–89; Ops Manager, P&O Bulk Carriers, 1989–91; Gen. Manager, 1991–94, Marine Dir, 1994–98, P&O Bulk Shipping; Marine Dir, Associated Bulk Carriers, 1998–2001; Dep. Dir, Bahamas Maritime Authy, 2002–04; Dep. Chief Inspector, Maritime Accident Investigation Br., DfT, 2004–10. Chairman: Marine Accident Investigator's Internat. Forum, 2012–; EU Permanent Co-op. Framework, 2012–. Trustee, CHIRP, 2010–. *Recreations:* theatre, walking, fine art. *Address:* Marine Accident Investigation Branch, Mountbatten House, Grosvenor Square, Southampton SO15 2JV. *T:* (023) 8039 5529. *E:* steve.clinch@dft.gsi.gov.uk.

CLINES, Prof. David John Alfred; Professor of Biblical Studies, University of Sheffield, 1985–2003, now Emeritus; Director: Dictionary of Classical Hebrew Ltd, since 2001; Sheffield Phoenix Press, since 2004; *b* 21 Nov. 1938; *s* of Alfred William and Ruby Coral Clines; *m* 1st, 1963, Dawn Naomi Joseph; one *s* one *d*; 2nd, 1989, Heather Ann McKay. *Educ:* Univ. of Sydney (BA Hons 1960); St John's Coll., Cambridge (BA 1963; MA 1967). University of Sheffield: Asst Lectr in Biblical History and Literature, 1964–67; Lectr, 1967–73, Sen. Lectr, 1973–79, Reader, 1979–85, in Biblical Studies. Co-Founder and Partner, JSOT Press, 1976–87; Dir, Sheffield Acad. Press, 1987–2001 (Chm., 1987–92). President: SOTS, 1996; Soc. of Biblical Literature, 2009. Hon. PhD Amsterdam, 2001. *Publications:* I, He, We and They: a literary approach to Isaiah 53, 1976; The Theme of the Pentateuch, 1978, 2nd edn 1997; Ezra, Nehemiah, Esther, 1984; The Esther Scroll; the story of the story, 1984; Job 1–20, 1990; What Does Eve Do to Help? and Other Readerly Questions to the Old Testament, 1990; Interested Parties: the ideology of writers and readers of the Hebrew Bible, 1995; The Bible and the Modern World, 1997; The Sheffield Manual for Authors and Editors in Biblical Studies, 1997; On the Way to the Postmodern: Old Testament essays 1967–1998, 1998; Job 21–37, 2006; On Psalms, 2008; Job 38–42, 2011; *edited:* The Dictionary of Classical Hebrew: vol. 1, 1993, vol. 2, 1995, vol. 3, 1996, vol. 4, 1998, vol. 5, 2001, vol. 6, 2006, vol. 7, 2010, vol. 8, 2011; The Poetical Books: a Sheffield reader, 1997; The Concise Dictionary of Classical Hebrew, 2009; *edited jointly:* Art and Meaning: rhetoric in biblical literature, 1982; Midian, Moab and Edom: the history and archaeology of late Bronze and Iron Age Jordan and North-West Arabia, 1983; The Bible in Three Dimensions (essays), 1990; Telling Queen Michal's Story: an experiment in comparative interpretation, 1991; Among the Prophets: imagery, language and structure in the prophetic writings, 1993; Of Prophets' Visions and the Wisdom of Sages (essays), 1993; The New Literary Criticism and the Hebrew Bible, 1993; The Bible in Human Society (essays), 1995; The World of Genesis: persons, places, perspectives, 1998; Auguries: the Jubilee volume of the Department of Biblical Studies, 1998; Weisheit in Israel, 2003; The Centre and the Periphery, 2010; A Critical Engagement, 2011; Making a Difference, 2012; The Reception of the Hebrew Bible in the Septuagint and the New Testament, 2013; articles in learned jls. *Recreations:* congresses, spreadsheets. *Address:* Department of Biblical Studies, University of Sheffield, Sheffield S3 7QB. *T:* (0114) 255 0562. *E:* d.clines@shef.ac.uk.

CLINK, Rear Adm. John Robert Hamilton, OBE 2002; Flag Officer Sea Training, since 2015; *b* Hillingdon, 18 Feb. 1964; *s* of Michael and Jennifer Clink; *m* 1988, Jacqueline Sayce; two *s*. *Educ:* Cheltenham Grammar Sch.; Britannia Royal Naval Coll.; King's Coll. London (MA Internat. Security and Strategy 2012). Joined RN, 1983; in Command: HMS Archer, 1991–93; HMS Kent, 1999–2002; HMS Ark Royal, 2008–10; Dep. Comdr, UK Maritime

Forces, 2011–12; Comdr, British Forces Gibraltar, 2012–14; Flag Officer, Scotland and NI, 2014–15. *Recreations:* golf, sailing, ski-ing, cycling. *Address:* c/o Naval Secretary, Fleet Headquarters, Whale Island, Portsmouth PO2 8BY. *Club:* Royal Navy of 1765 and 1785.

CLINTON; *see* Fiennes-Clinton, family name of Earl of Lincoln.

CLINTON, 22nd Baron *cr* 1299 (title abeyant 1957–65); **Gerard Nevile Mark Fane Trefusis;** DL; landowner; *b* 7 Oct. 1934; *s* of Capt. Charles Fane (killed in action, 1940); assumed by deed poll, 1958, surname of Trefusis in addition to patronymic; *m* 1959, Nicola Harriette Purdon Coote; one *s* two *d. Educ:* Gordonstoun. Took seat in House of Lords, 1965. Mem., Prince of Wales's Councils, 1968–79. JP Bideford, 1963–83; DL Devon, 1977. *Recreations:* shooting, fishing, forestry. *Heir: s* Hon. Charles Patrick Rolle Fane Trefusis [*b* 21 March 1962; *m* 1992, Rosanna, *yr d* of John Izat; three *s*]. *Address:* Heanton Satchville, near Okehampton, North Devon EX20 3QE. *T:* (01805) 804224. *Clubs:* Boodle's, Royal Yacht Squadron, Turf.

CLINTON, Bill; *see* Clinton, W. J.

CLINTON, Hillary Diane Rodham, JD; Secretary of State, United States of America, 2009–13; *b* Chicago, 26 Oct. 1947; *d* of late Hugh Ellsworth and Dorothy Howell Rodham; *m* 1975, William Jefferson, (Bill), Clinton, *qv*; one *d. Educ:* Wellesley Coll.; Yale Univ. Law Sch. (JD 1973). Attorney, Children's Defense Fund, Cambridge, Mass and Washington, 1973–74; legal consultant, Carnegie Counsel on Children, New Haven, 1973–74; legal counsel, Nixon impeachment inquiry, Judiciary Cttee, US House of Reps, 1974; Asst Prof. of Law and Dir, Legal Aid Clinic, Univ. of Arkansas, Fayetteville, 1974–77; Partner, Rose Law Firm, 1977–92; Asst Prof. of Law, Univ. of Arkansas, Little Rock, 1979–80. Hd, Presidential Task Force on Nat. Health Care Reform, 1993. US Senator from NY State, 2001–09. Numerous awards for humanitarian work. *Publications:* It Takes a Village, 1996; Dear Socks, Dear Buddy, 1998; Living History, 2003; Hard Choices, 2014; contribs to professional jls.

CLINTON, Robert George, CVO 2008; Senior Partner, Farrer & Co., 2002–08; *b* 19 Aug. 1948; *s* of George Thomas and Mary Josephine Clinton; *m* 1981, Annita Louise Bennett; one *s* one *d. Educ:* Beaumont Coll.; Brasenose Coll., Oxford (MA 1975). Admitted solicitor, 1975; Partner, Farrer & Co., 1979–2008. Dir, Early Resolution CIC, 2011–. Chm., Tony Blair Faith Foundn, 2007–14. Trustee, Wessex Youth Trust, 2002–. *Recreations:* sailing, travel. *Address:* 85 Richmond Avenue, N1 0LX. *T:* (020) 7609 8336. *Club:* Garrick.

CLINTON, William Jefferson, (Bill), JD; President of the United States of America, 1993–2001; *b* 19 Aug. 1946; *s* of late Virginia Kelly; *m* 1975, Hillary Diane Rodham (*see* H. D. R. Clinton); one *d. Educ:* Georgetown Univ. (BS 1968); University Coll., Oxford (Rhodes Schol.; Hon. Fellow, 1993; DCL by Diploma, 1994); Yale Univ. Law Sch. (JD 1973). Prof., Univ. of Arkansas Law Sch., 1974–76; Attorney Gen., Arkansas, 1977–79; with Wright, Lindsey & Jennings, law firm, 1981–83; Governor of Arkansas, 1979–81 and 1983–92. Chairman: Educn Commn of the States, 1986–87; Nat. Governors' Assoc., 1986–87 (Co-Chm., Task Force on Educn, 1990–91); Democratic Governors' Assoc., 1989–90 (Vice Chm., 1987–88); Democratic Leadership Council, 1990–91. UN Special Envoy to Haiti, 2009–. Democrat. Hon. DCL Oxford, 1994. *Publications:* Between Hope and History, 1996; My Life, 2004; Giving: how each of us can change the world, 2007; Back to Work: why we need smart government for a strong economy, 2011. *Address:* (office) 55 West 125th Street, New York, NY 10027, USA.

CLINTON-DAVIS, family name of **Baron Clinton-Davis.**

CLINTON-DAVIS, Baron *cr* 1990 (Life Peer), of Hackney in the London Borough of Hackney; **Stanley Clinton Clinton-Davis;** PC 1998; *b* 6 Dec. 1928; *s* of Sidney Davis; name changed to Clinton-Davis by deed poll, 1990; *m* 1954, Frances Jane Lucas; one *s* three *d. Educ:* Hackney Downs Sch.; Mercers' Sch.; King's Coll., London University (LLB 1950; FKC 1996). Admitted Solicitor, 1953; in practice, 1953–70; consultant, S. J. Berwin & Co., later S. J. Berwin LLP, 1989–97, 1998–. Mem. Exec. Council, Nat. Assoc. of Labour Student Organisations, 1949–50. Councillor, London Borough of Hackney, 1959; Mayor of Hackney, 1968. Contested (Lab): Langstone Div. of Portsmouth, 1955; Yarmouth, 1959 and 1964. MP (Lab) Hackney Central, 1970–83; Parly Under-Sec. of State, Dept of Trade, 1974–79; Opposition spokesman on trade, prices and consumer protection, 1979–81, on foreign affairs, 1981–83; Opposition frontbench spokesman on transport, H of L, 1990–97; Minister of State, DTI, 1997–98. Vice Chm., Parly Envmt Gp. Mem., Commn of EC, 1985–89. Chm., Adv. Cttee on Protection of the Sea, 1984–85, 1989–97; Pres., Refugee Council, 1989–97. Pres., AMA, 1992–97. Vice Pres., Lab. Finance and Industry Gp, 1993–. Member: RIIA; Council and Exec. Cttee, Justice; UN Selection Cttee for Sasakawa, Envmt Project; Adv. Bd, Centre of European Law, KCL; formerly Mem., Bd of Deputies of British Jews; Parly Relations Sub-Cttee of the Law Soc.; Hon. Mem., London Criminal Courts Solicitors' Assoc. Mem. Council, British Maritime League, 1989–97. Jt Pres., Soc. of Labour Lawyers, 1991–; President: UK Pilots Assoc. (Marine), 1991; BALPA, 1994; Inst. of Travel Management; Aviation Envmt Fedn; Vice-Pres., Chartered Instn of Envmtl Health Officers, 1991–. Pres., Hackney Br., Multiple Sclerosis Soc.; Vice-Pres., Hackney Assoc. for Disabled; Hon. Mem. Rotary Club, Hackney. Hon. Mem., 1979, and former Trustee, NUMAST (formerly Merchant Navy and Airline Officers' Assoc.); Hon. Fellow, QMW, 1993; Hon. FCIWEM; FRSA 1992 (Mem. Acad. Bd for Internat. Trade). Hon. Dr *hc* Polytechnical Inst., Bucharest, 1993. First Medal for Outstanding Services to Animal Welfare in Europe, Eurogroup for Animal Welfare, 1988. Grand Cross, Order of Leopold II, Belgium (for services to EC), 1990. *Recreations:* golf, Association football, reading biographical histories. *Address:* House of Lords, SW1A 0PW.

CLITHEROE, 2nd Baron *cr* 1955, of Downham; **Ralph John Assheton;** Bt 1945; Chairman, Yorkshire Bank, 1990–99; Vice Lord-Lieutenant of Lancashire, 1995–99; *b* 3 Nov. 1929; *s* of 1st Baron Clitheroe, KCVO, PC, FSA, and Sylvia Benita Frances, Lady Clitheroe, FRICS, FLAS, (*d* 1991), *d* of 6th Baron Hotham; *S* father, 1984; *m* 1961, Juliet, *d* of Lt-Col Christopher Lionel Hanbury, MBE, TD; two *s* one *d. Educ:* Eton; Christ Church, Oxford (Scholar, MA). FCIB 1991. Served as 2nd Lieut Life Guards, 1948–49. Chairman: RTZ Chemicals Ltd, 1973–87; RTZ Borax Ltd, 1979–89; US Borax and Chemical Corp., 1980–89; RTZ Oil & Gas Ltd, 1983–88; Director: Borax Consolidated, 1960–89; RTZ Corp., 1968–89; First Interstate Bank of California, 1981–89; TR Natural Resources Investment Trust, 1982–87; American Mining Congress, 1982–89; Halliburton Co., Texas, 1987–2002. Mem., Council, Chemical Industries Assoc., 1984–88. Liveryman, Skinners' Co. DL Lancs, 1986. *Heir: s* Hon. Ralph Christopher Assheton [*b* 19 March 1962; *m* 1996, Olivia, *o d* of Anthony Warrington]. *Address:* The Lidgett House, Downham, Clitheroe, Lancs BB7 4BL. *Clubs:* Boodle's, Royal Automobile.

CLITHEROW, Rev. Canon Andrew; Chaplain to the Queen, since 2007; Chaplain, University of Central Lancashire, since 2012; *b* Guildford, 18 Nov. 1950; *s* of late Rt Rev. Richard George Clitherow and of Diana Clitherow; *m* 2002, Rebekah Clare Eames (marr. diss.); two *s* two *d*; *m* 2011, Nicola Howard. *Educ:* Ellesmere Coll., Shropshire; St Chad's Coll., Durham Univ. (BA Hons 1972); Salisbury and Wells Theol Coll.; Exeter Univ. (MPhil 1987). Ordained deacon, 1979, priest, 1980; Hon. Curate, Christ Church, Bedford, 1979–84; Asst Chaplain, Bedford Sch., 1979–84; Chaplain, Caldicott Sch., 1984–85; Res. Minister, St James, Acton Trussell and All Saints', Bednall, and Curate, St Michael and All Angels, Penkridge, 1985–88; Chaplain and Hd of Religious Studies, Rossall Sch., 1989–94; Vicar, St Paul's, Scotforth, 1994–2000; Res. Canon, Blackburn Cathedral, 2000–07; Dir of Trng, Dio. of Blackburn, 2000–07; Priest in Charge: St Cuthbert's, Lytham, 2007–11; St John's, Lytham, 2008–11. *Publications:* Into Your Hands: prayer and the call to holiness in everyday ministry and life, 2001; Renewing Faith in Ordained Ministry, 2004; Creative Love in Tough Times, 2007; Desire, Love and the Rule of St Benedict, 2008; Prayer: the embrace of love, 2009. *Recreations:* walking, cycling, music, reading, fishing, cooking. *Address:* 31 Mythrop Avenue, Lytham, Lancs FY8 4HZ. *E:* clitherow814@btinternet.com.

CLIVE, Viscount; Jonathan Nicholas William Herbert; *b* 5 Dec. 1979; *s* and *heir* of Earl of Powis, *qv*.

CLIVE, Eric McCredie, CBE 1999; FRSE; Honorary Professor, University of Edinburgh, since 2014 (Visiting Professor, 1999–2014); *b* 24 July 1938; *s* of Robert M. Clive and Mary L. D. Clive; *m* 1962, Kay M. McLeman; one *s* two *d* (and one *d* decd). *Educ:* Univs of Edinburgh (MA, LLB with dist.); Michigan (LLM); Virginia (SJD). Solicitor. Lecturer 1962–69, Sen. Lectr 1969–75, Reader 1975–77, Professor of Scots Law 1977–81, Univ. of Edinburgh; a Scottish Law Comr, 1981–99. FRSE 1999. Hon. Dr Osnabrück, 2008. *Publications:* Law of Husband and Wife in Scotland, 1974, 4th edn 1997; (ed jtly) Principles, Definitions and Model Rules of European Contract Law, 2009; articles and notes in legal jls. *Address:* 14 York Road, Edinburgh EH5 3EH. *T:* (0131) 552 2875.

CLOGGIE, Angela Thomson; *see* Grahame, A. T.

CLOGHER, Bishop of, since 2011; **Rt Rev. (Francis) John McDowell;** *b* Belfast, 20 Jan. 1956; *s* of James McDowell and Elizabeth McDowell; *m* 1986, Dorothy Mary Jackson; one *d. Educ:* Annadale Grammar Sch.; Queen's Univ., Belfast (BA Hons Hist. 1978); London Sch. of Econs and Pol Sci. (DBS 1984); Trinity Coll., Dublin (BTh 1996). Ordained deacon, 1996, priest, 1997; Sen. Mgt, Short Brothers Missile Div., 1980–87; Asst Dir, CBI, NI, 1987–91. Curate, Antrim Parish, 1996–99; Rector: Kildollagh and Ballyrashane, 1999–2002; Dundela, 2002–11. Hon. Sec., Gen. Synod of C of I, 2008–11. *Recreations:* literature, theology, history, walking, admiring other people's gardens. *Address:* The See House, Fivemiletown, Co. Tyrone BT75 0QP. *E:* bishop@clogher.anglican.org.

CLOGHER, Bishop of, (RC), since 2010; **Most Rev. Liam Sean MacDaid;** *b* Dublin, 19 July 1945; *s* of William MacDaid and Mary Ellen MacDaid (*née* Kerrigan). *Educ:* St Patrick's Coll., Maynooth (BA 1965; BD 1968; HDipEd 1970; DD 2010); University Coll. Dublin (Dip. Career Guidance and Counselling 1978). Ordained priest, 1969; Tutor, Accord, Omagh, 1979–85 (Vice Pres., 2011); Pres., St Macartan's Coll., Monaghan, 1981–89; Diocese of Clogher: Diocesan Sec., 1993–2010; Chancellor, 1993–2010. Chair, Council for Marriage and the Family, 2013–; Mem. Bd, Towards Healing, 2012–. Chm., Council of Priests, Clogher, 1979–89; Regl Chair, Assoc. of Mgt of Catholic Secondary Schs, 1984–89. *Recreations:* swimming, cycling, walking, theatre, music. *Address:* Bishop's House, Monaghan, Ireland. *T:* (47) 81019, *Fax:* (47) 84773. *E:* diocesanoffice@clogherdiocese.ie.

CLOKE, Prof. (Frederick) Geoffrey (Nethersole), DPhil; FRS 2007; Professor of Chemistry, University of Sussex, since 1994; *b* 12 April 1953; *s* of late Frederick and Cecelia Cloke; partner, Siobhan Mehaffy. *Educ:* Balliol Coll., Oxford (BA Hons 1975; DPhil 1978; MA 1981). SERC Postdoctoral Fellow, Inorganic Chemistry Lab., Oxford, 1978–79; Jun. Res. Fellow, Balliol Coll., Oxford, 1979–83; Postdoctoral Associate, MIT, Cambridge, 1981–82; University of Sussex: SERC Advanced Fellowship, 1983–84; New Blood Lectr in Inorganic Chem., 1984–89; Sen. Lectr in Chem., 1989–90; Reader in Chem., 1990–94. *Publications:* over 150 res. papers in learned jls inc. Science, Jl of Amer. Chemical Soc., Angewandte Chemie, Chemical Communications. *Recreations:* sport—golf (playing), cricket (now only watching!), mountain walking/scrambling, woodworking, movies, jazz and 70s music. *Address:* Department of Chemistry, Chichester Building, University of Sussex, Brighton BN1 9QJ. *T:* (01273) 678735, *Fax:* (01273) 677196. *E:* f.g.cloke@sussex.ac.uk.

CLOKE, Prof. Paul John, PhD; DSc; FBA 2009; Professor of Geography, University of Exeter, since 2006; *b* 17 Feb. 1953; *s* of William and Iris Cloke (*née* Tinton); *m* 1974, Vivien Jane Hewitt; one *s* one *d. Educ:* Southampton Univ. (BA); Wye Coll., London (PhD); Bristol Univ. (DSc). Lectr, Reader, then Prof. of Geog., Univ. of Wales, Lampeter, 1977–92; Reader, 1992–93, Prof. of Geog., 1993–2005, Univ. of Bristol. Founder Ed., Jl of Rural Studies. *Publications:* Key Settlements in Rural Areas, 1979; Introduction to Rural Settlement Planning, 1983; (with C. Park) Rural Resource Management, 1985; Rural Planning, 1987; Policies and Plans for Rural People, 1988; Rural Land Use Planning, 1989; (with P. Bell) Deregulation and Transport, 1990; (with J. Little) The Rural State, 1990; (with C. Philo and D. Sadler) Approaching Human Geography, 1991; Policy and Change in Thatcher's Britain, 1992; (jtly) Writing the Rural, 1994; (ed jtly) Contested Countryside Cultures, 1997; Rural Wales, 1997; (ed jtly) Introducing Human Geographies, 1999, 3rd edn 2013; (with P. Milbourne and R. Widdowfield) Rural Homelessness, 2002; (with O. Jones) The Culture of Trees, 2002; Country Visions, 2003; (jtly) Practising Human Geography, 2004; (ed jtly) Envisioning Human Geographies, 2004; (ed jtly) Spaces of Geographic Thought, 2005; (ed jtly) Handbook of Rural Studies, 2006; (ed jtly) International Perspectives on Rural Homelessness, 2006; (with J. May and S. Johnsen) Swept Up Lives, 2010; (with C. Barnett, N. Clarke and A. Malpass) Globalizing Responsibility, 2011; (with V. del Casino, M. Thomas and R. Panelli) A Companion to Social Geography, 2011; (with J. Beaumont) Faith-Based Organisations, Welfare and Exclusion in European Cities, 2012; (with J. Beaumont and A. Williams) Working Faith, 2013. *Recreations:* Christian music, countryside walking, Tottenham Hotspur Football Club. *Address:* College of Life and Environmental Sciences, University of Exeter, Amory Building, Rennes Drive, Exeter EX4 4RJ. *T:* (01392) 724522, *Fax:* (01392) 263342. *E:* p.cloke@exeter.ac.uk.

CLOONEY, George Timothy; actor, director and producer; *b* 6 May 1961; *s* of Nicholas Clooney and Nina Bruce Clooney (*née* Warren); *m* 1989, Talia Balsam (marr. diss. 1993); *m* 2014, Amal Alamuddin. *Educ:* Northern Kentucky Univ. *Television series: actor:* E/R, 1984–85; The Facts of Life, 1985–86; Roseanne, 1988–89; Sunset Beat, 1990; Baby Talk, 1991; Bodies of Evidence, 1992; Sisters, 1992–94; ER, 1994–99; *director and producer:* K Street, 2003; Unscripted, 2005; *actor in television films:* Combat High, 1986; Fail Safe (also prod.), 2000. *Films: actor:* Return of the Killer Tomatoes, 1988; Red Surf, 1990; Unbecoming Age, 1993; From Dusk Till Dawn, One Fine Day, 1996; Batman and Robin, 1997; The Peacemaker, Out of Sight, The Thin Red Line, 1998; Three Kings, 1999; The Perfect Storm, O Brother, Where Art Thou? (Best Actor, Golden Globe Awards, 2001), 2000; Spy Kids, 2001; Ocean's Eleven, Welcome to Collinwood (also prod.), 2002; Solaris, Confessions of a Dangerous Mind (also dir), Intolerable Cruelty, 2003; Ocean's Twelve, 2005; Syriana (also prod.) (Best Supporting Actor, Golden Globe and Academy Awards, 2006), Good Night, and Good Luck (also writer and dir), 2006; The Good German (also prod.), Ocean's Thirteen, Michael Clayton, 2007; Leatherheads (also dir), Burn After Reading, 2008; The Men Who Stare at Goats, 2009; Up in the Air, The American, 2010; The Descendants, 2011 (Best Actor, Golden Globe Awards, 2012); Gravity, 2013; The Monuments Men (also co-writer, dir and prod.), 2014; Tomorrowland: a world beyond, 2015; *producer:* Rock Star, 2001; Insomnia, Far From Heaven, 2002; Criminal, 2004; The Jacket, The Big Empty, Rumour Has It, 2005; PU-239, A Scanner Darkly, 2006. *Address:* c/o Creative Artists Agency, 2000 Avenue of the Stars, Los Angeles, CA 90067, USA.

CLORE, Melanie; Chairman, Sotheby's Europe, since 2011; Co-Chairman Worldwide, Impressionist and Modern Art Department, Sotheby's, since 2000; *b* 28 Jan. 1960; *d* of Martin and Cynthia Clore; *m* 1992, Yaron Meshoulam; one *s* one *d. Educ:* Channing Sch., Highgate;

Univ. of Manchester (BA Hons Hist. of Art 1981). Became an auctioneer, 1985; Sotheby's: Hd, Impressionist and Modern Art Dept, 1991–; Member: European Bd, 1995–; Exec. Mgt Cttee, 1995–; Dep. Chm., Sotheby's Europe, 1997–2011. Trustee: Tate, 2004–08; Clore Duffield Foundn, 2012–. *Recreations:* going to the movies, pottering in the garden. *Address:* Sotheby's, 34–35 New Bond Street, W1A 2AA. *T:* (020) 7293 5394, *Fax:* (020) 7293 5932.

CLOSE, Anthony Stephen, CBE 1997; Chairman, Health Education Authority, 1994–99; *b* 9 Aug. 1931; *s* of Steven John Henry Close and Marion Lily Close (*née* Matthews); *m* 1961, Josephine Oakey; one *d. Educ:* Colston's Sch.; Queen's Coll., Oxford (MA); Birkbeck Coll., London (MSc). AFBPsS. Shell International Petroleum Co.; BOAC; Beecham Group; Grand Metropolitan, 1973–83; Group Dir of Personnel, Trusthouse Forte, 1983–93. Director: BIOSS Internat., 1993–; EAR Ltd, 1997–2001. Member: FEFC, 1992–95; Adv. Bd, Public Concern at Work, 1993–; Adv. Bd, QMC Public Policy Seminars, 1995–2002; Adv. Bd, Centre for Public Policy Seminars, 2002–06. MInstD (Mem. Council, 1985–2001). *Recreations:* walking, opera, golf, cooking. *Address:* Danes, Cox Green Lane, Maidenhead SL6 3EY. *T:* (01628) 622910. *Club:* Savile.

CLOSE, Prof. Francis Edwin, OBE 2000; FInstP; Professor of Theoretical Physics, University of Oxford, 2001–10, now Emeritus; Fellow, Exeter College, Oxford, since 2001; *b* 24 July 1945; *s* of Frederick Archibald Close and Frances Moreton Close; *m* 1969, Gillian Matilda Boyce; two *d. Educ:* King's Sch., Peterborough; St Andrews Univ. (BSc 1967); Magdalen Coll., Oxford (DPhil 1970). FInstP 1991. Research Fellow: Stanford Linear Accelerator, Calif, 1970–72; Daresbury Lab., 1973; CERN, Geneva, 1973–75; Res. Scientist, 1975–2000, and Head of Theoretical Physics Div., 1991–2000, Rutherford Appleton Lab. Dist. Scientist, Oak Ridge Nat. Lab. and Univ. of Tennessee, 1988–90; Vis. Prof., Birmingham Univ., 1996–2002; Sen. Scientist, CERN, 1997–2000; Gresham Prof. of Astronomy, 2000–03. Mem. Council, Royal Instn, 1997–99 (Christmas Lectr, 1993); Vice-Pres., BAAS, 1993–99. Chm., British Physics Olympiad, 2003–05. Fellow, APS, 1992; Fellow in Public Understanding of Physics, Inst. Physics, 1995–97. Kelvin Medal, Inst. Physics, 1996; Faraday Medal, Royal Soc., 2013. *Publications:* Introduction to Quarks and Partons, 1979; The Cosmic Onion, 1983; The Particle Explosion, 1987; End, 1988; Too Hot to Handle, 1991; Lucifer's Legacy, 2000; The Particle Odyssey, 2002; The Void, 2007; Antimatter, 2009; Neutrino, 2010; The Infinity Puzzle, 2012; Half-Life, 2015; numerous res. papers on theoretical physics, and articles on science in The Guardian. *Recreations:* writing, singing, travel, Real tennis, chasing solar eclipses. *Address:* Exeter College, Oxford OX1 3DP. *Club:* Oxford University Real Tennis.

CLOSE, Glenn; actress; *b* 19 March 1947; *d* of William and Bettine Close; *m* 1st, 1969, Cabot Wade (marr. diss.); 2nd, 1984, James Marlas (marr. diss.); 3rd, 2006, David Shaw; one *d* by John Starke. *Educ:* William and Mary Coll. (BA 1974). With New Phoenix Repertory Co., 1974–75; *theatre* includes: New York: Love for Love, 1974; A Streetcar Named Desire; The Crucifer of Blood, 1978–79; Barnum, 1980–81; The Real Thing, 1984 (Tony Award); Benefactors, 1986; Death and the Maiden, 1992 (Tony Award); Sunset Boulevard, LA, 1993–94, NY, 1994–95 (Tony Award); A Streetcar Named Desire, NT, 2002; A Delicate Balance, NY, 2014; *films* include: The World According to Garp, 1982; The Natural, 1984; Fatal Attraction, 1987; Dangerous Liaisons, 1989; Hamlet, 1991; The House of Spirits, 1994; Serving in Silence: the Margarethe Cammermeyer story, 1995; Air Force One, 1997; Paradise Road, 1997; Cookie's Fortune, 1999; Things You Can Just Tell by Looking at Her, 2000; 102 Dalmatians, 2000; The Safety of Objects, 2003; The Stepford Wives, 2004; The Chumscrubber, Evening, 2007; Albert Nobbs, 2012 (also prod. and co-writer); numerous TV appearances incl. The Shield (series), 2005; Damages (series), 2007–12. *Address:* c/o CAA, 2000 Avenue of the Stars, Los Angeles, CA 90067, USA.

CLOSE, Seamus Anthony, OBE 1996; Member (Alliance) Lagan Valley, Northern Ireland Assembly, 1998–2007; *b* 12 Aug. 1947; *s* of late James and of Kathleen Close; *m* 1978, Deirdre McCann; three *s* one *d. Educ:* St Malachy's Coll.; Belfast Coll. of Business Studies. Company Sec., 1970–85; Financial Dir, 1985–. Mem. (Alliance), Lisburn CC (formerly Lisburn BC), 1973–2011 (Mayor, 1993–94); Mem. (Alliance) NI Assembly, 1982–86; Negotiator: Brooke/Mayhew Talks, 1991–92; Good Friday Agreement, 1998. Dep. Leader, Alliance Party, 1991–2001. Contested (Alliance): Fermanagh and S Tyrone, Aug. 1981; S Antrim, 1983; Lagan Valley, 1987, 1992, 1997, 2001, 2005. Chm., Lisburn City Dist Policing Partnership, 2005–06. Freedom, City of Lisburn, 2010. *Recreations:* sports, family, current affairs. *Address:* 123 Moira Road, Lisburn, Northern Ireland BT28 1RJ. *T:* (028) 9267 0639.

CLOTHIER, Richard John; Chairman: Robinson plc, since 2004; Spearhead International Ltd, since 2005; Aqua Bounty Technologies plc, since 2006; Exosect, since 2012; *b* 4 July 1945; *s* of J. Neil Clothier and Barbara Clothier; *m* 1st, 1972, Ingrid Hafner (*d* 1994); two *s*; 2nd, 1995, Sarah (*née* Riley). *Educ:* Peterhouse, Zimbabwe; Univ. of Natal (BSc Agric.); Harvard (AMP). Milk Marketing Board, 1971–77; Dalgety Agriculture, 1977–88; Chief Executive: Pig Improvement Co., 1988–92; Dalgety plc, 1993–97; Plantation & Gen. Investments, later PGI Gp, 1998–2005; Director: Granada Gp, 1996–2004; PGI Gp, 2005–06. *Publications:* The Bundu Book, 1969. *Recreations:* yacht racing, field sports, painting and drawing. *Address:* 23 St Luke's Street, SW3 3RP. *T:* (020) 7351 2140. *Clubs:* Farmers, Royal Thames Yacht, Royal Ocean Racing.

CLOUDER, Fiona Jennifer; HM Diplomatic Service; Ambassador to Chile, since 2014. *Educ:* University Coll. London (BSc Human Scis and Neuroscis 1985); Henley Mgt Coll. (Dip. Mgt). Science and Engineering Research Council: Cttee Sec., Physical Scis, 1985–88; Regl Co-ordinator, Manufg Engrg, 1988–91; Private Sec. to Chm. and Chief Exec., 1991–94; Dep. Hd, Internat. Relns, BBSRC, 1994–96; Hd, UK Office, UK Res. Office, Brussels, 1996–97; Hd, Internat. Relns, 1997–2001, Hd of Strategy, 2001, BBSRC; entered FCO, 2001; Dep. Hd, Sci. and Technol., 2001–02, Hd, Sci. and Innovation, 2002–06, FCO; Dir, Corporate Services, New Delhi, 2006–09; Dep. Dir, 2009–11, Actg Dir, 2011, Migration, FCO; Dep. Dir, Americas and Hd, S America Dept, FCO, 2011–13. *Address:* c/o Foreign and Commonwealth Office, King Charles Street, SW1A 2AH.

CLOUGH, Alan; *see* Clough, J. A.

CLOUGH, Christopher George, FRCP; Consultant Neurologist, King's College Hospital, since 1995; Chairman, National Clinical Advisory Team; *b* 30 Aug. 1953; *s* of George and Daisy Clough; *m* 1979, Lyn Sylvia Griffiths; two *s* one *d. Educ:* Manchester Univ. (MB ChB). FRCP 1992. Royal Alexandra Hosp., Rhyl, 1975–76; Hull Royal Infirmary, 1976–79; Leeds Gen. Infirmary, 1979–80; Mount Sinai Med. Centre, 1980–81; Queen Elizabeth Med. Centre, Birmingham, and Midlands Centre for Neurology and Neurosurgery, Smethwick, 1981–89; Cons. Neurologist, Brook Regl Neuroscience Centre and Bromley Hosps, 1989–95; Dir, Regl Neuroscis Centre, 1991–98; Med. Dir, KCH, 1998–2003; Chief Med. Advr, SE London Strategic HA, 2003–06; Dir, Jt Cttee on Higher Med. Trng, RCP, later RCP Trng Bd, 2005–08. Hon. Sen. Lectr, KCL. Neurology Advr, DoH. Member: Fabian Soc.; Labour Party. *Publications:* pubns on Parkinson's Disease, headache and restless legs. *Recreations:* tennis, music, lifelong Spurs fan. *Address:* 17 Blenheim Road, Bickley BR1 2EX.

CLOUGH, (John) Alan, CBE 1972; MC 1945; Chairman, British Mohair Holdings plc (formerly British Mohair Spinners Ltd), 1980–84 (Deputy Chairman, 1970–80, Chief Executive, 1977–80, Joint Managing Director, 1980–83); *b* 20 March 1924; *s* of late John Clough and Yvonne (*née* Dollfus); *m* 1st, 1949, Margaret Joy Catton (marr. diss.); one *s* two *d*; 2nd, 1961, Mary Cowan Catherwood; one *s* one *d. Educ:* Marlborough Coll.; Leeds Univ. HM Forces, Queen's Bays, 1942–47, N Africa and Italy (Captain); TA Major, Yorkshire Hussars, 1947–55. Mayor, Co. of Merchants of Staple of England, 1969–70. Chairman: Wool Industries Res. Assoc., 1967–69; Wool Textile Delegn, 1969–72; Textile Res. Council, 1984–89; Member: Wool Textile EDC, 1967–72; Jt Textile Cttee, NEDO, 1972–74. President: Comitextil (Co-ordinating Cttee for Textile Industries in EEC), Brussels, 1975–77; British Textile Confedn, 1974–77; Textile Inst., 1979–81; Confedn of British Wool Textiles, 1982–84. Chm., Instant Muscle Ltd, 1989–94. CompTI 1975. Hon. DSc Bradford, 1987. *Recreations:* fishing, gardening, travel.

CLOUGH, Mark Gerard; QC 1999; Senior Counsel, Dentons Europe LLP, Brussels, since 2014; independent consultant, since 2014; *b* 13 May 1953; *s* of late Philip Gerard Clough and Mary Elizabeth Clough (*née* Carter); one *d*; *m* 1989, Joanne Elizabeth Dishington; two *s. Educ:* Ampleforth Coll.; St Andrews Univ. (MA 1976). Called to the Bar, Gray's Inn, 1978; admitted Solicitor, 1995, Scotland, 2013; Solicitor Advocate, 1996; Partner: Ashurst Morris Crisp, then Ashurst, 1995–2006; Addleshaw Goddard, 2006–10; Brodies LLP, 2011–13. Chm., Solicitors Assoc. of Higher Ct Advocates, 2003–06; Member: Adv. Bd, British Inst. of Internat. and Comparative Law Competition Law Forum, 2003–10; Bd, European Maritime Law Orgn, 2004–; Scottish Competition Law Forum, 2011–. Owner, Wynd Th., Melrose, 2009–. Trustee: Slynn Foundn, 1997–; Camden People's Th., 2000–; Children in Need India (UK), 2004–13; Melrose Arts Trust, 2009–. Mem., Editl Bd, Internat. Trade Law and Regulation Jl, 1996–. *Publications:* EC Competition Law and Shipping, 1990; EC Merger Regulation, 1995; (contrib.) Vaughan's Laws of the European Communities, 1997; Trade and Telecoms, 2002; (ed) Collective Dominance: the contribution of the Community Courts, 2003; (contrib.) A True European—essays for Judge David Edward, 2004; articles on EU Law and competition law. *Recreations:* theatre, poetry, shooting, tennis, golf. *Clubs:* Travellers; New (Edinburgh).

CLOUGH, Susanna Patricia; *see* FitzGerald, S. P.

CLOUT, Prof. Hugh Donald, PhD, DLit; FBA 1997; Professor of Geography, University College London, 1987–2007, now Emeritus; *b* 29 April 1944; *s* of Donald Clout and Florence (*née* Allwood). *Educ:* University College London (BA, MPhil, PhD 1979, DLit 2000); Univ. de Paris I (Dr de l'Université 1983). Lectr, 1967–81, Reader, 1981–87, in Geography, UCL. Fellow, UCL, 2008. Hon. Dr Geog. Paris IV, 2004. *Publications:* (ed) Regional Development in Western Europe, 1975, 3rd edn 1987; (ed) Themes in the Historical Geography of France, 1977; Agriculture in France on the Eve of the Railway Age, 1980; The Land of France 1815–1914, 1982; (ed) Western Europe: geographical perspectives, 1985, 3rd edn 1994; (ed) Times London History Atlas, 1991, 5th edn, as The Times History of London, 2007; After the Ruins: restoring the countryside of northern France after the Great War, 1996; (ed) Contemporary Rural Geographies, 2007; Patronage and the Production of Geographical Knowledge in France, 2009. *Address:* Department of Geography, University College London, Gower Street, WC1E 6BT.

CLOVER, (Anne) Sarah; Partner, since 1992, and Head, Professional and Commercial Disputes, since 2013, Clyde & Co. LLP (formerly Barlow Lyde & Gilbert); *b* London, 9 Sept. 1958; *d* of John Pinder and Sheila Pinder (*née* Keogh); *m* 1993, Anthony Clover; three *d. Educ:* St Leonards-Mayfield Sch.; University Coll. London (LLB 1981). Admitted as solicitor, 1983. *Address:* Clyde & Co. LLP, St Botolph Building, 138 Houndsditch, EC3A 7AR. *T:* (020) 7876 5000. *E:* Sarah.Clover@clydeco.com.

CLOW, Sarah Jane; *see* Mitchell, S. J.

CLOWES, Alfred William; General Secretary, Ceramic and Allied Trades Union, 1980–95; *b* 17 Dec. 1931. Joined the Industry on leaving school; Asst Gen. Sec., Ceramic and Allied Trades Union, 1975–80. Hon. Freeman, City of Stoke-on-Trent, 1995. *Address:* 22 Meadow Avenue, Wetley Rocks, Stoke-on-Trent ST9 0BD.

CLUCKIE, Prof. Ian David, FREng, FCIWEM; FICE; Pro-Vice-Chancellor (Science and Engineering), Swansea University, since 2008; *b* Edinburgh, 20 July 1949; *m* 1972; one *s* one *d. Educ:* Univ. of Surrey (BSc); Univ. of Birmingham (MSc, PhD). CEng, FREng (FEng 1997); FIWEM 1983; FICE 1988; FRMetS 1979. W. S. Atkins, Swansea, 1966–72; Central Water Planning Unit, Reading, 1974–76; Lectr, Univ. of Birmingham, 1976–88; Salford University: Prof. of Water Resources, 1988–97; Chm., Dept of Civil Engrg, 1991–96; Dir, Telford Res. Inst., 1993–94, 1996–97; Acad. Dir, Salford Civil Engineering Ltd, 1989–97; Prof. of Hydrology and Water Mgt, and Dir, Water and Envmtl Mgt Res. Centre, Bristol Univ., 1997–2007. Visiting Professor: Sun Yat-Sen Univ., 2004–; Anhui Univ., 2014–; Hohai Univ., 2014; Vis. Chair, Nat. Inst. of Hydraulic Res., Nanjing, 2012–. Natural Environment Research Council: Mem., AAPS Res. Grants and Trng Awards Cttee, 1988–91; Chm., AAPS Cttee, 1991–94; Mem., Terrestrial and Freshwater Scis, Marine Scis, Atmospheric Scis and Higher Educn Affairs Cttees, 1991–94; Chm., EPSRC Flood Risk Mgt Res. Consortium, 2004–12. Chm., UK IAHS Cttee, 2006–12; Pres., Internat. Commn on Remote Sensing, IAHS, 2009–14. FRSA 1993. *Publications:* (with C. G. Collier) Hydrological Applications of Weather Radar, 1991; (jtly) Radar Hydrology for Real-time Flood Forecasting, 2001; contribs to learned jls. *Recreations:* sailing, hill walking.

CLUFF, John Gordon, (Algy); DL; Chairman and Chief Executive, Cluff Natural Resources plc, since 2012; Chairman: Cluff Geothermal, 2009–14; Cluff Africa Associates, since 2010; Chairman, The Spectator, 1985–2005 (Proprietor, 1981–85); *b* 19 April 1940; *o s* of late Harold Cluff and Freda Cluff, Waldeshare House, Waldeshare, Kent; *m* 1993, Blondel Hodge, Anguilla, WI; three *s. Educ:* Stowe Sch. 2/Lieut, Grenadier Guards, 1959; Captain, Guards Independent Parachute Co., 1963; served W Africa, Cyprus, Malaysia, retd 1965. Founded Cluff Oil, subseq. Cluff Resources, 1971, Chief Exec., 1971, Chm., 1979; founded Cluff Mining, 1996, Chm., 1996–2004, Chief Exec., 1996–2003; founded Cluff Gold, 2004, Chief Exec., 2004–10, Exec. Chm., 2004–11, non-exec. Chm., 2011–12. Contested (C) Ardwick Div. of Manchester, 1966. Chm., Cons. Commn on the Commonwealth, 2000. A Dir, Centre for Policy Studies, 1998–2005. Governor: Commonwealth Inst., 1994–2009; Stowe Sch., 1998–2010. Chm., Nat. Army Mus. Foundn, 2013–; Mem. Council, Nat. Army Mus., 2013–; Pres., ATC, Kent, 2007–; Vice Pres., Army Benevolent Fund, Kent, 2007–. Trustee, Stowe House Preservation Trust, 1999–2011; Chm. Trustees, War Memorials Trust, 2003–14; Trustee, Commonwealth Educn Trust, 2009–. Hon. Col, 3rd Bn, Princess of Wales's Royal Regt, 2010–. DL Kent, 2009. Chevalier de l'Ordre Nat. (Burkina Faso), 2009. *Address:* c/o Cluff Natural Resources plc, 5–8 The Sanctuary, SW1P 3JS. *Clubs:* White's, Beefsteak, Brooks's, Pratt's, City of London, Turf, Special Forces; Royal Yacht Squadron; Travellers (Paris); Brook, Racquet and Tennis (New York).

CLUNAS, Prof. Craig, PhD; FBA 2004; Professor of the History of Art, and Fellow of Trinity College, University of Oxford, since 2007; *b* 1 Dec. 1954; *s* of Charles Clunas and Elizabeth Clunas (*née* Robertson); one *s. Educ:* Aberdeen Grammar Sch.; King's Coll., Cambridge (BA 1st cl. (Chinese Studies) 1977); SOAS, Univ. of London (PhD 1983). Res. Asst, Far Eastern Dept, 1979–93, Sen. Res. Fellow in Chinese Studies, 1993–94, V&A Mus.; Sen. Lectr in Hist. of Art, 1994–97, Prof. of Hist. of Art, 1997–2003, Univ. of Sussex; Percival David Prof. of Chinese and East Asian Art, SOAS, Univ. of London, 2003–07. A. W. Mellon Lectr in Fine Arts, Center for Advanced Study in Visual Arts, Nat. Gall. of Art, Washington, DC, 2012. MAE 2013. Hon. DLitt Warwick, 2010. *Publications:* Chinese Export Watercolours, 1984; Chinese Furniture, 1989; Superfluous Things: social status and material culture in Early Modern China, 1991; Fruitful Sites: garden culture in Ming Dynasty China, 1996; Art in China, 1997; Pictures and Visuality in Early Modern China, 1997; Elegant Debts: the social art of Wen Zhengming, 2004; Empire of Great Brightness: visual and material cultures of Ming China, 2007; Screen of Kings: royal art and power in Ming China, 2013; numerous articles in learned jls. *Address:* History of Art Department, Littlegate House, St Ebbe's, Oxford OX1 1PT. *E:* craig.clunas@hoa.ox.ac.uk.

CLUNES, Martin Alexander, OBE 2015; actor; *b* 28 Nov. 1961; *s* of late Alec Sheriff de Moro Clunes and Daphne (*née* Acott); *m* 1st, Lucy Aston (marr. diss. 1993); 2nd, 1997, Philippa Braithwaite; one *d.* Founder: Big Arts, 1990; Buffalo, prodn co. *Theatre includes:* The Henrys, ESC; The Admirable Crichton, Th. Royal, Haymarket; Much Ado About Nothing, Julius Caesar, Open Air Th., Regent's Park; Party Tricks, Nottingham Playhouse (dir), 1995; Tartuffe, NT, 2002. *Television includes:* No Place Like Home, 1983; All At Number 20, 1986; Men Behaving Badly, 1991–98; Jeeves and Wooster, 1991; If You See God, Tell Him, 1993; Demob, 1993; Harry Enfield and Chums, 1994; An Evening with Gary Lineker, 1994; Born to Be Wild, 1999; Gormenghast, 2000; Men Down Under, 2000; Lorna Doone, 2000; William and Mary, 2003; Doc Martin, 2004, 2005, 2007, 2009, 2011, 2013, 2015; Reggie Perrin, 2009; A Mother's Son, The Town, 2012; presenter, Martin Clunes: The Lemurs of Madagascar, 2012; Arthur and George, 2015; *television films:* Over Here, 1996; Neville's Island, 1998; Touch and Go, 1998; Hunting Venus (also dir), 1999; Sex 'n' Death, 1999; Dirty Tricks, 2000; A is for Acid, 2002; Goodbye Mr Chips, 2002; Beauty, 2004. *Films:* The Russia House, 1990; Carry on Columbus, 1992; Swing Kids, 1993; Staggered (also dir), 1994; Sweet Revenge, 1998; Shakespeare in Love, 1998; The Acid House, 1998; Saving Grace, 2000; Global Heresy, 2002.

CLUNIES ROSS, Prof. Margaret Beryl, (Mrs J. R. Green); McCaughey Professor of English Language and Early English Literature, 1990–2007, now Emeritus, and Honorary Professor, Medieval and Early Modern Studies Centre (formerly Centre for Medieval Studies), since 2009, University of Sydney; President, National Academies Forum, 1998; *b* 24 April 1942; *d* of Ernest Phillips Tidemann and Beryl Chudleigh Tidemann (*née* Birch); *m* 1st, 1964, Bruce Axel Clunies Ross; 2nd, 1971, Lester Richard Hiatt; one *s* one *d*; 3rd, 1990, John Richard Green. *Educ:* Walford Girls' Grammar Sch., Adelaide; Univ. of Adelaide (BA Hons 1963); Somerville Coll., Oxford (MA 1970; BLitt 1973). George Murray Overseas Scholar, Univ. of Adelaide at Somerville Coll., Oxford, 1963–65; Lectr in Medieval English Lang. and Lit., St Hilda's Coll. and LMH, Oxford, 1965–68; Alice B. Horsman Travelling Fellow, Somerville Coll., Oxford, at Arnamagnaean Inst. for Icelandic Studies, Copenhagen Univ., 1968–69; University of Sydney: Lectr, Dept of Early Eng. Lit. and Lang., 1969–73; Sen. Lectr, English Dept, 1974–83; Associate Prof., 1984–90; Head, Dept of English, 1993–94; Dir, Centre for Medieval Studies, 1997–2007. Vis. Mem., Linacre Coll., Oxford and Hon. Res. Associate, UCL, 1979–80; Guest researcher, Univ. of Munich, 1986–87; Vis. Scholar, Univ. of N Carolina, Chapel Hill, 1991–92; Visiting Professor: McMaster Univ., Ont and Vis. Scholar, Pontifical Inst. of Mediaeval Studies, Toronto, 1995; Centre for Medieval Studies, Univ. of Bergen, 2011; Exchange scholar, Kungl. Vitterhetsakademien, Sweden 1996; Quatercentenary Vis. Fellow, Emmanuel Coll., Cambridge, 1997; Vis. Scholar, Humboldt Univ., Berlin, 2002–03; Vis. Fellow, All Souls Coll., Oxford, 2003; Hon. Res. Associate, Dept of Anglo-Saxon, Norse and Celtic, Univ. of Cambridge, 2011–14. Mem., Australian Res. Council, 1995–97. Mem., Nat. Bd of Employment, Educn and Trng, 1995–97. Pres., Aust. Acad. of Humanities, 1995–98. Fellow, Royal Gustavus Adolphus Acad., Uppsala, 2001. Hon. DPhil Göteborg Univ., 2000. Centenary Medal, Commonwealth of Australia, 2003. *Film:* (jtly) Waiting for Harry, 1980 (1st Prize, RAI film comp., 1982). *Publications:* (with S. A. Wild) Djambidj: an Aboriginal song series from Northern Australia, 1982; (ed jtly) Songs of Aboriginal Australia, 1987; Skáldskaparmál: Snorri Sturluson's ars poetica and medieval theories of language, 1987; (with J. Mundrugmundrug) Goyulan the Morning Star: an Aboriginal clan song series from North Central Arnhem Land, 1988; Prolonged Echoes: Old Norse myths in Medieval northern society, Vol. 1: The Myths, 1994; Vol. 2: The Reception of Myth in Medieval Iceland, 1998; (ed jtly) Old Norse Studies in the New World, 1994; The Norse Muse in Britain 1750–1820, 1998; (ed) Old Icelandic Literature and Society, 2000; The Old Norse Poetic Translations of Thomas Percy, 2001; (ed) Old Norse Myths, Literature and Society, 2003; (ed jtly) The Correspondence of Edward Lye, 2004; A History of Old Norse Poetry and Poetics, 2005; (ed) Skaldic Poetry of the Scandinavian Middle Ages, vol. 7: poetry on Christian subjects (2 parts), 2007; The Cambridge Introduction to the Old Norse-Icelandic Saga, 2010; (ed with Jonas Wellendorf) The Fourth Grammatical Treatise, 2014; contrib. numerous articles in learned jls and chapters in books of essays. *Recreations:* family history, walking, visiting children and grandchildren. *Address:* Department of English, University of Sydney, NSW 2006, Australia. *T:* (2) 93516832.

CLUTTERBUCK, Andrew Maurice Gray; QC 2014. *Educ:* Worth Sch.; Lincoln Coll., Oxford (BA). Served RM, 1986–90. Called to the Bar: Middle Temple, 1992. *Address:* 4 Stone Buildings, Lincoln's Inn, WC2A 3XT. *Club:* Buck's.

CLUTTON, James Charles; Director of Opera, and Producer, Opera Holland Park, since 2000; *b* London, 18 Jan. 1966; *s* of Ernest James Clutton and Margaret Rose Clutton; *m* 2007, Angela Edwards. *Educ:* St Francis de Sales, Tottenham; St Ignatius Coll., Enfield. Ind. theatre producer, London, 1995–97; Associate Producer: Bill Kenwright Ltd, 1998–2000; UNICEF Fest., Kosovo, 1999. Compositions include: Oscar (musical, co-written with Damian Landi), 1995; Great Things (Thomas Hardy poem set to music), 1997. *Recreations:* running (London Marathon, 2012), mixology, 'The West Wing', The Beatles, Bob Dylan, painting, walking in Lake District, family history. *Address:* Opera Holland Park, 37 Pembroke Road, W8 6PW. *E:* james.clutton@operahollandpark.com.

CLUTTON-BROCK, Prof. Timothy Hugh, PhD; ScD; FRS 1993; Prince Philip Professor of Ecology and Evolutionary Biology, University of Cambridge, 2007–14, Director of Research, since 2014 (Professor of Animal Ecology, 1994–2007); *b* 13 Aug. 1946; *s* of Hugh Alan Clutton-Brock and late Eileen Mary Stableforth; *m* 1980, Dafila Kathleen Scott; one *s* one *d.* *Educ:* Rugby Sch.; Magdalene Coll., Cambridge (BA, MA, PhD, ScD). NERC res. fellowship, Animal Behaviour Res. Gp, Oxford, 1972; Lectr in Ethology, Univ. of Sussex, 1973; Cambridge University: Sen. Res. Fellow in Behavioural Ecology, King's Coll., 1976; SERC Advanced Fellow, Dept of Zoology, 1981; Royal Soc. Res. Fellow in Biology, 1983; Lectr in Zoology, 1987–91; Reader in Animal Ecology, 1991–94. Extraordinary Prof., Mammal Res. Inst., Univ. of Pretoria, 2000; Hon. Prof., Univ. of Exeter, 2011. Chm., IUCN Deer Specialist Gp, 1980–90. Jt Editor, Princeton Monographs in Behavioral Ecology, 1982–. Hon. Mem., Amer. Soc. of Mammalogists, 2009. Hon. Dr: Zurich, 2013; Pretoria, 2013. Scientific Medal, 1984, Frink Medal, 1998, Zoological Soc. of London; Hart Merriam Award, Mammal Soc. of America, 1991; Marsh Award, British Ecol Soc., 1998; William Bate Hardy Prize, Cambridge Philosophical Soc., 1999; Darwin Medal, Royal Soc., 2013. *Publications:* (ed) Primate Ecology, 1977; (ed) Readings in Sociobiology, 1978; Red Deer: the behaviour and ecology of two sexes, 1982; (ed) Rhum, Natural History of an Island, 1987; (ed) Reproductive Success, 1988; Red Deer in the Highlands, 1989; The Evolution of Parental Care, 1991; Meerkat Manor: flower of the Kalahari, 2007; approx. 250 sci. papers on animal behaviour, ecology and evolution in Nature, Jl Animal Ecol., Evolution, Amer. Naturalist, Jl of Zoology, Animal Behaviour, Behaviour, Behavioral Ecol. and Sociobiol., Folia Primatologica and other jls. *Recreations:* bird watching, fish watching, fishing. *Address:* Department of Zoology, Downing Street, Cambridge CB2 3EJ. *T:* (01223) 336618.

CLWYD, 4th Baron *cr* 1919, of Abergele, co. Denbigh; **John Murray Roberts;** Bt 1908; *b* 27 Aug. 1971; *e s* of 3rd Baron Clwyd and of Geraldine (*née* Cannons); *S* father, 2006; *m* 2004, Lea-Anne Margaret Henry; one *s* one *d.* *Heir:* *s* Hon. John David Roberts, *b* 16 June 2006.

CLWYD, Rt Hon. Ann; PC 2004; MP (Lab) Cynon Valley, since May 1984; journalist and broadcaster; *b* 21 March 1937; *d* of Gwilym Henri Lewis and Elizabeth Ann Lewis; *m* 1963, Owen Dryhurst Roberts (*d* 2012), TV director and producer. *Educ:* Halkyn Primary Sch.; Holywell Grammar Sch.; The Queen's Sch., Chester; University Coll., Bangor. Former: Student-teacher, Hope Sch., Flintshire; BBC Studio Manager; freelance reporter, producer; Welsh corresp., The Guardian and The Observer, 1964–79; Vice-Chm., Welsh Arts Council, 1975–79. Member: Welsh Hospital Board, 1970–74; Cardiff Community Health Council, 1975–79; Royal Commn on NHS, 1976–79; Working Party, report, Organisation of Out-Patient Care, for Welsh Hosp. Bd; Working Party, Bilingualism in the Hospital Service; Labour Party Study Gp, People and the Media; Arts Council of Gt Britain, 1975–80; Labour Party NEC, 1983–84; PLP Exec., 1997–2006 (Vice Chm., 2001–05; Chm., 2005–06); Chm., Cardiff Anti-Racialism Cttee, 1978–80. Chm., Labour back bench cttee on Health and Social Security, 1985–87; Vice-Chm., Labour back bench cttee on Defence, 1985–87; Opposition front bench spokesperson on women, 1987–88, on educn, 1987–88, on overseas develt and co-operation, 1989–92, on Wales, 1992, on Nat. Heritage, 1992–93, on employment, 1993–94, on foreign affairs, 1994–95. Member: Shadow Cabinet, 1989–93; Select Cttee on Internat. Develt, 1997–2005, on Foreign Affairs, 2010–. Chm., All Party Gp on Human Rights, 1997–; Special Envoy to the Prime Minister on Human Rights in Iraq, 2003–10; apptd by the Prime Minister to lead review into NHS, 2013–. Chair, Indict, 2003–. Member: NUJ; TGWU. Contested (Lab): Denbigh, 1970; Gloucester, Oct. 1974; Mem. (Lab) Mid and West Wales, European Parlt, 1979–84. Hon. Fellow: Univ. of Wales, Bangor; N Wales Inst. of Higher Educn. Hon. Dr Wales; Hon. LLD Trinity Coll., Carmarthen. White Robe, Gorsedd of Bards, Nat. Eisteddfod of Wales, 1991. Backbencher of the Year, House Magazine and Spectator Parly Awards, 2003; Campaigning MP of the Year, Channel 4 Political Awards, 2003. *Address:* (office) 4th Floor, Crown Buildings, Aberdare, Mid Glam CF44 7HU. *T:* (01685) 871394.

CLYDE, (Samuel) Wilson; Member (DUP) Antrim South, Northern Ireland Assembly, 1998–2007; *b* 8 April 1934; *m* 1970, Margaret Evelyn; one *s.* *Educ:* Shane's Castle Primary Sch. Farmer, 1948–98. Mem. (DUP), Antrim BC, 1981–2005. *Recreations:* go-karting, motor cycling. *Address:* 21 Groggan Road, Randalstown, Antrim BT41 3HA. *T:* (028) 9447 8370.

CLYDESMUIR, 3rd Baron *cr* 1948, of Braidwood, co. Lanark; **David Ronald Colville;** *b* 8 April 1949; *e s* of 2nd Baron Clydesmuir, KT, CB, MBE, TD and Joan Marguerita, *d* of late Lt-Col E. B. Booth, DSO; *S* father, 1996; *m* 1978, Aline Frances, *er d* of Peter Merriam; two *s* two *d.* *Educ:* Charterhouse. Dir, BDB Ltd, Lloyd's Brokers, 2001–. *Heir:* *s* Hon. Richard Colville, *b* 21 Oct. 1980. *Address:* 40 Ritherdon Road, SW17 8QF.

COACKLEY, Richard James, CBE 2014; CEng, FICE; FCIWEM; Director: URS Corporation Ltd, since 2012; AECOM I & E UK Ltd, since 2014; Chairman, CEEQUAL Ltd, since 2013; President, Institution of Civil Engineers, 2011–12; *b* Hexham, Northumberland, 8 Dec. 1954; *s* of Dr Peter Coackley and Marion Coackley; *m* 1978, Isabella Margaret Christina McArthur; two *s.* *Educ:* Bearsden Acad.; Univ. of Glasgow (BSc 1st Cl. Hons Civil Engrg). CEng 1980; FICE 1998; FCIWEM (CWEM 1998). Vice Pres., Binnie Black & Veatch, 1975–2000; Director: Mouchel Parkman, 2000–06; White Young Green, 2006–10; Scott Wilson, 2010–12. Chairman: Nuclear Construction Best Practice Forum, 2012–; Smoothing Financial Cyclicality in the Water Industry AMP Cycle. Freeman: Water Conservators' Co., 1999; City of London, 2000. Smeatonian Soc. of Civil Engrs, 2014. *Recreations:* sailing, vine growing, double bass playing. *Address:* Institution of Civil Engineers, One Great George Street, Westminster, SW1P 3AA. *T:* 07753 628126. *E:* coackleyrj@btinternet.com.

COADY, Frances Rachel; Literary Agent, Aragi Inc., since 2015; *b* 16 June 1958; *d* of Matthew and Patricia Coady; *m* 2007, Peter Philip Carey, *qv.* *Educ:* Streatham Hill and Clapham High Sch.; Bromley High Sch.; Univ. of Sussex (BA Hons English Lit. 1980); Univ. of Essex (MA English Lit. 1981). Faber and Faber, 1982–86, Sen. Non-Fiction Commng Editor, 1983–86; Researcher for Alan Yentob, Head of Dept of Music and Arts, BBC TV, 1986; Random House, 1986–95: Editl Dir, Jonathan Cape, 1986–89; Founder Publisher, Vintage Paperbacks, 1989–93; Publisher, overseeing Jonathan Cape, Chatto & Windus, Pimlico and Vintage, 1993–95; Publisher, Granta Books, 1995–99; Vice-Pres. and Publisher, Picador USA, 2000–12; Editor At Large, Macmillan, 2007–12; Pres. and Publisher, Atavist Books, 2012–15. *Recreations:* looking at art, theatre, cinema, reading.

COAKER, Vernon Rodney; MP (Lab) Gedling, since 1997; *b* 17 June 1953; *s* of Edwin Coaker; *m* 1978, Jacqueline Heaton; one *s* one *d.* *Educ:* Drayton Manor Grammar Sch., London; Warwick Univ. (BA Hons); Trent Poly. (PGCE). Hist. Teacher, Manvers Pierrepont Sch., 1976–82; Hd of Dept, Arnold Hill Sch., 1982–88; Sen. Teacher, Bramcote Pk Sch., 1989–95; Dep. Headteacher, Big Wood Sch., 1995–97. Mem., Rushcliffe BC, 1983–97 (Leader, 1987–97). PPS to Minister of State for Social Security, 1999, to Financial Sec. to HM Treasury, 1999–2001, to Minister of State (Minister for School Standards), DfES, 2001–02, to Sec. of State for Culture, Media and Sport, 2002–03; an Asst Govt Whip, 2003–05; a Lord Comr of HM Treasury (Govt Whip), 2005–06; Parly Under-Sec. of State, 2006–08, Minister of State, 2008–09, Home Office; Minister of State (Minister for Schs and Learners), DCSF, 2009–10; Shadow Sec. of State for NI, 2011–13, 2015–, for Defence, 2013–15. Contested (Lab): Rushcliffe, 1983; Gedling, 1987, 1992. *Address:* House of Commons, SW1A 0AA.

COAKLEY, Rev. Canon Prof. Sarah Anne; Norris-Hulse Professor of Divinity, University of Cambridge, since 2007 (Deputy Chair, Arts and Humanities, 2011–14); Fellow, Murray Edwards College (formerly New Hall), since 2007; *b* 10 Sept. 1951; *d* of (Frank) Robert Furber, *qv* and late Anne Wilson Furber; *m* 1975, Dr James Farwell Coakley; two *d.* *Educ:* Blackheath High Sch.; New Hall, Cambridge (BA 1973; MA, PhD 1983); Harvard Divinity Sch. (ThM 1975). Harkness Fellow, 1973–75; Univ. Lectr in Religious Studies, 1976–90, Sen. Lectr, 1990–91, Lancaster Univ.; Tutorial Fellow in Theology, Oriel Coll., and Univ. Lectr in Theology, Oxford, 1991–93; Prof. of Christian Theology, 1993–95, Edward Mallinckrodt, Jr, Prof. of Divinity, 1995–2007, Vis. Prof. of Systematic and Philosophical Theology, 2007–08, Harvard Univ. Vis. Professorial Fellow, Princeton Univ., 2003–04. Select Preacher, Oxford Univ., 1991, 2014; Hulsean Lectr, Cambridge Univ., 1991–92, 2010; Henry Luce III Fellow, 1994–95; Hulsean Preacher, Cambridge Univ., 1996; Mulligan Preacher, Gray's Inn, 2003. Lectures: Samuel Ferguson, Manchester Univ., 1997, 2010; Riddell, Newcastle Univ., 1999; Tate-Willson, Southern Methodist Univ., 1999; Prideaux, Exeter Univ., 2000; Jellema, Calvin Coll., 2001; Stone, Princeton Theol Seminary, 2002; Cheney, Berkeley Divinity Sch. at Yale, 2002; Hensley Henson, Oxford Univ., 2005; J. A. Hall, Univ. of Victoria, BC, 2007; Paddock, Gen. Theol Seminary, NY, 2009; Gifford, Aberdeen Univ., 2012; Warfield, Princeton Theol Seminary, 2015; DuBose, Sewanee, 2015; Stob, Calvin Coll., 2015. Pres., British Soc. for Philos. of Religion, 2013–15. Ordained deacon, 2000, priest, 2001; Asst Curate, SS Mary and Nicholas, Littlemore, 2000–07; Assoc. Priest, The Good Shepherd, Waban, MA, 2001–08; licensed to officiate, Ely Dio., 2008–; Asst Priest, 2008–10, Minor Canon, 2010, Hon. Canon, 2011–, Ely Cathedral. Consultant to C of E Doctrine Commn, 1982–84, Mem., 1984–92. ThD *hc* Lund, 2006; DD *hc*: Gen. Theol Seminary, NY, 2008; St Andrews, 2014. *Publications:* Christ Without Absolutes: a study of the Christology of Ernst Troeltsch, 1988; (ed with David A. Pailin) The Making and Remaking of Christian Doctrine, 1993; (ed) Religion and the Body, 1997; Powers and Submissions: spirituality, philosophy and gender, 2002; (ed) Re-thinking Gregory of Nyssa, 2003; (ed with Kay Kaufman Shelemay) Pain and Its Transformations: the interface of biology and culture, 2007; (ed with Samuel Wells) Praying for England: priestly presence in contemporary culture,

2008; (ed with Charles M. Stang) Re-thinking Dionysius the Areopagite, 2009; (ed with Paul Garilyuk) The Spiritual Senses, 2011; Sacrifice Regained: reconsidering the rationality of Christian belief, 2011; (ed with F. Ward) Fear and Friendship: Anglicans engaging with Islam, 2012; God, Sexuality and the Self: an essay on the Trinity, 2013; (ed with Martin A. Nowak) Evolution, Games and God: the principle of cooperation, 2013; contrib. to C of E reports and to theol. jls. *Recreations:* musical activities, thinking about the garden, picking up litter. *Address:* Faculty of Divinity, University of Cambridge, West Road, Cambridge CB3 9BS.

See also R. J. Furber, W. J. Furber.

COATES, Prof. Andrew John, DPhil; FRAS; Head, Planetary Science, since 2005, Professor of Physics, since 2007, and Co-Director (Solar System), since 2011, Mullard Space Science Laboratory, University College London; *b* Heswall, 26 Aug. 1957; *s* of late Thomas Theodore Coates and of Audrey Coates; *m* 1983, Katherine Ann Cooke; two *d. Educ:* Bancroft's Sch., Woodford Green, Essex; Univ. of Manchester Inst. of Sci. and Technol. (BSc Pure Applied Physics 1978); Keble Coll., Oxford (MSc Sci. and Application of Electric Plasmas 1979; DPhil Plasma Physics 1982). FRAS 1993. Mullard Space Science Laboratory, University College London: post doctoral res. asst, 1982–88; Sen. Exptl Officer, 1988–89; Royal Soc. Univ. Res. Fellow, 1989–99; Reader in Physics, 1996–2007; Hd, Space Plasma Physics, 1999–2005 (space mission contribs incl. Cassini Plasma Spectrometer (lead co-investigator, electron spectrometer), ExoMars Rover (principal investigator, PanCam), JUICE, Venus Express, Mars Express, Rosetta, Bepi Colombo, Cluster, Double Star, Magnetospheric Multiscale, Beagle 2, Active Magnetospheric Particle Tracer Explorer, Giotto (co-investigator)); Dep. Dir, 2007–11. Hon. Prof. of Physics, Univ. of Aberystwyth, 2007–; Visiting Scientist: Max Planck Inst. for Solar System Physics, 1987–88; Bartol Res. Inst., Univ. of Delaware, 1994. Mem., ESA Solar System Wkg Gp, 1999–2001. BA Media Fellow, BBC World Service, 1994. *Publications:* contribs to learned jls in plasma interaction with solar system objects, magnetospheres and ionospheres, planetary surfaces and space instrumentation. *Recreations:* family, travel, ski-ing, popularising science, Leyton Orient. *Address:* Mullard Space Science Laboratory, University College London, Holmbury St Mary, Dorking, Surrey RH5 6NT. *T:* (01483) 204145. *E:* a.coates@ucl.ac.uk.

COATES, Sir Anthony Robert M.; *see* Milnes Coates.

COATES, David; HM Diplomatic Service, retired; independent analyst, money laundering and sanctions requirements, since 2008; *b* 13 Nov. 1947; *s* of late Matthew Coates and Margaret Ann Davies Coates (*née* Ross); *m* 1974, Joanna Kay Weil (marr. diss. 2010); two *d. Educ:* Dame Allan's Boys' Sch., Newcastle; Univ. of Bristol (BA Hist.); Univ. of Hawaii; Joint Univ. Centre, Taiwan. FCO, 1974–77; language training, Hong Kong, 1977–78; First Sec., Peking, 1978–81; Iran Desk, FCO, 1981–83; Asst Head, S America Dept, 1983–86; First Sec., UKMIS, Geneva, 1986–89; Counsellor and Head, Political Section, Peking, 1989–92; Head, Jt Assistance Unit, Central and E Europe, FCO, 1993–95; Head, Far Eastern and Pacific Dept, FCO, 1995–98; Dir Gen., British Trade and Cultural Office, Taipei, 1999–2002; Estate Modernisation Man., FCO, 2002–04; Ambassador to Côte d'Ivoire, 2004–06. Dir, Financial Crime, BBA, 2006–08. Associate Prof., Tamkang Univ., Taiwan, 2009–14. *Recreations:* ski-ing, theatre, hill-walking, leeks. *E:* david.coates@live.co.uk.

COATES, David, PhD; CBiol, FRSB, FLS; Professor and Dean, School of Learning and Teaching, College of Life Sciences, University of Dundee, since 2009; *b* Wallsend upon Tyne, 8 May 1957; *s* of Jack and Eva Coates; *m* 1981, Janice Whatley; one *s* one *d. Educ:* Ipswich Sch.; Univ. of Leeds (BSc Hons Genetics 1978); Univ. of E Anglia (PhD 1983). Res. Fellow, Purdue Univ., Indiana, 1983–85; Demonstrator in Genetics, Oxford Univ., 1985–89; Snow Tutorial Fellow in Plant Develt, Magdalen Coll., Oxford, 1988–89; Lectr in Applied Biol., 1989–99, Hd, Sch. of Biol., 2000–04, Univ. of Leeds; Dean, Sch. of Life Scis, Univ. of Bradford, 2004–09; Dep. Principal, Learning and Teaching, Univ. of Dundee, 2011–13. Vis. Prof., Coll. de France and INSERM 36, Paris, 1986–87. Chair, Heads of Univ. Biol Scis, 2005–12. Vice Pres., Inst. of Biol., 2004–09. Hon. Sec., Soc. of Biol., 2009–12. *Recreations:* reading, history, supporting Diabetes UK. *Address:* School of Learning and Teaching, College of Life Sciences, University of Dundee, Dow Street, Dundee DD1 5EH. *E:* d.coates@dundee.ac.uk.

COATES, Sir David (Charlton Frederick), 3rd Bt *cr* 1921, of Haypark, City of Belfast; *b* 16 Feb. 1948; *o s* of Sir Frederick Gregory Lindsay Coates, 2nd Bt and Joan Nugent, *d* of Maj.-Gen. Sir Charlton Spinks, KBE, DSO; *S* father, 1994; *m* 1973, Christine Helen, *d* of Lewis F. Marshall; two *s. Educ:* Millfield. *Heir: s* James Gregory David Coates [*b* 12 March 1977; *m* 2004, Laura Claire, *er d* of Gordon and Margaret Bennett; one *s*]. *Address:* Launchfield House, Briantspuddle, Dorchester, Dorset DT2 7HN.

COATES, Dudley James; consultant and writer; Head of Environment Group, Ministry of Agriculture, Fisheries and Food, 1996–2001; Vice President, Methodist Conference, 2006; *b* 15 Sept. 1946; *o s* of late Edward and Margot Coates; *m* 1969, Rev. Canon Dr Jean Walsingham; two *d. Educ:* Westcliff High School for Boys; Univ. of Sussex (BA (Hons)); STETS (MA Univ. of Surrey). Joined MAFF as Asst Principal, 1968; Second Sec., UK Delegn to the EC, Brussels, 1970–72; Principal, MAFF, 1973; Lectr, Civil Service Coll., 1978–81; Head of Animal Health Div. II, 1981–83, Head of Financial Management Team, 1983–87, MAFF; Dir Gen. of Corporate Services, Intervention Bd for Agricultural Produce, 1987–89; Dir, Regl Services, MAFF, 1989–96. Public Mem., Network Rail, 2002–10. Methodist local preacher, 1970–; Member: Methodist Conf., 1988, 1989, 1993–2004, 2006–08, 2010, 2012, 2014–15; Methodist Council, 2004–08, 2009–10; Chair, Methodist Publishing House, 1996–2004; Methodist ecumenical representative: Gen. Synod of C of E, 2001–07; Baptist Union Council, 2012–13; Southampton Methodist District: Mem., Ecumenical Team (formerly Ecumenical Action Team), 2009–; Dist Ecumenical Officer, 2010–; Sec., Policy Exec., 2010–. Gov., 2002–11, Trustee, 2011–15, STETS. *Publications:* (contrib.) Policies into Practice (ed David Lewis and Helen Wallace), 1984; Shades of Grey, 2006. *Recreations:* Christian activities, singing, cycling, model railways. *E:* coatesdudley@gmail.com.

COATES, James Richard, CB 1992; FCILT; Under Secretary, Urban and Local Transport Directorate, Department of Transport, 1994; *b* 18 Oct. 1935; *s* of William Richard Coates and Doris Coral (*née* Richmond); *m* 1969, Helen Rosamund Rimington; one *s* one *d. Educ:* Nottingham High Sch.; Clare Coll., Cambridge (MA). Joined Ministry of Transport, 1959; Private Sec. to Permanent Sec., 1962–63; Principal, 1963; Private Sec. to Secretary of State for Local Govt and Regional Planning, 1969, and to Minister of Transport, 1970–71; Asst Sec., DoE, 1971; Under Secretary, 1977; Dir, London Reg., PSA, 1979–83; Department of Transport: Highways Policy and Prog. Directorate, 1983–85; Rlys Directorate, 1985–91; Urban and Gen. Directorate, 1991–93. FCILT (FCIT 1996; Mem., Policies Cttee). *Recreations:* reading, listening to music, looking at buildings, gardening. *Address:* 10 Alwyne Road, N1 2HH.

COATES, John Dowling, AC 2006 (AO 1995; AM 1989); President, Australian Olympic Committee, since 1990; Vice President, International Olympic Committee, since 2013 (Member, since 2001; Executive Board Member, 2009–13); *b* 7 May 1950; *s* of Sidney Dowling Coates and Valerie Irene Coates; *m* 1981, Pauline Frances Kahl (marr. diss. 2005); five *s* one *d. Educ:* Homebush Boys' High Sch.; Sydney Univ. (LLB). Joined Greaves Wannan & Williams, 1971: Partner, 1977–87 and 1991–2001; Consultant, 1987–91; Partner, 2001–09, Special Counsel, 2010–, Kemp Strang Lawyers. Man. Dir, Austus Properties Ltd, 1987–90 (Dir, 1990–91); Chairman: Reef Casino Trust, 1993–97; Triplecee Retail Investment Trust, 1994–99; Accord Pacific Hldgs Ltd, 1994–2002; Australian Olympic Foundn Ltd, 1996–; Burson-Marsteller Australia, 2000–04; William Inglis & Son Ltd, 2007–; Dep. Chm., Kengfu Properties Pte Ltd, 1997–2002; Dir, 1995–2012, Dep. Chm., 2003–12, David Jones Ltd; Member: Grant Samuel Adv. Bd, 2002– (Dir, managers, Grant Samuel Laundy Pub Fund, 2005–07); Sydney Olympic Park Authy, 2005–; Director: United Customer Solutions Pty Ltd, 2004–06; Grosvenor Australia Properties Pty Ltd, 2005–10 (Consultant, 2004–05); Grosvenor Australia Investments Ltd, 2005–10; Events NSW Pty Ltd, 2007–09. Mem., Eur. Australian Business Council, 2009–. Dir, Australian Inst. of Sport, 1985–86 (Dep. Chm., 1986–89); Dep. Chm., Australian Sports Commn, 1989–98 (Mem., 1987–89); Mem. Council, Internat. Rowing Fedn, 1992–2014; President: Internat. Council of Arbitration for Sport, 2011– (Vice Pres., 1994–2011); Court of Arbitration for Sport, 2011–. Australian Olympic Committee: Mem., Exec. Bd, 1982–85; Vice-Pres., 1985–90; Exec. Dir, 1992 Olympic Games Bid, Brisbane CC, 1985–86; Vice Pres., Sydney Olympics 2000 Bid Ltd, 1991–93; Sen. Vice Pres., Sydney Organising Cttee for Olympic Games, 1999–2000. International Olympic Committee: Member: Olympic Games Study Commn, 2002–03; TV Rights and New Media Commn, 2005–; Chair: Juridical Commn (Mem., 2002–); Sport and Law Commn; Member, Co-ordination Commission: Games of XXX Olympiad, London 2012, 2005–12; Games of XXXI Olympiad, Rio de Janeiro 2016, 2010–; Games of XXXII Olympiad, Tokyo, 2020. Dir, Roseville Coll. Foundn Ltd, 1997–2003. Rowing Manager, Australian Team, Montreal Olympics, 1976; Admin. Dir, Australian Team, Moscow Olympics, 1980; Asst Gen. Manager, Australian Team, Los Angeles Olympics, 1984; Chef de Mission, Australian Olympic Team: Seoul, 1988; Barcelona, 1992; Atlanta, 1996; Sydney, 2000; Athens, 2004; Beijing, 2008. Hon. Life Member: NSW Olympic Council Inc., 1990; Australian Rowing Council Inc., 1993; NSW Rowing Assoc. Inc., 1994; Australian Olympic Cttee, 1997. IOC Centennial Trophy, 1994; Olympic Order in Gold, 2000; FISA Medal of Honour, 2000; Australian Sports Medal, 2001; Centenary Medal, Australia, 2003. *Recreations:* golf, swimming, rowing, other sports, the Olympic movement. *Address:* c/o Australian Olympic Committee Inc., Level 4, Museum of Contemporary Art, 140 George Street, Sydney, NSW 2000, Australia. *Clubs:* Commonwealth (Canberra); Sydney Rowing (Hon. Life Mem.), Carbine (past Chm.), Australian Turf; Drummoyne Sailing, Concord Golf.

COATES, Prof. John Henry, FRS 1985; Sadleirian Professor of Pure Mathematics, Cambridge University, 1986–2012; Fellow of Emmanuel College, Cambridge, since 1986; *b* 26 Jan. 1945; *s* of J. R. Coates and Beryl (*née* Lee); *m* 1966, Julie Turner; three *s. Educ:* Australian National Univ. (BSc); Trinity Coll., Cambridge (PhD). Assistant Prof., Harvard Univ., 1969–72; Associate Prof., Stanford Univ., 1972–74; Univ. Lectr, Cambridge, and Fellow, Emmanuel Coll., 1974–77; Prof., ANU, 1977–78; Prof. of Maths, Univ. de Paris, Orsay, 1978–86, Ecole Normale Supérieure, Paris, 1985–86; Hd of Dept of Pure Maths and Math. Stats, Cambridge Univ., 1991–97. Pres., London Math. Soc., 1988–90; Vice-Pres., Internat. Mathematical Union, 1991–95; Mem. Council, Royal Soc., 1992–94. Dr *hc:* Ecole Normale Supérieure, 1997; Heidelberg, 2012. *Address:* Emmanuel College, Cambridge CB1 2EA; 104 Mawson Road, Cambridge CB1 2EA. *T:* (01223) 740260.

COATES, His Honour Marten Frank; a Circuit Judge, 1997–2013; a Judge of the Mental Health Tribunal, since 2013; *b* 26 March 1947; *s* of Frank and Violet Coates; *m* 1973, Susan Anton-Stephens; three *d. Educ:* Pocklington Sch., York; Durham Univ. (BA Hons 1972); Cert. Biblical Studies. Called to the Bar, Inner Temple, 1972; Asst Recorder, Midland and Oxford Circuit, 1989–93; Recorder, 1993–97. Chancellor, Dio. Lichfield, 2006–11.

COATES, Prof. Nigel Martin; Professor of Architectural Design and Head of Department of Architecture, Royal College of Art, 1995–2011, now Professor Emeritus; Founder and Director, Nigel Coates Ltd, since 2009; Art Director, Slamp, since 2009; *b* 2 March 1949; *s* of Douglas Coates and Margaret Coates (*née* Trigg). *Educ:* Hanley Castle Grammar Sch., Malvern; Univ. of Nottingham (BA Arch Hons); Architectural Assoc. (AA Dip (Year Prize)); Univ. of Rome (Italian Govt Scholar). Unit Master, AA, 1979–89. Course Master, Bennington Coll., Vt, 1980–81. Jt Founder and Co-dir, Branson Coates Architecture Ltd, 1985–2006. Founder Mem., Narrative Architecture Today, 1979–89. Mem., Adv. Bd, ICA, 1987–89. Architecture columnist, Independent on Sunday, 2003–05. Trustee, Architecture Foundn, 2000–13. External Examiner: Bartlett Sch. of Architecture and AA, 1993–94; Dept of Architecture, Univ. of Cambridge, 2000–02. Presenter, 1989, advr and subject, 1992, TV documentaries. Lectures world-wide. Branson Coates' projects include: Katharine Hamnett shop, London, 1988; Café Bongo 1985, Arca di Noe 1988, Hotel Otaru Marittimo 1989, Nishi Azabu Wall 1990 and Art Silo 1993, in Japan; (built projects) Taxim Nightpark 1991 and Key fihan 1999, in Turkey; shops for Jigsaw in UK, Ireland and Japan, 1988–96; new depts for Liberty, Regent St, branches and airport shops, 1992–96; La Forêt and Nautilus Restaurants, Schiphol Airport, Amsterdam, 1993; Bargo Bar, Bass Taverns, 1996; Oyster House and Powerhouse::uk, London, 1998; New Gall. Bldg, Geffrye Mus., 1998; Nat. Centre for Popular Music, Sheffield, 1998; British Expo Pavilion, Lisbon 98; Body Zone, Millennium Dome, London, 2000; Inside Out, travelling exhibn, British Council, 2001; Mktg Suite and Roman Amphitheatre display, Guildhall, London, 2002; House to Home, Houses of Parliament, 2004; (shop design) Charles Fish, London, 2006. Branson Coates' exhibition design projects include: (contrib.) Living Bridges Exhibn, RA, 1996; (contrib.) Erotic Design Exhibn, Design Mus., 1997; Look Inside! New British Public Interiors, internat. tour, 1997; Colani Exhibn, Design Mus., 2007. Nigel Coates Ltd's projects include Middle and Over Wallop Restaurant, Glyndebourne, 2009. Nigel Coates designs include: Metropole and Jazz furniture collections, 1986; Noah collection, 1988; Female, He-man and She-woman mannequins, 1988; Tongue chair, 1989; Carpet collection, 1990; Gallo collection, Poltronova, 1991; Slipper chair, 1994; glass vase collection, Simon Moore, 1996; Oxo furniture, Hitch Mylius; Oyster furniture, Lloyd Loom; Fiesolani vases, Salviati; Slamp:ville, Slamp; Big Shoom, Alessi; Tête-a-Tête collection, Fornasetti; G-love chair, Contempo, 2006; Bodypark Tiles, Bardelli, 2006; lighting collections, Slamp, 2005–; Veneziani collections, AV Mazzega, 2008–; Scubism collection, Fratelli Boffi, 2008–; Pandada table, Pandamonium auction, WWF; Cloudelier, Swarovski Crystal Palace; Rollover and Loop collections, Varaschin; Tulipino vases, Simon Moore, 2009; Animalia, Fratelli Boffi, 2010; Faretto and Chapeau collections, Slamp, Rome, 2011; Angel Falls, Terzani Spa, 2012; Carry Artid Vases, Secondo Me Edizioni, 2012; Illuminati, Crocco and Punctum Collections, Slamp, 2013; Tetrapetal, Xilo, 2014; Fornasetti-Combacio Sofa System, 2014; Baciamano Easy Chair, 2014; Gebruder Thonet Vienna-Lehnstuhl, 2014. Exhibitions: Gamma City, Air Gall., 1985; (one-person) Ark Albion, AA, 1984; Ecstacity, AA, 1992; British Pavilion, Venice Biennale, 2000; Latent Utopias, Graz, 2002; Micro Utopias, Valencia Biannual, 2003; Vextacity, Fabbrica Europa, Florence, 2003; Greetings from London, Selfridges and Architecture Foundn, 2004; Babylon:don, 10th Internat. Architecture Exhibn, Venice Biennale, 2006; FutureCities, Barbican Art Gall., 2006; Hypnerotosphere, Venice Biennale, 2008; Battersea Gods Home, Super Contemp. Exhibn, Design Mus., 2009; (one-person) Baroccabilly, Nigel Coates Studio, London, Galleria Carlo Madesami, Milan, 2010, Cristina Grajales Inc., NY, 2011; Poltronova Connection, Nigel Coates Studio, 2010; Postmodernism, V&A, 2011; Neo-mio Chandelier, Superdesign, London, 2011; British Design, V&A, 2012; Handblown, 2013; Exploded, London Design Fest., 2013; Springboard, Nigel Coates Studio, London, 2014; (co-curator) Pavilion of Art and Design, RCA, 2010; work in collections of V&A Mus.; Casa Reale, Entratalibera, Milano, 2012, London Design Fest., 2012; Kama: Sesso, E Design, Triennale Design Mus., Milano, 2012–13; Fonds Régional d'Art Contemporain du Centre, Orléans, France; work exhibited in UK, Europe, US and Japan. Mem., Soc. of Authors. Inter-Design Award for Contribution to Japanese cities, Japan Inter-Design Forum, 1990; Outstanding Lifetime Contribn to Design Award, FX mag., 2011; Annie Spink Award, RIBA, 2012. *Publications:* Ecstacity, 1992; Guide to Ecstacity, 2003; Collidoscope, 2004; Narrative Architecture, 2011. *Recreations:* contemporary art, video-making, Italian culture, riding. *Address:* Nigel Coates Ltd, 13 Great James Street, WC1N 3DN. *W:* www.nigelcoates.com. *Clubs:* Chelsea Arts, Groucho.

COATES, Ralph Douglas; Finance Director, Bank of England, since 2013; *b* Cape Town, SA, 28 Oct. 1972; *s* of John Coates and Jennifer Cluver; *m* 2002, Alexa Morrell; two *d. Educ:* Univ. of Cape Town (BCom; Postgrad. Dip. Accountancy). ACA CA (SA). With Price Waterhouse, then PricewaterhouseCoopers: SA, 1996–99; Sen. Manager in Transaction Services, London, 2000–04; Finance Dir, UK Retail and Business Bank, Barclays Bank, 2004–13. *T:* (020) 7601 3432. *E:* ralph.coates@bankofengland.co.uk.

COATES, Dame Sally (Anne), (Dame Sally Cefai), DBE 2013; Director, Southern Academies, United Learning Trust, since 2014; *b* London, 15 April 1953; *d* of Francis Coates and Emilie Coates (*née* McConnell); *m* 1995, Serge Cefai; three *s* one *d. Educ:* Convent of the Sacred Heart, Maidstone; Maidstone Girls' Grammar; Furzedown Coll. (Cert Ed); Inst. of Educn, Univ. of London (BEd); South Bank Univ. (MA). Dep. Hd, 1989–2004, Headteacher, 2004–08, Sacred Heart Sch.; Principal, Burlington Danes Acad., 2008–14. *Recreations:* reading, travelling. *Address:* 124 Amyand Park Road, Twickenham, Middx TW1 3HP. *T:* (020) 8891 3388, 07824 368526.

COATES, Her Honour Suzanne; a Circuit Judge, 1998–2013; *b* 2 Aug. 1949; *d* of late Jack Coates and of Elsie Coates (now Brown); *m* 1980, John Brian Camille Tanzer, *qv*; two *s. Educ:* Skipton Girls' High Sch.; Guy's Hosp.; South Bank Poly. (HVCert 1972); Queen Mary Coll., London Univ. (LLB 1977). SRN, Guy's Hosp., 1968–71; Health Visitor, Bromley LBC, 1972–74; called to the Bar, Gray's Inn, 1978; Asst Recorder, 1992–96; a Recorder, 1996–98. *Recreations:* music, reading, walking, football (watching), gardening, travel, cooking.

COATS, Sir Alastair Francis Stuart, 4th Bt *cr* 1905; *b* 18 Nov. 1921; *s* of Lieut-Col Sir James Stuart Coats, MC, 3rd Bt and Lady Amy Coats (*d* 1975), *er d* of 8th Duke of Richmond and Gordon; *S* father, 1966; *m* 1947, Lukyn (*d* 2006), *d* of Capt. Charles Gordon; one *s* one *d. Educ:* Eton. Served War of 1939–45, Coldstream Guards (Capt.). *Heir: s* Alexander James Coats [*b* 6 July 1951; *m* 1999, Clara, *d* of Ernesto Abril de Vivero]. *Address:* 122 Pelham Road, Wimbledon, SW19 1PA. *T:* (020) 8540 8349.

COATS, David Richard Graham; Director, WorkMatters Consulting Ltd, since 2010; Research Fellow, Smith Institute, since 2010; Visiting Professor, Centre for Sustainable Work and Employment Futures, University of Leicester, since 2014; *b* 28 Aug. 1962; *s* of Frank Alexander Coats and Doreen Coats. *Educ:* Portway Sch., Bristol; University Coll. London (LLB 1983; LLM 1986); Inns of Court Sch. of Law. Called to the Bar, Inner Temple, 1985; Trades Union Congress: Policy Officer, Orgn and Industrial Relns Dept, 1989–94; Sen. Policy Officer, 1994–99, Head, 1999–2004, Econ. and Social Affairs Dept. Mem., Low Pay Commn, 2000–04; Associate Dir - Policy, Work Foundn, 2004–10. Member: Partnership Fund Assessment Panel, DTI, 2000–04; Central Arbitration Cttee, 2005–; Nat. Stakeholder Council on Health, Work and Well-Being, DWP, 2006–10. Member, Advisory Board: ESRC Future of Work Prog., 2000–05; Industrial Relns Res. Unit, Univ. of Warwick, 2000–; Mem., Exec. Cttee, Involvement and Participation Assoc., 2000–; Mem., Global Agenda Council on Employment, WEF, 2012–14. Mem. (Lab) Haringey BC, 1990–98. *Recreations:* walking, travel, reading, cooking. *Address:* WorkMatters Consulting Ltd, 10 Albion Drive, Haggerston, E8 4ET. *T:* (020) 7241 1587. *E:* dcoats@workmattersconsulting.co.uk.

COBB, Henry Nichols; Partner, Pei Cobb Freed & Partners, Architects, since 1960; *b* 8 April 1926; *s* of Charles Kane Cobb and Elsie Quincy Cobb; *m* 1953, Joan Stewart Spaulding; three *d. Educ:* Harvard College (AB 1947); Harvard Graduate Sch. of Design (MArch 1949). Architectural Div., Webb & Knapp, 1950–60; Pei Cobb Freed & Partners (formerly I. M. Pei & Partners), 1960–. Sch. of Architecture, Yale University: William Henry Bishop Vis. Prof., 1973, 1978; Charlotte Sheperd Davenport Vis. Prof., 1975; Graduate School of Design, Harvard: Studio Prof. and Chm., Dept of Architecture, 1980–85; Adjunct Prof. of Architecture and Urban Design, 1985–88. Hon. DFA Bowdoin Coll., 1985; Dr Technical Scis *hc*, Swiss Fed. Inst. of Technol., 1990. Topaz Medallion for Excellence in Architectural Educn, Assoc. of Collegiate Schs of Architecture/AIA, 1995; Lynn S. Beedle Lifetime Achievement Award, Council on Tall Buildings and Urban Habitat, 2013. *Publications:* Where I Stand, 1980; Architecture and the University, 1985. *Address:* Pei Cobb Freed & Partners, 88 Pine Street, New York, NY 10005–1801, USA. *T:* (212) 8724020.

COBB, Henry Stephen, CBE 1991; FSA; FRHistS; Clerk of the Records, House of Lords, 1981–91; *b* 17 Nov. 1926; *y s* of Ernest Cobb and Violet Kate Cobb (*née* Sleath), Wallasey; *m* 1969, Eileen Margaret Downer. *Educ:* Birkenhead Sch.; London School of Economics (BA, MA); Liverpool Univ. (Dip. Archive Admin). Archivist, Church Missionary Soc., 1951–53; Asst Archivist, House of Lords, 1953–59, Asst Clerk of the Records, 1959–73, Dep. Clerk, 1973–81. Lecturer in Palaeography, School of Librarianship, North London Polytechnic, 1973–77. Pres., Soc. of Archivists, 1992–96 (Mem. Council, 1970–82; Chm., 1982–84); Mem. Council, British Records Assoc., 1978–81; Chm., London Record Soc., 1984–2005. Mem. Cttee of Management, Inst. of Historical Research, 1986–90. Hon. Archivist, Hampstead Garden Suburb, 1992–2010. FSA 1967; FRHistS 1970. *Publications:* (ed) The Local Port Book of Southampton 1439–40, 1961; (ed with D. J. Johnson) Guide to the Parliament and the Glorious Revolution Exhibition, 1988; (ed) The Overseas Trade of London: Exchequer Petty Customs Accounts 1480–1, 1990; A Handlist of the Braye Manuscripts in the House of Lords Record Office, 1993; contribs to Economic History Rev., Jl of Soc. of Archivists, Archives, etc. *Recreations:* historical research, music, orchestral concerts, oratorio, opera, ballet, art, historical exhibitions. *Address:* 1 Child's Way, Hampstead Garden Suburb, NW11 6XU. *T:* (020) 8458 3688.

COBB, Prof. Justin Peter, FRCS; Professor of Orthopaedics, Imperial College London, since 2005; Orthopaedic Surgeon to the Queen, since 2008; *b* 15 March 1958; *s* of Capt. Peter Cobb, OBE and Jennifer Cobb (*née* Martin); *m* 1985, Iona Stormonth Darling; three *s* one *d. Educ:* Sherborne Sch.; Magdalen Coll., Oxford (BM BCh 1982; MCh 1991). FRCS 1986. Registrar, St Thomas' Hosp., 1985–87; Sen. Registrar, Middlesex Hosp. and Royal Nat. Orthopaedic Hosp., 1987–91; Consultant Orthopaedic Surgeon: UCL Hosps NHS Trust, 1991–2005; King Edward VII's Hosp. Sister Agnes (formerly King Edward VII's Hosp. for Officers), 1995–. Dir, Stanmore Implants Worldwide, 1995–2008; Founder, 1999, Dir, 2001–, Acrobot Co. Ltd. *Publications:* pubns in computer-assisted and robotic surgery of the hip and knee. *Recreations:* sailing, ski-ing, golf, but mainly work. *Address:* St Johns House, Chiswick Mall, W4 2PS. *E:* j.cobb@imperial.ac.uk. *Clubs:* Hurlingham; St Albans Medical; Swinley Forest Golf (Ascot).

COBB, Piers Andrew Conrad R.; *see* Russell-Cobb.

COBB, Hon. Sir Stephen (William Scott), Kt 2013; **Hon. Mr Justice Cobb;** a Judge of the High Court, Family Division, since 2013; Family Division Liaison Judge, North Eastern Circuit, since 2015; *b* 12 April 1962; *s* of Hon. Sir John Francis Scott Cobb and of Lady (Joan Mary) Cobb; *m* 1989, Samantha Cowling; two *s* one *d. Educ:* Winchester Coll.; Liverpool Univ. (LLB Hons 1984). Called to the Bar, Inner Temple, 1985, Bencher, 2011; QC 2003; a Recorder, 2004–13; Head of Chambers, One Garden Court, 2007–13; a Dep. High Ct Judge, 2009–13. Mem., Family Justice Council, 2004–09. Chm., Family Law Bar Assoc., 2010–11. Fellow, Internat. Acad. of Matrimonial Lawyers, 2007. *Publications:* (ed) Essential Family Practice, 2000; (ed) Clarke, Hall and Morrison, On Children, 2004–09; (contrib.) A Handbook for Expert Witnesses in Children Act Cases, 2nd edn, 2007; (contrib.) Halsbury's Laws of England, vol. 3, 2008. *Recreation:* family. *Address:* Royal Courts of Justice, Strand, WC2A 2LL. *Clubs:* Hurlingham; Bembridge Sailing.

COBBETT, David John, ERD 1962; TD 1973; FCILT; railway and transportation management consultant; *b* 9 Dec. 1928; *m* 1952, Beatrix Jane Ogilvie Cockburn; three *s. Educ:* Royal Masonic Sch. FCILT (FILT 1999). Gen. Railway admin. and managerial positions, 1949–67; Divl Movements Manager, Liverpool Street, 1967; Divl Manager, Norwich (British Railways Bd), 1968–70; Asst Managing Dir, Freightliners Ltd, 1970–73; Dep. Gen. Manager, British Railways Bd Scottish Region, 1973; Gen. Manager, British Railways Scottish Region, 1974–76; Chm., British Transport Ship Management, Scotland, 1974–76; Gen. Manager, BR Eastern Region, 1976–77; British Railways Board: Export Dir (Special Projects), 1977–78; Dir, Strategic Studies, 1978–83; Dir, Information Systems and Technology, 1983–85. Dir, Transmark, 1978. Mem. Bd, Railway Benevolent Instn, 1974–99 (Dep. Chm., 1981–84; Chm., 1984–98; Vice Pres., 2000–). Dir, Dachaidh Respite Care, Kingussie (formerly Aviemore), 1993– (Sec. and Treas., 1993–2008; Finance Dir, 2012–). Bt Col, Royal Corps of Transport (RARO), 1974. *Recreations:* military matters, historical reading, games. *Address:* Ballytruim, Newtonmore, Inverness-shire PH20 1DS. *T:* and *Fax:* (01540) 673269. *Clubs:* Army and Navy, MCC.

COBBOLD; *see* Lytton Cobbold, family name of Baron Cobbold.

COBBOLD, 2nd Baron *cr* 1960, of Knebworth; **David Antony Fromanteel Lytton Cobbold;** DL; Chairman and Managing Director, Lytton Enterprises Ltd, Knebworth House, since 1971; *b* 14 July 1937; *s* of 1st Baron Cobbold, KG, GCVO, PC, and Lady Hermione Bulwer-Lytton, *er d* of 2nd Earl of Lytton, KG, GCSI, GCIE, PC; assumed by deed poll, 1960, additional surname of Lytton; *S* father, 1987; *m* 1961, Christine Elizabeth, 3rd *d* of Major Sir Dennis Frederic Bankes Stucley, 5th Bt; three *s* one *d. Educ:* Eton College; Trinity Coll., Cambridge (BA Hons Moral Sciences). Fellow, Assoc. of Corporate Treasurers. PO, RAF, 1955–57. NATO Flying Training Scheme, Canada, 1956–57. Morgan Guaranty Trust Co., New York, 1961–62; Bank of London and South America Ltd, London, Zürich, Barcelona, 1962–72; Treasurer, Finance for Industry Ltd, 1974–79; Manager Treasury Div., BP Finance International, The British Petroleum Co. plc, 1979–87; Gen. Manager Financial Markets, TSB England & Wales plc, 1987–88; Dir, Hill Samuel Bank Ltd, and Head of TSB-Hill Samuel Treasury Div., 1988–89; Man. Dir, Gaiacorp Currency Managers, 1991–94 (Dir, 1989–94); Director: Close Brothers Gp plc, 1993–2000; Stevenage Leisure Ltd, 1999–2002. Mem., Assoc. for Monetary Union in Europe, 1992–2002. Mem., Finance and Policy Cttee, HHA, 1973–97 (Hon. Treas., 1988–97); Gov., Union of European HHAs, 1993–97. Chm., Stevenage Community Trust, 1990–2006; Trustee, Pilgrim Trust, 1993–2010; Director: Shuttleworth Trust, 1998–2002; English Sinfonia Orch. Ltd, 1998–2002. Elected Mem., H of L, 2000–14, crossbencher. Contested (L): Bishop Auckland, Oct. 1974; Hertfordshire, European Parly Election, 1979. DL Herts, 1993. *Recreation:* travel. *Heir: s* Hon. Henry Fromanteel Lytton Cobbold [*b* 12 May 1962; *m* 1987, Martha Frances, *d* of James Buford Boone, Jr; one *s* one *d*].

COBBOLD, Rear-Adm. Richard Francis, CB 1994; Chief Executive Officer, C2S2, since 2008; *b* 25 June 1942; *s* of Geoffrey Francis and Elizabeth Mary Cobbold; *m* 1975, Anne Marika Hjörne (marr. diss. 1995); one *s* one *d. Educ:* Bryanston Sch.; BRNC Dartmouth. Early service, RN: HMS Kent; Staff of FO Naval Flying Training; HMS Juno; HMS Hermes; loan to RAN; RN Staff College 1973; Arctic Flight in comd, 1973–74; 820 Sqdn, Sen. Observer, 1974–75; MoD, 1975–77; HMS Mohawk in comd, 1977–79; MoD, 1979–83; RCDS 1984; HMS Brazen in comd, 1985–86; Dir of Defence Concepts, MoD, 1987–88; Captain 2nd Frigate Sqdn, 1989–90; ACDS Op. Requirements (Sea), 1991–94, and for Jt Systems, 1992–94; Dir, RUSI, 1994–2007. Specialist Adviser: H of C Defence Cttee, 1997–2007; H of C Foreign Affairs Cttee, 2003; Sen. Policy Advr, Ocean Security Initiative, 2005–08. Vice Pres., Strategic Develt, Duos Technologies Internat. Inc., 2007–08. FRAeS 1994. Governor, London Nautical Sch., 1997–. *Recreations:* gardening, naval and military history. *Club:* Army and Navy.

COBHAM, 12th Viscount *cr* 1718; **Christopher Charles Lyttelton;** DL; landowner; Bt 1618; Baron Cobham 1718; Lord Lyttelton, Baron of Frankley 1756 (renewed 1794); Baron Westcote (Ire.) 1776; *b* 23 Oct. 1947; 2nd *s* of 10th Viscount Cobham, KG, GCMG, GCVO, TD, PC and Elizabeth Alison, *d* of J. R. Makeig-Jones, CBE; *S* brother, 2006; *m* 1973, Tessa Mary, *d* of late Col A. G. Readman, DSO; one *s* one *d. Educ:* Eton. Wood Gundy Ltd, 1969–85; Chm. and Chief Exec., NCL Investments, 1985–2002; Dep. Chm., 2002–07, Consultant, 2007–11, Smith & Williamson. Elder Brother, Trinity House, 2003–. DL Worcs, 2010. *Heir: s* Hon. Oliver Christopher Lyttelton, *b* 24 Feb. 1976.

See also Hon. R. C. Lyttelton.

COBHAM, Penelope, Viscountess; Penelope Ann Lyttelton, CBE 2014; Chairman, VisitEngland, since 2009 (Deputy Chairman, VisitBritain, 2005–09); *b* 2 Jan. 1954; *d* of late Roy and Dorothy Cooper; *m* 1974, 11th Viscount Cobham (marr. diss. 1995; he *d* 2006). *Educ:* St James's Sch., Malvern. Chairman: British Casino Assoc., 1999–2009; Civic Trust, 1999–2003. Comr, Museums and Galls Commn, 1993–2000; Trustee, V&A, 1993–2003; Member: LDDC, 1993–98; Historic Royal Palaces Ministerial Adv. Bd, 1990–98; Exec. Council, HHA, 1985–; Council, Nat. Trust, 2004–10. Co. Dir and Consultant incl. Chm., Heart of England Radio Ltd, subseq. Chrysalis Radio Midlands, 1993–2007. Consultant: Ernst & Young, 1997–2009; GI Partners (UK) Ltd, 2007–08; aAIM Infrastructure, 2007–08; Advr, Citi Pvte Bank, 2010–11; Chm., Adv. Bd, Highland Gp Internat., 2010–13; Dep. Chm., Adv. Bd, Pagefield Communications Ltd, 2013–; Mem., Strategy Bd, Linley. Guardian, Birmingham Assay Office, 1990–. Chm., Mus. Prize Trust, 2001–. Trustee: Birmingham Mus Trust, 2012–; Shakespeare Birthplace Trust, 2013–. Pres., governor and patron, numerous civic, charitable and educnl bodies. Freeman: City of London; Goldsmiths' Co. DL West Midlands, 1994–95. FRSA. *Address:* (office) 198 Hagley Road, Stourbridge, W Midlands DY8 2JN. *T:* (01384) 377517.

COBURN, David Adam; Member (UK Ind) Scotland, European Parliament, since 2014; *b* Glasgow, 11 Feb. 1959; *s* of Adam Coburn and Matilda Coburn (*née* Sprott Black); partner, Crawford Austin. *Educ:* Glasgow High Sch.; Univ. of Leeds. Former trader, London and NY commodity and financial futures markets, 1981–92; co-founder and co-owner, air freight forwarding company. Freeman, City of Glasgow, 1980. Contested (UK Ind) Falkirk, 2015. Mem., Gadfly Club. *Recreations:* arts and antiques, archaeology, country pursuits, gardening, vintage cars, bibliophile. *Address:* European Parliament, Rue Wiertz, Brussels 1047, Belgium. *T:* 07904 864249. *E:* david.coburn@ukip.org.

COBURN, Michael Jeremy Patrick; QC 2010; barrister; *b* Manila, 28 March 1966; *s* of Jeremy Coburn and Rosemary Coburn; *m* 2006, Jennifer Manuel; two *d. Educ:* Charterhouse; Worcester Coll., Oxford (BA Lit.Hum.); City Univ., London (DipLaw). Called to the Bar, Inner Temple, 1990; in practice as a barrister, specialising in commercial law, 1991–. *Recreations:* cooking, cycling. *Address:* 20 Essex Street, WC2R 3AL. *T:* (020) 7842 1200. *E:* mcoburn@20essexst.com.

COCHRANE, family name of **Earl of Dundonald** and **Baron Cochrane of Cults**.

COCHRANE, Lord; Archie Iain Thomas Blair Cochrane; *b* 14 March 1991; *s* and *heir* of Earl of Dundonald, *qv. Educ:* Ampleforth Coll. Working for technol. start-up company, Bogotá, Colombia. *Recreations:* sailing, ski-ing, trial biking, country sports, travelling. *Address:* Lochnell Castle, Benderloch, Argyll PA37 1QT.

COCHRANE OF CULTS, 4th Baron *cr* 1919; **(Ralph Henry) Vere Cochrane;** DL; Chairman, Craigtoun Meadows Ltd, since 1972; *b* 20 Sept. 1926; 2nd *s* of 2nd Baron Cochrane of Cults, DSO and Hon. Elin Douglas-Pennant (*d* 1934), *y d* of 2nd Baron Penrhyn; *S* brother, 1990; *m* 1956, Janet Mary Watson, *d* of late William Hunter Watson Cheyne, MB, MRCS, LRCP; two *s*. *Educ:* Eton; King's Coll., Cambridge (MA). Served RE, 1945–48 (Lieut). Formerly: Vice-Chm., Cupar-Fife Savings Bank; Dir for Fife, Tayside Savings Bank. Underwriting Mem. of Lloyds, 1965–96. Gen. Comr for Income Tax. Mem., Queen's Body Guard for Scotland (Royal Co. of Archers), 1962–. DL Fife 1976. *Heir: s* Hon. Thomas Hunter Vere Cochrane, LLB, ACII [*b* 7 Sept. 1957; *m* 2008, Silke, *d* of late Peter Quandt, of Berlin]. *Club:* New (Edinburgh).

COCHRANE, Alannah Elizabeth W.; *see* Weston Cochrane, A. E.

COCHRANE, (Alexander John) Cameron, MBE 1987; MA; National Education Officer, Atlantic Council of UK, 2001–03; *b* 19 July 1933; *s* of late Dr Alexander Younger Cochrane and Jenny Johnstone Cochrane; *m* 1958, Rosemary Aline (*d* 2014), *d* of late Robert Alexander Ogg and Aline Mary Ogg; one *s* two *d*. *Educ:* The Edinburgh Academy; University Coll., Oxford. National Service in RA, 1952–54. Asst Master, St Edward's Sch., Oxford, 1957–66; Warden, Brathay Hall, Ambleside, Cumbria, 1966–70; Asst Dir of Educn, City of Edinburgh, 1970–74; Headmaster, Arnold Sch., Blackpool, 1974–79; Headmaster, Fettes Coll., Edinburgh, 1979–88; first Principal, Prince Willem-Alexander Coll., Holland, 1988–91; Principal, British Internat. Sch., Cairo, 1992–95. Consultant, Dutch and Internat. Educn Services, 1996–2006. Member: Lancashire CC Educn Cttee, 1976–79; Council, Outward Bound Trust, 1979–88; Admiralty Interview Bd, 1979–88; Scottish Cttee, Duke of Edinburgh's Award, 1981–86; Chairman: Outward Bound Ullswater, 1979–84; Outward Bound Loch Eil, 1984–88; Lothian Fedn of Boys' Clubs, 1981–84; HMC Services Cttee, 1982–88. Commandant, XIII Commonwealth Games Village, Edinburgh, 1986. Governor: Aiglon Coll., 1985–94; Pocklington Sch., 1985–2002. Session Clerk, Auchtertool Kirk, 1998–2004. CFM 1988. *Recreations:* games, the countryside, photography, friends, family, France. *Address:* 4/6 Spylaw Road, Edinburgh EH10 5BH. *T:* (0131) 445 1437. *Clubs:* East India, MCC; Vincent's (Oxford).

COCHRANE, Sir (Henry) Marc (Sursock), 4th Bt *cr* 1903; *b* 23 Oct. 1946; *s* of Sir Desmond Oriel Alastair George Weston Cochrane, 3rd Bt, and of Yvonne Lady Cochrane (*née* Sursock); *S* father, 1979; *m* 1969, Hala (*née* Es-Said); two *s* one *d*. *Educ:* Eton; Trinity Coll., Dublin (BBS, MA). Director: Hambros Bank Ltd, 1979–85; GT Management PLC, subseq. LGT Asset Management, 1985–98; INVESCO, 1998–99; Henderson Global Investors, 2000–05. Hon. Consul General of Ireland in Beirut, 1979–84. Trustee, Chester Beatty Library and Gall. of Oriental Art, Dublin. *Recreations:* ski-ing, target shooting, electronics. *Heir: s* Alexander Desmond Sursock Cochrane [*b* 7 May 1973; *m* 2007, Alannah Elizabeth Weston (*see* A. E. Weston Cochrane); two *d*]. *Address:* Woodbrook, Bray, Co. Wicklow, Ireland. *T:* (1) 2821421; Beit as-Saifi, Mar Maroun Street, Mar Maroun/Saifi District, Beirut, Lebanon. *T:* (1) 565368/9.

COCHRANE, Keith Robertson; Chief Executive, Weir Group PLC, since 2009 (Group Finance Director, 2006–09); *b* 11 Feb. 1965; *m* 1998, Fiona Margaret Armstrong; one *s* one *d*. *Educ:* Dunblane High Sch.; Univ. of Glasgow (BAcc 1st Cl. Hons). CA 1989; Audit Manager, Arthur Andersen, 1990–93; Gp Financial Controller and Co. Sec., 1993–96, Gp Financial Dir, 1996–2000, Stagecoach Holdings plc; Chief Exec., Stagecoach Gp, 2000–02; Dir of Gp Financial Reporting, 2003–04, Gp Controller, 2004–05, Gp Dir of Finance, 2005–06, Scottish Power plc. Mem. Council, Glenalmond Coll., 2013–. Hon. Treas., Royal Scottish Nat. Orch., 2008–. Hon. DSc Strathclyde, 2013. *Recreations:* golf, music, travel, reading. *Address:* Weir Group PLC, 20 Waterloo Street, Glasgow G2 6DB.

COCHRANE, Malcolm Ralph, MBE 2012; Vice Lord-Lieutenant of Oxfordshire, 1999–2009; *b* 8 Aug. 1938; *s* of Air Chief Marshal Hon. Sir Ralph Cochrane, GBE, KCB, AFC and Hilda (*née* Wiggin); *m* 1972, Mary Anne Scrope, *d* of Ralph Scrope and Lady Beatrice Scrope, *d* of 6th Earl of Mexborough; one *s* two *d*. *Educ:* Eton Coll.; Balliol Coll., Oxford. Nat. Service, Scots Guards, 1957–58. Design Research Unit, 1962–65; Design Panel, BRB, 1965–72; Director: Cochranes of Oxford Ltd, 1972–2007; Cults Lime Ltd, 1976–. High Sheriff, 1996, DL 1998, Oxon. *Recreations:* arts, gardening, watching sport. *Address:* Grove Farmhouse, Shipton-under-Wychwood, Oxon OX7 6DG. *T:* (01993) 830742.

COCHRANE, Sir Marc; *see* Cochrane, Sir H. M. S.

COCHRANE, Peter, OBE 1999; PhD, DSc; FREng, FIET, FIEEE; Co-Founder and Chairman, Cochrane Associates, since 2005; consultant to government and international companies; *b* 11 July 1946; *s* of Colin Cochrane and Gladys Cochrane; *m* 1971, Brenda Cheetham (*d* 2003); two *s* two *d*; *m* 2005, Jane Tromans. *Educ:* Trent Poly. (BSc Electrical Engrg 1973); Essex Univ. (MSc Telecommunications 1976; PhD Transmission Systems 1979; DSc Systems Design 1991). CGIA 1975; CEng 1977; FIET (FIEE 1987; MIEE 1977); FIEEE 1992 (MIEEE 1983); FREng (FEng 1994). General Post Office: Technician, System Maintenance, 1962–69; Student Engr, 1969–73; Exec. Engr, GPO Res. Labs, 1973–79; BT Laboratories: Head of Gp, 1979–83; Head of Section, 1983–87; Head, Optical Networks Div., 1987–91; Head, Systems Res., 1991–93; Head, Advance Res., 1993–94; Head of Res., 1994–99; Chief Technologist, BT, 1999–2000; Co-Founder and CEO, ConceptLabs, Calif., 2000–06. Mem. Adv. Bd, Computer Scis Corp. Vanguard Prog., 1996–98. Technical Advr, Motorola, 2002–08; Adviser: IRDETO, 2004–12; PMC Sierra, 2005–09. Visiting Professor: CNET, Lannion Univ., France, 1978; NE London Poly., 1980–90; Essex Univ., 1988–; Southampton Univ., 1991–94; Kent Univ., 1991–96; UCL, 1994–99; QMUL (formerly QMW), 1999–2006; Univ. of Hertfordshire, 2012–. Mem., NY Acad. of Scis, 1995. FRSA. Hon. DTech Stafford, 1996. Holds 14 original patents. *Publications:* (with J. E. Flood) Transmission Systems, 1991; (with D. J. T. Heatley) Modelling Telecommunication Systems, 1995; Tips for Time Travellers, 1997; Uncommon Sense, 2004; numerous professional papers and articles in IEE, IEEE, and other jls. *Recreations:* music, running, mathematics, philosophy, my family, fly fishing, reading, cycling. *Address:* Cochrane Associates, c/o Ensors, Cardinal House, 46 St Nicholas Street, Ipswich, Suffolk IP1 1TT.

COCHRANE-DYET, Fergus John, OBE 2015; HM Diplomatic Service; Ambassador to Liberia, 2013–15; *b* 16 Jan. 1965; *s* of Lt-Col Iain Cochrane-Dyet and Rosemary Cochrane-Dyet; *m* 1987, Susie Emma Jane Aram; three *s*. *Educ:* Felsted Sch.; Jesus Coll., Oxford; Durham Univ. (BA Hons); Sch. of Oriental and African Studies, Univ. of London; Univ. of Exeter. Joined HM Diplomatic Service, 1987; Third Sec. (Political), Lagos, 1990–93; Second Sec. (Political), Abuja, 1993–94; First Secretary: Hd, N Africa Section, FCO, 1994–96; Hd, British Interests Section, Tripoli, 1996–97; Hd, Commercial, Jakarta, 1998; Dir, Trade and Investment Promotion for Australia, and Dep. Consul Gen., Sydney, 1998–2001; Chargé d'Affaires, Conakry, 2001–02; Dep. Hd of Mission, Kabul, 2002; Dep. Hd, Africa Dept (Southern), FCO, 2002–04; Dep. High Comr, Lusaka, 2004–07; Dep. Hd, Helmand, Afghanistan, 2007; High Comr to Seychelles, 2007–09, to Malawi, 2009–11; Dep. Hd of Mission, Helmand, Afghanistan, 2012. *Recreations:* running, scuba diving, films. *Address:* c/o Foreign and Commonwealth Office, King Charles Street, SW1A 2AH.

COCKBURN, Sir Charles (Christopher), 13th Bt of that Ilk, *cr* 1671; Chairman, Portcullis Group Ltd, since 2015; *b* Ross-on-Wye, Herefordshire, 19 Nov. 1950; *s* of Sir John Elliot Cockburn, 12th Bt of that Ilk and Glory Patricia Cockburn (*née* Mullings); *S* father 2015, but his name does not appear on the Official Roll of the Baronetage; *m* 1st, 1978, Beverly Jane Stangroom (marr. diss. 1984; she *d* 1999); 2nd, 1985, Margaret Ruth, *d* of Samuel Bell; two *s* one *d* (of whom one *s* one *d* are twins). *Educ:* Lindisfarne Coll.; Emanuel Sch.; City of London Poly. (BA Govt and Politics); Garnet Coll. (PGCE). Rock 'n' roll (the lost years), 1970–78; teacher in further educn, 1981–84; with Lloyd Hughes Associates, public policy consultants, 1984–87; founding Ed., Financial Regulation Review, 1987–89; Chm., Portcullis Research Ltd, 1989–. MInstD. *Recreations:* cycling, song-writing. *Heir: s* Christopher Samuel Alexander Cockburn, *b* 24 March 1986. *Address:* Portcullis Public Affairs, 11 Haymarket, SW1Y 4BP. *T:* (020) 7368 3100. *E:* charles.cockburn@portcullispublicaffairs.com. *Club:* Twickenham Rowing.

COCKBURN, David; The Certification Officer for Trade Unions and Employers' Associations, since 2001; (part-time) Employment Judge (formerly Chairman, Employment Tribunals), 2001–12; *b* 30 Nov. 1948; *s* of John William Cockburn and Nora Cockburn (*née* Carr); *m* 1976, Polly Dickey; one *s* two *d*. *Educ:* King's Sch., Pontefract; LSE (LLB 1970; MSc (Econ) 1972). Admitted solicitor, 1975; Partner, Pattinson & Brewer, solicitors, 1978–2001; Chm., Code Compliance Panel, PhonepayPlus, 2008–14. Chairman: Industrial Law Soc., 1983–86 (Vice-Pres., 1986–); Employment Lawyers' Assoc., 1994–96; Employment Law Cttee, Law Soc., 1995–99; Treas., Inst. of Employment Rights, 1995–2001. Vis. Prof., Middlesex Univ., 2002–. Member, Editorial Committee: Industrial Law Jl, 1986–; Encyclopaedia of Employment Law, 1990–. *Publications:* (contrib.) Justice for a Generation, 1985; (contrib.) Labour Law in Britain, 1986; (jtly) Know-how in Employment Law, 1995; (contrib.) The Changing Institutional Face of British Employment Relations, 2006; articles on labour law in learned jls. *Recreations:* jogging, cycling, sailing, ski-ing, jazz, theatre. *Address:* Certification Officer for Trade Unions and Employers' Associations, 22nd Floor, Euston Tower, 286 Euston Road, NW1 3JJ. *T:* (020) 7210 3734, *Fax:* (020) 7210 3612. *E:* info@certoffice.org.

COCKBURN, Prof. Forrester, CBE 1996; MD; FRCPE, FRCPGlas; FRSE; Samson Gemmell Professor of Child Health, University of Glasgow, 1977–96, now Emeritus Professor; Chairman, Yorkhill NHS Trust, 1997–2001; *b* 13 Oct. 1934; *s* of Forrester Cockburn and Violet E. Bunce; *m* 1960, Alison Fisher Grieve; two *s*. *Educ:* Leith Acad.; Univ. of Edinburgh (MB ChB 1959; MD *cum laude* 1966); DCH Glasgow 1961. FRCPE 1971; FRCPGlas 1978; FRSE 1999. Med. trng, Royal Infirmary of Edinburgh, Royal Hosp. for Sick Children, and Simpson Memorial Maternity Pavilion, Edinburgh, 1959–63; Huntingdon Hertford Foundn Res. Fellow, Boston Univ., Mass, 1963–65; Nuffield Sen. Res. Fellow, Univ. of Oxford, 1965–66; Wellcome Trust Sen. Med. Res. Fellow, Univ. of Edin. and Simpson Meml Maternity Pavilion, 1966–71; Sen. Lectr, Dept of Child Life and Health, Univ. of Edin., 1971–77. Chm., Panel on Child Nutrition and Wkg Gp on Weaning Diet, Cttee on Med. Aspects of Food Policy (Report, 1994). Founder FRCPCH 1996, Hon. FRCPCH 1997; Hon. FRCSE 2000. James Spence Medal, RCPCH, 1998. *Publications:* Neonatal Medicine, 1974; The Cultured Cell in Inherited Metabolic Disease, 1977; Inborn Errors of Metabolism in Humans, 1980; (with O. P. Gray) Children—A Handbook for Children's Doctors, 1984; (with J. H. Hutchison) Practical Paediatric Problems, 6th edn 1986; (with T. L. Turner and J. Douglas) Craig's Care of the Newly Born Infant, 8th edn 1988; Fetal and Neonatal Growth, 1988; (ed jtly and contrib.) Diseases of the Fetus and Newborn, 1989, 2nd edn 1995; (jtly) Children's Medicine and Surgery, 1996; around 200 articles mainly on fetal and neonatal nutrition and inherited metabolic disease. *Recreations:* sailing, gardening, painting. *Address:* University Department of Child Health, Royal Hospital for Sick Children, Yorkhill, Glasgow G3 8SJ. *T:* (0141) 201 0000.

COCKBURN, Patrick Oliver; Iraq correspondent, The Independent, since 2003; *b* Cork, 5 March 1950; *s* of late Claud Cockburn, journalist and Patricia Cockburn; *m* 1981, Jan Montefiore; two *s*. *Educ:* St Stephen's, Dublin; Glenalmond, Perth; Trinity Coll., Oxford (BA Hist.). Financial Times: on Middle East staff, 1980–84; Moscow corresp., 1984–87; Associate, Carnegie Endowment for Internat. Peace, 1988–89; The Independent: Middle East Ed., 1990–92; Washington corresp., 1992–95; Jerusalem corresp., 1995–99; Moscow corresp., 1999–2002. *Publications:* (with Andrew Cockburn) Out of the Ashes: the resurrection of Saddam Hussein, 1999; The Broken Boy, 2005; The Occupation: war and resistance in Iraq, 2006; Muqtada al-Sadr and the Battle for the Future of Iraq, 2008; (with Henry Cockburn) Henry's Demons, 2011; The Jihadis Return: Isis and the New Sunni uprising, 2014, 2nd edn as The Rise of Islamic State: Isis and the new Sunni revolution, 2015. *Address:* The Independent, 2 Derry Street, W8 5HF. *T:* (020) 7005 2810. *E:* patrickcockburn2@gmail.com. *Clubs:* Reform, Frontline, Groucho.

COCKBURN, William, CBE 1989; TD 1980; Deputy Chairman, UK Mail Group (formerly Business Post) plc, 2002–12; *b* 28 Feb. 1943. Entered Post Office, 1961; held various junior and middle management positions; apptd Mem., PO Board, 1981, Mem. for Finance, Counter Services and Planning, 1982–84; Mem. for Royal Mail Operations, 1984–86; Man. Dir, Royal Mail, 1986–92; Chief Executive: The Post Office, 1992–95; W. H. Smith Gp PLC, 1996–97; Gp Man. Dir, BT UK, 1997–2001; Chm., Parity Gp plc, 2001–03; Dep. Chm., AWG, 2003–06. Chm., Internat. Post Corp., 1994–95; non-executive Director: Lex Service plc, 1993–2002; Centrica plc, 1997–99; Army Bd, 2008–11. Member: Bd, BITC, 1990–2003; Council, Industrial Soc., 1992–2002; Chairman: Sch. Teachers' Review Body, 2002–08; Senior Salaries Review Body, 2008–. Pres., Inst. of Direct Marketing, 2001–06. Col, RE Postal and Courier Service (V), 1986–91; Hon. Col, RE Postal and Courier Service, 1992–94; Hon. Col Comdt, RLC, 1996–2006. FCIT 1993; FRSA; CCMI (CIMgt 1993). Freeman, City of London.

COCKBURN-CAMPBELL, Sir Alexander (Thomas), 7th Bt *cr* 1821, of Gartsford, Ross-shire; Facilities Manager, Colliers International, 2012–14; *b* 16 March 1945; *o s* of Sir Thomas Cockburn-Campbell, 6th Bt and of Josephine Zoi Cockburn-Campbell (*née* Forward); *S* father, 1999; *m* 1969, Kerry Ann, *e d* of Sgt K. Johnson; one *s* one *d*. *Educ:* Edwards Business Coll. (Adv. Cert. Mktg/Mgt). Prodn Mgr, 1980–90; Maintenance Manager, Uniting Church Homes, 1995–2000; Building Ops Supervisor, Knight Frank Facilities Managers, Perth, WA, 2000–12. Protestant Lay Minister, 1980– (Dip. Ministry). *Recreation:* surf-board riding. *Heir: s* Thomas Justin Cockburn-Campbell, *b* 10 Feb. 1974. *Address:* 103 Waterperry Drive, Canning Vale, WA 6155, Australia. *T:* (8) 92562049.

COCKCROFT, Barry Michael, CBE 2010; dental surgeon; Chief Dental Officer, NHS England, Department of Health, Health Education England, 2013–15; *b* 6 Nov. 1950; *s* of late Harry and Margaret Cockcroft; *m* 1973, Diane Lay; one *s* two *d*. *Educ:* De La Salle Coll., Salford; Univ. of Birmingham (BDS 1973; Charles Greene Prize, 1973). Sen. House Officer, Coventry & Warwickshire Hosp., 1974; general dental practitioner: Coventry, 1975–79; Rugby, 1979–2002; Dep. Chief Dental Officer, 2002–06, Chief Dental Officer, 2006–13, DoH. JP Rugby, 1992–2000. Hon. FDS RCS 2007; Hon. FFGDP(UK) 2011. DDS Plymouth. *Recreations:* getting home at weekends, live music and theatre, watching Rugby RFC, supporting Bolton Wanderers FC. *Address:* Highview, Hillmorton Lane, Clifton Upon Dunsmore, Rugby CV23 0BL. *E:* bmc397237@gmail.com.

COCKCROFT, John Hoyle; author and journalist; Director, International Conflict Resolution, 1990–2006; writer and political and corporate adviser; various electronics directorships, since 1977; *b* 6 July 1934; *s* of late Lionel Fielden Cockcroft and Jenny Hoyle; *m* 1971, Tessa Fay Shepley; three *d*. *Educ:* Primary, Trearddur House; Oundle; St John's Coll., Cambridge (Sen. Maj. Scholar (History), 1953). MA Hons History and Econs 1958; Pres., Cambridge Union, 1958. Royal Artillery, 2nd Lieut, 1953–55. Feature writer, Financial Times, 1959–61; Economist, GKN, 1962–67; seconded to Treasury, Public Enterprises Div. (transport), 1965–66; Econ. Editor, Daily Telegraph, 1967–74. MP (C) Nantwich, Feb.

1974–1979; Mem. Select Cttee on Nationalised Industries (transport), 1975–79; Company Secretaries Bill (Private Member's), 1978. Duff Stoop & Co., stockbrokers (corporate finance), 1978–86; Laurence Prust, stockbrokers (corporate finance), 1986–90; Dir, BR (Eastern Region), 1984–89; Consultant: GKN, 1971–76; Mail Users' Assoc., 1976–79; Inst. of Chartered Secretaries, 1977–79; BR, 1979–84; Cray Electronics, 1982–84; Dowty, 1983–86; Wedgwood, 1983–84; Crystalate, 1983–86; Commed Ltd, 1983–93; MAP Securities (corporate finance), 1992–95; Heathmere (UK), 1996–; ESL & N, 2006–. Consultant: NEI History Archives, 1980–85; GKN History Archives, 2002–. Member Council: European Movement, 1973–74, 1983–84; Conservative Gp for Europe, 1980–87. Member: RUSI; UNA/European-Atlantic Gp. Trustee, Sanderson Trust (Oundle), 1992–. Leader-writer, Sunday Telegraph, 1981–86; Columnist: Microscope, 1982–85; electronic money transmission, Banking World, 1984–86; Westminster Watch, Electronics Times, 1985–90. *Publications:* (jtly) Reforming the Constitution, 1968; (jtly) Self-Help Reborn, 1969; Why England Sleeps, 1971; (jtly) An Internal History of Guest Keen and Nettlefolds, 1976; Microelectronics, 1982; Microtechnology in Banking, 1984; articles in The European, The Scotsman, Jl of Contemp. British Hist., Essex Chronicle, 1979–. Politics interviewer, BBC Radio Essex, 2011–. Probus Luncheon Club speaker, 2014–. *Recreations:* walking, reading, writing, entertaining. *Address:* 315 Broomfield Road, Chelmsford CM1 4DU.

COCKELL, Sir Merrick (Richard), Kt 2010; Member (C), since 1986, and Leader of the Council, 2000–13, Royal Borough of Kensington and Chelsea; Executive Chairman, Cratus Communications Ltd, since 2014; *b* 16 June 1957; *s* of late Peter Colvile Cockell and of Hildegard Christina Gaskell (*née* Kern); *m* 1986, Karen Libby; two *d. Educ:* Pierrepont Sch. Trader, F. M. Barshall Ltd, Ghana, Togo, Sierra Leone, The Gambia, then in China, 1977–82; Founder Dir, Abingdon Cockell Ltd, 1982–2006. Sen. Advr, PA Consulting Gp, 2014–. Royal Borough of Kensington and Chelsea: Chm., Educn Authy, 1992–95; Chief Whip, 1995–2000. Member: London Governance Commn, 2004–06; Audit Commn, 2009–11; Bd, London Pensions Fund Authy, 2011– (Dep. Chm., 2013–). Chairman: London Councils (formerly Assoc. of London Govt), 2006–10; LGA, 2011–14; UK Municipal Bonds Agency, 2015–. Chairman: Cons. Councillors' Assoc., 2008–11 (Dep. Chm., 2005–08); Bd, Cons. Party, 2008–11. Chm., Localis Res. Ltd, 2009–. Trustee, 2020 Public Services Trust (formerly Public Services Res. Gp), 2008–11. Gov., Kensington Aldridge Acad., 2014–. Freeman, City of London, 2008. Hon. Col 41 (Princess Louise's Kensington) Sqdn, 38 Signal Regt (Vol.), 2012–. *Recreations:* opera, travel (reading and actual), family and dogs. *Address:* c/o London Pensions Fund Authority, 2nd Floor, 169 Union Street, SE1 0LL. *T:* (020) 7369 6006. *E:* mrc@cockell.co. *Club:* Chelsea Arts.

COCKELL, Michael Henry; a Deputy Chairman of Lloyd's, 1986; *b* 30 Aug. 1933; *s* of Charles and Elise Seaton; *m* 1961, Elizabeth Janet Meikle; one *s* three *d. Educ:* Harrow School. Survey officer, 1st Regt HAC (RHA), 1955–59. Underwriter for G. N. Rouse Syndicate 570, 1968–90; Chm., M. H. Cockell & Co., 1978; Senior Partner, M. H. Cockell & Partners, 1986; Chm., Atrium Cockell Underwriting Ltd, 1997–98; Dir, Medway plc, 1997–2000. Dep. Chm., Lloyd's Non-Marine Assoc., 1982, Chm., 1983–; Mem. Council, Lloyd's, 1984–87, 1990–93 and 1995–96. *Recreations:* all sport (especially cricket), ornithology, melodic music, gardening, countryside. *Address:* Court Horeham, Cowbeech, Herstmonceaux, E Sussex BN27 4JN. *T:* (01323) 833171. *Clubs:* City of London, MCC; IZ.

COCKER, (Peter) Mark; author, naturalist and environmental activist; *b* Buxton; *s* of Peter Cocker and Anne Cocker; *m* 1989, Mary Muir; two *d. Educ:* Buxton Coll.; Univ. of East Anglia (BA Eng. 1982). Conservation work, RSPB, Nature Conservancy Council, Birdlife Internat., 1985–88; wildlife tour guide, Naturetrek, Limosa, 1988–2001; freelance journalism, mainly for Guardian, Guardian Weekly, Times Newspapers, Eastern Daily Press, 1988–. Founder Mem. Council, Oriental Bird Club, 1984–88; Mem. Council, African Bird Club, 1994–2000; Pres., Norfolk and Norwich Naturalists' Soc., 2007–08. Co-Founder, New Networks for Nature, 2008–13. *Publications:* A Himalayan Ornithologist: the life and work of Brian Houghton Hodgson (with Carol Inskipp), 1988; Richard Meinertzhalen: soldier, scientist and spy, 1989; Loneliness and Time, 1992; Rivers of Blood, Rivers of Gold: Europe's conflict with tribal peoples, 1998; Birders: tales of a tribe, 2001; Birds Britannica, 2005; A Tiger in the Sand, 2006; Crow Country, 2007 (New Angle Prize for Literature, 2009); (with David Tipling) Birds and People, 2013; Claxton: field notes from a small planet, 2014. *Recreations:* birds, insects, flowers, photography, reading, growing things, filling notebooks with scribble. *Address:* c/o Rogers, Coleridge and White, 20 Powis Mews, W11 1TN. *T:* (020) 7221 3717. *E:* mark.cocker@virgin.net.

COCKER, Victor, CBE 2000; Chairman, Aga Foodservice Group, 2004–08; *b* 30 Oct. 1940; *s* of Harold Nathan Cocker and Marjorie Cocker; *m* 1963, Jennifer Nicholls; two *d. Educ:* King Edward VII Sch., Sheffield; Nottingham Univ. (BA Econ Hons); Harvard Business Sch. (Internat. SMP 1990). FCIWEM. NW Gas Board, 1962–68; West Midlands Gas, 1968–74; Severn Trent Water Authy, 1974–89; Man. Dir, Severn Trent Water Ltd, 1991–95; Gp Chief Exec., Severn Trent plc (formerly Chief Exec., Severn Trent Water), 1995–2000. Non-executive Director: Aquafin NV, 1993–2000; Railtrack Gp, 1999–2002; Aga Foodservice Gp (formerly Glynwed Internat.), 2000–08; Modern Waste, 2008. Founder Chm., Waste and Resources Action Prog., 2000–08. Water Aid: Trustee, 1996–2007; Vice Chm., 1998–2001; Chm., 2001–07; Chm., Severn Trent Region, 1997–2000. Dir, Midlands Excellence, 1996–2000. Member: Adv. Cttee on Business in Environment, 1996–2003; World Business Council for Sustainable Develt, 1997–2000. Chm., Forward Birmingham RNLI Lifeboat Campaign, 1994–96; Member: RNLI Cttee of Mgt, 1996–2002; RNLI Council, 2003–10 (Vice Pres., 2010–); RSA Council, 2004–10. Birmingham City University: Mem., 2009–, Dep. Chm., 2011–15, Bd of Govs; Pro Chancellor, 2011–15. CCMI. Hon. FCIWM 2004. DUniv Central England, 2006. *Recreations:* Fakenham Ramblers (Gp Sec.), Holt U3A Thinkers Group, National Hunt. *Address:* Aldercarr, Bayfield, Holt, Norfolk NR25 7JW. *T:* (01263) 713613.

COCKERAM, Eric (Paul); JP; *b* 4 July 1924; *er s* of Mr and Mrs J. W. Cockeram; *m* 1949, Frances Irving; two *s* two *d. Educ:* The Leys Sch., Cambridge. Served War, 1942–46: Captain The Gloucestershire Regt; "D Day" landings (wounded and later discharged). MP (C): Bebington, 1970–Feb. 1974; Ludlow, 1979–87. PPS: to Minister for Industry, 1970–72; to Minister for Posts and Telecommunications, 1972; to Chancellor of Exchequer, 1972–74. Mem., Select Cttee on Corporation Tax, 1971, on Industry and Trade, 1979–87; Mem., Public Accounts Cttee, 1983–87. Pres., Menswear Assoc. of Britain, 1964–65. Mem., Bd of Governors, United Liverpool Hosps, 1965–74; Chm., Liverpool NHS Exec. Council, 1970. Chairman: Watson Prickard Ltd, 1966–2001; Johnson Fry (Northern) Ltd, 1988–94; Director: TSB (NW), 1968–83; TSB (Wales & Border Counties), 1983–88; Liverpool Building Soc., 1975–82 (Vice-Chm., 1981–82); Midshires Building Soc., 1982–88; Muller Group (UK) Ltd, 1983–94. Member of Lloyd's. Liveryman, Worshipful Co. of Glovers, 1969–, Mem. Court, 1979–89. Freeman: City of London; City of Springfield, Ill. JP, City of Liverpool, 1960. *Recreations:* bridge, golf, shooting, country walking. *Address:* Fairway Lodge, Caldy, Wirral, Cheshire CH48 1NB. *T:* (0151) 625 1100. *Clubs:* Carlton, Army and Navy.

COCKERELL, Michael Roger Lewis; political documentary maker, author, broadcaster; *b* 26 Aug. 1940; *s* of Prof. Hugh Cockerell and Fanny Cockerell (*née* Jochelman); *m* 1st, 1970, Anne Faber (marr. diss. 1980); one *s* one *d*; 2nd, 1984, Bridget Heathcoat-Amory (marr. diss. 1990); two *d*; 3rd, 2011, Anna Lloyd; three *d. Educ:* Kilburn Grammar Sch.; Heidelberg Univ.; Corpus Christi Coll., Oxford (MA PPE; Hon. Fellow, 2012). Magazine journalist, 1962–66; Producer, BBC African Service, 1966–68; Current Affairs, BBC TV, 1968–87: Producer, 24 Hours, 1968–72; reporter: Midweek, 1972–75; Panorama, 1975–87; freelance TV reporter and documentary maker, 1987–: *programmes* include: investigations into political lobbying, the Honours system, the Whips, and the Cabinet; How to Be series; profiles of Alan Clark, James Callaghan, Edward Heath, Enoch Powell, Barbara Castle, Roy Jenkins, Betty Boothroyd, Stella Rimington, The Rivals (Gordon Brown and Michael Portillo); Tony Blair's Thousand Days, 2000; News from Number Ten: Alastair Campbell and the media, 2000; Trust Me, I'm a Politician, 2003; With Friends Like These: Britain's relations with France, Germany and US, 2003; The Downing Street Patient: Health of PMs, 2004; Do You Still Believe in Tony?, 2004; The Brown-Blair Affair, 2004; Michael Howard: No More Mr Nasty, 2005; How We Fell for Europe, 2005; How to be Tory Leader, 2005; Tony's Tight Spot, 2006; Blair: the inside story (three-part series), How to be ex-Prime Minister, 2007; Dave Cameron's Incredible Journey, 2007; The Making of the Iron Lady, 2008; Great Offices of State (trilogy on Treasury, Home Office and FCO), 2010; How to Win the TV Debate, 2010; The Secret World of Whitehall (trilogy on Prime Minister's Office, Cabinet Office and Special Political Advrs), 2011; The Lost World of the Seventies, 2012; Boris Johnson: The Irresistible Rise, 2013; Inside the Commons (4-part series), 2015; BBC Radio 4 documentaries: The Trial of David Irving, 2004; Tales from the Cutting Room, 2006; Profile: Conrad Black, 2007 and 2010; Speaker Michael Martin, 2008. Vis. Prof. of Politics, Nottingham Univ., 2011–; Vis. Lectr, LSE, 1998–, Nuffield Coll., Oxford, 2001–04. Huw Wheldon Lect., BBC2, 2000. Consultant, Oxford DNB, 2000–. Hon. DCL UEA, 2007. Emmy Award, 1980; Best Documentary Award, RTS, 1982; Golden Nymph Award, Monte Carlo, 1988; Judges' Award for Special Contrib. to Politics, Pol Studies Assoc., 2008; James Cameron Special Award, 2010. *Publications:* (jtly) Sources Close to the Prime Minister, 1984; Live from Number Ten: the inside story of Prime Ministers and TV, 1988; (contrib.) The Blair Effect, 2001; (contrib.) Where the Truth Lies, 2006; articles in newspapers. *Recreations:* cricket, tennis, merry-making. *Address:* 27 Arundel Gardens, W11 2LW. *T:* (020) 7727 8035, 07747 031940. *E:* michael.cockerell@gmail.com. *Clubs:* MCC (playing mem.), Lord's Taverners, Bushmen.

COCKERHAM, David, CBE 1995; HM Diplomatic Service, retired; International Director, Invest.UK (formerly Invest in Britain Bureau), 1999–2001; *b* 14 May 1944; *s* of late Henry Cockerham and Eleanor Cockerham (*née* Nicholls); *m* 1967, Ann Lesley Smith; two *s. Educ:* Leeds Central High Sch. Joined FO, 1962; Saigon, 1967–68; Japanese studies, Tokyo, 1969–71; Vice-Consul: Yokohama, 1971–72; Tokyo, 1972–75; FCO, 1975–79; Vice-Consul (Commercial Inf.), British Inf. Services, NY, 1979–81; Consul (Commercial) and Exec. Asst to Dir-Gen. of Trade Develt, USA, British Trade Develt Office, NY, 1981–83; First Sec. (Commercial), Tokyo, 1983–87; Hd, Exports to Japan Unit, DTI, 1987–90 (on secondment); Dir of Ops, Migration and Visa Dept, FCO, 1990–91; Dep. High Comr, Madras, 1991–94; Consul-Gen. and Dir of Trade Promotion, Osaka, 1994–98. Member: FCO Assoc., 2000–; Bearsted and Thurnham Soc. (Vice-Chm. and Sec., 2005–07). *Recreations:* grape cultivation, wine making, jazz clarinet and soprano saxophone.

COCKERILL, Geoffrey Fairfax, CB 1980; Secretary, University Grants Committee, 1978–82; *b* 14 May 1922; *e s* of late Walter B. Cockerill and Mary W. Cockerill (*née* Buffery); *m* 1959, Janet Agnes Walters, JP, MA (*d* 2006); two *s. Educ:* Humberstone Foundation Sch.; UC Nottingham. BA London 1947. Royal Artillery, 1941–45 (Captain). Min. of Labour, 1947; Min. of Educn, 1952; Private Sec. to last Minister of Educn and Secs of State for Educn and Science, 1963–65; Asst Sec., 1964; Sec., Public Schools Commn, 1966–68; Jt Sec., Schools Council for Curriculum and Examinations, 1970–72; Under-Sec., DES, 1972–77; Dep. Sec., 1978. Chairman: Anglo-Amer. Primary Educ. Project, 1970–72; Working Party on Nutritional Aspects of School Meals, 1973–75; Kingston-upon-Thames CAB, 1985–88; Member: Adv. Gp on London Health Services, 1980–81; RCN Commn on Nursing Educn, 1984–85; RCN Strategy Gp, 1985–87; UGC, Univ. of S Pacific, 1984–87; Vice-Pres., Experiment in Internat. Living, 1989–98. Reviewed for Government: Central Bureau for Educational Visits and Exchanges, 1982; Youth Exchanges, 1983; Nat. Youth Bureau, 1983; Consultant to Cttee of Vice-Chancellors and Principals, 1984–85. Hon. Senior Research Fellow, KCL, 1982–86. *Recreations:* gardening, photography. *Address:* 29 Lovelace Road, Surbiton, Surrey KT6 6NS. *T:* (020) 8399 0125. *Club:* Athenæum.

COCKERILL, Sara Elizabeth, (Mrs N. T. Eaton); QC 2011; *b* Weston Super Mare, 7 Nov. 1968; *d* of Alan Cockerill and Lilian Cockerill; *m* 1997, Nigel Trevor Eaton, QC. *Educ:* Lady Eleanor Holles Sch.; St Anne's Coll., Oxford (BA 1989; Eldon Schol.). Called to the Bar, Lincoln's Inn, 1990; in practice as a barrister, specialising in commercial law, 1990–. *Publications:* (Contributing Ed.) (Commercial Court and Arbitration) Civil Procedure (The White Book), 2011–; The Law and Practice of Compelled Evidence in Civil Proceedings, 2011; Eleanor of Castile: the shadow queen, 2014. *Recreations:* medieval history, cycling, running, C19 fiction, waiting on cat. *Address:* Essex Court Chambers, 24 Lincoln's Inn Fields, WC2A 3EG. *T:* (020) 7813 8000, *Fax:* (020) 7813 8080. *E:* scockerill@essexcourt.net. *W:* www.saracockerill.com.

COCKERTON, Rev. Canon John Clifford Penn; Rector of Wheldrake with Thorganby, 1985–92 (Rector of Wheldrake, 1978–85); Canon of York (Prebend of Dunnington), 1987–92, Canon Emeritus 1992; *b* 27 June 1927; *s* of late William Penn Cockerton and Eleanor Cockerton; *m* 1974, Diana Margaret Smith (*d* 1987), *d* of Mr and Mrs W. Smith, Upper Poppleton, York. *Educ:* Wirral Grammar Sch.; Univ. of Liverpool; St Catherine's Society, Oxford; Wycliffe Hall, Oxford. Deacon 1954; Priest 1955; Asst Curate, St Helens Parish Church, 1954–58; Tutor 1958–60, Chaplain 1960–63, Cranmer Hall, Durham; Vice-Principal, St John's Coll., Durham, 1963–70; Principal, St John's College and Cranmer Hall, Durham, 1970–78. Examining Chaplain to Bishop of Durham, 1971–73; Proctor in Convocation, 1980–85. *Recreation:* music.

COCKETT, Ven. Elwin Wesley; Archdeacon of West Ham, since 2007; *b* Kotagiri, Tamil Nadu, India, 24 May 1959; *s* of late Dr Norman Cockett and Janet Cockett (*née* Graham, then Slade); *m* 1977, Susan Mary Jones; one *s* two *d. Educ:* St Paul's Cath. Choir Sch.; Forest Sch., Snaresbrook; Oak Hill Theological Coll. (BA Theol. and Pastoral Studies 1991). Practice Manager, Bethnal Green Med. Mission, 1983–88; ordained deacon, 1991, priest, 1992; Curate, St Chad's, Chadwell Heath, 1991–94; Curate i/c, 1994–95, Priest i/c, 1995–97, Vicar, 1997–2000, St Paul's, Harold Hill; Team Rector, Billericay and Little Burstead, 2000–07; Rural Dean, Basildon, 2004–07. Chair, Chelmsford Diocesan Bd of Educn. Club Chaplain, West Ham UFC, 1992–2011. Dir, Aston Mansfield, 2009–. Gov., Forest Sch., Snaresbrook, 2011–. *Recreations:* music, motorcycling, sailing, enjoying the delights of Exmoor. *Address:* 86 Aldersbrook Road, E12 5DH. *T:* (020) 8989 8557, *Fax:* (020) 8530 1311. *E:* a.westham@chelmsford.anglican.org, elwin@cockett.org.

COCKETT, Geoffrey Howard; consultant; Chief Scientific Officer, Ministry of Defence, and Deputy Director, Royal Armament Research and Development Establishment, 1983–86; *b* 18 March 1926; *s* of late William Cockett and Edith (*née* Dinham); *m* 1951, Elizabeth Bagshaw; two *d. Educ:* King Edward VI Sch., Southampton; Univ. of Southampton (BSc, Hons Maths, and Hons Physics). MRI; FInstP; CPhys. Royal Aircraft Establishment, 1948–52; Armament Research Estabt, Woolwich, 1952–62; RARDE, 1962–68; ASC 1965; Supt of Physics Div., Chemical Defence Estabt, 1968–71; RARDE: Supt, Optics and Surveillance Systems Div., 1971–76; Head, Applied Physics Group, 1976–83. Chm., Sci. Recruitment Bds, CS Commn, 1985–94; Consultant, Directorate of Sci. (Land), MoD, 1986–98. FLS 2012. (Jtly) Gold Medal, Congrès des Matériaux Résistants à Chaud, Paris, 1951. *Publications:* official reports; scientific and technical papers in various learned jls. *Recreations:* computing, photography, supporting activities at Charles Darwin's home and laboratory. *E:* ghc1uk@yahoo.co.uk. *Club:* Civil Service.

COCKING, Prof. Edward Charles Daniel, FRS 1983; Professor of Botany, University of Nottingham, 1969–97, now Professor Emeritus; *b* 26 Sept. 1931; *y s* of late Charles Cocking and Mary (*née* Murray); *m* 1960, Bernadette Keane; one *s* one *d*. *Educ:* Buckhurst Hill County High Sch., Essex; Univ. of Bristol (BSc, PhD, DSc). FRSB. Civil Service Commission Research Fellow, 1956–59; Nottingham University: Lectr in Plant Physiology, 1959–66; Reader, 1966–69; Head of Dept of Botany, 1969. Leverhulme Trust Res. Fellow, 1995–97. S. Yoshida Meml Lecture, Hangzhou Univ., China, 1987. Member: Lawes Agricl Trust Cttee, Rothamsted Experimental Stn, 1987–91 (Mem., Governing Body, 1991–2013; Chm., 1999–2003); Adv. Cttee on Forest Res., Forestry Commn, 1987–95; Council, Royal Soc., 1986–88; AFRC, 1990–94 (Royal Soc. Assessor, 1988–90); Lawes Agriculture Trust Co., 2000–. Mem., Bd of Trustees, Royal Botanic Gardens, Kew, 1983–93; Member, Governing Body: Glasshouse Crops Res. Inst., 1983–87; British Soc. Horticultural Res., 1987–89. Pres., Sect. K, BAAS, 1983. Royal Soc. Trustee, Uppingham Sch., 1997–2007. MAE 1993. Hon. Mem., Hungarian Acad. Scis, 1995; Fellow: Indian Acad. of Agricl Scis, 2000; World Innovation Foundn, 2003. Lifetime Achievement Award, Univ. of Toledo, USA, 2004. *Publications:* Introduction to the Principles of Plant Physiology (with W. Stiles, FRS), 3rd edn 1969; numerous scientific papers in botanical/genetics jls on plant genetic manipulations and nitrogen fixation. *Recreations:* walking, travelling, especially by train, occasional chess. *Address:* Centre for Crop Nitrogen Fixation, Life Sciences Building, School of Biosciences, University of Nottingham, University Park, Nottingham NG7 2RD. *T:* (0115) 951 3056, *Fax:* (0115) 951 6334. *E:* edward.cocking@nottingham.ac.uk; 30 Patterdale Road, Woodthorpe, Nottingham NG5 4LQ. *T:* (0115) 926 2452.

COCKLE, Ted; President, Virgin EMI, since 2013; *b* Wendover, Bucks; *s* of John Cockle and Josie Cockle; *m* 2011, Joanne Reid; one *s* one *d*. *Educ:* Aylesbury Grammar Sch.; Univ. of Bristol (BSocSci 1995). Mktg Dir, Sony Music Ops, 1995–2005; Mktg Dir, 2005–07, Co-Pres., 2007–13, Island Records. *Address:* Virgin EMI, Universal Music, 364 Kensington High Street, W14 8NS.

COCKROFT, His Honour (Peter) John; a Circuit Judge, 1993–2013; *b* 24 Sept. 1947; *s* of late Walter Philip Barron Cockroft and Nora Cockroft (*née* Collett); *m* 1975, Maria Eugenia Coromina Perandones; one *s* two *d*. *Educ:* Queen Elizabeth I Grammar Sch., Darlington; Queens' Coll., Cambridge (BA, LLB). Called to the Bar, Middle Temple, 1970 (Astbury Scholar); practised NE Circuit; Asst Recorder, 1985–89; Recorder, 1989–93. *Recreations:* visiting Spain, gardening. *Address:* Brackenwell Cottage, North Rigton, N Yorks LS17 0DG. *T:* (01423) 734585. *Clubs:* Yorkshire County Cricket; Yorkshire Rugby Football Union.

COCKS, family name of **Baron Somers**.

COCKS, Hon. Anna Gwenllian S.; *see* Somers Cocks.

COCKS, Clifford Christopher, CB 2008; FRS 2015; Chief Mathematician, Government Communications Headquarters, 2001–09; *b* Cheshire, 28 Dec. 1950; *s* of William Cocks and Joan Cocks; *m* 1979, Gillian White; one *s* one *d*. *Educ:* King's Coll., Cambridge (BA 1971). CMath 1998; FIMA 1998. Civil Service: SO, 1973; SSO, 1979; Sen. Civil Service, 1998. Visiting Fellow: Univ. of Bristol, 2005; Merton Coll., Oxford, 2006; Vis. Prof., KCL, 2015–. Treas., Playhouse Co., 2014–. Hon. DSc: Bristol, 2008; UEA, 2008; Birmingham, 2015. *Recreations:* Reader (Anglican), amateur dramatics. *E:* cliffcocks@outlook.com.

COCKS, Freda Mary, CBE 1999 (OBE 1972); JP; Deputy Leader, Birmingham City Council, 1982–86; *b* 30 July 1915; *d* of Frank and Mary Wood; *m* 1942, Donald Francis Melvin, *s* of Melvin J. Cocks; one *d* (and one *d* decd). *Educ:* St Peter's Sch., Harborne; Queen's Coll., Birmingham. Birmingham Council, 1953–78: Alderman, 1965–74; Lord Mayor of Birmingham, 1977–78; Dep. Chm., Housing Cttee, 1968–70, Chm. 1970–72. Founder Sec., Birmingham Sanatoria League of Friends, 1950–68; Founder and Chm., Birm. Hosps Broadcasting Assoc., 1952–78; Member: Little Bromwich Hosp. Management Cttee, 1953–68; West Birmingham Health Authority, 1981–92; Vice-Pres. and Mem., Nat. Careers Assoc., 1985–. Conservative Women's Central Council: Chm., 1968–71; Chm., Gen. Purposes Cttee, 1978; service on housing, finance, policies, and land cttees; Vice Pres., Edgbaston Conservative Assoc., 1992– (Pres., 1980–92). Member: Focus Housing Assoc.; Civic Housing Assoc.; Birmingham Blind Action Forum; Council Mem., Birmingham Rathbone Soc. (Patron, 1998). Pres., Missions to Seamen, subseq. Mission to Seafarers, Birmingham, 1981–2003 (Patron, 2003–). Patron, Pulse Trust, 1997–. JP Birmingham, 1968. Hon. Freeman: City of Birmingham, 1986; Du-Panne, Belgium, 1978. *Recreation:* hospitals and housing. *Address:* 49 Timber Mill Court, Serpentine Road, Harborne, Birmingham B17 9RD. *T:* (0121) 427 9123.

COCKS, Dr Leonard Robert Morrison, (Dr Robin Cocks), OBE 1999; TD 1979; Keeper of Palaeontology, Natural History Museum (formerly British Museum (Natural History)), 1986–98; *b* 17 June 1938; *s* of late Ralph Morrison Cocks and Lucille Mary Cocks (*née* Blackler); *m* 1963, Elaine Margaret Sturdy; one *s* two *d*. *Educ:* Felsted School; Hertford College, Oxford (BA, MA, DPhil, DSc). FGS; CGeol. Commissioned Royal Artillery 1958; active service Malaya, 1958–59; DSIR Research Student, Oxford Univ., 1962–65; British Museum (Nat. Hist.), 1965–; Dep. Keeper of Palaeontology, 1980–86. Geologist, Royal Engineers, 1970–83. President: Palaeontographical Soc., 1994–98; GA, 2004–06 (Vice-Pres., 2003–04, 2006–07); Member: Council, Palaeontological Assoc., 1969–82, 1986–88 (Editor, 1971–82, Pres., 1986–88; Lapworth Medal, 2010); Council, Geological Soc., 1982–89, 1997–2000 (Sec., 1985–89; Pres., 1998–2000; Coke Medal, 1995); NERC Geological Res. Grants Cttee, 1978–81, 1984. Comr, Internat. Commn on Zoological Nomenclature, 1982–2000. Vis. Fellow, Southampton Univ., 1988–95; Vis. Prof., Imperial Coll., London, 1997–2001. Visitor, Oxford Univ. Mus. of Natural Hist., 1997–2008. Dumont Medal, Belgian Geol Soc., 2003. *Publications:* The Evolving Earth, 1979; (ed) Encyclopedia of Geology, 5 vols, 2005; papers in sci. jls, on Ordovician-Silurian biostratigraphy and brachiopods, esp. from Britain, Canada, Norway, Russia, China. *Recreation:* country pursuits. *Address:* Department of Earth Sciences, Natural History Museum, Cromwell Road, SW7 5BD. *T:* (020) 7942 5140. *E:* r.cocks@nhm.ac.uk.

COCKSHAW, Sir Alan, Kt 1992; FREng; FICE; Chairman: Cibitas (formerly Cibitas Investments) Ltd, since 2003; HPR Holdings Ltd, since 2003; English Partnerships (formerly English Partnerships, and Commission for New Towns), 1998–2001; *b* 14 July 1937; *s* of John and Maud Cockshaw; *m* 1960, Brenda Payne; one *s* three *d*. *Educ:* Farnworth Grammar Sch.; Leeds Univ. (BSc). FCIHT (FIHT 1968); FICE 1985; FREng (FEng 1986). Chief Executive: Fairclough Civil Engrg, 1978–85; Fairclough Parkinson-Mining, 1982–85; Fairclough Engrg, 1983–84; Gp Chief Exec., 1984–88, Chm., 1988–97, AMEC plc; Chairman: Manchester Millennium Ltd, 1996–2003; Roxboro Gp, 1997–2005; British Airways Regl, 2000–03; New East Manchester Ltd, 2000–02. Non-exec. Dep. Chm., Norweb plc, 1992–95; non-executive Director: New Millennium Experience Co., 1997–2000; Pidemco Land, then CapitaLand, Singapore, 1999–2005. Chairman: Overseas Projects Bd, DTI, 1992–95; Oil and Gas Projects and Supplies Office, DTI, 1994–97; Mem., BOTB, 1992–95; Dep. Chm., NW Business Leadership Team, 1990–97 (Life Pres., 1997). Chm., Major Projects Assoc., 1998–2004. Pres., ICE, 1997–98. Hon. DEng UMIST, 1997; Hon. DSc Salford, 1998. *Recreations:* Rugby (both codes), cricket, walking, gardening. *Address:* Hanover House, 30–32 Charlotte Street, Manchester M1 4FD.

COCKSHUT, Gillian Elise, (Mrs A. O. J. Cockshut); *see* Avery, G. E.

COCKSWORTH, Rt Rev. Christopher John; *see* Coventry, Bishop of.

CODD, Geoffrey; *see* Codd, R. G.

CODD, Michael Henry, AC 1991; Chancellor, University of Wollongong, 1997–2009; *b* 2 Dec. 1939; *s* of Ernest Applebee Codd and Nell Gregory (*née* Pavy). *Educ:* Univ. of Adelaid (BEc Hons). Statistician, 1962–69; joined Dept of Prime Minister, Australia, 1969; Unde Sec., Dept of Prime Minister and Cabinet, 1979–81; Sec., Dept of Employment and In Relns, 1981–83; Chm., Industries Assistance Commn, 1983–85; Sec., Dept of Communi Services, 1985–86; Head, Dept of Prime Minister and Cabinet and Sec. to Cabinet, 1986–9 Non-executive Director: Qantas, 1992–2009; Telstra Ltd, 1992–99; Australian Nucle Science and Technol. Orgn, 1996–2001; MLC Ltd, 1996–2011; CitiPower, 1999–200 Ingeus, 2003–09 (Chm., 2006–09). *Address:* 586 Williamsdale Road, Williamsdale, NSW 2620, Australia. *T:* (2) 62350160.

CODD, (Ronald) Geoffrey, CEng; CITP; FBCS; change professional, since 1957; autho since 2004; *b* 20 Aug. 1932; *s* of Thomas Reuben Codd and Betty Leyster Codd (*née* Sturt *m* 1960, Christine Ellen Léone Robertson; one *s* two *d*. *Educ:* Cathedral Sch., Llandaff; Th College, Llandovery. CEng 1990. Dip. in Company Direction, 1989. Served RAF, Transpo Comd, 1952–57. Rolls Royce, Aero-Engine Div., 1957–58; International Computer 1958–61; Marconi Co., 1961–70; J. Bibby & Sons, Liverpool, 1970–74; Weir Gp, Glasgow 1974–80; Brooke Bond Gp, 1981–86; Under Sec. and Dir, Information and Risk Management, ECGD, 1986–90; Managing Partner, InterChange Associates, 1990–2004. D Randolph Enterprise, 1992–98. Advr to Bd, HM Customs and Excise, 1992–96. Associat Wentworth Res., 1992–. Mem., ELITE Forum, BCS, 1991–. Chairman: Community Pla Steering Gp, 2009–11; Osmington Soc., 2009–11; White Horse Ancient Monumen Restoration Gp, 2009–12. FInstD 1984. Freeman, City of London, 1990; Liveryman, Co. Inf. Technologists, 1990. *Publications:* The Drowning Director, 2007; The Diligent Direct in a Digital Business World, 2014; contributor to business magazines. *Recreations:* competitiv and leisure sailing, theatre, practical pastimes. *Address:* The White House, Church Lan Osmington, Dorset DT3 6EJ. *Clubs:* City Livery; Royal Dorset Yacht; Goodwood Aero.

CODRINGTON, Sir Christopher (George Wayne), 4th Bt *cr* 1876, of Dodingto Gloucestershire; *b* 20 Feb. 1960; *s* of Sir Simon Codrington, 3rd Bt and of Pamela Joy Hallida Codrington (*née* Wise); *S* father, 2005; *m* 1991, Noelle Lynne, *d* of Dale Leverson; one *s* or *d* (and one *s* decd). *Educ:* Millfield; RAC Cirencester. *Heir:* *s* William George Bethe Codrington, *b* 14 April 2003. *Address:* Springfield House, Fordwells, Witney, Oxon OX2 9PP.

CODRINGTON, Sir (Giles) Peter, 9th Bt *cr* 1721, of Dodington, Gloucestershire; *b* 28 Oc 1943; *s* of Sir William Richard Codrington, 7th Bt, and Joan Kathleen Birelli, *e d* of Percy Nicholas; *S* brother, 2006; *m* 1989, Shirley Linda Duke; two *s* one *d*. *Recreation:* yachting. *He* (to Btcy) *s* Daniel Peter Codrington, *b* 8 Feb. 1993. *Clubs:* Monaco Yacht; Antigua Yacht.

CODRINGTON, Richard John; HM Diplomatic Service, retired; *b* 18 Dec. 1953; *s* of Cap Christopher Thomas Codrington, RN and Anna Maria (*née* Hanscomb); *m* 1985, Jul Elizabeth Nolan; two *s*. *Educ:* Ampleforth; Lincoln Coll., Oxford (BA). MoD, 1975–7 entered HM Diplomatic Service, 1978: FCO, 1978–79; 2nd, later 1st, Sec., Dar es Salaam 1980–82; FCO, 1983–85; 1st Sec., New Delhi, 1985–88; Asst Hd, S Asian Dept, FCO 1989–92; on loan to S. G. Warburg & Co. Ltd, 1992–94; on loan, as Hd, Cross-med ownership review team, DNH, 1994; Dir of Trade Promotion and Investment, Pari 1995–99; Dep. High Comr, Ottawa, 1999–2003; Hd, Online Communications Dept, FCO 2003–04; RCDS, 2004; Hd, Afghanistan Gp, FCO, 2005–08; reviewed UK Trade Investment's worldwide inward investment activity, 2008; based in Jakarta, 2009–13, Ottaw 2013–. *Recreations:* photography, family history, diving, ski-ing. *Address:* BFPO 550 (Ottawa), Foreign and Commonwealth Office, West End Road, Ruislip HA4 6EP.

CODRON, Sir Michael (Victor), Kt 2014; CBE 1989; theatrical producer; *b* 8 June 193 *s* of I. A. Codron and Lily (*née* Morgenstern). *Educ:* St Paul's Sch.; Worcester Coll., Oxfo (MA; Hon. Fellow 2012). Director: Aldwych Theatre; Cameron Mackintosh Prof. Contemporary Theatre, Oxford Univ., 1993. Emeritus Fellow, St Catherine's Coll., Oxfor 2003. Productions include: Share My Lettuce, Breath of Spring, 1957; Dock Brief and Wh Shall We Tell Caroline?, The Birthday Party, Valmouth, 1958; Pieces of Eight, 1959; Th Wrong Side of the Park, The Caretaker, 1960; Three, Stop It Whoever You Are, One Ov the Eight, The Tenth Man, Big Soft Nellie, 1961; Two Stars for Comfort, Everything in th Garden, Rattle of a Simple Man, 1962; Next Time I'll sing to You, Private Lives (revival The Lovers and the Dwarfs, Cockade, 1963; Poor Bitos, The Formation Dancer Entertaining Mr Sloane, 1964; Loot, The Killing of Sister George, Ride a Cock Horse, 196 Little Malcolm and his Struggle against the Eunuchs, The Anniversary, There's a Girl in m Soup, Big Bad Mouse, 1966; The Judge, The Flip Side, Wise Child, The Boy Friend (revival 1967; Not Now Darling, The Real Inspector Hound, 1968; The Contractor, Slag, The Tw of Us, The Philanthropist, 1970; The Foursome, Butley, A Voyage Round my Father, Th Changing Room, 1971; Veterans, Time and Time Again, Crown Matrimonial, My F Friend, 1972; Collaborators, Savages, Habeas Corpus, Absurd Person Singular, 197 Knuckle, Flowers, Golden Pathway Annual, The Norman Conquests, John Paul Georg Ringo… and Bert, 1974; A Family and A Fortune, Alphabetical Order, A Far Better Husban Ashes, Absent Friends, Otherwise Engaged, Stripwell, 1975; Funny Peculiar, Treat Donkey's Years, Confusions, Teeth 'n' Smiles, Yahoo, 1976; Dusa, Stas, Fish & Vi, Ju Between Ourselves, Oh, Mr Porter, Breezeblock Park, The Bells of Hell, The Old Countr 1977; The Rear Column, Ten Times Table, The Unvarnished Truth, The Homecomir (revival), Alice's Boys, Night and Day, 1978; Joking Apart, Tishoo, Stage Struck, 1979; D Faustus, Make and Break, The Dresser, Taking Steps, Enjoy, 1980; Hinge and Bracket at th Globe, Rowan Atkinson in Revue, House Guest, Quartermaine's Terms, 1981; Season Greetings, Noises Off, Funny Turns, The Real Thing, 1982; The Hard Shoulder, 198 Benefactors, 1984; Why Me?, Jumpers, Who Plays Wins, Look, No Hans!, 1985; Made i Bangkok, Woman in Mind, 1986; Three Sisters, A View from the Bridge, 1987; Hapgoo Uncle Vanya, Re: Joyce, The Sneeze, Henceforward, 1988; The Cherry Orchard, 1989; Ma of the Moment, Look Look, Hidden Laughter, Private Lives, 1990; What the Butler Saw, 7 Girls 70, The Revengers' Comedies, 1991; The Rise and Fall of Little Voice, 1992; Time My Life, Jamais Vu, 1993; Kit and the Widow, Dead Funny, Arcadia, The Sisters Rosensweig 1994; Indian Ink, Dealer's Choice, 1995; The Shakespeare Revue, A Talent to Amuse, 199 Tom and Clem, Silhouette, Heritage, 1997; Things We Do for Love, Alarms and Excursion The Invention of Love, 1998; Copenhagen, Comic Potential, 1999; Peggy for You, 200 Blue/Orange, 2001; Life After George, Bedroom Farce, Damsels in Distress, 2002; M Brilliant Divorce, Dinner, 2003; Democracy, 2004; Ying Tong, Losing Louis, 200 Glorious!, 2006; Entertaining Angels, 2006; The Bargain, 2006; Quartermaine's Terms, 201 *film:* Clockwise, 1986. *Recreation:* collecting Caroline of Brunswick memorabilia. *Addres* Aldwych Theatre Offices, Aldwych, WC2B 4DF. *Club:* Garrick.

COE, family name of **Baron Coe**.

COE, Baron *cr* 2000 (Life Peer), of Ranmore in the co. of Surrey; **Sebastian Newbold Coe** CH 2013; KBE 2006 (OBE 1990; MBE 1982); Global Adviser, Nike International, sinc 2001; Chairman, British Olympic Association, since 2012; President, Internation Association of Athletics Federations, since 2015 (Council Member, since 2003; Vic President, 2007–15); *b* 29 Sept. 1956; *s* of late Peter and Angela Coe; *m* 1990, Nicola McIrvin (marr. diss.); two *s* two *d*; *m* 2011, Mrs Carole Annett, *d* of M. J. K. Smith. *Edu* Loughborough University (BSc Hons Economics and Social History). Won gold medal fo running 1500m and silver medal for 800m at Moscow Olympics, 1980; gold medal for 1500m and silver medal for 800m at Los Angeles Olympics, 1984; European Champion for 800m, Stuttgart, 1986; set world records at 800m, 1000m and mile, 1981. Research Assistant, Loughborough Univ., 1981–84. Sports Council: Mem., 1983–89; Vice-Chm., 1986–89; Chm., Olympic Review Gp, 1984–85. Member: HEA, 1987–92; Olympic Cttee, Medical Commn, 1987–93; Athletes Commn, IOC, Lausanne (first Chm., 1981–92); Olympic Cttee, Sport for All Commn, 1997–. Chairman: London 2012 Olympic Bid, 2004–05 (Vice-Chm., 2003–04); LOCOG, 2005–13; Olympic Legacy Ambassador, 2012–. Steward, BBB of C, 1995–97; Chm., FIFA Ethics Cttee, 2006–; Mem. Bd, England 2018 FIFA World Cup Bid, 2009–. Chairman: Diadora (UK), 1987–94; Complete Leisure Group Ltd, 2005–13; CSM Sport & Entertainment, 2013–; non-exec. Dir, Chime Communications, 2014–. Sebastian Coe Health Clubs, Jarvis Hotel Group, 1994. MP (C) Falmouth and Camborne, 1992–97; contested (C) same seat, 1997. PPS to Ministers of State for Defence Procurement and for Armed Forces, MoD, 1994–95, to Dep. Prime Minister, 1995–96; a Govt Whip, 1996–97. Dep. Chief of Staff, 1997, Private Sec., 1997–2001, to Leader of Conservative Party. Pres., AAA of England, 2000–; Founder Mem., Laureus World Sports Acad., 2000–; Assoc. Mem., Académie des Sports, France. Sports columnist, The Daily Telegraph, 2000–. Hon. DTech Loughborough, 1985; Hon. DSc Hull, 1988. Lifetime Achievement Award, BBC Sports Personality of the Year Awards, 2012. Principe de Asturias award (Spain), 1987. *Publications:* (with David Miller) Running Free, 1981; (with Peter Coe) Running for Fitness, 1983; (with Nicholas Mason) The Olympians, 1984, 2nd edn 1996; Running My Life (autobiog.), 2012. *Recreations:* listening to recorded or preferably live jazz, theatre. *Address:* House of Lords, SW1A 0PW. *Clubs:* East India, Sportsman's.

COE, Albert Henry, (Harry); Chairman: Travelsphere Holdings Ltd, 2000–06; Jaycare Holdings Ltd, 2000–04; Leisure Ventures plc, 2002–04; *b* 28 May 1944; *m* Beryl Margaret; two *d*. Supervisor, Coopers & Lybrand, 1967–70; Gp Financial Controller, Aerialite Ltd, 1970–72; Gp Finance Dir, London Scottish Bank, 1972–75; Finance Director: (print and packaging), Smurfit Ltd, 1975–81; Granada TV, 1981–88; Airtours plc: Gp Finance Dir, 1988–96; Dep. Chief Exec., 1996–97; Gp Man. Dir, 1997–99; non-exec. Dir, 1999–2001. Non-executive Director: Britannia Bldg Soc., 2000–03; Capital Ideas plc, 2004–07. *Recreations:* cricket, tennis, golf, ski-ing, stock market, current affairs. *Address:* Finvara, Wilmslow Road, Mottram St Andrew, Cheshire SK10 4QT.

COE, Jonathan, PhD; FRSL; writer, since 1987; *b* 19 Aug. 1961; *s* of Roger and Janet Coe; *m* 1989, Janine McKeown; two *d*. *Educ:* Trinity Coll., Cambridge (BA); Warwick Univ. (MA, PhD 1986). FRSL 2012. Hon. Dr: UCE, 2002; Birmingham, 2006; Hon. DLitt Wolverhampton, 2006. Chevalier, Ordre des Arts et des Lettres (France), 2004. *Publications:* The Accidental Woman, 1987; A Touch of Love, 1989; The Dwarves of Death, 1990; Humphrey Bogart: take it and like it, 1991; James Stewart: leading man, 1994; What a Carve Up!, 1994 (Prix du Meilleur Livre Etranger, 1995); The House of Sleep, 1997 (Prix Médicis Etranger, 1998); The Rotters' Club, 2001 (Bollinger Everyman Wodehouse Prize, 2001; Premio Arcebispo Juan de San Clemente, 2004) (televised 2005); Like a Fiery Elephant: the story of B. S. Johnson, 2004 (Samuel Johnson Prize, 2005); The Closed Circle, 2004; The Rain Before It Falls, 2007; The Terrible Privacy of Maxwell Sim, 2010; La Storia di Gulliver, 2011; Lo Specchio dei Desideri, 2012; Expo 58, 2013. *Recreations:* music, cycling. *Address:* c/o Peake Associates, PO Box 66726, NW5 9FE. *T:* (020) 7681 4307.

COE, Rosalind; QC 2008; **Her Honour Judge Coe;** a Circuit Judge, since 2011; *b* Nottingham, 2 Sept. 1959; *d* of late James Thompson; *m* 1980, David Lockhart Coe; one *s* one *d*. *Educ:* Nottingham Univ. (LLB 1981); Inns of Court Sch. of Law. Called to the Bar, Middle Temple, 1983, Bencher, 2013; Recorder, 2003–11. *Recreations:* family, films, holidays. *Address:* Sheffield Combined Court Centre, The Law Courts, 50 West Bar, Sheffield S3 8PH.

COELHO, Paulo; writer; *b* Rio de Janeiro, 28 Aug. 1947; *m* Christina Oiticica. Composer of popular songs, with Raul Seixas, 1973–82. Special Counsellor for Intercultural Dialogues and Spiritual Convergences, UNESCO, 2007; UN Messenger of Peace, 2007. Mem., Brazilian Acad. of Letters, 2002. *Publications:* The Pilgrimage, 1987; The Alchemist, 1988; Brida, 1990; O Dom Supremo: the gift, 1991; The Valkyries, 1992; Maktub, 1994; By the River Piedra I Sat Down and Wept, 1994; The Fifth Mountain, 1996; Love Letters from a Prophet, 1997; The Manual of the Warrior of Light, 1997; Veronika Decides to Die, 1998; The Devil and Miss Prym, 2000; Father, Sons and Grandsons, 2001; Eleven Minutes, 2003; The Genie and the Roses, 2004; The Zahir, 2005; Like the Flowing River, 2006; The Witch of Portobello, 2006; The Winner Stands Alone, 2008; Aleph, 2010; Manuscript Found in Accra, 2012; Adultery, 2014. *Recreations:* reading, travelling, computers, the Internet, music, football, walking, practising Kyudu. *Address:* Sant Jordi Asociados, Agencia Literaria S. L. U., Paseig de Gràcia 89, 08008 Barcelona, Spain. *T:* (93) 2240107, *Fax:* (93) 3562696. *E:* mail@santjordi-asociados.com.

COELLO, Judith Elaine; Her Honour Judge Coello; a Circuit Judge, since 2010; *b* 7 Jan. 1959; *d* of Anthony John Banks and Avrielle Doreen Mary Banks; *m* 1st, 1986, Timothy William Nichols (*d* 1999); 2nd, 2010, Kenneth R. Coello. *Educ:* Bridlington High Sch. for Girls; Liverpool Poly. (BA Hons); Christleton Coll. of Law, Chester. Admitted solicitor, 1983; Asst Solicitor, London Bor. of Sutton, 1983–85; Prosecuting Solicitor, Cambs CC, 1985–87; Principal Legal Advr, Richmond upon Thames Magistrates' Court, 1987–93; Hd of Legal Services, Uxbridge Magistrates' Court, 1993–2000; Dep. Dist Judge (Magistrates' Courts), 1997–2007; pt-time Immigration Adjudicator, 1997–2000; Immigration Judge, 2000–05, Designated Immigration Judge, 2005–06; a Judge of the Upper Tribunal (Immigration and Asylum Chamber) and Sen. Immigration Judge (formerly a Sen. Immigration Judge, Asylum and Immigration Tribunal), 2006–10; Recorder, 2007–10. Pres., Council of Immigration Judges, 2004–05. *Recreations:* gardening, walking, theatre, ballet. *E:* HHJudge.Coello@judiciary.gsi.gov.uk.

COEN, Prof. Enrico Sandro, CBE 2003; PhD; FRS 1998; John Innes Professor, John Innes Centre and School of Biology, University of East Anglia, since 1999; *b* 29 Sept. 1957; *s* of Ernesto Coen and Dorothea Coen (*née* Cattani); *m* 1984, Lucinda, *d* of late Alexander Poliakoff, OBE; two *s* one *d*. *Educ:* King's Coll., Cambridge (BA 1979; PhD Genetics 1982). SERC Postdoctoral Fellow, Cambridge, 1982–84; Res. Fellow, St John's Coll., Cambridge, 1982–85; Res. Scientist, John Innes Centre, BBSRC, 1984–99. Foreign Associate, US Nat. Acad. of Scis, 2001. EMBO Medal, Rome, 1996; Science for Art Prize, LVMH, Moët Hennessy, Paris, 1996; Linnean Medal, 1997; Darwin Medal, Royal Soc., 2004. *Publications:* papers in Nature, Cell, Science. *Recreation:* painting. *Address:* Department of Cell and Developmental Biology, John Innes Centre, Norwich Research Park, Norwich NR4 7UH. *T:* (01603) 450274.

See also Sir M. Poliakoff, S. Poliakoff.

COEN, (Thomas) Paul; Director, Paul Coen Ltd, since 2014; *b* 21 Dec. 1953; *s* of Patrick Coen and Anne Coen (*née* O'Neil); *m* 1974, Kate Knox (*d* 2009); two *s* two *d*. *Educ:* Manchester Univ. (BA Econ Hons Govt). NCB, later British Coal, 1977–89; Hertfordshire County Council, 1990–95: Dir, Commercial Services, 1990–91; Dir, Business Services, 1991–94; Dep. Chief Exec., 1995; Chief Executive: Surrey CC, 1995–2004; Essex CC, 2005–06; Local Govt Assoc., 2006–09; Man. Dir and Vice-Chm., UK Public Sector Gp, Citigroup, 2010–13. Chm., Ashridge Business Sch., 2014– (Vice-Chm., 2012–14). *Recreations:* reading, cycling, walking, cooking.

COEN, Yvonne Anne, (Mrs John Pini); QC 2000; a Recorder, since 2000; *d* of John and Bernadette Coen; *m* 1991, John Peter Julian Pini, *qv*; one *s* one *d*. *Educ:* Loreto Coll., St Albans; St Catherine's Coll., Oxford (MA Hons Jurisp.). Called to the Bar, Lincoln's Inn, 1982 (Hardwicke Schol. and Eastham Schol.), Bencher, 2008; criminal practitioner, Midland and Oxford Circuit, 1982–; an Asst Recorder, 1997–2000. Mem., Bar Council, 1987–90. *Recreation:* Stamford Shoestring Theatre. *Address:* 7 Bedford Row, WC1R 4BS. *T:* (020) 7242 3555.

COETZEE, Prof. John Maxwell; writer; Professor of Literature, University of Adelaide, since 2011; *b* 9 Feb. 1940; one *d* (one *s* decd). *Educ:* Univ. of Cape Town (MA); Univ. of Texas (PhD). FRSL 1988. Assistant Professor of English, State University of New York at Buffalo, 1968–71; Lectr in English, 1972–82, Prof. of Gen. Lit., 1983–98, Dist. Prof. of Lit., 1999–2001, Univ. of Cape Town; Res. Fellow, Univ. of Adelaide, 2002–10. Butler Prof. of English, State Univ. of New York at Buffalo, 1984; Hinkley Prof. of English, Johns Hopkins Univ., 1986, 1989; Visiting Professor of English: Harvard Univ., 1991; Univ. of Texas, 1995; Dist. Service Prof. of Social Thought, Univ. of Chicago, 1996–2003. Hon. Fellow, MLA, 1989. Hon. DLitt: Strathclyde, 1985; SUNY, 1989; Cape Town, 1995; Natal, 1996; Rhodes, 1999; Oxford, 2002; La Trobe, 2004; Adelaide, 2005. Nobel Prize for Literature, 2003. Order of Mapungubwe (Gold) (S Africa), 2005. *Publications:* Dusklands, 1974; In the Heart of the Country, 1977 (CNA Literary Award, 1977; filmed as Dust, 1986); Waiting for the Barbarians, 1980 (CNA Literary Award, 1980; James Tait Black Prize, 1980; Geoffrey Faber Award, 1980); Life and Times of Michael K, 1983 (CNA Literary Award, 1983; Booker-McConnell Prize, 1983; Prix Femina Etranger, 1985); Foe, 1986 (Jerusalem Prize, 1987); (ed with André Brink) A Land Apart, 1986; White Writing, 1988; Age of Iron, 1990 (Sunday Express Award, 1990); Doubling the Point, 1992; The Master of Petersburg, 1994 (Irish Times Internat. Fiction Award, 1995); Giving Offence, 1996; Boyhood, 1997; The Lives of Animals, 1999; Disgrace, 1999 (Booker Prize, 1999); Stranger Shores, 2001; Youth, 2002; Elizabeth Costello, 2003 (Qld Premier's Literary Award, 2004); Slow Man, 2005; Inner Workings: essays, 2007; Diary of a Bad Year, 2007; Summertime, 2009; Scenes from Provincial Life, 2011; The Childhood of Jesus, 2013; (with A. Kurtz) The Good Story: exchanges on truth, fiction and psychotherapy, 2015; essays in Comp. Lit., Jl of Mod. Lit., Linguistics, Mod. Lang. Notes, Pubns of MLA, etc. *Address:* PO Box 3045, Newton, SA 5074, Australia.

COEY, Prof. (John) Michael (David), PhD; FRS 2003; Erasmus Smith's Professor of Natural and Experimental Philosophy, 2007–12, Professor Emeritus, 2013, and Fellow, since 1982, Trinity College, Dublin (Professor of Experimental Physics, 1987–2007); *b* 24 Feb. 1945; *s* of David Stuart Coey and Joan Elizabeth Coey (*née* Newsam); *m* 1973, Wong May; two *s*. *Educ:* Jesus Coll., Cambridge (BA 1966); Univ. of Manitoba (PhD 1971). Chargé de Recherche, CNRS, Grenoble, 1971–78; Trinity College, Dublin: Lectr, 1978–84; Associate Prof., 1984–87. Visiting Scientist: IBM, Yorktown Heights, 1979; CEN Grenoble, 1985; Applied Physics Lab., Johns Hopkins, 1986; Visiting Professor: Inst. of Physics, Peking, 1980; McGill Univ., 1982; Univ. of Bordeaux, 1984; Univ. of Paris VI, 1992; UCSD, 1997; Florida State Univ., 1998; Univ. of Paris XI, 1998; Le Mans Univ., 1999, 2001, 2003; Univ. of Strasbourg, 2006, 2015 (Gutenberg Prize, 2015); Albert Einstein Prof., Chinese Acad. of Scis, 2011; NUS, 2012. Fulbright Fellow, 1997. Founder/Dir, Magnetic Solutions Ltd, 1994–2006. Chm., Magnetism Commn, Internat. Union of Pure and Applied Physics, 2002–05. Co-ordinator, Concerted European Action on Magnets, 1985–94. MRIA 1982 (Vice Pres., 1989–90; Gold Medal, 2005); Mem., Eur. Acad. Sci., 2013. FInstP 1984 (Charles Chree Medal and Prize, 1997). Fellow: American Mineralog. Soc., 1995; APS, 2000. Foreign Associate, Nat. Acad. of Scis, USA, 2005. Dr *hc* Inst. Nat. Poly., Grenoble, 1994. Advisory Editor: Jl of Magnetism and Magnetic Materials, 1990–; Physical Rev. Letters, 1999–2005. Humboldt Prize, Alexander von Humboldt Foundn, 2013. *Publications:* (with K. Moorjani) Magnetic Glasses, 1984; Rare Earth Iron Permanent Magnets, 1996; (with R. Skomski) Permanent Magnetism, 1999; Magnetism and Magnetic Materials, 2010; numerous articles on magnetism and electronic properties of solids in learned jls. *Recreation:* gardening. *Address:* School of Physics and CRANN, Trinity College, Dublin 2, Ireland. *T:* (1) 8961470. *E:* jcoey@tcd.ie.

COFFEY, Ann; *see* Coffey, M. A.

COFFEY, Rev. David Roy, OBE 2008; General Secretary, Baptist Union of Great Britain, 1991–2006; Global Ambassador, BMS World Mission, since 2010; *b* 13 Nov. 1941; *s* of Arthur Coffey and Elsie Maud Willis; *m* 1966, Janet Anne Dunbar; one *s* one *d*. *Educ:* Spurgeon's Coll., London (BA). Ordained, 1967; Minister: Whetstone Baptist Church, Leicester, 1967–72; North Cheam Baptist Ch, London, 1972–80; Sen. Minister, Upton Vale Baptist Ch, Torquay, 1980–88; Sec. for Evangelism, BUGB, 1988–91. President: BUGB, 1986–87; European Baptist Fedn, 1997–99; Vice Pres., 2000–05, Pres., 2005–10, Baptist World Alliance; Free Churches Moderator and a co-Pres., Churches Together in England, 2003–07; Vice Pres., CCJ, 2009–. Gov., 2007–, Chm. Council, 2012–, Spurgeon's Coll. Patron: Embrace (formerly Biblelands), 2009–; SAT-7, 2009–. Hon. DD: Dallas Baptist Univ., Texas, 2007; Palmer Seminary, Philadelphia, 2008. *Publications:* Build that Bridge—a Study in Conflict and Reconciliation, 1986; Discovering Romans, 2000; Joy to the World, 2008; All One in Christ Jesus: a passionate appeal for Evangelical Unity, 2009. *Recreations:* Elgar Society, Chelsea FC, armchair sportsman, grandchildren, music, political biography. *Address:* 129 Broadway, Didcot, Oxon OX11 8XD. *T:* (01235) 517700.

COFFEY, John Joseph; QC 1996; a Recorder, since 1989; *b* 29 July 1948; *s* of John and Hannah Coffey; *m* 1970, Patricia Anne Long; three *s* (and one *s* decd). *Educ:* Bishop Ward Secondary Modern Sch., Dagenham; Mid-Essex Coll. of Technology (LLB Hons London). Called to the Bar, Middle Temple, 1970; Asst Recorder, 1985. Hd of Chambers, 1993–. *Recreation:* supporting West Ham United. *Address:* 3 Temple Gardens, Temple, EC4Y 9AU. *T:* (020) 7353 3102.

COFFEY, (Margaret) Ann; MP (Lab) Stockport, since 1992; *b* 31 Aug. 1946; *d* of late John Brown, MBE, and of Marie Brown; *m* 1973 (marr. diss. 1989); one *d*; *m* 1998, Peter Saraga. *Educ:* Poly. of South Bank (BSc); Manchester Univ. (MSc). Trainee Social Worker, Walsall Social Services Dept, 1971–72; Social Worker: Birmingham, 1972–73; Gwynedd, 1973–74; Wolverhampton, 1974–75; Stockport, 1977–82; Cheshire, 1982–88; Team Leader, Fostering, Oldham Social Services Dept, 1988–92. Mem. (Lab) Stockport MBC, 1984–92 (Leader, Labour Group, 1988–92). Contested (Lab) Cheadle, 1987. An Opposition Whip, 1995–96; Opposition spokeswoman on health, 1996–97; PPS to Prime Minister, 1997–98, to Sec. of State for Social Security, 1998–2001, to Sec. of State for Work and Pensions, 2001–02, to Sec. of State for Transport, 2002–06, to Sec. of State for Trade and Industry, 2006–07, to Chancellor of the Exchequer, 2007–10. Mem., Trade and Industry Select Cttee, 1993–95. *Address:* House of Commons, SW1A 0AA.

COFFEY, Dr Therese Anne; MP (C) Suffolk Coastal, since 2010; Parliamentary Secretary (Deputy Leader), Office of the Leader of the House of Commons, since 2015; *b* Billinge, 18 Nov. 1971; *d* of late Tom Coffey and of Sally Coffey. *Educ:* St Mary's Coll., Crosby; St Edward's Coll., Liverpool; University Coll., London (BSc 1993; PhD Chem. 1997). Mgt Accountant. Various posts with Mars UK Ltd, 1997–2007; Finance Dir, Mars Drinks UK, 2007–09; Property Finance Manager, BBC, 2009–10. Mem. (C) Whitchurch Town Council, 1999–2003. An Asst Govt Whip, 2014–15. Contested (C): SE England, EP, 2004, 2009; Wrexham, 2005. *Recreations:* dog walking, sudoku, pub quizzes, live music. *Address:* House of Commons, SW1A 0AA. *T:* (020) 7219 7164. *E:* therese.coffey.mp@parliament.uk.

COFFIN, Rt Rev. Peter Robert; Bishop Ordinary (Anglican) to Canadian Forces, since 2004; *b* 31 May 1946; *s* of Gerald R. A. Coffin and Jean Mary Thorburn Coffin (*née* Edwards); *m* 1972, Deborah Creighton; one *d*. *Educ:* Univ. of King's Coll., Halifax, NS (BA); Trinity

Coll., Toronto (STB); Carleton Univ., Ottawa (MA Internat. Affairs). Ordained deacon, 1971, priest 1971; Asst Curate, St Matthew's, Ottawa, 1971–73; Lectr, House of the Epiphany, Kuching, Sarawak, E Malaysia, 1973–76; Incumbent, Parish of Hull, Quebec, 1976–84; Archdeacon of W Quebec, 1978–84; Incumbent, Christ Church, Bell's Corners, Ottawa (Nepean), 1984–90; Archdeacon of Carleton, 1986–90; Rector of Christ Church Cathedral, Ottawa and Dean of Ottawa, 1990–99; Bishop of Ottawa, 1999–2007. Chm., Interfaith Cttee on Canadian Military Chaplaincy, 2008–10. Hon. DD: Univ. of King's Coll., Halifax, NS, 1998; Trinity Coll., Toronto, 2004. *Address:* 42 Bridle Park Drive, Kanata, Ottawa, ON K2M 2E2, Canada.

COGBILL, Vivienne Margaret; *see* Dews, V. M.

COGDELL, Prof. Richard John, PhD; FRS 2007; FRSE; Hooker Professor of Botany, University of Glasgow, since 1993 (Titular Professor, 1988–93); *b* 4 Feb. 1949; *s* of Harry William Frank Cogdell and Evelyn Cogdell; *m* 1970, Barbara Lippold; one *s* one *d. Educ:* Royal Grammar Sch., Guildford; Univ. of Bristol (BSc Hons Biochem. 1970; PhD Biochem. 1973). Postdoctoral res., Cornell Univ., Ithaca, and Univ. of Washington, Seattle, 1973–75; Lectr, Dept of Botany, Univ. of Glasgow, 1975–88. Visiting Professor: UCLA, 1979; Univ. of Paris-Sud, 2004; Adjunct Prof., Chinese Nat. Acad. of Scis Inst. of Biophysics, Beijing, 2005–07. Mem., BBSRC, 2014–. FRSE 1991; FRSA 2009. Alexander von Humboldt Res. Prize, 1995; Daiwa-Adrian Prize for Anglo-Japanese Res., 2002. *Publications:* over 250 scientific papers in learned jls. *Recreations:* playing cricket, going to opera and theatre, Scottish country dancing. *Address:* 152 Hyndland Road, Glasgow G12 9PN. *T:* (0141) 330 4232, *Fax:* (0141) 330 4620. *E:* R.Cogdell@bio.gla.ac.uk.

COGGINS, Prof. John Richard, OBE 2008; PhD; FRSE; FRSB; Professor of Molecular Enzymology, 1995–2009, now Emeritus, and Vice-Principal, Life Sciences, Medicine and Veterinary Medicine, 2006–09, University of Glasgow; *b* 15 Jan. 1944; *s* of Cecil Rex Coggins and Pamela Mary Coggins (*née* Burnet); *m* 1970, Lesley Frances Watson; one *s* one *d. Educ:* Bristol GS; Queen's Coll., Oxford (MA); Univ. of Ottawa (PhD). FRSE 1988. Research Fellow: Brookhaven Nat. Lab., USA, 1970–72; Cambridge Univ., 1972–74; Glasgow University: Lectr, 1974–78; Sen. Lectr, 1978–86; Prof. of Biochemistry, 1986–95; Dir, Grad. Sch. of Biomedical and Life Scis, 1995–97; Hd, Div. of Biochemistry and Molecular Biology, 1997–98; Res. Dir, 1998–2000, Dir and Dean, 2000–05, Inst. of Biomed. and Life Scis; Chm., Hds of Univ. Biol Sci. Depts, 2003–07. Chm., Biochem. and Biophys. Cttee, 1985–88, Mem., Biotechnol. Directorate Management Cttee, 1987–90, SERC; Member: Liby and Inf. Services Cttee, Scotland, 1982–88; Biotechnol. Jt Adv. Bd, 1989–94; Wkg Party on Biotechnol., NEDO, 1990–92; AFRC, 1991–94; Council, Hannah Res. Inst., 1994–2005; Scottish Sci. Adv. Cttee, 2002–07; BBSRC, 2008–14; Governing Mem., 1994–2007, Chm., 2007–10, Caledonian Res. Foundn; Advr for Biochem., UFC, 1989–92; Chm., HEFCE RAE Panel for Biochemistry, 1995–96; Vice-Pres. (Life Scis), RSE, 2003–06 (Res. Awards Convener, 1999–2002). Chm., Molecular Enzymol. Gp, 1981–85, Policy Cttee, 2004–08, Biochemical Soc. Chm., Portland Press Ltd, 2009–13. Dir, Ops and Strategy, Glasgow City of Sci., 2011–13. Trustee, 2004–10, Vice Chm., 2010–16, Glasgow Sci. Centre. Mem. Adv. Bd, Research Inf. Network, 2005–12. *Publications:* Multidomain Proteins: structure and evolution, 1986; contribs on enzymes and on plant and microbial biochem. to Biochem. Jl, Jl of Biol Chem., Jl Molecular Biol., etc. *Recreations:* sailing, travel, good food, reading. *Address:* 5 Chapelton Gardens, Bearsden, Glasgow G61 2DH. *T:* (0141) 942 5082. *Club:* New (Edinburgh).

COGGON, Prof. David Noel Murray, OBE 2002; PhD, DM; FRCP, FFOM, FFPH, FMedSci; Professor of Occupational and Environmental Medicine, MRC Lifecourse Epidemiology Unit (formerly Environmental Epidemiology Unit, then Epidemiology Resource Centre), University of Southampton, since 1997; *b* 25 Dec. 1950; *s* of Frederick and Annette Coggon; *m* 1976, Sarah (*née* Cole); one *s* four *d. Educ:* Clare Coll., Cambridge (BA 1972; MA 1976); New Coll., Oxford (BM BCh 1976; DM 1993); Univ. of Southampton (PhD 1984). MRCP 1978, FRCP 1992; FFOM 1993; FFPH 2005. Clinical Scientist, MRC Envmtl Epidemiol. Unit, Univ. of Southampton, 1980–97. Chairman: Depleted Uranium Oversight Bd, 2001–07; Mobile Telecommns and Health Res. Prog. Mgt Cttee, 2008–12; Member: Industrial Injuries Adv. Council, 1988–2003; Adv. Cttee on Pesticides, 1997–2000 (Chm., 2000–05); Ind. Expert Gp on Mobile Phones, 1999–2000; Adv. Gp on Non-ionising Radiation, 2001–09; Plant Protection Products and Residues Panel, Eur. Food Safety Authy, 2006–09; Cttee on Toxicity of Chemicals in Food, Consumer Products and the Envmt, 2007– (Chm., 2008–). Pres., Faculty of Occupational Medicine, RCP, 2008–11. FMedSci 1998. *Publications:* Statistics in Clinical Practice, 1995, 2nd edn 2002; (jtly) Epidemiology for the Uninitiated, 3rd edn 1993 to 5th edn 2003. *Recreations:* rambling, gardening, cabinet making, choral singing. *Address:* MRC Lifecourse Epidemiology Unit, Southampton General Hospital, Southampton SO16 6YD. *T:* (023) 8077 7624, *Fax:* (023) 8070 4021. *E:* dnc@mrc.soton.ac.uk.

COGHER, Michael Patrick; Comptroller and City Solicitor, City of London Corporation, since 2012; *b* Prestatyn, Denbighshire, 1 Nov. 1966; *s* of Anthony and Eileen Cogher; *m* 1994, Penelope Martin; two *d. Educ:* Ruthin Sch., Denbighshire; Manchester Poly. (LLB Hons); Coll. of Law. Dip. Local Govt Law and Practice. Trainee solicitor, London Bor. of Richmond upon Thames, 1989–91; admitted as solicitor, 1991; London Borough of Merton: Asst Solicitor, 1991–95; Sen. Solicitor, 1995–96; Principal Solicitor, 1996–98; Hd, Legal Services, 1998–2000; Hd, Legal Services, Peterborough CC, 2000–01; Dir, Legal and Democratic Services, London Bor. of Hammersmith and Fulham, 2001–09; Shared Dir of Legal Services, RBKC, 2009–12. *Recreations:* sailing, ski-ing, hill-walking, theatre. *Address:* City of London, PO Box 270, Guildhall, EC2P 2EJ. *T:* (020) 7332 3699, *Fax:* (020) 7332 1634. *E:* michael.cogher@cityoflondon.gov.uk.

COGHILL, Sir Patrick Kendal Farley, 9th Bt *cr* 1778, of Coghill, Yorkshire; *b* 3 Nov. 1960; *o s* of Sir Toby Coghill, 8th Bt; *S* father, 2000. *Heir: cousin* John Kendal Plunket Coghill, OBE [*b* 17 July 1929; *m* 1951, Diana Mary Callen; three *d*].

COGHLAN, Terence Augustine; QC 1993; *b* 17 Aug. 1945; *s* of late Austin Frances Coghlan and of Ruby Coghlan (*née* Comrie); *m* 1973, Angela Agatha Westmacott; one *s* two *d. Educ:* Downside; Perugia; New Coll., Oxford; Inns of Court. Called to the Bar, Inner Temple, 1968 (Scholar; Bencher, 2004); Recorder, 1989–2009. Pt-time Judge, Mental Health Review Tribunal, 2000–. Film extra, 1968 (incl. German Heinkel bomber pilot in film, Battle of Britain, 1969); Director: City of London Sinfonia, 1975–2010; Temple Music Foundn, 2004–13. Chairman: St Endellion Fests Trust, 2007–; Temple Church Cttee, 2011–13. *Publications:* Meningitis, 1998; medico-legal articles. *Recreations:* wandering around buildings with Pevsner, wine, walking, cycling, theatre, opera, performing music badly. *Address:* 1 Crown Office Row, Temple, EC4Y 7HH. *T:* (020) 7797 7500. *Clubs:* Omar Khayyam, Les Six, MCC.

COGHLIN, Rt Hon. Sir Patrick, Kt 1997; PC 2009; a Lord Justice of Appeal, Supreme Court of Judicature, Northern Ireland, 2008–15; President, Lands Tribunal, Northern Ireland, 1999–2015; *b* 7 Nov. 1945; *s* of late James Edwin Coghlin and Margaret Van Hovenberg Coghlin; *m* 1971, Patricia Ann Elizabeth Young; one *s* three *d. Educ:* Royal Belfast Academical Instn; Queen's Univ., Belfast (LLB Hons); Christ's Coll., Cambridge (Dip. Criminology). Called to the Bar: NI, 1970; Gray's Inn, 1975 (Hon. Bencher 2000); NSW, 1992; Republic of Ireland, 1995; Jun. Crown Counsel for NI, 1983–85; QC (NI) 1985; Dep. County Court Judge, 1983–94; Sen. Crown Counsel, NI, 1993–97; Judge, High Ct of Justice, NI, 1997–2008. Vice-Chm., Mental Health Review Tribunal, 1987–97; Mem., Law Reform Adv. Cttee, NI, 1988–93; Vice-Pres., VAT Tribunal, NI, 1990–93; Dep. Chm., Boundar Commn, NI, 1999–2008. Chm., NI Bar Council, 1991–93. *Recreations:* Rugby, socce squash, reading, music, travel. *Clubs:* Kildare Street and University (Dublin); Royal Ulste Yacht, Ballyholme Yacht; Bangor Rugby, Perennials Rugby; Ballyholme Bombers FC.

COGLEY, Stephen William; QC 2011; *b* Hants, 13 Aug. 1961; *s* of William and Lorett Cogley; *m* Sally Jane; two *s* two *d. Educ:* Ripon Grammar Sch.; Newcastle Univ (LLB Hons). Called to the Bar, Gray's Inn, 1984; in practice as a barrister, specialisin in commercial law. *Recreations:* marching to my own drum, tinkering with the engin on my ship. *Address:* Quadrant Chambers, 10 Fleet Street, EC4Y 1AU. *E:* stephen.cogley@quadrantchambers.com.

COHAN, Robert Paul, CBE 1989; Founder Artistic Director, Contemporary Dance Trus *b* 27 March 1925; *s* of Walter and Billie Cohan; British citizen, 1989. *Educ:* Martha Grahan Sch., NYC. Joined Martha Graham Co., 1946; Partner, 1950; Co-Dir, Martha Graham Co 1966; Artistic Dir, Contemporary Dance Trust Ltd, 1967; Artistic Dir and Principa Choreographer, 1969–87, Dir, 1987–89, London Contemporary Dance Theatre; Artisti Advr, Batsheva Co., Israel, 1980–90; Director: York Univ., Toronto Choreographic Summe Sch., 1977; Gulbenkian Choreographic Summer Sch., Univ. of Surrey, 1978, 1979, 1982 Banff Sch. of Fine Arts Choreographic Seminar, Canada, 1980; New Zealand Choreographi Seminar, 1982; Choreographic Seminar, Simon Fraser Univ., Vancouver, 1985; Interna Dance Course for Professional Choreographers and Composers, Surrey Univ., 1985, 1989 With London Contemporary Dance Theatre toured Britain, E and W Europe, S America, N Africa and USA; major works created: Cell, 1969 (recorded for BBC TV, 1982); Stages, 1971 Waterless Method of Swimming Instruction, 1974 (recorded for BBC TV); Class, 1975 Stabat Mater, 1975 (recorded for BBC TV); Masque of Separation, 1975; Khamsin, 1976 Nympheas, 1976 (recorded for BBC TV, 1983); Forest, 1977 (recorded for BBC TV); Eos 1978; Songs, Lamentations and Praises, 1979; Dances of Love and Death, 1981; Agora, 1984 A Mass for Man, 1985 (recorded for BBC TV); Ceremony, 1986; Interrogations, 1986; Vide Life, 1986; Phantasmagoria, 1987; A Midsummer Night's Dream, 1993; The Four Seasons 1996; Aladdin, 2000. Editor, Choreography and Dance, 1988–2000. Hon. Fellow, York Univ., Toronto. Hon. DLitt: Exeter, 1993; Kent, 1996; DUniv: Middlesex, 1994 Winchester, 2006. Evening Standard Award for most outstanding achievement in ballet, 1975 Soc. of West End Theatres Award for most outstanding achievement in ballet, 1978; UK Dance Critics' Circle Cttee Award for Lifetime Achievement, 2005. *Publications:* The Danc Workshop, 1986. *Recreation:* dancing. *Address:* The Place, 17 Dukes Road, WC1H 9PY. *T* (020) 7121 1000.

COHEN, family name of **Baroness Cohen of Pimlico**.

COHEN OF PIMLICO, Baroness *cr* 2000 (Life Peer), of Pimlico in the City of Westminster **Janet Cohen;** Senior Advisor, BPP Holdings, since 2010; *b* 4 July 1940; *d* of late Georg Edric Neel and Mary Isabel Neel (*née* Budge); *m* 1971, James Lionel Cohen; two *s* one *d. Educ* Newnham Coll., Cambridge (BA Hons Law 1962; Associate Fellow, 1988–91). Article clerk, Frere Cholmeley, 1963–65; admitted solicitor, 1965; Consultant: ABT Associates USA, 1965–67; John Laing Construction, 1968–69; Department of Trade and Industry Principal, 1969–78; Asst Sec., 1978–82; Asst Dir, 1982–88, Dir, 1988–2000, Charterhous Bank Ltd. Chm., Café Pelican Ltd, 1984–90; Vice Chm., Yorks Building Soc., 1994–99 (Dir 1991–94); non-executive Director: Waddington plc (formerly John Waddington), 1994–97 London & Manchester Gp plc, 1997–98; United Assce Gp, 1998–99; BPP Hldgs, 1994–200 (Chm., 2002–06); London Stock Exchange, 2001–13; MCG plc, 2003–11; Chairman InviseoMedia Hldgs Ltd, 2007–09; Trillium Hldgs, 2008–10. Mem., Schools Exam. an Assessment Council, 1990–93. Mem. Bd, Sheffield Develt Corp., 1993–97. Pres., BP University Coll. (formerly Coll.) of Professional Studies, 2008–13; Chancellor, BPP Univ. 2013–. A Governor, BBC, 1994–99. Mem., EU Scrutiny Cttee, H of L, 2006– (Chm., Sub Cttee A). Chairman: Parlt Choir, 2006–08; Cambridge Arts Th., 2007–15. Hon. Fellow: S Edmund's Coll., Cambridge, 2000; Lucy Cavendish Coll., Cambridge, 2007. Hon. DLit Humberside, 1995. *Publications:* as Janet Neel: Death's Bright Angel, 1988; Death on Site 1989; Death of a Partner, 1991; Death among the Dons, 1993; A Timely Death, 1996; To Die For, 1998; O Gentle Death, 2000; Ticket to Ride, 2005; as Janet Cohen: The Highes Bidder, 1992; Children of a Harsh Winter, 1994. *Recreation:* writing.

COHEN, Prof. Anthony Paul, CBE 2008; PhD; FRSE; Principal and Vice-Chancellor Queen Margaret University (formerly Queen Margaret University College), 2003–09, now Emeritus Professor of Social and Cultural Anthropology; Hon. Professor of Socia Anthropology, University of Edinburgh, since 2003; *b* 3 Aug. 1946; *s* of Mark Cohen and Mary Cohen (*née* Nissenbaum); *m* 1968, Prof. Bronwen J. Steel, OBE; three *s. Educ:* Univ. o Southampton (BA Hons; MSocSc; PhD 1973). Res. Fellow, Meml Univ. of Newfoundland 1968–70; Asst Prof., Queen's Univ. at Kingston, Ont., 1970–71; Lectr, then Sen. Lectr in Social Anthropol., Univ. of Manchester, 1971–89; University of Edinburgh: Prof. of Socia Anthropol., 1989–2003; Provost of Law and Social Scis, and Dean of Social Scis, 1997–2002 FRSE 1995. Hon. DSc Edinburgh, 2005. *Publications:* The Management of Myths: the politic of legitimation in a Newfoundland community, 1975; (ed) Belonging: identity and socia organisation in British rural cultures, 1982; The Symbolic Construction of Community (CHOICE Award for Outstanding Book of the Year), 1985 (trans. Turkish and Japanese); (ed) Symbolising Boundaries: identity and diversity in British cultures, 1986; Whalsay: symbol segment and boundary in a Shetland Island community, 1987; (ed with K. Fukui) Humanisin the City?: social contexts of urban life at the turn of the Millennium, 1993 (trans. Japanese) (jtly) Villages Anglais, Ecossaises, Irlandaises, 1993; Self Consciousness: an alternativ anthropology of identity, 1994 (trans. Danish); (ed with N. J. Rapport) Questions o Consciousness, 1995; (ed) Signifying Identities: anthropological perspectives on boundarie and contested values, 2000; papers and chapters in books. *Recreations:* music, reading. *Club* New (Edinburgh).

COHEN, Prof. Bernard Woolf; Slade Professor, and Chair of Fine Art, University o London, 1988–2000, now Emeritus Slade Professor; *b* 28 July 1933; *s* of Victor and Leal Cohen; *m* 1959, Jean Britton; one *s* one *d. Educ:* Slade School of Fine Art, University Coll London (Dip. Fine Art). Head of Painting, Wimbledon Sch. of Art, 1980–87. Vis. Prof. Univ. of New Mexico, USA, 1969–70. Fellow: UCL, 1992; Kent Inst. of Art and Design 1998. First one man exhibn, Gimpel Fils Gall., 1958, again in 1960; other exhibitions: Moltor Gall., 1962; Kasmin Gall., Bond Street, 1963, 1964, 1967; Waddington Gall., 1974, 1977 1979, 1990; First New York exhibn, Betty Parsons Gall., 1967; major retrospective, Haywar Gall., 1972; print retrospective, Tate Gall., 1976; drawing retrospective, Ben Uri Gall., 1994 paintings, Tate Gall., 1995; paintings of the 90s, Flowers East Gall., London, 1998, Flower West Gall., Santa Monica, 1999; Flowers Central, London, 2001, 2004, six new larg lithographs, 2012; paintings, 2006, paintings retrospective, 2011, Flowers Gall., NY; painting from the 60s, Flowers East Gall., 2007; paintings of six decades, Flowers East Gall., 2009; 80t birthday, Flowers Central, London, 2013; represented GB at Venice Biennale, 1966. Work i collections of Tate Gall., Mus. of Modern Art, New York; Fogg Mus., Mass; Minneapoli Walker Art Centre; Carnegie Inst., Pittsburgh, and others. *Relevant publication:* Bernar Cohen: work of six decades, by Norbert Lynton and Ian McKay, 2009. *Recreations:* travel music. *Address:* 80 Camberwell Grove, SE5 8RF.

COHEN, Betty; *see* Jackson, B.

COHEN, Ven. Clive Ronald Franklin; Archdeacon of Bodmin, 2000–11, now Archdeaco Emeritus; Acting Archdeacon of Totnes, 2014–15; *b* 30 Jan. 1946; *s* of Ronald Arthur Wilfre

Cohen, MBE, and Janet Ruth Lindsay Cohen (*née* Macdonald); *m* 1969, (Elizabeth) June Kingsley Kefford; three *s* one *d* (and one *s* decd). *Educ:* Salisbury and Wells Theol Coll. (Gen. Ministerial Exam.). ACIB 1971. Asst Master, Edinburgh House Sch., 1965–67; Midland Bank plc, 1967–79; ordained deacon, 1981, priest, 1982; Asst Curate, Esher, Surrey, 1981–85; Rector, Winterslow, Wilts, 1985–2000; Rural Dean, Alderbury, Wilts, 1989–93; Non-Residentiary Canon and Prebendary, Salisbury Cathedral, 1992–2000. Ex officio Mem., Coll. of Canons, Truro Cathedral, 2000–11; Chapter Canon, Exeter Cathedral, 2011–. *Publications:* Crying in the Wilderness, 1994; So Great a Cloud, 1995; contrib. Jl of Army Histl Res. Soc. *Address:* 86 Moor View Drive, Teignmouth, Devon TQ14 9UZ.

COHEN, Daniel; Director of Television, BBC, since 2013; *b* London, 15 Jan. 1974; *s* of Ernie and Rosalind Cohen; *m* 2012, Prof. Noreena Tamar Hertz, *qv*. *Educ:* City of London Sch.; Lady Margaret Hall, Oxford (BA Hons Double First English Lit.). Channel 4: Commissioning Ed., Documentaries, 2001–04; Head of Documentaries, 2004–06; Head of E4, 2006–07; Controller: BBC Three, 2007–10; BBC One, 2010–13. *Recreations:* football, cricket, English literature, TV and new media, pickle, current affairs, meditation, giraffes, contemporary art. *Address:* c/o BBC, 6th Floor, New Broadcasting House, Portland Place, W1A 1AA. *E:* danny.cohen@bbc.co.uk. *Club:* Groucho.

COHEN, Frank; art collector; Founder, Initial Access, since 2007; Co-Founder, The Dairy Art Centre, since 2013; *b* Manchester, 15 Oct. 1943; *s* of Louis and Minnie Cohen; *m* 1972, Cherryl Garson; one *s* one *d*. *Educ:* Chorlton Grammar Sch. Founder and Owner, Glyn Webb Home Improvement Stores, 1977–99; Dir, Home Improvement Co. Ltd, 1997. Member, Advisory Board: Bonhams, 2008–; Art 13, 2012–; Art 14, 2013–14. Judge: Jerwood Prize, 2002; Turner Prize, 2003. *Recreations:* art, opera, wine, boxing. *Address:* Brindlow House, 32 Prestbury Road, Wilmslow, Cheshire SK9 2LL. *T:* (01625) 527100, 07768 875522. *E:* frankc@1st4arts.com. *Clubs:* Arts, Academicians, 5 Hertford Street, Annabel's, George, Ivy, Harry's Bar, Alfred's.

COHEN, Gabrielle Ann; an Assistant Auditor General, National Audit Office, since 2005; *b* 25 May 1961; *d* of David Michael Cowell and Gloria Ethel Cowell; three *s*. *Educ:* Univ. of Kent (BA Hons Hist. and Pol.). CPFA. National Audit Office, 1987–: Head of Press Office, 1996–2000; Dir, Communications and Corporate Affairs, 2000–05. *Recreations:* current affairs, reading, theatre, cinema, football. *Address:* National Audit Office, 157–197 Buckingham Palace Road, SW1W 9SP. *T:* (020) 7798 7782. *E:* Gabrielle.Cohen@nao.gsi.gov.uk.

COHEN, Harry Michael; accountant; *b* 10 Dec. 1949; *m* 1978, Ellen Hussain; one step *s* one step *d*. Mem., Waltham Forest Borough Council, 1972–83 (formerly Chm., Planning Cttee and Sec., Labour Group). MP (Lab) Leyton, 1983–97, Leyton and Wanstead, 1997–2010. Mem., Select Cttee on Defence, 1997–2001; Sec., All-Party Parly Gp on Race and Community. Mem., N Atlantic Assembly, 1992–2010 (Rapporteur; Chm. sub-cttee for Economic Co-operation and Convergence with Central & Eastern Europe, 1996–2000). Mem., UNISON. Vice Pres., Royal Coll. of Midwives.

COHEN, Sir Ivor (Harold), Kt 1992; CBE 1985; TD 1968; Chairman: Remploy Ltd, 1987–93; Japan Electronics Business Association, 1991–2002; *b* 28 April 1931; *s* of Jack Cohen and Anne (*née* Victor); *m* 1963, Betty Edith, *yr d* of Reginald George and Mabel Appleby; one *d*. *Educ:* Central Foundation Sch., EC2; University Coll. London (BA (Hons) Mod. Hist.; Fellow, 1987). Nat. Service, Royal Signals, 1952–54 (2nd Lieut); TA, Royal Signals, 1954–69 (Major 1964). Engrg industry, 1954–57; range of managerial posts, Mullard Ltd (subsid. of Philips (UK)), 1957–77; Dir, Philips Lighting, 1977–79; Man. Dir, Mullard Ltd, 1979–87; Dir, Philips Electronics (UK) Ltd, 1984–87. Non-executive Director: AB Electronic Products Gp plc, 1987–93; Océ (UK) Ltd, 1988–2001; PA Holdings Ltd, 1989–2001; Redifon Holdings Ltd, 1989–94; Magnetic Materials Gp plc, 1992; Electron Technologies Ltd, 1994–97; Deltron Electronics, 1995–2003; Russell Partnership Ltd, 1996–97; Chairman: Optima Group Ltd, 1995–96; Sira Ltd, 1998–2001; Cons., Comet Gp plc, 1987–90; Advr, Apax & Co. Ventures (formerly Alan Patricof Associates), 1987–93; Mem., Adv. Cttee, Mitsubishi Electric Europe BV (formerly Mitsubishi Electric (UK) Ltd), 1991–2002. Member: IT Adv. Panel, 1981–86; Teletext and Viewdata Steering Gp, DTI, 1981–86; Electronic Components EDC, NEDO, 1980–88; Electronics Ind. EDC, NEDO, 1982–86; Steering Cttee, Telecom. Infrastructure, DTI, 1987–88; Computing Software and Communications Requirements Bd, DTI, 1984–88; Steering Bd, Radiocommunications Agency, DTI, 1990–95; Electronics Ind. Sector Gp, NEDO, 1988–92 (Chm., 1990–92); Chairman: Electronic Applications Sector Gp, NEDO, 1988–90; Measurement Adv. Cttee, DTI, 1994–97; Member Council: Electronic Components Ind. Fedn, 1980–87; European Electronic Components Assoc., 1985–87; Dir, Radio Industries Council, 1980–87. Mem., Schs Examinations and Assessment Council, 1988–90; British Schools Technology: Mem. Council of Management, 1984–87, Trustee Dir, 1987–89; Mem., Management Adv. Gp IT Res. Inst., Brighton Poly., 1987–90. FIET (CompIEE 1988); CompInstMC 1997; Hon. Mem. CGLI, 1989; FInstD 1988–2003; FRSA 1984; Hon. FREng (Hon. FEng 1992). Freeman, City of London, 1982; Liveryman, Sci. Instrument Makers' Co., 1982– (Master, 1997). Hon. DSc City, 1998. Mem., Editl Bd, Nat. Electronics Review, 1987–90. *Publications:* articles on electronics policy and marketing and use of inf. technology in the technical press. *Recreations:* opera, reading, occasional sculpting, walking in towns, video film making. *Address:* c/o Lloyds Bank, 137 North End, Croydon CR0 1TN. *Clubs:* East India, Reform.

COHEN, Janet; *see* Baroness Cohen of Pimlico.

COHEN, Prof. Jonathan, FRCP, FRCPE, FRCPath; FMedSci; FFICM; Foundation Dean, Brighton and Sussex Medical School, University of Sussex, 2003–13, now Emeritus Professor; *b* 11 Oct. 1949; *s* of Norman and Ruth Cohen; *m* 1973, Noëmi Weingarten; one *s* one *d*. *Educ:* William Ellis Grammar Sch., London; Charing Cross Hosp. Med. Sch. (MB, BS). FRCP 1987; FRCPath 1992; FRCPE 1997; FFICM 2014. Jun. trng appts at Whittington Hosp., LSHTM, and Duke Univ. Med. Center, NC, USA, 1975–85; Wellcome Sen. Lectr in Infectious Diseases, RPMS, 1985–92; Prof. and Hd of Dept of Infectious Diseases, 1992–2002, Vis. Prof., 2002–, RPMS, later Imperial Coll., London. Forbes Fellow, Univ. of Melbourne, 2011. Member: Jt Commn on Vaccination and Immunisation, 2000–05; Nat. Expert Panel on New and Emerging Infections, 2004–07. Member: SE England Sci. and Technol. Adv. Council, 2003–08; Infections and Immunity Bd, MRC, 2004–07. Academy of Medical Sciences: Fellow, 2000; Mem. Council, 2002–05. Chm., Clin. Trials Adv. and Awards Cttee, CRUK, 2006–09; Panel Mem., RAE, 2008; Member: Exec. Cttee, Med. Schs Council, 2008– (Vice Chm., 2009–12); Undergrad. Bd, GMC, 2009–12; Clinical Med. Panel, REF, 2011–14; Med. Vice Chm., SE Region, Adv. Cttee on Clin. Excellence Awards, 2009–13. President: Eur. Congress Clin. Microbiol. and Infectious Diseases, 2012–13; Internat. Soc. of Infectious Diseases, 2014– (Mem. Council, 2006–; Mem. Exec., 2008–). Non-executive Director: Brighton and Sussex Univ. Hosps Trust, 2004–10; Sussex Partnership NHS Trust, 2010–13; E Sussex NHS Trust, 2014–. Chairman: British Med. and Dental Students' Trust, 2012–; Fellowship Cttee, Arthritis Res. UK, 2013–14 (Trustee and Chair, Scientific Cttee, 2014–); Member: Scientific Adv. Bd, Lister Inst., 2013–; Adv. Council, Coll. of Medicine, 2015–. Member Editorial Board: Lancet Infectious Diseases, 2000–; PLoS Medicine, 2004–; Ed.-in-Chief, Internat. Jl Infectious Diseases, 2001–06. *Publications:* (ed jtly) Infectious Diseases, 1999, 3rd edn 2010; contrib. scientific papers on infection, immunity and sepsis. *Recreations:* family, photography, ski-ing, pipe-smoking. *Address:* Brighton and Sussex Medical School, University of Sussex, Brighton, E Sussex BN1 9PX. *T:* (01273) 877577. *E:* j.cohen@bsms.ac.uk.

COHEN, Jonathan Lionel; QC 1997; a Recorder, since 1997; a Deputy High Court Judge (Family Division), since 2005; *b* 8 May 1951; *s* of late Hon. Leonard Harold Lionel Cohen, OBE and Eleanor Lucy Quixano Cohen (*née* Henriques); *m* 1983, Bryony Frances Carfrae; two *s* one *d*. *Educ:* Eton Coll.; Univ. of Kent at Canterbury (BA Hons). Called to the Bar, Lincoln's Inn, 1974, Bencher, 2004; SE Circuit; Hd of Chambers, 4 Paper Buildings, 2003–12. Mem., Mental Health Review Tribunal, 2000–. Liveryman, Skinners' Co., 1978– (Master, 2005–06). Governor: Skinners' Co.'s Sch. for Girls, Hackney, 1994–2002; Judd Sch., Tonbridge, 2002–06; Tonbridge Sch., 2006– (Chm., 2007–); Mem., Develt Bd, LAMDA, 2004–07. *Recreations:* playing sport badly, theatre. *Address:* 4 Paper Buildings, Temple, EC4Y 7EX. *Clubs:* Garrick, MCC; Swinley Forest Golf; Refreshers Cricket.

COHEN, Leonard, CC 2002 (OC 1991); GOQ 2008; writer and composer; *b* Montreal, 21 Sept. 1934. *Educ:* McGill Univ. Composer and singer: Songs of Leonard Cohen, 1967; Songs from a Room, 1969; Songs of Love and Hate, 1971; Live Songs, 1972; New Skin for the Old Ceremony, 1973; The Best of Leonard Cohen, 1975; Death of a Ladies' Man, 1977; Recent Songs, 1979; Various Positions, 1985; I'm Your Man, 1987; The Future, 1992; Cohen Live, 1994; More Best Of, 1997; Field Commander Cohen: tour of 1979, 2001; Ten New Songs, 2001; The Essential Leonard Cohen, 2002; Dear Heather, 2004; Blue Alert, 2006; Live in London, 2009; Old Ideas, 2012; Popular Problems, 2014; Can't Forget: a souvenir of the grand tour, 2015; composer, lyrics, for Night Magic, the musical, 1985. Inducted into Rock and Roll Hall of Fame, 2008, US Songwriters Hall of Fame, 2010; Grammy Lifetime Achievement Award, 2010; Prince of Asturias Award for Literature, Prince Asturias Foundn, 2011; Glenn Gould Prize, Glenn Gould Foundn, 2011; Song Lyrics of Literary Excellence Award, PEN New England, 2012. *Publications: poetry:* Let us Compare Mythologies, 1956; The Spice Box of Earth, 1961; Flowers for Hitler, 1964; Parasites of Heaven, 1966; Selected Poems 1965–68, 1968; The Energy of Slaves, 1972; Stranger Music: selected poems and songs, 1993; The Book of Longing, 2006; *novels:* The Favourite Game, 1963; Beautiful Losers, 1966; Death of a Lady's Man, 1978; Book of Mercy, 1984. *Address:* c/o R. K. Management LLC, 9300 Wilshire Boulevard, Suite 200, Beverly Hills, CA 90212, USA.

COHEN, Lt-Col Mordaunt, TD 1954; DL; Regional Chairman of Industrial Tribunals, 1976–89 (Chairman, 1974–76); *b* 6 Aug. 1916; *s* of Israel Ellis Cohen and Sophie Cohen; *m* 1953, Myrella Cohen (Her Honour Myrella Cohen, QC) (*d* 2002); one *s* one *d*. *Educ:* Bede Collegiate Sch. for Boys, Sunderland. Admitted solicitor, 1938; admitted Nigerian Bar (Mil. Advocate), 1942. Served War, RA, 1940–46: seconded RWAFF; despatches, Burma campaign; served TA, 1947–55: CO 463(M) HAA Regt, RA(TA), 1954–55. Alderman, Sunderland Co. Bor. Council, 1967–74; Chm., Sunderland Educn Cttee, 1970–72; Chm., NE Council of Educn Cttees, 1971; Councillor, Tyne and Wear CC, 1973–74; Dep. Chm., Northern Traffic Comrs, 1973–74. Chm., Mental Health Review Tribunal, 1967–76. Chm. of Governors, Sunderland Polytechnic, 1969–72; Mem. Court, Univ. of Newcastle upon Tyne, 1968–72. Pres., Sunderland Law Soc., 1970; Hon. Life Pres., Sunderland Hebrew Congregation, 1988; Mem., Bd of Deputies of British Jews, 1964–2006 (Chm., Provincial Cttee, 1985–91; Dir, Central Enquiry Desk, 1990–2000); former Mem., Chief Rabbinate Council; Vice Pres., AJEX, 1995– (Chm., 1993–95); Pres., Friends of Jewish Servicemen and Women, 2009–; Life Pres., Sunderland Br., AJEX, 1970; Trustee, AJEX Charitable Foundn, 2000–. Chm. of Govs, Edgware Sch., 1991–96. FRSA 1998. DL Tyne and Wear, 1986. *Recreations:* watching sport; communal service, promoting inter-faith understanding. *Address:* Flat 1, Peters Lodge, 2 Stonegrove, Edgware, Middlesex HA8 7TY. *Clubs:* Ashbrooke Cricket and Rugby Football (Sunderland); Durham County Cricket (Life Mem.).

COHEN, Sir Philip, Kt 1998; PhD; FRS 1984; FRSE 1984; Professor of Enzymology, since 2010, Director, Medical Research Council Protein Phosphorylation Unit, 1990–2012, and Director, Scottish Institute for Cell Signalling, 2008–12, University of Dundee; *b* 22 July 1945; *s* of Jacob Davis Cohen and Fanny (*née* Bragman); *m* 1969, Patricia Townsend Wade; one *s* one *d*. *Educ:* Hendon County Grammar Sch.; University Coll. London (BSc 1st Cl. Hons (Biochemistry Special), 1966; PhD Biochem., 1969; Fellow, 1993). SRC/NATO Postdoctoral Res. Fellow, Dept of Biochem., Univ. of Washington, Seattle, USA, 1969–71; Univ. of Dundee: Lectr in Biochem., 1971–78; Reader in Biochem., 1978–81; Prof. of Enzymology, 1981–84; Royal Soc. Res. Prof., 1984–2010; Dir, Wellcome Trust Biocentre, 1997–2007. Croonian Lectr, Royal Soc., 1998. Pres., British Biochemical Soc., 2006–08 (Hon. Mem., 2003). Mem., Eur. Molecular Biology Orgn, 1982–; MAE 1990. Hon. Mem., Amer. Soc. of Toxicol., 2010. Founder FMedSci 1998. Hon. FRCPath 1998. Foreign Associate, US NAS, 2008; Corresp. Fellow, Aust. Acad. of Sci., 2013. Hon. DSc: Abertay, 1998; Strathclyde, 1999; St Andrews, 2005; Hon. MD Linköping, 2004; Hon. LLD: Debrecen, 2004; Dundee, 2007. Anniversary Prize, Fedn of Eur. Biochemical Socs, 1977; Colworth Medal, 1978, CIBA medal and prize, 1992, British Biochem. Soc.; Prix van Gysel, Belgian Royal Acads of Medicine, 1992; Dundee City of Discovery Rosebowl Award, 1993; Bruce Preller Prize, RSE, 1993; Special Achievement Award, 1996, Dist. Service Award, 2005, Miami Biotech. Winter Symposium; Louis-Jeantet Prize for Medicine, 1997; Pfizer Award for Innovative Sci., 1999; Sir Hans Krebs Medal, Fedn of Eur. Biochem. Socs, 2001; Bristol Myers Squibb Dist. Achievement Award in Metabolic Res., 2002; Royal Medal, RSE, 2004; Debrecen Award for Molecular Medicine, 2004; Rolf Luft Prize, Karolinska Inst., Stockholm, 2006; Royal Medal, Royal Soc., 2008; Achievement Award, Soc. for Biomolecular Sci., 2009; Award for Leading Individual Contribn to Life Scis in Scot., Scottish Enterprise Life Scis, 2009; Millennium Medal, MRC, 2013; Albert Einstein World Award of Sci., World Cultural Council, 2014. Hon. Mem., Dundee Rotary Club, 2006. Man. Editor, Biochimica et Biophysica Acta, 1981–92. *Publications:* Control of Enzyme Activity, 1976, 2nd edn 1983; (ed series) Molecular Aspects of Cellular Regulation: vol. 1, 1980; vol. 2, 1982; vol. 3, 1984; vol. 4, 1985; vol. 5, 1988; vol. 6, 1991; over 500 original papers and revs in scientific jls. *Recreations:* chess, bridge, golf, natural history. *Address:* MRC Protein Phosphorylation and Ubiquitylation Unit, The Sir James Black Centre, University of Dundee, , Dow Street, Dundee DD1 5EH; Inverbay Bramblings, Waterside, Invergowrie, Dundee DD2 5DQ. *T:* (01382) 562328. *Clubs:* Downfield Golf; Isle of Harris Golf; Dundee Bridge; Royal & Ancient Golf (St Andrews).

COHEN, Robert; cellist, conductor and teacher; *b* London, 15 June 1959; *s* of late Raymond Cohen, violinist and of Anthya Cohen (*née* Rael); *m* 1987, Rachel Smith; four *s*. *Educ:* Purcell Sch.; Guildhall Sch. of Music; cello studies with William Pleeth, André Navarra, Jacqueline du Pré and Mstislav Rostropovich. Started playing cello, aged 5; début at RFH (Boccherini Concerto), aged 12; London recital début, Wigmore Hall, aged 17; ESU scholarship to Tanglewood Fest., USA, 1978; recording début, 1979; concerts with major orchestras in USA, Europe and worldwide, 1979–; cellist, Fine Arts Quartet, 2012–. Conductor: various chamber orchestras, 1990–; symphony orchestras, 1997–. Dir, Charleston Manor Fest., E Sussex, 1989–. Prof., Royal Acad. of Music, 1998–; Prof. of Advanced Cello Studies, Conservatorio della Svizzera Italiana di Lugano, 2000–11; Fellow, Purcell Sch. for Young Musicians, 1992–. Curator, HiBrow.TV, 2009–; radio series, On That Note, USA, 2014. Launched Cello Clinic and Cohen Pod Talks, 2009–; lectr, Royal Acad. of Music, 2014. Has made numerous recordings; internat. radio broadcasts and TV appearances. Hon. RAM 2009. Winner: Suggia Prize, Musicians Benevolent Fund, UK, 1970–75 (annually); Young Concert Artists Internat. Comp., NY, 1978; Piatigorsky Prize, Tanglewood Fest., 1978; UNESCO Internat. Comp., Czechoslovakia, 1981; Robert Helpmann Award, Live Performance Australia, 2004. *Recreations:* photography, alternative medicine, healing, philosophy. *E:* office@robertcohen.info. *W:* www.robertcohen.info, www.fineartsquartet.com.

COHEN, Sir Ronald (Mourad), Kt 2001; Chairman, The Portland Trust, since 2005; Founder, 1972, Chairman, 1972–2005, Apax Partners Worldwide LLP (formerly Apax Partners Holdings Ltd); *b* 1 Aug. 1945; *s* of late Michel Mourad Cohen and of Sonia Sophie Cohen (*née* Douek); *m* 1st, 1972, Carol Marylene Belmont (marr. diss. 1975); 2nd, 1983, Claire Whitmore Enders (marr. diss. 1986); 3rd, 1987, Sharon Ruth Harel; one *s* one *d*. *Educ:* Orange Hill GS; Exeter Coll., Oxford (Exhibnr, MA; Hon. Fellow, 2000; Pres., Oxford Union Soc.); Harvard Business Sch. (MBA; Henry Fellowship). Consultant, McKinsey & Co. (UK and Italy), 1969–71; Chargé de mission, Institut de Développement Industriel France, 1971–72. Founder Director: British Venture Capital Assoc., 1983 (Chm., 1985–86); Eur. Venture Capital Assoc., 1985; City Gp for Smaller Cos, 1992; a Founder and Vice-Chm., Eur. Assoc. Securities Dealers Automated Quotation, 1995–2001; Dir, NASDAQ Europe, 2001–03. Chairman: Social Investment Task Force, 2000–10; Bridges Ventures Ltd, 2002–; Commn on Unclaimed Assets, 2005–10; Portland Capital LLP, 2006–10; Big Society Capital Ltd, 2012–13; Social Impact Investment Task Force, 2013–; Founder and Dir, Social Finance Ltd, 2009–11; Dir, Social Finance US, 2011–; Member: Wkg Party on Smaller Cos, Stock Exchange, 1993; UK Competitiveness Cttee, DTI, 1998–2000. Member: Exec. Cttee, Centre for Econ. Policy Res., 1996–99; Finance Cttee, Inst. for Social and Econ. Policy in ME, Kennedy Sch., Harvard Univ., 1997–98; Adv. Bd, Fulbright Commn, 1997–99; Franco-British Council, 1997–99; Dean's Adv. Bd, Harvard Business Sch., 2005; Bd of Overseers, Harvard Univ., 2007–; Investment Cttee, Oxford Univ., 2007–; Trustee Mem., Exec. Cttee, IISS, 2005–10. Mem., Internat. Council, Tate Gall., 2004–; Trustee, BM, 2005–12. Mem., Adv. Bd, InterAction, 1986–; Hon. Pres., Community Develt Finance Assoc., 2005–07. Contested (L): Kensington N, 1974; London W, EP elecn, 1979. Vice-Chm., Ben-Gurion Univ. Innovation Award for innovation in social finance, Rockefeller Foundn, 2012. *Publications:* The Second Bounce of the Ball: turning risk into opportunity, 2007. *Recreations:* music, art, theatre, cinema, tennis. *Address:* The Portland Trust, 42 Portland Place, W1B 1NB. *T:* (020) 7182 7800, *Fax:* (020) 7182 7897. *Clubs:* Athenæum, Royal Automobile, Queen's.

COHEN, Prof. Simon B.; *see* Baron-Cohen, S.

COHEN, Prof. Stanley; Distinguished Professor, Department of Biochemistry, Vanderbilt University School of Medicine, 1986–2000, now Emeritus; *b* 17 Nov. 1922; *s* of Louis Cohen and Fruma Feitel; *m* 1st, 1951, Olivia Larson; three *s*; 2nd, 1981, Jan Elizabeth Jordan. *Educ:* Brooklyn Coll., NY; Oberlin Coll., Ohio; Univ. of Michigan (BA, PhD). Teaching Fellow, Dept of Biochem., Univ. of Michigan, 1946–48; Instructor, Depts of Biochem. and Pediatrics, Univ. of Colorado Sch. of Medicine, 1948–52; Fellow, Amer. Cancer Soc., Dept of Radiology, Washington Univ., St Louis, 1952–53; Associate Prof., Dept of Zoology, Washington Univ., 1953–59; Vanderbilt University School of Medicine, Nashville: Asst Prof. of Biochem., 1959–62; Associate Prof., 1962; Prof. 1967–86. Mem., Editl Bds of learned jls. Mem., Nat. Acad. of Science, and other sci. bodies. Hon. DSc Chicago, 1985. Nobel Prize for Physiology or Medicine, 1986 (jtly); other prizes and awards. *Publications:* papers in learned jls on biochemistry, cell biology, human developmental biology, embryology. *Address:* 106 Mint Spring Circle, Brentwood, TN 37027, USA. *E:* stancohen@earthlink.net.

COHEN, Sir Stephen Harry W.; *see* Waley-Cohen.

COHEN, Dr Stephen Michael, FRS 2008; Chief Executive Officer and Temasek Senior Investigator, Temasek Life Sciences Laboratory, Singapore, since 2007; Adjunct Professor, Department of Biological Sciences, National University of Singapore, since 2007. *Educ:* Univ. of Toronto; Princeton Univ. (PhD 1983). Postdoctoral Fellow: MIT; Max Planck Inst. for Develtl Biol., Germany; Asst Investigator, Howard Hughes Med. Inst. and Asst Prof., Baylor Coll. of Medicine, Houston, 1990–93; Gp Leader, 1993–2007, Co-ordinator, Develtl Biol. Unit, 1996–2007, EMBL, Germany. *Publications:* articles in jls. *Address:* Temasek Life Sciences Laboratory Ltd, 1 Research Link, National University of Singapore, Singapore 117604.

COHEN, Prof. Sydney, CBE 1978; FRS 1978; Professor of Chemical Pathology, Guy's Hospital Medical School, 1965–86, now Emeritus Professor, University of London; *b* Johannesburg, SA, 18 Sept. 1921; *s* of Morris and Pauline Cohen; *m* 1st, 1950, June Bernice Adler (*d* 1999); one *s* one *d*; 2nd, 1999, Deirdre Maureen Ann Boyd. *Educ:* King Edward VII Sch., Johannesburg; Witwatersrand and London Univs. MD, PhD. EMS, UK, 1944–45. Lectr, Dept of Physiology, Witwatersrand Univ., 1947–53; Scientific Staff, Nat. Inst. for Med. Research, London, 1954–60; Reader, Dept of Immunology, St Mary's Hosp. Med. Sch., 1960–65. Mem., MRC, 1974–76; Chm., Tropical Med. Research Bd, MRC, 1974–76; Chm., WHO Scientific Gp on Immunity to Malaria, 1976–81; Mem., WHO expert adv. panel on malaria, 1977–89; Mem. Council, Royal Soc., 1981–83; Royal Soc. Assessor, MRC, 1982–84. Nuffield Dominion Fellow in Medicine, 1954; Founder Fellow, RCPath, 1964. Hon. DSc Witwatersrand, 1987. *Publications:* papers on immunology and parasitic diseases in sci. jls. *Recreations:* golf, gardening, forestry. *Address:* 8 Gibson Place, St Andrews, Fife KY16 9JE. *Club:* Royal and Ancient (St Andrews).

COHEN-TANNOUDJI, Prof. Claude, PhD; Grand Officier, Légion d'Honneur; Commandeur, Ordre National du Mérite; Professor of Atomic and Molecular Physics, Collège de France, Paris, 1973–2004; *b* 1 April 1933; *s* of Abraham Cohen-Tannoudji and Sarah Sebbah; *m* 1958, Jacqueline Veyrat; one *s* one *d* (and one *s* decd). *Educ:* Ecole Normale Supérieure, Paris; Univ. of Paris (PhD Physics 1962). Researcher, CNRS, 1960–64; Associate Prof., 1964–67, Prof., 1967–73, Univ. of Paris. Member: Académie des Sciences, Paris, 1981; NAS, USA, 1994. (Jtly) Nobel Prize for Physics, 1997. *Publications:* (jtly) Quantum Mechanics, Vols I and II, 1977; Atoms in Electromagnetic Fields, 1994; with J. Dupont-Roc and G. Grynberg: Photons and Atoms: introduction to Q.E.D., 1989; Atom-photon Interactions, 1992; Advances in Atomic Physics: an overview, 2011. *Recreation:* music. *Address:* Laboratoire Kastler-Brossel, Département de Physique de l'ENS, 24 rue Lhomond, 75231 Paris Cedex 05, France. *T:* (1) 47077783.

COHN-SHERBOK, Rabbi Prof. Dan; Professor of Judaism, University of Wales, Lampeter, 1997–2009, Professor Emeritus, 2010; *b* 1 Feb. 1945; *s* of Dr Bernard Sherbok and Ruth Sherbok (*née* Goldstein), Denver, Colo; *m* 1976, Lavinia Charlotte Heath. *Educ:* Williams Coll., Mass (BA); Hebrew Union Coll., Ohio (BHL, MAHL); Wolfson Coll., Cambridge (MLitt, PhD). Served as rabbi in US, Australia, SA and England, 1970–75; Chaplain, Colorado Hse of Representatives, 1971; Lectr in Jewish Theology, Univ. of Kent, 1975–97; Dir, Centre for Study of Religion and Society, Univ. of Kent, 1982–90; Dir, Centre for Study of World's Religions, Univ. of Wales, Lampeter, 2003–08. Mem., AHRC Peer Review Coll., 2007–. Visiting Professor: Univ. of Essex, 1993–94; of Inter-Faith Dialogue, Univ. of Middx, 1995–; of Judaism, Univ. of Wales at Lampeter, 1995–97; Univ. of St Andrews, 1995; Univ. of Wales, Bangor, 1998; Vilnius Univ., 2000; Univ. of Durham, 2002; Trinity Univ. Coll. (formerly Trinity Coll.), Carmarthen, 2007–10, Univ. of Wales Trinity St David, 2010–; St Mary's Univ. (formerly UC), Twickenham, 2007–; Charles Univ., Prague, 2008; York St John Univ., 2011–; Vis. Schol., Sarum Coll., 2005–; Visiting Research Fellow: Heythrop Coll., Univ. of London, 2011–; Centre of Religions for Peace and Reconciliation, Univ. of Winchester, 2013–; Hon. Prof., Aberystwyth Univ., 2010–. Hon. DD Hebrew Union Coll., 1996. Hon. Col ADC, New Mexico, 1957. *Publications:* On Earth as it is in Heaven, 1987; (ed) Exploring Reality, 1987; The Jewish Heritage, 1988; Holocaust Theology, 1989; Jewish Petitionary Prayer, 1989; God and the Holocaust, 1989; Rabbinic Perspectives on the New Testament, 1990; (ed) The Canterbury Papers, 1990; (ed) The Salman Rushdie Controversy, 1990; (ed) Essays on Religion and Society, 1990; (ed) Using the Bible Today, 1991; (ed) A Traditional Quest, 1991; (ed) The Sayings of Moses, 1991; (ed) Tradition and Unity, 1991; (ed) Problems in Contemporary Jewish Philosophy, 1991; A Dictionary of Judaism and Christianity, 1991; Issues in Contemporary Judaism, 1991; (ed) Islam in a World of Diverse Faiths, 1991; The Blackwell Dictionary of Judaica, 1992; Israel: the history of an idea, 1992; Exodus, 1992; (ed) Many Mansions, 1992; (ed) World Religions and Human Liberation, 1992; (ed) Religion in Public Life, 1992; (ed) Torah and Revelation, 1992; Atlas of Jewish History, 1993; The Jewish Faith, 1993; Not a Job for a Nice Jewish Boy, 1993; Judaism and Other Faiths, 1994; The Future of Judaism, 1994; Jewish and Christian Mysticism, 1994; The American Jew, 1994; (ed) Glimpses of God, 1994; (jtly) A Short History of Judaism, 1994; Jewish Mysticism, 1995; (jtly) A Popular Dictionary of Judaism, 1995; (ed) Beyond Death: theological and philosophical reflections on life after death, 1995; (ed) Divine Interventions and Miracles, 1996; Medieval Jewish Philosophy, 1996; The Hebrew Bible, 1996; Modern Judaism, 1996; Biblical Hebrew for Beginners, 1996; (ed) The Liberation Debate, 1996; (jtly) A Short Reader in Judaism, 1996; Fifty Key Jewish Thinkers, 1997; The Jewish Messiah, 1997; After Noah, 1997; (ed) Theodicy, 1997; The Crucified Jew, 1997; Concise Encyclopedia of Judaism, 1998; Understanding the Holocaust, 1999; (ed) The Future of Jewish Christian Dialogue, 1999; (ed) The Future of Religion, 1999; Judaism, 1999; Jews, Christians and Religious Pluralism, 1999; Messianic Judaism, 2000; Interfaith Theology, 2001; (jtly) The Palestine-Israeli Conflict, 2001; (ed) Voices of Messianic Judaism, 2001; (ed) Religious Diversity in the Graeco-Roman World, 2001; Anti-Semitism, 2002; Holocaust Theology: a reader, 2002; Judaism: history, belief and practice, 2003; What's a Nice Jewish Boy Like You Doing in a Place Like This?, 2003; (ed) A Life of Courage: Sherwin Wine and Humanistic Judaism, 2003; The Vision of Judaism: wrestling with God, 2004; (jtly) An Encyclopedia of Judaism and Christianity, 2004; Dictionary of Jewish Biography, 2005; (jtly) Pursuing the Dream: a Jewish-Christian conversation, 2005; The Paradox of Antisemitism, 2006; The Politics of Apocalypse, 2006; Kabbalah and Jewish Mysticism, 2006; What Do You Do When Your Parents Live Forever?, 2007; Dictionary of Kabbalah and Kabbalists, 2009; Judaism Today, 2010; Introduction to Zionism and Israel, 2011; The Palestinian State: solving the unsolvable, 2012; The Illustrated Guide to Judaism, 2013; (jtly) Love, Sex and Marriage: insights from Judaism, Christianity and Islam, 2013; The Athenæum: sketches, 2014; (jtly) Why Can't They Get Along?, 2014; (jtly) Sensible Religion, 2014; (jtly) Debating Palestine and Israel, 2014; Illustrated History of the Jewish Faith, 2015; numerous articles to learned jls. *Recreations:* keeping cats, walking, drawing cartoons. *Address:* The Old Coach House, Bwlchllan, Wales SA48 8QJ. *E:* cohnsherbok@googlemail.com. *Clubs:* Athenæum, Lansdowne; Aberaeron Yacht.

COHRS, (William) Michael; Member of Court, Bank of England, since 2011; *b* Midland, Mich; *s* of William and Lois Cohrs; *m* 1984, Arlene; two *s*. *Educ:* Harvard Univ. (BA Econ; MBA). Deutsche Bank, 1995–2010: Hd, Global Banking, 2004–10; Mem., Mgt Bd, 2009–10. Non-exec. Dir, Surfcast, 2010–; Advr, EQT, 2012–. *Recreations:* football, fishing.

COID, Dr Donald Routledge; consultant and specialist in medical administration and public health medicine, since 1985; Director, Donald Coid Consultants Pty Ltd, since 2012; *b* 1 June 1953; *s* of Charles Routledge Coid and late Marjory Macdonald Coid (*née* Keay); *m* 1985, Susan Kathleen Ramus (*née* Crocker); three *d*. *Educ:* Bromley Grammar Sch. for Boys; Harrow County Sch. for Boys; Univ. of Nottingham (BMedSci; BM, BS); LSHTM (MSc 1981). MRCP 1979; MFCM 1985, MFPHM 1989, FFPH (FFPHM 1996); FRACMA 1985; FAFPHM 1991; FRCPE 1998; FRSPH (FRIPHH 1998). Hse Physician, Nottingham City Hosp., 1976; Hse Surgeon, Nottingham Gen. Hosp., 1977; Sen. Hse Officer, Brook Gen. Hosp., London, 1977–78; Res. Asst, Middlesex Hosp. Med. Sch., 1979; Field Med. Officer, Royal Flying Doctor Service, Australia, Eastern Goldfields Sect., 1979–80; MO, Community Health Services, WA, 1981–82; Regl Dir of Public Health, Eastern Goldfields, WA, 1982–85; Med. Supt, Kalgoorlie Reg. Hosp., WA, 1984–85; Fife Health Board: Cons. in Public Health, 1985–92; Asst Gen. Manager, 1992–93; Chief Admin. MO, Dir of Public Health and Exec. Dir, Tayside Health Bd, 1994–98; Consultant in Health Services Res., Ninewells Hosp. and Med. Sch., Dundee, 1998–2000; Public Health Consultant, Grampian Health Bd, 2000–01; Dir of Med. Services, Armadale Health Service, WA, 2001–06; Exec. Dir of Med. Services, Wide Bay Health Service (formerly Wide Bay Health Service Dist), Qld, 2006–09; Public Health Physician, Population Health Services, Qld, 2009–10; Med. Advr, Travel Doctor–TMVC, Perth, WA, 2010; Med. Dir, Clinics and Assistance, Internat. SOS, Beijing, 2010–11; Regl Med. Dir, Mainland China, Taiwan and Remote Territories, International SOS, 2011–12. Consultant to: Govt of Qatar, 1999; WHO, 2000; overseas projects, Corp. of Victoria, 2003. Hon. Sen. Lectr, Dundee Univ., 1994–2001. *Publications:* on public health and related topics in learned jls. *Recreations:* golf, cricket, piano, singing, cycling, swimming. *Address:* 131 Churchill Avenue, Subiaco, WA 6008, Australia. *T:* (61) 893822496. *Clubs:* Royal & Ancient Golf, New Golf (St Andrews); Cottesloe Golf (WA).

COJOCARU, Alina; ballet dancer; Principal, English National Ballet, since 2013; *b* Bucharest, 27 May 1981; *d* of Gheorge Cojocaru and Nina Cojocaru. *Educ:* Ukrainian State Ballet Sch.; Royal Ballet Sch. With Kiev Ballet, 1998; joined Royal Ballet, 1999, Principal, 2001–13. Guest dancer with Mariinsky Ballet, American Ballet Th., Royal Danish Ballet, Hungarian Nat. Ballet, Paris Opera Ballet, Romanian Nat. Ballet, Bolshoi Ballet, Hamburg Ballet, Nat. Ballet of Cuba, Teatro Colon, South African Ballet, Kremlin Ballet, Sarasota Ballet, Zagreb Ballet, Australian Ballet. Performances include main rôles in The Nutcracker, Romeo and Juliet, Giselle, Don Quixote, Swan Lake, Sleeping Beauty, Cinderella, Onegin, Manon, Coppelia, Mayerling and Le Corsaire, Lady of the Camellias, A Month in the Country, A Midsummer Night's Dream, Etudes, La Bayadère, Jewels, Symphonic Variations, La Sylphide, In the Night, Las Hermanas, Scènes de Ballet, Gong, Symphony in C, Daphnis and Chloë, No Man's Land, La Fille mal gardée, Second Breath, The Lesson, Duo Concertant, The Leaves are Fading, Other Dances, Voices of Spring, Beyond Bach, Tombeaux, Ondine, Vertiginous Thrill Of Exactitude, Raymond act 3, Dances at a Gathering, Radio and Juliet. Trustee, Hospices of Hope, 2008–. Prix de Lausanne, 1997; Best Female Dancer, Critics' Circle Dance Award, 2002; Ballerina of the Decade, Moscow, 2010; Dancer of the Year, German Dance Critics Award, 2012; Best Female Dancer, Benois de la Danse, 2004, 2013; Cavalier of Romania, 2002. *Address:* c/o English National Ballet, Markova House, 39 Jay Mews, SW7 2ES.

COKAYNE, family name of **Baron Cullen of Ashbourne**.

COKE, family name of **Earl of Leicester**.

COKE, Viscount; Edward Horatio Coke; *b* 11 June 2003; *s* and *heir* of Earl of Leicester, *q*.

COKER, Jane Elizabeth; a Judge of the Upper Tribunal, Immigration and Asylum Chamber, since 2011; *b* Saltburn, 11 July 1954; *d* of Frank Percival Charles Coker and Mary Coker; one *s* two *d*. *Educ:* Cheadle Hulme Sch.; Westfield Coll., Univ. of London (BSc Biol Scis). Admitted as solicitor, 1980; Founder Partner, Coker Vis Solicitors, 1982–2002; Immigration Judge (formerly Immigration Adjudicator), 2002–11 (pt-time, 2002–07). *Address:* Immigration and Asylum Chamber, Field House, 15–25 Breams Buildings, EC4A 1DZ. *E:* UpperTribunalJudge.Coker@eJudiciary.net.

COKER, Naaz; Chair, St George's Healthcare NHS Trust, 2003–11; independent management consultant (part-time), since 2002; *b* 14 Oct. 1948; *d* of Rahemtula and Shirin Suleman; *m* 1973, Raymond Coker. *Educ:* Portsmouth Univ. (BSc Pharm.); Chelsea Coll., London Univ. (MSc); Open Univ. (MBA). Chief Pharmacist, Royal Marsden Hosp., Sutton, 1973–76; Principal Pharmacist, Bromley & Beckenham Hosps, 1976–79; Dist Pharmaceutical Officer, Lewisham Health Dist, 1979–87; Guy's and Lewisham NHS Trust: Dir, Pharmacy and Med. Supplies, 1988–90; Clinical Dir, Clinical Support Services, 1990–92; Actg Unit Gen. Manager, 1992; King's Fund: Fellow, Leadership Develt, 1992–2002; Dir, Race and

Diversity, 1998–2002. Hon. Clinical Lectr, Dept of Pharmacy, Univ. of Brighton, 1992–96. Chair: British Refugee Council, 1998–2005; Shelter, 2007–08; Mem., Race Equality Adv. Panel, Home Office, 2003–06. Non-exec. Dir, Nat. Audit Office, 2012–. Chm., Aga Khan Health Bd UK (for Ismaili Muslim community), 1990–93; Mem., Ismaili Council for EU, 1999–2005. Mem. Council, St George's, Univ. of London, 2006–11. Chm., First Steps Nursery Sch., Streatham and London, 1985–87; Mem., Mgt Cttee, St Cecilia's Leonard Cheshire Foundn Home, Bromley, 1996–2000. Non-exec. Dir, Ethical Property Co., 2009–13. Trustee: Media Trust, 2001–05; Ashoka Trust, 2002–03; RSA, 2004–11 (Vice Chm., 2009–10); Clore Social Leadership Prog., 2010–; RCOG, 2013–. Hon. DSc Leeds Metropolitan, 2005; DUniv UCE, 2007. Asian Woman of Year: Asia Mktg Gp, 2000; Asian Guild, 2003; Asian Women of Achievement Award, 2004; Lifetime Achievement Award, Lloyds TSB/KPMG Jewel Awards, 2009. *Publications:* (ed) Racism in Medicine, 2001; interviews and book reviews; numerous articles, chapters and reports in med., pharmaceutical and mgt jls. *Recreations:* reading, gardening, walking, cooking.

COKER, Paul; Managing Director, Ranks Hovis McDougall, 1992–93; *b* 27 July 1938; *s* of Leslie and Mabel Coker; *m* 1966, Delphine Rostron Baden; twin *s* one *d*. *Educ:* Merchant Taylors' Sch. Joined Ranks Hovis McDougall (Cerebos Group), 1964: Man. Dir, General Products, 1982–87; Planning Dir, 1987–89; Dep. Man. Dir, 1989–91; Finance Dir, 1991–92. *Recreations:* golf, cricket, gardening, theatre. *Address:* Courtlands, Nightingales Lane, Chalfont St Giles, Bucks HP8 4SL. *T:* (01494) 762040.

COKER, William John; QC 1994; *b* 19 July 1950; *s* of Edgar and Peggy Coker; *m* 1977, Ruth Elaine Pull; one *s* one *d*. *Educ:* Bedford Sch.; Manchester Univ. (LLB). Called to the Bar, Gray's Inn, 1973. *Recreations:* golf, fishing.

COLBORN, (Leslie) Nigel; freelance writer and journalist, since 1986; *b* Nottingham, 20 Feb. 1944; *s* of late Leslie Colborn and Anne Colborn; *m* 1972, Rosamund Hewlett; two *s* two *d*. *Educ:* King's Sch., Ely; Cornell Univ. (BS). Dir, Colborn Gp, 1972–76; farmer, 1976–86. Presenter, Gardeners' World, BBC TV, 1988–91; Panellist, Gardeners' Question Time, BBC Radio, 1996–2003. Gardening Corresp., Daily Mail, 2009–. Royal Horticultural Society: Trustee, 2002–10; Vice-Chm., Council, 2006–09 (Mem., 1998–). FRSA. Lifetime Achievement Award, Garden Media Guild, 2012; VMH 2013. *Publications:* (with Ursula Buchan) The Classic Horticulturist, 1987; This Gardening Business, 1988; Exposed Gardens, 1989; Leisurely Gardening, 1989; Family Piles, 1990; The Container Garden, 1990; The Good Old Fashioned Gardener, 1993; Annuals and Bedding Plants, 1994; A Flower for Every Day, 1996; Great Plants for Small Gardens, 1997; Nigel Colborn's Garden Magic, 1998; The Garden Floor, 2000; Wisley: inspiration for all seasons, 2006; Plant Solutions, 2006; A Garden Under Glass, 2007; *novels:* The Kirkland Acres, 1994; The Congregation, 1996; Weather of the Heart, 1997. *Recreations:* nature, theatre, photography, ornithology, travel, music. *Address:* Wakefields, 14 Hall Road, Haconby, Bourne, Lincs PE10 0UY. *E:* ncolborn@btinternet.com. *Club:* Farmers.

COLCHESTER, Area Bishop of, since 2014; **Rt Rev. Roger Anthony Brett Morris;** *b* Hereford, 18 July 1968; *s* of Anthony Edward Morris and Eirwen Morris; *m* 1991, Sally Jane; two *d*. *Educ:* Imperial Coll. London (BSc; ARCS 1989); Trinity Coll., Cambridge (BA 1992; MA); Ridley Hall Theol Coll. Ordained deacon, 1993, priest, 1994; Asst Curate, Northleach Gp of Parishes, 1993–96; Rector, Coln River Gp of Parishes incl. Sevenhampton, 1996–2003; Dir of Parish Develt and Evangelism, Dio. of Coventry, 2003–08; Archdeacon of Worcester, 2008–14. *Recreations:* supporting Bristol Rovers, music, films, Greenbelt Festival, walking the dogs. *Address:* The Bishop's Office, 1 Fitzwalter Road, Lexden, Colchester CO3 3SS. *E:* roger.morris@me.com.

COLCHESTER, Archdeacon of; *see* Cooper, Ven. A. J.

COLCLOUGH, Prof. Christopher Louis, PhD; Commonwealth Professor of Education and Development, and Director, Centre for Education and Development, University of Cambridge, 2008–13, Professor Emeritus, 2014 (Professor of the Economics of Education and Director, Centre for Commonwealth Education, 2005–08); Fellow, Corpus Christi College, Cambridge, 2006–13, now Life Fellow; *b* 10 July 1946; *s* of Frederick and Margaret Colclough; *m* 1992, Sarah Elizabeth Butler; one *s*. *Educ:* Univ. of Bristol (BA Philosophy and Econs 1967); PhD Econs Cambridge 1971. Econ. Advr, Min. of Finance and Develt Planning, Botswana Govt, 1971–75; Fellow, 1975–94, Professorial Fellow, 1994–2004, Inst. of Develt Studies, Univ. of Sussex (Emeritus Fellow, 2014); Dir, Educn for All Global Monitoring Report, UNESCO, Paris, 2002–04. Advisor: to UK Parly Select Cttee on Overseas Aid and Develt, 1980–81; to govts of PNG and Botswana on wages and incomes policy, 1981–83; to UNICEF on educn financing, 1989–90; to S African Govt on educn policy, 1994–2000; Chief, UNDP Tech. Co-operation Mission to Zambia, 1986. Pres., British Assoc. for Internat. and Comparative Educn, 2004–05. Man. Ed., Jl of Develt Studies, 1989–2002. FAcSS (AcSS 2005). FRSA 2004. Dr *hc* Katholieke Univ. Leuven, 2010. *Publications:* (jtly) The Political Economy of Botswana: a study of growth and distribution, 1980; (ed jtly) States or Markets, 1991; (jtly) Educating All the Children: strategies for primary schooling in the South, 1993; (ed) Public Sector Pay and Adjustment, 1997; (ed) Marketizing Education and Health in Developing Countries, 1997; (jtly) Achieving Schooling for All in Africa: costs, commitment and gender, 2003; (ed) Education Outcomes and Poverty: a reassessment, 2012. *Recreations:* playing the piano and 'cello, opera, walking in the Pennines. *Address:* Little Hallands, Norton, Seaford, E Sussex BN25 2UN. *T:* (01323) 896101. *E:* cc413@cam.ac.uk.

COLCLOUGH, Rt Rev. Michael John; an Honorary Assistant Bishop, Diocese of London and Diocese in Europe, since 2013; *b* 29 Dec. 1944; *s* of Joseph and Beryl Colclough; *m* 1983, Cynthia Flora Mary De Sousa; two *s*. *Educ:* Leeds Univ. (BA Hons English and Religious Studies); Cuddesdon Coll., Oxford. Ordained deacon, 1971, priest, 1972; Curate: St Werburgh, Burslem, 1971–75; St Mary, S Ruislip, 1975–79; Vicar, St Anselm, Hayes, 1979–86; Area Dean of Hillingdon, 1985–92; Team Rector, Uxbridge, 1986–92; Archdeacon of Northolt, 1992–94; personal asst to Bp of London (Archdeacon at London House), 1994–96; Priest-in-Charge: St Vedast-alias-Foster, 1994–96; St Magnus the Martyr, London Bridge, 1995–96; Dep. Priest in Ordinary to the Queen, 1995–96; Area Bishop of Kensington, 1996–2008; a Residentiary Canon, St Paul's Cathedral, 2008–13. Chaplain to Mercers' Co., 2010–. Chm. Mission, Evangelism and Renewal in England Cttee, C of E, 1999–2003. Patron: Micro Loan Foundn, 1999–2008; London Care Connections, 2003–08; Shooting Star Trust, 2005–08; W London Action for Children, 2005–08; Hoffman Foundn for Autism, 2005–. *Recreations:* travel, walking in the English countryside, reading, people. *Address:* 12 Grosvenor Court, Sloane Street, SW1X 9PF. *T:* (020) 3612 3135. *E:* michaeljcolclough@gmail.com.

COLDSTREAM, John Richard Francis; writer; Literary Editor, The Daily Telegraph, 1991–99; *b* 19 Dec. 1947; *s* of Gerald Coldstream and Marian Gatehouse; *m* 1977, Susan Elizabeth Pealing. *Educ:* Bradfield Coll.; Univ. of Nice; Univ. of Sussex. Evening Echo, Hemel Hempstead, 1971–74; joined Daily Telegraph, Peterborough column, 1974; Dep. Literary Editor, Daily Telegraph, 1984–91 and Sunday Telegraph, 1989–91. Member: Arts Council Literature Adv. Panel, 1992–97; Man Booker (formerly Booker) Prize Adv. Cttee, 1996–2004. *Publications:* (ed) The Daily Telegraph Book of Contemporary Short Stories, 1995; Dirk Bogarde: the authorised biography, 2004; (ed) Ever, Dirk: the Bogarde letters, 2008; Victim, 2011; Restored, Refreshed, Renewed, 2015. *Recreation:* theatre. *E:* johncoldstream@btinternet.com. *Club:* Garrick.

COLE, family name of **Earl of Enniskillen**.

COLE, Allan Gordon Halliwell, FRCA; Consultant Anaesthetist, University Hospitals of Leicester NHS Trust (formerly Glenfield Hospital and Leicester Royal Infirmary), since 1985; *b* 20 Feb. 1949; *s* of late Robert Randle Cole and Anne Dorothy Cole; *m* 1st, 1974, Stacey Elizabeth Gregg (marr. diss.); 2nd, 1979, Penelope Gaye Cole (marr. diss.); one *s* one *d*; 3rd, 2007, Jennifer, *widow* of Prof. David Marsden, FRS. *Educ:* Marlborough Coll.; St Bartholomew's Hosp. (MB BS 1973). MRCS, LRCP 1973; FRCA (FFARCS 1979). SHO, then Registrar in Anaesthesia, St Bartholomew's Hosp., 1976–80; Sen. Registrar in Anaesthesia, John Radcliffe Hosp., Oxford, 1980–85; Medical Director: Glenfield Hosp., Leicester, 1993–2000; University Hosps of Leicester NHS Trust, 2000–09; Sen. Clin. Advr, Nat. Clin. Assessment Service, 2010; Med. Dir, NHS Revalidation Support Team, 2010–11. Chm., British Assoc. of Med. Managers, 2003–05. *Publications:* papers in peer-reviewed jls of anaesthesia and med. mgt. *Recreations:* golf, singing (choir), gliding. *Address:* 42 Groby Lane, Newtown, Linford, Leics LE6 0HH. *T:* (01530) 244375. *E:* coleallan@doctors.org.uk.

COLE, Babette S.; author and illustrator of children's books; *b* Jersey, 10 Sept. 1950. *Educ:* convent, Jersey; Canterbury Coll. of Educn (BA 1st Cl. Hons Illustration and Audio Visual 1973). Worked for BBC Children's TV. Member: BSJA; SSA. Side Saddle Rider of the Year, 1998; Side Saddle Nat. Champion (Working Hunter), 2002, 2003. Consultant, Authors and Artists Bookshop Ltd, 2010–; Dir, InkySprat.com, 2013–. Fellow, Kent Inst. of Art and Design, 2003. DVD, Writing and Illustrating a Children's Picture Book, 2008. *Publications:* include: Hairy Book, 1984; Slimy Book, 1985; Smelly Book, 1987; Silly Book, 1989; Trouble with Grandad, 1989; Cupid, 1989; Three Cheers for Errol, 1992; Princess Smartypants, 1992; Mummy Laid an Egg (BRIT Award Best Illustrated Children's Bk of Year), 1993 (trans. 73 languages); Prince Cinders, 1993; Hurrah for Ethelyn, 1993; Tarzanna, 1993; Trouble with Mum, 1993; Trouble with Uncle, 1994; Dr Dog, 1994 (TV series); Trouble with Dad, 1995; Winni Allfours, 1995; Drop Dead, 1996; Trouble with Gran, 1997; Two of Everything, 1997; Bad Good Manners Book, 1997; King Change-a-lot, 1998; Hair in Funny Places, 1999; Bad Habits!, 1999; Animals Scare Me Stiff, 2000; Truelove, 2001; Lady Lupin's Book of Etiquette, 2002; Mummy Never Told Me, 2003; The Sprog Owner's Manual, 2004; Long Live Princess Smartypants, 2004; That's Why, 2006; A Dose of Dr Dog, 2007; Princess Smartypants Breaks the Rules, 2009; Fetlocks Hall: the unicorn princess, 2010; Fetlocks Hall: the ghostly blinkers, 2010; Fetlocks Hall: the curse of the pony vampires, 2011; Fetlocks Hall: the enchanted pony, 2011; The Wildest West Country Tale of James Rabbit and the Giggleberries, 2014; *illustrated*: Richard Hamilton, If I Were You, 2008. *Recreations:* breeding and showing show hunters, sailing. *Address:* c/o Lauren Pearson, Curtis Brown, Haymarket House, 28–29 Haymarket, SW1Y 4SP. *T:* (020) 7393 4400. *W:* www.babette-cole.co.uk.

COLE, Caroline Louise; *see* Flint, Rt Hon. C. L.

COLE, Gordon Stewart; QC 2006; *b* 25 March 1956; *s* of Dermott and Jean Cole; *m* 1989, Sarah, (Sally), Cooper; one *s* one *d*. *Educ:* John Moores Univ., Liverpool (BA Hons Law); Inns of Court Sch. of Law. Called to the Bar, Inner Temple, 1979; in practice as barrister, 1979–, specialising in criminal law. *Recreations:* fly fishing, tennis, golf, shooting, Liverpool FC, skiing, tractor driving. *Address:* c/o Exchange Chambers, Pearl Assurance House, Derby Square, Liverpool L2 9XX. *T:* (0151) 236 7747. *E:* coleqc@exchangechambers.co.uk; c/o Furnival Chambers, 30–32 Furnival Street, EC4A 1JQ.

COLE, Harry; Contributing Editor, The Spectator, since 2012; *b* Kent, 27 April 1986; *s* of Robert and Denise Cole. *Educ:* Tonbridge Sch.; Univ. of Edinburgh (MA 2009). News Ed., Guido Fawkes Blog, 2009–; Columnist: Daily Star, 2011–12; GQ and Sun on Sunday, 2012–. *Recreation:* gossip. *T:* 07826 855190. *E:* hcole@spectator.co.uk.

COLE, Prof. John Peter; Professor of Human and Regional Geography (formerly of Regional Geography), University of Nottingham, 1975–94, Emeritus since 1994; *b* Sydney, Australia, 9 Dec. 1928; *s* of Philip and Marjorie Cecelia Cole; *m* 1st, 1952, Isabel Jesús (*née* Urrunaga) (*d* 2007); two *s*; 2nd, 2008, Karen Jean (*née* De Bres). *Educ:* Bromley Grammar Sch.; Univ. of Nottingham (State Schol., BA, MA, PhD, DLitt); Collegio Borromeo, Pavia Univ., Italy (British Council Schol.). Demonstrator, Univ. of Nottingham, 1951–52; Nat. Service with RN, Jt Services Sch. for Linguists, Russian Language Interpreter, 1952–54 (Lt Comdr RNR, retired); Oficina Nacional de Planeamiento y Urbanismo, Lima, Peru, 1954–55; Lectr in Geography, Univ. of Reading, 1955–56; Lectr in Geography, Univ. of Nottingham, 1956–69. Reader, 1969–75; Vis. Lectr or Prof., Univs of Washington, Columbia, Mexico, Valparaíso, Nanjing, Beijing. *Publications:* Geography of World Affairs, 1959, 6th edn 1983; (with F. C. German) Geography of the USSR, 1961, 2nd edn 1970; Italy, 1964; Latin America, 1965, 2nd edn 1975; (with C. A. M. King) Quantitative Geography, 1968; (with N. J. Beynon) New Ways in Geography, 1968, 2nd edn 1982; Situations in Human Geography, 1975; The Development Gap, 1981; Geography of the Soviet Union, 1984; China 1950–2000 Performance and Prospects, 1985; The Poverty of Marxism in Contemporary Geographical Applications and Research, 1986; Development and Underdevelopment, 1987; (with T. Buck) Modern Soviet Economic Performance, 1987; (with F. J. Cole) The Geography of the European Community, 1993, 2nd edn 1997; Geography of the World's Major Regions, 1996; Global 2050: a basis for speculation, 1999; Geography at Nottingham 1922–1970: a record, 2000; contribs to learned jls, UK and overseas. *Recreations:* travel, languages, pen drawing and painting, gardening. *Address:* 10 Ranmore Close, Beeston, Nottingham NG9 3FR. *T:* (0115) 925 0409.

COLE, Justin Mark; His Honour Judge Cole; a Circuit Judge, since 2014. *Educ:* Univ. of Nottingham (LLB); Chester Coll. of Law (Solicitor's Finals). Admitted solicitor, 1990; called to the Bar, Inner Temple, 1992; a Dep. Dist Judge, Magistrates' Court, 2005–10; a Recorder, 2009–14. *Address:* Aylesbury Crown Court, County Hall, Market Square, Aylesbury, Bucks HP20 1XD.

COLE, Margaret Rose, (Mrs Graeme Cooke); General Counsel, PricewaterhouseCoopers LLP UK, since 2012 (Member, UK Executive Board, since 2012); *b* Preston, Lancs, 17 June 1961; *d* of late Herbert and Patricia Cole; *m* 1998, Graeme Cooke. *Educ:* Winckley Sq. Convent Sch., Preston; New Hall, Cambridge (BA 1982); Coll. of Law, Lancaster Gate. Admitted solicitor, 1985. Stephenson Harwood: articled clerk, 1983; Asst Solicitor, 1985–90; Partner, 1990–95; Partner, White & Case, 1995–2005; Dir, Enforcement, 2005–10, Man. Dir, Enforcement, Financial Crime and Markets, 2010–12, FSA. Mem., Inst. for Fiscal Studies, 2012. Hon. Dr of Laws Coll. of Law, 2012. *Publications:* (contrib.) A Practitioner's Guide to FSA Investigations and Enforcement, 2nd edn 2007. *Recreations:* horse riding, travel, opera. *Address:* PricewaterhouseCoopers LLP, 1 Embankment Place, WC2N 6RH.

COLE, Martina; author; *b* Aveley, Essex, 30 March 1959; *d* of Christopher and Ellen Whiteside; one *s* one *d*. Hon. DLitt Anglia Ruskin, 2008. *Publications:* Dangerous Lady, 1992 (adapted for TV, 1995); The Ladykiller, 1993; Goodnight Lady, 1994; The Jump, 1995 (adapted for TV, 1996); The Runaway, 1997 (adapted for TV, 2010); Two Women, 1999; Broken, 2000; Faceless, 2001; Maura's Game, 2002; The Know, 2003; The Graft, 2004; The Take, 2005 (adapted for TV, 2009); Close, 2006; Faces, 2007; The Business, 2008; Hard Girls, 2009; The Family, 2010; The Faithless, 2011. *Recreation:* voracious reader. *Address:* c/o Darley Anderson Literary, TV & Film Agency, Estelle House, 11 Eustace Road, SW6 1JB. *T:* 07917 335263. *E:* chris@littlefreddie.tv.

COLE, Prof. Peter Geoffrey; journalist; Professor of Journalism, University of Sheffield, 2000–10, now Emeritus; *b* 16 Dec. 1945; *s* of Arthur and Elizabeth Cole; *m* 1982, Jane Ellison; three *s* one *d*. *Educ:* Tonbridge Sch.; Queens' Coll., Cambridge. Reporter, Evening News, 1968–72; Diary Editor, Evening Standard, 1976–78; News Editor, Deputy Editor, The

Guardian, 1978–88; Editor, Sunday Correspondent, 1988–90; News Review Editor, The Sunday Times, 1990–93; Prof. of Journalism, Univ. of Central Lancs, 1993–2000. *Publications:* (with Peter Pringle) Can You Positively Identify This Man?, 1975; (with Tony Harcup) Newspaper Journalism, 2010. *Address:* Department of Journalism, University of Sheffield, 9 Mappin Street, Sheffield S1 4DT. *Clubs:* Garrick; Plymouth Argyle Supporters' (London Branch); Lancashire County Cricket.

COLE, His Honour Richard Raymond Buxton; DL; a Circuit Judge, 1984–2007; *b* 11 June 1937; *s* of late Raymond Buxton Cole, DSO, TD, DL, and Edith Mary Cole; *m* 1962, Sheila Joy Rumbold; one *s* one *d*. *Educ:* Dragon School; St Edward's, Oxford. Admitted as solicitor 1960; Partner in Cole & Cole Solicitors, Oxford, 1962–84; Recorder, 1976–84; Hon. Recorder, City of Coventry, 1999–2007. Mem., Parole Bd, 1981–83. President: Berks, Bucks and Oxon Law Soc., 1981–82; Council of HM Circuit Judges, 2001. Mem. Governing Body, Dragon Sch., 1975–92, Chm., 1986–92. Chm., Burford Parish Council, 1976–79, first Town Mayor, 1979. Master, Upholders' Co., 1992–93. Hon. Pres., Assoc. of Master Upholsterers, 1993–. DL Warwickshire, 2001. Chancellor's Medal, Univ. of Warwick, 2011. *Publications:* Bunny Cole: an Oxford man, 2010. *Recreations:* sport, gardening. *Club:* Frewen (Oxford).

COLE, Sir (Robert) William, Kt 1981; Director, Legal and General, Australia, 1987–91; *b* 16 Sept. 1926; *s* of James Henry and Rita Sarah Cole; *m* 1956, Margaret Noleen Martin; one *s* one *d*. *Educ:* Univ. of Melbourne (BCom). Joined Australian Public Service, 1952; Res. Officer, Treasury, 1952–57; Technical Asst, IMF, Washington, 1957–59; various positions, Treasury, 1959–70; Dir, Bureau of Transport Econs, Dept of Shipping and Transport, 1970–72; First Asst Sec., Gen. Financial and Economic Policy Div., Treasury, 1972–76; Australian Statistician, 1976; Sec., Dept of Finance, 1977–78; Chm., Public Service Bd, 1978–83; Sec., Defence Dept, 1983–86. Hon. Treas., Winston Churchill Meml Trust. *Recreations:* reading, fishing, wine. *Address:* 120/7 Dean Street, Claremont, WA 6010, Australia.

COLE, Stephanie, (Mrs Peter Birrel), OBE 2005; actress; *b* 5 Oct. 1941; *d* of June Sheldon; *m* 1st, 1973, Henry Marshall (marr. diss.); one *d*; 2nd, 1998, Peter Birrel. *Educ:* Clifton High Sch., Bristol; Bristol Old Vic Sch. Work in repertory theatre, and with Old Vic, etc; *television:* Soldiering On (Alan Bennett Talking Heads monologue), 1988; The Lady Vanishes (TV film), 2013; *series:* Tenko, 1980–84; Waiting for God, 1989–94; Keeping Mum, 1997–99; Life As We Know It, 2001; Doc Martin, 2004–09; Coronation Street, 2011–13 (Best Comedy Actress, British Soap Awards, 2012); Still Open All Hours, 2014; Man Down, 2014–15; *theatre* includes: A Passionate Woman, Comedy, 1995; Quartet, Albery, 1999; So Long Life, Th. Royal, Bath, 2001; The Shell Seekers, tour, 2003–04; Blithe Spirit, Savoy, 2005; The Rivals, Th. Royal, Bath, 2005; Born in the Gardens, Th. Royal, Bath, 2008; Separate Tables, 2009, Pygmalion, 2010, Chichester Festival Th.; This May Hurt a Bit, tour and London, 2014; Talking Heads, Th. Royal, Bath, 2015; *films* include: Grey Owl, 2000; *radio* includes: Cabin Pressure (4 series), 2008–14; Ed Rearden's Week (8 series), 2005–15. Best TV Comedy Actress, 1992; Best TV Comedy Performance, 1999. *Publications:* A Passionate Life, 1998. *Recreations:* reading, gardening, painting, walking, theatre-going. *Address:* c/o John Grant, Conway van Gelder Grant Ltd, 8–12 Broadwick Street, W1F 8HW. *T:* (020) 7287 0077.

COLE, Prof. Stewart Thomas, PhD; FRS 2007; Director, Global Health Institute, Ecole Polytechnique Fédérale de Lausanne, Switzerland, since 2007; *b* 14 Jan. 1955; *s* of Leonard Thomas Cole and Jean Margaret Cole; *m* 1980, Lesley Curnick; one *s* one *d*. *Educ:* University Coll., Cardiff (BSc Hons 1976); Univ. of Sheffield (PhD 1979). Res. Asst, Max-Planck Institut for Biology, Tübingen, 1980–83; Institut Pasteur, Paris: staff scientist, 1984–89; Hd, Unité de Génétique Moléculaire Bactérienne, 1989–2007; Dir, Strategic Technol., 2000–04; Scientific Dir, 2004–05. Nat. Acad. of Pharmacy (France), 2014. Kochon Prize, Stop TB Partnership, 2009; Behring Prize, 2014. Chevalier de la Légion d'Honneur (France), 2004. *Publications:* (ed jtly) Tuberculosis and the Tubercle Bacillus, 2005; over 330 scientific articles. *Recreations:* fly fishing, ski-ing, opera, Rugby. *Address:* Global Health Institute, Ecole Polytechnique Fédérale de Lausanne, Station 19, 1015 Lausanne, Switzerland. *T:* (21) 6931851, *Fax:* (21) 6931790. *E:* stewart.cole@epfl.ch.

COLE, Timothy Marcus; HM Diplomatic Service; Ambassador to Cuba, since 2012; *b* Cuckfield, 2 May 1965; *s* of John Chantler Cole and Elsie Anne Cole; *m* 1997, Clare Elizabeth Parkes; one *s* one *d*. *Educ:* Durham Univ. (BA Hons). Christian Aid: Asst Eur. Community Officer, 1993–95; Sen. Prog. Officer, then Hd, Great Lakes Reg., 1995–99; Prog. Dir, Democratic Republic of Congo, Save the Children, 1999–2001; entered FCO, 2001; Head: Global Econ. Issues, FCO, 2001–02; Pan-African Policy Unit, FCO, 2003–05; Deputy Head of Mission: Mozambique, 2006–09; Zimbabwe, 2009–12. Gov., Internat. Sch. Havana, 2012–13. *Recreations:* golf, Rugby, ski-ing. *Address:* c/o Foreign and Commonwealth Office, King Charles Street, SW1A 2AH.

COLE, Sir William; *see* Cole, Sir R. W.

COLE-HAMILTON, (Arthur) Richard, CBE 1993; BA; CA; FCIBS; Chairman, Stakis PLC, 1995–98 (Deputy Chairman, 1994–95); Chief Executive, Clydesdale Bank PLC, 1982–92; *b* 8 May 1935; *s* of late John Cole-Hamilton, CBE; *m* 1963, Prudence Ann; one *s* two *d*. *Educ:* Ardrossan Academy; Loretto School; Cambridge Univ. (BA). Commissioned Argyll and Sutherland Highlanders, 1960–62. Brechin Cole-Hamilton & Co. (Chartered Accountants), 1962–67; Clydesdale Bank, 1967–92: Manager, Finance Corp. and Money Market, 1971; Asst Manager, Chief London Office, 1971; Supt of Branches, 1974; Head Office Manager, 1976; Asst Gen. Manager, 1978; Gen. Manager, 1979; Dep. Chief Gen. Manager, Feb. 1982; Dir, 1984–92. Chm., Cttee of Scottish Clearing Bankers, 1985–87, and 1991–92; Vice-Pres., Scottish Council for Develt and Industry, 1992–96; Dir, Glasgow Chamber of Commerce, 1985–91; Pres., Ayrshire Chamber of Commerce and Industry, 1992–96. Pres., Inst. of Bankers in Scotland, 1988–90. Mem. Council, Inst. of Chartered Accts of Scotland, 1981–85. Trustee: Nat. Galls of Scotland, 1986–96; Princess Royal Trust for Carers, 1991–98; Mem. Exec. Cttee, Erskine Hosp., 1976–2004. *Recreation:* golf. *Address:* 28 South Beach, Troon, Ayrshire KA10 6EF. *T:* (01292) 310603. *Clubs:* Western (Glasgow); Highland Brigade; Royal and Ancient Golf (Capt., 2004–05), Prestwick Golf.

COLEBY, Anthony Laurie; Executive Director, Bank of England, 1990–94; *b* 27 April 1935; *s* of Dr Leslie James Moger Coleby and Laurie Coleby (*née* Shuttleworth); *m* 1966, Rosemary Melian Elisabeth, *d* of Sir Peter Garran, KCMG; one *s* two *d*. *Educ:* Winchester; Corpus Christi, Cambridge (BAEcon, MA). Bank of England: joined, 1961; Personal Asst to Man. Dir, IMF, 1964–67; Assistant Chief, Overseas Dept, 1969; Adviser, Overseas Dept, 1972; Dep. Chief Cashier, 1973; Asst Dir, 1980–86; Chief Monetary Advr to the Governor, 1986–90; Exec. Dir, 1990–94. Non-executive Director: Halifax Building Soc., subseq. Halifax plc, 1994–2001; Anglo Irish Bank Corp., 1994–2001; Italian Internat. Bank, 1994–99. *Recreations:* choral singing, railways and transport. *Address:* 1 Maynard House, Moat Park, Great Easton, Essex CM6 2DL.

COLECLOUGH, Stephen Donald Gillings; Consultant, Mishcon de Reya, Solicitors, since 2014; Chairman, European Branch, Chartered Institute of Taxation, since 2013 (President, 2013–14); *b* W Bromwich, 6 April 1962; *s* of late Donald Derek Coleclough and of Vera Rosemary Coleclough; *m* 1997, Sarah Jane Gillings; two *d*. *Educ:* King Edward VI Sch., Lichfield; Sheffield Univ. (LLB Hons); Coll. of Law, Chester. CTA (Fellow); Assoc. of Taxation Technicians; Trust and Estate Practitioner. Articled clerk, Graham & Rosen, 1984–86; admitted solicitor, 1986; Solicitor, 1987–91, Partner, 1991–96, Simmons & Simmons; Partner, PricewaterhouseCoopers LLP, 1997–2013. Consultant, Expert Evidence Ltd, 2013–. Chartered Institute of Taxation: Mem. Council, 2000–; Chairman: Indirect Taxes Cttee, 2001–05; Tech. Cttee, 2005–08; Vice Pres., 2011–12; Dep. Pres., 2012–13. Confédération Fiscale Européene: Chm., Tech. Cttee and Bd Mem., 2005–08; Pres. and Chief Exec., 2009–12; Sec. Gen., 2014–. Mem., VAT Practitioners Gp, 1989–. Consultant, Butterworths Company Law Service, 1991–96. FICPD 1997; FIIT 2008. FRSA. *Publications:* (Tax Ed.) Knight on Private Company Acquisitions, 4th edn 1985; (jtly) Law Society VAT Guide, 1991; (contrib.) Commercial Leases, 2nd edn 1996; Tax Content of Companies vol., Butterworths Encyclopaedia of Forms and Precedents; (contrib.) The CFE at 50 Years, 2009; (contrib.) Sharing Information Across Border in Indirect Tax and Direct Tax, 2010; (contrib.) The Permanent Establishment in International Tax Law, 2011. *Recreations:* golf, guitar playing, gardening. *Address:* Mishcon de Reya, Summit House, 12 Red Lion Square, WC1R 4QD. *T:* 07802 878045. *E:* stephen.coleclough@mishcon.com, stephen.coleclough@hotmail.co.uk. *Club:* Stowe Golf.

COLEGATE, Isabel Diana, (Mrs Michael Briggs); writer; *b* 10 Sept. 1931; *d* of Sir Arthur Colegate, sometime MP, and Winifred Mary, *d* of Sir William Worsley, 3rd Bt; *m* 1953, Michael Briggs; two *s* one *d*. *Educ:* Runton Hill Sch., Norfolk. Worked as literary agent at Anthony Blond (London) Ltd, 1952–57. FRSL 1981. Hon. MA Bath, 1988. *Publications:* The Blackmailer, 1958; A Man of Power, 1960; The Great Occasion, 1962 (re-issued as Three Novels, 1983); Statues in a Garden, 1964; Orlando King, 1968; Orlando at the Brazen Threshold, 1971; Agatha, 1973 (re-issued as The Orlando Trilogy, 1984); News from the City of the Sun, 1979; The Shooting Party, 1980 (W. H. Smith Literary Award, 1980; filmed, 1985); A Glimpse of Sion's Glory, 1985; Deceits of Time, 1988; The Summer of the Royal Visit, 1991; Winter Journey, 1995; A Pelican in the Wilderness: hermits, solitaries and recluses, 2002. *Recreation:* walking the dog. *Address:* Rashwood Cottage, Mells, Frome, Somerset BA11 3PX.

COLELLA, Anton; Chief Executive, Institute of Chartered Accountants of Scotland, since 2006; Hon. Professor of Education, University of Glasgow, since 2012; *b* 25 May 1961; *s* of Dominic Colella and Anna Colella (*née* Bruno); *m* 1988, Angela Cooney; two *s* two *d*. *Educ:* St Mungo's Acad., Glasgow; Stirling Univ. (BA Hons 1983; DipEd). Teacher of RE, Holyrood Secondary Sch., Glasgow, 1983–87; Principal Teacher of RE, St Columba's High Sch., Gourock, 1987–92; Principal Teacher of RE, 1992–96, Asst Hd Teacher, 1996–99, Holyrood Secondary Sch.; Depute Hd Teacher, St Margaret Mary's Secondary Sch., Glasgow, 1999–2001, seconded to SQA, 2001; Dir of Qualifications, 2002–03, Chief Exec., 2003–06, SQA. Chairman: Scottish Council of Ind. Schs, 2010–; Global Accounting Alliance, 2011–; Exec. Bd, Scottish Catholic Educn Service, 2015–. Mem., QAA Scotland Cttee, 2001–09; Member Board: Scottish Further Educn Unit, 2001–07; CBI Scotland, 2008– (Mem. Council, 2011–). Member: Bd, Glasgow Coll. of Nautical Studies, 1998–2007; Bd of Trustees, Columba 1400, 2007–; Adv. Bd, Adam Smith Business Sch., 2011–. Hon. DBA BPP Univ., 2014. *Recreations:* family, playing guitar, Rugby, fishing, eating out. *Address:* Institute of Chartered Accountants of Scotland, CA House, 21 Haymarket Yards, Edinburgh EH12 5BH.

COLEMAN, Prof. Alice Mary; Professor of Geography, King's College, London, 1987–96, now Emeritus; *b* 8 June 1923; *d* of Bertie Coleman and Elizabeth Mary (*née* White). *Educ:* Clarendon House Sch.; Furzedown Training Coll. (Cert. of Educn); Birkbeck Coll., Univ. of London (BA Hons 1st Cl.); King's Coll., Univ. of London (MA with Mark of Distinction). FKC 1980. Geography Teacher, Northfleet Central Sch. for Girls, 1943–48; Geography Dept, King's Coll., London: Asst Lectr, 1948; Lectr, 1951; Sen. Lectr, 1963; Reader, 1965. Vis. Prof. for Distinguished Women Social Scientists, Univ. of Western Ontario, 1976; BC/Mombusho Prof. of Geog., Hokkaido Univ. of Educn at Asahikawa, 1985. Initiated and directed Second Land Utilisation Survey of Britain, 1960–; Dir, Design Improvement Controlled Experiment, 1988–94. Editor, Graphological Magazine, 1995. Gill Meml Award, RGS, 1963; The Times-Veuve Clicquot Award, 1974; Busk Award, RGS, 1987. *Publications:* The Planning Challenge of the Ottawa Area, 1969; Utopia on Trial, 1985; PACE Graphological Thesaurus, 1985; Scapes and Fringes: environmental territories of England and Wales, 2000; (English lang. ed. and designer) Graphology Across Cultures, 2003; (with Mona McNee) The Great Reading Disaster, 2007; 120 land-use maps in eleven colours at the scale of 1:25,000; over 300 academic papers. *Recreations:* reading, graphology. *Address:* 19 Giles Coppice, SE19 1XF. *T:* (020) 8244 6733.

COLEMAN, Brian John; Member (C) Barnet London Borough Council, 1998–2014; *b* 25 June 1961; *s* of John Francis Coleman and Gladys Coleman (*née* Cramp). *Educ:* Queen Elizabeth Boys' Sch., Barnet. Mills Allen Ltd, advertising co., 1989–99. Mem., Barnet CHC, 1991–94. Barnet London Borough Council: Cabinet Mem. for Envmt, 2002–04, for Community Safety and Community Engagement, 2006–08, for Envmt and Transport, 2010; Dep. Mayor, 2004–05; Mayor, 2009–10. London Assembly, Greater London Authority: Mem. (C) Barnet and Camden, 2000–12; contested (C) same seat, 2012; Chm., 2004–05 and 2006–07; Dep. Chm., 2005–06 and 2007–May 2008. Dep. Leader, Cons. Gp, GLA, 2002–04; Conservative Group Leader: London Fire and Emergency Planning Authy, 2000–12 (Dep. Chm., 2000–05; Vice Chm., 2005–08; Chm., 2008–12); N London Waste Authy, 2002–08 and 2010–12 (Chm., 2006–08; Vice Chm., 2012–). Chairman: Fire Services Mgt Cttee, LGA, 2009–; Local Govt Fire Service Employers, 2009–10. Hon. Pres., London Home and Water Safety Council, 2001–. Vice President: Chipping Barnet Cons. Assoc., 2002; Hendon Cons. Assoc., 2002. Governor: Christchurch Secondary Sch., 1993–2005 (Chm., 1999–2000); Ravenscroft Sch., 1996–2011; Queen Elizabeth's Boys' Sch., 2005–10. Vice Pres., Friern Barnet Summer Show (Chm., 1995–99); Trustee: Finchley Charities, 2000–; Eleanor Palmer Trust, 2012–. President: Hendon and Edgware Dist Scouts, 2004–08; Bor. of Barnet Dist Scouts, 2008–11. FRSA 2004. Freeman: City of London, 2003; Farriers' Co., 2008. Paul Harris Fellow, Rotary Internat., 2006. Hon. Dr Middlesex, 2008. *Recreations:* opera, theatre. *Club:* Barnet Rotary (Pres., 2014–15).

COLEMAN, Christopher Lewis; Managing Director, and Group Head of Banking, Rothschild, since 2015; *b* London, 25 June 1968; *s* of John and Anne Marie Coleman; *m* 1997, Vivienne Lundgren; two *s*. *Educ:* Westminster Sch.; London Sch. of Econs and Pol Sci. (BSc Econ.). With Rothschild, 1989–: Financial Services, Banking, 1990–93; Treasury Credit, 1993–94; Acquisition Finance, Banking, 1994–99; Hd, Natural Resources, Banking, 1999–2004; Chief Operating Officer, Banking, 2002–08; Co-Head of Banking, 2008–13; Hd of Banking, 2013–15. Non-executive Director: Merchant Bank of Central Africa, 2001–08; Randgold Resources, 2008–14 (non-exec. Chm., 2014–); Papa John's Internat., Inc., 2012–. *Address:* Rothschild, New Court, St Swithin's Lane, EC4N 8AL. *T:* (020) 7280 5000. *E:* christopher.coleman@rothschild.com, christopher.coleman@randgold.com.

COLEMAN, David Frederick, QPM 2004; DL; Chief Constable, Derbyshire Constabulary, 2001–07; *b* 4 Oct. 1952; *s* of Frederick and Margaret Elizabeth Coleman; *m* 1974, Hilary Grace Taylor; two *s*. *Educ:* Univ. of Manchester (BA Hons Geog.). Joined Derbyshire Constabulary, 1975; Divl Comdr, Derby, 1994–95; Asst Chief Constable, Leics Constabulary, 1996–2000. Pres., Peak Dist Mt Rescue Orgn, 2007–. DL Derbys, 2007, High Sheriff Derbys, 2014–15. *Recreations:* golf, reading, watching football, gardening, sailing, hill walking.

COLEMAN, Prof. Dulcie Vivien, MD; FRCPath; Professor Emeritus of Cell Pathology, Imperial College School of Medicine, London University, since 1998 (Head of Department of Cytopathology and Cytogenetics, St Mary's Hospital, London, 1972–98; Professor of Cell Pathology, St Mary's Hospital Medical School, 1988–98); *b* 19 Oct. 1932; *d* of Dr Frank Stuart

Coleman and Celia Coleman (*née* Walsman); *m* 1957, Jacob Benjamin Poznansky; three *s* one *d*. *Educ:* Bournemouth Sch. for Girls; Roedean Sch.; St Bartholomew's Hosp. Med. Sch. (MB, BS 1956; MD 1972). MRCPath 1980, FRCPath 1992. Hse Surgeon, Churchill Hosp., Oxford, 1956–57; Hse Physician, Plaistow Hosp., Essex, 1957–58; GP locums, 1959–64; Med. Asst (part-time), RPMS, 1967–70; Clin. Asst (part-time) (Cytopathol. and Cytogenetics), St Mary's Hosp., London, 1964–72; St Mary's Hospital Medical School: Sen. Lectr and Hon. Consultant in Cytopathol. and Cytogenetics, 1972–83; Reader in Cell Pathology, 1983–88; Hon. Consultant Cytopathologist, Hammersmith Hosps NHS Trust, 1998–. Member: Wkg Party on Safety of Chronic Villus sampling, MRC, 1987–90; Jt Wkg Party on Cytology Trng, DHSS, Inst. of Med. Lab. Scis and British Soc. for Clin. Cytol., 1988–90; Panel of Advrs, ACU, 1991–; Chairman: Wkg Party on Cervical Cancer Screening, Europe Against Cancer, 1990–; Wkg Party on Eur. Guidelines for Quality Assce in Cervical Screening (report pub. 1993); Cttee for Quality Assce, European Fedn of Cytology Socs, 1993–. Chm., Brit. Soc. for Clinical Cytology, 1989–92; Pres., Oncology section, RSM, 1988. Editor-in-Chief, Cytopathology, 1989–; Member, Editorial Board: Analytical Cellular Pathol.; Prenatal Diagnosis. Examr in Cytopathol. and Cytogenetics, Univs of London and Brunel, and RCPath. Hon. Member: Greek Cytology Soc.; CERDEC, France. Fellow, Internat. Acad. of Cytology. Morgani Medal, Italian Soc. of Pathology and Cytology, 1998. *Publications:* (with L. G. Koss) Advances in Clinical Cytology, Vol. 1 1981, Vol. 2 1984; (with D. M. D. Evans) Biopsy Pathology and Cytology of the Cervix, 1988, 2nd edn, 1999; (with P. C. Chapman) Clinical Cytotechnology, 1989; numerous papers, chapters, reviews on human polyomaviruses, human papillomaviruses, and other virus cytopathol. and prenatal diagnosis, incl. new techniques for cytodiagnosis of malignant disease, also on automated analysis of cervical smears. *Recreations:* gardening, swimming, nature walks. *Address:* Flat 12, 24 Hyde Park Square, W2 2NN. *T:* (020) 7262 0240.

COLEMAN, Iain; *b* 18 Jan. 1958; *m* 1996, Sally Powell (*see* Dame S. A. V. Powell); one *s*. *Educ:* Tonbridge Sch. Former Local Govt Officer. Mem. (Lab), Hammersmith and Fulham BC, 1986–97 and 2010–14 (Leader, 1991–96; Mayor, 1996–97). MP (Lab) Hammersmith and Fulham, 1997–2005.

COLEMAN, Isobel Mary; *see* Plumstead, I. M.

COLEMAN, Jeremy Barrington; a District Judge (Magistrates' Courts) (formerly Metropolitan Stipendiary Magistrate), since 1995; *b* 9 June 1951; *s* of late Neville Coleman and Pauline Coleman; *m* 1975, Margot; one *s* one *d*. *Educ:* Coll. of Law, London. Admitted solicitor, 1975; Partner in family firm, Samuel Coleman, 1975–95. Mem., Law Soc. Children's Panel, 1990. Mem., RPS (LRPS 1982). *Publications:* (contributing ed.) Archbold Magistrates' Court Criminal Practice, 2004. *Recreations:* photography, cricket, archaeology. *Address:* Hammersmith Magistrates' Court, 181 Talgarth Road, W6 8DN. *Club:* Middlesex CC.

COLEMAN, Hon. Dr Jonathan David; MP (Nat.) Northcote, New Zealand, since 2005; Minister of Health and Minister for Sport and Recreation, New Zealand, since 2014; *b* Auckland, 23 Sept. 1966; *s* of Ronald Douglas Coleman and Patricia Kathleen Ruby Coleman; *m* 2006, Sandra Jane Keaney; one *s* one *d*. *Educ:* Auckland Grammar Sch.; Auckland Univ. (BHB; MB ChB 1991; DObst 1993); London Business Sch. (MBA 2000). Jun. hosp. doctor, various posts in NZ and UK, 1991–94; GP Registrar, Oxford Vocational Trng Scheme, Oxford, 1995–96; Royal Flying Doctors Service, Broken Hill, NSW, 1996; Gen. Med. Practitioner, Islington, 1997–99; Mgt Consultant, Booz Allen and Hamilton, London, 2000–01; Med. Practitioner, Auckland, 2002–05; Mgt Consultant, PricewaterhouseCoopers, Auckland, 2003–05. Minister of Immigration, Minister of Broadcasting, Associate Minister of Health and Associate Minister of Tourism, 2008–11; Minister of Defence, Minister of State Services and Associate Minister of Finance, 2011–14. *Recreations:* travel, reading, tennis, fitness, Rugby, cricket, cycling. *Address:* c/o Parliament Buildings, Wellington 6160, New Zealand. *T:* (4) 4719999. *E:* jonathan.coleman@parliament.govt.nz.
See also R. J. L. Coleman.

COLEMAN, Katharine, MBE 2009; freelance glass artist and engraver; *b* 30 Jan. 1949; *d* of Hector Colin Beardmore Mackenzie and Frances Mackenzie; *m* 1974, David Edward Coleman; one *s* one *d*. *Educ:* Roedean Sch.; Girton Coll., Cambridge (BA Geog 1970; MA 1974). Regd Artist/Maker, Crafts Council. Solo exhibitions: Scottish Gall., Edinburgh, 2008, 2011; Galerie Porée, Paris, 2009, 2012. Work in public collections: Corning Mus. of Glass, USA; Cheltenham Art Gall. and Mus.; Nat. Mus of Scotland, Edinburgh; Shipley Art Gall., Gateshead; Birmingham City; Lybster, Caithness; Kamenicky Šenov; V&A; Broadfield House Glass Mus.; Kunstsammlungen Veste Coburg; Alexander Tutsek Collection, Munich; Norwich Castle Mus. Chm., Guild of Glass Engravers, 2002–05; FGE (FGGE 1992). Member: Contemp. Applied Arts, 2004; Art Workers Guild, 2004. Hon. Liveryman, Glass Sellers' Co., 2015. Adrian Sassoon Prize for Arts of the Kiln, 2004; Hon. Mention Prize, Coburg Glass Prize, 2006; (first) Glass Sellers' Prize for Engraving on Glass, 2007; Pearsons Prize for Best Use of Engraving on Glass, 2008. *Recreations:* other people's gardens, opera, antique glass. *Address:* 261 Cromwell Tower, Barbican, EC2Y 8DD. *T:* (020) 7628 6552. *E:* katharine@katharinecoleman.co.uk. *W:* www.katharinecoleman.co.uk.

COLEMAN, Lucy Madeline; *see* Stone, L. M.

COLEMAN, Martin Andrew; Partner, since 1991 and Global Head, Antitrust, Regulation and Competition, Norton Rose Fulbright LLP (formerly Norton Rose Group); *b* London, 19 Nov. 1952; *s* of Joseph Coleman and Betty Coleman; *m* 1991, Ishbel; one *s* two *d*. *Educ:* Preston Manor High Sch., Wembley; Worcester Coll., Oxford (BA, BCL). Lectr in Law, Brunel Univ., 1979–89; Associate, Norton Rose, 1989–91. Mem. Bd, Solicitors Regulatory Authy, 2010–. Mem., ESRC, 2010–. *Publications:* (with Michael Grenfell) The Competition Act 1998: law and practice, 1999. *Recreations:* reading, travel, cinema. *Address:* Norton Rose Fulbright LLP, 3 More London Riverside, SE1 2AQ. *T:* (020) 7444 3347. *E:* martin.coleman@nortonrosefulbright.com.

COLEMAN, His Honour Nicholas John; a Circuit Judge, 1998–2015; *b* 12 Aug. 1947; *s* of late Leslie Ernest Coleman and Joyce Coleman; *m* 1971, Isobel Mary Plumstead, *qv*; one *s* two *d*. *Educ:* Royal Pinner Sch.; Liverpool Univ. (LLB Hons). Called to the Bar, Inner Temple, 1970, Bencher, 2005; practised SE Circuit, 1972–98; a Recorder, 1989–98; Resident Judge, Peterborough Combined Court, 2001–09. Lectr, 1970–72, Examr, 1972–76, Inns of Court Sch. of Law. Judicial Member: Parole Bd, 2004–14; Restricted Patients Panel, 2011–15. *Recreations:* sport, travel, theatre, cinema. *Clubs:* MCC; Hampstead and Westminster Hockey; Hunstanton Golf.

COLEMAN, Peter Anthony; Secretary General, European Parliamentary Labour Party, 1997–2004; *b* 10 Oct. 1945; *s* of late William and Maggie Coleman; *m* 1966, Dorothy Edith Lawrence; two *d*. *Educ:* Avenue Primary Sch., Wellingborough; Park Road Junior Sch., Kettering; Kettering Sch. for Boys; Kettering Boot and Shoe Tech. Coll. (ABBSI). Progress chaser: Holyoake Footwear, 1961–64; Wilson & Watsons, 1964–66; Labour Party: organiser: Peterborough, 1967–71; Nottingham, 1972–76; SE Derbys, 1976–78; Asst Regl Organiser, E Midland, 1978–83, Regl Dir, 1983–93; Nat. Dir of Orgn and Devlt, 1993–97. Nat. Vice-Pres., Nat. Union of Labour Organisers, 1977–78; Nat. Chair, Computing for Labour, 2003–06. Member: Exec. Cttee, Fabian Soc., 1994–95; Mgt Cttee, H. S. Chapman Soc., 2000–04. Trustee, 2009–, Nat. Vice Chair, 2012–, Labour Party Superannuation Soc. Chm., Friends of Shanklin Th., 2011–. *Publications:* (ed) Labour's Fundraising Guide, 1984; pamphlets on electoral law, Labour Party regeneration and polling-day systems. *Recreations:* theatre, travel, watching cricket and football. *Clubs:* Hampshire CC; Newclose CC.

COLEMAN, Richard James Lee; QC 2012; *b* Auckland, NZ, 1968; *s* of Ronald Douglas Coleman and Patricia Kathleen Ruby Lee; *m* 2007, Rachel Jane Avery; two *s* one *d*. *Educ:* Auckland Grammar Sch.; Corpus Christi Coll., Cambridge (BA Double 1st Cl. Hons 1990); Yale Univ. (LLM 1991). Called to the Bar: Lincoln's Inn, 1994; NY, 1995; in practice as a barrister specialising in commercial law. *Publications:* (contrib.) Law of Bank Payments, 1996, 4th edn 2010. *Recreations:* spending time with family and friends, reading, following the All Blacks. *Address:* Fountain Court Chambers, Temple, EC4Y 9DH. *T:* (020) 7583 3335, *Fax:* (020) 7353 0329. *E:* rjc@fountaincourt.co.uk.
See also Hon. J. D. Coleman.

COLEMAN, Sir Robert (John), KCMG 2005; Visiting Professor, University of Plymouth, since 2006; *b* 8 Sept. 1943; *s* of Frederick and Kathleen Coleman; *m* 1966, Malinda Tigay Cutler; two *d*. *Educ:* Univ. of Oxford (MA); Univ. of Chicago (JD). Called to the Bar, Inner Temple, 1969. Lectr in Law, Univ. of Birmingham, 1967–70; Barrister at Law, 1970–73; European Commission: Administrator, subseq. Principal Administrator, 1974–82; Dep. Head of Div., safeguard measures and removal of non-tariff barriers, 1983; Head of Div., Intellectual Property and Unfair Competition, 1984–87; Dir, Public Procurement, 1987–90; Dir, Approximation of Laws, Freedom of Estabt, and Freedom to Provide Services, 1990–91; Director General: Transport, 1991–99; Health and Consumer Protection, 1999–2003. EU Liaison Officer, Baltic and Internat. Maritime Council, 2005–13; Mem., Admin. Bd, Eur. Maritime Safety Agency, 2007–12. Sen. Practitioner Fellow, 2003–04, Sen. Res. Fellow, 2004–06, Inst. of Governance, QUB. Visiting Professor: Univ. of East London, 1997–2003; World Maritime Univ., Malmo, 2006–12; Maritime Law Inst., Malta, 2006–12. Mem. Adv. Bd, Sch. of Mgt, Univ. of Bath, 2001–03. *Publications:* contribs and articles on legal and policy issues, concerning corporate accounting, employee participation, intellectual property and transport. *Recreations:* cycling, music. *Address:* Flete House, Apt 3, Ivybridge, Devon PL21 9NX.

COLEMAN, Roger, FRCA; Co-Director, Helen Hamlyn Centre for Design (formerly Research Centre), 1999–2008, and Professor of Inclusive Design, 2002–08, now Emeritus, Royal College of Art; *b* 20 March 1943; *s* of Ronald Charles Coleman and Margaret Grace Coleman (*née* Thomas); *m* 1st, 1965, Alison Fell (marr. diss. 1967); one *s*; 2nd, 1995, Sally Reilly. *Educ:* Ealing Grammar Sch. for Boys; Edinburgh Sch. of Art and Edinburgh Univ. (Andrew Grant Schol.; MA Hons Fine Art). Lectr, Leeds Sch. of Art and Design, and Vis. Lectr, Bradford Sch. of Art and Design, 1967–70; Sen. Lectr, St Martin's Sch. of Art and Design, 1970–72; Partner, Community Press, London, 1972–73; freelance designer and maker, 1973–84; Director: Community, Construction and Design Ltd, 1984–91; London Innovation Ltd, 1985–2003; Dir, DesignAge prog., RCA, 1991–98. Co-ordinator, Eur. Design for Ageing Network, 1994–98. Jury Chm., RSA Student Design Awards, 1992–2008. Founder and Mem. Council, Welfare State Internat. (perf. community arts gp), 1968–2008. Exhibitions: One Rock, Lanternhouse, Ulverston, 2003; Flat Earth, 2006, A Short Walk on the Lark, 2008, New Departures, 2012, Between Countries, 2014, Old Fire Engine House, Ely; Flat Earth 2007, EXHIBIT, London, 2007; Vendanges des Images, Sancerre, France, 2010; travelling exhibn, A Husk of Hares, Wisbech, March and Ely, 2013. FRCA 1996; FRSA 2000. Hon. Dr Catholic Univ. Leuven, 2012. Sir Misha Black Award for Innovation in Design Educn, 2001. *Publications:* The Art of Work: an epitaph to skill, 1988, rev. Japanese edn 1998; Designing for our Future Selves, 1993; Design Research for our Future Selves, 1994; Working Together: a new approach to design, 1997; (jtly, also ed) Design für die Zukunft, 1997; Living Longer: the new context for design, 2001; (jtly) Inclusive Design: design for the whole population, 2003; (jtly) Design for Patient Safety: a system-wide design-led approach to tackling patient safety in the NHS, 2003; (jtly) Design for Patient Safety: future ambulances, 2007; (jtly) Design for Inclusivity, 2007. *Recreation:* fen watching and imaginary punt-gunning - waiting for the seas to rise. *Address:* c/o Helen Hamlyn Centre for Design, Royal College of Art, Kensington Gore, SW7 2EU. *E:* roger.coleman@hon.rca.ac.uk. *W:* www.rogercolemanphotography.com.

COLEMAN, Terry, (Terence Francis Frank); reporter and author; *b* 13 Feb. 1931; *s* of J. and D. I. B. Coleman; *m* 1st, 1954, Lesley Fox-Strangeways Vane (marr. diss.); two *d*; 2nd, 1981, Vivien Rosemary Lumsdaine Wallace; one *s* one *d*. *Educ:* 14 schs incl. Poole Grammar Sch. LLB London. Formerly: Reporter, Poole Herald; Editor, Savoir Faire; Sub-editor, Sunday Mercury, and Birmingham Post; Reporter and then Arts Corresp., The Guardian, 1961–70, Chief Feature Writer, 1970–74; Special Writer with Daily Mail, 1974–76; The Guardian: Chief Feature Writer, 1976–79, writing mainly political interviews, incl. last eight British Prime Ministers; NY Correspondent, 1981; special corresp., 1982–89; Associate Editor, The Independent, 1989–91. FRSA. Feature Writer of the Year, British Press Awards, 1982; Journalist of the Year, Granada Awards, 1987. *Publications:* The Railway Navvies, 1965 (Yorkshire Post prize for best first book of year), rev. edn 2015; A Girl for the Afternoons, 1965; (with Lois Deacon) Providence and Mr Hardy, 1966; The Only True History: collected journalism, 1969; Passage to America, 1972, rev. edn 2000; (ed) An Indiscretion in the Life of an Heiress (Hardy's first novel), 1976; The Liners, 1976; The Scented Brawl: collected journalism, 1978; Southern Cross, 1979; Thanksgiving, 1981; Movers and Shakers: collected interviews, 1987; Thatcher's Britain, 1987; Empire, 1993; Nelson: the man and the legend, 2001, US edn as The Nelson Touch, 2002; Olivier: the authorised biography, 2005; The Old Vic: the history of a great theatre, 2014. *Recreations:* cricket, opera, circumnavigation. *Address:* c/o Peters, Fraser & Dunlop, Drury House, 34–43 Russell Street, WC2B 5HA. *T:* (020) 7720 2651. *E:* colemanterry@hotmail.co.uk. *Club:* MCC.

COLEMAN, Victor Paul; freelance travel and features writer, 2007–14; Deputy Director, Corporate Science and Analytical Services, Health and Safety Executive, 2006–07; *b* 28 Feb. 1952; *s* of Richard William Coleman and Edna Grace Coleman; *m* 1978, Eleanor Jane Kirkwood. *Educ:* Greenford Co. Grammar Sch.; King's Coll., Cambridge (MA); Univ. of Aston in Birmingham (Dip. Occupational Safety and Health). HM Inspector of Factories, 1973–83; Health and Safety Executive: Principal Inspector of Factories, 1983–92; Hd, Railway Safety Policy, 1992–94; Dep. Chief Inspector of Railways, 1995–98; Chief Inspector of Railways, 1998–2002; Hd of Policy for Hazardous Industries, 2002–03; Hd of Finance and Planning, 2003–06. Chm., Railways Industry Adv. Cttee, HSC, 1998–2001; Mem., Channel Tunnel Safety Authy, 1995–98. *Recreations:* theatre, walking, writing.

COLENSO-JONES, Maj. (Gilmore) Mervyn (Boyce); one of HM Body Guard, Honourable Corps of Gentlemen-at-Arms, 1982–2000 (Harbinger, 1997–2000); *b* 4 Sept. 1930; *s* of late Dr Gilmore Leonard Colenso Colenso-Jones and Kathleen Edwina Colenso-Jones (*née* Macartney); *m* 1968, Rosamond Anne Bowen. *Educ:* Rugby Sch. Commnd Royal Welch Fusiliers, 1950: served at home and abroad; jssc, Latimer, 1968–69; Brit. Exchange Officer, US Continental Army Comd, Va, 1969–70; retd 1972, in rank of Maj.; Regtl Sec., RWF, 1972–81. Mem., S Glamorgan HA, 1981–84. CStJ 1981 (Priory Sec. for Wales, 1981–84). *Recreations:* country pursuits, oil and water-colour painting. *Address:* 18 Bearwater, Hungerford, Berks RG17 0NN. *T:* (01488) 683250.

COLERAINE, 2nd Baron *cr* 1954, of Haltemprice; **James Martin Bonar Law;** *b* 8 Aug. 1931; *s* of 1st Baron Coleraine, PC, *y s* of Rt Hon. Andrew Bonar Law, and Mary Virginia (*d* 1978), *d* of A. F. Nellis, Rochester, NY; *S* father, 1980; *m* 1st, 1958, Emma Elizabeth Richards (marr. diss.); two *d*; 2nd, 1966, Anne Patricia, (Tomt) (*d* 1993), *yr d* of Major-Gen. R. H. Farrant, CB; one *s* one *d* (and one *d* decd); 3rd, 1998, Marion Robina, (Bobbie), *d* of

Sir Thomas Ferens, CBE and *widow* of Peter Smyth. *Educ:* Eton; Trinity College, Oxford. Formerly in practice as a solicitor. Hon. Consultant, Fedn of Private Residents' Assocs, 1994–. *Heir: s* Hon. James Peter Bonar Law, *b* 23 Feb. 1975. *Address:* 4 Ashdown Lodge, Chepstow Villas, W11 3EE. *T:* (020) 7221 4148; The Dower House, Sunderlandwick, Driffield, E Yorks YO25 9AD. *T:* (01377) 253535.

See also Baron Ironside, J. R. O'Grady.

COLERIDGE, family name of **Baron Coleridge**.

COLERIDGE, 5th Baron *cr* 1873, of Ottery St Mary; **William Duke Coleridge;** *b* 18 June 1937; *s* of 4th Baron Coleridge, KBE, and Cecilia Rosamund (*d* 1991), *d* of Adm. Sir William Wordsworth Fisher, GCB, GCVO; *S* father, 1984; *m* 1st, 1962, Everild Tania (marr. diss. 1977), *d* of Lt-Col Beauchamp Hambrough, OBE; one *s* two *d*; 2nd, 1977, Pamela, *d* of late G. W. Baker, CBE, VRD; two *d*. *Educ:* Eton; RMA Sandhurst. Commissioned into Coldstream Guards, 1958; served King's African Rifles, 1962–64; commanded Guards Independent Parachute Company, 1970–72. Director: Abercrombie & Kent, 1978–90; Larchpark Properties Ltd, 1987–92; Chairman: Universal Energy Ltd, 1984–90; European Leisure Estates plc, 1988–90; Advr, Nat. Marine Aquarium, 1990–. Gov., Royal West of England Residential Sch. for the Deaf, 1984–. *Heir: s* Hon. James Duke Coleridge, *b* 5 June 1967. *Address:* The Manor House, Ottery St Mary, Devon EX11 1DR. *T:* (01404) 812564.

COLERIDGE, David Ean; Chairman of Lloyd's, 1991, 1992 (Deputy Chairman, 1985, 1988, 1989); *b* 7 June 1932; *s* of Guy Cecil Richard Coleridge, MC and Katherine Cicely Stewart Smith; *m* 1955, Susan Senior; three *s*. *Educ:* Eton. Glanvill Enthoven, 1950–57; R. W. Sturge & Co., 1957–95: Dir, 1966–95; Chm., A. L. Sturge (Holdings) Ltd (now Sturge Holdings PLC), 1978–95. Chm., Oxford Agency Hldgs Ltd, 1987–90; Director: R. A. Edwards (Holdings) Ltd, 1985–90; Wise Speke Hldgs Ltd, 1987–94; Ockham Hldgs, subseq. Highway Insurance, 1995–2006 (Chm., 1995). Mem., Council and Cttee of Lloyd's, 1983–92. *Recreations:* golf, racing, gardening, family. *Address:* 37 Egerton Terrace, SW3 2BU. *T:* (020) 7581 1756.

See also N. D. Coleridge.

COLERIDGE, Geraldine Margaret, (Gill), (Mrs D. R. Leeming); Chairman, Rogers Coleridge and White, Literary Agency, since 2014 (Director, since 1988); *b* 26 May 1948; *d* of Antony Duke Coleridge and June Marian Caswell; *m* 1974, David Roger Leeming; two *s*. *Educ:* Queen Anne's School, Caversham; Marlborough Secretarial College, Oxford. BPC Partworks, Sidgwick & Jackson, Bedford Square Book Bang, to 1971; Publicity Manager, Chatto & Windus, 1971–72; Dir and Literary Agent, Anthony Sheil Associates, 1973–88. Pres., Assoc. of Authors' Agents, 1988–91. Mem. Cttee, Royal Literary Fund, 2008–. *Recreations:* music, reading, gardening. *Address:* The Warrens, Hartest, Bury St Edmunds, Suffolk IP29 4EB.

COLERIDGE, Most Rev. Mark Benedict; *see* Brisbane, Archbishop of, (RC).

COLERIDGE, Nicholas David, CBE 2009; President, Condé Nast International Ltd, since 2012 (Vice-President, 1999–2011); Managing Director: Condé Nast Publications, since 1992 (Editorial Director, 1989–91); Condé Nast Digital (formerly CondéNet) Ltd, since 1999; Director: Les Publications Condé Nast, since 1994; Condé Nast India, since 2006; Condé Nast Zao, since 2012; *b* 4 March 1957; *s* of David Ean Coleridge, *qv*; *m* 1989, Georgia Metcalfe; three *s* one *d*. *Educ:* Eton; Trinity Coll., Cambridge. Associate Editor, Tatler, 1979–81; Columnist, Evening Standard, 1981–84; Features Editor, Harpers and Queen, 1985–86, Editor, 1986–89. Chm., Periodical Publishers Assoc., 2004–06; Dir, Press Bd of Finance, 2006–. Chairman: British Fashion Council, 2000–03; Fashion Rocks for the Prince's Trust, RAH, 2003; Director: Prince's Trust Trading Bd, 2004–07; Adv. Bd, Concert for Diana, Wembley Stadium, 2007; Ambassador: Creative Industries, c&binet, DCMS, 2008–10; Landmark Trust, 2014–; Chm., Campaign for Wool, 2013– (Vice Chm., 2009–13). Council Mem., RCA, 1995–2000; Trustee, V&A Mus., 2013– (Chm., 2015–). Patron, Elephant Family, 2013–. Young Journalist of the Year, British Press Awards, 1983; Mark Boxer Award, BSME, 2001; Marcus Morris Award, PPA, 2013. *Publications:* Tunnel Vision, collected journalism, 1982; Around the World in 78 Days, 1984; Shooting Stars, 1984; The Fashion Conspiracy, 1988; How I Met My Wife and other stories, 1991; Paper Tigers, 1993; With Friends Like These, 1997; Streetsmart, 1999; Godchildren, 2002; A Much Married Man, 2006; Deadly Sins, 2009; The Adventuress, 2012. *Address:* Wolverton Hall, Pershore, Worcs WR10 2AU. *T:* (01905) 841697; 29 Royal Avenue, SW3 4QE. *T:* (020) 7730 5998.

COLERIDGE, Hon. Sir Paul (James Duke), Kt 2000; a Judge of the High Court, Family Division, 2000–14; Founder and Chairman, Marriage Foundation, since 2012; *b* 30 May 1949; *s* of late James Bernard and Jane Evelina Coleridge; *m* 1973, Judith Elizabeth Rossiter; two *s* one *d*. *Educ:* Cranleigh Sch., Surrey; College of Law, London. Called to the Bar, Middle Temple, 1970, Bencher, 2000; in practice at the Bar, 1970–85; Internat. Legal Advr to Baron Hans Heinrich Thyssen-Bornemisza, Switzerland, 1985–89; private practice, 1989–2000; QC 1993; a Recorder, 1996–2000; Family Div. Liaison Judge, Western Circuit, 2002–11. *Recreations:* Dorset, gardening, motor-bikes. *Address:* Marriage Foundation, PO Box 1230, Cambridge CB1 0XD. *E:* p.coleridge@marriagefoundation.org.uk. *Club:* MCC.

COLES, Adrian Michael, OBE 2011; Director-General, Building Societies Association, 1993–2013; *b* 19 April 1954; *s* of Kenneth Ernest Coles and Constance Mary (*née* Sykes); *m* 1981, Marion Alma Hoare; one *s* one *d*. *Educ:* Holly Lodge Grammar Sch., Smethwick; Univ. of Nottingham (BA Hons); Univ. of Sheffield (MA). Economist, Electricity Council, 1976–79; Building Societies Association: Economist, 1979–81; Head: Econs and Stats, 1981–86; External Relns, 1986–93; Dir-Gen., Council of Mortgage Lenders, 1993–96. Chm., Thames Valley Housing Assoc., 1990–93; Director: Housing Securities Ltd, 1994–; Banking Code Standards Bd Ltd, 1999–2009; Parsons Mead Educnl Trust Ltd, 2000–07; Communicate Mutuality Ltd, 2001–13; Independent Housing Ombudsman, 2001–04; Lending Standards Bd Ltd, 2009–13; Reclaim Fund Ltd, 2011–; Progressive Bldg Soc., 2014–; BSA Pension Trustees Ltd, 2014–. Sec. Gen., Internat. Union for Housing Finance, 2001–09; Chm., Commn on Co-operative and Mutual Housing, 2007–09. Mem., Financial Services Commn, Gibraltar, 2014–. Trustee, Money Advice Trust, 1994–2004. *Publications:* (with Mark Boleat) The Mortgage Market, 1987; numerous articles in housing and housing finance jls. *Recreations:* gym, walking, reading, family.

COLES, Alec, OBE 2010; Chief Executive Officer, Western Australian Museum, since 2010; Adjunct Associate Professor, School of Social Sciences, University of Western Australia, since 2014; *b* Wolverhampton, 3 Jan. 1959; *s* of William John and Kathleen Audrey Coles. *Educ:* Univ. of Leicester (BSc Hons Biol Scis); Univ. of Newcastle upon Tyne (Post Grad. Cert. Cultural Mgt); Univ. of E Anglia (Mus. Leadership Prog.). AMA (by Dip.) 1986. Asst Curator, 1980–86, Dep. Curator, 1986–88, Woodspring Mus.; Sen. Museums Officer, Tyne & Wear Museums, 1988–92; Curator, Hancock Mus., Newcastle upon Tyne, 1992–96; Sen. Curator, Tyne & Wear Museums, 1996–2000; Chief Exec., Northumberland Wildlife Trust, 2000–02; Director: Tyne & Wear Museums, 2002–09; Tyne & Wear Archives & Museums, 2009–10. Hon. Treas., Museums Assoc., 2006–. MAICD 2014. FLS 1990; FRSA 2009. *Recreations:* natural history (botany), music. *Address:* Western Australian Museum, 49 Kew Street, Welshpool, WA 6106, Australia. *T:* (8) 65527801. *E:* alec.coles@museum.wa.gov.au.

COLES, Sir (Arthur) John, GCMG 1997 (KCMG 1989; CMG 1984); HM Diplomatic Service, retired; Permanent Under-Secretary of State, Foreign and Commonwealth Office, and Head of the Diplomatic Service, 1994–97; *b* 13 Nov. 1937; *s* of Arthur Strixton Coles and Doris Gwendoline Coles; *m* 1965, Anne Mary Sutherland Graham; two *s* one *d*. *Educ:* Magdalen Coll. Sch., Brackley; Magdalen Coll., Oxford (BA 1960, MA). Served HM Forces 1955–57. Joined HM Diplomatic Service, 1960; Middle Eastern Centre for Arabic Studies Lebanon, 1960–62; Third Sec., Khartoum, 1962–64; FO (later FCO), 1964–68; Asst Political Agent, Trucial States (Dubai), 1968–71; FCO, 1971–75; Head of Chancery, Cairo, 1975–77 Counsellor (Developing Countries), UK Perm. Mission to EEC, 1977–80; Head of S Asia Dept, FCO, 1980–81; Private Sec. to Prime Minister, 1981–84; Ambassador to Jordan 1984–88; High Commissioner to Australia, 1988–91; Dep. Under-Sec. of State, FCO 1991–94. Non-exec. Dir, BG plc, 1998–2008. Chm., Sight Savers Internat., 2001–07 Trustee, Imperial War Mus., 1999–2004. Vis. Fellow, All Souls Coll., Oxford, 1998–99 Gov., Ditchley Foundn, 1997–12; Mem. Council, Atlantic Coll., 2001–03. President, FCO Assoc., 2000–02. Gov., Sutton's Hosp. in Charterhouse, 2003–05. *Publications:* British Influence and the Euro, 1999; Making Foreign Policy: a certain idea of Britain, 2000 Blindness and The Visionary: the life and work of John Wilson, 2006. *Recreations:* walking cricket, bird-watching, reading, music. *Address:* Kelham, Dock Lane, Beaulieu, Hants SO4 7YH. *Club:* Oxford and Cambridge.

COLES, Bruce; *see* Coles, His Honour N. B. C.

COLES, Prof. Bryony Jean, FBA 2007; FSA; Professor of Prehistoric Archaeology University of Exeter, 1996–2008, now Emeritus; *b* 12 Aug. 1946; *d* of John Samuel Orme CB, OBE, and Jean Esther Orme (*née* Harris); *m* 1985, John Morton Coles, *qv*. *Educ:* High Wycombe High Sch.; Univ. of Bristol (BA Hist. 1968); Inst. of Archaeology, Univ. of London (Postgrad. Dip. Archaeol. 1970); University Coll. London (MPhil Anthropol. 1972) FSA 1975. University of Exeter: Lectr, 1972–89; Sen. Lectr, 1989; Reader, 1990; British Acad. Res. Readership, 1991–94. Co-Dir (with J. M. Coles), Somerset Levels Proj., 1973–89 Dir, Wetland Archaeol. Res. Proj., 1989–. Editor, Jl of Wetland Archaeol., 2000–. Mem. Archaeol. Adv. Panel, Nat. Mus. and Galls of Wales, 1991–2003; Vice Pres., Prehistoric Soc. 1994–97; Chm., NW Wetland Survey, 1994–98. Mem., Scientific Adv. Council Netherlands Archaeol. Res. Sch., 1997–2008. Pres., Devon Archaeol Soc., 2006–08. Bagulee Award, Prehistoric Soc., 1990, 1999; George Stephenson Medal, ICE, 1995; (jtly) British Archaeol Award, 1986, 1988, 1998. *Publications:* Anthropology for Archaeologists, 1981 Beavers in Britain's Past, 2006; with J. M. Coles: Prehistory of the Somerset Levels, 1980 Sweet Track to Glastonbury: the Somerset Levels in prehistory, 1986; People of the Wetlands 1989; Enlarging the Past: the contribution of wetland archaeology (Rhind Lects 1994–95) 1996; contribs to Wetland Archaeol. Res. Proj. occasional papers, British and Europ. conf procs and learned jls. *Recreations:* walking, wildlife and wetlands, gardening, reading. *Address* c/o Department of Archaeology, University of Exeter, Laver Building, North Park Road Exeter EX4 4QE. *T:* (01392) 264350.

See also J. D. Orme.

COLES, Rt Rev. Dr David John; Bishop of Christchurch, 1990–2008; Vicar of Wakatipu Queenstown, 2008–14; *b* 23 March 1943; *s* of Samuel Arthur and Evelyn Ann Coles; *m* 1st 1970, Ceridwyn Mary Parr (marr. diss.); one *s* one *d*; 2nd, 2001, Joy Woodley. *Educ:* Auckland Grammar Sch.; Univ. of Auckland (MA Hons 1967); Univ. of Otago (BD 1969 MTh 1971); Univ. of Manchester (PhD 1974); Melbourne Coll. of Divinity (Dip. Religious Educn). Deacon 1968, priest 1969; Curate, St Mark, Remuera, Auckland, 1968–70; Asst Chaplain, Selwyn Coll., Dunedin, 1970–71; Curate, Fallowfield, 1972–73; Chaplain, Hulme Hall, Univ. of Manchester, 1973–74; Vicar of: Glenfield, 1974–76; Takapuna, 1976–80 Examining Chaplain to Bp of Auckland, 1974–80; Dean and Vicar of St John's Cathedral Napier, Dio. of Waiapu, 1980–84; Dean of Christchurch and Vicar-General, Dio. of Christchurch, 1984–90; Locum Chaplain, Copenhagen, 2014–15. Pres., Conf. of Churches of Aotearoa-NZ, 1991. *Recreations:* music, ski-ing, tramping. *Address:* 88 Canon Street, St Albans, Christchurch 8014, New Zealand.

COLES, Dominic Peter; Chief Operating Officer and Chief Financial Officer, Discovery Networks Western Europe, since 2014; *b* London, 22 Dec. 1964; *s* of Peter and Dianne Coles *m* 1991, Karen Ash; one *s* one *d*. *Educ:* Keele Univ. (BA Hons PPE 1987); Harvard Business Sch. (AMP 2010). ACA 1991. Manager, Touche Ross & Co., 1988–92; Sen. Manager Deloitte & Touche Corporate Finance, 1993–96; Investment Manager, Baltic Investments 1996–97; BBC: Hd of Investment, 1997–99; Dir, Sports Rights and Finance, BBC Sport 1999–2007; Chief Operating Officer: News and Nations, 2007–12; London 2012 Olympics 2008–12; Dir of Ops, 2012–14. Mem., Adv. Cttee, Sport Relief, 2008–. Olympic torchbearer, London 2012. *Recreations:* family first, then walking in the Lakes and Cornwall running (everywhere), harvesting chillis, an enduring fan of Liverpool and Harlequin FCs *Address:* Discovery Networks, Chiswick Park Building 2, 566 Chiswick High Road, W4 5YB. *T:* (020) 8811 3000. *E:* dominic_coles@discovery.com.

COLES, Prof. Harry James, PhD, DSc; FInstP; Professor of Photonics of Molecular Materials, and Director, Centre of Molecular Materials for Photonics and Electronics Electrical Engineering Division, University of Cambridge, 2002–13, now Professor Emeritus Fellow of St Catharine's College, Cambridge, 2006–13; *b* 28 Aug. 1946; *s* of William and Audrey Joan Coles; *m* 1st, 1968, Janet Phillips (marr. diss. 2008); one *s*; 2nd, 2009, Leon Marie Hope (*née* Averis). *Educ:* Tal Handaq Grammar Sch., Malta; Trowbridge Boys' High Sch.; Queen Elizabeth Coll., Univ. of London (BSc Hons); Brunel Univ. (PhD 1975) Victoria Univ. of Manchester (DSc 1985). FInstP 1985. Maître de Recherche, Univ. Louis Pasteur, Strasbourg, 1975–79; Victoria University of Manchester: Lectr, 1980–85; Sen. Lectr 1985–87; Reader, 1988–90; Prof., 1991–95; Prof., Univ. of Southampton, and Dir Southampton Liquid Crystal Inst., 1995–2002. Visiting Professor: Berlin, 1990; Tokyo, 1990 Directeur de Recherche, Strasbourg, 1991. George Gray Medal, British Liquid Crystal Soc. 2003. *Publications:* (jtly) Liquid Crystal Handbook, Vol. IIB, 1998; contrib. over 350 papers to learned jls; 35 internat. patents; over 450 presentations to scientific confs. *Recreations:* running gardening, oil painting, Charlton Athletic FC, fast cars. *Address:* CMMPE, Electrical Engineering Division, Department of Engineering, University of Cambridge, 9 JJ Thomson Avenue, Cambridge CB3 0FA. *E:* hjc37@cam.ac.uk.

COLES, Jenny; *see* Joseph, Jenny.

COLES, Sir John; *see* Coles, Sir A. J.

COLES, John David, CB 2005; FREng; RCNC; Consultant, Harcourt Coles Ltd, since 2006; *b* 10 May 1945; *s* of William Frederick Coles and Alice Marie Coles; *m* 1967, Judith Ann Baker (*d* 1992); two *d*. *Educ:* University Coll. London (BSc 1969; MSc 1970). FRINA 1998; FREng 2004. RCNC 1971–2005; Staff Constructor to Flag Officer Submarines 1978–82; Head of British Admiralty Office, USA, 1982–85; Assistant Director: Future Projects, 1985–88; Dir Gen. Submarines, 1988–92; Dir of Works, Strategic Systems, 1992–94 rcds, 1994; Supt Ships, Devonport, MoD, 1995–97; Dir Gen., Equipment Support (Sea) Chief Exec., Ships, then Warship, Support Agency, and Head of RCNC, 1998–2007; Carrier Vehicle Future Integrated Project Team Leader, Defence Procurement Agency, MoD 2005–07. Hon. DEng Bath.

COLES, John Morton, ScD, PhD; FBA 1978; Professor of European Prehistory, University of Cambridge, 1980–86; Fellow of Fitzwilliam College, since 1963, Hon. Fellow, 1987; *b* 25 March 1930; *s* of Edward John Langdon Coles and Alice Margaret (*née* Brown); *m* 1985 Bryony Jean Orme (*see* B. J. Coles); two *s* two *d* of previous marr. *Educ:* Woodstock, Ontario Univ. of Toronto (BA; tennis colours 1952); Univ. of Cambridge (MA, ScD); Univ. of Edinburgh (PhD; Scottish Tennis Cup 1959). Carnegie Scholar and Research Fellow, Univ of Edinburgh, 1959–60; Asst Lectr, 1960–65, Lectr, 1965–76, Reader, 1976–80, Univ. of Cambridge. Fellow, McDonald Inst. for Archaeological Res., Univ. of Cambridge, 1992–96; Hon. Res. Prof., Univ. of Exeter, 1993–2003. President, Prehistoric Soc., 1978–82. Member: Royal Commn on Ancient and Historical Monuments of Scotland, 1992–2002; Directorate, Discovery Prog. Ireland, 2001–06. MAE 1989; Hon. Corresp. Mem., Deutsches Archäologisches Institut, 1979; Hon. MIFA 1991; Hon. MRIA 2005. FSA 1963 (Vice-Pres., 1982–86); Hon. FSAScot 2000. Hon. FilDr Uppsala Univ., 1997. Grahame Clark Medal, British Acad., 1995; ICI Medal, British Archaeol Awards, 1998; Europa Prize for Prehistory, Prehistoric Soc., 2000; Gold Medal, Soc. of Antiquaries of London, 2002; European Archaeol Heritage Prize, 2006; Rajewski Medal, Nat. Mus., Warsaw, 2007; Gold Medal, Royal Swedish Acad. of Letters, History and Antiquities, 2009. *Publications:* The Archaeology of Early Man (with E. Higgs), 1969; Field Archaeology in Britain, 1972; Archaeology by Experiment, 1973; (with A. Harding) The Bronze Age in Europe, 1979; Experimental Archaeology, 1979; (with B. Orme) Prehistory of the Somerset Levels, 1980; The Archaeology of Wetlands, 1984; (with B. J. Coles) Sweet Track to Glastonbury: the Somerset Levels in prehistory, 1986; (ed with A. Lawson) European Wetlands in Prehistory, 1987; Meare Village East, 1987; (with B. J. Coles) People of the Wetlands, 1989; Images of the Past, 1990; From the Waters of Oblivion, 1991; (with A. Goodall and S. Minnitt) Arthur Bulleid and the Glastonbury Lake Village 1892–1992, 1992; (with D. Hall) Fenland Survey, 1994; Rock Carvings of Uppland, 1994; (with S. Minnitt) Industrious and Fairly Civilised: the Glastonbury lake village, 1995; (with B. Coles) Enlarging the Past: the contribution of wetland archaeology, 1996; (with S. Minnitt) The Lake Villages of Somerset, 1996; (with D. Hall) Changing Landscapes: the ancient Fenland, 1998; (ed jtly) World Prehistory: studies in memory of Grahame Clark, 1999; (ed jtly) Bog Bodies, Sacred Sites and Wetland Archaeology, 1999; Patterns in a Rocky Land: rock carvings in South West Uppland, Sweden, 2000; (jtly) Ceremony and Display: the South Cadbury Bronze Age shield, 2000; Shadows of a Northern Past: rock carvings of Bohuslän and Østfold, 2005; (ed jtly) Grahame Clark and his Legacy, 2010; contrib. Proc. Prehist. Soc., Antiquaries Jl, Antiquity, Somerset Levels Papers, etc. *Recreations:* music, ancient art, wetlands, woodlands. *Address:* Fursdon Mill Cottage, Cadbury, Devon EX5 5JS. *T:* (01392) 860125.

COLES, Jonathan Andrew; Chief Executive, United Learning (formerly United Church Schools Trust and United Learning Trust), since 2012; *b* 5 May 1972; *s* of Robert and Josephine Coles; *m* 1995, Rachel Brooks; one *s* two *d*. *Educ:* Judd Sch., Tonbridge; Mansfield Coll., Oxford (BA); St Catharine's Coll., Cambridge (PGCE); York Univ. (MA). Head, Class Size Unit, DfEE, 1998–99; Perf. and Innovation Unit, Cabinet Office, 1999–2000; Head, Educn Green Paper, White Paper and Bill, 2000–02, Dir, London Challenge, 2002–05, DfES; Dir, 14–9 Reform, DfES, later DCSF, 2005–08; Dir Gen., Schs, DCSF, later DFE, 2008–10; Dir Gen., Educn Standards, DFE, 2010–11. Chm., Challenge Partners, 2012–. Trustee: Prince's Teaching Inst., 2012–; Educn Media Centre, 2013–. *Address:* (office) Fairline House, Nene Valley Business Park, Oundle, Peterborough PE8 4HN. *E:* jon.coles@unitedlearning.org.uk.

COLES, Kenneth George, AM 2000; BE; FIEAust; CEng, FIMechE; Chairman, Conveyor Co. of Australia Pty Ltd, 1957–91; *b* Melbourne, 30 June 1926; *s* of Sir Kenneth Coles; *m* 1st, 1950, Thalia Helen Goddard (marr. diss. 1980); one *s* two *d*; 2nd, 1985, Rowena Danziger. *Educ:* The King's Sch., Parramatta, NSW; Sydney Univ. (BE 1948). FIE(Aust) 1986; FIMechE 1969; FAIM 1959. Gained engrg experience in appliance manufacturing and automotive industries Nuffield Aust. Pty Ltd, Gen. Motors Holdens Pty Ltd and Frigidaire, before commencing own business manufacturing conveyors, 1955; Chm. and Man. Dir, K. G. Coles & Co. Pty Ltd, 1955–76, Chm. 1976–95; Chm. and Man. Dir, KGC Magnetic Tape Pty Ltd, 1973–80. Director: Australian Oil & Gas Corp. Ltd, 1969–89 (Dep. Chm., 1984–89); A. O. G. Minerals Ltd, 1969–87 (Dep. Chm., 1984–87); Coles Myer Ltd (formerly G. J. Coles & Coy Ltd), 1976–94; Electrical Equipment Ltd, 1976–84; Permanent Trustee Co. Ltd, 1978–94 (Vice Chm., 1990–91; Chm., 1991–94); Chatham Investment Co. Ltd, 1987–94; NRMA Insurance Ltd, 1989–90; Stockland Trust Group, 1990–95; Chairman: Innovation Council of NSW Ltd, 1984–89 (Dir, 1982–89); Nat. Engrg (now Metal and Engrg) Training Bd, 1988–99. Metal Trades Industry Association: Gen. Councillor, NSW Br., 1976–94; Nat. Councillor, 1988–94; Mem. Bd, Sir William Tyree MTIA Foundn, 1995–2002. Chm., Lizard Island Reef Res. Foundn, 1994–2012 (Dir, 1992–). Member: Internat. Solar Energy Soc., 1957–97; Science & Industry Forum, Australian Academy of Science, 1983–94; Mem. and Employers' Rep., NSW Bd of Secondary Educn, 1987–90. Mem. Council, Nat. Roads and Motorists Assoc., NSW, 1986–90. Councillor and Mem. Bd of Governors, Ascham Sch., 1972–82; Employers' Rep., NSW Secondary Schs Bd, 1979–83. Sydney University: Fellow, Senate, 1983–97; Chairman: Internat. House, 2001–03 (Mem. Council 1993–2003); Save Sight Inst., 2001–10 (Mem. Council, 1998–2010); Mem., Bd of Advice, Sydney Conservatorium of Music, 2007–11. Hon. Associate, Med. Sch., Sydney Univ., 2011–. Co. Sec., Visionsearch Pty Ltd, 2011–. Hon. Dr Univ. Sydney, 1999. *Publications:* Branching Out: the George Coles family tree, 2001, 2nd edn 2015. *Address:* 501/170 Ocean Street, Edgecliff, NSW 2027, Australia. *T:* (2) 93286084, *Fax:* (2) 93274010. *Clubs:* Union, Australian, Sydney Rotary; Royal Sydney Golf; Rose Bay Surf.

COLES, His Honour (Norman) Bruce (Cameron); QC 1984; a Circuit Judge, 1997–2006; *b* 28 Feb. 1937; *s* of Sir Norman Coles and of Dorothy Verna (*née* Deague); *m* 1961, Sally Fenella Freeman; one *s* three *d*; *m* 2007, Alison Clifton Barnard. *Educ:* Melbourne Grammar Sch.; Univ. of Melbourne (LLB); Magdalen Coll., Oxford Univ. (BCL). 2nd Lieut, 6th Bn Royal Melbourne Regt, 1956–59. Associate to Sir Owen Dixon, Chief Justice of High Court of Australia, 1959–60; called to English Bar, Middle Temple, 1963, Bencher, 1991; admitted to Bar of Supreme Court of Victoria, 1964. Assistant Recorder, 1982–86; Recorder, 1986–97; Dep. Official Referee, 1992–97. Chm., Bar Race Relations Cttee, 1994–97; Mem., Equal Treatment Adv. Cttee, Judicial Studies Bd, 1999. Mem. Council, Oxfam, 1985–98. Mem., Synod, Dio. of Gloucester, 2011–; Lay Chair, N Cotswold Deanery, 2012–. Chm., Glenfall Hse Trust, 2010–; Trustee, Intrac, 2010–. Chm . of Govs, Enstone Co. Primary Sch., 1993–2000. *Recreations:* mountaineering, cycling, theatre, music. *E:* brucecoles@btinternet.com.

COLES, Sadie; Proprietor, Sadie Coles HQ gallery, since 1997; *b* Portsmouth, 13 Feb. 1963; *m* 2004, Juergen Teller; one *s*. *Educ:* Middlesex Poly. (BA). Jun. asst to Sir John Tooley, Royal Opera Hse, 1986–87; Mktg Asst, NT, 1987–89; Asst Dir, Arnolfini Art Centre, 1989–90; Dir, Anthony D'Offay Gall., 1990–96. *Publications:* (contrib.) Some Kind of Heaven, 1997; (contrib.) Art, Money, Parties: new institutions in the political economy of contemporary art, 2005; (contrib.) Collecting Contemporary, 2006. *Address:* Sadie Coles HQ, 69 South Audley Street, W1K 2QZ. *T:* (020) 7493 8611, *Fax:* (020) 7499 4878. *E:* info@sadiecoles.com.

COLES, Sir Sherard (Louis) C.; *see* Cowper-Coles.

COLEY, Dr Graham Douglas; Group Director Compliance, QinetiQ Ltd, 2006–08 (Business Continuity Director, 2001–06); *b* 16 Nov. 1946; *s* of late Douglas Leonard Coley and of Phyllis Adeline Coley (*née* Hughes); *m* 1972, Susan Elizabeth Thackery. *Educ:* Halesowen Grammar Sch.; Birmingham Univ. (BSc 1st Cl. Hons); Darwin Coll., Cambridge (PhD 1971). FIET (FIEE 1994); FInstP 1998. Midlands Res. Station, Gas Council, 1967–68; Atomic Weapons Research Establishment, Aldermaston, 1968–87: Supt, Explosives Technol. Br., 1982–85; Head, Chemical Technol. Div., 1985–87; Dir, Nuclear Resources, MoD PE, 1987–90; Dep. Head, Efficiency Unit, Prime Minister's Office, 1990–92; Asst Chief Scientific Advr (Projects), MoD, 1992–94; Man. Dir, Protection and Life Scis Div., 1994–97, Man. Dir, Science, 1997–2000, Business Continuity Dir, 2000–01, DERA. Trustee, Wild Trout Trust, 2003–. Non-executive Director: Upper Oykel Ltd, 2010–; Oykel Bridge Hotel Ltd, 2011–. *Publications:* papers in technical jls and internat. conf. proc. *Recreations:* flyfishing, shooting, gardening (auriculas). *Club:* Flyfishers'.

COLFER, Eoin; author; *b* 14 May 1965; *s* of Billy and Noreen Colfer; *m* 1991, Jacqueline Power; two *s*. *Educ:* Carysfort Coll. of Educn (BEd). Teacher: Scoil Mhuire Primary Sch., Wexford, 1986–94; Jeddah Private Acad., Saudi Arabia, 1994–95; Internat. Sch. of Martina Franca, Italy, 1995–96; Sfat Internat. Sch., Tunisia, 1996–98; Scoil Mhuire Primary Sch., 1998–2002. *Publications:* Benny and Omar, 1998; Benny and Babe, 1999; Going Potty, 1999; The Wish List, 2000; Ed's Funny Feet, 2000; Ed's Bed, 2001; Artemis Fowl, 2001; Artemis Fowl and the Arctic Incident, 2002; Artemis Fowl and the Eternity Code, 2003; Spud Murphy, 2004; The Supernaturalist, 2004; Artemis Fowl and the Opal Deception, 2005; Half Moon Investigations, 2006; Captain Crow's Teeth, 2006; Artemis Fowl and the Lost Colony, 2006; The Worst Boy in the World, 2007; Airman, 2008; Artemis Fowl and the Time Paradox, 2008; And Another Thing…: Douglas Adams's Hitchhiker's Guide to the Galaxy: Part Six of Three, 2009; Artemis Fowl and the Atlantis Complex, 2010; Plugged, 2011. *Address:* c/o Ed Victor Ltd, 6 Bayley Street, Bedford Square, WC1B 3HB.

COLGAN, Michael Anthony, Hon. OBE 2010; Artistic Director and Member Board, Gate Theatre, Dublin, since 1983; *b* Dublin, 17 July 1950; *s* of James Colgan and Josephine Colgan (*née* Geoghegan). *Educ:* Trinity Coll., Dublin (BA). Dir, Abbey Th., Dublin, 1974–78; Co-Manager, Irish Th. Co., 1977–78; Dublin Theatre Festival: Manager, 1978–80; Artistic Dir, 1981–83; Mem., Bd of Dirs, 1983–2015. Exec. Dir, Little Bird Films, 1986–; Co-Founder, Blue Angel Films Co., 1999. Artistic Dir, Parma Fest., 1982; Chm., St Patrick's Fest., 1996–99; Mem. Bd, Millennium Festivals Ltd, Laura Pels Foundn, NY, 2000–04. Mem., Irish Arts Council, 1989–94. Mem., Gov. Authy, Dublin City Univ. Theatre productions include: Faith Healer, Dublin, NY and Edinburgh; No Man's Land, Dublin and London; I'll Go On; Juno and the Paycock; Salomé; 19 Beckett Stage Plays; six Beckett Fests, Dublin, NY, London and Sydney; four Pinter Fests, Dublin and NY. World premières incl. The Birds, Molly Sweeney, Afterplay, Shining City, The Home Place. Director: First Love; Faith Healer; Krapp's Last Tape. Television Producer: Troubles, 1986; Two Lives, 1993; Beckett Film Project, 2000; Celebration, 2006. Member, Board of Directors: Lir Acad. of Dramatic Arts; Dublin Festival Th.; Blue Angel Films Ltd. Hon. LLD TCD. Sunday Independent Arts Award, 1985, 1987; Nat. Entertainment Award, 1996; People of the Year Award, 1999; Irish Times Theatre Lifetime Achievement Award, 2006. Chevalier, Ordre des Arts et des Lettres, 2007. *Recreations:* middle distance running, chamber music. *Address:* Gate Theatre, 1 Cavendish Row, Parnell Square, Dublin 1, Ireland. *T:* (1) 8744369, *Fax:* (1) 8745373. *E:* info@gate-theatre.ie. *Clubs:* Ivy; Residence (Dublin).

COLGAN, His Honour Samuel Hezlett; a Circuit Judge, 1990–2010; *b* 10 June 1945; *s* of late Henry George Colgan and of Jane Swan Hezlett. *Educ:* Foyle College, Londonderry; Trinity College Dublin (MA, LLB). Called to the Bar, Middle Temple, 1969; a Recorder, SE Circuit, 1987. *Recreations:* travelling, the arts, reading, tennis.

COLGRAIN, 4th Baron *cr* 1946, of Everlands, co. Kent; **Alastair Colin Leckie Campbell;** *b* 16 Sept. 1951; *s* of 3rd Baron Colgrain and of Veronica Margaret, *d* of late Lt-Col William Leckie Webster, RAMC; *S* father, 2008; *m* 1979, Annabel Rose, *yr d* of late Hon. Robin Hugh Warrender; two *s*. *Educ:* Eton; Trinity Coll., Cambridge (BA 1973). High Sheriff, Kent, 2013–14. *Heir:* *s* Hon. Thomas Colin Donald Campbell, *b* 9 Feb. 1984.

COLIN-THOMÉ, David Geoffrey, OBE 1997; FRCGP, FFPH, FRCP; General Practitioner, Castlefields, Runcorn, 1971–2007; National Director for Primary Care, 2001–10, and Medical Director for Commissioning and System Management Directorate, 2007–10, Department of Health; independent healthcare consultant, since 2010; *b* 5 Oct. 1943; *s* of William James Charles Colin-Thomé and Pearl Erin Colin-Thomé; *m* 1969, Christine Mary Simpson; one *s* one *d*. *Educ:* Hutton Grammar Sch., Preston; Newcastle upon Tyne Medical Sch. (MB BS 1966). FRCGP 1990; MHSM 1998; FFPH (FFPHM 2002); FRCP 2006. Dir Primary Care, NW Regl Office, NHS Exec., DoH, 1994–96; SMO, Scottish Office, 1997–98; Dir Primary Care, London Region, DoH, 1998–2001. Hon. Visiting Professor: Centre for Public Policy and Mgt, Manchester Univ., 2002–; Sch. of Health, Durham Univ., 2004–. Hon. FFGDP(UK) 2005; Hon. FQNI 2009. *Recreations:* eclectic interests in theatre, dance, books and sport; devoted grandfather to Amber, Jacob, Luca, Ryan, Beth and Zachary; supporter of Everton FC. *Address:* Hunter House, Bainbridge Lane, Eshott, Northumberland NE65 9FD.

COLL, Dame Elizabeth Anne Loosemore E.; *see* Esteve-Coll.

COLLARBONE, Dame Patricia, DBE 1998; EdD; Director, Creating Tomorrow Ltd, since 2009; Executive Director for Development, Training and Development Agency, 2006–07 (on secondment from Institute of Education). *Educ:* MBA 1995; EdD Lincolnshire and Humberside Univ. 1999. Headteacher, Haggerston Sch., Hackney, 1990–96; Founding Dir, London Leadership Centre, Inst. of Education, Univ. of London, 1997–2002; Dir of Leadership Progs, Nat. Coll. for Sch. Leadership, Nottingham, 2002–04; Dir, Nat. Remodelling Team, Nat. Coll. for Sch. Leadership, then TTA, 2003–06. Manager, London Regl Assessment Centre, 1996–98, London Regl Trng and Development Centre, 1998–99, NPQH. Advr, on rôle of the Headteacher, Govt 9th Select Cttee, 1998; Special Advr, on headship and leadership issues, DfEE, 1999–2001. Former Member: SCAA Key Stage 3 Adv. Gp; DfEE Adv. Cttee on Improving Schs; Educn Summit. Member: DfEE Sch. Improvement Team; NPQH Mgt Develt Gp, TTA. London Pres., NAHT. Fellow: Univ. of Lincolnshire and Humberside; Hull Univ., 2000. FRSA. *Publications:* Understanding Systems Leadership, 2008; (with John West-Burnham) Creating Tomorrow: planning, developing and sustaining change in education and other public services, 2009.

COLLARD, Dr Ian Frank; HM Diplomatic Service; Ambassador to Panama, since 2013; *b* 13 April 1976; *m* Tamara Renée; four *d*. *Educ:* King Edward VI Grammar Sch., Chelmsford; King's Coll., Cambridge (BA 1st Cl. Physical and Biol Anthropol. 1997; PhD Ecol. and Evolutionary Biol. 2002). Paralegal Associate, Imperial Oil, Canada, 1997; reporter, Lloyd's List, 1998; Res. Associate, Human Diversity Project, King's Coll. Res. Centre, Univ. of Cambridge, 1998–99; entered FCO, 2002; Desk Officer, ME Dept, 2002–03, UN/Internat. Orgns Dept, 2003–04, FCO; Second Sec. (Pol), UKMIS to UN, NY, 2005–08; First Sec. (Pol), Washington, 2008–11; Hd, N America Dept, FCO, 2011–12; Silver Comd, Olympics Security, Counter-Terrorism Dept, FCO, 2012; Hd, N America Dept, FCO, 2012–13. *Address:* c/o Foreign and Commonwealth Office, King Charles Street, SW1A 2AH.

COLLARD, Paul Anthony Carthew; Chief Executive, Creativity, Culture and Education, since 2009; *b* 17 Aug. 1954; *s* of late Douglas Reginald Collard, OBE and Eleni Cubitt; *m* 1983, Hilary Porter; three *s* one *d*. *Educ:* Ampleforth Coll., York; Trinity Coll., Cambridge (BA Hons). Exec. Sec., Friends of Cyprus, 1976–80; Administrator, Aga Khan Award for Architecture, 1980–82; Gen. Manager, ICA, 1983–87; Dep. Controller, BFI, South Bank, 1988–92; Director: UK Year of Visual Arts, 1993–97; Internat. Fest. of Arts and Ideas, New Haven, CT, 1997–2001; Hd, Programme Develt, Newcastle Gateshead Initiative, 2001–04; Nat. Dir, Creative Partnerships, 2005–09. Programme Co-ordinator, Newcastle Gateshead Bid for European Capital of Culture, 2001–03. David Goldman Prof. of Business Innovation, Univ. of Newcastle upon Tyne, 2003–04. Mem., Arts Council of England, subseq. Arts Council England, 2002–04 (Chm., NE Regl Arts Council, 2002–04). *Recreation:* arguing with the children. *Address:* Creativity, Culture and Education, 20 Portland Terrace, Newcastle upon Tyne NE2 1QS.

COLLAS, Sir Richard (John), Kt 2014; Bailiff of Guernsey, since 2012 (Deputy Bailiff, 2005–12); a Judge of the Court of Appeal of Jersey, since 2012; Acting Deemster, Isle of Man, since 2014; *b* 27 May 1953; *s* of Peter Renouf Collas and Nora Kathleen Collas (*née* Turner); *m* 1986, Amanda Judith Kenmir (*d* 2010); two *s* one *d*. *Educ:* Jesus Coll., Oxford (BA Engrg Sci. 1975); City Univ., London (Dip. Law 1981). Lever Brothers Ltd, 1975–80. Called to the Bar, Gray's Inn, 1982, Guernsey, 1983; Collas Day Advocates, 1983–2005. *Recreations:* family, boating. *Address:* Bailiff's Chambers, Royal Court House, St James Street, St Peter Port, Guernsey GY1 2NZ. *T:* (01481) 726161, *Fax:* (01481) 713861. *Clubs:* United (Guernsey); Guernsey Yacht, Royal Channel Islands Yacht.

COLLECOTT, Dr Peter Salmon, CMG 2002; HM Diplomatic Service, retired; consultant on international diplomacy and business, since 2009; Founding Partner, Ambassador Partnership (formerly ADRg Ambassadors LLP), since 2011; *b* 8 Oct. 1950; *s* of late George William Collecott and Nancie Alice Collecott (*née* Salmon); *m* 1982, Judith Patricia Pead. *Educ:* Chigwell Sch., Essex; St John's Coll., Cambridge (MA 1976; PhD 1976); MIT (Kennedy Schol. 1972). Royal Soc. Fellow, Max Planck Inst. for Physics and Astrophysics, Munich, 1976–77; joined HM Diplomatic Service, 1977: FCO, 1977–78; MECAS, Lebanon, later London, 1978–80; 1st Secretary: (Political), Khartoum, 1980–82; (Econ., Commercial, Agricl), Canberra, 1982–86; Head, Iran/Iraq Section, ME Dept, FCO, 1986–88; Asst Head, EC Dept (Ext.), FCO, 1988–89; Counsellor, Head of Chancery and Consul Gen., later Dep. Head of Mission, Jakarta, 1989–93; Counsellor (EU and Econ.), Bonn, 1994–98; Hd, Admin. Restructuring Rev. Team, FCO, 1998–99; Dir, Resources, FCO, 1999–2001; Dep. Under-Sec. of State and Chief Clerk, subseq. Dir Gen., Corporate Affairs, FCO, 2001–03; Ambassador to Brazil, 2004–08. Special Advr to Internat. Sustainability Unit, Prince of Wales' Charities, 2010–. *Publications:* papers on theoretical physics in learned jls. *Recreations:* gardening, reading.

COLLENDER, Andrew Robert; QC 1991; **His Honour Judge Collender;** a Circuit Judge, since 2006; *b* 11 Aug. 1946; *s* of John and Kathleen Collender; *m* 1974, Titia Tybout (*d* 2013); two *s*. *Educ:* Mt Pleasant Boys High Sch., Zimbabwe; Univ. of Bristol (LLB Hons). Called to the Bar, Lincoln's Inn, 1969, Bencher, 2000; a Recorder, 1993–2006; a Dep. High Ct Judge, 1998–; Head of Chambers, 2 Temple Gardens, 2002–05; a Sen. Judge, 2007–, Presiding Sen. Judge, 2014–, Sovereign Base Areas, Cyprus. *Recreations:* playing the violin, sailing. *Address:* Mayor's and City of London Court, Guildhall Buildings, Basinghall Street, EC2V 5AR. *Club:* Bosham Sailing.

COLLENETTE, Hon. David (Michael); PC (Canada) 1983; FCILT; Senior Counsel, Hill & Knowlton, Canada, since 2008; Distinguished Fellow, Glendon College, York University, Toronto, since 2004; Distinguished Visiting Fellow, Ryerson University, Toronto, since 2014; *b* 24 June 1946; *s* of David Henry and Sarah Margaret Collenette; *m* 1975, Penny Hossack; one *s*. *Educ:* Glendon Coll., York Univ. (BA Hons; MA). FCILT 2009. Admin. Officer, Marketing Div., Internat. Life Assurance Co., UK, 1970–72; Exec. Vice-Pres., Mandrake Management Consultants, Canada, 1987–93. Advr, Intergraph Corp., 2005–. MP (L): York East, 1974–79 and 1980–84; Don Valley East, 1993–2004; Minister of State for Multiculturalism, 1983–84; Minister of Nat. Defence and of Veterans' Affairs, 1993–96; Minister of Transport, 1997–2003. Sec.-Gen., Liberal Party of Canada, 1985–87 (Exec. Dir, Toronto, 1969–70, Ontario, 1972–74). Chm., CILT (N America), 2011–; Vice-Pres., CILT (Internat.), 2010–. Dir, Harbourfront Corp., Toronto, 2009–. Member: Internat. Adv. Council, Inst. for Internat. Studies, Stanford Univ., 1999–2005; Canadian Adv. Bd, Parsons Brinckerhoff, 2011–. Mem., Royal Canadian Military Inst. *Recreations:* swimming, theatre, classical music. *Address:* Suite 1100, 55 Metcalfe Street, Ottawa, ON K1P 6L5, Canada. *E:* david.collenette@hillandknowlton.ca, dcollenette@glendon.yorku.ca. *Club:* National (Toronto).

COLLENS, Rupert; *see* Mackeson, Sir R. H.

COLLETT, Sir Ian (Seymour), 3rd Bt *cr* 1934; *b* 5 Oct. 1953; *s* of David Seymour Collett (*d* 1962), and of Sheila Joan Collett (who *m* 1980, Sir James William Miskin, QC), *o d* of late Harold Scott; *S* grandfather, 1971; *m* 1982, Philippa, *o d* of late James R. I. Hawkins, Preston St Mary, Suffolk; one *s* one *d*. *Educ:* Lancing College, Sussex. Mem., Internat. Inst. of Marine Surveyors, 1998. *Recreations:* golf, fishing, cricket, shooting. *Heir:* *s* Anthony Seymour Collett [*b* 27 Feb. 1984; *m* 2011, Sophie Elizabeth Mary Williams]. *Clubs:* MCC; Aldeburgh Golf; Aldeburgh Yacht.

COLLETT, Michael John; QC 2013; *b* Bristol, 11 Dec. 1971; *s* of John and Bridget Collett; *m* 1998, Melissa Manes; one *s* one *d*. *Educ:* Queen Elizabeth's Hosp., Bristol; St John's Coll., Oxford (BA 1st Cl. Hons Lit. Hum.); City Univ. (DipLaw (Dist.)). MCIArb 2005. Called to the Bar, Gray's Inn, 1995; in practice as barrister, specialising in commercial law, 1997–. *Publications:* (contrib.) Arbitration in England, 2013. *Recreation:* classic cars. *Address:* 20 Essex Street, WC2R 3AL. *T:* (020) 7842 1200, *Fax:* (020) 7842 1270. *E:* clerks@20essexst.com.

COLLEY, Maj.-Gen. (David) Bryan (Hall), CB 1988; CBE 1982 (OBE 1977; MBE 1968); FCILT; Director-General, Road Haulage Association, 1988–97; *b* 5 June 1934; *s* of Lawson and Alice Colley; *m* 1957, Marie Thérèse (*née* Préfontaine); one *s* one *d*. *Educ:* King Edward's Sch., Birmingham; RMA, Sandhurst. Commissioned: RASC, 1954; RCT, 1965; regimental appts in Germany, Belgium, UK, Hong Kong and Singapore; Student, Staff Coll., Camberley, 1964; JSSC Latimer, 1970; CO Gurkha Transport Regt and 31 Regt, RCT, 1971–74; Staff HQ 1st (British) Corps, 1974–77; Comd Logistic Support Gp, 1977–80; Col Adjutant and Quartermaster (Ops and Plans) and Dir Admin. Planning, MoD (Army), 1980–82; Comd Transport 1st (British) Corps and Comdr Bielefeld Garrison, 1983–86; Dir Gen., Transport and Movts (Army), 1986–88, retired. Col Comdt, RCT, 1988–93; Col Comdt, Royal Logistic Corps, 1993–2000. Pres., RASC and RCT Benevolent Fund, 2006–11. Freeman, City of London, 1986; Hon. Liveryman, Worshipful Co. of Carmen, 1986. *Recreations:* travel, information technology, military history. *Address:* c/o HSBC, Redditch, Worcs B97 4EA. *Club:* Army and Navy.

COLLEY, Kitty; *see* Ussher, K.

COLLEY, Prof. Linda Jane, CBE 2009; PhD; FRHistS; FBA 1999; FRSL; Shelby M. C. Davis 1958 Professor of History, Princeton University, since 2003 (Old Dominion Professor in the Humanities, 2013–14); *b* 13 Sept. 1949; *d* of Roy Colley and Marjorie (*née* Hughes); *m* 1982, David Nicholas Cannadine (*see* Sir David Cannadine); one *d* decd. *Educ:* Bristol Univ. (BA); Cambridge Univ. (MA, PhD). University of Cambridge: Eugenie Strong Research Fellow, Girton Coll., 1975–78; Fellow: Newnham Coll., 1978–79; Christ's Coll., 1979–81 (Hon. Fellow, 2006); Yale University: Dir, Lewis Walpole Liby, 1982–96; Asst Prof., History, 1982–85; Associate Prof., 1985–90; Prof., History, 1990–92; Richard M. Colgate Prof. of History, 1992–98. Sch. Prof. in History and Leverhulme Personal Res. Prof., European Inst., LSE, 1998–2003. Hooker Distinguished Vis. Prof., McMaster Univ., 1999; Glaxo Smith Kline Sen. Fellow, Nat. Humanities Center, NC, 2006; Adjunct Prof., Humanities Res. Centre, ANU, 2006–; Fletcher Jones Distinguished Fellow, Huntington Liby, Calif, 2010; Birkelund Fellow, Cullman Center for Scholars and Writers, NY Public Liby, 2013–14. Journalism and work on radio and TV; writer and presenter, Acts of Union and Disunion series, BBC Radio 4, 2014. Lectures: Anstey, Univ. of Kent, 1994; William Church Meml, Brown Univ., 1994; Dist. (in British Hist.), Univ. of Texas at Austin, 1995; Trevelyan, Cambridge Univ., 1997; Wiles, QUB, 1997; Hayes Robinson, Royal Holloway, Univ. of London, 1998; Ford Special, Oxford Univ., 1998; Bliss Carnochan, Stanford Humanities Center, 1998; Prime Minister's Millennium, 1999; Ena H. Thompson, Pomona Coll., Calif, 2001; Raleigh, British Acad., 2002; Nehru, London, 2003; Bateson, Oxford Univ., 2003; Chancellor Dunning Trust, Queen's Univ., Ont., 2004; Byrn, Vanderbilt Univ., 2005; Annual Internat. Hist., LSE, 2006; C. P. Snow, Christ's Coll., Cambridge, 2007; Political Sci. Quarterly, 2007; Victoria County Hist., 2007; President's, Princeton Univ., 2007; Gordon B. Hinkley in British Studies, Univ. of Utah, 2010; Bosley-Warnock, Univ. of Delaware, 2010; Martin Wright, Univ. of Sussex, 2011; Kayser, George Washington Univ., 2011; Indian Social and Econ. Hist. Rev., Delhi, 2011; Ubbelohde, Case Western Univ., 2011; Max Weber, Eur. Univ., Florence, 2012; John Coffin Meml, Univ. of London, 2012; Iredell, Univ. of Lancaster, 2012; Macmillan, Univ. of Toronto, 2013; Ralph Miliband, LSE, 2014; Gomes, Emmanuel Coll., Cambridge, 2015; Robbs, Univ. of Auckland, 2015; Aylmer, Univ. of York, 2015; Donald W. Sutherland Lect. in Legal Hist., Univ. of Iowa, 2015. Guest Curator, exhibn, Taking Liberties: the struggle for Britain's freedoms and rights, BL, 2008–09. Member: Council, Tate Gall. of British Art, 1999–2003; BL Bd, 1999–2003; Adv. Council, Paul Mellon Centre for British Art, 1998–2003; Bd, Princeton Univ. Press, 2007–; Res. Cttee, BM, 2012–. MAE 2010. FRHistS 1988; FRSL 2004. Hon. DLitt: South Bank, 1998; UEA, 2005; Bristol, 2006; Hull, 2012; DUniv Essex, 2004. *Publications:* In Defiance of Oligarchy: The Tory Party 1714–60, 1982; Namier, 1989; Crown Pictorial: art and the British monarchy, 1990; Britons: forging the nation 1707–1837, 1992 (Wolfson History Prize, 1993); Captives: Britain, Empire and the world 1600–1850, 2002; The Ordeal of Elizabeth Marsh, 2007; Taking Stock of Taking Liberties, 2008; Acts of Union and Disunion, 2014; numerous articles and reviews in UK and USA jls. *Recreations:* travel, looking at art, politics. *Address:* Department of History, Princeton University, 129 Dickinson Hall, Princeton, NJ 08544–1017, USA; c/o Gill Coleridge, 20 Powis Mews, W11 1JN. *W:* www.lindacolley.com.

COLLIER, family name of **Baron Monkswell**.

COLLIER, Andrew James, CB 1976; Deputy Secretary, Department of Health and Social Security, 1973–82; *b* 12 July 1923; *s* of Joseph Veasy Collier and Dorothy Murray; *m* 1950, Bridget (*d* 2012), *d* of George and Edith Eberstadt, London; two *d*. *Educ:* Harrow; Christ Church, Oxford. Served Army, RHA, 1943–46. Entered HM Treasury, 1948; Private Sec. to successive Chancellors of the Exchequer, 1956–59; Asst Sec., 1961; Under-Sec., 1967; Under-Secretary: Civil Service Dept, 1968–71; DHSS, 1971–73. *Address:* 12 Oxford House, 52 Parkside, Wimbledon, SW19 5NE. *T:* (020) 8946 4220. *Club:* Athenæum.

COLLIER, Andrew John, CBE 1995; Schools Adjudicator, 1999–2005; General Secretary, Society of Education Officers, 1996–99 (Treasurer, 1987–92; President, 1990); *b* 29 Oct. 1939; *s* of Francis George Collier and Margaret Nancy (*née* Nockles); *m* 1964, Gillian Ann (*née* Churchill); two *d*. *Educ:* University College Sch.; St John's Coll., Cambridge (MA). Assistant Master, Winchester Coll., 1962–68; Hampshire County Educn Dept, 1968–71; Buckinghamshire County Educn Dept, 1971–77; Dep. Chief Educn Officer, 1977–80, Chief Educn Officer, 1980–96, Lancashire CC. Member: Open Univ. Vis. Cttee, 1982–88; Council for Accreditation of Teacher Educn, 1984–89; Nat. Training Task Force, 1989–92; Gen. Synod Bd of Educn, 1993–2001; Educn Cttee, Royal Soc., 1995–2000; Chm., County Educn Officers' Soc., 1987–88; Treas., Schools Curriculum Award, 1987–92. Chm., Assoc. of Educn Cttees Trust, 2010–. Liveryman, Worshipful Company of Wheelwrights, 1972–2002. Mem. Council, Univ. of Lancaster, 1981–86, 1988–94, 1996–99; Governor: Myerscough Coll., 1996–2003; St Martin's Coll., Lancaster, 2001–07; Whitechapel Primary Sch., 2002–05 (Chm. of Govs, 2003–04); Univ. of Cumbria, 2007–10. Pres., Lancs Fedn of Young Farmers' Clubs, 1985–88. *Publications:* (contrib.) New Directions for County Government, 1989; articles in jls. *Recreations:* music, walking, boating. *Clubs:* Athenæum; Leander (Henley-on-Thames); Salcombe Yacht; Warrington Rowing.

COLLIER, Air Vice-Marshal Andy; *see* Collier, Air Vice-Marshal J. A.

COLLIER, Prof. Christopher George, PhD, DSc; CMet, CEnv; Professor of Atmospheric Science, since 2009, and Head of Strategic Partnerships, National Centre for Atmospheric Science, since 2009, University of Leeds; *b* 10 Sept. 1946; *s* of George and Barbara Collier; *m* 1969, Cynthia Dawson; two *s*. *Educ:* Hyde County Grammar Sch.; Imperial Coll., London (BSc Hons Physics 1968; ARCS); Univ. of Salford (PhD 1999; DSc 2008). CMet 1995; CEnv 2005. Meteorological Office, 1968–95; University of Salford, 1995–2009: Dir, Telford Res. Inst., 1997–98; Dean, Fac. of Sci., Engrg and Envmt, 1999–2003; Prof. of Envmtl Remote Sensing, 1995–2009. Chm., EU COST-73 Internat. Radar Networking Mgt Cttee, 1986–91. FRMetS 1967 (Pres., 2004–06; Hon. FRMetS 2012); Member: British Hydrological Soc.; CIWEM; Amer. Meteorological Soc. Robert Hugh Mill Medal, RMetS, 1982; L. G. Groves Prize, Met. Office, 1984; first Vaisala Prize, WMO, 1986. *Publications:* Applications of Weather Radar Systems, 1996; over 90 refereed scientific pubns and over 200 conf. papers and reports. *Recreations:* swimming, reading, gardening, writing, Church of England. *Address:* School of Earth and Environment, Maths/Earth and Environment Building, University of Leeds, Leeds LS2 9JT.

COLLIER, David Gordon, OBE 2015; Chief Executive, England and Wales Cricket Board, 2005–14; *b* 22 April 1955; *s* of John and Pat Collier; *m* 1980, Jennifer Pendleton; two *s* one *d*. *Educ:* Loughborough Grammar Sch.; Loughborough Univ. (BSc Hons Sports Sci. and Recreation Mgt). Dep. Manager, Adams Sports Centre, Wem, 1979–80; Dep. Sec. Gen. and Manager, Essex CCC, 1980–83; Chief Exec., Glos CCC, 1983–86; Mktg Manager, Sema Gp plc, 1986–88; Sen. Vice-Pres., American Airlines, 1988–92; Man. Dir, Servisair plc, 1992–93; Chief Executive: Leics CCC, 1993–99; Notts CCC, 1999–2004. Internat. hockey umpire, 1985–2002. Member: European Hockey Fedn, 2000–04; Fedn of Internat. Hockey, 2002– (Mem. Exec. Bd, 2008–12; Chm., Audit Cttee, 2011); Ind. Mem., Major Events Panel, UK Sport, 2011–. Chm., Internat. Hockey Rules Bd, 2008–. Sydney Friskin Award, Hockey Writers, 2003. DUniv Loughborough, 2014. *Recreations:* cricket, hockey, golf.

COLLIER, Declan; Chief Executive Officer, London City Airport, since 2012; *b* Dublin, 14 June 1955; *s* of John and Margaret Collier; *m* 1985, Jan Winter; one *d*. *Educ:* Catholic Univ. Sch., Dublin; Trinity Coll., Dublin (BA Mod (Econ); MSc (Econ) Econs). Sen. exec. and mgt posts with ExxonMobil, 1980–99; Chm., Esso Ireland, 1999–2002; Alternative Fuels Manager/Eur. Dist Heating Manager, ExxonMobil, 2002–05; CEO, Dublin Airport Authy, 2005–12; Chm., AerRianta Internat., 2005–12. Non-exec. Dir, Allied Irish Banks (UK) plc, 2012–. President: Airports Council Internat., Europe, 2011–13; Airports Council Internat., World, 2015– (Vice-Chair, 2013–15); Mem. Bd, Airport Operators Assoc., UK, 2012–. Chairman: Dublin Th. Fest., 2011–; Irish Th. Trust, 2011–. *Recreations:* cycling, hill walking, Rugby, theatre, family. *Address:* London City Airport, City Aviation House, Royal Docks, E16 2PB. *T:* (020) 7646 0011. *E:* declan.collier@londoncityairport.com. *Clubs:* Naval and Military; Dun Laoghaire Golf.

COLLIER, Air Vice-Marshal James Andrew, (Andy), CB 2005; CBE 1995; Deputy Commander-in-Chief Personnel and Training Command and Chief of Staff to Air Member for Personnel, 2003–05; *b* 6 July 1951; *s* of late Charles Robert Collier and Cynthia Collier (*née* Walsh), and step *s* of late Paul Scott; *m* 1972, Judith Arnold; one *d*. *Educ:* Headlands Sch., Swindon; Univ. of Durham (BSc 1972). Commnd RAF 1972; Sqn Ldr 1980; Wing Comdr 1987; Gp Capt. 1991; Air Cdre 1998; Air Vice-Marshal 2003. *Recreations:* golf, following sport (especially international Rugby and cricket), reading science, philosophy, religion, historical fiction. *Club:* Royal Air Force.

COLLIER, John Spencer, FCA; Consultant, Grosvenor Clive & Stokes, since 2014 (Partner, 2011–13); *b* 4 March 1945; *s* of James Bradburn Collier and Phyllis Mary Collier; *m* 1972,

Theresa Mary Peers; two *s* one *d*. *Educ:* Trinity Coll., Cambridge (BA Geography 1967). FCA 1973. Tutor, King's Coll., London, 1967–69; joined Price Waterhouse, 1969: various posts, incl. Sen. Manager, 1969–81; Partner, 1981–92; Chief Executive: Newcastle Initiative, 1992–95; Lowes Gp plc, 1995–96; Finance Dir, Earth Centre, 1996–97; Sec. Gen., ICAEW, 1997–2002. Dir, Clive & Stokes Internat., 2004–11. Dir, Tyne and Wear Enterprise Agency, 1992–97; Chm., Dance City, Newcastle upon Tyne, 1994–97. Chm., Practice Regulation Directorate, ICAEW, 1993–97. Gov., Newcastle Coll., 1994–97. Chm., Friends of Richmond Park, 2004–07; Treas., Wordsworth Trust, 2004–; Trustee, British Pregnancy Adv. Service, 2013–. *Publications:* The Corporate Environment: the financial consequences for business, 1995. *Recreations:* mountains, marathons, painting, drawing. *Address:* 114 Lupus Street, SW1V 4AJ. *T:* (020) 7828 3412. *Club:* Travellers.

COLLIER, Lesley Faye, CBE 1993; Répétiteur, Royal Ballet, since 2000; Principal Dancer with the Royal Ballet, 1972–95; *b* 13 March 1947; *d* of Roy and Mavis Collier; twin *s*. *Educ:* The Royal Ballet School, White Lodge, Richmond. Joined Royal Ballet, 1965; has danced most principal roles in the Royal repertory; Ballet Mistress, 1995–99, Mem., Classical Ballet Staff, 1999–2000, Royal Ballet Sch. Evening Standard Ballet Award, 1987. *Address:* Royal Ballet, Royal Opera House, Covent Garden, WC2E 9DD.

COLLIER, Prof. Melvyn William; Director, Leuven University Library, Belgium, 2005–12, now Emeritus Professor, Leuven University; *b* 31 July 1947; *s* of late James Collier and Jessie Collier (*née* Siddall); *m* 1st, 1968, Anne Nightingale (*d* 2004); one *s* one *d*; 2nd, 2010, Hedwig Schwall. *Educ:* Bolton Sch.; Univ. of St Andrews (MA); Strathclyde Univ. (DipLib). FCLIP (ALA 1981; MIInfSc 1990, FIInfSc 1997). Academic Librarian posts at St Andrews Univ., UC, Cardiff and Hatfield Poly., 1970–79; Dep. Hd, Liby Services, PCL, 1980–84; Librarian, Leicester Poly., 1985–89; Hd, Div. of Learning Develt, and Prof. of Information Mgt, De Montfort Univ., 1989–97; Director: Strategic and Operational Planning, Dawson Hldgs, 1997–2000; Tilburg Univ. Liby, Netherlands, 2001–03. Vis. Prof., De Montfort Univ., 1997–2001; part-time Prof., Univ. of Northumbria, 2000–06. Mem., Liby and Inf. Commn, 1996–2000 (Chm., Res. Cttee, 1996–2000); Chairman: Liby and Inf. Adv. Cttee, British Council, 1995–2001; UK Office for Liby Networking, 1995–97; Mem., Jt Inf. Systems Cttee, HEFCs, 1996–97. Director: Open Learning Foundn, 1995–97; Information For All, 1997–99. Hon. DLitt Strathclyde, 2006. Medal, Hungarian Liby Assoc., 1992. *Publications:* Local Area Networks: the implications for library and information science, 1984; (ed) Case Studies in Software for Information Management, 1986; (ed) Telecommunications for Information Management and Transfer, 1987; (jtly) Decision Support Systems in Academic Libraries, 1991; (jtly) Decision Support Systems and Performance Assessment in Academic Libraries, 1993; (ed) Electronic Library and Visual Information Research: ELVIRA 1, 1995, ELVIRA 2, 1996; (ed) Business Planning for Digital Libraries: international approaches, 2010; numerous jl articles and res. reports. *Recreations:* golf, hill-walking. *Address:* Naamsestraat 145, 3000 Leuven, Belgium.

COLLIER, Sir Paul, Kt 2014; CBE 2008; DPhil; Professor of Economics, since 1993, and Co-Director, Centre for Study of African Economies (Director, 1991), Oxford University (on leave of absence, 1998–2003); Fellow, St Antony's College, Oxford, since 1986; *b* 23 April 1949; *s* of Charles and Doris Collier; *m* 1998, Pauline Boerma; one *s*. *Educ:* King Edward VII Grammar Sch., Sheffield; Trinity Coll., Oxford (MA 1970); Nuffield Coll., Oxford (DPhil 1975). Oxford University: Fellow, Keble Coll. and Research Officer, Inst. of Econs and Stats, 1976–86; Univ. Lectr in Econs, 1986–89; Reader in Econs, 1989–92; Dir, Res. Dept, World Bank, Washington, 1998–2003. Prof. Invité, Centre d'Études et de Recherches sur le Développement Internat., Univ. d'Auvergne, 1989–; Vis. Prof., Kennedy Sch. of Govt, Harvard, 1992–96; Fellow, Centre for Economic Policy Res., 1993–; Associate, Tinbergen Inst., 1994–95. Lectures: Rausig, Moscow, 2000; Summers, Pa, 2001. Member: Overseas Develt Council, Program Associates Gp, Washington, 1994–96; Africa Panel, SSRC, NY, 1993–96; ESCOR Cttee, ODA then DFID, 1996–98. Man. Editor, Jl of African Economies, 1992–. Edgar Graham Prize, SOAS, 1988; Distinction Award, 1996, 1998. *Publications:* Labour and Poverty in Kenya, 1986; Labour and Poverty in Rural Tanzania, 1986, 2nd edn 1991; Peasants and Governments, 1989; Controlled Open Economies, 1990, 2nd edn 1994; The Bottom Billion: why the poorest countries are failing and what can be done about it, 2007; Wars, Guns and Votes: democracy in dangerous places, 2009; The Plundered Planet: how to reconcile prosperity with nature, 2010; Exodus: immigration and multiculturalism in the 21st century, 2013. *Address:* Centre for the Study of African Economies, Department of Economics, University of Oxford, Manor Road, Oxford OX1 3UQ.

COLLIER, Peter Neville; QC 1992; **His Honour Judge Collier;** a Senior Circuit Judge, since 2007; Resident Judge, Leeds Combined Court Centre, since 2007; *b* 1 June 1948; *s* of late Arthur Neville Collier and of Joan Audrey Collier (*née* Brewer); *m* 1972, Susan Margaret Williamson; two *s*. *Educ:* Hymers Coll., Hull; Selwyn Coll., Cambridge (MA). Called to the Bar, Inner Temple, 1970, Bencher, 2002; Leader, NE Circuit, 2002–05. A Recorder, 1988–2007; a Dep. High Court Judge (Family Div.), 1998–2007; Hon. Recorder of Leeds, 2007. Chancellor: dio. of Wakefield, 1992–2006; dio. of Lincoln, 1998–2006; dio. of York, 2006–. Mem., Bar Council, 2000–07. Lay Canon, York Minster, 2001–; Chm., York Minster Council, 2005–. Vicar Gen., Province of York, 2008–. *Recreations:* long distance walking, reading, music. *Address:* Leeds Combined Court Centre, 1 Oxford Row, Leeds LS1 3BG.

COLLIER-KEYWOOD, Richard David; Network Vice Chairman, PricewaterhouseCoopers, since 2011; *b* Nottingham, 21 July 1961; *s* of John Richard Collier-Keywood and Eirwen Harris; *m* 1984, Karen Ann Bradford; two *s* two *d*. *Educ:* Warwick Univ. (LLB). FCA 1986. Called to the Bar. PricewaterhouseCoopers: Partner, 1992–; UK Hd of Tax, 2003–08; UK Man. Partner, and Global Hd of Tax, 2008–11. Trustee: NGM; Mango; Chasan Trust. *Recreations:* tennis, sailing. *Address:* PricewaterhouseCoopers LLP, One Embankment Place, WC2N 6RH. *T:* (020) 7213 3997. *E:* richard.collier-keywood@uk.pwc.com.

COLLIN, Jack, MA, MD; FRCS; Consultant Surgeon, John Radcliffe Hospital, Oxford, 1980–2010; Fellow of Trinity College, Oxford, since 1980; *b* 23 April 1945; *s* of John Collin and Amy Maud Collin; *m* 1971, Christine Frances Proud; three *s* one *d*. *Educ:* Univ. of Newcastle (MB BS, MD); Mayo Clinic, Minn. University of Newcastle: Demonstrator in Anatomy, 1969–70; Sen. Res. Associate, 1973–75; Registrar in Surgery, Royal Victoria Infirmary, Newcastle, 1971–80; Clin. Reader in Surgery, 1980–2001, Chm., Faculty of Clin. Medicine, 1990–92, Univ. of Oxford. Mayo Foundn Fellow, Mayo Clinic, Minn, 1977. Moynihan Fellow, Assoc. of Surgeons of GB and Ire., 1980; James IV Fellow, James IV Assoc. of Surgeons Inc., NY, 1993. Royal College of Surgeons: Arris and Gale Lectr, 1976; Jacksonian Prize, 1977; Hunterian Prof., 1988–89. Non-exec. Dir, Nuffield Orthopaedic Centre NHS Trust, 1990–93. Member: Internat. Soc. of Surgery, 1994–; European Surgical Assoc., 1994–. Jobst Prize, Vascular Surgical Soc. of GB and Ireland, 1990. *Publications:* papers on vascular surgery, intestinal myoelectrical activity and absorption, parenteral nutrition and pancreatic and intestinal transplantation. *Recreations:* gardening, walking. *Address:* Trinity College, Oxford OX1 3BH.

COLLIN, (John) Richard (Olaf), FRCS; Consultant Surgeon: Moorfields Eye Hospital, since 1981; King Edward VII's Hospital, Sister Agnes (formerly King Edward VII Hospital for Officers), since 1993; Hon. Consultant Ophthalmic Surgeon, Great Ormond Street Hospital for Sick Children, since 1983; Honorary Professor of Ophthalmology, Institute of Ophthalmology, University College London, since 2008; *b* 1 May 1943; *s* of late John Olaf Collin and Ellen Vera (*née* Knudsen); *m* 1st, 1979, Theresa Pedemonte (marr. diss. 1982); 2nd, 1993, Geraldine O'Sullivan (*d* 2013); two *d*. *Educ:* Charterhouse; Sidney Sussex Coll., Cambridge (MA); Westminster Med. Sch. (MB BChir). FRCS 1972. House surgeon and house physician, Westminster Hosp., 1967–68; ship's surgeon, P&O, 1969–70; Ophthalmology Registrar, Moorfields Eye Hosp., 1972–75; Fellow in Ophthalmic Plastic and Reconstructive Surgery, Univ. of Calif, San Francisco, 1976–77; Lectr, then Sen. Lectr, Professorial Unit, Moorfields Eye Hosp., 1978–81. Master, Oxford Ophthalmol Congress, 1997–98. President: British Ocular Plastic Surgery Soc., 2002–05; European Soc. Oculo Plastic and Reconstructive Surgery, 2003–05. *Publications:* A Manual of Systematic Eyelid Surgery, 1983, 3rd edn 2006; (with A. G. Tyers) A Colour Atlas of Ophthalmic Plastic Surgery, 1995, 3rd edn 2008; articles on ophthalmic, plastic and reconstructive surgery topics. *Recreations:* sailing, shooting, tennis, hunting, fishing, theatre, opera. *Address:* 67 Harley Street, W1G 8QZ. *T:* (020) 7486 2699; 32 Old Queen Street, SW1H 9HP. *T:* (020) 7222 0582. *Clubs:* Royal Ocean Racing, Hurlingham; Beaulieu River Sailing (Beaulieu).

COLLINGE, Prof. John, CBE 2004; MD; FRS 2005; Professor of Neurology and Head, Department of Neurodegenerative Disease, Institute of Neurology, University College London, since 2001; *b* 25 Jan. 1958; *s* of late Robert Collinge and of Edna Collinge; *m* 1986, Donna Anne Keel (marr. diss. 1990). *Educ:* Burnley Grammar Sch.; St John's Coll., Cambridge; Univ. of Bristol (BSc Hons 1981; MB ChB 1984; MD 1992). MRCP 1988, FRCP 1998; FRCPath 1999. Bristol Royal Infirmary: House Surg., 1984–85; House Physician, 1985; Hon. Sen. House Officer in Pathology, 1985–86; Demonstrator in Pathology, Univ. of Bristol, 1985–86; Med. Rotation, Westminster Hosp., 1986–87; Senior House Officer: in Medicine, Hammersmith Hosp., 1987; in Neurology, Nat. Hosp. for Neurology and Neurosurgery, 1987–88; Merck, Sharp and Dohme Fellow, 1988, Clin. Scientific Staff, 1988–90, MRC Div. of Psychiatry, Clin. Res. Centre, Harrow; Hon. Registrar in Psychiatry, Northwick Park Hosp., 1988–90; Clin. Res. Fellow, Dept of Biochemistry and Molecular Genetics, St Mary's Hosp. Med Sch., 1990–91; St Mary's Hospital: Hon. Registrar, 1990–91, Hon. Sen. Registrar, 1991–94, in Neurology; Hon. Consultant in Neurology and Molecular Genetics, 1994–; Imperial College School of Medicine at St Mary's (formerly St Mary's Hospital Medical School): Wellcome Sen. Res. Fellow, 1992–96, Prin. Res. Fellow, 1996–2000, in Clin. Scis; Prof. of Molecular Neurogenetics and Hd, Dept of Neurogenetics, 1994–2001; Hon. Consultant Neurologist, Nat. Hosp. for Neurology and Neurosurgery, 1996–; Hon. Dir, MRC Prion Unit, 1998–. Inaugural Sen. Investigator of Faculty, Nat. Inst. for Health Res., 2008. Member: Neuroscis Panel, Wellcome Trust, 1994–97; Spongiform Encephalopathy Adv. Cttee, 1996–2002, 2007–11; Dep. Chm., High-level Gp on BSE, EU, 1996–97; Chm., Res. Adv. Panel, MND Assoc., 1997–2000 (Mem., 1994–97). Member: Amer. Acad. of Neurology, 1993; Clin. Genetics Soc., 1993; Assoc. of British Neurologists, 1995. Founder FMedSci 1998. Hon. DSc Bristol, 2008. Linacre Medal, 1992, Graham Bull Prize in Clin. Sci., 1993, Jean Hunter Prize, 2004, RCP; Alfred Meyer Medal, British Neuropathol Soc., 1997; Howard Taylor Ricketts Medal, Univ. of Chicago, 2001. *Publications:* (ed jtly) Prion Diseases of Humans and Animals, 1992; (ed jtly) Prion Diseases, 1997; papers on prion diseases, neurodegenerative diseases and neurogenetics. *Recreations:* mountain walking, sailing. *Address:* MRC Prion Unit, Department of Neurodegenerative Disease, National Hospital for Neurology and Neurosurgery, Queen Square, WC1N 3BG. *T:* (020) 7837 4888. *Club:* Athenæum.

COLLINGE, John Gregory; High Commissioner for New Zealand in the United Kingdom, 1994–97, and concurrently High Commissioner in Nigeria and Ambassador to the Republic of Ireland; *b* 10 May 1939; *s* of Norman Gregory Collinge and Hilary Winifred Fendall; *m* 2003, Margaret Elaine Postlethwaite; two *d* by a previous marriage. *Educ:* Auckland Univ. (LLB); University Coll., Oxford (MLitt). Called to the Bar, 1963, and admitted Solicitor, 1963, High Court of NZ; called to the Bar, 1966, and admitted Solicitor, 1966, High Court of Australia. Sen. Lectr in Law, Melbourne Univ., 1967–70; Partner, law firm, Melbourne, Wellington and Auckland, 1969–2005. Pres., NZ National Party, 1989–94. Chairman: Policy and Finance Cttee, Auckland Regl Authy, 1983–86; Commerce Commn, 1984–89; Alcohol Adv. Council of NZ, 1991–94; Nat. Civil Defence Energy Planning Cttee, 1992–94. Member: Auckland Electric Power Bd, 1977–80, 1992–93 (Chm., 1980–92); Electrical Develt Assoc. of NZ, 1990–91 (Pres., 1991–94); Council, Electricity Supply Assoc. of NZ, 1991–92. Chairman: New Zealand Pelagic Fisheries Ltd, 1975–81; United Distillers (NZ) Ltd, 1991 (Dir, 1986–91); Director: Mercury Energy Ltd, 1998–99; Vector Ltd, 2002–04 (Dep. Chm., 2002–04). Pres., Auckland Citizens and Ratepayers Inc., 1999–2004; Trustee, Auckland Energy Consumer Trust, 2000–06 (Dep. Chm., 2001–04). Alternate Gov., EBRD, 1994–97. Comr, Commonwealth War Graves Commn, 1994–97; Gov., Commonwealth Foundn, 1994–97; Mem. Bd of Govs, Commonwealth Inst., 1994–97. Vice-Pres., Royal Over-Seas League, 1994–97; Trustee, Waitangi Foundn, 1994–97; Patron: Captain Cook Birthplace Trust, 1994–97; Shakespeare Globe Trust, 1994–97; British NZ Business Assoc. (formerly British/NZ Trade Council), 1994–. Commemoration Medal, NZ, 1990. *Publications:* Restrictive Trade Practices and Monopolies in New Zealand, 1969, 2nd edn 1982; Tutorials in Contract, 1985, 4th edn 1989; The Law of Marketing in Australia and New Zealand, 1989, 2nd edn 1990; An Identity for New Zealand?, 2010. *Recreations:* New Zealand history, restoring colonial houses and colonial antiques, Rugby, cricket. *Address:* 10 London Street, St Mary's Bay, Auckland, New Zealand. *T:* 93608951; Frog Pond Farm, Ansty, Wilts SP3 5PY. *Clubs:* Vincent's (Oxford); Wellington (NZ).

COLLINGRIDGE, Prof. Graham Leon, PhD; FRS 2001; Professor of Neuroscience in Anatomy, School of Physiology and Pharmacology, University of Bristol, since 1994; *b* 1 Feb. 1955; *s* of Cyril Leon Collingridge and Marjorie May Caesar; *m* 1st, 1992, Catherine Rose (marr. diss. 2009); one *s* two *d*; 2nd, 2011, Clarrisa Ann Bradley; one *s*. *Educ:* Enfield GS; Univ. of Bristol (BSc 1977); Sch. of Pharmacy, London Univ. (PhD 1980). CBiol, FRSB (FIBiol 1997). Res. Fellow in Physiology, Univ. of British Columbia, 1980–82; Sen. Res. Officer, Dept of Physiology and Pharmacology, Univ. of NSW, 1983; Lectr, 1983–90, Reader, 1990, Dept of Pharmacology, Univ. of Bristol; Prof., and Head of Dept of Pharmacology, Univ. of Birmingham, 1990–94; University of Bristol: Head of Dept of Anatomy, 1996–98; Dir, MRC Centre for Synaptic Plasticity, 1999–2012. WCU Prof., Dept of Brain and Cognitive Scis, Seoul Nat. Univ., 2009–13. Founder, European Dana Alliance for the Brain, 1997. Pres., British Neurosci. Assoc., 2007–09. Founder FMedSci 1998. Editor-in-Chief, Neuropharmacology, 1993–2010. *Publications:* numerous papers in scientific jls, such as Nature, Neuron, Nature Neuroscience on the neural basis of learning and memory and other aspects of neuroscience. *Recreations:* ski-ing, snow-boarding, soccer, running, golf, travel. *Address:* School of Physiology and Pharmacology, University of Bristol, Dorothy Hodgkin Building, Whitson Street, Bristol BS1 3NY. *T:* (0117) 331 3153.

COLLINGRIDGE, Jean Mary; *see* King, Jean M.

COLLINGS, Juliet Jeanne d'Auvergne; *see* Campbell, J. J. d'A.

COLLINGS, Matthew Glynn Burkinshaw; QC 2006; *b* 13 Aug. 1961; *s* of Frederick, (Burke), Collings and Beryl Collings; *m* 1984, Amanda Maine-Tucker; two *s*. *Educ:* Colston's Sch., Bristol; London Sch. of Econs (LLB). Called to the Bar: Lincoln's Inn, 1985; BVI, 2011; Cayman, 2012; in practice as barrister, 1986–, specialising in company, insolvency and commercial law. Former Mem., Insolvency Rules Adv. Cttee. Chm., Oxfordshire and Bucks Cons. Party, 2006–09. Contested (C) Newport E, 2005. *Recreations:* vintage cars, opera, ski-ing. *Address:* Maitland Chambers, 7 Stone Buildings, Lincoln's Inn, WC2A 3SZ. *T:* (020) 7406 1200, *Fax:* (020) 7406 1300. *E:* mcollings@maitlandchambers.com.

COLLINI, Prof. Stefan Anthony, PhD; FRHistS; FBA 2000; Professor of Intellectual History and English Literature, Cambridge University, 2000–14, now Emeritus; Fellow, Clare Hall, Cambridge, 1986–2014, now Emeritus; *b* 6 Sept. 1947; *s* of Raymond Collini and Hilda May (*née* Brown); *m* 1971, Ruth Karen Morse. *Educ:* St Joseph's Coll., Beulah Hill; Jesus Coll., Cambridge (BA 1969, MA 1973; Thirlwall Prize and Seeley Medal 1973; PhD 1977); Yale Univ. (MA 1970). FRHistS 1981. Res. Fellow, St John's Coll., Cambridge, 1973–74; University of Sussex: Lectr in Intellectual Hist., 1974–82; Reader, 1982–86; Cambridge University: Asst Lectr in English, 1986–90; Lectr, 1990–94; Reader, 1994–2000. Visiting Fellow: History of Ideas Unit, ANU, 1982–83 and 1987; Clare Hall, Cambridge, 1986; Vis. Prof., Inst. Internacional de Estudios Avanzados, Caracas, 1983; Dir d'études associé, Ecole des Hautes Etudes en Scis Sociales, Paris, 1986 and 1991; Mem., Inst. for Advanced Study, Princeton, 1994–95; British Studies Fellow, Ransom Humanities Res. Center, Austin, Tex., 1995; Sen. Res. Fellowship, British Acad., 1999–2000; Leverhulme Major Res. Fellowship, 2007–10; Birkelund Fellowship, Nat. Humanities Center, NC, 2012–13. Co-ed., Cambridge Rev., 1986–93. *Publications:* Liberalism and Sociology, 1979; (jtly) That Noble Science of Politics, 1983; Arnold, 1988, 2nd edn 1994; (ed) On Liberty, by J. S. Mill, 1989; Public Moralists, 1991; (ed) Interpretation and Overinterpretation, by Umberto Eco, 1992; (ed) Culture and Anarchy, by Matthew Arnold, 1993; (ed) The Two Cultures, by C. P. Snow, 1993; English Pasts: essays in history and culture, 1999; (ed jtly) Economy, Polity, and Society, 2000; (ed jtly) History, Religion, and Culture: British Intellectual History 1750–1950, 2000; Absent Minds: intellectuals in Britain, 2006; Common Reading: critics, historians, publics, 2008; That's Offensive!: criticism, identity, respect, 2011; What Are Universities For?, 2012; (ed) Two Cultures?, by F. R. Leavis, 2013; contrib. essays and reviews in jls, incl. TLS, London Rev. of Books, etc. *Address:* Faculty of English, Cambridge University, 9 West Road, Cambridge CB3 9DP. *T:* (01223) 335082.

COLLINS, family name of **Baron Collins of Mapesbury**.

COLLINS OF HIGHBURY, Baron *cr* 2011 (Life Peer), of Highbury in the London Borough of Islington; **Raymond Edward Harry Collins;** *b* Newport, IoW, 21 Dec. 1954; *s* of Harry Collins and Isobel Collins; civil partnership 2005, *m* 2014, Rafael Ballesteros. *Educ:* Univ. of Kent, Canterbury (BA Hons Industrial Relns and Pols 1980). Transport and General Workers' Union: Asst Librarian, 1972–74; Specialist Asst, Educn, 1974–77; Policy Advr and Special Asst to Gen. Sec., 1980–85; Nat. Admin. Officer, 1985–98; Asst Gen. Sec., TGWU, subseq. Unite, 1998–2008; Gen. Sec., Labour Party, 2008–11. An Opposition Whip, 2011–; opposition spokesman on internat. devel, H of L, 2012–. Labour Party: Mem., 1970–; Mem., Nat. Policy Forum, 1997–2003, Nat. Constitution Cttee, 2001–08. Mem., Unite (formerly TGWU), 1972–. *Recreations:* Spanish history, swimming, Arsenal FC. *Address:* House of Lords, SW1A 0PW. *W:* www.twitter.com/Lord_Collins.

COLLINS OF MAPESBURY, Baron *cr* 2009 (Life Peer), of Hampstead Town in the London Borough of Camden; **Lawrence Antony Collins,** Kt 2000; PC 2007; LLD; FBA 1994; a Justice of the Supreme Court of the United Kingdom, 2009–11, Acting Justice, since 2011 (formerly a Lord of Appeal in Ordinary); non-permanent Judge, Hong Kong Court of Final Appeal, since 2011; Fellow of Wolfson College, Cambridge, 1975–2008, now Emeritus (Honorary Fellow, 2009); Professor of Law, University College London, since 2011; international arbitrator; *b* 7 May 1941; *s* of late Sol Collins and Phoebe (*née* Barnett); *m* 1st, 1982, Sara Shamni (marr. diss. 2003); one *s* one *d*; 2nd, 2012, Patti Langton. *Educ:* City of London Sch.; Downing Coll., Cambridge (BA, George Long Prize, McNair Schol., 1963; LLB, Whewell Schol., 1964; LLD 1994; Hon. Fellow, 2000); Columbia Univ. (LLM 1965). Mem. Inst de Droit Internat., 1989. Admitted solicitor, 1968; Partner, Herbert Smith, solicitors, 1971–2000 (Hd, Litigation and Arbitration Dept, 1995–98); QC 1997; a Dep. High Court Judge, 1997–2000; a Judge of High Court of Justice, Chancery Div., 2000–07; a Lord Justice of Appeal, 2007–09. Bencher, Inner Temple, 2001. Visiting Professor: QMUL (formerly QMC, then QMW), 1982–; Columbia Law Sch., 2012; Vis. Prof., 2012, 2014, Adjunct Prof., 2015–, NY Univ. Sch. of Law. Lectr, Hague Acad. of Internat. Law, 1991, 1998, 2007; Graveson Meml Lectr, KCL, 1995; F. A. Mann Lectr, British Inst. of Internat. and Comparative Law, 2001; Lionel Cohen Lectr, Hebrew Univ., Jerusalem, 2007; Freshfields Arbitration Lectr, 2009; Chancery Bar Assoc. Lectr, 2010; Commercial Bar Assoc. Lectr, 2010; Ian Borrin Vis. Fellow, Victoria Univ. of Wellington, NZ, 2011; Clarendon Law Lectr, 2012; Herbert Smith Freehills Internat. Arbitration Lectr, Singapore, 2013. Member: Lord Chancellor's Wkg Party on Foreign Judgments, 1979–81; Bar and Law Soc. Jt Wkg Party on UK-US Judgments Convention, 1980–82; Law Commn Jt Wkg Party on Torts in Private Internat. Law, 1982–84; Ministry of Justice (formerly DCA) Adv. Cttee on Private Internat. Law, 2004–. Dep. Chm., Takeover Appeal Bd, 2013–. Hon. Sec., British Br., 1983–88, Chm., Cttee on Internat. Securities Regulation, 1988–94, Internat. Law Assoc. Member: Adv. Council, Centre for Commercial Law Studies, QMUL (formerly QMW), 1989–; Adv. Bd, Cambridge Univ. Centre for European Legal Studies, 1993–97; Council of Advrs, Singapore Internat. Arbitration Centre, 2010–. Mem., Amer. Law Inst., 2010–. Hon. Member: SPTL, 1993; British Inst. of Internat. and Comparative Law, 2008– (Mem., Council of Mgt, 1992–2006; Mem., Adv. Council, 2006–10; Vice-Pres., 2011–); Hon. Life Mem., 2000, Lifetime Achievement Award, 2011, Law Soc. Lifetime Achievement Award, Solicitors' Co., 2009. Member: Editl Adv. Cttee, Law Qly Rev., 1988–; Bd of Eds, Internat. and Comparative Law Qly, 1988–2009; Editl Cttee, British Yearbook of Internat. Law, 1991– (Chair, 2011–); Editl Bd, Civil Justice Qly, 2005–; Adv. Ed., Civil Procedure, 2002–09. *Publications:* European Community Law in the United Kingdom, 1975, 4th edn 1990; Civil Jurisdiction and Judgments Act 1982, 1983; Essays in International Litigation and the Conflict of Laws, 1994; (Gen. Ed.) Dicey & Morris (now Dicey, Morris & Collins), Conflict of Laws, 11th edn 1987 to 15th edn 2012. *Address:* Essex Court Chambers, 24 Lincoln's Inn Fields, WC2A 3EG.

COLLINS, Sir Alan (Stanley), KCVO 2005; CMG 1998; HM Diplomatic Service, retired; Managing Director, Olympic Legacy, UK Trade & Investment, 2011–12; *b* 1 April 1948; *s* of Stanley Arthur Collins and Rose Elizabeth Collins; *m* 1971, Ann Dorothy Roberts; two *s* one *d*. *Educ:* Strand GS; London School of Economics and Political Science (BSc Econs). Joined MoD, 1970; Private Sec. to Vice Chief of Air Staff, 1973–75; joined FCO, 1981; Deputy Head of Mission: Addis Ababa, 1986–90; Manila, 1990–93; Counsellor, FCO, 1993–95; Dir-Gen., British Trade and Cultural Office, Taipei, 1995–98; Ambassador, Philippines, 1998–2002; (on secondment) Vice-Pres. for Internat. Relns, Shell, 2002–03; High Comr, Singapore, 2003–07; Consul-Gen., New York and Dir-Gen., Trade and Investment in the US, 2007–11. *Recreations:* sport, antiques, reading, walking.

COLLINS, Hon. Sir Andrew (David), Kt 1994; **Hon. Mr Justice Collins;** a Judge of the High Court of Justice, Queen's Bench Division, since 1994; *b* 19 July 1942; *s* of late Rev. Canon Lewis John Collins, MA, and Dame Diana Clavering Collins, DBE; *m* 1970, Nicolette Anne Sandford-Saville; one *s* one *d*. *Educ:* Eton; King's Coll., Cambridge (BA, MA). Called to the Bar, Middle Temple, 1965, Bencher, 1992; QC 1985; a Recorder, 1986–94. Pres., Immigration Appeal Tribunal, 1999–2002; Lead Judge, Administrative Court, 2004–07. *Address:* Royal Courts of Justice, Strand, WC2A 2LL.

COLLINS, Arthur John, OBE 1973; HM Diplomatic Service, retired; Representative of the Secretary of State, Foreign and Commonwealth Office, 1988–2006; *b* 17 May 1931; *s* of Reginald and Margery Collins; *m* 1952, Enid Maureen, *d* of Charles Stableford, FRIBA and Sarah Stableford; one *s* one *d*. *Educ:* Purley Grammar Sch. Served RAF, 1949–51. Min. of Health, 1951–68 (Private Sec. to Perm. Sec., 1960–61, and to Parly Sec., 1962–63); transf. to HM Diplomatic Service, 1968; FCO, 1968–69; First Secretary and Head of Chancery: Dhaka, 1970–71; Brasilia, 1972–74; Asst Head of Latin America and Caribbean Depts, FCO, 1974–77; Counsellor, UK Delegn to OECD, Paris, 1978–81; High Comr, Papua New Guinea, 1982–85; adviser on management, FCO, 1986–88; Consultant, EBRD, 1991; Assessor, VSO, 1993–99. Pres., Brighton and Hove Archaeol Soc., 1996–99. Chm., Brighton Hove and Dist, 1998–2004 and 2012–, SE Region, 2009–14, ESU. *Publications:* papers on early colonialism in New Guinea. *Address:* 60 Dean Court Road, Rottingdean, Sussex BN2 7DJ. *Club:* Hove (Hove).

COLLINS, Prof. Brian Stanley, CB 2011; DPhil; CEng, FREng, FInstP, FIET, FICE, FBCS; Professor of Engineering Policy, University College London, since 2011; *b* 3 Oct. 1945; *s* of James and Maud Collins; *m* 1st (marr. diss.); one *s* one *d*; *m* 2nd (marr. diss.); partner, Gillian Sowerby. *Educ:* Chislehurst and Sidcup Grammar Sch.; St Peter's Coll., Oxford (Open Schol.; BA Physics 1967, MA); DPhil Astrophysics Oxon 1971. FInstP 1984; CEng 1988; FIET (FIEE 1988); FBCS 2000; CITP 2000; FREng 2009; FICE 2009. Res. Scientist, 1973–85, Dep. Dir, 1987, RSRE; rcds 1986; Chief Scientist and Dir, Technol. (Grade 3), GCHQ, 1987–91; Partner, KPMG, 1991–92; IT Dir, Wellcome Trust, 1994–97; Global Chief Inf. Officer, Clifford Chance, 1999–2001; Prof. of Information Systems, Cranfield Univ., 2003–11. Chief Scientific Adviser: DfT, 2006–11; BERR, then BIS, 2008–11. Vice President: IEE, 1999–2002; BCS, 2003–06. Mem., Court of Assts, Co. of Information Technologists, 2004–. FRSA 1997. *Publications:* (ed with Prof. R. Mansell) Trust and Crime in Information Societies, 2004. *Recreations:* golf (learning), cricket and Rugby (watching), country walks, ballet, music, reading. *Address:* Faculty of Engineering Science, University College London, Gower Street, WC1E 6BT. *E:* brian.collins@ucl.ac.uk.

COLLINS, Sir Bryan (Thomas Alfred), Kt 1997; OBE 1989; QFSM 1983; HM Chief Inspector of Fire Services, 1994–98; *b* 4 June 1933; *m* 1959, Terry Skuce; one *s* one *d*. *Educ:* Queen Mary's Sch. RAF, 1951–53; with Fire Service, 1954–98; Chief Fire Officer, Humberside, 1979–89; Inspector of Fire Services: Northern Area, 1989–93; Midlands and Wales, 1993–94. *Address:* Gwelo, Thatcher Stanfords Close, Melbourn, S Cambs SG8 6DT.

COLLINS, Christopher Douglas; Chairman, Hanson plc, 1998–2005 (Director, 1991–2005; Vice-Chairman, 1995–97); *b* 19 Jan. 1940; *s* of Douglas and Patricia Collins; *m* 1976, Susan Ann Lumb; one *s* one *d*. *Educ:* Eton Coll. Chartered Accountant. Articled clerk, Peat Marwick Mitchell, 1958–65; Goya Ltd: Man. Dir, 1968–75; Dir, 1975–80; with Hanson plc, 1989–2005. Chairman: Forth Ports PLC, 2000–09; Old Mutual plc, 2005–09 (non-exec. Dir, 1999–2005). Amateur steeplechase jockey, 1965–75; represented GB in 3-day equestrian events, 1974–80; Chm., British Team Selection Cttee, 1981–84; Jockey Club Steward, 1980–81; Mem., Horse Race Betting Levy Bd, 1982–84. Chairman: Aintree Racecourse Ltd, 1983–88; National Stud, 1986–88; Jockey Club Racecourses (formerly Racecourse Hldgs Trust), 2005–08. *Recreations:* reading, gardening, equestrian sport. *Clubs:* Jockey, White's, Pratt's.

COLLINS, Crispian Hilary Vincent; Chairman, Schroder Global Real Estate Securities Ltd (formerly ING Global Real Estate Securities Ltd, then Investors in Global Real Estate Ltd), since 2006; *b* 22 Jan. 1948; *s* of late Bernard John Collins, CBE, and Gretel Elisabeth Collins (*née* Piehler); *m* 1974, Diane Barbara Bromley; one *s* two *d*. *Educ:* Ampleforth Coll.; University Coll., Oxford (BA Hons Modern History). Joined Phillips & Drew, 1969; Fund Manager, Pension Funds, 1975–98; Partner, 1981–85; Dir, 1985–2002; Chief Exec., 1998–2000; Chm., 1999–2002; Mem., Mgt Cttee, Phillips & Drew Fund Mgt, 1994–2000; Chm., European (formerly Matrix) Real Estate Investment Trust Ltd, 2007–14; Vice Chm., UBS (later UBS Global) Asset Management, 2000–03. Director: Salvation Army Trustee Co., 2003–08; The Children's Mutual, 2003–09; Chm., Thai Children's Trust, 2009–. Chm. of Govs, St Leonards-Mayfield Sch., 2003–09. *Recreations:* golf, watching sport, opera, gardens. *E:* crispiancollins@btinternet.com.

COLLINS, Damian Noel Thomas; MP (C) Folkestone and Hythe, since 2010; *b* Northampton, 4 Feb. 1974; *s* of Fearghal and Diane Collins; *m* 2004, Sarah Richardson; one *s* one *d*. *Educ:* St Mary's High Sch., Herefordshire; Belmont Abbey Sch., Hereford; St Benet's Hall, Oxford (BA Hons Modern Hist.). Cons. Res. Dept and Press Officer, 1996–99; Dir, M & C Saatchi, 1999–2008; Sen. Counsel, Lexington Communications, 2008–10. PPS to Sec. of State for NI, 2012–14, to Foreign Sec., 2014–. Mem., H of C Select Cttee on Culture, Media and Sport, 2010–12. Pres., Oxford Univ. Cons. Assoc., 1995. *Publications:* (contrib.) Conservative Revival, 2006; (contrib.) The New Blue, 2008. *Recreations:* cricket, football, Rugby (watching), walking in Kent, cooking with Jamie Oliver. *Address:* House of Commons, SW1A 0AA. *T:* (020) 7219 7072. *E:* damian.collins.mp@parliament.uk. *Clubs:* Lord's Taverners, MCC; Manchester United.

COLLINS, Prof. David John, PhD; CPsychol, CSci; Professor of Coaching and Performance, University of Central Lancashire, since 2010; Director, Grey Matters Performance Ltd, since 2010; *b* 31 Dec. 1953; *s* of Arthur and Ivy Collins; *m* 2003, Helen Brooker; two *d*, and one *s* two *d* from previous marriage. *Educ:* Borough Rd Coll. (CertEd, BEd Hons); Pennsylvania State Univ. (MSc); Univ. of Surrey (PhD 1990); BASES accredited Sport Psychologist; BOA registered Sport Psychologist; Practitioner Psychologist, Health and Care Professionals Council, 2009. CPsychol 2009; CSci 2009; AFBPsS 2010. Commn RM, 1972–76. Teacher: Stowe Sch., 1978–79; Bucks CC, 1979–80 and 1981–85; Sen. Lectr, St Mary's Coll., Twickenham, 1985–93; Reader, then Prof., Manchester Metropolitan Univ., 1993–98; Prof. of Physical Educn and Sport Performance, 1998–2005, Adjunct Prof., 2005–, Univ. of Edinburgh; Performance Dir, UK Athletics, 2005–08. Sport Psychologist: RFU, 1990–91; Olympic Weightlifting, 1992–97; Short Track Speed Skating, 1993–99; Scottish Judo, 1999–2004; Scottish Curling, 1999–2004; UK Athletics, 1999–2005; Dir of Coaching, iZone Driver Performance, 2012–. Director: P^2E, 2002–09; Rugby Coaches Assoc., 2012–. Founding Fellow, British Soc. of Martial Arts, 1998; Fellow, BASES, 2010. *Publications:* The Use of Physiological Measures in Sport Psychology: a handbook, 1982; (jtly) Working with Teams, 1990; (jtly) Get Ready for Squash, 1990; Sport Psychology and Motor Control, 1992; Applying Psychological Research for Coaching and Performance Enhancement, 1993; (jtly) Talent Identification and Development: an academic review, 2002; (jtly) Rugby Tough, 2002; Performance Psychology: a practitioners' guide, 2008; chapters in books; contribs to learned jls. *Recreations:* scuba and technical diving, outdoor pursuits, curry consumption. *Clubs:* Romford Rugby, Saracens, Bedford Rugby, Northampton and Brackley Rugby; Royal Canoe (Teddington); Busen Martial Arts (Twickenham).

COLLINS, Dr David John, CBE 2005; Further Education Commissioner, since 2013; *b* 1 Nov. 1949; *s* of Leslie Reginald Collins and Vera Collins (*née* Harvey); *m* 1972, Linda Patterson; two *s*. *Educ:* Humphry Davy Grammar Sch., Penzance; Univ. of Edinburgh (MA Hons; PhD). Res. Asst, Univ. of Edinburgh, 1972–73; Educn Co-ordinator, HM YOI and HM Prison Edinburgh, 1973–75; Hd of Dept, 1975–85, Coll. Devel Officer, 1985–88, Redditch Coll.; Vice-Principal, Sandwell Coll., 1988–92; on secondment as Principal and Chief Exec., Bolton Coll., 1999–2000; Principal and Chief Exec., S Cheshire Coll., 1993–2009; Chief Exec., Learning and Skills Improvement Service, 2009–11; Principal and Chief Exec., Guildford Coll. of Further and Higher Educn, 2011–12. Vis. Professorial Fellow, Univ. of Lancaster, 2005–09. Member, Board: Cheshire and Warrington LSC, 2004–07; Assoc. of Colls, 2006–09 (Pres., 2008–09); Learning and Skills Network, 2006–08; Abingdon and Witney Coll., 2012–13. FRSA 2005. Hon. DBA Chester, 2008. *Publications:* A Survival Guide for College Leaders and Managers, 2006; The Role of the Principal, 2008. *Recreations:* travel, writing, sport. *Address:* Park House, Windrush, Burford OX18 4TT.

COLLINS, Deborah; Strategic Director, Environment and Leisure, Southwark Council, since 2012; *b* 18 April 1963; *d* of Brig. Kenelm John and Angela Charlotte Hathaway; *m* 1991, Tim Collins (marr. diss. 2013); one *s* one *d*. *Educ:* Worcester Coll., Oxford (BA (Jurisprudence) 1984). Articled Clerk, Coward Chance, 1985–87, Solicitor, Clifford Chance, 1987–88; merchant banker, J. Henry Schroder Wagg & Co. Ltd, 1988–91; Govt Legal Service: DTI, 1991–97; European Secretariat, Cabinet Office Legal Advrs, 1997–99; Divl Manager, DFEE Legal, 1999–2002; Legal Advr to Highways Agency, 2002–03; Dir, Legal Services Gp, DTI, 2003–06; Dir, Legal (Ops), HMRC, 2006–07; Strategic Dir, Communities, Law and Governance (formerly Dir, Legal and Democratic Services), Southwark Council, 2007–12. *Recreations:* shoes, ski-ing, walking, cooking, watching plants grow in my garden. *Address:* Environment and Leisure, Southwark Council, 160 Tooley Street, SE1 2TZ. *T:* (020) 7525 7630. *E:* deborah.collins@southwark.gov.uk.

COLLINS, Francis Sellers, MD; PhD; Director, National Institutes of Health, USA, since 2009; *b* 14 April 1950; *s* of Fletcher and Margaret Collins; *m* 1998, Diane Lynn Baker; two *d*. *Educ:* Univ. of Virginia, Charlottesville (BS Highest Hons 1970); Yale Univ. (MPhil, PhD Physical Chem. 1974); Univ. of N Carolina Sch. of Medicine (MD Hons 1977). University of Michigan: Asst Prof. of Internal Medicine and Human Genetics, Med. Sch., Ann Arbor, 1984–88; Chief, Div. of Med. Genetics, Dept of Internal Medicine and Human Genetics, 1988–91; Prof. of Internal Medicine and Human Genetics, 1991–93 (on leave, 1993–2003); Dir, Nat. Human Genome Res. Inst., Bethesda, Maryland, 1993–2008. Asst Investigator, 1987–88, Investigator, 1991–93, Howard Hughes Med. Inst., Ann Arbor, Mich. Presidential Medal of Freedom (USA), 2007; Nat. Medal of Sci. (USA), 2009. *Publications:* The Language of Life: DNA and the revolution of personalised medicine, 2010. *Address:* National Institutes of Health, 9000 Rockville Pike, Bethesda, MD 20892, USA.

COLLINS, Ven. Gavin Andrew; Archdeacon of The Meon, since 2011; *b* 31 Dec. 1966; *s* of John Collins and Margaret Collins; *m* 1994, Christina Kidd; one *s* two *d*. *Educ:* Trinity Hall, Cambridge (BA 1989; MA 1993); Trinity Coll., Bristol (BA 1996; MA 1997). Ordained deacon, 1997, priest, 1998; Asst Curate, St Barnabas, Cambridge, 1997–2002; Vicar, Christ Church, Chorleywood, 2002–11; Rural Dean, Rickmansworth, 2006–11. Hon. Canon, St Albans Cathedral, 2009–11. *Recreations:* cycling, running, time with my family, engagement in political debate. *Address:* Victoria Lodge, 36 Osborn Road, Fareham PO16 7DS. *T:* (01329) 608895.

COLLINS, Gerard; *see* Collins, J. G.

COLLINS, Prof. Harold Maurice, PhD; FBA 2012; Distinguished Research Professor, and Director, Centre for Study of Knowledge, Expertise and Science, School of Social Sciences, Cardiff University, since 1997; *b* Hitchin, 13 June 1943; *s* of Sidney and Sadie Collins; *m* 2010, Susan Carter; one *s* one *d* and one step *s* one step *d*. *Educ:* Hitchin Grammar Sch.; BSc (Econ) London ext. 1967; Univ. of Essex (MA 1971); Univ. of Bath (PhD 1981). Lectr in Sociol., Liverpool Coll. of Commerce, 1968–70; University of Bath: Lectr, Sen. Lectr, then Reader in Sociol., 1973–89; Dir, Sci. Studies Centre, 1981–85; Prof. of Sociol., 1989–95; Hd, Sch. of Social Scis, 1990–92; Prof. of Sociol., Univ. of Southampton, 1995–97; Affiliated Res. Schol., Dept of Hist. and Philosophy of Sci., Cambridge Univ., 1999. Guest, Xerox Park, Palo Alto, 1987; Visiting Professor: Univ. of Limburg, 1988–90; UCSD, 1993; Tayuan Univ., China, 2006; Univ. of Minas Geras, Belo Horizonte, Brazil, 2008; Andrew W. Mellon Vis. Prof. of Hist., CIT, 2003; Visiting Research Fellow: Dept of Sci. and Technol. Studies, Cornell Univ., 2001; Max Planck Inst. for Hist. of Sci., Berlin, 2002. Pres., Soc. for Social Studies of Sci., 1991–93. J. D. Bernal Award, Soc. for Social Studies of Sci., 1997. *Publications:* (with T. J. Pinch) Frames of Meaning: the social construction of extraordinary science, 1982; Changing Order: replication and induction in scientific practice, 1985, 2nd edn 1992; Artificial Experts: social knowledge and intelligent machines, 1990; (with T. J. Pinch) The Golem: what everyone should know about science, 1993, 2nd edn 1998 (Robert K. Merton Book Prize, Amer. Sociol Assoc., 1995); (with M. Kusch) The Shape of Actions: what humans and machines can do, 1998; (with T. J. Pinch) The Golem at Large: what you should know about technology, 1998; (ed jtly) The One Culture?: a conversation about science, 2001; Gravity's Shadow: the search for gravitational waves, 2004; (with T. J. Pinch) Dr Golem: how to think about medicine, 2005; (with R. Evans) Rethinking Expertise, 2007; Tacit and Explicit Knowledge, 2010; Gravity's Ghost: scientific discovery in the twenty-first century, 2011; Gravity's Ghost and Big Dog: scientific discovery and social analysis in the twenty-first century, 2013; Are We All Scientific Experts Now?, 2014. *Recreations:* making unnecessary things with wood taken from skips, banter. *Address:* School of Social Sciences, Cardiff University, Cardiff CF10 3WT. *T:* (029) 2140 9637. *E:* CollinsHM@cf.ac.uk.

COLLINS, Prof. Hugh Graham, FBA 2006; Vinerian Professor of English Law, University of Oxford, since 2013; Fellow, All Souls College, Oxford, since 2013; *b* 21 June 1953; *s* of Richard and Joan Collins; *m* 1983, Prof. Emily Simonoff; two *d*. *Educ:* Pembroke Coll., Oxford (MA, BCL); Harvard Law Sch. (LLM). Fellow, Brasenose Coll., Oxford, 1976–91; Prof. of English Law, 1991–2013, Hd, Dept of Law, 1994–97 and 2006–09, LSE; Acting Dean, Faculty of Law, Univ. of Oxford, 2015. Mem., Adv. Forum on Impact of Employment Policies, DTI, later BERR, then BIS, 2006–10. Member, Editorial Committee: Industrial Law Jl, 1982–; Modern Law Rev., 1992–; Eur. Rev. of Contract Law, 2005–. *Publications:* Marxism and Law, 1982; The Law of Contract, 1986, 4th edn 2003; Justice in Dismissal, 1992; Regulating Contracts, 1999; Employment Law, 2003, 2nd edn 2010; Labour Law: texts and materials, 2001, 2nd edn 2005; The European Civil Code, 2008; (with G. Teubner) Networks as Connected Contracts, 2011; (jtly) Labour Law, 2012. *Recreations:* opera, theatre, modern art, painting, sailing, building walls. *Address:* All Souls College, Oxford OX1 4AL. *T:* (01865) 279379.

COLLINS, Jacqueline Jill, (Jackie), OBE 2013; writer; *b* London, 4 Oct.; *d* of late Joseph Collins and Elsa (*née* Bessant); *m* Wallace Austin (marr. diss.); one *d*; *m* 1966, Oscar Lerman (*d* 1992); two *d*. Formerly TV and film actress. *Publications:* The World is Full of Married Men, 1968; The Stud, 1969 (filmed, 1978); Sunday Simmons and Charlie Brick, 1971 (new edn as Sinners, 1984); Lovehead, 1974; The World is Full of Divorced Women, 1975; Lovers and Gamblers, 1977; The Bitch, 1979 (filmed, 1979); Chances, 1981 (televised, 1990); Hollywood Wives, 1983 (televised); Lucky, 1985 (televised); Hollywood Husbands, 1986; Rock Star, 1988; Love Killers, 1989; Lady Boss, 1990 (televised); American Star, 1993; Hollywood Kids, 1994; Vendetta: Lucky's revenge, 1996; Thrill, 1998; LA Connections (four parts), 1998; Dangerous Kiss, 1999; Lethal Seduction, 2000; Hollywood Wives: the new generation, 2001; Hollywood Divorces, 2003; Lovers and Players, 2005; Drop Dead Beautiful, 2007; Married Lovers, 2008; Poor Little Bitch Girl, 2009; Goddess of Vengeance, 2011; The Power Trip, 2012; Confessions of a Wild Child, 2013. *Address:* c/o Simon and Schuster, 1st Floor, 222 Gray's Inn Road, WC1X 8HB.

See also Dame J. H. Collins.

COLLINS, James Douglas; QC 2012; *b* Bristol, 8 Dec. 1969; *s* of Charles Douglas Collins and Jhoann Temlett Collins; *m* 2001, Sharmila Vijayanti Nikapota; four *d*. *Educ:* Sherborne Sch., Dorset; Downing Coll., Cambridge (BA 1993). Called to the Bar, Gray's Inn, 1995; in practice as barrister, specialising in commercial litigation and arbitration, 1995–. *Address:* Essex Court Chambers, 24 Lincoln's Inn Fields, WC2A 3EG.

COLLINS, (James) Gerard; Member, European Parliament, 1994–2004; *b* Abbeyfeale, Co. Limerick, 16 Oct. 1938; *s* of late James J. Collins, TD and Margaret Collins; *m* 1969, Hilary Tattan. *Educ:* University Coll., Dublin (BA). Teacher. Asst Gen. Sec., Fianna Fáil, 1965–67. TD (FF) Limerick W, 1967–97; Parly Sec. to Ministers for Industry and Commerce and for the Gaeltacht, 1969–70; Minister for Posts and Telegraphs, 1970–73; opposition front-bench spokesman on agriculture, 1973–75; spokesman on justice, 1975–77; Minister for Justice, 1977–81; Minister for Foreign Affairs, March–Dec. 1982; opposition front-bench spokesman on foreign affairs, 1983–87; Minister for Justice, 1987–89; Minister for Foreign Affairs, 1989–92. Mem., Consultative Assembly, Council of Europe, 1973–77; Chm., Parly Cttee on Secondary Legislation of European Communities, 1983–87. Mem., Limerick CC, 1974–77. *Address:* The Hill, Abbeyfeale, Co. Limerick, Ireland.

COLLINS, Dr Jane Elizabeth, (Mrs David Evans), FRCP, FRCPCH; Chief Executive, Marie Curie Cancer Care, since 2012; *b* 19 Oct. 1954; *d* of Thomas and Betsy Collins; *m* 1978, David Evans; one *s* one *d*. *Educ:* Portsmouth High Sch.; Univ. of London (MSc Clin. Biochem. 1985); Univ. of Birmingham (MB ChB 1978; MD 1988). FRCP 1994; FRCPCH 1996. Consultant Paediatric Neurologist, Guy's Hosp., 1991–94; Consultant Paediatric Neurologist, 1994–96, Consultant in Metabolic Medicine, 1996–2001, Gt Ormond St Hosp.; Med. Dir, Gt Ormond St Hosp. NHS Trust, 1999–2001; Chief Exec., Great Ormond Street Hosp. NHS Trust and Great Ormond Street Hosp. Children's Charity, 2001–12. Paediatric consultant (formerly Children's Doctor columnist), The Times, 1999–2007. Chm., London Clinical Senate Council, 2013–; Mem., Gen. Adv. Council, King's Fund, 2013–. Hon. Fellow, UCL, 2011. *Address:* Marie Curie Cancer Care, 89 Albert Embankment, SE1 7TP. *T:* (020) 7599 7130.

COLLINS, Jane Maria; Member (UK Ind) Yorkshire and the Humber Region, European Parliament, since 2014; *b* East Hardwick, near Pontefract, 17 Feb. 1962. *Educ:* Pontefract Girls' High Sch. Head Girl, with Robert Ward, racehorse trainer, Doncaster, 1980–85; with Alex Stewart, trainer, Newmarket, 1985, subseq. at family stable yard, Selby; equine physiotherapist, 1995–2004. Contested (UK Ind): Scunthorpe, 2010; Barnsley, March 2011; Rotherham, Nov. 2012, 2015. *Address:* European Parliament, 60 Rue Wiertz, 1047 Brussels, Belgium.

COLLINS, Prof. Jeffrey Hamilton, FRSE; FREng; Professor and Specialist Advisor to Vice-Chancellor, Napier University, 1994–97; *b* 22 April 1930; *s* of Ernest Frederick and Dora Gladys Collins; *m* 1956, Sally Parfitt; two *s*. *Educ:* London Univ. (BSc, MSc, DSc). FIET (FIEE 1973), CPhys 1974, FInstP 1974, FIEEE 1980; CEng 1973, FREng (FEng 1981), FRSE 1983. GEC Research Laboratories, London, 1951–56; Ferranti Ltd, Edinburgh, 1956–57; Univ. of Glasgow, 1957–66; Research Engr, Stanford Univ., Calif, 1966–68; Dir of Physical Electronics, Rockwell International, Calif, 1968–70; University of Edinburgh: Research Prof., 1970–73; Prof. of Industrial Electronics, 1973–77; Prof. of Electrical Engrg and Hd of Dept, 1977–84; Emeritus Prof., 1984; Chm., Parallel Computing Centre, 1991–94. Dir, Automation and Robotics Res. Inst., and Prof. of Electrical Engrg, Univ. of Texas at Arlington, 1976–77 and 1987–90; Sen. Technical Specialist, Lothian Regl Council, 1991–93. Member: Electronics Res. Council, 1979; Computer Bd for Univs and Res. Councils, 1985–86; Information Systems Cttee, UFC, 1992–93; Jt Information Systems Cttee, HEFCs, 1993–94. Director: MESL, 1970–79; Racal-MESL, 1979–81; Advent Technology, 1981–86; Filtronics Components, 1981–85; Burr-Brown Ltd, 1985; River Bend Bank, Fort Worth, 1987–90. Member Honour Societies: Eta Kappa Nu; Tau Beta Pi; Upsilon Pi Epsilon; Phi Beta Delta. Hon. DEng Napier, 1997. *Publications:* Computer-Aided Design of Surface Acoustic Wave Devices, 1976; 197 articles in learned soc. electrical engrg jls. *Recreations:* music, DIY, tennis.

COLLINS, Dame Joan (Henrietta), DBE 2015 (OBE 1997); actress and writer; *b* 23 May; *er d* of late Joseph Collins and Elsa (*née* Bessant); *m* 1st, 1954, Maxwell Reed (marr. diss. 1957; he *d* 1974); 2nd, 1963, (George) Anthony Newley (marr. diss. 1970; he *d* 1999); one *s* one *d*; 3rd, 1972, Ronald S. Kass (marr. diss. 1983; he *d* 1986); one *d*; 4th, 1985, Peter Holm (marr. diss. 1987); 5th, 2002, Percy Gibson. *Educ:* Francis Holland Sch.; RADA. *Films include:* Lady Godiva Rides Again, I Believe in You, 1952; Our Girl Friday, The Square Ring, 1953; The Good Die Young, Turn the Key Softly, 1954; Land of the Pharaohs, The Virgin Queen, The Girl in the Red Velvet Swing, 1955; The Opposite Sex, 1956; The Wayward Bus, Island in the Sun, Sea Wife, 1957; The Bravados, 1958; Rally Round the Flag, Boys, 1959; Esther and the King, Seven Thieves, 1960; Road to Hong Kong, 1962; Warning Shot, The Subterfuge, 1967; Can Hieronymus Merkin Ever Forget Mercy Humppe and Find True Happiness?, Drive Hard Drive Fast, 1969; Up in the Cellar, The Executioner, 1970; Quest for Love, Revenge, 1971; Tales from the Crypt, Fear in the Night, 1972; Tales that witness Madness, 1973; Dark Places, Alfie Darling, 1974; The Call of the Wolf, I don't want to be born, 1975; The Devil within Her, 1976; Empire of the Ants, 1977; The Big Sleep, 1978; Sunburn, The Stud, 1979; The Bitch, 1980; The Nutcracker, 1984; The Cartier Affair, 1985; Decadence, 1994; In the Bleak Midwinter, 1995; The Clandestine Marriage, 1998; Joseph and the Amazing Technicolor Dreamcoat, 1999; The Flintstones in Viva Rock Vegas, 2000; Those Old Broads, 2000; Ellis in Glamourland, 2005; Fetish, 2010 (Best Actress, NY City Internat. Film Fest.); *stage includes:* The Last of Mrs Cheyney, Cambridge Th., 1980; Private Lives, Aldwych, 1990, US tour and NY, 1992; Love Letters, US, 2000; Over the Moon, Old Vic, 2001; Full Circle, UK tour, 2004; An Evening with Joan Collins, UK tour, 2006, NY, 2010; Legends, US tour, 2006–07; Dick Whittington, Birmingham Hippodrome, 2010; One Night with Joan Collins, Leicester Sq. Th., 2013, 2014; *television includes:* serials: Dynasty, 1981–89; Sins, 1986; Monte Carlo, 1986; Pacific Palisades, 1997; Guiding Light, 2002; Footballers' Wives, 2006; Benidorm, 2014; series: Tonight at 8.30, 1991; film: Annie: A Royal Adventure, 1995; documentary: Joan Does Glamour, 2009; also appearances in plays and series. Awards: Best TV Actress, Golden Globe, 1982; Hollywood Women's Press Club, 1982; Favourite TV Performer, People's Choice, 1985. *Publications:* Past Imperfect (autobiog.), 1978; The Joan Collins Beauty Book, 1980; Katy: a fight for life, 1982; My Secrets, 1994; Second Act (autobiog.), 1996; My Friends' Secrets, 2000; Joan's Way, 2002; The Art of Living Well, 2007; The World According to Joan, 2011; Passion for Life (autobiog.), 2013; *novels:* Prime Time, 1988; Love and Desire and Hate, 1990; Too Damn Famous, 1995; Star Quality, 2002; Misfortune's Daughters, 2004.

See also J. J. Collins.

COLLINS, Sir John (Alexander), Kt 1993; Chairman, DSG international (formerly Dixons Group) plc, 2002–09 (Deputy Chairman, 2001–02); *b* 10 Dec. 1941; *s* of John Constantine Collins and Nancy Isobel Mitchell; *m* 1965, Susan Mary Hooper. *Educ:* Campbell Coll., Belfast; Reading Univ. Joined Shell, 1964; various appointments in Shell in Kenya, Nigeria, Colombia and UK; Chm. and Chief Exec., Shell UK, 1990–93; Chief Exec., Vestey Gp, 1994–2001; Chm., National Power, 1997–2000. Non-executive Director: BSkyB, 1994–97; N. M. Rothschild & Sons, 1995–2005; LSO, 1997–2000; P&O, 1998–2006; Stoll Moss Theatres Ltd, 1999–2000; Rothschild Continuation Hldgs AG, 1999–2010; 3i Infrastructure plc, 2009–14; Blue Diamond Gp, 2014–. Chm., Cantab Pharmaceuticals plc, 1996–99. Chairman: Adv. Cttee on Business and Envmt, 1991–93; Energy Adv. Panel, DTI, 2001–03; Sustainable Energy Policy Adv. Bd, DTI/DEFRA, 2004–07. Mem., Supervisory sub-cttee, Treasury and Resources, States of Guernsey Govt Dept., 2013–. Pres., The Energy Institute, 2005–07. Gov., Wellington Coll., 1995–99. *Recreations:* theatre, sailing. *Address:* Le Repos Au Coin, La Fosse, St Martin, Guernsey GY4 6EB. *Clubs:* Royal Yacht Squadron (Cowes); United (Guernsey).

COLLINS, John Morris; a Recorder of the Crown Court, 1980–98; *b* 25 June 1931; *s* of late Emmanuel Cohen, MBE, and Ruby Cohen; *m* 1968, Sheila Brummer; one *d*. *Educ:* Leeds Grammar Sch.; The Queen's Coll., Oxford (MA LitHum). Called to Bar, Middle Temple, 1956, Member of North Eastern Circuit; Hd of Chambers, 1966–2001, Jt Hd of Chambers, 2001–02; a Deputy Circuit Judge, 1970–80. Pres., Leeds Jewish Representative Council,

1986–89. *Publications:* Summary Justice, 1963; various articles in legal periodicals, etc. *Recreation:* walking. *Address:* (home) 14 Sandhill Oval, Leeds LS17 8EA. *T:* (0113) 268 6008; (chambers) Zenith Chambers, 10 Park Square, Leeds LS1 2LH. *T:* (0113) 245 5438, *Fax:* (0113) 242 3515.

COLLINS, John Vincent, MD; FRCP; Consultant Physician, since 1973; Consultant Physician and Director of Education and Professional Development, Benenden Hospital, Kent, 2007–12; Medical Director, Lister Hospital, since 2008; *b* 16 July 1938; *s* of Thomas Ernest Vincent Collins and Zillah Phoebe Collins; *m* 1st, 1963, Helen Eluned Cash (marr. diss. 2008); one *s* one *d*; 2nd, 2009, Hilary Anne Booker. *Educ:* Guy's Hosp. Med. and Dental Sch. (BDS 1961; MD 1974). FRCP 1981. Dental and Medical Schs, Guy's Hosp., 1956–66; Guy's, St Mary's, Royal Brompton and Westminster Hosps, 1967–72; Hon. Consultant Physician and Sen. Lectr, St Bartholomew's Hosp. Med. Sch., London, 1973–76; Consultant Physician: Royal Brompton Hosp., 1976–2003; St Stephen's Hosp., 1979–89; Westminster Hosp., 1989–93; Chelsea & Westminster Hosp., 1993–2003 (Med. Dir, 1994–2003); Hon. Consultant, In Pensioners, Royal Hosp., Chelsea, 1980–2003. Sen. Med. Advr, Benenden Healthcare Soc., 1979–2011; Gp Med. Advr, Smith & Nephew plc, 1987–2010. Chm., Clinical Standards Cttee, RCP, 2000–03. Mem., Soc. of Apothecaries. *Publications:* more than 150 papers, two monographs, and contribs to books. *Recreations:* painting, travel, tennis. *Address:* Royal Brompton Hospital, Fulham Road, SW3 6NP; The Lister Hospital, Chelsea Bridge Road, SW1W 8RH.

COLLINS, Judith, (Mrs R. J. H. Collins); *see* McClure, J.

COLLINS, Karen Ann; *see* Hammond, K. A.

COLLINS, Kathleen Joyce, (Kate), (Mrs D. A. L. Cooke); Director, Career Development and Assessment, Home Office, 2006–07; *b* 12 March 1952; *d* of Norman Jeffrey Collins and Phyllis Laura Collins (*née* Yardley); *m* 1984, David Arthur Lawrence Cooke, *qv*. *Educ:* Lady Margaret Hall, Oxford (BA Mod. Langs 1973; MA 1974). Joined Home Office as Immigration Officer, 1975; Admin. Trainee, 1977; Principal, 1982; Dep. Chief Insp., 1988–91, Dir (Ports), 1991–94, Immigration Service; Cabinet Office, 1994–96; Home Office: Police Dept, 1997; Dep. Dir Gen., Immigration and Nationality Directorate, 1998–2000; Director: Organised Crime, 2000–03; Adelphi Prog., 2003–06. *Recreations:* music, reading, countryside.

COLLINS, Sir Kenneth Darlingston, (Sir Ken), Kt 2003; Chairman, Scottish Environment Protection Agency, 1999–2007; *b* 12 Aug. 1939; *s* of Nicholas Collins and Ellen Williamson; *m* 1966, Georgina Frances Pollard; one *s* one *d*. *Educ:* St John's Grammar Sch.; Hamilton Acad.; Glasgow Univ. (BSc Hons); Strathclyde Univ. (MSc). FRSGS 1993. Left school, 1956; steelworks apprentice, 1956–59; univ., 1960–65; planning officer, 1965–66; WEA Tutor-Organiser, 1966–67; Lecturer: Glasgow Coll. of Bldg, 1967–69; Paisley Coll. of Technol., 1969–79. MEP (Lab) Strathclyde E, 1979–99. European Parliament: Dep. Leader, Labour Gp, 1979–84; Socialist spokesman on envmt, public health and consumer protection, 1984–89; Chm., Cttee on Envmt, Public Health and Consumer Protection, 1979–84 and 1989–99 (Vice Chm., 1984–87); Chm., Conf. of Cttee Chairmen, 1993–99. Dir, Inst. for Eur. Envmt Policy, London, 1991–99 (Bd Mem., 1999–2006). Member: EU High-Level Gp on Competitiveness, Energy and the Envmt, 2005–08; Adv. Bd, ESRC Genomics Policy and Res. Forum, 2006–08; Professional Practices Panel, Eur. Public Affairs Consultancies' Assoc., 2006–09. Member: East Kilbride Town and Dist Council, 1973–79; Lanark CC, 1973–75; East Kilbride Develt Corp., 1976–79; Bd, Forward Scotland, 1996–2003; Bd, EEA, 2000–05; Chairman: NE Glasgow Children's Panel, 1974–76; Central Scotland Forest (formerly Countryside) Trust, 1998–2001; Adv. Cttee, Scottish Alliance for Geoscis, Envmt and Society, 2008–10. Hon. Sen. Res. Fellow, Dept of Geography, Lancaster Univ., 1991–98; Associate Fellow, Eur. Centre for Public Affairs, 1999–. Vice-Pres., Assoc. of Drainage Authorities. Hon. Mem., Landscape Inst. Member: Fabian Soc.; Amnesty Internat.; Labour Movement in Europe; Hon. Pres., Scottish Assoc. of Geography Teachers, 2003–06; Hon. Vice-President: Royal Envmtl Health Inst. of Scotland, 1983–2009; Internat. Fedn on Envmtl Health, 1987; Inst. of Trading Standards Admin; Inst. of Environmental Health Officers; Nat. Soc. for Clean Air; Town and Country Planning Assoc. Chm., Tak Tent Cancer Support Charity, 1999–2002; Ambassador, Nat. Asthma Campaign Scotland, 2002. Fellow, Industry and Parlt Trust, 1984. Hon. FCIWEM 1994; Hon. FCIWM 2001. Mem. Adv. Bd, Jl Water Law. DUniv Paisley, 2004; Hon. DSc Glasgow, 2009. *Publications:* contributed to European Parliament reports; various articles on European envmt policy. *Recreations:* listening to music, playing the piano, dog walking, gardening. *Address:* 11 Stuarton Park, East Kilbride, Lanarkshire G74 4LA. *T:* (01355) 221345.

COLLINS, Lesley Elizabeth; *see* Appleby, L. E.

COLLINS, Margaret Elizabeth, CBE 1983; RRC; Matron-in-Chief, Queen Alexandra's Royal Naval Nursing Service, 1980–83; *b* 13 Feb. 1927; *d* of James Henry Collins and Amy Collins. *Educ:* St Anne's Convent Grammar Sch., Southampton. RRC 1978 (ARRC 1965). Royal Victoria Hosp., Bournemouth, SRN 1949; West Middlesex Hosp., CMB Part 1; entered QARNNS as Nursing Sister, 1953; accepted for permanent service, 1958; Matron, 1972; Principal Matron, 1976. SSStJ 1978. QHNS, 1980–83. *Recreations:* gardening, theatre-going. *Address:* Lancastria, 5 First Marine Avenue, Barton-on-Sea, Hants BH25 6DP. *T:* (01425) 612374.

COLLINS, Mark; *see* Collins, N. M.

COLLINS, Michael; aerospace consultant; Vice President, LTV Aerospace and Defense Company (formerly Vought Corporation), 1980–85; former NASA Astronaut; Command Module Pilot, Apollo 11 rocket flight to the Moon, July 1969; *b* Rome, Italy, 31 Oct. 1930; *s* of Maj.-Gen. and Mrs James L. Collins, Washington, DC, USA; *m* 1957, Patricia M. Finnegan, Boston, Mass; one *s* two *d*. *Educ:* St Albans Sch., Washington, DC (grad.). US Mil. Academy, West Point, NY (BSc); advanced through grades to Colonel; Harvard Business Sch. (AMP), 1974. Served as an experimental flight test officer, Air Force Flight Test Center, Edwards Air Force Base, Calif; he was one of the third group of astronauts named by NASA in Oct. 1963; served as backup pilot for Gemini 7 mission; as pilot with John Young on the 3-day 44-revolution Gemini 10 mission, launched 18 July 1966, he shared record-setting flight (successful rendezvous and docking with a separately launched Agena target vehicle; completed two periods of extravehicular activity); Command Module Pilot for Apollo flight, first lunar landing, in orbit 20 July 1969, when Neil Armstrong and Edwin Aldrin landed on the Moon. Asst Sec. of State for Public Affairs, US, 1970–71; Dir, Nat. Air and Space Museum, Smithsonian Institution, 1971–78; Under Sec., Smithsonian Inst., 1978–80. Maj. Gen. Air Force Reserve, retired. Fellow, Soc. of Experimental Test Pilots. Member, Order of Daedalians. Hon. degrees from: Stonehill Coll.; St Michael's Coll.; Northeastern Univ.; Southeastern Univ. Presidential Medal of Freedom, NASA; FAI Gold Space Medal; DSM (NASA); DSM (AF); Exceptional Service Medal (NASA); Astronaut Wings; DFC; Congressional Gold Medal, 2011. *Publications:* Carrying the Fire (autobiog.), 1974; Flying to the Moon and Other Strange Places (for children), 1976; Liftoff, 1988; Mission to Mars, 1990. *Recreations:* fishing, painting.

COLLINS, Michael Brendan, OBE 1983 (MBE 1969); HM Diplomatic Service, retired; HM Consul-General, Istanbul, 1988–92; *b* 9 Sept. 1932; *s* of Daniel James Collins, GM and Mary Bridget Collins (*née* Kennedy); *m* 1959, Maria Elena Lozar. *Educ:* St Illtyd's College, Cardiff; University College London. HM Forces, 1953–55. FO 1956; Santiago, Chile, 1959; Consul, Santiago, Cuba, 1962; FO, 1964; Second, later First, Sec. (Admin.) and Consul, Prague, 1967; Dep. High Comr, Bathurst, The Gambia, 1970; Head of Chancery, Algiers, 1972; First Sec., FCO, 1975; Consul Commercial, Montreal, 1978; Consul for Atlantic Provinces of Canada, Halifax, 1981; Counsellor (Economic and Commercial), Brussels, 198[illegible] *Recreations:* fishing, golf, walking, reading, music. *Club:* Royal Over-Seas League.

COLLINS, Michael Geoffrey; QC 1988; barrister, arbitrator and mediator; *b* 4 March 194[illegible] *s* of late Francis Geoffrey Collins and Margaret Isabelle Collins; *m* 1985, Bonnie Gayle Bir[illegible] *Educ:* Peterhouse, Rhodesia (now Zimbabwe); Exeter Univ. (LLB). Called to the Bar, Gray's Inn, 1971, Bencher, 1999. A Recorder, 1997–2001. Special Legal Consultant: Fulbright & Jaworski LLP, Washington, 2002–06; Crandall, Hanscom & Collins PA, Rockland, ME 2006–. *Publications:* contributor, Private International Litigation, 1988. *Recreations:* golf, tennis, watercolours, amateur dramatics. *Address:* 9304 Belmart Road, Potomac, MD 20854, USA. *T:* (301) 9830024; Essex Court Chambers, 24 Lincoln's Inn Fields, WC2A 3EG. *T:* (020) 7813 8000.

COLLINS, Michael John, MBE 2015; clarinettist; Professor, Royal College of Music, sinc[e] 1983; *b* 27 Jan. 1962; *s* of Gwendoline Violet and Fred Allenby Collins; *m* 1997, Isabelle va[n] Keulen (marr. diss. 2008); one *s* one *d*. *Educ:* Royal Coll. of Music (ARCM, Clarinet an[d] Piano with Hons). FRCM 2010. BBC Young Musician of the Year, 1978. Principal clarinet[,] London Sinfonietta, 1982–2002; Nash Ensemble, 1982–2002; Philharmonia Orchestra, 1988–95; Dir, London Winds Ensemble, 1988–; Principal Conductor, City of London Sinfonia, 2010–. Many solo recordings. Hon. RAM 1997. Musicians' Co. Medal, 1980; competition winner: Leeds, 1980; Concert Artists' Guild, NY, 1982 (Amcon Award); Internat. Rostrum of Young Performers, Unesco, 1985; Tagore Gold Medal, 1982. *Recreations:* walking, driving, wildlife.

COLLINS, Neil Adam; Columnist: FT Alphaville, since 2010; Financial Times, since 2012; *s* of late Clive and Joan Collins; *m* 1981, Vivien Goldsmith (marr. diss. 1994); one *d*; *m* 1999, Julia Frances Barnes; one *s* one *d*. *Educ:* Uppingham School; Selwyn College, Cambridge (MA). City Editor: Evening Standard, 1979–84; Sunday Times, 1984–86; Daily Telegraph, 1986–2005; Flyfishing correspondent, The Spectator, 2002–04; Columnist: Evening Standard, 2005–09; Reuters, 2009–10. Director: Templeton Emerging Markets Investment Trust plc, 2006–; Dyson James Ltd, 2006–07; Finsbury Growth & Income Trust, 2008–. Gov., St Andrew's School, Eastbourne, 1999–2003. Financial Journalist of the Year, British Press Awards, 2002. *Recreations:* walking, wine, fly fishing, opera. *Address:* 12 Gertrude Street, SW10 0JN. *T:* (020) 7352 9595, 07836 256674.

COLLINS, (Nicholas) Mark, PhD; Chairman, Galapagos Conservation Trust, since 201[illegible] (Trustee, since 2006); Vice-Chairman, Earthwatch Europe, since 2012; *b* 23 April 1952; *s* o[f] late John Anthony Collins and of Mary Collins (*née* Humphries); *m* 1982, Melanie Margaret Stephens; one *s* one *d*. *Educ:* Wadham Coll., Oxford (BA 1973, MA 1974); Imperial Coll. London (DIC 1977; PhD 1977); MBA Open Univ. 1999. Centre for Overseas Pest Res. Nigeria and Sarawak, 1974–80; Internat. Centre for Insect Physiol. and Ecol., Kenya, 1980–82; IUCN, 1982–88; World Conservation Monitoring Centre, 1988–2000 (Dir 1994–2000); UNEP, Cambridge and Kenya, 2000–05; Dir, Commonwealth Foundn, 2005–11. Vis. Fellow, Univ. of Westminster, 2011–12. HM Inspector of Zoos, 1990–2000. Trustee: FFI, 1989–98; Wildscreen Trust, 1997–2004; Total Foundn, 2003–06; Member, Darwin Initiative Adv. Cttee, 2001–06; Darwin Expert Cttee, 2012–. Chairman: Cambridge Sustainable City, 1996–2002; Cambridge and Peterborough Sustainable Develt Round Table, 2003–04. Mem., Commonwealth Scholarship Commn, 2008–11. Gov., Meridian Co. Primary Sch., 1996–99. Member: Royal Entomol Soc.; RGS. Busk Medal, RGS, 200[illegible] *Publications:* (jtly) The IUCN Invertebrate Red Data Book, 1983; (with M. G. Morris) Threatened Swallowtail Butterflies of the World, 1985; (ed jtly) Kora: an ecological inventory of the Kora National Reserve, Kenya, 1986; (ed jtly) Insect-Fungus Interactions, 1988; (ed) The Management and Welfare of Invertebrates in Captivity, 1989; The Last Rainforests, 1990; (ed jtly) The Conservation of Insects and their Habitats, 1991; The Conservation Atlas of Tropical Forests: (ed jtly) Asia, 1991, (ed jtly) Africa, 1992; (editl advr and co-ordinator) Encyclopedia of the Biosphere, Vol. II, Tropical Rainforests, 2000; (ed jtly) From Hook to Plate: the state of marine fisheries, 2010; numerous contribs to learned jls. *Recreations:* boating, countryside. *Address:* 49 West Street, Comberton, Cambridge CB23 7DS. *T:* (01223) 262458. *E:* collinsmark@gmail.com.

COLLINS, Nina; *see* Lowry, Her Honour Noreen M.

COLLINS, Patrick Michael; Chief Sports Writer, Mail on Sunday, 1982–2014; *b* 23 Nov. 1943; *s* of Patrick and Julia Collins (*née* Canty); *m* 1969, Julie Kathleen Grundon; three *s* one *d*. *Educ:* St Joseph's Acad., Blackheath, London. Reporter, Kentish Mercury, 1962–65; sports writer: Sunday Citizen, 1965–67; News of the World, 1967–78; sports columnist: London Evening News, 1978–80; London Evening Standard, 1980–82; Punch, 1990–92. Mem., English Sports Council, 1999–2002. British Sports Journalism Awards: British Sports Journalist of the Year, 1989, 1990, 1997, 2002, 2008; Sports Feature Writer of the Year, 1993, 2002; Sports Columnist of the Year, 1999, 2000, 2004, 2006, 2012. *Publications:* (with Pat Pocock) Percy, 1987; The Sportswriter, 1996; Among the Fans: a year of watching the watchers, 2011. *Recreations:* watching cricket, reading modern history, family.

COLLINS, His Honour Paul Howard, CBE 1999; a Circuit Judge, 1991–2010; Senior Circuit Judge, Central London Civil Justice Centre, 2001–10; a Deputy Circuit Judge, 2010–12; *b* 31 Jan. 1944; *s* of Michael and Madie Collins; *m* 1987, Sue Fallows; one step *s*. *Educ:* Orange Hill Grammar Sch.; St Catherine's Coll., Oxford (MA). Called to the Bar, Lincoln's Inn, 1966 (Bencher, 2000); a Recorder, 1989. Designated Civil Judge for London Gp of County Cts, 2001–08. Mem., Parole Bd, 2010–14. Dir of Studies, Judicial Studies Bd, 1997–99. Chm., Council, Inns of Court Disciplinary Tribunals, 2010–13. *E:* paulhowardcollins@gmail.com. *Clubs:* Athenæum, Questors.

COLLINS, Pauline, OBE 2001; actress (stage and television); *b* Exmouth, Devon, 3 Sept. 1940; *d* of William Henry Collins and Mary Honora Callanan; *m* John Alderton, *qv*; two *s* one *d*. *Educ:* Convent of the Sacred Heart, Hammersmith, London; Central Sch. of Speech and Drama. *Stage:* 1st appearance in A Gazelle in Park Lane, Theatre Royal, Windsor, 1962; 1st London appearance in Passion Flower Hotel, Prince of Wales, 1965; The Erpingham Camp, Royal Court, 1967; The Happy Apple, Hampstead, 1967, and Apollo, 1970; Importance of Being Earnest, Haymarket, 1968; The Night I chased the Women with an Eel, 1969; Come As You Are (3 parts), New, 1970; Judies, Comedy, 1974; Engaged, National Theatre, Old Vic, 1975; Confusions, Apollo, 1976; Rattle of a Simple Man, Savoy, 1980; Romantic Comedy, Apollo, 1983; Shirley Valentine, Vaudeville, 1988, NY, 1989 (Tony Award, Best Actress, 1989); Shades, Albery, 1992; *television*, 1962–: series: Upstairs Downstairs; No Honestly; P. G. Wodehouse; Thomas and Sarah; The Black Tower; Forever Green; The Ambassador; Mount Pleasant; plays: Long Distance Information, 1979; Knockback, 1984; Man and Boy, 2002; Sparkling Cyanide, 2003; Famous Last, 2009; film: What We Did on Our Holiday, 2006; *films:* Shirley Valentine, 1989 (Evening Standard Film Actress of the Year, 1989; BAFTA Best Actress Award, 1990); City of Joy, 1992; My Mother's Courage, 1997; Paradise Road, 1997; Mrs Caldicot's Cabbage War, 2002; You Will Meet a Tall Dark Stranger, 2011; Albert Nobbs, 2012; Quartet, 2013. Dr *hc* Liverpool Poly., 1991. *Publications:* Letter to Louise, 1992. *Address:* c/o Independent Talent Group Ltd, 40 Whitfield Street, W1T 2RH.

COLLINS, Peter; *see* Collins, V. P.

COLLINS, Peter G., RSA 1974 (ARSA 1966); painter in oil; *b* Inverness, 21 June 1935; *s* of E. G. Collins, FRCSE; *m* 1959, Myra Mackintosh (marr. diss. 1978); one *s* one *d*. *Educ:* Fettes Coll., Edinburgh; Edinburgh Coll. of Art. Studied in Italy, on Andrew Grant Major Travelling Scholarship, 1957–58. Work in permanent collections: Aberdeen Civic; Glasgow Civic; Holyrood Palace. *Recreations:* music, art-historical research. *Address:* Royal Scottish Academy, The Mound, Edinburgh EH2 2EL; The Cottage, Hilltown of Ballindean, Inchture, Perthshire PH14 9QS.

COLLINS, Air Vice-Marshal Peter Spencer, CB 1985; AFC 1961; *b* 19 March 1930; *s* of Frederick Wildbore Collins, OBE and Mary (*née* Spencer); *m* 1953, Sheila Mary (*née* Perks) (*d* 2000); three *s* one *d*. *Educ:* Royal Grammar Sch., High Wycombe; Univ. of Birmingham (BA (Hons) History). Joined RAF, 1951; flying tours incl. service on squadron nos: 63, 141, 41, AWDS, AFDS; RAF Handling Sqdn, nos 23 and 11; commanded: 111 Sqdn, 1970–72; RAF Gütersloh, 1974–76; staff tours include: Air Ministry, 1962–64; Strike Comd HQ, 1968–70 and 1972–74; Dir of Forward Policy (RAF), 1978–81; SASO, HQ 11 Gp, 1981–83; DG, Communications, Inf. Systems and Orgn (RAF), 1983–85; psc 1965, rcds 1977; retired 1985. Marconi Radar Systems: Dir, Business Develt, 1986–88; Consultant Dir, 1988–95; Consultant, GEC-Marconi Res. Centre, 1989–95. Hon. Pres., Essex Wing, ATC, 2001–10; Vice-Pres., Chelmsford Br., RAFA, 1998–; Pres., United Services Assoc., Chelmsford & Dist, 2000–. CCMI (FBIM 1979). *Publications:* contribs to service jls and to Seaford House Papers, 1978. *Recreations:* golf, music, gardening. *Address:* 2 Doubleday Gardens, Braintree, Essex CM7 9SW. *Club:* Royal Air Force.

COLLINS, Philip, LVO 1994; singer, drummer, songwriter, actor and record producer; Trustee, Prince's Trust, since 1983; patron of numerous charities; *b* 30 Jan. 1951; *s* of Greville and June Collins; *m* 1st, 1976 (marr. diss.); one *s* one *d*; 2nd, 1984, Jill Tavelman (marr. diss. 1995); one *d*; 3rd, 1999, Orianne Cevey (marr. diss. 2008); two *s*. *Educ:* primary and secondary schs; Barbara Speake Stage Sch. Played parts in various television, film and stage productions, 1965–67; mem. of various rock groups, 1967–70; drummer, 1970–96, lead singer, 1975–96, Genesis; started writing songs, 1976; toured Japan, USA and Europe, 1978, 1987; reunion tour, Europe and N America, 2007; first solo album, 1981; solo world tours, 1985, 1990; started producing records for other artists, 1981. *Albums* include: *with Genesis:* Nursery Cryme, 1971; Foxtrot, 1972; Genesis Live, 1973; Selling England by the Pound, 1973; The Lamb Lies Down on Broadway, 1974; A Trick of the Tail, 1976; Genesis Rock Roots, 1976; Wind and Wuthering, 1977; Genesis Seconds Out, 1977; And Then There Were Three, 1978; Duke, 1980; Abacab, 1981; Three Sides Live, 1982; Genesis, 1983; Invisible Touch, 1986; We Can't Dance, 1991; *solo:* Face Value, 1981; Hello … I must be Going, 1982; No Jacket Required, 1985; But Seriously, 1989; Both Sides, 1993; Dance into the Light, 1996; Hits, 1998; Testify, 2002; Going Back, 2010. *Films:* Buster (lead role), 1988; Frauds, 1993. Numerous awards, incl. Grammy (eight), Ivor Novello (six), Brit (four), Variety Club of GB (two), Silver Clef (two), Academy Award, and Elvis awards.

COLLINS, Philip James; columnist and Chief Leader Writer, The Times, since 2013 (Deputy Chief Leader Writer, 2009–13); *b* 16 May 1967; *s* of Frederick John Collins and Jennifer Anne Collins (*née* Taylor, now Dawson); *m* 2002, Geeta Guru-Murthy; two *s*. *Educ:* Birmingham Univ. (BA Hons 1988); Birkbeck Coll., London (MSc Dist. 1991); St John's Coll., Cambridge. Res. Officer, London Weekend TV, 1988–89; Political Asst to Frank Field, MP, 1989–92; Research Officer: Inst. of Educn, London Univ., 1992; Fleming Investment Mgt, 1995–97; Equity Strategist: HSBC James Capel, 1997–99; Dresdner Kleinwort Benson, 1999–2000; Dir, Social Mkt Foundn, 2000–05; Chief Speech Writer, Prime Minister's Policy Directorate, 2005–07; Sen. Vis. Fellow, LSE, 2007–09; Vis. Fellow, Dept of Public Policy, Univ. of Oxford, 2010–. Chm. Trustees, Demos, 2008–. FRSA. *Publications:* (ed) An Authority in Education, 2001; The Men from the Boys, 2002; (ed) Culture or Anarchy?, 2002; Bobby Dazzler, 2003; (ed) Reinventing Government Again, 2004; (with R. Reeves) Liberal Republic, 2009; The Art of Speeches and Presentations, 2012. *Recreations:* music, cricket, football, poetry, television, philosophy. *Address:* The Times, 1 London Bridge Street, SE1 9GF. *E:* phil.collins@thetimes.co.uk.

COLLINS, Richard Edward Charles, FRCS; Vice President, Royal College of Surgeons of England, 2009–11; *b* Moncton, NB, 9 Jan. 1943; *s* of Edward Collins and Jessie Collins (*née* Charles); *m* 1971, Valerie Margaret Celba; three *d*. *Educ:* Chigwell Sch.; St George's Hosp. Med. Sch., London (MB BS 1967); Harvard Med. Sch. MRCS 1967, FRCS 1971; LRCP 1967. Consultant Surgeon, Kent and Canterbury, and Thanet Hosps, then East Kent Hosps NHS Trust, 1976–2008. Member, Council: Assoc. of Surgeons of GB and Ire., 1996–2002; RCS, 2002–11; Pres., British Assoc. of Endocrine Surgeons, 2002–03. Chm., Gen. Surgery, Intercollegiate Exam. Bd, 1998–2001. Kent Ambassador, 2007 (Chm., 2012–). FRCSEd *ad hominem* 2000; FRSocMed 1977. Freeman, City of London, 2002; Liveryman, Barbers' Co., 2006. Member: Kent Ornithological Soc., 1971–; Lord's Taverners, 2012–. *Publications:* (contrib.) Birds of Kent, 1981; chapters in various surgical textbooks on thrombosis, prophylaxis and endocrine surgery; papers on endocrine surgery, surgical trng and orgn of surgical and trauma services. *Recreations:* cricket, birdwatching, fly-fishing. *Address:* Seatonden, Ickham, Canterbury, Kent CT3 1SL. *Clubs:* MCC; Kent County Cricket (Pres., 2005; Vice-Chm., 2013–); Surgical 60 Travelling.

COLLINS, Sir Rory (Edwards), Kt 2011; FMedSci; FRS 2015; Co-director, Clinical Trial Service Unit and Epidemiological Studies Unit, since 1986, British Heart Foundation Professor of Medicine and Epidemiology, since 1996, and Head, Nuffield Department of Population Health, since 2013, University of Oxford; *b* Hong Kong, 3 Jan. 1955; *s* of Jack Collins and Catherine Collins (*née* Burke). *Educ:* Dulwich Coll., London; George Washington Univ., USA (BSc Stats 1977); St Thomas's Hosp. Med. Sch., London (MB BS 1981); St Peter's Coll., Oxford (MSc Stats 1983). FRCPE 2002. Res. Fellow, Dept of Cardiovascular Medicine and Clin. Trial Service Unit, Univ. of Oxford, 1981–86. FMedSci 2004. *Recreation:* tennis. *Address:* Clinical Trial Service Unit and Epidemiological Studies Unit, Nuffield Department of Population Health, Richard Doll Building, Old Road Campus, Roosevelt Drive, Oxford OX3 7LF. *T:* (01865) 743743, *Fax:* (01865) 743985. *E:* rory.collins@ndph.ox.ac.uk.

COLLINS, Sarah; *see* Veale, S.

COLLINS, Simon C.; *see* Crawford Collins.

COLLINS, Simon Jeremy; Partner, since 1999, and Chairman and Senior Partner, since 2012, KPMG LLP; *b* London, 13 April 1960; *s* of Bernard and Sylvia Collins; *m* 1986, Simone Bersinski; one *s* one *d*. *Educ:* Haberdashers' Aske's Sch., Elstree; Victoria Univ. of Manchester (BA (Econ) 1982). ACA 1986. Trng contract, Price Waterhouse, 1982–87; Sen. Manager, S. G. Warburg & Co., 1987–91; Man. Dir and Hd, Debt Structuring, Nat West, 1991–98. Trustee, Pancreatic Cancer UK, 2012–. Mem., Chartered Accountants' Co., 2013–. Mem., Global Leadership Bd, Manchester Univ., 2013–. *Recreations:* family, opera, motoring, art deco objects. *Address:* KPMG LLP, 15 Canada Square, E14 5GL. *T:* (020) 7311 8959. *E:* simon.collins@kpmg.co.uk.

COLLINS, Prof. Susan Alexis Regine, PhD; artist; Slade Professor, since 2013, Slade Director and Professor of Fine Art, since 2010, and Director, Slade Centre for Electronic Media in Fine Art, since 1995, Slade School of Fine Art, University College London; *b* London, 15 Jan. 1964; *d* of Dennis S. Collins and Helene M. Collins (*née* Davis); partner, 1998, Tim Head. *Educ:* St Paul's Girls' Sch.; Chelsea Coll. of Art (Foundn); Slade Sch. of Fine Art, University Coll. London (BA Hons Fine Art 1987); Univ. of Reading (PhD Fine Art 2001). Amer. Assoc. of Univ. Women Rose Sidgwick Meml Fellow, Sch. of Art Inst. of Chicago, 1990–91 (Fulbright Travel Award); Lectr in Computer Arts and Animation, Columbia Coll., Chicago, 1991–92; Res. Fellow in Interactive Media, W Surrey Coll. of Art and Design, 1992–94; Sessional Lectr (pt-time) in Fine Art, Univ. of Reading, 1994–95; Hd, Electronic Media, Slade Centre for Electronic Media in Fine Art, 1995–2010, Hd, Undergrad. Fine Art Media, 2005–10, Slade Sch. of Fine Art, UCL. *Works include:* Woolwich Foot Tunnel, 1993; Pedestrian Gestures, 1994; Touched, 1996; In Conversation, Brighton, Amsterdam, Helsinki, Cardiff, Berlin, 1997–2001; Transporting Skies, 2002; Tate in Space, commnd for Tate Online, 2002; The Spectrascope, 2004; Fenlandia, 2004–05; Glenlandia, 2005–06; Underglow, 2005; Seascape, De La Warr Pavilion, 2009; Love Brid, 2009; Brighter Later, 2013. Mem., BAFTA. FRSA. *Publications:* contributor: A Directory of British Film and Video Artists, 1996; New Media: practice and content in Britain 1994–2004, 2004; Networked Narrative Environments, 2004; Spatialities: geographies of art and architecture, 2012. *Recreations:* art, film, books, travel, food, social media. *Address:* Slade School of Fine Art, University College London, Gower Street, WC1E 6BT. *T:* (020) 7679 7040, *Fax:* (020) 7679 7801. *E:* susan.collins@ucl.ac.uk.

COLLINS, His Eminence Cardinal Thomas; *see* Toronto, Archbishop of, (RC).

COLLINS, Timothy William George, CBE 1996; Chairman, Bell Pottinger Political, since 2013; Partner, Bell Pottinger LLP, since 2013; *b* 7 May 1964; *s* of late William and of Diana Collins; *m* 1997, Clare, *d* of Geoffrey and Auriel Benson; one *s*. *Educ:* Chigwell Sch., Essex; LSE (BSc); KCL (MA). Cons. Res. Dept, 1986–89; Advr to Secs of State for the Envmt, 1989–90, for Employment, 1990–92; Press Sec. to Prime Minister, 1992; Dir of Communications, Cons. Party, 1992–95; Mem., Prime Minister's Policy Unit, 1995; Sen. Strategy Consultant, WCT Ltd, 1995–97. MP (C) Westmorland and Lonsdale, 1997–2005; contested (C) same seat, 2005. An Opposition Whip, 1998–99; Shadow Minister for the Cabinet Office, 2001–02; Shadow Secretary of State: for Transport, 2002–03; for Educn, 2003–05. Vice-Chm., Cons. Party, 1999–2001. Man. Dir, 2009–12, Chm., 2012–13, Bell Pottinger Public Affairs Ltd. *Address:* (office) Holborn Gate, 330 High Holborn, WC1V 7QD.

COLLINS, Prof. (Vincent) Peter, MD, PhD; FRCPath, FMedSci, FHEA; Professor of Histopathology, University of Cambridge, 1997–2014, now Emeritus; Hon. Consultant Pathologist, Addenbrooke's Hospital, 1997–2014; *b* 3 Dec. 1947; *s* of James Vincent Collins and Mary Ann Collins (*née* Blanche). *Educ:* University Coll., Dublin (MB, BCh, BAO 1971); Karolinska Inst., Stockholm (MD; PhD 1978); MA (Cantab). MRCPath 1988, FRCPath 1996. House appts, Mater Hosp., Dublin, 1972–73; junior appts, 1974–82, Cons. Pathologist, 1982–90, Sen. Cons. Pathologist, 1994–97, Karolinska Inst.; Head of Clin. Res., Ludwig Inst. for Cancer Res., Stockholm Br., 1986–98; Prof. of Neuropathology, Univ. of Gothenburg, 1990–94; Sen. Cons. Pathologist, Sahlgrenska Univ. Hosp., Gothenburg, 1990–94; Prof. of Tumour Pathology, Karolinska Inst., 1994–97. Foreign Adjunct Prof., Karolinska Inst., 1998–. FMedSci 2002. *Publications:* over 300 papers on human brain tumours. *Recreations:* sailing, ski-ing, music. *Address:* Department of Histopathology, Box 235, Addenbrooke's Hospital, Cambridge CB2 0QQ. *T:* (01223) 336072.

COLLINS, William Janson, MBE 2004; Chairman, William Collins Sons & Co. (Holdings) Ltd, 1976–81; *b* 10 June 1929; *s* of late Sir William Alexander Roy Collins, CBE, and Lady Collins (Priscilla Marian, *d* of late S. J. Lloyd); *m* 1951, Lady Sara Elena Hely-Hutchinson (*d* 2013), *d* of 7th Earl of Donoughmore; one *s* three *d*. *Educ:* Magdalen Coll., Oxford (BA). Joined William Collins Sons & Co. Ltd, 1952; Dir, then Man. Dir, 1967; Vice-Chm., 1971; Chm., 1976. *Recreations:* Royal tennis, shooting, fishing, tennis, golf. *Club:* All England Lawn Tennis and Croquet.

COLLINS RICE, Rowena; Director-General, Attorney General's Office, since 2013; *b* 24 April 1960; *d* of John Frederick, (Jack), Collins and Hilda Collins (*née* Campbell); *m* 1986, Hugh Robert Collins Rice; two *s*. *Educ:* Westbourne Sch., Glasgow; Hertford Coll., Oxford (BA 1st Cl. Hons Jurisprudence 1981). Home Office, 1985–91; Treasury Solicitor's Dept, 1992–95; admitted solicitor, 1995; Home Office, 1995–2003; DCA, 2003–05; HMRC, 2005–07, Dir, Legal (Tax Law); Legal Dir, 2007–08, Dir Gen., Democracy, Constitution and Law, and Chief Legal Officer, 2008–10, DCA, later MoJ; Dir Gen., Constitutional, Dep. Prime Minister's Gp, Cabinet Office, 2010–11; Sec., Leveson Inquiry, 2011–12. *Address:* Attorney General's Office, 20 Victoria Street, SW1H 0NF. *T:* (020) 7271 2401. *E:* rowena.collins-rice@attorneygeneral.gsi.gov.uk.

COLLINSON, Anne Elizabeth; *see* Aitken, A. E.

COLLINSON, Rev. Nigel Thomas; Methodist Minister; Secretary, Methodist Conference, 1999–2003 (President, 1996–97); *b* 14 March 1941; *s* of Tom and Agnes Collinson; *m* 1964, Lorna Ebrill; two *d*. *Educ:* Forster Street Sch., Tunstall; Hanley High Sch., Stoke on Trent; Hull Univ. (BA Theol 1962); Wesley House, Cambridge (MA Theol 1964). Ordained 1967; Methodist Minister: Clifton and Redland Circuit, Bristol, 1964–67; Stroud and Cirencester Circuit, 1967–72; Wolverhampton Trinity Circuit, 1972–80; Supt, Oxford Circuit and Methodist Chaplain to Univ. students, 1980–88; Chm., Southampton Dist, 1988–98. Hon. Chaplain, British and Internat. Sailors' Soc., 2005. Hon. DD Hull, 1997. *Publications:* The Opening Door, 1986; (with David Matthews) Facing Illness, 1986; The Land of Unlikeness, 1996. *Recreations:* golf, fishing, gardening, the arts.

COLLINSON, Prof. Simon Charles, DPhil; Director and Dean, Birmingham Business School, and Professor of International Business and Strategy, University of Birmingham, since 2012; *b* Mwanza, Tanzania, 23 April 1964; *s* of Michael and Norma Collinson; *m* 1993, Carol Bryce; three *s*. *Educ:* Univ. of Leeds (BA Jt Hons); Univ. of Florida (MA Hons); Sussex Univ. (DPhil 1991). University of Edinburgh: Asst Dir and Sen. Res. Fellow, Inst. for Japanese-Eur. Technol. Studies, 1991–98; Lectr in Internat. Business Studies, Mgt Sch. and Dept of Business Studies, 1998–2000; Warwick Business School, University of Warwick: Sen. Lectr, 2000–05; Associate Dean, MBAs, 2004–05; Reader in Internat. Business, 2006–08; Hd, Mktg and Strategy Gp, 2007–09; Prof. of Internat. Business and Innovation, 2008–11; Dep. Dean, 2009–10; Prof. of Internat. Business and Innovation, Henley Business Sch., Univ. of Reading, 2011–12. Guangbiao Prof., Sch. of Econs and Mgt, Zhejiang Univ., China, 2010–13; Academic Associate, Centre for Internat. Business and Mgt, Judge Business Sch., Univ. of Cambridge, 2008–. Mem., ESRC, 2011–. Member: Bd of Dirs, Advanced Inst. of Mgt, 2007–11; Council, British Acad. of Mgt, 2011–13; Exec. Bd, UK Assoc. of Business Schs, 2013–; Bd, Gtr Birmingham Chamber of Commerce, 2014–. FRSA 2014. *Publications:* Small and Successful in Japan, 1995; (with A. Rugman) International Business, 5th edn 2008, 6th edn 2012; (ed with G. Morgan) Images of the Multinational Firm, 2009; contrib. papers to learned jls. *Recreations:* squash, ski-ing, sailing, golf, tennis, travel. *Address:* Birmingham Business School, University House, Edgbaston Park Road, Birmingham B15 2TY.

COLLIS, His Honour Ian; a Circuit Judge, 2000–09; *b* 21 Feb. 1946; *s* of late Harold Collis and Florence Collis; *m* 1968, Julia Georgina Cure; three *s*. *Educ:* Dartford Grammar Sch.; LLB (Hons) London. Admitted Solicitor, 1970; District Judge, 1987–2000; a Recorder, 1996–2000. *Recreations:* gardening, walking dog.

COLLIS, Peter George, CB 2005; Chief Land Registrar and Chief Executive, HM Land Registry, 1999–2010; *b* 13 Oct. 1953; *s* of Martin Arthur Collis and Margaret Sophie Collis; *m* 1978, Linda Jean Worssam (marr. diss. 1999); one *s* one *d*; *m* 2000, Jan Morgan; one step *s*. *Educ:* Univ. of Aston in Birmingham (BSc 1st Cl. Hons Communication Sci. and Linguistics 1975). Joined Civil Service, 1975; admin trainee, Depts of Trade, Industry and Prices and

Consumer Protection, 1975–78; Personal Asst to Chm. and Dep. Chm., NEB, 1978–80; Principal, Dept of Trade, 1980–83; Mktg Exec., Balfour Beatty, 1983–85 (on secondment); Principal, Dept of Transport, 1985–88; Head, Driver Licensing Div., DVLA, 1988–91; Head, Finance Exec. Agencies 2 Div., 1991–92, Highways Resource Mgt Div., 1992–94, Dept of Transport; Strategy and Private Finance Dir, Highways Agency, 1994–97; Business Develt Dir, Dept of Transport, 1997; Finance and Commercial Policy Dir, Employment Service, 1997–99. Non-exec. Dir, GLE Gp, 2012–. Lay Mem., Governance, and Dep. Chm., Surrey Downs CCG, 2013–. Hon. RICS 2003 (Mem., Governing Council, 2006–12). *Recreations:* family, enjoying the coast and the countryside, Germany.

COLLIS, Sarah Lilian; *see* Anderson, S. L.

COLLIS, Simon Paul, CMG 2014; HM Diplomatic Service; Ambassador to Saudi Arabia, since 2015; *b* 23 Feb. 1956. *Educ:* King Edward VII Sch., Sheffield; Christ's Coll., Cambridge (BA Hons). Joined HM Diplomatic Service, 1978: FCO, 1978–80; Arabic lang. trng, 1980–81; 3rd, later 2nd, Sec., Bahrain, 1981–83; 1st Secretary: FCO, 1984–85; UK Mission to UN, NY, 1986; Head, India Section, S Asia Dept, FCO, 1987–88; Head of Chancery, Tunis, 1988–90; Gulf War Emergency Unit, FCO, 1990–91; New Delhi, 1991–94; Asst Head, Near East and N Africa Dept, FCO, 1994–96; Dep. Hd of Mission, Amman, 1996–99; on secondment to BP, 1999–2000; Consul General: Dubai, 2000–04; Basra, 2004–05; Ambassador to Qatar, 2005–07; Ambassador to Syria, 2007–12; Ambassador to Iraq, 2012–14. *Address:* c/o Foreign and Commonwealth Office, King Charles Street, SW1A 2AH.

COLLON, Nicholas William Hyde; Principal Conductor and Artistic Director, Aurora Orchestra, since 2005; *b* Kingston-upon-Thames, 7 Feb. 1983; *s* of Michael and Jo Collon; *m* 2010, Jane Mitchell; one *s*. *Educ:* Eton Coll.; Clare Coll., Cambridge (BA Music). Guest conducting débuts: BBC Proms, Opera North, BBC SO, Aldeburgh Fest., 2009; Glyndebourne, LSO, 2010; London Philharmonic, BBC Scottish SO, Bregenz Fest., Stavanger SO, Royal Northern Sinfonia, Birmingham Contemp. Music Gp, 2011; Philharmonia Orch., London Mozart Players, BBC Nat. Orch. of Wales, Munich Chamber Orch., ENO, Bremen Music Fest., BBC Philharmonic Orch., Bournemouth SO, 2012; Hallé Orch., RPO, Spanish Nat. Orch., Acad. Ancient Music, Auckland Philharmonia, Ensemble Intercontemporain, Lucerne Fest., Glyndebourne on Tour, 2013; Bamberg SO, Orch. du Capitole de Toulouse, Orch. Nat. de Lyon, Zurich Tonhalle, Residentie Orch., Brussels Philharmonic Orch., Wroclaw Philharmonic Orch., Ulster Orch., Prague Radio SO, Les Violons du Roy, Trondheim SO, 2014. *Address:* c/o Janet Marsden, International Classical Artists, Dunstan House, 14a St Cross Street, EC1N 8XA. *T:* (020) 7539 2632, *Fax:* (020) 7404 0150. *E:* jmarsden@icartists.co.uk.

COLLYEAR, Sir John (Gowen), Kt 1986; FREng; Chairman, AE plc, 1981–86; *b* 19 Feb. 1927; *s* of John Robert Collyear and late Amy Elizabeth Collyear (*née* Gowen); *m* 1953, Catherine Barbara Newman; one *s* two *d*. *Educ:* Leeds Univ. (BSc). FIMechE (Hon. FIMechE 1995); FIMMM (Hon. FIMMM 2002), FIET; FREng (FEng 1979). Served RE Lieut 6th Airborne Div., Far and Middle East, 1944–48. Graduate apprentice and Production Engr, Joseph Lucas Industries, 1951; Glacier Metal Company Ltd: Production Engr, 1953; Production Manager, 1956; Chief Production Engr, 1956; Factory Gen. Manager, 1959; Managing Director, 1969; Bearings Div. Man. Dir, Associated Engineering Ltd, 1972; Group Man. Dir, AE plc, 1975. Chairman: MK Electric Gp PLC, 1987–88; Fulmer Ltd, 1987–91; USM Texon Ltd (formerly United Machinery Gp), 1987–95. Chm., Technology Requirements Bd, DTI, 1985–88. President: Motor Industry's Res. Assoc., 1987–97; Inst. of Materials, 1992–94. Hon. Bencher, Gray's Inn, 2000. *Publications:* Management Precepts, 1975; The Practice of First Level Management, 1976. *Recreations:* golf, bridge, piano music. *Address:* Donnington House, Cotswold Heights, Lower Swell Road, Stow-on-the-Wold, Cheltenham, Glos GL54 1LT. *T:* (01451) 830565. *Club:* Athenæum.

COLMAN, Hon. Sir Anthony (David), Kt 1992; a Judge of the High Court of Justice, Queen's Bench Division, Commercial Court, 1992–2007; Deputy Chief Justice, Court of Dubai International Financial Centre, since 2010 (Judge, 2007–10); commercial arbitrator, since 2007; *b* 27 May 1938; *s* of late Solomon and Helen Colman, Manchester; *m* 1964, Angela Glynn; two *d*. *Educ:* Harrogate Grammar Sch.; Trinity Hall, Cambridge (Aldis Schol.; Double First in Law Tripos; MA). FCIArb 1978. Chartered Arbitrator, 2007. Called to the Bar, Gray's Inn, 1962, Master of the Bench, 1986; QC 1977; a Recorder, 1986–92; Judge in charge of Commercial Court, 1996–97. Mem., Bar Council, 1990–92 (Chm., Central and E European Sub-Cttee, 1991–92); Chairman: Commercial Bar Assoc., 1991–92 (Treasurer, 1989–91); Lloyd's Disciplinary Cttee for PCW and Minet, 1984; Mem., Cttee of Enquiry into Fidentia at Lloyd's, 1982–83; conducted Investigation into loss of MV Derbyshire, 1999–2000. Special Advr to Govt of Czech Republic on civil litigation procedure, 2000–01; accession advr to EC for Czech Republic, 2002, and for Slovakia, 2003; sole Comr of Govt of Trinidad and Tobago, Commn of Enquiry into failure of CL Financial Ltd and Hindu Credit Union Co-operative Soc., 2010–. Co-Founder and Consultant, Eur. Commercial Judges Forum, 2003–07. Principal, Faculty of Mediation, Acad. of Experts, 2004–. Chm., AIDA Reinsurance and Insurance Assoc., 2009–. Hon. Pres., Italian Soc. of Mediation and Conciliation, 2002–. Gratias Agit Award from Czech Republic for services to judicial reform, 2006. *Publications:* Mathew's Practice of the Commercial Court (1902), 2nd edn, 1967; The Practice and Procedure of the Commercial Court, 1983, 6th edn 2008; (Gen. Editor and contrib.) Encyclopedia of International Commercial Litigation, 1991. *Recreations:* tennis, music, gardening, the 17th Century, Sifnos, the River Chess. *Address:* 24 Lincoln's Inn Fields, WC2A 3EG. *E:* acolman@londonarbitrators.net.

COLMAN, Anthony John, PhD; Research Associate, since 2013 and Visiting Fellow, since 2014, University of East Anglia; non-executive Chairman, PupilAsset.com; *b* 24 July 1943; *s* of late William Benjamin Colman and Beatrice (*née* Hudson); *m* Juliet Annabelle, *d* of Alec and June Owen; two *s*, and four *s* two *d* by prev. marriages. *Educ:* Paston Grammar Sch.; Magdalene Coll., Cambridge (BA 1964; MA); Univ. of E Africa, 1964–66; LSE, 1966; Univ. of East Anglia (MA 2009; PhD 2013). Unilever (United Africa Co.), 1964–69; Burton Group, 1969–90: Merchandise Manager, 1971–74, Buying and Merchandising Dir, 1974–76, Top Shop; Asst Man. Dir, Womenswear Sector, 1976–81; Director: Burton Menswear, 1976–81; Top Man, 1976–81; Dorothy Perkins, 1979–81; Dir, 1981–90. Director: GLE, 1990–97 (Chm., GLE Development Capital, 1990–97); Aztec, 1990–98; London First Centre Ltd, 1994–2002. Mem. (Lab) Merton LBC, 1990–98 (Leader of Council, 1991–97). Chair, Local Govt Superannuation Funds Cttee (incl. Police, Fire Bde and Teachers), 1992–98. Vice-Chm., ALA, 1991–95. Contested (Lab), SW Herts, 1979. MP (Lab) Putney, 1997–2005; contested (Lab) same seat, 2005. PPS to Minister of State, NI Office, 1998–2000. Member: Treasury Select Cttee, 1997–98; Internat. Develt Select Cttee, 2000–05; Chairman: All Party Gp on Socially Responsible Investment, 1998–2005; All Party Gp on Mgt, 2001–05; All Party UN Gp, 2002–05; PLP Trade and Industry Cttee, 1997–99. Chairman: Low Pay Unit, 1990–98; London Res. Centre, 1994–97; Dir, Public Private Partnerships Prog. Ltd, 1998–2001 (Chm., 1996–98); Member: Price Commn, 1977–79; Labour Finance & Industry Gp, 1973–; Labour Party Enquiry into Educn & Trng in Europe, 1991–93; Exec. Cttee, UNED, subseq. Stakeholder Forum for Our Common Future, 1995–2005; Adv. Bd, African Venture Capital Assoc., 2005–08. Assoc. Dir, 2005–09, non-exec. Dir, 2009–, Africa Practice Ltd. Pres., UNA UK SE Reg., 2005–07 (Deleg. to UN Gen. Assembly Millennium Develt Goals, 2005); Smart Partner, Commonwealth Partnership for Technology Mgt, 2008–. Member of Council: VSO, 2000–07; Chatham House, 2001–07; ODI, 2006–14; World Future Council, 2007–. Chm., One World Trust, 2007–10; Trustee, New Economics Foundn, 2005–08. One People Oration, Westminster Abbey, 2006. Chm., Wimbledon Theatre Trust, 1991–96; Dir, London Arts Bd, 1994–98; Trustee, Nelson Mus., 2009- Patron: Friends of Africa, 2004–07; Friends of Ahmadiyya Muslim Assoc., 2005–07. Loc preacher, Methodist Ch, 2005–. Industrial Fellow, Kingston Univ. (formerly Poly.), 1983- Fellow, Southlands Coll., Roehampton Univ., 2003; Associate Fellow, Governance of Clea Develt Proj., ESRC/UEA, 2010–; Vis. Scholar, New Sch., NY, 2013–. Adjunct Sen. Re Scientist, Earth Inst., Columbia Univ., NY, 2013–; Hon. Vis. Res. Fellow, Univ. of Cap Town, 2014–. Liveryman, Horners' Co., 2009. FRSA 1983; FRGS 2003; CCMI 200 *Publications:* Missing Power, 2009. *Clubs:* Reform; Cromer and Sheringham Rotar (Norfolk); Norfolk.

COLMAN, (Bernard) Trevor; Member (UK Ind) South West, European Parliament, Oc 2008–2014; *b* St Breward, Cornwall, 27 Aug. 1941. *Educ:* Camelford Grammar Sch Tavistock Grammar Sch. Court clerk, Magistrate's Clerks office, Tavistock, 1958–62; polic officer, Devon Constabulary, then Devon and Cornwall Constabulary, 1962–95. Scrip advisor to Wycliffe, TV series, 1994–99. *Publications:* Incident into Evidence, 1989; sho stories; articles in magazines.

COLMAN, Jeremy Gye; Auditor General for Wales, 2005–10; *b* 9 April 1948; *s* of Phili Colman and Georgina Maude Colman (*née* Gye); *m* 1st, 1978, Patricia Ann Stewart, *qv* (mar diss. 1996); 2nd, 1997, Gillian Margaret Carless. *Educ:* John Lyon Sch., Harrow; Peterhous Cambridge (BA Mathematical Tripos 1969, MA 1973); Imperial Coll., London (MSc; DI 1972); Open Univ. (PGDCCI 2001). Home Civil Service, 1971–88: CSD, 1971–75, Privat Sec. to Second Perm. Sec., 1973–74; Principal, Industrial Policy: HM Treasury, 1975–7 CSD, 1978–81; Private Sec. to successive heads of Home Civil Service, 1980–82; Principa Health Finance, 1982–84, Asst Sec., Public Enterprises, 1984–88, HM Treasury; Dir, C NatWest Ltd, 1988–90; Partner, Privatisation Services, London, 1991, Head of Corp. Financ practice, Prague, 1992–93, Price Waterhouse; Dir, 1993–98, Asst Auditor Gen., 1999–200 National Audit Office. Freeman, Ironmongers' Co., 1991. *Recreations:* cookery, fine furniture making. *Club:* Oxford and Cambridge (Chm., 1992–94).

COLMAN, Sir Michael (Jeremiah), 3rd Bt *cr* 1907; Chairman, Reckitt and Colman pl 1986–95; First Church Estates Commissioner, 1993–99; *b* 7 July 1928; *s* of Sir Jeremia Colman, 2nd Bt, and Edith Gwendolyn Tritton; *S* father, 1961; *m* 1955, Judith Jean Wallo JP, DL, *d* of Vice-Adm. Sir Peveril William-Powlett, KCB, KCMG, CBE, DSO; two *s* thre *d*. *Educ:* Eton. Director: Reckitt & Colman plc, 1970–95; Foreign and Colonial Ventur Advisors Ltd, 1988–99; Foreign and Colonial Private Equity Trust, 1995–2002. Membe Council of Royal Warrant Holders, 1977–2012, Pres., 1984–85; Trinity House Lighthous Bd, 1985–94 (Younger Brother, 1994). Member: Council, Chemical Industries Assoc 1982–84; Bd, UK Centre for Econ. and Environmental Develt, 1985–99 (Chm., 1996–99 Mem., Council, Scout Assoc., 1985–2000. Mem. Gen. Council and Mem. Finance Ctte King Edward's Hosp. Fund for London, 1978–2004; Special Trustee, St Mary's Hosp 1988–99; Trustee: Royal Foundn of Grey Coat Hosp., 1989–2004; Allchurches Trust Lt 1994–2008. Capt., Yorks Yeomanry, RARO, 1967. Mem. Ct, Skinners' Co., 1985–200 (Master, 1991–92). Hon. LLD Hull, 1993. Cross of St Augustine, 1999. *Recreations:* farmin shooting. *Heir: s* Jeremiah Michael Powlett Colman [*b* 23 Jan. 1958; *m* 1981, Susan Elizabet *yr d* of John Henry Britland, York; two *s* one *d*]. *Address:* Dairy Hill House, Malshange Basingstoke, Hants RG23 7ET; 40 Chester Square, SW1W 9HT; Tarvie, Bridge of Cally Blairgowrie, Perthshire PH10 7PJ. *Clubs:* Cavalry and Guards, Boodle's.

COLMAN, Dr Peter Malcolm, FRS 2014; FAA, FTSE; Head, Structural Biology Divisio Walter and Eliza Hall Institute of Medical Research, Melbourne, since 2001; *b* 3 April 194 *s* of Clement Colman and Kathleen Colman (*née* Malcolm); *m* 1967, Anne Elizabeth Smit two *s*. *Educ:* University of Adelaide (BSc 1st Cl. Hons 1966; PhD 1970). FAA 1989; FTS 1997. Postdoctoral Fellow: Univ. of Oregon, 1969–72; Max Planck Inst., Munich, 1972–7 Queen Elizabeth II Fellow, 1975–77, Principal Investigator, NH&MRC, 1977–78, Univ. c Sydney; Scientist, 1978–89, Chief, Div. of Biomolecular Engrg, 1989–97, CSIRO; Di Biomolecular Res. Inst., Melbourne, 1991–2000. Scientific Founder and non-exec. Dir, Bio Hldgs Ltd, 1985–91. Performed res. which determined the 3-dimensional structure c influenza virus neuraminidase and established and led the group which subsequentl discovered Relenza, the first neuraminidase inhibitor to be approved for use in treatment c influenza. Mem., Asia-Pacific Internat. Molecular Biol. Network, 1998–. Vice Pres., Interna Union of Crystallography, 2008–11. Hon. DSc Sydney, 2000; DUniv Adelaide, 2010. (Jtl Australia Prize, 1996; Victoria Prize, Govt of Vic, Australia, 2008. *Publications:* contribs t scientific jls on structural biol., influenza virus and drug discovery, apoptosis. *Recreation:* music *Address:* PO Box 321, E Melbourne, Vic 8002, Australia.

COLMAN, Sir Timothy (James Alan), KG 1996; Lord-Lieutenant for Norfolk 1978–2004; *b* 19 Sept. 1929; 2nd but *o* surv. *s* of late Captain Geoffrey Russell Rees Colma and Lettice Elizabeth Evelyn Colman, Norwich; *m* 1951, Lady Mary Cecilia (Extra Lady i Waiting to Princess Alexandra), twin *d* of late Lt-Col Hon. Michael Claude Hamilton Bow Lyon and Elizabeth Margaret, Glamis; two *s* three *d*. *Educ:* RNC, Dartmouth and Greenwic Lieut RN, 1950, retd 1953. Chm., Eastern Counties Newspapers Group Ltd, 1969–9 Director: Reckitt & Colman plc, 1978–89; Whitbread & Co. PLC, 1980–86; Angli Television Group PLC, 1987–94; Life Trustee, Carnegie UK Trust, 1966–2000 (Chm 1982–87). Member: Countryside Commn, 1971–76; Water Space Amenity Commr 1973–76; Adv. Cttee for England, Nature Conservancy Council, 1974–80; Eastern Region Cttee, National Trust, 1967–71. Pro-Chancellor, Univ. of E Anglia, 1974–2000 (Chm Council, 1973–86). Chairman: Trustees, Norfolk and Norwich Festival, 1974–2002; Roy Norfolk Agricl Assoc., 1985–96 (Pres., 1982, 1997); Trustees, E Anglia Art Foundr 1993–2005; Trustees, Norwich Cathedral Trust, 1998–2009. President: Norfolk Naturalis Trust, 1962–78; Friends of Norwich Museums, 1978–2009. Pres., E. Anglian TAVRA 1989–95. FRSA 1995. JP 1958, DL 1968, High Sheriff, 1970, Norfolk. Hon. Fellow, UEA 2004. Hon. DCL UEA, 1973; DUniv Anglia Poly., 1999. KStJ 1979. *Address:* Bixley Mano Norwich, Norfolk NR14 8SJ. *T:* (01603) 625298. *Clubs:* Turf, Pratt's; Norfolk (Norwich). *See also S. R. Troughton.*

COLMAN, Trevor; *see* Colman, B. T.

COLMER, Ven. Malcolm John; Archdeacon of Hereford, 2005–10, now Archdeaco Emeritus; *b* 15 Feb. 1945; *s* of late Frederick Colmer, OBE and Gladys Colmer; *m* 196 Kathleen Elizabeth Colmer (*née* Wade); one *s* three *d*. *Educ:* Sussex Univ. (BSc (Maths); MS (Fluid Mechs)); Nottingham Univ. (BA (Theol.)). Scientific Officer, RAE, 1967–7 ordained deacon, 1973, priest, 1974; Assistant Curate: St John the Baptist, Egham, 1973–7 St Mary, Chadwell, 1976–79; Vicar: St Michael, S Malling, Lewes, 1979–85; St Mar Hornsey Rise, 1985–87; Team Rector, Hornsey Rise, Whitehall Park Team, 1987–9 Archdeacon of Middx, 1996–2005. Area Dean of Islington, 1990–95. *Recreations:* music painting, natural history, gardening. *E:* malcolm_colmer@hotmail.com.

COLQUHOUN, Andrew John, PhD; Chairman, National Horticultural Forum, 2002–1 Director General, Royal Horticultural Society, 1999–2006; *b* 21 Sept. 1949; *s* of late Kennet James Colquhoun, MC, and of Christine Mary Colquhoun (*née* Morris); *m* 1st, 1975, Patrici Beardall (marr. diss. 2010); one *s* one *d*; 2nd, 2011, Stephanie Donaldson. *Educ:* Tiffin Sch Nottingham Univ. (BSc 1st Cl. Hons 1971); Glasgow Univ. (PhD 1974); City Univ. Busine Sch. (MBA Dist. 1987); Roehampton Univ. (Postgrad. Dip. Counselling and Psychotherap 2009). Joined HM Diplomatic Service, 1974; Third Sec., FCO, 1974–75; Second Sec MECAS, 1975–77; Second, later First, Sec., Damascus, 1977–79; First Sec., Tel Avi 1979–81; Principal, Cabinet Office, 1981–83; Planning Staff, FCO, 1983–84; Shandwic

Consultants (on secondment to ICA), 1984–86; Dir of Educn and Trng, 1987–90; Sec. and Chief Exec., 1990–97, ICAEW. Sec., Consultative Cttee of Accountancy Bodies, 1990–97. Chm., Investigation Cttee, ICAEW, 2009–. Non-executive Director: NERC, 2007–12; Office of the Health Professions Adjudicator, 2009–12. Member: Audit Cttee, Edexcel Foundn, 1997–2002; BITC Headteacher Mentoring Prog., 1998–2013; Mid Sussex Literacy Project, 1998–2004; Rail Passengers (formerly Rail Users Consultative) Cttee for Southern England, 1999–2003; Chairman: SEEDA Horticulture Wkg Gp, 2006–10; Farming and Rural Issues Gp for the SE, 2010–. Mem. Council, Nottingham Univ., 1999–2006. *Publications:* various articles on accountancy, professions, educn, horticulture and recruitment in nat., educnl and professional press. *Recreations:* bird watching, gardening, country life, reading. *Address:* Studio House, 64 Croft Road, Hastings, Sussex TN34 3HE.

COLQUHOUN, Prof. David, FRS 1985; Professor of Pharmacology, since 1983 (A. J. Clark Professor of Pharmacology, 1985–2004), Director, Wellcome Laboratory for Molecular Pharmacology, 1993–2004, and Hon. Fellow, 2004, University College London; *b* 19 July 1936; *s* of Gilbert Colquhoun and Kathleen Mary (*née* Chambers); *m* 1976, Margaret Ann Boultwood; one *s*. *Educ:* Birkenhead Sch.; Liverpool Technical Coll.; Leeds Univ. (BSc); Edinburgh Univ. (PhD). Lectr, Dept of Pharmacol., UCL, 1964–70; Vis. Asst, then Associate Prof., Dept of Pharmacol., Yale Univ. Med. Sch., 1970–72; Sen. Lectr, Dept of Pharmacol., Univ. of Southampton Med. Sch., 1972–75; Sen. Lectr, Dept of Pharmacol., St George's Hosp. Med. Sch., 1975–79; Reader, Dept of Pharmacol., UCL, 1979–83. Guest Prof., Max-Planck-Institut für Medizinische Forschung, Heidelberg, 1990–91. Lectures: Krantz, Univ. of Maryland, 1987; Tony Birmingham Meml, Univ. of Nottingham, 2011. Trustee, Sir Ronald Fisher Meml Cttee, 1975–. Alexander von Humboldt Prize, 1990; HealthWatch Award, 2010; (jtly) UK Sci. Blog Prize, Good Thinking Soc., 2012. Member Editorial Board: Jl of Physiology, 1974–81; Jl Gen. Physiology, 1998–; Series B, Proceedings of Royal Soc. Blog, DC'S Improbable Science, www.dscience.net. *Publications:* Lectures on Biostatistics, 1971; articles in Jl of Physiology, Nature, British Jl of Pharmacology, Proc. of Royal Soc., etc. *Recreations:* walking, linear algebra, blogging, investigative journalism. *Address:* Chiddingstone, Common Lane, Kings Langley, Herts WD4 8BL. *T:* (01923) 266154. *E:* d.colquhoun@ucl.ac.uk.

COLQUHOUN of Luss, Sir Malcolm (Rory), 9th Bt *cr* 1786, of Luss, Dumbarton; Chief of the Clan; Joint Principal, Broomwood Hall and Northcote Lodge Schools, since 1984; Chairman, Luss Estates Co., since 2008; *b* 20 Dec. 1947; s of Sir Ivar Iain Colquhoun, 8th Bt and Kathleen Colquhoun (*née* Duncan); *S* father, 2008; *m* 1st, 1978, Susan Timmerman (marr. diss. 1983); one *s*; 2nd, 1989, Katharine Mears; one *s* one *d*. *Educ:* Eton; Univ. of Reading (BSc Est. Man.). *Recreations:* opera, travel, piano, beautifying things. *Heir: s* Patrick John Colquhoun [*b* 17 Dec. 1980; *m* 2010, Charlotte Murphy; two *s*]. *Address:* 74 Nightingale Lane, SW12 8NR. *E:* m.colquhoun@northwoodschools.com; Camstraddan, Luss, Argyllshire G83 8NX. *E:* sirmalcolm@lussestates.co.uk. *Clubs:* White's, Turf; New (Edinburgh).

COLQUHOUN, Ms Maureen Morfydd; political researcher and writer; Chief Executive, North West Government Relations, since 1994; *b* 12 Aug. 1928; *m* 1949, Keith Colquhoun (marr. diss. 1980); two *s* one *d*; partner, 1975, *m* 2015, Barbara Todd; extended family, two *d*. Mem. Labour Party, 1945–; Member: Shoreham UDC, 1965–74; Adur District Council, 1973–74; West Sussex CC, 1971–74; Hackney BC, 1982–90; Lakes Parish Council, 1994–98, 2006–. MP (Lab) Northampton North, Feb. 1974–1979. Information Officer, Gingerbread, 1980–82. Hon. Sec., All-Party Parly Gp on AIDS, 1987–88; Chm., Secretaries and Assistants' Council, H of C, 1992–93. Mem., Assoc. of Former MPs, 2005– (Mem., Exec. Cttee, 2006–). Founder and Chairman: Historic Ambleside Trust, 1992–; Pensions Lobbying, 1996–; Co-Founder, Lakes Vision Gp, 1997; Mem. Exec. Cttee, Ambleside Civic Trust, 1993–; Sec. of State Appointee, Lake Dist Nat. Park Authy, 1998–2006. Co-Founder and Chairperson to Trustees, Harriet Martineau Foundn, 2000. *Publications:* A Woman In the House, 1980; Inside the Westminster Parliament, 1992; New Labour–New Lobbying, 1998. *Recreations:* jazz, opera, theatre. *Address:* South Knoll, Rydal Road, Ambleside, Cumbria LA22 9AY. *E:* maureencolquhoun@btopenworld.com. *Club:* University Women's.

COLSTON, His Honour Colin Charles; QC 1980; a Circuit Judge, 1983–2003; *b* 2 Oct. 1937; *yr s* of late Eric Colston, JP, and Catherine Colston; *m* 1963, Edith Helga, *d* of late Med. Rat Dr Wilhelm and Frau Gisela Hille, St Oswald/Freistadt, Austria; two *s* one *d*. *Educ:* Rugby Sch.; The Gunnery, Washington, Conn, USA; Trinity Hall, Cambridge (MA). National Service, RN, 1956–58; commissioned, RNR, 1958–64. Called to the Bar, Gray's Inn, 1962; Midland and Oxford Circuit (formerly Midland Circuit); Recorder of Midland Circuit, 1968–69; Member, Senate of Inns of Court and Bar, 1977–80; Recorder of the Crown Court, 1978–83; Resident Judge, St Albans, 1989–2000. Lay Judge, Court of Arches, Canterbury, 1992–2012. Member: Criminal Cttee, Judicial Studies Bd, 1989–92; Parole Bd for England & Wales, 2004–07. Chm., St Albans Diocesan Bd of Patronage, 1987–2000. Hon. Canon, St Albans Cathedral, 2002–07, Canon Emeritus, 2007–.

COLSTON, Michael; Chairman, Ewelme Park Farm Ltd, since 1996; *b* 24 July 1932; *s* of Sir Charles Blampied Colston, CBE, MC, DCM, FCGI and Lady (Eliza Foster) Colston, MBE; *m* 1st, 1956, Jane Olivia Kilham Roberts (marr. diss.); three *d*; 2nd, 1977, Judith Angela Briggs. *Educ:* Ridley Coll., Canada; Stowe; Gonville and Caius Coll., Cambridge. Joined 17th/21st Lancers, 1952; later seconded to 1st Royal Tank Regt for service in Korea. Founder Dir, Charles Colston Group Ltd (formerly Colston Appliances Ltd) together with late Sir Charles Colston, 1955, Chm. and Man. Dir, 1969–89; Chm. and Man. Dir, Colston Domestic Appliances Ltd, 1969–79. Chairman: Colston Consultants Ltd, 1989–93; Tallent Engineering Ltd, 1969–89; Tallent Holdings plc, 1989–90; ITS Rubber Ltd, 1969–85; Quit Ltd, 1989–93; Dishwasher Council, 1970–75. Dir, Farming and Wildlife Adv. Gp, 1991–2002. Chm., Assoc. Manufrs of Domestic Electrical Appliances, 1976–79. Member Council: Inst. of Directors, 1977–93 (Pres., Thames Valley Br., 1983–93); CBI, 1984–90 (Chm., S Regl Council, 1986–88); British Electrotechnical Approvals Bd, 1976–79; SMMT, 1987–90. Chm., Dogwatch, 2006–13. Trustee, Hawk and Owl Trust, 1991–96. *Recreations:* fishing, shooting, tennis; founder Cambridge Univ. Water Ski Club. *Address:* C6 Albany, Piccadilly, W1J 0AW. *T:* (020) 7734 2452.

COLT, Sir Edward (William Dutton), 10th Bt *cr* 1694; MB, FRCP, FACP; Attending Physician, Mount Sinai-St Luke's Roosevelt Hospital, New York; *b* 22 Sept. 1936; *s* of Major John Rochfort Colt, North Staffs Regt (*d* 1944), and of Angela Miriam Phyllis (*née* Kyan; she *m* 1946, Capt. Robert Leslie Cock); *S* uncle, 1951; *m* 1st, 1966, Jane Caroline (marr. diss. 1972), *d* of James Histed Lewis, Geneva and Washington, DC; 2nd, 1979, Suzanne Nelson (*née* Knickerbocker); one *d* (one *s* decd). *Educ:* Stoke House, Seaford; Douai Sch.; University Coll., London. Lately: Medical Registrar, UCH; House Physician, Brompton Hosp.; Associate Clinical Professor of Medicine: Icahn Sch. of Medicine at Mount Sinai (formerly Mount Sinai Sch. of Medicine), New York, until 2015; Columbia Univ., until 2014. *Publications:* contribs, especially on sports medicine, particularly running, to British and American med. jls. *Recreations:* golf, ski-ing. *Heir:* none.

COLTART, Christopher McCallum; QC 2014; *b* London, 19 March 1968; *s* of Timothy McCallum Coltart and Eileen Elizabeth Anne Coltart; *m* 2003, Kirsty Ealand; two *s* one *d*. *Educ:* Dulwich Coll.; St Edmund Hall, Oxford (MA PPE 1990). Admitted Solicitor, 1993; Trainee solicitor, 1993–95, Solicitor, 1995–98, Manches & Co.; called to the Bar, Inner Temple, 1998; in practice as barrister, specialising in white collar crime and fraud, 1998–. *Recreations:* armchair sportsman, walking, fishing, ski-ing, birdwatching, cooking. *Address:* 2 Hare Court, Temple, EC4Y 7BH. *T:* (020) 7353 5324, 07866 628136. *E:* christophercoltartqc@2harecourt.com.

COLTART, Simon Stewart; His Honour Judge Coltart; a Circuit Judge, since 1991; *b* 3 Sept. 1946; *s* of late Gilbert McCallum Coltart and Mary Louise (*née* Kemp); *m* 1973, Sarah Victoria Birts; three *s*. *Educ:* Epsom Coll.; Leeds Univ. (LLB). Called to the Bar, Lincoln's Inn, 1969 (Eastham Scholar); a Recorder, 1987–91. Mem., Parole Bd, 1997–2003. Mem., Court of Assts, Grocers' Co., 1991– (Master, 1999). Governor: Stoke Brunswick Sch., 1991–2006; Oundle Sch., 2003–09. *Recreations:* sailing, golf, shooting, fishing. *Address:* Lewes Combined Court, Lewes, East Sussex BN7 1YB. *Clubs:* Boodle's; Sussex; Bar Yacht, Royal Yacht Squadron; Rye Golf.

COLTHURST, Sir Charles (St John), 10th Bt *cr* 1744, of Ardrum, co. Cork; *b* 21 May 1955; *s* of Sir Richard La Touche Colthurst, 9th Bt and Janet Georgina (*née* Wilson-Wright) (*d* 2007); *S* father, 2003; *m* 1987, Nora Mary (separated 2005), *d* of Mortimer Kelleher; one *s* three *d*. *Educ:* Eton; Magdalene Coll., Cambridge (MA); University Coll., Dublin. Solicitor. *Heir: s* John Conway La Touche Colthurst, *b* 13 Oct. 1988. *Address:* Blarney Castle, Blarney, Co. Cork, Ireland. *Clubs:* MCC; Royal Irish Automobile, Kildare Street (Dublin).

COLTMAN, Anne Clare, (Mrs T. C. Coltman); *see* Riches, A. C.

COLTON, Rt Rev. (William) Paul; *see* Cork, Cloyne and Ross, Bishop of.

COLTRANE, Robbie, OBE 2006; actor and director; *b* Glasgow, 31 March 1950; *m* 1999, Rhona Irene Gemmell; one *s* one *d*. *Educ:* Trinity Coll., Glenalmond; Glasgow Sch. of Art (DA Drawing and Painting). *Television* includes: Laugh? I nearly paid my licence fee!, 1985; Hooray for Holyrood, 1986; Tutti Frutti, 1986; The Miners' Strike, 1987; Mistero Buffo, 1990; Coltrane in a Cadillac, 1992; Cracker (3 series), 1993, 1994, 1995, (TV films) White Ghost, 1996, Cracker, 2006; The Ebb Tide, 1997; Coltrane's Planes and Automobiles, 1997; The Plan Man, 2003; Frazier, 2004; Robbie Coltrane: B-Road Britain (2 series), 2007, 2008; Murderland, 2009; The Gruffalo (voice), 2009; *films* include: Absolute Beginners, 1985; Mona Lisa, 1985; Danny Champion of the World, 1988; Henry V, 1988; Nuns on the Run, 1989; The Pope Must Die, 1990; Oh, What a Night, 1991; Huck Finn, 1992; Goldeneye, 1995; Buddy, 1996; Montana, 1997; Frogs for Snakes, 1997; Message in a Bottle, 1999; The World Is Not Enough, 1999; Harry Potter and the Philosopher's Stone, 2001; From Hell, 2002; Harry Potter and The Chamber of Secrets, 2002; Harry Potter and the Prisoner of Azkaban, 2004; Ocean's Twelve, 2005; Harry Potter and the Goblet of Fire, 2005; Harry Potter and the Order of the Phoenix, 2006; Provoked, 2007; Bloom Brothers, 2007; Harry Potter and the Half-Blood Prince, 2009; Harry Potter and the Deathly Hallows, Pt 1, 2010, Pt 2, 2011; Great Expectations, 2012; Brave, 2012; Effie Gray, 2014; *theatre:* has appeared and toured with Traverse Theatre Co. and Borderline Theatre Co., 1976–, incl. Mistero Buffo, 1990; Yr Obedient Servant, Lyric, 1987. Silver Rose Award, Montreux TV Fest., 1987; Evening Standard Peter Sellers Award, 1991; TV Best Actor Awards: BAFTA, 1994, 1995, 1996; Silver Nymph, Monte Carlo, 1994; BPG, 1994; RTS, 1994; FIPA (French Acad.), 1994; Cable Ace, 1994; Cannes TV Fest., 1994. *Publications:* Coltrane in a Cadillac, 1993; (with John Binias) Planes and Automobiles, 1997; Robbie Coltrane's B-Road Britain, 2008; newspaper and magazine articles. *Recreations:* politics, drawing, vintage cars, reading, sailing, piano, fishing, film, ships. *Address:* c/o CDA, 167–169 Kensington High Street, W8 6SH. *T:* (020) 7937 2749. *Clubs:* Groucho, Soho House, Chelsea Arts, Marzipan; Glasgow Arts.

COLVER, Hugh Bernard, CBE 1991; public affairs and business development consultant; Group Communications Director, BAE SYSTEMS, 2000–05; *b* 22 Aug. 1945; *s* of late Rev. Canon John Lawrence Colver and Diana Irene (*née* Bartlett); *m* 1970, Gillian Ogilvie (marr. diss. 2001), *y d* of late Morris and Dorothy Graham, Christchurch, NZ; one *s* one *d*; one *s* by Penny Studholme; *m* 2013, Winnie Marques. *Educ:* King Edward VI Grammar Sch., Louth, Lincs. Reporter: Market Rasen Mail, 1961–63; Hereford Times and Hereford Evening News, 1963–67; Asst Editor, Helicopter World and Hovercraft World, 1967–68; Journalist, FT Surveys, Financial Times, 1968–71; freelance journalist, writer and PR consultant, 1971–75; Press Officer, MoD, 1975–78; PRO, RAE, 1978–79; Staff PRO to Flag Officer, Scotland and NI, 1979–81; Press Officer, Prime Minister's Office, 1981–82; Chief Press Officer, Dept of Employment, 1982–84; Dep. Dir of Information, Metropolitan Police, 1984–85; Ministry of Defence: Dep. Chief of PR, 1985–87; Chief of PR, 1987–92; Public Affairs Dir, British Aerospace Defence Ltd, 1992–95; Dir of Communications, Cons. Central Office, 1995. Non-executive Chairman: Europac Gp Ltd, 2000–10 (Dir, 1997–2010); Defence Public Affairs Consultants, 2000–10 (Dir, 1997–2010); Dir, Global Venture Solutions Ltd, 2014–; Member: Strategic Adv. Gp, Qucomhaps Ltd, 2012–; Steering Gp, Conservative Alumni, 2014–. Hon. Col, Media Ops Gp (Vols), TA, 2002–06. FRAeS 1998; FRSA. Pres., Pen and Sword Club, 2006–. Liveryman, Bowyers' Co., 2005 (Court Asst, 2011); Hon. Freeman, Guild of PR Practitioners, 2015. *Publications:* This is the Hovercraft, 1972. *Recreations:* motoring, motor racing, walking.

COLVILE, Oliver Newton; MP (C) Plymouth, Sutton and Devonport, since 2010; *b* 26 Aug. 1959. *Educ:* Stowe Sch. Agent, Cons. Party, 1981–93; Account Dir, Rowland Sallingbury Casey, 1993, 1995–96; Dir, PR co., 1993–95; Proprietor, Oliver Colvile and Associates, 1996–2010. Dir, Polity Communications, 2005–10. Mem., NI Select Cttee, 2010–; Chm., All Party Parly Gp for Excellence in the Built Envmt, 2012– (Vice Chm., 2010–12); Vice Chairman: All Party Parly Gp: for the Armed Forces (RM), 2010–; on Pharmacy, 2010–; for Zambia and Malawi, 2011–; for Zimbabwe; Sec., All Party Parly Gp on Integrated Health, 2010–. Contested (C) Plymouth Sutton, 2001, 2005. *Address:* House of Commons, SW1A 0AA.

COLVILLE, family name of **Viscount Colville of Culross** and of **Baron Clydesmuir**.

COLVILLE OF CULROSS, 5th Viscount *cr* 1902; **Charles Mark Townshend Colville;** Lord (Scot.) 1604; Baron (UK) 1885; producer, BBC, since 1994; *b* 5 Sept. 1959; *e s* of 4th Viscount Colville of Culross, QC and of Mary Elizabeth (*née* Webb-Bowen); *S* father, 2010. *Educ:* Rugby; Univ. of Durham. Elected Mem., H of L, 2011. Trustee, Tree Council, 2014–. *Heir: b* Hon. (Richmond) James Innys Colville [*b* 9 June 1961; *m* 1993, Aurea Katherine Dowson; two *s*].

COLVIN, Andrew James; Comptroller and City Solicitor, City of London Corporation (formerly Corporation of London), 1989–2012; *b* 28 April 1947; *s* of Gilbert Russell Colvin, OBE, MA, and Dr Beatrice Colvin, MRCS, LRCP, DPH; *m* 1971, Helen Mary Ryan; one *s* three *d*. *Educ:* qualified Solicitor, 1975; LLM Leicester Univ., 1996. Articled to Borough Solicitor, subseq. Asst Town Clerk, London Borough of Ealing, 1971–82; Dep. Town Clerk and Borough Solicitor, Royal Borough of Kensington and Chelsea, 1982–89. Legal Advr, Assoc. of London Govt, subseq. London Councils, 1996–2012 (London Boroughs' Assoc., 1984–96); Advr, English Nat. Stadium Trust, 1997–2012. Governor: St Gregory's RC Sch., 1989–93; Cardinal Wiseman RC Sch., 1992–99 (Chm., 1994–99). Freeman: City of London, 1989; City of London Solicitors' Co., 1996. *Recreations:* sailing, music, cycling.

COLVIN, David, CBE 1991; Chief Adviser in Social Work, The Scottish Office, 1980–91; Scottish Secretary, British Association of Social Workers, 1992–97; *b* 31 Jan. 1931; *s* of James Colvin and Mrs Crawford Colvin; *m* 1957, Elma Findlay, artist; two *s* three *d*. *Educ:* Whitehill Sch., Glasgow; Glasgow and Edinburgh Univs. Probation Officer, Glasgow City, 1955–60; Psychiatric Social Worker, Scottish Prison and Borstal Service, 1960–61; Sen. Psychiatric Social Worker, Crichton Royal Hosp., Child Psychiatric Unit, 1961–65; Director, Family

Casework Unit, Paisley, 1965; Social Work Adviser, Scottish Office, 1966, and subseq.; Interim Dir of Social Work, Shetland Islands Council, 1991. At various times held office in Howard League for Penal Reform, Assoc. of Social Workers and Inst. for Study and Treatment of Delinquency. Sen. Associate Research Fellow, Brunel Univ., 1978. Chm., Dumfries Constituency Labour Party, 1963–65. Chairman: Scotland Cttee, Nat. Children's Homes, 1991–97; Marriage Council, Scotland, 1991–95; SACRO, 1997–2003; Vice-Chm., Scottish Consortium on Criminal Justice, 1998–2003; Vice-Pres., Scottish Carers Assoc., 1998–2001. Governor, Nat. Inst. for Social Work, 1986–89; Hon. Adviser, British Red Cross, 1982–90. Gov., St Columba's Hospice, 1998–2004; Trustee, Scottish Disability Foundn, 1998–2004. Chm., Exhibiting Socs of Scottish Artists, 1999–2008. Member: Labour Party, 1949–2001; SNP, 2007–. Hon. Mem., Soc. of Scottish Artists. DUniv Stirling, 1998. *Recreations:* collector; swimming, climbing, the arts, social affairs. *Address:* 2 Morton Street, Joppa, Edinburgh EH15 2EN. *E:* davidcolvin@gmail.com.

COLVIN, David Hugh, CMG 1993; HM Diplomatic Service, retired; *b* 23 Jan. 1941; 3rd *s* of late Major Leslie Hubert Boyd Colvin, MC, and of Edna Mary (*née* Parrott); *m* 1971, (Diana) Caroline Carew, *y d* of Gordon MacPherson Lang Smith and Mildred (*née* Carew-Gibson); one *s* one *d. Educ:* Lincoln Sch.; Trinity Coll., Oxford (MA). Assistant Principal, Board of Trade, 1966. Joined HM Foreign (later Diplomatic) Service, 1967; Central Dept, FO, 1967; Second Secretary, Bangkok, 1968–71; European Integration Dept, FCO, 1971–75; First Sec., Paris, 1975–77; First Sec. (Press and Inf.), UK Permanent Representation to the European Community, 1977–82; Asst Sec., Cabinet Office, 1982–85; Counsellor and Hd of Chancery, Budapest, 1985–88; Hd, SE Asian Dept, FCO, 1988–91; Minister, Rome, 1992–96; Ambassador to Belgium, 1996–2001. Diplomatic Communications Consultant, Adam Smith Inst., 2001–03. Consultant, SCS Ltd, 2003–; Exec. Dir, Jordan Internat. Bank plc, 2005–10. Mem., New Europe Adv. Council, 2001–06; Vice-Pres., European-Atlantic Gp, 2001–06. Chairman: British-Italian Soc., 2001–06; Anglo-Belgian Soc., 2001–13; Patron, Drones Club of Belgium (P. G. Wodehouse Soc.), 1997–2001. Trustee, Prospect Burma, 2001–. Freeman, City of London, 2002. Commendatore, Ordine della Stella della Solidarietà Italiana (Italy), 2003; Commandeur de l'Ordre de la Couronne (Belgium), 2009. *Recreations:* military history, tennis, shooting, rallying old cars. *Address:* 15 Westmoreland Terrace, SW1V 4AG. *T:* (020) 7630 8349. *Club:* Travellers.

COLVIN, Kathryn Frances, CVO 2002; FCIL; HM Diplomatic Service, retired; Ambassador to the Holy See, 2002–05; *b* 11 Sept. 1945; *d* of Ernest Osborne and Frances Joy Osborne; *m* 1971, Prof. Brian Colvin. *Educ:* Walthamstow Hall, Sevenoaks; Bristol Univ. (BA Hons 1967); Bordeaux Univ. (Diplôme d'Etudes Supérieures 1965). FCIL (FIL 1968). Joined FO (later FCO), 1968; Res. Analyst, Western and Central Europe, 1968–94: Inf. Res. Dept, 1968–77; Res. Dept, 1977–94; Mem., UK Delegn to UN Commn on Human Rights, 1980–90; Temp. Duty as 1st Sec., Political, Rome, 1988 and 1991, and Paris, 1992; Deputy Head: OSCE Dept, 1994–95; Western Eur. Dept, 1995–98; Whitehall Liaison Dept, 1998–99; Vice-Marshal of the Diplomatic Corps, and Head, Protocol Div., FCO, 1999–2002. Sen. Clerk to EU Foreign Affairs, Defence and Develt Policy Sub-Cttee, H of L, 2006–13. Mem., London Cttee, 2006–11, Nat. Cttee, 2007–, UN Women UK (formerly UNIFEM UK). Ind. Mem., Hons and Awards Cttee, Order of St John, 2007–. Officier, Légion d'Honneur (France), 1996. *Recreations:* art, design, opera, theatre, cinema, swimming.

See also Ven. H. J. Osborne.

COLVIN, Prof. Sarah Jean, DPhil; Schröder Professor of German, University of Cambridge, since 2014; Fellow, Jesus College, Cambridge, since 2014; *b* Singapore, 13 July 1967; *d* of Charles Alexander and Jean Colvin; partner Cary Parker; one *s. Educ:* Dauntsey's Sch., Devizes; Exeter Coll., Oxford (BA 1st Cl. Hons); Christ Church, Oxford (DPhil 1995). Jun. Res. Fellow, St John's Coll., Oxford, 1995–97; University of Edinburgh: Lectr, 1997–2002; Reader, 2002–04; Eudo C. Mason Chair of German, 2004–10; Prof. in Study of Contemp. Germany and Dir, Inst. for German Studies, Univ. of Birmingham, 2010–12; Prof. of German, Univ. of Warwick, 2013–14. *Publications:* The Rhetorical Feminine: gender and orient on the German stage, 1999; Women and German Drama, 2002; Ulrike Meinhof and West German Terrorism, 2009; The Routledge Handbook of German Politics and Culture, 2015. *Recreations:* theatre, National Alliance for Arts in Criminal Justice. *Address:* Jesus College, Cambridge CB5 8BL. *E:* sjc269@cam.ac.uk.

COLWYN, 3rd Baron *cr* 1917; **Ian Anthony Hamilton-Smith,** CBE 1989; Bt 1912; dental surgeon, 1966–2006; bandleader, 1970–2004; *b* 1 Jan. 1942; *s* of 2nd Baron Colwyn and Miriam Gwendoline (*d* 1996), *d* of Victor Ferguson; *S* father 1966; *m* 1st, 1964, Sonia Jane (marr. diss. 1977; she *d* 2006), *d* of P. H. G. Morgan; one *s* one *d*; 2nd, 1977, Nicola Jeanne, *d* of Arthur Tyers, The Avenue, Sunbury-on-Thames; two *d. Educ:* Cheltenham Coll.; St Bartholomew's Hosp. and Royal Dental Hosp., Univ. of London. BDS London 1965; LDS, RCS 1966. Dir, Dental Protection Ltd, 1990–2001 (Chm., 1996–2001). Non-exec. Dir, Project Hope UK, 1998–2001; Chm., Campbell Montague Internat., 2005–08; Dir, London Sedation Services Ltd, 2007–08. President: Natural Medicines Soc., 1989–2005; Huntington's Disease Assoc., 1991–98; Arterial Health Foundn, 1992–2004; Soc. for Advancement of Anaesthesia in Dentistry, 1994–97; Mem. Council, Med. Protection Soc., 1994–2001. Mem., H of L Sci. and Technol. Select Cttee, 2006–10; Pres., All Party Parly Gp for Complementary and Integrated Healthcare (formerly Alternative and Complementary Medicine), 1989–; Co-Chm., All Party Parly Jazz Gp, 1994–; Vice Chm., All Party Parly Gp on Dentistry, 1998–; Chm., All Party Parly Gp for Emergency Ambulance and Paramedic Services, 2010–12; Chm., 1997–2004, Mem., 2012–, Refreshment Cttee, H of L; a Dep. Speaker and Dep. Chm. of Cttees, 2007–; elected Mem., H of L, 1999. Patron: Res. Council for Complementary Medicine; Blackie Foundn. Fellow, BDA, 2007. *Recreations:* riparian activities, music, jazz, golf, Rugby. *Heir: s* Hon. Craig Peter Hamilton-Smith [*b* 13 Oct. 1968; *m* 2003, Louise Vanessa, *d* of Callum Barney; one *s* one *d*]. *Address:* House of Lords, SW1A 0PW. *T:* (020) 7219 3184.

COLYER, His Honour John Stuart; QC 1976; a Circuit Judge, 1991–2000; *b* 25 April 1935; *s* of late Stanley Herbert Colyer, MBE, and Louisa (*née* Randle); *m* 1961, Emily Warner, *o d* of late Stanley Leland Dutrow and Mrs Dutrow, Blue Ridge Summit, Pa, USA; two *d. Educ:* Dudley Grammar Sch.; Shrewsbury; Worcester Coll., Oxford (Open History Scholarship; BA 1958, MA 1961). 2nd Lieut RA, 1954–55. Called to the Bar, Middle Temple, 1959 (Bencher, 1983); Instructor, Univ. of Pennsylvania, Philadelphia, 1959–60, Asst Prof., 1960–61; practised English Bar, Midland and Oxford Circuit (formerly Oxford Circuit), 1961–91; a Recorder, 1986–91. Hon. Reader, 1985–91, and Mem. Council, 1985–91, Council of Legal Educn (Lectr (Law of Landlord and Tenant), 1970–89); Vice-Pres., Lawyers' Christian Fellowship, 1993–2010 (Chm., 1981–89); Mem., Anglo-American Real Property Inst., 1980– (Treasurer, 1984). Blundell Meml Lectr, 1977, 1982, 1986. Chm., Selection Cttee, Margaret Parkinson Scholarship, RCN, 1998–2009, RCN Foundn, 2009–; Trustee and Gov., Royal Sch. for Deaf Children, Margate, 2000– (Chm., 2005–08, 2009–; Chm., 2008–09, Dir, 2009–, John Townsend Trust); Trustee, RCN Foundn, 2010–. *Publications:* (ed jtly) Encyclopaedia of Forms and Precedents (Landlord and Tenant), vol. XI, 1965, vol. XII, 1966; A Modern View of the Law of Torts, 1966; Landlord and Tenant, in Halsbury's Laws of England, 4th edn, 1981, new edn, 1994; Gen. Ed., Megarry's The Rent Acts, 11th edn, 1988; articles in Conveyancer and other professional jls. *Recreations:* entertaining my family, opera, cultivation of cacti and of succulents (esp. Lithops), gardening generally, travel, education and welfare of the profoundly deaf. *Address:* c/o Falcon Chambers, Falcon Court, EC4Y 1AA. *T:* (020) 7353 2484, *Fax:* (020) 7353 1261.

COLYTON, 2nd Baron *cr* 1956, of Farway, Devon and of Taunton, Somerset; **Alisdair John Munro Hopkinson;** *b* 7 May 1958; *s* of Hon. Nicholas Henry Eno Hopkinson (*d* 1991), *o s* of 1st Baron Colyton, PC, CMG and Fiona Margaret (*d* 1996), *o d* of Sir Thomas Torquil Alphonso Munro, 5th Bt; *S* grandfather, 1996; *m* 1980, Philippa, *d* of P. J. Bell; two *s* one *d. Heir: s* Hon. James Patrick Munro Hopkinson, *b* 8 May 1983. *Address:* Lindertis, by Kirriemuir, Angus DD8 5NT.

COMBER, Ven. Anthony James; Archdeacon of Leeds, 1982–92, now Archdeacon Emeritus; *b* 20 April 1927; *s* of late Norman Mederson Comber and Nellie Comber. *Educ:* Leeds Grammar School; Leeds Univ. (MSc Mining); St Chad's Coll., Durham (DipTh); Munich Univ. Colliery underground official, 1951–53. Vicar: Oulton, 1960–69; Hunslet, 1969–77; Rector of Farnley, 1977–82. *Publications:* (contrib.) Today's Church and Today's World, 1977. *Recreations:* politics; walking in Bavaria. *Address:* 28 Blayds Garth, Woodlesford, Leeds LS26 8WN. *T:* (0113) 288 0489.

COMBERMERE, 6th Viscount *cr* 1827; **Thomas Robert Wellington Stapleton-Cotton;** Bt 1677; Baron 1814; *b* 30 Aug. 1969; *o s* of 5th Viscount Combermere; *S* father, 2000; *m* 2005, Caroline Sarah, *o d* of late Charles Leonard Anthony Irby; one *s* one *d. Heir: s* Hon. Laszlo Michael Wellington Stapleton-Cotton, *b* 20 Aug. 2010.

COMBES, Ven. Roger Matthew; Archdeacon of Horsham, 2003–14; *b* 12 June 1947; *m* 1983, Christine Mary Keiller; two *d. Educ:* King's Coll., London (LLB 1969); Ridley Hall, Cambridge. Ordained deacon, 1974, priest, 1975; Curate: St Paul's, Onslow Square, 1974–77; Holy Trinity, Brompton, 1976–77; Holy Sepulchre with All Saints, Cambridge, 1977–86; Rector, St Matthew's, Silverhill, 1986–2003; RD, Hastings, 1998–2002. *Address:* 3 Aldingbourne Close, Ifield, Crawley RH11 0QJ.

COMINS, David; Rector, Glasgow Academy, 1994–2005; *b* 1 March 1948; *s* of Jack Comins and Marjorie Mabel (*née* Rowbotham); *m* 1972, Christine Anne Speak; one *s* two *d. Educ:* Scarborough Boys' High Sch.; Downing Coll., Cambridge (BA, MA, PGCE). Assistant Mathematics Teacher: Mill Hill Sch., 1971–75; Strathallan Sch., Perthshire, 1975–76; Glenalmond College, Perthshire: Asst Maths Teacher, 1976–80; Head of Maths, 1980–85; Dir of Studies, 1985–89; Dep. Head, Queen's Coll., Taunton, 1989–94. Teacher of Maths, Shenzhen Coll. of Internat. Educn, Shenzhen, 2005–07. Churchill Fellow, 1981. *Recreations:* mountaineering, ballet, music, crosswords, sudoku. *Address:* Flat 6, Block 8, Kirklee Gate, Glasgow G12 0SZ. *Club:* Alpine.

COMNINOS, Sophie Henrietta; *see* Turner Laing, S. H.

COMPAGNONI, Marco; Partner, Weil Gotshal & Manges, since 2006; *b* Haltwhistle, Northumberland, 3 May 1962; *s* of Peter Compagnoni and Santina Margherita Compagnoni. *Educ:* Queen Elizabeth Grammar Sch., Hexham; Univ. of Newcastle upon Tyne (LLB Hons). Admitted solicitor, 1987; joined Lovell, White & King, later Lovell White Durrant, then Lovells, 1985, Partner, 1993–2006 (Hd, Internat. Private Equity Practice, 2002–06; Mem., Partnership Bd, 1996–99 and 2001–04). Trustee: Serpentine Gall., 2000–; Royal Opera Hse, Covent Gdn, 2000–07; Royal Opera Hse Benevolent Fund, 2000–07; Gov., Royal Ballet Co., 2001–07; Dir, Sadler's Wells Trust Ltd, 2009–; Pres., Serpentine Galleries of the Americas, 2014–; Mem. Council, Friends of Covent Gdn, 1995– (Chm., 2000–07). Mem., Law Panel, The Times, 2006–09. *Recreations:* opera, dance, contemporary art, shooting, Parson Jack Russell terriers, eating, wine, Scotland, Belted Galloway cattle. *Address:* c/o Weil, Gotshal & Manges, 110 Fetter Lane, EC4A 1AY.

COMPSTON, Alastair; *see* Compston, D. A. S.

COMPSTON, His Honour Christopher Dean, MA; a Circuit Judge, 1986–2013; *b* 5 May 1940; *s* of Vice Adm. Sir Peter Maxwell Compston, KCB and Valerie Bocquet; *m* 1st, 1968, Bronwen Henniker Gotley (marr. diss. 1982); one *d* (and two *s* decd); 2nd, 1983, Caroline Philippa, *d* of Paul Odgers, CB, MBE, TD; two *s* one *d. Educ:* Epsom Coll. (Prae Sum.); Magdalen Coll., Oxford (MA). Called to the Bar, Middle Temple, 1965, Bencher, 2006; a Recorder, 1982–86. Mem. Senate, Inns of Court, 1983–86. Trustee: Fund for Epilepsy, 2000–05; Prison Fellowship, 2001–07; ZANE, 2012–; Patron: Second Chance, 2008–; Compassionate Friends, 2014–. *Publications:* Recovery from Divorce: a practical guide, 1993; (contrib.) Relational Justice, 1994; Cracking up without Breaking up, 1998. *Recreations:* the arts, writing, family, travel, gardening, selling second hand books for charity. *Address:* c/o Royal Courts of Justice, Strand, WC2A 2LL. *Club:* Seaview Yacht.

COMPSTON, Prof. (David) Alastair (Standish), FRCP, FMedSci, FRSB; Professor of Neurology, University of Cambridge, 1989–2015, now Emeritus; Fellow of Jesus College, Cambridge, 1990–2015, now Emeritus; *b* 23 Jan. 1948; *s* of late Nigel Dean Compston and of Diana Mary Compston (*née* Standish); *m* 1973, Juliet Elizabeth Page (*see* J. E. Compston); one *d. Educ:* Rugby Sch.; Middlesex Hospital Med. Sch., London Univ. (MB BS (Hons); PhD). FRCP 1986. Jun. Hosp. appts, Nat. Hosp. for Nervous Diseases, 1972–82; Cons. Neurologist, University Hosp. of Wales, 1982–87; Prof. of Neurology, Univ. of Wales Coll. of Medicine, 1987–88. Editor, 2004–13, Editor Emeritus, 2014, Brain. Pres., Assoc. of British Neurologists, 2009–11. For. Mem., Nat. Acad. of Scis, Germany, 2008; For. Associate Mem., Inst. of Medicine, Nat. Academies, USA, 2012. Founder FMedSci 1998; FRSB (FIBiol 2000). FRSA 1997. Internat. Prize for Multiple Sclerosis Res., Sobek Foundn, 2002; Charcot Award, Multiple Sclerosis Internat. Fedn, 2007; Zülch Prize, Max Planck Soc., 2010; Medal for Scientific Achievement in Neurol., World Fedn of Neurol., 2013; John Dystel Prize, Amer. Acad. of Neurology, 2015. *Publications:* (ed) McAlpine's Multiple Sclerosis, 4th edn 2005; contribs to human and experimental demyelinating diseases, in learned jls. *Recreations:* being outside, antiquarian books. *Address:* Mead House, West Wickham Road, Horseheath, Cambridge CB21 4QA. *T:* (01223) 893414. *Club:* Garrick.

COMPSTON, Prof. Juliet Elizabeth, OBE 2014; MD; FRCP, FRCPath, FRCPE, FMedSci; Professor of Bone Medicine, University of Cambridge, 2003–12, now Emeritus; *b* 18 Dec. 1945; *d* of Sir Denys Lionel Page, FBA and Katharine Elizabeth Page; *m* 1973, (David) Alastair (Standish) Compston, *qv*; one *d. Educ:* Middlesex Hosp. Med. Sch., London Univ. (BSc 1967; MB BS 1970; MD 1979). FRCP 1988; FRCPath 1996; FRCPE 2011. Sen. Lectr and Hon. Consultant, Univ. Hosp. of Wales; Lectr in Medicine, then Reader in Metabolic Bone Disease, 1999–2003, Univ. of Cambridge. Hon. Consultant Physician, Addenbrooke's Hospital, Cambridge. Ed.-in-Chief, Jl Bone and Mineral Res., 2013–. FMedSci 1999. Kohn Foundn Award, Nat. Osteoporosis Soc., 2006; John G. Haddad Award, Internat. Bone and Mineral Soc., 2009; Frederic C. Bartter Award, Amer. Soc. for Bone and Mineral Res., 2009. *Publications:* (ed) Osteoporosis: new perspectives on causes, prevention and treatment, 1996; (with Clifford Rosen) Osteoporosis, 1997, 2nd edn 2001; Understanding Osteoporosis, 1998; (with Ignac Fogelman) Key Advances in the Effective Management of Osteoporosis, 1999; (ed jtly) HRT and the Menopause: current therapy, 2002; (jtly) Osteoporosis: best medicine for osteoporosis, 2005; (ed jtly) Bone Disease of Organ Transplantation, 2005; 385 articles in peer-reviewed jls. *Address:* Department of Medicine, University of Cambridge Clinical School, Addenbrooke's Hospital, Hills Road, Cambridge CB2 0QQ; Mead House, West Wickham Road, Horseheath, Cambridge CB21 4QA.

COMPSTON, Prof. William, PhD; FRS 1987; FAA; FTSE; Australian National University: Professor in Isotope Geochemistry, 1987–96, now Emeritus; Consultant, Research School of Earth Sciences, 1997–99 and since 2002; University Fellow, 2000–01, Visiting Fellow, since 2002; *b* 19 Feb. 1931; *s* of late J. A. Compston; *m* 1952, Elizabeth Blair; three *s* one *d. Educ:* Christian Brothers' Coll., Fremantle; Univ. of WA (BSc (Hons); PhD). Res. Fellow, CIT,

1956–58; Res. Fellow, Dept of Terrestrial Magnetism, Carnegie Inst. of Washington, 1958; Lectr, Univ. of WA, 1959–60; Australian National University: Fellow, then Sen. Fellow, 1961–74; Professorial Fellow, 1974–87. Lectures: Mawson, 1988, Flinders, 1998, Australian Acad. of Sci.; Hallimond, Mineralogical Soc., 1998. Hon. Fellow, Chinese Acad. of Geol Scis, 2006. Hon. DSc Western Australia, 1988. Stillwell Award, Geol Soc. of Australia, 1990; Clunies Ross Award, Clunies Ross Meml Foundn, 1995; Friendship Award, State Admin of Foreign Experts Affairs, China, 2006. *Address:* Research School of Earth Sciences, Australian National University, Canberra, ACT 0200, Australia; 8 Wells Gardens, Manuka, ACT 2603, Australia.

COMPTON, family name of **Marquess of Northampton**.

COMPTON, Earl; Daniel Bingham Compton; *b* 16 Jan. 1973; *s* and *heir* of Marquess of Northampton, *qv*; *m* 2001, Lucy (marr. diss. 2008), 5th *d* of Lt-Col Benedict Cardozo; two *d*. *Address:* Castle Ashby, Northants NN7 1LF.

COMPTON, Benjamin Edward; QC 2011; *b* Taunton, 11 May 1956; *s* of David Compton and Susan Compton; *m* 1991, Belinda Grice; one *s* two *d*. *Educ:* Harrow Sch.; Inns of Court Sch. of Law. Called to the Bar, Lincoln's Inn, 1979; in practice as barrister, specialising in health and safety and clinical negligence. *Recreations:* walking in mountains, ski-ing, running a small farm in Wiltshire. *Address:* Corsley House, Corsley, Warminster, Wilts BA12 7PH. *T:* (01373) 832229; Outer Temple Chambers, 222 The Strand, WC2R 1BA. *T:* (020) 7353 6381. *E:* Ben.Compton@outertemple.com. *Club:* Soho House.

COMPTON, Prof. Richard Guy, DPhil; Professor of Chemistry, since 1996, and Aldrichian Praelector, since 2011, University of Oxford; Tutorial Fellow, St John's College, Oxford, since 1985; *b* Scunthorpe, 10 March 1955; *s* of Joseph Compton and Doreen Compton. *Educ:* Frome Grammar Sch.; University Coll., Oxford (MA; DPhil 1981). Lecturer in Chemistry: Univ. of Liverpool, 1981–85; Univ. of Oxford, 1985–96. Lifelong Hon. Prof., Sichuan Univ., 2004–; Chinese Acad. of Scis Vis. Prof., Inst. of Physical Scis, Hefei, 2011–Nov. 2016. *Publications:* Electrode Potentials, 1996; Foundations of Physical Chemistry, 1996; Understanding Voltammetry, 2007, 2nd edn 2011; A G Stromberg: first class scientist, second class citizen, 2011; Understanding Voltammetry: problems and solutions, 2012; Simulation of Electrode Processes, 2014; over 1200 papers in jls incl. Electroanalysis, ChemPhysChem, Angewandte Chimie. *Recreations:* reading, travel. *Address:* St John's College, Oxford OX1 3JP. *T:* (01865) 275957, *Fax:* (01865) 275410. *E:* richard.compton@chem.ox.ac.uk.

COMYNS, Jacqueline Roberta; a District Judge (Magistrates' Courts) (formerly a Metropolitan Stipendiary Magistrate), 1982–2013; *b* 27 April 1943; *d* of late Jack and Belle Fisher; *m* 1963, Malcolm John Comyns, medical practitioner; one *s*. *Educ:* Hendon County Grammar Sch.; London Sch. of Econs and Pol Science (LLB Hons 1964). Called to the Bar, Inner Temple, 1969; practised on South Eastern Circuit; a Recorder, 1991–2002. *Recreations:* theatre, travel, swimming.

CONAGHAN, Geoffrey; Agent General for Victoria, Australia, in London, since 2013; *b* Australia, 1958; *s* of John Conaghan and Amirisa, (Amy), Conaghan (*née* Stavrianou); partner, Mathew Erbs. *Educ:* Holy Cross Coll., Ryde, Sydney; Australian Nat. Univ. (BA). Exec. Dir, Tourism Trng, Victoria, 1987–94; Gen. Manager, Corporate Affairs, Melbourne Airport, 1994–2009; Comr of Victoria to India, Victorian Govt Business Office, 2009–13. Comr, Tourism Victoria Bd, 1998–2009. *Address:* Office of the Agent General for Victoria, Australia Centre, Melbourne Place, Strand, WC2B 4LG. *T:* (020) 7836 2656. *E:* geoffrey.conaghan@invest.vic.gov.au. *Clubs:* Royal Over-Seas League; Castellorizian (Melbourne).

CONANT, Sir John (Ernest Michael), 2nd Bt *cr* 1954; farmer and landowner, since 1949; *b* 24 April 1923; *s* of Sir Roger Conant, 1st Bt, CVO, and Daphne, Lady Conant, *d* of A. E. Learoyd; *S* father, 1973; *m* 1st, 1950, Periwinkle Elizabeth (*d* 1985), *d* of late Dudley Thorp, Kimbolton, Hunts; two *s* two *d* (and one *s* decd); 2nd, 1992, Mrs Clare Attwater, *yr d* of W. E. Madden. *Educ:* Eton; Corpus Christi Coll., Cambridge (BA Agric). Served in Grenadier Guards, 1942–45; at CCC Cambridge, 1946–49. Farming in Rutland, 1950–; High Sheriff of Rutland, 1960. *Recreations:* fishing, shooting, tennis. *Heir:* *s* Simon Edward Christopher Conant [*b* 13 Oct. 1958; *m* 2000, Justine Sarah Preston]. *Address:* Periwinkle Cottage, Lyndon, Oakham, Rutland LE15 8TU. *T:* (01572) 737275.

CONCANNON, Dr Harcourt Martin Grant; President, Pensions Appeal Tribunals for England and Wales, 1998–2008; *s* of Edwin Martin Joseph Concannon and Caroline Elizabeth Margaret Concannon (*née* Grant); *m* 1978, Elaine Baldwin; one *s* one *d*. *Educ:* University Coll. Sch.; University College London (LLB, LLM, PhD). Solicitor. Articled to Town Clerk, London Borough of Bexley, 1960–64; Lectr in Law, Nottingham Poly., 1964–68; Senior Lecturer: Sheffield City Poly., 1968–71; Univ. of Salford, 1972–93; Full-time Chm., Independent Tribunal Service, 1993–98. *Recreations:* languages, painting, walking.

CONDON, family name of **Baron Condon**.

CONDON, Baron *cr* 2001 (Life Peer), of Langton Green in the County of Kent; **Paul Leslie Condon,** Kt 1994; QPM 1989; DL; Commissioner, Metropolitan Police, 1993–2000; Chairman, Anti-Corruption and Security (formerly Anti-Corruption) Unit, International Cricket Council, 2003–10 (Director, 2000–03); *m*; two *s* one *d*. *Educ:* St Peter's Coll., Oxford (Bramshill Scholar; MA; Hon. Fellow). Joined Metropolitan Police, 1967; Inspector, 1975–78; Chief Inspector, 1978–81; Superintendent, Bethnal Green, 1981–82; Staff Officer to Comr as Superintendent, then as Chief Superintendent, 1982–84; Asst Chief Constable, Kent Constabulary, 1984–87; Dep. Asst Comr, 1987–88, Asst Comr, 1988–89, Metropolitan Police; Chief Constable, Kent Constabulary, 1989–92. Pres., BSIA, 2003–06. Non-exec. Dir, G4S (formerly Securicor, then Group 4 Securicor), 2000–13 (Dep. Chm., 2006). CCMI (CIMgt 1991); FRSA 1992. DL Kent, 2001.

CONDRY, Rt Rev. Edward Francis; *see* Ramsbury, Bishop Suffragan of.

CONEFREY, Stella; *see* Bruzzi, Stella.

CONGDON, David Leonard; Head of Campaigns and Policies (formerly Director of Public Affairs, then Head of External Relations), MENCAP, 1998–2012; *b* 16 Oct. 1949; *s* of Archibald George Congdon and late Marjorie Congdon; *m* 1972, Teresa Winifred Hill; one *d*. *Educ:* Alleyn's Sch.; Thames Polytechnic (BSc Hons Econ.). Graduate Systems Analyst, ICL, 1970; Philips Electronics: Systems Analyst, 1973–85; Computer Consultant, 1985–92. London Borough of Croydon: Councillor, 1976–92; Vice-Chm., Educn Cttee, 1979–83; Chm., Social Services, 1983–86, 1990–91; Dep. Leader, 1986–92; Chm., Finance Sub-Cttee. Vice-Chm., local Cons. Assocs, 1979–82. MP (C) Croydon North East, 1992–97; contested (C) Croydon Central, 1997, 2001. PPS to Minister of State for Social Security, 1995–97. Mem., Select Cttee on Health, 1992–95. Lay Mem., E Surrey CCG. Governor, Croydon Coll., 1979–92. *Recreations:* tennis, badminton, reading political biographies, listening to music; lapsed Fulham fan. *Address:* 56 Keston Avenue, Old Coulsdon, Surrey CR5 1HN.

CONGDON, Timothy George, CBE 1997; Director, Institute of International Monetary Research and Professor of Economics, University of Buckingham, since 2014; Founder and Chief Executive, International Monetary Research Ltd, 2009–13; *b* 28 April 1951; *s* of D. G. Congdon and Olive Emma Congdon (*née* Good); *m* 1988, Dorianne Preston-Lowe; one *d*. *Educ:* Univ. of Oxford (BA 1st cl. Hons Mod. Hist. and Econs). MCSI. On economics staff, The Times, 1973–76; Chief Economist, L. Messel & Co., 1976–86 (Partner, 1980–86); Chief London Economist, Shearson Lehman, 1986–88; Founder, Man. Dir, 1989–2001, Chief Economist, 2001–05, Lombard Street Research. Non-exec. Chm., SBW Insurance Research, 1994–97. Mem., Treasury Panel of Independent Forecasters, 1993–97. Hon. Prof., Cardiff Business Sch., 1990–2006; Vis. Prof., Sir John Cass Business Sch., City of London (formerly City Univ. Business Sch.), 1998–2004; Vis. Fellow, LSE, 2005–07. Econs columnist, Standpoint mag., 2008–. Econs spokesman, UKIP, 2010–14. Contested (UK Ind) Forest of Dean, 2010. Chm., Freedom Assoc., 2011–14. Hon. Sec., Political Economy Club, 1999–2011. FRSA 1991; Fellow, Soc. of Business Economists, 2000. Hon. FIA 2002. *Publications:* Monetary Control in Britain, 1982; The Debt Threat, 1988; Reflections on Monetarism, 1992; Money and Asset Prices in Boom and Bust, 2005; Keynes, the Keynesians and Monetarism, 2007; Central Banking in a Free Society, 2009; How to Stop the Recession, 2009; Money in a Free Society, 2011. *Recreations:* reading, walking, chess, opera. *Address:* Huntley Manor, Huntley, Glos GL19 3HQ. *Club:* Royal Automobile.

CONGLETON, 8th Baron *cr* 1841; **Christopher Patrick Parnell;** Bt 1766; *b* 11 March 1930; 3rd *s* of 6th Baron Congleton (*d* 1932) and Hon. Edith Mary Palmer Howard (MBE 1941) (she *m* 2nd, 1946, Flight Lieut A. E. R. Aldridge, who died 1950), *d* of late R. J. B. Howard and late Lady Strathcona and Mount Royal; *S* brother, 1967; *m* 1955, Anna Hedvig, *d* of G. A. Sommerfelt, Oslo, Norway; two *s* three *d*. *Educ:* Eton; New Coll., Oxford (MA). Mem., Salisbury and Wilton RDC, 1964–74; Vice-President: RDCA, 1973–74; Assoc. of District Councils, 1974–79. Chm., Salisbury and S Wilts Museum, 1972–77; Mem., Adv. Bd for Redundant Churches, 1981–87. President: Nat. Ski Fedn of GB, 1976–81; Ski Club of GB, 1991–97; Mem., Eligibility Cttee, Internat. Ski Fedn, 1976–88. Trustee: Sandroyd Sch. Trust, 1975–92 (Chm., 1980–84); Wessex Med. Trust, 1984–90 (Chm., 1996–2000); Southampton Univ. Devlt Trust, 1986–95. Hon. LLD Southampton, 1990. *Recreations:* music, fishing. *Heir:* *s* Hon. John Patrick Christian Parnell [*b* 17 March 1959; *m* 1985, Marjorie-Anne, *o d* of John Hobdell, Cobham, Surrey; two *s* one *d*]. *Address:* West End Lodge, Ebbesbourne Wake, Salisbury, Wilts SP5 5JR.

CONGO, Sonia, (Mrs C. W. Congo); *see* Lawson, S.

CONINGHAM, Prof. Robin Andrew Evelyn, PhD; FRAS; Professor of Early Medieval Archaeology, since 2005, UNESCO Professor in Archaeological Ethics and Practice in Cultural Heritage, since 2014, and Pro Vice Chancellor and Head, Faculty of Social Sciences and Health, since 2008, Durham University; *b* Pembury, 2 Dec. 1965; *s* of late Simon Coningham and of Stephanie Coningham; *m* 1990, Paula Geake; two *s*. *Educ:* Tunbridge Wells Tech. High Sch.; Tonbridge Sch.; King's Coll., Cambridge (BA Archaeol. and Anthropol. 1988; PhD Archaeol. 1994). FRAS 1994. Grad. Schol., British Inst. in Eastern Africa, Nairobi, 1989–94; Department of Archaeological Sciences, University of Bradford: Lectr, 1994–99; Sen. Lectr, 1999–2001; Reader, 2001–04; Prof. of S Asian Archaeol., 2004–05; Hd of Dept, 2004–05; Hd, Dept of Archaeol., Durham Univ., 2007–08. Consultant, World Heritage Centre, 1997–2002 and 2009–, Expert Mem., Internat. Scientific Steering Cttee for Lumbini, 2010–, UNESCO. Mem., Edtl Bd, S Asian Studies, 2010–. Quality Assurance Agency for Higher Education: Specialist Reviewer, 1995–2001; Rev. Chair, 2000–02; Mem., Pearson World Class Qualifications Expert Panel, 2012–. Arts and Humanities Research Council: Mem., Peer Rev. Coll., 2004–06, 2009–; Mem., Res. Panel 1, 2006–08. British Academy: Mem., Sponsored Insts and Socs Cttee, 2009–; Mem., Internat. Engagement Cttee, 2011–. Hon. Sec., British Inst. Persian Studies, 2006–09. Gov., N Tees and Hartlepool NHS Foundn Trust, 2011–14. Trustee: Ancient Indian and Iran Trust, 1999–2010; Antiquity Trust, 2010–. *Publications:* Anuradhapura: the British-Sri Lankan Excavations at Anuradhapura Salgaha Watta, vol. 1, The Site, 1999, vol. 2, The Artefacts, 2006, (with P. Gunawardhana) vol. 3, The Hinterland, 2013; (with J.-F. Milou) UNESCO Reactive Monitoring Mission to Lumbini, Birthplace of Lord Buddha: report and recommendations of a UNESCO mission to Nepal, 2001; (with P. Gunawardhana) Essays in Archaeology, 2005; (with I. Ali) Charsadda: the British-Pakistani excavations at the Bala Hisar, 2007; (with P. Gunawardhana) Essays in Archaeology 2, 2010; (with G. Scarre) The Ethics of Archaeology: appropriating the past, 2013; contrib. popular, learned and scientific articles and book chapters on archaeol. of Buddhism, S Asia and Iran. *Recreations:* table-tennis, table-football, lap-dogs, typing with two fingers. *Address:* Department of Archaeology, Durham University, South Road, Durham DH1 3LE. *T:* (0191) 334 2904, *Fax:* (0191) 334 2905. *E:* r.a.e.coningham@durham.ac.uk. *Club:* Travellers.

CONINGSBY, His Honour Thomas Arthur Charles; QC 1986; a Circuit Judge, 1992–2006; Designated Civil Judge, 1999–2006; Vicar General of the Province of York, 1980–2008; *b* 21 April 1933; *s* of Francis Charles and Eilleen Rowena Coningsby; *m* 1959, Elaine Mary Coningsby; two *s* three *d*. *Educ:* Epsom; Queens' Coll., Cambridge (MA). Called to the Bar, Gray's Inn, 1957; Mem., Inner Temple, 1988. A Recorder, 1986–92; Head of Chambers, 3 Dr Johnson's Building, Temple, 1988–92; Dep. High Court Judge, 1992–2006; Liaison Judge, 1995–2005. Chancellor: Dio. of York, 1977–2006; Dio. of Peterborough, 1989–2006. Member: Lord Chancellor's Matrimonial Causes Rule Cttee, 1986–89; Gen. Council of the Bar, 1988–90; Supreme Court Procedure Cttee, 1988–92; Chm., Family Law Bar Assoc., 1988–90 (Sec., 1986–88); Pres., SE London Magistrates' Assoc., 1996–2006. Member, General Synod, 1970–2008 (Member: Legal Adv. Commn, 1975–2008; Fees Adv. Commn, 1979–2008). Mem. Governing Body, SPCK, 1990–92. Pres., Chipstead Decorative and Fine Arts Soc., 2014– (Chm., 2011–14). *Recreation:* lawn tennis. *Address:* Leyfields, Chipstead, Surrey CR5 3SG. *T:* (01737) 553304. *Club:* Athenæum.

CONLEY, Brian Paul; entertainer, host, actor and singer; *b* Paddington, London, 7 Aug. 1961; *s* of Colin and Pauline Conley; *m* 1996, Anne-Marie Aindow; two *d*. *Educ:* Wembley High Sch.; Barbara Speakes Stage Sch. *Television:* as host: Brian Conley This Way Up, 1989–90; Brian Conley Show, 1992–95 and 2000–02; Brian Conley Alive & Dangerous, 1996; National Lottery: We've Got Your Number, 1999; Royal Variety Performance, 1999; An Audience With…, 2002; Judgement Day, 2003; Let Me Entertain You, 2006–07; Dirty Rotten Cheater, 2007; Timeline, 2014; The TV That Made Me, 2015; as actor: Survivors, 1977; Outside Chance, 1993; Time after Time, 1994–95; The Grimleys, 1999–2000; The Life and Times of Vivienne Vyle, 2007; *film:* Circus, 2000; Dream, 2001; Arthur's Dyke, 2001; Cruise of the Gods, 2002; Equilibrium, 2002; I am Bob, 2007; for television: Hotel!, 2001; *theatre:* eight Royal Variety Performances, 1988–99; pantomimes, 1991–2015; Me and My Girl, Adelphi, 1991; Jolson (as Jolson), Victoria Palace, 1995–98; Elton John's Glasses, Queen's, 1998; Chitty Chitty Bang Bang, Palladium, 2005; The Music Man, Chichester, 2008 (Best Performance in a Musical, Theatrical Mgt Assoc.); Hairspray, Shaftesbury, 2009–10; Brother Love's Travelling Salvation Show, UK tour, 2011; Oliver!, UK tour, 2012; Barnum, UK tour, 2014; *albums:* Stage to Stage, 1996; Songs from the Shows, 2002; Brian Conley Sings, 2002; Let the Good Times Roll, 2002. Nat. TV Award for Most Popular Comedy Performer, 1995; Most Popular Performer, Manchester Evening News Th. Awards, 2004. Patron, Hire a Hero. *Recreations:* walking the dogs, cinema and theatre, being a dad. *Address:* c/o Sue Latimer, ARG Talent, 4a Exmoor Street, W10 6BD. *T:* (020) 7436 6400. *E:* latimer@argtalent.com.

CONLEY, Rosemary Jean Neil, CBE 2004; DL; diet and fitness expert; Partner, Rosemary Conley Enterprises, since 1986; Co-Founder and Chairman, Rosemary Conley Licences Ltd, since 2003; *b* 19 Dec. 1946; *d* of Oswald Neil Weston and Edith Cecilia Weston; *m* 1st, 1968, Philip Conley (marr. diss. 1983); one *d*; 2nd, 1986, Michael John Rimmington. *Educ:* Bushloe High Sch., Wigston. RSA Exercise to Music. Secretary, then founded own slimming club business, Slimming and Good Grooming, 1971; sold business to IPC Magazines, 1981; Man. Dir, Successful Slimming and Good Grooming Clubs Ltd, subsid. of IPC, 1981–85; (with Mike Rimmington): founder: Rosemary Conley Enterprises, 1986; Rosemary Conley Diet and Fitness Clubs Ltd, 1993 (Chm., 1993–2014); Rosemary Conley Diet and Fitness magazine, Quorn House Publishing Ltd, 1996 (Chm., 1996–2014); Quorn House Media, 2008 (Chm., 2008–14). Patron: Breast Cancer Campaign; Shaftesbury Soc.; Mildmay; Send a Cow; Laura Centre, Leicester; STEPS Conductive Educn Sch., Shepshed, Leics; FareShare E Midlands, 2015–. Pres., Leics. Young Enterprise, 2005–. Ambassador, Prince's Initiative for Mature Enterprise. DL Leics, 1999. Hon. Freeman, City of Leicester, 2001. *Publications:* Eat Yourself Slim, 1982; Eat and Stay Slim, 1983; Positive Living, 1984; Rosemary Conley's Hip and Thigh Diet, 1988, 2nd edn 1992; Rosemary Conley's Complete Hip and Thigh Diet, 1989, 2nd edn 2002; Looking Good, Feeling Great, 1989; Rosemary Conley's Inch Loss Plan, 1990, 2nd edn 1998; Whole Body Programme, 1992; Rosemary Conley's Metabolism Booster Diet, 1991; (with Patricia Bourne) Rosemary Conley's New Hip and Thigh Diet Cookbook, 1993; Shape Up For Summer, 1993; Rosemary Conley's Flat Stomach Plan, 1994; Rosemary Conley's Beach Body Plan, 1994; Be Slim, Be Fit, 1995; Rosemary Conley's Complete Flat Stomach Plan, 1996, 2nd edn 2002; Rosemary Conley's New Body Plan, 1997, 2nd edn 2002; Rosemary Conley's Low Fat Cookbook, 1999; Rosemary Conley's Low Fat Cookbook 2, 2000; Rosemary Conley's Red Wine Diet, 2000; Eat Yourself Slim, 2001; Rosemary Conley's GI Jeans Diet, 2006; Rosemary Conley's Ultimate GI Jeans Diet, 2007; GI Hip and Thigh Diet, 2008; Slim to Win: diet and cookbook, 2008; Rosemary Conley's Amazing Inch Loss Plan, 2010; My Kitchen Table, 2011; The Secrets of Staying Young, 2011; The FAB Diet, 2013; presented 31 fitness videos. *Recreations:* ski-ing, ice skating (celebrity contestant, Dancing on Ice, ITV, 2012), walking our dogs, home making, cooking, flower arranging, writing, speaking about and sharing my Christian testimony. *Address:* Rosemary Conley Enterprises, PO Box 10368, Melton Mowbray, Leics LE13 9EP. *T:* (01664) 840367. *E:* rosemary@rosemaryconley.com.

CONLON, Michael Anthony; QC 2002; Head of Indirect Tax, Hogan Lovells International LLP, since 2012; *b* 26 Nov. 1951; *s* of Thomas Reginald Conlon and Barbara (*née* Capper); *m* 1974, Pamela Carter; one *s* one *d*. *Educ:* Enfield Grammar Sch.; Queens' Coll., Cambridge (BA 1973, MA 1977). Called to the Bar, Inner Temple, 1974; in practice at the Bar, 1974–76; government lawyer, 1976–86; tax partner in accounting firms, 1986–91; solicitor, 1992–97; Partner, Allen & Overy, 1993–97; returned to the Bar, 1997. Mem., Tax Law Rev. Cttee, 1994–2007. Nat. Pres., VAT Practitioners Gp, 1998–; Pres., Inst. of Indirect Taxation, 1999–2012 (Fellow, 1998). FTII 1997; Fellow, Soc. of Advanced Legal Studies, 1999. Liveryman: Co. of Tax Advisers, 2006– (Mem., Ct of Assts, 1999–2008); Co. of Spectacle Makers, 2006– (Mem., Ct of Assts, 2008–12). Exec. Ed., VAT Intelligence, 1993–2006; Member Editorial Board: De Voil Indirect Tax Service, 1999–; Tax Jl, 2000–. *Publications:* numerous technical articles. *Recreations:* art, music, literature. *Address:* Hogan Lovells International LLP, Atlantic House, Holborn Viaduct, EC1A 2FG. *T:* (020) 7296 2404, *Fax:* (020) 7296 2001. *E:* michael.conlon@hoganlovells.com.

CONNAGHAN, John, CBE 2015; Director of Workforce and Performance (formerly Director of Health Delivery), Scottish Government (formerly Scottish Executive), since 2004; Chief Operating Officer, NHS Scotland, since 2015; *b* Glasgow, 2 Sept. 1954; *s* of John Connaghan and Mary Connaghan; *m* 1983, Evelyn Joyce Steven; three *s* one *d*. *Educ:* Glasgow Caledonian Univ. (BA Business Studies 1976); Univ. of Strathclyde (DMS 1980; MBA 1984). Gen. Manager, Charles Letts & Co. Ltd, 1979–87; Chief Executive: Victoria Infirmary NHS Trust, 1987–94; Western General NHS Trust, 1995–2000; Fife Acute Hosps Trust, 2000–04; Acting Dir Gen. for Health and Social Care, Scottish Govt, 2013–14. Chm., OPEX Ltd, 1998–. Dir, Maggie's Centres, 1994–2005. *Recreations:* golf, photography, hockey (current member Scotland Men's Veterans team). *Address:* 54A St Albans Road, Edinburgh EH9 2LX. *T:* 07836 704107. *E:* connaghan2000@yahoo.com. *Clubs:* Blairgowrie Golf, Fidra Lions Hockey, Scotland Masters Hockey.

CONNAL, (Robert) Craig; QC (Scot.) 2002; Partner, since 1980, and Head of Advocacy in Litigation and Compliance, since 2014, Pinsent Masons LLP (formerly McGrigor Donald, then McGrigors); *b* 7 July 1954; *s* of James Brownlee Connal and Jean Elizabeth Polley or Connal; *m* 1976, Mary Ferguson Bowie; two *d*. *Educ:* Hamilton Acad.; Glasgow Univ. (LLB 1st Cl. Hons). Admitted Solicitor, Scotland, 1977, England and Wales, 2006; Solicitor Advocate: (civil), 1996, (criminal), 2004, Scotland; (all courts), England and Wales, 2006. McGrigor Donald, then McGrigors: Hd, Commercial Litigation, 2002–07; Senior Litigation Partner, 2007–12; Hd of Advocacy, 2007. Ext. Examr in Law, Dept of Land Econ., Aberdeen Univ., 2001–05. Mem., Wkg Party on Partnership Law, Scottish Law Commn, 2000–03. Vice Chm. (Scotland), British and Irish Commercial Bar Assoc. Member, Council: Royal Faculty of Procurators in Glasgow, 1995–98; SSC, 1999–. Convenor, Rights of Audience Course (Civil), Law Soc. of Scotland, 2004–. Solicitor Advocate of the Year, Law Soc. of England and Wales, 2012. *Publications:* (contrib.) Stair Memorial Encyclopaedia of Scots Law, 1986; contrib. articles to learned jls incl. Jl Law Soc. of Scotland, Jl Planning & Envmtl Law, Estates Gazette, Scottish Planning and Envmt Law, Scots Law Times, Tax Advr, Scottish Criminal Law, Juridical Rev.; contribs to general press. *Recreations:* Rugby referee, food and wine, gardens (but not gardening). *Address:* Pinsent Masons LLP, 141 Bothwell Street, Glasgow G2 7EQ. *T:* (0141) 567 8400, *Fax:* (0141) 567 8401. *E:* craig.connal@pinsentmasons.com. *Club:* Whitecraigs Rugby.

CONNARTY, Michael; *b* 3 Sept. 1947; *m* 1969, Margaret Doran; one *s* one *d*. *Educ:* St Patrick's High Sch., Coatbridge; Stirling and Glasgow Univs (Student Pres., Stirling Univ., 1970–71); Jordanhill Coll. of Educn (BA; DCE). Teacher of econs and modern studies (secondary and special needs), 1976–92. Exec. Mem., Central region, EIS, 1978–84 (Pres., 1982–83). Rector, Stirling Univ., 1983–84. Mem. (Lab) Stirling DC, 1977–90 (Leader of Council, 1980–90); Chm., Lab. Party Scottish Local Govt Cttee, 1988–90. Mem., Lab. Party Scottish Exec., 1981, 1983–92. Contested (Lab) Stirling, 1983, 1987. MP (Lab) Falkirk E, 1992–2005, Linlithgow and E Falkirk, 2005–15; contested (Lab) same seat, 2015. PPS to Minister of State for Film and Tourism, 1997–98. Member: Information Select Cttee, 1997–2001; European Scrutiny Select Cttee, 1998–2015 (Chm., 2006–10); Parly Assembly, Council of Europe, 2010–15 (Mem., Educn, Culture and Scis Cttee, 2010–15; Chm., 2012–14, Vice Chm., 2014–15, Educn, Youth and Sport Sub Cttee). Chm., Parly Jazz Appreciation Gp, 2001–15; Secretary: Offshore Oil & Gas Industry Gp, 1998–2015; All Party Parly Gp on Nuclear Energy; Vice-Chm., All-Party Parly Gp on Chemical Industries, 2010–15 (Treas., 1994–97; Chm., 1997–2000; Sec., 2000–10); Sec., PLP Sci. and Technol. Cttee, 1992–97; Co-ordinator, PLP Scottish Task Force, Skills and Trng, Youths and Students, 1994–97; Vice Chm., Scottish PLP Gp, 1996–98 (Chm., 1998–99). Mem. Bd, POST, 1997–2015. JP 1977–90.

CONNELL, His Eminence Cardinal Desmond, DD; Archbishop of Dublin, and Primate of Ireland, (RC), 1988–2004; *b* 24 March 1926; *s* of John Connell and Maisie Connell (*née* Lacy). *Educ:* St Peter's National School, Phibsborough; Belvedere College; Clonliffe College; University Coll., Dublin (MA); St Patrick's Coll., Maynooth; Louvain Univ., Belgium (DPhil); DLitt NUI, 1981. University College, Dublin: Dept of Metaphysics, 1953–72; Prof. of General Metaphysics, 1972–88; Dean, Faculty of Philosophy and Sociology, 1983–88. Chaplain: Poor Clares, Donnybrook, 1953–55; Carmelites, Drumcondra, 1955–66; Carmelites, Blackrock, 1966–88. Prelate of Honour, 1984; Cardinal, 2001. *Publications:* The Vision in God, 1967; articles in reviews. *Address:* c/o Archbishop's House, Drumcondra, Dublin 9, Ireland.

CONNELL, George Edward, OC 1987; PhD; FCIC; FRSC; President, University of Toronto, 1984–90; *b* 20 June 1930; *m* 1955, Sheila Horan; two *s* two *d*. *Educ:* Univ. of Toronto (BA, PhD Biochemistry). FCIC 1971; FRSC 1975. Post-doctoral Fellow, Div. of Applied Biol., National Res. Council, Ottawa, Ont, 1955–56; Fellow, National Science Foundn (US), Dept of Biochem., New York University Coll. of Medicine, 1956–57; University of Toronto: Asst Prof. of Biochem., 1957–62; Associate Prof. of Biochem., 1962–65; Prof. and Chm. Dept of Biochem., 1965–70; Associate Dean, Faculty of Med., 1972–74; Vice-Pres., Res. and Planning, 1974–77; Pres. and Vice-Chancellor, Univ. of Western Ontario, 1977–84. Prin. Advr, Commn of Enquiry on Blood System of Canada, 1993–95; Sen. Policy Advr, Canada Foundn for Innovation, 1997; Mem., Res. Adv. Panel, Walkerton Inquiry, 2000–01. Chairman: Exec. Cttee, Internat. Congress of Biochem., 1979; Nat. Round Table on the Envmt and Economy, 1991–95; Technical Cttee 207 (Envmt Management), ISO, 1993–96; Task Force on Funding and Delivery of Med. Care in Ontario, 1995–96; Canadian Prostate Cancer Res. Initiative, 2000–; Vice-Chairman: Envmt Assessment Bd, Ontario, 1990–93; Sustainable Cities Foundn, 1993–98; Protein Engrg Nat. Centre of Excellence, 1995–97; Mem. Bd of Dirs, Lake Simcoe Region Conservation Foundn, 2001–. Member: MRC of Canada, 1966–70; Ont Council of Health, 1978–84; Bd of Dirs and Nat. Exec. Cttee, Canadian Arthritis and Rheumatism Soc., 1965–75; Bd of Dirs, Nat. Inst. of Nutrition, 1984–91; Bd of Res. Inst., Toronto Hosp., 1994–96; Council, Ont. Univs, 1977–90 (Chm., 1981–83); Bd of Governors, Upper Canada Coll., 1982–90; Bd of Trustees, Royal Ont Mus., 1984–90; Trustee, R. Samuel McLaughlin Foundn, 1996–2001; Mem., Ontario Press Council, 1996–. Member, Board of Directors: Southam Inc., 1985–93; Allelix Biopharmaceuticals Inc., 1995–99. Hon. LLD: Trent, 1984; Univ. of Western Ont., 1985; McGill, 1987; Hon. DSc Toronto, 1993. *Publications:* scientific papers in jls incl. Canadian Jl of Biochem., Biochemical Jl (UK), and Jl of Immunol. *Recreations:* ski-ing, tennis, wilderness canoe trips. *Address:* 904–130 Carlton Street, Toronto, ON M5A 4K3, Canada. *E:* george.connell@sympatico.ca. *Club:* Badminton and Racquet (Toronto).

CONNELL, Prof. John Jeffrey, CBE 1985; PhD; FRSE; FIFST; Director, Torry Research Station, Aberdeen (Ministry of Agriculture, Fisheries and Food), 1979–87 (Assistant Director, 1969–79); Emeritus Professor, Aberdeen University, 1987; *b* 2 July 1927; *s* of John Edward Connell and Margaret Connell; *m* 1950, Margaret Parsons; one *s* two *d* (and one *d* decd). *Educ:* Burnage High Sch.; Univ. of Manchester (BSc 1947); Univ. of Edinburgh (PhD 1950). FIFST 1970; FRSE 1984. Torry Research Station: Scientific Officer, 1950; Sen. Sci. Officer, 1955; Principal Sci. Officer, 1961; Dep. Chief Sci. Officer, 1979; Officer i/c Humber Lab., Hull (Sen. Principal Sci. Officer), 1968–69. Res. Associate, 1969–79 and Hon. Res. Lectr, 1979–83, Aberdeen Univ. Mem., Fisheries Res. and Develt Bd, 1979–84. *Publications:* Control of Fish Quality, 1975, 4th edn 1995 (Spanish edn 1978); Trends in Fish Utilisation, 1982; scientific and technical papers related to use of fish as food. *Recreations:* music, hill walking. *Address:* 61 Burnieboozle Crescent, Aberdeen AB15 8NR. *T:* (01224) 315852.

CONNELL, Prof. John Muir Cochrane, MD; FRCPGlas, FRCPE, FMedSci; FRSE; Professor of Endocrinology, since 2009, and Vice Principal and Head, College of Medicine, Dentistry and Nursing, since 2012, University of Dundee; *b* 10 Oct. 1954; *s* of William and Betty Connell; *m* 1978, Lesley Elizabeth Armstrong; three *s* one *d*. *Educ:* Spiers Sch., Beith, Ayrshire; Hutchesons' Grammar Sch., Glasgow; Univ. of Glasgow (MB ChB 1977; MD 1986). MRCP 1979; FRCPGlas 1989. Clin. Scientist, 1983–87, Sen. Clin. Scientist, 1987–94, MRC Blood Pressure Unit, Western Infirmary, Glasgow; MRC Travelling Fellow, Howard Florey Inst., Melbourne, 1986–87; University of Glasgow: Hon. Prof. in Medicine, 1994–95; Prof. of Endocrinol., 1995–2009; Hd, Grad. Sch., 2006–09, Faculty of Medicine; Dean of Medicine, Univ. of Dundee, 2009–11. Chm., Educn Trng Adv. Bd, GMC, 2013–. Sec., 2000–03, Treas., 2003–07, Assoc. of Physicians of GB and Ireland; Mem. Council, Acad. of Med. Scis, 2008–11. Gov., Hutchesons' GS, 2001–04. FMedSci 1999; FRSE 2002; FRCPE 2002. *Publications:* (contrib. with A. F. Dominiczak) Handbook of Hypertension, Vol. 44, 2007; contrib. learned articles on aspects of endocrinology and genetics of cardiovascular disease. *Recreations:* family, golf, travel, literature. *Address:* College of Medicine, Dentistry and Nursing, Ninewells Hospital and Medical School, University of Dundee, Dundee DD1 9SY. *T:* (01382) 632032. *E:* j.m.connell@dundee.ac.uk. *Clubs:* New (Edinburgh); New Golf (St Andrews).

CONNELL, Margaret Mary, MA; Principal, Queen's College, London, 1999–2009; *b* 3 Jan. 1949; *d* of late Leo Connell and Margaret Isobel Connell. *Educ:* Lady Margaret Hall, Oxford (MA). Physics teacher, Headington Sch., Oxford, 1970–76; maths teacher, North London Collegiate Sch., 1976–86; Dep. Headmistress, Bromley High Sch. (GPDST), 1986–91; Headmistress, More House Sch., 1991–99. *Recreations:* music, travel, reading. *Address:* 3 Cranford Mews, Bromley, Kent BR2 8GA. *T:* (020) 8295 1572. *Club:* University Women's.

CONNELLY, Brian Norman, OBE 2002; HM Diplomatic Service, retired; High Commissioner, Kingdom of Tonga, and Consul for Pacific Islands under American sovereignty South of the Equator, 1999–2001; *b* 25 Dec. 1941; *s* of late Bernard Connelly and Julia Connelly (*née* Murphy); *m* 1965, Theresa, (Terrie), Hughes; one *s* one *d*. *Educ:* Holycross Acad., Edinburgh. Joined FO, 1967; Budapest, 1969–71; Montevideo, 1971–74; FCO, 1974–76; Kuwait, 1976–80; Seoul, 1980–84; First Sec., FCO, 1984–86; First Sec. (Commercial), Dhaka, 1987–90; Adminr and Chief Magistrate, Ascension Island, 1991–95; High Comr, Solomon Is, 1996–98. *Recreations:* golf, tennis, snorkelling. *Address:* 24 Latimer, Stony Stratford, Bucks MK11 1HY.

CONNELLY, Christine Kerr; Director General Informatics, Department of Health, 2008–11; *b* Hamilton, 28 Dec. 1958; *d* of Thomas Connelly and Margaret Connelly (*née* Kerr); *m* 1985, Derek Ball. *Educ:* Holy Cross High Sch., Hamilton; Aberdeen Univ. (BSc Hons 1980). BP plc, 1984–2004; Chief Information Officer, Cadbury Schweppes, 2004–07. *Recreations:* netball, golf, theatre. *Club:* Stoke Park (Stoke Poges).

CONNELLY, Iain Miller; President, Royal Incorporation of Architects in Scotland, 2013–15; *b* Dunfermline, Fife, 2 Nov. 1954; *s* of Dr James Connelly and Susanne Connelly; partner, Christine Harper; two *s* one *d*. *Educ:* Dunfermline High Sch.; Edinburgh Coll. of Art (BArch Hons 1977, DipArch 1978, Heriot-Watt Univ.). Architect: Sir Frank Mears & Partners, 1978–79; Kenneth Oliver Architects, Dunfermline, 1979–83; Architect, then Principal Architect, Dunfermline DC, 1983–96; Property Services Manager, Fife Council, 1996–2012. Editorial, RIAS Qly mag., 2013–. Scottish Pres., Soc. of Chief Architects in Local Authorities, 2004–06. Mem. Council, RIAS, 2004–. Mem., Scottish Soc. of Architect Artists, 2012–. *Recreations:* golf, cycling, music (playing piano), reading, photography, watching world go by with a glass of red. *Address:* 5 Adia Road, Torryburn, Dunfermline, Fife KY12 8LB. *T:* (01383) 881763, 07711 993430. *E:* iainconnelly1@sky.com, iain.connelly@rias.org.uk. *Club:* Dunfermline Golf.

CONNER, Rt Rev. David John, KCVO 2010; Dean of Windsor, since 1998; Register, Order of the Garter, since 1998; Domestic Chaplain to the Queen, since 1998; *b* 6 April 1947; *s* of late William Ernest Conner and Joan Millington Conner; *m* 1969, Jayne Maria Evans; two *s*. *Educ:* Erith Grammar School; Exeter College, Oxford (Symes Exhibnr; MA); St Stephen's House, Oxford. Asst Chaplain, St Edward's School, Oxford, 1971–73, Chaplain, 1973–80; Team Vicar, Wolvercote with Summertown, Oxford, 1976–80; Senior Chaplain, Winchester College, 1980–86; Vicar, St Mary the Great with St Michael, Cambridge, 1987–94; RD of Cambridge, 1989–94; Bishop Suffragan of Lynn, 1994–98; Bishop to the Forces, 2001–09. Hon. Fellow, Girton Coll., Cambridge, 1995. Hon. Chaplain, The Pilgrims, 2002–12. *Address:* The Deanery, Windsor Castle, Berks SL4 1NJ. *T:* (01753) 848707, *Fax:* (01753) 819002.

CONNERY, Sir Sean, Kt 2000; actor; *b* 25 Aug. 1930; *s* of Joseph and Euphamia Connery; named Thomas; adopted stage name of Sean, 1953; *m* 1st, 1962, Diane Cilento (marr. diss

1974; she *d* 2011); one *s*; 2nd, 1975, Micheline Roquebrune; two step *s* one step *d*. Served Royal Navy. Has appeared in films: No Road Back, 1956; Action of the Tiger, 1957; Another Time, Another Place, 1957; Hell Drivers, 1958; Tarzan's Greatest Adventure, 1959; Darby O'Gill and the Little People, 1959; On the Fiddle, 1961; The Longest Day, 1962; The Frightened City, 1962; Woman of Straw, 1964; The Hill, 1965; A Fine Madness, 1966; Shalako, 1968; The Molly Maguires, 1968; The Red Tent (1st Russian co-production), 1969; The Anderson Tapes, 1970; The Offence, 1973; Zardoz, 1973; Ransom, 1974; Murder on the Orient Express, 1974; The Wind and the Lion, 1975; The Man Who Would Be King, 1975; Robin and Marian, 1976; The First Great Train Robbery, 1978; Cuba, 1978; Meteor, 1979; Outland, 1981; The Man with the Deadly Lens, 1982; Wrong is Right, 1982; Five Days One Summer, 1982; Highlander, 1986; The Name of the Rose, 1987 (BAFTA Award for Best Actor, 1988); The Untouchables, 1987 (Best Supporting Actor, Academy Awards, 1988; Golden Globe Award); The Presidio, 1989; Indiana Jones and the Last Crusade, 1989; Family Business, 1990; The Hunt for Red October, 1990; The Russia House, 1991; Highlander II–The Quickening, 1991; Medicine Man, 1992; Rising Sun, 1993; A Good Man in Africa, 1994; First Knight, 1995; Just Cause, 1995; The Rock, 1996; Dragonheart, 1996; The Avengers, 1998; Entrapment, 1999; Playing by Heart, 1999; Finding Forrester, 2001; League of Extraordinary Gentlemen, 2003; as James Bond: Dr No, 1963; From Russia With Love, 1964; Goldfinger, 1965; Thunderball, 1965; You Only Live Twice, 1967; Diamonds are Forever, 1971; Never Say Never Again, 1983. Producer, Art, Wyndhams, 1996 (Tony Award, 1998). FRSAMD 1984. Fellow, BAFTA, 1998. Freedom of City of Edinburgh, 1991. Hon. DLitt: Heriot-Watt, 1981; St Andrews, 1988. BAFTA Life Time Achievement Award, 1990; Man of Culture Award, 1990; Scot of the Year Award, BBC Scotland, 1991; American Cinematique Award, 1992; Rudolph Valentino Award, 1992; Nat. Board of Review Award, 1994; Golden Globe Cecil B. De Mille Award, 1996; Lifetime Achievement Award, European Film Awards, 2005. Commander, Order of Arts and Literature (France), 1987; Légion d'Honneur. *Publications:* (with Murray Grigor) Being A Scot, 2008. *Recreations:* golf, tennis, reading.

CONNING, David Michael, OBE 1994; FRCPath; FRSB; Director-General, British Nutrition Foundation, 1985–94; *b* 27 Aug. 1932; *s* of Walter Henry Conning and Phyllis Elsie Conning (*née* Lovell); *m* 1st, 1956, Betty Sleightholme (marr. diss. 1991); three *s* one *d*; 2nd, 1991, Lesley Myra Yeomans (*née* Beresford). *Educ:* Dame Allan's Boys' Sch., Newcastle upon Tyne; Med. Sch., King's Coll., Univ. of Durham (MB, BS). FRCPath 1982; FRSB (FIBiol 1984); FIFST 1988. RAMC, 1956–59. SMO Pathology, Middlesbrough Gen. Hosp., 1959–61; Lectr in Pathology, Royal Victoria Infirmary, 1961–65; Hon. Consultant Pathologist, Newcastle and Dist Hosps, 1963–65; Dep. Dir, Central Toxicol. Lab., ICI plc, 1966–78; Dir, BIBRA, 1978–85. Chm., Brit. Toxicol Soc., 1981. Hon. Mem., European Toxicol Soc. (Pres., 1983–86). Hon. Prof. of Toxicology, Surrey Univ., 1977–86. *Publications:* Toxic Hazards in Foods, 1983; Experimental Toxicology, 1988, 2nd edn 1993; contrib. book chapters and articles in jls of toxicol. and nutrition. *Recreation:* mending things. *Address:* Blacksmith's Cottage, Totnor, Brockhampton, Hereford HR1 4TJ. *T:* (01989) 740303.

CONNOCK, Alexander; Managing Director, Shine North and Shine ON, since 2012; *b* June 1965; *s* of late Michael and Caroline Connock; *m* 1998, Sumitra; one *d*. *Educ:* Manchester Grammar Sch.; St John's Coll., Oxford (BA Hons Politics and Econs); Columbia Univ. (MA Journalism); INSEAD (MBA). Researcher, Granada TV, 1989–90; asst producer, BBC, 1990–92; Planet TV: producer: The Word, 1992–93; The Big Breakfast, 1993–96; Man. Dir, Planet TV Radio, 1996–99; Co-Founder and Chief Exec., Ten Alps plc, factual media co., 1999–2011. Member: RTS 2007– (Chm., RTS North West, 2010–); BAFTA, 2013–. Vis. Prof., Univ. of Sunderland, 2012–; Visiting Fellow: Reuters Inst., Univ. of Oxford, 2012–; Manchester Business Sch., 2012–; Creative Dir, Digital Innovation, Manchester Metropolitan Univ., 2012–. *Recreations:* piano, photography. *Address:* c/o Shine, 109 Regent's Park Road, NW1 8UR. *Clubs:* Groucho, Soho House.

CONNOLLY, Barbara Winifred; QC 2011; *b* London, 12 Oct. 1955; *d* of John Thomas Murphy and Brigid, (Delia), Joyce; *m* (marr. diss.); two *s*. *Educ:* LLB Hons. Called to the Bar, Inner Temple, 1986; in practice as a barrister, specialising in family and civil law. *Recreations:* family, friends, walking, books, theatre. *Address:* 7 Bedford Row, WC1R 4BS. *T:* (020) 7242 3555, *Fax:* (020) 7242 2511. *E:* bconnolly@7br.co.uk.

CONNOLLY, Billy, CBE 2003; stand-up comedian, actor; *b* 24 Nov. 1942; *m* 1st, Iris (marr. diss. 1985); one *s* one *d*; 2nd, 1990, Pamela Stephenson; three *d*. Welder, Clyde shipyards; (with Gerry Rafferty) formed folk duo, Humblebums; first solo concert, 1971; *theatre* includes: writer, The Red Runner, Edinburgh, 1979; performer: Die Fledermaus, Scottish Opera, 1978; The Pick of Billy Connolly, Cambridge, 1981; The Beastly Beatitudes of Balthazar B, Duke of York's, 1982; one-man show, London Palladium, 1985; Hammersmith Apollo, 2004; Billy Connolly Live In New York, 2005; What About Dick?, 2007; tours: Rebel Without a Clue, world tour, 1987; UK, 1992; Northern UK, 1997; Hammersmith Apollo, Australia, NZ, 1999; Aberdeen, Canada, 2000; England, Ireland, 2001; Scotland, 2005; Too Old to Die Young, Australia, 2006; NY, Canada, 2006; Montreal, UK, 2007; Ireland, San Francisco, 2008; Scotland, NZ, 2009; Seattle, Hammersmith Apollo, 2010; Canada, 2010; The Man, Australia, 2011, England and Wales, 2012; High Horse, Scotland, 2014; *films* include: Big Banana Feet, 1976; Absolution, 1979; Bullshot, 1983; Water, 1985; The Big Man, 1990; Down Among the Big Boys, 1993; Pocahontas, 1995; Muppet Treasure Island, 1996; Mrs Brown, Ship of Fools, Paws, Deacon Brodie, 1997; Still Crazy, The Changeling, Boon Dock Saints, 1998; The Debt Collector, The Imposters, 1999; Beautiful Joe, 2000; Cletis Tout, 2000; An Everlasting Piece, Gabriel and Me, 2001; The Man Who Sued God, Timeline, 2003; The Last Samurai, Lemony Snicket's A Series of Unfortunate Events, 2004; Good Sharma, 2005; Fido, Open Season, Garfield 2, 2006; The X-Files: I Want to Believe, 2008; Boondock Saints II, 2008; Gulliver's Travels, 2010; Brave, The Hobbit, 2012; Quartet, 2013; What We Did on our Holiday, The Hobbit: The Battle of the Five Armies, 2014; *television* includes: Head of the Class (series, USA), 1990–92; Billy (series, USA), 1992; Billy Connolly's World Tour of Scotland (series), 1994; A Scot in the Arctic, 1995; Pearl (US series), 1997; Billy Connolly's World Tour of Australia (series), 1996; Erect for 30 Years, 1998; Gentlemen's Relish, 2000; White Oleander, 2001; Billy Connolly's World Tour of England, Ireland and Wales, 2002; Billy Connolly's World Tour of New Zealand (series), 2004; Billy Connolly: Journey to the Edge of the World (series), 2009; Billy Connolly's Route 66 (series), 2011; Billy Connolly's Big Send Off, 2014; presenter, The Bigger Picture, 1994; *play:* Androcles and the Lion, 1984. Numerous recordings and DVDs. *Publications:* Gullible's Travels, 1982; Billy Connolly's World Tour of Australia, 1996; Journey to the Edge of the World, 2009. *Address:* c/o Tickety-boo Ltd, 2 Triq Il-Barriera, Balzan BZN 1200, Malta. *T:* 21556166.

CONNOLLY, Edward Thomas; Regional Chairman of Industrial Tribunals, Manchester, 1988–98; *b* 5 Sept. 1935; *s* of Edward Connolly and Alice Joyce; *m* 1962, Dr Pamela Marie Hagan; one *s* one *d*. *Educ:* St Mary's Coll., Crosby; Prior Park Coll.; Liverpool Univ. (LLB). Qualified as solicitor, 1960. Asst Solicitor, Lancs CC, 1960–63; Asst Prosecuting Solicitor, Liverpool City Council, 1963–65; Dep. Chief Legal Officer, Skelmersdale Develt Corp., 1965–68; Asst Clerk of the Peace, Lancs CC, 1968–71; Dep. Circuit Administrator, Northern Circuit, 1971–76; Chm. of Industrial Tribunals, 1976–88.

CONNOLLY, John Patrick, FCA; non-executive Chairman: AMEC plc, since 2011; G4S, since 2012; Chief Executive and Senior Partner, Deloitte, 1999–2011; Global Chairman, Deloitte Touche Tohmatsu, 2007–11 (Global Managing Director, 2003–07); *b* 29 Aug. 1950; *s* of John Connolly and Mary Connolly (*née* Morrison); *m* 1992, Odile Lesley Griffith; one *s* one *d* (and one *s* decd) from former marriage. *Educ:* St Bede's Coll., Manchester. FCA 1971. Partner: Mann Judd, Chartered Accountants, 1977; Touche Ross, 1980: Regl Partner i/c North, 1983–87; Man. Partner, Regl Offices, 1987–90, London and South, 1990–95; Man. Partner, Deloitte & Touche, 1995–99. Non-executive Chairman: Metric Capital Partners, 2011–; Quest Topco Ltd, 2011–; Elian, 2014–; Man. Partner, Sports Investment Partners, 2011–. Mem., Bd of Govs, London Business Sch., 2011–. Chm., Appeal Bd, Centre for Children's Rare Disease Res., Gt Ormond St Hosp., 2012–. *Recreations:* Manchester United, horseracing, opera, country pursuits, wine, sport. *Address:* G4S plc, The Peak, 5 Wilton Road, SW1V 1AN.

CONNOLLY, Joseph; novelist and author; *b* 23 March 1950; *s* of Joseph Connolly and Lena Connolly (*née* Forte); *m* 1970, Patricia Quinn; one *s* one *d*. *Educ:* Oratory Sch. Apprentice, then Ed., Hutchinson Publishers, 1969–71; owner, Flask Bookshop, Hampstead, 1975–88; columnist, The Times, 1984–88; regular contributor, The Times, Daily Telegraph and other nat. newspapers, 1984–; occasional writer, Spectator, Independent, Daily Telegraph, Sunday Telegraph and others; Restaurant Critic, Hampstead & Highgate Express, 2009–. Founder Mem., Useless Inf. Soc., 1994–. Member: Soc. of Authors, 1983; RSL, 2007. Hon. Life Mem., Wodehouse Soc. Mem., Devonshire Soc., 2009–. Patron, Royal Free Charity, 2011–. *Publications:* Collecting Modern First Editions, 1977; P. G. Wodehouse: an illustrated biography, 1979; Jerome K. Jerome: a critical biography, 1981; Modern First Editions: their value to collectors, 1984; The Penguin Book Quiz Book, 1985; Children's Modern First Editions, 1988; Beside the Seaside, 1999; All Shook Up: a flash of the Fifties, 2000; Christmas and How to Survive It, 2003; Wodehouse, 2004; Faber and Faber: eighty years of book cover design, 2009; The A–Z of Eating Out, 2014; *novels:* Poor Souls, 1995; This Is It, 1996; Stuff, 1997; Summer Things, 1998 (filmed as Embrassez qui vous voudrez, and, in English, as Summer Things, 2002); Winter Breaks, 1999; It Can't Go On, 2000; SOS, 2001; The Works, 2003; Love is Strange, 2005; Jack the Lad and Bloody Mary, 2007; England's Lane, 2012; Boys and Girls, 2014; Style, 2015; *contributor:* My Life and Times, by Jerome K. Jerome, 1992; Booker 30: a celebration of 30 years of the Booker Prize for Fiction 1969–1998, 1998; British Greats, 2000; The Book of Useless Information, 2002; The Man Booker Prize: 35 years of the best in contemporary fiction 1969–2003, 2003; British Comedy Greats, 2003; Icons in the Fire: the decline and fall of almost everybody in the British film industry 1984–2000, by Alexander Walker, 2004; Private Passions, by Michael Berkeley, 2005; Folio 60: a bibliography of the Folio Society 1947–2006, 2007; A Hedonist's Guide to Life, 2007; On the Art of Making Up One's Mind, by Jerome K. Jerome, 2009; Christmas Pudding, by Nancy Mitford, 2011. *Recreations:* books, Times crossword, wine, lunching and loafing. *Address:* c/o Jonathan Lloyd, Curtis Brown Group Ltd, Haymarket House, 28–29 Haymarket, SW1Y 4SP. *T:* (020) 7393 4400, *Fax:* (020) 7393 4401. *E:* cb@curtisbrown.co.uk. *W:* www.josephconnolly.co.uk. *Clubs:* Garrick, Chelsea Arts, Groucho.

CONNOLLY, Sarah Patricia, CBE 2010; opera singer; mezzo-soprano; *b* 13 June 1963; *d* of Gerald Connolly and Jane Connolly (*née* Widdowson); *m* Carl Randolph Talbot; one *d*. *Educ:* Raventhorpe Sch., Darlington; Queen Margaret's Sch., Escrick; Royal Coll. of Music (Dip RCM Piano; Dip RCM Singing). Rôles include: English National Opera: Dido in The Trojans, 2004; Sesto in La clemenza di Tito, 2005; title rôle in Agrippina, 2007; title rôle in Medea, 2013; title rôle in Giulio Cesare, Glyndebourne, 2005; début, Metropolitan Opera, as Annio in La clemenza di Tito; début, La Scala, Milan as Dido; Octavian in Der Rosenkavalier, Scottish Opera, 2006; Romeo in I Capuleti e i Montecchi, Opera North, 2008; Nerone in L'incoronazione de Poppea, Barcelona, 2009; Dido in Dido and Aeneas, ROH, 2009; Der Komponist in Ariadne auf Naxos, Metropolitan Opera, 2010; Mary Queen of Scots in Mary Stuart, Opera North, 2010; David in Saul, Barbican, 2011; Phaedra in Hippolyte et Aricie, Glyndebourne, 2013; Brangane in Tristan und Isolde, ROH, 2014; concert appearances include: Salzburg Fest., Tanglewood Fest., Vienna Konzerthaus, Berlin Philharmonie, Zankel Hall, NY and Concertgebouw, Amsterdam; soloist in Last Night of the Proms, 2009. *Recreations:* reading, teaching, cooking, gardening. *Address:* c/o Askonas Holt Ltd, Lincoln House, 300 High Holborn, WC1V 7JH. *E:* keiron.cooke@askonasholt.co.uk.

CONNOR, Bishop of, since 2007; **Rt Rev. Alan Francis Abernethy;** *b* 12 April 1957; *s* of Walter Abernethy and Margaret (*née* Sloan); *m* 1983, Liz Forster; one *s* one *d*. *Educ:* Harding Meml Primary, Belfast; Grosvenor High Sch., Belfast; Queen's Univ., Belfast (BA 1978; BD 1989); Trinity Coll., Dublin (DipTh 1981). Ordained deacon, 1981, priest, 1982; Assistant Curate: St Elizabeth's, Dundonald, 1981–84; Lecale Gp of Parishes, 1984–87; Officiating Chaplain, RAF Bishopscourt, 1984–87; Rector: St John's, Helen's Bay, 1987–90; St Columbanus, Ballyholme, 1990–2007. Canon, Down Cath., 2000–07. Religious Advr, Downtown Radio, 1985–90. *Publications:* Fulfilment and Frustration, 2002; Shadows on the Journey, 2011. *Recreations:* tennis, cycling, family holidays, reading, cooking. *Address:* Bishop's House, 3 Upper Malone Road, Belfast BT8 6TD. *T:* (office) (028) 9082 8870, *Fax:* (028) 9031 0138. *E:* bishop@connor.anglican.org.

CONNOR, Clare Joanne, OBE 2006 (MBE 2004); Head of England Women's Cricket, England and Wales Cricket Board, since 2008; *b* Brighton, 1 Sept. 1976; *d* of Michael and Norma Connor; *m* 2006, Roger Nicholson. *Educ:* Brighton Coll.; Manchester Univ. (BA Hons English 1998). Neuro-Linguistic Programming Practitioner, 2011. Mem., England Women's Cricket team, 1995–2006 (Captain, 2000–06; team regained The Ashes, 2005). English teacher, Housemistress and Hd of PR, Brighton Coll., 1999–2007; on sabbatical, 2003–05, as presenter, The Cricket Show, Channel 4, columnist, The Observer and radio cricket summariser, Test Match Special, BBC Radio 4. Mem., Commn on Future of Women's Sport, 2009–. Member, Board: Sussex CCC, 2008–; Sport England, 2010–; Mem., Women's Cttee, 2008– (Chair, 2011–), Cricket Cttee, 2009–, Develt Cttee, 2011–, ICC. *Recreations:* keeping fit, reading, time with family, cinema, theatre. *Address:* 6A Amesbury Crescent, Hove, E Sussex BN3 5RD. *T:* 07721 728394. *E:* clare.connor@ecb.co.uk. *Club:* MCC (Hon. Life Mem. 2009).

CONNOR, Rt Rev. George Howard Douglas; Bishop of Dunedin, 2005–09; *b* 27 Feb. 1942; *s* of George Sherwood Connor and Elizabeth Agnes (*née* Gordon); step *s* of John Edward Marshall Ball; *m* 1967, Nonie Saxby; two *s* two *d*. *Educ:* St John's Coll., Auckland; LTh (1st cl. Hons) 1965, LTh (Aotearoa) 1992; Massey Univ. (Postgrad. Dip. Arts (History) 2011; MA History 2012). Ordained deacon, 1965, priest, 1966; Theol Tutor, Ch of Melanesia, 1967–73; Maori Mission priest, Waiapu dio., 1975–86; Archdeacon of Waiapu, 1981–86, Canon Theologian Emeritus, 1986; Regional Bishop in the Bay of Plenty, 1989–2005. Protector Gen., SSF, 2001–08. *Address:* 47 Pacific Parade, Surfdale, Waiheke Island 1081, New Zealand.

CONNOR, Prof. James Michael, MD, DSc; FRCPGlas; Burton Professor of Medical Genetics, Glasgow University, 1987–2011; *b* 18 June 1951; *s* of James Connor and Mona Connor (*née* Hall); *m* 1979, Dr Rachel Alyson Clare Brooks; two *d*. *Educ:* Liverpool Univ. (BSc (Hons); MB ChB (Hons); MD; DSc). MRCP 1977; FRCPGlas 1988; FRCPE 1990. Gen. med. professional trng in various Liverpool hosps, 1975–77; Resident in Internal Medicine, Johns Hopkins Hosp., Baltimore, 1977–78; Univ. Res. Fellow, Dept of Medicine, Liverpool Univ., 1978–81; Instr in Med. Genetics, John Hopkins Hosp., 1981–82; Cons. in Med. Genetics, 1982–84, Wellcome Trust Sen. Lectr in Med. Genetics, 1984–87, Duncan Guthrie Inst. of Med. Genetics, Glasgow. *Publications:* Essential Medical Genetics, 1984, 6th edn 2011; Prenatal Diagnosis in Obstetric Practice, 1989, 2nd edn 1995; (ed jtly) Emery and Rimoin's Principles and Practice of Medical Genetics, 3rd edn 1996 to 5th edn 2007; articles on pathophysiology and prevention of genetic disease. *Recreations:* mountain biking, cycle touring, sea kayaking, classic cars.

CONNOR, His Honour Jeremy George; a Circuit Judge, 1996–2004; *b* 14 Dec. 1938; *s* of Joseph Connor and Mabel Emmeline (*née* Adams), ARCA. *Educ:* Beaumont; University Coll., London (LLB; DRS); Heythrop Coll., Univ. of London (MA 2005); King's Coll. London (DTh 2011). Called to the Bar, Middle Temple, 1961, Bencher, 2003; S Eastern Circuit. Apptd to Treasury List, Central Criminal Court, 1973; Metropolitan Stipendiary Magistrate, 1979–96; a Recorder, 1986–96; a Chm., Inner London Youth Cts (formerly Juvenile Cts), 1980–96; Chairman: Family Proceedings Court, 1991–94; Inner London and City Probation Cttee, 1989–96; Member: Exec. Cttee, Central Council of Probation for England and Wales, 1982–89; Parole Bd, 1998–2004; Lord Chancellor's Adv. Cttee on Legal Educn and Conduct, 1996–99; Student Conduct Cttee, Inns of Court, 2005–10. Referee, Mental Health Foundn, 1993–2004. Mem., Judicial Studies Bd, 1990–95. Pres., British Acad. of Forensic Scis, 1989–90 (Chm., Exec. Council, 1983–86; Mem. Council, 1982–93); Chm., Inst. for Study of Treatment of Delinquency, 1992–93. Trustee: Grubb Inst. of Social Studies, 1995–2004; Stapleford Trust for Drug Treatment and Res., 1995–98; London Action Trust, 1996–2005; Assoc. of Blind Catholics, 1996–2004; Rainer Foundn, 1997–98 (Mem. Council, 1996–97); New Lease Trust, 1997–99; Royal Philanthropic Soc., 1998–99; Frontiers Th. Ltd, 2013–. Vice-Patron, Blind in Business, 1999–. Fellow, Soc. of Advanced Legal Studies, 1999. Freeman, City of London, 1980; Liveryman, Fanmakers' Co., 1981 (Mem., Livery Cttee, 1987–90; Master, 2007–08). *Publications:* chapter in Archbold, Criminal Pleading, Evidence and Practice, 38th and 39th edns. *Recreations:* travel, theatre, occasional broadcasting. *Clubs:* Garrick, Royal Society of Medicine.

CONNOR, John William, PhD; FRS 2010; CPhys, FInstP; Senior Consultant in plasma theory, Culham Centre for Fusion Energy, 2007–15, now Honorary Consultant; *b* Crewe, Cheshire, 6 Nov. 1942; *s* of John Connor and Mabel Connor, Cheshire; *m* 1965, Rachel Christine Hicks; one *s* one *d*. *Educ:* Crewe Co. Grammar Sch.; Univ. of Birmingham (BSc 1st Cl. 1964; PhD 1967). CPhys 1992, FInstP 1992. Research in field of theoretical plasma physics, UKAEA Culham Lab., 1967–89; Hd, Theory and Modelling Dept, UKAEA Fusion Culham Lab., 1989–2007. Vis. Scientist, Princeton Plasma Physics Lab., NJ, 1980; Vis. Prof., 2007–13, Dist. Res. Fellow, 2013–, Imperial Coll. London. Hannes Alfven Prize, Eur. Phys. Soc., 2004; Payne-Gaposchkin Prize, Inst. of Physics, 2007. *Publications:* approx. 150 papers in Nature, Procs Royal Soc., Physics of Fluids, Physics of Plasmas, Physical Rev. Letters, Plasma Physics and Controlled Fusion, Nuclear Fusion, etc. *Recreations:* amateur history, reading, crosswords, art history, walking. *Address:* Culham Centre for Fusion Energy, Culham Science Centre, Abingdon OX14 3DB. *T:* (01235) 466922, 07854 044258, *Fax:* (01235) 466435. *E:* jack.connor@ccfe.ac.uk, rachel@pennsbury.co.uk.

CONNOR, Michael Henry; HM Diplomatic Service, retired; Director of Trade Promotion, and Commercial Counsellor, Madrid, 1995–2000; *b* 5 Aug. 1942; *s* of late Henry Connor and Agnes Cecilia Connor (*née* Lindsey); *m* 1964, Valerie Jannita Cunningham; three *s*. *Educ:* St John's Coll., Portsmouth. Joined HM Diplomatic Service, 1964; FO, 1964–68; Attaché, Cairo, 1968–70; Commercial Officer, Vienna, 1970–73; Second Sec. (Commercial/Aid), Kathmandu, 1973–76; FCO, 1976–81; First Sec., 1979; Havana: First Sec. (Commercial) and Consul, 1981–82; First Sec. and Hd of Chancery, 1982–83; Hd of Chancery, Ottawa, 1983–88; First Sec., FCO, 1988–91; Ambassador, El Salvador, 1991–95. *Recreations:* swimming, photography, trekking, theatre.

CONNOR, His Honour Roger David; DL; a Circuit Judge, 1991–2005; *b* 8 June 1939; *s* of Thomas Bernard Connor and Susie Violet Connor (*née* Spittlehouse); *m* 1967, Sandra Home Holmes; two *s*. *Educ:* Merchant Taylors' School; Brunel College of Advanced Science and Technology; The College of Law. Solicitor; articled to J. R. Hodder, 1963–68; Asst Solicitor, 1968–70; Partner, Hodders, 1970–83; Metropolitan Stipendiary Magistrate, 1983–91; a Recorder, 1987–91. DL Bucks, 2005. *Recreations:* music, golf, gardening. *Address:* Bourn's Meadow, Little Missenden, Amersham, Bucks HP7 0RF. *Club:* Beaconsfield Golf.

CONNOR, (Ryan) Stephen, OBE 2013; Chief Executive Officer, National Centre for Domestic Violence, since 2002; *b* Aylesbury, 6 March 1974. *Educ:* Aylesbury Grammar Sch.; Surrey Univ. (LLB); City Univ. London (BVC; Postgrad. Dip. Legal Skills). Trainer, Judicial Studies Bd, 2009–. Chm., Hate Crime Scrutiny Panel, Crown Prosecution, 2009–12. Fellow, City Univ. London, 2008. *Recreations:* carp fishing, motor-cross. *Address:* National Centre for Domestic Violence, Edgeborough House, Upper Edgeborough Road, Guildford, Surrey GU1 2BJ. *T:* 0844 8044999, 07961 199999. *E:* steve.connor@ncdv.org.uk.

CONNOR, Prof. Steven Kevin, DPhil; Grace 2 Professor of English, University of Cambridge, since 2012; Fellow, Peterhouse, Cambridge, since 2012; *b* Chichester, 11 Feb. 1955; *s* of George Leslie Connor and Geraldine Vivien Connor; *m* 1st, 1984, Lindsey Richardson (marr. diss. 1988); one *d*; 2nd, 2005, Lynda Nead; two *s*. *Educ:* Christ's Hosp., Horsham; Bognor Regis Comprehensive Sch.; Wadham Coll., Oxford (BA English 1976; DPhil 1979). Birkbeck College, University of London: Lectr in English, 1979–89; Sen. Lectr in English, 1990–91; Reader in Modern English Lit., 1991–93; Prof. of Modern Lit. and Theory, 1994–2012. *Publications:* Charles Dickens, 1985; Samuel Beckett: repetition, theory and text, 1988; Postmodernist Culture: an introduction to theories of the contemporary, 1989, 2nd rev. and enlarged edn 1996; Theory and Cultural Value, 1992; (ed) Samuel Beckett's Waiting for Godot and Endgame: a new casebook, 1992; (ed) Charles Dickens, Oliver Twist, 1994; The English Novel in History, 1950 to 1995, 1995; James Joyce, 1996, 2nd edn 2012; (ed) Charles Dickens, The Mystery of Edwin Drood, 1996; (ed) Charles Dickens, 1996; Dumbstruck: a cultural history of ventriloquism, 2000; The Book of Skin, 2004; (ed) The Cambridge Companion to Postmodernism, 2004; Fly, 2006; The Matter of Air: science and art of the ethereal, 2010; Paraphernalia: the curious lives of magical things, 2011; A Philosophy of Sport, 2011; Beyond Words: sobs, hums, stutters and other vocalizations, 2014; Beckett, Modernism and the Material Imagination, 2014. *Recreations:* gardening, running. *Address:* Peterhouse, Trumpington Street, Cambridge CB2 1RD.

CONNOR, Sir William Joseph, (Sir Bill), Kt 2003; General Secretary, Union of Shop Distributive and Allied Workers, 1997–2004; Chair, British Acupuncture Federation, since 2013; *b* 21 May 1941; *s* of William and Mary Connor; *m* 1962, Carol Ann Beattie; one *s* one *d*. Union of Shop Distributive and Allied Workers: Area Organiser, 1971–78; Nat. Officer, 1978–89; Dep. Gen. Sec., 1989–97. Member: TUC Gen. Council and Exec. Cttee, 1997–2004; Partnership Fund Assessment Panel, 1998–2004; Central Arbitration Cttee, 2000–10. Dir, Unity Bank, 1997–2004. Chairman: Nat. Register of Hypnotherapists and Psychotherapists, 2004–09; Supervisory Bd, Union Modernisation Fund, 2005–10. *Recreations:* music, reading, computers, digital photography. *Address:* 25 Abington Drive, Banks, Southport, Merseyside PR9 8FL.

CONNORS, James Scott, (Jimmy); tennis player; tennis commentator, CBS television; *b* 2 Sept. 1952; *s* of late James Scott Connors and Gloria Thompson Connors; *m* 1978, Patti McGuire; one *s* one *d*. *Educ:* Univ. of California at Los Angeles. Amateur tennis player, 1970–72, professional, 1972; major Championships won: Australia, 1974; Wimbledon, 1974, 1982; USA, 1974, 1976, 1978, 1982, 1983; South Africa, 1973, 1974; WCT, 1977, 1980; Grand Prix, 1978; played for USA, Davis Cup, 1976, 1981. Champions Tour, 1993–99. BBC Overseas Sports Personality, 1982. *Publications:* The Outsider: my autobiography, 2013.

CONOLLY, Mrs Yvonne Cecile; consultant in primary education; Head of Inspection and Monitoring, London Borough of Islington, 1995–99 (Senior Inspector for Primary Education, 1989–95); *b* 12 June 1939; *d* of Hugh Augustus and Blanche Foster; *m* 1965, Michael Patrick Conolly (marr. diss. 1996); one *d*. *Educ:* Westwood High Sch., Jamaica; Shortwood Coll., Jamaica (Teachers' CertEd); Polytechnic, N London (BEd Hons Primary Educn). Primary school teacher: Jamaica, 1960–63; London, 1963–68; Head Teacher, London, 1969–78; ILEA Inspector, Multi-ethnic Education, 1978–81; Inspector of Primary Schools, 1981–90, Dis Primary Inspector, 1988–90, ILEA. Member: Home Secretary's Adv. Council on Race Relations, 1977–86; IBA, 1982–86; Consumer Protection Adv. Cttee, 1974–75. Governor former Centre for Information and Advice on Educnl Disadvantage, 1975–80; (first) Chm. Caribbean Teachers' Assoc., 1974–76. Registered Inspector, OFSTED, 1993–2000 Governor: Stroud Green Primary Sch., 1992–2004; Park View Community Coll. (formerly Langham Sch.), 1997–2004. Chaplaincy Visitor, Whittington Hosp., 2007–11. Mem. Soroptimist Internat. of Gtr London, 2001–13 (Hon. Sec., 2003–04; Pres., 2005–06). *Publications:* (contrib.) Mango Spice, book of 44 Caribbean songs for schools, 1981; (contrib. Against the Tide—Black Experience in the ILEA, 1990. *Recreations:* writing, theatre, classical music.

CONOLLY-CAREW, family name of **Baron Carew**.

CONRAD, His Honour Alan David; QC 1999; a Circuit Judge, since 2013; *b* 10 Dec 1953; *s* of Maurice and Peggy Conrad; *m* 1st, 1982 (marr. diss. 1998); one *s* one *d*; 2nd, 2002 Julie Whittle. *Educ:* Bury Grammar Sch.; Brasenose Coll., Oxford (BA Hons Jurisp.). Called to the Bar, Middle Temple, 1976; Asst Recorder, 1993–97; Recorder 1997–2013. *Recreations* travel, reading, music, motor cars, cricket, cookery, dogs. *Address:* Liverpool Crown Court Queen Elizabeth II Law Courts, Derby Square, Liverpool L2 1XA. *Club:* Lancashire County Cricket.

CONRAD, Peter John; writer; Student, and Tutor in English Literature, Christ Church Oxford, 1973–2011; *b* 11 Feb. 1948; *s* of Eric and Pearl Conrad. *Educ:* Hobart High Sch. Univ. of Tasmania (BA); New Coll., Oxford (MA). Fellow, All Souls Coll., Oxford, 1970–73 Boyer Lectr, ABC, 2004. Hon. DLitt Tasmania, 1993. *Publications:* The Victorian Treasure-House, 1973; Romantic Opera and Literary Form, 1977; Shandyism, 1978; Imagining America, 1980; Television: the medium and its manners, 1982; The Art of the City: views and versions of New York, 1984; The Everyman History of English Literature, 1985; A Song of Love and Death: the meaning of opera, 1987; Down Home: revisiting Tasmania, 1988 Where I Fell to Earth, 1990; Underworld, 1992; Feasting with Panthers, 1994; To Be Continued, 1995; Modern Times, Modern Places, 1998; The Hitchcock Murders, 2000 Orson Welles: the stories of his life, 2003; At Home in Australia, 2003; Tales of Two Hemispheres, 2004; Creation: artists, gods and origins, 2007; Islands, 2009; Verdi and/or Wagner, 2011; How the World Was Won, 2014. *Address:* 19 Offley Road, SW9 0LR. *T:* (020) 7735 1422.

CONRAN, Elizabeth Margaret, OBE 1994; MA, FMA; Curator, The Bowes Museum Barnard Castle, 1979–2001; *b* 5 May 1939; *d* of James Johnston and Elizabeth Russell Wilson *m* 1970, George Loraine Conran (*d* 1986); one *d*. *Educ:* Falkirk High Sch.; Glasgow Univ (MA). FMA 1969. Res. Asst, Dept of History of Fine Art, Glasgow Univ., 1959–60; Ass Curator, The Iveagh Bequest, Kenwood, 1960–63; Keeper of Paintings, City Art Galls Manchester, 1963–74; Arts Adviser, Greater Manchester Council, 1974–79. FRSA 1987 *Publications:* exhibn catalogues; articles in art and museum jls. *Recreations:* gardens, ballet *Address:* 31 Thorngate, Barnard Castle, Co. Durham DL12 8QB. *T:* (01833) 631055.

CONRAN, Jasper Alexander Thirlby, OBE 2008; Designer (clothing, accessories and bridalwear, ceramics, crystal, furniture, fragrances, luggage, theatre), Chairman and Chief Executive Officer, Jasper Conran Holdings Ltd; Director, Conran Holdings, since 2009 Creative Director, since 2011, and Chairman, since 2012, The Conran Shop Ltd; *b* 12 Dec 1959; *s* of Sir Terence Orby Conran, *qv* and Shirley Ida Conran, *qv*. *Educ:* Bryanston School Dorset; Parsons School of Art and Design, New York. First womenswear collection, 1978 menswear introd 1985; J by Jasper Conran collection at Debenhams, launched 1996 Costumes for: Anouilh's The Rehearsal, 1990 (Laurence Olivier Award, 1991); My Fair Lady 1992; (also sets), Bintley's Tombeaux, Royal Opera House, 1993; Sleeping Beauty, Scottish Ballet, 1994; The Nutcracker Sweeties, 1996, Edward II, 1997, Arthur, 2000, Birmingham Royal Ballet; Maria Stuarda, ENO, 1998. Vis. Prof., Univ. of the Arts London, 2007– Trustee: Wallace Collection, 2007–; Architecture Foundn. Gov., Bryanston Sch., 2007– Hon. DLitt Heriot-Watt, 2004; Hon. DCL East Anglia, 2006. Fil d'Or (Internat. Linen Award), 1982 and 1983; British Fashion Council Designer of the Year Award, 1986–87; Fashion Group of America Award, 1987; British Collections Award, 1991; Prince's Medal Homes and Gardens Classic Design Awards, 2003. *Address:* 1–7 Rostrevor Mews, Fulham SW6 5AZ. *T:* (020) 7384 0800. *E:* info@jasperconran.com.

CONRAN, Sebastian Orby; industrial designer; Managing Director, Sebastian Conran Associates, since 2009; *b* London, 5 April 1956; *s* of Sir Terence Orby Conran, *qv* and Shirley Ida Conran, *qv*; *m* 2008, Gertrude Maria Thoma; two *s*. *Educ:* Bryanston Sch.; Central Sch of Art and Design (Industrial Design). Wolff Olins, 1978–81; Hd of Design, Mothercare 1981–86; Founder, Sebastian Conran Associates, 1986, later merged with Conran Gp to form Conran & Partners, 1999; Man. Dir, Studio Conran, 2008–09. Taught furniture design RCA, 1994–97; Vis. Prof., Univ. of the Arts, London, 2009–12; Designer in Residence Sheffield Univ. Sci. Faculty, 2011–13. Leader, Design and Technol. Alliance against Crime 2008–; Chairman: Adv. Bd, Creative Industries Technols Innovation Network, 2009–; Design in Action Scotland, 2012–; Design Special Interest Gp, 2013–. Trustee: Design Council; D&AD; Design Mus.; Conran Foundn. Ambassador for: ICAN; ACID. Gov. Bryanston Sch., Dorset, 2011–. FCSD 2008; FRSA. Hon. FRCA 2008. Hon. DTech Loughborough, 2012; Hon. DArts Hertfordshire, 2012. *Publications:* Contemporary Furniture, 1999; Contemporary Lighting, 1999. *Address:* 2 Munden Street, W14 0RH. *E:* studio@sebastianconran.com.

See also J. A. T. Conran.

CONRAN, Shirley Ida, OBE 2004; writer; *b* 21 Sept. 1932; *d* of W. Thirlby Pearce and Ida Pearce; *m* 1955, Sir Terence Conran (marr. diss. 1962); two *s*. *Educ:* St Paul's Girls' Sch.; Southern College of Art, Portsmouth; Chelsea Poly.; Central St Martins Coll. of Art and Design. Fabric Designer and Director of Conran Fabrics, 1956–62; Member, Selection Cttee, Design Centre, 1961–69. Journalist; (first) Woman's Editor, Observer Colour Magazine, 1964; Woman's Editor, Daily Mail, 1969; Life and Style Editor, Over 21, 1972–74. Founder President: Mothers in Management, later Work-Life Balance Trust, 1998–2005; Maths Action, 2004–. Advr to DFE, 2014–. *Publications:* Superwoman, 1975, revd edn as Down with Superwoman, 1990; Superwoman Year Book, 1976; Superwoman in Action, 1977; (with E Sidney) Futurewoman, 1979; The Magic Garden, 1983; The Amazing Umbrella Shop, 1990; *novels:* Lace, 1982; Lace 2, 1985; Savages, 1987; Crimson, 1991; Tiger Eyes, 1994; The Revenge, 1997. *Recreations:* reading, iPad.

See also J. A. T. Conran, S. O. Conran.

CONRAN, Sir Terence (Orby), Kt 1983; RDI 2010; Chairman: The Conran Shop Ltd, 1976–2012; Conran Ltd, since 1990; Conran Holdings Ltd, since 1993; Conran & Partners (formerly C. D. Partnership), since 1993; *b* 4 Oct. 1931; *m*; two *s*; *m* 1963, Caroline Herbert (marr. diss. 1996); two *s* one *d*; *m* 2000, Vicki Davis. *Educ:* Bryanston, Dorset. Chm., Conran Holdings Ltd, 1965–68; Jt Chm., Ryman Conran Ltd, 1968–71; Chairman: Habitat Group Ltd, 1971–88; RSCG Conran Design (formerly Conran Design Group/Conran Associates), 1971–92; Habitat France SA, 1973–88; Conran Stores Inc., 1977–88; J. Hepworth & Son Ltd, 1981–83 (Dir, 1979–83); Habitat Mothercare Ltd, 1982–88; Jasper Conran Ltd, 1982–99; Heal & Sons Ltd, 1983–87; Richard Shops, 1983–87; Storehouse plc, 1986–90 (Chief Exec., 1986–88; non-exec. Dir, 1990); Butlers Wharf Ltd, 1984–90; Bibendum Restaurant Ltd, 1986–; Benchmark Woodworking Ltd, 1989–; Blue Print Café Ltd, 1989–2006; Conran

Shop Holdings Ltd, 1990–; Le Pont de La Tour Ltd, 1991–2006; Conran Shop SA, 1991–; Butlers Wharf Chop House Ltd, 1993–2006; Quaglino's Restaurant Ltd, 1991–2006; Bluebird Store Ltd, 1994–2006; Conran Restaurants Ltd, 1994; Mezzo Ltd, 1995–2006; Conran Shop Marylebone, 1995–; Gustavino's Inc., 1997–; Conran Collection Ltd, 1997–; Conran Shop Manhattan Inc., 1997–; Coq d'Argent Ltd, 1997–2006; Orrery Restaurant Ltd, 1997–2006; The Great Eastern Hotel Co. Ltd, 1997–2006; Sartoria Restaurant Ltd, 1997–2006; Zinc Bar & Grill Ltd, 1997–2005; Atlantic Blue SNC, 1998–; Conran Finance Ltd, 1998–; Almeida Restaurant Ltd, 2001–; Boundary Hotel, 2009–; Director: Conran Ink Ltd, 1969–; The Neal Street Restaurant, 1972–89; Conran Octopus, 1983–98; Bhs plc, 1986–88; Savacentre Ltd, 1986–88; Michelin House Investment Co. Ltd, 1989–; Vice-Pres., FNAC, 1985–89. Launched: Conran Exclusive Design for Marks & Spencer, 2011; Paint by Conran, with Master Paintmakers, 2014. Estabd Conran Foundn for Design Educn and Research, 1981–. Mem., Royal Commn on Environmental Pollution, 1973–76. Member: Council, RCA, 1978–81, 1986– (Provost); Adv. Council, V&A Mus., 1979–83; Trustee: V&A Museum, 1984–90; Internat. Design (formerly Design) Museum, 1989– (Chm., 1992). Gov., Bryanston Sch., 1992–2005. RSA Presidential Medal for Design Management to Conran Group; RSA Presidential Award for Design Management to Habitat Designs Ltd, 1975; SIAD Medal, 1981; Assoc. for Business Sponsorship of the Arts and Daily Telegraph Award to Habitat Mothercare, 1982; RSA Bicentenary Medal, 1982; President's Award, D&AD, 1989. Hon. FRIBA 1984. Commandeur de l'Ordre des Arts et des Lettres (France), 1991. *Publications:* The House Book, 1974; The Kitchen Book, 1977; The Bedroom & Bathroom Book, 1978; (with Caroline Conran) The Cook Book, 1980, rev. edn as The Conran Cookbook, 1997; The New House Book, 1985; Conran Directory of Design, 1985; Plants at Home, 1986; The Soft Furnishings Book, 1986; Terence Conran's France, 1987; Terence Conran's DIY by Design, 1989; Terence Conran's Garden DIY, 1990; Toys and Children's Furniture, 1992; Terence Conran's Kitchen Book, 1993; Terence Conran's DIY Book, 1994; The Essential House Book, 1994; Terence Conran on Design, 1996; (with Dan Pearson) The Essential Garden Book, 1998; Easy Living, 1999; Chef's Garden, 1999; Terence Conran on Restaurants, 2000; Terence Conran on London, 2000; Terence Conran on Small Spaces, 2001; Q & A: a sort of autobiography, 2001; Kitchens: the hub of the home, 2002; Classic Conran, 2003; Eco House Book, 2009. *Recreations:* gardening, cooking, cigar smoking. *Address:* 22 Shad Thames, SE1 2YU. *T:* (020) 7378 1161, *Fax:* (020) 7403 4309.

See also J. A. T. Conran, S. O. Conran.

CONROY, Paul Martin; music consultant; Chief Executive Officer, Adventures in Music Ltd, since 2002; *b* Surbiton, 14 June 1949; *s* of late D. and M. Conroy; *m* 1st, 1980, Maxine Felstead (marr. diss. 1989); one *s*; 2nd, 1993, Katie Rennie; one *d*. *Educ:* John Fisher Sch., Purley; Ewell Technical Coll.; Newman Coll., Birmingham. Has worked in various areas of music business, 1971–: agent: Terry King Associates, 1971–73; Charisma Artistes, 1973–75; Manager, Kursaal Flyers, 1975–77; Gen. Manager, Stiff Records, 1977–83; Man. Dir, US Div., WEA Records, 1983–89; President: Chrysalis Records, 1989–92; Virgin Records UK Ltd, 1992–2002. Dir, Matey Boys Prodns Ltd, 2007–. Chm., BRIT Awards, 1998, 1999, 2000. Mem. Cttee, Mus. of Childhood, Bethnal Green, 2004–10. Patron, Tech Music Sch., Acton, 2009–. President's Award, Country Music Assoc. of USA, 1987. *Recreations:* cycling, supporting Chelsea, cricket, antique collecting. *E:* paul@adventuresin-music.com.

CONRY, Rt Rev. Kieran Thomas; Bishop of Arundel and Brighton, (RC), 2001–14; *b* 1 Feb. 1951. *Educ:* Cotton Coll., N Staffs; Ven. English Coll., Rome; Gregorian Univ., Rome (PhB, STB). Ordained 1975; Teacher, Cotton Coll., 1976–80; Private Sec. to Apostolic Delegate to the Court of St James's, 1980–88; Parish Priest, Leek, 1988–90; Administrator, St Chad's Cathedral, 1990–94; Dir, Catholic Media Office, 1994–2001; Parish Priest, St Austin's, Stafford, 2001. Ecumenical Associate, Guildford Cath., 2013–. Mem., 1988–93, Vice-Chm., 1992–93, Nat. Conf. of Priests; Chm., Birmingham City Centre Churches, 1992–93.

CONS, Sir Derek, Kt 1990; SPMB; President, Court of Appeal, Brunei, 2003–06; *b* 15 July 1928; *s* of Alfred Henry Cons and Elsie Margaret (*née* Neville); *m* 1952, Mary Roberta Upton Wilkes. *Educ:* Rutlish; Birmingham Univ. (LLB (Hons)). Called to Bar, Gray's Inn, 1953. RASC (2nd Lieut), 1946–48. Hong Kong: Magistrate, 1955–62, Principal Magistrate, 1962–66; District Judge, 1966–72; Judge of Supreme Court, 1972–80, Justice of Appeal, 1980–86, Vice Pres., Court of Appeal, 1986–93; Comr of the Supreme Court, Brunei, 1974–2003; Justice of Appeal, Bermuda, 1994–2002; Mem., Court of Final Appeal, Hong Kong, 1997–2006. SPMB (Negara Brunei Darussalam), 2003. *Recreation:* walking. *Address:* Mulberry Mews, Church Street, Fordingbridge, Hants SP6 1BE; RS2, Rosalp, 1972 Anzere, Switzerland. *Club:* Bramshaw Golf (Hants).

CONSIDINE, Craig Anthony; Headmaster, Millfield School, since 2008; *b* Traralgon, Australia, 18 June 1959; *s* of Francis John and Pamela Joy Considine; *m* 1991, Penelope; one *s* four *d*. *Educ:* Royal Melbourne Inst. of Technol. (BASc); Melbourne Univ. (DipEd); Charles Sturt Univ. (MEd). Redden Coll., 1981–83; Geelong Coll., 1984–99; Hd of Boarding, Scotch Oakburn Coll., 1999–2000; Dir, Co Curriculum, Geelong GS, 2001–03; Headmaster, Wanganui Collegiate Sch., 2004–08. *Recreations:* golf, restaurants. *Address:* Springbok, Keens Elm Lane, Street, Som BA16 0ST. *T:* (01458) 444402. *E:* headmaster@millfieldschool.com.

CONSTABLE, Adam Michael; QC 2011; a Recorder, since 2010; *b* Croydon, 26 Jan. 1973; *s* of Paul Constable and Katrina Constable; *m* 1999, Lucy (*née* Rutherford); three *d*. *Educ:* Trinity Sch., Croydon; Balliol Coll., Oxford (BA 1st cl. Juris.; MA). Called to the Bar, Inner Temple, 1995, Bencher, 2012; Treasury Counsel, 2002–07. Chm., Putney Common Assoc., 2012–. Chm., Bd of Govs, Fairley House Sch., 2012–. Co-Editor, Construction Law Reports, 2010–. *Publications:* (ed) Keating on JCT Contracts, 2006; Building Defects, 2006; Construction Claims, 2007; Keating on NEC; (ed) Keating on Offshore Construction and Marine Engineering, 2015. *Recreations:* family, Rugby, golf, magic. *Club:* Winchester House.

CONSTABLE, Sir Frederic S.; *see* Strickland-Constable.

CONSTABLE, John Robert; Principal Pianist, London Sinfonietta, since 1968; Principal Harpsichordist, Academy of St Martin in the Fields, since 1984; Professor, Royal College of Music, since 1984; *b* 5 Oct. 1934; *s* of Ernest Charles William Constable and May Jane Constable (*née* Rippin); *m* 1956, Kate Ingham; two *d*. *Educ:* Leighton Park Sch., Reading; Royal Acad. of Music (pupil of Harold Craxton; LRAM and Recital Dip.; FRAM 1986). Pianist, piano accompanist and harpsichordist, music from medieval and baroque to modern; repetiteur, Royal Opera House, 1960–72; concerts at Wigmore Hall, Queen Elizabeth Hall, Royal Opera House and in major European, USA and Japanese cities; numerous TV and radio appearances; many records incl. lieder, chansons, Spanish songs, Victorian ballads, song cycles, chamber music, harpsichord concertos and harpsichord continuo in operas. *Recreations:* travel, looking at paintings, watching cricket. *Address:* 13 Denbigh Terrace, W11 2QJ. *T:* (020) 7229 4603.

CONSTABLE, Neil Ernest Alexander; Chief Executive, Shakespeare's Globe, since 2010; *b* Frimley, 15 Aug. 1965; *s* of Ernest and Patricia Constable; civil partnership 2010, Christopher Martin. *Educ:* Clifton Coll., Bristol; Guildhall Sch. of Music and Drama (FGS (FGSM 1985)). Royal Shakespeare Company: stage and co. manager, 1985–96; London Manager, 1997–2000; Gen. Adminr, 2000–02; Exec. Dir, Almeida Th., 2003–10. Governor: GSMD, 2008–; Clifton Coll., 2010–. Mem., Soc. of London Theatres, 2002–. Trustee: Shakespeare's Birthplace, 2012–; Royal Theatrical Support Trust, 2013–. CCMI 2012. *Recreations:* gardening, vintage cars, 20th century architecture. *Address:* Shakespeare's Globe, 21 New Globe Walk, Bankside, SE1 9DT. *T:* (020) 7902 1440. *E:* neil.c@shakespearesglobe.com. *Club:* Soho House.

CONSTABLE, Paule; lighting designer; Associate Director, Royal National Theatre, since 2015 (Technical Associate, 2006–15); Associate: Lyric Theatre, Hammersmith, since 2005; New Adventures, since 2007; *b* 9 Nov. 1966; *d* of Paul and Lyn Constable; partner, Ian Richards; one *s* one *d*. *Educ:* Stamford High Sch.; Goldsmiths' Coll., Univ. of London (BA Drama and English; Hon. Fellow, 2008). Productions for: RNT; Glyndebourne; Royal Opera House; ENO; RSC; Donmar Th.; productions include: Street of Crocodiles, 1993, The 3 Lives of Lucie Cabrol, 1995, Théâtre de Complicité; His Dark Materials, RNT, 2005 (Olivier Award for Best Lighting Design, 2005); Don Carlos, Gielgud, 2005 (Olivier Award for Best Lighting Design, 2006); Evita, Adelphi, 2006; Satyagraha, ENO, 2007; St Joan, RNT, 2007; Warhorse, RNT, 2007, Broadway, 2011 (Tony Award for Best Lighting); Othello, Donmar Warehouse, 2007; Ivanov, Wyndham's, 2008; Chalk Garden, Donmar, 2008 (Olivier Award for Best Lighting Design, 2009); Oliver, Drury Lane, 2009; Phedre, RNT, 2009; Billy Budd, Glyndebourne, 2010; Meistersinger, Glyndebourne, 2011; Anna Bolena, Don Giovanni, Metropolitan Opera, 2011; The Curious Incident of the Dog in the Night-Time, RNT, 2012 (White Light Award for Best Lighting Design, Olivier Awards, 2013); Britten Canticles, Aldeburgh and ROH, 2013; The Light Princess, RNT, 2013; Wolf Hall, RSC, 2014; for BBC: Carmen, 2003; Magic Flute, 2003; Giulio Cesare, 2005; Marriage of Figaro, 2006; Così Fan Tutti, 2006. Founder, Women in Stage Entertainment, 2011–. Mem., Assoc. Lighting Designers. Hon. Fellow: Rose Bruford Coll., 2010; Central Sch. of Speech and Drama, 2010. Hospital Award for Contribn to Theatre, Hosp. Club, 2006. *Recreations:* surfing, cycling, walking, digging the allotment, being with the kids. *Address:* c/o Mel Kenyon, Casarotto Ramsay and Associates, Waverley House, 7–12 Noel Street, W1F 8GQ. *T:* (020) 7287 4450.

CONSTANCE, Angela; Member (SNP) Almond Valley, Scottish Parliament, since 2011 (Livingston, 2007–11); Cabinet Secretary for Education and Lifelong Learning, since 2014; *b* 15 July 1970; *d* of Sonny Constance and Mary (*née* Colquhoun); *m* 2000, Garry Knox; one *s*. *Educ:* Univ. of Glasgow (MA Soc. Sci.); Univ. of Stirling (MSocSc Soc. Work). Social Worker (Criminal Justice): Clackmannanshire Council, 1998; Perth and Kinross Council, 1999; Social Worker (Mental Health), S Lanarks Council, 2001–07. Mem. (SNP), W Lothian Council, 1997–2007. Minister for Skills and Lifelong Learning, 2010–11, for Children and Young People, 2011, for Youth Employment, 2011–14, Scottish Parlt. *Recreations:* jogging, eating out, cinema. *Address:* Scottish Parliament, Edinburgh EH99 1SP. *T:* (0131) 348 6751. *E:* angela.constance.msp@scottish.parliament.uk.

CONSTÂNCIO, Vítor Manuel Ribeiro; Vice-President, European Central Bank, since 2010 (Member, Governing Council, 2000–09); *b* Lisbon, Portugal, 12 Oct. 1943. *Educ:* Technical Univ. of Lisbon (Econs degree 1965); Univ. of Bristol (postgrad. studies). Asst Prof. of Econs, Technical Univ. of Lisbon, 1965–73; Hd of Dept, Econ. Models and Global Programming, Centre of Planning Studies, and Prof., Instituto Superior do Serviço Social, 1972–73; Prof., Catholic Univ. of Portugal, 1980–81. Banco de Portugal: Hd, Res. Dept, 1975; Dep. Gov., 1977, 1979, 1981–84; Gov., 1985–86; Sen Advr, 1989–94; Exec. Dir, Banco Português de Investimento, 1995–2000; Gov., Banco de Portugal, 2000–10. MP, Portugal, 1976, 1980–81, 1987–88. Sec. of State, Planning, 1974–75, Budget and Planning, 1976; Minister of Finance, 1978. President: Commn for Eur. Integration, 1977, 1979; Parly Commn on Eur. Affairs, 1980–81; Portuguese Sect., Eur. Movement, 1980–81. Mem., Conselho de Estado, 1995–99. Non-exec. Dir, EDP, 1998–2000. Guest Prof., Univ. Nova de Lisbon, 1982–84; Guest Prof. of Econs, Instituto Superior de Economia e Gestão, Technical Univ. of Lisbon, 1989–2009. *Address:* Directorate General of Communications and Language Services, Press and Information Division, European Central Bank, Sonnemannstrasse 20, 60314 Frankfurt am Main, Germany. *T:* (69) 13447455, *Fax:* (69) 13447404. *E:* info@ecb.europa.eu.

CONSTANT, Charles Kenvyn ff.; *see* ffrench-Constant.

CONSTANTINE, David Peter, MBE 2010; DL; Co-Founder and President (formerly Executive Officer), Motivation Charitable Trust, since 1992; *b* 14 July 1960; *s* of William Geoffrey Constantine and Jean Virginia Constantine. *Educ:* Writtle Agricl Coll. (DipAgr 1982); Oxford Brookes Univ. (BSc Hons 1986); Royal Coll. of Art (MDes 1990; Hon. FRCA 1999; Sen. FRCA 2008). Programmer, IBM, 1986–88. Founded Motivation to help people with mobility disabilities, creating sustainable projects in low-income, countries. Mem., Internat. Cttee, Leonard Cheshire, 1997–2006; Trustee and Director: Design Mus., 1999–; Calvert Trust, Exmoor, 2004–10; Arnolfini Gall., Bristol, 2007–14. DL City of Bristol, 2014. Hon. FRSA and Bicentenary Medal for Design, RSA, 2010. Hon. MA Bristol, 2003; DUniv Oxford Brookes, 2006; Hon. Dr Essex, 2014. *Recreations:* photography, travel, cinema, modern history, kite flying, rowing. *Address:* Motivation, Brockley Academy, Brockley Lane, Backwell, Bristol BS48 4AQ. *T:* (01275) 464012. *E:* info@motivation.org.uk.

CONTE-HELM, Marie Theresa, (Mrs A. W. Purdue), OBE 2011; Executive Director, UK-Japan 21st Century Group, since 2011; *b* 13 Nov. 1949; *d* of Angelo and Santa Conte; *m* 1979, Arthur William Purdue; one *d*. *Educ:* CUNY (BA Art History 1971); East-West Center, Univ. of Hawaii (MA Asian Art 1973). Cultural Officer, Embassy of Japan, 1975–79; Lectr in Art History, Sunderland Poly., 1979–86; Head of Japanese Studies Div., and Reader in Japanese Studies, Sunderland Poly., subseq. Univ. of Sunderland, 1986–94; Reader in Japanese Studies and Dir, East Asian Affairs, Univ. of Northumbria at Newcastle, 1994–99. Dir Gen., Daiwa Anglo-Japanese Foundn, 2000–11. Vis. Prof., Univ. of Northumbria at Newcastle, 1999–. Mem., Bd of Govs, Univ. for Creative Arts, 2011–. Commendation, Japanese Minister of Foreign Affairs, 2009. *Publications:* Japan and the North East of England: from 1862 to the present day, 1989 (trans. Japanese 1991); The Japanese and Europe: economic and cultural encounters, 1996; academic papers, articles and book reviews. *Recreations:* theatre, film, outdoor swimming, walking. *Address:* The Old Rectory, Allendale, near Hexham, Northumberland NE47 9DA. *T:* (01434) 683350; 176A Leighton Road, NW5 2RE. *E:* marie@conte-helm.co.uk.

CONTI, Most Rev. Mario Joseph; Archbishop of Glasgow, (RC), 2002–12, now Archbishop Emeritus; *b* Elgin, Moray, 20 March 1934; *s* of Louis Joseph Conti and Josephine Quintilia Panicali. *Educ:* St Marie's Convent School and Springfield, Elgin; Blairs Coll., Aberdeen; Pontifical Gregorian Univ. (Scots College), Rome. PhL 1955, STL 1959. Ordained, Rome, 1958; Curate, St Mary's Cathedral, Aberdeen, 1959–62; Parish Priest, St Joachim's, Wick and St Anne's, Thurso (joint charge), 1962–77; Bishop of Aberdeen, 1977–2002. Chairman: Scottish Catholic Heritage Commn, 1980–2014; Commn for the Pastoral Care of Migrant Workers and Tourists (incl. Apostleship of the Sea, Scotland), 1978–85; Pres.-Treasurer, Scottish Catholic Internat. Aid Fund, 1978–85; Pres., National Liturgy Commn, 1981–85; Scottish Mem., Episcopal Bd, Internat. Commn for English in the Liturgy, 1978–87; Mem., Bishops' Jt Bio-ethics Cttee (formerly Cttee for Bio-ethical Issues), 1982–2012; Catholic Bishops' Conference of Scotland: Pres., Commn for Christian Doctrine and Unity, 1985–2012; Vice Pres., 2002–12; Chair, Cttee for Inter-religious Dialogue, 2006–; Consultor-Mem., Secretariat, later Council, for Promotion of Christian Unity (Rome), 1984–2014; Convener, Action of Churches Together in Scotland, 1990–93; Co-moderator, Jt Working Gp, WCC and RC Church, 1996–2006; Hd, Catholic Delegn, 8th Assembly of WCC, Harare, 1998; Member: Pontifical Commn for Cultural Heritage of the Church, Rome, 1994–2004; Jt Commn on Doctrine (RC Church and C of S), 2000–; Historic Bldgs

Council of Scotland, 2000–03. Conventual Chaplain *ad honorem*, British Assoc., SMO Malta, 1991– (Principal Chaplain, 1995–2000, 2005–15). FRSE 1995. Hon. Mem., Merchants' House of Glasgow, 2012. Hon. DD: Aberdeen, 1989; Glasgow, 2010. KCHS 1989. Commendatore, Order of Merit of the Italian Republic, 1981; Grande Ufficiale, Ordine della Stella della Solidarietà Italiana, 2007. *Publications:* Oh Help!: the making of an Archbishop, 2003; numerous articles in defence of the tradition of faith and Christian morality. *Recreations:* music, art, book browsing, TV, travel, swimming. *Address:* 40 Newlands Road, Glasgow G43 2JD.

CONTI, Tom; actor, since 1960; director; *b* Scotland, 1942; *m* Kara Wilson; one *d*. London appearances include: Savages, Royal Court and Comedy, 1973; Other People, The Black and White Minstrels, Hampstead; The Devil's Disciple, RSC Aldwych, 1976; Whose Life is it Anyway?, Mermaid and Savoy, 1978, NY 1979 (SWET Award for Best Actor in a new play, Variety Club of GB Award for Best Stage Actor, 1978, Tony Award for Best Actor, 1979); They're Playing Our Song, Shaftesbury, 1980; Romantic Comedy, Apollo, 1983; An Italian Straw Hat, Shaftesbury, 1986; Otherwise Engaged (also dir), Theatre Royal, Windsor, 1990; The Ride Down Mount Morgan, Wyndham's, 1991; Present Laughter (also dir), Globe, 1993; Chapter Two, Gielgud, 1996; Jesus, My Boy, Apollo, 1998; Jeffrey Bernard is Unwell, Garrick, 2006; Romantic Comedy (also dir), UK tour, 2007; Wife After Death, UK tour, 2010; Smash, Menier Chocolate Factory, 2011; Rough Justice, UK tour, 2012; Twelve Angry Men, Garrick, 2014, UK tour, 2015; *directed:* Last Licks, Broadway, 1979; Before the Party, Oxford Playhouse and Queen's, 1980; The Housekeeper, Apollo, 1982; Treats, Hampstead, 1989; *films include:* Galileo, Flame, 1974; Eclipse, 1975; Full Circle, The Duellists, 1977; The Wall, 1980; Merry Christmas, Mr Lawrence, 1983; Reuben, Reuben, 1983; American Dreamer, 1985; Miracles, 1985; Saving Grace, 1986; Heavenly Pursuits, 1987; Beyond Therapy, 1987; The Dumb Waiter (USA); White Roses; Shirley Valentine, 1989; Two Brothers Running; Someone Else's America, 1997; Sub Down, 1997; Out of Control, 1997; Something To Believe In, 1997; Don't Go Breaking My Heart, 1998; A Closed Book, 2010; The Tempest, 2010; Streetdance 2, 2012; City Slackers, 2012; The Dark Knight Rises, 2012; *television appearances include:* Madame Bovary, The Norman Conquests, Glittering Prizes, The Beate Klarsfeld Story, Fatal Dosage, The Quick and the Dead, Blade on the Feather, Wright Verdicts, Friends, The Cosby Show, I Was a Rat, Deadline, Donovan; Four Seasons, Ten Days to War, 2008. *Publications:* The Doctor (novel), 2004. *Club:* Garrick.

CONTRERAS, Dame (Carmen) Marcela, DBE 2007; MD; FRCP, FRCPE, FRCPath; Professor of Transfusion Medicine, UCL Medical School (formerly Royal Free and University College Medical School), University College London, 1998; Director, Diagnostics, Development and Research, National Blood Service, 1999–2007; *b* 4 Jan. 1942; *d* of Dr Juan Eduardo Contreras and Elena Mireya (*née* Arriagada); *m* 1968, Dr Roberto Jaime Guiloff (marr. diss. 1997); one *s* one *d*. *Educ:* Dunalastair British Sch. for Girls, Santiago; Sch. of Medicine, Univ. of Chile (BSc 1963; LMed 1967; MD 1972). MRCPath 1988, FRCPath 1997; FRCPE 1992; FRCP 1998. British Council Schol., RPMS and MRC Blood Gp Unit, London, 1972–74; SSO, 1974–76, Med. Asst in Blood Transfusion, 1976–78, N London Blood Transfusion Centre, Edgware; Sen. Registrar in Haematology, St Mary's Hosp., London, 1978–80; Dep. Dir, 1980–84, Chief Exec. and Med. Dir, 1984–95, N London Blood Transfusion Centre; Exec. Dir, London and SE Zone, Nat. Blood Service, 1995–99. Vis. Prof., Faculty of Applied Scis, UWE, 2004–. Hon. Mem., MRC Blood Gp Unit, 1987–95. President: Internat. Soc. of Blood Transfusion, 1996–98; British Blood Transfusion Soc., 2001–03. Review Editor, Vox Sanguinis, 1989–96, 2003– (Ed.-in-Chief, 1996–2003); Member, Editorial Board: Transfusion Medicine, 1990–; Transfusion Medicine Reviews, 1993–; Blood Reviews, 1995–; Transfusion Alternatives in Transfusion Medicine, 1999–. FMedSci 2003. *Publications:* (jtly) Blood Transfusion in Clinical Medicine, 8th edn 1987, 10th edn 1997; ABC of Transfusion, 1990, 3rd edn 1998; Blood Transfusion: the impact of new technologies, 1990; contrib. numerous papers and chapters in the field of transfusion medicine. *Recreations:* theatre, travelling, opera, horse riding, walking, training in developing countries.

CONVILLE, Clare Benedicta; literary agent; Director, Conville & Walsh, since 2000; *b* London, 14 Oct. 1959; *d* of David Henry Conville, *qv*, and late Jean Margaret Bury; two *s* one *d*. *Educ:* Garden House; Bute House; Cranbourne Chase Sch. for Girls; Westminster Sch.; Bristol Univ. (BA Hons). Publicity Officer, Penguin Books, 1986–87; an editor, Random House, 1987–93; agent, AP Watt, 1993–2000. *Publications:* (jtly) Dangerous Women: a guide to modern life, 2011. *Recreations:* organising arts festivals, going to prison, throwing poetry parties too big for my house. *Address:* Conville & Walsh, 5th Floor, Haymarket House, 28–29 Haymarket, SW1Y 4SP. *Clubs:* Academy, Quo Vadis Upstairs, Chelsea Arts.

CONVILLE, David Henry, OBE 1983; theatre director and producer; *b* 4 June 1929; *s* of Lt Col Leopold Henry George Conville, CBE and Katherine Mary Conville; *m* 1st, 1956, Jean Margaret Bury (*d* 1967); one *d*; 2nd, 1970, Philippa Falcke (*d* 1999); one *s*. *Educ:* Marlborough Coll.; St John's Coll., Oxford; RADA (Dip.). Commnd Royal W African Frontier Force, Royal Welch Fusiliers, 1948–49. *Actor:* Ipswich Rep. Co., 1952; Colchester Rep. Co., 1953; Dial M for Murder, Dundee Rep. Co. (tour), 1954; King Lear and Much Ado About Nothing (European, London and provincial tour), 1955, Titus Andronicus (European and London tour), 1957, Stratford Meml Theatre Co.; Folkestone and Richmond Rep. Cos, and TV, 1956; Dry Rot, Brian Rix Co. (London and tour), 1957; The Reluctant Débutante, 1957, Not in the Book, 1959, tours with Jack Hulbert; Surgical Spirit, Granada TV, 1988–95; *producer:* provincial tours, then several West End prodns, 1959–61; Toad of Toad Hall, London, Dec.–Jan., 1960–84; founded New Shakespeare Co., Open Air Theatre, Regent's Park, 1962 (Chm., 1987–); prod./dir of more than 100 classical prodns, 1962–87; *writer: plays:* Chetwode, Sandy and Co., Orange Tree Theatre, 1985; Wind in the Willows, London, 1986–87, Chichester, 1989; Look Here Old Son, BBC Radio, 1987; Obituaries, King's Head Theatre and BBC 1, 1989; Births, King's Head Theatre, 1990. Pres., SWET, 1975–76, 1982. Coronation Medal, 1953. *Publications:* The Park: the story of the Open Air Theatre, 2007. *Recreations:* Real tennis, walking, travel. *Address:* Briar Cottage, Holwell, Sherborne, Dorset DT9 5LN. *T:* (01963) 23022. *Clubs:* Garrick; Royal Tennis Court, Canford Tennis.

See also C. B. Conville.

CONWAY, Christopher John; Chief Executive, 1993–98, Chairman, 1994–98, Digital Equipment Co. Ltd; *b* 3 Nov. 1944; *s* of John Francis Conway and Monica Conway (*née* Hawksworth); *m* 1969, Gillian May Burrow; two *s* one *d*. *Educ:* Univ. of S Africa (BA Hons 1967). IBM (UK) Ltd, 1969–93: Dir, Financial Services, 1992–93. Non-executive Director: Brammer plc, 1997–2006; Detica plc, 2000–08 (Chm., 2001–08); Kofax (formerly DICOM) plc, 2004–. *Recreations:* golf, tennis, music.

CONWAY, (David) Martin; President, Selly Oak Colleges, Birmingham, 1986–97; *b* 22 Aug. 1935; *s* of Geoffrey S. and Dr Elsie Conway; *m* 1962, Ruth, *d* of Rev. Richard Daniel; one *s* two *d*. *Educ:* Sedbergh Sch.; Gonville and Caius Coll., Cambridge (BA, MA); and by friends and fellow Christians in many different cultures. Internat. Sec., SCM of GB and Ire., 1958–61; Study Sec., World Student Christian Fedn, Geneva, 1961–67; Sec. for Chaplaincies in Higher Educn, Gen. Synod of C of E, 1967–70; Publications Sec., WCC, 1970–74; Asst Gen. Sec. for Ecumenical Affairs, BCC, 1974–83; Dir, Oxford Inst. for Church and Society, and Tutor, Ripon Coll., Cuddesdon, Oxford, 1983–86. Simultaneous interpreter at assemblies and major world confs of WCC, 1961–; Consultant, Faith and Order Commn, WCC, 1971–82; Consultant, 1974–83, and Mem., 1986–91, C of E Bd for Mission and Unity. Chairman: Bd for Social Responsibility, Dio. of Oxford, 2000–10; Soc. of Ecumenical Studies, 2001–10; Trustees, Centennial Fund, World Student Christian Fedn, 2009–11. DLitt Lambeth, 1994. Editor: The Ecumenical Review, 1972–74; Christians Together, 1983–91; Oxford Papers on Contemporary Society, 1984–86. *Publications:* The Undivided Vision, 1966; (ed) University Chaplain?, 1969; The Christian Enterprise in Higher Education, 1971; Seeing Education Whole, 1971; Look Listen Care, 1983; That's When the Body Works, 1991; Journeying Together Towards Jubilee, 1999; Introducing the World Council of Churches, 2001; World Christianity in the 20th Century, 2 vols, 2008; contribs to Student World, New Christian, Audenshaw Papers, Internat. Rev. of Mission, etc. *Recreations:* other people—family, friends, colleagues; travel, music. *Address:* 303 Cowley Road, Oxford OX4 2AQ. *T:* (01865) 723085.

CONWAY, Derek Leslie, TD 1990; *b* 15 Feb. 1953; *s* of Leslie and Florence Conway; *m* 1980, Colette Elizabeth Mary (*née* Lamb); two *s* one *d*. *Educ:* Beacon Hill Boys' School. Principal Organiser, Action Research for the Crippled Child, 1974–83; Chief Exec., Cats Protection League, 1998–2003. Borough Councillor and Dep. Leader of the Opposition, Gateshead Metropolitan Borough Council, 1974–78; Mem., Tyne and Wear Metropolitan County Council, 1977–83 (Leader, 1979–82); Member Board: Washington Develt Corp., 1979–83; North of England Develt Council, 1979–83; Newcastle Airport, 1980–83; Northern Arts, 1980–83. Non-exec. Dir, Foreign & Colonial Gp Investment Fund, 1997–2001. MP (C) Shrewsbury and Atcham, 1983–97; contested (C) same seat, 1997; MP Old Bexley and Sidcup, 2001–10 (C, 2001–08; Ind C, 2008–10). PPS to Minister of State: Welsh Office, 1988–91; Dept of Employment, 1992–93; an Asst Govt Whip, 1993–94; a Lord Comr of HM Treasury (Govt Whip), 1994–96; Vice Chamberlain of HM Household, 1996–97. Mem., Speaker's Panel of Chairmen, 2001–08; Member, Select Committee: on Agric., 1987; on Transport, 1987–88; on Armed Forces Discipline, 1991; Liaison, 2001–08; Finance and Services, 2001–08; on Defence, 2005–07; Chm., Select Cttee on Accommodation and Works, 2001–08. Chairman: British-Morocco Parly Gp, 1984–92, 2001–10; British-Venezuelan Gp, 1987–93; Mem. Exec., British American Parly Gp, 2001–08; Vice Chm., Cons. backbench Defence Cttee, 1991–97. Treas., IPU, 2001–08 (Mem. Exec. Cttee, 1986–97; Vice-Chm., British Gp, 1992–93); Vice-Chm., CPA, 2004–08. Member, Conservative Party Committees: Nat. Exec. Cttee, 1971–81; Nat. Gen. Purposes Cttee, 1972–74; Nat. Local Govt Cttee, 1979–83; Nat. Vice-Chm., Young Conservatives, 1972–74. Mem. Exec. Cttee, British Venezuela Soc., 1987–93. Crown Estates Paving Comr, 1994–96. Commnd RMA Sandhurst into Royal Regt of Fusiliers; Major, 5th Bn (TA) Light Infantry. MInstD. Kt Comdr, Royal Order of Al-Alaoui (Morocco), 2004. *Recreation:* historical fiction.

CONWAY, Donald Hugh Stevenson; a Judge of the Upper Tribunal (Immigration and Asylum Chamber), since 2010, and Resident Judge of the First-tier Tribunal, since 2011; *b* Paisley, 31 Oct. 1954; *s* of Dr Hugh Conway, FRCP and Dr Lilian Conway (*née* Donald); *m* 1998, Isabella Sutherland; two *s*. *Educ:* Paisley Grammar Sch.; Glasgow Acad.; Cardonald Coll.; Univ. of Edinburgh (BA 1976; LLB 1978); Univ. of Glasgow (MPhil 1992). Admitted solicitor, 1980, NP, 1981; Reporter, Children's Panel, Glasgow, 1980–83; Procurator Fiscal Depute, Hamilton, Kilmarnock, Glasgow, 1983–89; admitted Faculty of Advocates, 1991; in practice as an advocate, 1991–96; Immigration Adjudicator, pt-time, 1994–96, full-time, 1996–2003; Regl Immigration Adjudicator, N Shields, 2003–05; Resident Senior Immigration Judge: N Shields, 2005–07; Manchester, 2007–11; Resident Judge, Hatton Cross, 2011–. *Recreations:* books, dogs, walking. *Address:* Upper Tribunal (Immigration and Asylum Chamber), York House, 2/3 Dukes Green Avenue, Feltham, Middx TW14 0LR. *T:* (020) 8831 3545. *E:* donald.conway@judiciary.gsi.gov.uk.

CONWAY, Edmund Alexander; Economics Editor, Sky News, since 2011; *b* London, 10 Nov. 1979; *s* of Cyril and Caroline Conway. *Educ:* Westminster Cathedral Choir Sch.; Oratory Sch.; Pembroke Coll., Oxford (BA English); Harvard Univ. (Fulbright Alistair Cooke Schol.; Shorenstein Schol.; MPA 2011). Reporter, Daily Telegraph, 2003–05; Econs Corresp., Daily Mail, 2005–06; Econs Ed., Daily Telegraph and Sunday Telegraph, 2006–10. Gov., NIESR, 2014–. *Publications:* 50 Economics Ideas You Really Need to Know, 2009; The Summit, 2014. *Recreations:* reading economic history, DJing (tech house, disco). *Address:* Sky News, Four Millbank, SW1P 3JA. *E:* ed.conway@bskyb.com.

CONWAY, Sir Gordon (Richard), KCMG 2005; FRS 2004; FRSB; Professor of International Development, Imperial College, London, since 2005; Chief Scientific Adviser, Department for International Development, 2005–09; *b* 6 July 1938; *s* of Cyril Conway and Thelma (*née* Goodwin); *m* 1965, Susan Mary Mumford; one *s* two *d*. *Educ:* Kingston Grammar Sch.; Kingston Polytechnic; University Coll. of North Wales, Bangor (BSc 1959). DipAgricSci, Cambridge, 1960; DTA University Coll. of West Indies, Trinidad, 1961; PhD Univ. of California, Davis, 1969; FIBiol 1978, Hon. FRSB (Hon. FIBiol 2001). Research Officer (Entomology), Agric. Res. Centre, State of Sabah, Malaysia, 1961–66; Statistician, Inst. Ecology, Univ. of California, Davis, 1966–69; Imperial College, London: Res. Fellow and Lectr, Dept of Zoology and Applied Entomology, 1970–76; Dir, 1977–80, Chm., 1980–86, Centre for Envmtl Technol.; Reader in Environmental Management, Univ. of London, 1976–80; Prof. of Environmental Technol., 1980–88; Rep. for India, Nepal and Sri Lanka, Ford Foundn, 1989–92; Vice-Chancellor, 1992–98, Emeritus Prof., 2003–, Univ. of Sussex. Pres., Rockefeller Foundn, 1998–2004. Vis. Prof., Imperial Coll., 1989–2004. Pres., RGS, 2006–09. Director: Sustainable Agric. Prog., Internat. Inst. for Envmt and Develt, 1986–88; BOC Foundn, 1994–97; Sussex Enterprise, 1995–98; RSA, 2005–06; African Agricl Technol. Foundn, 2009–; Lawes Agricl Trust, 2011–. Mem., Royal Commn on Environmental Pollution, 1984–88. Chm. Bd, Inst. Develt Studies, 1992–98; Member: Internat. Inst. for Envmt and Develt, 1993–97; Bd, Internat. Food Policy Res. Inst., Washington, 1994–97; Council, World Food Prize, 2002–; Bd, Meridian Inst., 2013–; Kirkhouse Trust, 2013–. Chairman: Runnymede Trust Commn on Muslims in Britain, 1996–97; Living Cities (formerly Nat. Community Develt Initiative), 2000–04; Visiting Arts, 2004–09; UK Collaborative on Develt Scis, 2007–09; Montpellier Panel, 2010–. DL E Sussex, 2006. FCGI 2006; Fellow, Amer. Acad. of Arts and Scis, 2000; Hon. FREng 2007. Hon. Fellow, Univ. of Wales, Bangor, 1997. Hon. LLD Sussex, 1998; Hon. DSc: W Indies, 1999; Brighton, 2001; DUniv Open, 2004. *Publications:* Pest and Pathogen Control, 1984; (jtly) After the Green Revolution, 1990; (jtly) Unwelcome Harvest, 1991; Doubly Green Revolution: food for all in the 21st century, 1997; (jtly) Science and Innovation for Development, 2010; One Billion Hungry: can we feed the world?, 2012; papers and reports on agricl ecology. *Recreations:* travel, movies, music. *Address:* Imperial College, SW7 1NA. *Club:* Reform.

CONWAY, James L.; General Director, English Touring Opera, since 2002; *b* Granby, Quebec, Canada, 10 Feb. 1956; *s* of Frederick L. Conway and Catherine P. McBride; partner, 2006, Jonathan Peter Kenny. *Educ:* Univ. of Toronto (BA Hons; Gold Medallist in Philosophy; MA Hons English); University Coll. Dublin (DipEd); City Univ., London (MA Arts Policy/Mgt). Gen. Dir, Opera Th. Co., Dublin, 1987–2003. Opera Specialist, Arts Council Ireland, 2003–06. Hon. RCM. *Publications:* The Christians of Malabar, 1991. *Recreation:* music. *Address:* English Touring Opera, 63 Charterhouse Street, EC1M 6HJ. *T:* (020) 7833 2555. *E:* jconway@englishtouringopera.org.uk.

CONWAY, Prof. John Horton, FRS 1981; John von Neumann Professor of Mathematics, Princeton University, USA, 1986, now Emeritus. *Educ:* Gonville and Caius Coll., Cambridge (BA 1959; MA 1963; PhD 1964). Cambridge University: Lectr in Pure Maths, to 1973; Reader in Pure Mathematics and Mathematical Statistics, 1973–83; Prof. of Maths, 1983–87; Fellow: Sidney Sussex Coll., 1964–70; Gonville and Caius Coll., 1970–87. Hon. DSc Liverpool, 2001. Polya Prize, London Mathematical Soc., 1987; Frederic Esser Nemmers

Prize, Northwestern Univ., 1999; Steele Prize, AMS, 1999; Joseph Priestley Award, 2001. *Publications:* Regular Algebra and Finite Machines, 1971; On Numbers and Games, 1976; Atlas of Finite Groups, 1985; The Book of Numbers, 1996; The Sensual Quadratic Form, 1997. *Address:* Department of Mathematics, Princeton University, Fine Hall, Washington Road, Princeton, NJ 08544–1000, USA.

CONWAY, Martin; *see* Conway, D. M.

CONWAY, Peter; *see* Gautier-Smith, P. C.

CONWAY, Rt Rev. Stephen David; *see* Ely, Bishop of.

CONWAY MORRIS, Prof. Simon, PhD; FRS 1990; Professor of Evolutionary Palaeobiology, since 1995, and Fellow of St John's College, since 1987, Cambridge University; *b* 6 Nov. 1951; *s* of Richard Conway Morris and Barbara Louise Maxwell; *m* 1975, Zoë Helen James; two *s*. *Educ:* Univ. of Bristol (BSc Hons); Univ. of Cambridge (PhD). Research Fellow, St John's Coll., Cambridge, 1975–79; Lectr, Open Univ., 1979–83; Lectr in Palaeontology, 1983–91, Reader in Evolutionary Palaeobiology, 1991–95, Cambridge Univ. Gallagher Vis. Scientist, Univ. of Calgary, 1981; Nuffield Sci. Res. Fellowship, 1987–88; Merrill W. Haas Vis. Dist. Prof., Univ. of Kansas, 1988; Selby Fellow, Aust. Acad. of Scis, 1992; Cecil H. and Ida Green Vis. Prof., Univ. of British Columbia, 2008–. Member Council: Systematics Assoc., 1981–85; NERC, 1996–2002; Cambridge Philosophical Soc., 2014–. Royal Instn Christmas Lectr, 1996; Gifford Lectr, Univ. of Edinburgh, 2007. Hon. Fellow, Eur. Union of Geoscis, 1997. Hon. DPhil Uppsala, 1993; Hon. DSc Hull, 2008. Walcott Medal, Nat. Acad. of Scis, 1987; Charles Schuchert Award, Paleontol. Soc., 1989; George Gaylord Simpson Prize, Yale Univ., 1992; Lyell Medal, Geol Soc. of London, 1998; Kelvin Medal, Royal Philosophical Soc. of Glasgow, 2007; Ide and Luella Prize, Coll. of Sci., A&M Univ., Texas, 2007; William Bate Hardy Prize, Cambridge Philosophical Soc., 2010. *Publications:* The Crucible of Creation, 1998; Life's Solution, 2003; The Runes of Evolution, 2015; contribs to professional jls. *Recreations:* G. K. Chesterton, wine, punting. *Address:* Department of Earth Sciences, Downing Street, Cambridge CB2 3EQ. *T:* (01223) 333400.

CONYNGHAM, family name of **Marquess Conyngham**.

CONYNGHAM, 8th Marquess *cr* 1816; **Henry Vivian Pierpoint Conyngham;** *b* 23 May 1951; *s* of 7th Marquess Conyngham and Eileen Wren (*née* Newsam); *S* father, 2009; *m* 1st, 1971, Juliet Ann, *yr d* of Robert Kitson (marr. diss. 1985); one *s* one *d*; 2nd, 1985, Lady Iona Grimston, *yr d* of 6th Earl of Verulam; one *d*. *Educ:* Harrow; Harvard Univ. Irish Rep., 1976–78, Consultant, 1978–84, Sotheby's; Chairman: Slane Castle Ltd; Slane Castle Productions. Dir, CityArts (formerly Grapevine Arts Centre), Dublin. Columnist, Irish Daily Mirror, 2002–. *Heir: s* Earl of Mount Charles, *qv*. *Address:* Slane Castle, Co. Meath, Eire; Beau Parc House, Navan, Co. Meath, Eire. *Club:* Kildare Street and University (Dublin).

COODE-ADAMS, (John) Giles Selby, OBE 1998; DL; President, Royal Horticultural Society, 2008–10 (Member, Council, 2002–10); *b* 30 Aug. 1938; *s* of Geoffrey Coode-Adams and Cynthia Mildred Coode-Adams (*née* Selby-Bigge); *m* 1960, Sonia Elizabeth, *d* of Laurence Frederick York; one *s* one *d*. *Educ:* Eton. 2nd Lieut, 16/5 Queen's Royal Lancers, 1956–58. Joined L. Messel, 1959, Partner, 1967–86; Man. Dir, then Sen. Advr, Lehman Bros, 1986–99; Director: Guardian Media Gp plc, 1999–2008; Rathbone Bros plc, 1999–2008; Trades Media Gp plc, 2003–07. Chm., Westonbirt and Bedgebury Adv. Cttee, Forestry Commn, 2006–; Mem., Adv. Cttee, Hillier Arboretum, 2010–. Chief Exec., Royal Botanic Gdns Kew Foundn, 1991–97 (Trustee, 2011–); Mem., Gdns Cttee, English Heritage, 1997–2002. Former Mem. Council, Univ. of Essex. High Sheriff, 2000–01, DL, Essex. Freeman: City of London; Merchant Taylors' Co. *Recreations:* fishing, music, gardening. *Address:* Feeringbury Manor, Feering, Colchester, Essex CO5 9RB. *T:* (01376) 561946, *Fax:* (01376) 562481. *E:* jgsca@btinternet.com. *Club:* Boodle's.

COOGAN, Ven. Robert Arthur William; Archdeacon of Hampstead, 1985–94, now Archdeacon Emeritus; *b* 11 July 1929; *s* of Ronald Dudley Coogan and Joyce Elizabeth Coogan (*née* Roberts). *Educ:* Univ. of Tasmania (BA); Univ. of Durham (DipTheol). Asst Curate, St Andrew, Plaistow, 1953–56; Rector of Bothwell, Tasmania, 1956–62; Vicar: North Woolwich, 1962–73; St Stephen, Hampstead, 1973–77; Priest in Charge, All Hallows, Gospel Oak, 1974–77; Vicar of St Stephen with All Hallows, Hampstead, 1977–85; Priest in Charge: Old St Pancras with St Matthew, 1976–80; St Martin with St Andrew, Gospel Oak, 1978–81; Area Dean, South Camden 1975–81, North Camden 1978–83; Prebendary of St Paul's Cathedral, 1982–85. Commissary for Bishop of Tasmania, 1968–88; Exam. Chaplain to Bishop of Edmonton, 1985–94. *Recreations:* reading, gardening, travel. *Address:* Salters Hall West, Stour Street, Sudbury, Suffolk CO10 2AX. *T:* (01787) 370026. *Club:* Oriental.

COOGAN, Steve; actor, writer and producer; *b* 14 Oct. 1965; one *d* by Anna Cole; *m* 2002, Caroline Hickman (marr. diss. 2005). *Educ:* Manchester Poly. Sch. of Theatre. Partner, Baby Cow Prodns Ltd, 1999–. *Radio:* On The Hour, 1992; Knowing Me, Knowing You, with Alan Partridge, 1992; *television* includes: Spitting Image, 1984; The Day Today (also writer), 1994; Knowing Me, Knowing You, with Alan Partridge (also writer), 1995; Coogan's Run (also writer), 1995; I'm Alan Partridge (also writer), 1997, 2002; The Fix, 1997; Alice Through the Looking Glass, 1998; Dr Terrible's House of Horrible (also writer and prod.), 2001; The Private Life of Samuel Pepys (also prod.), 2003; Saxondale (also writer and prod.), 2006, 2007; The Trip, 2010 (Best Male Perf. in a Comedy Role, BAFTA, 2011); Mid Morning Matters with Alan Partridge, 2010–11; Moone Boy, 2012; Welcome to the Places of My Life, 2013 (Best Male Perf. in a Comedy Prog., BAFTA, 2013); The Trip to Italy, 2014; Happyish, 2015; *films:* The Wind in the Willows, 1996; The Parole Officer (also writer), 2001; 24 Hour Party People, 2002; Coffee and Cigarettes, 2003; Around the World in 80 Days, 2004; Happy Endings, A Cock and Bull Story, 2005; The Alibi, Marie Antoinette, Night at the Museum, 2006; Hot Fuzz, 2007; Night at the Museum 2, 2009; The Look of Love, Alan Partridge: Alpha Papa, Philomena (also prod. and co-writer), 2013; Northern Soul, 2014; Night at the Museum: Secret of the Tomb, 2014; *theatre:* The Man Who Thinks He's It (tour), 1998. *Publications:* (jtly) I, Partridge: we need to talk about Alan, 2011. *Address:* Baby Cow Productions Ltd, 33 Foley Street, W1W 7TL; c/o Independent Talent Group Ltd, 40 Whitfield Street, W1T 2RH.

COOK; *see* Curnock Cook.

COOK, Alan Ronald, CBE 2006; FCII; Chairman: Permanent TSB Group Holdings (formerly Irish Life and Permanent Group Holdings), since 2011; Action for ME, since 2010; Deputy Chairman, Sainsbury's Bank, since 2014 (non-executive Director, 2011–13); *b* 23 Sept. 1953; *s* of Ronald Joseph Cook and Dorothy May Cook; *m* 1975, Anita Patricia Kelleher; two *s* one *d*. *Educ:* Ealing Grammar Sch. for Boys. FCII 1975. Prudential Assce Co. Ltd, 1970–93; Sen. Vice Pres., Jackson Nat. Life, USA, 1993–96; Prudential Assurance Co. Ltd: Acquisitions Dir, 1996–97; Man. Dir, Gen. Insce, 1997–99; Man. Dir, Retail Insce Ops, 1999–2000; Chief Exec., Insce Services, 2000–01; Chief Operating Officer, UK and Europe, 2001–02; CEO, Nat. Savings & Investments, 2002–06; Man. Dir, Post Office Ltd, 2006–10. Chm., Highways Agency, 2011–14; Gov., Inst. of Financial Services, 2005–08; non-executive Director: Financial Ombudsman Service, 2008–11; DfT, 2009–14; OFT, 2010–11; MetLife Europe, 2013–. Vice-Chm. Govs, Luton Univ., 2003–05; Ind. Gov., Univ. of Bedfordshire, 2010– (Chm., 2011–). FRSA 2000; FCMI 2005. Freeman, City of London, 2003; Mem., Co. of Insurers, 2005–. Hon. DBA Bedfordshire, 2006. *Recreations:* fell-walking, swimming. *Address:* Orchard Grange, 28 Church End Road, Shenley Brook End, Milton Keynes MK5 7AB. *E:* Alan.Cook@orchard-grange.co.uk.

COOK, Allan Edward, CBE 2008; FREng; FRAeS; Chairman, W. S. Atkins, since 2010; Deputy Chairman, Marshalls Holding Group, since 2011; *b* 27 Sept. 1949; *s* of late Stanley Livingston Porter and of Sarah Neve; *m* 1970, Kathleen Pegg; two *d*. *Educ:* Sunderland Coll. of FE; Sunderland Poly. (DMS; Full Technol. Cert); Sunderland Univ. (BSc Hons Electronics). Chief Exec., Hughes Aircraft (Europe), 1995; Man. Dir, GEC-Marconi Avionics, 1998–2000; Gp Man. Dir Progs and Man. Dir Eurofighter, BAE Systems, 2000–01; Chief Exec., Cobham plc, 2001–09. Chairman: Selex ES (formerly Selex Galileo), 2011–14; Finmeccanica UK, 2012–14. Director: Manufg Forum, 2006; Ministerial Adv. Gp for Manufg, 2008–; Chairman: Nat. Skills Acad. for Manufg, 2008–; SEMTA, 2010–; Skills and Job Retention Gp, BIS, 2010–; Lead non-exec. Mem. Bd, BIS, 2014–. President: SBAC, 2007–09; AeroSpace and Defence Industries Assoc. of Europe, 2008–09; Vice Pres., Royal Acad. of Engrg, 2014–. FREng 2010; FRAeS 1998. *Recreations:* squash, music, walking, theatre, wine. *Clubs:* Royal Automobile, Royal Air Force.

COOK, Andrew John, CBE 1996; Chairman and Chief Executive, William Cook Holdings Ltd, since 1982; *b* 11 Oct. 1949; *s* of late Andrew McTurk Cook and Barbara Jean (*née* Gale); *m* 1st, 1987, Alison Jane Lincoln (marr. diss. 2011); one *s* three *d*; 2nd, 2013, Angelika Hirsch-Stronstorff. *Educ:* High Storrs Grammar Sch., Sheffield; University Coll. London (LLB). Called to the Bar, Gray's Inn, 1972. Dir, William Cook & Sons (Sheffield) Ltd, 1974–82. *Publications:* Thrice Through the Fire: the history of the William Cook company 1985–1998, 1999; Ashes and Dust: a business autobiography 1997–2009, 2010; (with Andrew Rhys Thompson) Coal, Steam and Comfort: 141R568 and the Swiss classic train, 2010. *Recreations:* boats, mountains, my children, history, trains, planes, bikes. *Address:* William Cook Holdings Ltd, Parkway Avenue, Sheffield S9 4UL. *Clubs:* Royal Thames Yacht; Sheffield Sports Cycling.

COOK, Ann; *see* Christopher, A.

COOK, Brian Francis, FSA; classical archaeologist; Keeper of Greek and Roman Antiquities, British Museum, 1976–93; *b* 13 Feb. 1933; *yr s* of late Harry Cook and Renia Cook; *m* 1962, Veronica Dewhirst. *Educ:* St Bede's Grammar Sch., Bradford; Univ. of Manchester (BA); Downing Coll. and St Edmund's House, Cambridge (MA); British Sch. at Athens. FSA 1971. NCO 16/5 Lancers, 1956–58. Dept of Greek and Roman Art, Metropolitan Museum of Art, New York: Curatorial Asst, 1960; Asst Curator, 1961; Associate Curator, 1965–69; Asst Keeper, Dept of Greek and Roman Antiquities, BM, 1969–76. Corresp. Mem., German Archaeol. Inst., 1977. Hon. Member: Anglo-Hellenic League, 1981; Caryatids, 1992. *Publications:* Inscribed Hadra Vases in the Metropolitan Museum of Art, 1966; Greek and Roman Art in the British Museum, 1976; The Elgin Marbles, 1984 (Spanish edn 2000), 2nd edn 1997; The Townley Marbles, 1985; Greek Inscriptions, 1987 (Dutch edn 1990, French edn 1994, Japanese edn 1996); (ed) The Rogozen Treasure, 1989; (jtly) Relief Sculpture of the Mausoleum at Halicarnassus, 2005; articles and revs on Greek, Etruscan and Roman antiquities in Brit. and foreign periodicals, conf. reports, hon. vols and encyclopædic works. *Recreation:* reading.

COOK, Sir Christopher Wymondham Rayner Herbert, 5th Bt *cr* 1886; company director, since 1979; Director, Diamond Guarantees Ltd, 1980–91; *b* 24 March 1938; *s* of Sir Francis Ferdinand Maurice Cook, 4th Bt and Joan Loraine, *d* of John Aloysius Ashton-Case; *S* father, 1978; *m* 1st, 1958, Mrs Malina Gunasekera (from whom he obtained a divorce, 1975; she *d* 2010); one *s* one *d*; 2nd, 1975, Mrs Margaret Miller, *d* of late John Murray; one *s* one *d*. *Educ:* King's School, Canterbury. *Recreations:* reading, philately, painting. *Heir: s* Richard Herbert Aster Maurice Cook [*b* 30 June 1959; *m* 1996, Corinne Solange Andrée, *d* of René Daniel Dayras; one *s* two *d*]. *Address:* La Fosse Equierre, Bouillon Road, St Andrew's, Guernsey GY6 8YN.

COOK, David; *see* Cook, J. D.

COOK, David Julian, CB 2015; Second Parliamentary Counsel, since 2007; *b* 15 July 1962; *s* of Stanley and Dorothy Mary Cook; *m* 1988, Christine Margaret Alice Barnard; two *s* one *d*. *Educ:* Merton Coll., Oxford (BA Classics 1985, MA); Coll. of Law (CPE 1986; Law Finals 1987). Articled Clerk, then Solicitor, Freshfields, 1988–91; Office of Parliamentary Counsel: Asst Parly Counsel, 1991–95; Sen. Asst Parly Counsel, 1995–99; Dep. Parly Counsel, 1999–2003; Parly Counsel, 2003–; Hd of Drafting Team, Tax Law Rewrite Project, Bd of Inland Revenue, 2003–05 (on secondment). *Recreations:* archaeology, walking, Victorian novels.

COOK, David Somerville; solicitor; Senior Partner, Messrs Sheldon & Stewart, Solicitors, Belfast; Chairman, Police Authority for Northern Ireland, 1994–96; Lord Mayor of Belfast, 1978–79; *b* 25 Jan. 1944; *s* of late Francis John Granville Cook and Jocelyn McKay (*née* Stewart); *m* 1972, Mary Fionnuala Ann Deeny (*see* M. F. A. Cook); four *s* one *d*. *Educ:* Campbell Coll., Belfast; Pembroke Coll., Cambridge (MA). Alliance Party of Northern Ireland: Founder Member, 1970; Hon. Treasurer, 1972–75; Central Executive Cttee, 1970–78, 1980–85; Dep. Leader, 1980–84; Pres., 1992–93. Chm., NI Voluntary Trust, 1979–99. Mem., Belfast City Council, 1973–85; Mem. (Alliance) for Belfast S, NI Assembly, 1982–86; contested (Alliance): Belfast South, Feb. 1974, by-elections March 1982 and Jan. 1986, gen. election, 1987; N Ireland, European Parly elecn, 1984. Trustee: Ulster Museum, 1974–85; The Buttle Trust, 1991–2001; Brontë Memorial Cottage, Drumballyroney, Co. Down, 1995–; Vice Pres., NI Council on Alcohol, 1978–83; Member: NI Council, European Movement, 1980–84; Cttee, Charity Know How Fund, 1991–94; Exec. Cttee, Assoc. of Community Trusts and Foundns, 1992–98 (Chm., 1994–95); Exec. Cttee, Clanmil Housing Assoc. (formerly RBL Housing Assoc. Ltd), 1994–99; Chm., Craigavon and Banbridge Community Health and Social Services Trust, 1994–2001. Director: Ulster Actors' Co. Ltd, 1981–85; Crescent Arts Centre, Belfast, 1994–96; C21 Theatre Co., 2008–. Pres., Belfast Lit. Soc., 2012–13. Mem., Royal Naval Assoc. Gov., Brownlow Coll. (Integrated Secondary Sch.), 1994–98. Obtained Orders of Mandamus and fines for contempt of court against Belfast City Council, following its unlawful protest against the Anglo-Irish Agreement, 1986, 1987. Chm., West Down Beagles Hunt Club, 2003–13. *Publications:* Blocking the Slippery Slope, 1997; (contrib.) The Republican Ideal, ed Norman Porter, 1998. *Recreations:* fieldsports, marmalade making, observing politicians. *Address:* Sheldon & Stewart, 70 Donegall Pass, Belfast BT7 1BU. *Club:* Ulster Reform (Belfast).

COOK, Derek Edward, TD 1967; Deputy Chairman, 1987–92, and Group Managing Director, 1990–92, Pilkington plc (Director, 1984–92); *b* 7 Dec. 1931; 2nd *s* of late Hubert Edward Cook and Doris Ann Cook (*née* Appleyard); *m* 1968, Prudence Carolyn Wilson; one *s* one *d*. *Educ:* Fyling Hall; Denstone Coll.; Corpus Christi Coll., Oxford (MA); Salford Univ.; Huddersfield Tech. Coll. FSS; CText, FTI. Commissioned Z Battery, BAOR, 1951; W Riding Artillery, 1952–68. Tootal Ltd, 1955–61; John Emsley Ltd, 1961–63; Man. Dir, A. & S. Henry & Co. Ltd (Bradford), 1963–70; Man. Dir, 1971–75, Chm., 1976–79, Fibreglass Pilkington Ltd, India; Chm. and Man. Dir, Hindusthan-Pilkington Glass Works Ltd, India, 1976–79; Director: R. H. Windsor Ltd, India, 1976–79; Killick Halco Ltd, India, 1977–79; Chm. and Man. Dir, Pilkington Cos, S Africa and Zimbabwe, 1979–84, incl. Pilkington Bros S Africa Pty, Armour Plate Safety Glass Pty, and Glass S Africa Pty; Director: Pilkington Glass Ltd, 1982–85 (Chm., 1984–85); Pilkington Holdings Inc., 1984–89; Triplex Safety Glass Co. Ltd, 1984–85 (Chm.); Pilkington Floatglas AB, 1985–87; Flachglas AG, 1985–89. Chm., Pilkington Superannuation Scheme, 1987–2003; Director: Rowntree plc, 1987–88; Libby-Owens-Ford Co., USA, 1987–92; Charter Consolidated plc, 1988–93; Charter plc, 1993–97; Powell Duffryn plc, 1989–98; Leeds Permanent Building Soc., 1991–95; MFI (Furniture Group) plc, 1992–99; Littlewoods Organisation plc, 1992–99; D. E. Cook (Consultants),

1992–2008 (Sen. Consultant, 1992–2008); Kwik Save Gp plc, 1993–98; Halifax Bldg Soc., 1995–97; Halifax plc, 1996–98; Somerfield plc, 1998–99; Hobart Pension Trustee Ltd, 1993–97; Littlewoods Pension Trust Ltd, 1994–2001; Trustee: MFI Pension Plan, 1994–99; Halifax plc (formerly Bldg Soc.) Retirement Fund, 1995–98; Kwik Save Retirement Fund, 1997–2000 (Chm., 1998–2000). Member: Council of Industry and Parlt Trust, 1987–92; Council, CBI, 1988–92; Council, Textile Inst., 1994–99; Court, Univ. of Leeds, 1989–2001; Dir, Leeds Univ. Foundn Ltd, 1989–2002. Gov., Cathedral Sch., Bombay, 1974–79; Dir, Breach Candy Hosp. Trust, 1974–79. Trustee, W Riding Artillery Trust, 2001–13. Mem., Cook Soc., 1985–2002. Holder of Royal Warrant of Appointment, 1984–85. Hon. Life FInstD. CCMI; FRSA. Freeman, City of London; Liveryman, Glass Sellers' Co., 1991–. *Recreations:* sailing (British Admirals Cup team, 1967), general sporting and country life interests. *Address:* Cherchebi House, Main Street, Kirkby Overblow, N Yorks HG3 1HD. *T:* (01423) 870 840. *Clubs:* Cavalry and Guards, East India, Royal Over-Seas League (Hon. Life Mem.), Royal Thames, Royal Ocean Racing; New (Edinburgh); Royal Yorkshire Yacht (Bridlington); Leander (Henley); Racquets (Manchester); Lansdowne; Royal Bombay Yacht (Cdre, 1977–78).

COOK, Fionnuala; *see* Cook, M. F. A.

COOK, Gordon Charles, DSc, MD; FRCP; physician with special interest in tropical and infectious diseases, and medical historian; Visiting Professor, University College London, since 2002; *b* Wimbledon, 17 Feb. 1932; *e s* of late Charles Francis Cook and Kate Cook (*née* Kraninger, then Grainger); *m* 1963, Elizabeth Jane, *d* of late Rev. Stephen Noel Agg-Large; one *s* three *d*. *Educ:* Wellingborough, Kingston-upon-Thames and Raynes Park Grammar Schs; Royal Free Hosp. Sch. of Medicine, London Univ. (BSc Physiol 1955; MB BS 1957; MD 1965; Charlotte Brown Prize, 1965; Cunning Award, 1967; Legg Award, 1969; DSc 1976). MRCS; LRCP 1957, MRCP 1960, FRCP 1972; FRACP 1978; FLS 1989; FRCPE 2002. Commissioned RAMC (Capt.), seconded to Royal Nigerian Army, 1960–62. Hosp. appts, Royal Free, Hampstead Gen., Royal Northern, Brompton, St George's, 1958–63; Lectr, Royal Free Hosp. Sch. of Medicine and Makerere Univ. Coll., Uganda, 1963–69; Prof. of Medicine and Cons. Physician, Univs of Zambia, 1969–74, Riyadh, 1974–75, Papua New Guinea, 1978–81; Sen. MO, MRC, 1975–76; Sen. Lectr in Clinical Scis, LSHTM, 1976–97; University College London: Hon. Sen. Lectr in Medicine (Infectious Diseases), 1981–2002; Sen. Res. Fellow, Wellcome Trust Centre for History of Medicine, 1997–2002. Hon. Consultant Physician: Hosp. for Trop. Diseases and UCL Hosps, 1976–97; St Luke's Hosp. for the Clergy, 1988–2009; Hon. Lectr in Clinical Parasitology, St Bart's Hosp. Med. Coll., 1992–. Vis. Prof., Univs of Basra, Mosul, Doha. Consultant, advr and mem., professional and learned bodies; Mem., Jt Cttee on Higher Med. Trng, 1987–93. Member: Assoc. of Physicians of GB and Ireland, 1973–; Exec. Council, Med. Writers Gp, Soc. of Authors, 1994–99 (Chm., 1997–99); Mem. Exec. Cttee and Examiner, Faculty of Hist. and Philosophy of Medicine and Pharmacy, Soc. of Apothecaries, 1997–; Examiner for membership of RCP, 1977–84. Lectures: Ahmed Hafez Moussa Meml, 1994; Stanley Browne Meml, 1995; Monckton Copeman, Soc. of Apothecaries, 2000; Denny, Barber-Surgeons' Co., 2003. President: RSTM&H, 1993–95; Osler Club, London, 1993–95; Baconian Club of St Albans, 1995–96; History of Medicine Sect., RSM, 2003–04 (Vice-Pres., 1994–96); Fellowship of Postgrad. Medicine, 2000–07; Founder and Chm., Erasmus Darwin Foundn, Lichfield, 1994–2011 (Vice-Pres., 2011–); Trustee, BookPower (formerly Educnl Low-priced Sponsored Texts), 1996–2011; Member: Council, Galton Inst., 2005–10; Cttee, Friends of Florence Nightingale Mus., 2005–09 (Vice-Chm., 2006–09). Hon. Archivist, Seamen's Hosp. Soc., 2002– (Hon. Life Gov., 2007–); Hon. Res. Associate, Greenwich Maritime Inst., 2003–. Mem. Council, Cathedral and Abbey Church of St Alban, 1983–88. Liveryman, Apothecaries' Co., 1981–. Editor, Jl of Infection, 1995–97; mem., editl bds, med. jls. Frederick Murgatroyd Meml Prize, RCP, 1973; Hugh L'Etang Prize, RSM, 1999. *Publications:* (ed jtly) Acute Renal Failure, 1964; Tropical Gastroenterology, 1980; (jtly) 100 Clinical Problems in Tropical Medicine, 1987, 2nd edn 1998; Communicable and Tropical Diseases, 1988; Parasitic Disease in Clinical Practice, 1990; From the Greenwich Hulks to Old St Pancras: a history of tropical disease in London, 1992; (ed) Gastroenterological Problems from the Tropics, 1995; (ed) Travel-associated disease, 1995; (ed) Manson's Tropical Diseases, 20th edn, 1996 to 22nd edn, 2009; Victorian Incurables: a history of the Royal Hospital for Neuro-Disability, Putney, 2004; John MacAlister's Other Vision: a history of the Fellowship of Postgraduate Medicine, 2005; The Incurables Movement: an illustrated history of the British home, 2006; Tropical Medicine: an illustrated history of the pioneers, 2007; Disease in the Merchant Navy: a history of the Seamen's Hospital Society, 2007; Health-Care for All: history of a third-world dilemma, 2009; Caribbean Diseases: Doctor George Low's expedition in 1901–02, 2009; Twenty-Six Portland Place: the early years of the Royal Society of Tropical Medicine and Hygiene, 2011; Torrid Disease: memoirs of a tropical physician in the late twentieth century, 2011; Origin of a Medical Specialty: the Seamen's Hospital Society and tropical medicine, 2012; The Tropical Disease that never existed: a history of 'Sprue', 2013; The Rise and Fall of a Medical Specialty: London's clinical tropical medicine, 2014; National Service Fifty Years Ago: life of a medical conscript in West Africa, 2014; Before the 'Germ Theory': a history of cause and management of infectious disease before 1900, 2015; The Milk Enzyme: adventures with the human lactase polymorphism, 2015; numerous research papers, chapters, reviews and editorials. *Recreations:* cricket, walking, listening to baroque and classical music, medical/scientific history. *Address:* 11 Old London Road, St Albans, Herts AL1 1QE. *T:* (01727) 869000. *Clubs:* Athenæum, MCC.

COOK, (Jeremy) David; Master of the Senior Court, Queen's Bench Division, since 2011; *b* 18 May 1958; *s* of Brian and Pauline Cook; *m* 1990, Katherine Bayer; two *d*. *Educ:* Keele Univ. (BA Hons 1981). Accredited Mediator, Sch. of Psychotherapy and Counselling, 2005. Called to the Bar, Gray's Inn, 1982, Bencher, 2009; in practice at the Bar, specialising in common law, 1983–2011. Legally Qualified Mem., CICAP, later Tribunal Judge (Criminal Injuries), 2005–11. *Publications:* (contrib.) Civil Appeals, 2nd edn, 2013; (contrib.) Powers and Harris Clinical Negligence, 5th edn, 2015; (contrib.) Civil Procedure. *Recreations:* theatre, literature, sailing. *Address:* Royal Courts of Justice, Strand, WC2A 2LL.

COOK, John, FRCSEd; FRSE 1970; Consultant Surgeon, Eastern General Hospital, Edinburgh, 1964–87; *b* 9 May 1926; *s* of George Cook and Katherine Ferncroft (*née* Gauss); *m* 1st, 1953, Patricia Mary Bligh (*d* 1998); one *s* four *d*; 2nd, 2005, Judith Mary Strangward Hill. *Educ:* Fettes Coll., Edinburgh; Edinburgh Univ. (MB 1949, ChM 1963). FRCSEd 1954. Served Med. Br., RAF, 1950–52 (Flt Lieut). House Surgeon, Royal Infirmary, Edinburgh, 1949; Res. Asst, Radcliffe Infirm., Oxford, 1954–55; First Asst, Dept of Surg., Makerere University Coll., Uganda, 1955–64 (Reader in Surg., 1962–64). Royal Coll. of Surgeons of Edinburgh: Hon. Sec., 1969–72; Mem. Council, 1974–84. Representative Mem., GMC, 1982–86; Hon. Sec., Internat. Fedn of Surgical Colls, 1974–84. *Publications:* contrib. surgical jls. *Recreation:* music.

COOK, Dr John Barry; Headmaster, Epsom College, 1982–92; *b* 9 May 1940; *er s* of late Albert Edward and Beatrice Irene Cook, Gloucester; *m* 1964, Vivien Margaret Roxana Lamb, *o d* of late Victor and Marjorie Lamb, St Albans; two *s* one *d*. *Educ:* Sir Thomas Rich's Sch., Gloucester; King's Coll., Univ. of London (BSc 1961, AKC 1961); Guy's Hosp. Med. Sch. (PhD 1965). Guy's Hospital Medical School: Biophysics research, 1961–64; Lectr in Physics, 1964–65; Haileybury College: Asst Master, 1965–72; Senior Science Master and Head of Physics Dept, 1967–72; Headmaster, Christ Coll., Brecon, 1973–82. Dir, Inner Cities Young People's Project, 1992–95; Principal, King George VI & Queen Elizabeth Foundn of St Catharine's at Cumberland Lodge, 1995–2000; educnl consultant, 2000–. Church in Wales: Mem. Governing Body, 1976–83; Coll. of Episcopal Electors, 1980–83. Chairman: S Wales ISIS, 1978–82; Academic Policy Cttee, HMC, 1985–88. Children's Hospice Association for South-East: Chm., 1995–97; Trustee, 1995–2002. Chm. Governors, Royal School, Great Park, Windsor, 1998–2000. Liveryman, Barbers' Co., 1999– (Chm., 700th Anniv. Appeal, 2008–). *Publications:* (jtly) Solid State Biophysics, 1969; Multiple Choice Questions in A-level Physics, 1969; Multiple Choice Questions in O-level Physics, 1970; papers in Nature, Molecular Physics, Internat. Jl of Radiation Biology, Jl of Scientific Instruments, Educn in Science, Conference and Trends in Education. *Recreations:* sports, photography, philately. *Address:* 6 Chantry Road, Bagshot, Surrey GU19 5DB. *T:* (01276) 475843.

COOK, Prof. Jon; Professor of Literature, University of East Anglia, since 2005 (Dean, Faculty of Arts and Humanities, 2004–10); *b* Bristol, 14 March 1949; *s* of late Max William Jesse Cook and of Phylis Cook (*née* Jackman); *m* 1st, 1977 (separated 2007; marr. diss. 2012); one *d*; 2nd, 2012, Katherine Hope Skala. *Educ:* Sevenoaks Sch.; Queens' Coll., Cambridge (BA Hons Eng. 1970; MA 1974); Univ. of East Anglia (MA Studies in Fiction 1971). Lectr, 1972–92, Sen. Lectr, 1992–2005, in English, UEA. Vis. Associate Prof., Dept of English, Univ. of Minnesota, 1976; Vis. Lectr, English Seminar, Free Univ. of Berlin, 1983; Hurst Vis. Prof., Dept of English, Univ. of Washington, 2006. Member: Arts Council England, 2008– (Chairman: East, 2008; South East, 2013–); Arts and Humanities Res. Council Strategy Gp, 2011–13. Judge: Caine Prize for African Writing, 2009–10; Ind. Foreign Fiction Prize, 2011–12; Mem., Academy, Folio Prize for Literature, 2013–. *Publications:* Romanticism and Ideology, 1981; William Hazlitt: selected writings, 1991; Poetry in Theory, 2004; Hazlitt in Love, 2007; After Sebald: essays and illuminations, 2014. *Recreations:* walking, music, wandering in cities. *Address:* School of Literature, Drama and Creative Writing, Faculty of Arts and Humanities, University of East Anglia, Norwich NR4 7TJ. *T:* (01603) 592793, *Fax:* (01603) 507721. *E:* j.cook@uea.ac.uk.

COOK, Leonard Warren, CBE 2005; CRSNZ 2005; National Statistician and Registrar General for England and Wales, 2000–05; *b* 13 April 1949; *s* of late Archie Cook and of Jean (*née* Paterson). *Educ:* Univ. of Otago, New Zealand (BA Hons Maths and Stats). Department of Statistics, New Zealand: Res. Officer, 1971–79; Dir, Statistical Methods, 1979–82; Asst Govt Statistician, 1982–86; Dep. Govt Statistician, 1986–91; Govt Statistician, 1992–2000. Secretariat, Task Force on Tax Reform, NZ, 1981; Mem., Royal Commn on Social Policy, NZ, 1987–88; Chm., Medical Training Bd, 2007–09. Vis. Prof., UCL, 2005–10. *Publications:* contribs to NZ Population Review, Proceedings of ISI. *Recreations:* fly fishing, travel. *Address:* 71 Glen Road, Kelburn, Wellington, New Zealand.

COOK, Lucy L.; *see* Lumsden-Cook.

COOK, Prof. Malcolm Charles, PhD; Professor of French Eighteenth-Century Studies, University of Exeter, 1994–2008, now Emeritus; *b* 19 May 1947; *s* of Francis H. Cook and Betty J. G. Cook; *m* 1974, Odile Jaffré; two *s* one *d*. *Educ:* Univ. of Warwick (BA 1969; PhD 1974). Assistant associé, Université de Paris X, Nanterre, 1972–76; Lectr in French, Westfield Coll., London, 1977–78; Exeter University: Lectr in French, 1978–88; Sen. Lectr, 1988–93; Reader, 1993–94; Dep. Vice-Chancellor, 2001–04. Chm., MHRA, 1999–. Gen. Editor, MLR, 1994–2001 (French Ed., 1987–93). Officier, Ordre des Palmes Académiques (France), 2008. *Publications:* Fictional France, 1993; (ed) French Culture since 1945, 1993; (ed) Journalisme et Fiction au 18e siècle, 1999; (ed) Modern France: society in transition, 1999; (ed) Anecdotes, Faits-Divers, Contes, Nouvelles, 1700–1820, 2000; Critical Inventory of the Correspondence of Bernardin de Saint-Pierre, 2001; (ed) Réécritures 1700–1820, 2002; Bernardin de Saint-Pierre: a life of culture, 2006; (ed) Critique, Critiques, 2006; La Correspondance de Bernardin de Saint-Pierre, édition critique, 2007. *Recreations:* swimming, walking, watching soccer and cricket. *Address:* Myrtle Cottage, 10 East Terrace, Budleigh Salterton, Devon EX9 6PG. *T:* (01395) 446854.

COOK, Margaret Stella; *see* Singh, M. S.

COOK, (Mary) Fionnuala (Ann), OBE 2002; Chairwoman, Southern Health and Social Services Board, Northern Ireland, 2003–09; Vice Lord-Lieutenant, Co. Down, since 2009; *b* 3 May 1946; *d* of late Dr Donnell McLarnon Deeny and Annie Deeny (*née* McGinley); *m* 1972, David Somerville Cook, *qv*; four *s* one *d*. *Educ:* Loreto Abbey, Rathfarnham, Dublin; University Coll., Dublin (BA 1968). Member: Gen. Adv. Council, BBC, 1979–85; Bd, NI Housing Exec., 1985–91; Gen. Consumer Council, NI, 2002–08. Chairwoman, Southern HSS Council, NI, 1991–2001. Mem., Gen. Osteopathic Council of UK, 2002–09 (Actg Chair, 2003–05). Pres., Hosp. Caterers Assoc., 2012–; Trustee, British Red Cross, 2014–. Founding Gov., Integrated Educn Fund, 1992–97. Chairwoman, Bd of Govs, Bridge Integrated Primary Sch., 2003–08. High Sheriff, Co. Down, 2006. Mem., Loughbrickland WI. *Recreations:* gardening, gossip. *Address:* 8 Main Street, Loughbrickland, Banbridge, Co. Down BT32 3NQ. *T:* (028) 4066 9669.

See also Hon. Sir D. J. P. Deeny, M. E. McL. Deeny.

COOK, Michael Edgar, CMG 2000; HM Diplomatic Service, retired; High Commissioner, Kampala, 1997–2000; *b* 13 May 1941; *s* of FO Aubrey Edgar Cook, RAFVR (killed in action, 1944) and late Muriel Constance Molly Bateman (*née* Wemyss); *m* 1st, 1970, Astri Edel Wiborg (marr. diss. 1983); one *s* one *d*; 2nd, 1983, Annebritt Maria Aslund (*d* 2013); two step *d*; 3rd, 2014, Patricia Ann Dearlove; one step *d*. *Educ:* Bishop's Stortford Coll.; Fitzwilliam Coll., Cambridge (MA Hons); Regent St Poly. (Dip. Mgt Studies). Export Manager, Young's Sea Foods, 1964–66; joined FCO, 1966; 3rd Sec., Commercial, Oslo, 1967–70; FCO, 1970–73; 1st Sec. then Head of Chancery, Accra, 1973–77; 1st Sec., Commercial, Stockholm, 1977–81; Head of Chancery and Dep. High Comr, Port of Spain, 1981–84; Counsellor and Dep. High Comr, Dar es Salaam, 1984–87; FCO, 1987–92; Consul Gen., Istanbul, 1992–97. Area Dir for Brighton and Hove, Sussex Enterprise, 2001–03; non-exec. Chm., Orient Bank Ltd, Uganda, 2006–; Dir/Trustee, Concordia (YSV) Ltd, 2006–10. Mem., Conservative Party Globalisation and Global Poverty Gp, 2006–07. *Recreations:* wine, cooking, jazz. *Address:* 17 Denmark Villas, Hove, E Sussex BN3 3TD.

COOK, His Honour Michael John; a Circuit Judge, 1986–2003; consultant solicitor, 2005–11; legal author and speaker; *b* 20 June 1930; *s* of George Henry Cook and Nora Wilson Cook (*née* Mackman); *m* 1st, 1958, Anne Margaret Vaughan; three *s* one *d*; 2nd, 1974, Patricia Anne Sturdy; one *d*. *Educ:* Leeds Grammar Sch.; Worksop Coll.; Univ. of Leeds (LLB 2(1) Cl. Hons). Admitted Solicitor, 1953. National Service, commnd Royal Artillery, 1954. Willey Hargrave & Co., Solicitors, to 1957; Ward Bowie, Solicitors, 1957–86 (Senior Partner, 1965–86); a Recorder, 1980–86; Designated Family Judge for Surrey (formerly Designated Child Care Judge), Guildford County Ct, 1995–2003. Consultant, Horsey Lightly Fynn, Solicitors, 2007–11. Founder Mem., Holborn and City of Westminster Law Socs, 1962–; Past Hon. Sec. and Pres., London Solicitors' Litigation Assoc.; Hon. Pres., Assoc. of Law Costs Draftsmen, 1997–2003; Member: Solicitors Disciplinary Tribunal, 1975–86; Law Society sub-cttees and working parties. Chm., 2000–06, Mem. Bd, 2006–12, Royal Med. Foundn. Gov., Epsom Coll., 1990–2007. Patron: Assoc. for Families who have Adopted from Abroad, 1995–2012; Surrey Family Mediation Service, 2003–12. Freeman, City of London, 1990. General Editor: The Litigation Letter, 1981–; Butterworths Costs Service, 1991–2013. *Publications:* The Courts and You, 1976; The Taxation of Contentious Costs, 1979; The Taxation of Solicitors Costs, 1986; Cook on Costs, 1991, annually, 2000–13; (jtly) The New Civil Costs Regime, 1999; contrib. to: Cordery on Legal Services (formerly Cordery on Solicitors), 1995–; Butterworths Personal Injury Litigation Service, 1995–2013; Civil Justice Qly, 2002–13; The Civil Court Practice, 2012–13. *Recreations:* gardening, theatre. *Clubs:* Law Society; St George's Hill Tennis.

COOK, Michael John, PhD; FREng; Director, Buro Happold Engineers Ltd, since 2008; Chairman, Happold LLP, since 2011; *b* Epsom, 19 Feb. 1955; *s* of Jack Cook and Mary Cook; *m* 1981, Sue Martin. *Educ:* Rutlish Sch., Merton; Gonville and Caius Coll., Cambridge (BA Engrg 1977); Univ. of Bath (PhD 1983). CEng 1987; FIStructE 2004; FREng 2010. Joined Buro Happold, 1982; Dir (London), 1996–2003; Dir of Structural Engrg, 2003–08; Dir of Buildings, 2008–. Adjunct Prof., Dept of Civil and Envmtl Engrg, Imperial Coll. London, 2007–. Chm., Timber Res. and Develt Assoc., 2010–12. Trustee: IStructE Educnl Trust, 2005–13; Happold Foundn, 2011–. Vice-Pres., IStructE, 2015–. *Publications:* articles in Structural Engineer and NCE Jl. *Recreations:* live performance (especially opera), travel (cities), buildings, cooking, playing piano. *Address:* Buro Happold Ltd, 17 Newman Street, W1T 1PD. *T:* (020) 7927 9700. *E:* mike.cook@burohappold.com. *Club:* Athenæum.

COOK, Prof. Nicholas (John), PhD; FBA 2001; 1684 Professor of Music, University of Cambridge, since 2009; British Academy Wolfson Research Professor, 2014–Dec. 2016; *b* Athens, 5 June 1950; *s* of late Prof. John Manuel Cook, FBA and Enid May Cook (*née* Robertson); *m* 1975, Catherine Bridget Louise Elgie; one *s* one *d*. *Educ:* King's Coll., Cambridge (BA 1971, MA 1976; PhD 1983); Univ. of Southampton (BA 1977). Lectr in Music, Univ. of Hong Kong, 1982–90; Prof. of Music, 1990–99, Dean of Arts, 1996–98, Res. Prof. of Music, 1999–2003, Univ. of Southampton; Prof. of Music, 2004–05, Professorial Res. Fellow in Music, 2005–09, Royal Holloway, Univ. of London; Dir, AHRC (formerly AHRB) Res. Centre for the History and Analysis of Recorded Music, 2004–09. Chair, Music Panel, HEFC RAE 2001. MAE 2010. Hon. DHL Chicago, 2013. Ed., Jl Royal Musical Assoc., 1999–2004. *Publications:* A Guide to Musical Analysis, 1987; Music, Imagination and Culture, 1990; Beethoven: Symphony No 9, 1993; Analysis Through Composition: principles of the classical style, 1996; Analysing Musical Multimedia, 1998; Music: a very short introduction, 1998; (ed jtly) The Cambridge History of Twentieth-Century Music, 2004; (ed jtly) Empirical Musicology: aims, methods, prospects, 2004; The Schenker Project: culture, race, and music theory in fin-de-siècle Vienna, 2007 (Wallace Berry Award, Soc. for Music Theory, 2010); (ed jtly) The Cambridge Companion to Recorded Music, 2009; Beyond the Score: music as performance, 2013; contrib. articles in most major musicological jls. *Address:* Old School House, School Hill, Alderbury, Salisbury SP5 3DR. *T:* (01722) 710012. *E:* NJC69@cam.ac.uk.

COOK, Prof. Paul Derek, MBE 1985; PhD; CEng; Chairman and Managing Director, Scientifica-Cook Ltd, since 1962; Professor of Laser Science, Brunel University, 1986–97; *b* 12 March 1934; *s* of James Walter Cook and Florence Jefferay; *m* 1954, Frances Ann James; four *d*. *Educ:* Queen Mary Coll., London (BSc Hons; PhD 1963; Sir John Johnson Scholar, 1959). Res. Scientist: MRC, 1960–62; Middlesex Hosp. Med. Sch., 1962–65. Prof. of Laser Physics, Brunel Univ., 1986–91. Scientific Adviser to: Minister for the Envmt and Countryside, DoE, 1990–92; British Gas, 1990–92; Laser Consultant, BAe, 1986–; former Consultant, W Midlands Police, 1991–92; Scientific Advr to Lady Olga Maitland, 1992–96. Responsible for design and develt of numerous laser systems used in med. and mil. estabts throughout world, incl. ophthalmic LaserSpec; originator and inventor of Laser Guidance Systems for weapon alignment in each Tornado; major contrib. to Europe's first laser gyroscope in 1970s; invention of laser instrument that improves safety of motorists by detecting and correcting night myopia; estab. world's first Night Vision Clinic for treating night blindness disorders. Dep. Chm., Conserve, 1990–93; Founder/President: British Science and Technol. Trust, 1985–96; Science and Technol. Trust, 2002–; UK Pres., Japanese Zen Nippon Airinkai, 1978–81. *Recreations:* breeding and rearing exotic Japanese carp, cultivating Japanese bonsai, inventing, experimenting with ideas, especially those related to improving safety on the roads, passion for early automobile number plates. *Address:* 252A Acton Lane, Chiswick, W4 5DJ.

COOK, Sir Peter (Frederic Chester), Kt 2007; RA 2003; RIBA; Bartlett Professor of Architecture, University College London, 1990–2005 (Chairman, Bartlett School of Architecture, 1990–2004); Joint Professor of Architecture, Royal Academy, since 2005; Design Principal, HOK International, since 2004; Director, Cook-Robotham Architecture Bureau, since 2004; *b* 22 Oct. 1936; *s* of Major Frederick William Cook and Ada Cook (*née* Shaw); *m* 1st, 1960, Hazel Aimee Fennell (marr. diss. 1989); 2nd, 1990, Dr Yael Reisner; one *s*. *Educ:* Bournemouth Coll. of Art; Architectural Assoc. (AA Dip. 1960). Tutor, Architectural Assoc., 1964–90; Prof. of Arch., HBK Städelschule, Frankfurt am Main, 1984–2002. Director: ICA, 1969–71; Art Net, 1972–79. Visiting Professor: UCLA, 1968–69; Southern Calif Inst. of Arch., 1980, 1983, 1992; Oslo Sch. of Arch., 1982; Univ. of Qld, 1993; Nihon Univ., Tokyo, 1994; Tech. Univ., Vienna, 1997, 1999, 2001, 2002; Lund Univ., 2004–; Kenzo Tange Vis. Prof., Harvard Grad. Sch. of Design, 2014. Cook-Robotham Architecture Bureau projects: (completed) Verbania Th., Italy, 2008; Law and Admin Bldg, Univ. of Economics, Vienna, 2014; Abedian Sch. of Arch., Bond Univ., Qld, 2014; (current) Drawing Studio, Arts Univ. Bournemouth. Founder Mem., Archigram, 1961–76. Mem., European Acad. of Sci. and Art; Bund Deutscher Architekten. FRCA 2006; FRSA. Fellow, Bournemouth Arts Inst., 2008; Hon. Fellow, UCL, 2009. Hon. Dr Lund, 2009. Royal Gold Medal in Arch., RIBA, 2002; Gustav Eiffel Prize, Ecole Spéciale d'architecture, Paris, 2005; Mario Pani Award for Arch., Mexico City, 2010. Commandeur, Ordre des Arts et des Lettres (France), 2002. *Publications:* Architecture: action and plan, 1972; Experimental Architecture, 1982; (with R. Llewellyn-Jones) New Spirit in Architecture, 1992; Peter Cook: six conversations, 1993; Primer, 1996; (with N. Spiller) The Power of Contemporary Architecture, 1999; (with N. Spiller) The Paradox of Contemporary Architecture, 2001; The City: as a garden of ideas, 2003; Drawing: the motive force of architecture, 2008; Peter Cook Workbook, 2015. *Recreations:* music, observing towns. *Address:* 54 Compayne Gardens, NW6 3RY. *T:* and *Fax:* (020) 7372 3784. *E:* peter.cook@ucl.ac.uk; Cook-Robotham Architecture Bureau, 83 Essex Road, N1 2SF. *E:* info@crabstudio.net.

COOK, Prof. Peter John, CBE 1996; FTSE; Professorial Fellow, University of Melbourne, since 2011; Director, PJC International, since 1998; *b* 15 Oct. 1938; *s* of John and Rose Cook; *m* 1961, Norma Irene Walker; two *s*. *Educ:* Durham Univ. (BSc Hons, DSc); ANU (MSc); Univ. of Colorado (PhD). FTSE 1998. Geologist to Sen. Geologist, BMR, Canberra, 1961–76; Sen. Res. Fellow, ANU Res. Sch. of Earth Sci., 1976–82 (Vis. Fellow, 1982–90); Chief of Div./Chief Res. Scientist, BMR, 1982–90 (Prof., Univ. Louis Pasteur, Strasbourg, 1989); Dir, British Geol Survey, 1990–98; Dir, Australian Petroleum Co-op. Res. Centre, 1998–2003; Chief Exec., Co-op. Res. Centre for Greenhouse Gas Technologies, 2003–11. Adrian Fellow, Univ. of Leicester, 1992–98. Chairman: Consortium for Ocean Geosci., 1980–82; Commonwealth/State Hydrogeol. Cttee, 1983–88; Intergovtl Oceanographic Commn, Prog. Ocean Sci. and Non-Living Resources, 1984–2001; Dir, MineXchange, 1999–2015; Member: Adv. Cttee, Aust. Nuclear Sci. and Tech. Orgn, 1984–90; Geol. Adv. Panel, BM (Nat. Hist.), 1990–98; Earth Scis Cttee, 1990–94, Earth Scis Tech. Bd, 1995–98, NERC; Chm., Forum of European Geol Surveys, 1996–97. President: EuroGeoSurveys, 1995–96; Aust.-French Assoc. of Scientists, 2000–03; Member: Council, MIRO, 1991–98; Adv. Cttee for Protection of the Seas, 1997–99; Nat. Carbon Capture and Storage Council, 2010–12. Fellow, Geol Soc. of Aust., 2007. Major John Coke Medal, Geol Soc., London, 1997; Lewis G. Weeks Gold Medal, Australian Petroleum and Exploration Assoc., 2004; Leopold von Buch Medal, Geol Soc., Germany, 2004. Centenary Medal, Australia, 2001; Greenman Award, Internat. Energy Agency (GHG Prog.), 2010. Order of Merit, France, 2005. *Publications:* Clean Energy, Climate and Carbon, 2012; Geologically Storing Carbon, 2014; more than 150 contribs to books and learned jls, on energy and sustainability, greenhouse gas technologies, phosphate deposits, marine mineral resources, coastal zone studies, palaeogeography, science management and science policy. *Recreations:* ski-ing, hiking, travel, history, farming. *T:* (2) 2396504, *Fax:* (2) 62396049. *E:* pjcook@co2crc.com.au. *Club:* Commonwealth (Canberra).

COOK, Robert Barclay; Chief Executive, Village Hotels, De Vere Group, 2012–14; *b* Torphins, Aberdeenshire, 30 Jan. 1966; *s* of Thomas Barclay Cook and Ethel Cook; *m* 1995, Deborah Anne Elisabeth; one *s*. *Educ:* Robert Gordon's Inst. of Technol. (HND Hotel and Catering 1987). Ops Dir, Malmaison, 1998–2000; Man. Dir, Columbus and Dakota Hotels, 2000–04; CEO, Malmaison and Hotel du Vin Gps, 2004–11. Member: Global Scot; l'Académie du Champagne. Hon. DBA Robert Gordon, 2007. *Recreations:* golf (6 handicap), shooting.

COOK, Robert Edward L.; *see* Longley-Cook.

COOK, Roger James; investigative journalist; broadcaster: The Cook Report, ITV, 1985–97; Cook Report Specials, ITV, 1998–2004; *b* 6 April 1943; *s* of Alfred and Linda Cook; *m* 1st, 1966, Madeline Koh (marr. diss. 1974); 2nd, 1982, Frances Alice Knox; one *d*. *Educ:* Hurlstone Agricl Coll.; Sydney Univ. TV and radio reporter, ABC (Australia), 1960–66; TV and radio dir, Warnock Sandford Advertising (Aust.), 1966–68; reporter, BBC Radio 4, World at One, World This Weekend, PM, 1968–76; freelance documentary dir, 1968–72; creator and presenter, Checkpoint, Radio 4, 1973–85; presenter and reporter, Radio 4 documentary series: Time for Action; Real Evidence; investigative reporter, BBC TV: Nationwide; Newsnight, 1972–84. Vis. Prof., Centre for Broadcast Journalism, Nottingham Trent Univ., 1997–2011, now Emeritus. Hon. DLitt Nottingham Trent, 2004. BPG Award, for outstanding contrib. to radio, 1978; Pye (now Sony) Radio Personality of the Year, 1979; Ross McWhirter Foundn Award, for courageous reporting, 1980; Valiant for Truth Award, 1988; TV and Radio Industries Award, for best ITV prog., 1993, and Special Award, for outstanding contrib. to broadcasting, 1998; RTS (Midlands) Best On-Screen Personality, 1996; Houston Worldfest Silver Award, for best interview, 1997; Charleston Worldfest Gold Award, for best investigative prog., 1997; Brigitte Bardot Internat. Award (Genesis Awards), for best campaigning wildlife prog., 1997; British Acad. Special Award, for outstanding investigative reporting, 1998. *Publications:* (with Tim Tate) What's Wrong With Your Rights?, 1988; (with Howard Foster) Dangerous Ground, 1999; More Dangerous Ground, 2011. *Recreations:* film, music, motor sport.

COOK, Rosemary Grace, CBE 2008; Chief Executive Officer, Institute of Physics and Engineering in Medicine, since 2012; *b* London, 24 Feb. 1959; *d* of John Rogers and late Gladys Rogers; civil partnership 2006, Alison Norman; two *d*. *Educ:* Stafford Girls' High Sch.; Bradford Sch. of Nursing; Aston Univ. (MA Public Sector Mgt (Dist.)); Univ. of Manchester (Postgrad. Dip. Applied Social Res.). SRN 1980; RGN 1989; FQNI 2013. Registered Nurse, St Luke's Hosp., Bradford, and Stafford Dist Gen. Hosp., 1980–91; Primary Care Facilitator, N Staffs HA/Staffs Family HSA, 1991–97; Audit and Quality Manager, Manchester Audit and Quality Gp, 1997–99; Nursing Officer, DoH, 1999–2003; Hd, Working Time Directive Prog., NHS Modernisation Agency, DoH, 2003–05; Dir, Queen's Nursing Inst., 2005–12. Vis. Prof. of Enterprise, Northumberland Univ., 2008–11; Hon. Prof., Buckinghamshire New Univ., 2012. Hon. DLitt Manchester Metropolitan, 2008. *Publications:* A Nurse's Survival Guide to Primary Care, 1999; The Writer's Manual, 1999; Awareness and Influence in Health and Social Care, 2006; The Nightingale Shore Murder, 2011. *Recreations:* reading, writing, theatre, eating out. *Address:* Institute of Physics and Engineering in Medicine, Fairmount House, 230 Tadcaster Road, York YO24 1ES. *T:* (01904) 610821, *Fax:* (01904) 612279. *E:* rosemary.cook@ipem.ac.uk. *Club:* Penn.

COOK, Prof. Stephen Arthur, PhD; FRS 1998; FRSC 1984; University Professor, Department of Computer Science, University of Toronto, 1985–2005, now Emeritus; *b* 1939; *s* of Gerhard A. Cook and Lura Cook; *m* 1968, Linda; two *s*. *Educ:* Univ. of Michigan (BSc Math. 1961); Harvard Univ. (SM Math. 1962; PhD Math. 1966). Asst Prof., Math. and Computer Science, Univ. of Calif at Berkeley, 1966–70; University of Toronto: Associate Prof., 1970–75, Prof., 1975–85, Dept of Computer Science. Member: Nat. Acad. of Scis (US), 1985; Amer. Acad. of Arts and Scis, 1986. A. M. Turing Award, ACM, 1982. *Publications:* numerous papers in jls. *Recreation:* sailing. *Address:* Department of Computer Science, University of Toronto, Toronto, ON M5S 3G4, Canada. *T:* (416) 9785183. *Club:* Royal Canadian Yacht.

COOK, Timothy, OBE 1997; Clerk to the Trustees, City Parochial Foundation, 1986–98; *b* 25 April 1938; *s* of late Stephen Cook and Kathleen (*née* Henwood); *m* 1967, Margaret Taylor; one *s* one *d*. *Educ:* Loughborough Grammar Sch.; Trinity Hall, Cambridge (BA); Brunel Univ. (MA). Called to the Bar, Middle Temple, 1961. Asst Lectr in Law, Sheffield Univ., 1960–61; Asst Warden, Norman House, 1962–64; Prison Welfare Officer, HM Prison, Blundeston, 1964–66; Dir, Alcoholics Recovery Project, 1966–74; Hd, Cambridge House and Talbot, 1975–77; Dir, Family Service Units, 1978–85. *Publications:* Vagrant Alcoholics, 1975; (ed jtly) The Drunkenness Offence, 1969; (ed) Vagrancy, 1979; Merfyn Turner: practical compassion, 1999; (jtly) A Management Companion for the Voluntary Sector, 2000; Reflections on Good Grant Making, 2000; History of the Carers' Movement, 2007; (jtly) The Cohen Interviews, 2013. *Recreations:* cinema, reading, theatre. *Address:* 26 Criffel Avenue, SW2 4AZ. *T:* (020) 8674 3141.

COOK, Tina Gail, (Mrs Justin Goad); QC 2011; *b* Lancs, 23 Sept. 1964; *d* of Peter Cook and Pauline Cook; *m* 1997, Justin Goad; one *s* two *d*. *Educ:* Queen Elizabeth Grammar Sch., Blackburn; Exeter Coll., Oxford (BA Jurisprudence; MA). Called to the Bar, Middle Temple, 1988; in practice as a barrister, specialising in public law child care, 1988–. Dir, Giraffe Media, 2011–14. Trustee, Families for Children, 2008–. *Recreations:* buying wine, my children, my husband, lunching and parties (any kind). *Address:* 42 Bedford Row, WC1R 4LL. *E:* tc@42br.com.

COOK, William Birkett, MA; Master of Magdalen College School, Oxford, 1972–91; *b* 30 Aug. 1931; *e s* of late William James and Mildred Elizabeth Cook, Headington, Oxford; *m* 1958, Marianne Ruth, *yr d* of late A. E. Taylor, The Schools, Shrewsbury; one *s* one *d* (and one *d* decd). *Educ:* Dragon Sch.; Eton (King's Schol.); Trinity Coll., Cambridge (Schol.). National Service, 1950–51 (commnd in RA). Porson Prizeman, 1953; 1st cl. Classical Tripos Pt I, 1953, Pt II, 1954; Henry Arthur Thomas Student, 1954; MA Oxon by incorporation, 1972. Asst Master, Shrewsbury Sch., 1955–67, and Head of Classical Faculty, 1960–67; Headmaster of Durham Sch., 1967–72. Governor: Oxford High Sch., 1979–2000; Bedford Modern Sch., 1992–2001. Administrator, Choir Schools' Assoc. Bursary Trust, 1987–92; Dir, Thomas Wall Trust, 1992–2002; Gov., Ewelme Exhibn Endowment, 1993–2008 (Chm., 1999–2008). *Recreations:* music, gardening, Scottish country dancing. *Address:* 2 Cannon's Field, Old Marston, Oxford OX3 0QR. *T:* (01865) 250882.

COOKE, Prof. Anne, DPhil; FMedSci, FRSB; Professor of Immunobiology, University of Cambridge, 2000–13, now Emeritus; Fellow, King's College, Cambridge, 1992–2013, now Emeritus; *b* South Shields, 14 Nov. 1945; *d* of William and Margaret Syme; *m* 1969, Jonathan Cooke; two *s*. *Educ:* Univ. of Glasgow (BSc Hons 1967); Univ. of Sussex (DPhil 1970). SRC Postdoctoral Fellow, Univ. of Sussex, 1970–72; Postdoctoral Fellow, Univ. of Illinois, 1972–73; ARC Postdoctoral Fellow, Middx Hosp., 1973–78; Wellcome Trust Sen. Res. Fellow, Middx Hosp. Medical Sch., 1978–81; Wellcome Trust Sen. Lectr, University Coll. and Middx Schs of Medicine, 1981–88; Reader in Exptl Immunol., UCL, 1988–90; Lectr, 1990–96, Reader in Immunol., 1996–2000, Cambridge Univ. Poll Vis. Prof., Univ. of Seattle, 1999. Member, Grant Committees for: Arthritis Res. UK (formerly Arthritis Res.

Campaign), 1988– (Mem., Adv. Bd, Centre for Adolescent Rheumatol., 2012–); Diabetes UK, 1992–95; Leukaemia Res. Fund, 1993–96; Action Res., 1998–; MRC Fellowship, 1999–2004; Finnish Acad. of Scis, 2003–07; Hong Kong Univ., 2006–; Member: Res. Grants Council of HK, 2009–; Dorothy Hodgkin Fellowship Selection Cttee, 2010–13. FMedSci 2007; FRSB (FSB 2011). Hon. Fellow UCL, 2006. Hon. Dr Copenhagen, 2010. Member, Editorial Board: Trends in Parasitology; Diabetes; Autoimmunity; Scandinavian Jl Immunol.; Internat. Jl of Exptl Path.; Biology Direct; Rev. of Diabetic Studies; Assoc. Ed., Internat. Immunol. *Publications:* (jtly) Advanced Immunology, 1987, 3rd edn 1995; contrib. res. articles to jls incl. Nature, Jl Clin. Investigation, Diabetes, Jl Immunol., reviews for jls incl. Trends in Immunol., Parasitol. *Recreations:* walking in mountains, listening to music, reading, photography, travel, art. *Address:* Department of Pathology, University of Cambridge, Tennis Court Road, Cambridge CB2 1QP. *T:* (01223) 333907, *Fax:* (01223) 333914. *E:* ac416@cam.ac.uk; 10 Danvers Road, N8 7HH.

COOKE, Rear-Adm. Anthony John, CB 1980; Private Secretary to Lord Mayor of London, 1981–92; *b* 21 Sept. 1927; *s* of Rear-Adm. John Ernest Cooke, CB and late Kathleen Mary Cooke; *m* 1st, 1951, Margaret Anne (marr. diss. 1994; she *d* 2010), *d* of late Frederick Charles Hynard; one *s* three *d* (and one *s* decd); 2nd, 1995, Patricia Sinclair Stewart, *d* of late William Sinclair Stewart and of Margaret Jane Stewart; one step *s* two step *d*. *Educ:* St Edward's Sch., Oxford. Entered RN 1945; specialised in navigation, 1953; Army Staff Coll., 1958; Sqdn Navigating Officer, HMS Daring, Second Destroyer Sqdn, 1959–61; Staff Navigating Officer to Flag Officer, Sea Trng, 1961; Comdr 1961; Directorate of Naval Ops and Trade, 1961–63; i/c HMS Brighton, 1964–66; Directorate of Navigation and Tactical Control, 1966; Captain 1966; Captain of Dockyard and Queen's Harbourmaster, Singapore, 1967–69; Captain 1st Destroyer Sqdn, Far East, later Divl Comdr 3rd Div. Western Fleet, i/c HMS Galatea, 1969–71; Dir, Royal Naval Staff Coll., 1971–73; Cdre Clyde i/c Clyde Submarine Base, 1973–75; Rear-Adm. 1976; Senior Naval Mem., Directing Staff, RCDS, 1975–78; Adm. Pres., RNC Greenwich, 1978–80, retd. Police Foundn, 1980–81. A Younger Brother, Trinity House, 1974. Freeman: City of London, 1979; Shipwrights' Co., 1980. OStJ 1990. *Recreation:* keeping up with twenty-one grandchildren. *Address:* Sinclair House, 4 Amherst Road, Ealing, W13 8ND. *T:* (020) 8997 2620.

COOKE, Anthony Roderick Chichester Bancroft; Director, 1999–2007, and Chairman, 2005–07, Baltic Exchange Ltd; *b* 24 July 1941; *s* of Maj.-Gen. Ronald Basil Bowen Bancroft Cooke, CB, CBE, DSO and Joan, *d* of Maj. Claude O. Chichester; *m* 1972, Daryll, *d* of David Aird Ross; two *s* one *d*. *Educ:* Ampleforth Coll.; London Business Sch. (MSc 1970). FCA 1964. With Binder Hamlyn & Co., 1960–68; Manager, Jessel Securities plc, 1970–72; Man. Dir, London Australian & Gen. Exploration Co., 1972–75; Ellerman Lines plc, 1975–91: Chief Exec., Investment Services, 1975–78; Chief Exec., City Liners, 1978–85; Chief Executive and Chairman: Ellerman Lines plc, 1985–87; Cunard Ellerman, 1987–91; Gp Chief Exec., Andrew Weir & Co. Ltd, 1991–99. Director: James Fisher & Sons plc, 2002–11; West of England Shipowners Insce Assoc. Ltd, 2002–12. Mem., Adv. Bd, Inst. of Statecraft, 2013–. President: Chamber of Shipping, 1996–97; Inst. of Chartered Shipbrokers, 2002–04. Chm., NE Hants Cons. Assoc., 2012–13. High Sheriff, Hampshire, 2001–02. FRSA 1980. *Recreation:* active sports. *Address:* Poland Court, Odiham, Hampshire RG29 1JL. *T:* (01256) 702060. *Club:* Boodle's.

COOKE, Brian; Circuit Administrator, South Eastern Circuit, 1989–95; *b* 16 Jan. 1935; *s* of Norman and Edith Cooke; *m* 1958, Edith Mary Palmer; two *s* one *d*. *Educ:* Manchester Grammar Sch.; University Coll. London (LLB). Served Royal Air Force, 1956–59. Called to Bar, Lincoln's Inn, 1959; Dept of Director of Public Prosecutions, 1960–68; Deputy Clerk of the Peace, Inner London Quarter Sessions, 1968–71; Dep. Circuit Administrator, North Eastern Circuit, 1971–81, Circuit Administrator, 1981–82; Sec. of Commissions, 1982–88, Hd of Judicial Appointments Gp, 1987–88, Lord Chancellor's Dept. Part-time Pres., Mental Health Rev. Tribunals, 1996–2003. JP Middx, 1985–99. *Recreations:* golf, walking, theatre, music, the arts. *Address:* 12 The Pryors, East Heath Road, NW3 1BS. *Club:* Hampstead Golf.

COOKE, Colin Ivor; non-executive Chairman: Fenner PLC, 1993–2011; Dowlis Corporate Solutions plc, 2005–13; Energybuild Group plc, 2007–10; *b* 17 Dec. 1939; *m* 1983, Sheila Handley; four *s* one *d*. *Educ:* Cardiff High Sch.; Advanced Coll. of Technology, Newport (HND Metallurgy). GKN, 1956–63; Hepworth Ceramic, 1963–71; RTZ, 1971–72; Du-Port, 1972–80, Main Bd Dir, 1982–86; Dir, WDA, 1987–89; Dir, 1989–98, Chm., 1991–98, Triplex Lloyd. Dir, Dynacast Internat., 1999–2003; non-executive Director: Ash & Lacy, 1987–97; British Dredging, 1990–93; Yorkshire Water, 1995–97; Oystertec plc, 2002–. Chm., Tipton City Challenge, 1993–98. FIMMM (FIM 1996). Freeman, City of London, 1996; Liveryman, Founders' Co., 1996–. *Recreations:* golf, swimming, military history. *Clubs:* Royal Porthcawl Golf; Cardiff County.

COOKE, Cynthia Felicity Joan, CBE 1975; RRC 1969; Matron-in-Chief, Queen Alexandra's Royal Naval Nursing Service, 1973–76; *b* 11 June 1919; *d* of late Frank Alexander Cooke, MBE, DCM, and of Ethel May (*née* Buckle). *Educ:* Streatham Secondary Sch. for Girls; Victoria Hosp. for Children, Tite Street, Chelsea; RSCN, 1940; University Coll. Hosp., London, SRN, 1942; Univ. of London, Sister Tutor Diploma, 1949. Joined QARNNS, 1943; served in: Australia, 1944–45; Hong Kong, 1956–58; Malta, 1964–66. HMS: Collingwood, Gosling, Goldcrest; RN Hospitals: Chatham, Plymouth, Haslar. Principal Tutor, Royal Naval School of Nursing, 1967–70; Principal Matron, RN Hosp., Haslar, 1970–73. QHNS 1973–76. CStJ 1975. *Address:* The Banquet House, Kings Head Mews, The Pightle, Needham Market, Suffolk IP6 8AQ.

COOKE, David Arthur Lawrence; Director, British Board of Film Classification, since 2004; *b* 11 March 1956; *s* of James Robert Cooke and Verity Cooke (*née* Brandrick); *m* 1984, Kathleen Joyce Collins, *qv*. *Educ:* University Coll., Oxford (BA 1st Cl. Hons Mod Hist.; MA). Home Office: admin trainee, 1977–81; Private Sec. to Patrick Mayhew, MP (Minister of State), 1981–82; Principal, Prisons, Drugs and Broadcasting Depts, 1982–89; G5, Broadcasting Dept, 1990; on loan to other govt depts, 1990–93; Dir, Asylum, and Immigration Service Enforcement, Home Office, 1994–97; G3, Constitution Secretariat, Cabinet Office, 1997; Director: Central Inf. Technol. Unit, Cabinet Office, 1997–2000; Criminal Policy Gp, Home Office, 2000–02; Associate Pol Dir, NI Office, 2002–04. *Recreations:* film, music, sport, cooking. *Address:* British Board of Film Classification, 3 Soho Square, W1D 3HD. *Club:* Athenæum.

COOKE, David Charles; Consultant, Pinsent Masons (formerly Pinsents), Solicitors, 2002–06; *b* 22 March 1938; *s* of F. J. E. Cooke and Hilda Cooke. *Educ:* Bolton Sch.; Accrington Grammar Sch.; Manchester Univ. (LLB). Hall Brydon & Co., Manchester, 1961–64; King & Partridge, Madras, 1964–67; Pinsent & Co., Birmingham, then Pinsent Curtis, subseq. Pinsent Curtis Biddle, solicitors: Asst Solicitor, 1967; Partner, 1969–86; Sen. Partner, 1986–94. *Recreations:* classical music, fell walking, theatre, reading. *Address:* c/o Pinsent Masons, 3 Colmore Circus, Birmingham B4 6BH. *T:* (0121) 200 1050. *Club:* Oriental.

COOKE, David John, OBE 1995; Director, British Council, Brazil, 2002–05; *b* 4 Jan. 1947; *s* of late Dennis and of Bessie Cooke; *m* 1970, Lindsey Ram; two *d*. *Educ:* Oxford Coll. of Technology (ONC 1967, HNC Applied Biology 1968); Univ. of Leicester (BSc Biological Sci. 1971; PhD Genetics 1974). Jun. Technician, Dept of Biochemistry, Oxford Univ., 1963–65; Site Services Operator, UKAEA Culham, 1965–66; Scientific Asst, UKAEA Harwell, 1966–68; SRC/NATO Res. Fellow, Univ. of Tromsø, Norway, 1974–76; Res. Fellow and Lectr in Genetics, Univ. of Sheffield, 1976–78; British Council: Sci. Advr, London, 1978–81; Sci. Officer, Belgrade, 1981–84; First Sec. (Sci.), British High Commn New Delhi, 1984–87; Dir, Project Develt Dept, 1989–91; Educn Attaché, British Embassy Washington, 1991–94; Dep. Dir, Manchester, 1994–99; Dir, Develt and Training Services and Mem., Sen. Mgt Strategy Team, 1999–2002. Chm., Eastbourne Br., Eur. Movt, 2013– (Vice Chm., 2010–13). *Recreations:* walking, cycling, cross-country ski-ing, gardening. *E:* cooke.dave@gmail.com.

COOKE, David John; His Honour Judge David Cooke; Specialist Chancery Judge, since 2008; *b* Rugby, 23 Aug. 1956; *s* of Matthew and Margaret Cooke; *m* 1979, Susan George one *s* one *d*. *Educ:* Lawrence Sheriff Sch., Rugby; Trinity Coll., Cambridge (BA 1978) Admitted Solicitor, 1981; Partner, Pinsent & Co., Solicitors, 1983–2001; Dep. Dist Judge 1997–2001; Dist Judge, 2001–08. *Recreations:* competitive swimming, sailing, golf. *Address* Birmingham Civil Justice Centre, Bull Street, Birmingham B4 6DS.

COOKE, Col Sir David (William Perceval), 12th Bt *cr* 1661; freelance consultant/researcher, now retired; *b* 28 April 1935; *s* of Sir Charles Arthur John Cooke, 11th Bt, and Diana (*d* 1989), *o d* of late Maj.-Gen. Sir Edward Maxwell Perceval, KCB, DSO; *S* father 1978; *m* 1959, Margaret Frances (*d* 2013), *o d* of Herbert Skinner, Knutsford, Cheshire; three *d*. *Educ:* Wellington College; RMA Sandhurst; Open Univ. (BA). FCILT; FCMI; Associate Internat. Inst. of Risk and Safety Management. Commissioned 4/7 Royal Dragoon Guards 1955; served BAOR, 1955–58; transferred to RASC, 1958; served: BAOR, 1958–60; France 1960–62; Far East, 1962–65; UK. Transferred to RCT on formation, 1965, and served UK 1965–76, and BAOR, 1976–80; AQMG, MoD, 1980–82; Comdr, Transport and Movements, HQ British Forces, Hong Kong, 1982–84; Comdr, Transport and Movts, NW Dist, Western Dist and Wales, 1984–87; Col, Movements 1 (Army), MoD, 1987–90 Operational service: Brunei, 1962; Malay Peninsula, 1964–65; N Ireland, 1971–72. Attended Staff Coll., Camberley, 1968 and Advanced Transport Course, 1973–74. Col 1984. Dir of Finance and Resources, Bradford City Technol. Coll., 1990–92. Silver Jubilee Medal, 1977 *Recreations:* ornithology, military history. *Heir: cousin* Anthony Edmund Cooke-Yarborough [*b* 6 Aug. 1956; *m* 1990, Joanna Susan Northrop; one *s* two *d*]. *Address:* c/o HSBC, Knutsford Cheshire WA16 6BZ.

COOKE, Del; *see* Cooke, S. D.

COOKE, Dominic, CBE 2014; Artistic Director, Royal Court Theatre, 2007–13; Associate Artist, Royal Shakespeare Company, since 2012 (Associate Director, 2002–07); *b* 1966; *s* of Malcolm Cooke and Gloria Solomon (*née* Turower). *Educ:* Westminster City Sch.; Univ. of Warwick (BA Hons Eng. and Theatre Studies 1988). Associate Dir, Royal Court Th. 1998–2002; productions include: *Royal Court:* Other People, Fireface, 2000; Spinning into Butter, Redundant, Fucking Games, 2001; Plasticine, The People are Friendly, This is a Chair (co-dir), Identical Twins, 2002; Rhinoceros, The Pain and the Itch, 2007; Now or Later, Wig Out!, 2008; Seven Jewish Children, The Fever, Aunt Dan and Lemon, 2009; Clybourne Park 2010; Chicken Soup with Barley, 2011; In Basildon, Choir Boy, In the Republic of Happiness, 2012; The Low Road, 2013; *Royal Shakespeare Co.:* The Malcontent, 2002 Cymbeline, 2003; Macbeth, 2004; As You Like It, Postcards From America, 2005; The Crucible, The Winter's Tale, Pericles, 2006; Noughts and Crosses, 2007; Arabian Nights 2009; The Comedy of Errors, NT, 2011. *Publications:* Arabian Nights (adaptation), 1998 Noughts and Crosses (adaptation), 2007.

COOKE, Prof. Elizabeth Jane; a Principal Judge, Land Registration Division of the First-tier Tribunal (Property Chamber), since 2015; *b* Uxbridge, 29 April 1962; *d* of Jean Finney (*née* Pegler), and adopted *d* of Gerald Coppin and Mary Coppin (*née* Netherwood); *m* 1985 John Cooke; one *s* one *d* (and one *s* one *d* decd). *Educ:* Magdalen Coll., Oxford (BA); Univ of Reading (LLM). Admitted solicitor, 1988; Assistant Solicitor: Withers, 1988; Barrett & Thomson, 1989–91; University of Reading: Lectr, 1992–2001; Reader, 2001–03; Prof. of Law, 2003–15. A Law Comr, 2008–15. *Publications:* (jtly) The Family, Law and Society, 4th edn 1996 to 6th edn 2008; The Modern Law of Estoppel, 2000; The New Law of Land Registration, 2003; Land Law, 2006, 2nd edn 2012; Modern Studies in Property Law, 2001 4th edn 2007. *Recreations:* friendship, climbing, making music (organ, recorders, piano, singing), walking, watching the children and the garden grow. *Address:* 10 Alfred Place WC1E 7LR.

COOKE, Gregory Alan; Chairman, BNP Paribas Real Estate UK (formerly ATIS Real Weatheralls, then Atisreal), since 2001 (Senior Partner, Weatherall Green & Smith 1998–2001); *b* 28 April 1949; *m* Elizabeth; one *s* two *d*. *Educ:* Trent Coll. (BSc). MRICS Henley Sch. of Business Studies. Capital & Counties Property Co. Ltd, 1972–73; with Weatherall Green & Smith, subseq. ATIS Real Weatheralls, then Atisreal, later BNP Paribas Real Estate UK, 1973–. Mem., Mgt Bd, BNP Paribas Real Estate, 2004–. *Recreations:* ski-ing sailing, tennis. *Address:* BNP Paribas Real Estate, 5 Aldermanbury Square, EC2V 7BP. *Club* Royal Automobile.

COOKE, Helen Jane; freelance integrative and nutritional health adviser; Director: Health Designs, since 2006; The Soul Food Company, since 2010; Innovations Network Lead College of Medicine, since 2011; *b* 20 Sept. 1963; *d* of Dr Michael Cooke and Mary Cooke (now Brash). *Educ:* Orme Girls' Sch., Newcastle, Staffs; St Bartholomew's Hosp., London (RGN Cert.); Univ. of Exeter (MA Complementary Health Studies 2001); Thames Valley Univ. (BSc Nutritional Medicine 2009). Staff Nurse, St Bartholomew's Hosp., London, 1987 Hd of Nursing, Promis Recovery Centre, 1988–90; Sister, Abbotsleigh Nursing Home 1990–92; Bristol Cancer Help Centre, later Penny Brohn Cancer Care: Therapy Manager then Patient Services Manager, 1992–2000; Dir of Therapy, 2000–05; Hd, Inf. and Res. 2005–08. Integrative Health Advr, Sixpartswater; Nutrition Lead, Portland Centre for Integrative Medicine, 2014–. *Publications:* The Bristol Approach to Living with Cancer, 2003 *Recreations:* stained glass design, art, travel, walking, laughing. *E:* helen.cooke2@btinternet.com.

COOKE, Hon. Sir Jeremy (Lionel), Kt 2001; **Hon. Mr Justice Cooke;** a Judge of the High Court, Queen's Bench Division, since 2001; Judge in Charge of the Commercial Court 2012–14 (a Judge of the Commercial Court, 2003–12); Presiding Judge, South Eastern Circuit, 2007–11; *b* 28 April 1949; *s* of late Eric Edwin Cooke and Margaret Lilian Cooke; *m* 1972, Barbara Helen Willey; one *s* two *d*. *Educ:* Whitgift Sch., Croydon; St Edmund Hall Oxford (Open Exhibn, 1967; MA Jurisprudence, 1st cl. Hons 1970; Rugby blue, 1968, 1969) Harlequins RFC, 1970–75. Admitted Solicitor, 1973; with Coward Chance, 1973–76; called to the Bar, Lincoln's Inn (Droop Schol.), 1976, Bencher, 2001; QC 1990; an Asst Recorder 1994–98; a Recorder, 1998–2001; Hd of Chambers, 7 King's Bench Walk, 1999–2001. Pres. E Sussex Magistrates' Assoc., 2009–13. Vice-Pres., Lawyers' Christian Fellowship, 2003–11 Vice Chm., LICC Ltd (formerly London Inst. for Contemp. Christianity), 2004–14 (Mem Council, 1997–2014). Member, Council: WBT Ltd, 1977–89; Internat. Assoc. of English in Law and Insurance, 2013–. Youth club leader, 1972–92; Elder and congregation leader 1992–97. Asst leader, LDN Camps, 2014–. Reader, C of E, 2001–. *Recreations:* foozling at golf, learning to sing. *Address:* Royal Courts of Justice, Strand, WC2A 2LL. *Clubs:* National (Vice Pres., 2007–); Vincent's (Oxford).

COOKE, John Arthur; international economic relations consultant, since 2003; *b* 13 April 1943; *er s* of late Dr Arthur Hafford Cooke, MBE and Ilse Cooke (*née* Sachs); *m* 1970, Tania Frances, 2nd *d* of A. C. Crichton; one *s* two *d*. *Educ:* Dragon Sch.; Magdalen Coll. Sch., Oxford; Univ. of Heidelberg; King's Coll., Cambridge (Exhibnr, Sen. Scholar, BA History 1964, MA 1968); LSE. Mem., Cambridge Univ. expedition to Seistan, 1966. Asst Principal,

Board of Trade, 1966; Second, later First, Sec., UK Delegn to European Communities, 1969–73; DTI, 1973–76; Office of UK Perm. Rep. to European Communities, 1976–77; Dept of Trade, 1977–80 (at Inst. Internat. d'Administration Publique, Paris, 1979); Asst Sec., Dept of Trade, 1980–84; seconded to Morgan Grenfell & Co. as Asst Dir, 1984–85; Department of Trade and Industry, 1985–97: Under Sec., Overseas Trade Div. 2, 1987–89; Head of Central Unit, 1989–92; Dir, Deregulation Unit, 1990–92; Head of Internat. Trade Policy Div., 1992–96; Dir and Advr on Trade Policy, 1996–97; Leader, UK delegn to 9th UN Conf. on Trade and Develt, 1996; Chm., OECD Trade Cttee, 1996–97; Hd of Internat. Relations, ABI, 1997–2003. Non-executive Director: RTZ Pillar Ltd, 1990–93; W Middx Univ. Hosp. NHS Trust, 1996–98; Bd Sec., ENO, 1996–. Chairman: Financial Leaders' Wkg Gp Insurance Evaluation Team, 2002–13; Liberalisation of Trade in Services Cttee, TheCityUK (formerly Internat. Financial Services, London), 2006–; European Co-Chm., Financial Leaders' Wkg Gp, 2006–; Dep. Chm., SITPRO Ltd, 2006–11. Member: Exec. Bd, Anglo-Irish Encounter, 2004–08; Adv. Council, Federal Trust, 2004– (Treas., 2009–); Adv. Bd, Eur. Centre for Internat. Political Economy, 2008–. Trustee, St Luke's Community Trust, 1983–93 and 1996–2000 (Vice-Chm., 1991–93; Patron, 2000–); Member: Council, Marie Curie Cancer Care (formerly Marie Curie Meml Foundn), 1992–2008 (Vice Pres., 2008–); Bd, Marie Curie Trading Ltd, 1999–2002. Trustee, ENO Benevolent Fund, 2001– (Chm., 2008–). Mem. Editl Bd, Internat. Trade Law Reports, 1997–. *Publications:* articles and contribs to seminars, mainly on internat. trade in financial services. *Recreations:* reading, travelling, looking at buildings. *Address:* 29 The Avenue, Kew, Richmond, Surrey TW9 2AL. *T:* (020) 8940 6712. *Clubs:* Oxford and Cambridge; Cambridge Union.

COOKE, Kathleen Joyce; *see* Collins, K. J.

COOKE, Margaret Rose; *see* Cole, M. R.

COOKE, Prof. Michael John, CBE 2011; Professor of Practice, Healthcare Leadership and Innovation, Warwick Business School; *b* Coalville, 25 Oct. 1959; *s* of Albert Cooke and Dorothy Cooke; *m* 2001, Amanda Claire Blackwood; one *d*. *Educ:* Leeds Grammar Sch.; Loughborough Univ. (BSc 1983); Sheffield Univ. (DipHSM 1986). AHSM 1986. Dep. Chief Exec., Huddersfield NHS Trust, 1993–99; Chief Executive: Halton Gen. Hosps, 1999–2001; S Staffordshire and Shropshire NHS Foundn Trust, 2001–07; Nottinghamshire Healthcare NHS Trust, 2007–14. Special Prof. in Healthcare Innovation and Learning, Nottingham Univ., 2009. Chair, MindTech NIHR Health Technol. Co-operative. Hon. DLitt Staffordshire. *Recreations:* family, sport, Italy, wine. *Address:* Hagg Bridge House, Storwood, York YO42 4TF. *E:* mikecooke7@icloud.com.

COOKE, Nicholas Orton; QC 1998; **His Honour Judge Cooke;** a Senior Circuit Judge, since 2007; a Deputy High Court Judge, Queen's Bench Division, since 2010; a Judge of the Central Criminal Court, since 2012; *b* 1 July 1955; 2nd and *o* surv. *s* of B. O. Cooke and V. Cooke; *m* 1979, Jean Ann Tucker; two *d*. *Educ:* King Edward's Sch., Birmingham; UC Wales, Aberystwyth (Sweet and Maxwell Prize; LLB 1st Cl. Hons 1976). Called to the Bar, Middle Temple, 1977 (Blackstone Entrance Exhibn 1976), Bencher, 2010; in practice at the Bar, 1978–2007; Asst Recorder, 1994–97; Recorder, 1997–2007; Leader, Wales and Chester Circuit, 2007; Recorder of Cardiff, 2008–12. Dep. Pres., Mental Health Review Tribunal, Wales, 1999–. Judge of the Provincial Court of the Church in Wales, 2004–; Chancellor, Dio. of St Davids, 2005–. *Recreations:* hockey, theatre. *Address:* Central Criminal Court, Old Bailey, EC4M 7EH.

COOKE, Peter; *see* Cooke, W. P.

COOKE, Prof. Richard William Ingram, MD; FRCP, FRCPH, FMedSci; Professor of Neonatal Medicine, University of Liverpool, 1988–90 and 1998–2012, now Emeritus; *b* 23 May 1947; *s* of Edward Ingram Cooke and Pauline Ellen Ross Cooke (*née* Foster); *m* 1977, Theresa Elizabeth Reardon Garside; one *s* three *d*. *Educ:* Colfe's Sch.; Charing Cross Hosp. Med. Sch. (qual. 1971; MD 1979); Univ. of Exeter (MA Medieval Studies 2014). DCH 1973; FRCP 1986; FRCPCH 1997. Research Fellow, then Lectr, Oxford Univ., 1976–78; Staff Paediatrician, Sophia Kinderziekenhuis, Rotterdam, 1978–79; University of Liverpool: Sen. Lectr in Child Health, 1980–83; Reader, 1983–87; Prof. of Paediatric Medicine, 1991–98. President: British Assoc. Perinatal Paediatrics, 1990–92; Neonatal Soc., 1997–2000; Vice-Pres., RCPCH, 1997– (Actg Pres., 1999–2000). Founder FMedSci 1998. *Publications:* (ed jtly) Chemical Trade Names and Synonyms, 1978; (jtly) The Very Immature Infant, 1989; (ed jtly) The Baby under 1000 grams, 1989; (ed jtly) Practical Perinatal Care, 1999; numerous articles and papers on neonatal medicine. *Recreations:* jazz, contemporary painting, sailing. *Address:* 6 Market Street, Dartmouth TQ6 9QE.

COOKE, His Honour Roger Arnold; a Circuit Judge, 1989–2005; Deputy Circuit Judge, 2005–07; *b* 30 Nov. 1939; *s* of late Stanley Gordon and Frances Mabel Cooke; *m* 1970, Hilary Robertson; two *s* two *d*. *Educ:* Repton; Magdalen Coll., Oxford (BA 1961; MA 1966). Astbury Scholar, Middle Temple, 1962; called to the Bar, Middle Temple, 1962, *ad eund* Lincoln's Inn, 1967 (Bencher, 1994); in practice, Chancery Bar, 1963–89; Asst Recorder, 1982–87; Recorder, 1987–89; authorised to sit as a Judge of the High Court, Chancery Div., 1993, QBD, 1995. Sec., Chancery Bar Assoc., 1979–89; Member: Bar Disciplinary Tribunal, 1988–89; Inns of Court Advocacy Trng Cttee, 1995–2004; Advocacy Studies Bd, 1996–2000. Mem., Inst. of Conveyancers, 1983–; MRI 1962–2012. *Publications:* (contrib.) A Portrait of Lincoln's Inn, 2007. *Recreations:* gardening, photography, history, old buildings, travel. *Address:* c/o Radcliffe Chambers, 11 New Square, Lincoln's Inn, WC2A 3QB. *Club:* Athenæum.

COOKE, Roger Malcolm; Partner in charge, Administration, Arthur Andersen, 1995–98; *b* 12 March 1945; *s* of Sidney and Elsie Cooke; *m* 1st, 1968, Antoinette (*d* 2012); one *s* one *d*; 2nd, 2013, Susan. FCA, CTA (Fellow). Qualified Chartered Accountant, 1968; Arthur Andersen & Co.: joined 1968, Tax Div.; Partner, 1976; Head, London Tax Div., 1979–89; area co-ordinator, tax practice, Europe, Middle East, Africa and India, 1989–93; Dep. Man. Partner, UK, 1989–93; Man. Partner-Chief Financial Officer, Chicago, 1993–95. Mem., Exec. Bd, 2006–, Dep. Chm., 2010–13, Chm., 2013–, Glos CCC (Hon. Treas., 2007–10). Vice-Pres., Wooden Spoon Soc., 2012– (Hon. Treas., 1999–2006; Trustee, 1999–2012). *Publications:* Establishing a Business in the United Kingdom, 1978. *Recreations:* playing tennis, travel, ski-ing, cricket, football, good food. *Address:* Madoreen, Larch Avenue, Sunninghill SL5 0AP. *Club:* Royal Berkshire Racquets and Health.

COOKE, Prof. Sir Ronald Urwick, Kt 2002; DL; PhD, DSc; FAcSS; Vice-Chancellor, University of York, 1993–2002 (Member, Court, since 2003); *b* 1 Sept. 1941; *y s* of Ernest Cooke and Lillian (*née* Mount), Maidstone, Kent; *m* 1968, Barbara Anne, *d* of A. Baldwin; one *s* one *d*. *Educ:* Ashford Grammar Sch.; University College London, Univ. of London (BSc 1st Cl. Hons, MSc, PhD, DSc; Fellow, 1994). Lectr, UCL, 1961–75; Prof. of Geography, 1975–81, Dean of Science, 1978–80, and Vice-Principal, 1979–80, Bedford Coll., Univ. of London; Prof. and Hd of Dept of Geography, 1981–93, Dean of Arts, 1991–92, and Vice-Provost, 1991–93, UCL. Dir, UCL Press, 1990–95. Amer. Council of Learned Societies Fellow, UCLA, 1964–65 and 1973; Visiting Professor: UCLA, 1968; Univ. of Arizona, Tucson, 1970; Arizona State Univ., Tempe, 1988. Desert research in N and S America, N Africa and ME. Chm. and co-Founder, Geomorphological Services Ltd, 1986–90. Member: US-UK Fulbright Commn, 1995–2000; HEFCE, 1996–2003; Chm., Jt Information Systems Cttee, 2003–08. Chm., British Geomorphological Res. Group, 1979; Pres., RGS, 2000–03 (Mem. Council, 1980–83; Back Grant, 1977; Founder's Medal, 1994); Mem. Council, Inst. of British Geographers, 1973–75 (Pres., 1991–92). Hon. Sec., York Archaeological Trust, 1994–96; Chairman: Castle Howard Arboretum Trust, 2002–11; York Local Strategic Partnership, 2007–12 (Dep. Chm., 2012–); Dir, Visit York, 2012–; Ind. Chm., Reinvigorate York, 2011–; Trustee: Laurence Sterne Trust, 1994–2006; Nat. Mus. of Science and Industry, 2002–10; York Museums Trust, 2002–08; York Civic Trust, 2002– (Chm., 2009–12); St Leonard's Hospice, York, 2003–08. Patron: York Early Music Fest., 1995–; Elvington Air Mus., 1999–; Dir, Ryedale Fest., 2015–. Mem., Co. of Merchant Adventurers of City of York. DL N Yorks, 2002. Hon. Freeman, City of York, 2006. Fellow, RHBNC, 1993. Hon. DCL Kent, 2004; Hon. DPhil Glos, 2004; DUniv York, 2005. *Publications:* (ed with J. H. Johnson) Trends in Geography, 1969; (with A. Warren) Geomorphology in Deserts, 1973; (with J. C. Doornkamp) Geomorphology in Environmental Management, 1974, 2nd edn 1990; (with R. W. Reeves) Arroyos and Environmental Change in the American Southwest, 1976; (contrib.) Geology, Geomorphology and Pedology of Bahrain, 1980; (contrib.) Urban Geomorphology in Drylands, 1982; Geomorphological Hazards in Los Angeles, 1984; (with A. Warren and A. S. Goudie) Desert Geomorphology, 1993; (with G. B. Gibbs) Crumbling Heritage?, 1993; Why York is Special, 2006; contribs mainly on desert and applied geomorphology in prof. jls.

COOKE, (Sally) Del; Head, Henrietta Barnett School, since 2014; *b* London, 3 Sept. 1958; *d* of Eirwyn and Marlene Rowlands; *m* 1980, David Cooke; three *s*. *Educ:* Godolphin and Latymer Sch.; Bristol Univ. (BSc Maths and Stats 1979); Nottingham Univ. (PGCE 1980); Leicester Univ. (MBA Educnl Leadership 2005); Nat. Coll. of Sch. Leadership (NPQH 2006). Teacher, 1980–81, Hd of Year, 1981–82, T. P. Riley Community Sch.; private tutor, maths and clarinet, 1983–; teacher: adult educn, Horsham, 1989–93; Coll. of Richard Collyer, 1990–96; Cranleigh School: teacher, 1993–98; Hd of Maths, 1998–2001; Housemistress, 2001–02; Dep. Hd (and Actg Hd), 2002–07; Hd, Sir William Perkins's Sch., 2007–14. Team Inspector, Ind. Schs Inspectorate, 2007–14. Vice-Chair, Educn Cttee, Girls Schs Assoc., 2010–14; Mem., Jt Assocs Curriculum Gp, 2010–14. Gov., Halstead Prep. Sch., 2007–14. *Recreations:* family, books, competitive games, bassoon, church. *Address:* Henrietta Barnett School, Central Square, Hampstead Garden Suburb, NW11 7BN. *E:* dcooke@hbschool.org.uk.

COOKE, (William) Peter, CBE 1997; *b* 1 Feb. 1932; *s* of late Douglas Edgar Cooke, MC and Florence May (*née* Mills); *m* 1st, 1957, Maureen Elizabeth (*d* 1999), *er d* of late Dr E. A. Haslam-Fox; two *s* two *d*; 2nd, 2005, Mrs Julia Mary Bain (*née* Warrack). *Educ:* Royal Grammar Sch., High Wycombe; Kingswood Sch., Bath; Merton Coll., Oxford (MA; Hon. Fellow 1997). Entered Bank of England, 1955; Bank for Internat. Settlements, Basel, 1958–59; Personal Asst to Man. Dir, IMF, Washington, DC, 1961–65; Sec., City Panel on Takeovers and Mergers, 1968–69; First Dep. Chief Cashier, Bank of England, 1970–73; Adviser to Governors, 1973–76; Hd of Banking Supervision, 1976–85; Associate Dir, 1982–88; Chm., Price Waterhouse Regulatory Adv. Practice, 1989–96; Advr, Price Waterhouse, subseq. PricewaterhouseCoopers, 1997–2002. Housing Corporation: Mem. Bd, 1988–97; Dep. Chm., 1994–97; Chm., 1997. Chairman: City EEC Cttee, 1973–80; Group of Ten Cttee on Banking Regulations and Supervisory Practices at BIS, Basel, 1977–88. Director: Safra Republic Holdings SA, 1989–99; Financial Security Assce (UK), 1994–2009; Alexander & Alexander Services Inc., 1994–96; Bank of China Internat. Hldgs Ltd, 1997–98; Housing Finance Corp., 1997–2003; State Street Bank (Europe) Ltd, 1998–2006; Bank of China Internat. UK Ltd, 1999–; HSBC Republic Holdings SA, 2000–01; Bank of China Ltd, 2004–07; Medi Capital Hldgs, 2006–10; Assured Guaranty (UK), 2009–12; BMCE Internat. (Hldgs), 2010–11. Dir, Church Housing Trust, 1984–2006. Member: Nat. Cttee, English Churches Housing Group, 1977–94; Council, Chatham House (RIIA), 1992–2005 (Dep. Chm., 1998–2005). Governor: Pangbourne Coll., 1982–2002; Kingswood Sch., 1991–2002; Gayhurst Sch., 2010–14 (Chm., 2011–14). Pres., Merton Soc., 1995–98. *Recreations:* music, golf, travel. *Address:* Oak Lodge, Maltmans Lane, Gerrards Cross, Bucks SL9 8RP. *Clubs:* Reform; Denham Golf.

COOKE-PRIEST, Rear Adm. Colin Herbert Dickinson, CB 1993; CVO 2009; Chief Executive, The Trident Trust, 1994–99; an Extra Gentleman Usher to the Queen, since 2009 (a Gentleman Usher to the Queen, 1994–2009); *b* 17 March 1939; *s* of Dr William Hereward Dickinson Priest and Harriet Lesley Josephine Priest (*née* Cooke); *m* 1965, Susan Mary Diana Hobler; two *s* two *d*. *Educ:* St Piran's, Maidenhead; Marlborough Coll.; BRNC, Dartmouth. Entered RN, 1957; Lieut, 1960; exchange service with RAN, 1968–70; commanded: HMS Plymouth, 1975–76; HMS Berwick, 1976; Airwarfare Directorate, Naval Staff, MoD, 1977–79; Naval Asst to C-in-C Fleet, 1979–81; Asst Dir, Naval Air Warfare, 1981–82; CO, HMS Boxer, 1983–85; Dir, Maritime Tactical Sch., 1985–87; CO, HMS Brilliant and Capt. Second Frigate Sqn, 1987–89; Dep. Asst Chief of Staff (Ops) to Supreme Allied Comdr Europe, 1989–90; Flag Officer, Naval Aviation, 1990–93. Chm., FAA Officers' Assoc., 1998–2005. Pres., Fly Navy Heritage Trust, 2014–. FRAeS 1992. Freeman, City of London, 1985; Hon. Liveryman, Coachmakers' and Coach Harness Makers' Co., 1985; Liveryman, Hon. Co. of Air Pilots (formerly GAPAN), 1999– (Master, 2009–10). *Address:* Northwood Farmhouse, Northwood Lane, Hayling Island, Hants PO11 0LR.

COOKSEY, Sir David (James Scott), GBE 2007; Kt 1993; Chairman: Bechtel Ltd, since 2008; Francis Crick Institute, since 2008; *b* 14 May 1940; *s* of Dr Frank S. Cooksey, CBE, and Muriel M. Cooksey; *m* 1st, 1973, Janet Wardell-Yerburgh (marr. diss. 2003); one *s* one *d*; 2nd, 2011, Mrs Mary Ann Lutyens. *Educ:* Westminster Sch.; St Edmund Hall, Oxford Univ. (MA; Hon. Fellow 1995). Dir of Manufacturing, Formica International, 1969–71; Man. Dir, Intercobra Ltd, 1971–80; Man. Dir, 1981–87, Chm., 1987–2006, Advent Venture Partners; Director: Advent International Corp., 1985–90; Electra Risk Capital, 1981–90; Bespak plc, 1993–2004 (Chm., 1995–2004); William Baird plc, 1995–2002; Establishment Investment Trust plc, 2002–15 (Chm., 2011–15); Diamond Light Source Ltd, 2002–08 (Chm.); Resolution plc (formerly Resolution Life Gp), 2004–08; Chairman: London & Continental Railways Ltd, 2006–11; Quadrille Publishing Ltd, 2007–13; Eurasian Natural Resources Corp. plc, 2007–09; UK Financial Investments Ltd, 2009–12; Aegate Hldgs Ltd, 2013–. Chairman: Audit Commn, 1986–95; Local Govt Commn for England, 1995–96; Dir, Bank of England, 1994–2005 (Chm., non-exec. Dirs Cttee, 2001–05). Member: Council, CBI, 1976–88; Scottish Economic Council, 1980–87; Council, British Venture Capital Assoc., 1983–89 (Chm., 1983–84; Hon. Life Pres., 2012); Innovation Adv. Bd, DTI, 1988–93; Adv. Bd, SVP Global, 2012–; Dir, Eur. Private Equity and Venture Capital Assoc., 2004–07 (Chm., 2005–06); Chairman: MRC/DoH Jt Health Res. Delivery Gp, 2004–06; DoH UK Clinical Res. Collaboration Industry Reference Gp, 2004–10; HM Treasury Cooksey Review of UK Health Res., 2006; UK Govt Rep., Global Dementia Discovery Fund, 2015–. Chairman: Small Business Investment Taskforce, DTI, 2000–04; Biosci. and Innovation Growth Taskforce, DoH/DTI, 2003–09. Chm., State Honours Cttee, 2005–10; Mem., Main Honours Cttee, 2005–10. Mem. Council, 1993–2003, Pro Chancellor, 2008–13, Southampton Univ. Trustee: Mary Rose Trust, 1994–2001 (Chm., 1996–2001); Gov., Wellcome Trust, 1995–99. Hon. FMedSci 2004; Hon. Fellow, BAAS, 2004. Hon. Fellow: Univ. of Wales, Cardiff, 1998; Imperial Coll. London, 2007; Hon. FKC 2012. Hon. DBA Kingston, 1996; Hon. DSc: Southampton, 2008; UCL, 2011. *Recreations:* sailing, music, theatre. *Address:* c/o Francis Crick Institute, Gibbs Building, 215 Euston Road, NW1 2BE. *Clubs:* Boodle's, Royal Thames Yacht; Royal Yacht Squadron.

COOKSEY, Ian Alexander; Headmaster, Watford Grammar School for Boys, since 2015; *b* Sutton Coldfield, 25 Oct. 1974; *s* of Geoff Cooksey and Diana Cooksey (later Hillcox); *m* 2001, Eleanor Croft; one *s* one *d*. *Educ:* Queen Mary's Grammar Sch.; Magdalen Coll., Oxford (MA 1st Cl. Biol Scis 1997; PGCE 1998); Inst. of Educn, Univ. of London (NPQH

2007; MA with Dist. 2010). Teacher of Science, Furamera Secondary Sch., Zimbabwe (Project Trust), 1993–94; Teacher of Biology and Rowing, 1998–2003, Asst Hd, 2003–07, Tiffin Sch.; Vice Principal, Tomlinscote Sch., 2007–10; Hd of Coll., King's Internat. Coll., 2010–11; Hd, Dr Challoner's High Sch., 2011–15. FRGS 1999. *Publications:* (contrib.) Mkomazi: the ecology, biodiversity and conservation of a Tanzania savanna, 1999. *Recreations:* Munro-bagging, opera, cinema, cricket, gardening, bird-watching, travel. *Address:* Watford Grammar School for Boys, Rickmansworth Road, Watford, Herts WD18 7JF. *T:* (01923) 208900, *Fax:* (01923) 208901. *E:* BrownC@watfordboys.org. *Club:* Lansdowne.

COOKSEY, Janet Clouston Bewley, (Poppy), (Lady Cooksey), OBE 2004; PhD; art historian and picture restorer, since 1978; *b* 15 Feb. 1940; *d* of late Dr Ian Aysgarth Bewley Cathie and Dr Marian Josephine Cunning; *m* 1966, Hugh Arthur Wardell-Yerburgh (*d* 1970); one *d*; *m* 1973, Sir David Cooksey, *qv* (marr. diss. 2003); one *s* one *d*. *Educ:* Cheltenham Ladies' Coll.; Univ. of London (BSc ext.); Univ. of St Andrews (PhD Fine Arts). Amateur fencer, 1956–72, 1998–: Jun. Schs Champion, 1954 and 1955; Sen. Schs and under-20 Champion, 1956; British Ladies Foil Champion, 1965, 1967 and 1969–72; winner: De Beaumont International, 1967, 1971 and 1972; Desprez Cup, 1964–67, 1969 and 1972; Jubilee Bowl, 1964–67, 1970–72; double gold medallist, Commonwealth Games, 1966 and 1970; repr. GB in Olympic fencing teams, 1964, 1968, 1972 and in World Championships, 1963–72; veteran competitions include: double gold medallist (foil and epée individual and team) Commonwealth Games, Johannesburg, 1999, Wales, 2001; double gold medallist (foil and epée), World Championships, Budapest, 2000, Martinique, 2001, Tampa, Fla, 2002, Porec, 2010; double gold medallist (foil and epée), European Champs, Cologne, 2001 and France, 2011 (also silver medal, sabre); double gold medallist (foil and epée), World Championships, Croatia, 2011; triple gold medallist (foil, epée, sabre), Commonwealth Games, Singapore, 2012; double gold medallist (foil and epée), Commonwealth Games, Glasgow, 2014. Lectr, extra-mural studies, Univ. of St Andrews, 1975–78, and Dir, Alexander Nasmyth exhibn, 1979; Dir, Special Projects, Univ. of Southampton, 1993–96. Mem., Bd of Trustees, Royal Armouries, 1993–99 (Mem., Design Cttee, 1994–99). Chairman: RNLI Crew Training Appeal, 1996–2000; Countess Mountbatten Hospice Appeal, 1996–2000; Gift of Sight Appeal, Southampton Gen. Hosp., 1998–2001; Area Chm., Children's Hospice Appeal, 1994–96. Member: Corporate Develt Bd, NSPCC, 1997–2008; Bd Trustees, Mental Health Foundn, 1997–2000; Nat. Appeal Bd, Marie Curie Cancer Care, 1997–2000; Scrutiny Panel for N and Mid Hants HA, 2000. Trustee, British Fencing Assoc., 2000–. FRSA 1986. Freeman, City of London, 2004; Guild of Freemen: Mem. Ct, 2002–; Mem., Finance and Gen. Purposes Cttee, 2011–; Master, 2015–March 2016. DL Hants, 1998–2005. *Publications:* The Pleasure of Antiques, 1973; Alexander Nasmyth 1758–1840 (exhibn catalogue), 1979; Alexander Nasmyth: a man of the Scottish Renaissance, 1991; contributed to: The Dictionary of Art, 1996; Oxford DNB, 2004. *Recreations:* entertaining, reading, gardens, the arts, travel, tennis, fencing. *Address:* Uplands House, Upton, Banbury, Oxon OX15 6HJ. *Club:* Salle Paul Fencing.

COOKSLEY, Nigel James; QC 2002; *b* 2 April 1953; *s* of Norman Cooksley and Diana Margaret Barnes Cooksley; *m* 1980, Stephanie Jupe; one *s* one *d*. *Educ:* Felsted Sch.; Queens' Coll., Cambridge (MA Law). Called to the Bar, Inner Temple, 1975; in practice, specialising in personal injury, clinical negligence, professional negligence, health and safety work; Jt Hd of Chambers, 2009–. Mem., Civil Justice Council, 2002–04; former Chm., Personal Injuries Bar Assoc. *Recreations:* travel, golf, football, cricket, Rugby, horse racing. *Address:* Old Square Chambers, 10–11 Bedford Row, WC1R 4BU. *T:* (020) 7269 0300, *Fax:* (020) 7405 1387. *E:* cooksley@oldsquare.co.uk; 3 Orchard Court, St Augustine's Yard, Bristol BS1 5DP. *Clubs:* Chesfield Downs Golf, Weston Cricket.

COOKSON, Brian; *see* Cookson, M. B.

COOKSON, Clive Michael; Science Editor, Financial Times, since 1991; *b* London, 13 Feb. 1952; *s* of Prof. Richard Clive Cookson, FRS; *m* 1978, Caroline Davidson; one *s* one *d*. *Educ:* Winchester Coll.; Brasenose Coll., Oxford (BSc 1st Cl. Hons Chem.). Trainee journalist, Luton Evening Post, 1974–76; Sci. corresp., THES, 1976–77; American Ed., Times supplements, 1977–81; Technol. corresp., The Times, 1981–83; Sci. corresp., BBC Radio, 1983–87; Technol. Ed., 1987–90, Pharmaceuticals corresp., 1990–91, FT. *Address:* Financial Times, 1 Southwark Bridge, SE1 9HL. *E:* clive.cookson@ft.com.

COOKSON, (Michael) Brian, OBE 2008; President, Union Cycliste Internationale, since 2013; *b* Preston, 22 June 1951; *s* of Kenneth and Dorothy Cookson; *m* 1973, Sian Talbot; two *s* one *d*. *Educ:* Hutton Grammar Sch.; Manchester Poly. (Dip. Landscape Architecture 1973). Chartered Landscape Architect 1975. Landscape architect and regeneration manager, 1973–2004; Exec. Dir (Regeneration), Pendle BC, 2004–13. Pres., British Cycling, 1996–2013 (Life Mem.); Mem., Swiss Cycling, 2014–. *Recreations:* cycling, playing guitar (badly). *Address:* 1860 Aigle, Switzerland. *T:* (24) 4685811, *Fax:* (24) 4685854. *E:* brian.cookson@uci.ch.

COOKSON, Thomas Richard, MA; Headmaster, Winchester College, 2003–05; *b* 7 July 1942; *s* of Samuel Harold Cookson, MD, FRCP and Elizabeth Mary Cookson; *m* 1972, Carol Hayley (*d* 2009); three *d*. *Educ:* Winchester Coll.; Balliol Coll., Oxford (MA Eng. Lit.). Assistant Master: Winchester, 1964–65; Hopkins Grammar Sch., New Haven, USA, 1965–67; Winchester, 1967–72; Manchester Grammar Sch., 1972–74; Head of English, Winchester, 1974–83, Housemaster, 1983–90; Headmaster: King Edward VI Sch., Southampton, 1990–96; Sevenoaks School, 1996–2001; Principal, British Sch. in Colombo, 2002. Governor: Rugby Sch., 2005–12; English Coll. in Prague, 2005–09; New Sch. at W Heath, 2006–10; Wellington Coll., 2011–; Dorton House Coll., 2011–. Chm., Physics-S3, 2007–. *Publications:* John Keats, 1972; Bernard Shaw, 1972. *Recreation:* golf. *Address:* Chapel Cottage, Kemsing Road, Wrotham, Kent TN15 7BU.

COOLING, Vice Adm. Robert George, CB 2011; President, HMS Illustrious Association, 2012–13; *b* 11 July 1957; *s* of Edwin and Rosalind Cooling; *m* 1984, Helen Smith; two *s*. *Educ:* Christ Church Cathedral Sch., Oxford; King's Sch., Canterbury; Keele Univ. (BA Hons Internat. Relns 1978); BRNC, Dartmouth, 1978. Commnd RN, 1978; comd, HMS Sandpiper, 1985–86; Instructor in Navigation, US Naval Acad., Annapolis, 1990–92; comd HMS Battleaxe, 1992–93; jssc 1993; COS to Comdr UK Task Gp, 1997–98; comd HMS Montrose and 6th Frigate Sqn, 1998–2000; Dir Naval Staff, MoD, 2002–03; hcsc 2004; comd HMS Illustrious, 2004–06 (Carrier Strike Gp Comdr); has served in ops in Arctic Circle, ME and Gulf reg., Indian Ocean, Mediterranean, S China Sea and Atlantic; comd UK Task Gp evacuation operation from Beirut, 2006; Dep. Comdr, Striking and Support Force, NATO, 2006–08; ACNS, MoD, 2008–09; COS to NATO Supreme Allied Comdr Transformation, 2009–11. Dir, Northfield Leadership. Non-exec. dir in financial services, logistics and technol. sectors. Voluntary work in support of Armed Forces personnel. Freeman, City of London, 2007; Hon. Mem., Co. of Lightmongers, 2004. *Recreations:* travel, country pursuits, conservation work. *Club:* Royal Navy of 1765 and 1785.

COOMBE, Andrew Jackson, FCA; Lord-Lieutenant of South Yorkshire, since 2015; *b* Sheffield, 5 Nov. 1946; *s* of Major Richard Jackson Coombe, TD and Anne Jocelyn Coombe; *m* 1973, Susan Mary Lockwood; one *s* one *d*. *Educ:* Glengorse Prep. Sch., Battle; Wellington Coll., Crowthorne; Caer Rhun Hall, Conway; Coll. of Law, Guildford and Christelton. FCA 1969. Chartered Accountant, Cooper Brothers & Co., 1965–71; trainee solicitor, Wake Smith & Co., 1971–76; admitted solicitor, 1976; Wagon Finance Corporation plc: first in-house Solicitor, 1976–80; Dir, Bank of Europe and Wagon Finance Ltd, 1980–86; Dir, 1982–86; Dep. Man. Dir, 1984–86; Man. Dir, 1986; Keeble Hawson, solicitors: Partner, 1986–2008; Finance Partner, 1986–2008; Hd, Corporate Finance Dept, 1991–2006. Dir, Propland Hldgs Ltd, 1990–97; non-exec. Dir, VHE plc, 1998–2002. Sec., Claremont Nursing Home Th. Appeal, 1974–2005; Trustee: St Luke's Hospice, 1976–2011 (Chm., 2001–09; Vice Pres., 2012–); Bluecoat Educnl Trust, 1983–2000; Freshgate Foundn, 1987–2000; Ashdell Prep. Sch., 1990–95 (Chm., 1993–95); Broomgrove Trust, 2005–10 (Chm., 2005–09). Chairman: Mgt Cttee, Claremont Hosp., 1991–98; Our Story Our Community - Cohesion Gp, 2012–15; Council, Sheffield Cathedral, 2013–; Sec., S Yorks Muslim Community Forum, 2014–15. Non-executive Director: Sheffield (Students in Free Enterprise) Ltd, 2005–09; Univ. of Sheffield Students Union, 2007–10. Vice President: S and W Yorks, RBL, 2015–; Sheffield Chamber of Commerce and Ind., 2015–. Lieut, B Sqdn (SRY), Royal Yeo. Regt and Royal Yeo., TA, 1970–76. DL 1995, High Sheriff 2011, S Yorks. *Recreations:* golf, fishing (trout and salmon), cooking, hill walking, visiting house and family in SW France, reading. *Address:* 79 Slayleigh Lane, Sheffield S10 3RG. *T:* (0114) 230 5515, 07932 152365. *E:* drewcoombe@gmail.com. *Clubs:* Cavalry and Guards; Lindrick Golf (Hon. Treas., 1988–91), Royal and Ancient Golf (St Andrews); Derwent Fly Fishing, Cressbrook and Litton Flyfishers.

COOMBE, His Honour Gerald Hugh; a Circuit Judge, 1986–98; *b* 16 Dec. 1925; *s* of William Stafford Coombe and Mabel Florence Coombe; *m* 1957, Zoë Margaret Richards; one *s* one *d*. *Educ:* Alleyn's School, Dulwich; Hele's School, Exeter; Exeter College, Oxford MA 1950. RAF (Navigator), 1944–48; Solicitor, 1953; Partner, Whitehead Monckton, Maidstone, 1956–86; HM Coroner, Maidstone, 1962–86; a Recorder, 1983–86. *Club:* Royal Air Force.

COOMBE, John David, FCA; Chairman, Home Retail Group plc, since 2012 (non-executive Director, since 2005); *b* London, 17 March 1945; *s* of Sidney and Phyllis Coombe; *m* 1970, Gail Alicia Brazier; three *d*. *Educ:* Haberdashers' Aske's Sch., Elstree; City of London Coll. (BSc Econ.). FCA 1970. Dixon Wilson & Co., Chartered Accountants, 1966–71; Mgt Accountant, Head Office, 1971–72, Investment Analyst, 1972–73, British Oxygen Gp Ltd; Asst Chief Accountant, 1973–76, Gp Treas., 1976–84, Charterhouse Gp Ltd; Finance Manager, Charter Consolidated plc, 1984–86; Gp Financial Controller, Glaxo Hldgs plc, 1986–92; Gp Finance Dir, Glaxo Hldgs, later Glaxo Wellcome plc, 1992–2000; Chief Financial Officer, GlaxoSmithKline plc, 2000–05. Chm., Hogg Robinson Gp plc, 2006–16; Mem., Supervisory Bd, Siemens AG, 2003–08; non-exec. Dir, HSBC Holdings plc, 2005–14. Member: UK Accounting Standards Bd, 1996–2003; Code Cttee, Panel on Takeovers and Mergers, 2001–07. Mem., Cttee on Corporate Governance, ICAEW, 2003–09. Mem., Hundred Gp, 1992– (Chm., 1999–2001). Mem. Council, Royal Acad. of Arts, 2007–12; Trustee, Royal Acad. Trust, 2004–11. *Recreations:* golf, bridge. *Club:* Carlton.

COOMBER, Judith Amanda Jane; *see* Gleeson, J. A. J.

COOMBES, Prof. (Raoul) Charles (Dalmedo Stuart), MD; PhD; FRCP, FMedSci; Director of Cancer Research UK (formerly Imperial College Cancer Research (UK)) Laboratories, since 1999, and Head, Cancer Research UK Centre and Biomedical Research Centre Theme Leader for Cancer, since 2009, Imperial College Faculty of Medicine, Hammersmith Hospital; *b* 20 April 1949; *s* of late Raoul Coombes and Doreen Coombes; *m* 1984, Caroline Sarah Oakes; two *s* two *d*. *Educ:* Douai Sch.; St George's Hosp. Med. Sch. (MB BS); Inst. of Cancer Res., London (PhD 1978; MD 1981). MRCP 1973, FRCP 1990. MRC Clinical Res. Fellow, 1974–77; Sen. Registrar, 1977–80, Hon. Consultant, 1980–83, Royal Marsden Hosp.; Sen. Clinical Scientist, Ludwig Inst. for Cancer Res., 1980–83; Consultant Physician, St George's Hosp., 1983–90; Prof. and Hd of Dept of Med. Oncology, 1990–97, Dean of Res., 1993–97, Charing Cross and Westminster Med. Sch.; Dir of Cancer Services, Hammersmith Hosps NHS Trust, 1995–2006; Prof. of Med. Oncology, 1997–2012, Hd, Dept of Cancer Med., 1997–2012, Imperial Coll. Faculty of Medicine, Hammersmith Hosp. Civilian Consultant, RAF, 1993–. FMedSci 2001. Ed., Therapeutic Advances in Med. Oncology, 2009–. *Publications:* Breast Cancer Management, 1981; The New Endocrinology of Cancer, 1987; New Targets in Cancer Therapy, 1994; numerous papers and articles in professional jls. *Recreations:* painting, walking. *Address:* 13 Dorlcote Road, SW18 3RT. *Club:* Chelsea Arts.

COOMBS, Anthony Michael Vincent; Chairman, S & U plc, since 2008 (Managing Director, 1999–2008); Director, Grevayne Properties Ltd, since 1972; *b* 18 Nov. 1952; *s* of late Clifford Keith Coombs and of Celia Mary Gostling (*née* Vincent); *m* 1984, Andrea Caroline (*née* Pritchard); one *s*. *Educ:* Bilton Grange Sch.; Charterhouse; Worcester Coll., Oxford (MA). Birmingham City Council: Mem., 1978–88: Deputy Chairman: Educn Cttee, 1982–84; Social Services Cttee, 1982–84; Cons. spokesman on educn, Birmingham MDC, 1984–86. MP (C) Wyre Forest, 1987–97; contested (C) same seat, 1997. PPS to Rt Hon. David Mellor, MP, 1989–92, to Rt Hon. Gillian Shephard, MP, 1995–96; an Asst Govt Whip, 1996–97. Vice-Chairman: Cons. Back-Bench Educn Cttee, 1993–97 (Sec., 1987–93); Cons Parly Educn Cttee, 1993–97; All Party Parly Sports Cttee, 1993–97; Parly Human Rights Gp, 1993–97 (Sec., 1987–93); Parly Social Scis Gp, 1994–97; Sec., Cons. Parly Finance Cttee, 1994–96. Mem., Exec. Cttee, Conservative Team 1000, 1997–2001; Treas., Cons Party, 2004–05; Chm., Productivity Forum, Cons. Policy Forum, 2013–14. Chairman: Businessesforsale.com plc, 2000–02; Cubana Restaurants Ltd, 2002–. Chm., PR Cttee, Consumer Credit Assoc., 2006–. Member: Bd, Develt Cttee, Worcester Coll., Oxford, 1996–98; Bd, Birmingham Royal Ballet Develt Trust, 1998–2006; Business Council, Politeia, 2011–. Dir, Schools Outreach, 1997–2003. Pres., Wyre Forest "Solidarity" Campaign, 1987–97; Mem., One Nation Gp. Vice-Chm., Friends of Cyprus, 1992–97. Chm. of Governors, Perry Common Sch., Birmingham, 1978–93; Governor: King Edward Foundn, 1982–88; Birmingham Coll. of Tourism, 1982–88; Ind. Primary and Secondary Educn Trust, 1997–2007. Chm. of Trustees, Nat. Inst. for Conductive Educn, 2001–15 (Trustee, 1998–); Trustee: Scholarships for Kids (Kenya), 2008–14; Premier Christian Media Trust, 2014–. *Publications:* Bow Group papers, numerous articles in newspapers and jls. *Recreations:* golf, tennis, occasional football, music, theatre, ballet. *Address:* 18 Cheyne Walk, SW3 5RA. *Clubs:* Royal Automobile, Annabel's; Little Aston Golf.

COOMBS, Kay, OBE 2005; HM Diplomatic Service, retired; Ambassador to Honduras, 2002–04; *b* 8 July 1945; *d* of late William Tom Coombs and Beatrice Mabel Coombs (*née* Angel). *Educ:* Univ. of Newcastle upon Tyne (BA Hons). Joined FCO, 1967; Bonn, 1971–73; Latin American floater, 1974–75; Zagreb, 1976–79; FCO, 1979–82; La Paz, 1982–86; Rome, 1987–91; FCO, 1991–95; Beijing, 1995–98; Ambassador to Mongolia, 1999–2001. Hon. Mem., Queen's Messenger Corps, 2001. *Recreations:* listening to classical music, reading, flora, Garden Museum.

COOMBS, Ven. Peter Bertram; Archdeacon of Reigate, 1988–95, now Emeritus; *b* 30 Nov. 1928; *s* of Bertram Robert and Margaret Ann Coombs; *m* 1953, Catherine Ann (*née* Buckwell); one *s* one *d*. *Educ:* Reading Sch.; Bristol Univ. (MA 1960); Clifton Theological Coll. Curate, Christ Church, Beckenham, 1960–64; Rector, St Nicholas, Nottingham, 1964–68; Vicar, Christ Church, New Malden, 1968–75; Rural Dean of Kingston upon Thames, 1970–75; Archdeacon of Wandsworth, 1975–88. *Recreations:* walking, sketching. *Address:* 92 Locks Heath Park Road, Locks Heath, Southampton SO31 6LZ. *T:* (01489) 577288.

COOMBS, Simon Christopher; Managing Agent, South Swindon Conservative Association, 2001–04; *b* 21 Feb. 1947; *s* of late Ian Peter Coombs and of Rachel Robins Coombs; *m* 1983, Kathryn Lee Coe Royce (marr. diss. 2003; she *d* 2011). *Educ:* Wycliffe Coll.; Reading University (BA, MPhil). Marketing Executive, British Telecom and Post

Office, Data and Telex, 1970–82; Marketing Manager, Telex Networks, British Telecom, 1982–83; Business Develt Advr, Inst. of Customer Service, 1997–2001. Mem., Southern Electricity Consultative Council, 1981–84. Reading Borough Council: Mem., 1969–84; Chm., Transportation Cttee, 1976–83; Vice-Chm., Policy Cttee, 1976–83; Dep. Leader, 1976–81; Chief Whip, 1983. MP (C) Swindon, 1983–97; contested (C) Swindon South, 1997, 2001. PPS to Minister of State for Industry and IT, 1984–85, to Parly Under-Sec. of State DoE, and Minister of State for the Environment, 1985, to Sec. of State for Scotland, 1993–95, to Pres. of BoT, 1995–97. Member: Select Cttee on Employment, 1987–92; British-American Parly Gp, 1983–; CPA, 1983–97; Chairman: Cable TV Gp, 1987–97 (Sec., 1986–87); British Malaŵi Parly Gp, 1985–93 (Sec., 1985–89); Pres., Parly Food and Health Forum, 1993–97 (Chm., 1989–93; Sec., 1985–89); Treasurer: Parly IT Cttee, 1987–97; Anglo-Malta Parly Gp, 1994–97; Sec., Anglo-Tunisia Parly Gp, 1994–97. Vice-Chairman: Cons. Tourism Cttee, 1988–92 (Chm., 1992–97); All Party Tourism Cttee, 1992–97; All Party Manuf. Gp, 1993–97; All Party Exports Gp, 1993–97; Sec., Cons. Employment Cttee, 1991; Chm., Cons. Party, Wessex Area, 1980–83; Chm., Wessex Area Young Conservatives, 1973–76; Pres., Wilts Young Conservatives, 1984–97. Pres., Swindon Music Fest., 1987–2004; Vice-Chm., 1997–2014, Chm., 2014–, Ralph Vaughan Williams Soc.; Mem. Cttee, English Music Fest., 2002–05. Gov., Wycliffe Coll., 1995–2006. Proj. Manager, Blandford Railway Arches Trust, 2014–. *Recreations:* music, cricket, philately, reading, book-collecting, photography. *Address:* 24 Wellsworth Lane, Rowlands Castle, Hants PO9 6BY. *Club:* Hampshire Cricket.

COONEY, David John; Ambassador of Ireland to Spain, Tunisia and Andorra, since 2014; *b* London, 29 April 1954; *m* Geraldine O'Kelly; one *s* three *d. Educ:* Univ. of Keele (BA Hons Politics and Hist.). Exec. Officer, Dept of Agric., Ireland, 1976–78; Admin. Officer, Dept of Public Service, 1978–79; Department of Foreign Affairs: Third Secretary: Inf. Sect., 1979–80; Develt Cooperation Div., 1980–81; Sec., Embassy to the Holy See, 1981–85; Third Sec., Political Div., 1985–86; Private Sec. to Sec.-Gen., 1986–88; Sec., Embassy of Ireland, Vienna, 1988–89; First Secretary: Econ. Div., 1989–90; (Antici), Perm. Repn to EU, Brussels, 1990–93; Counsellor, Eur. Corresp., 1994; Coordinator of White Paper on Irish For. Policy, 1994–95; Counsellor: Hd, Political Sect., Anglo-Irish Div. (participated in negotiation of Good Friday Agreement), 1995–98; Dep. Perm. Rep. to OECD, Paris, 1998–2000; Minister-Counsellor, Paris, 2000; Ambassador, Dep. Perm. Rep. to UN, NY, 2000–01; Political Dir, Asst Sec.-Gen., 2001–05; Perm. Rep. to UN, NY, 2005–07; Ambassador to Court of St James's, 2007–09; Sec. Gen., Dept of For. Affairs and Trade (formerly Dept of For. Affairs), 2009–14; Ambassador to the Holy See, 2012–14. *Address:* Embassy of Ireland, Pajeo de la Castellana 46–4, 28046 Madrid, Spain.

COONEY, Lorna; *see* Fitzsimons, L.

COONEY, Raymond George Alfred, (Ray), OBE 2005; actor, author, director, theatrical producer; created Theatre of Comedy at Shaftesbury Theatre, and Little Theatre of Comedy at Ambassadors Theatre, 1983; purchased The Playhouse, London, 1992; *b* 30 May 1932; *s* of Gerard Cooney and Olive (*née* Clarke); *m* 1962, Linda Dixon; two *s. Educ:* Alleyn's Sch., Dulwich. First appeared in Song of Norway, Palace, 1946; toured in Wales, 1954–56; subseq. played in: Dry Rot and Simple Spymen, Whitehall; Mousetrap, Ambassador; Charlie Girl, Adelphi; Not Now Darling, Savoy (also film); Not Now Comrade (film); Run for your Wife, Guildford; Two into One, Leicester and Guildford; Caught in the Net, Windsor; (and dir) It Runs in the Family, Playhouse, 1992; (and dir) Funny Money, Playhouse, 1995; The Chiltern Hundreds, Vaudeville, 1999. Productions (some jointly) include: Thark (revival); Doctor at Sea; The Queen's Highland Servant; My Giddy Aunt; Move Over Mrs Markham; The Mating Game; Lloyd George Knew My Father; That's No Lady-That's My Husband; Say Goodnight to Grandma; Two and Two Make Sex; At the End of the Day; Why Not Stay for Breakfast?; A Ghost on Tiptoe; My Son's Father; The Sacking of Norman Banks; The Bedwinner; The Little Hut; Springtime for Henry; Saint Joan; The Trials of Oscar Wilde; The Dame of Sark; Jack the Ripper; There Goes the Bride (and played leading role, Ambassadors, 1974); Ipi Tombi; What's a Nice Country Like US Doing In a State Like This?; Some of My Best Friends Are Husbands; Banana Ridge; Fire Angel; Elvis; Whose Life is it Anyway? (London and NY); Clouds; Chicago; Bodies; Beatlemania; Not Now Darling (revival); Hello Dolly (revival); Duet for One (London and NY); They're Playing Our Song; Children of a Lesser God; Run for your Wife; Aladdin; See How They Run; Pygmalion; Two Into One (revival, 2014); Passion Play; Loot (revival); Intimate Exchanges; Wife Begins at Forty; An Italian Straw Hat (revival); It Runs in the Family; Out of Order; Fools Rush In; Run for your Wife 2; Caught in the Net; Over the Moon; Twice Upon a Time; Stop Dreamin'. *Publications:* (with H. and M. Williams) Charlie Girl, 1965; *plays:* (with Tony Hilton) One for the Pot, 1961; Chase Me Comrade, 1964; (with Tony Hilton) Stand by your Bedouin, 1966; (with John Chapman) Not Now Darling, 1967; (with John Chapman) My Giddy Aunt, 1968; (with John Chapman) Move Over Mrs Markham, 1969; (with Gene Stone) Why Not Stay for Breakfast?, 1970; (with John Chapman) There Goes the Bride, 1973; Run for Your Wife, 1981; Two into One, 1983; Wife Begins at Forty, 1986; It Runs in the Family, 1989; Out of Order, 1990; Funny Money, 1996; Caught in the Net, 2000; (with Michael Cooney) Tom, Dick and Harry, 2003; Twice in a Lifetime, 2010. *Recreations:* tennis, swimming. *Address:* Ridge House, Forest Side, Epping, Essex CM16 4ED.

COOPER; *see* Ashley-Cooper, family name of Earl of Shaftesbury.

COOPER, family name of **Viscount Norwich** and **Baron Cooper of Windrush**.

COOPER OF WINDRUSH, Baron *cr* 2014 (Life Peer), of Chipping Norton in the County of Oxfordshire; **Andrew Timothy Cooper;** Founder and Director, Populus Group Ltd, since 2003; *b* Twickenham, Middx, 9 June 1963; *s* of late Ian Roger and Brenda Muriel Cooper; *m* 2000, Elizabeth Fiona (*née* Campbell); three *d. Educ:* Reigate Grammar Sch.; London Sch. of Econs and Political Sci. (BSc Econ 1985). Policy Researcher, SDP, 1986–87; Political Advr to Rt Hon. David Owen, MP, 1987–90; Hd of Res., Social Market Foundn, 1994–95; Dep. Dir of Res., 1995–97, Dir of Political Strategy, 1997–99, Cons. Party; Dir, Live Strategy Ltd, 2000; Dir of Strategy, Prime Minister's Office, 2011–13. *Publications:* contributed to: Blue Tomorrow, 2001; The Blue Book on Health, 2002; The Blue Book on Transport, 2002; Philip Gould: an unfinished life, 2012. *Recreations:* watching Manchester Utd, visiting the USA, cooking Spanish food. *Address:* House of Lords, SW1A 0PW; Populus, 10 Northburgh Street, EC1V 0AT. *T:* (020) 7253 9900, *Fax:* (020) 7253 9911.

COOPER, Adam; dancer, choreographer and actor; *b* 1971; *m* 2000, Sarah Wildor, *qv*; one *d. Educ:* Arts Educational Sch.; Royal Ballet Sch. Royal Ballet, 1989–97: Principal Dancer, 1994; main rôles include: Prince Rudolf, in Mayerling; Kings of the North and South, in Prince of the Pagodas; Romeo, and Tybalt, in Romeo and Juliet; Lescaut, in Manon; Espada, in Don Quixote; created rôles in Bloodlines, Ebony Concerto, Tombeaux, Firstext, Room of Cooks; with Adventures in Motion Pictures: The Swan, in Swan Lake, 1995; The Pilot, in Cinderella, 1998; On Your Toes (also choreog.), Leicester Haymarket, 2002, RFH, 2003; Singin' in the Rain, Sadler's Wells, 2004, Chichester, 2011, Palace Th., 2012; Sky Masterson, in Guys and Dolls, Piccadilly, 2006; The Wizard of Oz, RFH, 2008; Shall We Dance (also choreog.), Sadler's Wells, 2009; with Adam Cooper Productions, Les Liaisons Dangereuses (also choreog.), Japan, then Sadler's Wells, 2005; *choreography* includes, Grand Hotel, Donmar Warehouse, 2004; Candide, Menier Chocolate Factory, 2013; for Scottish Ballet: Elegy for Two; Reflections for Images of Dance; Sunny Afternoon, Harold Pinter Th., 2014; *television:* Madame Bovary, 2000. Dir, musical, Simply Cinderella, Curve, Leicester, 2008. Dir of Boys, London Studio Theatre. *Address:* c/o Jean Diamond, Diamond Management, 31 Percy Street, W1T 2DD.

COOPER, Sir Adrian; *see* Cooper, Sir R. A.

COOPER, Prof. Aldwyn John Richard, PhD; Vice Chancellor and Chief Executive, Regent's University London, since 2013; *b* Dulwich, 27 May 1949; *s* of Robert and May Cooper; *m* 1973, Rosalind Patricia Meyer; one *s* two *d. Educ:* Dulwich Coll.; Sir John Cass Coll., subseq. City of London Poly. (BSc 1st Cl. Special Psychol. 1972); Bristol Univ. (PhD Cognitive Psychol. 1975). Jun. Engr, Mott, Hay and Anderson, 1969; Demonstrator in Psychol., Bristol Univ., 1973–75; Harkness Fellow, Stanford and Berkeley Univs, 1975–76; Sen. Lectr, Open Univ., 1976–80; Prof. of Information Systems, Henley Mgt Coll., 1980–87; Man. Dir, Henley Distance Learning, 1983–87; Business Gp Dir, Open Coll., 1987–90; Man. Dir, Workhouse Television, 1990–99; Pro Vice Chancellor, Univ. of Glamorgan, 2000–07; Dean, Glamorgan Business Sch., 2004–06; Principal, Regent's Coll., London, 2007–13. Hon. DHumLit Webster, St Louis, Mo, 2011. FRSA. *Publications:* (with M. Blakstad) The Communicating Organisation, 2005. *Recreations:* reading, theatre, travel, wine, gastronomy, perfumes, teddy bears, flying. *Address:* South Lodge, Regent's University London, Inner Circle, Regent's Park, NW1 4NS. *T:* (020) 7487 7506. *E:* coopera@regents.ac.uk.

COOPER, Sir Alexander (Paston Astley), 7th Bt *cr* 1821, of Gadebridge, Hertfordshire; *b* 1 Feb. 1943; *o s* of Sir Patrick Graham Astley Cooper, 6th Bt and Audrey Anne Jervoise, *d* of Major D. P. J. Collas; *S* father, 2002; *m* 1974, Minnie Margaret, *d* of Charles Harrison. *Heir: kinsman* Gerald Nigel Astley Cooper [*b* 8 June 1916; *m* 1st, 1941, Mary Constance Piercy (marr. diss. 1945); one *d*; 2nd, 1951, Joan Ryland, *d* of Dr Bernard Wall; one *s* one *d*]. *Address:* 8 Berkshire Close, Leigh-on-Sea, Essex SS9 4RT.

COOPER, Ven. Annette Joy; Archdeacon of Colchester, since 2004; *b* 15 Nov. 1953; *d* of Harry Whitaker and Grace Mary Whitaker (*née* Parnham, later James); *m* 1972, Andrew John Cooper; two *s. Educ:* Lilley and Stone Newark Girls' High Sch.; Open Univ. (BA 1980); London Univ. (CQSW, DipSW 1985, ext.); Dip. Religious Studies, Southwark Ordination Course, 1988; Durham Univ. (MA Theol. and Ministry 2013). Local Authority social worker, 1979–88. Ordained deacon, 1988, priest, 1994; NSM, St Peter, Pembury, and full-time Asst Chaplain, Tunbridge Wells HA, 1988–91; full-time Chaplain, Bassetlaw Hosp. and Community Services NHS Trust, 1991–96; Priest i/c Edwinstowe St Mary, 1996–2004. Chaplain: Center Parcs, Sherwood, 1996–2000; Southwell Diocesan Mothers' Union, 1996–99; Area Dean, Worksop, 1999–2004. Hon. Canon: Southwell Minster, 2002–04; Chelmsford Cathedral, 2004–. Regl Rep. to House of Bishops, 2013–. Non-exec. Dir, Allchurches Trust Ltd, 2008–. *Publications:* It's Hard to Say Goodbye, 1994. *Recreations:* sailing, singing, entertaining family and friends. *Address:* 63 Powers Hall End, Witham, Essex CM8 1NH. *T:* (01376) 513130, *Fax:* (01376) 500789. *E:* a.colchester@chelmsford.anglican.org.

COOPER, Anthony; *see* Cooper, Derek A.

COOPER, Anthony William, CBE 2003; Principal, Aldercar Community Language College, 1995–2014; *b* 22 Sept. 1952; *s* of Lawrence and Mary Cooper; *m* 1985, Susan Margaret Howard; four *d. Educ:* Leeds Univ. (BEd Hons 1975); Nottingham Univ. (MEd 1982). Teacher of Geog., 1975–81, Hd of Humanities, 1981–89, Western Mere Sch., Derbys; Hd of Humanities, High View Community Tech. Sch., Derbys, 1989–90; Dep. Hd, Aldercar Sch., Derbys, 1990–95. Mem., E Midlands Judging Panel, The Teaching Awards, 2001–. FRSA 2003. Nat. Award for Secondary Sch. Leadership, The Teaching Awards, 2000. *Recreations:* reading, antique collections, theatre and concerts, holidays with 5 girls (including Sue).

COOPER, Artemis Clare Antonia; writer; *b* London, 22 April 1953; *d* of Viscount Norwich, *qv*; *m* 1986, Antony James Beevor, *qv*. *Educ:* Camden Sch. for Girls; St Hugh's Coll., Oxford (BA English Lang. and Lit.). Administrator, Duff Cooper Prize, 1993–. Trustee, 999 Club, Deptford, 2006–13. Chevalier, Ordre des Arts et des Lettres (France), 1997. *Publications:* (ed) A Durable Fire: the letters of Duff and Diana Cooper, 1913–1950, 1983; Cairo in the War, 1939–1945, 1989; Mr Wu and Mrs Stitch: the letters of Evelyn Waugh and Diana Cooper, 1991; Watching in the Dark: a child's fight for life, 1992; (with Antony Beevor) Paris After the Liberation, 1944–49, 1994; Writing at the Kitchen Table: the authorized biography of Elizabeth David, 1999; (ed) Words of Mercury: Patrick Leigh Fermor, 2003; Patrick Leigh Fermor: an adventure, 2012; (ed jtly) The Broken Road: from the Iron Gates to Mount Athos, by Patrick Leigh Fermor, 2013. *Recreations:* reading, cooking, walking, peering through other people's windows. *Address:* c/o Felicity Bryan Literary Agency, 2A North Parade, Oxford OX2 6LX. *T:* (01865) 513816. *E:* agency@felicitybryan.com.

COOPER, Air Cdre Barbara, CBE 2003 (OBE 2001); Member of Council, National Trust, since 2013; *b* Kingston, Ont, 23 Nov. 1958; *d* of William Donald and Eva Paxton; *m* 1981, William Cooper. *Educ:* Staffordshire Univ. (Postgrad. Dip. HR 2013). Commnd Air Traffic Control Br., RAF, 1978–85; on sabbatical, 1985–87; personnel rôles, RAF Admin (Sec.) Br., 1987–93; SO to CAS, 1993–97; ascs 1998; OC, Base Support Wing, RAF Lyneham, 1998–2000; Directing Staff, Advanced Comd and Staff Course, Shrivenham, 2000–02; Dep. Dir, Service Personnel Policy (Operational Welfare) and Hd, UK Prisoner of War Inf. Bureau, 2002–05; Dir, RAF Div., JSCSC, Shrivenham, 2005–06; rcds 2007; ACOS Personnel Strategy and Manpower, 2008–10; Comdt, Air Cadets, 2010–12. Hon. Pres., Stroud, Tetbury and Cirencester Air Cadets, 2012. FCIPD 2012. *Recreations:* family and friends, visiting NT properties, theatre, cycling, mentoring, gardening and growing more veg than the family can politely eat. *Address:* c/o National Trust, Heelis, Kemble Drive, Swindon SN2 2NA. *Club:* Royal Air Force.

COOPER, Rt Rev. Carl Norman; Chief Executive Officer, Powys Association of Voluntary Organisations, since 2008; *b* 4 Aug. 1960; *s* of Joseph and Kathleen Mary Cooper; *m* 2011, Amanda Clare Williams; one *s* two *d* by a former marriage. *Educ:* St David's University Coll., Lampeter (BA Hons French 1982); Wycliffe Hall, Oxford; Trinity Coll., Carmarthen (MPhil Wales 1999); Univ. of Wales Inst., Cardiff (Postgrad. Cert. Leadership for Collaboration 2010). Ordained deacon, 1985, priest, 1986; Curate, Llanelli, 1985–87; Priest i/c, 1987–88, Rector, 1988–93, Ciliau Aeron, Llannerch Aeron, Dihewyd and Mydroilyn; Rector, Rectorial Benefice of Dolgellau, 1993–2002; Diocesan Warden of Ordinands, Bangor, 1999–2001; Archdeacon of Meirionnydd, 2000–02; Bishop of St Davids, 2002–08. *Address:* Powys Association of Voluntary Organisations, 30 Ddole Road Industrial Estate/Ystâd Ddiwydiannol Heol Ddole, Llandrindod Wells, Powys LD1 6DF.

COOPER, Sir Cary (Lynn), Kt 2014; CBE 2001; Professor of Organizational Psychology and Health, Lancaster University Management School, 2003–08, now Distinguished Professor; Pro Vice-Chancellor, Lancaster University, 2004–10 and since 2012; *b* 28 April 1940; adopted British nationality, 1993; *s* of Harry and Caroline Cooper; *m* 1984, Rachel Faith Cooper; two *d*; one *s* one *d* from previous marr. *Educ:* Univ. of California, Los Angeles (BS, MBA); Univ. of Leeds (PhD). FBPsS 1982. Lectr in Psychology, Univ. of Southampton, 1967–73; University of Manchester Institute of Science and Technology: Prof. of Organizational Psychol., subseq. BUPA Prof. of Organizational Psychol. and Health, 1975–2003; Pro-Vice-Chancellor, 1995–2000; Dep. Vice-Chancellor, 2000–02. Advr to WHO and ILO, 1982–84. Founding Editor, Jl of Organizational Behavior, 1980–; Co-Ed., Internat. Jl Mgt Reviews, 1999–2001; Ed., Stress and Health (formerly Stress Medicine), 2009– (Associate Ed., 1987–92; Co-Ed., 1992–2009). Member: Bd of Trustees, Amer. Inst.

of Stress, 1984–; Adv. Council, Nat. Inst. of Clin. Applications of Behavioral Medicine, USA; ESRC Research Priorities Bd, 1998–2000; Pres., British Acad. of Management, 1987–90, 1997–2004, 2015– (Fellow, 1995); Chairman: Sunningdale Inst., Nat. Sch. of Govt, 2004–09; World Econ. Forum Global Agenda Council, on Chronic Disease and Wellbeing, 2009–10, on Mental Health, 2011–. President: Inst. of Welfare Officers, 1998–; Internat. Stress Mgt Assoc. (UK), 2000–11; British Assoc. of Counselling and Psychotherapy, 2007–12 (Vice Pres., 2000–06); Relate, 2009–. Ambassador, The Samaritans, 2000–10. Myers Lectr, BPsS, 1986; Apothecaries Lect., Soc. of Occupational Medicine, 2001. FRSA 1990; FRSocMed 1995; FRSPH (FRSH 1997); Fellow, Amer. Acad. of Mgt, 1997 (Mem. Bd of Govs, 2000–03; Dist. Service Award, 1998); CCMI (CIMgt 1997); FAcSS (AcSS 2001) (Chm., 2009–15). Hon. Mem., Soc. of Psychosom. Res.; Hon. FFOM 2005; Hon. FRCP 2006; Hon. FRCPI 2008; Hon. FBPsS 2010; Hon. Fellow: Eur. Acad. of Occupational Health Psychol., 2010; IOSH, 2012. MSc Manchester, 1979; Hon. DLitt Heriot-Watt, 1998; Hon. DBA Wolverhampton, 1999; Hon. DSc: Aston, 2002; Sheffield, 2011; DUniv Middx, 2003; DLaws Bath, 2014. Lifetime Achievement Award, Div. of Occupational Psychol., BPsS, 2007; Lord Dearing Lifetime Achievement Award for Higher Educn, Times Higher Educn Awards, 2010. *Publications:* (jtly) T-Groups, 1971; Group Training for Individual and Organizational Development, 1973; Theories of Group Processes, 1975; Developing Social Skills in Managers, 1976; OD in the US and UK, 1977; (jtly) Understanding Executive Stress, 1978; Advances in Experiential Social Processes, vol. 1, 1978, vol. 2, 1980; (jtly) Stress at Work, 1978; (jtly) Executives under Pressure, 1978; Behavioural Problems in Organizations, 1979; (jtly) The Quality of Working Life in Western and Eastern Europe, 1979; Learning from Others in Groups, 1979; The Executive Gypsy, 1979; Current Concerns in Occupational Stress, 1980; Developing Managers for the 1980's, 1980; (jtly) Combating Managerial Obsolescence, 1980; The Stress Check, 1980; White Collar and Professional Stress, 1981; Improving Interpersonal Relations, 1981; (jtly) Groups at Work, 1981; Executive Families Under Stress, 1981; (jtly) After Forty, 1981; Coping with Stress at Work, 1982; Psychology and Management, 1982; (jtly) Management Education, 1982; (jtly) Introducing Organization Behaviour, 1982; (jtly) High Pressure, 1982; Stress Research, 1983; (jtly) Human Behaviour in Organizations, 1983; (jtly) Stress and the Woman Manager, 1983; Public Faces, Private Lives, 1984; (jtly) Working Women, 1984; (jtly) Psychology for Managers, 1984; Psychosocial Stress and Cancer, 1984; (jtly) Women in Management, 1984; (jtly) The Change Makers, 1985; (jtly) Job Stress and Blue Collar Work, 1985; (jtly) International Review of Industrial and Organizational Psychology, annually 1986–2004; (jtly) Man and Accidents Offshore, 1986; (jtly) Stress and the Nurse Manager, 1986; (jtly) Pilots under Stress, 1986; (jtly) Psychosocial Factors at Work, 1987; (jtly) Retirement in Industrialized Societies, 1987; Living with Stress, 1988; Stress and Breast Cancer, 1988; (jtly) High Fliers, 1988; (jtly) Early Retirement, 1989; (jtly) Career Couples: contemporary lifestyles and how to manage them, 1989; (jtly) Understanding Stress: health care professionals, 1990; (jtly) Managing People at Work, 1990; Industrial and Organizational Psychology: critical writings, 1991; (jtly) Stress Survivors, 1991; (jtly) Cancer and Stress, 1991; (jtly) Work Psychology, 1991, 2nd edn 1997; (jtly) Stress and Accidents in the Offshore Oil and Gas Industry, 1991; Managing Organizations in 1992, 1991; (jtly) On the Move: the psychology of change and transitions, 1991; Personality and Stress, 1991; (jtly) Mergers and Acquisitions: the human factor, 1992; (jtly) Shattering the Glass Ceiling: the woman manager, 1992; (jtly) Relax: dealing with stress, 1992; (jtly) Women's Career Development, 1992; (jtly) Total Quality and Human Resources, 1992; (jtly) Successful Stress Management, 1993; (jtly) Stress in the Dealing Room, 1993; (jtly) The Workplace Revolution, 1993; (jtly) No Hassle: taking the stress out of work, 1994; (jtly) Business Elites, 1994; Handbook on Stress Medicine and Health, 1995; Trends in Organizational Behaviour, 1995; (jtly) Stress and Employer Liability, 1996, 2nd edn 2001; (jtly) Organizations and the Psychological Contract, 1996; (ed jtly) Blackwell Encyclopedia of Management, 1997; (jtly) Creating Tomorrow's Organizations, 1997; (jtly) Balancing Work, Life and Family, 1998; (ed jtly) Concise Encyclopedia of Management, 1998; (ed) Theories of Organizational Stress, 1998; (jtly) Stress and Strain, 1999; (ed) Who's Who in the Management Sciences, 2000; (ed jtly) Cancer and the Family, 2000; (jtly) Conquer your Stress, 2000; (ed) Classics in Management Thought, 2000; (jtly) Strategic Stress Management, 2000; (jtly) Organizational Stress, 2001; (jtly) Occupational Health Psychology, 2001; (jtly) New World of Work, 2001; (jtly) Emotions at Work, 2001; (ed jtly) International Handbook of Organizational Culture and Climate, 2001; Fundamentals of Organizational Behaviour (4 vols), 2002; (jtly) FT Guide to Executive Health, 2002; (jtly) Workplace Bullying, 2002; (ed jtly) Advances in Mergers and Acquisitions, 2003; (ed jtly) Bullying and Emotional Abuse in the Workplace, 2003; (jtly) Creating a Balance, 2003; (jtly) Destressing Doctors, 2003; (jtly) The Employment Relationship, 2003; (jtly) Managing the Risk of Workplace Stress, 2004; (jtly) Stress: a brief history, 2004; (jtly) Work-Life Integration, 2005; (ed) Leadership and Management in the 21st Century, 2005; (ed) Handbook of Stress Medicine and Health, 2005; (ed jtly) Work, 6 vols, 2005; (ed jtly) Workplace Violence, 2005; (ed jtly) Reinventing Human Resource Management, 2005; Managing Emotions in Mergers and Acquisitions, 2005; (ed jtly) Inspiring Leaders, 2006; (jtly) Managing Value-based Organizations, 2006; (jtly) Happy Performing Managers, 2006; (ed jtly) Positive Organizational Behavior, 2007; (jtly) How to Deal with Stress, 2007, 2010; (jtly) Detox Your Desk, 2007; (jtly) Managing Executive Health, 2008; (jtly) Positively Responsible, 2008; (jtly) Organizational and Work Psychology, 2008; (ed jtly) Research Companion to Emotions in Organizations, 2008; (ed jtly) Building More Effective Organizations, 2008; (ed jtly) Employee Wellbeing Support, 2008; (ed jtly) Long Working Hours Culture, 2008; (jtly) Open Source Leadership, 2009; (jtly) Workplace Psychological Health, 2009; (jtly) Missing Pieces: employee wellbeing, 2009; (jtly) Employee Morale, 2009; (ed jtly) Oxford Handbook of Organizational Wellbeing, 2009; (ed jtly) Oxford Handbook of Personnel Psychology, 2009; (ed jtly) Handbook of Organizational Behavior, 2 vols, 2009; (ed) New Directions in OB, 4 vols, 2009; (ed jtly) Research Companion to Corruption in Organizations, 2009; (ed jtly) International Handbook of Work and Organizational Psychology, 2009; (ed jtly) Handbook of Managerial Behavior and Occupational Health, 2009; (jtly) Leading HR, 2010; (jtly) Coping with Work Stress, 2010; (jtly) Organizational Stress Management, 2010; (jtly) The Science of Occupation Health, 2010; (ed jtly) Risk Business, 2010; (ed jtly) Bullying and Harassment in the Workplace, 2011; (ed jtly) Women and Management, 2011; (ed jtly) Crime and Corruption in Organizations, 2011; (jtly) Wellbeing, 2011; (jtly) Doing the Right Thing, 2011; (jtly) Stress in Turbulent Times, 2012; (jtly) Wellbeing and Work, 2012; (jtly) High Engagement Work Culture, 2012; (jtly) OB for Dummies, 2012; (jtly) Downsizing, 2012; From Stress to Wellbeing, 2013; (ed jtly) How Can HR Drive Success, 2013; (ed jtly) Building Resilience for Success, 2013; (ed jtly) Wellbeing (6 vols), 2014; (jtly) Solving the Strategy Delusion, 2015; The Economic Crisis and Occupational Stress, 2015; (jtly) Do We Need HR, 2015; (jtly) Why the Social Sciences Matter, 2015; articles on social science and medicine, stress medicine. *Recreations:* reading 19th century Russian fiction, living in hope with Manchester City football, enjoying my four children and five grandchildren! *Address:* Lancaster University Management School, Bailrigg, Lancaster LA1 4YX; 25 Lostock Hall Road, Poynton, Cheshire SK12 1DP. *T:* (01625) 871450.

COOPER, Prof. Cyrus, OBE 2015; DM; FRCP, FFPH; Professor of Musculoskeletal Science, University of Oxford, since 2011 (Norman Collisson Professor of Musculoskeletal Sciences, 2007–11); Fellow of St Peter's College, Oxford, since 2007; *b* 14 Feb. 1957; *s* of Dr Sarosh Cooper and Khorshed Cooper; *m* 1984, Margaret O'Donovan; two *s. Educ:* Gonville and Caius Coll., Cambridge (BA 1977); St Bartholomew's Hosp., London (MB BS 1980); DM Soton 1985. FRCP 1996; FFPH 2005. Sen. Registrar, Bristol Royal Infirmary, 1988–90; Asst Prof., Mayo Clinic, Minn, 1990–92; University of Southampton: Sen. Lectr in Rheumatol., 1992–97; Prof. of Rheumatol., 1997–; Dir, MRC Lifecourse Epidemiol. Unit (formerly MRC Epidemiol. Resource Centre), 2003–. Chm., Bd of Trustees, Nat. Osteoporosis Soc., 2004–07. FMedSci 2000. *Publications:* (jtly) Prevention and Treatment of Osteoporosis: a clinician's guide, 2005; original res. contribs to learned jls on epidemiology of osteoporosis, osteoarthritis and other rheumatic disorders, studies into develt origins of coronary heart disease and metabolic syndrome. *Recreation:* cricket. *Address:* c/o Nuffield Department of Orthopaedic Surgery, University of Oxford, Nuffield Orthopaedic Centre, Windmill Road, Oxford OX3 7LD. *Club:* Hampshire County Cricket.

COOPER, David Antony; a District Judge (Magistrates' Courts) (formerly Metropolitan Stipendiary Magistrate), 1991–2010; a Deputy District Judge (Magistrates' Courts), 2010–14; *b* 12 June 1945; *s* of Rev. Stanley Francis Cooper and Jane Anne Cooper; *m* 1968, Françoise Armandine Henriette Fourré; three *s. Educ:* Sandown Grammar Sch., IoW; Exeter Univ. (LLB); College of Law. Articled to David Rule Pyott, Freshfields, London, 1966–69; admitted Solicitor, 1969; with Heppenstalls, Lymington, 1969–71; Solicitor and Partner in charge of criminal litigation, Ellison & Co., Colchester, 1971–91. *Recreations:* undisturbed reading, boating, walking on Mull.

COOPER, Prof. David Edward; Professor of Philosophy, University of Durham, 1986–2008; *b* 1 Oct. 1942; *s* of late Edward Cooper and Lilian Doris Cooper (*née* Turner); *m* 1st, 1971, Patricia Patterson; 2nd, 1980, Sheila Ann Armstrong, *qv* (marr. diss. 1998); 3rd, 2000, Joy Palmer. *Educ:* Highgate Sch.; St Edmund Hall, Oxford; Nuffield Coll., Oxford (MA, BPhil). Lectr in Philosophy, Pembroke and Jesus Colls, Oxford, 1966–69; Asst Prof. of Philosophy, Univ. of Miami, 1969–72; Lectr in Phil. of Educn, Univ. of London Inst. of Educn, 1972–74; Reader in Phil., Univ. of Surrey, 1974–85. Associate Dir, Project Sri Lanka, Durham Univ., 2008–11; Sec. and Trustee, Project Sri Lanka Charity, 2010–. Visiting Professor, Universities of: Khartoum, 1975; Minnesota, 1977; Cape Town, 1979; Heidelberg and Tübingen, 1985; Trinity (Texas), 1986; Alberta, 1987; Vanderbilt, 1990; Malta, 1994; Ruhuna, Sri Lanka, 2006–09; Rivers Distinguished Vis. Prof. of the Humanities, E Carolina Univ., 1998; Vis. Sen. Res. Fellow, KCL, 1991–94; Leverhulme Res. Fellow, 1996–97; AHRB Res. Fellow, 1999–2000; Leverhulme res. grant, 2002–03, 2006–07. Fellow, Internat. Soc. for Intercultural Studies and Res., India, 1993–. Chairman: Phil. of Educn Soc., 1987–90; Friedrich Nietzsche Soc., 1991–94; President: Mind Assoc., 1991; Aristotelian Soc., 1993–94; Member: Council, Royal Inst. of Philosophy, 1995–; Exec. Cttee, Royal Inst. of Phil., 1997–2009. Hon. Diploma, Univ. Nacional de Educación a Distancia, Madrid, 1992. *Publications:* Philosophy and the Nature of Language, 1973; Presupposition, 1974; Knowledge of Language, 1975; (ed) The Manson Murders, 1975; Illusions of Equality, 1980; Authenticity and Learning, 1983; Metaphor, 1986; (ed) Education, Values and Mind, 1986; Existentialism: a reconstruction, 1990, 2nd rev. edn 1999; (ed jtly) The Environment in Question, 1992; (ed) Blackwell's Companion to Aesthetics, 1993; (ed jtly) Just Environments, 1995; World Philosophies: an historical introduction, 1995, 2nd edn 2002; Heidegger, 1996; (ed) Aesthetics: the classic readings, 1997; (ed) Ethics: the classic readings, 1998; (ed) Epistemology: the classic readings, 1998; (ed jtly) Spirit of the Environment, 1998; (ed) Metaphysics: the classic readings, 1999; The Measure of Things: humanism, humility and mystery, 2002; Meaning, 2003; (with S. P. James) Buddhism, Virtue and Environment, 2005; A Philosophy of Gardens, 2006; (ed jtly) Philosophy: the classic readings, 2009; Convergence with Nature: a Daoist perspective, 2012; Sunlight on the Sea: reflecting on reflections, 2013. *Recreations:* music, walking, wildlife. *Address:* The Bererns, 8 New Road, Chatton, Northumberland NE66 5PU. *E:* davide.cooper@yahoo.co.uk.

COOPER, (Derek) Anthony; Member, Nuclear Decommissioning Authority, 2005–11; *b* 11 Dec. 1943; *s* of Donald Cooper and Freda Cooper (*née* Sheridan); *m* 1967, June Iley; one *s* two *d*; one *s. Educ:* Whitehaven Grammar Sch.; Edinburgh Univ. (BSc Forestry and Wild Life Mgt). Forest Officer, Forestry Commn, 1967–76; Institution of Professionals, Managers and Specialists: Negotiations Officer, 1976–79; Asst Sec., 1979–82; Asst Gen. Sec., 1982–87; Dep. Gen. Sec., 1987–91; Gen. Sec., Engrs and Managers Assoc., 1991–2001; Jt Gen. Sec., Prospect, 2001–02; Chm., Nuclear Industry Assoc. (formerly British Nuclear Industry Forum), 2002–05. Chairman: Aid Tspt Ltd, 1993–98; 4U@work Ltd, 2000–03; PPP Consultancy Ltd, 2002–06; Chairman of Trustees: Combined Nuclear Industry Pension Plan Ltd, 2006–13; Magnox Electric Gp of Electricity Supply Pension Scheme Ltd, 2009–15; Trustee, BNFL Gp Pension Scheme Ltd, 2008–12; Dir, Way Ahead Training Ltd, 1999–2003. Commissioner: Postal Services Commn, 2000–10; Forestry Commn, 2001–06. Member: Govt Energy Adv. Panel, 1993–2003; EU Energy Consultative Cttee, 1998–2001; Strategy Bd, 2002–04, Investment Cttee, 2003–04, Nuclear Decommissioning Agency Prog. Bd, 2003–04, DTI. Mem., Gen. Council, TUC, 1997–2000. Trustee: Power Aid Logistics, 1993–98; Royal Hosp. for Neuro-disability, Putney, 1995–97. *Recreations:* reading, sailing, walking. *Address:* 55 Rivulet Gardens, Devan Grove, N4 2GS.

See also Rt Hon. Y. Cooper.

COOPER, Wing Comdr Donald Arthur, CBE 1990; AFC 1961; Chief Inspector, Air Accidents Investigation Branch, Department of Transport, 1986–90; *b* 27 Sept. 1930; *s* of A. A. Cooper and E. B. Cooper (*née* Edmonds); *m* 1958, Belinda, 3rd *d* of Adm. Sir Charles Woodhouse, KCB and Lady Woodhouse; three *s. Educ:* Queen's Coll., British Guiana; RAF Coll., Cranwell; BA Open. ATPL (H) 1961, ATPL (A) 1972. FRAeS. Served on fighter and trng sqdns, 1952–56; Empire Test Pilot's Sch., 1957; RAE Farnborough, 1958–60; RAF sc 1961; Sqdn Comdr CFS Helicopter Wing, 1962–64; HQ FTC, 1964–66; Defence Operational Requirements Staff, MoD, 1966–70; joined Accidents Investigation Br., BoT, on retirement, 1970. *Recreations:* walking, ballroom dancing, amateur dramatics. *Address:* 7 Lynch Road, Farnham, Surrey GU9 8BZ.

COOPER, Edward James Oswald; Partner, since 1988, and National Practice Group Head, since 2012, Slater & Gordon Lawyers (formerly Russell Jones & Walker LLP); *b* London, 12 June 1959; *s* of Derek Oswald Cooper and Julia Mary Cooper; *m* 1993, Atinuke Olubunmi Alake, (Bobbie); three *s. Educ:* Winchester House Sch., Sevenoaks; Tonbridge Sch.; Bristol Univ. (LLB). Admitted solicitor, 1984; Trainee Solicitor, then Asst Solicitor, Simmons & Simmons, 1982–85; Asst Solicitor, 1985–88, Nat. Hd, Employment Dept, 1990, Russell Jones & Walker. Member: Employment Lawyers' Assoc.; Professional Negligence Lawyers' Assoc. *Recreations:* cricket, tennis, reading, jazz. *Address:* Slater & Gordon Lawyers, 50–52 Chancery Lane, WC2A 1HL. *T:* (020) 7657 1506, *Fax:* (020) 7657 1546. *E:* ECooper@slatergordon.co.uk. *Clubs:* MCC; Crocodiles Cricket.

COOPER, (Edward) John; Chief Executive, Hammersmith Hospitals NHS Trust, 1994–2001; *b* 21 April 1943; *s* of John and Rosalind Cooper; *m* 1977, Susan Hitchin. *Educ:* Malvern Coll.; Nottingham Univ. (BA); Manchester Business Sch. (MBA 1971). AHSM 1969. Nat. Admin. Trng Scheme, NHS, 1965–66; United Liverpool Hosps, 1966–67; Univ. Hosp., S Manchester, 1967–69; various posts, Llewelyn-Davies Internat., 1971–78; S Australian Health Commn, 1978–85 (Dep. Chm. and Comr, 1983–85); Dist Gen. Manager, Hampstead HA, 1985–91; Chief Exec., Royal Free Hampstead NHS Trust, 1991–94. Mem. Council, RCP, 2004–08. Hon. FRCP 2008. *Recreations:* performing arts, travel. *Address:* 74 High Street, Hemingford Grey, Cambs PE28 9BN.

COOPER, Eileen, RA 2001; RE 2002; Keeper of the Royal Academy, since 2011; *b* 10 June 1953; *d* of John Lawrence and Marjorie Cooper; *m* 1983, David Malcolm Southward; two *s. Educ:* Goldsmiths' Coll., London (DipAD); RCA (MA Painting; FRCA 2006, Hon. FRCA 2011). Part-time Tutor, Printmaking: RCA, 1994–2008; Royal Acad. Schs, 2005–; Artist in Residence, Dulwich Picture Gall., 1998–99. Solo exhibitions include: at Art First, London:

Open Secrets, 1998; Raw Material Part II, 2000; Works on Paper, 2002; Eileen Cooper 50 New Works, 2003; Time of Your Life, 2005; Deeper Water, 2007; Dreams of Elsewhere, 2009; Showing Off, 2011; Edge to Edge, 2013; Second Skin: Eileen Cooper in the 80's and 90's, touring show, 1999; Raw Material Part I, Dulwich Picture Gall., 2000; Passions: new work on paper, Art First, NY, 2002; A Celebration, Art First Projects, NY, 2003; Collages, Royal Acad. Friends Room, 2010; In the Garden, Rabley Drawing Centre, 2015; Hide and Seek, work on paper 1977–2014, RA. Numerous gp exhibns in Britain, Europe, USA and Asia; works in public and private collections worldwide. Curator: Confluence, APT Gallery, 2009; RA Summer Show, 2009–14; Encounter, Royal Acad. in Asia, 2012, Royal Acad. in Middle E, Doha, 2013. Hon. DArt Southampton Solent, 2013. *Publications:* (cover) Women who Run with the Wolves, by Clarissa Pinkola Estés, 1998; (cover and illus.) Meeting Midnight, by Carol Ann Duffy, 1999; *relevant publication:* Between the Lines, by Martin Gayford and Sara Lee, 2015. *Recreation:* reading. *Address:* Royal Academy of Arts, Burlington House, Piccadilly, W1J 0BD.

COOPER, Prof. (Elizabeth) Helen, PhD, DLitt; FBA 2006; Professor of Medieval and Renaissance English, University of Cambridge, 2004–14; Fellow, Magdalene College, Cambridge, 2004–14, now Life Fellow; *b* 6 Feb. 1947; *d* of Sir Percy Edward, (Sir Peter), Kent, FRS and (Margaret) Betty Kent; *m* 1970, Michael George Cooper (*d* 2007); two *d. Educ:* New Hall, Cambridge (BA 1968, MA; PhD 1972); DLitt Oxford 1996. Jun. Res. Fellow, New Hall, Cambridge, 1971–74; Beaverbrook Tutorial Fellow in English and Univ. CUF Lectr, University Coll., Oxford, 1978–2004, now Emeritus Fellow (Hon. Fellow, 2014). Editor for Old and Middle English, Medium Ævum, 1989–2002. Pres., New Chaucer Soc., 2000–02. Trustee: Prince's Teaching Inst. 2013–; Shakespeare's Birthplace Trust, 2013–. Hon. DLitt Washington and Lee, 2001. *Publications:* Pastoral: Mediaeval into Renaissance, 1978; Great-Grandmother Goose, 1978; The Structure of the Canterbury Tales, 1983; Oxford Guides to Chaucer: The Canterbury Tales, 1989, 2nd edn 1996; (ed) Sir Thomas Malory: Le Morte Darthur, 1998; The English Romance in Time, 2004; Shakespeare and the Medieval World, 2010; numerous articles in books and periodicals. *Address:* Magdalene College, Cambridge CB3 0AG. *E:* ehc31@cam.ac.uk.

COOPER, Sir (Frederick Howard) Michael C.; *see* Craig-Cooper.

COOPER, Gareth; *see* Cooper, W. G.

COOPER, George A.; marketing and business consultant; Chairman, Independent Television Publications Ltd, 1971–89; *b* 9 Oct. 1915; *s* of late Joseph Cooper; *m* 1944, Irene Burns; one *d.* Exec. with internat. publishing gp; served War of 1939–45, Royal Artillery (Captain); Exec., Hulton Press, 1949–55; Director: ABC Television Ltd, 1955–77; Thames Television Ltd, 1968 (Man. Dir, 1974–77); Independent Television News, 1976–77; Chm., Network Programme Cttee of Independent Television, 1975–77. FRTS 1987. *Address:* 43 Rivermill, 151 Grosvenor Road, SW1V 3JN. *T:* (020) 7821 9305. *Club:* Royal Automobile.

COOPER, Gen. Sir George (Leslie Conroy), GCB 1984 (KCB 1979); MC 1953; DL; Chief Royal Engineer, 1987–93; *b* 10 Aug. 1925; *s* of late Lt-Col G. C. Cooper and Mrs Y. V. Cooper, Bulmer Tye House, Sudbury; *m* 1957, Cynthia Mary Hume; one *s* one *d. Educ:* Downside Sch.; Trinity Coll., Cambridge (wartime short course). Commnd 1945; served with Bengal Sappers and Miners, 1945–48; Korea, 1952–53; psc 1956; jssc 1959; Instructor, RMA Sandhurst, 1959–62 and Staff Coll., Camberley, 1964; Brevet Lt-Col, 1964; GSO1, 1st Div., 1964–66; CRE, 4th Div., 1966–68; MoD, 1968–69; Comdr, 19th Airportable Bde, 1969–71; Royal Coll. of Defence Studies, 1972; Dep. Dir Army Trng, 1973–74; GOC SW District, 1974–75; Dir, Army Staff Duties, 1976–79; GOC SE District, 1979–81; Adjt-Gen., 1981–84, retd. ADC General to the Queen, 1982–84. Mem., UK Bd of Management, and Dir of Management Develt, GEC, 1985–86. Colonel Commandant: RE, 1980–93; RPC, 1981–85; Col, Queen's Gurkha Engineers, 1981–91. Mem. Council, Nat. Army Mus., 1981–95. Chm., Knightstone Syndicate Management (formerly HGP Managing Agency), 1991–93 (Dir, 1990–91). Lay Rep., Senate and Bar Council Disciplinary Bodies, 1984–90. Chm., 1980–95, Jt Pres., 1995–2002, Jt Patron, 2002–, Infantile Hypercalcæmia Foundn, later Williams Syndrome Foundation; Chm., Princess Alexandra's NHS Hosp. Trust, 1994–96; Mem. Council, Action Research (formerly Nat. Fund for Res. into Crippling Diseases), 1982–95; Trustee, Harlow War Meml Inst., 1990–2014; Patron, Pahar Trust, 1993–2010. DL Essex, 1990. *Publications:* (with D. A. Alexander) The Bengal Sappers 1803–2003, 2003; Fight, Dig and Live: the story of the Royal Engineers in the Korean War, 2011; articles and book reviews. *Recreations:* writing, gardening, fighting old age. *Address:* 37 Mulberry Green, Old Harlow, Essex CM17 0EY. *T:* (01279) 427214. *Club:* Army and Navy.

COOPER, Gilead Patrick; QC 2006; *b* 24 April 1955; *s* of Lionel and Lily Cooper. *Educ:* Haileybury; Christ Church, Oxford (MA); City Univ. (Dip. Law). Called to the Bar, Middle Temple, 1983; in practice specialising in Chancery law. *Publications:* contributed: Tolley's Pensions Law; Palmer on Bailment, 2009. *Recreation:* anything other than sport. *Address:* 3 Stone Buildings, Lincoln's Inn, WC2A 3XL. *T:* (020) 7242 4937, *Fax:* (020) 7405 3896. *E:* sibyl@cumae.me. *Club:* Garrick.

COOPER, Helen; *see* Cooper, E. H.

COOPER, Imogen, CBE 2007; concert pianist; *b* 28 Aug. 1949; *d* of late Martin Du Pré Cooper, CBE and Mary Cooper (*née* Stewart); *m* 1982, John Alexander Batten (marr. diss. 2002). *Educ:* Paris Conservatoire, with Jacques Février and Yvonne Lefébure, 1961–67 (Premier Prix, 1967); Vienna, with Alfred Brendel, 1970. Plays regularly with all major British orchestras; regular appearances at Proms, 1975–; first British pianist, and woman, to have appeared in South Bank Piano Series, 1975; British festivals include Bath, Cheltenham, Harrogate, Brighton, Edinburgh and Aldeburgh. Overseas engagements incl. concerts with Berlin, Vienna, New York and Los Angeles Philharmonic Orchestras, and regular tours to Australasia, Holland, France, Scandinavia, USA and Japan. Humanitas Vis. Prof. of Classical Music and Music Educn, St John's Coll., Oxford, 2012–13. Recordings include: Schubert's late works; Schubert lieder (with Wolfgang Holzmair), Brahms and Schumann; Mozart's Concerti for Two and Three Pianos, with Alfred Brendel and Acad. of St Martin in the Fields; solo Mozart concerti; Wigmore Hall Live Series. Hon. RAM. Mozart Meml Prize, 1969. *Recreations:* architecture, cooking, walking. *Address:* c/o Askonas Holt, Lincoln House, 300 High Holborn, WC1V 7JH. *T:* (020) 7400 1700.

COOPER, Jane Elizabeth Louise; Director of Communications and Brand (formerly Director of Communications), UNICEF UK, since 2011; *b* New York City, 9 Aug. 1958; *d* of Bryan Cooper and Patricia Cooper; *m* 2005, David Robertson; one *s* one *d. Educ:* Leeds Univ. (BA Hons Eng. Lit. 1979); Univ. of London (MA Hist. of Art 2007). Editl Asst, BT Batsford, 1981–87; Sec., All Party Human Rights Gp, 1987–89; Hd, Govt Relns, Amnesty Internat., 1989–95; Dir, Westminster Strategy, 1995–2001; communications consultant, 2001–05; Head of Communications: Leigh Day & Co., 2001–05; Enforcement and Compliance, HMRC, 2005–08; Director of Communications: DCSF, 2008–09; DCMS, 2009–10. Dir, Death Penalty Proj., 2007–13. Trustee, Internat. Broadcast Trust, 2013–. Gov., City Lit, London, 2011–. *Publications:* International Human Rights (with David Mepham), 2004. *Recreations:* swimming, scuba diving. *Address:* 69 Queen Elizabeth's Walk, N16 5UG. *T:* (020) 8800 4906. *E:* jane.cooper4@btinternet.com.

COOPER, Jilly, (Mrs Leo Cooper), OBE 2004; author; *b* 21 Feb. 1937; *d* of Brig. W. B. Sallitt, OBE, and Mary Elaine Whincup; *m* 1961, Leo Cooper (*d* 2013); one *s* one *d. Educ:* Godolphin Sch., Salisbury. Reporter, Middlesex Independent, Brentford, 1957–59; followed by numerous short-lived jobs as account executive, copy writer, publisher's reader, receptionist, puppy fat model, switchboard wrecker, and very temporary typist. Columnist: Sunday Times, 1969–82; Mail on Sunday, 1982–87. Hon. DLitt: Gloucester, 2009; Anglia Ruskin, 2011. *Publications:* How to Stay Married, 1969, rev. edn 2011; How to Survive from Nine to Five, 1970 (new edn as Work and Wedlock, 1978); Jolly Super, 1971; Men and Super Men, 1972; Jolly Super Too, 1973; Women and Super Women, 1974 (new edn as Super Men and Super Women, 1977); Jolly Superlative, 1975; Super Jilly, 1977; Class, 1979; The British in Love, 1980; (with Tom Hartman) Violets and Vinegar, 1980; Supercooper, 1980; Intelligent and Loyal, 1981, re-issued as Mongrel Magic, 1981; Jolly Marsupial, 1982; (with Imperial War Museum) Animals in War, 1983; The Common Years, 1984; Leo and Jilly Cooper on Cricket, 1985; (with Patrick Lichfield) Hot Foot to Zabrieskie Point, the Unipart Calendar Book, 1985; How to Survive Christmas, 1986; Leo and Jilly Cooper on Horse Mania, 1986; Turn Right at the Spotted Dog, 1987; Angels Rush In, 1990; *novels:* Emily, 1975; Bella, 1976; Harriet, 1976; Octavia, 1977; Prudence, 1978; Imogen, 1978; Riders, 1985 (televised, 1993); Rivals, 1988; Polo, 1991; The Man who made Husbands Jealous, 1993 (televised, 1995); Araminta's Wedding, 1993; Appassionata, 1996; Score, 1999; Pandora, 2002; Wicked!, 2006; Jump!, 2010; *short stories:* Love and Other Heartaches, 1981, re-printed as Lisa and Co., 1982; *for children:* Little Mabel, 1980; Little Mabel's Great Escape, 1981; Little Mabel Wins, 1982; Little Mabel Saves the Day, 1985. *Recreations:* merry-making, wild flowers, music, mongrels, greyhounds. *Address:* c/o Curtis Brown, Haymarket House, 28–29 Haymarket, SW1Y 4SP.

COOPER, John; *see* Cooper, E. J.

COOPER, John Gordon; QC 2010; barrister; writer and broadcaster; Hon. Visiting Professor of Law, Cardiff University, since 2010; *b* Wolverhampton, 15 Sept. 1958; *s* of John Cooper and Mary Cooper. *Educ:* Regis Comp. Sch., Wolverhampton; Univ. of Newcastle (LLB Hons; Butterworth's Law Prizeman 1980). Called to the Bar: Middle Temple, 1983, Bencher, 2012; NSW and Vic, Australia, 1989; Gibraltar, 2013; lawyer, Clifford Chance, London, 1988–89. Member: Cttee, Criminal Bar Assoc., 2001–12; Bar Council, 2007–14 (Vice-Chm., Public Affairs Cttee, 2008–11); Cttee, SE Circuit, 2010–15; Dir of Educn, 2012–15. Chm., Iran Tribunal, 2010–13. Pres., League Against Cruel Sports, 2011– (Chm., 1992–2012). Mem., Working Pty, Nudge Global, 2012–15. Chm., Adv. Bd, Trust the Mkt, 2015–. Mem., Bd of Trustees, Prisoners of Conscience, 2010–. Sen. Legal Advr, Home Affairs Select Cttee, 2014–; Legal Advr to Shadow Attorney Gen. and Solicitor Gen., 2015–. Mem., Adv. Bd, Newcastle Univ. Law Sch., 2012–. Mem. Labour Party, 1984–. Contested (Lab): NW Surrey, 1987; Amber Valley, 1992. Mem. (Lab) Watford BC, 1991–94 (Vice Chm., Civic Amenities, 1993–94). FRSA 2009. Freeman, City of London, 2011–; Mem., Coopers' Co. Broadcaster on TV and radio, 1982–, incl. presenter and contrib. to progs on BBC, ITV, Sky, Channel 4, Al Jazeera, Radio 4. Writer: plays: The Cure, Royal Court, 1982; The Burning Point, Tricycle, 1987; television: The Law Lord, 1991; The Advocates, 1992. Columnist: The Times, 1999–2009; Independent, 2012–; writer, Observer, 2009–; Ed., Criminal Bar Qly, 2004–; Consultant Ed., Criminal Law and Justice Weekly, 2010–. *Publications:* Encyclopedia of Data Protection and Privacy (contrib.), 1998–; Cruelty: an analysis of Article 3, 2003; The Link Between Animal Abuse and Human Violence, 2009; Inquests, 2010; (contrib.) Cases That Changed our Lives, 2010; contrib. articles and feature writer for most legal pubns incl. New Law Jl, Criminal Law Rev., Solicitors Jl and nat. newspapers. *Recreations:* photography, history, Wolverhampton Wanderers, pedalling on a bicycle in the gym but going nowhere. *Address:* Parsonage Farm, Dairy Way, Abbots Langley, Herts WD5 0QJ. *T:* 07973 908288; 25 Bedford Row, WC1R 4HD; (literary) c/o Paul Stevens, Independent Talent, 40 Whitfield Street, W1T 2RH. *E:* johncooperqc@sky.com. *W:* www.john-cooper.info, www.twitter.com/john_cooper_qc. *Clubs:* Groucho, Chelsea Arts, Home House, Royal Gibraltar Yacht.

COOPER, Rev. Canon John Leslie; Archdeacon of Coleshill, 1990–93; *b* 16 Dec. 1933; *s* of Iris and Leslie Cooper; *m* 1959, Gillian Mary Dodds; two *s* one *d. Educ:* Tiffin School, Kingston, Surrey; Chichester Theological Coll. BD 1965, MPhil 1978, London Univ. (External Student). National Service, RA; commissioned, 1952–54. General Electric Co. management trainee, 1954–59; Chichester Theol Coll., 1959–62; Asst Curate, All Saints, Kings Heath, Birmingham, 1962–65; Asst Chaplain, HM Prison, Wandsworth, 1965–66; Chaplain: HM Borstal, Portland, Dorset, 1966–68; HM Prison, Bristol, 1968–72; Research Fellow, Queen's Coll., Birmingham, 1972–73; Priest-in-Charge 1973–81, Vicar 1981–82, St Paul's, Balsall Heath, Birmingham. Examining Chaplain to Bishop of Birmingham, 1981–82; Archdeacon of Aston, and Canon Residentiary, St Philip's Cathedral, Birmingham, 1982–90; Asst Curate, Holy Trinity, Sutton Coldfield, 1993–96. Hon. Canon, Birmingham Cathedral, 1993–97, now Canon Emeritus. *Recreations:* music, reading, travel, carpentry, photography, cookery, painting. *Address:* 4 Ireton Court, Kirk Ireton, Ashbourne, Derbys DE6 3JP. *T:* (01335) 370459.

COOPER, John Michael; QC 2014; *b* Newcastle upon Tyne, 14 Aug. 1960; *s* of Michael and Angela Cooper; *m* 1993, Romina; two *d. Educ:* Mt St Mary's Coll., Spinkhill; Reading Univ. (LLB). Called to the Bar, Inner Temple, 1985; in practice as barrister, specialising in health and safety and envmtl law, London, 1986–99, Manchester, 1999–2003, London, 2003–. *Recreations:* running marathons, cricket, shooting, wine. *Address:* Crown Office Chambers, 2 Crown Office Row, Temple, EC4Y 7HJ. *T:* (020) 7797 8100. *E:* cooper@crownofficechambers.com. *Club:* MCC.

COOPER, Rear-Adm. John Spencer, OBE 1974; *b* 5 April 1933; *s* of Harold Spencer Cooper and Barbara (*née* Highet); *m* 1966, Jacqueline Street (*née* Taylor); two *d. Educ:* St Edward's Sch., Oxford; Clare Coll., Cambridge (MA 1959). Joined RN, 1951; served as Lieut on HM Ships Ceylon and Ark Royal; joined Submarines 1966, Polaris Systems Officer in HMS Renown; Comdr 1969; MoD, 1970–73; Flag Officer, Submarines Staff, 1974–76; Captain 1976; Director, Trials, Chevaline programme, 1976–78; Special Proj., RN, Washington, 1978–80; Cdre 1981; Dir, Weapons (Strategic Systems), 1981–83; Dir Gen., Strategic Weapon Systems, 1983–85; Chief Strategic Systems Exec., MoD, 1985–88. Operations Manager: Naval Command and Control Div., Ferranti International, 1988–90; Ferranti Naval Systems, 1990–93.

COOPER, Julie Elizabeth; MP (Lab) Burnley, since 2015; *b* 20 June 1960; *d* of Robert Calder and Teresa Fletcher; *m* 1984, Brian Cooper; one *s* one *d. Educ:* Colne Park High Sch., Colne; Edge Hill Coll., Ormskirk (BA Hons Eng. Lang. and Lit.). English teacher, Birkdale High Sch., Dewsbury, 1982–84; Librarian, Hagergham High Sch., Burnley, 1990–92; Dir, Coopers Chemist, Burnley, 1992–2010. Mem. (Lab), Burnley BC, 2005– (Leader, 2012–14). *Recreations:* travel, film, music, reading. *Address:* House of Commons, SW1A 0AA. *T:* (01282) 425744.

COOPER, Kenneth Reginald, CB 1991; Chief Executive, The British Library, 1984–91; *b* 28 June 1931; *s* of Reginald and Louisa May Cooper; *m* 1955, Olga Ruth (*née* Harvey); two *s* two *d. Educ:* Queen Elizabeth's Grammar Sch., Barnet; New Coll., Oxford (MA). FIPM; FITD (Pres., 1981–83); FIInfSc (Pres., 1988–89). Various appointments, Min. of Labour, 1954–62; Principal, HM Treasury, 1962–65; Principal Private Secretary to Minister of Labour, 1966–67; Asst Sec. for Industrial Training, Min. of Labour, 1967–70; Chief Executive: Employment Services Agency, 1971–75; Training Services Agency, 1975–79; Dir Gen., Nat. Fedn of Building Trades Employers, 1979–84. Vis. Prof., Strathclyde Univ.,

1987–91. Dep. Chm., CICI, 1988–92; Dir, Book Trust, 1988–93. CCMI (CBIM 1989); FRSA 1987. Hon. Fellow, Brighton Poly., 1991. Hon. FCLIP 2002. *Recreations:* music, Rugby football.

COOPER, Prof. Leon N., PhD; Thomas J. Watson, Sr, Professor of Science, Brown University, Providence, RI, since 1974; Director, Institute for Brain and Neural Systems, since 1991, and Director, Brain Science Program, since 2000, Brown University; *b* NYC, 28 Feb. 1930; *s* of Irving Cooper and Anna Cooper (*née* Zola); *m* 1969, Kay Anne Allard; two *d*. *Educ:* Columbia Univ. (AB 1951, AM 1953, PhD 1954). Nat. Sci. Foundn post-doctoral Fellow, and Mem., Inst. for Advanced Study, 1954–55; Res. Associate, Univ. of Illinois, 1955–57; Asst Prof., Ohio State Univ., 1957–58; Associate Prof., Brown Univ., 1958–62, Prof., 1962–66, Henry Ledyard Goddard Prof., 1966–74. Consultant, various governmental agencies, industrial and educational organizations. Lectr, Summer Sch., Varenna, Italy, 1955; Visiting Professor: Brandeis Summer Inst., 1959; Bergen Internat. Sch. Physics, Norway, 1961; Scuola Internazionale di Fisica, Erice, Italy, 1965; Ecole Normale Supérieure, Centre Universitaire Internat., Paris, 1966; Cargèse Summer Sch., 1966; Radiation Lab., Univ. of Calif at Berkeley, 1969; Faculty of Scis, Quai St Bernard, Paris, 1970, 1971; Brookhaven Nat. Lab., 1972; Chair of Math. Models of Nervous System, Fondation de France, 1977–83; Mem., Conseil Supérieur de la Recherche, l'Université René Descartes, Paris, 1981–87. Alfred P. Sloan Foundn Res. Fellow, 1959–66; John Simon Guggenheim Meml Foundn Fellow, 1965–66. Co-Chm., Bd of Dirs, Nestor Inc. Fellow: Amer. Physical Soc.; Amer. Acad. of Arts and Sciences. Member: Amer. Philosoph. Soc.; National Acad. of Sciences; Sponsor Fedn of Amer. Scientists; Soc. for Neuroscience, Amer. Assoc. for Advancement of Science; Defense Science Bd, 1989–93. Mem. Bd of Govs, Internat. Neural Network Soc., 1989–94. (Jtly) Comstock Prize, Nat. Acad. of Scis, 1968; (jtly) Nobel Prize for Physics, 1972; Award of Excellence, Grad. Fac. Alumni, Columbia Univ., 1974; Déscartes Medal, Acad. de Paris, Univ. René Déscartes, 1977; Yrjö Reenpää Medal, Finnish Cultural Foundn, 1982; John Jay Award, 1985, Award for Distinguished Achievement, 1989, Columbia Univ.; Alexander Hamilton Award, Columbia Coll., 1996; Rosenberger Medal, Brown Univ., 2013. Hon. DSc: Columbia, 1973; Sussex, 1973; Illinois, 1974; Brown, 1974; Gustavus Adolphus Coll., 1975; Ohio State Univ., 1976; Univ. Pierre et Marie Curie, Paris, 1977. Public lectures, internat. confs, symposia. *Publications:* Introduction to the Meaning and Structure of Physics, 1968; (contrib.) The Physicist's Conception of Nature, 1973; How We Learn, How We Remember: toward an understanding of brain and neural systems, 1995; contrib. The Many Body Problem, 1963; (jtly) Theory of Cortical Plasticity, 2004; (ed jtly) BCS: 50 years, 2011; contrib. to numerous jls incl. Physics Rev., Amer. Jl Physics, Biological Cybernetics, Jl of Neurosci., Jl of Neurophysiol., Procs of the US Nat. Acad. of Scis. *Recreations:* music, theatre, ski-ing. *Address:* Physics Department, Brown University, Providence, RI 02912–1843, USA. *T:* (401) 8632172. *Clubs:* University, Faculty (Providence, RI).

COOPER, Sir Louis Jacques B.; *see* Blom-Cooper.

COOPER, Mark; Head of Music Television, BBC, since 2013; *b* London, 14 Nov. 1952; *s* of Rt Hon. Sir Frank Cooper, GCB, CMG, PC and Peggie Cooper; *m* 2003, Sian Davies; three *s* one *d*. *Educ:* Cranbrook Sch.; Jesus Coll., Cambridge (BA English Lit. 1974); Sussex Univ. (MA American Studies 1976); Univ. of Calif, Santa Barbara. Music journalist, Record Mirror, Number 1, 1980–84; freelance music journalist, Q, Mojo, Word, Guardian, Telegraph, 1984–2000; Press Officer, Virgin Records, 1984–86; Internat. Liaison, Polygram, 1987–88; Researcher, Initial TV, 1988–89; joined BBC TV, 1990; Asst Prod., The Late Show (music); est. and Exec. Prod., Later with Jools Holland, 1992–; est. and oversees BBC TV Glastonbury coverage, 1997–; Creative Hd, BBC Music Entertainment, 2001–13; Executive Producer: BBC 4 music documentaries, incl. Britannia strand (jazz, punk, reggae etc), Blues America, The Joy of Abba/Easy Listening, The Joy of Mozart; BBC 2 documentary series, incl. Girls and Boys, I'm a Rock n Roll Band!, Reginald D. Hunter's Songs of the South; BBC 1 documentaries, incl. Fleetwood Mac, The Carpenters, Agnetha; BBC 1 and BBC 4 music sessions, incl. Tom Jones, Richard Thompson; Top of the Pops Christmas; Top of the Pops 2; BBC Classical output incl. The Proms on TV and documentaries incl. Good Swan Bad Swan: Dancing Swan Lake; Sir Simon Rattle: The Making of a Maestro; The Duke and the Composer: Monteverdi in Mantua. *Recreations:* cricket, supporting QPR, literature. *Address:* 6 Layer Gardens, Acton, W3 9PR. *T:* (020) 8993 3021. *E:* mark.cooper@bbc.co.uk. *Club:* Millfields Cricket.

See also V. Glastonbury.

COOPER, Mary Helen; *see* Lazarus, M. H.

COOPER, Michael John; Director General, British Diabetic Association, 1992–98; *b* 24 July 1937; *s* of Frederick Walton Cooper and Ivy Kathleen (*née* Harris); *m* 1961, Kathy Cockett; two *s* one *d*. *Educ:* King's Sch., Rochester; Univ. of Exeter (BA 1960); Oberlin Coll., Ohio; Internat. Management Devlt Inst., Switzerland (MBA 1970). RAF, 1955–57. Shell Internat. Petroleum Co. Ltd, 1961–69; Panocean-Anco Ltd, 1970–83 (Man. Dir, 1980–83); Dir, Burmah Castrol PLC, 1983–91. Vice-Chm., E Sussex HA, 1996–2000 (Dir, 1992–2000). Vis. Prof., Univ. of Westminster, 1992–2001. Chm., Care for the Carers, Sussex, 2000–07. Vice-Chm., Queen's Nursing Inst., 2003–13 (Trustee, 2002–); Trustee: Music in Hosps (formerly Council for Music in Hosps), 2001–; Diabetes Network Internat., 2002–07. Member: Exec. Cttee, Lib Dem Wealden Constituency, 2000–08 (Vice Chm., 2004–06); Exec. Cttee, Lib Dem European Gp, 2006–. Mem. Bd, Conservators of Ashdown Forest, 2002–. Gov., High Hurstwood C of E Primary Sch., 1995– (Chm., 1998–2007). *Recreations:* music, walking, cricket, tennis, travel. *Address:* Old Hall Cottage, High Hurstwood, Uckfield, E Sussex TN22 4AD. *T:* (01825) 733268, 07836 221261; Flat 5, 130 Belgrave Road, SW1V 2BL; Le Gouttat, 71520 Clermain, France. *Club:* Oriental.

COOPER, Michael John, OBE 1997; CBiol; Staff Development Adviser and Trainer, Voluntary Service Overseas, 2005–07; *b* 5 April 1949; *s* of Stanley and Evelyn Cooper; *m* 1975, Gillian Isted; two *s*. *Educ:* Sutton High Sch., Plymouth; York Univ. (BA). CBiol, MRSB (MIBiol 1971). VSO, Chassa Secondary Sch., Zambia, 1972; Mill Hill Sch., London, 1973–78 (Dir of Biol., 1974–78); Dep. Head, Upper Sch., Moulsham High Sch., Chelmsford, 1978–81; Dep. Headteacher, Valley Sch., Worksop, 1982–85; Headmaster, Hillcrest Sch., Hastings, 1985–90; Principal, British Sch. in the Netherlands, 1990–99; Headmaster, Latymer Sch., 1999–2005. Selector, VSO, 1975–90. Governor: Middx Univ., 2003–06; Enfield Coll., 2003–06; Truro Coll., 2014–. Trustee, CAB Cornwall, 2014–. FRSA 1991. *Recreations:* walking, gardening, swimming, reading. *Address:* Blue Ocean, Chapel Point Lane, Cornwall PL26 6PP. *T:* (01726) 842955. *Club:* Victory.

COOPER, Morris; a District Judge (Magistrates' Court), 2004–15; *b* 10 Oct. 1948; *s* of Arthur Cooper and Elsie Cooper; *m* 1989, Vivien Joy Hallam; one *s* two *d*. Called to the Bar, Gray's Inn, 1979; Clerk to the Justices: for Burton-on-Trent and Uttoxeter, 1980–88; for N Staffs, 1988–89; in practice as a barrister, 1991–2004; actg Stipendiary Magistrate, 1999, subseq. Dep. Dist Judge (Magistrates' Court), 2000–04. *Recreation:* playing guitar.

COOPER, Nigel Cookson; Co-ordinator, Wimbledon Tennis Championships, 1988–95; *b* 7 May 1929; *s* of Richard and Violet Sarah Cooper; *m* 1972, Elizabeth Gillian Smith; two *s* one *d*. *Educ:* Leeds Training Coll., Leeds Univ. (LLB); State Univ. of Iowa, USA (MA). Teacher, primary and secondary schools, 1950–59; Lecturer: Trent Park Training Coll., 1959–61; Loughborough Training Coll., 1961–64; Provincial Supervisor (Schools and Community) for Nova Scotia, Canada, 1964–65; County Organiser of Schools for Norfolk, 1965–68; Asst Education Officer for Oldham, 1970–72; Asst Director of Educn for British Families Educn Service in Europe, 1972–78; Registrar, Kelvin Grove College of Advanced Education, Brisbane, Australia, 1978–82; Gen. Sec., BAAB, 1982–87. Mem., Elmbridge BC, 1999– (Dep. Mayor, 2007–08, Mayor, 2008–09). *Recreations:* playing the trumpet, squash, jogging. *Address:* 24 Southfields, East Molesey, Surrey KT8 0BP. *T:* and *Fax:* (020) 8224 0712.

COOPER, Philip John, CB 1989; Comptroller-General of Patents, Designs and Trade Marks, Department of Trade and Industry, 1986–89; *b* 15 Sept. 1929; *s* of Charles Cooper and Mildred Annie Marlow; *m* 1st, 1953, Dorothy Joan Chapman (*d* 1982); two *d*; 2nd, 1986 Pamela Mary Pysden (*d* 1988); 3rd, 1993, Antoinette Erasmus. *Educ:* Deacon's Sch. Peterborough; University Coll., Leicester. BSc (Chem. 1st Cl. Hons). CChem, FRSC. Joined Dept (later Laboratory) of Govt Chemist, 1952; Nat. Service, 2nd Lt, R Signals, 1953–55. Dept of Scientific and Ind. Res., 1956–67; Principal, Min. of Technology, 1967; Prin. Private Sec. to Minister for Industrial Develt, 1972–73; Asst Sec., 1973–79, Under Sec., 1979–89 DoI and DTI; Dir, Warren Spring Lab., DTI, 1984–85. *Publications:* various papers on analytical and chemical matters. *Address:* 12 The Lye, Tadworth, Surrey KT20 5RS.

COOPER, Sir (Richard) Adrian, 6th Bt *cr* 1905, of Shenstone Court, co. Stafford; *b* 21 Aug 1960; *o s* of Sir Richard Powell Cooper, 5th Bt and Angela Marjorie (*née* Wilson); *S* father, 2006; *m* 1994, Belinda Potter. *Educ:* Millfield Sch. *Heir:* none. *Address:* Hill Farm, Swalcliffe Banbury, Oxon OX15 5EN.

COOPER, Rev. Canon Richard Thomas; Rector of Richmond, North Yorkshire 1998–2009; Chaplain to the Queen, since 2003; *b* 7 March 1946; *s* of Frank and Margaret Cooper, Littlethorpe; *m* 1978, Janet Johnston; one *s* one *d*. *Educ:* Ripon Grammar Sch.; Leeds Univ. (BA 1969); Coll. of the Resurrection, Mirfield. Ordained deacon, 1971, priest, 1972. Assistant Curate: Rothwell, 1971–75; Adel, Leeds, 1975–78; Priest i/c, Holy Trinity Knaresborough, 1978–81; Vicar: Middleton Tyas, Croft and Eryholme, 1981–90; Aldborough with Boroughbridge and Roecliffe, 1990–98. RD, Richmond, 1986–90; Area Dean, Ripon, 1990–93; Chaplain, The Green Howards, 2002–; Regtl Chaplain, Yorks Regt, 2007–12; Officiating Chaplain to the Military, 2009–12. Hon. Canon, Ripon Cathedral, 1997–. Proctor in Convocation and Mem., Gen. Synod of C of E, 1986–90; Chm., House of Clergy, dio. Ripon, 1993–2001. Freeman and Chaplain: Mercers', Grocers' and Haberdashers' Co., Richmond, 1991– (Warden, 2007); Fellmongers' Co., Richmond, 1998–. *Recreations:* choral singing, cycling, fishing. *Address:* 26 The Springs, Middleham, Leyburn DL8 4RB.

COOPER, Sir Robert (Francis), KCMG 2013 (CMG 1997); MVO 1975; HM Diplomatic Service, retired; Counsellor, European External Action Service, European Union, 2010–12; *b* 28 Aug. 1947; *s* of late Norman and Frances Cooper. *Educ:* Delamere Sch., Nairobi; Worcester Coll., Oxford (BA); Univ. of Pennsylvania (MA). Joined FCO 1970; Tokyo 1972. London 1977; seconded to Bank of England, 1982; UK Rep. to EC, 1984; Head of Management Review Staff, FCO, 1987; Head of Far Eastern Dept, FCO, 1987; Hd of Policy Planning Staff, FCO, 1989; Counsellor, 1993, Minister and Dep. Hd of Mission, 1996–98, Bonn; Dir, Asia, FCO, 1998–99; Hd, Defence and Overseas Secretariat, Cabinet Office (on secondment), 1999–2001; Govt's special rep. for Afghanistan, 2001–02; Dir Gen. for Ext Affairs, Council Secretariat of EU, 2002–10. Special Advr to EU High Rep., 2012–. Vis. Prof., LSE, 2012–. *Publications:* The Postmodern State and the World Order, 1996; The Breaking of Nations, 2003. *Recreations:* Shakespeare, ballroom dancing, bicycling.

COOPER, Prof. Robin Hayes, PhD; FBA 1993; Professor of Computational Linguistics, University of Gothenburg, 1995–2012, now Emeritus; Director, Swedish National Graduate School of Language Technology, 2001–12; *b* 23 Dec. 1947; *s* of Dennis J. Cooper and Marjorie (*née* Wilding); *m* 1985, Elisabet B. Engdahl; two *d*. *Educ:* Corpus Christi Coll., Cambridge (MA); Univ. of Massachusetts at Amherst (PhD). Lektor, Universität Freiburg, 1969–71; Assistant Professor: Univ. of Texas at Austin, 1975–76; Univ. of Massachusetts at Amherst, 1976–77; Univ. of Wisconsin, Madison, 1977–81, Associate Prof., 1981–87 Docent, Lund Univ., 1984–87; University of Edinburgh: Lectr, 1986–89; Reader in Cognitive Sci., 1989–96. Mellon Fellow, Stanford Univ., 1980–81; Fellow, Center for Advanced Study in Behavioral Scis, Stanford, 1981–82; Guggenheim Fellow, Edinburgh and Stanford, 1986–87. Fellow, Royal Soc. of Arts and Scis, Gothenburg, 1996. MAE 2009. FilDr *hc* Uppsala, 2006. *Publications:* Quantification and Syntactic Theory, 1983; (ed jtly) Situation Theory and its Applications, Vol. 1, 1990; (ed jtly) Language in Flux: dialogue coordination, language variation, change and evolution, 2008; contribs to numerous books, contrib. Computational Intelligence, Ethnomusicology, Jl Logic, Lang. and Information, Jl Logic and Computation, Lang., Linguistics and Philosophy, Musique en Jeu, Nordic Jl Linguistics, Res on Lang. and Computation, Dialogue and Discourse. *Recreations:* yoga, music. *Address:* Department of Philosophy, Linguistics and Theory of Science, University of Gothenburg, Box 200, 40530 Göteborg, Sweden; Bigatan 1, 43139 Mölndal, Sweden.

COOPER, Rosemary; *see* Martin, R.

COOPER, Rosemary Elizabeth; MP (Lab) West Lancashire, since 2005; *b* 5 Sept. 1950; *d* of William and Rose Cooper. *Educ:* Bellerive Convent GS; Liverpool Univ. W. Cooper Ltd 1973–80; Littlewoods Organisation: merchandiser, 1980–92; PR Manager, Littlewoods Internat., 1994–95; Gp Corporate Communications Manager, 1995–2001; EOC, 1999–2000 Mem. and Vice-Chm., Liverpool HA, 1994–96; Chm., Liverpool Women's Hosp. NHS Trust, 1996–2005. Mem. (Lib Dem, then Lab), Liverpool CC, 1973–2000; Lord Mayor of Liverpool, 1992–93. Contested (Lib Dem): Knowsley N, Nov. 1986, 1987; Liverpool Garston, 1983; Liverpool Broadgreen, 1992; contested (Lab) NW Reg., EP elecns, 2004 Former Director: Merseyside Centre for Deaf People; Roy Castle Foundn. *Address:* House of Commons, SW1A 0AA.

COOPER, Russell; *see* Cooper, T. R.

COOPER, Maj.-Gen. Sir Simon (Christie), GCVO 2000 (KCVO 1991); Master of HM's Household, 1992–2000; *b* 5 Feb. 1936; *s* of Maj.-Gen. Kenneth Christie Cooper, CB, DSO, OBE and Barbara Harding-Newman; *m* 1967, Juliet Elizabeth Palmer; one *s* one *d*. *Educ:* Winchester College; rcds, psc. Commissioned Life Guards, 1956; served Aden, London, BAOR, 1957–63; Captain-Adjt, Household Cavalry Regt, 1963–65; ADC to CDS Earl Mountbatten of Burma, 1965–66; Borneo, Malaya, 1966–67; Staff Coll., 1968; BAOR, 1969–75; CO Life Guards, 1974–76; GSO1, Staff Coll., 1976–78; OC Household Cavalry and Silver Stick in Waiting, 1978–81; Commander, RAC Centre, 1981–82; RCDS, 1983; Dir, RAC, 1984–87; Comdt, RMA, Sandhurst, 1987–89; GOC London Dist and Maj.-Gen Commanding Household Div., 1989–91. Trustee, Royal Armouries, 2004–11. Pres. 2005–12, Vice Pres., 2012–, SSAFA (formerly SSAFA Forces Help), Wilts. Hon. Colonel Westminster Dragoons, 1987–97; Royal Yeomanry, 1987–97. *Recreations:* cricket, ski-ing, sailing, shooting. *Clubs:* Army and Navy, MCC.

COOPER, Simon Nicholas; a District Judge (Magistrates' Courts), since 2002; *b* 2 Sept 1953; *s* of Lt Comdr Alan Geoffrey Cooper and Wendy Anne Cooper (*née* Mcleod); *m* 1998 Philippa Mason. *Educ:* Kelly Coll.; Bristol Univ. (LLB Hons); RNC Dartmouth; Inns of Court Sch. of Law. Joined RN, 1972; served HMS Wilton, Rhyl, Intrepid, Hecate and Yarmouth; called to the Bar, Middle Temple, 1982; RN Judge Advocate, 1988; Comdr 1994; Dep. Chief Naval Judge Advocate, 1994–97 and 2001–02; retd from RN, 2002. Recorder, 2002–12. *Recreations:* fly fishing, golf, choral singing. *Address:* North West Wiltshire Magistrates' Court, The Court House, Pewsham Way, Chippenham, Wilts SN15 3BF. *T:* (01249) 466203. *Club:* Army and Navy.

COOPER, Prof. Susan, PhD; Professor of Experimental Physics, and Fellow of St Catherine's College, University of Oxford, 1995–2015; *b* USA, 1949. *Educ:* Colby Coll., USA (BA); Univ. of California at Berkeley (PhD). Guest Physicist, Deutsches Elektronen-Synchrotron, Germany, 1980–83; Research Associate, Stanford Linear Accelerator Center, USA, 1984–86; Asst Prof., MIT, 1987–89; Group leader, Max Planck Inst. of Physics, Munich, 1989–96. *Publications:* numerous papers in sci. jls.

COOPER, (Theo) Russell, AM 2012; MLA (National Party) Crows Nest, Queensland, 1992–2001 (Roma, Queensland, 1983–92); *b* 4 Feb. 1941; *s* of Theo Beverley Cooper and Muriel Frances Cooper; *m* 1965, Penelope Anne Parkinson; one *s* three *d*. *Educ:* Surfers Paradise State Sch.; Correspondence Sch.; Toowoomba Prep. Sch.; King's Sch., Parramatta. Councillor, 1976–88, Dep. Chm., 1982–86, Bendemere Shire Council; Dep. Chm., Roma Electorate NP Council, 1980–83; Chm., Wallumbilla-Yuleba Branch, NP, 1974–83. Minister for: Corrective Services and Admin. Services, 1987–89; Police and Emergency Services, 1989; Premier of Qld, Sept.–Dec. 1989; Leader of the Opposition, 1989–91; Opposition spokesman for police and corrective services, 1992–96; Minister for Police and Corrective Services and for Racing, 1996–98; Opposition spokesman on Primary Industries, 1998–2000. Vice-Pres., Maranoa Graziers Assoc., 1979–80 (Chm., Wallumbilla Br.); Pres., Roma and Dist Amateur Race Club, 1981–83. *Recreations:* golf, tennis (active), Rugby League, Rugby Union, cricket. *Address:* 10 Somerset Drive, Buderim, Qld 4556, Australia. *Clubs:* Queensland; Headland Golf.

COOPER, Dame Trelise (Pamela), DNZM 2014 (MNZM 2004); fashion designer; Director, Trelise Cooper Group, since 1997; *b* Auckland, 21 Dec. 1957; *d* of Joseph and Pamela Neill; *m* 1984, Jack Cooper; one *s* and one step *s* one step *d*. *Educ:* Henderson High Sch. Estabd Trelise Cooper Ltd Editions, 1985–89 (two boutiques, Auckland and Wellington); estabd Trelise Cooper Gp, 1997. *Recreations:* family, travel, opera, charity. *Address:* Trelise Cooper Group, 8 Lion Place, Newmarket, Auckland 1023, New Zealand. *T:* 93795005. *E:* enquiry@trelisecooper.co.nz.

COOPER, Hon. Warren Ernest, CNZM 1997; MP (National Party) Otago, 1975–96; Minister of Defence and Minister responsible for War Pensions, New Zealand, 1990–96, also Minister of Civil Defence and of Internal Affairs, 1993–96; *b* Dunedin, 21 Feb. 1933; *s* of William Cooper; *m* 1959, Lorraine Margaret, *d* of Angus T. Rees; three *s* two *d*. *Educ:* Musselburgh Sch.; King's High Sch., Dunedin. Formerly Minister of Tourism, Minister of Regional Develt, Minister in charge of Publicity and in charge of Govt Printing Office; Postmaster Gen., 1980; Minister of Broadcasting and Assoc. Minister of Finance, 1981; Minister of Foreign Affairs and Overseas Trade, 1981–84; Minister of Local Govt and of Radio and Television, 1990–93. Mem., Cabinet Cttees on Expenditure Control and Revenue, State Sector, Appts and Honours, Social and Family Policy, Treaty of Waitangi Issues, 1990–96. Member Executive: S Island Publicity Assoc., 1971; NZ Municipal Assoc. Life Mem. and former Pres., Queenstown Jaycees. Mayor of Queenstown, 1968–75 and 1995–2001. JP Queenstown. Silver Jubilee Medal, 1977. *Address:* 8 Park Street, Queenstown 9300, New Zealand.

COOPER, Sir William (Daniel Charles), 6th Bt *cr* 1863, of Woollahra; *b* 5 March 1955; *s* of Sir Charles Eric Daniel Cooper, 5th Bt, and Mary Elisabeth (*d* 1999), *e d* of Captain J. Graham Clarke; *S* father, 1984; *m* 1988, Julia Nicholson. *Educ:* Northease Manor, Lewes, Sussex. *Heir: b* George John Cooper, *b* 28 June 1956.

COOPER, (William) Gareth, FCILT; Chairman, Stena Line, 1997–2006; *b* 19 Aug. 1943; *s* of William Alderson Cooper and Florence Morwen Cooper (*née* Matthews); *m* 1966, Carole Roberta Davies; one *s* one *d*. *Educ:* University Coll., Swansea (BScEng). Managing Director: Wallington Weston Co. Ltd, 1977–83; Weston Hyde Products Ltd, 1983–87; Crown Berger Ltd, 1987–91; Stena Line UK Ltd, 1991–97; Chairman: White Young Green plc, 1997–2004; Arriva plc, 1999–2004. *Recreations:* opera, travel, photography. *Address:* 5 Oak Park, Alderley Edge, Cheshire SK9 7GS.

COOPER, William Robert Patrick W.; *see* White-Cooper.

COOPER, Rt Hon. Yvette; PC 2007; MP (Lab) Normanton, Pontefract and Castleford, since 2010 (Pontefract and Castleford, 1997–2010); *b* 20 March 1969; *d* of (Derek) Anthony Cooper, *qv* and June Cooper (*née* Iley); *m* 1998, Rt Hon. Edward Michael Balls, *qv*; one *s* two *d*. *Educ:* Eggars Comprehensive Sch., Hants; Balliol Coll., Oxford (BA 1st Cl. Hons PPE 1990); Harvard Univ.; London Sch. of Econs (MSc Econs 1995). Economic researcher for Rt Hon. John Smith, MP, 1991–92; Domestic Policy specialist, Clinton Presidential Campaign, Arkansas, 1992; Policy Advr to Labour's Treasury Team, 1992–95; leader writer and economic columnist, The Independent, 1995–97. Parliamentary Under-Secretary of State: for Public Health, DoH, 1999–2002; Lord Chancellor's Dept, 2002–03; (Social Exclusion Minister), ODPM, 2003–05; Minister of State (Minister for Housing and Planning), ODPM, later DCLG, 2005–07; Minister for Housing, DCLG, 2007–08; Chief Sec. to HM Treasury, 2008–09; Sec. of State for Work and Pensions, 2009–10; Shadow Sec. of State for Work and Pensions, 2010; Shadow Minister for Women and Equalities, 2010–13; Shadow Sec. of State for Foreign and Commonwealth Affairs, 2010–11, for the Home Dept, 2011–15. Member: Select Cttee on Educn and Employment, 1997–99; Intelligence and Security Cttee, 1997–99. *Address:* House of Commons, SW1A 0AA. *T:* (020) 7219 5080.

COOTE, Anna; policy analyst and writer; Head of Social Policy, New Economics Foundation, since 2008; Commissioner for Health, UK Sustainable Development Commission, 2000–09; *b* 1 April 1947; *d* of Capt. J. O. Coote and Sylvia Coote; one *d*. *Educ:* Edinburgh Univ. (MA). Feature Writer, Observer, 1968–72; Dep. Editor, New Statesman, 1978–82; Editor, Diverse Reports, Channel 4, 1982–86; Res. Fellow, IPPR, 1989–91; Sen. Lectr, Goldsmiths' Coll., London Univ., 1991–93; Dep. Dir, IPPR, 1993–98; Dir of Health Policy, King's Fund, 1998–2005; Hd of Patient and Public Involvement, Healthcare Commn, 2005–08. Mem., London Health Commn, 2000–05. Trustee, Help the Aged, 2001–06. Hon. DLitt Bath, 1999. *Publications: include:* (jtly) Civil Liberty: the NCCL guide, 1972; (jtly) Women's Rights: a practical guide, 1974; (jtly) Sweet Freedom, 1987; (jtly) Power and Prejudice, 1990; (ed) The Welfare of Citizens, 1992; (jtly) Citizens' Juries, 1994; New Gender Agenda, 2000; (ed) Claiming the Health Dividend, 2002; Finding Out What Works, 2004; (jtly) Green Well Fair, 2009; (jtly) 21 Hours, 2010; Cutting It, 2010. *Recreations:* cycling, walking, cinema, theatre. *Address:* 8/51 Surrey Row, SE1 0BZ.

COOTE, Sir Christopher (John), 15th Bt *cr* 1621; Senior Baronetcy of Ireland in use; *b* 22 Sept. 1928; *s* of Rear Adm. Sir John Ralph Coote, 14th Bt, CB, CBE, DSC, and Noreen Una (*d* 1996), *o d* of late Wilfred Tighe; *S* father, 1978; *m* 1952, Anne Georgiana, *d* of Lt-Col Donald Handford; one *s* one *d*. *Educ:* Winchester; Christ Church, Oxford (MA 1957). *Heir: s* Nicholas Patrick Coote [*b* 28 July 1953; *m* 1980, Mona, *d* of late Moushegh Bedelian; one *s* one *d*].

COOTE, Prof. John Haven; Bowman Professor, 1987–2003, and Head of Department of Physiology, 1984–2003, University of Birmingham, now Professor Emeritus; *b* 5 Jan. 1937; *m* 1976, Susan Hylton; one *s* two *d*. *Educ:* Royal Free Hosp. Sch. of Medicine (BSc (Hons) Physiol.; PhD London); DSc Birmingham 1980. CBiol, FRSB (FIBiol 1988). Birmingham University: Prof. of Physiology, 1984–2003; Hd of Sch. of Basic Med. Scis, 1988–91. Vis. Scientist, Inst. de Medicina Experimental, Univ. of Caracas, Venezuela, 1971; Visiting Professor: Inst. of Gerontology, Tokyo, 1974–75; Inst. of Physiological Scis, Warsaw, 1977–78; Shanghai Univ., 1988; Chicago Univ., 1988; Leicester Univ., 2003; Warwick Univ., 2003; Nankai and Tiansin Univs, China, 2004. Carl Ludwig Dist. Lectr, Fedn of Amer. Socs for Experimental Biol., 2003; Paton Lectr, Physiol. Soc., 2005. Chm., Human Scis Ethics Cttee, DERA/QinetiQ, 1998–; Member: Internat. Adv. Bd, Acta Physiologica Sinica, 2002–; Defence Sci. Adv. Council, 2003–. Member: AAAS, 1989; NY Acad. of Scis, 1991. Mem. Council, BHF, 1998–2003. Civil Consultant, Applied Physiol., RAF Centre for Aviation Medicine, 2002–. Hon. Mem., Physiol Soc., 2004. Chm. Editorial Bd, Experimental Physiology, 2000–06. FRGS 2004; Hon. FBPhS (Hon. FBPharmacolS 2012). Hon. DipMed Krakow, 1995. *Publications:* contribs to Jl of Physiol., Jl of the Autonomic Nervous System, Brain Res., Exptl Physiol., Neurosci., Ann. Thoracic Surgery, Circ. Cardiovascular Res., British Jl Pharmacol., Ann. Neurol. *Recreation:* mountaineering. *Address:* College of Medical and Dental Science, School of Clinical and Experimental Medicine, University of Birmingham, Birmingham B15 2TT.

COPE, family name of **Baron Cope of Berkeley**.

COPE OF BERKELEY, Baron *cr* 1997 (Life Peer), of Berkeley in the co. of Gloucestershire; **John Ambrose Cope,** Kt 1991; PC 1988; *b* 13 May 1937; *s* of George Cope, MC, FRIBA, Leicester; *m* 1969, Djemila Lovell Payne, *d* of late Col P. V. L. Payne, Martinstown, Dorset and Mrs Tanetta Blackden, Amer. Colony of Jerusalem; two *d*. *Educ:* Oakham Sch., Rutland. Chartered Accountant; Company Director. Commnd RA and RE, Nat Service and TA. Contested (C) Woolwich East, 1970; MP (C) South Gloucestershire, Feb. 1974–1983, Northavon, 1983–97; contested (C) Northavon, 1997. A Govt Whip, 1979–87, and Lord Comr of HM Treasury, 1981–83; Treas. of HM Household and Dep. Chief Whip, 1983–87; Minister of State: Dept of Employment and Minister for Small Businesses, 1987–89; NI Office, 1989–90; Dep. Chm. and Jt Treas., Cons. Party, 1990–92; HM Paymaster Gen., 1992–94; Opposition spokesman on NI, 1997–98, on home affairs, 1998–2001, H of L; Opposition Chief Whip, H of L, 2001–07. Chm., H of L Select Cttee on Small and Medium Sized Enterprises, 2012–13. Mem., British-Irish Parly Assembly, 2008–11. Sen. Comr, Royal Hospital Chelsea, 1992–94. Pres., Inst. of Business Counsellors, 1988–90; Dep. Chm., Small Business Bureau, 1995–2001; Pres., S Glos Chamber of Commerce, 1993–2001. Chm., Horse and Pony Taxation Cttee, 1994–2000. Vice Pres., Royal Soc. of St George, 1998–. Trustee: War Memls Trust (formerly Friends of War Memls), 1997–; Conservative Party Archive, Bodleian Liby, 2008–; Friends of Edward Saïd Nat. Conservatory of Music UK, 2013–. Patron: Avon Riding for the Disabled, 1985–2012; Friends of Royal Nat. Hosp. for Rheumatic Diseases, Bath, 2003–. *Publications:* (with Bernard Weatherill) Acorns to Oaks (Policy for Small Business), 1967; (ed) A Funny Thing Happened, 1991; I'm sorry you were in when I called, 1992. *Recreations:* woodwork, a Derby Bentley motor car, church bell ringing. *Address:* House of Lords, SW1A 0PW. *Clubs:* Carlton (Chm., 2004–10), Pratt's, Beefsteak; Tudor House (Chipping Sodbury).

COPE, Alan, CPFA, FCCA; County Treasurer, Cheshire County Council, 1997–2001; *b* 8 Oct. 1946; *s* of John William Cope and Bertha Cope; *m* 1969, Gillian Mary Kirk; two *s*. *Educ:* Swanwick Hall Grammar Sch.; Univ. of Liverpool (MA 2004). CPFA 1968; FCCA 1981. Accountant, Derbyshire CC, 1963–69; Cheshire County Council: Sen. Auditor, 1969–72; Technical Accountant, 1972–74; Gp Accountant, 1974–78; Chief Accountant, 1978–85; Asst Dir, Policy Unit, 1985–87; Asst Co. Treas., 1987–89; Co. Finance Officer, 1989–97. Treasurer: Cheshire Fire Authy, 1997–2001; Cheshire Probation Service, 1997–2001; Cheshire Police Authy, 1998–2001. Non-exec. Mem., Finance Cttee, Royal Mencap Soc., 2004–12. *Address:* The Meadows, 19 Dee Crescent, Farndon, Chester CH3 6QJ. *T:* (01829) 270602.

COPE, David Robert, MA; education and recruitment consultant; *b* 24 Oct. 1944; *yr s* of late Dr Cuthbert Cope, FRCP and Eileen Cope (*née* Putt); *m* 1st, 1966, Gillian Margaret Peck (marr. diss. 1994); one *s* two *d*; 2nd, 1996, Juliet Caroline, *e d* of Prof. Richard Swinburne, *qv*; two *s*. *Educ:* Winchester Coll. (Scholar); Clare Coll., Cambridge (Scholar). 1st Cl. Hons Hist. Tripos Part II, 1965; BA 1965; MA 1972. Asst Master, Eton Coll., 1965–67; Asst British Council Rep. (Cultural Attaché), Mexico City, 1968–70; Asst Master, Bryanston Sch., 1970–73; Headmaster: Dover College, 1973–81; British Sch. of Paris, 1981–86; Master of Marlborough Coll., 1986–93; Field Dir, Zambia, VSO, 1994–97. Director: Ashoka (UK) Trust, 1998–2001; Application Research Ltd, 2002–08; Sen. Associate, Search Associates, 2002– (Vice-Pres., 2009–). Trustee: Assoc. for Educn and Guardianship of Internat. Students, 2005–15; SoundAffects, 2008–12. FRSA. *Recreations:* music, running, books, travel. *Address:* Berry House, 41 High Street, Over, Cambridge CB24 5NB. *T:* (01954) 231130. *Club:* Athenæum.

COPE, David Robert; Director, Parliamentary Office of Science and Technology, 1998–2012; *b* 7 July 1946; *s* of Lawrence William and Ethel Anne Cope; *m* 1992, Reiko Takashina. *Educ:* Fitzwilliam Coll., Cambridge Univ. (MA); London School of Economics (MScEcon, with dist.). Res. Officer, University Coll. London, 1969–70; Lectr, Nottingham Univ., 1970–81; Environment Team Leader, Internat. Energy Agency Coal Unit, 1981–86; Exec. Dir, UK CEED, 1986–97; Prof. of Energy Econs, Doshisha Univ., Kyoto, Japan, 1997–98. Special Lectr in Energy and Environment Studies, Nottingham Univ., 1985–94; Vis. Lectr, Cambridge Univ., 1988–95; First Caltex Green Fund Fellow, 1992, and Ext. Examiner, 1992–, Centre of Urban Planning and Envmtl Mgt, Univ. of Hong Kong; Associate, Clare Hall, Cambridge Univ., 2005–. Member: Council, Nat. Soc. for Clean Air, 1990–98; Standing Cttee on the Envmt, ACOST, 1990–92; Climate Change Wkg Gp, 1993; Packaging Standards Council (formerly Packaging Council), 1992–96; Envmtl Stats Adv. Cttee, DoE, later DETR, 1994–98. Chm., Europe-Japan Experts' Assoc., 2002–. Hon. PhD N London, 2001. *Publications:* (with P. Hills and P. James) Energy Policy and Land Use Planning, 1984; (with S. Owens) Land Use Planning Policy and Climate Change, 1992; numerous papers on energy and environmental policy topics. *Recreations:* amateur volcanology, hill walking, woodworking.

COPE, Jeremy Ewart; Managing Director, UK, Royal Mail Group, 2002–03; *b* 30 Nov. 1951; *s* of late Michael Ewart Cope and Maureen Ann Cope (*née* Casey); *m* 1985, Dianne Elizabeth Gilmour; one *s*. *Educ:* St Paul's Sch.; Jesus Coll., Cambridge (MA); Warwick Univ. (MSc). MCIPD. Joined Post Office as management trainee, 1973; Asst Head Postmaster, Southend, 1980; Dir of Personnel, Royal Mail, 1986; Gen. Manager, London, 1988; Dir of Strategy, Royal Mail, 1989; Dir of Strategy and Commercial Develt, Post Office, 1992; Man. Dir, Strategy and Personnel, Post Office, 1995; Mem. for Strategy and Personnel, Post Office Bd, 1996–99; Gp Man. Dir, Post Office, subseq. Consignia, then Royal Mail Gp, 1999–2003. Dir, Camelot plc, 2000–03; Chm., Celyn Hldgs (formerly HRS Ltd, then T-Three Ltd), 2004–; non-exec. Dir, GCDA, 2007–12. Chairman: Prison Service Pay Review Body, 2005–11; NHS Pay Review Body, 2011–. Chm., London Regl Cttee, FEFC, 2000–01. Dir, English Bridge Union, 2011–; Chm., English Bridge Educn and Develt, 2014–. Gov., Kingston Univ., 1999–2007 (Chm., 2002–07); Chm., London South Bank Univ., 2015–. *Recreations:* bridge, supporting Fulham FC, cooking, theatre, avoiding the gardening. *Address:* 24 Auckland Road, SE19 2DJ. *Club:* Hurlingham.

COPE, Jonathan, CBE 2003; Répétiteur, Royal Ballet Company, since 2005 (Principal, 1987–90 and 1992–2006); *b* 1963; *m* Maria Almeida; one *s* one *d*. *Educ:* Royal Ballet Sch. Joined Royal Ballet Co., 1982; Soloist, 1985–86; property business, 1990–92. Leading rôles include: Cinderella, Pursuit, Giselle, Swan Lake, Prince of the Pagodas, Fearful Symmetries, The Sons of Horus, Romeo and Juliet, Sleeping Beauty, La Bayadère, Different Drummer,

Frankenstein, Fleeting Figures, The Modern Prometheus, Words Apart, Manon, The Nutcracker, Ondine, Mayerling, The Judas Tree, Aminta, in Sylvia. *Address:* c/o Royal Ballet Company, Royal Opera House, Covent Garden, WC2E 9DD.

COPE, Wendy Mary, OBE 2010; FRSL; writer, freelance since 1986; *b* 21 July 1945; *d* of Fred Stanley Cope and Alice Mary (*née* Hand). *Educ:* Farringtons Sch.; St Hilda's Coll., Oxford (MA); Westminster College of Education, Oxford (DipEd). Teacher in London primary schs, 1967–81 and 1984–86; Arts editor, ILEA Contact, 1982–84; Television columnist, The Spectator, 1986–90. FRSL 1992. Hon. Fellow, Goldsmiths, Univ. of London, 2013. Hon. DLitt: Southampton, 1999; Oxford Brookes, 2003. Cholmondeley Award for Poetry, 1987; Michael Braude Award, Amer. Acad. of Arts and Letters, 1995. *Publications:* Making Cocoa for Kingsley Amis (poems), 1986; Twiddling Your Thumbs (rhymes for children), 1988; (ed) Is That The New Moon?, 1989; The River Girl, 1991; Serious Concerns (poems), 1992; (ed) The Orchard Book of Funny Poems, 1993; (ed) The Funny Side, 1998; (ed) The Faber Book of Bedtime Stories, 2000; If I Don't Know (poems), 2001; (ed) Heaven on Earth: 101 happy poems, 2001; (ed) George Herbert, Verse and Prose, 2002; Two Cures for Love: selected poems 1979–2006, 2008; The Audience (with music by Roxanna Panufnik), 2009; Going for a Drive (poems for children), 2010; Family Values (poems), 2011; Time for School (poems for children), 2013; Life, Love and The Archers: recollections, reviews and other prose, 2014. *Recreation:* playing the piano. *Address:* c/o Faber and Faber, Bloomsbury House, 74–77 Great Russell Street, WC1B 3DA.

COPELAND, Maj. Gen. Ian Martin, CB 2013; FCILT; Associate Consultant, Systems Consultant Services Ltd, since 2015; *b* Weston-super-Mare, 6 Oct. 1959; *s* of Peter Wilfred Norman Copeland and Ann Copeland; *m* 1982, Sallyann Horlick; one *s* one *d*. *Educ:* Bristol Grammar Sch.; Royal Military Acad. Sandhurst. FCILT 2013. Joined Army, 1979; Troop Comdr, 1 Sqdn, 1980–81, Jun. Leaders' Regt, 1981–83, RCT; Transport Control Officer (New Territories Hong Kong), Gurkha Transport Regt, 1984–86; Regtl Ops Officer, 4 Armd Div., Transport Regt, RCT, 1986–88; Adjutant, 155 (Wessex) Transport Regt RCT (Vol.), 1988–89; Army Command and Staff Course, 1990; psc 1991; Dep. COS 19 Mechanised Bde, 1992–94; Directing Staff, Army Comd and Staff Coll., 1997–99; CO 10 Transport Regt RLC and Comdr Queen's Own Gurkha Logistic Regt, 1999–2001; Dep. Asst COS Orgn, HQ Land Forces, 2001–04; hcsc 2004; Comdr 101 Logistic Bde, 2004–06; Dir Logistics (Army), 2006–09; Hd Defence Support Chain Ops and Movements, 2009–10; Dir Jt Support Chain, Defence Equipment and Support, 2010–13; Man. Dir and Vice Pres., DynCorp Internat. UK, 2014–15. Hon. Col, 155 (Wessex) Transport Regt RLC (Vol.), 2010–14. President: RLC Cricket Club, 2005–; RLC Shooting Club, 2005–; RLC Golf Soc., 2008–; RLC Regtl Assoc., 2012–. *Recreations:* golf, keeping fit, walking the dog, gardening, travel. *E:* ian.copeland59@gmail.com.

COPELAND, Michael Stewart; Member (UU) Belfast East, Northern Ireland Assembly, 2003–07 and since 2011; *b* Belfast, 23 June 1954; *s* of George and Emily Copeland; *m* Sonia; one *s* one *d*. *Educ:* Lisnasharragh High Sch.; RMA, Sandhurst. Apprentice joiner, then site manager, William Copeland & Son Ltd; Dir, then Man. Dir, Modarc, Copeland Gp. Rifleman, then Commnd Officer, UDR. Mem. (UU) Castlereagh BC, 2001–. GSM Clasp (NI). *Address:* Northern Ireland Assembly, 276 Parliament Buildings, Stormont, Belfast BT4 3XX; (office) 174 Albertbridge Road, Ballymacarrett, Belfast BT5 4GS. *T:* (028) 9046 3900. *E:* michael.copeland@mla.niassembly.gov.uk.

COPISAROW, Sir Alcon (Charles), Kt 1988; DUP; FInstP; FIET; Chairman of Trustees, Eden Project, 1996–2000; *b* 25 June 1920; *o s* of late Dr Maurice Copisarow, Manchester; *m* 1953, Diana (OBE 2004), *y d* of Ellis James Castello, MC, Bucklebury, Berks; two *s* two *d*. *Educ:* Manchester Central Grammar Sch.; University of Manchester; Imperial Coll. of Science and Technology; Sorbonne, Paris (DUP 1960). Council of Europe Research Fellow. Served War, 1942–47; Lieut RN, 1943–47; British Admiralty Delegn, Washington, 1945. Home Civil Service, 1946–66; Office of Minister of Defence, 1947–54. Scientific Counsellor, British Embassy, Paris, 1954–60. Dir, Forest Products Research Laboratory, Dept of Scientific and Industrial Research, 1960–62; Chief Technical Officer, Nat. Economic Development Council, 1962–64; Chief Scientific Officer, Min. of Technology, 1964–66. Dir, McKinsey & Co. Inc., 1966–76; non-exec. Dir, British Leyland, 1976–77; Dir, TR Technol. and Hldgs, 1976–96; Mem., BNOC, 1980–83; Chm., APAX Venture Capital Funds, 1981–94. Special Advr, Ernst & Young, 1993–99; Chm., ARINSO Internat., 2000–03. Academic Fellow, Churchill Coll., Cambridge, 2005. Chairman: Commonwealth Forest Products Pre-Conf., Nairobi, 1962; CENTO Conf. on Investment in Science, Teheran, 1963; Member: Scientific Manpower Cttee, Advisory Council on Scientific Policy, 1963–64; Econ. Develt Cttees for Electronics Industry and for Heavy Electrical Industry; Trop. Prod. Adv. Cttee, 1965–66; Press Council, 1975–81. A Chm., Gen. Comrs for Income Tax, 1975–95. External Mem., Council of Lloyd's, 1982–90; Dep. Chm., Lloyd's Tercentenary Trust, 1989– (Chm., 1988 and 2007; Hon. Lloyd's Fellow 2008). Dep. Chm., Bd of Governors, English-Speaking Union, 1976–83; Chm., Youth Business Initiative, subseq. The Prince's Youth Business Trust, 1982–87. Dir, Windsor Fest., 1983–2000. Trustee: Duke of Edinburgh's Award, 1978–84; FMI, 1995–2001; Member Council: Royal Jubilee Trusts, 1981–87; Zoological Soc., 1990–91. Patron: Société des Ingénieurs et des Scientifiques de France, 1992–2013; Assoc. of MBAs, 2007–. Governor, Benenden Sch., 1976–86. Freeman, City of London, 1981. Hon. FTCL. *Publications:* Unplanned Journey: from Moss Side to Eden (memoir), 2014. *Address:* Flat 5, 7/8 Southwell Gardens, SW7 4SB. *Clubs:* Athenæum (Chm. and Sen. Trustee, 1989–2008), Beefsteak.

COPLAND, Geoffrey Malcolm, CBE 2007; DPhil; CPhys, FInstP; consultant on higher education, since 2007; Rector and Vice-Chancellor, University of Westminster, 1996–2007; *b* 28 June 1942; *s* of late Cyril Charles Copland and Jessie Palmer Copland; *m* 1st, 1967, Janet Mary Todd (marr. diss. 1985); one *s* one *d*; 2nd, 1985, Dorothy Joy Harrison. *Educ:* Fitzmaurice Grammar Sch., Bradford-on-Avon; Merton Coll., Oxford (MA, DPhil 1967). MInstP 1973; CPhys 1973; FInstP 2003. Post-doctoral scientist, Yale Univ., 1967–69; University of London: Researcher and Lectr in Physics, QMC, 1969–71; Lectr in Physics, Queen Elizabeth Coll., 1971–80; Dean of Studies, Goldsmiths' Coll., 1981–87; Dep. Rector, Poly. of Central London, later Univ. of Westminster, 1987–95. Mem. Council, UUK (formerly CVCP), 1998–2007 (Vice-Pres. and Chm., England and NI Council, 2003–07). Member Board: Edexcel Foundn, 1998–2003; PSI, 1998–2007; Central London Partnership, 2001–07; Central London LSC, 2005–07; Chm. Bd, Univs and Colls Employers Assoc., 2002–06. Pres., Assoc. of ASET, 2006–. Mem., Council for Industry and Higher Educn, 1999–2007 (Trustee, 2001–07); Chm., Thomas Wall Trust, 1999–; Trustee: Regent St Polytechnic Trust, 1996–2007; Quintin Hogg Trust, 1996–; Quintin Hogg Meml Fund, 1996–; Internat. Student House, 2000–; Learning from Experience Trust, 2000– (Chair, 2011–); Helena Kennedy Foundn, 2008–13. Governor: Trinity Laban, 2007– (Vice-Chm., 2012–); Univ. of Bedfordshire, 2008–14. Mem. Council, Trinity Coll. London, 2012–. FRSA 1991; FGCL 2000; Hon. FTCL 2000. Hon. Fellow, Univ. of Bedfordshire, 2014. Hon DSc Westminster, 2008. *Publications:* research papers in physics and higher educn in various jls. *Recreations:* walking, cricket, gardening. *Address:* 24 The Broadway, Wheathampstead, St Albans AL4 8LN. *T:* (01438) 833663. *Club:* Oxford and Cambridge.

COPLEY, John (Michael Harold), CBE 2014; opera director; *b* 12 June 1933; *s* of Ernest Harold Copley and Lilian Forbes; civil partnership 2006, John Hugh Chadwyck-Healey (*d* 2014). *Educ:* King Edward's, Five Ways, Birmingham; Sadler's Wells Ballet Sch.; Central Sch. of Arts and Crafts, London (Dip. with Hons in Theatre Design). Appeared as the apprentice in Britten's Peter Grimes for Covent Garden Opera Co., 1950; stage managed: both opera and ballet companies at Sadler's Wells, in Rosebery Avenue, 1953–57; also various musicals, plays etc, in London's West End, incl. The World of Paul Slickey and My Fair Lady. Joined Covent Garden Opera Co.: Dep. Stage Manager, 1960; Asst Resident Producer, 1963; Associate Resident Producer, 1966; Resident Producer, 1972; Prin. Resident Producer, 1975–88. *Productions include: at Covent Garden:* Suor Angelica, 1965; Così fan Tutte, 1968, 1981; Orpheo ed Euridice, 1969; Le Nozze di Figaro, 1971, 1985; Don Giovanni, 1973; La Bohème, 1974, 1985, 2012, 2015; Faust, 1974; L'elisir d'amore, 1975, 1981, 1985; Benvenuto Cellini, 1976; Ariadne auf Naxos, 1976; Maria Stuarda; Royal Silver Jubilee Gala, 1977; Werther, 1979; La Traviata, Lucrezia Borgia, 1980; Alceste, 1981; Semele, 1982, 1988, 1996; Norma, 1987; L'elisir d'amore, 1992; *at London Coliseum (for Sadler's Wells, subseq. ENO):* Carmen, Il Seraglio, Il Trovatore, La Traviata, Mary Stuart; Rosenkavalier, La Belle Hélène, 1975; Werther, 1977; Manon, Aida, Julius Caesar, Les Mamelles de Tirésias, 1979; The Merry Widow, 2008; *Athens Festival:* Macbeth; *Netherlands Opera:* Lucia; *Opera National de Belge:* Lucia; *Wexford Festival:* La Clemenza di Tito; L'Infedelta delusa; *Dallas Civic Opera:* Lucia; Hansel and Gretel, 1991; Elektra, Il Trovatore, 1996; Ariodante, 1998; *Chicago Lyric Opera:* Lucia; La Bohème, 1983; Orlando, 1986; Tancredi, 1989; The Barber of Seville, 1989; Peter Grimes, Idomeneo, 1997; Gioconda, 1998; Die Fledermaus, 1999; *Canadian Opera, Toronto:* Lucia; Falstaff; La Bohème, 1984; Adriana Lecouvreur, La Forza del Destino, 1987; *Greek Nat. Opera:* Madame Butterfly; Otello; *Australian Opera:* Fidelio, Nozze di Figaro, Rigoletto, Magic Flute, Jenufa, Ariadne auf Naxos, Madame Butterfly, Fra Diavolo, Macbeth, La Traviata, Manon Lescaut, Lucia di Lammermoor, Tosca, Manon; Adriana Lecouvreur, 1984; Peter Grimes, 1986; Carmen, 1987; La Forza del Destino, 1988; *Victoria State Opera:* Don Carlos, 1984; La Bohème, 1985; *WNO:* La Traviata, Falstaff, Peter Grimes, Tosca; Peter Grimes, 1983; *Opera North:* Les Mamelles de Tirésias, Madama Butterfly; *Scottish Opera:* Lucia; Ballo in Maschera, Dido and Aeneas; Acis and Galatea for English Opera Group in Stockholm, Paris, Aldeburgh Fest.; *New York City Opera:* Le Nozze di Figaro; Der Freischutz; Don Quichotte; *Santa Fé Opera:* Ariodanie, 1987; Così fan tutte, 1988; Der Rosenkavalier, La Traviata, 1989; La Bohème, 1990; Tosca, 1994; Semele, 1997; Idomeneo, 1999; *Ottawa Festival:* Midsummer Night's Dream; Eugene Onegin, 1983; *Vancouver Opera:* Carmen; *San Francisco Opera:* Julius Caesar; The Midsummer Marriage, 1983; Don Giovanni, 1984; Orlando, 1985; Le Nozze di Figaro, Eugene Onegin, 1986; La Traviata, 1987; Idomeneo, 1989; Midsummer Night's Dream, 1992; Pique Dame, 1993; Peter Grimes, 1998; *San Diego Opera:* Eugene Onegin, 1985; Le Nozze di Figaro, 1986; Così fan tutte, 1991; *Staatsoper, Munich:* Adriana Lecouvreur, 1984; *Teatro La Fenice, Venice:* Semele, 1991 and 1992; *Deutsche Oper, Berlin:* L'Elisir d'amore, 1988; *Metropolitan Opera, NY:* Julius Caesar, 1988; Semiramide, 1990; L'Elisir d'amore, 1991; Norma, 2001; Le Pirata, 2002; *Opera Theatre of St Louis:* La Rondine, 1996. Sang as soloist in Bach's St John Passion, Bremen, Germany, 1965; appeared as Ferdy in John Osborne's play, A Patriot for Me, at Royal Court Theatre, 1965. Co-directed (with Patrick Garland): Fanfare for Europe Gala, Covent Garden, 3 Jan. 1973; Fanfare for Elizabeth gala, Covent Garden, 21 April 1986. Hon. RAM 1999; Hon. RCM 2002. *Recreation:* cooking. *Address:* 9D Thistle Grove, SW10 9RR.

COPLEY, Tom; Member (Lab) London Assembly, Greater London Authority, since 2012; *b* 11 May 1985. *Educ:* Univ. of Nottingham (BA Politics). Worked for Labour Party, HPA and Searchlight Educnl Trust. Greater London Authority: Member: Econ. Cttee, 2012–; Housing and Regeneration Cttee, 2012–13; Transport Cttee, 2012–; Dep. Chm., Housing Cttee, 2013–. Trustee, British Humanist Assoc., 2013–. *Address:* Greater London Authority, City Hall, Queen's Walk, SE1 2AA.

COPP, Prof. Andrew John, DPhil; FRCPath; FMedSci, FRSB; Professor of Developmental Neurobiology, since 1996, and Head, Developmental Biology and Cancer Academic Programme, since 2013, Institute of Child Health, University College London; *b* 27 Feb. 1954; *s* of Frederick John Copp and Doreen Ann Copp (*née* Crouch). *Educ:* St Peter's Coll., Oxford (BA 1st Cl. Hons (Zool.) 1975); Wolfson Coll., Oxford (DPhil (Exptl Embryol.) 1978); Guy's Hosp. Med. Sch., London Univ. (MB BS 1983). FRCPath 2003. Fogarty Internat. Res. Fellow, Dept of Paediatrics, Stanford Univ. Med. Sch., Calif, 1984–86; Res. Scientist, ICRF, Univ. of Oxford, 1986–92; Sen. Lectr, then Reader, Inst. of Child Health, UCL, and Wellcome Sen. Res. Fellow in Clin. Sci., 1992–96; Dir, Inst. of Child Health, UCL, 2003–12. Mem., Neuroscis & Mental Health Bd, 2003–07, Career Develt Award and Sen. Non-clinical Fellowship Panel, 2012–, MRC. Non-exec. Dir, Gt Ormond St Hosp. NHS Trust, 2003–12. Mem., Med. Adv. Bd, SPARKS, 1999–2004. Pres., Develtl Pathol. Soc., UK, 1993–97. Mem. Bd of Advrs, Foulkes Foundn, 2000–; Mem. Bd, 2004–07, Hon. Dir of Res., 2007–14, Children's Trust Tadworth; Mem. Bd, Bo Hjelt Foundn, 2010–. FMedSci 2000; FRSB (FSB 2012). Man. Ed., Anatomy and Embryology, 1998–2003; Associate Ed., Birth Defects Res. A: Clinical and Molecular Teratology, 2002–12. *Publications:* (with D. L. Cockcroft) Postimplantation Mammalian Embryos: a practical approach, 1990; more than 180 peer-reviewed articles in acad. jls on birth defects, esp. neural tube defects such as spina bifida, develtl biol., genetics. *Address:* UCL Institute of Child Health, 30 Guilford Street, WC1N 1EH. *T:* (020) 7905 2355, *Fax:* (020) 7905 2953. *E:* a.copp@ucl.ac.uk.

COPPEL, Andrew Maxwell, CBE 2008; FCA; Group Chief Executive, De Vere Group, 2011–15 (Chairman, Alternative Hotel Group, later De Vere Group, 2010–12); *b* 22 Aug. 1950; *s* of Isaac Coppel and Marjorie Coppel; *m* 1974, June Vanessa Gillespie; one *s* one *d*. *Educ:* Belfast Royal Acad.; Queen's Univ., Belfast (LLB Hons). FCA 1982. With Coopers & Lybrand, 1973–77; Asst Dir, Morgan Grenfell & Co. Ltd, 1977–86; Finance Dir, Ratners Gp plc, 1986–90; Chief Executive: Sale Tilney plc, 1990–92; Queens Moat Houses plc, 1993–2003; Racecourse Hldgs Trust, later Jockey Club Racecourses, 2004–07; McCambridge Gp, 2008–10. Ind. Dir, Crest Nicholson Hldgs Ltd, 2009–11. Mem., Adv. Bd on Ireland, Lloyds Bank, 2012. Chairman: Tourism Ireland Ltd, 2001–07; London Irish Hldgs Ltd, 2008–11. Vice Pres., Queen's Univ. Assoc., London, 2000– (Mem. Council, 1980–). *Recreations:* Rugby, golf, tennis, cinema, reading action novels. *E:* acop@btinternet.com. *Clubs:* Hurlingham, Arts; Claygate Tennis, St George's Hill Golf (Surrey); Malone Golf (Belfast).

COPPEL, Philip Antony; QC 2009; *b* London, 5 Jan. 1960; *s* of William Andrew and Maria Antonietta Coppel; *m* 1991, Francesca Maria Gallo; one *s* two *d*. *Educ:* Daramalan Coll. Canberra; Australian Nat. Univ. (BA Hons Hist., LLB). Barrister and solicitor, Canberra, 1984–91; Solicitor, McKenna & Co., London, 1991–94; called to the Bar, Lincoln's Inn, 1994; barrister, Gray's Inn, specialising in govt, regulatory and commercial law, 1994–. *Publications:* Information Rights, 2004, 5th edn 2016; (contrib.) Halsbury's Laws of England, 2001, 2002; (contrib.) Atkin's Court Forms, 2007, 2008, 2011, 2012, 2015; (contrib.) Jordan's Tribunal Practice, 2012. *Recreation:* classical music. *Address:* 2–3 Gray's Inn Square, Gray's Inn, WC1R 5JH. *T:* (020) 7421 1860, *Fax:* (020) 7405 1166. *E:* philipc@cornerstonebarristers.com.

COPPEL, Yvonne Ruth; Her Honour Judge Coppel; a Circuit Judge, since 2007; *b* Salford, 24 July 1954; *d* of Hyman and Hilda Coppel; *m* 1988; one *s* one *d*. *Educ:* N. Manchester High Sch. for Girls; Univ. of Birmingham (LLB Hons). Called to the Bar, Inner Temple, 1976; Asst Recorder, 1996–2000; Recorder, 2000–07. *Recreations:* cinema, fell walking, theatre. *Address:* Liverpool Civil and Family Courts, 35 Vernon Street, Liverpool L2 2BX. *T:* (0151) 296 2200.

COPPEN, Dr Alec James, MD, DSc; FRCP, FRCPsych; Director, Medical Research Council Neuropsychiatry Laboratory, and Emeritus Consultant Psychiatrist, West Park Hospital, Epsom, Surrey, 1974–89, retired; *b* 29 Jan. 1923; *y s* of late Herbert John Wardle Coppen and Marguerite Mary Annie Coppen; *m* 1952, Gunhild Margareta (*d* 2007), *y d* of late Albert and Sigrid Andersson, Båstad, Sweden; one *s. Educ:* Dulwich Coll.; Univ. of Bristol (MB, ChB 1953; MD 1958; DSc 1978); Maudsley Hosp.; Univ. of London (DPM 1957); MRCP 1975, FRCP 1980, FRCPsych 1971 (Hon. FRCPsych 1995). Registrar, then Sen. Registrar, Maudsley Hosp., 1954–59; MRC Neuropsychiatry Research Unit, 1959–74, MRC External Staff, 1974–89; Consultant Psychiatrist: St Ebba's Hosp., 1959–64; West Park Hosp., 1964–89; Hon. Cons. Psychiatrist, St George's Hosp., 1965–70. Head of WHO designated Centre for Biological Psychiatry in UK, 1974–89; Consultant, WHO, 1977–89; Examiner, Royal Coll. of Psychiatry, 1973–77; Andrew Woods Vis. Prof., Univ. of Iowa, 1981; Lectr to learned socs and univs in Europe, N and S America, Asia and Africa. Mem. Council, RMPA (Chm., Research and Clinical Section), 1965–70; Chairman, Biolog. Psychiatry Section, World Psychiatric Assoc., 1972; President, British Assoc. of Psychopharmacology, 1975; Member: Internat. Coll. Neuropsychopharm., 1960– (Mem. Council, 1979; Pres., 1988–90); RSM, 1960–; British Pharmacol. Soc., 1977–; Special Health Authy, Bethlem Royal and Maudsley Hosp., 1982–87; Hon. Member: Mexican Soc. for Biolog. Psychiatry, 1973–; Mexican Inst. of Culture, 1974–; Swedish Psychiatric Assoc., 1977–; European Collegium Neuro-Psychopharmacologicum, 1987–; Corresponding Member: Amer. Coll. of Neuropsychopharm., 1977–; Deutsche Gesellschaft für Psychiatrie und Nervenheilkunde; Distinguished Fellow, APA, 1981. Freeman, City of London, 1980; Soc. of Apothecaries: Yeoman, 1980; Liveryman 1985. Anna Monika Prize, 1969; European Prize for Psychopharmacology, 1991; Lifetime Achievement Gold Medal, British Assoc. of Psychopharmacology, 1998; Pioneer in Psychopharmacology Award, Collegium Internat. Neuro-Psychopharmacologicum, 2000; Award, American Assoc. for Suicide Prevention, 2004. *Publications:* (jtly) Recent Developments in Schizophrenia, 1967; (jtly) Recent Developments in Affective Disorders, 1968; (jtly) Psychopharmacology of Affective Disorders, 1979; contribs to text books; papers in Nature, Lancet, BMJ, etc (Current Contents Citation Classic, 1978, Biochemistry of the Affective Disorders). *Recreations:* golf, opera. *Address:* 5 Walnut Close, Epsom, Surrey KT18 5JL. *T:* (01372) 720800. *Clubs:* Athenæum, Royal Automobile.

COPPEN, Luke Benjamin Edward; Editor, The Catholic Herald, since 2004; *b* 8 Feb. 1976; *s* of Rev. Canon Martin Coppen and Christine Coppen (*née* Stevens); *m* 2004, Marlena Marciniszyn; two *d. Educ:* Testbourne Community Sch., Whitchurch, Hants; Cricklade Coll., Andover; Sch. of Oriental and African Studies, Univ. of London (BA Study of Religions and Politics); Univ. of Wales, Cardiff (Postgrad. Dip. Journalism Studies). Film Ed., London Student mag., 1996–97; reporter, 1998–2000, Dep. Ed., 2000–04, Catholic Herald; Faith in Brief columnist, The Times, 2001–05. *Recreations:* cinema, cycling, rabbit-keeping. *Address:* The Catholic Herald, Herald House, Lambs Passage, Bunhill Row, EC1Y 8TQ. *T:* (020) 7448 3606, *Fax:* (020) 7256 9728. *E:* luke@catholicherald.co.uk.

COPPIN, Alan Charles; a Crown Representative, Cabinet Office, since 2013; Chairman, Campaign Board, and Trustee, Royal Air Force Museum, since 2013; *b* 4 June 1950; *s* of Charles and Vera Coppin; *m* 1975, Gaynor Hilary Wareham; one *s. Educ:* Westlain Grammar Sch., Brighton; Brighton Poly. Mgt posts with cos incl. Strutt & Parker, THF Leisure, Associated Leisure and Bembom Group, 1971–86; Sen. Mgt Consultant, KPMG, 1986–88; Chief Exec., Wembley Stadium Ltd, 1988–95, Wembley plc, 1995–98; Chief Exec., Historic Royal Palaces, 1999–2003. Associate, Prime Minister's Delivery Unit, Cabinet Office, 2002–04. Chm., Sports Ground Safety Authy, 2015–. Chairman: Danoptra Hldgs, 2002–06; Redstone plc, 2006–09; Timeless Mgt Gp, 2009–12; Aeternum Ltd, 2010–14; Venue Retail Ltd, 2010–12; The Coffee Mob CIC, 2011–; Mem. Exec. Bd, Compass Gp plc, 1998–99; non-executive Director: Metroline plc, 1997–2000; Carillion plc, 1999–2002; Expocentric plc, 2000–02; Protocol n. v., 2002–04; Capital & Regional plc, 2004–10; Berkeley Gp Hldgs plc, 2006–13; Marshalls plc, 2010–. Non-executive Director: Air Force Operating and Performance Gp (formerly Air Comd), RAF, 2007–13; RAF Bd, 2009–13; Ind. Mem., Air Rank Appts Bd, RAF, 2011–13; Ind. Panel Mem., Public Appts, DCMS, 2015–. Chairman: NW London TEC, 1990–92; Stadium and Arena Mgt Project, 1994–95. Chairman: Include, nat. children's charity, 1997–2000; Robinia Care Gp, 2003–04; Prince's Foundn for Built Envmt, 2004–06 (Trustee, 2003–04); Trustee, Greenwich Foundn, 2003–04. Mem., Adv. Forum, Saïd Business Sch., Oxford Univ., 2002–07. Patron, Windsor Leadership Trust, 2003–. Hon. Vis. Prof., Business Sch., Univ. of N London, 1998–2003. CCMI (CIMgt 1997). FRSA 2003–05. *Publications:* (jtly) Timeless Management, 2002; Great Britons on Success, 2009. *Recreations:* family activities, cinema, writing. *Club:* Royal Air Force.

COPPLE, Philip; Executive Director, since 2011, and Director of Public Sector Prisons, since 2013, National Offender Management Service, Ministry of Justice; *b* Ashton under Lyne, Manchester, 30 May 1969; *s* of Anthony and Eleanor Copple; *m* 1992, Gabrielle Reddington; two *s* one *d. Educ:* St Joseph's RC High Sch., Whitefield; Holy Cross Sixth Form Coll., Bury; Univ. of Durham (BA 1st Cl. Hons Politics). Prison Officer, HMP Leeds, 1990–92; Principal Officer, HMP Wakefield, 1992–94; Gov. 5, Office of Dir of Security and Progs, HM Prison Service HQ, 1994–95; Gov. 5, HMP Wealstun, 1995–96; Gov. 4, 1997–98, Dep. Gov., 1999–2000, HMP Frankland; Governor: HM YOI Deerbolt, 2000–02; HMP Frankland, 2002–06; Area Manager, NE Prisons, 2006–09; Dir, Offender Mgt, NE, 2009–11; Dir, Nat. Operational Services, 2011, Dir, High Security, 2011–12, Nat. Offender Mgt Service, MoJ. *Recreations:* family, friends, swimming, cinema. *Address:* National Offender Management Service HQ, Clive House, 70 Petty France, SW1H 9EX. *T:* 0300 047 5709. *E:* phil.copple@noms.gsi.gov.uk.

COPPOLA, Francis Ford; Artistic Director, Zoetrope Studios, since 1969; *b* 7 April 1939; *s* of late Carmine Coppola and of Italia Pennino; *m* 1963, Eleanor Neil; one *s* one *d* (and one *s* decd). *Educ:* Hofstra Univ. (BA); Univ. of Calif, LA (MFA). Films directed: Dementia 13, 1963; You're a Big Boy Now, 1967; Finian's Rainbow, 1968; The Rain People, 1969; The Godfather, 1972 (2 Acad. Awards, 1973); The Conversation, 1974; The Godfather Part II, 1974 (3 Acad. Awards, 1975); Apocalypse Now, 1979; One From the Heart, 1981; The Outsiders, 1983; Rumble Fish, 1983; The Cotton Club, 1984; Peggy Sue Got Married, 1987; Gardens of Stone, 1988; Tucker: The Man and his Dream, 1988; New York Stories (Life Without Zoe), 1989; The Godfather Part III, 1991; Bram Stoker's Dracula, 1993; Jack, 1996; John Grisham's The Rainmaker, 1998; Apocalypse Now Redux, 2001; Youth Without Youth, 2007; Tetro (also prod. and writer), 2010; executive producer: Black Stallion, 1979; Hammett, 1983; Lionheart, 1987; The Secret Garden, 1993; Mary Shelley's Frankenstein, 1994. Irving G. Thalberg Meml Award, Academy Awards, 2011. Commandeur, Ordre des Arts et des Lettres, 1983. *Recreations:* reading, writing, scientific discovery. *Address:* Zoetrope Studios, 916 Kearny Street, San Francisco, CA 94133–5138, USA. *T:* (415) 7887500.

COPPS, Hon. Sheila Maureen, OC 2012; PC (Can.) 1993; President, Sheila Copps & Associates; radio and television presenter; newspaper columnist; actress; *b* 27 Nov. 1952; *d* of Vic Copps and Geraldine (*née* Guthro); one *d. Educ:* Univ. of Western Ontario (BA Hons English and French); Univ. of Rouen; McMaster Univ. Journalist, 1974–77. MPP (L) Ontario, 1981–84; MP (L) Hamilton E, Canada, 1984–2004. Official Opposition Critic for: Housing and Labour, 1984–87; Health and Welfare and Fitness and Amateur Sport, 1987–89; Envmt and Co-Critic for Social Policy, 1989–90; Industry, 1990–91; Dep. Leader of Opposition, 1991–93; Minister of the Envmt, 1993–96; Dep. Prime Minister, 1993–97; Minister of Canadian Heritage, 1996–2003. *Publications:* Nobody's Baby, 1986; Worth Fighting For, 2004.

COPSON, Andrew James William; Chief Executive, British Humanist Association, since 2010; *b* Nuneaton, 19 Nov. 1980; *s* of David Copson and Julia Heather Cunningham; civil partnership 2011, Mark John Wardrop. *Educ:* King Henry VIII Sch., Coventry; Balliol Coll., Oxford (BA Hons 1st cl. Ancient and Mod. Hist. 2004); Chartered Inst. of Public Relations (Dip. Public Relns 2008). Vice Pres., Welfare and Equal Opportunities, Oxford Univ. Student Union, 2002–03; Parly Liaison Officer, Citizenship Foundn, 2004–05; British Humanist Association: Educn and Public Affairs Officer, 2005–07, on part-time secondment as Researcher, Office of Baron Macdonald of Tradeston, 2005–07; Hd, Educn and Public Affairs, 2007–09. Member: RE Consultants Gp, QCA, 2006–10; Standing Adv. Council on RE, City of Westminster, 2006– (Chm., 2010–); Census Diversity Adv. Gp, ONS, 2007–09; Steering Gp for New Guidance on RE, DCSF, 2008–09; Humanities Diploma Adv. Gp, 2008–10; Standing Adv. Conference on Religion and Belief, BBC, 2009–; Steering Gp on Spiritual, Moral, Social and Cultural Educn in FE, Learning and Skills Improvement Service, 2009–10; Ind. Schs Practitioners' Gp on Spiritual, Moral, Social and Cultural Educn, DCSF, 2009–10; Equality Reference Gp, DWP, 2010–11; Faith, Belief and Meaning Gp, Nat. Council for Palliative Care, 2010–12; Non-religion and Secularity Res. Network, 2010–; Nat. Adv. Panel, Equality Matters for Children, 2011–12; Community Accountability Forum, CPS, 2011–13; Adv. Panel on Equality and Inclusion, Ofqual, 2011–; Steering Gp, Religious Educn (England) Subject Review, 2011–13; Commn on Religion and Belief in British Public Life, 2013–15; Freedom of Religion and Belief Adv. Gp, FCO, 2014–. Trustee: Oxford Pride, 2004–05; Values Educn Council, 2005–08 (Chm., 2006–08); Gay and Lesbian Humanist Assoc., 2005–10 (Chm., 2008–10); Pink Triangle Trust, 2006–08; Religious Educn Council of England and Wales, 2006–15; Conway Hall Ethical Soc. (formerly South Place Ethical Soc.), 2007–13; Eur. Humanist Fedn, 2007–10; Nat. Council of Faiths and Beliefs in Further Educn, 2008–13 (Vice Chm., 2008–13); Internat. Humanist Trust, 2011–; All Faiths and None, 2011–13; Actors of Dionysus, 2014–; Pres., Internat. Humanist and Ethical Union, 2015– (Vice Pres., 2010–15, First Vice Pres., 2012–15). Exec. Cttee, Labour Humanists, 2007–09. Associate: Centre for Law and Religion, Cardiff Univ., 2008–; Equality and Diversity Forum Res. Network, 2012–. MCIPR 2005; FCMI 2014; FRSA 2006. *Publications:* The Wiley-Blackwell Handbook on Humanism (ed with A. C. Grayling), 2015. *Recreations:* American science fiction, English novels, Roman and Greek history, Greek drama. *Address:* British Humanist Association, 39 Moreland Street, EC1V 8BB. *T:* (020) 7324 3066, *Fax:* (020) 7324 306. *E:* andrew@humanism.org.uk.

CORBEN, Albert Edward; Assistant Under Secretary of State, Radio Regulatory Department, Home Office (and subsequently with Department of Trade and Industry), 1980–83, retired; *b* 25 Nov. 1923; *s* of Ebenezer Joseph James Corben and Frances Flora (*née* Orchard); *m* 1953, Doris Dodd; two *s. Educ:* Portsmouth Grammar Sch.; Sir John Cass Technical Inst. Served Royal Artillery, 1943–47. Entered Home Office, as Executive Officer, 1947; Higher Executive Officer, 1955–62; Sen. Executive Officer, 1962–66; Principal, 1966–72; Secretary to Advisory Council on Penal System, 1966–68; Sen. Principal, 1972–73; Asst Sec., 1973–80. *Recreations:* swimming, dancing, walking. *Address:* The Gables, 30 Kingswood Road, Bromley, Kent BR2 0NF. *T:* (020) 8460 4106.

CORBET, Dr Gordon Barclay; zoologist; *b* 4 March 1933; *s* of George and Mary Corbet; *m* 1959, Elizabeth Urquhart; one *s* one *d. Educ:* Morgan Acad., Dundee; Univ. of St Andrews. BSc, PhD. Asst Lectr in Biology, Sir John Cass Coll., London, 1958–59; British Museum (Natural History): Sen., later Principal, Scientific Officer, Dept of Zoology, 1960–71; Dep. Keeper of Zoology, 1971–76; Hd, Dept of Central Services, 1976–88. *Publications:* The Terrestrial Mammals of Western Europe, 1966; Finding and Identifying Mammals in Britain, 1975; The Handbook of British Mammals, 2nd edn (with H. N. Southern), 1977, 3rd edn (with S. Harris), 1991; The Mammals of the Palaearctic Region, 1978; The Mammals of Britain and Europe, 1980; A World List of Mammalian Species (with J. E. Hill), 1980, 3rd edn 1991; The Mammals of the Indomalayan Region (with J. E. Hill), 1992; The Nature of Fife, 1998. *Recreations:* wildlife on sand dunes, family history. *Address:* Little Dumbarnie, Newburn, Upper Largo, Fife KY8 6JG. *T:* (01333) 340634.

CORBETT, family name of **Baron Rowallan**.

CORBETT, Dame Antoinette; *see* Sibley, Dame A.

CORBETT, Bernie; General Secretary, Writers' Guild of Great Britain, since 2000; *b* Cuckfield, Sussex, 17 Sept. 1952; *s* of Wally Corbett and Liz Corbett (*née* Smoker); partner, Jane Pickard; one *s. Educ:* Haywards Heath Grammar Sch., Sussex. Reporter: W Sussex County Times, 1969–73; Evening Argus, Brighton, 1973–74; Dep. Chief Sub-Ed., Birmingham Post, 1974–80; Chief Sub-Ed., Guardian, 1980–85; Ed., The Journalist (NUJ), 1985–87; freelance journalist, 1987–90; Chief Features Sub-Ed., Independent, 1990–94; Nat. Organiser, NUJ, 1995–2000. *Address:* Writers' Guild of Great Britain, 134 Tooley Street, SE1 2TU. *T:* (020) 7833 0777. *E:* corbett@writersguild.org.uk.

CORBETT, Gerald Michael Nolan; DL; Chairman: Britvic PLC, since 2005; Betfair, since 2012; Numis Securities plc, since 2014 (non-executive Director, 2009–14); *b* 7 Sept. 1951; *s* of late John Michael Nolan Corbett and of Pamela Muriel Corbett (*née* Gay); *m* 1976, Virginia Moore Newsum; one *s* three *d. Educ:* Tonbridge Sch.; Pembroke Coll., Cambridge (Foundn Schol.; MA); London Business Sch. (MSc with Dist.); Harvard Business Sch. (Exchange Schol.). Boston Consulting Gp, 1975–82; Dixons Group plc: Gp Finance Controller, 1982–85; Corporate Finance Dir, 1985–87; Group Finance Director: Redland plc, 1987–94; Grand Metropolitan plc, 1994–97; Chief Exec., Railtrack Gp plc, 1997–2000. Chairman: Woolworths Gp plc, 2001–07; Holmes Place plc, 2003–06; SSL International PLC, 2005–10; Moneysupermarket.com plc, 2007–14; Towry Hldgs, 2012–14; non-executive Director: MEPC Plc, 1995–98; Burmah Castrol Plc, 1998–2000; Greencore Gp plc, 2004–10. Chm., RNID, 2007–13. Chm. Govs, Abbot's Hill Sch., 1997–2002; Gov., Luton Univ., 2002–05. Vice Chm., Herts Community Foundn, 2010–13 (Chm., 2013–); Chm., St Albans Cathedral Music Trust, 2010–. Mem. Council, High Sheriffs Assoc., 2008–11. Freeman, City of London, 1989. High Sheriff, 2010–11, DL, 2015, Herts. FRSA 2006. *Recreations:* country pursuits, golf, ski-ing, bridge. *Address:* Holtsmere End Farm, Redbourn, Herts AL3 7AW. *Clubs:* Oxford and Cambridge, MCC (Chm., 2015–).

CORBETT, Graham; *see* Corbett, P. G.

CORBETT, Prof. Greville George, PhD; FBA 1997; FAcSS; Distinguished Professor (formerly Professor) of Linguistics, University of Surrey, since 1988; *b* 23 Dec. 1947; *s* of George Pilsbury Corbett and Elsie Mary Bates; three *s. Educ:* Univ. of Birmingham (BA 1970; MA 1971; PhD 1976). Lectr, 1974–85, Reader, 1985–88, Univ. of Surrey. Pres., Linguistics Assoc. of GB, 1994–97. FAcSS (AcSS 2000). MAE 2008. Hon. Mem., Linguistic Soc. of America, 2014. *Publications:* Predicate Agreement in Russian, 1979; Hierarchies, Targets and Controllers: agreement patterns in Slavic, 1983; (jtly) Computers, Language Learning and Language Teaching, 1985; Gender, 1991; (ed jtly) Heads in Grammatical Theory, 1993; (ed jtly) The Slavonic Languages, 1993; Number, 2000; (jtly) The Syntax-Morphology Interface: a study of syncretism, 2005; Agreement, 2006; (ed jtly) Deponency and Morphological Mismatches, 2007; (jtly) A Dictionary of Archi: Archi-Russian-English, 2007; (ed jtly) Defective Paradigms: missing forms and what they tell us, 2010; (ed jtly) Case and Grammatical Relations: studies in honor of Bernard Comrie, 2008; (ed jtly) Features: perspectives on a key notion in linguistics, 2010; Features, 2012; (ed jtly) Canonical Morphology and Syntax, 2012; (ed jtly) Periphrasis: the role of syntax and morphology in paradigms, 2013; (ed) The Expression of Gender, 2014. *Recreation:* music. *Address:* Surrey Morphology Group, School of English and Languages, Faculty of Arts and Human Sciences, University of Surrey, Guildford, Surrey GU2 7XH.

CORBETT, James Patrick; QC 1999; FCIArb; Trust and Estate Practitioner, since 2005; a Deputy High Court Judge and Deputy Mercantile Judge, since 2007; *b* 10 May 1952; *s* of late Patrick Francis Corbett and Kathleen Mary Corbett (*née* O'Callaghan); *m* 1979, Barbara Janet Willett; one *s* four *d*. *Educ:* Sloane Sch., Chelsea; Univ. of Exeter (LLB 1973; LLM European Legal Studies 1975); Inns of Court Sch. of Law. FCIArb 1997; Chartered Arbitrator, 2001. Called to the Bar, Inner Temple, 1975, Bencher, 2008, Lincoln's Inn, *ad eundem*, 1998; Lectr in Law, Univ. of Leicester, 1975–77; in practice at the Bar, 1977–2010; joined Midland and Oxford Circuit, 1979; called to Irish Bar, 1981, Northern Irish Bar, 1994, NSW Bar, 2002, Anguilla Bar, 2002, St Kitts and Nevis Bar, 2004, BVI Bar, 2004, Turks and Caicos Bar, 2007, Cayman Is Bar, 2010, Gibraltar Bar, 2013, Bahamas Bar, 2015; in practice with Kobre & Kim LLP, 2010–. Asst Recorder, 1996–2000; Recorder, 2000–10. CEDR Registered Mediator, 2000. Mem., Soc. of Trust and Estate Practitioners, 2005–. Contested (SDP): Erewash, Derbys, 1983; Cheshire E, 1984; Staffs Moorlands, 1987. Liveryman: Arbitrators' Co., 2000–; Bowyers' Co., 2003–. *Publications:* articles in legal and arbitration jls. *Recreations:* jazz, the cinema, Rugby League, cricket. *Address:* Kobre & Kim (UK) LLP, Tower 42, 25 Old Broad Street, EC2N 1HQ. *Club:* Garrick.

CORBETT, Michelle Jane, (Mrs Michael O'Gorman); Her Honour Judge Corbett; a Circuit Judge, since 2009; *b* Salford, 9 Feb. 1965; *d* of Michael Corbett and Carol Lowry (*née* Seddon); *m* 1993, Michael O'Gorman, JP; two *d*. *Educ:* Manchester High Sch. for Girls; Univ. of Leeds (LLB Hons). Called to the Bar, Inner Temple, 1987 (Profumo Award); barrister, 1987–2009; Recorder, 2007–09. *Recreations:* my two children, marmalade making, running, Manchester United Football Club. *Address:* West London Family Court, Dukes Green Avenue, Feltham, Middx TW14 0LR. *E:* HHJudge.Corbett@judiciary.gsi.gov.uk.

CORBETT, (Peter) Graham, CBE 1994; Chairman, Rica (Consumer Research for Older and Disabled People) (formerly Ricability (Research and Information for Consumers with Disabilities)), since 1998; *b* 6 Nov. 1934; *s* of John and Greta Corbett; *m* 1964, Anne (*née* James), PhD, Res. Fellow, Eur. Inst., LSE; two *s*. *Educ:* Stowe Sch. ACA 1957, FCA 1962. Peat Marwick, London, 1959–75; Sen. Partner, Peat Marwick Continental Europe, 1975–87; Chief Financial Officer, Eurotunnel plc and Eurotunnel SA, 1987–96. Dep. Chm., Monopolies and Mergers, then Competition Commn, 1997–2000; Chm., Postal Services Commn, 2000–04. Non-executive Director: Kier Gp plc, 1996–2000; Remploy Ltd, 2004–10. Trustee, Franco-British Council, 1995–99. CCMI (CIMgt 1994); FRSA 1999. DUniv Brunel 1995. *Address:* 95 Coleherne Court, Old Brompton Road, SW5 0ED. *T:* (020) 7373 9878.

CORBETT, Dr Richard Graham; Member (Lab) Yorkshire and the Humber Region, European Parliament, 1999–2009 and since 2014 (Merseyside West, Dec. 1996–1999); *b* 6 Jan. 1955; *s* of Harry Graham Corbett and Kathleen Zita Corbett (*née* Bryant); *m* 1st, 1984, Inge van Gaal (marr. diss.); one *s*; 2nd, 1989, Anne de Malsche (separated); two *d*. *Educ:* Farnborough Rd Sch., Southport; Internat. Sch., Geneva; Trinity Coll., Oxford (BA Hons PPE); Univ. of Hull (Extra Mural Doctorate 1995). Stagiare, Socialist Gp, European Parlt, 1976; UK Labour Delegn, 1977; Commn (Regl Policy), 1977; Sec. Gen., European Co-ordination Bureau, Internat. Youth Orgns, 1977–81; European civil servant, 1981–89; European Parliament: political advr, 1989–94, Dep. Gen. Sec., 1995–96, Socialist Gp; Vice Pres., Cttee on Instnl Affairs, 1997–99; Labour Party and Socialist Gp spokesman on constitutional affairs, 1999–2009; Dep. Leader, Labour MEPs, 2006–09; Mem. Bd, Britain in Europe, 2001–05. Mem., Cabinet of Herman Van Rompuy, Pres. of European Council, 2010–14. Mem. Regl Bd, Yorks, 1999–2001 and 2007–09, Mem., Nat. Policy Forum, 2008–09, Labour Party. *Publications:* A Socialist Policy for Europe, 1985; The European Parliament, 1990, 7th edn 2007; The Treaty of Maastricht: from conception to ratification, 1993; The European Parliament's Role in closer EU integration, 1998; The European Union: how does it work?, 3rd edn, 2012; contrib. Annual Rev. on Instnl Devels in EU for Jl Common Mkt Studies. *Recreations:* cycling, ski-ing, watching football, reading. *Address:* European Parliament, Rue Wiertz, 1047 Brussels, Belgium.

CORBETT, Maj.-Gen. Sir Robert (John Swan), KCVO 1994; CB 1991; lecturer in history, since 2003; Director, Hart International, since 2003; *b* 16 May 1940; *s* of Robert Hugh Swan Corbett and Patricia Elizabeth Corbett (*née* Cavan-Lambart); *m* 1966, Susan Margaret Anne O'Cock; three *s*. *Educ:* Woodcote House; Shrewsbury School; Royal Mil. Coll. of Sci., 1972; Army Staff Coll., 1973; US Armed Forces Staff Coll., 1980. Joined Army in ranks, 1958, commissioned Irish Guards, 1959; served UK, Cyprus, Hong Kong, Falkland Is, Belize, BAOR; Brigade Major, HQ Household Div., 1980–81; CO, 1st Bn Irish Guards (4 Armoured Brigade, BAOR), 1981–84; Chief of Staff and Dep. Comdr, British Forces Falkland Is, 1984–85; Comdr, 5th Airborne Brigade, 1985–87; rcds 1987; Dir, Defence Programme, MoD, 1987–89; GOC Berlin (British Sector) and British Comdt, Berlin, 1989–3 Oct. 1990 (German re-unification); attached HQ BAOR, 1990–91; GOC London Dist, and Maj. Gen. Comdg Household Div., 1991–94. Mem. Adv. Bd, Deutsche Bank Berlin AG, 1991–2000. Chairman: Guards Chapel Adv. Cttee, 1993–2011; Berlin Infantry Bde Meml Trust Fund, 1992–99. Dir, Dulverton Trust, 1994–2003. Regtl Lt-Col, Irish Guards, 1988–91. Hon. Col, London Irish Rifles, 1993–2000. Liveryman, Vintners' Co., 1968. Hon. Citizen, 1993, Mem., Conseil Municipal, 2000–04, Pierrefeu, France. Order of Merit, Berlin, 1990; Hon. Grand Officier, Ordre de Mérite (Luxembourg), 1994; Hon. Grande Oficial, Ordem do Infante Dom Henrique (Portugal), 1994; Hon. Dato Paduka, Order of Crown of Brunei, 1993. *Publications:* Berlin and the British Ally 1945–1990, 1993. *Recreations:* travel, reading (especially military history), walking, English church history and architecture. *Address:* c/o RHQ Irish Guards, Wellington Barracks, SW1E 6HQ. *Clubs:* Pratt's, Buck's.

CORBETT, Ronald Balfour, CBE 2012 (OBE 1978); comedian/character actor; *b* 4 Dec. 1930; *s* of William Balfour Corbett and Anne Elizabeth Corbett; *m* 1965, Anne Hart; two *d*. *Educ:* James Gillespie Sch., Edinburgh; Royal High Sch., Edinburgh. *Films:* Top of the Form; You're Only Young Once; Casino Royale, 1966; No Sex Please, We're British, 1974; Fierce Creatures, 1997; Burke and Hare, 2010; *television:* Frost Report, 1966–67; Frost on Sunday, 1968–69; The Two Ronnies (12 in series), 1971–85, 2005; The Two Ronnies Christmas Special, 1982, 1987; Variety Specials, 1977; Sorry! (8 in series), 1981–88; Small Talk (3 series), 1994–96; Ronnie's Animal Crackers, 2013; *theatre:* Twang (Lionel Bart musical), 1965; Cinderella, London Palladium, Christmas 1971–72; two seasons at London Palladium, 1978, 1983; The Dressmaker (Feydeau), 1990; Out of Order, UK and Australian tour, 1992–93; *radio:* When the Dog Dies (4 series), 2010–11. *Publications:* Small Man's Guide to Life; Armchair Golf, 1986; High Hopes (autobiog.), 2000; And It's Goodnight from Him: the autobiography of the two Ronnies, 2006. *Recreations:* golf, racing, soccer, cooking. *Clubs:* Saints and Sinners; Addington Golf (Surrey); Gullane Golf (East Lothian); Hon. Company of Edinburgh Golfers (Muirfield).

CORBIN, Christopher John, OBE 2014; hotelier and restaurateur; *b* 1 March 1952; *s* of Frederick Christopher Corbin and Vera Corbin (*née* Copperwaite); *m* 1982, Francine Checinski; one *s* one *d* (twins). *Educ:* St Christopher's, Bournemouth; Westminster Tech. Coll. Co-founder and Director (with Jeremy King): Caprice Hldgs Ltd, 1982–2002; Caprice Events Ltd, 1995–2000; Dir, Rex Restaurant Associates, 2003–; co-proprietor (with Jeremy King): restaurants: Le Caprice, 1981–2004; The Ivy, 1990–2004; J. Sheekey, 1998–; The Wolseley, 2003–; St Alban, 2006–09; bar, Monkey Bar, NY, 2009–10; The Delaunay, 2011–; Brasserie Zédel, 2012–; Colbert, 2012–; Fischer's, 2014; hotel, The Beaumont, 2014–. Restaurateur of Year, Caterer and Hotelkeeper, 1993. *Recreations:* eating, British modern art, art history, France and the French, modern music. *Clubs:* Royal Automobile, Groucho.

CORBITT, Air Vice Marshal Ian Stafford; Chief Executive, RAF Training Group Defence Agency, and Air Officer Commanding, RAF Training Group, 1999–2002; *b* 30 July 1947; *s* of John Kellock Corbitt and Hilda Mary Corbitt; *m* 1976, Anne Lucille Worthy; two *d*. *Educ:* Simon Langton Grammar Sch., Canterbury; Quaid-i-Azam Univ., Islamabad (MSc Defence and Strategic Studies 1993). ACCA; CDipAF 1999. No 48 Sqdn, RAF Changi Singapore, 1970–72; qualified Flying Instructor, RAF Leeming, 1973; ADC to AOC 46 Gp RAF Upavon, 1973–75; Flt Comdr, No 30 Sqdn, 1976–77, OC Hercules Conversion Sqdn 1977–79, RAF Lyneham; Staff Coll., Bracknell, 1980; HQ British Forces, Hong Kong 1981–83; OC 242 OCU, RAF Lyneham, 1983–86; Flt Examr, USAF, Scott AFB, Ill 1986–88; OC RAF Lyneham, 1989–91; HCSC, 1992; Nat. Defence Coll., Rawalpindi 1992–93; Contingency Plans, HQ STC, 1993–95; Air Cdre, Policy and Plans, HQ PTC 1995–99. *Club:* Royal Air Force.

CORBOULD, Christopher Charles, OBE 2014; special effects supervisor in film industry since 1988; *b* London, 5 March 1958; *s* of Clifford and Jean Corbould; *m* 1986, Lynne Margaret Buckley; three *d*. *Educ:* Colfe's Grammar Sch. MIExpE 2003. Special effects asst 1975–80; special effects technician/sen. technician, 1980–88; *films* include: Superman II, 1980; For Your Eyes Only, 1981; Superman III, 1983; A View to Kill, 1985; The Living Daylights, 1987; Willow, 1988; special effects supervisor/director, 1988–; *films* include: Licence to kill, 1989; Shadowlands, 1993; Interview with a Vampire: The Vampire Chronicles, 1994; GoldenEye, 1995; Tomorrow Never Dies, 1997; The Mummy, The World is Not Enough, 1999; Lara Croft: Tomb Raider, 2001; Die Another Day, 2002; Lara Croft Tomb Raider: The Cradle of Life, 2003; Casino Royale, 2006; The Dark Knight, Quantum of Solace, 2008; Inception, 2010 ((jtly) Academy Award, BAFTA Award, 2011); X Men: First Class, 2011; The Dark Knight Rises, Skyfall, 2012. Hon. DTech Southampton Solent, 2009; Hon. DA Hertfordshire, 2010. *Recreations:* guitar, horse riding, theatre, music, family.

CORBY, Mary Margaret; *see* Reilly, M. M.

CORBYN, Rt Hon. Jeremy (Bernard); PC 2015; MP (Lab) Islington North, since 1983; Leader of the Labour Party and Leader of the Opposition, since 2015; *b* 26 May 1949; *s* of David Benjamin Corbyn. *Educ:* Adams Grammar Sch., Newport, Shropshire. NUPE Official, 1975–83; sponsored NUPE, then UNISON, MP. Mem., Haringey Borough Council, 1974–84 (Chm., Community Develt Cttee 1975–78, Public Works 1978–79, Planning Cttee 1980–81, 1982–83). Member: Select Cttee on Social Security, 1990–97; Justice Select Cttee, 2011–15; Chair, London Gp of Lab MPs, 1993–96 (Vice-Chair, 1985–93); All Party Parliamentary Groups: Chair, Mexico, Chagos Islands; Jt Vice Chair, Human Rights; Vice Chair, Latin America, African Great Lakes; Sec., Bolivia, Dalits; Mem., traveller law reform, cycling; Member, Parliamentary Groups: RMT; CWU; Justice Unions; Socialist Campaign; CND (Chair). Chair: Liberation; Stop the War Coalition; Vice Chair, Nat. Council, CND. Trustee: Highbury Vale Blackstock Trust; Dalit Solidarity Campaign. Patron, Mitford Under Fives. *Address:* House of Commons, SW1A 0AA. *T:* (020) 7219 3545.

CORBYN, Stuart Alan; Chairman, Pollen Estate Trustee Company, 2008–14; *b* Inverness, 9 Feb. 1945; *s* of late Gp Capt. Donald Corbyn, CBE and Frances Corbyn (*née* Anderson); *m* 1st, 1985, Mary Moolan Feroze (*d* 2003); 2nd, 2005, Gillian Louise Nunn. *Educ:* Haileybury. FRICS 1982. Gooch & Wagstaff, 1972–82; Sole Principal, Surveyors Consultancy Services, 1982–86; Chief Exec., Cadogan Estates Ltd, 1986–2008. Chm., Get Living London, 2013–; non-executive Director: Derwent London plc, 2006–; Long Acre Estates, 2008–. Pres., British Property Fedn, 1997–98. Church Comr, 2001–06; Mem., Royal Commn for the Exhibn of 1851, 2009–. Trustee: Royal Parks Foundn, 2003–06; Chelsea Physic Garden, 2008–14; Sloane Stanley Estate, 2009–11; Somerset House Trust, 2009–12; Naunton Dovecote Trust (formerly Naunton Village Trust), 2011–; Young Dementia UK Homes, 2014–; Queen Alexandra's Housing Assoc., 2015–; Comr, Royal Hosp. Chelsea, 2008–. Chm., Chelsea Soc., 2009–12. Non playing Dir, RPO, 2006–12. Mem. Council, Royal Albert Hall, 2010–. *Recreations:* architecture, art, fishing, gardening, music, travel. *Clubs:* Chelsea Arts, Sloane.

CORCORAN, Alexander Martin Desmond; Chairman, Lefevre Fine Art Ltd, since 2001; *b* London, 28 Feb. 1968; *s* of Desmond Corcoran and Judith Keppel; *m* (marr. diss.); one *s* one *d*. *Educ:* Ampleforth Coll., Yorks; British Inst., Florence; City & Guilds of London Art Sch. Waddington Galls, London, 1986–88; Partner, Alex Reid and Lefevre Ltd (Lefevre Gall.), 1995–2000. *Recreations:* cycling, walking. *Address:* Lefevre Fine Art Ltd, 31 Bruton Street, W1J 6QS. *T:* (020) 7493 2107. *E:* amdc@lefevrefineart.com.

CORCORAN, Prof. Neil, FEA; King Alfred Professor of English Literature, University of Liverpool, 2004–10, now Emeritus; *b* 23 Sept. 1948; *s* of John Patrick Corcoran and Angela (*née* Attwood); *m* 1979, Gillian Anne Jeffs; three *s*. *Educ:* Austin Friars Sch., Carlisle; St Edmund Hall, and Wolfson Coll., Oxford (MA, MLitt). Lectr, then Sen. Lectr in English, Sheffield Univ., 1974–94; Professor of English: Univ. of Wales, Swansea, 1994–96; Univ. of St Andrews, 1996–2004. FEA 2001. *Publications:* The Song of Deeds: a study of The Anathemata of David Jones, 1982; Seamus Heaney, 1986; (ed) The Chosen Ground: essays on the contemporary poetry of Northern Ireland, 1992; English Poetry since 1940, 1993; After Yeats and Joyce, 1997; The Poetry of Seamus Heaney: a critical study, 1998; Poets of Modern Ireland: text, context, intertext, 1999; (ed) Do You, Mr Jones?: Bob Dylan with the poets and professors, 2002; Elizabeth Bowen: the enforced return, 2004; (ed) Cambridge Companion to Twentieth-Century English Poetry, 2007; Shakespeare and the Modern Poet, 2010; Poetry & Responsibility, 2014. *Recreations:* swimming, cycling, listening to various kinds of music, looking at paintings. *Address:* School of English, University of Liverpool, Liverpool L69 7ZR. *T:* (0151) 794 2720. *E:* nc23@liverpool.ac.uk.

CORDARA, Roderick Charles; QC 1994; *b* 26 March 1953; *s* of Carlo and Silvia Cordara; *m* 1997, Tsambika Anastasas; one *d*. *Educ:* City of London Sch.; Trinity Hall, Cambridge. Called to the Bar, Middle Temple, 1975; SC (NSW) 2001. *Address:* Essex Court Chambers, 24 Lincoln's Inn Fields, WC2A 3EG. *Clubs:* Oxford and Cambridge, Royal Automobile, Hospital.

CORDER, Vice Adm. Ian Fergus, CB 2013; UK Military Representative to NATO, since 2013; *b* Nuneaton, 6 Aug. 1960; *s* of William and Colleen Corder; *m* 1984, Kathryn Alison Snoad; two *s*. *Educ:* Rugby Sch.; Peterhouse, Cambridge (BA Maths 1981; MA). Joined RN, 1978; various operational submarine appts, 1982–88; Submarine Comd Course, 1989; EO, HMS Sceptre, 1990–91; Commanding Officer: HMS Oracle, 1991–92; HMS Splendid, 1996–98; Naval Asst to First Sea Lord, 1999–2001; CO, HMS Cumberland, 2001–02; Dep. Dir, Policy on Internat. Orgns, MoD, 2002–03; Chief of Strategic Systems Exec., 2004–06; Dir, Naval Personnel Strategy, 2006–08; Dep. Comdr Striking Force NATO, 2009–11; Comdr Ops and Rear Adm. Submarines as Hd of Fighting Arms, 2011–13. *Recreations:* reading, music, running, travel. *Address:* c/o Naval Secretary, Leach Building, Navy Headquarters, Whale Island, Portsmouth PO2 8BY.

CORDEROY, Rev. Graham Thomas; Minister, Hutton and Shenfield Union Church, 1987–96; *b* 15 April 1931; *s* of Thomas and Gladys Corderoy; *m* 1957, Edna Marian Barnes; six *d*. *Educ:* Emanuel Sch., London; Manchester Univ. (BA Theology 1957). Ordained 1957; King's Lynn, 1957–62; commissioned RAF Chaplain, 1962; Principal Chaplain, Church of Scotland and Free Churches, and Hon. Chaplain to the Queen, 1984–87. Inst. of Alcohol

Studies Bd, 1986–2006. *Recreations:* Rugby referee 1964–87, Gilbert and Sullivan buff. *Address:* Longmead, 66 Hardwick Lane, Bury St Edmunds, Suffolk IP33 2RB. *Club:* Royal Air Force.

CORDINGLEY, David; Director South Africa, British Council, 2010–13; *b* 27 Oct. 1952; *s* of Robert and Annie Burrell Cordingley; *m* 1992, Patricia Lobo; one *s*. *Educ:* Lancaster Royal Grammar Sch.; St Peter's Coll., Oxford (BA Physics 1973, MA 1977; PGCE 1974); Univ. of E Anglia (MA Develt Studies 1993). VSO, St Kitts, WI, 1974–76; teacher, Tonbridge Sch., 1977–79; Hd of Sci., Navrongo Secondary Sch., Ghana, 1979–81; teacher, Island Sch., Hong Kong, 1981–86; joined British Council, 1986: Asst Rep., Malawi, 1987–88; First Sec. (Sci. and Health), British Council Div., High Commn, New Delhi, 1988–92; Contract Dir, Manchester, 1993–97; Project Manager, Nairobi, 1997–2000; Dir, Vietnam, 2000–04; Regl Dir, Americas and Australasia, 2004–05; Dir, Brazil, 2005–09. *Recreations:* transport (railways, motoring, aviation), sport (walking, cycling, soccer), travel, photography. *Address:* Billingshurst, West Sussex. *E:* dcordingley@btinternet.com.

CORDINGLEY, Maj.-Gen. Patrick Anthony John, DSO 1991; Chairman, MMI Research, 2001–08; *b* 6 Oct. 1944; *s* of Maj.-Gen. John Edward Cordingley, OBE and Ruth Pamela St John Carpendale; *m* 1968, Melissa Crawley; two *d*. *Educ:* Sherborne School. Commissioned into 5th Royal Inniskilling Dragoon Guards, 1965; commanded, 1984–87; commanded 7th Armoured Brigade, 1988–91; served Libya, Cyprus, UK, BAOR, Gulf; Comdr, Combined Arms Trng Centre, 1991–92; GOC Eastern Dist, 1992–95; GOC 2nd Div., 1995–96; Sen. British Loan Service Officer, Sultanate of Oman, 1996–2000. Col, Royal Dragoon Guards, 2000–05; Hon. Col, Bristol Univ. OTC, 2000–05. Chm., Defence and Security Forum, 2002–. Chm. Trustees, Gilbert White House and Oates Mus., 2002–08; Chm., Nat. Meml Arboretum Future Foundns Appeal, 2007–. Gov., Sherborne Sch., 2001– (Chm., Internat. Coll., 2007–). Mem. Ct, Ironmongers' Co., 2000– (Master, 2010–11). FRGS 1986. Hon. DSc Hull, 2007. OStJ 1993. USA Bronze Star, 1991; Order of Oman, 2000. *Publications:* Captain Oates: soldier and explorer, 1984, 3rd edn 2009; In the Eye of the Storm, 1996, 2nd edn 1997. *Recreations:* country pursuits, whale-watching. *Club:* Cavalry and Guards (Chm., 2002–04).

CORDINGLY, David Michael Bradley, DPhil; writer; *b* 5 Dec. 1938; *s* of late Rt Rev. Eric Cordingly, MBE, sometime Bishop of Thetford, and of Mary Mathews; *m* 1971, Shirley Elizabeth Robin; one *s* one *d*. *Educ:* Christ's Hosp., Horsham; Oriel Coll., Oxford; (MA); Univ. of Sussex (DPhil). Graphic designer, 1960–68; Exhibn designer at BM, 1968–71; Keeper of Art Gall., Royal Pavilion and Museums, Brighton, 1971–78; Asst Dir, Mus. of London, 1978–80; National Maritime Museum: Asst Keeper, 1980–82; Dep. Keeper, 1982–86; Keeper of Pictures, 1986–88; Head of Exhibns, 1988–93. Guest Curator, Mariners' Mus., Va, 2000–01. Exhibns organised include: Looking at London, 1980; Sea Finland, 1986; Captain Cook, Brisbane Expo, 1988; Mutiny on the Bounty, 1989; Henry VIII at Greenwich, 1991; Pirates: Fact and Fiction, 1992. FRSA 1974. Order of the White Rose of Finland, 1986. *Publications:* Marine Painting in England, 1974; Painters of the Sea, 1979; (with W. Percival Prescott) The Art of the Van de Veldes, 1982; Nicholas Pocock, 1986; Captain James Cook, Navigator, 1988; Pirates: fact and fiction, 1992; Life Among the Pirates, 1995; Pirates: an illustrated history, 1996; Ships and Seascapes, 1997; Heroines and Harlots: women at sea in the great age of sail, 2001; Billy Ruffian: the Bellerophon and the downfall of Napoleon, 2003; Cochrane the Dauntless: the life and adventures of Thomas Cochrane, 2007; Spanish Gold: Captain Woodes Rogers and the Pirates of the Caribbean, 2011. *Recreations:* sailing, carpentry. *Address:* 2 Vine Place, Brighton, Sussex BN1 3HE. *Clubs:* Athenæum; Chichester Yacht.

CORDY, Timothy Soames; Director, TSC-Europe, since 2010; Senior Consultant, Global to Local Ltd, 2009–10 (Consultant, 2000–05; Director, 2006–08); *b* 17 May 1949; *s* of late John Knutt Cordy and of Margaret Winifred Cordy (*née* Sheward); *m* 1974, Dr Jill Margaret Tattersall; one *s* one *d*. *Educ:* Dragon Sch., Oxford; Sherborne Sch.; Durham Univ. (BA); Glasgow Univ. (MPhil). MRTPI 1976. Leicester City Council, 1974–85 (Asst City Planning Officer, 1980–85); Communauté Urbaine de Strasbourg, 1978–79; Asst Chief Exec., Bolton MBC, 1985–87; Chief Exec., RSNC, 1987–94. Director: UK 2000, 1987–95; Volunteer Centre UK, 1989–95; TCPA, 1995–97; Envmtl Trng Orgn, 1996–98. *Publications:* Planning and Environmental Protection, 2002; articles on housing renewal, local economic develt, biodiversity, sustainability. *Recreations:* music, France, food. *Address:* 49 Hove Park Villas, Hove BN3 6HH.

CORDY-SIMPSON, Lt-Gen. Sir Roderick (Alexander), KBE 1998 (OBE 1984); CB 1993; DL; President, Royal British Legion, 2000–04; *b* 29 Feb. 1944; *s* of late Col John Roger Cordy-Simpson, CBE, MC and Ursula Margaret Cordy-Simpson; *m* 1974, Virginia Rosemary Lewis; one *s* one *d*. *Educ:* Radley College. Commissioned 1963, commanded, 1983–86, 13th/18th Royal Hussars (QMO); Comd 4th Armoured Brigade, 1988–90; COS, UN Bosnia Hercegovina, 1992–93; COS BAOR, 1993–94; GOC 1st (UK) Armd Div., 1994–96; Dep. Force Comdr, Bosnia Hercegovina, 1996–97; retd 1998. Lieut, HM Tower of London, 2001–04. Hon. Colonel: Light Dragoons, 2000–08; Wilts ACF, 2014. Pres., Regular Forces Employment Assoc., 2002–07 (Chm., 1999–2002); Chm., Services Sound and Vision Corp., 2004–08. DL Wilts, 2004. Order of Al Istiqual (1st Class), 2008. *Recreations:* ski-ing, shooting, reading, fishing. *Address:* c/o Coutts & Co., 440 Strand, WC2R 0QS. *Club:* Cavalry and Guards.

COREN, Giles Robin Patrick; opinion columnist, since 1999, Restaurant Critic, since 2002, The Times; *b* 29 July 1969; *s* of late Alan Coren, writer and broadcaster, and of Anne Coren (*née* Kasriel); *m* 2010, Esther Walker; one *s* one *d*. *Educ:* Westminster Sch.; Keble Coll., Oxford (BA Hons English Lit.). The Times: feature writer, 1993–96; Ed., Times Diary, 2000–01; columnist, Tatler, and Ed., Tatler About Town, 1998–99; columnist: Match of the Day mag., 1996–99; Mail on Sunday, 1997–98; Sunday Times, 2002–06; GQ mag., 2004–07; Esquire mag., 2011–; Time Out, 2014–; restaurant critic, Independent on Sunday, 1999–2000; television: co-presenter: The F-word, 2005; Our Food, 2012; Pressure Cooker, 2014–15; presenter: Movie Lounge, 2006; Animal Farm, 2007; Edwardian Supersize Me, 2007; The Supersizers Go… (2 series), 2008, 2009; Giles and Sue Live the Good Life, 2010; The Twelve Drinks of Christmas, 2013; Million Dollar Critic, 2014–15; Back in Time for Dinner, 2015; writer and presenter: Tax the Fat, 2006; Eat to Live Forever with Giles Coren, 2015. *Publications:* Against the Odds: James Dyson, an autobiography, 1997; Winkler, 2005; Anger Management for Beginners, 2010; How to Eat Out, 2012; (ed jtly) Chocolate and Cuckoo Clocks: the essential Alan Coren, 2008. *Recreations:* Eton fives, cricket, writing fiction, daily afternoon naps. *Address:* The Times, 1 London Bridge Street, SE1 9GF. *T:* (020) 7782 5000. *Clubs:* Groucho, Soho House; MCC (Assoc. Mem.); Old Westminster Cricket.

See also D. J. S. Mitchell.

COREY, Prof. Elias James, PhD; Professor of Chemistry, 1959–68, Sheldon Emory Professor of Chemistry, 1968–98, Harvard University, now Emeritus; *b* 12 July 1928; *s* of Elias Corey and Tina Corey (*née* Hasham); *m* 1961, Claire Higham; two *s* one *d*. *Educ:* MIT (BS 1948; PhD 1951). University of Illinois, Urbana-Champaign: Instructor, 1951; Asst Prof., 1953–55; Prof. of Chemistry, 1955–59. Former Member: Bd of Dirs, physical sciences, Alfred P. Sloan Foundn; Sci. Adv. Bd, Robert A. Welch Foundn. Foreign Mem., Royal Soc., 1998. Hon. DSc: Chicago, 1968; Hofstra, 1974; Oxford, 1982; Liège, 1985; Illinois, 1985; Hon. ScD Cantab, 2000; Hon. AM Harvard, 1959. Numerous awards, medals and prizes from univs and learned bodies in USA, Europe and Asia, incl. US Nat. Medal of Science, 1988 and Nobel Prize for Chemistry, 1990. *Publications:* numerous papers in learned jls on pure and synthetic chemistry, esp. on development of methods of organic synthesis, making possible mass production of medicinal and other products, based on natural materials. *Address:* Department of Chemistry, Harvard University, 12 Oxford Street, Cambridge, MA 02138, USA.

CORFIELD, Sir Kenneth (George), Kt 1980; FREng; Chairman, 1979–85, and Managing Director, 1969–85, STC PLC (formerly Standard Telephones & Cables plc); Chairman, Tanks Consolidated Investments, since 1990; *b* 27 Jan. 1924; *s* of Stanley Corfield and Dorothy Elizabeth (*née* Mason); *m* 1960; one *d*. *Educ:* South Staffs Coll. of Advanced Technology. FREng (FEng 1979); FIMechE. Management Develt, ICI Metals Div., 1946–50; Man. Dir, K. G. Corfield Ltd, 1950–60; Exec. Dir, Parkinson Cowan, 1960–66; Dep. Chm., STC Ltd, 1969–79; Sen. Officer, ITT Corp. (UK), 1974–84. Chairman: Standard Telephones and Cables (NI), 1974–85; Distributed Information Processing Ltd, 1987–; Vice-Pres., ITT Europe Inc., 1967–85; Director: Midland Bank Ltd, 1979–91; Britoil PLC, 1982–88; Octagon Investment Management, 1987–95. Chairman: EDC for Ferrous Foundries Industry, 1975–78; British Engrg Council, 1981–85; Defence Spectrum Review, 1985–88; Radio Spectrum Review, 1990–93; Mem., ACARD, 1981–84. President: TEMA, 1974–80; BAIE, 1975–79; Vice-Pres., Engineering Employers' Fedn, 1979–85; Member Council: CBI, 1971–85; Inst. of Dirs, 1981– (Pres. 1984–85); BIM, 1978– (Vice-Pres. 1978–83). Trustee, Science Museum, 1984–92 (Mem. Adv. Council, 1975–83). CCMI; FIEE (CompIEE 1974), Hon. FIET (Hon. FIEE 1985). Hon. Fellow: Sheffield Polytechnic, 1983; Wolverhampton Polytechnic, 1986. DUniv: Surrey, 1976; Open, 1985; Hon. DSc: City, 1981; Bath, 1982; Aston in Birmingham, 1985; Hon. DScEng London, 1982; Hon. DSc (Engrg) QUB, 1982; Hon. LLD Strathclyde, 1982; Hon. DTech Loughborough, 1983; Hon. DEng Bradford, 1984. Bicentennial Medal for design, RSA, 1985. *Publications:* Product Design, Report for NEDO, 1979; No Man An Island, 1982 (SIAD Award). *Recreations:* photography, music. *Address:* 14 Elm Walk, Hampstead, NW3 7UP.

CORK AND ORRERY, 15th Earl of, *cr* 1620; **John Richard Boyle, (Jonathan);** Baron Boyle of Youghal, 1616; Viscount Dungarvan, 1620; Baron Boyle of Broghill, 1621; Viscount Boyle of Kinalmeaky and Baron of Bandon Bridge, 1627; Earl of Orrery, 1660 (all Ire.); Baron Boyle of Marston (GB) 1711; Chairman, Maritime Investment Holdings Pte Ltd, Singapore, 1986–2014; *b* 3 Nov. 1945; *e s* of 14th Earl of Cork and Orrery, DSC, VRD; *S* father, 2003; *m* 1973, Hon. Rebecca Juliet Noble, *y d* of Baron Glenkinglas (Life Peer), PC; one *s* two *d* (of whom one *s* one *d* are twins). *Educ:* Harrow; RNC Dartmouth. Lt-Comdr RN, retd. Dir, E. D. & F. Man Sugar Ltd, London, 1994–2006. Life Governor, Soc. for the Advancement of the Christian Faith. Mem. Council, Internat. Dendrol. Soc., 2007–. Chm., Chichester Cathedral Restoration and Develt Trust, 2008–15; Trustee, MapAction, 2007–14. *Recreations:* country pursuits, sailing, ski-ing, classic cars, cathedrals. *Heir:* *s* Viscount Dungarvan, *qv*. *Address:* Lickfold House, Petworth, West Sussex GU28 9EY. *Clubs:* Boodle's; Royal Yacht Squadron, Royal Northern and Clyde Yacht; Castaways.

See also Baron Middleton.

CORK, CLOYNE, AND ROSS, Bishop of, since 1999; **Rt Rev. (William) Paul Colton;** *b* 13 March 1960; *s* of George Henry Colton and Kathleen Mary Colton (*née* Jenkins); *m* 1986, Susan Margaret Good; two *s*. *Educ:* Ashton Sch., Cork; Lester B. Pearson Coll. of the Pacific, BC, Canada; University Coll., Cork (BCL Hons); Trinity Coll., Dublin (DipTh, MPhil); Univ. of Wales, Cardiff (LLM 2006; PhD 2013). Curate, St Paul, Lisburn, dio. Connor, 1984–87; Domestic Chaplain to Bp of Connor, 1985–90; Vicar Choral, Belfast Cathedral, 1987–90, Minor Canon, 1989–90; Priest Vicar, Registrar and Chapter Clerk, Christ Church Cathedral, Dublin, 1990–95; Co-ordinator of Religious Programmes (Protestant), RTE, 1993–99; Incumbent of Castleknock and Mulhuddart with Clonsilla, dio. Dublin, 1990–99; Canon, Christ Church Cathedral, Dublin, 1997–99. Associate, Centre for Law and Religion, Cardiff Univ., 2006–. Clerical Hon. Sec., Gen. Synod of C of I, 1999. *Recreations:* piano, organ, music, walking, reading, computers, Manchester United Football Club. *Address:* The Palace, Bishop Street, Cork, Ireland. *T:* (21) 5005080. *Club:* Kildare Street and University (Dublin).

CORK, Adam James; freelance composer, since 1997; Associate Artist, Royal Shakespeare Company, since 2012; *b* London, 16 Jan. 1974; *s* of Richard Graham Cork, *qv*; partner, Lorna Heavey; one *s*. *Educ:* Hampstead Sch.; Camden Sch. for Girls (6th Form); Trinity Hall, Cambridge (BA Hons Music 1995). Composer: *radio* includes: Losing Rosalind, 2000; Don Carlos, 2005; The Luneberg Variation, 2006; Othello, The Chalk Garden, 2008; *television* includes: Re-ignited, 2003; Frances Tuesday, 2004; Macbeth, 2010; The Hollow Crown: Richard II, 2012; *films*: Bust, 2002; Tripletake, 2003; The Three Rules of Infidelity, 2004. *Theatre*: composer and sound designer: Don Carlos, Sheffield Crucible, Gielgud, 2004; Suddenly Last Summer, Sheffield Crucible, Albery, 2004; The Late Henry Moss, Tom and Viv, Almeida, 2006; The Tempest, RSC, 2006; Frost/Nixon, Gielgud, 2006, transf. NY, 2007; The Cherry Orchard, Sheffield Crucible, 2007; Macbeth, Chichester, Gielgud, transf. NY, 2007; No Man's Land, Duke of York's, 2008; Ivanov, Wyndhams, 2008; The Last Days of Judas Iscariot, Almeida, 2008; The Chalk Garden, Creditors, Donmar, 2008; (and lyricist) Enron, Chichester, Royal Court, Noël Coward, 2009, transf. NY, 2010; Time and the Conways, Phèdre, NT, 2009; A View from the Bridge, Duke of York's, 2009; A Streetcar Named Desire, Donmar, 2009; Madame de Sade, Wyndhams, 2009; Hamlet, Wyndhams, transf. NY, 2009; Red, Donmar, 2009, transf. NY, 2010 (Tony Award for Best Sound Design of a Play); Romeo and Juliet, RSC, 2010, transf. NY, 2011; Danton's Death, NT, 2010; King Lear, Donmar, 2010 (Olivier Award for Best Sound, 2011; Evening Standard Award for Best Design, 2011); Luise Miller, Donmar, 2011; Anna Christie, Donmar, 2011 (Evening Standard Award for Best Design); Decade, Headlong, 2011; Richard II, Donmar, 2011; Cat on a Hot Tin Roof, Broadway, 2013; Peter & Alice, Henry V, Noël Coward, 2013; composer: All's Well That Ends Well, NT, 2009; (and co-lyricist) London Road, Cottesloe, 2011, transf. Olivier, 2012 (Critics Circle Award for Best Musical); The Merchant of Venice, RSC, 2011; (and lyricist and sound score) The Lion, the Witch and the Wardrobe, Kensington Gardens, 2012. *Publications:* London Road, 2011. *Address:* c/o United Agents, 12–26 Lexington Street, W1F 0LE. *T:* (020) 3214 0873. *E:* RCobbe@unitedagents.co.uk.

CORK, Richard Graham; art critic, art historian, broadcaster and exhibition organiser; *b* 25 March 1947; *s* of Hubert Henry Cork and Beatrice Hester Cork; *m* 1970, Vena Jackson; two *s* two *d*. *Educ:* Kingswood Sch., Bath; Trinity Hall, Cambridge (MA, PhD). Art critic, Evening Standard, 1969–77, 1980–83; Editor, Studio International, 1975–79; art critic, The Listener, 1984–90; Chief Art Critic, The Times, 1991–2002; Art Critic, New Statesman, 2003–06. Slade Prof. of Fine Art, Cambridge, 1989–90; Lethaby Lectr, RCA, 1974; Durning-Lawrence Lectr, UCL, 1987; Henry Moore Foundn Sen. Fellow, Courtauld Inst. of Art, 1992–95. Former Member: Hayward Gall. Advisory Panel; Fine Arts Advisory Cttee, British Council; Cttee, 1995, Contemp. Art Soc.; Mem., Arts Council of England, 1995–98 (Chm., Visual Art Panel, 1995–98). Curator: Critic's Choice, 1973; Vorticism and its Allies, 1974; Beyond Painting and Sculpture, 1974; Sculpture Now: Dissolution or Redefinition?, 1974; Arte Inglese Oggi, 1976; Art for Whom?, 1978; Art for Society, 1978; Un Certain Art Anglais, 1979; British Art in the 20th Century, 1987; David Bomberg retrospective, 1988; A Bitter Truth: Avant-Garde Art and the Great War, 1994; British Art Show, 1995; A Life of Their Own, Lismore Castle, 2008; Wild Thing: Jacob Epstein, Henri Gaudier-Brzeska and Eric Gill, RA, 2009–10; Selector: Turner Prize, 1988; Citibank Photography Prize, 1997; Natwest Art Prize, 1998; North Meadow Millennium Dome Sculpture Project, 1998–2000; Sunderland Gateway Commn, 1999–; John Moores Painting Prize, 1999; Times/Artangel Open, 1999–2000; Jerwood Drawing Prize, 2001; Elector, Slade Professorship of Fine Art, Univ. of Cambridge, 1999–2004; Member: Trafalgar Sq. Plinth Adv. Gp, 1999–2000; Selection Cttee, New St Paul's Cathedral Font, 1999; Adv. Council, Paul Mellon Centre for British Art, 1999–2005;

Design Cttee, Diana, Princess of Wales Meml Fountain, 2000–02; BBC Churchill Commn, 2003–; St Martin-in-the-Fields Crib Sculpture Cttee, 2004; Maggie's Arts Gp, 2009–; Internat. Adv. Bd, Ben Uri Mus., 2011–; Editl Bd, RA Mag., 2009–; Chm. of Judges, Rouse Kent Public Art Award, 2006 and 2007; Judge: BlindArt, 2006; St Martin-in-the-Fields East Window, 2006; Chichester Open Art Exhibn, 2007; Darwin Ceiling Commn, Nat. History Mus., 2008; Sculpture Shock, Royal British Soc. of Sculptors, 2012–13; British Watercolour Soc. Competition, 2015. Syndic, Fitzwilliam Mus., Cambridge, 2002–14. Patron, Paintings in Hosps, 2012–. Trustee, Public Art Develt Trust, 1988–95. Organiser of many exhibns, incl. shows in Milan, Paris, Berlin and at Hayward Gall., Tate Gall. and RA. Frequent broadcaster on radio and television. Hon. FRA 2011. John Llewellyn Rhys Meml Prize, 1976; Sir Banister Fletcher Award, 1986; Art Fund Award, 1995. *Publications:* Vorticism and Abstract Art in the First Machine Age, vol. I: Origins and Development, 1975, vol. II: Synthesis and Decline, 1976; The Social Role of Art, 1979; Art Beyond the Gallery in Early Twentieth Century England, 1985; David Bomberg, 1987; Architect's Choice, 1992; A Bitter Truth: Avant-Garde Art and the Great War, 1994; Bottle of Notes: Claes Oldenburg and Coosje van Bruggen, 1997; Jacob Epstein, 1999; Everything Seemed Possible: art in the 1970s, 2003; New Spirit, New Sculpture, New Money: art in the 1980s, 2003; Breaking Down the Barriers: art in the 1990s, 2003; Annus Mirabilis?: art in the year 2000, 2003; Michael Craig-Martin, 2006; Wild Thing: Epstein, Gaudier-Brzeska, Gill, 2009; The Healing Presence of Art: a history of Western art in hospitals, 2012; Peter Prendergast, 2013; Face to Face: interviews with artists, 2015; contribs to art magazines and exhibn catalogues. *Recreations:* enjoying family, looking at art, walking. *Address:* 24 Milman Road, NW6 6EG. *T:* (020) 8960 2671.

See also A. J. Cork.

CORKE, Donald Stevenson; Sheriff of Lothian and Borders at Edinburgh, since 2013; *b* Salisbury, Southern Rhodesia, 5 Aug. 1959; *s* of Robert and Marion Corke; *m* 1989, Helen White; one *s* two *d. Educ:* Mount Pleasant Sch., Salisbury, Southern Rhodesia; Univ. of Cape Town (BA); Univ. of the Witwatersrand (LLB). Advocate of Supreme Court of SA, 1985; Mem., Faculty of Advocates, Edinburgh, 1988; Advocate, Scottish Bar, 1988–2000; called to the Bar, Middle Temple, 1995; pt-time Immigration Adjudicator, 1997–2000; Immigration Adjudicator, 2000–05; Immigration Judge, 2005–09; pt-time Sheriff, 2005–09; Sheriff of: S Strathclyde, Dumfries and Galloway at Airdrie, 2009–11; Lothian and Borders at Jedburgh, 2011–13. Dep. Dist Chm., Appeals Service, 1998–2001. *Address:* Sheriff Court House, 27 Chambers Street, Edinburgh EH1 1LB.

CORKERY, Michael; QC 1981; *b* 20 May 1926; *o s* of late Charles Timothy Corkery and of Nellie Marie Corkery; *m* 1967, Juliet Foulkes, *o d* of late Harold Glyn Foulkes; one *s* one *d. Educ:* The King's Sch., Canterbury. Grenadier Guards, 1944; Commissioned in Welsh Guards, 1945; served until 1948. Called to Bar, Lincoln's Inn, 1949 (Bencher 1973, Master of the Library, 1991, Treasurer, 1992). Mem., South Eastern Circuit; 3rd Junior Prosecuting Counsel to the Crown at the Central Criminal Court, 1959; 1st Junior Prosecuting Counsel to the Crown, 1964; 5th Senior Prosecuting Counsel to the Crown, 1970; 3rd Sen. Prosecuting Counsel, 1971; 2nd Sen. Prosecuting Counsel, 1974; 1st Sen. Prosecuting Counsel, 1977–81. *Recreations:* shooting, sailing, gardening, music. *Address:* c/o 5 Paper Buildings, Temple, EC4Y 7HB. *Clubs:* Cavalry and Guards, Garrick, Hurlingham, Sloane; Itchenor Sailing; Household Div. Yacht; Friends of Arundel Castle Cricket.

CORKUM, Paul Bruce, OC 2007; PhD; FRSC 1996; FRS 2005; Director, Attosecond Science Program, National Research Council of Canada; *b* 30 Oct. 1943. *Educ:* Acadia Univ., Nova Scotia (BSc 1965); Lehigh Univ., Penn (MS 1967; PhD 1972). Joined Nat. Research Council of Canada, 1973. Gold Medal, Canadian Assoc. of Physicists, 1996; Killam Prize, 2006. Golden Jubilee Medal, 2002. *Publications:* articles in learned jls. *Address:* Steacie Institute for Molecular Sciences, National Research Council of Canada, 100 Sussex Drive, Ottawa, ON K1A 0R6, Canada; 15 Rothwell Drive, Ottawa, ON K1J 7G3, Canada.

CORLETT, Andrew Thomas Kaneen; His Honour Deemster Corlett; HM Second Deemster, Isle of Man, since 2011; *b* Douglas, I of M, 2 March 1959; *s* of William Thomas Kaneen Corlett and Jean Mary Corlett; *m* 1989, Angelina Tehan; one *s* one *d. Educ:* King William's Coll., Isle of Man; Pembroke Coll., Oxford (MA). Called to the Bar, Gray's Inn, 1984; admitted to the Manx Bar, 1984; Partner, Dickinson Cruickshank & Co., Advocates, 1985–95; Government Advocate, Attorney General's Chambers, Douglas, 1995–2001; Dir, Simcocks, Advocates, 2001–07; Dep. Deemster, 2007–11. *Recreations:* walking, sporadic gym attendance, cinema, theatre, visual arts, London. *Address:* Isle of Man Courts of Justice, Deemsters Walk, Bucks Road, Douglas, Isle of Man IM1 3AR.

CORLETT, Clive William, CB 1995; Deputy Chairman, Board of Inland Revenue, 1994–98 (Under Secretary, 1985–92; Director General, 1992–94); *b* 14 June 1938; *s* of F. William and Hanna Corlett; *m* 1964, Margaret Catherine Jones; one *s. Educ:* Birkenhead Sch.; Brasenose Coll., Oxford (BA PPE). Merchant Navy, 1957. Joined Inland Revenue, 1960; seconded to: Civil Service Selection Bd, 1970; HM Treasury, 1972–74 (as Private Sec. to Chancellor of Exchequer) and 1979–81. Mem. Cttee, Friends of Greenwich Park, 2001–. Hon. Treas., Old Colfeians RFC, 2000–13.

CORLETT, Gerald Lingham; Chairman, Higsons Brewery plc, 1980–88; *b* 8 May 1925; *s* of Alfred Lingham Corlett and Nancy Eileen Bremner; *m* 1957, Helen Bromfield Williamson; three *s* one *d. Educ:* Rossall School; Aberdeen University (short war-time course). RA, 1943–47 (Lieut, Royal Indian Artillery). Higsons Brewery, 1947–88. Director: Westminster (Liverpool) Trust Co., 1960–2001 (Chm., 1995–2001); Midshires Building Soc. (Northern Bd), 1977–87; Radio City (Sound of Merseyside), 1982–88 (Chm., 1985–88); Boddington Gp, 1985–88; Watson Prickard, 1991–96 (Chm., 1991–96). Member, Council: Brewers' Soc., 1964–88; Rossall Sch., 1956–95. Mem., Brewers' Co., 1983–2006. *Recreation:* family. *Address:* Kirk House, 4 Abbey Road, West Kirby, Wirral CH48 7EW. *T:* (0151) 625 5425. *Club:* Royal Liverpool Golf.

CORLETT, William John Howarth; QC (I of M) 1999; Attorney General, Isle of Man, 1998–2011; *b* 25 March 1950; *s* of William Thomas Kaneen Corlett and Jean Mary Corlett; *m* 1974, Janice Mary Crowe; one *s. Educ:* King William's Coll., Isle of Man; Univ. of Nottingham (LLB). Called to the Bar, Gray's Inn, 1972; admitted to Manx Bar, 1974; Partner, Dickinson Cruickshank & Co., Advocates, 1975–92; Sen. Partner, Corlett Bolton & Co., Advocates, 1992–98. *Recreations:* golf, salmon fishing. *Address:* Close Jairg, Old Church Road, Crosby, Isle of Man IM4 2HA. *T:* (01624) 852119.

See also A. T. K. Corlett.

CORLEY, Elizabeth Pauline Lucy, CBE 2015; Chief Executive Officer, Allianz Global Investors, since 2012; *b* Luton, 19 Oct. 1956; *d* of Robert Cooper Trown and Yvonne Celina-Rose Trown; *m* 1986, Michael Charles Corley; one step *d. Educ:* Horsham High Sch. for Girls; Postgrad. Dip. Mgt 1984. FCII 1980. Sun Alliance Life & Pensions, 1975–85; Consultant, then Partner, Coopers & Lybrand Mgt Consultancy, 1985–93; Dir, 1993–98, Man. Dir, 1998–2004, Mercury Asset Mgt, subseq. Merrill Lynch Investment Managers; CEO, Europe, Allianz Global Investors, 2005–12. Non-executive Director: Financial Reporting Council, 2011–; Pearson plc, 2014–. FRSA. *Publications:* Requiem Mass, 1998; Fatal Legacy, 2000; Grave Doubts, 2006; Innocent Blood, 2008; Dead of Winter, 2014. *Recreations:* thriller writing, music, travel, gardening. *Address:* Allianz Global Investors, 155 Bishopsgate, EC2M 3AD.

CORLEY, Paul John; media consultant, since 2008; *b* 23 Dec. 1950; *s* of Robert Charles Corley and Margaret Dorothy Corley. *Educ:* Worcester Coll., Oxford (BA Hons Modern Hist.). Journalist, Westminster Press, 1972–76; News and Current Affairs, BBC TV, 1976–81; Producer, The Tube, Tyne Tees TV, 1982–84; Director of Programmes: Border TV, 1984–91; Granada Gp, NE TV, 1991–92; Controller: Factual Progs, Carlton TV, and Man. Dir, Carlton Broadcasting, 1992–96; Network Factual Progs, ITV Network Centre, 1996–98; Chief Exec., Border TV, 1998–2000; Man. Dir, GMTV, 2001–08. *Recreations:* television, music, ski-ing. *Clubs:* Groucho, Soho House.

CORLEY, Peter Maurice Sinclair; Chairman, Community Library, Painswick, 2011–13; *b* 15 June 1933; *s* of Rev. James Maurice Corley, MLitt and Mrs Barbara Shearer Corley; *m* 1961, Dr Marjorie Constance Doddridge; two *d. Educ:* Marlborough Coll.; King's Coll., Cambridge (MA). Min. of Power, 1957–61; Min. of Transport, 1961–65; BoT, 1965–69; Commercial Sec., Brussels, 1969–71; Asst Sec., DTI, 1972–75; Dir Gen., Econ. Co-operation Office, Riyadh, 1976–78; Dept of Industry, 1978–81; Under Sec., DTI, 1981–93. Consultant, Year of Engineering Success, 1993–96. *Recreations:* painting, travel. *Club:* Oxford and Cambridge.

CORLEY, Roger David, CBE 1993; Director, Clerical, Medical and General Life Assurance Society, 1975–97 (Managing Director, 1982–95); *b* 13 April 1933; *s* of Thomas Arthur and Erica Trent Corley; *m* 1964, Brigitte (*née* Roeder), PhD, FSA, FRSA; three *s. Educ:* Hymers College, Hull; Univ. of Manchester (BSc). FIA 1960. Joined Clerical Medical, 1956: Investment Manager, 1961–72; Actuary, 1972–80; Dep. Gen. Manager and Actuary, 1980–82. Chairman: Pharos SA, 1995–2006; St Andrew's Gp, 1995–2003; Director: Korea Asia Fund Ltd, 1990–2000; Nat. Westminster Life Assce Ltd, 1992–95; Lands Improvement Hldgs, 1994–99; City of Westminster Arts Council, 1994–2003; British Heart Foundn, 1995–2004; Medical Defence Union Ltd, 1996–2004; FIL (formerly Fidelity Investments) Life Insurance Ltd, 1997–2012; RGA Reinsurance UK Ltd, 1999–2012. Mem., Financial Services Commn of Gibraltar, 1995–2000. Pres., Inst. of Actuaries, 1988–90 (Mem. Council, 1976–94; Hon. Sec., 1980–82; Vice-Pres., 1985–88); Vice Pres., Internat. Actuarial Assoc., 1990–98 (Mem. Council, 1983–98; Nat. Correspondent for England, 1984–90); Mem., Deutsche Gesellschaft für Finanz- und Versicherungsmathematik (formerly für Versicherungsmathematik), 1975–. Master, Actuaries' Co., 1992–93 (Mem. Court, 1985–). FRSA 1990. *Recreations:* theatre, travel, music.

CORMACK, family name of **Baron Cormack**.

CORMACK, Baron *cr* 2010 (Life Peer), of Enville in the County of Staffordshire; **Patrick Thomas Cormack,** Kt 1995; DL; *b* 18 May 1939; *s* of Thomas Charles and Kathleen Mary Cormack, Grimsby; *m* 1967, Kathleen Mary McDonald; two *s. Educ:* St James' Choir School and Havelock School, Grimsby; Univ. of Hull. Second Master, St James' Choir School, Grimsby, 1961–66; Company Education and Training Officer, Ross Group Ltd, Grimsby, 1966–67; Assistant Housemaster, Wrekin College, Shropshire, 1967–69; Head of History, Brewood Grammar School, Stafford, 1969–70. Vis. Lectr, Univ. of Texas, 1984. Dir, Historic House Hotels Ltd, 1981–89; Chm., Aitken Dott Ltd (The Scottish Gallery), 1983–89. Trustee, Tradescant Trust, 1980–2001; President: Staffs Historic Buildings Trust, 1983–; Staffs Historic Churches Trust, 1997–2012; Staffs Parks and Gdns Trust, 2006–14; Prayer Book Soc., 2011–; Vice-President: Lincs Old Churches Trust, 1997–; Nat. Churches Trust (formerly Historic Churches Preservation Trust, 2005– (Trustee, 1972–2006); Member: Historic Buildings Council, 1979–84; Faculty Jurisdiction Commn, 1979–84; Heritage in Danger (Vice-Chm., 1974–2000); Council for British Archaeology, 1979–89; Royal Commn on Historical Manuscripts, 1981–2003; Council for Independent Educn (Chm., 1979–97); Lord Chancellor's Adv. Cttee on Public Records, 1979–84; Council, Georgian Gp, 1985–; Council, Winston Churchill Meml Trust, 1983–93; Adv. Council on Nat. Records and Archives, 2003–06. Chairman: William Morris Craft Fellowship, 1988–; Adv. Council, Nat. Fisheries Mus., 1997–2000; Historic Lincoln Trust, 2012–; Ambassador, Nat. Forest, 2005–10. MP (C) Cannock, 1970–74, Staffs SW, 1974–83, Staffs S, 1983–2010. Dep. Shadow Leader of H of C and spokesman on constitutional affairs, 1997–2000. Member: Select Cttee on Educn, Science and Arts, 1979–84; Select Cttee on Foreign Affairs, 2001–03; Chairman's Panel, H of C, 1983–97; Chairman: H of C Works of Art Cttee, 1987–2001; NI Affairs Select Cttee, 2005–10; Mem., H of C Commn, 2001–05. Member: All Party Arts and Heritage Gp (Chm. 1979–2010; Pres., 2010–); Cons. Party Arts and Heritage Cttee, 1979–84 (Chm.); H of L Works of Art Cttee, 2012–; Chm., Cons. Party Adv. Cttee on Arts and Heritage, 1988–99; Treas., CPA, 2000–03; Mem. Exec., 1922 Cttee, 2002–05; Dir, Parly Broadcasting Unit, 2002–10; Chm., Campaign for an Effective Second Chamber, 2003–. Chairman: British-Finnish Parly Gp, 1992–2010; British-Bosnian Parly Gp, 1992–97, 2001–10; British-Croatian Parly Gp, 1992–97. Sen. Associate Mem., St Antony's Coll., Oxford, 1996– (Vis. Parly Fellow, 1994–95); Vis. Schol., Hull Univ., 1995–. Trustee, 1983–, Chm., 2001–, History of Parlt Trust. Chm. Editorial Bd, Parliamentary Publications, 1983–; Ed., The House Magazine, 1983–2005 (Chm. Editl Bd, 1978–; Life Pres., 2005); Internat. Pres., First mag., 1994–. FSA 1978 (Vice Pres., 1994–98). Rector's Warden, 1978–90, Parly Warden, 1990–92, St Margaret's Church, Westminster; Churchwarden, St Mary's, Enville, 1992–2009; Mem., Gen. Synod of C of E, 1995–2005. Governor, ESU, 1999–2006 (Vice-Pres., Lincs Br., 2013–). Vice-President: Royal Stuart Soc., 2002–; Tennyson Soc., 2012–; Sen. Vice Pres., Public Monuments and Sculpture Assoc., 2010–. FRHistS 2010. Mem., Worshipful Co. of Glaziers, 1979–; Freeman, City of London, 1979. DL Staffs, 2011. Hon. FHA 2010. Hon. Dr Catholic Univ. of America, 2010; Hon. DLitt Hull, 2010. Hon. Citizen of Texas, 1985. Commander, Order of the Lion (Finland), 1998. *Publications:* Heritage in Danger, 1976; Right Turn, 1978; Westminster: Palace and Parliament, 1981; Castles of Britain, 1982; Wilberforce—the Nation's Conscience, 1983; Cathedrals of England, 1984; Responsible Capitalism, 2010. *Recreations:* fighting philistines, walking, visiting old churches, avoiding sitting on fences. *Address:* House of Lords, SW1A 0PW. *Clubs:* Athenæum, Arts (Hon. Mem.).

CORMACK, Dr Douglas; independent consultant on environment and management; *b* 10 Jan. 1939; *s* of Douglas Cormack and Mary Hutton (*née* Bain); *m* 1966, Barbara Ann Jones (*d* 2004); two *s. Educ:* Gourock High Sch.; Greenock High Sch.; Univ. of Glasgow (BSc 1961; PhD Physical Chemistry 1964). Res. Associate, Chemical Oceanography, Woods Hole Oceanographic Instn, Mass, USA, 1964–67; Warren Spring Laboratory, Department of Trade and Industry: SSO, 1967–72; PSO, 1972–74; Sen. Principal and Hd, Oil Pollution Div., 1974–79; Scientific Advr, Marine Pollution Control Unit, Depts of Trade and Industry and Transport, 1979–86; Warren Spring Laboratory, Department of Trade and Industry: Dep. Dir with responsibility for Envmtl Res. and Personnel, 1986–89; Dep. Dir and Business Manager, 1989–92; Chief Exec., 1992–94; Dir, Envmt, British Maritime Technology, 1994–96. Chm., British Oil Spill Control Assoc., 2000–04; Mem., UK Accreditation Exec. Gp, 2003–04; Chm., ISAA, 2003–. Mem. Bd, Soc. of Maritime Industries (formerly British Marine Equipment Council), 2000–04. Vice-Chm., Adv. Cttee on Protection of the Sea, 1992–95. Associate, Paragon Associates, Envmtl Consultants, 1994–97; Ind. Consultant, Cormack Associates, 1997–. Hon. Fellow, Internat. Spill Control Orgn, 2009. Mem., Council, RNLI, 2003–. FRSA 1988; Founding Fellow, Inst. of Contemp. Scotland, 2001. Editor, Jl of Oil and Chem. Pollution, 1985–91. *Publications:* Response to Oil and Chemical Marine Pollution, Applied Science, 1983; Response to Marine Oil Pollution—Review and Assessment, 1999; The Rational Trinity: imagination, belief and knowledge, 2010; numerous scientific papers and reports on catalytic processes, atmospheric pollution abatement, marine pollution prevention and response, waste recycling, final disposal and remediation of contaminated land.

Recreations: sailing, beagling, reading philosophy, politics, history and science. *Address:* 1 Flint Copse, Redbourn, Herts AL3 7QE. *Clubs:* Civil Service; Royal Gourock Yacht.

CORMACK, John, CB 1982; Director, Parliamentary and Law, Institute of Chartered Accountants of Scotland, 1987–88 (Assistant Director, 1984–87); Fisheries Secretary, Department of Agriculture and Fisheries for Scotland, 1976–82; *b* 27 Aug. 1922; *yr s* of late Donald Cormack and Anne Hunter Cormack (*née* Gair); *m* 1947, Jessie Margaret Bain; one *s* one *d* (and one *d* decd). *Educ:* Royal High Sch., Edinburgh. Served RAPC, 1941–46; Captain and Command Cashier, CMF, 1946. Entered Department of Agriculture for Scotland, 1939: Principal, 1959; Private Sec. to Sec. of State for Scotland, 1967–69; Asst Sec., 1969; Under Sec., 1976. *Recreations:* golf, music. *Address:* 9/1 Murrayfield Road, Edinburgh EH12 6EW.

CORMACK, Robert Linklater Burke, CMG 1988; DL; HM Diplomatic Service, retired; *b* 29 Aug. 1935; *s* of late Frederick Eunson Cormack, CIE, and Elspeth Mary (*née* Linklater), Dounby, Orkney; *m* 1962, Eivor Dorotea Kumlin; one *s* two *d*. *Educ:* Trinity Coll., Glenalmond; Trinity Hall, Cambridge (BA Agric.). National Service, 2nd Lieut, The Black Watch, 1954–56. Dist Officer, Kenya (HMOCS), 1960–64; entered CRO (subseq. Diplomatic Service), 1964: Private Sec. to Minister of State, 1964–66; 1st Secretary: Saigon, 1966–68; Bombay, 1969–70; Delhi, 1970–72; FCO, 1972–77; Counsellor and Consul-Gen., Kinshasa, 1977–79; RCDS, 1980; Counsellor (Economic and Commercial), Stockholm, 1981–85; Hd of Information Technology Dept, FCO, 1985–87; Ambassador, Zaire and (non-resident) Rwanda and Burundi, 1987–91; Ambassador, Sweden, 1991–95. Hon. Consul for Sweden in Orkney, 1996–2006. Mem. (Ind.), Orkney Is Council, 1997–2003. DL Orkney, 1996; JP Orkney, 2002–07. Comdr, Order of North Star (Sweden), 1983. *Address:* Westness House, Rousay, Orkney KW17 2PT.

CORMACK, Prof. Robin Sinclair, PhD; FSA; Professor in the History of Art, Courtauld Institute of Art, London University, 1991–2004, now Emeritus; *b* 27 Sept. 1938; *s* of James Menzies Cormack and Meryl Joyce Cormack (*née* Pendred); *m* 1st, 1961, Annabel Shackleton (marr. diss. 1985); one *s* one *d*; 2nd, 1985, (Winifred) Mary Beard, *qv*; one *s* one *d*. *Educ:* Bristol Grammar Sch.; Exeter Coll., Oxford (BA Lit.Hum. 1961; MA 1965); Courtauld Inst. of Art, London Univ. (AcDip 1964; PhD 1968). FSA 1975. Gall. Manager, ICA, 1961–62; Lectr in History of Slavonic and E European Art, SSEES and Courtauld Inst. of Art, London Univ., 1966–73; Vis. Fellow, Dumbarton Oaks, Center for Byzantine Studies, Harvard Univ., 1972–73; Lectr in History of Art, Courtauld Inst., London Univ., 1973–82; British Academy Reader, Warburg Inst., London Univ., 1982–85; Bye Fellow, Robinson Coll., Cambridge, 1984–85 (Sen. Mem., 1985–); Reader in History of Art, 1986–90, Dep. Dir, 1999–2002, Courtauld Inst., London Univ. Geddes-Harrower Prof. of Greek Art and Archaeology, Aberdeen Univ., 2001–02; Leverhulme Emeritus Fellow, 2004–06; Getty Scholar, Res. Inst., The Getty, Los Angeles, 2005–06; Special Prof. in Classics, Univ. of Nottingham, 2005–08; Lecturing Asst, Faculty of Classics, Univ. of Cambridge, 2010–. Vis. Schol. in Byzantine Studies, Dumbarton Oaks, Washington DC, 2011. Consultant to RA for Byzantium 330–1453 exhibn, 2008–09. *Publications:* Writing in Gold, 1985 (trans. French, Icones et Société à Byzance, 1993); The Church of S Demetrios of Thessaloniki, 1985; The Byzantine Eye, 1989; Painting the Soul, 1998 (Runciman Award, Anglo-Hellenic League and Onassis Foundn); Byzantine Art, 2000; Icons, 2007, 2nd edn 2014; Byzantium 330–1453, 2008; Oxford Handbook of Byzantine Studies, 2008. *Recreations:* learning to play the spinet and use Photoshop. *Address:* 120 Huntingdon Road, Cambridge CB3 0HL. *T:* (01223) 312734.

CORMACK, (Winifred) Mary; *see* Beard, W. M.

CORNELIUS, David Frederick, FCIHT; transport and research consultant; *b* 7 May 1932; *s* of Frederick M. N. and Florence K. Cornelius; *m* 1956, Susan (*née* Austin); two *s* two *d*. *Educ:* Teignmouth Grammar Sch.; Exeter University Coll. (BSc (Hons) Physics). Royal Naval Scientific Service, 1953–58; UKAEA, 1958–64; Research Manager, Road Research Laboratory, 1964–72; Asst Director, Building Research Estabt, 1973–78; Head, Research, Transport and Special Programmes, 1978–80, Transport Science Policy Unit, 1980–82, Dept of Transport; Asst Dir, 1982–84, Dep. Dir, 1984–88, Actg Dir, 1988–89, Dir, 1989–91, Transport and Road Res. Lab. Initiated formation of European Forum of Highway Res. Labs in 1990, leading to successful collaboration between members in highway res., road safety and traffic engrg. FRSA. *Publications:* Path of Duty (biog.), 2000, 2nd edn 2014; scientific papers to nat. and internat. confs and in jls of various professional instns on range of topics in tribology, highway transportation and internat. collaboration in res. *Recreations:* touring Europe, Africa and Australia by motorhome, swimming, cycling, world travel by container ships, sea and river cruises, observing and taking pleasure from the career progression of offspring in fields of commerce, science, the arts and academia; member of Emsworth Methodist Church Council, member of Hayling Island U3A. *Address:* White Poplars, 40 Webb Lane, Hayling Island, Hants PO11 9JE. *T:* (023) 9246 7212.

CORNELL, Eric Allin, PhD; Adjoint Professor, Department of Physics, University of Colorado, Boulder, since 1995 (Assistant Adjoint Professor, 1992–95); Fellow, Joint Institute for Laboratory Astrophysics and National Institute of Standards and Technology, since 1994; *b* Palo Alto, Calif, 1961; *s* of Prof. Allin Cornell and Elizabeth Cornell (*née* Greenberg); *m* 1995, Celeste Landry; two *d*. *Educ:* Stanford Univ. (BS 1985); MIT (PhD 1990). Postdoctoral res. asst, Jt Inst. for Lab. Astrophysics, Boulder, 1990–92; Sen. Scientist, Nat. Inst. of Standards and Technol., Boulder, 1992–. (Jtly) Nobel Prize for Physics, 2001. *Publications:* articles in jls. *Address:* Joint Institute for Laboratory Astrophysics, University of Colorado, Campus Box 440, Boulder, CO 80309–0440, USA.

CORNELL, Jim Scott, CEng, FREng; FICE; FCILT; Executive Director, Railway Heritage Trust, 1996–2009; *b* 3 Aug. 1939; *s* of James William Cornell and Annie Cornell (*née* Scott); *m* 1962, Winifred Eileen Rayner; one *s* one *d*. *Educ:* Thirsk Grammar Sch.; Bradford Inst. of Technol. CEng 1967; FICE 1983; FCILT (FCIT 1986); FREng (FEng 1992). With British Rail, 1959–96: jun. and middle mgt civil engrg posts, 1959–76; Divisional Civil Engineer: King's Cross, 1976–78; Newcastle, 1978–81; Asst Regl Civil Engr, York, 1981–83; Regl Civil Engr, Scotland, 1983–84; Dep. Gen. Manager, 1984–86, Gen. Manager, 1986–87, ScotRail; Dir, Civil Engrg, 1987–92; Man. Dir, Regl Railways, 1992–93; Man. Dir, BR Infrastructure Services, 1993–96. Non-exec. Dir, Railtrack plc, subseq. Network Rail, 2002–09. FCMI (FIMgt 1987). *Recreations:* tennis, gardening. *T:* (01525) 851070.

CORNELL, Peter; Founder, Cornell Partners, 2011; Founder Partner, Metric Capital Partners, since 2011; *b* 5 Oct. 1952; *s* of Dr Sydney Page Cornell and Marjorie Joan Cornell; *m* 1981, Bernadette Conway; one *s* three *d*. *Educ:* Tonbridge Sch., Kent; Exeter Univ.; Chester Law Coll. SSC. Admitted solicitor, 1975; joined Clifford Chance, 1975: on secondment to Philip Morris, Lausanne, 1978–79; opened Singapore office, 1981; returned to London office, 1986; Man. Partner, Madrid office, 1989–2001; opened Barcelona office, 1993; Eur. Man. Partner, 1996–2001; Global Managing Partner, 2001–07; Man. Dir, Stakeholder Relations, Terra Firma Capital Partners Ltd, later Terra Firma Capital Mgt Ltd, 2007–11. Mem. Council, 2009–11, Vice-Chm., Global Buyout Cttee, 2009–11, BVCA. Non-exec. Dir, Circle Hldgs plc, 2011–13. Chm., Legal Bd, Ogier, 2011–. Mem., Internat. Adv. Bd, IE Business Sch., Madrid, 2006–. Accredited Mediator, CEDR, 2010. Legal Business Lawyer of the Year, 2007. *Recreations:* family, sport, tennis, golf, squash, ski-ing, surfing. *Address:* Horizons, York Way, Fort George, St Peter Port, Guernsey GY1 2SY. *Clubs:* Royal Automobile, Royal Channel Yacht; Royal Guernsey Golf; La Moraleja (Madrid).

CORNER, Diane Louise; HM Diplomatic Service; Deputy Special Representative and Deputy Head, United Nations Multidimensional Integrated Stabilization Mission in the Central African Republic, since 2014; *b* 29 Sept. 1959; *d* of Captain Alaric John Corner and Marjorie Corner (*née* Ashcroft); *m* 1986, Peter Timothy Stocker; four *d*. *Educ:* Winchester Co. High Sch. for Girls; Peter Symonds Coll.; Univ. of Bristol (BA Hons French and Politics). Entered FCO, 1982; Second Sec. (Chancery), Kuala Lumpur, 1985–88; First Sec., FCO, 1989–91; Cabinet Office (on secondment), 1991–93; Dep. Hd of Mission, Berlin, 1994–98; First Sec., FCO, 1998–2000; NATO Defence Coll., Rome, 2000; Counsellor and Dep. High Comr, Harare, 2001–03; Counsellor, FCO, 2003–04; on loan to Cabinet Office as Chief Assessor, CSSB, 2004–05; Dir, Prism Change Prog., 2005–06, Shared Services Prog., 2007–08, FCO; Catlin Underwriting (on loan), 2008; Actg High Comr, Sierra Leone, 2008–09; High Comr, Tanzania, 2009–13; Ambassador to Democratic Republic of Congo and Republic of Congo, 2013–14. *Recreations:* reading, trying to keep fit.

CORNER, Prof. Frances Marie, OBE 2009; DPhil; Head of College, since 2005, and Professor of Arts and Design Education, since 2009, London College of Fashion; Pro Vice-Chancellor, University of the Arts London, since 2013; *b* Aden, 25 Feb. 1959; *d* of Ernest James Agnew and Joanna Southworth Agnew (*née* Kelly); *m* 1980, Anthony Peter Corner; one *s*. *Educ:* St Maurs Convent, Weybridge; St Martin's Sch. of Art (BA Hons 1981); Chelsea Coll. of Art (MA Fine Art 1984); Kellogg Coll., Oxford (DPhil 2004). University of Gloucestershire: Sen. Lectr, 1991–94; Hd, Div. of Arts, 1994–95; Hd, Dept of Arts, 1995–98; Associate Dean, Faculty of Arts and Humanities, 1998–2001; Hd, Sir John Cass Dept of Art, Media and Design, London Metropolitan Univ., 2001–05. London Leader, Sustainability, London Sustainable Develt Commn, 2008. Member: Steering Gp, Gp for Learning in Art and Design, 2002–07; Adv. Bd, British Fashion Council, 2011–; Exec. Cttee, Internat. Foundn of Fashion Technology Institutes, 2011– (Chair, 2014–). Chair, Council for Higher Educn in Art and Design, 2006–09 (Vice Chair, 2005–06). Trustee, Wallace Collection, 2009–. FRSA. *Recreations:* yoga, running, reading, travel. *Address:* London College of Fashion, 20 John Princes Street, W1G 0BJ. *T:* (020) 7514 7402. *E:* f.corner@fashion.arts.ac.uk. *Clubs:* Groucho, House of St Barnabas.

CORNER, Dame Jessica (Lois), DBE 2014; PhD; Dean of Health Sciences, University of Southampton, since 2008; Chief Clinician, Macmillan Cancer Support, since 2008 (Director for Improving Cancer Services, 2005–08); *b* 22 March 1961; *d* of Rodney, (Bunny), Corner and Judith Corner; *m* 1st, 1985, Cameron Findlay (marr. diss. 1998); one *d*; 2nd, 1999, Christopher Bailey; one *d*. *Educ:* Chelsea Coll., London (BSc Hons Nursing Studies 1983); King's Coll., London (PhD 1990). RN 1983; Oncology Nurse Cert. 1985; Mem. Inst. for Learning and Teaching. 2002. Staff Nurse: Cardiothoracic Unit, St George's Hosp., London, 1983–84; Royal Marsden Hosp., London, 1984–85; Nursing Studies Department, King's College, London: Res. Asst, 1985; Postgrad. Researcher, 1985–87; Macmillan Lectr in Cancer and Palliative Care, 1987–90; Sen. Macmillan Lectr and Hd, Academic Nursing Unit, Inst. of Cancer Res. and Royal Marsden Hosp., 1990–94; Institute of Cancer Research, London: Dir and Dep. Dean (Nursing), Centre for Cancer and Palliative Care Studies, 1994–2002; Prof. of Cancer Nursing, 1996–2002; Prof. of Cancer and Palliative Care, Univ. of Southampton, 2002–08. *Publications:* Becoming a Staff Nurse, 1991; Cancer Nursing: care in context, 2001, 2nd edn 2008; Researching Palliative Care, 2001; over 100 acad. papers in books and jls. *Recreations:* a very amateur gardener and flautist, walking in the Lake District, chaotic family life with two daughters born 12 years apart. *Address:* Health Sciences, University of Southampton, Highfield, Southampton SO17 1BJ. *E:* j.l.corner@soton.ac.uk.

CORNER, Philip; Director General of Quality Assurance, Ministry of Defence Procurement Executive, 1975–84, retired; Chairman, Institute of Quality Assurance's Management Board (for qualification and registration scheme for lead assessors of quality assurance management system), 1984–92; *b* 7 Aug. 1924; *s* of late William Henry Corner and Dora (*née* Smailes); *m* 1948, Nora Pipes (*d* 1984); no *c*; *m* 1985, Paula Mason. *Educ:* Dame Allan's Boys' Sch., Newcastle upon Tyne; Bradford Technical Coll.; RNEC Manadon; Battersea Polytechnic. BScEng (London); CEng 1966; MIMechE 1952; MIET (MIEE 1957); Hon. FCQI (Hon. FIQA 1985). Short Bros (Aeronautical Engrs), 1942–43; Air Br., RN, Sub-Lieut RNVR, 1944–46; LNER Co., 1946–47; Min. of Works, 1947–50; Min. of Supply, 1950; Ministry of Defence: Dir of Guided Weapons Prodn, 1968–72; Dir of Quality Assurance (Technical), 1972–75. Member: Metrology and Standards Requirements Bd, DoI, 1974–84; Adv. Council for Calibration and Measurement, DoI, 1975–84; BSI Quality Assurance Council, 1979–84; BSI Bd, 1980–84. *Recreations:* reading, listening to music. *Address:* 8 Kingsway Court, Queens Gardens, Hove, E Sussex BN3 2LP.

CORNER, Timothy Frank; QC 2002; a Recorder, since 2004; a Deputy High Court Judge, since 2008; *b* 25 July 1958; *s* of Frank and June Corner. *Educ:* Bolton Sch.; Magdalen Coll., Oxford (Demy (Open Scholar); BCL; MA (Jurisprudence)). Called to the Bar, Gray's Inn, 1981, Bencher, 2007; Junior Counsel to the Crown, A Panel, 1999–2002. Chm., Adv. Panel on Standards for the Planning Inspectorate, 2006–10. Chm., Planning and Envmt Bar Assoc., 2008–12. *Publications:* contrib. Jl of Planning and Envmt Law. *Recreations:* singing, walking, books, travel. *Address:* Landmark Chambers, 180 Fleet Street, EC4A 2HG. *T:* (020) 7430 1221. *E:* tcorner@landmarkchambers.co.uk. *Club:* Athenæum.

CORNESS, Sir Colin (Ross), Kt 1986; Chairman, Glaxo Wellcome plc, 1995–97; *b* 9 Oct. 1931; *s* of late Thomas Corness and Mary Evlyne Corness. *Educ:* Uppingham Sch.; Magdalene Coll., Cambridge (BA 1954, MA 1958; Hon. Fellow, 2001); Graduate Sch. of Business Admin, Harvard, USA (Advanced Management Program Dip. 1970). Called to the Bar, Inner Temple, 1956. Dir, Taylor Woodrow Construction Ltd, 1961–64; Man. Dir, Redland Tiles Ltd, 1965–70; Redland PLC: Man. Dir, 1967–82; Chief Exec., 1977–91; Chm., 1977–95. Chm., Nationwide Building Soc., 1991–96. Director: Chubb & Son PLC, 1974–84 (Dep. Chm., 1984); W. H. Smith & Son (Holdings) PLC, 1980–87; Gordon Russell PLC, 1985–89; Courtaulds PLC, 1986–91; S. G. Warburg Gp, 1987–95; Unitech, 1987–95; Union Camp Corp., 1991–99; Chubb Security, 1992–97; Taylor Woodrow plc, 1997–2001. A Dir, Bank of England, 1987–95. Chm., Building Centre, 1974–77; Pres., Nat. Council of Building Material Producers, 1985–87; Member: EDC for Building, 1980–84; Industrial Develt Adv. Bd, 1982–84. Trustee, Uppingham Sch., 1996–99; Observer/Trustee, Nottingham RC Dio., 2007–12. Hon. DBA Kingston, 1994. *Recreations:* gardening, travel, music.

CORNICK, Rev. Dr David George; General Secretary, Churches Together in England, since 2008; Fellow of Robinson College, Cambridge, since 1997; *b* 12 Sept. 1954; *s* of Cecil George Cornick and Thelma (*née* Le Brun); *m* 1977, Mary Hammond; two *s*. *Educ:* Hertford and Mansfield Colls, Oxford (MA); King's Coll., London (BD; PhD 1982); Open Univ. (MBA 2008). United Reformed Church: Minister, Radlett and Borehamwood, 1981–84; Chaplain, Robinson Coll., Cambridge, 1984–87; Trng Officer, South-Western Province, 1987–92; Dir of Studies in Church Hist., 1992–2001, Principal, 1996–2001, Westminster Coll., Cambridge; Gen. Sec., URC, 2001–08. Select Preacher, Univ. of Cambridge, 2003. *Publications:* Under God's Good Hand, 1998; (contrib. and ed jtly) From Cambridge to Sinai: the worlds of Agnes Smith Lewis and Margaret Dunlop Gibson, 2006; Letting God be God: the reformed tradition, 2008. *Recreations:* music, walking, embroidery. *Address:* Churches Together in England, 27 Tavistock Square, WC1H 9HH. *T:* (020) 7529 8131; Robinson College, Grange Road, Cambridge CB3 9AN.

CORNISH, Prof. Alan Richard Henry, PhD; CEng, FIChemE; Ramsay Memorial Professor of Chemical Engineering and Head of Department of Chemical and Biochemical Engineering, University College London, 1990–96, now Professor Emeritus; *b* 14 March 1931; *s* of late Richard Heard Cornish and Evelyn Jennie Cornish (*née* Hatton); *m* 1957, Rita Ellen Wright; one *s* one *d*. *Educ:* Emanuel Sch.; Westminster Tech. Coll. (Ordinary and

Higher Certs in Gas Engrg (supply)); Wandsworth Tech. Coll. (Ordinary and Higher Nat. Certs in Mech. Engrg); Illinois Inst. of Technology (PhD Chem. Engrg 1962). CEng; MIChemE 1965, FIChemE 1986; MIGEM; MEI; CSci 2004. Staff pupil, South Eastern Gas Bd, 1948–53; Nat. Service, REME; Asst Industrial Engr, South Eastern Gas Bd, 1955–56; King George VI Meml Fellow, ESU, 1956–57; Shell Oil Fellow, 1959–61; Imperial College, London: Asst Lectr, Lectr, Sen. Lectr, 1962–88; Dir of Studies, 1982–88, Dep. Hd of Dept, 1985–88, Dept of Chem. Engrg and Chem. Technol.; Prof. of Chemical Engineering, Univ. of Bradford, 1988–90; Crabtree Scholar, UCL, 1990. Drapers' Co. Vis. Lectr, Univ. of Sydney, 1974; Vis. Prof., Univ. de Pau et des Pays de l'Adour, 1994, 1997, 1998. Pres., Ramsay Soc., 1990–96; Mem. Council, 1991–94, Hon. Treas., 1997–2000, IChemE. FRSA 1986. Mem., Athenæum Club, 1991–2010. Freeman, City of London, 1996; Liveryman, Engineers' Co., 1996–2010. Dr *hc* L'Institut Nat. Polytechnique de Toulouse, 1999. Morgan Crucible Prize in Mech. Engrg, Morgan Crucible Co. Ltd, 1951; Whitworth Prize, Whitworth Soc., 1951; Arnold Greene Medal, IChemE, 2000. *Publications:* contribs to professional jls incl. on heat and mass transfer from particles and drops, drying of solids, and of foodstuffs, heat and mass transfer in closed beds of solid particles, design of heat exchanger networks for energy recovery in process plants, design of perforated plate extraction columns.

CORNISH, Charles T.; Group Chief Executive, Manchester Airports Group, since 2010; *b* Hamilton, Scotland; *s* of Charlie Cornish and Isabel Cornish; *m* 1992, Margo; one *s* three *d*. *Educ:* Hamilton Grammar Sch.; Univ. of Strathclyde (BA 1980); Postgrad. Dip. Personnel and Develt. Customer Services Dir, 1997–99, Chief Exec., 1999–2000, West of Scotland Water; Global Business Performance Dir, 2000–01, Chief Operating Officer, 2001–02, Thames Water, later RWE/Thames Water; Man. Dir and Bd Dir, United Utilities plc, 2002–10. *Recreations:* golf, football. *E:* Charlie.Cornish@manairport.co.uk. *Club:* Oriental.

CORNISH, Francis; *see* Cornish, R. F.

CORNISH, Iain Charles Andrew; Chairman, Shawbrook Bank, since 2015; *m* Josette; two *d*. *Educ:* Univ. of Southampton (BSc 1982). Statistician, DTI; Sen. Consultant, Strategy Services Consultancy Practice, KPMG; Corporate Planner, Bradford & Bingley Bldg Soc.; Corporate Develt Manager, 1992, later Gen. Mktg Manager, Chief Exec., 2003–11, Yorks Bldg Soc. Dep. Chm., 2006–07, Chm., 2007–08, Building Societies' Assoc. Chm., Financial Services Practitioner Panel, 2009–11; non-exec. Dir, Prudential Regulation Authy, 2013–15. Ind. non-exec. Dir, St James's Place, 2011–.

CORNISH, James Easton; Director and European Market Strategist, BT Alex. Brown (formerly NatWest Securities), 1990–99; *b* 5 Aug. 1939; *s* of Eric Easton Cornish and Ivie Hedworth (*née* McCulloch); *m* 1968, Ursula Pink; one *s*. *Educ:* Eton Coll.; Wadham Coll., Oxford (BA); Harvard. Joined FO, 1961; Bonn, 1963; British Mil. Govt, Berlin, 1965; FCO, 1968; Washington, 1973; Dep. Head of Planning Staff, FCO, 1977; Central Policy Rev. Staff, 1980; seconded to Phillips & Drew, 1982; resigned HM Diplomatic Service, 1985; Manager, Internat. Dept, Phillips & Drew, 1982–87; Asst Dir, subseq. Associate Dir, County Securities Ltd, 1987–90.

CORNISH, (Robert) Francis, CMG 1994; LVO 1978; HM Diplomatic Service, retired; Chairman, South West Tourism Ltd, 2003–09; *b* 18 May 1942; *s* of late Charles Derrick Cornish and Catherine Cornish; *m* 1964, Alison Jane Dundas; three *d*. *Educ:* Charterhouse; RMA Sandhurst. Commissioned 14th/20th King's Hussars, 1962–68; HM Diplomatic Service 1968; served Kuala Lumpur, Jakarta and FCO, 1969–76; First Sec., Bonn, 1976–80; Asst Private Sec. to HRH the Prince of Wales, 1980–83; High Comr, Brunei, 1983–86; Counsellor (Inf.), Washington, and Dir, British Inf. Services, NY, 1986–90; Head of News Dept, and Spokesman, FCO, 1990–93; Sen. British Trade Comr, Hong Kong, 1993–97; Consul-Gen., HKSAR, 1997; Sen. Directing Staff, RCDS, 1998; Ambassador to Israel, 1998–2001. FRSA 2003. Director: Gross Hill Properties Ltd, 2002–10; Sydney & London Properties Ltd, 2003–10. Trustee, Brewhouse Th., Taunton, 2010–13. *Club:* Cavalry and Guards.

CORNISH, Sophie, MBE 2013; Co-Founder and Director, notonthehighstreet.com, since 2006; *b* London, 11 Aug. 1965; *d* of Paul and Penny Vincenzi; *m* 2001, Simon Cornish; one *s* one *d*. *Educ:* Kingston Grammar Sch. Writer and ed., Cosmopolitan, Hearst Mags, 1984–86; Creative Brand Manager, No 7 and 17 Cosmetics, BA Associates, 1986–88; beauty writer and ed., Good Housekeeping, Hearst Mags, 1988–90; New Business Manager, GGK London, 1990–94; Account Dir, Publicis London, 1994–99; Channel Ed., BEME.com, IPC Media/Time Inc. UK, 2000; freelance writer, stylist, mktg consultant, 2001–05. Mem. Bd, CRUK Women of Influence, 2012–. Gov., Surbiton High Sch., 2012–. *Publications:* Your Wedding Your Way, 2003; (jtly) Build a Business from Your Kitchen Table, 2012; (jtly) Shape Up Your Business, 2014. *Recreations:* CrossFit, running, entrepreneurship.

CORNISH, Prof. William Rodolph, CMG 2013; FBA 1984; Herchel Smith Professor of Intellectual Property Law, Cambridge University, 1995–2004, now Emeritus (Professor of Law, 1990–95); Fellow, Magdalene College, Cambridge, since 1990 (President, 1998–2001); *b* 9 Aug. 1937; *s* of Jack R. and Elizabeth E. Cornish, Adelaide, S Australia; *m* 1964, Lovedy E. Moule; one *s* two *d*. *Educ:* Univs of Adelaide (LLB) and Oxford (BCL); LLD Cantab, 1996. Lectr in Law, LSE, 1962–68; Reader in Law, Queen Mary Coll., London, 1969–70; Prof. of English Law, LSE, 1970–90. Ext. Acad. Mem., Max Planck Inst. for Innovation and Competition (formerly for Patent, Copyright and Competition Law, then for Intellectual Property, Competition and Tax Law, subseq. for Intellectual Property and Competition Law), Munich, 1989–. Hon. QC 1997; Bencher, Gray's Inn, 1998. Hon. Mem., Chartered Inst. of Patent Agents, 2005. Hon. Fellow, LSE, 1996. Hon. LLD Edinburgh, 2005. *Publications:* The Jury, 1968; (Jt Editor) Sutton and Shannon on Contracts, 1970; (jtly) Encyclopedia of United Kingdom and European Patent Law, 1977; Intellectual Property, 1981, 8th edn (jtly) 2013; Law and Society in England 1750–1950, 1989; (jtly) Oxford History of the Laws of England, vols XI-XIII 1820–1914, 2010; articles etc in legal periodicals. *Address:* Magdalene College, Cambridge CB3 0AG.

CORNOCK, Maj.-Gen. Archibald Rae, CB 1975; OBE 1968; FIMgt; Chairman, London Electricity Consultative Council, 1980; *b* 4 May 1920; *s* of Matthew Cornock and Mrs Mary Munro MacRae; *m* 1951, Dorothy Margaret Cecilia; two *d*. *Educ:* Coatbridge. NW Frontier, 1940–42; Burma, 1942–43; transf. Royal Indian Navy, 1943; Burma (Arakan), 1944–46; Gordon Highlanders, 1947–50; transf. RAOC, 1950; psc 1954; GSO2 Intelligence, 1955–57; DAQMG Northern Army Gp, 1959–61; comd 16 Bn RAOC, 1961–64; SEATO Planning Staff, Bangkok, 1964; Defence Attaché, Budapest, 1965–67; Comdt 15 Base Ordnance Depot, 1967; DDOS Strategic Comd, 1968–70; Brig. Q (Maint.), MoD, 1970–72; Dir of Clothing Procurement, 1972; Dir of Army Quartering, 1973–75. Col Comdt, RAOC, 1976–80. Pres., Mahratta LI Regtl Assoc., 2000–. Chm., Army Athletic Assoc., 1968–75; Mem. Council, Back Pain Assoc., 1979–. FCMI (MBIM 1965). *Recreations:* sailing, opera, golf. *Clubs:* Royal Thames Yacht, Roehampton; Royal Scots (Edinburgh); Highland Brigade.

CORNOCK, Maj.-Gen. Charles Gordon, (Bill), CB 1988; MBE 1974; Bursar, Cranleigh School, 1989–95; *b* 25 April 1935; *s* of Gordon Wallace Cornock and Edith Mary (née Keeley); *m* 1963, Kay Smith; two *s*. *Educ:* King Alfred Sch., Plön, Germany; RMA, Sandhurst. Commnd RA, 1956; served, 1957–71: 33 Para Lt Regt; 1 RHA; RMA, Sandhurst; Staff Coll., Camberley; BMRA; Armed Forces Staff Coll., Norfolk, Va; Second in Comd, 1972–74 and CO 1974–76, 7 Para RHA; GSO1 DS Staff Coll., Camberley, 1977–78; Col GS HQ UKLF, 1979; CRA 3rd Armoured Div., 1980–81; RCDS, 1982; Dep. Comdt, Staff Coll., Camberley, 1983; Dir, RA, 1984–86; C of S and Head of UK Delegn, Live Oak, SHAPE, 1986–89. Col Comdt RA, 1986–94; Rep. Col Comdt, RA, 1991–92. Chm., Confedn of British Service and Ex-Service Orgns, 1996–99. Comdr, St John Ambulance (Jersey) 1999–2004. Mem., Police Complaints Authy (Jersey), 2001–05. President: RA Golfing Soc. 1989–98; Jersey Scout Assoc., 2005–11; Mem. Cttee, Jersey Blind Soc., 2006–; Vice-Pres. Combined Services and Army Hockey Assoc. Trustee, Jersey Army Cadet Force, 2010–. Mem., Sen. Golfers' Soc. FCMI. *Recreations:* hockey, tennis, golf, ski-ing, water ski-ing. *Address:* Upton, Trinity, Jersey JE3 5DT. *Clubs:* Army and Navy; La Moye Golf (Jersey).

CORNS, Prof. Thomas Nicholas, DPhil; FBA 2015; Professor of English Literature, Bangor University (formerly University College of North Wales, then University of Wales, Bangor) 1994–2014, now Emeritus; *b* Prescot, Lancs; *s* of Joseph Richard Corns and Martha Lily Corns; *m* 1972, Patricia Allen; two *s*. *Educ:* Prescot Grammar Sch.; Brasenose Coll., Oxford (BA 1972); Maximilianeum Foundn, Munich; University Coll., Oxford (DPhil 1978) University College of North Wales, subseq. University of Wales, Bangor: Lectr, 1975–87 Sen. Lectr, 1987–92, Reader, 1992–94, of English Lit.; Pro-Vice-Chancellor, 2004–07 Founder and Co-Convener, British Milton Seminar, 1990–2014; Hon. Sec., Standing Cttee Internat. Milton Symposium, 1995–2015. *Publications:* The Development of Milton's Prose Style, 1982; Milton's Language, 1990; Uncloistered Virtue: English political literature 1640–1660, 1992; (ed) The Cambridge Companion to English Poetry, Donne to Marvell 1993; Regaining Paradise Lost, 1994; John Milton: the prose works, 1998; (ed) The Royal Image: representations of Charles I, 1999; (ed) Blackwell Companion to Milton, 2001; A History of Seventeenth-Century English Literature, 2006; (jtly) John Milton and the Manuscript of De Doctrina Christiana, 2007; John Milton: life, work and thought, 2008; (ed jtly) The Complete Works of Gerrard Winstanley, 2009; (ed) The Milton Encyclopedia 2012. *Recreations:* golf, bird watching, dog walking. *Address:* School of English Literature Bangor University, Gwynedd LL57 2DG. *T:* (01248) 382102. *E:* els009@bangor.ac.uk. *Club* Henllys Golf (Beaumaris).

CORNWALL, Archdeacon of; *see* Stuart-White, Ven. W. R.

CORNWALL, Christopher John; His Honour Judge Cornwall; a Circuit Judge, since 2002; *b* 20 Dec. 1950; *s* of Geoffrey and Joan Cornwall; *m* 1977, Elizabeth Dunbar Cliff; two *s* one *d*. *Educ:* Shrewsbury Sch.; St Catherine's Coll., Oxford (BA Hons). Called to the Bar Lincoln's Inn, 1975; Asst Recorder, 1990–94; a Recorder, 1994–2002. *Recreations:* hill-walking, gardening, European literature, classical music, the visual arts. *Address:* Preston Combined Court Centre, Openshaw Place, Ring Way, Preston PR1 2LL. *T:* (01772) 844700, *Fax:* (01772) 844759. *E:* HHJudge.Cornwall@judiciary.gsi.gov.uk.

CORNWALL, Hugo; *see* Sommer, P. M.

CORNWALL-LEGH, family name of **Baron Grey of Codnor**.

CORNWALLIS, family name of **Baron Cornwallis**.

CORNWALLIS, 4th Baron *cr* 1927, of Linton, Kent; **(Fiennes Wykeham) Jeremy Cornwallis;** *b* Tunbridge Wells, 25 May 1946; *s* of 3rd Baron Cornwallis, OBE and Judith Lacy Scott (*d* 2009); *S* father, 2010; *m* 1969, Sara Gray de Neufville, *d* of Lt-Col Nigel Stockwell, Benenden, Kent; one *s* two *d*. *Educ:* Eton; Royal Agricultural Coll., Cirencester. *Recreations:* golf, cricket. *Heir:* *s* Hon. (Fiennes) Alexander (Wykeham Martin) Cornwallis, *b* 25 Nov. 1987. *Address:* Dundurn, St Fillans, Crieff, Perthshire PH6 2NH. *T:* (01764) 685252. *E:* cornwallis46@btinternet.com. *Clubs:* MCC, I Zingari, Eton Ramblers; Rye Golf Machrihannish Golf.

CORNWELL, Alison Margaret; creative industries finance executive; Chief Financial Officer, Vue Entertainment International Group, since 2014; *b* Glasgow, 30 June 1966; *d* of Dr Harold John Campbell Cornwell and Jane Helen Cornwell (*née* Begg); *m* 1993, Norman Macleod; three *s* one *d*. *Educ:* Univ. of Glasgow (BAcc 1987). CA 1990. Sen. Manager, Coopers & Lybrand Corporate Finance, 1990–95; Sen. Vice Pres. Finance, Walt Disney TV Internat., 1995–2005; Chief Financial Officer: Sparrowhawk Media Gp, 2005–08; Alliance Films Gp, 2008–13. Gov., BFI, 2013– (Chm., Audit Cttee, 2013–). Columnist, ICAS mag. 2013–14. *Recreations:* music, photography, film, cycling. *Address:* Frieth, Henley on Thames Bharcasaig, Isle of Skye. *E:* alison_cornwell@msn.com.

CORNWELL, Bernard, OBE 2006; novelist, since 1980; *b* 23 Feb. 1944; *s* of William Oughtred and Dorothy Rose Cornwell and adopted *s* of late Joseph and Margery Wiggins; *m* 1st, 1967, Lindsay Leworthy (marr. diss. 1976); one *d*; 2nd, 1980, Judy Cashdollar. *Educ:* Monkton Combe Sch.; London Univ. (BA ext.). Producer, BBC TV, 1970–76; Hd, Current Affairs TV, BBC NI, 1976–78; Ed., Thames TV News, 1978–80. Dir, Amer. Associates of Nat. Army Mus. Mem., Charleston Liby Soc. *Publications:* Sharpe's Eagle, 1981; Sharpe's Gold, 1981; Sharpe's Company, 1982; Sharpe's Sword, 1983; Sharpe's Enemy, 1984; Sharpe's Honour, 1985; Sharpe's Regiment, 1986; Sharpe's Siege, 1987; Redcoat, 1987; Sharpe's Rifles, 1988; Wildtrack, 1988; Sharpe's Revenge, 1989; Sea Lord, 1989; Sharpe's Waterloo, 1990; Crackdown, 1990; Stormchild, 1991; Sharpe's Devil, 1992; Scoundrel, 1992; Rebel, 1993; Copperhead, 1994; Sharpe's Battle, 1995; Battle Flag, 1995; The Winter King, 1995; The Bloody Ground, 1996; Enemy of God, 1996; Sharpe's Tiger, 1997; Excalibur, 1997; Sharpe's Triumph, 1998; Sharpe's Fortress, 1999; Stonehenge, 2000 BC, 1999; Sharpe's Trafalgar, 2000; Harlequin, 2000; Sharpe's Prey, 2001; Gallows Thief, 2001; Vagabond, 2002; Sharpe's Havoc, 2003; Heretic, 2003; Sharpe's Escape, 2004; The Last Kingdom, 2004; The Pale Horseman, 2005; Sharpe's Fury, 2006; Lords of the North, 2006; Sword Song, 2007; Azincourt, 2008; The Burning Land, 2009; The Fort, 2010; Death of Kings, 2011; 1356, 2012; The Pagan Lord, 2013; The Empty Throne, 2014; *non-fiction*: Waterloo: the true story of four days, three armies and three battles, 2014. *Recreations:* sailing, acting with Monomoy Theatre (Chatham, Mass). *Address:* PO Box 168, West Chatham, MA 02669, USA. *Clubs:* Stage Harbor Yacht (Chatham, Mass), Carolina Yacht (Charleston, SC).

CORNWELL, David John Moore, (John le Carré); writer; *b* 19 Oct. 1931; *s* of late Ronald Thomas Archibald Cornwell and Olive (*née* Glassey); *m* 1954, Alison Ann Veronica Sharp (marr. diss. 1971; she *d* 2009); three *s*; *m* 1972, Valerie Jane Eustace; one *s*. *Educ:* Sherborne; Berne Univ.; Lincoln Coll., Oxford (1st cl. Modern Languages; Hon. Fellow 1984). Taught at Eton, 1956–58. Mem. of HM Foreign Service, 1960–64. Hon. DLitt: Exeter, 1990; St Andrews, 1996; Southampton, 1997; Bath, 1998; Hon. Dr Berne, 2008; Hon. DLitt Oxford, 2012. Cartier Diamond Dagger, CWA, 1988; Goethe Medal, Goethe Inst., 2011. Comdr, Ordre des Arts et des Lettres (France), 2005. *Publications:* Call for the Dead, 1961 (filmed as The Deadly Affair, 1967); A Murder of Quality, 1962; The Spy Who Came in from the Cold, 1963 (Somerset Maugham Award; Crime Writers' Assoc. Gold Dagger, 1963, Dagger of Daggers, 2005) (filmed); The Looking-Glass War, 1965 (filmed); A Small Town in Germany, 1968; The Naïve and Sentimental Lover, 1971; Tinker, Tailor, Soldier, Spy, 1974 (televised 1979; filmed 2011); The Honourable Schoolboy, 1977 (James Tait Black Meml Prize; Crime Writers' Assoc. Gold Dagger); Smiley's People, 1980 (televised 1982); The Little Drummer Girl, 1983 (filmed 1985); A Perfect Spy, 1986 (televised 1987); The Russia House, 1989 (filmed 1991); The Secret Pilgrim, 1991; The Night Manager, 1993; Our Game, 1995; The Tailor of Panama, 1996 (filmed 2001); Single & Single, 1999; The Constant Gardener, 2001 (filmed 2005); Absolute Friends, 2003; The Mission Song, 2006; A Most Wanted Man, 2008 (filmed 2014); Our Kind of Traitor, 2010; A Delicate Truth, 2013. *Address:* c/o Jonny Geller, Curtis Brown Group Ltd, Haymarket House, 28–29 Haymarket, SW1Y 4SP.

CORNWELL, Patricia D(aniels); American crime novelist; *b* 9 June 1956; *d* of Sam and Marilyn Daniels; *m* 1980, Charles Cornwell (marr. diss. 1990). *Educ:* Davidson Coll., N Carolina (BA English 1979). Crime Reporter, Charlotte Observer, 1979–81 (N Carolina Press Assoc. Award, 1980); Technical Writer, then Computer Analyst, Office of Chief Med. Examr, Richmond, Va, 1984–90; Volunteer Police Officer. *Publications: non-fiction:* A Time For Remembering: the story of Ruth Bell Graham, 1983, re-issued as Ruth—a Portrait, 1997; Portrait of a Killer: Jack the Ripper—case closed, 2002; *fiction:* Hornet's Nest, 1997; Southern Cross, 1999; Isle of Dogs, 2001; At Risk, 2006; The Front, 2007; Dr Kay Scarpetta novels: Postmortem, 1990 (John Creasey Meml Award, CWA; Edgar Award, MWA; Anthony Award, Boucheron Award, World Mystery Convention; MacAvity Award, Mystery Readers Internat.); Body of Evidence, 1991; All That Remains, 1992; Cruel and Unusual, 1993; The Body Farm, 1994; From Potter's Field, 1995; Cause of Death, 1996; Unnatural Exposure, 1997; Point of Origin, 1998; Black Notice, 1999; The Last Precinct, 2000; Blow Fly, 2003; Predator, 2005; Trace, 2005; Book of the Dead, 2007; Scarpetta, 2008; The Scarpetta Factor, 2009; Port Mortuary, 2010; Red Mist, 2011; The Bone Bed, 2012; Dust, 2013; Flesh and Blood, 2014. *Address:* c/o Curtis Brown Group Ltd, Haymarket House, 28–29 Haymarket, SW1Y 4SP; c/o ICM Partners, 730 Fifth Avenue, New York, NY 10019, USA.

CORP, Maj.-Gen. Philip James Gladstone, CB 1996; CEng, FIMechE; *b* 23 June 1942; *s* of Wilfred James Corp and Janet Maude Corp (*née* Gladstone); *m* 1st, 1965, Penelope Joan Smith (marr. diss.); two *s*; 2nd, 1978, Dawn Phyllis Durrant (*née* Holder); one step *s* two step *d*. *Educ:* Warwick Sch.; Queen Elizabeth GS, Crediton; Pembroke Coll., Cambridge (MA Mech. Scis and Law). Commissioned REME from RMA Sandhurst, 1962; RMCS and Staff Coll., 1973–74; Op. Requirements, MoD, 1975–76; Comd 3 Field Workshop, 1977–78; REME Combat Develt, 1979–80; Dep. Project Manager, MoD (PE), 1981–83; Comd 7 Armd Workshop, BAOR, 1984–86; QMG Staff, MoD, 1987–89; Comdt, REME Officers' Sch., 1990; Dir, Equipment Engrg, MoD, 1990–93; Dir-Gen. Equipment Support (Army), 1993–97; Chief Exec., IRTE, subseq. Soc. of Ops Engrs, 1998–2002. Col Comdt, REME, 1996–2000. Mem. Bd, Engrg Council (UK), 2002–08. Vice-Pres., C&G, 2008–11. Trustee: Army Rifle Assoc., 1996–2011; Council for Cadet Rifle Shooting, 1998–. Hon. FSOE 2001; Hon. FCGI 2011. *Recreations:* music, furniture restoration, idleness. *Address:* RHQ REME, MoD Lyneham, Lyneham, Chippenham SN15 9HB.

CORP, Rev. Ronald Geoffrey, OBE 2012; SSC; freelance conductor and composer; *b* 4 Jan. 1951; *s* of Geoffrey Charles Corp and Elsie Grace (*née* Kinchin). *Educ:* Blue Sch., Wells; Christ Church, Oxford (MA); Southern Theol Educn and Trng Scheme (DipTheol). Librarian, producer and presenter, BBC Radio 3, 1973–87; freelance, 1987–: Conductor: Highgate Choral Soc., 1984–; London Chorus (formerly London Choral Soc.), 1985–; New London Orch., 1988–; New London Children's Choir, 1991–; has conducted: BBC Singers, BBC Concert Orch., Cape Philharmonic Orch., Leipzig Philharmonic Orch., Brussels Radio and TV Orch., Royal Scottish Nat. Orch., BBC Scottish SO and at BBC Promenade concerts. Numerous recordings. Trustee, Help Musicians UK (formerly Musicians Benevolent Fund), 2000– (Chm., Educn Cttee, 2002); Vice-Pres., Sullivan Soc., 2001–; Pres., Bracknell Choral Soc., 2006–11 (Patron); Patron, Oundle Fest. Ordained deacon, 1998, priest, 1999; NSM, St James, Hampstead and St Mary with All Souls, Kilburn, 1998–2002; Assistant Curate (non-stipendiary): Christ Church, Hendon, 2002–07; St Alban's, Holborn, 2007–. Freeman, City of London, 2007; Freeman, Musicians' Co., 2007. *Compositions:* And All The Trumpets Sounded (cantata), 1989; Laudamus, 1994; Cornucopia, 1997; Piano Concerto, 1997; A New Song (cantata), 1999; Mary's Song, 2001; Adonai Echad, 2001; Kaleidoscope, 2002; Missa San Marco, 2002; Dover Beach, 2003; Forever Child, 2004; Waters of Time, 2006; String Quartet no 1 The Bustard, 2007; Jubilate Deo, 2008; String Quartet no 2, 2009; Symphony, 2009; The Hound of Heaven, 2009; The Ice Mountain (children's opera), 2010; Dhammapada, 2010; String Quartet no 3, 2011; The Wayfarer, 2011; Things I Didn't Say, 2011; Songs of the Elder Sisters, 2011; The Yellow Wallpaper, 2011; Crawhall (clarinet quintet), 2012; Lullaby for a Lost Soul, 2012; Cello Concerto, 2014. Hon. DMus Anglia Ruskin, 2012; Hon. DMus Hull, 2014. *Publications:* The Choral Singer's Companion, 1987, 3rd edn 2006. *Recreation:* reading. *Address:* Bulford Mill, Bulford Mill Lane, Cressing, Essex CM77 8NS.

CORRALL, Prof. Sheila Mary, (Mrs R. G. Lester); Professor and Chair, Library and Information Science Program, University of Pittsburgh, since 2012; *b* 11 Sept. 1950; *d* of Baron Lowry, PC, PC (NI) and Mary Audrey Lowry (*née* Martin); *m* 1st, 1974, Jonathan Austyn Corrall (marr. diss. 1995); 2nd, 1996, Raymond George Lester. *Educ:* Richmond Lodge Sch., Belfast; Girton Coll., Cambridge (BA Classical Tripos 1974, MA 1977); Poly. of N London (Postgrad. DipLib (CNAA) 1976); Roffey Park Mgt Inst. (MBA Sussex 1992); Univ. of Southampton (MSc Inf. Systems 2002); Univ. of Sheffield (Postgrad. Cert. Higher Educn 2006). ALA 1977, FLA 1999, MIInfSc 1986, FCLIP 2002, Hon. FCLIP 2012. Hd, Inf. Services, Sci. Ref. and Inf. Service, BL, 1988–90; Dir, Liby and Inf. Services, Aston Univ., 1991–95; Librarian, Univ. of Reading, 1995–2001; Dir, Acad. Services, Univ. of Southampton, 2001–03; Prof. of Librarianship and Inf. Mgt, 2004–12, Hd, Dept of Inf. Studies, Univ. of Sheffield, 2006–10. Chairman: Adv. Cttee, UKOLN, 1995–98; Inf. Services NTO, 1999–2001; Mgt Bd, MIMAS (formerly Manchester Inf. and Associated Services), 2006–10; Hds of Schs and Depts Cttee, British Assoc. for Inf. and Liby Educn and Res., 2006–10; Member: Cttee on Electronic Inf., 1994–98, Learning and Teaching Cttee, 2005–08, JISC; Libraries and Inf. Adv. Cttee, British Council, 1995–98; AHRC Peer Rev. Coll., 2006–. Mem., Presidential Cttee for Internat. Agenda on Lifelong Literacy, IFLA, 2005. Pres., Chartered Inst. of Liby and Inf. Professionals, 2002–03. FRSA 1996; MIMgt 1998; FCMI 2003. Lifetime Achievement Award, Internat. Inf. Industries, 2003. *Publications:* (ed) Collection Development: options for effective management, 1988; Strategic Planning for Library and Information Services, 1994; (with A. Brewerton) The New Professional's Handbook: your guide to information services management, 1999; Strategic Management of Information Services: a planning handbook, 2000; contrib. numerous articles and book chapters on liby and inf. mgt. *Recreations:* walking, theatre. *Address:* University of Pittsburgh, 135 North Bellefield Avenue, Information Sciences Building, Room 605c, Pittsburgh, PA 15260, USA. *T:* (412) 6249317, *Fax:* (412) 6487001.

CORRAN, Anne Jane; *see* Mills, Dame A. J.

CORRIE, John Alexander; consultant on African affairs and development, and financial advisor to developing countries, since 2004; Chairman, Polymer Training Ltd, 2007–10; Member (C) West Midlands Region, European Parliament, 1999–2004 (Worcestershire and South Warwickshire, 1994–99); *b* 29 July 1935; *s* of John Corrie and Helen Brown; *m* 1965, Sandra Hardie; one *s* two *d*. *Educ:* Kirkcudbright Acad.; George Watson's Coll.; Lincoln Agric. Coll., NZ. Farming in NZ, 1955–59, in Selkirk, 1959–65 and in Kirkcudbright, 1965–. Lectr for British Wool Marketing Bd and Agric. Trng Bd, 1966–74; Mem. Cttee, NFU, SW Scotland, 1964–74 (Vice-Chm. Apprenticeship Council, 1971–74); Nuffield Scholar in Agriculture, 1972. Dist Officer, Rotary Internat., 1973–74 (Community service). Nat. Chm., Scottish Young Conservatives, 1964. Contested (C): North Lanark, 1964; Central Ayr, 1966; Cunninghame N, 1987; Argyll and Bute, 1992. MP (C): Bute and N Ayr, Feb. 1974–1983; Cunninghame N, 1983–87. Opposition spokesman on educn in Scotland, Oct. 1974–75; an Opposition Scottish Whip, 1975–76 (resigned over Devolution); PPS to Sec. of State for Scotland, 1979–81; Mem., Council of Europe and WEU, 1982–87. Treas., Scottish Cons. Back Bench Cttee, 1980, Chm. 1981–82; Leader, Cons. Gp on Scottish Affairs, 1982–84; Sec., Cons. Back Bench Fish-farming Cttee, 1982–86; brought in Pvte Mem.'s Bill, Diseases of Fish, 1983. Mem. European Parlt, 1975–76 and 1977–79 (Mem. Cttees of Agriculture, Reg. Develt and Transport, 1977–79). Vice-President: EEC-Turkey Cttee, 1975–76; EEC Fisheries Cttee, 1977–79; EEC Mediterranean Agricl Cttee, 1977–79; Rapporteur for EEC Fisheries Policy, 1977–78. European Parliament: Chief Whip of Cons. Gp, 1997–99; Member: Employment and Social Affairs, 1998–99; Agric. and Budgets Cttees, 1999; Chm., 1979 Back Bench Cttee; Dir, Human Rights Cttee, 1994–99; Dir, Animal Rights and Sustainable Develt Intergp, 1994–99; Chm., Pensions Cttee, 1999–2004; Co-ordinator, Develt Cttee, 1999–2004; Co-Pres., ACP/EU Jt Parly Assembly, 1999–2002 (Vice-Pres., 2002–04, Hon. Life Pres., 2002–). Pres., European Sustainable Develt Gp, 2004–; Mem., Council, AWEPA European Parliamentarians for Africa, 2004–. Mem., N/S Cttee, Council of Europe. Chm., Transport Users' Consultative Cttee for Scotland, 1989–94; Mem., Central Transport Consultative Cttee, 1989–94 (Vice Chm., 1992–94; Mem., Railways Industry Adv. Cttee, 1993–94; Mem., Health Safety Cttee, 1993–94). Member: Council, Scottish Landowners Fedn, 1990–94 (Vice Chm., SW Reg., 1992–94); Judges Panel for Belted Galloway Soc., 1991– (Council Mem., 2004–; Vice Chm., 2008–11; Chm., 2011–14); Timber Growers UK (SW), 1991–94; Dir, Ayr Agricl Soc., 1990–95; Pres., Rigget Cattle Soc., 2008–14. Industry and Parlt Trust Fellowship with Conoco (UK) Ltd, 1986–87. *Publications:* (jtly) Towards a European Rural Policy, 1978; Towards a Community Forestry Policy, 1979; Fish Farming in Europe, 1979; The Importance of Forestry in the World Economy, 1980. *Recreations:* shooting, fishing. *Address:* Park House, Tongland, Kirkcudbright DG6 4NE. *T:* (01557) 820232. *E:* j.corrie126@btinternet.com.

CORRIE, His Honour Thomas Graham Edgar; a Circuit Judge, 1994–2014; *b* 18 Dec. 1946; *s* of late John Alexander Galloway Corrie, OBE, MC and Barbara Phyllis Corrie (*née* Turner); *m* 1971, Anna Cathinca Logsdail; one *s* two *d*. *Educ:* Eton (King's Schol.); Brasenose Coll., Oxford (MA). Called to the Bar, Gray's Inn, 1969; Midland and Oxford Circuit, 1971–94; a Recorder, 1988–94; Designated Family Judge, Oxford, 2001–05. Chm., Oxfordshire Family Mediation, 1996–2007. Chm., 1999–2011, Pres., 2011–, Oxford Med. and Legal Soc. *Recreation:* cycling. *Address:* c/o 2 Harcourt Buildings, Temple, EC4Y 9DB. *Club:* Frewen (Oxford).

CORRIE, Timothy David; Agent, United Agents, since 2008; *b* 8 Dec. 1940; *s* of Robert Corrie and Peggy Rose Corrie; *m* 1966, Helene Desgouilles; two *s* one *d*. *Educ:* Reed's Sch.; Univ. of Bristol (BA Hons French and Drama). Paramount Pictures, 1970–71; Agent: at Fraser & Dunlop, subseq. Peters, Fraser & Dunlop, 1971–2008. Chm., BAFTA, 2010–12 (Dep. Chm., 2009–10, 2012–13). *Recreations:* playing awful golf and watching films, good, bad and indifferent. *Address:* Top of the Hill, 29 South Road, Chorleywood, Herts WD3 5AS. *T:* (01923) 283540. *E:* tcorrie@unitedagents.co.uk. *Clubs:* Groucho; Chorleywood Golf.

CORRIGAN, Prof. (Francis) Edward, PhD; FRS 1995; Professor of Mathematics, University of York, since 2011; *b* 10 Aug. 1946; *s* of late Anthony Corrigan and Eileen Corrigan (*née* Ryan); *m* 1970, Jane Mary Halton; two *s* two *d*. *Educ:* St Bede's Coll., Manchester; Christ's Coll., Cambridge (MA, PhD). A. J. Wheeler Fellow, Durham, 1972–74; CERN Fellow, Geneva, 1974–76; Durham University: Lectr, Sen. Lectr and Reader, 1976–92; Prof. of Maths, 1992–99; Hd, Dept of Math. Scis, 1996–98; University of York: Prof. of Maths, 1999–2007; Hd, Dept of Maths, 1999–2004, 2005–07; Prof. of Maths and Principal, Collingwood Coll., Durham Univ., 2008–11; Hd, Dept of Maths, Univ. of York, 2011–15. Joliot-Curie Fellow, ENS Paris, 1977–78; Vis. Associate, CIT, 1978–79; Vis. Fellow, Dept of Applied Maths and Theoretical Physics, Cambridge, 1983; Derman Christopherson Fellow, Durham Univ., 1983–84; Visiting Professor: Centre for Particle Theory, Durham Univ., 1999–2002; Kyoto Univ., 2005. Life Mem., Clare Hall, Cambridge. Hon. Ed., Jl of Physics A, 1999–2003. *Publications:* articles on elementary particle theory and mathematical physics in learned jls. *Recreations:* playing and listening to music, squash. *Address:* Department of Mathematics, University of York, York YO10 5DD. *T:* (01904) 323074. *E:* edward.corrigan@york.ac.uk.

CORRIGAN, Margaret Mary; Teacher: of children with special needs, Beechwood School, Aberdeen, 2007–08; of children with additional support needs, Mile End School, Aberdeen, 2010–11; *d* of Joseph Hamilton and Mary Anna (*née* Monaghan); *m* 1979, Gerard Michael Corrigan; one *s* two *d*. *Educ:* Univ. of Strathclyde (BA Hons English); Edinburgh Univ. (PGCE 2005). Trainee journalist with newspaper/magazine publishers D. C. Thomson, Dundee, 1977–78; Advertising Copywriter and Acct Exec., Austin Knight Advertising, Glasgow, 1978–81; Depute Dir of Public Relns, Cumbernauld Develt Corp., 1981–83; Mktg and Communications Officer/Lectr, Falkirk Coll. of Further and Higher Educn, 1999–2004; Teacher of English, Mearns Acad., Aberdeenshire, 2005–07. Mem., Radio Authority, 1990–95. *Recreations:* swimming, music, theatre, dancing.

CORRIGAN, Thomas Stephen, OBE 1999; Chairman, 2change, 2003–10; *b* 2 July 1932; *s* of late Thomas Corrigan and Renée Victorine Chaborel; *m* 1963, Sally Margaret Everitt; two *d*. *Educ:* Beulah Hill; Chartered Accountant (Scottish Inst.). Nat. Service, Army (2nd Lieut), 1955–57. Chief Accountant, Lobitos Oilfields, 1957–62; Exec., Keyser Ullmann, 1962–64; Inveresk Group: Finance Dir, 1964–71; Man. Dir, 1971–74; Chm., 1974–83. Chairman: Havelock Europa, 1983–89; Rex Stewart Gp Ltd, 1987–90; dir of other cos. Pres., British Paper and Board Industry Fedn, 1975–77; Vice-Pres., European Confedn of Pulp, Paper and Board Industries, 1982–83; Mem., NEDC (Tripartite Sector Working Party on paper industry), 1976–77. Chairman: POUNC, 1984–94; Direct Mail Accreditation and Recognition Centre, 1995–97. Advr and Chief Assessor, 1994–2000, Mem. Ind. Panel of Judges, 2001–03, Charter Mark Awards, Cabinet Office; Chief Assessor, Queen's Awards for Internat. Trade, 2002–11; Mem., London Award Panel, Prince's Trust, 2002–; Mem., Investment Cttee, Printing Charity (formerly Printers' Charitable Corp.), 2006–. Master: Makers of Playing Cards Co., 1978–79; Stationers and Newspaper Makers' Co., 1990–91; Marketors' Co., 1995. FRSA. *Recreations:* golf, bridge, tennis, travel. *Address:* 57 Marsham Court, Marsham Street, SW1P 4JZ. *T:* (020) 7828 2078. *Clubs:* MCC, Royal Automobile, City Livery; Royal & Ancient Golf (St Andrews); Walton Heath Golf.

CORRIGAN-MAGUIRE, Mairead; Co-Founder, Northern Ireland Peace Movement, later Community of the Peace People, 1976 (Hon. Life President); *b* 27 Jan. 1944; *d* of Andrew and Margaret Corrigan; *m* 1981, Jackie Maguire; two *s* and three step *c*. *Educ:* St Vincent's Primary Sch., Falls Road, Belfast; Miss Gordon's Commercial Coll., Belfast. Secretarial qualification. Confidential Sec. to Managing Director, A. Guinness Son & Co. (Belfast) Ltd, Brewers, Belfast. Initiator of Peace Movement in Northern Ireland, Aug. 1976; Chm., Peace People Organisation, 1980–81; Co-founder, Nobel Women's Initiative. Hon. Dr of Law, Yale Univ., 1976; Nobel Prize for Peace (jtly), 1976; Carl-Von-Ossietzky Medaille for Courage, Berlin, 1976. *Publications:* The Vision of Peace: faith and hope in Northern Ireland, 1999. *Address:* c/o The Peace People, 224 Lisburn Road, Belfast, N Ireland BT9 6GE. *T:* (028) 9066 3465, *Fax:* (028) 9068 3947. *E:* info@peacepeople.com.

CORRIN, His Honour John William, CBE 1995; Chairman, BlackRock (Isle of Man) Ltd (formerly Merrill Lynch Investment Managers (Isle of Man) Ltd), 1998–2008; *b* 6 Jan. 1932; *s* of Evan Cain Corrin and Dorothy Mildred Corrin; *m* 1961, Dorothy Patricia, *d* of late J. S. Lace; one *d*. *Educ:* Murrays Road Primary Sch., Douglas; King William's Coll., IOM. Admitted to Manx Bar, 1954. Attorney Gen., IOM, 1974–80; Second Deemster, 1980–88; HM's First Deemster, Clerk of the Rolls, and Dep. Governor, IOM, 1988–98. Chairman (all IOM): Criminal Injuries Compensation Tribunal, 1980–88; Licensing Appeal Court, 1980–88; Prevention of Fraud (Unit Trust) Tribunal, 1980–88; Income Tax Appeal Comrs, 1988–2007; Tynwald Ceremony Arrangements Cttee, 1988–98. Chairman: Manx Blind Welfare Soc., 1980–2012; Manx Workshop for the Disabled, 1982–2010; Hon. Member: IOM Med. Soc.; IOM Law Soc.; President: IOM Br., Crossroads Care, 1988–2013; Lon

Dhoo Male Voice Choir; IOM Br., SSAFA, 1989–2009; IOM Alcohol Adv. Council; Patron: Cruse Bereavement Care (IOM), 1988–2013; Sailing for the Disabled, 2000–09. Freeman, Borough of Douglas, 1998. Paul Harris Fellow, Rotary Internat., 2007. Tynwald Honour, I of M, 2012. *Recreations:* music, gardening, bridge. *Address:* Cummal Cheh, 11 Devonshire Road, Douglas, Isle of Man IM2 3QY. *T:* (01624) 621806.

CORRIS, Prof. Paul Anthony, FRCP; Professor of Thoracic Medicine, Newcastle University, since 2000; Deputy Director, Institute of Transplantation, Newcastle University and Newcastle Hospitals NHS Foundation Trust, since 2012; *b* Bebington, Cheshire, 20 May 1953; *s* of Ronald George and Gladys Corris; *m* 1980, Elizabeth Ann Hill; one *s* one *d*. *Educ:* Birkenhead Sch.; University Coll. and Westminster Med. Sch., Univ. of London (MB BS 1976). FRCP 1991. House Physician, Westminster Hosp., 1976; Postgrad. Trng, London, Leicester and Newcastle, 1976–86; Consultant Respiratory Physician, Newcastle upon Tyne Hosps, 1986–. Clinical Respiratory Lead, NHS North (formerly Respiratory Lead, NHS NE), 2010–; Chm., Clinical Ref. Gp, 2010–, Res. Lead, 2012–, Nat. Pulmonary Hypertension Service. President: Eur. Soc. for Heart and Lung Transplantation, 2006; Internat. Soc. for Heart and Lung Transplantation, 2007; British Thoracic Soc., 2009; N of England Thoracic Soc., 2010; Pulmonary Vascular Res. Inst., 2016–. Gov., Newcastle Hosps NHS Foundn Trust, 2013–. Mem., Literary and Philosophical Soc. of Newcastle. *Publications:* (ed) Heart and Heart Lung Transplantation, 1999; contrib. 275 papers to jls incl. New England Jl Medicine, Lancet, BMJ, Amer. Jl Respiratory and Critical Care Medicine, Thorax; 50 book chapters. *Recreations:* cinema, theatre, opera, wine, Rugby, soccer, ski-ing, mountain walking, literature, art and design. *Address:* Department of Respiratory Medicine, Freeman Hospital, High Heaton, Newcastle upon Tyne NE7 7DN. *T:* (0191) 223 1084, *Fax:* (0191) 223 1321. *E:* paul.corris@ncl.ac.uk.

CORRY; *see* Lowry-Corry, family name of Earl of Belmore.

CORRY, Viscount; John Armar Galbraith Lowry-Corry; *b* 2 Nov. 1985; *s* and *heir* of Earl of Belmore, *qv*. *Address:* The Garden House, Castle Coole, Enniskillen, N Ireland BT74 6JY.

CORRY, Daniel Richard; Chief Executive, New Philanthropy Capital, since 2011; *b* London, 4 Dec. 1959; *s* of Bernard Corry and Marilyn Corry; one *s* one *d* by Dinah Roake. *Educ:* University Coll., Oxford (BA 1st Cl. PPE); Queen's Univ., Canada (MA Econs). Economist, Dept of Employment and HM Treasury, 1984–89; Hd, Labour Party Econ. Secretariat, 1989–92; Sen. Economist, IPPR, 1992–97; Special Adviser: DTI, 1997–2001; DTLR, 2001–02; Dir, New Local Govt Network, 2002–05; Special Advr to Sec. of State for Educn, 2005–06; Chm., Council of Econ. Advrs, HM Treasury, 2006–07; Hd, Downing St Policy Unit, 2007–08; Sen. Econ. Advr to the Prime Minister, 2007–10; Dir in Econs Segment, FTI Consulting, 2011. Vis. Fellow, Univ. of Southampton, 2011–. Mem., Financial Adv. Cttee, FA, 2002–07; Member, Advisory Board: Centre for Public Scrutiny, 2005–; CentreForum, 2010–. Trustee, 19 Princelet Street, 2011–. *Publications:* (with Gerry Holtham) Growth With Stability: progressive macroeconomic policy, 1995; Public Expenditure: effective management and control, 1997; (jtly) Public/Private Partnerships, 1997; (with Gerry Stoker) New Localism, 2002; (jtly) UK Economic Performance since 1997, 2011. *Recreations:* Chelsea FC, jazz, writing. *E:* dan.corry@thinknpc.org.

CORRY, Sir James (Michael), 5th Bt *cr* 1885, of Dunraven, co. Antrim; Manager, LPG Operations, BP Nederland VOF, Netherlands, 1992–2001; *b* 3 Oct. 1946; *e s* of Sir William James Corry, 4th Bt and of Diana Pamela Mary Corry (*née* Lapsley); *S* father, 2000; *m* 1973, Sheridan Lorraine, *d* of A. P. Ashbourne; three *s*. *Educ:* Downside Sch. Joined Shell-Mex and BP Ltd, 1966; British Petroleum Co. Ltd, 1976; BP Nederland BV, 1992. Admin Officer, DWP, 2009–13. *Heir: s* William James Alexander Corry, *b* 7 Dec. 1981. *Address:* Chackeridge Cottage, Ashbrittle, Wellington, Somerset TA21 0LJ. *T:* (01823) 672993. *E:* james.corry@btopenworld.com.

CORSAR, Hon. Dame Mary (Drummond), DBE 1993; FRSE; Chairman: TSB Foundation Scotland, 1994–97 (Trustee, 1992–97); Women's Royal Voluntary Service, 1988–93; *b* 8 July 1927; *o d* of Lord Balerno, CBE, TD, DL and Mary Kathleen Smith; *m* 1953, Col Charles Herbert Kenneth Corsar, LVO, OBE, TD (*d* 2012); two *s* two *d* (and one *d* decd). *Educ:* Westbourne, Glasgow; St Denis, Edinburgh; Edinburgh Univ. (MA Hons). Dep. Chief Comr, Girl Guides, Scotland, 1972–77; Chm., Scotland WRVS, 1981–88. Member: Vis. Cttee, Glenochil Young Offenders Instn, 1976–94; Parole Bd for Scotland, 1982–89. Hon. Pres., Scottish Women's AAA, 1973–91. Member: Exec. Cttee, Trefoil Centre for Handicapped, 1975–2002; Convocation, Heriot-Watt Univ., 1986–96; Royal Anniversary Trust, 1990–93. Gov., Fettes Coll., 1984–99. FRSE 1997. *Recreations:* countryside, hand crafts. *Address:* Flat 4, 85 South Oswald Road, Edinburgh EH9 2HH. *T:* (0131) 662 0194. *Clubs:* New (Edinburgh); Scottish Ladies Climbing.

CORSTON, Baroness *cr* 2005 (Life Peer), of St George in the County and City of Bristol; **Jean Ann Corston;** PC 2003; *b* 5 May 1942; *d* of late Charles Lawrence Parkin and Eileen Ada Parkin; *m* 1st, 1961, Christopher John Davy Corston; one *s* one *d*; 2nd, 1985, Prof. Peter Brereton Townsend, FBA (*d* 2009). *Educ:* LSE (LLB 1989). Labour Party posts: Asst Regl Organiser, 1976, Regl Organiser, 1981, South West; Asst National Agent, London, 1985–86. Called to the Bar, Inner Temple, 1991; Bristol chambers. MP (Lab) Bristol East, 1992–2005 (sponsored by TGWU). PPS to Sec. of State for Educn and Employment, 1997–2001. Mem., Select Cttee on Agric., 1992–95, on Home Affairs, 1995–97; Chair, All Party Parly Gp for Women in Penal System, 2009–. Chm., Jt Cttee on Human Rights, 2001–05; Member: Jt Cttee on Privacy and Injunctions, 2011–12; EU Cttee on Justice, Institutions and Consumer Protection, 2012 (Chair, 2013–14); Co-Chm., PLP Women's Gp, 1992–97; Chairman: PLP Civil Liberties Gp, 1997–2005; PLP, 2001–05 (Dep. Chm., 1997–98 and 1999–2000; Mem., Parly Cttee, 1997–2005). Chm., Commonwealth Women Parliamentarians, 2000; Mem., Exec. Cttee, 1998–2005, Mem., UK Exec. Cttee, 2011–, CPA. Vice Chair, Parliament Choir, 2011–. FRSA 2008. *Recreations:* gardening, reading, walking. *Address:* House of Lords, SW1A 0PW.

CORTAZZI, Sir (Henry Arthur) Hugh, GCMG 1984 (KCMG 1980; CMG 1969); HM Diplomatic Service, retired; *b* 2 May 1924; *m* 1956, Elizabeth Esther Montagu; one *s* two *d*. *Educ:* Sedbergh Sch.; St Andrews and London Univs. Served in RAF, 1943–47; joined Foreign Office, 1949; Third Sec., Singapore, 1950–51; Third/Second Sec., Tokyo, 1951–54; FO, 1954–58; First Sec., Bonn, 1958–60; First Sec., later Head of Chancery, Tokyo, 1961–65; FO, 1965–66; Counsellor (Commercial), Tokyo, 1966–70; Royal Coll. of Defence Studies, 1971–72; Minister (Commercial), Washington, 1972–75; Dep. Under-Sec. of State, FCO, 1975–80; Ambassador to Japan, 1980–84. Director: Hill Samuel & Co., later Hill Samuel Bank, 1984–91; Foreign and Colonial Pacific Investment Trust, 1984–98; GT Japan Investment Trust plc, 1984–99. Senior Adviser: Mitsukoshi Ltd, 1984–99; NEC Corp., Japan, 1992–98; Dai-ichi Kangyo Bank, Japan, 1992–99; Bank of Kyoto, 1992–99; Matsuura Machinery Corp., 1994–2000; Wilde Sapte, solicitors, 1992–99; PIFC, 1993–99. Mem., ESRC, 1984–89. Pres., Asiatic Soc. of Japan, 1982–83; Chm., Japan Soc., of London, 1985–95. Mem., Council and Court, Sussex Univ., 1985–92. Hon. Fellow, Robinson Coll., Cambridge, 1988. Hon. Dr Stirling, 1988; Hon. DLitt East Anglia, 2007. Yamagata Banto Prize, Osaka, 1991. Grand Cordon, Order of the Sacred Treasure (Japan), 1995. *Publications:* trans. from Japanese, Genji Keita: The Ogre and other stories of the Japanese Salarymen, 1972; The Guardian God of Golf and other humorous stories, 1972, reprinted as The Lucky One, 1980; (ed) Mary Crawford Fraser, A Diplomat's Wife in Japan: sketches at the turn of the century, 1982; Isles of Gold: antique maps of Japan, 1983; Higashi No Shimaguni, Nishi No Shimaguni (collection of articles and speeches in Japanese), 1984; Dr Willis in Japan, 1985; (ed) Mitford's Japan, 1985; Victorians in Japan: in and around the Treaty Ports, 1987; for Japanese students of English: Thoughts from a Sussex Garden (essays), 1984; Second Thoughts (essays), 1986; Japanese Encounter, 1987; Zoku, Higashi no Shimaguni, Nishi no Shimaguni, 1987; (ed with George Webb) Kipling's Japan, 1988; The Japanese Achievement: a short history of Japan and Japanese culture, 1990; (ed) A British Artist in Meiji Japan, by Sir Alfred East, 1991; (ed) Building Japan 1868–1876, by Richard Henry Brunton, 1991; (ed with Gordon Daniels) Britain and Japan 1859–1991, 1991; Themes and Personalities, 1991; Modern Japan: a concise survey, 1993; (ed with Terry Bennett) Caught in Time: Japan, 1995; Japan and Back and Places Elsewhere, 1998; Collected Writings, 2000; (compiled and ed) Japan Experiences: Fifty Years, One Hundred Views: post-war Japan through British eyes, 2001; (ed) Biographical Portraits of Anglo-Japanese Personalities, vol. IV, 2002, vol. V, 2004, vol. VI, 2007, vol. VII, 2010, vol. VIII, 2012, vol. IX, 2015; (ed) British Envoys in Japan 1859–1972, 2004; Britain and the 're-opening' of Japan: the Treaty of Yedo and the Elgin Mission, 2008; Japan in Late Victorian London: the Japanese village in Knightsbridge and the Mikado 1885, 2009; Images of Japan 1885–1912: scenes, tales and flowers, 2011; A Miscellany of Japanese Sketch Books and Print Albums 1840–1908, 2013; (ed) The Growing Power of Japan, 1967–1972: analysis and assessments from John Pilcher and the British Embassy, Tokyo, 2014; trans., Crown Prince Naruhito: The Thames and I: a memoir of two years at Oxford, 2005; articles on Japanese themes in English and Japanese pubns. *Recreations:* Japanese studies, the arts including antiques, opera. *Address:* Ballsocks, Vines Cross, Heathfield, E Sussex TN21 9ET. *Club:* Royal Air Force.

CORVEDALE, Viscount; Benedict Alexander Stanley Baldwin; *b* 28 Dec. 1973; *s* and *heir* of 4th Earl Baldwin of Bewdley, *qv*. *Educ:* Newcastle Univ. (BMus 1996).

CORY, Sir (Clinton Charles) Donald, 5th Bt *cr* 1919, of Coryton, Whitchurch, Glamorgan; *b* 13 Sept. 1937; *s* of Sir Clinton James Donald Cory, 4th Bt and Mary, *o d* of Dr Arthur Douglas Hunt; *S* father, 1991. *Educ:* Brighton Coll.; abroad. *Recreations:* collecting antiques, travel, gardening. *Heir: kinsman* James Maurice Perkins-Cory [*b* 10 May 1966; *m* 1998, Alexandra Dudfield; two *d*]. *Address:* 18 Cloisters Road, Letchworth Garden City, Herts SG6 3JS. *T:* (01462) 677206; PO Box 167, Mpemba, Malawi, Central Africa.

CORY, Prof. Suzanne, AC 1999; PhD; FRS 1992; FAA; Honorary Distinguished Professorial Fellow, Molecular Genetics of Cancer Division, Walter and Eliza Hall Institute of Medical Research, University of Melbourne, since 2009 (Vice Chancellor's Fellow, 2010–14); *b* 11 March 1942; *d* of Desmond and Joy Cory; *m* 1969, Prof. Jerry Adams; two *d*. *Educ:* Univ. of Melbourne (BSc, MSc); Wolfson Coll., Cambridge (PhD 1968; Hon. Fellow, 2000). Rothmans Fellow, Univ. of Geneva, 1969–71; Walter and Eliza Hall Institute of Medical Research, 1971–: Sen. Principal Res. Fellow, 1988–; Jt Head, Molecular Genetics of Cancer Div., 1988–2005; Dir, 1996–2009; Prof. of Medical Biol., Univ. of Melbourne, 1996–2009. Internat. Res. Schol., Howard Hughes Med. Inst., 1992–97. FAA 1986 (Pres. 2010–14); Fellow, Inaugural Class, Amer. Assoc. Cancer Res. Acad., 2013. Foreign Mem., NAS, USA, 1997; Foreign Hon. Mem., Amer. Acad. of Arts and Scis, 2001; Assoc. Foreign Mem., French Acad. Sci., 2002; Academician, Pontifical Acad. of Scis, 2004; Assoc. Mem., EMBO, 2007; Hon. Mem., Japan Acad., 2013. Hon. DSc: Sydney, 2000; Oxford, 2004. Lemberg Medal, Australian Soc. Biochem. and Molecular Biol., 1995; Burnet Medal, Australian Acad. Sci., 1997; (jtly) Australia Prize, 1998; (jtly) Charles S. Mott Prize, General Motors Cancer Res. Foundn, 1998; Women in Science Award, L'Oréal-UNESCO, 2001; Royal Medal, Royal Soc., 2002; Pearl Meister Greengard Prize, Rockefeller Univ., 2009; Colin Thomson Medal for Cancer Res., Assoc. for Internat. Cancer Res., UK, 2011; Eureka Prize for Leadership in Sci., Australian Mus., 2012; Lifetime Achievement Award, Fac. of Medicine, Nursing and Health Scis, Monash Univ., 2014. Chevalier de la Légion d'Honneur (France), 2009. *Publications:* numerous scientific papers and reviews. *Recreations:* camping, hiking, swimming, wilderness photography, ski-ing. *Address:* Walter and Eliza Hall Institute of Medical Research, 1G Royal Parade, Parkville, Vic 3052, Australia. *T:* (3) 93452490.

CORY-WRIGHT, Sir Richard (Michael), 4th Bt *cr* 1903; *b* 17 Jan. 1944; *s* of Capt. A. J. J. Cory-Wright (killed in action, 1944), and Susan Esterel (*d* 1993; she *m* 2nd, 1949, Lt-Col J. E. Gurney, DSO, MC), *d* of Robert Elwes; *S* grandfather, 1969; *m* 1st, 1976, Veronica Bolton (marr. diss. 1994); three *s*; 2nd, 1998, Helga Wright, *e d* of George Godfrey. *Educ:* Eton; Birmingham Univ. *Heir: s* Roland Anthony Cory-Wright, *b* 11 March 1979.

COSCELLI, Dr Andrea; Executive Director, Markets and Mergers, Competition and Markets Authority, since 2013; *b* Parma, Italy, 11 Feb. 1969; *s* of Carlo and Brenna Alinovi Coscelli; *m* 1996, Giovanna Bertazzoni; one *s*. *Educ:* Bocconi Univ. (Laurea in Econs 1992); Stanford Univ. (PhD Econs 1998). Trng and Mobility of Researchers Fellow, UCL, 1997–98; Consultant, Nat. Economic Res. Associates, 1998–2002; Associate Dir, Lexecon Ltd, 2002–05; Vice Pres., Charles River Associates, 2005–08; Dir, Competition Economics, Ofcom, 2008–13. *Address:* Competition and Markets Authority, Victoria House, Southampton Row, WC1B 4AD. *T:* (020) 3738 6105. *E:* andrea.coscelli@cma.gsi.gov.uk.

COSFORD, Paul Anthony, FFPHM; Director for Health Protection and Medical Director, Public Health England, since 2013; *b* 20 May 1963; *s* of Brian and Judith Cosford; *m* 2006, Dr Gillian Catherine Leng, *qv*; two step *d*, and one *s* one *d* (and one *s* decd) from a previous marriage. *Educ:* Exmouth Ch Primary Sch.; Exeter Sch.; St Mary's Hosp. Med. Sch., Univ. of London (BSc Hons 1984; MB BS (Hons in Pathol.) 1987); St George's Hosp. Med. Sch., Univ. of London (MSc Public Health 1994). MRCPsych 1991; MFPHM 1995, FFPHM 2001; Cert. of Completion of Specialist Trng 1996. Lectr and Hon. Registrar in Psychiatry, St Mary's Hosp. Med. Sch., 1990–92; Consultant in Public Health: Herts, 1996–97; Beds, 1997–2000; Dir of Public Health, Northants HA, 2000–02; Dir, Health Strategy and Public Health, Leics, Northants and Rutland Strategic HA, 2002–06; Medical Dir, E of England Strategic HA, 2006–10; Regl Dir of Public Health, East of England, DoH, 2006–10; Exec. Dir of Health Protection Services, HPA (on secondment), 2010–13. Hon. Sen. Lectr, Univ. of Leicester, 2005–; Hon. Sen. Fellow, Univ. of Cambridge, 2007–. *Publications:* contribs on health protection, screening and public health to learned jls. *Recreations:* amateur dramatics, golf, gardening, walking. cycling. *Address:* 3 Park Palings Walk, Haynes, Beds MK45 3PY. *E:* paulcosford@doctors.org.uk.

COSGRAVE, Liam, SC; *b* April 1920; *s* of late William T. Cosgrave; *m* 1952, Vera Osborne; two *s* one *d*. *Educ:* Synge Street Christian Brothers; Castlenock College, Dublin; King's Inns. Served in Army during Emergency. Barrister-at-Law, 1943; Senior Counsel, 1958. Member, Dail Eireann, 1943–81; Chairman Public Accounts Committee, 1945; Parliamentary Secretary to Taoiseach and Minister for Industry and Commerce, 1948–51; Minister for External Affairs, 1954–57; Leader, Fine Gael Party, 1965–77; Taoiseach (Head of Govt of Ireland), 1973–77; Minister for Defence, 1976. Leader first delegation from Ireland to the UN Assembly, 1956. Hon. LLD: Duquesne Univ., Pittsburg, Pa, and St John's Univ., Brooklyn, 1956; de Paul Univ., Chicago, 1958; NUI, 1974; Dublin Univ., 1974. Knight Grand Cross of Pius IX, 1956. *Address:* Beechpark, Templeogue, Co. Dublin, Ireland.

COSGROVE, Rt Hon. Lady; Hazel Josephine Cosgrove, CBE 2004; PC 2003; a Senator of the College of Justice in Scotland, 1996–2006; *b* 12 Jan. 1946; *d* of late Moses Aron Aronson and Julia Tobias; *m* 1967, John Allan Cosgrove, dental surgeon; one *s* one *d*. *Educ:* Glasgow High Sch. for Girls; Univ. of Glasgow (LLB). Advocate at the Scottish Bar. Admitted to Fac. of Advocates, 1968; QC (Scot.) 1991; Standing Junior Counsel to Dept of Trade, 1977–79; Sheriff of Glasgow and Strathkelvin, 1979–83; Sheriff of Lothian and Borders at Edinburgh, 1983–96. Temporary Judge, High Court and Court of Session, Scotland, 1992–96. Mem.,

Parole Bd for Scotland, 1988–91; Chairman: Mental Welfare Commn for Scotland, 1991–96; Expert Panel on Sex Offending, Scotland, 1997–2001; Dep. Chm., Boundary Commn for Scotland, 1997–2006. Hon. Fellow, Harris Manchester Coll., Oxford, 2001. Hon. LLD: Napier, 1997; Glasgow, 2002; Strathclyde, 2002; St Andrews, 2003; DUniv Stirling, 2004. *Recreations:* foreign travel, opera, swimming, walking, reading, being a grandmother. *E:* hazelcosgrove@uk2.net.

COSGROVE, Brian Joseph; artist and sculptor; Executive Producer and Co-Founder, Cosgrove Hall Fitzpatrick, since 2011; *b* 6 April 1934; *s* of Denis Cosgrove and Martha Cosgrove (*née* Hesketh); *m* 1963, Angela Helen Dyson; two *d. Educ:* Manchester Coll. of Art. Nat. Service, Army, 1952–54 (Malayan campaign). TV Graphic Designer, 1967–72; TV Programme Dir, 1972–76; Founder (with Mark Hall), Cosgrove Hall Productions, to produce animated films, 1976–95, Jt Man. Dir, 1995–2002 (BAFTA Award, 1982, 1983, 1985, 1986, 1987, 2000, 2004; Prix Jeunesse, Munich Film Fest., 1982; Internat. Emmy, 1984, 1991; Prix Danube, Bratislava Film Fest., 1990; 2 Observer Children's Film Awards, 1990; RTS Award, 1999, 2002). Mem., MENSA. Hon. DA Manchester Metropolitan, 2010; Hon. DLitt Chester, 2015. Special Award, 2012, Lifetime Achievement Award, 2013, BAFTA. *Recreations:* writing, painting, sculpture, gardening, computer graphic art. *Address:* B. & A. Cosgrove Ltd, Longlea Cottage, Kidderton Lane, Brindley, Nantwich, Cheshire CW5 8JD. *T:* (01270) 524550.

COSGROVE, Hazel Josephine; *see* Cosgrove, Rt Hon. Lady.

COSGROVE, Gen. Hon. Sir Peter (John), AK 2014 (AM 1985; AC 2000); MC 1970; CNZM 2000; Governor-General of Australia, since 2014; *b* Sydney, NSW, 28 July 1947; *s* of John Francis and Ellen Mary Cosgrove; *m* 1976, Lynne Elizabeth Payne; three *s. Educ:* Waverley Coll., Sydney; RMC, Duntroon (Dip. Mil. Studies); US Marine Corps Comd and Staff Coll., Quantico; Nat. Defence Coll., New Delhi. Platoon Comdr, 9th Bn, Royal Australian Regt, S Vietnam, 1969–70; ADC to Gov.-Gen., 1972; Adjt and Co. Comdr, 5th/7th Bn, Royal Australian Regt, 1973–75; Instructor, Inf. Centre, 1976–78; psc (US) 1979; SO, HQ Field Force Command, 1979–82; CO, 1st Bn, Royal Australian Regt, 1983–84; Instructor, British Army Staff Coll., 1984–86; MA to CGS, 1987; jssc, Canberra, 1988; Dir Information, and Comdt, Information Centre, 1990–91; Comdr, 6th Bde, 1992–93; Comdt, Australian Defence Force Warfare Centre, 1995–96, RMC, 1997; Commander: 1st Div. and Deployable Jt Force, HQ Australian Army, 1998–99; InterFET Force (E Timor), 1999–2000; Land Comdr, Australia, 2000; Chief of Army, 2000–02; Chief, Australian Defence Force, 2002–05. Hd, Operation Recovery Taskforce after Cyclone Larry, Qld, 2006. Chm., SA Defence Adv. Bd, 2006–14. Chm., Australian War Meml Council, 2007–12. Chm., Augusta Westland Australia, 2006–13; Director: Qantas Airways Ltd, 2005–14; Qantas Superannuation Plan, 2005–14; Cardno Ltd, 2007–14. Chancellor, Australian Catholic Univ., 2010–14. FAICD 2009; Paul Harris Fellow, Rotary Internat., 2001. DUniv: Northern Territory, 2001; Griffith, 2006; Australian Catholic, 2009. GCSG 2013; KStJ 2014. Order of Nat. Merit Tong-Il Medal (Republic of Korea), 2001; Legion of Merit Medal (USA), 2001; Order of Prince Henry (Portugal), 2001; Centenary Medal (Australia), 2003; DSO (Singapore), 2004; Officier, Légion d'Honneur (France), 2005; Grand Collar, Order of Timor Leste (Portugal), 2009. Australian of Year, 2001. *Publications:* My Story (autobiog.), 2006; Boyer Lectures, 2009. *Recreations:* golf, cricket, Rugby, music, literature. *Address:* Government House, Dunrossil Drive, Yarralumla, ACT 2600, Australia.

COSSONS, Sir Neil, Kt 1994; OBE 1982; Director, Science Museum, 1986–2000; Chairman, English Heritage, 2000–07; *b* 15 Jan. 1939; *s* of Arthur Cossons and Evelyn (*née* Bettle); *m* 1965, Veronica Edwards (MBE 2015; DL); two *s* one *d. Educ:* Henry Mellish Grammar Sch., Nottingham; Univ. of Liverpool (MA). FSA 1968; FMA 1970. Curator of Technology, Bristol City Museum, 1964; Dep. Dir, City of Liverpool Museums, 1969; Dir, Ironbridge Gorge Museum Trust, 1971; Dir, Nat. Maritime Mus., 1983–86. Comr, Historic Buildings and Monuments Commn for England (English Heritage), 1989–95, and 1999–2000 (Mem., Ancient Monuments Adv. Cttee, 1984–98; Mem., Adv. Cttee, English Heritage, later Historic England, 2013–); Chm., RCHME, 2000–03. Member: Curatorium Internat. Committee for the Conservation of the Industrial Heritage, 1973–78; BBC General Adv. Council, 1987–90; NEDO Tourism and Leisure Industries Sector Gp (formerly Leisure Industries EDC), 1987–90; Council, RCA, 1989–2015 (Pro-Provost and Chm. of Council, 2007–15); Design Council, 1990–94; Comité Scientifique, Conservatoire Nat. des Arts et Métiers, 1991–2000. President: Assoc. for Industrial Archaeology, 1977–80; Assoc. of Independent Museums, 1983– (Chm., 1978–83); Museums Assoc., 1981–82; ASE, 1996; RGS-IBG, 2003–06; Member, Council: Newcomen Soc. for Study of Hist. of Engrg and Technol., 1992–2006 (Mem., 1963; Pres., 2001–03; Fellow 2010); FMI, 1993–98. Mem., British Waterways Bd, 1995–2001. Trustee, Civic Trust, 1987–93. Gov., Imperial Coll. of Sci., Technology and Medicine, 1989–93. Collier Prof. in the Public Understanding of Sci., Univ. of Bristol, 2001–02. Hon. Prof., Univ. of Birmingham, 1994–. Hon. FRCA, 1987, Sen. FRCA, 2015; Hon. FRIBA 2002; Hon. FCIWEM 2002; Hon. Fellow, BAAS, 2007; Comp IEE, 1991; CCMI (CIMgt 1996); Hon. Mem., SCI, 2002; Hon. CRAeS 1996. Hon. DSocSc Birmingham, 1979; DUniv: Open, 1984; Sheffield Hallam, 1995; York, 1998; Hon. DLitt: Liverpool, 1989; Bradford, 1991; Nottingham Trent, 1994; UWE, 1995; Bath, 1997; Greenwich, 2004; Hon. DSc: Leicester, 1995; Nottingham, 2000; Hon. DArts De Montfort, 1997. Norton Medlicott Medal, Historical Assoc., 1991; President's Medal, Royal Acad. of Engrg, 1993; Dickinson Meml Medal, Newcomen Soc., 2001; Maitland Medal, IStructE, 2002. Series Editor, England's Landscape, 2006. *Publications:* (with R. A. Buchanan) Industrial Archaeology of the Bristol Region, 1968; (with K. Hudson) Industrial Archaeologists' Guide, 1969, 2nd edn 1971; Industrial Archaeology, 1975, 3rd edn 1993; (ed) Transactions of the First International Congress on the Conservation of Industrial Monuments, 1975; (ed) Rees's Manufacturing Industry, 1975; (with H. Sowden) Ironbridge—Landscape of Industry, 1977; (with B. S. Trinder) The Iron Bridge—Symbol of the Industrial Revolution, 1979, 2nd edn (Japanese) 1989, (English) 2002; (ed) Management of Change in Museums, 1985; (ed) Making of the Modern World, 1992; (ed) Perspectives on Industrial Archaeology, 2000; numerous papers, articles and reviews. *Recreations:* travel, design, industrial archaeology. *Address:* The Old Rectory, Rushbury, Shropshire SY6 7EB. *T:* (01694) 771603. *E:* nc@cossons.org.uk. *Club:* Athenæum.

COSTA, Alberto Castrenze; MP (C) South Leicestershire, since 2015.

COSTA, Antonio Maria, PhD; Executive Director, United Nations Office on Drugs and Crime, and Director-General, United Nations Office, Vienna, 2002–10; Editor-in-Chief, Journal of Policy Modeling, since 1975; *b* 16 June 1941; *s* of Francesco Costa and Maria (*née* Contratto); *m* 1971, Patricia Wallace; two *s* one *d. Educ:* Turin Univ. (degree in political sci. 1964); Acad. of Scis, Moscow (Math. Econs 1967); Univ. of Calif at Berkeley (MA Econs 1969; PhD Econs 1971). Sen. Economic Advr, UN, NY, 1971–83; Dep. Sec. Gen. (Special Counsellor), OECD, 1983–87; Dir Gen. for Econs and Finance, Special Advr to Pres., and Mem., Monetary Cttee, EU, Brussels, 1987–92; Dir Gen. for Strategic Planning, Ferrero Gp, 1992–93; Sec. Gen., EBRD, 1994–2002. Member: Wkg Party for Co-ordination of Macroeconomic Policies of G10 Countries, OECD; Bd of Dirs, EIB; EU Rapporteur to EP; financial Sherpa for G8 meetings, 1987–92. Vis. Prof. of Econs, Moscow Univ. and Acad. of Scis, Moscow, 1963–64; Adjunct Professor of Economics: Univ. of Calif at Berkeley, 1968–70; CU NY, 1970–76; New York Univ., 1976–87; Vis. Prof., Free Univ., Brussels, 1990–94. *Publications:* Checkmate: a fictional rendering of the European financial crisis, 2013. *E:* Editor@EconModels.com.

COSTA, Kenneth Johann; Chairman, London Connection, St Paul's Institute, since 2011; *b* 31 Oct. 1949; *s* of late Joseph Costa and of Martha Costa; *m* 1982, Fiona Morgan Williams; two *s* two *d. Educ:* Univ. of Witwatersrand (BA, LLB); Queens' Coll., Cambridge (LLM, Cert. in Theology). Joined S. G. Warburg, subseq. UBS Investment Bank, 1976: Dep. Chm., 1993; Chm., Investment Banking Bd, Hd of Global Mergers and Acquisitions, 1995; Vice-Chm., 1996–2007; Chm., Investment Banking for Europe, ME and Africa, 2004–07; Chm., Lazard Internat., 2007–11. Dir, Songbird Estates plc, 2014–. Gresham Prof. of Commerce, Gresham Coll., 2009–12. Chm. Adv. Bd, LSO, 2000–09. Chm., fund raising gp, Gt Ormond Street Hosp., 2006–09; Trustee, Nelson Mandela Children's Trust UK. Chm., Alpha Internat.; Church Warden, Holy Trinity, Brompton. *Publications:* God at Work, 2007; contrib. articles to Wall St Jl, FT, The Times. *Recreations:* country activities, politics, music, theology.

COSTA-LOBO, António; Ambassador of Portugal to the Court of St James's, 1995–97; *b* 22 May 1932; *s* of Gumersindo da Costa Lobo and Maria Magdalena Teixeira Leal da Costa Lobo; *m* 1980, Maria Catarina de Locher Machado. *Educ:* Univ. of Coimbra, Portugal (Law degree). Joined Ministry of Foreign Affairs, Portugal, 1956: served Havana, 1961–63; The Hague, 1964–66; Consul-Gen., San Francisco, 1966–70; Perm. Mission to UN, NY, 1973–77; Council of Europe, 1980–82; Ambassador to China, 1982–85; Perm. Mission, Geneva, 1985–90; Ambassador to Russia, 1990–93; Sec. Gen., Ministry of Foreign Affairs, 1993–95. Head of Portugal delegation: Diplomatic Conf. on establishment of Internat. Criminal Court, 1998; Meetings of Preparatory Commn for Internat. Criminal Court, 1999–2002. Visiting Professor: Univ. Católica Portuguese, 1978–80 and 2001–; Univ. Técnica de Lisboa, 1998–2002; Lectr, Univ. Nova de Lisboa, 2003–. Grã-Cruz da Ordem do Infante Dom Henrique (Portugal), 1985; Grã-Cruz da Ordem Militar de Cristo (Portugal), 1997. *Publications:* As Operações de Paz das Nações Unidas, 1969. *Recreations:* reading, bridge, tennis. *Address:* Av. D. Nuno Álvares Pereira 41, 2765-261 Estoril, Portugal. *T:* and *Fax:* (21) 4680508. *E:* acostalobo@netcabo.pt. *Club:* Grémio Literário (Lisbon).

COSTAIN, Janice Elizabeth; *see* Hall, J. E.

COSTAIN, Peter John, FCA; Deputy Chairman, Costain Group Plc, 1995–97 (Group Chief Executive, 1980–95); Director: Pearl Group, 1989–2005; London Life Ltd, 1994–2005; Hendersons (formerly AMP UK, then HHG) plc, 1994–2005; *b* 2 April 1938; *s* of Sir Albert Costain; *m* 1963, Victoria M. Pope; three *s. Educ:* Charterhouse. Peat Marwick Mitchell & Co., 1956–63; Richard Costain Ltd, 1963–65; Costain Australia Ltd, 1965–92: Board Member, 1967; Managing Director, 1971; Chief Executive, 1973. Dir, Wessex Water Services Ltd, 1999–2014. Mem., London Adv. Bd, Westpac Banking Corp., 1981–86. Mem. Bd, CITB, 1989–93. Chm., Tenterden Day Care Centre for the Disabled and Elderly, 2007–. FAIB. Prime Warden, Basketmakers' Co., 1998–99. *Recreations:* sailing, ski-ing, golf. *Clubs:* Royal Thames Yacht; Athenæum (Melbourne); Rye Golf, Royal St George's Golf.

COSTELLO, Elvis; *see* McManus, D. P. A.

COSTELLO, John Francis, MD; FRCP, FRCPI; Consultant Physician: Cromwell Hospital, SW5, since 1983; London Clinic, since 2005; Chairman, Capital Hospitals Ltd, since 2006; *b* 22 Sept. 1944; *s* of late William and Sarah Costello; *m* 1972, Dr Christine Ellen McGregor White (marr. diss.); three *s*; *m* 1996, Susanna Clarke; two *s. Educ:* Belvedere Coll., Dublin; University Coll., Dublin (MB BCh, BAO Hons 1968; MD 1987). MRCP 1972, FRCP 1982; MRCPI 1995, FRCPI 1996. Hospital appts, Mater Hosp., Dublin, St Stephen's, and Royal Northern; RPMS, 1970–72; Registrar, Brompton Hosp., 1972–73; Lectr, Univ. of Edinburgh, Edinburgh Royal Infirmary, 1973–75; Asst Prof. of Medicine, and attending physician, Univ. of California, San Francisco, 1975–77; King's College Hospital: Consultant Physician, 1977–2003, now Hon. Consultant Physician; Chm. of Consultants, 1989–91; Med. Clinical Dir, Acute Services, 1989–93; Dir, Respiratory Medicine, King's Coll. Sch. of Medicine and Dentistry, 1982–98; Med. Dir, King's Healthcare NHS Trust, 1991–94; Dir of Medicine, King's Healthcare, subseq. KCH, NHS Trust, 1997–2003. Vis. Fellow, KCL, 2003–. Mem. Bd, Health Care Projects, 2008–12. Examr in Medicine, Conjoint Bd, 1979–83; Examr, MRCPI, 2004–12; Med. Vice Chm., SE Thames/S London Regl Cttee for Distinction Awards, 1997–2002. Chm., Educn Trust, Ind. Doctors Fedn, 2007–. Founder Pres., Respiratory Sect., RSocMed, 1991–93; Mem. Council, British Thoracic Soc., 1996. *Publications:* (ed jtly) Beta Agonists in the Treatment of Asthma, 1992; (ed) Methylxanthines and Phosphodiesterase Inhibitors, 1994; (jtly) A Colour Atlas of Lung Infections, 1996; (ed) Sympathomimetic Enantiomers in the Treatment of Asthma, 1997; (contrib.) Horizons in Medicine, 2002; papers, reviews and chapters on lung disease, esp. asthma, and early detection of lung cancer, bowel cancer and coronary heart disease. *Recreations:* opera, golf. *Address:* 12 Melville Avenue, Wimbledon, SW20 0NS. *T:* (020) 8879 1309. *E:* jfcostello@btinternet.com. *Clubs:* Garrick; Royal Wimbledon Golf.

COSTELLO, Hon. Peter Howard, AC 2011; Chairman, ECG Financial, since 2013; *b* 14 Aug. 1957; *s* of Russell and Anne Costello; *m* 1982, Tanya Pamela Coleman; one *s* two *d. Educ:* Carey Baptist Grammar Sch.; Monash Univ. (LLB Hons, BA). Solicitor, 1981–84; Barrister, 1984–90. MP (L) Higgins, Vic, 1990–2009; Shadow Minister for Corporate Law Reform and Consumer Affairs, 1990–92; Shadow Attorney Gen. and Shadow Minister for Justice, 1992–93; Shadow Minister for Finance, 1993–94; Shadow Treasurer, 1994–96; Dep. Leader of Opposition, 1994–96; Treasurer, 1996–2007; Dep. Leader, Liberal Party, 1994–2007. Man. Dir, BKK Partners, 2009–12; Chm., Qld Commn of Audit, 2012–13. Chairman: OECD, 2000; G20 Finance Ministers and Central Bankers, 2006. World Bank: Gov., 1996–2007; Mem., 2008–11, Chm., 2011–14, Ind. Adv. Bd; Governor: IMF, 1996–2007; Asian Develt Bank, 1996–2007. Guardian, Australian Future Fund, 2009–13 (Chm., 2014–). Mem., Internat. Adv. Bd, Allianz SE, 2011–; Dir, Nine Entertainment Co., 2013–. Trustee, Melbourne Cricket Ground, 2013–. Co-Chairman: Third Australia-China Forum, 2013; Australia-China High Level Dialogue, 2014–. Hon. LLD Monash, 2013. *Publications:* (jtly) Arbitration in Contempt, 1986; (with P. Coleman) The Costello Memoirs, 2008. *Recreations:* swimming, football, reading. *Clubs:* Australian (Melbourne); Melbourne Cricket (Trustee, 2013–); Essendon Football.

COTRUBAS, Ileana, (Mme Manfred Ramin); opera singer, retired 1990; *b* Rumania; *d* of Vasile and Maria Cotrubas; *m* 1972, Manfred Ramin. *Educ:* Conservatorul Ciprian Porumbescu, Bucharest. Opera and concert engagements all over Europe, N America and Japan. Formerly permanent guest at Royal Opera House, Covent Garden; Member, Vienna State Opera (Hon. Mem., 1991); also frequently sang in Scala, Milan, Munich, Berlin, Paris, Chicago, NY Metropolitan Opera. Main operatic roles: Susanna, Pamina, Gilda, Traviata, Manon, Tatyana, Mimi, Melisande, Amina, Elisabetta, Nedda, Marguerite. Has made numerous recordings. Hon. Citizen, Bucharest, 1993. Kammersängerin, Austria, 1981; Grand Officer: Sant Iago da Espada (Portugal), 1990; Steaua României (Romania), 2000. *Publications:* Opernwahrheiten, 1998.

COTTAGE, Rosina; QC 2011; a Recorder, since 2012; *b* London, 29 Dec. 1965; *d* of Peter Cottage and Josephine Cottage; partner, Andrew Davidson; one *s* one *d. Educ:* Dunottar Sch. for Girls; Epsom Coll.; Univ. of Bristol (LLB); Coll. of Law. Called to the Bar, Inner Temple, 1988; in practice as a barrister, specialising in crime and family, 9–12 Bell Yard, 1989–98, 9 Gough Square, 1998–2013, Red Lion Chambers, 2013–. *Recreations:* family, friends, domestic animal husbandry. *Address:* 18 Red Lion Court, EC4A 3EB.

COTTAM, Harold; Founding Partner, Investor Relations Development LLP, 2002–08; Managing Director, Pentwyn Renewables Ltd, since 2012; *b* 12 Oct. 1938; *s* of Rev. Canon

Frank and Elizabeth Cottam; *m* 1962, Lyn Minton; two *d*. *Educ:* Bedford School. FCA. Deloitte & Co., Tanganyika and Peru, 1960–64; Smith Kline UK, 1964–66; Simon Engineering Group, Spain, 1966–68; Ernst & Whinney, subseq. Ernst & Young, 1968–92; UK Man. Partner, 1987–92; Chairman: Ernst & Young Case Services (Internat.), 1992–93; Ernst & Young Pan-European Consulting Gp, 1992–93; Haden MacLellan Hldgs, 1992–97; Anglo United (Coalite Products, Charrington and Falkland Is Gp), 1993–96; Rebus Gp, 1996–99; Britannic plc, subseq. Britannic Gp plc, 1996–2004. Dir, Allied Colloids Gp, 1992–97. *Recreations:* piano, opera, tennis. *Address:* 8a Burton Mews, SW1W 9EP.

COTTAM, Maj.-Gen. Nicholas Jeremy, CB 2007; OBE 1990; Registrar, St Paul's Cathedral, 2009–15; *b* 17 Feb. 1951; *s* of late Brig. H. W. Donald Cottam, OBE and Diana Cottam; *m* 1982, Susan Habberfield-Bateman; one *s* one *d*. *Educ:* Univ. of Durham (BA Hons). VSO, 1969. Commnd Royal Green Jackets, 1973: CO, 2nd RGJ, 1990–93 (despatches 1993); Comd, 8th Inf. Bde, 1995–96; rcds 1997: Director: Intelligence, MoD, 1998–2000; Personal Services (Army), MoD, 2000–02; GOC 5th Div., 2003–05; Mil. Sec., 2005–08; Reserve Forces Study Team Leader, 2008. Col Comdt, 2nd RGJ, 2002–07. *Recreation:* mountaineering. *Club:* Alpine.

COTTENHAM, 9th Earl of, *cr* 1850; **Mark John Henry Pepys;** Bt 1784 and 1801; Baron Cottenham 1836; Viscount Crowhurst 1850; Partner, Bridging the Gap China LLP, since 2011; *b* 11 Oct. 1983; *s* of 8th Earl of Cottenham; *S* father, 2000. *Educ:* Eton; Bristol Univ. *Heir: b* Hon. Sam Richard Pepys, *b* 26 April 1986.

COTTER, family name of **Baron Cotter**.

COTTER, Baron *cr* 2006 (Life Peer), of Congresbury in the County of Somerset; **Brian Joseph Michael Cotter;** *b* 24 Aug. 1936; *s* of Michael Joseph Cotter and Mary Cotter; *m* 1963, Eyleen Patricia Wade; two *s* one *d*. *Educ:* Downside Sch., Somerset. Sales Manager, then Man. Dir, Plasticable Ltd, 1989–2003. MP (Lib Dem) Weston-super-Mare, 1997–2005; contested (Lib Dem) same seat, 2005. Lib Dem spokesman on small businesses, 1997–2005. Lib Dem spokesman in H of L for small businesses, 2006–, for skills and apprenticeships, 2007–. Sec., All-Party Parly China Gp. National Patron: SURF (charity for Rwandan widows), 1998–; YMCA; Patron, Somewhere To Go (charity for homeless people, N Som). *Recreations:* reading, gardening, films. *Address:* 52 Eddington Court, 30 Beach Road, Weston-Super-Mare, Som BS23 1DM. *T:* (01934) 832755; House of Lords, SW1A 0PW.

COTTER, Barry Paul; QC 2006; **His Honour Judge Cotter;** a Circuit Judge, since 2010; Designated Civil Judge for Devon and Cornwall, since 2010; a Deputy High Court Judge, since 2010; *b* 30 July 1963; *s* of Austin and Angela Cotter; *m* 1996, Catherine Maskell; one *s* two *d*. *Educ:* St Theresa's Primary Sch., St Helens; West Park High Sch., St Helens; University Coll. London (LLB 1984). Called to the Bar, Lincoln's Inn, 1985; Recorder, 2002–10; Dep. Hd, Old Sq. Chambers, 2003–10. Mem. Cttee, Personal Injury Bar Assoc., 1995–99 and 2001–03. Personal Injury Barrister of Yr, Eclipse Proclaim Personal Injury Awards, 2009. *Publications:* Cotter: Defective and Unsafe Products: Law and Practice, 1996; (Gen. Ed.) Munkman on Employer's Liability, 14th edn 2006, 15th edn 2009. *Recreations:* family life, running, walking, Rugby. *Address:* Exeter Combined Court Centre, Southernhay Gardens, Exeter, Devon EX1 1UH. *T:* (01392) 415300.

COTTER, Sir Patrick Laurence Delaval, 7th Bt *cr* 1763, of Rockforest, Cork; *b* 21 Nov. 1941; *s* of Laurence Stopford Llewelyn Cotter; *S* uncle, 2001; *m* 1967, Janet, *d* of George Potter, Barnstaple; one *s* two *d*. *Educ:* Blundell's; RAC Cirencester. *Heir: s* Julius Laurence George Cotter, *b* 5 Jan. 1968.

COTTER, Suzanne Maree; Director, Museum of Contemporary Art, Serralves Foundation, Porto, since 2013; *b* Melbourne, Australia, 20 April 1961; *d* of James and Elaine Cotter; *m* 1987, Bruce Manson. *Educ:* Star of the Sea High Sch., Southport, Qld; Queensland Inst. of Technol., Brisbane (Dip. Applied Sci. 1981); Univ. of Melbourne; École du Louvre, Paris (Dip. du Premier Cycle 1994); Courtauld Inst. of Art (MA 1995); City Univ. (Post-grad. Dip. Cultural Leadership 2007). Asst to Australian Cultural Attaché, Paris, 1991–94; Exhibn Organiser, Serpentine Gall., London, 1996–98; Curator, Whitechapel Gall., London, 1998; Exhibns Curator, Hayward Gall., London, 1998–2002; Sen. Curator, Modern Art Oxford, 2002–07; Dep. Dir and Sen. Curator, then Curator at Large, Modern Art Oxford, 2008–09; Curator, Abu Dhabi Project, Solomon R. Guggenheim Foundn, 2010–12. Co-Curator, Sharjah Biennial 10, 2011. Ext. Examr, MA in Curating Contemp. Art, RCA, 2007–10. Trustee: Paris Calling charity, 2005–10; Peer, London, 2005–09. Judge, Turner Prize, 2008. FRSA 2005. Chevalier, Ordre des Arts et des Lettres (France), 2005. *Publications:* (contrib.) Vox Populi, by Fiona Tan, 2006; (ed) Out of Beirut, 2006; (ed) Transmission Interrupted, 2009; (ed) Michael Clark, 2011; (contrib) Defining Contemporary Art: 25 years in 200 pivotal artworks, 2011; Joana Hadjithomas and Khalil Joreige, 2013; Imran Qureishi: artist of the year, 2013; exhibn catalogues. *Recreations:* tennis, ski-ing, swimming, reading, theatre, films, art.

COTTERELL, Sir John (Henry Geers), 6th Bt *cr* 1805; Vice Lord-Lieutenant, Herefordshire, 1998–2010; Chairman: Radio Wyvern, 1980–97; Herefordshire Community Health NHS Trust, 1991–97; *b* 8 May 1935; *s* of Sir Richard Charles Geers Cotterell, 5th Bt, CBE, and Lady Lettice Cotterell (*d* 1973), *d* of 7th Earl Beauchamp; *S* father, 1978; *m* 1959, Vanda Alexandra Clare (MBE 1997) (*d* 2005), *d* of Major Philip Alexander Clement Bridgewater; three *s* one *d*. *Educ:* Eton; RMA Sandhurst. Officer, Royal Horse Guards, 1955–61. Vice-Chm. Hereford and Worcs CC, 1973–77, Chm., 1977–81. Pres., Nat. Fedn of Young Farmers Clubs, 1986–91 (Dep. Pres., 1979–86); Mem., Jockey Club, 1990–. Chairman: Hereford Mappa Mundi Trust, 1987–2007; Rural Voice, 1991–92. *Recreations:* cricket, shooting. *Heir: s* Henry Richard Geers Cotterell, OBE [*b* 22 Aug. 1961; *m* 1st, 1986, Carolyn (*d* 1999), *er d* of John Beckwith-Smith, Maybanks Manor, Rudgwick, Sussex; two *s* one *d*; 2nd, 2002, Katherine Bromley; one *s*]. *Address:* Downshill House, Bishopstone, Herefordshire HR4 7JT. *T:* (01981) 590232.

COTTERILL, Kenneth William, CMG 1976; Chairman, Commercial and Political Risk Consultants Ltd, 1986–98 (Deputy Chairman, 1981–86); *b* 5 June 1921; *s* of William and Ada May Cotterill; *m* 1948, Janet Hilda Cox; one *d*. *Educ:* Sutton County Sch.; London School of Economics, BSc (Econ). Served War in Royal Navy, 1941–46. After the war, joined ECGD; Principal, 1956; Asst Sec., 1966; Under Sec., 1970; Dep. Head of Dept, 1976–81. Dir, Tarmac Internat., 1981–86; Consultant: NEI International, 1981–87; Barclays Bank, 1981–87. *Address:* 61 Willow Court, Campion Gardens, Clyne Common, Swansea SA3 3JB. *T:* (01792) 235261.

COTTERRELL, Prof. Roger Brian Melvyn, LLD; FBA 2005; FAcSS; Anniversary Professor of Legal Theory, Queen Mary University of London, since 2005; *b* 30 Nov. 1946; *s* of Walter Leslie Cotterrell and Hilda Margaret Cotterrell (*née* Randle); *m* 1969, Ann Zillah Poyner; one *s* one *d*. *Educ:* King Edward VI Camp Hill Sch., Birmingham; University Coll. London (LLB 1968; LLM 1969); Birkbeck Coll., Univ. of London (MScSoc 1977); LLD London 1988. Lectr in Law, Univ. of Leicester, 1969–74; Queen Mary College, then Queen Mary and Westfield College, subseq. Queen Mary, University of London: Lectr in Law, 1974–78; Sen. Lectr in Law, 1978–85; Reader in Legal Theory, 1985–90; Prof. of Legal Theory, 1990–2005; Actg Hd, 1989–90, Hd, 1990–91, Dept of Law; Dean, Faculty of Laws, 1993–96. Vis. Prof. and Jay H. Brown Centennial Faculty Fellow in Law, Univ. of Texas, Austin, 1989; George Lurcy Lectr, Amherst Coll., Mass, 1989; Visiting Professor: Univ. of Lund, 1996; Katholieke Univ. Brussel and Facultés Universitaires St Louis, Brussels, 1996, 1997; Internat. Inst. for the Sociol. of Law, Onati, Spain, 2003, 2004. Mem., Cttee of Hds of Univ. Law Schs, 1993–96. Mem., Law Panel, RAE, 1999–2001, 2005–08. Trustee, 1996–99, Chm., Articles Prize Cttee, 1999–2000, Law and Soc. Assoc. Mem. Ct, Univ. of Leicester, 2000–03. FAcSS 2014. *Publications:* The Sociology of Law: an introduction, 1984 (trans. Chinese 1989, Spanish 1991, Korean 1992), 2nd edn 1992 (trans. Lithuanian 1997); (ed jtly) Law, Democracy and Social Justice, 1988; The Politics of Jurisprudence: a critical introduction to legal philosophy, 1989, 2nd edn 2003; (ed) Law and Society, 1994; (ed) Process and Substance: Butterworth lectures on comparative law, 1994; Law's Community: legal theory in sociological perspective, 1995; Emile Durkheim: law in a moral domain, 1999; (ed) Sociological Perspectives on Law, 2 vols, 2001; (with Coleridge Goode) Bass Lines: a life in jazz, 2002; Law, Culture and Society: legal ideas in the mirror of social theory, 2006; (ed) Law in Social Theory, 2006; Living Law: studies in legal and social theory, 2008; (ed) Emile Durkheim: justice, morality and politics, 2010; contribs to symposia and jls on law, social sci. and phil. *Recreations:* listening to and writing about music, exploring cities, European cinema. *Address:* Law School, Queen Mary University of London, Mile End Road, E1 4NS. *T:* (020) 7882 3946, *Fax:* (020) 8981 8733. *E:* r.b.m.cotterrell@qmul.ac.uk.

COTTESLOE, 5th Baron (UK) *cr* 1874; **Comdr John Tapling Fremantle,** RN (retired); JP; DL; Bt 1821; Baron of Austrian Empire 1816; Lord-Lieutenant of Buckinghamshire, 1984–97; *b* 22 Jan. 1927; *s* of 4th Baron Cottesloe, GBE and his 1st wife, Lady Elizabeth Harris (*d* 1983), *o d* of 5th Earl of Malmesbury; *S* father, 1994; *m* 1958, Elizabeth Ann (*d* 2013), *e d* of late Lt-Col H. S. Barker, DSO; one *s* two *d*. *Educ:* Summer Fields, Hastings; Eton College. Joined RN, 1944; CO HMS Palliser, 1959–61; retired at own request, 1966. Governor, Stowe School, 1983–89. Chm., Radcliffe Trust, 1997–2006 (Trustee, 1983–). Vice President: British Assoc. for Shooting and Conservation, 1975–; Hospital Saving Assoc., 1979–2001; Bucks County Agricl Assoc., 1988–; Bucks Guide Assoc., 1996–; Bucks Fedn of Young Farmers' Clubs, 1997–2000 (Trustee, 1985–96); Dep. Pres., RASE, 1995–96; President: Bucks Br., CLA, 1983–97; HMS Concord Assoc., 1984–; Bucks Assoc. for the Blind, 1997– (Trustee, 1984–96); Bucks Farming and Wildlife Adv. Gp, 1997–2000; Bucks County Rifle Assoc.; Chm., Oxon Bucks Div., Royal Forestry Soc., 1981–83. Councillor, Winslow RDC, 1971–74; Hon. Treas., Aylesbury Vale Assoc. of Local Councils, 1974–84. Patron: RN Assoc. Aylesbury (No 1) Br.; Ferris Foundn. High Sheriff, 1969–70, JP 1984, DL 1978–84, 1997, Bucks. KStJ 1984. DUniv Buckingham, 1993. *Recreations:* shooting, crosswords, steam railways, Sherlock Holmes. *Heir: s* Hon. Thomas Francis Henry Fremantle, *b* 17 March 1966. *Address:* Athawes Farm House, 15 Nearton End, Swanbourne, Milton Keynes, Bucks MK17 0SL. *T:* (home) (01296) 720263, *T:* and *Fax:* (office) (01296) 720256. *Club:* Travellers.

See also Rt Hon. G. I. Duncan Smith.

COTTHAM, (George) William; Chairman, CentreWest London Buses Ltd, 1995–97; *b* 11 July 1944; *s* of George William and Elizabeth Cottham; *m* 1967, Joan Thomas; two *d*. *Educ:* Univ. of London; Polytechnic of Liverpool; Liverpool Coll. of Commerce. BSc 1st Cl. Hons, LLB 2nd Cl. Hons. FCILT. Various posts, Liverpool City Transport, 1960–74; District Transport Manager, St Helens, 1974–77; Transport General Manager, Newport, 1977–80; Gen. Manager, Cleveland Transit, 1980–83; Dir Gen., W Yorks PTE, 1983–86; Chairman and Managing Director: Yorkshire Rider, 1986–94; Rider Hldgs, 1988–94; Rider York, 1990–94. *Recreations:* family, home, garden, music, photography. *Address:* Bismarckia, 1438 Palm Grove Villas, Four Seasons Resort Estates, Nevis, West Indies; Vila Fonte, Algarve, Portugal; Naples Lakes, Naples, FL 34112, USA.

COTTINGHAM, Barrie, FCA; Deputy Chairman, Pinelog Group Ltd, 1997–2013; *b* 5 Oct. 1933; *s* of John and Eleanor Cottingham; *m* 1st, 1957, Kathleen Morton (marr. diss. 2008); one *s* (and one *d* decd); 2nd, 2012, Nicola Lesley Scahill McMullan. *Educ:* Carfield Sch. ATII. Coopers & Lybrand: joined, 1957; Partner, 1964–95; Exec. Partner, i/c Regl Practice, 1986–93; Mem. UK Bd, 1974–93. Chairman: SIG plc, 1993–2004; Cattles plc, 1995–2006; Dep. Chm., Dew Pitchmastic plc, 1997–2005; non-exec. Dir, VP plc, 1996–2009. Pres., Sheffield and District, Soc. of Chartered Accountants, 1964. Mem., Investment Gp and Pension Fund Sub-cttee, Univ. of Sheffield, 2002–13. Dir and Trustee, Autism Plus, 2010–12. Pres., Boys and Girls Clubs S Yorks, 1964–. *Recreations:* racketball, golf, watching Rugby and soccer, theatre, opera. *Address:* Waterstones, 2 Beckside, Cawthorne, Barnsley S75 4EP. *T:* (01226) 791395.

COTTON; *see* Stapleton-Cotton, family name of Viscount Combermere.

COTTON, Christopher John Pott; Chief Executive, Royal Albert Hall, since 2010; *b* Edinburgh, 27 Jan. 1950; *s* of Tom and Phyllis Alexander Cotton; *m* 1983, Elizabeth Meriol Trevor; one *d* and one step *s*. *Educ:* Malvern Coll.; Architectural Assoc. RIBA. Whinney Mackay Lewis Partnership, 1974–2000; Aros Architects, 2000–05; Royal Albert Hall: Building and Ops Dir, 2005–10; Exhibition Rd Cultural Gp Dir, 2010–12. Dir, Julie's Bicycle, 2011–. *Recreations:* sailing, architecture, music, visual arts. *Address:* Royal Albert Hall, Kensington Gore, SW7 2AP. *T:* (020) 7589 3203. *E:* chrisc@royalalberthall.com. *Club:* Capital.

COTTON, Diana Rosemary, (Mrs R. B. Allan); QC 1983; a Recorder, 1982–2011; *b* 30 Nov. 1941; *d* of Arthur Frank Edward and Muriel Cotton; *m* 1966, Richard Bellerby Allan; two *s* one *d*. *Educ:* Berkhamsted School for Girls; Lady Margaret Hall, Oxford (MA). Joined Middle Temple, 1961; called to Bar, 1964; Bencher, 1990; Member, Midland Circuit; a Dep. High Ct Judge, 1993–2011. Mem., Criminal Injuries Compensation Bd, 1989–2000; a Judge of First-tier Tribunal: Criminal Injuries Compensation (formerly Mem., Criminal Injuries Compensation Appeal Panel), 1996–2013; Mental Health (formerly Pres., Mental Health Ind. Rev. Tribunal for restricted patients), 1997–2011; Asst Boundary Comr, 2000–05. *Recreation:* her family and other animals.

COTTON, Jane Catherine; Human Resources Director, Oxfam, 1999–2014; *b* 10 Jan. 1959; *d* of Tony and Jean Alderson; *m* 1980, Stephen Paul Cotton. *Educ:* Girton Coll., Cambridge (MA). Department of Transport: graduate trainee posts, 1979–83; Aviation Policy, 1983–88; Personnel, 1989–92; Railways Policy/Finances, 1992–93; Hd of Resources, Charity Commn, 1993–96; Sec. to Board, Dept of Transport, 1996–97; Personnel Dir, DETR, 1997–99. Trustee: Canal and River Trust, 2012–; WWF, 2014–. *Recreations:* gardening, walking, football (spectator), theatre.

COTTON, His Honour John Anthony; a Circuit Judge, 1973–93; *b* 6 March 1926; *s* of Frederick Thomas Hooley Cotton and Catherine Mary Cotton; *m* 1960, Johanna Aritia van Lookeren Campagne; three *s* two *d*. *Educ:* Stonyhurst Coll.; Lincoln Coll., Oxford. Called to the Bar, Middle Temple, 1949; Dep. Chm., W Riding of Yorks QS, 1967–71; Recorder of Halifax, 1971; a Recorder and Hon. Recorder of Halifax, 1972–73. Mem., Parole Bd, 1995–2001. *Recreation:* golf. *Address:* Myrtle Garth, Rossett Beck Close, Harrogate HG2 9NU.

COTTON, Richard Selkirk; Commercial Consultant, Iraq Britain Business Council, since 2014; *b* 29 March 1947; *s* of Albert George Cotton and Vera May Cotton. *Educ:* Coll. of Estate Mgt (BSc (Estate Mgt) London); Wye Coll., London Univ. (Dip. Farm Business Admin). Cluttons, subseq. Cluttons LLP, 1970–2009: Partner, 1976; Sen. Partner, 2003–09; Dir, Cluttons Private Finance Ltd, 2006–09. Property Dir, Residential Land, 2010–12; Hd, Mktg and Leasing, Basra Internat. Oil and Gas Free Zone, 2012–14. Non-exec. Dir, Go Native, 2009–; Chm., First Penthouse plc, 2009–. Chm., UAE Br., 1980–83, Mem., Brooke Rev. Cttee, 2004, Mem., Mgt Bd, 2009–Jan. 2016, RICS. Mem., Chartered Surveyors' Co., 1997– (Master, 2006–07). *Recreations:* golf, walking, bridge, travel, theatre. *Address:* 21C Sunderland Terrace, W2 5PA. *T:* 07885 807816.

COTTRELL, Amanda Arianwen Cecilia, OBE 2011; DL; Chairman, Visit Kent, since 2007; *b* Windsor, Berks, 22 Sept. 1941; *d* of Stafford Vaughan Stephen Howard and Mary Gracia Howard (*née* Neville); *m* 1967, Michael Noel Francis Cottrell; two *s* two *d*. *Educ:* St George's Sch., Clarens, Montreux; Sch. of Mus. of Fine Arts, Boston, Mass (Dip.). Magistrate, 1983–2006, High Sheriff 2006–07, DL 2011, Kent. Patron: Produced in Kent, 2006–; Hadlow Coll., 2013–; Trustee, Canterbury Cath., 2007–; Mem. Bd, Visit England, 2011–. Chm., Communities and Partnerships Framework, Dio. of Canterbury, 2013–. County Pres., Kent, Guide Assoc., 2003–. Kent Ambassador, 2006–. Hon. Fellow, Canterbury Christchurch Univ., 2010. Hon. DCL Kent, 2011. *Recreations:* painting, gardening, walking. *Address:* Visit Kent, 28–30 St Peter's Street, Canterbury, Kent CT1 2BQ. *T:* (01227) 812900. *E:* chairman@visitkent.co.uk.

COTTRELL, Prof. David John, FRCPsych; Professor of Child and Adolescent Psychiatry, since 1994, and Dean of Medicine, 2008–13, University of Leeds; *b* Leigh-on-Sea, 22 June 1956; *s* of John Geoffrey and Eileen Beatrice Cottrell; *m* 1985, Amanda Caroline Stroud; two *s*. *Educ:* Westcliff High Sch. for Boys; Hertford Coll., Oxford (BA Hons Physiol Sci. 1976; MA 1984); Westminster Med. Sch., Univ. of London (MB BS 1979). MRCPsych 1983, FRCPsych 1999. Lectr in Child and Adolescent Psychiatry, St George's Hosp. Med. Sch., Univ. of London, 1984–87; Sen. Lectr in Child and Adolescent Psychiatry, London Hosp. Med. Coll., 1987–93; Dir, Learning and Teaching, Sch. of Medicine, Univ. of Leeds, 1999–2006. Non-exec. Dir, Bradford Teaching Hosps Foundn Trust, 2008–12. Trustee and Director: YoungMinds, 2005–; Nat. Youth Adv. Service, 2013–. *Publications:* (jtly) What Works for Whom: a critical review of treatments for children and adolescents, 2002, 2nd edn 2014; (jtly) Developing Multi-professional Teamwork for Integrated Children's Services, 2006, 2nd edn 2010; contrib. articles to scientific med. jls on child and adolescent psychiatry. *Recreations:* rowing, reading, France.
See also Bishop of Chelmsford.

COTTRELL, Peter John Waraker, AO 1987; OBE 1978; Director, SAHF Enterprises, 2004–08; *b* 25 May 1928; *s* of Knowles Waraker Cottrell and Elmira Grenfell Cottrell; *m* 1952, Barbara Jean Wheeler (*d* 2011); two *s* two *d*. *Educ:* Sydney Univ. (BEng, MEng; Univ. Medal (Mech. Eng) 1951); Birmingham Univ. (Postgrad. Dip. in Mgt). Cadet, Qld Irrigation Commn, 1945–46; cadet, then engr, Australian Dept of Munitions, 1947–60; Email Ltd: Manager, 1960–74; Man. Dir, 1974–92; Chm., 1993–98. Chairman: Export Finance & Insurance Corp., 1983–86; Pacifica Gp Ltd, 1989–95; Scania Australia Pty Ltd, 1991–2003; Adelaide Steamship Co. Ltd, 1992–99; Boral Ltd, 1994–2000; Adsteam Marine Ltd, 1997–2001; Dep. Chm., Australian Telecommunications Commn, 1982–87; Dir, Nat. Australia Bank, 1985–98. Vice-Pres., Business Council of Australia, 1991–92. Hon. FIEAust 1994. Hon. Life Mem., Sydney Adventist Hosp. Fedn, 2008. Hon. DBus Charles Sturt Univ., 1996. Sir James Kirby Medal, IProdE, 1986; Sir Charles McGrath Award, Aust. Marketing Inst., 1989. *Recreations:* golf, family activities. *Address:* 4 Canberra Avenue, Turramurra, NSW 2074, Australia. *T:* (2) 99839836. *Clubs:* Royal Sydney Yacht Squadron; Pymble Golf (Sydney).

COTTRELL, Richard John; author and internet journalist; *b* 11 July 1943; *s* of John Cottrell and Winifred (*née* Barter); *m* 1st, 1965, Dinah Louise (*née* David) (marr. diss. 1986); two *d*; 2nd, 1987, Tracy Katherine (*née* Wade) (marr. diss. 1996); one *d*; 3rd, 1997, Liliana (*née* Velitchkova) (marr. diss. 2000); 4th, 2001, Diana (*née* Kiebdoj); two *d*. *Educ:* Court Fields Sch., Wellington, Somerset. Journalist: Wellington Weekly News, 1958; South Devon Jl, 1960; Topic (internat. news weekly), 1962; Evening Argus, Brighton, 1963; Lincolnshire Standard, 1964; Evening Post, Bristol, 1965; TWW, subseq. HTV, 1967–79. Chairman: RCA Ltd, 1989–94; Rail Central Europe, 1994–2002. Contested (C) Bristol, European Parly elecn, 1989. MEP (C) Bristol, 1979–89; Sec., backbench cttee, European Dem. Gp, 1979; Member: Transport Cttee, 1979–83; External Econ. Relns Cttee, 1979–82; Information Cttee, 1981–84; ACP-EEC Convention, 1981–84; Agriculture Cttee, 1982–86; Rules Cttee, 1982–89; Environment Cttee, 1983–89; Budget Cttee, 1983–86; Energy Cttee, 1986–88; deleg. to China, 1987. Pres., Euroconsult Ltd, 2002–08. Ed., Warsaw Business Jl, 2004–05. *Publications:* Energy, the Burning Question for Europe (jtly), 1981; (ed and contrib.) Transport for Europe, 1982; Blood on their Hands: the killing of Ann Chapman, 1987; The Sacred Cow, 1987; Gladio: NATO's dagger at the heart of Europe, 2011; Doctor Who?: atomic bomber Beeching and his war on the railways, 2013; Love Story: how Thatcher and Blair made the new British nationalism; contribs to Encounter, Contemporary Review, Foreign Policy Jl, End the Lie. *Recreations:* travel, reading, transport studies, appreciation of real ale, astronomy, ornithology, maintenance of a large private library, philosophy, psychoanalysis, cooking, economics.

COTTRELL, Rt Rev. Stephen Geoffrey; *see* Chelmsford, Bishop of.

COTTRELL-BOYCE, Frank; writer; Professor of Reading and Communication, Liverpool Hope University, since 2012; *b* Liverpool, 23 Sept. 1959; *s* of Francis and Joan Boyce; *m* 1983, Denise Cottrell; four *s* three *d*. *Educ:* W Park High Sch., St Helens; Keble Coll., Oxford (BA, DPhil). Screenplays: Forget About Me, 1990; Butterfly Kiss, 1995; Welcome to Sarajevo, 1997; Hilary and Jackie, 1998; The Claim, 2000; 24 Hour Party People, 2002; Code 46, 2003; Millions, 2004 (Best Screenplay, BIFA, 2005); A Cock and Bull Story, 2005; Grow Your Own, 2007; scriptwriter, London 2012 Olympics opening ceremony; *television* includes: God on Trial, 2008; Framed, 2009. FRSA. *Publications:* The Claim (play), 2001; novels for children: Millions, 2004 (Carnegie Medal, CLIP, 2005); Framed, 2006; Cosmic, 2008; Desirable, 2008; The Unforgotten Coat, 2011 (Guardian Children's Fiction Prize, 2012); Chitty Chitty Bang Bang Flies Again, 2011; Chitty Chitty Bang Bang and the Race Against Time, 2013; Chitty Chitty Bang Bang Over the Moon, 2014; The Astounding Broccoli Boy, 2015. *Recreations:* running, fencing, desk avoidance, involved in many community projects including Plaza Community Cinema, Liverpool. *Address:* c/o Greg Hunt, Independent Talent Group, 40 Whitfield Street, W1T 2RH.

COTTS, Sir Richard Crichton Mitchell, 4th Bt *cr* 1921, of Coldharbour Wood, Rogate, Sussex; *b* 26 July 1946; *er s* of Sir Robert Crichton Mitchell Cotts, 3rd Bt and Barbara Mary Winifrede (*d* 1982), *o d* of Captain H. J. A. Throckmorton, RN; *S* father, 1995, but his name does not appear on the Official Roll of the Baronetage. *Educ:* Oratory Sch. *Heir: b* Hamish William Anthony Mitchell Cotts [*b* 15 Sept. 1951; *m* 1995, Merlyn Mattiuzzo; three *s* three *d*].

COUCHER, Iain Michael; Managing Director, Alvarez & Marsal Corporate Solutions (Europe) LLP, since 2012; *b* 22 Aug. 1961; *s* of Brian and Daphne Coucher; *m* 1993, Tanya Nightingale; one *s* one *d*. *Educ:* Ashville Coll., Harrogate; Imperial Coll., London (BSc Eng Hons Aeronautical Engrg); Henley Mgt Coll. (MBA). Defence project design, Hunting Engrg, and Marconi, 1982–85; project manager and dir, then Head of Transport, EDS, then SD-Scicon, 1985–97; Chief Executive: TranSys Consortium, 1997–99; Tube Lines Gp, 1999–2001; Network Rail: Man. Dir, Jan.–Sept. 2002; Dep. Chief Exec., 2002–07; Chief. Exec., 2007–10; Chief Exec., LBC Tank Terminals, 2014–15. Dir, Rly Safety and Standards Bd, 2003–10. *Recreations:* cycling, birdwatching, films. *Address:* Alvarez & Marsal Corporate Solutions (Europe) LLP, 1 Finsbury Circus, EC2M 7EB.

COUCHMAN, James Randall; *b* 11 Feb. 1942; *s* of Stanley Randall Couchman and Alison Margaret Couchman; *m* 1967, Barbara Jean (*née* Heilbrun); one *s* one *d*. *Educ:* Cranleigh School; King's College, Newcastle upon Tyne; Univ. of Durham. Oil industry, 1964–70; Public House Manager, family company, 1970–74; Gen. Manager, family licensed trade co., 1974–80, Director, 1980–95. Member (C): Bexley LBC, 1974–82 (Chm., Social Services, 1975–78, 1980–82); Oxford CC, 2005–13 (Cabinet Mem. for Adult Social Services, 2006–10, for Finance and Property, 2010–12). Chm., Bexley HA, 1981–83. Member: Assoc. of Metropolitan Authorities Social Services Cttee, 1975–80; Central Council for Educn and Training of Social Workers, 1976–80; Governor, Nat. Inst. for Social Workers, 1976–80. MP (C) Gillingham, 1983–97; contested (C) same seat, 1997. PPS to Minister of State for Social Security, 1984–86, to Minister of Health, 1986–88, to Chancellor of Duchy of Lancaster, 1988–89, to Sec. of State for Social Security, 1989–90, to Lord Pres. of the Council and Leader of the House, 1995–97. Member: Social Services Select Cttee, 1983–85; Select Cttee on Health, 1990–92; Public Accounts Cttee, 1992–95; Select Cttee on NI, 1995–97. Fellow, Industry and Parlt Trust, 1987. Mem., Vintners' Co. *Recreations:* travel, reading, listening to music, politics. *Address:* 4 Shelley Close, Banstead, Surrey SM7 1EE. *T:* (01737) 363020.

COUCHMAN, Martin, OBE 2005; Deputy Chief Executive, British Hospitality Association, since 1993; *b* 28 Sept. 1947; *s* of late Frederick Alfred James Couchman and Pamela Mary Couchman (*née* Argent); *m* 1983, Carolyn Mary Constance Roberts; three *s* one *d*. *Educ:* Sutton Valence Sch.; Exeter Coll., Oxford (BA Jurisprudence). Building Industry, 1970–77; National Economic Development Office, 1977–92: Industrial Advr, 1977–84; Hd of Administration, 1984–87; on secondment as UK Dir of European Year of the Environment, 1987–88; Sec., NEDC, 1988–92. Chm., Social Affairs, HOTREC, Hospitality Europe (formerly European Confedn of Nat. Assocs of Hotels, Restaurants, Cafés and Similar Estabts), 2001–13 (Mem. Exec. Cttee, 1997–2000); Chm., CBI Sectoral Employment Issues Cttee, 2000–10. Mem., Green Alliance, 1988–. FRSA 1988. *Recreations:* Anglo-Saxon history, armchair archaeology, amateur dramatics. *Address:* British Hospitality Association, Queens House, 55–56 Lincoln's Inn Fields, WC2A 3BH.

COUGHLAN, John Joseph, CBE 2009; Director of Children's Services, since 2005, and Deputy Chief Executive, since 2009, Hampshire County Council; Director of Children's Services, Isle of Wight Council, since 2013; *b* Birmingham, 19 April 1960; *s* of James Coughlan and Philomena Coughlan (*née* Swann); *m* 1994, Madeleine O'Connor; one *s* one *d*. *Educ:* Univ. of Leeds (BA Jt Hons 1982); Selly Oak Colls, Birmingham (CQSW 1988); Univ. of Birmingham (MBA 2001). Birmingham CC, 1982–97; Asst Dir, Social Services Dept, Dudley MBC, 1997–2001; Corporate Dir, Telford and Wrekin Council, 2001–05; on secondment as Interim Dir, Children and Young People, Haringey LBC, 2008. Pres., ADSS, 2006–07; Jt Pres., Assoc. of Dirs of Children's Services, 2007–08. *Recreations:* swimming, reading, walking, Birmingham City Football Club. *Address:* Hampshire County Council, Castle Avenue, Winchester SO23 8UG. *E:* john.coughlan@hants.gov.uk.

COUGHLIN, Michael Charles; Group Managing Director, Bathroom Brands Holdings (UK) Ltd, since 2014; *b* London, 13 May 1959; *s* of Dennis and Jean Louise Dorothy Coughlin; *m* 1986, Christine Ann Hance; two *s* one *d*. *Educ:* Thomas Bennett Sch.; Portsmouth Poly. (BA Hons Social Admin); Loughborough Univ. (Dip. ILAM); Croydon Coll. (Dip. Mgt Studies, Dip. CI Mktg). Recreation Officer, Crawley BC, 1981–84; Leisure Manager, Bexley London Bor., 1984–87; Hd of Leisure and Community Services, Elmbridge BC, 1987–97; Dir, Leisure and Cultural Services, 1997–2000, Planning and Envmt, 2000–02, Royal Bor. Windsor and Maidenhead; Chief Executive: Crawley BC, 2002–08; Reading BC, 2008–12. Exec. Dir, LGA, 2012–14. *Recreations:* music - playing guitar and bass, songwriting, performing, singing, squash - team and league, ballroom and latin dancing, family, friends and holidays, cooking. *Address:* Bathroom Brands Holdings (UK) Ltd, Lake View House, Rennie Drive, Dartford, Kent DA1 5FU. *T:* 07771 957640. *E:* michael.coughlin@crosswater.co.uk.

COUGHLIN, Vincent William; QC 2003; *b* 6 May 1957; *s* of Cornelius and Maureen Coughlin; *m* 1988, Elizabeth Anne Ray; one *s* two *d*. *Educ:* Christ's Hospital, Horsham; Queen Mary Coll., London (LLB Hons). Called to the Bar, Middle Temple, 1980; in practice, SE Circuit, specialising in criminal law and white collar fraud. *Recreations:* gypsy jazz guitar, classical guitar, cycling, mountain biking, sailing, home cooking. *Address:* 4 Breams Buildings, Chancery Lane, EC4A 1HP. *T:* (020) 7092 1900, *Fax:* (020) 7092 1999. *E:* clerks@4bb.co.uk. *Clubs:* Essex; Blackwater Sailing.

COULING, Neil William, CBE 2013; Director General, Universal Credit, Department for Work and Pensions, since 2014; *b* Ware, Herts, 12 Feb. 1964; *s* of Donald and Valerie Couling; *m* 1993, Kate Lloyd Jones; three *s* one *d*. *Educ:* Richard Hale Sch., Hertford; Univ. of Manchester (BA Hons Politics and Modern Hist. 1985). Admin. rôles, DHSS, then DSS, 1986–99; Principal Private Sec. to Sec. of State for DSS, then DWP, 2000–03; Director: Jobcentre Plus SE, 2003–06; Jobcentre Plus Benefit and Fraud, 2006–09; Benefit Strategy, 2009–12; Work Services and Hd, Jobcentre Plus, 2012–14. Non-executive Director: Govt Office of SE, 2004–06; Pension and Disability Carers Service, 2009–11. *Recreations:* walking in the Welsh hills and South Downs, my children, watching sci-fi; Secretary of Milland Tractor Appreciation Soc., 2014–. *Address:* Department for Work and Pensions, Caxton House, Tothill Street, SW1H 9NA. *E:* neil.couling@dwp.gsi.gov.uk.

COULL, Prof. Alexander, PhD; DSc; FRSE; FICE; Regius Professor of Civil Engineering, University of Glasgow, 1977–92; *b* 20 June 1931; *s* of William Coull and Jane Ritchie (*née* Reid); *m* 1962, Frances Bruce Moir; one *s* two *d*. *Educ:* Peterhead Acad.; Univ. of Aberdeen (BScEng, PhD; DSc 1983). FRSE 1971; FICE 1972, FIStructE 1973; Res. Asst, MIT, USA, 1955; Struct. Engr, English Electric Co. Ltd, 1955–57; Lectr in Engrg, Univ. of Aberdeen, 1957–62; Lectr in Civil Engrg, Univ. of Southampton, 1962–66; Prof. of Struct. Engrg, Univ. of Strathclyde, 1966–76. Chm., Clyde Estuary Amenity Council, 1981–86. *Publications:* Tall Buildings, 1967; Fundamentals of Structural Theory, 1972; (with B. Stafford Smith) Tall Building Structures: Planning Analysis and Design, 1991; author or co-author of 130 res. papers in scientific jls. *Recreations:* golf, hill walking. *Address:* 4 Monaltrie Way, Ballater, Aberdeenshire AB35 5PS. *T:* (01339) 755766.

COULL, Ian David, FRICS; Chairman, Galliford Try plc, since 2011 (non-executive Director, since 2010); *b* 7 June 1950; *s* of John and Davina Coull; *m* 1971, Linda Shepherd; one *s* two *d*. *Educ:* Perth Acad.; Coll. of Estate Management. FRICS 1984. Dir, J. Sainsbury plc, 1988–2002; Chief Exec., Slough Estates, later Segro plc, 2003–10. Mem., London Regl Bd, Royal and Sun Alliance, 2001–11; non-exec. Dir, House of Fraser, 2003–06; non-exec. Mem., Pendragon plc, 2010–13. Co-Chair, London Sustainable Develt Commn, 2002–04; Member: Sustainable Construction Task Gp, 2003–04; Code for Sustainable Bldgs Sen. Steering Gp, 2004–11. Non-exec. Mem., Duchy of Lancaster Council, 2014–. Pres., British Property Fedn, 2005–06. Chm., P3 plc, 2012–. Chm., South Bank Employers Gp, 1994–2003. FRSA. *Recreations:* Rugby, golf, family. *Address:* Galliford Try plc, Cowley Business Park, Cowley, Uxbridge, Middx UB8 2AL. *Clubs:* Temple Golf; London Scottish Rugby; Marlow Rugby.

COULL, Maj.-Gen. John Taylor, CB 1992; FRCS; FRCSE; Medico-Legal Adviser, Army Medical Directorate, Ministry of Defence, 1992–97; *b* 4 March 1934; *s* of late John Sandeman Coull and Ethel Marjory (*née* Taylor); *m* 1958, Mildred Macfarlane; three *s*. *Educ:* Robert Gordon's College; Aberdeen Univ. Med. Sch. MB ChB. House appts, Aberdeen Royal Infirmary, 1958–60; Commissioned RAMC, 1960; Surgeon: Colchester Mil. Hosp., 1960–63; Queen Alexandra Mil. Hosp., 1963; Sen. Registrar, Edinburgh East Gen. Hosp., 1963–65; Royal Herbert Hosp., 1965–67; Sen. Registrar, Birmingham Accident Hosp., 1967; Consultant Surgeon, BMH Singapore, 1967–70; Lectr, Dept of Orthopaedics, Univ. of Edinburgh, 1970–71; Consultant Orthopaedic Surgeon, BAOR, 1971–77; Consultant Adviser in Orthop. Surgery and Sen. Consultant, Queen Elizabeth Mil. Hosp., 1977–86; Consulting Surgeon, HQ BAOR, 1986–88; Dir of Army Surgery, 1988–92. Hon. Col 202 (Midland) Field Hosp. RAMC (V), 1992–97; Col Comdt, RAMC, 1994–99. Mitchiner Meml Lectr, RAMC, 2001. QHS 1988–92. Mitchiner Medal, RCS, 1980. OStJ. GSM N

Ireland, 1976. *Publications:* chapters in: Field Pocket Surgery, 1981; R. Smith's The Hand, 1985; Trauma, 1989; articles in learned jls. *Recreations:* home maintenance, carpentry, gardening, travel. *Address:* Sheigra, 25 Braemar Road, Ballater AB35 5RL. *Club:* Royal Northern and University (Aberdeen).

COULSFIELD, Rt Hon. Lord; John Taylor Cameron; PC 2000; a Senator of the College of Justice in Scotland, 1987–2002; *b* 24 April 1934; *s* of late John Reid Cameron, MA, formerly Director of Education, Dundee; *m* 1964, Bridget Deirdre Sloan; no *c. Educ:* Fettes Coll.; Corpus Christi Coll., Oxford; Edinburgh Univ. BA (Oxon), LLB (Edinburgh). Admitted to Faculty of Advocates, 1960. Lecturer in Public Law, Edinburgh Univ., 1960–64. QC (Scot.) 1973; Keeper of the Advocates' Library, 1977–87; an Advocate-Depute, 1977–79. Judge, Courts of Appeal of Jersey and Guernsey, 1986–87; a Judge, Employment Appeal Tribunal, 1992–96; Mem., Scottish Court in the Netherlands, 2000–01; Judge of Appeal, Botswana, 2005–09. Chm., Medical Appeal Tribunals, 1985–87. Editor, Scottish Law and Practice Qly, 1995–2003. Chm., Esmée Fairbairn Foundn Inquiry, Alternatives to Prison, 2003–04. Chairman: Jt Standing Cttee on Legal Educn in Scotland, 1998–2003; Scottish Council for Internat. Arbitration, 2003–11. Trustee, Nat. Liby of Scotland, 2000–09. Hon. Mem., Soc. of Legal Scholars, 2006. *Publications:* Report Disclosures, Scots Criminal Law, 2007; (ed jtly) Gloag and Henderson, The Law of Scotland, 12th edn, 2007; articles in legal jls.

COULSHED, Brian Thomas; Headmaster, Parmiter's School, Hertfordshire, 1993–2010, now Emeritus Headmaster; *b* St Helens, Lancs, 11 March 1950; *s* of Thomas Cyril and Mary Ann Coulshed; *m* 1982, Gillian Margaret Dunsire; two *s. Educ:* West Park Grammar Sch., St Helens; Univ. of Manchester (BA Hons, PGCE). Asst teacher, then Hd of Year, Longdean Sch., Hemel Hempstead, 1972–79; Hd of Dept, then Hd of Year, Hemel Hempstead Sch., 1979–86; Dep. Headmaster, Goffs Sch., 1986–92. Vis. Fellow, St Catharine's Coll., Cambridge, 2000. Chm., SW Herts Heads' Assoc., 1999–2010. Pres., Herts Schs FA, 2004–. Vice-Chm., Parmiter's Almshouse Foundn, 2010–. Mem., 1912 Club. Gov., St Margaret's Sch., Bushey, 2011–. Freeman, City of London, 2015. Headteacher of the Year, 2007. *Publications:* The History of the Parmiter's Estates Foundation, 1997; The History of the Parmiter's Foundation, 2000, 2nd edn 2008. *Recreations:* cricket (playing mem., Leverstock Green CC, 1973–; mem., Herts Over 60s County XI), football, Rugby League (lifelong supporter of Liverpool FC and St Helens Rugby League FC). *E:* briancoulshed@hotmail.co.uk. *Clubs:* Leverstock Green Cricket (Pres., 2003–), Middx County Cricket.

COULSON, Mrs Ann Margaret; Chairman, Leamington Hastings Consolidated Charity, 1998–2011 (Trustee, 1992–2011); *b* 11 March 1935; *d* of Sidney Herbert Wood and Ada (*née* Mills); *m* 1958, Peter James Coulson; two *s* one *d. Educ:* The Grammar Sch., Chippenham, Wilts; UCL (BScEcon); Univ. of Manchester (DSA); Wolverhampton Technical Teachers' Coll. (CertEd). Hosp. Admin, 1956–62; Lectr in Econs and Management, Bromsgrove Coll. of Further Educn, 1968–76; Asst Dir, North Worcestershire Coll., 1976–80; Service Planning and Develt Co-ordinator, 1980–83, Regl Planning Administrator, 1983–88, Dir of Planning, 1988–91, W Midlands RHA; Gen. Manager, Age Concern, Solihull, 1991–94. City of Birmingham Dist Council, 1973–79; special interest in Social Services. Mem., IBA, 1976–81. Trustee, Age Concern, Warwicks, 1996–2007. *Recreations:* sailing, cooking, music, theatre. *Address:* Rowans, Leamington Hastings, near Rugby, Warwicks CV23 8DY. *T:* (01926) 633264.

COULSON, Frances Elaine; Managing Partner, Moon Beever, Solicitors, since 2000 (Partner, since 1988); *b* Sheffield, 23 Dec. 1961; *d* of Richard and Faith Gilbert; *m* 1983, Philip Coulson; three *d. Educ:* Sheffield High Sch. for Girls; King's Coll. London (LLB Hons 1983; Dip. EC Law 1991). Admitted as solicitor, 1986. Chm., Appeals Cttee, ACCA, 2006–12. Mem., Charity Cttee, Co. of Blacksmiths, 2009–. Pres., R3, 2011–12 (Chm., Fraud Gp, 2011–). Trustee, Fraud Adv. Panel, 2012–. Mem., Remuneration Panel, Braintree DC, 2014–. *Recreations:* equestrian, walking, reading. *Address:* Moon Beever, Bedford House, 21a John Street, WC1N 2BF. *T:* (020) 7400 7770, *Fax:* (020) 7400 7799. *E:* fcoulson@moonbeever.com. *Clubs:* Carlton, Adam Street.

COULSON, Hon. Sir Peter (David William), Kt 2008; **Hon. Mr Justice Coulson;** a Judge of the High Court of Justice, Queen's Bench Division, since 2008; Judge in Charge of Estates; *b* 31 March 1958; *s* of David Coulson and Pamela Coulson (*née* Shorter); *m* 1985, Veronica Lachkovic; one *s* two *d. Educ:* Lord Wandsworth Coll.; Univ. of Keele (BA Hons 1980). Called to the Bar, Gray's Inn, 1982 (Sir Malcolm Hilbery Award, 1982; Bencher, 2006); in practice, 1984–2004; QC 2001; Recorder, 2002–04; Sen. Circuit Judge, 2004–07; Presiding Judge, NE Circuit, 2011–14. Trustee, Orchard Vale Trust, 1999–. Mem. Bd, Acad. of St Martin in the Fields, 2009. Contributor, Lloyd's Law Reports: Professional Negligence, 1999–2000. Hon. DLaws Keele, 2012. *Publications:* (jtly) Professional Negligence and Liability, 2000; The Technology and Construction Court, 2006; Construction Adjudication, 2007, 3rd edn 2015. *Recreations:* British art 1750–1950, comedy, music, cricket, Watford FC. *Address:* Royal Courts of Justice, Strand, WC2A 2LL. *Club:* Travellers.

COULSON, Sarah April Louise; *see* Baxter, S. A. L.

COULSON, Prof. Timothy Neal, PhD; Professor of Zoology, University of Oxford, since 2013; Fellow, Jesus College, Oxford, since 2013; *b* Cambridge, 31 July 1968; *s* of Patrick Coulson and Anne Coulson; one *s* two *d. Educ:* Barton C of E Prim. Sch.; Comberton Village Coll., Cambridge; Hill Road Sixth Form Coll., Cambridge; Univ. of York (BSc Biol. 1990); Imperial Coll. London (PhD 1994). Res. Fellow, Inst. of Zool., 1994–2000; Res. Fellow, 2000–03, Lectr in Zool., 2003–04, Univ. of Cambridge; Imperial College London: Sen. Lectr, 2004–05; Reader, 2005–07; Prof. of Population Biol., 2007–12. *Publications:* 150 articles in scientific jls. *Recreations:* cycling, hiking, cooking, fieldwork. *Address:* 122 Southfield Road, Oxford OX4 1PA. *T:* 07872 850090. *E:* timothy.coulson@zoo.ox.ac.uk.

COULTER, Rev. Dr David George; QHC 2010; Chaplain General HM Land Forces, since 2014; *b* Belfast, 29 Dec. 1957; *s* of George Coulter and Elizabeth Coulter; *m* 1981, Grace Woods; two *s. Educ:* Regent House Sch.; Queen's Univ., Belfast (BA Hons); Univ. of St Andrews (BD Hons); Cranfield Univ. (MDA); Univ. of Edinburgh (PhD 1998). Officer, Royal Irish Rangers, 1976–85; Minister, C of S, 1989–; Chaplain, Royal Army Chaplains' Dept, 1989–. QCVS 1996. SBStJ 2011. *Recreations:* sailing, Nordic walking. *Address:* Headquarters Land Forces, MoD Chaplains (Army), Marlborough Lines, Andover, Hants SP11 8HJ. *T:* (01264) 381840. *E:* ArmyCG-CG@mod.uk. *Club:* Royal Air Force.

COULTER, Rev. Robert James, MBE 2010; Member (UU) Antrim North, Northern Ireland Assembly, 1998–2011; *b* 23 Oct. 1929; *m* 1956, Elizabeth Holmes; one *s* one *d. Educ:* Trinity Coll., Dublin (BA, MA, BD); Univ. of Ulster (MA Educn). Ordained, 1963, Minister, 1963–76, Presbyterian Church in Ireland; Lectr in Further and Higher Educn, 1976–93. Mem. (UU), Ballymena BC, 1985–2001; Mayor of Ballymena, 1993–96. Mem., NI Assembly Commn, 2007–11. *Recreation:* vintage vehicles. *Address:* 18 Springmount Road, Clough, Ballymena, Co. Antrim BT44 9QQ. *T:* (028) 2568 5694.

COULTON, Very Rev. Nicholas Guy; Residentiary Canon and Sub-Dean, Christ Church, Oxford, 2003–08, Canon Emeritus, since 2012; *b* 14 June 1940; *s* of Nicholas Guy Coulton and Audrey Florence Furneaux Coulton (*née* Luscombe); *m* 1978, Edith Mary Gainford; one *s* two *d. Educ:* Blundell's School, Tiverton; Cuddesdon Coll., Oxford; BD London (ext.) 1972; MA Oxon 2007. Admitted Solicitor, 1962; Asst Solicitor, Burges, Salmon & Co., Bristol, 1962–65. Ordination training, 1965–67; Curate of Pershore Abbey with Birlingham, Wick and Pinvin, 1967–71; Domestic Chaplain to Bishop of St Albans, 1971–75; Vicar of St Paul's, Bedford, 1975–90; part-time Industrial Chaplain, 1976–89; Provost, subseq. Dean, St Nicholas' Cathedral, Newcastle upon Tyne, 1990–2003, now Dean Emeritus. Proctor in Convocation, 1985–90; Hon. Canon of St Alban's Cathedral, 1989–90. Member: Gen. Synod of C of E, 1998–2003; Legal Adv. Commn of C of E, 2001–11. Mem., USPG Delegn to Province of West Indies, 1999. Chm., NE CCJ, 1991–2002; Member: NE Assembly, 2002–03; Churches' Refugee Network, 2008–. Dir, Ecclesiastical Insurance Gp, 1997–2005. Governor: Newcastle upon Tyne Church High Sch., 1990–2003; Dame Allan's Schs, 1990–2003; Ripon Coll., Cuddesdon, 2002–08; Christ Church Cathedral Sch., 2003–08. Pres., Friends of Pershore Abbey, 2006–11. OStJ 2002. *Publications:* Twelve Years of Prayer, 1989; (ed) The Bible, The Church and Homosexuality, 2005; contrib. articles and book reviews in Ecclesiastical Law Jl, 2010–15. *Recreations:* gardening, reading, listening to music, historical exploration, national asylum work for the churches. *Address:* 123 Merewood Avenue, Oxford OX3 8EQ.

COUNSELL, Her Honour Hazel Rosemary; *see* Fallon, Her Honour H. R.

COUNT, Dr Brian Morrison; Chairman: Jacoma Estates Ltd, since 2008; InfraCo Africa Ltd, since 2014; *b* 18 Feb. 1951; *s* of Douglas John Count and Ethel Sarah Count; *m* 1975, Jane Elizabeth Hudson; three *s. Educ:* King's College, Cambridge (MA Maths); Exeter Univ. (PhD Physics). Central Electricity Generating Board: Research Dept, 1974–84; Planning Dept, 1984–90; National Power: Project Develt Dir, 1990–95; Dir of Ops, 1995–96; Mem. Bd, 1996–2000; Man. Dir, UK, 1999–2000; Innogy Holdings: Chief Operating Officer, 2000–01; Chief Exec., 2001–03; CEO, RWE Trading, 2003–05. Non-executive Director: Eskom, 2002–08; Sterecycle Ltd, 2008–. Mem., Industrial Develt Adv. Bd, DTI, later BERR, then BIS, 2004–10. *Recreations:* golf, Rugby, entertaining. *Address:* Oakwood House, Blindmans Gate, Woolton Hill, Newbury, Berks RG20 9XD.

COUPER, Prof. Alastair Dougal; Research Professor, Seafarers International Research Centre for Safety and Occupational Health, University of Wales Cardiff, 1997–98 (Director, 1995–97); Emeritus Professor, University of Cardiff, since 1999; *b* 4 June 1931; *s* of Daniel Alexander Couper and Davina Couper (*née* Rilley); *m* 1958, Norma Milton; two *s* two *d. Educ:* Robert Gordon's School of Navigation (Master Mariner); Univ. of Aberdeen (MA, DipEd); Australian National Univ. (PhD). FNI 1979. Cadet and Navigating Officer, Merchant Navy, 1947–57; student, Univ. of Aberdeen, 1958–62, postgraduate teaching course, 1962–63; Research Schol., Sch. of Pacific Studies, ANU, Canberra, 1963–66; Lectr, Univ. of Durham, 1967–70; Prof. of Maritime Studies, UWIST, then UWCC, 1970–97; Prof., World Maritime Univ. (UN), Malmö, Sweden, 1987–89 (on secondment). UN Consultant, 1972–98; Chm., Maritime Bd, CNAA, 1978–85; Assessor, Chartered Inst. of Transport, 1976–85; Founder Mem., Council, British Maritime League, 1982–85; Member: Exec. Bd, Law of the Sea Inst., USA, 1989–95; British Commn, Internat. Commn for Maritime History, 1996–99; Adv. Bd, Seafarers' Rights Internat., 2010–; Adv. Bd, Internat. Ocean Inst., 2011–. Thomas Gray Meml Lectr, RSA, 2003. Pres., Neptune Assoc. of Maritime Res. Insts, 1997–98. Trustee, Nat. Maritime Mus., 1992–2000. Editor (and Founder), Journal of Maritime Policy and Management, 1973–84. Hon. DSc Plymouth, 1995. *Publications:* Geography of Sea Transport, 1971; The Law of the Sea, 1978; (ed) Times Atlas of the Oceans, 1983; contrib. Pacific, in World Atlas of Agriculture, 1969; Pacific in Transition (ed Brookfield), 1973; New Cargo Handling Techniques: implications for port employment and skills, 1986; (ed) Development and Social Change in the Pacific, 1988; (ed) The Shipping Revolution, 1992; Voyages of Abuse: Seafarers, Human Rights and International Shipping, 1999; (contrib.) Seafarers' Rights, 2005; Sailors and Traders: a maritime history of the Pacific peoples, 2009; several UN Reports, UNCTAD, ILO, IMO; articles in jls; conf. papers. *Recreations:* hill walking, sailing, archaeology, Pacific history. *Address:* 91 Bishops Walk, Llandaff, Cardiff CF5 2HB. *T:* (029) 2055 5178.

COUPER, Heather Anita, CBE 2007; CPhys, FInstP; FRAS; science broadcaster and author, since 1983; Director, Pioneer TV Productions, 1988–99; *b* 2 June 1949; *o d* of late George Couper Elder Couper and Anita Couper (*née* Taylor). *Educ:* St Mary's Grammar Sch., Northwood, Middx; Univ. of Leicester (BSc Hons Astronomy and Physics); Linacre Coll., Oxford. FRAS 1970; CPhys 1999; FInstP 1999. Management trainee, Peter Robinson Ltd, 1967–69; Res. Asst, Cambridge Observatories, 1969–70; Lectr, Greenwich Planetarium, Old Royal Observ., 1977–83. Gresham Prof. of Astronomy, 1993–96. Mem., Millennium Commn, 1994–2006. President: Brit. Astron. Assoc., 1984–86; Jun. Astron. Soc., 1987–89. Presenter on television: Heavens Above, 1981; Spacewatch, 1983; The Planets, 1985; The Stars, 1988; The Neptune Encounter, 1989; A Close Encounter of the Second Kind, 1992; Stephen Hawking: a profile, 2002; producer/narrator: ET—Please Phone Earth, 1992; Space Shuttle Discovery, 1993; Electric Skies, 1994; Arthur C. Clarke: the Visionary, 1995; On Jupiter, 1996; Black Holes, 1997; narrator/presenter: Rendezvous in Space, and Avalanche, 1995; Raging Planet, 1997; The Sci-Fi Files, Killer Earth, and Stormforce, 1998; producer, Universe, 1999; presenter/producer, Space Shuttle: human time bomb?, 2003; presenter on radio: Science Now, 1983; Cosmic Pursuits, 1985; Seeing Stars, 1991–2001; ET on Trial, 1993; Starwatch, 1996; Sun Science, 1999; The Essential Guide to the 21st Century (series), 2000; Red Planet (series), 2003; Worlds Beyond (series), 2005; Arthur C. Clarke: the Science Behind the Fiction, 2005; A Brief Guide to Infinity, 2006; Britain's Space Race, 2007; Cosmic Quest (series), 2008; also appearances and interviews on wide variety of television and radio progs. Astronomy columnist: The Independent; BBC Focus Mag. Hon. DLitt Loughborough, 1991; Hon. DSc: Hertfordshire, 1994; Leicester, 1997. *Publications:* Exploring Space, 1980; (jtly) Heavens Above, 1981; Journey into Space, 1984; (jtly) Starfinder, 1984; (jtly) The Halley's Comet Pop-Up Book, 1985; (jtly) The Universe: a 3-dimensional study, 1985; Space Scientist series, 1985–87: Comets and Meteors; The Planets; The Stars; jointly: The Sun; The Moon; Galaxies and Quasars; Satellites and Spaceprobes; Telescopes and Observatories; *with Nigel Henbest:* Space Frontiers, 1978; The Restless Universe, 1982; Physics, 1983; Astronomy, 1983; The Planets, 1985; The Stars, 1988; The Space Atlas, 1992; Guide to the Galaxy, 1994; How the Universe Works, 1994; Black Holes, 1996; Big Bang, 1997; Is Anybody Out There?, 1998; To the Ends of the Universe, 1998; Space Encyclopedia, 1999; Universe, 1999; Mars: the inside story of the red planet, 2001; Extreme Universe, 2001; Philip's Stargazing, annually 2004–; Out of this World, 2007; Universe, 2007; The History of Astronomy, 2007; The Story of Astronomy, 2012; The Secret Life of Space, 2015; The Astronomy Bible, 2015; numerous articles in nat. newspapers and magazines. *Recreations:* travel, the English countryside, classical music; wine, food and winemaking. *Address:* David Higham Associates, 7th Floor, Waverley House, 7–12 Noel Street, W1F 8GQ. *Club:* Groucho.

COUPER, Sir James George, 7th Bt *cr* 1841; *b* 27 Oct. 1977; *o s* of Sir Nicholas Couper, 6th Bt and of his 1st wife, Kirsten Henrietta, *d* of Major George Burrell MacKean; *S* father 2002. *Heir: cousin* Jonathan Every Couper [*b* 26 Feb. 1931; *m* 1986, Heather Agnes Heath].

COUPLAND, George, PhD; FRS 2007; Director, Max Planck Institute for Plant Breeding Research, Cologne, since 2001; *b* 20 Dec. 1959; *s* of Walter Archibald Coupland and Margaret Coupland; *m* 1991, Jane Parker; one *s* one *d. Educ:* Univ. of Glasgow (BSc 1st Cl. Hons Microbiol. 1981); Univ. of Edinburgh (PhD 1984). Postdoctoral experience, Inst. for Genetics, Univ. of Cologne and Max Planck Inst. for Plant Breeding Res., Cologne, 1985–88; res. gp leader, Plant Breeding Inst., Cambridge and Cambridge Lab., John Innes Centre, Norwich, 1987–2001. Hon. Lectr, UEA, 1993–2001; Hon. Prof., Univ. of Cologne, 2003–. Cttee, Genetical Soc. of UK, 1997–2001; Cttee, UK RAE, 2007–08. Mem., EMBO, 2001; Associate Member: Class of Scis, Royal Acad. of Belgium, 2006; NAS, USA, 2012. *Publications:* articles in learned jls incl. Nature, Science, Cell. *Recreations:* ornithology, travel.

Address: Max Planck Institute for Plant Breeding Research, Plant Developmental Biology, Carl von Linné Weg 10, 50829 Köln, Germany. *T:* (221) 5062205, *Fax:* (221) 5062207. *E:* coupland@mpipz.mpg.de.

COURAGE, Maj.-Gen. Walter James, CB 1994; MBE 1979; Director, The Risk Advisory Group plc (formerly Ltd), since 1997; *b* 25 Sept. 1940; *s* of late Walter Henry Phipps and of Nancy Mary Courage (*née* Reeves, who *m* 3rd, John Frederick Gardner), and step *s* of late Lt-Col Nigel Anthony Courage, MC; *m* 1964, Lavinia Patricia, *d* of late John Emerson Crawhall Wood; one *s* one *d. Educ:* Abingdon Sch.; RMA, Sandhurst. Commnd 5th Royal Inniskilling Dragoon Guards, 1961; served BAOR, Libya and Canada, 1961–81; commanded Regt, 1982–84; Div. Col Staff Coll., 1985; Comdr 4th Armoured Bde, 1985–88; Chief of Staff, UN Force in Cyprus, 1988–90; Chief Joint Services Liaison Officer, BAOR, Bonn, 1990–94; Chief, Ext. Affairs Div., Germany, 1994–95; Dir-Gen., TA, 1995–96. Member: Bd, British American Business Inc., 2001–; Adv. Bd, Moore, Clayton & Co., 2002–07; Dir, Janusian Security Risk Mgt, 2002–07; Chm., Future Digital Footprint. Consultant: AMEC Project Investments Ltd, 1997–2004; DLA, 2000–04. Trustee, Shotover Estate, 2005–. FCMI. *Recreations:* shooting, cricket, ski-ing, polo, fine art. *Address:* Brigmerston Farm House, Brigmerston, Salisbury, Wilts SP4 8HX. *Clubs:* Cavalry and Guards, MCC; I Zingari.

COURCY; *see* de Courcy, family name of Baron Kingsale.

COURT, Rt Rev. David; *see* Grimsby, Bishop Suffragan of.

COURT, Hon. Richard Fairfax, AC 2003; Premier of Western Australia, Treasurer and Minister for Public Sector Management and for Federal Affairs, 1993–2001; *b* 27 Sept. 1947; *s* of Hon. Sir Charles Walter Michael Court, AK, KCMG, OBE; *m* 1989, Joanne, *d* of B. Moffat; one *d*, and one *s* one *d* by previous marriage. *Educ:* Univ. of Western Australia (BCom). Man. Dir, Court Marine Pty, 1974–82. MLA (L) Nedlands, WA, 1982–2001; Shadow Minister for Small Business, 1986; Dep. Leader, Parly Lib. Party, 1987–90; Shadow Minister for: Resources, Develt, Mines, Fuel and Energy, NW and Goldfields, 1990–91; Resource and Industrial Develt, Mines and Aboriginal Affairs, 1991–92; Public Sector Management, also Leader of the Opposition and Shadow Treas., 1992–93; Minister for: Tourism, 1994–95; Youth, 1996–97. Chm., Resource Investment Strategy Consultants, 2001–. Non-exec. Dir, Iron Ore Hldgs Ltd, 2007–.

COURT, Robert Vernon; Global Head of External Affairs, Rio Tinto, since 2009; *b* 28 Jan. 1958; *s* of Derrick and Catherine Court; *m* 1983, Rebecca Ophelia Sholl; three *s* one *d. Educ:* Churchill Coll., Cambridge (MA). Entered FCO, 1981; Bangkok, 1983–86; First Sec., FCO, 1986–88; Private Sec. to Minister of State, 1988–90; First Secretary: UK Delegn to NATO, 1990–93; UK Perm. Repn to EU, 1993–96; PA to Chm. and CEO, 1997–99, Gp Co-ordinator for Sustainable Develt, 2000–01, Rio Tinto plc; Dep. High Comr, Canberra, 2001–05; Vice-Pres., Govt Affairs Internat., GlaxoSmithKline, 2005–09. *Recreations:* sub-aqua diving, swimming, travel. *Address:* c/o Rio Tinto, 2 Eastbourne Terrace, W2 6LG. *E:* robert.v.court@gmail.com. *Club:* Royal Automobile.

COURTAULD, George; Vice Lord-Lieutenant of Essex, 2003–13; landowner and farmer; *b* 2 May 1938; *s* of George Courtauld and Claudine Suzanne (*née* Booth); *m* 1962, Dominie Jennifer Faith Mirren Riley-Smith; two *s* two *d. Educ:* Gordonstoun; Pembroke Coll., Cambridge (BA 1961). Commnd Grenadier Guards, 1957. With textile manufacturer, Courtaulds Ltd, 1962–83. Queen's Messenger, 1985–2000. Chairman: Haven Gateway Partnership, 2002–08 (Pres., 2008–); NE Essex Strategic LSC, 2004; Harwich Regeneration Gp, 2005–10; Essex Br., Prince's Trust, 2005–08; Essex Envmt Trust, 2005–; Essex Women's Adv. Gp, 2007–; Rural Community Council, Essex, 2008–; Harwich and Stour Valley Area Bd, 2010–12. President: Friends of Essex Churches, 2002–14; Chelmsford and Mid Essex Samaritans, 2003–14; Halstead Allotment Holders and Leisure Gardeners Assoc., 2006–; Essex Br., SSAFA, 2008–; Vice President: Essex Co. Scout Council, 2002–13; Essex Community Foundn, 2004–. Master Patron, Public Catalogue Foundn, Essex, 2006–. Member: Halstead RDC, 1967–74; Braintree DC, 1974–85. Freeman, City of London, 1959; Liveryman: Weavers' Co., 1961–; Goldsmiths' Co., 1970–. High Sheriff, 2001–02, DL 2002, Essex. *Publications:* An Axe, A Spade and Ten Acres, 1983; Odd Noises from the Barn, 1985; The Travels of a Fat Bulldog, 1995; The Fat Bulldog Roams Again, 1998; The Last Travels of a Fat Bulldog, 2000; (ed) Essex Girl's Limericks, 2010. *Recreations:* travel, plant collecting, forestry. *Address:* Knight's Barn, Colne Engaine, Earls Colne, Essex CO6 2JG. *Clubs:* White's, Special Forces; Essex.

COURTENAY, family name of **Earl of Devon**.

COURTENAY, Lord; Jack Haydon Langer Courtenay; *b* 16 Aug. 2009; *s* and *heir* of Earl of Devon, *qv*.

COURTENAY, Ralph Andrew, RIBA; FCSD; Managing Director, 1992–2007, Senior Vice President, 1998–2007, HOK Europe; *b* 21 Feb. 1943; *s* of Reginald William James Courtenay and Joyce Louisa Courtenay; *m* 1969, Brenda Ruth Caudle; two *d. Educ:* Abbey Sch., London; NE London Poly. (Dist. in Thesis). RIBA 1972; FCSD 1984. Austin-Smith, London, 1978–89: Partner, 1980–89; Man. Partner, 1984–89; own practice, Ralph Courtenay Associates, 1989–92; joined HOK, London, 1992, Man. Dir, 1995–2007; Dir, HOK Worldwide, 1996–2007; Chm., HOK European Architects Network, 2000–07. Mem., Soc. of Architectural Illustrators, 1982. *Publications:* contrib. articles to Building Design, Architects Jl and Architectural Rev. *Recreations:* marathon running, golf, tennis, ski-ing, painting, music, opera. *Address:* 1 The Orchards, Mill Road, Winchelsea, E Sussex TN36 4HJ. *Clubs:* Royal Automobile, Arts; Hemstead Forest Golf, Sissinghurst Tennis.

COURTENAY, Sir Thomas Daniel, (Sir Tom), Kt 2001; actor; *b* 25 Feb. 1937; *s* of late Thomas Henry Courtenay and Annie Eliza Quest; *m* 1st, 1973, Cheryl Kennedy (marr. diss. 1982); 2nd, 1988, Isabel Crossley. *Educ:* Kingston High Sch., Hull; University Coll., London (Fellow 1994). RADA, 1958–60; started acting professionally, 1960; Old Vic, 1960–61: Konstantin Treplieff, Poins, Feste and Puck; Billy Liar, Cambridge Theatre, June 1961–Feb. 1962 and on tour; Andorra, National Theatre (guest), 1964; The Cherry Orchard, and Macbeth, Chichester, 1966; joined 69 Theatre Co., Manchester, 1966: Charley's Aunt, 1966; Romeo, Playboy of the Western World, 1967; Hamlet (Edinburgh Festival), 1968; She Stoops to Conquer, (transferred to Garrick), 1969; Peer Gynt, 1970; Charley's Aunt, Apollo, 1971; Time and Time Again, Comedy, 1972 (Variety Club of GB Stage Actor Award, 1972); The Norman Conquests, Globe, 1974; The Fool, Royal Court, 1975; Prince of Homburg, The Rivals, Manchester (opening prods of The Royal Exchange), 1976; Otherwise Engaged, NY, 1977; Clouds, Duke of York's, 1978; Crime and Punishment, Manchester, 1978; The Dresser, Manchester and Queen's, 1980 (Drama Critics Award and New Standard Award for best actor, 1980), NY 1981; The Misanthrope, Manchester and Round House, 1981; Andy Capp, Manchester and Aldwych, 1982; Jumpers, Manchester, 1984; Rookery Nook, Shaftesbury, 1986; The Hypochondriac, Lyric, Hammersmith, 1987; Dealing with Clair, Richmond, 1988; The Miser, Manchester, 1991; Moscow Stations (one-man show), Traverse Theatre, Edinburgh, 1993, 1994, Garrick, 1994 (Evening Standard and Critics Circle Award), NY, 1995; Poison Pen, Manchester, 1993; Uncle Vanya, NY, 1995, Manchester, 2001; Art, Wyndham's, 1996; King Lear, Manchester, 1999; Pretending to be Me (one-man show), W Yorks Playhouse, 2002, Comedy, 2003; The Home Place, Gate, Dublin, transf. Comedy, 2005; UK and Ireland tour, Pretending to be Me, 2010–11. Began acting in films, 1962. *Films:* The Loneliness of the Long Distance Runner, Private Potter, 1962; Billy Liar, 1963; King and Country, 1964 (Volpi Cup, 1964); Operation Crossbow, King Rat, Dr Zhivago, 1965; The Night of the Generals, The Day the Fish Came Out, 1967; A Dandy in Aspic, 1968; Otley, 1969; One Day in the Life of Ivan Denisovich, 1970; Catch Me a Spy, 1971; The Dresser, 1983 (Golden Globe Award); The Last Butterfly, 1990; Let Him Have It, 1991; The Boy from Mercury, 1996; Whatever Happened to Harold Smith?, 1999; Last Orders, 2002; Nicholas Nickleby, 2003; The Golden Compass, 2007; Gambit, 2012; Quartet, 2013; Night Train to Lisbon, 2014; 45 Years, 2015 (Silver Bear for best actor, Berlin Film Fest., 2015); 45 Years, 2015; *television* includes: Redemption, 1991; Old Curiosity Shop (film), 1995; A Rather English Marriage, 1998 (BAFTA Award); The Flood, 2007; Little Dorrit, Royle Family Christmas Special, 2008. Best Actor Award, Prague Festival, 1968; TV Drama Award (for Oswald in Ghosts), 1968. *Publications:* Dear Tom: letters from home (memoirs), 2000. *Recreations:* listening to music (mainly classical, romantic and jazz), watching sport (and occasionally taking part in it, in a light-hearted manner), the countryside, playing the ukelele. *Address:* Putney. *Club:* Garrick.

COURTNEY, Prof. Edward, MA; Gildersleeve Professor of Classics, University of Virginia, 1993–2002, now Emeritus; *b* 22 March 1932; *s* of George and Kathleen Courtney; *m* 1962, Brenda Virginia Meek; two *s. Educ:* Royal Belfast Academical Instn; Trinity Coll., Dublin (BA); BA (by incorporation) 1955, MA 1957, Oxford. University studentship, Dublin, 1954–55; Research Lectr, Christ Church, Oxford, 1955–59; Lectr in Classics, 1959, Reader in Classics, 1970, Prof. of Latin, 1977, King's Coll., London; Prof. of Classics, 1982–93, Leonard Ely Prof. of Humanistic Studies, 1986–93, Stanford Univ. *Publications:* (ed) Valerius Flaccus, Argonautica (Leipzig), 1970; (ed jtly) Juvenal, Satires 1, 3, 10, 1977; (ed jtly) Ovid, Fasti (Leipzig), 1978, 4th edn 1997; A Commentary on the Satires of Juvenal, 1980, repr. 2014; (ed) Juvenal, The Satires, a text, 1984; (ed) Statius, Silvae, 1990; The Poems of Petronius, 1991; The Fragmentary Roman Poets, 1993, 2nd edn 2003; Musa Lapidaria: a selection of Latin verse inscriptions, 1995; Archaic Latin Prose, 1999; A Companion to Petronius, 2002; many articles and reviews. *Recreation:* chess (schoolboy champion of Ireland, 1950). *Address:* 1500 West Pines Drive, Charlottesville, VA 22901, USA.

COURTNEY, Roger Graham, CPhys, FInstP; CEng, FCIBSE; consultant, construction research and innovation; *b* 11 July 1946; *s* of late Ronald Samuel Courtney and Marjorie Dixon Courtney; *m* 1973, Rosemary Madeleine Westlake; four *d. Educ:* Roan School for Boys, SE3; Trinity Coll., Cambridge (MA); Univ. of Bristol (MSc); Brunel Univ. (MTech(OR)). CPhys 1991, FInstP 1991; MCIOB 1993; FCIBSE 1993; CEng 1994. Building Research Station, later Building Research Establishment, 1969–77: res. on bldg and urban services and energy conservation; Sci. Officer, 1969–72; Sen. Sci. Officer, 1972–75; PSO, 1975–81; Inner Cities Directorate, DoE, 1977–78; Sci. and Technology Secretariat, Cabinet Office, 1978–84 (Sec. to ACARD and IT Adv. Panel); SPSO, 1981–83; DCSO, 1983–86; Technical Dir, Energy Efficiency Office, Dept of Energy, 1984–86; Dep. Dir, 1986–88, Dir, 1988–90, Chief Exec., 1990–97, BRE, DoE; Dep. Chm., BRE Ltd, 1997–99. Chm., Dacortium Ltd, 2013–. Professorial Fellow in Construction Innovation, 2001–08, Professorial Res. Fellow, Sch. of Mechanical, Aerospace and Civil Engrg, 2008–12, Univ. of Manchester (formerly UMIST); Vis. Prof., Bartlett Sch. of Construction and Project Mgt, 2005–12, Bartlett Sch. of Graduate Studies, 2013–, UCL. *Publications:* papers in sci. and professional jls. *Address:* 89 Parkside Drive, Watford WD17 3AY. *T:* (01923) 221715.

COURTOWN, 9th Earl of, *cr* 1762; **James Patrick Montagu Burgoyne Winthrop Stopford;** Baron Courtown (Ire.), 1758; Viscount Stopford, 1762; Baron Saltersford (GB), 1796; a Lord in Waiting (Government Whip), since 2015; *b* 19 March 1954; *s* of 8th Earl of Courtown, OBE, TD, DL, and Patricia, 3rd *d* of Harry S. Winthrop, Auckland, NZ; *S* father, 1975; *m* 1985, Elisabeth, *yr d* of I. R. Dunnett, Broad Campden, Glos; one *s* two *d. Educ:* Eton College; Berkshire Coll. of Agriculture; RAC, Cirencester. A Lord in Waiting (Govt Whip), 1995–97; an Opposition Whip, 1997–2000; elected Mem., H of L, 1999. *Heir: s* Viscount Stopford, *qv. Address:* House of Lords, SW1A 0PW.

See also Lady E. C. Godsal.

COUSE, Philip Edward, FCA; Partner, Coopers & Lybrand, 1966–91; *b* 24 March 1936; *s* of Oliver and Marion Couse; *m* 1st (marr. diss. 1973); two *s* one *d*; 2nd, Carol Ann Johannessen Pruitt; one step *d. Educ:* Uppingham Sch.; Hackley Sch., USA. Qualified as Chartered Accountant, 1961. Birmingham Chartered Accountants' Students Society: Sec., 1958–59; Chm., 1967–69; Pres., 1977–78; Birmingham and West Midlands Soc. of Chartered Accountants: Mem. Cttee, 1974–92, Pres., 1982–83; Institute of Chartered Accountants: Mem. Council, 1978–92; Chm. of various cttees; Pres., 1989–90; Chartered Accountants' Dining Club: Mem. Cttee, 1981–92; Treas., 1985–89; Pres., 1989–91. Director: Birmingham Heartlands and Solihull Hosp. NHS Trust, 1991–2000; William King Ltd, 1993–99. Part-time Comr, Friendly Socs Commn, 1992–97. Dir, Hillstone Sch. Trust, Malvern, 1971–86; Chairman: Edgbaston C of E Coll. for Girls, 1982–88; Birmingham Rep. Theatre Foundn, 1991–96; Dir, Birmingham Rep. Th., 1991–96; Chm., Birmingham Dio. Bd of Finance, 1992–2000, and Mem. of various cttees; Mem., C of E Pensions Bd, 1998–99. Mem., Council of Management, Ironbridge Heritage Foundn, 1991–2005 (Treas., 1991–2003); Trustee, Birmingham Eye Foundn, 1981–91 (Treas., 1981–91). Liveryman, Co. of Chartered Accountants in England and Wales, 1977–2014 (Mem., Court, 1987–90). *Recreations:* music, horse racing, woodwork, theatre going. *Address:* 23 Frederick Road, Edgbaston, Birmingham B15 1JN; 715 Greenwood Manor Circle, West Melbourne, FL 32904, USA.

COUSINS, Air Chief Marshal Sir David, KCB 1996 (CB 1991); AFC 1980; Air Member for Personnel, and Air Officer Commanding-in-Chief, Personnel and Training Command, 1995–98; *b* 20 Jan. 1942; *s* of late Peter and Irene Cousins; *m* 1st, 1966, Mary Edith McMurray (marr. diss. 2003); two *s* one *d*; 2nd, 2006, Maggie Broadbent. *Educ:* St Edward's Coll., Malta; Prince Rupert's Sch., Wilhelmshaven; RAF College; Open Univ. (BA 1992). 92 Sqn (Lightnings), 1965–68; ADC to CAS, 1968–70; 15 Sqn (Buccaneers), 1970–73; Air Plans, HQ RAF Germany, 1973; RAF Staff Coll., 1974; Staff Officer to ACAS (OR), 1975–77; OC 16 Sqn (Buccaneers), 1977–80; Central Trials and Tactics Orgn, 1980; PSO to CAS, 1981–83; OC RAF Laarbruch, 1983–85; RCDS 1986; Dir, Air Offensive, MoD, 1987–89; Dir Gen. Aircraft 2, MoD (PE), 1989–91; AOC and Comdt, RAF Coll., Cranwell, 1992–94; AOC No 38 Gp, and SASO Strike Comd, 1994–95. Controller, RAF Benevolent Fund, 1998–2006. ADC to the Queen, 1984–85. Hon. Air Cdre, 7630 Sqn RAuxAF, 2008–. Pres., Buccaneer Aircrew Assoc., 2014–. Mem. Appeal Council, Nat. Meml Arboretum, 2008–. *Recreations:* dinghy sailing, golf, horology. *Club:* Royal Air Force.

COUSINS, James Mackay; *b* 23 Feb. 1944; *m*; two *s*, and one step *s* one step *d. Educ:* New Coll., Oxford (Schol.); London School of Economics. Contract Researcher, and Lectr in job markets, Commn on Industrial Relns and Depts of Employment and the Environment. Member: Wallsend Borough Council, 1969–73; Tyne and Wear County Council, 1973–86 (Dep. Leader, 1981–86). MP (Lab) Newcastle upon Tyne Central, 1987–2010. Mem., Treasury Select Cttee, 1997–2010. Member: CND; Amicus.

COUSINS, Jeremy Vincent; QC 1999; a Recorder, since 2000; *b* 25 Feb. 1955; *s* of Eric Cousins and Joyce Cousins; *m* 1993, Jane Owens; two *s* one *d. Educ:* Oxford Sch.; Warwick Univ. Called to the Bar, Middle Temple, 1977; in practice at the Bar, 1977–; an Asst Recorder, 1996–2000; a Dep. High Ct Judge, 2007–. Chm., Midland Chancery and Commercial Bar Assoc., 2002–05. *Publications:* (consultant ed.) Third Party Litigation Funding, 2014. *Recreations:* walking in Scotland, travelling in Europe. *Address:* 11 Stone Buildings, Lincoln's Inn, WC2A 3TG.

COUSINS, John Peter; Chairman, Crown Asset Management Ltd, Hong Kong, since 1994; *b* 31 Oct. 1931; *s* of Rt Hon. Frank Cousins, PC; *m* 1976, Pauline Cousins (*née* Hubbard);

three *d.* *Educ:* Doncaster Central Sch. Motor engineering apprentice, 1947–52; RAF Engineering, 1952–55; BOAC cabin crew and clerical work, 1955–63; Full Time Official, TGWU, 1963–75, Nat. Sec., 1966–75; Dir of Manpower and Industrial Relations, NEDO, 1975–79; Dir of Personnel, Plessey Telecommunications and Office Systems Ltd, 1979–81; Dir of Personnel and Industrial Relns, John Brown PLC, 1981–83; Gen. Sec., Clearing Bank Union, 1983–86; Head of Personnel, Scottish Daily Record & Sunday Mail (1986) Ltd, 1987; Personnel Dir, Maxwell Pergamon Publishing Corp., 1988–89; Sen. Consultant, Contract 2000, 1989–90; Man. Dir, Cousins Financial Services Ltd (Gibraltar), 1990–95. Mem., Transport and Local Govt Cttees, TUC; UK Deleg., ILO; International Transport Workers Federation: Member: Aviation Sect.; Local Govt Cttee; Chemical Cttee; Civil Aviation Cttee; Mem. Industrial Training Bds. Member: Countryside Commn, 1972–84; New Towns Commn, 1975–79; Sandford Cttee to review National Parks in England and Wales, 1972–73; Council, RSPB, 1982; Bd of Trustees, Royal Botanic Gardens, Kew, 1983–88. Chm., British Council of Productivity Assocs, 1977–82. Travelling Fellow, Kingston Reg. Management Centre, 1977–88. FCMI. *Recreation:* music.

COUSINS, Richard John; Chief Executive, Compass Group PLC, since 2006; *b* 29 March 1959; *s* of late Philip Cousins and Marian Cousins; *m* 1982, Caroline Thorpe; two *s.* *Educ:* Sheffield Univ. (BSc Maths and Stats); Lancaster Univ. (MA Operational Res.). OR Dept, Cadbury Schweppes plc, 1981–84; BTR (Newey and Eyre) Corporate Planning, 1984–90; with BPB plc, 1990–2005: Corporate Planning, 1990–92; Gp Financial Controller, 1992–95; Gen. Manager, Packaging, 1995–96; Man. Dir, Abertay, 1996–98; Pres., BPB Westroc (Canada), 1998–2000; Chief Exec., 2000–05. Non-executive Director: P&O plc, 2005–06; HBOS plc, 2007–09; Reckitt Benckiser, 2009–14; Tesco plc, 2014– (Sen. Ind. Dir., 2015–). *Recreations:* cricket, walking, Scotland, boating. *Address:* Compass Group PLC, Compass House, Guildford Street, Chertsey, Surrey KT16 9BQ.

COUSSINS, Baroness *cr* 2007 (Life Peer), of Whitehall Park in the London Borough of Islington; **Jean Elizabeth Coussins;** independent consultant on corporate responsibility, since 2006; *b* 26 Oct. 1950; *d* of Walter Leonard Coussins and Jessica Coussins (*née* Hughes); *m* 1976, Roger Hamilton (marr. diss. 1985); one *s* one *d*; one *d.* *Educ:* Godolphin and Latymer Girls' Sch.; Newnham Coll., Cambridge (BA (Medieval and Modern Langs) 1973; MA 1976; Hon. Fellow, 2014). Sec., UN Youth and Student Assoc., 1973–75; Women's Rights Officer, NCCL, 1975–80; Dep. Dir, Child Poverty Action Gp, 1980–83; Sen. Educn Officer, ILEA, 1983–88; Dir, Social Policy Div., 1988–94, Equality Assurance Div., 1994–96, CRE; Chief Exec., Portman Gp, 1996–2006. Non-exec. Dir and Council Mem., ASA, 2003–09. Founder Mem. and Chm., Maternity Alliance, 1980–81. Member: Crime Prevention Panel, Foresight Prog., DTI, 2000–03; Scottish Ministerial Adv. Cttee on Alcohol Problems, 2001–06; Adv. Gp on alcohol harm reduction, PM's Strategy Unit, 2003–04; Expert Taskforce on Consumers and Markets, DoH, 2004. Ind. Mem. Adv. Council, BBFC, 2002–05; Comr, Better Regulation Commn, 2004–07. Chm., All-Party Parly Gp on Modern Langs, 2008–; Member: H of L Information Cttee, 2007–12; Sub-Cttee on External Affairs, H of L EU Select Cttee, 2013–. Mem., Corporate Responsibility Bd (formerly Adv. Panel on Corporate Responsibility), Camelot Gp, 2011–. Trustee: Inst. for Citizenship, 1994–99; Drinkaware Trust, 2001–06; Alcohol Educn and Res. Council, 2004–07; Pres., Money Advice Trust, 2010–. Parent Gov., Ashmount Sch., 1980s; Associate Fellow and Mem. Governing Body, Newnham Coll., Cambridge, 2002–05; Mem., Bd Govs, Channing Sch., 2007–12. Pres., Peru Support Gp, 2012–. Patron, On the Shoulders of Giants Th. Co.; Vice-Patron, British Sch. of Osteopathy. Hon. Fellow: Chartered Inst. of Linguists, 2010 (Vice-Pres., 2012–); UCL, 2010. *Publications:* Taking Liberties, 1978; (jtly) Shattering Illusions: West Indians in British politics, 1986; (contrib.) Policing Black People, 1990; pamphlets and booklets on equality and maternity rights. *Recreations:* family, travel, food, swimming, football, crosswords. *Address:* House of Lords, SW1A 0PW. *T:* (020) 7219 5353. *E:* coussinsj@parliament.uk. *Club:* Fulham Football.

COUSSIOS, Prof. Constantin-Cassios, PhD; Professor of Biomedical Engineering, University of Oxford, since 2011; Fellow of Magdalen College, Oxford, since 2004; *b* Athens, 21 March 1977; *s* of Dimitrios Coussios and Elissabeth Coussiou; *m* 2005, Agathoniki Trigoni; three *s.* *Educ:* Pembroke Coll., Cambridge (BA 1998; MEng 1998; MA 2001; PhD 2002). Engrg undergrad. trainee, Balfour Beatty Civil Engrg Ltd, 1995; engrg intern, Centre d'Essais Aéronautique de Toulouse, 1995; military service, Hellenic Air Force, 1997 and 1998; Post-doctoral Res. Fellow, Dept of Biomed. Engrg, Univ. of Cincinnati, 2001–02; Lectr and Res. Associate, Dept of Aerospace and Mechanical Engrg, Boston Univ., 2002–03; University of Oxford: Lectr in Biomed. Engrg, Dept of Engrg Sci., 2004–06; Founder and Hd, Biomed. Ultrasonics, Biotherapy and Biopharmaceuticals Lab., Oxford Inst. of Biomed. Engrg, 2004–; Bellhouse Foundn Reader in Biomed. Engrg, 2006–10. Tech. Dir, OrganOx Ltd, 2008–. Sec. Gen. and Mem. Bd, Internat. Soc. for Therapeutic Ultrasound, 2006–10. Fellow, Acoustical Soc. of Amer., 2009 (F. V. Hunt Postdoctoral Fellow, 2002–03; R. Bruce Lindsay Award, 2012). Hamilton Prize, Univ. of Cambridge, 2001; Young Person's Award for Innovation in Acoustical Engrg, Inst. of Acoustics, 2007; Frederic Lizzi Early Career Award, Internat. Soc. for Therapeutic Ultrasound, 2012. *Publications:* (contrib.) Methods in Engineering, 2011; articles in learned jls. *Recreations:* piano, basketball, tennis. *Address:* Institute of Biomedical Engineering, Old Road Campus, Research Building, Headington, Oxford OX3 7DQ. *T:* (01865) 617727, *Fax:* (01865) 617728. *E:* constantin.coussios@eng.ox.ac.uk.

COUTTIE, Philippa Marion; *see* Roe, P. M.

COUTTS; *see* Money-Coutts, family name of Baron Latymer.

COUTTS, Anne Jane, MEd; Principal, Canberra Girls' Grammar School, since 2011; *b* Watford, 9 April 1956; *d* of Alistair and Mysie Sutherland; *m* 1978, Ian Alexander Coutts; two *d.* *Educ:* King's High Sch., Warwick; Aspley Grammar Sch.; Univ. of Warwick (BSc, PGCE, MEd). Res. Asst, Nuffield Inst. for Med. Res. and Oxford Inst. of Virol., 1978–80; Teacher of Chemistry: Coventry LEA, 1981–83; Hereford and Worcester LEA, 1983–86; Hd of Gen. Studies, Trent Coll., 1986–88; Dep. Hd, then Actg Hd, Edgbaston Coll. of Educn, 1988–92; Head: Eothen Sch., Caterham, 1992–95; Sutton High Sch., 1995–2003; Headington Sch., 2003–10. Mem., QCDA (formerly QCA) Adv. Gp for Res. in Assessment and Qualifications Cttee, HMC Council, 2007–12. *Recreations:* photography, singing, saxophone, cooking, reading. *Address:* Canberra Girls' Grammar School, Melbourne Avenue, Deakin, ACT 2600, Australia.

COUTTS, Gordon; *see* Coutts, T. G.

COUTTS, Herbert, MBE 2008; FSAScot; FMA; Director of Culture and Leisure (formerly of Recreation), City of Edinburgh Council, 2001–07; *b* 9 March 1944; *s* of late Herbert and Agnes Coutts, Dundee; *m* 1970, Angela Elizabeth Mason Smith; one *s* three *d.* *Educ:* Morgan Acad., Dundee. FSAScot 1965; AMA 1970, FMA 1976. Asst Keeper of Antiquities and Bygones, Dundee City Museums, 1965–68, Keeper, 1968–71; Supt, Edinburgh City Museums, 1971–73; City Curator, City of Edinburgh Museums and Art Galls, 1973–96; City of Edinburgh Council: Hd of Museums and Galls, 1996–97; Hd of Heritage and Arts, 1997–99; Dir of Recreation, 1999–2001. Vice Pres., Museums Assts Gp, 1967–70; Member: Bd, Scottish Museums Council, 1971–74, and 1986–88; Govt Cttee on Future of Scotland's Nat. Museums and Galleries, 1979–80 (report pub. 1981); Bd, Museums Trng Inst., 1995–2000; Bd, Cultural Heritage NTO, 2000–04; Bd of Trustees, Nat. Galleries of Scotland, 2007–11. Member, Council: Museums Assoc., 1977–78, 1987–88; Soc. of Antiquaries of Scotland, 1981–82; Museums Advr, COSLA Arts and Recreation Cttee, 1985–90, 1995–99. Member: Paxton House Trust, 1988–2002, 2006–; E Lothian Community Devel Trust, 1989–2010; Scottish Catholic Heritage Commn, 2006–; Bd, Order of Malta Dial-a-Journey Ltd, 2007– (Chm., 2011–) (Mem. Bd, 2010–, Chm., 2011–, Wheelchair Vehicle Enterprise Ltd); Dunbar Community Council, 2007–; Bd, Dunbar Community Develt Co., 2007–; Bd, Battle of Prestonpans Heritage Trust, 2007– (Vice Chm., 2011–). Trustee, Scottish Catholic Heritage Collections Trust, 2011–. External Examr, St Andrews Univ., 1993–97. Building Projects: City of Edinburgh Art Centre (opened 1980); Museum of Childhood Extension (opened 1986); People's Story Museum (opened 1989); City of Edinburgh Art Centre Extension (opened 1992); Makars' Court, Scotland's Poets' Corner (opened 1998); Scott Monument Restoration (completed 1999); Usher Hall Renovation (completed 2000). Exhibitions at City of Edinburgh Art Centre: The Emperor's Warriors, 1985; Gold of the Pharaohs, 1988; Gold of Peru, 1990; Golden Warriors of the Ukrainian Steppes, 1993; Star Trek—The Exhibition, 1995; Quest for a Pirate, 1996; Gateway to the Silk Road, 1996. Contested (Lab) Angus South, 1970. Founding Fellow, Inst. of Contemp. Scotland, 1999. SBStJ 1977; KM 2009. Bailie of Dolphinstoun, 2008–. *Publications:* (jtly) Broughty Castle, 1970; Ancient Monuments of Tayside, 1970; Tayside Before History, 1971; (with Robin Hill) Edinburgh Crafts, 1974; Aince a Bailie, Aye a Bailie, 1974; Edinburgh: an illustrated history, 1975; (ed) Amber in Polish History, 1978; (with John Heyes) Museum of Childhood, 1980; Huntly House, 1980; Lady Stair's House, 1980; (ed) The Emperor's Warriors, 1985; (ed) Gold of the Pharaohs, 1988; The Pharaoh's Gold Mask, 1988; (ed) Dinosaurs Alive, 1990; (ed) Gold of Peru, 1990; (ed) Golden Warriors of the Ukrainian Steppes, 1993; (ed) Star Trek—The Exhibition, 1995; (ed) Gateway to the Silk Road, 1996; (ed) Quest for a Pirate, 1996; (ed) Faster, Higher, Stronger, 1997; exhibn catalogues; contrib. Museums Jl and archaeol jls. *Recreations:* relaxing with family, gardening, going to the opera, writing, reading, walking. *Address:* Kirkhill House, Queen's Road, Dunbar, East Lothian EH42 1LN. *T:* (01368) 863113.

COUTTS, Sir Russell, KNZM 2009 (DCNZM 2000); CBE 1995 (MBE 1985); yachtsman; *b* 1 March 1962; *s* of late Allan and of Beverley Coutts; *m* 1999, Jennifer Little; three *s* one *d.* *Educ:* Auckland Univ. (BEng). Gold Medal, Finn Cl., Olympic Games, LA, 1984; World Champion, Match Racing, 1992, 1993 and 1996; ranked No 1, Match Racing Circuit, 1994; winner, Brut Sailing series, 1996; Helmsman: Admiral's Cup winner, Pinta, 1993; America's Cup winners, Black Magic, San Diego, 1995 and Team NZ, Auckland, 2000; World Title, S Australia, 2001; 1st Swedish Match Cup, Marstrand, 2001; winner, World Title, Farr 40, 2001 and 2006; Skipper and Exec. Dir, America's Cup winner, Alinghi Team, Switzerland, 2003; designer, new boat, RC 44, 2005; winner, World Title, TP 52, 2007; CEO and Skipper, Oracle Team USA (formerly BMW Oracle Racing), 2007– (winner, America's Cup in Yacht USA, 2010). Yachtsman of the Year, NZ, 1984; Sperry World Sailor of the Year, 1995; Trophée Fabergé, Match Racing, 1996. *Publications:* The Course to Victory, 1996; America's Cup 2000, 1999; Challenge 2000: the race to win the America's Cup, 1999. *Recreation:* golf. *Clubs:* Société Nautique de Genève; New York Yacht; Royal New Zealand Yacht; North Shore Golf, Titirangi Golf (Auckland).

COUTTS, T(homas) Gordon; QC (Scotland) 1973; *b* 5 July 1933; *s* of Thomas Coutts and Evelyn Gordon Coutts; *m* 1959, Winifred Katherine Scott, PhD; one *d* (one *s* decd). *Educ:* Aberdeen Grammar Sch.; Aberdeen Univ. (MA, LLB). Admitted Faculty of Advocates, 1959; Standing Junior Counsel to Dept Agric. (Scot.), 1965–73; called to the Bar, Lincoln's Inn, 1995. Temporary Judge, Court of Session, Scotland, 1991–2004; Vice Pres. (Scot.), VAT and Duties Tribunals, 1996–2008. Part-time Chairman: Industrial Tribunals, 1972–2003; Medical Appeal Tribunal, 1984–2006; VAT Tribunal, 1990–96; Financial Services and Markets Tribunal, 2001–08; Pension Regulator Appeal Tribunal, 2005–08. Mem., Panel of Arbitrators, 1995. FCIArb 1994; Chartered Arbitrator, 1999. *Recreations:* travel, stamp collecting. *Address:* 6 Heriot Row, Edinburgh EH3 6HU. *Club:* New (Edinburgh).

COUTTS, William Walter B.; *see* Burdett-Coutts.

COUTURE, Most Rev. Maurice, GOQ 2003; Archbishop of Québec, (RC), and Primate of Canada, 1990–2002; *b* 3 Nov. 1926. Perpetual vows with Vincentian Fathers, 1948; ordained priest, 1951; Patros de la Baie, Plessisville, Port Alfred and Bagotville, 1952–55; in charge of Minor Seminary of his Congregation, 1955–65; founder and Rector, Inter-Congregational Seminary, Cap-Rouge, 1965–70; Provincial Superior, 1970–76, Superior General of Congregation, 1976–82; Titular Bishop of Talattula and Auxiliary Bishop of Québec, 1982–88; Bishop of Baie-Comeau, 1988–90. *Address:* c/o Diocèse de Québec, 1073 Boulevard René Levesque Ouest, Québec, QC G1S 4R5, Canada.

COUTURIER, Hernán Antonio; Ambassador of Peru to the Court of St James's, 2010–11; *b* 9 Dec. 1943; *s* of Hernán Couturier and Josefina Mariátegui; *m* 1996, Sonia Labarthe; two *s* two *d.* *Educ:* Champagnat Marist Sch., Peru; Leoncio Prado Military Sch.; Catholic Univ. of Peru; San Marcos Univ. of Peru; Diplomatic Acad. of Peru (Bachelor Internat. Relns). Joined Min. of Foreign Affairs as Third Sec., 1968; Third Sec., Chile, 1968; Second Sec., Perm. Mission to OAS, 1971; Second, then First Sec., USA, 1973–74; First Sec., Foreign Policy Under-Secretariat, 1975, Hd, S Amer. Dept of Pol and Diplomatic Div., 1976, Min. of Foreign Affairs; First Sec., then Counsellor, Colombia, 1977–80; Counsellor, Perm. Mission to UN, 1980; Minister Counsellor, Dep. Perm. Rep. to UN, 1981; Dir, 1984–86, Dir Gen., 1986–87, Policy Planning, Min. of Foreign Affairs; Ambassador to Zimbabwe, 1987–89; Consul Gen., NY, 1989–92; Dir Gen. for Special Pol Affairs, 1993, for Pol Affairs, 1994, Sec.-Gen., 1994, Min. of Foreign Affairs; Ambassador to Canada, 1994–2000; Nat. Dir for Border Develt and Borderlines, 2000, Under-Sec. for Multilateral and Special Affairs, 2000–01, Min. of Foreign Affairs; Ambassador to Bolivia, 2001–04, to Brazil, 2004–07, and non-resident to Guyana, 2005–07; Ministry of Foreign Affairs: Under-Sec. for Eur. Affairs, 2007–08; Gen. Co-ordinator, Latin Amer., Caribbean-EU V Summit, 2007; Under-Sec. for Amer. Affairs, 2009–10. Mem., Peruvian Soc. of Internat. Law, 1977; Associated Mem., Peruvian Centre for Internat. Studies, 1993. Professor: Diplomatic Acad. of Peru, 1975–76, 1985–86, 2009–10; San Martin de Porres Univ., Peru, 2008; Peruvian Univ. of Applied Scis, 2009–10; lectr on internat. issues in academic, professional and mil. instns. Mem. of Soc. of Founders of Independence of Peru, 1993. Officer: Orden Bernardo O'Higgins (Chile), 1975; Orden Rio Branco (Brazil), 1976; Grand Cross: Orden de San Carlos (Colombia), 1979; Orden, Libertador Simón Bolívar (Bolivia), 1995; Orden del Cóndor de los Andes (Bolivia), 2004; Orden al Mérito por Servicios Distinguidos (Peru), 2004; Orden Cruzeiro do Sul (Brazil), 2007; Orden del Mérito Civil (Spain), 2008; Orden José Gregorio Paz Soldán (Peru), 2008. *Publications:* articles, monographs and lectures on foreign policy issues in newspapers and mags. *Recreations:* tennis, cycling, hunting, reading. *Clubs:* Travellers; Tennis Las Terrazas, Los Inkas Golf (Lima).

COUZENS, Air Vice-Marshal David Cyril, CEng, FIMechE, FRAeS; Senior Directing Staff (Air), Royal College of Defence Studies, 2003–04; *b* 15 Oct. 1949; *s* of Cyril Couzens and Joyce Couzens (*née* Walker); *m* 1977, Deborah Cawse; one *s* one *d.* *Educ:* Ecclesbourne Sch.; Churchill Coll., Cambridge (MA); Open Univ. Business Sch. (MBA); Loughborough Univ. (Postgrad. Dip). CEng 1979; FIMechE 1991; FRAeS 1995. Joined Royal Air Force, 1968: initial and professional trng, 1968–72; practical aircraft/weapon system appts, 1972–88; personnel mgt, 1988–89; Gp Captain 1990; Superintendent of Armament, 1990–91; Dep. Dir Support Policy (Op. Requirements) (RAF), MoD Policy, 1991–94; rcds 1994; Air Cdre 1995; Air Cdre, CIS, HQ Strike Comd, 1995–97; Dir, Logistic Inf. Strategy (RAF), MoD, 1997–98; AO, Logistic Inf. Strategy and Industrial Interface Study, MoD, 1998–99; Air Vice-Marshal 1999; Dir Gen., Defence Logistics (Communications and Inf. Systems), 1999–2001, Defence Logistics Capability, 2001–02, MoD; COS to Surgeon Gen., MoD, 2002–03. Pres., RAeS, 2010–11 (Mem. Council, 2006–12; Chm., Professional Standards Bd, 2006–09);

Mem. Bd, Engrg Council, 2008–15. Trustee, RAF Benevolent Fund, 2003–04, 2006–14. President: RAF Rugby League, 1999–2004; Combined Services Rugby League, 2002–04. *Recreations:* hill-walking, gardening, music. *Club:* Royal Air Force (Chm., 2003–04).

COVENEY, Michael William; theatre critic and author; *b* 24 July 1948; *s* of William Coveney and Violet Amy Coveney (*née* Perry); *m* 1977, Susan Monica Hyman; one *s*. *Educ:* St Ignatius College, London; Worcester College, Oxford. Editor, Plays and Players, 1975–78; theatre critic: Financial Times, 1981–89; The Observer, 1990–97; Daily Mail, 1997–2004. *Publications:* The Citz, 1990; Maggie Smith, 1992; The Aisle is Full of Noises, 1994; (with Robert Stephens) Knight Errant: memoirs of a vagabond actor, 1995; The World According to Mike Leigh, 1996; Cats on a Chandelier: the Andrew Lloyd Webber story, 1999; Ken Campbell: the great caper, 2011. *Recreations:* music, running, travel. *Address:* 11 Shirlock Road, NW3 2HR.

COVENTRY, family name of **Earl of Coventry**.

COVENTRY, 13th Earl of, *cr* 1697; **George William Coventry;** Viscount Deerhurst 1697; *b* 5 Oct. 1939; *s* of Comdr Cecil Dick Bluett Coventry, DSC, RD, RNR; *S* kinsman, 2004; *m* 1965, Gillian Frances, *d* of F. W. R. Randall; one *d*. *Educ:* Prince of Wales Sch., Nairobi. *Heir: nephew* David Duncan Sherwood Coventry [*b* 5 March 1973; *m* 2003, Sarah Sadie Bishop; one *s*].

COVENTRY, Bishop of, since 2008; **Rt Rev. Dr Christopher John Cocksworth;** *b* 12 Jan. 1959; *s* of Stanley John Cocksworth and Auriol Gwyneth Cocksworth; *m* 1979, Charlotte Mary Pytches; five *s*. *Educ:* Manchester Univ. (BA (1st cl. Hons) Theol., 1980; PhD 1989); Didsbury Sch. of Educn, Manchester Poly. (PGCE 1981); St John's Theol Coll., Nottingham. Teacher and House Tutor, King Edward's Sch., Witley, Surrey, 1981–84; doctoral res. student, 1986–88. Ordained deacon, 1988, priest, 1989; Asst Curate, Christ Church, Epsom, 1988–92; Chaplain, RHBNC, Univ. of London, 1992–97; Dir, STETS, 1997–2001; Principal, Ridley Hall, Cambridge, 2001–08. Hon. Canon, Guildford Cathedral, 2000–01, now Canon Emeritus. Mem., C of E Liturgical Commn, 1996–2006; Jt Chair, Jt Implementation Commn of Anglican-Methodist Covenant, 2009–; Chm., C of E Faith and Order Commn, 2012–. Mem., H of L, 2013–. Hon. DD Royal Holloway, Univ. of London, 2009. *Publications:* Evangelical Eucharistic Thought in the Church of England, 1993; (with Paul Roberts) Renewing Daily Prayer, 1993; (with Alan Wilkinson) An Anglican Companion, 1996, 2nd edn 2001; Holy, Holy, Holy: worshipping the Trinitarian God, 1997; Prayer and the Departed, 1997; (with Jeremy Fletcher) The Spirit and Liturgy, 1998; (with Rosalind Brown) Being a Priest Today, 2002, 2nd edn 2006; Wisdom: the Spirit's gift, 2003; Holding Together: Gospel, Church and Spirit, 2008; Seeing Jesus and Being Seen by Him, 2014; various articles in bks and learned jls. *Recreations:* hill-walking, cycling, swimming, film watching, organic vegetable gardening. *Address:* Bishop's House, 23 Davenport Road, Coventry CV5 6PW. *T:* (024) 7667 2244.

COVENTRY, Dean of; *see* Witcombe, Very Rev. J. J.

COVENTRY, Archdeacon of; *see* Green, Ven. J.

COVEY, Donna May, CBE 2014; Director, Against Violence and Abuse, since 2014; *b* 20 June 1961; *d* of Mrs Cynthia Covey. *Educ:* Univ. of Warwick (BSc); Birkbeck Coll., London (Postgrad. Dip. Mgt). Nat. Officer, GMB, 1988–98; Dir, Assoc. of CHCs for England and Wales, 1998–2001; Chief Executive: Nat. Asthma Campaign, subseq. Asthma UK, 2001–07; Refugee Council, 2007–12. Chm., London Food Commn, 1986–87; Vice Chm., Wandsworth CHC, 1987–88. Member: Gen. Council, TUC, 1988–98; Nat. Women's Cttee, Labour Party, 1992–98; Migration Impacts Forum, 2007–09. Mem. Bd, Eur. Fedn of Allergy and Airway Diseases Patients Assocs, 2003–07 (Vice-Pres. 2006–07); Trustee: Long Term Conditions Alliance, 2005–07; Equality and Diversity Forum, 2010–12; Counterpoints Arts, 2012–. FRSA. *Publications:* contributed to: Waiting for Change, 1986; Visions of Primary Care, 1999; NHS Frontline: visions for 2010, 2000; A Practical Guide to Primary Care Groups and Trusts, 2001. *Recreations:* rambling, murder mysteries, Tate Gallery, yoga. *E:* donna_covey@hotmail.com.

COVILLE, Air Marshal Sir Christopher (Charles Cotton), KCB 2000 (CB 1995); Chairman, C4 Defence & Security Ltd, since 2010; *b* 2 June 1945; *s* of Henry and Anna Coville; *m* 1967, Irene Johnson; one *s* two *d*. *Educ:* De La Salle Grammar Sch., Liverpool; RAF Coll., Cranwell. BA Open. Lightning Pilot and Instructor, 1969–73; Phantom Pilot and Instructor, 1973–78; Central Tactics and Trials Orgn, 1978–80; Personal Staff Officer to UK Mil. Rep., Brussels, 1981–83; OC Ops Wing, RAF Stanley, 1983; OC 111 Fighter Sqn, 1983–85; Gp Capt. Air, HQ 11 Fighter Group, 1985–86; OC RAF Coningsby, 1986–88; RCDS 1989; Air Cdre Flying Training, HQ RAF Support Command, 1990–92; AO Trng and AOC Trng Gp, 1992–94; Chief Exec., Trng Gp Defence Agency, Apr.–Sept. 1994; ACDS, Op. Requirements (Air), 1994–98; Dep. C-in-C, AFCENT, 1998–2000; Dep. C-in-C, AFNORTH, 2000–01; Air Mem. for Personnel, and C-in-C, PTC, 2001–03. Chairman: Westland Helicopters, 2005–11; Forces Pension Soc., 2011–14; Sen. Defence and Security Advr, EMC UK, 2007–15; non-exec. Dir, Arizona Gp Ltd, 2011–12. President: RAF Microlight Assoc., 1992–2000; RAF Football Assoc., 1996–2002; Vice-Pres., RAFA, 2001–. FCIPD (FITD 1993); FRAeS 1994. *Recreations:* mountaineering, shooting, fishing. *Clubs:* Royal Air Force, Mosimann's.

COVINGTON, Nicholas; Director, Office of Manpower Economics, 1986–89; *b* 9 June 1929; *s* of late Cyril Tim Covington and Margaret Joan (*née* Bray); *m* 1st, 1953, Pat Sillitoe; one *s* two *d*; 2nd, 1983, Kathy Hegarty. *Educ:* Cranleigh Sch.; Oriel Coll., Oxford. RAF, 1947–49; TA Commn, 1952. Metal Box Co. Ltd, South Africa, 1952–57; Gen. Manager and Dir, Garnier & Co. Ltd, 1957–66; entered Min. of Labour, 1966; Asst Sec., 1971; Industrial Relns Div., Dept of Employment, 1976–86. *Address:* Dovecote House, Lower Slaughter, near Cheltenham, Glos GL54 2HY.

COWAN, Annella Marie; Sheriff of Grampian, Highland and Islands at Aberdeen, since 1997; *b* 14 Nov. 1953; *m* 1979, James Temple Cowan (marr. diss. 1995). *Educ:* Elgin Acad.; Edinburgh Univ. (LLB 1976; MSc 1984). Admitted Solicitor, 1978; Procurator Fiscal Depute, 1978–86; seconded to Scottish Law Commn, 1984–86; admitted Faculty of Advocates, 1987; Temp. Sheriff, 1991; Sheriff of Tayside, Central and Fife at Stirling, 1993–97. *Recreations:* equestrianism, foreign travel. *Address:* Sheriff's Chambers, Sheriff Court, Aberdeen AB10 1WP. *T:* (01224) 657200.

COWAN, Dr George Osborne, OBE 1986; FRCP, FRCPE; Medical Director, Joint Committee on Higher Medical Training, Royal Colleges of Physicians of UK, 2001–05; *b* 5 Sept. 1939; *s* of late John Jardine Cowan and Marion Ramsay Cowan (*née* Corrie); *m* 1981, Beatrice Mary Hill, MA, MPhil, MLitt, *d* of late Leonard Charles Hill, OBE, DSC, FRGS and Joyce (*née* Snelus). *Educ:* Merchiston Castle Sch., Edinburgh; Univ. of St Andrews (MB ChB 1963); Open Univ. (Dip. Music, 2004; BA 1st Cl. Hons Humanities with Music, 2007). MRCPE 1967, FRCPE 1978; DTM&H 1968; MRCP 1967, FRCP 1983. Commissioned RAMC, 1962; served Australia, Hong Kong, Malaysia, Singapore, Nepal, The Gambia, Germany and NI; Consultant Physician in Army Hosps, 1973–96; Prof. of Mil. Medicine, RAMC, 1987–92; Dir of Army Medicine, 1992–93; Comdt and Post-Grad. Dean, Royal Army Med. Coll., 1993–96; QHP 1992–96; retired in rank of Maj.-Gen., 1996. Dean of Postgrad. Medicine, Univ. of London (N Thames) (formerly N Thames (E) Region), 1996–2001. Hon. Sen. Lectr, Bute Med. Sch., subseq. Sch. of Med. and Biol Scis, Univ. of St Andrews, 2008–14. Cohen Lectr, Univ. of Liverpool, 1991; Grundy Lectr (and Medal), RCP and RAMC, 2013. Pres., RSTM&H, 1995–97 (Vice-Pres., 1993–95). Hon. FRCPI 2003; Hon. FRCPGlas 2005; Hon. Life Fellow, Soc. for Acute Medicine, 2011. MD *hc* St Andrews, 2008. Mitchiner Medal, RCS, 1992. OStJ 1994. *Publications:* (ed) Atlas of Medical Helminthology and Protozoology, 3rd edn, 1991; (with B. J. Heap) Clinical Tropical Medicine, 1993; (with N. R. H. Burgess) Atlas of Medical Entomology, 1993. *Recreations:* golf, music, medical history. *Clubs:* Army and Navy; Royal & Ancient Golf (St Andrews).

COWAN, Lionel David, (Nick Cowan); Chairman, West Lambeth Health Authority, 1982–86; *b* 18 Dec. 1929; *m* 1953, Pamela Ida, *e d* of Hubert and Winifred Williams, Totton, Hants; one *s* two *d*. *Educ:* Surbiton County Grammar Sch.; King's Coll., London (BA Hons Spanish, 1995); Univ. of Salamanca (Dip. in Hispanic Studies, 1994). CCIPD (CIPM 1979; AMIPM 1965). Served Royal Navy, 1945–61: Fleet Air Arm Aircrew (Lieut), 1953; Sen. Instr, RAN, 1958–60. Training Officer, Shoe and Allied Trades Res. Assoc., 1961–62; Perkins Engines Gp, 1962–72; Dir of Personnel, Philips Electronic and Associated Industries, 1972–78; Gp Personnel Dir, Unigate Ltd, 1978–79; Dir and Sec., Fedn of London Clearing Bank Employers, 1980–87; Personnel Dir, TSB England & Wales, 1987–89. Personnel mgt consultant, 1989–2005. Member: Employment Appeal Tribunal, 1976–2000; Editorial Panel, Industrial Relns Law Reports, 1977–; Civil Service Arbitration Tribunal, 1979–; Central Arbitration Cttee, 1984–2000; Equal Opportunities Commn, 1988–91; NEDO Enquiry, Industrial Relns Trng for Managers, 1976, Supply and Demand for Skilled Manpower, 1977. Vice-Pres. (Employee Relations), IPM, 1977–79. Director, Oxford Univ. Business Summer Sch., 1980. *Publications:* Personnel Management and Banking, 1983; The Clearing Banks and the Trade Unions, 1984. *Recreations:* things Spanish, music and opera, bridge. *Address:* 3 Oaks Way, Ripley, Woking, Surrey GU23 6LT. *T:* (01483) 479665.

COWAN, Robert Charles; writer and broadcaster; *b* 14 April 1948; *s* of Maurice Bernard Cowan and Vera Cowan; *m* 1971, Georgina Gilmour; two *d*. *Educ:* Fern Bank Primary Sch.; Leas House Sch.; Pitman's Coll. Asst, Lewis Cranston Public Relns, 1965; Advertising Dept, Pergamon Press, 1966–68; Asst Librarian, BBC Record Liby and Concerts Mgt, 1968–69; Advertising Manager, 1970–78, Archivist, 1978–89, Boosey & Hawkes Music Publishers Ltd. Ed., Music Diary, 1982–89; contrib. 1985–, Ed., 1989–91, CD Rev. mag.; Ed., Classics mag., 1991–93; contrib., 1993–, Contributing Ed., 1999–, Gramophone; writer, The Independent, 1993–; radio: co-presenter, Classic Verdict, 1992–95; presenter: Our Musical Yesterdays, 1993; Off the Record, 1996; CD Choice, 1998–2000; CD Masters, 2001–07; The Cowan Collection, 2003–07; Radio 3 (formerly Rob Cowan) Breakfast, 2007–11; Radio 3 Essential Classics, 2011–; Radio 3 Sunday Morning, 2011–. Mem., Royal Soc. of Musicians, 2014. Grammy Award, 1995. *Publications:* The Guinness Classical 1000, 1997. *Recreations:* walking, listening, reading, collecting, travelling, writing (for fun), spending time with my family. *Address:* 2 Merry Hill Mount, Bushey, Herts WD23 1DJ.

COWAN, Ronald Jack; MP (SNP) Inverclyde, since 2015; *b* Greenock, 6 Sept. 1959; *s* of James Clews Cowan and May Harper Cowan; one *s* two *d*. *Educ:* Greenock Acad. Systems Analyst, Playtex, 1978–86; IT Consultant, Campbell Lee Computer Services, 1986–2001; Man. Dir, Ronnie Cowan Solutions, 2001–15. *Recreations:* art (appreciation), sport (watching), sleeping (with optional snoring). *Address:* House of Commons, SW1A 0AA. *E:* ronnie.cowan.mp@parliament.uk. *Club:* Greenock Wanderers Rugby Football.

COWAN, Gen. Sir Samuel, KCB 1997; CBE 1988 (OBE 1983); Chief of Defence Logistics, Ministry of Defence, 1998–2002; Aide-de-camp to the Queen, 2000–02; *b* 9 Oct. 1941; *s* of late Samuel Cowan and Rachel Cowan; *m* 1971, Anne Gretton; one *s* one *d*. *Educ:* Lisburn Technical Coll.; Open Univ. (BA 1980). Commissioned Royal Signals, 1963; CO 2 Armd Div. HQ and Signal Regt, 1980–82; Comdr Communications and Comdr 1 Signal Brigade, 1 (BR) Corps, 1985–87; Director of Public Relations (Army), 1987–88; Comdt, RMCS, 1989–91; ACDS OR (Land), 1991–94; Inspector Gen. Training, MoD, 1995–96; QMG, MoD, 1996–98. Col Comdt, Brigade of Gurkhas, 1994–2003; Master of Signals, 2003–08. President: Gurkha Bde Assoc., 2004–13; Oxfordshire Br., SSAFA (formerly SSAFA-Forces Help), 2008–; Dep. Grand Pres., Royal Commonwealth Ex-Services League, 2003–13. Trustee, Racing Welfare, 2009–13. Hon. FCIPS 2000; Hon. FCILT (Hon. FILT 2000). Hon. DSc Cranfield, 1999. *Recreations:* sport, walking. *Address:* c/o RHQ Royal Signals, Blandford Camp, Dorset DT11 8RH. *T:* (01258) 482082.

COWANS, David; Chief Executive, Places for People Group, since 1999; *b* 3 May 1957; *s* of Harry and Margaret Cowans; *m* 1997, Julie Brewerton (*d* 2011); one *s* two *d*. *Educ:* St Cuthbert's Grammar Sch., Newcastle upon Tyne; New Coll., Durham (Dip. Housing Studies); Birmingham Univ. (MBA). CDir 2010; FRICS 2013; MIRPM 2014. Neighbourhood Officer, Walsall MBC, 1979–82; Area Manager, Sheffield CC, 1982–86; Asst Dir of Housing, Leicester CC, 1986–88; Gen. Manager, 1988–94, Dir of Housing, 1994–97, Birmingham CC; Gp Chief Exec., N British Housing Gp, 1997–99. Mem. Exec. Council, Nat. Housing Fedn, 1998–2001. *Recreations:* cinema, music, my children, social history, gardening, walking, economic history. *Address:* Galtres House, 11 Rawcliffe Lane, Clifton, York YO30 6NP. *T:* (01904) 650150. *E:* david.cowans@placesforpeople.co.uk.

COWARD, Lt Gen. Sir Gary (Robert), KBE 2012 (OBE 1996); CB 2008; Chairman, Redline Aviation Security Ltd, since 2013; *b* 26 Aug. 1955; *s* of Robert Vacey and Marion Avril Coward; *m* 1978, Chrissie Hamerton; one *s*. *Educ:* Duke of York's Royal Mil. Sch.; RMA Sandhurst. Served RA, 1974–82; transf. to AAC, 1983; OC 656 Sqdn, 1991–93; UN mil. spokesman (UNPROFOR), 1994–95; CO 1 Regt, 1996–98; Sec., Chiefs of Staff Cttee, MoD, 1998–2000; Dep. Comdr, Jt Helicopter Comd, 2000–03; Dir, Equipt Capability (Air and Littoral Manoeuvre), MoD, 2003–05; Comdr, Jt Helicopter Command, 2005–08; COS (Jt Welfare Develt), 2008–09; Chief of Materiel (Land), Defence Equipment and Support, 2009–12; Quartermaster Gen., 2009–12. CGIA 1988.

COWARD, Vice Adm. Sir John (Francis), KCB 1990; DSO 1982; Lieutenant Governor and Commander-in-Chief of Guernsey, Channel Islands, 1994–2000; *b* 11 Oct. 1937; *s* of Reginald John Coward and Isabelle (*née* Foreman); *m* 1963, Diana (*née* Taylor); two *s*. *Educ:* Downside; RNC, Dartmouth. Served submarines, 1959–76, i/c HMS Oracle and HMS Valiant; Naval Asst to First Sea Lord, 1978–80; i/c HMS Brilliant, 1980–82; S Atlantic, 1982; Dir, Naval Operational Requirements, 1984; Flag Officer: Sea Trng, 1987–88; Flotilla One, 1988–89; Submarines, and Comdr Submarines Eastern Atlantic, 1989–91; Comdt, RCDS, 1992–94. Rear Adm. 1987; Vice Adm. 1989; retd 1994. Mem. Bd, N. M. Rothschild (CI) Ltd, 2000–07; Chm., Luxury Brands Gp, 2001–02. Underwriting Mem. of Lloyd's, 1978–. Mem., Council, RNLI, 1998–2008. *Recreations:* sailing, gardening, cricket, golf. *Address:* South Wilcove, Torpoint, Cornwall PL11 2PE. *T:* (01752) 814331. *Clubs:* Royal Navy of 1919, Royal Navy of 1765 and 1785, Sloane; Royal Yacht Squadron.

COWARD, Nicholas; General Secretary, Premier League, since 2011; *b* 13 Feb. 1966; *s* of John and Jane Coward; *m* 2007, Vivien Lyle; one *s* one *d*. *Educ:* Shrewsbury Sch.; Bristol Univ. (LLB 1989); Guildford Coll. of Law. Solicitor, Freshfields, 1990–96; Football Association: Co. Solicitor, 1996–98; Dir, Legal and Corporate Affairs, 1998–2004; Actg Chief Exec., 1998–2000 and 2002–03; Dir, Wembley Stadium, 1999–2001; Dep. Chm., A. S. Biss & Co., 2004–07; Chief Exec., British Horseracing Authy, 2007–11. Chm., Sports Rights Owners Coalition, 2005–10; Director: European Professional Football Leagues, 2013–; FA, 2014–; UEFA Professional Football Strategy Council, 2014–. Treas., CCPR, 2004–07. *Address:* Premier League, 30 Gloucester Place, W1U 8PL. *Clubs:* MCC; Royal Cinque Ports Golf (Deal).

COWARD, Dame Pamela (Sarah), DBE 2003; education consultant, 2004–09; Headteacher, Middleton Technology School, 1991–2004; *b* 18 Jan. 1944; *d* of late Henry and Faith Coward; one *s*, and one step *s* one step *d*. *Educ:* City of Leeds Trng Coll. (Teachers' Cert. 1969); Open Univ. (BA 1979; Advanced Dip. in Mgt 1988); Manchester Univ. (Advanced Dip. in Guidance in Educn 1981). Special Needs Co-ordinator, Heywood Community Sch., 1984–88. Council Mem., Specialist Schools' Trust, 1998–2004; Chm. Govs, Rochdale Sixth Form Coll., 2009–. FRSA 1993. *Recreations:* theatre, evenings out, reading, playing with two granddaughters.

COWARD, Richard Edgar; retired; Director for Library Planning, OCLC Inc., 1980–81; *b* 19 April 1927; *s* of Edgar Frank Coward and Jean (*née* McIntyre); *m* 1949, Audrey Scott Lintern; one *s* two *d*. *Educ:* Richmond Grammar Sch., Surrey. FCLIP. Dir Gen., Bibliographic Servs Div., British Library, 1975–79. Member: Adv. Cttee on BBC Archives, 1976–79; Library Adv. Council (England), 1976–. *Address:* Allfarthings, West Street, Mayfield, E Sussex TN20 6DT.

COWBURN, Norman; Chairman, Britannia Building Society, 1987–90 (Managing Director, 1970–84; Deputy Chairman, 1986–87); *b* 5 Jan. 1920; *s* of Harold and Edith Cowburn; *m* 1945, Edna Margaret Heatley; two *s* one *d*. *Educ:* Queen Elizabeth's Grammar Sch., Blackburn. FCIS, FCIB. Burnley Building Soc., 1936. Served War, 1940–46. Burnley Building Soc., 1946; Leek and Westbourne Building Soc., 1954 (re-named Britannia Building Soc., Dec. 1975). *Recreations:* golf, gardening. *Address:* Greywoods, Cheddleton Road, Birchall, Leek, Staffs ST13 5QZ. *T:* (01538) 383214.

COWBURN, Prof. Russell Paul, PhD; FRS 2010; Professor of Experimental Physics, University of Cambridge, since 2010; *b* Newcastle-upon-Tyne, 1971; *s* of Frank and Dorothy Cowburn; *m* 1996, Rebecca Wade. *Educ:* Dame Allan's Boys' Sch., Newcastle-upon-Tyne; St John's Coll., Cambridge (BA Natural Scis 1993; PhD Exptl Condensed Matter Physics 1996). Res. Fellow, St John's Coll., Cambridge, 1997–2000; Reader, Durham Univ., 2000–04; Prof. of Nanotechnol., Imperial Coll. London, 2005–10. *Publications:* contribs to Nature, Science, Physical Rev. Letters, Applied Physics Letters. *Address:* Department of Physics, Cavendish Laboratory, University of Cambridge, J. J. Thomson Avenue, Cambridge CB3 0HE. *E:* rpc12@cam.ac.uk.

COWDRAY, 4th Viscount *cr* 1917; **Michael Orlando Weetman Pearson;** Bt 1894; Baron 1910; *b* 17 June 1944; *s* of 3rd Viscount Cowdray and of his 1st wife, Lady Anne Pamela Bridgeman, *d* of 5th Earl of Bradford; *S* father, 1995; one *s* by Barbara Page; *m* 1st, 1977, Ellen (marr. diss. 1984), *d* of Hermann Erhardt; 2nd, 1987, Marina Rose, *d* of late John H. Cordle and of Mrs H. J. Ross Skinner; two *s* three *d*. *Educ:* Gordonstoun. *Recreation:* historic motor racing. *Heir:* *s* Hon. Peregrine John Dickinson Pearson, *b* 27 Oct. 1994. *Address:* Greenhill House, Vann Road, Fernhurst, Haslemere GU27 3NL. *Club:* White's.

COWELL, (Andrew John Hulke) Hamish; HM Diplomatic Service; Ambassador to Tunisia, since 2013; *b* Richmond, N Yorks, 31 Jan. 1965; *s* of Barry Hulke Cowell and Anne Roberta Cowell (*née* Menzies); *m* 2000, Shadi Akhtar Khankasmai; three *d*. *Educ:* Madras Coll., St Andrews; Wadham Coll., Oxford (BA 1st Cl. Hons Oriental Studies (Persian and Islamic Studies); Oriental Studies Faculty Prize). Entered FCO, 1987; ME Dept, 1987–88; Second Sec., Colombo, 1989–92; First Sec. and Dep. Hd of Mission, Tehran, 1992–94; EU Directorate, 1994–96; Hd, Pol and Econ. Sections, Cairo, 1996–99; Foreign Sec.'s Speechwriter, 1999–2000; Press Office, 10 Downing St, 2000; First Sec., UK Representation, Brussels (ME/N Africa), 2001–04; on secondment to Quai d'Orsay, 2004; Hd, Internat. Policy, Paris, 2005–09; Private Sec. to Minister of State, FCO, 2010–11; Head: Libya Crisis Unit, 2011–12; N Africa Dept, 2012–13. *Recreations:* fishing, reading, tennis, walking. *Address:* BFPO 5304, Ruislip, Middx HA4 6EP. *T:* (Tunisia) 71108700. *E:* Hamish.cowell@fco.gov.uk.

COWELL, His Honour Peter Reginald; a Circuit Judge, 1996–2012; *b* 9 March 1942; *s* of Reginald Ernest Cowell and Philippa Eleanor Frances Anne Cowell (*née* Prettejohn); *m* 1975, Penelope Jane Bowring; two *s* one *d*. *Educ:* Bedford Sch.; Gonville and Caius Coll., Cambridge. Called to the Bar, Middle Temple, 1964, Bencher, 1997 (Master of the Revels, 2001–13; Autumn Reader, 2008); Asst Recorder, 1985–92; Recorder, 1992–96. Mem. Senate, Inns of Court, 1975–78. *Recreations:* acting (Mem., Old Stagers, 1970–), sculling, genealogy. *Address:* c/o Middle Temple Treasury, Middle Temple Lane, EC4Y 9AT. *Club:* Garrick.

COWELL, Prof. Raymond, CBE 2004; Vice-Chancellor, Nottingham Trent University, 1992–2003 (Director and Chief Executive, Trent Polytechnic, Nottingham, then Nottingham Polytechnic, 1987–92); *b* 3 Sept. 1937; *s* of Cecil Cowell and Susan Cowell (*née* Green); *m* 1963, Sheila (*née* Bolton); one *s* one *d*. *Educ:* St Aidan's Grammar Sch., Sunderland; Bristol Univ. (BA, PhD); Cambridge Univ. (PGCE). Head of English, Nottingham Coll. of Educn, 1970–73; Dean of Humanities 1974–81, Dep. Rector 1981–87, Sunderland Polytechnic. Member: CNAA, 1974–77 and 1981–85; Unit for Develt of Adult and Continuing Educn, 1986–90; British Council Cttee for Internat. Co-op. in Higher Educn, 1990–2000; Bd, Greater Nottingham TEC, 1990–93; Directing Gp, Prog. on Instnl Management in Higher Educn, OECD, 1990–97; Council, NCVQ, 1991–97; Bd, Higher Educn Business Enterprise, 1993–95; Policy Liaison Gp, Open Learning Foundn, 1993–95; Adv. Panel, Nat. Reading Initiative, DNH, 1996–97; E Midlands Business Leadership Team, BITC, 2001–03. Chairman: Staff and Educnl Develt Assoc., 1993–99; CVCP working gp on vocational higher educn, 1993–96; Management Bd and Members Adv. Gp, Univs and Colls Staff Develt Agency (formerly Univs Staff Develt Unit), 1993–95; E Midlands Arts Bd Ltd, 1995–2001 (Mem., Arts Council of England, 1996–98). Board Member: Nottingham City Challenge, 1991–93; Opera North, 2000–10; Nottingham Bldg Soc., 2003–08 (Vice-Chm., 2004–08); Chair, Bd, Viva Chamber Orch., 2005–09. Trustee: Djanogly City Acad., 2008– (Mem. Bd of Govs, 2005–08); Nottingham Contemporary, 2008–12. FRSA 1996. DL Notts, 1996. Midlander of the Year, Carlton TV, 2002. *Publications:* Twelve Modern Dramatists, 1967; W. B. Yeats, 1969; (ed) Richard II, 1969; Critics on Yeats, 1971; Critics on Wordsworth, 1973; The Critical Enterprise, 1975; articles and reviews on higher education. *Recreations:* books, music, theatre.

COWELL, Simon Phillip; music executive and television producer; *b* Brighton, 7 Oct. 1959; *s* of late Eric Cowell and of Julie Cowell; one *s* by Lauren Silverman. Various posts, EMI Music Publishing; co-founder, E&S Music; co-founder, Fanfare Records; A&R Consultant, BMG, later Sony BMG, then Sony Music, 1989–; signed acts incl. Curiosity Killed the Cat, Five, Westlife, Robson and Jerome; founder, Syco Music and Syco TV, 2002; artists incl. Leona Lewis, Il Divo, Susan Boyle and Alexandra Burke; producer and judge of TV talent shows; creator of Got Talent and X Factor formats; *judge:* Pop Idol, 2001–03; American Idol, 2002–10; *executive producer:* Cupid, 2003; Celebrity Duets, 2006; American Inventor, 2006–07; Grease is the Word, 2007; *creator and executive producer:* America's Got Talent, 2006–08; Australia's Got Talent, 2007; *creator and judge:* X Factor, 2004–10, 2014–; Britain's Got Talent, 2007–; X Factor USA, 2011; *creator:* Red or Black?, 2011. Special Award, BAFTA, 2010; Internat. Emmy Founders Award, 2010. *Publications:* I Don't Mean to be Rude, but…, 2003. *Address:* c/o Syco Entertainment, Sony, 9 Derry Street, W8 5HY.

COWEN, Brian; Member (FF) of the Dáil (TD) for Laois-Offaly, June 1984–2011; Taoiseach (Prime Minister of Ireland), 2008–11; President, Fianna Fáil, 2008–11; *b* 10 Jan. 1960; *s* of late Bernard Cowen; *m* 1990, Mary Molloy; two *d*. *Educ:* Cistercian Coll., Roscrea; University Coll., Dublin. Solicitor. Minister: for Labour, 1991–92; for Transport, Energy and Communications, 1992–94; for Health and Children, 1997–2000; for Foreign Affairs, 2000–04; for Finance, 2004–08; Tánaiste (Dep. Prime Minister), 2007–08. *Recreation:* all sports.

COWEN, Prof. Philip John, MD; FRCPsych; FMedSci; MRC Clinical Scientist and Hon Consultant Psychiatrist, Department of Psychiatry, since 1983, and Professor of Psychopharmacology, since 1997, University of Oxford; *b* Romford, Essex, 26 April 1951; *s* of Dennis D. Cowen and Judith Cowen (*née* Elks); *m* 1983, Stephanie Ruth Marsh; one *s* three *d*. *Educ:* Brentwood Sch.; University Coll. London (BSc 1971); University Coll. Hosp (MB BS 1974); Univ. of London (MD 1984). FRCPsych 1991. Hse Physician, UCH, 1974–75; Hse Surgeon, Wycombe Gen. Hosp., 1975–76; Registrar, Rotational Trng Scheme in Psychiatry, KCH, 1976–79; Fellow in Clin. Pharmacol., MRC Clin. Pharmacol. Unit, Oxford, 1979–83. Member: Guideline Panel on Generalized Anxiety Disorder, NICE, 2010–11; MRC Neurosci. and Mental Health Bd, 2011–15. FMedSci 2000. *Publications:* (jtly) Shorter Oxford Textbook of Psychiatry, 1995, 6th edn 2012; contribs to learned jls on psychopharmacol. and psychiatry. *Recreations:* sport (spectator), philosophy, family. *Address:* Department of Psychiatry, Warneford Hospital, Oxford OX3 7JX. *T:* (01865) 226394. *E:* phil.cowen@psych.ox.ac.uk.

COWGILL, Peter Alan; Executive Chairman, JD Sports Fashion plc, since 2004; *b* 18 March 1953; *s* of John Cowgill and Kathleen Cowgill; *m* Lindsay; one *s* two *d*. *Educ:* De La Salle Grammar Sch., Manchester; Hull Univ. (BSc). FCA 1981. Sen. Partner, Cowgill Holloway LLP, chartered accountants, 1983–; Finance Dir, JD Sports plc, 1996–2001. Non-executive Chairman: United Carpets plc, 2005–; MBL Gp plc, 2006–. *Address:* JD Sports Fashion plc, Hollinsbrook Way, Pilsworth, Bury BL9 8RR. *T:* (0161) 767 1620, *Fax:* (0161) 767 1759. *E:* peter.cowgill@jdplc.com.

COWIE, Hon. Lord; William Lorn Kerr Cowie; a Senator of the College of Justice in Scotland, 1977–94; a Judge of the Court of Appeal, Botswana, 1995–98; *b* 1 June 1926; *s* of late Charles Rennie Cowie, MBE and Norah Slimmon Kerr; *m* 1958, Camilla Henrietta Grizel Hoyle; twin *s* two *d*. *Educ:* Fettes Coll.; Clare Coll., Cambridge; Glasgow Univ. Sub-Lieut RNVR, 1944–47; Cambridge, 1947–49; Glasgow Univ., 1949–51; Mem., Faculty of Advocates, 1952; QC (Scotland) 1967. *Address:* 61/6 Grange Loan, Edinburgh EH9 2EG. *T:* (0131) 667 8238. *Club:* New (Edinburgh).

COWIE, Andrew Graeme; Assistant HM Inspector of Constabulary for Scotland, since 2013; *b* Edinburgh, 1 July 1966; *s* of Alan Cowie and Eleanor Cowie; *m* 1988, Alison Macleod; one *s* two *d*. *Educ:* Onthank Prim. Sch., Kilmarnock; Mile End Prim. Sch., Aberdeen; Aberdeen Grammar Sch.; Univ. of Aberdeen (MA Hons Internat. Relns and Politics 1987); Open Univ. (MBA 2003). Patrol Officer, then Sgt, Metropolitan Police, 1988–94; Northern Constabulary: Patrol Officer, 1994–97; Patrol Sgt, 1997–99; Emergency Planning Officer, 2000; Partnership Develt, 2002; Area Comdr, Shetland, 2003–06; Supt, Corporate Services, 2006–09; Chief Supt, 2009–11; Dep. Chief Constable, 2011–13. *Recreations:* family, cycling, time trialling, cinema, travelling. *Address:* HM Inspectorate for Constabulary in Scotland, 1st Floor, St Andrew's House, Regent Road, Edinburgh EH1 3DG. *T:* (0131) 244 5610.

COWIE, Ian McGregor; journalist; columnist, Sunday Times, since 2013; *b* 15 Sept. 1958; *s* of Joseph Cowie and Mary (*née* Proctor); *m* 1987, Susan Carole Fleming; one *s*. *Educ:* William Ellis Sch.; Univ. of York (BA Hons); City Univ. (Postgrad. Dip.). Daily Telegraph: City Reporter, 1986–89; Personal Finance Ed., 1989–2010; Head of Personal Finance, 2008–13. Columnist, Spectator Business, 2008–10. Personal Finance Journalist of the Year: Golden Pen Awards, 1996; Assoc. of British Insurers Awards, 1996, 1997, 1998; Wincott Award, 2007; Consumer Journalist of the Year, London Press Club Awards, 2011. *Publications:* Daily Telegraph Guides series on savings and investments, 1996–2013; contrib. Spectator. *Recreation:* sailing close to the wind. *E:* ian.cowie@sunday-times.co.uk. *Club:* Royal Ocean Racing.

COWIE, Dr Lennox Lauchlan, FRS 2004; Astronomer, University of Hawaii, since 1997; *b* 18 Oct. 1950. *Educ:* Edinburgh Univ. (BSc 1st cl.); Harvard Univ. (PhD 1976). Res. Astronomer, with rank of Associate Prof., Princeton Univ., 1979–81; Associate Prof. of Physics, MIT, 1981–84; Chief, Acad. Affairs Br., Space Telescope Sci. Inst., and Prof., Johns Hopkins Univ., 1984–86; Associate Dir, Inst. for Astronomy, Univ. of Hawaii, 1986–97. *Publications:* numerous papers in refereed learned jls. *Address:* Institute for Astronomy, University of Hawaii, 2680 Woodlawn Drive, Honolulu, HI 96822–1839, USA.

COWIE, William Lorn Kerr; *see* Cowie, Hon. Lord.

COWLEY, 7th Earl *cr* 1857; **Garret Graham Wellesley;** Baron Cowley, 1828; Viscount Dangan, 1857; Senior Investment Partner, Thos R. Miller & Son (Bermuda), Isle of Man, 1990–2000; *b* 30 July 1934; 3rd *s* of 4th Earl Cowley (*d* 1962) and Mary (Elsie May), Countess Cowley (*d* 1992); *S* nephew, 1975; *m* 1st, 1960 Suzanne Lennon (marr. diss. 1967), S Carolina; one *s* one *d*; 2nd, 1968, Isabelle O'Bready (marr. diss. 1981), Quebec; 3rd, 1981, Paige Deming (*d* 2008), Reno, Nevada; 4th, 2012, Carola Marion, *er d* of Sir Robert Erskine-Hill, 2nd Bt and *widow* of Robin Stormonth Darling. *Educ:* Univ. of S California (BSc Finance 1957); Harvard Univ. (MBA 1962). Investment Research Analyst: Wells Fargo Bank, San Francisco, 1962–64; Dodge & Cox, San Francisco, 1964–66; Asst Head, Investment Research Dept, Wells Fargo Bank, 1966–67; Vice-Pres., Investment Counsel, Thorndike, Doran, Paine & Lewis, Los Angeles, 1967–69; Sen. Vice-Pres., Exec. Cttee Mem., Securities, Real Estate and Company Acquisition Advisor, Shareholders Capital Corp., Los Angeles, 1969–74; Vice-Pres., and Sen. Investment Manager, Trust Dept, Bank of America, San Francisco, 1974–78; Gp Vice-Pres. and Dir, Internat. Investment Management Service, Bank of America NT & SA, 1980–85; Director: Bank of America Internat., London, 1978–85; BankAmerica Trust Co. (Hong Kong), 1980–85; Bank of America Banking & Trust Co. (Gibraltar), 1981–85; Bank of America Trust Co. (Jersey), 1982–85; Bank of America Banking & Trust Co. (Nassau), 1982–85; Bank of America Banking & Trust Co. (Cayman), 1982–85; ind. financial advr and co. dir, 1985–90; Director: Duncan Lawrie (IOM) Ltd, 1993–2001; Scottish Provident Internat. Ltd, 1998–2009; L-R Global Fund (New York), 2003–09; Kazimir Russia Growth Fund (Moscow), 2005–; Mem., Gen. Cttee of Trustees, 2006–, Mem., Audit Cttee, 2006–15, Chm., Investment Cttee, 2011–15, Lloyds Register Gp. Served US Army Counter Intelligence Corps, primarily in France, 1957–60. Member: Assoc. of Conservative Peers, 1981–; Parly Arts and Heritage Gp, 1981–99, Defence Gp, 1982–99, and Anglo-Amer. Gp, 1987–99, H of L. *Heir:* *s* Viscount Dangan, *qv*. *Clubs:* Brooks's; Pilgrims, Philippics; Harvard (San Francisco).

COWLEY, Prof. Alan Herbert, FRS 1988; FRSC; Robert A. Welch Professor of Chemistry, University of Texas at Austin, since 1991; *b* 29 Jan. 1934; *s* of late Herbert Cowley and Dora Cowley; *m* 1975, Deborah Elaine Cole; two *s* three *d*. *Educ:* Univ. of Manchester (BSc, MSc; Dalton Chem. Schol., 1956–58; PhD 1958). Technical Officer, ICI, 1960–61; University of Texas at Austin: Asst Prof. of Chemistry, 1962–67; Associate Prof., 1967–70; Prof., 1970–84; George W. Watt Centennial Prof., 1984–88; Richard J. V. Johnson Regents Prof. of Chemistry, 1989–91; Sir Edward Frankland Prof. of Inorganic Chem., Imperial Coll., London, 1988–89. Deutsche Akademische Austauschdienst Fellow, 1973; Guggenheim Fellow, 1976–77; von Humboldt Sen. Fellow, 1996; Lectures: Jeremy I. Musher Meml, Hebrew Univ., Jerusalem, 1979; Mobay, Univ. of New Hampshire, 1985; Karcher, Univ. of Oklahoma, 1985; Reilly, Univ. of Notre Dame, 1987; Fischel, Vanderbilt Univ., 1991; Baxter, Northern Illinois Univ., 1992; Etter Meml, Univ. of Minnesota, 1995; Vis. Prof., Univ. of Western Ont., 1987; Gauss Prof., Göttinger Acad. of Scis, 2005. Member: Chem.

Soc., subseq. RSC, 1961 (Award for Main-Gp Element Chem., 1980; Centenary Medal and Lectureship, 1986); Amer. Chem. Soc., 1962 (Southwest Regl Award, 1986); Eur. Acad. of Scis, 2009; Corresp. Member: Mexican Acad. of Scis, 2004; Göttingen Acad. of Scis, 2007; Eur. Acad. of Scis and Arts, 2007. Stiefvater Meml Award and Lectureship, Univ. of Nebraska, 1987; Chemical Pioneer Award, Amer. Inst. of Chemists, 1994; C. N. R. Rao Award, Chem. Res. Soc. of India, 2007; Award for Dist. Service in Advancement of Inorganic Chem., ACS, 2009. Mem. Bd of Trustees, Gordon Res. Confs, 1989–98 (Chm., 1994–95). Member, Editorial Board: Inorganic Chemistry, 1979–83; Chemical Reviews, 1984–88; Polyhedron, 1984–2000; Jl of Amer. Chem. Soc., 1986–91; Jl of Organometallic Chemistry, 1987–2008; Organometallics, 1988–91; Dalton Trans., 1997–2000; Mem. Bd, Inorganic Syntheses, 1983– (Ed.-in-Chief, vol. 31). FRSC 2004. Dr *hc* Bordeaux I, 2003. *Publications:* over 500 pubns in learned jls. *Recreations:* squash, sailing, music. *Address:* Department of Chemistry and Biochemistry, University of Texas at Austin, 1 University Station A5300, Austin, TX 78712, USA. *Clubs:* Athenæum; Headliners (Austin).

COWLEY, Jason; journalist, magazine editor and cultural critic; Editor, New Statesman, since 2008; *b* Harlow, Essex, 1965; *s* of Anthony Frank Cowley and Lilian Ella Edith Cowley (*née* Shears); *m* 1998, Sarah Jane Kernohan; one *s*. *Educ:* Univ. of Southampton (BA 1st Cl. Hons English and Philosophy). Reporter, then News Ed., The Bookseller, 1992–95; staff feature writer, The Times, 1996–98; Literary Ed., New Statesman, 1999–2002; Sen. Ed. and writer, Observer, 2003–07; Ed., Granta, 2007–08. Founder Mem. Council, Caine Prize for African Writing, 1997; Booker Prize judge, 1997. Ed. of Year, current affairs and specialist mags, 2009, Ed. of Year, current affairs and newspaper magazines, 2011, British Soc. of Mag. Editors. *Publications:* Unknown Pleasures: a novel, 2000; The Last Game: love, death and football, 2009. *Recreations:* reading, writing, walking, watching football. *Address:* New Statesman, 20 Farringdon Road, EC1M 3HE. *E:* jcowley@newstatesman.co.uk. *Clubs:* Garrick; Arsenal; Hatfield Heath Cricket.

COWLEY, Kenneth Edward, AO 1988; Chairman, R. M. Williams Holdings Ltd, since 1994; *b* 17 Nov. 1934; *s* of Edward Clegg Cowley and Patricia Bertha (*née* Curran); *m* 1958, Maureen Yvonne Manahan; one *s* one *d*. Sen. Exec., The Australian, 1964–97; Director: News Ltd, 1976–97; Internat. Bd, News Corp., 1980–2011; Chief Exec., 1980–97, Chm., 1992–96, Exec. Chm., 1996–97, News Ltd; Chairman: PMP Communications (formerly Pacific Magazines and Printing) Ltd, 1991–2001; Ansett Transport Industries, then Ansett Australia Hldgs, 1992–98 (Dir, 1997–2000); Ansett Internat., 1997–2000; Tasman Pacific Airways (traded as Ansett NZ, then Qantas NZ), 1997–2000; Ind. Newspapers Ltd (NZ), 2001–04 (Dir, 1990–2005). Director: Qld Press Ltd, 1987–97; Commonwealth Bank of Australia, 1997–2001; Tower Estate plc, 1998–. Councillor, Royal Agricl Soc. of NSW, 1979–. Life Gov., Art Gall. of NSW, 1997 (Trustee, 1986–97); Patron, Australian Stockman's Hall of Fame & Outback Heritage Centre, 2009– (Chm., 1976–2009). Hon. DBus NSW, 2008. *Address:* R. M. Williams Holdings Pty Ltd, Level 11, 52 Alfred Street, Milsons Point, NSW 2061, Australia. *T:* (2) 90285412. *Club:* Union (Sydney).

COWLEY, Lesley Ruth, OBE 2011; consultant and coach; Chair, Driver and Vehicle Licensing Agency, since 2014; *b* Bristol, 30 June 1960; *d* of John Mawson and Heather Mawson; *m* 1989, David Cowley; one *s*. *Educ:* St Ursula's High Sch., Bristol; Univ. of West of England, Bristol (MBA Dist.). Asst to Insolvency Partner, Monahans, 1988–90; Dir, New Coll., Swindon, 1990–99; Nominet: Ops Dir, 1999–2001; Man. Dir, 2002–04; CEO, Nominet, 2004–14. Non-exec. Dir, Public Policy, AQL, 2014–. Member: Council, Country Code Names Supporting Orgn, 2007–; Policy and Public Affairs Bd, BCS, 2013–; Surveillance Rev. Panel, RUSI, 2014. FCMI 2005; FICM 2005; FBCS 2008; FRSA 2010; FInstD 2011. *Recreations:* Tiffany glass and glass fusing, competitive gardening. *W:* www.lesleycowley.me.uk.

COWLEY, Dame Sarah (Ann), DBE 2013; PhD; Professor of Community Practice Development, Florence Nightingale School of Nursing and Midwifery, King's College London, 1997–2012, now Emeritus Professor; *b* St Helier, Jersey, 6 Feb. 1948; *d* of Charles Lyn and Margaret Handley; *m* 1971, Ernest Michael Leonard Cowley (marr. diss. 1974); one *s*. *Educ:* Perse Sch. for Girls, Cambridge; St Mary's Hosp., London (RN 1969); Brighton Poly. (RHV 1981); Open Univ. (BA Hons 1984); Brighton Poly. (PhD 1991). Staff Nurse, St Mary's Hosp., 1969–70; Ward Sister, Marple Dale Hosp., 1971; Night Sister, Bromley Hosp., 1972–74; Clinical Teacher, Farnborough Sch. of Nursing, 1975–80; Health Visitor, 1981–86, Field Work Teacher, 1986–92, Eastbourne HA; Lectr, Dept of Nursing Studies, 1992–95, Sen. Lectr, 1995–97, KCL. Trustee, Inst. of Health Visiting, 2012–. *Publications:* (ed with I. Norman) The Changing Nature of Nursing in a Managerial Age, 1999; (ed with J. Appleton) The Search for Health Needs: research for health visiting practice, 2000; (ed) Public Health Policy and Practice: a sourcebook for health visitors and community nurses, 2002; (with M. Frost) The Principles of Health Visiting, 2006; (ed) Public Health in Policy and Practice: a sourcebook for health visitors and community nurses, 2002, 2nd edn as Policy and Practice in Community Public Health: a sourcebook, 2008; contrib. peer-reviewed acad. papers. *Recreation:* walking on Bournemouth beach and in New Forest with dog and grandchildren. *Address:* Florence Nightingale School of Nursing and Midwifery, King's College London, 57 Waterloo Road, SE1 8WA. *E:* sarah.cowley@kcl.ac.uk.

COWLEY, Sarah Julie; HM Diplomatic Service; Ambassador to Latvia, since 2013; *b* Norfolk, 19 Nov. 1977; *d* of Paul and Julie Cowley; *m* 2007, Paul Hamilton Boschi; one *d*. *Educ:* Wisbech Grammar Sch.; University Coll. London (BA Hons Hist.); Open Univ. (MBA). With KPMG, 2003–04; DLA Piper, 2004–05; entered FCO, 2005; Asst Private Sec. to Minister of State, 2007–09; Private Sec. to UK Special Rep. for Afghanistan and Pakistan, 2009–10; Political Advr to Hd, EU Delegn in Kabul, 2010–11; Head: of Communications, Islamabad, 2011–12; of Olympic and Paralympic Co-ordination Centre, FCO, 2012; Commercial Diplomacy, FCO, 2012–13. *Recreations:* mountaineering, travel. *Address:* British Embassy, Alunana iela 5, Riga 1010, Latvia. *E:* sarah.cowley@fco.gov.uk.

COWLEY, Prof. Stanley William Herbert, FRS 2011; Professor of Solar-Planetary (formerly Space Plasma) Physics, and Head, Radio and Space Plasma Physics Group, Department of Physics and Astronomy, University of Leicester, since 1996; *b* 11 April 1947; *s* of late Herbert William Leslie Cowley and Annie Jenny Cowley (*née* Clark); *m* 1970, Lynn Doreen Moore; two *s* one *d*. *Educ:* Imperial Coll., Univ. of London (BSc, ARCS, PhD, DIC). FBIS 1975; MInstP 1975, FInstP 2011; FRAS 1986; CPhys 1989. Imperial College, University of London: SERC Advanced Fellow, 1977–82; Lectr, 1982–85; Reader, 1985–88; Prof. of Physics, 1988–95; Head, Space and Atmospheric Physics Gp, Blackett Lab., 1990–95; PPARC Sen. Fellow, 2001–04; Royal Soc. Leverhulme Trust Sen. Res. Fellow, 2006–07. Mem., PPARC, 1994–96. Fellow, Amer. Geophysical Union, 1995. Chapman Medal, 1991, Gold Medal, 2006, RAS; Bartels Medal, Eur. Geoscis Union, 2006. *Publications:* contrib. numerous papers in solar system plasma physics in learned jls. *Recreation:* walking the dog. *Address:* Department of Physics and Astronomy, University of Leicester, University Road, Leicester LE1 7RH. *T:* (0116) 223 1331, (0116) 252 3563.

COWLEY, Prof. Steven, PhD; FRS 2014; FInstP, FREng; Director, Culham Centre for Fusion Energy, since 2008; Chief Executive Officer, United Kingdom Atomic Energy Authority, since 2009. *Educ:* Corpus Christi Coll., Oxford (BA Physics 1981); Princeton Univ. (MA 1983; PhD 1985). FInstP 2004; FREng 2014. Harkness Fellow, 1981–83; postdoctoral res., Culham Lab., 1985–87; Princeton Univ., 1987–93; UCLA, 1993–2001 (Prof., 2000–01); Leader, Plasma Physics Gp, Imperial Coll. London, 2001–03; Dir, Center for Multi-scale Plasma Dynamics, UCLA, 2004–08; Prof. of Plasma Physics (pt-time), Imperial Coll. London. Mem., Prime Minister's Council for Sci. and Technol., 2011–. Fellow, Amer. Physical Soc., 1998. Glazebrook Medal, Inst. of Physics, 2012. *Publications:* contribs to learned jls incl. Physical Rev. Letters, Physics of Plasmas, Nuclear Fusion, New Jl of Physics. *Address:* United Kingdom Atomic Energy Authority, Culham Science Centre, Abingdon, Oxon OX14 3DB.

COWLING, Gareth; *see* Cowling, His Honour T. G.

COWLING, Peter John; Director, Falmouth Quay Consultants, 2003–13; *b* 11 Nov. 1944; *s* of Harold Cowling and Irene (*née* Phillips); *m* 1979, Sara Fox; one *d* (and one *d* decd). *Educ:* Bletchley Grammar Sch.; Britannia Royal Naval Coll. Joined RN 1963; commanded: HMS Naiad, 1979; HMS York and 3rd Destroyer Sqdn, 1988; Sen. Naval Officer, Middle East, 1991; Dir, Naval Ops, MoD, 1992; retired 1994. Dir, RSA, 1994–96; Head of Corporate Relns, Proshare, 1997–98; Dir, Nat. Maritime Mus. Cornwall, 1998–2003. Chm., Cornwall SSAFA, 2006–15; SSAFA SW Regl Rep., 2015–. Younger Brother, Trinity House, 1981– (Pilgrim, 1996–). Queen's Gold Medal, 1967. *Recreations:* sailing, gardening, tennis. *Address:* Parc Vean, Mylor Churchtown, Cornwall TR11 5UD.

COWLING, Sharon Katherine; *see* Phillips, S. K.

COWLING, His Honour (Thomas) Gareth; a Circuit Judge, 2004–09; *b* 12 Nov. 1944; *s* of late Clifford Cowling and Beryl Elizabeth Cowling (*née* Thomas); *m* 1970, Jill Ann Stephens; one *s* one *d*. *Educ:* Eastbourne Coll.; College of Law. Articled to Clifford Cowling, of Clifford Cowling & Co., Hampshire, 1964; admitted Solicitor of Supreme Court, 1969; Solicitor, Solicitor's Dept, New Scotland Yard, 1969–72; called to Bar, Middle Temple, 1972; private practice at Bar, London and Winchester, Western Circuit, 1972–88; Metropolitan Stipendiary Magistrate, 1988–89; Stipendiary Magistrate, subseq. Dist Judge (Magistrates' Courts), Hampshire, 1989–2004; a Recorder, 1998–2004. Mem., Parole Bd, 2007. *Recreations:* eating and drinking with family and friends, trying to play golf.

COWMAN, Prof. Alan Frederick, PhD; FRS 2011; Head, Division of Infection and Immunity, Walter and Eliza Hall Institute of Medical Research, since 1999; *b* Brisbane, 27 Dec. 1954. *Educ:* Griffith Univ. (BSc Hons 1979); Univ. of Melbourne (PhD Molecular Parasitol. 1984). FAA 2001. Postdoctoral res. at Univ. of Calif, Berkeley, 1984–86; Walter and Eliza Hall Inst. Med. Res., 1986–. Wellcome Trust Australian Sen. Res. Fellow, 1988; Internat. Res. Schol., 1992, 1993–97, 2000–10, Sen. Internat. Res. Schol., 2012–, Howard Hughes Med. Inst. NHMRC Australia Fellow, 2011. Boehringer-Mannheim Medal, 1994, Lemberg Medal, 2006, Australian Soc. Biochem. and Molecular Biol. *Publications:* contribs to scientific jls incl. Nature, Cell, Blood, Science, Traffic. *Address:* Walter and Eliza Hall Institute of Medical Research, WEHI Biotechnology Centre, 4 Research Avenue, La Trobe R&D Park, Bundoora, Vic 3086, Australia.

COWPER-COLES, Sir Sherard (Louis), KCMG 2004 (CMG 1997); LVO 1991; Group Head of Government Affairs, HSBC Holdings plc, since 2015 (Senior Adviser to Group Chairman and Group Chief Executive, 2013–15); *b* 8 Jan. 1955; *s* of late Sherard Hamilton Cowper-Coles and Dorothy (*née* Short); *m* 1st, 1982, Bridget Mary Elliott (marr. diss. 2011); four *s* one *d*; 2nd, 2012, Jasmine Zerinini; one *d*. *Educ:* Freston Lodge Sch.; New Beacon Sch.; Tonbridge Sch. (Scholar); Hertford Coll., Oxford (Classical Scholar; MA; Hon. Fellow, 2002). HM Diplomatic Service, 1977–2010: Third, later Second, Sec., Cairo, 1980–83; First Sec., Planning Staff, FCO, 1983–85; Private Sec. to Perm. Under-Sec. of State, 1985–87; First Sec., Washington, 1987–91; Asst, Security Policy Dept, FCO, 1991–93; Res. Associate, IISS, 1993–94; Head, Hong Kong Dept, FCO, 1994–97; Counsellor (Political) Paris, 1997–99; Prin. Private Sec. to Sec. of State for For. and Commonwealth Affairs, 1999–2001; Ambassador to: Israel, 2001–03; Saudi Arabia, 2003–07; Afghanistan, 2007–09; Special Rep. for Afghanistan and Pakistan, FCO, 2009–10; Business Develt Dir, Internat., BAE Systems, 2011–13. Chm., Financial Inclusion Commn, 2014–; Mem. Bd, China Britain Business Council, 2014–. Chm., Saudi-British Soc., 2011–. Mem., Internat. Engagement Cttee, British Acad., 2014–. Pres., Jane Austen Soc., 2015–. Chm., Pitzhanger Manor Trust, 2012–. Hon. Prof., Nottingham Univ., 2011–; Hon. Fellow, Exeter Univ., 2011–. CRAeS 2011. Liveryman, Skinners' Co., 1988. Hon. DLitt Westminster, 2014. *Publications:* Cables from Kabul: the inside story of the West's Afghanistan campaign, 2011; Ever the Diplomat: confessions of a Foreign Office mandarin, 2012; contrib. Survival (IISS jl). *Address:* HSBC Holdings plc, 8 Canada Square, E14 5HQ. *Club:* Brooks's.

COX, family name of **Baroness Cox**.

COX, Baroness *cr* 1982 (Life Peer), of Queensbury in Greater London; **Caroline Anne Cox;** a Deputy Speaker, House of Lords, 1986–2006; Chief Executive Officer, Humanitarian Aid Relief Trust, since 2004; *b* 6 July 1937; *d* of Robert John McNeill Love, MS, FRCS and Dorothy Ida Borland; *m* 1959, Dr Murray Cox, FRCPsych (*d* 1997); two *s* one *d*. *Educ:* Channing School; London Univ. (BSc (Sociology, 1st Cl. Hons) 1967, MSc (Economics) 1969). FRCN 1985. SRN, London Hosp., 1958; Staff Nurse, Edgware Gen. Hosp., 1960; Research Associate, Univ. of Newcastle upon Tyne, 1967–68; Department of Sociology, Polytechnic of North London: Lecturer, Senior Lectr, Principal Lectr, 1969–74; Head of Department, 1974–77; Dir, Nursing Educn Res. Unit, Chelsea Coll., London Univ., 1977–84. Dir, Centre for Policy Studies, 1983–85; Co-Dir, Educn Res. Trust, 1980–2010. A Baroness in Waiting, April–Aug. 1985. Chancellor: Bournemouth Univ., 1992–2001; Liverpool Hope Univ., 2006–13. Vice President: RCN, 1990–; Liverpool Sch. of Tropical Medicine, 2006–. Chm., Exec. Bd, Internat. Islamic Christian Orgn for Reconciliation and Reconstruction. Pres., Tushinskaya Children's Hosp. Trust; Patron, Medical Aid for Poland Fund. Fellow, Goodenough Coll., 2005. Hon. FRCS 1996. Hon. PhD Polish Univ. in London, 1988; Hon. LLD CNAA; DUniv: Surrey; UCE, 1998; Hon. DH Utah; Hon. Dr Yerevan; Hon. DSS QUB, 1996; Hon. DSc: City, 1999; Wolverhampton, 1999. Internat. Mother Teresa Award, All India Christian Council, 2005; Mkhitar Gosh Medal, Republic of Armenia, 2005; 25th Anniv. Medal, Polish Solidarity Movt, 2005; Medal of Gratitude, Eur. Solidarity Centre, Poland 2012. Commander's Cross, Order of Merit (Poland), 1990. *Publications:* (ed jtly) A Sociology of Medical Practice, 1975; (jtly) Rape of Reason: The Corruption of the Polytechnic of North London, 1975; (jtly) The Right to Learn, 1982; Sociology: A Guide for Nurses, Midwives and Health Visitors, 1983; (jtly) The Insolence of Office, 1989; (jtly) Choosing a State School: how to find the best education for your child, 1989; Trajectories of Despair: misdiagnosis and maltreatment of Soviet orphans, 1991; (with John Eibner) Ethnic Cleansing in Progress: war in Nagorno Karabakh, 1993; (jtly) Made to Care: the case for residential and village communities for people with a mental handicap, 1995; (contrib.) Remorse and Reparation, ed Murray Cox, 1998; (jtly) The West, Islam and Islamism, 2003, 2nd edn 2006; (with Catherine Butcher) Cox's Book of Modern Saints and Martyrs, 2006; (with John Marks) This Immoral Trade: slavery in the 21st century, 2006, 2nd edn 2013; (with B. Rogers) The Very Stones Cry Out: the persecuted Church: pain, passion and praise, 2011. *Recreations:* campanology, tennis, hill walking. *Address:* House of Lords, SW1A 0PW. *T:* (office) (020) 8204 7336, *Fax:* (020) 8204 5661. *Club:* Royal Over-Seas League.

COX, Sir Alan (George), Kt 1994; CBE 1988; FCA; FCMA; Chief Executive, ASW Holdings PLC, 1981–96; *b* 23 Aug. 1936; *s* of late George Henry Cox and Florence Ivy Cox; *m* 1994, Rosamund Shelley. *Educ:* Oldbury Grammar Sch. FCA 1959; ACMA 1961. Chm. and Chief Exec., GKN Rolled and Bright Steel Ltd, 1978–80; Corporate Management Dir, GKN, PLC, 1980–81; Director: Morgan Crucible Co. plc, 1995–2004; Meggitt plc, 1996–2011; Henry Ivy Associates Ltd, 2000–. Founder Chairman: Wales Millennium Centre

Ltd, 1996–2001; The Public Ltd (formerly Jubilee/c/Plex Arts), 2001–04. Member: Bd, Cardiff Bay Develt Corp., 1987–2000; School Teachers Review Body, 1991–95; Financial Reporting Council, 1996–99. Chm., Mountview Acad. of Theatre Arts Ltd, 2004–07. *Recreations:* cookery, opera, walking. *Address:* PO Box 27, Chepstow, Monmouthshire NP16 6EY. *Club:* Cardiff and County.

COX, Alistair Richard; Chief Executive, Hays plc, since 2007; *b* 25 Feb. 1961; *s* of Gerald and Jean Cox; *m* 1988, Merete Oftedahl; two *s*. *Educ:* Univ. of Salford (BSc Hons Aeronautical Engrg, Dip. Engrg); Stanford Grad. Sch. of Business (MBA). Aeronautical Engr, British Aerospace UK, 1978–83; Engr and Manager, Schlumberger Wireline Services, Norway and USA, 1983–90; Consultant and Manager, McKinsey & Co., 1990–94; Gp Strategy Dir, 1994–98, Regl Pres. Asia, 1998–2002, Blue Circle Industries, subseq. Lafarge; Chief Exec., Xansa plc, 2002–07. Non-exec. Dir, 3i, 2009–. *Recreations:* scuba diving, mountaineering, sailing, wake boarding, motorsports. *Address:* Hays plc, Hays, 250 Euston Road, NW1 2AF. *T:* (020) 7383 2266, *Fax:* (020) 7388 4367.

COX, Alister Stransom, MA; Headmaster, Royal Grammar School, Newcastle upon Tyne, 1972–94; *b* 21 May 1934; *s* of Rev. Roland L. Cox and F. Ruth Cox; *m* 1960, Janet (*née* Williams); one *s* two *d*. *Educ:* Kingswood School, Bath; New College, Oxford (Scholar). Hon. Mods (1st Class); Lit. Hum. BA 1957, MA 1961. Sixth Form Master, Clifton Coll., 1957–63; Head of Classics, Wellington Coll., 1963–69; Dep. Head, Arnold Sch., Blackpool, 1969–72. Vis. Lectr in Greek, Bristol Univ., 1968. Founder Mem., Sinfonia Chorus, Northern Sinfonia of England, 1973–94 (Mem., Management Cttee, 1980–85). FRSA 1982. *Publications:* Lucretius on Matter and Man, 1967; Didactic Poetry, in Greek and Latin Literature (ed Higginbotham), 1969; articles in Greece and Rome, Times Educnl Supp. and educnl jls. *Recreations:* music, especially singing; French life and politics; touring lecturer Alliance Française. *Address:* 3 Lower Gale, Ambleside, Cumbria LA22 0BD. *T:* (015394) 32634.

COX, Gen. André; General of the Salvation Army, since 2013; *b* Salisbury, Fedn of Rhodesia and Nyasaland, 12 July 1954; *s* of Ronald Cox and Hilda Cox; *m* 1976, Silvia Volet; three *d*. *Educ:* Nat. Retail Distribution Cert. Salvation Army: Corps Officer, Switzerland, 1979–87; PR Officer, Zimbabwe, 1987–92; Financial Officer, Zimbabwe, 1992–97; PR Officer, Switzerland, 1997–2001; Business Officer, Switzerland, 2001–05; Territorial Commander: Finland and Estonia, 2005–08; S Africa, 2008–12; UK and Ire., 2012–13; COS, 2013. *Recreations:* photography, reading, walking. *Address:* Salvation Army, 101 Queen Victoria Street, EC4V 4EH.

COX, Anthony Robert, PhD, CEng; adviser on science and technology, since 1998; *b* 30 Nov. 1938; *s* of Robert George Cox and Gladys Cox; *m* 1963, Constance Jean Hammond; one *s* two *d*. *Educ:* Brockley County School; Imperial College, London. BScEng (Metallurgy). ARSM, MIMMM. RARDE, 1960–69; Exchange Scientist, US Naval Research Lab., Washington, 1969–71; Dep. Materials Supt, RARDE, 1971–75; Asst Dir, Armour and Materials, Military Vehicle Engineering Estab., 1975–80; MoD Central Staffs Defence Science, 1980–83; Counsellor, Science and Technol., Washington, 1983–87; Superintendent, Radiation Sci. and Acoustics, NPL, 1988–92; Counsellor, Sci. and Technol., Tokyo, 1993–98. Dir, Asia Pacific Technology Network, 1999–2003. Business Mentor, Prince's Trust, 2001–05. *Publications:* papers on refractory metals, structure and strengthening mechanism on high strength steel, fractography, explosive effects, archaeological artefacts corrosion, composites, space, robotics, science policy, metrology. *Recreations:* sailing, foreign travel, gardening, industrial archaeology, University of the Third Age.

COX, Archibald, Jr; Chairman: Sextant Group Inc., since 1993; Ayablu Inc., since 2011; EyeLock Inc., since 2012; *b* 13 July 1940; *s* of late Prof. Archibald Cox and Phyllis Ames; *m* 1962, Cornelia Sharp; one *s* one *d*; *m* 2005, Judy Gordon. *Educ:* Harvard Coll. (ABEcon 1962); Harvard Business Sch. (MBA 1964). Associate 1964–70, Vice Pres. 1971–72, Man. Dir, 1973–88, Morgan Stanley & Co. Incorp.; Man. Dir and Head of London Office, Morgan Stanley Internat., 1977–88; President and Chief Executive Officer: First Boston Corp., 1990–93; Magnequench Internat., 1995–2005. Chairman: Neo Material Technologies Inc., 2005–06; Precision Magnetics Singapore, 2007–10; Barclays Americas, 2008–11. Director: Diamar Interactive Corp., 1995–2000; Hutchinson Technol. Inc., 1996–2009; Harris Chemical Gp, 1997–98; BidClerk Inc., 2004–; Micell Technologies Inc., 2007–; Unifi Inc., 2008–; Simphotek Inc., 2010–; ImpulseSave Inc., 2011–; MediaMerx Inc., 2011–; SponsorHub Inc., 2011–. Man. Mem., Courant Capital Mgt LLC, 2010–. Dir, Amer. Mus. of Natural Hist., 2011–. Member: Securities and Investments Board, 1986–88; Bd, Securities Industry Assoc., 1990–93; Chm., Foreign Policy Assoc., 2010–14. Trustee, St Paul's Sch., Concord, NH, 2012–. *Recreations:* cycling, rowing, hiking, sailing. *Clubs:* Links (New York); Bucks Harbor Yacht (Brooksville, Maine); Kollegewidgwok Yacht (Blue Hill, Maine); Blue Hill Country (Blue Hill, Maine).

COX, Barry; *see* Cox, C. B.

COX, Barry Geoffrey, CBE 2013; Chairman: Digital UK, 2005–12; Deputy Chairman, Channel Four, 1999–2006; *b* 25 May 1942; *s* of Leonard William Cox and Daisy Miriam; *m* 1st, 1963, Pamela Ann Doran (marr. diss. 1977); two *s* two *d*; 2nd, 1984, Kathryn Diane Kay (marr. diss. 1994); 3rd, 2001, Fiona Pamela Hillary. *Educ:* Tiffin Sch., Kingston-upon-Thames; Magdalen Coll., Oxford (BA Hons). Reporter: The Scotsman, 1965–67; Sunday Telegraph, 1967–70; Producer and Dir, Granada TV, 1970–74; London Weekend Television: Editor, then Controller, 1974–87; Dir, Corporate Affairs, 1987–94; Dir, ITV Assoc., 1995–98; Chairman: Digital TV Stakeholders' Gp, 2002–05; Digital Radio Working Gp, 2008. News Internat. Vis. Prof. of Broadcast Media, Oxford Univ., 2003. Treas., Inst. of Educn, London Univ., 2000–08. Chm., Oval House Theatre, 2001–07. Life Mem., BAFTA. *Publications:* Civil Liberties in Britain, 1975; The Fall of Scotland Yard, 1977; Free For All?, 2004. *Address:* Mapledene TV Productions Ltd, 72 Wilton Road, SW1V 1DE. *E:* Barry.cox3@btopenworld.com.

COX, Brian Denis, CBE 2003; actor, director, teacher and writer; *b* 1 June 1946; *s* of Charles Mcardle Campbell Cox and Mary Ann Gillerline (*née* Mccann); *m* 1st, 1968, Caroline Burt (marr. diss. 1987); one *s* one *d*; 2nd, 2001, Nicole Elisabeth Ansari; two *s*. *Educ:* LAMDA. *Stage appearances:* début, Dundee Rep., 1961; Royal Lyceum, Edinburgh, 1965–66; Birmingham Rep., 1966–68; As You Like It, Birmingham and Vaudeville (London début), 1967; title rôle, Peer Gynt, Birmingham, 1967; When We Dead Awaken, Edinburgh Fest., 1968; In Celebration, Royal Court, 1969; The Wild Duck, Edinburgh Festival, 1969; The Big Romance, Royal Court, 1970; Don't Start Without Me, Garrick, 1971; Mirandolina, Brighton, 1971; Getting On, Queen's, 1971; The Creditors, Open Space, 1972; Hedda Gabler, Royal Court, 1972; Playhouse, Nottingham: Love's Labour's Lost, title rôle, Brand, What The Butler Saw, The Three Musketeers, 1972; Cromwell, Royal Court, 1973; Royal Exchange, Manchester: Arms and the Man, 1974; The Cocktail Party, 1975; Pilgrims Progress, Prospect Th., 1975; Emigrés, Nat. Theatre Co., Young Vic, 1976; Olivier Theatre: Tamburlaine The Great, 1976; Julius Caesar, 1977; The Changeling, Riverside Studios, 1978; National Theatre: title rôle, Herod, The Putney Debates, 1978; On Top, Royal Court, 1979; Macbeth, Cambridge Th. and tour of India, 1980; Summer Party, Crucible, 1980; Have You Anything to Declare?, Manchester then Round House, 1981; title rôle, Danton's Death, Nat. Theatre Co., Olivier, 1982; Strange Interlude, Duke of York, 1984 (Drama Mag. Best Actor Award, 1985), Nederlander, NY, 1985; Rat in the Skull, Royal Court, 1984 (Drama Mag. and Olivier Best Actor Awards, 1985) and NY, 1985; Fashion, The Danton Affair, Misalliance, Penny for a Song, 1986, The Taming of the Shrew, Titus Andronicus (title rôle), 1987, The Three Sisters, 1989, RSC, and Titus Andronicus on tour, Madrid, Paris, Copenhagen, 1988 (Olivier Award, Best Actor in a Revival, and Drama Mag. Best Actor Award for RSC 1988 season); Frankie and Johnny in the Clare-de-Lune, Comedy, 1989; Richard III, and title rôle, King Lear, National and world tour, 1990–91; The Master Builder, Edinburgh, 1993, Riverside, 1994; St Nicholas, Bush, 1997, NY, 1998 (Lucille Lortel Award, 1998); Skylight, LA, 1997; Art, NY, 1998; Dublin Carol, Old Vic, and Royal Court, 2000; Uncle Varrick, Edinburgh Royal Lyceum, 2004; Rock 'n' Roll, Royal Court, 2006, NY, 2007; Lolita, NT, 2009; That Championship Season, NY, 2011; The Weir, Donmar Warehouse, 2013, transf. Wyndhams, 2014; Waiting for Godot, Royal Lyceum, Edinburgh, 2015; *films:* Nicholas and Alexandra, 1971; In Celebration, 1975; Manhunter, Shoot for the Sun, 1986; Hidden Agenda, 1990; Braveheart, The Cutter, 1994; Rob Roy, 1995; Chain Reaction, The Glimmer Man, Long Kiss Goodnight, 1996; Desperate Measures, Food for Ravens, Poodle Spring, 1997; The Boxer, The Corruptor, Mad About Mamba, The Minus Man, Rushmore, 1998; The Biographer, 2000; Saltwater, Strictly Sinatra, The Affair of the Necklace, 2001; Morality Play, The Rookie, Adaptation, The Bourne Identity, L.I.E., Super Troopers, 2002; 25th Hour, X-Men 2, The Ring, 2003; Troy, The Reckoning, The Bourne Supremacy, 2004; Red-eye, Woman in Winter, The Ringer, 2005; Match Point, Fourth Wall, Running with Scissors, 2006; The Flying Scotsman, Zodiac, Terra, The Waterhorse: legend of the deep, 2007; The Escapist, Agent Crush, Shoot on Sight, 2008; Tell-Tale, The Good Heart, 2009; Red, Wide Blue Yonder, 2010; Ironclad, Rise of the Planet of the Apes, 2011; Coriolanus, The Campaign, Blood, 2012; Theatre of Dreams, Red 2, 2013; Believe, Forsaken, 2014; The Anomaly, 2014; Pixels, 2015; *TV appearances:* Churchill's People: The Wallace, 1972; The Master of Ballantrae, 1975; Henry II, in The Devil's Crown, 1978; Thérèse Raquin, 1979; Dalhousie's Luck, Bothwell, 1980; Bach, 1981; Pope John Paul II, 1984; Florence Nightingale, 1985; Beryl Markham: a shadow in the sun, 1988; Secret Weapon, Acting in Tragedy (BBC Masterclass), 1990; The Lost Language of Cranes, The Cloning of Joanna May, The Big Battalions, 1992; The Negotiator, 1994; Witness for Hitler, Blow Your Mind See A Play, 1995; Nuremberg (best supporting actor, Emmy Award), 2001; Frasier, 2002; The Strange Case of Sherlock Holmes and Arthur Conan Doyle, Blue/Orange, 2005; Deadwood, 2006; The Outsiders, The Secret of the Nutcracker, 2007; The Day of the Triffids, Marple: They Do It with Mirrors, 2009; On Expenses, 2010; The Sinking of the Laconia, 2011; The Straits, A Touch of Cloth, Addicted to Pleasure, 2012; An Adventure in Space and Time, 2013; Bob Servant, 2013–15; Shetland, The Game, 2014; War and Peace, 2015; *radio:* McLevy, 2001–15; *directed:* Edinburgh Festival: The Man with a Flower in his Mouth, The Stronger, 1973; Orange Tree, Richmond: I Love My Love, 1982; Mrs Warren's Profession, 1989; The Crucible, Moscow Art Theatre, London and Edinburgh, 1988–89; The Philanderer, Hampstead Th. Club, 1991 (world première of complete version); Richard III, Regent's Park Open Air Th., 1995. Rector, Dundee Univ., 2010–. Hon. LLD Dundee, 1994; Hon. DLitt: Queen Margaret, 2007; Kingston, 2011; Hon. DDra, RSAMD, 2007; Hon. Dr Napier, 2008. Internat. Theatre Inst. Award, 1990. *Publications:* Salem to Moscow: an actor's Odyssey, 1991; The Lear Diaries, 1992. *Recreations:* keeping fit, tango. *Address:* c/o Conway van Gelder Grant Ltd, 8–12 Broadwick Street, W1F 8HW. *T:* (020) 7287 0077. *Clubs:* Savile, Garrick, Groucho.

COX, Prof. Brian Edward, OBE 2010; PhD; Professor of Particle Physics, University of Manchester, since 2009; *b* Oldham, 3 March 1968; *m* 2003, Gia Milinovich; one *s*, and one step *s*. *Educ:* Hulme Grammar Sch.; Univ. of Manchester (BSc 1st Cl. Hons Physics; PhD). Keyboard player, rock band: Dare, 1986–92; D:Ream, 1993–97. University of Manchester: Mem., High Energy Physics Gp; PPARC Advanced Fellow; Royal Soc. Univ. Res. Fellow, 2005; researcher, ATLAS experiment, Large Hadron Collider, CERN, 2004–. Television: presenter: Wonders of the Solar System, 2010; Wonders of the Universe, 2011; Wonders of Life, 2013; Science Britannica, 2013; Human Universe, 2014; Six Degrees of Separation, 2015; co-presenter, Stargazing Live, 2011–; radio: co-presenter, The Infinite Monkey Cage, 2009–. Michael Faraday Award, Royal Soc., 2012. *Publications:* (with Jeff Forshaw) Why Does $E=mc^2$?, 2010; (with Andrew Cohen) Wonders of the Solar System, 2010; (with Andrew Cohen) Wonders of the Universe, 2011; (with Jeff Forshaw) The Quantum Universe: everything that can happen does happen, 2012; (with Andrew Cohen) Wonders of Life, 2013; (with Andrew Cohen) Human Universe, 2014. *Address:* School of Physics and Astronomy, University of Manchester, Oxford Road, Manchester M13 9PL; c/o Sue Rider Management Ltd, Unit C219, Trident Business Centre, 89 Bickersteth Road, SW17 9SH.

COX, Brian (Robert) Escott; QC 1974; a Recorder of the Crown Court, 1972–98; *b* 30 Sept. 1932; *yr s* of late George Robert Escott Cox, solicitor, and Doris Cox; *m* 1st, 1956; one *s* two *d*; 2nd, 1969, Noelle Gilormini; one *s* one *d*. *Educ:* Rugby Sch.; Oriel Coll., Oxford (BA Jurisprudence). Called to the Bar, Lincoln's Inn, 1954, Bencher, 1985; Midland and Oxford Circuit; a Dep. High Court Judge, 1980–98. *Recreation:* listening to and playing jazz. *Address:* 14 The Butts, Warwick CV34 4SS.

COX, (Charles) Geoffrey; QC 2003; MP (C) Torridge and West Devon, since 2005; *b* 30 April 1960; *s* of Michael and Diane Cox; *m* 1985, Jeanie (*née* McDonald); two *s* one *d*. *Educ:* Downing Coll., Cambridge (BA). Called to the Bar, Middle Temple, 1982; in practice, specialising in criminal law, human rights, constitutional, commercial and defamation law; Hd of Chambers, Thomas More Chambers, 2003–. Contested (C) Torridge and W Devon, 2001. *Recreations:* walking, swimming, theatre, literature, political history, enjoying rural life. *Address:* Thomas More Chambers, 7 Lincoln's Inn Fields, WC2A 3BP. *T:* (020) 7404 7000, *Fax:* (020) 7831 4606. *E:* clerks@thomasmore.co.uk; House of Commons, SW1A 0AA.

COX, Prof. (Christopher) Barry, PhD, DSc; Professor, Division of Life Sciences, and Assistant Principal, King's College London, 1989–96; *b* 29 July 1931; *s* of Herbert Ernest Cox and May Cox; *m* 1st, 1961, Sheila (*née* Morgan) (*d* 1996); two *s* one *d*; 2nd, 1998, Marie-Hélène (*née* Forges). *Educ:* St Paul's Sch., Kensington (Sen. Foundn Scholar); Balliol Coll., Oxford (MA); St John's Coll., Cambridge (PhD); DSc London. Asst Lectr in Zoology, King's Coll. London, 1956–59; Harkness Fellow of Commonwealth Fund, at Mus. of Comparative Zoology, Harvard, 1959–60; King's College London: Lectr in Zoology, 1959–66; Sen. Lectr, 1966–69; Reader, 1970–76; Prof., 1976–96; Head: Dept of Zoology, 1982–85; Dept of Biology, 1985–88; Fulbright Schol., Stanford Univ., Calif, 1988–89. Mem. Council, Palaeontological Assoc., 1967–69, 1974 (Vice-Pres., 1969–81). Editor: Palaeontology, 1975–79; Proc. of Leatherhead & Dist Local Hist. Soc., 2005–. Palaeontological collecting expedns to Central Africa, 1963; Argentina, 1967; N Brazil, 1972; Qld, Aust., 1978. *Publications:* Prehistoric Animals, 1969; (with P. D. Moore) Biogeography—an ecological and evolutionary approach, 1973, 8th edn 2010; (jtly) The Prehistoric World, 1975; (jtly) Illustrated Encyclopedia of Dinosaurs and Prehistoric Animals, 1988; (jtly) Atlas of The Living World, 1989; research papers on vertebrate palaeontology and historical biogeography, in Phil. Trans. Royal Soc., Proc. Zool. Soc., Nature, Bull. Brit. Mus. (Nat. Hist.), Jl Biogeog., etc. *Recreations:* theatre, old Surrey buildings (Chm., Domestic Bldgs Res. Gp, 2000–05; Sec., Surrey Dendrochronology Project, 2002–).

COX, Prof. Sir David (Roxbee), Kt 1985; PhD; FRS 1973; FRSC; Warden of Nuffield College, Oxford, 1988–94, Hon. Fellow, 1994; *b* 15 July 1924; *s* of S. R. Cox, Handsworth, Birmingham; *m* 1948, Joyce (*née* Drummond), Keighley, Yorks; three *s* one *d*. *Educ:* Handsworth Grammar Sch., Birmingham; St John's Coll., Cambridge (MA). PhD Leeds, 1949. Posts at Royal Aircraft Establishment, 1944–46; Wool Industries Research Assoc., 1946–50; Statistical Laboratory, Cambridge, 1950–55; Visiting Prof., University of N Carolina, 1955–56; Reader in Statistics, 1956–60, Professor of Statistics, 1961–66, Birkbeck Coll. (Fellow, 2001); Prof. of Statistics, 1966–88 and Head of Dept of Maths, 1970–74, Imperial Coll. of Sci. and Technology. SERC Sen. Res. Fellow, 1983–88. President:

Bernoulli Soc., 1979–81; Royal Statistical Soc., 1980–82; Pres., ISI, 1995–97. Foreign Member: Royal Danish Acad. of Scis and Letters, 1983; Indian Acad. of Scis, 1997; For. Hon. Mem., Amer. Acad. of Arts and Sciences, 1974; For. Associate, Nat. Acad. of Scis, USA, 1988. FIC 1994; FRSC 2010. Hon. FIA 1991; Hon. FBA 1997; Hon. FRSE 2013. Hon. DSc: Reading, 1982; Bradford, 1982; Helsinki, 1986; Heriot-Watt, 1987; Limburg's Univ. Centrum, 1988; Queen's Univ., Kingston, Ont, 1989; Waterloo, 1991; Neuchâtel, 1992; Padua, 1994; Minnesota, 1994; Toronto, 1994; Abertay Dundee, 1995; Tech. Univ. of Crete, 1996; Athens Univ. of Economics, 1998; Bordeaux II, 1999; Harvard, 1999; Elche, 1999; Rio de Janeiro, 2000; Leeds, 2005; Southampton, 2006; Gothenburg, 2007; Glasgow, 2011. Weldon Meml Prize, Univ. of Oxford, 1984; Kettering Medal, General Motors Cancer Foundn, 1990; (jtly) Max Planck Forschungspreis, 1993; Copley Medal, Royal Soc., 2010. Editor of Biometrika, 1966–91. *Publications:* Statistical Methods in the Textile Industry, 1949 (jt author); Planning of Experiments, 1958; (jtly) Queues, 1961; Renewal Theory, 1962; (jtly) Theory of Stochastic Processes, 1965; (jtly) Statistical Analysis of Series of Events, 1966; Analysis of Binary Data, 1970, 2nd edn 1989; (jtly) Theoretical Statistics, 1974; (jtly) Problems and Solutions in Theoretical Statistics, 1978; (jtly) Point Processes, 1980; (jtly) Applied Statistics, 1981; (jtly) Analysis of Survival Data, 1984; (jtly) Asymptotic Methods, 1989; (jtly) Inference and Asymptotics, 1994; (jtly) Multivariate Dependencies, 1996; (jtly) Theory of Design of Experiments, 2000; (jtly) Components of Variance, 2002; Selected Papers, two vols, 2005; Principles of Statistical Inference, 2006; (jtly) Principles of Applied Statistics, 2011; (jtly) Case-Control Studies, 2014; papers in Jl of Royal Statistical Society, Biometrika, etc. *Address:* Nuffield College, Oxford OX1 1NF.

COX, Dame Elizabeth (Louise); *see* Neville, Dame E. L.

COX, Geoffrey; *see* Cox, C. G.

COX, Sir George (Edwin), Kt 2005; Chairman, Design Council, 2004–07; *b* 28 May 1940; *s* of George Herbert Cox and Beatrice Mary Cox; *m* 1st, 1963, Gillian Mary Mannings (marr. diss. 1996); two *s*; 2nd, 1996, Lorna Janet Peach; two *d*. *Educ:* Quintin Sch.; Queen Mary Coll., Univ. of London (BScAeEng). Engineer, BAC, 1962–64; Molins Machine Co.: Systems Designer, 1964–67; Manufacturing Manager, 1967–69; Management Consultant, Urwick Orr & Partners, 1969–73; UK Dir, Diebold Gp, 1973–77; Man. Dir, Butler Cox, 1977–92; Chm., 1992–94, Chief Exec., 1993–94, P-E International; Chief Exec., 1995–96, Chm., 1996–99, Unisys Ltd; Man. Dir, Unisys Inf. Services, Europe, 1996–99; Dir Gen., Inst. of Dirs, 1999–2004 (Hon. Life Fellow, 2004). Non-exec. Dir, 2000–07, Sen. Ind. Dir, 2003–07, Bradford & Bingley plc; Member: Bd, Shorts, 2000–; Supervisory Bd, Euronext, 2002–07; Bd, NYSE-Euronext, 2007–13. Cox Review of Creativity in Business, for HM Treasury, reported 2005; Author, Overcoming Short-termism within British Business, reported 2013. Chm., Merlin (Med. Emergency Relief Internat.), 2001–07. Mem. Bd, LIFFE, 1995–2002. Mem. Bd of Inland Revenue, 1996–99. Vis. Prof., Royal Holloway, Univ. of London, 1995–98. Pres., Management Consultancies Assoc., 1991. President: Royal Coll. of Speech and Lang. Therapists, 2008– (Hon. Fellow, 2011); IED, 2010–14 (Hon. FIED 2007). Mem. Adv. Bd, Warwick Business Sch., 2001– (Chm., 2006–10); Pro-Chancellor, 2010–, Chm. Council, 2011–, Univ. of Warwick. Trustee: VSO, 2004–07; Culham Languages and Sci. Sch., 2009–11. Mem., Information Technologists Co., 1992–; Master, Guild of Mgt Consultants, 1997–98. CCMI (CIMgt 1992); CRAeS 2008. Hon. Fellow, Queen Mary, Univ. of London, 2007. DUniv Middlesex, 2002; Hon. DBA Wolverhampton, 2004; Hon. DDes De Montfort, 2007; Hon. DCL Northumbria, 2007; Hon. DSc: Huddersfield, 2008; Cranfield, 2011. *Publications:* contribs to various jls. *Recreations:* theatre, rowing (Chief Coach, Univ. of London Boat Club, 1976–78, Chm. of Selectors, GB Men's Rowing, 1978–80), gliding, history of aviation. *Address:* University of Warwick, University House, Coventry CV4 8UW. *Club:* Leander (Pres., 2008–13).

COX, Gilbert Kirkwood, CVO 2010; MBE 1996; JP; Lord-Lieutenant of Lanarkshire, 2000–10; *b* 24 Aug. 1935; *s* of William and Mary Bryce Cox; *m* 1959, Marjory Moir Ross Taylor; two *s* one *d*. *Educ:* Airdrie Acad.; Glasgow Royal Tech. Coll. NCB, 1953–63; David A. McPhail & Sons Ltd, 1963–71; Gen. Manager, Scotland, Associated Perforators & Weavers Ltd, 1971–97. Dir, Airdrie Savings Bank, 1985–2012 (Chm., 1995–97). Chm. Bd of Mgt, Coatbridge Coll., 1996–2000. JP N Lanarks, 1984; DL, 1989, Hon. Sheriff, 2002–, Lanarks. *Recreations:* golf, photography, travel. *Address:* Bedford House, 29 Commonhead Street, Airdrie, N Lanarkshire ML6 6NS. *T:* (01236) 763331.

COX, Helen Joanne, (Jo); MP (Lab) Batley and Spen, since 2015; *b* Batley; *m* Brendan Cox; two *c*. *Educ:* Heckmondwike Grammar Sch.; Pembroke Coll., Cambridge (BA Social and Pol Studies 1995); London Sch. of Econs and Pol Sci. Pol Advr, Joan Walley, MP, 1995–97; Hd, Key Campaigns, Britain in Europe, 1998–99; Pol Advr, Glenys Kinnock, MEP, 2000–02; Head, EU Office, 2002–05, Policy and Advocacy, 2005–07, Humanitarian Campaigning, 2007–09, Oxfam; Dir, Maternal Mortality Campaign, 2009–11; Strategy Consultant: Save the Children, 2012; NSPCC, 2012; Dir of Strategy, White Ribbon Alliance for Safe Motherhood, 2012; CEO and Founder, UK Women, 2013–14; Strategic Adviser: Freedom Fund, 2014; Bill and Melinda Gates Foundn, 2014–15. Chair, Labour Women's Network, 2010–14. *Address:* House of Commons, SW1A 0AA.

COX, John; freelance director of plays, opera, revue and musicals in Britain and abroad; *b* 12 March 1935; *s* of Leonard John Cox and Ethel Minnie May Cox (*née* McGill). *Educ:* Queen Elizabeth's Hosp., Bristol; St Edmund Hall, Oxford (MA; Hon. Fellow, 1991). Vis. Fellow, European Humanities Res. Centre, Oxford, 1995. Freelance dir, 1959–; Dir of Prodn, Glyndebourne Festival Opera, 1971–81; Gen. Adminr, 1981–85, Artistic Dir, 1985–86, Scottish Opera; Prodn Dir, Royal Opera House, Covent Gdn, 1988–94. Productions include: *Glyndebourne:* Richard Strauss cycle, Rake's Progress, The Magic Flute, La Cenerentola; *ENO:* Così fan tutte, Patience; *Scottish Opera:* L'Egisto, Manon Lescaut, Marriage of Figaro, Lulu, Don Giovanni; *Royal Opera:* Manon, Die Fledermaus, Guillaume Tell, Capriccio, Die Meistersinger, Il Viaggio a Reims, Die Frau ohne Schatten, Tosca, Eugene Onegin; *Garsington Opera:* Così fan tutte, Nozze di Figaro, Philosopher's Stone, Fidelio; *Australian Opera:* Barber of Seville, Albert Herring, Patience, Masked Ball, Capriccio (Olympic Arts Fest.), Arabella; *Santa Fe Opera:* L'Egisto, La Calisto, Marriage of Figaro, Arabella; *Monte Carlo Opera:* Rake's Progress, Hamlet, Eugene Onegin, Picture of Dorian Gray (world première), Vanessa, Così fan tutte, Otello; *Salzburg Opera:* Il Re Pastore, Ariadne auf Naxos, Rake's Progress, Der Freischutz, La Traviata; *Madrid:* Eugene Onegin, La Cenerentola, Rake's Progress, Capriccio; *Drottningholm:* Zemire et Azor, Tom Jones; *San Francisco:* Arabella, Magic Flute, Rake's Progress, Capriccio, Don Carlos, Ariadne auf Naxos, Così fan tutte; *Metropolitan, NY:* Barber of Seville, Magic Flute, Capriccio, Werther, Thaïs; *La Scala, Milan:* Rake's Progress, Magic Flute; *Amsterdam:* Der Rosenkavalier, Tannhäuser, Intermezzo; *Chicago Lyric Opera:* Thaïs, Capriccio, Ariadne auf Naxos, Così fan tutte; *Copenhagen:* Hamlet, Falstaff; also opera in Brussels, Stockholm, Cologne, Frankfurt, Munich, Florence, Turin, Parma, Nice, Strasbourg, Toulouse, Lisbon, Vienna, Leeds, Dallas, San Diego, Los Angeles, Washington, Houston, Wexford, Melbourne, Vancouver, etc. Jt Librettist, Oscar, Santa Fe Opera, 2013 (world première). Mem., Adv. Bd, Youth At Risk, 2005–. *Address:* 7 West Grove, SE10 8QT. *T:* (020) 8692 2450.

See also S. J. Cox.

COX, John Colin Leslie, CBE 1994; Chief Executive, Pensions, Protection and Investment Accreditation Board, 2000; Chairman, London Europe Gateway Ltd, since 1996; *b* 23 Oct. 1933; *s* of late Dr Leslie Reginald Cox, OBE, FRS, and Hilda Cecilia Cox; *m* 1983, Avril Joyce Butt; one *s* one *d*. *Educ:* University College Sch., London; Queens' Coll., Cambridge (BA). National Service, 2nd Lieut, 2nd 10th Princess Mary's Own Gurkha Rifles, 1956–58 (GSM Malaya 1958). Joined Shell Group, 1958: Executive positions in Shell Ghana, 1962–65, and in Shell Gp in London, 1966–77; Shell Chemicals UK: Personnel Dir, 1978–81; Dir, Business Develt, and chm. of subsid. cos, 1981–86; Dir Gen., CIA, 1987–95; Chief Exec., London First Centre, 1995–96. Member: Armed Forces Pay Review Body, 1993–99; Steering Bd, Lab. of the Govt Chemist, 1992–96; Adv. Cttee, European Movement, 1994–; Bd, UK CEED, 1996 (Chm., 1999); Bd, PHLS, 1997; Standards Bd, Edexcel Foundn, 1997; Envmt Cttee, Knightsbridge Assoc., 1997–; Vice Chm., Defence and Security Forum, 1996–. Mem. (C), Westminster CC, 1998 (Vice Chm., PFI Cttee, 1998, Planning and Licensing Cttee, 2000). Chairman: Governing Body, Westminster Adult Educn Service, 1998; Edge Foundn, 2009–; Gov., City of Westminster Coll., 2000. Mem., Caux Round Table, 1991–. FRSA 1989. *Recreations:* sailing, antiques, country pursuits, photography. *Address:* London Europe Gateway Ltd, 138 Brompton Road, SW3 1HY. *T:* (020) 7581 9510. *Clubs:* Army and Navy, Hurlingham; Leander (Henley on Thames); Royal Solent Yacht (IoW).

COX, Ven. John Stuart; Archdeacon of Sudbury, 1995–2006, now Archdeacon Emeritus; *b* 13 Sept. 1940; *s* of Arthur F. W. Cox and Clarice M. Cox; *m* Mary Diane Williams; one *s* one *d*. *Educ:* Fitzwilliam House, Cambridge (MA); Linacre Coll., and Wycliffe Hall, Oxford (BA); Birmingham Univ. (DPS). Ordained deacon, 1968, priest, 1969; Assistant Curate: St Mary's, Prescot, 1968–71; St George, Newtown, Birmingham, 1971–73; Rector, St George, Newtown, Birmingham, 1973–78; Selection Sec., ACCM, 1978–83 (Sen. Selection Sec., 1979–83); Canon Residentiary, Southwark Cathedral, 1983–91; Diocesan Dir of Ordinands and Dir of Post-Ordination Training, Southwark, 1983–91; Vicar, Holy Trinity Church in the Ecumenical Parish of Roehampton, 1991–95; Diocesan Dir of Educn, St Edmundsbury and Ipswich, 2006–10. *Publications:* (contrib.) Religion and Medicine, Vol. 1, 1970; (contrib.) Say One for Me, 1992; A Risk Worth Taking, 2007; In All Senses, 2008; Fast and Feast, 2008; Cross Examined, 2009; Relationships, 2010; More than Caring and Sharing, 2011; The Voice of the Prophet, 2011; Dreams and Visions, 2011; Life is Not a Game of Perfect, 2012; The Week That Changed the World, 2012; Critical Friend, 2013; Light to the Nations, 2013; What do Christians Believe?, 2014; It's Not Your Fault You're Stressed, 2014. *Recreations:* music, reading, theatre, golf, wine-making. *Address:* 2 Bullen Close, Bury St Edmunds, Suffolk IP33 3JP. *T:* and *Fax:* (01284) 766796.

COX, Jonathan Mark, PhD; Headmaster, Royal Grammar School, Guildford, since 2007; *b* 25 Feb. 1966; *s* of Darrell and Nita Cox; *m* 1993, Rosemary Bruce; one *s* two *d*. *Educ:* Charlton Prep. Sch.; St Mary's Coll., Southampton; Univ. of Southampton (BSc Hons Physiol. with Pharmacol. 1987; PhD Biochem. 1992); Royal Coll. of Music (Cert. Advanced Performance 1988). Whitgift School: Biology Teacher, 1992–98; Hd of Sixth Form, 1998–2001; Second Master, 2001–06. *Recreations:* classical music and close-up magic, enjoying the company of my children, listening to opera, visiting auctions, drinking my father-in-law's fine wine. *Address:* c/o The Royal Grammar School, High Street, Guildford, Surrey GU1 3BB. *T:* (01483) 880608, *Fax:* (01483) 306127. *E:* j.cox@rgs-guildford.co.uk. *Clubs:* East India, MCC.

COX, Jonson; Chairman: Coalfield Resources plc (formerly UK Coal plc), since 2010; Water Services Regulation Authority, since 2012; *b* 11 Oct. 1956; *s* of Peter Cox and Bobbie Cox (*née* Sutton); partner, Barbara Kennedy Wight; one *s* two *d*. *Educ:* King Edward VI Sch., Totnes; Clare Coll., Cambridge (BA Hons Econs; MA). Royal Dutch/Shell Gp, 1979–92; Man. Dir and Chm., Yorkshire Envmtl, 1993–96; Managing Director: and Mem. Bd, Kelda Gp plc, 1994–2000; Yorkshire Water, 1996–2000; Chief Operating Officer, Railtrack plc, 2000–01; Chief Exec., Valpak Ltd, 2002–04; Gp Chief Exec., Anglian Water Gp plc, 2004–10 (Dep. Chm., 2010). Non-exec. Dir, Wincanton plc, 2005–; Advr, RWE Npower, 2011–. *Recreation:* outdoor activities. *Address:* Water Services Regulation Authority, Centre City Tower, 7 Hill Street, Birmingham B5 4UA. *T:* (0121) 644 7750. *E:* jonson.cox@gmail.com.

COX, Josephine; writer; *b* 15 July 1940; *d* of Bernard and Mary Jane Brindle; *m* Kenneth George Cox; two *s*. Formerly: clerk, Milton Keynes Devel Council; secretarial and teaching posts, incl. Lectr in Sociol. and History, Bletchley Coll., Milton Keynes; Partner, family landscaping co. *Publications:* as Josephine Cox: Her Father's Sins, 1986; Let Loose the Tigers, 1988; Take This Woman, 1989; Angels Cry Sometimes, 1990; Whistledown Woman, 1990; Outcast, 1991; Alley Urchin, 1991; Don't Cry Alone, 1992; Vagabonds; Jessica's Girl, 1993; Nobody's Darling, 1993; More Than Riches, 1994; Born to Serve, 1994; Little Badness, 1995; Living a Lie, 1995; A Time For Us, 1996; The Devil You Know, 1996; Miss You Forever, 1997; Cradle of Thorns, 1997; Love Me or Leave Me, 1998; Tomorrow the World, 1998; Gilded Cage, 1999; Somewhere, Someday, 1999; Rainbow Days, 2000; Looking Back, 2000; Let It Shine, 2001; The Woman Who Left, 2001; Child of the North: memories of a northern childhood (autobiog.), 2001; Jinnie, 2002; Bad Boy Jack, 2002; The Beachcomber, 2003; Lovers and Liars, 2004; Live the Dream, 2004; The Journey, 2005; Journey's End, 2006; The Loner, 2007; Songbird, 2008; Born Bad, 2009; Divorced and Deadly, 2009; Blood Brothers, 2010; Midnight, 2011; Three Letters, 2012; The Broken Man, 2013; The Runaway Woman, 2014; Lonely Girl; as Jane Brindle: Scarlet, 1991; No Mercy, 1992; The Tallow Image, 1994; No Heaven, No Hell, 1995; The Seeker, 1997; Hiding Game, 1998. *Address:* c/o LBA, 91 Great Russell Street, WC1B 3PS.

COX, Hon. Dame Laura (Mary), DBE 2002; **Hon. Mrs Justice Cox;** a Judge of the High Court of Justice, Queen's Bench Division, since 2002; *b* 8 Nov. 1951; *d* of John Arthur Bryant and Mary Eileen Bryant (*née* Clarke); *m* 1970, David Cox; three *s*. *Educ:* Queen Mary Coll., Univ. of London (LLB 1973; LLM 1975). Called to the Bar, Inner Temple, 1975, Bencher, 1999; in practice at the Bar, 1976–2002; QC 1994; Head of Chambers, 1996–2002. A Recorder, 1995–2002. Chairman: Equal Opportunities Cttee, Bar Council, 2000–02; Equal Treatment Adv. Cttee, Judicial Studies Bd, 2003–10; Mem., Justice, 1997–. British Mem., ILO Cttee of Experts, 1998–2013. Chm. Bd, Interights, 2002–05. Pres., Assoc. of Women Barristers, 2005–; Vice-Pres., UK Assoc. of Women Judges, 2013–. Hon. Life Pres., Univ. of Essex Law Soc. Hon. Fellow, Queen Mary, Univ. of London, 2005. *Recreations:* music, theatre, cinema, watching football, cooking, novels, walking, arguing with sons! *Address:* Royal Courts of Justice, Strand, WC2A 2LL.

COX, Nigel John; HM Diplomatic Service, retired; Sensitivity Reviewer, Archives Management Department, Foreign and Commonwealth Office, since 2015; *b* 23 April 1954; *s* of late Basil Cox, DFC and Anne (*née* Webber); *m* 1992, Olivia Jane, *d* of Lt-Col Sir Julian Paget, *qv*. *Educ:* The High Sch., Dublin; Trinity Coll., Dublin (BA, LLB); Ecole Nat. d'Administration, Paris. FCO 1975; Chinese lang trng, Cambridge and Hong Kong, 1976–78; Second Sec., Peking, 1978–81; Second, later First, Sec., FCO, 1981–84; Asst Political Advr, Hong Kong, 1984; First Sec., Paris, 1985–90; Assistant Head: Western European Dept, FCO, 1990–91; Hong Kong Dept, FCO, 1991–92; Counsellor, Peking, 1992–96; Hd of SE Asian Dept, FCO, 1996–99; Minister, Peking, 2000–02; Dir, Asia-Pacific, FCO, 2003–05; Sen. Advr to Chief Exec., P&O Gp, 2005–06 (on secondment). Sen. Advr, E Asia, International Power plc, 2007–08; Mem. Adv. Panel, PricewaterhouseCoopers LLP, 2007–09. Clerk, Fishmongers' Co., 2009–13. Gov., Gresham's Sch., 2009–13. *Recreations:* sinological claptrap, irony. *Club:* Travellers.

COX, Patricia Ann, CB 1989; Under Secretary, Scottish Home and Health Department, 1985–88, retired; *b* 25 May 1931; *d* of Sir (Ernest) Gordon Cox, KBE, TD, FRS. *Educ:* Leeds Girls' High Sch.; Newnham Coll., Cambridge (MA). Asst Principal, Dept of Health for Scotland, 1953; Principal: SHHD, 1959–62; HM Treasury, 1962–65; SHHD, 1965–67; Asst

Sec., 1967–76, Under Sec., 1976–85, Scottish Educn Dept. *Publications:* Sandal Ash (novel for children), 1950. *Recreations:* archaeology, needlework, botanical painting. *Address:* 2 Gloucester Place, Edinburgh EH3 6EF. *T:* (0131) 225 6370.

COX, Patricia Anne, (Mrs Roger Cox); *see* Edwards, P. A.

COX, Patrick; President: International European Movement, 2005–11; Jean Monnet Foundation for Europe, since 2015; Member (ELDR), Munster, 1989–2004, and President, 2002–04, European Parliament; *b* 29 Nov. 1952; *m* 1974, Kathleen Tighe; two *s* four *d*. *Educ:* Trinity Coll., Dublin (BA Mod. Econs 1974). Lecturer in Economics: Inst. of Public Admin, Dublin, 1974–76; Nat. Inst. for Higher Educn, Limerick, 1976–82; TV current affairs reporter and presenter, Today Tonight, Dublin, 1982–86. TD (Progressive Democrats), Cork S Central, 1992–94; Leader, Liberal Gp, European Parlt, 1998–2002. Gen. Sec., Progressive Democrat Party, 1985–89. Dir, Tiger Develts Europe; Member: Eur. Adv. Council, Microsoft; Eur. Adv. Council, Pfizer; Conseil de Surveillance, Michelin. Comr Gen., Europalia, Brussels, 2006, 2008. Pres., European Parlt Former Members' Assoc., 2010–14. EU Project Coordinator, Scandinavian-Mediterranean TEN-T Core Network Corridor, 2014–. Member: Bd, Michael Smurfit Grad. Sch. of Business, UCD; Pres.'s Adv. Bd, Univ. Coll. Cork. Member, Board of Trustees: Crisis Gp; Friends of Europe; Edmund Rice Schs Trust. Patron: Blue Box Creative Learning Centre, Limerick; Fedn for Victim Assistance. Hon. Life Mem., Irish Inst. of Trng and Develt, 2002. Hon. Fellow, Irish Auctioneers and Valuers Instn, 2002. Freeman, Limerick City, 2002. Hon. LLD NUI, 2002; Hon. DHL American Coll., Dublin/Lynn Univ., Florida, 2002. President's Medal, Univ. of Limerick, 2002; European Movt/Aer Rianta European of Year Award, 2002; Charlemagne Prize, 2004.

COX, Paul William; freelance artist and illustrator, since 1982; *b* 31 July 1957; *s* of late Oliver Jasper Cox, CBE, RIBA and Jean Cox; *m* 1987, Julia Claire Nichol; one *s* one *d*. *Educ:* Port Regis and Stanbridge Earls School; Camberwell Sch. of Art and Crafts (BA Hons); Royal Coll. of Art (MA). Contributor to: The Times, Daily Telegraph, Independent, Express, Spectator, Punch, Sunday Times, Observer, Guardian, New Yorker, Vanity Fair, Town and Country, Wall St Journal, Traditional Home, Chatelaine, Business Week, House Beautiful, Country Life, Elle Decor; founder contributor to Blueprint, 1984; designed: PO stamps for Lord Mayor's Show, 1989; mural for Eleanor Davies Colley Lect. Th., RCS, 2004; sets for 50th anniv. prodn of Salad Days, 2005; 15 paintings for St Charles Hosp., 2007; exhibns of watercolour drawings: Workshop Gallery, 1984; Illustrators' Gallery, 1985; Chris Beetles Gallery, 1989, 1993, 2001, 2006, 2009, 2010, 2011, major retrospective 2013; Molesworth Gall., Dublin, 2001; Durrell Wildlife Conservation Trusts, 2006; historical illustrations for Drama and Debate exhibn, Hampton Ct Palace, 2004; 65 covers for International Living, 2010–15; 15 illustrations, Anderson & Sheppard, 2011; illustrated Today Prog. for opening of House of Illustration, 2014. Vis. Lectr in Illustration, Camberwell Sch. of Art and Crafts, 1982–90; Sen. Tutor, West Dean Coll., 2009–11. *Publications:* illustrated books: Experiences of an Irish RM, 1984; The Common Years, 1984; A Varied Life, 1984; The Outing, 1985; The Character of Cricket, 1986; Romantic Gardens, 1988; Evacuee, 1988; Rebuilding the Globe, 1989; Dear Boy, 1989; Leave it to Psmith, 1989; Three Men in a Boat, 1989; The Cricket Match, 1991; Honourable Estates, 1992; The Darling Buds of May, 1992; The Russian Tea Room, 1993; The Wind in the Willows, 1993; Rumpole, 1994; Look out London, 1995; Jeeves & Wooster, 1996; The Plumbs of P. G. Wodehouse, 1997; Three Men on the Bummel, 1998; Tinkerbill, 1999; Jeeves & Wooster II, 2000; Best After-Dinner Stories, 2003; The Giver, 2003; The Train To Glasgow, 2003; The Best of Blandings, 2004; The Folio Book of Comic Short Stories, 2005; My Family and Other Animals, 2006; The Elevator Man, 2008; Absolute Corkers, 2008; Jeeves & Wooster III, 2010; Gay and Lesbian Etiquette, 2011; Running is Flying, 2012; Did I Mention the Free Wine, 2012. *Address:* 23 Bromwich Avenue, Highgate, N6 6QH. *T:* (020) 8347 9515. *E:* paulwcox@gmail.com. *Clubs:* Chelsea Arts; Bembridge Sailing.

COX, Pauline Victoria, MA; Head Teacher, The Tiffin Girls' School, 1994–2010; *b* 9 Oct. 1948; *d* of Harold and Lily Greenwood; *m* 1970, Stephen James Cox, *qv*; one *s* one *d*. *Educ:* High Storrs Girls' Grammar Sch., Sheffield; Birmingham Univ. (BA Hons Geography 1970); Inst. of Education, London Univ. (PGCE 1973); W London Inst. of HE (RSA Dip. TEFL 1981); MA London 1983. Asst Editor, Polish News Bulletin of British and American Embassies, Warsaw, 1971–72; Teacher, subseq. also Head of Geography, Wandsworth Boys' Sch., 1973–75; Teacher of Geography, Lady Eleanor Holles Sch., Hampton, 1976–77; Lectr in ESL, Univ. of Legon, Accra, Ghana, 1978–80; Teacher of Geography: Tiffin Girls' Sch., 1981–83; Teddington Sch., 1983–84; Head of Geography, Waldegrave Sch. for Girls, Twickenham, 1984–87; Dep. Head, Cranford Community Sch., Hounslow, 1987–94; Exec. Hd Teacher, Tiffin Boys' Sch., Jan.–Aug. 2009. Mem. Council, London South LSC, 2001–04. Judge, Teaching Awards, 2005–06. Trustee: Smallpeice Trust, 2007– (Chm., 2014–); Arkwright Scholarships Trust, 2007– (Chm., 2014–); Mus. of Richmond, 2010–. FRGS 1988. *Recreations:* reading crime fiction, listening to the Archers, watching sport.

COX, Peter Arthur, BSc Eng; FREng, FICE; FCGI; FIC; consulting engineer; *b* 30 Oct. 1922; *m* 1944, Rosemary; one *s* two *d*. *Educ:* Westcliff High Sch., Essex; City and Guilds Coll., Imperial Coll., London (FIC 1991). Commissioned, Royal Engineers, 1942 (despatches). Lewis & Duvivier, 1947; Rendel Palmer & Tritton, 1952; Peter Lind & Co. Ltd, 1954; Sir Bruce White Wolfe Barry & Partners, 1955; Rendel Palmer & Tritton Ltd, Consulting Engineers, 1956, Partner, 1966, Sen. Partner, 1978–85, Chm., 1985–88. Chm., Ceemaid Ltd, 1984–85. Member: Dover Harbour Bd, 1983–89; Nat. Maritime Inst. Ltd, 1983–85; British Maritime Technology Ltd, 1986–93. Institution of Civil Engineers: Pres., 1980–81; Mem., Infrastructure Policy (formerly Planning) Gp, 1981–92 (Chm. 1981–84); Chm., Legal Affairs Cttee, 1988–92; Member: Smeatonian Soc. of Civil Engrs, 1980–; British Acad. of Experts, 1991–96. Mem., Commonwealth Scholarship Commn, 1982–88. Pres., Old Centralians, 1989–90. Governor, Westminster Coll., Wandsworth, 1990–92. *Publications:* papers to Instn of Civil Engrs on Leith Harbour and Belfast Dry Dock; many papers to conferences. *Recreations:* walking, gardening. *Address:* 22 Manor Court, Swan Road, Pewsey SN9 5DW. *Club:* East India.

COX, Peter Frederick; Head of Information & Archives (formerly of Libraries), BBC, 1993–98; *b* 1 Dec. 1945; *s* of George William and Edna May Cox; *m* 1968, Gillian Mary Stevens; two *d*. *Educ:* Bedford Sch.; University Coll. London (BA); Univ. of Herts (MSc 1999). MCLIP (ALA 1968; MIInfSc). Chartered Librarian, 1968; Sen. Asst County Librarian, Herts, 1979–88; City of Westminster: City Librarian, 1989–92; Asst Dir (Leisure and Libraries), 1992–93. Member: Library and Information Services Council for England and Wales, 1992–95; Cttee on Public Library Objectives, 1992; Adv. Cttee, Nat. Sound Archive, 1996–98. FRSA 1991. JP Stevenage, 1980–88. *Publications:* professional articles and symposia papers. *Recreations:* sailing, painting. *Address:* 14 Ellis Grove, Norton Fitzwarren, Taunton, Somerset TA2 6SY. *T:* (01823) 284780.

COX, Philip Ardagh R.; *see* Roxbee Cox.

COX, Philip Christopher; Chief Executive, Cheshire and Warrington Local Enterprise Partnership, since 2014; *b* Hertford, 30 Dec. 1963; *s* of Leonard and Jean Cox; *m* 1988, Gillian Plews; two *s* one *d*. *Educ:* Univ. of Durham (BA Hons Econs); Queen Mary Coll., Univ. of London (MSc Econ.). Economist, DSS, 1985–93; Economist, 1993–96, Hd, Railways Econs and Finance, 1996–98, Dept of Transport; Head: Housing and Urban Econs, DETR, 1998–2001; Millennium Dome Sale Unit, 2001–02, Regl Econ. Performance, 2003–05, ODPM; Principal Private Sec. to Dep. Prime Minister, 2005–07; Department for Communities and Local Government: Director: Homes and Communities Agency Implementation, 2007–08; Thames Gateway and Olympics, 2009–10; Olympics, Thames Gateway and Regeneration, 2010; Local Economies, Regeneration and European Progs, 2011–14. *Recreations:* walking, Member of Scout Association. *Address:* Cheshire and Warrington Local Enterprise Partnership, Richmond House, Gadbrook Business Park, Rudheath, Northwich CW9 7TN.

COX, Philip Gotsall, CBE 2013; Chief Executive Officer, GDF SUEZ Energy International (formerly International Power plc), 2003–13; *b* 22 Sept. 1951; *m* 1976, Brenda Sadler; one *s* one *d*. *Educ:* Queens' Coll., Cambridge (BA 1973; MA). Gp Controller, 1989–98, Chief Financial Officer, 1998–99, Siebe plc; Sen. Vice-Pres., Ops, Invensys plc, 1999–2000; Chief Financial Officer, International Power plc, 2000–03. Chm., Drax Gp, 2014–; Sen. Ind. Dir, Wm Morrison Supermarkets, 2009– (Chm., Audit Cttee, 2009–); non-executive Director: Meggit plc, 2012–15; PPL, 2013–. Former Mem., CBI President's Cttee. *Recreations:* golf, football. *T:* 07712 279757. *E:* philipgcox51@gmail.com.

COX, Raymond Edwin; QC 2002; *b* 6 May 1959; s of Edwin David Cox and Catherine (*née* Mook Lan, now Deverill-West); *m* 1990, Alexandra Clare Howell; two *s* two *d*. *Educ:* Mansfield Coll., Oxford (BA Hons Jurisprudence (1st cl.); Eldon Schol.). Called to the Bar, Gray's Inn (Arden Schol.), 1982, Bencher, 2008. Consultant Editor, Civil Procedure Reports, 2005–. *Publications:* (ed jtly) Commercial Court Procedure, 2000; (ed jtly) Law of Bank Payments, 4th edn, 2010; Private International Law of Reinsurance and Insurance, 2006. *Recreations:* music, ski-ing. *Address:* Fountain Court Chambers, Temple, EC4Y 9DH. *T:* (020) 7583 3335, *Fax:* (020) 7353 0329. *E:* rc@fountaincourt.co.uk.

COX, Richard T.; *see* Temple Cox.

COX, Dr Roger; Director, Centre for Radiation, Chemical and Environmental Hazards, Health Protection Agency, 2005–09; *b* 26 May 1947; *s* of Thomas and Leonora Cox; *m* 1971, Susan Whisstock; one *s* one *d*. *Educ:* Univ. of Reading (BSc Hons Microbiol. 1968; PhD Microbial Genetics 1973). With MRC, 1971–90; Hd of Dept, and Div. Hd, 1990–2003, Dir, 2003–05, NRPB. Hon. Prof., Brunel Univ., 1999–. Delegate to UN Scientific Cttee on Effects of Atomic Radiation, 2001–09. Member: Internat. Commn on Radiological Protection, 1996–2009 (Vice Chm., 2003–09); Biol Effects of Ionizing Radiation VII Cttee, NAS, 1999–2005. Hon. Mem., ARR, 2011. FMedSci 2006. Hon. Fellow, Soc. for Radiological Protection, 2007. (Jtly) Weiss Medal, ARR, 1992. *Publications:* (jtly) Health Risks from Exposure to Low Levels of Ionizing Radiation, 2005; numerous contribs to radiation sci. and cell/molecular biol. jls and reports. *Recreations:* family life, boats, fishing, cinema. *E:* rogercoxis@btinternet.com.

COX, Roy Arthur, CBE 1987; JDipMA; FCA, FCMA, FCBSI; Chief General Manager, 1970–85, Director, 1976–89, Alliance and Leicester (formerly Alliance) Building Society; *b* 30 Nov. 1925; *s* of J. W. Arthur Cox; *m* 1st, 1951, Joy (*née* Dunsford); one *s* one *d*; 2nd, 1980, Audrey (*née* Brayham); 3rd, 2007, Audrey (*née* Smith). *Educ:* Isleworth Grammar Sch. FCA 1953; FCMA 1957; FCBSI (FBS 1971). War Service, 1944–47. Wells & Partners, Chartered Accountants, 1942–49; Colombo Commercial Co. Ltd, 1950–61; Urwick, Orr & Partners, Management Consultants, 1961–65; Alliance Building Society: Sec., 1965; Gen. Man., 1967. Dir, Southern Bd, Legal & General Assce Soc. Ltd, 1972–86. Building Societies Association: Chm., S Eastern Assoc., 1972–74; Mem. Council, 1973–87; Chm., Gen. Purposes and Public Relations Cttee, 1975–77; Dep. Chm., Council, 1983–85; Chm., Council, 1985–87; Vice-Pres., 1987–2002. Mem., Royal Commn on Distribution of Income and Wealth, 1974–78; Dir, SE Electricity Bd, 1983–90; Dep. Chm., Seeboard plc, 1990–96; Chairman: PO Staff Superannuation Scheme, 1986–95; PO Pension Scheme, 1987–95; Siebe Pension Trustee Ltd, 1992–2000; Dir, Hermes Pensions Management Ltd, 1995–98. CCMI (CBIM 1980). *Recreations:* golf, snooker, bridge.

COX, Sarah Elizabeth; Senior Responsible Owner, State Pensions Reform, Department for Work and Pensions; *b* 19 May 1967; *d* of Dr Joseph Cox and Dr Barbara Cox (*née* Smith). *Educ:* Arnold Sch., Blackpool; Univ. of Birmingham (BCom Hons 1988). APMI 1991. Commercial Union Assce Co., later CGU and Aviva, 1991–2001: operational mgt, 1991–95; Prog. Dir, 1995–98; IT Service Centre Manager, 1996–98; Sen. Consultant, 1998–2000; Business Develt Manager, Norwich Union Internat., Aviva plc, 2000–01; Partner, Business Change and Delivery, Barclays Solutions, Barclays plc, 2001–04; Dir, Business Change and Delivery, ODPM, 2004–06; a Dir, Capability Rev. Team, Prime Minister's Delivery Unit, 2006–07, Dir, Strategy, Planning and Performance, 2007–10, Cabinet Office; Hd, Business Planning and Prog. Mgt, London 2012 Olympic Games, 2010–12; Dir, Universal Credit Prog., DWP, 2013. DUniv Birmingham, 2012. *Recreations:* golf, season ticket holder at Chelsea FC. *Club:* Woodcote Park Golf (Lady Captain, 2013).

COX, Sebert Leslie, OBE 1994; Partner, Kingston Reid Consulting, since 2001; Chairman, Key Real Estate Ltd, since 2004; *b* 27 Dec. 1950; *s* of late Maunsell Newton Cox and Anna Louise Cox (*née* Reid); *m* 1974, Christine Lesley Hall; two *d*. *Educ:* Univ. of Lancaster (MSc). Granada Gp Ltd, 1967–70; Ford Motor Co. Ltd, 1970–72; Easton House Trust, 1972–73; Springboard Trust, 1973–76; Northumbria Probation Service, 1976–90; Develt Advr, Home Office, 1990–2001; Chairman: Thames Gateway Ltd Partnership, 2003–05; NNTLIFTCo Ltd, 2004–09. Chairman: N British Housing Assoc., subseq. Places for People Gp, 1997–2004; Co. Durham Probation Bd, 2007–10; Durham Tees Valley Probation Trust, 2010–14; Probation Assoc., 2010–15; Derwentside Homes Ltd, 2013–. Mem., Inst. of Dirs, 1996. *Recreations:* cooking and entertaining, gardening, walking, visiting historic buildings. *Address:* Spurtop House, Whitehall Lane, Iveston, Co. Durham DH8 7TA.

COX, Stephen James, CVO 1997; Executive Director (formerly Executive Secretary), Royal Society, 1997–2011; *b* 5 Dec. 1946; *s* of late Harold James West Cox and of Norah Cox (*née* Wilkinson); *m* 1970, Pauline Victoria Greenwood (*see* P. V. Cox); one *s* one *d*. *Educ:* Queen Elizabeth Grammar Sch., Blackburn; Atlantic Coll.; Birmingham Univ. (BA Hons Geography 1969); Leeds Univ. (Postgrad. Dip. ESL 1970); Sussex Univ. (MA Educn 1977). VSO, Bolivia, 1965–66. British Council: Warsaw, 1970; Western Europe Dept, London, 1974; Accra, 1977; Staff Training Dept, 1981; Chm., British Council Whitley Council, Trade Union Side, 1981–84; Educn Attaché, Washington DC, 1984–85; Asst Sec., Royal Society, 1985–91; Dir Gen., Commonwealth Inst., 1991–97; Chief Exec., Westminster Foundn for Democracy, 1995–97. Member: Jt Commonwealth Socs Council, 1992–97; Court, RCA, 1993–99; Council, Parly and Scientific Cttee, 1997–2011 (Vice-Pres., 2004–08); Council, British Sci. Assoc. (formerly BAAS), 1997–2010; Crown Estate Paving Commn, 2002–14. Trustee: Council for Assisting Refugee Academics, 1997–2010; Internat. Polar Foundn, 2006–. Chm., Richmond Duke of Edinburgh Awards Forum, 2003–07. Mem. Bd of Govs, 2002–09, and Chair, Audit Cttee, 2004–08, Kingston Univ.; Chm. of Govs, Atlantic Coll., 2010–; Chm. Council, Royal Holloway, Univ. of London, 2011–. FRGS (Member: Sci. and Public Affairs Cttee, 1994–96; Educn Cttee, 1996–98; Expedn and Field Work Cttee, 1998–2004). Mem., 1994–, Chm., 2002–06, Editl Bd, Commonwealth Round Table. Hon. DSc Lancaster, 2003. *Recreations:* cricket, travel, visiting galleries, architecture. *Address:* 25 Trowlock Avenue, Teddington, Middx TW11 9QT. *Clubs:* Royal Over-Seas League, Geographical; Middlesex County Cricket.

COX, Stephen Joseph, RA 2010; artist; *b* Bristol, 16 Sept. 1946; *s* of late Leonard John Cox and Ethel Minnie May Cox (*née* McGill); *m* 1996, Judith Atkins; two *d*. *Educ:* St Mary Redcliffe, Bristol; W of England Coll. of Art; Loughborough Coll. of Art; Central Sch. of Art and Design (DipAD Hons). Lectr, Brighton Poly., 1980–81; part-time Lectr, Coventry Coll. of Art, 1968–72; Stourbridge Coll. of Art, 1973–75; Newport Coll. of Art, 1975–77;

Birmingham Poly., 1977–79, 1980–81. Sen. Res. Fellow, Wimbledon Sch. of Art, 1995–96. First Vis. Montgomery Fellow in Sculpture, Lincoln Coll., Oxford, 2009. Hon. Fellow, Hereford Coll. of Art, 2010. *Solo exhibitions* include: Gallerie Swart, Amsterdam, 1978; Gallerie La Salita, Rome, 1982; 25th Festivale dei Due Mondi, Spoleto, 1982; Tate Gall., Lisson Gall., Greenwood Gall., 1982; Villa Romana, Florence, 1983; Casa di Masacchio, San Giovanni Valdarno, 1984; Arnolfini Gall., Bristol, 1985; UK Rep., Indian Triennale, 1986; Gallerie Carini, Florence, 1987, 1989, Bath Fest. Artsite Gall., 1988; Art Now, Gothenberg, 1991; Mus. of Egyptian Modern Art, Cairo, 1995; Henry Moore Inst., 1995; Michael Hue-Williams Fine Art, 1995, 1996, 1998–99; Royal Botanic Gdns, Kew, 1995–96; An Indian Decade, three exhibitions, Art Today Gall., Ajanta Gall. and Jamali Kamali Gdns, 1996; Dulwich Picture Gall., 1997; Glyndebourne Opera Hse, 1998; Santa Maria Della Scala, Siena, 1999; Mus. Archeologico, Aosta, Italy, 2000; Culture Gall., NY, 2001; Eyestorm Gall., London, 2004; Mappa Mundi, Hereford Cathedral and Meadow Gall., Burford, 2004; San Francesco Della Scarpa, Bari, 2005; Bristol City Mus. and Art Gall., 2006; Lincoln Coll., Oxford, 2009; Drawing Gall., Ludlow Castle, 2011; Yogini Drawings, Chelsea Arts Club, 2012; *group exhibitions* include: Paris Biennale, 1977; Hayward Gall., 1978, 1983; Whitechapel Art Gall., 1981; Venice Biennale, 1982, 1984; Kunstmuseum, Lucerne, 1982; Tate Gall., 1983, 1985, 1992, 1994, 1997; Internat. Garden Fest., Liverpool, 1984; MOMA, NY, 1984; Summer Exhibn, RA 1988 (Goldhill Prize for Sculpture); MOMA, Brussels, 1992; BM and Museo Egizio Torino, 1994–95; Hathill Foundn, Goodwood, 1997; Schloss Ambrass, Innsbruck, Jesus Coll., Cambridge, 1999; Gori Collection, Japan, Nat. Gall., Winchester Cathedral, 2000; Guggenheim, Venice, Cass Sculpture Foundn, 2002; Summer Exhibn, Burghley Hse, Lincs, 2003; *work in collections* includes: Tate Gall., V&A, BM, British Council, Arts Council, Walker Art Gall., Liverpool, Henry Moore Centre for Sculpture, Hunterian Art Gall., Groningen Mus., Netherlands, Fogg Mus., USA, Hakone Open Air Mus., Japan; *commissions* include: Atyeo, Baltic Wharf, Bristol, 1987; Cairo Opera Hse, 1989; Ganapathi and Devi, Broadgate, 1989; Osirisisis, Stockley Park, nr Heathrow, 1991; Hymn, Univ. of Kent at Canterbury, 1991; Mantra, British Council bldg, New Delhi, 1992; Echo, Fleet Place, Ludgate Hill, 1993; Reredos, altar, font and stations of the cross, Ch of St Paul Haringey, 1995; Rajiv Gandhi Samadi, New Delhi (central feature), 1997; Adam and Eve vessels, St Luke's, Chelsea, 1996; Eucharist, Cathedral Ch of St Nicholas, Newcastle upon Tyne, 1997; Tribute sculpture, British High Commn, Canberra, 1997; Faceted Column, Finsbury Pavement, 1999; altar, St Anselm's Chapel, Canterbury Cathedral, consecrated 2006 (Art and Christianity Enquiry Award for Art in a Religious Context, 2007); Tribute to St Anselm, Aosta Cathedral, 2009; Peregrine sculpture, Goodwood, 2009; Virgin Mary and St Mildred, Tower Gateway, Lincoln Coll., Oxford, 2009; Holy Water Stoup, Canterbury Cathedral, 2010; Willoughby Meml, St Michael and All Angels Church, Edenham, Lincs, 2011; Elemental Head, St James' Gateway, London, 2013; Relief, Apple Tree Yard, 8 St James's Sq., 2015. *Relevant Publication*: The Sculpture of Stephen Cox, by Stephen Bann, 1995. *Address:* Lower House Farm, Coreley, Ludlow, Shropshire SY8 3AS. *T:* (01584) 891532. *E:* coxstepstone@aol.com. *Clubs:* Arts, Chelsea Arts.
See also J. Cox.

COX, Prof. Susan Jean, OBE 2011; Professor of Safety and Risk Management and Dean, Lancaster University Management School, Lancaster University, since 2001; *b* 17 Oct. 1947; *d* of late Derric and Jean Minshall; *m* 1969, Thomas Rodford Cox, CBE; two *d. Educ:* Univ. of Nottingham (BSc (Chemistry and Psychol.) 1969; MPhil (Psychol.) 1988). Loughborough University: Director: Centre for Extension Studies, 1993–94; Centre for Hazard and Risk Mgt, 1994–97; Loughborough Business Sch., 1997–2001. Chm., Assoc. of Business Schs, 2002–04; Mem., Res. Priorities Bd, ESRC, 2003–07; Dir, Inspire Learning, 2003–06. *Publications:* (with Robin Tait) Reliability, Safety and Risk Management: an integrated approach, 1991, 2nd edn 1998; (with Tom Cox) Safety, Systems and People, 1996. *Recreations:* gardening, theatre, walking, football (Stoke City supporter), reading, travel. *Address:* Walnut Lodge, Rose Grove, Keyworth, Notts NG12 5HE. *T:* (0115) 937 5947, *Fax:* (office) (01524) 594720. *E:* s.cox@lancaster.ac.uk.

COX, Thomas Michael; *b* London, 19 Jan. 1930. *Educ:* state schools; London Sch. of Economics. Electrical worker. Former Mem., Fulham Borough Council; contested (Lab) GLC elections, 1967; contested (Lab) Stroud, 1966. MP (Lab): Wandsworth Central, 1970–74; Wandsworth Tooting, 1974–83; Tooting, 1983–2005. An Asst Govt Whip, 1974–77; a Lord Comr of the Treasury, 1977–79. Member: ETU; Co-operative Party.

COX, Timothy Blakiston; Lord-Lieutenant of Warwickshire, since 2013; *b* Shrewsbury, 8 Sept. 1955; *s* of William Peter Cox and June Eleanor Cox; *m* 1984, Penny Roodhouse; one *s* one *d. Educ:* Shrewsbury Sch. MRICS 1980. With Chesshire Gibson & Co., 1974–86; founder, Tim Cox Associates, chartered surveyors, 1986–. High Sheriff, Warwicks, 2011–12. *Recreations:* sport, golf and tennis. *Address:* Tim Cox Associates, 37 Guild Street, Stratford upon Avon, Warks CV37 6QY.

COX, Prof. Timothy Martin, MD; FRCP, FMedSci; Professor of Medicine, 1989–2015, now Emeritus, and Director of Research, Department of Medicine, since 2015, University of Cambridge; Fellow of Sidney Sussex College, Cambridge, 1990–2015, now Life Fellow; *b* 10 May 1948; *s* of late William Neville Cox and Joan Desirée Cox (*née* Ward); *m* 1975, Susan Ruth Mason; three *s* one *d. Educ:* Oundle Sch.; London Hosp. Med. Coll., Univ. of London (Price Entrance Scholar; James Anderson Prize; MB 1971, MSc 1978, MD 1979); MA Cantab 1990, MD Cantab 1991. FRCP 1984. Junior posts, Med. Unit, Royal London Hosp., 1971; Dept of Morbid Anatomy, Bernard Baron Inst., Hammersmith and United Oxford Hosps, 1972–77; Royal Postgraduate Medical School, London University: MRC Training Fellow, Cell Biology Unit, 1977–79; Wellcome Sen. Clinical Fellow and Sen. Lectr, Dept of Medicine, 1979–87; Sen. Lectr, Depts of Haematology and Medicine, 1987–89. Hon. Consultant Physician, Addenbrooke's Hosp., 1989–. Vis. Scientist, Dept of Biology, MIT, 1983–84. Vis. Prof., Weizmann Inst. of Sci., Rehovot, Israel, 2012. Pres., Translational Medicine Cttee, L'Agence nationale de la recherche, Paris, 2013–15. Lectures: A. J. S. McFadzean, Univ. of Hong Kong, 1990; Schorstein Meml, London Hosp. Med Coll., 1994; Bradshaw, RCP, 1996; Flynn, RCPath, 2001 and 2009; Opening Lect., Gordon Res. Conf. on Lysosomal Diseases, Galveston, 2011; Hunterian Oration, Hunterian Soc., 2012; Benoziyo, Weizmann Inst., 2012; 17th McFadzean Oration, Hong Kong Coll. of Physicians, 2012 (Gold Medal). External examiner in Medicine: Univ. of Hong Kong, 1990; Univ. of London, 1993–97; RCSI, 1995–97; Chinese Univ. of HK, 2001; Univ. of Oxford, 2001–05. Member: MRC Grants Cttee, 1990–94; MRC Clin. Trng Career Develt Panel, 2000–03. Mem., Vet. Panel, Wellcome Trust, 1996–98. Trustee, Croucher Foundn, HK, 2001– (Vice-Chm., 2013–). Mem., Assoc. of Physicians of GB and Ire., 1984– (Mem., Exec. Cttee, 1995–97); Cambridge Philosophical Society: Mem. Council, 1994–; Vice Pres., 1999–2002, 2005–; Pres., 2002–03; Sen. Vice Pres., 2003–05. Fellow and Mem. Council, Galton Inst., 2007–. Founder FMedSci 1998; MRSocMed 2009. FRSA 2000. Syndic, CUP, 1998–; Mem., Editl Bd, Qly Jl of Medicine; Ed.-in-Chief, Expert Reviews in Molecular Medicine, 2013–. *Publications:* Oxford Textbook of Medicine, (contrib.) 3rd edn, 1995, (ed jtly) 6th edn, 2016; (ed jtly) Molecular Biology in Medicine, 1997 (trans. Spanish 1998, Serbo-Croat 2000); contribs to sci. and med. jls on inborn errors metabolism, incl. Cell, New England Jl of Med., Lancet, Jl of Clin. Investigation, Jl Biol. Chem., Nature Reviews Genetics, Proc. Nat. Acad. Sci. (USA), Medicine (Baltimore), Nature Medicine, Jl of Pathology. *Recreations:* natural history, piano, making cider. *Address:* Department of Medicine, University of Cambridge School of Clinical Medicine, Hills Road, Cambridge CB2 0QQ. *T:* (01223) 336864.

COX, Vivienne; Executive Vice President, and Chief Executive Officer, Alternative Energy, BP plc, 2008–09; *b* 29 May 1959; *d* of Ewart Arthur Cox and Doreen Olive Cox (*née* Merchant); *m* 2007, Eric Vischer; two *d. Educ:* St Catherine's Coll., Oxford (BSc 1981, MA); INSEAD (MBA 1989). Joined BP, 1981; Chief Exec., Air BP, 1997–99; Group Vice President: Refining and Mkting, 1999–2001; Integrated Supply and Trading, 2001–05; Exec. Vice Pres., Gas Power and Renewables, 2005–08. Non-executive Director: Rio Tinto, 2005–14; Climate Change Capital, 2008–12 (Chm., 2009–12); Vallourec, 2010–14; DFID, 2010–; Pearson plc, 2012–; BG Gp, 2012–. Mem., Internat. Council and Bd, INSEAD, 2009–; Adjunct Prof., Imperial Coll. London. Patron, St Francis Hospice, 2006–. Hon. DSc Hull, 2009. *Recreations:* sailing, swimming, gardening.

COX, Hon. William John Ellis, AC 1999; RFD 1985; ED 1968; Governor, Tasmania, 2004–08; *b* 1 April 1936; *s* of Hon. William Ellis Cox, CBE, MC, and Alice Mary Cox; *m* 1970, Jocelyn Fay Wallace; two *s* one *d. Educ:* Xavier Coll., Melbourne; Univ. of Tasmania (BA, LLB). Called to the Bar, Tasmania, 1960; Partner, Dobson, Mitchell & Allport, 1961–76; Magistrate, Hobart, 1976–77; Crown Advocate, Tasmania, 1977–82; QC 1978; Judge, Supreme Court of Tasmania, 1982–95; Chief Justice, Tasmania, 1995–2004; Lieut Gov., Tasmania, 1996–2004. Dep. Pres., Defence Force Discipline Appeal Tribunal, 1988–95. Pres., Bar Assoc. of Tasmania, 1973–75. Lt Col, Army Reserve; CO, 6 Field Regt, RAA, 1972–75; Hon. Col Comdt, RAA (Tas), 1993–97. Dir, Winston Churchill Meml Trust, 1988– (Nat. Chm., 2000–04). Pres., St John Ambulance, Australia (Tas), 2002–04. Hon. LLD Tasmania, 2005. KStJ 2002. *Recreations:* bush walking, gardening. *Address:* 214 Davey Street, Hobart, Tas 7004, Australia. *Club:* Tasmanian.

COX, William Trevor; *see* Trevor, W.

COYLE, Prof. Andrew Gerard, CMG 2003; PhD; Visiting Professor, University of Essex, since 2011; *b* 17 June 1944; *m* 1st, Joyce Hamilton (marr. diss.); one *s* three *d*; 2nd, Vivien Stern (*see* Baroness Stern). *Educ:* Real Colegio Escocés, Valladolid; Open Univ. (BA); Univ. of Edinburgh (PhD 1986). Scottish Prison Service and HM Prison Service, 1973–97: Assistant Governor: Edinburgh Prison, 1973–76; Polmont Borstal, 1976–78; Dep. Gov., Shotts Prison, 1978–81; Head of Ops, Scottish Prison Service HQ, 1981–86; Governor: Greenock Prison, 1986–88; Peterhead Prison, 1988–90; Shotts Prison, 1990–91; Brixton Prison, 1991–97; Prof. of Prison Studies, 2003–10, now Emeritus, and Dir, Internat. Centre for Prison Studies, 1997–2005, KCL. Expert consultant on prison matters: to Office of UN High Comr for Human Rights, 1992–; to Council of Europe, 1992–. Member: Foreign Sec.'s Panel on Torture, 2003–10; Nat. Adv. Body on Offender Mgt, 2006–10; Judicial Appts Bd for Scotland, 2009–14; Administrative Justice and Tribunals Council, 2009–13; undertook Review of Ind. Prison Monitoring for Scottish Govt, 2012–13. Chairman: Scottish Assoc. for Study of Delinquency, 1989–91; Inst. for Study and Treatment of Delinquency, 1993–97; Vice Pres., Nat. Assoc. of Prison Visitors, 1999–. Mem. Editl Bd, Punishment & Society, 1997–. Winston Churchill Travelling Fellow, 1984; University of Edinburgh: Associate Mem., Centre for Law and Society, 1988; Mem., Centre for Theol. and Public Issues, 1993–; Hon. Prof., Min. of Justice Acad. of Law and Mgt, Russia, 2000–. Pres., Howard League Scotland, 2013–; Patron: Unlock, Assoc. of Former Prisoners, 1997–; Prisoners Abroad, 2013– (Trustee, 1999–2007). Trustee: Unit for Arts and Offenders, 2000–05; Royal London Aid Soc., 2002–05; Internat. Centre for Prison Studies, 2010–. Bd Mem., Eisenhower Foundn, Washington, 2004–08. FRSA 1993; FKC 2004. Medal: Russian Penitentiary Service, 2001; Min. of Justice, Russian Fedn, 2002. *Publications:* Inside: rethinking Scotland's prisons, 1991; The Prisons We Deserve, 1994; Managing Prisons in a Time of Change, 2002; Human Rights Approach to Prison Management: handbook for prison staff, 2002; (ed) Capitalist Punishment: prison privatisation and human rights, 2003; Humanity in Prison, 2003; Understanding Prisons, 2005; contrib. numerous articles to learned jls on human rights, prisons, prison mgt and alternatives to prison. *Address:* International Centre for Prison Studies, 42 Store Street, WC1E 7DB. *E:* andrew.coyle@prisonstudies.org.

COYLE, Dr Diane, OBE 2009; Director, Enlightenment Economics, since 2001; Professor of Economics, University of Manchester, since 2014; *b* Feb. 1961; *d* of Joseph and Kathleen Coyle; *m* 1990, (Nicholas) Rory Cellan-Jones, *qv*; two *s. Educ:* Brasenose Coll., Oxford (BA Hons PPE 1981); Harvard Univ. (PhD Econs 1985). Sen. Econ. Asst, HM Treasury, 1985–86; Sen. Economist, DRI Europe, 1986–89; Eur. Ed. and features writer, Investors' Chronicle, 1989–93; Econs Ed., The Independent, 1993–2001. Member: Competition Commn, 2001–09; Migration Adv. Cttee, UK Border Agency, 2007–12; BBC Trust, 2007–15 (Vice Chair, 2011–15); Browne Rev. of Higher Educn Funding, 2009–10. *Publications:* The Weightless World, 1996 (US edn 1997); Governing the World Economy, 2000; Paradoxes of Prosperity, 2001; Sex, Drugs and Economics, 2002; New Wealth for Old Nations, 2005; The Soulful Science, 2007; The Economics of Enough, 2011; GDP: a brief but affectionate history, 2014; contrib. chapters in books and articles to jls. *Recreations:* classical ballet, reading. *Address:* Department of Economics, University of Manchester, Oxford Road, Manchester M13 9PL. *T:* (0161) 306 6000. *E:* diane@enlightenmenteconomics.com, diane.coyle@manchester.ac.uk.

COYLE, Eurfron Gwynne, (Mrs Michael Coyle); *see* Jones, E. G.

COYLE, Neil; MP (Lab) Bermondsey and Old Southwark, since 2015; *b* Luton, Dec. 1978; *s* of Alan Coyle and Mary Coyle (*née* Wesson); *m* 2014, Sarah Lindars. *Educ:* Hull Univ. (BA Hons). Lived in China, 2001–03; Disability Rights Commn, 2003–07, latterly as Policy Manager for health and social care; Hd of Policy, Nat. Centre for Ind. Living, 2007–09; Dir of Policy, Disability Alliance, 2009–12; Dir of Policy and Campaigns, DRUK, 2012–13. Mem. (Lab), Southwark LBC, 2010–15; Dep. Mayor of Southwark, 2014–15. Vice Chm., Walworth Community Council, 2010–11. Trustee, N Southwark Envmt Trust. *Address:* House of Commons, SW1A 0AA.

COYNE, Prof. John; Vice-Chancellor, University of Derby, 2004–15; *b* Barnsley, 27 Sept. 1951; *m* Julie; two *d. Educ:* Univ. of Nottingham (BA). University of Nottingham, 1985–90: Lectr, then Sen. Lectr, Dept of Industrial Econs, subseq. Dept of Industrial Econs, Accountancy and Insurance; Warden of Cripps Hall; Co-Dir, Centre for Mgt Buy-out Res.; De Montfort University: Prof. of Business, 1990–2000 (Bass Prof., 1990–93); Hd, Leicester Sch. of Business, 1990–97; Dean, Faculty of Business and Law, 1997–2000; Pro-Vice-Chancellor, 2000–04. Mem., UK Commn for Employment and Skills, 2011–.

COZENS, Andrew Geoffrey, CBE 2005; Director, Acainn Ltd, since 2012; independent social care and health policy and improvement specialist, since 2012; *b* 3 June 1955; *s* of late Geoffrey Cozens and Iris Cozens (*née* Hammett). *Educ:* Peter Symonds Sch., Winchester; Magdalene Coll., Cambridge (BA 1977); Green Coll., Oxford (MSc, CQSW 1981). Social Worker, N Yorks CC, 1981–84; Develt Officer, N Yorks Forum for Vol. Orgns, 1984–88; North Yorkshire County Council: Principal Officer, 1988–90; Asst Dir, 1990–94; Sen. Asst Dir, 1994–96; Dir of Social Services, Glos CC, 1996–2000; Dir of Social Services, then of Social Care and Health, and Dep. Chief Exec., Leicester CC, 2000–06; Strategic Advr, Children, Adults and Health Services, Improvement and Develt Agency, subseq. Local Govt Improvement and Develt, 2006–12. Pres., Assoc. of Dirs of Social Services, 2003–04. Chm., Carers Trust, 2012–. Publishing Editor: Platform Mag., 1972–77; Green Horse Pubns, 1974–77; Avalon Editions, 1978–82. Hon. Fellow, Cheltenham and Gloucester Coll. of Higher Educn, 1998. *Recreations:* hill walking, the arts, reading, watching sport, travel. *Address:* 67 Knighton Drive, Leicester LE2 3HD.

COZENS, Robert William, CBE 1989; QPM 1981; Chief Constable, West Mercia Constabulary (Hereford, Worcester and Shropshire), 1981–85, retired; *b* 10 Nov. 1927; *s* of Sydney Robert and Rose Elizabeth Cozens; *m* 1952, Jean Dorothy Banfield; one *s* one *d*. *Educ:* Stoke C of E Sch., Guildford. Constable to Chief Superintendent, Surrey Constabulary, 1954–72; Asst Dir, Command Courses, Police Staff Coll., Bramshill, 1972–74; Asst Chief Constable, S Yorks Police, 1974–78; seconded to Federal Judicial Police in Mexico for advisory duties, 1975; Dep. Chief Constable, Lincs Police, 1978–81. Dir, Police Requirements for Sci. and Technol., Home Office, 1985–88. *Recreations:* making friends, volunteer with Witness Service, working at Guildford Crown and Magistrates' Court, Guide at Farnham Castle, doing my best to keep active. *Club:* Farnham Weyside Rotary.

CRABB, Rt Hon. Stephen; PC 2014; MP (C) Preseli Pembrokeshire, since 2005; Secretary of State for Wales, since 2014; *b* 20 Jan. 1973; *m* 1996, Béatrice Alice Claude Odile Monnier; one *s* one *d*. *Educ:* Bristol Univ. (BSc Hons 1995); London Business Sch. (MBA 2004). Res. Asst to Andrew Rowe, MP, 1995–96; Parly Officer, Nat. Council for Voluntary Youth Services, 1996–98; Policy and Campaigns Manager, LCCI, 1998–2002; mktg consultant, 2003–05. An Opposition Whip, 2009–10; an Asst Govt Whip, 2010–12; a Lord Comr of HM Treasury (Govt Whip), 2012–14; Parly Under-Sec. of State, Wales Office, 2012–14. *Recreations:* Rugby, cooking, spending time with family. *Address:* House of Commons, SW1A 0AA. *T:* (020) 7219 3000. *E:* crabbs@parliament.uk. *Clubs:* Balfour, Haverfordwest Co. Assoc. Football (Haverfordwest).

CRABB, Tony William; General Manager, CCT Productions Ltd, 1995–97; *b* 27 June 1933; *s* of William Harold Crabb and Ellen Emily Crabb; *m* 1957, Brenda Margaret (*née* Sullman) (*d* 2013); one *s* one *d*. *Educ:* Chiswick Grammar School; London School of Economics (BScEcon); Intelligence Corps Russian Interpreters Course, 1952–54. BBC, 1957–88; seconded as news adviser to Govt of Libya, 1968–69; Managing Editor: BBC TV News, 1979–82; BBC Breakfast Time, 1982–84; Controller, Corporate News Services, BBC, 1984–87; Special Asst, News and Current Affairs, BBC, 1987–88; Dep. Dir of Broadcasting, Radio TV Hong Kong, 1988–92. Mem. (Lib Dem) Spelthorne BC, 1999–2003 and 2008–11. FRTS (Mem. Council, 2002–06). *Address:* 38 The Avenue, Sunbury-on-Thames, Middx TW16 5ES. *E:* tony.crabb@tiscali.co.uk.

CRABBIE, Christopher Donald, CMG 1995; HM Diplomatic Service, retired; UK Permanent Representative to OECD, Paris, (with rank of Ambassador), 1999–2003; *b* 17 Jan. 1946; *s* of late William George Crabbie and of Jane (*née* Coe). *Educ:* Rugby Sch.; Newcastle Univ.; Liverpool Univ.; Corpus Christi Coll., Oxford. Second Sec., FCO, 1973–75; First Secretary: Nairobi, 1975–79; Washington, 1979–83; FCO, 1983–85; Counsellor and Hd of European Communities Div., HM Treasury, 1985–87; Counsellor, FCO, 1987–90; Dep. UK Perm. Rep., OECD, Paris, 1990; Counsellor, British Embassy, Paris, 1990–94; Ambassador: to Algeria, 1994–95; to Romania, 1996–99; to Moldova, 1999. *Recreations:* ski-ing, bridge, sailing, gardening.

CRABTREE, Maj.-Gen. Derek Thomas, CB 1983; *b* 21 Jan. 1930; *s* of late William Edward Crabtree and Winifred Hilda Burton; *m* 1960, Daphne Christine Mason; one *s* one *d*. *Educ:* St Brendan's Coll., Bristol. Commissioned, 1953; Regimental Service: 13th/18th Royal Hussars (QMO), 1953–56; Royal Berkshire Regt, 1956–59; Technical Staff Course, RMCS, 1960–62; sc Camberley, 1964; BM 11 Inf. Bde, BAOR, 1965–67; CO 1st Bn Duke of Edinburgh's Royal Regt, UK and Berlin, 1970–72; Col GS, MGO Secretariat, MoD, 1974–76; Dep. Comdr and Chief of Staff Headquarters British Forces Hong Kong, 1976–79; Dep. Comdt RMCS, 1979–80; Dir Gen. of Weapons (Army), MoD, 1980–84. Sen. Mil. Advr, Short Bros, 1984–86; Gen. Manager, Regular Forces Employment Assoc., 1987–94. Col, Duke of Edinburgh's Royal Regt, 1982–87, 1988–89. *Recreations:* golf, computing, gardening. *Address:* 53 High Street, Shrivenham, Swindon SN6 8AW. *Club:* Army and Navy.

CRABTREE, Harriet Mary, OBE 2008; ThD; Director, Inter Faith Network for the UK, since 2007; *b* London, 25 Nov. 1958; *d* of His Honour Jonathan Crabtree and of Caroline Ruth Keigwin Crabtree (*née* Oliver, now Baden-Powell); *m* 1984, James Stewart (marr. diss. 1990). *Educ:* Mill Mount Grammar Sch. for Girls, York; Lewes Priory Comp. Sch.; King's Coll. London (BD); Harvard Divinity Sch. (ThM; ThD 1989). Coordinator, Progs and Develt, Center for Study of World Religions, Harvard Divinity Sch., 1988–89; Lectr in Study of Religion, Faculty of Arts and Scis, Harvard Univ., 1989–90; Asst Dir, Inter Faith Network, 1991–94; Dep. Dir, Inter Faith Network for UK, 1994–2007. Vis. Lectr, Univ. of Massachusetts, Boston, 1986–87. Mem., Commn on Integration and Cohesion, 2006–07; Trustee, UNICEF UK, 2007–13. *Publications:* The Christian Life: traditional metaphors and contemporary theologies, 1991; Inter Faith Activity in the UK: a survey, 2003; pubns for Inter Faith Network; contribs to jls. *Recreations:* time with family and other good company, music, history, woods and their preservation, railways. *Address:* Inter Faith Network for the UK, 2 Grosvenor Gardens, SW1W 0DH. *T:* (020) 7730 0410. *E:* harriet.crabtree@interfaith.org.uk. *Club:* Athenæum.

CRABTREE, Peter Dixon, OBE 1997; **His Honour Judge Crabtree;** a Circuit Judge, since 2014; *b* 2 March 1956; *s* of Kenneth and Elizabeth Crabtree; *m* 1981, Ann Davina Cooper; three *d*. *Educ:* Liverpool Coll.; Manchester Poly. (BA Hons); Univ. of Bristol (LLM); Inns of Court Sch. of Law. ACIS. Royal Navy, 1979–2005: served HMSs Fearless, Minerva, Ark Royal, Invincible; Captain. Called to the Bar, Gray's Inn, 1985; a District Judge (Magistrates' Courts), 2005–14; a Recorder, 2009–14. *Recreations:* walking, climbing, reading, family. *Address:* Courts of Justice, London Road, Southampton, Hampshire SO15 2XQ. *Club:* Royal Scots (Edinburgh).

CRACKETT, Maj. Gen. John, CB 2015; TD 1993; CEng; Assistant Chief of Defence Staff (Reserves and Cadets), since 2013; *b* Newcastle upon Tyne, 19 Dec. 1958; *s* of John Thomas Morton and Yvonne Crackett; *m* 1987, Claire Luckhurst; two *d*. *Educ:* Hymers Coll.; Churchill Coll., Cambridge (BA Engrg 1981). CEng 1988; FIEE 1998; FIMechE 2004. Power stn design and project mgt engr, CEGB, 1978–90; National Power plc: Stn Develt and Consents Manager, 1990–95; Engrg Manager, Ironbridge Power Stn, 1995–97; TXU Europe Ltd: Stn Manager, Ironbridge, Rugeley and Drakelow Power Stns, 1997–2000; Hd of Prodn, 2000–02; E.ON UK: Managing Director: Shared Services, 2002–05; Energy Services, 2005–07; Central Networks, 2007–11. Trustee, E.ON UK Pension Scheme, 2003–06. Ind. Bd Mem., Office of Nuclear Regulation, 2011–; non-exec. Mem., Strategy Bd, Arqiva, 2011–13. Trustee, Marches Energy Agency, 1997–2015. Territorial Army: enlisted Cambridge Univ. OTC, 1978; commnd 1980; troop and sqdn officer, 37 Signals Regt, then o/c 57 Signals Sqdn, 1982–95; SO2 2 Signals Bde, 1995–96; o/c 55 Signals Sqdn, 1996–98; CO, 39 Signals Regt, 1998–2000; DS JSCSC, 2000–02; Dep. Comdr 143 Bde, 2002–06; TA Col Royal Signals, 2007–09; Asst Comdr 5 Div., 2009–12; AComd Army Recruiting and Trng Div., 2012–13; Col Comdt Royal Corps of Signals, 2014–. Mem., Engr and Logistic Staff Corps, 2003–; Hon. Col, 37 Signals Regt, 2011–. Liveryman: Co. of Engrs, 2001–; and Trustee, Shrewsbury Co. of Drapers, 2003–. *Recreations:* flying, walking, riding, DIY. *Address:* c/o Ministry of Defence, Reserves and Cadets, Main Building, Whitehall, SW1A 2HB. *T:* (020) 7218 8000. *Club:* Army and Navy.

CRACKNELL, David John; Founder and Director, Big Tent Communications, since 2008; *b* 5 June 1968; *s* of David Lewis and Norma Rose Cracknell; *m* 1998, Rachel Laurent; one *s* two *d*. *Educ:* Southampton Univ. (LLB); Pembroke Coll., Oxford (BCL). Reporter, Coventry Evening Telegraph, 1993–95; Lobby Corresp., Press Assoc., 1995–98; Political Ed., Sunday Business, 1998–99; Dep. Political Ed., Sunday Telegraph, 1999–2001; Political Ed., Sunday Times, 2001–08; Chm., FD-LLM, 2008. *E:* david@bigtentcommunications.com.

CRACKNELL, James Edward, OBE 2005 (MBE 2001); Olympic oarsman, retired 2006; adventurer, broadcaster and journalist; *b* 5 May 1972; *s* of John David and Jennifer Ann Cracknell; *m* 2002, Beverley Anne Turner; one *s* two *d*. *Educ:* Kingston Grammar Sch.; Reading Univ. (BSc Geog.); Inst. of Educn, London Univ. (PGCE); Brunel Univ. (MSc). Gold Medal, Jun. World Championships, 1990; Mem., British rowing team, 1991–2006; winner: World Championships: Gold Medal, coxless fours, 1997, 1998 and 1999; (with Matthew Pinsent) Gold Medal, coxed pairs, 2001; Gold Medal, coxless pairs, 2001 and 2002; Gold Medal, coxless fours, Olympic Games, Sydney, 2000 and Athens, 2004. Journalist and columnist, Daily Telegraph, 1998–; broadcaster, ITV and Channel 4, 2005–. Contested (C) SW England and Gibraltar, EP, 2014. Pres., London Road Safety Council, 2015–. *Publications:* James Cracknell's No-Gym Health Plan, 2006; (with Ben Fogle) The Crossing: conquering the Atlantic in the world's toughest rowing race, 2006; (with Ben Fogle) Race to the Pole, 2009; (with Beverley Turner) Touching Distance, 2012. *Recreations:* motorbikes, surfboards. *Address:* James Grant Group Ltd, 94 Strand On The Green, W4 3NN. *Club:* Leander (Captain, 2000–05) (Henley-on-Thames).

CRACKNELL, His Honour Malcolm Thomas; a Circuit Judge, 1989–2009; Member, Parole Board for England and Wales, since 2009; *b* 12 Dec. 1943; *s* of late Percy Thomas Cracknell and Doris Louise Cracknell; *m* 1st, 1968, Ann Carrington (*née* Gooding) (marr. diss. 1980); one *s* one *d*; 2nd, 1988, Felicity Anne Davies; two *s* one *d*. *Educ:* Royal Liberty Sch., Romford; Hull Univ. (LLB); King's Coll., London (LLM). Called to Bar, Middle Temple, 1969. Lectr in Law, Univ. of Hull, 1968–74; Barrister, NE Circuit, 1970–89; a Recorder, 1988; Designated Family Judge, Hull Combined Court Centre, 1994–2007. *Recreations:* golf, gardening, cricket, reading.

CRACROFT-BRENNAN, (Stephen) Patrick, FCA; sole practitioner, Bambury & Co., since 1989; *b* Kingston-upon-Hull, 29 April 1951; *s* of Harry Brennan and Mildred Zadie Brennan (*née* Cracroft); *m* 1974, Angela Jane (separated 1975, marr. diss. 1981), *d* of Kenneth Archer Easby, FCA and Joan Mary Easby (*née* Hudson). *Educ:* Hull Grammar Sch. ACA 1974, FCA 1984. Served articles, Hodgson Harris, 1969–72; Dutton Moore, 1972–74; Sen. Manager, Kenneth Easby & Co., 1974–75; Accountant, Alton Computer Services Ltd, 1975–81; Computer Manager, Finnies, 1981–84; Financial Controller, Baronsmead Associates Ltd, 1984–87; Gp Chief Internal Auditor, Taylor Woodrow plc, 1987–89; Finance Manager, Servite Housing, 1995–97; Hd of Finance, Threshold Tennant Trust, 1998–2001; Hd of Finance and Admin, Office of Immigration Services Comr, 2006–10. Sole practitioner, Patrick Cracroft-Brennan & Co., 1975–89. Exec. Dir and Sec., Magistrates's Assoc., 2010–12. Man. Editor, Cracroft's Peerage Online, 1998–; Founder and Trustee, Peerage Research Trust, 2004–. Director: Heraldic Media Ltd; Heraldic Graphics Ltd; Heraldic China Ltd; Heraldry.com Ltd; Heraldic Genealogy.com Ltd; Cracroft's Peerage Ltd; Complete Peerage Ltd; Bambury Secretary Ltd; London Will Co. Ltd; Peerage Research Trust. Heraldry Society: Hon. Treas., 1983–88, 2012–; Mem. Council, 1988–97, 2001–10, 2012–; Hon. FHS 1988. St John Ambulance: Pres., Wimbledon Div., 1987–91; Mem., 1988–2012, Hospitaller, 1988–93, 1998–, St John Council for London; Pres., Crystal Palace and Anerley Div., 2001–13; Mem., London Regl Priory Gp, 2012–. Freeman, City of London, 1986; Liveryman, Scriveners' Co., 1988 (Court Asst, 2013). SBStJ 1991. *Recreations:* heraldry, genealogy, classical music, international travel, cooking, baking, supporting and promoting gay Rugby. *Address:* The Bungalow, Parsonage Farm, Upper Street, Tingewick, Bucks MK18 4QG. *Club:* Cheap Ward.

CRADDOCK, Timothy James; HM Diplomatic Service, retired; a Director and Trustee, UK National Commission for UNESCO, 2008–10; *b* 27 June 1956; *s* of James Vincent Craddock and Kathleen Mary Craddock (*née* Twigg). *Educ:* King Edward's Sch., Birmingham; Gonville and Caius Coll., Cambridge (Exhibnr; MA); School of Oriental and African Studies, London Univ. Entered FCO, 1979; Third Sec. and Vice-Consul, Chad, 1979–80; Vice-Consul, Istanbul, 1981–82; Second Sec., Ankara, 1982–85; Hd of Section, South America Dept, FCO, 1985–87; Sec., FCO Bd of Mgt, 1988–90; First Sec., Paris, 1990–94; Dep. Hd, Aid Policy and Resources Dept, FCO, 1995–97; Ambassador to Estonia, 1997–2000; Hd, Africa Gt Lakes and Horn Dept, DFID (on secondment), 2000–03; UK Perm. Delegate to UNESCO, 2003–07. Exec. Mem. and Trustee, Norwich Soc., 2011–. *Recreations:* hill walking, opera, London, gardening in France. *Address:* 56 St Faith's Lane, Norwich, Norfolk NR1 1NN; 52 rue du Bourg Voisin, 21140 Semur-en-Auxois, France.

CRAFT, Sir Alan (William), Kt 2004; MD; FRCP, FRCPE, FRCPI, FRCPCH, FMedSci, FRCR, FRCA; Director, Northern Institute for Cancer Research, 2007–09, and Sir James Spence Professor of Child Health, 1993–2007, now Emeritus, University of Newcastle upon Tyne; *b* 6 July 1946; *s* of William and Yvonne Craft; *m* 1st, 1968, Dorothy Noble (decd); one *s*; 2nd, 1992, Anne Nicholson. *Educ:* Rutherford Grammar Sch., Newcastle upon Tyne; Univ. of Newcastle upon Tyne (MB, BS; MD). FRCP 1982; FRCPCH 1997; FFPH (FFPHM 2001); FRCPE 2003; FRCPI 2003; FAAP 2003; FIAP 2003; FAMM 2003; FACP 2005; FRCR 2006; FRCA 2006. House Officer, Royal Victoria Infirmary, Newcastle upon Tyne, 1969–70; Sen. House Officer, then Registrar and Sen. Registrar, Newcastle Hosps, 1970–77; MRC Trng Fellow, Royal Marsden Hosp., 1976–77; Consultant Paediatrician: N Tyneside Hosp., 1977–86; Royal Victoria Infirmary, 1977–; Prof. of Paediatric Oncology, Univ. of Newcastle upon Tyne, 1991–93. Chm., European Osteosarcoma Intergroup, 1994–97; Sec. Gen., 1993–99, Pres., 2002–05, Internat. Paediatric Oncology Soc.; President: RCPCH, 2003–06 (Vice-Pres., 1998–2002); Assoc. for Care of Terminally Ill Children, 2001–. Chm., Academy of Med. Royal Colls, 2004–06. Mem. Bd, Med. Defence Union, 2010–. FMedSci 2003. Chm., Scout Assoc., 2009–15; Pres., Northumberland Scouts, 2011–. Hon. FRCN 2013. *Publications:* papers on childhood cancer and other childhood disorders in BMJ, Lancet, Archives of Disease in Childhood, etc. *Recreations:* marathon running, orienteering, crosswords, scouting. *Address:* 1 The Villas, Embleton, Northumberland NE66 3XG. *T:* (01665) 576619. *Club:* Athenæum.

CRAFT, Prof. Ian Logan, FRCS; FRCOG; Director, London Gynaecology and Fertility Centre, 1990–2009; *b* 11 July 1937; *s* of Reginald Thomas Craft and Lois Mary (*née* Logan); *m* 1959, Jacqueline Rivers Symmons; two *s*. *Educ:* Owen's Sch., London; Westminster Med. Sch., Univ. of London (MB, BS). FRCS 1966; MRCOG 1970, FRCOG 1986. Sen. Registrar, Westminster Hosp. Teaching Gp (Westminster Hosp. and Kingston Hosp.), 1970–72; Sen. Lectr and Consultant, Inst. of Obstetrics and Gynaecology, Queen Charlotte's Hosp., London, 1972–76; Prof. of Obstetrics and Gynaecology, Royal Free Hosp., London, 1976–82; Dir of Gynaecology, Cromwell Hosp., 1982–85; Dir of Fertility and Obstetric Studies, Humana Hosp. Wellington, 1985–90. Vis Prof., UCL. *Publications:* contrib. BMJ, Lancet and other medical jls. *Recreations:* art, music, ornithology, sports of most types.

CRAFT, Prof. Maurice, PhD, DLitt; Emeritus Professor of Education, University of Nottingham; *b* 4 May 1932; *er s* of Jack and Polly Craft, London; *m* 1957, Alma, *y d* of Elio and Dinah Sampson, Dublin; one *d* (and one *d* decd). *Educ:* LCC Elem. Sch. and Colfe's Grammar Sch., SE13; LSE, Univ. of London (BSc Econ); Sch. of Education, Trinity Coll., Univ. of Dublin (HDipEd); Inst. of Education, Univ. of London (AcadDipEd); Dept of Sociology, Univ. of Liverpool (PhD 1972); Sch. of Education, Univ. of Nottingham (DLitt 1990). 2/Lt RAOC (Nat. Service), 1953–55. Asst Master, Catford Secondary Sch., SE6, 1956–60; Princ. Lectr and Head of Dept of Sociology, Edge Hill Coll. of Education, Ormskirk, Lancs, 1960–67; Sen. Lectr in Education, i/c Advanced Courses, Univ. of Exeter, 1967–73; Sub-Dean, Faculty of Educn, 1969–73; Prof. of Education, and Chairman, Centre for the Study of Urban Education, La Trobe Univ., Melbourne, 1973–75; Goldsmiths' Prof. of Education, Inst. of Educn, Univ. of London, and Head of Dept of Advanced Studies in

Education, Goldsmiths' Coll., 1976–80; University of Nottingham: Prof. of Educn, and Hd, Div. of Advanced Studies, 1980–89; Dean, Faculty of Educn, 1981–83; Chm., Sch. of Educn, 1983–85, 1988–89; Pro-Vice-Chancellor, 1983–87; Foundn Dean of Humanities and Social Science, Hong Kong Univ. of Science and Technol., 1989–92; Foundn Prof. of Educn, Open Univ. of Hong Kong, 1992–94; Res. Prof. in Educn, Univ. of Greenwich, 1994–97; Vis Prof. of Educn, Goldsmiths' Coll., Univ. of London, 1997–2002. Adviser: Devon CC, 1970–72; Aust. Federal Poverty Commn, 1974–75; ACU, 1976, 1979; CNAA, 1978–89; Centre for Advice and Inf. on Educn Disadvantage (Chm., Teacher Educn Working Gp, 1979–80); Schools Council, 1979; CRE (Chm., Teacher Educn Adv. Gp, 1980–84); H of C Home Affairs Cttee, 1981; Swann Cttee, 1982–84; Leverhulme Trust, 1982–90; Macquarie Univ., Aust., 1982; Council for Educn and Trng in Youth and Community Work (Chm., In-service Wkg Gp, 1983); UNESCO, 1985; QUB, 1986; Univ. of Kuwait, 1988; Peshawar Univ., Pakistan, 1988; Hong Kong Council for Academic Accreditation, 1991; Hong Kong Educn Commn, 1991; Lagos Univ., Nigeria, 1991; City Polytechnic of Hong Kong, 1992; Hong Kong Baptist Univ., 1994; Griffith Univ., Aust., 1996; Hong Kong Govt Res. Grants Council, 1996–; Commonwealth of Learning, Vancouver, 1996; ESRC, 1997; Hong Kong Inst. of Educn, 1997; Southampton Univ., 1999; Chester UC, 2000; Surrey Univ., 2000–04; Lewisham PCT, 2003–14. Mem., UK Delegn to EEC Colloquium on Ethnic Min. Educn, Brussels, 1979, 1982; UK delegate to: Council of Europe Seminars on Intercultural Trng of Teachers, Lisbon, 1981, Rome, 1982, Strasbourg, 1983; UNESCO Colloquium on Educnl Disadvantage, Thessalonika, 1984. Member: Council of Validating Univs, 1982–89 (Vice-Chm., 1987–89); E Midlands Reg. Consultative Gp on Teacher Educn, 1980–84 (Chm., 1980–84); Exec. Cttee, Univs Council for Educn of Teachers, 1984–88 (Chm., Standing Cttee on Validation, 1984–87); Cttee on Validation, CVCP, 1986–88; Hong Kong Govt Bd of Inquiry in Educn, 1992; Hong Kong Govt Adv. Cttee on Teacher Educn and Qualifications, 1993; Exec. Cttee, Soc. for Educnl Studies, 1996–2002 (Chm., Res. sub-cttee, 1999–2002); Froebel Trust Council, 2000– (Chm., Res. Cttee, 2004–06; Chm., Educn Cttee, 2009–). Chm., Blackheath Cator Estate Community Assoc., 2003–06. Non-exec. Dir, Greenwich PCT, 2007–09; Mem., Exceptional Treatment Panel, 2006–09, Chm., Cardiol. Clin. Panel, 2008–10, Lewisham PCT. Member, Editorial Board: Sociology of Educn Abstracts, 1965–; Jl of Multilingual and Multicultural Develt, 1979–96; Multicultural Educn Abstracts, 1981–; Internat. Studies in Sociology of Educn, 1991–; British Jl of Educnl Studies, 1996–2002. FRSA 1989. *Publications:* (ed jtly) Linking Home and School, 1967, 3rd edn 1980; (ed jtly) Guidance and Counselling in British Schools, 1969, 2nd edn 1974; (ed) Family, Class and Education: a Reader, 1970; Urban Education—a Dublin case study, 1974; School Welfare Provision in Australia, 1977; (ed) Teaching in a Multicultural Society: the Task for Teacher Education, 1981; (jtly) Training Teachers of Ethnic Minority Community Languages, 1983; (ed jtly) Change in Teacher Education, 1984; (ed) Education and Cultural Pluralism, 1984; The Democratisation of Education, 1985; Teacher Education in a Multicultural Society, 1986; (ed jtly) Ethnic Relations and Schooling, 1995; (ed) Teacher Education in Plural Societies, 1996; contrib. to numerous books and to the following jls: Educnl Research, Internat. Review of Educn, Internat. Jl of Educnl Develt, Educnl Review, Social and Econ. Admin, Cambridge Jl of Educn, Educn for Teaching, British Jl of In-Service Educn, Internat. Social Work, Aust. Jl of Social Work, Aust. Educnl Researcher, THES, Higher Educn Jl, New Society, Education, Administration, New Era, Studies. *Recreations:* music, walking. *T:* (020) 8852 7611. *E:* almacraft@hotmail.com. *Club:* Royal Over-Seas League.

CRAFTS, Prof. Nicholas Francis Robert, CBE 2014; FBA 1992; Professor of Economic History, since 2006, and Director of ESRC Research Centre on Competitive Advantage in the Global Economy, since 2010, University of Warwick; *b* 9 March 1949; *s* of Alfred Hedley Crafts and Flora Geraldine Mary Crafts; *m* 1969, Barbara Daynes; one *s* two *d*. *Educ:* Brunts Grammar Sch., Mansfield; Trinity Coll., Cambridge (BA Econs 1st cl., 1970). Lectr in Econ. Hist., Exeter Univ., 1971–72; Lectr in Econs, Univ. of Warwick, 1972–77; Fellow in Econs, University Coll., Oxford, 1977–86; Professor of Economic History: Leeds Univ., 1987–88; Univ. of Warwick, 1988–95 (Hon. Prof., 1995–2006); LSE, 1995–2005. Vis. Asst Prof. of Econs, Univ. of Calif., Berkeley, 1974–76; Vis. Prof. of Econs, Stanford Univ., 1982–83. *Publications:* British Economic Growth during the Industrial Revolution, 1985; contrib. to Economic Jl, Jl of Economic Hist., Economic Policy, Population Studies, etc. *Recreations:* betting on horses, drinking beer. *Address:* Department of Economics, University of Warwick, Coventry CV4 7AL. *T:* (024) 7652 3468. *E:* n.crafts@warwick.ac.uk.

CRAGG, Prof. Anthony Douglas, CBE 2002; RA 1994; sculptor; Hon. Member, Kunstakademie, Düsseldorf, since 2015 (Professor of Sculpture, 2006–14; Director, 2009–13); *b* 9 April 1949; *m* 1990, Tatjana (*née* Verhasselt); one *s* one *d*, and two *s* by former *m*. *Educ:* Wimbledon Sch. of Art (BA); Royal Coll. of Art (MA). Prof., l'Ecole des Beaux Arts de Metz, 1976; teacher, 1978–88, Prof., 1989–2001, Co-Dir, 1989–2001, Kunstakademie, Düsseldorf; Prof., Univ. der Künste, Berlin, 2001–06. *One-man exhibitions include:* Lisson Gall., 1979, 1980, 1985, 1991, 1992, 1997, 1998, 2001, 2010; Whitechapel Art Gall., 1981, 1997; Kanrasha Gall., Tokyo, 1982, 1984, 1989, 1990; Konrad Fischer, Düsseldorf, 1982, 1986, 1989, 1990; Marian Goodman, NY, 1982, 1983, 1986, 1987, 1989; Palais des Beaux-Arts, Brussels, 1985; Brooklyn Mus. of Art, NY, 1986; Venice Biennale, 1986, 1988, 1997; Hayward Gall., 1987; Tate Gall., Liverpool, 1988, 2000; Tate Gall., 1989; Stedelijk Van Abbemus., Eindhoven, 1989, 1991; Corcoran Gall. of Art, Washington, 1991; Wiener Secession, 1991; IVAM, Valencia, 1992; Kunst- und Ausstellungshalle BRD, Bonn, 2003; Goodwood Sculpture Park, 2005; Das Potential der Dinge, Berlin, 2006; Tony Cragg versus Franz Messerschmidt, Belvedere, Vienna, 2008; Second Nature, Karlsruhe, 2009; Louvre, Paris, 2011; Scottish Nat. Gall. of Modern Art, 2011; CAFAM, Beijing, 2011; Mus. of Contemp. Art, Chengdu, 2011; Himalayas Art Mus., Shanghai, 2012; Exhibition Road, London, 2012; Nat. Taiwan Mus., 2013; *group exhibitions:* Documenta 7, Documenta 8, 1987, Kassel; Mus. van Hedendaagse Kunst, Ghent, 1980; Bienal de São Paulo, 1983; Tate Gall., 1983, 1985; Sydney Biennale, 1984, 1990; Hayward Gall., 1985, 1990; and many others throughout Europe, US, Japan and Australia. Turner Prize, 1988; Shakespeare Prize, 2001; Praemium Imperiale for Sculpture, Japan Art Assoc., 2007. Chevalier des Arts et des Lettres (France), 1992; Order of Merit (1st cl.) (Germany), 2012. *Address:* Lise Meitner Strasse 33, 42119 Wuppertal, Germany.

CRAGG, Anthony John, CMG 2000; JP; consultant, international security affairs; *b* 16 May 1943; *s* of late Leslie Cragg and Gwendolen Cragg (*née* Pevler); *m* 1971, Jeanette Ann Rix; two *d*. *Educ:* Hastings Grammar School; Lincoln College, Oxford (Open Schol.). Ministry of Defence, 1966–2003: Asst Private Sec. to Sec. of State for Defence, 1974; UK Delegn to NATO, 1977; Asst Sec., 1979; Chief Officer, Sovereign Base Areas, Cyprus, 1983–85; RCDS 1988; Asst Under Sec. of State, 1990; Chm., Defence Organisation Planning Team, 1991–92; Asst Sec. Gen. for Defence Planning and Policy, then Ops, NATO, 1993–99; Dep. Chief, Defence Intelligence Staff, MoD, and Mem., Jt Intelligence Cttee, 1999–2003. Sen. Associate Res. Fellow, Centre for Defence Studies, KCL, 2003–10; Associate Fellow, RUSI, 2003. Visiting Lecturer: NATO Defence Coll., 2003–; Geneva Centre for Security Policy, 2005–12. Chm., MoD Grievance Appeal Panel, 2004–10. Lay Mem., First-tier Tribunal (Immigration and Asylum Chamber) (formerly Immigration Appeal Tribunal, then Asylum and Immigration Tribunal), 2003–13. JP London, 2005. *Publications:* (contrib.) Global Monitoring for Security and Stability, 2008; (contrib.) Remote Sensing From Space, 2009; articles on internat. security issues in press and specialised jls. *Recreations:* the performing arts, swimming, walking, reading.

CRAGG, Dr Martin Robert; Chief Executive and Secretary, Institution of Highways and Transportation, 1990–2001; *b* 8 June 1941; *s* of Robert Brooks Cragg and Hilda Cragg (*née* Bateman); *m* 1966, Pamela Watts; one *s* two *d*. *Educ:* Dixie Grammar Sch., Market Bosworth; Sheffield Univ. (BSc Hons Chem.; PhD Fuel Technol. 1966); London Business Sch. (Sloan Fellow). Industrial Advr, NEDO, 1979–88; Dir, then Dir-Gen. and Chief Exec., Business Equipt and Information Technol. Assoc., 1988–89, then Sen. Exec., Electronic and Business Equipt Assoc., 1989–90. *Recreations:* golf, fly fishing. *Address:* 10 Woodside Road, New Malden, Surrey KT3 3AH. *T:* (020) 8942 8008.

CRAGG, Stephen James; QC 2013; *b* Wisbech, 16 Dec. 1961; *s* of John Maurice Cragg and Audrey Anne Cragg; *m* 2000, Deborah Tripley; two *d*. *Educ:* King's Coll. London (LLB 1984); Brunel Univ. (MA Sociol. and Law 1986). Articled clerk, Christian Fisher & Co., 1987–89; admitted solicitor, 1989; solicitor: Hackney Law Centre, 1989–93; Public Law Project, 1993–96; called to the Bar, Middle Temple, 1996; in practice as barrister, 1996–. Chair, Public Law Project, 2007–. Pt-time Judge, Mental Health Tribunals, 2007–. Mem., Ind. Adv. Panel on Deaths in Custody, 2014–. *Publications:* (jtly) Police Misconduct: legal remedies, 2nd edn 1987 to 5th edn 2016. *Recreations:* walking, cycling and running in London, cinema, theatre, Proust, parenting. *Address:* Monckton Chambers, 1–2 Raymond Buildings, Gray's Inn, WC1R 5NR. *E:* scragg@monckton.com.

CRAGGS, Madeleine Jennifer; Chief Executive and Registrar, General Osteopathic Council, 1997–2007; *b* 28 Dec. 1945; *d* of René Beaumont-Craggs and Muriel (*née* Robinson). *Educ:* Couvent des Ursulines, Brussels; Alexandra Grammar Sch., Singapore; WRAC Coll., Camberley. MCMI. Commnd WRAC, 1965; served in UK and Germany, incl. staff appts, MoD and HQ BAOR; Maj., 1970; WRAC Advr, 16th Signal Regt, 1973–75; Battery Comdr, Royal Sch. Artillery, 1975–77; SO2(A), HQ York Dist, 1977–79; Chief Instructor, WRAC Trng Centre, 1979–81; Detachment Comdr, Manning and Records Office, Chester, 1981–82; SO2 (Manpower & Planning), WRAC Directorate, MoD, 1982–84; Develt Dir, St Bartholomew's Hosp. Med. Coll., 1984–90; Sec., ICRF, 1991–97. *Recreations:* travel, good wine, good food, good company. *Address:* Orchard House, Ranscombe Lane, Glynde, Lewes BN8 6RP.

CRAIG, family name of **Viscount Craigavon** and of **Baron Craig of Radley**.

CRAIG OF RADLEY, Baron *cr* 1991 (Life Peer), of Helhoughton in the County of Norfolk; **Marshal of the Royal Air Force David Brownrigg Craig,** GCB 1984 (KCB 1981; CB 1978); OBE 1967; Chief of the Defence Staff, 1988–91; *b* 17 Sept. 1929; *s* of Major Francis Brownrigg Craig and Mrs Olive Craig; *m* 1955, Elisabeth June Derenburg; one *s* one *d*. *Educ:* Radley Coll.; Lincoln Coll., Oxford (MA; Hon. Fellow 1984). FRAeS 1986. Commnd in RAF, 1951; OC RAF Cranwell, 1968–70; ADC to the Queen, 1969–71; Dir, Plans and Ops, HQ Far East Comd, 1970–71; OC RAF Akrotiri, 1972–73; ACAS (Ops), MoD, 1975–78; AOC No 1 Group, RAF Strike Command, 1978–80; Vice-Chief of Air Staff, 1980–82; AOC-in-C, RAF Strike Command and C-in-C, UK Air Forces, 1982–85; CAS, 1985–88. Air ADC to the Queen, 1985–88. Dir, M. L. Holdings plc, 1991–92. Mem., H of L Select Cttee for Sci. and Technology, 1993–99; Convenor, Cross Bench Peers, 1999–2004. Chm. Council, King Edward VII's Hosp. (Sister Agnes) (formerly King Edward VII's Hosp. for Officers), 1998–2004. Dep. Chm. Council, RAF Benevolent Fund, 1996–2013. Pres., Not Forgotten Assoc., 1996–2014. Hon. DSc Cranfield, 1988. *Recreations:* fishing, shooting. *Address:* House of Lords, SW1A 0PW. *Club:* Royal Air Force (Pres., 2002–13).

CRAIG, Rev. Canon Alan Stuart; Chaplain to the Bishop of Newcastle and Diocesan Director of Ordinands, 1999–2002; Chaplain to the Queen, 1995–2008; *b* 7 Feb. 1938; *s* of Dr John Gray Craig and Grace Craig (*née* Kay); *m* 1962, Marjorie (*née* Bell); one *s* two *d*. *Educ:* Uppingham Sch.; Leeds Univ. (BA (Hons)); Cranmer Hall, Durham Univ. (DipTh). Ordained deacon, Lichfield, 1961, priest, 1962; Assistant Curate: St Giles, Newcastle under Lyme, 1961–65; St Mary's, Scarborough, 1965–67; Vicar, Werrington, Stoke-on-Trent, 1967–72; Asst Chaplain, Manchester Prison, 1972–73; Chaplain: Hindley Borstal, 1973–78; Acklington Prison, 1978–84; Vicar, Longhirst and Hebron, Newcastle, 1984–90; Rector of Morpeth, 1990–99; Rural Dean of Morpeth, 1984–95. Hon. Canon, Newcastle Cathedral, 1990–2002. Chm., Newcastle Diocesan Pastoral Cttee, 1994–99. *Recreations:* music, theatre, fell-walking, visual arts. *Address:* 5 Springfield Meadow, Alnwick, Northumberland NE66 2NY. *T:* (01665) 602806. *E:* as.m.craig@talktalk.net.

CRAIG, Sir (Albert) James (Macqueen), GCMG 1984 (KCMG 1981; CMG 1975); HM Diplomatic Service, retired; President, Middle East Association, 1993–2011 (Director General, 1985–93); *b* 13 July 1924; *s* of James Craig and Florence Morris; *m* 1st, 1952, Margaret Hutchinson (*d* 2001); three *s* one *d*; 2nd, 2002, Bernadette Hartley Lane. *Educ:* Liverpool Institute High Sch.; Queen's Coll., Oxford (Exhibr), 1942; 1st cl. Hon. Mods Classics, 1943 (Hon. Schol.); Hon. Fellow, 2007. Army, 1943–44; 1st cl. Oriental Studies (Arabic and Persian), 1947; Sen. Demy, Magdalen Coll., 1947–48; student, Cairo Univ., 1950–51. Lectr in Arabic, Durham Univ., 1948–55; seconded to FO, 1955 as Principal Instructor at Middle East Centre for Arab Studies, Lebanon; joined Foreign Service substantively, 1956; served: FO, 1958–61; HM Political Agent, Trucial States, 1961–64; 1st Sec., Beirut, 1964–67; Counsellor and Head of Chancery, Jedda, 1967–70; Supernumerary Fellow, St Antony's Coll., Oxford, 1970–71; Head of Near East and N Africa Dept, FCO, 1971–75; Dep. High Comr, Kuala Lumpur, 1975–76; Ambassador to: Syria, 1976–79; Saudi Arabia, 1979–84. Vis. Prof. in Arabic, and Lectr, Pembroke Coll., Univ. of Oxford, 1985–91. Director: Saudi-British Bank, 1985–94; Hong Kong Egyptian Bank, 1987–94; Special Adviser, Hong Kong Bank Gp, 1985–92; Chm., Roxby Engineering Internat., 1988–99. Pres., British Soc. for ME Studies, 1987–94; Vice-Chm., Middle East Internat., 1990–2005. Vice-Chm., Saudi-British Soc., 1986–2003; Chm., Anglo-Arab Assoc., 2000–03. Sen. Associate Mem., St Antony's Coll., Oxford, 1989 (Hon. Fellow, 2008). Hon. Fellow, Middle East Centre, Durham Univ., 1987–. OStJ 1985; Mem. Council, Order of St John, 1985–90. *Publications:* Shemlan: a history of the Middle East Centre for Arab Studies, 1998; (ed jtly) MECAS Memoirs: vol. 1, The Arabists of Shemlan, 2006, vol. 2, Envoys to the Arab World, 2009; various articles on the Arab world. *Address:* Old Well Cottage, 2 High Street, Standlake, Oxon OX29 7RY. *Club:* Travellers.

CRAIG, Surgeon Rear-Admiral Alexander; Member, Criminal Injuries Compensation Appeal Panel, 1997–2007; *b* 22 Nov. 1943; *s* of Rev. Dr Albert Craig and Agnes Nicol (*née* Wards); *m* 1968, Kate Margaret Elliott; one *s* two *d*. *Educ:* George Watson's Boys' Coll., Edinburgh; Edinburgh Univ. (MB ChB 1967). Royal Infirmary, Edinburgh, 1968; Regimental MO, 45 Commando, RM, 1969–72; Jt Services Families Clinic, Malta, 1972–74; OC Med. Sqn, CDO LOG Regt, 1974–78; MoD, 1978–80, NDC 1981; UK Support Unit, Naples, 1981–83; CSO to Surgeon Cdre (NMT), 1983–86; PMO, HMS Sultan, 1986–87; CSO to SRA (OMS), 1987–89; MO i/c, Inst. of Naval Medicine, 1989–90; Dir, Med. Organisation, MoD, 1990–93; Surg. Rear-Adm. Support Med. Services, 1993–94; Med. Dir Gen. (Naval), 1994–97. Non-exec. Dir, IoW Healthcare NHS Trust, 1997–99. QHP, 1992–97. CStJ 1996. *Recreation:* travel. *Address:* Home Cottage, Seven Sisters Road, St Lawrence, Isle of Wight PO38 1UY.

CRAIG, Andrew Hugh; Agent-General for Queensland in London, 2008–11; *b* Sydney, 28 Feb. 1943; *s* of late Hugh Dempster Craig and Berenice Norma Craig; *m* 1st, 1971, Mary Prudence Dunlop (*d* 1992); three *s* one *d*; 2nd, 1998, Susan Elizabeth Cantamessa; one step *s* two step *d*. *Educ:* Melbourne Grammar Sch.; Royal Australian Naval Coll.; BRNC Dartmouth; Deakin Univ. (MBA 1986). Royal Australian Navy: flying trng, 1966–67; Helicopter Flight, Vietnam, 817 Sqdn, 1968–69; CO 817 Sqdn, 1978–79; Lieut 1966; Lieut

Comdr 1974; Comdr 1979; Capt. 1985; retd, 1988. Man. Dir, Sikorsky Aircraft Australia, 1988; CEO, Clayton UTZ (Brisbane), 1989–94. Exec. Dir, Queensland br., Australian Red Cross, 1997–99; CEO, Queensland Chamber of Commerce and Industry, 2000–02; Queensland Dir, Australian Industry Gp, 2003–06; Queensland Comr, Los Angeles, 2007. Freeman, City of London, 2010. *Recreations:* music, travel, life. *Clubs:* Queensland, United Service (Brisbane).

CRAIG, Anne Gwendoline, (Wendy); actress; *b* 20 June 1934; *d* of late George Dixon Craig and Anne Lindsay; *m* 1955, John Alexander, Jack, Bentley (*d* 1994); two *s. Educ:* Durham High Sch. for Girls; Darlington High Sch.; Yarm Grammar Sch.; Central Sch. of Speech and Drama. *Theatre includes:* Ipswich Rep. Theatre, 1953; Royal Court season, 1957; The Wrong Side of the Park, 1960; The Ginger Man, Royal Court, 1964; Ride a Cock Horse, Piccadilly, 1965; I Love You Mrs Patterson; Finishing Touches; Peter Pan; Beyond Reasonable Doubt, Queen's, 1987; Easy Virtue, Chichester Fest., 1999; The Rivals, RSC, 2000; The Circle, Queen's, 2002; The Importance of Being Earnest, nat. tour, 2003; *television includes:* Not in Front of the Children, 1967–70; And Mother Makes Three, 1971–74; And Mother Makes Five, 1974–76; Butterflies, 1978–82; Nanny, 1981–83; Brighton Belles, 1993; The Forsyte Saga, Midsomer Murders, 2002; The Royal, 2002–06; Reggie Perrin, 2010; *films include:* The Servant, The Mind Benders, 1963; The Nanny, 1965; Just Like a Woman, 1966; I'll Never Forget Whatsisname, 1967; Joseph Andrews, 1977. Awards incl. BAFTA award for best actress, 1968; BBC Personality of the Year, 1969. Hon. MA Teesside 1994; Hon. BA Sunderland, 2009. *Publications:* Happy Endings, 1972; The Busy Mums Cook Book, 1983; The Busy Mums Baking Book, 1986; Show Me the Way, 2006. *Recreations:* music, walking, reading, gardening.

CRAIG, Cairns; *see* Craig, R. C.

CRAIG, Christopher John Sinclair, CB 1991; DSC 1982; RN retired; *b* 18 May 1941; *s* of Richard Michael Craig and Barbara Mary Craig; *m* 1973, Daphne Joan Underwood; two *s. Educ:* Portchester Sch., Bournemouth. Joined RN, 1959; BRNC Dartmouth, 1959–62; qualified as anti-submarine helicopter pilot, 1963; HMS Eagle, 1964–66; HMS Dido, 1967–69; in command: HMS Monkton, 1970–72; naval air sqdns, 705, 1973–74, and 826, 1975; HMS London, 1976–77; Asst Sec. to Chiefs of Staff, 1978–79; in command: HMS Alacrity, 1980–82 (incl. Falklands War); HMS Avenger and Fourth Frigate Sqdn, 1985–86; RNAS Portland/HMS Osprey, 1986–87; HMS Drake, 1987–89; Comdr, RN Task Gp (Gulf War), 1990–91; COS to FONA, 1991–93; retd 1994. Chm., Brooke, Evelyn and Thistlethwaite Trust, 2011–. US Bronze Star, 1991. *Publications:* Call for Fire: Sea Combat in the Falklands and the Gulf War, 1995. *Recreations:* watercolour painting, classical music, reading. *Address:* Greencroft, East Grimstead, near Salisbury, Wilts SP5 3SA.

CRAIG, Daniel; actor. *Theatre* includes: Angels in America, A Number, RNT; Hurly Burly, Old Vic; A Steady Rain, Gerald Schoenfeld Th., NY, 2009; Betrayal, Ethel Barrymore Th., NY, 2013; *films* include: The Power of One, 1992; Obsession, 1997; Love and Rage, Elizabeth, Love is the Devil, 1998; The Trench, 1999; I Dreamed of Africa, Some Voices, Hotel Splendide, 2000; Lara Croft: Tomb Raider, 2001; Road to Perdition, Ten Minutes Older: The Cello, Occasional, Strong, 2002; The Mother, Sylvia, 2003; Enduring Love, Layer Cake, 2004; The Jacket, Sorstalanság, Munich, 2005; Casino Royale, 2006; The Golden Compass, Infamous, 2007; Flashbacks of a Fool, Quantum of Solace, 2008; Defiance, 2009; Cowboys and Aliens, Dream House, The Girl with the Dragon Tattoo, 2011; Skyfall, 2012; Spectre, 2015; *television* includes: Our Friends in the North, 1996; Sword of Honour, 2001; Copenhagen, 2002; Archangel, 2005.

CRAIG, (David) Jonathan; Member (DemU) Lagan Valley, Northern Ireland Assembly, since 2007; *b* 2 Feb. 1965; *s* of David and Deborah Craig; *m* 1991, S. G. Yvonne; one *s* one *d. Educ:* Univ. of Ulster (HND with Dist. Mech. Engrg). Tool design engr, Shorts Bombardier, 1987–2007. Mem. Educn Cttee, NI Assembly, 2011–. Mem., Policing Bd, NI, 2011–. Mem. (DemU) Lisburn CC, 2001– (Mayor, 2005–06). *Recreations:* following motorbike racing, building computers, home DIY. *Address:* (office) 29 Castle Street, Lisburn, Co. Antrim BT27 4DH. *T:* (028) 9266 8378.

CRAIG, David Mark; QC 2015; *b* London, 24 July 1972; *s* of Graham Craig and Rosalind Simmons (*née* Montague); *m* 2000, Ruth Elana Jonas; one *s* three *d. Educ:* University Coll. Sch., London; Manchester Univ. (BSc 1st Cl. Hons Psychol.); Queen's Coll., Cambridge (MPhil Criminol. 1995); City Univ. (CPE). Called to the Bar, Inner Temple, 1997; in practice as barrister, 1997–. *Publications:* (contrib.) Violence, Culture and Censure, 1997; (jtly) The Law of Reinsurance, 2004. *Recreations:* family, sport, theatre. *Address:* Essex Court Chambers, 24 Lincoln's Inn Fields, WC2A 3EG. *T:* (020) 7813 8000, *Fax:* (020) 7813 8080. *E:* dcraig@essexcourt.com.

CRAIG, Prof. David Parker, AO 1985; FRS 1968; FAA 1969; FRSC; FRSN; University Fellow and Emeritus Professor, Australian National University, since 1985; *b* 23 Dec. 1919; *s* of Andrew Hunter Craig, Manchester and Sydney, and Mary Jane (*née* Parker); *m* 1948, Veronica, *d* of Cyril Bryden-Brown, Market Harborough and Sydney; three *s* one *d. Educ:* Sydney Church of England Grammar Sch.; University of Sydney; University Coll., London. MSc (Sydney) 1941, PhD (London) 1950, DSc (London) 1956. Commonwealth Science Scholar, 1940. War Service: Capt., Australian Imperial Force, 1941–44. Lectr in Chemistry, University of Sydney, 1944–46; Turner and Newall Research Fellow, 1946–49, and Lectr in Chemistry, University Coll., London, 1949–52; Prof. of Physical Chemistry, Univ. of Sydney, 1952–56; Prof. of Chemistry, University Coll., London, 1956–67; Prof. of Chemistry, 1967–85, Dean, Research Sch. of Chemistry, 1970–73 and 1977–81, ANU. Vis. Prof., UCL, 1968–90; Firth Vis. Prof., Univ. of Sheffield, 1973; Vis. Prof., University Coll., Cardiff, 1975–89. Part-time Mem., CSIRO Exec., 1980–85. Chm., Adv. Cttee, Aust. Nat. Botanic Gdns, 1986–89. Pres., Australian Acad. of Sci., 1990–94. Fellow of University Coll., London, 1964–. FRSN 2010; Hon. FRSC 1987. Hon. Dr Chem. Bologna, 1985; Hon. DSc Sydney, 1985. *Publications:* books and original papers on chemistry in scientific periodicals. *Address:* 216 Dryandra Street, O'Connor, ACT 2602, Australia. *Club:* Athenæum.

CRAIG, Prof. Edward John, FBA 1993; Knightbridge Professor of Philosophy, University of Cambridge, 1998–2005; Fellow, Churchill College, Cambridge, since 1966; *b* 26 March 1942; *s* of Charles William Craig and Annie (*née* Taylor); *m* 1st, 1973, Isabel Nina Barnard (marr. diss. 1986); two *d*; 2nd, 1987, Gillian Helen Elizabeth Edwards. *Educ:* Charterhouse; Trinity Coll., Cambridge (MA 1966; PhD 1970). Cricket for Cambridge Univ. and Lancs CCC, 1961–63; Cambridge University: Asst Lectr and Univ. Lectr in Philosophy, 1966–92; Reader in Modern Philosophy, 1992–98. Visiting University appointments: Melbourne, 1974; Hamburg, 1977–78; Heidelberg, 1981; Indian Inst. of Advanced Studies, 1996. General Editor: Routledge Encyclopedia of Philosophy, 1991–2011; Routledge Encyclopedia of Philosophy Online, 2000–11 Editor, Ratio, 1988–92. *Publications:* David Hume: eine Einführung in seine Philosophie, 1979; The Mind of God and the Works of Man, 1987; Knowledge and the State of Nature, 1990; Pragmatische Untersuchungen zum Wissensbegriff, 1993; Hume on Religion, 1997; Philosophy: a very short introduction, 2002. *Recreations:* music, golf. *Address:* Churchill College, Cambridge CB3 0DS. *T:* (01223) 336000.

CRAIG, George Charles Graham; Senior Director, Social Affairs (formerly Social Policy and Land Affairs), Welsh Assembly Government, 1999–2003; *b* 8 May 1946; *s* of late George Craig and of E. S. Craig (*née* Milne); *m* 1968, (Ethne) Marian, *er d* of late H. H. A. Gallagher and of E. F. Gallagher; two *s* one *d. Educ:* Brockley County Grammar Sch.; Nottingham Univ. (BA). Asst Principal, Min. of Transport, 1967; Welsh Office: Private Sec. to Minister of State, 1970–72; Principal, 1972; Private Sec. to Sec. of State for Wales, 1978–80; Asst Sec., 1980; Under Sec., 1986; Dep. Sec., 1999. *Address:* c/o Brian J. Harries, 1/3 The Sidings, Victoria Avenue, Swanage, Dorset BH19 1AU.

CRAIG, Gloria Linda, CB 2010; Director (formerly Director-General), International Security Policy, Ministry of Defence, 2007–11 (Director General, Security Policy Jan.–June 2011, Special Studies, July–Aug. 2011); *b* 23 Nov. 1948; *née* Kristler; adopted *d* of late George Edward Franklin and of Victoria Franklin; *m* 1st, 1987, Gordon Montgomery Craig (marr. diss. 2001); 2nd, 2012, Robert Lee Ayers. *Educ:* St Martin-in-the-Fields High Sch. for Girls; Lady Margaret Hall, Oxford (MA). GB-USSR Assoc., 1970–71; joined MoD, 1971; Private Sec. to Parly Under Sec. of State (Navy), 1975–76; Planning Staff, FCO, 1979–81; Asst Sec., 1984; RCDS 1988; Dep. Dir, Cabinet Office, 1989–92, 1995–99; Ministry of Defence: Director General: Security and Safety, 1999–2003; Defence Export Services, 2003–07. Non-executive Member Board: Family Housing Assoc., 1999–2004; CS Healthcare, 2011–; Trustee, Somerset Army Cadet Force, 2013–. Mentor, RCDS, 2013–. Ehrenkreuz der Bundeswehr in Gold, Germany, 2011. *Publications:* papers and lectures on defence and public service issues, white papers and best practice guides. *Recreations:* antiques, music, travel, animals, gardening.

CRAIG, Rev. Gordon Thomas, QHC 2007; Chaplain, UK Offshore Oil and Gas Industry Association, since 2012; *b* Glasgow, 1959; *s* of John Craig and Elizabeth Craig; *m* 1984, Rhona; three *c. Educ:* Paisley Grammar Sch.; Univ. of Glasgow (BD 1985). RAF Chaplain: RAF Marham, 1988–91; RAF St Athan, 1991–93; RAF Lossiemouth, 1993–96; RAF Laarbruch, 1996–99; Senior Chaplain: RAF Coll. Cranwell, 1999–2002; RAF Cosford, 2002–04; RAF Cottesmore, 2004–06; Air Command, 2006–11; Principal Chaplain, Church of Scotland and Free Churches, RAF, 2009–12; Principal, Armed Forces Chaplaincy Centre, 2011–12. Hon. Chaplain: to RAF Widows' Assoc., 1991–2011; to War Widows' Assoc. of GB, 2007–09. *Recreation:* playing very loud bass guitar. *Club:* Royal Air Force.

CRAIG, Sir James; *see* Craig, Sir A. J. M.

CRAIG, Dr (James) Oscar (Max Clark), FRCS, FRCP, FRCSI, FRCR, FRCGP; Consultant Radiologist since 1963, and Hon. Senior Clinical Lecturer, since 1987, St Mary's Hospital, London; President, Royal College of Radiologists, 1989–92; *b* 7 May 1927; *s* of James Oscar Max Clark Craig and Olivia Craig; *m* 1st, 1950, Louise Burleigh (*d* 2008); four *d*; 2nd, 2009, Mary Gillian Sprange. *Educ:* Royal College of Surgeons in Ireland. LRCP&SI 1950; FRCSI 1956; DMRD 1959; FRCR (FFR 1962); FRCS 1982; MRCP 1989, FRCP 1993; FRCGP 1991. Asst GP, 1950–51; Ho. Surg., St Helier Hosp., Carshalton, 1951–52; Gen. practice, Sutton, 1952–54. Surg., RAF, 1954–56. Sen. Ho. Officer, Surgery, Hammersmith Hosp., 1956–57; Registrar and Sen. Registrar, Dept of Radiology, St Mary's Hosp., London, 1957–63; Lectr in Radiology, London Univ., 1963–87; Dir of Clinical Studies, 1969–75, Dir of Post Grad. Studies, 1979–81, St Mary's Hosp. Med. Sch. Visiting Professor: UBC, Canada, 1977; Univ. of Queensland, 1984; Concord Hosp., Sydney, 1988. Chm., Cases Cttee, Med. Protection Soc., 1986–92. Pres., Harveian Soc. of London, 2002. Hon. Pres., British Med. Students Assoc. Fellow, Med Soc. of London, 2001. Hon. Member: Radiological Soc. of N America, 1993; British Soc. Interventional Radiologists. Hon. FFR RCSI 1985; Hon. Fellow, Hong Kong Coll. of Radiologists, 1995. Lifetime Achievement Award, Imperial Coll. London, 2012. *Publications:* A Life in Medicine (autobiog.), 2000; Medical Memoirs (autobiog.), 2006; Doctors at War, 2007; Can't You See the Seagulls?, 2008; Come Sit with Me Awhile, 2011; Reflections: the collected poems of Dr Oscar Craig, 2012; numerous papers and chapters in books on clinical radiology, phlebography, lymphangiography, gastro-intestinal radiology, medico-legal medicine and the develt of digital radiology. *Recreation:* country-walking. *Address:* 62 Burdon Lane, Cheam, Surrey SM2 7BY. *T:* (020) 8642 2696. *Clubs:* Royal Society of Medicine, MCC.

CRAIG, John Frazer, CB 1994; Director, Economic Affairs (formerly Head of Economic and Industrial Affairs), Welsh Office, 1990–97; *b* 8 Nov. 1943; *s* of late John Frazer Craig and Margaret Jane Gibson Craig; *m* 1st, 1963, Ann Bardo (marr. diss. 1972); two *s* one *d*; 2nd, 1973, Janet Elizabeth. *Educ:* Robert Richardson Grammar Sch., Sunderland. Customs and Excise, 1961–69; Nat. Bd for Prices and Incomes, 1969–70; Welsh Office, 1970–97: Private Sec. to Perm. Sec., 1972–74; Private Sec. to Sec. of State for Wales, 1980–82; Asst Sec., 1982–85, Under Sec. (Dir), 1985–87, Industry Dept; Under Sec. (Principal Finance Officer), Welsh Office, 1987–90; Dep. Sec., 1990–97.

CRAIG, Jonathan; *see* Craig, D. J.

CRAIG, Jonathan Laurie; Chief Political Correspondent, Sky News, since 2006; *b* Eastham, Cheshire, 9 Aug. 1957; *s* of late James Royan Craig and Muriel Craig (*née* Webb); *m* 1st, 1980, Jane Isobel Simons (marr. diss. 1987); 2nd, 1987, Fiona Mary Walsh (marr. diss. 1998); 3rd, 2013, Caroline Audrey Rachel Edmondson. *Educ:* King's Sch., Macclesfield; Wetherby High Sch.; Tadcaster Grammar Sch.; Southampton Univ. (LLB Hons). Pres., Students' Union, Southampton Univ., 1978–79. Trainee journalist, N Eastern Evening Gazette, 1979–81; Parly corresp., 1982–85, Sen. Political corresp., 1985–86, Thomson Regl Newspapers; Home Affairs corresp., Sunday Times, 1986–89; Political corresp., Today, 1989–92; Political Ed., Daily Express, 1992–96; Dep. Political Ed., The Express, 1996–98; Political Editor: Sunday Express, 1998–2001; BBC London, 2001–03; Political corresp., Sky News, 2003–06. Columnist, Public Affairs News, 2008–. *Publications:* contrib. articles to Tribune. *Recreations:* films, theatre, music, country walks, watching sport. *Address:* Sky News, 2nd Floor, 4 Millbank, SW1P 3JA. *T:* (020) 7032 2805, *Fax:* (020) 7032 2801. *E:* jon.craig@bskyb.com. *Clubs:* Le Beaujolais, Phoenix Artist.

CRAIG, Kenneth Allen; a Judge of the Upper Tribunal (Asylum and Immigration Chamber), since 2011; *b* 19 Aug. 1950; *yr s* of Seymour Craig and Nancie Craig (*née* Livingstone); *m* 1971, Linda Lambert; two *s. Educ:* Haberdashers' Aske's Sch., Elstree; Sussex Univ. (BA Hons American Studies); Council of Legal Educn (Prize for obtaining only 1st in Bar Pt 1 Exams 1974). Called to the Bar, Lincoln's Inn, 1975, Bencher, 1999; in private practice as barrister, 1975–2011; Founder Mem., Hardwicke Bldg, 1990. Legal Mem. (and pt-time Chm.), Immigration and Asylum Tribunal, 2004–06; fee-paid Immigration Judge, 2006–11; Dep. Judge, Upper Tribunal (Asylum and Immigration Chamber), 2010–11. Mem., Bar Council, 1994–2011. *Recreations:* spending time with his grandchildren, theatre, travel, telling good jokes badly. *Address:* Asylum and Immigration Chamber, Field House, 15–25 Breams Buildings, EC4A 1DZ. *E:* ken.craig@judiciary.gsi.gov.uk. *Clubs:* Athenæum, MCC; Tottenham Hotspur.

CRAIG, Mary Elizabeth, OBE 2010; Chief Executive, Lloyds TSB Foundation for Scotland, since 2009; *b* Bellshill, Lanarks, 24 Oct. 1950. *Educ:* St Patrick's High Sch., Coatbridge. Trustee Savings Bank, later Lloyds TSB: admin posts, 1969–87; bank manager, 1987–92; Customer Service Manager, 1992–94; Area Manager, 1994–97; Dep. Chief Exec., Lloyds TSB Foundn for Scotland, 1997–2009. Gov., Glasgow Caledonian Univ., 2012–13. FCIBS 1997; FRSA 2010. *Recreations:* gardening, holidays, especially to Florida! *Address:* Lloyds TSB Foundation for Scotland, Riverside House, 501 Gorgie Road, Edinburgh EH11 3AF. *T:* (0131) 444 4020, *Fax:* (0131) 444 4099. *E:* mec@ltsbfoundationforscotland.org.uk.

CRAIG, Oscar; *see* Craig, J. O. M. C.

CRAIG, Pamela Tudor; *see* Wedgwood, Pamela, Lady.

CRAIG, Prof. Paul Philip, FBA 1998; Professor of English Law, since 1998 (Professor of Law, 1996–98), and Fellow of St John's College, since 1998, University of Oxford; *b* 27 Sept. 1951; *s* of Maurice and Beatrice Craig; *m* 1991, Dr Anita Cooper; one *s*. *Educ:* Worcester Coll., Oxford (MA, BCL). University of Oxford: Fellow, Worcester Coll., 1976–98, now Emeritus; Reader in Law, 1990–96. Vis. Prof. in Univs of Virginia, Cornell, Connecticut, York (Osgoode Hall) Canada, Indiana, Queensland. Hon. QC 2000. Hon. DLaws Maastricht, 2014. *Publications:* Administrative Law, 1983, 7th edn 2012; Public Law and Democracy in the United Kingdom and the United States of America, 1990; Text, Cases and Materials on Community Law, 1995, 5th edn 2011; Law Making in the European Union, 1998; The Evolution of EU Law, 1999, 2nd edn 2011; EU Administrative Law, 2006, 2nd edn 2012; The Lisbon Treaty: law, politics and treaty reform, 2010; UK, EU and Global Administrative Law: foundations and challenges, 2015; articles in jls. *Recreations:* riding, ski-ing, theatre, acting, ballet. *Address:* St John's College, Oxford OX1 3JP. *T:* (01865) 277340.

CRAIG, Maj.-Gen. Peter; *see* Craig, Maj.-Gen. R. P.

CRAIG, Prof. R. Cairns, OBE 2007; PhD; FBA 2005; FRSE; Glucksman Professor of Irish and Scottish Studies and Director, Research Institute of Irish and Scottish Studies, since 2005, and Director of AHRC Centre for Irish and Scottish Studies, 2006–10, University of Aberdeen; *b* 16 Feb. 1949. Lectr, Dept of English, Univ. of Aberdeen; Department of English Literature, University of Edinburgh: Lectr; Sen. Lectr; Reader; Prof. of Scottish and Modern Literature; Hd of Dept, 1997–2003; Dir, Centre for History of Ideas in Scotland. Hon. Prof. and Chm., Academic Adv. Bd, AHRC Centre for Irish and Scottish Studies, Univ. of Aberdeen, 2001–06. FRSE 2003. *Publications:* Yeats, Eliot, Pound and the Politics of Poetry: richest to the richest, 1982; Out of History: narrative paradigms in Scottish and English Culture, 1996; The Modern Scottish Novel: narrative and the national imagination, 1999; Iain Banks's Complicity: a reader's guide, 2002; Intending Scotland, 2009; Associationism and the Literary Imagination: from the phantasmal chaos, 2007. *Address:* Research Institute of Irish and Scottish Studies, Humanity Manse, 19 College Bounds, Aberdeen AB24 3UG.

CRAIG, Maj.-Gen. (Robert) Peter, MD; FRCS, FRCEM; expert medical witness, since 2001; Chairman, Queen Mary's Roehampton Trust, 2002–12; *b* 24 June 1940; *s* of late Dr Robert Theodore Gilpin Craig, TD, MB BS, MRCGP and Jessie Craig (*née* McKinstry); *m* 1971, Jean Toft, MA; one *s* two *d*. *Educ:* George Watson's Boys' Coll.; Durham Univ. Med. Sch. (MB BS 1964); MD Newcastle upon Tyne 1987; FRCS 1972; FRCEM (FFAEM 1994). Commissioned RA (TA) 1958; RAMC 1963; Royal Victoria Infirmary, Newcastle, 1964–65; RMO 1/2 Gurkha Rifles, 1966–68; Queen Alexandra Mil. Hosp.; Birmingham Accident Hosp.; Dept of Surgery, Univ. of Newcastle upon Tyne; BMH Rinteln; Guy's Hosp., 1974–78; Consultant Surgeon: BMH Hong Kong, 1979–81; Queen Elizabeth Mil. Hosp., 1981–86; Sen. Lectr in Mil. Surgery, Royal Army Med. Coll., 1981–86; BMH Rinteln, 1986–89, CO, 1987–89; Comd Med., 4th Armoured Div., 1989–90; Comd Surgeon, HQ BAOR, 1990–92; Dir of Army Surgery, 1992–93; Comdr Medical, UKLF, 1993–94; Consultant in A & E Medicine, Wansbeck Gen. Hosp., 1994–96. Medical Member: War Pensions and Armed Forces Compensation Chamber, Pensions Appeals Tribunals, then First-tier Tribunal, 1997–2010 (Med. Chm., 2000–01); The Appeals Service, 1998–2008. QHS 1992–94. Liveryman, Soc. of Apothecaries, 2003–. Montefiore Meml Medal, 1979; Leishman Meml Medal, 1987. OStJ 1993. GSM Oman 1973, NI 1979. *Publications:* contribs to surgical jls. *Recreations:* golf, bridge, military history. *Address:* 162 New Kent Road, SE1 4YS. *T:* (020) 7701 6553. *E:* rpetercraig12@gmail.com. *Clubs:* Athenæum, Royal Society of Medicine; Northumberland Golf; Wildernesse (Sevenoaks).

CRAIG, Sheenagh; *see* Adams, Sheenagh.

CRAIG, Stuart (Norman), OBE 2003; RDI 2004; film production designer; *b* 14 April 1942; *s* of Norman and Kate Craig; *m* 1965, Patricia Stangroom; two *d*. *Educ:* Royal Coll. of Art. *Films:* The Elephant Man, 1980 (BAFTA Award); Gandhi, 1982 (Acad. Award); Greystoke, 1984; Cal, 1984; The Mission, 1986; Cry Freedom, 1987; Dangerous Liaisons, 1988 (Acad. Award); Memphis Belle, 1990; Chaplin, 1992; The Secret Garden, 1993; Shadowlands, 1993; Mary Reilly, 1996; The English Patient, 1996 (Acad. Award); In Love and War, 1996; The Avengers, 1998; Notting Hill, 1999; The Legend of Bagger Vance, 2000; Harry Potter I–VIII, 2001–11; Gambit, 2012. *Address:* c/o The Skouras Agency, 1149 Third Street, Santa Monica, CA 90403, USA.

CRAIG, Susan Ann; Sheriff of Lothian and Borders at Livingston, since 2013; *b* Stirling, Scotland; *d* of Alasdair and Tove Fraser; four *s*. *Educ:* Univ. of Aberdeen (LLB; DipLP 1984). NP, 1986; Solicitor Advocate (Civil), 1994; WS, 1997; an Employment Judge, 2003–13; Sheriff (pt-time), 2011–13. *Recreations:* running, music, travel. *Address:* Livingston Sheriff Court, Howden South Road, Livingston, W Lothian EH54 6FF.

CRAIG, Wendy; *see* Craig, A. G.

CRAIG-COOPER, Sir (Frederick Howard) Michael, Kt 1991; CBE 1982; TD 1968 (3 bars); Director: Craig-Lloyd, since 1968; National Bank of Kuwait (International) plc, since 1993; Vice Lord-Lieutenant of Greater London, 2005–11; *b* 28 Jan. 1936; *s* of late Frederick William Valentine Craig-Cooper and Elizabeth Oliver-Thompson Craig-Cooper (*née* Macdonald) (she *m* 1978, Col J. H. Carroll-Leahy, MC (decd)); *m* 1968, Elizabeth Snagge, MVO; one *s*. *Educ:* Horris Hill; Stowe; College of Law. Solicitor, 1961. National Service, RA, 1954–56; TA, 1956–88; Comdr, Naval Gunfire Liaison Unit, 29 Commando Regt, RA, 1972–75; Mem., Greater London TAVRA (Chm., Employers Support Cttee, 1987–90). Jaques & Co., 1956–61; Allen & Overy, 1962–64; Inco, 1964–85; Director: Paul Ray Internat., 1984–92 (merged with Carre Orban & Partners, 1989); Tichborne Enterprises Ltd, 1993–; non-executive Director: Ely Place Holdings Ltd, 1994–2010; Craigmyle & Co. Ltd, 1995–2009; Westminster Forum (formerly WIB Publications) Ltd, 1996–. Royal Borough of Kensington & Chelsea: Councillor, 1968–74; Chief Whip, 1971–74; Chm. Finance Cttee, 1972–74; Alderman, 1974–78; Mem. Investment Cttee, 1973–. Contested (C) Houghton-le-Spring, 1966, 1970; Chm., Cons. Nat. Property Adv. Cttee, 1986–93 (Mem., 1993–); Pres., Kensington and Chelsea (formerly Chelsea), Cons. Assoc., 1983–2005 (Chm., 1974–77). Trustee: Copper Devel Trust Fund, 1974–85; Order of Malta Homes Trust, 1980–2003; Orders of St John Trust, 1988–2003; Thames Diamond Jubilee Pageant Foundn, 2011–14. Mem. Council, Mining Assoc., 1977–82; Chm. Disciplinary Appeal Cttee, CIMA, 1994–2005. Comr, Royal Hosp. Chelsea, 1998–2005 (Pres., Friends of Royal Hosp. Chelsea, 2009–). Pres., Boys' Brigade (London Dist), 2002–05. Vice Pres., RFCA, Greater London, 2005–. Freeman, City of London, 1964; Liveryman, Drapers' Co., 1970– (Mem. Court of Assistants, 1987–; Master, 1997–98); Hon. Freeman, Royal Bor. of Kensington and Chelsea, 2011. DL Greater London, 1986; Rep. DL Kensington & Chelsea, 1987–2006. FCIArb 1992. KStJ 1990 (Chm., Council for London, 1990–94; Mem., Chapter-Gen., 1993–99). Comdr, SMO Malta, 2001. *Publications:* (with Philippe De Backer) Management Audit: how to create an effective management team, 1993; (jtly) Maw on Corporate Governance, 1994; (jtly) Maximum Leadership, 1995, revd edn as Maximum Leadership 2000, 1997. *Recreation:* admiring wife's gardening. *Clubs:* Beefsteak, Pratt's, White's.

CRAIG-McFEELY, Comdt Elizabeth Sarah Ann, (Mrs C. C. H. Dunlop), CB 1982; DL; Director, Women's Royal Naval Service, 1979–82; *b* 28 April 1927; *d* of late Lt-Col Cecil Michael Craig McFeely, DSO, OBE, MC, and Nancy Sarah (*née* Mann, later Roberts); *m* 1995, Rear-Adm. Colin Charles Harrison Dunlop, CB, CBE (*d* 2009). *Educ:* St Rose's Convent, Stroud, Glos; Anstey College of Physical Educn, Birmingham. DipPE London. Taught PE at St Angela's Ursuline Convent Sch., 1948–52; joined WRNS, 1952; Third Officer, 1953; served in various Royal Naval, Royal Marines and Royal Naval Reserve Estabts, 1952–67; in charge, WRNS, Far Eastern Fleet, 1967–69; various appts, MoD (Navy), 1969–74; HMS Centurion, 1974–76; Supt WRNS, 1977. Naval member, NAAFI Bd of Management, 1977–79; Hon. ADC to the Queen, 1979–82; retired 1982. DL Kent, 1996–2005. *Recreation:* gardening and country pursuits. *Address:* 1 The Gatehouse, Elliscombe Park, Holton, Wincanton, Somerset BA9 8EA. *T:* (01963) 31534.

CRAIG-MARTIN, Prof. Michael, CBE 2001; RA 2006; artist; *b* 28 Aug. 1941; *s* of Paul and Rhona Craig-Martin; *m* 1963, Janice Lucia Hashey (separated); one *d*. *Educ:* Priory Sch., Washington; Yale Univ. Artist in Residence, King's Coll., Cambridge, 1970–72; Sen. Lectr, 1974–79, Prin. Lectr, 1979–88, Millard Prof. of Fine Art, 1994–2000, Goldsmiths' Coll., London (Hon. Fellow, 2001). Trustee, Tate Gall., 1989–99. *Exhibitions* include: Hayward Gall., 1972; Tate Gall., 1972; IX Biennale des Jeunes Artistes, Paris, 1975; Sydney Biennale, 1976, 1990; Whitechapel Art Gall., 1995; MOMA, NY, 1999; *one-man exhibitions* include: Whitechapel Art Gall., 1989 (retrospective); MOMA, NY, 1991; Centre Pompidou, Paris, 1994; Hannover Kunstverein, 1998; São Paulo Bienal, 1998; Stuttgart Kunstverein, 1999; Peter Blum, NY, 1999; Waddington Galls, 2000, 2002; IVAM, Valencia, Spain, 2000; Irish Mus. of Modern Art, 2006 (retrospective); Nat. Art Centre, Tokyo, 2007; Alan Cristea Gall., London, 2008, 2014; New Paintings and Sculptures, New Art Centre, Roche Court, Wilts, 2011; Sculptures, Chatsworth House, Derbys, 2014; *curated:* Master Works, Alan Cristea Gall., London, 2014.

CRAIGAVON, 3rd Viscount *cr* 1927, of Stormont, Co. Down; **Janric Fraser Craig;** Bt 1918; *b* 9 June 1944; *s* of 2nd Viscount Craigavon; *S* father, 1974. *Educ:* Eton; London Univ. (BA, BSc). FCA. Elected Mem., H of L, 1999. *Heir:* none.

CRAIGEN, James Mark; Director and Secretary, Scottish Federation of Housing Associations, 1988–90; freelance writer; *b* 2 Aug. 1938; *e s* of James Craigen, MA and Isabel Craigen; *m* 1971, Sheena Millar. *Educ:* Shawlands Academy, Glasgow; Strathclyde University; MLitt Heriot-Watt 1974. Compositor, 1954–61. Industrial Relations Asst, Scottish Gas Bd, 1963–64; Head of Organisation and Social Services at Scottish TUC, 1964–68; Asst Sec., and Industrial Liaison Officer, Scottish Business Educn Council, 1968–74. Glasgow City Councillor, 1965–68, Magistrate, 1966–68. Member: Scottish Ambulance Service Bd, 1966–71; Race Relations Bd, Scottish Conciliation Cttee, 1967–70; Police Adv. Bd for Scotland, 1970–74; ITC Viewer Consultative Council for Scotland, 1990–93; S Scotland Electricity Consumers' Cttee, 1994–97. Contested Ayr constituency, 1970. MP (Lab and Co-op) Glasgow Maryhill, Feb. 1974–1987 (retired on grounds of experience, not age); PPS to Rt Hon. William Ross, MBE, MP, Sec. of State for Scotland, 1974–76; Opposition Spokesman on Scottish Affairs, 1983–85. Member: Select Cttee on Employment, 1979–83 (Chm., 1982–83); Select Cttee on Scottish Affairs, 1987; Chairman: Co-op. Party Parly Group, 1978–79; Scottish Group, Labour MPs, 1978–79; PLP Employment Gp, 1981–83. Member: UK Delegn to Council of Europe Assembly, 1976–80; Extra Parly Panel, Private Legislation Procedure (Scotland) Act 1936, 1996–2005. Trustee, Industry and Parliament Trust, 1983–88 (Fellow, 1978–79). Mem., Bd of Trustees, Nat. Museums of Scotland, 1985–91. Hon. Vice-Pres., Building Societies Assoc., 1985–88. Hon. Lectr, Strathclyde Univ., 1980–85; Fellow, Inst. of Advanced Studies in Humanities, Edinburgh Univ., 1990–91. JP: Glasgow, 1966; Edinburgh, 1975–2007. CCMI. *Publications:* (contrib.) Forward! Labour Politics in Scotland 1888–1988, 1989; contribs to Co-operative News. *Address:* 38 Downie Grove, Edinburgh EH12 7AX.

CRAIGIE, Cathie; Member (Lab) Cumbernauld and Kilsyth, Scottish Parliament, 1999–2011; *b* Stirling, 14 April 1954; *d* of George Mitchell and Marion (*née* Mandelkau); *m* 1978, Arthur Craigie; one *s* one *d*. *Educ:* Kilsyth Acad. Mem., Ext. Audit Team for Chartered Accountants, 1970–80. Parly Asst to MP, 1992–97. Member (Lab): Cumbernauld and Kilsyth DC, 1984–96: Council Leader, 1994–96; Chm., Planning, Housing, Policy & Resources and Equal Opportunities Cttees, 1984–96; N Lanarks Council, 1995–99: Vice-Chm., Housing, 1995–98; Chairman: Envmtl Services, 1998–99; Kilsyth Local Area Cttee, 1998–99; Cumbernauld Housing Partnership, 1997–98. Scottish Parliament: Member: Audit Cttee, 1999–2000; Social Inclusion, Housing and Voluntary Sector Cttee, 1999–2000; Social Justice Cttee, 2001. Contested (Lab) Cumbernauld and Kilsyth, Scottish Parlt, 2011. Labour Party: Mem., 1974–; Constituency Party Sec., 1992–99; Mem., Nat. Policy Forum, 1998–. *Recreations:* cycling, reading, family holidays.

CRAIGMYLE, 4th Baron *cr* 1929, of Craigmyle, co. Aberdeen; **Thomas Columba Shaw;** *b* 19 Oct. 1960; *s* of 3rd Baron Craigmyle and of Anthea Esther Christine (*née* Rich); *S* father, 1998; *m* 1987, (Katherine) Alice (*née* Floyd); four *s*. *Heir: e s* Hon. Alexander Francis Shaw, *b* 1 July 1988.

CRAIK, Prof. Fergus Ian Muirden, PhD; FRS 2008; FRSC; psychologist; University Professor, University of Toronto, 1997–2000, now Emeritus; Senior Scientist, Rotman Research Institute, Baycrest Centre, Toronto, since 1989; *b* Edinburgh, 17 April 1935; *s* of late George Craik and of Frances Craik; *m* 1961, Anne, *d* of Jack and Rita Catherall; one *s* one *d*. *Educ:* George Watson's Boys' Coll., Edinburgh; Univ. of Edinburgh (BSc 1960); Univ. of Liverpool (PhD 1965). Lectr in Psychol., Birkbeck Coll., Univ. of London, 1965–71; University of Toronto: Associate Prof. of Psychol., 1971–75; Prof. of Psychol., 1975–97; Chm. of Psychol., 1985–90; Glassman Prof. of Neuropsychol., 1996–2000. Fellow, Center for Advanced Study in Behavioral Scis, Stanford Univ., 1982–83; Killam Res. Fellow, 1982–84; Guggenheim Fellow, 1982–83. Ed., Jl of Verbal Learning and Verbal Behavior, 1980–84. Mem., Soc. of Experimental Psychologists; Fellow: Canadian Psychol. Assoc. (Hon. Pres., 1997–98); Amer. Psychol. Assoc. FRSC 1985. Hon. Dr Bordeaux 2, 2006; Hon. DSocSc Edinburgh, 2012; Hon. Dr Saarland, 2013. Dist. Scientific Contribution Award, Canadian Psychol. Assoc., 1987; William James Fellow Award, Amer. Psychol. Soc., 1993; Hebb Award, Canadian Soc. for Brain, Behaviour and Cognitive Sci., 1998; Killam Prize, 2000; Anderson Lifetime Achievement Award, Soc. of Experimental Psychologists, 2009. *Publications:* (ed jtly) Levels of Processing in Human Memory, 1979; Aging and Cognitive Processes, 1982; Varieties of Memory and Consciousness, 1989; The Handbook of Aging and Cognition, 1992, 3rd edn 2008; The Oxford Handbook of Memory, 2000; Lifespan Cognition: mechanisms of change, 2006; Mind and the Frontal Lobes: cognition, behavior, and brain imaging, 2012. *Recreations:* reading, walking, music, tennis. *Address:* Rotman Research Institute of Baycrest, 3560 Bathurst Street, Toronto, ON M6A 2E1, Canada.

See also R. G. Craik.

CRAIK, Roger George; QC (Scot.) 1981; Sheriff of Lothian and Borders, 1984–2005; *b* 22 Nov. 1940; *s* of late George and of Frances Craik; *m* 1964, Helen Sinclair Sutherland; one *s* one *d*. *Educ:* Lockerbie Academy; Breadalbane Academy, Aberfeldy; George Watson's Boys' Coll.; Edinburgh Univ. (MA 1960, LLB 1962). Qualified as solicitor, 1962; worked for Orr Dignam & Co., Solicitors, Pakistan, 1963–65; called to Scottish Bar, 1966. Standing junior counsel to Min. of Defence (Army), 1974–80; Advocate Depute, 1980–83. Temp. Court of Session Judge, 2004–10. Mem., Sheriff Court Rules Council, 1990–95. *Publications:* The Advocates' Library 1689–1989, 1989; James Boswell: the Scottish perspective, 1994; Parliament House Portraits: the art collection of the Faculty of Advocates, 2000. *Recreations:* Scottish antiquities, modern jazz. *Address:* 9 York Road, Trinity, Edinburgh EH5 3EJ.

See also F. I. M. Craik.

CRAM, Stephen, CBE 2015 (MBE 1986); former middle distance runner; athletics presenter and commentator, BBC TV, since 1999; Chairman, English Institute of Sport, 2002–13; *b* 14 Oct. 1960; *s* of William Frank Cram and Maria Helene (*née* Korte); *m* 1983, Karen Anne

Waters (marr. diss. 2005); one *s* one *d. Educ:* Jarrow Grammar Sch.; Newcastle Poly. (BA). Commonwealth Games: Gold Medal for 1500m, 1982, 1986; Gold Medal for 800m, 1986; European Championships: Gold Medal for 1500m, 1982, 1986; Bronze Medal for 800m, 1986; Gold Medal for 1500m, World Championships, 1983; Silver Medal for 1500m, Olympic Games, 1984; Member, British Olympic Squad, 1980, 1984, 1988; former world record for mile, 1500m and 2000m, 1985. Regular contributor, BBC Radio 5 Live, 1995–; athletics columnist, Guardian; motivational speaker and sports consultant. Chm. and Trustee, Northumberland Sport. Chm. and Dir, Comrades of Children Overseas, 1998–. Patron, Macmillan Cancer Relief. Chancellor, Sunderland Univ., 2008– (Hon. Fellow 1986). DUniv: Staffordshire, 2001; Sheffield Hallam, 2001. BBC Sports Personality of the Year, 1983. *Recreations:* golf, football, snooker. *Address:* Extra Mile Media and Events, Kiln Rigg, Wall, Hexham, Northumberland NE46 4EQ. *T:* 07900 223563. *E:* steve@extramileme.com. *Clubs:* Jarrow and Hebburn Athletic; Sunderland Association Football (Pres. London and Southern England Br., Supporters' Assoc.).

CRAMER, Shirley Christine, CBE 2009; Chief Executive, Royal Society for Public Health, since 2013; *b* Whitehaven, 11 April 1955; *d* of Joseph and Jean Tyson; *m* 1979, Carl Cramer; two *d. Educ:* Cockermouth Grammar Sch.; Univ. of Bradford (BA CQSW 1978); Columbia Univ., NY (MSc Social Admin 1985). Exec. Dir, Nat. Center for Learning Disabilities, NY, 1992–95; Dir, Coordinated Campaign for Learning Disabilities, USA, 1995–99; Chief Exec., Dyslexia Action, 2000–11; Interim CEO, Alzheimer's Res. UK, 2012. Chairman: Equality and Diversity Ext. Adv. Gp, 2009–13; British Future Think Tank, 2013–. Mem., Nat. Council, LSC, 2002–08. *Publications:* Learning Disabilities: lifelong issues, 1996. *Recreations:* ski-ing, walking, opera, theatre, art, singing in a choir. *Address:* 2 Little Dormers, 15 South Park Crescent, Gerrards Cross, Bucks SL9 8HJ. *T:* (01753) 899189, 07841 672081. *E:* scramer@rsph.org.uk, scramer0@gmail.com.

CRAMOND, Ronald Duncan, CBE 1987; Secretary and Founding Trustee, Intellectual Access Trust, 1995–2011; *b* 22 March 1927; *s* of Adam and Margaret Cramond; *m* 1st, 1954, Constance MacGregor (*d* 1985); one *s* one *d*; 2nd, 1999, Ann Rayner. *Educ:* George Heriot's Sch.; Edinburgh Univ. (MA 1949; MPhil by research 2011). Sen. Medallist History 1949. FSAScot 1978. Commnd Royal Scots, 1950. Entered War Office, 1951; Private Sec. to Parly Under-Sec. of State, Scottish Office, 1956; Principal, Dept of Health for Scotland, 1957; Mactaggart Fellow (Applied Econs), Glasgow Univ., 1962; Haldane Medallist in Public Admin, 1964; Asst Sec., Scottish Develt Dept, 1966, Under Sec., 1973; Under Sec., Dept of Agric. and Fisheries for Scotland, 1977; Dep. Chm., Highlands and Islands Develt Bd, 1983–88. Chairman: Strathclyde Greenbelt Co., then Scottish Greenbelt Foundn, 1992–2000 (Mem., 1992–2005); Greenbelt Foundn, 1999–2002. Dir, Cairngorm Chairlift Co., 1988–90. Chairman: Scottish Museums Council, 1990–93; LandTrust, 1997–98; Member: Scottish Museums Adv. Bd, 1984–85; Scottish Tourist Board, 1985–88; CCS, 1988–92; Trustee: Nat. Museums of Scotland, 1985–96; Scottish Civic Trust, 1988–95; Scottish Fisheries Mus., 2001–04; Vice-Pres., Architectural Heritage Soc. of Scotland, 1988–93. *Publications:* Housing Policy in Scotland, 1966. *Recreations:* showing visitors round the Museum of Scotland, researching Scottish History.

CRAMP, Leslie Thomas, CBE 2011; Deputy Chief Executive, Insolvency Service, 2010–13; *b* 25 Oct. 1949; *s* of Noel Clifford Cramp and Doris Nellie Irene Cramp; *m* 1974, Linda Ann Lipscomb; one *s* one *d. Educ:* Maidstone Grammar Sch. Local govt post, 1968–70; Insolvency Service, Department of Trade and Industry, later Department for Business, Enterprise and Regulatory Reform, then Department for Business, Innovation and Skills, 1970–2013: Companies Winding-up, London, 1970–82; Principal Examr, Policy Unit, 1982–88; Official Receiver, High Court, London, 1988–96; Manager, Anglia Reg., 1996–98; Dep. Inspector Gen. and Sen. Official Receiver, 1998–2010. *Recreations:* music, football, reading, gardening.

CRAMP, Dame Rosemary Jean, DBE 2011 (CBE 1987); FBA 2006; Professor of Archaeology, University of Durham, 1971–90, now Emeritus; *b* 6 May 1929; *er d* of Robert Kingston and Vera Cramp, Cranoe Grange, Leics. *Educ:* Market Harborough Grammar Sch.; St Anne's Coll., Oxford (MA, BLitt). Lectr, St Anne's Coll., Oxford, 1950–55; Lectr, Durham Univ., 1955, Sen. Lectr, 1966. Vis. Fellow, All Souls Coll., Oxford, 1992. Commissioner: Royal Commn on Ancient and Historical Monuments of Scotland, 1975–99; Historic Bldgs and Monuments Commn, 1984–89 (Mem., Adv. Cttee (Archaeology), 1984–89). Trustee, BM, 1978–98. Member: Adv. Bd for Redundant Churches, 1984–98; Validation Panel, Museums' Trng Inst., 1993–97; Reviewing Cttee on Export of Works of Art, 1994–2003. Chm., Archaeology Data Service, 1996–2001. President: Council for British Archaeology, 1989–92 (Hon. Vice-Pres., 1992–); Cumberland and Westmorland Antiquarian and Archaeol Soc., 1984–87; Soc. for Church Archaeology, 1996–2001; Soc. of Antiquaries of London, 2001–04 (Hon. Vice-Pres., 2004–); Vice-Pres., Royal Archaeol Inst., 1992–97; Hon. Vice Pres., Soc. for Medieval Archaeol., 2004–. Gen. Editor, Corpus of Anglo-Saxon Stone Sculpture, 1974–. Hon. DSc: Durham, 1995; Bradford, 2002; Hon. DLitt: NUI, 2003; Leicester, 2004. *Publications:* Corpus of Anglo-Saxon Stone Sculpture, vol. I, Durham and Northumberland, 1984, vol. 2, (with R. N. Bailey) Cumberland and Westmorland, 1986, vol. 7, South West England, 2006; Wearmouth and Jarrow Monastic Sites, vol. 1, 2005, vol. 2, 2006; The Hirsel Excavations, 2014; contribs in the field of early monasticism, early medieval sculpture and glass, and northern archaeology. *Address:* 5 Leazes Place, Durham DH1 1RE.

CRAMPIN, Peter; QC 1993; *b* 7 July 1946; *s* of late John Hames Crampin and of Gwendoline Edith (*née* Richardson); *m* 1975, Frida Yvonne Schoemann; one *s. Educ:* St Albans Sch.; University Coll., Oxford (Open Exhibnr; MA). Admitted Solicitor, 1973; called to the Bar, Middle Temple, 1976; in practice at Chancery Bar, 1978–; an Asst Recorder, 1990–95; a Recorder, 1995; 2nd Jun. Counsel to Attorney General in Charity Matters, 1988–93. *Address:* 3 Stone Buildings, Lincoln's Inn, WC2A 3XL. *T:* (020) 7242 4937.

CRAMPTON, Prof. Julian Moray, CBE; PhD; CBiol, FRSB; DL; Vice-Chancellor, and Professor of Molecular Biology, University of Brighton, since 2005; *b* 1 Nov. 1952; *s* of late Sqdn Ldr Roy A. V. Crampton and of Jean D. Crampton (*née* Macnair); partner, Dr Teresa F. Knapp. *Educ:* Univ. of Sussex (BSc Biol. 1975); Univ. of Warwick (PhD 1978). CBiol, MIBiol 1997, FRSB (FIBiol 2004). MRC Postdoctoral Res. Fellow, St Mary's Hosp. Med. Sch., 1978–83; Liverpool School of Tropical Medicine, University of Liverpool: Hd, Wolfson Unit of Molecular Genetics, 1983–96; Wellcome Trust Sen. Res. Fellow, 1986–96; Hd, Div. of Molecular Biol. and Immunol., 1994–96; University of Liverpool: Prof. of Molecular Biol., 1991–2005; Hd, Sch. of Biol Scis, 1996–2000; Pro-Vice-Chancellor, 2000–04. Chairman: Higher Educn SE, 2006–10; Hastings and Bexhill Renaissance Ltd, 2006–; Member: SE England Sci. Engrg and Technol. Adv. Council, 2006–11; Innovation, Sci. and Technol. Cttee, CBI, 2010–11; Member, Board: UUK, 2005– (Treas., 2008–12); Nat. Centre for Univs and Business (formerly Council for Industry and Higher Educn), 2010–. Member: Bd, SE England Develt Agency, 2009–12; Bd, 2010–, Exec. Gp, 2012–, SE Local Enterprise Partnership; Bd, Inst. for Employment Studies, 2012–; Nat. Growth Bd, 2013–. Chm. and Dir, E Sussex Energy, Infrastructure and Develt Ltd, 2011–; Member Board: NHS Postgrad. Deanery for Kent, Surrey and Sussex, 2011–13; Health Educn Kent, Surrey and Sussex (formerly Local Educn Trng Bd for Kent, Surrey and Sussex), 2012–. Chair and Director: Hastings Academies Trust, 2010–; Univ. of Brighton Academies Trust, 2014–; Trustee and Governor, Friends of Royal Pavilion and Mus, 2006–; Chm. and Trustee, Royal Pavilion and Mus Foundn, 2006–; Trustee, Brighton Dome and Fest. Ltd, 2007–. DL E Sussex, 2012. Ed., Insect Molecular Biol., 1989–99 (Mem., Editl Bd, 1999–). FRSTM&H 1984; FRES 1989 (Hon. FRES 2002). FRSA 2001. *Publications:* (ed jtly) Insect Molecular Science, 1992; (ed jtly) The Molecular Biology of Insect Disease Vector, 1996; numerous contribs to learned jls. *Recreations:* photography, hill-walking, music, kayaking. *Address:* University of Brighton, Mithras House, Lewes Road, Brighton BN2 4AT. *T:* (01273) 642001.

CRAMPTON, Prof. Richard John, PhD; Professor of East European History, University of Oxford, 1996–2006; Fellow of St Edmund Hall, Oxford, 1990–2006, now Emeritus; *b* 23 Nov. 1940; *s* of John Donald Crampton and Norah Crampton (*née* Haden); *m* 1965, Celia Harriss; two *s. Educ:* Univ. of Dublin (MA); MA Oxon; SSEES, Univ. of London (PhD). University of Kent at Canterbury: Lectr, 1967–78; Sen. Lectr, 1978–88; Prof. of East European History, 1988–90; Lectr in History, Univ. of Oxford, 1990–96. Fellow, Woodrow Wilson Internat. Center for Scholars, Washington, 1998–99. Dr *hc* Sofia, 2000. *Publications:* The Hollow Détente, 1981; Bulgaria 1878–1918: a history, 1984; Short History of Modern Bulgaria, 1987; Eastern Europe in the Twentieth Century, 1994; (with Ben Crampton) Atlas of Eastern Europe in the 20th Century, 1996; Concise History of Bulgaria, 1997; The Balkans since the Second World War, 2002; Bulgaria: Oxford History of Modern Europe, 2007; Aleksandŭr Stamboliĭski: Bulgaria, 2009. *Recreations:* pure mathematics, trying to avoid pop music and mobile phones. *Address:* St Edmund Hall, Oxford OX1 4AR. *T:* (01865) 279000.

CRAN, James Douglas; *b* 28 Jan. 1944; *s* of James Cran and Jane McDonald Cran, Aberdeenshire; *m* 1973, Penelope Barbara Wilson; one *d. Educ:* Ruthrieston Sch., Aberdeen; Aberdeen Coll. of Commerce; King's Coll., Univ. of Aberdeen (MA Hons). Researcher, Cons. Res. Dept, 1970–71; Sec., 1971–73, Chief. Exec., 1973–79, Nat. Assoc. of Pension Funds; Northern Dir, 1979–84, West Midlands Dir, 1984–87, CBI. Councillor (C), London Borough of Sutton, 1974–79 (Chm., Health and Housing Cttee). MP (C) Beverley, 1987–97, Beverley and Holderness, 1997–2005. PPS to Sec. of State for NI, 1995–96; an Opposition Whip, 1997–2001 (Pairing Whip, 1998–2000); Opposition Asst Chief Whip, 2001. Member: Select Cttee on Trade and Industry, 1987–92, on NI, 1994–95, on Administration, 1997–98, on Selection, 1998–2001, on Defence, 2001–05; Chairmen's Panel, 2001–05; Vice Chairman: Cons. Backbench NI Cttee, 1992–95; All-Party Anglo-Mongolian Gp, 1993–94; Order of St John All-Party Gp, 1994–95; Secretary: Cons. Backbench Cttee on Constitutional Affairs, 1989–91, on European Affairs, 1989–91; All-Party Anglo-Malta Gp, 1992–94; Co-Founder, Parly Gp on Occupational Pensions, 1992. Mem., Council of Europe and WEU, 2001–02. Mem., NI Grand Cttee, 1996–2001. Fellow: Armed Forces Parly Scheme, attached to RM, 1992; Parlt and Industry Trust, 1994. Parly consultant, Lincoln Nat. (UK) plc, 1994–98. Treas., European Res. Gp, 1994–97; Mem., 92 Gp Steering Cttee, 2001–04. Vice-Pres., Beverley Combined Div., St John Ambulance. Council Mem., Pension Trustees Forum, 1992–95. Member of Court: Univ. of Birmingham, 1984–87; Univ. of Hull, 1987–2005. Dux Medallion, City of Aberdeen, 1959; Daily Mirror Nat. Speaking Trophy, 1969. OStJ. *Recreations:* travelling, reading biographies, autobiographies and military history. *Address:* The Mill House, Ashkirk, Selkirkshire TD7 4NY; Apartment 11, The Waterfront, Triq Stella Maris, San Pawl, Il-Bahar, Malta.

CRAN, Mark Dyson Gordon; QC 1988; a Recorder, since 2000; *b* 18 May 1948; *s* of William Broadbent Gordon Cran and Diana Rosemary Cran (*née* Mallinson); *m* 1983, Prudence Elizabeth Binning (marr. diss.). *Educ:* Gordonstoun; Millfield; Bristol Univ. (LLB). Called to the Bar, Gray's Inn, 1973, Bencher, 2009. *Recreations:* country sports, long walks, convivial disputation, wine and food, performing arts. *Address:* Brick Court Chambers, 7–8 Essex Street, WC2R 3LD. *T:* (020) 7379 3550; Crawford House, 50 Cedar Avenue, PO Box HM2879, Hamilton HMLX, Bermuda. *T:* 2956500. *Clubs:* Brooks's, MCC.

CRANBORNE, Viscount; Robert Edward William Gascoyne-Cecil; *b* 18 Dec. 1970; *s* and *heir* of Marquess of Salisbury, *qv*; one *d* by Camilla Mary Davidson.

CRANBROOK, 5th Earl of, *cr* 1892; **Gathorne Gathorne-Hardy;** Viscount Cranbrook, 1878; Baron Medway, 1892; Adjunct Senior Research Fellow, School of Geography and Environmental Science, Monash University; *b* 20 June 1933; *er s* of 4th Earl of Cranbrook, CBE, and the Dowager Countess of Cranbrook (Fidelity, OBE 1972, *o d* of late Hugh E. Seebohm) (*d* 2009); *S* father, 1978; *m* 1967, Caroline (OBE 2006), *o d* of Col Ralph G. E. Jarvis, Doddington Hall, Lincoln; two *s* one *d. Educ:* Eton; Corpus Christi Coll., Cambridge (MA); University of Birmingham (PhD). Asst, Sarawak Museum, 1956–58; Fellow, Yayasan Siswa Lokantara (Indonesia), 1960–61; Asst Lectr, subseq. Lectr then Sen. Lectr in Zoology, Univ. of Malaya, 1961–70. Editor of Ibis, 1973–80. Mem., H of L Select Cttee on EC, then EU, three terms, 1979–99 (Mem., Envmt Sub-Cttee, 1979–85, 1987–90 (Chm., 1980–83, 1987–90), Chm., Envmt, Public Health and Consumer Protection Sub-Cttee, 1998–99). Bd Mem., Anglian Water Authy, 1987–89; non-exec. Dir, Anglian Water, 1989–98. Chairman: English Nature, 1990–98; ENTRUST, Envmtl Trusts Scheme Regulatory Body, 1996–2002; Member: Royal Commn on Environmental Pollution, 1981–92; NERC, 1982–88; Foundn for Eur. Envmtl Policy, 1987–98 (Chm., 1990–98); UK Round Table on Sustainable Develt, 1994–98; Broads Authy, 1988–99; Harwich Haven Authy, 1989–97 (Vice Chm., 1995–97); NCC, 1990–91; Suffolk Coastal DC, 1974–83; Pres., Suffolk Wildlife Trust (formerly Suffolk Trust for Nature Conservation), 1979–2014; Chm. Adv. Cttee, NERC Centre for Ecology and Hydrology, 1998–2005; Pres., Haven Gateway Partnership, 2001–08. Advr, Ironwood Foundn (Yayasan Ulin), Indonesia, 2009–. Chm., Long Shop Project Trust, 1981–; Trustee, BM (Natural History), 1982–86. Skinner and Freeman of the City of London. DL Suffolk, 1984. FZS; FRGS; FRSB; MBOU. Hon. FCIWEM; Hon. FIWM; Hon. FLS 2006. Hon. DSc: Aberdeen, 1989; Cranfield, 1996. Founder's Medal, RGS, 1995. OStJ. Hon. Johan Bintang Sarawak, 1997; Hon. Panglima Negara Bintang Sarawak, 2005; WWF Internat. Duke of Edinburgh Gold Medal, 2014; Merdeka Award (Malaysia), 2014. *Publications:* Mammals of Borneo, 1965, 2nd edn 1977; Mammals of Malaya, 1969, 2nd edn 1978; (with D. R. Wells) Birds of the Malay Peninsula, 1976; Riches of the Wild: mammals of South East Asia, 1987, 2nd edn 1991; (ed) Key Environments: Malaysia, 1988; (with D. S. Edwards) Belalong: a tropical rain forest, 1994; Wonders of Nature in South-East Asia, 1997; (trans.) The Ballad of Jerjezang, 2001; (with C. K. Lim) Swiftlets of Borneo: builders of edible nests, 2002, 2nd edn 2014. *Heir: s* Lord Medway, *qv. Fax:* (home) (01728) 663339.

CRANE, Nicholas Peter; writer and broadcaster, since 1979; *b* 9 May 1954; *s* of Harold and Naomi Crane; *m* 1991, Annabel Huxley; one *s* two *d. Educ:* St Cedd's Primary Sch., Chelmsford; Ketteringham Hall Prep. Sch.; Town Close House Prep. Sch., Norwich; Wymondham Coll.; Cambridgeshire Coll. of Arts & Technol., Cambridge (BA Hons Geog., Univ. of London). Information Officer, Cyclists Touring Club, 1976–78. Presenter: documentaries, BBC Radio 4: Journey to the Centre of the Earth, 1987; Forbidden Journey, 1989; From Ancient Sparta to the Gates of Hell, 1990; BBC television: Blazing Pedals, 1990; The Pyrenees (for Wilderness Walks series), 1998; Map Man, Series 1, 2004, Series 2, 2005; Coast, Series 1 (BAFTA Award for Interactivity, 2005), Christmas Special, 2005, Series 2, 2006, Series 3, 2007, Series 4, 2009, Series 5, 2010, Series 6, 2011, Series 7, 2012, Series 8, 2013, Series 9, 2014, Series 10, 2015; Great British Journeys, 2007; Down the Line, 2008; Nicholas Crane's Britannia, 2009; In Search of England's Green and Pleasant Land, 2009; Munro: mountain man, 2009; Town with Nicholas Crane, 2011, 2013; producer, High Trails to Istanbul, 1995. Pres., Globetrotters Club, 1990–93; Mem. Mgt Cttee, Soc. of Authors, 2000–03; Mem. RSL 1998; Vice-Pres., CPRE, 2008–13. FRGS 1987 (Chm., Ind. Travellers' Seminar, 1989–90; Mem. Council, 2004–07). Editl Adv. Gp, Geographical magazine, 1999–. Come to Britain Trophy, BTA, 1977; Mungo Park Medal, RSGS, 1993; journalism award, British Guild of Travel Writers, 1996; Ness Award, RGS. *Publications:* (with Christa Gausden) The CTC Route Guide to Cycling in Britain & Ireland, 1980; Cycling in Europe, 1984; (with Richard Crane) Bicycles up Kilimanjaro, 1985; (with Richard Crane) Journey to the Centre of the Earth, 1987; The Great Bicycle Adventure, 1987; Nick Crane's Action Sports, 1989; Atlas Biker, 1990; Clear Waters Rising: a mountain walk across Europe, 1996 (Thomas

Cook/Daily Telegraph Travel Book Award, 1997); Two Degrees West: a walk along England's Meridian, 1999; Mercator: the man who mapped the planet, 2002; Great British Journeys, 2007; Coast, 2010; World Atlas, 2011. *Recreations:* walking, cycling, boating. *Address:* c/o A. P. Watt Ltd, United Agents, 12–26 Lexington Street, W1F 0LE.

CRANE, Sir Peter (Robert), Kt 2004; PhD; FRS 1998; Carl W. Knobloch Jr Dean, School of Forestry and Environmental Studies, Yale University, since 2009; *b* 18 July 1954; *s* of Walter Robert Crane and Dorothy Mary Crane; *m* 1986, Elinor Margaret Hamer; one *s* one *d. Educ:* Univ. of Reading (BSc 1975; PhD 1981). Lectr, Dept of Botany, Univ. of Reading, 1978–81; Post-doctoral Res. Schol., Indiana Univ., 1981–82; Field Museum, Chicago: Curator, Dept of Geology, 1982–92; Vice Pres., Acad. Affairs, 1992–99; Dir, 1995–99; Dir, Royal Botanic Gardens, Kew, 1999–2006; John and Marion Sullivan Prof., Dept of Geophys. Scis, Univ. of Chicago, 2006–09. Visiting Professor: Univ. of Reading, 1999–2006; Royal Holloway, Univ. of London, 2000–06; ICSTM, 2003–06. President: Paleontol Soc., 1998–2000; Palaeontol Assoc., 2004–06. Foreign Associate, Nat Acad. of Scis, USA, 2001; Foreign Member: Royal Swedish Acad. of Scis, 2002; Acad. Leopoldina, 2004; Royal Soc. of Arts and Sci., Göteborg, 2005; Amer. Acad. of Arts and Scis, 2008. Hon. DSc: Cambridge, 2009; Connecticut, 2011. Internat. Prize for Biology, 2014. *Publications:* (ed jtly) The Origins of Angiosperms and their Biological Consequences, 1987; (ed jtly) The Evolution, Systematics and Fossil History of the Hamamelidae, vols 1 and 2, 1989; (jtly) The Origin and Diversification of Land Plants, 1997; (jtly) Early Flowers and Angiosperm Evolution, 2011; Ginkgo: the tree that time forgot, 2013. *Address:* School of Forestry and Environmental Studies, Yale University, 195 Prospect Street, New Haven, CT 06511, USA.

CRANE, Prof. Timothy Martin, PhD; Knightbridge Professor of Philosophy, University of Cambridge, since 2009; Fellow, Peterhouse, Cambridge, since 2009; *b* Oxford, 17 Oct. 1962; *s* of Walter and Ann Crane; *m* 2000, Katalin Farkas. *Educ:* Durham Univ. (BA Hons Phil. 1984); York Univ. (MA Phil. 1985); Peterhouse, Cambridge (PhD 1989). University College London: Lectr in Philosophy, 1990–96; Reader, 1996–2002; Prof. of Philosophy, 2002–09; Dir, Inst. of Philosophy, Univ. of London, 2005–08. MAE 2008. *Publications:* The Contents of Experience, 1992; The Mechanical Mind, 1995, 2nd edn 2004; A Debate on Dispositions, 1996; History of the Mind-Body Problem, 2000; Elements of Mind, 2001; Metaphysics, 2004; Intentionalität als Merkmal des Geistigen, 2007; The Objects of Thought, 2013; Aspects of Psychologism, 2014. *Recreations:* music, wine. *Address:* Faculty of Philosophy, University of Cambridge, Sidgwick Avenue, Cambridge CB3 9DA. *E:* tc102@cam.ac.uk. *W:* www.timcrane.com. *Club:* Blacks.

CRANSTON, David Alan, CBE 1993; Director General, National Association of Pension Funds, 2000–01; *b* 20 Oct. 1945; *s* of Stanley Cranston and Mary Cranston (*née* Fitzherbert); *m* 1968, Pippa Ann Reynolds; three *d. Educ:* Strathallan Sch., Perthshire; RMA, Sandhurst. Commnd RA, 1966; Army Staff Course, 1979–80; transf. to AAC, 1981; COS HQ, British Forces, Belize, 1983; DS, RMCS Shrivenham, 1984–86; Comd, 4th Regt, AAC, 1986–88; COS, 2nd Inf. Div., 1988–90; Higher Comd and Staff Course, 1990; Comd, British Army Aviation, Germany, 1990–92; Dep. Head of Mission, EC Monitor Mission to former Yugoslavia, 1992; rcds, 1993; Dep. Comdr, Multinational Airmobile Div., 1994–95. Head of Mem. Relns, PIA, 1995–97; Head of Gp Compliance, Royal Bank of Scotland, 1997–2000. Non-exec. Dir, National Olympic Cttee, 2001–10, Mem., Exec. Bd, 2007–10, British Olympic Assoc. Non-executive Director: Skandia UK, 2002–08 (Chm. Pension Trustee Bd, 2002–); Forces Pension Soc. Investment Co., 2002–13; Bankhall Investment Mgt, 2003–08; Voller Energy, 2005–09; Chairman, Pension Trustee Board: Austin Reed, 2002–; Sibelco UK, 2007–; MRC, 2010–. Chm., British Biathlon Union, 1996–2011. *Recreations:* gardening, reading, tennis, ski-ing. *Club:* Army and Navy.

CRANSTON, Hon. Sir Ross (Frederick), Kt 2007; FBA 2007; **Hon. Mr Justice Cranston;** a Judge of the High Court of Justice, Queen's Bench Division, since 2007; *b* 23 July 1948; *s* of late Frederick Hugh Cranston and of Edna Elizabeth Cranston (*née* Davies); *m* 1st, 1976, Prof. Jane Stapleton (marr. diss. 1985); 2nd, 1988, Anna Whyatt (marr. diss. 1998); one *d*; 3rd, 2007, Hazel Phillips. *Educ:* Univ. of Queensland (BA 1970; LLB 1971); Harvard Law Sch. (LLM 1973); Oxford (DPhil 1976; DCL 1998). Called to the Bar, Gray's Inn, 1976, Bencher, 1998; Asst Recorder, 1991–97; Recorder, 1997–2007; QC 1998. Lectr, Univ. of Warwick, 1975–77; Res. Fellow, 1978–81, Sen. Lectr, then Reader, 1981–86, Assoc. Dean, 1984–86, Faculty of Law, ANU Canberra; W. G. Hart Sen. Fellow, QMC, 1983–84; Queen Mary and Westfield College, London University: Sir John Lubbock Prof. of Banking Law, 1986–92; Dean, Faculty of Laws, 1988–91; Dir, Centre for Commercial Law Studies, 1989–92; London School of Economics and Political Science: Cassel Prof. of Commercial Law, 1993–97; Vis. Prof., 1997–2005, 2007–; Centennial Prof. of Law, 2005–07. Acad. Consultant, Woolf Inquiry into Access to Justice, 1994–96; Assessor, Jackson Rev. of Civil Litigation Costs, 2009; Consultant to various international bodies including World Bank, IMF, UN Conf. on Trade and Develt, Commonwealth Secretariat, 1988–96. Contested (Lab) Richmond, Yorks, 1992. MP (Lab) Dudley North, 1997–2005. Solicitor-Gen., 1998–2001. Chairman: All-Party Parly Gp on Alcohol Misuse, 2002–05; All-Party Parly Gp for the Bar, 2002–05. Judiciary Assessment Mission, Turkey, 2005, Justice and Home Affairs Peer Rev. Mission, Bulgaria, 2006, Croatia, 2007, Romania, 2012, 2013, Eur. Commn. Vice Pres., 1991–92, Pres., 1992–93, SPTL. Dep. Chm., 1993–96, Chm., 1996–97, Bd of Trustees, Public Concern at Work. Trustee: Build IT Internat., 2006–13; NOFAS-UK, 2006–12. Chair, Soc. of Labour Lawyers, 2003–06; Pres., Internat. Acad. of Commercial and Consumer Law, 2004–06. Mem., American Law Inst., 1999. FCIArb 2006. *Publications:* Consumers and the Law, 1978, 3rd edn, as Cranston's Consumers and the Law, 2000; Regulating Business, 1979; Legal Foundations of the Welfare State, 1985; Law, Government and Public Policy, 1987; (ed) Banks, Liability and Risk, 1990, 2nd edn 1995; (ed) The Single Market and the Law of Banking, 1991, 2nd edn 1995; (ed with R. M. Goode) Contemporary Issues in International Commercial Law, 1993; (ed) European Banking Law, 1993, 2nd edn 1999; (ed) Legal Ethics and Professional Responsibility, 1995; (ed with A. Zuckerman) Reform of the Administration of Civil Justice, 1995; (ed) Making Commercial Law, 1997; Principles of Banking Law, 1997, 2nd edn 2002; How Law Works, 2006. *Address:* Royal Courts of Justice, Strand, WC2A 2LL.

CRANWORTH, 3rd Baron *cr* 1899; **Philip Bertram Gurdon;** Lieutenant, Royal Wiltshire Yeomanry; *b* 24 May 1940; *s* of Hon. Robin Gurdon (killed in action, 1942) and Hon. Yoskyl Pearson (she *m* 2nd, 1944, as his 2nd wife, Lieut-Col Alistair Gibb, and 3rd, 1962, as his 2nd wife, 1st Baron McCorquodale of Newton, PC, KCVO; she *d* 1979), *d* of 2nd Viscount Cowdray; *S* grandfather, 1964; *m* 1st, 1968, Frances Henrietta Montagu Douglas Scott (*d* 2000), *d* of late Lord William Scott and Lady William Scott; two *s* one *d*; 2nd, 2006, Cameron Vail Noble. *Educ:* Eton; Magdalene Coll., Cambridge. *Heir: s* Hon. Sacha William Robin Gurdon, [*b* 12 Aug. 1970; *m* 2001, Susannah, *d* of Martin Bates; one *s*]. *Address:* Boulge House, Woodbridge IP13 6BW.

See also Marquess of Huntly.

CRASNOW, Rachel; QC 2015; *b* Cambridge, 24 May 1970; *d* of E. and J. A. Crasnow; partner, Matthew Dodd; one *s* two *d. Educ:* Univ. of Oxford (BA Hons); City Univ., London (DipLaw 1993). Called to the Bar, Middle Temple, 1994. Chm., Police Appeals Tribunal, 2015–. Legal Advr to UK Bd for Health Care Chaplaincy. Chm., Legislation and Guidance Cttee, Mem., Equality and Diversity Cttee, Bar Council. Mem. Cttee, Employment Law Bar Assoc. Member: Employment Lawyers Assoc.; ELAAS; Discrimination Law Assoc.; Industrial Law Soc.; Human Rights Lawyers' Assoc. Editor, Case Commentaries, Educnl Law Jl, until 2004. *Publications:* (jtly) Employment Law and Human Rights, 2nd edn 2007; (jtly) Blackstone's Guide to the Equality Act, 2010; (jtly and ed) Family Rights in Employment Law, 2012; (contrib. and ed) Human Rights and ECJ sections in Bullen and Leake and Jacob's Precedents of Pleadings. *Recreations:* camping, travel, walking, family. *Address:* Cloisters Chambers, 1 Pump Court, Temple, EC4Y 7AA. *T:* (020) 7827 4000.

CRASTON, Rev. Canon (Richard) Colin; Vicar, then Rector, St Paul with Emmanuel, Bolton, 1977–93, retired; Hon. Canon, Manchester Cathedral, 1968–95, Canon Emeritus, since 1995; Chaplain to the Queen, 1985–92; *b* 31 Dec. 1922; *s* of Albert Edward Craston and Ethel Craston; *m* 1st, 1948, Ruth Taggart (*d* 1992); one *s* one *d*; 2nd, 1993, Rev. Brenda H. Fullalove. *Educ:* Preston Grammar Sch.; Univ. of Bristol (BA Hons); Univ. of London (BD Hons); Tyndale Hall, Bristol. Served War, RN, 1941–46. Ordained 1951; Curate, St Nicholas, Durham, 1951–54; Vicar, St Paul, Bolton, 1954–76; Priest i/c, 1964–66, Vicar, 1966–76, Emmanuel, Bolton; Area Dean of Bolton, 1972–92. Chm., House of Clergy, Dio. of Manchester, 1982–94; Member: Gen. Synod, 1970–95 (Mem., Standing Cttee, 1975–95; Chm., Business Sub-Cttee, 1991–95); ACC, 1981–96 (Mem., Standing Cttee, 1981–96; Vice-Chm., 1986–90; Chm., 1990–96); Crown Appts Commn, 1982–92. Order of William Temple, Dio. of Manchester, 2011. DD Lambeth, 1992. *Publications:* Biblical Headship and the Ordination of Women, 1986; (ed) Open to the Spirit—Essays on Renewal, 1987; (contrib.) Authority in the Anglican Communion, 1987; (jtly) Anglicanism and the Universal Church, 1990; (ed) By Word and Deed, 1992; Debtor to Grace, 1998; The Silence of Eternity, 2003; Evangelical and Evolving: following the gospel in a changing world, 2006; Heaven Science and the Last Things, 2011; contrib. Anvil. *Address:* 12 Lever Park Avenue, Horwich, Bolton BL6 7LE. *T:* (01204) 699972. *E:* colbren@craston.fsnet.co.uk. *Club:* Union Jack.

CRATHORNE, 2nd Baron *cr* 1959; **(Charles) James Dugdale,** KCVO 2013; FSA; Bt 1945; Lord-Lieutenant of North Yorkshire, 1999–2014; *b* 12 Sept. 1939; *s* of 1st Baron Crathorne, PC, TD, and Nancy, OBE (*d* 1969), *d* of Sir Charles Tennant, 1st Bt; *S* father, 1977; *m* 1970, Sylvia Mary (*d* 2009), *yr d* of Brig. Arthur Herbert Montgomery, OBE, TD; one *s* two *d. Educ:* Eton College; Trinity Coll., Cambridge. MA Cantab (Fine Arts). FSA 2009. Impressionist and Modern Painting Dept, Sotheby & Co., 1963–66; Assistant to the President, Parke-Bernet, New York, 1966–69; James Dugdale & Associates, London, Independent Fine Art Consultancy Service, 1969–77; James Crathorne & Associates, 1977–; Director: Woodhouse Securities, 1989–99; Cliveden Ltd, 1999–2002; Hand Picked Hotels Ltd, 2001–02. Member: Yorks Regl Cttee, NT, 1978–84 and 1988–94; Council, RSA, 1982–88; Exec. Cttee, Georgian Gp, 1985–99 (Chm., 1990–99); Cons. Adv. Gp on Arts and Heritage, 1988–98; Chm., Jt Cttee, Nat. Amenity Socs, 1996–99 (Dep. Chm., 1993–96); President: Cleveland Assoc., NT, 1982–96; Hambledon Dist, CPRE, 1988–; Cleveland Family History Soc., 1988–; Middlesbrough Sea Cadets, 1988–2014; Cleveland and N Yorks Br., 1997–2003, Cleveland and S Durham Br., 2003–14, Magistrates' Assoc.; Cleveland Search and Rescue Team, 1998–; Yorks and Humberside RFCA, 2005–08 (Vice Pres., 1999–2005); Yorks Agricultural Soc., 2014–15; Vice President: Cleveland Wildlife Trust, 1990–; Public Monuments and Sculpture Assoc., 1997–; N Yorks County Scouts, 1998–2014; N of England RFCA, 2001–14; Patron, Cleveland Community Foundn, 1990–. Member: Works of Art Sub-Cttee, H of L, 1983–2001 (Chm., 2004–07); Editorial Bd, House Magazine, 1983–; Hon. Secretary: All-Party Parly Arts and Heritage Gp, 1981– (Chm., 2010–); All-Party Photography Gp, 1997–; elected Mem., H of L, 1999. Trustee: Captain Cook Trust, 1978– (Chm., 1993–); Georgian Theatre Royal, Richmond, Yorks, 1970–; Nat. Heritage Meml Fund, 1992–95; Patron: Attingham Trust for Study of the British Country House, 1991–; Middlesbrough Inst. of Modern Art, 2012–; Hon. Patron, Friends of Yorks Sculpture Park, 1992–2009. Church Warden, All Saints, Crathorne, 1977–. Annual lecture tours to America, 1970–90; lecture series, Metropolitan Mus., NY, 1981; Australian Bicentennial Lecture Tour, 1988. Member Court: Univ. of Leeds, 1985–97; Univ. of York, 1999–; Univ. of Hull, 1999–2014; Gov., Queen Margaret's Sch. York Ltd, 1986–99. FRSA 1972. DL Cleveland, 1983, N Yorks, 1996; JP N Yorks, 1999. Freeman: Town of Richmond, N Yorks, 2014; City of York, 2015. Hon. LLD Teesside, 2013. KStJ 1999. Golden Jubilee Medal, 2002; Diamond Jubilee Medal, 2012. *Exhibitions:* Photographs: Middlesbrough Art Gall., 1980; Georgian Th. Royal, Richmond, N Yorks, 2005; All Party Photography Gp annual exhibn, Westminster and touring, 1992–. *Publications:* Edouard Vuillard, 1967; (co-author) Tennant's Stalk, 1973; (co-author) A Present from Crathorne, 1989; Cliveden: the place and the people, 1995; The Royal Crescent Book of Bath, 1998; (co-photographer) Parliament in Pictures, 1999; contribs to Apollo and The Connoisseur. *Recreations:* photography, travel, collecting, country pursuits, jazz. *Heir: s* Hon. Thomas Arthur John Dugdale, *b* 30 Sept. 1977. *Address:* Crathorne House, Yarm, N Yorks TS15 0AT. *T:* (01642) 700431; House of Lords, SW1A 0PW. *T:* (020) 7219 5224. *E:* crathornej@parliament.uk, james.crathorne@btconnect.com. *Clubs:* Garrick, Pratt's.

CRAUFURD, Sir Robert (James), 9th Bt *cr* 1781; *b* 18 March 1937; *s* of Sir James Gregan Craufurd, 8th Bt and Ruth Marjorie (*d* 1998), *d* of Frederic Corder; *S* father, 1970; *m* 1st, 1964, Catherine Penelope (marr. diss.), *yr d* of late Captain Horatio Westmacott, Torquay; three *d*; 2nd, 1987, Georgina Anne, *d* of late John D. Russell, Lymington. *Educ:* Harrow; University College, Oxford. Elected Member of the London Stock Exchange, 1969. *Address:* East Grove, Grove Road, Lymington, Hants SO41 3RF.

CRAUSBY, David Anthony; MP (Lab) Bolton North East, since 1997; *b* 17 June 1946; *s* of Thomas Crausby and Kathleen Lavin; *m* 1965, Enid Anne Noon; two *s. Educ:* Derby Grammar Sch., Bury. Apprentice centre lathe turner, 1962, skilled turner, 1967; Works Convenor, AEEU (formerly AEU), 1978–97. Mem (Lab) Bury MDC, 1979–92. Contested (Lab): Bury N, 1987; Bolton NE, 1992. *Recreations:* football, walking, cinema. *Address:* (office) 426 Blackburn Road, Bolton BL1 8NL. *T:* (01204) 303340.

CRAVEN, family name of **Earl of Craven.**

CRAVEN, 9th Earl of, *cr* 1801; **Benjamin Robert Joseph Craven;** Baron Craven, 1665; Viscount Uffington, 1801; *b* 13 June 1989; *s* of 8th Earl and of Teresa Maria Bernadette Craven; *S* father, 1990. *Heir: cousin* Rupert José Evelyn Craven, Lt-Comdr RN [*b* 22 March 1926; *m* 1st, 1955, Margaret Campbell (*d* 1985), *d* of Alexander Smith, MBE; 2nd, 2000, Susan Lilian Margaret Eaton].

CRAVEN, Janet; *see* Morrison, J. R.

CRAVEN, Sir John (Anthony), Kt 1996; Member, Board of Managing Directors, Deutsche Bank AG, Frankfurt, 1990–96; Chairman, Morgan Grenfell, later Deutsche Morgan Grenfell, Group PLC, 1989–97 (Chief Executive, 1987–89); *b* 23 Oct. 1940; *s* of William Herbert Craven and Hilda Lucy Craven; *m* 1st, 1961, Gillian Margaret (*née* Murray); one *s* one *d*; 2nd, 1970, Jane Frances (*née* Stiles-Allen); three *s*; 3rd, 2005, Ning Chang (*d* 2009). *Educ:* Michaelhouse, S Africa; Jesus Coll., Cambridge (BA Hons Law); Queen's Univ., Kingston, Ont. Clarkson Gordon & Co., Toronto, Chartered Accountants, 1961–64; Wood Gundy, Investment Bankers, 1964–67; S. G. Warburg & Co., 1967–73, Dir 1969–73; Gp Chief Exec., White Weld & Co. Ltd, 1973–78; Vice Chm., S. G. Warburg & Co., 1979; Founder and Chm., Phoenix Securities Ltd, 1981–89; Dir, Mercury Securities Ltd, 1979. Non-executive Chairman: Tootal Group PLC, 1985–91; Lonmin plc (formerly Lonrho), 1997–2009; GEMS Funds, HK, 1998–; Fleming Family & Partners, 2003–07 (non-exec. Dir, 2000); Patagonia Gold plc, 2004–13; Director: Rothmans Internat. NV, 1993–95; Rothmans Internat. BV, 1995–99; non-executive Director: Reuters plc, 1997–2004; Robert Fleming Hldgs Ltd, 1999–2000; Ducati Motor Hldgs SpA, 1999–2000. Mem., Conseil d'Administration, Société

Générale de Surveillance, Switzerland, 1989–98; Dir, SIB, 1990–93. Mem. Bd, Royal Marsden NHS Trust, 2008–15. Former Member: Ontario Inst. of Chartered Accts; Canadian Inst. of Chartered Accountants. *Recreation:* ski-ing. *Club:* White's.

CRAVEN, Prof. John Anthony George, CBE 2013; Vice-Chancellor, University of Portsmouth, 1997–2013; *b* 17 June 1949; *s* of late George Marriott Craven and Dorothy Maude Craven (*née* Walford); *m* 1974, Laura Elizabeth Loftis; one *s* one *d*. *Educ:* Pinner GS; King's Coll., Cambridge (BA 1970; MA 1974). Kennedy Meml Schol., MIT, 1970–71; University of Kent at Canterbury: Lectr in Econs, 1971–76; Sen. Lectr, 1976–80; Reader, 1980–86; Prof., 1986–96; Dean of Faculty, Social Scis, 1987–91; Pro Vice-Chancellor, 1991–93; Dep. Vice-Chancellor, 1993–96. Vis. Associate Prof., Univ. of Guelph, 1982–83. Chm., University Alliance, 2006–09; Mem. Bd, UUK, 2006–12. Mem., Archbishops' Council, 2006–13. Chair, St Martin's Trust for the Homeless, 1987–96. Governor: South Kent Coll., 1991–96; Highbury Coll., 1997–2003; St Luke's Sch., Portsmouth, 2002–09; Mem. Bd, UWE, 2014–. Dir, New Th. Royal, Portsmouth, 1999–2010; Mem. Bd, Nat. Mus. of the Royal Navy, 2008–. FRSA. Hon. DSc: Univ. Teknologi, Malaysia; Southampton, 2013; Hon. DLaws Portsmouth, 2013. *Publications:* The Distribution of the Product, 1979; Introduction to Economics, 1984, 2nd edn 1990; Social Choice, 1992; articles in learned jls. *Recreations:* gardening, choral singing, house restoration. *Address:* Fyning Cross, Rogate, Petersfield GU31 5EF. *T:* (01730) 821392. *E:* jagcraven@yahoo.com.

CRAVEN, Sir Philip (Lee), Kt 2005; MBE 1991; President, International Paralympic Committee, since 2001; *b* 4 July 1950; *s* of Herbert and Hilda Craven; *m* 1974, Jocelyne Halgand; one *s* one *d*. *Educ:* Manchester Univ. (BA Hons (Geog.) 1972). Hd of Secretariat, British Coal Corp., 1986–91; Pres., 1989–2002, CEO, 1994–98, Internat. Wheelchair Basketball Fedn; Performance Dir, GB Men's Wheelchair Basketball Team, 1998–2001. Played wheelchair basketball for GB, 1969–93: Team Captain, 1982–88; Gold Medal, Commonwealth Games, 1970; European Championships: Bronze Medal, 1970; Gold Medal, 1971, 1973, 1974; Silver Medal, 1993; 4th Place, Paralympic Games, 1974; Bronze Medal, World Championship, 1975; Silver Medal, Internat. Stoke Mandeville Games, 1986; Gold Medal, European Champions Cup, 1994; Nat. Table Tennis Champion, 1977. Chm., GB Wheelchair Basketball Assoc., 1977–80, 1984–87 and 1989–94. International Olympic Committee: Mem., 2003–; Member: Sport and Envmt Commn, 2002–05; 2008 Beijing Co-ordination Commn, 2002–08; Culture and Olympic Educn Commn, 2005–; Bd, LOCOG, 2005–13. Foundn Bd Mem., World Anti-Doping Agency, 2002–12. Hon. Fellow, Liverpool John Moores Univ., 2009. Hon. DSc: Manchester Metropolitan, 2006; Stirling, 2010; Hon. LLD: Nottingham, 2007; York St John, 2013; DUniv: Staffordshire, 2008; Manchester, 2012; Bolton, 2013; Chester, 2015; Hon. Dr Worcester, 2012. Sports Industry Awards—Lifetime Achievement, 2012. Medaille d'argent de la Jeunesse et des Sports (France), 1973; Gold Medal: City of Athens, 2004; City of Turin, 2006; Key to City of Beijing, 2008. Grande Ufficiale, Order of Merit (Italy), 2006; Chevalier, Ordre Ducal de la Croix de Bourgogne (France), 2007; Order of Friendship (Russia), 2012; Order of Honour (Russia), 2014; Officier de la Légion d'Honneur (France), 2014. *Recreations:* playing wheelchair basketball, gardening, the culture of wine. *Address:* International Paralympic Committee, Adenauerallee 212–214, 53113 Bonn, Germany. *T:* (228) 2097200, *Fax:* (228) 2097209. *E:* info@paralympic.org.

CRAWFORD, 29th Earl of, *cr* 1398, **AND BALCARRES**, 12th Earl of, *cr* 1651; **Robert Alexander Lindsay,** KT 1996; GCVO 2002; PC 1972; Lord Lindsay of Crawford, before 1143; Lord Lindsay of Balcarres, 1633; Lord Balniel, 1651; Baron Wigan (UK), 1826; Baron Balniel (Life Peer), 1974; Premier Earl of Scotland; Head of House of Lindsay; Lord Chamberlain to the Queen Mother, 1992–2002; *b* 5 March 1927; *er s* of 28th Earl of Crawford and 11th of Balcarres, KT, GBE, and Mary (*d* 1994), 3rd *d* of late Lord Richard Cavendish, PC, CB, CMG; *S* father, 1975; *m* 1949, Ruth Beatrice, *d* of Leo Meyer-Bechtler, Zürich; two *s* two *d*. *Educ:* Eton; Trinity College, Cambridge. Served with Grenadier Guards, 1945–49. MP (C) Hertford, 1955–74, Welwyn and Hatfield, Feb.–Sept. 1974; Parliamentary Private Secretary: to Financial Secretary of Treasury, 1955–57; to Minister of Housing and Local Government, 1957–60; Opposition front-bench spokesman on health and social security, 1967–70; Minister of State for Defence, 1970–72; Minister of State for Foreign and Commonwealth Affairs, 1972–74. First Crown Estate Comr, 1980–85. Chairman: Lombard North Central Bank, 1976–80; Abela Hldgs (UK), 1983–95; Director: Nat. Westminster Bank, 1975–88; Scottish American Investment Co., 1978–88; a Vice-Chm., Sun Alliance & London Insurance Gp, 1975–91. President, Rural District Councils Assoc., 1959–65; Chairman: National Association for Mental Health, 1963–70; Historic Buildings Council for Scotland, 1976–83; Royal Commn on Ancient and Historical Monuments of Scotland, 1985–95; Bd of Trustees, Nat. Library of Scotland, 1990–2000. Hon. FRIAS; Hon. Fellow, Nat. Library of Scotland, 2012. DL Fife, 1976–2003. *Heir: s* Lord Balniel, *qv*. *Address:* House of Lords, SW1A 0PW.

CRAWFORD, Alex Christine, OBE 2012; Special Correspondent, based in Africa, Sky TV News, since 2011; *b* UK, 15 April 1962; *d* of Max Crawford and Emma Crawford (*née* Hale); *m* 1988, Richard Edmondson; one *s* three *d*. *Educ:* St John's Convent, Kitwe, Zambia; Chisipite Sch., Harare, Zimbabwe; Cobham Hall Sch., Kent; Open Univ.; Thomson Regl Newspapers Trng, Newcastle; Nat. Council for Trng of Journalists; BBC TV and Radio Trng, London. Reporter: Wokingham Times, 1981–83; BBC Radio Nottingham, 1983–85; BBC Radio News, London, 1985–86; sub-editor, BBC TV, London, 1986–88; producer, TV-am, 1988–89; Sky News: news producer, 1989–91; news corresp., 1991–2004; news corresp., Channel 5, 2004–05; Asia corresp., based in India, Sky News, 2005–10; Special corresp., based in UAE, Sky TV News, 2010–11. Hon. Dr Univ. of Arts London, 2012. Journalist of Year, RTS, 2007, 2009, 2010, 2011; Golden Nymph Award, Monte Carlo, 2010, 2011, 2012; News and Factual Award, 2010, Achievement of the Year, 2011, Women in Film and TV; Internat. Emmy Award for News Coverage, 2010; Story of the Year, For. Press Assoc., 2011; James Cameron Award, 2011; Broadcasting Journalist of Year, London Press Club, 2011; Bayeux War Corresp. Winner, 2011; Red's Hot Women Award, Red Mag., 2011. *Publications:* Colonel Gaddafi's Hat, 2012. *Recreations:* scuba diving, swimming, tennis, horse riding, running, parachuting, ski-ing, trekking, cycling, exploring, painting, writing, obsessively checking Blackberry. *Address:* c/o Sky TV News, 6 Centaurs Business Park, Grant Way, Osterley, Isleworth, Middx TW7 5QD. *T:* (020) 7705 3000. *E:* alex.crawford@bskyb.com.

CRAWFORD, Alistair Stephen; Chairman: Access IS, since 2013; FutureGov Ltd, since 2014; *b* 4 Jan. 1953; *s* of late Daniel Clark Crawford and Joan Crawford; *m* 1981, Susan Potter; two *d*. *Educ:* Oriel Coll., Oxford (MA Jurisprudence). Pres. and CEO, Computer Sciences Corp. (UK), 1989–94; Sen. Vice Pres., Oracle Corp., 1995–2000; Chief Operating Officer, CMG plc, 2001; CEO, Logica CMG plc, 2002–03; Chief Exec., Psion, 2003–06; Chm., Lysanda Ltd, 2008–11. *Club:* Reform.

CRAWFORD, Prof. Andrew Charles, FRS 1990; Professor of Neurophysiology, Cambridge University, since 1992; Fellow of Trinity College, Cambridge, since 1974; *b* 12 Jan. 1949; *s* of Charles and Vera Crawford; *m* 1974, Catherine Jones; one *s* one *d*. *Educ:* King Edward VI Camp Hill Sch., Birmingham; Downing Coll., Cambridge (BA 1970); Emmanuel Coll., Cambridge (MA, PhD 1974). Cambridge University: Research Fellow, Emmanuel Coll., 1972; Univ. Demonstrator, 1974; Lectr, 1977; Reader in Sensory Physiology, 1987. *Publications:* contribs on physiology of hearing, in learned jls. *Address:* Department of Physiology, Development and Neuroscience, Physiological Laboratory, Downing Street, Cambridge CB2 3EG. *T:* (01223) 333879.

CRAWFORD, Bruce; *see* Crawford, R. H. B.

CRAWFORD, Prof. Carolin Susan, PhD; Public Astronomer (formerly Outreach Officer), Institute of Astronomy, University of Cambridge, since 2005; Fellow and College Lecturer, Emmanuel College, Cambridge, since 2004; Gresham Professor of Astronomy, since 2011; *b* Guildford, 10 Dec. 1963; *d* of Laurence and Elsie Crawford; *m* 1991, Prof. Andrew Christopher Fabian, *qv*; two *s*. *Educ:* Newnham Coll., Cambridge (BA Hons 1985; PhD 1988). Skynner-Radcliffe Res. Fellow, Balliol Coll., Oxford, 1988–91; Res. Fellow, Trinity Hall, Cambridge, 1991–94; University of Cambridge: SERC Postdoctoral Fellow, 1991–93, PPARC Advanced Fellow, 1994–96, Inst. of Astronomy; Royal Soc. Res. Fellow, 1996–2007; Associate Lectr in Astronomy, Newnham Coll., Cambridge, 2002–04. *Recreations:* reading, gardening. *Address:* Emmanuel College, St Andrews Street, Cambridge CB2 3AP; Institute of Astronomy, Madingley Road, Cambridge CB3 0HA. *T:* (01223) 337510. *E:* csc@ast.cam.ac.uk.

CRAWFORD, Charles Graham, CMG 1998; HM Diplomatic Service, retired; professional mediator, since 2008; speechwriter, negotiations expert and communication skills consultant, since 2008; *b* 22 May 1954; *s* of Graham Wellington James Crawford and Edith Ellen Crawford; *m* 1990, Helen Margaret Walsh; two *s* one *d*. *Educ:* St John's Coll., Oxford (BA Hons Jurisprudence 1976); Lincoln's Inn (part II Bar exams 1977); Fletcher Sch. of Law and Diplomacy, Boston, USA (MA 1979). Entered FCO, 1979; Second, later First Sec., Belgrade, 1981–84; FCO (air services then speechwriter), 1984–87; First Sec., Pretoria/Cape Town, 1987–91; FCO, 1991–93; Political Counsellor, Moscow, 1993–96; Ambassador to Bosnia and Herzegovina, 1996–98; Weatherhead Center for Internat. Affairs, Harvard Univ., 1998–99; Dep. Political Dir, FCO, 1999–2000; Dir, SE Europe, FCO, 2000; Ambassador to Federal Republic of Yugoslavia, subseq. Serbia and Montenegro, 2001–03; Ambassador to Poland, 2003–07. Qualified Mediator, 2007. Founder Partner, Ambassador Partnership (formerly ADRg Ambassadors), 2010–. *Recreations:* chess, music, writing/website. *E:* charlescrawf@gmail.com. *W:* www.charlescrawford.biz.

CRAWFORD, Sir Frederick (William), Kt 1986; DL; FREng; Chairman, Criminal Cases Review Commission, 1996–2003; Vice-Chancellor, Aston University, 1980–96; *b* 28 July 1931; *s* of William and Victoria Maud Crawford; *m* 1963, Béatrice M. J. Hutter, LèsL, MA, PhD, Paris; one *d* (one *s* decd). *Educ:* George Dixon Grammar Sch., Birmingham; Univ. of London (BSc Eng (1st cl. hons) 1952; MSc 1958; DSc 1975); Univ. of Liverpool (DipEd 1956; PhD 1955; DEng 1965); Open Univ. (DipStat 2006; BA Maths (1st cl. hons) 2007; MSc Maths 2015). Pres., Guild of Undergraduates, 1955–56, Mem. Court, 1955–62 and 1981–2013, Univ. of Liverpool; Treas., NUS, 1957–59; Winner, NUS-Observer Fifth Nat. Student Debating Tourn., 1958, followed by ESU debating tour of USA. FInstP 1964; FAPS 1965; FIET (FIEE 1965); FIEEE 1972; FIMA 1978; FREng (FEng 1985). Research Trainee, J. Lucas Ltd, 1948–52; Scientist, NCB Mining Res. Estabt, 1956–57; Sen. Lectr in Elec. Engrg, CAT Birmingham, 1958–59; Stanford University, California, 1959–82: Res. Associate, W. W. Hansen Labs of Physics, 1959–64; Institute for Plasma Research: Prof. (Research), 1964–67; Associate Prof., 1967–69; Prof., 1969–82; Consulting Prof., 1983–84; Chm., 1974–80; Dir, Centre for Interdisciplinary Res., 1973–77. Vis. Scientist, French Atomic Energy Commn, and Cons. to Comp. Française Thomson-Houston, 1961–62; Visiting Professor: Japan, 1969; Univ. of Paris, 1971; Australia, 1972; Mathematical Inst., Oxford Univ., 1977–78; Vis. Fellow, St Catherine's Coll., Oxford, 1977–78, 1996–97. Union Radio-Scientifique Internationale: Mem., US Nat. Cttee, 1975–81, UK Nat. Cttee, 1980–84; Commn H (Waves in Plasmas): US Chm., 1975–78; Internat. Chm., 1978–81; UK Rep., 1982–84; Chm. Internat. Sci. Cttee, Internat. Conf. on Phenomena in Ionised Gases, 1979–81; Universities Space Research Association: Member: Council, 1973–81 (Chm. 1977–78); Bd of Trustees, 1975–81 (Chm. 1976–77). Dir, Sigma Xi, 1976–78; Mem. Council, Amer. Assoc. of Univ. Profs, 1980–82; Vice-Chm., CVCP, 1993–95; Dir, HEQC, 1994–96; Vice-Pres., Parly and Scientific Cttee, 1992–95 (Vice-Chm., 1989–92). Member: Council, IEE, 1985–88, 1989–92 and 1993–96; Smeatonian Soc. of Civil Engrs, 1995. Director: Birmingham Technology Ltd, 1982–96; West Midlands Technology Transfer Centre, 1985–93; Legal & General Gp plc, 1988–97; Rexam (formerly Bowater) plc, 1989–97; PowerGen plc, 1990–2002. Member: US-UK Educnl (Fulbright) Commn, 1981–84; British-North American Cttee, 1987–2013; Franco-British Council, 1987–98; Vice-President: Birmingham Civic Soc., 1990– (Chm., 1983–88). Founder Mem., Lunar Soc., Birmingham, 1991–. Freeman, City of London, 1986; Master: Co. of Engineers, 1996; Co. of Information Technologists, 2000. High Sheriff, W Midlands, 1995, DL W Midlands, 1995. Hon. Bencher, Inner Temple, 1996. CCMI (CBIM 1986; Special Award for Univ. Mgt, 1992). Hon. FCIL (Hon. FIL 1987). Hon. DSc Buckingham, 1996. *Publications:* numerous papers on plasma physics and higher educn. *Address:* 47 Charlbury Road, Oxford OX2 6UX. *T:* (01865) 554 707. *Club:* Athenæum.

CRAWFORD, Geoffrey Douglas, CVO 2000 (LVO 1995); Director of Strategy and Communications, Australian Broadcasting Corporation, 2003–05; *b* 29 Sept. 1950; *s* of late Rev. Canon Douglas Crawford and Edna Crawford; *m* 1st, 1980 (marr. diss.); one *s* two *d*; 2nd, 1998, Catherine Banks. *Educ:* King's Sch., Parramatta, NSW; Univ. of Sydney (BA Hons); American Univ., Cairo. Entered Australian Dept of Foreign Affairs, 1974: Third Sec., Port Moresby, 1974–75; Vice-Consul, Lae, 1975–76; lang. trng, Cairo, 1978–80; Second Sec., then First Sec., Jeddah, 1980–82; First Sec., Baghdad, 1983–84; seconded as Asst Press Sec. to the Queen, 1988–93; transferred to Civil List, 1991; Dep. Press Sec., 1993–97, Press Sec. to the Queen, 1997–2000; Consultant, Edelman Public Relations Worldwide (Sydney), 2001–02; Dir, Corp. Affairs, Australian Broadcasting Corp., 2002–03. *Recreations:* cricket, classical and jazz music, reading, swimming. *Address:* Villa 1, The Maples, 117 Bowral Street, Bowral, NSW 2576, Australia.

CRAWFORD, Iain; Director, Veterinary Field Service, Ministry of Agriculture, Fisheries and Food, 1988–98; *b* 8 April 1938; *s* of James and Agnes Crawford, Baillieston, Glasgow; *m* 1962, Janette Mary Allan; two *s* one *d*. *Educ:* Coatbridge High Sch., Lanarks; Glasgow Univ. (BVMS). MRCVS 1961. Entered private vet. practice, 1961; joined MAFF as a Vet. Officer, 1968; Dep. Regl Vet. Officer, Bristol, 1981; Vet. Head of Sect. (Regl Vet. Officer), 1983; Asst Chief Vet. Officer, 1986. *Recreations:* sailing, walking.

CRAWFORD, Prof. Ian Andrew, PhD; FRAS; Professor of Planetary Science and Astrobiology, Birkbeck, University of London, since 2012; *b* Warrington, Cheshire, 13 Aug. 1961; *s* of Anthony Crawford and Joan Crawford (*née* Heighway); *m* 1988, Naoko Yamagata; one *s*. *Educ:* North Cestrian Grammar Sch., Altrincham; University Coll. London (BSc 1982; PhD 1988); Univ. of Newcastle upon Tyne (MSc 1983). FRAS 1984. Royal Soc. Overseas Res. Fellow, Mt Stromlo Observatory, Canberra, 1989; Res. Fellow, UCL, 1990–92; Royal Soc. Overseas Fellow, Anglo-Australian Observatory, Sydney, 1993; Sen. Res. Fellow, UCL, 1994–2002; Lectr, 2003–07, Sen. Lectr, 2007–09, Reader, 2009–12, Birkbeck, Univ. of London. Pres., Soc. for Popular Astronomy, 2006–08; Geophysical Sec., 2007–11, Sen. Sec., 2011–, RAS. Member: Eur. Space Scis Cttee, 2008–14; Human Spaceflight and Exploration Sci. Adv. Cttee, ESA, 2014–. *Publications:* contrib. over 150 papers to scientific and professional jls on astronomy, planetary sci., astrobiol. and space exploration. *Recreations:* reading, squash, classical music. *Address:* Department of Earth and Planetary Sciences, Birkbeck, University of London, Malet Street, WC1E 7HX. *T:* (020) 3073 8026. *E:* i.crawford@bbk.ac.uk.

CRAWFORD, Ian James; Director, Scottish Enterprise, 2008–12; *b* Peterborough, 27 July 1954; *s* of Henderson Crawford and Jane Crawford; *m* 1977, Sheila McNicol. *Educ:* John

Neilson High Sch., Paisley; Glasgow Univ. (BAcc 1975). Joined IBM UK Ltd, 1972; Site Dir, IBM Greenock, 1994–98; Vice Pres. Procurement, IBM Corp., 1998–2007. Mem., Mgt Cttee, Kilmarnock FC, 2009–13; Dir, Riverside Inverclyde, 2009–13. *Publications:* Clyde Shipwrecks, 1988, 3rd edn 2004; Argyll Shipwrecks, 1994, 2nd edn 2003. *Recreations:* golf, music, shipwreck research. *E:* ianjcrawfordvp@btinternet.com. *Clubs:* Loch Lomond Golf, Kilmacolm Golf; Los Flamingos Golf (Spain).

CRAWFORD, Prof. James Richard, AC 2013; DPhil, LLD; FBA 2000; a Judge, International Court of Justice, since 2015; Whewell Professor of International Law, University of Cambridge, 1992–2015; Fellow of Jesus College, Cambridge, 1992–2015, now Emeritus; *b* 14 Nov. 1948; *s* of James Allen and Josephine Margaret Crawford; *m* 1st, 1971, Marisa Luigina (marr. diss. 1991); two *d*; 2nd, 1992, Patricia Hyndman (marr. diss. 1998); two *d*; 3rd, 1998, Joanna Gomula (marr. diss. 2014); one *s*; 4th, 2014, Freya Baetens; one *s*. *Educ:* Adelaide Univ. (LLB Hons; BA 1971); Oxford Univ. (DPhil 1977); LLD Cantab 2004. Called to the Bar, High Court of Australia, 1979; SC, NSW, 1997. University of Adelaide: Lectr, 1974; Sen. Lectr, 1977; Reader, 1982; Prof. of Law, 1983; Challis Prof. of Internat. Law, 1986–92, Dean, Faculty of Law, 1990–92, Univ. of Sydney. Chm., Faculty Bd of Law, Univ. of Cambridge, 2003–06. Res. Prof. (pt-time), La Trobe Univ., 2011–14. Comr, Australian Law Reform Commn, 1982–90; Mem., UN Internat. Law Commn, 1992–2001. *Publications:* The Creation of States in International Law, 1979, 2nd edn 2006; Australian Courts of Law, 1982, 4th edn 2003; (ed) The Rights of Peoples, 1988; The International Law Commission's Articles on State Responsibility, 2002; International Law as an Open System, 2002; (ed) The Law of International Responsibility, 2010; (ed jtly) Cambridge Companion to International Law, 2012; Brownlie's Principles of International Law, 8th edn 2012; State Responsibility: the general part, 2012; Chance, Order, Change: the course of international law, 2014. *Recreations:* cricket, reading. *Address:* International Court of Justice, Carnegieplein, The Hague 2517 KJ, Netherlands. *E:* JRC3000@aol.com.

CRAWFORD, (Jeremy) Patrick (Stewart), CB 2013; Chief Executive, The Charity Bank Ltd, since 2012; *b* 16 Sept. 1952; *s* of Sir (Robert) Stewart Crawford, GCMG, CVO and Mary Katharine (*née* Corbett); *m* 1980, Charlotte Elizabeth Cecily Burnaby-Atkins; one *s* three *d*. *Educ:* Worcester Coll., Oxford (BA Juris.). Called to the Bar, Middle Temple, 1975; Morgan Grenfell & Co. Ltd, then Deutsche Morgan Grenfell, subseq. Deutsche Bank AG, 1976–2002: Man. Dir and Global Hd, Project and Export Finance, 1998–2001; Global Hd, Project Finance, 2001–02; Man. Dir, Emerging Africa Advisers, fund manager of Emerging Africa Infrastructure Fund, 2002–04; Chief Exec., ECGD, 2004–12. Non-executive Director: Crossrail Ltd, 2008–11; UK Trade and Investment, 2011–12; Caxton Trust, 2014–; Community Develt Finance Assoc., 2015–; Emerging Africa Infrastructure Fund Ltd, 2015–. *Address:* The Charity Bank Ltd, Fosse House, 182 High Street, Tonbridge, Kent TN9 1BE.

See also M. J. Crawford.

CRAWFORD, Lesley Jane; *see* Anderson, L. J.

CRAWFORD, Lionel Vivian, FRS 1988; Principal Scientist, Imperial Cancer Research Fund Tumour Virus Group, Department of Pathology, Cambridge University, 1988–95; *b* 30 April 1932; *s* of John Mitchell Crawford and Fanny May Crawford (*née* Barnett); *m* 1957, Elizabeth Minnie (*née* Green); one *d*. *Educ:* Rendcomb College, Cirencester; Emmanuel College, Cambridge (BA, MA, PhD). Virus Lab., Berkeley, Calif., 1958–59; Calif. Inst. of Technology, 1959–60; Inst. of Virology, Glasgow, 1960–68; Molecular Virology Lab., Imperial Cancer Res. Fund, 1968–88. Mem., EMBO. FRSE 1970. Gabor Medal, Royal Soc., 2005. *Publications:* numerous scientific articles. *Recreation:* wood-turning.

CRAWFORD, Prof. Michael Hewson, FBA 1980; Professor of Ancient History, University College London, 1986–2005, now Emeritus (Honorary Fellow, 2009–10); *b* 7 Dec. 1939; *s* of late Brian Hewson Crawford and Margarethe Bettina (*née* Nagel). *Educ:* St Paul's School; Oriel College, Oxford (BA, MA). Scholar, British School at Rome, 1962–64; Jane Eliza Procter Visiting Fellow, Princeton Univ., 1964–65; Cambridge University: Research Fellow, 1964–69, Fellow, 1969–86, Christ's Coll.; Lectr, 1969–86. Visiting Professor: Univ. of Pavia, 1983, 1992; Ecole Normale Supérieure, Paris, 1984; Univ. of Padua, 1986; Sorbonne, Paris, 1989; San Marino, 1989; Milan, 1990; L'Aquila, 1990; Ecole des Hautes Etudes, Paris, 1997; Ecole des Hautes Etudes en Sciences Sociales, Paris, 1999; Trento, 2007; Naples, 2009; Joseph Crabtree Orator, UCL, 2000. Joint Director: Excavations of Fregellae, 1980–86; Valpolcevera Project, 1987–93; Velleia Project, 1994–95; San Martino Project, 1996–99. Mem. Bd, UK Research Reserve, 2010–. Chm., JACT, 1992–95 (Chm., Ancient History Cttee, 1978–84); Vice-Pres., Roman Soc., 1981–. Membro Straniero, Istituto Lombardo, 1990; MAE 1995; Mem., Reial Acadèmia de Bones Lletres, 1998; Corresp. Member: Accademia Petrarca, 2004; Académie des Inscriptions et Belles Lettres, 2006. Editor: Papers of the British Sch. at Rome, 1975–79; Jl of Roman Studies, 1980–84. Officier, Ordre des Palmes Académiques (France), 2001. *Publications:* Roman Republican Coin Hoards, 1969; Roman Republican Coinage, 1974; The Roman Republic, 1978; La Moneta in Grecia e a Roma, 1981; (with D. Whitehead) Archaic and Classical Greece, 1982; Sources for Ancient History, 1983; Coinage and Money under the Roman Republic, 1985; (with M. Beard) Rome in the Late Republic, 1985; L'impero romano e la struttura economica e sociale delle province, 1986; (with A. M. Burnett) The Coinage of the Roman World in the Late Republic, 1987; (with C. Ligota and J. B. Trapp) Medals and Coins from Budé to Mommsen, 1990; (ed) Antonio Agustín between Renaissance and Counter-reform, 1993; (ed) Roman Statutes, 1995; (jtly) The Customs Law of Asia, 2008; Imagines Italicae, 2012; contribs to Annales, Athenaeum, Economic History Rev., Jl of Roman Studies, etc. *Address:* Department of History, University College London, Gower Street, WC1E 6BT.

CRAWFORD, Michael James, CMG 2008; HM Diplomatic Service, retired; independent consultant and writer; *b* London, 3 Feb. 1954; *s* of Sir (Robert) Stewart Crawford, GCMG, CVO and Mary Katharine Crawford (*née* Corbett); *m* 1984, Georgia Anne Moylan; two *s* one *d* (of whom one *s* one *d* are twins). *Educ:* University Coll., Oxford (BA Juris. 1975); St Antony's Coll., Oxford (MPhil Mid. Eastern Studies 1980). Called to the Bar, Inner Temple, 1978; joined FCO, 1981; Second, then First Sec., Cairo, 1983–84; First Secretary: Sana'a, 1985–86; Riyadh, 1986–90; FCO, 1990–92; Warsaw, 1992–95; FCO, 1995–99; Counsellor: Islamabad, 1999–2001; FCO, 2001–09. Vis. Fellow, Near East Dept, Princeton Univ., 2009; Consulting Sen. Fellow, IISS, 2010–11. *Recreations:* travel, reading and writing on Middle East and Islam, second-hand bookshops.

See also J. P. S. Crawford.

CRAWFORD, Michael Patrick, CBE 2014 (OBE 1987); actor, since 1955; *b* 19 Jan. 1942. *Educ:* St Michael's Coll., Bexley; Oakfield Sch., Dulwich. In orig. prodn of Britten's Noyes Fludde and of Let's Make an Opera; *stage appearances include:* Come Blow Your Horn, Prince of Wales, 1961; Travelling Light, 1965; The Anniversary, 1966; No Sex Please, We're British, Strand, 1971; Billy, Drury Lane, 1974; Same Time, Next Year, Prince of Wales, 1976; Flowers for Algernon, Queen's, 1979; Barnum, Palladium, 1981, 1983, Victoria Palace, 1985–86 (Olivier Award; Show Business Personality of the Year, Variety Club of GB); The Phantom of the Opera, Her Majesty's, 1986 (Olivier Award, Best Actor in a Musical), NY, 1988 (Tony Award, Best Actor in a Musical), Los Angeles, 1989; The Music of Andrew Lloyd Webber (concert tour), USA, Australia and UK, 1991–92; EFX, Las Vegas, 1995–96; Dance of the Vampires, NY, 2002–03; The Woman in White, Palace, 2004; The Wizard of Oz, London Palladium, 2011. *Films include:* Soap Box Derby; Blow Your Own Trumpet; Two Left Feet; The War Lover; Two Living, One Dead; The Knack, 1964 (Variety Club Award for Most Promising Newcomer); A Funny Thing Happened on the Way to the Forum, 1965; The Jokers, How I Won the War, 1966; Hello Dolly, 1968; The Games, 1969; Hello and Goodbye, 1970; Alice in Wonderland, 1972; The Condorman, 1980. Numerous radio broadcasts and TV appearances; *TV series include:* Some Mothers Do 'Ave 'Em; Chalk and Cheese. *Publications:* Parcel Arrived Safely: Tied with String (autobiog.), 1999. *Address:* c/o Knight Ayton Management, 35 Great James Street, WC1N 3HB. *T:* (020) 7831 4400.

CRAWFORD, Patrick; *see* Crawford, J. P. S.

CRAWFORD, His Honour Peter John; QC 1976; a Senior Circuit Judge, 1992–2002 (a Circuit Judge, 1988–92); *b* 23 June 1930; *s* of William Gordon Robertson and Doris Victoria Robertson (*née* Mann, subseq. Crawford); *m* 1st, 1955, Jocelyn Lavender (marr. diss.; she *d* 2004); two *s* two *d*; 2nd, 1979, Ann Allen Travis. *Educ:* Berkhamsted Sch.; Brasenose Coll., Oxford (MA). Intelligence Corps (Field Security, Hong Kong), 1948–49. Called to Bar, Lincoln's Inn, 1953; Bencher, 1984; a Recorder, 1974–88; Resident Judge, Oxford Crown Court, 1991–92; Recorder of Birmingham, 1992–2001; Additional Judge, Court of Appeal (Criminal Div.), 1995–2002; Hon. Recorder of Oxford, 2001–02. Pres., Trent Region, Mental Health Review Tribunal, 1986–2002; Vice Chm., Appeal Cttee, ICA, 1987–88; Member: Council of Justice, 1986–88; Parole Bd, 1992–96. Chm., Disciplinary Ct, Univ. of Oxford, 2004–10. Associate, Kathryn Redway Associates, 2004–. Mem., Paddington Borough Council, 1962–65; Chm., W London Family Service Unit, 1972–79; Mem., Family Service Units Nat. Council, 1975–81. Hon. Pres., English Nat. Sect., Internat. Assoc. of Penal Law, 1998–2002. *Recreation:* gardening. *Address:* Wheatsheaf House, The Green, Culworth, Banbury OX17 2BB. *E:* pj.crawford@btinternet.com. *Club:* Royal Over-Seas League.

CRAWFORD, Prof. Robert, DPhil; FBA 2011; FRSE, FEA; Professor of Modern Scottish Literature, since 1995, and Bishop Wardlaw Professor of Poetry, since 2011, School of English, University of St Andrews; *b* 23 Feb. 1959; *s* of Robert Alexander Nelson Crawford and Elizabeth Menzies Crawford; *m* 1988, Alice Wales; one *s* one *d*. *Educ:* Hutchesons' Grammar Sch., Glasgow; Univ. of Glasgow (MA Hons 1981); Balliol Coll., Oxford (DPhil 1985). Elizabeth Wordsworth Jun. Res. Fellow, St Hugh's Coll., Oxford, 1984–87; British Acad. Postdoctoral Res. Fellow, Univ. of Glasgow, 1987–89; University of St Andrews: Lectr in Modern Scottish Lit., 1989–95; Hd, Sch. of English, 2002–05. Ed., Verse mag., 1984–95; Poetry Ed., Polygon, 1991–99. FRSE 1999; FEA 1999. *Publications:* The Savage and the City in the Works of T. S. Eliot, 1987; A Scottish Assembly, 1990; (with W. N. Herbert) Sharawaggi, 1990; (ed) Other Tongues, 1990; (ed jtly) About Edwin Morgan, 1990; The Arts of Alasdair Gray, 1991; Talkies, 1992; Devolving English Literature, 1992, 2nd edn 2000; (ed jtly) Reading Douglas Dunn, 1992; Identifying Poets, 1993; (ed jtly) Liz Lochhead's Voices, 1993; (ed jtly) Talking Verse, 1995; Literature in Twentieth-Century Scotland, 1995; Masculinity, 1996; (ed) Robert Burns and Cultural Authority, 1997; (ed) The Scottish Invention of English Literature, 1998; (ed jtly) The Penguin Book of Poetry from Britain and Ireland since 1945, 1998; Spirit Machines, 1999; (ed jtly) The New Penguin Book of Scottish Verse, 2000; (ed jtly) Scottish Religious Poetry, 2000; The Modern Poet, 2001; The Tip of My Tongue, 2003; (ed) Heaven-Taught Fergusson, 2003; Selected Poems, 2005; (ed) The Book of St Andrews, 2005; (ed) Apollos of the North, 2006; (ed) Contemporary Poetry and Contemporary Science, 2006; Scotland's Books: the Penguin history of Scottish literature, 2007; Full Volume, 2008; The Bard, Robert Burns, a Biography, 2009; (ed jtly) The Best Laid Schemes, 2009; (ed) New Poems, Chiefly in the Scottish Dialect, 2009; The Beginning and the End of the World, 2011; Simonides, 2011; On Glasgow and Edinburgh, 2013; Bannockburns, 2014; Testament, 2014; Young Eliot: from St Louis to 'The Waste Land', 2015. *Recreations:* walking, Scottish nationalism, internationalism, Anglophilia. *Address:* School of English, University of St Andrews, St Andrews, Fife KY16 9AL. *T:* (01334) 462666, *Fax:* (01334) 462655.

CRAWFORD, (Robert Hardie) Bruce; JP; Member (SNP) Stirling, Scottish Parliament, since 2007 (Scotland Mid and Fife, 1999–2007); *b* 16 Feb. 1955; *s* of Robert and Wilma Crawford; *m* 1980, Jacqueline Hamilton Scott; three *s*. *Educ:* Kinross High Sch.; Perth High Sch. Personnel Officer, then Equal Opportunities Officer, later Develt Advr, Scottish Office, 1974–99. Member (SNP): Perth and Kinross DC, 1988–96; Perth and Kinross Council, 1995–99 (Leader, 1995–99). Scottish Parliament: Opposition Chief Whip, 1999; Opposition frontbench spokesman on transport and the envmt, 2000–01, on envmt and energy, 2001–03, on Parliament, 2003–07; Minister for Parly Business, 2007–11; Cabinet Sec. for Parly Business and Govt Strategy, 2011–12. Business Convenor, SNP, 2005–. Member Board: Scottish Enterprise Tayside, 1996–99; Perthshire Tourist Bd, 1996–99; Perth Coll., 1996–99. Chairman: Perth and Kinross Recreational Facilities Ltd, 1996–99; Kinross-shire Partnership Ltd, 1998–99. JP Perth, Kinross, 1993. *Recreations:* politics, golf, football. *Address:* Scottish Parliament, Edinburgh EH99 1SP. *T:* (0131) 348 5686.

CRAWFORD, Prof. Robert James, (Roy), CNZM 2015; FREng; Vice-Chancellor, University of Waikato, since 2005; *b* 6 April 1949; *s* of Robert James Crawford and Teresa Harriet Crawford; *m* 1974, Isobel Catherine Allen; two *s* one *d*. *Educ:* Queen's Univ., Belfast (BSc 1st cl. Hons Mech. Engrg 1970; PhD 1973; DSc 1987). FREng 1997; FIPENZ 2006. Queen's University, Belfast: Asst Lectr in Engrg, 1972–74; Lectr, 1974–82; Sen. Lectr, 1982–84; Reader, 1984–89; Prof. of Engrg Materials, 1989–2005; Dir, Sch. of Mechanical and Process Engrg, 1989–97; Dir, Polymer Processing Res. Centre, 1996–2005; Pro-Vice-Chancellor, 2001–05. Director: Rotosystems Ltd, 1991–2005; Hughes & McLeod Ltd, 1993–. *Publications:* Plastics Engineering, 1981, 3rd edn 1998; Mechanics of Engineering Materials, 1987, 2nd edn 1996; Rotational Moulding of Plastics, 1992, 2nd edn 1996; (with J. L. Throne) Rotational Molding Technology, 2002; (with M. P. Kearns) Practical Guide to Rotational Moulding, 2003, 2nd edn 2012. *Recreations:* reading, golf. *Address:* Vice-Chancellor's Office, University of Waikato, Private Bag 3105, Hamilton, New Zealand.

CRAWFORD, Dr Robert McKay, CBE 2004; Chairman, Economic Development Association Scotland, since 2014; *b* 14 June 1951; *s* of Robert and Catherine Crawford; *m* 1975, Linda Acheson; one *s* one *d*. *Educ:* Strathclyde Univ. (BA Hons Politics); Harvard Univ. (John F. Kennedy Schol.); Glasgow Univ. (PhD Govt 1982). Leverhulme Fellow, Fraser of Allander Inst., Strathclyde Univ., 1983–85; Develt Exec., 1985–87, Manager of US Desk, 1987–89, SDA; Dir, N America, 1989–91, Dir, 1991–94, Locate in Scotland; Man. Dir, Scottish Enterprise Ops, 1994–96; Sen. Specialist in Investment, World Bank, 1996–98; Partner, Ernst & Young, 1998–2000; Chief Exec., Scottish Enterprise, 2000–04; Hd of Strategy and Special Projects, Wood Gp, 2004–05; Chief Exec., Mersey Partnership, 2005–06; Exec. Dir, Business Develt and Commercialisation, Glasgow Caledonian Univ., 2006–08; Gp Exec. Dir, Ops, SEEDA, 2008; Dir, Orgnl Develt, States of Jersey, 2012–14. Chm., Invest Thames Gateway, 2010. FRSA 1995. *Recreations:* running, reading, modern history, economics, biography.

CRAWFORD, Sir Robert (William Kenneth), Kt 2007; CBE 2002; Director-General, Imperial War Museum, 1995–2008 (Deputy Director-General, 1982–95); *b* 3 July 1945; *s* of late Hugh Merrall Crawford, FCA, and Mary Crawford (*née* Percival); *m* 1975, Vivienne Sylvia Polakowski; one *d* one *s*. *Educ:* Culford Sch.; Pembroke Coll., Oxford (Cleoburey Schol.; BA). Joined Imperial War Museum as Research Asst, 1968: Head of Research and Information Office, 1971–89; Keeper, Dept of Photographs, 1975–83; Asst Director, 1979–82. Chairman: UK Nat. Inventory of War Memorials, 1995–2008; Nat. Mus. Dirs' Conf., 2000–06; Member: British Nat. Cttee for History of Second World War, 1995–2008; Bd, Museum Documentation Assoc., 1998–2006; Nat. Historic Ships Cttee, 2000–06. Trustee: Imperial War Mus. Trust, 1982–2008; Sir Winston Churchill Archives Trust, 1995–2006; Florence Nightingale Mus. Trust, 1999–2011; Royal Logistic Corps Mus. Trust,

2000–13; Fleet Air Arm Mus., 2000–10; Horniman Mus. and Public Park Trust, 2001–13; Greenwich Foundn for Old Royal Naval Coll., 2007–14 (Chm., 2011–14); Chatham Historic Dockyard Trust, 2008–; Nat. Maritime Mus., 2008–; Nat. Mus. of the Royal Navy, 2008–; Nat. Museums Liverpool, 2009–15; British Empire and Commonwealth Mus., 2010–13. Vice-Pres., Fedn of Merchant Mariners, 2005–. Vice-Patron, Army Museums Ogilby Trust, 2009–; Patron, Evacuees Reunion Assoc., 1997–. Freeman, City of London, 1998; Liveryman, Glovers' Co., 1998–. *Address:* 55 Marlborough Crescent, Riverhead, Sevenoaks, Kent TN13 2HL. *Clubs:* Special Forces, Royal Over-Seas League.

CRAWFORD, Ruth; QC (Scot.) 2008; *b* Glasgow, 17 July 1965; *d* of George Douglas Crawford and Joan Burnie. *Educ:* Cranley Sch. for Girls, Edinburgh; George Heriot's Sch., Edinburgh; Aberdeen Univ. (LLB Hons 1986; DipLP 1987). Called to Scottish Bar, 1993; Second Standing Jun. Counsel to Scottish Exec., 2000–08; ad hoc Advocate Depute, 2006–. *Recreation:* relaxing in France. *Address:* Advocates' Library, Parliament House, Edinburgh EH1 1RF. *T:* (0131) 226 5071. *E:* ruth.crawford@axiomadvocates.com.

CRAWFORD, Prof. Vincent Paul, PhD; FBA 2012; Drummond Professor of Political Economy, University of Oxford, since 2010; Fellow, All Souls College, Oxford, since 2010; *b* Springfield, Ohio, 6 April 1950; *s* of David James Crawford, III and Marjorie Piga Crain, and adopted *s* of Bennett Crain; *m* 1985, Zoë Marie Clark. *Educ:* Princeton Univ. (AB *summa cum laude* Econs 1972); Massachusetts Inst. of Technol. (PhD Econs 1976). University of California, San Diego: Asst Prof., 1976–81; Associate Prof., 1981–85; Prof., 1985–97; Dist. Prof. of Econs, 1997–2009, now Emeritus. Vis. Prof. of Econs and Vis. Res. Associate, Industrial Relns Section, Princeton Univ., 1985–86. Guggenheim Fellow, 1997–98. Associate Editor: Jl of Econ. Theory, 1986–96, 1998–2004; Econometrica, 2004–07; Co-Ed., Amer. Econ. Rev., 2005–09; Ed., Games and Econ. Behavior, 2011– (Mem. Editl Bd, 1988–); Member: Editl Adv. Bd, NZ Econ. Papers, 2007–; Editl Bd, Jl of Econ. Literature, 2010–12. Fellow: Econometric Soc., 1990; Amer. Acad. of Arts and Scis, 2003. *Publications:* Essays in Economic Theory, 1983; International Lending, Long-Term Credit Relationships and Dynamic Contract Theory, 1987; contrib. articles to professional jls. *Recreations:* hiking, bicycling, sailing. *Address:* All Souls College, Oxford OX1 4AL. *T:* (01865) 279339; Department of Economics, Manor Road Building, Manor Road, Oxford OX1 3UQ. *E:* vincent.crawford@economics.ox.ac.uk.

CRAWFORD, His Honour William Hamilton Raymund, QC 1980; a Circuit Judge, 1986–2001; *b* 10 Nov. 1936; *s* of late Col Mervyn Crawford, DSO, DL, JP, and Martha Hamilton Crawford; *m* 1965, Marilyn Jean Colville; one *s* two *d*. *Educ:* West Downs, Winchester; Winchester Coll.; Emmanuel Coll., Cambridge (BA). Commnd 2nd Lt, Royal Scots Greys, 1955–57. Called to the Bar, Inner Temple, 1964; Dep. Chm., Agricultural Land Tribunal, 1978; a Recorder, 1979–86. Pres., Royal Scottish Forestry Soc., 2013–15 (Vice Pres., 2010–13). Chm., Dunscore Community Council, 2009–12. *Recreations:* hill farming, fishing, shooting (shot for GB in Kolapore Match, and for Scotland in Elcho and Twenty Matches on several occasions; mem., Scottish Rifle Team, Commonwealth Games, Jamaica, 1966). *Club:* Northern Counties (Newcastle).

See also Earl of Kinnoull.

CRAWFORD COLLINS, Simon; Managing Director, Slim Film and Television, since 2011; *b* London, 5 April 1967; *s* of David and Ann Crawford Collins; *m*; one *s* one *d*. *Educ:* Oriel Coll., Oxford (BA Mod. Hist. 1989). Kudos Film and Television Ltd: joined, 2001; Dir, Drama, 2005–08; Jt Man. Dir, 2008. *Address:* Slim Film and Television, 33 Foley Street, W1W 7TL.

CRAWLEY, family name of **Baroness Crawley**.

CRAWLEY, Baroness *cr* 1998 (Life Peer), of Edgbaston in the co. of West Midlands; **Christine Mary Crawley;** *b* 9 Jan. 1950; *d* of Thomas Louis Quinn and Joan Ryan; *m*; one *s* two *d* (incl. twins). *Educ:* Notre Dame Catholic Secondary Girls' School, Plymouth; Digby Stuart Training College, Roehampton. Formerly teacher; S Oxfordshire District Council; contested (Lab) Staffordshire SE, gen. election, 1983. MEP (Lab) Birmingham E, 1984–99; Dep. Leader, Eur. PLP, 1994–99. Govt spokesman, H of L, on foreign affairs, 2002–05, defence, 2002–08, internat. devlt, 2002–04 and 2008–10, transport, 2004–05 and 2007–08, N Ireland, 2007–08. A Baroness in Waiting (Govt Whip), 2002–08 and 2009–10. Chm., European Parlt Women's Rights Cttee, 1989–94. Chm., Women's Nat. Commn, 1999–2002. Dir, Northfield Regeneration Forum; Chm., W Midlands Regl Cultural Consortium, 1999–2002. Patron: Orgn for Sickle Cell Anaemia Relief; Women's Returners Network. FRSA. *Address:* House of Lords, SW1A 0PW.

CRAWLEY, Angela; MP (SNP) Lanark and Hamilton East, since 2015; *b* Hamilton, 3 June 1987. *Educ:* John Ogilvie High Sch.; Stirling Univ. (BA Hons Politics 2009); Univ. of Glasgow (LLB 2015). Parly Asst, Scottish Parlt, 2007–09; Tour Co-ordinator and Sen. Gp Leader, Educn Travel Gp, 2009–11; Parly Asst and Researcher, Scottish Parlt, 2011–13; Legal Asst, Aamer Anwar & Co., Solicitors, 2014. Mem. (SNP), S Lanarkshire Council, 2012–15. SNP spokesperson for Equalities, Women and Children, 2015–. Nat. Convenor, Young Scots for Independence, 2014–. *Address:* House of Commons, SW1A 0AA.

CRAWLEY, David Jonathan; Director, Scottish Executive European Union Office, Brussels, 2005–06; *b* 6 May 1951; *s* of Frederick John Crawley and Olive Elizabeth Crawley (*née* Bunce); *m* 1983, Anne Anderson; one *s* two *d*. *Educ:* Chichester High Sch.; Christ Church, Oxford (BA Modern Hist. 1972; MA 1973). Scottish Office, 1972–81; Dept of Energy, 1981–84; Asst Sec., Scottish Educn Dept, 1984–87; Principal Private Sec. to Sec. of State for Scotland, 1987–89; Counsellor, UK Representation to EU, Brussels, 1990–94; Asst Dir, Finance, and Hd, Private Finance Unit, 1994–97, Hd, Powers and Functions, Constitution Gp, 1997–98, Scottish Office; Hd of Schs Gp, Scottish Office, then Scottish Exec., Educn Dept, 1998–99; Hd of Agriculture, Rural Affairs, then Envmt and Rural Affairs, Dept, Scottish Exec., 1999–2002; Hd of Dept, Scotland Office, 2002–05. Chm., Audit Cttee, Wales Office, 2005–15. Member: Bd, Scottish Natural Heritage, 2006–12; Jt Nature Conservation Cttee, 2007–12; Chm., Central Scotland Forest Trust, 2008–13. Treas., St Fillan's Episcopal Ch, 1998–99. Comr, Queen Victoria Sch., Dunblane, 2006–11. *Recreations:* gardening, music, travel to warm places. *Address:* Blackberry Cottage, Hundon, Sudbury, Suffolk CO10 8DW.

CRAWLEY, Most Rev. David Perry; Archbishop of Kootenay and Metropolitan of British Columbia and Yukon, 1994–2004; *b* 26 July 1937; *s* of Rev. Canon George Antony Crawley, LTh and Lucy Lillian Crawley (*née* Ball); *m* 1st, 1959, Frances Mary Louise Wilmot; two *d*; 2nd, 1986, Joan Alice Bubbs; one *d* (and one *d* decd). *Educ:* Univ. of Manitoba (BA 1958); St John's Coll., Winnipeg (LTh 1961; DD 1990); Univ. of Kent at Canterbury (MA 1967). Ordained Deacon 1961, Priest 1962. Incumbent, St Thomas', Sherwood Park, Edmonton, 1961–66; Canon Missioner, All Saints Cathedral, Edmonton, 1967–70; Rector, St Matthew's, Winnipeg, 1971–77; Archdeacon of Winnipeg, 1974–77; Archdeacon of Rupert's Land, 1977–81; Lectr, St John's College, Winnipeg, 1981–82; Rector, St Michael and All Angels, Regina, 1982–85; Rector, St Paul's, Vancouver, 1985–90; Bishop of Kootenay, 1990–2004. *Recreations:* ski-ing, hiking. *Address:* c/o Diocese of Kootenay, 1876 Richter Street, Kelowna, BC V1Y 2M9, Canada.

CRAWLEY, John Maurice, CB 1992; Under Secretary, Inland Revenue, 1979–93; *b* 27 Sept. 1933; *s* of late Charles William and Kathleen Elizabeth Crawley; *m* 1978, Jane Meadows Rendel; three *s*. *Educ:* Rugby Sch.; New Coll., Oxford (MA). Assistant Principal, Inland Revenue, 1959; Principal, 1963; Asst Secretary, 1969; Under Sec., 1979; seconded to Cabinet Office (Central Policy Review Staff), 1973–76 and 1979–81. *Recreations:* music, walking, book-binding.

CRAWLEY, Prof. Michael John, PhD; FRS 2002; Professor of Plant Ecology, Imperial College London (formerly Imperial College, London University), since 1994; *b* 9 March 1949; *s* of John and Isabel Crawley; *m* 1971, Greer Anne Williams. *Educ:* Dukes Grammar Sch., Alnwick; Edinburgh Univ. (BSc Hons 1st Cl. 1970); Imperial Coll., London (DIC, PhD 1973). Lectr, Univ. of Bradford, 1973–79; Lectr, 1979–89, Reader, 1989–94, Imperial Coll., London. Trustee, Royal Botanic Gardens, Kew, 1996–2002, 2011–14. *Publications:* Herbivory, 1983; Plant Ecology, 1986; Colonization, Succession and Stability, 1987; Natural Enemies, 1992; GLIM for Ecologists, 1993; Statistical Computing, 2002; The Flora of Berkshire, 2005; The R Book, 2007; papers on plant-herbivore interactions and biological invasions. *Recreations:* BSBI plant recorder for Berkshire and East Sutherland, mountains, croquet, Newcastle United. *Address:* Department of Biological Sciences, Silwood Park, Ascot, Berks SL5 7PY. *T:* (020) 7594 2216, *Fax:* (020) 7594 2339. *E:* m.crawley@imperial.ac.uk.

CRAWLEY-BOEVEY, Sir Thomas (Michael Blake), 8th Bt *cr* 1784; *b* 29 Sept. 1928; *er s* of Sir Launcelot Valentine Hyde Crawley-Boevey, 7th Bt, and Elizabeth Goodeth (*d* 1976), *d* of Herbert d'Auvergne Innes, late Indian Police; *S* father, 1968; *m* 1st, 1957, Laura Coelingh (*d* 1979); two *s*; 2nd, 2003, Judith Tillotson. *Educ:* Wellington Coll.; St John's Coll., Cambridge (BA 1952, MA 1956). 2nd Lieut, Durham Light Infantry, 1948. With Shipping Agents, 1952–61; with Consumers' Association, 1961–82; Editor: Money Which?, 1968–76; Which?, 1976–82; Editor-in-Chief, Which? magazines, 1980–82. Master, Girdlers' Co., 1992–93. *Heir: er s* Thomas Hyde Crawley-Boevey [*b* 26 June 1958; *m* 1992, Lynette Claire Gilbert; two *s*]. *Address:* 47 Belvoir Road, Cambridge CB4 1JH. *T:* (01223) 368698.

CRAWSHAW, 5th Baron *cr* 1892, of Crawshaw, co. Lancaster and of Whatton, co. Leics; **David Gerald Brooks;** Bt 1891; *b* 14 Sept. 1934; *s* of 3rd Baron Crawshaw and Sheila (*d* 1964), *o d* of Lt-Col P. R. Clifton, CMG, DSO; *S* brother, 1997; *m* 1970, Belinda Mary, *d* of George Burgess; four *d*. *Educ:* Eton; RAC, Cirencester. President: NW Leics Cons. Assoc., 2000–; Leics Agricl Soc., 2009–13. High Sheriff, Leics, 1984–85. *Heir: b* Hon. John Patrick Brooks [*b* 17 March 1938; *m* 1967, Rosemary Vans Agnew, *o d* of C. Vans Agnew Frank; one *s* one *d*].

CRAWSHAW, Steven John; Group Chief Executive, Bradford & Bingley plc, 2004–08; *b* 15 April 1961; *s* of John Crawshaw and Serena Gillean Crawshaw; *m* 1991, Brigid Rushmore; two *s*. *Educ:* Eastbourne Coll.; Univ. of Leicester (LLB); Cranfield Univ. (MBA). Articled clerk and Asst Solicitor, Hewitson Becke & Shaw, 1984–88; Partner, Froggatt & Co., 1988–89; Manager, Legal Dept, 1990–95, Strategic Planner, 1995–96, Hd of Strategy, 1996–97, Cheltenham & Gloucester plc; PA to Gp Dir, Customer Finance, Lloyds TSB plc, 1997–98; Bradford & Bingley plc, 1999–2008, Gp Strategy, HR and IT Dir, 2002–04. *Recreations:* family, hill walking, cooking.

CRAWSHAY, Elisabeth Mary Boyd, (Lady Crawshay), CBE 1986; Chairman, Local Government Boundary Commission, Wales, 1981–94; Deputy Chief Commissioner, St John's Ambulance Brigade, Wales, 1979–84; *b* 2 July 1927; *d* of Lt-Col Guy Franklin Reynolds, late 9th Lancers, and Katherine Isobel (*née* Macdonell); *m* 1950, Col Sir William (Robert) Crawshay, DSO, ERD, TD. *Educ:* Convent of Sacred Heart, Roehampton; St Anne's Coll., Oxford (MA). Mem., Mental Health Act Commn, 1983–88. DL Gwent 1978–90; JP Abergavenny, 1972–96 (Chm., Juvenile Bench, 1980–95; Mem., Borstal Board of Visitors, 1975–84). DStJ 1970. *Address:* Ty Carreg, Govilon, Abergavenny, Mon NP7 9PT. *T:* (01873) 832220.

CRAXTON, Christine Elizabeth; *see* Gamble, C. E.

CRAXTON, (Katharine) Jane; *see* Carmichael, K. J.

CRAY, Rt Rev. Graham Alan; Archbishops' Missioner, and Team Leader, Fresh Expressions, 2009–14; an Honorary Assistant Bishop: Diocese of York, since 2009; Diocese of Rochester, since 2011; *b* 21 April 1947; *s* of late Alan Cray and Doris Mary Kathleen Cray; *m* 1973, Jacqueline Webster; two *d*. *Educ:* Leeds Univ. (BA 1968); St John's Coll., Nottingham. Ordained deacon, 1971, priest, 1972; Asst Curate, St Mark, Gillingham, 1971–75; N Area Co-ordinator, Youth Dept, CPAS, 1975–78; Asst Curate, 1978–82, Vicar, 1982–92, St Michael-le-Belfrey, York; Principal, Ridley Hall Theol Coll., 1992–2001; Bishop Suffragan of Maidstone, 2001–09; an Hon. Asst Bishop, Dio. of Canterbury, 2009–14. *Publications:* The Post Evangelical Debate, 1997; Postmodern Culture and Youth Discipleship, 1998; (with Paul Simmonds) Being Culturally Relevant, 2000; Youth Congregations and the Emerging Church, 2002; (ed) Mission-Shaped Church, 2004, rev. edn 2009; (jtly) Making Sense of Generation Y, 2006; (with Tim Sudworth and Chris Russell) Mission-shaped Youth, 2007; Disciples and Citizens, 2007; Discerning Leadership, 2010; Who's Shaping You?, 2010; (ed jtly) New Monasticism as Fresh Expression of Church, 2011; (ed jtly and contrib.) Fresh Expressions and the Kingdom of God, 2012; Making Disciples in Fresh Expression of Church, 2013; contributor: Mass Culture, 1999; Mission as Transformation, 1999; Christ and Consumerism, 2000; Beholding the Glory, 2000; Fanning the Flame, 2003; The Future of the Parish System, 2006; The Heart of Faith, 2008; Faith in the Future, 2008; The Art of Compassion, 2008; The Holy Spirit in the World Today, 2011; The Gospel after Christendom, 2012. *Recreations:* listening to rock music, following sport, reading theology.

CRAY, Timothy James; Senior Treasury Counsel (Criminal), Central Criminal Court, since 2014; *b* Belfast, 1966; *s* of John and Florence Cray; *m* (marr. diss.); one *s* one *d*. *Educ:* Down High Sch., Downpatrick; Univ. of Durham (BA Hons Law). Called to the Bar, Inner Temple, 1989; in practice as barrister, 1989–. *Recreations:* golf, shooting. *Address:* 6KBW College Hill, 21 College Hill, EC4R 2PR. *T:* (020) 3301 0910. *E:* timothy.cray@6kbw.com.

CREAGH, Mary Helen; MP (Lab) Wakefield, since 2005; *b* 2 Dec. 1967; *d* of Thomas and Elizabeth Creagh; *m* 2001, Adrian Pulham; one *s* one *d*. *Educ:* Pembroke Coll., Oxford (BA Jt Hons Modern Langs (French and Italian)); London Sch. of Econs (MSc Eur. Studies). Press Officer: Youth Forum of EU, 1991–95; London Enterprise Agency, 1995–97; Lectr in Entrepreneurship, Cranfield Sch. of Mgt, 1997–2005. Mem. (Lab) Islington BC, 1998–2005 (Leader, Labour Gp, 2000–04). An Asst Govt Whip, 2009–10; Shadow Sec. of State for Envmt, Food and Rural Affairs, 2010–13, for Transport, 2013–14, for Internat. Devlt, 2014–15. Trustee, Rathbone Trng, 1997–2004. *Recreations:* cycling, cooking, theatre, friends and family, pop music. *Address:* House of Commons, SW1A 0AA. *T:* (020) 7219 6984. *E:* mary@marycreagh.co.uk. *Club:* Red Shed (Wakefield).

CREALLY, Eugene Patrick, PhD; QC (Scot.) 2011; *b* Dungannon, Co. Tyrone, 3 Feb. 1961; *s* of Joseph Creally and Annie Creally (*née* Quinn); *m* 2004, Ailsa Mhairi Wilson; one step *s*. *Educ:* Queen's Univ. Belfast (LLB Hons 1983); Edinburgh Univ. (DipLP 1988; PhD 1991). Admitted as solicitor, 1990; Solicitor, Bird Semple Fyfe Ireland, 1990–92; Advocate, 1993–; Standing Counsel: to Lord Advocate, 1998–2005; to Advocate Gen. for Scotland, 2009–11. Clerk to Faculty of Advocates, 1999–2003. Vice Convenor, Free Legal Services Unit, 2003–. *Publications:* Judicial Review of Anti Dumping and Other Safeguard Measures in the European Community, 1992. *Recreations:* golf, tennis, hill walking. *Address:* Advocates Library, Parliament House, Edinburgh EH1 1RF. *T:* (0131) 226 5071. *E:* eugene.creally@advocates.org.uk.

CREAN, Anthony Joseph Daniel; QC 2006; *b* 9 June 1962; *s* of Michael and Patricia Crean; *m* 2003, Angela Roberts; two *s* three *d*. *Educ:* Univ. of Essex (BA); Univ. of Manchester (MPhil). Called to the Bar, Gray's Inn, 1987; in practice as barrister, 1987–, specialising in planning law. FRGS 2003. *Recreations:* hanging out with Alice, Laura, Francis, Lawrence and Hilary, scuba-diving, poetry, ski-ing, swimming, chess. *Address:* Kings Chambers, Embassy House, 60 Church Street, Birmingham B3 2DJ.

CREAN, Hon. Simon (Findlay); Director, Ashley Services Group Ltd, since 2014; *b* 26 Feb. 1949; *s* of late Hon. Francis Daniel Crean and of Mary Isobel Crean, AM; *m* 1973, Carole (*née* Lamb); two *d*. *Educ:* Middle Park Central, Melbourne; Melbourne High Sch.; Monash Univ. (BEc, LLB). Trade Union Official, Federated Storemen and Packers Union of Australia, 1970–85; Pres., ACTU, 1985–90. MP (ALP) Hotham, Vic, 1990–2013. Federal Minister for: Science and Technology, 1990; Primary Industries and Energy, 1991–93; Employment, Educn and Training, 1993–96; Dep. Leader of the Opposition, 1998–2001; Leader of the Opposition, 2001–03; Shadow Treasurer, 1998–2001, 2003–04; Shadow Trade Minister, 2004–07; Minister for Trade, 2007–10; Minister for Regl Australia, Regl Develt and Local Govt, and Minister for the Arts, 2010–13. Patron, North Melbourne FC. *Recreations:* bushwalking, tennis. *Club:* North Melbourne Football.

CREASY, Dr Stella Judith; MP (Lab Co-op) Walthamstow, since 2010; *b* 1977. *Educ:* Colchester High Sch.; Magdalene Coll., Cambridge; London Sch. of Econs (PhD Social Psychol.). Formerly: researcher to Douglas Alexander, MP, Charles Clarke, MP and Ross Cranston, MP; Dep. Dir, Involve think tank; Hd, Public Affairs and Campaigns, Scout Assoc. Formerly Mem. (Lab Co-op) Waltham Forest LBC (Dep. Mayor, then Mayor). Shadow Minister: for Home Affairs, 2011–13; BIS, 2013–15. *Address:* House of Commons, SW1A 0AA.

CREDITON, Bishop Suffragan of, since 2015; **Rt Rev. Dame Sarah Elisabeth Mullally,** DBE 2005; *b* 26 March 1962; *d* of Michael Frederick Mills Bowser and Ann Dorothy Bowser; *m* 1987, Eamonn James Mullally; one *s* one *d*. *Educ:* Nightingale Sch. of Nursing; S Bank Poly. (BSc Hons Nursing and RGN 1984); MSc Interprofessional Health and Welfare, S Bank Univ., 1992; DipTh Kent 2001; MA Pastoral Theol., Heythrop Coll., London Univ., 2006. Staff Nurse: St Thomas' Hosp., 1984–86; Royal Marsden Hosp., 1986–88; Ward Sister, Westminster Hosp., 1988–90; Sen. Nurse, Riverside HA, 1990–92; Asst Chief Nurse, Riverside Hosps, 1992–94; Dir of Nursing and Dep. Chief Exec., Chelsea and Westminster Healthcare Trust, 1994–99; Chief Nursing Officer, DoH, 1999–2004. Ordained deacon, 2001; NSM, Battersea Fields, 2001–04; Asst Curate, St George, St Saviour and All Saints, Battersea Fields, 2004–06; Team Rector, Sutton, Surrey, 2006–12; Canon Res. and Treas., Salisbury Cathedral, 2012–15. Non-executive Director: Royal Marsden NHS Foundn Trust, 2005–13; Salisbury NHS Foundn Trust, 2013–. Ind. Gov., S Bank Univ., 2005–15. Hon. Fellow: S Bank Univ., 2000; Christ Church, Canterbury, 2006. Hon. Dr Health Sci.: Bournemouth, 2001; Wolverhampton, 2004; Hon. DSc Herts, 2005.

CREECH, Rt Hon. Wyatt (Beetham), CNZM 2003; PC 1999; Deputy Prime Minister of New Zealand, 1998–99; *b* Oceanside, Calif, 13 Oct. 1946; *s* of Jesse Wyatt Creech and Ellanora Sophia (*née* Beetham); arrived in NZ, 1947; *m* 1981, Diana, (Danny), Marie Rose; three *s*. *Educ:* Hadlow Prep. Sch., Masterton; Wanganui Collegiate Sch.; Massey Univ. (Dip. Sheep Farming); Victoria Univ. (BA Pol Sci. and Internat. Politics). Farmer, Wairarapa, 1974–79; horticulturalist (vineyard developer), 1979–88; Accountant, Masterton, 1983–87. MP (Nat.) Wairarapa, NZ, 1988–99, List Seat, 1999–2002; Minister: of Revenue, 1990–95; of Customs, i/c Public Trust Office and responsible for Govt Superannuation Fund, 1990–91; for Sen. Citizens, and Associate Minister of Finance and of Social Welfare, 1991–93; for State Owned Enterprises, 1993; of Employment, 1993–96; of Revenue and Dep. Minister of Finance, 1993–96; Leader of the House, 1996–98; Minister of Educn, 1996–99; Minister of Courts and of Ministerial Services, 1997–98. Dep. Leader, Nat. Party, 1997–2001; Ind. Dir, Blue Chip NZ, 2004–06. Mem., Parly Services Commn; Chm., NZ Fire Service Commn, 2011–12. Chm., NZ Windfarms Ltd; Director: Kaimai Cheese Co. Ltd; Seales Ltd; Healthcare NZ Ltd. Dir, Cognition Educn Trust. *Recreations:* outdoor pursuits, wine-tasting, gardening, traditional acoustic music. *Address:* 43 Kandy Crescent, Khandallah, Wellington 6035, New Zealand.

CREED, Prof. Francis Hunter, MD; FRCP, FRCPsych, FMedSci; Professor of Psychological Medicine, University of Manchester, 1997–2012, now Emeritus; *b* 22 Feb. 1947; *s* of late Albert Lowry Creed and Joyce Marian Creed; *m* 1972, Ruth Alison Kaye; two *s* two *d*. *Educ:* Kingswood Sch., Bath; Downing Coll., Cambridge (Pilley Schol.; MB BChir 1971; MA; MD 1985); St Thomas' Hosp. Med. Sch., London. FRCP 1991; FRCPsych 1991. Registrar, Maudsley Hosp., 1974–76; Sen. Registrar, Maudsley and London Hosps, 1976–78; Mental Health Leverhulme Res. Fellow, 1978–80; Sen. Lectr, Univ. of Manchester and Consultant Psychiatrist, Manchester Royal Infirmary, 1980–92; Prof. of Community Psychiatry, 1992–97, Res. Dean, Faculty of Medicine, Dentistry, Nursing and Pharmacy, 1997–2001, Univ. of Manchester; Hon. Consultant Psychiatrist, Manchester Royal Infirmary, subseq. Central Manchester Healthcare Trust, then Central Manchester and Manchester Children's Univ. Hosps NHS Trust, 1981–2012. Co-chair, Psychosocial Cttee, Rome Working Team Report on Functional Bowel Disorders, 2000, 2006. Treas., Eur. Assoc. of Consultation-Liaison Psychiatry and Psychosomatics, 2004–11 (Pres., 2000–04). Churchill Travelling Fellow, 1993. FRSocMed 1980; FMedSci 2000. Ed., Jl of Psychosomatic Res., 1999–2011. Hackett Award, Acad. Psychosomatic Medicine, 2009. *Publications:* Medicine and Psychiatry, 1981; Psychiatry in Medical Practice, 1989, 2nd edn 1994; (ed jtly) Medically Unexplained Symptoms, Somatisation and Bodily Distress: developing better clinical services, 2011; over 250 articles in learned jls on psychological aspects of medicine and Community Psychiatry. *Recreations:* hill walking, swimming, travelling. *Address:* Department of Psychiatry, Manchester University, Rawnsley Building, Manchester Royal Infirmary, Oxford Road, Manchester M13 9WL. *T:* (0161) 276 5331.

CREED, Martin; artist; *b* 21 Oct. 1968; *s* of John Creed and Gisela Grosscurth. *Educ:* Slade Sch. of Fine Art, London (BA Hons Fine Art 1990). Exhibitions include: Martin Creed Works (organised by Southampton City Art Gall.), Leeds City Art Gall., Bluecoat Gall., Liverpool, Camden Arts Centre, London, 2000; Art Now: Martin Creed, Tate Britain, London, 2000; Martin Creed: Down Over Up, Fruitmarket Gall., Edinburgh, 2010; Mothers, Hauser & Wirth, London, 2011; Martin Creed: What's the point of it?, Hayward Gall., 2014. Works include: Work#227: The lights going on and off (Turner Prize, 2001); Work#1197: All the bells in a country rung as quickly and loudly as possible for three minutes, 2012. *Publications:* the whole world + the work = the whole world, 1996; Martin Creed Works, 2010. *E:* mail@martincreed.com.

CREED, Murray Laurence; His Honour Judge Creed; a Circuit Judge, since 2010; *b* Solihull, 21 Jan. 1955; *s* of Brian Creed and Pamela Creed; *m* 1982, Jacqueline Burbridge; one *s* two *d*. *Educ:* Tudor Grange Grammar Sch., Solihull; University Coll. London (LLB). Called to the Bar, Lincoln's Inn, 1978; in private practice as a barrister, 1978–95; a Chm., Employment Tribunals, 1992–95; an Employment Judge, 1995–2010; an Asst Recorder, 2000; a Recorder, 2000–10. *Recreations:* music, family, walking, hockey, ski-ing, gardening.

CREEDON, Michael Francis, QPM 2011; Chief Constable, Derbyshire Constabulary, since 2007; *b* London, 14 June 1958; *s* of Raymond and Elizabeth Creedon; *m* 1994, Sally Deans; two *s* one *d*. *Educ:* City of Leicester Boys' Sch.; Univ. of Manchester (BA Hons Hist. and Econs); Univ. of Leicester (MA Criminol.). Leicestershire Constabulary, 1980–2003: served as detective in every rank; Basic Comd Unit Comdr, S Area, 2001–03; Derbyshire Constabulary: Asst Chief Constable (Ops), 2003–06; Dep. Chief Constable for ACPO, Nat. Co-ordinator for Serious and Organised Crime, 2006–07. Holder, ACPO portfolio for asset recovery and policy lead for serious and organised crime, financial investigation and proceeds of crime, investigative interviewing and for kidnap and extortion, 2005–. *Recreations:* Middlesbrough Football Club, family, cookery (oriental especially), painting and decorating, running. *Address:* Derbyshire Constabulary HQ, Butterley Hall, Ripley, Derbys DE5 3RS.

CREEDON, Roger, CBE 2005; Chief Executive, Electoral Commission, 2000–04; *b* 31 Dec. 1946; *s* of late Patrick Michael Creedon and Norah Creedon (*née* Rice); *m* 1969, Shirley Ann Clay; two *s*. Joined Home Office, 1964; Police Directorate, 1969–77; Asst Sec., Cttee on Obscenity and Film Censorship, 1977–80; Forensic Sci. Service, 1980–83; Gaming Bd, 1983–87; Home Office Finance Directorate, 1987–90; Police Sci. and Technology Gp, 1990–93; Dir, Nat. Criminal Intelligence Service, 1993–96; Corporate Resources and Constitutional Directorates, Home Office 1996–2000. Election Observer for Commonwealth Secretariat, 2005. Lay Member: First-tier Tribunal (Information Rights) (formerly Information Tribunal), 2006–; GMC Fitness to Practise Panel, 2006–13; Rules and Ethics/Standards Cttee, SRA, 2007–12; Standards Cttee, Bar Standards Bd, 2008–10; Fitness to Practise Panel, NMC, 2008–; General Chiropractic Council, 2009–; Fitness to Practise Panel, GDC, 2011–. Mem., Kentish Opera Council, 2005–11. *Recreations:* oil painting, reading. *E:* rcreedon@ntlworld.com.

CREELMAN, Graham Murray, OBE 2006; Managing Director, Anglia Television, 1996–2006; Director, Regional Programming, ITV, 2003–06; *b* 20 May 1947; *s* of late Robert Kelly Creelman and Jean Murray Creelman; *m* 1st, 1969, Eleanor McCulloch McAuslan (marr. diss. 1984); two *d*; 2nd, 1984, Sarah Katharine Bruce-Lockhart (marr. diss. 1996); two *d*; 3rd, 1997, Francesca Vivica Parsons; one step *s* one step *d*. *Educ:* Greenock Acad.; Univ. of Sussex (BA Hons). Journalist, Scotsman, 1969–70; journalist and producer, BBC Scotland, 1970–78; producer and dir documentaries, Anglia TV, 1978–89; Exec. Dir, Survival Anglia Ltd, 1989–94; Dir of Programmes, Anglia TV, 1994–96; Chm., Anglia Multimedia, 1999–2001. Founder, Creelman Associates Ltd, 2006. Dir, Eastern Arts Bd, 1995–2002; Chairman: Eastern Screen Commn, 1997–2002; East of England Cultural Consortium, 1999–2009; Screen East, 2001–06; Council Mem., Arts Council England, East, 2002–08; (and Founder) East of England Prodn Innovation Centre, 2010–. Mem., Ofcom Adv. Cttee for England, 2009–. Mem., E of England Regl Assembly, 2001–09. Bd Associate, Govt Office for E of England, 2006–09. Trustee/Dir, Wildscreen Trustees, 1993–2001; Director: Writers' Centre Norwich (formerly New Writing Partnership), 2004– (Dep. Chm., 2008–12; Chm., 2012–); Norwich Heritage Economic and Regeneration Trust, 2004–; Chm., Norwich Partnership, 2006–10; Sen. Ind. Dir/Dep. Chair, Norfolk and Suffolk Foundn Trust, 2008–15; Dep. Chair, Norfolk Strategic Partnership for Older People's Services, 2014–. Dep. Chm., United Wildlife, 1997–2001. Norwich University of the Arts (formerly School of Art and Design, then Norwich University College of the Arts): Gov., 2004– (Vice-Chm., 2006; Chm., 2007–13; Pro-Chancellor, 2013–); Vis. Prof. of Media, 2012–. Sheriff of Norwich, 2013–14. *Publications:* contribs to New Statesman, The Listener. *Recreations:* walking in Scotland, fly fishing, Schubert, the books of John Buchan, playing the ukelele. *Address:* 22 Christchurch Road, Norwich NR2 2AE. *Club:* Norfolk (Norwich).

CREESE, Nigel Arthur Holloway, AM 1988; Executive Officer, Association of Heads of Independent Schools of Australia, 1989–95 (Chairman, 1985–87); *b* 4 June 1927; *s* of late H. R. Creese; *m* 1951, Valdai (*née* Walters); two *s* two *d*. *Educ:* Blundell's Sch.; Brasenose Coll., Oxford. Assistant Master: Bromsgrove Sch., 1952–55; Rugby Sch., 1955–63; Headmaster: Christ's Coll., Christchurch, NZ, 1963–70; Melbourne Grammar Sch., 1970–87. *Address:* 75 Charles Street, Kew, Vic 3101, Australia. *E:* n.creese@bigpond.com. *Clubs:* East India and Public Schools; Melbourne (Melbourne).

CREESE, Prof. Sadie, DPhil; Professor of Cybersecurity, University of Oxford, since 2011; Fellow, Worcester College, Oxford, since 2011; *b* Gloucester, 6 Dec. 1973; *d* of Peter Creese and Vicky Creese; one *d*. *Educ:* Univ. of North London (BSc Hons 1st Cl. Maths and Philos. 1996); Worcester Coll., Oxford (MSc Computation 1997; DPhil Computer Sci. 2001). Sen. Res. Scientist, 2000–05, Dir, Strategic Progs, Trusted Information Systems Div., 2005–07, QinetiQ; Prof. and Dir of e-Security, Univ. of Warwick, 2007–11; Dir, Cyber Security Centre, 2012–15, Global Capacity Centre, 2013–, Univ. of Oxford. *Address:* Department of Computer Science, University of Oxford, Robert Hooke Building, Parks Road, Oxford OX1 3PR. *T:* (01865) 273616. *E:* sadie.creese@cs.ox.ac.uk.

CREIGHTON, Alan Joseph, CEng, FRINA; RCNC; Chief Underwater Systems Executive, Ministry of Defence, 1989–91, retired; *b* 21 Nov. 1936; *s* of Joseph Kenneth and Iris Mary Creighton; *m* 1959, Judith Bayford; two *d*. *Educ:* Gillingham County Grammar School; Royal Naval College, Greenwich. Joined Admiralty, 1953; Cadetship to Royal Corps of Naval Constructors, 1957; pass out, RNC Greenwich, 1961; RCDS 1980; Technical Dir, Yarrow Shipbuilders, 1981 (on secondment); resumed MoD (PE) career, 1984; Dir Gen., Surface Ships, 1986–89. *Recreations:* music, golf, computers, website design, cabinet making. *Address:* Rose Cottage, West Littleton, Chippenham SN14 8JE. *T:* (01225) 891021.

CREIGHTON, Robert Mandell; Managing Director, Creighton Consulting and Management Services, since 2013; *b* 18 Feb. 1950; *s* of Hugh Creighton and Christian Creighton (*née* Barclay); *m* 1st, 1977, Sok-Chzeng Ong (marr. diss. 1983); 2nd, 1985, Rosanne Jelley; two *d*. *Educ:* Marlborough Coll.; King's Coll., Cambridge (MA Hist.); King's Coll. London (PGCE). Teacher, King's Coll. Sch., Wimbledon, 1974–78; Internat. Sec., United World Colls, 1978–88; Department of Health: Principal, 1988–91; Asst Sec., 1991–95; Principal Private Sec. to Sec. of State for Health, 1992–94; Chief Exec., Great Ormond Street Hosp. for Children NHS Trust, 1995–2000; Chief Executive: Ealing PCT, 2002–10; Ealing, Hillingdon and Hounslow PCT, 2010–11; Dir, London Public Health Transition, later London Health Transition and Legacy Prog., NHS London, 2011–13. Chm., London Primary Care Trusts Gp, 2006–11; Mem., Family Mediation Standards Bd, 2015–. Hon. Sen. Lectr, LSHTM, 2012–. Trustee: Waterford Sch. Trust, 1988–; Imperial Coll. Healthcare Charity, 2013–. *Recreations:* tennis, opera, painting. *Address:* 50 Thurleigh Road, SW12 8UD. *Club:* Wimbledon Tennis.

CRELLIN, Adrian Mark, FRCR, FRCP; Consultant Clinical Oncologist, St James's University Hospital, Leeds, since 1990; National Clinical Lead for Proton Beam Therapy programme, Department of Health and NHS England, since 2012; *b* London, 11 Nov. 1954; *s* of Vivian Henry Crellin and Eileen Maud Crellin (*née* Bodkin); *m* 1981, Sarah Anne Humphreys; one *s* one *d*. *Educ:* Hitchin Grammar Sch.; Christ's Coll., Cambridge (MB 1979, BChir 1980; MA); St Bartholomew's Hosp. Med. Sch. FRCR 1988; FRCP 1997. Hse Officer and SHO, 1980–85; Registrar and Sen. Registrar, Middx Hosp. and Mt Vernon Hosp., 1985–90. Chair: Proton Nat. Clin. Reference Panel, 2008–; NHS England Radiotherapy Clinical Reference Gp; Co-Chair, Nat. Radiotherapy Implementation Gp, 2012–13. Dean, Faculty of Clin. Oncol. and Vice Pres., RCR, 2010–12. Mem. Council, Bd of Trustees, CRUK, 2012–. *Recreations:* country sports, photography. *Address:* St James's Institute of Oncology, Level 4 Bexley Wing, St James's University Hospital, Beckett Street, Leeds LS9 7TF. *T:* (0113) 206 8602. *E:* adrian.crellin@nhs.net.

CREMONA, Hon. John Joseph; Judge, 1965–92, Vice-President, 1986–92, European Court of Human Rights; Judge, 1985–92, Vice-President, 1987–92, European Tribunal in matters of State immunity; Emeritus Professor, University of Malta, since 1965; Chief Justice of Malta and President of the Constitutional Court, Court of Appeal and Court of Criminal Appeal, 1971–81; *b* 6 Jan. 1918; *s* of late Dr Antonio Cremona, KM, MD and Anne (*née*

Camilleri); *m* 1949, Marchioness Beatrice Barbaro of St George (*d* 2001); one *s* two *d*. *Educ:* Malta Univ. (BA 1936, LLD *cum laude* 1942); Rome Univ. (DLitt 1939); London Univ. (BA 1st Cl. Hons 1946, PhD in Laws 1951). DJur Trieste, 1972. Crown Counsel, 1947; Lectr in Constitutional Law, Malta Univ., 1947–65, Prof. of Criminal Law, 1959–65; Attorney-Gen., 1957–64; Vice-Pres., Constitutional Court and Court of Appeal, 1965–71; sometime Actg Governor General and Actg Pres., Republic of Malta. Chm., UN Cttee on Elimination of Racial Discrimination (CERD), 1986–88 (Mem., 1984–88). Chairman: Human Rights Section, World Assoc. of Lawyers; Planning Council, Foundn for Internat. Studies, Malta Univ.; Malta Human Rights Assoc.; Vice-Pres., Internat. Inst. of Studies, Documentation and Info. for the Protection of Envmt, Italy; Member: Cttee of Experts on Human Rights and Cttee of Experts on State Immunity, Council of Europe, Strasbourg; Inst Internat. de Droits de l'Homme, Strasbourg; Scientific Council, Revue des Droits de l'Homme, Paris; Scientific Council, Centro Internazionale per la Protezione dei Diritti dell'Uomo, Pesaro, Italy; Scientific Council, Faculty of Law, Université de Saint Esprit, Lebanon; Editorial Adv. Board: Checklist of Human Rights Documents, NY; Rivista Internazionale dei diritti dell'Uomo, Milan; delegate and rapporteur, internat. confs. FRHistS; Fellow *ex titulo*, Internat. Acad. of Legal Medicine and Social Medicine; Hon. Fellow, LSE; Hon. Mem., Real Acad. de Jurisprudencia y Legislación, Madrid. KStJ 1984 (Chm., St John Council, Malta, 1983–). KSG 1972. Kt, 1966, Commendatore al Merito Melitense, 2004, Sovereign Military Order of Malta; Companion, Order of Merit (Malta), 1994. Kt Comdr, 1968, Grand Officier, 1989, Kt Grand Cross, 1995, Order of Merit (Italy); Kt Comdr, 1971, Grand Cross of Merit, 1981, Constantinian Order of St George; Chevalier de la Légion d'Honneur (France), 1990. *Publications:* The Treatment of Young Offenders in Malta, 1956; The Malta Constitution of 1835, 1959; The Doctrine of Entrapment in Theft, 1959; The Legal Consequences of a Conviction, 1962; The Constitutional Development of Malta, 1963; From the Declaration of Rights to Independence, 1965; Human Rights Documentation in Malta, 1966; Selected Papers 1946–1989, 1990, vol. II, 1990–2000, 2002; The Maltese Constitution and Constitutional History, 1994; Malta and Britain: the early constitutions, 1996; six poetry books; articles in French, German, Italian, Portuguese and American law jls. *Recreation:* gardening. *Address:* Villa Barbaro, Zejtun Road, Tarxien, Malta. *T:* 21826414.

CRERAR, Prof. Lorne Donald; Founding Partner and Chairman, Harper Macleod LLP, since 1987; Professor of Banking Law, University of Glasgow, since 1997; *b* Renfrew, 29 July 1954; *s* of Ronald Crerar and Isobel Scott (*née* Pollock); *m* 2013, Taroub Zahran. *Educ:* Kelvinside Acad., Glasgow; Univ. of Glasgow (LLB Hons). NP 1980; FCIBS 1999. Partner, Mackenzie Robertson & Co., 1979–87. Chairman, Discipline: for Scottish Rugby Union, 1995–; for European Rugby Cup Ltd, 1999–; for 6 Nations Ltd, 1999–; Judicial Officer, Internat. Rugby Bd, 1995–. Dep. Chm., Scottish Enterprise Glasgow, 2000–03; Chairman: Sub-Gp, Housing Improvement Task Force, 2001–03; Ind. Review of Audit, Inspection, Regulation and Complaints Handling in the Public Sector (Crerar Review), 2006–08; Highlands and Is Enterprise, 2011– (Mem. Bd, 2007–11); Highlands and Is Audit Cttee, 2011–12; Convener, Standards Commn for Scotland, 2003–07; non-exec. Dir, Scottish Govt Justice Dept, 2004–11; Ind. Mem., Purchasers Information Adv. Gp, 2005–08; Ind. Reviewer, Lending Code, 2010–11. Mem., Adv. Bd, Scottish Investment Bank, 2011–. *Publications:* The Law of Banking in Scotland, 1999, 2nd edn 2007; (contrib.) Stair Memorial Encyclopaedia, 2000. *Recreations:* West Highlands of Scotland and its history, hillwalking, fishing, sailing. *Address:* Harper Macleod LLP, Ca'd'oro Building, 45 Gordon Street, Glasgow G1 3PE. *T:* (0141) 227 9377. *E:* lorne.crerar@harpermacleod.co.uk; Tigh-na-mara, Fasaich, Lonemore, Gairloch, Wester Ross IV21 2DB.

CRESSON, Edith; Commandeur du Mérite Agricole, 1983; Chevalier de la Légion d'Honneur; Grand Croix de l'Ordre National du Mérite, 1991; Member, European Commission, 1995–99; *b* 27 Jan. 1934; *née* Campion; *m* Jacques Cresson (*d* 2001); two *d*. *Educ:* Diplômée de l'Ecole des Hautes Etudes Commerciales; Dr en démographie (doctoral thesis: the life of women in a rural district of Guémené-Penfao, Loire-Atlantique). Mem., Convention des Institutions Républicaines (responsible for agricl problems), 1966; Dir of Studies, Bureau des Etudes Economiques privés (dealing especially with industrial investment); National Secretary, Parti Socialiste (in charge of youth organisation), 1974; Mem. Directing Cttee, Parti Socialiste; contested (for Parti Socialiste) Châtellerault, 1975; Mem., Eur. Parlt, 1979–81 (Mem., Cttee on Agriculture); elected Deputy, Vienne, 1981–93; Minister: of Agriculture, France, 1981–83; of For. Trade and Tourism, 1983–84; for Industrial Redeployment and Foreign Trade, 1984–86; for European Affairs, 1988–90; Pres.-Dir Gen., Schneider Industries Services Internat., 1990–91; Prime Minister of France, 1991–92; Pres. Dir Gen., Services Industries Strategies Internat. et Envmt, 1993–94. Consultant, Agence pour le Développement de l'Innovation et de la Technologie, 2008–. President: Inst d'Etudes Européennes de Paris 8, 2000–; Fondation des Ecoles de la Deuxième Chance, 2002–; Commission Scientifique de la Fondation France Israël, 2007–. Pres., Assoc. Démocratique des Français à l'Etranger, 1986–91. Member, Conseil Général of Vienne, 1978–98; Mayor of Châtellerault, Vienne, 1983–97 (Dep. Mayor, 1997–2008). Dr *hc* Weizmann Inst., Israel, 1999; DUniv Open, 1999. *Publications:* Avec le soleil, 1976; Innover ou subir, 1998; Histoires Françaises, 2007.

CRESSWELL, Rev. Amos Samuel; Chairman, Plymouth and Exeter District of the Methodist Church, 1976–91; President of the Methodist Conference, 1983–84; *b* Walsall Wood, 21 April 1926; *s* of Amos and Jane Cresswell; *m* 1956, Evelyn Rosemary Marchbanks; two *s* one *d*. *Educ:* Queen Mary's Grammar School, Walsall; University College, Durham Univ.; Wesley House, and Fitzwilliam Coll., Cambridge; Theological Seminary, Bethel bei Bielefeld, Westphalia. BA (Dunelm), Classics, 1947; BA (Cantab), Theology, 1952, MA (Cantab) 1956. Teacher of English and Latin, High School for Boys, Colchester, 1947–49; Methodist Minister, Clitheroe Circuit, 1949–50; Asst Tutor in New Testament, Richmond Coll., London, 1953–56; Minister in Darlaston (Slater St), 1956–61; Tutor in New Testament, Cliff Coll., Derbyshire, 1961–66; Minister in Bramhall Circuit (Cheadle Hulme), 1966–73; Superintendent Minister, Welwyn Garden City, 1973–76. Pres., Devonshire Assoc., 1985–86. Editor, Advance (religious weekly, formerly Joyful News), 1961–63; (with Evelyn Cresswell), Founder, Vigo Press, 1991. *Publications:* The Story of Cliff (a history of Cliff College), 1965, 2nd edn 1983; The Story They Told (a short study of the Passion Narratives in the Gospels), 1966, 2nd edn 1992; Life, Power and Hope—a study of the Holy Spirit, 1972; Lord! I've had enough! (a collection of sermons), 1991; I've Told You Twice (sermons), 1995; (with Maxwell Tow) Dr Franz Hildebrandt: Mr Valiant-for-Truth (biog.), 2000; (ed jtly) Methodist Hymns, Old and New, 2001; Whispers of Love (poems), 2004; More Whispers of Love (poems), 2010. *Recreations:* compulsive watching of sport (especially West Bromwich Albion), collecting Roman Imperial coins, reading about American Civil War, listening to music and to Shakespeare, family and friends, research into German church struggle of 1930s and 1940s. *Address:* 2 Sage Park Road, Braunton, North Devon EX33 1HH. *T:* (01271) 813835.

CRESSWELL, Jeremy Michael, CVO 1996; HM Diplomatic Service, retired; Director, Foreign Service Programme, University of Oxford, since 2010; Fellow, Kellogg College, Oxford, since 2010; *b* 1 Oct. 1949; *s* of late John Cresswell and of Jean Cresswell; *m* 1st, 1974, Petra Forwick (marr. diss. 2006); two *c*; 2nd, 2009, Dr Barbara Munske. *Educ:* Eton Coll. Choir Sch.; Sir William Borlase's Sch., Marlow; Exeter Coll., Oxford (BA Hons); Johannes-Gutenberg Univ., Mainz, Germany. Entered FCO, 1972: Brussels, 1973–77; Kuala Lumpur, 1977–78; FCO, 1978–82 (Private Sec. to Minister of State, 1980–82); Dep. Pol Advr, BMG, Berlin, 1982–86; Dep. Head, News Dept, 1986–88, Asst Head, S America Dept, 1988–90, FCO; Counsellor (Political), UK Delegn to NATO, 1990–94; Dep. Head of Mission, Prague, 1995–98; Sen. Directing Staff, RCDS, 1998; Hd of EU Dept (Bilateral), FCO, 1999–2001; Minister and Dep. Hd of Mission, Berlin, 2001–05; High Comr to Jamaica and the Commonwealth of the Bahamas, 2005–09. *Recreations:* tennis, music. *Address:* Foreign Service Programme, Department for Continuing Education, Rewley House, 1 Wellington Square, Oxford OX1 2JA. *T:* (01865) 270366. *E:* jeremy.cresswell@conted.ox.ac.uk.

CRESSWELL, John Harold; Chief Executive Officer, Arqiva, 2011–15. *Educ:* Peter Symonds Sch., Winchester; Univ. of Keele (BA Hons Econs and Pols 1983). Practice Dept, KPMG, 1983–87; Gp Financial Accountant, latterly Financial Controller, TVS, 1987–92; United Broadcasting and Entertainment Ltd: Financial Dir, Meridian Broadcasting, 1992–95, Financial Dir, 1996–98; Chief Op. Officer, 1998–2000; Granada Content: Dir of Ops, 2000–01; Chief Op. Officer, 2001–05; ITV plc: Chief Op. Officer, 2005–06, 2007–10; Interim CEO, 2006–07, 2010; Finance Dir, 2006–08. Non-executive Director: Liverpool FC and Athletics Ground plc, 2003–07; Ambassador Theatre Gp, 2004–06. *Recreations:* tennis, sport, family.

CRESSWELL, Michael John, CBE 2010; PhD; Director General, Assessment and Qualifications Alliance, 2003–10; consultant in educational assessment, since 2010; *b* 11 Dec. 1950; *s* of Sidney Walter Cresswell and Marjorie Mary Cresswell; *m* 1980, Lowena Orchard; one *s* one *d*. *Educ:* Chelsea Coll., London (BSc 1972; PGCE 1973); Inst. of Educn, London (PhD 1997). Various res. posts, NFER, 1973–80; Res. Officer, then Hd of Res., Associated Examining Bd, 1980–2000; Assessment and Qualifications Alliance: Hd of Res., 2000–02; Dir of Exams, 2002–03. Special Advr, Select Cttee on Educn, 2011–12. Visiting Professor: of Educn, Inst. of Educn, London, 2000–09; Bristol Univ., 2010–. Member, Board: TDA, 2010–12; Ofqual, 2013–. *Publications:* (with D. Vincent) Reading Tests in the Classroom, 1976; (with J. Gubb) The Second International Mathematics Study in England and Wales, 1987; (with F. Good) Grading the GCSE, 1988; Research Studies in Public Examining, 2000; over 50 other articles and papers in learned jls and other pubns. *Recreations:* birding, philosophy, theatre, music, croquet, board and computer games.

CRESSWELL, Prof. Peter, PhD; FRS 2000; Eugene Higgins Professor of Immunobiology, since 2009, and Investigator at Howard Hughes Medical Institute, since 1991, Yale University (Professor of Immunobiology, 1991); *b* 6 March 1945; *s* of Maurice and Mary Cresswell; *m* 1969, Ann K. Cooney; two *s*. *Educ:* Univ. of Newcastle upon Tyne (BSc, MSc); Guy's Hosp. Med. Sch., Univ. of London (PhD 1971). Post-doctoral Fellow, Harvard Univ., 1971–73; Duke University: Asst Prof., 1973–78; Associate Prof., 1978–85; Prof., 1985–91. *Address:* Department of Immunobiology, Howard Hughes Medical Institute, Yale University School of Medicine, PO Box 208011, New Haven, CT 06520–8011, USA. *T:* (203) 7855176.

CRESSWELL, Hon. Sir Peter (John), Kt 1991; DL; a Judge of the High Court of Justice, Queen's Bench Division, 1991–2008; arbitrator and mediator, since 2008; *b* 24 April 1944; *s* of late Jack Joseph Cresswell and Madeleine Cresswell; *m* 1972, Caroline Ward (*d* 2003); one *s* (and one *s* decd). *Educ:* St John's Sch., Leatherhead; Queens' Coll., Cambridge (MA, LLM). Called to the Bar, Gray's Inn, 1966 (Malcolm Hilbery Award), Bencher, 1989; QC 1983; a Recorder, 1986–91; Nominated Commercial List Judge, 1991–2008 (Judge in Charge, 1993–94). Mem., Senate of Inns of Court and Bar, 1981–84, 1985–86; Chm., Common Law and Commercial Bar Assoc., 1985–87; Mem., 1987–88, Vice Chm., 1989, Chm., 1990, Gen. Council of the Bar. Mem., Civil Justice Council, 1999–2003. Trustee and Mem. Bd, Cystic Fibrosis Trust, 2002–13. Patron, Soc. of Mediators, 2014–; Companion, Acad. of Experts, 2014. Hon. Mem., Canadian Bar Assoc., 1990. DL Hants, 2008. *Publications:* Encyclopaedia of Banking Law, 1982, and subseq. service issues. *Recreations:* fly-fishing, river management, the Outer Hebrides. *Club:* Flyfishers' (Pres., 2003–05).

CRETNEY, Stephen Michael, DCL; FBA 1985; Fellow of All Souls College, Oxford, 1993–2001, now Emeritus; *b* 25 Feb. 1936; *yr s* of late Fred and Winifred M. V. Cretney; *m* 1973, Rev. Antonia Lois Vanrenen, *o d* of late Lt-Comdr A. G. G. Vanrenen, RN; two *s*. *Educ:* Cheadle Hulme Sch.; Magdalen Coll., Oxford; DCL Oxon 1985. Nat. Service, 1954–56. Admitted as solicitor, 1962; Partner, Macfarlanes, London, 1964; Lecturer: Kenya Sch. of Law, Nairobi, 1966; Southampton Univ., 1968; Fellow and Tutor, Exeter Coll., Oxford, 1969–78; a Gen. Comr of Income Tax, 1970–78; a Law Comr, 1978–83; Prof. of Law, 1984–93, and Dean, Faculty of Law, 1984–88, Univ. of Bristol. Pt-time Chm. of Social Security and other Appeal Tribunals, 1985–96. Member: Departmental Cttee on Prison Disciplinary System, 1984–85; Family and Civil Cttee, Judicial Studies Bd, 1985–90; Lord Chancellor's Adv. Cttee on Legal Educn, 1987–88; President's Ancillary Relief Adv. Gp, 2000–03. Chm., Cttee of Heads of Univ. Law Schs, 1986–88. Bencher (Academic), Inner Temple, 2006. Hon. QC 1992; Hon. LLD Bristol, 2007. *Publications:* Theobald on Wills, (ed jtly) 13th edn 1970; Principles of Family Law, 1974, 7th edn (ed jtly) 2002; Family Law (Teach Yourself series), 1982; Enduring Powers of Attorney, 1986, 4th edn (ed jtly) 1996; Elements of Family Law, 1987, 4th edn 2000; (jtly) Simple Quarrels, 1994; (jtly) Divorce—the New Law, 1996; Law, Law Reform and the Family, 1998; (ed) Family Law at the Millennium, 2000; Family Law in the 20th Century: a history, 2003; Same Sex Relationships: from 'odious crime' to 'gay marriage', 2006; *contributed to:* English Private Law, 2000, 2nd edn 2007; Halsbury's Laws of England, 4th edn; Oxford DNB, 2004; The Judicial House of Lords, 2nd edn 2009; Oxford International Encyclopedia of Legal History, 2009; articles and notes in legal jls. *Address:* 8 Elm Farm Close, Wantage, Oxon OX12 9FD. *T:* (01235) 763192. *Club:* Oxford and Cambridge.

CREW, Sir Edward (Michael), Kt 2001; QPM 1991; DL; Chairman, Surrey Health NHS Clinical Commissioning Group, 2013–14; *b* 13 Jan. 1946; *s* of Joseph Edwin Crew and Cecilia May Crew (*née* Davis); *m* 1967, Gillian Glover; one *s* one *d*. *Educ:* Haberdashers' Aske's Hatcham Sch. for Boys; Police Staff Coll. Joined Metropolitan Police from Cadet Corps, 1965; Inspector, 1970; Mem., investigation team into breach of security at Buckingham Palace, 1982; Chief Supt, comdg SE London Traffic Div., 1982–84; Asst Chief Constable, 1984–89, Dep. Chief Constable, 1989–93, Kent County Constabulary; rcds, 1988; Chief Constable: Northants, 1993–96; W Midlands Police, 1996–2002. Advr to Ind. Rev. of Police Service Pay and Conditions, 2011. DL West Midlands, 1999. CCMI 2001. Hon. LLD Birmingham, 2001. OStJ 1989. *Recreations:* good food, walking, gardening, travel.

CREWE, Sir Ivor (Martin), Kt 2006; DL; Master, University College, Oxford, since 2008; *b* 15 Dec. 1945; *s* of Francis and Lilly Crewe; *m* 1968, Jill Barbara (*née* Gadian); two *s* one *d*. *Educ:* Manchester Grammar Sch.; Exeter Coll., Oxford (MA; Hon. Fellow, 1998); London School of Economics (MScEcon). Assistant Lecturer, Univ. of Lancaster, 1967–69; Junior Research Fellow, Nuffield Coll., Oxford, 1969–71; Lectr, Dept of Govt, Univ. of Essex, 1971–74; Dir SSRC Data Archive, 1974–82; University of Essex: Prof. of Govt, 1982–2007; Pro-Vice-Chancellor (Academic), 1992–95; Vice-Chancellor, 1995–2007; Res. Prof., 2007–09; Vis. Prof., 2009–. Member: Exec. Cttee and UK Council, UUK, 2000–07 (Chm., England and NI Bd, 2001–03; Pres., 2003–05); Bd, Univ. and Colls Employers Assoc., 2001–07; Bd, Leadership Foundn, 2003–09; Adv. Bd, Office of Fair Access, 2013–; Governing Body: SOAS, 2007–; Univ. of the Arts, London, 2008–; Trustee, Higher Educn Policy Inst., 2007– (Chair, 2015–). Pres., Acad. of Social Scis, 2014–. Member: High Council, Eur. Univ. Inst., Florence, 1998–; Internat. Adv. Bd, Freie Universität Berlin, 2008–. Dir, USS Ltd, 2006–07. Co-Dir, Feb. 1974, Oct. 1974, 1979 British Election Studies; elections analyst for: BBC TV, 1982–89; The Times, 1990–92; BBC World TV, 1997, 2001, 2005. High Steward, Colchester, 2003–09. Editor, 1977–82, Co-editor, 1984–92, British Journal of Political Science. DL Essex, 2002. Hon. Fellow, Nuffield Coll., Oxford, 2008. Hon. DLitt Salford, 1999; DUniv Essex, 2009. *Publications:* (with A. H. Halsey) Social Survey of the Civil

Service (HMSO), 1969; ed, British Political Sociology Yearbook, vol. 1 1974, vol. 2 1975; (with Bo Sarlvik) Decade of Dealignment, 1983; (with Anthony Fox) British Parliamentary Constituencies, 1984; (ed jtly) Electoral Change in Western Democracies, 1985; (ed jtly) Political Communications: the general election campaign of 1983, 1986, of 1987, 1989, of 1992, 1995, of 1997, 1998; (with Anthony Fox and Neil Day) The British Electorate 1963–87, 1991, 2nd edn as The British Electorate 1963–92, 1992; (with Anthony King) SDP: the birth, life and death of the Social Democratic Party, 1995; (jtly) The New British Politics, 1998, 3rd edn 2004; (with Anthony King) The Blunders of Our Governments, 2013; articles in various academic jls on public opinion, parties and elections in Britain. *Recreations:* music, mountain walking, ski-ing, friends, family. *Address:* University College, Oxford OX1 4BH.

CREWE, Susan Anne; Editor, House and Garden, 1994–2014; *b* 31 Aug. 1949; *d* of late Richard Cavendish and Pamela Cavendish; *m* 1st, 1970, Quentin Crewe (marr. diss.; he *d* 1998); one *s* one *d*; 2nd, 1984, (Christopher) Nigel (John) Ryan, CBE (marr. diss.; he *d* 2014). *Educ:* St Mary's Sch., Wantage; Cheshire Coll. of Agriculture. Harpers & Queen magazine, 1986–92: shopping editor, 1987; consultant editor, 1990; social editor, 1991–92; subseq. freelance writer, broadcaster, journalist; contribs to The Times, Daily Telegraph, Daily Mail, Evening Standard and Literary Review. *Recreations:* gardening, sea-swimming, music. *Address:* Ladysyke House, Haverthwaite, Ulverston, Cumbria LA12 8PQ. *Club:* Academy.

See also Baron Cavendish of Furness.

CRIBB, Derek Wayne, FCA; FRSM; Chief Executive, Institute and Faculty of Actuaries, since 2011; *b* Swansea, 5 July 1966; *s* of Albert John Cribb and Rita Cribb; *m* 1993, Tessa Julie Stone; one *s* one *d*. *Educ:* Ringwood Comp.; Canford Sch.; Imperial Coll. London (BSc Hons Chem.). ACA 1992, FCA 2012. Audit Manager, Touche Ross & Co., 1989–93; Internat. Audit, Saudi Internat. Bank, 1993–94; Projects, Central Transport Rental Gp, 1994–96; Business Support Manager, EMI Records, 1996–97; Gp Hd of Corporate Planning and Investor Relns, Booker plc, 1997–2000; Consultant, Cisco Systems Europe, 2000–01; Chief Financial Officer, Customers and Products, Barclays plc, 2001–04; Gp Finance Consultant, Serco plc, 2004–05; Chief Financial Officer, Public Sector, Liberata plc, 2005; Finance and Ops Dir, Navigant Consulting Europe, 2006–07; Chief Operating Officer, Pension Protection Fund, 2007–09. Trustee, Hockering Residents' Assoc., 2011–. FRSocMed 2012. *Recreations:* good food, good wine, bad golf. *Address:* Institute and Faculty of Actuaries, 7th Floor, Holborn Gate, 326–330 High Holborn, WC1 7PP. *T:* (020) 7632 2190. *E:* derek.cribb@actuaries.org.uk. *Club:* Wisley Golf.

CRIBB, Joseph Edmond; Keeper of Coins and Medals, British Museum, 2003–10; *b* 30 Oct. 1947; *s* of Peter William Cribb and Rewa Annie Cribb (*née* Bloor); *m* 1971, Margaret Morrison Moore; two *s* two *d*. *Educ:* Queen Mary Coll., London (BA Hons Latin). British Museum: Curator of Asian coins, Dept of Coins and Medals, 1970–2003; Curator, HSBC Money Gall., 1997. Hon. Sec., 1983–94, Pres., 2004–09, RNS; Sec. Gen., Oriental Numismatic Soc., 2011–. Trustee: Ditchling Mus., 2000–; Living Archive, Milton Keynes, 2014–; Milton Keynes Mus., 2015–. Hon. Res. Associate, Ashmolean Mus., Oxford, 2011–. Hirayama Inst. of Silk Road Studies (Kamakura) Award, 1997; Silver Medal, RNS, 1999; Archer M. Huntington Medal, Amer. Numismatic Soc., 2009; Nelson Wright Medal, Indian Numismatic Soc., 2010. *Publications:* Money, from Cowrie Shells to Credit Cards, 1986; Money Fun Book, 1986; Money in the Bank, 1987; The Coin Atlas, 1990, 2nd edn 2003; Eyewitness Guide: Money, 1990, 2nd edn 1999; Collected Papers of Nicholas Lowick, vol. I, 1990, vol. II, 1991; Crossroads of Asia, 1992; A Catalogue of Sycee in the British Museum, Chinese Silver Currency Ingots *c*.1750–1933, 1992; Studies in Silk Road Coins and Culture, 1997; Magic Coins of Java, Bali and the Malay Peninsula, 1999; The Order of Industrial Heroism - Eric Gill's Medal for the Daily Herald, 2000; The Chand Collection - Ancient Indian Coins, 2003; The Indian Coinage Tradition, 2005; After Alexander: Central Asia before Islam, 2007; Eric Gill and Ditchling: the workshop tradition, 2007; Coins from Kashmir Smast, 2008; Eric Gill: lust for letter and line, 2011; Kushan, Kushano-Sasanian and Kidarite Coins from the Collection of the American Numismatic Society, 2015. *Recreations:* history of the Guild of St Joseph and St Dominic, Ditchling, numismatic research, grandchildren. *Address:* 141 Windsor Street, Wolverton, Milton Keynes MK12 5AW. *E:* joecribb@btinternet.com.

See also P. J. W. Cribb.

CRIBB, Phillip James William, PhD; botanist; Deputy Keeper of Herbarium, 1989–2006, Hon. Research Fellow, since 2006, Royal Botanic Gardens, Kew; *b* 12 March 1946; *s* of Peter William Cribb and Rewa Annie, (Nancy), Cribb (*née* Bloor); *m* 1984, Marianne Gafafer. *Educ:* Christ's Coll., Cambridge (BA 1968); Univ. of Birmingham (PhD 1972). Joined Royal Botanic Gardens, Kew, as Higher Scientific Officer, 1974. Hon. Research Associate: Harvard Univ., 1979–90; Royal Holloway and Bedford New Coll., Univ. of London, 2006–. Trustee: Gilbert White & Oates Mus., Selborne, 1993–2006; Jany Renz Foundn, Univ. of Basel, 2003–. Veitch Meml Medal, RHS, 2006; Linnean Medal for Botany, 2007. *Publications:* The Genus Paphiopedilum, 1987; The Genus Cypripedium, 1997; (jtly) Slipper Orchids of Vietnam, 2003; (with M. Tibbs) A Very Victorian Passion, 2004; (with C. Grey-Wilson) Guide to the Flowers of Western China, 2011; (contrib. and ed jtly) Genera Orchidacearum, 6 Vols, 1999–2014; (with Werner Frosch) Hardy Cypripedium, 2012. *Recreations:* natural history, travel. *Address:* The Herbarium, Royal Botanic Gardens, Kew, Richmond, Surrey TW9 3AE. *T:* (020) 8332 5245, *Fax:* (020) 8332 5278. *E:* p.cribb@kew.co.org.

See also J. E. Cribb.

CRICH, Michael Arthur, FCMA; Corporate Director, Economy, Enterprise and Environment, Cornwall Council, since 2014 (Corporate Director, Resources, 2010–14, Environment, Planning and Economy, 2013); *b* 9 Jan. 1957; *s* of Arthur Crich and Elizabeth Crich; *m* 1980, Gillian Anne Chamberlain; three *s* one *d*. *Educ:* Slough Grammar Sch.; Univ. of Hull; Emile Woolf Coll.; Warwick Business Sch., Univ. of Warwick (MBA 2002). FCMA 1991; CGMA. Financial Controller, Wendy Restaurants (UK) Ltd, 1981–84; Sketchley Dry Cleaning: Finance Manager, 1984–86; Financial Controller, 1986–87; Financial Dir, 1987–91; London Borough of Brent: Gen. Manager, Contract Services, 1992–93; Dir, Brent Business Support, 1993–96; Exec. Dir, Finance and Corporate Services, London Borough of Lambeth, 1996–2001; Dir of Resources, English Heritage, 2002–07; Corporate Dir, Resources, Advantage W Midlands, 2008–09; Dir, Michael Crich Associates Ltd, 2009–10. *Publications:* (contrib.) Local Government Governance, 2001. *Recreations:* food and wine, live music, motor racing, le parkour. *Address:* Cornwall Council, The Exchange, New County Hall, Treyew Road, Truro TR1 3AY.

CRICHTON, family name of **Earl of Erne**.

CRICHTON, Viscount; John Henry Michael Ninian Crichton; Founder Director, John Crichton Property, since 2008; *b* 19 June 1971; *s* and *heir* of Earl of Erne, *qv*. *Educ:* Sunningdale Prep. Sch.; Shiplake Coll.; L'Institut de Touraine, Tours. Douglas & Gordon Ltd, 1992–98; Associate Dir, Lane Fox Residential Ltd, 1998–2007. Trustee, Hope for Youth, NI (formerly Women Caring Trust for NI), 2009–. *Recreations:* theatre, amateur dramatics, shooting, ski-ing. *Address:* Flat 1, 42 Redcliffe Road, SW10 9NJ; West Wing, Crom Castle, Newtownbutler, Co. Fermanagh, N Ireland. *Club:* White's.

CRICHTON, Nicholas, CBE 2012; a District Judge (Magistrates' Courts) (formerly Metropolitan Stipendiary Magistrate), 1987–2014; a Recorder, 1995–2014; *b* 23 Oct. 1943; *s* of late Charles Ainslie Crichton and Vera Pearl McCallum; *m* 1st, 1973, Ann Valerie (*née* Jackson) (marr. diss. 2008); two *s*; 2nd, 2014, Mrs Jane Maskell. *Educ:* Haileybury & ISC; Queen's Univ., Belfast (LLB, 2nd Cl. Hons). Schoolmaster, Pembroke House Sch., Gilgil, Kenya, 1963; cowhand, Montana, USA, 1966; articled to late T. J. Burrows, Currey & Co., SW1, 1968–70; Assistant Solicitor: Currey & Co., 1970–71; Nicholls Christie & Crocker, 1972–74; Partner, Nicholls Christie & Crocker, 1974–86. An Asst Recorder, 1991–95. Mem., Family Justice Council, 2004–14. *Recreations:* cricket, golf, watching rugby, gardening, walking, reading, bird watching, photography.

CRICHTON-STUART, family name of **Marquess of Bute**.

CRICK, Michael Lawrence; broadcaster and writer; Political Correspondent, Channel 4 News, since 2011; *b* 21 May 1958; *s* of John Fairhurst Crick and late Patricia Margaret Crick (*née* Wright); *m* 1985, Beatrice Margaret Sarah Hounsell (marr. diss. 2008); one *d*; partner, Lucy Katharine Anna Hetherington; one *d*. *Educ:* Manchester Grammar Sch. (Foundn Schol.); New Coll., Oxford (BA 1st Cl. Hons PPE 1979). Pres., Oxford Union, 1979. Trainee journalist, ITN, 1980–82; Channel 4 News: producer, 1982–84; reporter, 1984–88; Washington Corresp., 1988–90; BBC: reporter, Panorama, 1990–92; reporter, 1992–2007, Political Editor, 2007–11, Newsnight. Chm., Young Fabian Gp, 1980–81. Organiser, Shareholders United, 1998–99 (Vice-Chm., 1999–2001). Lay Gov., Univ. of Manchester, 2012–; Bd Mem., Manchester University Press, 2013–. Mem., Manchester United Fans' Forum, 2000–02. Specialist Journalist of the Year 2012–13, RTS, 2014; Journalist of the Year, Political Studies Assoc., 2014. *Publications:* (Founder Ed.) Oxford Handbook, 1978; (Founder Ed.) Oxbridge Careers Handbook, 1979; Militant, 1984; Scargill and the Miners, 1985; (with D. Smith) Manchester United: the betrayal of a legend, 1989; Jeffrey Archer: stranger than fiction, 1995; The Complete Manchester United Trivia Factbook, 1996; Michael Heseltine: a biography, 1997; The Boss: the many sides of Alex Ferguson, 2002; In Search of Michael Howard, 2005. *Recreations:* following Manchester United, swimming, hill-walking, collecting political and football books and memorabilia. *Address:* Channel 4 News, ITN, 4 Millbank, SW1P 3JA. *E:* michael.crick@itn.co.uk. *W:* www.twitter.com/MichaelLCrick.

CRICKHOWELL, Baron *cr* 1987 (Life Peer), of Pont Esgob in the Black Mountains and County of Powys; **Roger Nicholas Edwards;** PC 1979; Chairman, ITNET Plc, 1995–2004; *b* 25 Feb. 1934; *s* of late (H. C.) Ralph Edwards, CBE, FSA, and Marjorie Ingham Brooke; *m* 1963, Ankaret Healing; one *s* two *d*. *Educ:* Westminster Sch.; Trinity Coll., Cambridge, 1954–57; read History: BA 1957, MA 1968. Served 1st Bn, RWF, 1952–54 (2nd Lt). Member of Lloyds, 1965–2002. Director: Brandt's Insce Gp, 1957–76; A L Sturge Ltd, 1970–76; Brandt's Ltd, 1974–76; Globtik Tankers Ltd, 1976–79; P A Internat. & Sturge Underwriting Agency Ltd, 1977–79; Dir, 1987–97, Chm., 1997–2002, HTV Ltd; Dir, Associated British Ports Hldgs, 1988–99; Vice-Chm., Anglesey Mining, 1988–2000; Chm., Cameron May, 1992–94. MP (C) Pembroke, 1970–87. Opposition spokesman on Welsh affairs, 1975–79; Sec. of State for Wales, 1979–87. House of Lords: Mem., EU Sub-Cttee D, 2000–05; EU Sub-Cttee C, 2006–10; Sci. and Technol. Cttee, 2007–12; Constitution Cttee, 2010–. Chm., NRA, 1989–96 (Chm., Adv. Cttee, 1988–89). Pres., Univ. of Wales, Cardiff (formerly Univ. of Wales Coll. of Cardiff), 1988–98 (Hon. Fellow, UC, Cardiff, 1985). Dir, WNO, 1988–92; Chm., Cardiff Bay Opera Trust, 1994–96. President: Contemporary Art Society for Wales, 1988–93; SE Wales Arts Assoc., 1988–94; Mem., Cttee, AA, 1988–98. Hon. LLD Glamorgan, 2001. *Publications:* Opera House Lottery, 1997; Westminster, Wales and Water, 1999; The Rivers Join, 2009; articles and reviews in The Connoisseur and other jls. *Recreations:* fishing, gardening, collecting watercolours and drawings. *Address:* Y Cwt Mochyn, Manson Lane, Monmouth NP25 5RD; 4 Henning Street, SW11 3DR. *Club:* Brooks's.

CRICKMAY, Anthony John; photographer, since 1961; *b* 20 May 1937; *s* of Jack and Peggy Crickmay. *Educ:* Belmont Sch., Dorking. Photographer, specialising in theatre, portraits, fashion, reportage; work has appeared in many publications throughout the world; has photographed personalities and stars incl. the Queen, the Queen Mother, the Prime Minister and family, etc. *Publications:* The Principles of Classical Dance, 1979; Lynn Seymour, 1980; Dancers, 1982. *Recreations:* swimming, tennis, but most of all, photography. *Address:* c/o Camera Press, 21 Queen Elizabeth Street, SE1 2PD. *T:* (020) 7378 1300.

CRIDLAND, John Robert, CBE 2006; Director-General, Confederation of British Industry, 2011–15 (Deputy Director-General, 2000–11); *b* 3 Feb. 1961; *s* of Walter and Doreen Cridland; *m* 1987, Denise Yates; one *s* one *d*. *Educ:* Christ's Coll., Cambridge (MA). Confederation of British Industry, 1982–2015: Director: Envmtl Affairs, 1991–95; Human Resources Policy, 1995–2000. Member: Low Pay Commn, 1997–2007; UK Commn for Employment and Skills, 2011–15; Vice Chair, LSC, 2007–10; Councillor, ACAS, 1998–2007; Dir, Business in the Community, 2011–15. Mem. Council, Cranfield Univ., 2008–14. *Recreations:* history, cinema, castles. *Address:* c/o Confederation of British Industry, Cannon Place, 78 Cannon Street, EC4N 6HN.

CRIGMAN, David Ian; QC 1989; *b* 16 Aug. 1945; *s* of late Jack Crigman and of Sylvia Crigman; *m* 1980, Judith Ann Penny; one *s*. *Educ:* King Edward's Sch., Birmingham; Univ. of Leeds (LLB Hons). Called to the Bar, Gray's Inn, 1969; a Recorder, 1985. *Publications: novels:* What's Truth Got To Do With It?, 2006; The Molecule Man, 2008; In Death We Trust, 2009; The Hangman's Fracture, 2011. *Recreations:* tennis, ski-ing, writing, travel. *Address:* St Philips Chambers, 55 Temple Row, Birmingham B2 5LS. *T:* (0121) 246 7000.

CRINE, Simon John Geoffrey; Interim Director of Communications, Ofgem; Senior Advisor, UK Statistics Authority, since 2013; *b* Weston-super-Mare, 30 Nov. 1955; *s* of Geoffrey V. Crine and Ruby E. Crine; *m* Alison Blom-Cooper; one *s* one *d*. *Educ:* Weston-super-Mare Grammar Sch.; Univ. of York (BA Hons Hist.). Various political and public policy appts, 1979–84; Dir, Nat. Campaign for the Arts, 1985–90; Gen. Sec., Fabian Soc., 1990–96; Dir, Public Affairs, APCO UK, 1997–2004; Dir, England and Industry, Ofcom, 2004–06; Dir of Corporate Affairs, Digital UK, 2006–12. Trustee, Money Advice Trust, 2013–. Mem., Adv. Bd, Social Market Foundn, 2000–09. Harkness Fellow, Washington, DC, 1993–94. *Publications:* various Fabian, WEA and Low Pay Unit reports; occasional journalism. *Recreations:* reading the papers, ball games, outdoors, arts, history, politics and public affairs. *T:* 07711 066378. *E:* simonjgcrine@gmail.com.

CRIPPS, family name of **Baron Parmoor**.

CRIPPS, Prof. Martin William, PhD; FBA 2011; Professor of Economics, University College London, since 2006; *b* London, 25 April 1960; *s* of Leonard Albert Cripps and Shirley Anne Cripps; *m* 1989, Louise Pincombe; two *s* two *d*. *Educ:* London Sch. of Econs and Pol Sci. (BSc Econs; MSc Econs; PhD Econs). Lectr, 1987–97, Prof. of Econs, 1997–2000, Univ. of Warwick; Wallace Dist. Prof. of Econs, Washington Univ., St Louis, 2000–06. Mem. Council, Game Theory Soc., 2007. Fellow, Econometric Soc., 2008. *Recreations:* squash, cycling, walking. *Address:* Department of Economics, University College London, Gower Street, WC1E 6BT. *E:* m.cripps@ucl.ac.uk.

CRISHAM, Catherine Ann; lawyer, Treasury Solicitor's Department, 2003–07; *b* 29 April 1950; *d* of Air Vice-Marshal W. J. Crisham, CB, CBE and late Maureen Teresa Crisham (*née* Bergin). *Educ:* St Anne's Coll., Oxford (BA); Exeter Univ. (LLM). Lecturer in European Community Law: Leiden Univ., 1977–80; London Univ., 1980–82; called to the Bar, Gray's Inn, 1981; private practice, 1982–84; lawyer, MAFF, 1984–88 and 1991–94; Legal Sec., European Court of Justice, 1988–90; Hd, Legal Directorate, MAFF, subseq. DEFRA, 1994–2003. *Recreations:* classical studies, theatre, walking.

CRISP, family name of **Baron Crisp**.

CRISP, Baron *cr* 2006 (Life Peer), of Eaglescliffe in the County of Durham; **Edmund Nigel Ramsay Crisp,** KCB 2003; consultant and author on global health and international development; *b* 14 Jan. 1952; *s* of late Edmund Theodore Crisp and Dorothy Sheppard Crisp (*née* Ramsay); *m* 1976, Siân Elaine Jenkins; one *s* one *d*. *Educ:* Uppingham Sch.; St John's Coll., Cambridge (BA Hons 1973; MA 1976; Hon. Fellow 2008). Dep. Dir, Halewood Community Council, 1973; Production Manager, Trebor, 1978; Dir, Cambs Community Council, 1981; Unit Gen. Manager, E Berks HA, 1986; Chief Executive: Heatherwood and Wexham Park Hosps, 1988; Oxford Radcliffe Hosp. NHS Trust, 1993–97; Regl Dir, S Thames, 1977–98, London, 1999–2000, NHS Exec., DoH; Permanent Sec. and Chief Exec., DoH and NHS, 2000–06. Co-Chm., All Party Parly Global Health, 2011–. Hon. Prof., LSHTM, 2007–; Sen. Fellow, Inst. of Healthcare Improvement, Cambridge, Mass, 2007–; Dist. Vis. Fellow, Harvard Sch. of Public Health, 2010–; Regents' Lectr, Univ. of Calif, Berkeley, 2014. Chm., Sightsavers Internat., 2008–15; Mem. Council, BHF, 2008–10. Advr, HLM Architects, 2007–. Trustee: Florence Nightingale Mus., 2007–10; Rand Europe, 2008–. Co-Chair: Zambia UK Health Alliance, 2009–; Uganda UK Health Alliance, 2013–. For. Associate, Inst. of Medicine, USA, 2012. CCMI 2002; Companion, Inst. of Healthcare Mgt, 2003. Hon. FRCP, 2004; Hon. FRCPath 2010; Hon. FRCOG 2011. Hon. DSc City, 2001. *Publications:* Global Health Partnerships, 2007; Scaling Up, Saving Lives, 2008; Turning the World Upside Down: the search for global health in the 21st century, 2010; 24 Hours to Save the NHS: the Chief Executive's account of reform 2000 to 2006, 2011; (ed with Francis Omaswa) African Health Leaders: making change and claiming the future, 2014; articles in various jls incl. Lancet, BMJ and New England Jl of Medicine. *Recreation:* the countryside. *Address:* House of Lords, SW1A 0PW. *Club:* Reform.

CRISP, Clement Andrew, OBE 2005; contributor, since 1956, and Dance Critic, since 1970, Financial Times; *b* 21 Sept. 1931; *s* of Charles Evelyn Gifford Crisp and Bertha Dorothy (*née* Dean). *Educ:* Oxted Sch.; Bordeaux Univ.; Keble Coll., Oxford Univ. (BA). Critic and dance writer to various jls, 1956–; Ballet Critic, The Spectator, 1966–70. Lectr, Librarian and Archivist to Royal Acad. of Dancing, 1963–85, Archivist, 1985–2001. Associate Prof., Univ. of Notre Dame (London Faculty), 1997–2008. Queen Elizabeth II Coronation Award, Royal Acad. of Dancing, 1992; Vaslav Nijinsky Medal, Poland, 1995. Knight, Order of Dannebrog (Denmark), 1992. *Publications:* (with Peter Brinson) Ballet for All, 1971, rev. edn 1980; with Mary Clarke: Ballet: an illustrated history, 1973, rev. edn 1992; Making a Ballet, 1974; Ballet in Art, 1976; Design for Ballet, 1978; Introducing Ballet, 1978; Ballet-goer's Guide, 1981; History of Dance, 1981; How to Enjoy Ballet, 1983, 2nd edn 1987; Dancer, 1984; Ballerina, 1987; London Contemporary Dance, 1989. *Recreations:* avoiding noise, gardening, despair about dancing. *Address:* 82 Marsham Court, Marsham Street, SW1P 4LA.

CRISP, Sir John Charles, 5th Bt *cr* 1913, of Bungay, Suffolk; *b* 10 Dec. 1955; *s* of Sir (John) Peter Crisp, 4th Bt and Judith Mary Crisp (*née* Gillett); *S* father, 2005; *m* 1992, Mary Jo, *e d* of Dr and Mrs D. MacAuley; one *s*. *Educ:* Radley; Birmingham Univ. *Heir:* *s* George Peter Daniel Crisp, *b* 17 Sept. 1993.

CRISP, June Frances; *see* de Moller, J. F.

CRISPIN, Prof. Sheila Margaret, PhD; FRCVS; independent consultant; Visiting Professorial Fellow, University of Bristol, since 2004; *b* 21 Jan. 1944; *d* of William George Crispin and Winifred Margaret Crispin. *Educ:* Ulverston Grammar Sch.; University Coll. of N Wales (Bangor) (BSc Hons Zool. 1967); Girton Coll., Cambridge (ARC Vet. Trng Schol.; MA, VetMB 1972 (Dist.); Grad. Schol.); Univ. of Edinburgh (PhD 1984). DVA 1976; DVOphthal 1985; DipECVO 1993; FRCVS 1999. In private practice, Cumbria, 1972; Clin. Schol., then Univ. House Surgeon, Univ. of Cambridge, 1972–75; Bye-Fellow and Dir of Studies in Vet. Medicine, Girton Coll., Cambridge, 1974–75; Lectr, Univ. of Edinburgh, 1975–83; University of Bristol: Lectr, 1983–91; Sen. Lectr, 1991–2000; Reader, 2000–02; Prof. of Comparative Ophthalmol., 2002–04; Res. Fellow, 2003–04. Share-Jones Lectr, RCVS, 1991. Bull Fellow, Univ. of Guelph, Canada, 2000. Co-Chm., Quinquennial Sci. Audit, DEFRA Lab. Sci. Agencies, 2005–07; Mem., Sci. Adv. Council, DEFRA, 2005–09. Chief Panellist, BVA/Kennel Club/Internat. Sheep Dog Soc. Eye Scheme, 1992–96, 1998–99 and 2008–09. Chm., Dog Welfare Rev. Bd, 2010; Founding Chm., Adv. Council on Welfare Issues of Dog Breeding, 2010–14. Member: Vet. Services Adv. Cttee, BVA, 1995–98; Council, RCVS, 1997–2015 (Univ. Rep., 1997–2003; Chm. of various cttees; Pres., 2006–07); Sci. Adv. Cttee, Animal Health Trust, 1998–; Adv. Gp, Ind. Inquiry into Dog Breeding, 2009–10; Companion Animal Welfare Council, 2009–. Chm., British Assoc. for Vet. Ophthalmol., 1983–86. Trustee, Wildlife Information Network, 2007–09. Sen. Affiliate MRCOphth (Associate MRCOphth 1990). Simon Award, 1989, Life Mem., 2014, British Small Animal Vet. Assoc.; Lifetime Achievement Award, British Assoc. of Vet. Ophthalmologists, 2013; J. A. Wight Meml Award, 2015. *Publications:* (ed and contrib. with S. M. Petersen-Jones) Manual of Small Animal Ophthalmology, 1993, 2nd edn 2002; (ed jtly and contrib.) A Colour Atlas and Text of Equine Ophthalmology, 1995, 2nd edn 2004; (ed and contrib. with K. C. Barnett) Feline Ophthalmology: an atlas and text, 1998; Notes on Veterinary Ophthalmology, 2005; contribs mainly in the field of comparative ophthalmology; peer-reviewed papers and book chapters. *Recreations:* sport (Univ. of Wales gold (Captain, athletics and hockey); Univ. of Cambridge blue (Captain, hockey and cricket); Captain, Combined Univs hockey team; Mem., British Univs Sports Fedn hockey team; Wales sen. hockey squad), mountaineering, sailing, classical music, environmental stewardship, moral philosophy. *Address:* Cold Harbour Farm, Underbarrow, Kendal, Cumbria LA8 8HD. *T:* and *Fax:* (01539) 568637. *E:* s.m.crispin@bris.ac.uk, s.crispin@rcvs.org.uk, sheilacrispin6@gmail.com. *Clubs:* Farmers, Kennel; Pinnacle.

CRITCHETT, Sir Charles George Montague, 4th Bt *cr* 1908, of Harley Street, St Marylebone; engineer, W. S. Atkins, since 1998; *b* 2 April 1965; *s* of Sir Ian George Lorraine Critchett, 3rd Bt and of Jocelyn Daphne Margret Critchett (*née* Hall); *S* father, 2004; *m* 2004, Joanna Jane Sugden, *d* of late Dr H. J. S. Sugden and of Mrs Pamela Morrow; two *s*. *Educ:* Harrow; Univ. of Bristol (BEng 1st Cl. Aeronautical Engrg); Wolfson Coll., Cambridge (PGCE Design, Mfr and Mgt). Aerodynamicist and Project Mgr, British Aerospace, 1990–97. *Heir:* *s* Ralph Henry Anderson Critchett, *b* 22 Jan. 2006.

CRITCHLEY, Philip, CB 1990; consultant, Martin Jack & Co., 1991–2005; *b* 31 Jan. 1931; *s* of Henry Stephen and Edith Adela Critchley; *m* 1962, Stella Ann Barnes; two *s* one *d*. *Educ:* Manchester Grammar Sch.; Balliol Coll., Oxford (MA, 2nd Classical Mods and Greats). National Service, Intelligence Corps, 1953–55. Joined Min. of Housing and Local Govt, later Dept of Environment, 1955: Principal, 1960; Asst Sec., 1969; Under Sec., 1980; Dir of Waste Disposal, 1983; Dir of Contracts, Highways Administration and Maintenance, 1985–90; Dir of Network Mgt and Maintenance, 1990–91, Dept of Transport. Volunteer, Ulverston Br., MIND, 1996–2013. Mem., Cttee, S Cumbria Mental Health User and Carer Forum, 2004–09; Advr, Cumbria Mental Health Gp, 2009–13. FRSA 1990. *Recreations:* philosophy, writing poetry. *Address:* Infield House, Kendall Ground, Lowick, Ulverston, Cumbria LA12 8ER. *T:* (01229) 885254. *Clubs:* Blackheath Harriers; Oxford Union Society.

CRITCHLOW, Christopher Allan; His Honour Judge Critchlow; DL; a Circuit Judge, since 2000; Resident Judge, Guildford Crown Court, since 2008; *b* 8 July 1951; *s* of late Charles Brandon Critchlow and Eileen Margerie (*née* Bowers); *m* 1974, Wendy Anne Lucey; one *s* two *d*. *Educ:* Royal Grammar Sch., Lancaster; Exeter Univ. (LLB). FCIArb 1994. Called to the Bar, Inner Temple, 1973, Bencher, 2003; Mem., Western Circuit; Asst Recorder, 1987–91; a Recorder, 1991–2000. Hon. Recorder of Guildford, 2010. Gov., RGS Guildford, 2004– (Vice-Chm.). DL Surrey, 2009. *Recreations:* golf, bridge, listening to music, reading history. *Address:* Guildford Crown Court, Bedford Road, Guildford, Surrey GU1 4ST. *Club:* Reform.

CROALL, Simon Martin; QC 2008; *b* Bramhall, Cheshire, 12 Feb. 1963; *s* of Alan and Jean Croall; 1st, 1989 (marr. diss. 2010); one *s* one *d*; 2nd, 2013, Davina Richardson. *Educ:* Stockport Grammar Sch.; Emmanuel Coll., Cambridge (BA Law 1985; MA). Called to the Bar, Middle Temple, 1986; in practice as barrister, 1986–. Mem., Professional Conduct and Complaints Cttee, Bar Council of England and Wales, 2001–04. Gov., Stanley Infant Sch., 1997–2001. *Publications:* (contrib.) Butterworth's Commercial Court & Arbitration Pleadings, 2005. *Recreations:* travel, golf, walking, tennis. *Address:* Quadrant Chambers, 10 Fleet Street, EC4Y 1AU. *T:* (020) 7583 4444, *Fax:* (020) 7583 4455. *E:* simon.croall@quadrantchambers.com.

CROCKARD, Prof. (Hugh) Alan, DSc; FRCS, FRCP; FDS RCS; National Director for Modernising Medical Careers, Department of Health, 2004–07; Professor of Surgical Neurology, Institute of Neurology, University College London, 2001–06, now Professor Emeritus; Consultant Neurosurgeon, National Hospital for Neurology and Neurosurgery, 1978–2006, now Hon. Consultant; *b* 24 Jan. 1943; *s* of Hugh and Mary Crockard; *m* 1977, Dr Caroline Orr; two *s*. *Educ:* Royal Belfast Academical Instn; Queen's Univ., Belfast (MB BCh, BAO 1966; DSc 2000). FRCSEd 1970; FRCS 1971; FDS RCS 2001; FRCP 2003. Wellcome Surgical Fellow, 1973; Hunterian Prof., RCS, 1974; Fogarty Internat. Fellow, 1974, Asst Prof., 1975, Univ. of Chicago; Sen. Lectr, QUB, 1975–78. Dir, Raven Dept of Educn, RCS, 1998–2003. Vis. Prof. of Surgical Neurology, Univ. of WA, 2000. Co-Founder, Hill Surgical Workshops, 1990. Chm., Global Spinal Tumour Study Gp, 2011–. President: British Cervical Spine Soc., 1997–99 (Co-Founder, 1986); Eur. Cervical Spine Res. Soc., 1999–2001; Member: British Soc. of Neurological Surgeons; Amer. Acad. of Neurological Surgeons. Sinclair Medal for Surgery, QUB, 1966; Olivecrona Lectr, Karolinska Inst., Stockholm, 1995; Harrington Medal, Scoliosis Res. Soc., USA, 1995; Arnott Demonstr, RCS, 1995. *Publications:* (jtly) Trauma Care, 1981; (jtly) Neurosurgery: scientific basis of clinical practice, 1985, 3rd edn 2000; more than 300 papers. *Recreations:* sailing, photography, birdwatching, travel, music. *Address:* Victor Horsley Department of Neurosurgery, National Hospital for Neurology and Neurosurgery, Queen Square, WC1N 3BG. *Clubs:* Athenæum, Royal Ocean Racing; Ocean Cruising.

CROCKART, Michael; *b* Perth, 19 March 1966; *m*; two *s*. *Educ:* Perth High Sch.; Edinburgh Univ. (BSc Social Scis 1987). Police Constable, Lothians and Borders Police, 1990–98; Standard Life Assurance Co.: systems developer, 1998–2005; Lead Business Service Developer, 2006–07; IT Project Manager, 2007–10. Contested (Lib Dem): Edinburgh N and Leith, 2005; Edinburgh N and Leith, Scottish Parlt, 2007. MP (Lib Dem) Edinburgh W, 2010–15; contested (Lib Dem) same seat, 2015. PPS to Sec. of State for Scotland, 2010. Convenor, Edinburgh W Lib Dems, 2009–.

CROCKER, His Honour John Fraser; a Circuit Judge, 1995–2010; *b* 27 May 1943; *o s* of late Noel John Fraser Crocker and Marjorie Jean Crocker (*née* Heaton); *m* 1969, Janet Butteriss; one *s* twin *d*. *Educ:* The Leys, Cambridge; Christ's Coll., Cambridge (MA). Admitted Solicitor, 1969; called to the Bar, Inner Temple, 1973; a Recorder, 1991–95. Resident Judge: Isleworth Crown Court, 1999–2003; Guildford Crown Court, 2004–08. *Recreations:* reading thrillers, avoiding gardening.

CROFT, family name of **Baron Croft**.

CROFT, 3rd Baron *cr* 1940, of Bournemouth, co. Southampton; **Bernard William Henry Page Croft;** Bt 1924; publisher; *b* 28 Aug. 1949; *s* of 2nd Baron Croft and Lady Antoinette Conyngham (*d* 1959), *o d* of 6th Marquess Conyngham; *S* father, 1997; *m* 1993, Elizabeth Mary Richardson, *o d* of late James Richardson, Co. Tyrone. *Educ:* Stowe; UCW, Cardiff (BScEcon). *Recreations:* shooting, fishing, ski-ing. *Address:* Croft Castle, Leominster, Herefordshire HR6 9PW; 29 Musgrave Crescent, SW6 4QE. *Clubs:* Naval and Military, Hurlingham.

CROFT, Charles Beresford, FRCS, FRCSE; Consultant Surgeon, Royal National Throat, Nose and Ear Hospital, and Royal Free Hospital, 1979–2004, now Emeritus; *b* 14 Jan. 1943; *s* of Arthur James Croft and Margaret Bays Croft (later Conyers); *m* 1968, Hilary Louise Whitaker; one *d*. *Educ:* Worksop Coll., Notts; Leeds Univ. Med. Sch. (MB BCh Hons 1965). FRCS 1970; FRCSE 1972; Dip. Amer. Bd Otolaryngology, 1979. House Surg., then Physician, Leeds Gen. Infirmary, 1966–68; Demonstrator in Anatomy, Leeds Med. Sch., 1968–69; Surgical Registrar, 1969–73, Sen. Registrar, Otolaryngology, 1971–73, Leeds Gen. Infirmary; Fellow in Head and Neck Surgery, Albert Einstein Med. Sch., NY, 1973–76; Associate Prof. in Otolaryngology, Albert Einstein Med. Sch. and Montefiore Hosp., NY, 1976–79. Civil Consultant Laryngologist, RAF, 1984–2004. FRSocMed. Arnott Demonstrator and Medal, RCS, 1988. *Publications:* chapters and papers on mgt of head and neck tumours, surgery of sleep breathing disorders and sleep apnoea in textbooks on tumour mgt and otolaryngology. *Recreations:* golf, fly fishing, bridge. *Address:* Westward Barn, Woodcock Hill, Rickmansworth, Herts WD3 1PX. *T:* (01923) 897187. *Clubs:* MCC; Moor Park Golf.

CROFT, David Michael Bruce; Director, Carat, since 2012; *b* 2 April 1955; *s* of late Eric David Croft and of Catherine Margaret Croft (*née* Kelly); *m* 2001, Angela Jane Murray; two *s*. *Educ:* Epsom Coll.; Magdalen Coll., Oxford (MA Hons Modern Hist.). Ocean Transport & Trading; NFC; Thames TV; Channel Four TV; Dir, 1998–2009, Man. Dir, 2002–09, Yorkshire TV Ltd; Director: Tyne Tees TV, 1998–2007; Granada TV, 1998–2007; Meridian Broadcasting, 2001–07; Border TV, 2001–07; Anglia TV, 2001–07; Central Independent TV, 2004–07; HTV Gp, 2004–07; Westcountry TV, 2004–07; Dir, Regl Sales, ITV plc, 2009–11; Founder and Man. Partner, David Croft and Associates Ltd, 2011–12. Hon. Consul for S Africa in Yorks, 2006–. *Recreations:* golf, horse-racing, travel, wine. *Address:* Shamrock Cottage, Foxcovert Lane, Lower Peover, Knutsford, Cheshire WA16 9QP. *E:* Dmbcroft@hotmail.com. *Club:* Royal Liverpool Golf.

CROFT, Frederick Lister; Deputy Legal Adviser, Department for Communities and Local Government (formerly Office of the Deputy Prime Minister), 2004–11; *b* 13 April 1951; *s* of Frederick Croft and Eirian Croft (*née* Spickett); *m* 1975, Elizabeth May Cohen; two *s* one *d*. *Educ:* Highgate Sch.; Jesus Coll., Oxford (MA). Called to the Bar, Middle Temple, 1975; Treasury Solicitor's Department: Litigation Div., 1977–84; Dept of Energy Div., 1984–86; HM Treasury Div., 1986–87, 1989–91; DES Div., 1987–89; Dep. Head of Litigation, 1991–97; Under Sec., 1997; Legal Adviser: DfEE, 1997–98; BBC, 1998–2000; Divl Manager, Legal Gp, DETR, subseq. DTLR, 2000–02, ODPM and Dept of Transport, 2002–04. *Recreations:* reading, theatre, running. *Club:* Thames Hare and Hounds.

CROFT, Giles Laurance; Artistic Director, Nottingham Playhouse, since 1999; *b* 20 June 1957; *s* of John Rothschild Croft and Myrtle Maud Croft (*née* Geal). *Educ:* Monkton Combe Sch. Artistic Director: Bath Young People's Th. Co., 1978–80; Gate Th., London, 1985–89; Literary Manager, Nat. Th., 1989–95; Artistic Dir, Palace Th., Watford, 1995–99. Director of plays including: Hinkemann, 1983; Naomi, 1987; (and adaptor) Kind Hearts and Coronets, 1997; Polygraph, 2001; Rat Pack Confidential, 2002; The Man Who, 2003; The White Album, 2006; Garage Band, 2009; (and adaptor) Forever Young, 2009; Private Lives, 2011; The Kite Runner, 2013; adapted: The Ladykillers, 1999; Loving April, 2010. Chair, Th. Writing Panel, Arts Council, 2000–03; Vice Pres., Eur. Th. Convention, 2003–12. FRSA

1993. *Recreations:* reading, music. *Address:* Nottingham Playhouse, Wellington Circus, Nottingham NG1 5AF. *T:* (0115) 947 4361. *E:* gilesc@nottinghamplayhouse.co.uk. *Club:* Blacks.

CROFT, (Ivor) John, CBE 1982; painter; Head of Home Office Research and Planning Unit, 1981–83 (Head, Home Office Research Unit, 1972–81); *b* 6 Jan. 1923; *s* of Oswald Croft and Doris (*née* Phillips). *Educ:* Westminster Sch.; Christ Church, Oxford (Hinchcliffe Scholar in Mod. Hist.; MA); Inst. of Education, Univ. of London (MA); LSE. Temp. jun. admin. officer, FO, 1942–45 (at GCHQ (Bletchley Park) and Govt Communications Bureau, London); asst teacher, LCC, 1949–51; Inspector, Home Office Children's Dept, 1952–66; Sen. Research Officer, Home Office Research Unit, 1966–72. Member: Criminological Scientific Council, Council of Europe, 1978–83, Chm., 1981–83; Conservative Study Gp on Crime, 1983–87; Kensington Crime Prevention Panel, 1984–87; Tribunal under I of M Interception of Communications Act, 1989–94. Mem., Crime Policy Gp, Centre for Policy Studies, 2001–04. Governor, ILEA Secondary Schs, 1959–68. Mem. Exec. Cttee, English Assoc., 1966–77 (Hon. Treas. 1972–75); Chairman: Pembridge Assoc., 1985–87; Peel Heritage Trust, 1991–93 (Mem. Cttee, 1989–93); Circus Area Residents' Assoc., 1997–99 (Mem. Cttee, 1996–99); Commn on Community Safety, Bath and NE Somerset Council, 1996–97; Working Gp on Evening Economy, Bath, 2004–05. Group shows, 1958, 1963, 1967, 1968, 1969, 1973, 1992, 1993, 2002, 2010, 2014; one-man shows, 1970, 1971, 2007. *Publications:* booklets, pamphlets and articles, and various studies of crime, criminological research and the administration of justice. *Address:* 15 Circus Mews, Bath BA1 2PW. *Club:* Reform.

CROFT, Sir Owen (Glendower), 14th Bt *cr* 1671; grazier; *b* 26 April 1932; *s* of Sir Bernard Hugh Denman Croft, 13th Bt, and of Helen Margaret (*née* Weaver); *S* father, 1984; *m* 1959, Sally Patricia, *d* of Dr T. M. Mansfield, Brisbane; one *s* two *d*. *Educ:* Armidale School, NSW. Mem., State Council of Advice to Rural Lands Protection Bds of NSW, 1983–96; Member: NSW Feral Animal Control Council, 1983–96; NSW Footrot Strategic Plan Steering Cttee, 1986–96; NSW Non-Indigenous Species Adv. Cttee; Armidale Rural Lands Protection Bd, 1978–2001; NSW National Parks and Wildlife Service: Chm., Armidale Dist Adv. Cttee, 1988–2000; Chm., Northern Tablelands Region Adv. Cttee, 2000–04. *Recreations:* tennis; National Trust activities. *Heir: s* Thomas Jasper Croft [*b* 3 Nov. 1962; *m* 1989, Catherine Fiona, *d* of Graham William White; two *d*]. *Address:* Australia.

CROFT, Rt Rev. Dr Steven John Lindsey; *see* Sheffield, Bishop of.

CROFT, Prof. Stuart John, PhD; Professor of International Security, since 2007, and Provost, since 2013, University of Warwick; *b* Leicester, 7 March 1963; *s* of John Croft and Margaret Croft; *m* 1994, Jane Usherwood; one *s*. *Educ:* Univ. of Southampton (BSc, MSc; PhD 1989). Prof. of Internat. Relns, 1996–2007, Hd, Sch. of Social Scis, 2000–03, Univ. of Birmingham; Pro Vice Chancellor for Res. (Arts and Soc. Scis), Univ. of Warwick, 2011–13. Mem., ESRC, 2011–14. Series Ed., New Security Challenges, 2009–. *Publications:* (ed) British Security Policy, 1991; (ed jtly) European Security without the Soviet Union, 1992; (ed) The Treaty on Conventional Armed Forces in Europe: the Cold War endgame, 1994; The End of British Superpower: Foreign Office conceptions of a changing world, 1945–51, 1994; Strategies of Arms Control: a history and typology, 1996; (jtly) The Enlargement of Europe, 1999; (jtly) Security Studies Today, 1999; (jtly) Britain and Defence, 1945–2000: a policy re-evaluation, 2001; (ed jtly) Critical Reflections on Security and Change, 2001; Culture, Crisis and America's War on Terror, 2006; (ed jtly) Comparative Regional Security Governance, 2012; Securitizing Islam, 2013. *Recreation:* football. *Address:* Provost's Office, University of Warwick, Coventry CV4 7AL. *T:* (024) 7657 4951, *Fax:* (024) 7652 4578. *E:* s.croft@warwick.ac.uk.

CROFT, Sir Thomas (Stephen Hutton), 6th Bt *cr* 1818, of Cowling Hall, Yorkshire; Principal, Thomas Croft, Architects, since 1988; *b* 12 June 1959; *o s* of Major Sir John Croft, 5th Bt and Lucy Elizabeth, *d* of late Major William Dallas Loney Jupp, OBE; *S* father, 1990; *m* 2001, Maxine Julia, *d* of Antonio Benato and Mrs Jean Sichel; one *d*. *Educ:* King's Sch., Canterbury; University Coll., London (BSc); Royal Coll. of Art, London (MA). Architect, Richard Meier & Partners, Architects, New York, 1985–86; Project Architect, Rick Mather, Architects, London, 1986–88. Completed buildings include Royal Yacht Squadron Pavilion, Cowes, 2000. *Address:* (office) 9 Ivebury Court, 325 Latimer Road, W10 6RA. *T:* (020) 8962 0066, *Fax:* (020) 8962 0088. *E:* email@thomascroft.com.

CROFT, Trevor Anthony; Reporter, Scottish Government Directorate for Planning and Environmental Appeals (formerly Scottish Executive Inquiry Reporters Unit), since 2002; *b* 9 June 1948; *s* of late Kenneth Edward Croft and Gladys (*née* Bartle); *m* 1980, Janet Frances Halley; two *d*. *Educ:* Belle Vue Boys' GS, Bradford; Hull Univ. (BSc 1969); Sheffield Univ. (DipTRP 1971). MRTPI 1974. Sen. Asst Planning Officer, Min. of Develt, NI, 1971–72; Asst Planning Officer, Countryside Commn for Scotland, 1972–75; Physical Planning Officer, Office of the President, Malaŵi, 1976–78; Parks Planning Officer, Dept of Nat. Parks and Wildlife, Malaŵi, 1978–82; National Trust for Scotland: Planning Officer, 1982–84; Head of Policy Res., 1984–88; Regl Dir, 1988–95; Dep. Dir and Dir of Countryside, 1995–97; Dir, 1997–2001; Consultant, 2001–03. Mem., Regl Adv. Cttee, S Scotland, Forestry Commn, 1987–90. Member Council: RSGS, 1998–2001, 2003–05 (Mem., Finance Cttee, 2003–08; Chm., Dunfermline Br., 1993–96); Europa Nostra, 1999–2001. Chm., British Equestrian Vaulting Ltd, 2002–03; Mem. Bd, BEF, 2002–03. Chm. Awards Panel, Kinross Civic Trust, 2005–09. Associate, RSGS, 1995; FRSA 1997. *Recreations:* travel, motorcycling, restoring Srs 1 Land Rover. *Address:* Glenside, Tillyrie, Kinross KY13 0RW. *T:* (01577) 864105. *Club:* Royal Scots (Edinburgh).

CROFTON, family name of **Baron Crofton**.

CROFTON, 8th Baron *cr* 1797 (Ire.); **Edward Harry Piers Crofton;** Bt 1758; civil and structural engineer; *b* 23 Jan. 1988; *er* twin *s* of 7th Baron Crofton and of Gillian Crofton (*née* Bass); *S* father, 2007. *Educ:* Sandroyd Sch.; Stowe Sch.; Univ. of Bristol. *Recreations:* travel, popular music, outdoor sports. *Heir: yr* twin *b* Hon. Charles Marcus George Crofton, *b* 23 Jan. 1988. *E:* hcrofton@gmail.com.

CROFTON, (Sir) Hugh Dennis, (8th Bt *cr* 1801, of Mohill); *S* nephew, 1987, but does not use the title and his name does not appear on the Official Roll of the Baronetage. *Heir: b* Major Edward Morgan Crofton.

CROFTON, Sir Julian (Malby), 7th Bt *cr* 1838, of Longford House, Sligo; *b* 26 Nov. 1958; *s* of Sir Melville Crofton, 6th Bt, MBE and of Mary Brigid Crofton (*née* Riddle), OBE; *S* father, 2003, but his name does not appear on the Official Roll of the Baronetage; *m* 1989, Hilary, *d* of T. J. Twort; two *s* one *d*. *Heir: s* William Robert Malby Crofton, *b* 5 Jan. 1996. *Address:* Broomfield House, Broomfield Park, Ascot, Berks SL5 0JT.

CROFTS, Max Osborn, FRICS; Consultant, Jones Lang LaSalle (formerly J. P. Sturge & Sons, then King Sturge LLP), since 2011 (Partner, 1981–2011); President, Royal Institution of Chartered Surveyors, 2009–10; *b* Northampton, 3 June 1950; *s* of Geoffrey Albert Crofts and Daphne Beryl Crofts; *m* 1973, Angela Clare Heazle; one *s* two *d*. *Educ:* King Edward VI Camp Hill, Birmingham; Keynsham Grammar Sch., Bristol; Coll. of Estate Mgt, Reading Univ. (BSc). FRICS 1983. Joined J. P. Sturge & Sons, Bristol, 1970. Royal Institution of Chartered Surveyors: Mem., Nat. Cttee, 1972–83, Nat. Chm., 1981, RICS Jun. Orgn; Mem. Council, 1977–83 and 1997–2010; Member: Pres.'s Panel of Arbitrators, 1990–2011; Standards and Practice Cttee, 1995–2000; Chairman: Compulsory Professional Indemnity Insce Wkg Party, 1995–2000; Public Affairs Policy Cttee, 2000–03; Members' Support Service Mgt Bd, 2003–09; Vice Chm., Ethics, Conduct and Consumer Policy Cttee, 2003–08; Mem., Commn on Major Disaster Mgt, 2005–08; Vice-Pres., 2006–09. Chm., Standards Setting Cttee, Internat. Property Measurement Standards Coalition, 2013–. Chm., Somerset Fedn of Young Farmers Clubs, 1976 (Pres., 1996–97); Pres., Bath Chamber of Commerce, 1980. Liveryman, Chartered Surveyors' Co., 1992. Hon. MA UWE, 2010. *Recreations:* supporting Bath Rugby, National Hunt Racing, village and family activities, reading newspapers, canal boating and restoration of Wilts and Berks Canal. *Address:* Glenacre, The Hollow, Dunkerton, Bath BA2 8BG. *T:* (01761) 436723. *E:* max.crofts@eu.jll.com. *Clubs:* Carlton; Bath Rugby.

CROFTS, Roger Stanley, CBE 1999; FRSE; independent environment and management adviser; Chief Executive, Scottish Natural Heritage, 1991–2002; *b* 17 Jan. 1944; *s* of Stanley Crofts and Violet May Crofts (*née* Dawson); *m* 1996, Lindsay Manson; one *s* one *d* by previous marriage. *Educ:* Hinckley Grammar Sch.; Liverpool Univ. (BA); Leicester Univ. (PGCE); Aberdeen Univ. (MLitt). Res. Asst to Prof. K. Walton, Aberdeen Univ., 1966–72; British Geomorphological Res. Gp, UCL, 1972–74; Central Res. Unit, Scottish Office, 1974–84; Scottish Office: Head of Highlands and Tourism, 1984–88; Head of Rural Affairs, 1988–91. Visiting Professor: of Geography, 1992–95, of Envmtl Mgt, 1997–2004, Royal Holloway, Univ. of London; of Geoscience, Univ. of Edinburgh, 2004–08; of Geog. and Envmt, Univ. of Aberdeen, 2008–; Hon. Professor: of Geography and Environment, Univ. of Aberdeen, 1997–2008; of Geoscience, Univ. of Edinburgh, 2008–. Dir, Fieldfare Internat. Ecol Develt plc, 2005–. Chairman: UK Cttee, IUCN, 1999–2002; Europe Cttee, IUCN World Commn on Protected Areas, 2001–08, Emeritus, 2010; Southern Ayrshire and Galloway Biosphere Partnership Bd, 2011–; National Trust for Scotland: Member: Council, 1992–2004 and 2005–10; Exec. Cttee, 2003–04; Bd, 2004–09; Convener, Conservation Cttee, 2004–09. Chm., Dalry Bird Town Steering Gp, 2010–. Member: Council, Scottish Wildlife Trust, 1992–97; Scottish Assoc. for Marine Science, 1995–2005; Board Member and Trustee: Plantlife Internat., 2001–10 (Chm., 2007–10); Scottish Agricl Coll., 2002–10; Bd, Crichton Carbon Centre, 2009–14 (Fellow, 2014); Chairman: Sibthorp Trust, 2003–13; RSGS, 2014– (Mem., 1994–2000). Hon. Pres., Scottish Assoc. of Geography Teachers, 1994–95 (Patron, 2002–). FRSA 1997; FRSE 2001; FRSGS 2001; FRGS 2002; FCIEEM (FIEEM 2008). Hon DSc: St Andrews, 2004; Glasgow, 2013. Knight's Cross, Order of the Falcon (Iceland), 2014. *Publications:* (with A. McKirdy) Scotland: the creation of its natural landscape, 1999; (ed) Scotland's Environment: the future, 2000; (ed) Conserving Nature: Scotland and the wider world, 2005; (with A. McKirdy and J. Gordon) Land of Mountain and Flood: the geology and landforms of Scotland, 2007; (ed jtly) Ecosystems and Health: a UK perspective, 2009; (ed) Climate Change Action After Copenhagen and Cancun: what next?, 2011; Healing the Land: the story of land reclamation and soil conservation in Iceland (Icelandic Soil Conservation Medal, Icelandic Soil Conservation Service), 2011; contribs to books on marginal regions, geomorph. mapping, second homes, field studies, conservation, envmtl policy; numerous articles. *Recreations:* designing gardens, choral singing, flower photography, cooking, hill walking. *Address:* 6 Eskside West, Musselburgh EH21 6HZ. *T:* (0131) 665 0788. *W:* www.rogercrofts.net.

CROISDALE-APPLEBY, Lindsay; HM Diplomatic Service; Europe Director, Foreign and Commonwealth Office, since 2015; *b* Amersham, 12 May 1973; *s* of David and Carolyn Croisdale-Appleby; *m* Barbara Maria; one *s* one *d*. *Educ:* Univ. of Oxford (BA Hons Modern Hist.); Univ. of Lancaster (MA Hons Internat. Relns and Internat. Law). Entered FCO, 1996; Desk Officer for Nigeria, FCO, 1996–97; ME Section, UK Mission to UN, 1997–98; Second Sec., Caracas, 1998–2001; Desk Officer, Afghanistan Emergency Unit, FCO, 2001–02; DEFRA, 2002; First Sec., UK Perm. Repn to EU, 2002–08; Asst Dir for Recruitment and Develt, Human Resources Directorate, FCO, 2008–10; Principal Private Sec. to Sec. of State for Foreign and Commonwealth Affairs, 2010–12; Ambassador to Colombia, 2013–15. *Recreations:* reading, swimming, art, history. *Address:* c/o Foreign and Commonwealth Office, King Charles Street, SW1A 2AH. *Club:* El Nogal (Bogota).

CROLL, Prof. James George Arthur, FREng; Professor of Civil Engineering, University College London, 2003–09, now Emeritus; *b* 16 Oct. 1943; *s* of late Keith Waghorn Croll and Jean Croll; *m* 1st, 1966, Elisabeth Joan (*née* Sprackett) (marr. diss. 1997; she *d* 2007); one *s* one *d*; 2nd, 2005, Patricia Jean Hepker (*née* Hindmarsh); three step *d*. *Educ:* Palmerston North Boys' High Sch., NZ; Univ. of Canterbury, NZ (BE 1st cl. Hons, PhD). FIStructE, FICE, FIMA; CEng 1970, FREng (FEng 1990); CMath. Asst Engineer, Min. of Works, NZ, 1962–67; University College London: Res. Fellow, 1967–70; Lectr, 1970–81; Reader in Structural Engrg, 1981–85; Prof. of Structural Engrg, 1985–92; Chadwick Prof. of Civil Engrg, and Hd, Dept of Civil and Envmtl Engrg, 1992–2003. Director: Synchromesh Systems Ltd, 2010–; Kapiti Engrg Ltd, 2012–. Vis. Fellow, Princeton, 1979; Visiting Professor: Fed. Univ. of Rio de Janeiro, 1973, 1981, 1984; Univ. of Hong Kong, 1985, 2000. FRSA. *Publications:* Elements of Structural Stability, 1972; Force Systems and Equilibrium, 1974; contrib. jl and conf. papers. *Recreations:* singing, piano, painting, drawing, sailing, ski-ing, travel. *Address:* 53 Mount View Road, Crouch Hill, N4 4SS. *T:* (020) 8341 7994. *Club:* Natural Science (UCL).

CROLL, (Mary) Louise, CBE 1995; HM Diplomatic Service, retired; Ambassador to Costa Rica, 1992–95; *b* 10 Sept. 1935. Joined FO, subseq. FCO, 1953; Bahrain, 1957; Addis Ababa, 1959; UK Mission, NY, 1961; FO, 1964; S America floater, 1967; Bilbao, 1969; Lusaka, 1972; First Sec., Madrid, 1979, FCO, 1984; Consul, Florence, 1988.

CROMARTIE, 5th Earl of, *cr* 1861; **John Ruaridh Grant Mackenzie,** MIExpE; Viscount Tarbat, Baron Castlehaven, Baron MacLeod, 1861; Chief of the Clan Mackenzie; explosives engineer; *b* 12 June 1948; *s* of 4th Earl of Cromartie, MC, TD and Olga (*d* 1996), *d* of late Stuart Laurance; *S* father, 1989; *m* 1973, Helen, *d* of John Murray; (one *s* decd); *m* 1985, Janet Clare, *d* of Christopher J. Harley; two *s*. *Educ:* Rannoch School, Perthshire; Strathclyde University. Pres., Mountaineering Council of Scotland, 2003–07 (Mem. Council, 1995–2007); Trustee, John Muir Trust, 2001–07. *Publications:* Selected Climbs in Skye, 1982; articles in Classic Rock Climbs and Cold Climbs. *Recreations:* mountaineering, art, astronomy, geology. *Heir: s* Viscount Tarbat, *qv*. *Address:* Castle Leod, Strathpeffer, Ross-shire IV14 9AA. *Clubs:* Army and Navy; Scottish Mountaineering (Pres., 2013–).

CROMBIE, Sir Alexander Maxwell, (Sir Sandy), Kt 2009; FFA; Senior Independent Director, Royal Bank of Scotland, since 2009; Chairman, Creative Scotland, 2010–14. *Educ:* Buckhaven High Sch., Fife. FFA 1973. Joined Standard Life as trainee actuary, 1966; Chief Investment Manager, 1994; Chief Exec., Standard Life Investments Ltd, 1998–2004; Dep. Gp Chief Exec., Standard Life Assurance Co., 2002–04; Gp Chief Exec., Standard Life Assurance Co., later Standard Life plc, 2004–09. Chm., Edinburgh UNESCO City of Literature Trust, 2006–10; Vice-Chm., Bd of Govs, RSAMD, later Royal Conservatoire of Scotland, 2007–; Pres., Cockburn Assoc., 2009–. *Address:* Royal Bank of Scotland, Gogarburn, Edinburgh EH2 1HQ.

CROME, Prof. Ilana Belle, MD; FRCPsych; Professor of Addiction Psychiatry, 2002–11, now Emeritus, and Academic Director of Psychiatry, 2002–11, University of Keele; Hon. Consultant Addiction Psychiatrist, South Staffordshire and Shropshire NHS Foundation Trust, since 2009; *b* 2 Feb. 1951; *d* of late Solomon Glass and Yette Glass (*née* Golombick); *m* 1989, Prof. Peter Crome, *qv*; one *s*, and one step *s* one step *d*. *Educ:* Redhill Sch., Johannesburg; Lauriston Sch., Melbourne; Damelin Coll., Johannesburg; Univ. of Witwatersrand; New Hall, Cambridge (BA 1972, MA 1974); Univ. of Birmingham (MB ChB

1975; MD 1996). FRCPsych 1997. Sen. Lectr, Inst. of Psychiatry and Hon. Consultant, Maudsley and Bethlem Royal Hosp. and KCH, 1989–93; Sen. Lectr and Consultant Psychiatrist, St Bartholomew's Hosp. Med. Coll. and Barts NHS Trust, 1994; Consultant in Gen. Hosp. Liaison Psychiatry, City Gen. Hosp., Stoke-on-Trent, 1994–97; Prof. of Addiction Studies, 1997–98, Prof. and Hd, Dept of Psychiatry, 1998–2002, Univ. of Wolverhampton; Consultant Addiction Psychiatrist: Wolverhampton Healthcare Trust, 1997–2002; N Staffs Combined Healthcare Trust, Stoke-on-Trent, 2002–09. Associate, Drug and Alcohol Centre, Middx Univ., 2014. Vis. Prof., St George's, Univ. of London, 2015. Hon. Prof., QMUL, 2014–. Member: Soc. for the Study of Addiction, 1994–2010; Scientific Cttee on Tobacco and Health, DoH, 2001–; Alcohol Educn and Res. Council, 2001–; Adv. Council on Misuse of Drugs, 2002–10. Trustee, Ind. Scientific Cttee on Drugs, 2012–. Chair, Faculty of Substance Misuse, RCPsych, 1998–2002. Pres., Drug and Alcohol Section, Assoc. of European Psychiatrists, 2006–08 (Pres.-elect, 2004–06); Vice-Pres., Profs of Psychiatry Club, 2012– (Hon. Sec., 2003–12). Internat. Ed., American Jl of Addictions, 2002–; Ed., Drugs Educn, Prevention & Policy, 2002–11; Member, International Advisory Board: Addiction; Jl Psychopharmacol.; British Jl Psychiatry. *Publications:* International Handbook of Addiction Behaviour, 1991; Young People and Substance Misuse, 2004; Psychological Disorders in Obstetrics and Gynaecology, 2006; (jtly) Substance Misuse and Older People, 2014; (Lead Ed.), Substance Use and Older People, 2015; (contrib. and Section Ed.) Textbook of Addiction Treatment: international perspectives; contrib. book chapters; contrib. papers to Addiction, Drug & Alcohol Dependence, Anaesthesia, Psychiatric Bull., Alcohol & Alcoholism, Acta Psychiatrica Scandinavica, British Jl Psychiatry, Psychol Medicine, Neuropharmacol., Lancet, Psychoneuroendocrinol. Reviews in Gerontology, BMJ, Eur. Jl of Psychiatry, Canadian Jl of Addiction, Advances in Psychiatric Treatment. *Recreations:* painting and paintings, plays and playing, pots and pottering, but not pot! *E:* ilana.crome@btinternet.com, i.crome@keele.ac.uk.

CROME, Prof. Peter, MD, PhD, DSc; FRCPE, FRCP, FRCPGlas; FFPM; FBPhS; Professor of Geriatric Medicine, Keele University, 1994–2012, now Emeritus; *b* 4 Feb. 1947; *s* of Leonard Crome, MC, FRCPE, FRCPath and Helena Crome (*née* Huttner); *m* 1989, Ilana Belle Glass (*see* I. B. Crome); one *s*, and one *s* one *d* from a former marr. *Educ:* Dulwich Coll.; King's Coll. London; King's Coll. Hosp. Med. Sch. (MB BS 1970; MD 1980; PhD 1995); Keele Univ. (DSc 2009). LRCP 1970, MRCP 1974, FRCP 1990; MRCS 1970; DObstRCOG 1973; FRCPE 1988; FFPM 1992; FRCPGlas 1995; FBPhS (FBPharmacolS 2012). Consultant Geriatrician, Orpington Hosp., 1981–91; Sen. Lectr, King's Coll. Sch. of Medicine and Dentistry, 1991–94; Keele University: Dep. Head, 2001–05, Head, 2005, Med. Sch.; Head of Postgrad. Medicine, 2001–08. Hon. Consultant: Guy's and St Thomas' Hosp., 1988–2003; King's Healthcare NHS Trust, 1991–94. Dir, Shropshire and Staffs Strategic HA, 2003–06. President: Section of Geriatrics and Gerontol., RSocMed, 2001–03; British Geriatrics Soc., 2006–08 (Pres.-elect, 2004–06); Mem. Council, RCP, 2006–08; Sec.-Gen., Clinical Sect., Internat. Assoc. of Gerontol. and Geriatrics, 2007–15. Hon. Prof., Dept of Primary Care and Population Health, UCL, 2012. *Publications:* (with G. A. Ford) Drugs and the Older Population, 2001; (jtly) Pain in Older People, 2006; Substance Use and Older People, 2015; contrib. papers on geriatric medicine, stroke and clinical pharmacol. *Recreations:* travel, food, especially cheese. *Address:* 62 Redington Road, NW3 7RS. *T:* (020) 7209 4219. *E:* p.crome@ucl.ac.uk, p.crome@keele.ac.uk. *Club:* Royal Society of Medicine.

CROMER, 4th Earl of, *cr* 1901; **Evelyn Rowland Esmond Baring;** Baron Cromer, 1892; Viscount Cromer, 1899; Viscount Errington, 1901; Chief Executive, Cromer Associates Ltd, since 1994; *b* 3 June 1946; *e s* of 3rd Earl of Cromer, KG, GCMG, MBE, PC and Hon. Esmé Harmsworth, CVO, *d* of 2nd Viscount Rothermere; *S* father, 1991; *m* 1971, Plern Isarangkun Na Ayudhya (marr. diss. 1993); 2nd, 1993, Shelley Hu Cheng-Yu, *e d* of Hu Guoquin, Shanghai; one *s* one *d*. *Educ:* Eton; INSEAD. Managing Director: Inchcape (China) Ltd, 1979–94; Inchcape Vietnam Ltd, 1987–94; Inchcape Special Markets Ltd, 1990–94; Dir, Inchcape Pacific Ltd, 1985–94. Chairman: Lloyd George Standard Chartered China Fund Ltd (Hong Kong), 1994–2006; Jardine Fleming China Region Fund Inc. (USA), 1994–; Korea Asia Fund Ltd, 1996–2000; Philippine Discovery Investment Co. Ltd, 1997–2006; Cambridge Asia Fund Ltd, 2001–08; Western Provident Assoc., 2004–; China IPO Gp Ltd, 2005–09; Pedder St Asia Absolute Return Fund Ltd, 2006–; London Asia Capital plc, 2008–10; LG Asia Plus Fund Ltd, 2009–; LG India Plus Fund, 2010–; Director: Cluff Oil China Ltd (Hong Kong), 1990–99; China & Eastern Investments Ltd, 1991–96; Schroder AsiaPacific Fund Ltd, 1995–2011; Pacific Basin Shipping Ltd, 2004–08; Japan High Yield Property Fund Ltd, 2005–09; Cheetah Korea Value Fund, 2010–. Dir, Somerset TEC, 1999–2001; Chm., Business Link Somerset, 1999–2008. Chm., Cromer Foundn for Chinese Contemp. Art, 2009–. Mem. St John's Council (Hong Kong), 1980–85. *Publications:* The Son from the West, 2007. *Recreations:* mountain climbing, deep sea diving. *Heir: s* Viscount Errington, *qv*. *Address:* 6 Sloane Terrace Mansions, SW1X 9DG; Kinnaree, 9/32 Katamanda, Katanoi Road, Karon, Phuket 83100, Thailand; Dragoneye, CPO Box 3187, Central Post Office, Muscat 111, Sultanate of Oman. *Clubs:* White's, Oriental; Hong Kong (Hong Kong), Royal Yacht Squadron.

CROMIE, Sharon Nadine; Headteacher, Wycombe High School, since 2009; *b* Carlisle, 6 Oct. 1965; *s* of Norman Mulholland and Daphne Mulholland; *m* 1990, Alistair Cromie; one *s* one *d*. *Educ:* Victoria Coll., Belfast; Queen's Univ., Belfast (LLB Hons 1988); Reading Univ. (CertEd 1994). IT Mgt Consultant, Arthur Andersen, 1988–90; Quality Assurance Manager, EPG Computer Services, 1990–93; Lectr and Curriculum Manager, Reading Coll., 1993–97; Lectr and Business Develt Manager, Henley Coll., 1997–2000; Asst Headteacher and Business Manager, Wycombe High Sch., 2003–07; Dep. Hd, John Hampden Grammar Sch., 2007–09. *Recreations:* family, reading, travelling. *Address:* Wycombe High School, Marlow Road, High Wycombe HP11 1TB. *T:* (01494) 523961, *Fax:* (01494) 510354. *E:* office@whs.bucks.sch.uk.

CROMPTON, Sir Dan, Kt 2003; CBE 1996; QPM 1990; HM Inspector of Constabulary, North of England and Northern Ireland, 1995–2002; *b* 15 Feb. 1941; *s* of Arthur and Elizabeth Crompton; *m* 1962, Olive Ramsden; one *s*. *Educ:* Didsbury Technical Sch., Manchester. Manchester City Police, 1960–68; Manchester and Salford Police, 1968–74; Greater Manchester Police, 1974–87; Nottinghamshire Constabulary, 1987–95 (Chief Constable, 1990–95). *Recreations:* reading, popular classics, gardening, cricket, Rugby. *Address:* 1 Half Acre Lane, Rochdale, Lancs OL11 4BY.

CROMPTON, Prof. Gareth, FRCP, FFPH; Professor of Public Health Medicine, University of Wales College of Medicine, 1989–97, now Emeritus; Hon. Fellow, Cardiff Metropolitan University (formerly University of Wales Institute, Cardiff), since 1997; *b* 9 Jan. 1937; *s* of late Edward and Annie Jane Crompton, Drefach-Felindre, Carmarthenshire; *m* 1965; one *d*. *Educ:* Llandysul Grammar Sch.; Welsh Nat. Sch. of Medicine. MB, BCh Wales, 1960; DObstRCOG 1962; DPH Wales, 1964; FFPH (FFCM 1976); FRCP 1986 (MRCP 1980). County Med. Officer, County Welfare Officer and Principal Sch. Med. Officer, Anglesey CC, 1966–73; Area Med. Officer, Gwynedd Health Authority, 1974–77; CMO, Welsh Office, 1978–89; Chief Admin. MO and Dir of Public Health Medicine, S Glam HA, 1989–96. Specialty Advr, Health Service Comr for England and Wales, 1974–77; Advr in Wales, Faculty of Community Medicine, 1974–77. Chm., Anglesey Disablement Adv. Cttee, 1969–77; Sec., Fluoridation Study Gp, Soc. of Med. Officers of Health, 1969–73; Mem., Welsh Hosp. Bd, 1970–74. Member: GMC, 1981–83 and 1987–89; Bd, PHLS, 1990–97; Exec. Bd, FPHM, 1990–95. Med. Fellow, Council of Europe, 1971. Jt Life Pres., Bargod Rangers AFC, 2014–. QHP 1984–87. Hon. MD Wales, 1999. Alwyn Smith Prize Medal, Faculty of Public Health, RCP, 2000. *Publications:* papers on the effects of fluoridated water supplies on dental caries, and the epidemiology and management of chronic sickness and disablement. *Recreations:* bowls, watching Rugby football and cricket, reading contemporary Welsh verse. *Address:* 19 Kenilworth House, Castle Court, Westgate Street, Cardiff CF10 1DJ. *T:* (029) 2075 6704.

CROMPTON, Kenneth Charles; Chief Executive, General Sir John Monash Foundation, 2002–09; solicitor, now retired; *b* 19 July 1948; *s* of late Charles Frederic Crompton and of Margaret Joan Crompton; *m* 1971, Elizabeth Anne Meek; one *s* two *d*. *Educ:* Melbourne Univ. (LLB). Solicitor, Morris Komesaroff, Aarons & Co., 1971–75; Seton Williams & Smyth, 1975–79; Gen. Manager, Legal and Technical Services, Victorian Chamber of Manufactures, 1979–87; Dir, Industrial Relations, 1987–88, Chief Exec. (Vic.), 1988–92, Aust. Chamber of Manufactures; Agent-Gen. for Victoria in London, 1993–96. Dir, Corporate Counsel Pty Ltd. *Recreations:* golf, photography. *Address:* 104 Scenic Crescent, Eltham, Vic 3095, Australia. *Clubs:* Athenæum (Melbourne); Melbourne Cricket.

CROMWELL, 7th Baron *cr* 1375 (called out of abeyance, 1923); **Godfrey John Bewicke-Copley;** *b* 4 March 1960; *s* of 6th Baron Cromwell and of Vivian, *y d* of late Hugh de Lisle Penfold, Isle of Man; *S* father, 1982; *m* 1990, Elizabeth, *d* of John Hawksley; three *s* (incl. twins) one *d*. *Educ:* Eton; Selwyn Coll., Cambridge (BA 1982; MA 1986). Elected Mem., H of L, 2014. *Heir: s* Hon. David Godfrey Bewicke-Copley, *b* 21 Sept. 1997.

CRONEY, Alan Malcolm, FRICS; Director, Enbornewood Consulting Ltd, since 2012; *b* Stoke Newington, London, 4 March 1955; *s* of Charles Frederick Croney and Joan Croney; one *s*. *Educ:* Latymer Sch., Edmonton, London. FRICS 1985. Estates Manager, London Docklands Develt Corp., 1981–86; Gp Property Manager, Thames Water, 1986–90; Gen. Manager Estates, WH Smith plc, 1990–96; Exec. Dir, London First, 1997–2000; Dir, i-Scraper UK, 2000–02; Dir, Property Services, Metropolitan Police Service, 2002–09; Global Dir, Estates and Security, FCO, 2009–11; Interim Dir, Serco UK and Europe Ltd, 2012–14. Sen. Civil Mem., ACPO, 2004–09. Former specialist panel mem. on water industry and town centre mgt, RICS. FRSA 2006. *Recreation:* country walking. *Address:* Enborne Wood Cottage, Newbury, Berks RG20 0HA. *T:* 07771 817519.

CRONEY, Prof. Paul; Vice-Chancellor and Chief Executive, Teesside University, since 2015; *b* Newcastle upon Tyne, 29 June 1963; *s* of William Turner Croney and Georgina Gibson Croney; *m* 1988, Pamela; one *s* one *d*. *Educ:* Manor Park Comp. Sch.; Sheffield City Poly. (BA Hons Business Studies); Univ. of Warwick (MA Industrial Relns). Chartered MCIPD. Officer, Barclays Bank plc, 1979–82; researcher, AUT, 1986–87; Academic Staff: Leeds Poly., 1988–90; Sheffield City Poly., subseq. Sheffield Hallam Univ., 1990–99; Northumbria University: Academic Staff, 1999–2003; Dean, Newcastle Business Sch., 2003–10; Pro-Vice-Chancellor (Learning and Teaching), 2010–13; Dep. Vice-Chancellor, 2013–15. Honorary Professor: State Univ. of Management, Moscow, 2003–; Sinerghia Econs and Finance Inst., 2006. *Recreations:* cycling, swimming, running.

CRONIN, Prof. Leroy, (Lee), DPhil; FRSE; Regius Professor of Chemistry, University of Glasgow, since 2013; *b* Ipswich, 1 June 1973; *s* of Liam and Jill Cronin; *m* 1999, Deborah Aitken Porter; two *s*. *Educ:* Copleston High Sch., Ipswich; Northgate Sixth Form, Ipswich; York Univ. (BSc 1st Cl. Chem. 1994; DPhil Chem. 1997). Res. Fellow, Univ. of Edinburgh, 1997–99; Alexander von Humboldt Res. Fellow, Univ. of Bielefeld, Germany, 1999–2000; Lectr, Univ. of Birmingham, 2000–02; University of Glasgow: Lectr, 2002–05; Reader, 2005–06; Prof., 2006–09; Gardiner Prof., 2009–13. FRSE 2009. *Publications:* contribs to peer-reviewed jls. *Recreations:* running, walking, sailing, science history, philosophy. *Address:* School of Chemistry, University of Glasgow, University Avenue, Glasgow G12 8QQ. *T:* (0141) 330 6650. *E:* lee.cronin@glasgow.ac.uk.

CROOK, family name of **Baron Crook**.

CROOK, 3rd Baron *cr* 1947, of Carshalton, Surrey; **Robert Douglas Edwin Crook;** Chief Executive Officer, Exoma Energy Ltd, Brisbane; *b* 19 May 1955; *S* father, 2001; *m* 1981, Suzanne Jane Robinson, BA, LLB; two *s*. *Educ:* Sir William Borlase's Sch., Marlow; Newcastle Univ. (BSc Mining Engrg); Queensland Univ. (MBA). MIE (Aust); CPEng. *Heir: s* Hon. Matthew Robert Crook, *b* 28 May 1990.

CROOK, (Alan) Peter, MA; Head of Music, Repton Senior School Dubai, since 2012; *b* 1954; *s* of Donald Hartley Crook and Constance Crook (*née* Llewellyn); *m* 1981, Elaine Joyce Scragg; two *s*. *Educ:* Rydal Sch.; Charterhouse; Royal Acad. Music (BMus Hons; ARCO, ARAM); Univ. of London Inst. of Educn (PGCE); Univ. of Durham (MA). Asst Dir of Music, 1979–83, Dir of Music, 1983–85, Loretto Sch.; Dir of Music, 1985–2003, Co-ordinator of Performing Arts, 2003–07, Rugby Sch.; Headmaster, Purcell Sch., 2007–11. Conductor: Loretto Choral Soc., 1983–85; Rugby Philharmonic Choir and Orch., 1985–2007. FRSA 2007. *Publications:* hymn tunes and arrangements in various hymnals. *Recreations:* family, fiction, fly fishing, over-seas travel. *E:* crookp@gmail.com. *Club:* Royal Over-Seas League.

CROOK, Colin, FREng; special advisor to business, academia, governments and non-governmental organisations on advanced thinking for complex problems; Senior Fellow, Wharton School, University of Pennsylvania, since 1997; *b* 1 June 1942; *s* of Richard and Ruth Crook; *m* 1965, Dorothy Jean Taylor; two *d*. *Educ:* Harris Coll., Preston; Liverpool Polytechnic (ACT Hons; Dip. Elec. Engrg). CEng 1977, FREng (FEng 1981); MIET (MIEE 1976); MIERE 1976; MIEEE 1976; MACM 1977. Electronics Engr, Canadian Marconi, 1962–64; Computer Designer, The Plessey Co., 1964–68; Systems Engr, Eli Lilly Co., 1968–69; sen. appts, Motorola Semiconductor Div., Switzerland and USA, 1969–79; sen. appts, The Rank Organisation, 1979–83, including: Man. Dir, RPI, 1979–81; Man. Dir, Zynar, CEO Nestar Systems, USA, 1981–83; Mem. of Bd, British Telecom, and Man. Dir, BT Enterprises, 1983–84; Sen. Vice Pres., Data General Corp., 1984–89; Sen. Technol. Officer (formerly Chm., Corporate Technol. Cttee), Citicorp, 1990–97. Mem., various NAS adv. cttees, USA; advr to various global cos; Member: Bd, Onsett Internat., Boston, 1998–; Adv. Bd, Rein Capital, NJ, 1999–; Advr, IDAnalytics, San Diego, 1999–. Mem. Editl Bd, Emergence Jl, NY. *Publications:* The Power of Impossible Thinking, 2004; articles and learned papers on electronics and computers. *Recreations:* photography, walking, reading, wine, sailing. *Address:* Penberen House, Seifton, Shropshire SY7 9BY.

CROOK, Frances Rachel, OBE 2010; Chief Executive, Howard League for Penal Reform, since 1986; *b* 18 Dec. 1952; *d* of Sheila Sibson-Turnbull and Maurice Crook; one *d*. *Educ:* Camden School; Liverpool University (BA Hons History). Historical Researcher, Liverpool, 1977–78; Teacher, 1978–79; Campaign Co-ordinator, Amnesty International, 1980–85. Sen. Vis. Fellow, LSE, 2010–; Vis. Fellow, Leicester Univ., 2014–. Councillor (Lab) Barnet, 1982–90. Mem. Court, Greenwich Univ., 1996–2002 (Chm., Staffing and Gen. Cttee, 1997–2002). Mem., Sch. Food Trust, 2005–08. Non-exec. Dir, NHS Barnet, 2009–. Chm., Old Barn Youth and Community Centre, Finchley, 1996–97. Freeman, City of London, 1997. Perrie Award, Perrie Lectures Cttee, 2005. *Recreation:* demonstrations. *Address:* The Howard League, 1 Ardleigh Road, N1 4HS. *T:* (020) 7249 7373.

CROOK, Maj.-Gen. James Cooper, MD, FRCPath; late RAMC, retired 1981; Civilian Medical Practitioner, Army Blood Supply Depot, Aldershot, 1982–88; *b* 19 March 1923; *s* of late Francis William Crook and late Mary Catherine Perry, *d* of late Sir Edwin Cooper Perry, GCVO, MD, Superintendent of Guy's Hospital and Vice-Chancellor of London Univ.; *m* 1950, Ruth (*d* 2015), *d* of late W. A. Bellamy of Santa Cruz, Tenerife; one *s* two *d*. *Educ:*

Worksop Coll.; Guy's Hosp. Med. Sch., Univ. of London. MB BS 1946, MD 1953; DTM&H 1952; FRCPath 1968. Guy's and Pembury Hosps, 1946; Commnd RAMC 1946; served Egypt and N Africa, 1946–49; Pathologist, Queen Alexandra's Mil. Hosp., 1950; David Bruce Laboratories, 1953; med. liaison officer to MRC Radiobiology Unit, AERE, Harwell, 1954; Asst Dir of Pathology, Middle East, 1957; Cons. in Pathology, 1958; RAMC Specialist, Chem. Defence Estab., Porton, 1960; Asst Dir of Pathology, Eastern Comd, 1963; ADGMS, 1966; Comd Cons. in Pathology, BAOR, 1969; Prof. of Pathology, Royal Army Med. Coll., 1974; Dir of Army Pathology and Consulting Pathologist to the Army, 1976–81; Hon. Physician to HM The Queen, 1978–81. Hon. Col, 380 Blood Supply Unit RAMC, TAVR, 1982–86. *Publications:* articles in Jl of Clinical Path., Nature, Med. Sci. and the Law, Jl of RAMC, British Jl of Radiology. *Recreations:* gardening, beekeeping. *Address:* Egloshayle, Fore Street, Kingsand, Torpoint, Cornwall PL10 1NB. *T:* (01752) 823666.

CROOK, Rt Rev. John Michael; Bishop of Moray, Ross and Caithness, 1999–2006; *b* 11 June 1940; *s* of late John Hadley Crook and Ada Crook; *m* 1965, Judith Christine, *d* of late Rev. John Angles Barber and Dorothy Barber; one *s* three *d*. *Educ:* Argyle Hse Sch., Sunderland; Dame Allan's Sch., Newcastle upon Tyne; William Hulme's GS, Manchester; St David's Coll., Lampeter (BA 1962); Coll. of the Resurrection, Mirfield. Ordained deacon, 1964, priest, 1965; Curate: Horninglow, 1964–66; Bloxwich, 1966–70; Rector: St Michael, Inverness, 1970–78; St John, Inverness, 1974–78; Aberfoyle, and Callander, and Doune, 1978–87; Bridge of Allan, 1987–99; Canon, St Ninian's Cathedral, Perth, 1985–99. Diocesan Synod Clerk, St Andrews, 1997–99. *Recreations:* bird-watching, music, history. *Address:* 8 Buccleuch Court, Dunblane, Perthshire FK15 0AR.

CROOK, Prof. Joseph Mordaunt, CBE 2003; DPhil; FBA 1988; FSA; Professor of Architectural History, University of London at Royal Holloway and Bedford New College (formerly at Bedford College), 1981–99, now Emeritus; *b* 27 Feb. 1937; *e s* of late Austin Mordaunt Crook and late Irene Woolfenden; *m* 1st, 1964, Margaret, *o d* of late James Mulholland; 2nd, 1975, Susan, *o d* of late F. H. Mayor. *Educ:* Wimbledon Coll.; Brasenose Coll., Oxford (BA (1st cl. Mod. Hist.) 1958; DPhil 1961, MA 1962; Hon. Fellow, 2010). FSA 1972. Research Fellow: Inst. of Historical Res., 1961–62; Bedford Coll., London, 1962–63; Warburg Inst., London, 1970–71; Asst Lectr, Univ. of Leicester, 1963–65; Lectr, Bedford Coll., London, 1965–75, Reader in Architectural Hist., 1975–81; Dir, Victorian Studies Centre, RHBNC, 1990–99. Slade Prof. of Fine Art, Oxford Univ., 1979–80; Vis. Fellow: Brasenose Coll., Oxford, 1979–80; Humanities Res. Centre, ANU, Canberra, 1985; Waynflete Lectr and Vis. Fellow, Magdalen Coll., Oxford, 1984–85; Vis. Fellow, Gonville and Caius Coll., Cambridge, 1986; Humanities Fellow, Princeton Univ., 1990; Supernumerary Fellow, Brasenose Coll., Oxford, 2002–10. Public Orator, Univ. of London, 1988–90. Member: Exec. Cttee, Soc. Architect. Historians of Gt Britain, 1964–77 (Pres., 1980–84); RIBA Drawings Cttee, 1969–75; Exec. Cttee, Georgian Gp, 1970–77; Exec. Cttee, Victorian Soc., 1970–77, Council, 1978–88; Historic Buildings Council for England, 1974–80; Council, Soc. of Antiquaries, 1980–82; Adv. Council, Paul Mellon Centre for Studies in British Art, 1985–90; Gen. Cttee, Incorp. Church Building Soc., 1987–99; Council, British Acad., 1989–92; Adv. Bd for Redundant Churches, 1991–99; Westminster Abbey Architectural Adv. Panel, 1993–99 and Fabric Commn, 2000– (Vice-Chm., 2002–10). Freeman, 1979, Liveryman, 1984, Worshipful Co. of Goldsmiths. Hon. DLit London, 2004. Editor, Architectural History, 1967–75. *Publications:* The Greek Revival, 1968; Victorian Architecture: A Visual Anthology, 1971; The British Museum, 1972, 2nd edn 1973; The Greek Revival: Neo-Classical Attitudes in British Architecture 1760–1870, 1972, 2nd edn 1995; The Reform Club, 1973; (jtly) The History of the King's Works, Vol. VI, 1782–1851, 1973 (Hitchcock Medallion, 1974), Vol. V, 1660–1782, 1976; William Burges and the High Victorian Dream, 1981, rev. edn 2013; (jtly) Axel Haig and The Victorian Vision of the Middle Ages, 1984; The Dilemma of Style: architectural ideas from the picturesque to the post-modern, 1987, 2nd edn 1989; John Carter and the Mind of the Gothic Revival, 1995; The Rise of the Nouveaux Riches: style and status in Victorian and Edwardian architecture, 1999, 2nd edn 2000; London's Arcadia: John Nash and the Planning of Regent's Park, 2001; The Architect's Secret: Victorian critics and the image of gravity, 2003; Brasenose: the biography of an Oxford college, 2008, 2nd edn 2010; *edited:* Eastlake, A History of the Gothic Revival, 1970, rev. edn, 1978; Emmet, Six Essays, 1972; Kerr, The Gentleman's House, 1972; The Strange Genius of William Burges, 1981; Clark, The Gothic Revival, 1995; Bedford College: memories of 150 years, 2001; *contrib. to:* Concerning Architecture, 1967; The Country Seat, 1970; The Age of Neo-Classicism, 1972; The Building of Early America, 1976; Seven Victorian Architects, 1976; The Ruskin Polygon, 1982; In Search of Modern Architecture, 1983; Rediscovering Hellenism, 1989; The University of London and the World of Learning 1836–1986, 1990; Brooks's: a social history, 1991; London: World City 1800–1840, 1992; Scottish Country Houses, 1995; The Question of Style in Philosophy and the Arts, 1995; Armchair Athenians, 2001; The Impact of the Railway on Society in Britain, 2003; All Souls and the Wider World, 2011; Brooks's, 1764–2014: the story of a Whig club, 2013; John Nash: architect of the picturesque, 2013; Architectural History After Colvin, 2014; numerous articles in Architect. History, Architect. Review, Country Life, History Today, Jl Royal Soc. Arts, RIBA Jl, Antiquaries Jl, TLS, Architect Design, etc. *Recreation:* strolling. *Address:* D4, Albany, Piccadilly, W1J 0AP; West Wing, Maristow, near Roborough, Devon PL6 7BZ. *T:* (01752) 696648. *Clubs:* Athenæum, Brooks's.

CROOK, Pamela June, (PJ Crook), MBE 2011; RWA 1987; artist (painter and sculptor); *b* Cheltenham, 28 June 1945; *d* of John, (Jack), Albert Hagland and Jessie Edith Hagland (*née* Birch); *m* 1969, Dr Geoff Crook (marr. diss. 1980); one *s* one *d*; partner, 1983, Richard Parker. *Educ:* Gloucestershire Coll. of Art and Design (NDD 1965). *Major solo exhibitions:* Portal Gall., London, 1980–94; Cheltenham Art Gall. and Mus., 1986, 1996, 2006; Lee Drexler, NY, 1989; Galerie Alain Blondel, Paris, 1991, 1993, 1995, 1997, 2002, 2008, 2011; Montpelier Sandelson, London, 1994–96; Musée Paul Valery, Séte, 1996; RWA, 1997; Brian Sinfield Gall., 1997, 1999, 2004, 2007, 2009, 2011; Nancy Poole Gall., Toronto, 1998; Theo Waddington Fine Art, London, 1998, Florida, 2000; Barry Friedman, NY at ArtChicago, 1998–99; Morohashi MOMA, Japan, 2001, 2006, 2012, 2016; Gloucester City Mus., 2002, 2006, 2012; Robert Sandelson Gall., London, 2003; Draakon Galerii, Tallinn, 2006; Loch Gall., Toronto, 2007, 2010; Vaal Galerii, Tallinn, 2010; Hay Hill Gall., London, 2010; Alpha Gall., London, 2012, 2013; Panter & Hall, London, 2014, 2015; *major group exhibitions:* RWA, 1978– (First Prize, 1984); RA Summer Exhibn, 1978–2011 (World of Newspapers, RA/Sotheby's Prize, 1982); Salisbury Fest., 1986; British Council tour of Far East, 1988; Contemporary Icons, Royal Albert Meml Mus., Exeter, 1992; Lincoln Mus. and Art Gall. tour, 1993–94; contemp. paintings from perm. collection, Imperial War Mus., 1995; Mairie de Paris, 1995; Realismus der gegenwart, Berlin, 1996; Holbourne Mus. of Art, Bath, 2010; works in major museums, corporate and private collections, incl. Imperial War Mus., Morohashi MOMA, Japan, Cheltenham Art Gall. and Mus., ALJ, Jeddah, Gloucester City Mus., Standard Chartered Bank, Open Mus., Leics, crucifixion for St Michael and All Angels, Bishop's Cleeve, Gloucester Royal Hosp., RWA, Ralli Mus., Caesarea, JP Morgan Inc., Longleat House. Dir, Artists' Collecting Soc., 2007–13. Pres., Friends of Cheltenham Art Gall. and Mus., 2007–; Hon. Vice Pres., Gloucester Coll., 2012. Trustee: Forest of Dean Sculpture Trail, 2011–13; Aston Project, 2015–. Patron: Nat. Star Coll., 1992–; Cheltenham Open Studios, 2011–; Linc, 2013–; Artshape, 2013–. Mem., Manchester Acad. of Fine Art, 1992. Hon. DArt Glos, 2010. FRSA 2010. *Relevant Publications:* P. J. Crook, ed Raymond Daussy, 1993; P. J. Crook, ed Jon Bennington, 1996; P. J. Crook, by Martin Bailey, 2003. *Recreations:* painting is all-embracing, entwined around my family and everything that I do; writing, hatching schemes and ideas in the early hours. *Address:* The Old Police Station, 39 Priory Lane, Bishop's Cleeve, Cheltenham, Glos GL52 8JL. *T:* (01242) 675963; Panter & Hall, 11–12 Pall Mall, SW1Y 5LU; Brian Sinfield Gallery, 127 High Street, Burford OX18 4RE. *E:* pj@pjcrook.com. *W:* www.pjcrook.com. *Club:* Chelsea Arts.

CROOK, Peter; *see* Crook, A. P.

CROOKALL, Ian; Chief Executive, Buckinghamshire County Council, 1995–2001; *b* 28 Dec. 1944; *s* of F. Harold Crookall and M. Ida Crookall (*née* Stubbs); *m* 1974, Georgina; one *s*. *Educ:* Arnold Sch., Blackpool; University Coll. London (LLB Hons). Admitted Solicitor, 1969; Asst Solicitor, N Yorks CC, 1974–82; Asst Clerk, Norfolk CC, 1982–85; Dep. County Solicitor, Dorset CC, 1985–89; Buckinghamshire County Council: County Secretary and Solicitor, 1989–95. *Recreations:* tennis, swimming, walking, theatre. *Address:* Flemings House, Old School, High Street, Wendover HP22 6DU. *T:* (01296) 696410.

CROOKE, Alastair Warren, CMG 2004; Founder, 2004, and Director, since 2005, Conflicts Forum; *b* 30 June 1949; *s* of Frederick Montague Warren and Shona Ann Crooke (*née* Thomson); *m* 1976, Carole Cecilia (*née* Flaxman) (marr. diss.); three *s*; *m* 2012, Aisling Byrne; one *s* one *d*. *Educ:* Aiglon Coll., Switzerland; St Andrews Univ. (MA Hons Pol Economy and Philos.). Contrib. to mediation, mgt and resolution of conflict in Ireland, Namibia, Afghanistan, Cambodia and Colombia; co-ordinated hostage negotiations in four overseas locations; Security Adviser: to EU Special Rep. for ME peace process, 1997–2003; to EU High Rep., Javier Solana, 1999–2003; Mem., US Senator George Mitchell's Fact Finding Cttee into causes of Palestinian Intifada, 2000–01; facilitated Israeli/Palestinian ceasefires, 2002, 2003; mediated negotiations that led to ending of siege of Church of Nativity, Bethlehem, 2002; instrumental in negotiations that led to ceasefire declared by Hamas and Islamic Jihad, 2003; initiated bringing together Islamist movts with European and US non-official participants, 2005–. Has made TV documentaries and broadcasts. *Publications:* Resistance: the essence of the Islamist Revolution, 2009; various articles in jls and newspapers on ME and Islamic affairs. *Recreations:* scuba diving instructing, climbing, ski-ing, study of 18th century art, architecture and furniture. *E:* exchange@conflictsforum.com.

CROOKENDEN, Simon Robert; QC 1996; a Recorder, since 1998; a Deputy High Court Judge, since 2010; *b* 27 Sept. 1946; *s* of late Spencer Crookenden and Jean Phyllis (formerly Carter, *née* Dewing); *m* 1983, Sarah Anne Georgina Margaret Pragnell; one *s* two *d*. *Educ:* Winchester Coll.; Corpus Christi Coll., Cambridge (MA Mech. Scis). Management trainee, Westland Aircraft, 1968–69; various posts, incl. Brand Manager, Unilever, 1969–72; Brand Manager, Express Dairies, 1972–74; called to the Bar, Gray's Inn, 1975, Bencher, 2003; in practice as barrister, 1975–; Asst Recorder, 1994–98. *Recreations:* ski-ing, rowing, sailing. *Address:* Essex Court Chambers, 24 Lincoln's Inn Fields, WC2A 3EG. *T:* (020) 7813 8000.

CROOKHAM, Ian; Chief Executive, Kingston upon Hull City Council, 1995–2002; *b* 7 Oct. 1952; *s* of George Edward Crookham and Jean Crookham; *m* 1977, Shirley Ann Green; four *s*. *Educ:* St Margaret's Sch., Liverpool (BA Hons). CPFA 1979. Graduate trainee, Liverpool CC, 1974–77; various finance posts, Gtr Manchester Council, 1977–86; Chief Accountant, Trafford MBC, 1986–88; Asst Dir of Finance, 1988, Sen. Asst Dir of Finance, 1988–94, Humberside CC; Dir of Finance, Hull CC, 1994–95. Clerk to: Hull and Goole Port HA, 1995–2002; Humber Bridge Bd, 1996–2002; Humberside Police Authy, 1997–2002. Co. Sec., Hull City Vision, 1995–2002. Audit Cttee, Univ. of Hull Council, 2003–08. Chm. Governors, South Cave Sch., 1993–2005. *Recreations:* aviation, military history, reading.

CROOKS, Air Marshal David Manson, CB 1985; OBE 1969; FRAeS; Chief of Defence Staff, New Zealand Armed Forces, 1986–87, retired; aviation and defence industry consultant, 1988–99; *b* 8 Dec. 1931; *s* of James and Gladys Meta Crooks; *m* 1954, Barbara Naismith McDougall; four *d*. *Educ:* Rangiora, NZ. Joined RNZAF, 1951; Head, NZ Defence Liaison Staff, Singapore, 1967–70; Commanding Officer: RNZAF Base: Ohakea, 1971–72; Wigram, 1973–74; RCDS, UK, 1974–75; AOC RNZAF Ops Gp, 1978–80; DCAS, 1980–83; CAS, RNZAF, 1983–86. President: RNZAF Assoc., 1990–2000; Air Cadet League; Chairman: Patriotic Fund Bd; RNZAF Mus. Trust Bd. *Recreations:* gardening, reading, vintage motoring, sailing. *Address:* 13 Burrows Avenue, Karori, Wellington 6012, New Zealand. *T:* (4) 4764588. *Club:* Wellington (Wellington, NZ).

CROOKS, Emily Jane; *see* Bell, E. J.

CROPPER, Sir James (Anthony), KCVO 2011; FCA; Director, James Cropper PLC, 1967–2013, now Honorary President (Chairman, 1971–2010); Lord-Lieutenant of Cumbria, 1994–2012 (Vice Lord-Lieutenant, 1991–94); *b* 22 Dec. 1938; *s* of Anthony Charles Cropper and Philippa Mary Gloria (*née* Clutterbuck); *m* 1967, Susan Rosemary, *y d* of Col F. J. N. Davis; one *s* one *d* (and one *s* decd). *Educ:* Eton; Magdalene Coll., Cambridge (BA). FCA 1966. James Cropper, 1966–; Dir, East Lancashire Paper Group, 1982–84. Member: Lancs River Authority, 1968–74; NW Water Authority, 1973–80, 1983–89; Dir, NW Water Group, 1989–90. Dir, Cumbria Rural Enterprise Agency, 1986–2010; Mem., NW Business Leadership Team, 1991–98. Pres., British Paper and Bd Fedn, 1988–90. Chm., Frieda Scott Charitable Trust, 1981–94; Trustee, Lakeland Arts Trust (formerly Abbot Hall Art Gall. and Mus.), 1992–2010 (Chm. Govs, 1983–88). Member (Indep.): S Westmorland RDC, 1967–74; S Lakeland DC, 1974–77. High Sheriff of Westmorland, 1971; DL Cumbria, 1985. KStJ 1997; CMLJ 2005. Commander, Order of the Lion (Finland), 1991. *Recreations:* shooting, golf. *Address:* Tolson Hall, Kendal, Cumbria LA9 5SE. *T:* (01539) 722011.

CROPPER, Peter John, CBE 1988; Special Adviser: to Chief Secretary to the Treasury, 1979–82; to Chancellor of the Exchequer, 1984–88; *b* 18 June 1927; *s* of late Walter Cecil Cropper and Kathleen Cropper; *m* 1965, Rosemary Winning (*d* 2014); one *s*. *Educ:* Hitchin Grammar Sch.; Gonville and Caius Coll., Cambridge (MA). Served Royal Artillery, 1945–48. Conservative Research Dept, 1951–53, 1975–79, Dir, 1982–84. *Address:* 77 Hadlow Road, Tonbridge, Kent TN9 1QB. *Club:* Reform.

CRORKIN, Colin Wynn, MBE 1993; HM Diplomatic Service; Ambassador to The Gambia, since 2014; *b* Edinburgh, 31 Jan. 1957; *s* of Daniel and Elizabeth Crorkin; *m* 1991, Joanne Lynn Finnamore; two *s* one *d*. *Educ:* Rowlinson Sch., Sheffield. Entered FCO, 1975; Finance Dept, FCO, 1975–77; Chancery Officer, Rome, 1977–79; Visa Officer, Beirut, 1980–82; Asst Press Officer, UK Representation to EU, Brussels, 1983–84; Personnel Dept, FCO, 1984–87; Mgt Officer, then Dep. Hd of Mission, Kinshasa, 1987–91; British Trade and Investment Office, NY, 1992–94; Near East and N Africa Dept and HR, FCO, 1994–97; Sen. Mgt Officer, Lagos, 1997–2002; Dep. Hd of Mission, Tripoli, 2002–04; Sen. Mgt Officer, Baghdad, 2004–05; Consul Gen., Kirkuk, 2005–06; Dep. Hd of Mission, Manila, 2006–11; Consul Gen., Kabul, 2012–14. *Recreations:* sport, walking. *Address:* c/o Foreign and Commonwealth Office, King Charles Street, SW1A 2AH.

CROSBIE, Annette, OBE 1998; actress; *b* 12 Feb. 1934; *m* Michael Griffiths; one *s* one *d*. *Educ:* Bristol Old Vic Theatre Sch. *Stage* includes: Citizens' Theatre, Glasgow: A View from the Bridge; The Crucible; The Cherry Orchard; Bristol Old Vic: Romeo and Juliet; The Tempest; A Taste of Honey; Comedy Theatre: Tinker; A Singular Man; The Winslow Boy, New, 1970; Mr Bolfry, Aldwych; The Changeling, Royal Court; The Family Dance, Criterion, 1976; The Trojan War Will Not Take Place, NT, 1983; Curtains, Whitehall, 1988; I Thought I Heard a Rustling, Theatre Royal Stratford, 1991; A Delicate Balance, Haymarket, 1997; The Night Season, NT, 2004; *television* includes: *series and serials:* The Six Wives of Henry VIII, 1970 (BAFTA Award for best actress); Edward VII, 1975 (BAFTA Award for best actress); Lillie, 1978; Paradise Postponed, 1986; Take Me Home, 1989; Summer's Lease, 1989; One Foot in the Grave, 1989–2000; Dr Finlay (Scottish TV Award for best actress), 1993; An Unsuitable Job for a Woman, 1997; Little Dorrit, 2008; Hope Springs, 2009; *plays:* The Seagull; Waste, 1977; Richard III; Beyond the Pale, 1989; radio plays and serials; *films* include: The Slipper and the Rose (Eve. News British Film Award for best actress), 1975; Ordeal by Innocence; The Pope Must Die, 1990; Calendar Girls, 2003. Founding Mem., Greyhounds UK, 1998; Vice Pres., League Against Cruel Sports (Pres., 2002–11). Hon. DVMS Glasgow, 2000. *Address:* c/o Independent Talent Group Ltd, 40 Whitfield Street, W1T 2RH.

CROSBIE, Hon. John Carnell; PC (Canada) 1979; OC 1998; QC; Counsel, Cox and Palmer (formerly Patterson Palmer Hunt Murphy, then Patterson Palmer), Atlantic Canada lawyers, 1994–2008; Lieutenant Governor of Newfoundland and Labrador, 2008–13; *b* 30 Jan. 1931; *s* of Chesley Arthur Crosbie and Jessie Carnell; *m* 1952, Jane Furneaux; two *s* one *d*. *Educ:* Bishop Feild Coll., St John's, Nfld; St Andrew's Coll., Aurora, Ont.; Queen's Univ., Kingston, Ont. (Pol Sci. and Econs); Dalhousie Univ., Halifax, NS (Law); LSE, London, Eng. Joined Newfoundland Law Soc. and Newfoundland Bar; entered law practice, St John's, 1957; Mem. City Council, St John's, 1965; Dep. Mayor, 1966; Minister of Municipal Affairs and Housing, Province of Newfoundland, (Lib. Admin), July 1966; MHA, Prov. of Newfoundland, Sept. 1966; Minister of Health, 1967; resigned from Govt, 1968; re-elected Member for St John's West (Progressive Conservative), Provincial election, 1971; Minister of Finance, Pres. of Treasury Bd and Minister of Econ. Develt, 1972–74; Minister of Fisheries, Min. for Intergovtl Affairs and Govt House Leader, 1974–75; Minister of Mines and Energy and Minister for Intergovtl Affairs, 1975–76; resigned from Newfoundland Govt, Sept. 1976; elected to House of Commons, Oct. 1976; MP (PC) St John's West, Newfoundland, 1976–93; Chm. of Progressive Conservative Caucus Cttee on Energy, 1977; PC parly critic for Industry, Trade and Commerce, 1977–79; Minister of Finance, 1979–80; Party Finance Critic, 1980; Party External Affairs Critic, 1981–83; Minister of Justice and Attorney General, 1984–86; Minister of Transport, 1986–88; Minister for International Trade, 1988–91; Minister for Fisheries and Oceans and for Atlantic Canada Opportunities Agency, 1991–93. Dir, Atlantic Inst. of Market Studies, 1996–2008. Hon. Consul of Mexico in Newfoundland and Labrador, 1996–2008. Chancellor, Meml Univ. of Newfoundland, 1994–2008. *Publications:* No Holds Barred (memoirs), 1997.

CROSBY, James Robert; Senior Independent Director, Compass Group plc, 2007–13; *b* 14 March 1956; *m*; four *d*. *Educ:* Lancaster Royal Grammar Sch.; Brasenose Coll., Oxford (BA Maths). FFA 1980. With Scottish Amicable, 1977–94: posts incl. Investment Dir, 1983, and Hd of Marketing and Finance; Man. Dir, Halifax Life, Halifax Bldg Soc., 1994–96; Dir, Financial Services and Insurance, 1996–99, Chief Exec., 1999–2001, Halifax plc; Gp Chief Exec., HBOS plc, 2001–06. Sen. Ind. Dir, ITV (formerly Granada) plc, 2008–09 (non-exec. Dir, 2002–09); Chm., Misys plc, 2009–12. Member: Eur. Adv. Bd, Bridgepoint Capital, 2006–13; Finance Cttee of the Delegacy, OUP, 2006. Dep. Chm., FSA, 2007–09 (non-exec. Dir, 2004–09). Chairman: Public Private Forum on Identity Mgt, 2006–08 (report, Opportunities and Challenges in Identity Assurance, 2008); Private Investment Commn, North Way, 2008–09; Wkg Gp, Housing Finance Rev., HM Treasury, 2008–09. Trustee, CRUK, 2008–13.

CROSBY, Lynton Keith, AO 2005; Managing Director, Crosby/Textor, since 2002; Co-Founder, CTF Partners (UK), since 2010; Campaign Consultant, Conservative Party, since 2013; *b* 23 Aug. 1956; *s* of Dudley Keith and Sheila Evelyn Crosby; *m* 1978, Dawn Heinrich; two *d*. *Educ:* Kadina Meml High Sch.; Univ. of Adelaide (BEc). Mkt analyst, Golden Fleece Petroleum, 1976–78; Executive Assistant: to Minister for Educn and Aboriginal Affairs, SA, 1980–82; to Leader of Opposition in Legislative Council, SA, 1982–86; Sen. Planning Officer, Santos Ltd, 1986–89; Manager, PR and Mktg Support, Elders Ltd, 1989–91; Liberal Party of Australia: State Dir, Qld Div., 1991–93; Dep. Federal Dir, 1994–97; Federal Dir, 1997–2002; Campaign Director: for Prime Minister of Australia, John Howard, 1998 and 2001 Gen. Elections; for Cons. Party, UK, 2005 Gen. Election and 2008 and 2012 London Mayoral Elections. *Recreations:* reading, tennis, hockey, politics. *Address:* CTF Partners, Sixth Floor, 7 Old Park Lane, W1K 1QR.

CROSLAND, Neisha, (Mrs S. Perche), RDI 2006; wallpaper and fabric designer with own business, since 1994; *b* 11 Jan. 1960; *d* of C. R. H. Crosland and Felicity Crosland (*née* d'Abreu); *m* 2002, Stephane Perche; two *s*. *Educ:* Camberwell Sch. of Arts and Crafts (BA 1st Cl. Hons Textile Design); Royal Coll. of Art (MA Printed Textiles). Freelance designer and teaching appointments: Glasgow Sch. of Art, 1989–90; Winchester Sch. of Art, 1991–92; Northbrooke Coll., 1992; freelance designer: designed: Romagna collection for Osborne & Little, 1988; Carnaval collection of wallpaper and fabrics for Harlequin Wall Coverings Ltd, 1990–94; contrib. First Eleven Portfolio, textile agency, 1991; launched: Neisha Crosland Scarves, 1994; Neisha at Debenhams, 1998; Ginka Ready to Wear and own Neisha Crosland Wallpaper Collection, 1999; home decorative and stationery collection and opened first retail outlet, London, 2000–01; licensed collection of scarves and fashion accessories for Hank Yu, Japan, 2002; first collection of home furnishing fabrics, 2003; collaboration with Rug Co., 2005–; designed: scarves and ties for Reed Employment, 2007; tiles for De Ferranti, 2008; range of home furnishings for John Lewis, 2009; hand embroidered fabrics for Chelsea Textiles, 2010; hand crafted stationery for Harris & jones, 2011; vinyl flooring collection for Harvey Maria, 2011; secured UK distribn, 2009, worldwide fabric and wallpaper distribn, 2011, with Turnell & Gigon. Ext. Examr, RCA, 2007. Mem. Panel, RSA Design Bursary Award, 2006–. *Recreations:* food, wine, films, arts, music. *Address:* 29 Oberstein Road, SW11 2AE. *T:* (020) 7657 1150, *Fax:* (020) 7288 0346. *E:* info@neishacrosland.com. *Club:* Chelsea Arts.

CROSS, Alistair Robert Sinclair B.; *see* Bassett Cross.

CROSS, Prof. Anthony Glenn, FBA 1989; Professor of Slavonic Studies, 1985–2004, now Emeritus, and Fellow of Fitzwilliam College, 1986–2004, Cambridge University; *b* 21 Oct. 1936; *s* of Walter Sidney Cross and Ada Cross; *m* 1960, Margaret (*née* Elson); two *d*. *Educ:* High Pavement Sch., Nottingham; Trinity Hall, Cambridge (BA 1960, MA 1964, PhD 1966); Harvard Univ. (AM 1961); LittD East Anglia 1981; LittD Cambridge 1997. Frank Knox Fellow, Harvard Univ., 1960–61; Univ. of East Anglia: Lectr in Russian, 1964–69; Sen. Lectr in Russian, 1969–72; Reader, 1972–81; Roberts Prof. of Russian, Univ. of Leeds, 1981–85. Vis. Fellow: Univ. of Illinois, 1969–70; All Souls Coll., Oxford, 1977–78. Leverhulme Emeritus Fellow, 2008. Pres., British Univs Assoc. of Slavists, 1982–84; Chm., British Academic Cttee for Liaison with Soviet Archives, 1983–95. Mem., Russian Acad. of Humanities, 1996. General Editor: Russia through European Eyes, 1966–68; Anglo-Russian Affinities, 1992–95; Reviews Editor, Jl of European Studies, 1971–; Editor, Study Group on Eighteenth-Century Russia Newsletter, 1973–2009. Hon. Dr, Inst. of Russian Lit., St Petersburg, 2008. Nove Prize, 1997; Antsiferov Prize, St Petersburg, 1998; Dashkova medal, Moscow, 2003. *Publications:* N. M. Karamzin, 1971; Russia Under Western Eyes 1517–1825, 1971; (ed) Russian Literature in the Age of Catherine the Great, 1976; Anglo-Russian Relations in the Eighteenth Century, 1977; (ed) Great Britain and Russia in the Eighteenth Century, 1979; By the Banks of the Thames, 1980; (ed) Russia and the West in the Eighteenth Century, 1981; The Tale of the Russian Daughter and her Suffocated Lover, 1982; (ed jtly) Eighteenth Century Russian Literature, Culture and Thought: a bibliography, 1984; The Russian Theme in English Literature, 1985; (ed jtly) Russia and the World of the Eighteenth Century, 1988; (ed) An English Lady at the Court of Catherine the Great, 1989; Anglophilia on the Throne: the British and the Russians in the age of Catherine II, 1992; (ed) Engraved in the Memory: James Walker, engraver to Catherine the Great and his Russian anecdotes, 1993; Anglo-Russica: aspects of Anglo-Russian cultural relations in the eighteenth and early nineteenth centuries, 1993; (ed jtly) Literature, Lives and Legality in Catherine's Russia, 1994; By the Banks of the Neva: chapters from the lives of the British in eighteenth-century Russia, 1996; (ed) Russia in the Reign of Peter the Great: old and new perspectives, 1998; (ed jtly) Britain and Russia in the Age of Peter the Great: historical documents, 1998; Peter the Great through British Eyes: perceptions and representations of the tsar since 1698, 2000; Catherine the Great and the British, 2001; (ed) St Petersburg 1703–1825: a collection of essays, 2003; (ed) Anglo-Russian Cultural Encounters and Collisions in the Nineteenth and Early Twentieth Centuries, 2005; (ed) Days from the Reigns of Eighteenth-Century Russian Rulers, 2007; St Petersburg and the British: the city through the eyes of British visitors and residents, 2008; (ed) A People Passing Rude: British responses to Russian culture, 2012; In the Lands of the Romanovs: an annotated bibliography of first-hand English-language accounts of the Russian empire 1613–1907, 2014. *Recreations:* book collecting, cricket watching. *Address:* Fitzwilliam College, Storey's Way, Cambridge CB2 0DG. *T:* (01223) 332000. *E:* agc28@cam.ac.uk.

CROSS, Anthony Maurice; QC 2006; a Recorder of the Crown Court, since 2002; a Deemster, Isle of Man, since 2012; *b* 16 June 1958; *s* of Maurice and Mia Cross; *m* 1982, Joanne Corrin; one *s* two *d*. *Educ:* St Mary's Marist Coll., Blackburn; Univ. of Manchester (LLB Hons 1980). Called to the Bar, Middle Temple, 1982; in practice as a barrister, Manchester. Chm., Criminal Bar Assoc., 2014–15 (Vice Chm., 2013–14). Registered Lawyer, FA. *Recreations:* travel, fashion, theatre, film, football, golf, cricket, physical fitness. *Address:* Lincoln House Chambers, Tower 12, The Avenue North, Spinningfields, 18–20 Bridge Street, Manchester M3 3BZ. *T:* (0161) 832 5701, *Fax:* (0161) 832 0839. *E:* anthony.cross@lincolnhousechambers.com; Garden Court Chambers, 57–60 Lincoln's Inn Fields, WC2A 3LJ. *Club:* Burnley Football.

CROSS, Prof. George Alan Martin, FRS 1984; André and Bella Meyer Professor of Molecular Parasitology, 1982–2013, now Emeritus, and Dean of Graduate and Postgraduate Studies, 1995–99, Rockefeller University, New York; *b* 27 Sept. 1942; *s* of George Bernard and Beatrice Mary Cross; *m*; one *s*. *Educ:* Cheadle Hulme Sch.; Downing Coll., Univ. of Cambridge (BA, PhD). ICI Postdoctoral Fellow, Biochemistry, Cambridge, 1967–69; Research Fellow, Fitzwilliam Coll., Cambridge, 1967–70; Scientist, MRC Biochemical Parasitology Unit, Molteno Inst., Cambridge, 1969–77; Head, Dept of Immunochemistry, Wellcome Research Laboratories, 1977–82. Fleming Lectr, Soc. for General Microbiology, 1978; Leeuwenhoek Lectr, Royal Soc., 1998. Chalmers Medal, Royal Soc. for Tropical Medicine and Hygiene, 1983; (jtly) Paul Ehrlich and Ludwig Darmstaedter Prize, 1984. *Publications:* in journals of parasitology, biochemistry, microbiology and molecular biology. *Recreations:* sailing, tennis, building projects, observing people. *Address:* Rockefeller University, 1230 York Avenue, New York, NY 10065–6399, USA. *T:* (212) 3277571. *E:* george.cross@rockefeller.edu.

CROSS, Gillian Clare, DPhil; author; *b* 1945; *d* of James Eric Arnold and Joan Emma (*née* Manton); *m* 1967, Martin Francis Cross; two *s* two *d*. *Educ:* North London Collegiate Sch. for Girls; Somerville Coll., Oxford (MA); Univ. of Sussex (DPhil). Mem., Adv. Council on Libraries, 1995–2000. Mem., Soc. of Authors, 1978–. Member: Octavian Droobers, 1990–2009; Wimborne Orienteering Club, 2010–. Freeman, 2007–13, Liveryman, 2013–, Guild of Educators. Hon. DLitt Glamorgan, 2008. *Publications:* The Runaway, 1979; The Iron Way, 1979; Revolt at Ratcliffe's Rags, 1980; Save Our School, 1981; A Whisper of Lace, 1981; The Dark Behind the Curtain, 1982; The Demon Headmaster, 1982; Born of the Sun, 1983; The Mintyglo Kid, 1983; On the Edge, 1984; The Prime Minister's Brain, 1985; Chartbreak, 1986 (USA as Chartbreaker, 1987); Swimathon, 1986; Roscoe's Leap, 1987; A Map of Nowhere, 1988; Rescuing Gloria, 1989; Wolf, 1990 (Carnegie Medal, LA, 1990); The Monster from Underground, 1990; Twin and Super-Twin, 1990; Gobbo The Great, 1991; Rent-A-Genius, 1991; The Great Elephant Chase, 1992 (Smarties Book Prize and Whitbread Children's Novel Award, 1992); Beware Olga!, 1993; Furry Maccaloo, 1993; The Tree House, 1993; Hunky Parker is Watching You, 1994; What will Emily Do?, 1994; New World, 1994; The Crazy Shoe Shuffle, 1995; Posh Watson, 1995; The Roman Beanfeast, 1996; Pictures in the Dark, 1996; The Demon Headmaster Strikes Again, 1996; The Demon Headmaster Takes Over, 1997; The Goose Girl, 1998; Tightrope, 1999; Down with the Dirty Danes, 2000; The Treasure in the Mud, 2001; Calling a Dead Man, 2001, US edn as Phoning a Dead Man, 2002; Beware of the Demon Headmaster, 2002; Facing the Demon Headmaster, 2002; The Dark Ground, 2004; The Black Room, 2005; The Nightmare Game, 2006; Brother Aelred's Feet, 2007; Where I Belong, 2010; The Odyssey (retold), 2012; The Monster Snowman, 2012; After Tomorrow, 2013; The Cupcake Wedding, 2013; The Mystery of the Man with the Black Beard, 2014; Mozart's Banana, 2014; Shadow Cat, 2015. *Recreations:* playing the piano, orienteering. *Address:* c/o Oxford Children's Books, Oxford University Press, Great Clarendon Street, Oxford OX2 6DP.

CROSS, James Edward Michael; QC 2006; *b* 18 March 1962; *s* of Michael Cross and Mary (*née* Wright); *m* 1994, Victoria, *d* of Sir John Henry Lambert, KCVO, CMG; two *s*. *Educ:* Shrewsbury Sch.; Magdalen Coll., Oxford (MA Juris; Academical Clerk). Called to the Bar, Gray's Inn, 1985, Bencher, 2010; in practice specialising in construction and engrg law, professional negligence and liability, insurance and product liability. Member: Monitoring of Pupillage Review Panel, Bar Council, 1999–2002; Cttee, London Common Law and Commercial Bar Assoc., 2002–08; Cttee, Professional Negligence Bar Assoc., 2008–12; Chm., Pupillage Cttee, 4 Pump Ct, 2003–06. Lectr in Law, Magdalen Coll., Oxford, 1985–88. Trustee, Shrewsbury Foundn, 2011–. *Publications:* (contrib.) The Architect's Legal Handbook, 9th edn 2010. *Recreations:* singing (Mem., Vasari Singers, since 1992, Chm., 2004–07), hill walking, gardening. *Address:* 4 Pump Court, Temple, EC4Y 7AN. *Club:* Roehampton.

CROSS, James Michael; Chief Executive Officer, Natural England, since 2014; *b* Stockton on Tees, 7 Nov. 1974; *s* of Michael Arthur Cross and Winifred Cross (*née* Brown); partner, Karen Purvis; one *s* one *d* (and one *s* decd). *Educ:* Univ. of Teesside (BA Hons Business Econs); Inst. of Dirs (Dip. Company Direction). CMgr 2013. Asst Chief Inspector of Court Admin in England and Wales, HM Inspectorate of Court Admin, 2005–10; CEO, Marine Mgt Orgn, 2010–14. Mem., Assoc. of Chief Execs, 2010–. FCMI 2013; FInstD 2015. *Recreations:* being with my family, being outdoors, sailing, camping, hiking. *Address:* Natural England, Foss House, 1–2 Peasholme Green, York YO1 7PX. *T:* 0300 060 1106. *E:* james.cross@naturalengland.org.uk.

CROSS, James Richard, (Jasper), CMG 1971; Under-Secretary, Principal Establishment Officer, Department of Energy, 1978–80; *b* 29 Sept. 1921; *s* of J. P. Cross and Dinah Cross (*née* Hodgins); *m* 1945, Barbara Dagg; one *d*. *Educ:* King's Hosp., Dublin; Trinity Coll., Dublin. Scholar, First Cl. Moderatorship Economics and Pol Science. RE (Lieut). Asst Principal, Bd of Trade, 1947; Private Sec. to Parly Sec., 1947–49; Principal, 1950; Trade Commissioner: New Delhi, 1953–56; Halifax, 1957–60; Winnipeg, 1960–62; Asst Sec., 1962; Sen. Trade Comr, Kuala Lumpur, 1962–66; Bd of Trade, 1966–67; Under Sec., 1968; Sen. British Trade Comr, Montreal, 1968–70 (kidnapped by terrorists and held for 59 days, Oct.–Dec. 1970); Under-Sec., Export Planning and Develt Div., DTI, 1971–73; Coal Div., DTI, later Dept of Energy, 1973–78. *Recreations:* theatre, bridge. *Address:* 4 Crouchfield Close, Crooked Lane, Seaford, East Sussex BN25 1QE.

CROSS, Jane Elizabeth; QC 2010; *b* Sussex, 13 Nov. 1958; *d* of Ernest Leonard Cross and Patricia Mary Cross (*née* Baldwin); *m* 1986, Charles Garth McDonald; two *d* (and one *d* decd). *Educ:* Winckley Sq. Convent Sch.; Liverpool Univ. (LLB). Called to the Bar, Middle Temple,

1982; in practice as barrister, specialising in family law, Northern Circuit, 1982–. *Recreations:* art, opera, the outdoors. *Address:* Deans Court Chambers, 24 St John Street, Manchester M3 4DF. *T:* (0161) 214 6000, *Fax:* (0161) 214 6001. *E:* cross@deanscourt.co.uk.

CROSS, Jasper; *see* Cross, J. R.

CROSS, Julia; *see* Black, J.

CROSS, Linda Mary, MBE 2004; HM Diplomatic Service, retired; Ambassador to El Salvador, 2012–14; *b* Dundee, 15 March 1956; *d* of late W. Gordon Guild and Elizabeth Mary Guild; *m* 1989, Michael Cross. *Educ:* Leeds Metropolitan Univ. (BA Hons 1st Cl. Hospitality and Business Mgt). Entered FCO, 1978; Rabat, 1978–81; Prague, 1981–82; Quito, 1983–85; Paris, 1985–88; FCO, 1988–91; Third Sec., Chancery, and Vice-Consul, Vienna, 1992–94; Third Sec., UK Mission to UN, NY, 1995–97; Dep. Hd of Mission, Azerbaijan, 1998–2001; Consul Gen., Yekaterinburg, 2001–05; FCO, 2005–08; Ambassador to Ecuador, 2008–12. *Recreations:* music, reading, swimming, learning languages.

CROSS, Dame Margaret Natalie; *see* Smith, Dame Maggie.

CROSS, Dr Nigel; consultant in international development; *b* 9 March 1953; *s* of Sir Barry Albert Cross, CBE, FRS and of Audrey Lilian Cross; *m* 1st, 1980, Dr Caroline Dakers (marr. diss. 2010); two *d*; 2nd, 2014, Josephine Namusisi. *Educ:* Univ. of Sussex (BA English 1974); University Coll. London (PhD 1980). Archivist, Royal Literary Fund, 1975–80; Leverhulme Res. Fellow, 1980–81; tutor-counsellor and tutor, third world studies, Open Univ., 1981–87; Sec., British Cttee, SOS Sahel-Internat., 1983–85; Director: SOS Sahel UK, 1985–95; Panos Inst., 1995–99; Dir, 1999–2003, Consultant, 2003–04, Internat. Inst. for Envmt and Develt; Professorial Res. Fellow, Dept of Develt Studies, SOAS, Univ. of London, 2005–08; Dir, Netherlands Develt Orgn, Sudan, 2008–11; Dir, Windle Trust Internat., S Sudan, 2012. Consultant: IDL Gp, 2004–07; Creative Exchange, 2006–08. Board Member: FARM Africa, 1989–94; Inst. for Develt Policy and Mgt, Univ. of Manchester, 1992–95; Agency for Co-op. and Res. in Develt (ACORD Africa), 1996–2002 (Chm., 1998–2000); Inst. for Global Envmtl Strategies, Japan, 1999–2003. Ext. collaborator, ILO, Geneva, 1984–86; Member: NGO Consultative Gp, IFAD, Rome, 1991–96 (Co-Chm., 1991–92); Adv. Bd, Grid Arendal, Norway, 2000–02. *Publications:* The Common Writer, 1985; (with N. Ardill) Undocumented Lives, 1987; The Sahel: the people's right to development, 1990; (with R. Barker) At The Desert's Edge: oral histories from the Sahel, 1991; (contributing ed.) Listening for a Change, 1993; (ed) Evidence for Hope: the search for sustainable development, 2003; contribs on literature and develt to various newspapers and specialist jls. *E:* nigelcross@ncross.plus.com.

CROSS, Peter H.; *see* Hulme Cross.

CROSS, Philippa Jane, (Mrs Graham Lee); Director, CrossDay Productions, since 2002; *b* Ipswich, 13 May 1956; *d* of Robert and Jill Cross; *m* 1982, Graham Lee; one *s* one *d*. *Educ:* Ipswich High Sch.; St Anne's Coll., Oxford (BA 1st Cl. English Lang. and Lit. 1977). Asst Entertainments Manager, Wembley Conf. Centre, 1978–80; Manager: Granada TV, 1980–85; TVS, 1985–88; Hd of Develt, 1988–93, Hd, 1993–2002, Granada Film; credits incl. My Left Foot, The Field, Jack and Sarah, Rogue Trader, House of Mirth, Longitude, Bloody Sunday; CrossDay Prodns credits incl. Shooting Dogs, Heartless, Chalet Girl, Summer in February, Desert Dancer, A Hundred Streets. Member: Screen South, 2003–12; UK Film Council, 2009–10. *Recreations:* family, theatre, winter sports. *Address:* CrossDay Productions, 14 Rathbone Place, W1T 1HT. *T:* (020) 7637 0182. *E:* pippacro@aol.com.

CROSS, Stefan Tylney; Senior Partner, Stefan Cross Solicitors, 2002–13; *b* Chiswick, 5 Oct. 1960; *s* of Brian Cross and Jacqueline Ann Pilling; *m* 1986, Dr Alison Mary Steele; two *s* two *d*. *Educ:* Univ. of Southampton (LLB 1982); Univ. of Leicester (LLM 1990). Admitted solicitor, 1985; trainee solicitor, GA Mooring Aldridge and Brownlee, 1983–86; Partner: Brian Thompson and Partners, 1986–90; Thompsons Solicitors, 1990–2002. Part-time Chm., Employment Tribunal, subseq. Employment Judge, 2005–08. Director: Action4Equality Scotland Ltd, 2005–; Fox Cross Solicitors, 2009–11. Mem. (Lab) Newcastle CC, 1990–98. Hon. QC 2013. Campaigner for equal pay for women. *Recreations:* Newcastle United Football Club, trashy crime novels, indie rock music, travel, politics. *Address:* 23 Montagu Avenue, Newcastle upon Tyne NE3 4HY. *T:* (0191) 285 6110. *E:* Stc@stefancross.co.uk.

CROSS, Maj.-Gen. Timothy, CBE 2000; Chief Executive Officer, CROSSTC Ltd, since 2007 (Director, since 2006); *b* 19 April 1951; *s* of Sidney George and Patricia Mary Cross; *m* 1972, Christine Mary Pelly; two *s* one *d*. *Educ:* Welbeck; RMA, Sandhurst; RMCS Shrivenham (BSc Hons, MSc); ato. NI, 1978; Adjt 1 Ordnance Bn, 1979–80; UN, Cyprus, 1981; Army Staff Coll., 1982–83 (psc); British Liaison Bureaux, Paris, 1984–85; Co. Comdr, 1 Ordnance Bn, 1986–87; Directing Staff, Army Staff Coll., 1988–90; CO, 1 Ordnance Bn, 1990–92; deployed to Kuwait/Iraq, 1990–91; Comdr, Logistic Support 3 (UK) Div., 1992–96; deployed to Balkans (IFOR), 1995–96; HCSC, 1995; Dir, Materiel Support (Army), 1996–97; Comdr, 101 Logistic Bde, 1998–2000; deployed to Balkans/Kosovo, 1998 (SFOR), 2000 (KFOR); rcds 2000; Dir Gen., Defence Supply Chain (formerly Defence Logistic Support), 2000–03; deployed to Kuwait/Iraq as UK Deputy in ORHA/CPA, 2003; GOC Theatre Troops, 2004–06. Col Comdt RLC, 2003–11; Hon. Col 168 Pioneer Regt, RLC (V), 2007–13. Army Advr, Defence Cttee, H of C, 2007–11, 2013–14. Pres., Inst. of Civil Protection and Emergency Mgt, 2009–. Defence Advisor: Fujitsu, 2007–11; Harmonic, 2007–; Senior Military Adviser: Coker Logistic Solutions, 2007–14; Husons, 2008–; SC Skills, 2009–; Advr, Imeon Logistics. Mem., Ethics Cttee, Ultra Electronics, 2011–. Has lectured in UK and abroad; Visiting Professor: Nottingham Univ., 2007–; Cranfield Univ., 2007–; Reading Univ., 2008–. Director: Centre for Internat. Humanitarian Co-operation, 2004–11; Humanitarian Internat. Services Gp, 2008–; Caring for Ex-Offenders, 2011–12; William Wilberforce Trust, 2013–; Agility Defence and Govt Services Bd, 2014–; Mem., Mgt Bd, Theos, 2007– (Chm., 2012–); Trustee, Leadership Trust Foundn, 2003–14. Lay Reader, C of E. Trustee: British and Foreign Bible Soc., 2007–12; Accts Mil. Ministries Internat., 2007–12. *Publications:* contribs chapters and articles to books and jls. *Recreations:* golf, walking, reading, writing.

CROSS BROWN, Tom; Chairman, Just Retirement Group plc, since 2006; *b* Oxford, 22 Dec. 1947; *s* of Christopher James and Georgina Cross Brown; *m* 1972, Susan Rosemary Jackson; three *d* (one *s* decd). *Educ:* Uppingham Sch.; Brasenose Coll., Oxford (MA); INSEAD (MBA). Nat. and Grindlays Bank Ltd, 1970–75; Lazard Brothers & Co. Ltd, 1976–97: Dir, 1985–97, Man. Dir, 1994–97; Chief Exec., Lazard Brothers Asset Mgt Ltd, 1994–97; Chm., 1997–2003, Global Chief Exec., 2000–03, ABN AMRO Asset Mgt Ltd. Non-executive Chairman: Pearl Assce plc, 2005–09; National Provident Life Ltd, 2005–09; NPI Ltd, 2005–09; London Life Ltd, 2005–09; Ignis Asset Mgt Ltd, 2008–10; non-executive Director: Whitegate Leisure plc, 1987–91; Artemis Investment Mgt Ltd, 2002–06; Quintain Estates and Develt plc, 2005–06; BlueBay Asset Mgt plc, 2006–10; Artemis Alpha Trust plc, 2006–; Phoenix Gp Hldgs, 2009–; Artemis Investment Mgt LLP, 2011–. Dir, P. A. T. Pensions Ltd, 2005–08. Dir, Financial Planning Standards Bd, 2011–. Chm., Heathfield Sch., 2005–14 (Gov., 1999–). Trustee: Cancer Care and Haematol. Fund, Stoke Mandeville Hosp., 2004–14; Lazard Dirs' Pension Scheme, 2007–14. Mem., Finance and Gen. Purposes Cttee, VSO, 1979–82. Pres., INSEAD Alumni Assoc. UK, 1977–82. Hon. Sec., Benedict Soc., 2005–12 (Mem., 2001). *Recreations:* opera, shooting, gardening. *Address:* Shipton Old Farm, Winslow, Buckingham MK18 3JL.

CROSSE, Gordon; composer; *b* 1 Dec. 1937; *s* of Percy and Marie Crosse; *m* 1965, Elizabeth Bunch. *Educ:* Cheadle Hulme Sch.; St Edmund Hall, Oxford; Accademia di S Cecilia, Rome. Music Fellow, Essex Univ., 1969–74; Composer in residence, King's Coll., Cambridge, 1974–76; Vis. Lectr, Univ. of Calif at Santa Barbara, 1977–78. Hon. RAM 1980. *Operas:* Purgatory, 1966; The Grace of Todd, 1967; The Story of Vasco, 1970; Potter Thompson, 1973; *ballets:* Playground, 1979; Wildboy, 1981; *other compositions:* Concerto da Camera, 1962; Meet My Folks, 1963; "Symphonies", 1964; Second Violin Concerto, 1970; Memories of Morning: Night, 1972; Ariadne, 1973; Symphony 2, 1975; Wildboy (clarinet concerto), Play Ground, 1977; Dreamsongs, 1978; Cello Concerto, 1979; String Quartet, 1980; Trio for clarinet, cello and piano, 1980; Dreamcanon (chorus), 1981; Trio for piano, violin and cello, 1986; Trumpet Concerto, 1986; Rhyming with Everything for oboe, violin and cello, 2009; Fantasia on Ca' The Yowes for flute, harp (or clarsach) and strings, 2009; Brief Encounter for oboe d'amore, recorder and strings, 2009; Ad Patrem, 3rd elegy for small orchestra, 2009; Spring Awakening for 5 male voices and speaker, 2009; String Quartet No 2, Good to be Here, 2010; Sabbath Rest, anthem for TrATB and organ, 2010; Hey the Gift, Ho the Gift for SATB a capella, 2010; much other orchestral, vocal and chamber music. *Address:* Brant's Cottage, Blackheath, Wenhaston, Halesworth, Suffolk IP19 9EX.

CROSSETT, Robert Nelson, (Tom), DPhil; Chairman: National Flood Forum, 2004–06 (Director, 2003–06); Thames Flood Forum, 2005–08; *b* 27 May 1938; *s* of Robert Crossett and Mary Nelson; *m* 1966, Susan Marjorie Legg; two *s*. *Educ:* British School, Hamburg; Campbell College, Belfast; Queen's Univ., Belfast (BSc, BAgr); Lincoln College, Oxford (DPhil); Univ. of East Anglia. Group Leader Environmental Studies, Aust. Atomic Energy Commn, 1966; Sen. Sci. Officer, ARC Letcombe Lab., 1969; Develt Officer (Crops), Scottish Agricl Develt Council, 1972; PSO, Dept of Agric. and Fisheries for Scotland, 1975; Ministry of Agriculture, Fisheries and Food: Sci. Liaison Officer (Horticulture and Soils), 1978; Head, Food Sci. Div., 1984; Chief Scientist (Fisheries and Food), 1985–89; Head of Envmtl Policy, 1989–90, Envmt Dir, 1990–91, National Power; Sec. Gen., Nat. Soc. for Clean Air and Envmtl Protection, 1992–96; Dir-Gen., Internat. Union of Air Pollution Prevention Assocs, 1996–98. Chairman: Southern Regional Envmtl Protection Adv. Cttee, EA, 1996–2002; SE Water Resources Forum, 2005–08. Consultant, SE Inst. of Public Health, 1998–2000. Member: NERC, 1985–89; AFRC, 1985–89; UK Delegn, Tripartite Meetings on Food and Drugs, 1985–88; Cttee on Med. Aspects of Food Policy, 1985–89; Adv. Gp to Sec. of State for Envmt on Eco-Management and Audit, 1994–96; UK Round Table on Sustainable Develt, 1995–97. Vis. Fellow, Sci. Policy Res. Unit, Univ. of Sussex, 1997–2000; Sen. Vis. Fellow, Sch. of Health and Life Scis, KCL, 2000–05. *Publications:* papers in plant physiology, marine biology, food science and envmtl management. *Recreations:* walking, gardening, orienteering, boats.

CROSSICK, Prof. Geoffrey Joel, PhD; FRHistS; Distinguished Professor of the Humanities, School of Advanced Study, University of London, since 2013; *b* 13 June 1946; *s* of Louis Crossick and Rebecca Naomi (*née* Backen); *m* 1973, Rita Geraldine Vaudrey, JP; two *s*. *Educ:* Haberdashers' Aske's Sch., Elstree; Gonville and Caius Coll., Cambridge (BA Hist. 1967); Birkbeck Coll., London (PhD Hist. 1976). FRHistS 1993. Res. Fellow in Hist., Emmanuel Coll., Cambridge, 1970–73; Lectr in Social Hist., Univ. of Hull, 1973–78; University of Essex: Lectr in Hist., 1979–83; Sen. Lectr, 1983–86; Reader, 1986–91; Prof. of Hist., 1991–2002; Dean: Comparative Studies, 1992–95; Grad. Sch., 1996–97; Pro-Vice-Chancellor, 1997–2002; Chief Exec., AHRB, 2002–05; Warden, Goldsmiths Coll., later Goldsmiths, Univ. of London, 2005–10 (Hon. Fellow, 2012); Vice-Chancellor, Univ. of London, 2010–12. Vis. Prof., Univ. of Lyon 2, 1990–91. Member: Business and Community Strategy Cttee, then Enterprise and Skills Strategy Cttee, HEFCE, 2005–12; Bd, UUK, 2006–12. Dir, AHRC Cultural Value Project, 2012–. Member: British Library Adv. Council, 2004–14; Council, Royal Coll. Music, 2005–10; Bd, UCEA, 2007–09; Governing Body, Courtauld Inst., 2007–; Council, Agence d'évaluation de la recherche et de l'enseignement supérieur, 2012–13; Chairman: Financial Sustainability Strategy Gp, 2008–12; Bd of Governance, Trinity Long Room Hub, TCD, 2010–; Crafts Council, 2014–. Trustee: Nat. Maritime Mus., 2010–; Samuel Courtauld Trust, 2010–; Horniman Mus. and Gardens, 2013–; Goldsmiths Centre. Hon. Fellow, Emmanuel Coll., Cambridge, 2004. FRSA 2009. *Publications:* (ed) The Lower Middle Class in Britain, 1976; An Artisan Elite in Victorian Society, 1978; (ed jtly) Shopkeepers and Master Artisans in 19th Century Europe, 1984; (ed jtly) The Power of the Past: essays for Eric Hobsbawm, 1984; (with H. G. Haupt) The Petite Bourgeoisie in Europe 1780–1914, 1995; (ed) The Artisan and the European Town, 1997; (ed jtly) Cathedrals of Consumption: the European department store 1850–1939, 1998; Knowledge Transfer without Widgets: the challenge of the creative economy, 2006; contrib. articles to learned jls. *Recreations:* Tottenham Hotspur, music. *E:* geoffrey.crossick@london.ac.uk.

CROSSLAND, Anthony, FRCO; Organist and Master of the Choristers, Wells Cathedral, 1971–96; *b* 4 Aug. 1931; *s* of Ernest Thomas and Frances Elizabeth Crossland; *m* 1960, Barbara Helen Pullar-Strecker; one *s* two *d*. *Educ:* Christ Church, Oxford. MA, BMus (Oxon), FRCO (CHM), ARCM. Asst Organist: Christ Church Cathedral, Oxford, 1957–61; Wells Cathedral, 1961–71. Conductor: Wells Cathedral Oratorio Soc., 1966–96; Wells Sinfonietta, 1985–96; Organs Advr to dio. of Bath and Wells, 1971–96. Pres., Cathedral Organists' Assoc., 1983–85. Chief Theory Moderator, Associated Bd of Royal Schs of Music, 2009–13. DMus Lambeth, 1994. *Recreations:* reading, photography, armchair travelling. *Address:* Barton End, 10b Newtown, Bradford-on-Avon, Wilts BA15 1NE. *T:* (01225) 864496.

CROSSLEY, family name of **Baron Somerleyton**.

CROSSLEY, Prof. Gary; Principal, Central School of Speech and Drama, 2000–07; *b* 11 Jan. 1946; *s* of John and Patricia Crossley; *m* 1981, Yvonne Stapleton-Henthorne; one *d*. *Educ:* Portsmouth Coll. of Art (BA Hons); Hornsey Sch. of Art (PG Dip.). Hd of Dept, E Ham Coll., 1979–85; Vice Principal, W Surrey Coll. of Art and Design, 1985–89; Dep. Dir, Surrey Inst. of Art and Design, 1989–98; Founding Chm., Consortium of Arts and Design Instns in Southern England, 1998–2000. Mem. Bd, 2000–05, Exec. Council, 2005–07, Standing Conf. of Principals. Mem., Univ. Choice TV Adv. Bd, 2004. *Recreations:* theatre, film, flyfishing. *Club:* Savile.

CROSSLEY, Paul Christopher Richard, CBE 1993; concert pianist; Artistic Director, London Sinfonietta, 1988–94; *b* 17 May 1944; *s* of late Frank Crossley and Myra Crossley (*née* Barrowcliffe). *Educ:* Silcoates Sch., Wakefield; Mansfield Coll., Oxford (BA, MA; Hon. Fellow, 1992). International concert pianist; recitals and concerts with all major orchestras; numerous recordings and films for TV. *Recreations:* Mah-Jongg, reading, crosswords. *Address:* 39 Henry Tate Mews, SW16 3HA. *T:* (020) 8769 4471. *E:* pcr.crossley@btinternet.com.

CROSSLEY, Sir Sloan (Nicholas), 6th Bt *cr* 1909, of Glenfield, Dunham Massey, Chester; Managing Director, Pull Scar Estates (Pty) Ltd, White River, South Africa; *b* 20 March 1958; *s* of late Wing Comdr Michael Nicholson Crossley, RAF, DSO, OBE, DFC and Sylvia Constance Crossley; *S* cousin, 2003; *m* 1999, Jane Elizabeth, *d* of late Henry Cecil Twycross and Katherine Elizabeth Twycross. *Educ:* St Alban's Coll., Pretoria; Kingston Polytech., London; Central Sch. of Art and Design, London (BSc Hons Industrial Design (Eng)). *Address:* Pull Scar Estate, PO Box 121, White River, 1240 Mpumalanga, South Africa.

CROSSLEY-HOLLAND, Kevin John William, FRSL; author; President, School Library Association, since 2012; *b* 7 Feb. 1941; *s* of late Prof. Peter Charles Crossley-Holland and Joan Mary Crossley-Holland (*née* Cowper), MBE; *m* 1st, 1963, Caroline Fendall, *er d* of Prof. L. M. Thompson; two *s*; 2nd, 1972, Ruth, *er d* of John Marris; 3rd, 1982, Gillian Paula, *er d* of

Peter Cook; two *d*; 4th, 1999, Linda Marie, *d* of Abner Jones. *Educ:* Bryanston Sch.; St Edmund Hall, Oxford (MA Hons; Hon. Fellow, 2001). FRSL 1998. Editor, Macmillan & Co., 1962–69; Gregory Fellow in Poetry, Univ. of Leeds, 1969–71; Talks Producer, BBC, 1972; Editl Dir, Victor Gollancz, 1972–77; Lectr in English: Tufts-in-London Program, 1967–78; Regensburg Univ., 1978–80; Arts Council Fellow in Writing, Winchester Sch. of Art, 1983 and 1984; Vis. Prof. of English and Fulbright Scholar, St Olaf Coll., Minnesota, 1987–90; Prof. and Endowed Chair in Humanities and Fine Arts, Univ. of St Thomas, Minnesota, 1991–95; Vis. Lectr for British Council in Germany, Iceland, India, Malawi, Yugoslavia, Slovakia. Editl Consultant, Boydell & Brewer, 1983–90. Chm., Literature Panel, Eastern Arts Assoc., 1986–89; Trustee, Wingfield Coll., 1989–99 (Chm., Friends, 1989–91). Dir, American Composers Forum, 1993–97. Chm., Poetry-next-the-Sea, 1999–2006. Patron: Thomas Lovell Beddoes Soc., 1999–2011; Soc. for Storytelling, 2002–; Publishing House Me, 2008–; European Storytelling Archive, 2009–; Story Mus., 2013–. Contribs to radio (incl. drama), TV (incl. educnl series), and musical works. Hon. DLitt: Anglia Ruskin, 2011; Worcester, 2013. *Publications: poetry:* The Rain-Giver, 1972; The Dream-House, 1976; Time's Oriel, 1983; Waterslain, 1986; The Painting-Room, 1988; New and Selected Poems, 1991; The Language of Yes, 1996; Poems from East Anglia, 1997; Selected Poems, 2001; (with Norman Ackroyd) Moored Man, 2006; The Mountains of Norfolk: new and selected poems, 2011; Attraction Water, 2012; The Breaking Hour, 2015; *for children:* Havelok the Dane, 1964; King Horn, 1965; The Green Children, 1966 (Arts Council Award); The Callow Pit Coffer, 1968; (with Jill Paton Walsh) Wordhoard, 1969; Storm and Other Old English Riddles, 1970; The Pedlar of Swaffham, 1971; The Sea Stranger, 1973; The Fire-Brother, 1974; Green Blades Rising, 1975; The Earth-Father, 1976; The Wildman, 1976; The Dead Moon, 1982; (with Charles Keeping) Beowulf, 1982; (with Gwyn Thomas) The Mabinogion, 1984; Axe-Age, Wolf-Age, 1985; Storm, 1985 (Carnegie Medal); (with Susanne Lugert) The Fox and the Cat, 1985; British Folk Tales, 1987, reissued as The Magic Lands, 2001; Wulf, 1988; (with Gwyn Thomas) The Quest for Olwen, 1988; Piper and Pooka, 1988; Small Tooth Dog, 1988; Boo!, 1988; Dathera Dad, 1989; (with Ian Penney) Under the Sun and Over the Moon, 1989; Sleeping Nanna, 1989; Sea Tongue, 1991; Tales from Europe, 1991; Long Tom and The Dead Hand, 1992; (with Gwyn Thomas) Taliesin, 1992; The Labours of Herakles, 1993; Norse Myths, 1993; The Green Children, 1994; The Dark Horseman, 1995; The Old Stories, 1997; Short!, 1998; The King Who Was and Will Be, 1998; Enchantment, 2000; The Seeing Stone, 2000 (Guardian Children's Fiction Prize; Tir na n-Og Award); At the Crossing-Places, 2001; (with Meilo So) The Ugly Duckling, 2001; Viking!, 2002; King of the Middle March, 2003; (with Peter Malone) How Many Miles to Bethlehem?, 2004; King Arthur's World, 2004; Outsiders, 2005; Gatty's Tale, 2006; Thor and the Master of Magic, 2007; Waterslain Angels, 2008; Short Too!, 2011; Bracelet of Bones, 2011; Scramasax, 2012; (with Jane Ray) Heartsong, 2015; *play:* (with Ivan Cutting) The Wuffings, 1999; *travel:* Pieces of Land, 1972; *mythology:* The Norse Myths, 1980; *history:* (with Andrew Rafferty) The Stones Remain, 1989; *translations from Old English:* (with Bruce Mitchell) The Battle of Maldon, 1965; (with Bruce Mitchell) Beowulf, 1968; The Exeter Book Riddles, 1978; The Illustrated Beowulf, 1987; The Anglo-Saxon Elegies, 1988; *edited:* Running to Paradise, 1967; Winter's Tales for Children 3, 1967; Winter's Tales 14, 1968; (with Patricia Beer) New Poetry 2, 1976; The Faber Book of Northern Legends, 1977; The Faber Book of Northern Folk-Tales, 1980; The Anglo-Saxon World, 1982; The Riddle Book, 1982; Folk-Tales of the British Isles, 1985; The Oxford Book of Travel Verse, 1986; Northern Lights, 1987; Medieval Lovers, 1988; Medieval Gardens, 1990; Peter Grimes by George Crabbe, 1990; The Young Oxford Book of Folk-Tales, 1998; (with Lawrence Sail) The New Exeter Book of Riddles, 1999; (with Lawrence Sail) Light Unlocked: Christmas card poems, 2005; *operas:* (with Nicola LeFanu): The Green Children, 1990; The Wildman, 1995; (with Rupert Bawden) The Sailor's Tale, 2002; *memoir:* The Hidden Roads, 2009. *Recreations:* walks, wine, opera, the company of friends, appreciating East Anglia. *Address:* Chalk Hill, Burnham Market, Norfolk PE31 8JR; c/o The Agency, 24 Pottery Lane, Holland Park, W11 4LZ. *Club:* Garrick.

CROSSMAN, Prof. David Christopher, MD; FRCP; Dean of Medicine, University of St Andrews, since 2014; *b* Gravesend, 20 July 1957; *s* of William George Crossman and Charmian Jeanette Crossman; *m* 1988, Moira Katherine Brigid Whyte, *qv*; two *s*. *Educ:* Sedbergh Sch.; St Bartholomew's Med. Sch., London (BSc Physiol. 1979; MB BS 1982; MD 1991). MRCP 1985, FRCP 1998; FACC 1999; FESC 2000. MRC Clin. Trng Fellow, 1988–91; Sen. Registrar, Cardiol., Hammersmith and St Mary's Hosps, 1991–94; Prof. of Cardiol., Univ. of Sheffield, 1994–2010; Dean of Medicine, Norwich Med. Sch., UEA, 2011–14. *Recreations:* running, classical music, motor bikes, fishing. *Address:* School of Medicine, University of St Andrews, North Haugh, St Andrews, Fife KY16 9TF. *T:* (01334) 463502, *Fax:* (01334) 463482. *E:* medical.dean@st-andrews.ac.uk.

CROSSMAN, Moira Katherine Brigid; *see* Whyte, M. K. B.

CROTHERS, William, CB 2014; commercial adviser, Cabinet Office, since 2015; *b* Thirsk, Yorks, 9 Nov. 1960; *s* of Morland Crothers and Violet Crothers; *m* 2009, Lucy Bloem; four *d*. *Educ:* Belfast Royal Acad.; Univ. of Manchester (BSc 1st Cl. Hons Computer Sci. and Accounting 1982). FCA 1985; FBCS 2009; FCIPS 2012. Chartered Accountant, Peat Marwick, 1982–85; Mgt Consultant, Andersen Consulting, subseq. Accenture, 1985–2006, Partner and Mem. UK Bd, 1995–2006; Exec. Dir, Identity and Passport Service, 2007–10; Commercial Dir, Home Office, 2010–12; Crown Rep., 2010–12; Chm., Crown Commercial Service, 2014; Govt Chief Commercial (formerly Procurement) Officer, and Dir Gen., Commercial, Cabinet Office, 2012–15. Mem. Bd, Nat. Citizen Service, 2015–. Trustee, UK Youth, 2005–13 (Chm., 2010–13). Governor: Woldingham Sch. for Girls, 2010–; Hazelwood Sch., 2014–. *Recreations:* spending time with family and friends, enjoying sun, sea and sand of the south coast of England (West Sussex).

CROUCH, Prof. Colin John, DPhil; FBA 2005; FAcSS; Professor of Governance and Public Management, Warwick Business School, University of Warwick, 2005–11, now Emeritus; *b* 1 March 1944; *s* of Charles and Doris Crouch; *m* 1970, Joan Ann Freedman; two *s*. *Educ:* Latymer Upper Sch.; London School of Economics (BASoc; Pres., Students Union, 1968; Hobhouse Prize, 1969); Nuffield Coll., Oxford (MA; DPhil 1975). Lecturer in Sociology: LSE, 1969–70; Univ. of Bath, 1972–73; Lectr, 1973–79, Sen. Lectr 1979–80, Reader 1980–85, in Sociology, LSE; University of Oxford: Fellow and Tutor in Politics, Trinity Coll., Oxford, 1985–98; Prof. of Sociol., 1996–98; Curator, Bodleian Liby, 1991–95; Jun. Proctor, 1990–91; Deleg., OUP, 1992–98; European University Institute, Florence: Prof. of Comparative Social Instns, 1995–2004; Chm., Dept of Social and Political Scis, 2001–04. External Scientific Mem., Max-Planck Institut für Gesellschaftsforschung, Cologne, 1997–. Mem., Exec. Cttee, Fabian Soc., 1969–78 (Chm., 1976); Dir, Andrew Shonfield Soc., 1989–95. Vice Pres., British Acad., 2012–. Member: Standing Cttee, Court of Govs, LSE, 1980–84; Scientific Adv. Bd, Univ. of Vienna, 2007–. Fellow, Sunningdale Inst., 2005–09. Chm. Editl Bd, The Political Qly, 1999–2009 (Joint Editor, 1985–95). FAcSS (AcSS 2008). *Publications:* The Student Revolt, 1970; (ed jtly) Stress and Contradiction in Modern Capitalism, 1975; (ed) British Political Sociology Year Book, vol. III, 1977; Class Conflict and the Industrial Relations Crisis, 1977; (ed jtly) The Resurgence of Class Conflict in Western Europe since 1968, 2 vols, 1978; (ed) State and Economy in Contemporary Capitalism, 1979; The Politics of Industrial Relations, 1979, 2nd edn 1982; Trade Unions: the logic of collective action, 1982; (ed jtly) International Yearbook of Organizational Democracy, vol. I, 1983; (ed jtly) The New Centralism: Britain out of step in Europe?, 1989; (ed jtly) European Industrial Relations: the challenge of flexibility, 1990; (ed jtly) Corporatism and Accountability: organised interests in British public life, 1990; (ed jtly) The Politics of 1992: beyond the single European market, 1990; (ed jtly) Towards Greater Europe?, 1992; Industrial Relations and European State Traditions, 1993 (Political Studies Assoc. Book Prize, 1993); (ed jtly) Ethics and Markets: co-operation and competition in capitalist economies, 1993; (ed jtly) Reinventing Collective Action: the global and the local, 1995; (ed jtly) Organized Industrial Relations in Europe: what future?, 1995; (ed jtly) Les capitalismes en Europe, 1996; (ed jtly) Political Economy of Modern Capitalism, 1997; (jtly) Are Skills the Answer?, 1999; Social Change in Western Europe, 1999; (ed jtly) After the Euro, 2000; (ed jtly) Citizenship, Markets and the State, 2001; (ed) Coping with Post-Democracy, 2001; (jtly) Local Production Systems in Europe: rise or demise?, 2001; Commercialisation or Citizenship, 2003; Postdemocrazia, 2003, trans. English as Postdemocracy, 2004; (jtly) Changing Governance of Local Economies: responses of European local production systems, 2004; Capitalist Diversity and Change, 2005; (jtly) Innovation in Local Economies: Germany in comparative text, 2009; The Strange Non-Death of Neoliberalism, 2011; (ed jtly) The Responsible Corporation, 2011; Making Capitalism Fit for Society, 2013; Governing Social Risks in Post-Crisis Europe, 2015; The Knowledge Corrupters: hidden consequences of the financial takeover of public life, 2015; numerous articles on industrial relns, politics, economic sociology and social structure in Britain and Western Europe. *Recreations:* playing violin, music, gardening, watching and refereeing football matches. *Address:* Warwick Business School, University of Warwick, Coventry CV4 7AL.

CROUCH, Prof. David Bruce, PhD; FBA 2014; FRHistS; Professor of Medieval History, University of Hull, since 2000; *b* Cardiff, 31 Oct. 1953; *s* of Ronald Desmond Crouch and Elsie Mary Crouch (*née* Skipper); *m* 1987, Linda Helen Smith (separated); two *s*. *Educ:* Cantonian High Sch., Cardiff; University Coll., Cardiff (BA Hist. 1975); Univ. of Wales, Cardiff (PhD 1983). Secondary sch. teacher, Mountain Ash Comprehensive Sch., 1976–82; researcher, Inst. of Histl Res., 1983–89; Sen. Lectr, N Riding Coll., 1990–93; Prof. of Hist., University Coll., Scarborough, 1993–2000. FRHistS 1986. *Publications:* The Beaumont Twins, 1986; William Marshal, 1990, 2nd edn 2002; The Image of Aristocracy in Britain, 1992; The Reign of King Stephen, 2002; The Birth of Nobility, 2005; Tournament, 2005; The English Aristocracy, 1070–1272, 2011; Lost Letters of Medieval Life, 2013; The Newburgh Earldom of Warwick, 2015. *Address:* Department of History, University of Hull, Cottingham Road, Hull HU6 7RX. *T:* (01482) 465613. *E:* d.crouch@hull.ac.uk.

CROUCH, Sybil Edith; Director, Taliesin Arts Centre, Swansea University (formerly University College of Swansea, then University of Wales, Swansea), since 1990; *b* 9 Aug. 1953; *d* of David George and Lilian Crouch; *m* 2010, David Phillips. *Educ:* Birkenhead High Sch. for Girls; Swansea Coll. of Art. Specialist Art Teacher. Dep. Dir, W Wales Assoc. for the Arts, 1979–90. Chm., Arts Council of Wales, 1999–2003. Mem. (Lab) Swansea CC, 2012– (Cabinet Mem. for Sustainability, 2012–). *Recreation:* the company of friends. *Address:* Taliesin Arts Centre, Swansea University, Singleton Park, Swansea SA2 8PZ.

CROUCH, Tracey Elizabeth Anne; MP (C) Chatham and Aylesford, since 2010; Parliamentary Under-Secretary of State for Sport and Tourism, Department for Culture, Media and Sport, since 2015; *b* Ashford, Kent, 24 July 1975; *d* of Kenneth Allen Crouch and Sallyanne Crouch (*née* French). *Educ:* Folkestone Sch. for Girls; Hull Univ. (BA Jt Hons Law and Pols 1996). Parly Researcher, 1996–98; Sen. Public Affairs Manager, Harcourt Public Affairs, 1999–2000; Westminster Strategy, 2000–03; COS to Shadow Educn Sec., then Shadow Transport Sec., 2003; COS to Shadow Home Sec., 2003–05; Hd, Public Affairs, Aviva, 2005–10. Mem., Culture, Media and Sport Select Cttee, 2012–15. Chm., All Party Parly Gp on Alcohol Misuse, 2011–14 (Vice Chm., 2010–11); Vice Chm., All Party Parly Gp on Athletics, 2010–, on Dementia, 2010–; Sec., All Party Parly Gp on Insce and Financial Services, 2010–11. Mem., British delegn, OSCE, 2010–; Parly Ambassador, Us Girls, 2011–. Mem., Exec., 1922 Cttee, 2010–12. Trustee, Women's Sport and Fitness Foundn, 2013. Pres., RSPCA Medway, 2010–; Chm., Pet Adv. Cttee, 2011–; Patron: Chatham Town FC, 2011–; Nat. Osteoporosis Soc. Hon. MInstRE 2011. *Recreations:* sport, travel, manager of Meridian Girls FC. *Address:* House of Commons, SW1A 0AA. *E:* tracey.crouch.mp@parliament.uk.

CROW, Jonathan Rupert; QC 2006; Attorney General to the Prince of Wales, since 2006; a Judge of the Courts of Appeal of Jersey and Guernsey, since 2011; *b* 25 June 1958; *s* of Michael Frederick Crow and Edith Mae Crow; *m* 1998, Claudia Jane Turner; three *s* one *d*. *Educ:* St Paul's Sch.; Magdalen Coll., Oxford (BA Modern Hist.). Called to the Bar, Lincoln's Inn, 1981; Treasury Counsel (Chancery), 1994–98; First Treasury Counsel (Chancery), 1998–2006; Dep. High Court Judge, 2001–. *Address:* 4 Stone Buildings, Lincoln's Inn, WC2A 3XT. *T:* (020) 7242 5524, *Fax:* (020) 7831 7907. *E:* clerks@4stonebuildings.com. *Club:* Athenæum.

CROW, Prof. Timothy John, PhD; FRCP, FRCPsych, FMedSci; Hon. Scientific Director, SANE Prince of Wales Centre for Research into Schizophrenia and Depression, University Department of Psychiatry, Warneford Hospital, Oxford, 1995; Titular Professor of Psychiatry, University of Oxford, 1998–2007, now Emeritus; *b* 7 June 1938; *s* of late Percy Arthur Crow and Barbara Bonner Davies; *m* 1966, Julie Carol Carter; one *s* one *d*. *Educ:* Shrewsbury Sch.; London Hosp. Med. Coll. MB BS, PhD, DPM. Maudsley Hosp., 1966; University of Aberdeen: Lectr in Physiology, 1966–70; Lectr in Mental Health, 1970–72; Sen. Lectr in Psychiatry, Univ. of Manchester, 1972–73; Head, Div. of Psychiatry, Clinical Res. Centre, Northwick Park Hosp., 1974–94. Part-time Mem., Sci. Staff, Div. Neurophysiology and Neuropharmacology, Nat. Inst. for Med. Res., 1974–83; Dep. Dir, Clinical Res. Centre, 1984–89. Member: MRC Neuroscis Projects Grants Cttee, 1978–80; Neuroscis Bd, 1986–90; Chm., Biol. Psych. Gp, RCPsych, 1983–88 (Sec., 1980–83). Andrew W. Woods Vis. Prof., Univ. of Iowa, 1980; Lectures: St George's Hosp., 1980; St Louis, 1981; Univ. of Minnesota, 1981; Univ. of Ohio, 1986; RSocMed, 1988; Roche, RCPsych, Dublin, 1988; Stockholm, 1988; Maudsley, RCPsych, 1989; APA Internat. Scholars, 1990; Univ. of Oregon, 1991. Founder FMedSci 1998. A. P. Noyes Award, 1988; US Nat. Alliance Lieber Award, 1989; Res. Prize, World Fedn of Socs of Biol Psychiatry, 1991; Alexander Gralnick Award, Amer. Psych. Foundn, 2000; Kurt Schneider Award, 2006; Lifetime Achievement Award, British Assoc. Psychopharmacol., 2011. *Publications:* (ed) Disorders of Neurohumoral Transmission, 1982; (ed) Recurrent and Chronic Psychoses, 1987; (ed) The Speciation of Modern Homo Sapiens, 2002; papers on brain reward mechanisms, learning, evolution of language, speciation of Homo Sapiens, and schizophrenia in sci. and med. jls. *Recreations:* sciolistic archaeology, anthropology. *Address:* 16 Northwick Circle, Kenton, Middx HA3 0EJ. *T:* (020) 8907 6124. *Club:* Royal Society of Medicine.

CROWCROFT, Prof. Jonathan Andrew, PhD; FRS 2013; FREng, FIET, FBCS; Marconi Professor of Communications Systems, since 2001, and Associate Fellow, Centre for Science and Policy, University of Cambridge; Fellow, Wolfson College, Cambridge, since 2003; *b* 23 Nov. 1957; *s* of late Dr Andrew Crowcroft and of Prof. Kyla Crowcroft (*née* Greenbaum); *m* 1988, Noreen McKeever; two *s* one *d*. *Educ:* Trinity Coll., Cambridge (BA 1979); University Coll. London (PhD 1997). FREng 1999; FIET (FIEE 1999); FBCS 2000. Sen. Lectr, 1996–97, Prof. of Networked Systems, 1997–2001, UCL. FIEEE 2003 (SMIEE 1992); FACM 2004 (MACM 1988). *Publications:* WWW: beneath the surf, 1994; Open Distributed Systems, 1997; Internet Multimedia, 2000; Linux Internet Protocols, 2001. *Recreation:* classical guitar. *Address:* The Computer Laboratory, William Gates Building, 15 J. J. Thomson Avenue, Cambridge CB3 0FD. *T:* (01223) 763633, *Fax:* (01223) 334678. *E:* jon.crowcroft@cl.cam.ac.uk.

CROWDEN, James Gee Pascoe, CVO 2003; JP; FRICS, FCIArb; Senior Partner, Grounds & Co., 1974–88; Lord-Lieutenant and Custos Rotulorum of Cambridgeshire, 1992–2002; *b*

14 Nov. 1927; *yr s* of late Lt-Col R. J. C. Crowden, MC, and Nina Mary (*née* Gee), Peterborough; *m* 1st, 1955, Kathleen Mary (*d* 1989), *widow* of Captain F. A. Grounds and *d* of late Mr and Mrs J. W. Loughlin, Upwell; (one *s* decd), and one step *s*; 2nd, 2001, Margaret (*d* 2009), *widow* of J. R. Crowden and *d* of late Rev. Wilfred Cole, Oundle; four step *d*. *Educ:* Bedford Sch.; Pembroke Coll., Cambridge (MA; Hon. Fellow, 1993). Chartered surveyor; FRICS 1959; FCIArb 1977. Commissioned Royal Lincs Regt, 1947. Rowed in Oxford and Cambridge Boat Race, 1951 and 1952 (Pres., 1952); Captain, Great Britain VIII, European Championships, Macon, 1951 (Gold Medallists); also rowed in European Championships, Milan, 1950 (Bronze Medallists) and Helsinki Olympics, 1952; coached 20 Cambridge crews, 1953–75; Steward, Henley Royal Regatta, 1959– (Mem., Cttee of Management, 1964–92); Mem. Council, Amateur Rowing Assoc., 1957–77; Hon. Mem. of Court and Freeman, Co. of Watermen and Lightermen of the River Thames (Master, 1991–92). Vice-Pres., British Olympic Assoc., 1988–; Chairman: Cambridgeshire Olympic Appeals, 1984, 1988, 1992, 1996 and 2000; Appeal Exec. Cttee, Peterborough Cathedral, 1979–80; Member: Ely Diocesan Pastoral Cttee, 1969–89; Ely Cathedral Fabric Cttee, 1986–90. Chm., Order of St Etheldreda, 1992–2002. Former Pres., Agricl Valuers' Assocs for Herts, Beds and Bucks, Lincs, Norfolk, Cambs, and Wisbech. Dep. Pres., E of England Agricl Soc., 2001; President: Cambs Fedn of Young Farmers, 1971–73; Cambs Scouts, 1992–2002; Cambs TAVR and Cadet Cttee, 1992–2002; E Anglia TAVRA, 1996–2000 (Vice-Pres., 1992–96 and 2000–02); Hon. Col, Cambs ACF, 1996–2002. Patron: Cambs RBL, 1992–2006; Cambs Red Cross, 1992–2002; Duke of Edinburgh's Award County Cttee, 1992–2002; Cambs St John Ambulance, 1993–2002; Cambs Regt Old Comrades' Assoc., 1998–. Governor: March Grammar Sch., 1960–70 (Chm., 1967–70); King's Sch., Peterborough, 1980–90; St Hugh's Sch., Woodhall Spa, 1981–92. Church Warden, All Saints', Walsoken, 1964–76 and 1983–84. Pres., Old Bedfordians' Club, 1996–98. JP Wisbech, 1969; DL 1971, Vice Lord-Lieut, 1985–92, Cambridgeshire; High Sheriff, Cambridgeshire and Isle of Ely, 1970. Freeman: Town of Wisbech, 2001; Tri-Base (Alconbury, Molesworth and Upwood), USAF, 2001; City of Peterborough, 2007. FRSA 1990. KStJ 1992. *Recreations:* rowing, shooting. *Clubs:* Sette of Odd Volumes; Hawks, University Pitt, Cambridge County (Cambridge); Leander (Henley-on-Thames).

CROWE, Sir Brian (Lee), KCMG 2002 (CMG 1985); Director General for External and Defence Affairs, Council of the European Union, 1994–2002; *b* 5 Jan. 1938; *s* of Eric Crowe and Virginia Crowe; *m* 1969, Virginia Willis; two *s*. *Educ:* Sherborne; Magdalen Coll., Oxford (1st Cl. Hons PPE). Joined FO, 1961; served: Moscow, 1962–64; London, 1965–67; Aden, 1967; Washington, 1968–73; Bonn, 1973–76; Counsellor and Hd of Policy Planning Staff, FCO, 1976–78; Hd of Chancery, UK Perm. Representation to EEC, Brussels, 1979–81; Counsellor and Hd of EEC Dept (External), FCO, 1982–84; Minister, Commercial, Washington, 1985–89; Ambassador to Austria, 1989–92; Dep. Under-Sec. of State (Dir Gen.) for Econ. Affairs, FCO, 1992–94. Dir, ITT Defence Ltd, 2006–12. Mem. Council, Chatham House, 2003–09 (Dep. Chm., 2005–09); Eur. Dir, Centre for Political and Diplomatic Studies, Oxford, 2003–. *Recreations:* winter sports, tennis, riding, swimming. *Address:* 55 Ashley Gardens, Ambrosden Avenue, SW1P 1QF. *E:* blcrowe@gmail.com.

CROWE, Frank Richard; Sheriff of Lothian and Borders at Edinburgh, since 2009; *b* 15 March 1952; *s* of James Crowe and Helen Mary Harle or Crowe; *m* 1975, Alison Margaret Purdom or Crowe (separated 1997); two *d*; partner, Margaret Elizabeth Scott (*see* Hon. Lady Scott); one *s*. *Educ:* Valley and West Primary Schs, Kirkcaldy; Kirkcaldy High Sch.; Royal High Sch., Edinburgh; Dundee Univ. (LLB). Admitted solicitor, 1975, NP 1991, Solicitor Advocate, 1995; law apprentice, N of Scotland Hydro-Electric Bd, 1973–75; Procurator Fiscal Depute: Dundee, 1975–78; Glasgow, 1978–81; Sen. Legal Asst, Crown Office, 1981–83; Sen. Depute Procurator Fiscal, Edinburgh, 1983–87; Crown Office: Sen. Depute i/c Fraud Unit, 1987–88; Asst Solicitor i/c High Court Unit, 1988–91; Procurator Fiscal, Kirkcaldy, 1991–96; Regl Procurator Fiscal, Hamilton, 1996–99; Deputy Crown Agent, Crown Office, 1999–2001; Sheriff of Tayside Central and Fife, at Dundee, 2001–04; Dir of Judicial Studies in Scotland, 2004–08. Mem., Stephen Lawrence Steering Gp, Scottish Exec., 1999–2001; Chm., Adv. Gp to Zone Trng for New Futures, Dundee, 2002–04; consultant to Criminal Justice Oversight Comr, NI, 2003–07; Mem., Res. Adv. Gp on Breach of Community Orders, Univ. of Strathclyde for Scottish Govt, 2013–. Mem. Council, Law Soc. of Scotland, 1996–99. Mem. and Vice Chm., Lothian Victim Support Scheme, 1983–89; Mem. Bd, Apex Scotland, 2014–. Chm. Bd, Stockbridge Primary Sch., 2006–08. Pres., Royal High Sch. Former Pupils Club, 2013. *Publications:* (jtly) Criminal Procedure, 1989, 2nd edn, as part of Stair Memorial Encyclopaedia of the Laws of Scotland, 2002; Justices of the Peace Bench Book and Legal Advisors' Manual, 2008. *Recreations:* golf, music, walking, racing, analysis. *Address:* Sheriff's Chambers, Sheriff Court House, 27 Chambers Street, Edinburgh EH1 1LB. *T:* (0131) 225 2525, *Fax:* (0131) 225 2288. *E:* sheriff.frcrowe@scotcourts.gov.uk.

CROWE, Lucy Mary Elizabeth; opera singer (soprano); *b* Burton upon Trent, 24 Dec. 1978; *d* of Charles John Crowe and Jeannie Crowe; *m* 2008, Joseph Nicholas Sidney Walters; one *s* one *d*. *Educ:* Denstone Coll.; Royal Acad. of Music (BMus 1st Cl. Hons; Dip. RAM; LRAM; ARAM; FRAM). Opera debuts: ENO, 2007; Royal Opera House, Covent Garden, 2009; Glyndebourne, 2010; Deutsche Oper Berlin, 2010; Chicago Lyric Opera, 2011; Bayerische Staatsoper, 2011; Metropolitan Opera, NY, 2012; major rôles include: Sophie in Der Rosenkavalier; Susanna in Le Nozze di Figaro; Poppea in Agrippine; Dorinda in Orlando; Iole in Hercules; Servilia in Clemenza di Tito; Rosina in Barber of Seville; Gilda in Rigoletto; Adina in L'Elisir d'amore; Eurydice in Orphée et Eurydice. *Recreations:* charity work (Songbound), cooking, cinema, tennis, baking. *Address:* c/o Askonas Holt, Lincoln House, 300 High Holborn, WC1V 7JH. *T:* (020) 7400 1715. *E:* lucycrowe@hotmail.com.

CROWE, Dr Michael John, DM; FRCP, FRCPsych; Consultant Psychiatrist, Bethlem Royal and Maudsley Hospital, London, 1978–2002; psychiatrist in private practice, 1978–2012; *b* 16 Oct. 1937; *s* of Robert James Crowe and Olive (*née* Kingston-Jones); *m* 1968, Diane Jordan; one *s* one *d*. *Educ:* St Paul's Sch., London; Exeter Coll., Oxford (MA, BM 1963); London Hosp. Med. Coll. MPhil London, 1970; DM Oxon, 1977. MRCP 1967; MRCPsych 1973; FRCPsych 1984; FRCP 1992. House Officer: London Hosp., 1964; Chelmsford and Essex Hosp., 1964; Senior House Officer: Addenbrooke's Hosp., 1965–66; London Hosp., 1966–67; Maudsley Hospital: Registrar, 1967–69; Sen. Registrar, Res. Worker and Lectr, 1970–74; Sen. Lectr, Inst. of Psychiatry, 1974–77 (Course Leader, Couple Therapy Dip. Course, 1989–2002). Vis. Fellow, Univ. of Vermont, USA, 1969. Lectr on behavioural and couple therapy, USA, Trinidad, Denmark, Italy, etc. Founder Mem., Inst. of Family Therapy, London, 1976–2002. Chm., Assoc. of Sexual and Marital Therapists, 1986–88. Gaskell Gold Medal, RCPsych, 1972. *Publications:* (with J. Ridley) Therapy with Couples, 1990, 2nd edn 2000; Overcoming Relationship Problems, 2005; papers in med. and psychol. jls on behaviour therapy, couple therapy and sexual dysfunctions. *Recreations:* music (performing and listening), poetry, literature, languages, walking. *Address:* 66 Palace View, Shirley, Croydon CR0 8QN. *T:* (020) 8777 4823.

CROWE, Rev. Philip Anthony; Director, St Asaph Ministry Training Scheme, 1995–2001; *b* 16 Aug. 1936; *s* of late Frederick Francis Crowe and of Hilda Crowe; *m* 1963, Freda Maureen Gill; two *s* one *d*. *Educ:* Repton School; Selwyn Coll., Cambridge; Ridley Hall, Cambridge. National service, RA, 1955–57. Tutor in NT Greek and Mission, Oak Hill, 1962–67; Curate at Christchurch, Cockfosters, 1962–65; Editor, Church of England Newspaper, 1967–70; Sec., Bursary Scheme for Overseas Students, 1967–70; Senior Staff Member, St Martin in the Bull Ring, Birmingham, 1970–76; Rector of Breadsall, Derby, 1977–88; Derby Diocesan Missioner, 1977–83; Tutor in Ethics, St John's Coll., Nottingham, 1986–88; Principal, Salisbury and Wells Theol Coll., 1988–94; Rector, Overton, Penley and Erbistock, 1995–97; Hon. Canon, Salisbury Cathedral, 1991–95. Mem., Gen. Synod, C of E, 1992–95. *Publications:* (contrib.) Mission in the Modern World, Church and Sacraments, 1977; Pastoral Reorganisation, 1978; Christian Baptism, 1980; The Use and Abuse of Alcohol, 1980; A Whisper will be Heard, 1994; Strange Design, 1999. *Recreations:* gardening, music, squash, walking, caravanning. *Address:* Alderlea, Babbinswood, Whittington, Shropshire SY11 4PQ. *T:* and *Fax:* (01691) 671698.

CROWE, Stuart Davison; Corporate Director, Resources, Durham County Council, 2008–10; *b* Blackhill, Consett, 28 March 1950; *s* of late Andrew Braid Crowe and Margaret Crowe; *m* 1980, Mary Jane Armstrong; one *s* one *d*. *Educ:* Blackfyne Secondary Sch., Consett; New Coll., Durham (CIPFA). Dep. County Treas., 1989–2002, County Treas., 2002–08, Durham CC. Treasurer: Durham and Darlington Fire and Rescue Authy, 2002–10; Durham Police Authy, 2002–09; Durham Charter Trustees, 2009–10. Consultant, 2011–13. Mem., Town and Gown Soc., Durham. *Recreations:* walking, photography, ornithology, gardening, stick making, Member of National Trust, Durham Wildlife Trust, Durham Photographic Society, Border Stick Dressers Association.

CROWLEY, Graham Neil; Professor of Painting, and Head, Department of Painting, Royal College of Art, 1998–2006; *b* 3 May 1950; *s* of Victor Matthew Crowley and Violet Mary Crowley (*née* Lee); *m* 1978, Sally Ann Townshend; two *s*. *Educ:* St Martin's Sch. of Art (DipAD); Royal Coll. of Art (MA). Vis. Lectr, Painting, Royal Coll. of Art, 1978–85; Artist-in-Residence, Oxford Univ. and Fellow, St Edmund Hall, Oxford, 1982–83; Vis. Lectr, Goldsmiths' Coll., London, 1984–86; Sen. Fellow in Painting, S Glamorgan Inst. of Higher Educn, Cardiff, 1986–89; Artist-in-Residence: Riverscape Project, Cleveland, 1991–92; Dulwich Picture Gall., London, 1994–95; Hd of Fine Art, C&G, 1996–98. *One-man exhibitions* include: In Living Memory, Orchard Gall., Derry, and touring, 1987; Millfield Gall., Som, 1993; The Last Decade, Lamont Gall., London, 1995; A Drift, RCA, 1999; Familiar Ground, Beaux Arts, London, 2001; Are you serious?, Wolsey Art Gall., Ipswich, 2002; Graham Crowley, Beaux Arts, 2003, 2005; W Cork Arts Centre, Skibbereen, 2008; Churchill Coll., Cambridge, Atkinson Gall., Millfield, 2011; *group exhibitions* include: Arnolfini Gall., Bristol, 1977; Open Attitudes, MOMA, Oxford, 1979; South Bank Show, Hayward Gall. and Paris Biennale, 1982; Venice Biennale, 1984; Artists Against Apartheid, RFH, 1985; Edward Totah Gall., London, 1986, 1987; New British Painting, Queens Mus., NY, 1990; Royal Acad. Summer Exhibn, 1990, 1991, 1992; British Liby, 1994; Flowers E Gall., London, annually 1994–98, 2001, 2002; Summer Shows, 2000–02, Art 2001, Art 2002, Beaux Arts; The Discerning Eye, Mall Galls, London, 2000, 2001; British Art Fair, Beaux Arts, RCA, 2001, Commonwealth Inst., 2002; Govt Art Collection, Whitechapel Gall., 2011; *work in public collections* includes: Imperial War Mus.; V&A Mus.; Contemporary Arts Soc.; Kettles Yard, Cambridge; Castle Mus., Nottingham; Mus. of Auckland, NZ. Selector, John Moores 24 Painting Competition, 2008. Prizewinner, John Moores 24 Painting Competition, 2006. *Publications:* (with S. Hood) De Sade for Beginners, 1995; *relevant publication*: Graham Crowley, by Martin Holman, 2009. *Recreations:* painting, classic motorcycles, writing, reading. *W:* www.grahamcrowley.com.

CROWLEY, Jane Elizabeth Rosser; QC 1998; a Recorder, since 1995; *b* 5 Aug. 1953; *d* of Robert Jenkyn Rosser and Marion Rosser (*née* Davies); *m* 1986, (Jonathan) Mark Crowley; one *s* one *d*. *Educ:* Howell's Sch., Llandaff, Cardiff; King's Coll. London (LLB 1975). Called to the Bar, Gray's Inn, 1976; Bencher, 2004; in practice at the Bar, 1976–. Dep. High Ct Judge, Family Div., 1999–. Legal Mem., Mental Health Tribunal Restricted Order Panel, 2000–. *Recreations:* family, music, Pembrokeshire coast, supporting Wales Rugby, Glamorgan County Cricket Club, good friends, good wine. *Address:* 30 Park Place, Cardiff CF10 3BA. *T:* (029) 2039 8421; 1 Garden Court, Temple, EC4Y 9BJ. *T:* (020) 7797 7900.

CROWLEY, Rt Rev. John; Bishop of Middlesbrough, (RC), 1993–2007; *b* Newbury, 23 June 1941. Ordained priest, 1965; Holy Trinity Parish, Brook Green, W6, 1965–68; Catholic Missionary Soc., 1968–74; Private Sec. to Cardinal Hume, 1974–82; Vicar Gen. for Westminster dio., 1982–86; Auxiliary Bishop of Westminster (Bishop in Central London), and Titular Bishop of Tala, 1986–92. Chairman, Catholic Fund for Overseas Development, 1988–2000. Rep. of Bishops' Conf. of England and Wales to Conf. of European Bishops within EU, 2001. *Address:* Our Lady of Lourdes Church, 1 Kirkwick Avenue, Harpenden, Herts AL5 2QH.

CROWLEY, John Desmond; QC 1982; a Recorder of the Crown Court, 1980–2004; a Deputy Judge of the High Court, 1991–2004; *b* 25 June 1938; *s* of late John Joseph Crowley and Anne Marie (*née* Fallon); *m* 1977, Sarah Maria, *er d* of late Christopher Gage Jacobs and Joan Zara (*née* Atkinson); two *d*. *Educ:* St Edmund's College, Ware; Christ's College, Cambridge (BA 1961, LLB 1962). National Service, 2/Lieut 6th Royal Tank Regt, 1957–58. Called to the Bar, Inner Temple, 1962, Bencher, 1989. Member: Criminal Injuries Compensation Bd, 1985–2000; Criminal Injuries Compensation Appeal Panel, 2000–02. Chm., Appeal Cttee, ICAEW, 2000–04. *Recreations:* music, the turf, wine. *Address:* 37 Viceroy Road, SW8 2HA.

CROWLEY, Robert, RDI 1997; set and costume designer for theatre, opera, ballet and film; *b* Cork, 1952. *Educ:* Crawford Municipal Sch. of Fine Art; Bristol Old Vic Theatre Sch. *Productions* include: *theatre:* Royal Shakespeare Company: Love's Labour's Lost, 1984; As You Like It, 1985; Les Liaisons Dangereuses, 1986, transf. Ambassadors, NY, LA, Tokyo; Macbeth, A Penny for a Song, Principia Scriptoriae, 1986; The Plantagenets, 1988; Othello, 1989; Hamlet, 1992; National Theatre, later Royal National Theatre: Ghetto (Laurence Olivier Award for Designer of the Year, 1990), Hedda Gabler, Ma Rainey's Black Bottom, 1989; White Chameleon, Murmuring Judges, 1991; Carousel, 1992, transf. Shaftesbury, 1993, NY (Tony Award, 1994); Mourning Becomes Electra, 2003; The History Boys, 2004, NY (Tony Award, 2006); The Coast of Utopia, 2007, NY (Tony Award, 2007); Gethsemane, Fram, 2008; The Year of Magical Thinking, 2008, NY 2007; Every Boy Deserves Favour, Phèdre, 2009; Power of Yes, 2009; The Habit of Art, 2009; Collaborators, 2011; Travelling Light, People, 2012; The Hard Problem, 2015; Bristol Old Vic: Timon of Athens; A View from the Bridge; Destiny; Women All Over, King's, Edinburgh, 1985; Two Way Mirror, Young Vic, 1989; The Three Sisters, Gate, Dublin, 1990; The Cure at Troy, Guildhall, Derry, then Lyric, Belfast, 1990 (also Jt Dir); Saint Oscar, Field Day Theatre Co., Derry (Dir); Madame de Sade, Tokyo; No Man's Land, Almeida, 1992; When She Danced, Globe; Cunning Little Vixen, Châtelet, Paris; The Judas Kiss, Playhouse, then NY, 1998; The Capeman, NY, 1998; Twelfth Night, NY, 1998; Into the Woods, Donmar Warehouse, 1998; The Seagull, NY, 2001; Sweet Smell of Success, NY, 2002; Mary Poppins, Prince Edward, 2004 (Best Designer, Evening Standard Theatre Awards, 2005; Tony Award, 2007); Moon for the Misbegotten, Old Vic, 2006, transf. NY, 2007; Love Never Dies, Adelphi, 2010; Juno and the Paycock, Abbey Th., Dublin, 2011; Once (musical), NY, 2012, transf. Phoenix Th., 2013; The Dark Earth and the Light Sky, Almeida, 2012; The Audience, Gielgud Th., 2013; The Glass Menagerie, NY, 2013; *opera:* Don Giovanni, Kent Opera; The Magic Flute, ENO, 1988, 1997, 2012; Aida, NY (Tony Award), 2001, Japan, 2009; Don Carlos, NY, 2010; Royal Opera: costumes, The King Goes Forth to France, 1987; The Knot Garden, 1988; La Traviata, 1994; Don Carlo, 2008, 2013; *ballet:* Anastasia, Pavane, Royal Ballet; Naked, Sadler's Wells, 2005; Alice's Adventures in Wonderland, Royal Ballet and Nat. Ballet of Canada, 2011; The Winter's Tale, Royal Ballet, 2014; *musical:* An American in Paris, Châtelet, Paris, 2014; *films:* Othello; Tales of Hollywood; Suddenly Last Summer, 1993; The

Crucible, 1997. Robert L. B. Tobin Award for Lifetime Achievement, Th. Develt Fund/ Irene Sharaff Awards, NY, 2009. *Address:* c/o Simpson Fox Associates Ltd, 6 Beauchamp Place, SW3 1NG.

CROWN, Dr June Madge, CBE 1998; FRCP, FFPH; President, Faculty of Public Health Medicine, Royal College of Physicians, 1995–98; *b* 5 June 1938; *d* of late Edward Downes and Madge Edith Downes; *m* 1964, Sidney Crown (*d* 2009); two *s* one *d*. *Educ:* Pate's Grammar Sch. for Girls, Cheltenham; Newnham Coll., Cambridge (MA); Middlesex Hosp. Med. Sch. (MB, BChir); London Sch. of Hygiene and Tropical Medicine (MSc). FFPH (FFPHM 1986); FRCP 1991. Area MO, Brent and Harrow AHA, 1980–82; Dir of Public Health, Bloomsbury HA, 1982–91. Dir, SE Inst. of Public Health, UMDS, 1991–99. Chairman: DoH Adv. Gp on Nurse Prescribing, 1988–89; DoH Rev. of Prescribing, 1996–98; Member: Standing Med. Adv. Cttee, DoH, 1984–88 and 1995–98; Clinical Standards Adv. Gp, DoH, 1995–99. Advr to WHO, 1984–; Consultant on Health Sector Mgt Develt to Czech Republic and Slovakia, 1992–93; Advr to NZ Govt and Health Bds on Health Care Reforms, 1992; Chm., UK Inquiry into Mental Health and Well-Being in Later Life, 2005–07. President: Sect. of Epidemiology and Public Health, RSocMed, 1994–96; Medical Action for Global Security (MEDACT), 1993–. Chm., 1998–2002, Vice Pres., 2002–09, Age Concern, England; Vice-Pres., Chartered Inst. of Envmtl Health, 2001. Chm., Queen's Nursing Inst., 2002–03 (Mem. Council, 1982–; Vice Pres., 2003–); Member: Bd of Govs, Royal Nat. Orthopaedic Hosp., 1976–82 (Vice-Chm., 1980–82); Inst. of Orthopaedics, Univ. of London, 1978–88 (Chm., 1982–88); Bd of Mgt and Court of Govs, LSHTM, 1983–94; Dep. Chm., Bd of Govs, Univ. of Brighton, 2002– (Mem., 2000–02). Trustee, Help the Aged, 2004–09. Chm., Fitzrovia Youth in Action, 2000–. Associate, Newnham Coll., Cambridge, 1992– (Associate Fellow, 1997–99; Chm., Associates, 1998–2000). Hon. Fellow: Soc. of Chiropodists, 1986; Australasian Faculty of Public Health Medicine, 1996; Faculty of Public Health Med., RCPI, 1997; RCPE, 1998; Hon. FDSRCS 2005; Hon. MCSP 2011. Hon. DSc Brighton, 2009. *Publications:* Health for All: revised targets, 1993; (with J. Connelly) Homelessness and Ill Health, 1995; Epidemiologically Based Needs Assessment: child and adolescent mental health, 1995. *Recreations:* family, opera, fine art, theatre, travel, jogging. *Address:* 118 Whitfield Street, W1T 5EG. *T:* (020) 7387 6787.

CROWNE, Stephen Thomas; Chief Executive, The Bar Council, since 2013; *b* 9 Aug. 1957; *s* of late Charles and Beatrice Crowne; *m* 1979, Elizabeth; three *s*. *Educ:* Queens' Coll., Cambridge (BA (Hist.) 1978). Principal Private Sec. to Sec. of State for Educn, 1989–91; Hd, 16–19 Policy, DFEE, 1991–94; Chief Exec., Further Educn Develt Agency, 1994–98; Department for Education and Skills: Hd, Special Educnl Needs Div., 1998–2000; Dep. Dir, then Actg Dir, Standards and Effectiveness Unit, 2001–02; Dir, Sch. Resources, 2002–06; Chief Exec., British Educnl Commns and Technol. Agency, 2006–11; Dir, Global Education, Cisco Systems Inc., 2011–13. Dir, Partnership for Schs, 2004–06. *Address:* The Bar Council, 289–293 High Holborn, WC1V 7HZ. *T:* (020) 7242 0082, *Fax:* (020) 7831 9217. *E:* scrowne@barcouncil.org.uk.

CROWSON, Howard Keith; His Honour Judge Crowson; a Circuit Judge, since 2010; *b* Belper, Derbys, 30 Dec. 1964; *s* of David John Crowson and Kathleen Cooper Crowson; *m* 1988, Alison Dawn Morritt (*d* 2012); one *s* one *d*. *Educ:* Ecclesbourne Sch., Duffield; Leeds Univ. (LLB Hons). Called to the Bar, Inner Temple, 1987; in practice at the Bar, St Paul's Chambers, Leeds, specialising in crime and fraud, 1987–2010; Recorder, 2002–10. *Recreations:* Rugby Union, walking. *Address:* c/o Teesside Combined Court Centre, Russell Street, Middlesbrough TS1 2AE. *Club:* Selby Rugby Union Football.

CROWSON, Richard Borman, CMG 1986; HM Diplomatic Service, retired; Chairman, Uweso UK Trust, 1996–2007; *s* of late Clarence Borman Crowson and Cecilia May Crowson; *m* 1st, 1960, Sylvia Cavalier (marr. diss. 1974); one *s* one *d*; 2nd, 1983, Judith Elaine Turner; one step *s*. *Educ:* Downing Coll., Cambridge (MA). FCIS. HMOCS, Uganda, 1955–62; Foreign Office, 1962–63; First Sec. (Commercial), Tokyo, 1963–68; Dep. High Commissioner, Barbados, 1968–70; FCO, 1970–75; Counsellor (Commercial and Aid), Jakarta, 1975–77; Counsellor for Hong Kong Affairs, Washington, 1977–82; Counsellor and Head of Chancery, Berne, 1983–85; High Comr in Mauritius, 1985–89, and Ambassador (non-resident) to Federal Islamic Republic of the Comoros, 1986–89. *Recreations:* music, drama, travel. *Address:* 67 Crofton Road, Orpington, Kent BR6 8HU. *T:* (01689) 891320.

CROWTHER, (David) Bruce, MBE 2009; Executive Director, The FIG Tree, International Fair Trade Centre, St John's Church, Lancaster, since 2015; International Fair Trade Towns Ambassador (part-time), since 2013; *b* 19 Oct. 1959; *s* of late John and Florence Crowther; *m* 1992, (Nancy) Jane Bamber; two *s* one *d*. *Educ:* Queen's Park High Sch., Chester; Liverpool Univ. Vet. Coll. (BVSc 1985). Dep. Vet. Officer, Min. of Agric., Dungannon, NI, 1985; Vet. Surgeon, 1986–2003; Vet. Surgeon (pt-time), 2003–12. Started campaigning for Oxfam, 1984; founded Garstang Oxfam Gp, 1992 (Chm., 1992–2002); led campaign to make Garstang the world's first Fairtrade Town, 2000; instigated twinning of Garstang with New Koforidua (a cocoa farming community) in Ghana, 2002; Fairtrade Towns Advr (formerly Co-ordinator) for Fairtrade Foundn (pt-time), 2003–12; Exec. Dir, The FIG Tree, Internat. Fair Trade Visitor Centre, Garstang, 2011–14. Assoc. Mem., Oxfam, 2001–06. Mem., Calder Bridge Meeting of Religious Soc. of Friends. Hon. Citizen and Sub-Chief (Nana Kwado Osafo I) of New Koforidua, 2004. Beacon Fellow for Creative Giving, 2004. *Recreations:* persuading people to buy, sell or use Fair Trade products, travelling, watching Manchester United FC live or on TV. *Address:* c/o The FIG Tree, St John's Church, North Road, Lancaster, Lancs LA1 1PA. *T:* (home) (01995) 602637. *E:* brucecrowther300@gmail.com.

CROWTHER, Prof. Derek, PhD; FRCP, FRCR; Professor and Director, Cancer Research Campaign Department of Medical Oncology, Christie Hospital and Manchester University, 1974–97, now Professor Emeritus; *b* 1 July 1937; *s* of Robinson Westgarth Crowther and Gladys Hannah Crowther; *m* 1959, Margaret Frances Dickinson; two *d* (one *s* decd). *Educ:* City of London Sch.; Clare Coll., Cambridge (Foundn Scholar; MB, BChir, MA 1963); Baylor Univ., Texas (Fulbright Scholar, 1959–60); Royal Postgraduate Medical Sch., London (PhD 1968); Royal Marsden Hosp. MSc Manchester, 1977. FRCP 1976; FRCR 1993. Sen. Registrar and Dep. Dir of Med. Oncology, St Bartholomew's Hosp., 1972–74. CMO, Friends Provident, 1995–2006. Chairman: Leukaemia Res. Fund, Clinical Trials Adv. Panel, 2000–06; London Cancer Res. Mapping Working Gp, 2000–01; Co-Chm., CRUK (formerly CRC) Central Instnl Review Bd, 2001–04; Mem., Statutory Gene Therapy Adv. Cttee, 1994–97. Pres., Assoc. of Cancer Physicians, 1999–2007. Mem. Council, Manchester Lit. & Phil. Soc., 2002–. Hon. MRSocMed. Prizes in medicine, paediatrics, and pathology, incl. Gold Medal in Obstetrics and Gynaecology, St Bartholomew's Hosp.; Glyn Evans Gold Medal, RCR, 1980; Award of Distinction, CRC, 1997; Lifetime Achievement in Cancer award, Cancer BACUP, 1999. *Publications:* edited: Manual of Cancer Chemotherapy, 1978 (trans. several langs); Interferons, 1991; more than 300 publications in the field of anti-cancer therapy. *Recreations:* gardening, travel, cosmology, oriental and modern art.

CROWTHER, John Anthony; Chief Executive, Vickers Defence Systems, 1994–96; Chief Executive, 1997–2006, Consultant, 2006–11, Lawn Tennis Association; *b* 16 Oct. 1951; *s* of Charles Alec Crowther and Joan Sylvia (*née* Boddam-Whetham); *m* 1975, Lorraine Ann Chadwick; three *s*. *Educ:* Malvern Coll.; Imperial Coll., London (BSc Eng). ACGI. British Aerospace PLC, 1970–77; Delta Neu Ltd, 1977–78; Panavia Aircraft GmbH, 1978–79; British Aerospace PLC, 1979–90; Vickers Defence Systems: Commercial Dir, 1990–92; Man. Dir, 1992–94. Confederation of British Industry: Chm., Contracts Panel, 1990–92; Regl Council Mem., Yorks & Humberside, 1994–96. Chm., Leeds Career Guidance, 1995–96. Dir, 2002–03, Chm., Major Spectator Sports Div., 2001–03 (Dep. Chm., 1999–2001), Treas., 2007–11, CCPR. Non-executive Director: Sports Leaders UK, 2002–09; N Yorks Sport, 2007– (Chm., 2009–); Yorks Culture, 2007–08; Chairman: Sports Leaders Foundn, 2009; Amateur Swimming Assoc., 2009–13; Yorks Lawn Tennis Assoc., 2015–. Mem., Major Match Gp, ECB, 2006–. *Recreations:* piano, tennis, golf, bridge, walking.

CROWTHER, Prof. Richard, PhD; CEng; FRAeS; Chief Engineer, UK Space Agency, since 2011; *b* Salisbury, Wilts, 5 Dec. 1960; *s* of William James Crowther and Shirley Gladys Crowther; partner, Dr Wendy Alison Holden; two *s*. *Educ:* Bishop Wordsworth's Sch., Salisbury; Univ. of Southampton (BSc Hons 1983; PhD 1989). CEng 1993; FRAeS 1998. PSO, RAE, 1991–98; Sen. Principal Consultant, DERA, 1998–2003; Head: Space Technol. Div., STFC, 2003–07; Internat. Relns, BNSC, 2007–11. Vis. Prof., Univ. of Southampton, 2005–. Hd, UK Delegn to UN Cttee on Peaceful Uses of Outer Space, 2007–. Member: Internat. Inst. of Space Law, 2008–; Adv. Bd, London Inst. of Space Policy and Law, 2010–; Internat. Inst. for Strategic Studies, 2013–; Mem. Council, RAeS, 2013–. Associate Ed., Aerospace Jl, 2004–08; Mem., Editl Bd, Encyclopedia Aerospace Engrg, 2010–. Expert, UN Gp of Govtl Experts on Transparency and Confidence Bldg Measures in Outer Space, 2012–13. Academician, Internat. Acad. of Astronautics, 2012–. *Publications:* contrib. papers to peer reviewed jls, incl. Philosophical Trans Royal Soc. *Recreations:* family, sailing, walking, gardening. *Address:* UK Space Agency, Polaris House, North Star Avenue, Swindon SN2 1SZ. *T:* (01793) 418071. *E:* richard.crowther@ukspaceagency.bis.gsi.gov.uk. *Club:* Royal Air Force.

CROWTHER, Dr Richard Anthony, FRS 1993; Member of Scientific Staff, 1969–2007, Visiting Scientist, since 2007, Medical Research Council Laboratory of Molecular Biology, Cambridge; Fellow of Peterhouse, Cambridge, 1981–2009, now Emeritus; *b* 26 July 1942; *s* of Albert Crowther and Joyce Edith Crowther (*née* Anthony); *m* 1964, Susan Elizabeth Hope; two *s*. *Educ:* Manchester Grammar Sch.; Jesus Coll., Cambridge (BA); PhD Cantab. Res. Fellow, Edinburgh Univ., 1968. FMedSci 2007. *Publications:* research papers and reviews in sci. jls. *Recreations:* walking, bird watching. *Address:* MRC Laboratory of Molecular Biology, Francis Crick Avenue, Cambridge CB2 0QH. *T:* (01223) 267815.

CROWTHER, Thomas Edward; QC 2013; **His Honour Judge Crowther;** a Circuit Judge, since 2013; *b* Newport, Mon, 25 May 1970; *s* of His Honour Thomas Rowland Crowther, *qv*; *m* 2003, Molly Ratna Das; two *d*. *Educ:* Croesyceiliog Comprehensive Sch.; Exeter Univ. (BSc; BA). Called to the Bar, Inner Temple, 1993; in practice at the Bar, 1993–2013; Founder Mem., Apex Chambers, 2007, Hd of Chambers, 2012–13; a Recorder, 2009–13. An Immigration Judge, 2006–13. Mem., Bar Council, 2006–08 and 2010–12. *Address:* The Law Courts, Cathays Park, Cardiff CF10 3PG.

CROWTHER, His Honour Thomas Rowland; QC 1981; a Circuit Judge, 1985–2010; a Senior Circuit Judge, 2001–10; *b* 11 Sept. 1937; *s* of late Kenneth Vincent Crowther, MB, BCh, and Winifred Anita Crowther, MPS; *m* 1969, Gillian Jane (*née* Prince); one *s* one *d*. *Educ:* Newport High Sch.; Keble Coll., Oxford (MA). President, Oxford Univ. Liberal Club, 1957; Editor, Oxford Guardian, 1957. Called to the Bar, Inner Temple, 1961, Bencher, 2005; Junior and Wine Steward, Wales and Chester Circuit, 1974. A Recorder, 1980–85. Hon. Recorder, Bristol, 2001. Contested (L) General Elections: Oswestry, 1964 and 1966; Hereford, 1970. Founder Mem., Gwent Area Broadcasting, 1981. *Recreations:* garden, trout fishing. *Address:* Lansor, Llandegfedd, Caerleon NP18 1LS. *T:* (01633) 450224.

See also T. E. Crowther.

CROWTHER, William Ronald Hilton; QC 1980; a Recorder, 1984–96; *b* 7 May 1941; *s* of Ronald Crowther and Ann Bourne Crowther; *m* 1964, Valerie Meredith (*née* Richards); one *s*. *Educ:* Oundle Sch.; Univ. of Oxford (BA Jurisprudence). Called to the Bar, Inner Temple, 1963, Bencher, 1985–96. *Recreation:* bird-watching and all aspects of natural history.

CROXALL, Prof. John Patrick, CBE 2004; PhD; FRS 2005; Chair, BirdLife International Marine Programme (formally Global Seabird Programme), since 2006; *b* 19 Jan. 1946; *s* of Harold Eli Croxall and Marjorie (*née* Jones); partner, Alison Jane Stattersfield. *Educ:* King Edward's Sch., Birmingham; Queen's Coll., Oxford (Open Schol.; BA 1st Cl. Hons Zool. 1968; MA 1987); Univ. of Auckland, NZ (Commonwealth Schol.; PhD 1971). Dir, Oiled Seabird Res. Unit and Sen. Res. Associate in Zool., Univ. of Newcastle upon Tyne, 1972–75; British Antarctic Survey: Hd, Birds and Mammals Section, 1976–85; SPSO, 1985; Hd, Higher Predator Section, 1986–2001; DCSO, 1992; Hd of Conservation Biology, 2001–06. Hon. Professor: Univ. of Birmingham, 1998–; Univ. of Durham, 1998–. Mem., Royal Soc. Interdisciplinary Cttee on Antarctic Res., 1997–2001 and 2005–. Scientific Committee for Antarctic Research: Member, Group of Specialists: on Seals, 1984–90; on Southern Ocean Ecol., 1986–96; Mem., Wkg Gp on Biol., 1986–2000; Mem., 1978–, Sec., 1980–85, Chm., 1986–94, Bird Biol Sub Cttee. Chm., Seabird Gp, 1984–87; Mem., 1990–, Mem. Perm. Exec., 1998–2006, Internat. Ornithol Cttee; British Ornithologists' Union: Mem. Council, 1974–78; Vice-Pres., 1987–91; Pres., 1995–99; Royal Society for the Protection of Birds: Mem. Council, 1989–2003 (Chm., 1998–2003); Chm., Conservation Cttee, 1993–98; Falklands Conservation: Trustee, 1987–; Chm., 1993–98; Trustee, S Georgia Heritage Trust, 2005– (Vice Chm., 2008–10). Vice-Chair, World Seabird Union, 2010–12. Scientific Medal, 1984, Marsh Award for Conservation, 2002, Zool Soc. of London; Polar Medal, 1992, clasp, 2004; President's Medal, British Ecol Soc., 1995; Robert Cushman and Murphy Prize and Medal, Internat. Waterbird Soc., 1997; Godman-Salvin Medal, 2004, Union Medal, 2015, BOU; Lifetime Achievement Award, Pacific Seabird Gp, 2008. *Publications:* (ed jtly) Status and Conservation of the World's Seabirds, 1984; (ed) Seabirds: feeding ecology and role in marine ecosystems, 1987; (ed with R. L. Gentry) Status, Biology and Ecology of Fur Seals, 1987; Seabird Status and Conservation: a supplement, 1991; contrib. numerous scientific papers and reports. *Recreations:* birdwatching, conservation, pteridology, French wines and countryside. *Address:* BirdLife International, Wellbrook Court, Girton Road, Cambridge CB3 0NA. *T:* (01223) 277318, *Fax:* (01223) 277200. *E:* john.croxall@birdlife.org.

CROXFORD, Ian Lionel; QC 1993; *b* 23 July 1953; *s* of Peter Patrick Croxford, BEM, and Mary Helen Croxford (*née* Richardson); *m* 1976, Sandra McCord; one *s* one *d*. *Educ:* Westcliff High Sch. for Boys; Univ. of Leicester (LLB 1st Cl. Hons). Called to the Bar, Gray's Inn, 1976 (Bacon Schol.), Bencher, 2001; Lincoln's Inn, *ad eundem*, 1977. Mem. Council, Medical Protection Soc., 2007–. Gov., Westcliff High Sch. for Boys, 1990– (Chm. Govs, 1995–). *Recreation:* watching sport. *Address:* Wilberforce Chambers, 8 New Square, Lincoln's Inn, WC2A 3QP. *T:* (020) 7306 0102.

CROYDON, Area Bishop of, since 2012; **Rt Rev. Jonathan Clark;** *b* Southend, 13 Feb. 1961; *s* of George and Elizabeth Clark; *m* 1984, Alison Walker; one *s* one *d*. *Educ:* Alleyn's Sch., Dulwich; Univ. of Exeter (BA Eng. Lit. 1983); Univ. of Bristol (MLitt Theol. 1990); Univ. of Southampton (MA Adult Educn 1999). Ordained deacon, 1988, priest, 1989; Curate, Stanwix, Carlisle, 1988–92; Chaplain, Univ. of Bristol, 1992–93; Dir of Studies, Southern Dioceses Ministerial Trng Scheme, 1994–97; Chaplain, London Metropolitan Univ., 1997–2003; Area Dean, Islington, 1999–2003; Rector, St Mary's, Stoke Newington, 2003–12. *Publications:* The Republic of Heaven, 2008. *Recreations:* visiting Westray, contemporary art and dance, poetry. *Address:* St Matthew's House, 100 George Street, Croydon CR0 1PE. *T:* (020) 8256 9630. *E:* bishop.jonathan@southwark.anglican.org.

CROYDON, Archdeacon of; *see* Skilton, Ven. C. J.

CROYDON, Rear-Adm. John Edward Kenneth; JP; DL; CEng, FIET; *b* 25 Feb. 1929; *s* of late Kenneth P. Croydon and Elizabeth V. Croydon; *m* 1953, Brenda Joyce Buss, MA; one *s* two *d*. *Educ:* King Edward's Sch., Birmingham; Selwyn Coll., Cambridge (MA). BA London; CEng, FIET (FIEE 1975); jssc 1969. RN Special Entry Cadet (L), 1947; HMS Verulam and HMS Undine, 1954–55; Royal Naval Coll., Dartmouth, 1959–61; HMS Devonshire, 1961–64; HMS London, 1970–72; MoD, 1972–74; Captain Weapon Trials, 1974–77; Dir, Underwater Weapon Projects (Naval), 1978–80; Dir Gen. Weapons (Naval), 1981–83; Dep. Controller, Warships Equipment, MoD (Navy), 1983–84, retd. Rear Cdre (Dinghies), Royal Naval Sailing Assoc., 1980. Gov., Milton Abbey Sch., 1985–2002. Chm. Bd of Visitors, HMP Weare, 1997–2000. Trustee, Weldmar Cancercare Dorset, 2002–06. County Comr for Scouts, Dorset, 1986–93. JP Weymouth, 1985; DL Dorset, 1993. *Recreations:* sailing, music, restacking the dishwasher. *Address:* Hillside, Plaisters Lane, Sutton Poyntz, Weymouth, Dorset DT3 6LQ. *Clubs:* Royal Naval Sailing Association; Weymouth Sailing.

CROZIER, Adam Alexander; Chief Executive, ITV plc, since 2010; *b* 26 Jan. 1964; *s* of Robert and Elinor Crozier; *m* 1994, Annette Edwards; two *d*. *Educ:* Heriot-Watt Univ. (BA Business Orgn). Pedigree Petfoods, Mars (UK) Ltd, 1984–86; Daily Telegraph, 1986–88; Saatchi & Saatchi, 1988–99: Dir, 1990; Media Dir, 1992; Vice Chm., 1994; Chief Exec., 1995; Chief Executive: FA, 2000–02; Royal Mail Group plc, 2003–10. *Recreations:* football, golf, my children. *Address:* ITV plc, Upper Ground, SE1 9LT.

CRUDDAS, Jon, PhD; MP (Lab) Dagenham and Rainham, since 2010 (Dagenham, 2001–10); *b* 7 April 1962; *s* of John and Pat Cruddas; *m* 1992, Anna Mary Healy (*see* Baroness Healy of Primrose Hill); one *s*. *Educ:* Oaklands RC Comprehensive Sch., Waterlooville; Warwick Univ. (BSc, MA; PhD 1991). Labour Party: Policy Officer, 1989–94; Chief Asst to Gen. Sec., 1994–97; Dep. Political Sec., Prime Minister's Office, 1997–2001. Policy Rev. Co-ordinator, Labour Party, 2012–15. Mem., White Hart Angling Soc., 2000–. Mem., Dagenham Royal Naval Assoc., 2000–. *Publications:* Blue Labour: forging a new politics, 2015. *Recreations:* golf, angling. *Address:* House of Commons, SW1A 0AA. *Club:* Dagenham Working Men's.

CRUICKSHANK, Alistair Ronald; Trustee, since 2001, and Chair, since 2007, EcoLocal (formerly Centre for Environmental Initiatives); *b* 2 Oct. 1944; *s* of late Francis John Cruickshank and Kate Cameron Cruickshank (*née* Brittain); *m* 1967, Sandra Mary Noble; three *d*. *Educ:* Aberdeen Grammar School; Aberdeen University (MA). Joined MAFF as Assistant Principal, 1966; Principal, 1970; Asst Secretary, 1978; Under Sec. (Animal Health), 1986; Principal Finance Officer, 1989–94; Under Sec. (Agricl Inputs), 1995–96. Chairman: Surrey Organic Gardening Gp, 1997–2012; Sutton Future Network, subseq. Sutton Envmt Network, 2000–13; Carshalton Lavender, 2004–; Dir, EcoLocal Services Ltd, 2003–; Mem., Standards Bd, Soil Assoc., 2008–13. Vice Pres., London, CPRE, 2004–06. *Recreations:* gardening, looking at old buildings, various church activities. *Club:* Royal Over-Seas League.

CRUICKSHANK, David Charles, CA, CPFA; independent management consultant; *b* Christchurch, NZ, 22 April 1954; *s* of Clarence Albert Shepperd and Eunice Caroline Cruickshank (formerly Shepperd, *née* Wilson); *m* 1974, Linda Friel; one *d*. *Educ:* Queen Charlotte Coll., Picton, NZ; Victoria Univ. of Wellington (BCA 1979). Audit Dir, Audit NZ, 1977–98; Chief Financial Officer, Wellington CC, 1998–2002; Dir of Finance, Islington LBC, 2002–05. Mem., Inst. of Chartered Accountants of NZ, 1980– (Chm., Public Sector Cttee, 1997–2002); CPFA 2003. *Publications:* contrib. auditing and accounting articles to Accountants Jl. *Recreations:* cycling, family, golf, mountain biking. *Clubs:* Wellington; Manor Park Golf.

CRUICKSHANK, David John Ogilvie, CA; Chairman, Deloitte Global, since 2015 (Chairman, Deloitte UK, 2007–15); *b* Ellon, Aberdeenshire, 20 Feb. 1959; *s* of Ogilvie and Rosemary Cruickshank; *m* 1984, Rona; two *d*. *Educ:* Univ. of Edinburgh (BCom 1979). CA 1982. With Deloitte, 1979–: trainee, Edinburgh, 1979–82; Tax Manager, London, 1982–88; Tax Partner, London, 1988; partner i/c Tax, London office, 1995–98; Man. Partner, Tax, 1998–2006. Chair, Educn and Employer Taskforce, 2012– (Jt Chair, 2011). Mem. Council, Heart of the City, 2007–; Business Leader, Community Links, 2011–. Founder Chair, 30% Club, 2010–. *Recreations:* work, family, golf, tennis, watching sport, travel, reading, charity support. *Address:* Deloitte, 2 New Street Square, EC4A 3BZ. *T:* (020) 7007 1826. *E:* dcruickshank@deloitte.co.uk. *Clubs:* Caledonian; Newtonmore Golf, Isle of Purbeck Golf, Coombe Hill Golf.

CRUICKSHANK, Sir Donald Gordon, (Sir Don), Kt 2006; Director, Qualcomm Inc., since 2005; Chairman, Audioboo Ltd, 2010–14; *b* 17 Sept. 1942; *s* of Donald Campbell Cruickshank and Margaret Buchan Cruickshank (*née* Morrison); *m* 1964, Elizabeth Buchan Taylor; one *s* one *d*. *Educ:* Univ. of Aberdeen (MA); Inst. of Chartered Accountants of Scotland (CA); Manchester Business School (MBA). McKinsey & Co., 1972–77; Times Newspapers, 1977–80; Pearson, 1980–84; Man. Dir, Virgin Group, 1984–89; Chief Exec., NHS in Scotland, 1989–93; Dir Gen., Oftel, 1993–98; Chairman: Scottish Media Gp, subseq. SMG plc, 1999–2004; London Stock Exchange, 2000–03; Formscape Gp Ltd, 2003–06; Taylor & Francis plc, 2004–05; Clinovia Gp Ltd, 2004–06; 7digital plc, 2014–. Non-exec. Dir, Christian Salvesen, 1994–95. Chairman: Wandsworth HA, 1986–89; Action 2000, 1997–2000; UK Banking Review, 1998–2000. Mem. Court, Univ. of Aberdeen, 2005–11. Hon. LLD Aberdeen, 2001. *Recreations:* education, sport, golf, opera. *E:* don.cruickshank@btopenworld.com.

CRUICKSHANK, Prof. Garth Stuart, PhD; FRCS, FRCSE; Professor of Neurosurgery, University of Birmingham and Queen Elizabeth Hospital, since 1997; *b* 24 Jan. 1951; *s* of Lt Col Alfred, (Jimmy), Cruickshank and Peggy Lillian Cruickshank (*née* Rushton); *m* 1979, Ros Fitzgerald; two *s* two *d*. *Educ:* Wellington Coll., Berks; Univ. of London (BSc Hons 1974); Royal Free Hosp. (PhD 1979; MB BS 1984). FRCS 1989; FRCSE 1989; FRCS (Surgical Neurol.) 1993. Institute of Neurological Sciences, Glasgow: Registrar, 1989–93; Sen. Lectr in Neurosurgery, 1993–97. Member: NCRI Brain Tumour Gp, 1998–; DVLA Adv. Panel, 2001– (Chair, Neurol. Panel, 2010). *Publications:* publications in the area of brain tumour res., gene therapy and imaging. *Recreation:* sailing. *Address:* Queen Elizabeth Hospital, Edgbaston, Birmingham B15 2TH. *T:* (0121) 697 8225, *Fax:* (0121) 697 8248. *E:* g.s.cruickshank@bham.ac.uk.

CRUICKSHANK, Flight-Lieut John Alexander, VC 1944; ED 1947; late RAF; with Grindlay's Bank Ltd, London, 1952–76; retired; Administrator, Northern Division, North West Securities Ltd, 1977–85; *b* 20 May 1920; *s* of James C. Cruickshank, Aberdeen, and Alice Bow, Macduff, Banffshire; *m* 1955, Marion R. Beverley (*d* 1985), Toronto, Canada. *Educ:* Aberdeen Grammar Sch.; Daniel Stewart's Coll., Edinburgh. Entered Commercial Bank of Scotland, 1938; returned to banking, 1946. Mem. of Territorial Army and called for service, Aug. 1939, in RA; transferred to RAF 1941 and commissioned in 1942; all RAF service was with Coastal Command. ADC to Lord High Commissioner to the Gen. Assembly of the Church of Scotland, 1946–48. *Clubs:* Naval and Military; Royal Northern and University (Aberdeen); Royal Scots (Edinburgh); Merchants of Edinburgh Golf.

CRUICKSHANK, Sheena Carlin, CVO 2011; JP; Lord-Lieutenant of Clackmannanshire, 2001–11; *b* 26 March 1936; *d* of David Irons Brown and Janet Cameron Carlin Brown; *m* 1957, Alistair Booth Cruickshank; two *s* one *d*. *Educ:* High Sch. of Stirling. Hon. Sheriff, Alloa Sheriff Court, 1996. JP Clackmannan, 1989. *Recreations:* quilting, travel.

CRUISE MAPOTHER, Thomas, IV, (Tom Cruise); actor and producer; *b* 3 July 1962; *s* of late Thomas Cruise Mapother, III and of Mary Lee Cruise Mapother (*née* Pfeiffer); *m* 1st, 1987, Mimi Rogers (marr. diss. 1990); 2nd, 1990, Nicole Mary Kidman, *qv* (marr. diss. 2001); one adopted *s* one adopted *d*; 3rd, 2006, Katie Holmes (marr. diss. 2012); one *d*. *Educ:* Glen Ridge High Sch., NJ. *Films:* actor: Endless Love, Taps, 1981; Losin' It, The Outsiders, Risky Business, All the Right Moves, 1983; Legend, 1985; Top Gun, The Color of Money, 1986; Rain Man, 1988; Cocktail, Born on the Fourth of July, 1989; Days of Thunder, 1990; Far and Away, A Few Good Men, 1992; The Firm, 1993; Interview with the Vampire, 1994; Jerry Maguire, 1996; Eyes Wide Shut, 1999; Magnolia, 2000; Vanilla Sky, Minority Report, 2002; Collateral, 2004; War of the Worlds, 2005; Rock of Ages, 2012; Oblivion, 2013; Edge of Tomorrow, 2014; actor and producer: Mission Impossible, 1996; Mission Impossible 2, 2000; The Last Samurai, 2003; Mission Impossible 3, 2006; Lions for Lambs, 2007; Valkyrie, 2009; Knight and Day, 2010; Mission: Impossible - Ghost Protocol, 2011; Jack Reacher, 2012; Mission Impossible: Rogue Nation, 2015; producer: Without Limits, 1998; The Others, 2001; co-producer: Ask the Dust, 2006. *Address:* c/o CAA, 2000 Avenue of the Stars, Los Angeles, CA 90067, USA.

CRUM, Douglas Vernon E.; *see* Erskine Crum.

CRUMP, Bernard John, FRCP, FFPH; Director, BC Healthcare Solutions Ltd, since 2011; Chief Executive Officer, NHS Institute for Innovation and Improvement, 2005–11; *b* 10 Nov. 1956; *s* of Vincent and Bridget Crump; *m* 1990, Izabela Kuncewicz; one *s* one *d*. *Educ:* Burton Grammar Sch.; Univ. of Birmingham (MB ChB). FFPH 1999; FRCP 2005. Engaged in clin. medicine, res. and public health trng, W Midlands and London, 1980–91; Director of Public Health: South Birmingham HA, 1991–95; Leicestershire HA, 1995–2002; CEO, Shropshire and Staffs Strategic HA, 2002–05. Vis. Prof., Public Health and Epidemiology, Univ. of Leicester, 2000–; Hon. Prof., Medical Leadership, Univ. of Warwick, 2012–. Sen. Associate, Nuffield Trust. MInstD. *Publications:* (with M. Drummond) Evaluating Clinical Evidence: a handbook for managers, 1993; articles in health and social care jls. *Recreations:* skiing, golf. *Club:* Leicestershire Golf (Leicester).

CRUMP, Douglas Woodward; fee-paid Employment Judge, Birmingham, 2011–15; fee-paid Tribunal Judge, Stoke, 2011–15; *b* W Bromwich, 26 May 1944; *s* of W. R. A. Crump and E. M. Crump; *m* 1971, Jennifer Ann Snape; two *d*. Legal practice, 1968–93; Chm., Employment Tribunals, 1993–2007; Regl Employment Judge (formerly Regl Chm., Employment Tribunals), Birmingham, 2007–11. *Recreations:* music, fly fishing.

CRUMPLER, Rev. Peter George; Curate, St Leonard's Church, Sandridge, since 2013; Director of Communications, Archbishops' Council of Church of England, 2004–11; *b* 27 Aug. 1956; *m* 1977, Linda Charmaine Smith; one *s* two *d*. *Educ:* Chiswick Sch.; Harlow Coll., Essex (CAM Foundn Dip. in PR 1983). Journalist, Acton Gazette Series, 1975–77; Press Officer, London Bor. of Hillingdon, 1977–79; Press Officer, London Bor. of Hounslow, 1979–81; communications posts with N Thames Gas, 1981–89; PR Manager, British Gas Eastern, 1989–91; Internat. Public Affairs Manager, British Gas, 1991–97; Head: Ext. Affairs, Internat., BG plc, 1997–2000; Communications, BG Gp plc, 2000–01; Communications Officer, Dio. of St Albans, 2001–04. Lay Reader, Dio. of St Albans, 2008–13; training for Ordination, 2011–13; ordained deacon, 2013, priest, 2014. MIPR 1984, FCIPR (FIPR 2002). *Publications:* Making Friends with the Media, 1989; Keep in Touch!, 1993. *Recreations:* family, films, studying, Brentford FC. *Address:* c/o St Leonard's Church, Church End, Sandridge, St Albans AL4 9DL. *E:* sandridgecurate@gmail.com.

CRUMPTON, Michael Joseph, CBE 1992; PhD; FRS 1979; Director of Research (Laboratories), Imperial Cancer Research Fund Laboratories, London, 1991–93, retired (Deputy Director of Research, 1979–91); *b* 7 June 1929; *s* of Charles E. and Edith Crumpton; *m* 1960, Janet Elizabeth Dean; one *s* two *d*. *Educ:* Poole Grammar Sch., Poole; University Coll., Southampton; Lister Inst. of Preventive Medicine, London. BSc, PhD, London. National Service, RAMC, 1953–55. Member, scientific staff, Microbiological Research Estabt, Porton, Wilts, 1955–60; Visiting Scientist Fellowship, Nat. Insts of Health, Bethesda, Maryland, USA, 1959–60; Research Fellow, Dept of Immunology, St Mary's Hosp. Med. Sch., London, 1960–66; Mem., scientific staff, Nat. Inst. for Med. Research, Mill Hill, 1966–79, Head of Biochemistry Div., 1976–79. Visiting Fellow, John Curtin Sch. of Med. Research, ANU, Canberra, 1973–74. Non-exec. Dir, Imperial Cancer Research Technology Ltd, 1989–99 (Chief Operating Officer, 1993–94). Member: WHO Steering Cttee for Encapsulated Bacteria, 1984–91 (Chm., 1988–91); Cell Board, MRC, 1979–83; Scientific Adv. Cttee, Lister Inst., 1986–91; Sloan Cttee, General Motors Res. Foundn, 1986–88 (Chm., 1988); MRC AIDS Directed Prog. Steering Cttee, 1987–91; Scientific Cttee, Swiss Inst. for Experimental Cancer Res., 1989–96; DTI/SERC Biotech. Jt Adv. Bd, 1989–93. Member Council: Royal Instn, 1986–90 (Mem., Davy Faraday Lab. Cttee, 1985–90, Chm. of Cttee, 1988–90); MRC, 1986–90; Royal Soc., 1990–92; Mem. Sci. Council, Celltech Ltd, 1980–90; Chairman: Sci. Adv. Bd, Biomed. Res. Centre, Univ. of British Columbia, Vancouver, 1987–91; DoH/HSE Adv. Cttee on Dangerous Pathogens, 1991–98; Mem. Sci. Adv. Bd, Ciba Foundn, 1990–94. Chm., InferMed Ltd, 1998–2000; non-executive Director: Amersham Internat., 1990–97; Amersham Pharmacia Biotech Ltd, 1997–2001; Amersham Pharmacia Biotech Inc., 2001–02. Mem. Council, Inst. of Cancer Res., 1994–2001; Member, Governing Body: Imperial Coll. of Sci., Technol. and Medicine, 1994–98; BPMF, 1987–95; Gov., Strangeways Res. Lab., 1993–2000. Mem., EMBO, 1982; MAE, 1996; Hon. Mem., Amer. Assoc. of Immunologists, 1995. Trustee: EMF Biol Res. Trust, 1995–2007 (Chm., 2005–07; Chm., Sci. Adv. Cttee, 1995–2005); Breakthrough Breast Cancer, 1997–2004 (Hon. Fellow, 2009). Fellow, Inst. of Cancer Res., 2001. Bernal Lectr, Royal Soc., 2004. Founder FMedSci 1998. Hon. FRCPath 2000. Mem. Editorial Board: Biochemical Jl, 1966–73 (Dep. Chm., 1969–72); Eur. Jl of Immunology, 1972–86; Immunochemistry, 1975–79; Immunogenetics, 1979–85; Biochemistry Internat., 1980–86; Molecular Biol. and Medicine, 1983–86; Human Immunology, 1985–96; Regional Editor, Molecular Immunology, 1982–86. Biochem. Soc. Vis. Lectr, Australia, 1983. Sen. Treas., Royal Soc. Club, 1988–89. *Publications:* contribs to learned scientific jls. *Recreations:* gardening, reading. *Address:* 8 Ticknell Piece Road, Charlbury, Chipping Norton OX7 3TW. *T:* (01608) 811845.

CRUSH, His Honour Harvey Michael; aviation arbitrator and mediator, since 2001; a Circuit Judge, 1995–2001; *b* 12 April 1939; *s* of late George Stanley Crush, Chislehurst, and Alison Isabel Crush; *m* 1st, 1965, Diana Bassett (marr. diss. 1982); one *s* one *d*; 2nd, 1982, Maggie, *d* of Nicholas Dixson. *Educ:* Chigwell Sch. Admitted solicitor, 1963; Partner, Norton Rose, 1968–91; Asst Recorder, 1987–92; Recorder, 1992–95; Higher Courts Advocate, 1994; Dep. Circuit Judge, 2001–04; called to the Bar, 2001. Dir, TOSG Trust Fund Ltd, 1970–95. Mem., Supreme Court Rule Cttee, 1984–88. Mem., Law Soc., 1963–; Vice-Pres., City of London Law Soc., 1989–91. Hon. Solicitor, British Assoc. Aviation Consultants, 1990–95 (Mem. Council, 1991–95, 2001–14; Chm., 2002–04). FRAeS 2004 (MRAeS 1980; Mem. Council, 2011–14; Trustee, 2012–14). Hon. Life Member: Solicitors' Assoc. of Higher Ct Advocates (formerly Solicitors' Higher Courts Advocacy Assoc.); London Solicitors' Litigation Assoc. Liveryman: Co. of Solicitors, 1982 (Mem. Court, 1987–; Master, 1994–95); Co. of Farriers, 1984 (Mem. Court, 1997–2003); Hon. Co. of Air Pilots (formerly GAPAN), 2000 (Freeman, 1991). Hon. Life Mem., Sevenoaks & Dist Motor Club (Chm., 1968–71). *Publications:* (jtly) The British Manual of International Air Carriage, 2009. *Recreations:* flying light aircraft, travel, Spain. *Address:* Arbitrators at 10 Fleet Street, EC4Y 1AU. *T:* 0845 262 0310. *E:* harvey.crush@quadrantchambers.com.

CRUTCHLOW, John Adrian; Director of Finance, Metropolitan Police, 1986–96, retired; *b* 30 March 1946; *s* of James William Crutchlow and Elsie Nellie Crutchlow (*née* King); *m* 1971, Valerie Elizabeth Farage. *Educ:* Finchley County Grammar Sch.; HNC (with dist.) in Business Studies; BA Open; postgraduate Dip. Management Studies. Paymaster General's Office, 1962–65; Metropolitan Police Civil Staff, 1965–96; Principal, 1974–81; Dep. Dir of Finance, 1981–84; Dep. Estabt Officer, 1984–86; Asst Sec., 1986–92; Asst Under-Sec. of State, 1992–96; Dep. to Receiver, Metropolitan Police Dist, 1994–96. President: New Scotland Yard Civil Staff Assoc., 1994–96; Metropolitan Police Former (formerly Metropolitan Police Retired) Civil Staff Assoc., 1996–. FCMI (FBIM 1992); FInstAM 1995. *Recreations:* reading, gardening, golf, renovating old houses. *Address:* 16 Edward Square, Surrey Quays, SE16 5EE.

CRUTE, Prof. Ian Richard, CBE 2010; PhD; Chief Scientist, Agriculture and Horticulture Development Board, 2009–14 (non-executive Director, since 2015); *b* 3 June 1949; *s* of Walter and Rose Crute; *m* 1973, J. Elizabeth Harden; two *d*. *Educ:* Univ. of Newcastle upon Tyne (BSc Hons Botany 1970; PhD 1973). Research Leader, Nat. Vegetable Res. Station, Wellesbourne, Warwick, 1973–86; Horticulture Research International: Head, Crop and Envmt Protection Dept, E Malling, Kent, 1987–93; Head, Plant Pathology Dept, 1993–95, Dir, 1995–99, Wellesbourne; Dir, Rothamsted Research (formerly Inst. of Arable Crops Research), 1999–2009. Fulbright Fellow, Univ. of Wisconsin, 1986; Vis. Prof. in Plant Pathol., Faculty of Biol Scis, Univ. of Oxford, 1997–. Trustee Director: E Malling Trust, 2010–15; John Innes Foundn, 2012–. Hon. Fellow, RASE 2010. Hon. DSc Harper Adams UC, 2010. *Publications:* numerous papers on plant pathol. genetics and sustainable agriculture in scientific jls. *Recreations:* gardening, golf, walking, theatre. *Address:* Agriculture and Horticulture Development Board, Stoneleigh Park, Kenilworth, Warwicks CV8 2TL. *T:* (024) 7669 2051.

CRUTHERS, Sir James (Winter), Kt 1980; AO 2008; Vice-Chairman and Executive Vice-President, News America Publishing Inc., 1984–90 (Director, 1983); Vice-Chairman, News America Holdings Inc., 1984–90 (Director, 1984); *b* 20 Dec. 1924; *s* of James William and Kate Cruthers; *m* 1950, Alwyn Sheila Della (*d* 2011); one *s* one *d*. *Educ:* Claremont Central State Sch.; Perth Technical College. Started as junior in Perth Daily News, 1939; war service, AIF and RAAF (Pilot), 1942; Journalist, Perth Daily News, 1946; Editor, Weekly Publications, West Australian Newspapers Ltd, 1953; TVW Enterprises Ltd: General Manager, 1958; Managing Director, 1969; Dep. Chm., 1974; Chm., 1976–81; Chm., Australian Film Commn, 1982–83. Director: News Corp. Ltd, 1981–92; Satellite Television plc, 1984–90 (Chm., 1985–88). Western Australian Citizen Of The Year, Industry and Commerce, 1980. *Recreations:* golf, jogging. *Clubs:* Weld, Lake Karrinyup Country (Perth).

CRUTZEN, Prof. Dr Paul; Director, Atmospheric Chemistry Division, Max-Planck Institute for Chemistry, Germany, 1980–2000; *b* Amsterdam, 3 Dec. 1933; *m* 1958, Terttu Crutzen (*née* Soininen); two *d*. *Educ:* Stockholm Univ. (PhD 1968; DSc 1973). Member: Royal Swedish Acad. of Scis; Royal Swedish Acad. of Engrg Scis; Academia Europaea. Foreign Mem., Royal Soc., 2006. (Jtly) Nobel Prize for Chemistry, 1995. *Address:* c/o Max-Planck Institute for Chemistry, PO Box 3060, 55020 Mainz, Germany.

CRWYS-WILLIAMS, Air Vice-Marshal David Owen, CB 1990; Managing Director, Services Sound and Vision Corporation (SSVC), 1994–2005 (Deputy Managing Director, 1993–94); *b* 24 Dec. 1940; *s* of Gareth Crwys-Williams and Frances Ellen Crwys-Williams (*née* Strange); *m* 1st, 1964, Jennifer Jean (*née* Pearce) (marr. diss. 1971); one *s* one *d*; 2nd, 1973, Irene Thompson (Suzie) (*née* Whan); one *s* two *d*. *Educ:* Oakham Sch.; RAF Coll., Cranwell. Commnd as pilot, RAF, 1961; served No 30 Sqn, Kenya, 1962–64, No 47 Sqn, Abingdon, 1964–66; ADC to C-in-C RAF Trng Comd, 1966–68; OC 46 Sqn, 1969; RAF Masirah, 1972; Army Staff Coll., 1973; Personal Staff Officer to C-in-C NEAF, 1974–75; OC No 230 Sqn, 1976–77; Air Sec. Dept, MoD, 1977–78; Dep. Dir Air Plans, MoD, 1979–82; OC RAF Shawbury, 1983–84; RCDS 1985; Dir of Air Support and Dir of Air Staff Duties, MoD, 1986–88; Comdr, British Forces Falkland Is, 1988–89; Dir Gen., RAF Personal Services, MoD, 1989–92. Gp Captain 1979; Air Cdre 1985; Air Vice-Marshal 1988. Executive Chairman: SSVC Services Ltd, 1994–99; Columbia Communications Europe, 1994–98; VISUA Ltd, 1996–99; Man. Dir, Teleport London Internat., 1994–98; Director: Forces Events Ltd, 1999–; Amersham Business Centre, 2001–09; RAF Museum Enterprises Ltd, 2008–10; RAF Museum Investments Ltd, 2008–10; HDFDP Trading Ltd, 2008–. Council Mem., Cinema and Television Benevolent Fund, 1994–2005. Chm., New Island South Conservation Trust, 1995–. Trustee: British Forces Foundn, 1999–; RAF Museum, 2002–10 (Chm., Finance Cttee, 2003–10); Hearing Dogs for Deaf People, 2006– (Hon. Treas., 2008–). Gov., Amersham and Wycombe Coll., 1997–2009 (Vice-Chm., 1998–2000; Chm., 2000–03). Freeman, City of London, 2002; Liveryman, Hon. Co. of Air Pilots (formerly GAPAN), 2001–. MInstD; FICPD (FIPM 1991); FCMI (FIMgt 1993). *Recreations:* walking, travelling the world, building, fishing. *Address:* Ashendon, Bucks HP18 0HB. *Club:* Royal Air Force.

CRYAN, Donald Michael; His Honour Judge Cryan; a Circuit Judge, since 1996; authorised to sit as a Judge of the High Court, Family Division, since 1996; *b* 18 Jan. 1948; *s* of late Thomas Joseph Cryan and Helen McBeath Cryan (*née* Munro); *m* 1973, Pamela; two *s*. *Educ:* Salvatorian Coll.; UCL (LLB (Hons)). Called to the Bar, Inner Temple, 1970 (Bencher, 1992; Master of the House, 1993–98; Master of Marshals, 2002–14; Master of Silver, 2013–14; Reader, 2015; Treas., 2016); a Recorder, 1993–96; SE Circuit. Designated Family Judge, Medway, 2001–04, Kent, 2004–08. Chm., Working Party on Delay in Family Proceedings Courts, LCD, 2002; Member: Lord Chancellor's Children Act Judicial Case Mgt Adv. Cttee, 2002–04; Unified Admin Judicial Cttee, 2003–05; various cttees/sub-cttees, Judicial Studies Bd, 2003–07 (Vice Chm., 2005, Chm., 2005–07, Magisterial and Family sub-cttee); Working Party on Authorisation of Magistrates, DCA, 2004–05; Judicial Mem., Courts Bd for Kent, 2005–08; Chm., Family Justice Council for Kent, 2005–08. Freeman, City of London, 1978; Liveryman, Co. of Fruiterers, 1978 (Master, 1999–2000). Member, Committee: Marshall Hall Trust, 1991–2005; Centre for Child and Family Law Reform, City Univ., 1999–2014 (Chm., 2010–14); Chm., Adv. Bd, Law Sch., City Univ., 2010–15. Mem., founding Cttee, IFLA, 2010–12 (Chm., Adv. Cttee, 2012–). Hon. LLD City, 2012. *Recreations:* walking, two granddaughters. *Address:* 4 Paper Buildings, Temple, EC4Y 7EX. *T:* (020) 7583 0816. *E:* HHJudge.Cryan@Judiciary.gsi.gov.uk. *Club:* Royal Automobile.

CRYER, (Constance) Ann; JP; *b* 14 Dec. 1939; *d* of Allen Place and Margaret Ann Place; *m* 1st, 1963, George Robert, (Bob), Cryer, MP (*d* 1994); one *s* one *d*; 2nd, 2003, Rev. John Hammersley (*d* 2004); one step *s* one step *d*. *Educ:* St John's Primary Sch.; Spring Bank Secondary Mod. Sch., Darwen; Bolton Tech. Coll.; Keighley Tech. Coll. Clerk, ICI, 1955–60; telephonist, GPO, 1960–64; researcher, Social Hist. Dept, Essex Univ., 1969; PA to Bob Cryer, MP and MEP, 1974–94. MP (Lab) Keighley, 1997–2010. Member: Home Affairs Select Cttee, 2004–10; Parly Cttee, PLP, 2005–10; Jt Ecclesiastical Cttee, 2008–10; Speaker's Conf. on Diversity in H of C, 2008–10; Chair, All Party Parly Gp on Gardening and Horticulture, 2009–10; Vice Chair, PLP, 2008–10. Rep. of UK on Council of Europe, 1997–2003. Mem. (Lab), Darwen BC, 1962–65. Mem., Cathedral Council, 1999–, Hon. Lay Canon, 2005–12, Bradford Cathedral. Pres., Keighley and Worth Valley Railway Preservation Soc., 2003–; Vice President: Friends of Settle to Carlisle Line, 2001–; Yorks Dales Soc., 2006–; Women and the Church; Cruse Bereavement Care. JP Bradford, 1996. DUniv Bradford, 2009. *Publications:* (contrib.) Boldness be My Friend: remembering Bob Cryer, 1997. *Recreations:* gardening, cinema, theatre, time with my 6 grandchildren and 3 step grandchildren. *Address:* 32 Kendall Avenue, Shipley, W Yorks BD18 4DY. *T:* (01274) 584701.

See also J. R. Cryer.

CRYER, John Robert; MP (Lab) Leyton and Wanstead, since 2010; *b* 11 April 1964; *s* of late (George) Robert Cryer, MP and of Ann Cryer, *qv*; *m* 1994, Narinder Bains (marr. diss. 2012), *d* of Shiv Singh Bains and Bakhshish Bains; two *s* one *d*; *m* 2012, Ellie Reeves. *Educ:* Oakbank Sch., Keighley; Hatfield Poly. (BA). Underwriter, 1986–88; Journalist, Morning Star, 1989–92; Editor, Labour Briefing, 1992–93; Journalist: GPMU Jl, 1992–93; Tribune, 1993–96; Lloyd's of London Pubns, 1996–97; Pol Officer, ASLEF, 2005–06; Nat. Pol Officer, T&G section of Unite - the union (formerly TGWU), 2006–10. MP (Lab) Hornchurch, 1997–2005; contested (Lab) same seat, 2005. Mem., Treasury Select Cttee, 2010–11. Chm., Parly Labour Party, 2015–. Chm., Labour Against the Superstate. Trustee, Thames Chase Community Forest. Mem., Editl Bd, Tribune. *Publications:* (jtly) Boldness be My Friend: remembering Bob Cryer, 1997. *Recreations:* most sports, reading, cinema, old cars. *Address:* House of Commons, SW1A 0AA.

CRYNE, Christine; Chief Executive, Brainwave, 2008–11; *b* 5 March 1955; *d* of William George and Irene Ethel Austin; *m* 1978, John Michael Cryne. *Educ:* Univ. of Reading (BSc Hons Chem. Physics with Maths). Researcher, Unilever Res., 1977–82; Product Develt Exec., Schweppes, 1982–85; commercial and new product develt roles, RHM Foods, 1985–90; Gp Product Manager, Sharwoods, 1990–92; Marketing Manager, IPC Mags, 1992–94; Hd, Corporate, Trading and Develt, 1994–97, Mktg Dir, 1997–2001, Help the Aged; Exec. Dir, Muscular Dystrophy Campaign, 2001–04; Chief Exec., CIM, 2005–06; Sen. Dir, Consumer Direct, OFT, 2006–08. Non-exec. Dir, Dimensions, 2013–. A Dir, CAMRA, 1987–98 and 2011–; Mem., British Guild of Beer Writers, 1998–. MInstD 2000. *Recreations:* swimming, tutored beer tastings, cooking. *Address:* 10 Sneyd Road, NW2 6AN. *E:* c.cryne@btinternet.com.

CRYSTAL, Prof. David, OBE 1995; FBA 2000; author, lecturer, broadcaster on language and linguistics, and reference books editor; Hon. Professorial Fellow, Bangor University (formerly University College of North Wales, then University of Wales, Bangor), since 1985; *b* 6 July 1941; *s* of late Samuel Cyril Crystal, OBE and Mary Agnes Morris; *m* 1st, 1964, Molly Irene Stack (*d* 1976); one *s* two *d* (and one *s* decd); 2nd, 1976, Hilary Frances Norman; one *s*. *Educ:* St Mary's Coll., Liverpool; University Coll. London (BA 1962; Hon. Fellow, 1998); London Univ. (PhD 1966). Res. Asst, UCL, 1962–63; Asst Lectr, UCNW, 1963–65; University of Reading: Lectr, 1965–69; Reader, 1969–75; Prof., 1975–85. Vis. Prof., Bowling Green State Univ., 1969. Dir, Ucheldre Centre, Holyhead, 1991–. Member Board: British Council, 1996–2001; ESU, 2001–06. Chm., 2001–06, Hd, R&D, 2006–09, Crystal Reference Systems. Sec., Linguistics Assoc. of GB, 1965–70; Chm., Nat. Literacy Assoc., 1995–2003 (Patron, 2004–); Vice-President: Chartered Inst. of Linguists (formerly Inst. of Linguistics), 1998–; Soc. for Eds and Proofreaders, 2004–; Pres., Johnson Soc., 2005–06. Hon. Vice-Pres., Royal Coll. of Speech and Lang. Therapists, 1995– (Mem., Academic Bd, Coll. of Speech Therapists, 1972–79); FRCSLT (FCST 1983). Hon. President: Nat. Assoc. of Professionals concerned with Lang. Impaired Children, 1985–2002; Internat. Assoc. of Forensic Phonetics, 1991–94; Soc. of Indexers, 1992–95; Patron: Internat. Assoc. of Teachers of English as a Foreign Lang., 1995–; Assoc. for Language Learning, 2006–. Sam Wanamaker Fellow, Shakespeare's Globe, 2003. FRSA 1983; FLSW 2010. Hon. FTCL 2003; Hon. Fellow, Wolfson Coll., Cambridge, 2005. Hon. DSc Queen Margaret UC, Edinburgh, 1997; Hon. DLitt: Cambridge, 2005; Winchester, 2010; Memorial Univ., Newfoundland, 2011; Lancaster, 2013; DUniv Open, 2007; Hon. Dr Huddersfield, 2014. Editor: Language Res. in Progress, 1966–70; Jl of Child Language, 1973–85; The Language Library, 1978–2008; Applied Language Studies, 1980–84; Child Language Teaching and Therapy, 1985–96; Linguistics Abstracts, 1985–96; Blackwells Applied Language Studies, 1986–95; Consultant Editor, English Today, 1985–94; Adv. Editor, Penguin Linguistics, 1968–75; Associate Editor, Jl of Linguistics, 1970–73; Co-Editor, Studies in Language Disability, 1974–2006. Regular BBC broadcasts on English language and linguistics. DVD, Introduction to Language, 2011. *Publications:* Systems of prosodic and paralinguistic features in English (with R. Quirk), 1964; Linguistics, language and religion, 1965; (ed jtly) Proceedings, Modern approaches to language teaching at university level, 1967; What is linguistics?, 1968, 5th edn 1985; Prosodic systems and intonation in English, 1969; (with D. Davy) Investigating English style, 1969; (ed with W. Bolton) The English language, vol. 2, 1969; Linguistics, 1971, 2nd edn 1985; Basic linguistics, 1973; Language acquisition, 1973; The English tone of voice, 1975; (with D. Davy) Advanced conversational English, 1975; (with J. Bevington) Skylarks, 1975; (jtly) The grammatical analysis of language disability, 1976, 2nd edn 1989; Child language, learning and linguistics, 1976, 2nd edn 1987; Working with LARSP, 1979; Introduction to language pathology, 1980, 4th edn (with R. Varley) 1998; A first dictionary of linguistics and phonetics, 1980, 6th edn 2008; (ed) Eric Partridge: in his own words, 1980; Clinical linguistics, 1981; Directions in applied linguistics, 1981; Profiling linguistic disability, 1982, 2nd edn 1992; (ed) Linguistic controversies, 1982; Who cares about English usage?, 1984, 2nd edn 2000; Language handicap in children, 1984; Linguistic encounters with language handicap, 1984; Listen to your child, 1986; (ed with W. Bolton) The English language, 1987; Cambridge Encyclopedia of Language, 1987, 3rd edn 2010; Rediscover grammar, 1988, 3rd edn 2004; The English Language, 1988, 2nd edn 2002; Pilgrimage, 1988; (with J. C. Davies) Convent, 1989; (ed) Cambridge Encyclopedia, 1990, 4th edn 2000; Language A to Z, 1991; Making Sense of English Usage, 1991; Nineties Knowledge, 1992; Introducing Linguistics, 1992; An Encyclopedic Dictionary of Language and Languages, 1992, 2nd edn, as The Penguin Dictionary of Language, 1999; (ed) Cambridge Concise Encyclopedia, 1992, 2nd edn 1995; (ed) Cambridge Paperback Encyclopedia, 1993, 3rd edn 1999; (ed) Cambridge Factfinder, 1993, 4th edn 2000; (ed) Cambridge Biographical Encyclopedia, 1994, 2nd edn 1998; Cambridge Encyclopedia of the English Language, 1995, 2nd edn 2003; Discover Grammar, 1996; (ed) John Bradburne, Songs of the Vagabond, 1996; Cambridge Biographical Dictionary, 1996; English as a Global Language, 1997, 2nd edn 2003; Language Play, 1998; (with H. Crystal) Words on Words, 2000 (Wheatley Medal, LA, 2001); Language Death, 2000; (with H. Crystal) John Bradburne's Mutemwa, 2000; Happenings, 2000; Language and the Internet, 2001, 2nd edn 2006; (with Ben Crystal) Shakespeare's Words, 2002; (ed) The New Penguin Encyclopedia, 2002, 3rd edn, as The Penguin Encyclopedia, 2006; (ed) The New Penguin Factfinder, 2003, 3rd edn, as The Penguin Factfinder, 2007; (ed) The Concise Penguin Encyclopedia, 2003, 3rd edn 2007; The Stories of English, 2004; Making Sense of Grammar, 2004; The Language Revolution, 2004; A Glossary of Netspeak and Textspeak, 2004; John Bradburne's Book of Days, 2004; Pronouncing Shakespeare, 2005; (with Ben Crystal) The Shakespeare Miscellany, 2005; Johnson's Dictionary: an anthology, 2005; Words, Words, Words, 2006; How Language Works, 2006; The Fight for English, 2006; As They Say in Zanzibar, 2006; By Hook or by Crook, 2007; (ed) John Bradburne's Birds, Bees and Beasts, 2007; The Ucheldre Story, 2007; Think on my Words: exploring Shakespeare's language, 2008; Txtng: the Gr8 Db8, 2008; Just a Phrase I'm Going Through: my life in language, 2009; The Future of Language, 2009; (ed) Fowler's Dictionary of Modern English Usage, 2009; (ed) John Bradburne on Love, 2009; A Little Book of Language, 2010; Begat: the King James Bible and the English language, 2010; Evolving English, 2010; (ed jtly) From International to Local English - and Back Again, 2010; Internet Linguistics, 2011; The Story of English in 100 Words, 2011; (ed jtly) Assessing Grammar: the languages of LARSP, 2012; Spell it Out: the singular story of English spelling, 2012; (with Hilary Crystal) Wordsmiths and Warriors: the English language tourist's guide to

Britain, 2013; Words in Time and Place: exploring the historical thesaurus of the Oxford English Dictionary, 2014; (with Ben Crystal) You Say Potato, 2014; (with Ben Crystal) The Oxford Illustrated Shakespeare Dictionary, 2015; The Disappearing Dictionary, 2015; Making a Point: the pernickety story of English punctuation, 2015; (with J. L. Foster) Databank series: Heat, Light, Sound, Roads, Railways, Canals, Manors, Castles, Money, Monasteries, Parliament, Newspapers, 1979; The Romans, The Greeks, The Ancient Egyptians, 1981; Air, Food, Volcanoes, 1982; Deserts, Dinosaurs and Electricity, 1983; Motorcycles, Computers, Horses and Ponies, Normans, Vikings, Anglo-Saxons, Celts, 1984; The Stone Age, Fishing, 1985; (with J. L. Foster) Datasearch series: Air and Breathing, Heating and Cooling, Light and Seeing, Sound and Hearing, 1991; contributions to: The Library of Modern Knowledge, 1978; A Dictionary of Modern Thought, 1978, 2nd edn 1987; Reader's Digest Great Illustrated Dictionary, 1984; Reader's Digest Book of Facts, 1985; A Comprehensive Grammar of the English Language, 1985; International Encyclopedia of Linguistics, 1992; William Shakespeare: the Complete Works (ed Wells and Taylor), 2005; and to numerous volumes on language, style, prosody, communication, religion, handicap, teaching and reading; symposia and proceedings of learned socs; articles and reviews in jls on linguistics, English language, Shakespeare, speech pathology and education. *Recreations:* cinema, music, bibliophily, development of the arts. *Address:* Akaroa, Gors Avenue, Holyhead, Anglesey LL65 1PB. *T:* (01407) 762764. *E:* davidcrystal2@googlemail.com. *W:* www.davidcrystal.com, http://david-crystal.blogspot.com.

CRYSTAL, Michael; QC 1984; a Deputy High Court Judge, since 1995; Senior Visiting Fellow, Centre for Commercial Law Studies, Queen Mary (formerly Queen Mary College, then Queen Mary and Westfield College), University of London, since 1996 (Hon. Senior Visiting Fellow, 1987–96); *b* 5 March 1948; *s* of late Dr Samuel Cyril Crystal, OBE, and Rachel Ettel Crystal; *m* 1972, Susan Felicia Sniderman; one *s* one *d*. *Educ:* Leeds Grammar Sch.; Queen Mary Coll., Univ. of London (LLB Hons; Hon. Fellow, QMW, 1996); Magdalen Coll., Oxford (BCL). Called to the Bar, Middle Temple, 1970, Bencher, 1993 (Autumn Reader, 2012); called to the Bar *ad eundem*, Gray's Inn, 1989; Lecturer in Law, Pembroke Coll., Oxford, 1971–76. Vis. Prof., Dept of Laws, UCL, 2002–. DTI Inspector into County NatWest Ltd and County NatWest Securities Ltd, 1988–89, and into National Westminster Bank plc, 1992. Member: Insolvency Rules Adv. Cttee, 1993–97; Financial Law Panel, 1996–2002; FA Premier League Panel, 2004–; Internat. Insolvency Inst., 2005–. Mem., Adv. Council, Centre for Commercial Law Studies, QMUL (formerly QMC, then QMW), 1996–. Gov., 1988–2006, Hon. Gov., 2007–, RSC. Trustee: British Friends of Haifa Univ., 2007–10; Israel Philharmonic Orchestra Foundn, 2009–. Fellow: Royal Instn, 2004; Amer. Coll. of Bankruptcy, 2006–. Hon. Fellow, Soc. for Advanced Legal Studies, 1997. *Publications:* various legal text books. *Recreations:* travel, music, theatre. *Clubs:* Royal Automobile, MCC.

CSÁK, János; Ambassador of Hungary to the Court of St James's, 2011–14; *b* Budapest, 15 Oct. 1962; *s* of János Csák and Erzsébet Holozsi; *m* 1986, Júlia Márton; three *s* one *d*. *Educ:* Corvinus Univ. (MSc Finance and Sociol. 1987). Finance Dir, MATÁV Hungarian Telecom, 1993–2000; Chairman: MOL Hungarian Oil and Gas Co., 1999–2000; T-Mobile Hungary, 1999–2001; Mem., Gp Exec. Bd, CreditAnstalt Investment Bank, 2001–03; CEO, Mobilnet, Finance and Strategy Advisory, 2003–10; Owner, Helikon Book Publishing, 2003–10. Treasury Advr, Ameritech Corp., Chicago, 1996; Advr to Pres. of Hungary, 2007–10. Vis. Fellow, Heritage Foundn, 2009–10. Founder, Széll Kálmán Club, 2003; Trustee, Saint Francis Children's Foundn, 2004–. Comdr's Cross, Order of Merit (Hungary), 2010. *Recreations:* family and friends, reading, football, travelling, walking. *Clubs:* Athenæum; Széll Kálmán (Budapest).

CSOKA, Simon; QC 2011; *b* Blackburn, 12 April 1968; *s* of Béla Csoka and Kathleen Csoka; *m* 1996, Elizabeth Baker; three *s*. *Educ:* Stonyhurst; Fitzwilliam Coll., Cambridge (BA 1990). Called to the Bar, Gray's Inn, 1991. *Recreations:* live music, hill walking. *Address:* Lincoln House Chambers, Tower 12, The Avenue North, Spinningfields, 18–22 Bridge Street, Manchester M3 3BZ. *T:* (0161) 832 5701, *Fax:* (0161) 832 0839. *E:* simon.csoka@lincolnhousechambers.com.

CUBIE, Sir Andrew, Kt 2009; CBE 2001; FRSE; consultant to Fyfe Ireland LLP, since 2003 (Senior Partner, 1994–2003); *b* 24 Aug. 1946; *s* of late Dr Alexander Cubie and Elsie B. C. Cubie (*née* Thorburn); *m* 1968, Heather Ann Muir (*see* H. A. Cubie); one *s* two *d*. *Educ:* Dollar Acad.; Edinburgh Univ. (LLB Hons). WS. Admitted solicitor, 1969; NP; Partner: Fyfe Ireland & Co., WS, 1971–87; Bird Semple Fyfe Ireland, WS, 1987–94 (Chm., 1991–94). Non-exec. Chm. or Dir, Blas Ltd, ESPC Ltd, Kinloch Anderson Ltd and other private cos. Advr, World Bank, Washington. Chairman: CBI Scotland, 1995–97; Regl Chairmen of CBI, 1996–97; Scotland's Health at Work, 1996–2005; Independent Cttee of Inquiry into Student Finance, 1999–2000; Quality Scotland Foundn, 1999–; Scottish Credit and Qualification Framework, 2001–; British Council, Scotland, 2002–08; Centre for Healthy Working Lives, 2005–; Jt Negotiating Cttee, USS, 2008–. Member, Board: Education Scotland; Scotland's Futures Forum; Scottish Cancer Foundation; Scottish Chamber Orchestra; Chm., Scotland's Garden Trust. Member: Consultative Steering Gp, Scottish Parliament, 1997–98; McIntosh Commn in respect of Scottish Local Govt, 1998–99. Fulbright Comr, 2005–08; Chm., Cttee of Univ. Chairmen, 2007–08. Chm., Northern Lighthouse Bd, 2009– (Vice Chm., 2007–09). Vice-Pres., 2000–, Dep. Chm., 2009–, RNLI (Chm., Scottish Council, 1997–); Chm., UK Cttee, VSO, 2006–14 (Vice-Pres., 2001–04, Chm., 2004–05, BESO); Trustee, Common Purpose, 2003–. Chairman: Governing Council, George Watson's Coll., 1994–99; Court, Napier Univ., 2001–08. FRSE 2001; FCGI 2012; FRSA. Hon. FRCPSGlas 2006. Hon. DBA Queen Margaret UC, Edinburgh, 2000; Hon. LLD: Edinburgh, 2001; Glasgow, 2001; Glasgow Caledonian, 2001; DUniv Edinburgh Napier, 2009. *Recreations:* sailing, gardening. *Address:* The Garden Flat, 14 Moray Place, Edinburgh EH3 6DT. *T:* (0131) 221 9222. *E:* andrew@cubie-edinburgh.com. *Clubs:* New (Edinburgh); Royal Highland Yacht.
See also G. Cubie.

CUBIE, Andrew MacInnes; Sheriff of Glasgow and Strathkelvin at Glasgow, since 2010; Deputy Director, Judicial Institute for Scotland; *b* 12 Feb. 1963; *s* of John Pattison Cubie and Mary Moira Keir Cubie; *m* 1987, Joan Crockett; two *s* one *d*. *Educ:* Univ. of Glasgow (LLB 1st Cl. Hons; DLP). Admitted solicitor, 1986; Partner, Maxwell MacLaurin (Solicitors), Glasgow, until 2003. Temp. Sheriff, 1997–99; Floating Sheriff, 2003–04; Sheriff of Tayside, Central and Fife at Stirling, 2004–10. Lectr (pt-time), Centre for Professional Legal Studies, Univ. of Strathclyde, 1993–2003. *Publications:* (contrib. ed.) Butterworth's Family Law Service; (contrib.) MacPhail, Sheriff Court Practice, 2006; Scots Criminal Law, rev. 3rd edn, 2010; contrib. articles to Scots Law Time, Green's Family Law Bulletin and Jl Law Soc. of Scotland. *Recreations:* family, sports, music, travel, the M8s. *Address:* Glasgow Sheriff Court, 1 Carlton Place, Glasgow G5 9DA. *T:* (0141) 429 8888.

CUBIE, George, CB 2003; Clerk of Committees, House of Commons, 2001–05; *b* 30 Aug. 1943; *s* of late Dr Alexander Cubie and Elsie B. C. Cubie (*née* Thorburn); *m* 1966, Kathleen S. Mullan; one *s*. *Educ:* Dollar Acad.; Edinburgh Univ. (MA Hons). Clerk in H of C, 1966; Clerk of Financial Cttees, H of C, 1987–89; Sec. to Public Accounts Commn, 1987–89; Clerk of Select Cttees, H of C, 1989–91; Clerk of the Overseas Office, 1991–95; Principal Clerk, Table Office, 1995–97; Clerk Asst, H of C, 1998–2001. *Publications:* (contrib.) Erskine May's Parliamentary Practice, 22nd edn, 1997; (contrib.) Halsbury's Laws of England, 5th edn. *Recreation:* walking. *Address:* 10 Lower Westport, Wareham, Dorset BH20 4FE. *T:* (01929) 554246.
See also Sir A. Cubie.

CUBIE, Prof. Heather Ann, (Lady Cubie), MBE 2012; PhD; FRSE; Senior Advisor, Global Health Academy, University of Edinburgh, since 2014; *b* Dunfermline, 8 Dec. 1946; *d* of William Muir and Freida Muir; *m* 1968, Sir Andrew Cubie, *qv*; one *s* two *d*. *Educ:* Dunfermline High Sch.; Univ. of Edinburgh (BSc 1st Cl. Hons 1968; MSc by thesis 1972; PhD 1989); Moray House (PGTCSE). FRCPath 2000. NHS Lothian: Consultant Clinical Scientist in Virology, 1993–2008 (pt-time, 1995–2008); Dir, R&D, 1995–2008; Dir, Scottish HPV Reference Lab., 2008–12; University of Edinburgh: Hd, HPV Res. Gp and Scottish HPV Archive, 2012–14; Hon. Prof. Trustee, Girl Guiding Scotland, 2009–14; Elder and Trustee, Mayfield Salisbury Parish Ch. FRSE 2012. *Publications:* (jtly) Viral Warts, 2nd edn 1992; (contrib.) Medical Microbiology: a guide to microbial infections, 15th edn 1997 to 18th edn 2011; over 80 articles in academic jls. *Recreations:* gardening, walking. *Address:* Flat 4, 4 The Cedars, Colinton Road, Edinburgh EH13 0PL. *T:* (0131) 441 9079. *E:* heather.cubie@ed.ac.uk.

CUBITT, family name of **Baron Ashcombe**.

CUBITT, Sir Hugh (Guy), Kt 1983; CBE 1977; JP; DL; FRICS; Chairman, Peabody Trust, 1998–2003 (Governor, 1991–2003); Director, PSIT PLC (formerly Property Security Investment Trust PLC), 1962–97; *b* 2 July 1928; *s* of late Col Hon. (Charles) Guy Cubitt, CBE, DSO, TD, and Rosamond Mary Edith, *d* of Sir Montagu Cholmeley, 4th Bt; *m* 1958, Linda Ishbel, *d* of late Hon. Angus Campbell, CBE; one *s* two *d*. *Educ:* RNC Dartmouth and Greenwich. Lieut RN, 1949; served in Korea, HMS Charity, 1949–51; Flag Lieut to Adm., BJSM Washington, 1952 and to C-in-C Nore, 1953; retd 1953. Qual. Chartered Auctioneer and Estate Agent, 1958; Chartered Surveyor (FRICS) 1970. Partner: Rogers Chapman & Thomas, 1958–67; Cubitt & West, 1962–79. Regl Dir, 1970–77, Dir, 1977–90, Mem., UK Adv. Bd, 1990–91, National Westminster Bank; Chairman: Lombard North Central PLC, 1980–91; The Housing Corp., 1980–90; Rea Brothers Group PLC, 1996–98. Comr, and Chm., London Adv. Cttee, English Heritage, 1988–94. Mem. Westminster City Council, 1963–78; Leader of Council, 1972–76; Alderman, 1974–78; Lord Mayor and Dep. High Steward of Westminster, 1977–78. Pres., London Chamber of Commerce, 1988–91. Chairman: Anchor Trust (formerly Anchor Gp of Housing Assocs), 1991–98; Housing Assocs' Charitable Trust, 1991–97; Chairman of Governors: West Heath Sch., 1978–91; Cranleigh Sch., 1981–95; Dir and Mem. Governing Body, RAM, 1978–98. Hon. Steward, Westminster Abbey, 1978–2002 (Chief Steward, 1997–2002). Mem., Bd of Green Cloth Verge of Palaces, 1980–98. Trustee, Titsey Foundn, 1983–. FRSA; Hon. FRAM 1985. JP Surrey, 1964; Chairman: Dorking PSD, 1991–93; SE Surrey PSD, 1993–95. High Sheriff of Surrey, 1983–84; DL Greater London, 1978. *Recreations:* travel, photography, painting. *Address:* Chapel House, Westhumble, Dorking, Surrey RH5 6AY. *T:* (01306) 882994. *Club:* Boodle's.

CUBITT, Maj. Gen. Sir William (George), KCVO 2011; CBE 2005 (OBE 2000); farmer and landowner; General Officer Commanding, London District, and Major General Commanding Household Division, 2007–11; *b* 19 Feb. 1959; *m* 1990, Lucy Jane Brooking (*née* Pym); two *s* one *d*. *Educ:* Beechwood Park, Herts; Stowe Sch., Bucks; Univ. of Edinburgh (BSc Hons Agric.). Served Coldstream Guards, 1977–98; regtl appts in 1st Bn in London, New Zealand (attached 2/1 RNZIR), N Ireland, Cyprus, Falkland Is and Hong Kong; Trng Officer, Mozambique Trng Team, Zimbabwe, 1989; acsc 1991–92; Military Asst 2 to Chief of GS, 1992–94; commanded No 2 Co. in Germany, Bosnia and Canada, 1994–96; Lt Col 1996; seconded to Cabinet Office 1996–98; transf. to Irish Guards, 1998–2011; commanded 1st Bn in Germany, Macedonia, Kosovo and Poland, 1998–2001; Col 2001; commanded Land Warfare School; hcsc 2002; commanded 8th Infantry Bde, N Ireland, 2002–04; Dir of Gen. Staff, 2004–07. Regtl Lt Col, Irish Guards and Chm Trustees, Irish Guards Charities, 2008–12. Member: Norfolk Cttee, CLA, 2011– (Vice Chm., 2013–15; Chm., 2015–); Norfolk Churches Trust Cttee, 2012–; Gallipoli Assoc., 2012–; Pres., Norfolk Br., RBL, 2014–. Member: Royal Forestry Soc.; Nat. Trust; British Assoc. of Shooting and Conservation; British Deer Soc.; Woodland Heritage; Game and Wildlife Conservation Trust; Inst. of Advanced Motorists. Trustee, E Anglian Air Ambulance, 2015–. Freeman, City of London, 2012. Class IV, Order of St Olav (Norway), 1988. *Clubs:* Cavalry and Guards, Norfolk.

CUCKNEY, Lady; *see* Newell, Dame P. J.

CUDDIGAN, Hugo Jonathan Patrick; QC 2015; *b* London, 22 Feb. 1971; *s* of Dr Jeremy Cuddigan and Jacqueline Cuddigan; *m* 2007, Jemma Louise Whicheloe; one *s* two *d*. *Educ:* Ampleforth Coll.; Trinity Coll., Cambridge (BA Engrg 1993; MA); Univ. of Westminster (DipLaw). Called to the Bar, Middle Temple, 1995; in practice as a barrister, specialising in intellectual property, 1997–. *Recreations:* sailing, ski-ing, Arsenal Football Club. *Address:* 11 South Square, Gray's Inn, WC1R 5EY. *T:* (020) 7405 1222. *E:* clerks@11southsquare.com. *Clubs:* Soho House; Hawks' (Cambridge); Royal Yacht Squadron, Bembridge Sailing; Worthless Athletic Football.

CUDMORE, Harold; yachtsman/businessman; *b* 21 April 1944; *s* of late Harold Cudmore, LLD and Sheila Coleman; *m* 1993, Lauren E. Dagge; two *d*. Skipper, White Crusader, British challenger, America's Cup, 1986; Manager and sailor, British Admiral's Cup winning team, 1989; Adviser and Coach, America 3, America's Cup winning team, 1992; racing, worldwide, Maxi Yachts, 1979–, Internat. Twelve Metres, 1981–, Heritage/Classic Yachts, 1991–, and superyachts, 2006–. Winner of many world championships, internat. match-racing regattas and major events. *Recreations:* other sports, walking, travelling, socialising. *Address:* 4 Queen's Road, Cowes, Isle of Wight PO31 8BQ. *T:* (01983) 291376, 07710 270952. *E:* haroldcudmore@aol.com. *Clubs:* Royal Thames Yacht, Royal Ocean Racing; Royal Cork Yacht, Island Sailing, Royal Corinthian Yacht, Irish Cruising, Fort Worth Boat.

CUI, Prof. Zhanfeng, PhD, DSc; CEng, FREng; Donald Pollock Professor of Chemical Engineering, and Fellow of Hertford College, Oxford University, since 2000; *b* 16 Nov. 1962; *s* of Chun-Ting Cui and Su-e Li; *m* 1985, Dr Jing Yu; one *s* one *d*. *Educ:* Inner Mongolia Poly. Univ., China (BSc 1982); Dalian Univ. of Technol., China (MSc 1984; PhD 1987); MA 1994, DSc 2009, Oxon. CEng 1997; FREng 2013. Res. Fellow, Univ. of Strathclyde, 1988–91; Lectr in Chemical Engrg, Edinburgh Univ., 1991–94; Oxford University: Lectr in Engrg Sci., 1994–99; Reader, 1999–2000; Fellow, Keble Coll., 1994–2000. Visiting Professor: Georgia Inst. of Technol., Atlanta, 1999; Univ. of Minnesota, 2004; (also Chang Jiang Scholar) Dalian Univ. of Technol., China, 2005. *Publications:* contrib. numerous res. articles to professional jls, as sole or jt author. *Recreations:* bridge, basketball. *Address:* Department of Engineering Science, Oxford University, Parks Road, Oxford OX1 3PJ. *T:* (01865) 617693.

CULHAM, Michael John, CB 1992; Assistant Under Secretary of State (Civilian Management (Administrators)), Ministry of Defence, 1987–92, retired; *b* 24 June 1933; *s* of Cecil and Constance Culham; *m* 1963, Christine Mary Daish; one *s* two *d*. *Educ:* Reading Sch.; Lincoln Coll., Oxford (MA); Open Univ. (Dip. French, 1997). National Service, Queen's Own Royal West Kent Regt, RAEC, 1952–54. Exec. Officer, WO, 1957–61; Asst Principal, Air Min., 1962; Private Sec. to Under-Sec. of State for Air, 1962–64; Principal, MoD, 1964–72; Jt Services Staff Coll., 1969; 1st Sec. (Defence), UK Delegn to NATO, Brussels, 1972–74; Asst Sec., MoD, 1974–82; Asst Under-Sec. of State (Adjt-Gen.), MoD, 1982–87. Member: Royal Patriotic Fund Corp., 1983–87; Adv. Council, RMCS, Shrivenham, 1983–87. Commissioner: Duke of York's Royal Mil. Sch., 1982–87; Queen Victoria Sch., 1982–87; Welbeck Coll., 1985–87; Royal Hosp. Chelsea, 1985–88. Chm., Defence Sports and Recreation (formerly MoD Recreation) Assoc., 1985–92; Vice President: CS RFU, 1992–; Farnham Town Boys' FC, 1987– (Chm., 1983–85). Trustee, Nat. Army

Mus., 1985–88. *Recreations:* music, sailing, walking, watching cricket. *Address:* 39 Waverley Lane, Farnham, Surrey GU9 8BH. *Clubs:* Civil Service; Surrey County Cricket; Hampshire County Cricket.

CULHANE, Prof. (John) Leonard, FRS 1985; Professor of Physics, 1981–2005, now Emeritus, Director, Mullard Space Science Laboratory, 1983–2003, and Head of Department of Space and Climate Physics, 1993–2003, University College London; Director, International Space Science Institute, Bern, 2010–13; *b* 14 Oct. 1937; *s* of late John Thomas Culhane and Mary Agnes Culhane; *m* 1961, Mary Brigid, *d* of James Smith; two *s*. *Educ:* Clongowes Wood College, Co. Kildare; University College Dublin (BSc Phys 1959; MSc Phys 1960); UCL (PhD Phys 1966). FRAS 1970; FInstP 1991. Physics Department, University College London: Res. Asst, 1963; Lectr, 1967; Reader, 1976; Prof., 1981. Sen. Scientist, Lockheed Palo Alto Res. Lab., 1969–70; Vis. Prof., Inst. of Space and Astronautical Sci., Tokyo, 1997. Chairman: SERC/BNSC Space Sci. Prog. Bd, 1989–92 (Vice-Pres., and UK Deleg., ESA Sci. Prog. Cttee, 1990–94); Royal Soc. Space Res. Cttee, 1990–93; COSPAR Commn E, 1994–2002; Eur. Space Sci. Cttee, ESF, 1997–2002; Member: Council, RAS, 1975–78; Space Sci. Adv. Cttee, ESA, 1985–89 (Chm., Astrophysics Working Group, 1985–89); SERC/BNSC Earth Obs. Prog. Bd, 1986–88; SERC Astronomy and Planetary Sci. Bd, 1989–92; Adv. Panel, ESA Space Sci. Dept, 1995–2000; PPARC, 1996–2000; Sci. Oversight Cttee, Internat. Space Sci. Inst., Bern, 2004–09. Mem. Council, Surrey Univ., 1985–90. MAE 2001; Member: IAU; Amer. Astronomical Soc.; Amer. Geophys. Union; Internat. Acad. of Astronautics; For. Mem., Norwegian Acad. of Scis and Letters, 1966. Fellow, UCL, 2008. Hon. DSc Wroclaw, 1993. Silver Award and Pardoe Space Prize, RAeS, 2005; Gold Medal in Astronomy, Royal Astronomical Soc., 2007. *Publications:* X-ray Astronomy (with P. W. Sanford), 1981; over 400 papers on solar physics, X-ray astronomy, X-ray instrumentation and plasma spectroscopy. *Recreations:* music, racing cars. *Address:* Mullard Space Science Laboratory, Holmbury St Mary, Dorking RH5 6NT. *T:* (01483) 204100. *E:* j.culhane@ucl.ac.uk.

CULHANE, Simon Hugh Desmond, Chartered FCSI; Chief Executive, Chartered Institute for Securities & Investment (formerly Securities Institute, then Securities & Investment Institute), since 2004; *b* 15 Feb. 1960; *m* 1985, Sarah; three *s* one *d*. *Educ:* St Paul's Sch.; Univ. of Surrey (BSc Hons Econs and Stats). ACIB 1984; Chartered FCSI 2010 (FSI 2005). Lloyds TSB Bank, 1981–95; Dep. Dir, Prime Minister's Efficiency Unit, Cabinet Office, 1995–98; Dir, Chairman's Office, Deutsche Bank AG, London, 1998–2002; Foundn Trust Project Dir, UCLH, 2003–04. Non-exec. Dir, Efficiency Project Prog. Bd, Office of Govt Commerce, 2004–07. MInstD 2004–09. *Recreations:* sailing, badminton, following AFC Wimbledon. *Address:* Chartered Institute for Securities & Investment, 8 Eastcheap, EC3M 1AE. *T:* (020) 7645 0605, *Fax:* (020) 7626 3068. *E:* simon.culhane@cisi.org. *Club:* Cornhill.

CULL-CANDY, Prof. Stuart Graham, PhD; FMedSci, FBPhS; FRS 2002; Gaddum Chair of Pharmacology and Professor of Neuroscience, University College London, since 2006; *b* 2 Nov. 1946; *s* of late Stanley William Cull-Candy and Margaret Cull-Candy; *m* Dr Barbara Paterson Fulton; one *d*. *Educ:* Royal Holloway Coll., Univ. of London (BSc Hons Biology 1969); UCL (MSc Physiology and Biophysics 1971); Univ. of Glasgow (PhD Synaptic Physiology 1974). FBPhS (FBPharmacolS 2005). Royal Society European Exchange Prog. Fellow, Inst. of Pharmacology, Univ. of Lund, Sweden, 1974–75; University College London: Beit Meml Res. Fellow, and MRC Associate Res. Staff, Dept of Biophysics, 1975–82; Wellcome Trust Reader in Pharmacology, Dept of Pharmacology, 1982–90; Prof. of Pharmacology, 1990–2003; Royal Soc.—Wolfson Res. post, 2002–08; Prof. of Neuroscience, 2003–06. Japan Soc. for Promotion of Sci. Vis. Prof., Dept of Physiol., Kyoto Univ. Med. Sch., 1990; Internat. Res. Scholar, Howard Hughes Medical Inst., 1993–98. Mem., Neurosci. Cttee, MRC, 1987–91; Founder Mem., Wellcome Trust Internat. Interest Gp, 1991–97; Expert Advr, Scientific Bd, INSERM, France, 2007–. Member: Royal Soc. Univ. Res. Fellowships Grants Cttee, 2003–, Res. Grants Bd, 2005–; Panel, Leverhulme Trust Sen. Res. Fellowships, 2006–; Panel, REF 2014 sub-panel 5: Biol Scis, 2011–. Mem., Faculty of 1000, 2006–. External Editl Advr in Neuroscience, Nature, 1993–97; Editor: Jl of Physiology, 1987–95; European Jl of Neuroscience, 1988–; Neuron, 1994–98; Reviewing Ed., Jl of Neuroscience, 2000–; Associate Ed., Molecular Pharmacology, 2012–; Guest Ed., Current Opinions in Neurobiology, 2007–; Mem., Adv. Bd for F1000 Medicine Reports, 2009–. FMedSci 2004. G. L. Brown Prize, Physiological Soc., 1996; Wolfson Res. Award, Royal Soc., 2003. *Publications:* various book chapters; numerous basic research articles on fast excitatory synaptic transmission mediated by glutamate, the most important excitatory transmitter between nerve cells in the brain; research articles on glutamate receptors involved in nerve cell signalling in the brain and spinal cord, and role of NMDA receptors, AMPA receptors and associated proteins that underlie normal nerve cell signalling and certain important neurol disorders, in scientific jls Nature, Neuron, Jl of Neuroscience, Jl of Physiology, Nature Neuroscience and Science. *Recreations:* the Arts and Crafts movement, architecture, antiquarian books, jazz and blues music, natural history. *Address:* Department of Neuroscience, Physiology and Pharmacology, University College London, Medical Sciences Building, University College London, Gower Street, WC1E 6BT. *T:* (020) 7679 3766. *E:* s.cull-candy@ucl.ac.uk.

CULLEN, family name of **Baron Cullen of Whitekirk**.

CULLEN OF ASHBOURNE, 3rd Baron *cr* 1920, of Roehampton, co. Surrey; **Edmund Willoughby Marsham Cokayne;** *b* 18 May 1916; 2nd *s* of 1st Baron Cullen of Ashbourne, KBE and Grace Margaret (*née* Marsham); *S* brother, 2000; *m* 1943, Janet Muirhead Manson (*née* Watson) (*d* 2006); (one adopted *d* decd). *Educ:* Eton; Royal Sch. of Mines. PEng. Served War, Pilot (Flt-Lt) RAF, 1940–46. Jun. Engr, Sons of Gwalia Mine and Zinc Corp., Australia, 1937–40; Chief Engineer: Central Patricia Gold Mine, Ont, Canada, 1946–51; Algoma Ore Properties, Ont, 1951–65; Chief Engr, Mine Supt then Mine Mgr, Craigmont Mines, BC, 1965–76; Mine Mgr then Gen. Mgr, Lakeshore Mine, Casa Grande, Arizona, USA, 1976–84. *Publications:* technical papers. *Recreations:* music, gardening, volunteering. *Heir: nephew* Michael John Cokayne [*b* 28 Nov. 1950; *m* 1st, 1976, Baudilia Medina Negrin (marr. diss. 1985); 2nd, 1986, Yvette Santana (marr. diss. 1994); 3rd, 2001, Ljubov Gruntal]. *Address:* 15–1901 Maxwell Avenue, Merritt, BC V1K 1L9, Canada. *T:* (250) 3789462.

CULLEN OF WHITEKIRK, Baron *cr* 2003 (Life Peer), of Whitekirk in East Lothian; **William Douglas Cullen,** KT 2007; PC 1997; Lord Justice-General of Scotland and Lord President of the Court of Session, 2001–05; *b* 18 Nov. 1935; *s* of late Sheriff K. D. Cullen and Mrs G. M. Cullen; *m* 1961, Rosamond Mary Downer (MBE 2007); two *s* two *d*. *Educ:* Dundee High Sch.; St Andrews Univ. (MA); Edinburgh Univ. (LLB). FRSE 1993. Called to the Scottish Bar, 1960. Standing Jun. Counsel to HM Customs and Excise, 1970–73; QC (Scot.) 1973; Advocate-depute, 1978–81; a Senator of the Coll. of Justice in Scotland, 1986–2005; Lord Justice-Clerk and Pres. of the Second Div. of the Court of Session, 1997–2001. A Justice, Qatar Financial Centre Civil and Commercial Court, 2007–. Chairman: Medical Appeal Tribunal, 1977–86; Inquiry into the Piper Alpha disaster, 1988–90; Review of Business of the Outer House of the Court of Session, 1995; Tribunal of Inquiry into the shootings at Dunblane Primary Sch., 1996; Ladbroke Grove Rail Inquiry, 1999–2001; Rev. of fatal accident legislation, 2008–09. Chm., Bd of Dirs, The Signet Accreditation Ltd, 2007–. Member: Scottish Valuation Adv. Council, 1980–86; Royal Commn on Ancient and Historical Monuments of Scotland, 1987–97. President: SACRO, 2000–; Saltire Soc., 2005–11. Chancellor, Abertay Univ. (formerly Univ. of Abertay, Dundee), 2009–. Chairman: Council, Cockburn Assoc. (Edinburgh Civic Trust), 1984–86; Govs, St Margaret's Sch., Edinburgh, 1994–2001; Mem. Court, Napier Univ., 1996–2005. Hon. Bencher: Inner Temple, 2001; Inn of Court of NI, 2002. Hon. FREng (Hon. FEng 1995); Hon. FSaRS 2002; Hon. FRCSEd 2006; FRCPEd 2010. Hon. LLD: Aberdeen, 1992; St Andrews, 1997; Dundee, Edinburgh, Glasgow Caledonian, 2000; DUniv Heriot-Watt, 1995. *Publications:* The Faculty Digest Supplement 1951–60, 1965; non-legal booklets on buildings in Edinburgh. *Recreations:* gardening, natural history. *Address:* House of Lords, SW1A 0PW. *Clubs:* Caledonian; New (Edinburgh).

CULLEN, Edmund William Hector; QC 2012; *b* 29 Sept. 1966; *s* of Terence Lindsay Graham Cullen, QC and of Muriel Elisabeth Cullen; *m* 1994, Emma; three *d*. *Educ:* Winchester Coll.; Bristol Univ. (BA Philosophy). Called to the Bar, Lincoln's Inn, 1990; in practice as barrister, 1991–. *Recreations:* horse racing, opera, weeding. *Address:* Maitland Chambers, 7 Stone Buildings, Lincoln's Inn, WC2A 3SZ. *T:* (020) 7406 1200.

CULLEN, Sir (Edward) John, Kt 1991; PhD; FREng; Chairman, Health and Safety Commission, 1983–93; *b* 19 Oct. 1926; *s* of William Henry Pearson Cullen and Ellen Emma Cullen; *m* 1954, Betty Davall Hopkins (*d* 2006); two *s* two *d*. *Educ:* Cambridge Univ. (MA 1952, PhD 1956); Univ. of Texas (MS 1953). UKAEA, 1956–58; ICI, 1958–67; Rohm and Haas Co., 1967–83: Eur. Dir for Engrg and Regulatory Affairs, 1981–83; Dep. Chm., Rohm and Haas (UK) Ltd, 1981–83. Chm., British Nat. Cttee for Internat. Engrg Affairs, 1990–96; President: Pipeline Industries Guild, 1996–98; FEANI, 1996–99 (Vice-Pres., 1995–96); British Safety Industries Fedn, 1997–2007; Mem., Engrg Council, 1990–96. FREng (FEng 1987; Mem. Council, 1991–94); Pres., IChemE, 1988–89. Mem., 1995–99, Chm., 1999–2002, McRobert Award Cttee. MInstD 1978; FRSA 1988. Liveryman, Engineers' Co., 1989–. Hon. DSc Exeter, 1993. *Publications:* articles on gas absorption, in Trans Faraday Soc., Trans IChemE, Chem. Engrg Science; numerous articles on health and safety. *Recreations:* reading (detective stories), photography, swimming, gardening. *Club:* Athenæum.

CULLEN, Felicity Ann; QC 2008; *b* Talgarth, 5 March 1962; *d* of John Milton and Mary Christine London; *m* 1986, Christopher Cullen; two *s*. *Educ:* Holy Trinity Convent, Kidderminster; St David's Ursuline Convent, Brecon; Brecon High Sch.; Univ. of Birmingham (LLB 1983); Queens' Coll., Cambridge (LLM 1984). Called to the Bar, Lincoln's Inn, 1985; in practice as barrister, specialising in revenue law; Mem., Gray's Inn Tax Chambers, 1986–; CEDR Accredited Mediator, 2012. *Recreations:* arts, entertaining, architecture and design, adventure travel, sport. *Address:* Gray's Inn Tax Chambers, 26 Queen Street, EC4R 1BN. *T:* (020) 7242 2642.

CULLEN, Sir John; *see* Cullen, Sir E. J.

CULLEN, Hon. Sir Michael (John), KNZM 2012; PhD; Chairman, New Zealand Post, since 2010 (Deputy Chairman, 2009–10); *b* London, 5 Feb. 1945; adopted NZ citizenship, 1975; *s* of John Joseph Thomas Cullen and Ivy May Cullen; *m* 1st, 1967, Rowena Joy Knight (marr. diss. 1987); two *d*; 2nd, 1989, Lowson Anne Collins. *Educ:* Christ's Coll., Christchurch; Canterbury Univ. (BA 1965; MA Hist. 1967); Edinburgh Univ. (PhD Social and Economic Hist.). Asst Lectr, Univ. of Canterbury; Tutor, Univ. of Stirling; Sen. Lectr, Univ. of Otago. MP (Lab) St Kilda, 1981–96, Dunedin S, 1996–99, List MP (Lab), 1999–2009. Sen. Govt Whip, 1984–87; Associate Minister of Finance, 1987–90; Minister of Social Welfare, 1987–90; Associate Minister of Health, 1988–90; Associate Minister of Labour, 1989–90; opposition spokesperson on social welfare, war pensions and Accident Compensation Corp., 1990–91, on finance, 1991; Minister of Revenue, 1999–2005; Treasurer, Minister of Finance and Leader of the House, 1999–2008; Dep. Prime Minister, 2002–08; Minister for Tertiary Education, 2005–08; Attorney General, 2005–08. Dep. Leader, NZ Labour Party, 1996. Vis. Fellow, ANU. Hon. LLD Otago, 2010. *Publications:* The Statistical Movement in Early Victorian Britain, 1974; Lawfully Occupied, 1979; articles in jls. *Recreations:* music, reading, golf, house renovation. *Address:* New Zealand Post, Level 12, New Zealand Post House, 7 Waterloo Quay, Wellington 6011, New Zealand.

CULLEN, Paul Benedict; *see* Pentland, Hon. Lord.

CULLEY, Ronald; author; Director: Liberabit UK, since 2010; Liberabit International, since 2013; *b* 2 Feb. 1950; *s* of Ronald Frank Culley and Mary McTavish Culley (*née* McLeod); *m* 1st, 1973, Margaret Ferguson (marr. diss. 1985); two *s*; 2nd, 1994, Jean Pollock; two *s*. *Educ:* Craigbank Comprehensive Sch.; Jordanhill Coll. of Educn (Dip. YCS); Moray House Coll. of Educn (CQSW, CSW); Univ. of Glasgow (Cert. Supervisory Mgt); Univ. of Strathclyde (MSc); Univ. of St Andrews (CTS). Various social work and social policy posts, Strathclyde Regl Council, 1975–87; Chief Executive: Govan Initiative Ltd, 1987–2000; Scottish Enterprise Glasgow, 2000–06; Strathclyde Partnership for Transport, 2006–10. Mem. Bd, Police Adv. Bd for Scotland, 1999–2005. Member Board: Scottish Urban Regeneration Foundn, 1992–2006; Quality Scotland, 1999–2000; Glasgow Alliance, 2000–06; Glasgow Economic Forum, 2001–06; Prince's Trust Glasgow, 2002–06; Wise Gp, 2003–10; Glasgow Community Planning Partnership, 2004–10; Clyde Valley Community Planning Partnership, 2004–10; Glasgow Sci. Centre, 2004–06. Sec., Ibrox Community Trust, 1990–99. Panel Mem., Investors in People, 1999–2002. Mem., British Transport Police Authy, 2008–10. Dir, 2011–, Trustee, 2013–, Harmony Row Developments Ltd. Dir, Bd of Trustees, Humanist Soc. of Scotland, 2014–15. Contested (SLP) Scotland W, Scottish Parly elecns, 1999. Gov., Scottish Police Trng Coll., 1999–2004. Hon. Mem., Harmony Row Youth Club, 2000–. *Publications:* The New Guards, 1999; I Belong to Glasgow, 2009, 2nd edn 2010; The Kaibab Resolution, 2010; Glasgow Belongs To Me, 2011; A Confusion of Mandarins 2011; The Patriot Game, 2013; Shoeshine Man, 2014; One Year, 2015. *Recreations:* family and friends, music, Association football (particularly Manchester United), socialising, reading biographies, Scottish, American and Irish politics, irreverence, song-writing, Glasgow memorabilia, convivial temulence, oenology, Humanism. *Address:* Liberabit UK, Garret Studios, Sutherland Drive, Glasgow G46 6PL. *T:* 07860 530972. *E:* author@ronculley.com. *W:* www.ronculley.com, www.twitter.com/lblogtoglasgow. *Clubs:* Griffin, Potstill (Glasgow).

CULLIMORE, Charles Augustine Kaye, CMG 1993; HM Diplomatic Service, retired; *b* 2 Oct. 1933; *s* of Rev. Canon Charles Cullimore and Constance Alicia Kaye Cullimore (*née* Grimshaw); *m* 1956, Val Elizabeth Margot (*née* Willemsen); one *s* one *d*. *Educ:* Portora Royal Sch., Enniskillen; Trinity Coll., Oxford (MA). N Ireland Short Service Commn, 1955–57. HMOCS, Tanganyika, 1958–61; ICI Ltd, 1961–71; joined HM Diplomatic Service, 1971; FCO, 1971–73; Bonn, 1973–77; FCO, 1977–79; Counsellor, New Delhi, 1979–82; Dep. High Comr, Canberra, 1982–86; FCO, 1986–89; High Comr, Uganda, 1989–93. Chief Exec., Southern Africa Business Assoc., 1995–2001; Chm., British African Business Assoc., 2001–09. Dir, Transparency Internat. (UK), 1996–99. Council Member: Royal African Soc., 2000–10; Overseas Service Pensioners' Assoc., 2004– (Vice Chm., 2011; Chm., 2013). Hon. Pres., Business Council for Africa UK, 2009–. Member: The Pilgrims, 1993–; RIIA, 1996–; Britain-Australia Soc. *Publications:* (contrib.) Portora - The School on the Hill: a quatercentenary history 1608–2008, 2009; contrib. Jl of Mod. African Studies. *Recreations:* theatre, walking, travel. *Address:* Deacon House, Bidborough, Kent TN3 0UP. *Club:* Royal Over-Seas League.

CULLIMORE, Colin Stuart, CBE 1978; DL; Chairman, Lincoln Cathedral Council, 2000–07 (Member, Transitional Council, 1998–2000); *b* 13 July 1931; *s* of Reginald Victor Cullimore and May Maria Cullimore; *m* 1952, Kathleen Anyta Lamming; one *s*. *Educ:* Westminster Sch.; Grenoble Univ.; National Coll. of Food Technol. Commnd Royal Scots Fusiliers, 1951; seconded Parachute Regt; transf. when perm. officer cadre formed; Major 1956; 10th Bn Parachute Regt TA, 1960. Gen. Man., Payne & Son (Butchers) Ltd, 1960; Asst Gen. Man., J. H. Dewhurst Ltd, 1965, Gen. Man., 1969, Man. Dir, 1976–90; Dir of External

Affairs, Vestey Gp, 1990–92; Dir, Airborne Initiative Holdings Ltd, 1991–93; Chm., NAAFI, 1993–96 (non-exec. Dir, 1984–96); Director: Longhurst Housing Assoc., 1996–2001; Longhurst Gp, 2000–02 (Chm., Audit Cttee, 2000–02). Trustee, Western United Gp Pension Scheme, 1986–2010. Chairman: Retail Consortium Food Cttee, 1973–74; Multiple Shops Fedn, 1977–78; Vice-Chairman: Multiple Food Retailers Assoc., 1972–74; Retail Consortium, 1982–88 (Vice-Pres., 1990–92); Pres., British Retailers Assoc., 1984–89 (Vice Pres., 1978–84); Dep. Chm., Meat Promotion Exec., 1975–78; Vice Pres., Bd of Admin, CECD (European Retailers), 1986–88 (Mem., 1981–85); Gov., Coll. for Distributive Trades, 1976–79 (Vice Chm.), 1984–88. Member: EDC for Distribn Trades, 1972–80; Council and Management Cttee, Inst. of Meat (Vice-Chm., 1981–83); Cttee of Commerce and Distribn, EEC, 1984–93; Council, Industry & Parlt Trust, 1987–93. Chm. Council, Westminster Sch. Soc., 1999–2007 (Mem., 1990–2008). Vice Pres., Royal Smithfield Club, 1991– (Mem. Council, 1993–95). Gov., Court of London Inst., 1984–87 and 1989–90; Exec. Trustee, Airborne Assault Normandy Trust, 1983–2004; Chm., Reserve Forces Ulysses Trust, 1992–96; Member: Regtl Council, Parachute Regt, 1991–97; Lincoln Diocese Trust and Bd of Finances, 1993–2001 (Chm. Resources Cttee, 1994–96). FInstD 1979; CCMI (CBIM 1984); FRSA 1987. Liveryman, Butchers' Co. (Mem. Court, 1992–2007; Warden, 1998–2003; Providitor, 2002–03; Master, 2004–05). DL Lincs, 1998. Gold Medal: Inst. of Meat, 1956; Butchers' Co., 1956. OStJ 1988. *Address:* 20 Minster Yard, Lincoln LN2 1PY. *T:* (01522) 569581, *Fax:* (01522) 524205. *E:* colincullimore@yahoo.co.uk. *Clubs:* Naval and Military, Farmers.

CULLINAN, Edward Horder, CBE 1987; RA 1991; RDI 2010; Chairman, Cullinan Studio (formerly Edward Cullinan Architects Ltd), since 1989 (Founder, 1965, and Senior Partner, 1965–89, Edward Cullinan Architects); *b* 17 July 1931; *s* of Dr Edward Cullinan and Joy (*née* Horder); *m* 1961, Rosalind Yeates; one *s* two *d*. *Educ:* Ampleforth Coll.; Cambridge Univ. (Anderson and Webb Schol., 1951; BA); Univ. of California at Berkeley (George VI Meml Fellow, 1956). AADip; RIBA. With Denys Lasdun, 1958–65. Bannister Fletcher Prof., UCL, 1978–79; Graham Willis Prof., Univ. of Sheffield, 1985–87; George Simpson Prof., Univ. of Edinburgh, 1987–90; Special Prof., Univ. of Nottingham, 2004–09. Mem., Royal Fine Art Commn, 1996–99. Designed and built: Horder House, Hampshire, 1959–60; Minster Lovell Mill, 1969–72; Parish Ch. of St Mary, Barnes, 1978–84; Lambeth Community Care Centre, 1979–84; RMC Internat. HQ, 1985–90; Fountains Abbey visitor centre and landscape, 1987–92; Archeolink Visitor Centre, Oyne, Aberdeenshire, 1994–97; Faculty of Divinity, 1995–2000, Centre for Mathematical Scis, 1996–2002, Cambridge Univ.; Univ. of East London, 1997–99; Downland Gridshell, Weald and Downland Open Air Mus., 1997–2002; Greenwich Millennium Sch. and Health Centre, 1998–2001; Singapore Mgt Univ., 2000–; Clink St, Southwark, 2000–09; Stonebridge Hillside Hub, W London, 2005–09; Maggie's Centre, Freeman Hospital, Newcastle upon Tyne, 2010. Masterplans: Univ. of N Carolina, 1996; Bristol Harbourside, 2000–; Masshouse, Birmingham, 2002–; Chinese Univ., Hong Kong, 2007–09; Shahat Garden City, Libya, 2009–11; all have received awards and been published internationally. FRSA 1984; Hon. FRIAS 1995; Hon. RIAI 2011; Hon. RAIC 2012. Royal Gold Medal, RIBA, 2008. *Publications:* Edward Cullinan, Architects, 1984; (with K. Powell) Edward Cullinan, Architect, 1995; *relevant publication:* Ends Middles Beginnings: Edward Cullinan Architects, by Jonathan Hale, 2005; contribs to many architectural jls. *Recreations:* horticulture, travel, building, history, geography. *Address:* 5 Baldwin Terrace, N1 7RU. *T:* (020) 7704 1975.

CULLINAN, Nicholas Robert, PhD; Director, National Portrait Gallery, since 2015; *b* New Haven, Conn, 29 Dec. 1977; *s* of Brian Cullinan and Valerie Cullinan. *Educ:* Courtauld Inst. of Art, Univ. of London (BA Hist. of Art 2002; MA Hist. of Art 2003; PhD 2010). Curator: Internat. Modern Art, Tate Modern, London, 2007–13; Modern and Contemp. Art, Metropolitan Mus. of Art, NY, 2013–15. Thaw Sen. Fellow, Morgan Liby and Mus., NY, 2013. *Recreations:* travel, reading, opera. *Address:* National Portrait Gallery, St Martin's Place, WC2H 0HE. *E:* ncullinan@npg.org.uk.

CULLINGFORD, Martin James; Editor, since 2011, and Publisher, since 2014, Gramophone; *b* Frimley, 3 Aug. 1978; *s* of Rodney and Jacqueline Cullingford; *m* 2001, Jasmine Wan; one *d*. *Educ:* Kirkley High Sch., Lowestoft; Girton Coll., Cambridge (BA Hist. 2000). Staff writer, Pensions Mgt, 2000–02; Gramophone: News and Online Ed., 2002–04; Features Ed., 2005–06; Dep. Ed., 2006–10; Ed., Gramophone Online, 2010–11. *Recreations:* classical guitar, seeking out off-the-beaten-path museums and galleries, road cycling (riding and cheering), church music and architecture, real ale. *Address:* Gramophone, Mark Allen Group, St Jude's Church, Dulwich Road, SE24 0PB. *T:* (020) 7501 6361. *E:* martin.cullingford@markallengroup.com.

CULLIS, Prof. Anthony George, DPhil, DSc; FRS 2004; Professor of Semiconductor Nanocharacterisation (formerly of Electronic and Electrical Engineering), University of Sheffield, 1995, now Emeritus; *b* 16 Jan. 1946; *s* of late George Thomas Cullis and Doris Mary Cullis; *m* 1979, Ruth Edith Allen; one *s* one *d*. *Educ:* Royal Grammar Sch., Worcester; Wadham Coll., Oxford (MA, DPhil, DSc). Mem. Tech. Staff, Bell Labs, Murray Hill, USA, 1972–75; posts to SPSO (Individual Merit), DERA/QinetiQ, Malvern, 1975–95. Chairman: Electron Microscopy and Analysis Gp, Inst. of Physics, 1980–82; Wkg Party on Transient Annealing, DoI, 1981–84; SERC MSEC Instrumentation Panel, 1988–93; Mem., Functional Materials Coll., EPSRC, 1997–. Pres., Scientific Council, TASC Italian Nat. Lab., Trieste, 2001–03. Ed., Procs vols for Microscopy of Semiconducting Materials internat. conf. series, 1979–; Co-ordinating Ed., Materials Sci. and Engrg Reports, 1994–. Holliday Award, IMMM, 1984. *Publications:* numerous refereed scientific papers in learned jls and other media. *Recreations:* philately, armchair archaeology, motoring. *Address:* Department of Electronic and Electrical Engineering, University of Sheffield, Mappin Street, Sheffield S1 3JD. *T:* (0114) 222 5407, *Fax:* (0114) 272 6391. *E:* a.g.cullis@sheffield.ac.uk.

CULLIS, Prof. Charles Fowler; Professor of Physical Chemistry, City University, 1967–84, now Emeritus (Head, Chemistry Department, 1973–84; Pro-Vice-Chancellor, 1980–84; Saddlers' Research Professor, 1984–87; Leverhulme Emeritus Research Fellow, 1987–89); *b* 31 Aug. 1922; 2nd *s* of late Prof. C. G. Cullis, Prof. of Mining Geology, Univ. of London, and Mrs W. J. Cullis (*née* Fowler); *m* 1958, Marjorie Elizabeth, *er d* of late Sir Austin and Lady Anderson; two *s* two *d*. *Educ:* Stowe Sch. (Open Schol.); Trinity Coll., Oxford. BA 1944, BSc 1st Cl. Hons Chem. 1945, DPhil 1948, MA 1948, DSc 1960; FRSC (FRIC 1958); FRSA. ICI Research Fellow in Chem., Oxford, 1947–50; Lectr in Phys. Chem., Imperial Coll., London, 1950–59; Sen. Lectr in Chem. Engrg and Chem. Tech., Imperial Coll., 1959–64; Reader in Combustion Chemistry, Univ. of London, 1964–66. Vis. Prof., College of Chem., Univ. of California, Berkeley, 1966; Vis. Scientist, CSIRO, Sydney, 1970. Mem. Council, Chem. Soc., 1969–72, 1975–78; Hon. Sec., Brit. Sect. of Combustion Inst., 1969–74; Mem., Rockets Sub-cttee, 1968–73, and of Combustion Sub-cttee, 1969–72, Aeronautical Research Council; Member: Navy Dept Fuels and Lubricants Adv. Cttee (Fire and Explosion Hazards Working Gp), 1967–83; Safety in Mines Research Adv. Bd, 1973–88 (Chm., 1980–88); Chem. Cttee, Defence Sci. Adv. Council, 1979–82; Chem. Bd, 1982–87, Phys. Sci. Cttee, 1987–89, CNAA. Scientific Editor, Internat. Union of Pure and Applied Chem., 1976–78. Non-exec. Dir, City Technology Ltd, 1977–91. Mem., Mid Sussex DC, 1986–95. Mem. Council, Sussex Univ., 1993–95; Governor, City of London Polytechnic, 1982–84. Trustee, Sino-British Fellowship Trust, 1992–2002. Freeman, City of London, 1983; Liveryman, Bakers' Co., 1983. Joseph Priestley Award, 1974, Combustion Chem. Medal and Award, 1978, Chem. Soc. *Publications:* The Combustion of Organic Polymers (jtly with M. M. Hirschler), 1981; numerous sci. papers in Proc. Royal Soc., Trans Faraday Soc., Jl Chem. Soc., etc, mainly concerned with chemistry of combustion reactions. *Recreations:* music, travel. *Address:* Church Farm Barn, Coombe Bissett, Salisbury SP5 4LR. *T:* (01722) 718006. *Club:* Athenæum.

CULLODEN, Lord; Xan Richard Anders Windsor; *b* 12 March 2007; *o s* and heir of Earl of Ulster, *qv*.

CULLOTY, James Hugh; racehorse trainer, since 2006; *b* 18 Dec. 1973; *s* of Donal and Maureen Culloty; *m* 2004, Susannah Samworth; two *s* one *d*. *Educ:* St Brendan's Coll., Killarney. Stable jockey to Miss Henrietta Knight, 1996–2005; winner: Grand National, on Bindaree, 2002; Cheltenham Gold Cup, on Best Mate, 2002, 2003, 2004; Irish Grand National, on Timbera, 2003; Cheltenham Gold Cup, on Lord Windermere, 2014. *Recreations:* golf, farming. *Address:* Mount Corbitt, Churchtown, Mallow, Co. Cork, Ireland. *T:* (22) 49776. *W:* www.jimculloty.net.

CULLUM, Prof. Dame Nicola Anne, (Prof. Dame Nicky), DBE 2013; PhD; FMedSci; Professor of Nursing, since 2011, and Head, School of Nursing, Midwifery and Social Care, since 2015, University of Manchester; *b* Leeds, 6 June 1962; *d* of Ian and Brenda Cullum; *m* 1998, Deepak Popli; one *s* one *d*. *Educ:* Univ. of Liverpool (BSc Hons Pharmacol. 1984; PhD Pharmacol. 1990). RGN 1985. Res. Fellow, Nursing Practice Res. Unit, Univ. of Surrey, 1988–90; Lectr, Dept of Nursing, Univ. of Liverpool, 1990–94; University of York: Res. Fellow, Centre for Health Econs, 1994–96; Reader, 1996–2001, Prof., 2001–11, Dept of Health Scis. Prof., 2011, Hon. Prof., 2014–, Sch. of Nursing and Midwifery, Griffith Univ., Qld; Hon. Vis. Prof., Dept of Health Scis, Univ. of York, 2011–. NIHR Sen. Investigator, 2008–. FMedSci 2012; FAAN 2012. *Publications:* contrib. articles to jls on wounds, wound care and evidence-based nursing. *Recreations:* family, music, art, watching basketball. *Address:* School of Nursing, Midwifery and Social Work, University of Manchester, Jean McFarlane Building, Oxford Road, Manchester M13 9PL. *T:* (0161) 306 7779. *E:* nicky.cullum@manchester.ac.uk.

CULLUM, Peter Geoffrey, CBE 2011; FCII; non-executive Deputy Chairman, Towergate Partnership Ltd, since 2011 (founding Executive Chairman, 1997–2011); *b* Norwich; *s* of Geoffrey and Doreen Cullum; *m* 2000, Ann Fulton; one *s* two *d*. *Educ:* City of Norwich Grammar Sch. for Boys; Cass Business Sch., City Univ., London (MSc, DSc; PhD Business Admin 2008); City Business Sch. (MBA 1975). FCII 1971; ACIM 2002. Inspector, Royal Insce, 1969–74; Commercial Union: Mktg Exec., 1975–82; Mktg Dir, London and Edinburgh, 1987–91; CEO, Economic Insce, 1991–96; Mktg Dir, Hiscox plc, 1996–97. Chairman: Global Risk Partners Ltd, 2013–; Minority Venture Partners Ltd, 2013–. Vice Pres., Nat. Autistic Soc., 2012–. FRSA. *Publications:* Panic, Passion and Power, 2007; contrib. articles to insce sector jls. *Recreations:* golf, tennis, reading, spectator at most sports. *Address:* Towergate Partnership Ltd, Towergate House, Eclipse Park, Sittingbourne Road, Maidstone, Kent ME14 3EN.

CULME-SEYMOUR, Sir Michael Patrick; *see* Seymour.

CULPIN, Sir Robert (Paul), Kt 2001; Managing Director, Budget and Public Finances, HM Treasury, 1998–2003. *Educ:* Christ's Coll., Cambridge (BA 1968); Harvard Univ.; California Univ. HM Treasury, 1965–2003; Press Sec. and Hd of Information, 1984–87; Under-Sec., Fiscal Policy Div., 1987–93; Dep. Sec., Public Finance, 1993–94; Second Permanent Sec., 1994; Dir, Public Expenditure, then Public Spending, 1994–98. *Address:* c/o HM Treasury, 1 Horse Guards Road, SW1A 2HQ.

CULSHAW, John Douglas; Assistant Chief Scientific Adviser (Capabilities), Ministry of Defence, 1985–87; *b* 22 Oct. 1927; *s* of Alfred Henry Douglas Culshaw and Dorothy Yeats Culshaw (*née* Hogarth); *m* 1951, Hazel Speirs Alexander (*d* 1998); one *s* one *d*. *Educ:* Washington Alderman Smith Grammar Sch., Co. Durham; University Coll., Nottingham. BSc London 1949; MSc Nottingham 1950. Joined Weapons Dept, Royal Aircraft Estabt, Min. of Supply, Farnborough, 1950; OC (Scientific) 6 Joint Services Trials Unit RAF (UK), 1956; OC (Sci.) 16 JSTU RA Weapons Research Estabt, Salisbury, S Australia, 1961; Co-ordinating Research and Development Authority Technical Project Officer, RAE, 1964; Supt Mine Warfare Br., Royal Armament R&D Estabt, MoD, Sevenoaks, 1967; Director, Scientific Adv. Br., Home Office, 1970; Dept of Chief Scientific Adviser (Army), 1972; Head of Mathematics and Assessment Dept, RARDE, MoD, Sevenoaks, 1974; Head of Defence Science II, MoD, 1975; RCDS 1976; Dep. Dir, Scientific and Technical Intelligence, 1977; Dir, Defence Operational Analysis Estabt and Asst Chief Scientific Advr (Studies), MoD, 1979–84. *Recreation:* historical research. *Club:* Civil Service.

CULSHAW, Robert Nicholas, MVO 1979; Deputy Director, British Antarctic Survey, 2006–12; HM Diplomatic Service, retired; *b* 22 Dec. 1952; *s* of late Ivan Culshaw and Edith Marjorie Jose Barnard; *m* 1977, Elaine Ritchie Clegg; one *s*. *Educ:* University Coll. Sch., Hampstead; King's Coll., Cambridge (BA 1st Cl. Hons Classics 1974; Major Univ. Scholarship for Classics, 1974; MA 1977). FCO, 1974–75; MECAS, Lebanon and Jordan, 1975–77; 3rd Sec., Muscat, 1977–79; 2nd Sec., Khartoum, 1979–80; 1st Sec., Rome, 1980–84; FCO, 1984–88; Head of Chancery, 1988–90, Dep. Hd of Mission and Consul-Gen., 1991–93, Athens; FCO Spokesman and Hd of News Dept, 1993–95; Minister-Counsellor, Washington, 1995–99; Consul Gen., Chicago, 1999–2003; Dir, Americas and Overseas Territories, FCO, 2003–05. Churchill Fellow, Westminster Coll., Fulton, 2001. Mem. Bd, US Friends of Leonard Cheshire, 1998–2005; Trustee, Lady Ryder of Warsaw Foundn (formerly Bouverie Foundn), 2007–10. Mem. Bd, Cambridge Leisure and Ice Centre, 2013–. Vice Chm., Cambridge Univ. Music Soc., 2008–10 (Singing Mem., 2005–). MCIL (MIL 2004); FRSA 1995; FRGS 2007. *Recreations:* ski-ing, singing, cricket, poetry, languages. *Address:* Piney Lodge, 66 Cow Lane, Fulbourn, Cambridge CB21 5HB. *E:* robert.culshaw@me.com.

CULVER, John Howard, LVO 2000; HM Diplomatic Service, retired; *b* 17 July 1947; *s* of late Frank and Peggy Culver; *m* 1973, Margaret Ann Davis; two *s* one *d*. Entered FO, 1968; Moscow, 1974–76; La Paz, 1977–80; FCO, 1980–83; Rome, 1983–87; Head of Chancery, Dhaka, 1987–90; FCO, 1990–92; Ambassador to Nicaragua, 1992–97; Consul-General, Naples, 1997–99; Rome, 2000; Ambassador to Iceland, 2001–04; Hd of Resources, Europe Directorate-Gen., FCO, 2004–05; Chargé d'Affaires *ai*, Holy See, 2005. *E:* john@theculvers.com.

CULYER, Prof. Anthony John, CBE 1999; Professor of Economics, University of York, 1979–2014, on leave of absence, 2003–06, now Emeritus (Director of Health Development, 1997–2001); Chief Scientist, Institute for Work and Health, Toronto, 2003–06; Adjunct Professor, University of Toronto, since 2014 (Ontario Research Chair in Health Policy and System Design, 2007–14); *b* 1 July 1942; *s* of late Thomas Reginald Culyer and Betty Ely (*née* Headland); *m* 1966, Sieglinde Birgit (*d* 2011); one *s* one *d*. *Educ:* King's Sch., Worcester; Exeter Univ. (BA Hons); Univ. of California at Los Angeles. Tutor and Asst Lectr, Exeter Univ., 1965–69; York University: Lectr, Sen. Lectr and Reader, 1969–79; Dep. Dir, Inst. of Social and Economic Research, 1971–82; Hd, Dept of Econs and Related Studies, 1986–2001; Pro-Vice-Chancellor, 1991–94; Dep. Vice-Chancellor, 1994–97. University of Toronto: Status-only Prof., 1989–2001 and Adjunct Prof., 2003–07. Sen. Research Associate, Ontario Economic Council, 1976, Vis. Professorial Lectr, Queen's Univ., Kingston, 1976; William Evans Vis. Professor, Otago Univ., 1979; Vis. Fellow, Australian National Univ., 1979; Visiting Professor: Trent Univ., 1985–86; Inst. für Med. Informatik und Systemforschung, Munich, 1990–91; Toronto Univ., 1991; Central Inst. of Technology, NZ,

1996; Adjunct Scientist, Inst. for Work & Health, Toronto, 2007–. Lectures: Woodward, Univ. of BC, 1986; Perey, McMaster Univ., and Champlain, Trent Univ., Canada, 1990; Francis Fraser, BPMF, 1994; Sinclair, Queen's Univ., Kingston, 2005. Member: Value Focus Gp on cost and benefit perspective of NICE, DoH, 2008; Policy Res. Units Commng Panel, DoH, DoH, 2009–. Member: Standing Cttee, Conf. of Heads of Univ. Depts of Econs, 1988–2001; Coll. Cttee, King's Fund Coll., London, 1989–92; Res. Adv. Cttee, 1990–2002, Sci. Adv. Cttee, 2002–03 (Sen. Scientist, 2006–07), Inst. for Work and Health, Toronto; Adv. Cttee for Centre for Health and Society, UCL, 1992–99; Rev. Adv. Cttee on London SHAs, 1992–93; Adv. Cttee, Canadian Inst. for Advanced Res., 1992–2002; Future Health Care Options Wkg Pty, IHSM, 1992–93; British Council Health Adv. Cttee, 1995–97; Academic Adv. Council, Univ. of Buckingham, 1996–2004; Chm., Res. Adv. Council, Workers' Safety and Insurance Bd, Ontario, 2006–08; Vice Chm., Nat. Inst. for Clinical Excellence, 1999–2003. Royal School of Church Music: Chm., York Dist, 1984–95, NE Yorks Area, 1995–2003; Mem. Adv. Bd, 2002–; Mem. Council, and Trustee, 2003–10. Mem., 1982–90, non-exec. Mem., 1990–92, Northallerton HA; Dep. Chm., N Yorks HA, 1995–99 (non-exec. Mem., 1994–99); Member: Yorks RHA R&D Cttee, 1992–94; Northern and Yorks Regl R&D Adv. Cttee, 1995–; Central R&D Cttee, NHS, 1991–2001; NHS Standing Gp on Health Technol., 1992–97; R&D Cttee of High Security Psychiatric Hosps Commissioning Bd, 1995–99; Chair: Methodology Panel, NHS Standing Gp on Health Technol., 1993–97; NHS Task Force on Supporting R&D in NHS, 1994; Advr to NHS Dir of R&D, 1997–99; Chm., R&D Cttee, NICE, 2007–10; Mem. Adv. Cttee, NICE Internat., 2009– (Chair, 2011–). Chm., Office of Health Econs, 2001–13 (Chm., Editl Bd, 1997–); Mem., Economics Adv. Panel, Home Office, 2005–08. Ontario Ministry of Health and Long Term Care: Member: Equity Editl Bd, 2006; Career Scientist Relevance Rev. Panel, 2007–; Health Res. Adv. Council, 2007–; Ext. Adv. Gp, Health System Strategy Div., 2009–; Adv. Gp on Productivity, 2009–; Steering Cttee for Partnerships for Health System Improvement, 2009–; Bd, Canadian Agency for Drugs and Technologies in Health, 2013–; Special Advr, Canada Health Council, 2005–07; Sen. Economic Advr, Cancer Care Ontario, 2006–07; Chair, Res. Adv. Council, Workplace Safety and Insce Bd (Ontario), 2006–10. Trustee, Canadian Health Services Res. Foundn, 2000–03. Pres., Econs Section, BAAS, 1994. Founder FMedSci 1998. Ed.-in-Chief, Elsevier online Encyclopedia of Health Econs, 2009–; Co-Editor, Jl of Health Econs, 1982–2013; Member, Editorial Board: Econ. Rev., 1983–95; Med. Law Internat., 1992–; BMJ, 1995–2000; Mem. Managing Cttee, Jl of Med. Ethics, 1994–2001. Hon. DEc Stockholm Sch. of Econs, 1999. *Publications:* The Economics of Social Policy, 1973; (ed with M. H. Cooper) Health Economics, 1973; (ed) Economic Policies and Social Goals, 1974; Need and the National Health Service, 1976; (with J. Wiseman and A. Walker) Annotated Bibliography of Health Economics, 1977; (ed with V. Halberstadt) Human Resources and Public Finance, 1977; Measuring Health: Lessons for Ontario, 1978; (ed with K. G. Wright) Economic Aspects of Health Services, 1978; The Political Economy of Social Policy, 1980; (ed) Health Indicators, 1983; (ed with B. Horisberger) Economic and Medical Evaluation of Health Care Technologies, 1983; Economics, 1985; (ed with G. Terny) Public Finance and Social Policy, 1985; (ed with B. Jonsson) Public and Private Health Services: complementarities and conflicts, 1986; (jtly) The International Bibliography of Health Economics: a comprehensive annotated guide to English language sources since 1914, 1986; Canadian Health Care Expenditures: myth and reality, past and future, 1988; (ed) Standards for the Socio-economic Evaluation of Health Care Products and Services, 1990; (ed jtly) Competition in Health Care: reforming the NHS, 1990; (ed) The Economics of Health, 1991; (ed jtly) Some Recent Developments in Health Economics, 1992; (ed jtly) Swedish Health Care: the best in the world?, 1993; (ed jtly) Reforming Health Care Systems: experiments with the NHS, 1996; (ed jtly) Being Reasonable about the Economics of Health: selected essays by Alan Williams, 1997; (ed jtly) Handbook of Health Economics, 2001; The Dictionary of Health Economics, 2005, 3rd edn 2014; Health Economics: critical perspectives on the world economy, 4 vols, 2006; (jtly) Economic Evaluation of Interventions for Occupational Health and Safety, 2008; The Humble Economist: Tony Culyer on health, health care and social decision making, 2012; (ed jtly) Portrait of a Health Economist: festschrift in honour of Bengt Jönsson, 2014; articles in Oxford Econ. Papers, Economica, Scottish Jl of Political Economy, Public Finance, Jl of Public Economics, Kyklos, Qly Jl of Economics, Jl Royal Statistical Soc., Jl of Health Economics, Health Econs, BMJ, Jl Med Ethics, and others. *Recreations:* church music (Organist and Choir Director, St Catherine's, Barmby Moor, 1971–2003), music generally. *Address:* Centre for Health Economics, University of York, York YO10 5DD. *E:* tony.culyer@york.ac.uk; Department of Health Policy Management and Evaluation, University of Toronto, 155 College Street, Toronto, ON M5T 3M6, Canada.

CUMANI, Luca Matteo; racehorse trainer; *b* 7 April 1949; *s* of Sergio Cumani and Elena Cardini Cumani; *m* 1979, Sara Doon Plunket; one *s* one *d*. *Educ:* Milan. Riding career: 85 winners in Italy, France and UK; champion amateur, Italy, 1972; won Moët and Chandon on Meissen, 1972; Prix Paul Noël de la Houtre on Harland, 1970, 1972, 1973; Asst to Sergio Cumani and to H. R. A. Cecil, 1974–75; first held licence, 1976; numerous major races won, incl. St Leger (Commanche Run), 1984; Derby and Irish Sweeps Derby, 1988 (Kahyasi); Breeders Cup Mile, 1994 (Barathea); Derby, 1998 (High Rise); Coral Eclipse Stakes, Sandown, 2003 (Falbrav); Juddmonte Internat. Stakes, 2003 (Falbrav); Queen Elizabeth II Stakes, Ascot, 2003 (Falbrav); Prix du Moulin, Longchamp, 2005 (Starcraft); Japan Cup, 2005 (Alkaased); Queen Elizabeth Cup, Hong Kong, 2009 (Presvis); Dubai Duty Free, 2011 (Presvis); King George VI and Queen Elizabeth Stakes, Ascot, 2015 (Postponed); Qatar Prix Foy, Longchamp, 2015 (Postponed). *Address:* Bedford House Stables, Bury Road, Newmarket, Suffolk CB8 7BX. *T:* (01638) 665432.

CUMBERLEGE, family name of **Baroness Cumberlege**.

CUMBERLEGE, Baroness *cr* 1990 (Life Peer), of Newick in the County of East Sussex; **Julia Frances Cumberlege,** CBE 1985; FRCP, FRCGP; Founder and Director: Cumberlege Connections Ltd, since 2001; Cumberlege Eden and Partners, since 2013; Director, Assuring Better Practice (UK) Ltd, 2004–07; Associate, Quo Health, 2001–05; *b* 27 Jan. 1943; *d* of late Dr L. U. Camm and M. G. G. Camm; *m* 1961, Patrick Francis Howard Cumberlege; three *s*. *Educ:* Convent of the Sacred Heart, Tunbridge Wells. FRCP 2007; FRCGP 2007; FRCOG 2013. Mem., East Sussex AHA, 1977–81; Chairman: Brighton HA, 1981–88; SW Thames RHA, 1988–92; Mem. Council, NAHA, 1982–88 (Vice-Chm., 1984–87; Chm., 1987–88). Member (C): Lewes DC, 1966–79 (Leader, 1977–78); East Sussex CC, 1974–85 (Chm., Social Services Cttee, 1979–82). Chairman: Review of Community Nursing for England, 1985 (report, Neighbourhood Nursing—a focus for care, 1986); Expert Maternity Gp, 1993 (report, Changing Childbirth, 1993). Member: Social Security Adv. Cttee, 1980–82; DHSS Expert Adv. Gp on AIDS, 1987–89; Council, UK Central Council for Nursing, Midwifery and Health Visiting, 1989–92; NHS Policy Bd, 1989–97. Parly Under-Sec. of State, DoH, 1992–97; Co-Chm., Associate Parly Health Gp, 2001–; Jt Chm., All Party Parly Osteoporosis Gp, 2000–; Jt Chm., All Party Parly Gp on Maternity, 2000–. Exec. Dir, MJM Healthcare Solutions, 1997–2001; Dir, Huntsworth plc, 2001–03. Chairman: AMRC, 2007–12; Adv. Bd, Humana Europe, 2008–09. Lay Mem., 1977–83, Mem. Appts Commn, 1984–90, Press Council. Vice President: RCN, 1989– (Hon. FRCN 2010); Royal Coll. of Midwives, 2001–; Pres., Age UK (formerly Age Concern), E Sussex, 1995–; Mem. Council, ICRF, subseq. Cancer Res. UK, 1998–2007; Trustee: Princess Royal Trust for Carers, 1992–93; Life Education Centres, 1997–99; Patron: Nat. Childbirth Trust; Assoc. for Nurse Prescribing. Sen. Associate, King's Fund. Member Council: Brighton Poly., 1987–89; Univ. of Sussex, 2001–09; Chm. Trustees, Chailey Heritage Sch., 1997– (Governor, 1982–88); Chm. Council, St George's, Univ. of London (formerly St George's Hosp. Med. Sch.), 2000–07; Trustee, Leeds Castle Foundn, 2005–. Governor: Chailey Comprehensive Sch., 1972–86; Ringmer Comprehensive Sch., 1979–85; Newick Primary Sch., 1977–85; Lancing Coll., 2013–. Founder: Newick Playgp; Newick Youth Club. Fellow, Royal Coll. of Chiropractors, 2013. FRSA 1989. DL 1986, Vice Lord-Lieut, 1992, E Sussex; JP East Sussex, 1973–85. DUniv: Surrey, 1990; Brighton, 1994; Northampton, 2009; Hon. DSc (Med.) London, 2006. *Recreations:* bicycling, other people's gardens. *Address:* Snells Cottage, The Green, Newick, Lewes, East Sussex BN8 4LA. *T:* (01825) 722154, *Fax:* (01825) 723873. *Club:* Royal Society of Medicine.

CUMING, Frederick George Rees, RA 1974 (ARA 1969); ARCA 1954; NDD 1948; NEAC 1960; painter; *b* 16 Feb. 1930; *m* 1962, Audrey Lee Cuming; one *s* one *d*. *Educ:* University School, Bexley Heath; Sidcup Art School; Royal College of Art; travelling schol., Italy. Exhibns in Redfern, Walker, New Grafton, Thackeray, Fieldborne Galleries; Group shows at NEAC, RA, Schools' Exhibn, John Moores London Group; One Man exhibns at Thackeray Gall., galls in Chichester, Lewes, Eastbourne, Guildford, Durham, Chester, Folkestone, Canterbury, New York; featured artist, RA Summer Exhibn, 2001; artist in residence, Christchurch Coll., Canterbury, 2015; works in collections: DoE; Treasury; Chantrey Bequest; RA; Kendal Mus.; Scunthorpe Mus.; Bradford; Carlisle; Nat. Mus. of Wales; Brighton and Hove Mus.; Maidstone Mus.; Towner Gall., Eastbourne; Monte Carlo Mus.; St John's Coll., Oxford; Worcester Coll., Oxford; Faringdon Trust, Oxon; ITV collection; Southend Mus.; Preston Mus.; Nat. Trust collection; Barings Bank; Lloyd's; Guinness collection; W. H. Smith; Nat. Portrait Gall.; City private collections; portrait of Prof. Stephen Hawking, NPG; works in galls in America, Argentina, Canada, Chile, France, Germany, Greece, Holland, Hong Kong and S Africa. Hon. ROI 1992; Hon. RBA. Hon. DLitt Kent, 2005. Grand Prix, Art Contemporaine, Monte Carlo. *Publications:* Figure in a Landscape, 2000; Another Figure in the Landscape, 2014. *Address:* The Gables, Wittersham Road, Iden, near Rye, E Sussex TN31 7UY. *T:* (01797) 280322.

CUMMINES, Robert, OBE 2011; Chief Executive, Unlock, 2002–12 (Deputy Chief Executive, 1999–2002); Founder and Chief Executive, MIDAS Association for Disadvantaged People; *b* Islington, 23 Nov. 1951; *s* of Frederick George Francis Cummines and Mary Cummines (*née* Passmore); *m* 2009, Ayumi Yokozéki; one step *s*; one *d* (and one *d* decd) from previous marriage. Criminal and prisoner, 1969–88; volunteer, SOVA: Supporting Others through Volunteer Action, 1989–90; Purchasing Manager, Van Gell Systems, Holland, 1991–93; Mem., On-call Critical Response Team, Stonham Housing Assoc., 1993–99. Sessional Lectr, Kent Univ. Formerly: Mem., Adv. Gp, ODPM; Specialist Advr, Zahid Mubarek Public Inquiry; Mem., H of C Home Affairs Select Cttee Inquiry on Rehabilitation of Offenders Act; Expert Witness to H of C Home Affairs Select Cttee on Prisoner Educn. Mem., SE Regl Reducing Re-offending Delivery Bd, Nat. Offender Mgt Service, MoJ; former Mem., Mgt Bd, Exodus: Ex-Offenders Discharged Under Supervision. Contrib. to BBC, ITV and Sky TV, radio and nat. newspapers. FRSA. MUniv Open, 2012. *Publications:* I Am Not a Gangster (autobiog.), 2014. *Club:* National Liberal.

CUMMING, Alexander James; Chief Executive (formerly Project Director), IMMPACT (Initiative for Maternal Mortality Project), since 2004; *b* 7 March 1947; *s* of Alexander George Cumming and Jean Campbell (*née* McWilliam); *m* 1973, Margaret Ada Callan; one *s* two *d*. *Educ:* Fordyce Acad., Banffshire; Robert Gordon's Coll., Aberdeen; Univ. of Aberdeen (MA). Mem., CIMA; IPFA. Volunteer teacher, VSO, India, 1968–70; Trainee Accountant, Wiggins Teape, Papermakers, 1970–72; Company Sec., Glen Gordon Ltd, Aberdeen, 1972–74; Chief Accountant, BOC Offshore, 1974–75; Accountant, then Dir of Finance, Grampian Health Bd, 1975–93; Actg Dir of Finance, Mgt Exec., Scottish Health Service, 1994; Chief Exec., Acute Services Div., NHS Grampian (formerly Aberdeen Royal Hosps, later Grampian Univ. Hosps NHS Trust), 1994–2004. Chm., Langstane Housing Assoc., 1997–2002 (Hon. Treas., 1984–97). *Recreations:* music, literature, history, the outdoors. *Address:* (office) IMMPACT, University of Aberdeen, Health Sciences Building, Foresterhill, Aberdeen AB25 2ZD.

CUMMING, Sir Alexander Penrose G.; *see* Gordon Cumming.

CUMMING, Maj. Gen. Andrew Alexander John Rennie, CBE 1993; Controller, Soldiers, Sailors, Airmen and Families Association—Forces Help, 2004–12; *b* 12 March 1948; *s* of Donald Alexander Cumming and Evelyn Julia (*née* Rennie); *m* 1979, Gilly Thompson; three *d*. *Educ:* Hawtreys Prep. Sch.; Bradfield Coll.; Army Staff Coll. In command 17th/21st Lancers, 1988–90; hcsc 1992; Commander: 20 Armd Bde, 1992; 11 Armd Bde/British Forces, Croatia and Bosnia-Herzegovina, 1992–93; ACOS Ops, HQ LAND, 1993–95; Chief Jt Ops Centre, Intervention Force (IFOR), 1995–96; Comdr, Initial Trng Gp, 1996–99; Comdr, Land Warfare Centre, 1999–2002; UK Co-ordinator, Kosovo Protection Corps, 2002–04. Col, Queen's Royal Lancers, 2006–11. Dir, Wincanton Race Course, 2004–11. Trustee, Southern Spinal Injuries Trust, 2014–. *Recreations:* field sports, racing, walking, sailing, ski-ing, reading, piano playing. *E:* aajrc@tiscali.co.uk. *Club:* Cavalry and Guards.

CUMMING, Valerie Lynn, FMA; writer and lecturer; Deputy Director, Museum of London, 1988–97; *b* 11 Oct. 1946; *d* of late John Gunson Carter and Edna Ruth Carter (*née* Willis); *m* 1972, John Lawrence Cumming. *Educ:* Abbey Sch., Reading; Univ. of Leicester (BA); Courtauld Inst. of Art (Courtauld Cert. in History of Dress). Admin. trainee, Univ. of Surrey, 1968–69; Asst, Chertsey Mus., 1971–73; Res. Asst, 1973–75, Sen. Asst Keeper, 1975–78, Mus. of London; Curator, Court Dress Collection, Kensington Palace, 1978–81; Asst Dir, Mus. of London, 1981–88. Trustee: Olive Matthews Collection, Chertsey Mus., Surrey, 1983– (Chm., 2003–); Costume Soc., 2001–04 (Chm., 2004–09); Bullard and Callow Trusts, Museums Assoc., 1992–. Curatorial advr, Chartered Insurance Inst., 1991–98. Vis. Lectr, 1997 and 2007, External Examr, 2003–06, Courtauld Inst. of Art. Editor, Costume, jl of Costume Soc., 2014–. *Publications:* Exploring Costume History 1500–1900, 1981; Gloves, 1982; A Visual History of Costume: the Seventeenth Century, 1984; (with Aileen Ribeiro) The Visual History of Costume, 1989; Royal Dress, 1989; The Visual History of Accessories, 1998; Understanding Fashion History, 2004; (consulting ed.) Berg Encyclopedia of World Dress and Fashion, vol. 8: West Europe, 2010; (revising ed.) The Dictionary of Fashion History, 2010; contributed to: Tradescant's Rarities, 1983; The Late King's Goods, 1989; London—World City 1800–1840, 1992; The Oxford Companion to the Body, 2001; The Oxford Encyclopedia of Theatre and Performance, 2003; City Merchants and the Arts 1670–1720, 2004. *Recreations:* gardening, watching cricket. *Address:* 7 Frere Street, SW11 2JA. *T:* (020) 7223 1380.

CUMMINGS, Prof. Alan John, FRCA; higher education consultant and lecturer, since 2011; Pro-Rector and Director of Academic Development, Royal College of Art, 2000–11, now Emeritus Professor; *b* South Shields, 17 April 1950; *s* of Alan and Elizabeth Cummings; *m* 2002, Sarah Cove; two *s* two *d*. *Educ:* S Shields Grammar Tech. Sch. for Boys; Imperial Coll. London (BSc Hons 1971; ARCS); Courtauld Inst. of Art, London (Postgrad. Dip. Conservation of Paintings 1974). FRCA 1991. Freelance conservator of paintings for NPG, NT, English Heritage and others, 1975–98; Lectr in Conservation of Paintings, Courtauld Inst. of Art, 1984–85; Royal College of Art: Hd of Dept, RCA/V&A Conservation, 1988–2001; Hd, Sch. of Humanities, 1998–2001. Vis. Prof., Faculty of Engrg, Imperial Coll. London, 2011–. Dir and Trustee, Creative Mentors Foundn, 2009–; Gov., Nat. Film and TV Sch., 2011–. FHEA 2000; FCGI 2010. FRSA 2004. *Publications:* contribs to conservation and higher educn jls. *Recreations:* playing guitar, songwriting and recording, tennis, swimming, cycling, scuba-diving. *E:* alan.cummings@network.rca.ac.uk.

CUMMINGS, Brian; QC 2008; a Recorder, since 2005; *b* Belfast, 10 April 1965; *s* of late Wilbur Cummings and of Shirley Cummings (*née* Drum). *Educ:* Trinity Coll., Cambridge (BA 1987). Called to the Bar, Lincoln's Inn, 1988; in practice at the Bar, Liverpool, 1989–. *Recreations:* cycling, hill-walking/mountaineering, Rugby, cricket, foreign travel, foreign languages, reading. *Address:* Exchange Chambers, Pearl Assurance House, Derby Square, Liverpool L2 9XX. *T:* (0151) 236 7747, *Fax:* (0151) 236 3433. *E:* cummingsqc@exchangechambers.co.uk.

CUMMINGS, John Scott; *b* 6 July 1943; *s* of late George Scott Cummings and Mary (*née* Cain); unmarried. *Educ:* Murton Council Infants, Jun. and Sen. Schs; Easington Technical Coll. Colliery apprentice electrician, 1958–63, colliery electrician, 1963–87, Murton Colliery. Vice-Chm., Coalfields Community Campaign, 1985–87; Member: Northumbrian Water Authority, 1977–83; Aycliffe and Peterlee Develt Corp., 1980–87; Easington RDC, 1970–73; Easington DC, 1973–87 (Chm., 1975–76; Leader, 1979–87). MP (Lab) Easington, 1987–2010. Member: Envmt, Transport and Regions Select Cttee, 1997–2001; ODPM Select Cttee, 2002–10; Speaker's Panel of Chairmen, 2000–10; Chm., All-Party Czech and Slovak Gp, 1997–2010; Vice-Chm., All-Party Aluminium Gp, 1999. Mem., Council of Europe, 1992–97. Hon. Parliamentary Adviser: Nat. Assoc. of Councillors; Nat. Assoc. of Licensed House Managers. *Recreations:* Jack Russell terriers, walking, travel. *Address:* 18 Grasmere Terrace, Murton, Seaham, Co. Durham SR7 9NU. *T:* (0191) 526 1142. *Clubs:* Murton Victoria, Democratic, Ex-Servicemen's (Murton); Peterlee Labour; Thornley Catholic.

CUMMINGS, Prof. Keith Richard; Professor of Glass Studies, School of Art and Design, University of Wolverhampton, 1991–2014, now Emeritus; *b* 15 July 1940; *s* of Henry Gordon Cummings and Kathleen Cummings; *m* 1963, Pamela Anne Cornall; two *s*. *Educ:* Univ. of Durham (BA Hons Fine Art). Sen. Lectr in Glass, Stourbridge Coll. of Art, 1967–85; Tutor, Sch. of Ceramics and Glass, RCA, 1986–89; Principal Lectr, Sch. of Art and Design, Univ. of Wolverhampton, 1989–94. Work exhibited in nat. and internat. collections, incl. V&A, Mus. of Decorative Art, Paris. *Publications:* Techniques of Glassforming, 1980; Techniques of Kiln-Formed Glass, 1997, 3rd edn 2007; A History of Glassforming, 2002; Contemporary Kiln-formed Glass, 2009. *Recreations:* reading, gardening, table-tennis. *Address:* The Granary, Thicknall Lane, Clent, Stourbridge, W Midlands DY9 0HP. *E:* kr.cummings@tiscali.co.uk.

CUMMINGS, Laurence Alexander, FRCO, FRCM; harpsichordist and conductor; William Crotch Professor of Historical Performance, Royal Academy of Music, since 2012 (Head of Historical Performance, 1997–2012); Musical Director: London Handel Society, since 2002; Casa da Música Baroque Orchestra, since 2004; Göttingen Handel Society, since 2012; *b* 25 May 1968; *s* of Geoffrey Victor and Maureen Cummings; civil partnership 2012, Martin Parr. *Educ:* Christ Church, Oxford (MA); Royal Coll. of Music (ARCM). FRCO 1985. Freelance harpsichordist, 1989–. Guest Conductor: ENO (Semele, 2004; Orfeo, 2006; Poppea, 2007; Messiah, 2009; Radamisto, 2010; The Indian Queen, 2015); Glyndebourne Fest. Opera (Giulio Cesare, 2005 and 2009; The Fairy Queen, 2009 and 2012; Saul, 2015); Gothenburg Opera (Giulio Cesare, 2008; Alcina, 2011; Orfeo ed Euridice, 2014); Opera de Lyon (Messiah, 2012); Opernhaus Zurich (Sale, 2012, 2013); Opera North (Poppea, 2014). Co-director: London Handel Fest., 1999–2002; Tilford Bach Fest., 1999–2002. Trustee, Handel House Mus., London, 2002–. Has made recordings. Hon. RAM (Hon. ARAM 2001). *Recreations:* travelling, reading, walking. *Address:* 42 Larkhall Lane, SW4 6SP.

CUMMINGS, Peter Joseph; Chief Executive, Corporate, HBOS plc, 2006–09 (Director, 2005–09); *b* Dumbarton, 19 July 1955; *m* 1978, Margaret Mary Docherty. *Educ:* St Patrick's High Sch., Dumbarton; Glasgow Coll. of Technol.; Univ. of Strathclyde (MBA). Joined Bank of Scotland, 1973; worked in branches in W of Scotland; Chief Manager, Glasgow Chief Office, 1982–85; Advances Manager, Corporate Div., 1985–90; Hd, Corporate Recovery, 1990–93; Regl Manager, N of England, 1993–95; Dir, Corporate Banking, Bank of Scotland, subseq. HBOS plc, 1995–2005; Dep. Chief Exec., Corporate, HBOS plc, 2005–06. Mem., Adv. Cttee, Edinburgh Univ. Business Sch., 2008. Dir, Maggie's Cancer Care Centres, 2005. FCIBS 2000. *Recreations:* scuba-diving, swimming, football, music. *Clubs:* Mark's, George.

CUMMINS, Gus, RA 1992; artist; *b* 28 Jan. 1943; *s* of Harold George Cummins and Honor Cecilia (*née* Bird); *m* 1968, Angela Braven; two *s* one *d*. *Educ:* Sutton and Wimbledon Schs of Art; RCA (NDD, MA). Part-time teacher at nine art schs and colls, 1969–; currently at RA schs. Exhibns, mainly in UK, also Norway, Holland, UAE and USA, 1980–; 7 solo exhibns, 1991–. Henry Moore Prize, London Gp, 1982; Spirit of London 2nd Prize, 1983; Daler-Rowney Prize, RA, 1987; Hunting Gp 1st Prize, Mall Gall., 1990, RCA, 1999; House & Garden Prize and Blackstone Award, RA Summer Show, 1992; RWS Prize, 2001; Jack Goldhill Sculpture Award, RA, 2005. *Recreations:* music, poetry, literature, swimming, cycling, pubs, snooker. *Address:* Harpsichord House, Cobourg Place, Hastings, Sussex TN34 3HY. *T:* (01424) 426429. *W:* www.guscummins.com.

CUMMINS, Judith; MP (Lab) Bradford South, since 2015; *b* W Yorks; one *s* one *d*. *Educ:* Ruskin Coll.; Univ. of Leeds. Former Mem. (Lab) Bradford MDC; Mem. (Lab), Leeds CC, 2012–. *Address:* House of Commons, SW1A 0AA. *T:* (020) 7219 8607. *E:* judith.cummins.mp@parliament.uk.

CUMMINS, Sir Michael (John Austin), Kt 2003; Serjeant at Arms, House of Commons, 2000–04; *b* 26 Nov. 1939; *s* of Harold Leslie Cummins and Florence Gladys Cummins (*née* Austin); *m* 1st, 1964, Mary Isobel Farman (marr. diss. 1995); two *s*; 2nd, 1995, Catherine Ellen Lamb; one step *d*. *Educ:* Queen Mary Sch.; RMA Sandhurst; psc. Commnd 3rd Carabiniers (POW DG), 1959; Royal Scots Dragoon Guards, 1971–81. Serjeant at Arms Dept, H of C, 1981–2004; Dep. Serjeant at Arms, 1995–99. Trustee, Selwood Foundn, 1986–. *Publications:* (with Sir Peter Thorne) Serjeant for the Commons, 1994, 2nd edn 1999. *Recreations:* equitation, gardening, tennis, tapestry. *Address:* 140A Ashley Gardens, Westminster, SW1P 1HN. *Club:* Cavalry and Guards.

CUMPSTY, Prof. Nicholas Alexander, PhD, FREng; Professor of Mechanical Engineering, Imperial College, London, 2005–08, now Emeritus; *b* 13 Jan. 1943; *s* of Norman and Edith Cumpsty; *m* 1st, 1966, Annette Tischler (*d* 1982); one *s* one *d*; 2nd, 1983, Mary Cecily Hamer (*née* Turner); two step *d*. *Educ:* Haberdashers' Aske's Sch., Hampstead; Imperial Coll., London (BScEng 1964); Trinity Coll. and Peterhouse, Cambridge (PhD 1967; MA 1968). Post Office Student Apprentice, 1960–64; Peterhouse Research Fellow, 1966–69; Rolls-Royce, 1969–71; Cambridge University: Sen. Asst in Research, Lectr, then Reader, Dept of Engineering, 1972–89; Prof. of Aerothermal Technology, 1989–99; Fellow of Peterhouse, 1972–99, now Emeritus; Chief Technologist, Rolls-Royce plc, 2000–05. Hunsaker Vis. Prof., Dept of Aeronautics and Astronautics, MIT, 1991–92. Mem., Royal Commn on Envmtl Pollution, 2005–09. Mem., Defence Scientific Adv. Council, 2005–11. FREng (FEng 1995). *Publications:* Compressor Aerodynamics, 1989; Jet Propulsion, 1997; numerous papers on aerodynamics, esp. relating to jet engines. *Recreations:* reading, music, walking. *Address:* Imperial College, London, SW7 2AZ. *T:* (020) 7594 2099. *E:* n.cumpsty@imperial.ac.uk.

CUNINGHAME, Sir John Christopher Foggo M.; *see* Montgomery Cuninghame.

CUNINGHAME, Sir Robert Henry F.; *see* Fairlie-Cuninghame.

CUNLIFFE, family name of **Baron Cunliffe.**

CUNLIFFE, 3rd Baron *cr* 1914, of Headley; **Roger Cunliffe,** RIBA; MCMI; farmer; writer; *b* 12 Jan. 1932; *s* of 2nd Baron and Joan Catherine Lubbock (*d* 1980); *S* father, 1963; *m* 1957, Clemency Ann Hoare; two *s* one *d*. *Educ:* Eton; Loughborough Tech. Coll.; Trinity Coll., Cambridge (MA); Architectural Association (AA Dipl.); Open Univ. With various architectural firms in UK and USA, 1957–65; Associate, Robert Matthew, Johnson-Marshall & Partners, 1966–69; Dir, Architectural Assoc., 1969–71; Partner, SCP, 1973–78; own practice as architectural, planning and management consultant, 1977–2002; Dir, Exhibition Consultants Ltd, 1981–2004. Member: Urban Motorways Cttee, 1969–72; Council, British Consultants Bureau, 1986–90. Member: Council, Lancing Coll., 1967–85; Delegacy, Goldsmiths' Coll., 1972–78; Bd, Coll. of Estate Management, 1992–2006 (Hon. Fellow, 2007); Vis. Sen. Fellow, Univ. Campus Suffolk, 2011–. Chm., Suffolk Craft Soc., 1994–97. Mem. Ct, Goldsmiths' Co., 1986–2012 (Prime Warden, 1997). DUniv Univ. Campus Suffolk (UEA and Essex), 2008. *Publications:* (with Leonard Manasseh) Office Buildings, 1962; (with Santa Raymond) Tomorrow's Office, 1996; contrib. various professional jls. *Recreations:* making pots and pottering, baking bread and loafing. *Heir: s* Hon. Henry Cunliffe [*b* 9 March 1962; *m* (marr. diss.)]. *Address:* The Broadhurst, Brandeston, Woodbridge, Suffolk IP13 7AG.

CUNLIFFE, Sir Barrington Windsor, (Sir Barry), Kt 2006; CBE 1994; FBA 1979; FSA; Professor of European Archaeology, Oxford University, 1972–2007, now Emeritus; Fellow of Keble College, Oxford, 1972–2007; *b* 10 Dec. 1939. *Educ:* Portsmouth; St John's Coll., Cambridge (MA, PhD, LittD). Lecturer, Univ. of Bristol, 1963–66; Prof. of Archæology, Univ. of Southampton, 1966–72. O'Donnell Lectr in Celtic Studies, Oxford Univ., 1983–84. Member: Ancient Monuments Bd for England, 1976–84; Historic Bldgs and Monuments Commn for England, 1987–92 (Mem., Ancient Monuments Adv. Cttee, 1984–); Comr, English Heritage, 2006–14 (Interim Chm., 2008–09). President: Council for British Archaeology, 1976–79; Soc. of Antiquaries, 1991–95 (Vice-Pres., 1982–86). Gov., Mus. of London, 1995–99; Trustee: British Mus., 2000–09; BM Trust, 2011–; English Heritage Foundn, 2011–15. Hon. DLitt: Sussex, 1983; Southampton, 2009; Kent, 2010; Hon. DSc Bath, 1984; DUniv Open, 1995; Bradford, 2014. *Publications:* Fishbourne, a Roman Palace and its Garden, 1971; Roman Bath Discovered, 1971, rev. edn 1984; The Cradle of England, 1972; The Making of the English, 1973; The Regni, 1973; Iron Age Communities in Britain, 1974, 4th edn 2005; Rome and the Barbarians, 1975; Hengistbury Head, 1978; Rome and her Empire, 1978; The Celtic World, 1979; Danebury: the anatomy of an Iron Age hillfort, 1984; The City of Bath, 1986; Greeks, Romans and Barbarians, 1988; Wessex before AD 1000, 1991; (ed) The Oxford Illustrated Prehistory of Europe, 1994; Iron Age Britain, 1995; The Ancient Celts, 1997; Facing the Ocean: the Atlantic and its peoples, 2001 (Wolfson History Prize, 2002); The Extraordinary Voyage of Pytheas the Greek, 2001; The Celts: a very short introduction, 2003; (ed) England's Landscape: the west, 2006; Europe Between the Oceans: 9000 BC to AD 1000, 2008; The Druids: a very short introduction, 2010; Britain Begins, 2013; contribs to several major excavation reports and articles to Soc. of Antiquaries, and in other learned jls. *Recreation:* mild self-indulgence. *Address:* Institute of Archaeology, 36 Beaumont Street, Oxford OX1 2PG.

CUNLIFFE, Ven. Christopher John, DPhil; Archdeacon of Derby, since 2006; *b* 25 Sept. 1955; *s* of Joseph and Margaret Cunliffe; *m* 1979, Helen Margaret Ketley (*see* Ven. H. M. Cunliffe); two *s*. *Educ:* Charterhouse; Christ Church, Oxford (MA, DPhil 1981); Trinity Coll., Cambridge (MA 1986); Westcott House, Cambridge. ARHistS 1993. Ordained deacon, 1983, priest, 1984; Asst Curate, Chesterfield, 1983–85; Chaplain and Jun. Res. Fellow, Lincoln Coll., Oxford, 1985–89; Chaplain, City Univ. and Guildhall Sch. of Music and Drama, 1989–91; Selection Sec. and Vocations Officer, Adv. Bd of Ministry, 1991–96; Bp of London's Advr for Ordained Ministry, 1997–2003; Chaplain to Bp of Bradwell, 2004–06; Canon Residentiary, Derby Cathedral, 2006–08. Commissary of the Bishop of Angola, 2013–. Clerk, All Saints Educnl Trust, 2004. *Publications:* (ed) Joseph Butler's Moral and Religious Thought, 1992. *Recreations:* walking, reading, listening to music, watching sport, fly-fishing. *Address:* Derby Church House, Full Street, Derby DE1 3DR. *T:* (01332) 388676, *Fax:* (01332) 292969. *E:* archderby@derby.anglican.org.

CUNLIFFE, Sir David Ellis, 9th Bt *cr* 1759; business development manager; *b* 29 Oct. 1957; *s* of Sir Cyril Henley Cunliffe, 8th Bt and of Eileen Lady Cunliffe, *d* of Frederick William and Nora Anne Parkins; *S* father, 1969; *m* 1983, Linda Carol, *d* of John Sidney and Ella Mary Batchelor; three *d*. *Educ:* St Albans Grammar School. *Heir: b* Andrew Mark Cunliffe [*b* 17 April 1959; *m* 1980, Janice Elizabeth, *d* of Ronald William Kyle; one *s* three *d*].

CUNLIFFE, Ven. Helen Margaret; Archdeacon of St Albans, 2003–07, now Emeritus; *b* 1954; *m* 1979, Ven. Christopher John Cunliffe, *qv*; two *s*. *Educ:* Homelands Sch., Derby; St Hilda's Coll., Oxford (BA 1977, MA 1978); Westcott House, Cambridge. Ordained deaconess, 1983, deacon, 1987, priest, 1994; Curate, St Mary and All Saints, Chesterfield, 1983–85; Dss, 1986–87, Parish Deacon, 1987–89, St Mary the Virgin with St Cross and St Peter, Oxford; Chaplain, Nuffield Coll., Oxford, 1986–89; Team Deacon, 1989–94, Team Vicar, 1994–96, Clapham Team Ministry; Residentiary Canon, Southwark Cathedral, 1996–2002; Diocesan Advr for Women in Ministry, Southwark, 1996–2002. Chaplain, Welcare, 1996–2002. Chair, USPG, 1997–2000. *Recreations:* walking, gardening, watching football, dogs, especially Lagotto Romagnolo. *Address:* 1 Thatch Close, Derby DE22 1EA.

CUNLIFFE, Sir Jonathan (Stephen), Kt 2010; CB 2001; a Deputy Governor and Member, Monetary Policy Committee, Bank of England, since 2013; *b* 2 June 1953; *s* of Ralph and Cynthia Cunliffe; *m* 1984, Naomi Brandler; two *d*. *Educ:* St Marylebone GS, London; Manchester Univ. (BA Eng. 1975; MA 1976). Lectr in English and Drama, Univ. of Western Ontario, 1976–79; res. student, 1979–80; joined Civil Service, 1980; DoE, 1980–85; Department of Transport: Principal, 1985; Pvte Sec. to Sec. of State, 1985–88; Transport Industry Finance, 1988–90; HM Treasury: Asst Sec., Pay Gp, 1990–93; Internat. Financial Instns, and UK Alternate Dir, EBRD (on secondment), 1993–95; Debt and Reserves Mgt, 1995–97; Dep. Dir, Macroeconomic Policy and Prospects, 1997–98; Dep. Dir, then Dir, Internat. Finance, later Macroeconomic Policy and Internat. Finance, 1998–2001; Managing Director: Financial Regulation and Industry, 2001–02; Macroecon. Policy and Internat. Finance, 2002–05; Perm. Sec., Macroecon. Policy and Internat. Finance, subseq. Internat. and Finance, 2005–07; Prime Minister's Advr on Europe and global issues, G8 and G20 Sherpa, and Hd, Europe and Global Issues Secretariat, 2007–11; UK Perm. Rep. to EU, Brussels, 2012–13. UK Alternate Mem., EU Monetary Cttee, 1996–98; UK Mem., EU Economic and Financial Cttee and G7 Treaty, 2002–. *Address:* Bank of England, Threadneedle Street, EC2R 8AH.

CUNLIFFE, Lawrence Francis; *b* 25 March 1929; *m* 1950, Winifred (marr. diss. 1985), *d* of William Haslem; three *s* two *d*. *Educ:* St Edmund's RC Sch., Worsley, Manchester. Engr, NCB, 1949–79. Member (Lab): Farnworth BC, 1964–74 (Mayor 1968–69); Bolton MDC, 1974–79. Contested (Lab) Rochdale, Oct. 1972 and Feb. 1974. MP (Lab) Leigh, 1979–2001. An Opposition Whip, 1985–87. Hon. Alderman, Bolton, 1996. JP 1967–79.

CUNLIFFE, Peter Whalley, CBE 1980; Chairman: Pharmaceuticals Division, Imperial Chemical Industries PLC, 1976–87; British Pharma Group, 1987–90; *b* 29 Oct. 1926; *s* of Fred Cunliffe and Lillie Whalley; *m* 1951, Alice Thérèse Emma Brunel; one *d*. *Educ:* Queen Elizabeth's Grammar Sch., Blackburn; Trinity Hall, Cambridge (Scholar; BA 1st Class Hons, 1948). Joined ICI Ltd, Pharmaceuticals Div., 1950; Services Dir, 1968; Overseas Dir, 1970; Dep. Chm., 1971. Pres., Assoc. of British Pharmaceutical Industry, 1981–83; Member:

Council, Internat. Fedn of Pharmaceutical Manufrs Assoc., 1979–87 (Vice Pres., 1982–84, Pres. 1984–86); Exec. Cttee, European Fedn of Pharmaceutical Industries Assocs, 1982–85. *Address:* 38 Admirals Tower, 8 Dowells Street, SE10 9FQ.

CUNLIFFE-LISTER, family name of **Earl of Swinton** and **Baroness Masham of Ilton**.

CUNLIFFE-OWEN, Sir Hugo Dudley, 3rd Bt *cr* 1920, of Bray; *b* 16 May 1966; *s* of Sir Dudley Herbert Cunliffe-Owen, 2nd Bt, and Jean (*d* 2015), *o d* of late Surg.-Comdr A. N. Forsyth, RN; *S* father, 1983; *m* 2005, Leanda Jane, *d* of Malcolm Harris. *Heir:* none.

CUNNAH, Michael Graeme; Chairman, iSportconnect.com, since 2011; Chief Executive Officer, Stadium Management Systems Ltd, since 2012; Managing Director, International Services Group, since 2009; Mobsventures, since 2011; *b* 26 Feb. 1958; *s* of Alan and Irene Cunnah; *m* 1984, Julie Kendrew; one *s* one *d*. *Educ:* Univ. of Aston in Birmingham (BSc Managerial and Admin. Studies). FCMA 1997. Guinness Plc, 1987–96: Financial Controller, Guinness GB, 1987–91; Dir, Corporate Finance, GBW, 1991–92; Finance Dir, Africa/Americas Region, 1992–93; Vice Pres., Finance, Desnoes & Geddes Ltd, Jamaica, 1993–95; Hd, Internal Audit, 1996; Corporate Finance Dir, Coca-Cola Schweppes, 1996–98; Finance Dir, FA, 1998–2002; CEO, Wembley Stadium, 2002–06; Director: Aston Villa FC, 2007–08; Internat. Media Content, 2011–14. Fellow, Aston Univ. Business Sch., 2006. *Recreations:* football, music, cricket, golf, reading. *E:* michaelcunnah@me.com.

CUNNINGHAM, family name of **Baron Cunningham of Felling**.

CUNNINGHAM OF FELLING, Baron *cr* 2005 (Life Peer), of Felling, in the county of Tyne and Wear; **John Anderson, (Jack), Cunningham;** PC 1993; DL; PhD; *b* 4 Aug. 1939; *s* of late Andrew and May Freda Cunningham; *m* 1964, Maureen; one *s* two *d*. *Educ:* Jarrow Grammar Sch.; Bede Coll., Durham Univ. Hons Chemistry, 1962; PhD Chemistry, 1966. Formerly: Research Fellow in Chemistry, Durham Univ.; School Teacher; Trades Union Officer. MP (Lab) Whitehaven, Cumbria, 1970–83, Copeland, 1983–2005. PPS to Rt Hon. James Callaghan, 1972–76; Parly Under-Sec. of State, Dept of Energy, 1976–79; opposition spokesman on industry, 1979–83; Mem., Shadow Cabinet, 1983–95 and 1996–97; spokesman on the environment, 1983–89; Shadow Leader, H of C, 1989–92; opposition front bench spokesman on foreign and Commonwealth affairs, 1992–94; on trade and industry, 1994–95; on national heritage, 1995–97; Minister of Agriculture, Fisheries and Food, 1997–98; Minister for the Cabinet Office and Chancellor of the Duchy of Lancaster, 1998–99. Mem., H of L Select Cttee on Sci. and Technol., 2008–. DL Cumbria, 1991. *Recreations:* fell walking, fly-fishing, gardening, shooting, classical and folk music, reading, listening to other people's opinions. *Address:* House of Lords, SW1A 0PW.

CUNNINGHAM, Alex; MP (Lab) Stockton North, since 2010; *b* 1 May 1955; *s* of John and Jean Cunningham; *m* 1977, Evaline; two *s*. *Educ:* Branksome Comprehensive Sch., Darlington; Queen Elizabeth Sixth Form Coll., Darlington; Darlington Coll. of Technol. (Cert. Journalism 1976). Journalist: Darlington and Stockton Times, 1974–76; The Mail, Hartlepool, 1976–77; Radio Tees, 1977–79; Radio Clyde, 1979; Evening Gazette, 1979–84; PR officer, British Gas, 1984–89; Transco: communications advr, 1995–2000; Hd of Communications, 2000–02; Man. Dir, Tees Valley Communicators, 2002–10. Chm., NE Mus. and Libraries Council, 1993–99; Member: NE Regl Bd, Arts Council England, 1992–2000; Bd, One North East, 2008–10; non-exec. Dir, N Tees and Hartlepool NHS Foundn Trust, 2008–10. PPS to Shadow Lord Chancellor and Sec. of State for Justice, 2010–. Member (Lab): Cleveland CC, 1989–96; Stockton on Tees BC, 1999–2010. Mem. Council, MLA, 2008–09. *Address:* House of Commons, SW1A 0AA; Unit 142, Stockton Business Centre, 70–74 Brunswick Street, Stockton on Tees TS18 1DW.

CUNNINGHAM, Carey Louise; *see* Bennet, C. L.

CUNNINGHAM, George; *b* June 1931; *s* of Harry Jackson Cunningham and Christina Cunningham, Dunfermline; *m* 1957, Mavis Walton; one *s* one *d*. *Educ:* Univ. of Manchester (BA 1952); Univ. of London (BSc(Econ) ext. 1969). Nat. Service in Royal Artillery (2nd Lieut), 1954–56; Commonwealth Relations Office, 1956–63; 2nd Sec., British High Commn, Ottawa, 1958–60; Commonwealth Officer of Labour Party, 1963–66; Min. of Overseas Development, 1966–69; Chief Exec., Library Assoc., 1984–92. MP South West Islington, 1970–74, Islington South and Finsbury, 1974–83 (Lab, 1970–81, Ind, 1981–82, SDP, 1982–83). Opposition front bench spokesman (Lab) on home affairs, 1979–81. Contested: (Lab) Henley, 1966; (SDP) Islington South and Finsbury, 1983, 1987. Mem., Parlt of European Community, 1978–79. Pres., Study of Parlt Gp, 2000–03. Chm., Gen. Council for Massage Therapy, 2002–04; Treas., Trigeminal Neuralgia Assoc., 2008–11. Mem. Council, Hansard Soc., 1984–2003. Trustee, Children's Aid Direct, 1994–2002. Hon. FCLIP (Hon. FLA 1992). *Publications:* (Fabian pamphlet) Rhodesia, the Last Chance, 1966; (ed) Britain and the World in the Seventies, 1970; The Management of Aid Agencies, 1974; Careers in Politics, 1984. *Address:* 28 Manor Gardens, Hampton, Middlesex TW12 2TU. *T:* (020) 8979 6221.

CUNNINGHAM, Lt-Gen. Sir Hugh (Patrick), KBE 1975 (OBE 1966); *b* 4 Nov. 1921; *s* of late Sir Charles Banks Cunningham, CSI; *m* 1st, 1955, Jill (*d* 1992), *d* of J. S. Jeffrey, East Knoyle; two *s* two *d*; 2nd, 1995, Zoë Simpson (*née* Andrew), Constantia, Cape Town, S Africa. *Educ:* Charterhouse. 2nd Lieut, RE, 1942; served War of 1939–45, India, New Guinea, Burma; Greece, 1950–51; Egypt, 1951–53; Instructor, Sch. of Infantry, 1955–57, RMA Sandhurst, 1957–60; Cameroons, 1960–61; CRE 3 Div., Cyprus and Aden, 1963–66; comd 11 Engr Bde, BAOR, 1967–69; comd Mons OCS, 1969–70; Nat. Defence Coll., Canada, 1970–71; GOC SW District, 1971–74; ACGS (OR), 1974–75; DCDS (OR), 1976–78, retired. Lieutenant of Tower of London, 1983–86. Col, Queen's Gurkha Engineers (formerly Gurkha Engrs), 1976–81; Col Comdt, RE, 1976–81; Col, Bristol Univ. OTC, 1977–87. Director: Fairey Holdings Ltd, 1978–86; Fairey Engineering, 1981–86; MEL, 1982–89; TREND Communications Ltd, 1984–86, 1990–93; Chairman: LL Consultants Ltd, 1984–89; TREND Group, 1986–90. Pres., Old Carthusian Soc., 1982–87. Master, Glass Sellers' Co., 1981. Chm. of Governors, Port Regis School, 1982–94; Gov., Suttons Hosp. in Charterhouse, 1984–96. *Recreations:* bird-watching, opera, golf. *Address:* Granary Mill House, Fontmell Magna, Shaftesbury, Dorset SP7 0NY. *T:* (01747) 812025. *Club:* Army and Navy.

CUNNINGHAM, James Dolan; MP (Lab) Coventry South, since 1997 (Coventry South East, 1992–97); *b* Coatbridge, 4 Feb. 1941; *s* of Adam and Elizabeth Cunningham; *m* 1985, Marion Douglas; one *s* one *d* and one step *s* one step *d*. *Educ:* St Columba High Sch., Coatbridge. Trade Union Diplomas in Industrial Law and Social Sciences. Engineer, 1964–88. Mem. (Lab) Coventry CC, 1972–92 (Leader, 1988–92; formerly Dep. Leader, Chief Whip, Chm. and Vice Chm. of Cttees). Chm., W Midlands Jt Cttee of Local Authority, 1990–92; Sec., AMA, 1991–92. PPS to Solicitor Gen., 2005–07, to Minister of State, DWP, 2007–10. Chm., HM Treasury Back Bench Cttee, 1997–2010. Chm., W Midland Gp of MPs, 2005–10. Mem., MSF. *Address:* House of Commons, SW1A 0AA.

CUNNINGHAM, Prof. John, KCVO 2014 (CVO 2008); DM, FRCP; Professor of Nephrology, University College London, and Consultant Nephrologist, Royal Free Hospital and University College London Hospitals, since 2003; Physician to the Queen and Head of HM Medical Household, 2005–14 (Physician to the Royal Household, 1993–2005); Physician, King Edward VII's Hospital Sister Agnes (formerly King Edward VII's Hospital for Officers), since 1993; *b* 27 June 1949; *s* of late Daniel John Chapman Cunningham and of Judith (*née* Hill); *m* 1st, 1970, Deborah Alison Yeates (marr. diss. 1996); three *s*; 2nd, 2001, Caroline Ann Hughes Hewitt; one *d*. *Educ:* Magdalen Coll. Sch., Oxford; Trinity Hall, Cambridge (BA 1970); St John's Coll., Oxford (BM, BCh 1973; DM 1988). FRCP 1988. Junior appointments, 1973–77: Radcliffe Infirmary, Oxford; Whittington Hosp., London; Brompton Hosp., London; Central Middx Hosp., London; Lectr in Medicine, London Hosp. Med. Coll., 1977–80; Res. Fellow, Washington Univ. Sch. of Medicine, St Louis, USA, 1980–82; Consultant Physician, London, subseq. Royal London, Hosp., 1982–2003; Sub-Dean for Med. Student Admissions, London Hosp. Med. Coll., 1990–97; Prof. of Renal and Metabolic Medicine, Queen Mary, Univ. of London, 2001–03. Special Trustee, Royal London Hosp., 1985–. Jan Brod Meml Lecture, Prague, 1993, and other invited lectures. *Publications:* contrib. chapters in books, reviews and numerous articles in scientific jls. *Recreations:* music, sport, walking. *Address:* 31A King Henry's Road, NW3 3QR. *T:* (020) 7722 3883. *Club:* MCC.

CUNNINGHAM, Rt Rev. John, JCD; Bishop of Galloway, (RC), 2004–14, now Bishop Emeritus; *b* 22 Feb. 1938. *Educ:* Blairs Coll.; St Peter's Coll., Cardross; Pontifical Scots Coll., Rome; Pontifical Gregorian Univ. (JCD). Ordained priest, 1961; Asst, Our Lady of Lourdes, Bishopton, 1964–69; Chaplain, Moredun Convent, 1969–74; Asst Priest, St Columba's, Renfrew, 1974–86; Officialis, Scottish Nat. Tribunal, 1986–92; Parish Priest, St Patrick's, Greenock, 1992–2004; VG Paisley, 1997. Prelate of Honour, 1999. *Address:* 24 Johnstone Terrace, Greenock PA16 8BD.

CUNNINGHAM, Mark James; QC 2001; *b* 6 June 1956; *s* of late James Arthur Cunningham and Carole Kathleen Cunningham; *m* 1980 (marr. diss. 1995); two *s* two *d*. *Educ:* Stonyhurst Coll.; Magdalen Coll., Oxford (BA Hons Modern Hist.); Poly. of Central London (Dip. Law). Called to the Bar: Inner Temple, 1980; E Caribbean, 2005; Junior Counsel to the Crown: Chancery, 1991–99; A Panel, 1999–2001; DTI Inspector, 1998–99. *Recreations:* cricket, tennis, horses, food, travel. *Address:* Maitland Chambers, 7 Stone Buildings, Lincoln's Inn, WC2A 3SZ. *T:* (020) 7406 1200, *Fax:* (020) 7406 1300. *E:* mcunningham@maitlandchambers.com. *Clubs:* Pegasus, Drayton Parslow Cricket, Stewkley Tennis.

CUNNINGHAM, Michael Bernard, QPM 2013; HM Inspector of Constabulary, since 2014; *b* Crosby, 14 July 1961; *s* of Terence and Shirley Cunningham; *m* 1986, Felicity Carroll; two *s*. *Educ:* St Mary's Coll., Crosby; Univ. of Durham (BA Hons Theol.). Joined Lancs Police, 1987; held a variety of uniform and CID posts across the force, 1987–2002; Chief Superintendent and Divl Comdr, Western Div., 2002–05; Asst Chief Constable, 2005–07; Dep. Chief Constable, 2007–09; Chief Constable, Staffordshire Police, 2009–14. *Recreations:* hill walking, cycling. *Address:* HM Inspectorate of Constabulary, Unit 2, Wakefield Office Village, Fryers Way, Silkwood Park, Wakefield WF5 9TJ.

CUNNINGHAM, Phyllis Margaret, CBE 1997; Chief Executive, Royal Marsden NHS Trust, 1994–98 (Chief Executive, Royal Marsden Hospital Special Health Authority, 1980–94); *b* 15 Sept. 1937; *d* of late Andrew Cunningham and of Minnie Cunningham (*née* Rees). *Educ:* Chorlton Central Sch., Manchester; Loreburn Coll., Manchester (Dip. in Business Studies, 1956). Trainee Adminr, Withington Hosp., Manchester, 1956–59; PA/Res. Asst to Med. Dir, Geigy Pharmaceutical Co., 1959–62; Unit Adminr, Roosevelt Hosp., NY, 1962–64; Planning Officer, Royal Free Hosp., London, 1964–74; Dep. House Gov./Sec. to Board, Royal Marsden Hosp., 1974–80. Mem., Ministerial Adv. Bd, Med. Devices Agency, 2001–03. Trustee and Mem. Council, St Christopher's Hospice, Sydenham, 1999–2013; Trustee: Headley Court Trust, 2001–13; Lady Capel's Charity, 2003–; Trustee/Chm., Abbeyfield Richmond, Thames and Dist Soc. Ltd, 2002–04; Trustee/Bd Mem., Abbeyfield UK, 2004–07. Governor: Christ's Sch., Richmond, 1996–99; Queen's Sch., Richmond, 2002–. FRSA 1992. *Recreations:* current affairs, travel, theatre, music, gardening. *Address:* 12 Augustus Close, Brentford Dock, Brentford, Middx TW8 8QE. *T:* (020) 8847 1067.

CUNNINGHAM, Roseanna; Member (SNP) Perthshire South and Kinross-shire, Scottish Parliament, since 2011 (Perth, 1999–2011); Cabinet Secretary for Fair Work, Skills and Training, since 2014; *b* 27 July 1951; *d* of Hugh and Catherine Cunningham. *Educ:* Univ. of Western Australia (BA Hons Politics 1975); Edinburgh Univ. (LLB 1982); Aberdeen Univ. (Dip. Legal Practice 1983). SNP Research Asst, 1977–79; Solicitor, 1983–90; admitted Faculty of Advocates, 1990; in practice, 1990–95. MP (SNP) Perth and Kinross, May 1995–1997, Perth, 1997–2001. Scottish Parliament: Minister for Envmt, 2009–11, for Envmt and Climate Change, 2010–11, for Community Safety and Legal Affairs, 2011–14; Convener: Health and Community Care Cttee, 2004–07; Rural Affairs and Envmt Cttee, 2007–09. Dep. Leader, SNP, 2000–04. *Recreations:* hill walking, music, reading, stirring up trouble. *Address:* Scottish Parliament, Edinburgh EH99 1SP.

CUNNINGHAM, Rt Rev. Seamus; *see* Hexham and Newcastle, Bishop of, (RC).

CUNNINGHAM, Sir Thomas Anthony, (Sir Tony), Kt 2012; *b* 16 Sept. 1952; *s* of late Daniel Cunningham and of Bessie Cunningham; *m* 1985, Anne Gilmore; one *s* one *d*, and one step *s* one step *d*. *Educ:* Workington GS; Liverpool Univ. (BA Hons). Mem., Allerdale DC, then BC, 1987–94 (Leader, 1992–94); Mayor of Workington, 1990–91. MEP (Lab) Cumbria and Lancs N, 1994–99; contested (Lab) NW Reg., 1999. MP (Lab) Workington, 2001–15. An Asst Govt Whip, 2005–08; a Lord Comr of HM Treasury (Govt Whip), 2008–10; Shadow Minister for Internat. Develt, 2011–13. *Address:* 17 Carlton Road, Workington, Cumbria CA14 4BX. *T:* (01900) 605799.

CUNNINGHAM, Prof. Valentine David, DPhil; Professor of English Language and Literature, University of Oxford, since 1996; Lecturer in English Literature, Corpus Christi College, Oxford, since 2014 (Fellow and Tutor in English, 1972–2012, Senior Research Fellow, 2012–14); *b* 28 Oct. 1944; *s* of Rev. Valentine Cunningham and Alma Lilian Cunningham (*née* Alexander); *m* 1966, Carol Ann Shaw; two *s*. *Educ:* Lawrence Sheriff Sch., Rugby; Keble Coll., Oxford (BA); St John's Coll., Oxford (MA, DPhil 1972). University of Oxford: Jun. Res. Fellow, St John's Coll., 1969–72; Dean, 1980–91, Sen. Tutor, 1991–94, Vice-Pres., 2008–12, Corpus Christi Coll.; Special Lectr, English Faculty, 1996–97. Visiting Professor: Univ. of Massachusetts, 1979–80; Konstanz Univ., 1980, 1983, 1989–90, 1992–93; Scholar-in-Residence, Univ. of Western Australia, 1985; Ständigergastprof., Konstanz Univ., 1994–2001; Fellow, Centre for British Studies, Humboldt Univ., Berlin, 2012–; Hon. Prof., Univ. of Bucharest, 2013–. *Publications:* Everywhere Spoken Against: dissent in the Victorian novel, 1975, 2nd edn 1977; (ed) The Penguin Book of Spanish Civil War Verse, 1979; (ed) Spanish Front: writers on the Civil War, 1986; British Writers of the Thirties, 1988; (ed) Cinco Escritores Britannicos/Five British Writers (bilingual text), 1990; In the Reading Gaol: postmodernity, texts and history, 1994; (ed) Adam Bede, 1996; (ed) The Victorians: an anthology of poetry and poetics, 2000; Reading After Theory, 2002; Victorian Poetry Now: poets, poems, poetics, 2011; The Connell Guide to Shakespeare's King Lear, 2012; (ed) Victorian Poets: a critical reader, 2014. *Recreations:* playing piano and trumpet (Leader, Dark Blues Jazz Band), listening to jazz, haunting bookshops, going to the cinema, reading bad novels, going to church. *Address:* 26 Frenchay Road, Oxford OX2 6TG. *T:* (01865) 556128. *E:* valentine.cunningham@ccc.ox.ac.uk. *Club:* Oxford and Cambridge.

CUNO, James, PhD; President and Chief Executive Officer, J. Paul Getty Trust, since 2011; *b* St Louis, Mo, 4 April 1951. *Educ:* Willamette Univ. (BA Hist. 1973); Univ. of Oregon (MA Hist. of Art 1978); Harvard Univ. (AM Fine Arts 1980; PhD Fine Arts 1985). Asst Curator of Prints, Fogg Art Mus., Harvard Univ., 1980–83; Asst Prof., Dept of Art, Vassar Coll., 1983–86; Adjunct Asst Prof., Dept of Art Hist., and Dir, Grunwald Center for Graphic Arts, UCLA, 1986–89; Adjunct Prof. of Art Hist., and Dir, Hood Mus. of Art, Dartmouth Coll., 1989–91; Prof. of Hist. of Art, Harvard Univ., and Elizabeth and John Moors Cabot Dir, Harvard Univ. Art Mus., 1991–2002; Dir and Märit Rausing Prof., Courtauld Inst. of Art,

2003–04; Pres. and Dir, Art Inst. of Chicago, 2004–11. Mem., Nat. Cttee for Hist. of Art, 1998. Association of Art Museum Directors: Mem., 1990; Trustee, 1999; Treas., 1999–2000; Vice-Pres., 2000–01; Pres., 2001–02. Trustee: Mus. of Fine Arts, Boston, 1991–2000; Wadsworth Atheneum Mus. of Art, Hartford, 2000. Fellow, Amer. Acad. Arts and Scis, 2001. *Publications:* (ed and contrib.) Foirades/Fizzles: echo and allusion in the art of Jasper Johns, 1987; (ed and contrib.) Politics and Polemics: French caricature and the Revolution 1789–1799, 1988; Who Owns Antiquity?: museums and the battle over our ancient heritage, 2008; contrib. numerous articles, reviews and papers to learned jls. *Address:* J. Paul Getty Trust, 1200 Getty Center Drive, Los Angeles, CA 90049–1679, USA.

CUNY, Jean-Pierre; Président Directeur Général, Bigot Mécanique Sopram, since 2011; *b* 8 April 1940; *s* of Robert Cuny and Marie Louise Marchal; *m* 1968, Anne-Marie Fousse; two *d. Educ:* Ecole Centrale de Paris (Ingénieur); Massachusetts Inst. of Technol. (MSc). Ingénieur, Serete, 1965–68; Director: Firmin Didot, 1968–73; DAFSA, 1973–76; Project Manager, CGA, 1976–78; joined Placoplatre, France, 1978: Prodn Dir, 1978–82; Commercial Dir, 1982–86; Pres. Dir Gen., BPB France, 1986–92; Dir, 1988–99, Chief Exec., 1994–99, BPB plc; Chm., St Eloi Finance, 2000–05; President-Director General: Bigot Mécanique, 2002–11; Sopram, 2003–11. Chevalier de la Légion d'Honneur, 1994. *Recreations:* ski-ing, photography.

CUNYNGHAME, Sir Andrew (David Francis), 12th Bt *cr* 1702; FCA; *b* 25 Dec. 1942; *s* of Sir (Henry) David St Leger Brooke Selwyn Cunynghame, 11th Bt, and of Hon. Pamela Margaret Stanley (*d* 1991), *d* of 5th Lord Stanley of Alderley; *S* father, 1978; *m* 1st, 1972, Harriet Ann, *d* of late C. T. Dupont, Montreal; two *d*; 2nd, 1989, Isabella King, *d* of late Edward Everett Watts, Jr and of Isabella Hardy Watts. *Educ:* Eton. *Heir: b* John Philip Henry Michael Selwyn Cunynghame [*b* 9 Sept. 1944; *m* 1981, Marjatta, *d* of Martti Markus; one *s* one *d*]. *Address:* 12 Vicarage Gardens, W8 4AH. *Club:* Brooks's.

CUPITT, Rev. Don; Fellow of Emmanuel College, 1965–96, now Life Fellow (Dean, 1966–91) and University Lecturer in Divinity, 1973–96, Cambridge; *b* 22 May 1934; *s* of late Robert and Norah Cupitt; *m* 1963, Susan Marianne (*née* Day); one *s* two *d. Educ:* Charterhouse; Trinity Hall, Cambridge; Westcott House, Cambridge. Curate, St Philip's Church, Salford, 1959–62; Vice-Principal, Westcott House, Cambridge, 1962–65. Writer and presenter, BBC TV series: The Big Question, 1973; Who Was Jesus?, 1976; The Sea of Faith, 1984. Hon. DLitt Bristol, 1985. *Publications:* Christ and the Hiddenness of God, 1971; Crisis of Moral Authority, 1972; The Leap of Reason, 1976; The Worlds of Science and Religion, 1976; (with Peter Armstrong) Who Was Jesus?, 1977; Jesus and the Gospel of God, 1979; The Nature of Man, 1979; The Debate about Christ, 1979; Explorations in Theology, 1979; Taking Leave of God, 1980; The World to Come, 1982; The Sea of Faith, 1984; Only Human, 1985; Life Lines, 1986; The Long-Legged Fly, 1987; The New Christian Ethics, 1988; Radicals and the Future of the Church, 1989; Creation Out of Nothing, 1990; What is a Story?, 1991; Rethinking Religion, 1992; The Time Being, 1992; After All, 1994; The Last Philosophy, 1995; Solar Ethics, 1995; After God, 1997; Mysticism After Modernity, 1998; The Religion of Being, 1998; The Revelation of Being, 1998; The New Religion of Life in Everyday Speech, 1999; The Meaning of It All in Everyday Speech, 1999; Kingdom Come in Everyday Speech, 2000; Philosophy's Own Religion, 2000; Reforming Christianity, 2001; Emptiness and Brightness, 2002; Is Nothing Sacred?, 2002; Life, Life, 2003; The Way to Happiness, 2005; The Great Questions of Life, 2006; Radical Theology, 2006; The Old Creed and the New, 2006; Impossible Loves, 2007; Above Us Only Sky, 2008; The Meaning of the West, 2008; The Method of Religious Studies (in Chinese), 2008; Jesus and Philosophy, 2009; Theology's Strange Return, 2010; A New Great Story, 2010; The Fountain, 2010; Turns of Phrase, 2011; The Last Testament, 2012; Creative Faith, 2015. *Address:* Emmanuel College, Cambridge CB2 3AP. *T:* (01223) 334200.

CURA, José; singer, composer, conductor and stage director; *b* Rosario, Argentina, 5 Dec. 1962; *m* 1985, Silvia Ibarra; two *s* one *d. Educ:* Nat. Univ. of Rosario; Sch. of Arts, Teatro Colon, Buenos Aires. Débuts: Father, in Pollicino, Verona, 1992; Stiffelio (title rôle), Royal Opera, Covent Garden, 1995; La Gioconda, La Scala, Milan, 1997; Otello (title rôle), Teatro Regio, Torino, 1997; other rôles include: Cavaradossi, in Tosca; Samson, in Samson et Dalila; Don José, in Carmen; Rhadames, in Aida; Don Carlo; Alfredo, in La Traviata; Manrico, in Il Trovatore; Calaf, in Turandot; Dick Johnson, in La Fanciulla del West. Début as Stage Dir, Samson et Dalila, Badisches Staatstheater, Karlsruhe, 2010. Principal Guest Conductor, Sinfonia Varsovia, 2001–04. Founder and Pres., Cuibar Productions, 2001–. Recordings include: all tenor arias from Puccini's operas; Annelo, Argentine songs; Verismo Arias; Samson et Dalila. *Address:* c/o Cuibar Productions SL, Ronda de la Abubilla 30b, 28043 Madrid, Spain. *W:* www.josecura.com.

CURDS, Prof. Colin Robert, DSc, PhD; Keeper of Zoology, 1991–97, Research Associate, since 1997, Natural History Museum; *b* 16 Sept. 1937; *s* of Robert Redvers Curds and Daisy Violet Curds (*née* Howsam); *m* 1961, Pauline (Polly) Armitage; one *s* one *d. Educ:* East Ham Grammar Sch.; Univ. of London (BSc 1960; PhD 1963; DSc 1978). FRSB (FIBiol 1979), CBiol 1982. Jun. Res. Fellow, Water Pollution Res. Lab., 1963–65; Min. of Technology, 1965–71; British Museum (Natural History), 1971–: Dep. Keeper of Zoology, 1976–89; Acting Keeper of Zoology, 1989–91. Visiting Lecturer: Chelsea Coll., 1965–73; Aston Univ., 1967–75; Surrey Univ., 1971–85; Vis. Prof., Mexico Univ., 1989–. Former mem., biol. and microbiol. cttees, 1972–; Member: Publications Policy Cttee, Inst. Biol., 1979–85; Council of Management, Project Urquhart, 1991–. Hon. Mem., Soc. of Protozoology, 1999–. Gov., Powell-Cotton Mus., 1992–97. *Publications:* (ed jtly) Ecological Aspects of Used-water Treatment Processes, vol. 1, 1979, vols 2 and 3, 1983; British and other freshwater ciliated protozoa, Pt 1, 1982, Pt 2 (jtly), 1983; Protozoa in the Water Industry, 1992; contribs to professional jls. *Recreations:* family life, furniture design, cabinet-making, France, cats, snorkelling, genealogy. *Address:* Department of Zoology, Natural History Museum, Cromwell Road, SW7 5BD. *T:* (home) (01825) 791796. *E:* colin.curds@googlemail.com.

CURL, His Honour Philip; a Circuit Judge, 1996–2015; *b* 31 Oct. 1947; *s* of Dr Oliver Curl and Joan Curl; *m* 1983, Nicola Ruth Gurney; two *d. Educ:* Radley Coll.; Southampton Univ. (LLB). Called to the Bar, Gray's Inn, 1970; Asst Recorder, 1991–95; Recorder, 1995–96; Designated Family Judge, Norwich, 1998–2007. Legal Mem., Mental Health Review Tribunal (Restricted Patients Panel), 2002–. Mem., Disciplinary Panel, BHA, 2011–. Mem. Council, Norwich Cathedral, 2002–12. Local Steward: Gt Yarmouth and Fakenham Racecourses, 2004–; Newmarket Racecourse, 2007–. Patron, Childhood First, 2014–. *Recreations:* playing and watching sport, art, travel. *Clubs:* Boodle's, MCC; Norfolk (Norwich).

CURL, Prof. Robert Floyd, PhD; Kenneth S. Pitzer-Schlumberger Professor of Natural Sciences and University Professor, Rice University, Houston, 2003–05, now Emeritus; *b* 23 Aug. 1933; *s* of Robert Floyd Curl and Lessie Waldeen Curl; *m* 1955, Jonel Whipple; two *s. Educ:* Rice Inst. (BA 1954); Univ. of Calif, Berkeley (PhD 1957). Res. Fellow, Harvard, 1957–58; Rice Institute, then Rice University: Asst Prof., 1958–63; Associate Prof., 1963–67; Prof. of Chemistry, 1967–96; Chm., Chemistry Dept, 1992–96; Harry C. and Olga K. Wiess Prof. of Natural Scis, 1996–2003; Master, Lovett Coll., 1968–72. Dr (*hc*): Buenos Aires, 1997; Littoral, 2003; Bar Ilan, 2010. (Jtly) Clayton Prize, IMechE, 1958; (jtly) APS Prize for New Materials, 1992; (jtly) Nobel Prize for Chemistry, 1996; (jtly) Texas Distinguished Scientist, Texas Acad. of Sci., 1997; (jtly) Achievement in Carbon Science, Amer. Carbon Soc., 1997; (jtly) Order of the Golden Plate, Amer. Acad. of Achievement, 1997. *Publications:* numerous contribs to scientific jls. *Recreations:* contract bridge, squash. *Address:* Chemistry Department, Rice University, Houston, TX 77005, USA. *T:* (713) 3484816; 1824 Bolsover Road, Houston, TX 77005–1728, USA.

CURLE, James Leonard; Member and Managing Director, Civil Aviation Authority, 1984–87; *b* 14 Nov. 1925; *s* of Leonard and Mary Curle; *m* 1952, Gloria Madaleine Roch; one *s* one *d. Educ:* St Joseph's Academy, Blackheath; SE London Technical College; Borough Polytechnic. CEng, MIET. Royal Signals, 1944–48; joined Telecommunications Div., MTCA, 1957; Dir Telecommunications, ATS, 1976–79; Dir Gen. Telecommunications, NATS, 1979–84. *Address:* 6 Nightingale Lane, Bickley, Kent BR1 2QH. *T:* (020) 8460 8023.

CURNOCK COOK, Jeremy Laurence; Chairman: AmpliPhi Bioscience Corporation (formerly Targeted Genetics inc.), since 1998; International Bioscience Managers Ltd, since 2001; Deputy Chairman, Rex Bionics plc, since 2015; Managing Director, Bioscience Managers Pty Ltd, since 2007; *b* 3 Sept. 1949; *s* of Colin Curnock Cook and Doris (*née* Wolsey); *m* 1st, 1975, Elizabeth Joanna Badgett (marr. diss. 1981); 2nd, 1987, Mary Elizabeth Thomasson (*see* M. E. Curnock Cook) (marr. diss. 1997); one *s* two *d*; 3rd, 2007, Sara Jane Stickland. *Educ:* Lycée Français de Londres; Westminster Sch.; Trinity Coll., Dublin (MA Natural Scis). Res. Scientist, Inst. Cancer Res., London, 1972–73; Managing Director: Badgett-Cook Biochems Ltd, London, 1973–75; Internat. Biochems Ltd, Dublin, London, 1975–87; Rothschild Asset Mgt (Biosci. Unit), 1987–2000. Non-executive Director: Cantab Pharmaceuticals plc, 1990–2001; Biocompatibles Internat. plc, 1992–2011; Vernalis, 1995–2001; Angiotech Pharmaceuticals Inc., 1995–2001; Amrad Corp., 1995–2002; Sirna Therapeutics Inc., 2003–06; Q chip, 2004–06; Silence Therapeutics (formerly S. R. Pharma) plc, 2005–10; Excalibur Group Holdings Ltd, 2005–; Osteologix Inc., 2006–10; Eacom Timber Corp. Inc. (formerly Inflazyme Pharmaceuticals Inc.), 2006–13 (Chm., 2006–10); Aegera Therapeutics Inc., 2008–11; Topigen Pharmaceuticals Inc., 2008–10; Bioxyne Ltd (formerly Hunter Immunology Ltd), 2010–14; Virgin Health Bank QSTP LLC, 2011–13; Phylogica Ltd, 2012–; Avita Medical Ltd, Perth, Aust., 2012–; Sea Dragon Ltd, Nelson, NZ, 2012–; Nexus6 Ltd, Auckland, NZ, 2013–; Arthurian Life Sciences Ltd, 2013–; Smart Matrix Ltd, 2013–; Avena Therapeutics Ltd, 2013– (Chm., 2012–); CEO, Rex Bionics plc (formerly Union MedTech plc), 2012–14. Mem., Biosci. Futures Forum, 2005–08. Mem., Soc. for Gen. Microbiol., 1971–. FInstD 1988; FRSA 1994. *Recreations:* keeping fit, music, ski-ing, hanging out in France. *Address:* 56 Chiswick Green Studios, Evershed Walk, Chiswick, W4 5BW. *Clubs:* Kildare Street and University (Dublin); Royal Automobile of Victoria (Melbourne).

CURNOCK COOK, Mary Elizabeth, OBE 2000; Chief Executive, Universities and Colleges Admissions Service, since 2010; *b* London, 10 Oct. 1958; *d* of Christopher Thomasson and Bryony Thomasson; *m* 1987, Jeremy Laurence Curnock Cook, *qv* (marr. diss. 1997); one *s* two *d. Educ:* Convent of the Sacred Heart, Woldingham; London Business Sch. (MSc Gen. Mgt). Sales and Mktg Dir, International Biochemicals, 1980–88; Mktg Dir, Food from Britain, 1989–93; Chief Exec., BII, 1994–2001; Dir, Qualifications and Skills, QCA, 2003–09. Mem., FEFC, 1997–2001. Non-executive Director: Creative Learning Media, 2002–05; Laurel Pub Co., 2002–05. Gov., Swindon Acad., 2006–. Trustee: Access Proj., 2013–; National Star Coll., 2013–. *Recreations:* fine food and wine, tennis, sailing. *Address:* Universities and Colleges Admissions Service, Rosehill, New Barn Lane, Cheltenham, Glos GL52 3LZ. *T:* (01242) 544990. *E:* m.curnockcook@ucas.ac.uk. *Club:* Blacks.

CURNOW, Rt Rev. Andrew William; *see* Bendigo, Bishop of.

CURR, Surgeon Rear Adm. Ralph Donaldson, FRCGP; Medical Director General (Naval), Ministry of Defence, 2002–03; *b* 25 Sept. 1943; *s* of George and Florence Curr; *m* 1972, Susan Brereton; two *s* three *d. Educ:* Dulwich Coll.; King's Coll. Hosp. (MB BS; AKC). LRCP, MRCS 1969; DRCOG 1975; FRCGP 1992. Joined RN 1969; HMS Mohawk, 1969; HMS Cleopatra, 1971; Malta, 1972–74; GP, NHS and RNR, HMS Vivid, 1975–76; Clyde Submarine Base, 1976–79; Gibraltar, 1979–81; PMO, HMS Raleigh, 1981–84; HK, 1984–86; HMS Intrepid, 1986–88; Dean of Naval Medicine, 1988–90; PMO, HMS Drake, 1990–95; Dir of Naval Personnel, MoD, 1995–97; COS to Med. Dir Gen. (Naval), MoD, 1997–2000; Dir, Med. Ops, CINCFLEET, 2000–02. QHP 2000–03. Civilian Med. Practitioner, HMS Raleigh, Torpoint, 2004–12. Founder Mem., DefenceSynergia, 2010–. Chm., Kosovo Mammography Project, 2007–08; Provost, Tamar Faculty, RCGP, 2011– (Sec., 2005–11). Director: Lord Caradon Trust, 2007–; UK Nat. Defence Assoc., 2008–10. Member: Britannia Assoc., 2004–; St Austell Bay Rotary Club, 2006– (Pres., 2009–11; Gov., Rotary District 1290, 2014–15, and Med. Dir, Overseas Project Team); Chm., St Austell Sea Cadets, 2006–. Dir, Clergy Cottage Trust, 2004–. Mem., Parish Council, 2009–, and Churchwarden, All Saints, Pentewan. OStJ 2001. *Recreations:* walking, church, tennis, medical and defence politics. *Address:* Sea Garth, Pentewan Hill, Pentewan, St Austell, Cornwall PL26 6DD. *T:* (01726) 843106. *E:* rdcurr@hotmail.com. *Club:* Naval.

CURRAN, Edmund Russell, OBE 2006; Editor-in-Chief, Independent News and Media (Northern Ireland), 2005–09; Columnist, Belfast Telegraph, 2009–14; *b* 29 Sept. 1944; *s* of William John Curran and Elizabeth (*née* Russell); *m* 1st, 1968, Romaine Carmichael (marr. diss. 1991); two *s* two *d*; 2nd, 1994, Pauline Hall. *Educ:* Royal Sch., Dungannon; Queen's Univ., Belfast (BSc, DipEd). Dep. Editor, Belfast Telegraph, 1974–88; Editor, Sunday Life (NI), 1988–92; Actg Editor, Wales on Sunday, 1991; Editor, Belfast Telegraph, 1993–2005. Dir, Alpha Newspapers Ltd, 1983–. Mem. Bd, NCTJ, 2005–12. Mem., Press Complaints Commn, 2002–06. Fellow, Soc. of Editors, 2011 (Pres., 2001). Newspaper Focus UK Regl Newspaper Editor of Year, 1991. Hon. DLitt Ulster, 2012. *Recreations:* golf, tennis, reading newspapers. *Address:* c/o Independent News and Media (Northern Ireland), 124/144 Royal Avenue, Belfast BT1 1EB. *T:* (028) 9026 4400. *E:* Edmund.Curran@belfasttelegraph.co.uk. *Clubs:* Ulster Reform; Belvoir Park Golf, Belfast Boat (Belfast); Royal County Down Golf (Newcastle).

CURRAN, Frances; Member (Scot. Socialist) Scotland West, Scottish Parliament, 2003–07; *b* 21 May 1961. *Educ:* St Brendan's Sch., Linwood; St Andrew's Secondary Sch., Carntyne, Glasgow. Mem., NEC, Labour Party, 1984–86; worked for campaigns incl. red wedge, anti-poll tax, youth against racism in Europe; involved in launching Scottish Socialist Alliance, 1995, Scottish Socialist Party, 1998. Contested (Scot. Socialist) Glasgow E, July 2008, 2010. *Recreations:* reading, bingo, caravanning, socialising.

CURRAN, His Honour John Terence; a Circuit Judge, 1996–2012; Resident Judge, Merthyr Tydfil Combined Court Centre, 1998–2012; acting Resident Judge, Cardiff Crown Court, 2012; *b* 31 Oct. 1941; *s* of Eugene Curran, OBE and Joan Curran; *m* 1971, Elizabeth Ann Bowcott; one *s* one *d. Educ:* Ratcliffe; Jesus Coll., Cambridge (MA). Hallinans, solicitors, Cardiff: articled clerk, 1963–68; admitted solicitor, 1968; Partner, 1968–83; called to the Bar, Gray's Inn, 1983; Asst Recorder, 1989–93; Actg Stipendiary Magistrate, 1989; Provincial Stipendiary Magistrate (Mid-Glam), 1990–96; a Recorder, 1993–96. *Recreations:* walking, gardening, history, supporting Cardiff RFC, looking for my spectacles. *Address:* Law Courts, Cathays Park, Cardiff CF10 3PG. *Club:* Cardiff and County.

CURRAN, Kevin Barry; Chair, Central London Hotel Workers, Unite, since 2008; *b* 20 Aug. 1954; *s* of John and Maureen Curran; *m* 1977, June Bartholomew; one *s* one *d.* GMB (formerly General, Municipal, Boilermakers and Allied Trades Union): joined 1975; Health and Safety Officer, London Region, 1988; Regl Organiser, 1990, Regl Industrial Organiser, 1996, Southern Region; Regl Sec., Northern Region, 1997; Gen. Sec., 2003–05; Internat. Co-ordinator, IUF, 2005–07. Living Wage Advr, London Citizens, 2007–. Tree surgeon,

2007–. *Recreations:* football, running, blacksmithing, woodlands, reading, allotment gardening, keeping fit, keeping the foes of working people on their toes. *Club:* Crystal Palace Football.

CURRAN, Maj. Gen. Liam Diarmuid, CB 2001; independent consultant, 2001–06; Engineering Adviser to Defence Procurement Agency and President of the Ordnance Board, 1998–2001; *b* 31 March 1946; *s* of late William James Curran and Genevieve Curran (*née* Lavery); *m* 1971, Evelyn Mary Elizabeth Strang; two *d. Educ:* Presentation Coll., Reading; Welbeck Coll.; Royal Military Acad., Sandhurst; Fitzwilliam Coll., Cambridge (MA 1970). CEng 1980; FIEE 1990. CO, 7 Armd Workshop, REME and Comdr, Fallingbostel Station, 1986–89; Equipt Support Manager on staff of QMG, 1989–91; Project Manager for Light Armd Vehicles, 1991–93; Equipt Support Dir on staff of QMG, 1993–96; Vice-Pres., Ordnance Bd, 1996–98. Col Comdt, REME, 2000–05. *Recreations:* walking, gardening, National Trust. *Address:* c/o Lloyds Bank, 38 Market Place, East Dereham, Norfolk NR19 2AT.

CURRAN, Margaret Patricia; *b* 24 Nov. 1958; *d* of James Curran and Rose McConnellogue; *m* Robert Murray; two *s. Educ:* Glasgow Univ. (MA Hons Hist. and Econ. Hist.); Cert. Community Educn. Welfare rights officer, 1982–83; community worker, 1983–87, sen. community worker, 1987–89, Strathclyde Regl Council; Lectr, Dept of Community Educn, Univ. of Strathclyde, 1989–99. Mem. (Lab) Glasgow Baillieston, Scottish Parlt, 1999–2011; Dep. Minister for Social Justice, 2001–02; Minister: for Social Justice, 2002–03; for Communities, 2003–04; for Parly Business, 2004–07. Contested (Lab) Glasgow E, July 2008. MP (Lab) Glasgow E, 2010–15; contested (Lab) same seat, 2015. Shadow Sec. of State for Scotland, 2011–15. *Recreations:* reading, theatre, American politics, spending time with my sons.

CURRAN, Patrick David; QC 1995; **His Honour Judge Curran;** a Circuit Judge, since 2007; a Deputy Judge of the High Court, Queen's Bench Division, since 2008; *s* of late David Curran and Noreen Curran; *m* 1976; two *s* two *d. Educ:* Ratcliffe; Queen's Coll., Oxford (MA). Called to the Bar, Gray's Inn, 1972, Bencher, 2005; Asst Recorder, 1988–92; Recorder, 1992–2007; admitted to Bar of Ireland, 1993. Asst Comr, Parly Boundary Commn for Wales, 1994–2007. Legal Mem., Mental Health Review Tribunal for Wales, 1995–2008. Legal Assessor, GMC, 2002–07. Governor, Westminster Cathedral Choir Sch., 2000–09. FRSocMed 2007–10. Editor, 1992–2004, Consultant Editor, 2004–, Personal Injuries and Quantum Reports. *Publications:* Personal Injury Pleadings, 1994, 5th edn 2014; (contrib.) Criminal Law and Forensic Psychiatry, 1995; (ed and contrib.) Personal Injury Handbook, 1997. *Address:* The Law Courts, Cathays Park, Cardiff CF10 3PG. *Club:* Athenæum.
See also Dame D. J. Hine.

CURRAN, Prof. Paul James, PhD, DSc; CGeog, FRGS; Vice-Chancellor, and Professor of Physical Geography, City University London, since 2010; *b* 17 May 1955; *s* of late James Patrick Curran and Betty Doreen (*née* Bott); *m* 1978, Helen Patricia Palin; one *d. Educ:* Longslade Upper Sch., Birstall, Leics; Univ. of Sheffield (BSc Hons Geog. 1976); Univ. of Bristol (PhD 1979, DSc 1991); Univ. of Southampton (MBA Dist. 1998). FRGS 1979; CGeog 2002. Lectr, Univ. of Reading, 1979–81; Lectr, then Sen. Lectr, Univ. of Sheffield, 1981–89; Sen. Res. Associate, NASA Ames Res. Center, Calif, 1988–89; Prof. of Physical Geog., UC of Swansea, 1990–93; University of Southampton: Prof. of Physical Geog., 1993–2005; Hd, Dept of Geog., 1995–99; Dean of Sci., 2000–03; Hd, Winchester Sch. of Art, 2003–04; Dep. Vice Chancellor, 2004–05; Vis. Prof., 2005–; Vice-Chancellor, and Prof. of Physical Geog., Bournemouth Univ., 2005–10. Vis. Res. Fellow, Univ. of NSW, 1986. Member: NERC, 2006–14 (Mem., Terrestrial Life Scis Cttee, 1989–92; Mem., 2007–11, Chm., 2011–, Audit and Risk Assurance Cttee; Mem., Remuneration Cttee, 2012–); Bd, QAA, 2006–11 (Mem., Audit Cttee, 2007–11, Remuneration Cttee, 2007–11); Bd, UCEA, 2010– (Chm., 2011–; Chm. employers' negotiating team in nat. pay negotiations, 2011–); Chm., Nat. Review Body on Doctors' and Dentists' Remuneration, 2013–. Member: Sci. Adv. Gp, ESA, 1990–2009; Earth Observation Prog. Bd, BNSC, 1995–98; Sci. Adv. Cttee, ISPRS, 1999–; Wkg Party on Terrestrial Carbon Sinks, Royal Soc., 2000–01; Geog. Panel, 2001 RAE, HEFCE; Employability, Business and Industry Policy Cttee, 2005–, Research Policy Cttee, 2006–, UUK; Chairman: Wkg Gp on Global Ecosystem Monitoring, ISPRS, 1992–2000; Higher Educn Workforce Steering Gp (formerly High Level Academic Workforce), HEFCE, 2007–10; Pres., Remote Sensing and Photogrammetry Soc., 2009–. FRSPS 1995; FCIM 1999. Otto van Gruber Medal, ISPRS, 1988; Cuthbert Peek Award (1883), RGS, 1998; Gold Medal, Remote Sensing Soc., 2000; Patron's Medal, RGS, 2007. *Publications:* Principles of Remote Sensing, 1985; (jtly) Remote Sensing of Soils and Vegetation in the USSR, 1990; (ed) Environmental Remote Sensing from Regional to Global Scales, 1994; Remote Sensing in Biosphere Studies, 1994; Remote Sensing in Action, 1995; Scaling-up from Cell to Landscape, 1997; contrib. chapters in books and articles to conf. proc. and learned jls. *Recreations:* running, travel, family, art, sea. *Address:* City University London, Northampton Square, EC1V 0HB. *T:* (020) 7040 8002, *Fax:* (020) 7040 8596. *E:* vice-chancellor@city.ac.uk. *Clubs:* Athenæum, Geographical; Royal Motor Yacht.

CURRAN, Terence Dominic; HM Diplomatic Service, retired; Consul-General, Toronto, and Director-General of Trade and Investment in Canada, 1996–2000; *b* 14 June 1940; *m* 1969, Penelope Anne Ford; two *s* one *d.* Joined HM Diplomatic Service, 1966; DSAO, 1966–68; Peking, 1968–69; Consul, Dakar, 1970–73; Asst Trade Comr, then Consul (Commercial), Edmonton, 1973–78; FCO, 1978–80; First Sec., Pretoria, 1980–84; FCO, 1984–87; Counsellor (Commercial and Economic), Singapore, 1987–90; Head of Training, FCO, 1990–93; Dep. High Comr, Bombay, 1993–96. *Address:* Rother House, Nyewood, Petersfield, Hants GU31 5HY.

CURRAN, Prof. Thomas, PhD; FRS 2005; Deputy Scientific Director, since 2006, and Director of Basic Scientific Research, Center for Childhood Cancer Research, since 2007, Children's Hospital of Philadelphia Research Institute (formerly Joseph Stokes Jr Research Institute at the Children's Hospital of Philadelphia); Professor of Pathology and Laboratory Medicine, since 2006, and Professor of Cell and Developmental Biology, since 2008, Perelman School of Medicine, University of Pennsylvania; *b* 14 Feb. 1956; *s* of Thomas and Jane Curran; *m* (marr. diss.); one *s* one *d. Educ:* Univ. of Edinburgh (BS 1st cl. Hons Biol Sci. 1978; Ashworth Prize in Zool., 1978); ICRF Labs and University Coll. London (PhD 1982). Postdoctoral Damon Runyon Fellow, Salk Inst., San Diego, Calif, 1982–84; Sen. Scientist, Hoffman-La Roche, Inc., NJ, 1984–85; Asst Mem., 1985–86, Associate Mem., 1986–88, Full Mem., 1988–95, Associate Dir, 1991–95, Roche Inst., Molecular Biol., NJ; Prof. of Anatomy and Neurobiol., Univ. of Tennessee, 1995–2006; Mem. and Chm., Dept of Develtl Neurobiol., St Jude Children's Res. Hosp., Tenn, 1995–2006. Adjunct Prof., Columbia Univ., NY, 1989–95. Mem., Bd of Scientific Advrs, Nat. Cancer Inst., Washington, 2000–05. Litchfield Lectr, Oxford Univ., 1993; W. W. Sutow Vis. Lectr in Pediatric Oncology, Univ. of Texas MD Anderson Cancer Centre, Houston, 2009. Lectures: Marguerite Vogt, Salk Inst., San Diego, 2006; Colleen Giblin Meml, Columbia Univ., NY, 2006. Pres., Amer. Assoc. for Cancer Res., Philadelphia, 2002. Fellow: Amer. Acad. of Microbiol., 1994; Amer. Assoc. for Cancer Res. Acad., 2013; FAAAS 1994; Mem., Inst. Medicine, 2009; Fellow: Amer. Acad. of Arts and Scis, 2012; Amer. Assoc. for Cancer Res. Acad., 2013. Tenovus-Scotland Medal, Glasgow, 1991; Rita Levi Montalcini Award in Neuroscis, 1992; Passano Foundn Young Scientist Award, Baltimore, 1992; Outstanding Achievement in Cancer Res. Award, Amer. Assoc. for Cancer Res., 1993; Golgi Award, Italian Acad. Neurosci., Brescia, 1994; Javitz Neurosci. Investigator Award, Nat. Inst. of Neurol Disorder and Stroke, NIH, 2001; Peter M. Steck Meml Award and Lecture, Houston, Texas, 2002; LIMA Internat. Award for Excellence in Pediatric Brain Tumour Res., PBT Foundn, NY, 2004. *Publications:* (as Tom Curran): (ed) The Oncogene Handbook, 1988; Origins of Human Cancer, 1991; (ed jtly) Two Faces of Evil: cancer and neurodegeneration, 2011; contrib. to books and over 270 articles in scientific jls. *Address:* Children's Hospital of Philadelphia Research Institute, Colket Translational Research Building, 3501 Civic Center Boulevard, Philadelphia, PA 19104–4318, USA. *T:* (267) 4262819, *Fax:* (267) 4262791. *E:* currant@email.chop.edu.

CURRIE, family name of **Baron Currie of Marylebone**.

CURRIE OF MARYLEBONE, Baron *cr* 1996 (Life Peer), of Marylebone in the City of Westminster; **David Anthony Currie;** Chairman, Competition and Markets Authority, since 2012; *b* 9 Dec. 1946; *s* of Kennedy Moir Currie and Marjorie Currie (*née* Thompson); *m* 1st, 1975, Shaziye Gazioglu Currie (marr. diss. 1992); two *s*; 2nd, 1995, Angela Mary Piers Dumas. *Educ:* Battersea Grammar Sch.; Univ. of Manchester (BSc 1st cl. Maths); Univ. of Birmingham (MSocSci Econs); PhD Econs London. Economist: Hoare Govett, 1971–72; Economic Models, 1972; Lectr, Reader and Prof. of Economics, Queen Mary College, Univ. of London, 1972–88; London Business School: Prof. of Econs, 1988–2000; Res. Dean, 1989–92; Gov., 1989–95; Dep. Principal, 1992–95; Dep. Dean for External Relations, 1999–2000; Dir, Centre for Econ. Forecasting, 1988–95; Dean, City Univ. Business Sch., subseq. Cass Business Sch., City of London, 2001–07. Res. Fellow, Centre for Economic Policy Research, 1983–. Houblon-Norman Res. Fellow, Bank of England, 1985–86; Vis. Scholar, IMF, 1987. Member: Treasury's Panel of Independent Forecasters, 1992–95; Gas and Electricity Mkts Authy, 2000–02; Bd, Dubai FSA, 2004–; Chairman: Office of Communications, 2002–09; ICFR, 2009–12. Assessor, Leveson Inquiry into culture, practice and ethics of the press, 2011–12. Dir and Chm. Exec. Cttee, 1993–97, Charter 88; Dir, Abbey National plc, 2001–02. Non-executive Director: BDO (formerly BDO Stoy Hayward), 2008–12; Royal Mail, 2009–12; IG Group, 2010–12. Chm., Semperian PPP Investment Partners, 2008–12. Mem., Bd, LPO, 2007–12. Trustee, Joseph Rowntree Reform Trust, 1989–2002. Hon. Fellow, QMW, 1997. Hon. DLitt Glasgow, 1998; Hon. DSc City, 2012; Hon. Dr Essex, 2014. *Publications:* Advances in Monetary Economics, 1985; (with Charles Goodhart and David Llewellyn) The Operation and Regulation of Financial Markets, 1986; (with David Vines) Macroeconomic Interactions Between North and South, 1988; (with Paul Levine) Rules, Reputation and Macroeconomic Policy Co-ordination, 1993; (with David Vines) North-South Linkages and International Macroeconomic Policy, 1995; The Pros and Cons of EMU, 1997; Will the Euro Work?: the ins and outs of EMU, 1998; articles in jls. *Recreations:* music, literature, swimming. *Address:* House of Lords, SW1A 0PW.

CURRIE, Btcy *cr* 1847; succession to this Baronetcy has not yet been established following the death of the 7th Bt in 2014; no name has yet been entered on the Official Roll of the Baronetage.

CURRIE, Maj. Gen. Archibald Peter Neil, CB 2001; CBE 2014; Lieutenant Governor, Royal Hospital, Chelsea, 2005–14; *b* Dar es Salaam, 30 June 1948; *s* of Donald and Ysobel Currie; *m* 1974, Angela Margaret Howell; two *s. Educ:* Sao Hill Sch., Tanzania; Monkton Combe Sch.; RMA, Sandhurst; Nottingham Univ. (BA Hons Hist. 1973). 2nd Regt, RA, 1970–75; 22 Regt, RA, 1975–79; RMCS, Shrivenham, 1980; psc, 1981; Operational Requirements, MoD, 1982–83; Batt. Comdr, 22 Regt, RA, 1984–86; Army Staff Duties, MoD, 1986–87; CO, 12 Regt, RA, 1987–90; Instr, Staff Coll., Camberley, 1990–91; Col, Mil. Ops 1, MoD, 1991–93; HCSC, 1993; Comdr Artillery, HQ ARRC, 1994; Dep. Comdr, Multinat. Div. Central (Airmobile), 1995; DPS (Army), MoD, 1996–98; Mil. Advr to High Rep. in Bosnia Herzegovina, 1998–99; COS to Adjt Gen., 1999–2001; Dep. Adjt Gen., MoD, 2001–02. Has served in NI, Falkland Is and Bosnia. Advr to Sunday Mirror, 2003–05. Dir, Blue Force Gp, 2003–06. Non-exec. Dir, Close Brothers Mil. Services, 2004–06. Member: Bd, Services Sound and Vision Corp., 2003–09; Council, Forces Pension Soc., 2003–; Trustee, Combat Stress, 2006–13 (Chm., 2007–13). *Recreations:* ski-ing, tennis, opera, walking in wild places, Persian rugs.

CURRIE, Austin; *see* Currie, J. A.

CURRIE, Brian Murdoch; President, Institute of Chartered Accountants in England and Wales, 1996–97 (Vice-President, 1994–95; Deputy President, 1995–96); *b* 20 Dec. 1934; *s* of William Murdoch Currie and Dorothy (*née* Holloway); *m* 1961, Patricia Maria, *d* of Capt. Frederick Eaton-Farr; three *s* one *d. Educ:* Blundell's Sch. (Scholar); Oriel Coll., Oxford (Open Scholar; MA). ACA 1963, FCA 1973; MIMC 1968, FIMC 1990. Commnd RTR, 1957–59; Arthur Andersen Chartered Accountants and Andersen Consulting, 1959–90: Partner, 1970–90; Man. Partner, London, 1977–82; Chm., Partnership Council, 1983–85. Dist Auditor, 1982–87. Dept of Trade Inspector, Fourth City and other cos, 1978; Mem., Foster Cttee of Inquiry into Road Haulage Licensing, 1977. Member: Management Bd, HMSO, 1972–74; Restrictive Practices Court, 1979–2004; Takeover Panel, 1989–97; Lay Mem., GDC, 1994–99; Dep. Chm., Financial Reporting Council, 1996–98. Institute of Chartered Accountants in England and Wales: Mem. Council, 1988–99; Chm., Practice Regulation, 1993; Chm., Chartered Accountants Jt Ethics Cttee, 1994–95; Mem., IFAC Compliance Cttee, 2000–02. Trustee, Oriel Coll. Develt Trust, 1980–94. Chm., Peter Blundell Soc., 1997–2002; Member, Committee: Exmoor Soc., 1993–2002 (Founder's Award, 2002); Glass Assoc., 1998–2003. Gov., Blundell's Sch., 2000–02. Jt Ed., Glass Cone, 1999–2005. *Publications:* A Principle-based Framework for Professional Independence, 1992; official public reports; papers and articles in professional and technical pubns. *Recreations:* natural history, Exmoor, church (lay assisting). *Address:* Westbrook House, Bampton, Tiverton, Devon EX16 9HU. *T:* (01398) 331418. *Club:* Athenæum.

CURRIE, Dr Christopher Richard John, FRHistS, FSA; Senior Research Fellow, Institute of Historical Research, 2002–08 and since 2008; Gazette Editor, Church Times, since 2002 (Deputy Web Editor, 2002–09); *b* 3 March 1948; *s* of George Samson Currie, MC and Norah Currie (*née* Kennedy); *m* 1981, Katherine Ruth Gommon; one *s* one *d. Educ:* Winchester; Balliol Coll., Oxford (MA 1976, DPhil 1976). FRHistS 1979; FSA 1984. Victoria County History: Asst Editor, Staffs, 1972–78; Dep. Editor, 1978–94; Gen. Editor, 1994–2000; Consultant Editor, 2000–02. Mem. Council, RHistS, 1996–2000. Pres., 2007–11, Vice Pres., 2011–14, Vernacular Architecture Gp; Hon. Editor, Vernacular Architecture, 1980–82. *Publications:* (ed with C. P. Lewis) English County Histories: a guide, 1994; articles in Victoria County Hist. and learned jls. *Recreation:* sleep. *Address:* 14 Keston Road, N17 6PN. *T:* (020) 8801 2185.

CURRIE, Edwina, (Edwina Currie Jones); *b* 13 Oct. 1946; *m* 1st, 1972, Raymond F. Currie, BA, FCA (marr. diss. 2001); two *d*; 2nd, 2001, John Benjamin Paul Jones, former Det. Supt, Met. Police; four step *s. Educ:* Liverpool Inst. for Girls; St Anne's Coll., Oxford (scholar; MA 1972); London Sch. of Econs and Pol Science (MSc 1972). Teaching and lecturing posts in econs, econ. history and business studies, 1972–81. Birmingham City Council: Mem., 1975–86; Chm., Social Services Cttee, 1979–80; Chm., Housing Cttee, 1982–83. Chm., Central Birmingham HA, 1981–83. MP (C) Derbyshire South, 1983–97; contested (C) same seat, 1997. PPS to Sec. of State for Educn and Science, 1985–86; Parly Under-Sec. of State (Health), DHSS, later Dept of Health, 1986–88. Member: European Movement, 1992– (Vice Chm., 1995–98); Cons. Gp for Europe, 1992– (Chm., 1995–97); Dir, Future of Europe Trust, 1992–97 (Jt Chm., 1994–97). Contested (C) Bedfordshire and Milton Keynes, Eur. Parly elecns, 1994. Regular contributor to nat. newspapers and magazines; presenter: Sunday Supplement, TV, 1993; Espresso, TV, 1997; various radio progs, incl. Late Night Currie, 1998–2003, BBC Radio Five Live. Trustee: Marie Curie Cancer Care, 1992–94; VOICE (UK) (Chm., 1994–97); The Patients Assoc., 2006–08; Patron: Reigate and Banstead Women's Aid, 2005–11; MRSA Action UK, 2007–; Pres., Tideswell Male Voice Choir,

2012–. Dir, Future of Europe Trust (Jt Chm., 1994–97). Speaker of the Year, Assoc. of Speakers' Clubs, 1990; Campaigner of the Year, Spectator Awards, 1994. *Publications:* Financing our Cities (Bow Group pamphlet), 1976; Life Lines, 1989; What Women Want, 1990; (jtly) Three-Line Quips, 1992; Edwina Currie Diaries: 1987–92, 2002, vol. II, 1992–97, 2012; *novels:* A Parliamentary Affair, 1994; A Woman's Place, 1996; She's Leaving Home, 1997; The Ambassador, 1999; Chasing Men, 2000; This Honourable House, 2001. *Recreations:* earning a living, theatre, reading other people's books, keeping up with nine grandchildren and three great-grandchildren. *Address:* c/o CJA Ltd, Whaley Bridge, Derbys SK23 7BA.

CURRIE, Dr Graham Alan, MD; FRCP, FRCPath; Research Director, Marie Curie, 1982–2002; *b* 17 Aug. 1939; *s* of Alan Currie and Dorothy Currie; *m* 1964, Dr Angela Wright; one *s* three *d*. *Educ:* Charing Cross Hosp. Med. Sch. (MB BS; Univ. of London Prize Medal, 1963; MD 1974). FRCPath 1982; FRCP 1984. Jun. appts, Charing Cross Hosp., 1963–69; staff mem., Chester Beatty Res. Inst., 1969–74; Sen. Lectr, Ludwig Inst. for Cancer Res., 1974–82; Hon. Consultant Physician, Royal Marsden Hosp., 1974–82. Saltwell Res. Scholar, RCP, 1966; Wellcome Res. Fellow, Charing Cross Hosp., 1968. Founding Ed., Oncogene, 1987. *Publications:* Cancer and the Immune Response, 1974, 2nd edn 1980; numerous papers and reviews in learned jls. *Recreations:* art, music, gardens, sleep. *Address:* Hunters, Forest Lodge, Epsom Road, Ashtead, Surrey KT21 1JX. *T:* (01372) 278707.

CURRIE, Heriot Whitson; QC (Scot.) 1992; *b* 23 June 1952; *s* of Heriot Clunas Currie and Evelyn Whitson; *m* 1st, 1975, Susan Carolyn Hodge (marr. diss. 2001); three *d*; 2nd, 2003, Paula Maria Christian. *Educ:* Edinburgh Academy; Wadham Coll., Oxford (MA); Edinburgh Univ. (LLB). Admitted to Faculty of Advocates, 1979; practice as Advocate, 1979–; called to the Bar, Gray's Inn, 1991; Mem., Monckton Chambers, 2005–14. Chm. (pt-time), Competition Appeal Tribunal, 2013–. *Recreations:* chamber music, cinema, golf, foreign languages. *Address:* 2 Doune Terrace, Edinburgh EH3 6DY; 1 & 2 Raymond Buildings, Gray's Inn, WC1R 5NR. *Clubs:* New (Edinburgh); Honourable Company of Edinburgh Golfers, Royal Burgess Golfing Society (Edinburgh).

CURRIE, James McGill; Director-General (Environment, Climate and Nuclear Safety), European Commission, 1997–2001; *b* 17 Nov. 1941; *s* of late David Currie and of Mary (*née* Smith); *m* 1968, Evelyn Barbara MacIntyre; one *s* one *d*. *Educ:* St Joseph's High Sch., Kilmarnock; Blairs Coll., Aberdeen; Royal Scots Coll., Valladolid; Univ. of Glasgow (MA). Asst Principal, Scottish Home and Health Dept, 1968–72; Principal, Scottish Educn Dept, 1972–75; Secretary, Management Gp, Scottish Office, 1975–77; Scottish Development Dept: Principal, 1977–79; Asst Sec., 1979–81; Asst Sec., Scottish Economic Planning Dept, 1981–82; Counsellor, UK Perm. Representation to EEC, 1982–87; Dir of Regional Policy, EEC, 1987–89; Chef de Cabinet to Leon Brittan, EEC, 1989–92; Dep. Head, EC Delegn to USA, 1993–96; Dir-Gen. (Customs and Indirect Taxation), EC, 1996–97. Vis. Prof. of Law, Georgetown Law Center, Washington, 1997–2005. Chm., Davaar Associates, 2002–13; Chm. and Sen. Advr, Burson-Marsteller Brussels, 2007–. Non-executive Director: Royal Bank of Scotland, 2001–09; Total UK, 2004–; Vimetco NV, 2007–; Met Office, 2007–11. FRSA 2007. Hon. DLitt Glasgow, 2001. *Recreations:* tennis, golf, guitar, good food. *Club:* New (Edinburgh).

CURRIE, (Joseph) Austin; retired politician and author; Minister of State, Departments of Health, Education and Justice, Irish Parliament, 1994–97; only person to have been elected to both Irish Parliaments and to have served as a Minister in both; *b* 11 Oct. 1939; *s* of John Currie and Mary (*née* O'Donnell); *m* 1968, Anne Ita Lynch; two *s* three *d*. *Educ:* Edendork Sch.; St Patrick's Academy, Dungannon; Queen's Univ., Belfast (BA). MP (Nat) Tyrone, Parlt of N Ireland, 1964–72; Founder Mem., SDLP, 1970; Mem. (SDLP), Fermanagh and S Tyrone, NI Assembly, 1973–75, NI Constitutional Convention, 1975–76, NI Assembly, 1982–86; Minister of Housing, Planning and Local Govt, 1974. Contested (FG) Presidency of Ireland, 1990. Irish Parliament: TD (FG), Dublin W, Dail Eireann, 1989–2002. Mem., Anglo-Irish Parly tier; frontbench spokesperson: on communications, 1991–93; on equality and law reform, 1993–94; spokesperson on energy, 1997–2001; dep. spokesperson on foreign affairs, 2001–02. Mem., Forum for Peace and Reconciliation, 1995–. Mem. Bd, Caranua, 2013–. Advr to Eur. Commn, 1984–87. *Publications:* All Hell Will Break Loose (autobiog.), 2004. *Recreations:* Gaelic football, golf, snooker, reading. *Address:* Tullydraw, Derrymullen, Robertstown, Naas, Co. Kildare, Ireland.

CURRIE JONES, Edwina; *see* Currie, E.

CURRIMBHOY, Sir Mohamed; *see* Ebrahim, Sir M. C.

CURRY, family name of **Baron Curry of Kirkharle**.

CURRY OF KIRKHARLE, Baron *cr* 2011 (Life Peer), of Kirkharle in the County of Northumberland; **Donald Thomas Younger Curry,** Kt 2001; CBE 1997; Chairman: Leckford Estate, Waitrose, since 2009; Better Regulation Executive, Department for Business, Innovation and Skills, since 2009; Royal Veterinary College, since 2012; Cawood Scientific, since 2014; *b* 4 April 1944; *s* of Robert Thomas Younger Curry and Barbara Ramsey Curry; *m* 1966, Rhoda Mary Murdie; two *s* one *d*. *Educ:* Northumberland Coll. of Agric. Estabd farming business, 1971; farms 450 acres in Northumberland (C&G Farm Mgt and Orgn). Comr, MLC, 1986–2001 (Dep. Chm., 1992–93; Chm., 1993–2001); Crown Estate Comr, 2000–07; Chm., NFU Mutual Insurance Soc., 2003–11 (non-exec. Dir, 1997–2011; Vice-Chm., 2000–03). Chm., Commn on the Future of Farming and Food, 2001–02. Founder/Chairman: N Country Primestock (livestock mktg co-op.), 1990–2002; At Home in the Community (provides residential homes for people with a learning disability), 1992–2013. Trustee: Clinton Devon Estate, 2009–; Lawes Trust (Rothamsted Research) 2009–; Anglican Internat. Develt, 2010–; Prospects, 2013–. Hon. BSc Cranfield, 2004; Hon. Dr Gloucester, 2005; Hon. DCL Newcastle, 2008. *Recreations:* church responsibilities, photography, travel, gardening. *Address:* Middle Farm, Barrasford, Hexham, Northumberland NE48 4DA. *Club:* Farmers.

CURRY, Prof. Anne Elizabeth, (Mrs J. G. Painter), PhD; FRHistS, FSA, FHA; Professor of Medieval History, since 2004, and Dean, Faculty of Humanities, since 2010, University of Southampton; *b* Chester-le-Street, Co. Durham, 27 May 1954; *d* of Ralph Curry and Jean Mary Curry (*née* Whittaker); *m* 1979, John Geoffrey Painter; one *s*. *Educ:* Deanery Secondary Sch., Chester-le-Street; Univ. of Manchester (BA 1st Cl. Hist. 1975; MA 1977); CNAA (Teesside Poly.) (PhD 1985). FRHistS 1986. Res. Asst, Teesside Poly., 1976–78; University of Reading: Lectr in Hist., 1978–94; Sen. Lectr, 1994–2001; Prof., 2001–04. Ed., Jl Medieval Hist., 2001–08. Dep. Chair, Hist. Sub-panel, REF 2014. Mem., Battlefields Panel, English Heritage, 2012–. Co-Chair, Agincourt 600, 2012–. Pres., Histl Assoc., 2008–11; Vice-Pres., RHistS, 2006–09. Trustee, Royal Armouries, 2014–. Member: Soc. de l'Histoire de France, 1980; Soc. des Antiquaires de Normandie, 2014. FSA 1996; FHA 2006. Liveryman, Fletchers' Co., 2013. *Publications:* The Hundred Years War, 1993, 2nd edn 2003; The Battle of Agincourt: sources and interpretations, 2000, 2nd edn 2009; Essential Histories: the Hundred Years War, 2002; Agincourt: a new history, 2005, 2nd edn 2006; The Parliament Rolls of Medieval England, X, XI and XII (1422–1453), 2005; (with G. Foard) Bosworth: a battlefield rediscovered, 2013; (jtly) The Soldier in Later Medieval England, 2013; Great Battles: Agincourt, 2015; Henry V, 2015. *Recreations:* classical music, singing, escaping to the fifteenth century. *Address:* Faculty of Humanities, University of Southampton, Southampton SO17 1BF. *T:* (023) 8059 5419, *Fax:* (023) 8059 3868. *E:* a.e.curry@soton.ac.uk. *Club:* Athenæum.

CURRY, Rt Hon. David (Maurice); PC 1996; *b* 13 June 1944; *s* of late Thomas Harold Curry and Florence Joan (*née* Tyerman); *m* 1971, Anne Helene Maud Roullet; one *s* two *d*. *Educ:* Ripon Grammar Sch.; Corpus Christi Coll., Oxford (MA Hons); Kennedy Sch. of Govt, Harvard (Kennedy Scholar, 1966–67). Reporter, Newcastle Jl, 1967–70; Financial Times: Trade Editor, Internat. Cos Editor, Brussels Corresp., Paris Corresp., and European News Editor, 1970–79. Sec., Anglo-American Press Assoc. of Paris, 1978; Founder, Paris Conservative Assoc., 1977. MEP (C) Essex NE, 1979–89; Chm., Agriculture Cttee, 1982–84; Vice-Chm., Budgets Cttee, 1984–85; spokesman on budgetary matters for European Democratic Gp, 1985–89; Gen. Rapporteur for EEC's 1987 budget. MP (C) Skipton and Ripon, 1987–2010. Parly Sec., 1989–92, Minister of State, 1992–93, MAFF; Minister of State, DoE, 1993–97; Shadow Sec. of State for Local and Devolved Govt Affairs, 2003–04. Chairman, Select Committee: on agriculture, 1999–2001; on envmt, food and rural affairs, 2001–03; Member: Public Accounts Cttee, 2004–10; Cttee on Standards & Privileges, 2007–10. Chm., Dairy UK, 2005–08. Chm., Internat. Develt Enterprises, subsistence farming charity, 2013– (Vice Chm., 2010–13). *Publications:* The Food War: the EEC, the US and the battle for world food markets, 1982; (ed) The Conservative Tradition in Europe, 1998; Lobbying Government, 1999. *Recreations:* digging, windsurfing. *Address:* Newland End, Arkesden, Essex CB11 4HF. *T:* (01799) 550368.

CURRY, Dr Gordon Barrett; Senior University Teacher, School of Geographical and Earth Sciences, University of Glasgow, since 2013; *b* 27 June 1954; *s* of Robert and Violet Curry; *m* 1983, Gillian. *Educ:* Masonic Sch., Dublin; Trinity Coll., Dublin (BA Mod.); Imperial Coll. London (PhD, DIC). University of Glasgow: Research Asst to Sir Alwyn Williams, 1980–84; Royal Soc. Res. Fellow, 1984–92; Reader, Dept of Geol. and Applied Geol., then Div. of Earth Scis, subseq. Sch. of Geographical and Earth Scis, 1992–2013; Dep. Dir, Human Identification Centre, 1995–98; Project Manager, Taxonomy Prog., 1996–99; Chief Advr for Sci., Coll. of Sci. and Engrg, 2011–13. Treas., Systematics Assoc., 1996–2004. President's Award, Geol Soc., 1985; Clough Award, Edinburgh Geol Soc., 1985–86; Wollaston Fund, Geol Soc., 1989. *Publications:* (jtly) British Brachiopods, 1979; (ed) Allochthonous Terranes, 1991; (jtly) Molecules through Time: fossil molecules and biochemical systematics, 1991; Biology of Living Brachiopods, 1992; (ed) Biodiversity Databases, 2007; (ed) Evolution and Development of the Brachiopod Shell, 2010; numerous contribs to learned jls. *Recreations:* music, walking, swimming, cricket, golf, travel. *Address:* School of Geographical and Earth Sciences, Gregory Building, University of Glasgow, Lilybank Gardens, Glasgow G12 8QQ. *T:* (0141) 330 5444. *E:* Gordon.Curry@glasgow.ac.uk.

CURRY, John Arthur Hugh, CBE 1997; Chairman, All England Lawn Tennis Ground plc, 1990–2011; *b* 7 June 1938; *s* of Alfred Robert and Mercia Beatrice Curry; *m* 1962, Anne Rosemary Lewis; three *s* one *d*. *Educ:* King's College School, Wimbledon; St Edmund Hall, Oxford (MA); Harvard Univ. Graduate College (MBA). FCA. Arthur Andersen, 1962–64; Man. Dir, Unitech, 1966–86 (non-exec. Dir, 1986–96); Exec. Chm., 1986–2001, non-exec. Chm., 2001–05, ACAL. Dir and Chm. of private cos, 1976–. Non-executive Director: Dixons, 1993–2001; Foreign & Colonial Smaller Cos PLC, 1996–2004 (Chm., 2002–04); Terence Chapman Group plc, 1999–2003; Chm., Invicta Leisure Gp, 1999–2002. *Publications:* Partners for Profit, 1966. *Recreations:* tennis, Rugby. *Address:* Stokewood Park House, Sheardley Lane, Droxford, Hants SO32 3QY. *Clubs:* Farmers, Institute of Directors; All England Lawn Tennis and Croquet (Chm., 1989–99, Mem. Cttee, 1979–99, Vice Pres., 2000–); International Lawn Tennis of GB (Hon. Treas., 1977–86); Oxford University Lawn Tennis (Pres., 2003–10).

CURRY, Judith Penelope; Chief Executive, Commonwealth Education Trust, since 2007; *b* Cambridge, 7 Aug. 1952; *d* of Sir Denys Haigh Wilkinson, *qv*; *m* 1981, Philip Curry; two *d*. *Educ:* Oxford High Sch.; Somerville Coll., Oxford (BA Maths 1973); Laban Art of Movement Studio (Dip. Dance Th. 1975); Cass Business Sch. (MSc Math. Trading and Finance 2001). ACA 1982. Scientific Sub-Editor, Academic Press, 1977–78; Computer Audit Senior and Trainee Accountant, Hill Vellacott, 1979–82; Mem., Micro Computer Adv. Service, Peat Marwick, 1982–83; Finance and Inf. Manager, Univ. Centre, Cambridge, 1996; Supervisor, 1997, Manager, 1998, Sen. Manager, 1999–2000, Global Risk Mgt Solutions, Coopers & Lybrand, later PricewaterhouseCoopers; Finance Dir, 2000–02, Finance Dir and Sec., 2003–07, Commonwealth Inst. Chair, Thirty Bird Prodns, 1998–2011. Member: Adv. Bd, Caribbean Poetry Project, 2010–, Southern African Poetry Project, 2013–, Cambridge Univ.; Cttee, Oxford Educn Soc., 2012– (Treas., 2013–). Mem., Clavering Players, 2008– (Mem., Cttee, 2012–; Treas., 2014–). Mem., 100 Women in Hedge Funds, 2010–. *Recreations:* travel, hiking, dance, drama. *Address:* Commonwealth Education Trust, New Zealand House, 80 Haymarket, SW1Y 4TE. *T:* (020) 7024 9822. *E:* jcurry@cet1886.org.

CURRYER, Ian; Chief Executive, Nottingham City Council, since 2013; *b* Stevenage, Herts, 19 Sept. 1962; *s* of Dennis and Barbara Curryer; *m* 1991, Margaret Figures; two *s*. *Educ:* Nobel Sch., Stevenage; Nottingham Trent Univ. (BEd Hons Primary Generalist). Accredited OFSTED Inspector, 2002. Teacher: Crossdale Drive Primary Sch., 1986–88; Claremont Primary and Nursery Sch., 1988–91; Head Teacher, Forest Fields Primary Sch., 1991–99; Nottingham City Council: Primary Sch. Advr, 1999–2002; Asst Dir, Equalities, Regeneration and Partnerships, 2002–04; Asst Dir, Economic and Social Regeneration, 2004; Asst Dir, Inclusion and Family Services, 2004–06; Dir, Schs Services, 2006–07; Dir, Targeted Services for Children and Young People, 2007–08; Corporate Dir for Children and Families, 2008–11. *Publications:* Strategies for Building School Improvement, 2002; Grasping the Nettle: early intervention for children and families, 2011. *Recreations:* ski-ing, cycling, cookery, travel, football. *Address:* Nottingham City Council, Loxley House, Station Street, Nottingham NG2 3NG. *T:* (0115) 876 3600. *E:* ian.curryer@nottinghamcity.gov.uk.

CURTEIS, Ian Bayley, FSA; dramatist; *b* 1 May 1935; *m* 1st, 1964, Mrs (Dorothy) Joan Macdonald (marr. diss.; she *d* 2009); two *s*; 2nd, 1985, Joanna Trollope, *qv* (marr. diss. 2001); two step *d*; 3rd, 2001, Lady Deirdre Freda Mary Hare, *e d* of 5th Earl of Listowel, GCMG, PC and *widow* of 7th Baron Grantley, MC; two step *s*. *Educ:* Iver Council Sch.; Slough Grammar Sch.; Slough Trading Estate; London Univ. FSA 2011. Director and actor in theatres all over Great Britain, and BBC-tv script reader, 1956–63; BBC and ATV staff director (drama), directing plays by John Betjeman, John Hopkins, William Trevor and others, 1963–67. Pres., Writers' Guild of GB, 1998–2001 (Mem. Exec. Council and Chm. various cttees, 1979–2001). Founder and Trustee, Joanna Trollope Charitable Trust, 1995–2003. *Television plays:* Beethoven, Sir Alexander Fleming (BBC's entry at 1973 Prague Fest.), Mr Rolls and Mr Royce, Long Voyage out of War (trilogy), The Folly, The Haunting, Second Time Round, A Distinct Chill, The Portland Millions, Philby, Burgess and Maclean (British entry 1978 Monte Carlo Fest., BAFTA nomination), Hess, The Atom Spies, Churchill and the Generals (BAFTA nomination; Grand Prize, Best Programme of 1980, NY Internat. Film and TV Fest.), Suez 1956 (BAFTA nomination), Miss Morison's Ghosts (British entry 1982 Monte Carlo Fest.), The Mitford Girls, BB and Joe (trilogy), Lost Empires (adapted from J. B. Priestley), The Trials of Lady Sackville, Eureka (1st Euroserial simultaneously shown in UK, West Germany, Austria, Switzerland, Italy and France), The Nightmare Years, The Zimmerman Telegram, The Choir (dramatisation of Joanna Trollope novel), The Falklands Play; also originated and wrote numerous popular television drama series; *film screenplays:* Andre Malraux's La Condition humaine, 1982; Graham Greene's The Man Within, 1983; Tom Paine (for Sir Richard Attenborough), 1983; *plays:* A Personal Affair, Globe, 1982; The Bargain, Bath and nat. tour, 2007; Lafayette, NY, 2015; *radio plays:* Eroica, 2000; Love, 2001; The Falklands Play, 2002; After the Break, 2002; More Love, 2003; Yet More Love, 2004; Miss Morison's Ghosts, 2004; Boscobel, 2008; Last Tsar, 2009; The Road to Yalta, 2014.

Publications: plays: Long Voyage out of War (trilogy), 1971; Churchill and the Generals, 1979; Suez 1956, 1980; The Falklands Play, 1987; numerous articles and speeches on the ethics and politics of broadcasting. *Recreations:* history of art, history of architecture, country pursuits. *Address:* Markenfield Hall, Ripon, N Yorks HG4 3AD. *T:* (01765) 603411; 2 Warwick Square, SW1V 2AA. *T:* (020) 7821 8606. *Clubs:* Beefsteak, Garrick.

See also T. A. Curteis.

CURTEIS, Tobit Armstrong, FIIC; FSA; architectural conservator, Tobit Curteis Associates LLP, since 1996; *b* 2 March 1966; *s* of Ian Bayley Curteis, *qv* and late Dorothy Joan Curteis; *m* 1996, Victoria Ellen Kaye; one *s* one *d. Educ:* King's Sch., Canterbury; Univ. of Warwick (BA Hons Hist. of Art 1988); Courtauld Inst. of Art, Univ. of London (Dip. Conservation of Wall Paintings 1991). FIIC 2003. Research and treatment projects include: Winchester Cathedral, 1995, 2012–; Hill Hall (English Heritage), 1995–2005; Chartwell (NT), 1998–2005; Fitzwilliam Mus., Cambridge, 1999–2001; Peterborough Cathedral, 1999–2005; Cormac's Chapel, Cashel, Ireland, 2001–; St John's Coll., Cambridge, 2002; Golden Temple, Amritsar, 2003; Worcester Cathedral, 2003–06; Hampton Court Palace, 2004–; Chinese Palace, St Petersburg, Russia (World Monument Fund), 2004–08; Blickling Hall, Norfolk (NT), 2005; Lincoln Cathedral, 2006; Canterbury Cathedral, 2008–; Windsor Castle, 2009–10; King's Coll. Chapel, Cambridge, 2010–; Westminster Cathedral, 2011–; Hypogeum Hal Saflieni, Malta, 2011–13; Knole, Kent (NT), 2011–; York Minster, 2011–; Rochester Cathedral, 2011–; Westminster Abbey, 2013–; Exeter Cathedral, 2013–; Durham Cathedral, 2013–; St Paul's Cathedral, 2013–; Coventry Cathedral, 2014–. Consultant to English Heritage on conservation of wall paintings, 2002–; Wall Paintings Advr to NT, 2005–. *Publications:* (ed jtly) Building Environment, 2014; contrib. numerous articles and published lectures to conf. proc. and professional jls. *Recreations:* paragliding, hill walking, cooking. *Address:* Tobit Curteis Associates LLP, 33 Cavendish Avenue, Cambridge CB1 7UR. *T:* (01223) 501958, *Fax:* (01223) 790225. *E:* tc@tcassociates.co.uk.

CURTICE, Prof. John Kevin, FBA 2014; FRSE; FAcSS; Professor of Politics, University of Strathclyde, since 1998; *b* Redruth, Cornwall, 10 Dec. 1953; *s* of Thomas John and Mildred Winifred Curtice; *m* 1978, Dr Lisa Joan Riding; one *d. Educ:* Truro Sch.; Magdalen Coll., Oxford (MA). Gwilym Gibbon Prize Res. Fellow, Nuffield Coll., Oxford, 1981–83; Lectr in Politics, Univ. of Liverpool, 1983–88; University of Strathclyde: Lectr in Politics, 1988–89; Sen. Lectr in Politics, 1989–96; Reader in Politics, 1997; Dir, Social Stats Lab., 1989–2009. Fellow in Residence, Netherlands Inst. for Advanced Study, 1988–89. Co-Dir, British Election Study, 1983–98. Res. Consultant, NatCen/ScotCen Social Res., 2001–. Freelance broadcaster and newspaper commentator, 1979–. President: British Polling Council, 2008–; British Politics Gp, 2012–. FRSA 1992; FRSE 2004; FAcSS (AcSS 2013). *Publications:* (jtly) How Britain Votes, 1985; (jtly) Understanding Political Change, 1991; (ed jtly) British Social Attitudes Reports, annually, 1994–; (ed jtly) Labour's Last Chance, 1994; (jtly) On Message, 1999; (jtly) The Rise of New Labour, 2001; (jtly) New Scotland, New Politics, 2001; (jtly) New Scotland, New Society?, 2002; (ed jtly) Devolution: Scottish answers to Scottish questions?, 2003; (ed jtly) Has Devolution Delivered?, 2006; (ed jtly) Has Devolution Worked?, 2009; (jtly) Revolution or Evolution? The 2007 Scottish Elections, 2009; contribs to ed books and contrib. papers to academic jls. *Recreations:* music, theatre, gardening, walking. *Address:* School of Government and Public Policy, University of Strathclyde, 16 Richmond Street, Glasgow G1 1XQ. *T:* 07710 348755. *E:* J.Curtice@strath.ac.uk. *Club:* National Liberal.

CURTIS, Prof. Adam Sebastian Genevieve, PhD; Professor of Cell Biology, University of Glasgow, 1967–2004, now Emeritus; *b* 3 Jan. 1934; *s* of Herbert Lewis Curtis and Nora Patricia Curtis (*née* Stevens); *m* 1958, Ann Park; two *d. Educ:* Aldenham Sch.; King's Coll., Cambridge (BA 1955; MA); Univ. of Edinburgh (PhD 1957). University College London: Hon. Research Asst, 1957–62; Lectr in Zool., 1962–67; University of Glasgow: Head, Molecular and Cellular Biol. Planning Unit, 1991–94; Head, Molecular and Cellular Biol. Div., 1994–95; Jt Dir, Centre for Cell Engrg, 1996–2004. Pres., Tissue & Cell Engrg Soc., 2001–03. Editor in Chief, Exptl Biology Online, 1996–99; Ed., IEEE Trans in Nanobioscience, 2002–08. Cuvier Medal, Zool Soc. of France, 1972; Chapman Meml Medal, IMMM, 2008. *Publications:* The Cell Surface, 1967; (with J. M. Lackie) Measuring Cell Adhesion, 1991; numerous articles in scientific jls; also articles on scuba diving. *Recreations:* scuba diving, oil painting, gardening. *Address:* 2 Kirklee Circus, Glasgow G12 0TW. *T:* (0141) 339 2152.

See also P. Curtis.

CURTIS, Sir Barry (John), Kt 1992; Mayor of Manukau, New Zealand, 1983–2007; *b* 27 Feb. 1939; *s* of John Dixon Cory Curtis, Donaghadee, NI, and Vera Gladys Curtis (*née* Johnson); *m* 1961, Miriam Ann Brooke (marr. diss. 1991); three *d. Educ:* Otahuhu College; Univ. of Auckland (Dip. TP). MRICS, MNZIS, MNZPI. Town Planner, Chartered and Registered Surveyor. Manukau City Councillor, 1968–83; Member: Auckland Regl Authy, 1971–84 (Chm., Regl Planning Cttee, 1977–83); Prime Minister's Safer Communities Council, 1990–96; Chairman: Hillary Commn Task Force on Recreation, 1988; Jean Batten Meml Trust, 1989; Manukau Healthy City Cttee, 1989–93; Manukau Safer Community Council, 1990–93; Auckland Mayors' Forum, 1990–96, 2004–05; Electoral Coll., Infrastructure Auckland, 1998–2004; Auckland Regl Econ. Develt Strategy Establishment Gp, 2002–04; Nat. Taskforce for Community Violence Reduction Leaders Gp, 2005–07; Dep. Chm., Auckland Regl Growth Strategy Forum, 1996–2007; Dir, NZ Food Innovation (Auckland) Ltd, 2010–13. Past Pres., NZ Sister Cities Cttee. A Dir, XIVth Commonwealth Games Ltd, 1989–92 (Mem. Exec. Bd, 1989–90). Pres., Auckland Football Fedn, 2010–. Patron, Auckland Hockey Assoc. Valedictory Award, NZ Pacific Business Council, 2007. Seiuli (High Chief Matai title) conferred by HE Malietoa Tanumafili II, Western Samoa, 1993; Kaumatua conferred by Tuhoe and Te Arawa tribes, Aotearoa, 2007; Hon. Residence, Cook Islands, 2005. *Recreations:* jogging, surfing, gardening, follower of Rugby, hockey, cricket, tennis, yachting. *Address:* 1/1A The Esplanade, Eastern Beach, Manukau 2012, Auckland, New Zealand. *T:* (9) 5348153, *Fax:* (9) 5349153.

CURTIS, Bronwen Mary, CBE 2008; Director of Human Resources and Organisation Development, Northamptonshire Healthcare NHS Foundation Trust, since 2011; *b* 17 May 1955; *d* of Hywel Arwyn Hughes and Doris Winifred Hughes (*née* Billingham); *m* 1990, Alan Curtis (marr. diss. 2002); one *s* (one *d* decd). *Educ:* Sheffield Poly. (HND Business Studies (Dist.)); University Coll., Cardiff (Postgrad. Dip. Personnel Mgt). Avon Cosmetics: Dir, UK Manufg, 1988–90; Vice President: Manufg, 1990–92; Planning and Develt, 1993–95; HR, 1995–2001. Chairman: Two Shires Ambulance Trust, 1995–98; Northampton Gen. Hosp. NHS Trust, 1998–2007. Home Sec.'s Rep., Northants Police Authy Selection Panel, 1997–2003; a Civil Service Comr, 2001–07; Ind. Mem., Sen. Salaries Rev. Bd, DCMS, 2005–08; Mem., Prison Service Pay Rev. Body, 2007–12. Chm., Appts Cttee, GDC, 2010–12. Non-executive Director: Nat. Archives, 2007–12; Northants Healthcare Trust, 2007–12; Service Personnel and Veterans Agency, 2009–12. Mem., Forum UK, 1990–. Midlands Businesswoman of Year, Winged Fellowship Trust, 1990. *Recreations:* playing and watching sport, learning from others, solving complex problems and making life easier for others.

CURTIS, Bronwyn Nanette, OBE 2008; Head of Global Research, HSBC Bank plc, 2008–13; Vice Chairman, Society of Business Economists, since 2013 (Chairman, 2006–13); *b* Bendigo, Australia; *d* of Edward J. and Loris M. Schlotterlein; *m* Paul G. Curtis (*d* 2011); one *s* one *d. Educ:* La Trobe Univ., Australia (BEc Hons); London Sch. of Econs (MSc Econ.). Sen. Manager, Mars Confectionery, 1977–82; Chief Economist, Gill and Duffus plc, 1982–84; Res. Dir, Landell Mills Commodities Studies, 1984–87; Global Hd, Currency and Fixed Income Strategy, Deutsche Bank, 1987–97; Chief Economist, Nomura Internat., 1997–99; Managing Ed. and Hd, Eur. Broadcasting, Bloomberg LP, 1999–2006; Econ. Advr, Arch Financial Products, LLP, 2006–08. Non-executive Director: JP Morgan Asian Investment Trust plc, 2013–; Scottish Amer. Investment Trust plc, 2014–. Chief Econ. Advr, Official Monetary and Financial Instns Forum, 2014–. Consultant: UN, 1984–87; World Bank, 1984–87. Vis. Prof., Cass Business Sch., 1997–2005. Non-exec. Dir, OFT, 2007–08. Member: ESRC, 1998–2003; Bd of Mgt, NIESR, 2005–. Gov., 2002–, Mem. Council, 2009–12, LSE. *Publications:* Cocoa, A Trader's Guide, 1987. *Recreations:* yacht racing and cruising, ballet. *Address:* Society of Business Economists, Dean House, Vernham Dean, Andover, Hants SP11 0JZ. *T:* (01264) 737552. *E:* admin@sbe.co.uk. *Clubs:* Royal Thames Yacht, Royal Southern Yacht.

CURTIS, Cathleen, (Kate); *see* Purkiss, C.

CURTIS, Prof. Charles David, OBE 2001; Independent Member, Repository Development Management Board, Nuclear Decommissioning Authority, since 2008; *b* 11 Nov. 1939; *s* of Charles Frederick Curtis and Kate Margaret Curtis (*née* Jackson); *m* 1963, Dr Diana Joy Saxty; two *d. Educ:* Imperial College London; Univ. of Sheffield (BSc, PhD). University of Sheffield: Lectr, Sen. Lectr, Reader, 1965–83; Personal Chair in Geochem., 1983–88; University of Manchester: Professor of Geochemistry, 1988–2004, now Emeritus; Hd, Dept of Geology, 1989–92; Res. Dean, Faculty of Science and Engrg, 1994–2000. Hd of Res. and Develt Strategy, UK Nirex Ltd, 2004–07; Hd of Res. and Develt Strategy, Radioactive Waste Mgt Directorate, Nuclear Decommng Authy, 2007–08. Ind. non-exec. Mem. Bd, Dounreay Site Restoration Ltd, 2008–12; Ind. non-exec. Dir, Radioactive Waste Mgt Ltd, 2014–. Vis. Prof., Dept of Geology and Geophys., UCLA, 1970–71; Res. Associate, British Petroleum Res. Centre, 1987–88; Hon. Res. Fellow, Natural Hist. Mus., 1999–. Member: Council, NERC, 1990–93; Radioactive Waste Mgt Adv. Cttee, 1994–2004 (Chm., 1999–2004); Radioactivity Res. and Envmtl Monitoring Cttee, 1995–2004; Bd Assurance Cttee, UKAEA, 2002–. Pres., Geological Soc., 1992–94. Murchison Medal, Geological Soc., 1987. *Publications:* numerous articles in learned jls. *Recreations:* mountaineering, gardening, photography. *Address:* Townhead Cottage, Edale Road, Hope, Derbyshire S33 6SF. *T:* (01433) 620724.

CURTIS, Colin Hinton Thomson, CVO 1970; ISO 1970; retired; Chairman, Metropolitan Public Abattoir Board, 1971–81; Member, Queensland Meat Industry Authority, 1972–78; *b* 25 June 1920; *s* of A. Curtis, Brisbane; *m* 1943, Anne Catherline Drevesen; one *s. Educ:* Brisbane Grammar School. RANR Overseas Service, 1940–45. Sec. and Investigation Officer to Chm., Sugar Cane Prices Board, 1948–49; Asst Sec. to Central Sugar Cane Prices Board, 1949; Sec. to Premier of Queensland, 1950–64; Mem., Qld Trade Missions to SE Asia, 1963 and 1964; Asst Under-Sec., Premier's Dept, 1961–64; Assoc. Dir and Dir of Industrial Development, 1964–66; Under-Sec., Premier's Dept and Clerk of Exec. Council, 1966–70; State Dir, Royal Visit, 1970; Agent-General for Queensland in London, 1970–71. *Address:* 57 Daru Avenue, Runaway Bay, Gold Coast, Qld 4216, Australia. *Club:* RSL Memorial (Queensland).

CURTIS, Daniel Nicholas Mansfield; a District Judge (Magistrates' Courts), since 2005; *b* 15 May 1963; *s* of late Cyril Frank Paul Curtis and of Joyce Mary Curtis (*née* Bailey); two *s* two *d. Educ:* Boston Spa Comp. Sch.; King's Coll., London (LLB Hons). Partner, Tates, solicitors, 1992–2005; a Dep. District Judge, 2003–05. *Recreations:* travel, running (almost as slowly as District Judge Browne), golf, playing the drums. *Address:* Grimsby Magistrates' Court, Victoria Street, Grimsby, Lincs DN31 1PE. *T:* (01472) 320444, *Fax:* (01472) 320440. *E:* districtjudge.curtis@judiciary.gsi.gov.uk.

CURTIS, Prof. David Roderick, AC 1992; FRACP 1987; FRS 1974; FAA 1965; Emeritus Professor, Australian National University, since 1993; *b* 3 June 1927; *s* of E. D. and E. V. Curtis; *m* 1951, Lauri Sewell; one *s* one *d. Educ:* Univ. of Melbourne; Australian National Univ. MB, BS Melbourne 1950, PhD ANU 1957. John Curtin School of Medical Research, Australian National University: Department of Physiology: Research Scholar, 1954–56; Research Fellow, 1956–57; Fellow, 1957–59; Sen. Fellow, 1959–62; Professorial Fellow, 1962–66; Prof. of Pharmacology, 1966–68; Prof. of Neuropharmacology, 1968–73; Prof. and Foundn Head, Dept of Pharmacology, 1973–88; Chm., Div. of Physiol Sciences, 1988–89; Howard Florey Prof. of Med. Res., and Dir of the Sch., 1989–92; University Fellow, 1993–95. President: Aust. Acad. of Sci., 1986–90 (Burnet Medal, 1983); Australian Physiol and Pharmacol Soc., 1992–95; Chairman: Res. Adv. Bd, Nat. Multiple Sclerosis Soc., Australia, 1978–83, 1993–96; Inaugural Australia Prize Cttee, 1989–90. Centenary Medal, 2003. *Publications:* (with F. J. Fenner) The John Curtin School of Medical Research: the first fifty years, 2001; papers in fields of neurophysiology, neuropharmacology in Jl Physiology, Jl Neurophysiol., Brain Research, Exper. Brain Research. *Recreations:* woodwork, wombling. *Address:* 7 Patey Street, Campbell, Canberra, ACT 2612, Australia. *T:* (2) 62485664.

CURTIS, Major Sir Edward (Philip), 8th Bt *cr* 1802, of Cullands Grove, Middlesex; *b* Livingstone, Northern Rhodesia, 25 June 1940; *s* of late Gerald Edward Curtis and Philippa Curtis (*née* Alcock); *S* cousin, 2014; *m* 1978, Catherine Mary (*née* Armstrong) (*d* 2015); two *s* two *d. Educ:* Bradfield Coll.; RMA Sandhurst. Commnd 16th/5th Queen's Royal Lancers, 1961; Adjt, 1970–71; Sqn Ldr, 1971–73; Co. Comdr, RMA Sandhurst, 1973–75; retired from Army, 1977. Stockbroker, 1981–2002. *Recreations:* cricket, fishing, shooting. *Heir: s* George Edward Curtis, *b* 31 Oct. 1980. *Clubs:* I Zingari, Free Foresters.

CURTIS, Frank; *see* Curtis, R. F.

CURTIS, James William Ockford; QC 1993; a Recorder, since 1991; *b* 2 Sept. 1946; *s* of late Eric William Curtis, MC, TD and Margaret Joan Curtis (*née* Blunt); *m* 1985, Genevra Fiona Penelope Victoria Caws, QC (*d* 1997); one *d. Educ:* Bedford Sch.; Worcester Coll., Oxford (MA Jurisp). Called to the Bar, Inner Temple, 1970. *Recreations:* farming, field sports, ski-ing, classics. *Address:* 21 College Hill, EC4R 2RP. *T:* (020) 3301 0910. *Clubs:* Reform, Flyfishers'.

CURTIS, Most Rev. John Barry; Honorary Assistant, St Matthew's Anglican Church, Ottawa, since 2008; Archbishop of Calgary, 1994–99; Metropolitan of Rupert's Land, 1994–99; *b* 19 June 1933; *s* of Harold Boyd Curtis and Eva B. Curtis (*née* Saunders); *m* 1959, Patricia Emily (*née* Simpson) (decd); two *s* two *d. Educ:* Trinity Coll., Univ. of Toronto (BA 1955, LTh 1958); Theological Coll., Chichester, Sussex. Deacon 1958, priest 1959; Asst Curate, Holy Trinity, Pembroke, Ont, 1958–61; Rector: Parish of March, Kanata, Ont, 1961–65; St Stephen's Church, Buckingham, Que, 1965–69; Church School Consultant, Diocese of Ottawa, 1969; Rector, All Saints (Westboro), Ottawa, 1969–78; Director of Programme, Diocese of Ottawa, 1978–80; Rector, Christ Church, Elbow Park, Calgary, Alta, 1980–83; Bishop of Calgary, 1983–99. Member, Governing Board: Canadian Council of Churches, 1994 (Pres., 1999); Habitat for Humanity Canada, 1994. Hon. DD Trinity Coll., Toronto, 1985. *Recreations:* reading, hiking, ski-ing, cycling. *Address:* 205 Clearview Avenue, Ottawa, ON K1Z 1A8, Canada. *T:* (613) 317 0334. *Club:* Ranchmen's (Calgary, Alta).

CURTIS, John Edward, OBE 2006; PhD; FBA 2003; FSA; Keeper, Department of Middle East (formerly Department of Western Asiatic Antiquities, then of Ancient Near East), British Museum, 1989–2011; Chief Executive Officer, Iran Heritage Foundation, since 2014; *b* 23 June 1946; *yr s* of late Arthur Norman Curtis and of Laura Letitia Ladd (*née* Thomas); *m* 1977, Vesta Sarkhosh; one *s* one *d. Educ:* Collyer's Grammar Sch., Horsham; Univ. of Bristol (BA);

Inst. of Archaeology, Univ. of London (Postgrad. Diploma in Western Asiatic Archaeology; PhD 1979). FSA 1984. Fellow, British Sch. of Archaeology in Iraq, 1969–71; Res. Asst, Dept of Western Asiatic Antiquities, British Museum, 1971–74, Asst Keeper, 1974–89. Chm., British Assoc. for Near Eastern Archaeol., 1996–2001; Member, Governing Council: British Sch. of Archaeol. in Iraq, 1980–2001 and 2002–08; British Inst. of Persian Studies, 1991–2001, 2002–05 and 2012–; Pres., British Inst. for Study of Iraq, 2012–. Corresponding Member: German Archaeol Inst., 2010; Archaeol Inst. of America, 2013. Trustee: Ancient Persia Fund, 1987–; Honor Frost Foundn, 2012–. Iran Heritage Foundn Award, 2005 and 2013; Persian Golden Lioness Award for Outstanding Research, 2008. *Publications:* (ed) Fifty Years of Mesopotamian Discovery, 1982; Nush-i Jan III: the Small Finds, 1984; (ed) Bronzeworking Centres of Western Asia *c* 1000–539 BC, 1988; Excavations at Qasrij Cliff and Khirbet Qasrij, 1989; Ancient Persia, 1989, 2nd edn 2000; (ed) Early Mesopotamia and Iran: Contact and Conflict 3500–1600 BC, 1993; (ed with J. E. Reade) Art and Empire: treasures from Assyria in the British Museum, 1995; (ed) Later Mesopotamia and Iran: tribes and empires 1600–539 BC, 1995; (ed) Mesopotamia and Iran in the Persian period: conquest and imperialism 539–331 BC, 1997; (with A. R. Green) Excavations at Khirbet Khatuniyeh, 1997; (ed) Mesopotamia and Iran in the Parthian and Sasanian periods: rejection and revival *c* 238 BC–AD 642, 2000; (with M. Kruszyński) Ancient Caucasian and Related Material in the British Museum, 2002; (ed with N. Tallis) Forgotten Empire: the world of Ancient Persia, 2005 (Book of the Yr Prize, Islamic Republic of Iran, 2009); (ed with N. Tallis) The Balawat Gates of Ashurnasirpal II, 2008; (ed jtly) New Light on Nimrud, 2008; (ed with St John Simpson) The World of Achaemenid Persia: history, art and society in Iran and the Ancient Near East, 2010; (with N. Tallis) The Horse: from Arabia to Royal Ascot, 2012; (ed with R. Matthews) Proceedings of the 7th International Congress on the Archaeology of the Ancient Near East, 3 vols, 2012; An Examination of Late Assyrian Metalwork, 2013; The Cyrus Cylinder and Ancient Persia, 2013; articles in learned jls. *Address:* 4 Hillfield Road, NW6 1QE. *T:* (020) 7435 6153; 1 Francis Cottage, Sandy Hill Road, Saundersfoot, Dyfed SA69 9HW.

CURTIS, Michael Alexander; QC 2008; *b* Birmingham, 4 July 1959; *s* of Frank and Ann Curtis; *m* 1992, Cathleen Purkiss, *qv*; one *s* two *d*. *Educ:* King Henry VIII Sch., Coventry; Brasenose Coll., Oxford (MA); King's Coll. London (MSc). Called to the Bar, Middle Temple, 1982; in practice as barrister, specialising in construction, commercial and public law, 1982–. *Publications:* (ed) Emden's Construction Law. *Recreation:* watching football. *Address:* Crown Office Chambers, 2 Crown Office Row, Temple, EC4Y 7HJ. *T:* (020) 7797 8100, *Fax:* (020) 7797 8101. *E:* curtis@crownofficechambers.com. *Club:* Arsenal Football.

CURTIS, Michael John; Director of Finance, Islington Council, since 2006; *b* 2 Aug. 1961; *s* of John and Sylvia Curtis; *m* 1992, Julie Thompson; two *s*. *Educ:* Portsmouth Poly. (BA Hons 1982); Miami Univ., Ohio (MA 1984); St Antony's Coll., Oxford. CPFA 1989. Trainee Accountant, 1986–89, Finance Manager, 1989–90, Kent CC; Projects Consultant, Berks CC, 1990–93; Manager, CSL Managed Services, 1993–95; Head of Financial Services, 1996–98, Dir of Finance, 1998–2001, Broxbourne BC; Asst Dir, Adult Care Services, Herts CC, 2001–06. Bd Mem., Broxbourne Housing Assoc., 2005– (Chm., Audit Cttee). Trustee and Treas., One World Action, 2006–12; Treasurer: Highfield Park Trust, 2011–; Old Albanians RFC, 2012–. *Recreations:* travel, walking, reading, cricket, football, Rugby, theatre, music. *Address:* Islington Council, 7 Newington Barrow Way, N7 7EP. *T:* (020) 7527 2294. *E:* mike.curtis@islington.gov.uk.

CURTIS, Monica Anne; Head, Chelmsford County High School for Girls, 1997–2006; *b* 26 May 1946; *d* of H. L. Seale; *m* 1968, Timothy Chaytor Curtis (*d* 1986), former Dep. Dir, Lancashire Poly.; two *s*. *Educ:* Manchester Univ. (BA English and History of Art 1968). Teacher: Urmston Grammar Sch. for Girls, 1968–70; various schs in Newcastle upon Tyne, 1970–80; Lancaster Girls' Grammar Sch., 1980–89; Kesteven and Grantham Girls' Sch., 1989–97. Gov., Felsted Sch., Essex, 2003–13 (Chm., Govs' Academic Cttee, 2009–13). *Address:* Apartment 8, Devonshire Court, Derbyshire Road South, Sale, Cheshire M33 3YN.

CURTIS, Prof. Paul Tyrrel, PhD; FREng; FRAS; Senior Fellow, Defence Science and Technology Laboratory (formerly Defence Evaluation and Research Agency), Ministry of Defence, since 1997; *b* London; *s* of Noel Curtis and Constance Curtis; *m* 1977, Anne Denise Clark; one *s* three *d*. *Educ:* Christ's Coll., Cambridge (BA Hons Nat. Scis 1973); Univ. of Surrey (PhD 1976). FIMMM 1998; FRAeS 2004; FREng 2013; FRAS 2013. Joined Royal Aircraft Establishment, Farnborough, 1978; Principal Scientific Officer, DRA, Farnborough, 1991; Res. Fellow, Surrey Univ., 1997. Vis. Prof., 1997–, Sen. Res. Investigator (pt time), 2011–, Imperial Coll. London; Vis. Prof., Univ. of Bristol, 2004–. *Publications:* over 150 articles in learned jls. *Recreations:* Andover Astronomical Society (Chm.), gardening (Clatford Valley Gardening Club), family, walking. *Address:* Aeronautics Department, Imperial College London, Prince Consort Road, SW7 2AZ. *T:* (020) 7594 5040. *E:* p.curtis@imperial.ac.uk. *W:* www.amateurastronomy.co.uk.

CURTIS, Dr Penelope; Director, Museu Calouste Gulbenkian, Lisbon, since 2015; *b* London, 24 Aug. 1961; *d* of Prof. Adam Sebastian Genevieve Curtis, *qv*. *Educ:* Westbourne Sch., Glasgow; Corpus Christi Coll., Oxford (BA Mod. Hist. 1982); Courtauld Inst. of Art, London (MA Art Hist. 1985; PhD 1989). Exhibns Curator, Tate Gall., Liverpool, 1988–94; Hd, 1994–99, Curator, 1999–2010, Henry Moore Centre for the Study of Sculpture, later Henry Moore Inst., Leeds; Dir, Tate Britain, 2010–15. *Publications:* Barbara Hepworth, 1998, 5th edn 2010; Sculpture 1900–1945: after Rodin, 1999; Patio and Pavilion: the place of sculpture in modern architecture, 2007. *Recreations:* the Hebrides, modern architecture, 19th-century novels. *Address:* Museu Calouste Gulbenkian, Avenida de Berna 45A, 1067–001 Lisbon, Portugal.

CURTIS, Hon. Sir Richard Herbert, Kt 1992; a Judge of the High Court of Justice, Queen's Bench Division, 1992–2005; Presiding Judge, Wales and Chester Circuit, 1994–97. *Educ:* Oxford Univ. (MA). Called to Bar, Inner Temple, 1958, Bencher, 1985; QC 1977; a Recorder, 1974–89; Recorder of Birmingham, 1989–92; Hon. Recorder, City of Hereford, 1981–92; Sen. Circuit Judge, Oxford and Midland Circuit, 1989–92. *Address:* c/o Royal Courts of Justice, Strand, WC2A 2LL.

CURTIS, Richard Whalley Anthony, CBE 2000 (MBE 1995); freelance writer; *b* 8 Nov. 1956; *s* of late Anthony J. Curtis and Glynness S. Curtis; partner, Emma Vallencey Freud, *qv*; three *s* one *d*. *Educ:* Papplewick Sch.; Harrow Sch.; Christ Church, Oxford (BA). Freelance writer: *television:* Not the Nine O'clock News (four series), 1979–83; Blackadder (four series), 1984–89; Mr Bean, 1989–95; Bernard and the Genie, 1993; The Vicar of Dibley, 1994–2000; The Girl in the Café, 2005 (Emmy Award, 2006); Mary and Martha, 2013; Esio Trot, 2015; *films:* The Tall Guy, 1988; Four Weddings and a Funeral, 1994; Bean, 1997; Notting Hill, 1999; (jtly) Bridget Jones's Diary, 2001 ((jtly) Best Screenplay, Evening Standard British Film Awards, 2002); (also dir) Love Actually, 2003; (jtly) Bridget Jones: The Edge of Reason, 2004; (also dir) The Boat that Rocked, 2009; (jtly) War Horse, 2012; (also dir) About Time, 2013; producer, Comic Relief, 1985–2003. Campaigner, Make Poverty History and Live 8, 2005. Fellow, BAFTA, 2007. Outstanding Contribn to British Film and TV Award, Dirs' Guild of GB, 2004. *Recreations:* too much TV, too many films, too much pop music. *Address:* c/o United Agents, 12–26 Lexington Street, W1F 0LE.

CURTIS, Prof. (Robert) Frank, CBE 1985; PhD, DSc; Chairman, Norfolk Mental Health Care NHS Trust, 1994–98; Professor, University of East Anglia, 1977–88, Hon. Professor, 1988–2001; *b* 8 Oct. 1926; *s* of late William John Curtis, Somerset, and Ethel Irene Curtis, Bath; *m* 1954, Sheila Rose, *y d* of Bruce Rose, Huddersfield; two *s* one *d*. *Educ:* City of Bath Sch.; Univ. of Bristol (BSc 1949, PhD 1952, DSc 1972). FRIC 1966; FIFST 1977. Johns Hopkins University: W. H. Grafflin Fellow, 1952; Instr in Chemistry, 1953; Technical Officer, ICI Ltd, Manchester, 1954–56; Res. Fellow, Univ. of WI, 1956–57; Lectr in Chem., University Coll., Swansea, 1957–62, Sen. Lectr, 1962–69; Reader, Univ. of Wales, 1969–70; Head, Chem. Div., 1970–77, Dir, 1977–85, ARC Food Res. Inst.; Dir, AFRC Inst. of Food Res., Reading, 1985–88. Chm., Food Adv. Cttee, MAFF, 1983–88 (Chm., Food Standards Cttee, 1979–83); Mem. Management Bd, AFRC, 1987–88. Mem., Norwich HA, 1989–94 (Vice-Chm., 1993–94); Mem. Council, RVC, 1991–2000. Hon. ScD UEA, 1988. *Publications:* res. papers on chemistry and food science in jls of learned socs. *Address:* Manor Barn, Colton, Norwich NR9 5BZ. *T:* (01603) 880379.

CURTIS, Prof. Sarah Elizabeth, DPhil; FBA 2014; FRGS; Executive Director, Institute of Hazard Risk and Resilience, since 2006, and Professor of Health and Risk, since 2012, Durham University; *d* of Dr Leonard Curtis and Diana Curtis; *m* Brian Blundell. *Educ:* Redland High Sch. for Girls, Bristol; St Hilda's Coll., Oxford (BA Geog.); Univ. of Kent at Canterbury (DPhil Urban and Regl Studies 1981). Res. Associate, Personal Social Services Res. Unit, Univ. of Kent, 1979–81; Department of Geography, Queen Mary College, subseq. Queen Mary and Westfield College, then Queen Mary, University of London: Res. Fellow, 1981–84; Sen. Res. Fellow, 1984–88; Lectr, 1988–91; Sen. Lectr, 1991–95; Reader in Geog., 1995–99; Prof. of Geog., 1999–2006. MRSocMed; Mem., Soc. of Social Medicine. FAcSS; FHEA. *Publications:* Health and Inequality: geographical perspectives, 2004; Space, Place and Mental Health, 2010; contribs to learned jls incl. Social Sci. and Medicine, Health and Place, Envmt and Planning. *Recreations:* music, gardening, campanology. *Address:* Department of Geography, Durham University, Lower Mountjoy, South Road, Durham DH1 3LE.

CURTIS, Stephen Russell; Chairman, Association of Company Registration Agents Ltd, since 2009; *b* 27 Feb. 1948; *s* of Barry Russell and Joyce Muriel (*née* Smith); *m* 1972, Gillian Mary Pitkin; three *s* one *d*. *Educ:* Forest Sch., E17; Exeter Univ. (BA Econs and Stats). Asst Statistician, Business Stats Office, 1970–72; DTI, 1972–78, Statistician, Export Stats, 1975–78; Statistician, 1978–83, Chief Statistician, 1983–85, Business Stats Office; Registrar of Companies, 1985–90, and Chief Exec., 1988–90, Companies House; Chief Exec., DVLA, 1990–95; Man. Dir, Professional Services Div., Jordans Ltd, 1997–2003; Statistician, 2004–. *Recreations:* travel, photography, walking.

CURTIS-RALEIGH, Dr Jean Margaret Macdonald, FRCPsych; Consultant Psychiatrist, Queen Mary's University Hospital, Roehampton, 1979–98; *b* 12 July 1933; *d* of late Dr Harry Hubert Steadman and Janet Gilchrist Steadman (*née* Macdonald); *m* 1964, His Honour Judge Nigel Hugh Curtis-Raleigh (*d* 1986); five *s*. *Educ:* Convent of the Sacred Heart, Epsom, Surrey; Sutton High Sch. for Girls; Guy's Hospital Med. Sch. (MB BS). DPM 1965; MRCPsych 1973, FRCPsych 1996. Psychiatric trng, Maudsley and Bethlem Royal Hosps, 1963–66. Med. Mem., Mental Health Review Tribunal, 1994–2006. Mem., Broadcasting Standards Council, 1988–95. *Recreations:* opera, gardening, walking.

See also J. H. Steadman.

CURTIS-THOMAS, Claire; Chief Executive, British Board of Agrément, since 2013; *b* 30 April 1958; *d* of late Joyce Curtis; *m* Michael Louis Jakub; one *s* two *d*. *Educ:* Mynyddbach Comp. Sch. for Girls, Swansea; UC Cardiff (BSc); Aston Univ. (MBA). CEng; FIMechE 1995; FIET (FIEE 2000). Shell Chemicals, 1990–92; Hd, Strategic Planning, 1992–93, Hd R&D Lab., 1993–95, Birmingham CC; Dean, Faculty of Business and Engrg, Univ. of Wales Coll. Newport (formerly Gwent Coll. of Higher Educn), 1996–97. MP (Lab) Crosby, 1997–2010. Member: Home Affairs Select Cttee, 2003–05; Sci. and Technology Select Cttee, 1997–2002. CEO, Instn of Gas Engineers and Managers, 2011–13. Senator, Engrg Council, 1996–2002; Mem., Engrg Technol. Bd, 2002–08. Chair: Waterloo Partnership, 2006–08; Construction and Develt Partnership, 2008–. Pres., Instn of Engrg Designers, 2003–06 (Hon. FIED). Pres., SETup (Promotion of Science Engrg and Technol.), 1997–2005; Patron Trustee, Severn Bridges Trust; Trustee, IMechE, 2005–10. FICES 2000; FCGI 2001. Hon. PhD Staffordshire Univ., 1999. *Address:* British Board of Agrément, Bucknalls Lane, Watford, Herts WD25 9BA. *E:* curtisthomasc@gmail.com.

CURWEN, Peter Stewart; Director, Europe, HM Treasury, since 2008; *b* 25 Oct. 1963; *s* of late Brian Stewart Curwen and Pamela Westgarth Curwen (*née* Jones); *m* 1996, Helene Radcliffe; one *s* one *d*. *Educ:* King Edward VI Grammar Sch. for Boys, Aston; Manchester Univ. (BA Econ Hons); Warwick Univ. (MA Econs). Economist, MSC, 1985–87; HM Treasury: Macroeconomist, 1987–90; World economy forecaster, Econ. Advr, 1991–94; EU co-ordination and strategy, 1994–96; Dep. Hd, Communications, 1996–97; Head: Communications, 1997–99; EU and Internat. Tax Team, 1999–2002; on secondment to FCO, as Counsellor, Econs, Finance and Tax, UK Perm. Repn to EU, 2002–06; Dir, Budget and Tax Policy, 2006–08. *Recreations:* golf, tennis, ski-ing, campanology. *Address:* HM Treasury, 1 Horse Guards Road, SW1A 2HQ. *T:* (020) 7270 4470. *E:* peter.curwen@hmtreasury.gsi.gov.uk. *Club:* Sandy Lodge Golf (Northwood, Middx).

CURZON; *see* Roper-Curzon, family name of Baron Teynham.

CURZON, family name of **Earl Howe** and **Viscount Scarsdale**.

CURZON, Viscount; Thomas Edward Penn Curzon; *b* 22 Oct. 1994; *s* and *heir* of Earl Howe, *qv*.

CUSACK, Niamh; actress; *b* 20 Oct. 1959; *d* of late Cyril James Cusack and Mary Margaret, (Maureen), Cusack (*née* Kiely); *m* Finbar Lynch; one *s*. *Educ:* Scoil Lorcáin; Coláiste Iosagáin; Royal Acad. of Music; Guildhall Sch. of Music and Drama. Actress in theatre, television, film and radio; *theatre* includes: Royal Shakespeare Company: Othello, 1985; Romeo and Juliet, 1986; As You Like It, 1996; National Theatre: His Dark Materials, 2003–04; The Enchantment, 2007; The Curious Incident of the Dog in the Night-Time, 2012, transf. West End, 2013; other productions: Three Sisters, Gate, Dublin, then Royal Court, 1990; Playboy of the Western World, Old Vic, 1991; A Doll's House, 1993, Ghosts, 2007, Gate, Dublin; Dancing at Lughnasa, 2009, Cause Célèbre, 2011, Old Vic; Juno and the Paycock, Bristol Old Vic, then Liverpool Playhouse, 2014; Afterplay, Crucible, Sheffield, 2014; The Rehearsal, Minerva, Chichester, 2015; *television* series: Heartbeat, 1992–95; Always and Everyone, 1999–2002; The Hollow Crown, 2012; *films:* Fools of Fortune, 1990; The Playboys, 1992; The Closer You Get, 2000; Hereafter, 2011; Departure, ChickLit, 2015. *Recreations:* walking, reading, people watching. *Address:* c/o Independent Talent Group, 40 Whitfield Street, W1T 2RH.

CUSCHIERI, Prof. Sir Alfred, Kt 1998; MD; FRCS, FRCSE; FRSE; Professor of Surgery, Scuola Superiore S'Anna di Studi Universitari, Pisa, since 2003; Chief Scientific Advisor, Institute for Medical Science and Technology, University of Dundee, since 2008; *b* 30 Sept. 1938; *s* of Saviour and Angela Cuschieri; *m* 1966, Marguerite Holley; three *d*. *Educ:* Univ. of Malta (MD 1961); Univ. of Liverpool (ChM 1968). FRCSE 1965; FRCS 1967; FRSE 1998. University of Liverpool: Sen. Lectr in Surgery, 1970–74; Reader, 1974–76; Prof., and Hd of Dept of Surgery, Univ. of Dundee, 1976–2003. Dir, Minimal Access Therapy Unit for Scotland, 1992–2000. Mem. Council, RCSE, 1980–; President: Internat. Hepatobiliary Pancreatic Assoc., 1992–93; European Assoc. Endoscopic Surgeons, 1995–97. Founder FMedSci 1998. Hon. FRCSGlas 1996; Hon. FRCSI 1996. Hon. MD Liverpool, 1997; Hon. DSc: Abertay, 2002; St Andrews, 2007; Hon. LLD Dundee, 2007. Gold Medal, Scandinavian Soc. Gastroenterology, 1990; Society Prize for pioneering work in minimal access surgery, Internat. Soc. of Surgery, 1993. *Publications:* Essential Surgical Practice, 1986, 4th edn 2001;

contrib. to learned jls incl. Brit. Jl Surgery, Surgical Endoscopy, Lancet, Annals of Surgery, Archives of Surgery. *Recreations:* music, fly-fishing, carving. *Address:* Denbrae Mill, Strathkinness Low Road, St Andrews, Fife KY16 9TY. *T:* (01334) 475046. *Club:* Athenæum.

CUSENS, Prof. Anthony Ralph, OBE 1989; PhD; FRSE; FREng; FICE, FIStructE; Professor of Civil Engineering, University of Leeds, 1979–92, now Emeritus (Dean, Faculty of Engineering, 1989–91); *b* 24 Sept. 1927; *s* of James Henry Cusens and May Edith (*née* Thomas); *m* 1953, Pauline Shirin German; three *d. Educ:* St John's Coll., Southsea; Portsmouth Municipal Coll.; University Coll. London (BSc Eng; PhD 1955). FICE 1966; FIStructE 1972; FASCE 1972; FREng (FEng 1988). FRSE 1974. Res. Engr, British Cast Concrete Fedn, 1952–54; Sen. Lectr, RMCS, Shrivenham, 1954–56; Sen. Lectr, Univ. of Khartoum, Sudan, 1956–60; Prof. of Structl Engrg, Asian Inst. of Technol., Bangkok, 1960–65; Prof. of Civil Engineering: Univ. of St Andrews, 1965–67; Univ. of Dundee, 1967–78. Visitor, Transport and Road Res. Lab., 1982–88; President: Concrete Soc., 1983–84; IStructE, 1991–92; Chairman: Jt Bd of Moderators of ICE, IStructE and CIBSE, 1986–89; UK Certifying Authy for Reinforcing Steels, 1994–2001. Hon. DSc Aston, 1993. *Publications:* (jtly) Bridge Deck Analysis, 1975; Finite Strip Method in Bridge Engineering, 1978; res. papers on concrete technol. and structures. *Recreations:* golf, gardening, family history. *Address:* Old Hall Cottage, Bramham, West Yorks LS23 6QR.

CUSHING, Penny; Her Honour Judge Cushing; a Circuit Judge, since 2013; *b* 10 April 1950; *d* of George Norman Cushing and Doris Cushing. *Educ:* Birkenhead High Sch. (GPDST); University Coll., London (LLB Hons 1971). Admitted solicitor, 1974; Solicitor: London Bor. of Harrow, 1974–75; Camden Community Law Centre, 1975–80; Trng Officer, Law Centres Fedn, 1980–83; Partner, Cushing & Kelly, subseq. Clinton Davis Cushing & Kelly, solicitors, 1983–90; Mem., Mental Health Act Commn, 1991–94; District Judge, Principal Registry, Family Div., 1994–2013. Performed in: Medea, Edinburgh Fringe, 2008; Blue Remembered Hills, 2012; dir, The Tempest, 2012. *Recreations:* theatre, reading, gardening, walking, allotmenteering. *Address:* Guildford County Court, The Law Courts, Mary Road, Guildford, Surrey GU1 4PS.

CUSHING, Philip Edward; Chairman, Loyalty Street, since 2014; *b* 9 Sept. 1950; *s* of Cyril Edward Willis Cushing and Marguerite Ellen Cushing (*née* Whaite); *m* 1st, 1972, Margareta Barbro Westin (marr. diss.); one *s* one *d*; 2nd, 2000, Ruth Christine Clarke. *Educ:* Highgate Sch.; Christ's Coll., Cambridge (BA 1st Cl. Hons Econs). Marketing Manager, Norprint Ltd, 1972–78; Man. Dir, Modulex Systems, 1978–84; Norton Opax plc: Marketing Dir, 1984–86; Chief Exec., Internat. Ops, 1986–89; Inchcape plc: Chief Exec., Inchcape Berhad, 1990–92; Dir, Services, 1992–95; Gp Man. Dir, 1995–96; Gp Chief Exec., 1996–99; Chief Exec., Vitec, 2000–01. Chairman: Paragon Print and Packaging Ltd, 2002–13; DCI Biologicals Inc., 2002–11; Strix Investments Ltd, 2007–08; Wrapfilm Systems Ltd, 2008–13; American Golf Ltd, 2010–12; Dir, Ikon Office Solutions, 1998–2008. *Recreations:* golf, reading, bridge, cricket, travel, music.

CUSHING, Sir Selwyn (John), KNZM 1999; CMG 1994; FCA; Chairman: Skellerup Holdings Ltd, since 2007; New Zealand Rural Property Trust Management Ltd; Rural Equities Ltd; *b* 1 Sept. 1936; *s* of Cyril John Cushing and Henrietta Marjory Belle Cushing; *m* 1964, Kaye Dorothy Anderson; two *s. Educ:* Hastings High Sch.; Univ. of NZ. FCA 1957; ACIS 1958; CMA 1959. Dir, Esam Cushing & Co., later Forsyth Barr Esam Cushing, sharebrokers, Hastings, 1960–2011 (Partner, 1960–86); Brierley Investments Ltd: Exec. Dir, 1986–93; Chm. and Chief Exec., 1999–2001; Chairman: Carter Holt Harvey Ltd, 1991–93; Electricity Corp. of NZ, 1993–99; Director: Air New Zealand (Dep. Chm., 1988–98; Chm., 1998–2001); PGG Wrightson, 2005–. Chm., NZ Symphony Orch. Ltd, 1996–2002. *Recreations:* cricket, music. *Address:* 1 Beatson Road, Hastings 4122, New Zealand. *T:* (6) 8786160. *Clubs:* Wellington; Auckland; Dunedin.

CUSHLEY, Most Rev. Leo; *see* St Andrews and Edinburgh, Archbishop of, (RC).

CUSINE, Douglas James; Sheriff of Grampian, Highland and Islands at Aberdeen, 2001–11 (at Peterhead, 2000–01); *b* 2 Sept. 1946; *s* of James Fechnie Cusine and Catherine Cusine (*née* McLean); *m* 1973, Marilyn Calvert Ramsay; one *s* one *d. Educ:* Hutchesons' Boys' Grammar Sch.; Univ. of Glasgow (LLB (Hons)). Admitted Solicitor, 1971; in private practice, 1971–74; Lectr in Private Law, Univ. of Glasgow, 1974–76; University of Aberdeen: Lectr in Private Law, 1976–82; Sen. Lectr in Conveyancing and Professional Practice of Law, 1982–90; Prof. (personal), 1990–92; Hugh McLennan Prof. of Conveyancing, 1990–2000. Temp. Sheriff, 1998–99; Hon. Sheriff: Aberdeen; Stonehaven. Member: Council, Law Soc. of Scotland, 1988–2000; Lord President's Adv. Council on Messengers-at-Arms and Sheriff Officers, 1989–2000; Legal Practice Course Bd, Law Soc. (England and Wales), 1993–97; Adv. Cttee on Feudal System, 1997–2000, Adv. Cttee on Real Burdens, 1998–2000, Scottish Law Commn; UK Mem., CCBE, 1997–2000; Rep., Internat. Union of Latin Notaries, 1989–97. Examiner, Messengers-at-Arms and Sheriff Officers, 1989–92; Examiner in Conveyancing, Faculty of Advocates, 1992–2011. Mem., AID sub-cttee, RCOG, 1976–79. Mem., 1978, Fellow, 1981, Galton Inst. (formerly Eugenics Soc.). Review Ed., Jl Law Soc. of Scotland, 1988–98. *Publications:* (ed jtly) The Impact of Marine Pollution: law and practice, 1980; (ed jtly) Scottish Cases and Materials in Commercial Law, 1987, 2nd edn 2002; (ed) A Scots Conveyancing Miscellany: essays in honour of Professor Halliday, 1988; New Reproductive Techniques: a legal perspective, 1988; (jtly) The Law and Practice of Diligence, 1990; (ed jtly) Reproductive Medicine and the Law, 1990; (ed) The Conveyancing Opinions of Professor Halliday, 1992; Standard Securities, 1991, 2nd edn (jtly) 2002; (jtly) Missives, 1993, 2nd edn 1999; (jtly) The Requirements of Writing, 1995; (ed) Green's Practice Styles, vol. 1, 1996; (ed jtly) McDonald's Conveyancing Manual, 6th edn 1997; (jtly) Servitudes and Rights of Way, 1998; articles in legal journals. *Recreations:* golf, swimming, walking, bird watching, photography. *Address:* The Brae, Gurney Street, Stonehaven, Kincardineshire AB39 2EB.

CUSK, Rachel Emma; novelist and writer; *b* Saskatchewan, 8 Feb. 1967; *d* of Peter Cusk and Carolyn Cusk (*née* Woods); *m* 2001, Adrian Clarke (separated); two *d*, and one step *d. Educ:* St Mary's Convent, Cambridge; New Coll., Oxford (BA). Reader in Creative Writing, Kingston Univ. *Publications:* novels: Saving Agnes, 1992 (Whitbread First Novel Award, 1993); The Temporary, 1995; The Country Life (Somerset Maugham Award), 1997; The Lucky Ones, 2003; In the Fold, 2005; Arlington Park, 2006; The Bradshaw Variations, 2009; Outline, 2014; A Life's Work: on becoming a mother (autobiog.), 2001; Aftermath: on marriage and separation (autobiog.), 2012; The Last Supper: a summer in Italy, 2009; numerous articles and short stories; contrib. The Times, The Guardian, Daily Telegraph, Evening Standard, etc. *Address:* c/o The Wylie Agency, 17 Bedford Square, WC1B 3JA. *T:* (020) 7908 5900.

CUST, family name of **Baron Brownlow**.

CUSTIS, Patrick James, CBE 1981; FCA, FCMA, FCIS; director of companies; *b* 19 March 1921; *er s* of late Alfred and Amy Custis; *m* 1954, Rita, *yr d* of late Percy and Annie Rayner; one *s. Educ:* The High Sch., Dublin. JDipMA. FCA 1951; FCMA 1950; FCIS 1945. Served articles with Josolyne Miles & Co., Chartered Accountants, Cheapside, London, 1946–51; Asst to Gen. Man., Rio Tinto Co. Ltd, London, 1952–54; Gp Chief Accountant and Dir of subsid. cos, Glynwed Ltd, W Midlands, 1955–67; Guest Keen & Nettlefolds Ltd, W Midlands, 1967–81 (Dir of Finance, 1974–81); various sen. appts prior to 1974. Mem., Midlands and N Wales Reg. Bd (formerly Birmingham and W Midlands Reg. Bd), Lloyds Bank plc, 1979–91; Director: New Court Property Fund Managers Ltd, 1978–91; Associated Heat Services plc, 1981–90; Leigh Interests PLC, 1982–96 (Dep. Chm., 1990–93; Chm., 1993–96); Wolseley plc, 1982–90; Birmingham Technology Ltd, 1983–93; Wyko Group PLC, 1985–94; Benford Concrete Machinery plc, 1985–86; Chm., MCD Gp plc, 1983–86. Member: Monopolies and Mergers Commn, 1981–82; HM Prisons Bd, Home Office, 1980–85. Chm., Midlands Indust. Gp of Finance Dirs, 1977–80. Trustee, Bi-Centenary Appeal, Birmingham Gen. Hosp., 1978–89. Co-opted Mem. Council, Inst. of Chartered Accountants in England and Wales, 1979–85; Liveryman, Worshipful Co. of Chartered Accountants in England and Wales; Pres., Wolverhampton Soc. of Chartered Accountants, 1985–86. FRSA 1987. *Address:* 18 Richmond Village, Stroud Road, Painswick, Glos GL6 6UH.

See also R. A. Custis.

CUSTIS, Ronald Alfred; Director General, Energy Industries Council, 1981–92; *b* 28 Feb. 1931; *yr s* of late Alfred and Amy Custis, Dublin; *m* 1st, 1957, Enid Rowe (*d* 1984); one *s* one *d*; 2nd, 1986, Valerie Mackett (*née* Holbrook). *Educ:* The High Sch., Dublin. Joined HM Treasury, 1947; DES, 1964; Min. of Technology, 1964–70: Private Sec. to Permanent Under Sec., 1964–66; Principal, 1967; Sec. to Cttee of Inquiry into the Brain Drain, 1967–68; Min. of Aviation Supply, later MoD (Procurement Exec.), 1970–74: Private Sec. to Sec. of State for Defence, 1971–73; Asst Sec., 1973; Dept of Energy, 1974–81: Private Sec. to successive Secs of State for Energy, 1974–75; Under Sec., 1978; Dir Gen., Offshore Supplies Office, 1980–81. *Recreations:* reading, walking public footpaths, listening to music, gardening. *Address:* 11 Chantry Hall, Foxbury Lane, Westbourne, W Sussex PO10 8FG. *T:* (01243) 371450.

See also P. J. Custis.

CUSWORTH, Nicholas Neville Grylls; QC 2009; a Recorder, since 2006; a Deputy High Court Judge, since 2011; *b* Barnes, London, 20 March 1964; *s* of Neville Cusworth and Susan Cusworth; *m* 1994, Rachel Platts; one *s* one *d. Educ:* St Paul's Sch., London; Christ Church, Oxford (BA Juris. 1985; MA). Called to the Bar, Lincoln's Inn, 1986; barrister specialising in matrimonial finance. Hd of Chambers, 1 Hare Ct, 2011–. Mem. Cttee, Family Law Bar Assoc., 1998– (Vice Chair, 2010–11; Chair, 2012–13); Member: Training for the Bar Cttee, Bar Council, 2006–11 (Chm., Recruitment and Entry Sub-Cttee, 2009–11); Money and Property Sub-Cttee, Family Justice Council, 2007–11. Liveryman, Stationers' Co., 1994. *Publications:* (contrib.) Essential Family Practice, 2000–02; (contrib.) Financial Provision in Family Matters, 2003–. *Recreations:* Queens Park Rangers FC, works of Bob Dylan. *Address:* 1 Hare Court, Temple, EC4Y 7BE. *T:* (020) 7797 7070. *E:* cusworth@1hc.com. *Club:* Garrick.

CUTHBERT, Prof. Alan William, ScD; FMedSci; FRS 1982; Sheild Professor of Pharmacology, 1979–99, and Deputy Vice-Chancellor, 1995–99, University of Cambridge; Master of Fitzwilliam College, Cambridge, 1990–99 (Hon. Fellow, 1999); *b* 7 May 1932; *s* of late Thomas William Cuthbert and Florence Mary (*née* Griffin); *m* 1957, Harriet Jane Webster; two *s. Educ:* Leicester Coll. of Technol.; St Andrews Univ. (BSc); London Univ. (BPharm, PhD); MA, ScD Cantab. Instructor Lieut, RN, 1956–59. Res. Fellow, then Asst Lectr, Dept of Pharmacology, Sch. of Pharmacy, Univ. of London, 1959–63; Demonstrator in Pharmacol., 1963–66, Lectr, 1966–73, and Reader, 1973–79, Dept of Pharmacol., Univ. of Cambridge; Fellow of Jesus Coll., Cambridge, 1968–90 (Hon. Fellow, 1991). Chm. Editorial Bd, British Jl of Pharmacology, 1974–82. For. Sec., British Pharmacol Soc., 1997–2000 (Hon. Mem., 2000; Hon. Fellow, 2004); Pres., Fedn of European Pharmacol Socs, 2002–04. Member: AFRC, 1988–90; Council, Royal Soc., 1986–88; Council, Zool Soc. of London, 1988–91. Gov., De Montfort Univ., 1998–2005. Mem., Académie Royale de Médecine de Belgique, 1996–; MAE, 1996; Founder FMedSci 1998. Fellow, Sch. of Pharmacy, Univ. of London, 1996. Hon. Fellow, Gonville and Caius Coll., Cambridge, 2008. Hon. DSc: De Montfort, 1993; Aston, 1995; Hon. LLD Dundee, 1995. Pereira Medal in Materia Medica, Pharmaceutical Soc. of GB, 1953; Sir James Irvine Medal in Chemistry, St Andrews Univ., 1955; Wellcome Gold Medal, 2005. *Publications:* scientific papers in pharmacol and physiol jls. *Recreations:* travel, painting, growing orchids. *Address:* Department of Medicine, University of Cambridge, Addenbrooke's Hospital, Hills Road, Cambridge CB2 2QQ; 7 Longstanton Road, Oakington, Cambridge CB24 3BB. *T:* (01223) 233676.

CUTHBERT, Ceri Jayne; *see* Jones, C. J.

CUTHBERT, Sir Ian Holm; *see* Holm, Sir Ian.

CUTHBERT, Jeffrey Hambley; Member (Lab) Caerphilly, National Assembly for Wales, since 2003; *b* 4 June 1948; *s* of William and Jennie Cuthbert; *m* 1985, Catherine (marr. diss.); one *s* four *d. Educ:* University Coll., Cardiff (BSc Hons; Pres., Students' Union, 1974–75). Mining surveyor, Saudi Arabia, 1978–81, Libya, 1981–82, NCB. Sen. Consultant, Welsh Jt Educn Cttee; Principal (pt-time), Aberbargoed Adult Educn Centre. Dep. Minister for Skills, 2011–13, for Skills and Technol., 2013; Minister for Communities and Tackling Poverty, 2013–14. *Recreations:* reading, politics and trade union studies, walking, travel. *Address:* National Assembly for Wales, Cardiff Bay, Cardiff CF99 1NA. *E:* jeff.cuthbert@assembly.wales.

CUTHBERT, Stephen Colin, CBE 2005; FCA; Chief Executive, Port of London Authority, 1999–2004; *b* 27 Oct. 1942; *s* of Colin Samuel Cuthbert and Helen Mary Cuthbert (*née* Scott); *m* 1st, 1969, Jane Elizabeth Bluett (marr. diss. 1984); two *s* one *d*; 2nd, 1987, Susan Melanie Shepherd; one step *s* two step *d. Educ:* Trinity Sch. of John Whitgift; Bristol Univ. (BScEng). FCA 1968. Voluntary Service, UNRWA, Jordan, 1964–65; Price Waterhouse, London, 1965–76; Finance Dir, 1976–79, Chief Exec., 1980–93, Brent International plc; Dir Gen., Chartered Inst. of Marketing, 1994–99. Chm., UK Major Ports Gp, 2002–04. Dir, London Chamber of Commerce and Industry, 2000–02. Mem. Council, 1989–99, Chm. Southern Reg., 1992–93, CBI. Chm., Iain Rennie Grove House Hospice Care (formerly Iain Rennie Hospice at Home), 2006–13. Freeman: City of London, 1998; Co. of Watermen and Lightermen, 2000; Liveryman: Co. of Marketors, 1998–2006; Co. of Shipwrights, 2003–. *Recreations:* opera, gardening, family pursuits.

CUTHBERTSON, Lauren Louise; Principal Dancer, Royal Ballet, since 2008; *b* Torquay, 11 June 1984. *Educ:* Royal Ballet Sch. Joined Royal Ballet, 2002; soloist, 2003, first soloist, 2006. Awards include: Lynn Seymour Award, 2000, Phyllis Bedell Prize, 2000, Royal Ballet Sch.; Young British Dancer of Year, Ricki Gail Conway, 2001; Critics Circle Award, 2004; Silver Medal, Varna Internat. Competition, 2006; Arts and Culture Woman of Future Award, Woman of the Future Awards, 2007. Patron: London Children's Ballet, 2007–; Nat. Youth Ballet, 2012–. *Recreations:* theatre, music, cinema, art galleries. *Clubs:* Ivy, Hospital.

CUTIFANI, Mark; Chief Executive, Anglo American plc, since 2013; *b* Wollongong, Australia, 2 May 1958; *m* 1994, Luana Morgante; two *s* two *d*; one *s* two *d* from previous marriage. *Educ:* Wollongong Univ., NSW (BSc 1st Cl. Hons Engrg). Trainee engr to Manager, Ops, CRA (Rio Tinto), Kembla Coal and Coke, 1976–88; Gen. Manager, Ops, Kalgoorlie Consolidated Gold Mines, 1988–93; Gen. Manager, Ops and CEO, Liddell Jt Venture Savage Resources, 1993–94; Ops Manager, Nickel Div., then Gp Manager, Project Mgt, Western Mining Corp., 1994–98; Gp Exec., Normandy Mining, 1998–2000; Man. Dir, Sons of Gwalia, 2000–03; Vice Pres., CanUK Div., then Pres., N America/Europe, later Chief Operating Officer, INCO, 2003–06; Chief Operating Officer, CVRD-INCO, 2006–07; CEO, Anglo Gold Ashanti, 2007–13. Chm., Internat. Council on Mining and Metals, 2013–15; Pres., SA Chamber of Mines; Dir, World Gold Council. Member: Internat. Adv. Council, Fundação Dom Cabral Brasil Univ.; Internat. Adv. Cttee, Kellogg Innovation Network, Northwestern Univ.; Adv. Bd, Grad. Sch. of Business, Univ. of Cape Town; Advr on global trends in sustainable business practices, Columbia Univ. Hon. Chair, World Mining Congress, 2013. Fellow, Australasian Inst. of Mining and Metallurgy, 2000. Rotary Paul

Harris Fellowship Award, 2006. *Recreations:* Rugby, cricket, family. *Address:* Anglo American plc, 20 Carlton House Terrace, SW1Y 5AN. *T:* (020) 7968 8542.

CUTLER, Prof. (Elizabeth) Anne, PhD; FRS 2015; Research Professor, MARCS Institute, University of Western Sydney, since 2006 (part time, 2006–13, full time, since 2013); Director, Max Planck Institute of Psycholinguistics, Nijmegen, 1993–2013, now Emeritus Director; *b* Melbourne, 17 Jan. 1945; *d* of Clifford Ian Cutler and Betty Cutler (*née* O'Loghlen); *m* 1979, Anthony William Sloman. *Educ:* Univ. of Melbourne (BA 1964; DipEd 1966; MA 1971); Univ. of Texas, Austin (PhD 1975). Research Assistant: Univ. of Melbourne, 1966–67; Univ. of Bonn, 1968–69; Teaching Fellow, then Sen. Teaching Fellow, Monash Univ., 1969–71; Res. Asst and Teaching Asst, Univ. of Texas, Austin, 1972–75; Postdoctoral Fellow, MIT, 1975–76; Res. Fellow, Univ. of Sussex, 1976–82; Res. Scientist, MRC Applied Psychol. Unit, Cambridge, 1982–93; Prof. of Comparative Psycholinguistics, Radboud Univ. Nijmegen, 1995–2013. MAE 1999; Mem., Netherlands Royal Acad. of Scis, 2000; MNAS 2008. FAHA 2005; FASSA 2009. *Publications:* Native Listening, 2012; approx. 400 articles. *Recreation:* learning more (especially about food and wine). *Address:* MARCS Institute, University of Western Sydney, Locked Bag 1797, Penrith South DC, NSW 2751, Australia.

CUTLER, Keith Charles, CBE 2010; **His Honour Judge Cutler;** a Senior Circuit Judge, since 2009; Resident Judge of Winchester and Salisbury, since 2009; Hon. Recorder of Salisbury, 2007–10 and of Winchester, since 2009; *b* 14 Aug. 1950; *s* of Henry Walter Cutler and Evelyn Constance Cutler; *m* 1975, Judith Mary Haddy; one *s* one *d. Educ:* Bristol Univ. (LLB Hons). Called to the Bar, Lincoln's Inn, 1972 (Bencher, 2005); Asst Recorder, 1989; Recorder, 1993–96; Circuit Judge, 1996–2009; Resident Judge, Salisbury, 2003–09; Additional Judge, Court of Appeal Criminal Div., 2013–. Asst Dep. Coroner for Inquest into death of Mark Duggan, 2013–14. Dep. Chancellor, dio. of Portsmouth, 2003–; Wilts Magistrates Liaison Judge, 2006–09. Judicial Member: Parole Bd, 2001–04; Wilts Courts Bd, 2004–07; Chm., Salisbury and Dist, Mediation, 2001–09. Mem., Judges' Council, 2005–09 and 2012– (Chm., Standing Cttee on Communications and Media, 2009–); Pres., Council of HM Circuit Judges, 2012 (Asst Sec., 2003–04, 2009–10; Hon. Sec., 2005–09; Jun. Vice-Pres., 2010; Sen. Vice-Pres., 2011). Lay Canon, Salisbury Cathedral, 2009–14, now Lay Canon Emeritus. *Recreations:* church music and history, maps, travel. *Address:* Winchester Combined Court Centre, Winchester SO23 9EL. *T:* (01962) 814100.

CUTLER, Timothy Robert, (Robin), CBE 1995; Director-General and Deputy Chairman, Forestry Commission, 1990–95; *b* 24 July 1934; *s* of Frank Raymond Cutler and Jeannie Evelyn Cutler (*née* Badenoch); *m* 1958, Ishbel Primrose; one *s* one *d. Educ:* Banff Academy; Aberdeen Univ. (BSc Forestry 1956). National Service, Royal Engineers, 1956–58. Colonial Forest Service, Kenya, 1958–64; New Zealand Forest Service: joined 1964; Dir of Forest Management, 1978; Dep. Dir-Gen., 1986; Chief Exec., Min. of Forestry, 1988–90. Hon. DSc Aberdeen, 1992. *Recreations:* golf, gardening, stamps. *Address:* 14 Swanston Road, Fairmilehead, Edinburgh EH10 7BB.

CUTTELL, Very Rev. Dr Jeffrey Charles; Dean of Derby, 2008–10; Rector, Astbury with Smallwood, 1999–2008 and since 2015; *b* Giltbrook, Notts, 1959; *s* of late Vernon Howard Cuttell and Joan Cuttell (*née* Brown); *m* 1981, Dr Elizabeth Jane Beton; one *s* one *d. Educ:* Broadoak Comp. Sch., Weston-Super-Mare; Birmingham Univ. (BSc 1980; PhD 1983); Trinity Theol Coll., Bristol (DipHE 1986); Sheffield Univ. (MA 1991). Res. Student, AERE Harwell, Oxon, 1980–83; ordained deacon, 1987, priest, 1988; Asst Curate, 1987–91, Vicar, 1991–95, Normanton; producer and presenter, BBC Religious Progs, 1995–99. Associate Lectr, Cardiff Univ., 2001–06; Tutor, St Michael's Theol Coll., Cardiff, 2001–06. Chaplain: 4th Bn Parachute Regt Res., 1997–2006; HM Young Offender Instn, Werrington, 2011–15. *Recreation:* walking with large dogs in lonely places. *Address:* Corner Cottage, Pools Lane, Smallwood, Sandbach, Cheshire CW11 2XD. *E:* jeffrey.cuttell@btinternet.com.

CUTTER, David John; Group Chief Executive, Skipton Building Society, since 2009; Chairman, Building Societies Association, since 2013; *b* Bradford, 1 Jan. 1962; *s* of Geoffrey and Valerie Cutter; *m* 1987, Carol Ingham; three *s. Educ:* Malsis Sch.; Rugby Sch.; Durham Univ. (BA). ACA 1987. Grad. trainee to Sen. Audit Manager, KPMG, 1983–93; Skipton Building Society: Hd, Internal Audit, 1993–96; Gen. Manager, 1996–99; Exec. Dir, 2000–08. *Recreations:* hockey, golf, piano. *Address:* Skipton Building Society, The Bailey, Skipton, N Yorks BD23 1DN. *T:* (01756) 705509. *E:* David.Cutter@skipton.co.uk. *Clubs:* Ben Rhydding Hockey, Ilkley Golf.

CUTTING, Ven. Alastair Murray; Archdeacon of Lewisham and Greenwich, since 2013; *b* Birmingham, 29 May 1960; *s* of William Alexander Murray Cutting and Margaret, (Margot), McLean Cutting (*née* Manderson); *m* 1984, Kay Elizabeth Greenhalgh; two *d. Educ:* George Watson's Coll., Edinburgh; Lushington Boys Sch., Ootacamund, S India; Watford Grammar Sch. for Boys; Westhill Coll., Birmingham (BEd 1983); St John's Coll., Nottingham (LTh; DPS 1987); Heythrop Coll., Univ. of London (MA 2003). Ordained deacon, 1987, priest, 1988; Curate: Woodlands, Doncaster, 1987–88; Wadsley, Sheffield, 1989–91; Chaplain to The Nave and Town Centre, Uxbridge, 1991–96; Vicar: Copthorne, W Sussex, 1996–2010; Henfield with Shermanbury and Woodmancote, W Sussex, 2010–13. *Recreations:* family and friends, South Indian food, Kiwiana. *Address:* Trinity House, 4 Chapel Court, Borough High Street, SE1 1HW. *T:* (020) 7939 9408, 07736 676106. *E:* Alastair.Cutting@southwark.anglican.org.

CUTTS, Johannah; QC 2008; **Her Honour Judge Cutts;** a Circuit Judge, since 2011; *b* Taplow, 13 Jan. 1964; *d* of Anthony and Jacqueline Cutts. *Educ:* Sch. of St Helen and St Katharine, Abingdon; Chelmer Inst. of Higher Educn (LLB Hons). Called to the Bar, Inner Temple, 1986; in practice as barrister, specialising in criminal law, particularly in cases involving vulnerable witnesses, 1986–2011; a Recorder, 2002–11. *Publications:* (contrib.) Rook and Ward on Sexual Offences, 2003, 4th edn 2011. *Recreations:* walking my dogs in Somerset, travelling with my niece, relaxing and eating with friends. *Address:* Reading Crown Court, Old Shire Hall, The Forbury, Reading, Berks RG1 3EH.

CYPRUS AND THE GULF, Bishop in, since 2007; **Rt Rev. Michael Augustine Owen Lewis;** *b* 8 June 1953; *er s* of John Lewis, Swaythling, Hants, and Jean Lewis (*née* Pope); *m* 1979, Julia Donneky (*née* Lennox); two *s* one *d. Educ:* King Edward VI Sch., Southampton; Merton Coll., Oxford (Postmaster; BA Oriental Studies 1975; MA 1979); Cuddesdon Coll. (BA Theology, Oxon 1977). Ordained deacon, 1978, priest, 1979; Curate, Salfords, 1978–80; Chaplain, Thames Poly., 1980–84; Vicar, Welling, 1984–91; Team Rector, Worcester SE Team Ministry, 1991–99; Rural Dean, Worcester E, 1993–99; Canon, Worcester Cathedral, 1998–99; Bishop of Middleton, 1999–2007. Chairman: House of Clergy, Worcester Diocesan Synod, 1997–99; Diocesan Adv. Cttee, Worcester, 1998–99; Manchester Diocesan Bd of Educn, 2000–07; Jt Adv. Cttee, Church Colls and Univs, 2005–07; C of E Bd of Educn HE Panel, 2006–07; Member: Bd, Al-Amana Interfaith Centre, Muscat, Oman, 2008–; Internat. Commn for Anglican-Orthodox Theol Dialogue, 2009–; Anglican Consultative Council, 2012–. Warden of Readers and Lay Assts, dio. of Manchester, 2001–07. Visitor, Community of the Sisters of the Love of God, Fairacres, Oxford, 2006–; Governing Trustee, St Michael's Coll., Llandaff, 2006–07. *Recreations:* enjoying architecture, food and drink, Middle Eastern and Caucasian travel. *Address:* Bishop's Office, St Paul's Cathedral, 2 Grigori Afxentiou, PO Box 22075, Nicosia 1517, Cyprus. *T:* (22) 671220, *Fax:* (22) 674553. *E:* bishop@spidernet.com.cy.

CYPRUS AND THE GULF, Archdeacon for; *see* Holdsworth, Ven. J. I.

CZAKÓ, Borbála; Global Partner and Global Director, Ernst & Young Global Ltd, since 2010; *b* Budapest, 22 Nov. 1953; *d* of Jozsef Serfozo and Ilona Bock; two *d. Educ:* Budapest Tech. Coll. (BA 1975); Univ. of Econs, Budapest (MA 1987); Tulane Univ., New Orleans (MBA 1991). CDir 2011. Sen. Manager, Ernst & Young Hungary, 1989–91; Chief of Mission and Investment Officer, World Bank and IFC, 1991–2002; Man. Partner and Hd of Corporate Finance, Ernst & Young Hungary, 2002–07; Dep. Man. Partner, Central Europe and South, Ernst & Young, 2003–07; Ambassador of Hungary to the UK, 2007–10. Pres., Hungarian Business Leaders Forum, 2003–. Mem., Bd of Dirs, Central European Univ., 2003–06. Pro-Europe Award, 2005. *Recreations:* reading, theatre, gardening, cooking. *Address:* Ernst & Young Global Ltd, Becket House, 1 Lambeth Palace Road, SE1 7EU.

CZERNIN, family name of **Baroness Howard de Walden.**

CZERNIN, Hon. Peter John Joseph; Co-Founder and Producer, Blueprint Pictures Ltd, since 2005; *b* London, 1 Jan. 1966; *s* of late Count Joseph Czernin and of Baroness Howard de Walden, *qv*; *m* 1994, Lucinda Wright; one *s* one *d. Educ:* Eton Coll.; Univ. of Bristol (BA Hons 1988). Producer of films: In Bruges, 2008; The Best Exotic Marigold Hotel, 2011; Seven Psychopaths, Now is Good, 2012; The Riot Club, 2014; The Second Best Marigold Hotel, 2015. Gov., BFI, 2014–. *Recreations:* Liverpool FC, the Turf, fishing, shooting, travel, literature, pop music, pursuit of the best martini ever. *Address:* Duxford Grange, Grange Road, Duxford CB22 4WF. *T:* (01763) 208850.

CZYZAK-DANNENBAUM, Peggy Scott; President, British Friends of Verbier Festival, since 2009; Member, Board, American Friends of Covent Garden, since 2007; *b* Cleveland, Ohio, 29 March 1947; *d* of John Joseph Czyzak and Marjorie Czyzak (*née* Kemp); *m* 1973, Karl Hermann Dannenbaum; four *s. Educ:* Wellesley Coll. (BA Hist. of Art 1969); London Business Sch. (MSc 1976; Alumni Achievement Award 1993; Alumni Service Award, 2011). Man. Dir, La Fornaia Ltd, 1985–95. Director: Thornton's plc, 1994–2002 (Chm., Audit Cttee, 1996–2002); Cavaghan & Grey Ltd, 1997–98; Village du Pain, 2002–09; Maison Madeleine Ltd, 2011– (Chm., 2013–); Member Advisory Board: Sapphire Partners, 2006–; Hubbub Online Ltd, 2009–. Vice Chm., Wellhouse NHS Trust, 1991–94; Mem., Assessment Panel, 1993–96, Adv. Bd, 1996–99, Business Link. London Business School: Chm., UK Regl Adv. Bd, 1999–2009; Gov., 2001–07; Chm., Capital Soc., 2006–09; Mem., Global Adv. Council, 2009–. Vice Chm., Brogdale Horticl Trust, 2002–09. Member, Board of Trustees: Royal Opera House, 2006–10 (Chm., Friends Adv. Council, 2007–11); Florida Grand Opera, 2010–13. Mem., Develt Bd, World Wide Web Foundn, 2013–. FRSA. *Recreations:* opera, ballet, theatre, travelling, mountain hiking, reading, cooking (plus London Marathon, 2007). *Address:* Albany, I6, Piccadilly, W1J 0AZ. *T:* 07831 527755. *E:* peggy@czyzak.com; 6899 Collins Avenue, Miami Beach, FL 33141, USA. *Club:* Reform.

D

DABBOUS, Oliver Elie; Chef and Owner: Dabbous, since 2012; Barnyard, since 2014; *b* Kuwait City, 5 Oct. 1980; *s* of Gilbert Dabbous and Jan Dabbous. *Educ:* Cranleigh Sch. Commis to Sen. Chef de Partie, Le Manoir aux Quat'Saisons, Oxon, 2000–04; Sous Chef, Hibiscus, Ludlow, 2005; Chef de Partie, Mugaritz, San Sebastian, 2006; Hd Chef, Texture, 2007–09; freelance chef, 2009–11. *Publications:* Dabbous: the cookbook, 2014. *Address:* Dabbous, 39 Whitfield Street, W1T 2SF. *T:* (020) 7323 1544. *E:* info@dabbous.co.uk.

DABER, Timothy Mark; a District Judge (Magistrates' Courts), since 2007; *b* Manchester, 24 Feb. 1958; *s* of Dr Keith Daber and Patricia Daber; *m* 2005, Karen Sonja Vanterpool; one *d*. *Educ:* William Hulme's Grammar Sch., Manchester; Sch. of Oriental and African Studies, Univ. of London (LLB Hons); Univ. of Portsmouth (Dip. Mgt Studies with dist.). Called to the Bar, Gray's Inn, 1981; Principal Court Clerk, SE Hants Magistrates' Courts, 1982–87; Principal Asst, S Hants Magistrates' Courts, 1987–98; Dep. Clerk to Justices, N Hants Magistrates' Courts, 1989–96; Clerk to N Cambs Justices, 1996–2000, to Cambs Justices, 2000–07; Dep. Dist Judge (Magistrates' Courts), 2000–07. *Recreations:* golf, ski-ing, boating. *Address:* Leicester Magistrates' Court, 15 Pocklingtons Walk, Leicester LE1 6BT.

DACOMBE, William John Armstrong; *b* 21 Sept. 1934; *s* of late John Christian Dacombe and of Eileen Elizabeth Dacombe; *m* 1962, Margaretta Joanna (*née* Barrington); two *d*. *Educ:* Felsted School; Corpus Christi College, Oxford (MA). Kleinwort Benson, 1961–65; N. M. Rothschild & Sons, 1965–73 (Dir, 1970–73); Dir, 1973–84, Asst Chief Exec., 1979–82, Williams & Glyn's Bank; Group Exec. Dir, Royal Bank of Scotland Group, 1982–84; Chief Exec. Dir, Rea Brothers Group, 1984–88. Co-founder and Partner, Campbell Lutyens and Co., 1988; Chairman: Brown Shipley Holdings, 1991–2005; Postern Ltd, 1996–2002; Albert E. Sharp Hldgs, 1997–98. Mem., Export Guarantees Adv. Council, 1982–86 (Dep. Chm., 1985–86). *Recreations:* art, historic buildings, reading. *Address:* Mullion Cottage, Well Lane, SW14 7AJ. *T:* (020) 8876 4336. *Clubs:* Brooks's, City of London.

DACRE, Baroness (29th in line) *cr* 1321; **Emily Douglas-Home;** *b* 7 Feb. 1983; *o d* of 28th Baron Dacre and Christine Douglas-Home (*née* Stephenson) (*d* 2008); *S* father, 2014. *Heir: co-heiresses: aunts* Hon. Sarah [*b* 4 July 1954; *m* 1977, Nicholas Charles Dent; two *s* two *d*]; Hon. Gian Leila [*b* 23 June 1958; one s]; Hon. Dinah Lilian [*b* 22 Jan. 1964; *m* 1989, Harry Marriott; three *s* one *d*].

DACRE, Prof. Jane Elizabeth, MD; FRCP, FRCPGlas, FRCPE; Professor of Medical Education, since 2001, Vice Dean, since 2005, and Director, UCL Medical School (formerly Division of Medical Education), since 2008, University College London; President, Royal College of Physicians, since 2014; *b* 11 Nov. 1955; *d* of late Peter Verrill and Christine Verrill; *m* 1979, Nigel Dacre, *qv*; one *s* two *d*. *Educ:* Univ. Coll. Hosp. Med. Sch. (BSc 1977; MB BS 1980; MD 1992). MRCP 1983, FRCP 1994; FRCPGlas 1999. Sen. Lectr in Clin. Skills and Consultant Physician and Rheumatologist, St Bartholomew's Med. Coll., 1980–95. Academic Vice-Pres., RCP, 2006–08. Mem., GMC, 2009–13. FHEA 2007. Woman of Achievement Award for Medicine and Healthcare, Women in the City, 2012. *Publications:* (with M. Nicol) Clinical Skills: the learning matrix for students of medicine and nursing, 1996; (with P. Kopelman) Handbook of Clinical Skills, 2002; articles on med. educn, assessment, fitness to practice and women in medicine. *Recreations:* family life, all things French. *Address:* University College London Medical School, 134 Medical School Building, 74 Huntley Street, WC1E 6AU. *T:* (020) 7679 0894. *E:* j.dacre@ucl.ac.uk; Royal College of Physicians, 11 St Andrews Place, Regent's Park, NW1 4LE. *T:* (020) 3075 1233. *E:* jane.dacre@rcplondon.ac.uk.

DACRE, Nigel; Chief Executive, Inclusive Digital Ltd, since 2008; *b* 3 Sept. 1956; *s* of late Peter and of Joan Dacre; *m* 1979, Jane Verrill (*see* Prof. Jane Elizabeth Dacre); one *s* two *d*. *Educ:* St John's Coll., Oxford (MA, PPE). BBC News Trainee, 1978; Regl Journalist, BBC Bristol, 1980; ITN, 1982–2002: ITN Scriptwriter, 1982; Programme Editor, Super Channel News, 1986; Editor, World News, 1987; Editor, News at One, 1989; Head of Programme Output and Exec. Producer, News at Ten, 1992; Dep. Editor, News Programmes, 1993–95; Editor, ITN News on ITV, subseq. ITV News, 1995–2002; Dean, Sch. of Media, London Coll. of Printing, 2003; Chief Exec., Educn Digital Mgt Ltd (Teachers' TV), 2003–06; Man. Dir, Ten Alps Digital, 2007. Chm., Local TV Network, 2013–15; Dir, Notts TV Ltd, 2012–. Editor, Centenary News, 2011–.

See also P. M. Dacre.

DACRE, Paul Michael; Editor in Chief, Associated Newspapers, since 1998; Editor, Daily Mail, since 1992; *b* 14 Nov. 1948; *s* of Joan and late Peter Dacre; *m* 1973, Kathleen Thomson; two *s*. *Educ:* University College Sch.; Leeds Univ. (Hons English). Reporter, feature writer, Associate Features Editor, Daily Express, 1970–76; Washington and NY corresp., Daily Express, 1976–79; Daily Mail: NY Bureau Chief, 1980; News Editor, 1981–85; Asst Editor (News and Foreign), 1986; Exec. Editor (Features), 1987; Associate Editor, 1989–91; Editor, Evening Standard, 1991–92. Director: Associated Newspaper Holdings, 1991–; Daily Mail & General Trust plc, 1998–; Teletext Hldgs Ltd, 2000–02; Chairman: Bd, Mail Newspapers, 2010–; Mail Online Adv. Bd, 2013–. Member: Press Complaints Commn, 1998–2008; Press Bd of Finance, 2004–; Chairman: Editors' Code of Practice Cttee, 2008–; Govt Rev. into 30 year Rule, 2008. Ambassador for Alzheimer's Soc., 2007–. Cudlipp Lect., London Coll. of Communication, 2007. FRSA 2007. Hon. Mem., NSPCC, 2009. *Address:* Daily Mail, Northcliffe House, 2 Derry Street, W8 5TT. *T:* (020) 7938 6000. *Club:* Garrick.

See also N. Dacre.

DADSON, Prof. Trevor John, PhD; FBA 2008; Professor of Hispanic Studies, Queen Mary University of London, since 2004 (Vice-Principal, 2006–10); *b* 7 Oct. 1947; *s* of Leonard John Dadson and Chrissie Vera (*née* Black); *m* 1975, Maria Angeles Gimeno; two *s*. *Educ:* Borden Grammar Sch., Sittingbourne; Univ. of Leeds (BA Hons); Univ. of Durham (PGCE); Emmanuel Coll., Cambridge (PhD 1974). Queen's University, Belfast: Lectr, 1978–86; Reader, 1986–88; Prof., 1988–90; University of Birmingham: Prof. of Hispanic Studies, 1990–2004; Head, Sch. of Modern Langs, 1993–97; Dir, Centre for European Langs and Culture, 2001–02. Pres., Assoc. of Hispanists of GB and Ire., 2011–15. *Publications:* The Genoese in Spain, 1983; Avisos a un Cortesano, 1985; (ed) G. Bocángel, La Lira de las Musas, 1985; (ed) D. Silva y Mendoza, Antología Poética, 1985; (ed) A. Barros, Filosofía Cortesana, 1987; Una Familia Hispano-Genovesa, 1991; Libros, lectores y lecturas: bibliotecas particulares españolas del Siglo de Oro, 1998; (gen. ed) Actas del XII Congreso de la AIH, 1998; (ed) Ludisimo e intertextualidad en la lírica española moderna, 1998; (ed) Voces subversivas: poesía bajo el Régimen, 2000; (ed) G. Bocángel, Obra Completa, 2001; (ed) La poesía española del siglo XX y la tradición literaria, 2003; Estudios sobre poesía española contemporánea, 2005; Los moriscos de Villarrubia de los Ojos, siglos XV–XVIII, 2007, 2nd edn 2015; Historia de la impresión de las Rimas de Lupercio y Bartolomé Leonardo de Argensola, 2010; Diego de Silva y Mendoza: poeta y político en la corte de Felipe III, 2011; (ed) La España del siglo XIX vista por dos inglesas: Lady Holland y la novelista George Eliot (1802–1804 y 1867), 2012; (ed) Epistolario e historia documental de Ana de Mendoza y de la Cerda, princesa de Éboli, 2013; Tolerance and Co-existence in Early Modern Spain: Old Christians and Moriscos in the Campo de Calatreva, 2014; (ed) Britain, Spain and the Treaty of Utrecht 1713–2013, 2014; (ed) Diego de Silva y Mendoza, Conde de Salinas y Marqués de Alenquer: cartas y memoriales (1584–1630), 2015; Cautiva del rey: Vida de Ana de Mendoza y de la Cerda, princesa de Éboli, 2015; (ed) Conde de Salinas. Obra completa: La poesía desconocida, 2015; numerous articles. *Recreations:* ski-ing, walking, tennis, reading.

DAFFERN, Paul George; Chief Financial Officer, Greengate Holdings (formerly Greengate Management Services) Ltd, 2008–12; *b* 5 May 1953; *s* of late George Thomas Daffern and Kathleen Esther Daffern; *m* 1984, Hilary Margaret Jenkins; one *s* one *d*. *Educ:* Foxford School, Coventry. Unbrako Ltd, 1969–73; Massey-Ferguson UK, 1973–75; Chrysler UK, 1975–77; Lucas Service UK, 1978–79; National Freight Co., 1980–88; Autoglass, 1988–91; Exec. Dir, Finance, AEA Technology, 1991–95; Chief Financial Officer, X/Open Co. Ltd, 1995–97; Finance Dir, Autoglass Ltd, 1998–2000; Dir, IMS, 2000–02; Gp Finance Dir, PD Ports, Logistics and Shipping Gp, then PD Ports Gp Ltd, subseq. PD Ports plc, 2002–06; Finance Dir, Infinis Ltd, 2006–07. Gov., St Hugh's Sch., Faringdon, 2005–. *Recreations:* golf, reading.

DAFIS, Cynog Glyndwr; Member (Plaid Cymru) Mid and West Wales, National Assembly for Wales, 1999–2003; *b* 1 April 1938; *s* of Annie and George Davies; *m* 1963, Llinos Iorwerth Jones; two *s* one *d*. *Educ:* Aberaeron County Secondary Sch.; Neath Boys' Grammar Sch.; UCW Aberystwyth (BA Hons English, MEd). Teacher of English: Coll. of Further Educn, Pontardawe, 1960–62; Newcastle Emlyn Secondary Modern Sch., 1962–80; Aberaeron Comprehensive Sch., 1980–84; Dyffryn Teifi Comprehensive Sch., Llandysul, 1984–91; Research Officer, Dept of Adult Continuing Educn, UC Swansea, 1991–92. Contested (Plaid Cymru) Ceredigion and Pembroke North, 1983 and 1987. MP (Plaid Cymru) Ceredigion and Pembroke N, 1992–97, Ceredigion, 1997–Jan. 2000. Member: Select Cttee, Welsh Affairs, 1995–97; Envmtl Audit Cttee, 1997–2000. National Assembly for Wales: Chair: Post-16 Educn and Culture Cttee, 1999–2000; Educn and Lifelong Learning Cttee, 2000–02. Dir of Policy, Plaid Cymru, 1997–2003. Vice Chm., Cymru Yfory/Tomorrow's Wales. Fellow: Univ. of Aberystwyth; Univ. of Wales Trinity St David. *Publications:* Mab y Pregethwr (autobiog.), 2005; pamphlets and booklet (in Welsh) on bilingualism and Welsh politics. *Recreations:* walking, jogging, reading, listening to music. *Address:* Cedrwydd, Llandre, Bow Street, Ceredigion SY24 5AB. *T:* (01970) 828262.

DAGLISH, Simon Edward De Guingand; Group Commercial Director, ITV plc, since 2011; *b* London, 29 Aug. 1965; *s* of Richard and Sarah Daglish; *m* 1998, Emma Charlotte Suter; two *s*. *Educ:* Holmwood House Prep. Sch.; Duke of York's Royal Mil. Sch.; RMA Sandhurst. Asst, Daily Express, 1988–90; Gp Hd, Telegraph Gp, 1990–95; Sales Dir, Independent Magazines, 1995–99; Sales Dir, Classic FM, 1999–2002; Commercial Dir, GCAP Media, 2002–09; Vice Pres., Commercial, Fox Internat., 2009–11. Jt Founder, Walking with the Wounded charity, 2010. *Publications:* Walking with the Wounded, 2011. *Recreations:* polar travel, adventure, Rugby, cricket, polar history. *Address:* 40 Westbridge Road, Battersea, SW11 3PW. *T:* (020) 7350 2247, 07833 234069. *E:* simon.daglish@me.com.

DAGWORTHY, Prof. Wendy, OBE 2011; Professor, 1998–2014, and Dean, School of Material, 2011–14, Royal College of Art (Head, Department of Fashion, 1998–2000; Head, School of Fashion and Textiles, 2000–11); *b* Gravesend, 4 March 1950. *Educ:* Medway Coll. of Art (Foundn and Pre-Dip. 1968); Middx Poly. (Hornsey Coll. of Art) (DipAD 1st Cl. Hons 1971). Designer, Radley (Quorum), 1971–72; designer and Dir, Wendy Dagworthy Ltd, 1972–88; Dir, London Design Collections, 1982–90; Central St Martins College of Art and Design: Course Dir, BA Hons Fashion, 1989–98; Fashion Prof., 1998; Actg Dean, Sch. of Fashion and Textiles, 1998. Consultant: fashion course, Temask Poly., Singapore, 1992; Export Promotion Bd, Pakistan, 1993–94; Crown Paints Fashion for Walls range, 2006–; Designer/Consultant: Laura Ashley, 1992; Liberty Retail and Internat., 1997–99; Design Consultant, Betty Jackson, 1996–2011. Guest Ed., Good Housekeeping, 2002–. Member: Adv. Bd, British Fashion Council, 1991–; Assoc. of Degree Courses in Fashion and Textile Design, 1999–. Has lectured at colls of art and design; external assessor for Foundn, BA Hons and MA Hons Fashion courses at univs and colls, 1982–, including: Domus Acad., Milan, 2004–; UCE, Birmingham, 2005–; Univ. of Westminster, 2006–; judge of art and design projects, awards and competitions. Outfits on display: exhibn at V&A Mus., 1997–; Cutting Edge Exhibn, V&A Mus., 1997; Matter in Hand Exhibn, London Inst. Gall., 1999–2000; outfits archived at V&A Mus., Brighton Mus., Manchester City Galls, Mus. of London, Bath Mus. of Fashion. Curated Club to Catwalk Exhibn, V&A Mus., 2013. *Publications:* contrib. articles to newspapers and mags, incl. Woman & Home, Good Housekeeping, Wall St Jl, The Times, Mail on Sunday, Guardian, Independent.

DAHL, Mildred; *see* Gordon, M.

DAIN, Sir David (John Michael), KCVO 1997; CMG 1991; HM Diplomatic Service, retired; High Commissioner to Pakistan, 1997–2000; *b* 30 Oct. 1940; *s* of late John Gordon Dain and Joan (*née* Connop); *m* 1969, Susan Kathleen Moss; one *s* four *d*. *Educ:* Merchant Taylors' Sch.; St John's Coll., Oxford (MA Lit.Hum.). Entered HM Diplomatic Service, 1963; Third, later Second Sec., Tehran and Kabul, 1964–68; seconded to Cabinet Office, 1969–72; First Sec., Bonn, 1972–75; FCO, 1975–78; Head of Chancery, Athens, 1978–81; Counsellor and Dep. High Comr, Nicosia, 1981–85; Head of Western European Dept,

FCO, 1985–89; on attachment to CSSB, 1989–90; High Comr, Cyprus, 1990–94; Asst Under-Sec. of State, then Dir, S Asian and SE Asian Depts, FCO, 1994–97. Chm., Anglo-Hellenic League, 2007–. FCIL (FIL 1986). Royal Order of Merit, Norway, 1988. *Recreations:* tennis, bridge, flying, golf, walking, natural history. *Address:* Manor Cottage, Frant, Tunbridge Wells, Kent TN3 9DR. *Clubs:* Oxford and Cambridge; Oxford Union Society.

DAINTITH, Prof. Terence Charles; Professor of Law: University of London, 1988–2002, now Professor Emeritus; University of Western Australia, since 2002; *b* 8 May 1942; *s* of Edward Terence and Irene May Daintith; *m* 1965, Christine Anne Bulport; one *s* one *d*. *Educ:* Wimbledon Coll.; St Edmund Hall, Oxford (BA Jurisp., MA); Univ. of Nancy (Leverhulme European Schol.). Called to the Bar, Lincoln's Inn, 1966; Bencher, 2000. Associate in Law, Univ. of California, Berkeley, 1963–64; Lectr in Constitutional and Admin. Law, Univ. of Edinburgh, 1964–72; University of Dundee: Prof. and Head of Dept of Public Law, 1972–83; Dir, Centre for Petroleum and Mineral Law Studies, 1977–83; Prof. of Law, European Univ. Inst., Florence, 1981–87; Dir, Inst. of Advanced Legal Studies, Univ. of London, 1988–95; Dean, Univ. of London Sch. of Advanced Study, 1994–2001. Sen. Fellow (formerly Vis. Fellow), Sch. of Law, Univ. of Melbourne, 2004–; Hon. Prof., Univ. of Dundee, 2014–. MAE 1989 (Chm., Law Cttee, 1993–96; Chm., Social Scis Section, 1996–98). Editor, Jl Energy and Natural Resources Law, 1983–92. Hon. LLD: De Montfort, 2001; Aberdeen, 2013. *Publications:* The Economic Law of the United Kingdom, 1974; (with G. Willoughby) United Kingdom Oil and Gas Law, 1977, 3rd edn (with A. D. G. Hill) 2000; (with L. Hancher) European Energy Strategy: the legal framework, 1986; (with S. Williams) The Legal Integration of Energy Markets, 1987; Law as an Instrument of Economic Policy, 1988; (with G. R. Baldwin) Harmonisation and Hazard, 1992; Implementing EC Law in the United Kingdom, 1995; (with A. C. Page) The Executive in the Constitution, 1999; Discretion in the Administration of Offshore Oil and Gas, 2006; Finders Keepers? How the Law of Capture Shaped the World Oil Industry, 2010; contribs to UK and foreign law jls. *Recreations:* cycling, carpentry. *Address:* Institute of Advanced Legal Studies, 17 Russell Square, WC1B 5DR.

DAINTON, Prof. John Bourke, DPhil; FRS 2002; CPhys, FInstP; Sir James Chadwick Professor of Physics, University of Liverpool, since 2002; Founding Director, Cockcroft Institute of Accelerator Science and Technology, 2005–07; *b* 10 Sept. 1947; *s* of Lord Dainton, FRS and Dr Barbara Hazlitt Dainton (*née* Wright); *m* 2008, Josephine Zilberkweit (*d* 2010). *Educ:* Merton Coll., Oxford (BA Hons 1969; MA, DPhil 1973). CPhys, FInstP, 1982. Lectr in Physics, Merton Coll., Oxford, 1972–73; Res. Associate, SRC Daresbury Lab., 1973–77; Lectr in Physics, Univ. of Glasgow, 1978–85; University of Liverpool: Lectr in Physics, 1986–88; Sen. Lectr in Physics, 1988–91; Reader in Physics, 1991–94; SERC Sen. Fellow, 1992–97; Prof. of Physics, 1994–2002. Vis. Scientist, DESY, Hamburg, 1980–82, 1997–99; Fellow, Alexander von Humboldt Stiftung, Germany, 2003. Chm., Super Proton Synchrotron and PS Cttee, CERN, 2003–09. Gov., Stockport Grammar Sch., 2008–. Freeman, City of London, 1982; Liveryman, Goldsmiths' Co., 1982–. FRSA 2003. Max Born Medal, Inst. of Physics and German Physical Soc., 1999. *Publications:* more than 250 articles in Zeitschrift für Physik C, European Jl of Physics, Nuclear Physics B, Physics Letters B, Jl of High Energy Physics, Jl of Physics G, Nuclear Instruments and Methods, Physics World, conf. proceedings, reports for SERC, PPARC and STFC, written evaluations for internat. sci. reviews. *Recreations:* music, travel, taking time to think. *Address:* Cockcroft Institute of Accelerator Science and Technology, Daresbury Science and Innovation Campus, Warrington WA4 4AD. *T:* (01925) 603820. *E:* John.Dainton@cockcroft.ac.uk; Oliver Lodge Laboratory, Department of Physics, University of Liverpool L69 7ZE. *T:* (0151) 794 7769, 07973 247769.

DAINTY, Prof. (John) Christopher, PhD; MRIA; Pilkington Professor of Applied Optics, Imperial College London, 1984–2012, Distinguished (formerly Senior) Research Fellow, since 2012; Professorial Research Associate, University College London, since 2013; *b* 22 Jan. 1947; *s* of late Jack Dainty and of Mary Elizabeth (*née* Elbeck); *m* 1978, Janice Hancock; one *s* one *d*. *Educ:* George Heriot's, Edinburgh; City of Norwich Sch.; Polytechnic of Central London (Diploma); Imperial Coll. of Science and Technol. (MSc; PhD 1972). Lectr, Queen Elizabeth Coll., Univ. of London, 1974–78; Associate Prof., Inst. of Optics, Univ. of Rochester, NY, USA, 1978–83. Sen. Res. Fellow, SERC, 1987–92; PPARC Sen. Res. Fellow, Imperial Coll., Univ. of London, 2001–02; Sci. Foundn Ireland Prof. of Experimental Phys, subseq. Prof. of Applied Phys, NUI, 2002–12, now Emeritus. President: Internat. Commn for Optics, 1990–93; European Optical Soc., 2002–04; Pres., Optical Soc. of America, 2011. MRIA 2008. Internat. Commn of Optics Prize, 1984; Thomas Young Medal and Prize, Inst. of Physics, 1993; Mees Medal and Prize, Optical Soc. of America, 2003. *Publications:* (with R. Shaw) Image Science, 1974; (ed) Laser Speckle and Related Phenomena, 1975, 2nd edn 1984; (ed with M. Nieto-Vesperinas) Scattering in Volumes and Surfaces, 1989; scientific papers. *Address:* UCL Insitute of Ophthalmology, 11–43 Bath Street, EC1V 9EL. *T:* (020) 7608 4057.

DAKIN, Nicholas; MP (Lab) Scunthorpe, since 2010; an Opposition Whip, since 2011; *b* 10 July 1955; *m* Audrey; three *c*. *Educ:* Longslade Upper Sch., Birstall, Leics; Hull Univ.; King's Coll. London. English teacher: Greatfield High Sch., Hull; Gävle, Sweden; John Leggott College, Scunthorpe: English teacher, then Vice Principal; Principal, 2007–10. Mem. (Lab) N Lincs Council, 1996–2007 (Leader, 1997–2003; Leader, Lab Gp, 2003–07). Mem., Select Cttee on Educn, 2010–11, on Procedure, 2011–. *Address:* House of Commons, SW1A 0AA.

DAKIN, Rt Rev. Timothy; *see* Winchester, Bishop of.

DALAI LAMA; *see* Tenzin Gyatso.

DALAL, Maneck Ardeshir Sohrab, OBE 1997; Director: Tata Ltd, SW1, since 1977 (Managing Director, 1977–88; Vice-Chairman, 1989–94); Tata Industries, Bombay, since 1979; *b* 24 Dec. 1918; *s* of Ardeshir Dalal, OBE and Amy Dalal; *m* 1947, Kathleen Gertrude Richardson; three *d*. *Educ:* Trinity Hall, Cambridge (MA). Cambridge Univ. Captain, tennis and squash rackets. Called to the Bar, Middle Temple, 1945. Manager: Air-India New Delhi, 1946–48; Air-India London, 1948–53; Regional Traffic Manager, 1953–59; Regional Director, 1959–77; Minister for Tourism and Civil Aviation, High Commn for India, 1973–77. President: Indian Chamber of Commerce in Great Britain, 1959–62; Indian Management Assoc. of UK, 1960–63; UK Pres., World Conf. on Religions and Peace, UK and Ireland Gp, 1985–; Vice-Pres., Friends of Vellore, 1979–; Chairman: Foreign Airlines Assoc. of UK, 1965–67; Indian YMCA, London, 1972–98; Bharatiya Vidhya Bhavan, London (Indian Cultural Inst. of Gt Britain), 1975–; Northbrook Soc., 1990– (Mem. Cttee, 1975–); Indian Women's Educn Assoc., 1985–95 (Mem. Cttee, 1975–95); Vice-Chm., Fest. of India in GB, 1980–81; Member: Sub-Cttee on Transport, Industrial Trng Bd of GB, 1975–77; Assembly, British Council of Churches, 1984–87; Internat. Bd, United World Colls, 1985–; Bd Govs, Nat. Inst. for Social Work, 1986–96; Chm. Central Council, Royal Over-Seas League, 1986–89 (Dep. Chm. Central Council, 1982–86; Mem., 1974–; Vice-Pres., 1989–). Patron: Internat. Centre for Child Studies, 1984–; Satyajit Ray Foundn, 1995–; Indian Professionals Assoc., UK, 1996–; Child in Need Internat. (UK), 2001–. FCILT (FCIT 1975); FCMI; FRSA 1997. Award for Asian leadership in promoting heritage and culture, Asian Who's Who, 2009; Gold Award for Community Service, Asian Achievers Awards, 2010. *Recreations:* reading, walking. *Address:* Tall Trees, Marlborough Road, Hampton, Middx TW12 3RX. *T:* (020) 8979 2065. *Clubs:* Hurlingham, Royal Over-Seas League, MCC; Hawks (Cambridge).

DALBY, Dr (Terry) David (Pereira); Reader in West African Languages, School of Oriental and African Studies, University of London, 1967–83, now Emeritus; Director, Linguasphere Observatory (Observatoire linguistique), since 1987; *b* 7 Jan. 1933; *s* of Ernest Edwin Dalby and Rose Cecilia Dalby; one *s* four *d*. *Educ:* Cardiff High Sch.; Queen Mary Coll., London (BA 1954, PhD 1961; Hon. Life Mem., Queen Mary Coll. Union Soc., 1954). Served to Lieut, Intell. Corps, 1954–56. United Africa Co. Ltd, London and W Africa, 1957–60; Lectr in Mod. Languages, University Coll. of Sierra Leone, 1961–62; Lectr in W African Langs, SOAS, Univ. of London, 1962–67; Hon. Res. Fellow, Adran y Gymraeg, Univ. of Wales, Cardiff, 1996–2005. Hanns Wolff Vis. Prof., Indiana Univ., 1969. Chm., Centre for Afr. Studies, Univ. of London, 1971–74; Dir, Internat. African Inst., 1974–80; Chairman: Internat. Conf. on Manding Studies, 1972, and Drought in Africa Conf., 1973; UK Standing Cttee on Univ. Studies of Africa, 1978–82 (Dep. Chm., 1975–78). Vice-Pres., Unesco Meeting on Cultural Specificity in Africa, Accra, 1980. Member: Governing Body, SOAS, 1969–70; Council, African Studies Assoc. of UK, 1970–73; Cttee of Management, British Inst. in Paris, 1975–82; Conseil Internat. de Recherche et d'Etude en Linguistique Fondamentale et Appliquée, 1980–86 (Président, 1984); Centre Internat. de Recherche sur le Bilinguisme, Laval Univ., Que, 1981–89; Eur. Council on African Studies, 1985–87; Centre Internat. des Industries de la Langue, Univ. Paris X, 1993–95; Comité Français des Etudes Africaines, 1993–94; BSI Cttee TS/1, 2001–06; ISO Cttee TC37, 2002–05; Carmarthen Family Centres Mgt Cttee, 2005–11; ISO 639 Jt Adv. Cttee, 2012–14. Hon. Mem., SOAS, 1983. Editor, African Language Review, 1962–72; Co-editor, Africa, 1976–80. Endowed Rhoswen Enfys awards, Nat. Eisteddfod Wales, 2002–08. *Publications:* Lexicon of the Mediaeval German Hunt, 1965; Black through White: patterns of communication in Africa and the New World, 1970; (ed) Language and History in Africa, 1970; (ed jtly) Drought in Africa, 1st vol. 1973, 2nd vol. 1978; Language Map of Africa and the adjacent islands, 1977; Clavier international de Niamey, 1984; (jtly) Les langues et l'espace du français, 1985; Afrique et la lettre, 1986; (jtly) Thesaurus of African Languages, 1987; Linguasphere Register of the World's Languages and Speech Communities, 2 vols, 2000; articles in linguistic and other jls. *Recreations:* keeping fit, campaigning for women's and children's rights.

DALDRY, Stephen David, CBE 2004; Director, Stephen Daldry Pictures, since 1998; Associate Director, Royal Court Theatre, since 1999; *b* 2 May 1961; *s* of late Patrick Daldry and Cherry (*née* Thompson); *m* 2001, Lucy Sexton; one *d*. *Educ:* Huish GS, Taunton; Univ. of Sheffield (BA). Trained with Il Circo di Nando Orfei, Italy; Artistic Dir, Metro Theatre, 1984–86; Associate Artist, Crucible Theatre, Sheffield, 1986–88; Artistic Director: Gate Theatre, Notting Hill, 1989–92; English Stage Co., Royal Court Theatre, 1992–99. Exec. Prod., Creative, London 2012 Ceremonies, 2010–12. Cameron Mackintosh Vis. Prof. of Contemp. Theatre, St Catherine's Coll., Oxford, 2002. Major productions include: Damned for Despair, Gate, 1991; An Inspector Calls, RNT, 1992, Aldwych, 1994, Garrick, 1995, NY, 1995, Playhouse, 2001; Machinal, RNT, 1993; The Audience, Gielgud Th., 2013, NY, 2015; Skylight, Wyndham's, 2014; Royal Court: The Kitchen, 1995; Via Dolorosa, 1998, NY, 1999, filmed 1999; Far Away, 2000, transf. Albery, 2001; A Number, 2002; Wall, 2009; Billy Elliot - the Musical, Victoria Palace, 2005, NY, 2008. *Films:* Eight (short), 1998; Billy Elliot, 2000; The Hours, 2003; The Reader, 2009; Extremely Loud and Incredibly Close, 2012; Trash, 2015. *Address:* c/o Stephen Daldry Pictures Ltd, Lion House, Red Lion Street, WC1R 4GB.

DALE, Barry Gordon, FCA; Partner, Baird Partners, and International Corporate Finance Group, since 2003; *b* 31 July 1938; *s* of Francis and Catherine Dale; *m* 1963, Margaret (*née* Fairbrother); one *s* one *d*. *Educ:* Queen Elizabeth Grammar Sch., Blackburn. Coopers Lybrand, Montreal, 1960–62; Pilkington Brothers Glass, St Helens, 1962–65; ICI, 1965–85: Mond Div., Cheshire, 1966–68; Head Office, 1968–72; Dep. Chief Acct, Mond Div., 1972–78; Finance Dir, ICI Latin America (Wilmington, USA), 1978–80; Chief Acct, Organics Div., Manchester, 1980–84; Bd Mem. for Finance, LRT, 1985–88; Gp Finance Dir, 1988–92, Gp Chief Exec., 1993–95, Littlewoods Orgn. Director: Ellis & Everard, 1978–81; Magadi Soda Co. (Kenya), 1980–82; Triplex Lloyd, 1994–98; London Buses Ltd, 1985–88; London Underground Ltd, 1985–88; LRT Bus Engineering Ltd, 1985–88; Greenalls, then De Vere, Gp, 1992–2000; Chairman: London Transport Trustee Co., 1985–88; London Transport Pension Fund Trustees, 1985–88; Datanetworks, 1987–88; Creightons, 1997–99. *Recreations:* golf, fell walking, other sports. *Address:* Tanglewood, Spinney Lane, Knutsford WA16 0NQ. *Clubs:* Carlton; Tatton (Knutsford); Knutsford Golf.

DALE, Iain Campbell; Founder and Managing Director, Biteback Publishing, since 2009; Presenter, LBC Radio, since 2010; *b* Cambridge, 15 July 1962; *s* of Garry Dale and late Jane Dale; civil partnership 2008, *m* 2015, John Simmons. *Educ:* Saffron Walden County High Sch.; Univ. of East Anglia (BA Hons German 1985). Researcher, H of C, 1985–87; Public Affairs Mgr, British Ports Fedn, 1987–89; Insce Corresp., Lloyd's List, 1990; Public Affairs Mgr, Waterfront Partnership, 1990–96; Founder and Man. Dir, Politico's Bookstore, 1996–2006; Man. Dir, Politico's Publishing, 1998–2003; COS to Rt Hon. David Davis, MP, 2005; Presenter, 18 Doughty Street TV, 2006–07; Publisher, Total Politics Magazine, 2008–12. Ed., Iain Dale's Diary, 2003–10; columnist, Daily Telegraph, 2007–09. Contested (C) N Norfolk, 2005. *Publications:* (edited): The End of the Dock Labour Scheme, 1991; Unofficial Book of Political Lists, 1997; As I Said to Denis: the Margaret Thatcher book of quotations, 1997; The Blair Necessities, 1998; Bill Clinton Joke Book, 1998; Tony Blair New Labour Joke Book, 1998; Dictionary of Conservative Quotations, 1999, 2nd edn 2013; Wit and Wisdom of Tony Banks, 1999; Labour Party General Election Manifestos 1900–97, 1999; Liberal Party General Election Manifestos 1990–97, 1999; Conservative Party General Election Manifestos 1990–97, 1999; Memories of Maggie, 2000; Directory of Political Websites, 2001; Directory of Think Tank Publications, 2001; Memories of the Falklands, 2002, 2nd edn 2012; Directory of Political Lobbying, 2003; (jtly) Prime Minister Portillo and Other Things That Never Happened, 2003; Times Guides to the House of Commons 1906–10, 2003; Times Guides to the House of Commons 1929–35, 2003; Politico's Book of the Dead, 2003; Margaret Thatcher: a tribute in words and pictures, 2005; Little Red Book of New Labour Sleaze, 2006; Big Red Book of New Labour Sleaze, 2007; 500 of the Most Witty, Acerbic and Erudite Things Ever Said About Politics, 2007; Guide to Political Blogging in the UK, 2007; Little Book of Boris, 2007; Total Politics Guide to the General Election, 2009; Total Politics Guide to Political Blogging 2010–11, 2010; Margaret Thatcher: in her own words, 2010; Talking Politics: political conversations with Iain Dale, 2010; West Ham United: when football was football, 2011; (jtly) Prime Minister Boris and Other Things That Never Happened, 2011; The Bigger Book of Boris, 2011; Norwich City: when football was football, 2012; Memories of Margaret Thatcher, 2013; Great Parliamentary Speeches 1978–2013, 2014; (author): The Blogfather, 2012; The NHS: things that need to be said, 2015. *Recreations:* politics, books, Jack Russells, Europop, golf, debating, radio, travel, Audis. *T:* (020) 7091 1260. *E:* iain@iaindale.com. *Club:* West Ham United.

DALE, Maj.-Gen. Ian Conway, CBE 2007; CEng; Director and Principal Consultant, SELIX Ltd, since 2012; Senior Defence Adviser, Glue Reply Ltd, since 2013; *b* Leicester, 8 Sept. 1957; *s* of Eric Dale and Gwendolen Dale (*née* Mann); *m* 1983, Karen Moore; two *d*. *Educ:* Gateway Grammar Sch., Leicester; Army Apprentices Coll., Arborfield; RMA, Sandhurst; Royal Mil. Coll. of Sci., Shrivenham (BSc Eng Hons 1983; MSc 1988). CEng 1987; FIET 2011 (MIET 1986). REME Apprenticeship, 1974–76; Lance-Corp., REME Wing, Royal Sch. of Artillery 1977; Troop Comd, 14/20 King's Hussars, Germany and Canada, 1979; 2IC Light Aid Detachment REME, 14/20 King's Hussars, Germany, 1980; Trng Officer, 20 Electronics Workshop REME, Germany, 1984; OC, 32 Regt RA Workshop REME, Germany, 1985–86; Adjt, Logistic Bn, Falkland Is, 1987; psc† 1989; Gen.

Staff, Directorate of CIS (Army), MoD, 1990–91; Co. Comd, 20 Electronics Workshop REME, Germany, 1992–93; Gen. Staff, HQ ARRC, Germany and Denmark, 1994–95; CO, 6 Bn REME, UK and Bosnia, 1996–97; COS Inspector REME, UK, 1998; Comdr Equipment Support, Germany, 1999–2000, DCS, Germany and Oman, 2001, 1 (UK) Armoured Div.; hcsc 2001; Commander: 101 Logistic Bde, UK, 2002–03; UK Jt Force Logistics Component, Kuwait and Iraq, 2003; Deputy Chief of Staff: ARRC, Germany, 2004–05; Internat. Security Assistance Force, Afghanistan, 2006; rcds 2007; Mil. Team Leader, Service Personnel Command Paper, MoD, 2008; Dir (formerly Dir Gen.) Land Equipment, Defence Equipment and Support, 2008–11. Global Mkt Advr, Inmarsat Global Govt, 2012–; Eur. Advr, Portafloor UK, 2012–. President: Army Rugby League, 2007–11; REME Winter Sports, 2008–12; Dep. Pres., Army Winter Sports, 2009–11. Chairman, Trustees: REME Central Charitable Trust, 2012–; Council for Cadet Rifle Shooting, 2012–. FCIM 2010. *Recreations:* mountain sports, ski-ing, deer management. *Address:* RHQ REME, MoD Lyneham, Lyneham, Chippenham SN15 9HB.

DALE, Jim, MBE 2003; actor, director, singer, composer, lyricist; *b* 15 Aug. 1935; *m*; three *s* one *d*. *Educ:* Kettering Grammar School. Music Hall comedian, 1951; singing, compèring, directing, 1951–61; *films*, 1965–, include: Lock Up Your Daughters, The Winter's Tale, The Biggest Dog in the World, National Health, Adolf Hitler—My Part in his Downfall, Joseph Andrews, Pete's Dragon, Hot Lead Cold Feet, Bloodshy, The Spaceman and King Arthur, Scandalous, Carry On films: Carry On Cabby, Carry On Cleo, Carry On Jack, Carry On Cowboy, Carry On Screaming, Carry On Spying, Carry On Constable, Carry On Doctor, Carry On Again Doctor, Carry On Don't Lose Your Head, Carry On Follow that Camel, Carry On Columbus. *Stage:* joined Frank Dunlop's Pop Theatre for Edinburgh Festival, 1967–68; National Theatre, 1969–71: main roles in National Health, Love's Labour's Lost, Merchant of Venice, Good-natured Man, Captain of Köpenick, The Architect and the Emperor of Assyria; also appeared at Young Vic in Taming of the Shrew, Scapino (title rôle and wrote music); title rôle in musical The Card, 1973; Compère of Sunday Night at the London Palladium, 1973–74; Scapino (title rôle), Broadway, 1974–75 (Drama Critics' and Outer Circle Awards for best actor; Tony award nomination for best actor); Privates on Parade, Long Wharf Theatre, New Haven, Conn, 1979; Barnum (title rôle), Broadway, 1980 (Tony award for best actor in a musical, Drama Desk Award); A Day in the Death of Joe Egg, NY, 1985 (Tony nomination for best actor; Outer Circle Award for best actor); Me and My Girl, NY, 1987–88; Privates on Parade, NY, 1989; Oliver!, London Palladium, 1995; The Music Man, Travels With My Aunt, NY (Drama Desk Award, Outer Circle Award and Critics Award, 1995); Comedians, NY, 2003; A Christmas Carol, NY, 2003–04; Address Unknown, NY, 2004; The Threepenny Opera, NY, 2006; Busker Alley, NY, 2006; The Oak Tree, NY, 2007; Don Juan in Hell, Williamstown, 2007; The Road to Mecca, NY, 2012; one-man show, Just Jim Dale, NY, transf. Vaudeville Th., 2015. *Television* includes: host of Ringling Brothers Barnum and Bailey Circus (TV special), 1985; Adventures of Huckleberry Finn, 1985; Pushing Daisies, 2007–08. Composed film music for: The Winter's Tale, Shalako, Twinky, Georgy Girl (nominated for Academy Award), Joseph Andrews. Audio recordings incl. Harry Potter series (Grammy Award, best children's audio recording: 2001, for Harry Potter and the Goblet of Fire; 2008, for Harry Potter and the Deathly Hallows), A Christmas Carol, 2004; Peter and the Wolf, The Shoe Bird, 2008. 10 Audie Awards, Audio Publishers Assoc.; 2 Earphones Awards, AudioFile Mag. *Address:* c/o Tom Celia, CED, 257 Park Avenue South, New York, NY 10010, USA; c/o Janet Glass, Eric Glass Ltd, 25 Ladbroke Crescent, W11 1PS.

DALE, John; editorial consultant; columnist, Press Gazette; Editor, Take a Break, 1991–2011; *b* Cleethorpes, Lincs, 1 May 1946; *s* of Ken Dale and Eileen Dale. *Educ:* Wintringham Grammar Sch., Grimsby. Reporter: Daily Mail, 1968–78; The Observer, 1978–79; Now!, 1979–81; London Ed., Sunday Standard (Scotland), 1981–83; freelance journalist, 1983–91. Editor of the Year, weekly women's mags, 1992, 1994, 1995, 1996, 1997, 2001, 2003, 2007, 2009, Innovation of the Year, 1998, 2002, BSME. *Publications:* The World Beneath My Wheels, 1976; The Prince and the Paranormal, 1986; 24 Hours in Journalism, 2012. *Recreations:* slow cycling, founder of the slow cycling movement. *Address:* Brentford, Middx. *T:* 07720 054626. *E:* johnkdale@msn.com. *Club:* Soho House.

DALE, Peter David; Founder, Rare Day Ltd, since 2008; *b* 25 July 1955; *s* of late David Howard Dale and Betty Marguerite Dale (*née* Rosser); *m* 1988, Victoria Francesca Pennington; one *s* two *d*. *Educ:* King Henry VIII Grammar Sch., Coventry; Liverpool Univ. (BA Hons English Lit. and Lang.). BBC Television: research asst trainee, 1980–82; Dir and Producer, 1982–98; Channel 4: Commissioning Ed., Documentaries, 1998–2000; Head of Documentaries, 2000–05; Head of More4, 2005–08. Non-exec. Dir, Fresh One Prodns, 2009–12. Dir, Sheffield Internat. Documentary Fest., 2002–04. Mem. Exec. Cttee, Guardian Edinburgh TV Fest., 2002–05. Associate Fellow, IPPR, 2009–. Trustee, Grierson Trust, 2007–11. Journalism Prize, Anglo-German Foundn, 1992; Best Documentary Award, 1994, Best Documentary Series, 1996, RTS; Producer of Year Award, Broadcast Mag., 1997; Grierson Award for Best British Documentary, BFI, 1997. *Recreations:* family, sailing.

DALE, Robert Alan; business consultant, retired; Director, Business Development, Lucas Industries plc, 1992–93; *b* 31 Oct. 1938; *s* of Horace and Alice Dale; *m* 1963, Sheila Mary Dursley; one *s* one *d*. *Educ:* West Bromwich Grammar Sch.; Birmingham Univ. (BA Hons). Joined Lucas Industries as graduate apprentice, 1960; first management appt, 1965; first Bd appt, 1971; Dir, Lucas CAV, 1972–77; Dir and Gen. Man., Lucas Batteries, 1978–81; joined Exec. Cttee of Lucas (Joseph Lucas Ltd), 1980; Managing Director: Lucas World Service, 1981–85; Lucas Electrical, 1985–87; Lucas Automotive, 1987–92; Dir, Lucas Industries, 1987–93. Vice-Pres., SMMT, 1989–92. *Recreations:* sport, photography, travel.

DALE, Spencer; Chief Economist, BP plc, since 2014; *b* London, 12 Jan. 1967; *s* of John James Dale and B Dale; *m* Natasha Cavill; one *s* one *d*. *Educ:* Exeter Coll.; University Coll. Cardiff (BSc Econs 1988); Univ. of Warwick (MSc Econs 1989). Bank of England, 1989–2014: Private Sec. to Mervyn King, 1997–99; Hd, Monetary Assessment and Strategy Div., 1999–2000; Hd, Conjunctural Assessment and Projects Div., 2000–06; on secondment as Vis. Sen. Advr, Bd of Govs, Federal Reserve System, USA, 2006–08; Chief Economist, and Mem., Monetary Policy Cttee, 2008–14; Exec. Dir, Financial Stability Strategy and Risk, 2014. Mem. Council, REconS, 2008–. Mem., Soc. of Business Economists, 2008–. *Publications:* numerous res. articles in acad. jls and central bank pubns. *Recreations:* running, theatre, tennis. *Address:* BP plc, 1 St James's Square, SW1Y 4PD.

DALES, Sir Richard (Nigel), KCVO 2001; CMG 1993; HM Diplomatic Service, retired; Ambassador to Norway, 1998–2002; *b* 26 Aug. 1942; *s* of late Kenneth Richard Frank Dales and Olwen Mary (*née* Preedy); *m* 1966, Elizabeth Margaret Martin; one *s* one *d*. *Educ:* Chigwell Sch.; St Catharine's Coll., Cambridge (BA 1964). Entered FO, 1964; Third Sec., Yaoundé, Cameroon, 1965–67; FCO, 1968–70; Second Sec., later First Sec., Copenhagen, 1970–73; FCO, 1973; Asst Private Sec. to Foreign and Commonwealth Sec., 1974–77; First Sec., Head of Chancery and Consul, Sofia, Bulgaria, 1977–81; FCO, 1981; Counsellor and Head of Chancery, Copenhagen, 1982–86; Dep. High Comr, Harare, 1986–89; Head of Southern Africa, later Central and Southern Africa, Dept, FCO, 1989–91; Resident Chm. (FCO), CSSB, 1991–92; High Comr, Zimbabwe, 1992–95; Asst Under-Sec. of State, later Dir, Africa and Commonwealth, FCO, 1995–98. Chm., Anglo-Norse Soc., 2003–; Trustee, Internat. Alert, 2005–10 (Chm., 2006–10). Mem. Bd, Norfolk and Norwich Fest., 2003–06. Mem. Council, UEA, 2004–13. *Recreations:* music, walking, cross-country ski-ing, grandchildren. *Club:* Oxford and Cambridge.

DALEY, Her Honour Judith Mary Philomena; a Circuit Judge, 1994–2013; *b* 12 Aug. 1948; *d* of James Patrick Daley and Mary Elizabeth Daley (*née* Rawcliffe), BA. *Educ:* Seafield Convent Grammar Sch., Crosby; King's Coll. London (LLB Hons). Called to the Bar, Gray's Inn, 1970; Asst Recorder, 1984; Recorder, 1989–94 (Northern Circuit). *Recreations:* opera, music, theatre, travel, gardening. *Club:* Athenæum (Liverpool).

DALGETY OF SIKOTILANI TONGA, Rt Hon. Lord, Life Peer of Tonga (*cr* 2008); **Rt Hon. Ramsay Robertson Dalgety;** PC (Tonga) 2008; a Law Lord, Tonga, since 2008; *b* 2 July 1945; *s* of James Robertson Dalgety and Georgia Dalgety (*née* Whyte); *m* 1971, Mary Margaret Bernard (*d* 2012); one *s* one *d*. *Educ:* High School of Dundee; Univ. of St Andrews (LLB Hons). Advocate, 1972; Temp. Sheriff, 1987–91; QC (Scot.) 1986. Dep. Traffic Comr for Scotland, 1988–93. Councillor, City of Edinburgh, 1974–80. Director/Chairman: Archer Transport Ltd and Archer Transport (London) Ltd, 1982–85; Venture Shipping Ltd, 1983–85. Director: Scottish Opera Ltd, 1980–90; Scottish Opera Theatre Trust Ltd, 1987–90; Chm., Opera Singers Pension Fund, 1990–92 (Dep. Chm., 1989–90; Trustee, 1983–92); Dep. Chm., Edinburgh Hibernian Shareholders Assoc., 1990–92. Judge of the Supreme Court, Tonga, 1991–95, and sometime Acting Chief Justice; Sec. Gen., Tonga Chamber of Commerce, 1998–2001. Chairman: Tonga Electric Power Bd, 2003–08; Electricity Commn, 2008–; Judicial Cttee, Privy Council, 2008–; Mem. Defence Bd, Tonga, 2011–. Vice-Pres. and Treas., Tonga Internat. Gamefishing Assoc., 1994–98; Pres., Tonga Archery Fedn, 1998–2010; Dep. Chef de Mission, Kingdom of Tonga team, Olympic Games, Athens, 2004. Grand Cross, Order of Queen Salote (Tonga), 2008; Coronation Medal (Tonga), 2008. *Recreations:* heraldry, opera, travel, cricket, football, archery. *Address:* PO Box 869, Nuku'alofa, Kingdom of Tonga, South Pacific. *T:* 8723400. *E:* lawlord.tonga@gmail.com. *Clubs:* Royal Over-Seas League; Royal Nuku'alofa (Tonga) (Mem. Cttee, 2003–13; Pres., 2015).

DALGLISH, Kenneth Mathieson, MBE 1985; Manager, Liverpool Football Club, 2011–12 (Carling Cup winners, 2012); *b* Glasgow, 4 March 1951; *m* 1974, Marina (MBE 2009); one *s* three *d*. Professional football player, 1968–89: Celtic FC, 1970–77; Liverpool FC, 1977–89 (also Manager, 1985–91) (winner, Eur. Cup, 1978, 1981, 1984, FA Cup, 1986, 1989); Scotland, 1971–86 (102 caps); Manager, 1991–95, Dir of Football, 1995–96, Blackburn Rovers FC; New Business Develt Manager, Carnegie Sports Internat., 1996; Manager, Newcastle Utd FC, 1997–98; Dir of Football Ops and Bd Mem., Celtic FC, 1999–2000; with Liverpool FC Acad., 2009–11. Non-exec. Dir, Liverpool FC, 2013–. Founder, Marina Dalglish Appeal, 2004. Football Writers' Footballer of Year, 1979, 1983; Player of Year, PFA, 1983; Manager of Year, 1986, 1988, 1990, 1995. Freeman, City of Glasgow, 1986. *Publications:* Kenny Dalglish (autobiog.), 1996; My Liverpool Home (autobiog.), 2010.

DALHOUSIE, 17th Earl of, *cr* 1633; **James Hubert Ramsay;** Baron Ramsay 1618; Lord Ramsay 1633; Baron Ramsay (UK) 1875; Vice Lord-Lieutenant, Angus, since 2002; Lord Steward of HM Household, since 2009; Director, Jamestown Investments Ltd, since 1987; *b* 17 Jan. 1948; *er s* of 16th Earl of Dalhousie, KT, GCVO, GBE, MC; *S* father, 1999; *m* 1973, Marilyn, *yr d* of Major Sir David Henry Butter, KCVO, MC; one *s* two *d*. *Educ:* Ampleforth. 2nd Bn Coldstream Guards, commnd 1968–71, RARO 1971. Director: Hambros Bank Ltd, 1981–82; (exec.) Enskilda Securities, 1982–87; Capel-Cure Myers Capital Management Ltd, 1988–91; Dunedin Smaller Cos Investment Trust, 1993–2015 (Chm., 1998–2015); Scottish Woodlands Ltd, 1993–2005 (Chm., 1998–2005). Chm., (Scotland) Mental Health Foundn, 2000–02. Capt., 2010–, Pres. Council and Silver Stick for Scotland, 2013, Royal Co. of Archers (The Queen's Body Guard for Scotland). Vice Chm., Game Conservancy Trust, 1994–2009; President: British Deer Soc., 1987–2010; Dundee and Angus Br., Scots Guards Assoc., 2008. DL Angus, 1993. CStJ 2012 (OStJ 2001). *Heir: s* Lord Ramsay, *qv*. *Address:* Brechin Castle, Brechin, Angus DD9 6SG. *Clubs:* White's, Pratt's, Caledonian (Pres., 1990–), Turf.

DALKEITH, Earl of; Walter John Francis Montagu Douglas Scott; *b* 2 Aug. 1984; *s* and *heir* of Duke of Buccleuch, *qv* and of Duchess of Buccleuch, *qv*; *m* 2014, Elizabeth Honor Cobbe. A Page of Honour to HM The Queen, 1996–99.

DALLAGLIO, Lawrence Bruno Nero, OBE 2008 (MBE 2004); professional Rugby Union player, 1995–2008; Sales Director, Serco Global Services (formerly The Listening Company); *b* 10 Aug. 1972; *s* of Vincenzo Dallaglio and late Eileen Dallaglio; *m* 2006, Alice Corbett; one *s* two *d*. *Educ:* Ampleforth Coll.; Kingston Univ. Debut, Wasps Rugby Union team, 1992, Capt., 1995–2008; Mem., British Lions touring teams, 1997, 2001, 2005; England team: debut, 1995; 85 caps, 1995–2007; Capt., 1997–99 and 2004; Mem., World Cup winning team, Australia, 2003. Dir, 2008–12, non-exec. Dir, 2015–, Wasps. Rugby Ambassador for: World Cup England 2015; Amlin. Lead Rugby expert, BT Sport, 2013–; columnist, Sunday Times. Founder, Dallaglio Foundn, 2009. *Publications:* Diary of a Season, 1997; Know the Modern Game, 1999; It's in the Blood: my life (autobiog.), 2007; Rugby Tales, 2009; World Cup Rugby Tales, 2011. *Recreations:* golf, cycling, Chelsea supporter. *Address:* c/o Serco Global Services, Oriel House, 26 The Quadrant, Richmond, Surrey TW9 1DL.

DALLAS, James; Partner, Dentons (formerly Denton Wilde Sapte, then SNR Denton), since 1985; Executive Director, Energy and Natural Resources Law Institute, Centre for Commercial Law Studies, Queen Mary University of London; *b* 21 April 1955; *m* 1979, Annabel Hope; one *s* two *d*. *Educ:* Eton; St Edmund Hall, Oxford (MA Jurisprudence). Trainee and asst solicitor, 1976–81; Sen. Legal Advr, Internat. Energy Develt Corp., 1981–84; Denton Hall, subseq. Denton Wilde Sapte, later SNR Denton: Solicitor, 1984–; Chm., 1996–2009; Sen. Partner, ME and Africa, 2009–12. Non-exec. Dir, AMEC plc, 1999–2007. Trustee, Thames Rivers Trust, 2005–; Mem., Action for the River Kennet, 2003–. *Recreations:* fishing, birdwatching, cricket. *Address:* Dentons, One Fleet Place, EC4M 7WS.

DALLAT, John James; Member (SDLP) East Londonderry, Northern Ireland Assembly, since 1998; *b* 24 March 1947; *s* of Daniel and Ellen Dallat; *m* 1975, Anne Philomena Long; two *s* one *d*. *Educ:* Coleraine Coll. of Further Educn (qual. teacher, commercial subjects, 1968); North West Inst., Derry (Business Studies Teacher's Dip., 1975); Univ. of Ulster (Dip. in Advanced Studies in Educn, 1979); UC, Galway (Dip. in Rural Studies, 1997). Teacher: Technical Coll., Carndonagh, 1968–74; St Paul's Coll., Kilrea, 1975–98. Mem. (SDLP) Coleraine BC, 1977–98; Mayor of Coleraine, 2001–02. Contested (SDLP) Londonderry East, 2001. Dep. Speaker, NI Assembly, 2007–. Chm., District Policing Partnership, 2007–08. *Recreations:* attending meetings!, walking, reading. *Address:* Northern Ireland Assembly, Stormont Castle, Belfast BT4 3XX. *T:* (028) 2554 0798, *Fax:* (028) 2554 1798.

DALLISTON, Very Rev. Christopher Charles; Dean of Newcastle, since 2003; *b* 2 April 1956; *s* of Gerald and Rosemary Dalliston; *m* 1989, Michelle Aleysha Caron; two *s* two *d*. *Educ:* Diss Grammar Sch.; Peterhouse, Cambridge (MA 1980); St Stephen's House, Oxford (BA 1984). Ford Motor Co., 1978–81. Ordained deacon, 1984, priest, 1985; Curate, Halstead, 1984–87; Domestic Chaplain to Bp of Chelmsford, 1987–91; Vicar, St Edmund, Forest Gate, 1991–95; St Botolph, Boston, 1995–2003. *Recreations:* choral music, folksong, theatre, Norwich City FC, walking. *Address:* The Cathedral Vicarage, 26 Mitchell Avenue, Jesmond, Newcastle upon Tyne NE2 3LA. *E:* dean@stnicnewcastle.co.uk.

DALLMAN, Prof. Margaret Jane, DPhil; FRSB; FCGI; Professor of Immunology, since 1999, and Associate Provost (Academic Partnerships), since 2015, Imperial College London; *b* Farnborough, Kent, 14 May 1957; *d* of James Philip Dallman and Margaret Florence Dallman (*née* Ware); *m* 1997, Andrew Christopher George Porter; one *s*. *Educ:* Ravensbourne Sch. for Girls; Univ. of Bristol (BSc Hons Cellular Pathol. 1978); Linacre Coll., Oxford

(DPhil 1982; MA 1985). FRSB (FSB 2011). Res. scientist, Wellcome Res. Labs, 1978–79; Post-doctoral Res. Fellow, Stanford Univ., 1982–84; Nuffield Foundn Jun. Res. Fellow, Hertford Coll., Oxford, 1984–87 (Emeritus Fellow, 1994); MRC Sen. Res. Fellow, Univ. of Oxford, 1987–94; Imperial College London: Lectr in Immunol., 1994–96; Reader in Immunoregulation, 1996–99; Dean, Faculty of Natural Scis, 2008–14. Chair, Basic Scis Underpinning Health Bd, BBSRC, 2011–14. Non-exec. Dir, Imperial Coll. Healthcare NHS Trust, 2010–11. Mem. Bd, Francis Crick Inst. (formerly UK Centre for Med. Res. and Innovation), 2011–. Member: Scientific Adv. Bd, Pirbright Inst. (formerly Inst. for Animal Health), 2010–; Bd, NC3Rs, 2010–; Res. and Innovation Strategic Adv. Cttee, HEFC, 2011–12; Strategic Adv. Cttee for Res. and Knowledge Exchange, HEFCE, 2012–; BBSRC, 2014–. Trustee and Chm., Wye Coll. Foundn Trust, 2009–14. FCGI 2011. *Publications:* contrib. papers, book chapters and reviews to scientific lit. in fields of immunol. and transplantation biol. *Recreations:* painting, reading, ski-ing, walking. *Address:* L2 Faculty Building, Imperial College London, SW7 2AZ. *T:* (020) 7594 5406. *E:* m.dallman@imperial.ac.uk.

DALMENY, Lord; Harry Ronald Neil Primrose; DL; Chairman, Sotheby's Private Clients, since 2013 (Director, Sotheby's, since 2001); *b* 20 Nov. 1967; *s* and *heir* of 7th Earl of Rosebery, *qv*; *m* 1994, Caroline (marr. diss. 2014), *e d* of Ronald Daglish and Mrs William Wyatt-Lowe; one *s* four *d* (incl. triplets). *Educ:* Dragon Sch., Oxford; Eton Coll.; Trinity Coll., Cambridge (BA Hons). Mem., Royal Co. of Archers, The Queen's Body Guard for Scotland, 2002–. Pres., Royal Scottish Corpn (Scotscare). DL Midlothian, 2006. *Heir: s* Hon. Caspian Albert Harry Primrose, *b* 8 Sept. 2005. *Address:* Dalmeny House, South Queensferry, West Lothian EH30 9TQ. *T:* (0131) 331 1784. *Clubs:* White's; University Pitt (Cambridge); Midlothian (Edinburgh); Royal Caledonian Hunt; St Moritz Tobogganing.

DALRYMPLE, family name of **Earl of Stair**.

DALRYMPLE, Viscount; John James Thomas Dalrymple; *b* 3 Jan. 2008; *s* and *heir* of Earl of Stair, *qv*.

DALRYMPLE, Sir Hew (Fleetwood) Hamilton-, 10th Bt *cr* 1697; GCVO 2001 (KCVO 1985; CVO 1974); JP; late Major, Grenadier Guards; Lord-Lieutenant of East Lothian, 1987–2001 (Vice-Lieutenant, 1973–87); *b* 9 April 1926; *er s* of Sir Hew (Clifford) Hamilton-Dalrymple, 9th Bt, JP; *S* father, 1959; *m* 1954, Lady Anne-Louise Mary Keppel, *d* of 9th Earl of Albemarle, MC, and (Diana Cicely), Diana, Countess of Albemarle, DBE; four *s*. *Educ:* Ampleforth. Commnd, Grenadier Guards, 1944; Staff Coll., Camberley, 1957; DAAG HQ 3rd Div., 1958–60; Regimental Adjt, Grenadier Guards, 1960–62; retd 1962. Adjt, 1964–85, Pres. of Council, 1988–96, and Captain General and Gold Stick, 1996–2004, Queen's Body Guard for Scotland (Royal Company of Archers). Vice-Chm., Scottish & Newcastle Breweries, 1983–86 (Dir, 1967–86); Chm., Scottish American Investment Co., 1985–91 (Dir, 1967–93). DL 1964, JP 1987, East Lothian. *Heir: e s* Hew Richard Hamilton-Dalrymple [*b* 3 Sept. 1955; *m* 1987, Jane Elizabeth, *yr d* of Lt-Col John Morris; one *s* three *d*. *Educ:* Ampleforth; Corpus Christi Coll., Oxford (MA); Clare Hall, Cambridge (MPhil); Birkbeck Coll., London (MSc). ODI Fellow, Swaziland, 1982–84]. *Address:* Leuchie, North Berwick, East Lothian EH39 5NT. *T:* (01620) 892903. *Club:* Cavalry and Guards.

See also W. B. H. Dalrymple.

DALRYMPLE, Prof. Mary Elizabeth, PhD; FBA 2013; Professor of Syntax, University of Oxford, since 2006; *b* Missouri, 9 March 1954; *d* of Thomas W. and Mary E. Dalrymple; *m* 1999, Kenneth M. Kahn; one step *s*. *Educ:* Cornell Coll. (BA Hons English 1976); Univ. of Texas at Austin (MA Linguistics 1984); Stanford Univ. (PhD Linguistics 1990). Mem., Res. Staff, 1990–2001, Sen. Mem., Res. Staff, 2001–02, Palo Alto Res. Center, Calif; Sen. Lectr, Dept of Computer Sci., KCL, 2003–04; Lectr in Gen. Linguistics, Univ. of Oxford, 2004–06. *Publications:* The Syntax of Anaphoric Binding, 1993; Lexical Functional Grammar, 2001; (with I. Nikolaeva) Objects and Information Structure, 2011; (with S. Mofu) Dusner, 2012. *Recreations:* cinema, theatre, swimming, travelling. *Address:* Centre for Linguistics and Philology, Walton Street, Oxford OX1 2HG. *T:* (01865) 280412, *Fax:* (01865) 280412. *E:* mary.dalrymple@ling-phil.ox.ac.uk.

DALRYMPLE, William Benedict Hamilton; writer; Co-Director, Jaipur Literature Festival, since 2005; *b* 20 March 1965; *s* of Sir Hew (Fleetwood) Hamilton-Dalrymple, *qv*; *m* 1991, Olivia Fraser; two *s* one *d*. *Educ:* Ampleforth Coll.; Trinity Coll., Cambridge (Exhibr; Sen. Hist. Schol., MA Hons 1992). Television series: Stones of the Raj, 1997; Indian Journeys, 2000 (Grierson Award, Best Documentary Series, 2001); Sufi Soul, 2005; radio series: Three Miles an Hour, 2002; The Long Search, 2002 (Sandford St Martin Prize for Religious Broadcasting), 2003. Exhibn, Princes and Painters in Mughal Delhi, 1707–1857, Asia Soc., NY, 2012. Whitney J. Oates Fellow in S Asian Studies, Princeton Univ., 2012. FRSL 1993; FRGS 1993; FRAS 1998. Hon. DLitt: St Andrews, 2006; Lucknow, 2007; Aberdeen, 2008; Bradford, 2012. Mungo Park Medal, RSGS, 2002; Sir Percy Sykes Meml Medal, RSAA, 2005; Col James Todd Award, Mewar Foundn, 2008. *Publications:* In Xanadu, 1989 (Yorks Post Best First Work Award, Scottish Arts Council Spring Book Award, 1990); City of Djinns, 1993 (Thomas Cook Travel Book Award, Sunday Times Young British Writer of Year Award, 1994); From the Holy Mountain (Scottish Arts Council Autumn Book Award), 1997; The Age of Kali (collected journalism), 1998 (Prix d'Astrolabe, 2005); White Mughals, 2002 (Wolfson Hist. Prize, 2003; Scottish Book of the Year Prize, 2003); The Last Mughal, 2006 (Duff Cooper Memorial Prize, 2007); Nine Lives: in search of the sacred in modern India, 2009 (Asia House Literary Award, 2010); (with Yuthika Sharma) Princes and Painters in Mughal Delhi, 1707–1857, 2012; Return of a King: the battle for Afghanistan 1835–42, 2012; contribs to jls incl. TLS, Granta, New Yorker, NY Review of Books, Guardian. *Address:* 1 & 2 Pages' Yard, Church Street, Old Chiswick, W4 2PA. *T:* (020) 8994 4500. *E:* williamdalrymple@gmail.com.

DALRYMPLE HAMILTON, (North) John (Frederick), OBE 1992; TD 1989; farmer, since 1982; Vice Lord-Lieutenant, Ayrshire and Arran, since 1998; *b* 7 May 1950; *s* of late Captain North Edward Frederick Dalrymple-Hamilton, CVO, MBE, DSC, RN and Hon. Mary Colville; *m* 1980, Sally Anne How; two *s* one *d*. *Educ:* Eton Coll.; Aberdeen Univ. (MA Hons 1972); E of Scotland Coll. of Agriculture (Cert. Agric. 1983). Sales Manager, Scottish & Newcastle Breweries, 1973–82; Bargany estate, 1983–; Chm., Gardening Leave, 2008–12. Commnd TA, 1970; CO, QOY, 1989–92; Dep. Comdr (Col), 52 Bde, 1993–94. Chm., Lowlands RFCA, 2003–07. DL Ayrshire and Arran, 1995–98. *Address:* Lovestone House, Bargany, Girvan, Ayrshire KA26 9RF. *T:* (01465) 871227. *Club:* New (Edinburgh).

DALRYMPLE-HAY, Sir Malcolm (John Robert), 8th Bt *cr* 1798, of Park Place, Wigtownshire; FRCS; Consultant Cardiac Surgeon, since 2001; *b* Epsom, 1 April 1966; *o s* of Sir John Hugh Dalrymple-Hay, 7th Bt and of Jennifer Phyllis, *d* of Brig. Robert Johnston, OBE; *S* father, 2009; *m* 1998, Vanessa Long; three *d*. *Educ:* Univ. of London (MB BS 1990; PhD 1997). FRCS 1999; FECTS 1999. *Recreations:* golf, ski-ing, running. *Heir: uncle* Ronald George Inglis Dalrymple-Hay [*b* 3 March 1933; *m* 1973, Anne Valerie, *d* of Bernard James Dawson; one *s*]. *E:* malcolm@dalrymple-hay.com.

DALRYMPLE-WHITE, Sir Jan Hew, 3rd Bt *cr* 1926, of High Mark, Wigtownshire; Director, Mia Online Ltd, since 2003; *b* 26 Nov. 1950; *o s* of Sir Henry Arthur Dalrymple-White, 2nd Bt and Mary (*née* Thomas); *S* father, 2006, but his name does not appear on the Official Roll of the Baronetage; *m* 1st, 1979, Elizabeth Wallis (marr. diss); 2nd, 1984, Angela Stevenson (marr. diss.); one *s*; 3rd, 1990, Elizabeth Smith. *Educ:* Stowe.

DALTON, Carol; *see* Monaghan, C.

DALTON, Daniel Anthony Thomas; Member (C) West Midlands Region, European Parliament, since 2015; *b* Oxford, 1974; *s* of Anthony Thomas Dalton and Anita Jirina Dalton; *m* 2010, Silue; one *s*. *Educ:* Warwick Sch.; Coventry Univ. (BA Hons Internat. Relns and Politics); Warwick Univ. (MA Internat. Politics of E Asia). Professional cricketer, Warwickshire CCC and cricket coach, 1996–2005. Hd of Office, Neil Parish, MEP, 2005–09; Policy Advr, Eur. Conservatives and Reformists Gp, EP, 2009–15. *Address:* European Parliament, Rue Wiertz, 1047 Brussels, Belgium. *T:* 22845897. *E:* daniel.dalton@europarl.europa.eu.

DALTON, Duncan Edward S.; *see* Shipley Dalton.

DALTON, Vice-Adm. Sir Geoffrey (Thomas James Oliver), KCB 1986; Secretary-General of Mencap, 1987–90; *b* 14 April 1931; *s* of late Jack Rowland Thomas Dalton and Margaret Kathleen Dalton; *m* 1957, Jane Hamilton (*née* Baynes); four *s*. *Educ:* Parkfield, Sussex; Reigate Grammar Sch.; RNC Dartmouth. Midshipman 1950; served in HM Ships Illustrious, Loch Alvie, Cockade, Virago, Flag Lieut to C-in-C The Nore, and HMS Maryton (in comd), 1950–61; served HMS Murray, RN Staff Course and HMS Dido, 1961–66; served HMS Relentless (in Comd), RN Sch. of PT, HMS Nubian (in Comd), Staff of Flag Officer Second in Comd Far East Fleet and Second Flotilla, 1966–72; Asst Dir of Naval Plans, 1972–74; RCDS, 1975; Captain RN Presentation Team, 1976–77; in Comd HMS Jupiter, 1977–79 and HMS Dryad, 1979–81; Asst Chief of Naval Staff (Policy), MoD, 1981–84; Dep. SACLANT, 1984–87. Commander, 1966; Captain, 1972; Rear-Adm. 1981; Vice-Adm. 1984. President: RBL, 1993–97; Regular Forces Employment Assoc., 1999–2002; Chm., Ex-Services Fellowship Centres, 1991–2006. Hon. Col 71st (Yeomanry) Signal Regt (Volunteers), 1998–2001. Gov., QMW, 1992–2002. Mem. Ct of Assts, Drapers' Co., 1989– (Master, 1996). FCMI (FBIM 1987). *Recreations:* tennis, ski-ing, fishing, gardening, motor cycling, walking. *Address:* Farm Cottage, Catherington, Waterlooville, Hants PO8 0TD.

DALTON, Graham Edward, CEng, FICE, FCIHT; Chief Executive, Highways Agency, 2008–15; *b* 24 Sept. 1960; *s* of John and Jocelyn Dalton; *m* 1985, Fiona Jane Iles; three *d*. *Educ:* Gillotts Sch., Henley-on-Thames; Imperial Coll., London (BSc 1st Cl. Civil Engrg 1983); Henley Mgt Coll. (MBA 2000). CEng 1989; FICE 2003; FCIHT 2013. Mgt trainee, BR, 1979–88; civil engr, L. G. Mouchel & Partners, 1988–95; Project Manager, Bovis Construction, 1995–2001; Project Dir, Strategic Rail Authy, 2001–05; Dir, Rail Projects, DfT, 2005–08. Mem. Council, ICE, 2004–07. *Recreations:* sailing, walking. *E:* graham.dalton@talk21.com. *Club:* Dell Quay Sailing (Chichester).

DALTON, Ian Mark Marshall, CBE 2011; President of Global Government and Health, BT Global Services, since 2014; *b* Welwyn Garden City, 14 Jan. 1964; *s* of Douglas Vivian Marshall Dalton and Helgard Dalton (*née* Herzog); *m* 1992, Juliet Kearsley; one *s* one *d*. *Educ:* Verulam Sch., St Albans; Univ. of York (BA Hons Econs; MA Mental Handicap Services); Univ. of Durham (MBA). Residential Care Officer, N Yorks CC, 1985–86; Project, 1986–88, Dist Officer, 1988–90, RSMHCA; Develt Manager, Community Mental Health, Durham CC, 1990–91; Policy Officer, Community Care, then Hd of Primary and Community Care, Northern and Yorks (formerly Northern) RHA, 1991–95; Hd, Primary and Community Care, 1995–96, Purchaser Perf. Develt, 1996–97, Northern & Yorks Regl Office, NHS Exec.; Dir, Planning and Develt, Hartlepool and E Durham NHS Trust, 1997–99; Dir, Acute Services, Planning and Develt, N Tees and Hartlepool NHS Trust, 1999–2000; Department of Health: Regl Dir of Perf. Mgt (Northern and Yorks), 2000–02; Dir of Perf. (N), 2002–03; Chief Executive: N Cheshire Hosps NHS Trust, 2003–05; N Tees and Hartlepool NHS Trust, 2005–07; NE Strategic HA, 2007–11 (on secondment as Nat. Dir for NHS Flu Resilience, DoH, 2009–10; on assignment as Man. Dir, Provider Develt, DoH, 2010–11); NHS North of England, 2011–12; Chief Operating Officer and Dep. Chief Exec., NHS Commissioning Bd, 2012–13; Pres., Global Health, BT Global Services, 2013–14. Hon. Col, (250) Med. Sqdn (V), 3 Med. Regt (formerly B (250) Med. Sqdn (V), 5 Gen. Med. Support Regt), RAMC, 2007–12. *Address:* BT Global Government and Health, BT Centre, 81 Newgate Street, EC1A 7AJ.

DALTON, Maurice Leonard, LVO 1986 (MVO 1981); OBE 1996; HM Diplomatic Service, retired; protocol consultant, since 2000; *b* 18 May 1944; *s* of late Albert William Dalton and Mildred Eliza (*née* Wraight); *m* 1982, Cathy Lee Parker. Joined FO, 1965; Enugu and Lagos, 1967–68; FCO, 1968–70; Attaché, Ankara, 1970–72; Third Secretary: E Berlin, 1973–74; Abu Dhabi, 1974–76; Second Sec., FCO, 1977–79; Second, later First Sec., Oslo, 1979–83; First Secretary: Kuala Lumpur, 1983–86; Peking, 1986; FCO, 1987–92; Asst Head of Protocol Dept, FCO, and HM Asst Marshal of Diplomatic Corps, 1992–96; Counsellor and Head of Conference Dept, FCO, 1996–98; Head of Protocol Dept, FCO, 1998–99; HM First Asst Marshal of Diplomatic Corps, 1998–2000; Protocol Consultant, FCO, 2001–05. Protocol Adviser: Jamaican Govt, 2010–12; St Lucia Gov.-Gen.'s Office, 2013–14. Chairman: Tenterden and Dist Nat. Trust Assoc., 2012– (Mem. Cttee, 2010–12); Smallhythe 500 Commemoration Cttee, 2013–. Royal Norwegian Order: of St Olav, 1981; of Merit, 1994. *Recreations:* National Trust volunteer, genealogy. *Address:* Brookside, Hope's Grove Lane, Smallhythe Road, Tenterden, Kent TN30 7LT.

DALTON, Sir Richard (John), KCMG 2005 (CMG 1996); HM Diplomatic Service, retired; Associate Fellow, Middle East and North Africa Programme, Royal Institute of International Affairs, since 2008; *b* 10 Oct. 1948; *s* of Maj.-Gen. John Cecil D'Arcy Dalton, CB, CBE and Pamela Frances (*née* Segrave); *m* 1972, Elisabeth Mary Keays; two *s* two *d* (and one *s* decd). *Educ:* Winchester Coll.; Magdalene Coll., Cambridge (BA). Joined HM Diplomatic Service, 1970: FCO, 1971; MECAS, 1971–73; 3rd Sec., Amman, 1973–75; 2nd, later 1st, Sec., Mission to UN, NY, 1975–79; FCO, 1979–83; Dep. Head of Mission, Muscat, 1983–87; Dep. Head, Southern African Dept, FCO, 1987–88; Head, Tropical Foods Div. and Ext. Relns and Trade Div., MAFF, 1988–91; Vis. Fellow, RIIA, 1991–92; Head, CSCE Unit, FCO, 1992–93; Consul Gen., Jerusalem, 1993–97; Dir (Personnel), FCO, 1998–99; Ambassador to: Libya, 1999–2002; Iran, 2003–06. Dir Gen., Libyan British Business Council, 2006–09. *Publications:* Peace in the Gulf: a long term view, 1992; (ed) Iran: breaking the nuclear deadlock, 2009; Iran's Nuclear Future, 2014. *Recreation:* land and woodland management. *Address:* Hauxwell Hall, Leyburn, N Yorks DL8 5LR.

DALTON, Air Chief Marshal Sir Stephen (Gary George), GCB 2012 (KCB 2009; CB 2006); FRAeS; Chief of the Air Staff, 2009–13; Air Aide-de-Camp to the Queen, 2009–13; *b* 23 April 1954. *Educ:* Univ. of Bath (BSc). Royal Air Force: exercises in Europe, USA and Canada; psc; qwi 1983; RAF Brockwell, 1990; Comdr, RAF Coltishall and Jaguar Force, 1997–99; Dir, Eurofighter Prog. Assurance Gp, MoD, 2000; hcsc, 2002; Dir Air Ops, MoD, 2002–03; Capability Manager (Information Superiority), 2003–04; Controller Aircraft, 2004–07; Dir Gen. Typhoon, 2006–07; Dep. C-in-C Personnel and Air Mem. for Personnel, HQ Air Comd, 2007–09. Hon. LLD Leicester. CCMI.

DALTON, William Robert Patrick, FCIB, FICB; Chief Executive, HSBC (formerly Midland) Bank plc, 1998–2004; *b* 8 Dec. 1943; *s* of Albert and Emily Dalton; *m* 1993, Starr Underhill; one *s* one *d*. *Educ:* Univ. of British Columbia (BComm 1971). FICB 1971; FCIB 1998. Joined Bank of Montreal, 1961; Wardley Canada Ltd, later HSBC Bank, Canada, 1980, Pres. and CEO, 1992–97; Director: HSBC Holdings, 1998–2004; HSBC Private Banking Hldgs (Suisse) SA, 2001–04; Crédit Commercial de France SA, 2000–04; AEGIS Insce Services Inc. (formerly AEGIS Ltd), 2004–. Non-executive Director: Mastercard Internat., 1998–2004; HSBC Finance Inc. (formerly Household Internat. Inc.), 2003–08; First Choice

Holidays plc, 2004–07; Swiss Re GB, 2005–08; Talisman Energy Inc., 2005–14; TUI Travel plc, 2007–12; HSBC Hldgs USA Inc., 2008–. Vice-Pres., CIB, 2001–. Pres., BBA, 2003–04. Chm., Young Enterprise UK, 1998–2004; Trustee: Crimestoppers Trust, 2000–04; Duke of Edinburgh's Commonwealth Study Confs (UK Fund), 2002–10; Centre for Study of Financial Innovation, 2003–13. Hon. Dr UCE, 2001.

DALTREY, Roger Harry, CBE 2005; singer; *b* Hammersmith, 1 March 1944; *s* of Harry and Irene Daltrey; *m* 1971, Heather Taylor; two *s* two *d*; one *s* by a previous marriage. *Educ:* Acton Co. Grammar Sch. Lead singer, The Detours, later The Who, 1964–84; solo singer, 1984–. Albums with The Who: My Generation, 1965; A Quick One, 1966; Happy Jack, 1967; The Who Sell Out, 1967; Magic Bus, 1968; Tommy, 1969; Who's Next, 1971; Meaty Beefy Big And Bouncy, 1971; Quadrophenia, 1973; The Who By Numbers, 1975; The Story of the Who, 1976; Who Are You, 1978; Face Dances, 1981; Hooligans, 1982; It's Hard, 1982; Once Upon A Time, 1983; Two's Missing, 1987; Endless Wire, 2006; solo albums: Daltrey, 1973; Ride A Rock Horse, 1975; One of the Boys, 1977; Parting Should Be Painless, 1984; Under a Raging Moon, 1985; Can't Wait to See the Movie, 1987; Rocks in the Head, 1992; (with Wilko Johnson) Going Back Home, 2014. Actor in films including: Tommy, 1974; Lisztomania, 1975; The Legacy, 1978; McVicar (also prod.), 1980; Mack the Knife, 1990; Buddy's Song (also prod.), 1991. *Address:* c/o Trinifold Management Ltd, 12 Oval Road, NW1 7DH.

DALY, Angela Josepha; *see* Garvey, A. J.

DALY, Hon. Francis Lenton; Judge of District Courts, Queensland, Australia, 1989–99; Judge of Planning and Environment Court, Queensland, 1994–99; *b* 23 June 1938; *s* of late Sydney Richard Daly and Lilian May Daly (*née* Lindholm); *m* 1964, Joyce Brenda (*née* Nicholls). *Educ:* Forest School; London School of Economics (LLB). Called to Bar, Gray's Inn, 1961 (Lord Justice Holker Exhibn). English Bar, 1961–66; Legal Secretary, Lord Chancellor's Office, 1966; Bermudian Bar, 1966–72; Asst Judge Advocate General to the Forces, UK, 1972–78; Principal Magistrate, Malaita, Solomon Islands, 1978; Attorney General, 1979, Chief Justice, 1980–84, Solomon Islands; Chief Justice, Nauru, 1983; admitted, Qld Bar, 1984. *Publications:* contribs to International and Comparative Law Qly, Commonwealth Judicial Jl. *Recreations:* yachting, rowing, reading. *Address:* 22 Booth Street, Balmain, NSW 2041, Australia.

See also O. L. Aikin.

DALY, James, CVO 1994; HM Diplomatic Service, retired; re-employed, Foreign and Commonwealth Office, since 2001; *b* 8 Sept. 1940; *s* of late Maurice Daly and Christina Daly; *m* 1970, Dorothy Lillian Powell; two *s*. *Educ:* St Thomas More, Chelsea; University College London (BSc Hons Econ). Served RM, 1958–67. Joined Foreign Office, 1968: Third Secretary: Accra, 1971–73; Moscow, 1973–76; Second Sec., Karachi, 1976–78; First Secretary: FCO, 1978–79; Sofia, 1979–86; Consul-Gen., Paris, 1986–92; Counsellor and Consul-Gen., Moscow, 1992–95; High Commissioner: Vanuatu, 1995–97; Mauritius, 1997–2000. Mem., Special Immigration Appeals Commn, 2002–. *Recreations:* reading, music, walking. *Address:* 44 Ashley Court, Morpeth Terrace, SW1P 1EN. *Club:* Naval and Military.

DALY, Rev. Mgr John Anthony; Parish Priest, St Mary's Oswaldtwistle, since 2008; Principal Roman Catholic Chaplain, Royal Air Force, 2004–07; *b* 23 Sept. 1952; *s* of Richard and Mary Daly. *Educ:* St Anne's RC Primary Sch., Stretford; St Mary's Secondary Sch., Stretford; Ushaw Coll., Durham. Ordained, 1977; Priest: St Osmund's, Breightmet, Bolton, 1977–83; St Mary's, Radcliffe, Bury, 1983–84; joined RAF, 1985; Gp Captain, 2004. QHC, 2004–07; Vicar General, 2004–07. Pres., Oswaldtwistle St Mary's FC, 2010–. *Recreations:* supporting Manchester United, ski-ing, golf, music, cooking. *Address:* St Mary's Presbytery, Catlow Hall Street, Oswaldtwistle, Accrington BB5 3EZ. *E:* jdmon.jady@gmail.com.

DALY, Margaret Elizabeth; *b* 26 Jan. 1938; *d* of Robert and Elizabeth Bell; *m* 1964, Kenneth Anthony Edward Daly; one *d*. *Educ:* Methodist Coll., Belfast. Departmental Head, Phoenix Assurance Co., 1956–60; Trade Union Official, Guild of Insurance Officials, later Union of Insurance Staffs, and subseq. merged with ASTMS, 1960–71; Consultant, Cons. Party, 1976–79; Nat. Dir of Cons. Trade Unionists, 1979–84. MEP (C) Somerset and Dorset W, 1984–94; contested (C) Somerset and N Devon, Eur. Parly elecns, 1994; Mem., Develt Cttee, Eur. Parlt, 1984–94 (Vice Chm., 1987–89; Cons. spokesman, 1989–94); Vice-Pres., Jt EEC/African Caribbean Pacific Lomé Assembly, 1988–94. Contested (C), Weston-super-Mare, 1997. Mem. Bd, Traidcraft PLC, 1995–98. Mem. Bd, South West in Europe, 2000–01; European Movement: Mem. Mgt Bd, 1999–2006; Vice-Pres., Somerset Br., 2002– (Chair, 1999–2001); Pres., Devon Br., 2005–. Direct Mem., EPP, 1990–. *Recreations:* swimming, music, travel, positive actions regarding the EU. *Address:* The Old School House, Aisholt, Bridgwater, Somerset TA5 1AR.

DALY, Michael Francis, CMG 1989; HM Diplomatic Service, retired; *b* 7 April 1931; *s* of late William Thomas Daly and Hilda Frances Daly; *m* 1st, 1963, Sally Malcolm Angwin (*d* 1966); one *d*; 2nd, 1971, Juliet Mary Siragusa (*née* Arning); one step *d*. *Educ:* Downside; Gonville and Caius Coll., Cambridge (Scholar; MA). Mil. Service, 1952–54; 2nd Lieut, Intell. Corps. E. D. Sassoon Banking Co., London, 1954; Transreef Industrial & Investment Co., Johannesburg, 1955–66; General Electric Co., London, 1966; HM Diplomatic Service: 1st Sec., FCO, 1967; 1st Sec. (Commercial), Rio de Janeiro, 1969; 1st Sec. (Inf.) and Head of Chancery, Dublin, 1973; Asst, Cultural Relations Dept, FCO, 1976; Counsellor, Consul-Gen. and Head of Chancery, Brasilia, 1977–78; Ambassador to Ivory Coast, Upper Volta and Niger, 1978–83; Head of West African Dept, FCO, and Ambassador (non-resident) to Chad, 1983–86; Ambassador: to Costa Rica and (non-resident) to Nicaragua, 1986–89; to Bolivia, 1989–91. Sec., Margaret Mee Fellowship Programme, 1993–. Kew Medal, 2002. *Recreations:* sailing, theatre, golf, watching cricket, am-dram. *Address:* 45 Priory Road, Kew, Surrey TW9 3DQ. *T:* (020) 8940 1272. *Club:* Canning.

DALY, Michael Vincent; Director, Corporate Services Transformation Programme, Department for Children, Schools and Families (formerly Efficiency and Reform Unit, Department for Education and Skills), 2006–09; *b* 23 July 1958; *s* of Michael Joseph Daly and Mary Anne Daly. *Educ:* St Philip's Grammar Sch., Edgbaston; Birmingham Univ. (DMS 1989). HEO (D), HSE, 1989; Second Sec. for Social Affairs, UK Repn to EC, 1990; Private Sec. to Parly Under Sec. of State, Dept of Employment, 1990–93; UK Rep. on Social Affairs to Council of Europe, Strasbourg, 1993–95; Divl Manager, DFEE, 1999–2001; Project Dir, No 10 Forward Strategy Unit, 2001–02; Hd, Learning Acad., 2002–04, Dir of Change, 2004–06, DFES. *Recreations:* pickle-ball, curate's egg golf, film, early science fiction novels.

DALYELL, Kathleen Mary Agnes, OBE 2005; National Trust for Scotland Administrator at The Binns, since 1972; Chairman, Royal Commission on Ancient and Historical Monuments of Scotland, 2000–05; *b* 17 Nov. 1937; *o d* of Rt Hon. Lord Wheatley and Agnes (Nancy) Lady Wheatley (*née* Nichol); *m* 1963, Tam Dalyell, *qv*; one *s* one *d*. *Educ:* Convent of the Sacred Heart, Aberdeen; Edinburgh Univ. (MA Hons History 1960); Craiglochart Teacher Trng Coll., Edinburgh. Teacher of History: St Augustine's Secondary Sch., Glasgow, 1961–62; James Gillespie's High Sch. for Girls, Edinburgh, 1962–63. Member: Historic Buildings Council for Scotland, 1975–87; Lady Provost of Edinburgh's Delegn to China, 1987; Nat. Cttee of Architectural Heritage Soc. for Scotland, 1983–89 (Vice-Chm., 1986–89); Ancient Monuments Bd for Scotland, 1989–99; Royal Fine Art Commn for Scotland, 1992–2001. Chm., Bo'ness Heritage Trust, 1988–93; Director: Heritage Educn Trust, 1987–2005; Weslo Housing Assoc., 1994–2003; Trustee: Paxton Trust, 1988–92; Carmont Settlement Trust, 1997–2013; Hopetoun Preservation Trust, 2005–; Mus. of Scotland Charitable Trust, 2005–. DL W Lothian, 2001. Mem. Ct, Stirling Univ., 2003–08. Hon. Dr: Edinburgh, 2006; Stirling, 2008. *Publications:* House of The Binns, 1973. *Recreations:* reading, travel, chess, hill walking. *Address:* The Binns, Blackness, Linlithgow, Scotland EH49 7NA. *T:* (01506) 834255.

DALYELL, Tam, FRSE; *b* 9 Aug. 1932; *s* of late Gordon and Eleanor Dalyell; *m* 1963, Kathleen Mary Agnes Wheatley (*see* K. M. A. Dalyell); one *s* one *d*. *Educ:* Eton; King's Coll., Cambridge; Moray House Teachers' Training Coll., Edinburgh. Trooper, Royal Scots Greys, 1950–52; Teacher, Bo'ness High Sch., 1956–60. Dep.-Dir of Studies on British India ship-school, Dunera, 1961–62. Contested (Lab) Roxburgh, Selkirk, and Peebles, 1959. MP (Lab) West Lothian, 1962–83, Linlithgow, 1983–2005. Member Public Accounts Cttee, House of Commons, 1962–66; Secretary, Labour Party Standing Conference on the Sciences, 1962–64; PPS to Rt Hon. Richard Crossman, Minister of Housing, Leader of H of C, Sec. of State for the Social Services, 1964–70; Opposition spokesman on science, 1980–82; Chairman: PLP Education Cttee, 1964–65; PLP Sports Group, 1964–74; PLP Foreign Affairs Gp, 1974–75; Vice-Chairman: PLP Defence and Foreign Affairs Gps, 1972–74; Scottish Labour Group of MPs, 1973–75; Parly Lab. Party, 1974–76; Sub-Cttee on Public Accounts; Mem., Labour Party NEC, 1986–87. Member: European Parlt, 1975–79; European Parlt Budget Cttee, 1976–79; European Parlt Energy Cttee, 1979; Member: House of Commons Select Cttee on Science and Technology, 1967–69; Liaison Cttee between Cabinet and Parly Labour Party, 1974–76; Chm., All-Pty Latin-America Gp, 1997–2005. Father, H of C, 2001–05. Leader, IPU Delegation: to Brazil, 1976; to Peru, 1999; to Bolivia, 2000; to Libya, 2001. Chm., *ad hoc* Cttee against war in Iraq, 1998. Trustee, History of Parlt Trust, 1999–2005; Mem., Council, National Trust for Scotland. Rector, Edinburgh Univ., 2003–06. Mem., Trade Delegn to China, Nov. 1971, Hon. Pres., 2005–08, Scottish Council for Develt and Industry. Political columnist, New Scientist, 1967–2005. FRSE 2003. Hon. DSc: Edinburgh, 1994; Heriot-Watt, 2011; Hon. DLitt City Univ., 1998; Hon. Dr: St Andrews, 2001; Northumbria, 2005; Napier, 2005; Stirling, 2006; DUniv Open, 2006. *Publications:* The Case of Ship-Schools, 1960; Ship-School Dunera, 1963; Devolution: the end of Britain?, 1977; One Man's Falklands, 1982; A Science Policy for Britain, 1983; Thatcher's Torpedo, 1983; Misrule, 1987; Dick Crossman: a portrait, 1989; The Importance of Being Awkward, 2011; 55 Years to the Referendum, 2015. *Recreations:* tennis, swimming. *Address:* The Binns, Linlithgow, Scotland EH49 7NA. *T:* (01506) 834255.

DALZELL PAYNE, Henry Salusbury Legh, (Harry), CBE 1973 (OBE 1970; MBE 1961); *b* 9 Aug. 1929; *m* 1963, Serena Helen (marr. diss. 1980), *d* of Col Clifford White Gourlay, MC, TD; two *d*. *Educ:* Cheltenham; RMA Sandhurst; Staff Coll.; RCDS. Commissioned, 7th Hussars, 1949; served Queen's Own Hussars, 1957–66; seconded to Sultan of Muscat's Armed Forces, 1959–60; commanded: 3rd Carabiniers, 1967–69; 6th Armoured Bde, 1974–75; 3rd Armoured Div., 1979–80; resigned in rank of Maj.-Gen., 1981. Dir, Nat. Securities and Res. Corp., USA, 1983–93; Dir/Trustee, Mutual Funds Complex, USA, 1993–2009. *Recreations:* travel, the turf, fine wines. *Clubs:* Cavalry and Guards, Turf, White's.

DALZIEL, Ian Martin; Head of Global Private Wealth, Threadneedle Asset Management Ltd, since 2009; Member, Advisory Board, Cerno Capital, 2010–12; *b* 21 June 1947; *s* of late John Calvin Dalziel and of Elizabeth Roy Dalziel, *e d* of Rev. Ian Bain, FRSE and Mrs Christian Stuart Fisher Bain, Gairloch; *m* 1972, Nadia Maria Iacovazzi; four *s*. *Educ:* Daniel Stewart's Coll., Edinburgh; St John's Coll., Cambridge; Université Libre de Bruxelles (Weiner Anspach Foundation Scholarship, 1970). Mullens & Co., 1970–72; Manufacturers Hanover Ltd, 1972–83. Mem., Richmond upon Thames Council, 1978–79. Mem. (C) Lothian, European Parlt, 1979–84. Chairman: Continental Assets Trust plc, 1989–98; Invesco Smaller Continental Cos Trust plc, 1998–2005; Director: Adam & Co. plc, 1983–92; Lepercq-Amcur Fund NV, 1989; Gen. Man., Devin SA, 1992–2008; Consultant, Primwest Hldg NV, 1992–2008. Mem., Queen's Body Guard for Scotland (Royal Company of Archers). *Recreations:* golf, shooting, tennis, ski-ing. *Address:* Stables House, Maxton, St Boswells, Roxburghshire TD6 0EX. *E:* imd4@mac.com. *Clubs:* Brooks's; New (Edinburgh); Hawks (Cambridge); Royal and Ancient Golf (St Andrews); Hon. Company of Edinburgh Golfers; Sunningdale Golf; Royal St George's Golf (Sandwich).

DALZIEL, Maureen, MD; FFPH; Director, MD health consultancy Ltd, since 2004; *b* 7 April 1952; *d* of late Peter and of Eileen Farrell; *m* 1974, Ian Dalziel. *Educ:* Notre Dame High Sch., Glasgow; Univ. of Glasgow (MB ChB); MD London 2004. MFCM 1985, FFPH (FFPHM 1990). Jun. hosp. posts, Glasgow and Lanarkshire Hosps, 1976–79; GP, E Kilbride, 1979–81; Registrar, then Sen. Registrar in Public Health Medicine: SW Herts HA, 1981–83; Brent HA, 1983–85; Consultant in Public Health Medicine, 1985–89, Associate Dir, 1989, NW Thames RHA; Chief Executive: SW Herts DHA, 1990–93 (Dir, Public Health, 1989–90); Hillingdon Health Agency, 1993–95; Regl Dir of Public Health and Med. Dir, N Thames Regl HA, then N Thames Regl Office, NHS Exec., DoH, 1995–99; Dir, Nat. Co-ordinating Centre for NHS Service Delivery and Orgn, LSHTM, 1999–2001; Med. Dir, NHS Litigation Authy, 1999–2000; Chief Exec., HFEA, 2001–02. Associate: Zenon Consulting, 2009–13; Hill Coates, 2009–13. Chair, Barking, Havering and Redbridge Univ. Hosps NHS Trust, 2014– (non-exec. Dir, Barking, Havering and Redbridge NHS Hosps Foundn Trust, 2012–14). Sec., Contract Skill Ltd, 2002–05; Sen. Consultant, Hoggett Bowers, 2008–09; Director: Solena Solutions, 2010–12; COC, 2010–13. Lectr in Public Health Medicine, 1981–85, Sen. Lectr, 1989–90, Hon. Sen. Lectr, 1999–, LSHTM. Mem., European Steering Gp, Mégapoles, 1997–2001; Chairman: Sub-network on Social Disadvantage, Mégapoles, 1997–2001; Migration Foundn, 2010–11. Member Board: Housing 21, 1995–2002; Intensive Care Nat. Audit and Res. Centre, 1997–; Refugee Housing Assoc., 2005–07; Metropolitan Support Trust, 2007–11 (Trustee, 2007–11; Vice Chair, 2010–11, Chair, 2010–11); Trustee, British Pregnancy Adv. Service, 2007–13 (Chair, Clinical Governance Cttee, 2010–13). *Publications:* numerous articles in learned jls and papers presented at nat. confs. *Recreations:* ski-ing, reading novels and biographies, golf (par 3), watching old films. *E:* dalziel@btinternet.com.

DAMANAKI, Maria; Global Managing Director for Oceans, Nature Conservancy, since 2014; *b* Crete, 1952; one *s* two *d*. *Educ:* Nat. Tech. Univ. of Athens (MSc Hons Chem. Engrg 1975); Lancaster Univ. Active in underground student opposition to dictatorship in Greece, 1970–74; leading role in coordination of activities and as speaker on clandestine radio transmitter, Nov. 1973; imprisoned, 1973–74. Engr, Pechiney Aluminium Industries, 1974; Adminr, Dept of Import-export Planning, Min. of Finance, Greece, 1975–76; Sect. Manager, Dept of Energy and Waste Mgt, Helector SA, 2003–04. MP 1977–93, 2000–03 and 2004–09; Vice Pres., Greek Parlt, 1986–90; Pres., Coalition of Left and Progress, 1991–93; Head, PASOK Group in Select Cttees on Educn and Culture, on Social Affairs, on Environment; Chm., Select Cttee on Foreign Affairs and Defence, 2009. Member, Parliamentary Assembly: Council of Europe; WEU; NATO. Member, Political Council, PASOK for educn, 2004–06, for social affairs, 2006–07, for culture, 2008–09. Mem., Inter-parly Union. Hd of Opposition, Athens CC. Mem., EC, 2010–14.

DAMATO, Bertil, PhD, MD; FRCOphth; Professor of Ophthalmology and Radiation Oncology, University of California, San Francisco, since 2013; *b* Malta, 8 Nov. 1953; *s* of Pierre Damato and Margareta Damato; *m* 1978, Frankanne Fenech; one *s* one *d*. *Educ:* St Edward's Coll., Malta; Univ. of Glasgow (PhD 1988); Univ. of Malta (MD 1989). MRCS, LRCP 1977; FRCSEd 1982; FRCOphth 1989; FRCSGlas 1990. Resident House Surgeon and Physician, 1978–79, Sen. House Officer in Pathol., 1979–80, Glasgow Royal Infirmary; Registrar in Ophthalmol., Glasgow Western Infirmary, 1980–83; Sen. Registrar in Ophthalmol., Glasgow Teaching Hosps, 1983–84; Lectr, 1984–87, Sen. Lectr, 1987–91,

Reader, 1991–92, in Ophthalmol., Univ. of Glasgow; Consultant Ophthalmic Surgeon, Royal Liverpool Univ. Hosp., 1993–2013. Hon. Prof., Univ. of Liverpool, 2000–. Member: Eur. Ophthalmic Oncology Gp, 1992– (Pres., 1995–97); Club Jules Gonin, 1995–; President: Eur. Vision and Eye Res. Assoc., 2001; Internat. Soc. of Ocular Oncology, 2011–13 (Vice-Pres., 2007–11; Pres., 2012–13). *Publications:* Ocular Tumours: diagnosis and treatment, 2000; over 50 chapters in textbooks; approx. 200 articles in learned jls. *Recreations:* sailing, running, hill walking, travelling, writing, music. *Address:* Department of Ophthalmology, University of California, San Francisco, 10 Koret Way, San Francisco, CA 94143–0644, USA.

DAMAZER, Mark David, CBE 2011; Master, St Peter's College, Oxford, since 2010; *b* 15 April 1955; *s* of Stanislaw and Suzanne Damazer; *m* 1981, Rosemary Jane Morgan; one *s* one *d*. *Educ:* Gonville & Caius Coll., Cambridge (BA History); Harvard Univ. Harkness Fellow, 1977–79; American Political Sci. Fellow, 1978–79. Trainee, ITN, 1979–81; Producer: BBC World Service, 1981–83; TV-AM, 1983–84; BBC: Six O'Clock News, 1984–86; Output Editor, Newsnight, 1986–88; Dep. Editor, 1988–89, Editor, 1989–94, Nine O'Clock News; Editor, TV News, 1994–96; Head: Current Affairs, 1996–98; Political Progs, 1998–2000; Asst Chief Exec. (Dir of Journalism), BBC News, 2000–01; Dep. Dir of News, BBC, 2001–04; Controller, BBC Radio 4 and BBC Radio 7 (formerly BBC7), 2004–10. Dep. Chm., Internat. Press Inst., 2005–10. Mem. Bd, Centre for Contemporary British Hist., Univ. of London, 2005–11. Trustee: Victoria and Albert Mus., 2011–; BBC Trust, 2015–. *Publications:* articles in various newspapers and periodicals. *Recreations:* opera, Tottenham Hotspur, Boston Red Sox, cycling, gardening, Italian painting, church architecture.

DAMER; *see* Dawson-Damer, family name of Earl of Portarlington.

DAMMERS, Dianna Patricia; *see* Melrose, D. P.

DANCE, Charles Walter, OBE 2006; actor; *b* 10 Oct. 1946; *s* of late Walter Dance and Eleanor Dance (*née* Perks); *m* 1970, Joanna Haythorn (marr. diss.); one *s* one *d*. *Educ:* Widey Tech. Sch.; Plymouth Sch. of Art; Leicester Poly. Rep. theatre at Nottingham, Leeds, Greenwich and Chichester Fest.; joined RSC, 1975; appeared in Henry IV, Hamlet, Richard III, Perkin Warbeck, As You Like It, The Changeling, Henry VI, title rôles in Henry V and Coriolanus; other *theatre* includes: Irma La Douce, 1978; The Heiress, 1980; Turning Over, 1982; Good, Donmar Warehouse, 1999; Long Day's Journey Into Night, Lyric, 2000; Shadowlands, Wyndham, 2007; *television:* Edward VII, 1973; The Fatal Spring, 1978; Little Eyolf, 1980; Frost in May, Nancy Astor, 1981; Saigon, the Last Day, The Jewel in the Crown, 1982; Rainy Day Women, The Secret Servant, 1984; Thunder Rock, The McGuffin, 1985; Out on a Limb, 1986; Out of the Shadows, First Born, 1988; Goldeneye, The Phantom of the Opera, 1989; Undertow, 1993; In the Presence of Mine Enemies, 1995; Rebecca, 1996; Randall & Hopkirk Deceased, Bloodlines, 1999; Justice in Wonderland, 2000; Nicholas Nickleby, 2001; Trial and Retribution, Henry VIII, Looking for Victoria, 2003; To the Ends of the Earth, Don Bosco, Last Rights, 2004; Bleak House, 2005; Fallen Angel, Consenting Adults, 2007; Trinity, 2008; Neverland, 2010; Game of Thrones, 2011, 2012, 2013, 2014; This September, 2010, 2011; Strike Back 3, Secret State, 2012; Common Ground, 2013; The Great Fire, 2014; *films:* For Your Eyes Only, 1979; Plenty, 1984; The Golden Child, Good Morning Babylon, 1985; White Mischief, Hidden City, 1986; Pascali's Island, Kalkstein, 1989; China Moon, 1990; Alien 3, 1991; Century, Last Action Hero, Exquisite Tenderness, 1992; Kabloonak (Best Actor, Paris Film Fest., 1994), Shortcut to Paradise, 1993; Michael Collins, Space Truckers, 1995; The Blood Oranges, Don't Go Breaking My Heart, What Rats Won't Do, 1997; Hilary and Jackie, 1998; Jurij, 1999; Dark Blue World, Gosford Park, Ali G Indahouse, 2002; Swimming Pool, 2003; Black and White, (writer and dir) Ladies in Lavender, 2004; Remake, Funny Farm, 2005; Starter for Ten, 2006; Going Postal, Your Highness, There Be Dragons, Ironclad, 2009; Winds of Change, 2011; Underworld 4: Awakening, Midnight's Children, St George's Day, 2012; Patrick, 2013; Dracula Untold, The Imitation Game, 2014; Woman in Gold, 2015. *Recreations:* tennis, swimming. *Address:* c/o Tavistock Wood, 45 Conduit Street, W1S 2YN. *T:* (020) 7494 4767. *Club:* Groucho.

DANCE, Sebastian; Member (Lab) London Region, European Parliament, since 2014; *b* London, 1 Dec. 1981; partner, Spencer Livermore. *Educ:* Univ. of Manchester. Communications Officer, Univ. of Manchester Students' Union; advr on campaigns in public, private and voluntary sector; Advr to Sec. of State for NI, 2007–09; campaigner, ActionAid UK. *Address:* European Parliament, 60 Rue Wiertz, 1047 Brussels, Belgium; (office) 46 Tower Bridge Road, SE1 4TR.

DANCER, Sir Eric, KCVO 2013; CBE 1991; JP; Lord-Lieutenant of Devon, 1998–2015; Managing Director, Dartington Crystal Ltd, 1986–2000; *b* 17 April 1940; *s* of Joseph Cyril Dancer and Mabel Dancer; *m* 1980, Carole Anne Moxon. *Educ:* King Edward VII Sch., Sheffield; Sheffield Poly. Buyer: Moorwood-Vulcan Ltd, 1959–63; Balfour-Darwins Ltd, 1963–67; Purchasing Officer, Brightside Foundry and Engineering Co. Ltd, 1965–67; Dep. Chief Buyer, Metro-Cammell Ltd, 1967–68; Chief Buyer, Chrysler Parts Div., 1968–69; Supplies Manager, Jensen Motors Ltd, 1969–72; Dir, Anglo Nordic Hldgs plc, 1972–80; Man. Dir, Dartington Hall Corp., 1980–87; Chm., English Country Crystal, 1983–87. Trustee, Dartington Hall Trust, 1984–87; Member: SW Regl IDB, 1984–91; Council, CBI, 1997–2000; Chairman: Devon Cttee, Rural Develt Commn, 1981–86; Devon and Cornwall TEC, 1989–93; Gp of 10, 1990–92; West Country Develt Corp., 1993–99; Nat. Assessor, TEC, 1993–98. Gov., Univ. of Plymouth, 1992–96. CCMI (CIMgt 1987); FCIPS 1990 (President's Prize, 1964); FInstD 1981 (Dip. 1989); FRSA 1984 (Mem. Council, 1994–98). Freeman, City of London, 1992; Liveryman, Co. of Glass Sellers, 1992–. JP Devon, 1998 (Chm., Adv. Cttee of Magistrates). Hon. Captain RNR, 2001. DUniv Sheffield Hallam, 1999; Hon. LLD Exeter, 2010; Hon. DBus Plymouth, 2010. KStJ 1998. *Recreations:* travel, reading, music. *Address:* The Roundhouse, Moreleigh, Totnes, Devon TQ9 7JN. *Clubs:* Army and Navy; Royal Dart Yacht (Dartmouth).

DANCEY, Roger Michael, MA; Chief Master, King Edward's School, Birmingham, and Educational Adviser, King Edward VI Foundation, 1998–2005; *b* 24 Nov. 1945; *s* of Michael and Rosalind Dancey; *m* 1988, Elizabeth Jane Shadbolt; one step *s* one step *d*. *Educ:* Lancing Coll.; Exeter Univ. (MA). Careers Master, Whitgift Sch., 1972–76; Head of Sixth Form, Greenshaw High Sch., 1976–81; Sen. Master, Royal Grammar Sch., Worcester, 1982–86; Headmaster: King Edward VI Camp Hill Sch. for Boys, 1986–95; City of London Sch., 1995–98. Mem. Council, 1999–2005, Dep. Pro Chancellor, 2005–09, Birmingham Univ. Vice Chm., Warwick Ind. Schools Foundn, 2007–09; Chm., Warwick Sch. Cttee, 2009–15. Gov., Lancing Coll., 2015–. DUniv Birmingham, 2008. *Recreations:* cricket, golf, theatre, cinema. *Address:* 7 Austen Place, Edgbaston, Birmingham B15 1NJ. *Club:* Edgbaston Golf.

d'ANCONA, John Edward William, CB 1994; consultant; Chairman, Maris International Ltd, 2001–04 (Chief Executive, 2000–03); *b* 28 May 1935; *o s* of late Adolph and Margaret d'Ancona; *m* 1958, Mary Helen (*d* 2014), *o d* of late Sqdn-Ldr R. T. Hunter and Mrs Hunter; three *s*. *Educ:* St Edward's Coll., Malta; St Cuthbert's Grammar Sch., Newcastle upon Tyne. BA (Hons) Mod. History, DipEd (Durham). Teacher, 1959–61; Civil Service, 1961–94: Asst Principal, Dept of Educn and Science, 1961; Private Sec. to Minister of State, DES, 1964–65; Principal: DES, 1965–67; Min. of Technology and DTI, 1967–74; Asst Sec., 1974, Under Sec., 1981, DoE; Dir Gen., Offshore Supplies Office, Dept of Energy, then DTI, 1981–94. Chm., UK Maritime Forum, 2000–. Pres., Soc. for Underwater Technol., 1997–99. *Recreations:* cricket, philately, wine-bibbing. *Address:* 33 Culverley Road, Catford, SE6 2LD.
See also M. R. R. d'Ancona.

d'ANCONA, Matthew Robert Ralph; political commentator and writer; Editor, The Spectator, 2006–09; *b* 27 Jan. 1968; *e s* of John Edward William d'Ancona, *qv*; *m* 2002, Sarah Schaefer (marr. diss.); two *s*. *Educ:* St Dunstan's Coll.; Magdalen Coll., Oxford (Demy; H. W. C. Davis Prize in Hist. 1987; BA 1st Cl. Hons Hist. 1989). Fellow, All Souls Coll., Oxford, 1989–96; The Times, 1991–95 (Asst Ed., 1994–95); Sunday Telegraph: Dep. Ed. (Comment), 1996–98; Dep. Ed., 1998–2006; Contributing Ed. and Political Columnist, GQ magazine, 2006–; Columnist: Evening Standard, 2009–; Internat. New York Times, 2013–. Res. Fellow, Sch. of Politics and Internat. Relns, QMUL, 2013–. Member: Bd of Dirs, Centre for Policy Studies, 1998–2006; Adv. Council, Demos, 1998–2006; Millennium Commn, 2001–06; Policy Adv. Bd, Social Market Foundn, 2002–06; Puttnam Commn on Parliament in the Public Eye, 2004–05; Steering Bd, Digital Britain, 2008–09; Chm., Bright Blue, 2014– (Mem., Adv. Bd, 2013). Mem., British Exec., IPI, 1998–2006. Trustee, Sci. Mus. Gp, 2015–. Philip Geddes Meml Lectr, St Edmund Hall, Oxford, 2006. FRSA 2004. Judge, Man Booker Prize, 2011. Charles Douglas-Home Meml Trust Prize, 1995; Political Journalist of the Year: British Press Awards, 2004; Political Studies Assoc. Awards, 2006; Ed. of the Year, Current Affairs Magazines, BSME, 2007; UK Commentator of the Year, Comment Awards, 2011. *Publications:* (with C. P. Thiede) The Jesus Papyrus, 1996; The Ties That Bind Us, 1996; (with C. P. Thiede) The Quest for the True Cross, 2000; Going East (novel), 2003; Tabatha's Code (novel), 2006; Confessions of a Hawkish Hack, 2006; Nothing to Fear (novel), 2008; (contrib.) Magdalen College Oxford: a history, 2008; (ed) Being British, 2009; (contrib.) Tory Modernisation 2.0, 2013; In It Together: the inside story of the coalition government, 2013. *Recreations:* cinema, opera. *Address:* The Old Forge, 79 Lauriston Road, E9 7HJ. *Club:* Ivy.

DANCY, Prof. John Christopher, MA; Professor of Education, University of Exeter, 1978–84, now Emeritus; *b* 13 Nov. 1920; *e s* of late Dr J. H. Dancy and Dr N. Dancy; *m* 1944, Angela Bryant (*d* 2013); two *s* one *d*. *Educ:* Winchester (Scholar); New Coll., Oxford (Scholar, MA). 1st Class, Classical Hon. Mods, 1940; Craven Scholar, 1946; Gaisford Greek Prose Prize, 1947; Hertford Scholar, 1947; Arnold Historical Essay Prize, 1949. Served in Rifle Brigade, 1941–46; Capt. GSO(3)I, 30 Corps, 1945; Major, GSO(2)I, 1 Airborne Corps, 1945–46. Lecturer in Classics, Wadham Coll., 1946–48; Asst Master, Winchester Coll., 1948–53; Headmaster of Lancing Coll., 1953–61; Master, Marlborough Coll., 1961–72; Principal, St Luke's Coll. of Educn, Exeter, 1972–78. Dir, St Luke's Coll. Foundn, 1978–86. Member, Public Schools' Commission, 1966–68. Chm., Higher Educn Foundn, 1981–86. Chm., British Accreditation Council for Independent Further and Higher Educn, 1984–93. *Publications:* Commentary on 1 Maccabees, 1954; The Public Schools and the Future, 1963; Commentary on Shorter Books of Apocrypha, 1972; Walter Oakeshott: a diversity of gifts, 1995; The Divine Drama: the Old Testament as literature, 2001. *Address:* Wharf House, Mousehole, Penzance, Cornwall TR19 6RX. *T:* (01736) 731137.

DANCZUK, Simon Christopher; MP (Lab) Rochdale, since 2010; *b* 24 Oct. 1966; *m* 1st (marr. diss.); one *s* one *d*; 2nd, 2012, Karen Burke; two *s*. *Educ:* Gawthorpe Comprehensive Sch., Padiham; Lancaster Univ. (BA Econs and Sociol. 1991). Prodn worker, Main Gas, Padiham, 1982–86; labourer, ICI factory, Darwen, 1986–88; barman, ICI Sports and Social Club, Darwen, 1988–91; res. asst, Sociol. Dept, Lancaster Univ., 1991–93; Res. Officer, Bolton Bury TEC, 1993–95; res. consultant, Opinion Res. Corp. Internat., 1995–97; Res. Co-ordinator, 1997–98, Media and PR Officer, 1998–99, Big Issue in N Trust; Co-founder and Dir, Vision Twentyone, 1999–2011. Mem. (Lab) Blackburn with Darwen BC, 1993–2001. *Publications:* (jtly) Smile for the Camera: the double life of Cyril Smith, 2014. *Address:* House of Commons, SW1A 0AA.

DANDEKER, Prof. Christopher, PhD; FAcSS; Professor of Military Sociology, King's College London, 1997–2015, now Emeritus; *b* 12 July 1950; *s* of Arjun Dandeker and Yvonne Florentina Margerat (*née* Bogaert); *m* 2011, Anna Felicity Alexander-Williams. *Educ:* Worthing High Sch. for Boys; Univ. of Leicester (BSc (Sociol.) 1971; PhD 1978). Lecturer: in Applied Social Studies, Hallam Univ., 1973–74; in Sociol., Univ. of Leicester, 1974–90; King's College London: Sen. Lectr in War Studies, 1990–97; Head, Dept of War Studies, 1997–2001; Co-Dir, King's Centre for Military Health Res., 2004–; Head, Sch. of Social Sci. and Public Policy, 2005–08; Fellow 2012. FAcSS (AcSS 2011). Morris Janowitz Career Achievement Award, Inter-Univ. Seminar on Armed Forces and Society, 2011. *Publications:* The Structure of Social Theory (jtly), 1984; Surveillance, Power and Modernity, 1990; (with B. Boene) Les Armées en Europe, 1998; Nationalism and Violence, 1998; Facing Uncertainty: Sweden in international perspective, 2000; (contrib.) Israel's Armed Forces in Comparative Perspective: the new citizen armies, 2009; (contrib.) Modern Warfare and the Utility of Force, 2010; contribs to jls inc. Armed Forces and Society, Political Quarterly, British Jl of Sociol., Sociol Rev., The Lancet, Commonwealth & Comparative Politics. *Recreations:* wine, food, walking, gardening, travel, classical music, being near the sea! *Address:* Department of War Studies, King's College London, Strand, WC2R 2LS. *T:* (020) 7848 2673, *Fax:* (020) 7848 2026. *E:* christophe.dandeker@kcl.ac.uk, christopherdndkr@aol.com, chrisdandeker@gmail.com. *Club:* Travellers.

DANDO, Stephen Gordon; Operating Partner, Bain Capital, since 2013; *b* 13 Feb. 1962; *s* of Douglas and Anne Dando; *m* 1985, Catherine Macquarrie Fraser; one *s* one *d*. *Educ:* Univ. of Strathclyde (BA Hons 1984); Univ. of Edinburgh (MBA 1990). Mgt Develt Dir, United Distillers, 1995–97; Gp Mgt Develt Dir, Diageo plc, 1997–99; Human Resources Director: (Europe), United Distillers & Vintners, 1999–2000; Guinness Ltd, 2000–01; Dir, Human Resources and Internal Communications, BBC, subseq. BBC People, 2001–06; Gp Human Resources Dir, Reuters, 2006–08; Exec. Vice-Pres. and Chief Human Resources Officer, Thomson Reuters, 2008–12. Chartered CCIPD 2004; FRSA. *Recreations:* family, keeping fit, golf, current affairs. *E:* stephen@dandomail.co.uk. *Clubs:* Roehampton; Elie Golf House.

DANDRIDGE, Nicola, CBE 2015; Chief Executive, Universities UK, since 2009; *d* of Lawrence and Dorothy Dandridge; *m* 1995, Andrew Nairne, *qv*; two *s*. *Educ:* Chichester High Sch. for Girls; Univ. of Oxford (BA Lit. Hum.); City of London Poly.; Glasgow Univ. Admitted Solicitor: England, 1987; Scotland, 1991; Partner, Thompsons Solicitors, 1989–2006; Chief Exec., Equality Challenge Unit, 2006–09. *Address:* Universities UK, Woburn House, 20 Tavistock Square, WC1H 9HQ. *T:* (020) 7419 5403. *E:* nicola.dandridge@universitiesuk.ac.uk.

DANDY, David James, MD; FRCS; Consultant Orthopaedic Surgeon: Addenbrooke's Hospital, Cambridge, 1975–2002; Newmarket General Hospital, 1975–2002; *b* 30 May 1940; *s* of late James Dandy, Great Shelford, Cambs, and Margaret Dandy (*née* Coe); *m* 1966, (Stephanie) Jane Essex; one *s* one *d*. *Educ:* Forest Sch.; Emmanuel Coll., Cambridge (Windsor Student, 1965; BA 1961, MA 1963; BChir 1964; MB 1965; MD 1990; MChir 1994); London Hosp. Med. Coll. (Robert Milne Prize for Surgery, 1995). LRCP, MRCS 1964, FRCS 1969. Surg. Registrar, St Andrew's Hosp., Bow, 1966–67; Surg., then Orthopaedic Registrar, London Hosp., 1967–69; Orthopaedic Registrar: Royal Nat. Orthopaedic Hosp., 1969–71; St Bartholomew's Hosp., 1971; Princess Alexandra Hosp., Harlow, 1971–72; Norfolk and Norwich Hosp., 1972–73; Sen. Registrar: St Bartholomew's Hosp., 1973–75; Hosp. for Sick Children, Gt Ormond St, 1974; Sen. Fellow, Toronto Gen. Hosp., 1973–74; Associate Lectr, Univ. of Cambridge, 1975–2007; Civilian Advr in Knee Surgery, RN and RAF, 1980–2006. Lectures: Mackenzie Crooks, RAF Hosp., Ely, 1980; Munsif Meml Orator, Bombay, 1987; Sir Ernest Finch Meml, Sheffield, 1990; William Gissane, Inst. of Accident Surgery, 1998; Bradshaw, 2004, Vicary, 2005, RCS. Director: Internat. Soc. of the Knee, 1989–93; European Soc. for Sports Traumatology, Knee Surgery, Sports Medicine and Arthroscopy, 1992–96; President: Internat. Arthroscopy Assoc., 1989–91; British Orthopaedic Sports Trauma Assoc., 1993–95; British Orthopaedic Assoc., 1998–99 (Robert Jones Prize and

Assoc. Medal, 1991; Naughton Dunn Lectr, 1991; Mem. Council, 1992–95); Combined Services Orthopaedic Soc., 2001–04; Mem. Council, RCS, 1994–2006 (James Berry Prize, 1985; Hunterian Prof., 1994; Treas., 2003–06; Vice-Pres., 2005–06; Cheselden Medal, 2009). Chm., Granta Decorative and Fine Arts Soc., 2007–11. Trustee, Gretton Court Ltd (formerly Barton Housing Assoc.), 2009–. Hon. FRCSE 1998; Hon. FFGDP(UK) 2007; Hon. Fellow, British Orthopaedic Assoc., 2011. *Publications:* Arthroscopy of the Knee, 1973; Arthroscopic Surgery of the Knee, 1981, rev. edn 1987; Arthroscopy of the Knee: a diagnostic atlas, 1984; Essentials of Orthopaedics and Trauma, 1989, rev. edn 2009; articles on surgery of the knee and arthroscopic surgery. *Recreations:* travel, ablative horticulture. *Address:* Steeple View, King's Mill Lane, Great Shelford, Cambridge CB22 5EN. *Clubs:* East India, Royal Society of Medicine.

DANESH, Prof. John Navid, DPhil; FRCP; FFPH; Professor of Epidemiology and Medicine, and Head, Department of Public Health and Primary Care, University of Cambridge, since 2001; *b* 21 April 1968; *s* of Dr Ali Danesh and Dr Mahtaban Danesh (*née* Safapour); *m* 2005, Nathalie Jacoby. *Educ:* Univ. of Otago Med. Sch., NZ (MB ChB Dist. 1992); London Sch. of Hygiene and Trop. Medicine (MSc Epidemiol. Dist. 1995); DPhil Epidemiol. Oxon 2000. MRCP (Dist.) 2005. House Officer, Royal Melbourne Hosp., 1993; Rhodes Schol., New Coll. and Balliol Coll., Oxford, 1994–97; Jun. Res. Fellow, Merton Coll., Oxford, 1997–99; Clin. Res. Fellow, Univ. of Oxford, 1999–2001. *Publications:* (jtly) Reason and Revelation, 2002; Search for Values, 2004; (jtly) The Baha'i Faith in Words and Images, 2008; contrib. articles to scientific jls on epidemiology of chronic diseases, particularly molecular risk factors in heart disease. *Recreations:* food, conversation. *Address:* Department of Public Health and Primary Care, University of Cambridge, Strangeways Research Laboratory, Wort's Causeway, Cambridge CB1 8RN. *T:* (01223) 748655, *Fax:* (01223) 748658. *E:* john.danesh@phpc.cam.ac.uk.

DANGAN, Viscount; Garret Graham Wellesley, (Jr); Group Chief Executive, Wellesley & Co., since 2013; *b* 30 March 1965; *s* and *heir* of 7th Earl Cowley, *qv*; *m* 1990, Claire Lorraine, *d* of P. W. Brighton, Stow Bridge, Norfolk; two *s* one *d*. *Educ:* Franklin Coll., Switzerland (Associate of Arts degree). Traded Options, Hoare Govett, 1985–88; Manager, Ing (London) Derivatives Ltd, 1991–94; CEO, IFX Ltd, 1995–2003; Gp Chief Exec., Zetters plc, then IFX Gp plc, 2000–03; Sen. Vice Pres., Index Futures Gp, 1995–2002; Chief Executive: ODL Securities Ltd, 2003–10; ODL Gp Ltd, 2003–10; Vice-Chm., FXCM Securities Ltd, 2010–13. Non-executive Chairman: Prestige Asset Management Ltd, 2008–; Eastern Counties Finance, 2008–. Non-exec. Chm., Children's Miracle Network UK, 2007–; Trustee, Redwings Horse Sanctuary, 2004–. *Heir: s* Hon. Henry Arthur Peter Wellesley, *b* 3 Dec. 1991. *Address:* Ashbourne Manor, High Street, Widford, Herts SG12 8SZ.

DANIEL, Brother; *see* Matthews, Brother D. F.

DANIEL, Caroline Frances; Editor, Weekend Financial Times, since 2010; *b* Aldershot, 10 March 1971; *d* of Peter Edward Burgoyne Daniel and Alison Taylor. *Educ:* St Helen's Sch., Northwood, Middx; St John's Ravenscourt Sch., Winnipeg; St John's Coll., Cambridge (BA 1st Cl. Hist. 1993). Non-exec. Dir Dip., FT, 2014. Researcher, Gordon Brown, MP, 1994–96; reporter, New Statesman, 1996–99; tech. corresp., 1999–2002; Financial Times: Chicago corresp., 2002–05; White House corresp., 2005–09; comment and analysis ed., 2009; Asst Ed., 2009; Consulting Ed., FT Events and Conferences, 2014. Mem., Trilateral Commn. Trustee, IPPR. *Recreations:* photography, swimming, reading. *Address:* c/o Financial Times, Number One, Southwark Bridge, SE1 9HL. *T:* (020) 7873 3166. *E:* caroline.daniel@ft.com.

DANIEL, Gareth John; Director, GDA Ltd, since 2013; consultant on public policy, partnerships and governance, since 2013; *b* 30 March 1954; *s* of late Evan John Daniel and Eileen Marie Daniel; partner, Margaret Wilson; three *s*. *Educ:* St Edward's Coll., Liverpool; Jesus Coll., Oxford (BA Hons); South Bank Poly. (DASS, CQSW). Pres., Oxford Univ. Students' Union, 1974–75. Social worker, London Borough of Ealing, 1976–83; London Borough of Brent, 1986–2012: Principal Develt Officer; Divl Manager, Strategy; Head, Central Policy Unit; Dir, Partnership and Res.; Chief Exec., 1998–2012. Member (Lab): Ealing LBC (Chm., Planning and Econ. Develt, 1986–90); Ealing North, GLC, 1981–86. Contested (Lab): Worcs S, 1979; Ealing, Acton, 1983. *Recreations:* family, hill-walking, foreign travel. *T:* 07774 738009.

DANIEL, His Honour (Gruffydd) Huw Morgan, CVO 2014; a Circuit Judge, 1986–2006; Lord-Lieutenant of Gwynedd, 2006–14; *b* 16 April 1939; *s* of Prof. John Edward Daniel, MA, and Catherine Megan Daniel (*née* Parry Hughes); *m* 1968, Phyllis Margaret (*née* Bermingham); one *d*. *Educ:* Ampleforth; University College of Wales (LLB; Pres., Students' Law Soc., 1962–63); Inns of Court School of Law. Commissioned 2nd Lieut First Bn Royal Welch Fusiliers, 1959; Captain 6/7 Bn Royal Welch Fusiliers (TA), 1965; served MELF, Cyprus. Called to the Bar, Gray's Inn, 1967; Wales and Chester Circuit (Circuit Junior, 1975); Hd of Chambers, Stanley Place, Chester, 1975–86; Recorder, 1980–86; Asst Liaison Judge, 1983–87, Liaison Judge, 1988–2006, Gwynedd; Liaison Judge for N Wales, 1998–2006; Dep. Sen. Judge, 1995–2002, Sen. Judge, 2002–06, Sovereign Base Area, Cyprus. Asst Parly Boundary Comr for Wales, 1981–82, 1985–86; Pres., Mental Health Appeals Tribunal, 2002–06. Chairman: N Wales Judicial Forum, 2005–06; Lord Chancellor's Adv. Cttee on JPs for N Wales, 2012–. President: Caerns Br., SSAFA, 1995–; St John's Council in Gwynedd, Anglesey and Conwy Co. Borough, 2006–; Custos rotulorum of Gwynedd, 2006–; Gwynedd Magistrates' Assoc., 2006–; Gwynedd SSAFA, 2013–; Vice Pres., RFCA Wales, 2006–; Trustee, St John Wales, 2006–. Member of Court: Bangor Univ., 2006–; Cardiff Univ., 2006–. Hon. Col, 6th Cadet Bn, Royal Welch Fusiliers, 1997–2003. DL Gwynedd, 1993. KStJ 2012 (CStJ 2006). *Recreation:* gardening. *Address:* (residence) Rhiwgoch, Pont y Pandy, Bangor, Gwynedd LL57 3AX. *Club:* Reform.

DANIEL, Hamish St Clair, CMG 2008; OBE 2004 (MBE 1992); HM Diplomatic Service, retired; Deputy High Commissioner, Karachi and UK Director of Trade and Investment, Pakistan, 2004–08; *b* 22 Aug. 1953; *s* of James Anderson Daniel and Charlotte Daniel; *m* 2002, Heather Ann Bull; one *s* one *d* from previous marriage. *Educ:* Lerwick Central Public Sch., Scotland. Joined FCO, 1973: Algiers, 1975–77; Prague, 1977; Lisbon, 1978–80; Islamabad, 1980–82; FCO, 1982–85; San Francisco, 1985–88; Second Secretary: Khartoum, 1989–92; FCO, 1992–94; Dep. Hd of Mission, Sana'a, 1994–96; Pol and Econ. Sec., Jakarta, 1997–2001; British Rep., Dili, 2001–02; Ambassador to E Timor, 2002–03. *Recreations:* sailing, golf, walking.

DANIEL, Huw Morgan; *see* Daniel, His Honour G. H. M.

DANIEL, Jack; *see* Daniel, R. J.

DANIEL, Joan; *see* Rodgers, J.

DANIEL, John, MA; Headmaster, Royal Grammar School, Guildford, 1977–92; *b* 7 March 1932; *s* of John Daniel and Mary (*née* Young); *m* 1st, 1956, Heather Joy Retey (marr. diss. 2001); two *d*; 2nd, 2001, Beatrice Miller McTighe. *Educ:* Truro Sch.; New Coll., Oxford (Hons Modern Langs 1955). Thomas Hedley & Son, 1955–57; Linton Lodge Hotel, Oxford, 1957–59; Hartford Motors, Oxford, 1959–62; Royal Grammar Sch., Worcester, 1963–65; Malvern Coll., 1965–72; Royal Grammar School, Guildford: Dep. Headmaster, 1972–75; Acting Headmaster, 1975–77. Chm. of Govs, Tormead Sch., Guildford, 1981–97. Asst Dir, Gap Activity Projects Ltd, 1994–2002. Chm., Guildford Symphony Orch., 1995–2002. *Recreations:* watching Rugby football, playing the piano. *Address:* 800 Truman Street NE, Albuquerque, NM 87110, USA. *E:* upalong32@gmail.com.

DANIEL, Sir John (Sagar), Kt 1994; OC 2013; DSc; President and Chief Executive Officer, Commonwealth of Learning, 2004–12; *b* 31 May 1942; *s* of John Edward Daniel and Winifred (*née* Sagar); *m* 1966, Kristin Anne Swanson (*d* 2011); one *s* two *d*. *Educ:* Christ's Hosp.; St Edmund Hall, Oxford (BA Metallurgy, MA; Hon. Fellow, 1990); Univ. of Paris (DSc Metallurgy); Thorneloe Univ., Ont (Associate 1992); Concordia Univ., Quebec (MA Educnl Technol. 1995). Asst Prof., then Associate Prof., Ecole Polytechnique, Montreal, 1969–73; Dir, Etudes Télé-Univ., Univ. of Quebec, 1973–77; Vice Pres., Learning Services, Athabasca Univ., Alberta, 1979–80; Vice-Rector, Academic Affairs, Concordia Univ., Montreal, 1980–84; Pres., Laurentian Univ., Sudbury, Ont, 1984–90; Vice-Chancellor, Open Univ., 1990–2001 (Hon. Fellow, 2002); Pres., US Open Univ., 1998–2001; Asst Dir-Gen. for Educn, UNESCO, 2001–04. Chairman: UNESCO-CEPES Adv. Council, 1990–92; Adv. Council for Develt of RN Personnel, 1996–2001; Member: HEQC, 1992–94; Council of Foundn, Internat. Baccalaureate, 1992–99; Council for Industry and Higher Educn, 1994–2001; British N American Cttee, 1995–2001, 2006–; Council, CBI, 1996–98; Steering Cttee, Defence Trng Rev., 1999–2001; Adv. Bd, Internat. Quality Gp, Council for Higher Educn Accreditation, USA, 2012–. Member: Bd of Govs, Commonwealth of Learning, 1988–90; Council, Univ. of Buckingham, 1994–; Council, Open Univ. of Hong Kong, 1996–; Bd, Univ. for Industry, 1999–2001 (Mem. Transition Bd, 1998–99); Canadian Council on Learning, 2005–; Member, Advisory Board: Whitney Internat. Univ. System, 2008–; Taylor's Univ., Malaysia, 2011–; Hamdan bin Mohammed e-Univ., Dubai, 2011–13; Educn Master, De Tao Masters Acad., China, 2011–; Chm., Internat. Bd, United World Colls, 2013–; Sen. Advr, Academic Partnerships Internat., USA, 2013–; Trustee, Carnegie Foundn for Advancement of Teaching, 1993–2001. Mem., Adv. Bd, Xerox, Canada, 1998–99; Dir, Blackwells Publishing, 1998–2001. Hon. Chair, Canadian Soc. for Trng and Develt, 2006–08. Licensed Reader: Montreal, 1980–84, Algoma, 1984–90, Anglican Ch of Canada; St Albans, 1990–2001, Europe, 2003–04, C of E. Forum Fellow, World Econ. Forum, 1998. Hon. Fellow, Commonwealth of Learning, 2002. CCMI (CIMgt 1997; Pres., Milton Keynes Br., 1998–2001). Hon. FCP 1997. Hon. DLitt: Deakin, Aust., 1985; Lincolnshire and Humberside, 1996; Athabasca, Canada, 1998; Indira Gandhi Nat. Open Univ., India, 2003; Thompson Rivers, Canada, 2005; Netaji Subhas Open Univ., India, 2005; Kota Open Univ., India, 2007; McGill, Canada, 2007; Hon. DHumLitt: Thomas Edison State Coll., USA, 1997; Richmond Coll., London, 1997; Hon. DSc: Royal Mil. Coll., St Jean, Canada, 1988; Open Univ., Sri Lanka, 1994; Paris VI, 2001; Univ. of Education, Winneba, Ghana, 2006; Hon. DEd: CNAA, 1992; Sukhothai Thammathirat Open Univ., Thailand, 1999; Open Univ. Malaysia, 2009; Hon. LLD: Univ. of Waterloo, Canada, 1993; Wales, 2002; Laurentian, Canada, 2006; Canada West, 2008; Univ. of Ghana, 2013; DUniv: Aberta, Portugal, 1996; Anadolu, Turkey, 1998; Québec, Derby, and New Bulgarian, 2000; Open Univ., Hong Kong, 2001; Stirling, 2002; de Montreal, 2008; Hon. DLitt and DPhil South Africa, 2010; Hon. LittD State Univ. NY, 2011. Individual Excellence Award, Commonwealth of Learning, 1995; Morris T. Keeton Award, Council for Adult and Experiential Learning, USA, 1999; Symons Medal, Assoc. of Commonwealth Univs, 2008; Res. Excellence Prize, China TVU System, 2011. Officier, Ordre des Palmes Académiques (France), 1991 (Chevalier, 1987); Golden Jubilee Medal, Canada, 2002. *Publications:* Learning at a Distance: a world perspective, 1982; Mega-universities and Knowledge Media, 1996; Mega-Schools, Technology and Teachers: achieving education for all, 2010; more than 350 articles to professional pubns. *E:* ODLSirJohn@gmail.com.

DANIEL, Nicholas; oboe soloist; conductor; *b* 9 Jan. 1962; *s* of late Jeremy Daniel and Margaret Louise Daniel; *m* 1986, Joy Farrall, clarinettist (marr. diss. 2011); two *s*. *Educ:* Salisbury Cathedral Sch.; Purcell Sch.; Royal Acad. of Music. ARAM 1986, FRAM 1987; FGS (FGSM 1996). Prof., GSMD, 1986–97; Oboe Prof., Indiana Univ., 1997–99; Prince Consort Lectr, RCM, 1999–2002; Prof., Trossingen Musikhochschule, 2004–. Artistic Director: Osnabrück Chamber Music Fest., 2001–04; Leicester Internat. Music Fest., 2004–; Barbirolli-Isle of Man Internat. Oboe Fest. and Competition, 2005–; Associate Artistic Dir, Britten Sinfonia, 2002–. Dedicatee and first performer of many new works; more than 30 recordings and many broadcasts. Internat. appearances in USA, Japan, Europe, Australasia. Competition prize winner: BBC Young Musician of Year, 1980; Munich, 1983; Graz, 1984; Duino, Italy, 1986. Member: Assoc. for Improvement of Maternity Services; Assoc. of Radical Midwives; Good Practice; JABS; The Informed Parent. The Queen's Medal for Music, 2012. *Recreations:* childbirth studies (home birth), music, literature, Star Trek, travel, cinema. *E:* nicholas@engage.plus.com.

DANIEL, Paul Wilson, CBE 2000; conductor; Chief Conductor and Artistic Advisor, Royal Philharmonic Orchestra of Galicia, since 2013; Music Director, Orchestre National Bordeaux Aquitaine, since 2013; *b* 5 July 1958; *s* of Alfred Daniel and Margaret Daniel (*née* Poole); *m* 1st, 1988, Joan Rodgers, *qv* (marr. diss. 2005); two *d*; 2nd, 2008 Sarah Walley. *Educ:* King Henry VIII Sch., Coventry; King's Coll., Cambridge; Guildhall Sch. of Music and Drama. Music Dir, Opera Factory, London, 1987–90; Artistic Dir, Opera North, 1990–97; Principal Conductor, English Northern Philharmonia, 1990–97; Music Dir, ENO, 1997–2005; Principal Conductor and Artistic Advr, West Australian SO, 2009–13. Has worked with ENO, Royal Opera House, Metropolitan Opera, New York, Bayerische Staatsoper, Munich, La Monnaie, Brussels, Geneva Opera and Teatro Real Madrid; has conducted many orchestras incl. Philharmonia, LSO, LPO, RPO, BBC SO, London Sinfonietta, CBSO, Scottish Chamber Orch., and ABC orchestras, Australia; has conducted many BBC Proms, including Last Night of the Proms 2005, and has also conducted in Germany, Holland, France and USA. Conductor: Gloriana (filmed), 2000; Lucrecia Borgia (filmed), 2011. Co-presenter, Harry Enfield's Guide to Opera, TV series, 1993. Has made numerous recordings. *Address:* c/o Ingpen & Williams, 7 St George's Court, 131 Putney Bridge Road, SW15 2PA. *T:* (020) 8874 3222.

DANIEL, (Reginald) Jack, OBE 1958; FREng, CEng, FRINA, FIMarEST; RCNC; *b* 27 Feb. 1920; *o s* of Reginald Daniel and Florence Emily (*née* Woods); *m* 1st, Joyce Earnshaw (marr. diss.); two *s*; 2nd, 1977, Elizabeth, *o d* of George Mitchell, Long Ashton, Som. *Educ:* Royal Naval Engrg Coll., Keyham; Royal Naval Coll., Greenwich. Grad., 1942; subseq. engaged in submarine design. Served War of 1939–45; Staff of C-in-C's Far East Fleet and Pacific Fleet, 1943–45. Atomic Bomb Tests, Bikini, 1946; Admty, Whitehall, 1947–49; Admty, Bath, Aircraft Carrier Design, 1949–52; Guided Missile Cruiser design, 1952–56; Nuclear and Polaris Submarine design, 1956–65; idc, 1966; Materials, R&D, 1967–68; Head of Forward Design, 1968–70; Director, Submarine Design and Production, 1970–74; Dir-Gen. Ships and Head of RCNC, MoD, 1974–79; British Shipbuilders: Bd Mem., 1979; Man. Dir, for Warshipbuilding, 1980–83; Dir (Training, Educn, Safety), 1981–85; Dir of Technology (Warships), British Shipbuilders, 1983–84; Dir, British Shipbuilders Australia Pty, 1983–86. Dep. Chm., Internationale Schiff Studien GmbH Hamburg, 1984–88; Man. Dir, Warship Design Services Ltd, 1984–87; VSEL Canadian Project Dir, 1987–91; Director: VSEL Australia Pty, 1986–91; VSEL Defence Systems Canada Inc., 1987–91; Chm., VSEL-CAP, 1987–91. Vice Pres., RINA, 1982. Parsons Meml Lect., 1976. Liveryman, Worshipful Co. of Shipwrights, 1980. Hon. Res. Fellow, UCL, 1974. FREng (Founder Fellow, Fellowship of Engineering, 1976). *Publications:* The End of an Era, 2003; Hawkridge series: Murder in the Park, 2006; Murder in Providence, 2006; It Couldn't Happen in Dorset, 2006; The Qatar Affair, 2006; Diamonds in Dorset, 2006; Bedsits in Bath, 2006; Problem in Portland, 2006; Nuclear. No! How?, 2006; Submarines and Swindlers, 2006; Requiem for a Sapper, 2006; Politics and Property, 2006; The Body in the Churchyard, 2006; Chain of Circumstances, 2007; Murder in the Theatre, 2007; The Irish Affair, 2007; The Spetisbury Mystery, 2007; Death Isn't Particular, 2007; Family Affairs, 2007; Nemesis, 2007; Satan's

Disciples, 2007; Tragedy in Downing Street, 2009; papers on warship design, technology and production. *Recreations:* gardening, motoring, music. *Address:* Meadowland, Cleveland Walk, Bath BA2 6JU.

DANIEL, William Wentworth, CBE 1997; independent social scientist; Director, Policy Studies Institute, 1986–93; *b* 19 Nov. 1938; *s* of late George Taylor Daniel and Margaret Elizabeth Daniel; *m* 1st, 1961, Lynda Mary Coles Garrett (marr. diss.); one *s* two *d*; 2nd, 1990, Eileen Mary Reid (*née* Loudfoot) (*d* 1996). *Educ:* Shebbear Coll., Devon; Victoria Univ. of Manchester (BA Hons); Univ. of Manchester Inst. of Science and Technology (MSc Tech). Directing Staff, Ashorne Hill Management Coll., 1963–65; Sen. Res. Officer, Research Services Ltd, 1965–67; Senior Research Fellow: Bath Univ., 1967–69; PSI (formerly PEP), 1969–81; Dep. Dir, PSI, 1981–86. Member: ESRC, 1992–96; Eur. Foundn for Improvement of Living and Wkg Conditions, Dublin, 1992–96. Dir, Holsworthy Biogas Ltd, 1999. Mem. Bd of Govs, Plymouth Univ., 2001. *Publications:* Racial Discrimination in England, 1968; Whatever Happened to the Workers in Woolwich?, 1972; The Right to Manage?, 1972; A National Survey of the Unemployed, 1974; Sandwich Courses in Higher Education, 1975; Pay Determination in Manufacturing Industry, 1976; Where Are They Now?: a follow-up survey of the unemployed, 1977; The Impact of Employment Protection Laws, 1978; Maternity Rights: the experience of women, 1980; Maternity Rights: the experience of employers, 1981; Workplace Industrial Relations in Britain, 1983; Workplace Industrial Relations and Technical Change, 1987; The Unemployed Flow, 1989; (with Terence Hogarth) Britain's New Industrial Gypsies, 1989. *Recreations:* golf, lawn tennis. *Address:* Bryn-Mor, 7 Maer Down Road, Bude, Cornwall EX23 8NG. *T:* (01288) 356678. *Clubs:* National Liberal; Bude & N Cornwall Golf; David Lloyd Slazenger Racquet (Heston).

DANIELL, Prof. David John, PhD; Professor of English, University College London, 1992–94, now Emeritus Professor; *b* 17 Feb. 1929; *s* of late Rev. Eric Herbert Daniell, MA, and Betty (*née* Heap); *m* 1956, Dorothy Mary Wells (*d* 2010); two *s*. *Educ:* Queen Elizabeth GS, Darlington; St Catherine's Coll., Oxford (BA English Lang. and Lit., MA; BA Theol.; Hon. Fellow, 2000); Univ. of Tübingen; UCL (PhD 1972). Radar fitter, RAF, 1947–49. Sixth Form Master, Apsley GS, 1958–69; Lectr, 1969–86, Sen. Lectr, 1986–92, English Dept, UCL. Vis. Prof., KCL, 1995; Vis. Fellow, Magdalen Coll., Oxford, 1996 (Hon. Mem., Sen. Common Room, 1996); Leverhulme Emeritus Fellow, 1997–99; Mayers Fellow, Henry E. Huntington Liby, Calif, 1998; Special Lectr, Magdalen Coll., Oxford, 1999; Oxford Univ. Sermon, 2000. Lectures: Beatrice Warde Meml, 1994; Lambeth Tyndale, 1994; A. G. Dickens, Univ. of Cambridge, 1994; Hertford Tyndale, 1994; Hilda Hulme Meml, 1994; Waynflete, Univ. of Oxford, 1996; Staley, Michigan, 1998; St Paul's Cathedral, 2003; Shakespeare Inst., Illinois, 2005. Asst Ed., The Year's Work in English Studies, 1976–84; Gen. Ed., John Buchan series, OUP World's Classics, 1993–2003; Founder and Ed., Reformation, 1995–97. Mem., Acad. Adv. Cttee, Internat. Shakespeare Globe Centre, 1981–91; Founder and organiser, biennial Oxford Internat. Tyndale Confs, 1994–; Founder and Chm., Tyndale Soc., 1995–. Curator, Let There Be Light Exhibn, British Liby, 1994–97 (London, Calif, NY and Washington). Frequent broadcaster, incl. Tyndale's New Testament, Radio 3, 1993. Lectures widely in UK, Europe and USA. Hon. Fellow, Hertford Coll., Oxford, 1998. *Publications:* The Interpreter's House, 1975; Coriolanus in Europe, 1980; The Best Short Stories of John Buchan, vol. 1, 1980, vol. 2, 1982; The Critics Debate: The Tempest, 1989; (ed) Tyndale's 1534 New Testament, 1989; (ed) Tyndale's Old Testament, 1992; William Tyndale: a biography, 1994; The Arden Shakespeare: Julius Caesar, 1998; (ed) Tyndale, the Obedience of a Christian Man, 2000; The Bible in English, 2003; William Tyndale, Selected Writings, 2003; contrib. Oxford DNB; numerous contribs to learned jls incl. Shakespeare Survey, TLS, The Year's Work in English Studies, MLR, Jl of Ecclesiastical Hist., Jl of Amer. Studies, Jl of Theol Studies, Reformation. *Recreations:* music, reading, hill-walking in Scotland. *Address:* 17 Crossfell Road, Leverstock Green, Hemel Hempstead, Herts HP3 8RF. *T:* (01442) 254766. *Clubs:* Arts, Authors'.

DANIELS, David; countertenor; *b* S Carolina, 12 March 1966. *Educ:* Cincinnati Conservatoire; Univ. of Michigan. Singing début, 1992; début with Metropolitan Opera, as Sesto in Giulio Cesare, 1999; *rôles* include: Rinaldo, Nerone in L'Incoronazione di Poppea, Didymus in Theodora, Hamor in Jeptha, Arsamenes in Xerxes, Oberon in A Midsummer Night's Dream; title rôles in Tamerlano, Giulio Cesare, Orfeo ed Euridice, Orlando, Radamisto; has performed with San Francisco SO, St Louis SO, New World SO, Philharmonia Baroque, San Francisco Opera, Florida Grand Opera, Bavarian State Opera, Glimmerglass Opera Fest., Brooklyn Acad. of Music, Royal Opera, Covent Gdn, Glyndebourne Fest., Salzburg Fest., Bayerische Staatsoper, NY City Opera, Canadian Opera Co., Lyric Opera of Chicago, Netherlands Opera, and Paris Opera; extensive recital and concert repertoire performed in US and Europe, incl. Promenade Concerts. Has made numerous recordings. Richard Tucker Award, 1997; Vocalist of Year Award, Musical America, 1999. *Recreations:* theatre, sports, especially baseball. *Address:* c/o Askonas Holt Ltd, Lincoln House, 300 High Holborn, WC1V 7JH. *T:* (020) 7400 1700.

DANIELS, Edward David, FREng, FIChemE; Executive Vice President, Commercial and New Business Development, Royal Dutch Shell plc, since 2014; *b* Haverfordwest, 26 Jan. 1966; *s* of Glyn Daniels and Meriel Daniels; *m* 1994, Laura Jane Stephens; three *d*. *Educ:* Sir Thomas Picton Sch., Haverfordwest; Imperial Coll. London (MEng 1988); Henley Management Coll. (MBA 1995). FIChemE 2010. Shell Europe Oil Products: Technologist, Project Mgt and Implementation, 1988–93; Refinery Technical Auditor and Economist, 1993–95; Mktg Co-ordination, Commercial Markets, 1995–96; Sales and Mktg Manager, Commercial Road Transport, 1996–97; Mktg Consultant, 1997; Mktg Manager, Eur. Fleet Business, 1998–2000; Shell International Oil Products: Consultancy Manager, Business Develt Consultancy, Singapore, 2000–03; Global Base Oil Business Gen. Manager, Shell Lubricants, 2003–06; Vice Pres. Commercial, Shell Global Solutions, 2006–09; Exec. Vice Pres., Global Solutions Downstream, Shell Projects and Technol., 2009–14; Chm., Shell UK Ltd, 2013–14. FREng 2014; FCGI 2015. *Recreations:* gardening, travel, fitness. *Address:* Shell International Exploration and Production BV, Carel van Bylandtlaan 23, 2596 HP The Hague, Netherlands. *T:* (office) (70) 3775535. *E:* e.daniels@shell.com.

DANIELS, Eric; *see* Daniels, J. E.

DANIELS, Prof. Harry Richard John, PhD; Professor of Education, University of Oxford, since 2013; Fellow, Green Templeton College, since 2013; *b* S Molton, Devon, 6 June 1951; *s* of Alfred Hart Daniels and Wendy Irene Daniels; *m* (marr. diss.); two *d*; partner, Jill Porter. *Educ:* King's Sch., Ottery St Mary, Devon; Univ. of Liverpool (BSc Computational and Statistical Sci. 1972; BSc Hons Genetics 1973); Univ. of Leicester (PGCE); Inst. of Educn, Univ. of London (Dip. Psychol. and Educn of Children with Special Needs 1982; PhD 1986). Asst teacher, Leysland High Sch., Countesthorpe, Leics, 1975–76; Hd, Disruptive Unit, Wreake Valley Coll., Syston, Leics, 1977–80; Dep. Hd, Gp 7(S), Temple Court Special (MLD) Sch., Guildford, 1980–84; Sen. Lectr in Special Educn, W London Inst. Higher Educn, 1984–87; Sen. Lectr, Dept of Educnl Psychol. and Special Educnl Needs, Univ. of London, Inst. of Educn, 1988–95; Prof. of Special Educn and Educnl Psychol., Dep. Hd of Sch., Dir of Res. and Dir, Centre for Sociocultural and Activity Theory Res., Sch. of Educn, Univ. of Birmingham, 1995–2004; Prof. of Educn, Culture and Pedagogy, and Dir, Centre for Sociocultural and Activity Theory Res. (Bath), Dept of Educn, Univ. of Bath, 2004–13. Adjunct Prof., Centre for Learning Res., Griffith Univ., Brisbane, 2006–; Research Professor: Centre for Human Activity Theory, Kansai Univ., Osaka, 2006–; in Cultural Histl Psychol., Moscow State Univ. of Psychol. and Educn, 2006–. *Publications:* (with S. Sandow) Child Study in Special Education: the teacher-researcher in action, 1985; (with J. Anghileri) Secondary School Mathematics and Special Educational Needs, 1995; (jtly) Teacher Support Teams in Primary and Secondary Schools, 1997; (jtly) Educational Support for Children with Mental Health Issues including the Emotionally Vulnerable, 1999; (jtly) Emotional and Behavioural Difficulty in Mainstream Schools, 1999; (jtly) The Framework for Intervention: identifying and promoting effective practice (Second Evaluation Report), 2000; Vygotsky and Pedagogy, 2001 (Spanish edn 2003; Brazilian edn 2003; Japanese edn 2006); (jtly) The Mental Health Needs of Young People with Emotional and Behavioural Difficulties - Bright Futures: working with vulnerable people, 2002; Study of Young People Permanently Excluded from School, 2003; (with A. Parrilla) Criação e desenvolvimento de grupos de apoio entre professores, 2004; (jtly) Disability Data Collection for Children's Services, 2008; Vygotsky and Research, 2008 (Brazilian edn 2011); (jtly) Improving Inter-professional Collaborations: multi-agency working for children's well being, 2009; (with A. Edwards) Leading for Learning: how the intelligent leader builds capacity, 2012; *edited:* Charting the Agenda: educational activity after Vygotsky, 1993 (Brazilian edns 1994, 2007); An Introduction to Vygotsky, 1996, 2nd edn 2005 (Brazilian edn 2002); (with P. Garner) Inclusive Education: World Yearbook of Education 1999, 1999; Special Education Re-formed: beyond rhetoric?, 2000; (jtly) Effecting Change for the Child with Special Educational Needs: a celebration of the contribution of Professor Ron Gulliford, 2000; (jtly) Towards a Sociology of Pedagogy: the contribution of Basil Bernstein to research, 2001; (jtly) Emotional and Behavioural Difficulty in Mainstream Schools, 2001; (with A. Edwards) The Routledge Falmer Reader in the Psychology of Education, 2004; (jtly) New Learning Challenges: going beyond the industrial age system of school and work, 2005; (with P. Garner) Inclusive Education: world yearbook of education (in Japanese), 2006; (jtly) Knowledge, Power and Educational Reform: applying the sociology of Basil Bernstein, 2006; (jtly) Cambridge Companion to Vygotsky, 2007; (jtly) Knowledge, Values and Educational Policy: a critical perspective, 2009; (jtly) Educational Theories, Cultures and Learning: a critical perspective, 2009; (jtly) Learning and Expanding with Activity Theory, 2009; (jtly) Activity Theory in Practice: promoting learning across boundaries and agencies, 2009; (with M. Hedegaard) Vygotsky and Special Needs Education: rethinking support for children and schools, 2011; Vygotsky and Sociology, 2012; (jtly) Transforming Troubled Lives: strategies and interventions for children with social, emotional and behavioural difficulties, 2012; (jtly) The Routledge International Companion to Emotional and Behavioural Difficulties, 2012. *Recreations:* cooking, walking, music. *Address:* Department of Education, University of Oxford, 15 Norham Gardens, Oxford OX2 6PY. *T:* (01865) 274041. *E:* harry.daniels@education.ox.ac.uk.

DANIELS, Hilary; Member, Conduct Committee, Financial Reporting Council, 2012–15 (Member, Professional Oversight Board, 2005–12); *b* Horsham, 1954; *m* 1995. *Educ:* High Sch. for Girls, Horsham; Southampton Univ. (BSc Hons Maths). CPFA 1981. Various posts, London Bor. of Barnet, 1975–86; Chief Accountant, London Fire and Civil Defence Authy, 1986–89; Dep. Treas., S Somerset DC, 1989–91; Dir of Finance, Cambridge CC; Dir of Finance and Inf., NW Anglia HA; Chief Exec., W Norfolk PCG, later PCT, 2000–06. Pres., CIPFA, 2003–04. Member Board: Olympic Lottery Distributor, 2006–13 (Chm., Audit Cttee); ILEX Professional Standards Ltd, 2008–14; Vice Chm., E Northants Standards Bd, 2009–12 (Mem., 2007–12); Independent Member: Audit and Risk Cttee, Gen. Pharmaceutical Council, 2010–; Audit and Risk Mgt Cttee, City of London, 2012–; Audit and Risk Cttee, S Lincs CCG, 2014–; Chm., Audit Cttee, 2014– (Ind. Mem., 2012–14), Trustee, 2014–, Peterborough Diocesan Bd of Finance. Churchwarden, Nassington Church, 2011–. *Recreations:* watching athletics, bellringing. *E:* hilarydaniels@btinternet.com.

DANIELS, (John) Eric; Chief Executive, Lloyds Banking Group (formerly Lloyds TSB Group) plc, 2003–11; Principal and Senior Adviser, StormHarbour, since 2012; *b* Montana, USA, 1951; *m*; one *s*. *Educ:* Cornell Univ. (BA 1973); Massachusetts Inst. of Technol. (MSc 1975). Joined Citibank, USA, 1975; Regl Hd, Citigroup Consumer Bank Europe, 1996; Chief Operating Officer, Citigroup Consumer Bank, 1998; Chm. and CEO, Travelers Life & Annuity, 1998–2000; Chm. and CEO, Zona Financiera, 2000–01; Exec. Dir, UK Retail Banking, Lloyds TSB Gp plc, 2001–03. Non-exec. Dir, BT, 2008–12. Trustee, Career Academies UK.

DANIELS, Ruth Sarah; *see* Farwell, R. S.

DANIELS, Prof. Stephen J., PhD; FBA 2010; Professor of Cultural Geography, University of Nottingham. *Educ:* Univ. of St Andrews (MA); Univ. of Wisconsin (MSc); Univ. of London (PhD). University of Nottingham, 1980–: Dir, AHRC Landscape and Envmt Prog., Sch. of Geog., 2005–. Vice Chancellor's Achievement Award, Univ. of Nottingham, 2010. *Publications:* Joseph Wright: art and enlightenment, 1999; Humphry Repton and the Geography of Georgian England, 1999; (jtly) Art of the Garden: the garden in British art, 1800 to the present day, 2004; contribs to jls incl. British Art Jl, Jl Histl Geog., Cultural Geographies, Jl Garden Hist. *Address:* School of Geography, University of Nottingham, University Park, Nottingham NG7 2RD.

DANKWORTH, Lady; *see* Laine, Dame C. D.

DANN, Mrs Jill; *b* 10 Sept. 1929; *d* of Harold Norman Cartwright and Marjorie Alice Thornton; *m* 1952, Anthony John Dann (*d* 2000); two *s* two *d* (and one *s* decd). *Educ:* Solihull High Sch. for Girls, Malvern Hall; Birmingham Univ. (LLB); St Hilda's Coll., Oxford (BCL). Called to the Bar, Inner Temple, 1952. Mayoress of Chippenham, 1964–65. Church Commissioner, 1968–93; Member: General Synod of Church of England, 1965–95 (Mem., Standing Cttee, 1971–90; Vice-Chm. House of Laity, 1985–90); Crown Appointments Commn, 1977–87; Chairman: House of Laity, Bristol Diocesan Synod, 1982–88; C of E Evangelical Council, 1985–89; Trustee, Church Urban Fund, 1987–95. Vice Chm., Trinity Coll., Bristol, 1990–2006; Pres. of Fellows, Cheltenham and Gloucester Coll. of Higher Educn, subseq. Univ. of Gloucestershire, 1988–2003. Director: Wiltshire Radio, 1981–88; ARK 2 TV Ltd, 1995–97. Pres., Inner Wheel, 1978–79. *Recreations:* reading, enjoying being a grandmother. *Address:* 47 The Cloisters, Pegasus Grange, Whitehouse Road, Oxford OX1 4QQ. *T:* (01865) 608009.

DANNATT, family name of **Baron Dannatt**.

DANNATT, Baron *cr* 2011 (Life Peer), of Keswick in the County of Norfolk; **Gen. (Francis) Richard Dannatt,** GCB 2009 (KCB 2004); CBE 1996; MC 1973; DL; Constable, HM Tower of London, since 2009; *b* 23 Dec. 1950; *s* of late Anthony Richard Dannatt and of Mary Juliet Dannatt (*née* Chilvers); *m* 1977, Philippa Margaret Gurney (MBE 2013); three *s* one *d*. *Educ:* Felsted Jun. Sch.; St Lawrence Coll.; RMA, Sandhurst; Univ. of Durham (BA Hons Econ. Hist. 1976). Commnd Green Howards, 1971; Army Comd and Staff Coll., Camberley, 1982; COS, 20th Armd Bde, 1983–84; MA to Minister of State for Armed Forces, 1986–89; CO, 1 Green Howards, 1989–91; Col Higher Comd and Staff Course, Staff Coll., Camberley, 1992–94; Comdr, 4th Armd Bde, 1994–96; Dir, Defence Progs, MoD, 1996–98; GOC 3rd UK Div., 1999–2000; Dep. Comdr Ops, HQ SFOR, 2000–01; ACGS, 2001–02; Comdr, Allied RRC, 2003–05; C-in-C Land Comd, 2005–06; Chief of Gen. Staff, 2006–09; ADC Gen. to the Queen, 2006–09. Col, Green Howards, 1994–2003; Dep. Col Comdt, AGC (RMP), 1999–2005; Colonel Commandant: King's Div., 2001–05; AAC, 2004–09. Vice Pres., Officers Christian Union, 1998–2012; President: Soldiers' and Airmen's Scripture Readers Assoc., 1999–; Army Rifle Assoc., 2000–08; Royal Norfolk Agricl Assoc., 2008; YMCA Norfolk, 2010; Norfolk Churches Trust, 2011; Chm., Strategic Adv. Bd, Durham Global Security Inst., 2010–; Trustee: Windsor Leadership Trust, 2005–12; Royal Armouries, 2009–; Patron, Hope and Homes for Children, 2006–; Founder Patron, Help for Heroes, 2007– (Pres., 2011–); Vice Patron, Blind Veterans UK (formerly St Dunstan's),

2010–. DL: Gtr London, 2010; Norfolk 2012. Hon. DCL: Durham, 2009; Kent, 2009; Hon. DTech Anglia Ruskin, 2010; Hon. DLitt Buckingham, 2012. *Publications:* Leading from the Front, 2010. *Recreations:* cricket, tennis, fishing, shooting, golf. *Address:* HM Tower of London, EC3N 4AB. *T:* (020) 3166 6200. *Clubs:* Army and Navy, Cavalry and Guards; Royal West Norfolk Golf.

DANNATT, Prof. (James) Trevor, MA; RA 1983 (ARA 1977); FRIBA; Consultant, since 2003, Partner, 1975–2003, Dannatt, Johnson Architects (formerly Trevor Dannatt & Partners); Professor of Architecture: Manchester University, 1975–86; Royal Academy, 1988–2005; *b* 15 Jan. 1920; *s* of George Herbert and Jane Ellen Dannatt; *m* 1st, 1953, Joan Howell Davies (marr. diss. 1991); one *s* one *d*; 2nd, 1994, Dr Ann Crawshaw (*née* Critchley). *Educ:* Colfe's Sch.; Sch. of Architecture, Regent Street Polytechnic (Dip. Arch.). Professional experience in office of Jane B. Drew and E. Maxwell Fry, 1943–48; Architects Dept, LCC (Royal Festival Hall Gp), 1948–52; commenced private practice, 1952. Vis. Prof., Washington Univ., St Louis, 1976 and 1987. Assessor for national and international architectural competitions. Member: Cathedrals Adv. Commn, 1986–91; Historic Bldgs Adv. Cttee, English Heritage, 1988–91 (Mem., Post War Listing Adv. Cttee, 1986–2003); Fabric Cttees of Cathedrals: Lichfield, 1985–97; Portsmouth, 1990–96; St Paul's, 1991–2006. Pres., 20th Century Soc., 2003–11. Trustee, DOCOMOMO (Documents of the Modern Movement), 1991–. Editor, Architects' Year Book, 1945–62. Exhibn of paintings and architecture, Whitworth Art Gall., 2006. Architectural work includes: private houses, housing, school buildings; university buildings (residences, Leicester, Hull; Trinity Hall Combination Room, Cambridge; Vaughan Coll. and Jewry Wall Mus., Leicester; develt plan and extensive works for Univ. of Greenwich, formerly Thames Polytechnic, inc. studies for occupation of Wren and Hawksmoor at RNC Greenwich, comprising conversion and refurbishment of Queen Anne Quarters and Dreadnought Seamen's Hosp., 1999, Queen Mary's Quarters, 2000 and King William's Quarters, 2001); works for Univ. of Westminster; welfare buildings and schools for London boroughs; conservation and restoration, interiors for private, corporate and public clients; Architects for British Embassy and Diplomatic Staff housing, Riyadh, 1985; Consultant Architects, Royal Botanic Gardens, Kew, 1989–2005; Victoria Gate visitor reception and facilities building; various restorations and new buildings; houses for Morden Coll., Blackheath, 2004; Walker House, W Sussex, 2010. Won internat. competition for Conference complex in Riyadh, Saudi Arabia, completed 1974. Hon. FAIA 1988. Hon. DDes Greenwich, 2002. *Publications:* Modern Architecture in Britain, 1959; Trevor Dannatt: Buildings and Interiors 1951–72, 1972; (Editorial Adviser, and foreword) Buildings and Ideas 1933–83 from the Studio of Leslie Martin, 1983; (with P. Carolin) Sir Leslie Martin: architecture, education, research, 1996; Maritime Greenwich Campus, 2002; contribs to Architectural Rev., Architects' Jl, and various foreign journals; *relevant publication:* Trevor Dannatt: works and words, by R. Stonehouse, 2008. *Recreations:* the arts, including architecture. *Address:* (office) 77 Great Suffolk Street, SE1 0BU. *T:* (020) 7357 7100. *E:* trevordannatt@djarchitects.co.uk. *W:* www.trevordannatt.co.uk. *Club:* Travellers.

DANNENBAUM, Peggy Scott C.; *see* Czyzak-Dannenbaum.

d'ANSEMBOURG, Count Jan Mark Vladimir Anton de Marchant et; *see* de Marchant et d'Ansembourg.

DANTON, Joanna Ruth; *see* Place, J. R.

DANTZIC, Roy Matthew, CA; Chairman, ISG (formerly Interior Services Group) plc, since 2004; *b* 4 July 1944; *s* of David and Renee Dantzic; *m* 1969, Diane Clapham; one *s* one *d*. *Educ:* Brighton Coll., Sussex. CA 1968. Coopers & Lybrand, 1962–69; Kleinwort, Benson Ltd, 1970–72; Drayton Corporation Ltd, 1972–74; Samuel Montagu & Co. Ltd, 1974–80 (Exec. Dir, 1975); Mem. for Finance, BNOC, subseq. Finance Dir, Britoil plc, 1980–84; Dir, Pallas SA, 1984–85; Dir, Wood Mackenzie & Co., 1985–89; Finance Dir, Stanhope Properties, 1989–95; Dir, Merrill Lynch Internat., 1995–96; Man. Dir, British Gas Properties, then BG Property Hldgs, subseq. SecondSite Property Hldgs, 1996–2003 (non-exec. Dir, 2003–04). Chairman: Premier Portfolio Ltd, 1985–92; Associated British Cinemas Ltd, 1998–2000; Development Securities plc, 2003–07; Dep. Chm., Spazio Investment NV, 2007–09; non-executive Director: Moor Park (1958) Ltd, 1980–90; Saxon Oil plc, 1984–85; Total Oil Holdings, 1995–96; Airplanes Ltd, 1996–; Blenheim Bishop Ltd, 2003–07. pt-time Mem., CEGB, 1984–87; Pt-time Dir, BNFL, 1987–91. Mem., Council of Mgt, Architectural Heritage Fund, 2001– (Dep. Chm., 2014–). Trustee, Portman Estate, 2005–. Governor, Brighton Coll., 1990–98. *Recreations:* cinema, theatre, playing golf, watching cricket. *Clubs:* MCC; Moor Park Golf.

DARBISHIRE, Adrian Munro; QC 2012; *b* Guildford, 11 Nov. 1966; *s* of David Hamilton Darbishire and Gaynor Darbishire. *Educ:* Charterhouse; Balliol Coll., Oxford (MA Hons 1988); City Univ. London (DipLaw 1993); King's Coll. London (LLM 1994). Called to the Bar, Lincoln's Inn, 1993; in practice as barrister, specialising in criminal law, 1995–. Treasury Counsel, Central Criminal Court, 2007–12. *Address:* QEB Hollis Whiteman, 1–2 Laurence Pountney Hill, EC4R 0EU. *T:* (020) 7933 8855. *E:* barristers@qebhw.co.uk. *Club:* Groucho.

DARBY, John Oliver Robertson; Chairman, Arthur Young, Chartered Accountants, 1974–87; *b* 5 Jan. 1930; *s* of Ralph Darby and Margaret Darby (*née* Robertson); *m* 1955, Valerie Leyland Cole; three *s*. *Educ:* Charterhouse. FCA 1953. Pilot Officer, RAF, 1953–55; Arthur Young, Chartered Accts, 1955–87, Partner, 1959–87. Chairman: Nat. Home Loans Hldgs PLC, 1985–92; Property Lending Trust, later Property Lending Bank, PLC, 1987–92; Ultramar, 1988–91; BREL Gp, later ABB Transportation (Hldgs) Ltd, 1989–94; Director: British Rail Engineering Ltd, 1986–89; Lightgraphix Ltd, 1996–2009. *Recreations:* racing, golf. *Address:* The Tithe Barn, Headley, Bordon, Hants GU35 8PW. *Clubs:* Garrick, Royal Thames Yacht; Royal & Ancient Golf (St Andrews); Liphook Golf.

DARBY, Dr Michael Douglas, FRES; taxonomic entomologist; Managing Director, Malthouse Books, since 2009; Scientific Associate, Department of Life Sciences, Natural History Museum, since 2015; *b* 2 Sept. 1944; *s* of Arthur Douglas Darby and Ilene Doris Darby (*née* Eatwell); *m* 1977, Elisabeth Susan Done; two *s*. *Educ:* Rugby School; Reading Univ. (PhD). FRES 1977, FRGS 1984; AMA 1990. Asst to Barbara Jones, 1963; Victoria and Albert Museum: Textiles Dept, 1964–72; Prints and Drawings Dept, 1973–76; Exhibitions Officer, 1977–83; Dep. Dir, 1983–87; Hd of Publications, Exhibitions and Design, 1988–89; Surveyor Gen., Carroll Art Collection, 1990–94. Member: Crafts Council, 1984–88; IoW Adv. Cttee, English Heritage, 1986–; Council, Royal Entomol Soc., 1988–90; Council, National Trust, 1989–93; Council, Wilts Archaeol and Natural Hist. Soc., 1996–2001; Council, British Entomol and Natural Hist. Soc., 2009–; Chm., Wilts Natural Hist. Pubns Trust, 2000–. Has described over 80 new species of beetle from across the world and has several named after him. FRSA 1989. Ed., Recording Wiltshire's Biodiversity, 1996–2004; Natural Hist. Ed., Wiltshire Studies, 2000–. *Publications:* Marble Halls, 1973; Early Railway Prints, 1974, 2nd edn 1979; British Art in the Victoria and Albert Museum, 1983; John Pollard Seddon, 1983; The Islamic Perspective, 1983; (as Nic Ryman) Bye Bye Pests, 2008; Wiltshire Beetles, 2009; articles in art, architectural and entomological periodicals. *Recreations:* beetles, books. *Address:* The Old Malthouse, Sutton Mandeville, near Salisbury, Wilts SP3 5LZ. *T:* (01722) 714295.

DARBYSHIRE, Jane Helen, (Mrs Jane Darbyshire-Walker), OBE 1994; Consultant, Jane Darbyshire and David Kendall Ltd, since 2000 (Director, 1995–2000); *b* 5 June 1948; *d* of Gordon Desmond Wroe and Patricia Keough; *m* 1st, 1973, David Darbyshire (marr. diss. 1987); one *d*; 2nd, 1993, Michael Walker. *Educ:* Univ. of Newcastle upon Tyne (BA Hons, BArch Hons). RIBA. Architect: Ryder and Yates, Newcastle upon Tyne, 1972–75; Barnett Winskell, 1975–79; Partner, Jane and David Darbyshire, 1979–87; Dir, Jane Darbyshire Associates, 1987–95. Ext. Examr, Newcastle upon Tyne Univ., 1993–95. Mem., RIBA Nat. Council, 1998–2001; Board Member: Tyne and Wear Develt Corp., 1992–98; NE Regl Cultural Consortium, 1999–2001. *Recreations:* classical music, horse riding, art, English and French literature. *Address:* Jane Darbyshire and David Kendall Ltd, Millmount, Ponteland Road, Newcastle upon Tyne NE5 3AL.

DARBYSHIRE, Prof. Janet Howard, (Mrs G. M. Scott), CBE 2010 (OBE 1996); FRCP, FFPH, FMedSci; Director, MRC Clinical Trials Unit, 1998–2010; Professor of Epidemiology, University College London, 1997–2010, now Emeritus; Joint Director, NIHR Clinical Research Network (formerly UK Clinical Research Network), 2005–10; *b* 16 Nov. 1947; *d* of Philip and Jean Darbyshire; *m* 1976, Dr Geoffrey M. Scott, FRCP, FRCPath. *Educ:* Manchester Univ. (MB ChB 1970); London Sch. of Hygiene and Tropical Medicine (MSc 1990). MRCP 1973, FRCP 1988; FFPH 2001; FMedSci 2005. Mem., Scientific Staff, MRC, 1974–2010. Hon. Professor: Dept of Pharmacol. and Therapeutics, Univ. of Liverpool, 1994–; LSHTM, 1999–; Univ. of Leeds, 2007–. Hon. Consultant Physician: Royal Brompton Hosp., 1982–2010; Camden PCT, 1997–2010. *Publications:* contribs on clinical trials and epidemiol studies in tuberculosis, HIV infection and other diseases. *Recreations:* music, horse-riding, walking, reading, cooking, flying. *Address:* Flat 64, County Hall North Block, 5 Chicheley Street, SE1 7PN.

DARCEY, Michael William; Chief Executive Officer, News UK, 2013–15; *b* Oxford, 10 June 1965; *s* of Dr Warwick Darcey and Yvonne Darcey; *m* 1994, Julie Bishop; one *s* one *d*. *Educ:* St Patrick's Coll., Wellington, NZ; Victoria Univ., Wellington (BSc Hons Maths); London Sch. of Econs and Pol Sci. (MSc Econs). Mgt Consultant, KPMG, Wellington, NZ and London, 1987–89; Res. Associate, Putnam, Hayes & Bartlett, 1989–91; Partner, Lexecon Ltd, 1991–98; Dir of Strategy, 1998–2006, Chief Operating Officer, 2006–12, BSkyB. Non-exec. Dir, Home Retail Gp, 2010– (Sen. Ind. Dir, 2012–). Chm., Bd of Trustees, RTS, 2010–12. *Recreation:* mountains and water.

DARCY DE KNAYTH, 19th Baron *cr* 1332; **Caspar David Ingrams;** consultant engineer, since 2005; *b* 5 Jan. 1962; *s* of late Rupert George Ingrams and Baroness Darcy de Knayth (18th in line); *S* mother, 2008; *m* 1996, Catherine Ann Baker (marr. diss. 2013); three *s*. *Educ:* Eton Coll.; Reading Univ. (BSc (Hons) Mech. Engrg). Ops Mgr, Howden Wade, 1987–98; Engrg Mgr, Airscrew Ltd, 1998–2004. *Recreations:* walking, opera, family. *Heir:* *s* Hon. Thomas Rupert Ingrams, *b* 23 Oct. 1999. *Address:* The Orchard, Rookery Lane, Broughton, Stockbridge SO20 8AZ. *T:* (01794) 301628. *Club:* Brooks's.

DARELL, Sir Guy Jeffrey Adair, 9th Bt *cr* 1795, of Richmond Hill, Surrey; Director, Tysers Insurance Brokers, since 1999; *b* London, 8 June 1961; *o s* of Brig. Sir Jeffrey Lionel Darell, 8th Bt, MC and of Bridget Mary Darell (*née* Adair); *S* father, 2013, but his name does not appear on the Official Roll of the Baronetage; *m* 1988, (Justine) Samantha Reynolds; one *s* two *d*. *Educ:* Eton Coll.; RMA Sandhurst. Coldstream Guards, 1980–83. J. H. Minet, 1984–90; Fenchurch Insce Brokers, 1994–97; Windsor Insce Brokers, 1997–99. *Recreations:* tennis, ski-ing, shooting. *Heir:* *s* Harry Thomas Adair Darell, *b* 10 May 1995. *Address:* 5 Norland Square, W11 4PX. *T:* (020) 7228 9036. *E:* guy.darell@tysers.com. *Clubs:* Lansdowne, Annabel's.

DARESBURY, 4th Baron *cr* 1927, of Walton, co. Chester; **Peter Gilbert Greenall;** DL; Bt 1876; Chairman, The De Vere (formerly Greenalls) Group plc, 2000–06 (Director, 1982–2006); *b* 18 July 1953; *e s* of 3rd Baron Daresbury and his 1st wife, Margaret Ada, *y d* of C. J. Crawford; *S* father, 1996; *m* 1982, Clare Alison, *d* of late Christopher Nicholas Weatherby; four *s*. *Educ:* Eton; Magdalene Coll., Cambridge (MA); London Business Sch. (Sloan Fellowship). Man. Dir, 1992–97, Chief Exec., 1997–2000, Greenalls Gp; Chairman: Aintree Racecourse Co. Ltd, 1988–2014; Highland Gold Mining Ltd, 2002–04; Kazakh Gold, 2005–07; Tewlint Services Ltd, 2005–11; Nasstar plc, 2005–; Mallett plc, 2008–14; Stellar Diamonds plc, 2008–; Haydock Park Racecourse, 2013–; non-executive Director: Evraz, 2005–06; Sumatra Copper & Gold Ltd, 2007–11; RusAnt, 2007–; Bespoke Hotels, 2011–; Auriant Mining AB, 2012–; Pesto Restaurants, 2012–. Steward, Jockey Club, 2013–. DL Cheshire, 1993. *Heir:* *s* Hon. Thomas Edward Greenall, *b* 6 Nov. 1984. *Address:* Manor Farm, Wychough, Cheshire SY14 7NQ. *T:* (home) (01948) 860963, (office) (01948) 861900, *Fax:* (01948) 861483. *E:* peter.daresbury@daresburyltd.co.uk. *Clubs:* Jockey, MCC; Royal & Ancient Golf (St Andrews).

See also J. R. Weatherby, R. N. Weatherby.

DARKE, Christopher; Director, Regional Services, British Medical Association, since 2010; *b* 5 Aug. 1949; *s* of late Derek Herbert Darke and Helen Navina Darke (*née* Davies); *m* 1st, 1976, Marian Dyson (marr. diss. 1982); one *s* one *d*; 2nd, 1992, Lorraine Julie Hinchliffe; two *d*. *Educ:* Handsworth Secondary Sch., Birmingham. Engrg apprentice, GEC, 1967–70; Engrg Draughtsman, Lucas Industries, 1970–77; TU Officer, AUEW-TASS, 1977–82; Nat. Officer, AUEW-TASS, later MSF, 1982–92; Gen. Sec., BALPA, 1992–2002; Hd, Regl Services (England), BMA, 2002–10. Mem., Competition (formerly Monopolies and Mergers) Commn, 1998–2005. *Recreations:* flying, travel, reading, gardening. *Address:* (office) BMA House, Tavistock Square, WC1H 9JP.

DARKE, Dr Wendy; Head, BBC Natural History Unit, since 2012; *b* Gloucester, 29 May 1965; *d* of Robert William Darke and Janet Mary Darke; *m* 1996, Stephen Anthony Batty; two *d*. *Educ:* Univ. of Bristol (BSc Jt Hons Geol. and Zool. 1986); James Cook Univ., N Qld (PhD Marine Biol. 1991). BBC Natural History Unit: Researcher and Asst Producer, 1991–95; Producer and Dir, 1995–2000; Series Producer, 2000–06; Exec. Producer, 2006–12. Hon. DSc Bristol, 2015; Hon. DArt UWE, 2015. *Recreations:* family, friends, coral reefs, tennis, ski-ing, travel, Cornwall. *Address:* BBC Natural History Unit, BBC Bristol, Whiteladies Road, Bristol BS8 2LR. *T:* (0117) 974 2164. *E:* wendy.darke@bbc.co.uk.

DARLEY, Gillian Mary, OBE 2015; FSA; architectural writer and biographer; *b* 28 Nov. 1947; *d* of Lt Col Robert Darley, MC and Caroline (*née* Swanston Ward); *m* 1986, Michael Horowitz, QC; one *d* (one *s* decd). *Educ:* Courtauld Inst. of Art, London Univ. (BA Hons 1969); Birkbeck Coll., London (MSc Politics and Admin 1986). Journalist and broadcaster; contributor to daily and Sunday newspapers, magazines and professional press, 1975–; Architectural correspondent, Observer, 1991–93. Dir, Landscape Foundn, 1994–98. Trustee, SPAB (Chm., 1997–2000); Member: Lottery Architecture Adv. Cttee, Arts Council of England, 1996–2001; Council, 2008–15, Architecture Panel, 2014–, NT; London Diocesan Adv. Cttee, 2008–13; English Heritage Blue Plaques Panel, 2012–14. Pres., Twentieth Century Soc., 2014–. FRSA 1995; FSA 2007. Esher Award, SPAB, 2014. *Publications:* Villages of Vision, 1975, 2nd edn 2007; The National Trust Book of the Farm, 1981; Built in Britain, 1984; (with P. Lewis) Dictionary of Ornament, 1986; Octavia Hill: a life, 1990, 2nd edn 2010; (with A. Saint) The Chronicles of London, 1994; John Soane: an accidental romantic, 1999; Factory, 2003; John Evelyn: living for ingenuity, 2006; Vesuvius: the most famous volcano in the world, 2011; (with D. McKie) Ian Nairn: words in place, 2013. *Recreations:* gardening in a small space, Jack Russell, spending time in the desert.

DARLEY, Kevin Paul; freelance flat race jockey, retired 2007; Chief Executive, Professional Jockeys Association, 2009–12; *b* 5 Aug. 1960; *s* of Clifford Darley and Dorothy Thelma Darley (*née* Newby); *m* 1983, Debby Ford; two *d*. *Educ:* Colton Hills Comprehensive Sch., Wolverhampton. Apprentice Jockey to Reg Hollinshead, 1976–78 (Champion apprentice, 1978, with 70 winners); has ridden over 2,400 winners, incl. 71 Group winners (24 in Gp 1) in Britain and Europe, and 158 in one season, 2001; winner: French Derby, 1995, on Celtic Swing; St Leger, 2002, on Bollin Eric; English and Irish 1,000 Guineas, on Attraction, 2004; Champion Jockey, 2000. Jt Pres., Jockeys' Assoc. of GB, 2003–07. *Recreations:* shooting, golf, hunting, ski-ing. *Address:* The Old Granary, Gale Road, Alne, York, N Yorks YO61 1TH. *T:* (01347) 833015.

DARLING, family name of **Baron Darling**.

DARLING, 3rd Baron *cr* 1924; **Robert Julian Henry Darling;** chartered surveyor in private practice, since 1990; *b* 29 April 1944; *s* of 2nd Baron Darling and Bridget Rosemary Whishaw Darling (*née* Dickson); *S* father, 2003; *m* 1970, Janet Rachel (*née* Mallinson); two *s* one *d*. *Educ:* Wellington Coll.; RAC Cirencester. FRICS. Nuffield Scholar, Australia and NZ, 1984. Partner, Smith-Woolley, Chartered Surveyors, 1970–89. Vice-Chairman: Norfolk Mental Healthcare NHS Trust, 1993–97; Nat. Assoc. of Prison Visitors, 2000. Chairman: Gt Yarmouth and Waveney, Mind, 2001–08; Rural Enterprise (formerly Land Use and Access) Panel, NT, 2007–13. Vice-Chm., Nuffield Farming Scholarships Trust, 2014–. *Recreations:* fishing, gardening. *Heir: s* Hon. (Robert) James (Cyprian) Darling, *b* 6 March 1972. *Address:* Wood, Bishopsteignton, S Devon TQ14 9TN. *T:* (01626) 774446, *Fax:* (01626) 776187. *E:* jdarling@paston.co.uk. *Club:* Norfolk.

DARLING, Rt Hon. Alistair (Maclean); PC 1997; *b* 28 Nov. 1953; *m* 1986, Margaret McQueen Vaughan; one *s* one *d*. *Educ:* Aberdeen Univ. Admitted to Faculty of Advocates, 1984. Member: Lothian Regl Council, 1982–87; Lothian and Borders Police Bd, 1982–86. MP (Lab) Edinburgh Central, 1987–2005, Edinburgh SW, 2005–15. Shadow Chief Sec. to HM Treasury, 1996–97; Chief Sec. to HM Treasury, 1997–98; Secretary of State: for Social Security, 1998–2001; for Work and Pensions, 2001–02; for Transport, 2002–06; for Scotland, 2003–06; for Trade and Industry, 2006–07; Chancellor of the Exchequer, 2007–10; Shadow Chancellor of the Exchequer, 2010. Chm., Better Together, 2012–14. Gov., Napier Coll., Edinburgh, 1982–87. *Publications:* Back from the Brink: 1,000 days at Number 11, 2011.

[Created a Baron (Life Peer) 2015 but title not yet gazetted at time of going to press.]

DARLING, Rt Rev. Edward Flewett; Bishop of Limerick and Killaloe, 1985–2000; *b* 24 July 1933; *s* of late Ven. Vivian W. Darling and Honor F. G. Darling; *m* 1958, E. E. Patricia Mann; three *s* two *d*. *Educ:* Cork Grammar School; Midleton Coll., Co. Cork; St John's School, Leatherhead, Surrey; Trinity Coll., Dublin (MA). Curate: St Luke's, Belfast, 1956–59; St John's, Orangefield, Belfast, 1959–62; Incumbent, St Gall's, Carnalea, Co. Down, 1962–72; Chaplain, Bangor Hosp., Co. Down, 1963–72; Rector, St John's, Malone, Belfast, 1972–85; Minor Canon, Belfast Cathedral, 1974–85; Chaplain, Ulster Independent Clinic, Belfast, 1981–85. ARSCM 2010. Hon. FGCM 2006. *Publications:* Choosing the Hymns, 1984; (ed) Irish Church Praise, 1990; Sing to the Word, 2000; (ed) Church Hymnal, 5th edn 2000; (jtly) Companion to Church Hymnal, 2005; Understanding Hymns, 2007. *Recreations:* music, gardening. *Address:* 15 Beechwood Park, Moira, Craigavon, Co. Armagh BT67 0LL. *T:* (028) 9261 2982.

DARLING, Ian Galen; His Honour Judge Darling; a Circuit Judge, since 2009; *b* Sunderland, 27 Oct. 1962; *s* of William Martindale Darling, *qv* and Ann Edith Darling, OBE; *m* 1st, 1990, Tessa Ross (*née* Thompson) (marr. diss. 1999); 2nd, 2002, Emma Charlotte Sillars (marr. diss. 2012); one *s* one *d*. *Educ:* Winchester Coll.; King's Coll., London (LLB 1984). Called to the Bar, Middle Temple, 1985; a Recorder, 2003–09. *Recreations:* Newcastle United Football Club, Harlequins Rugby Club. *Address:* Snaresbrook Crown Court, 75 Hollybush Hill, E11 1QW. *Club:* Westoe Rugby Football.

See also P. A. Darling.

DARLING, Ian Marshall, OBE 2015; FRICS; a Vice President, Royal Society for the Protection of Birds, since 2013 (Chairman of Council, 2008–12); *b* Perth, Scotland, 16 April 1945; *s* of John Darling and Nora Darling; *m* 1971, Kathryn Pearman; one *s* one *d*. *Educ:* Perth Acad.; Coll. of Estate Mgt; Wye Coll., London (Dip. Farm Business Admin 1969). ARICS 1966, FRICS 1978. Partner, Bell Ingram Chartered Surveyors, 1974–96 (Man. Dir, 1987–96); Dir, Chesterton (Scotland), 1996–2001. Chm., RICS Scotland, 1997–98. Non-exec. Dir, British Waterways, 2000–06. Mem., Lands Tribunal for Scotland, 2004–13. Mem. Council, British Trust for Ornithology, 1994–99; Pres., Scottish Ornithologist Club, 1996–99; Chm., Isle of May Bird Observatory, 1999–. Mem. Court, Univ. of Edinburgh, 2004–09. Master, Edinburgh Merchant Co., 2000–01. *Recreations:* travel, natural history, birding. *Club:* New (Edinburgh).

DARLING, Judith K.; *see* Kirton-Darling.

DARLING, Paul Antony, OBE 2015; QC 1999; *b* 15 March 1960; *s* of William Martindale Darling, *qv*, and Ann Edith Darling; *m* 1st, 1983 (marr. diss.); 2nd, 1994 (marr. diss.); 3rd, 2013, Anne Camilla Frances, *d* of Brian John Barker, *qv* and Anne Barker (*see* Rt Hon. Dame A. J. Rafferty). *Educ:* Tonstall Sch., Sunderland; Winchester Coll. (Schol.); St Edmund Hall, Oxford (BA Jurisp. 1981; BCL 1982). Treas., Oxford Union, 1980. Called to the Bar, Middle Temple, 1983, Bencher, 2004; in practice, 1985–; Hd, Keating Chambers, 2010–15. Chairman: Technol. and Construction Bar Assoc., 2003–07; Access to the Bar Cttee, Bar Council, 2007–09; Mem., Gen. Council of the Bar, 2007–08. Dir, J. M. & W. Darling Ltd (pharmaceutical chemists), 1978–. Non-exec. Dir, Horserace Totalisator Bd, 2006–08; Mem., Horse Racing Betting Levy Bd, 2008–14; Chairman: Football Licensing Authy, 2009–11; Sports Grounds Safety Authy, 2011–15; Assoc. of British Bookmakers, 2014–. Ed., Construction Industry Law Letter, 1990–94; Mem., editl team, Keating on Building Contracts, 5th edn 1991 to 8th edn 2006. Trustee, Free Repn Unit, 2004–12. *Recreations:* horse racing, Newcastle United, Apostrophe Chambers. *Address:* Keating Chambers, 15 Essex Street, WC2R 3AA. *T:* (020) 7544 2600. *E:* pdarling@keatingchambers.com. *Clubs:* Garrick, Arts; Royal Ascot Racing (Mem. Cttee, 2004–06); South Shields and Westoe (South Shields).

See also I. G. Darling.

DARLING, Peter S.; *see* Stormonth Darling.

DARLING, Susan; writer; *b* 1942; *d* of Eric Francis Justice Darling and Monica Darling. *Educ:* Nonsuch County Grammar Sch. for Girls, Cheam; King's Coll., London (BA Hons). Joined BoT as Asst Principal, 1963; transf. to FCO, 1965; Nairobi, 1967–69; Second, later First Sec., Econ. and Social Affairs, UK Mission to UN, 1969–73; FCO, 1973–74; resigned, 1974; reinstated, 1975; FCO, 1975–78; Dep. High Comr and Head of Chancery, Suva, 1981–84; FCO, 1984–87; Consul-Gen., Perth, WA, 1987–88; resigned FCO, 1988; Dept of Chief Minister, NT, Australia, 1989–90; Quaker Service Australia, 1991–93; Aboriginal and Torres Strait Islander Commn, 1994–96; Law Soc. of England and Wales, 2000–02. *Recreations:* countryside, working horse. *Address:* Mayor House Farm Cottages, Farley Heath, Surrey GU5 9EW.

DARLING, William Martindale, CBE 1988 (OBE 1972); DL; FRPharmS; Managing Director, J. M. & W. Darling Ltd, since 1957; Chairman, Gateshead and South Tyneside (formerly South Tyneside, then South of Tyne) Health Authority, 1974–2002; *b* 7 May 1934; *s* of William Darling, MPS and Muriel Darling; *m* 1958, Ann Edith Allen; two *s*. *Educ:* Mortimer Road Primary Sch.; Newcastle Royal Grammar Sch.; Sunderland Polytechnic Sch. of Pharmacy. MPS 1956. Member: Medicines Commn, 1971–79; Health Educn Council, 1972–80; Pharmacy Bd, CNAA, 1972–78; Cttee on Safety of Medicines, 1979–86; Cttee on Review of Medicines, 1987–90; Health Service Supply Council, 1975–84 (Chm. and Vice-Chm.); Mem., Ministerial Adv. Bd, 2000–08, Chm., Audit Cttee, 2005–, NHS Purchasing and Supply Agency; Lay Mem., GMC, 1995–99; Chairman: Standing Pharmaceutical Adv. Cttee, 1974–2001; Nat. Pharmaceutical Supplies Gp, 1984–2009; Head, UK Pharm. Delegn to EU, 1972–2003; Pres., Pharm. Gp, EU, 1985–86, 2002; Mem., Comité Consultatif pour formation des pharmaciens, 1988–2003. Chairman: Standards Cttee, S Tyneside MBC, 2000–; Nat. Jt Registry Steering Cttee, 2002–09; Counter Fraud and Security Mgt Special HA, 2003–06. Pharmaceutical, later Royal Pharmaceutical, Society of Great Britain: Mem. Council, 1962–2001; Vice-Pres., 1969–71; Pres., 1971–73; Treas., 1992–95; Chm., Code of Ethics and Health Wkg Pty, 1970–2001. Mem., Council, NAHA, 1974–90 (Chm., 1980–82; Hon. Treasurer, 1988–89); first Chm., Nat. Assoc. of Health Authorities and Trusts, 1990–93; Pres., Internat. Hosp. Fedn, 1997–2000 (Mem., Exec., 1994–2000). Gov., Univ. of Sunderland (formerly Sunderland Poly.), 1989–2003 (Chm., 1994–2003; Hon. Fellow, 1990). DL Tyne and Wear, 2000. Pharm. Soc. Gold Medal, 1985. *Recreations:* horse racing, eating good food, growing prize flowers and vegetables, foreign travel. *Address:* 21 Sunniside Terrace, Cleadon Village, Sunderland SR6 7XE. *T:* (0191) 536 8783.

See also I. G. Darling, P. A. Darling.

DARLINGTON, Joyce B.; *see* Blow Darlington.

DARLINGTON, Stephen Mark, FRCO; Organist and Official Student in Music, Christ Church, Oxford, since 1985; *b* 21 Sept. 1952; *s* of John Oliver Darlington and Bernice Constance Elizabeth (*née* Murphy); *m* 1975, Moira Ellen (*née* Hill); three *d*. *Educ:* King's Sch., Worcester; Christ Church, Oxford (Organ Schol.; MA). Asst Organist, Canterbury Cathedral, 1974–78; Master of the Music, St Albans Abbey, 1978–85. Artistic Dir, Internat. Organ Fest., 1979–85. Choragus, Oxford Univ., 2001–. Pres., RCO, 1998–2000. Chm., Ouseley Trust, 2007–. DMus Lambeth, 2001. *Publications:* (ed jtly) Composing Music for Worship, 2003. *Recreations:* travel, walking, punting, Italian food. *Address:* Christ Church, Oxford OX1 1DP. *T:* (01865) 276195.

DARLOW, Annabel Charlotte; QC 2015; a Recorder, since 2010; *b* London, 19 March 1970; *d* of Clive Darlow and Rita Darlow. *Educ:* St Paul's Girls' Sch.; Westminster Sch.; St John's Coll., Cambridge (BA Eng. Lit. 1991); City Univ., London (DipLaw). Called to the Bar, Middle Temple, 1993; in practice as a barrister, 6KBW College Hill (formerly 6 King's Bench Walk), 1993–. Standing Counsel to BIS, 2012–. Mem., Glyndebourne Festival Soc. *Publications:* (ed and contrib.) EU Law in Criminal Practice, 2013. *Recreations:* family, opera and theatre, travel. *Address:* 6KBW College Hill, 21 College Hill, EC4R 2RP.

DARLOW, Paul Manning; His Honour Judge Darlow; a Circuit Judge, since 1997; *b* 7 Feb. 1951; *s* of late Brig. Eric William Townsend Darlow, OBE and Elsie Joan Darlow, JP (*née* Ring); *m* 1985, Barbara Joan Speirs; one *d*. *Educ:* Audley House Prep. Sch.; St Edward's Sch., Oxford; Mount Hermon Sch., Massachusetts; King's Coll., London (LLB). Called to the Bar, Middle Temple, 1973; in practice as barrister, London, 1974–78, Bristol, 1978–97; Asst Recorder, 1991–94; a Recorder, 1994–97. *Recreations:* sailing, tennis, bridge, walking, ski-ing. *Address:* Plymouth Combined Court Centre, 10 Armada Way, Plymouth, Devon PL1 2ER.

DARNBROUGH, Monica Anne, CBE 2003; PhD; Head of Bioscience Unit, Department of Trade and Industry, 1998–2005; independent consultant, writer and speaker on science policy; photographer; *b* 14 Aug. 1951; *d* of Cecil Charles Webb and Marjorie Edyth (*née* Perring); *m* 1974, Geoffrey Darnbrough (marr. diss.; he *d* 2015). *Educ:* Univ. of Nottingham (BSc Jt Hons (Physiol. and Psychol.) 1972; PhD (Develtl Biol.) 1979). Police Scientific Develt Br., Home Office, 1975–79; Department of Industry: Res. and Technol. and Space Div., 1979–80; Rayner study of res. estabts, 1980; Office of Chief Engr and Scientist, 1980–81; Office of Govt Chief Scientific Advr, Cabinet Office, 1981–83; Sec. to ACARD, 1981–83; IT Div., 1984–88, Personnel Div., 1989–93, DTI; Counsellor for Sci. and Technol., FCO, Paris, 1994–98. Member: Council, BBSRC, 2002–04; Commonwealth Scholarship Commn, 2006–12. Founder Mem., and Mem. Bd, Newton's Apple Foundn (formerly Newton's Apple Science Think Tank), 2006–. Hon. Sec., Twickenham Choral Soc., 2010–. Mem., PCC, 2001–05, 2009–13, Church Warden, 2005–09, St Bartholomew the Great. *Publications:* (contrib.) Handbook of Medicinal Chemistry, 2006. *Recreations:* choral singing, photography (exhibitions in Hampstead, 2010, 2011, and Dore Abbey, annually, 2007–14), looking at mountains, exploring the rest of Europe, weaving. *E:* mondarn@gmail.com.

DARNLEY, 11th Earl of, *cr* 1725; **Adam Ivo Stuart Bligh;** DL; Baron Clifton of Leighton Bromswold, 1608; Baron Clifton of Rathmore, 1721; Viscount Darnley, 1723; *b* 8 Nov. 1941; *s* of 9th Earl of Darnley and of Rosemary, *d* of late Edmund Basil Potter; *S* half-brother, 1980; *m* 1965, Susan Elaine Anderson (*see* Countess of Darnley); one *s* one *d*. *Educ:* Harrow; Christ Church, Oxford. Dir, City of Birmingham Touring Opera, 1990–2000. Chm., Herefordshire Historic Churches Trust, 2003–. Governor: Cobham Hall Sch., 1981–2013 (Vice Chm., 1991–2013); Hereford Cathedral Sch., 2003–11 (Chm., 2006–11). DL Herefordshire, 2010. *Heir: s* Lord Clifton, *qv*. *Address:* Horndean, 22 Broomy Hill, Hereford, Herefordshire HR4 0LH. *Club:* MCC.

DARNLEY, Countess of; Susan Elaine Bligh; Lord-Lieutenant of Herefordshire, since 2008; *b* 4 Sept. 1945; *d* of Sir Donald Forsyth Anderson and Margaret Elaine Anderson (*née* Llewellyn); *m* 1965, Hon. Adam Ivo Stuart Bligh (*see* Earl of Darnley); one *s* one *d*. Member: Hereford Diocesan Synod; Bishop of Hereford's Council; Council, Hereford Cathedral; formerly: Mem., Hereford and Worcs Probation Cttee; Mem., Council for Social Responsibility; Vice Chm., Worcs Ethics and Standards Cttee. JP 1977–2005; DL Worcs, 2000–08. *Address:* Horndean, 22 Broomy Hill, Hereford, Herefordshire HR4 0LH.

See also Lord Clifton.

DARRINGTON, Sir Michael (John), Kt 2004; FCA; Group Managing Director, Greggs plc, 1984–2008 (non-executive Director, 2008–09); Founder and Lead Campaigner, Pro Business Against Greed, since 2011; *b* 8 March 1942; *s* of George and Kathleen Darrington; *m* 1965, Paula Setterington; one *s* two *d*. *Educ:* Lancing Coll.; Harvard Business Sch. (PMD 1974). FCA 1965. Josolyne Miles and Co., 1960–66; United Biscuits, 1966–83: posts incl. Gp Export Acct; Commercial Dir, Foods Div.; Man. Dir, Sayers Confectioners Ltd, 1978–83. Prince of Wales Regl Ambassador, NE, BITC, 2003–04; Regional Councillor: NE, CBI, 1990–2009; Princes Trust, 2007–. Founder and Owner, Common Sense Soc., 2009–. Mem. Ct, Newcastle Univ., 2007–. Hon. DBA Sunderland, 2011; Hon. DCL Northumbria, 2011. *Recreations:* sailing, golf, reading, pyrotechnics.

DARROCH, His Honour Alasdair Malcolm; a Circuit Judge, 2000–12; *b* 18 Feb. 1947; *s* of Ronald George Darroch and Diana Graburn Darroch; *m* 1972, Elizabeth Lesley Humphrey; one *s*. *Educ:* Harrow Sch.; Trinity Coll., Cambridge. Articled Mills & Reeve, Solicitors, Norwich, 1969; admitted as solicitor, 1971; Partner, Mills & Reeve, 1974–2000; a Recorder, 1996–2000. Pres., Norfolk and Norwich Incorporated Law Soc., 1996–97. *Publications:* contrib. articles to legal press. *Recreations:* gardening, European travel, real ale.

DARROCH, Sir (Nigel) Kim, KCMG 2008 (CMG 1998); HM Diplomatic Service; Ambassador to United States of America, from Jan. 2016; *b* 30 April 1954; *s* of Alastair Macphee Darroch and Enid Darroch (*née* Thompson); *m* 1978, Vanessa Claire Jackson; one *s* one *d*. *Educ:* Abingdon Sch.; Durham Univ. (BSc Zool 1975). Joined FCO, 1976; First Secretary: Tokyo, 1980–84; FCO, 1985–86; Private Sec. to Minister of State, FCO, 1987–89; First Sec., Rome, 1989–92; Dep. Head, European Integration Dept, FCO, 1993–95; Head, Eastern Adriatic Dept, FCO, 1995–97; Counsellor (External Affairs), UK Perm. Rep. to EU, Brussels, 1997–98; Foreign and Commonwealth Office: Head, News Dept, 1998–2000; Dir, EU Comd, 2000–03; Dir Gen., EU Directorate, 2003–04; EU Advr to the PM and Hd,

European Secretariat, 2004–07; UK Permanent Rep. to the EU, Brussels, 2007–11; Nat. Security Advr, 2012–15. *Recreations:* squash, ski-ing, sailing, cinema. *Address:* c/o Foreign and Commonwealth Office, King Charles Street, SW1A 2AH.

DART, Dr Edward Charles, CBE 1997; CBiol, FRSB; Chairman, Plant Bioscience Ltd (formerly John Innes Centre Innovations), since 1999 (non-executive Director, 1997–99); *b* 8 March 1941; *s* of late Arthur and Alice Dart; *m* 1964, Jean Ellen Long; one *s* two *d*. *Educ:* Univ. of Manchester Inst. of Science and Technol. (BSc 1962; PhD 1965); Univ. of Calif, LA; Univ. of Calif, Berkeley. Imperial Chemical Industries: Sen. Res. Scientist, Petrochemical and Polymer Lab. (and Lectr in Org. Chem., Univ. of Liverpool), 1968–71; Sen. Res. Scientist, Corporate Lab., 1971–73; Jt Gp Head, Bioscience Gp, 1973–75; Gp Head, Bioscience, 1975–78; Jt Lab. Manager, Corporate Lab. Policy Gp, 1981–83; Head, Corporate Bioscience and Colloids Lab., 1983–85; Associate Res. Dir, Plant Protection Div., 1985–86; Res. Dir, ZENECA (formerly ICI) Seeds, 1986–97; Chief Executive Officer: Norwich Res. Park, 1997–98; AdProTech plc, 1997–99. Chm., Novacta Biosystems Ltd, 2004–05; Board Member: Poalis AS, 2004–05; Rainbow Seed Fund, 2004–10. Science and Engineering Research Council: Mem., Biotechnol. Directorate, 1981–84, Chm., 1984–89; Member: Molecular Biology Sub Cttee, 1980–82; Science Bd, 1985–88. Member: BBSRC, 1994–98 (Chm., Technol. Interaction Bd, 1994–97; Mem., Appointments Cttee, 1998–; Mem., Strategy Bd, 2005–08); BBSRC/Science Mus. Consensus Conf. Steering Cttee, 1994. Chairman: Biotechnol. Jt Adv. Bd, 1992–94; Agric., Horticulture and Forestry Foresight Panel, 1997–99; Member: Adv. Cttee on Genetic Manipulation, 1984–96; DTI/MAFF Agro Food Quality Link Cttee, 1991–98; John Innes Council, 1986–94; MAFF/AFRC Arable Crops Sectoral Gp, 1991–93; Agric. and Envmt Biotechnology Commn, 2000–05; Mem., Internat. Adv. Bd, 2001–07, Exec. Advr, 2008–09, Kansai Res. Inst. Pres., Berks and Oxfordshire Assoc. for Science Educn, 1989–92. *Publications:* review articles in scientific books; papers in chemical and bioscience jls. *Recreations:* travel, books, music, golf, gardening.

DART, Geoffrey Stanley; Director, Office of Manpower Economics, 2010–14; *b* 2 Oct. 1952; *s* of Wilfrid Stanley Dart and Irene Jean Dart; *m* 1974, Rosemary Penelope Hinton; one *s* one *d*. *Educ:* Torquay Boys' Grammar Sch.; St Peter's Coll., Oxford (BA and MA Mod. Hist.). Researcher, Electricity Council, 1974–77; Department of Energy: Energy Policy, Offshore Supplies, Oil Policy, Gas, Asst Private Sec. to Sec. of State, to 1984; Cabinet Secretariat, 1984–85; Principal Private Sec. to Sec. of State for Energy, 1985–87; Asst Sec., Electricity Div., 1987–89; Offshore Safety Div., 1989–91; Estabt and Finance Div., 1991–92; Department of Trade and Industry, later Department for Business, Enterprise and Regulatory Reform, then Department for Business, Innovation and Skills: Competitiveness Div., 1992–94; Under Sec., 1994–2014; Dir, Deregulation Unit, 1994; Hd, Regl Develt Div., 1995–96; Shell UK (on secondment), 1996; Dir, Insurance, 1997–98; Dir, Oil and Gas, 1998–2002; Dir, Strategy, 2003–05; Dir of Corporate Law and Governance, 2005–09; Dir, Advanced Manufacturing Industries, 2009–10. Director: Laing Engineering, 1991–96; European Investment Bank, 1994–96. Trustee, Public Concern at Work, 2013–. Gov., Gwyn Jones Sch., 1996–99. FRSA 2001. *Recreations:* gardening, reading, music, films. *E:* geoffrey.dart@sky.com.

DARTMOUTH, 10th Earl of, *cr* 1711; **William Legge;** Baron Dartmouth 1682; Viscount Lewisham 1711; Member (UK Ind) South West Region, European Parliament, since 2009; Chartered Accountant; *b* 23 Sept. 1949; *e s* of 9th Earl of Dartmouth and of Raine, Countess Spencer, *qv*; *S* father, 1997; *m* 2009, Mrs Fiona Handbury (*née* Campbell). *Educ:* Eton; Christ Church, Oxford; Harvard Business Sch. Secretary, Oxford Union Soc., 1969. Contested (C): Leigh, Lancs, Feb. 1974; Stockport South, Oct. 1974; contested (C) Yorkshire and the Humber Region, Eur. Parly elecns, 1999. Mem., UKIP. Founder, Kirklees Cable. *Recreation:* tennis. *Heir:* *b* Hon. Rupert Legge [*b* 1 Jan. 1951; *m* 1984, Victoria, *d* of L. E. B. Ottley; one *s* one *d*]. *Address:* Blakelea House, Marsden, near Huddersfield, W Yorks HD7 5AU. *Clubs:* Buck's; Travellers (Paris).

DARTON, Prof. Richard Charles, OBE 2011; PhD; FREng, FIChemE; Professor of Engineering Science, University of Oxford, 2000–14, now Emeritus; Fellow, Keble College, Oxford, 1992–2014 (by special election, 1992–2001), now Emeritus; *b* 1 July 1948; *s* of Allan John Darton and Beryl Clare Darton (*née* Davies); *m* 1974, Diana Mildred Warrell; two *s* one *d*. *Educ:* King's Sch., Rochester; Univ. of Birmingham (BSc 1970); Downing Coll., Cambridge (PhD 1973). FIChemE 1987. ICI Post-doctoral Res. Fellow, Univ. of Cambridge, 1973–75; various appts, Shell Internat. Petroleum, Netherlands, 1975–91; on secondment to Univ. of Oxford, from Shell UK, 1991–99; Reader in Chem. Engrg, 2001–14, Head, Dept of Engrg Sci., 2004–09, Univ. of Oxford; Sen. Res. Fellow and Tutor, Keble Coll., Oxford, 2001–14. President: IChemE, 2008–09 (Council Medal, 2005; Dep. Pres., 2007–08); EFCE, 2010–13. FREng 2000. *Publications:* (ed jtly) Chemical Engineering: visions of the world, 2003. *Recreations:* Scottish country dancing, reading history. *Address:* Department of Engineering Science, University of Oxford, Parks Road, Oxford OX1 3PJ. *E:* richard.darton@eng.ox.ac.uk.

DARVILL, Keith Ernest; Partner, Kenneth Elliott & Rowe, Solicitors, since 1999; *b* 28 May 1948; *s* of Ernest Arthur James Darvill and Ellen May (*née* Clarke); *m* 1971, Julia Betina de Saran; two *s* one *d*. *Educ:* Coll. of Law, Chester. Admitted solicitor, 1981. Port of London Authority: clerical posts, 1967–73; Asst Solicitor, 1973–84; Partner, Duthie Hart and Duthie, Solicitors, 1984–93; sole practitioner, 1993–97. MP (Lab) Upminster, 1997–2001; contested (Lab) same seat, 2001 and 2005. Mem. (Lab), Havering LBC, 2002– (Leader, Labour Gp, 2006–). Chm., Havering Fabian Soc. Chm. Govs, Havering Sixth Form Coll., 2002–. *Recreations:* tennis, gardening. *Address:* Kenneth Elliott & Rowe, Enterprise House, 18 Eastern Road, Romford RM1 3PJ. *Club:* Cranston Park Lawn Tennis (Upminster).

DARWALL SMITH, His Honour Simon Crompton; a Circuit Judge, 1992–2012; *b* 13 April 1946; *s* of late Randle Darwall Smith and Barbara Darwall Smith (*née* Crompton); *m* 1968, Susan Patricia Moss (*see* S. P. Darwall Smith); two *d*. *Educ:* Charterhouse. Called to the Bar, Gray's Inn, 1968; in practice on Western Circuit, 1968–92; a Recorder, 1986–92. *Recreations:* opera, travel, ballet, theatre, concerts. *Club:* Army and Navy.

DARWALL SMITH, Her Honour Susan Patricia; DL; a Circuit Judge, 1992–2012; *b* 27 Oct. 1946; *d* of late George Kenneth Moss, JP and Jean Margaret Moss (*née* Johnston); *m* 1968, Simon Crompton Darwall Smith, *qv*; two *d*. *Educ:* Howell's Sch., Denbigh. Called to the Bar, Gray's Inn, 1968; in practice on Western Circuit, 1968–92; a Recorder, 1986–92. Pres., Grateful Soc., 2012–13. Chm., Bristol NSPCC, 2014–. Gov., Red Maids' Sch., Bristol, 1990–2010. Maître, Bristol Commanderie de Bordeaux, 2015–. DL Bristol, 2004. *Recreations:* travel, opera, ballet, theatre, gardening. *E:* su.darwallsm@gmail.com. *Club:* Army and Navy.

DARWEN, 4th Baron *cr* 1946, of Heys-in-Bowland; **(David) Paul (Cedric) Davies;** Design Consultant, Green Factory Ltd, since 2008; *b* London, 20 Feb. 1962; *er s* of 3rd Baron Darwen and of Gillian Irene (*née* Hardy); *S* father, 2011; one *s*; *m* 1996, Leilani N. Kamen; two *s* one *d*, and one step *d*. *Educ:* Oxford Brookes Univ. (BSc (Hons) Construction Mgt). Designer, Reed Educational Books, 1986–91; freelance book designer, 1992–2007. *Heir:* *s* Hon. Oscar Kamen Davies, *b* 24 April 1996. *Address:* Oxford. *E:* paulkdavies@yahoo.co.uk.

DARWENT, Rt Rev. Frederick Charles; JP; Bishop of Aberdeen and Orkney, 1978–92; *b* Liverpool, 20 April 1927; *y s* of Samuel Darwent and Edith Emily Darwent (*née* Malcolm); *m* 1st, 1949, Edna Lilian (*d* 1981), *oc* of David Waugh and Lily Elizabeth Waugh (*née* McIndoe); twin *d*; 2nd, 1983, Roma Evelyn, *er d* of John Michie and Evelyn Michie (*née* Stephen). *Educ:* Warbreck Sch., Liverpool; Ormskirk Grammar Sch., Lancs; Wells Theological Coll., Somerset. Followed a banking career, 1943–61; War service in Far East with Royal Inniskilling Fusiliers, 1945–48. Deacon 1963; priest 1964, Diocese of Liverpool; Curate of Pemberton, Wigan, 1963–65 (in charge of St Francis, Kitt Green, 1964–65); Rector of: Strichen, 1965–71; New Pitsligo, 1965–78; Fraserburgh, 1971–78; Canon of St Andrew's Cathedral, Aberdeen, 1971; Dean of Aberdeen and Orkney, 1973–78. JP Aberdeen City, 1988. Hon. LTh St Mark's Inst. of Theology, 1974. *Recreations:* amateur stage (acting and production), music (especially jazz), calligraphy. *Address:* 107 Osborne Place, Aberdeen AB25 2DD. *T:* (01224) 646497. *Clubs:* Rotary International; Club of Deir (Aberdeens).

DARWIN, Prof. John Gareth, FBA 2012; DPhil; Professor of Global and Imperial History, and Director, Oxford Centre for Global History, University of Oxford; Fellow, Nuffield College, Oxford, since 1984; *b* Exeter, 29 June 1948; *s* of Gerald Meredith Darwin and Maud Phyllis Darwin; *m* 1973, Caroline Atkinson; three *d*. *Educ:* Brockenhurst Grammar Sch.; St John's Coll., Oxford (BA; MA); Nuffield Coll., Oxford (DPhil 1978). Lectr in Hist., Univ. of Reading, 1972–84; Beit Lectr in Commonwealth Hist., Univ. of Oxford, 1984. *Publications:* Britain, Egypt and the Middle East, 1981; Britain and Decolonization, 1988; The End of the British Empire, 1991; After Tamerlane, 2007; The Empire Project, 2009; Unfinished Empire, 2012; contrib. articles to learned jls. *Recreations:* walking, unskilled gardening. *Address:* Nuffield College, Oxford OX1 1NF. *T:* (01865) 278500. *E:* john.darwin@nuffield.ox.ac.uk.

DARWIN, Kelyn Meher B.; *see* Bacon Darwin.

DARZI, family name of **Baron Darzi of Denham**.

DARZI OF DENHAM, Baron *cr* 2007 (Life Peer), of Gerrards Cross in the county of Buckinghamshire; **Ara Warkes Darzi,** KBE 2002; PC 2009; MD; FRCS, FRCSI, FACS, FRCPSGlas, FMedSci; FRS 2013; Professor of Surgery, since 1996, Paul Hamlyn Professor of Surgery, since 2005, and Chair, Institute of Global Health Innovation, since 2010, Imperial College London; Consultant Surgeon: St Mary's Hospital, Paddington, since 1994; Royal Marsden Hospital, since 2005; Executive Chair, World Innovation Summit for Health, Qatar Foundation, since 2013; Chairman, London Health Commission, 2014; *b* 7 May 1960; adopted British citizenship, 2002; *m* 1991, Wendy Hutchinson; one *s* one *d*. *Educ:* RCSI (MB BCh, BAO 1984); TCD (MD 1992). FRCSI 1992; FRCS 1995; FACS 1998; FRCPSGlas 2003; FMedSci 2003. Consultant Surgeon/Sen. Lectr, Central Middx Hosp., 1993–94; Hd, Div. of Surgery, Anaesthetics and Intensive Care, Imperial Coll., London, 2004–07. Parly Under-Sec. of State, DoH, 2007–09. UK Business Ambassador, 2009–12; Exec. Chair, Global Health Policy Summit, 2012; Chm., Imperial Coll. Healthcare NHS Trust-Academic Health Science Partnership, 2012–14; non-exec. Dir, NHS Monitor, 2015–. Mem., EPSRC, 2013–. FCGI 2004. Hon. FREng 2006; Hon. FRCSE 2005. Sash of Independence, Qatar, 2014. *Publications:* Laparoscopic Inguinal Hernia Repair, 1994; Laparoscopic Colorectal Surgery, 1995; Clinical Surgery, 1996, 2nd edn 2003; Atlas of Operative Laparoscopy, 1997; over 800 articles in learned jls. *Address:* Imperial College London, St Mary's Hospital Campus, 10th Floor, QEQM Building, Praed Street, W2 1NY. *T:* (020) 7886 1310, *Fax:* (020) 7886 6950. *E:* a.darzi@imperial.ac.uk. *Clubs:* Athenæum, Mosimann's.

DASGUPTA, Partha; Chairman, Pensions Advisory Service, 2010–14; *b* 23 Jan. 1969; *s* of Purnendu Dasgupta and Chandana Dasgupta; *m* 2000, Uttara Moorthy. *Educ:* Links Primary Sch., Edinburgh; Leith Acad.; Heriot-Watt Univ. (BSc 1st Cl. Maths 1990); Birkbeck, Univ. of London (Grad. Dip. Econs with Dist. 2011). Valuation Analyst, Prudential, 1991–94; Barclays Global Investors: Associate, 1994–98; Principal, 1998–2003; Man. Dir, 2003–05; Dir of Investment and Finance, 2005–06, CEO, 2006–09, Pension Protection Fund. Non-executive Member: Statistics Authy, 2008–14; Superannuation Arrangements of Univ. of London, 2010–14; Investment Cttee, Save the Children (UK), 2009–14. Hon. LittD Heriot-Watt, 2008. *Recreations:* reading, yoga, hill walking in Scotland.

DASGUPTA, Sir Partha (Sarathi), Kt 2002; PhD; FRS 2004; FBA 1989; Frank Ramsey Professor of Economics, Cambridge University, 1994–2010, now Emeritus (Professor of Economics, 1985–94); Fellow of St John's College, Cambridge, since 1985; *b* 17 Nov. 1942; *s* of late Prof. Amiya Dasgupta and Shanti Dasgupta, Santiniketan, India; *m* 1968, Carol Margaret, *d* of Prof. James Meade, CB, FBA; one *s* two *d*. *Educ:* Univ. of Delhi (BSc Hons 1962); Trinity Coll., Cambridge (BA 1965; PhD 1968; Stevenson Prize, 1967; Hon. Fellow, 2010). Res. Fellow, Trinity Hall, Cambridge, 1968–71, Supernumerary Fellow, 1971–74; Lectr, 1971–75, Reader, 1975–78, Prof. of Econs, 1978–84, LSE (Hon. Fellow, 1994); Prof. of Econs and Philosophy, Stanford Univ., 1989–92. Sen. Res. Fellow, Inst. for Policy Reform, 1992–94. Visiting Professor: Stanford Univ., 1974–75 and 1983–84; Delhi Univ., 1978; Harvard Univ., 1987; Princeton Univ., 1988; Andrew D. White Prof.-at-Large, Cornell Univ., 2007–13; Prof. of Envmtl and Develt Econs, later Professorial Res. Fellow, Sustainable Consumption Inst., Manchester Univ., 2008–13. Res. Advr, WIDER (UN Univ., 1989–94); Univ. Fellow, Resources for the Future, Washington, 1998–. Chairman: Beijer Internat. Inst. of Ecological Econs, Stockholm, 1991–97; Internat. Scientific Adv. Bd, Wittgenstein Centre, Vienna, 2011–; Scientific Bd, Internat. Human Dimensions Prog. on Global Envmtl Change, Bonn, 2011–; Govt of India Commn on Greening India's Nat. Accounts, 2011–13; Member: Science Cttee, Santa Fe Inst., 1992–96; External Adv. Council, World Bank Inst., 1999–2005; Millennium Ecosystem Assessment Panel, 2000–05; External Adv. Bd, Earth Inst., Columbia Univ., 2002–; Annual Meeting Scientific Prog. Cttee, AAAS, 2006–09; Adv. Bd on Econ. Develt to Chief Economist, World Bank, 2009–. President: European Econ. Assoc., 1999; REconS, 1998–2001; Sect. F, BAAS, 2006; European Assoc. of Environmental and Resource Economists, 2010–11. For. Hon. Mem., Amer. Acad. of Arts and Scis, 1991; For. Mem., Royal Swedish Acad. of Scis, 1991; Hon. Mem., Amer. Econ. Assoc., 1997; Mem., Pontifical Acad. of Social Scis, 1998; MAE 2009; For. Associate, US Nat. Acad. of Scis, 2001; Foreign Member: Amer. Phil Soc., 2005; Istituto Veneto di Scienze, Lettere ed Arti, 2009. Fellow: Econometric Soc., 1975; Third World Acad. of Sci., 2002; Soc. for Advancement of Econ. Theory, 2013; Dist. Fellow, Ludwig-Maximilians Univ., Munich, 2011. Dr *hc*: Wageningen, 2000; Catholic Univ. of Louvain, 2007; Faculté Univ. Saint-Louis, 2009; Bologna, 2010; Tillberg, 2012; Harvard, 2013. Jt winner, Volvo Envmt Prize, 2002; John Kenneth Galbraith Award, Amer. Agricl Econs Assoc., 2007; Zayed Internat. Envmtl Prize, Dubai, 2011; Eur. Lifetime Achievement Award in Envmtl Econs, Eur. Assoc. Envmtl and Resource Econs, 2014. *Publications:* (with S. Marglin and A. K. Sen) Guidelines for Project Evaluation, 1972; (with G. Heal) Economic Theory and Exhaustible Resources, 1979; The Control of Resources, 1982; (with K. Binmore) Economic Organizations as Games, 1986; (with K. Binmore) The Economics of Bargaining, 1987; (with P. Stoneman) Economic Policy and Technological Performance, 1987; An Inquiry into Well-Being and Destitution, 1993; (with K. G. Mäler) The Environment and Emerging Development Issues, vols 1 and 2, 1997; (with I. Serageldin) Social Capital: a multifaceted perspective, 1999; Human Well-Being and the Natural Environment, 2001; Economics: a very short introduction, 2007; Selected Papers: vol. 1, Institutions, Innovations and Human Values, 2010, vol. 2, Poverty, Population and Natural Resources, 2010; articles on develt planning, optimum population, taxation and trade, welfare and justice, nat. resources, game theory, indust. org. and technical progress, poverty and unemployment, in Econ. Jl, Econometrica, Rev. of Econ. Stud., etc; *festschrift:* (ed S. Barrett, K-G Mäler and E. Maskin) Environment and Development Economics: essays in honour of Sir Partha Dasgupta, 2014; (ed D. Southerton and A. Ulph) Sustainable Consumption: multi-disciplinary perspectives, in honour of Sir Partha Dasgupta, 2014. *Address:* 1 Dean Drive, Holbrook Road, Cambridge CB1 7SW. *T:* (01223) 212179. *Club:* MCC.

DASH, Penelope Jane; Partner, McKinsey & Co., since 2002; *b* 27 Jan. 1963; *d* of Hugo and Margaret Dash; *m* 1998, Guy Palmer; three *s*. *Educ:* Robinson Coll., Cambridge (BA Hons 1984); Middlesex Hosp. Med. Sch., London Univ. (MB BS 1987); LSHTM (MSc 1992); Stanford Univ. (MBA 1994). MRCP 1990. Jun. hosp. posts, UCH and Middlesex Hosps, 1987–88; Barnet Gen. Hosp., 1988; Northwich P Hosp., 1988–90; Registrar in Public Health Medicine, NW Thames RHA, 1990–92; Mgt Consultant, Boston Consulting Gp, 1994–99; Hd of Strategy and Planning, DoH, 2000–01.

DASHWOOD, Sir (Arthur) Alan, KCMG 2013; CBE 2004; QC 2010; Professor of European Law, University of Cambridge, 1995–2009, now Emeritus; Fellow, Sidney Sussex College, Cambridge, 1995–2009, now Emeritus (Vice-Master, 1997–2000); Professor of Law, City University, since 2012; *b* 18 Oct. 1941; *s* of late Alan Stanley Dashwood and of Dorothy Mary Dashwood (*née* Childe); *m* 1971, Julie Rosalind Pashley. *Educ:* Michaelhouse, Natal, SA; Rhodes Univ., Grahamstown, SA (BA Hons 1962); Oriel Coll., Oxford (MA). Called to the Bar, Inner Temple, 1969, Bencher, 2001. Asst Lectr, Dept of Civil Law, Univ. of Glasgow, 1966–67; Lecturer: Dept of Law, UCW, Aberystwyth, 1968–73; Centre of European Governmental Studies, Univ. of Edinburgh, 1973–75; Reader, Univ. of Sussex, 1975–78; Legal Sec. to Advocate General, Court of Justice of ECs, 1978–80; Prof. of Law, Univ. of Leicester, 1980–87; Dir, Legal Service, Council of EU, 1987–94. Editor: European Law Rev., 1975–91; Common Market Law Rev., 1995–2009. *Publications:* The Substantive Law of the EEC, 1980, 6th edn (with D. Wyatt *et al*) as Wyatt and Dashwood's European Union Law, 2011; contrib. to legal jls. *Recreation:* salmon and trout fishing. *Address:* Sidney Sussex College, Cambridge CB2 3HU. *T:* (01223) 338874; Henderson Chambers, 2 Harcourt Buildings, Temple, EC4Y 9DB. *T:* (020) 7583 9020. *Clubs:* Athenæum; Porcupines.

DASHWOOD, Sir Edward (John Francis), 12th Bt *cr* 1707, of West Wycombe, Buckinghamshire; Premier Baronet of Great Britain; *b* 25 Sept. 1964; *o s* of Sir Francis Dashwood, 11th Bt and Victoria Ann Elizabeth Gwynne (*née* de Rutzen); *S* father, 2000; *m* 1989, Lucinda Nell (*née* Miesegaes); two *s* one *d*. *Educ:* Eton; Reading Univ. (BSc Estate Mgt). MRICS. Land Agent. *Recreations:* shooting, fishing, tennis, bridge. *Heir:* *s* George Francis Dashwood, *b* 17 June 1992. *Address:* West Wycombe Park, High Wycombe, Bucks HP14 3AJ. *T:* (01494) 524411/2. *Clubs:* White's, Pitt, Daniel's; Shikar; Eton Ramblers.

DASHWOOD, Sir Frederick George Mahon, 10th Bt *cr* 1684, of Kirtlington Park, Oxfordshire; *b* 29 Jan. 1988; *s* of Sir Richard James Dashwood, 9th Bt, TD and Kathryn Ann Dashwood (*née* Mahon); *S* father, 2013.

da SILVA, Joanna Gabrielle, OBE 2011; FREng; Director, International Development, Arup, since 2006; *b* Washington, DC; *d* of John Burke da Silva, CMG and Jennifer Jane da Silva. *Educ:* Trinity Coll., Cambridge (BA Engrg 1988; MA). CEng; MIStructE 1994; MICE 1995, FICE 2014; FREng 2008. Associate Dir, Buildings, Arup, 2000–04; Sen. Shelter Co-ordinator, UNHCR, Colombo, 2005. Vis. Sen. Fellow, Centre for Sustainable Develt, Univ. of Cambridge, 2003–. *Recreation:* mountaineering. *Address:* 116 Grosvenor Road, N10 2DT. *T:* (020) 8341 7057. *E:* jodasilva01@gmail.com.

DAUBENY DE MOLEYNS, family name of **Baron Ventry**.

DAUNCEY, Brig. Michael Donald Keen, DSO 1945; DL; *b* 11 May 1920; *o s* of late Thomas Gough Dauncey and Alice Dauncey (*née* Keen); *m* 1945, Marjorie Kathleen (*d* 2014), *d* of H. W. Neep, FCA; one *s* two *d*. *Educ:* King Edward's School, Birmingham; Inter. Exam., Inst. of Chartered Accountants. Commissioned, 22nd (Cheshire) Regt, 1941; seconded to Glider Pilot Regt, 1943; Arnhem, 1944 (wounded three times; taken prisoner, later escaped); MA to GOC-in-C, Greece, 1946–47; seconded to Para. Regt, 1948–49; Staff Coll., 1950; Instructor, RMA, 1957–58; CO, 1st Bn 22nd (Cheshire) Regt, 1963–66, BAOR and UN peace keeping force, Cyprus; DS plans, JSSC, 1966–68; Comdt, Jungle Warfare Sch., 1968–69; Comdt, Support Weapons Wing, Sch. of Infantry, 1969–72; Defence and Military Attaché, Madrid, 1973–75; retired 1976. Col, 22nd (Cheshire) Regt, 1978–85; Hon. Col, 1st Cadet Bn, Glos Regt (ACF), 1981–90. President: Glider Pilot Regtl Assoc., 1994–98; Double Hills Arnhem Commemoration-1978, 1999–; Vice Pres., Arnhem 1944 Veterans' Club, 2007–10; Leader, Airborne Pilgrimage to Arnhem, 2000, 2008. Hon. Life Mem., Arnhem 1944 Fellowship. DL Glos 1983. *Recreations:* travelling, tennis; also under-gardener. *Address:* Uley Lodge Coach House, Uley, Dursley, Glos GL11 5SN. *T:* (01453) 860216. *Club:* Army and Navy.

DAUNT, Katherine Mary; *see* Steward, K. M.

DAUNT, Sir Timothy Lewis Achilles, KCMG 1989 (CMG 1982); HM Diplomatic Service, retired; Lieutenant-Governor of the Isle of Man, 1995–2000; *b* 11 Oct. 1935; *s* of L. H. G. Daunt and Margery (*née* Lewis Jones); *m* 1962, Patricia Susan Knight; one *s* two *d*. *Educ:* Sherborne; St Catharine's Coll., Cambridge. 8th KRI Hussars, 1954–56. Entered Foreign Office, 1959; Ankara, 1960; FO, 1964; Nicosia, 1967; Private Sec. to Permanent Under-Sec. of State, FCO, 1970; Bank of England, 1972; UK Mission, NY, 1973; Counsellor, OECD, Paris, 1975; Head of South European Dept, FCO, 1978–81; Associate at Centre d'études et de recherches internationales, Paris, 1982; Minister and Dep. UK Perm. Rep. to NATO, Brussels, 1982–85; Asst Under-Sec. of State (Defence), FCO, 1985–86; Ambassador to Turkey, 1986–92; Dep. Under-Sec. of State (Defence), FCO, 1992–95. Chm., British Inst. at Ankara, 1995–2006. Chairman: Anglo-Turkish Soc., 2001–09; Ottoman Fund Ltd, 2005–09. *Address:* 20 Ripplevale Grove, N1 1HU.
See also K. M. Steward.

DAUNTON, Prof. Martin James, PhD, LittD; FBA 1997; Professor of Economic History, 1997–2015, and Head, School of Humanities and Social Sciences, 2012–15, University of Cambridge; Master of Trinity Hall, Cambridge, 2004–14; Fellow, Churchill College, Cambridge, since 2014; *b* 7 Feb. 1949; *s* of Ronald James Daunton and Dorothy May Daunton (*née* Bellett); *m* 1984, Claire Hilda Gabriel Gobbi. *Educ:* Barry Grammar Sch.; Univ. of Nottingham (BA 1970); Univ. of Kent (PhD 1974); LittD Cambridge, 2005. Lectr in Economic History, Univ. of Durham, 1973–79; University College London: Lectr in Economic History, 1979–85; Reader, 1985–89; Prof. of Modern History, 1989–92; Astor Prof. of British History, 1992–97; University of Cambridge: Fellow, Churchill Coll., Cambridge, 1997–2004; Chm., Faculty of History, 2001–03, Sch. of Humanities and Soc. Scis, 2003–05; Chm., Colls' Cttee, 2009–11. Vis. Fellow, ANU, 1985, 1994; Vis. Prof., Nihon Univ., Tokyo, 2000. Trustee: Nat. Maritime Mus., 2002–10; Barings Archive, 2007–14; Chm., Fitzwilliam Mus., 2008–14 (Syndic, 2006–08). Pres., RHistS, 2004–08 (Hon. Treas., 1986–91; Vice-Pres., 1996–2000; Convener, Studies in History, 1994–2000). Chair: Inst. of Historical Res., 1994–98; Res. Awards Adv. Cttee, Leverhulme Trust, 2012– (Mem., 2009–12); Mem., Adv. Bd, Inst. of Advanced Studies, Univ. of Durham, 2006–11. Consultant Ed., Oxford DNB, 1993–98; Member: Editorial Board: Historical Jl, 2000–15; English Historical Rev., 2001–13. Comr, Historic England (formerly English Heritage), 2014–. Hon. DLitt: UCL, 2006; Nottingham, 2010; Kent, 2011. *Publications:* Coal Metropolis: Cardiff 1870–1914, 1977; House and Home in the Victorian City, 1983; Royal Mail: the Post Office since 1840, 1985; A Property Owning Democracy?, 1987; Progress and Poverty: an economic and social history of Britain 1700–1850, 1995; Cambridge Urban History of Britain, 2000; Trusting Leviathan: the politics of taxation in Britain 1799–1914, 2001; Just Taxes: the politics of taxation in Britain 1914–79, 2002; Organisation of Knowledge in Victorian Britain, 2005; Wealth and Welfare: an economic and social history of Britain 1851–1951, 2007; State and Market in Victorian Britain, 2008; articles in learned jls. *Recreations:* collecting modern ceramics, opera, architectural tourism. *Address:* Primrose Farm, Primrose Farm Road, Little Wilbraham, Cambridge CB21 5JZ. *E:* mjd42@cam.ac.uk. *Club:* Reform.

DAURIS, James Edward; HM Diplomatic Service; High Commissioner to Sri Lanka and (non-resident) to the Maldives, since 2015; *b* Harlow, Essex, 15 Jan. 1966; *s* of Colin James Dauris and Prudence Ann Dauris (*née* Butterworth); *m* 1995, Helen Claire Parker; three *d*. *Educ:* Haileybury; Downing Coll., Cambridge (MA); Coll. of Law, London. Admitted as solicitor, 1991; Solicitor, Ashurst Morris Crisp, 1991–95; entered FCO, 1995; FCO, 1995–98; First Sec. (Commercial), Moscow, 1998–2002; Dep. Hd, EU Dept, FCO, 2002–03; Dep. Hd, 2003–04, Hd, 2004–05, S Asia Dept, FCO; Dep. Hd of Mission, Bogota, 2005–09; Finance Directorate, FCO, 2009–10; Ambassador to Peru, 2010–14. *Recreations:* travel, bird watching, choral singing. *Address:* c/o Foreign and Commonwealth Office, King Charles Street, SW1A 2AH.

DAUTH, John Cecil, AO 2011; LVO 1980; High Commissioner of Australia in the United Kingdom, 2008–12; *b* Brisbane, 9 April 1947; *s* of Cecil Neville Dauth and Olga Maud Dauth (*née* Acworth). *Educ:* Gosford High Sch.; Wesley Coll.; Univ. of Sydney (BA Hons; Hon. Fellow 1996). Joined Dept of Ext. Affairs, Australia, 1969; External Affairs Office, then Foreign Affairs Office: Third, later Second Sec., Lagos, 1970–72; First Sec. and Dep. Hd of Mission, Islamabad, 1974–77; on secondment as Asst Press Sec. to the Queen and Press Sec. to the Prince of Wales, 1977–80; Hd, Commonwealth and Multilateral Orgns Section, 1980–82; Chargé d'Affaires, Tehran, 1983–85; Consul-Gen., New Caledonia, 1986–87; Department of Foreign Affairs and Trade: Asst Sec., Public Affairs, 1987–89; Principal Private Sec. to Minister for Foreign Affairs, 1989–91; First Asst Sec., Internat. Security Div., 1991–93; High Comr in Malaysia, 1993–96; First Asst Sec., S and SE Asia Div., 1996–98; Dep. Sec., 1998–2001; Ambassador and Perm. Rep. to UN, NY, 2001–06; High Comr in NZ, 2006–08. Chm., Menzies Centre for Australian Studies, KCL. Trustee, British Red Cross, 2014– (Dep. Chm.). *Recreations:* sport (golf, cricket), music. *Club:* Royal Automobile.

DAVAN WETTON, Hilary John; Principal Conductor, City of London Choir, since 1989; Associate Conductor, London Mozart Players, since 2010; Artistic Director, Leicester Philharmonic Choir, since 2013; freelance conductor and broadcaster; *b* 23 Dec. 1943; *s* of late Eric Davan Wetton, CBE and (Kathleen) Valerie Davan Wetton (*née* Edwards); *m* 1st, 1964, Elizabeth Jane Tayler; three *d*; 2nd, 1989, Alison Mary Moncrieff Kelly; one *s* one *d*; 3rd, 2003, Dr Antonia Louise Vincent; one *d*. *Educ:* Westminster Sch.; Royal Coll. of Music (ARCM); Brasenose Coll., Oxford (BA, MA, DipEd). Director of Music: St Alban's Sch., 1965–67; Cranleigh Sch., 1967–74; Stantonbury Music Centre, 1974–78; St Paul's Girls' Sch., 1978–93; Tonbridge Sch., 1993–2006. Conductor: Guildford Choral Soc., 1968–; Milton Keynes City Orch., 1974–2007; Holst Singers, 1978–91; Wren Orch., 1990–; Scottish Schools Orch., 1984–95; Edinburgh Youth Orch., 1994–97; Hastings Phil. Choir, 2008–12; Surrey Fest. Choir, 2009–13; guest conducting and recording with Philharmonia, LPO, Royal Phil. Orch., BBC Concert Orch., Ulster Orch., orchestras in Bulgaria, Iceland, USA, Australia. Prof. of Conducting, Guildhall Sch. of Music, 2012–. Presenter, Classic FM Masterclass. Member: RSA; Pepys Soc. Hon. Fellow, Birmingham Conservatoire, 2011. Hon. MA Open, 1984; Hon. DMus De Montfort, 1994. Diapason d'Or for Holst recording, 1994. *Publications:* contrib. musical jls, The Lady, Guardian and Daily Telegraph. *Recreation:* tennis. *Address:* 25 North End Road, Steeple Claydon, Bucks MK18 2PG. *Club:* Garrick.
See also P. H. D. Wetton.

DAVENPORT; *see* Bromley-Davenport.

DAVENPORT, Major (retd) David John Cecil, CBE 1989; DL; Member, Rural Development Commission, 1982–90 (Deputy Chairman, April–Oct. 1988); *b* 28 Oct. 1934; *s* of late Major John Lewes Davenport, DL, JP, and Louise Aline Davenport; *m* 1st, 1959, Jennifer Burness (marr. diss. 1969); two *d*; 2nd, 1971, Lindy Jane Baker; one *s*. *Educ:* Eton College; Royal Military Academy, Sandhurst. Commnd into Grenadier Guards, 1954, retired 1967. RAC, Cirencester, 1968–69. Chairman, Leominster District Council, 1975–76. Chm., CoSIRA, 1982–88. Chm., Regional Adv. Cttee of the Forestry Commn (SW), 1974–87; Pres., Royal Forestry Soc., 1991–93. DL, 1974, High Sheriff, 1989–90, Hereford and Worcester. *Address:* Mansel Lacy House, Hereford HR4 7HQ. *T:* (01981) 590224. *Clubs:* Boodle's, MCC.

DAVENPORT, Hugo Benedick; editorial consultant, writer, journalist, critic, broadcaster, since 2001; *b* 6 June 1953; *s* of late (Arthur) Nigel Davenport and Helena Davenport (*née* White); *m* 1988, Sarah Mollison; one *s* one *d*. *Educ:* Westminster Sch.; Univ. of Sussex (BA 1st Cl.). Trainee journalist, Liverpool Daily Post & Echo, 1977–80; reporter/diarist, Observer, 1981–84; feature writer, Mail on Sunday, 1985–87; op-ed news feature writer, then film critic, Daily Telegraph, 1987–96; contributor, BBC World Service, 1992–96; editor: FT New Media Markets, 1997–2000; Broadband Media, 2000–01; Sen. Communications Consultant, Caseworks Customer Interaction, 2005–. FRSA 2003. *Publications:* Days that Shook the World, 2003. *Address:* Flat 4, 2 Waldegrave Park, Twickenham TW1 4TE. *E:* hugodavenport1@gmail.com.
See also J. A. Davenport.

DAVENPORT, Rev. Canon Ian Arthan; a Chaplain to the Queen, since 2015; Rector, Malpas and Threapwood, since 2010, and Bickerton, since 2011; *b* Stockport, Cheshire, 30 Dec. 1954; *s* of Norman and Margaret Lyndon Davenport. *Educ:* Aston Trng Scheme; Lincoln Theol Coll. Ordained deacon, 1987, priest, 1988; Curate, Holy Trinity, Blacon, Chester, 1987–91; Vicar: St Michael and All Angels, Newton, W Kirby, 1991–97; St Saviour, Oxton, Birkenhead, 1997–2010; Chaplain, Birkenhead Sch., 2003–10; Rural Dean: of Birkenhead, 2005–10; of Malpas, 2014–. Hon. Canon, Chester Cathedral, 2006–. Wing Chaplain, Merseyside Wing, ATC; Regl Chaplain, Wales and W Reg., ATC. *Recreations:* classical music, opera, walking, reading, the countryside. *Address:* The Rectory, Church Street, Malpas, Cheshire SY14 8PP. *T:* (01948) 860922. *E:* malpas.iandavenport@live.co.uk.

DAVENPORT, Jack Arthur; actor, since 1991; *b* Wimbledon, 1 March 1973; *s* of late (Arthur) Nigel Davenport and Maria Aitken, *qv*; *m* 2000, Michelle Gomez; one *s*. *Educ:* Dragon Sch.; Cheltenham Coll.; Univ. of East Anglia (BA Hons). *Theatre* includes: Hamlet, 1991; Enemies, Almeida, 2006; *films* include: The Talented Mr Ripley, 2000; Pirates of the Caribbean: The Curse of the Black Pearl, 2003, Dead Man's Chest, 2006, At World's End, 2007; Kingsman: The Secret Service, 2014; *television series:* This Life, 1995–97; Coupling, 2000–04; Swingtown, 2008; FlashForward, 2010; Smash, 2012; Breathless, 2013; The Good Wife, 2014. Hon. LittD UEA, 2013. *Address:* c/o Hamilton Hodell Ltd, 20 Golden Square, W1F 9JL. *Club:* Stage Golfing Society.

DAVENPORT, Maurice Hopwood, FCIB; Director, First National Finance Corporation plc, 1985–95; *b* 19 March 1925; *s* of Richard and Elizabeth Davenport; *m* 1954, Sheila Timms (*d* 2008); one *s* two *d*. *Educ:* Rivington and Blackrod Grammar Sch. FIB 1982. Served RN, 1943–46. Joined Williams Deacon's Bank, 1940; Sec., 1960; Asst Gen. Man., 1969; Dir, 1978–85, Man. Dir, 1982–85, Williams & Glyn's Bank; Dir, Royal Bank of Scotland Gp and Royal Bank of Scotland, 1982–85. *Recreations:* walking, gardening, reading. *Address:* Pines, Dormans Park, East Grinstead, West Sussex RH19 2LX. *T:* (01342) 870439.

DAVENPORT, Michael Hayward, MBE 1994; HM Diplomatic Service; European Union Ambassador to Serbia, since 2013; *b* 25 Sept. 1961; *s* of late Montague Davenport and Olive Margaret Davenport (*née* Brabner); *m* 1992, Lavinia Sophia Braun; one *s* two *d*. *Educ:* Gonville and Caius Coll., Cambridge (BA 1983, MA 1985); Coll. of Law, London. Lectr, Graz Univ., Austria, 1983–84; with Macfarlanes, Solicitors, 1986–88; admitted solicitor, 1988; joined FCO, 1988: est. British Know-How Fund for Poland, Warsaw, 1990–93; Hd, Peacekeeping Section, FCO, 1993–95; First Sec. (Political), Moscow, 1996–99; Dir of Trade Promotion and Consul-Gen., Warsaw, 2000–03; Dep. Hd of Mission, Cairo, 2004–07; Dir for Russia, Central Asia and S Caucasus, FCO, 2007–10; Ambassador to Serbia, 2010–13. *Recreations:* tennis, German literature, cooking. *Address:* c/o Foreign and Commonwealth Office, King Charles Street, SW1A 2AH.

DAVENPORT, Sara Jane; Founder, The Haven (formerly Haven Trust, then Breast Cancer Haven), since 1997; *b* 11 March 1962; *d* of David Davenport and late Jennifer Davenport (*née* Burness, later Zuridis); *m* 1988, Adrian Kyriazi (marr. diss. 2002); two *d*. *Educ:* N Foreland Lodge; Fitzwilliam Coll., Cambridge (BA 1983; MA). Publicity Dept, Hodder & Stoughton, 1983–84; Manager, Cadogan Gall., 1985–87; Sara Davenport Gall., Walton St, London, 1987–97; founded Haven Trust (breast cancer charity), 1997; opened London Haven, 2000, Hereford Haven, 2004, Leeds Haven, 2008. *Recreations:* travel, friends, complementary medicine. *Address:* 76 Chelsea Park Gardens, SW3 6AE. *T:* (020) 7352 4032. *E:* saradavenport@hotmail.com.

DAVENPORT, Hon. Simon Nicholas; QC 2009; *b* Plymouth, 10 Oct. 1963; *s* of Keith Robin Davenport and Baroness Wilcox, *qv*; *m* 2001, Angelika Brozler; two *s* two *d*. *Educ:* Blundell's Sch., Devon; Leeds Univ. (LLB Hons); Birkbeck Coll., London (BA Hons). Called to the Bar, Inner Temple, 1987; in practice as barrister specialising in commercial and corporate recovery. *Recreations:* history of art, sailing, cricket, cooking. *Address:* 3 Hare Court, Temple, EC4Y 7BJ. *T:* (020) 7415 7800, *Fax:* (020) 7415 7811. *E:* sdavenport@3harecourt.com. *Clubs:* Lansdowne, Royal Automobile; Royal London Yacht, St Mawes Sailing.

DAVENPORT-HINES, Richard Peter Treadwell, FRSL, FRHistS; historian and biographer; *b* London, 21 June 1953; *m* 1978, Frances Jane Davenport; one *s* (and one *s* decd). *Educ:* St Paul's; Selwyn Coll., Cambridge (Corfield Exhibnr; BA 1975; PhD 1980). FRHistS 1984. Res. Fellow, LSE, 1982–86; slush-pile reader, Macmillan Publishers, 1987–89; Res. Associate, Oxford DNB, 1995–. Trustee: London Liby, 1996–2005; Royal Literary Fund, 2008–. Judge: Cosmo Davenport-Hines Prize for Poetry, 2008–; Tony Lothian Prize, Biographer's Club, 2008; PEN-Hessell Tiltman Prize, 2010; Ackerley Prize, 2011–; RSL Jerwood Prizes, 2012; Soc. of Authors' Travelling Scholarships, 2015–. FRSL 2003. *Publications:* Dudley Docker, 1984 (Wolfson Prize for Hist. and Biog., 1985; Wadsworth Prize, 1986); (ed) Speculators and Patriots, 1986; (ed) Markets and Bagmen, 1986; (ed) British Business in Asia since 1860, 1989; Sex, Death and Punishment, 1990; The Macmillans, 1992; Glaxo, 1992; Vice, 1993; Auden, 1995; Gothic, 1998; The Pursuit of Oblivion, 2001; A Night at the Majestic, 2006; (ed) Letters from Oxford: Hugh Trevor-Roper to Bernard Berenson, 2006; Ettie: the intimate life of Lady Desborough, 2008; (ed) Hugh Trevor-Roper's Wartime Journals, 2011; Titanic Lives, 2012; An English Affair, 2013 (Paddy Power Political History Book of the Year 2014); (ed) One Hundred Letters from Hugh Trevor-Roper, 2014; Universal Man: the seven lives of Maynard Keynes, 2015; Edward VII: the cosmopolitan king, 2016; *contributor:* Appleyard and Schedvin, Australian Financiers, 1988; Levy-Leboyer and Teichova, Historical Studies in International Corporate Business, 1989; Porter and Teich, Sexual Knowledge, Sexual Science, 1994; Bucknell and Jenkins, Auden Studies, 1994; Chen and Skidelsky, High Time for Reform, 2001; Parini, British Writers, 2002; Parini, World Writers in English, 2004; Stanford, The Death of a Child, 2011; Louis, Irrepressible Adventures with Britannia, 2013; contrib. reviews to Guardian, Literary Rev., Spectator, Sunday Times, TLS and other periodicals. *Recreations:* quelling Torschlusspanik, encouraging Europhilia. *Address:* 51 Elsham Road, W14 8HD; Le Meygris, 07200 Ailhon, France. *E:* richarddavenporthines@hotmail.com. *Clubs:* Athenæum, Brooks's, Cranium.

DAVENTRY, 4th Viscount *cr* 1943; **James Edward FitzRoy Newdegate;** R. K. Harrison Insurance Group Ltd, since 1998; *b* 27 July 1960; *s* of 3rd Viscount Daventry and Hon. Rosemary, *e d* of 1st Baron Norrie, GCMG, GCVO, CB, DSO, MC; *S* father, 2000; *m* 1994, Georgia, *yr d* of John Stuart Lodge; one *s* two *d*. *Educ:* Milton Abbey; RAC Cirencester (MRAC). Surveyor, Shakespear, McTurk and Graham, 1980–83; Bain Dawes plc, 1983–87; Penrose Forbes Ltd, 1987–98. Mem. Cttee, Warwicks County and Land Assoc., 2000–. Gov., The Lady Katherine Leveson Charity. Patron: Mary Ann Evans Hospice; George Eliot Fellowship. *Recreations:* shooting, fishing, racing, golf, farming, occasional gardening. *Heir:* *s* Hon. Humphrey John FitzRoy Newdegate, *b* 23 Nov. 1995. *Address:* Arbury, Nuneaton, Warwickshire CV10 7PT. *Clubs:* White's, Turf, MCC; Bean; Sunningdale, Trevose, Blackwell.

DAVEY, Alan, CBE 2015; Controller, BBC Radio 3, since 2015; *b* 12 Nov. 1960; *s* of late William Patrick Davey and Alwyn Davey (*née* Dorrington); partner, Patrick Feeny, *qv*. *Educ:* Univ. of Birmingham (BA Hons (English Lang. and Lit.) 1982); Merton Coll., Oxford (MLitt (English) 1985); Birkbeck Coll., London (MA Hist. 1998). Admin. Trainee, DHSS, 1985; Sec. to Inquiry into Child Abuse in Cleveland, 1987; Private Sec. to Minister of State for Health, 1988–90; Hd, AIDS Treatment and Care, DoH, 1990–92; Hd, Nat. Lottery Bill Team, DNH, 1992–93; Principal Private Sec. to Sec. of State for Nat. Heritage, 1993–94; Hd, European Business, Medicines Control Agency, 1995–97; Sec., Royal Commn on Long Term Care, 1997–99; Fulbright/Helen Hamlyn Scholar, 1999; Hd, Arts Div., 2001–03, Dir of Arts and Culture, subseq. of Culture, 2003–08, DCMS; Chief Exec., Arts Council England, 2008–15. Chm., Internat. Fedn of Arts Councils and Cultural Agencies, 2009–14; Member: Access to the Professions Working Forum, 2010–14; Creative Industries Council, 2011–14. Hon. DLitt Birmingham, 2011; Hon. DArt Teesside, 2012. *Recreations:* music, football, medieval Scandinavian literature, ancient history, cultural theory, Apple Macintosh computers. *Address:* BBC, Broadcasting House, W1A 1AA. *T:* (020) 7765 4928. *E:* alan.davey@bbc.co.uk. *Club:* Two Brydges.

DAVEY, Hon. Sir David Herbert P.; *see* Penry-Davey.

DAVEY, Rt Hon. Edward (Jonathan); PC 2012; *b* 25 Dec. 1965; *s* of late John George Davey and Nina Joan (*née* Stanbrook); *m* 2005, Emily Jane Gasson; one *s* one *d*. *Educ:* Nottingham High Sch.; Jesus Coll., Oxford (BA 1st Cl. Hons PPE); Birkbeck Coll., London (MSc Econs). Sen. Econs Advr to Lib Dem MPs, 1989–93; Mgt Consultant, Omega Partners, 1993–97. MP (Lib Dem) Kingston and Surbiton, 1997–2015; contested (Lib Dem) same seat, 2015. Lib Dem spokesman: on econ. affairs, 1997–2001; for London, 2000–01; on Treasury affairs, 2001–02; on ODPM affairs, 2002–05; for education and skills, 2005–06; for trade and industry, 2006; on foreign affairs, 2007–10; Parly Under-Sec. of State, BIS, 2010–12; Sec. of State for Energy and Climate Change, 2012–15; Chm., Lib Dem Campaigns and Communications, 2006–08; Chief of Staff to Lib Dem Leader, 2006–07. Mem., Treasury Select Cttee, 1999–2001. FRSA 2001. Hon. Testimonial, RHS, and Cert. of Commendation from Chief Constable of Brit. Transport Police (for rescuing a woman who had fallen on the track at Clapham Junction), 1995. *Recreations:* walking, music.

DAVEY, Eric; Chairman, Sea Fish Industry Authority, 1996–2002 (Deputy Chairman, 1990–96); *b* 16 Jan. 1933; *s* of William James Davey and Doris Evelynne Davey; *m* 1955, Janet Nicholson; two *d*. *Educ:* Woodbridge Sch.; Ilminster Sch. With Bank of England, 1953–88, Agent, Newcastle Br., 1980–88; Newcastle Building Society: Dir, 1988–2001; Dep. Chm., 1992–98; Chm., 1998–2001; Pres., 2001–04. *Recreations:* foreign travel, motoring, reading, theatre.

DAVEY, Francis, MA; Headmaster of Merchant Taylors' School, 1974–82; *b* 23 March 1932; *er s* of Wilfred Henry Davey, BSc and Olive (*née* Geeson); *m* 1st, 1960, Margaret Filby Lake, MA Oxon, AMA (marr. diss. 2004), *o d* of Harold Lake, DMus Oxon, FRCO; one *s* one *d*; 2nd, 2005, Patricia Quaife, *er d* of late Alfred Grover Quaife. *Educ:* Plymouth Coll.; New Coll., Oxford (Hon. Exhibr); Corpus Christi Coll., Cambridge (Schoolmaster Fellow Commoner). 1st cl. Class. Hon. Mods 1953, 2nd cl. Lit. Hum. 1955, BA 1955, MA 1958. RAF, 1950–51; Classical Upper Sixth Form Master, Dulwich Coll., 1955–60; Head of Classics Dept, Warwick Sch., 1960–66; Headmaster, Dr Morgan's Grammar Sch., Bridgwater, 1966–73. *Publications:* (with R. Pascoe) The Camino Portugués, 1997; William Wey, 2000; (with P. Quaife) The Camino Inglés, 2000; The Itineraries of William Wey, 2010; Richard of Lincoln: a medieval doctor travels to Jerusalem, 2013; Heart of Oak: the lost letters of Admiral Gardner, 2015; articles in Enciclopedia dello Spettacolo, Classical Review, Jl of Royal Instn of Cornwall, Devon and Cornwall Notes and Queries. *Recreations:* Rugby, swimming, gardening, travel. *Address:* 1 North Street, Topsham, Exeter, Devon EX3 0AP. *T:* (01392) 873251. *Clubs:* East India, Devonshire, Sports and Public Schools; Union (Oxford).

DAVEY, Grenville; artist; Visiting Professor, University of the Arts, London (formerly London Institute), since 1997; Artist in Residence, Isaac Newton Institute for Mathematical Sciences, University of Cambridge, since 2012; *b* 28 April 1961; *s* of Clifford Henry and Lillian Joyce Davey. *Educ:* Goldsmiths' Coll., London. Artist in Residence, Dept of Theoretical Physics, QMUL, 2010–11. Exhibitions: Lisson Gall., London, 1987; Stichting De Appel Foundn, Amsterdam, 1990; Kunsthalle, Berne, 1991; Kunstverein für die Rheinlande und Westfalen, Dusseldorf, 1992; Le Crypte Jules-Noriac, Limoges, 1993; Württembergischer Kunstverein, Stuttgart, 1994; Henry Moore Foundn, Dean Clough Foundn, 1994; Mus. of Modern Art, Vienna, Kunstverein, Hanover, 1996; Odense, Denmark, and Yorks Sculpture Park, 1999; Peggy Guggenheim, Venice, 2002; LSHTM, 2004; Tate Modern, 2005; William Morris Gall., London, 2006; No 1 Canada Square, London, 2007; Olympic Park, London, 2011; 'Chelsea Space', UAL, 2014. Turner Prize, 1992. *Recreation:* work.

DAVEY, Jon Colin; Chairman, Media Matrix Partnership, 1996–2003; *b* 16 June 1938; *s* of late Frederick John Davey and Dorothy Mary Davey; *m* 1962, Ann Patricia Streames; two *s* one *d*. *Educ:* Raynes Park Grammar Sch. Joined Home Office, 1957; served in Civil Defence, Immigration, Criminal Policy, Prison and Criminal Justice Depts; Asst Sec., Broadcasting Dept, 1981–85; Dir-Gen., Cable Authy, 1985–90; Dir of Cable and Satellite, ITC, 1991–96; Dir, Communications Equity Associates Internat., 1996–98. Asst Sec., Franks Cttee on Sect. 2 of Official Secrets Act, 1971–72; Secretary: Williams Cttee on Obscenity and Film Censorship, 1977–79; Hunt Inquiry into Cable Expansion and Broadcasting Policy, 1982. Vice-Chm., Media Policy Cttee, Council of Europe, 1983–84; Member: British Screen Adv. Council, 1990–96; Adv. Panel on Public Appointments, DCMS, 1999–2007. Ed., Insight, 1997–2008. Hon. Fellow, Soc. of Cable Television Engrs, 1994. Silver Medal, RTS, 1999. *Recreations:* lawnmaking, Bach, English countryside, theatre. *Address:* 71 Hare Lane, Claygate, Esher, Surrey KT10 0QX. *T:* (01372) 810106. *E:* joncdavey@ntlworld.com.

DAVEY, Julian; mountaineer and mountain leader, since 1998; adviser, Citizens Advice Bureau, since 2012; *b* 24 July 1946; *s* of Frederick Victor Davey and Dorothy Davey (*née* Stokes); *m* 1971, Prof. Katherine O'Donovan (marr. diss. 2004); one *d*; *m* 2007, Dr Kate Keohane. *Educ:* Kingston Grammar Sch.; Selwyn Coll., Cambridge; Inst. of Education, London Univ. (MA 1973). British Council: Ethiopia, 1969–72; E Africa Dept, 1973–75; Mgt Accountant, 1975–78; Malaysia, 1978–81; Dep. Controller, Finance, 1981–85; Dir, Hong Kong, 1985–90; Regl Dir, Asia-Pacific, 1992–94; Internat. Advr, Anglia Polytechnic Univ., 1994–97. Chm., Hesket Newmarket Brewery, 2000–10. *Recreations:* climbing, ski-ing, caving, running, furniture making, performing arts. *Address:* Potts Gill, Caldbeck, Cumbria CA7 8LB. *T:* (016974) 78773. *Clubs:* Alpine; Eagle Ski; Eden Valley Mountaineering; Kendal Caving; Hong Kong (Hong Kong).

DAVEY, Marcus John, OBE 2012; Artistic Director and Chief Executive Officer, The Roundhouse, since 1999; *b* Malvern, 5 July 1967; *s* of Robin and Ruth Davey; *m* 1997, Tatty Theo; two *s*. *Educ:* Dartington Coll. of Arts (BA Hons). Administrator, Dartington Internat. Summer Sch., 1989–95; Dir, Dartington Arts Centre, 1992–95; Artistic Dir, Norfolk and Norwich Fest., 1995–99. Chairman: Hackney Youth Orchestras Trust, 1991–97; PRS Foundn, 1999–2006; Dartington Internat. Summer Sch. Foundn, 2010–; Co-Chm., Adv. Council, Creative Industries Fedn; Member: Adv. Bd, Clore Leadership Foundn, 2004–10; Bd, Arts Council, 2011–; Barclays Life Skills Adv. Bd, 2014. Trustee, Longplayer Trust, 2010–. FRSA. *Recreations:* cooking, music, walking. *Address:* The Roundhouse, Chalk Farm Road, NW1 8EH. *T:* (020) 7424 9991, *Fax:* (020) 7424 9992. *E:* marcus.davey@roundhouse.org.uk. *Clubs:* Savile, Soho House.

DAVEY, Peter Gordon, CBE 1986; Partner, Crossfell Consultants, since 1998; *b* 6 Aug. 1935; *s* of late Lt-Col Frank Davey, Royal Signals and H. Jean Davey (*née* Robley); *m* 1961; two *s* two *d*. *Educ:* Winchester Coll.; Gonville and Caius Coll., Cambridge (1st Cl. Hons Mech. Scis Tripos, pt 2 Electrical; MA 1961). MIET; MBCS 1967. Engineer: GEC Applied Electronics Labs, Stanmore, 1958–61; Lawrence Radiation Lab., Berkeley, Calif, 1961–64; Guest Researcher, Heidelberg Univ., 1964–65; Oxford University: Project Engr, Nuclear Physics Lab., 1966–79; Co-ordinator, Indust. Robotics Research Prog., SERC, 1979–84; Head of Inter-active Computing Facility, Rutherford Lab., SRC, 1978–80; of Robot Welding Project, Engrg Sci. Lab., 1979–84; Sen. Res. Fellow, St Cross Coll., 1981–89. Tech. Dir, Electro Pneumatic Equipment Ltd, Letchworth, 1968–87; Man. Dir, Meta Machines Ltd, 1984–87 (Dir, 1984–91); Man. Dir, Oxford Intelligent Machines Ltd, 1990–98; Dep. Chm., Oxim Ltd, 1999–2000. Ed., Open University Press Industrial Robotics Series, 1982–92. Hon. Prof., UCW, Aberystwyth, 1988–93. Hon. DSc Hull, 1987. *Publications:* (with W. F. Clocksin) A Tutorial Introduction to Industrial Robotics: artificial intelligence skills, 1982; (contrib.) Robot Vision, 1982; contribs to learned jls on robotics and image analysis systems. *Recreations:* buildings restoration, Mousehole harbour lights, sailing. *Address:* Trewennack, Raginnis, Penzance, Cornwall TR19 6NJ.

DAVEY, Peter John, OBE 1998; architectural writer and critic; Editor, The Architectural Review, 1981–2005; *b* 28 Feb. 1940; *s* of John Davey and Mary (*née* Roberts); *m* 1968, Carolyn Pulford; two *s*. *Educ:* Oundle Sch.; Edinburgh University (BArch). RIBA. News and Features Editor, 1974, Man. Editor, 1978, Architects' Journal; Managing Editor, Architectural Review, 1980. Mem. Council, RIBA, 1990–93 (Vice Pres. and Hon. Librarian, 1991–93). Editl Dir, EMAP Construct, 1995–2005. Member Jury, including: RIBA Royal Gold Medal, 1990–95, 2007, 2008; Carlsberg Architecture Prize, 1992, 1995, 1998; Brunel Prize, 1996; Constitutional Court Competition, S Africa, 1997–98; Hellenic Inst. of Arch. Nat. Prize, 2000; competition for Oil Ministry HQ bldg, Tehran, Iran, 2002; Jury Chairman: Prague Castle Pheasantry (pleasure grounds) Competition, 1997; Emerging Architecture Awards, 1999–2007; Commonwealth Assoc. of Architects Student Comp., Wellington, NZ, 2000, Bloemfontein, S Africa, 2003, Dhaka, Bangladesh, 2007; Internat. Architectl Photography Comp., Stuttgart, 2005. Pierre Vago Award, Internat. Cttee of Architectl Critics, 2005; Médaille d'argent de l'Analyse Architecturale, Acad. d'Architecture, Paris, 2005; Jean Tschumi Prize for architectl criticism, Internat. Union of Architects, 2005. Kt 1st Cl., Order of White Rose (Finland), 1991. *Publications:* Architects' Journal Legal Handbook (ed), 1973; Arts and Crafts Architecture, 1980, 2nd edn 1995; Heikkinen & Komonen, 1997; Peter Zumthor, 1998; Exploring Boundaries: the architecture of Wilkinson Eyre, 2007; Engineering for a Finite Planet: sustainable solutions by Buro Happold, 2009; numerous articles in architectural jls and books. *Recreations:* pursuit of edible fungi, fishing, cooking, classical music, travelling in Italy, architecture. *Address:* 44 Hungerford Road, N7 9LP. *Club:* Athenæum.

DAVEY, Dr Ronald William, LVO 2001; Physician to the Queen, 1986–2001; *b* 25 Oct. 1943; *s* of Frederick George Davey and Cissy Beatrice Davey (*née* Lawday); *m* 1966; one *s* one *d*. *Educ:* Trinity School of John Whitgift; King's College London; King's College Hosp. (MB BS; FFHom; AKC); MD Imperial Coll., London, 1997. Gen. med. practice, 1970–77; research into electro-acupuncture, 1978–79; private med. and homoeopathic practice, 1980–2001; nutrition and counselling practice, 2001–. Under auspices of Blackie Foundation Trust, research into antibiotic properties of propolis, Nat. Heart and Lung Inst., Univ. of London, 1984–94; Hon. Med. Res. Dir, 1980–98, Vice Pres., 1998–, Blackie Foundation Trust. Vis. Schol., Green Coll., Oxford, 1998. Freeman, City of London, 1997; Liveryman, Barbers' Co., 2001– (Freeman, 1997). *Publications:* medical papers. *Recreations:* Scottish reeling, opera, reading, writing. *Address:* BM Box 4019, London, WC1N 3XX.

DAVEY, Valerie; *b* 16 April 1940; *m* 1966, Graham Davey; twin *d* one *s*. *Educ:* Birmingham Univ. (MA); London Univ. Inst. of Educn (PGCE). Teacher: Wolverhampton; Tanzania; FE Coll. Mem. (Lab) Avon CC, 1981–96. MP (Lab) Bristol West, 1997–2005; contested (Lab) same seat, 2005. Mem., Educn and Employment Select Cttee, 1997–2005. Exec. Chair, Council for Educn in the Commonwealth, 2005–10. Mem., Amnesty International. Hon. DEd UWE, 2008. *Recreations:* gardens, cooking esp. marmalade.

DAVEY SMITH, Prof. George, MD, DSc; FRSE; Professor of Clinical Epidemiology, University of Bristol, since 1994; *b* 9 May 1959; *s* of George Davey Smith and Irmgaard Davey Smith (*née* Beckmann). *Educ:* Stockton Heath Primary Sch.; Lymm Grammar Sch.; Queen's Coll., Oxford (BA 1981; DSc 2000); Jesus Coll., Cambridge (MB BChir 1984; MD 1991); London Sch. of Hygiene and Tropical Medicine (MSc 1988). Clinical Res. Fellow (Hon. Clinical Med. Officer), Welsh Heart Prog., Cardiff, 1985–86; Wellcome Res. Fellow in Clinical Epidemiol., Dept of Community Medicine, UCL and Middlesex Sch. of Medicine, 1986–89; Lectr in Epidemiol., LSHTM, 1989–92; Sen. Lectr in Public Health and Epidemiol., and Hon. Sen. Registrar, 1992–93, Consultant in Public Health Medicine, 1993–94, Univ. of Glasgow. Hon. Prof., Dept of Public Health, Univ. of Glasgow, 1996–. Vis. Prof., Dept of Epidemiol. and Popn Health, LSHTM, 1999–. FMedSci 2006; FRSE 2014. Foreign Associate, Inst. of Medicine, 2008. *Publications:* (ed jtly) The Sociology of Health Inequalities, 1998; (jtly) The Widening Gap: health inequalities and policy in Britain, 1999; (ed jtly) Inequalities in Health: the evidence presented to the independent inquiry into inequalities in health, 1999; (ed jtly) Systematic Reviews in Health Care: meta-analysis in context, 2nd edn, 2001; (ed jtly) Poverty, Inequality and Health in Britain, 1800–2000: a reader, 2001; Health Inequalities: lifecourse approaches, 2003; (with M. Shaw) Cultures of Health, Cultures of Illness, 2004; (jtly) The Handbook of Inequality and Socioeconomic Position: concepts and measures, 2007; over 1000 articles in jls. *Recreations:* poor squash, bad tennis and abysmal badminton. *Address:* MRC Integrative Epidemiology Unit, University of Bristol, Oakfield House, Oakfield Grove, Bristol BS8 2BN. *T:* (0117) 928 7329.

DAVID, Prof. Anthony Sion, MD; FRCP, FRCPGlas, FRCPsych, FMedSci; Professor of Cognitive Neuropsychiatry, since 1996, and Vice Dean, Academic Psychiatry, since 2014, King's College London; *b* 27 Sept. 1958. *Educ:* Univ. of Glasgow (MB ChB 1980; MD 1993); MSc Cognitive Neuropsychol. London 1990. FRCP 1994; FRCPGlas 1994; FRCPsych 1998; FMedSci 2002. Registrar: in Neurol., Southern Gen. Hosp., Glasgow, 1982–84; in Psychiatry, Maudsley Hosp., London, 1984–87; Institute of Psychiatry, University of London: Lectr, 1987–90; Sen. Lectr, 1990–94; Reader, 1994–96. *Publications:* (ed with X. Amador) Insight and Psychosis, 1998, 2nd edn 2004; (with T. Kircher) Self in Neuroscience and Psychiatry, 2003; (ed jtly) Lishman's Organic Psychiatry, 2009; contrib. scientific articles on schizophrenia and neuropsychol. *Recreations:* football, jazz piano. *Address:* Institute of Psychiatry, Psychology and Neuroscience, King's College London, PO Box 68, De Crespigny Park, SE5 8AF. *T:* (020) 7848 0138. *E:* anthony.david@kcl.ac.uk.

DAVID, George Alkiviades, OBE 2009; Chairman, Coca-Cola HBC AG, since 1981; *b* Petra, Cyprus, 1937; *s* of Alkiviades David and Kalliope David (*née* Leventis); *m* 1964, Kaity Hordovatzi; two *s* one *d*. *Educ:* English Sch., Nicosia; Lindisfarne Coll., Wales; Univ. of Edinburgh (BCom 1959). Gp Dir, A. G. Leventis Orgn, Nigeria, 1959–80. Chm., EFG Eurobank, 2013–14; Mem. Bd, Titan, 2001–13. Co-founder, Hellenic Initiative, 2012–. Mem., Bilderberg Gp, 1997–2010. Regent, Univ. of Edinburgh, 2012–. Chm. Bd, Centre for Asia Minor Studies, 2009–; Vice Chm. Council, Univ. of Cyprus, 2015–. Chm., Greek Cttee, A. G. Leventis Foundn, 1981–; Mem. Bd, Hellenic Foundn for Eur. and Foreign Policy, 1999–2013 (Mem., Hon. Cttee, 2013–). Chm., Bd of Trustees, Campion Sch., 2000–07, now Chm. Emeritus. Hon. Dr Nat. and Kapodistrian, Athens, 2013. Archon Maistor, Ecumenical Patriarchate of Constantinople, 2003. Mem., Order of Federal Republic (Nigeria), 2008. *Recreations:* golf, gardening, reading. *Address:* 40 Gladstone Street, 1095 Nicosia, Cyprus. *T:* 22667706, *Fax:* 22675002. *E:* george.david@leventis.net. *Club:* Loch Lomond Golf.

DAVID, Prof. (Julian) Saul Markham, PhD; writer, since 1991; Professor of Military History, University of Buckingham, since 2009; *b* Monmouth, 27 March 1966; *s* of Robin David and Cherry David (*née* Quinn); *m* 1995, Louise Harper; three *d*. *Educ:* Ampleforth Coll.; Univ. of Edinburgh (MA Hons); Univ. of Glasgow (PhD 2001). Staff writer, Haymarket Publishing, 1989–91; broadcaster, 1999– (TV series incl. Escape From…, Boots, Bullets and Bandages). Vis. Prof. of Mil. Hist., Hull Univ., 2007–08. Judge, Guggenheim-Lehrman Mil. Book Award, 2012–14. Mem., Acad. Adv. Cttee, Nat. Army Mus., 2013–. Trustee, RA Mus. *Publications:* Churchill's Sacrifice of the Highland Division, 1994; Mutiny at Salerno, 1995; The Homicidal Earl, 1997; Military Blunders, 1997; Prince of Pleasure, 1998; The Indian Mutiny, 2002; Zulu, 2004; Victoria's Wars, 2006; The Bengal Army and the Outbreak of the Indian Mutiny, 2009; Zulu Hart, 2009; Hart of Empire, 2010; All the King's Men, 2012; Mud and Bodies, 2013; 100 Days to Victory, 2013; Operation Thunderbolt, 2015. *Recreations:* tennis, ski-ing, sailing, Arsenal FC, playing bagatelle (with daughters), making cocktails, poker. *Address:* c/o Peter Robinson, Rogers, Coleridge and White, 20 Powis Mews, W11 1JN. *T:* (020) 7221 3717. *W:* www.sauldavid.co.uk. *Clubs:* Soho House, Frontline.

DAVID, Prof. Miriam Elizabeth, PhD; FAcSS; Professor of Sociology of Education, Institute of Education, University of London, 2006–10, now Emerita; Visiting Professor of Education, Centre for Higher Education Equity Research, University of Sussex, since 2010; *b* Keighley, Yorks, 9 Aug. 1945; *d* of Curt L. David and Esther L. David; *m* 1st, 1974, Prof. Robert Reiner (marr. diss. 1994); one *s* one *d*; 2nd, 2002, Prof. Jeffrey Duckett. *Educ:* Univ. of Leeds (BA Hons Sociol. 1966); Queen Mary Coll., Univ. of London (PhD 1975). Researcher: Univ. of London, at Inst. of Psychiatry, LSE and QMC, 1966–73; Harvard Univ. Grad. Sch. of Educn, 1972–73; Lectr in Social Admin, 1973–85, Grad. Studies Officer, 1982–85, Univ. of Bristol; Hd, Dept of Social Scis, 1986–92 (Prof., 1989), Prof. of Social Scis and Dir, Social Scis Res. Centre, 1992–97, South Bank Poly., later London South Bank Univ.; Dean of Res. and Prof., London Inst., 1997–99; University of Keele: Prof. of Policy Studies in Educn, 1999–2005; Dir, Grad. Sch. of Social Scis, 2002–04; Res. Dean, Faculty of Humanities and Social Scis, 2004–05; Associate Dir (Higher Educn), ESRC's Teaching and Learning Res. Prog., on secondment to Dept of Educn, Cambridge Univ., 2004–05, then Inst. of Educn, Univ. of London, 2005–09, Dir, 2009. Vis. Prof. of Policy Studies in Educn, Univ. of Keele, 2005–10; Vis. Res. Consultant, Centre for Med. Educn, St George's, Univ. of London, 2010–12. International Research Consultant: Acad. of Finland, 2010–; Eur. Res. Foundn, 2010–; Res. Council of Norway, 2010–; Univ. of Helsinki, 2010–. Mem., Exec. Editl Bd, British Jl Sociol. of Educn, 1990–2012; Co-Editor: Jl Social Policy, 1993–98; 21st Century Society, 2005–09. Member: Gender and Education Assoc., 2002– (Policy Officer, 2010–14); Governing Council, SRHE, 2005–11; Res. Grants Bd, ESRC, 2006–09. Trustee: British Shalom-Salaam Trust, 2004–12; Women's Therapy Centre, 2010– (Chair, 2010–). FAcSS (AcSS 1999) (Chair of Council, 2005–09). FRSA 1994. Hon. DEd Bedfordshire, 2009. *Publications:* School Rule in the USA, 1975; (jtly) Gambling Work and Leisure, 1976, re-issued 2013; Reform, Reaction and Resources, 1977; Half the Sky: an introduction to women's studies, 1979; The State, the Family and Education, 1980, re-issued 2015; (with C. New) For the Children's Sake, 1985; (jtly) Mothers and Education: inside out?, 1993; (jtly) Choosing a Secondary School, 1993; Parents, Gender and Education Reform, 1993; (jtly) Mother's Intuition? Choosing Secondary Schools, 1994; (ed) The Fragmenting Family: does it matter?, 1998; (ed with D. Woodward) Negotiating the Glass Ceiling: senior women in the academic world, 1998; (jtly) Closing the Gender Gap, 1999; Personal and Political: feminisms, sociology and family lives, 2003; (jtly) Degrees of Choice: social class, race and gender in higher education, 2005; (with P. Alldred) Get Real About Sex, 2007; (jtly) Improving Learning Through Widening Participation to Higher Education, 2010; Feminism, Gender and Universities: politics, passion and pedagogies, 2014; A Feminist Manifesto for Education, 2015. *Recreations:* travel, film, theatre, walking, esp. with my King Charles Cavalier, re-evaluation co-counselling. *Address:* (office) 20 Bedford Way, WC1H 0AL. *T:* (020) 7612 6825. *E:* miriam.david@ioe.ac.uk; 11 Hugo Road, N19 5EU. *E:* miriamedavid3@gmail.com.

DAVID, Prof. Paul Allan, PhD; FBA 1995; Professor of Economics, 1969–2005, now Emeritus, and Senior Fellow, Stanford Institute for Economic Policy Research, since 1990, Stanford University, California; Professor of Economics and Economic History, University of Oxford, 1994–2002, now Emeritus; Senior Research Fellow, All Souls College, Oxford, 1993–2002, now Emeritus Fellow; *b* 24 May 1935; *s* of Henry David and Evelyn (*née* Levinson); *m* 1st, 1958, Janet Williamson (marr. diss. 1982); one *s* one *d*; 2nd, 1982, Sheila Ryan Johansson; one step *s* one step *d*. *Educ:* High Sch. of Music and Art, NYC; Harvard Coll. (AB *summa cum laude* 1956); Pembroke Coll., Cambridge (Fulbright Schol.); Harvard Univ. (PhD 1973); MA Oxon. Stanford University, California: Asst Prof. of Econs, 1961–66; Associate Prof., 1966–69; William Robertson Coe Prof. of American Econ. Hist., 1978–94; Sen. Fellow, Oxford Internet Inst., 2002–08; Prof. Titulaire, Chaire Innovation et Régulation des Services Numérique, École Polytechnique and Telecom ParisTech, France, 2008–11. Vis. Fellow, All Souls Coll., Oxford, 1967–68 and 1992–93; Vis. Prof. of Econs, Harvard Univ., 1972–73; Pitt Prof. of American Hist. and Institutions, Univ. of Cambridge, 1977–78; Vis. Res. Prof. in Econs of Sci. and Technol., Rijksuniversiteit Limburg, 1993–95; Marshall Lectr, Univ. of Cambridge, 1992. Guggenheim Fellow, 1975–76; Fellow, Center for Advanced Study in the Behavioral Scis, 1978–79; Professorial Fellow, UN Univ. MERIT, 2004–. Dir, Cie Saint-Gobain, 2002–07. Pres.-Elect and Pres., Econ. Hist. Assoc., 1987–89 (Vice Pres., 1986); Past Pres., Western Econ. Assoc. Internat., 2011 (Vice Pres., 2009; Pres., 2010). Mem. Council, REconS, 1996–2002. Fellow: Internat. Econometrics Soc., 1975; Amer. Acad. Arts and Scis, 1979; Amer. Philos. Soc., 2003. Phi Beta Kappa, Harvard, 1956. Hon. Dr Inf. and Commns Scis, Torino, 2003. *Publications:* (ed) Households and Nations in Economic Growth, 1974; Technical Choice, Innovation and Economic Growth, 1975, 2nd edn 2003; Reckoning with Slavery, 1976; The Economic Future in Historical Perspective, 2003; over 200 articles, contribs to edited books and govt and internat. orgn reports. *Recreations:* photography, Chinese cooking, tennis, walking. *Address:* Department of Economics, Stanford University, Stanford, CA 94305–6072, USA. *Fax:* (650) 7255702. *E:* pad@stanford.edu.

DAVID, Robert Allan, MBE 2011; Head of International and Tourism Division, Department of Employment, 1989–91; *b* 27 April 1937; *s* of George David and Mabel Edith David; *m* 1961, Brenda Marshall; three *d*. *Educ:* Cathays High Sch., Cardiff. BoT, 1955–71; Dept of Employment, 1971–91. Mem. (Ind.), Tandridge DC, 2003–15. *Recreations:* badminton, tennis, gardening. *Address:* The Briars, Ninehams Road, Tatsfield, Westerham, Kent TN16 2AN. *T:* (01959) 577357.

DAVID, His Honour Sir Robert Daniel George, (Sir Robin), Kt 1995; QC 1968; DL; a Circuit Judge (formerly Chairman, Cheshire Quarter Sessions), 1968–97; *b* 30 April 1922; *s* of late Alexander Charles Robert David and late Edrica Doris Pole David (*née* Evans); *m* 1st, 1944, Edith Mary Marsh (*d* 1999); two *d*; 2nd, 2000, Zena (*née* Cooke). *Educ:* Christ Coll., Brecon; Ellesmere Coll., Salop. War Service, 1943–47, Captain, Royal Artillery. Called to Bar, Gray's Inn, 1949; joined Wales and Chester Circuit, 1949. Dep. Chairman, Cheshire QS, 1961; Dep. Chairman, Agricultural Land Tribunal (Wales), 1965–68; Commissioner of Assize, 1970; Dep. Presiding Judge, Judicial Trng, 1970–74; Mem., Parole Bd for England and Wales, 1971–74. DL Cheshire 1972. *Publications:* The Magistrate in the Crown Court, 1982. *Address:* Kings Bench House, 165 Springvale Road, Winchester, Hants SO23 7LF. *T:* (01962) 884555.

DAVID, Saul; *see* David, J. S. M.

DAVID, Prof. Timothy Joseph, PhD, MD; FRCP, FRCPCH; Professor of Child Health and Paediatrics, University of Manchester, and Hon. Consultant Paediatrician, Royal Manchester (formerly Booth Hall) Children's Hospital, Manchester, since 1991; two *s*. *Educ:* Clifton Coll., Bristol; Univ. of Bristol (MB ChB 1970; PhD 1975; MD 1981); DCH 1976 (RCP). MRCP 1976, FRCP 1986; FRCPCH 1997. Posts in Bristol, Taunton and Plymouth, 1970–78; Tutor/Lectr in Child Health, 1978–81, Sen. Lectr, Dept of Child Health, 1981–91, Univ. of Manchester. *Publications:* (jtly) Applied Paediatric Nursing, 1982; (ed) Cystic Fibrosis in Children, 1986; (ed) Recent Advances in Paediatrics, vol. 9, 1991–vol. 23, 2006; (ed) Role of the Cystic Fibrosis Nurse Specialist, 1992; Food and Food Additive Intolerance in Childhood, 1993; Symptoms of Disease in Childhood, 1995 (Dutch edn, 1999); (jtly) Eczema in Children, 1995; (ed) Major Controversies in Infant Nutrition, 1996; (jtly) Problem-based Learning in Medicine, 1999; author or editor of over 390 scientific and med. pubns, inc. conf. procs. *Recreations:* baseball, cricket, cricket umpiring, classical music, opera. *Address:* Royal Manchester Children's Hospital, Manchester M13 9WL. *T:* (0161) 276 1234, *Fax:* (0161) 904 9320.

DAVID, Wayne; MP (Lab) Caerphilly, since 2001; *b* 1 July 1957; *s* of late D. Haydn David and of Edna A. David; *m* 1991, Catherine Thomas (marr. diss. 2008). *Educ:* Cynffig Comprehensive Sch.; University Coll., Cardiff (BA Hons History; PGCE); University Coll., Swansea. History teacher, Brynteg Comprehensive Sch., Bridgend, 1983–85; Mid Glam Tutor Organiser, S Wales Dist, WEA, 1985–89. Policy Advr, Wales Youth Agency, 1999–2001. MEP (Lab) S Wales, 1989–94, S Wales Central, 1994–99. Treas., 1989–91, Leader, 1994–98, European Parly Labour Party (formerly British Labour Gp); 1st Vice-Pres., Regl Policy and Planning Cttee, Eur. Parlt, 1992–94; Sec., Tribune Gp of MEPs, 1992–94. Mem., Labour Party NEC, 1994–98. PPS to Minister of State for Armed Forces, 2005–06; an Asst Govt Whip, 2007–08; Parly Under-Sec. of State, Wales Office, 2008–10; Shadow Minister: for Europe, 2010–11; for Political and Constitutional Reform, 2011–13; PPS to Leader of the Opposition, 2013–15. Mem., European Scrutiny Select Cttee, 2001–07; Chm., All Party Parly Gp on EU, 2006–07. Sec., DWP Gp, 2002–07, Wales Gp, 2003–07, PLP; Sec., Labour Movt for Europe, 2003–07. Bd Mem., European Movt, 2002–07; Pres., Wales Council, European Movt, 2006–. Pres., Council for Wales of Voluntary Youth Services, 2001–; Vice-Pres., City of Cardiff Br., UNA, 1989–; Mem., Cefn Cribwr Community Council, 1985–91. President: Aber Valley Male Voice Choir, 2001–; Caerphilly Local Hist. Soc., 2006–; Lab Heritage, 2015–. Fellow, Univ. of Wales Coll. of Cardiff, 1995. *Publications:*

(contrib.) Oxford Companion to the Literature of Wales, 1986; Remaining True: a biography of Ness Edwards, 2006; three pamphlets; contrib. Llafur—Jl of Welsh Labour History, Gelligaer Hist. Soc. Jl. *Recreations:* music, reading. *Address:* c/o House of Commons, SW1A 0AA. *T:* (020) 7219 8152. *Club:* Bargoed Bowls (Pres., 2005–).

DAVID-WEILL, Michel Alexandre; Chairman, Lazard Frères & Co., LLC, New York, 1977–2005; Partner, Lazard Frères et Cie, Paris, 1965–2005; *b* 23 Nov. 1932; *s* of Berthe Haardt and Pierre David-Weill; *m* 1956, Hélène Lehideux; four *d. Educ:* Institut de Sciences Politiques, Paris; Lycée Français de New York. Brown Brothers Harriman, 1954–55; Lehman Brothers, NY, 1955–56; Lazard Frères & Co., NY, 1956–2005, Partner, 1961, Sen. Partner, 1977; Lazard Brothers & Co., London, Dir, 1965–2005; Chm., Lazard Partners, 1984–2005. Chm., Supervisory Bd, Eurazeo Investor Relations, 2003–. Dir, French Amer. Foundn, NY; Member Council: Musée de la Légion d'Honneur, Paris, 1975; Cité Internat. des Arts, Paris, 1976; Mem., Acad. des Beaux-Arts, 1983; Pres., Conseil Artistique de la Réunion des Musées Nationaux, Paris. Gov., NY Hosp. Officier, Legion of Honour (France), 1990. *Address:* c/o Eurazeo, 32 rue de Monceau, 75008 Paris, France.

DAVIDSON, family name of **Viscount Davidson**.

DAVIDSON, 3rd Viscount *cr* 1937, of Little Gaddesden; **Malcolm William Mackenzie Davidson;** *b* 28 Aug. 1934; *yr s* of 1st Viscount Davidson, GCVO, CH, CB, PC and Hon. Frances Joan Dickinson, (Baroness Northchurch (Life Peer), DBE), *yr d* of 1st Baron Dickinson, KBE, PC; *S* brother, 2012; *m* 1970, Mrs Evelyn Ann Carew Perfect (*d* 2011), *yr d* of William Blackmore Storey; one *s* one *d. Educ:* Westminster; Pembroke Coll., Cambridge (BA 1958; MA 1962). *Heir: s* Hon. John Nicolas Alexander Davidson [*b* 1971; *m* 2002, Venetia Sophie Maunsell; four *d*]. *Address:* Berwick Place, Hatfield Peverel, Essex CM3 2EY. *T:* (01245) 380321.

DAVIDSON OF GLEN CLOVA, Baron *cr* 2006 (Life Peer), of Glen Clova in Angus; **Neil Forbes Davidson;** QC (Scot.) 1993; *b* 13 Sept. 1950; *s* of John and Flora Davidson; *m* 1980, Regina Anne Sprissler, Philadelphia. *Educ:* Univs of Stirling (BA), Bradford (MSc), Edinburgh (LLB, LLM). Admitted Faculty of Advocates, 1979; called to the Bar, Inner Temple, 1990; Standing Jun. Counsel to Registrar Gen., 1982, to Depts of Health and Social Security, 1988; Solicitor Gen. for Scotland, 2000–01; Advocate Gen. for Scotland, 2006–10. Opposition Spokesman on Law and Treasury, H of L, 2010–. Dir, City Disputes Panel, 1993–2000. ICJ missions to Egypt, 1997, 1998. Reviewer, Davidson Review on UK Implementation of EU Legislation, 2005–06. Pres., Clan Davidson Assoc., 2004–. DUniv Stirling, 2012. *Publications:* (jtly) Judicial Review in Scotland, 1986; (contrib.) ADR in Scotland, 1995. *Address:* House of Lords, SW1A 0PW.

DAVIDSON, Amanda; Director, Baigrie Davies, since 2005; *b* London, 1 April 1955; *d* of His Honour Ian Thomas Rollo Davidson, QC and Gyöngyi Magdolna Davidson (*née* Anghi). *Educ:* Channing Sch.; Queen Elizabeth Coll., London Univ. (BSc). Dir, Chase de Vere, 1982–84; sole trader, 1986–88; Director: Holden Matthews Financial Services, 1988–92; Holden Meehan, 1992–2005. Personal Investment Authority: Mem., Membership and Disciplinary Cttee, 1994–2001; Mem. Bd, 1998–2001; Financial Services Authority: Mem., Regulatory Decisions Cttee, 2001–06, Financial Capability Steering Gp, 2008–10; Mem. Bd, 2010–13; non-exec. Dir, Financial Conduct Authy, 2013–. Mem. Council, Assoc. of Ind. Financial Advrs, 2000–10 (Dep. Chm., 2007–10). Certified Financial Planner, 2003. Gov., Channing Sch., 1997–2013. *Recreations:* violin, theatre, ballet, opera, travel, scuba diving. *Address:* Baigrie Davies, 25 City Road, EC1Y 1AA. *T:* (020) 7786 2000, *Fax:* (020) 7786 2020. *E:* amanda.davidson@baigriedavies.co.uk.

DAVIDSON, Arthur; QC 1978; *b* 7 Nov. 1928. *Educ:* Liverpool Coll.; King George V Sch., Southport; Trinity Coll., Cambridge. Served in Merchant Navy. Barrister, Middle Temple, 1953. Trinity Coll., Cambridge, 1959–62; Editor of the Granta. Legal Director: Associated Newspapers Hldgs, 1987–90; Mirror Gp, 1991–93. MP (Lab) Accrington, 1966–83; PPS to Solicitor-General, 1968–70; Chm., Home Affairs Gp, Parly Labour Party, 1971–74; Parly Sec., Law Officers' Dept, 1974–79; Opposition spokesman on Defence (Army), 1980–81, on legal affairs, 1981–83, Shadow Attorney-General, 1982–83; Member: Home Affairs Select Cttee, 1980–83; Armed Forces Bill Select Cttee, 1981–83. Contested (Lab): Blackpool S, 1955; Preston N, 1959; Hyndburn, 1983. Member: Council, Consumers' Association, 1970–74; Exec. Cttee, Soc. of Labour Lawyers, 1981; Nat. Exec., Fabian Soc.; Council, Nat. Youth Jazz Orchestra; Chm., House of Commons Jazz Club, 1973–83. *Recreations:* lawn tennis, ski-ing, theatre, listening to good jazz and playing bad jazz; formerly Member Cambridge Univ. athletics team. *Address:* Cloisters, 1st Floor, 1 Pump Court, Temple, EC4Y 7AA. *Clubs:* James Street Men's Working (Oswaldtwistle); Free Gardeners (Rishton); King Street, Marlborough Working Men's (Accrington).

DAVIDSON, Brian John; HM Diplomatic Service; Ambassador to Thailand, from June 2016; *b* Kingston, Jamaica, 28 April 1964; *s* of John Burton Davidson and Joan Margaret Davidson (*née* Stevenson); *m* 2014, Scott Kelly Chang. *Educ:* Sullivan Upper Grammar Sch., Holywood, Co. Down, NI; Trinity Coll., Cambridge (BA Hons 1985). Entered FCO, 1985; lang. trng (Mandarin Chinese), 1986–88; Second Sec., Beijing, 1988–92; Cabinet Office, 1992–94; Hd, China Section, FCO, 1994–96; First Sec., Canberra, 1996–2000; Dep. Hd of Mission, Vilnius, 2001–04; Dep. Chief Exec., Internat. Financial Services London (on secondment), 2005–06; Consul General: Guangzhou, 2006–10; Shanghai, 2011–15. *Recreations:* badminton, tennis, photography, travel, art, science fiction. *Address:* c/o Foreign and Commonwealth office, King Charles Street, SW1A 2AH.

DAVIDSON, Carolyn Jayne; HM Diplomatic Service; Ambassador (non-resident) to Honduras, since 2015; *b* Manchester, 18 April 1964; *d* of Derek Davidson and Barbara Wild (*née* Morris); *m* 1997, Thomas Henry Carter, *qv*; two *s. Educ:* Manchester High Sch. for Girls; Univ. of Bristol (BA Hons French and German); Sch. of Oriental and African Studies, Univ. of London (Japanese); Open Univ. (MBA). Entered FCO, 1986; Third Secretary: Tokyo, 1989–92; on secondment to EC Commn, 1993; Bonn, 1993–95; FCO, 1995–99; Jt Dep. Hd of Mission, Bratislava, 2004–08; Jt High Comr to Zambia, 2008–12; FCO, 2012–15. *Recreations:* sport (doing rather than watching), travel, family and friends. *Address:* c/o Foreign and Commonwealth Office, King Charles Street, SW1A 2AH.

DAVIDSON, Charles Peter Morton; a District Judge (Magistrates' Courts) (formerly Metropolitan Stipendiary Magistrate), 1984–2004; a Deputy District Judge (Magistrates' Courts), 2004–10; *b* 29 July 1938; *s* of late William Philip Morton Davidson, MD, and Muriel Maud Davidson (*née* Alderson); *m* 1966, Pamela Louise Campbell-Rose. *Educ:* Harrow; Trinity Coll., Dublin (MA, LLB). Called to the Bar, Inner Temple, 1963; employed by Legal and General Assurance Soc., 1963–65; in practice at Bar, 1966–84; a Recorder, 1991–99. Chairman, London Rent Assessment Panel, 1973–84; part-time Immigration Appeals Adjudicator, 1976–84; a Chairman: Inner London Juvenile Courts, 1985–88; Family Court, 1991–2004. Contested (C) North Battersea, 1966. Member: Wandsworth BC, 1964–68; Merton BC, 1968–71. *Recreations:* music, gardening. *Club:* Hurlingham.

DAVIDSON, Christopher Kenneth, CBE 2008; Director, Tax Management Consulting, KPMG UK, since 2014; *b* Leeds, 15 June 1957; *s* of Joseph Hector Davidson and Elinor Margery Kathleen Davidson (*née* Dibbs); *m* 1980, Ann Elizabeth Buckland; two *s. Educ:* Leeds Modern Sch.; Bradford Univ. Board of Inland Revenue, later HM Revenue and Customs: Tax Officer (Higher Grade), 1976–80; qualified as Tax Inspector, 1983; Tax Inspector, 1980–85; Inspector (P), 1985–92; Inspector (SP), 1992–97; Sen. Civil Servant, 1997–2014; Disclosure of Tax Avoidance Schemes, 2004–06; Dep. Dir, Tax Intermediaries Study, 2006–08; Nat. Business Dir, Large Business Service, 2008–11; Hd, Anti-Avoidance Group, 2011–14. Trustee, IFS, 2008–. Gov., Chelmer Valley High Sch., 2001–. Personality of Year, Taxation Awards, 2009. *Recreations:* listening to music, watching cricket (and occasionally playing), family and friends, Spain. *Address:* KPMG UK, 15 Canada Square, E14 5GL.

DAVIDSON, David; independent consultant in organisational strategy, governance and audit, since 2010; *b* 25 Jan. 1943; *s* of John and Marjory Davidson; *m* 1968, Christine Hunter; three *s* two *d. Educ:* Heriot-Watt Univ. (Pharmacy); Manchester Business Sch. (DipBA). MRPharmS. Manager, 1966–69, Proprietor, 1969–74, community pharmacy, Kent; developed gp of community pharmacies in Scotland and Northern England, 1974–93; Dir, Unichem Ltd, 1977–90; Regl Chm., Unichem plc, 1990–93. Managing Director: Earlston Ltd, 1984–2008; Carse Ltd, 1996–2008; Associate Dir, Caledonia Consulting, 2007–10. Non-exec. Dir, NHS Borders, 2010–; Director: Bill McLaren Park Ltd, 2013–; Home Basics Ltd, 2013–. Mem., Scottish Borders Jt Integration Bd for Health and Social Care, 2014–. Mem. (C) Stirling Council, 1995–99. MSP (C) Scotland NE, 1999–2007. Founder Chm., Assoc. Scottish Community Councils, 1993–95. Chair, Hawick Sports Initiative, 2010–. *Recreations:* travel, Rugby football development, reading, local history research. *Address:* Ravenslea, Sunnyhill Road, Hawick, Roxburghshire TD9 7HS. *T:* (01450) 372175.

DAVIDSON, Dennis Arthur; Principal, DDA Consulting, since 2013; *b* Chester, 11 March 1947; *s* of Arthur Davidson and Elizabeth Joan Morgan; *m* 1991, Janette Graydon Dickson; three *s* one *d. Educ:* Helsby Grammar Sch.; Ellesmere Port Grammar Sch. Associated British Picture Corp., 1964–70; Chm., DDA Public Relations Ltd, 1970–2013. Member: BAFTA, 1975; Acad. of Motion Picture Arts and Scis, 1980. FCIPR 1995; FRSA 2007; FInstD 2008. *Recreations:* tennis, cinema, food and wine consumption, Rugby Union. *Address:* Barrihurst House, Cranleigh, Surrey GU6 8LQ. *T:* (01483) 279779. *E:* dennis.davidson@ddaconsulting.co.uk. *Clubs:* Hurlingham, Groucho, Soho House.

DAVIDSON, Duncan Henry; Chairman, 1972–2006, Life President, since 2006, Persimmon plc; *b* 29 March 1941; *s* of late Col Colin Keppel Davidson, CIE, OBE, RA (killed in action 1943) and late Lady (Mary) Rachel Davidson (later Lady (Mary) Rachel Pepys, DCVO); *m* 1965, Sarah Wilson; four *d. Educ:* Ampleforth Coll. Lieut, Royal Scots Greys, 1959–63; Manager, George Wimpey plc, 1963–65; Founder and Chm., Ryedale Homes Ltd, 1965–72. *Recreation:* country pursuits. *Address:* Lilburn Tower, Alnwick, Northumberland NE66 4PQ. *T:* (01668) 217291. *Clubs:* White's, Turf; Northern Counties.

DAVIDSON, Edward Alan; QC 1994; *b* 12 July 1943; *o s* of late Alan T. Davidson and H. Muriel Davidson, Sheffield; *m* 1973, Hilary Jill, *er d* of late Major N. S. Fairman, MBE; two *s. Educ:* King's Sch., Canterbury; Gonville and Caius Coll., Cambridge (schol., Tapp Postgrad. Schol.; MA, LLB). Called to the Bar, Gray's Inn, 1966 (Atkin and Birkenhead Schol.), Bencher, 2002. Chm., Summer Fields Sch. Trust, 2007–13 (Gov., 1998–). *Recreations:* tennis, bridge, gardening. *Address:* Thatch End, Furneux Pelham, Buntingford, Herts SG9 0LW.

DAVIDSON, Ian Graham; *b* 8 Sept. 1950; *s* of Graham Davidson and Elizabeth Crowe; *m* 1978, Morag Mackinnon; one *s* one *d. Educ:* Jedburgh Grammar Sch.; Galashiels Acad.; Edinburgh Univ. (MA Hons); Jordanhill Coll. (Teacher Cert.). Chm., Nat. Orgn of Labour Students, 1973–74; Pres., Jordanhill Coll. Students' Assoc., 1975–76; PA/Researcher, Janey Buchan, MEP, 1978–85; Community Service Volunteers, 1985–92. Councillor, Strathclyde Region, 1978–92 (Chm., Educn Cttees, 1986–92). MP (Lab and Co-op) Glasgow, Govan, 1992–97, Glasgow Pollok, 1997–2005, Glasgow SW, 2005–15; contested (Lab and Co-op) same seat, 2015. Member: Public Accounts Select Cttee, 1997–2010; Select Cttee on Scottish Affairs, 2005–15 (Chm., 2010–15); Liaison Select Cttee, 2010–15; Chairman: MSF Parly Gp, 1996–97; Co-op Gp, 1998–99; Bermuda Gp, 1998–2015; Secretary: New Europe Parly Gp, 2001–15; British/German All Party Parly Gp, 1998–2002; British/Japanese All Party Parly Gp, 1998–2015; Aerospace All Party Parly Gp, 1998–2001; Ship Building and Repair All Party Parly Gp, 2000–15; Parly Rugby Union team, 1996–2015. Secretary: Tribune Gp of MPs, 1997–2015; Trade Union Gp of Lab MPs, 1998–2015; Vice Chm., Scotland Lab Gp; Chm., Lab Against the Euro. *Recreations:* running, swimming, family.

DAVIDSON, James Duncan Gordon, OBE 1984; MVO 1947; Chief Executive, Royal Highland and Agricultural Society of Scotland, 1970–92; *b* 10 Jan. 1927; *s* of Alastair Gordon Davidson and M. Valentine B. Davidson (*née* Osborne); *m* 1st, 1955, Catherine Ann Jamieson; one *s* two *d*; 2nd, 1973, Janet Stafford; one *s. Educ:* RN Coll., Dartmouth; Downing Coll., Cambridge. Active List, RN, 1944–55. Subseq. farming, and political work; contested (L) West Aberdeenshire, 1964; MP (L) West Aberdeenshire, 1966–70. FRAgS; MIEx. *Publications:* Scots and the Sea, 2003; Admiral Lord St Vincent: saint or tyrant?, 2006; Thinker, Sailor, Shepherd, Spy, 2009. *Recreations:* family, walking, music, forestry, naval history. *Address:* Coire Cas, Newtonmore, Inverness-shire PH20 1AR. *T:* (01540) 673322.

DAVIDSON, James Patton, CBE 1980; *b* 23 March 1928; *s* of Richard Davidson and Elizabeth Ferguson Carnichan; *m* 1st, 1953, Jean Stevenson Ferguson Anderson (marr. diss. 1981); two *s*; 2nd, 1981, Esmé Evelyn Ancill. *Educ:* Rutherglen Acad.; Glasgow Univ. (BL). Mil. service, commissioned RASC, 1948–50. Clyde Navigation Trust, 1950; Asst Gen. Manager, 1958. Clyde Port Authority: Gen. Manager, 1966; Managing Dir, 1974; Dep. Chm. and Man. Dir, 1976; Chm., 1980–83. Chairman: Ardrossan Harbour Co. Ltd, 1976–83; Clydeport Stevedoring Services Ltd, 1977–83; Clyde Container Services Ltd, 1968–83; S. & H. McCall Transport (Glasgow) Ltd, 1972–83; Rhu Marina Ltd, 1976–80; Scotway Haulage Ltd, 1976–81; R. & J. Strang Ltd, 1976–81; Nat. Assoc. of Port Employers, 1974–79; British Ports Assoc., 1980–83 (Dep. Chm., 1978–80); Port Employers' & Registered Dock Workers' Pension Fund Trustee Ltd, 1978–83; Pilotage Commn, 1983–91 (Mem., 1979–83); UK Dir, 1976–83 and Mem., Exec. Cttee, 1977–83, Hon. Mem., 1983, Internat. Assoc. of Ports and Harbours. Dir, Iron Trades Insurance Gp, 1981–94; Chm., Foods & Feeds (UK), 1982–83. FCIT, CCMI; FRSA. *Recreations:* golf, bridge, travel, reading.

DAVIDSON, Jane Barbara; *see* Stevenson, J. B.

DAVIDSON, Jane Elizabeth; Director of Sustainability, since 2011, and Associate Pro Vice Chancellor for External Engagement, since 2014, University of Wales Trinity Saint David; *b* 19 March 1957; *d* of Dr Lindsay Alexander Gordon Davidson and Dr Joyce Mary Davidson; *m* 1994, Guy Roger George Stoate; one *d,* and two step *s. Educ:* Malvern Girls' Coll.; Birmingham Univ. (BA 2nd Cl. Hons English); UCW, Aberystwyth (PGCE). Teacher, Cardigan and Pontypridd, 1981–83; Develt Officer, YHA, 1983–86; youth and community worker, Dinas Powys Youth Centre, 1986–89; researcher to Rhodri Morgan, MP, 1989–94; Welsh Co-ordinator, Nat. Local Govt Forum Against Poverty, 1994–96; Hd, Social Affairs, Welsh Local Govt Assoc., 1996–99. National Assembly for Wales: Mem. (Lab) Pontypridd, 1999–2011; Dep. Presiding Officer, 1999–2000; Sec., then Minister, for Educn and Lifelong Learning, subseq. Minister for Educn, Lifelong Learning and Skills, 2000–07; Minister for Sustainability and Rural Develt, 2007; Minister for Envmt, Sustainability and Housing, 2007–11. *Publications:* The Anti Poverty Implications of Local Government Reorganisation, 1990; (jtly) Freeing the Dragon, 1998; (contrib.) The One Planet Life, 2014; (contrib.) The Sustainable University, 2014; contrib. to social policy jls. *Recreations:* theatre, walking, cycling, sea kayaking.

DAVIDSON, Prof. John Frank, FRS 1974; FREng; Shell Professor of Chemical Engineering, University of Cambridge, 1978–93 (Professor of Chemical Engineering, 1975–78); Vice-Master, Trinity College, Cambridge, 1992–96; Adjunct Professor, Monash

University, Australia, 1996–99; *b* 7 Feb. 1926; *s* of John and Katie Davidson; *m* 1948, Susanne Hedwig Ostberg (*d* 2011); one *s* one *d*. *Educ:* Heaton Grammar Sch., Newcastle upon Tyne; Trinity Coll., Cambridge. MA, PhD, ScD; FIChemE, MIMechE. 1st cl. Mech. Scis Tripos, Cantab, 1946, BA 1947. Engrg work at Rolls Royce, Derby, 1947–50; Cambridge Univ.: Research Fellow, Trinity Coll., 1949; research, 1950–52; Univ. Demonstrator, 1952; Univ. Lectr, 1954; Steward of Trinity Coll., 1957–64; Reader in Chem. Engrg, Univ. of Cambridge, 1964–75. Visiting Professor: Univ. of Delaware, 1960; Univ. of Sydney, 1967. Member: Flixborough Ct of Inquiry, 1974–75; Adv. Cttee on Safety of Nuclear Installations, HSC, 1977–87. Pres., IChemE, 1970–71; Vice Pres. and Mem. Council, Royal Soc., 1988. FREng (Founder FEng, 1976). For. Associate, Nat. Acad. of Engrg, US, 1976; For. Fellow, Indian National Science Acad., 1990; For. Mem., Russian Engrg Acad., 1998. Dr *hc* Institut Nat. Polytech. de Toulouse, 1979; Hon. DSc Aston, 1989. Leverhulme Medal, Royal Soc., 1984; Messel Medal, Soc. of Chemical Industry, 1986; Royal Medal, Royal Soc., 1999; Prince Philip Medal, RAEng, 2010. *Publications:* (with D. Harrison): Fluidised Particles, 1963; Fluidization, 1971, 2nd edn (with R. Clift and D. Harrison), 1985; (with D. L. Keairns) Fluidization (Conference Procs), 1978. *Recreations:* gardening, upholstery, mending domestic artefacts. *Address:* 5 Luard Close, Cambridge CB2 8PL. *T:* (01223) 246104.

See also I. G. Letwin.

DAVIDSON, John Roderick, OBE 2004; Director of Administration, 1991–2004, Clerk of the Council, 1994–2004, University of London; *b* 29 Jan. 1937; *yr s* of late Alexander Ross Davidson and Jessie Maud (*née* Oakley). *Educ:* Portsmouth Northern Grammar Sch.; Univ. of Manchester (BA). Advr to students, Chelsea Sch. of Art, 1966–68; Asst Sch. Sec., RPMS, 1968–74; Imperial College of Science, Technology and Medicine: Asst Sec., 1974–77; Personnel Sec., 1977–85; Admin. Sec., 1985–89; London University: Clerk of Senate, 1989–94; Member: Exams and Assessment Council, 1991–2000; Bd, British Inst. in Paris, 1993–2004. Director: London E Anglian Gp, 1990–96; Superannuation Arrangements of Univ. of London Trustee Co., 1993–98; London and S Eastern Library Region, 1995–2001; Senate House Services Ltd, 1996–2004; Digital Preservation Coalition Ltd, 2002–04. Chm., Lansdowne (Putney) Ltd, 1999–. Trustee: Univ. of London Convocation Trust, 1997–2004; St Stephen's AIDS Trust, 2003– (Chm., Finance and Gen. Purposes Cttee, 2014–). Governor: Charterhouse Sch., 1994–2003; More House Sch., 2000–15 (Chm., 2005–14; Mem., More House Assoc., 2000–); Wimbledon High Sch., 2001–09. *Recreations:* theatre, opera, genealogy. *Address:* 10 Lansdowne, Carlton Drive, SW15 2BY. *T:* (020) 8789 0021. *Club:* Athenæum.

DAVIDSON, Katharine Mary, (Mrs Christopher Baylis); QC 2011; *b* Edinburgh, 19 June 1962; *d* of late Andrew Davidson and of Dorothy Davidson; *m* 2007, Christopher Baylis; two *s* one *d*. *Educ:* Epsom Coll.; Lincoln Coll., Oxford (BA Juris.; MA). Called to the Bar, Lincoln's Inn, 1987; in practice as a barrister, specialising in family law, 1 Mitre Court, then 1 Hare Court, 1988–. *Recreations:* family, ski-ing, art. *Address:* 1 Hare Court, Temple, EC4Y 7BE. *T:* (020) 7797 7070. *E:* clerks@1hc.com.

DAVIDSON, Sir Martin (Stuart), KCMG 2014 (CMG 2007); Chairman, Great Britain China Centre, since 2015 (Member of Board, since 2009); *b* 14 Oct. 1955; *s* of Westland Davidson and Freda (*née* Hill); *m* 1980, Elizabeth Fanner; two *s* one *d*. *Educ:* Royal Grammar Sch., Guildford; St Andrews Univ. (MA). Admin. Officer, Hong Kong Govt, 1979–83; British Council: Peking, 1984–87; Regl Officer, China, 1987–89; Dir, S China, 1989–93; Asst Regl Dir, E and S Europe, 1993–95; Cultural Counsellor and Dir, British Council, Peking, 1995–2000; Dir, E Asia and Americas, 2000–03; Dir, Europe, Americas and Middle East, 2003–05; Dep. Dir-Gen., 2006–07; Chief Exec., 2007–14. Internat. Trustee, Leonard Cheshire Disability, 2012–. Gov., Goodenough Coll. FRSA. *Recreations:* hill walking, reading, Rugby. *Address:* c/o Great Britain China Centre, 15 Belgrave Square, SW1X 8PS. *Club:* Foreign Correspondents' (Hong Kong).

DAVIDSON, Nicholas Ranking; QC 1993; a Deputy High Court Judge, since 2000; *b* 2 March 1951; *s* of late Brian Davidson, CBE and Priscilla Margaret (*née* Chilver); *m* 1978, Gillian Frances Watts; two *d*. *Educ:* Winchester (Schol.); Trinity Coll., Cambridge (Exhibnr; BA; MA). Called to the Bar, Inner Temple, 1974 (Treas.'s Prize, Hughes Parry Prize and Inner Temple Scholarship, 1974); Bencher, 1998. Chm., Professional Negligence Bar Assoc., 1997–99. MCIArb 2004. Trustee, St Mary's Sch., Ascot, 2012– (Gov., 1996–2006). *Publications:* (contrib.) Now and Then, 1999; (contrib.) Professional Negligence and Liability, 2000. *Recreations:* bridge, music, ski-ing. *Address:* 4 New Square, Lincoln's Inn, WC2A 3RJ. *T:* (020) 7822 2000.

DAVIDSON, Prof. Peter Robert Keith Andrew, PhD; Professor of Renaissance Studies and Scholar-Keeper of University Renaissance Collections, University of Aberdeen, since 2005; *b* 14 May 1957; *s* of Robert Ritchie Davidson and Daphne Davidson (*née* Sanderson); *m* 1989, Jane Barbara Stevenson, *qv*. *Educ:* Clare Coll., Cambridge (BA 1979; PhD 1986); Univ. of York (MA 1980). Lectr, Univ. of St Andrews, 1989–90; Docent in Lit. and Book Studies, Universiteit Leiden, Netherlands, 1990–92; University of Warwick: Lectr in English, 1992–97; Sen. Lectr, 1997–99; Reader, 1999–2000; Chalmers Regius Prof. of English, Aberdeen Univ., 2000–05. Dir, St Omers Press, 2013–. Academic Advr, Stonyhurst Coll. Christian Heritage Centre Trust, 2014–. Trustee, Scottish Catholic Heritage Trust, 2012–. *Publications:* (with A. H. van der Weel) Poems of Sir Constantijn Huygens, 1996; The Vocall Forest, 1996; The Poems and Translations of Sir Richard Fanshawe, vol. I, 1998, vol. II, 1999; Poetry and Revolution, 1998; (with Jane Stevenson) Early Modern Women's Verse, 2000; The Idea of North, 2005; (with Anne Sweeney) Collected Poems of St Robert Southwell, SJ, 2007; The Universal Baroque, 2007; (with Jill Bepler) The Triumphs of the Defeated, 2007; The Palace of Oblivion, 2008; (with Jane Stevenson) The Lost City, 2008; Winter Light, 2010; (with Iain Beavan and Jane Stevenson) The Library and Archive Collections of the University of Aberdeen, 2011; Distance and Memory, 2013; The Last of the Light, 2015. *Recreation:* casuistry. *Address:* Art History, King's College, Aberdeen AB24 3FX.

DAVIDSON, Prof. Robin, DPhil; Interim Chairman, UK SMART Recovery, since 2014; *b* Belfast, 4 July 1950; *s* of James and May Davidson; *m* 1975, Patricia Anderson; three *s*. *Educ:* Queen's Univ., Belfast (BSc, MSc); Univ. of Ulster (DPhil 1989). Consultant Clinical Psychologist: Leeds Addiction Service, 1980–84; NI DHSS, 1984–2008; Chm., Alcohol Res. UK (formerly Alcohol Educn and Res. Council), 2007–14. Lectr, Greenwich and S Bank Univs. Hon. Prof., Univ. of Ulster, 2002–; Hon. Lectr, Faculty of Medicine, QUB, 1992–. *Publications:* Alcoholism and Drug Addiction, 1985; Counselling Problem Drinkers, 1990. *Recreation:* motor cycling. *Address:* UK SMART Recovery, Box 123, 24 Station Square, Inverness IV1 1LD. *T:* 07783 729709.

DAVIDSON, Shearer Carroll; *see* West, S. C.

DAVIDSON, Stephen Robert; DL; Headmaster, Bradford Grammar School, 1996–2011; *b* 20 Oct. 1950; *er s* of Robert Davidson and late Joan Davidson, Tynemouth; *m* 1983, Carol, *d* of Ralston and Dorothy Smith, St Bees; one *s*. *Educ:* Univ. of Manchester Inst. of Sci. and Technol. (BSc Hons Engrg 1972); Univ. of Newcastle (PGCE 1974). Teacher, Lord Wandsworth Coll., 1974–83; Middle Sch. Master, Manchester Grammar Sch., 1983–96. DL 2001, High Sheriff 2012–13, W Yorks. *Recreations:* travel (especially USA), sport, civil aviation.

DAVIE, Jonathan Richard; Chairman, First Avenue Partners, since 2007; *b* Esher, 21 Sept. 1946; *s* of Richard Davie and Anne Davie; *m* 1986, Belinda Mary Blake; two *d*. *Educ:* Tonbridge Sch.; École de Commerce, Neuchatel. FCA 1969. Wedd Durlacher Mordaunt, 1969–86, Partner, 1975–86; Man. Dir, Barclays de Zoete Wedd, 1986–98; Vice Chm., Credit Suisse First Boston, 1998–2007; Chm., IG Gp Hldgs, 2004–14. Non-executive Director: Infrastata plc (formerly Portland Gas), 2008–10; Persimmon, 2010–; Hansa Trust plc, 2013–. Gov., Heathfield Sch., 2006–13. *Recreations:* golf, ski-ing, tennis, antiques. *Address:* c/o First Avenue Partners LLP, Swan House, 17–19 Stratford Place, W1C 1BQ. *T:* (020) 7016 6600, *Fax:* (020) 7016 6699. *E:* jdavie@firstavenue.com.

DAVIE, Sir Michael F.; *see* Ferguson Davie.

DAVIE, Rex; *see* Davie, S. R.

DAVIE, Ronald, PhD; FBPsS; Director, National Children's Bureau, 1981–90; *b* 25 Nov. 1929; *s* of late Thomas Edgar Davie and Gladys (*née* Powell); *m* 1957, Kathleen, *d* of William Wilkinson, Westhoughton, Lancs; one *s* one *d*. *Educ:* King Edward VI Grammar Sch., Aston, Birmingham; Univ. of Reading (BA 1954); Univ. of Manchester (PGCE and Dip. Deaf Educn 1955); Univ. of Birmingham (Dip. Educnl Psych. 1961); Univ. of London (PhD 1970). FBPsS 1973. Teacher, schs for mainstream and disabled children, 1955–60; Co. Educnl Psychologist, IoW, 1961–64; Nat. Children's Bureau, London: Sen. Res. Officer, 1964; Dep. Dir, 1968; Dir of Res., 1972; Prof. of Educnl Psychology, Dept of Educn, UC Cardiff, 1974–81. Mem., Special Educnl Needs Tribunal, 1994–2003. Visiting Professor: Oxford Poly., later Oxford Brookes Univ., 1991–97; Cheltenham and Gloucester Coll. of Higher Educn, later Univ. of Gloucestershire, 1997–2006; Visiting Fellow: Inst. of Educn, Univ. of London, 1985–93; Univ. of Newcastle, 1995–2006; Hon. Res. Fellow, UCL, 1991–2006. Co-Dir, Nat. Child Develt Study, 1968–77; Scientific Adviser: Local Authority Social Services Res. Liaison Gp, DHSS, 1975–77; Mental Handicap Res. Liaison Gp, DHSS, 1977–81; Prof. Advr, All Party Parly Gp for Children, 1983–91. President: Links Assoc., 1977–90; Child Develt Soc., 1990–91; Nat. Assoc. for Special Educnl Needs, 1992–94; Vice-Pres., British Assoc. for Early Childhood Educn, 1984–95, Young Minds, 1991–2007; Chairman: Trng and Educn Cttee, Nat. Assoc. Mental Health, 1969–72; Assoc. for Child Psychol. and Psychiatry, 1972–73 (Hon. Sec. 1965–70); Working Party, Children Appearing Before Juvenile Courts, Children's Reg. Planning Cttee for Wales, 1975–77; Wales Standing Conf. for Internat. Year of the Child, 1978–79; Steering Cttee, Child Health and Educn Study, 1979–84; Bd of Trustees, Eden Valley Hospice, 2000 (Trustee, 1998–2006; Vice Chm., 2001). Mem., Nat. Curriculum Council, 1988–90. Chm. Govs, Fellview Sch., 1998–2001. Church Warden, St Kentigern's, Caldbeck, 2004–11. FRSA 1991. Hon. FRCPCH 1996. Hon. DEd: CNAA, 1991; UWE, 1998; Hon. DLitt Birmingham, 1999. *Publications:* (co-author) 11,000 Seven-Year Olds, 1966; Directory of Voluntary Organisations concerned with Children, 1969; Living with Handicap, 1970; From Birth to Seven, 1972; Child Sexual Abuse: the way forward after Cleveland, 1989; Listening to Children in Education, 1996; The Voice of the Child, 1996; chapters in books and papers in sci. and other jls on special educn, psychol., child care health, effects of TV on children, and children's ownership and use of mobile phones. *Recreations:* photography, antiques, good music of all kinds. *Address:* Beck Rise, Upton, Caldbeck, Cumbria CA7 8EU.

DAVIE, (Stephen) Rex, CB 1993; Member: Council on Tribunals, 1995–2001; Civil Service Appeal Board, 1995–2001; Principal Establishment and Finance Officer (Under Secretary), Cabinet Office, 1989–93; *b* 11 June 1933; *s* of late Sydney and Dorothy Davie; *m* 1955, Christine Stockwell; one *s* one *d*. *Educ:* Ilfracombe Grammar Sch. Executive Officer, Inland Revenue, 1951. National Service, RAF, 1952–54. Office of Minister for Science, 1962; NEDO, 1967; CSD, 1970; Asst Sec. 1979; Cabinet Office, 1983; Sen. Sec., Security Commn, 1979–89. Mem. Council, Inst. of Cancer Res., 1993– (Vice Chm., then Dep. Chm., 1995–2003). *Recreations:* reading, family, travel, gardening. *Address:* 2 Linnet Close, Basingstoke, Hants RG22 5PD. *Clubs:* Athenæum, Civil Service.

DAVIE, Timothy Douglas; Chief Executive, BBC Worldwide and Director, Global, since 2013; *b* 25 April 1967; *s* of Douglas John Davie and Alicia Margaret Davie; *m* 1997, Anne Claire Shotbolt; three *s*. *Educ:* Selwyn Coll., Cambridge (BA 1989). Brand Manager, Procter and Gamble, 1989–93; Vice Pres., Pepsico, 1993–2005; Dir, Marketing, Communications and Audiences, BBC, 2005–08; Dir, BBC Audio and Music, 2008–12; Acting Dir-Gen., BBC, 2012–13. Mem., Mktg Gp of GB, 2001– (Chm., 2009–10). Chm., Comic Relief, 2013–; Vice Chair, Royal Television Soc., 2013–. *Recreations:* my young family, running, reading, ski-ing, live music, fresh air, strong coffee. *Address:* BBC Worldwide, The Media Centre, 201 Wood Lane, W12 7TQ. *T:* (020) 8433 3533. *E:* tim.davie@bbc.com. *Club:* Soho House.

DAVIES; *see* Prys-Davies.

DAVIES, family name of **Barons Darwen, Davies, Davies of Abersoch, Davies of Coity, Davies of Oldham** and **Davies of Stamford**.

DAVIES, 3rd Baron *cr* 1932, of Llandinam; **David Davies,** CEng, MICE; Vice Lord-Lieutenant of Powys, since 2004; Chairman, Welsh National Opera Company, 1975–2000; *b* 2 Oct. 1940; *s* of 2nd Baron and Ruth Eldrydd (*d* 1966), 3rd *d* of Major W. M. Dugdale, CB, DSO; *S* father (killed in action), 1944; *m* 1972, Beryl, *d* of W. J. Oliver; two *s* two *d*. *Educ:* Eton; King's Coll., Cambridge (MA); MBA. DL Powys, 1997. *Heir: s* Hon. David Daniel Davies [*b* 23 Oct. 1975; *m* 2001, Leyla Natasha, *d* of Martin and Elaine Pope]. *Address:* Maethfa, Llandinam, Powys SY17 5AB.

DAVIES OF ABERSOCH, Baron *cr* 2009 (Life Peer), of Abersoch in the County of Gwynedd; **(Evan) Mervyn Davies,** CBE 2002; FCIB; Chairman and Partner, Corsair Capital, since 2010 (Member, Advisory Board, 2007–09); Chairman, Advisory Board, and Senior Advisor to Chief Executive Officer, Moelis & Co., since 2010; *b* 21 Nov. 1952; *s* of Richard Aled Davies and Margaret Davies; *m* 1979, Jeanne Marie (*née* Gammie); one *s* one *d*. *Educ:* Rydal Sch., N Wales; Harvard Business Sch. (PMD). FCIB 1990. Man. Dir, UK Banking and Sen. Credit Officer, Citibank, 1983–93; Standard Chartered plc, 1993–2009: Dir, 1997–2009; Gp Chief Exec., 2001–06; Chm., 2006–09; Dir, Standard Chartered Bank, Hong Kong, 1997–2001. Minister of State, BIS (formerly BERR), and FCO, 2009–10. Chairman: Fleming Family and Partners, 2007–09; Nordic Windpower Ltd, 2008–09; PineBridge Investments, 2010–14; Chime Communications plc, 2012–; Jack Wills, 2014–; Dep. Chm., LetterOne, 2015–; Dir, FF&P Private Equity Ltd, 2007–09. Non-executive Director: Tesco plc, 2003–08; Tottenham Hotspur FC, 2004–09; Breakingviews Ltd, 2007–09; Bharti Airtel, 2010–12; Diageo plc, 2010–; J Rothschild Capital Mgt, 2012–. Past Member: Singapore Business Council; UK-India Forum; UK-China Forum; Asia House Internat. Adv. Council; UK-India Business Council; Dir, Hong Kong Assoc., 2006–; Chairman: Prime Minister's Business Council for Britain, 2007–08; Interim Exec. Cttee, ICFR, 2007–09. Former Chairman: British Chamber of Commerce, HK; HK Assoc. of Banks; HK Youth Arts Fest.; Asia Youth Orch.; Generations Appeal, Breakthrough Breast Cancer. Pres., Royal Soc. of Asian Affairs, 2013–. Mem., Roundhouse, 2008–09. Chm., Council, Bangor Univ., 2008–14. Chm., Garden Bridge Trust, 2013–; Trustee: Sir Kyffin Williams Trust, 2007–09; RA, 2008– (Chm., RA Trust, 2012–); Dir, Glyndebourne Prodns Ltd, 2012–. JP Hong Kong, 2000. *Recreations:* soccer, cricket, golf, Rugby, Welsh art, antiques. *Address:* House of Lords, SW1A 0PW. *T:* (020) 7152 6536. *Clubs:* Arts, George, Alfreds, Mark's; Hong Kong, Shek O (Hong Kong).

DAVIES OF COITY, Baron *cr* 1997 (Life Peer), of Penybont, in the co. of Mid Glamorgan; **David Garfield Davies,** CBE 1996; General Secretary, Union of Shop, Distributive and Allied Workers, 1986–97; *b* 24 June 1935; *s* of David John Davies and Lizzie Ann Davies; *m*

1960, Marian (*née* Jones); four *d.* *Educ:* Heolgam Secondary Modern School; Bridgend Tech. Coll. (part time). Served RAF, 1956–58. Junior operative, electrical apprentice and electrician, British Steel Corp., Port Talbot, 1950–69; Area Organiser, USDAW, Ipswich, 1969–73; Dep. Divl Officer, USDAW, London/Ipswich, 1973–78; Nat. Officer, USDAW, Manchester, 1978–85. Mem., TUC Gen. Council, 1986–97; Chm., TUC Internat. Cttee, 1992–94; TUC spokesperson on internat. affairs, 1994–97. Member: Exec. Bd, ICFTU, 1992–97; Exec. Cttee, ETUC, 1992–97. Mem., Employment Appeal Tribunal, 1991–2006. Governor, Birmingham Coll. of Food, Tourism and Creative Studies, 1995–99. JP 1972–79. President: Kidney Res. UK, 2002–; Manchester S Scout Council, 2004–; Seashell Trust (formerly Royal Sch. for the Deaf and Communication Disorders, Manchester), 2007– (Trustee, 2004–07); Stockport County AFC Ind. Supporters Club, 2007–. *Recreations:* swimming, reading, spectator sports (supporter, Stockport County FC); formerly soccer, cricket, Rugby. *Address:* 64 Dairyground Road, Bramhall, Stockport, Cheshire SK7 2QW. *T:* (0161) 439 9548. *Clubs:* Union Jack; Stockport County Football.

DAVIES OF OLDHAM, Baron *cr* 1997 (Life Peer), of Broxbourne in the co. of Hertfordshire; **Bryan Davies;** PC 2006; *b* 9 Nov. 1939; *s* of George William and Beryl Davies; *m* 1963, Monica Rosemary Mildred Shearing; two *s* one *d.* *Educ:* Redditch High Sch.; University Coll. London (BA Hons History); Inst. of Education (CertEd); London Sch. of Economics (BScEcons). Teacher, Latymer Sch., 1962–65; Lectr, Middlesex Polytechnic at Enfield, 1965–74. Sec., Parly Labour Party, 1979–92. Contested (Lab): Norfolk Central, 1966; Newport W, 1983. MP (Lab): Enfield North, Feb. 1974–1979; Oldham Central and Royton, 1992–97. An Asst Govt Whip, 1978–79; front bench spokesman on Further and Higher Educn, 1993–97. Member: Select Cttee on Public Expenditure, 1975–79; Select Cttee on Overseas Develt, 1975–79; Select Cttee on Nat. Heritage, 1992–93. A Lord in Waiting (Govt Whip), 2000–03; Captain of the Yeomen of the Guard (Dep. Govt Chief Whip), 2003–10; Parly Under-Sec. of State, DEFRA, 2009–10; Shadow Minister for Transport, 2010–; Opposition Treasury Spokesman, 2010–. Chm., FEFCE, 1998–2000. Mem., MRC, 1977–79. Pres., RoSPA, 1998–2000. *Recreations:* sport, literature. *Address:* 28 Churchfields, Broxbourne, Herts EN10 7JS. *T:* (01992) 410418.

DAVIES OF STAMFORD, Baron *cr* 2010 (Life Peer), of Stamford in the County of Lincolnshire; **(John) Quentin Davies;** *b* 29 May 1944; *e s* of late Dr Michael Ivor Davies and Thelma Davies (*née* Butler), Oxford; *m* 1983, Chantal, *e d* of late Lt-Col R. L. C. Tamplin, 17/21 Lancers, Military Kt of Windsor, and Claudine Tamplin (*née* Pleis); two *s.* *Educ:* Dragon Sch.; Leighton Park (exhibnr); Gonville and Caius Coll., Cambridge (Open Scholar; BA Hist. Tripos 1st cl. Hons 1966; MA); Harvard Univ. (Frank Knox Fellow, 1966–67). HM Diplomatic Service, 1967; 3rd Sec., FCO, 1967–69; 2nd Sec., Moscow, 1969–72; 1st Sec., FCO, 1973–74. Morgan Grenfell & Co.: Manager, later Asst Dir, 1974–78; Rep. in France, later Dir-Gen. and Pres., Morgan Grenfell France SA, 1978–81; Director (main bd), and Hd of Eur. Corporate Finance, 1981–87; Consultant, 1987–93. Director: Dewe Rogerson International, 1987–95; SGE, later Vinci SA, 1999–2001, 2003–08; Vinci UK (formerly Norwest Holst), 2001–08. Adviser: NatWest Securities, then NatWest Markets, 1993–99; Royal Bank of Scotland, 1999–2003. Mem. Council, Lloyds of London, 2004–07. Parly Advr, Chartered Inst. of Taxation, 1993–2008. Contested (C) Birmingham, Ladywood, Aug. 1977. MP Stamford and Spalding, 1987–97, Grantham and Stamford, 1997–2010 (C, 1987–2007, Lab, 2007–10). Parliamentary Private Secretary: to Minister of State for Educn, 1988–90; to Minister of State, Home Office, 1990–91; Opposition spokesman on social security and pensions, 1998–99; Shadow Paymaster-Gen., 1999–2000; Opposition spokesman on defence, 2000–01; Shadow NI Sec., 2001–03; Parly Under-Sec. of State (Minister for Defence Equipment and Support), MoD, 2008–10. Member: Treasury Select Cttee, 1992–98; Cttee on Standards and Privileges, 1995–98; Eur. Standing Cttee, 1991–97; Eur. Legislation Cttee, 1997–98; Internat. Develt Cttee, 2003–07; Chairman: British-German Parly Gp, 2005–08 (Jt Chm., 1997–2005); British-Romanian Parly Gp, 2011–; Vice Chairman: Anglo-French Parly Gp, 1997–2008; British-Netherlands Parly Gp, 1999–2008; British-Italian Parly Gp, 2005–08; Chm., Conservative Gp for Europe, 2006–07. Chm., Inquiry into Nat. Recognition of our Armed Forces, 2007 (report publd 2008). Chm., City in Europe Cttee, 1975. Parly Fellow, RCDS, 2012–13. Freeman, City of London; Liveryman, Goldsmiths' Co. Trustee and Mem. Council, Centre for Econ. Policy Res., 1996–2008. Freedom of Information Award, 1996; Guardian Backbencher of the Year Award, 1996; Spectator Parliamentarian of the Year Award, 1997. *Publications:* Britain and Europe: a Conservative view, 1996. *Recreations:* reading, walking, riding, ski-ing, travel, playing (bad) tennis, looking at art and architecture. *Address:* House of Lords, SW1A 0PW. *Clubs:* Brooks's, Beefsteak, Travellers.

DAVIES, Adele, (Mrs R. O. Davies); *see* Biss, A.

DAVIES, Alan Roger; actor and comedian; *b* 6 March 1966; *s* of Roy and Shirley Davies; *m* 2007, Katie Maskell; one *s* one *d.* *Educ:* Bancroft's Sch.; Loughton Coll. of Further Educn; Univ. of Kent (BA Hons 1988). Stand-up comedian, 1988–; Live at the Lyric (one-man show), 1994; Urban Trauma (one-man show), Duchess Th., 1998; Life is Pain (one-man show), Criterion Th., 2012; *television* series include: Jonathan Creek, 1996–2003, 2010, 2013, 2014; Bob and Rose, 2001; QI, 2003–; The Brief, 2004, 2005; Alan Davies' Teenage Revolution, 2010; Show Me The Funny, 2011; Alan Davies: As Yet Untitled, 2014; The Dog Rescuers with Alan Davies, 2014; *radio* series include: The Alan Davies Show, Radio 4, 1998; *films* include: Angus, Thongs and Perfect Snogging, 2008. Contributor: The Times, 2003–06; Wisden Cricket Monthly. Hon. DLitt Kent, 2003. *Publications:* My Favourite People and Me, 2009. *Recreations:* Arsenal FC, motor cycling, scuba diving. *Address:* c/o PBJ Management Ltd, 22 Rathbone Street, W1T 1LG.

DAVIES, Alan Seymour; JP; Headmaster, Copland Community School and Technology Centre Foundation, 1988–2009; *b* 21 Feb. 1947; *s* of Seymour George Davies and Sarah Louise Davies; *m* 1972, Frances Patricia Williamson; one *s* two *d.* *Educ:* Inst. of Educn, London Univ. (BEd, CertEd); NE London Poly. (MEd). Teacher, E Barnet Sch., 1972–75; Teacher, 1975–80, Dep. Head, 1980–86, McEntee Sen. High Sch.; Headteacher, Sidney Chaplin Sch., 1986–88; Acting Headteacher, Harlesden Primary Sch., 2000. Consultant Headteacher, London Leadership Challenge, 2003. Chm. of Govs, Chalkhill Primary Sch., 2003–09; Governor: Park Lane Primary Sch., 1998; Mitchell Brook Primary Sch., 1999; Harlesden Primary Sch., 2000. JP Barnet, 1984. Hon. DSc Westminster, 2007. *Recreation:* sport. *Address:* 39 Grants Close, Mill Hill, NW7 1DD. *T:* (020) 8349 9731.

DAVIES, Alun; Member (Lab) Blaenau Gwent, National Assembly for Wales, since 2011 (for Wales Mid and West, 2007–11); *b* Tredegar, 12 Feb. 1964; *s* of Thomas Rhys Davies and Mair Davies; one *s* one *d.* *Educ:* Tredegar Comprehensive Sch.; University Coll. of Wales, Aberystwyth (BSc Hons Econs). Campaigner on envmtl issues, WWF; poverty campaigner, Oxfam; Public and Corporate Affairs Manager, Hyder; Hd, Public Affairs, UKAEA; Dir, Corporate Affairs, S4C; founded Bute Communications, 2004. Dep. Minister for Agric., Fisheries and Eur. Progs, 2011–13, Minister for Natural Resources and Food, 2013–14, Welsh Govt. Contested: (Plaid Cymru-Green Alliance) Blaenau Gwent, 1992; (Plaid Cymru) Cynon Valley, 1997; (Lab) Ceredigion, 2005. *Address:* National Assembly for Wales, Cardiff Bay, Cardiff CF99 1NA.

DAVIES, Prof. Alun Millward, PhD; FMedSci; FRS 2011; FRSE, FLSW; Distinguished Research Professor, School of Biosciences, Cardiff University, since 2004; Wellcome Trust Senior Investigator, since 2014; *b* Newport, Gwent, 2 Aug. 1955; *s* of Gywnfryn Millward Davies and Nancy Eva Davies; partner, Christina Burch; two *s.* *Educ:* Pontllanfraith Grammar Tech. Sch.; Univ. of Liverpool Med. Sch. (MB ChB 1978); Univ. of Liverpool (BSc Cell Biol. and Biochem. 1979); Guy's Hosp. Med. Sch., Univ. of London (PhD Develtl Neurobiol. 1984). Lectr, Middlesex Hosp. Med. Sch., Univ. of London, 1982–83; Lectr, 1983–88, Sen. Lectr, 1988–89, Reader in Neurobiol., 1989–93, St George's Hosp. Med. Sch., Univ. of London; Prof. of Develtl Neurobiol., Sch. of Biol Scis, St Andrews Univ., 1993–2000; Prof. of Physiol., Royal (Dick) Sch. of Veterinary Studies, Edinburgh Univ., 2000–04. Exec. Vice Pres. of Res., Rinat Neuroscience Corp., Palo Alto, Calif, 2001–03. Mem., EMBO, 2000; MAE 2011. FRSE 2000; FMedSci 2010; FLSW 2011. *Publications:* articles in learned jls. *Recreations:* playing piano and harpsichord, portraiture, carpentry, single-handed sailing, scuba diving. *Address:* Life Sciences Building, School of Biosciences, Cardiff University, Museum Avenue, Cardiff CF10 3AT. *T:* (029) 2087 4303. *E:* daviesalun@cf.ac.uk.

DAVIES, Prof. Alwyn George, FRS 1989; Professor of Chemistry, University College London, 1969–91, now Emeritus; *b* 13 May 1926; *s* of John Lewis and Victoria May Davies; *m* 1956, Margaret Drake; one *s* one *d.* *Educ:* Hamond's Grammar Sch., Swaffham; University College London (BSc, PhD, DSc; Fellow 1991). CChem, FRSC. Lectr, Battersea Polytechnic, 1949; Lectr, 1953, Reader, 1964, UCL. Ingold Lectr, RSC, 1992–93. Medal for Organic Reaction Mechanism, RSC, 1989; Humboldt Prize, Freiburg Univ., 1994. *Publications:* Organic Peroxides, 1959; Organotin Chemistry, 1997, 2nd edn 2004; (ed jtly) Tin Chemistry, 2008; (with P. J. Garratt) UCL Chemistry Department 1828–1974, 2013; scientific papers on physical organic chemistry and organometallic chemistry in learned jls. *Address:* Chemistry Department, University College London, 20 Gordon Street, WC1H 0AJ. *T:* (020) 7679 4701. *E:* a.g.davies@ucl.ac.uk.

DAVIES, Andrew; *see* Davies, D. A.

DAVIES, Andrew L.; *see* Lloyd-Davies.

DAVIES, Andrew Oswell Bede; Chief Executive Officer, Wates Group, since 2014; *b* Wantage, 12 Oct. 1963; *m* Catherine Louise Hendry; two *s* one *d.* *Educ:* King Edward VI Sch., Norwich; Univ. of Sheffield (BA Hons Business Studies). With BAE Systems plc, 1985–2013 (Man. Dir, Land Systems Div.; Gp Strategy Dir and Mem., Exec. Cttee; Man. Dir, Maritime). *Address:* Wates Group Ltd, Wates House, Station Approach, Leatherhead, Surrey KT22 7SW. *T:* (01372) 861071, *Fax:* (01372) 861072. *E:* andrew.davies@wates.co.uk.

DAVIES, Andrew Robert Tudor; Member (C) South Wales Central, National Assembly for Wales, since 2007; Leader of the Opposition, since 2011; *b* 8 April 1968; *s* of Tudor John Davies and Margaret Elizabeth Rees Davies; *m* 1991, Julia Mary; two *s* two *d.* *Educ:* Balfour House Sch., St Athan; Wycliffe Coll., Stonehouse. Partner, family farming and agricl business. National Farmers Union: Chm., 2001, Pres., 2002, Glamorgan; Mem., Welsh Council, 2002–07; Mem., Nat. Combinable Crops Bd, 2004–07. Chm., Creative Rural Communities, 2003–04. Various positions in Cons Party. Gov., Llanfair Primary Sch., 2001–07. Chm., Llantrisant Young Farmers' Club, 1988. *Recreations:* work, travel, family. *Address:* Tudor Barn, The Garn Farm, St Hilary, Vale of Glamorgan CF71 7DP. *T:* 0300 200 7227. *E:* andrewrt.davies@assembly.wales. *Club:* Farmers (Glamorgan).

DAVIES, Andrew Wynford; writer; *b* Rhiwbina, Cardiff, 20 Sept. 1936; *e s* of Wynford and Hilda Davies; *m* 1960, Diana Lennox Huntley; one *s* one *d.* *Educ:* Whitchurch Grammar Sch., Cardiff; University College London. Teacher: St Clement Danes Grammar Sch., 1958–61; Woodberry Down Comprehensive Sch., 1961–63; Lecturer: Coventry Coll. of Educn, 1963–71; Univ. of Warwick, 1971–87. Hon. Fellow, Univ. of Wales, Cardiff, 1997. Hon. DLitt: Coventry, 1994; Warwick, 2004; UCL, 2006; Hon. DArts De Montfort, 2003; DUniv Open, 2004. Guardian Children's Fiction Award, 1979; Boston Globe Horn Award, 1979; BPG Award, 1980, 1990, 1995, 1997, 2000, 2006; Pye Colour TV Award, best children's writer, 1981; writer's awards: RTS, 1986–87, 2006; BAFTA, 1989, 1993, 1998, 2006 (Fellow 2002); Writers' Guild, 1991, 1992, 1996; Primetime Emmy, 1991. *Television includes:* To Serve Them All My Days, 1979; A Very Peculiar Practice, 1986–87; Mother Love, 1989; House of Cards, 1990; Filipina Dreamers, 1991; The Old Devils, Anglo-Saxon Attitudes, A Very Polish Practice, 1992; Anna Lee, Harnessing Peacocks, To Play the King, 1993; Middlemarch, 1994; Game On, Pride and Prejudice, The Final Cut, 1995; Emma, Moll Flanders, Wilderness, 1996; A Few Short Journeys of the Heart, Bill's New Frock, 1997; Getting Hurt, Vanity Fair, A Rather English Marriage, 1998; Wives and Daughters, 1999; Take a Girl Like You, 2000; Othello, The Way We Live Now, 2001; Tipping the Velvet, Dr Zhivago, Daniel Deronda, 2002; Boudica, 2003; He Knew He Was Right, 2004; Falling, Bleak House, 2005; The Chatterley Affair, The Line of Beauty, 2006; Northanger Abbey, The Diary of a Nobody, Fanny Hill, A Room With A View, 2007; Sense and Sensibility, Affinity, Sleep With Me, Little Dorrit (Emmy Award, 2009), 2008; South Riding, 2011; Mr Selfridge, 2013–15; Quirke, A Poet in New York, 2014; War and Peace, 2015; *stage plays:* Rose, 1981; Prin, 1990; *film screenplays:* Circle of Friends, 1995; B. Monkey, 1996; Bridget Jones's Diary, The Tailor of Panama, 2001; Bridget Jones: The Edge of Reason, 2004; The Three Musketeers, 2011; *radio:* The Purple Land, 2011. *Publications: for children:* The Fantastic Feats of Dr Boox, 1972; Conrad's War, 1978; Marmalade and Rufus, 1980; Marmalade Atkins in Space, 1981; Educating Marmalade, 1982; Danger Marmalade at Work, 1983; Marmalade Hits the Big Time, 1984; Alfonso Bonzo, 1987; Marmalade on the Ball, 1995; (with Diana Davies): Poonam's Pets, 1990; Raj in Charge, 1994; *fiction:* A Very Peculiar Practice, 1986; The New Frontier, 1987; Getting Hurt, 1989; Dirty Faxes, 1990; B. Monkey, 1992. *Recreation:* lunch. *Address:* c/o The Agency, 24 Pottery Lane, W11 4LZ.

DAVIES, Ven. Anthony; *see* Davies, Ven. V. A.

DAVIES, (Anthony) Roger; a District Judge (Magistrates' Courts) (formerly Metropolitan Stipendiary Magistrate), 1985–2005; Chairman, Family Courts, 1989–2005; a Recorder, 1993–2005; *b* 1 Sept. 1940; *er s* of late R. George Davies and Megan Davies, Penarth, Glam; *m* 1967, Clare, *e d* of Comdr W. A. Walters, RN; twin *s* one *d.* *Educ:* Bridgend; King's Coll., London. LLB (Hons); AKC. Called to the Bar, Gray's Inn, 1965 (Lord Justice Holker Sen. Schol.). Practised at Bar, London and SE Circuit, 1965–85. *Recreations:* reading (history, biography), music (especially opera), travel, family life. *Club:* Travellers.

DAVIES, Barry George, MBE 2005; broadcaster, BBC Television sport and events; *b* 24 Oct. 1937; *s* of Roy Charles Davies and Dorothy Davies; *m* 1968, Edna (Penny) Pegna; one *s* one *d.* *Educ:* Cranbrook Sch., Kent; London Univ. (King's Coll. Royal Dental Hosp.). Commnd RASC, 1960. Sub-editor/reporter, The Times, 1963–66; Independent Television, 1966–69; commentator, World Cup 1966, Olympic Games 1968; joined BBC Television, 1969; commentator, Match of the Day, 1969–2004; commentator and presenter covering variety of sports, including: World Cup, 1970–2002; Olympic Games, 1972–; Winter Olympics, 1978–2006; Commonwealth Games, 1978–; Wimbledon, 1983–; University Boat Race, 1993–2004; commentator, LBC, University Boat Race, 2008–09. Commentator: Lord Mayor's Show, 1996–2003; (last) Royal Tournament, 1999; All the Queen's Horses, 2003. Presenter, Maestro Series, 1985–87. *Publications:* Interesting, Very Interesting: the autobiography, 2007. *Recreations:* family, theatre, political biographies, all sports (enthusiasm way ahead of talent). *Address:* Luxton Harris Ltd, 104A Park Street, W1K 6NG. *Clubs:* Lord's Taverners; Hawks (Cambridge); Wentworth.

DAVIES, (Beverley) Jane, OBE 2010; self-employed management consultant in science parks and innovation, since 2012; Chief Executive, Manchester Science Parks Ltd, 2000–12; *b* Leeds, 3 June 1952; *d* of Peter Baxendale and Patricia Baxendale; *m* 1975, Wyn Davies. *Educ:*

Lawnswood High Sch., Leeds; St Anne's Coll., Oxford (MA Chem.). Plant Chemist, BP Chemicals, 1974–81; Section Leader, Supply, BP Oil Internat., 1981–84; Crude Oil Trader, BP N America, 1984–86; Policy Planner, FCO, 1986–88 (on secondment); Sen. Consultant, BP Corp. Inf. Systems, 1988–91; Regl Manager, Air BP, 1991–92; self-employed mgt consultant, 1992–94; Gen. Manager, Buxton Fest., 1994–98. Non-exec. Dir, NI Sci. Park, 2013–. Mem., Project Adv. Bd, Sci. Park Graz, Austria, 2014–. Pres., Adv. Council, Internat. Assoc. of Sci. Parks, 2009–13. Cavaliere, Ordine al Merito (Italy), 2006. *Recreations:* Italy, theatre, opera, music, travel, eating good food with good friends. *E:* jane.davies@polidori.co.uk.

DAVIES, Brian; *see* Davies, E. B.

DAVIES, Prof. Brian Lawrence, PhD, DSc; FREng, FIMechE; Professor of Medical Robotics, Imperial College, London, since 2000; *b* 18 July 1939; *s* of William and Elizabeth Davies; *m* 1975, Marcia Mills; one *d.* *Educ:* Harrow Grammar Sch.; UCL (MPhil 1970); Imperial Coll., London (PhD 1995; DSc 2001). CEng 1973, FREng 2005; FIMechE 1990. GEC Ltd: indentured apprenticeship, 1955–60; design engr, 1960–63; Res. Asst in Mech. Engrg, 1963–69, Lectr, 1969–83, UCL; Lectr, 1983–89, Sen. Lectr, 1989–93, Reader, 1993–2000, in Mech. Engrg, Imperial Coll., London. Founder and Tech. Dir, Acrobot Co. Ltd, 1999–2010. Institute of Mechanical Engineering: Mem. Bd, 1990–, Chm., 1998–2001, Med. Engrg Div.; Mem. Council, 1998–2001. Chm., Strategic Acad. Bd, Swiss Nat. Computer Aided Med. Engrg, 2001–13. *Publications:* Engineering Drawing and Computer Graphics, 1986; (jtly) Computer-aided Drawing and Design, 1991; Computer Integrated Surgery, 1995; over 200 refereed papers mainly on computer-aided surgery and med. robotics. *Recreations:* painting, walking. *Address:* Department of Mechanical Engineering, Imperial College, London, SW7 2AZ. *T:* (020) 7594 7054.

DAVIES, Brigid Catherine Brennan; *see* Gardner, B. C. B.

DAVIES, Bryn, CBE 1987 (MBE 1978); DL; Member, General Council, Wales Trades Union Congress, 1974–91 (Vice-Chairman, 1983–84, Chairman, 1984–85); *b* 22 Jan. 1932; *s* of Gomer and Ann Davies; *m* 1st, 1956, Esme Irene Gould (*d* 1988); two *s*; 2nd, 1991, Katherine Lewis. *Educ:* Cwmlai School, Tonyrefail. Served HM Forces (RAMC), 1949–51; Forestry Commn, 1951–56; South Wales and Hereford Organiser, Nat. Union of Agricultural and Allied Workers, subseq. TGWU (following merger), 1956–91. Chm., Mid Glamorgan AHA, 1978–94; Member: Welsh Council, 1965–81; Development Commn, 1975–81; Nat. Cttee (Wales), Forestry Commn, 1978–86; Nat. Water Council, 1982–85; Council, British Heart Foundn, 1986–. Trustee, Sir Geraint Evans Wales Heart Res. Inst. Patron, Mencap Jubilee Festival. DL Mid Glamorgan, 1992. *Recreations:* cricket, Rugby football. *Address:* 3 Lias Cottages, Porthcawl, Mid Glamorgan CF36 3AD. *T:* (01656) 785851. *Clubs:* Tonyrefail Rugby (Pres., 1985–88); Pyle and Kenfig Golf; Pyle Rugby; Pirates (Porthcawl).

DAVIES, Byron, OBE 2008; DL; CEng, FICE; FCMI; Managing Director, BD Consulting (UK) Ltd, since 2010; Welsh Government Commissioner, since 2011; *b* 23 April 1947; *s* of Cecil and Elizabeth Gwendoline Davies; *m* 1972, Sarah Kay Lott; one *s* one *d.* *Educ:* Swansea Univ. (BSc Hons); Univ. of Glamorgan (MPhil). CEng 1976; FICE 1992. Work in private sector orgns, 1968–72; with Swansea CC and Devon CC, 1972–77; South Glamorgan County Council, 1977–96: various sen. civil engrg, property develt and gen. mgt posts; Dir, Property Services, 1990–92, Chief Exec., 1992–96; Chief Exec., Cardiff CC, 1996–2009. Director: Cardiff-Wales Airport, 1992–2009; Millennium Stadium plc, 1996–2009; Cardiff Chamber of Trade and Commerce, 1999–2009; Cardiff Marketing, 1999–2009; Cardiff Initiative, 1999–2009. Chm., Wales Internat. Business Council (formerly Wales N America Business Chamber), 2010–. Clerk to Lieutenancy of S Glam, 1992–2009; Sec. to Lord Chancellor's Adv. Cttee for S Glam, 1992–2009. Sec., Soc. of Local Authority Chief Execs and Sen. Managers in Wales, 2004–09; Pres., Solace UK, 2007–08 (Jun. Vice-Pres., 2005–07); Pres., Union des Dirigeants Territoriaux de l'Europe, 2008–10 (Vice Pres., 2006–08). Ex-Officio Mem., Council and Court, Univ. of Wales, Cardiff, 1992–. FCMI (FIMgt 1992); Pres., Cardiff Inst. of Mgt, 1999–2000. DL S Glamorgan, 2011. *Publications:* contrib. on engrg and mgt to professional jls. *Recreations:* walking, sport, cinema, photography. *Address:* The Cottage, Ystradowen, Cowbridge CF71 7SZ.

DAVIES, Byron; *see* Davies, H. B.

DAVIES, Prof. Christine Tullis Hunter, OBE 2006; PhD; FInstP; FRSE; Professor of Physics, University of Glasgow, since 1999; *b* Clacton, 19 Nov. 1959; *d* of Crawford Stewart and Elizabeth Stewart (*née* Clachan); *m* 1982, John Davies; two *d.* *Educ:* Colchester Co. High Sch. for Girls; Churchill Coll., Cambridge (BA 1981; PhD 1984). FInstP 1988. Postdoctoral res. associate, Cornell Univ., NY, 1984–86; SERC Advanced Fellow, 1987–93; Lectr, 1993–96, Reader, 1996–99, Univ. of Glasgow. Fulbright Schol. and Leverhulme Trust Fellow, Univ. of Calif at Santa Barbara, 1997–98. Science and Technology Facilities Council: Mem., Particle Physics Grants Panel (theory), 2006–09; Mem., Educn, Trng and Careers Cttee, 2006–09; Chair, Project Mgt Bd, Distributed Res. utilising Adv. Computing, High Performance Computing Facility, 2011–14; Mem., Physics Rev. Panel, Res. Council UK, 2008. Mem. Council, Inst. of Physics, 2007–11 (Chm., Diversity Cttee, 2007–11). FRSE 2001. Rosalind Franklin Award, Royal Soc., 2005; Nuclear and Particle Physics Div. Prize, Inst. of Physics, 2011; Wolfson Res. Merit Award, Royal Soc., 2012–. *Publications:* contrib. jls on theoretical particle physics. *Recreations:* walking, photography. *Address:* Department of Physics and Astronomy, University of Glasgow, Glasgow G12 8QQ. *T:* (0141) 330 4710.

DAVIES, Christopher Graham, (Chris); Member (Lib Dem) North West Region, England, European Parliament, 1999–2014; *b* 7 July 1954; *s* of Caryl St John Davies and Margaret (*née* McLeod); *m* 1979, Carol Hancox; one *d.* *Educ:* Cheadle Hulme Sch.; Gonville and Caius Coll., Cambridge (BA 1975, MA 1978); Univ. of Kent. Member: Liverpool City Council, 1980–84 (Chm., Housing Cttee, 1982–83); Oldham MBC, 1994–98. Manager: Public Affairs Div., Extel, 1983–85; Northern PR, Liverpool, 1985–87; Dir, Abercromby Consultancy Ltd, 1988–91; marketing and communications consultant, 1991–95; Sen. Consultant, Concept Communications, 1997–99. Contested (Lib Dem) Littleborough and Saddleworth, 1987, 1992. MP (Lib Dem) Littleborough and Saddleworth, July 1995–1997; contested (Lib Dem) Oldham East and Saddleworth, 1997. Leader, British Lib Dem MEPs, 2004–06; Lib Dem spokesman on envmt and climate change, 1999–2014; EP rapporteur on carbon capture and storage, 2008–14; Alliance of Liberals and Democrats for Europe co-ordinator, Cttee for Envmt, Food Safety and Public Health, 2008–14; Mem., Cttee for Fisheries, 2012–14; Secretary: All-Party Fish for the Future Gp, 2011–14; Carbon Capture and Storage Gp, 2013–14; Mem., delegn to Palestinian Legislative Council, 2004–14; Sub-Mem., delegn to Israel, 2009–14. Chm., NW Liberal Democrats, 2015–. Contested (Lib Dem) NW England, EP, 2014. MEP of Year (Envmt), Parlt Mag., 2014; Parliamentarian of Year (MEP), Green Ribbon Pol Awards, 2015. *Recreations:* fell running, ultra distance running. *Address:* 4 Higher Kinders, Greenfield, Oldham OL3 7BH. *E:* chrisdavies@greenfield.org.uk.

DAVIES, Christopher Paul; MP (C) Brecon and Radnorshire, since 2015; *b* Swansea, 18 Aug. 1967; *s* of T. V. S. Davies and late M. G. Davies (*née* Morgan); *m* 2006, Elizabeth Mary Dwyer; two *d.* *Educ:* Morriston Sch., Swansea. Rural auctioneer and estate agent; Manager, Hay Vet. Gp, Hay-on-Wye, 2008–14. Mem., Brecon Beacons Nat. Park Authy, 2012–15. Asst Hon. Dir, Royal Welsh Show, 2014–. Mem. (C) Powys CC, 2012–15. Contested (C) Brecon and Radnorshire, Welsh Assembly, 2011. Gov., Gwernyfed High Sch., 2012–. *Recreation:* countryside activities. *Address:* Ty Gwyn, Brookside, Glasbury-on-Wye, Powys HR3 5NF. *T:* (01982) 559180. *E:* chris.davies.mp@parliament.uk.

DAVIES, Prof. Colin; architectural writer; Professor of Architectural Theory, London Metropolitan University (formerly University of North London), 2005 (Professor, 2000–05); *b* 24 March 1948; *s* of John and Hazel Davies; *m* 1st, 1973, Diana Lamont (marr. diss.); one *s*; 2nd, 1992, Susan Wallington. *Educ:* King Henry VIII Sch., Coventry; Oxford Polytechnic; Architectural Assoc.; University College London (MSc). AADip, RIBA. Asst Editor, Building Magazine, 1975–77; Associate Partner, Derek Stow and Partners, 1977–81; freelance journalist, 1981–88; Editor, Architects' Jl, 1989–90. Lecturer: Bartlett, Canterbury and Brighton Schs of Architecture, 1983–91; Univ. of North London, 1992–2000. *Publications:* High Tech Architecture, 1988; Century Tower, 1992; Hopkins, 1993; Commerzbank, Frankfurt, 1997; Hopkins 2, 2001; The Prefabricated Home, 2005; Key Houses of the Twentieth Century, 2006; Thinking About Architecture, 2010; contribs to arch. jls. *Recreation:* choral singing.

DAVIES, Colin Godfrey, CEng, FIET; FRAeS; Director (formerly Director General, Projects and Engineering), National Air Traffic Services, 1991–97; *b* 9 Nov. 1934; *s* of Thomas William Godfrey Davies and Kathleen Mabel Davies; *m* 1966, Enid Beryl Packham; two *s.* *Educ:* King's Sch., Bruton; Loughborough Univ. (BSc Hons 1964; BA Hons 2009). FIET (FIEE 1986); FRAeS 1995. RAF Flying Officer (Aircrew), 1952–54. Cable and Wireless, 1955–90: Radio Technician, 1955–59; student, 1960–64; Special Projects Engr, Engr-in-Chief's Dept, 1964–68; Project Manager, 1968–75; Manager Transmission, Omantel, 1975–76; Manager Engrg, Fintel, 1976–77; Chief Engr Long Distance Services, Emirtel, 1978–79; Manager Internat. Services, 1980–82, Gen. Manager, 1983–87, Qatar; Dir of Corporate Technology and of two associated cos, 1987–90; Dep. Dir, Communications, NATS, 1990–91. Sen. Advr, Frequentis, Vienna, 1998–2003. *Recreations:* sport (badminton, sailing, ski-ing), gardening, photography. *Address:* Ibex House, Church Lane, Worplesdon, Guildford, Surrey GU3 3RU. *T:* (01483) 233214.

DAVIES, Cynog Glyndwr; *see* Dafis, C. G.

DAVIES, Cyril James, CBE 1987; DL; Chief Executive, City of Newcastle upon Tyne, 1980–86; *b* 24 Aug. 1923; *s* of James and Frances Davies; *m* 1948, Elizabeth Leggett; two *s* two *d.* *Educ:* Heaton Grammar Sch. CIPFA. Served RN, Fleet Air Arm, 1942–46. Entered City Treasurer's Dept, Newcastle upon Tyne, 1940: Dep. City Treas., 1964; City Treas., 1969; Treas., Tyne and Wear Co., 1973–80. Mem. Council, 1982–99, Mem. Court, 1999–2005, Univ. of Newcastle upon Tyne. DL Tyne and Wear, 1989. Hon. DCL Newcastle, 1998. *Recreations:* theatre, walking, music. *Address:* 4 Montagu Court, Gosforth, Newcastle upon Tyne NE3 4JL. *T:* (0191) 285 9685.

DAVIES, Dai; *see* Davies, David Clifford.

DAVIES, Dr David; Director: Elmhirst Trust, 1987–2002; Open College of the Arts, 1989–99 (Administrative Director, 1988–89); *b* 11 Aug. 1939; *s* of late Trefor Alun and Kathleen Elsie Davies; *m* 1968, Joanna Rachel, *d* of late David Brian Peace, MBE; one *s* three *d.* *Educ:* Nottingham High Sch.; Peterhouse, Cambridge. MA, PhD. Res. Scientist, Dept of Geophysics, Cambridge, 1961–69; Leader, Seismic Discrimination Gp, MIT Lincoln Laboratory, 1970–73; Editor of Nature, 1973–79; Dir, Dartington N Devon Trust, 1980–87. Rapporteur, Seismic Study Gp of Stockholm Internat. Peace Res. Inst. (SIPRI), 1968–73; Chm., British Seismic Verification Res. Project, 1987–91. Member: Warnock Cttee on artificial human fertilisation, 1982–84; BMA Working Party on Surrogacy, 1988–89. Chm., Ivanhoe Trust, 1986–2001. Member Council: Internat. Disaster Inst., 1979; Beaford Arts Centre, 1980–87; Voluntary Arts Network, 1992–95; Trustee: Bristol Exploratory, 1983–90; Cooper Art Gall., Barnsley, 1994–2001; Yorks Organiser, Open Coll. of the Arts, 1987–89. Musical Director: Blackheath Opera Workshop, 1977–79; Winterbourne Opera, 2006–12; Conductor: Exmoor Chamber Orch., 1980–87; Cross Keys Orch., 2014–; Member: Musica Rustica, 2002–; Cross Keys Ensemble, 2006–13; Salisbury Baroque, 2010–; Producer: Ebblesway Opera, 2004–05; Opera at Chilmark, 2006–. Hon. Lectr, Bretton Hall Coll., 1987–2001. Hon. Fellow: Univ. of Leicester, 1988; Univ. of Leeds, 1989. *Publications:* Seismic Methods for Monitoring Underground Explosions, 1968; numerous scientific papers. *Recreation:* keyboard playing.

DAVIES, (David) Andrew; Chairman, Abertawe Bro Morgannwg University Health Board, since 2013; *b* 5 May 1952; *s* of Wallace Morton Davies and Elizabeth Muriel Jane Davies (*née* Baldwin); *m* 1978, Deborah Frost (marr. diss. 1991). *Educ:* UC, Swansea (BSc Econ 1979; PGCE 1981); Gwent Coll. of Higher Educn (Dip. Counselling). Lectr in Adult and Further Educn, Swansea Univ., WEA and Swansea Coll., 1980–84; Regl Official, Wales Labour Party, 1984–91; Head of Employee Develt and Assistance Prog., Ford Motor Co., 1991–96; Lectr, Swansea Coll., 1994–97; Special Projects Officer (Referendum), Wales Labour Party, 1997–98; Associate Dir, Welsh Context, 1998–99. National Assembly for Wales: Mem. (Lab) Swansea West, 1999–2011; Chief Whip, Labour Gp, 1999–2000; Business Manager, then Minister for Assembly Business, 1999–2002; Minister: for Econ. Develt, 2002–06; for Transport, 2003–06; for Enterprise, Innovation and Networks, 2006–07; for Social Justice and Public Service Delivery, 2007; for Finance and Public Service Delivery, 2007–09. Strategic Advr, Swansea Univ., 2012. Chairman: National Dance Co. Wales, 2010–; Welsh Commn on Co-operatives and Mutuals, 2012–15. Trustee, Charity Bank, 2010–13. *Recreations:* bird watching, cooking, gardening, the arts (especially contemporary dance and film).

DAVIES, David Clifford, (Dai); community worker in training and education, Blaenau Gwent; *b* 26 Nov. 1959; *m* 1996, Amanda Gearing; one *s.* *Educ:* secondary sch.; served electrical apprenticeship. Steelworker, British Steel, subseq. Corus, Blaenau Gwent, 1976–2002; work with trade unions, 2002–05. Researcher for Peter Law, MP, 2005–06. MP (Ind) Blaenau Gwent, June 2006–2010; contested (People's Voice) same seat, 2010.

DAVIES, David Cyril, BA, LLB; Headmaster, Crown Woods School, 1971–84; *b* 7 Oct. 1925; *s* of D. T. E. Davies and Mrs G. V. Davies, JP; *m* 1952, Joan Rogers, BSc; one *s* one *d.* *Educ:* Lewis Sch., Pengam; UCW Aberystwyth. Asst Master, Ebbw Vale GS, 1951–55; Head, Lower Sch., Netteswell Bilateral Sch., 1955–58; Sen. Master and Dep. Headmaster, Peckham Manor Sch., 1958–64; Headmaster: Greenway Comprehensive Sch., 1964–67; Woodberry Down Sch., 1967–71. Pres., Inverliever Lodge Trust, 1971–84. *Recreations:* reading, Rugby and roughing it. *Address:* 9 Plaxtol Close, Bromley, Kent BR1 3AU. *T:* (020) 8464 4187.

DAVIES, Sir David (Evan Naunton), Kt 1994; CBE 1986; PhD, DSc; FRS 1984; FREng; Chairman, Hazard Forum, 2003–10; President, Royal Academy of Engineering, 1996–2001; *b* 28 Oct. 1935; *s* of David Evan Davies and Sarah (*née* Samuel); *m* 1st, 1962, Enid Patilla (*d* 1990); two *s*; 2nd, 1992, Jennifer E., (Jenna), Rayner. *Educ:* Univ. of Birmingham (MSc 1958; PhD 1960; DSc 1968). FIET (FIEE 1969); FIERE 1975; FREng (FEng 1979). Lectr and Sen. Lectr in Elec. Engrg, Univ. of Birmingham, 1961–67 (also Hon. SPSO, RRE, Malvern, 1966–67); Asst Dir of Elec. Res., BR Bd, Derby, 1967–71; Vis. Industrial Prof. of Elec. Engrg, Loughborough Univ. of Technol., 1969–71; University College London: Prof. of Elec. Engrg, 1971–88; Pender Prof. and Hd of Dept of Electronic and Electrical Engrg, 1985–88; Vice-Provost, 1986–88; Vice-Chancellor, Loughborough Univ. of Technology, 1988–93; Chief Scientific Advr, MoD, 1993–99. Chm., Railway Safety, 2001–03; Safety Advr, Nat. Grid plc (formerly Nat. Grid Transco), 2002–08. Non-executive Director: Gaydon Technology (Rover Group), 1986–88; Loughborough Consultants, 1988–93; Inst. Consumer

Ergonomics, 1988–93; ERA Technology, 1996–2003; Lattice plc, 2000–02; ERA Foundn, 2002–07. Member: SERC, 1985–89; IT Adv. Bd, DTI, 1988–91; EPSRC, 1994–99; Bd, POST, 2006–; Chm., Defence Scientific Adv. Council, 1992–93. Pres., IEE, 1994–95; Vice Pres., Royal Acad. of Engrg, 1995–96. Pro Chancellor, Univ. of Sussex, 1998–2001. Liveryman, Engineers' Co., 1995 (Master Engineer, 2003–04). Hon. FIChemE 1997; Hon. FIMechE 1998; Hon. FIStructE 2001; Hon. FIEE 2002; Hon. Fellow UCL, 2006. Hon DSc: Birmingham, Loughborough, South Bank, 1994; Bradford, 1995; Surrey, 1996; Bath, Warwick, 1997; Heriot-Watt, 1999; Wales, 2002; Hon. DEng UMIST 2000. Rank Prize for Optoelectronics, 1984; Callendar Medal, Inst. of Measurement & Control, 1984; Faraday Medal, IEE, 1987; President's Medal, RAEng, 2006. *Publications:* technical papers and articles on radar, antennae and aspects of fibre optics. *Address:* Church Hill House, Church Lane, Danehill, Haywards Heath, W Sussex RH17 7EY. *T:* (01825) 790321.

DAVIES, (David) Hywel, MA, PhD; FREng; FIET; consultant; Deputy Director-General for Science, Research and Development, EEC, Brussels, 1982–86; *b* 28 March 1929; *s* of John and Maggie Davies; *m* 1961, Valerie Elizabeth Nott; one *s* two *d. Educ:* Cardiff High Sch.; Christ's Coll., Cambridge. Radar Research Estabt, 1956; Head of Airborne Radar Group, RRE, 1970; Head of Weapons Dept, Admty Surface Weapons Estabt, 1972; Asst Chief Scientific Advr (Projects), MoD, 1976–79; Dir, RARDE, MoD, 1979–80; Dep. Controller, Res. Programmes, MoD, 1980–82. Man. Dir, Topexpress Ltd, 1988–89. FREng (FEng 1988). *Publications:* papers on electronics, radar and remote sensing, in Proc. IEE, etc. *Recreations:* Europe, computing, knots. *Address:* 52 Brittains Lane, Sevenoaks, Kent TN13 2JP. *T:* (01732) 456359.

DAVIES, (David) Ian, MA; Headmaster, Brentwood School, since 2004; *b* 17 May 1959; *s* of Dillwyn and Morfydd Davies; *m* 1989, Sara Stern. *Educ:* St John's Coll., Oxford (MA 1980); Fitzwilliam Coll., Cambridge (PGCE 1981). Hd, Lower Sch., Latymer Upper Sch., 1992–98; Headmaster, St Dunstan's Coll., 1998–2004. Boarding Headmaster, Admiralty Bd, 2000–04; Ind. Schs Advr to Duke of Edinburgh's Award Scheme, 2004–13. Chm., London Div. (S), HMC, 2002. Chm., Brentwood Th. Trust. Gov., St Aubyn's Prep. Sch., Woodford Green. Liveryman, Co. of Wax Chandlers. *Recreations:* golf, tennis, cricket, reading, France. *Address:* Brentwood School, Brentwood, Essex CM15 8AS. *T:* (01277) 243243, *Fax:* (01277) 243299. *E:* headmaster@brentwood.essex.sch.uk. *Clubs:* East India; Thorndon Park Golf.

DAVIES, Sir David (John), Kt 1999; Chairman, Shaftesbury Asset Management Group, since 2007; *b* 1 April 1940; *s* of late Stanley Kenneth Davies, CBE and Stephanie Davies; *m* 1st, 1967, Deborah Frances Loeb (marr. diss.); one *s*; 2nd, 1985, Linda Wong Lin-Tye (marr. diss.); one *s* two *d. Educ:* Winchester Coll., Winchester; New Coll., Oxford (MA); Harvard Business Sch. (AMP). Chase Manhattan Bank, 1963–67; Hill Samuel Group, 1967–73: Dir, Hill Samuel Inc., New York, 1970–73; Dir, Hill Samuel Ltd, London, 1973; Finance Dir, 1973–83, and Vice-Chm., 1977–83, MEPC Ltd; Man. Dir, The Hongkong Land Co. Ltd, 1983–86; Director: Jardine Matheson Gp, 1983–86; Hong Kong Electric Co., 1983–86; Chairman: Hong Kong Land Property Co. Ltd, 1983–86; Mandarin Oriental Hotel Gp, 1983–86; Dairy Farm Ltd, 1983–86; Dir, 1986–88, Chief Exec. and Exec. Vice Chm., 1987–88, Hill Samuel Gp; Jt Chm., Hill Samuel & Co., 1987–88. Chm., 1990–98, Chief Exec., 1994–98, Johnson Matthey plc. Chairman: Wire Ropes Ltd, Wicklow, 1979–; Imry Merchant Developers (formerly Imry Internat.), 1987–89; Imry Holdings, 1992–98; MBO Partners Ltd, HK, 1992–2000; Semara (formerly Sketchley) PLC, 1990–2000; EFG Private Bank Ltd, 1999–2006; Dep. Chm., Charter Consolidated, 1988–89; Director: American Barrick Resources Corp., Toronto, 1986–94; Delaware North Cos Inc., Buffalo, NY, 1986–; Singapore Land Ltd, 1986–90; Fitzwilton PLC, Dublin, 1987–90; Asia Securities, Hong Kong, 1987–89; Hardwicke Ltd, Dublin, 1987–2007; TSB Group, 1987–89; First Pacific Co., Hong Kong, 1988–91; Irish Life Assce, 1991–97; The Wharf (Holdings) Ltd, Hong Kong, 1992–99; Wheelock NatWest, 1994–97; Glyndebourne Productions Ltd, 1990–2000; Hilton Gp (formerly Ladbroke Gp) plc, 1997–2001; General Enterprise Mgt Services Ltd, 1998–2001; European Financial Gp, EFG (Luxembourg) SA, 2006–12; Gluskin Sheff and Associates, Toronto, 2007–08. Chm., Adv. Cttee on Business and the Envmt, 1995–98 (Mem., 1993–98); Dep. Chm., Prince of Wales' Business Leaders Forum, 1997–98 (Dir, 1991–96); Mem., Prince of Wales Business and the Envmt Prog., 1993–99. Member: Council, Ireland Fund of GB, 1988–2002; Bd, Wales Millennium Centre, 2004–10; Governing Council, Centre for Study of Financial Innovation, 2004–13; Chm., Adv. Cttee, Global Leadership Foundn, 2004– (Chm., Global Leadership Foundn, UK, 2008–). Director: Irish Georgian Soc., 2002–09; Everard Read Gall., 2005–. Chm., Wexford Fest. UK Trust, 1997–; Pres., Wexford Fest. Trust, 2014–; Chm., Grange Park Opera, 1998–2005 (Chm., Adv. Council, 2005–); Vice-Pres., Leeds Internat. Piano Comp., 2004–12. Chairman: Irish Heritage Trust, 2006–12; Develt Bd, Saïd Business Sch., Univ. of Oxford, 2007–10; Member: Adv. Cttee for Fund Raising, Ashmolean Mus., 1991–96; New Coll. Develt Fund, 1995– (Chm., 2007–; Mem., New Coll. Endowment Cttee, 1994–2007); Winchester Coll. Develt Council, 2002–08; Dep. Chm., Campaign for Oxford, 2008–10; Trustee: Anglo-Hong Kong Trust, 1989–2004; Monteverdi Trust, 1991–97; Royal Opera House Trust, 1997–2001 (Mem., Appeal Cttee, 1997–2001); St Catherine Foundn, 2001–; World Monuments Fund in Britain, 2002–07; Cape Town Opera, 2004–11. *Recreations:* trees, walking, opera. *Address:* 1712 Tower One Times Square, 1 Matheson Street, Hong Kong. *Clubs:* Beefsteak, Garrick; All England Lawn Tennis; Cardiff and County (Cardiff); Kildare Street and University (Dublin); Hong Kong, China (Hong Kong).

DAVIES, Rt Hon. (David John) Denzil; PC 1978; *b* 9 Oct. 1938; *s* of G. Davies, Conwil Elfed, Carmarthen; *m* 1963, Mary Ann Finlay (marr. diss. 1988), Illinois; one *s* one *d. Educ:* Queen Elizabeth Grammar Sch., Carmarthen; Pembroke Coll., Oxford. Bacon Scholar, Gray's Inn, 1961; BA (1st cl. Law) 1962; Martin Wronker Prize (Law), 1962. Teaching Fellow, Univ. of Chicago, 1963; Lectr in Law, Leeds Univ., 1964; called to Bar, Gray's Inn, 1964. MP (Lab) Llanelli, 1970–2005. Member: Select Cttee on Corporation Tax, 1971; Jt Select Cttee (Commons and Lords) on Delegated Legislation, 1972; Public Accounts Cttee, 1974; PPS to the Secretary of State for Wales, 1974–76; Minister of State, HM Treasury, 1975–79; Opposition spokesman on Treasury matters, 1979–81, on foreign affairs, 1981–82, on defence, 1982–83; chief opposition spokesman: on Welsh affairs, 1983; on defence and disarmament, 1983–88. *Publications:* The Galilean and the Goose: how Christianity converted the Roman Empire, 2010.

DAVIES, Prof. David Roy, OBE 1995; PhD; Professor of Applied Genetics, University of East Anglia, 1968–94, now Professor Emeritus (Dean of School of Biological Sciences, 1985–91); Deputy Director, John Innes Institute, 1978–94; *b* 10 June 1932; *s* of late J. O. Davies and A. E. Davies; *m* 1957, Winifred Frances Davies, JP, BA (*née* Wills); two *s* two *d. Educ:* Llandyssul and Grove Park, Wrexham Grammar Schs; Univ. of Wales. BSc, PhD. UK Atomic Energy Authority, 1956–62 and 1963–68; US Atomic Energy Commn, 1962–63. Editor, Heredity, 1975–82. *Publications:* edited: The Plant Genome, 1980; Temperate Legumes, 1983; Peas: genetics, molecular biology and biotechnology, 1993; papers on radiobiology and plant genetics in scientific jls. *Address:* 57 Church Lane, Eaton, Norwich NR4 6NY. *T:* (01603) 451049.

DAVIES, His Honour David Theodore Alban; a Circuit Judge, 1994–2007; *b* 8 June 1940; *s* of late John Rhys Davies, Archdeacon of Merioneth, and Mabel Aeronwy Davies; *m* 1966, Janet Mary, *er d* of late Frank and Barbara Welburn, Cheadle Hulme, Cheshire; one *s* one *d. Educ:* Rossall School (Scholar); Magdalen College, Oxford (Exhibnr, 2nd cl. Mods 1960, 1st cl. Lit.Hum., 1962, BA 1962; Eldon Law Schol., 1963; MA 1967). Called to the Bar, Gray's Inn, 1964 (Entrance Schol., Arden Atkin and Mould Prize, Lord Justice Holker Sen. Schol.). Practised SE Circuit, 1965–83; Registrar, then a Dist Judge, Family Div., High Court, 1983–94; a Recorder, 1989–94; Designated Family Judge, Rhyl County Court, 1994–2007. Chancellor, dio. of Bangor, 1995–2012. Sec., Family Law Bar Assoc., 1976–80, Treasurer, 1980–83; Member: Senate Law Reform Cttee, 1979–83; Civil and Family Cttee, 1988–93, Main Bd, 1991–93, Judicial Studies Bd. *Publications:* (ed jtly) Jackson's Matrimonial Finance and Taxation, 2nd edn 1975, 5th edn 1992. *Recreations:* reading, walking, history. *Address:* c/o Rhyl County Court, Clwyd Street, Rhyl, Denbighshire LL18 3LA.

DAVIES, David Thomas Charles; MP (C) Monmouth, since 2005; *b* 26 June 1970; *s* of Peter Hugh Charles Davies and Kathleen Diane Davies (*née* Elton); *m* 2003, Aliz Harnisföger; one *s* two *d. Educ:* Clytha Sch., Newport; Bassaleg Sch., Newport. MInstTA; MILog; MIFF. BSC, 1988–89; Australia, 1989–91; Gen. Manager, Tea Importing and Shipping Co. (family business), 1991–99. Chm., Welsh Affairs Select Cttee, 2010–. Mem. (C) Monmouth, Nat. Assembly for Wales, 1999–2007. Contested (C) Bridgend, 1997. *Recreations:* running, surfing, white collar boxing (incl. charity bouts as 'The Tory Tornado'), salsa dancing, debunking climate change alarmism. *Address:* (constituency office) The Grange, 16 Maryport Street, Usk, Monmouthshire NP15 1AB; House of Commons, SW1A 0AA. *Clubs:* Abergavenny Conservative; Chepstow Conservative; Monmouth Conservative; Usk Conservative.

DAVIES, Deborah; *see* Arnott, D.

DAVIES, Rt Hon. Denzil; *see* Davies, Rt Hon. David J. D.

DAVIES, Dickie; television sports presenter, since 1964; *s* of Owen John Davies and Ellen Davies; *m* 1962, Elisabeth Ann Hastings Mann; twin *s. Educ:* William Ellis Sch., Highgate; Oldershaw Grammar Sch., Wallasey, Cheshire. Purser, Cunard Line, 1953–60; Television Announcer, Southern TV, 1960–63; World of Sport Presenter, 1964–85, Presenter: ITV Sport, 1985–89; Sportsmasters, 1988–92; The World of Golf, 1990; Classic FM, 1995–; Bobby Charlton's Football Scrapbook, Sky Sports TV, 1995–; Dickie Davies's Sporting Heroes, 1998–; World Cup Classics, 1999. *Recreations:* golf, walking our dogs.

DAVIES, Donald, CBE 1978 (OBE 1973); consultant; *b* 13 Feb. 1924; *s* of late Wilfred Lawson Davies and Alwyne Davies; *m* 1948, Mabel (*née* Hellyar); two *d. Educ:* Ebbw Vale Grammar Sch.; UC Cardiff (BSc). CEng, FIMinE. National Coal Board: Colliery Man., 1951–55; Gp Man., 1955–58; Dep. Prodn Man., 1958–60; Prodn Man., 1960–61; Area Gen. Man., 1961–67; Area Dir, 1967–73; Bd Mem., 1973–84; Chairman: Nat. Fuel Distributors, 1973–89; Southern Depot Co., 1973–89; NCB (Ancillaries), 1979–89; Horizon Exploration, 1981–89. *Recreations:* golf, walking. *Address:* Wendy Cottage, Dukes Wood Avenue, Gerrards Cross, Bucks SL9 7LA. *T:* (01753) 885083.

DAVIES, Rev. Prof. Douglas James, PhD, DLitt; Professor in the Study of Religion, since 2000, and Director, Centre for Death and Life Studies, since 2007, University of Durham (Head, Department of Theology, 2002–05); *b* 11 Feb. 1947; *s* of Llewelyn James Davies and Gladys Evelyn Davies (*née* Morgan). *Educ:* Lewis Sch., Pengam; St John's Coll., Durham (BA Anthropology 1969; BA Theology 1973); St Peter's Coll., Oxford (MLitt 1972); PhD Nottingham 1980; DLitt Oxon 2004. Ordained deacon 1975; priest 1976; University of Nottingham: Lectr in Theology, 1974–90; Sen. Lectr, 1990–93; Prof. of Religious Studies, 1993–97; Principal, Coll. of St Hild and St Bede, and Prof. of Theol., Univ. of Durham, 1997–2000. Vis. Res. Fellow, Rothermere American Inst., Oxford Univ., 2006; Mayers Fellow, Huntington Library, Calif, 2007; Res. Fellow, Collegium for Advanced Studies, Helsinki Univ., 2011; Vis. Fellow, Harris Manchester Coll., Oxford, 2014. Pres., British Assoc. for Study of Religion, 2009–12. FAcSS (AcSS 2009). FLSW 2012. Hon. DTheol Uppsala, 1998. SBStJ 2011. *Publications:* Meaning and Salvation in Religious Studies, 1984; Mormon Spirituality, 1987; (jtly) Church and Religion in Rural England, 1991; Frank Byron Jevons: an evolutionary realist, 1991; (jtly) Reusing Old Graves, 1995; (ed) Mormon Identities in Transition, 1996; Death, Ritual and Belief, 1997; The Mormon Culture of Salvation, 2000; Private Passions, 2000; Anthropology and Theology, 2002; Introduction to Mormonism, 2003; A Brief History of Death, 2004; (ed jtly) Encyclopedia of Cremation, 2005; (jtly) Studying Local Churches, 2005; (jtly) Bishops, Wives and Children: spiritual capital across the generations, 2007; The Theology of Death, 2008; Joseph Smith, Jesus and Satanic Opposition: atonement, evil and the Mormon vision, 2010; Emotion, Identity and Religion: hope, reciprocity and otherness, 2011; (ed jtly) Emotion, Identity and Death: mortality across disciplines, 2012; (jtly) Natural Burial: traditional-secular spiritualities and funeral innovation, 2012; (ed) Emotions and Religious Dynamics, 2013; (ed jtly) Sacred Selves, Sacred Settings: reflecting Hans Mol, 2015. *Recreations:* squash, cacti, gardening. *Address:* Department of Theology and Religion, Abbey House, Palace Green, Durham DH1 3RS. *Club:* Royal Over-Seas League.

DAVIES, Ednyfed Hudson, BA (Wales); MA (Oxon); barrister; Chairman, Lincs FM Group of Commercial Radio Stations (formerly Lincs FM plc), since 1991; *b* 4 Dec. 1929; *s* of Rev. E. Curig Davies and Enid Curig Davies (*née* Hughes); *m* 1972, Amanda, *d* of Peter and Elsa Barker-Mill (marr. diss. 1994); two *d*; partner, Dr Susan Owen. *Educ:* Friars Sch., Bangor; Dynevor Grammar Sch., Swansea; University College of Swansea; Balliol Coll., Oxford. Called to the Bar, Gray's Inn, 1975. Lecturer in Dept of Extra-Mural Studies, University of Wales, Aberystwyth, 1957–61; Lecturer in Political Thought, Welsh Coll. of Advanced Technology, Cardiff, 1961–66. MP: (Lab) Conway, 1966–70; Caerphilly, 1979–83 (Lab, 1979–81, SDP, 1981–83); Mem., H of C Select Cttee on Energy, 1980–83; Sec., H of C All-Party Tourism Cttee, 1979–83. Contested (SDP) Basingstoke, 1983. Part-time TV and radio commentator and interviewer on current affairs, 1962–66; on full-time contract to BBC presenting Welsh-language feature programmes on overseas countries, 1970–76; Chm., Wales Tourist Board, 1976–78. Dep. Chm., Ocean Sound Radio, 1989–94 (Dir, 1986–94); Dir, Southern Radio, 1989–94. Director: New Forest Butterfly Farm, 1984–94; New Forest Enterprise Centre (formerly New Forest Industrial Assoc. Ltd), 1989– (Chm., 2013–). Trustee: New Forest Ninth Centenary Trust and New Forest Centre, 1986– (Chm., 1994–2011; Pres., 2012–); Wessex Cultural (formerly Hants Mus and Galleries) Trust, 2007–. *Address:* Lincs FM Group Ltd, Witham Park, Waterside South, Lincoln LN5 7JN. *Clubs:* Royal Welsh Yacht (Caernarfon) (Cdre, 2002–03); Royal Anglesey Yacht; Royal Southampton Yacht.

DAVIES, Prof. (Edward) Brian, DPhil; FRS 1995; Professor of Mathematics, King's College London, 1981–2010, now Emeritus; *b* 13 June 1944; *s* of Arthur Granville Davies and Mary Davies (*née* Scudamore); *m* 1968, Jane Christine Phillips; one *s* one *d. Educ:* Jesus Coll., Oxford (BA 1965; MA); Brasenose Coll., Oxford (DPhil Maths 1968). Tutorial Fellow, St John's Coll., Oxford, 1970–81; Univ. Lectr, Oxford Univ., 1973–81; Head, Dept of Maths, KCL, 1990–93; FKC 1996. Pres., London Mathematical Soc., 2007–09. Editor, Qly Jl of Mathematics, 1973–81; Founding Editor, London Mathematical Soc. Student Text Series, 1983–90. *Publications:* Quantum Theory of Open Systems, 1976; One-Parameter Semigroups, 1980; Heat Kernels and Spectral Theory, 1989; Spectral Theory and Differential Operators, 1995; Science in the Looking Glass, 2003; Linear Operators and Their Spectra, 2007; Why Beliefs Matter, 2010. *Recreations:* family, scientific reading. *Address:* Department of Mathematics, King's College, Strand, WC2R 2LS.

DAVIES, (Edward) Hunter, OBE 2014; author, journalist; *b* Renfrew, Scotland, 7 Jan. 1936; *s* of late John Hunter Davies and Marion (*née* Brechin); *m* 1960, Margaret Forster, *qv*; one *s* two *d. Educ:* Creighton Sch., Carlisle; Carlisle Grammar Sch.; University Coll., Durham (BA 1957, DipEd 1958; Hon. Fellow 2007; Editor of Palatinate). Reporter: Manchester Evening Chronicle, 1958–59; Sunday Graphic, London, 1959–60; Sunday Times, 1960–84: Atticus,

1965–67; Chief Feature Writer, 1967; Editor, Sunday Times Magazine, 1975–77; Columnist: Punch, 1979–89; Stamp News, 1981–86; London Evening Standard, 1987; The Independent, 1989–93; New Statesman & Society, 1996–; Money section, Sunday Times, 1999–; Cumbria Life, 2008–. Presenter, Bookshelf, Radio 4, 1983–86. Mem., British Library Consultative Gp on Newspapers, 1987–89; Dir, Edinburgh Book Festival Bd, 1990–95; Chm., Cumbria Wildlife Trust, 1995–2008. Dep. Pro-Chancellor, Lancaster Univ., 1996–97. *Television:* The Playground (play), 1967; The Living Wall, 1974; George Stephenson, 1975; A Walk in the Lakes, 1979. Outstanding Achievement Award, Carnegie Sporting Words Awards, 2008. *Publications: fiction:* Here We Go, Round the Mulberry Bush, 1965 (filmed, 1968); The Rise and Fall of Jake Sullivan, 1970; (ed) I Knew Daisy Smuten, 1970; A Very Loving Couple, 1971; Body Charge, 1972; Flossie Teacake's Fur Coat, 1982; Flossie Teacake—Again!, 1983; Flossie Teacake Strikes Back, 1984; Come on Ossie!, 1985; Ossie Goes Supersonic, 1986; Ossie the Millionaire, 1987; Saturday Night, 1989; S.T.A.R.S (12 books in Penguin series), 1989–90; Snotty Bumstead, 1991; Striker, 1992; Snotty Bumstead and the Rent-a-Mum, 1993; Snotty the Hostage, 1995; Flossie Wins the Lottery, 1996; Flossie Teacake's Holiday, 2000; *non-fiction:* The Other Half, 1966; (ed) The New London Spy, 1966; The Beatles, 1968, illus. edn 2002, 3rd edn 2009; The Glory Game, 1972, 4th edn 2000; A Walk Along the Wall, 1974, 2nd edn 1984; George Stephenson, 1975, 2nd edn 2004; The Creighton Report, 1976; (ed) Sunday Times Book of Jubilee Year, 1977; A Walk Around the Lakes, 1979, 2nd edn 2000; William Wordsworth, 1980, 3rd edn 2009; The British Book of Lists, 1980; The Grades, 1981; Father's Day, 1981 (television series, 1983); Beaver Book of Lists, 1981; A Walk Along the Tracks, 1982, 2nd edn 2002; England!, 1982; (with Frank Herrmann) Great Britain: a celebration, 1982; A Walk Round London Parks, 1983; The Joy of Stamps, 1983; London at its Best, 1984; (also publisher) The Good Guide to the Lakes, 1984, 6th edn 2003; The Grand Tour, 1986; The Good Quiz Book to the Lakes, 1987; Back in the USSR, 1987; Beatrix Potter's Lakeland, 1988; My Life in Football, 1990; In Search of Columbus, 1991; Teller of Tales: in search of Robert Louis Stevenson, 1994; Hunting People: thirty years of interviews with the famous, 1994; Wainwright: the biography, 1995; Living on the Lottery, 1996; Born 1900, 1998; London to Loweswater, 1999; Dwight Yorke, 1999; A Walk Around the West Indies, 2000; Joe Kinnear: still crazy, 2000; The Quarrymen, 2001; The Eddie Stobart Story, 2001; Hurry, Hurry While Stocks Last, 2001; The Best of Lakeland, 2002; Relative Strangers, 2003; Boots, Balls and Haircuts, 2003; The Fan (anthol.), 2003; (jtly) Gazza—My Story, 2004; The Best of Wainwright, 2004; Strong Lad Wanted for Strong Lass, 2004; Mean With Money (anthol.), 2005; (jtly) Being Gazza, 2006; I Love Football, 2006; The Beatles, Football and Me: a memoir, 2006; The Second Half (anthol.), 2006; (jtly) Wayne Rooney, 2006; The Bumper Book of Football, 2007; (jtly) Prezza: my story - pulling no punches, 2008; Cold Meat and How to Disguise It, 2009; Confessions of a Collector, 2009; Behind the Scenes at the Museum of Baked Beans, 2010; Postcards from the Edge of Football, 2010; (ed) The Wainwright Letters, 2011; (ed) Sellafield Stories: life with Britain's first nuclear plant, 2012; (ed) The John Lennon Letters, 2012; The Biscuit Girls, 2014; The Beatles Lyrics, 2014. *Recreations:* walking, Lakeland books, Beatles memorabilia, swimming, football memorabilia. *Address:* 11 Boscastle Road, NW5 1EE; Grasmoor House, Loweswater, Cumbria CA13 0RU.

DAVIES, Edwin, CBE 2012 (OBE 2000); FCMA; investment advisor; *b* 18 June 1946; *s* of Edwin Davies and Hannah Davies (*née* Kelly); *m* 1989, Susan Chinn Crellin; one *s* one *d*. *Educ:* Farnworth Grammar Sch.; Durham Univ. (BA 1st Cl. Hons Maths). FCMA 1985; CCMI 2005. Asst Gp Man. Dir, Scapa Gp plc, 1968–84; Chm., Strix Gp Ltd, 1984–2006. Dir, Bolton Wanderers FC Ltd, 1999–. Mem. Adv. Council, Manchester Business Sch., Univ. of Manchester, 2010–. Trustee, V&A Mus., 2006–. Hon. DSocSc Manchester, 2008. *Recreations:* travel, archaeology, soccer. *Address:* Moorecroft, Crossag Road, Ballasalla, Isle of Man IM9 3EF. *T:* (01624) 828730, *Fax:* (01624) 824578.

DAVIES, Emrys Thomas, CMG 1988; HM Diplomatic Service, retired; *b* 8 Oct. 1934; *s* of Evan William Davies and Dinah Davies (*née* Jones); *m* 1960, Angela Audrey, *er d* of late Paul Robert Buchan May, ICS and of Esme May; one *s* two *d*. *Educ:* Parmiters Foundation Sch. RAF, 1953–55; commnd RAFVR, 1955. Sch. of Slavonic Studies, Cambridge Univ., 1954; Sch. of Oriental and African Studies, London Univ., 1955–56. Served Peking, 1956–59; FO, 1959–60; Bahrain, 1960–62; FO, 1962–63; Asst Political Adviser to Hong Kong Govt, 1963–68; First Sec., British High Commn, Ottawa, 1968–71; FCO, 1972–76; Commercial Counsellor, Peking, 1976–78 (Chargé, 1976 and 1978); Oxford Univ. Business Summer Sch., 1977; NATO Defense Coll., Rome, 1979; Dep. High Comr, Ottawa, 1979–82; Overseas Inspector, FCO, 1982–84; Dep. UK Perm. Rep. to OECD, and Counsellor (Econ. and Financial) to UK Delegn, Paris, 1984–87; Ambassador to Hanoi, 1987–90; High Comr, Barbados, Grenada, St Lucia, Dominica, Antigua and Barbuda, St Vincent and the Grenadines, and St Kitts and Nevis, 1990–94; Hd, UK Delegn to EC Monitoring Mission to former Yugoslavia, 1995 and 1998–99. Sec. Gen., Tripartite Commn for Restitution of Monetary Gold, Brussels, 1995–98. Appointments Advr to Welsh Office, 1997–2002; Pol Advr, EU Police Mission to Bosnia and Herzegovina, 2003. *Address:* Edinburgh House, 8 Alison Way, Winchester, Hants SO22 5BT. *Club:* Royal Air Force.

DAVIES, Dr Ernest Arthur; JP; management consultant and lecturer, retired 1987; *b* 25 Oct. 1926; *s* of Dan Davies and Ada (*née* Smith), Nuneaton; *m* 1st, 1956, Margaret Stephen Tait Gatt (marr. diss. 1967), *d* of H. Gatt, Gamesley, near Glossop; no *c*; 2nd, 1972, Patricia (marr. diss. 1980), *d* of S. Bates, Radford, Coventry; no *c*. *Educ:* Coventry Jun. Techn. Coll.; Westminster Trng Coll., London; St Salvator's Coll., University of St Andrews; St John's Coll., Cambridge. PhD Cantab 1959; MInstP 1959, CPhys 1986. RAF Aircraft Apprentice, 1942–43 (discharged on med. grounds). Westminster Trng Coll., 1946–48; Teacher, Foxford Sch., Coventry, 1948–50; University of St Andrews, 1950–54 (1st cl. hons Physics, Neil Arnott Prize, Carnegie Schol.); subseq. research in superconductivity, Royal Society Mond Lab., Cambridge; AEI Research Scientist, 1957–63; Lectr in Physics, Faculty of Technology, University of Manchester, 1963–66; Management Selection Consultant, MSL, 1970–81; Lectr in Business Studies, Hammersmith and West London Coll., 1981–87. MP (Lab) Stretford, 1966–70; Parliamentary Private Secretary to: PMG (Mr Edward Short), Nov.–Dec. 1967; Foreign Secretary (Mr George Brown), Jan.–March 1968; Foreign and Commonwealth Sec. (Mr Michael Stewart), 1968–69; Jt Parly Sec., Min. of Technology, 1969–70. Co-Vice-Chm., Parly Labour Party's Defence and Services Group; Mem., Select Cttee on Science and Technology, 1966–67, 1967–68, 1968–69; Parly Deleg. to 24th Gen. Assembly of UN (UK Rep. on 4th Cttee). Councillor: Borough of Stretford, 1961–67; Borough of Southwark, 1974–82. JP Lancs, 1962, Inner London, 1972. *Publications:* contribs to Proc. Royal Society, Jl of Physics and Chem. of Solids. *Recreations:* reading, art and design practice, writing family history. *Address:* 43 Frensham Drive, Nuneaton, Warwickshire CV10 9QH.

DAVIES, Prof. (Eurfil) Rhys, CBE 1990; FRCR, FRCPE; FFR (RCSI); FDSRCS; Professor of Clinical Radiology (formerly Radiodiagnosis), University of Bristol, 1981–93; *b* 18 April 1929; *s* of late Daniel Haydn Davies and Mary Davies; *m* 1962, Zoë Doreen Chamberlain; three *s*. *Educ:* Rhondda Grammar Sch.; Llandovery Coll.; Clare Coll., Cambridge (MB, BChir 1953; MA); St Mary's Hosp., London. FRCR (FFR 1964); FRCPE 1971; FFR (RCSI) 1978; FDSRCS 1989. Served RAMC, 1954–56 (Regtl MO 24 Regt). Sen. Registrar, St Mary's Hosp., 1963–66; Consultant Radiologist, United Bristol Hosps, 1966–81; Clinical Lectr, 1972–81, Hd, Clinical Sch., 1992–93, Univ. of Bristol. Vis. Sen. Lectr, Lagos Univ., 1971; Mayne Vis. Prof., Queensland Univ., 1982. Civilian Cons. Advr to RN, 1989–94. Mem., Bristol and Weston DHA, 1983–86. Member: Admin of Radio Active Substances Adv. Cttee, DHSS, 1978–83; Clin. Standards Adv. Cttee, 1991–93; GMC, 1989–93; Ionising Radiation Adv. Cttee, HSC, 1995–97 (Mem., Working Gp, 1987–95). Royal Coll. of Radiologists: Sen. Examr, 1973–74; Mem., Fellowship Bd, 1974–76; Registrar, 1976–81; Chm., Examining Bd, 1981–84; Warden of the Fellowship, 1984–86; Pres., 1986–89; Chm., Nuclear Medicine Cttee, 1972–78; Knox Lectr, 1990. Pres., Nuclear Medicine Soc., 1974–76 (Sec., 1972–74); Chm., Inter Collegiate Standing Cttee for Nuclear Medicine, 1982–84 (Sec., 1980–82). *Publications:* (contrib.) Textbook of Radiology, ed Sutton, 1969, Associate Editor, 6th edn 1998; (contrib.) Textbook of Urology, ed J. P. Blandy, 1974; (jtly) Radioisotopes in Radiodiagnosis, 1976; (contrib.) Radiological Atlas of Biliary and Pancreatic Disease, 1978; Textbook of Radiology by British Authors, 1984; (ed with W. E. G. Thomas) Nuclear Medicine for Surgeons, 1988; papers in Clin. Radiology, British Jl of Radiology, Lancet. *Recreations:* theatre, cooking, wine, travel. *Address:* 19 Hyland Grove, Bristol BS9 3NR.

DAVIES, (Evan) Huw; QC 2006; *b* 22 Jan. 1962; *s* of John and Joan Davies; *m* 1988, Alison Susan Keen; one *s* one *d*. *Educ:* Carr Lane Primary Sch., Hull; Wolfreton Comprehensive Sch., Hull; Imberhorne Comprehensive Sch., E Grinstead; University Coll., Cardiff (LLB 1st Cl. Hons). Called to the Bar, Gray's Inn, 1985; in practice, specialising in commercial litigation and arbitration. CEDR accredited mediator. *Recreations:* Rugby, ski-ing, mountaineering, cycling, golf (still learning), travel, food. *Address:* Essex Court Chambers, 24 Lincoln's Inn Fields, WC2A 3EG. *T:* (020) 7813 8000. *E:* hdavies@essexcourt.net.

DAVIES, Rt Rev. (Francis James) Saunders; Bishop of Bangor, 2000–04; *b* 30 Dec. 1937; *s* of Tom and Clara Davies; *m* 1963, (Marianne) Cynthia Young; one *s* one *d*. *Educ:* UCNW Bangor (BA Hons Welsh and accessory Hebrew 1960; Hon. Fellow, 2002); Selwyn Coll., Cambridge (MA Theol. 1966); St Michael's Coll., Llandaff; Bonn Univ., Germany. Ordained deacon, 1963, priest, 1964; Curate, Holyhead, 1963–67; Minor Canon, Bangor Cathedral and Hon. Staff Mem., SCM, 1967–69; Rector, Llanllyfni, 1969–75; Canon Missioner, Bangor Dio., 1975–78; Vicar, Gorseinon, 1978–86; Rural Dean, Llwchwr, 1983–86; Vicar, Eglwys Dewi Sant, Cardiff, 1986–93; Rector, Cricieth with Treflys and Archdeacon of Meirionnydd, 1993–2000; permission to officiate, dio. of St Davids, 2004–. Tutor: NSM Course, Llandaff Dio., 1987–93; for Continuing Educn, UC Cardiff, 1988–93. Vice-Chm., Cardiff Christian Adult Educn Centre, 1990–93. *Publications:* (ed jtly) Euros Bowen Poet-Priest/Bardd Offeiriad, 1993; Y Daith Anorfod: a commentary on St Luke's Gospel, 1993. *Recreations:* reading, travelling, listening to classical music, going to the theatre and the Nat. Eisteddfod of Wales. *Address:* 5 Maes-y-coed, Cardigan SA43 1AP.

DAVIES, Sir Frank (John), Kt 1999; CBE 1993; Chairman, Health and Safety Commission, 1993–99; *b* 24 Sept. 1931; *s* of late Lt-Col F. H. Davies and Veronica Josephine Davies; *m* 1956, Sheila Margaret Bailey; three *s*. *Educ:* Monmouth Sch.; UMIST. BPB Industries plc, 1953–63; RTZ Pillar Ltd, 1964–67; Alcan Aluminium (UK) Ltd, 1967–83: Div. Man. Dir, 1971–83; Dir, 1977–83; Dir, Alcan Booth, 1972–82; Gp Chief Exec., Rockware Gp, 1983–93. Chairman: Dartington Crystal, 1989–94; ACI Europe Ltd, 1991–93; Bardon Gp plc, 1994–97; Mediwatch plc, 2003–05; non-executive Director: Ian Proctor M. Masts, 1974–83; Ardagh plc, 1985–2003; BTR Nylex, 1991–94; Saltire (formerly Cannon St Investments), 1993–99; Aggregate Industries plc, 1997–2002; Investor Champions plc, 2000–04; Ardagh Glass Gp, 2003–10. Mem., Oxfordshire HA, 1981–90; Chm., Nuffield Orthopaedic Centre NHS Trust, 1990–98. Dep. Chm., Railway Safety, 2001–03; non-exec. Dir, Railway Safety and Standards Board, 2003–08. President: Glass Manufrs Fedn, 1985, 1986; Fédn Européene du Verre d'Emballage, 1987–88; Member: Council, Cttee Permanent Industrie du Verre, Brussels, 1984–86; Council, Aluminium Fedn, 1980–82; Council, CBI, 1985–93; Council, Industry Council for Packaging and the Envmt, 1986–93; Packaging Standards Council, 1992–93; Vice-President: Inst. of Packaging, 1992; Inst. of Occupational Safety & Health, 1995. Trustee, British Occupnl Health Res. Foundn, 1993–99; Chm. of Trustees, Back Care, 1998–2004. Governor: Inst. of Occupl Medicine, 2000–; British Safety Council, 2000–06 (Chm., 2001–06). CCMI (CBIM 1986); FRSA 1986. Freeman, City of London, 1986; Liveryman: Basketmakers' Co., 1987; Glass-Sellers' Co., 1990. OStJ 1977 (Mem., Council of St John, Oxfordshire, 1973–2000); Vice-Pres., Oxfordshire St John Ambulance, 1973–2000. *Recreations:* gardening, theatre, travel. *Address:* Stonewalls, Castle Street, Deddington, Banbury, Oxon OX15 0TE. *Club:* Carlton.

DAVIES, Col (Frederic) Nicolas (John), LVO 2002; JP; DL; Independent Member: Standards Committee, Surrey County Council, 2001–10 (Chairman, 2007–08); Standards Committee, Waverley Borough Council, 2001–11 (Chairman, 2002–09); Secretary for Appointments and Chief Clerk, Duchy of Lancaster, 1992–2002; *b* 11 May 1939; *s* of late Rev. William John Davies and Winifred Mary Davies (*née* Lewis); *m* 1970, Caroline Tweedie; one step *s* one step *d*, and one *s* one *d* by previous *m*. *Educ:* King's Coll., Taunton; RMA Sandhurst. Nat. Service, Queen's Royal Regt, 1957; commnd Royal Regt of Artillery, 1959; served in UK, Cyprus, Hong Kong and Germany; COS, Catterick Garrison, N Yorks, 1982–85; Defence and Military Attaché, Hungary, 1986–91; retd 1992. Non-exec. Dir, Guildford and Waverley PCT, 2003–06. Trustee, Queen's Royal Surrey Regtl Mus., 2003–11 (Chm., 2006–11). Member: St John Council for Surrey, 1995– (Pres., Haslemere Div., 2000; OStJ 2010); Court, Univ. of Surrey, 1997–. Mem., Ex-Services Mental Welfare Soc. (Combat Stress), 2007–. Mem., Pilgrims Soc., 1996–. Gov., Corp. of Sons of the Clergy, 1997– (Mem., Court of Assts, 1999–2005). JP Inner London 1997–2002, SW Surrey 2002 (supplemental list, 2009); DL Surrey, 1997. Hon. Mem., Order of Vitéz (Hungary), 1994. *Recreations:* walking, gardening, reading. *Club:* Army and Navy.

DAVIES, Gareth, CBE 1992; FCA; Group Chief Executive, 1984–93, Chairman, 1986–98, Glynwed International plc; *b* 13 Feb. 1930; *s* of Lewis and Margaret Ann Davies; *m* 1953, Joan Patricia Prosser; one *s*. *Educ:* King Edward's Grammar School, Aston, Birmingham. Joined Glynwed Group, 1957; Computer Manager, 1964; Financial Dir, 1969; Man. Dir, 1981. Non-executive Director: Midlands Electricity Plc, 1989–96; Midlands Ind. Newspapers plc, 1994–97; Lloyds Chemists plc, 1995–97. *Recreations:* music, gardening. *Address:* Berkley House, Barton-on-the-Heath, Morton-in-Marsh, Glos GL56 0PJ. *T:* (01608) 674043.

DAVIES, Gareth; *see* Davies, W. G.

DAVIES, His Honour Gareth Lewis; a Circuit Judge, 1990–2002; *b* 8 Sept. 1936; *s* of David Edward Davies and Glynwen Davies; *m* 1st, 1962; two *s* two *d*; 2nd, 2001, Emma Messenger. *Educ:* Brecon County Grammar Sch.; Univ. of Wales (LLB). National Service, RAF, 1954–56. Articled 1959, qualified Solicitor, 1962; Partner, Ottaways', Solicitors, St Albans, 1965–90; a Recorder, 1987. *Recreations:* sailing instructor, ski guide, classic cars, cycling. *Address:* Bronllys Castle, Bronllys, Brecon, Powys LD3 0HL. *T:* (01874) 711930.

DAVIES, Gareth Neil; Director General of Knowledge and Innovation, Department for Business, Innovation and Skills, since 2015; *b* Liverpool, 13 July 1973; *s* of Peter and Laraine Davies; *m* 2013, Emma Loxton. *Educ:* Wallasey Comprehensive Sch.; Christ Church, Oxford (BA PPE 1994; MA); London Sch. of Econs and Pol Sci. (MSc Econs 1999). Mgt consultant, Coopers and Lybrand, subseq. PriceWaterhouseCoopers, 1994–2002; Dep. Dir, Prime Minister's Strategy Unit, 2002–03; Sen. Advr, Downing St Policy Unit, 2003–07; Prog. Dir, DIUS, 2007–09; Exec. Dir, Cabinet Office, 2009–13; Dir, Gp Strategy, AIA Insce, 2013–15. Chm. Govs, Bolingbroke Acad., 2012–. *Recreations:* running, cycle touring, theatre, Liverpool Football Club. *Address:* Department for Business, Innovation and Skills, 1 Victoria Street, SW1H 0ET. *T:* (020) 7215 1219. *E:* gareth.davies@bis.gsi.gov.uk.

DAVIES, Gavyn, OBE 1979; Chairman, Fulcrum Asset Management; Principal, KKR Prisma (formerly Prisma Capital Partners), since 2005; *b* 27 Nov. 1950; *s* of W. J. F. Davies and M. G. Davies; *m* 1989, Susan Jane Nye (*see* Baroness Nye); two *s* one *d*. *Educ:* St John's Coll.,

Cambridge (BA); Balliol Coll., Oxford. Economic Advr, Policy Unit, 10 Downing Street, 1974–79; Economist, Phillips and Drew, 1979–81; Chief UK Economist, Simon & Coates, 1981–86; Goldman Sachs: Chief UK Economist, 1986–93; Partner, 1988–2001; Hd of Investment Res. (London), 1991–93; Head, later Co-Head, Eur. Investment Res., 1993–99; Chief Internat. Economist, 1993–2001; Chm., Investment Res. Dept, 1999–2001; Adv. Dir, 2001. Vis. Prof. of Economics, LSE, 1988–98. Principal Econs Commentator, The Independent, 1991–99. Mem., HM Treasury's Ind. Forecasting Panel, 1993–97. Chairman: Future Funding of the BBC (govt inquiry), 1999; Bd of Govs, BBC, 2001–04 (Vice-Chm., 2001). Fellow, Univ. of Wales, Aberystwyth, 2002. Hon. DSc (Social Sci.) Southampton, 1998; Hon. LLD Nottingham, 2002; Hon. Dr Middlesex, 2004. *Recreation:* Southampton FC.

DAVIES, George William; Chairman, FG4 Childrenswear and Ladieswear, since 2011; *b* 29 Oct. 1941; *s* of George Davies and late Mary Davies; *m* 1st, 1964, Anne; three *d*; 2nd, 1985, Liz; two *d*; 3rd, 1992, Fiona; two *s*. *Educ:* Netherton Moss Primary Sch.; Bootle Grammar Sch.; Birmingham Univ. Littlewoods, 1967–72; School Care (own business), 1972–75; Pippa Dee (subsid. of Rosgill Hldgs)—Party Plan/Lingerie, 1975–81; J. Hepworth & Son plc (responsible for launch of Next), 1981; Jt Gp Man. Dir, J. Hepworth & Son, 1984; Chief Exec., 1985–88, Chm., 1987–88, Next (name changed from J. Hepworth & Son); Managing Director: George Davies Partnership plc, 1989–2000; George Clothing, 1995–2000; Pres., Asda Gp, 1995–2000; Chm., Per Una clothing for Marks and Spencer plc, 2001–08 (Chief Exec., 2004–05). Chm., S'Porter Internat. Ltd (formerly S. Porter Ltd), 1995–. Sen. Fellow, RCA, 1988. FRSA 1987; Hon. FSDC 2004. Hon. DBA Liverpool Polytechnic, 1989; Hon. DDes: Nottingham Trent, 1996; Middlesex, 2002; De Montfort, 2006; Hon. DLitt Heriot-Watt, 2003; Hon. DCL Northumbria, 2005; Hon. DBA Edge Hill, 2012. Guardian Young Businessman of the Year, 1985; Wood Mackenzie Retailer of the Year, 1987; Marketing Personality of the Year, 1988; Lifetime Achievement Award, Drapers' Co., 2003; Designer of the Decade, Prima mag., 2004; Forum Award, Textil Wirtschaft mag., 2004. *Publications:* What Next? (autobiog.), 1989. *Recreations:* tennis, golf, cycling. *Clubs:* Formby Golf; Liverpool Ramblers; Blackwell Golf.

DAVIES, Geraint Rhys; Member (Plaid Cymru), Rhondda Cynon Taff County Borough Council, since 2012; *b* 1 Dec. 1948; *s* of John Davies and Sarah Olwen Davies; *m* 1973, Merril Margaret Williams; three *s* one *d*. *Educ:* Pentre Grammar Sch.; Chelsea Coll., London (BPharm). MRPharmS. Community pharmacist: Boots, Treorci, Rhondda, 1972–75; self-employed, 1975–. Member (Plaid Cymru): Rhondda CBC, 1983–95; Rhondda Cynon Taff CBC, 1995. Mem (Plaid Cymru), Nat. Assembly for Wales, 1999–2003. Contested (Plaid Cymru): Rhondda, Nat. Assembly for Wales, 2003; Rhondda, 2010. *Recreations:* playing tennis, listening to music, reading.

DAVIES, Geraint Richard; MP (Lab and Co-op) Swansea West, since 2010; *b* 3 May 1960; *s* of David Thomas Morgan Davies and Betty Ferrer Davies; *m* 1991, Dr Vanessa Catherine Fry; three *d*. *Educ:* Llanishen Comp. Sch., Cardiff; Jesus Coll., Oxford (JCR Pres.; BA Hons PPE, MA). Joined Brooke Bond Oxo as sales and mkting trainee, 1982; subseq. Gp Product Manager, Unilever; Marketing Manager, Colgate Palmolive Ltd; Founder, and Director: Pure Crete, 1989–2010; Pure Aviation, 1996–2010; Dir, Equity Creative Ltd, 1989–2001. Chair, Flood Risk Mgt Wales, 2005–10. Mem., Croydon BC, 1986–97 (Chm. of Housing, 1994–96; Leader of Council, 1996–97); Chm., London Boroughs Housing Cttee, 1994–96. Contested (Lab): Croydon S, 1987; Croydon Central, 1992. MP (Lab) Croydon Central, 1997–2005; contested (Lab) same seat, 2005. Team PPS, Dept of Constitutional Affairs, 2003–05. Member: Public Accounts Select Cttee, 1997–2003; Welsh Affairs Select Cttee, 2010–15; European Scrutiny Select Cttee, 2013–; Chairmen's Panel, 2015–. Sec., Parly Gp on Domestic Violence, 2003–05; Parly Ambassador, NSPCC, 2003–05. Chair: Lab. Finance and Industry Gp, 1998–2003 (Mem. Exec., 1994–; Vice Pres., 2003–); Deptl Cttee, Envmt, Transport and Regions, 1997–2003. Mem., Parly Assembly of the Council for Europe, 2010–15. Published parliamentary bills: Physical Punishment of Children (Prohibition) Bill, 2003; Regulation of Child Care Providers Bill, 2003; Regulation of Hormone Disrupting Chemicals Bill, 2004; School Meals and Nutrition Bill, 2005; Credit Card Regulation (Child Pornography) Bill, 2010; Multinational Motor Companies (duty of care to former employees) Bill, 2012; Regulation of Psychotherapists and Counsellors Bill, 2013; Sugar in Food and Drinks Bill, 2014; Bill criminalising Revenge Pornography, 2014 (incorporated into Criminal Justice and Courts Act, 2015); Electronic Cigarettes Bill, 2014; Internat. Trade Agreements (Security) Bill, 2014. *Recreations:* spending time with the family, singing. *Address:* House of Commons, SW1A 0AA.

DAVIES, Geraint Talfan, OBE 2014; DL; Chairman: Institute of Welsh Affairs, 1992–2014; Welsh National Opera, 2000–03 and since 2006; *b* 30 Dec. 1943; *s* of late Aneirin Talfan Davies, OBE and Mary Anne (*née* Evans); *m* 1967, Elizabeth Shân Vaughan (*née* Yorath); three *s*. *Educ:* Cardiff High Sch.; Jesus Coll., Oxford (MA; Hon. Fellow, 2013). Western Mail, Cardiff, 1966–71; The Journal, Newcastle upon Tyne, 1971–73; The Times, 1973; Asst Editor, Western Mail, Cardiff, 1974–78; HTV Wales: Head, News and Current Affairs, 1978–82; Asst Controller of Progs, 1982–87; Dir of Progs, Tyne Tees TV, 1987–90; Controller, BBC Wales, 1990–2000. Non-executive Director: Glas Cymru Cyf, 2000–11; Wales Millennium Centre, 2000–03, 2006–09; Shakespeare Schs Fest., 2014–; Mem., BT Wales Adv. Forum, 2001–09. Chairman: Newydd Housing Assoc., 1975–78; Cardiff Bay Arts Trust, 1997–2003; Wales Internat. Film Festival, 1998–2001; Arts Council of Wales, 2003–06. Mem., Prince of Wales' Cttee, 1993–95; Trustee: Tenovus Cancer Appeal, 1984–87; British Bone Marrow Donor Appeal, 1987–95; Media Standards Trust, 2006–. Member: Management Cttee, Northern Sinfonia, 1989–90; Radio Authy, 2001–04; UK Cttee, Eur. Cultural Foundn, 2005–09. Governor: Welsh Coll. of Music and Drama, 1993–97; UWIC, 2000–06. DL S Glamorgan, 2007. Hon. Fellow: UWIC, 2000; RIBA, 2000; Swansea Univ., 2011; Bangor Univ., 2013. Hon. Dr, Glamorgan, 1996. *Publications:* At Arm's Length, 2008; (ed) English is a Welsh Language, 2009. *Recreations:* theatre, music, architecture. *Address:* 15 The Parade, Whitchurch, Cardiff CF14 2EF. *T:* (029) 2062 6571. *E:* geraint.talfan@btopenworld.com.

See also R. T. Davies.

DAVIES, Geraldine; Principal, UCL Academy, since 2011; *b* London, 11 Sept. 1954; *d* of Charles and Mary Bayley; *m* 1978, Michael Davies; one *s*. *Educ:* St Victoire's Convent Grammar Sch.; St Mary's Coll., Twickenham (BSc Hons Botany and Chem.; Cert Ed); Inst. of Educn, Univ. of London (MBA Higher Educn Mgt). Teacher of chem. and sci., Holy Cross Convent, New Malden, 1977–87; Hd of Sci. and Sen. Teacher, Coombe Girls Sch., 1987–90; Dep. Headteacher, Bishop Thomas Grant, Streatham, 1990–2000; Headteacher, Douay Martyrs Sch., Ickenham, 2000–07; Hd, Sch. of Educn, St Mary's UC, Twickenham, 2007–11. *Recreations:* art, choir, ski-ing, sailing. *Address:* UCL Academy, Adelaide Road, Swiss Cottage, NW3 3AQ.

DAVIES, Prof. Gideon John, PhD; FRS 2010; FRSC; FMedSci; Professor of Chemistry, University of York, since 2001; *b* Great Sutton, Cheshire, 6 July 1964; *s* of Robert Edward Davies and Phyllis Dinah Davies (*née* Parker); *m* 1999, Dr Valérie Marie-Andrée Ducros; two *d*. *Educ:* Univ. of Bristol (BSc Hons Biochem. 1985; PhD 1990; DSc 2007). FRSC 2002. EMBO Res. Fellow, EMBL, Hamburg, 1990; Postdoctoral Fellow, Univ. of York, 1991–95; Royal Soc. Univ. Res. Fellow, 1996–2005. Peter Wall Catalytic Visitor, Univ. of BC, 2000. Mem., EMBO, 2010. FMedSci 2014. Carbohydrate Chem. Medal, 1998, Corday Morgan Medal, 2001, Proteins and Peptides Award, 2008, Khorana Prize, 2014, RSC; Whistler Prize, Internat. Carbohydrate Orgn, 2006; Wolfson Res. Merit Award, 2007, Gabor Medal, 2010, Royal Soc.; GlaxoSmithKline Award, Biochem. Soc., 2010. *Publications:* contrib. scientific papers. *Recreations:* music, sailing, fishing. *Address:* Department of Chemistry, York Structural Biology Laboratory, University of York, Heslington, York YO10 5DD. *T:* (01904) 328260, *Fax:* (01904) 328266. *E:* gideon.davies@york.ac.uk.

DAVIES, Dr Gillian; DL; barrister; Chairman, Technical Board of Appeal, European Patent Office, Munich, 1997–2005; *b* 5 April 1940; *d* of late Ninian Rhys Davies and Gweneth Elizabeth Davies (*née* Griffith). *Educ:* Cheltenham Ladies' Coll.; Grenoble Univ.; Univ. of Wales, Aberystwyth (PhD 1997). Called to the Bar, Lincoln's Inn, 1961; in practice at the Bar, 1961–63, and 2005–. Legal Assistant: De La Rue Co., 1963–65; United Internat. Bureaux for Protection of Intellectual Property, Geneva, 1965–70; Legal Advr, 1970–73, Asst Dir Gen., 1973–80, Associate Dir Gen. and Chief Legal Advr, 1980–91, IFPI. Res. Fellow, Max Planck Inst. for Foreign and Internat. Patent, Copyright, and Competition Law, Munich, 1990; Hon. Prof., Aberystwyth Univ. (formerly Univ. of Wales, Aberystwyth), 1994–; Vis. Prof., Centre for Commercial Law Studies, QMUL, 2007–. Bangor University: Member: Adv. Bd, Centre for Internat. Law, 2012–; Council, 2015–; Financial and Resources Cttee, 2015–. Mem., Wkg Gp on the Rôle of the State vis-à-vis the Cultural Industries, Council of Europe, 1980–86; Legal Mem., Bds of Appeal, 1991, Mem., Enlarged Bd of Appeal, 1996, European Patent Office. Chm., British Literary and Artistic Copyright Assoc., 2013– (Vice-Pres., 2010–13). DL Gwynedd, 2001. Liveryman, Livery Co. of Wales (formerly Welsh Livery Guild), 2007 (Court Asst, 2009; Sen. Court Asst, 2014–15; Jun. Warden, 2015–Oct. 2016; Mem., N Wales Cttee, 2008– (Chm., 2009–13)). *Publications:* Piracy of Phonograms, 1981, 2nd edn 1986; Private Copying of Sound and Audiovisual Recordings, 1984; (jtly) Challenges to Copyright and Related Rights in the European Community, 1983; (jtly) Music and Video Private Copying, 1993; Copyright and the Public Interest, 1994, 2nd edn 2002; Copinger and Skone James on Copyright, suppl. (jtly) 1994, 14th edn (ed jtly) 1999 to 16th edn (ed jtly) 2010, suppls (jtly) 2012, 2013; Clerk and Lindsell on Torts, suppl. (jtly) 2009, 20th edn (ed jtly) 2010, suppls (jtly) 2011, 2012, 2013, 21st edn (ed jtly) 2014; (jtly) Moral Rights, 2010; many articles in intellectual property law jls. *Recreations:* gardening, art, travel. *Address:* Hogarth Chambers, 5 New Square, Lincoln's Inn, WC2A 3RJ; Trefaes, Abersoch, Gwynedd LL53 7AD. *T:* (01758) 712426. *Clubs:* Athenæum, Hurlingham.

DAVIES, Most Rev. Glenn Naunton; *see* Sydney, Archbishop of.

DAVIES, Glyn; *see* Davies, R. H. G.

DAVIES, Glyn; MP (C) Montgomeryshire, since 2010; *b* 16 Feb. 1944; *m* 1969, Bobbie; three *s* one *d*. *Educ:* Caereinion High Sch.; UCW, Aberystwyth. Mem. (C) Montgomeryshire DC, 1985–88 (Chm.). Chm., Develt Bd for Rural Wales, 1989–94. Mem. (C) Mid & W Wales, Nat. Assembly for Wales, 1999–2007. Contested (C) Montgomeryshire, 1997. *Recreations:* countryside, sport. *Address:* Cil Farm, Berriew, Welshpool, Montgomeryshire, Mid Wales SY21 8AZ. *T:* (01686) 640698.

DAVIES, Prof. Glyn Arthur Owen, FRAeS; FCGI; Professor of Aeronautical Structures, 1985–99, and Senior Research Fellow and Senior Research Investigator in Aerostructures, 1999–2013, Imperial College London (formerly Imperial College of Science, Technology and Medicine, London) (Head of Department of Aeronautics, 1982–89; Pro-Rector (Resources), 1997–99); *b* 11 Feb. 1933; *s* of Arthur and Florence Davies; *m* 1959, Helen Rosemary (*née* Boot); two *d*. *Educ:* Liverpool Inst., Univ. of Liverpool (BEng); Cranfield Inst. of Technology (DCAe); PhD Sydney, 1966. Res. Asst, MIT, 1956; Advanced Project Engr, Brit. Aerospace, 1957–59; Lectr, Sen. Lectr, Dept of Aeronautics, Univ. of Sydney, 1959–66; Lectr, Sen. Lectr, Dept of Aeronautics, Imperial Coll. of Sci., Technol. and Medicine (formerly Imperial Coll. of Sci. and Technol.), 1966–85. Consultant to: ARC, 1975–81; MoD, 1980–2005; Nat. Agency for Finite Element Methods and Standards, 1983–95; SERC, 1986–90 (Supercomputing, 1991–93); The Computer Bd, 1989–91; ABRC (Supercomputing), 1991–94; UFC (IT), 1991–93; DTI (Aviation), 1991–2005; RAeS, 1994–2013; EPSRC, 1994–2005; OST (Foresight) Defence & Aerospace, 1994–2002. FRAeS 1987; FCGI 2000. Consultant Ed. (Aero Engrg), McGraw-Hill, 2009–13. *Publications:* Virtual Work in Structural Analysis, 1982; Mathematical Methods in Engineering, 1984; Finite Element Primer, 1986; Background to Benchmarks, 1993; Finite Element Modelling of Composite Materials and Structures, 2002; The Standard Handbook for Aeronautical and Astronautical Engineers, 2003; From Lysander to Lightning: Teddy Petter, aircraft designer, 2014. *Recreations:* photography, archaeology, painting and drawing life and portraits, theatre, music, allotment. *Address:* Hedsor School House, Bourne End, Bucks SL8 5JJ.

DAVIES, Sir Graeme (John), Kt 1996; FREng; FRSE; Vice-Chancellor, University of London, 2003–10; *b* 7 April 1937; *s* of Harry John Davies and Gladys Edna Davies (*née* Pratt); *m* 1959, Florence Isabelle Martin (*d* 2014); one *s* one *d*; *m* 2015, Svava Bjarnason. *Educ:* Mount Albert Grammar School, Auckland, NZ; Univ. of Auckland (BE, PhD); St Catharine's College, Cambridge (MA, ScD). FREng (FEng 1988). Junior Lectr, Univ. of Auckland, 1960–62; University of Cambridge: TI Research Fellow, 1962–64; Univ. Demonstrator in Metallurgy, 1964–66; Lectr, 1966–76; Fellow of St Catharine's Coll., 1967–77 (Hon. Fellow 1989); Prof. of Metallurgy, Univ. of Sheffield, 1978–86; Vice Chancellor, Univ. of Liverpool, 1986–91; Chief Executive: UFC, 1991–93; PCFC, 1992–93; HEFCE, 1992–95; Principal and Vice-Chancellor, Univ. of Glasgow, 1995–2003. Visiting Professor: Brazil, 1976–77; Israel, 1978; Argentina, 1980; China, 1981; Hon. Professor: Zhejiang Univ., China, 1985; Yantai Univ., China, 1996; Hon. Pres., British Univ., Vietnam, 2009–. Chm., Univs Superannuation Scheme, 1996–2006. Mem., ACOST, 1991–93. Member: Merseyside Enterprise Forum, 1986–90; London Economic Panel, 2004–10; Chairman: Scottish Educn and Trng, 1996–2001; Observatory on Borderless Higher Educn, 2001–10; Higher Educn Policy Inst., 2004–15 (Trustee, 2002–15). Guardian, Sheffield Assay Office, 1983–86; Chairman: CCLRC, 2001–07; Glasgow Sci. Centre, 2002–06, 2007–10; NZ-UK Link Foundn, 2011–; Member Council: Inst. Metals, 1981–86; Sheffield Metallurgical and Engineering Assoc., 1977–86 (Pres., 1984–85); ACU, 1987–91, 1998–2002, 2007–10; UUK (formerly CVCP), 1996–2010; Pres., Council of Military Educn Cttees, 2006–10. Trustee: Bluecoat Soc. of Arts, 1986–91; Museums and Galls on Merseyside, 1987–92; Iona Trust, 1995–2003; Carnegie Trust for the Univs of Scotland, 1995–2003; Scottish Science Trust, 1996–2003; Internat. Students House, 2005–; Cumberland Lodge, 2005–13; Foundn for Liver Research, 2009– (Chair, 2012–). Governor: Shrewsbury Sch., 1989–95; Glasgow Sch. of Art, 2004–08; Univ. of Seychelles, 2010–; Univ. of Herts, 2011–; Taylors Univ., Malaysia, 2012–. FRSA 1989; FRSE 1996; CCMI (CBIM 1991). Freeman, City of London, 1987; Liveryman, Co. of Ironmongers, 1989 (Mem., Court, 1992–; Master, 2005–06); Freeman and Burgess Holder, City of Glasgow, 1996. DL Merseyside, 1989–92. Hon. FRSNZ 1993; Hon. FTCL 1995; FRCPSGlas 1999; Hon. FCIPS 2003; Hon. FIPENZ 2007; Hon. FRVC 2011; Hon. Fellow, Sch. of Pharmacy, UCL, 2012. Hon. LLD: Liverpool, 1991; Strathclyde, 2000; Edinburgh, 2003; London, 2012; Hon. DSc: Nottingham, 1995; Ulster, 2004; Hon. DMet Sheffield, 1995; Hon. DEng: Manchester Metropolitan, 1996; Auckland, 2002; DUniv: Glasgow, 2004; Paisley, 2004; London South Bank, 2006; Hon. DLitt Bath Spa, 2010. Rosenhain Medal, Inst. of Metals, 1982. *Publications:* Solidification and Casting, 1973; Texture and Properties of Materials, 1976; Solidificação e Fundição de Metais e Suas Ligas, 1978; Hot Working and Forming Processes, 1980; Superplasticity, 1981; Essential Metallurgy for Engineers, 1985; Herding Cats, 2010; Herding Professional Cats, 2013; papers to learned jls. *Recreations:* cricket, birdwatching, golf, The Times crossword. *Address:* The Coach House, Fosse Road, Farndon, Newark NG24 3SF. *E:* graeme.davies@lon.ac.uk. *Club:* Athenæum.

DAVIES, Prof. Graham Ivor, PhD, DD; FBA 2003; Professor of Old Testament Studies, University of Cambridge, 2001–11, Fellow, Fitzwilliam College, Cambridge, since 1983; *b* 26 Sept. 1944; *s* of late Ivor Samuel Davies and Pauline Beryl Davies (*née* Serjeant); *m* 1971, Nicola Rina Galeski; three *s* one *d. Educ:* King's Coll. Sch., Wimbledon; Merton Coll., Oxford (Postmaster in Classics; BA 1st cl. hons Lit. Hum. 1967; 1st cl. hons Theol. 1969; MA 1970; DD 1998); Peterhouse, Cambridge (PhD 1975). FSA 1987. Asst Lectr, then Lectr, in Theol., Univ. of Nottingham, 1971–78; University of Cambridge: Lectr in Divinity, 1979–93; Reader in OT Studies, 1993–2001; Chm., Faculty Bd of Divinity, 1995–97. Director of Studies in Theology: Pembroke Coll., 1979–87; Peterhouse, 1979–88; Fitzwilliam Coll., 1983–2008; Director: Hebrew Inscriptions Project, 1987–2003; Cambridge Centre, Semantics of Ancient Hebrew Database, 1995– (Sec., ESF Network Co-ordinating Cttee, 1991–95). Mem., Exec. Cttee, Palestine Exploration Fund, 1981–2001, 2009–13; Sec., Fifteenth Congress, Internat. Orgn for Study of OT, Cambridge, 1995. Chm., Theol. and Religious Studies Section, British Acad., 2006–09. Macbride Sermon, Oxford, 1986; Schweich Centenary Lect., British Acad., 2008. Editor: Cities of the Biblical World series, 1981–96; Palestine Exploration Qly, 1990–2000; Internat. Critical Commentary (OT), 2004–; Mem. Editl Bd, Zeitschrift für die Alttestamentliche Wissenschaft, 2007–. *Publications:* The Way of the Wilderness, 1979; Megiddo (Cities of the Biblical World), 1986; Ancient Hebrew Inscriptions: corpus and concordance, vol. 1, 1991, vol. 2, 2004; Hosea (New Century Bible Commentary), 1992; Hosea (Old Testament Guide), 1993; (with A. N. S. Lane) John Calvin's The Bondage and Liberation of the Will, 1996; The Schweich Lectures and Biblical Archaeology, 2011; contrib. Vetus Testamentum, Palestine Exploration Qly, Jl of Semitic Studies and other learned jls and collections of essays. *Recreations:* steam trains, Rugby football, hill-walking, gardening, religious poetry. *Address:* Fitzwilliam College, Cambridge CB3 0DG. *T:* (01223) 763002, *Fax:* (01223) 763003. *E:* gid10@cam.ac.uk.

DAVIES, Prof. Graham James, PhD, DSc; CEng, FREng, FIET, FInstP, FIEAust, FIMMM, FTSE; Dean of Engineering, UNSW Australia (formerly University of New South Wales), since 2008; *b* 2 July 1946; *s* of William Thomas and Amy Davies; *m* 1975, Frances Vivienne Martin (marr. diss. 2010); two *s. Educ:* UCW Aberystwyth (BSc 1968; PhD 1971; DSc 1986). MRSC 1969; CEng, FIET (FIEE 1998); FInstP 1990; FIMMM 2002; FIEAust 2009; FTSE 2013. Res. Officer, KCL, 1971–72; Post Office Research: Jun. Res. Fellow, 1972–75; Hd of Gp, 1975–84; British Telecom Research Laboratories: Head: Advanced Materials and Devices Section, 1984–90; Competitor Analysis Section, 1990–93; Director: Corporate Res., 1993–98; Technol. Acquisition, 1998–2001; Sir James Timmins Chance Prof. of Engrg and Hd, Sch. of Engrg, Univ. of Birmingham, 2001–08. Chm., Foresight Materials Panel, DTI, 2000–04. Chm., Mining Educn Australia, 2012–. Director: Inst. of Physics Publishing, 2001–03; Birmingham R&D, 2001–08; Diamond Light Source, 2003–08; NSi Innovations, 2009–; Advanced Manufacturing, 2010–, CO2, 2010–, Collaborative Res. Centre. Member: Council, CCLRC, 2003–07; Bd, Collaborative Res. Centre for Advanced Manufg, 2010–; Bd, UNSW Foundn UK, 2014–. FREng 1999. Liveryman, Co. of Engrs, 2003. *Publications:* (with R. H. Williams) Semiconductor Growth, Surfaces and Interfaces, 1994; (jtly) Chemical Beam Epitaxy and Related Techniques, 1997; contrib. papers to peer-reviewed learned jls. *Recreations:* walking, music, golf, reading. *Address:* 2/149–151 Brook Street, Coogee, NSW 2034, Australia. *E:* g.davies@unsw.edu.au.

DAVIES, Prof. Graham Michael; Professor of Psychology, University of Leicester, 1989–2006, now Emeritus; Honorary Professor: University of Birmingham, since 2007; University of Coventry, since 2007; University of Nottingham, since 2013; *b* 19 Feb. 1943; *s* of Harold Cecil Davies and Mona Florence Daisy Wisbey; *m* 1st, 1966, Heather Jane Neale; one *s* one *d*; 2nd, 1987, Noelle Robertson; two *d. Educ:* Bodmin Grammar Sch.; Univ. of Hull (BA, PhD, DSc). CPsychol, FBPsS. Lectr in Psychology, 1967–77, Sen. Lectr, 1977–87, Univ. of Aberdeen; Prof. of Psychology, NE London Poly., 1987–89. Chm., Soc. for Applied Res. in Memory and Cognition, 1998–99; Pres., Eur. Assoc. for Psychology and Law, 2003–06. Founding Editor, Applied Cognitive Psychology, 1987. JP: Melton, Belvoir and Rutland, 2000; Loughborough, Melton, Belvoir and Rutland, 2011–13. Sen. Academic Award in Forensic Psychol., BPsS, 2012. *Publications:* edited jointly: Perceiving and Remembering Faces, 1981; Identification Evidence: a psychological evaluation, 1982; Memory in Context, 1988; Memory in Everyday life, 1993; Psychology, Law and Criminal Justice: international developments in research and practice, 1995; Recovered Memories: seeking the middle ground, 2001; Children's Testimony: a handbook of psychological research and forensic practice, 2002; Practical Psychology for Forensic Investigations and Prosecutions, 2006; Forensic Psychology, 2008; Current Issues in Applied Memory Research, 2010; Forensic Psychology: crime, justice, law and interventions, 2012; reports for the Home Office: (jtly) An evaluation of the live link for child witnesses, 1991; (jtly) Videotaping of Children's Evidence: an evaluation, 1995; (jtly) The training needs of officers investigating child sexual abuse, 1998; (jtly) Interviewing child witnesses under the 'Memorandum of Good Practice': a research review, 1999. *Recreations:* reading, walking, collecting modern first editions. *Address:* Forensic Psychology, University of Leicester, 106 New Walk, Leicester LE1 7EA. *T:* (home) (01664) 474708.

DAVIES, Grahame Brian; entrepreneur; Chairman, London Internet Exchange, 2000–14; *b* 6 May 1961; *s* of Brian and Joyce Davies; *m* 1990, Karen Uridge; two *s. Educ:* Haberdashers' Aske's Boys' Sch., Elstree. Computer operator, Unilever Computer Services Ltd, 1979–81; computer programmer, Impetus Computer Services, 1981–83; Dir, Demon Systems Ltd, 1983–95; Founder, Demon Internet, 1992; Gp Man. Dir, Easynet Gp plc, 1995–2001; Dir, Internet Watch Foundn, 1997–2002; Dir, Great Scores, digital sheet music, 2005–, and other internet start-ups; non-exec. Dir, Bytemark Hosting, 2012–; Dir, Agile Spice Ltd, 2012–; Chm., Simwood eSMS Ltd, 2013–; Chief Technology Officer: Boardroom Excellence, 2014–; PayDashboard Ltd, 2015–. *Recreations:* piano, running, tennis, golf, kart racing. *E:* grahame@tptb.co.uk.

DAVIES, (Gwilym) E(dnyfed) Hudson; *see* Davies, Ednyfed H.

DAVIES, Helen Louise; QC 2008; *b* Hampshire, 24 May 1969; *d* of Terence Alan Davies and Joan Davies; partner, Mark Philip Brealey, *qv*; one *s* one *d. Educ:* Emmanuel Coll., Cambridge (BA 1st Cl. Law 1990). Called to the Bar, Inner Temple, 1991, Bencher, 2010; in practice at the Bar, 1992–; Mem., B Panel to the Crown, 1999–2008. Stage, Competition Directorate, EC, 1993. *Recreations:* opera, theatre, ski-ing. *Address:* Brick Court Chambers, 7/8 Essex Street, WC2R 3LD. *T:* (020) 7379 3550.

DAVIES, (Henry) Byron; MP (C) Gower, since 2015; *b* Swansea, 4 Sept. 1952; *s* of William John Davies and Gladys Mary Davies; *m* 1978, Gill; one *s. Educ:* Gowerton Boys' Grammar Sch., Swansea; Univ. of West London (LLB Hons). Officer, Metropolitan Police, 1971–2003; owner and dir of consultancy co. advising foreign govts on organised crime, 2003–11. Mem. (C) S Wales W, Nat. Assembly for Wales, 2011–May 2015. *Recreations:* general aviation, private pilot, cycling, Rugby. *Address:* House of Commons, SW1A 0AA. *Clubs:* Royal Air Force; Gowerton Conservative and Unionist.

DAVIES, Howard; *see* Davies, S. H.

DAVIES, (Sir) Howard (John), Kt 2000; Chairman, Royal Bank of Scotland, since 2015; *b* 12 Feb. 1951; *s* of late Leslie Powell Davies and Marjorie Davies; *m* 1984, Prudence Mary Keely; two *s. Educ:* Manchester Grammar Sch.; Memorial Univ., Newfoundland; Merton Coll., Oxford (MA History and Mod. Langs); Stanford Graduate Sch. of Business, USA (MS Management Science). Foreign Office, 1973–74; Private Sec. to HM Ambassador, Paris, 1974–76; HM Treasury, 1976–82; McKinsey & Co. Inc., 1982–87 (Special Adviser to Chancellor of the Exchequer, 1985–86); Controller, Audit Commn, 1987–92; Dir Gen., CBI, 1992–95; Dep. Gov., 1995–97, Dir, 1998–2003, Bank of England; Chm., FSA, 1997–2003; Dir, London Sch. of Econs and Pol Sci., 2003–11. Chm., Phoenix Gp plc, 2012–15; Director: GKN plc, 1990–95; Morgan Stanley Inc., 2004–15; Paternoster Ltd, 2006–10; Prudential plc, 2010–; Mem., NatWest Internat. Adv. Bd, 1992–95. Director: BOTB, 1992–95; BITC, 1992–95. Chm., Airports Commn, 2012–15. Vis. Prof., Institut d'Etudes Politiques, Paris, 2011–. Dir, Nat. Theatre, 2004–; Trustee, Tate Gall., 2002–10. Pres., Age Concern England, 1994–98. Governor: De Montfort Univ. (formerly Leicester Polytechnic), 1988–95; Royal Acad. of Music, 2005–13. Chm. Judges, Man Booker Prize for Fiction, 2007. *Publications:* The Chancellors' Tales, 2006; Global Financial Regulation: the essential guide, 2008; Banking on the Future: the fall and rise of central banking, 2010; The Financial Crisis: who's to blame?, 2010; Can Financial Markets be Controlled?, 2015. *Recreations:* cricket, drama. *Clubs:* Barnes Common Cricket; Manchester City Supporters.

DAVIES, Hugh Curry, OBE 2011; QC 2013; *b* Pembury, 11 Jan. 1967; *s* of Roy and Ann Ursula Davies; *m* 1999, Claire Ellis; one *s* two *d. Educ:* Reading Sch.; Pembroke Coll., Oxford (BA Hons Juris.; Domus Schol.; Winter Williams Prize for Law 1988). Called to the Bar, Lincoln's Inn, 1990 (Walter Wigglesworth Maj. Schol. 1990); in practice as a barrister, specialising in criminal law, police misconduct and regulation, inquests, and child exploitation. Legal Advr to Child Exploitation and Online Protection Centre, 2006–. *Publications:* (with J. Beggs) Police Misconduct, Complaints and Public Regulation, 2009, 2nd edn 2014. *Recreations:* hill-walking, running. *Address:* 3 Raymond Buildings, Gray's Inn, WC1R 5BH. *T:* (020) 7400 6400. *Club:* MCC.

DAVIES, Hugh Llewelyn, CMG 1994; HM Diplomatic Service, retired; Senior Partner, Orient Asian Partners, since 2005; *b* 8 Nov. 1941; *s* of late Vincent Davies (formerly ICS), OBE, and Rose (*née* Temple); *m* 1968, Virginia Ann Lucius; one *d* one *s. Educ:* Rugby School; Churchill College, Cambridge (Hons History degree). HM Diplomatic Service, 1965–99: Chinese Language Studies, Hong Kong, 1966–68; Second Sec., Office of British Chargé d'Affaires, Peking, 1969–71; Far Eastern Dept, FCO, 1971–74; First Sec. (Econ.), Bonn, 1974–77; Head of Chancery, Singapore, 1977–79; Asst Head, Far Eastern Dept, FCO, 1979–82; on secondment, Barclays Bank International, 1982–83; Commercial Counsellor, Peking, 1984–87; Dep. British Permanent Rep., OECD, Paris, 1987–90; Hd, Far Eastern Dept, FCO, 1990–93; Sen. British Trade Comr, Hong Kong, June–Sept. 1993; British Sen. Rep., (Ambassador), Sino-British Jt Liaison Gp, Hong Kong, 1993–97; Special Enquiry on China Trade and Special Co-ordinator, China, Taiwan and Hong Kong, FCO, 1997–98; Exec. Dir, Prudential Corp. Asia, 1999–2005; Sen. Advr, China, Old Mutual, 2005–06. Chm., China Assoc., 2002–14; Mem. Bd, China Britain Trade Council, 1999–2013; Vice Chm., GB China Centre, 2003–. Mem., Adv. Bd, China Policy Inst., Univ. of Nottingham, 2008–. *Recreations:* writing and researching family history, watersports, sketching, travel, gardens, walking. *Address:* Church Farm, Cucklington, Wincanton, Somerset BA9 9PT.
See also Sir J. M. Davies.

DAVIES, Hunter; *see* Davies, Edward H.

DAVIES, Huw; QC 2001; **His Honour Judge Huw Davies;** a Circuit Judge, since 2008; *b* 25 Oct. 1955; *s* of Walter Stephen Davies and May Davies. *Educ:* UCW, Aberystwyth (LLB); Sidney Sussex Coll., Cambridge (MPhil). Called to the Bar, Gray's Inn, 1978; Asst Recorder, 1994–98; Recorder, 1998–2008; Standing Counsel to HM Customs and Excise, Wales and Chester Circuit, 1996–2001. *Address:* Swansea Crown Court, St Helen's Road, Swansea SA1 4PF. *T:* (01792) 637000. *Club:* Tiger.

DAVIES, Huw; *see* Davies, Evan H.

DAVIES, Huw Humphreys; Chief Executive, Channel Television, 2000–06; *b* Aug. 1940; *s* of William Davies and Sian Davies; *m* 1966, Elizabeth Shân Harries; two *d. Educ:* Llangynog Primary School; Llandovery College; Pembroke College, Oxford. MA (Lit.Hum.). Director/Producer: Television Wales and West, 1964; HTV, 1968; HTV Cymru/Wales: Asst Controller of Programmes, 1978; Controller of Programmes, 1979–81; Dir of Programmes, 1981–87; Chief Exec., 1987–91; Gp Dir of Television, HTV, 1989–94; Pres., HTV Internat., 1994–96; Chairman: Square Circle Prodns Ltd, 1996–2002; Content Media Corp., 2010–14 (Dir, Content Film, 2004–10); Dir, 1996–2003, Chm., 2003–04, Winchester Entertainment (formerly Winchester Multimedia). Produced and directed many programmes and series in English and Welsh; latterly numerous plays and drama-documentaries. Chm., Regional Controllers, ITV, 1987–88. Mem., Gorsedd of Bards. *Recreation:* driving around America. *Address:* Penarth, S Glamorgan CF64 3HY.

DAVIES, Hywel; *see* Davies, D. H.

DAVIES, Lt-Col Hywel William; *b* 28 June 1945; *s* of late William Lewis Davies, JP and Barbara Beatrice Eleanor Davies, JP, MFH, Pantyderi, Boncath, Pembs; *m* 1969, Patricia, *d* of late Lt-Col E. B. Thornhill, MC; one *s* one *d. Educ:* Harrow; Magdalene Coll., Cambridge (MA). Commnd RHG (The Blues, later Blues & Royals), 1965; Staff Coll., 1977; Operational Requirements, MoD, 1978–80; Defence Intelligence, MoD, 1982–84; CO, Blues & Royals, 1985–87; with Pilkington Optronics, 1988–89; Chief Executive: RHASS, 1991–98; BHS, 1998–2000. Chm., Peatland Gp, 2000–07; Man. Dir, Peatland Smokehouse Ltd, 2002–07; Director: G. D. Golding & Son Ltd, 1988–2015; Challenger Consultancy Ltd, 1987–91; Ingliston Hotels Ltd, 1997–98; Scottish Farming and Educnl Trust, 1991–98; Scottish Agricl & Rural Develt Centre Ltd, 1992–98; The Countryside Movt, 1995–97; Ingliston Develt Trust, 1996–98; British Horse Soc. Trading Co. Ltd, 1998–2000. Mem., Countryside Cttee, Countryside Alliance, 1997–99. Chairman: Assoc. of Show and Agricl Orgns, 1998–99 (Hon. Life Mem., 2000); Draught Horse Trng Cttee, 1998–2000; Royal Internat. Horse Show, 1998–2000. Mem. (C) S Ayrshire Council, 2003– (Convenor, Rural Affairs Cttee and HR Cttee, 2005–07; Sen. Councillor, Leadership Panel, Lifelong Learning portfolio, 2007–12). Chairman: Central Region, 1998, Ayr and Arran, 2004–12, Assoc. of Order of St John; W Lowland Cadet Force League, 2001–09; Vice Pres., Ayrshire and Arran Red Cross, 2002–04; Mem., Strathclyde Police Authy, 2012–13. Treas., St Brynach's Ch, Nevern, 2014–. ARAgS 1996. CStJ 2009 (OStJ 1997). *Recreations:* equestrian pursuits (Mem., Coaching Club; represented UK at Four-in-Hand Carriage Driving, 1984–87), shooting, fishing, gardening. *Address:* Shieldaig, Nevern, Newport, Pembrokeshire SA42 0NQ.

DAVIES, Ian; HM Diplomatic Service; Head, Home Estate Team, Estates and Security Department, Foreign and Commonwealth Office, since 2013; *b* 1 Aug. 1956; *s* of late John Davies and of Freda Mary Davies; *m* 1979, Purificación Bautista Hervias; two *d. Educ:* Queen Mary Coll., London (BSc Econs 1983); Birkbeck Coll., London (MSc Econs 1985); Open Univ. (MBA 2011). Joined FCO, 1976; Moscow, 1978–80; Protocol Dept, FCO, 1983–85; Paris, 1985–88; Moscow, 1988–90; Far Eastern Dept, FCO, 1990–93; Dep. Head of Mission, Bolivia, 1993–96; Consul Gen., Marseille, 1997–2001; Dep. Head of Mission, Peru, 2002–05; FCO Response Centre, FCO, 2005–08; project work, FCO, 2008–09; Hd, Chem. and Biol Weapons Conventions Team, 2010–13. *Recreations:* walking, classical music, cinema, theatre. *Address:* c/o Foreign and Commonwealth Office, King Charles Street, SW1A 2AH.

DAVIES, Ian; *see* Davies, D. I.

DAVIES, Iestyn Ioan, FRAM; countertenor singer; *b* York, 16 Sept. 1979; *s* of Dr Ioan Charles Davies and Diana Wood; partner, Gemma Lawley. *Educ:* Wells Cathedral Sch.; St John's Coll., Cambridge (BA Archaeol. and Anthropol. 2002); Royal Acad. of Music (PGDip; ARAM). Operatic début, Zurich, 2005; roles in operas by Handel, Britten, Adès and

Benjamin. Residency at Wigmore Hall, 2012–13. Music Award for Young Artist, Royal Philharmonic Soc., 2009; Gramophone Award for Recital Disc, 2012, 2014; Critics' Circle Award for Best Singer, 2013. *Recreations:* archaeology, Georgian architecture, football, wine collecting, baroque music, dogs. *Address:* c/o Askonas Holt Ltd, Lincoln House, 350 High Holborn, WC1V 7JH. *T:* (020) 7400 1700. *E:* sue.spence@askonasholt.co.uk.

DAVIES, (Ifor) Huw I.; *see* Irranca-Davies.

DAVIES, Isobel Mary M.; *see* Macdonald-Davies.

DAVIES, Prof. (Ivor) Norman (Richard), CMG 2001; PhD; FBA 1997; historian; Senior Research Associate, Oxford University, since 1997; Fellow, St Antony's College, Oxford, 2007–10, now Honorary; Supernumerary Fellow, Wolfson College, Oxford, 1998–2005; Professor of Polish History, School of Slavonic and East European Studies, University of London, 1985–96, now Emeritus; *b* Bolton, 8 June 1939; *s* of Richard Davies and Elizabeth Bolton; *m* 1st, 1966, Maria Zielińska; one *s*; 2nd, 1984, Maria Korzeniewicz; one *s*. *Educ:* Bolton Sch.; Grenoble Univ.; Magdalen Coll., Oxford (MA); Sussex Univ. (MA); Jagiellonian Univ., Cracow (PhD). Asst Master, St Paul's Sch., London, 1963–65; Alistair Horne Res. Fellow, St Antony's Coll., Oxford, 1969–71; Lectr, 1971–84, Reader, 1984–85, SSEES, London Univ. Visiting Professor: Columbia Univ., 1974; McGill Univ., 1977–78; Hokkaido Univ., 1982–83; Stanford Univ., 1985–86; Harvard Univ., 1991; Univ. of Adelaide, 1998; ANU, Canberra, 1999; Visiting Fellow: Clare Hall, Cambridge, 2006–07; Peterhouse, Cambridge, 2008–09. FRHistS 1974. Dr *hc*: Marie Curie-Skłodowska Univ., Lublin, 1993; Univ. of Gdańsk, 2000; Jagiellonian Univ., 2003; Sussex, 2006; Warsaw, 2007. Hon. Citizen: Cracow, 1999; Lublin, 2000; Wrocław, 2002; Warsaw, 2004. Kt Cross, Order of Polonia Restituta (Poland), 1984; Commander Cross, 1992, Grand Cross, 1998, Order of Merit (Poland); Medal of Bene Merito (Poland), 2010; Mem., Order of White Eagle (Poland), 2012. *Publications:* White Eagle, Red Star: the Polish-Soviet war of 1919–20, 1972; Poland Past and Present: a bibliography of works in English on Polish history, 1976; God's Playground: a history of Poland, 2 vols, 1981; Heart of Europe: a short history of Poland, 1984; (ed with A. Polonsky) The Jews in Eastern Poland and the Soviet Union 1939–45, 1991; Europe: a history, 1996; The Isles: a history, 1999; (with Roger Moorhouse) Microcosm: portrait of a central European city, 2002; Rising '44: the battle for Warsaw, 2003; Europe East & West, 2006; Europe at War 1939–1945: no simple victory, 2006; Vanished Kingdoms: the history of half-forgotten Europe, 2011; books trans. into most European langs and others, incl. Chinese and Japanese. *Recreation:* not writing. *Address:* St Antony's College, Oxford OX2 6JF.

DAVIES, Jacqueline, (Mrs P. N. R. Clark); Her Honour Judge Jacqueline Davies; a Circuit Judge, since 1993; *b* 21 May 1948; one *d*; *m* 1997, His Honour Paul Nicholas Rowntree Clark (*d* 2008). *Educ:* Manchester High Sch. for Girls; Univ. of Leeds (LLB Hons). Called to the Bar, Middle Temple, 1975, Bencher, 2004; a Recorder, 1991–93. Pres., Council of Circuit Judges, 2011– (Jun. Vice Pres., 2009; Sen. Vice Pres., 2010). *Address:* Doncaster Crown Court, College Road, Doncaster DN1 3HS.

DAVIES, James Michael; MP (C) Vale of Clwyd, since 2015; *b* St Asaph, 27 Feb. 1980; *s* of Michael Davies and Belinda Davies; *m* 2012, Nina Jones; one *s*. *Educ:* King's Sch., Chester; Christ's Coll., Cambridge (BA; MB BChir 2004; MA 2005). MRCGP 2008. Pre-registration House Officer, Glan Clwyd Hosp., 2004–05; Sen. House Officer, Countess of Chester Hosp., 2005–07; GP Registrar, City Walls Med. Centre, Chester, 2007–08; GP, Boughton Med. Gp, Chester, 2008–15, Partner, 2010–15. Mem. (C), Denbighshire CC, 2004–15. *Recreations:* travelling, walking, languages, local community regeneration, cinema, real ale and dining out, DIY. *Address:* House of Commons, SW1A 0AA. *T:* (020) 7219 4627. *E:* james.davies.mp@parliament.uk; (office) Hanover House, The Roe, St Asaph LL17 0LT. *T:* (01745) 583270. *Club:* Carlton.

DAVIES, James Selwyn, (Joe); Master of Haileybury, since 2009; *b* Harlech, 29 June 1956; *s* of John Selwyn Davies and Joan Davies; *m* 1981, Virginia Felicity Graham; three *s* one *d*. *Educ:* Christ Coll., Brecon; St John's Coll., Cambridge (BA 1977); University Coll., Cardiff (PGCE 1980). Housemaster, Tonbridge Sch., 1980–94, exchange teacher, Anglican Church Grammar Sch., Brisbane, 1988; Dep. Hd, St John's Sch., Leatherhead, 1994–2000; Headmaster, Sutton Valence Sch., 2001–09. Chm., Ind. Schs Teacher Induction Panel, 2014–. *Recreations:* Rugby football (Cambridge blue, London Welsh, Penarth), cricket, squash, marathon running, reading, cycling, camping. *Address:* Master's Lodge, Haileybury, Hertford SG13 7NU. *T:* (01992) 706200. *E:* j.davies@haileybury.com. *Clubs:* East India, Lansdowne; Hawks (Cambridge).

DAVIES, Jane; *see* Davies, B. J.

DAVIES, Janet; Member (Plaid Cymru) South Wales West, National Assembly for Wales, 1999–2007; *b* 29 May 1938; *d* of late David Rees and Jean Wardlaw Rees; *m* 1965, Basil Peter Ridley Davies (*d* 2000); one *s* one *d*. *Educ:* Howell's Sch., Llandaff; Trinity Coll., Carmarthen (BA); Open Univ. (BA Hons Social Scis). Mem. (Plaid Cymru) Taff Ely BC, 1983–96 (Leader, 1991–96); Mayor, Taff Ely, 1995–96. National Assembly for Wales: Plaid Cymru spokesperson on local govt, 1993–99, on housing, 1999–2002, for envmt, planning and transport, 2002, for transport, 2003–07; Plaid Cymru Chief Whip, 2003–07; Chm., Audit Cttee, 2003–07. Dir of Elections, Plaid Cymru, 1996–2001. Contested (Plaid Cymru) Brecon and Radnorshire, 2010.

DAVIES, Janet Mary H.; *see* Hewlett-Davies.

DAVIES, Jill Adrian; *see* Kraye, J. A.

DAVIES, Jocelyn Ann; Member (Plaid Cymru) South East Wales, National Assembly for Wales, since 1999; *b* 18 June 1959; *d* of Edward and Marjorie Davies; one *s* two *d* by Michael Davies. *Educ:* Harris Manchester Coll., Oxford. Work in local govt, Islwyn BC and Newport BC, 1976–80. Mem. (Plaid Cymru) Islwyn BC, 1987–91. Dep. Minister for Housing, 2007–09, for Housing and Regeneration, 2009–11, Nat. Assembly for Wales. *Recreations:* walking, people watching. *Address:* National Assembly for Wales, Cardiff Bay, Cardiff CF99 1NA. *T:* (constituency) (01633) 220022, *Fax:* (01633) 220603.

DAVIES, Joe; *see* Davies, James S.

DAVIES, Prof. John Brian, FREng; Professor of Electrical Engineering, University College London, 1985–97, now Emeritus Professor; *b* 2 May 1932; *s* of John Kendrick Davies and Agnes Ada Davies; *m* 1956, Shirley June (*née* Abrahart); one *s* two *d*. *Educ:* Jesus Coll., Cambridge (MA); Univ. of London (MSc, PhD, DSc Eng). Research Engineer, Mullard Res. Labs, Redhill, 1955–63; Lectr, Dept of Electrical Engineering, Univ. of Sheffield, 1963; Sen. Lectr 1967, Reader 1970–85, Dean of Engrg, 1989–91, University College London. Vis. Scientist, Nat. Bureau of Standards, Boulder, Colo, 1971–72; Visitor, Univ. of Oxford, 1983; Vis. Prof., Univ. of Colorado, 1988–89. FREng (FEng 1988). *Publications:* Electromagnetic Theory, vol. 2, 1972; (contrib.) Numerical Techniques for Microwave and Millimeter Wave Passive Structures, 1989. *Recreations:* fell walking, music.

DAVIES, Rt Rev. John David Edward; *see* Swansea and Brecon, Bishop of.

DAVIES, Rt Rev. John Dudley; Hon. Assistant Bishop: diocese of Lichfield, 1995–2005; diocese of St Asaph, since 2009; Bishop Suffragan, then Area Bishop, of Shrewsbury, 1987–94; *b* 12 Aug. 1927; *s* of Charles Edward Steedman Davies and Minnie Paton Davies; *m* 1956, Shirley Dorothy Gough; one *s* two *d*. *Educ:* Trinity Coll., Cambridge (BA 1951, MA 1963); Lincoln Theol Coll. Deacon 1953, priest 1954, dio. Ripon; Curate: Halton, Leeds, 1953–56; Yeoville, Johannesburg, 1957; Priest-in-Charge, Evander, dio. Johannesburg, 1957–61; Rector and Dir of Missions, Empangeni, dio. Zululand and Swaziland, 1961–63; Anglican Chaplain, Univ. of Witwatersrand and Johannesburg Coll. of Educn, 1963–70; Chm., Div. of Christian Educn, S African Council of Churches, 1964–70; Mem. Exec., Univ. Christian Movement of Southern Africa, 1966–69; Sec. for Chaplaincies of Higher Educn, C of E Bd of Educn, 1970–74; Vicar of Keele and Chaplain, Univ. of Keele, 1974–76; Principal, Coll. of Ascension, Selly Oak, 1976–81; Preb. of Sandiacre, Lichfield Cathedral, 1976–87; Diocesan Missioner, St Asaph, 1982–87; Canon Res. and Hellins Lectr, St Asaph, 1982–85; Vicar/Rector, Llanrhaeadr-ym-Mochnant, Llanarmon-Mynydd-Mawr, Pennant, Hirnant and Llangynog, 1985–87. *Publications:* Free to Be, 1970; Beginning Now, 1971; Good News in Galatians, 1975; Creed and Conflict, 1979; The Faith Abroad, 1983; (with John J. Vincent) Mark at Work, 1986; World on Loan, 1992; The Crisis of the Cross, 1997; Be Born in us Today, 1999; God at Work, 2001; Only Say the Word, 2002; A Song for Every Morning 2008; (jtly) Stilling the Storm, 2011; Acts in Practice, 2012; Leviticus in Practice, 2014, contribs to jls. *Address:* Nyddfa, By Pass Road, Gobowen, Oswestry SY11 3NG. *T:* (01691) 653434.

DAVIES, John Hamilton, OBE 2005; Chairman, Civil Service Appeal Board, 1999–2011; *b* 24 Nov. 1943; *s* of Albert Victor Davies and Betty Davies; *m* 1971, Helen Ruth Thomas; three *s*. *Educ:* Lewis Sch., Pengam, S Wales; Selwyn Coll., Cambridge (MA). ACIB 1970, FCIB 1991; FCIPD (FIPD 1991). With Barclays Bank, 1966–98: Local Dir, Chelmsford Reg., 1983–86; Hd, Career Planning, Gp Personnel, 1986–90; Dep. Dir, Gp Personnel, 1991–95; Dir, Personnel, Barclays UK Banking Services, 1995–98. Non-exec. Dir, ILX Gp (formerly Intellexis plc), 2001–06. Vis. Fellow, Cranfield Univ. Sch. of Mgt, 1998–2002. Board Member: Employers' Forum on Disability, 1991–96; BESO, 1991–98; Member: CBI Employment Policy Cttee, 1996–98; Armed Forces Pay Review Body, 1999–2005; Prison Service Pay Review Body, 2007–. Treas. and Mem., Exec. Bd, CIB, 1998–99. Gov., Felsted Sch., 1990–95 and 1998– (Chm., 2007–). Freeman, City of London, 2002; Liveryman, Curriers' Co., 2002–. *Recreations:* walking, Church of England, music, travel. *Address:* Denbies, Bardfield Saling, Essex CM7 5EG. *T:* (01371) 850735. *Clubs:* Oxford and Cambridge; Essex.

DAVIES, Very Rev. Dr John Harverd; DL; Dean of Derby, since 2010; *b* Bolton, Lancs, 29 Nov. 1957. *Educ:* Brentwood Sch.; Keble Coll., Oxford (MA 1984); Corpus Christi Coll., Cambridge (MPhil 1984); Lancaster Univ. (PhD); Westcott House, Cambridge. Ordained deacon, 1984, priest, 1985; Assistant Curate: Our Lady and St Nicholas with St Anne, Liverpool, 1984–87; St John the Baptist, Peterborough, 1987–90; Minor Canon, Peterborough Cathedral, 1988–90; Vicar, St Margaret's, Anfield, 1990–94; Chaplain, Fellow and Lectr, Keble Coll., Oxford, 1994–99; Vicar, St Michael, Melbourne, 1999–2010; Dir of Ordinands, Dio. of Derby, 2000–09. Hon. Canon, Derby Cathedral, 2010. Chm., Industrial Mission in Derbys, 2009–. DL Derbys, 2011. *Recreations:* reading, walking, musing. *Address:* Derby Cathedral Centre, 18–19 Iron Gate, Derby DE1 3GP. *T:* (01332) 341201. *E:* dean@derbycathedral.org.

DAVIES, Rev. Canon John Howard; Director of Theological and Religious Studies, University of Southampton, 1981–94; *b* 19 Feb. 1929; *s* of Jabez Howard and Sarah Violet Davies; *m* 1956, Ina Mary (*d* 1985), *d* of Stanley William and Olive Mary Bubb; two *s* (and two *s* decd). *Educ:* Southall Grammar Sch.; St John's Coll., Cambridge (MA); Westcott House, Cambridge; Univ. of Nottingham (BD); FRCO 1952. Ordained deacon, 1955, priest 1956. Succentor of Derby Cathedral, 1955; Chaplain of Westcott House, 1958; Lectr in Theology, Univ. of Southampton, 1963, Sen. Lectr 1974. Canon Theologian of Winchester, 1981–91. *Publications:* A Letter to Hebrews, 1967; (contrib.) Walter Frere, 2011. *Recreations:* music, architecture, the countryside. *Address:* 13 Glen Eyre Road, Southampton SO16 3GA. *T:* (023) 8067 9359.

DAVIES, John Irfon, CBE 1998 (MBE (mil.) 1963); Under Secretary, Welsh Office, 1985–90, retired; Chairman, Health Promotion Authority for Wales, 1992–99; *b* 8 June 1930; *s* of late Thomas M. Davies and Mary M. Davies (*née* Harris); *m* 1950, Jean Marion Anderson (*d* 2000); one *d*. *Educ:* Stanley School; Croydon Polytechnic. Joined RAF, 1948, commissioned 1950, Specialist Navigator 1957; psc 1963; MoD, 1964–66; Chief Navigation Instructor, Cranwell, 1967; OC Flying, Muharraq, 1967–69; awc 1970; MoD, 1970–72; Cabinet Office, 1972–74; retd from RAF, 1974; Principal, 1974, Asst Sec., 1978, Welsh Office; Private Sec. to Sec. of State for Wales, 1977–78. Mem., GMC, 1990–99. *Recreations:* golf, piano, fishing, books. *Address:* 7 Danybryn Close, Radyr, Cardiff CF15 8DJ. *Clubs:* Royal Air Force; Cardiff and County; Radyr Golf.

DAVIES, Prof. John Kenyon, MA, DPhil; FSA; FBA 1985; Rathbone Professor of Ancient History and Classical Archaeology, University of Liverpool, 1977–2003; *b* 19 Sept. 1937; *s* of Harold Edward Davies and Clarice Theresa (*née* Woodburn); *m* 1st, 1962, Anna Elbina Morpurgo (Prof. Anna Morpurgo Davies, Hon. DBE, FBA) (marr. diss. 1978; she *d* 2014); 2nd, 1978, Nicola Jane, *d* of Dr and Mrs R. M. S. Perrin; one *s* one *d*. *Educ:* Manchester Grammar Sch.; Wadham Coll., Oxford (BA 1959; MA 1962; DPhil 1966). FSA 1986. Harmsworth Sen. Scholar, Merton Coll., Oxford, 1960–61 and 1962–63; Jun. Fellow, Center for Hellenic Studies, Washington, DC, 1961–62; Dyson Jun. Res. Fellow, Balliol Coll., Oxford, 1963–65; Lectr in Ancient History, Univ. of St Andrews, 1965–68; Fellow and Tutor in Ancient History, Oriel Coll., Oxford, 1968–77; Pro-Vice-Chancellor, Univ. of Liverpool, 1986–90. Leverhulme Res. Prof., 1995–2000. Vis. Lectr, Univ. of Pennsylvania, 1971; Teaching Fellow, and Dir, Postgraduate residential course, British Sch. of Archaeology, Athens, 2004, 2006, 2008; Sen. Fellow, Istituto di Studi Avanzati, Univ. di Bologna, 2006; Onassis Foundn Vis. Fellow, Inst. of Greek and Roman Antiquity, Athens, 2010. Chairman: St Patrick's Isle (IOM) Archaeological Trust Ltd, 1982–86; NW Archaeol Trust, 1982–91. Chm., Adv. Cttee, Inst. of Classical Studies, Univ. of London, 2005–13; Expert Advr, Eur. Sci. Foundn, 2006–. Corresp. Mem., Deutsche Archäologische Institut, 2000. Editor: Jl of Hellenic Studies, 1972–77; Archaeol Reports, 1972–74. *Publications:* Athenian Propertied Families 600–300 BC, 1971; Democracy and Classical Greece, 1978, 2nd edn 1993 (Spanish trans. 1981, German and Italian trans. 1983, Polish trans. 2003, Russian trans. 2004); Wealth and the Power of Wealth in Classical Athens, 1981; (ed with L. Foxhall) The Trojan War: its historicity and context, 1984; (ed jtly) Cambridge Ancient History vol. 5, 2nd edn, 1992; (ed jtly) Hellenistic Economies, 2001; (ed jtly) Making, Moving, and Managing, 2005; (ed jtly) The Economies of Hellenistic Societies, Third to First Centuries BC, 2011; (ed jtly) Epigraphy and the Historical Sciences, 2012; articles and reviews in learned jls. *Recreations:* canal walking, choral music, mainland European railways. *Address:* 20 North Road, Grassendale Park, Liverpool L19 0LR. *T:* (0151) 427 2126.

DAVIES, Sir (John) Michael, KCB 2002; Clerk of the Parliaments, House of Lords, 1997–2003; *b* 2 Aug. 1940; *s* of late Vincent Ellis Davies, OBE and Rose Trench (*née* Temple); *m* 1971, Amanda Mary Atkinson; two *s* one *d*. *Educ:* The King's Sch., Canterbury; Peterhouse, Cambridge. Joined Parliament Office, House of Lords, 1964; seconded to Civil Service Dept as Private Sec. to Leader of House of Lords and Govt Chief Whip, 1971–74; Establishment Officer and Sec. to Chm. of Cttees, 1974–83; Principal Clerk, Overseas and European Office, 1983–85; Principal Clerk, Private Bill and Overseas Offices and Examiner of Petitions for Private Bills, 1985–88; Reading Clerk, 1988–90, and Clerk of Public Bills, 1988–94; Clerk Asst, 1991–97, and Principal Finance Officer, 1994–97. Secretary: Soc. of Clerks-at-the-Table in Commonwealth Parlts, and Jt Editor, The Table, 1967–83; Statute

Law Cttee, 1974–83. Pres., Assoc. of Secs-General of Parlts, 1997–2000. Chm., BACSA, 2008–. *Address:* 26 Northchurch Terrace, N1 4EG.

See also H. L. Davies.

DAVIES, Rt Rev. John Stewart; Bishop of St Asaph, 1999–2008; *b* 28 Feb. 1943; *s* of John Edward Davies and Dorothy Stewart Davies (*née* Jones); *m* 1965, Joan Patricia Lovatt; two *s*. *Educ:* St John's Sch., Leatherhead; UCNW, Bangor (BA Hebrew); Westcott House, Cambridge; Queens' Coll., Cambridge (MLitt 1974). Journalism, 1960–68; ordained deacon, 1974, priest, 1975; Curate, Hawarden, 1974–78; Vicar: Rhosymedre, 1978–87; Mold, 1987–92; Archdeacon of St Asaph, 1991–99. *Recreations:* hill walking, cycling.

DAVIES, John Thomas, FCIB; Director, 1990–98, a Deputy Chairman, 1995–98, Lloyds Bank plc; a Deputy Chairman, Lloyds TSB Group plc, 1995–98; *b* 9 Feb. 1933; *s* of Joseph Robert and Dorothy Mary Davies; *m* 1957, Margaret Ann Johnson; two *s* three *d*. *Educ:* King Edward's Grammar Sch., Camp Hill, Birmingham. FCIB. Joined Lloyds Bank, 1949; served RAF, 1951–53; Lloyds Bank: Manager of branches, 1963–78; Gen. Management, 1978–89; Dir, Internat. Banking Div., 1989–91; Asst Chief Exec., 1991–92; Dep. Chief Exec., 1992–94. Director: Nat. Bank of NZ, 1989–90 and 1995–98; Cheltenham & Gloucester Building Society, 1995–98; Dir, 1995–98, Chm., 1997–98, Lloyds Abbey Life, later Lloyds TSB Financial Hldgs plc. Chm. Bd, OBO Property (formerly Office of the Banking Ombudsman), 1995–2004. *Recreations:* opera, gardening, walking, reading.

DAVIES, Jonathan, OBE 2015 (MBE 1995); writer and commentator on Rugby Union and League football; *b* 24 Oct. 1962; *s* of late Len and of Diana Davies; *m* 1984, Karen Hopkins (*d* 1997); one *s* two *d*; *m* 2002, Helen Jones. *Educ:* Gwendraeth Grammar Sch. Rugby Union footballer to 1989; played for Neath and Llanelli; 37 Wales caps, 4 as Captain; transferred to Rugby League, 1989; with Widnes, 1989–93, Warrington, 1993–95; returned to Rugby Union, 1995; with Cardiff, 1995–97, retired. Player of the Year Award, 1991, 1994; Stones Bitter Man of Steel, 1994. Pres., Velindre Cancer Centre, 2009–. *Publications:* with Peter Corrigan: Jonathan (autobiog.), 1989; Codebreaker, 1996. *Recreations:* golf, football. *Address:* c/o Cardiff RUFC, Cardiff Arms Park, Cardiff CF10 1JL.

DAVIES, Prof. Julian Edmund, PhD; FRS 1994; FRSC 1996; Professor and Head of Department of Microbiology and Immunology, University of British Columbia, 1992–97, now Professor Emeritus; *b* 9 Jan. 1932; *s* of Norman Alfred Davies and Lilian Constance (*née* Clarke); *m* 1957, Dorothy Jean Olney; two *s* one *d*. *Educ:* Univ. of Nottingham (BSc Hons Chem., Maths and Phys.; PhD 1956). Lectr in Chem., Univ. of Manchester, 1959–62; Associate in Bacteriol., Harvard Univ., 1962–67; University of Wisconsin: Associate Prof. of Biochem., 1967–70; Prof., 1970–80; Biogen: Res. Dir, 1980–83; Pres., 1983–85; Prof., Inst. Pasteur, Paris, 1986–91; Dir, West-East Center, Univ. of BC, 1993–96; Chief Scientific Officer, and Vice-Pres. of Res., TerraGen Diversity Inc., 1996–2000; Exec. Vice-Pres. for Technology Develt, Cubist Pharmaceuticals, Vancouver, 2000–04; Dir, Life Scis Inst., Univ. of British Columbia, 2005–06. President: Amer. Soc. for Microbiol., 1999–2000; Internat. Union Microbiol. Soc., 2002–05. Foreign Associate, US NAS, 2014. Hon. DSc: UBC 2003; Nottingham, 2009; McGill, 2011; Guelph; McMaster, 2015. Hoechst-Roussel Award, 1986, Lifetime Achievement Award, 2012, Amer. Soc. for Microbiol.; Thom Award, Soc. for Industrial Microbiol., 1993; Scheele Prize, Swedish Acad. of Pharmaceutical Scis, 1997; Bristol Myers Squibb Award, 1999; Soc. of Gen. Microbiol. Medal, 2012. *Publications:* Elementary Biochemistry, 1980; Milestones in Biotechnology, 1992. *Recreations:* cycling, wine. *Address:* 202/5760 Hampton Place, Vancouver, BC V6T 2G1, Canada. *T:* (604) 2228235.

DAVIES, Julienne Elizabeth; *see* Meyer, J. E.

DAVIES, Karl; *see* Davies, R. K.

DAVIES, Dame Kay (Elizabeth), DBE 2008 (CBE 1995); DPhil; FMedSci; FRS 2003; Dr Lee's Professor of Anatomy, since 1998, Associate Head (Development, Impact and Equality), Medical Sciences Division, since 2011, University of Oxford; Fellow of Hertford College, Oxford, since 1998; Hon. Director, MRC Functional Genetics Unit, since 1999; Deputy Chairman, Wellcome Trust, since 2013; *b* 1 April 1951; *d* of Harry Partridge and Florence Partridge (*née* Farmer); *m* 1973, Stephen Graham Davies (marr. diss. 2000); one *s*. *Educ:* Stourbridge Girls' High Sch.; Somerville Coll., Oxford (BA, MA; DPhil; Hon. Fellow, 1995). MRCPath 1990, FRCPath 1997. Guy Newton Jun. Res. Fellow, Wolfson Coll., Oxford, 1976–78; Royal Soc. European Post-doctoral Fellow, Service de Biochimie, Centre d'Etudes, Gif-sur-Yvette, France, 1978–80; St Mary's Hospital Medical School: Cystic Fibrosis Res. Fellow, 1980–82; MRC Sen. Res. Fellow, 1982–84; Nuffield Department of Clinical Medicine, John Radcliffe Hospital, Oxford: MRC Sen. Res. Fellow, 1984–86; MRC Ext. Staff, 1986–92; Univ. Res. Lectr, 1990; MRC Ext. Staff, Inst. of Molecular Medicine, Oxford, 1989–95; Fellow of Green Coll., Oxford, 1990–95; MRC Res. Dir, MRC Clin. Scis Centre, Hammersmith Hosp., 1992–94; Oxford University: Prof. of Genetics, and Fellow, Keble Coll., 1995–98; Co-Dir, Oxford Centre for Gene Function, 2001; Hd, Dept of Physiol., Anatomy and Genetics, Med. Scis Div., 2008–11. Mem., MRC, 2002–. Mem., Royal Commn for Exhibn of 1851, 2011–. Editor (with S. Tilghman), Genome Analysis Reviews, 1990–. Bristol-Myers Prof., USA, 1986; 7th Annual Colleen Giblin Dist. Lectr, Columbia Univ., 1992; Dist. Lectr, Mayo Clinic, USA, 1994. Founder FMedSci 1998. Hon. FRCP 1994. Hon. DSc Victoria, Canada, 1990; DUniv Open, 1999. Wellcome Trust Award, 1996; SCI Medal, 1999. *Publications:* (with A. P. Read) Molecular Analysis of Inherited Diseases, 1988, rev. edn 1992; (ed) Human Genetics Diseases: a practical approach, 1988, rev. edn 1993; (ed) Genome Analysis: a practical approach, 1988; (ed) The Fragile X Syndrome, 1989; (ed) Application of Molecular Genetics to the Diagnosis of Inherited Diseases, 1989; numerous reviews and 400 peer-reviewed pubns. *Recreations:* sport, music, gardening. *Address:* Department of Physiology, Anatomy and Genetics, University of Oxford, Parks Road, Oxford OX1 3PT.

DAVIES, Keith Laurence M.; *see* Maitland Davies.

DAVIES, Keith Price; Member (Lab) Llanelli, National Assembly for Wales, since 2011; *b* Gwaun-Cae-Gurwen, 25 May 1940; *s* of James Glyn Davies and Elizabeth Iris Davies; *m* 1st, 1963, Margaret Legge (marr. diss. 1991); two *s* one *d*; 2nd, 1992, Heddyr Gregory; two *s*. *Educ:* Ystalyfera Grammar Sch.; University Coll. Swansea (BSc 1st Cl.; MSc); University Coll. of South Wales and Monmouthshire (PGCE). Hd of Maths, Maesteg Grammar Tech. Sch., 1963–65; Sen. Lectr, Cardiff Coll. of Educn, 1965–72; Advr in Maths, Glamorgan LEA, 1972–74; Mid Glamorgan County Council: Sen. Advr, Secondary, 1974–79; Chief Advr, 1979–94; Dir of Educn, 1994–96; Dir of Educn, Carmarthenshire CC, 1996–2000; Chief Exec. (pt-time), Birmingham Careers and Educn Business Partnership, 2000; Dir (pt-time), Welsh Baccalaureate Qualification, WJEC, 2003–08. *Recreations:* sport in general, reading. *Address:* Caedelyn, 2 Fen-y-Fai Lane, Llanelli SA15 4EN. *T:* 07540 964669, (Llanelli office) (01554) 774902, (Cardiff office) 0300 200 7101. *E:* keith.davies@assembly.wales.

DAVIES, Keith Robert, OBE 2009; Director, Sri Lanka, British Council, since 2013; *b* Frodsham, Cheshire, 9 May 1954; *s* of Robert Charles Davies and Mary Davies (*née* Briscoe); *m* 1994, Christine Loh; one *d*. *Educ:* Helsby Co. Grammar Sch. for Boys; Univ. of Hull (BA Hons Drama and English 1975); Poly. of Central London (Postgrad. Dip. Film Studies 1983). Joined British Council, 1976; Club Sec., British Council Students Centre, London, 1976–80; Acquisitions Officer, Film Dept, 1980–84; Asst Rep., Bahrain, 1985–88; Promotions Officer, Educn Counselling Service, London, 1988–90; Educn Counsellor, Malaysia, 1990–95; Dep. Dir, Thailand, 1995–99; Hd, Ops, China, 1999–2004; Director: Vietnam, 2004–08; Indonesia, 2009–13. *Recreations:* assiduously following the trials and tribulations and occasional triumphs of Everton Football Club, travel, cinema, exploring, reading, food, Asian cultures. *Address:* British Council Colombo, BFPO 5438, HA4 6EP. *E:* keithdaviesvn@yahoo.co.uk.

DAVIES, Dame Laura (Jane), DBE 2014 (CBE 2000; MBE 1988); professional golfer; *b* 5 Oct. 1963; *d* of David Thomas Davies and Rita Ann Davies (*née* Foskett). *Educ:* Fullbrook County Secondary Sch. Mem., Curtis Cup team, 1984; professional début, 1985; Mem., Solheim Cup team, 1990, 1992, 1994, 1996, 1998, 2000, 2002, 2003, 2005, 2007, 2009, 2011; Winner: Belgian Ladies' Open, 1985; Ladies' British Open, 1986; US Ladies' Open, 1987; Italian Open, 1987, 1988, 1996; Ford Classic, Woburn, 1988; Biarritz Ladies' Open, 1988; Itoki Classic, Japan, 1988; European Open, 1992; Thailand Ladies' Open, 1993, 1994; English Open, 1993, 1995; Australian Ladies' Masters, 1993, 1994, 2003; LPGA Championship, 1994, 1996; Irish Open, 1994, 1995; Scottish Open, 1994; French Masters, 1995; Danish Open, 1997; Championship of Europe, 1999; Norwegian Masters, 2002, 2006; Australian Open, 2004, 2009; Pegasus NZ Women's Open, 2010; German Open, 2010; Austrian Open, 2010; Spanish Open, 2010; Indian Open, 2010. Mem., Golf Foundn. *Publications:* Carefree Golf, 1991. *Address:* c/o IMG Golf, McCormack House, Hogarth Business Park, Burlington Lane, W4 2TH.

DAVIES, Leighton; *see* Davies, Robert L.

DAVIES, Her Honour Linda Hillary; a Circuit Judge, 1992–2009; *b* 31 May 1945; *d* of Lt-Col Robert Blowers and Doris Rhoda (*née* Hillary); *m* 1966, Michael Llewelyn Lifton Davies; two *d*. *Educ:* Folkestone Grammar Sch. for Girls; King's Coll., London (LLB Hons). Called to the Bar, Gray's Inn, 1969; Barrister, 1972–92, a Recorder, 1990–92, Western Circuit. Part-time Chm., Industrial Tribunals, 1986–92. Trustee, Roberts Centre, 2006–. Fine arts degree student, Chichester Univ., 2011–.

DAVIES, Lindsay Jane; Her Honour Judge Lindsay Davies; a Circuit Judge, since 2012; *b* Swansea, 9 Aug. 1952; *d* of Raymond Peter and Finvola Clifford Davies. *Educ:* Llwyn-y-bryn Sch., Swansea; University Coll. of Wales, Aberystwyth (LLB Hons). Called to the Bar, Gray's Inn, 1975. Mem., Fenners Chambers, Cambridge, 1977–2012. Mem., RSAA, 1984. *Recreation:* travel in Central Asia. *Address:* Luton County Court, Cresla House, Alma Road, Luton, Beds LU1 2PU. *E:* HHJudgeLindsay.Davies@judiciary.gsi.gov.uk.

DAVIES, Dr Lindsey Margaret, CBE 2004; FFPH; President, Faculty of Public Health, Royal Colleges of Physicians of the UK, 2010–13; *b* 21 May 1953; *d* of Dr Frank Newby and Margaret Newby; *m* 1974, Peter Davies (marr. diss. 1994); two *s*. *Educ:* Univ. of Nottingham (BM, BS). MHSM 1987; FFPH (FFPHM 1991); FRCP 2002; FRCPE 2013. Community paediatrics, 1976–82; trainee in public health medicine, 1982–85; Director of Public Health: Southern Derbys HA, 1985–89; Nottingham HA, 1989–92; Hd, Public Health Div., NHS Exec., DoH, 1992–94; Dir of Public Health, Trent RHA, 1994–96; Dir of Public Health and Med. Dir, Trent Regl Office, NHS Exec., DoH, 1996–2002; Regl Dir of Public Health, E Midlands, DoH, 2002–06; Nat. Dir of Pandemic Influenza Preparedness, DoH, 2006–10; Dir of Health, Olympics and Paralympics Prog., 2008–10; Interim Regl Dir of Public Health, NHS London, 2009–10. Hon. Prof. (formerly Special Prof.), Nottingham Univ. Med. Sch., 2001–. British Medical Association: Mem. Council, 1989–92; Chm., Cttee for Public Health Medicine and Community Health, 1990–92. Hon. FRCPI 2013. Hon. MD Sheffield, 2013. *Publications:* contribs to learned jls. *Recreations:* family life, gardening, walking.

DAVIES, Ven. Lorys Martin; Archdeacon of Bolton, 1992–2001, now Emeritus; *b* 14 June 1936; *s* of Evan Tudor Davies and Eigen Morfydd Davies; *m* 1960, Barbara Ethel (*née* Walkley); two *s*. *Educ:* Whitland Grammar Sch.; St David's Coll., Lampeter, Univ. of Wales (BA Hons); Philips Hist. Schol.; Organ Exhibnr. Wells Theol Coll. ALCM 1952. Ordained: deacon, 1959; priest, 1960; Curate, St Mary's, Tenby, 1959–61; Asst Chaplain, Brentwood Sch., 1962–66; Chaplain and Head of Dept, Solihull Sch., 1966–68; Vicar, St Mary's, Moseley, 1968–81; Residentiary Canon, Birmingham Cathedral, 1981–92; Diocesan Dir of Ordinands, Birmingham, 1982–90; Advr to Bishop of Manchester on Hosp. Chaplaincies, 1992–2001, Warden of Readers, 1994–2000, dio. of Manchester. Chm., House of Clergy, Birmingham Diocesan Synod, 1990–91; Proctor in Convocation, 1998–2001. Member: Nat. Stewardship Cttee, 2000–05; Hosp. Chaplaincies Council, 2000–05 (Vice-Chm., 2003–05). Reviewer: Community Health Improvement, 2001–04; Healthcare Commn, 2004–07. Midland Rep., Retired Clergy Assoc., 2009–12. JP Birmingham, 1978–92. *Recreations:* sport, theatre, music, reading. *Address:* Heolcerrig, 28 Penshurst Road, Bromsgrove, Worcestershire B60 2SN.

DAVIES, Lucy Alexandra; Executive Producer, Royal Court Theatre, since 2013; *b* Birmingham, 24 July 1970; *d* of Prof. Llewellyn, (Tony), Davies and Hon. Teresa Davies; *m* 2005, Jonathan Glynn; two *s*. *Educ:* Swanshurst Sch., Birmingham; Cadbury Coll., Birmingham; Univ. of Exeter (BA Hons 1st Cl. Drama); University Coll. London (MA Philos.). Asst Dir and Asst Administrator, Kneehigh Th., 1992–94; Donmar Warehouse: Carlton Donmar Trainee Dir, 1994–95; Literary Manager and Producer, New Writing Seasons, 1995–99; Asst to Jez Butterworth, Miramax/Film 4, 1999–2001; Hd of Develt, Fox Phillips, 2001–04; Hd of Studio, RNT, 2004–07; Exec Producer, Donmar Warehouse, 2007–09; Founding Exec. Producer, National Theatre Wales, 2009–13. FRSA. *Recreations:* politics, visual arts, literature, travel, cooking, cycling, swimming, yoga. *Address:* Royal Court Theatre, Sloane Square, SW1W 8AS.

DAVIES, Lynn, CBE 2006 (MBE 1967); President, UK Athletics, 2002–15; *b* Nantymoel, Wales, 20 May 1942; *s* of Tegfryn Davies and Gwladys Davies; *m* 1966, Meriel Griffiths; one *d*. *Educ:* Cardiff Coll. of Educn (DipPE; Cert Ed). Teacher, Bridgend Grammar Sch., 1964–66; Lectr in Sport and PE, Cardiff Coll. of Educn, 1966–72; Tech. Dir, Canadian athletics, 1972–76; Team Manager, British Athletics Team, 1978–84, incl. Moscow and LA Olympic Games; Sen. Lectr in Sport and PE, UWIC, 1996–2007. Mem., Sports Council Wales, 2000–06; Vice Pres., British Olympic Assoc., 2001. Athlete; gold medal for long jump: Tokyo Olympics, 1964; European Championships, 1966; Commonwealth Games, 1966, 1970; European Indoor Championships, 1967; silver medal for long jump: European Championships, 1969; European Indoor Championships, 1969. Hon. MA: Open 1992; Wales 2008. *Recreations:* gardening, golf, tennis, fitness, reading, cinema. *Address:* 1 Orchard Close, Marshfield, Cardiff CF3 2UA. *T:* (01633) 681672.

DAVIES, Rt Rev. Mark; *see* Middleton, Bishop Suffragan of.

DAVIES, Rt Rev. Mark; *see* Shrewsbury, Bishop of, (RC).

DAVIES, Mark Edward Trehearne; Chairman, Fleming Family & Partners Ltd, since 2015 (Chief Executive, 2008–14; Director, 2003–14); Director, Stonehage Fleming Family & Partners, since 2015; *b* 20 May 1948; *s* of late Denis Norman Davies and Patricia Helen (*née* Trehearne); *m* 1987, Antonia Catharine Chittenden; two *s* two *d*. *Educ:* Stowe. Chief Executive: Intercommodities Ltd, 1971–85; GNI Ltd, 1985–95; Gerrard Gp plc, 1995–2001 (Dir, 1986–2001); Chairman: Townhouse Hotel Investments Ltd, 1994–2006; Thornhill Nominees (formerly Thornhill Hldgs) Ltd, 2001–10; Director: Thornhill Investment Mgt Ltd, 2001–10; Thornhill Hldgs (formerly Thornhill Acquisitions) Ltd, 2001–10; Thornhill Unit Trust Managers Ltd, 2001–10; Ascot Authority (Hldgs) Ltd, 2002–; Caledonia Investments plc, 2002–12; FF&P Capital Mgt Ltd, 2004–10; Chairman: FF&P Asset Mgt Ltd, 2003–10; FF&P Advisory, 2015–; FF&P Private Equity, 2015–. Director: Rank Foundn Ltd, 1991–; Admington Hall Farms Ltd, 1995–; Racing Welfare, 2001–10; Racing Welfare

(Enterprises) Ltd, 2006–10. *Publications:* (jtly) Trading in Commodities, 1974. *Recreations:* hunting, racing. *Address:* 26 Chester Street, SW1X 7BL; Stonehage Fleming Family & Partners Ltd, 15 Suffolk Street, SW1Y 4HG. *Club:* White's.

DAVIES, Sir Michael; *see* Davies, Sir J. M.

DAVIES, Michael Jeremy Pugh, CBE 2000; RIBA; FICPD; Founder Director, 1977–2011, Senior Partner, since 2011, Rogers Stirk Harbour & Partners (formerly Richard Rogers Partnership), Architects; *b* 23 Jan. 1942; *er s* of late Leonard Gwerfyl Davies and of Nancy Hannah Davies; *m* 1st, 1967, Isabel Christina Hogg (marr. diss. 1977); 2nd, 1977, Elizabeth Renee Yvonne Escalmel; one *s* one *d*. *Educ:* Highgate Sch.; Architectural Assoc. (AA Dip.); UCLA (Charles Scott Fellow; MArch Urban Design). Dir, Airstructures Design, 1966–68; Partner, Chrysalis USA, 1969–72; Project architect, Piano and Rogers, 1972–77 (projects incl. Centre Pompidou and IRCAM, Paris, 1971–77); Partner, Chrysalis Architects (London), 1978–83. Richard Rogers Partnership projects incl. Lloyd's of London, 1978–86; Project Director: Masterplan Royal Albert Docks, 1983–85; INMOS, 1984; Greenwich Peninsula Masterplan, 1996–2000; Millennium Dome, London, 1996–2000; Terminal 5, Heathrow Airport, 1989–2008; Wood Wharf Masterplan, London, 2004–08; Grand Paris Masterplan, 2008–10; Masterplan Bercy Charenton, Paris, 2010–; Masterplan Charolais Rambouillet, Paris, 2012–. Dir, MustRD, 2010–. Trustee, Useful Simple Trust. Has lectured at univs, confs and schools of architecture worldwide. FRGS; FICPD 1998; FRSA; FRAS. Hon. Fellow, Goldsmiths, Univ. of London, 2007. Chevalier, Legion d'Honneur, 2010. *Publications:* contrib. articles and papers to professional jls. *Recreations:* astronomy, sailing. *Address:* Rogers Stirk Harbour & Partners, Thames Wharf, Rainville Road, W6 9HA. *T:* (020) 7385 1235.

DAVIES, Mims; MP (C) Eastleigh, since 2015; *b* Crawley, 2 June 1975; *m* Mark Davies; two *d*. *Educ:* Forest Grange Sch., Horsham; Royal Russell Sch., Croydon; Univ. of Swansea (BA Hons Politics with Internat. Relns). Radio presenter and events asst, The Wave, Swansea; radio presenter, Heartbeat FM, Knebworth; reporter and producer, BBC Southern Counties Radio; Communications Officer, Sussex Safer Roads Partnership. Member: Mid Sussex DC; Haywards Heath Town Council. *Recreations:* running, pop music, family time, sport. *Address:* House of Commons, SW1A 0AA. *T:* (020) 7219 6853. *E:* mims.davies.mp@parliament.uk. *W:* www.mimsdavies.org.uk. *Club:* Haywards Heath Harriers.

DAVIES, Prof. Nicholas Barry, DPhil; FRS 1994; Professor of Behavioural Ecology, University of Cambridge, since 1995, and Fellow of Pembroke College, Cambridge, since 1979; *b* 23 May 1952; *s* of Anthony Barry Davies and Joyce Margaret Davies; *m* 1979, Jan Parr; two *d*. *Educ:* Merchant Taylors' Sch., Crosby; Pembroke Coll., Cambridge (BA 1973, MA 1977); Edward Grey Inst., Oxford Univ. (DPhil 1976). Demonstrator, Dept of Zoology (Edward Grey Inst. of Field Ornithology), Oxford Univ., 1976–79, and Jun. Res. Fellow, Wolfson Coll., Oxford, 1977–79; Demonstrator and Lectr in Zoology, 1979–92, Reader in Behavioural Ecology, 1992–95, Univ. of Cambridge. Pres., Internat. Soc. for Behavioural Ecology, 2000–02 (Hamilton Prize Lect., 2010). Hon Dr Bielefeld, 2011. Scientific Medal, Zool Soc., 1987; Cambridge Foundn Teaching Prize, 1995; William Bate Hardy Prize, Cambridge Phil Soc., 1995; Medal, Assoc. Study Animal Behaviour, 1996; Frink Medal, Zool Soc. of London, 2001; Elliott Coues Award, Amer. Ornithologists' Union, 2005; Croonian Medal and Lect., Royal Soc., 2015. *Publications:* (ed with J. R. Krebs) Behavioural Ecology, 1978, 4th edn 1997; (with J. R. Krebs) An Introduction to Behavioural Ecology, 1981, 4th edn (with J. R. Krebs and S. A. West) 2012; Dunnock Behaviour and Social Evolution, 1992; Cuckoos, Cowbirds and other Cheats, 2000; Cuckoo: cheating by nature, 2015; contribs to learned jls. *Recreations:* bird watching, cricket. *Address:* Department of Zoology, Downing Street, Cambridge CB2 3EJ. *T:* (01223) 336600.

DAVIES, Hon. Dame Nicola (Velfor), DBE 2010; **Hon. Mrs Justice Nicola Davies;** a Judge of the High Court of Justice, Queen's Bench Division, since 2010; a Presiding Judge, Wales Circuit, since 2014; *b* 13 March 1953. *Educ:* Bridgend Girls' Grammar School; Birmingham Univ. (LLB). Called to the Bar, Gray's Inn, 1976, Bencher, 2001; QC 1992; Recorder, 1998–2010; Dep. High Ct Judge, 2003–10. Hon. Fellow, Cardiff Univ., 2012. Hon. LLD S Wales, 2014. *Address:* Royal Courts of Justice, Strand, WC2A 2LL.

DAVIES, Col Nicolas; *see* Davies, Col F. N. J.

DAVIES, Rev. Noel Anthony, OBE 2003; PhD; Minister, Swansea and Clydach Ecumenical Pastorate, 2000–05; Associate Lecturer, Cardiff University (formerly University of Wales, Cardiff), 2000–04; *b* 26 Dec. 1942; *s* of late Rev. Ronald Anthony Davies and Anne Davies; *m* 1968, Patricia Barter. *Educ:* UCNW, Bangor (BSc Chem. and Biochem.); Mansfield College, Oxford (BA Theol.); PhD Wales 1998; Open Univ. (BSc 2013). Ordained, 1968; Minister, Bryn Seion Welsh Congregational Church, Glanaman, 1968–77; General Secretary: Council of Churches for Wales and Commn of Covenanted Churches in Wales, 1977–90; Cytûn: Churches Together in Wales, 1990–98; Minister, Ebeneser Newydd Congregational Ch, Swansea, 1996–2013. Co-ordinator of Trng, Coll. of Welsh Independents, 2005–09. Pres., Union of Welsh Independents (Congregational), 1998–99 (Chm. Council, 1990–93); Moderator, Churches' Commn on Mission, CCBI, 1991–95. Dir, Welsh Nat. Centre for Ecumenical Studies, University of Wales Trinity Saint David (formerly Trinity Coll., then Trinity Univ. Coll., Carmarthen), 2001–. Trustee, 1998–2009, Vice-Chm., 2006–09, Christian Aid. *Publications:* Wales: language, nation, faith and witness, 1996; (ed jtly) Wales: a moral society?, 1996; Un er mwyn y byd (A History of Welsh Ecumenism), 1998; God in the Centre, 1999; Religion and Ethics, 2003; (with Martin Conway) World Christianity in the 20th Century, 2 vols, 2008; A History of Welsh Ecumenism, 2008; Moeseg Gristnogol Gyfoes: dylanwadau ecwmenaidd (Contemporary Christian Ethics: ecumenical influences), 2013; articles in ecumenical jls and Welsh language items. *Recreations:* classical music and hi-fi, gardening, West Highland White terriers, oriental cookery. *Address:* 16 Maple Crescent, Uplands, Swansea SA2 0QD.

DAVIES, (Norah) Olwen, MA; Headmistress, St Swithun's School, Winchester, 1973–86; *b* 21 March 1926; *d* of late Rev. and Mrs E. A. Davies. *Educ:* Tregaron County Sch.; Walthamstow Hall, Sevenoaks; Edinburgh Univ. (MA). DipEd Oxon. Staff of Girls' Remand Home, Essex, 1948–50; Russell Hill Sch., Purley, 1950–53; Woodford House, NZ, 1953–57 (Dep. Headmistress); Westonbirt Sch., 1957–65; Headmistress, St Mary's Hall, Brighton, 1965–73. Pres., Girls' Schools Association, 1981–82. *Address:* 28 Arle Gardens, Alresford, Hants SO24 9BA.

DAVIES, Norman; *see* Davies, I. N. R.

DAVIES, Col Norman Thomas, OBE 1996 (MBE (mil.) 1970); Registrar, General Dental Council, 1981–96; *b* 2 May 1933; *s* of late Edward Ernest Davies and Elsie Davies (*née* Scott); *m* 1961, Penelope Mary, *e d* of late Peter Graeme Agnew, MBE and (Mary) Diana Agnew; one *s* one *d*. *Educ:* Holywell; RMA, Sandhurst; Open Univ. (BA 1979). Commnd RA, 1954; Regtl and Staff Appts, Malaya, Germany and UK, 1954–64; ptsc 1966; psc 1967; Mil. Asst to C of S Northern Army Gp, 1968–69; Commanded C Bty RHA and 2IC 3RHA, 1970–72; GSO I (DS), Staff Coll., Camberley, and Canadian Land Forces Comd and Staff Coll., 1972–74; Commanded 4 Field Regt, RA, 1975–77; Mil. Dir of Studies, RMCS, Shrivenham, 1977–80. Mem., EEC Adv. Cttee on the Training of Dental Practitioners, 1983–96. Vice Pres., British Dental Hygienists Assoc., 1996–99. Hon. Mem., BDA, 1990; Hon. FDSRCS 1997. JP Hants, 1984–2003. *Recreations:* Rugby football (Treas., RARFC, 1984–2000), the renaissance of Welsh Rugby football, fly fishing, wine, keeping up with four grandchildren, battling with the computer. *Address:* 6 Weatherby Gardens, Hartley Wintney, Hook, Hants RG27 8PA. *T:* (01252) 843303.

DAVIES, Olwen; *see* Davies, N. O.

DAVIES, Owen Handel; QC 1999; **His Honour Judge Owen Davies;** a Circuit Judge, since 2011; *b* 22 Sept. 1949; *s* of Trevor Davies and Mary Davies (*née* Jacobs); *m* 1971, Dr Caroline Jane Smith; one *s* one *d*. *Educ:* Hazelwick Sch.; Magdalene Coll., Cambridge (MA). Called to the Bar, Inner Temple, 1973, Bencher, 2001; in practice at the Bar, 1974–2011; a Recorder, 2000–11; Jt Head of Chambers, 1980–2011. Chm., Admin. Law Bar Assoc., 2002–05; Mem., Bar Council, 1998–2002. *Publications:* numerous contribs on humanitarian laws of conflict, extradition, information technol. and legal practice. *Recreations:* silversmithing, stained glass windows, narrowboating. *Address:* 57–60 Lincoln's Inn Fields, WC2A 3LS; Basildon Combined Court Centre, The Gore, Basildon SS14 2BU. *Club:* India.

DAVIES, Patrick Taylor, CMG 1978; OBE 1967; HM Overseas Civil Service, retired; *b* 10 Aug. 1927; *s* of Andrew Taylor Davies and Olive Kathleen Mary Davies; *m* 1959, Marjorie Eileen (*née* Wilkinson); two *d*. *Educ:* Shrewsbury Sch.; St John's Coll., Cambridge (MA); Trinity Coll., Oxford. Lieut, RA, Nigeria, 1945–48. Colonial Admin. Service, Nigeria, 1952; Permanent Sec., Kano State, 1970; Chief Inspector, Area Courts, Kano State, 1972–79. *Address:* 1 Millfield Drive, Market Drayton, Shropshire TF9 1HS. *T:* (01630) 653408.

DAVIES, Paul; General Manager, St John's, Smith Square, 1985–2012; *b* 28 Dec. 1955; *s* of Thomas Rees Davies and Eirlys Davies. *Educ:* Gowerton Boys' Grammar Sch.; University Coll. London (BA Hons English). Asst, Camden Fest. and Shaw Theatre, 1978–79; Wigmore Hall: Concert Asst, 1979–84; Dep. Manager, 1984–85. *Recreations:* music, opera, theatre, reading.

DAVIES, Dr Paul Charles, CB 2006; JP; CEng, FRSC; Chief Scientist, and Director, Corporate Science and Analytical Services Directorate, Health and Safety Executive, 1999–2006; *b* 25 April 1948; *s* of Philip Davies and Edith Mary Davies (*née* Johnson); *m* 1970, Sheila Tatham; one *s* one *d*. *Educ:* James Watt Tech. High Sch., Smethwick; Leicester Poly. (BSc 1st Cl. Hons Applied Chem.); Univ. of Leicester (PhD 1974). FRSC 1990; CEng 1996. With Unilever, 1968–69; Health and Safety Executive, 1975–2006: Factory Inspector, 1975–83; Major Hazards Assessment Unit, 1983–86; Hazardous Installations Policy Unit, 1986–89; Area Dir, London, 1989–93; Hd, Occupational Health Br., 1993–96; Mem. Bd, and Hd, Chemical and Hazardous Installations Div., 1996–99; Dir, Hazardous Installations Directorate, 1999–2002. Mem., Internat. Adv. Cttee on Health & Safety, Govt of Singapore, 2006–09. Dir, Crosby Housing Assoc., 2005–. JP Ormskirk, 2004. *Publications:* contrib. papers on risk management. *Recreations:* walking, music, gardening, Aston Villa FC. *Address:* 18 Barrow Nook Lane, Bickerstaffe, Lancs L39 0ET.

DAVIES, Prof. Paul Charles William, AM 2007; PhD; Regents' Professor, since 2012, and Director, Beyond: Center for Fundamental Concepts in Science, since 2006, Arizona State University (College Professor, 2006–11); *b* London, 22 April 1946; *s* of Hugh Augustus Robert Davies and Pearl Vera Davies; *m* 2003, Pauline. *Educ:* University Coll. London (BSc 1st Cl. 1967; PhD 1970). Res. Fellow, Inst. of Theoretical Astronomy, Univ. of Cambridge, 1970–72; Lectr in Maths, KCL, 1972–80; Prof. of Theoretical Physics, Univ. of Newcastle upon Tyne, 1980–90; Prof. of Mathematical Physics, 1990–93, Prof. of Natural Philos., 1993–97, Univ. of Adelaide; Prof. of Natural Philos., Macquarie Univ., Sydney, 2001–06. Vis. Prof., Imperial Coll., London, 1998–2003; Adjunct Prof., Univ. of Queensland, 1998–. Hon. Fellow, UCL, 2011. Hon. DSc: Macquarie, 2006; Chapman, 2009. *Publications:* The Physics of Time Asymmetry, 1974; Space and Time in the Modern Universe, 1977; The Runaway Universe, 1978; The Forces of Nature, 1979, 2nd edn 1986; Other Worlds, 1980; The Search for Gravity Waves, 1980; The Edge of Infinity, 1981; The Accidental Universe, 1982; (with N. D. Birrell) Quantum Fields in Curved Space, 1982; God and the New Physics, 1983; Superforce, 1983; Quantum Mechanics, 1984, 2nd edn (with D. Betts) 1994; (with J. R. Brown) The Ghost in the Atom, 1986; Fireball, 1987; The Cosmic Blueprint, 1987, rev. edn 2004; (with J. R. Brown) Superstrings: a theory of everything?, 1988; (ed) The New Physics, 1989; (with J. Gribbin) The Matter Myth, 1991; The Mind of God, 1992; The Last Three Minutes, 1994; About Time: Einstein's unfinished revolution, 1995; Are We Alone?: the philosophical basis of the search for extraterrestrial life, 1995; (with Phillip Adams) The Big Questions, 1996; One Universe or Many Universes?, 1998; (with Phillip Adams) More Big Questions, 1998; The Fifth Miracle: the search for the origin of life, 1998, rev. edn as The Origin of Life, 2003; How to Build a Time Machine, 2001; (ed jtly) Science and Ultimate Reality, 2004; The Goldilocks Enigma: why is the universe just right for life?, 2006 (US title, Cosmic Jackpot, 2007); (ed with Philip Clayton) The Re-Emergence of Emergence, 2006; (ed jtly) Instruments, Methods and Missions for Astrobiology, 2007; The Eerie Silence: are we alone in the universe?, 2010. *Recreation:* keeping fit. *Address:* PO Box 3215, Tempe, Arizona 85280–3215, USA. *T:* (480) 3021066. *E:* deepthought@asu.edu. *Club:* Victory Services.

DAVIES, Prof. Paul Lyndon, FBA 2000; Allen and Overy Professor of Corporate Law, University of Oxford, 2009–14, now Emeritus; Fellow of Jesus College, Oxford, 2009–14, now Emeritus; Senior Research Fellow, Commercial Law Centre, Harris Manchester College, Oxford, since 2014; *b* 24 Sept. 1944; *s* of John Clifford Davies and Kathleen Gertrude Davies (*née* Webber); *m* 1973, Saphieh Ashtiany, *qv*; two *d*. *Educ:* Cardiff High Sch.; Balliol Coll., Oxford (BA, MA); London Sch. of Econs and Pol Sci. (LLM); Yale Univ. (LLM). Lectr, Univ. of Warwick, 1969–73; University of Oxford: CUF Lectr, 1973–91; Reader in Law of Enterprise, 1991–96, Prof., 1996–98; Chm. Bd, Faculty of Law, 1992–95; Balliol College: Fellow and Tutor in Law, 1973–98, Emeritus Fellow, 1998; Estates Bursar, 1983–86; Cassel Prof. of Commercial Law, LSE, 1998–2009. Mem., Steering Gp, Co. Law Rev., 1999–2001. Dep. Chm., Central Arbitration Cttee, 2001–. Vice-Pres., Industrial Law Soc., 2001. Hon. QC 2006; Hon. Bencher, Gray's Inn, 2008. *Publications:* (with K. W. Wedderburn) Employment Grievances and Disputes Procedures in Britain, 1969; Takeovers and Mergers, 1976; (with M. R. Freedland) Labour Law: text and materials, 1979, 2nd edn 1984; (with M. R. Freedland) Labour Legislation and Public Policy, 1993; (ed) Gower's Principles of Modern Company Law, 6th edn 1997, 9th edn 2012; Introduction to Company Law, 2002, 2nd edn 2010; (ed) Palmer's Company Law, 23rd edn 1982 to 25th edn 1992; (jtly) Anatomy of Corporate Law, 2004, 2nd edn 2009; (with M. R. Freedland) Towards a Flexible Labour Market, 2007. *Recreation:* walking. *Address:* Harris Manchester College, Mansfield Road, Oxford OX1 3TD.

DAVIES, Paul Windsor; Member (C) Preseli Pembrokeshire, National Assembly for Wales, since 2007; *b* 2 Jan. 1969; *s* of Timothy Iorwerth Davies and Mair Elizabeth Davies; *m* 2006, Julie Wheeler. *Educ:* Tregroes Primary Sch.; Llandysul Grammar Sch.; Newcastle Emlyn Comp. Sch. Lloyds Bank, subseq. Lloyds TSB, 1987–2007, Business Manager, Haverfordwest, 1994–2007. *Recreations:* reading, visiting historical attractions, Rugby. *Address:* National Assembly for Wales, Cardiff Bay, Cardiff CF99 1NA. *T:* 0300 200 7216. *E:* Paul.Davies2@assembly.wales.

DAVIES, Pauline Elizabeth, MEd; educational consultant, since 2010; Headmistress, Wycombe Abbey School, 1998–2008; *b* 8 April 1950; *d* of Gordon White and Petroula White (*née* Theohari); *m* 1970, Alan Henry Davies; two *s*. *Educ:* Univ. of Manchester (BSc Jt Hons 1971; PGCE 1972; MEd 1978). Teacher of Biology, 1972–77, Head of Dept, 1974–77, Urmston Girls' Grammar Sch.; various posts, incl. Dep. Head and Head of Middle Sch., King

Edward VI Grammar Sch. for Boys, Chelmsford, 1979–90; Headmistress, Croydon High Sch., 1990–98. Pres., GSA, 2003. Gov., St Paul's Girls' Sch., 2007–; Mem. Court, Whitgift Foundn, 2009–. *Recreations:* reading, theatre, music, travel.

DAVIES, Peter Douglas Royston, CMG 1994; HM Diplomatic Service, retired; *b* 29 Nov. 1936; *e s* of Douglas and Edna Davies; *m* 1967, Elizabeth Mary Lovett Williams; one *s* two *d. Educ:* Brockenhurst County High Sch.; LSE (BSc(Econ)). Joined HM Diplomatic Service, 1964; FO, 1964–66; Second Sec., Nicosia, 1966–67; FO, 1967–68; First Sec., Budapest, 1968–71; FCO, 1971–74; Consul (Commercial), Rio de Janeiro, 1974–78; Counsellor (Commercial): The Hague, 1978–82; Kuala Lumpur, 1982–83; Dep. High Comr, Kuala Lumpur, 1983–85; RCDS 1986; Head of Arms Control and Disarmament Dept, FCO, 1987–91; Consul-Gen., Toronto, and Dir-Gen. of Trade and Investment in Canada, 1991–96. Pres., Peter Davies Associates, 1997–2000. Mem. (C), S Northants DC, 2011–. Mem., British Malaysian Soc., 2006–. *Recreations:* golf, ski-ing, biography, travel. *Address:* South Wing, The Manor, Moreton Pinkney, Northants NN11 3SJ.

DAVIES, Sir Peter Maxwell; *see* Maxwell Davies.

DAVIES, Rear-Adm. Peter Roland, CB 2005; CBE 1996 (MBE 1984); part-time consultant and interim management, since 2011; *b* 2 April 1950; *s* of Roland and Winifred Davies; *m* 1974, Dianne Whittaker; one *s* one *d. Educ:* Thornleigh Grammar Sch., Bolton; King's Coll. London (BSc Elec. Engrg 1971); RMCS Shrivenham (MSc Guided Weapons Systems 1977). Naval service, 1973–89: Weapon Engineer Officer: HMS Opportune, 1973–75; HMS Narwhal, 1975–77; Submarine Harpoon Project, 1978–80; Weapon Engineer Officer: 3rd Submarine Sqn, 1980–82; HMS Courageous, 1982–84; 2nd Submarine Sqn, 1984–87; Submarine Senser's Commns Office Flag Officer Submarine Staff, 1987–89; Ministry of Defence: Future Projects, 1991–92; Res. Requirements, 1992–93; Project Manager: Sonar, 1993–95, Tomahawk, 1995–97, Procurement Exec.; Asst Dir, (Command, Control, Computers, Commns, Intel) Directorate of Communication & Inf. Systems (Navy), 1997–98; CO, HMS Collingwood, 1998–2001; FO Trng and Recruiting and Chief Exec., Naval Recruiting and Trng Agency, 2001–04. Principal and Chief Exec., City Literary Inst., 2004–11; Interim CEO, Educn and Trng Foundn, 2013–14. *Recreations:* music, sailing, swimming. *Clubs:* Royal Naval Sailing Assoc.; Royal Naval Swimming Assoc.

DAVIES, Maj.-Gen. Peter Ronald, CB 1992; Chairman, Marjan Centre for the Study of Conflict and Conservation, Department of War Studies, King's College London, since 2010; President, Eurogroup for Animals (formerly Animal Welfare), since 2012 (Director, 1992–2002); *b* 10 May 1938; *e s* of Lt-Col Charles Henry Davies and Joy Davies (*née* Moore); *m* 1960, (Rosemary) Julia, *er d* of late David Felice of Douglas, IoM; one *s* one *d. Educ:* Llandovery College; Welbeck College; RMA Sandhurst; RMCS 1969; Army Staff Coll., 1970; RCDS, 1985. Commissioned Royal Corps of Signals, 1958; service in BAOR, Berlin, Borneo, Cyprus and UK, 1958–68; OC Artillery Bde Sig. Sqn, 1971–72; Bde Maj., 20 Armd Bde, 1973–75; Directing Staff, Staff Coll., Camberley, 1975–76; CO 1 Armd Div. HQ and Signal Regt, 1976–79; Col GS SD, HQ UKLF, 1979–82; Brigade Comdr, 12 Armd Brigade, 1982–84; Dep. Comdt and Dir of Studies, Staff College, Camberley, 1985–86; Comdr Communications, BAOR, 1987–90; GOC Wales, 1990–91. Director-General: RSPCA, 1991–2002; WSPA, 2002–09 (Dir, 1992–2002; Vice-Pres., 1998–2000; Pres., 2000–02; Hon. Vice Pres., 2009–). Mem., Internat. Strategic Planning and Adv. Bd, Andrew Corp., USA, 1991–92. Consultant, NESS, 2011–12. Chairman: Brooke, 2009–13; Freedom Food Ltd, 1994–2002; Animals in War Meml Fund, 1996–2009; Trustee: Flora for Fauna Soc., 2000–10; Wildlife Inf. Network, 2002–04; Vier Pfoten (Four Paws), Vienna, 2012–. Colonel, King's Regt, 1986–94; Chm., Regtl Council and King's and Manchester Regts' Assoc., 1986–94; Col Comdt, RCS, 1990–96; Life Pres., Jullunder Bde Assoc., 1990. Member, Executive Committee: Lord Roberts Workshops and Forces Help Soc., 1994–96; Addaction (Drug and Alcohol Abuse), 1997–2000; Nat. Equine Forum, 2009–13. Gov., Welbeck Coll., 1980–81; Trustee, Llandovery Coll., 1992–2003. CCMI (CIMgt 1994); FIPD 1991; FRSA 2002. Queen Victoria Silver Medal, RSPCA, 2003; Angell Humanitarian Award, Mass Soc. for Prevention Cruelty to Animals, USA, 2003; Assisi Medal, NZ Companion Animals, 2007; Eurogroup for Animals Award, 2008. *Recreations:* Italy, wine, jazz music. *E:* pdavies@fastmail.fm. *Clubs:* Army and Navy; Fadeaways (Founder and Chm., 1992–).
See also T. D. H. Davies.

DAVIES, Peter Wilton, MBE 2009; DL; Chief Executive, Cornwall County Council, 1999–2002; *b* 7 March 1945; *s* of late John Finden Davies and Mary (*née* Harrison); *m* 1971, Ann Mary Dawn Jones; two *d. Educ:* Blundell's Sch.; Southampton Inst. FCIPD (FIPD 1979). Grad. trainee, Devon CC, 1964–67; Personnel Officer, Berkshire CC, 1967–69; Sen. Personnel Officer, Camden LBC, 1969–70; Industrial Relns Officer, Hampshire CC, 1970–74; Dep. County Personnel Officer, 1974–81, Dir of Personnel, 1981–99, Cornwall CC. Chairman: Central Cornwall PCT, 2002–06; Royal Cornwall Hosps NHS Trust, 2007–08; Mem., Exec. Bd, SW Strategic HA (NHS SW), 2006–09. Mem., Lord Chancellor's Adv. Cttee for Cornwall on JPs, 1998–2008. Chairman: Common Purpose Cornwall, 2001–06; Hall for Cornwall Th., 2002–11; Vice Chm., SW Regl Adv. Bd (formerly Devon and Cornwall Regl Cttee), NT, 2004–; Chm., Nat. Maritime Mus., 2014–. FCMI (FIMgt 1988); FRSA 1994. DL Cornwall, 2002. *Recreations:* walking, shooting, the arts. *Address:* Arundell, 1 Moresk Gardens, Truro, Cornwall TR1 1BJ. *T:* (01872) 274764.

DAVIES, Philip Andrew; MP (C) Shipley, since 2005; *b* 5 Jan. 1972; *s* of Peter Davies and Marilyn (*née* Johnson, now Lifsey); *m* 1994, Debbie Hemsley (marr. diss. 2012); two *s. Educ:* Univ. of Huddersfield (BA Hons Histl and Pol Studies). Asda: various positions, 1993–2000; Customer Service Project Manager, 2000–04; Mktg Manager, 2004–05. Contested (C) Colne Valley, 2001. Member: Culture, Media and Sport Select Cttee, 2006–15; Backbench Business Cttee, 2010–12; Chairmen's Panel, 2010–; Justice Select Cttee, 2015–. Mem. Exec. Cttee, 1922 Cttee, 2006–12. *Recreation:* horse racing. *Address:* House of Commons, SW1A 0AA. *E:* philip.davies.mp@parliament.uk.

DAVIES, Philip John, CB 2001; Deputy Counsel, House of Commons, since 2011; consultant legislative drafter, since 2011; *b* 19 Sept. 1954; *s* of late Glynn Davies and Mary Davies (*née* Adams); *m* 1981, Jacqueline Sara Boutcher; one *d. Educ:* St Julian's High Sch., Newport, S Wales; Hertford Coll., Oxford (MA, BCL). Called to the Bar, Middle Temple, 1981; Lectr in Law, Univ. of Manchester, 1977–82; Asst and Sen. Asst Parly Counsel, 1982–90; Dep. Parly Counsel, 1990–94 (seconded to Law Commn, 1992–94); Parly Counsel, 1994–2011. *Publications:* articles and notes in Law Qly Rev., Modern Law Rev. and other legal jls. *Recreations:* family, Welsh terriers, the garden. *Address:* Pinecroft, The Downs, Givons Grove, Leatherhead, Surrey KT22 8JY. *T:* (01372) 373915; 5 Glendower House, The Norton, Tenby, Pembrokeshire SA70 8AH. *T:* (01834) 842840. *E:* davies.pinecroft@hotmail.co.uk.

DAVIES, Maj.-Gen. Philip Middleton, OBE 1975; *b* 27 Oct. 1932; *s* of late Hugh Davies and Miriam Allen (*née* Tickler); *m* 1956, Mona Wallace; two *d. Educ:* Charterhouse; RMA, Sandhurst. Commnd Royal Scots, 1953; served Korea, Canal Zone, Cyprus, Suez, Berlin, Libya 1st Bn Royal Scots, 1953–63; Staff Coll., 1963; National Defence Coll., 1971; commanded 1st Bn Royal Scots, Norway, Cyprus, N Ireland (despatches), 1973–76; DS, Staff Coll., 1976–77; comd 19 Bde/7 Fd Force, 1977–79; RCDS, 1980; Comd Land Forces, Cyprus, 1981–83; GOC NW Dist, 1983–86; retired. *Recreations:* fishing, gardening.

DAVIES, Rhodri; *see* Davies, W. R.

DAVIES, Rhodri Talfan; Director, BBC Cymru Wales, since 2011; *b* Cardiff, 9 Feb. 1971; *s* of Geraint Talfan Davies, *qv*; two *s* one *d. Educ:* Ysgol Gyfun Gymraeg Glantaf, Cardiff; Royal Grammar Sch., Newcastle upon Tyne; Jesus Coll., Oxford (BA Hons); Cardiff Univ. (Post Grad. Dip. Journalism). Sub-editor, Western Mail, 1993; news trainee, BBC, 1993; news reporter and producer, BBC, 1994–99; Hd, Regl Progs, BBC West, 1999–2001; Dir, TV, Video Networks/Home Choice, 2001–05; Hd, TV Mktg, ntl, 2005–06; Hd, Strategy and Communications, BBC Cymru Wales, 2006–11. *Recreations:* Rugby, ski-ing, US politics, useless gadgets. *Address:* BBC Cymru Wales, Broadcasting House, Llandaf, Cardiff CF5 2YQ. *T:* (029) 2032 2001. *E:* rhodri.talfan.davies.pa@bbc.co.uk.

DAVIES, Rhys; *see* Davies, E. R.

DAVIES, His Honour Sir Rhys (Everson), Kt 2000; QC 1981; a Senior Circuit Judge, 1990–2003; retired; *b* 13 Jan. 1941; *s* of late Evan Davies and Nancy Caroline Davies; *m* 1963, Katharine Anne Yeates; one *s* one *d. Educ:* Cowbridge Grammar School; Neath Grammar School; Victoria University of Manchester. LLB (Hons). Called to the Bar, Gray's Inn, 1964, Bencher, 1993. Northern Circuit, 1964–90; a Recorder, 1980–90; Hon. Recorder of Manchester, 1990–2003. Mem., Sentencing Adv. Panel, 2000–05. Pres., Manchester and District Medico-Legal Soc., 2002–04 (Patron, 2004–). Ind. Monitor, Criminal Records Bureau, 2004–08. Mem. Court and Council, Victoria Univ. of Manchester, 1993–2004 (Dep. Chm. Council, 2000–04); Visitor, Univ. of Manchester, 2004–. *Recreations:* music, conversation.

DAVIES, Prof. Richard Bees, PhD; Vice-Chancellor, Swansea University (formerly University of Wales, Swansea), since 2003; *m*; three *c. Educ:* Milford Haven Grammar Sch.; Sidney Sussex Coll., Cambridge (MA); Univ. of Birmingham (MSc); Univ. of Bristol (PhD). Lectr, then Sen. Lectr, Dept of Town Planning, UWIST, subseq. UWCC; Univ. of Lancaster, 1989–2003: Prof. and Dir, Centre for Applied Statistics; Dean, Faculty of Engrg, Computing and Math. Scis; Pro-Vice-Chancellor. *Address:* Swansea University, Singleton Park, Swansea SA2 8PP.

DAVIES, Richard John; Management Board Director and Head, Department for Public Services and Performance, Welsh Assembly Government, 2006–09; *b* 12 Aug. 1949; *s* of Sydney John Davies and Valerie Reynolds Davies; *m* 1971, Margaret Mary Goddard; one *s* one *d. Educ:* King's Coll., Taunton; Univ. of Liverpool (BA Hons 1971; MA 1976). Teaching Asst, Dept of Political Theory and Instns, Liverpool Univ., 1972–73; entered Civil Service, 1973; MoD, FCO, MPO, etc, 1973–84; Welsh Office: Asst Sec., 1985; Head of Division: Health Mgt, Systems and Personnel, 1985–87; Health and Social Services Policy, 1987–89; Housing, 1989–94; School Performance, 1994–97; Gp Dir, Educn Dept, Welsh Office, subseq. Dept for Trng and Educn, Nat. Assembly for Wales, 1997–2006. Registered Comr, Infrastructure Planning Commn, 2010–12; Chair: Fitness to Practise Cttee, NMC, 2012–; Health Cttee, Gen. Osteopathic Council, 2013–; non-exec. Mem., Knowledge and Membership Bds, Ind. Appeals Panel, RICS, 2009–; Adjudicator, SRA, 2008–13; Lay Mem., Educn and Trng Cttee, Bar Standards Bd, 2012–; Lay Mem., Adv. Cttee, MPTS, 2014–; Associate: GMC, 2006–; Gen. Pharmaceutical Council, 2010–. Trustee: Nationwide Foundn, 2008–13; Carnegie (UK), 2009–; Regent's Coll., London, 2009–10. Vis. Prof., Univ. of Glamorgan, 2006–11. Nuffield-Leverhulme Fellow, 1990. *Recreations:* family, walking, swimming, music.

DAVIES, (Robert Harold) Glyn; HM Diplomatic Service, retired; Ambassador to Panama, 1999–2002; Records and Archive Management, Foreign and Commonwealth Office (part-time), since 2008; *b* 23 March 1942; *s* of late Robert Leach Davies and Edith Greenwood Davies (*née* Burgoyne); *m* 1968, Maria Del Carmen Diaz; one *s. Educ:* Hulme Grammar Sch., Oldham; St John's Coll., Cambridge. Joined FO, 1963; Havana, 1964; FO, 1964; Third, later Second Sec., Mexico, 1968; FCO, 1972; Consul (Commercial), Zagreb, 1980; First Sec., on loan to Cabinet Office, 1983; First Sec., Consul and Head of Chancery, Luanda, 1986; FCO, 1989; High Commissioner to Namibia, 1996–98. *Address:* c/o Knowledge Management Department, Foreign and Commonwealth Office, SW1A 2AH.

DAVIES, Dr Robert James; Partner, Masters-in-Science LLP, since 2011 (Partner, Masters-in-Science.com, then Managing Director, Masters-in-Science, 2004–11); *b* 24 Feb. 1943; *s* of late Rev. Canon Dilwyn Morgan Davies and Kate Davies (*née* Maltby); *m* 1st, 1969 (marr. diss. 1980); two *s*; 2nd, 1981, Karen, *d* of Dennis Henley. *Educ:* St Catharine's Coll., Cambridge (BA 1964); St Thomas's Hosp. Med. Sch. (BChir 1967; MB BS, MA 1968); Univ. of Cambridge (MD 1977); Univ. of Greenwich (MSc Computing and Info. Systems (Distinction) 2003; PGCE 2003). FRCP 1982. Res. Fellow, Brompton Hosp., 1971–73; Lectr in Medicine, St Thomas's Hosp., 1973–76; MRC Res. Fellow, Univ. of Tulane, New Orleans, 1976–77; St Bartholomew's Hospital: Consultant Physician, 1977–82; Dir, Asthma & Allergy Res. Dept, 1981–99; Reader in Respiratory Medicine, 1982–90; Dir, General and Emergency Medicine, 1994–96; Prof. of Respiratory Medicine, St Bartholomew's and Royal London Sch. of Medicine and Dentistry, QMW, London Univ., 1991–99; Cons. Physician, 1994–99, Dir of R&D, 1995–97, Royal Hosps NHS Trust. British Allergy Foundn: Founder and Chm., 1991–97; Pres., 1997–2002; Dir of Tech. and Educn, Allergy UK, 2000–02; Scientific Dir, Allergy Res. Ltd, 2000–02; Lectr in Computing, NW Kent Coll., 2003–11. Ed., Respiratory Medicine, 1988–95. Pres., Brit. Soc. for Allergy and Clin. Immunology, 1987–90; 2nd Vice Pres., Internat. Assoc. of Allergology and Clin. Immunology, 1997–99 (Treas., 1985–94); Chm., World Allergy Forum, 1996–99; Mem., Collegium Internationale Allergologicum, 1998–2000. Hon. Mem., Argentinian Assoc. of Allergy and Immunology, 1997. Fellow, Amer. Acad. Allergy, Asthma and Immunology, 1984. Medal, Faculty of Medicine, Univ. of Montpellier, 1981. *Publications:* Allergy The Facts, 1989; (ed) Formoterol: clinical profile of a new long acting inhaled B2-Agonist, 1990; Hay Fever and Other Allergies, 1995; contrib. Allergy. *Recreations:* hill-walking, mountain and moorland ponies. *Address:* 96 Vanbrugh Park, Blackheath, SE3 7AL.

DAVIES, Robert John; Chairman: Biffa plc, 2006–08; Euroports Holdings, SARL, 2010–13; Home Group, since 2012; Chief Executive, Arriva plc, 1999–2006; *b* 12 Oct. 1948; *s* of William Davies and Janet Davies (*née* Robinson); *m* 1971, Eileen Susan Littlefield; one *s. Educ:* Univ. of Edinburgh (LLB Law and Econs). FCMA 1976. With Ford Motor Co., in UK, USA and latterly as Finance Dir, Ford Spain, 1970–85; Coopers & Lybrand, 1985–87; Finance Director: Waterford Wedgwood plc, 1987–91; Ferranti Internat. plc, 1991–93; Finance Dir, 1994–97, Chief Exec., 1997–98, E Midlands Electricity plc. Non-executive Director: T & S Stores plc, 1998–2003; Geest plc, 1998–2004; Barratt Developments plc, 2004–12; British Energy, 2006–09; Northern Rock plc, 2008–09; Northern Rock (Asset Mgt) plc, 2010; Kelda Hldgs Ltd, 2012–; Chm., Countrywide PLC, 2013. Chm., NE Regl Council, CBI, 2007–08. Chm. Bd Govs, Sunderland Univ., 2003–09. *Recreations:* golf, vintage cars.

DAVIES, (Robert) Karl; Chief Adviser Wales (formerly Head, Governance and Accountability), BBC Trust, since 2007; *b* 26 July 1963; *s* of late R. Keith Davies and of Dilys Catherine Davies (*née* Hughes). *Educ:* Ysgol Glan Clwyd, St Asaph; University Coll. of Wales, Aberystwyth (BA). Editor, Tafod Y Ddraig, 1983–84; Chm., Welsh Lang. Soc., 1984–85; Res. Dir, Plaid Cymru, 1985–89; BBC Wales: Producer, Radio, 1989–90; Parly Editor, 1990–93; Chief Exec., Plaid Cymru, 1993–2002; Dir for Wales, NAHT, 2002–03; Sec., BBC Wales, 2003–06. Mem. Council, UCW, Aberystwyth, 1988–91. Fellow, British American Proj., 1996–. Trustee, Voices from Care, 2013–. *Publications:* Beth am Gynnau Tân?, 1985. *Recreations:* travel, cinema, gossip, Italy. *Address:* Room E5117, BBC Broadcasting House, Llandaff, Cardiff CF5 2YQ. *T:* (029) 2032 2004, *Fax:* (029) 2032 2280. *E:* karl.davies-cf@bbc.co.uk.

DAVIES, (Robert) Leighton; QC 1994; a Recorder, since 1994; a Deputy High Court Judge, since 2001; *b* 7 Sept. 1949; *s* of Robert Brinley Davies and Elizabeth Nesta Davies (*née* Jones); *m* 1979, Linda Fox; two *s* one *d*. *Educ:* Rhondda Co. Grammar Sch., Porth, Rhondda; Corpus Christi Coll., Oxford (MA, BCL; boxing blue, 1971–72); Inns of Court Sch. of Law. Called to the Bar, Gray's Inn, 1975, Bencher, 2002; practising on Wales and Chester Circuit, 1975–; Asst Recorder, 1990–94. *Recreations:* fly-fishing, gardening, military history. *Address:* Farrar's Building, Temple, EC4Y 7BD. *T:* (020) 7583 9241; Bryn Corun, Glyncoli Road, Treorchy, Rhondda CF42 6SB. *T:* (01443) 774559. *Club:* Vincent's (Oxford).

DAVIES, (Robert) Russell; freelance writer and broadcaster, since 1970; *b* 5 April 1946; *s* of late John Gwilym Davies and of Gladys Davies (*née* Davies); *m* 1972, Judith Anne Slater (marr. diss.); one *s*; *m* 2003, Emma Jane Kingsley; three *s*. *Educ:* Manchester Grammar Sch.; St John's Coll., Cambridge (Scholar; BA Mod. Langs). Comedy actor and TV presenter, 1970–71; literary reviewer and caricaturist, 1972–; football reporter, 1973–76, film critic, 1973–78, Observer; TV critic, Sunday Times, 1979–83; Dep. Editor and acting Editor, Punch, 1988; sports columnist, Sunday Telegraph, 1989–94. Presenter and feature-maker, 1979–: radio includes: When Housewives had the Choice; Turns of the Century; Word of Mouth (Premio Ondas, 1997); Jazz Century; Russell Davies Song Show, 1998–2013 (Gold Badge of Merit, BACS, 2001); Russell Davies with…, 2013; Chm., Brain of Britain, 2009–; television includes: What the Papers Say (also Annual Awards, 1989–97); jazz weeks and weekends; Saturday Review. *Publications:* (with Liz Ottaway) Vicky, 1987; Ronald Searle, 1990; (ed) The Kenneth Williams Diaries, 1993; (ed) The Kenneth Williams Letters, 1994; (with Wes Butters) Kenneth Williams Unseen, 2008. *Recreations:* playing trombone, bass saxophone, American crosswords, painting, visiting Wales. *Address:* c/o United Agents, 12–26 Lexington Street, W1F 0LE.

DAVIES, Prof. Rodney Deane, CBE 1995; DSc, PhD; FRS 1992; CPhys, FInstP; FRAS; Professor of Radio Astronomy, University of Manchester, 1976–97, now Professor Emeritus; Director, Nuffield Radio Astronomy Laboratories, Jodrell Bank, 1988–97; *b* 8 Jan. 1930; *s* of Holbin James Davies and Rena Irene (*née* March), Mallala, S Australia; *m* 1953, Valda Beth Treasure; one *s* two *d* (and one *s* decd). *Educ:* Adelaide High Sch.; Univ. of Adelaide (BSc Hons, MSc); Univ. of Manchester (PhD, DSc). Research Officer, Radiophysics Div., CSIRO, Sydney, 1951–53; Univ. of Manchester: Asst Lectr, 1953–56; Lectr, 1956–67; Reader, 1967–76. Visiting Astronomer, Radiophysics Div., CSIRO, Australia, 1963. Member: Internat. Astronomical Union, 1958; Org. Cttee and Working Gps of various Commns; Bd and various panels and cttees of Astronomy Space and Radio Bd and Science Bd of Science Research Council; British Nat. Cttee for Astronomy, 1974–77. Royal Astronomical Society: Mem. Council, 1972–75 and 1978–89; Sec., 1978–86; Vice-Pres., 1973–75 and 1986–87; Pres., 1987–89. *Publications:* Radio Studies of the Universe (with H. P. Palmer), 1959; Radio Astronomy Today (with H. P. Palmer and M. I. Large), 1963; The Crab Nebula (co-ed with F. G. Smith), 1971; numerous contribs to Monthly Notices of RAS and internat. jls on the galactic and extragalactic magnetic fields, structure and dynamics of the Galaxy and nearby external galaxies, use of radio spectral lines, the early Universe and studies of the Cosmic Microwave Background. *Recreations:* gardening, fell-walking. *Address:* University of Manchester, Jodrell Bank Observatory, Macclesfield, Cheshire SK11 9DL. *T:* (01477) 571321.

DAVIES, Roger; *see* Davies, Anthony R.

DAVIES, Roger John; Assisted Living Director, Castleoak, since 2015; *b* Altrincham, 29 Oct. 1959; *m* Helen; one *s* one *d*. *Educ:* Altrincham Grammar Sch.; Cheltenham Grammar Sch.; Leeds Poly. (HND Hotel Mgt). Chief Exec., Methodist Homes, 2001–14. Former non-executive Director: English Community Care Assoc.; Associated Retirement Community Operators; non-exec. Dir, Your Care Rating. FCMA. *Recreations:* yoga, wildlife, church.

DAVIES, Prof. Roger Llewelyn, PhD; FRAS; FInstP; Philip Wetton Professor of Astrophysics, since 2002, and Director, Centre for Astrophysical Surveys, since 2014, Oxford University; Student, since 2002, Dr Lee's Reader in Physics, since 2006, Christ Church, Oxford; *b* 13 Jan. 1954; *s* of Albert Edward Davies and Gwendoline Mary Davies; *m* 1982, Ioana Christina Westwater; one *s* one *d*. *Educ:* John Leggott Grammar Sch., Scunthorpe; University Coll. London (BSc Physics 1975); Inst. of Astronomy and Churchill Coll., Cambridge (PhD 1979). FRAS 1979; FInstP 2009. Lindemann Fellow, Lick Observatory, Calif, 1979–80; Res. Fellow, Christ's Coll., Cambridge, 1979–82; Staff Mem., US Nat. Optical Astronomy Observatories, Tucson, Arizona, 1982–88; Scientist, UK Gemini Project, 1988–96; Lectr in Physics, Oxford Univ. and Fellow, St Peter's Coll., Oxford, 1992–94; Prof. of Astronomy, Dept of Physics, Univ. of Durham, 1994–2002; Hd, Sub-Dept of Astrophysics, 2004–05, 2011–14, Chm. of Physics, 2005–10, Oxford Univ. PPARC Senior Res. Fellow, 2001–04 (Mem. Council, PPARC, 1999–2001, 2006–07). Vis. Prof., Beihang Univ., Beijing, 2006. Chairman: Anglo-Australian Telescope Bd, 1997–99 (Mem., 1996–99); Eur. Space Telescope Co-ordinating Facility Users Cttee, 2001–03; Gemini Telescopes Bd, 2002–03 (Mem., 2001–04; Chm., UK Gemini Telescopes Steering Cttee, 1996–99); Extremely Large Telescope Standing Review Cttee, ESO, 2006–12. Member: VISTA Telescope Bd, 1999–2001; Adv. Cttee, Australian Astronomical Observatory, 2011–; Council, Space Telescope Sci. Inst., 2011–; Pres., Commn 28, Galaxies, IAU, 2009–12. Pres., RAS, 2010–12 (Mem. Council, 2005–08; Vice Pres., 2006–08); Vice Pres. and Mem. Council, Eur. Astronomical Soc., 2012–. Member: IAU, 1980; AAS, 1980. Fellow, UCL, 2009. Dr *hc* Univ. Claude Bernard Lyon 1, 2006. Daiwa-Adrian Prize, Daiwa Anglo Japanese Foundn, 2001; RAS Gp Achievement Award for SAURON survey, 2013. *Publications:* contrib. papers to Astrophysical Jl, Monthly Notices of RAS, Astronomical Jl and conf. procs. *Recreations:* hiking, swimming, photography, films, listening to music, pilates. *Address:* Denys Wilkinson Building, Keble Road, Oxford OX1 3RH. *T:* (01865) 613973.

DAVIES, Roger Oliver; *b* 4 Jan. 1945; *s* of Griffith William Davies and Dorothy Anne Davies; *m* 1973, Adele Biss, *qv*; one *s*. *Educ:* Reading Sch.; Devonport High Sch.; London School of Economics (BScEcon). Marketing Dir, 1972, Man. Dir, 1977, Thomson Holidays; Man. Dir, 1982, Chm., 1984–90, Thomson Travel Gp; Chairman: Going Places, 1994–97; Sunway Travel, 1997–2000; Travel Chest.com, 2000; Dir, Airtours PLC, 1994–2000. Mem., Monopolies and Mergers Commn, 1989–98. Governor, LSE, 1995–. Commandeur de la République (Tunisia), 1987. *Recreations:* walking, ski-ing, reading. *Address:* 7 Elsworthy Road, NW3 3DS.

DAVIES, Rt Hon. Ronald; PC 1997; Commercial Manager, Bedwas Rugby Football Club, since 2012; *b* 6 Aug. 1946; *s* of late Ronald Davies; *m* 1981, Christina Elizabeth Rees (marr. diss. 2000); one *d*; *m* 2002, Lynne Hughes; one *d*. *Educ:* Bassaleg Grammar Sch.; Portsmouth Polytechnic; University Coll. of Wales, Cardiff. Schoolteacher, 1968–70; WEA Tutor/Organiser, 1970–74; Further Educn Adviser, Mid-Glamorgan LEA, 1974–83. Councillor, Rhymney Valley DC (formerly Bedwas and Machen UDC), 1969–84 (Vice-Chm.). MP (Lab) Caerphilly, 1983–2001. Opposition Whip, 1985–87; Opposition spokesman on agriculture and rural affairs, 1987–92, front bench spokesman on Wales, 1992–97; Sec. of State for Wales, May 1997–Oct. 1998. National Assembly for Wales: Mem. (Lab) Caerphilly, 1999–2003; Mem., Econ. Develt Cttee, 1999–2003 (Chm., 1999). Contested (Plaid Cymru) Caerphilly, Nat. Assembly for Wales, 2011. Mem. (Ind), Caerphilly CBC, 2008–12. Dir, Valleys Race Equality Council, 2003–. Highest Order, Gorsedd of the Bards, 1998. *Publications:* paper on devolution. *Address:* Wernddu House, Wernddu, Caerphilly CF83 3DA.

DAVIES, Rt Rev. Ross Owen; Bishop of The Murray, 2002–10; *b* 4 Feb. 1955; *s* of Rex John Davies and Margaret June Cooper; *m* 1983, Christine Fyfield; two *s* twin *d*. *Educ:* Melbourne Univ. (BA 1977, LLB 1979); St Barnabas Coll., ACT (ThL 1981). Ordained deacon, 1981, priest, 1982; Assistant Curate: St Peter's, Ballarat, 1981–83; St Lucia, Brisbane, 1984–85; Rector, Camperdown, Vic, 1985–91; Parish Priest, England: Mundford, 1991–93; Kingsdon, 1993–97; Rector, Hindmarsh, Vic, 1997–2000; Archdeacon of The Murray, 2000–02. *Recreations:* singing, gardening, reading.

DAVIES, Russell; *see* Davies, R. R.

DAVIES, Ryland; opera singer; tenor; Head of Vocal Department, Escuela Superior de Musica Reina Sofia, Madrid, since 2014; *b* 9 Feb. 1943; *s* of Gethin and Joan Davies; *m* 1st, 1966, Anne Elizabeth Howells, *qv* (marr. diss. 1981); 2nd, 1983, Deborah Rees; one *d*. *Educ:* Royal Manchester College of Music (Fellow, 1971) (studied with Frederic R. Cox, OBE). Voice teacher: RNCM, 1987–94; RCM 1989–2009; RAM, 2008–; teaches privately and gives masterclasses at home and abroad. Début as Almaviva in The Barber of Seville, WNO, 1964; Glyndebourne Fest. Chorus, 1964–66; has since sung with Royal Opera, Sadler's Wells Opera, WNO, Scottish Opera, at Glyndebourne, and in Brussels, Chicago, NY, San Francisco, Houston, Paris, Salzburg, Buenos Aires, Hong Kong, Berlin, Hamburg, Stuttgart, Munich and Milan; solo rôles include: Belmonte in Il Seraglio; Fenton, and Dr Caius, in Falstaff; Ferrando in Così Fan Tutte; Flamand in Capriccio; Tamino in The Magic Flute; Essex in Britten's Gloriana; Hylas in The Trojans; Don Ottavio in Don Giovanni; Cassio in Otello; Ernesto in Don Pasquale; Lysander in A Midsummer Night's Dream; title rôle in Werther; Prince in L'Amour des Trois Oranges; Nemorino in L'Elisir d'amore; Don Basilio in Le Nozze di Figaro; Rector in Peter Grimes; Triquet in Eugene Onegin; Alfredo in La Traviata, Pelléas in Pelléas et Melisande; Eneas in Esclarmonde; Jack in The Midsummer Marriage; Chaplin in Dialogues des Carmelites; Remendado in Carmen; Sellem in The Rake's Progress; Albazar in The Turk in Italy; Gaudenzio in Leoncavallo's La Bohème; Hauk Šendorf in The Makropulos Case; Francis Flute in A Midsummer Night's Dream; Ein Hirt in Tristan and Isolde; Monsieur Taupe in Capriccio. Many concerts at home with all major British orchestras, and abroad with such orchestras as: Boston Symphony, Cleveland Symphony, Chicago Symphony, Philadelphia, San Francisco, Los Angeles, Bavarian Radio and Vienna Symphony. Principal oratorio rôles include: Bach, B minor Mass; Beethoven: Mass in C; Berlioz, narrator in L'Enfance du Christ; Elgar, St John, in The Kingdom; Handel: Acis, in Acis and Galatea; title rôle, Judas Maccabaeus; Messiah; Jonathan, in Saul; Haydn: Nelson Mass; The Seasons; Mendelssohn: Obadiah, in Elijah; Hymn of Praise; Rossini, Messe Solennelle; Schubert, Lazarus; Tippett, Child of Our Time. Has sung in all major religious works including: Missa Solemnis, Verdi's Requiem, Dream of Gerontius, St Matthew Passion, The Creation. Many recordings incl. Il Seraglio, The Trojans, Saul, Così Fan Tutte, Thérèse, Monteverdi Madrigals, Idomeneo, Haydn's The Seasons, Messiah, L'Oracolo (Leone), Judas Maccabaeus, Il Matrimonio Segreto (Cimarosa), L'Amore dei Tre Re (Montemezzi), La Navarraise (Massenet), Lucia di Lammermoor (Donizetti). Hon. RAM, 2012. FRMCM; FRWCMD (FWCMD 1996). John Christie Award, 1965. *Recreations:* antiques, art, cinema, sport. *Address:* c/o Hazard Chase Ltd, 25 City Road, Cambridge CB1 1DP; Escuela Superior de Música Reina Sofía, Calle Requena 1, 28013 Madrid, Spain.

DAVIES, Dame Sally (Claire), DBE 2009; FRS 2014; Chief Scientific Adviser, since 2004, and Chief Medical Officer, since 2011, Department of Health; Emeritus Professor, Imperial College London, since 2011; *b* 24 Nov. 1949; *d* of John Gordon Davies and Emily Mary Davies (*née* Tordoff); *m* 1st, 1974, R. F. W. Skilbeck (marr. diss. 1982); 2nd, 1982, P. R. A. Vulliamy (*d* 1982); 3rd, 1989, W. H. Ouwehand; two *d*. *Educ:* Manchester Univ. (MB ChB); London Univ. (MSc). FRCP 1992; FRCPath 1997; FRCPCH 1997; FFPH (FFPHM 1999). House Phys. and Surg., and SHO, Manchester, 1972–74; clin. assistant in cardiology, Clínica la Concepción, Fundación Jimenez Díaz, Madrid, 1974–77; SHO in Paediatrics, Middlesex Hosp., 1978–79; Lectr, 1979–83, MRC Fellow in Recombinant DNA Technology, 1983–85, Middlesex Hosp. Med. Sch.; Consultant Haematologist, Central Middlesex Hosp., 1985–2011; Dep. Dir, 1997–2004, Dir Gen. (formerly Dir), Res. and Develt, DoH, 2004–11. Mem., MRC, 2009–. Wkg Gp on Haemoglobinopathies, European Haematology Assoc., 1999–. Non-exec. Dir, Genomics England Ltd. FMedSci 2002. Ed. for haemoglobinopathies, Internat. Cochrane Collaboration. Author, Annual Report of the CMO, 2011, 2012, 2013, 2014. Hon. Fellow: Imperial Coll. London Faculty of Medicine, 2009; Harris Manchester Coll., Oxford, 2012; Hon. Vis. Fellow, Trinity Coll., Oxford, 2013–. Hon. FRCOG 2013. Hon. DM: Southampton, 2007; Birmingham, 2008; Leeds, 2011; KCL, 2011; Hon. DSc: Sheffield, 2008; Cranfield, 2008; Liverpool, 2009; Lincoln, 2010; Exeter, 2010; Keele, 2011; Lancaster, 2011; Aston, 2012; Manchester, 2012; Brunel, 2013; Leicester, 2014; Loughborough, 2014; Nottingham Trent, 2014; Surrey, 2014; Warwick, 2015; DUniv York, 2012; Hon. DCL Newcastle, 2013. *Publications:* The Drugs Don't Work: a global threat, 2013; contribs to med. jls, mainly relating to research strategy and sickle cell disease and to antimicrobial resistance. *Recreations:* travel, opera, music, cooking, art, architecture. *Address:* Department of Health, Richmond House, 79 Whitehall, SW1A 2NS.

DAVIES, Saphié, (Sue); *see* Ashtiany, S.

DAVIES, Rt Rev. Saunders; *see* Davies, Rt Rev. F. J. S.

DAVIES, Siân; Co-founder, The Behavioural Architects, since 2011; *b* Long Eaton, 1 Aug. 1966; *d* of Alyn and Margaret Davies; *m* 2002, Chad Wollen; one *d*. *Educ:* Hertford Coll., Oxford (BA PPE). Mercer Mgt Consulting, 1988–96; Henley Centre: Associate Dir, 1996–97; Dir, 1998–2000; Man. Dir, 2000–01; Chief Exec., Henley Centre, then Henley Centre HeadlightVision, later The Futures Co., 2001–10. Mem., Mktg Soc. *Recreations:* contemporary art, photography. *E:* sian@thebearchitects.com.

DAVIES, Simon James; Chief People, Legal and Strategy Officer, Lloyds Banking Group, from Jan. 2016; *b* London, 29 May 1967; *s* of T. D. Davies and late M. J. Davies; *m* 2007, Minori Mano; two *d*. *Educ:* Emmanuel Coll., Cambridge (BA Law 1989). Admitted Solicitor, 1992; Linklaters: Solicitor, 1992–99; Partner, 1999–2003; Man. Partner, Asia, 2003–07; Firmwide Man. Partner, 2008–15. *Recreations:* theatre, Rugby, running. *Address:* Lloyds Banking Group, 25 Gresham Street, EC2V 7HN.

DAVIES, Simon Philip; Headmaster, Eastbourne College, since 2005; *b* 27 July 1964; *s* of late Ven. Philip Bertram Davies and of Jane Davies (*née* Richardson); *m* 1991, Robina Pelham Burn; two *s* one *d*. *Educ:* Radley Coll.; Lady Margaret Hall, Oxford (MA); Inst. of Educn, Univ. of London (PGCE 1994). Grad. trainee, Chase Manhattan Bank, 1986–87; Futures and Options Broker, James Capel, London and Goodbody James Capel, Dublin, 1987–92; Form Teacher, Hereward House Prep. Sch., 1992–93; Hd of Biol. and Sen. Housemaster, Abingdon Sch., 1994–2002; Vice Master and Usher, Bedford Sch., 2002–05. *Recreations:* walking, fly fishing. *Address:* Headmaster's House, Eastbourne College, Eastbourne, E Sussex BN21 4JX. *T:* (01323) 452320, *Fax:* (01323) 452327. *E:* spdavies@eastbourne-college.co.uk. *Club:* East India.

DAVIES, Siobhan; *see* Davies, Susan.

DAVIES, Col Stephen, MBE 1998; Managing Director, Conwy Adventure Leisure Ltd, since 2012; *b* Darwen, Lancs, 22 April 1959; *s* of Thomas Davies and Elsie Davies; *m* 1985, Ruth Lomax; one *s* one *d*. *Educ:* Bishop Rawstorne Sch., Croston; Royal Mil. Acad. Sandhurst; Army Staff Coll. Camberley. Joined Army, 1975; commnd, 1978; ADC to Quartermaster Gen., 1988–90; various appts, 1991–99; CO 1st Bn Queen's Lancashire Regt,

1999–2002; Chief G3 HQ 3rd Div., 2002–03; SO1 Comd and Staff Trainer (N), 2003–04; MoD Advr Sierra Leone, 2004–05; COS HQ 2nd Div., 2005–08. Director: Mus. of Sci. and Industry, Manchester, 2008–10; Nat. Railway Mus., 2010–12. Dep. Col, Duke of Lancaster's Regt, 2006–14; Trustee, Mus. of Queen's Lancashire Regt, 2006–. Pres. and Dir, 76084 Locomotive Co. Ltd, 2010–; Chm., Sierra Leone Nat. Railway Mus. Supporters Fund, 2010–. Pres., Friends of Darwen Cemetery, 2013–. QCVS 2002. *Recreations:* railways, military history, industrial archaeology, running to stave off old age. *Address:* Conwy Adventure Leisure Ltd, Oakland House, 21 Hope Carr Road, Leigh, Wigan WN7 3ET. *T:* (01942) 269791. *E:* s.davies@surfsnowdonia.co.uk. *Club:* Grand Junction.

DAVIES, (Stephen) Howard, CBE 2011; Associate Director, National Theatre, since 1989; *b* 26 April 1945; *s* of late Thomas Emrys Davies and (Eileen) Hilda Davies; *m* 1st, Susan Wall (marr. diss.); two *d*; 2nd, 2005, Clare Holman. *Educ:* Christ's Hosp.; Univ. of Durham; Univ. of Bristol. Associate Dir, Bristol Old Vic, 1971–73; Associate Dir, RSC, 1976–86; freelance dir, 1974–76; Founder, The Warehouse, RSC, 1977, Co. Dir, 1977–82. *Productions* include: Royal Shakespeare Company: Troilus and Cressida; Bandits, Bingo, 1977; The Jail Diary of Albie Sachs, 1979; Much Ado About Nothing, 1980; Piaf; Henry VIII, 1983; Les Liaisons Dangereuses, 1986; Royal National Theatre: The Shaughraun; Cat on a Hot Tin Roof, 1988; The Secret Rapture; Hedda Gabler, 1989; The Crucible, 1990; A Long Day's Journey into Night; Mary Stuart, 1996; Chips with Everything, 1997; Flight, 1998; Battle Royal, 1999; All My Sons, 2000 (Best Dir, Laurence Olivier Awards, 2001); The Talking Cure, 2003; Mourning Becomes Electra, 2003; Cyrano de Bergerac, 2004; The House of Bernarda Alba, 2005; The Life of Galileo, 2006; Philistines, 2007; Present Laughter, 2007; Never So Good, Her Naked Skin, 2008; Burnt by the Sun, 2009; The White Guard, 2010 (Best Dir, Lawrence Olivier Awards, 2011); Blood and Gifts, 2010; Juno and the Paycock, 2011; Children of the Sun, 2013; The Silver Tassie, 2014; 3 Winters, 2014; Almeida: Who's Afraid of Virginia Woolf?, 1996; The Iceman Cometh, 1998 (Best Dir, Evening Standard Awards, Lawrence Olivier Awards); Conversations After a Burial, 2000; Period of Adjustment, 2006; Albery: Vassa, 1999; Private Lives, 2001; The Breath of Life, Haymarket, 2002; A Moon for the Misbegotten, Old Vic, 2006, transf. NY, 2007; The House of Special Purpose, Minerva, Chichester, 2009; All My Sons, Apollo, 2010; Hay Fever, Noël Coward Th., 2012; 55 Days, Hampstead Th., 2012; The Herd, Bush Th., 2013; Drawing the Line, Hampstead Th., 2013; Temple, Donmar Warehouse, 2015; For Services Rendered, Minerva, Chichester, 2015. Director: film, The Secret Rapture, 1993; television: Tales from Hollywood, 1992; Armadillo, 2001; Copenhagen, 2002; Blue/Orange, 2005. FRSA. *Address:* c/o National Theatre, South Bank, SE1 9PX.

DAVIES, Stephen Rees; QC 2000; *b* 2 May 1960; *s* of John Stephen Davies and Auriol (*née* Huber, now Barriball); *m* 2010, Daisy Leticia Brown. *Educ:* Stanwell Comprehensive Sch.; Cowbridge Comprehensive Sch.; London Sch. of Economics (LLB 1981); Trinity Hall, Cambridge (LLB 1982). Called to the Bar, Gray's Inn, 1983, Bencher 2006; in practice at the Bar, 1983–. Trustee: CLIC, subseq. CLIC Sargent, 2003–06; Jessie May Trust, 2006–13. *Recreations:* music, poetry, Welsh Rugby. *Address:* 5–8 Broad Street, Bristol BS1 2HW. *E:* stephen.davies@guildhallchambers.co.uk.

DAVIES, Stephen Richard; His Honour Judge Stephen Davies; a Specialist Circuit Judge, Manchester Civil Justice Centre, since 2007; *b* 7 Feb. 1963; *s* of Robert Davies and Merle Davies; *m* 1996, April Marland; two *d*. *Educ:* Baines Sch., Poulton-le-Fylde, Lancs; Downing Coll., Cambridge (BA Law 1984). Called to the Bar, Middle Temple, 1985; in practice as barrister, 601 Royal Exchange, then 8 King St Chambers, Manchester, 1986–2007; a Recorder of the Crown Court, 2002–07. *Address:* Manchester Civil Justice Centre, 1 Bridge Street West, Manchester M60 9DJ.

DAVIES, Susan, (Siobhan), CBE 2002 (MBE 1995); freelance choreographer; Director, Siobhan Davies Dance Company, since 1988; *b* 18 Sept. 1950; *d* of Grahame Henry Wyatt Davies and Tempé Mary Davies (*née* Wallich); lives with David John Buckland, *qv*; one *s* one *d*. *Educ:* several schools, ending with Queensgate School for Girls; Hammersmith College of Art and Building. With London Contemporary Dance Theatre, 1967–87: first choreography, 1972; Associate Choreographer, 1971; Associate Dir, 1983. Formed Siobhan Davies and Dancers, 1980; Jt Dir, with Ian Spink and Richard Alston, Second Stride, 1981–86; Associate Choreographer, Rambert Dance Co., 1988–93. Choreographed works include: White Man Sleeps, 1988; Art of Touch, 1995; Eighty-Eight, 1998; 13 Different Keys, 1999; Wild Air, 1999; Of Oil and Water, 2000; Plants and Ghosts, 2002; Bird Song, 2004; In Plain Clothes, 2006; Two Quartets, 2007; (with Victoria Miro) The Collection, 2009; Rotor, 2010; (with Matthias Sperling) To hand, 2011; (with Helka Kaski) Manual, 2013; (jtly) Table of Contents, 2014; film work (with David Hinton) All This Can Happen, 2012. Hon. FTCL 1996. DUniv: Surrey, 1999; Leicester, 2003. Arts Award, Fulbright Commn, 1987, to travel and study in America; Digital Dance Award, 1988, 1989, 1990, 1992; Laurence Olivier Award for Outstanding Achievement in Dance, 1993, 1996; Prudential Award for Dance, Evening Standard Dance Award, 1996; Time Out Award, 1997; South Bank Show Award for Dance, Prudential Creative Britons Award, 2000. *Address:* Siobhan Davies Studios, 85 St George's Road, SE1 6ER.

DAVIES, Susan Elizabeth, (Mrs John Davies), OBE 1988; Founder and Director, Photographers' Gallery, 1971–91; freelance consultant; *b* 14 April 1933; *d* of Stanworth Wills Adey and Joan Mary Margaret Adey (*née* Charlesworth); *m* 1954, John Ross Twiston Davies (*d* 2004); two *d* (and one *d* decd). *Educ:* Nightingale Bamford Sch., NY; Eothen Sch., Caterham. Municipal Journal, 1952–54; local and voluntary work, 1960–67; Artists Placement Group, 1967–68; ICA, 1968–71. Curator, Istanbul Photo-Biennial, 1995–96. Mem. (Ind) S Bucks DC, 1995–99; Parish Councillor, Burnham, Bucks, 1995–2003. Hon. FRPS (President's Medal, 1982). Photokina Award, 1986; National Artist Karel Plicka Medal, Czechoslovakia, 1989. *Recreations:* jazz live and recorded, reading, gardening. *Address:* 57 Sandilands Road, Fulham, SW6 2BD. *Club:* Chelsea Arts.

DAVIES, Dr Susan Jane; Lecturer in Palaeography, Aberystwyth University (formerly University of Wales, Aberystwyth), 1979–2008; *b* 4 April 1941; *d* of Iorwerth Howells and Megan Howells; *m* 1966, Brian Harold Davies; one *s* one *d*. *Educ:* Queen Elizabeth Grammar Sch. for Girls, Carmarthen; University Coll. of Wales, Aberystwyth (BA Hist., Dip. in Palaeography and Archive Admin, PhD). Trustee, Nat. Mus. Wales (formerly Mem., Council and Court of Govs, Nat. Museums and Galls of Wales), 1994–2007 (Vice-Pres., 2002–07); Mem., Royal Commn on Historical Manuscripts, 1995–2003. *Address:* Department of History and Welsh History, Aberystwyth University, Aberystwyth SY23 3DY.

DAVIES, Prof. Trevor David, PhD; FRMetS; Professor of Environmental Sciences, since 1993, and Pro Vice-Chancellor, since 2011, University of East Anglia; Special Professor and Director, Fudan Tyndall Centre, Fudan University, Shanghai, since 2011; *b* 29 March 1946; *s* of David Vincent Davies and Alice Beatrice Davies (*née* Savage); *m* 1970, Sandra Patricia Rowles (marr. diss. 2007); one *s* one *d*. *Educ:* Saltley Grammar Sch., Birmingham; Univ. of Sheffield (BSc 1967, PhD 1970). FRMetS 1974. Res. Asst, Univ. of New England, Australia, 1967; University of East Anglia: Lectr in Meteorol., 1970–88; Reader in Atmospheric Scis, 1988–93; Dir, Climatic Res. Unit, 1993–98; Dean, Sch. of Envmtl Scis, 1998–2004; Pro Vice-Chancellor, Res., Enterprise and Engagement, 2004–11. Mem., NERC, 2001–08. *Publications:* contrib. numerous scientific papers to specialist jls. *Recreation:* many things. *Address:* Vice-Chancellor's Office, University of East Anglia, Norwich NR4 7TJ. *T:* (01603) 592836. *E:* t.d.davies@uea.ac.uk.

DAVIES, Tristan David Henry; Assistant Editor, Mail on Sunday, since 2012; *b* 26 Oct. 1961; *s* of Maj.-Gen. Peter Ronald Davies, *qv*; *m* 2006, Shane, *d* of Maj.-Gen. Andrew Linton Watson, *qv*; two *s* one *d* from a former marriage. *Educ:* Douai; Bristol Univ. (English and Hist. (failed)). Editor: Covent Gdn Courier, 1983–86; Piazza Mag., 1986–87; joined The Independent, 1987: Listings Ed., 1988–90; Arts and Weekend Ed., 1990–93; Dep. Features Ed., 1993–96; Asst Ed., Mail on Sunday, Night and Day Mag., 1996–98; Exec. Ed., The Independent, 1998–2001; Ed., Independent on Sunday, 2001–07; Exec. Ed., Sunday Times, 2008–12. *Recreations:* football, singing. *Address:* Mail on Sunday, Northcliffe House, 2 Derry Street, W8 5TT. *Club:* Groucho.

DAVIES, Ven. (Vincent) Anthony; Archdeacon of Croydon, 1994–2011, now Archdeacon Emeritus; *b* 15 Sept. 1946; *s* of Vincent Davies and Maud Mary Cecilia Davies (*née* Hackett); unmarried. *Educ:* Brasted Place Theol Coll.; St Michael and All Angels Theol Coll., Llandaff. Curate: St James, Owton Manor, dio. Durham, 1973–76; St Faith, Wandsworth, dio. Southwark, 1976–78; Parish Priest: St Faith, Wandsworth, 1978–81; St John, Walworth, 1981–94; RD of Southwark and Newington, 1988–93. Bishop's Advr for Healthcare Chaplaincy, dio. Southwark, 2000–11. FRSA. *Recreations:* walking, reading, country pubs, all things Italian. *Address:* 1 High Beeches, Worthing, W Sussex BN11 4TJ. *Club:* National Liberal.

DAVIES, Vivian; *see* Davies, W. V.

DAVIES, Prof. Wendy Elizabeth, OBE 2008; FSA, FRHistS, FLSW; FBA 1992; Professor of History, 1985–2007, now Emerita, and Pro-Provost, 1995–2007, University College London; *b* 28 Aug. 1942; *d* of Douglas Charles Davies and Lucy (*née* Evans). *Educ:* University Coll. London (BA, PhD). Temporary Lectr 1970, Res. Fellow 1971, Lectr 1972, Univ. of Birmingham; University College London: Lectr 1977; Reader 1981; Hd, Dept of Hist., 1987–92; Dean of Arts, 1991–94; Dean of Social and Historical Scis, 1994–95; Fellow, 1997. Dist. Vis. Prof., Univ. of Calif, Berkeley, 2001. Member: Ancient Monuments Bd for Wales, 1993–2003; Humanities Res. Bd, 1996–98. Vice-Pres., British Acad., 2003–05. UK Team Mem., Bologna Experts (formerly Promoters), 2004–08. Gov., Mus. of London, 1995–2001. FLSW 2010. Hon. DLit UCL, 2014. *Publications:* An Early Welsh Microcosm, 1978; The Llandaff Charters, 1979; Wales in the Early Middle Ages, 1982; (ed with P. Fouracre) Settlement of Disputes in Early Medieval Europe, 1986; Small Worlds: the village community in early medieval Brittany, 1988; Patterns of Power, 1990; (with G. Astill) The East Brittany Survey, Field Work and Field Data, 1994; (ed with P. Fouracre) Property and Power, 1995; (with G. Astill) A Breton Landscape, 1997; Inscriptions of Early Medieval Brittany, 2000; (ed) From the Vikings to the Normans, 2003; (ed jtly) People and Space, 2006; Acts of Giving: individual, community and church in tenth-century Christian Spain, 2007; Welsh History in the Early Middle Ages: texts and societies, 2009; Brittany in the Early Middle Ages: texts and societies, 2009; (ed with P. Fouracre) The Languages of Gift in the Early Middle Ages, 2010; papers in Eng. Historical Rev., Past and Present, Francia, Bull. of Bd of Celtic Studies, Etudes Celtiques, Hist. and Anthropology, Oxford Jl of Archaeology, etc. *Recreations:* walking, gardening, friends, early music, cello.

DAVIES, Dame Wendy (Patricia), DBE 2001; Head Teacher, Selly Park Technology College (formerly Selly Park School), 1986–2003; *b* 19 Dec. 1942; *d* of Cecil and Mary Trotter; *m* 1967, Mansel John Davies; one *s* (one *d* decd). *Educ:* Portsmouth High Sch., GPDST; UCNW (BSc Hons); DipEd Oxford Univ. Teacher, Birmingham LEA, 1966; Dep. Hd, 1969–74, Hd, 1974–80, Dept of Maths; Dep. Head Teacher, 1980–86. Associate Dir, Specialist Schs and Academies Trust (formerly Specialist Schs Trust), 2005–; Trustee, e-Learning Foundn. *Recreations:* maths, travelling, reading, ICT. *Address:* 82 Lugtrout Lane, Solihull, W Midlands B91 2SN. *T:* (0121) 624 2693. *Club:* Selly Park Technol. Coll. Saturday.

DAVIES, (William) Gareth; Chief Executive, Newport Gwent Dragons and Newport Rugby Football Club, since 2013; Chairman, Welsh Rugby Union Ltd, since 2014; *b* 29 Sept. 1955; *s* of late David Elvet Davies and Sarah Davies; *m* 1st, 1979, Helen (marr. diss. 2003); two *d*; 2nd, 2012, Fiona Neivandt. *Educ:* UWIST, Cardiff (BSc); Oxford Univ. Manager, Burnley Bldg Soc. (Nat. and Provincial Bldg Soc.), 1979–87; Asst Dir, CBI, Wales, 1987–89; Hd of Sport, BBC Wales, 1989–94; Chief Exec., Cardiff Rugby Club, 1994–99; Commissioning Ed., Sports and Events (formerly Sports Advr), S4C, 1999–2006; Dir for Welsh Affairs, Royal Mail Gp, 2003–06; Hd, Australia and NZ, Internat. Business Wales, 2006–09; Dean, Carnegie Faculty of Sport and Educn, later Carnegie Faculty, Leeds Metropolitan Univ., 2009–13. Chm., Sports Council for Wales, 1999–2003. Rugby journalist: Independent on Sunday, 1999; Sunday Times, 2002–06. Member, Board: Leeds Carnegie Rugby, 2009–13; Yorks CCC, 2011–13. Hon. Fellow, Cardiff Univ., 1995. *Publications:* Standing Off, 1985. *Recreations:* golf, wine (Burgundy and Bordeaux). *Address:* Newport Gwent Dragons, Rodney Parade, Newport, Gwent NP19 0UU. *Clubs:* MCC; Royal Porthcawl Golf, Moortown Golf.

DAVIES, William Llewellyn M.; *see* Monro Davies.

DAVIES, (William) Rhodri; QC 1999; a Recorder, since 2004; *b* 29 Jan. 1957; *s* of His Honour (Lewis) John Davies, QC; *m* 1984, Vicky Platt; three *d*. *Educ:* Winchester Coll.; Downing Coll., Cambridge (BA Hons Law). Called to the Bar, Middle Temple, 1979; Bencher, 2011; practising barrister, 1980–. *Recreations:* running, sailing, swimming. *Address:* 1 Essex Court, Temple, EC4Y 9AR. *T:* (020) 7583 2000. *Club:* Thames Hare and Hounds.

DAVIES, Rev. Dr William Rhys; Principal of Cliff College, Sheffield, 1983–94; Moderator of the Free Church Federal Council, 1991–92; *b* Blackpool, 31 May 1932; *m* 1955, Barbara; one *s* one *d*. *Educ:* Junior, Central Selective and Grammar schools, Blackpool; Hartley Victoria Methodist Coll., Manchester; Univ. of Manchester. BD London 1955; MA 1959, PhD 1965, Manchester. Junior Rating and Valuation Officer (Clerical), Blackpool Corp., 1950–51. Methodist Circuit Minister: Middleton, Manchester, 1955–60; Fleetwood, 1960–65; Stockton-on-Tees, 1965–66; Sen. Lectr in Religious Studies, Padgate Coll. of Higher Education, and Methodist Minister without pastoral charge on Warrington Circuit, 1966–79; Superintendent Minister, Bradford Methodist Mission, 1979–83. Nat. Advr, Aglow Internat. (GB), 1983–. Pres., Methodist Conf., 1987–88. Methodist Committees: Chairman: Cttee for Relations with People of Other Faiths, 1988–98; Ministerial Candidates Appeals Cttee, 1994–2004. Member: Cliff Coll. Gen. Cttee, 1974–77 and 1981–94; Faith and Order Cttee, 1975–82; Doctrinal Cttee, 1979–82; Divl Bd for Social Responsibility, 1982–85; Home Mission Bd, 1983–94. Mem. Council, Garden Tomb (Jerusalem) Assoc., 1992–95. Patron: Pen-y-Rhondda Trust, 2003–; Philippi Trust, 2007–. Co-Editor, Dunamis (renewal magazine for Methodists), 1972–94. *Publications:* (with Ross Peart) The Charismatic Movement and Methodism, 1973; Spirit Baptism and Spiritual Gifts in Early Methodism, (USA) 1974; Gathered into One (Archbishop of Canterbury's Lent Book), 1975; (with Ross Peart) What about the Charismatic Movement?, 1980; (contrib.) A Dictionary of Christian Spirituality, 1983; Rocking the Boat, 1986; Spirit without Measure, 1996; (contrib.) An Encyclopedia: Jesus in history, thought and culture, 2003; contribs to jls. *Recreations:* reading, sport (soccer). *Address:* 25 Grange Avenue, Thornton Cleveleys, Lancs FY5 4PA. *T:* (01253) 864678.

DAVIES, (William) Vivian, FSA 1980; Keeper, Ancient Egypt and Sudan (formerly Egyptian Antiquities), British Museum, 1988–2011; *b* 14 Oct. 1947; *s* of late Walter Percival Davies and Gwenllian Davies (*née* Evans); *m* 1970, Janet Olwen May Foat (marr. diss. 1994); one *s* one *d*; *m* 1996, Renée Frances Friedman. *Educ:* Llanelli Grammar Sch.; Jesus Coll.,

Oxford (BA, MA). Randall-MacIver Student in Archaeology, Queen's Coll., Oxford, 1973–74; Asst Keeper, 1974–81, Dep. Keeper, 1981–88, Dept of Egyptian Antiquities, BM. Vis. Prof. of Egyptology, Univ. of Heidelberg, 1984–85. Hon. Librarian, 1975–85, Gen. Ed. of Pubns, 1990–99, Egypt Exploration Soc.; Chm., Sudan Archaeol Res. Soc., 1991–2012; Member: Governing Council, British Inst. in Eastern Africa, 1989–2005; German Archaeol Inst., 1992–. Reviews Editor, Jl of Egyptian Archaeology, 1975–85. *Publications:* A Royal Statue Reattributed, 1981; (with T. G. H. James) Egyptian Sculpture, 1983; The statuette of Queen Tetisheri: a reconsideration, 1984; (with A. el-Khouli, A. B. Lloyd, A. J. Spencer) Saqqara Tombs, I: The Mastabas of Mereri and Wernu, 1984; (ed with J. Assmann and G. Burkard) Problems and Priorities in Egyptian Archaeology, 1987; Egyptian Hieroglyphs, 1987; Catalogue of Egyptian Antiquities in the British Museum, VII: Tools and Weapons—1: Axes, 1987; (ed) Egypt and Africa: Nubia from prehistory to Islam, 1991; (ed with R. Walker) Biological Anthropology and the Study of Ancient Egypt, 1993; (ed with J. Putnam) Time Machine: Ancient Egypt and contemporary art, 1994; (ed with L. Schofield) Egypt, the Aegean and the Levant: interconnections in the second millennium BC, 1995; (with R. Friedman) Egypt, 1998; (ed) Studies in Egyptian Antiquities: a tribute to T. G. H. James, 1999; (ed) Colour and Painting in Ancient Egypt, 2001; (ed with D. Welsby) Uncovering Ancient Sudan: a decade of discovery by the Sudan Archaeological Research Society, 2002; contribs to: Egypt's Golden Age: the art of living in the New Kingdom, 1982; Excavating in Egypt: The Egypt Exploration Society 1882–1982, 1982; Tanis: l'or des pharaons, 1987; Africa: the art of a continent, 1996; Sudan: ancient treasures, 2004; Hatshepsut, from Queen to Pharaoh, 2005; reviews and articles in learned jls.

DAVIES-JONES, Jonathan; QC 2013; *b* Sheffield, 10 June 1967; *s* of Dr Aelwyn Davies-Jones and Geraldine Davies-Jones; *m* 1997, Annette King; three *s*. *Educ:* Winchester Coll.; St John's Coll., Cambridge (BA 1988). Called to the Bar, Middle Temple, 1994; in practice as a barrister, specialising in commercial law. Chm. Govs, Balham Nursery Sch. and Children's Centre, 2010–. *Recreations:* family, walking, cycling, laughter. *Address:* 3 Verulam Buildings, Gray's Inn, WC1R 5NT. *T:* (020) 7831 8441, *Fax:* (020) 7831 8447. *E:* jdj@3vb.com.

DAVIGNON, Viscount Etienne; Minister of State and Ambassador of HM the King of the Belgians; Chairman: Foundation P. H. Spaak, since 1983; Institut Egmont (formerly Royal Institute for International Relations), since 1987; *b* Budapest, 4 Oct. 1932; *m* 1959, Françoise de Cumont; one *s* two *d*. *Educ:* University of Louvain (LLD). Diplomat; Head of Office of Minister for Foreign Affairs, Belgium, 1963; Political Director, Ministry for Foreign Affairs, Belgium, 1969; Chm., Gov. Board, Internat. Energy Agency, 1974. Mem., 1977–84 (with responsibility for internal mkt, customs, union and indust. affairs), and Vice-Pres., 1981–84 (with responsibility for industry, energy and research policies), EEC. Chairman: CMB (Belgium), 2002–; Recticel (Belgium), 2004–15; Brussels Airlines, Belgium; Vice-Chairman: Fortis, 1989–2004; ACCOR, 2000–09 (Dir, 1990–2000); Société Gén. de Belgique, 2001–03 (Chm., 1989–2001); Suez-Tractebel, 2003–10; Director: Umicore, 1989–92 and 2000–05 (Chm., 1992–2000); Suez, 1989–2010; Gilead (USA), 1990–. *Recreations:* tennis, golf. *Address:* 12 Avenue des Fleurs, 1150 Brussels, Belgium.

DAVIS; *see* Clinton-Davis.

DAVIS; *see* Hart-Davis.

DAVIS, Adam David; QC 2012; *b* London, 6 May 1963; *s* of Edgar Davis and Leila Davis; *m* 1994, Cheryl Fellerman; one *s* two *d*. *Educ:* Mill Hill Sch.; Queen Mary Coll., Univ. of London (LLB Hons). Called to the Bar, Inner Temple, 1985; in practice as barrister, specialising in crime and sports. Very High Cost Cases Appeals Cttee, 2003–; Sports Disputes Resolution Panel, 2005–09. *Recreations:* football (Tottenham Hotspur FC), golf, cricket, cinema. *Address:* 3 Temple Gardens, EC4Y 9AU. *T:* (020) 7353 3120. *E:* adqc@3TG.co.uk. *Clubs:* MCC; Hampstead Golf.

DAVIS, Prof. Adrian Charles, OBE 2007; PhD; Professor of Hearing and Communication, and Director, MRC Hearing and Communication Group, University of Manchester, 2004; *b* 21 March 1950; *s* of Albert H. W. Davis and G. H., (Trudy), Davis; *m* 1978, Kathryn Southworth; two *s* one *d*. *Educ:* Douai Sch.; University Coll. London (Dip. Theol. 1970; PhD Psychol. 1984); Univ. of Exeter (BSc Mathematical Stats and Psychol. 1973); Stirling Univ. (MSc Mathematical Psychol. 1974). Lectr in Community Medicine, St Thomas's Hosp. Med. Sch., 1977–78; SRC Res. Fellow (Psychol.), Lancaster Poly., 1978; Sen. Scientific Epidemiologist, MRC Inst. of Hearing Res., 1978–2004. Special Prof., Dept of Surgery, Univ. of Nottingham, 1996–; Hon. Consultant Clinical Scientist, Queens Med. Centre, Nottingham, 1996–; Hon. Consultant, Central Manchester and Manchester Children's Univ. NHS Trust, 2005–. Director: NHS Newborn Hearing Screening Prog., 2001–; NHS Clinical Audiology Res. Network, 2005–; DoH Advr, Audiology, 2005–; DoH Clinical/Scientific Audiology Champion for Physiol Measurement Strategy Gp, 2005–. Medal, Swedish Med. Assoc., 1992; Amer. Auditory Soc. Award, 1998; Thomas Simm Littler Prize, British Soc. of Audiology, 1999. *Publications:* Hearing in Adults, 1995; over 100 books, conf. papers and over 100 articles in scientific jls. *Recreations:* badminton, running.

DAVIS, Adrian Derek; Governor, Montserrat, 2011–15 (on secondment from Department for International Development); *b* London, 22 July 1950; *s* of Bernard and Betty Davis; *m* 1975, Sujue Sattayipiwat; two *s*. *Educ:* University Coll., London (BSc (Econ) 1971); London Sch. of Econs (MSc (Econ) 1974). Department for International Development, 1974–2015; First Secretary: (Econ.), Dhaka, 1977–79; Econ. Advr, SE Asia Develt Div., Bangkok, 1980–83; (Aid/Econ.), Cairo, 1984–87; Dep. Hd, FCO/DFID Know-How Fund for Eastern Europe, 1987–91; UK Exec. Dir, Asia Develt Bank, Manila, 1991–94 (on secondment); Hd, E Asia and Pacific Dept, 1994–96; Hd, Information and Services Dept, 1996–99; Hd, Envmt Dept, 1999–2003; Country Rep. for Cambodia, China, Indonesia, N Korea and Vietnam, 2003–11. *Recreations:* ten-pin bowling, table tennis, word games, reading, music.

DAVIS, Alan Henry; strategy consultant; Director of Neighbourhood Renewal Strategy, Department for Communities and Local Government (formerly Office of the Deputy Prime Minister), 2004–07; *b* 1 May 1948; *s* of Arthur Wallace Davis and Phyllis Marjorie Davis (*née* Grudgings); *m* 1st, 1972, Angela Joy Wells (marr. diss. 2003); two *s* one *d*; 2nd, 2012, Theresa Mary Crossley (*née* Short). *Educ:* Wyggeston Boys' Sch., Leicester; University Coll., Oxford (MA Chem. 1973). Joined DoE, 1973; on secondment to GLC, 1979–80; Private Sec. to successive Secs of State, 1983–85; Asst Sec., 1986; Head of Divs in Local Govt, Housing, Global Atmosphere; Principal Private Sec. to Sec. of State, 1994–97; Under-Sec., 1997; Director: Water and Land, DETR, 1997–2001; Integrated and Local Transport, DfT (formerly DETR, then DTLR), 2001–04. Churchwarden, St Paul's Ch, Winchmore Hill. *Recreations:* gardening, walking, watching sport. *Address:* 11 Old Park View, Enfield, Middx EN2 7EG. *T:* (020) 8364 4043.

DAVIS, Ven. Alan Norman; Archdeacon of West Cumberland, 1996–2004; *b* 27 July 1938; *s* of Arthur William and Bertha Eileen Davis; *m* 1966, Françoise Marguerite Blondet; one *s* two *d*. *Educ:* King Edward's Sch., Birmingham; Durham Univ.; Lichfield Theol Coll.; Open Univ. (BA). Ordained deacon, 1965, priest, 1966; Asst Curate, St Luke's Birmingham, 1965–68; Priest-in-charge, 1968–73, Vicar, 1973–75, St Paul, Wordsworth Avenue, Sheffield; Vicar, St James and St Christopher, Shiregreen, Sheffield, 1975–80; Team Rector, Maltby, Sheffield, 1980–89; Archbishop's Officer for Urban Priority Areas, 1990–92; Priest-in-charge, St Cuthbert, Carlisle, and Diocesan Communications Officer, 1992–96; Area Dean, Sparkenhoe W, Dio. Leicester, 2007–09. *Recreations:* French holidays, RSC Theatre Stratford, Aston Villa Football Club. *Address:* 71 North Street, Atherstone, Warwicks CV9 1JW. *T:* (01827) 718210.

DAVIS, Alan Roger M.; *see* Maryon Davis.

DAVIS, Andrew; Founder and Executive Chairman, von Essen group of companies, 1997–2011; Executive Chairman, PremiAir Aviation Services Ltd, 2007–12; *b* 22 Feb. 1964; *s* of Brendon G. F. Davis and Catharine Agnes Davis (*née* Smyth); one *s*. Farmer; property develt and investment; art consulting. *E:* andrew.davis@andrew-davis.co.uk.

DAVIS, Sir Andrew (Frank), Kt 1999; CBE 1992; conductor; Musical Director, Chicago Lyric Opera, since 2000; Chief Conductor, Melbourne Symphony Orchestra, since 2012; *b* 2 Feb. 1944; *m* 1989, Gianna Rolandi; one *s*. *Educ:* Watford Grammar Sch.; King's Coll. Cambridge (MA, BMus); Accademia di S Cecilia, Rome. Assistant Conductor, BBC Scottish Symphony Orchestra, 1970–72; Asst Conductor, New Philharmonia Orchestra, 1973–77; Artistic Dir and Chief Conductor, Toronto Symphony, 1975–88, now Conductor Laureate; Musical Dir, Glyndebourne Fest. Opera, 1988–2000; Chief Conductor, BBC SO, 1989–2000, now Conductor Laureate. Principal Guest Conductor: Royal Liverpool Philharmonic Orchestra, 1974–77; Royal Stockholm Philharmonic, 1995–2000. Has conducted major US orchestras: New York, Boston, Chicago, Cleveland, Philadelphia and LA. Particularly noted for interpretations of Strauss operas; conducts at: La Scala, Milan; Metropolitan Opera, NY; Chicago Lyric; San Francisco; Glyndebourne; Royal Opera House Covent Gdn; Bayreuth Fest. Toronto Symphony Orchestra tours: US Centres, China, Japan, 1978; Europe, 1983, 1986, incl. London, Helsinki, Bonn, Paris and Edinburgh Fest.; BBC SO tours: Far East, 1990; Europe, 1992 and 1996; Japan, 1993; N America, 1995 and 1998; Korea and Japan, 1997; Salzburg Fest., 1997; other tours include: Australia, 2002; LSO, 2002, 2004. Many commercial recordings include: complete Dvorak Symphonies, Philharmonia Orch.; Mendelssohn Symphonies, Bavarian Radio Symphony; Borodin Cycle, Holst's The Planets and Handel's Messiah, Toronto Symphony; Tippett's The Mask of Time, BBC SO and Chorus (Record of the Year, Gramophone Awards, 1987); The British Line (British Orchestral Series), BBC SO; world première of Elgar/Payne Symphony No 3. *Recreation:* the study of mediaeval stained glass. *Address:* c/o Opus 3 Artists, 470 Park Avenue South, 9th Floor North, New York, NY 10016, USA.

DAVIS, Ann-Louise; *see* Kinmonth, A.-L.

DAVIS, Prof. Anne Christine, PhD; FInstP; Professor of Mathematical Physics (1967), University of Cambridge, since 2013; Fellow, King's College, Cambridge, since 1986; *b* Bristol, 5 Feb. 1951; *d* of Albert and Esmé Davis; *m* (marr. diss.); one *d*. *Educ:* Ashton Park Sch., Bristol; Royal Holloway Coll., Univ. of London (BSc); Bristol Univ. (PhD 1975). FInstP 2001. Postdoctoral Res. Associate in Theoretical Physics: Durham Univ., 1976–78; Blackett Physics Lab., Imperial Coll. London, 1978–80; Fellow, Theory Div., CERN, Geneva, 1980–82; Mem., Inst. for Advanced Study, Princeton, USA, 1982–83; University of Cambridge: Res. Council Advanced Fellow, Dept of Applied Maths and Theoretical Physics, 1983–88; Coll. Teaching Officer, King's Coll., 1988–95; Department of Applied Mathematics and Theoretical Physics: Asst Dir of Res., 1995–96; Reader in Theoretical Physics, 1996–2002; Prof. of Theoretical Physics, 2002–13. Vis. Prof., Brown Univ., USA, 1989; CNRS Vis. Prof., Paris, 1996. MAE 2009. *Publications:* Formation and Interactions of Topological Defeats, 1995; contrib. papers on theoretical physics, incl. theoretical cosmol. and high energy physics. *Recreations:* walking and trekking, opera, theatre, ballet, time with my family, reading, travelling. *Address:* Department of Applied Mathematics and Theoretical Physics, Centre for Mathematical Sciences, University of Cambridge, Wilberforce Road, Cambridge CB3 0WA. *T:* (01223) 337878. *E:* acd@damtp.cam.ac.uk.

DAVIS, Anthony Ronald William James; media consultant, since 1990; *b* 26 July 1931; *e* *s* of Donald William Davis, Barnes and Mary Josephine Davis (*née* Nolan-Byrne), Templeogue Mill, Co. Dublin; *m* 1960, Yolande Mary June, *o* *d* of Patrick Leonard, retd civil engr; one *s* two *d* (and one *d* decd). *Educ:* Hamlet of Ratcliffe and Oratory; Regent Street Polytechnic; Joint Services School for Linguists on Russian course as National Serviceman (Army), 1953–55; Architectural Asst, Housing Dept, Middx County Architect's Dept, 1956–58; Sub-Editor, The Builder, 1959; Editor: Official Architecture and Planning, 1964–70; Building, 1970–74; Director, Building, 1972–77; Editor-in-Chief, New World Publishers Ltd, 1978–83; Editl Dir, New World Publishers Ltd, Middle East Construction and Saudi Arabian Construction, 1983–86; Editor, World Property, 1986–90. Member Board: Architecture and Planning Publications Ltd, 1966; Building (Publishers) Ltd, 1972. Mem. Council, Modular Soc., 1970–71. JP Berkshire, 1973–81. *Publications:* contribs to various, architectural and technical. *Recreations:* collecting porcelain, music and dreaming.

DAVIS, (Arthur) John, RD 1967; FCIB; Vice-Chairman, Lloyds Bank, 1984–91 (Chief General Manager, 1978–84); *b* 28 July 1924; *s* of Alan Wilfrid Davis and Emily Davis; *m* 1950, Jean Elizabeth Edna Hobbs (*d* 2004); one *s* one *d* (and one *d* decd). *Educ:* grammar schs. FCIB (FIB 1969). Served War, RN, 1942–46. Entered Lloyds Bank, 1941; Jt Gen. Manager, 1973; Asst Chief Gen. Man., 1973; Dep. Chief Gen. Man., 1976. Pres., Chartered Inst. of Bankers, 1985–87. *Recreations:* gardening, music, country pursuits. *Address:* The Granary, Stocks Road, Aldbury, Tring, Herts HP23 5RX. *T:* (01442) 851321.

DAVIS, Barbara Ann; *see* Cassani, B. A.

DAVIS, Prof. Benjamin Guy, DPhil; FRS 2015; Professor of Chemistry, University of Oxford, since 2005; Fellow, Pembroke College, Oxford, since 2001; *b* Hatfield, 8 Aug. 1970; *s* of Stanley Stewart Davis and Jennifer Margaret Morley. *Educ:* Nottingham High Sch.; Keble Coll., Oxford (BA Chem. 1st Cl. with Chem. Pharmacol. (Dist.) 1993; DPhil Chemistry 1997); Univ. of Durham (PGCHE 2001). Postdoctoral Researcher, Dept of Chem., Univ. of Toronto, 1997–98; Demonstrator and Lectr, Dept of Chem., Univ. of Durham, 1998–2001; Lectr, Univ. of Oxford, 2001–05. Vis. Prof., Pierre and Marie Curie Univ., Paris, 2011. *Publications:* Carbohydrate Chemistry, Oxford Chemistry Primer No. 99 (with A. J. Fairbanks), 2002; over 30 book chapters; over 200 scientific jl articles; over 30 patents. *Recreations:* rowing (Mem., Stewards' Enclosure, Henley Royal Regatta), open-water swimming, art. *Address:* Pembroke College, Oxford OX1 1DW. *Clubs:* City of Oxford Rowing, Pembroke College Boat (Sen. Mem.), Oxford University Lightweight Rowing (Sen. Mem.).

DAVIS, Dr Brian Elliott, CBE 2000; Chief Executive, Nationwide Building Society, 1994–2001; *b* 22 Sept. 1944; *s* of William and Bessie Davis; *m* 1972, Elizabeth Rose; one *s* two *d*. *Educ:* St John's Coll., Southsea; Sussex Univ. (BSc); Sheffield Univ. (PhD). FCIB 2000. With Esso Petroleum Co., 1969–86; joined Nationwide Building Soc., 1986; Gen. Manager (Technology), 1987; Resource Dir, 1989; Ops Dir, 1992. Chm., BSA, 1996–98. *Recreations:* sport, computing.

DAVIS, Maj.-Gen. Brian William, CB 1985; CBE 1980 (OBE 1974); Head of Public Affairs, Royal Ordnance plc, 1987–94 (Director, Product Support Group, 1985–87); *b* 28 Aug. 1930; *s* of late Edward William Davis, MBE, and Louise Jane Davis (*née* Webber); *m* 1954, Margaret Isobel Jenkins; one *s* one *d*. *Educ:* Weston-super-Mare Grammar Sch.; Mons OCS, Aldershot. Commissioned Royal Artillery, 1949; Regtl Duty, 1949–56 and 1960–61, UK/BAOR; Instr-in-Gunnery, 1956–59; Staff Coll. Camberley, 1962; DAA and QMG HQ 7 Armd Bde BAOR, 1963–66; GSO2 SD UN Force, Cyprus, 1966; Regtl Duty, 1967–69; Lt-Col 1969, Directing Staff, Staff Coll. Camberley, 1969–71; CO 32 Lt Regt RA BAOR/

England/N Ireland, 1971–74; Col AQ Ops HQ BAOR, 1975; Brig. 1975; CRA 3 Div., 1976–77; RCDS 1978; Chief of Staff N Ireland, 1979–80; Chief of Comdrs-in-Chief Mission to Soviet Forces in Germany, 1981–82; Maj. Gen., 1982; C of S, Logistic Exec. (Army), 1982–83; DGLP (A) (formerly VQMG), MoD, 1983–85, retired. Col Comdt RA, 1987–93. Mem., HAC, 1987–95. *Recreations:* Rugby (President, RARFC, 1975–78; Dep. Pres., Army Rugby Union, 1984–89), cricket, fishing, ornithology. *Clubs:* Special Forces, MCC; Army Rugby Union; Fadeaways; Piscatorial Society (Pres., 2003–07).

DAVIS, Carl, Hon. CBE 2005; composer; *b* 28 Oct. 1936; *s* of Isadore and Sara Davis; *m* 1971, Jean Boht; two *d*. *Educ:* New England Conservatory of Music; Bard Coll. (BA). Associate Conductor, London Philharmonic Orchestra, 1987–88; Principal Conductor, Bournemouth Pops, 1984–87; Principal Guest Conductor, Munich SO, 1990–93; Artistic Dir, Liverpool Philharmonic Summer Pops, 1993–2000; *major TV credits:* The Snow Goose, 1971; World at War (Emmy Award), 1972; The Naked Civil Servant, 1975; Marie Curie, 1977; Our Mutual Friend, 1978; Prince Regent, The Old Curiosity Shop, 1979; Hollywood, Oppenheimer, The Sailor's Return, Fair Stood the Wind for France, 1980; The Commanding Sea, Private Schulz, 1981; The Last Night of the Poms, Home Sweet Home, La Ronde, 1982; The Unknown Chaplin, The Tale of Beatrix Potter, The Far Pavilions, 1983; The Day the Universe Changed, 1985; Hotel du Lac, 1986; The Accountant (BAFTA Award), The Pied Piper, 1989; Flight Terminal, Secret Life of Ian Fleming, 1990; The Black Velvet Gown, Buried Mirror, Yellow Wallpaper, The Last of the Romantics, Ashenden, Separate But Equal, 1991; The Royal Collection, A Very Polish Practice, A Sense of History, Fame in the 20th Century, 1992; A Year in Provence, Genghis Cohen, Thatcher: the Downing Street Years, 1993; Red Eagle, Hope in the Year 2, 1994; Pride and Prejudice, 1995; A Dance to the Music of Time, 1997; Cold War, Good Night Mr Tom, Seesaw, Coming Home, 1998; The Great Gatsby, 2000; Christopher Columbus, 2002; Promoted by Glory, 2003; Upstairs Downstairs, 2012; *radio:* presenter, Carl Davis Classics, R2, 1997–2000; *scores:* for RSC, National Theatre and Birmingham Royal Ballet; *musicals:* The Projector, 1971; Pilgrim, 1975; Cranford, 1976; Alice in Wonderland, 1978; The Wind in the Willows, 1985; Kip's War, 1987; *opera:* Peace, 1978; *TV operas:* The Arrangement, 1967; Orpheus in the Underground, 1976; *West End:* Forty Years On, 1969; Habeas Corpus, 1973; *films:* The French Lieutenant's Woman (BAFTA Original Film Score Award), 1981; Champions, 1984; King David, 1985; Girl in a Swing, Scandal, The Rainbow, 1988; Frankenstein Unbound, Fragments of Isabella, 1989; Crucifer of Blood, Raft of the Medusa, 1991; The Voyage, 1992; The Trial, 1993; Widows Peak, 1994; Topsy-Turvy, 1999; Book of Eve, 2002; *silent films:* Napoleon, 1980, newly adapted, 2000, US premiere, San Francisco Silent Film Fest., 2012; The Crowd, 1981; Flesh and the Devil, Show People, How to Make Movies, 1982; Broken Blossoms, The Wind, The Musketeers of Pig Alley, An Unseen Enemy, 1983; Thief of Bagdad, 1984; The Big Parade, Greed, 1985; The General, Ben Hur, 1987; Mysterious Lady, Intolerance, City Lights (re-creation of Chaplin score), 1988; Safety Last, Kid Brother, 1989; The Immigrant, 1991; IT, The Four Horsemen of the Apocalypse, 1992; Wings; The Gold Rush (re-creation of Chaplin score), 1993; The Wedding March, 1998; Old Heidelberg, 1999; The Iron Mask, 1999; The Adventurer, 2000; The Rink, Behind the Screen (Chaplain short films), 2003; *ballets:* Dances of Love and Death, 1981; Fire and Ice (ice ballet for Torvill and Dean), 1986; The Portrait of Dorian Gray (for SWRB), 1987; A Simple Man (based on L. S. Lowry, for Northern Ballet Theatre), 1987; Liaisons Amoureuses, 1988; Lipizzaner (Northern Ballet Theatre), 1988; A Christmas Carol (Northern Ballet Theatre), 1992; Savoy Suite (English Nat. Ballet), 1993; Alice in Wonderland (English Nat. Ballet), 1995; Aladdin (Scottish Ballet), 2000; Cyrano (Birmingham Royal Ballet), 2007; The Lady of the Camellias (Ballet HNK, Croatia), 2008; *orchestral compositions:* Lines on London (symphony), 1984 (commnd by Capital Radio); Clarinet Concerto, 1984; Fantasy for flute, 1985 (commnd by Acad. of St Martin in the Fields); Glenlivet Firework Music, 1987; Beginners Please!, 1987; (with Paul McCartney) Paul McCartney's Liverpool Oratorio, 1991; On the Beach at Night Alone, 1999; Ballade for Cello and Orchestra, 2011 (commnd by Royal Liverpool Philharmonic Orch.); *choral:* The Last Train to Tomorrow, 2012. Has made numerous recordings. Formed Carl Davis Collection (with Jean Davis and Charles Padley) for promotion of recordings of own music, 2009. Mem. BAFTA, 1979–. First winner, BAFTA Award for Original TV Music, 1981; BAFTA Lifetime Achievement Award for Contribution to Film and TV, 2003. Chevalier de L'Ordre des Arts et des Lettres, 1983. *Publications:* sheet music of television themes. *Recreations:* reading, gardening, playing chamber music, cooking. *Address:* c/o Peter Hall, Musichall, Oast House, Crouch's Farm, Hollow Lane, E Hoathly, E Sussex BN8 6QX. *E:* peter@musichall.uk.com.

DAVIS, Christopher John; Headmaster, Sherborne School, 2010–14; *b* Middx, 27 April 1961; *s* of John Priddis Davis and Juliet Myfanwy Davis (*née* Stearns); *m* 1994, Innes Flora McLeod Fraser; two *d*. *Educ:* Eton Coll.; Corpus Christi Coll., Cambridge (BA 1984; MA). Asst Master, St Edmund's Sch., Canterbury, 1984–85; Bank of England: Internat. Div., 1986–90; on secondment to Cabinet Office, 1990–92; Editor, Qly Bulletin, 1992–94; Eton College: Asst Master, 1994–2001; House Master, 2001–10. *Recreations:* music, reading, sport, theatre, English literature.

DAVIS, Prof. (Conrad) Glyn, AC 2002; PhD; Vice-Chancellor and President, University of Melbourne, since 2005. *Educ:* Univ. of NSW (BA 1st Cl. Hons Pol Sci. 1981); ANU (PhD 1985). FIPAA 1995; FASSA 2003. Lectr in Politics and Public Policy, Griffith Univ., 1985; Harkness Fellow, Univ. of Calif, Berkeley, Brookings Instn, Washington and John F. Kennedy Sch. of Govt, Harvard, 1987–88; Griffith University: Aust. Res. Council QE II Res. Fellow, 1992–95, 1996–98; Prof., 1998; Vice-Chancellor and Pres., 2002–05; on secondment to Queensland Government: as Comr for Public Sector Equity, Qld Public Sector Mgt Commn, 1990–93; as Dir Gen., Office of the Cabinet, 1995–96; as Dir Gen., Qld Dept of the Premier and Cabinet, 1998–2002. Chm., Aust. and NZ Sch. of Govt, Univ. of Melbourne, 2002–06; Mem. Bd, Menzies Centre, KCL, 2007–. Chairman: Universities Australia, 2011–13; Educn and Curriculum Wkg Gp, Anzac Centenary Adv. Bd, 2012–. Director: South Bank Corp., 1998–2001; Qld Theatre Co., 2002–05; Melbourne Theatre Co., 2005–; Asialink, 2005–. DUniv Griffith, 2006. *Publications:* Breaking Up the ABC, 1988; A Government of Routines, 1995; (with P. Bridgman) The Australian Policy Handbook, 1998, 5th edn (with P. Bridgman and C. Althaus) 2012; (ed with M. Keating) The Future of Australian Governance: policy choices, 2000; (ed with P. Weller) Are You Being Served?: state, citizens and governance, 2001; The Republic of Learning: higher education transforms Australia, 2010. *Address:* Vice-Chancellor's Office, University of Melbourne, Vic 3010, Australia.

DAVIS, Sir Crispin Henry Lamert, Kt 2004; Chief Executive Officer, Reed Elsevier, 1999–2009; Chairman, StarBev B.V., 2010–12; *b* 19 March 1949; *s* of late Walter Patrick Carless Davis and Jane (*née* Lamert); *m* 1970, Anne Richardson; three *d*. *Educ:* Charterhouse; Oriel Coll., Oxford (MA Mod. Hist.). Joined Procter & Gamble, 1970: Man. Dir, Procter & Gamble Germany, 1981–84; Vice-Pres., Food Div., Procter & Gamble USA, 1984–90; European Man. Dir, 1990–92, Gp Man. Dir, 1992–94, United Distillers; CEO, Aegis plc, 1994–99. Non-executive Director: GlaxoSmithKline plc, 2003–; Vodafone, 2014–. Trustee, Nat. Trust, 2005–12. Mem. Council, Oxford Univ., 2009–. *Recreations:* sport: tennis, squash, golf, ski-ing; gardening, art, antique furniture. *Address:* Hills End, Titlarks Hill, Sunningdale, Berks SL5 0JD. *T:* (01344) 291233. *Clubs:* Royal Automobile, MCC; Sunningdale Golf.

See also I. E. L. Davis, Rt Hon. Sir N. A. L. Davis.

DAVIS, Prof. Daniel Michael, PhD; Professor of Immunology and Director of Research, Manchester Collaborative Centre for Inflammation Research, University of Manchester, since 2013; *b* London, 2 Aug. 1970; *s* of Gerald and Marilyn Davis; *m* 2000, Katie Nicholls; one *s* one *d*. *Educ:* Univ. of Manchester (BSc 1st Cl. Physics 1992); Strathclyde Univ. (PhD 1995). Postdoctoral Res. Fellow, Dept of Molecular and Cell Biol., Harvard Univ., 1996–99; Imperial College London: Lectr, Dept of Biol., 1999–2005; Prof. of Molecular Immunology, 2005–13; Hd, Immunology Sec., 2008–13. *Publications:* The Compatibility Gene, 2013; contrib. papers to scientific jls. *Recreation:* reading and collecting American super-hero comic books. *Address:* University of Manchester, CTF Building, 2nd Floor, 46 Grafton Street, Manchester M13 9NT. *T:* (0161) 275 5019. *E:* daniel.davis@manchester.ac.uk.

DAVIS, Rt Hon. David (Michael); PC 1997; MP (C) Haltemprice and Howden, 1997–June 2008 and since July 2008 (Boothferry, 1987–97); *b* 23 Dec. 1948; *s* of Ronald and Elizabeth Davis; *m* 1973, Doreen Margery Cook; one *s* two *d*. *Educ:* Warwick Univ. (BSc); London Business Sch. (MSc); Harvard (AMP). Joined Tate & Lyle, 1974: Strategic Planning Dir, 1984–87; Dir, 1987–89. PPS to Parly Under-Sec. of State, DTI, 1989–90; an Asst Govt Whip, 1990–93; Parly Sec., Office of Public Service and Science, Cabinet Office, 1993–94; Minister of State, FCO, 1994–97; Chm., Cons. Party, 2001–02; Shadow Sec. of State, ODPM, 2002–03; Shadow Home Sec., 2003–08. Chm., H of C Public Accounts Cttee, 1997–2001. Resigned seat June 2008 to contest by-election on civil liberties issue; re-elected July 2008. Non-exec. Dir, New City Agenda, 2014–. Mem., Financial Policy Cttee, CBI, 1977–79; Exec. Mem., Industrial Soc., 1985–87. Chm., Fedn of Cons. Students, 1973–74. *Recreations:* writing, flying, mountaineering. *Address:* House of Commons, SW1A 0AA.

DAVIS, Dennis Tyrone, CBE 2004 (OBE 1996); QFSM 1991; CEng, FIFireE; independent fire adviser, since 2004; HM Chief Inspector of Fire Services for Scotland, 1999–2004; *b* 10 Feb. 1947; *s* of Dennis and Winifred Davis; *m* 1968, Maureen; two *s*. *Educ:* Queen Mary's Grammar Sch., Walsall; MPhil Univ. of Central Lancs 2005. Joined Fire Bde, 1965; Walsall, 1965–71; Cheshire, 1971–99, Chief Fire Officer, 1986–99. Chm., Fire Confs and Exhibitions Ltd, 1990–2005 (Dir, 1990–2011). Chm., Fedn of British Fire Orgns, 2006–11 (Vice Chm., 2004–06); Vice Chm., Fire Sector Fedn, 2011–; Vice Pres., Internat. Assoc. Fire and Rescue Services, 2007–. FIFireE 1981 (Chm., 1988–2006; Life Fellow, 1999); CEng 1998; CCMI (CIMgt 1995). OStJ 1996. *Recreation:* old cars. *Address:* 11 Private Walk, Chester CH3 5XB.

DAVIS, Derek Alan, CEng; Director, World Energy Council Commission, 1990–93; *b* 5 Oct. 1929; *s* of Irene Davis (*née* Longstaff) and Sydney George Davis; *m* 1954, Ann Margery Willett; three *s*. *Educ:* private schools; Battersea Polytechnic; London University. BScEng (First Hons) 1950; MIMechE; CCMI. De Havilland Engine Co. Ltd: post-graduate apprentice, 1950–52; develt engineer, Gas Turbine Div., 1952–53, Rocket Div., 1953–56; Central Electricity Generating Board: Research Labs, 1956–60; Manager, Mech. and Civil Engineering, 1960–65; Group Head Fuel, 1965, System Econ. Engineer, 1970, System Planning Engineer, 1973–75, Planning Dept; Dir, Resource Planning, later Dir Production, NE Region, 1975–81; Dir Corporate Strategy Dept, 1981–84; Bd Mem., 1984–90. Member: SERC, 1989–94; Meteorology Cttee, MoD, 1986–99; ACORD, Dept of Energy, 1990–92. *Publications:* articles in tech. and engineering jls. *Recreations:* playing, now watching, sport; gardening, DIY, reading.

DAVIS, Derek Richard; Chairman, British Geological Survey, 2005–10 (Chairman, Commercialisation Strategy Group, 2009–10; Board Member, 2004); *b* 3 May 1945; *s* of late Stanley Lewis Davis, OBE and Rita Beatrice Rachel Davis (*née* Rosenheim), MBE; *m* 1987, Diana Levinson; one *s* one *d*. *Educ:* Clifton Coll., Bristol; Balliol Coll., Oxford (BA 1967; MA 2009). Asst Master, Scindia Sch., Gwalior, 1962–63. Asst Principal, BoT, 1967; Pvte Sec. to Perm. Sec., DTI, 1971–72; Principal, 1972; Asst Sec., Dept of Energy, 1977; Secretary: Energy Commn, 1977–79; NEDC Energy Task Force, 1981; seconded to NCB, 1982–83; Under Sec., Gas Div., 1985–87, Oil and Gas Div., 1987–93, Dept of Energy, subseq. DTI; Dir Gen., BNSC, 1993–99; Dir, Chemicals, Biotechnology, Consumer Goods and Posts, 1999–2002, Nuclear and Coal Liabilities, 2002–04, DTI. Member: BBSRC, 2000–02. Trustee: Nat. Space Sci. Centre, 1998–99; Royal Asiatic Soc., 2014–. *Publications:* contribs to Jl RAS, Trans Jewish Histl Soc. of England. *Address:* 6 Roman Road, Bedford Park, W4 1NA. *T:* (020) 8747 3931.

DAVIS, Lt Gen. Edward Grant Martin, CB 2014; CBE 2012 (OBE 2005; MBE 1996); Governor and Commander-in-Chief of Gibraltar, since 2016; *b* Hereford, 13 Feb. 1963; *s* of Robert and Heather Davis; *m* 1987, Lorraine Francine Ezra. *Educ:* Coleraine Academical Instn; King's Coll. London (MA Defence Studies). Joined Royal Marines, 1981; ACSC 1996; CO Commando Unit, 2002–04; Hd, Dept of Acquisition and Ops, MoD, 2005–09; HCSC 2009; Comdr 3 Commando Bde (incl. Task Force Helmand, Afghanistan), 2010–11; Comdt Gen., RM and Comdr, UK Amphibious Forces, 2011–14; Dep. Comdr Land Comd, Izmir, Turkey, 2014–15. Legion of Merit (USA), 2011. *Recreations:* gardening, enjoying the countryside.

DAVIS, Evan Harold; Presenter, Newsnight, since 2014; *b* 8 April 1962; *s* of Quintin Visser Davis and Hazel Noreen Davis. *Educ:* Ashcombe Sch., Dorking; St John's Coll., Oxford (PPE Hons 1984); Kennedy Sch. of Government, Harvard Univ. (MPA 1988). Res. Officer, Inst. for Fiscal Studies, 1984–86; Res. Fellow, London Business Sch., 1988–92; Res. Co-ordinator, Inst. for Fiscal Studies, 1992–93; Econs Correspondent, 1993–2001, Econs Ed., 2001–08, Presenter, Today prog., Radio 4, 2008–14, BBC. *Publications:* Public Spending, 1998; (jtly) Penguin Dictionary of Economics, 4th edn 1987 to 7th edn 2003; (jtly) New Penguin Dictionary of Business, 2003; Made in Britain: how the nation earns its living, 2011. *Address:* BBC News Centre, Broadcasting House, Portland Place, W1A 1AA. *E:* evan.davis@bbc.co.uk.

DAVIS, Gareth; Chairman: William Hill plc, since 2010; Wolseley plc, since 2011 (non-executive Director, since 2003); DS Smith plc, since 2012 (non-executive Director, since 2010); *b* 13 May 1950; *m* 1973, Andrea Allan; one *d* (and one *d* decd). *Educ:* Beal Grammar Sch., Ilford; Univ. of Sheffield (BA Hons Econ.). Mgt trainee, Imperial Tobacco, 1972; W. D. & H. O. Wills: Prodn Manager, Newcastle, 1973–79; Prodn Control Manager, Bristol, 1979–83; Factory Manager, Players, Nottingham, 1983–89; Mfg Dir, Imperial, 1987–95, and Man. Dir, Imperial Internat., 1988–95; CEO, Imperial Tobacco Gp plc, 1996–2010. *Recreations:* most sports, especially cricket, golf, soccer.

DAVIS, Glen Milton; QC 2011; *b* London, 11 Sept. 1956; *s* of David and June Davis; *m* 1st, 1986 (marr. diss.); 2nd, 2002, Mary Jane Aladren; two *s* two *d*. *Educ:* University Coll. Sch., Hampstead; Balliol Coll., Oxford (Goldsmith Schol.; BA 1st Cl. Hons English Lang. and Lit. 1979); City Univ., London (DipLaw 1991); London Business Sch. (Dip. Investment Mgt 1991); Inns of Court Sch. of Law (BVC 1992). CEDR Accredited Mediator, 1998; MCIArb 2011. Playwright (with Martin Bergman), Brown Rice with Everything, performed by Cambridge Footlights at Edinburgh Fest., 1979; researcher on TV prog., Police, and asst producer and studio dir, Newsnight and other progs, BBC TV, 1979–84; Brook Productions Ltd: Associate Producer, A Week in Politics, Channel 4, 1984–86; special asst to Jt Chief Execs, later Hd of Publicity and Dep. Hd of Marketing, ITV Superchannel Ltd, 1987–88. Called to the Bar: Middle Temple, 1992; Gibraltar (for specific cases); Eastern Caribbean Supreme Court (BVI), 2014; in practice at the Bar, specialising in insolvency, financial services and asset recovery, 1993–; licensed to practice in Courts of Dubai Internat. Financial Centre, 2014. Member: Users Cttee, Bankruptcy and Companies Courts (formerly Insolvency Courts), 2001–; Insolvency Rules Cttee, 2002–12; Panel of Sen. Decision Makers, Guernsey Financial Services Commn, 2014–. Society for Computers and Law: Chair, Media Bd,

2001–06; Trustee/Dir, 2002–06; Fellow, 2007. Chair, Africa Cttee, Commercial Bar Assoc., 2006–. Fellow, Assoc. of Business Recovery Professionals, 2010. *Publications:* Insolvent Partnerships, 1996; (ed) Butterworth's Insolvency Law Handbook, 4th edn 1997 to 16th edn 2014; (contrib.) Company Directors: duties, liabilities and remedies, ed Simon Mortimore, QC, 2009. *Recreations:* contemporary art, African music, football (Arsenal). *Address:* South Square, 3–4 South Square, Gray's Inn, WC1R 5HP. *T:* (020) 7696 9900, *Fax:* (020) 7696 9911. *E:* glendavis@southsquare.com. *W:* www.twitter.com/GDQC.

DAVIS, Prof. Glyn; *see* Davis, C. G.

DAVIS, Godfrey Pawle; non-executive Chairman, Mulberry Group plc, since 2012 (Chairman and Chief Executive, 2002–12); *b* Bristol, 27 Feb. 1949; *s* of late Granville Davis and of Pauline Davis; *m* 1971, Sally Ann; one *s* one *d. Educ:* Clifton Coll. FCA 1972. Arthur Andersen, 1974–88, Partner, 1986–88; Dir, Mulberry Gp plc, 1989–2012. *Recreations:* fishing, shooting, travel. *Address:* Mulberry Group plc, The Rookery, Chilcompton, Somerset BA3 4EH. *T:* (01761) 234501. *E:* godfreyd@mulberry.com.

DAVIS, Gray; *see* Davis, Joseph G.

DAVIS, Rt Hon. Helen Elizabeth; *see* Clark, Rt Hon. H. E.

DAVIS, Ian Edward Lamert; Chairman, Rolls-Royce plc, since 2013; *b* 10 March 1951; *s* of late Walter Patrick Carless Davis and Jane Davis (*née* Lamert); *m* 1st, 1977, Sally J. Fuller; one *s* one *d*; 2nd, 1994, Penny A. Thring. *Educ:* Charterhouse; Balliol Coll., Oxford (MA). Bowater, 1972–79; McKinsey & Company: Associate, 1979–85; Principal, 1985–90; Dir, 1990–2010; Man. Dir, UK, 1996–2003; Worldwide Man. Dir, 2003–09; Sen. Partner, 2009–10; Man. Dir Emeritus, 2010. Non-executive Director: BP plc, 2010–; Johnson & Johnson Inc., 2010–; Teach for All, 2010–. Non-exec. Mem. Bd, Cabinet Office, 2011–. *Recreations:* the Alps, watching cricket, golf, biographies. *Clubs:* Hurlingham, Queen's; Berkshire Golf.

See also Sir C. H. L. Davis, Rt Hon. Sir N. A. L. Davis.

DAVIS, Ian Paul, CEng; Operations Director, National House-Building Council, since 2006; *s* of George Davis and Margaret Davis; *m* 1978, Jane Fidell; two *d. Educ:* Grove Sch., Newark; Univ. of Liverpool (BEng 1976); Open Univ. (MBA 1999). CEng, MICE 1982. Site Engr, Head Wrightson Process Engrg, 1976–78; Design Engr, Simpson Coulson & Partners, 1978–80; Project Engr, Davy International, 1980–83; Regl Engr, 1983–90, Dir of Standards, 1990–94, Dep. Chief Exec., 1994–97, NHBC; Dir Gen., Fedn of Master Builders, 1997–2006. Chm., Soha Housing (formerly S Oxfordshire Housing Assoc.), 2000–03 (Dir, 1996–2005). *Address:* National House-Building Council, NHBC House, Davy Avenue, Knowl Hill, Milton Keynes MK5 8FP.

DAVIS, Ivan, OBE 2005; Member (UU) Lagan Valley, Northern Ireland Assembly, 1998–2003; *b* 16 April 1937; *s* of late James and Susan Davis; *m* 1960, Hannah Elizabeth (Betty), Murphy; three *s* one *d. Educ:* Lisburn Public Elementary Sch. Lisburn Borough Council: Mem., 1973–2002; Chairman: Police Liaison Cttee, 1977–81; Recreation and Allied Services, 1977–79, 1993–95; Housing Liaison Cttee, 1984–2002; Planning Cttee, 1987–89; Leisure Services Cttee, 1997–99; Capital Develt Cttee, 1997–99; Member: Health Cttee, 1994–96; Strategic Policy Cttee, 1997–99; Dep. Mayor of Lisburn, 1989–91, Mayor, 1991–93; Mem. (UU) Lisburn CC, 2002–10. Member: NI Assembly, 1982–86; NI Forum (Dep. Chm.), 1996–98. Northern Ireland Assembly: Dep. Whip, 1998–2002; Chief Whip, 2002; Member: Culture, Arts and Leisure Cttee; Business Cttee, 1998–2002; Cttee on Procedures, 2001–02. Member: UUP, 1987– (Mem. Exec. Cttee, 1993–99, 2000–); UU Council, 1993– (Mem., Exec. Cttee, 1993–99). Member: Sport Lisburn (formerly Lisburn Sports Adv. Council), 1989–; SE Educn and Liby Bd, 1993–95; Lisburn CAB, 1997–. Vice President: Lisburn Amateur Boxing Club, 1985–; Lisburn Swimming Club, 1989–. Freeman of Lisburn, 2010. *Address:* 29 Roseville Park, Lisburn BT27 4XT. *T:* (028) 9267 8164. *Club:* Lambeg Golf (Pres., 1998–2000).

DAVIS, James Gresham, CBE 1988; FCILT; FICS; Chairman: International Maritime Industries Forum, since 1981; British Committee, ClassNK, since 2003; *b* 20 July 1928; *s* of Col Robert Davis, OBE, JP and Josephine Davis (*née* Edwards); *m* 1973, Adriana Johanna Verhoef, Utrecht, Holland; three *d. Educ:* Bradfield Coll.; Clare Coll., Cambridge (MA). FCILT (FCIT 1969, FILT); FIEx; FInstLM (FISM 1989); FNI. Served RN, 1946–49. P&OSN Co., 1952–72: Calcutta, 1953; Kobe, Japan, 1954–56; Hong Kong, 1956–57; Director: P&O Lines, 1967–72; Kleinwort Benson Ltd, 1973–88; DFDS Ltd, 1975–97 (Chm., 1984–95; Advr, 1995–97); Pearl Cruises of Scandinavia Inc., 1982–86; Rodskog Shipbrokers (Hong Kong) Ltd, 1983–88; Associated British Ports Holdings plc, 1983–97; Transport Develt Gp plc, 1984–91; TIP Europe Plc, 1987–93 (Chm., 1990–93); Global Ocean Carriers Ltd, 1988– (Chm., 1996–); Sedgwick Energy & Marine Ltd, 1988–99; Sedgwick Gp Develt Ltd, 1991–99; Hempel Paints Ltd, 1992–2000; Tsavliris Salvage (International) Ltd, 1994–2000; 2M Invest AS (Copenhagen), 1996–2000; Catenas Ltd, 2000–02; Foresight Ltd, 2002–; Shipserve Ltd, 2002–; Chairman: Bromley Shipping, 1989–94; Trinitas Services Ltd, 1993–2006; Marine Risk Mgt Services, 1995–99; Liberia Maritime Adv. Bd, 1998–2001; Wigham Richardson Shipbrokers Ltd, 2003–08; Caterham Leasing Ltd, 2003–06; Dep. Chm., Hanjin Eurobulk Ltd, 2003–07; Member Advisory Board: J. Lauritzen A/S, Copenhagen, 1981–85; DFDS A/S, Copenhagen, 1981–85; Adviser, Tjaerborg (UK) Ltd, 1985–87. Mem. (part-time), British Transport Docks Bd, 1981–83; Chm., SITPRO, 1987–98; Dir, British Internat. Freight Assoc., 1989–; Chm., Danish-UK Chamber of Commerce, 1992–2001 (Pres., 2001–). Chairman: Friends of the World Maritime Univ., 1985–; Marine Soc., 1987–93 (Vice-Pres., 1993); Anglian Bd, BR, 1988–92; Trinitas Management Services Ltd (Trinity House), 1999–2006; Mem. Council, Missions to Seamen, subseq. Mission to Seafarers, 1981–2008 (Trustee, 2008–). President: World Ship Soc., 1969, 1971, 1984–86, 2003–08 (Vice Pres., 2008–); CIT, 1981–82; Inst. of Freight Forwarders, 1984–86; National Waterways Transport Assoc., 1986–91; Inst. of Supervisory Management, 1989–92; Inst. of Chartered Shipbrokers, 1990–92 (Vice-Pres., 1988–90); Inst. of Export, 1995–2001, 2008– (Vice Pres., 1991–95); Harwich Lifeboat, RNLI, 1984–; Vice-President: British Maritime League, 1984–88; British Maritime Charitable Foundn, 1992–; Member: Baltic Exchange, 1973–; Greenwich Forum, 1982–; Internat. and UK Cttees, Bureau Veritas, 1989–; Gen. Cttee, Lloyds Register, 1998–2006; Lloyds Register, 2008– (Trustee, Lloyds Register Hldgs, 2006–08). Trustee, Nat. Maritime Mus., 1993–98. UK Ambassador, Women's Internat. Shipping and Trading Assoc., 2008–. Lectures: Grout, CIT, 1975; Wakeford Meml, Southampton Univ., 1993; Thomas Gray Meml, RSA, 1990. FRSA 1986. Hon. FNI 1985; Hon. FIFF 1986. Hon. RSMA, 2006. Freeman, City of London, 1972; Liveryman and Mem., Court of Assts, Shipwrights' Co.; Master, World Traders' Co., 1996–97; Associate Mem., Master Mariners' Co., 1998. Younger Brother, Trinity House, 1989. Seatrade Personality of the Year, Seatrade Orgn, 2002; Lifetime Achievement Award, Lloyd's List, 2011. Knight Commander, Order of Dannebrog (Denmark), 1996. *Publications:* You and Your Ships (autobiog.), 2007. *Recreations:* golf, family, ships. *Address:* 115 Woodsford Square, W14 8DT. *T:* (020) 7602 0675; Summer Lawn, Dovercourt, Essex CO12 4EF. *T:* (01255) 502981. *Clubs:* Brooks's, Hurlingham, Golfers; Fanlingerers (Hong Kong); Harwich & Dovercourt Golf, Royal Calcutta Golf; Holland Park Lawn Tennis.

DAVIS, John; *see* Davis, A. J.

DAVIS, Prof. John Allen, MD, FRCP, FRCPCH; Professor of Paediatrics, and Fellow of Peterhouse, University of Cambridge, 1979–88, now Professor Emeritus and Fellow Emeritus; *b* 6 Aug. 1923; *s* of Major H. E. Davis, MC, and Mrs M. W. Davis; *m* 1st, 1957, Madeleine Elizabeth Vinicombe Ashlin (author with D. Wallbridge of Boundary and Space: introduction to the work of D. W. Winnicott, 1981) (*d* 1991); three *s* two *d*; 2nd, 2005, Prof. Ann-Louise Kinmonth, *qv. Educ:* Blundell's Sch., Tiverton (Scholar); St Mary's Hosp. Med. Sch. (Scholar; MB, BS 1946; London Univ. Gold Medal); MSc Manchester 1967; MA Cantab 1979, MD 1988. FRCP 1967. Army Service, BAOR, 1947–49. House Physician: St Mary's Hosp., 1947; Gt Ormond St Hosp. for Sick Children, 1950; Registrar/Sen. Registrar, St Mary's Paediatric Unit and Home Care Scheme, 1951–57; Sen. Asst Resident, Children's Med. Centre, Boston, Mass, and Harvard Teaching Fellow, 1953; Nuffield Res. Fellowship, Oxford, 1958–59; Sen. Lectr, Inst. of Child Health, and Reader, Hammersmith Hosp., 1960–67; Prof. of Paediatrics and Child Health, Victoria Univ. of Manchester, 1967–79. Second Vice Pres., RCP, 1986; Member: Assoc. of Physicians; Société française de pédiatrie; Hon. Member: BPA (former Chm., Academic Bd); Hungarian Acad. Paediatrics; Neonatal Soc.; Pres., Eur. Soc. for Pediatric Research, 1984–85; Patron: Arts for Health, 1989–; Squiggle Foundn, 1993–. Greenwood Lectr, Univ. of Exeter, 1981; Teale Lectr, RCP, 1990. Hon. FRSocMed 2006. Dawson Williams Prize, BMA, 1986; James Spence Medal, BPA, 1991; Hunterian Medal, Hunterian Soc., 1995. *Publications:* Scientific Foundations of Paediatrics (ed and contrib.), 1974 (2nd edn 1981); Place of Birth, 1978; (ed jtly) Parent-Baby Attachment in Premature Infants, 1984; Mortalia and Other Things (verse), 2003; Historiae et Fabulae (short stories), 2008; papers in various medical and scientific jls. *Recreations:* collecting and painting watercolours, gardening, reading, music. *Address:* Four Mile House, 1 Cambridge Road, Great Shelford, Cambridge CB22 5JE.

DAVIS, Sir John (Gilbert), 3rd Bt *cr* 1946; *b* 17 Aug. 1936; *s* of Sir Gilbert Davis, 2nd Bt, and of Kathleen, *d* of Sidney Deacon Ford; *S* father, 1973; *m* 1960, Elizabeth Margaret, *d* of Robert Smith Turnbull; one *s* two *d. Educ:* Oundle School; Britannia RNC, Dartmouth. RN, 1955–56. Joined Spicers Ltd, 1956; emigrated to Montreal, Canada, 1957; joined Inter City Papers and progressed through the company until becoming Pres., 1967; transf. to parent co., Abitibi-Price Inc., 1976 and held several exec. positions before retiring as Exec. Vice-Pres., 1989; co-developer, Greenfield de-inked pulp business, Château Thierry, France. *Recreations:* golf, tennis, music, reading. *Heir: s* Richard Charles Davis, *b* 11 April 1970. *Address:* 3900 Yonge Street, Apt 603, Toronto, ON M4N 3N6, Canada. *T:* (416) 2224916. *Clubs:* Donalda, Rosedale Golf (Toronto).

DAVIS, John Horsley Russell, PhD; FBA 1988; Warden of All Souls College, Oxford, 1995–2008; *b* 9 Sept. 1938; *s* of William Russell Davis and Jean (*née* Horsley); *m* 1981, Dymphna Gerarda Hermans (marr. diss. 2006); three *s. Educ:* University Coll., Oxford (BA); Univ. of London (PhD). University of Kent, 1966–90: progressively, Lectr, Sen. Lectr, Reader, Social Anthropology; Prof., 1982–90; Prof. of Social Anthropology, and Fellow of All Souls College, Univ. of Oxford, 1990–95. Chm., European Assoc. of Social Anthropologists, 1993–94; Pres., Royal Anthropological Inst., 1997–2001. *Publications:* Land and Family in Pisticci, 1973; People of the Mediterranean, 1977; Libyan Politics: tribe and revolution, 1987; Exchange, 1992; (with Scott Mandelbrote) The Warden's Punishment Book of All Souls College, Oxford, 2013. *Recreations:* gardens, music. *Address:* Beechwood House, Iffley Turn, Oxford OX4 4HW.

DAVIS, Jonathan; author, columnist and investment professional, since 1991; founder and Managing Director, Jonathan Davis & Associates, since 1991; *b* RAF Halton, Bucks, 17 Feb. 1954; *s* of Air Cdre John Frank Davis and Elaine Davis (*née* Smorthwaite); *m* 1st, 1982, Janet Prior (marr. diss.); one *s* one *d*; 2nd, 2008, Kristin van Santen. *Educ:* Winchester Coll. (Schol.); Gonville and Caius Coll., Cambridge (BA Hist. 1975; MA); Sloan Sch. of Mgt, Massachusetts Inst. of Technol. (MSc Mgt 1991). Grad. trainee, Westminster Press (editl staff, Durham Advertiser, Oxford Mail), 1975–78; City office, Sunday Telegraph, 1978–82; Energy, then Business Corresp., The Times, 1982–85; Energy Ed., The Economist, 1985–86; Dep. Business Ed., Independent, 1986–88; Hd of Public Affairs, Enterprise Oil plc, 1988–90; City Ed., The Week, 1995–98; columnist: Independent, 1995–2007; FT, 2007–. Founder, JDA Independent Investor LLP, 2006–12; Director: Genagro Services Ltd, 2008–; Smith & Williamson Investment Mgt, 2012–; non-executive Director: Hargreaves Lansdown plc, 2008–10; Jupiter Primadona Growth Trust, 2011–. MCSI. *Publications:* Learn Bridge in a Weekend, 1992; Money Makers, 1998, 2nd edn 2013; Investing with Anthony Botton, 2006, 2nd edn 2008; (with Dr S. Nairn) Templeton's Way with Money, 2012. *Recreations:* bridge, Real tennis, golf. *E:* jd@independent-investor.com. *W:* www.independent-investor.com. *Clubs:* Savile (Chm., 2002–08), Portland, Queen's; Huntercombe Golf.

DAVIS, Joseph Graham, (Gray), Jr; Counsel, Loeb & Loeb LLP, Los Angeles, since 2004; Governor of California, 1999–2003; *b* New York City, 26 Dec. 1942; *s* of Joseph G. and Doris Davis; *m* 1983, Sharon Ryer. *Educ:* Stanford Univ. (BA Hist. *cum laude*); Columbia Univ. Law Sch. (JD). Served US Army, 1967–69 (Bronze Star for Meritorious Service, Vietnam War). Chief of Staff to Gov. of Calif., Edmund G. Brown Jr, 1975–81; Mem. for Los Angeles, Calif. State Assembly, 1983–87; Controller, State of Calif., 1987–95; Lt Gov., Calif., 1995–99. Mem., Calif. State Bar, 1969–. Dist. Fellow, Sch. of Public Affairs, UCLA. *Recreations:* golf, reading.

DAVIS, Dame Karlene (Cecile), DBE 2001; General Secretary and Chief Executive, Royal College of Midwives, 1997–2008; *b* 10 Oct. 1946; *d* of late Herman Leiba and of Inez Leiba; *m* 1975, Victor Davis; one *s. Educ:* Titchfield Secondary Sch., Port Antonio, Jamaica; BEd Hons South Bank Poly. 1986; MA Inst. of Educn, London Univ. 1989. RN 1970; RM 1974; MTD 1980. SRN, 1967–70; SCM, 1973–74; Midwife Clinician, 1974–80; Midwife Tutor, Pembury Hosp., 1980–84; Sen. Midwife Teacher, Mayday Hosp., Croydon, 1984–87; Dir, Midwifery Educn, Olive Hayden Sch. of Midwifery, Guy's, St Thomas' and Lewisham Hosps, 1987–91; Regl Nurse, Midwifery Practice and Educn, SE Thames RHA, 1991–94; Dep. Gen. Sec., Royal Coll. of Midwives, 1994–97. Member: Modernisation Bd overseeing implementation of NHS plan, 2000–04; SOS Stakeholder Gp, 2005–08; Bevan Commn, 2010–. Dir, WHO Collaborating Centre for Midwifery, 1997–2008. Pres., 2005–08, Consultant, Sierra Leone, 2009–12, Internat. Confedn of Midwives. Vis. Prof. of Midwifery, London South Bank Univ., 2008–11. Non-exec. Dir, NUS, 2010–13. Consultant, Bounty, 2013. FRSocMed 1998. FRSA 2010. Hon. Fellow, London South Bank Univ., 2011. Hon. DSc: Brighton, 2001; Kingston, 2002; Greenwich, 2002; Nottingham, 2004; City, 2005; Wolverhampton, 2006; West Indies, 2008; Anglia Ruskin, 2009. *Recreations:* politics, reading political biographies, travel to experience different cultures. *T:* (020) 8239 0611.

DAVIS, Kenneth Joseph; Director of Children and Young People Services, London Borough of Bromley, 2006; *b* 19 March 1948; *s* of late Kenneth Sydney Joseph Davis and Dorothy May Davis (later Addison); *m* 1970, Susan Mary Thompson; one *s. Educ:* Mark Hall Sch., Harlow; City of Portsmouth Coll. of Education (BEd Hons 1971); Wolverhampton Poly. (DMS 1978); Inst. of Education, London Univ. (MA 1981). Computer operator, London & Manchester Assce Co., 1966–67; Asst Teacher, Brune Pk Comp. Sch., Gosport, 1971–73; Head of Physics, Darlaston Comp. Sch., Walsall, 1973–78; Professional Asst, E Sussex CC, 1978–80; Kent County Council: Asst Educn Officer, 1980–83; Divl Educn Officer, 1983–86; Area Educn Officer, 1986–89; Area Dir of Educn Services, 1989–96; Dir of Educn, 1996–2004, of Educn and Libraries, 2004–06, Bromley LBC. FCMI. *Recreations:* sailing, ski-ing. *Address:* Walmer, Deal, Kent. *Clubs:* Ski Club of Great Britain; Downs Sailing.

DAVIS, Dom Leo M.; *see* Maidlow Davis.

DAVIS, Leonard Andrew, (Leon), AO 2004; Chairman, Westpac Banking Corporation, 2000–07; *b* 3 April 1939; *s* of Leonard Harold Davis and Gladys Davis; *m* 1963, Annette Brakenridge; two *d. Educ:* S Australian Inst. of Technol. (Dip. in Primary Metallurgy). Man. Dir, Pacific Coal, 1984–89; Gp Exec., CRA Ltd, 1989–91; Mining Dir, RTZ Corp., 1991–94; Man. Dir and Chief Exec., CRA Ltd, 1994–95; Chief Operating Officer, RTZ-CRA, 1996; Chief Exec., 1997–2000, Dep. Chm., 2000–05, Rio Tinto. Dir, Codan Ltd, 2000–04. Bd Mem., Walter and Eliza Hall Inst. of Med. Res., 2001–13 (Pres., 2003–13); Gov., Ian Potter Foundn, 2007–. Hon. DSc: Curtin Univ., 1998; Qld Univ., 2004; DUniv S Australia, 2005. Centenary Medal, Australia, 2003. *Address:* Box 627 PO, East Melbourne, Vic 3002, Australia. *Clubs:* Melbourne; Melbourne Cricket.

DAVIS, Prof. Mark Herbert Ainsworth; Professor of Mathematics, Imperial College London, 2000–09 and 2011–12, now Emeritus; *b* 1 May 1945; *s* of Christopher A. Davis and Frances E. Davis (*née* Marsden); *m* 1988, Jessica I. C. Smith. *Educ:* Oundle Sch.; Clare College, Cambridge (BA 1966, MA 1970, ScD 1983); Univ. of California, Berkeley (PhD 1971). FSS 1985; FIMS 1994. Research Asst, Electronics Res. Lab., Univ. of California, Berkeley, 1969–71; Lectr, 1971–79, Reader, 1979–84, Prof. of System Theory, 1984–95, Imperial College, London; Hd of Res. and Product Develt, Tokyo-Mitsubishi Internat., 1995–99. Visiting appointments: Polish Acad. of Sciences, 1973; Harvard, 1974; MIT, 1978; Washington Univ., St Louis, 1979; ETH Zurich, 1984; Oslo Univ., 1991; Technical Univ., Vienna, 2000. Hon. FIA 2001. Editor, Stochastics and Stochastics Reports, 1978–95; Founding Co-Editor, Mathematical Finance, 1990–93. *Publications:* Linear Estimation and Stochastic Control, 1977, Russian edn 1984; (with R. B. Vinter) Stochastic Modelling and Control, 1985; Markov Models and Optimization, 1993; (with A. Etheridge) Louis Bachelier's Theory of Speculation: the origins of modern finance, 2006; (with S. Lleo) Risk-Sensitive Investment Management, 2014; jl articles on stochastic analysis, control theory, maths of finance. *Recreation:* classical music (violin and viola). *Address:* 11 Chartfield Avenue, SW15 6DT. *T:* (020) 8789 7677; Department of Mathematics, Imperial College London, SW7 2AZ. *T:* (020) 7594 8486.

DAVIS, Brig. Sir Miles Garth H.; *see* Hunt-Davis.

DAVIS, Rt Hon. Sir Nigel (Anthony Lamert), Kt 2001; PC 2011; **Rt Hon. Lord Justice Davis;** a Lord Justice of Appeal, since 2011; *b* 10 March 1951; *s* of late Walter Patrick Carless Davis and Jane (*née* Lamert); *m* 1st, 1977, Sheila Ann Gillies Nickel (marr. diss. 1992); three *d*; 2nd, 2001, Emma Douglas. *Educ:* Charterhouse; University Coll., Oxford (BA 1973; MA 1983). Called to the Bar, Lincoln's Inn, 1975 (Hardwicke Schol., Kennedy Schol.; Bencher, 2000). Jun. Counsel to Crown (Chancery), 1985–92; QC 1992; an Asst Recorder, 1995–98; a Recorder, 1998–2001; a Judge of the High Court, QBD, 2001–11; a Presiding Judge of Wales (formerly Wales and Chester) Circuit, 2006–09; Vice-Pres., QBD, 2014–. Counsel to inquiry of Bd of Banking Supervision into collapse of Barings Bank, 1995. *Address:* Royal Courts of Justice, Strand, WC2A 2LL. *Clubs:* MCC; Vincent's (Oxford).

See also Sir C. H. L. Davis, I. E. L. Davis.

DAVIS, Nira Y.; *see* Yuval-Davis, N.

DAVIS, Peter Anthony; Director General, National Lottery, 1993–98; *b* 10 Oct. 1941; *s* of late Stanley H. S. Davis and Betty H. Davis (*née* Back); *m* 1971, Vanessa C. E. Beale; two *s*. *Educ:* Winchester Coll.; Lincoln Coll., Oxford (MA Law). CA 1967. With Price Waterhouse, 1963–80, Gen. Audit Partner, 1974–80; Exec. Dep. Chm., Harris Queensway PLC, 1980–87; Sturge Holdings PLC: Gp Finance Dir, 1988–93; Dep. Chm., 1991–93; Abbey National PLC: non-exec. Dir, 1982–94; Dep. Chm., 1988–94; Chm., Audit Cttee, 1988–93, and Scottish Adv. Bd, 1989–92. Non-executive Director: Horne Bros, 1984–87; Symphony Gp, 1984–87; Avis Europe, 1987–89; Provident Financial, 1994–2000; Proned Holdings, 1992–94; Equitable Life Assurance Soc., 1995–2001; Boosey & Hawkes, 1998–2003; non-exec. Chm., Ascent Gp, 2001–. Institute of Chartered Accountants in England and Wales: Council Mem., 1989–95; Chm., Bd for Chartered Accountants in Business, 1991–94; Mem., Senate, 1989–99. MInstD 1993. *Recreations:* fishing, football, theatre. *Address:* 29 Arthur Road, SW19 7DN. *Club:* Hurlingham.

DAVIS, Sir Peter (John), Kt 1997; Chairman, Marie Curie Cancer Care, 2006–11, now Life Vice President; *b* 23 Dec. 1941; *s* of John Stephen Davis and Adriaantje de Baat; *m* 1968, Susan Hillman; two *s* one *d*. *Educ:* Shrewsbury Sch.; Grad. Inst. of Marketing (Drexler Travelling Schol., 1961). Management trainee and sales, Ditchburn Orgn, 1959–65; marketing and sales posts, General Foods Ltd, Banbury, 1965–72; Fitch Lovell Ltd, 1973–76: Marketing Dir, Key Markets; Man. Dir, Key Markets and David Greig; J. Sainsbury, 1976–86: Marketing Dir, 1977; Asst Man. Dir, 1979; Dep. Chief Exec., 1986, Chief Exec., 1986–92, Chm., 1990–94, Reed Internat.; Chief Exec., 1993, Chm., 1993–94, Reed Elsevier; Gp Chief Exec., Prudential Corp., 1995–2000; Chief Exec., 2000–04, Chm., 2004, J. Sainsbury plc. Director: Boots Co. PLC, 1991–2000; UBS AG, 2001–07; Mem., Adv. Bd, Permira Advisers Ltd, 2005–09; non-exec. Dir, Kind Consumer Ltd (Strategic Advr, 2009); Investment Partner, Vestra Wealth LLP, 2008–. Chairman: Basic Skills Agency (formerly Adult Literacy and Basic Skills Unit), 1989–97; Nat. Adv. Council for Educn and Training Targets, 1993–97; BITC, 1997–2002 (Dep. Chm., 1991–97); Welfare to Work New Deal Task Force, 1997–2000. Vice Pres., Chartered Inst. of Marketing, 1991–2010. Dir, Royal Opera House, 1999–2005 (Trustee, 1994–2005); Trustee, V&A Mus., 1994–97; Chm., Internat. Adv. Bd, 2011–, Mem. Bd, 2013–, WNO. Mem. Council, Bangor Univ., 2007– (Dep. Chm., 2012–; Vice-Pres., then Pro-Chancellor, 2007–12). Governor: Duncombe Sch., Hertford, 1976–2005; Queenswood Sch., 1993–95. FRSA. Hon. LLD Exon, 2000. Gold Medal, BIM, 2003. *Recreations:* sailing, reading, opera, wine. *Clubs:* Royal Thames Yacht; Trearddur Bay Sailing (Cdre, 1982–84).

See also C. V. Gipps.

DAVIS, Peter John; Director, Applied Economics Ltd, since 2004; Executive Vice President, Compass Lexecon, since 2013 (Senior Vice President, 2011–13); *b* Lincoln, 4 Aug. 1970; *s* of John and Joyce Davis; *m* 2006, Lara Sevanot; two *s* one *d*. *Educ:* London Sch. of Econs (BSc Stats); St Peter's Coll., Oxford (MPhil Econs); Yale Univ. (PhD Econs 1999). Asst Prof. of Applied Econs, MIT, 1998–2002; Leverhulme Lectr in Econs, LSE, 2002–06. Dep. Chm., Competition Commn, 2006–11. Vis. Prof., Faculty of Laws, UCL, 2012–. Pres., Assoc. of Competition Economists, 2009–11. *Publications:* Quantitative Techniques for Competition and Antitrust Analysis, 2010; contrib. articles to Jl Econometrics, Rand Jl Econs, Eur. Econ. Rev., Jl Industrial Econs, Jl Law and Econs, Internat. Jl Industrial Econs, Agricl Econs, Econ. Jl, Scandinavian Jl of Econs, Eur. Competition Law Rev., Concurrences. *Recreations:* keeping up with three young children, piano, French. *E:* peter_john_davis@yahoo.com.

DAVIS, Philip Michael; consumer representative and public interest adjudicator; *b* 15 May 1954; *o s* of late Ronald Davis and of Joan Davis; *m* 1977, Susan Jean Wolton; one *s* two *d*. *Educ:* Holly Lodge High Sch.; Southampton Univ. (BA Jt Hons Mod. Hist./Politics); Warwick Univ. (Master Ind. Relns). Full-time Officer, GMB, 1979–2000. Member (Lab): Wrekin DC, 1979–97 (Chm., Planning and Envmt Cttee, 1991–97); Telford and Wrekin Council, 1997–2006 (Leader, 2000–04); Birmingham CC, 2012– (City Heritage Lead and Chm., Heritage Strategy Gp, 2012–; Chm., Trusts and Charities Cttee, 2014–). Mem., Nat. Exec., Assoc. of Labour Councillors, 2013–. Chm., W Midlands Regl Assembly, 2001–03; Sen. Vice-Chm., W Midlands LGA, 2003–05 (Vice-Chm., 2000–01); Mem., LGA Regeneration Bd, 2004–06. Chairman: W Midlands Low Pay Unit, 1989–2000; W Midlands Regl Mus Council, 1995–2000; Midlands Rail Passengers' Cttee, 1999–2005; Campaign for English Regions, 2003–; Founder Chair, TravelWatch Midlands West, 2005–07; Mem., Nat. Rail Passengers' Council, 1999–2010 (Mem., Passenger Focus Bd, 2005–10); Public Mem., Network Rail, 2002–06; Network Dir, Regl Action W Midlands, 2006–07; Mem. Bd, Commn for Integrated Transport, 2007–10. Chair: NHS S Birmingham Community Health Pilot, 2008–10; Birmingham Community Healthcare NHS Trust, 2010–11. Non-exec. Dir, Birmingham Jewellery Quarter Develt Trust, 2011–. Lay Mem., Employment Tribunal, 2000–. Comr, English Heritage, 1999–2002. Pres., Eurotowns, 2001–04. Founder Chm., UK World Heritage Forum, 1995–2005 (Hon. Pres., 2005–07); Trustee, Ironbridge Mus. Trust, 1982– (Mem. Bd, 1982–2005). Contested (Lab): Ludlow, 1983; W Midlands, EP, 1999. *Address:* Islington Gates, Fleet Street, Birmingham B3 1JH.

DAVIS, Richard Cuthbert Tolley M., (Dom Leo M.); *see* Maidlow Davis.

DAVIS, Maj. Gen. Richard Roderick, CB 2015; CBE 2004 (MBE 1996); Managing Director, Nant Enterprises Ltd, since 2015; *b* Hampshire, 2 Aug. 1962; *s* of Peter and Cynthia Davis; *m* 1985, Martina Stewart; two *s*. *Educ:* Bloxham Sch.; RMCS Shrivenham (BSc Civil Engrg 1983); Cranfield Univ. (MSc Defence Technol. 2004). Joined Army, 1983; Staff Coll., 1993–94; OC 51 Field Sqn, 1995–96; DCOS 1 Mech. Bde, 1997–99; Instructor, RMCS Shrivenham, 1999–2001; CO, 22 Engr Regt, 2001–04; Comdr, UK Provincial Reconstruction Team, Mazar-e-Sharif, 2004; Col Strategy, HQ Army Recruiting and Trng Agency, 2004–05; Chief Engr, HQ ARRC, 2005–07; Dir Plans, Land Forces, 2007–09; COS Regl Comd (South), 2009–10; Dir Gen. Army Recruiting and Trng, 2011–13; Dir Gen. Personnel, Army HQ, 2013–14. Chairman: RE Mus., 2012–; RE Officers' Widows Soc., 2012–; Army Sports Control Bd, 2013–14; Vice Pres., Army Winter Sports Assoc., 2013–14. FCMI. Hon. Col, Royal Monmouthshire RE (Militia), 2014–. QCVS 2000, 2003, 2007, 2011. Bronze Star (USA), 2010. *Recreations:* mountaineering, mountain biking, cycling, ski-ing, following my sons up rock climbs.

DAVIS, (Richard) Simon; His Honour Judge Simon Davis; a Circuit Judge, since 2004; *b* 29 July 1956; *s* of Peter Richard Davis and Evelyn Davis; *m* 1980, Caroline Jane Neal; two *s* one *d*. *Educ:* Wellington Sch., Somerset; Univ. of Leicester (LLB Hons). Called to the Bar, Inner Temple, 1978, Bencher, 2007; a Recorder, 1998–2004. Judicial Mem., Parole Bd, 2009–; Jt Course Dir, Judicial Coll. Criminal Induction Course, 2013–14. Freeman, Haberdashers' Co., 2010 (Liveryman, 2013). *Recreations:* sport, theatre, travel. *Address:* Isleworth Crown Court, 36 Ridgeway Road, Isleworth TW7 5LP. *T:* (020) 8380 4500. *Clubs:* Roehampton; Rye Golf.

DAVIS, Robert Jonathan, MBE 2015; DL; Partner, Freeman Box Solicitors, since 1985; Deputy Leader, Westminster City Council, since 2008; *b* London, 27 Sept. 1957; *s* of late Gerald and Pamela Davis; civil partnership 2007, Sir Simon Henry Milton (*d* 2011). *Educ:* Brooklands Primary Sch., Finchley; Christ's Coll., Finchley; Gonville and Caius Coll., Cambridge (MA 1982); Wolfson Coll., Cambridge; Coll. of Law, London. Research Assistant: to Rt Hon. Peter Walker, MP, 1977–79; to John Watson, MP, 1979–80; admitted solicitor, 1983; Asst Solicitor, Freeman Box Solicitors, 1983–85. Westminster City Council: Mem. (C), 1982–; Chairman: Traffic and Works Cttee, 1987–90; Envmt Cttee, 1990–93; Planning and Transportation Cttee, 1993–95; Planning Sub-Cttee, 2000–; Customer Services Cttee, 2000–01; Gen. Purposes Cttee, 2000–08; Leader of Opposition, Parking Cttee for London, 1994–95; Cabinet Member: for Customer Services, 2001–06; for Planning, 2006–08; for Built Envmt, 2008–; Chief Whip, 2000–08; Lord Mayor of Westminster, 1996–97; Lord Mayor of Westminster Locum Tenens, 2003–. Chm., Regent's Park (formerly New Shakespeare) Theatre Ltd, 2009– (Dir, 1986–); Director: Soho Theatre Ltd, 1986–2004; Film and Video Develt Agency, 1992–93; London Film Commn, 1997–2002. Chm., Amusement Arcade Action Gp, 1983–96. Chm., Cambridge Univ. Tory Reform Gp, 1977–78; Nat. Sec., Tory Reform Gp, 1979–82. Exec. Producer and creator, West End Live, 2005–; Chief Curator, City of Westminster City of Sculpture Fest., 2010–; Chm., Westminster Partnership Public Realm Bd, 2013–. Chm., London Mayors' Assoc., 1998–. Pres., Westminster Guild Lectrs' Assoc., 2008–. Trustee: Savoy Educnl Trust, 2000–; Heritage of London Trust, 2005–14 (Vice Pres., 2014–); Founding Trustee, Sir Simon Milton Foundn, 2013–. Dir, Mousetrap Foundn for the Arts, 2011–. Internat. Goodwill Ambassador, London Parade, 1997–. Freeman: City of London, 1991; Watermen and Lightermen's Co., 1997; Liveryman, Fan Makers' Co., 1997. Mem., Guild of Freemen of City of London, 1993–. DL Gtr London, 2006. Cons. Councillor of the Year, Asian Voice, 2014. *Publications:* The Law of Amusement Arcades, 1979; Civic Ceremonial for Mayors of the London Boroughs, 2009. *Recreations:* the theatre, collecting miniature mayors. *Address:* 8 Bentinck Street, W1U 2BJ. *T:* (020) 7486 9041, *Fax:* (020) 7224 1336. *E:* rjd432@aol.com.

DAVIS, Air Vice-Marshal Robert Leslie, CB 1984; RAF, retired 1983; *b* 22 March 1930; *s* of Sidney and Florence Davis; *m* 1956, Diana, *d* of Edward William Bryant; one *s* one *d*. *Educ:* Wolsingham Grammar Sch., Co. Durham; Bede Collegiate Sch., Sunderland, Co. Durham; RAF Coll., Cranwell. Commnd, 1952; served fighter units, exchange posting, USAF, Staff Coll., OR and Ops appts, MoD, DS Staff Coll., 1953–69; comd No 19 Sqdn, 1970–72; Dep. Dir Ops Air Defence, MoD, 1972–75; comd RAF Leuchars, 1975–77; Comdr RAF Staff, and Air Attaché, British Defence Staff, Washington, DC, 1977–80; Comdr, British Forces Cyprus, and Administrator, Sovereign Base Areas, Cyprus, 1980–83, retired. Man. Dir, Bodenseewerk Geratetechnik/British Aerospace GmbH, 1983–86, retd. Chm. Durham Br., SSAFA Forces Help, 1993–2002. *Recreations:* golf, antiques, music. *Address:* High Garth Farm, Witton-le-Wear, Bishop Auckland, Co. Durham DL14 0BL.

DAVIS, Prof. Roger John, PhD; FRS 2002; Professor of Molecular Medicine and H. Arthur Smith Professor of Cancer Research, University of Massachusetts Medical School; Investigator, Howard Hughes Medical Institute, since 1990. *Educ:* Queens' Coll., Cambridge (BA 1979; MPhil Biochem.; PhD 1983). Damon Runyon-Walter Winchell Cancer Fund Fellow, Dept of Biochem. and Molecular Biol., Univ. of Massachusetts Med. Sch. Fellow, Amer. Acad. Microbiol. 2012. Steven C. Beering Award, Indiana Univ., 2013. *Address:* Program in Molecular Medicine, University of Massachusetts Medical School, 373 Plantation Street, Suite 309, Worcester, MA 01605, USA.

DAVIS, Simon; *see* Davis, R. S.

DAVIS, Prof. Stanley Stewart, CChem, FRSC; Lord Trent Professor of Pharmacy, Nottingham University, 1975–2003, now Emeritus Professor; *b* 17 Dec. 1942; *s* of William Stanley and Joan Davis; *m* 1984, Lisbeth Illum; three *s*. *Educ:* Warwick Sch.; London Univ. (BPharm, PhD, DSc). FRPharmS. Lecturer, London Univ., 1966–70; Sen. Lectr, Aston Univ., 1970–75. Fulbright Scholar, Univ. of Kansas, 1967–68; various periods as visiting scientist to pharmaceutical industry. Founder: Danbiosyst (UK) Ltd; Pharmaceutical Profiles Ltd. Mem., Medicines Commn, 1994–97. *Publications:* (co-ed) Radionuclide Imaging in Drug Research, 1982; (co-ed) Microspheres and Drug Therapy, 1984; (co-ed) Site Specific Drug Delivery, 1986; (co-ed) Polymers in Controlled Drug Delivery, 1988; (co-ed) Drug Delivery to the Gastrointestinal Tract, 1989; (co-ed) Pharmaceutical Application of Cell and Tissue Culture to Drug Transport, 1991; ed jtly over 700 research pubns in various scientific jls. *Recreations:* ski-ing, horse riding, painting, travel. *Address:* 19 Cavendish Crescent North, The Park, Nottingham NG7 1BA. *T:* (0115) 948 1866.

DAVIS, Steve, OBE 2000 (MBE 1988); snooker player and commentator; *b* 22 Aug. 1957; *s* of Harry George Davis and Jean Catherine Davis; *m* 1990, Judy Greig; two *s*. *Educ:* Alexander McLeod Primary School and Abbey Wood School, London. Became professional snooker player, 1978; has won numerous championships in UK and abroad; major titles include: UK Professional Champion, 1980, 1981, 1984, 1985, 1986, 1987; Masters Champion, 1981, 1982,

1988, 1997; International Champion, 1981, 1983, 1984, 1987, 1988, 1989; World Professional Champion, 1981, 1983, 1984, 1987, 1988, 1989. BBC Sports Personality of the Year, 1988. Mem. Bd, World Professional Billiards and Snooker Assoc., 1993–. *Publications:* Steve Davis, World Champion, 1981; Frame and Fortune, 1982; Successful Snooker, 1982; How to be Really Interesting, 1988. *Recreations:* chess, keep fit, listening to records (jazz/soul), Tom Sharpe books. *Address:* Mascalls, Mascalls Lane, Brentwood, Essex CM14 5LJ. *T:* (01277) 359900. *Club:* Matchroom (Romford).

DAVIS, Susan; *see* Gubbay, S.

DAVIS, Rt Hon. Terence Anthony Gordon, (Terry), CMG 2010; PC 1999; Secretary General, Council of Europe, 2004–09; *b* 5 Jan. 1938; *s* of Gordon Davis and Gladys (*née* Avery), Stourbridge, West Midlands; *m* 1963, Anne, *d* of F. B. Cooper, Newton-le-Willows, Lancs; one *s* one *d*. *Educ:* King Edward VI Grammar Sch., Stourbridge, Worcestershire; University Coll. London (LLB; Fellow 2007); Univ. of Michigan, USA (MBA). Company Executive, 1962–71. Motor Industry Manager, 1974–79. Joined Labour Party, 1965; contested (Lab): Bromsgrove, 1970, Feb. and Oct. 1974; Birmingham, Stechford, March 1977. MP (Lab): Bromsgrove, May 1971–Feb. 1974; Birmingham, Stechford, 1979–83; Birmingham, Hodge Hill, 1983–2004. Opposition Whip, 1979–80; opposition spokesman: on the health service and social services, 1980–83; on Treasury and economic affairs, 1983–86; on industry, 1986–87. Member: Public Accounts Cttee, 1987–94; Adv. Council on Public Records, 1989–94. Chm., Birmingham Lab. MPs, 1992–97. Leader: British delegn to WEU Assembly, 1997–2002 (Mem., 1992–2004; Leader, Lab. delegn, 1995–97; Pres., Socialist Gp, 1996–99; Vice Pres. Assembly, 1997–2001); British delegn to Council of Europe Assembly, 1997–2002 (Mem., 1992–2004; Leader, Labour delegn, 1995–97; Chairman: Econ. Affairs and Develt Cttee, 1995–98; Pol Affairs Cttee, 2000–02; Vice Pres. Assembly, 1997–2002; Pres., Socialist Gp, 2002–04); British Delegn to OSCE Assembly, 2002–04 (Mem., 1997–2004). Mem., MSF. Member, Yeovil Rural District Council, 1967–68. *Address:* Hermitage, The Green, Adderbury, Oxon OX17 3ND. *T:* (01295) 810813. *E:* rthonterrydavis@gmail.com.

DAVIS, Trevor Fraser C.; *see* Campbell Davis.

DAVIS, William; author, publisher, and columnist; Chairman: Abingdon Media Services Ltd, since 1980; Headway Publishing, 1999–2004; *b* 6 March 1933; *m* 1967, Sylvette Jouclas. *Educ:* City of London Coll. On staff of Financial Times, 1954–59; Editor, Investor's Guide, 1959–60; City Editor, Evening Standard, 1960–65 (with one year's break as City Editor, Sunday Express); Financial Editor, The Guardian, 1965–68; Editor, Punch, 1968–77; Editor-in-Chief: High Life, 1973–97; Financial Weekly, 1977–80. Presenter: Money Programme, BBC TV, 1967–69; World at One, BBC Radio, 1972–79. Chairman: Headway Publications, 1977–90; BTA, 1990–93; English Tourist Bd, 1990–93; Allied Leisure, 1993–94; Premier Magazines, 1992–99; Director: Fleet Publishing International, Morgan-Grampian, and Fleet Holdings, 1977–80; Thomas Cook, 1988–98; British Invisibles, 1990–93. Editor and Publr, Private Patient, 2000–02. Mem., Develt Council, Royal Nat. Theatre, 1990–92. Knight, Order of Merit of Italian Republic. *Publications:* Three Years Hard Labour: the road to devaluation, 1968; Merger Mania, 1970; Money Talks, 1972; Have Expenses, Will Travel, 1975; It's No Sin to be Rich, 1976; (ed) The Best of Everything, 1980; Money in the 1980s, 1981; The Rich: a study of the species, 1982; Fantasy: a practical guide to escapism, 1984; The Corporate Infighter's Handbook, 1984; (ed) The World's Best Business Hotels, 1985; The Supersalesman's Handbook, 1986; The Innovators, 1987; Children of the Rich, 1989; The Lucky Generation: a positive view of the 21st century, 1995; Great Myths of Business, 1997; Business Life: Wit and Wisdom, a treasury of international quotations, 1998; The Alien: an autobiography, 2003, 2nd edn 2012; How to be British, 2005; The Rich: a new study of the species, 2006; Caviar Dogs, 2008; The Luck Factor, 2012; (ed) Wit and Humour series, 2015. *Recreations:* pétanque, swimming, lunch. *E:* sylvetteandbill@aol.com. *Club:* Garrick.

DAVIS, Hon. Sir William (Easthope), Kt 2014; **Hon. Mr Justice Davis;** a Judge of the High Court of Justice, Queen's Bench Division, since 2014; Presiding Judge, Northern Circuit, from Jan. 2016; *b* 20 June 1954; *s* of Prof. Ralph Davis, FBA and Dorothy Davis (*née* Easthope); *m* 1990, Susan Virginia Smith; one *s* one *d*. *Educ:* Wyggeston Boys' Sch., Leicester; Queen Mary Coll., London (LLB 1974). Called to the Bar, Inner Temple, 1975, Bencher, 2007; Recorder, 1995–2008; QC 1998; a Circuit Judge, 2008–14; a Sen. Circuit Judge and Resident Judge, Birmingham Crown Court, 2009–14. Judicial Lead for Youth Justice in England in Wales, 2014–. Mem., Sentencing Council, 2012–15. Dir of Trng, Judicial Coll., 2014–. *Recreations:* Rosie and Ralph, writing and performing in sketches, wine. *Address:* Royal Courts of Justice, Strand, WC2A 2LL.

DAVIS, Hon. William Grenville; PC (Can.) 1982; CC (Canada) 1986; QC (Can.); barrister and solicitor; Counsel to Davis Webb LLP, Ontario, since 2010; Member of the Provincial Parliament, Ontario, 1959–85; Premier of Ontario, Canada, and President of the Council, Ontario, 1971–85; Leader, Progressive Conservative Party, 1971–85; *b* Brampton, Ont, 30 July 1929; *s* of Albert Grenville Davis and Vera M. Davis (*née* Hewetson); *m* 1st, 1953, Helen MacPhee (*d* 1962), *d* of Neil MacPhee, Windsor, Ontario; 2nd, 1963, Kathleen Louise, *d* of Dr R. P. Mackay, California; two *s* three *d*. *Educ:* Brampton High Sch.; University Coll., Univ. of Toronto (BA); Osgoode Hall Law Sch. (grad. 1955). Called to Bar of Ontario, 1955; practised gen. law, Brampton, 1955–59. Elected Mem. (C) Provincial Parlt (MPP) for Peel Riding, 1959, 1963, Peel North Riding, 1967, 1971, Brampton Riding, 1975, 1977, 1981. Minister of Educn, 1962–71; also Minister of Univ. Affairs, 1964–71; Special Envoy on Acid Rain, apptd by Prime Minister of Canada, 1985–86. Counsel, Torys LLP, 1985–2010. Director: First American Title Insurance Co.; Magellan Aerospace Corp.; BPO Properties Ltd; First American Financial Corp.; Home Capital Gp Inc. A Freemason. Chevalier, Légion d'Honneur. Holds hon. doctorates in Law from eight Ontario Univs: Waterloo Lutheran, W Ontario, Toronto, McMaster, Queen's, Windsor; Hon. Graduate: Albert Einstein Coll. of Med.; Yeshiva Univ. of NY; NUI; Ottawa; Tel Aviv. Amer. Transit Assoc. Man of the Year, 1973. *Publications:* Education in Ontario, 1965; The Government of Ontario and the Universities of the Province (Frank Gerstein Lectures, York Univ.), 1966; Building an Educated Society 1816–1966, 1966; Education for New Times, 1967. *Address:* 61 Main Street South, Brampton, ON L6Y 1M9, Canada; Davis Webb LLP, 24 Queen Street East, Suite 800, Brampton, ON L6V 1A4, Canada. *Clubs:* Kiwanis, Shriners, Masons, Albany (Ont.).

DAVIS, William Herbert, BSc; CEng, FIMechE; former executive with BL and Land Rover Ltd, retired 1983; *b* 27 July 1919; *s* of William and Dora Davis; *m* 1945, Barbara Mary Joan (*née* Sommerfield); one *d*. *Educ:* Waverley Grammar Sch.; Univ. of Aston in Birmingham (BSc). Army Service, France, Belgium, Egypt, Libya, Iraq, Cyprus and Italy, 1939–46. Austin Motor Co.: Engr Apprentice, 1935–39; Mech. Engr and Section Leader, Works Engrs, 1946–51; Supt Engr, 1951; Asst Production Manager, 1954; Production Manager, 1956; Dir and Gen. Works Manager, 1958. British Motor Corp. Ltd: Dir of Production, 1960; Dep. Managing Dir (Manufacture and Supply), 1961; Dep. Managing Dir, British Leyland (Austin-Morris Ltd), 1968; Chairman and Chief Executive, Triumph Motor Co. Ltd, 1969; Managing Dir, Rover Triumph BLUK Ltd, 1972; Dir (Manufacture), British Leyland Motor Corporation, 1973; Dir, Military Contracts and Govt Affairs, Leyland Cars, 1976–81; Consultant, BL and Land Rover Ltd, 1981–83; Dir, Land Rover Santana (Spain), 1976–83. Member: Engrg ITB, 1976–81; CBI Regl Council, 1978–83. Gov., Solihull Coll. of Technol., 1978–87. FIIM, SME(USA). Silver Jubilee Medal, 1977. *Recreations:* motoring, photography; interests in amateur boxing. *Address:* The Courtyard House, Marley, South Brent, Devon TQ10 9JX.

DAVIS-GOFF, Sir Robert William; *see* Goff.

DAVIS SMITH, Dr Justin, CBE 2011; Executive Director for Volunteering, National Council for Voluntary Organisations, since 2013; *b* Ilford, Essex, 3 Aug. 1961; *s* of Christopher and Barbara Smith; *m* 1986, Julia Davis. *Educ:* Ashlyns Sch., Berkhamsted; Loughborough Univ. (BA 1st Cl. Hons Modern Social Hist. 1982; PhD 1986). Pol Asst to Rt Hon. Sir James Callaghan, MP, 1986–87; Hd of Res., Nat. Centre for Volunteering, 1988–97; Founding Dir, Inst. for Volunteering Res., 1997–2008; Chief Exec., Volunteering England, 2008–13. Vis. Prof., Birkbeck, Univ. of London, 2005–13. Mem., Russell Commn on Youth Volunteering, 2004–05. Mem., ESRC, 2011–14. Chair, Nationwide Foundn, 2005–08. Assessor, Queen's Anniversary Awards Cttee for Further and Higher Educn, 2005–; Mem., Queen's Awards for Voluntary Service Cttee, 2005–. Chair, Volunteering Adv. Gp, Canal and River Trust, 2012–; Mem., Adv. Cttee, Step up to Serve, 2013–; Trustee: v (youth volunteering charity), 2005–09; Join-In Trust, 2012–; Watford FC Community, Sport and Educn Trust, 2013–. *Publications:* The Attlee and Churchill Administrations and Industrial Unrest, 1945–55, 1991; (ed jtly) Volunteering and Society: principles and practice, 1992; (ed jtly) An Introduction to the Voluntary Sector, 1994; (ed jtly) Volunteering and the Test of Time, 2007. *Recreations:* football, cricket, reading, walking, supporting Watford Football Club. *Address:* National Council for Voluntary Organisations, Society Building, 9 All Saints Street, N1 9RL. *T:* (020) 7520 2430. *E:* justin.davis-smith@ncvo.org.uk.

DAVIS-WHITE, Malcolm; QC 2003; a Recorder, since 2009; a Deputy Judge of the High Court, Chancery Division, since 2013; *b* 18 Sept. 1960; *m* 1989, Sarah O'Hara; two *s* one *d*. *Educ:* Hertford Coll., Oxford (BCL; MA). Called to the Bar, Middle Temple, 1984; Bencher, Lincoln's Inn, 2009; JC to the Crown (A Panel), 1994. Vice Chm., 2008–10, Chm., 2010–12, Chancery Bar Assoc. Mem., Panel of Sen. Decision Makers, Guernsey Financial Services Commn, 2014–. *Publications:* (with Adrian Walters) Directors' Disqualification and Bankruptcy Restrictions: law and practice, 1999, 3rd edn 2010; (contrib.) Atkin's Court Forms, vol. 9 Companies General, 1999, 2004, 2009, vol. 9 (2)-(4) Companies (Insolvency), 2000, 2006; (with Sandra Frisby) Kerr & Hunter on Receivers and Administrators, 19th edn, 2009. *Recreations:* walking, gardening, sailing, opera. *Address:* 24 Old Buildings, Lincoln's Inn, WC2A 3UP. *T:* (020) 7691 2424. *E:* mdw@xxiv.co.uk.

DAVISON, Prof. Alan, PhD; FRS 2000; Professor of Inorganic Chemistry, Massachusetts Institute of Technology, 1974–2005, now Emeritus; *b* 24 March 1936. *Educ:* UC, Swansea (BSc 1959); Imperial Coll. (PhD 1962; DIC). Lectr in Chemistry, Harvard Univ., 1962–64; Asst Prof., 1964–67, Associate Prof., 1967–74, MIT. Alfred P. Sloan Foundn Fellow, 1967–69. Amer. Chem. Soc. Award, 2006. *Publications:* articles in learned jls. *Address:* Department of Chemistry, Massachusetts Institute of Technology, 77 Massachusetts Avenue, Cambridge, MA 02139–4307, USA.

DAVISON, Alan John, EdD; Headteacher, Dame Alice Owen's School, since 2005; *b* 9 April 1956; *s* of Sydney and Margaret Davison; *m* 2002, Prof. Kholoud Porter; one *s* one *d*, and two step *s*. *Educ:* Durham Inst. of Educn (Cert Ed 1977); Univ. of Leicester (MBA 1994; EdD 1998). Headteacher: Notley High Sch., 1993–97; Mill Hill County High Sch., 1997–2003; Strategic Dir, London Leadership Strategy, London Challenge, 2003–05. Lectr (pt-time), Univ. of Leicester, 1999–2002. Advisor to Department for Education and Skills: Educn Action Zones, 1999; Teacher Threshold, 2000–02; Transforming Sch. Workforce Pathfinder Proj., 2002–04. *Publications:* (contrib.) Raising Boys' Achievement in Schools, 1998. *Recreations:* ski-ing, theatre, cinema, travel. *Address:* Dame Alice Owen's School, Dugdale Hill Lane, Potters Bar, Herts EN6 2DU. *E:* head@damealiceowens.herts.sch.uk.

DAVISON, Andrew Michael; a District Judge (Magistrates' Courts), since 2011; *b* Leeds, 26 July 1956; *s* of Charles Raymond Davison and Prudence Mary Davison; *m* 1977, Carol Ann Johnson; one *s* one *d*. *Educ:* Prince Henry's Grammar Sch., Otley; Bristol Poly. (DipLaw for Magistrates' Court Clerks with Dist. 1979); Manchester Metropolitan Univ. (CPE 1982). Called to the Bar, Middle Temple, 1986; Legal Advr, then Sen. Legal Advr, Leeds Magistrates' Court, 1979–87; Principal Legal Advr, Batley and Dewsbury Magistrates' Court, 1987–91; Dep. Justices' Clerk, Manchester City Magistrates' Court, 1991–95; Justices' Clerk and Justices' Chief Exec., Rotherham Magistrates' Court, 1995–2001; Justices' Clerk: Doncaster and Rotherham Magistrates' Courts, 2001–04; S Yorks, 2004–11; Dep. Dist Judge (Magistrates' Courts), 2000–11. Chm., S Yorks Criminal Justice Bd, 2007–11. Pres., Yorks and Humber Justices' Clerks' Soc., 1999–2000. *Recreations:* crown green bowling (over 100 caps for Yorks and S Yorks county sides), supporting Bradford City AFC, reading, cruising the world P&O style. *Address:* Chesterfield Magistrates' Court, The Courthouse, Tapton Lane, Chesterfield S41 7TW. *T:* (01246) 246505, *Fax:* (01246) 246510. *E:* DistrictJudge.A.Davison@judiciary.gsi.gov.uk.

DAVISON, Air Vice Marshal Christopher, MBE 1978; *b* 26 Sept. 1947; *s* of Dixon and Kathleen Lillian Davison; *m* 1971, Rosemary Stamper; one *s* one *d*. *Educ:* Tynemouth Grammar Technical Sch.; Borough Road Coll., London. Joined RAF Phys. Educn Br., 1970; RAF Halton, Inst. of Aviation Medicine, Farnborough and RAF Hereford, 1970–76; Comd, RAF Outdoor Activity Centre, Scotland, 1976–78; Sqn Leader, 1978; HQ Strike Comd, 1979–80; Chief Instr, RAF Sch. of Physical Trng, RAF Cosford, 1981–82; RAF Staff Coll., Bracknell, 1983; PSO to Controller Aircraft, MoD, 1984–85; Wing Comdr, 1985; OC Admin Wing, RAF Wattisham, 1985–87; Dep. Comdr, Support Gp, HQ AFCENT, 1987–89; Gp Capt., 1989; Admin. Trng, HQ Support Comd, 1989–91; OC RAF Swinderby, 1991–93; Head of Physical Educn Specialisation, RAF, 1994; Air Cdre, 1994; AOA and AOC Directly Administered Units, RAF HQ PTC, 1994–96 and 2000–01; Dir Personnel (Airmen) and Controller Reserve Forces, RAF, 1997–99; retd 2001. Dir, RAF Sports Bd, 2001–09. *Recreations:* golf, ski-ing, Rugby. *Address:* c/o National Westminster Bank plc, 225 High Street, Lincoln LN2 1AZ. *Club:* Royal Air Force.

DAVISON, Ian Frederic Hay, CBE 2003; Managing Partner, Arthur Andersen & Co., 1966–82; Deputy Chairman and Chief Executive, Lloyd's of London, 1983–86; *b* 30 June 1931; *s* of late Eric Hay Davison, FCA, and Inez Davison; *m* 1955, Maureen Patricia Blacker; one *s* two *d*. *Educ:* Dulwich Coll. (Fellow 2014); LSE (BScEcon; Hon. Fellow, 2004); Univ. of Mich. ACA 1956, FCA 1966. Chairman: Crédit Lyonnais Capital Markets, 1988–91; Storehouse plc, 1990–96; NMB Group plc, 1992–2000; McDonnell Information Systems, later Northgate plc, 1993–99; Director: Midland Bank, 1986–88; Newspaper Publishing, 1986–94 (Chm., 1993–94); Chloride plc, 1988–98; Cadbury-Schweppes plc, 1990–2000; CIBA plc, 1991–96. Chm., Ruffer LLP, 2002–11. Mem. Council, ICA, 1975–99; Chm., Accounting Standards Cttee, 1982–84. Mem., NEDC for Bldg Industry, 1971–77; Member: Price Commn, 1977–79; Audit Commn, 1983–85; Chairman: EDC for Food and Drink Manufg Industry, 1981–83; Securities Review Cttee, Hong Kong, 1987–88. Dept of Trade Inspector, London Capital Securities, 1975–77; Inspector, Grays Building Soc., 1978–79. Chm., Regulatory Council, Dubai FSA, 2002–04. Trustee: V&A Museum, 1984–93 (Chm., V&A Enterprises Ltd, 1993–2002); Holburne Mus., Bath, 2005–09; Mus. of E Asian Art, 2009–; Dir, Royal Opera House, 1984–86; Chm., 1979–84, Dir, 2013–15, Pres., 2015, Monteverdi Trust; Chm., Sadler's Wells Foundation, 1995–2003. Pres., Nat. Council for One-Parent Families, 1991–2004; Chairman: SANE, 2000–02; Railway Heritage Cttee, 2000–04. Council Mem., Nat. Trust, 1992–94. Governor, LSE, 1982–2007; Pro-Provost and Chm. Council, RCA, 1996–2007 (Sen. Fellow, 2007). Chairman: Wells Cathedral Trust, 1997–2009; Council, Exeter Cathedral, 2002–08. Councillor and Alderman, London Bor. of Greenwich, 1961–73. Hon. DSc Aston, 1985; Hon. LLD Bath, 1998. *Publications:* A View of the Room: Lloyd's change and disclosure, 1987. *Recreations:* opera, theatre, music, bell-ringing. *Address:* 13 Catharine Place, Bath BA1 2PR. *Clubs:* Athenæum, Beefsteak, MCC; Bath and County.

DAVISON, (John) Stanley, OBE 1981; Secretary General, World Federation of Scientific Workers, 1987–2001; *b* 26 Sept. 1922; *s* of George Davison and Rosie Davison (*née* Segger); *m* 1959, Margaret Smith; two *s* one *d*. *Educ:* Timothy Hackworth Sch., Shildon, Co. Durham; Shildon Senior Boys' Sch.; St Helens Tech. Coll. RAF, 1941–46. Civil Servant (Technical), 1946–52; Regional Organiser, 1953–60, Dep. Gen. Sec., 1960–68, Assoc. of Scientific Workers; Dep. Gen. Sec., ASTMS, 1968–87. Member: Engineering Council, 1986–94; Heavy Electrical NEDO, 1976–87; Exec. Council, CSEU, 1981–88; Exec. Council, Internat. Metalworkers' Fedn, 1986–87; All Party Energy Cttee, 1982–88; Chm., Trade Union Side, GEC NJC, 1965–87; Governor, Aston CAT, 1955–60; Mem. Council, Brunel Univ., 1989–2000. Mem., Henlow Amateur Theatre Soc. (RAF). MUniv Brunel, 2001. *Recreations:* science policy, amateur dramatics, bridge, caravanning. *Address:* 1 Hazel Close, Shefford, Beds SG17 5YE. *Clubs:* Players' Theatre; Addington Theatre Group (Hon. Mem.); Caravan.

DAVISON, Peter; *see* Moffett, P.

DAVISON, Rt Hon. Sir Ronald (Keith), GBE 1978; CMG 1975; PC 1978; Chief Justice of New Zealand, 1978–89; *b* 16 Nov. 1920; *s* of Joseph James Davison and Florence May Davison; *m* 1948, Jacqueline May Carr; one *s* one *d* (and one *s* decd). *Educ:* Auckland Univ. (LLB). Admitted as barrister and solicitor, 1948; QC (NZ) 1963. Chairman: Environmental Council, 1969–74; Legal Aid Bd, 1969–78; Member: Council, Auckland Dist Law Soc., 1960–65 (Pres., 1965–66); Council, NZ Law Soc., 1963–66; Auckland Electric Power Bd (13 yrs); Aircrew Indust. Tribunal, 1970–78. Chm., Montana Wines Ltd, 1971–78; Dir, NZ Insurance Co. Ltd, 1975–78. *Recreations:* golf, fishing, bowls. *Address:* 1 Lichfield Road, Parnell, Auckland, New Zealand. *T:* (9) 3020493. *Clubs:* Wellington; Northern (Auckland, NZ).

DAVISON, Stanley; *see* Davison, J. S.

DAVISON, Timothy Paul; Chief Executive, NHS Lothian, since 2012; *b* 4 June 1961; *s* of late John Paul Davison and of Patricia Davison; *m* 1st, 1984, Hilary Williamson Gillick (marr. diss. 2009); one *s*; 2nd, 2012, Fiona Jane Maguire. *Educ:* Univ. of Stirling (BA Hons Hist.); Univ. of Glasgow (MBA, MPH); DipHSM. NHS nat. mgt trainee, 1983–84; Gen. Services Manager, Stirling Royal Infirmary, 1984–86; Asst Unit Administrator, Royal Edinburgh Hosp., 1986–87; Patient Services Manager, Lothian Mental Health Unit, 1987–88; Hosp. Administrator, Glasgow Royal Infirmary, 1988–90; Sector Gen. Manager, Gartnavel Royal Hosp., 1990–91; Unit Gen. Manager, Gtr Glasgow Community and Mental Health Unit (formerly Gtr Glasgow Mental Health Unit), 1991–94; Chief Executive: Gtr Glasgow Community and Mental Health Services NHS Trust, 1994–99; Gtr Glasgow Primary Care NHS Trust, 1999–2002; NHS Gtr Glasgow, N Glasgow Univ. Hosps NHS Trust, subseq. N Glasgow Univ. Hosps Div., 2002–05; Chief Exec., NHS Lanarkshire, 2005–12. Non-exec. Dir, Clinical Standards Bd for Scotland, 1999–2002. Mem. Ct, UWS, 2007–09. *Recreations:* tennis, military and political history, motor-cycling. *Address:* Lothian NHS Board, Waverley Gate, 2–4 Waterloo Place, Edinburgh EH1 3EG.

d'AVRAY, Prof. David Levesley, DPhil; FBA 2005; Professor of History, University College London, since 1996; *b* 3 Feb. 1952; *s* of Hector Anthony d'Avray and Audrey Sabina d'Avray (*née* Atkinson); *m* 1985, Julia Caroline Walworth. *Educ:* St John's Coll., Cambridge (BA 1973, MA 1977); DPhil Oxon 1977. Lectr, 1977–93, Reader, 1993–96, UCL. *Publications:* The Preaching of the Friars, 1985; Death and the Prince, 1994; Medieval Marriage Sermons, 2001; Medieval Marriage, 2005; Medieval Religious Rationalities, 2010; Rationalities in History, 2010; Dissolving Royal Marriages, 2014. *Recreations:* alpine walking, domestic discussion of television. *Address:* Department of History, University College London, Gower Street, WC1E 6BJ. *E:* ucradav@ucl.ac.uk.

DAVSON, Sir George Trenchard Simon, 4th Bt *cr* 1927, of Berbice, British Guiana; *b* 5 June 1964; *s* of Sir Christopher Davson, 3rd Bt and of Evelyn Mary Davson (née Wardrop); *S* father, 2004; *m* 1985, Joanna (marr. diss. 1996), *e d* of Rev. Dr James Bentley; one *s* one *d*. *Educ:* Eton; Magdalen Coll., Oxford. *Heir: s* James Davson, *b* 23 Dec. 1990.

DAVY, Diana Margaret; *see* Green, D. M.

DAVY, Margaret Ruth; *see* Bowron, M. R.

DAW, Christopher; QC 2013; *b* Milton Keynes, 21 Jan. 1970; *s* of Alan Charles Daw and Sandra Daw; *m* 2002, Ruth Hannah; two *s* two *d*. *Educ:* Univ. of Manchester (LLB Hons 1992); Inns of Court Sch. of Law. Called to the Bar, Gray's Inn, 1993; in practice as barrister, 1993–. *Recreations:* food, wine, travel. *Address:* 25 Bedford Row, WC1R 4HD. *T:* (020) 7067 1500, *Fax:* 0870 458 0592. *E:* uklawyer@aol.com.

DAW, Roger Keith; Principal Policy Advisor to the Director of Public Prosecutions, Crown Prosecution Service, 2009–10; *b* 10 March 1959; *s* of Owen William Albert Daw and late Mavis Hilda Daw (*née* Elson); partner, Courtney David Spence. *Educ:* Tiffin Sch., Kingston-upon-Thames; Birmingham Univ. (LLB). Called to the Bar, Middle Temple, 1982. Chief Crown Prosecutor, Hants and IoW, 1999–2003; Speaker's Sec., H of C, 2003–04; Prog. Dir, Police Reform, 2005–07, Dir, Policy, 2007–10, CPS. *Recreations:* genealogy, theatre.

DAWANINCURA, Sir John (Norbert), Kt 1999; OBE 1992; President, Papua New Guinea Sports Federation and Olympic Committee, since 2012 (Vice President, 1983; Secretary General, 1994–2010); *b* 25 May 1945; *s* of Stephen Joe Frank Dawanincura and Giro Paulo; *m* Lenah; one *s* two *d*. *Educ:* Chevalier Coll., NSW. Dist Valuer, W Highlands Province, Valuer Gen.'s Office; Manager, E Highlands Province, Bureau of Mgt Services; Graemme Dunnage Real Estate, 1977–78; Partner, Property Mgt and Maintenance, 1979–85. Rugby Football Union Player, Papua New Guinea team, 1965–70; Gen. Team Manager, PNG Contingents, 1981–86; Chief of PNG Delegation: Olympic Games, 1984; Commonwealth Games, 1982–97, 1999; S Pacific Games, 1983–98 (Chm. of Sports, Organising Cttee, Port Moresby, 1991); Mini S Pacific Games, 1981; Mem., 1984–97, Vice Pres., 1993–97, 2001–04, Oceania Nat. Olympic Cttee (Chm., Develt Commn, 1993–97); Alternate Mem., PNG Sports Commn, 1992; Schol. Mem., Mgt Cttee, Oceania Olympic Trng Coll., 1993–97; Mem. Mgt Cttee, Australia S Pacific 2000 Prog., 1995–97; Mem., Assoc. of Nat. Olympic Cttees, 1993–97; Deleg., 1981–86, Bd Mem., 1987–91, Pres. and Chm., 1995–99, S Pacific Games Council; Mem., Nat. Coaching Council, 1988. Sir Buri Kidu Heart Inst., 1996. *Recreations:* golf, circuit training, fishing. *Clubs:* Carbine, Golf, Yacht (Papua New Guinea).

DAWBARN, Sir Simon (Yelverton), KCVO 1980; CMG 1976; HM Diplomatic Service, retired; *b* 16 Sept. 1923; *s* of Frederic Dawbarn and Maud Louise Mansell; *m* 1948, Shelby Montgomery Parker; one *s* two *d*. *Educ:* Oundle Sch.; Corpus Christi Coll., Cambridge. Served in HM Forces (Reconnaissance Corps), 1942–45. Reckitt & Colman (Overseas), 1948–49. Joined Foreign Service, 1949. Foreign Office, 1949–53; Brussels, 1953; Prague, 1955; Tehran, 1957; seconded to HM Treasury, 1959; Foreign Office, 1961; Algiers, 1965; Athens, 1968; FCO, 1971–75. Head of W African Dept and concurrently non-resident Ambassador to Chad, 1973–75; Consul-General, Montreal, 1975–78; Ambassador to Morocco, 1978–82. *Address:* 44 Canonbury Park North, N1 2JT. *T:* (020) 7226 0659.

DAWE, Howard Carlton; Chairman, Bellway plc, 1999–2013; *b* 7 April 1944; *s* of Sydney Carlton Dawe and Dorothy Dawe (*née* Cooke); *m* 1968, Kathryn Jennifer Adcock; one *s* two *d*. *Educ:* Newlands Sch., Newcastle; Durham Cathedral Choir Sch.; Newcastle Royal Grammar Sch.; various tech. colls. Joined Bellway, 1961; Man. Dir, 1984–99. *Recreations:* country pursuits, photography, environmental travel (particularly rainforests and Africa). *Address:* Fenham Grange, Fenham le Moor, Belford, Northumberland NE70 7PN.

DAWE, Roger James, CB 1988; OBE 1970; educational consultant; *b* 26 Feb. 1941; *s* of late Harry James and Edith Mary Dawe; *m* 1965, Ruth Day Jolliffe; one *s* one *d*. *Educ:* Hardyes Sch., Dorchester; Fitzwilliam House, Cambridge (MA; Hon. Fellow, Fitzwilliam Coll., 1996). Entered Min. of Labour, 1962; Dept of Economic Affairs, 1964–65; Private Sec. to Prime Minister, 1966–70; Principal, Dept of Employment, 1970; Private Sec. to Secretary of State for Employment, 1972–74; Asst Sec., Dept of Employment, 1974–81; Under Sec., MSC, 1981; Chief Exec., Trng Div., MSC, 1982–84; Dep. Sec., Dept of Employment, 1985–87; Dir Gen., MSC, then Training Commn, subseq. Training Agency, 1988–90; Dir Gen., Training, Enterprise and Educn Directorate, Dept of Employment, 1990–92; Dep. Sec., Further and Higher Educn, DFE, 1992–95; Dir Gen. for Further and Higher Educn and Youth Trng, DFEE, 1995–2000. Mem., Exec. Cttee, Better Govt Initiative, 2007–. Chm., Strategy and Resources Cttee, Methodist Church, 2000–06. Dep. Chm., Council, Open Univ., 2003–09 (Mem., 2001–09); Mem., Council, Roehampton Univ., 2010–; Chair, Bromley Coll. Corporation, 2013–. FRSA. Hon. DEd UWE, 2000; DUniv Open, 2010. *Recreations:* tennis, Plymouth Argyle supporter, music, theatre, cinema.

DAWE, Sandra, (Sandie), CBE 2015 (MBE 2008); Chief Executive, VisitBritain, 2009–14; *b* Colombo, Ceylon, 29 Sept. 1955; *d* of Peter Vincent Dawe and Mary Hood Dawe; *m* 1987, John Reid Meikle. *Educ:* St Margaret's Sch., Edinburgh; Univ. of Edinburgh (MA Hons German 1977); Univ. of Freiburg; Napier Coll. of Commerce, Edinburgh (Business Dip.); INSEAD (AMP 2009). MCIPR 1990. Sec. to Hd of German Lang. Service and Announcer/Translator, BBC World Service, 1978–80; Officer Manager, W S Wotherspoon, 1980–82; travelling and working, USA, Australia and Far East, 1982–83; Publicity Exec., Book Mktg Council, Publishers' Assoc., 1983–85; Press Officer, 1985–86, PR Manager, 1986–88, BTA and England Tourist Bd; Hd of PR, London Tourist Bd, 1988–91; Hd of PR, 1991–96, Press and PR Dir, 1997, BTA and England Tourist Bd; Mktg Communications Dir, BTA, 1999–2003; Strategy and Communications Dir, VisitBritain, 2003–08. Member, Board: Visit London, 2009–11; Visit England, 2009–14; Dir, London & Partners, 2014–. Trustee: Nat. Heritage Meml Fund, 2014–; Heritage Lottery Fund, 2014–; Chm., Bd of Trustees, Kids in Museums, 2014–. FTS 1988. FRSA. *Recreations:* yoga, swimming, sailing. *Address:* Kids in Museums, CAN Mezzanine, 49–51 East Road, N1 6AH. *Club:* Royal Automobile.

DAWES, Prof. Edwin Alfred, CBiol, FRSB; CChem, FRSC; Reckitt Professor of Biochemistry, University of Hull, 1963–90, now Emeritus; *b* 6 July 1925; *s* of late Harold Dawes and Maude Dawes (*née* Barker); *m* 1950, Amy Rogerson (*d* 2014); two *s*. *Educ:* Goole Grammar Sch.; Univ. of Leeds. (BSc, PhD, DSc). Asst Lectr, later Lectr, in Biochemistry, Univ. of Leeds, 1947–50; Lectr, later Sen. Lectr, Univ. of Glasgow, 1951–63; Hull University: Head of Biochemistry Dept, 1963–86; Dean of Science, 1968–70; Pro-Vice-Chancellor, 1977–80; Dir, Biomed. Res. Unit, 1981–92. Visiting Lecturer: Meml Univ., Newfoundland, Dalhousie Univ., 1959; Univ. of Brazil, 1960, 1972; Univ. of S California, 1962; Univ. of Rabat, 1967; Univ. of Göttingen, 1972; Osmania Univ., Hyderabad, 1986; Univ. of Massachusetts, Amherst, 1989; Univ. of Padua, 1991; Lectures: Biochemical Soc., Australia and NZ, 1975; Amer. Medical Alumni, Univ. of St Andrews, 1980–81; Biodegradable Plastics Soc., Japan, 1991. Editor, Biochemical Jl, 1958–65; Editor-in-Chief, Jl of Gen. Microbiol., 1976–81; Man. Editor, Fedn of European Microbiol Socs, and Editor-in-Chief, FEMS Microbiology Letters, 1982–90. Vice Chm., 1987–2009, Chm., Scientific Adv. Cttee, 1978–2006, Yorks Cancer Res. Campaign; Member: Scientific Adv. Cttee, Whyte-Watson-Turner Cancer Res. Trust, 1984–91; Adv. Gp for Cancer Res., Sheffield Univ., 1991–96. President: Hull Lit. Philosophical Soc., 1976–77; British Ring of Internat. Brotherhood of Magicians, 1972–73; Hon. President: Scottish Conjurers' Assoc., 1973–; Scottish Assoc. Magical Socs, 1996–; Hon. Vice-Pres., Magic Circle (Official Historian, 1987–; Mem., 1959–; Maskelyne Trophy, 1998; David Devant Internat. Award, 2002); Chm., Centre for the Magic Arts Ltd, 2005–09. Chm., Philip Larkin Soc., 1995–. Governor, Pocklington Sch., 1965–74; Member, Court: Leeds Univ., 1974–2002; Bradford Univ., 1985–2002. Mem., Hall of Fame and H. A. Smith Literary Award, Soc. Amer. Magicians, 1984, 1997; Literary Fellowship and Hon. Life Mem., Acad. Magical Arts, USA, 1985; Hon. Mem. Bd, Houdini Historical Center, Wisconsin, 1990–. Consultant, The Mysteries of Magic, Learning Channel, 1998. Hon DSc Hull, 1992. Maskelyne Literary Award, 1988, 2009; Literary Award, Milbourne Christopher Foundn, USA, 1999; Special Award for Hist. and Res., Fédn Internat. des Sociétés Magiques, 2006. *Publications:* Quantitative Problems in Biochemistry, 1956, 6th edn 1980; (jtly) Biochemistry of Bacterial Growth, 1968, 3rd edn 1982; The Great Illusionists, 1979; Isaac Fawkes: fame and fable, 1979; The Biochemist in a Microbial Wonderland, 1982; Vonetta, 1982; The Barrister in the Circle, 1983; (ed) Environmental Regulation of Microbial Metabolism, 1985; (ed) Enterobacterial Surface Antigens, 1985; Microbial Energetics, 1985; (jtly) The Book of Magic, 1986, re-issued as Making Magic, 1992; The Wizard Exposed, 1987; (ed) Continuous Culture in Biotechnology and Environment Conservation, 1988; (contrib.) Philip Larkin: the man and his work, 1989; Henri Robin: expositor of science and magic, 1990; (ed) Molecular Biology of Membrane-Bound Complexes in Photosynthetic Bacteria, 1990; (ed) Novel Biodegradable Microbial Polymers, 1990; The Magic of Britain, 1994; Charles Bertram: the court conjurer, 1997; Stodare: the Enigma variations, 1998; (ed jtly) The Annals of Conjuring, 2001; Stanley Collins: conjuror and iconoclast, 2002; Harry Leat, 2003; The Great Lyle, 2005; (ed jtly and contrib.) Circle Without End, 2005; (jtly) David Nixon: entertainer with the magic touch, 2009; (jtly) John Henry Anderson the Great Wizard of the North and his Magical Family: a revisionary biography, 2014; Henry Dean: eighteenth century best-selling magic author/compiler, 2015; numerous papers in scientific jls. *Recreations:* conjuring, book-collecting. *Address:* Dane Hill, 393 Beverley Road, Anlaby, E Yorkshire HU10 7BQ. *T:* (01482) 657998.

DAWES, Rev. Helen Elizabeth; Team Rector, Shaftesbury, Dorset, since 2015; *b* 5 Jan. 1974; *d* of John Bridger and Carolyn Bridger; *m* 1997, Jonathan Dawes; one *s* two *d*. *Educ:* S Wilts Grammar Sch., Salisbury; Trinity Coll., Cambridge (MA); Westcott House, Cambridge; Anglia Ruskin Univ. (MA). Analyst, Roland Berger and Partners, 1996–98; Res. Associate, Caminus Energy Ltd, 1998–99; ordained deacon, 2002, priest, 2003; Asst Curate, St Andrew's, Chesterton, Cambridge, 2002–05; Priest-in-charge, United Benefice of Sandon, Wallington and Rushden with Clothall, Herts, 2005–09; Archbishop of Canterbury's Dep. Sec. for Public Affairs, 2009–13; Archbishop of Canterbury's Social and Public Affairs Advr, 2013–15. *Recreations:* gardening, singing, cycling, reading. *Address:* Shaftesbury Team Office, 5 Gold Hill, Shaftesbury, Dorset SP7 8JW.

DAWES, Melanie Henrietta, CB 2013; Permanent Secretary, Department for Communities and Local Government, since 2015; *b* 9 March 1966; *d* of Nigel G. K. Dawes and Rosalie J. Dawes (*née* Wood); *m* 1992, Benedict Brogan; one *d*. *Educ:* Malvern Girls' Coll.; New Coll., Oxford (BA Hons); Birkbeck Coll., London (MSc Econ.). Econ. Asst, Dept of Transport, 1989–91; joined HM Treasury, 1991: Econ. Advr, then Team Leader, Econ. and Monetary Union, 1996–98; Head: Work Incentives and Poverty Analysis, 1998–2001; Educn and Culture, 2001–02; Dir (Europe), 2002–06; HM Revenue and Customs: Dir, Large Business Service, 2006–07; Dir Gen., Business Tax, and Commissioner, 2007–11; Dir Gen., Econ. and

Domestic Secretariat, Cabinet Office, 2011–15. Chair, Alcohol Recovery Project, 2003–05. Mem. Council, Which?, 2011–15. *Recreation:* gardening. *Address:* Department for Communities and Local Government, 2 Marsham Street, SW1P 4DF.

DAWES, Rt Rev. Peter Spencer; Bishop of Derby, 1988–95; *b* 5 Feb. 1928; *s* of Jason Spencer Dawes and Janet Dawes; *m* 1954, Ethel Marrin; two *s* two *d. Educ:* Bickley Hall School; Aldenham School; Hatfield Coll., Durham (BA); Tyndale Hall, Bristol. Assistant Curate: St Andrew's, Whitehall Park, 1954–57; St Ebbe's, Oxford, 1957–60; Tutor, Clifton Theological Coll., 1960–65; Vicar, Good Shepherd, Romford, 1965–80; Archdeacon of West Ham, 1980–88. Examining Chaplain to Bishop of Chelmsford, 1970–88. Member, General Synod, 1970–95. *Address:* 45 Arundell, Ely, Cambs CB6 1BQ. *T:* (01353) 661241.

DAWES, Prof. William Nicholas, PhD; FREng, FRAeS; Francis Mond Professor of Aeronautical Engineering, Cambridge University, since 1996; Fellow of Churchill College, Cambridge, since 1984; *b* 5 Sept. 1955; *s* of Kenneth Frederick Dawes and Doris Jacyntha Hulm; *m* 1980, Luigia Cuomo; two *d. Educ:* Churchill Coll., Cambridge (BA, MA, PhD). CEng; FRAeS 1997; FREng 2000. Res. Officer, CEGB, 1980–84; Sen. Res. Asst, 1984–86, Lectr, 1986–96, Engrg Dept, Cambridge Univ. Mem., Amer. Inst. Aeronautics and Astronautics, 1990. *Publications:* articles in professional jls. *Recreations:* Italy, good food and good wine. *Address:* Church Farm, 7 Church Lane, Little Eversden CB23 1HQ. *T:* (01223) 263318.

DAWID, Prof. (Alexander) Philip, ScD; Professor of Statistics, University of Cambridge, 2007–13, now Emeritus; Fellow, Darwin College, Cambridge, 2007–13, now Emeritus; *b* 1 Feb. 1946; *s* of Israel Dawid and Rita Dawid; *m* 1974, Fatemeh Elahe Madjd; one *s* one *d. Educ:* Trinity Hall and Darwin Coll., Cambridge (BA 1966; Dip. Math. Statistics 1967; ScD 1982). CStat 1993. Lectr, UCL, 1969–78; Prof. of Statistics, City Univ., 1978–81; University College London: Reader, 1981–82; Prof. of Statistics, 1982–2007; Hon. Prof., 2007–. Hon. Prof., Univ. of Hong Kong, 2009–; Vis. Fellow, Inst. of Criminology, Univ. of Cambridge, 2013–15. Editor: Jl of Royal Stat. Soc. Series B, 1992; Biometrika, 1992–96; Bayesian Analysis, 2005–09; Jl of Causal Inference, 2011–. *Publications:* (ed jtly) Bayesian Statistics 4, 1992, 5, 1996, 6, 1999, 7, 2003, 8, 2007; (jtly) Probabilistic Networks and Expert Systems, 1999; (ed jtly) Simplicity, Complexity and Modelling, 2011; (ed jtly) Evidence, Inference and Enquiry, 2011; (ed jtly) Beauty, 2013. *Recreation:* music. *Address:* Darwin College, Silver Street, Cambridge CB3 9EU. *E:* apd25@cam.ac.uk.

DAWKINS, Prof. (Clinton) Richard, FRS 2001; Charles Simonyi Professor of the Public Understanding of Science, University of Oxford, 1995–2008; Fellow, New College, Oxford, 1970–2008, now Emeritus; *b* 26 March 1941; *s* of late Clinton John Dawkins and of Jean Mary Vyvyan (*née* Ladner); *m*; one *d. Educ:* Oundle Sch.; Balliol Coll., Oxford (MA, DPhil, DSc; Hon. Fellow 2004). Asst Prof. of Zoology, Univ. of California, Berkeley, 1967–69; Oxford University: Lectr, 1970–89; Reader in Zoology, 1989–95. Gifford Lectr, Glasgow Univ., 1988; Sidgwick Meml Lectr, Newnham Coll., Cambridge, 1988; Kovler Vis. Fellow, Univ. of Chicago, 1990; Nelson Lectr, Univ. of California, Davis, 1990; Royal Instn Christmas Lects for Young People, 1991. Presenter, BBC TV Horizon progs, 1985, 1986. Editor: Animal Behaviour, 1974–78; Oxford Surveys in Evolutionary Biology, 1983–86. FRSL 1997. Hon. Fellow, Regent's Coll., London, 1988. Hon. DLitt: St Andrews, 1995; ANU, 1996; Hon. DSc: Westminster, 1997; Hull, 2001; DUniv Open, 2003. Silver Medal, Zool Soc., 1989; Michael Faraday Award, Royal Soc., 1990; Nakayama Prize, Nakayama Foundn for Human Scis, 1994; Internat. Cosmos Prize, 1997; Kistler Prize, Foundn for the Future, 2001; Shakespeare Prize, 2005; Lewis Thomas Prize, Rockefeller Univ., NY, 2007; Deschner Prize, Johann-Wolfgang-Goethe Univ., Frankfurt, 2007. *Publications:* The Selfish Gene, 1976, 2nd edn 1989; The Extended Phenotype, 1982; The Blind Watchmaker, 1986 (RSL Prize 1987; LA Times Lit. Prize 1987); River Out of Eden, 1995; Climbing Mount Improbable, 1996; Unweaving the Rainbow: science, delusion and the appetite for wonder, 1998; A Devil's Chaplain and Other Selected Essays, 2003; The Ancestor's Tale, 2004; The God Delusion, 2006 (Book of Year, Galaxy Book Awards, 2007); (ed) The Oxford Book of Modern Science Writing, 2008; The Greatest Show on Earth, 2009; The Magic of Reality, 2011; An Appetite for Wonder: the making of a scientist, 2013; Brief Candle in the Dark: my life in science, 2015. *Recreation:* the Apple Macintosh. *Address:* New College, Holywell Street, Oxford OX1 3BN.

DAWKINS, Douglas Alfred; Associate Director, Bank of England, 1985–87; *b* 17 Sept. 1927; *s* of Arthur Dawkins and Edith Annie Dawkins; *m* 1953, Diana Pauline (*née* Ormes); one *s* one *d. Educ:* Edmonton County Secondary Sch.; University Coll. London (Rosa Morison Scholar; BA Hons). Entered Bank of England, 1950; Bank for Internat. Settlements, 1953–54; Adviser to Governors, Bank of Libya, 1964–65; Asst Chief of Overseas Dept, 1970; First Dep. Chief of Exchange Control, 1972; Chief of Exchange Control, 1979; Asst Dir, 1980. *Address:* c/o Bank of England, Threadneedle Street, EC2R 8AH.
See also M. Dawkins.

DAWKINS, Hon. John Sydney, AO 2000; economist, consultant, company director; Chairman, John Dawkins & Co., since 1994; *b* 2 March 1947; *s* of Dr A. L. Dawkins and M. Dawkins (*née* Lee Steere); *m* 1987, Maggie Maruff; one *d*, one step *s*, and one *s* one *d* by previous marr. *Educ:* Roseworthy Agricl Coll., SA (RDA); Univ. of WA (BEc). MHR, Tangney, 1974–75; Press Officer, WA Trades and Labor Council, 1976–77; MP (ALP) Fremantle, WA, 1977–94; Shadow Minister for Educn, 1980–83; Minister: for Finance and assisting Prime Minister for Public Service Matters, 1983–84; for Trade and assisting Prime Minister for Youth Affairs, 1984–87; for Employment, Educn and Trng, 1987–91; Treasurer of Australia, 1991–93. Special investment rep., 1994–95; Chairman: Innisfree Australia Pty, 1994–; Elders Rural Bank, 1998–2006; Med. Corp. of Australasia, 1997–2000; Law Central, 2000–06; Retail Energy Market Co., 2003–09; Integrated Legal Hldgs Ltd, 2006–; Australian Qualification Council, 2008–; TVET Australia Pty, 2010–11; Archer Exploration Ltd, 2010–12; Australian Bauxite Ltd, 2011–; Sovereign Gold Ltd, 2010–; Nat. Skills Standards Council, 2011–13; Vocation Ltd, 2013–; Director: Sealcorp Hldgs, 1994–2004; Govt Relations Australia, 2000–; Genetic Technologies, 2004–07; MGM Wireless, 2007–10; M & C Saatchi Direct Ltd, 2009–. Chairman: Botanic Gardens of Adelaide, 2003–05; Inst. of Trade, 2005–13. Bd Mem., Fred Hollows Foundn, 1995–2004. Hon. Dr: Univ. of S Australia, 1996; Queensland Univ. of Technol., 1997; Ballarat, 2009. Centenary Medal, Australia, 2003. *Address:* PO Box 376, Walkerville, SA 5081, Australia.

DAWKINS, Prof. Marian Ellina Stamp, CBE 2014; DPhil; FRS 2014; Professor of Animal Behaviour, University of Oxford, since 1998; *b* Hereford, 13 Feb. 1945; *d* of Arthur Maxwell Stamp and (Alice) Mary Stamp (*née* Richards); *m* 1967, (Clinton) Richard Dawkins, *qv* (marr. diss. 1984). *Educ:* Queen's Coll., Harley St, London; Somerville Coll., Oxford (BA 1966; DPhil 1971). Pt-time res. asst to Prof. Niko Tinbergen, 1971–74; Deptl Demonstrator in Animal Behaviour, Dept of Zool., Oxford Univ., 1974–80; Mary Snow Fellow in Biol Scis, Somerville Coll., Oxford, 1980–2012, now Fellow Emeritus. *Publications:* Animal Suffering: the science of animal welfare, 1980; Unravelling Animal Behaviour, 1986, 2nd edn 1995; Through Our Eyes Only?: the search for animal consciousness, 1993; Observing Animal Behaviour, 2007; Why Animals Matter: animal consciousness and human well-being, 2012; (with A. Manning) An Introduction to Animal Behaviour, 2012. *Recreations:* photography, wind-surfing. *Address:* Department of Zoology, University of Oxford, South Parks Road, Oxford OX1 3PS. *T:* (01865) 271215. *E:* marian.dawkins@zoo.ox.ac.uk.

DAWKINS, Mark; Partner, Akin Gump Strauss Hauer & Feld LLP, since 2014; *b* 2 May 1960; *s* of Douglas Alfred Dawkins, *qv*; *m* 2002, Kim (*née* Taylor); two *s* two *d. Educ:* Exeter Univ. (LLB). Admitted solicitor, 1985; Simmons & Simmons: Partner, 1990–2011; Hd of Litigation, 1997–2000; Hd, Financial Mkts, 2000–05; Man. Partner, 2005–11; Partner, Bingham McCutchen, 2011–14. *Recreations:* family, tennis, squash, Southern African history, photography. *Address:* Akin Gump Strauss Hauer & Feld LLP, 41 Lothbury, EC2R 7HF. *T:* (020) 7661 5330.

DAWKINS, Richard; *see* Dawkins, C. R.

DAWKINS, Simon John Robert, MA; Headmaster, Merchant Taylors' School, Crosby, 1986–2005; *b* 9 July 1945; *s* of Col William John Dawkins, TD and Mary Doreen Dawkins (*née* King); *m* 1968, Janet Mary Stevens; one *s* one *d. Educ:* Solihull Sch.; Univ. of Nottingham (BA); Queens' Coll., Cambridge (PGCE); Birkbeck Coll. London (MA distn). Head of Economics: Eltham Coll., 1968–71; Dulwich Coll., 1971–86 (Housemaster, 1979–86). Headmasters' Conference: Chm. NW Div., 1996 (Sec., 1995); Member: Memship Cttee, 1996–99; Academic Policy Cttee, 2000–04. Gov., Arnold Sch., Blackpool, 2005–10. Freeman, Merchant Taylors' Co., 2005–. *Recreations:* physical exercise, tennis, golf, ski-ing, reading. *Address:* Brackenwood, St George's Road, Hightown, Liverpool L38 3RT. *T:* (0151) 929 3546. *Clubs:* Hightown (Lancs); Formby Golf, St Enodoc Golf.

DAWNAY, family name of **Viscount Downe**.

DAWNAY, (Charles) James (Payan); DL; Chairman, CCLA Investment Management Ltd, since 2004; *b* 7 Nov. 1946; *s* of late Capt. Oliver Dawnay, CVO and of Lady Margaret Dawnay (*née* Boyle, now Lady Margaret Stirling-Aird); *m* 1978, Sarah Stogdon; one *s* three *d. Educ:* Trinity Hall, Cambridge (BA 1968). Investment Manager, M & G Gp Ltd, 1969–78; Export Sales Dir, Alginate Industries Ltd, 1979–81; Man. Dir, Vannick Products Ltd, 1981–83; S G Warburg & Co. Ltd, 1983–87 (Dir, 1984–87); Dir, Mercury Asset Mgt Gp plc, 1987–92; Chm., Mercury Fund Managers Ltd, 1987–92; Business Develt Dir, 1992–99, Dep. Chm., 1999–2000, Martin Currie Ltd; Chairman: China Heartland Fund Ltd, 1997–2006; Northern Aim VCT plc, 2000–11; Gurr Johns Ltd, 2000–06; Investec High Income Trust plc, 2001–09; Resources Investment Trust plc, 2001–08; New Opportunities Investment Trust plc, 2002–06; Director: Govett Strategic Trust plc, 2000–03; Taiwan Opportunities Trust Ltd, 2001–. Mem. Bd of Trustees, Nat. Galls of Scotland, 2003–11. Mem., Finance Cttee, NT, 1991–2005; Mem. Finance Cttee, 1993–2005, Dir NTS Enterprises, 2001–05 and Chm. Commercial Develt Cttee, 2001–05, Nat. Trust for Scotland, 1993–2005. Chairman: Biggar Mus. Trust, 1993–; Penicuik House Preservation Trust, 2001–14. DL Lanarks, 2012. *Recreations:* collecting, conservation, country sports. *Address:* Symington House, by Biggar, Lanarkshire ML12 6LW. *T:* (01899) 308211, *Fax:* (01899) 308727. *E:* jdawnay@yahoo.co.uk. *Clubs:* Brooks's; Pratt's; Biggar.
See also R. S. Johnson.

DAWNAY, Lady Jane Meriel; Member of Board, Historic Buildings Council for Scotland, 1996–99; *b* 8 Feb. 1953; *yr d* of 5th Duke of Westminster, TD and Hon. Viola Maud Lyttelton (*d* 1987); *m* 1st, 1977, Duke of Roxburghe, *qv* (marr. diss. 1990); two *s* one *d*; 2nd, 1996, Edward William Dawnay. *Educ:* Collegiate Sch., Enniskillen; Sherborne Hill; Switzerland; Bedgebury Park; Paris. Vice Pres., Arthritis and Rheumatism Council for Res., 1998– (Regl Chm., 1983–98); Macmillan Cancer Relief (formerly Cancer Relief Macmillan Fund): Vice Pres., Scotland, 1994– (Dir and Bd Mem., 1990–94); Chm., Scotland and NI, 1989–94. Mem. Bd, Ancient Monuments Scotland, 1993–96; Member: Adv. Cttee, Royal Parks, 1994–99; Royal Highland & Agricultural Soc. of Scotland, 1998 (Pres., 1998–). Trustee, Atlantic Salmon Trust Scotland, 1995–. Dir, Radio Borders, 1992–98. Mem., Racehorse Owners' Assoc.; Partner, Hillington Hall Bloodstock Partnership, 2006–. Vice Pres., NW Norfolk Cons. Assoc. (Pres., 1999–2002). Pres., W Norfolk, King's Lynn and Wisbech Br., NSPCC, 2007–. Patron, British Lymphology Soc., 1998–2011; Life Patron, George Thomas Soc.; Vice Patron, Norfolk Community Foundn, 2006–. MInstD 1997. Freeman: City of Chester, 1997; City of London, 2012; Farriers' Co., 2009 (Liveryman, 2012). Queen Elizabeth the Queen Mother's Award for Envmt, Scotland, 1996. *Address:* Hillington Hall, Hillington, King's Lynn, Norfolk PE31 6BW; 48f Eaton Square, SW1W 9BD.
See also Marquis of Bowmont and Cessford, Viscount Grimston.

DAWNAY, Rachel Sabiha; *see* Johnson, R. S.

DAWS, Dr Christine; Director-General, Finance, Welsh Assembly Government, 2009–10 (Director of Finance, 2006–09); *b* Rugby, 3 Feb. 1955; *d* of Harold and Daphne Sellar; *m* 1993, Robert Daws (*d* 2001). *Educ:* Durham Univ. (BA Hons Econs); Loughborough Univ. (MSc Recreation Mgt); Texas A&M Univ. (PhD Agricl Econs 1982). Dir of Finance, Bucks HA, 1995–99; Dep. Dir of Finance, DoH, 1999–2003; Dir of Finance, NHS Wales Dept, 2003–06. Non-exec. Dir, Shared Services Audit Cttee, 2007–10, Shared Services Bd, 2009–10, DWP. Lay Mem., and Chm., Audit and Assurance Cttee, NHS Herefordshire CCG, 2012–. *Recreations:* gardening, golf.

DAWSON, (Archibald) Keith; educational consultant, since 1996; Headmaster, Haberdashers' Aske's School, Elstree, 1987–96; *b* 12 Jan. 1937; *s* of Wilfred Joseph and Alice Marjorie Dawson; *m* 1961, Marjorie Blakeson; two *d. Educ:* Nunthorpe Grammar School for Boys, York; The Queen's College, Oxford. MA, Dip Ed distinction. Ilford County High School for Boys, 1961–63; Haberdashers' Aske's Sch., 1963–71 (Head of History, 1965–71); Headmaster, John Mason Sch., Abingdon, 1971–79; Principal, Scarborough Sixth Form Coll., 1979–84; Principal, King James's College of Henley, 1984–87. Liveryman, Haberdashers' Co., 1996–. *Publications:* Society and Industry in 19th Century England (with Peter Wall), 1968; The Industrial Revolution, 1971. *Recreations:* theatre, 'cello, cricket, tending my fruit and vegetables, seeing Europe by rail. *Address:* Puffins, 77 Chapel Street, Sidbury, Sidmouth EX10 0RQ.

DAWSON, Celia Anne, (Mrs D. Charlton); a District Judge (Magistrates' Courts), since 2004; *b* 25 Sept. 1959; *d* of David and Jean Dawson; *m* 1983, Dr David Charlton; one *s* two *d. Educ:* Essex Univ. (BA Hons (Lit.) 1981); Coll. of Law. Admitted solicitor, 1983; Partner, Thompson Smith and Puxon, Solicitors, Colchester, 1987–91; Sen. Legal Advr, Essex Magistrates' Courts, 1991–98; Partner, Birkett Long, Solicitors, Colchester, 1998–2004; Dep. Dist Judge, Sussex, 2001–04. Mem. Bd, and Chm., Mgt Cttee, Colne Housing Soc., 1999–2004. Trustee: Coram Children's Legal Centre (formerly Children's Legal Centre), Univ. of Essex, 2007–; Coram Cambridge Adopt, 2014–. *Recreations:* obsessive sailing, unsuccessful garden taming, making a mess in the kitchen. *Address:* Ipswich Magistrates' Court, Elm Street, Ipswich, Suffolk IP1 4EY. *Clubs:* Brightlingsea Sailing, Colne Yacht.

DAWSON, Hon. Sir Daryl (Michael), AC 1988; KBE 1982; CB 1980; Justice of the High Court of Australia, 1982–97; Non-permanent Member, Hong Kong Court of Final Appeal, 1997–2003; Professorial Fellow, University of Melbourne, since 1998; *b* 12 Dec. 1933; *s* of Claude Charles Dawson and Elizabeth May Dawson; *m* 1971, Mary Louise Thomas. *Educ:* Canberra High Sch.; Ormond Coll., Univ. of Melbourne (LLB Hons); LLM Yale. Sterling Fellow, Yale Univ., 1955–56. QC 1971; Solicitor-General for Victoria, 1974–82. Mem. Council, Univ. of Melbourne, 1976–86; Chm. Council, Ormond Coll., Univ. of Melbourne, 1991–92. Adjunct Prof. of Law, Monash Univ., 1997–2006. Chairman: Australian Motor Sport Appeal Court, 1986–88 (Mem., 1970–86); Longford Royal Commn, 1998–99; Trade Practices Act Review Cttee, 2002–03. Chm., Menzies Foundn, 1998–2008; Gov., Ian Potter

Foundn, 1998–. Hon. LLD: Monash, 2006; Melbourne, 2008. *Recreation:* gardening. *Address:* PO Box 147, East Melbourne, Vic 8002, Australia. *Clubs:* Melbourne, Savage, RACV (Melbourne).

DAWSON, Dee; *see* Dawson, J. D.

DAWSON, Prof. Donald Andrew, PhD; FRS 2010; FRSC; FIMS; Professor Emeritus and Distinguished Research Professor, School of Mathematics and Statistics, Carleton University, Ottawa, since 1999; *b* Montreal, Canada, 4 June 1937. *Educ:* McGill Univ. (BSc Hons Maths and Physics 1958; MSc Maths 1959); Massachusetts Inst. of Technol. (PhD 1963). Sen. Res. Engr, Space Div., Raytheon Corp., Mass, 1962–63; Asst Prof., 1963–66, Associate Prof., 1967–70, Dept of Maths, McGill Univ.; Associate Prof., 1970–71, Prof. of Maths and Statistics, 1971–96, Carleton Univ.; Dir, Fields Inst. for Res. in Mathematical Scis, Toronto, 1996–2000; Adjunct Professor: Depts of Maths and Statistics, Univ. of Toronto, 1996–2000; Dept of Maths and Statistics, McGill Univ., 2000–10. Pres., Bernoulli Soc., 2003–05. FIMS 1977; FRSC 1987. Gold Medal, Statistical Soc. of Canada, 1991. *Publications:* over 100 articles in jls. *Address:* School of Mathematics and Statistics, Carleton University, 1125 Colonel By Drive, Ottawa, ON K1S 5B6, Canada.

DAWSON, (Edward) John; Assistant Chief Executive, 1989–90, and Director, 1989–91, Lloyds Bank; *b* 14 Oct. 1935; *s* of late Edward Dawson and Kathleen Dawson (*née* Naughton); *m* 1st, 1963, Ann Prudence (*née* Hicks) (marr. diss. 1997); one *s* one *d* (and one *s* decd); 2nd, 1998, Jill Solveig (*née* Linton). *Educ:* St Joseph's Coll., Blackpool; London Graduate Sch. of Business Studies (Sloan Fellow, 1969–70); Manchester Coll., Univ. of Oxford (BA Hons PPE 1994; MA 1998). FCIB. Entered Lloyds Bank, 1952; served RAF, 1954–56; General Manager, Lloyds Bank and Exec. Dir, Lloyds Bank International, 1982–84; Asst Chief Gen. Manager, 1985, Dir, UK Retail Banking, 1985–88, Lloyds Bank; Chairman: Lloyds Bowmaker Finance, 1988–90 (Dir, 1985–90); Black Horse Agencies, 1988–89 (Dir, 1985–89). Chm., Walsingham Community Homes Ltd, 1991–96. *Recreations:* life in South Africa during Northern winter, golf, cricket, choral singing, hiking, T'ai chi ch'uan. *Address:* c/o Lloyds Bank, Westminster House, 4 Dean Stanley Street, SW1P 3HU. *Clubs:* MCC; Wareham Golf.

DAWSON, Hilton; *see* Dawson, T. H.

DAWSON, Ian David; Assistant Under-Secretary of State (Policy), Ministry of Defence, 1991–93; *b* 24 Nov. 1934; *s* of Harry Newton Dawson and Margaret (*née* Aspinall); *m* 1955, Barbara (*née* Mather); two *s* one *d*. *Educ:* Hutton Grammar Sch.; Fitzwilliam House, Cambridge (MA). Directorate of Military Survey, 1958–71; Principal, MoD, 1971; Private Sec. to CAS, 1975–77; Asst Sec., Naval Staff, 1977–80; Sec., AWRE, 1980–83; RCDS, 1984; Dir, Defence and Security Agency, WEU, Paris, 1986–88; Asst Under-Sec. of State (Resources), MoD, 1988–90; Fellow, Center for Internat. Affairs, Harvard, 1990–91. *Recreations:* music, mountaineering, travel. *Address:* 15 Lingard Close, Liskeard, Cornwall PL14 6EY.

DAWSON, James Grant Forbes, CEng, FICE; Strategic Development Director, BST Consultants, since 2002; Chairman, Vilnius Consult, since 2002; Associate, First Class Partnerships, since 2003; *b* 6 Sept. 1940; *s* of William Maxwell Hume Dawson and Caroline Margaret Storey Dawson; *m* 2nd, 1993, Joan Margaret Davison. *Educ:* Edinburgh Univ. (BSc). FIPENZ (FNZIE); Eur Ing. GIBB Ltd: Chief Engr, 1975–78; Associate, 1978–80; Head of Transport, 1980–82; Partner, 1982; Director, 1989; Chm., 1995–2001; Chm. Emeritus, Jacobs GIBB Ltd, 2001–. Consultant: RSM Robson Rhodes, 2002–03; MVA, 2005–06. Member: DTI Cttee for S Africa Trade, 1998–2001; E Europe Trade Council, 1999–2001; Mem., ME and African Gp, 2001–03, Chm., Ports and Logistics Gp, British Trade Investments. Chm., ACE, 1999–2000. Liveryman, Engineers' Co., 2001–. *Recreations:* golf, gardening. *Address:* Woodpeckers, Pangbourne Hill, Pangbourne, Berks RG8 8JS. *Club:* East India.

DAWSON, Joan Denise, (Dee); Medical Director, Rhodes Farm Clinic, 1991–2011; *b* 17 Jan. 1947; *d* of Horace and Joan Webb; *m* 1st, 1969, Stephen Dawson (marr diss.); 2nd, 1979, Ian Dear (marr. diss.); one *s* four *d*; 3rd, 2002, Eberhard von Wick. *Educ:* Chelsea Coll., London Univ. (BSc); London Business Sch.; Royal Free Hosp. Sch. of Medicine (MB BS 1989). Voluntary Teacher, VSO, Madagascar, 1969–71; Mkt Res. Manager, Parker Ltd, 1974–75; Man. Dir, Dee Dawson Fashion Ltd, 1977–84; House Physician, 1989–90, House Surgeon, 1990–91, North Middx Hosp.; set up Rhodes Farm Clinic, first residential unit, incl. full-time school, dedicated solely to treatment of anorexic children, 1991. *Publications:* A Quick Guide to Eating Disorders, 1995; Anorexia and Bulimia - a parents' guide, 2001. *Recreations:* tennis, water ski-ing. *Address:* The Old House, Totteridge Green, N20 8PA.

DAWSON, John; *see* Dawson, E. J.

DAWSON, Prof. John Alan, FRSE; Professor of Marketing, University of Edinburgh, 1990–2009, now Emeritus; Professor of Retail Studies, University of Stirling, 2005–09, now Emeritus; *b* 19 Aug. 1944; *s* of Alan and Gladys Dawson; *m* 1967, Jocelyn M. P. Barker (marr. diss. 2007); one *s* one *d*. *Educ:* University College London (BSc, MPhil); University of Nottingham (PhD). Lectr, Univ. of Nottingham, 1967–71; Lectr, 1971, Sen. Lectr, 1974, Reader, 1981–83, Univ. of Wales, Lampeter; Fraser of Allander Prof. of Distributive Studies, and Dir, Inst. for Retail Studies, Univ. of Stirling, 1983–90. Vis. Lectr, Univ. of Western Australia, 1973; Vis. Res. Fellow, ANU, 1978; Vis. Prof., 2000–, Dist. Prof., 2003–11, Univ. of Mktg and Distribn Sci., Kobe; Visiting Professor: Florida State Univ., 1982; Chuo Univ., 1986; Univ. of S Africa, 1999; Sch. for Higher Mgt and Business Strategy, Barcelona, 2000–07; Bocconi Univ., Milan, 2000; Saitama Univ., 2002; Kobe Univ., 2010; Valencia Univ., 2010. Chm., Nat. Museums of Scotland Retailing Co., 1992–2003. Member: Distributive Trades EDC, 1984–87; Board, Cumbernauld Develt Corp., 1987–96. Hon. Sec., Inst. of British Geographers, 1985–88. FRSE 2003. Hon. DBA Abertay Dundee, 2010. *Publications:* Evaluating the Human Environment, 1973; Man and His World, 1975; Computing for Geographers, 1976; Small Scale Retailing in UK, 1979; Marketing Environment, 1979; Retail Geography, 1980; Commercial Distribution in Europe, 1982; Teach Yourself Geography, 1983; Shopping Centre Development, 1983; Computer Programming for Geographers, 1985; Shopping Centres Policies and Prospects, 1985; Evolution of European Retailing, 1989; Competition and Markets, 1991; Retail Environments in Developing Countries, 1991; Distribution Statistics, 1992; Internationalisation of Retailing in Asia, 2003; International Retailing Plans and Strategies in Asia, 2005; Strategic Issues in International Retailing, 2006; The Retail Reader, 2008; Global Strategies in Retailing, 2013; articles in geographical, management and marketing jls. *Recreations:* sport, travel. *Address:* University of Edinburgh Business School, Edinburgh EH8 9JS. *T:* (0131) 651 3220.

DAWSON, John Anthony Lawrence, FICE, FCIHT; Chairman, European Road Assessment Association, since 2005; Chairman, International Road Assessment Programme, since 2005; *m* 1980, Frances Anne Elizabeth Whelan; two *d*. *Educ:* Mill Hill Sch.; Southampton Univ. British Rail Engineering Scholar, 1968–72; Depts of Envmt and Transport, 1972–81; Overseas Transport Consultant, 1981–85; Dir (Transport), London Regl Office, Dept of Transport, 1985–88; Chief Road Engineer, Scottish Develt Dept, 1988; Dir of Roads and Chief Road Engr, Scottish Office, 1989–95; Automobile Association: Policy Dir, 1995–2004; Internat. Dir, 2003–04; Mem. Cttee, 1996–99; Man. Dir, AA Foundn for Road Safety Research, 1995–2004; Dir, AA Motoring Trust, 2003–04; Man. Exec., Road Safety Foundn, 2005–. Mem. Bd, Ertico, 1995–97, 1999–2002. Trustee, Air Ambulance Assoc., 1999–2002; Vice-Chm., FIA Foundn for Automobile and Soc., 2012– (Sec., 2001–12). *Recreations:* touring, music. *Address:* EuroRAP AISBL, Worting House, Basingstoke, Hants RG23 8PX. *T:* (01256) 345598.

DAWSON, John Kelvin, AM 2008; Agent-General for Queensland in London, and Commissioner, Europe, 2001–07; Adviser to: Russell Reynolds Associates; iCarehealth; Corporate Value Associates; *b* Melbourne, 15 Sept. 1943; *s* of John Inglis Dawson and Marie Victoria Dawson; one *s* one *d*. *Educ:* Ivanhoe Grammar Sch.; Univ. of Melbourne (BA). National Australia Bank Ltd: Gen. Manager, Strategic Develt, 1991–93; Man. Dir, UK and Europe, 1993–95; Gp Gen. Manager, Asian and Internat. Banking, 1995; CEO, Bank of Queensland Ltd, 1996–2001. Director: Clydesdale Bank, 1993–95; Nat. Irish Bank, 1993–95; Northern Bank, Belfast, 1993–95; Yorkshire Bank, 1993–95; Bank of Hawaii Internat., 1999–2001; Queensland Treasury Corp., 2008–11. Chm., Exec. Cttee, Aust. Bankers' Assoc., 1992–93. Dir, British-Aust. Soc., 2001–07. Freeman, City of London, 2004. *Recreations:* all sports, wine, reading. *Address:* Villa 2, Stradbroke Apartments, 2 Goodwin Street, Kangaroo Point, Qld 4169, Australia. *Clubs:* East India; Australian, Melbourne Cricket (Melbourne); Brisbane, Tattersalls (Qld); Hong Kong Foreign Correspondents'.

DAWSON, Keith; *see* Dawson, A. K.

DAWSON, Malcolm Edward, OBE 2008; Director, Yewdale Consulting Ltd, since 2014; *b* Harrogate, N Yorks, 8 April 1961; *s* of late Thomas Edward Dawson and of Ruth Dawson; *m* 1985, Tracey Anne Brewin; one *s*. *Educ:* Ashville Coll., Harrogate; Kingston Univ. (MA Human Resource Mgt). Procurement Officer, MoD, 1982–85; HM Customs and Excise: VAT Inspector, 1985–89; various HR rôles, 1989–94; Personnel Manager, Office of Nat. Lottery, 1994–97; Cabinet Office: Mgt Develt Advr, 1997–99; Project Advr, Prime Minister's Strategy Unit, 1999; Hd, Sen. Pay, 2000–02; Prog. Dir, Centre for Mgt and Policy Studies, 2002–03; Department for Constitutional Affairs, later Ministry of Justice: Hd, HR Strategy, 2003–06; Actg HR Dir, 2006–07; Dir, Workforce Reform, 2007–08; Dir, HR, 2008–11, Chief Land Registrar and Chief Exec., 2011–13, HM Land Registry; Dir, BIS, 2014. FCIPD 2010. FRSA. Hon. RICS 2012. *Publications:* (contrib.) Public Sector Leadership for the 21st Century, 2001. *Recreations:* badminton, golf, walking, family.

DAWSON, Sir Nicholas Antony Trevor, 5th Bt *cr* 1920, of Edgewarebury, co. Middlesex; *b* 17 Aug. 1957; *yr s* of Sir (Hugh Halliday) Trevor Dawson, 3rd Bt and Caroline Jane, *d* of William Antony Acton; *S* brother, 2007; *m* 1995, Gisela Bücherl.

DAWSON, Rev. Peter, OBE 1986; education consultant, since 1985; employment law consultant, since 2002; *b* 19 May 1933; *s* of Richard Dawson and Henrietta Kate Dawson (*née* Trueman); *m* 1957, Shirley Margaret Pentland Johnson; two *d*. *Educ:* Beckenham Technical Sch.; Beckenham Grammar Sch.; London School of Economics (BScEcon); Westminster Coll. (Postgrad. CertEd). Schoolmaster Fellow Commoner, Keble Coll., Oxford, 1969, and Corpus Christi Coll., Cambridge, 1979. Asst Master, Roan Grammar School for Boys, London, 1957–62; Head of Upper School, Sedgehill Sch., London, 1962–67; Second Master, Gateacre Comprehensive Sch., Liverpool, 1967–70; Headmaster, Eltham Green Sch., London, 1970–80; Gen. Sec., Professional Assoc. of Teachers, 1980–92; OFSTED Registered Inspector of Schs, 1993–2000. Methodist Minister, ordained 1985; Asst Minister, Queen's Hall Methodist Mission, Derby, 1984–87; Minister, Spondon Methodist Church, Derby, 1989–90; Free Church Minister, Church on Oakwood, Derby, 1990–94; Minister, Mayfield Rd Methodist Church, Derby, 1994–98. Member: Burnham Cttee, 1981–87; Council of Managerial and Professional Staffs, 1989–92 (Pres.); Econ. and Social Cttee, EC, 1990–94; Employment Appeal Tribunal, 1992–2004. Chairman: East Midlands RSA, 2004–06; Church Wilne Probus Club, 2003 (Sec., 2009–11). *Publications:* Making a Comprehensive Work, 1981; Teachers and Teaching, 1984; Why Preach?, 2000; A Short History of the Employment Appeal Tribunal, 2002, rev. and updated edn 2004; Messages and Other Short Stories, 2011; Never Was There Tale of Brighter Hue and Other Short Stories, 2013; The Grey Lady and Other Stories and Stuff, 2015. *Recreations:* reading, theatre, cinema, grandparenthood. *Address:* 30 Elm Street, Borrowash, Derby DE72 3HP. *T:* (01332) 672669. *E:* ockery@ntlworld.com.

DAWSON, Prof. Peter, PhD; FRCP, FRCR, FBIR, FInstP; Professor of Radiology and Consultant Radiologist, 1999–2009, Chairman and Clinical Director of Radiology, 2002–09, University College London Hospitals; *b* 17 May 1945; *s* of Frederick and May Dawson; *m* 1968, Hilary Sturley; one *s* one *d*. *Educ:* Firth Park Sch., Sheffield; King's Coll. London (BSc 1st Cl. Hons 1966; PhD 1970); Westminster Med. Sch. (MB BS 1978). FRCR 1984; FRCP 1994; FInstP 2005; FBIR 2007. Sen. Lectr and Reader in Radiology, 1985–96, Prof. of Med. Imaging, 1996–99, RPMS. Pres., BIR, 1994–95; Royal College of Radiologists: Roentgen Prof., 2002; Registrar, 2002–06. Mem., Internat. Commn on Radiation Units and Measurements, 1999–; Special Asst to IAEA, 2003–. Bd Mem., Internat. Soc. of Radiology, 2002–07; Mem. Res. Cttee, European Assoc. of Radiology, 2005–07. Barclay Prize, 1984, Barclay Medal, 1998, BIR; (jtly) Finzi Prize, RSM, 1991, 1993. *Publications:* Contrast Media in Practice, 1993; Functional CT, 1997; A Textbook of Contrast Media, 1999; Protocols for Multi-slice Computed Tomography, 2006; some 250 papers on physics and medical imaging in learned jls. *Recreations:* music, mathematics, wine, scuba diving. *Address:* Beechers, Green Lane, Chesham Bois, Bucks HP6 5LQ. *T:* (01494) 728222. *E:* peterxdawson@gmail.com. *Club:* Royal Society of Medicine.

DAWSON, Peter, OBE 2015; Secretary, Royal and Ancient Golf Club of St Andrews, 1999–2015; *b* 28 May 1948; *s* of George Dawson and Violet Dawson (*née* Smith); *m* 1969, Juliet Ann Bartlett; one *s* one *d*. *Educ:* Westcliff High Sch.; Corpus Christi Coll., Cambridge (MA). Managing Director: Grove Cranes, 1977–83; Blackwood Hodge (UK), 1983–89; Grove Europe, 1989–93; Thos Storey, 1994–97. Pres., Internat. Golf Fedn, 2011–Sept. 2016 (Jt Sec., 1999–2011). *Address:* Royal and Ancient Golf Club of St Andrews, Fife KY16 9JD. *T:* (01334) 460000. *Clubs:* Northumberland Golf; Royal Worlington and Newmarket Golf; Golf House (Elie).

DAWSON, Rex Malcolm Chaplin, FRS 1981; PhD, DSc; Deputy Director and Head of Biochemistry Department, Institute of Animal Physiology, Babraham, Cambridge, 1969–84, retired (Deputy Chief Scientific Officer, 1969–84); *b* 3 June 1924; *s* of late James Dawson and Ethel Mary Dawson (*née* Chaplin); *m* 1st, 1946, Emily Elizabeth Hodder (*d* 2005); one *s* one *d*; 2nd, 2009, June Margaret Buschman. *Educ:* Hinckley Grammar Sch.; University Coll., London (BSc 1946, DSc 1960); Univ. of Wales (PhD 1951). MRC Fellowship followed by Beit Meml Fellowship, Neuropsychiatric Res. Centre, Whitchurch Hosp., Cardiff, 1947–52; Betty Brookes Fellow, Dept of Biochemistry, Univ. of Oxford, 1952–55. Vis. Res. Fellow, Harvard Univ., 1959; Vis. Prof., Northwestern Univ., Chicago, 1974. International Lipid Prize, Amer. Oil Chemists' Assoc., 1981. *Publications:* Metabolism and Physiological Significance of Lipids, 1964; Data for Biochemical Research, 1959, 3rd edn 1986; Form and Function of Phospholipids, 1973; numerous papers on structure, turnover and role of phospholipids in cell membranes in various scientific jls. *Recreations:* mercantile marine history, sailing, gardening. *Address:* Kirn House, Holt Road, Langham, Norfolk NR25 7BX. *T:* (01328) 830396.

DAWSON, Ruth Mitchell; *see* McKernan, R. M.

DAWSON, Dame Sandra (June Noble), DBE 2004; KPMG Professor of Management Studies, University of Cambridge, 1995–2013, now Emeritus (Director, Judge Business School (formerly Judge Institute of Management Studies), 1995–2006; Deputy Vice

Chancellor, 2008–12); Fellow, Sidney Sussex College, Cambridge, since 2009 (Master, 1999–2009); *b* 4 June 1946; *d* of late Wilfred Denyer and Joy (*née* Noble); *m* 1969, Henry R. C. Dawson; one *s* two *d*. *Educ:* Dr Challoner's Grammar Sch., Amersham; Univ. of Keele (BA 1st Cl. Hons Hist. and Sociol. 1968). Research Officer, Govt Social Survey, 1968–69; Imperial College of Science, Technology and Medicine: Res. Officer, Lectr, then Sen. Lectr, Industrial Sociol. Unit, Dept of Social and Econ. Studies, 1969–90; Prof. of Organisational Behaviour, Mgt Sch., 1990–95; Fellow, Jesus Coll., Cambridge, 1995–99. Non-exec. Dir, Riverside HA, 1990–92; Chm., Riverside Mental Health Trust, 1992–95. Member: Res. Strategy Bd, Offshore Safety Div., HSE, 1991–95; Strategic Review Gp, PHLS, 1994; Sen. Salaries Review Body, 1997–2003; Futures and Innovation Bd, DTI, 1998–2002; Res. Priorities Bd, ESRC, 2000–03; Task Force on Accounting for People, 2003; Fire and Rescue Service Ministerial Adv. Gp, 2004–; Council for Sci. and Technol., 2011–14. Chm., Exec. Steering Cttee, ESRC Advanced Inst. of Mgt, 2007–11. Non-executive Director: Cambridge Econometrics, 1996–2007; Fleming Claverhouse Investment Trust, 1996–2003; PHLS, 1997–99; Soc. for Advancement of Mgt Studies, 1999–2003; Barclays plc, 2003–09; Oxfam, 2006–12; FSA, 2010–13; DRS plc, 2012–; Inst. for Govt, 2012– (Trustee, 2012–); Winton Capital Mgt, 2013–; TSB, 2014–. Mem. Adv. Bd, Alchemy Partners, 2000–04. Member: UK-India Roundtable, 2006–; Adv. Bd, UK India Business Council, 2007–; Social Sci. Res. Council, USA, 2009–. Trustee, RANDEurope (UK), 2001–04. Companion, Assoc. of Business Schs, 2007. Internat. Women's Forum Hall of Fame, 2007. *Publications:* Analysing Organisations, 1986, 3rd edn 1996; Safety at Work: the limits of self regulation, 1988; Managing in the NHS, 1995; (ed) Future Health Organisations and Systems, 2005; (ed) Policy Futures for UK Health, 2006; Engaging with Care: a vision for the health and care workforce of England, 2007; (ed) Future Public Health: burdens, challenges and opportunities, 2009; contribs to mgt learned jls. *Recreations:* music, walking, family. *Address:* Sidney Sussex College, Cambridge CB2 3HU.

DAWSON, Stephen Eric; His Honour Judge Dawson; a Circuit Judge, since 2010; *b* 16 Feb. 1952. Admitted Solicitor, 1977. Articled and subseq. Partner, Victor Lissack, solicitors, 1978–82; Partner, Reynolds Dawson, 1982–94; Metropolitan Stipendiary Magistrate, later District Judge (Magistrates' Courts), 1994–2010; Recorder, 2000–10. *Address:* Ministry of Justice, Judicial Division, 3rd Floor, Petty France, SW1H 9AJ.

DAWSON, (Thomas) Hilton; Director, Northumbria People, since 2013; *b* 30 Sept. 1953; *s* of late Harry Dawson and Sally Dawson; *m* 1973, Susan, *d* of Ellis and Alice Williams; two *d*. *Educ:* Warwick Univ. (BA Hons Philos. and Pols 1975); Lancaster Univ. (Dip. in Social Work 1982); Dip. Funeral Celebrancy 2013. Brickworks labourer, 1975; clerk, 1976; kibbutz volunteer, 1976; community worker, 1977; social worker, 1979; Lancs Social Services, 1982–97; youth justice worker, 1983; social work manager, 1989. Mem. (Lab) Lancaster CC, 1987–97. MP (Lab) Lancaster and Wyre, 1997–2005. Chief Exec., Shaftesbury Homes and Arethusa, subseq. Shaftesbury Young People, 2005–08; Develt Consultant, Serco Educn and Children's Services, 2008–09; Chm., Nat. Acad. for Parenting Practitioners, 2007–09; Chief Exec., BASW, 2009–13; Gen. Sec., Social Workers Union, 2011–13. Founding Chm., North East Party, 2014–. Columnist, The Journal, Newcastle, 2013–. Civil Funeral Celebrant. *Publications:* Frank Renner's Bairns: looking at the world through the lives of a Northumbrian family, 2013; (jtly) Newbiggin Resilient, 2014; Eddie, 2015. *Recreations:* family, four grandchildren, the arts, walking, keeping fit, politics, Chair of Newbiggin by the Sea Genealogy Project. *Address:* 36 Morwick Road, Warkworth, Northumberland NE65 0TD. *T:* (01665) 711817.

DAWSON-DAMER, family name of **Earl of Portarlington**.

DAWTRY, Sir Alan, Kt 1974; CBE 1968 (MBE (mil.) 1945); TD 1948; Chief Executive (formerly Town Clerk), Westminster City Council, 1956–77; Chairman: Sperry Rand Ltd, 1977–86; Sperry Rand (Ireland) Ltd, 1977–86; President, London Rent Assessment Panel, 1979–86; *b* 8 April 1915; *s* of Melancthon and Kate Nicholas Dawtry, Sheffield; *m* 1997, Sally Ann, *d* of Mr and Mrs D. P. Chalklin. *Educ:* King Edward VII Sch., Sheffield; Sheffield Univ. (LLB). Served War of 1939–45: commissioned RA; campaigns France, N Africa, Italy (MBE, despatches twice); released with rank of Lt-Col. Admitted Solicitor, 1938; Asst Solicitor, Sheffield, 1938–48; Deputy Town Clerk, Bolton, 1948–52; Deputy Town Clerk, Leicester, 1952–54; Town Clerk, Wolverhampton, 1954–56; Hon. Sec., London Boroughs Assoc., 1965–78. Member: Metrication Bd, 1969–74; Clean Air Council, 1960–75; Council of Management, Architectural Heritage Fund, 1977–89; CBI Council, 1982–86. Pres., Soc. of Local Authority Chief Execs, 1975–76. Vice-Chm., Dolphin Square Trust, 1985–99. FCMI (FBIM 1975); FRSA 1978. Hon. LLD Sheffield, 2007. Foreign Orders: The Star (Afghanistan); Golden Honour (Austria); Leopold II (Belgium); Rio Branco (Brazil); Merit (Chile); Legion of Honour (France); Merit (W Germany); the Phœnix (Greece); Merit (Italy); Homayoun (Iran); The Rising Sun (Japan); the Star (Jordan); African Redemption (Liberia); Oaken Crown (Luxembourg); Loyalty (Malaysia); the Right Hand (Nepal); Orange-Nassau (Netherlands); the Two Niles (Sudan); the Crown (Thailand); Zaire (Zaire). *Address:* 901 Grenville House, Dolphin Square, SW1V 3LR. *T:* (020) 7798 8100.

DAWTRY, Ven. Dr Anne Frances; Archdeacon of Halifax, since 2011; *b* Grantham, 25 Oct. 1957; *d* of Frederick Ewart Dawtry and Mary Josephine Dawtry. *Educ:* Westfield Coll., Univ. of London (BA Hons 1979; PhD 1985). Sen. Lectr, Univ. of Chester, 1983; ordained deacon, 1993, priest, 1994; Curate: St Hubert's, Corfe Mullen, 1993–96; St Peter's, Parkstone with Branksea, 1996–97; Sen. Chaplain, Bournemouth Univ., 1997–99; Principal, Ordained Local Ministry, Dio. of Salisbury, 1999–2003; Dir of Ministry Trng, Dio. of Manchester, 2003–06; Dir, Southern NW Trng Partnership, 2006–08; Rector, St Werburgh's, Chorlton cum Hardy, 2008–11; Warden of Readers, Dio. of Wakefield, 2012. Consultant, 2000–05, Mem., 2005–, Liturgical Commn. *Publications:* (contrib.) They Shaped our Worship, 1998; (contrib.) Companion to Common Worship, vol. 1, 2001, vol. 2, 2006; (jtly) Art and Worship, 2000, 2nd edn 2002; (contrib.) New Dictionary of Liturgy and Worship, 2002. *Recreations:* architecture, photography, stained glass design, gardening. *Address:* 2 Vicarage Gardens, Brighouse, W Yorks HD6 3HD. *T:* (01484) 714553. *E:* archdeacon.halifax@westyorkshiredales.anglican.org. *Club:* Army and Navy.

DAY, Prof. Alan Charles Lynn; Professor of Economics, London School of Economics, University of London, 1964–83, now Professor Emeritus; *b* 25 Oct. 1924; *s* of late Henry Charles Day, MBE, and Ruth Day; *m* 1962, Diana Hope Bocking (*d* 1980); no *c*; *m* 1982, Dr Shirley E. Jones. *Educ:* Chesterfield Grammar Sch.; Queens' Coll., Cambridge. Asst Lecturer, then Lecturer, LSE, 1949–54; Economic Adviser, HM Treas., 1954–56; Reader in Economics, London Univ., 1956–64. Ed., National Inst. Econ. Review, 1960–62; Econ. Correspondent, The Observer, intermittently, 1957–81. Economic Adviser on Civil Aviation, BoT, later Dept of Trade and Industry, 1968–72; Economic Adviser, Civil Aviation Authority, 1972–78. Member: Council, Consumers' Assoc., 1963–82; Board, British Airports Authority, 1965–68; SE Region Econ. Planning Council, 1966–69; Home Office Cttee on the London Taxicab Trade, 1967–70; Layfield Cttee on Local Govt Finance, 1974–76; Air Transport Users' Cttee, CAA, 1978–79; Home Office Adv. Panel on Satellite Broadcasting Standards, 1982. British Acad. Leverhulme Vis. Prof., Graduate Inst. for International Studies, Geneva, 1971. Governor, LSE, 1971–76, 1977–79, Pro-Director, 1979–83; Hon. Fellow, 1988. *Publications:* The Future of Sterling, 1954; Outline of Monetary Economics, 1956; The Economics of Money, 1959; (with S. T. Beza) Wealth and Income, 1960. *Address:* Chart Place, Chart Sutton, Maidstone, Kent ME17 3RE. *T:* (01622) 842236.

DAY, Andrew Christopher King, CBE 2003; Deputy Bailiff, 1999–2002, Lieutenant Bailiff, 2002–05, Guernsey; *b* 30 Oct. 1941; *m* José Guillemette; one *s* two *d*. *Educ:* Gresham's Sch., Holt; Magdalen Coll., Oxford (BA 1964); Inst. of Educn, London Univ. (Cert. Ed. 1965). Teacher, Kenya, 1965–69; called to the Bar, Gray's Inn, 1970; Advocate, Royal Court of Guernsey, 1971; in private practice, 1971–82; QC (Guernsey) 1989; Solicitor General, HM Comptroller, 1982–92, Attorney General, HM Procureur and Receiver General, 1992–99, Guernsey. *Address:* Sans Souci, Les Dunes, Vazon, Castel, Guernsey GY5 7LQ.

DAY, Anneliese Mary; QC 2012; *b* Edinburgh, 6 March 1973; *d* of Alan and Katherine Day; one *s* one *d*. *Educ:* Edinburgh Acad.; Clare Coll., Cambridge (BA 1994); Harvard Univ. (Kennedy Schol.; MA Law). Called to the Bar, Inner Temple, 1996; in practice as barrister, specialising in commercial, construction, insurance and professional liability, 1996–. Mem., Legal Services Bd, 2013–. *Publications:* (ed) Jackson & Powell on Professional Negligence, 1982, 7th edn 2012. *Recreations:* children, travel, bikram yoga. *Address:* 4 New Square, Lincoln's Inn, WC2A 3RJ. *T:* (020) 7822 2000, *Fax:* (020) 7822 2111. *E:* a.day@4newsquare.com.

DAY, Sir Barry (Stuart), Kt 2014; OBE 2007; Chief Executive, Greenwood Academies Trust, since 2009; *b* Stevenage, 12 June 1953; *s* of Sidney William Day and Peggy Joyce Day; *m* 1991, Brenda Partridge; two *d*. *Educ:* Alleyne's Grammar Sch., Stevenage; Loughborough Univ. (MSc). Teacher of Maths, Stonehill High Sch., Leicester, 1974–75; 2nd i/c Maths, Wreake Valley Coll., Leicester, 1975–81; Hd of Maths, Hamilton Community Coll., Leicester, 1981–85; Vice Principal, Mundella Community Coll., Leicester, 1985–91; Head Teacher, Greenwood Dale Sch., Nottingham, 1992–2008; Exec. Principal, Nottingham Acad., 2008–09. Hon. DEd Nottingham Trent, 2008. *Recreations:* walking, swimming, travel. *Address:* Greenwood House, Private Road No. 2, Colwick Quays Business Park, Colwick, Nottingham NG4 2JY. *T:* 07733 227244. *E:* barry.day@greenwoodacademies.org.

DAY, Bernard Maurice, CB 1987; Chairman, The Riverside (East Molesey) Management Co., 1996–99, 2004–05 (Director, 1999–2004); *b* 7 May 1928; *s* of M. J. Day and Mrs M. H. Day; *m* 1956, Ruth Elizabeth Stansfield (*d* 2010); two *s* one *d*. *Educ:* Bancroft's Sch.; London School of Economics (BScEcon). Army service, commnd RA, 1946–48. British Electric Traction Fedn, 1950–51; Asst Principal, Air Ministry, 1951; Private Sec. to Air Mem. for Supply and Organisation, 1954–56; Principal, 1956; Cabinet Secretariat, 1959–61; Asst Sec., 1965; Sec., Meteorological Office, 1965–69; Estabt Officer, Cabinet Office, 1969–72; Head of Air Staff Secretariat, MoD, 1972–74; Asst Under Sec. of State, MoD, 1974; Civilian Staff Management, 1974–76; Operational Requirements, 1976–80; Programmes and Budget, 1980–82; Supply and Orgn, Air, 1982–84; Resident Chm., CSSB, 1984–85; Asst Under-Sec. of State (Fleet Support), MoD, 1985–88. Panel Chm., CSSB, 1988–96. Chairman: MoD Branch, First Div. Assoc., 1983–84; MoD Liaison Cttee with CS Benevolent Fund, 1975–84. Pres., Fellowship Club, Weybridge, 2008–10 (Immediate Past Pres., 2010–11). *Recreations:* local church, arts and environment. *Address:* 26 The Riverside, Graburn Way, East Molesey, Surrey KT8 9BF. *T:* (020) 8941 4520.

DAY, Prof. Christopher, DPhil, DLitt; FAcSS; Professor, School of Education, University of Nottingham, 1993–2010, now Emeritus; *b* 3 May 1943; *s* of Walter Day and Patricia Jane Day; *m* 1984, Alison Jane Stewart; two *s*. *Educ:* St Luke's Coll., Exeter (Cert Ed 1964); Univ. of Sussex (MA 1976; DPhil 1979); Univ. of Nottingham (DLitt 2008). LRAM 1966. School teacher, 1964–68; Lectr, 1968–71; LEA Advr, London Borough of Barking and Dagenham, 1972–76; Associate Prof., Univ. of Calgary, Alberta, 1979–81; Lectr, Sen. Lectr and Reader, Univ. of Nottingham, 1981–93. Editor, Developing Teachers and Schools series, 1991–94; Founding Editor, Teachers and Teaching, 1995–; Co-Editor: Jl of In-Service Teacher Educn, 1975–2002; Educational Action Res. Jl, 1993–2011. FRSA 1972; FAcSS (AcSS 2013). Hon. PhD Linköping, Sweden, 1993. *Publications:* Developing Teachers: the challenges of lifelong learning, 1999; A Passion for Teaching, 2004; New Understandings of Teachers' Work: emotions and educational change, 2011; *jointly:* Managing Primary Schools, 1985; Appraisal and Professional Development in Primary Schools, 1987; Reconceptualising School-Based Curriculum Development, 1990; Managing Primary Schools in the 1990s, 1990; Leadership and Curriculum in Primary Schools, 1993; Developing Leadership in Primary Schools, 1998; Leading Schools in Times of Change, 2001; Effective Leadership for School Improvement, 2003; Teachers Matter: connecting work, lives and effectiveness, 2007; The New Lives of Teachers, 2010; School Leadership on Pupil Outcomes: building and sustaining success, 2011; Resilient Leaders, Resilient Schools, 2013; Leading Schools Successfully: stories from the field, 2014; *edited jointly:* Staff Development in Secondary Schools, 1986; Partnership in Educational Management, 1988; Insights into Teachers' Thinking and Practice, 1990; Managing the Professional Development of Teachers, 1991; Research on Teacher Thinking, 1993; Children and Youth at Risk and Urban Education, 1997; Teachers and Teaching: international perspectives on school reform and teacher education, 1997; The Life and Work of Teachers in Changing Times: international perspectives, 1999; Developing Teachers and Teaching Practice, 2002; Theory and Practice in Action Research, 2002; (and contrib.) International Handbook of the Continuing Professional Development of Teachers, 2004; Successful Principal Leadership in Times of Change: an international perspective, 2007; International Handbook on Teacher and School Development, 2012. *Recreations:* walking, tennis, reading, swimming. *Address:* School of Education, University of Nottingham, Jubilee Campus, Wollaton Road, Nottingham NG8 1BB. *T:* (0115) 951 4423.

DAY, Prof. Christopher Paul, MD, PhD; DL; FRCP, FRCPE, FMedSci; Professor of Liver Medicine, since 2000 and Pro Vice Chancellor, Faculty of Medical Sciences, since 2008, Newcastle University; *b* Darlington, 2 Feb. 1960; *s* of Raymond Day and June Day; two *s* one *d* by former marriage. *Educ:* Churchill Coll., Cambridge (BA 1981; MB BChir 1983); Univ. of Newcastle upon Tyne (MD (with commendation) 1994; PhD 1994). MRCP 1986, FRCP 1998; FRCPE 2005. University of Newcastle upon Tyne, later Newcastle University: MRC Trng Fellow and Clinician Scientist, 1990–97; Hd, Sch. of Clinical Med. Scis, 2004–08; Hon. Consultant Hepatologist, Freeman Hosp., then Newcastle upon Tyne Hosps NHS Foundn Trust, 1995–. Mem., MRC, 2010–. Vice Pres. (Clin.), Acad. of Med. Scis, 2014–. FMedSci 2008. DL Tyne and Wear, 2014. *Publications:* over 200 articles on all aspects of liver disease in jls incl. Lancet, New England Jl of Medicine, Nature Genetics; approx. 200 review articles. *Recreations:* playing guitar, tennis, golf. *Address:* Medical Sciences Faculty Office, The Medical School, Newcastle University, Framlington Place, Newcastle upon Tyne NE2 4HH. *T:* (0191) 222 7003, *Fax:* (0191) 222 6621. *E:* c.p.day@ncl.ac.uk. *Clubs:* Medical Pilgrims, 1942.

DAY, Rev. David Vivian; Principal, St John's College, University of Durham, 1993–99; non-stipendiary Curate, St Nicholas, Durham, since 1999; *b* 11 Aug. 1936; *s* of Frederick Vivian Day and Enid Blodwen (*née* Evans); *m* 1959, Lorna Rosemary Taylor; two *s* one *d*. *Educ:* The Grammar Sch., Tottenham; QMC, Univ. of London (BA Classics); Univ. of Nottingham (MEd, MTheol). Classics Master, Southgate County Sch., 1958–64; Head of Religious Education: Southgate Sch., 1964–66; Bilborough Sch., 1966–73; Sen. Lectr in Theol., Bishop Lonsdale Coll., Derby, 1973–79; Sen. Lectr in Educn, Univ. of Durham, 1979–97. Ordained deacon, 1999, priest, 2000. *Publications:* This Jesus, 1980, 2nd edn 1981; Jeremiah: speaking for God in a time of crisis, 1987; Teenage Beliefs, 1991; (ed jtly) The Contours of Christian Education, 1992; Beyond the Here and Now, 1996; A Preaching Workbook, 1998, 4th edn 2004; Pearl beyond Price, 2002; Christ Our Life, 2003; (ed jtly) A Reader on Preaching, 2005; Embodying the Word, 2005. *Recreations:* keeping fit, watching Rugby and soccer. *Address:* 35 Orchard Drive, The Sands, Durham DH1 1LA. *T:* (0191) 386 6909.

DAY, Douglas Henry; QC 1989; a Recorder, since 1987; *b* 11 Oct. 1943; *s* of James Henry Day and Nancy Day; *m* 1970, Elizabeth Margaret (*née* Jarman); two *s* one *d*. *Educ:* Bec Sch.; Selwyn Coll., Cambridge (MA). Called to the Bar, Lincoln's Inn, 1967, Bencher, 1996. Asst Parly Boundary Comr, 1994–. Treas., Gen. Council of the Bar, 1999–2001. *Address:* Farrar's Building, Temple, EC4Y 7BD. *T:* (020) 7583 9241. *Clubs:* Garrick; Bec Old Boys Rugby.

DAY, Sir Graham; *see* Day, Sir J. G.

DAY, (Henrietta Miriam) Ottoline; *see* Leyser, H. M. O.

DAY, John Leigh, MD; FRCP; Professor of Internal Medicine, Catholic University of Mozambique, since 2002; *b* 30 Nov. 1939; *s* of Peter Leigh Day and Jean Metcalfe Bailey; *m* 1972, Anne Pamela Northcote; two *s* one *d*. *Educ:* King's Coll., London (MD 1973). FRCP 1979. Medical Registrar: Ipswich and E Suffolk Hosp., 1966; KCH, 1967; Lectr in Medicine, KCL; Consultant Physician, 1972, now Emeritus, Clinical Dir of Medicine, 1998–2002, Ipswich Hosp. Advr on Educn, WHO, 1990–95. Chm., Educn Adv. Cttee, Diabetes UK, 1985–92; Pres., Diabetes Educn Study Gp, European Assoc. of Diabetes, 1985–92. Dir, Ipswich-Beira Health Initiative, 2003–. Hon. DSc UEA, 2000. *Publications:* Learning Diabetes Type 1, and Type 2 Diabetic, 1986, 3rd edn 2001; res. articles in Diabetes Educn and Care, Diabetes Medicine, Patient Educn and Counselling, BMJ. *Recreations:* golf, canal boating. *E:* days_bealings@hotmail.com.

DAY, Air Chief Marshal Sir John (Romney), KCB 1999; OBE 1985; FCGI; Senior Military Adviser, BAE Systems, 2003–10; *b* 15 July 1947; *er s* of John George Day and Daphne Myrtle Day (*née* Kelly); *m* 1969, Jane Richards; two *s*. *Educ:* King's Sch., Canterbury; Imperial Coll., Univ. of London (BSc Aer. Eng.). No 72 Sqn, 1970–73; Flying Instructor, RAF Linton-on-Ouse, 1973–76; OC Oxford Univ. Air Sqn, 1976–79; RAF Staff Coll., 1981; PSO to Air Mem. for Personnel, 1982–83; OC No 72 Sqn, 1983–85; OC RAF Odiham, 1987–89; RCDS, 1990; Dir, Air Force Plans and Progs, MoD, 1991–94; AOC No 1 Gp, 1994–97; DCDS (Commitments), MoD, 1997–2000; AMP and C-in-C, RAF PTC, 2000–01; C-in-C Strike Comd, 2001–03; Air ADC to the Queen, 2001–03. FCGI 2002. *Address:* c/o Lloyds Bank, Ashford, Kent TN24 8SS. *Club:* Royal Air Force.
See also Air Vice Marshal N. J. Day.

DAY, Jonathan Stephen, CBE 1999; Chairman, Joint Intelligence Committee, Cabinet Office, since 2012; *b* 23 April 1954; *s* of late Peter Alan John Day and of Josephine Day; *m* 1980, Sandra Ayres; one *d*. *Educ:* Marling Sch., Stroud; Univ. of Nottingham (LLB Hons 1976). Ministry of Defence: admin trainee, 1979; early posts included Naval, out-of-area and policy studies secretariats, and Asst Private Sec. to Armed Forces Minister; seconded: to FCO in UK Delegn to NATO, Brussels, 1988–92; to NATO as Hd, Force Planning, 1992–95; Dep. Comd Sec., Land Comd, 1995–97; Dir, Defence Policy, 1997–99; sabbatical, Harvard Univ., 1999–2000; seconded: to Cabinet Office as Chief, Jt Intelligence Cttee Assessments Staff, 2000–01; to NATO as Dir, Sec. Gen.'s Private Office, 2001–03; Comd Sec., Fleet Comd, 2004–06; Dir, Operational Policy, 2007–08, Dir Gen., then Dir, Security Policy, 2008–11, Second Permanent Sec., 2011–12, MoD. Hon. Prof., Strategy and Security Inst., Univ. of Exeter. *Publications:* Gloucester and Newbury 1643, Turning Point of the Civil War, 2007. *Recreations:* history, reading, theatre and cinema, cricket, walking, unsuitably juvenile loud music. *Address:* c/o Cabinet Office, 70 Whitehall, SW1A 2AS.

DAY, Sir (Judson) Graham, Kt 1989; OC 2014; Chairman, PowerGen, 1990–93 (Director, 1990–93); *b* 3 May 1933; *s* of Frank Charles Day and Edythe Grace (*née* Baker); *m* 1958, Leda Ann (*née* Creighton); one *s* two *d*. *Educ:* Queen Elizabeth High Sch., Halifax, NS; Dalhousie Univ., Halifax, NS (LLB). Private practice of Law, Windsor, Nova Scotia, 1956–64; Canadian Pacific Ltd, Montreal and Toronto, 1964–71; Chief Exec., Cammell Laird Shipbuilders Ltd, Birkenhead, Eng., 1971–75; Dep. Chm., Organising Cttee for British Shipbuilders and Dep. Chm. and Chief Exec. designate, British Shipbuilders, 1975–76; Prof. of Business Admin and Dir, Canadian Marine Transportation Centre, Dalhousie Univ., NS, 1977–81; Vice-Pres., Shipyards & Marine Develt, Dome Petroleum Ltd, 1981–83; Chm. and Chief Exec., British Shipbuilders, 1983–86; Chief Exec., 1986–88, Chm., 1986–91, BL, subseq. The Rover Gp Hldgs. Chm., Cadbury Schweppes, 1989–93 (Dir, 1988–93); Deputy Chairman: MAI plc, 1989–93 (Dir, 1988–93); Ugland Internat. Hldgs plc, 1997; Director: The Laird Gp plc, 1985; British Aerospace, 1986–92 (Chairman, 1991–92); Extendicare (formerly Crownx) Inc. (Canada), 1989; Bank of Nova Scotia (Canada), 1989–2004; NOVA Corp. of Alberta, 1990; EMI Gp, 1991; Empire Co. Ltd, 1991–2006; Sobeys Inc., 1998–2005. Counsel, Stewart McKelvey (formerly Stewart McKelvey Stirling Scales), 1991–. Pres., ISBA, 1991–93. Member: Nova Scotia Barristers' Soc.; Law Soc. of Upper Canada; Canadian Bar Assoc. Freeman, City of London. ARINA. Hon. Fellow, Univ. of Wales Coll. of Cardiff, 1990. Hon. doctorates: Dalhousie; City; CNAA; Cranfield; Aston; Warwick; Humberside; South Bank. Order of Nova Scotia, 2011. *Recreation:* reading. *Address:* 162 Avon Street, PO Box 422, Hantsport, NS B0P 1P0, Canada.

DAY, Lance Reginald; Keeper, Science Museum Library, 1976–87; *b* 2 Nov. 1927; *s* of late Reginald and Eileen Day; *m* 1959, Mary Ann Sheahan; one *s* two *d*. *Educ:* Sherrardswood Sch., Welwyn Garden City; Alleyne's Grammar Sch., Stevenage; Northern Polytechnic (BSc London); University Coll., London (MSc Hist. and Philos. of Sci.). Res. Asst, Science Museum Library, 1951–64, Asst Keeper 1964–70; Asst Keeper, Science Museum, Dept of Chemistry, 1970–74; Keeper, Science Museum, Dept of Communications and Electrical Engrg, 1974–76. Sec., Nat. Railway Museum Cttee, 1973–75; Newcomen Society: Hon. Sec., 1973–82; Hon. Mem., 1996; Ed., Trans of Newcomen Soc., 1990–2000 (Chm., Editl Bd, 1992–2000); Newcomen Fellow, 2010. *Publications:* Broad Gauge, 1985; (contrib.) Encyclopaedia of the History of Technology, 1990; (ed jtly and contrib.) Biographical Dictionary of the History of Technology, 1996; reviews and articles. *Recreation:* music. *Address:* 12 Rhinefield Close, Brockenhurst, Hants SO42 7SU. *T:* (01590) 622079.

DAY, Martyn; MP (SNP) Linlithgow and East Falkirk, since 2015; *b* Falkirk, 26 March 1971. Former bank worker. Mem. (SNP), W Lothian Council, 1999–2015. *Address:* House of Commons, SW1A 0AA.

DAY, Sir Michael (John), Kt 1992; OBE 1981; Chairman, Commission for Racial Equality, 1988–93; *b* 4 Sept. 1933; *s* of Albert Day and Ellen Florence (*née* Itter); *m* 1960, June Marjorie, *d* of late Dr John William and Edith Mackay; one *s* one *d*. *Educ:* University College Sch., Hampstead; Selwyn Coll., Cambridge (MA); London School of Economics (Cert. Social Work and Social Admin). Probation Officer, Surrey, 1960–64; Sen. Probation Officer, W Sussex, 1964–67; Asst Prin. Probation Officer, 1967–68, Chief Probation Officer, 1968–76, Surrey; Chief Probation Officer, W Midlands, 1976–88. Chm., Chief Probation Officers' Conf., 1974–77; First Chm., Assoc. Chief Officers of Probation, 1982–84. Member: Probation Adv. and Trng Bd, Home Office, 1970–73; Adv. Council for Probation and Aftercare, 1973–78. Member Council: Howard League for Penal Reform, 1966–73; Volunteer Centre, 1977–81; Grubb Inst., 1980–93. Dir, Shropshire and Mid Wales Hospice, 1998–2003. *Publications:* contribs to professional jls and others. *Recreations:* family and friends, gardening, the countryside, turning wood and pages. *Address:* 30 Broad Street, Ludlow, Shropshire SY8 1NJ.
See also R. M. Gordon Clark.

DAY, Michael Patrick, CVO 2015; Chief Executive, Historic Royal Palaces, since 2003; *b* 20 Feb. 1953; *s* of Harry and Anne Day; *m* 1998, Anne Murch; one *s* one *d*. *Educ:* Nottingham High Sch.; Univ. of Leeds (BA Hons (English) 1974). Graduate trainee, Mus. Asst, then Asst Keeper of Social Hist., Norfolk Mus Service, 1974–83; Curator of Social Hist., Ironbridge Gorge Mus. Trust, 1983–86; Dir, Jersey Heritage Trust, 1987–2003. Mem. Faculty, Mus. Leadership Prog., UEA, 1994–2011; Co-Dir, Nordic Mus. Leadership Prog., Copenhagen, 2001–08; Mem. Bd, Cultural Leadership Prog., 2009–11. Trustee, Alnwick Garden Trust, 2010–13; Chm., Battersea Arts Centre, 2012–. FMA 1994; FRSA 1995; FCMI (FIMgt 1999); CCMI 2007. Hon. DArts Kingston, 2010. *Recreations:* family and friends, ski-ing, sailing (Mem., National 12 Owners' Association), Aston Villa FC, real tennis, music, cinema. *Address:* Historic Royal Palaces, Apt 39, Hampton Court Palace, Surrey KT8 9AU. *T:* (020) 3166 6600. *E:* michael.day@hrp.org.uk. *Clubs:* Ski Club of Great Britain; Royal Tennis Court.

DAY, Prof. Nicholas Edward, CBE 2001; PhD; FRS 2004; FRCPath, FMedSci; MRC Research Professor in Epidemiology, 1999–2004, and Fellow of Hughes Hall, since 1992, University of Cambridge; *b* 24 Sept. 1939; *s* of late John King Day, TD and Mary Elizabeth (*née* Stinton); *m* 1961, Jocelyn Deanne Broughton; one *s* one *d*. *Educ:* Magdalen Coll., Oxford (BA Maths); Aberdeen Univ. (PhD Med. Stats). FRCPath 1997. Res. Fellow, Aberdeen Univ., 1962–66; Fellow, ANU, 1966–69; Statistician, 1969–78, Head, Unit of Biostats and Field Studies, 1979–86, Internat. Agency for Res. on Cancer, Lyon; Cancer Expert, Nat. Cancer Inst., USA, 1978–79; Dir, 1986–89, Hon. Dir, 1989–99, MRC Biostats Unit; Prof. of Public Health, Cambridge Univ., 1989–99; Fellow, Churchill Coll., Cambridge, 1986–92. Founder FMedSci 1998. *Publications:* Statistical Methods in Cancer Research, vol. 1 1980, vol. 2 1988; Screening for Cancer of the Uterine Cervix, 1986; Screening for Breast Cancer, 1988; over 300 articles in scientific jls. *Recreations:* sea fishing, fruit growing. *Address:* Seawinds Les Jardins, Rue de la Lague, St Pierre du Bois, Guernsey GY7 9BU. *T:* (01481) 267257.

DAY, Air Vice Marshal Nigel James, CBE 2000; FRAeS; Senior Defence Adviser, MBDA Missile Systems, 2004–13; *b* 13 Feb. 1949; *s* of John George Day and Daphne Myrtle Day (*née* Kelly); *m* 1971, Gillian Cronk; one *s* one *d*. *Educ:* King's Sch., Canterbury; Imperial Coll., Univ. of London (BSc). No 45 Sqn, 1974; No 17 Sqn, 1975–76; No 31 Sqn, 1976–78; No 725 Sqn, Royal Danish Air Force, 1979–81; Flight Comdr, No 226 (Jaguar) OCU, 1982–83; RAF Staff Coll., 1984; Operational Requirements Staff, MoD, 1985–87; OC No 617 (DamBusters) Sqn, 1987–90; Air Offensive Staff, MoD, 1990–93; OC RAF Lossiemouth, 1993–95; rcds, 1996; OC Brit. Forces, Gulf Region, 1997; Dir, Air Ops, Strike Command, 1997–99; Dep. UK Mil. Rep. to NATO, 1999–2001; Capability Manager (Strike), MoD, 2001–04. FRAeS 2004. *Publications:* contrib. to RUSI jl. *Recreations:* dog walking, sailing, painting. *Club:* Royal Air Force.
See also Air Chief Marshal Sir J. R. Day.

DAY, Penelope Jane, (Penny); *see* Dyer, P. J.

DAY, Prof. Peter, DPhil; FRS 1986; FRSC, FInstP; Fullerian Professor of Chemistry, Royal Institution, 1994–2008, now Emeritus; Emeritus Professor of Chemistry, University of London, since 2008; Royal Institution Professorial Research Fellow, University College London, since 1995 (Honorary Fellow, 2003); *b* 20 Aug. 1938; *s* of Edgar Day and Ethel Hilda Day (*née* Russell); *m* 1964, Frances Mary Elizabeth Anderson; one *s* one *d*. *Educ:* Maidstone Grammar School; Wadham College, Oxford (BA 1961; MA, DPhil 1965; Hon. Fellow, 1991). FInstP 1996. Cyanamid European Research Institute, Geneva, 1962; Jun. Res. Fellow, 1963–65, Official Fellow, 1965–91, Hon. Fellow, 1994, St John's College, Oxford; Departmental Demonstrator, 1965–67, Lectr in Inorganic Chemistry, 1967–89, *ad hominem* Prof. of Solid State Chemistry, 1989–91, Oxford Univ. Dir, Inst. Laue-Langevin, Grenoble, 1988–91 (on secondment); Royal Institution: Dir, 1991–98; Resident Prof. of Chemistry, 1991–94; Dir, Davy Faraday Res. Lab., 1991–98. Prof. Associé, Univ. de Paris-Sud, 1975; Prof. Invité, Univ. Rennes, 1997; Guest Prof., Univ. of Copenhagen, 1978; Iberdrola Prof., Univ. of Valencia, 2001. Vis. Fellow, ANU, 1980; Senior Research Fellow, SRC, 1977–82. Lectures: Du Pont, Indiana Univ., 1988; Royal Soc. Blackett Meml, 1994; Bakerian, 1999; ACL, Chinese Univ. Hong Kong, 1997; Birch, ANU, 1997; Humphry Davy, Royal Soc., 2002; Stefan, Stefan Inst., Ljubjana, 2010; Coochbehaar, Indian Assoc. for Cultivation of Sci., Kolkata, 2010. Science and Engineering Research Council: Member: Neutron Beam Res. Cttee, 1983–88; Chemistry Cttee, 1985–88; Molecular Electronics Cttee, 1987–88; Nat. Cttee on Superconductivity, 1987–88; Materials Commn, 1988–90. British Council: Mem., Sci. and Engrg Cttee, 1991–98; Chm., Anglo-French Res. Grants Cttee, 1995–98; Member: COPUS, 1991–98; EC DG Res. Infrastructures Panel, 1992–98; Phys. and Engrg Sci. Cttee, ESF, 1994–2000; Medicines Commn, 1998–2005; Adv. Council, RIKEN Advanced Sci. Inst., Tokyo, 2009–12; Council Member: Inst. for Molecular Scis, Okazaki, Japan, 1991–95; Parly and Scientific Cttee, 1992–98; Internat. Advr, Tohoku Univ., Sendai, 2008–10. Royal Society of Chemistry: Vice-Pres., Dalton Div., 1986–88; Sci. Adv. Ed., Jl of Material Chemistry, 1996–2004; Corday-Morgan Medal, 1971; Solid State Chem. Award, 1986; Daiwa Adrian Prize, Daiwa Foundn, 1998. Governor: Sevenoaks Sch., 1977–88; Birkbeck Coll., London, 1993–2001. Vice Pres., Jury, LABEX, Agence Nationale de Recherche, France, 2011. Mem., Academia Europaea, 1992 (Mem. Council, 2000–09; Treas., 2000–09; Trustee, 2002–09). Fellow, Internat. Union of Pure and Applied Chem., 2009. Hon. Foreign Mem., Indian Soc. of Materials Res., 1994. Hon. Fellow, Indian Acad. of Sci., 1995. Hon. DSc: Newcastle, 1994; Kent, 1999. *Publications:* Physical Methods in Advanced Inorganic Chemistry (ed with H. A. O. Hill), 1968; Electronic States of Inorganic Compounds, 1974; Emission and Scattering Techniques, 1980; Electronic Structure and Magnetism of Inorganic Compounds, vols 1–7, 1972–82; (ed with A. K. Cheetham) Solid State Chemistry, vol. 1 1987, vol. 2 1992; The Philosopher's Tree, 1999; Nature Not Mocked, 2006; Molecules into Materials, 2007; On the Cucumber Tree, 2012; papers in Jl Chem. Soc.; Inorg. Chem. *Recreation:* cultivating gardens (horticultural and Voltairean). *Address:* Department of Chemistry, University College London, 20 Gordon Street, WC1H 0AJ; 16 Dale Close, Oxford OX1 1TU.

DAY, Peter Rodney, PhD; Founding Director, Biotechnology Center for Agriculture and the Environment (formerly Center for Agricultural Molecular Biology), Rutgers University, New Jersey, 1987–2001; *b* 27 Dec. 1928; *s* of Roland Percy Day and Florence Kate (*née* Dixon); *m* 1950, Lois Elizabeth Rhodes; two *s* one *d*. *Educ:* Birkbeck Coll., Univ. of London (BSc, PhD). John Innes Institute, 1946–63; Associate Prof. of Botany, Ohio State Univ., 1963–64; Chief, Dept of Genetics, Connecticut Agricl Experiment Station, 1964–79; Dir, Plant Breeding Inst., Cambridge, 1979–87. Sec., Internat. Genetics Fedn, 1984–93. Special Prof. of Botany, Nottingham Univ., 1982–88. Commonwealth Fund Fellow, 1954; John Simon Guggenheim Meml Fellow, 1973. *Publications:* Fungal Genetics (with J. R. S. Fincham), 1963, 4th edn 1979; Genetics of Host-Parasite Interaction, 1974; (with H. H. Prell) Plant-Fungal Pathogen Interaction, 2001; contrib. Genetical Research, Genetics, Heredity, Nature, Proc. Nat. Acad. Sci., Phytopathology, etc. *Recreations:* Scottish country dancing, bird watching. *Address:* 8200 Tarsier Avenue, New Port Richey, FL 34653–6559, USA. *E:* p1rd@verizon.net.

DAY, Richard D.; *see* Digby Day.

DAY, Rosemary; Trustee, Chiswick House and Grounds Trust, since 2005; *b* 20 Sept. 1942; *d* of Albert Rich and Alice Rich (*née* Wren); *m* (marr. diss.). *Educ:* Bedford Coll., Univ. of London (BA Hons 1964); Birkbeck, Univ. of London (MA 2011). ATII 1978. Asst Dir Gen., GLC, 1964–83; Admin. Dir, London Transport, 1983–88; Ops Dir, Allied Dunbar, 1988–94; Chm., London Ambulance Service, 1995–99. Non-executive Director: Nationwide Building Soc., 1984–88; Milk Mktg Bd, 1993–95; London Transport, 1994–99; Govt Offices Mgt Bd, 1996–98; NATS, 1997–2001; UKAEA, 1999–2006; Picker Inst. Europe, 2002–05; NI Dept of Regl Develt, 2007–08. Member: Legal Aid Adv. Bd, 1992–94; Sen. Salaries Review Body, 1994–2000. Chm., Joyful Company of Singers, 1988–2001. Trustee, Railway Children, 1999–. Chm. Govs, Hounslow Town Primary Sch., 2001–10. CCMI (CBIM 1984); FRSA. *Recreations:* economic and architectural research, the arts, gardening, books. *Address:* 63a Barrowgate Road, W4 4QT.

DAY, Sir Simon (James), Kt 1997; farmer; *b* 22 Jan. 1935; *s* of late John Adam Day and Kathleen Day (*née* Hebditch); *m* 1959, Hilary Maureen Greenslade Gomm; two *s* (and one *s* decd). *Educ:* S Devon Tech. Coll.; Emmanuel Coll., Cambridge (MA Hist.). Nat. Service, RN, 1954–56. Devon County Council: Councillor, Modbury Div., 1964–74, Modbury and Salcombe Div., 1974–2005, Thurlestone, Salcombe and Allington Div., 2005–13; Whip, 1981–89; Dep. Leader, 1989, Leader, 1991–93; Opposition Leader, 1993–99; Chm., 2001–02. Non-exec. Dir, SW Water, 1989–98; Regl Dir, Portman Building Soc., 1989–91; Director: Plymouth Sound Radio, 1966–80; Plymouth Develt Corp., 1993–96; Exeter Internat. Airport, 1997–2006; Chm., West of England Newspapers Gp, 1981–86. Mem., Exec. Council, ACC, 1981–85, 1990–96 (Chm., Police Cttee, 1991–93; Dep. Leader, 1992; Vice Chm., 1993–95; Cons. Leader, 1993–95); Chm., Devon and Cornwall Police Authy, 1990–93; Member: Police Adv. Bd, Home Office, 1989–93; Police Negotiating Bd, 1989–93; Chairman: Devon Sea Fisheries Cttee, 1986–95; Assoc. of Sea Fisheries Cttees, England and Wales, 1993–96 (Vice-Chm., 1991–93); Mem., Govt Salmon Adv. Cttee, 1987–90; Chm., Devon and Cornwall Develt Bureau, 1989–91; Vice Chairman: Nat. Parks Cttee for England and Wales, 1981–83; Local Govt Finance Cttee, 1983–85; Member: Consultative Council, Local Govt Finance, 1983–85 and 1993; Standing Conf. of Local and Regl Authies, Council of Europe, 1990–97; Cttee of Regions, EU, 1994–97, 1998–2001, 2002–05, 2006–13 (Vice-Chm., UK Delegn, 2006–13); Chm., Cons. Nat. Local Govt Adv. Cttee, 1994–95; Cons. Leader, 2004, Vice Chm., 2004–08, Chm., 2008–09, SW Regl Assembly. President: S Devon Herd Book Soc., 1986; Devon Co. Show, 2006–07. Chm. Govs, Bicton Coll. of Agric., 1983–2000. Trustee, West Country Rivers Trust, 1997–. Mem. Court, Exeter Univ., 1964–2009. Pres., Devon County LTA, 2002–. Contested (C): Carmarthen, 1966, by-election 1966; N Cornwall, 1970. High Sheriff, Devon, 1999–2000. Hereditary Freeman, City of Norwich. *Recreations:* shooting, sailing, fishing. *Address:* Keaton House, near Ivybridge, Devon PL21 0LB. *T:* (01752) 691212. *Clubs:* Buck's, Beefsteak, Royal Thames Yacht; Royal Yacht Squadron; Hawks (Cambridge) (Hon. Mem., 1995).

DAY, Stephen Nicholas; a District Judge (Magistrates' Courts) (formerly Stipendiary Magistrate), Middlesex, since 1991; *b* 17 Aug. 1947; *s* of late Robert Weatherston Day and Margaret Diana (*née* McKenzie); *m* 1973, Shama (*née* Tak); one *s* one *d*. *Educ:* St Mary's Coll., Southampton; King Edward VI Sch., Southampton; Brasenose Coll., Oxford (MA). Called to the Bar, Middle Temple, 1972. Trainee, Berks Magistrates' Courts Cttee, 1969–73; Sen. Court Clerk, Nottingham, 1973–77; Justices Clerk, Abingdon, Didcot and Wantage, 1977–91. Member: Gtr London Magistrates' Courts Authy, 2002–05; Sentencing Adv. Panel, Sentencing Guidelines Council, 2006–08. *Address:* c/o Ealing Magistrates' Court, Green Man Lane, W13 0SD. *Club:* Oxford and Cambridge.

DAY, Stephen Peter, CMG 1989; HM Diplomatic Service, retired; consultant, Middle East affairs; *b* 19 Jan. 1938; *s* of Frank William and Mary Elizabeth Day; *m* 1965, Angela Doreen (*née* Waudby); one *s* two *d*. *Educ:* Bancroft's School; Corpus Christi Coll., Cambridge. MA. Entered HMOCS as Political Officer, Western Aden Protectorate, 1961, transf. to FO, 1965; Senior Political Officer, South Arabian Federation, 1964–67; FO, 1967–70; First Sec., Office of C-in-C, Far East, Singapore, 1970–71; First Sec. (Press), UK Mission to UN, NY, 1971–75; FCO, 1976–77; Counsellor, Beirut, 1977–78; Consul-Gen., Edmonton, 1979–81; Ambassador to Qatar, 1981–84; Head of ME Dept, FCO, 1984–87; attached to Household of the Prince of Wales, 1986; Ambassador to Tunisia, 1987–92; Sen. British Trade Comr, Hong Kong, 1992–93; Dir, Council for Advancement of Arab-British Understanding, 1993–94. Dir, Claremont Associates, 1995–. Mem., Exec. Cttee, Soc. for Arabian Studies, 1995–2000. Chairman: British-Tunisian Soc., 1993–2008; Palestine Exploration Fund, 1995–2000; British-Yemeni Soc., 1998–99; MBI Trust, SOAS, 2000–03; MBI Foundn, 2002–07. Governor, Qatar Academy, 1996–2002. Comdr, Order of the Republic (Tunisia), 2002. *Publications:* At Home in Carthage, 1991. *Recreations:* walking, family. *Address:* Stedham Lodge, The Highlands, East Horsley, Surrey KT24 5BG. *T:* (01483) 281880, 07971 806677. *E:* s.day@claremontassociates.net. *Club:* Hong Kong.

DAY, Stephen Richard; political columnist, Cyprus Today, since 2006; *b* 30 Oct. 1948; *s* of late Francis and of Anne Day; one *s* by former marriage. *Educ:* Otley Secondary Modern Sch.; Park Lane Coll., Leeds; Leeds Polytechnic. MIEx 1972. Sales Clerk, William Sinclair & Sons, stationery manufrs, Otley, W Yorks, 1965–70, Asst Sales Manager (working in Home and Export Depts), 1970–77; Sales Representative: Larkfield Printing Co. Ltd (part of Hunting Group), Brighouse, W Yorks, 1977–80; A. H. Leach & Co. (part of Hunting Gp), photographic processing lab., Brighouse, 1980–84; Sales Executive: PPL Chromacopy, photographic labs, Leeds and Manchester, 1984–86; Chromogene, photographic lab., Leeds, 1986–87; self-employed public affairs consultant, 2001–06. Vice-President: Stockport Chamber of Commerce, 1987–2001; Stockport and Dist Heart Foundn, 1985–2001. Chm., Yorks Area Cons. Political Centre, 1983–86; Vice-Chm., NW Leeds Constituency, 1983–86. Town Councillor, Otley, 1975–76 and 1979–83; City Councillor, Leeds, 1975–80. Contested (C): Bradford West, 1983; Cheadle, 2001; Prospective Parly Cand. (C) Cheadle, 2002–05. MP (C) Cheadle, 1987–2001. An Opposition Whip, 1997–2001. Member: Select Cttee on Social Security, 1990–97; Select Cttee on Envmt, Transport and Regions, 1997; Co-Chm., Parly Adv. Council for Transport Safety, 1989–97; Vice-Chm., All-Party Non-Profit-Making Clubs Gp, 1995–2001; Co-Chm., All-Party West Coast Main Line Gp, 1993–2001. Sponsor, Private Member's Bill to introduce compulsory wearing of rear car seat belts by children, enacted into law 1988. Mem., Cheadle Hulme Cons. Club, 1987–2006; Vice-Chm., CPA (UK), 1996–97; Nat. Chm., Assoc. of Cons. Clubs, 1997–2006 (Vice-Chm., 1995–97). Pres., Council of Registered Club Assocs, 2002–06. Mem., Bramhall and Woodford Rotary Club, 2001–06; Pres., Cheadle Hulme Br., RBL, 2001–06. Vice Chm., British Residents Soc. (N Cyprus), 2014– (Vice Chm., 2009–10; Actg Chm., 2010–11; Chm., 2011–12). *Publications:* pamphlets on Otley and on rate reform. *Recreations:* movies, music, history (particularly Roman).

DAY, William, PhD; CPhys; Editor-in-Chief, Biosystems Engineering, since 2007; Director, Silsoe Research Institute, BBSRC, 1999–2006; *b* 11 June 1949; *s* of late Arthur Thomas Day and Barbara Nan Day; *m* 1973, Virginia Lesley Elisabeth Playford; two *s* one *d*. *Educ:* Norwich Sch.; Gonville and Caius Coll., Cambridge (MA Natural Scis (Physics)); PhD Physics Cantab 1974. CPhys 1980. Higher Scientific Officer, SSO, then PSO, Physics Dept, Rothamsted Exptl Stn, 1974–81 Head: Envmtl Physiol. Gp, Long Ashton Res. Stn, 1982–83; Physiology and Envmtl Physics Dept, Rothamsted Exptl Stn, 1983–88; Process Engrg Div., Silsoe Res. Inst., 1988–99. Special Prof. of Agricl Engrg, Univ. of Nottingham, 1993–2002; Vis. Prof., Cranfield Univ. at Silsoe, 2003–07. *Publications:* contribs relating to interaction between biological systems and envmt in numerous jls, include. Jl Agricl Sci., Agricl and Forest Meteorol. and Phytopathol. *Recreations:* bird watching, choral singing, tandem-ing.

DAY, William Michael; Fellow, Cambridge Institute for Sustainability Leadership (formerly University of Cambridge Programme for Industry, then Cambridge Programme for Sustainability Leadership), since 2013 (Senior Associate, 2003–13); Sustainability Advisor, PricewaterhouseCoopers, since 2008; Chairman, Water and Sanitation for the Urban Poor, since 2006; *b* 26 June 1956; *s* of Sir Derek Malcolm Day, KCMG; *m* 1986, Kate Gardener; one *s* two *d*. *Educ:* Univ. of Exeter (BA). Save the Children Fund: Uganda, 1983; Ethiopia, 1983–84; Sudan, 1984–86; BBC World Service for Africa, 1986–87; Oxfam, Ethiopia, 1987–88; Grants Dir for Africa, Charity Projects/Comic Relief, 1988–94; Dir, Opportunity Trust, 1994–96; Chief Exec., CARE International UK, 1996–2004. Non-exec. Dir, S Kent Hosps NHS Trust, 1994–96. Public Appts Ind. Assessor, DCMS, 1999–2008; Member: Corporate Responsibility Adv. Gp, ICAEW, 2011–14; Corporate Responsibility Panel, British Land, 2012–14; Council, ODI, 2000–12 (Chm., 2012); Adv. Bd, SEE Change Net, 2012–; Special Advr, UNDP, 2004–11; Chm., Sustainable Develt Commn, 2009–11. Member: BBC Central Appeals Cttee, 1992–2003 (Chm., 1997–2003); Grants Council, Charities Aid Foundn, 1990–94; Globalisation and Global Poverty Commn, 2006; Ramphal Centre Commn on Migration and Develt, 2010–11; Council of Ambassadors, WWF (UK), 2011–; Co-Chair, Kent Local Nature Partnership, 2014–; Trustee: BBC Children in Need, 1998–2008 (Chm., 2006–08); Disasters Emergency Cttee, 1998–2004. *Address:* Pilgrims, Hastingleigh, Ashford, Kent TN25 5HP. *T:* (01233) 750196. *E:* william.day@phonecoop.coop.

DAY-LEWIS, Sir Daniel, Kt 2014; actor; *s* of late Cecil Day-Lewis, CBE, CLit and Jill Angela Henriette Balcon; *m* 1996, Rebecca, *d* of Arthur Miller, playwright; two *s*. *Educ:* Bedales; Bristol Old Vic Theatre Sch. *Stage:* The Recruiting Officer, Troilus and Cressida, Funny Peculiar, Old King Cole, A Midsummer Night's Dream, Class Enemy, Edward II, Oh! What a Lovely War, Look Back in Anger, Dracula, Another Country, Romeo and Juliet, The Futurists, Hamlet; *films:* Gandhi, 1981; The Saga of HMS Bounty, 1983; My Beautiful Laundrette, 1985; A Room With a View, 1985; Nanou, 1985; The Unbearable Lightness of Being, 1986; Stars and Bars, 1987; My Left Foot, 1988 (Oscar best actor and numerous other awards); Ever Smile New Jersey, 1988; Last of the Mohicans, 1991 (Variety Club best actor); Age of Innocence, 1992; In the Name of the Father, 1993; The Crucible, 1997; The Boxer, 1998; Gangs of New York, 2002; The Ballad of Jack and Rose, 2006; There Will Be Blood, 2008 (Oscar and BAFTA for best actor); Nine, 2009; Lincoln, 2013 (Oscar, BAFTA and Golden Globe for best actor); principal roles in TV. *Address:* c/o Julian Belfrage Associates, 3rd Floor, 9 Argyll Street, W1F 7TG.

DAY-LEWIS, Séan; journalist and author; *b* 3 Aug. 1931; *s* of late Cecil Day-Lewis, CBE, CLit and Mary Day-Lewis; *m* 1960, Anna Mott; one *s* one *d*. *Educ:* Allhallows Sch., Rousdon, Devon. National Service, RAF, 1949–51. Bridport News, 1952–53; Southern Times, Weymouth, 1953–54; Herts Advertiser, St Albans, 1954–56; Express and Star, Wolverhampton, 1956–60; The Daily Telegraph, 1960–86 (first nat. newspaper Arts Reporter, 1965–70; TV and Radio Editor, 1970–86); TV Editor, London Daily News, 1987; TV Critic, Country Life, 1989–2003. Arts Editor, Socialist Commentary, 1966–71; Founder-Chm., 1975, Chm., 1990–92, BPG; Vice Pres., Bulleid Soc., 1970; Member, BAFTA, 1976. *Publications:* Bulleid: last giant of steam, 1964; C. Day-Lewis: an English literary life, 1980; (ed) One Day in the Life of Television, 1989; TV Heaven: a review of British television from the 1930s to the 1990s, 1992; Talk of Drama: views of the television dramatist now and then, 1998. *Recreations:* music (J. S. Bach preferred), reading the Guardian and books, giving in to temptation. *Address:* Restorick Row, Rosemary Lane, Colyton, Devon EX24 6LW. *T:* (01297) 553039.

DAYAN, Edouard; Director General, International Bureau, Universal Postal Union, 2005–12. La Poste, France: Hd, Air Transport Bureau, 1984–86; Manager, Dept of Internat. Mail Mgt and Internat. Accounting, then Internat. Partnership Strategy Dept, 1986–92; European Commission: expert, 1992–93; Dep. Dir, 1993–97, Dir, 1998–2005, Eur. and Internat. Affairs. Chm., Eur. Social Dialogue Cttee for postal sector, 1994–; former Mem., Mgt Bd, PostEurop; Universal Postal Union: Chm., Tech. Co-operation Action Gp; Chm., Bd of Trustees, Quality Service Fund. Chevalier: Ordre national du Mérite (France), 1995; Légion d'Honneur (France), 2001. *Address:* c/o Universal Postal Union, Weltpoststrasse 4, 3000 Bern 15, Switzerland.

DAYKIN, Christopher David, CB 1993; FIA; Government Actuary, 1989–2007; *b* 18 July 1948; *s* of John Francis Daykin and Mona Daykin; *m* 1977, Kathryn Ruth (*née* Tingey); two *s* one *d*. *Educ:* Merchant Taylors' Sch., Northwood; Pembroke Coll., Cambridge (BA 1970, MA 1973). FIA 1973. Government Actuary's Department, 1970; VSO, Brunei, 1971; Govt Actuary's Dept, 1972–78; Principal (Health and Social Services), HM Treasury, 1978–80; Govt Actuary's Dept, 1980–2007, Principal Actuary, 1982–84, Directing Actuary (Social Security), 1985–89. Mem., Council, Inst. of Actuaries, 1985–99 (Hon. Sec., 1988–90; Vice Pres., 1993–94; Pres., 1994–96); Chm., Internat. Forum of Actuarial Assocs, 1996–97; Chm., Perm. Cttee for Statistical, Actuarial and Financial Studies, ISSA, 1992–2007; Vice Chm., 2008–10, Chm., 2010–11, Groupe Consultatif Actuariel Européen (Chm., Educn Cttee, 1992–2007). Mem. Pensions Observatory, EC Commn, 1992–96. Chm., CS Insce Soc., 1991–. Visiting Professor: City Univ., 1997–; Shanghai Univ. of Finance and Econs, 1998–. Treasurer, Emmanuel Church, Northwood, 1982–87 and 1998–; Chm., VSO Harrow and Hillingdon, 1976–91. Hon. DSc City, 1995. *Publications:* Practical Risk Theory, 1993; articles and papers on pensions, demography, consumer credit, social security and insurance. *Recreations:* travel, photography, languages. *Address:* c/o Institute and Faculty of Actuaries, 7th Floor, Holborn Gate, 326–330 High Holborn, WC1V 7PP.

DAYMAN, Stephen John, MBE 2011; Executive Founder, Meningitis Now, since 2013; *b* Dursley, Glos, 17 April 1948; *s* of Fredrick and Patricia Dayman; *m* 1968, Gloria Clements; three *s* two *d* (and one *s* decd). *Educ:* Wotton under Edge Secondary Modern Sch. Founding Chm., Meningitis Trust, 1986–89; Founder: Meningitis Res. Foundn, 1989–97; Spencer Dayman Meningitis UK, 1999–2013. *Recreation:* football (Manchester United and Bristol Rovers). *Address:* 4 Spencers Court, Alveston, Bristol BS35 3BA. *T:* (01454) 413344. *E:* Steve.Dayman@btinternet.com.

DAYMOND, Nicholas Joseph; Headmaster, Parmiter's School, since 2010; *b* London, 3 Jan. 1962; *s* of Mark and Margot Daymond; *m* 1992, Kate Randall; one *s* one *d*. *Educ:* St Paul's Sch., Barnes; Queens' Coll., Cambridge (BA Hons Langs and Theol. 1983); Homerton Coll., Cambridge (PGCE 1985). NPQH 2003. Teacher of Modern Foreign Langs, Goffs Sch., Cheshunt, 1985–98; Dep. Headteacher, Beaumont Sch., St Albans, 1999–2003; Headteacher, Roundwood Park Sch., Harpenden, 2004–10. Nat. Leader of Educn, 2012–. *Publications:* (contrib.) The Parentalk Guide to Secondary School, 2005. *Recreations:* theatre, cinema, reading, travel, watching cricket. *Address:* Parmiter's School, High Elms Lane, Garston, Watford, Herts WD25 0UU. *T:* (01923) 671424. *E:* head@parmiters.herts.sch.uk.

DEACON, Keith Vivian; international tax and management consultant, 1996–2004; Under Secretary, 1988–95, and Director of Quality Development, 1993–95, Inland Revenue; *b* 19 Nov. 1935; *s* of Vivian and Louisa Deacon; *m* 1960, Brenda Chater; one *s* one *d*. *Educ:* Sutton County Grammar School; Bristol Univ. (BA Hons English Lang. and Litt.). Entered Inland Revenue as Inspector of Taxes, 1962; Regional Controller, 1985; Dir, Technical Div. I until Head Office reorganisation, 1988; Dir, Insce and Specialist Div., 1988–91; Dir of Operations, 1991–93. Part time work for Civil Service Selection Board: Observer, 1969–72; Chairman, 1985–87. FRSA 1992. *Recreations:* keeping up with four grandchildren, photography, music, reading, art and architecture.

DEACON, Richard, CBE 1999; RA 1998; sculptor; *b* Bangor, 15 Aug. 1949; *s* of late Gp Capt. Edward William Deacon, RAF (retd) and Dr Joan Bullivant Winstanley; *m* 1977, Jacqueline Poncelet (marr. diss. 2000); one *s* one *d*. *Educ:* Somerset Coll. of Art; St Martin's Sch. of Art; RCA; Chelsea Sch. of Art. *Solo exhibitions* include: Orchard Gall., Londonderry, 1983; Lisson Gall., 1983, 1985, 1987, 1992, 1995, 1999, 2002, 2012; Riverside Studios, Chapter Arts Centre, Cardiff, and Fruitmarket Gall., Edinburgh, 1984; Tate Gall., 1985;

Marian Goodman Gall., NY, 1986, 1988, 1990, 1992, 1997, 2004, 2012; Whitechapel Art Gall., Musée Nat. d'Art Moderne, Paris, 1989; Kunstnernes Hus, Oslo, and Mala Galerija, Slovenia, 1990; Kunstverein Hanover, 1993; LA Louver, 1995, 2001, 2004, 2007; tour of South America, 1996–97; Musée de Rochechouart, 1997; Tate Gall., Liverpool, 1999; Dundee Contemp. Arts, 2001; PSI Center for Art and Urban Resources, NY, 2001; Museum Ludwig, Cologne, 2003; Atelier Brancusi, CNAC, Paris, 2003; Tate St Ives, 2005; Museo Artium, Vitoria-Gasteiz, Spain, 2005; Sara Hilden Art Mus., Tampere, Finland, 2005–06; Arp Mus., Remagen, Germany, 2006; Ikon Gall., Birmingham, 2007; New Art Centre, Salisbury, 2007, 2010; rep. Wales at the Venice Biennale, 2007; Gall. Thaddeus Ropac, Paris, 2007, 2010, Salzburg, 2010; Fondation Maeght, France, 2008; Madison Square Park, NY, 2008; Stedelijk Mus., s'Hertogenbosch, 2008; Gall. Thomas Schulte, Berlin, 2009; Musée d'Art Moderne et Contemporaine, Strasbourg, 2010; Sprengel Mus., Hannover, 2011; Univ. of New Mexico, 2011; Tyler Print Inst., Singapore, 2012; Centro de Arte Contemporáneo, Malaga, 2012; Tate Britain, 2014; (jtly with B. Woodrow) New Art Centre, Salisbury, 2014; represented in collections in: Tate Gall.; Mus. of Modern Art, NY; Art Gall. of NSW, Sydney; Musée Beaubourg, Paris; Bonnefanten Mus., Maastricht. Vis. Prof., Chelsea Sch. of Art, 1992–; Professor: Ecole Nat. Superieure des Beaux-Arts, Paris, 1998–2009; Kunstakademie, Dusseldorf, 2009–. Member: Grants to Artists Sub Cttee, 1986–92, Visual Arts Adv. Gp, 1990–93, British Council; Architecture Adv. Gp, Arts Council of England, 1996–2000; Trustee, Tate Gall., 1991–96; Vice Chm. Trustees, Baltic Flour Mills Centre for Contemporary Art, 1999–2004. Mem., Akademie der Kunst, Berlin, 2010. Hon. Fellow, Univ. of the Arts London, 2013. Turner Prize, 1987; Robert Jakobsen Prize, Mus. Wurth, Germany, 1995. Chevalier des Arts et des Lettres (France), 1997. *Publications:* Stuff Box Object, 1972, 1984; For Those Who Have Ears #2, 1985; Atlas: Gondwanaland & Laurasia, 1990; In Praise of Television, 1997; About the Size of It, 2005; Water Under The Bridge, 2008; I Met Paul, Out of the Woods, Judd-Like, 2009; In the Garden, 2010; Por Escrito 1970–2010, 2012; So, And, If, But: Richard Deacon writings 1970–2012, 2014; Transmission, Reception, Noise: abstract drawing, 2014. *Address:* c/o Lisson Gallery, 67 Lisson Street, NW1 5DA. *W:* www.richarddeacon.net.

DEACON, Prof. Susan Catherine; Assistant Principal Corporate Engagement and Professorial Fellow, University of Edinburgh, since 2012; speaker, facilitator and consultant on public policy, leadership and strategic change; *b* 2 Feb. 1964; *d* of James Deacon and Barbara Deacon (*née* Timmins); partner, John Boothman; one *s* one *d. Educ:* Edinburgh Univ. (MA Hons 1987; MBA 1992). Local Govt officer, 1987–94; sen. mgt consultant, 1994; Dir of MBA Programmes, Edinburgh Business Sch., Heriot-Watt Univ., 1994–98; business consultant, 1998–99. Mem. (Lab) Edinburgh E and Musselburgh, Scottish Parlt, 1999–2007; Minister for Health and Community Care, 1999–2001. Prof. of Social Change, Queen Margaret Univ., 2007–10. Mem., RSA Commn on Illegal Drugs, Communities and Public Policy, 2005–07. Mem., UK Adv. Bd, ScottishPower, 2007–09; non-exec. Dir, ScottishPower Renewables Ltd, 2009– (Chm., 2010–12). Mem. Bd, Traverse Th. Co., 2007–10. Chm., Hibernian Community Foundn, 2008–12; Mem. Bd, Pfizer UK Foundn, 2007–13; Trustee, Iberdrola Foundn, 2009–. Early Years Champion, Scottish Govt, 2010–11. Gov., Inst. of Occupational Medicine, 2013–. Hon. Prof., Sch. of Social and Political Sci., Univ. of Edinburgh, 2010–12. *E:* susan.deacon@ed.ac.uk.

DEAKIN, Prof. (John Francis) William, PhD; FRCPsych; Professor of Psychiatry, since 1990, and Director, Neuroscience and Psychiatry Unit, since 2000, Manchester University; *b* 5 July 1949; *s* of John Deakin and Kathleen Brown; *m* 1973, Hildur Jakobsdottir; three *d. Educ:* Eltham Coll., Kent; Leeds Univ. (BSc 1st Cl. Physiol. 1970; MB Hons, ChB dist. and prize 1973); PhD London 1982. MRCPsych 1984, FRCPsych 1990. MRC Trng Fellow, NIMR, Mill Hill, and Clin. Res. Centre, Harrow, 1974–83; Sen. Lectr, Manchester Univ., 1983–90. FMedSci 2000. *Publications:* contrib. numerous articles to learned jls on neuroscientific basis of mental illness and novel ways of imaging the action of drugs on the brain, especially the rôle of serotonin in neuroses. *Recreations:* jazz, playing classical guitar, the game of Go, astronomy, cycling. *Address:* 3 Chesham Place, Bowdon, Cheshire WA14 2JL. *T:* (0161) 941 6385.

DEAKIN, Michael; writer, documentary and film maker; Director, Gryphon Productions Ltd, 1985–2005; *b* 21 Feb. 1939; *s* of Sir William Deakin, DSO, and Margaret Hodson (*née* Beatson-Bell); civil partnership 2006, David Steele. *Educ:* Bryanston; Univ. d'Aix-Marseille; Emmanuel Coll., Cambridge (MA Hons). Founding Partner, Editions Alecto, Fine Art Publishers, 1960–64; Producer, BBC Radio Current Affairs Dept, 1964–68; Producer, then Editor, Yorkshire Television Documentary Unit, 1968–81; Sen. Vice-Pres., Paramount/Revcom, 1987–93. Documentary film productions include: Out of the Shadow into the Sun—The Eiger; Struggle for China; The Children on the Hill; Whicker's World—Way Out West; The Japanese Experience; The Good, the Bad and the Indifferent; Johnny Go Home (British Academy Award, 1976); David Frost's Global Village; The Frost Interview—The Shah; Rampton—The Secret Hospital; Painting With Light (co-prodn with BBC); other films: Act of Betrayal, 1987; Not a Penny More, Not a Penny Less, 1990 (TV mini series); Secret Weapon, 1990; The Supergun, 1994; Good King Wenceslas, 1994; The Human Bomb, 1996; The Place of Lions, 1997; Varian's War, 2001; also many others. Founding Mem., TV-am Breakfast Television Consortium, 1980; Consultant, TV-am, 1984–87 (Dir of Programmes, 1982–84; Bd Mem., 1984–85). *Publications:* Restif de la Bretonne—Les Nuits de Paris (critical edn and trans. with Nicholas Deakin), 1968; Gaetano Donizetti—a biography, 1968; (for children) Tom Grattan's War, 1970, 2nd edn 1971; The Children on the Hill, 1972, 9th edn 1982; (with John Willis) Johnny Go Home, 1976; (with Antony Thomas) The Arab Experience, 1975, 2nd edn 1976; Flame in the Desert, 1976; (with David Frost) I Could Have Kicked Myself, 1982, 2nd US edn 1983; (with David Frost) Who Wants to be a Millionaire, 1983; (with David Frost) If You'll Believe That You'll Believe Anything..., 1986. *Recreations:* travel, music, books, pictures. *Address:* 6 Glenhurst Avenue, NW5 1PS; La Marsaulaie, Saint Mathurin 49250, France. *Club:* Hat.

See also N. D. Deakin.

DEAKIN, Prof. Nicholas Dampier, CBE 1997; Professor of Social Policy and Administration, University of Birmingham, 1980–98, now Emeritus Professor (Dean, Faculty of Commerce and Social Science, 1986–89; Foundation Fellow, 2006); Visiting Professor: London School of Economics, 1998–2004; Warwick Business School, 1998–2001; *b* 5 June 1936; *s* of Sir (Frederick) William Deakin, DSO and Margaret Ogilvy Hodson; *m* 1st, 1961, Rose Albinia Donaldson (marr. diss. 1988), *d* of Baron Donaldson of Kingsbridge, OBE and Frances Donaldson; one *s* two *d*; 2nd, 1988, Lucy Moira, *d* of Jack and Moira Gaster. *Educ:* Westminster Sch.; Christ Church Coll., Oxford (BA (1st cl. Hons) 1959, MA 1963); DPhil Sussex 1972. Asst Principal, Home Office, 1959–63, Private Sec. to Minister of State, 1962–63; Asst Dir, Nuffield Foundn Survey of Race Relations in Britain, 1963–68; Res. Fellow, subseq. Lectr, Univ. of Sussex, 1968–72; Head of Social Studies, subseq. Head of Central Policy Unit, GLC, 1972–80. Scientific Advr, DHSS, later Dept of Health, 1986–91. Chm., Ind. Commn on Future of Voluntary Sector in England, 1995–96. Vice-Chm., Social Affairs Cttee, ESRC, 1984–86. Chair, Social Policy Assoc., 1989–92; Member: Exec. Cttee, NCVO, 1988–90; Council, RIPA, 1984–88; Governing Council, Family Policy Studies Centre, 1987–2001. Trustee: Nationwide Foundn, 1999–2005; Baring Foundn, 2005–10 (Vice Chm., 2008–10). Chair, Birmingham City Pride, 1998–2001. FAcSS 2015; FRSA 1996. *Publications:* (ed and trans.) Memoirs of the Comte de Gramont, 1965; Colour and the British Electorate 1964, 1965; Colour, Citizenship and British Society, 1969; (with Clare Ungerson) Leaving London, 1977; (jtly) Government and Urban Poverty, 1983; (ed) Policy Change in Government, 1986; The Politics of Welfare, 1987, 2nd edn 1994; (ed jtly) Consuming Public Services, 1990; (jtly) The Enterprise Culture and the Inner Cities, 1992; (ed jtly) The Costs of Welfare, 1993; (jtly) Public Welfare Services and Social Exclusion, 1995; (jtly) Contracting for Change, 1997; (with Richard Parry) The Treasury and Social Policy, 2000; In Search of Civil Society, 2001; (ed jtly) Welfare and the State, 2003; (contrib.) Angleterre ou Albion, entre fascination et répulsion, ed by G. Millat, 2006; (ed jtly and contrib.) Beveridge and Voluntary Action in Britain and the Wider British World, 2011; contribs to other vols and learned jls. *Recreations:* reading fiction, music. *Address:* Chedington, Lynmouth Road, N2 9LR.

See also M. Deakin.

DEAKIN, Richard Simon, CEng, FRAeS; Chief Executive Officer, NATS, 2010–15; *b* Ipswich, 25 Feb. 1964; *s* of Comdr David Deakin, RN and Mary Deakin; *m* 1997, Marian Whitelock; one *s* one *d. Educ:* Kingston Poly. (BSc Hons Aero Engrg 1987); Cranfield Univ. (MBA 1991). CEng 1990; FRAeS 1996. British Aerospace, 1982–91; TRW, 1999–2001; Gp Dir, Progs, GKN Aerospace, 2001–03; Man. Dir, Thales Aerospace, 2004–08; Sen. Vice-Pres., Thales Air Systems, 2008–10. Hon. DEng Kingston, 2008. *Publications:* Battlespace Technologies: network enabled information dominance, 2010. *Recreations:* sailing, clay pigeon shooting, photography.

DEAKIN, Prof. Simon Francis, PhD; FBA 2005; Professor of Law, University of Cambridge, since 2006; Fellow, Peterhouse, Cambridge, since 1990; *b* 26 March 1961; *s* of Anthony Francis and Elizabeth Mary Deakin; *m* 1989, Elaine Skidmore; one *s. Educ:* Netherthorpe Grammar Sch., Staveley; Peterhouse, Cambridge (BA 1983, MA 1985, PhD 1990). Res. Fellow, Peterhouse, Cambridge, 1985–88; Lectr in Law, QMC, 1987–90; Cambridge University: Asst Lectr, Lectr, then Reader in Law, 1990–2001; Asst Dir, 1994–2014, Dir, 2014–, Centre for Business Res.; Robert Monks Prof. of Corporate Governance, Judge Inst. of Mgt, subseq. Judge Business Sch., 2001–06. Bigelow Fellow, Univ. of Chicago Law Sch., 1986–87; Visiting Fellow: Univ. of Nantes, 1993, 1995; Univ. of Melbourne, 1996; European Univ. Inst., Florence, 2004; Doshisha Univ., Kyoto, 2004–; Vis. Prof., Columbia Univ., 2003, 2008; Francqui Vis. Prof., Univ. of Antwerp, 2013–14. Mem. Exec. Cttee, Inst. of Employment Rights, 1990–2002. Mem., Ind. Commn of Inquiry into Drug Testing at Work, 2003–05. Tanner Lectures, Oxford Univ., 2008; Mike Larkin Meml Lect., Univ. of Cape Town, 2009; V. V. Giri Meml Lect., New Delhi, 2013. Hon. Dr Univ. Catholique de Louvain, 2012. *Publications:* (with B. S. Markesinis) Tort Law, 3rd edn 1994, 4th edn 1999, 5th edn 2003, 6th edn (with A. Johnston) 2007; (with G. S. Morris) Labour Law, 1995, 5th edn 2009; (ed with J. Michie) Contracts, Co-operation and Competition, 1997; (ed with A. Hughes) Enterprise and Community, 1997; (with F. Wilkinson) The Law of the Labour Market: industrialization, employment and legal evolution, 2005; (ed with A. Supiot) Capacitas: contract law and the institutional preconditions of a market economy, 2009; (ed with D. H. Whittaker) Corporate Governance and Managerial Reform in Japan, 2009; (jtly) Hedge Fund Activism in Japan: the limits of shareholder primacy, 2012; contribs to jls in law, econs, corporate governance and industrial relns. *Recreation:* fell walking. *Address:* Peterhouse, Cambridge CB2 1RD. *T:* (01223) 338200, *Fax:* (01223) 337578. *E:* s.deakin@cbr.cam.ac.uk.

DEAKIN, William; *see* Deakin, J. F. W.

DEAKINS, Eric Petro; international public affairs consultant; *b* 7 Oct. 1932; *er s* of late Edward Deakins and Gladys Deakins; *m* 1990, Sandra Weaver; one *s* two *d. Educ:* Tottenham Grammar Sch.; London Sch. of Economics. BA (Hons) in History, 1953. Nat. Service (commn), 1953–55. Executive with FMC (Meat) Ltd, 1956; General Manager, Pigs Div., FMC (Meat) Ltd, 1969. Contested (Lab): Finchley, 1959; Chigwell, 1966; Walthamstow W, 1967. MP (Lab): Walthamstow W, 1970–74; Walthamstow, 1974–87. Parly Under-Sec. of State, Dept of Trade, 1974–76, DHSS, 1976–79. *Publications:* A Faith to Fight For, 1964; You and your MP, 1987; What Future for Labour?, 1988. *Recreations:* writing, cinema, yoga, football. *Address:* 36 Murray Mews, NW1 9RJ.

DEAL, Hon. Timothy Edward; Senior Vice President, United States Council for International Business, Washington, 1996–2010; *b* 17 Sept. 1940; *s* of Edward Deal and Loretta (*née* Fuemuller); *m* 1964, Jill Brady; two *s. Educ:* Univ. of California at Berkeley (AB Pol Sci.). First Lieut, US Army, 1963–65. Joined Foreign Service, US Dept of State, 1965; served Tegucigalpa, Honduras, Warsaw, Poland, and Washington, 1965–76; Sen. Staff Mem., Nat. Security Council, 1976–79 and 1980–81; Special Asst to Asst Sec. of State for European Affairs, 1979–80; Counsellor for Econ. Affairs, London, 1981–85; Dep. US Rep., OECD, Paris, 1985–88; Dir, Office of Eastern European Affairs, Washington, 1988–89; Special Asst to President and Sen. Dir for Internat. Econ. Affairs, Nat. Security Council, 1989–92; Minister and Dep. Chief of Mission, US Embassy, London, 1992–96. Presidential Awards for: Meritorious Service, 1991; Distinguished Service, 1993. *Recreations:* theatre, cinema, horse racing. *Address:* 5721 MacArthur Boulevard NW, Washington, DC 20016, USA.

DEALTRY, Prof. (Thomas) Richard; Managing Director: Intellectual Partnerships Consultancy Ltd, since 1999; Global Association of Corporate Universities and Academies, since 2004; independent real-time business development process designer; *b* 24 Nov. 1936; *s* of George Raymond Dealtry and Edith (*née* Gardner); *m* 1962, Pauline (*née* Sedgwick) (marr. diss. 1982); one *s* one *d. Educ:* Cranfield Inst. of Advanced Technol.; MBA. CEng, MIMechE; MInstM; FIMCB. National Service Commn, 1959–61: Temp. Captain 1960. Divl Exec., Tube Investments Ltd, 1967–71; Sen. Exec., Guest, Keen & Nettlefold Gp Corporate Staff, 1971–74; Dir, Simpson-Lawrence Ltd, and Man. Dir, BUKO BV, Holland, 1974–77; Under Sec./Industrial Adviser, Scottish Econ. Planning Dept, 1977–78; Director, Gulf Regional Planning, Gulf Org. for Industrial Consulting, 1978–82; Man. Dir, RBA Management Services Ltd, London and Kuwait, 1982–85; Regl Dir, Diverco Ltd, 1985–; Prof. of Strategic Mgt, Internat. Mgt Centres, Buckingham, 1989–97; Programmes Director: BAA plc, 1997–99; Univ. of Surrey Mgt Learning Partnership, 1997–99. Vis. Prof., Birmingham City Univ., 2008–. *Publications:* The Corporate University Blueprint, 2013. *Recreations:* golf, squash. *Address:* 43 Hunstanton Avenue, Harborne, Birmingham B17 8SX.

DEAN OF THORNTON-LE-FYLDE, Baroness *cr* 1993 (Life Peer), of Eccles in the Metropolitan County of Greater Manchester; **Brenda Dean;** PC 1998; Chairman, Housing Corporation, 1997–2003; *b* 29 April 1943; *d* of Hugh Dean and Lillian Dean; *m* 1988, Keith Desmond McDowall, *qv. Educ:* St Andrews Junior Sch., Eccles; Stretford High Sch. for Girls. Admin. Sec., SOGAT, 1959–72; SOGAT Manchester Branch: Asst Sec., 1972–76; Sec., 1976–83; Mem., Nat. Exec. Council, 1977–83; Pres., 1983–85, Gen.-Sec., 1985–91, SOGAT '82; Dep. Gen. Sec., Graphical, Paper and Media Union, 1991–92; Chm., ICSTIS, 1993–99 (Mem., 1991–93). Chm., Empiric Student Property plc, 2014–; non-executive Director: Inveresk plc, 1993–97; Chamberlain Phipps Gp plc, 1994–96; Takare plc, 1995–98; Assured British Meat, 1997–2001; George Wimpey plc, 2003–07; Dawsons plc, 2004–11; NATS, 2006–; Taylor Wimpey plc, 2007–13. Co-Chm., Women's Nat. Commn, 1985–87; Dep. Chm., UCL Hosps NHS Trust, 1993–98; Chairman: Armed Forces Pay Review Body, 1999–2004 (Mem., 1993–94); Covent Gdn Mkt Authy, 2005–13 (Mem., 2004–05); Member: Printing and Publishing Trng Bd, 1974–82; Supplementary Benefits Commn, 1976–80; Price Commn, 1977–79; Occupational Pensions Bd, 1983–87; Gen. Adv. Council, BBC, 1984–88; TUC Gen. Council, 1985–92; NEDC, 1989–92; Employment Appeal Tribunal, 1991–93; Broadcasting Complaints Commn, 1993–94; Press Complaints Commn, 1993–98; Nat. Cttee of Inquiry into Future of Higher Educn, 1996–97; Royal Commn on H of L reform, 1999; Bd, Gen. Insce Standards Council, 1999–2005; Sen. Salaries Review Body, 1999–2004; H of L Appts Commn, 2000–10; Regulated Bd of Places for People, 2014–. Mem. Council, ABSA, 1990–95. Member: Council, City Univ., 1991–96; Bar Council of

Legal Educn, 1992–95; Council, Open Univ., 1996–98; Court of Governors, LSE, 1996–98; Gov., Ditchley Foundn, 1992. Pres., Coll. of Occupational Therapy, 1995–2004. Mem. Adv. Bd of Mgt, PYBT, 1999–2002 (Trustee, 1996–99); Trustee, Prince's Foundn, 1999–. FRSA 1992. Hon. Fellow, Lancs Poly., 1991. Hon. MA: Salford, 1986; South Bank, 1995; Hon. DCL City, 1993; Hon. LLD: North London, 1996; Exeter, 1999; Hon. LLB De Montfort, 1998. *Recreations:* sailing, reading, relaxing, thinking! *Address:* House of Lords, SW1P 0PW. *Clubs:* Reform; Royal Cornwall Yacht.

DEAN, Caroline, OBE 2004; DPhil; FRS 2004; Project Leader, John Innes Centre, Norwich, since 1988; *b* 2 April 1957; *d* of late D. H. Dean and Alice Joy Dean; *m* 1991, Jonathan Dallas George Jones, *qv*; one *s* one *d*. *Educ:* Univ. of York (BA Hons (Biol.); DPhil (Biol.) 1982). Res. Scientist, Advanced Genetic Sciences, Oakland, Calif, 1983–88; Associate Res. Dir, John Innes Centre, Norwich, 1999–2008. Hon. Chair, UEA, 2000–. Foreign Mem., US NAS, 2008. Medal, Genetics Soc., 2007. *Publications:* numerous articles in learned jls, incl. Science, Cell, Plant Cell, Plant Jl, EMBO Jl, Nature, Nature Genetics. *Recreation:* sailing. *Address:* John Innes Centre, Norwich Research Park, Norwich, Norfolk NR4 7UH. *T:* (01603) 450526, *Fax:* (01603) 450045. *E:* caroline.dean@jic.ac.uk.

DEAN, (Catherine) Margaret, CVO 2013; HM Lord Lieutenant of Fife, 1999–2014; *b* 16 Nov. 1939; *d* of Thomas Day McNeil Scrimgeour and Catherine Forbes Scrimgeour (*née* Sunderland); *m* 1962, Brian Dean; three *d*. *Educ:* George Watson's Ladies' Coll., Edinburgh; Univ. of Edinburgh (MA). *Address:* Viewforth, 121 Rose Street, Dunfermline, Fife KY12 0QT. *T:* (01383) 722488, *Fax:* (01383) 738027.

DEAN, (Cecil) Roy; HM Diplomatic Service, retired; writer and composer; *b* 18 Feb. 1927; *s* of Arthur Dean and Flora Dean (*née* Clare); *m* 1954, Heather Sturtridge; three *s*. *Educ:* Watford Grammar Sch.; London Coll. of Printing and Graphic Arts (diploma); Coll. for Distributive Trades (MCIPR). Sec., Watford Boys' Club, 1943–45. Served RAF, 1945–48, SEAC; Central Office of Information, 1948–58; Second, later First Sec., Colombo, 1958–62; Vancouver, 1962–64; Lagos, 1964–68; FCO, 1968–71; Consul, Houston, 1971, Acting Consul-Gen., 1972–73; FCO, 1973–76; Dir, Arms Control and Disarmament Res. Unit, 1976–83; Dep. High Comr, Accra, 1983–86, Acting High Comr, 1984 and 1986; retd in rank of Asst Under-Sec. of State. Mem., UN Sec.-General's expert group on disarmament instns, 1980–81; UK Rep., UNESCO Conf. on Disarmament Educn, 1980. Contested (Lab) Bromley LBC, 1990 and 1994. Trustee, Urbanaid, 1987–96. Mem., RSL. Editor: Insight, 1964–68; Arms Control and Disarmament, 1979–83; author and presenter, The Poetry of Popular Song (BBC Radio Four series), 1989–91. Vice-Pres., Bromley Arts Council; Press Officer: Bromley Music Soc.; Biggin Hill Br., RAFA. *Compositions:* A Century of Song, 1996; A Shropshire Lass, 2000; Three Moons: a lyric suite, 2003; Hymn to the Laureate, 2004; Ceremonial March: Betjemania, 2005; A Somerset Lad, 2005. *Publications:* Peace and Disarmament, 1982; chapter in Ethics and Nuclear Deterrence, 1982; Mainly in Fun, 1998, enlarged edn 2002; A Simple Songbook, 2002; Great British Lyric Writers 1890–1950, 2006; Victor in the Battle of Britain, 2006; Translations from Eight French Poets, 2007; Diplomat with a Difference, 2008; Words and Music - a Late Harvest, 2012; numerous research papers; contribs to learned jls. *Recreations:* crosswords (Times national champion, 1970 and 1979, world record for fastest solution, 1970), humour, light verse, setting puzzles. *Address:* 39 Park End, Bromley, Kent BR1 4AN. *T:* (020) 8402 0743.

DEAN, Christopher Colin, OBE 2000 (MBE 1981); professional ice skater; *b* 27 July 1958; *s* of Colin Gordon Dean and Mavis (*née* Pearson) and step *s* of Mary Betty (*née* Chambers); *m* 1st, 1991, Isabelle Duchesnay (marr. diss. 1993); 2nd, 1994, Jill Trenary; two *s*. *Educ:* Calverton Manor Sch., Nottingham; Sir John Sherbrooke Sch., Nottingham; Col Frank Seely Sch., Nottingham. Police constable, 1974–80. Ice dancer, with Jayne Torvill, *qv*: British Champions, 1978, 1979, 1980, 1981, 1982, 1983, 1994; European Champions, 1981, 1982, 1984, 1994; World Champions, 1981, 1982, 1983, 1984; World Professional Champions, 1984, 1985, 1990, 1995 and 1996; Olympic Champions, 1984; Olympic Bronze Medallists, 1994. Choreographer, Encounters, English Nat. Ballet, 1996; trainer, choreographer and performer: Stars on Ice, USA, 1998–99, 1999–2000; Dancing on Ice, ITV, 2006, 2007, 2008, 2009, 2010, 2011, 2012, 2013, 2014; trainer, Ice Rink on the Estate, ITV, 2015. Hon. MA Nottingham Trent, 1993. With Jayne Torvill: BBC Sportsview Personality of the Year, 1983–84; Figure Skating Hall of Fame, 1989. *Publications:* (with Jayne Torvill) Facing the Music, 1995; (with Jayne Torvill) Our Life on Ice, 2014. *Recreations:* motor racing, films, dance. *Address:* PO Box 32, Heathfield, E Sussex TN21 0BW. *T:* (01435) 867825. *Club:* Groucho.

DEAN, Gillian Margaret; *see* Weeks, G. M.

DEAN, Janet Elizabeth Ann; *b* 28 Jan. 1949; *d* of late Harry Gibson and Mary Gibson (*née* Walley); *m* 1968, Alan Dean (*d* 1994); two *d*. *Educ:* Winsford Verdin County Grammar Sch., Cheshire. Clerk: Barclays Bank, 1965–69; Bass Charrington, 1969–70. Member (Lab): Staffordshire County Council, 1981–97; E Staffordshire BC, 1991–97; Uttoxeter Town Council, 1995–97. MP (Lab) Burton, 1997–2010. *Recreations:* dressmaking, reading.

DEAN, Margaret; *see* Dean, C. M.

DEAN, His Honour Michael; QC 1981; a Circuit Judge, 1991–2009; *b* 2 Feb. 1938; *m* 1st, 1967, Diane Ruth Griffiths; 2nd, 1992, Jane Isabel Glaister; one *s*. *Educ:* Altrincham Co. Grammar Sch.; Univ. of Nottingham (LLB 1st Cl. Hons 1959). Lectr in Law, Univ. of Manchester, 1959–62; called to the Bar, Gray's Inn, 1962 (Arden Scholar and Holker Sen. Scholarship, 1962); Northern Circuit, Manchester, 1962–65; Lectr in Law, LSE, 1965–67; practice at the Bar, London, 1968–91; an Asst Recorder, 1986–89; a Recorder, 1989–91. *Publications:* articles in various legal periodicals. *Recreations:* conversation, music, theatre, sailing, family life.

DEAN, Nicholas Arthur; QC 2003; **His Honour Judge Dean;** a Circuit Judge, since 2013; *b* 11 July 1960; *s* of John and Alwyne Dean; *m* 1987, Nicola Anne Kay Carslaw; one *s* one *d*. *Educ:* Wyggeston Boys' Sch.; Univ. of Leeds (LLB Hons). Called to the Bar, Lincoln's Inn, 1982; in practice specialising in crime, clinical negligence and commercial competition law; Recorder, 2001–13. *Recreations:* cycling, reading, keeping chickens, listening to the Archers. *Address:* Birmingham Crown Court, Queen Elizabeth II Law Courts, 1 Newton Street, Birmingham B4 7NA.

DEAN, Nigel Francis; a District Judge (Magistrates' Courts), since 2011; *b* Epping, 17 March 1956; *s* of Roger Dean and Paula Holmes (*née* Waller); *m* 1993, Megan Galliet; one *s* two *d*. *Educ:* Wellington Coll.; Univ. of Westminster (BA Hons). Admitted as solicitor, 1982; Asst Solicitor, Sowman Pinks & Co., 1982–84; Edward Fail Bradshaw & Waterson: Asst Solicitor, 1984–87; Partner, 1987–2011; a Dep. Dist Judge (Magistrates' Courts), 2005–11. *Recreations:* sports, classic cars, cinema, history, family. *Address:* Bromley Magistrates' Court, The Court House, 1 Bromley Road BR1 1RA.

DEAN, Dr Paul, CB 1981; Director, National Physical Laboratory, 1977–90 (Deputy Director, 1974–76); *b* 23 Jan. 1933; *s* of late Sydney and Rachel Dean; *m* 1961, Sheila Valerie Gamse; one *s* one *d*. *Educ:* Hackney Downs Grammar Sch.; Queen Mary Coll., Univ. of London (Fellow, 1984). BSc (1st cl. Hons Physics), PhD; CPhys; FInstP, FIMA, CMath. National Physical Laboratory: Sen. Sci. Officer, Math. Div., 1957; Principal Sci. Officer, 1963; Sen. Principal Sci. Officer (Individual Merit), 1967; Head of Central Computer Unit, 1967; Supt, Div. of Quantum Metrology, 1969; Under-Sec., DoI (Head of Space and Air Res. and R&D Contractors Divs), 1976–77; initiated testing lab. accreditation in UK, leading to NAMAS, 1985. Part-time Head, Res. Estabts Management Div., DoI, 1979–82; Exec. Dep. Chm., Council of Res. Estabts, 1979–82. Mem., Internat. Cttee of Weights and Measures, 1985–90; Pres., Comité Consultatif pour les Etalons de Mesure des Rayonnements Ionisants, 1987–90; Founder Pres., British Measurement and Testing Assoc., 1990–95; First Chm., EUROMET, 1988–90. *Publications:* papers and articles in learned, professional and popular jls. *Recreations:* scientific interests, chess, piano, bridge, table tennis. *Address:* Dorset.

DEAN, Peter Henry, CBE 1993; Chairman, Gambling Commission, 2005–07 (Chairman, Gaming Board for Great Britain, 1998–2005); *b* 24 July 1939; *s* of late Alan Walduck Dean and Gertrude (*née* Bürger); *m* 1965, Linda Louise Keating; one *d*. *Educ:* Rugby Sch.; London Univ. (LLB). Admitted Solicitor, 1962. Joined Rio Tinto-Zinc Corp., 1966; Sec., 1972–74; Dir, 1974–85; freelance business consultant, 1985–96. Director: Associated British Ports Holdings, 1982–2001 (Mem., British Transport Docks Bd, 1980–82); Liberty Life Assce Co., 1986–95; Seeboard, 1993–96. Chm., G. H. Dean & Co., 2001–14 (Dir, 1999–2014). Dep. Chm., Monopolies and Mergers Commn, 1990–97 (Mem., 1982–97); Investment Ombudsman, 1996–2001. Chm., Council of Management, Highgate Counselling Centre, 1991–2002 (Mem., 1985–2002); Chairman: English Baroque Choir, 1985–89, 1999–2000; City Chamber Choir, 2003–07. Trustee, Responsible Gambling Fund, 2009–11. *Recreations:* choral singing, ski-ing, tennis. *Address:* 52 Lanchester Road, Highgate, N6 4TA. *T:* (020) 8883 5417. *E:* phdean@blueyonder.co.uk.

DEAN, Robert John, CMG 2012; Chairman of Trustees, Kennet and Avon Canal Trust, since 2012; *b* Portsmouth, 21 May 1959; *s* of Albert and Margaret Dean; *m* 1981, Julie Margaret Stott; two *d*. *Educ:* Southern Grammar Sch., Portsmouth. ACMA 1996. Entered FCO, 1978; various roles incl. mgt services, personnel ops and IT develt, 1978–86; Second Sec., Copenhagen, 1987–92; Mgt Accountant and Hd of Finance, FCO, 1992–99; First Sec., Wellington, NZ, 1999–2004; Co-ordinator, Intelligence and Security Secretariat, Cabinet Office (on secondment), 2004–06; Dir, FCO, 2007–12. *Recreations:* inland waterways cruising, heritage restoration and management, conservation and woodland management, passenger boat master and trainer. *Address:* c/o Kennet and Avon Canal Trust, Couch Lane, Devizes, Wilts SN10 1EB. *T:* 07795 116223. *E:* chair@katrust.org.uk.

DEAN, Prof. Roger Thornton, DSc, DLitt, PhD; FAHA; Research Professor of Sonic Communication, MARCS Institute (formerly Macarthur Auditory Research Centre Sydney, then MARCS Auditory Laboratories), University of Western Sydney, since 2007; *b* UK, 6 Sept. 1948; *s* of Cyril Thornton Dean and Kathleen Ida Dean (*née* Harrington); *m* 1973, Dr Hazel Anne Smith. *Educ:* Corpus Christi Coll., Cambridge (BA 1970; PhD 1974); Brunel Univ. (DSc 1984, DLitt 2002). FRSB (FIBiol 1988). Post-Doctoral Fellow, Dept of Exptl Pathol., UCH Med. Sch., 1973–76; MRC Scientist, Div. of Cell Pathol., Clinical Res. Centre, London, 1976–79; Brunel University: Hd, Cell Biol. Res. Gp, and Reader in Applied Biol., 1979–84; Hd, Cell Biol. Res. Gp, and Prof. of Cell Biol., 1984–88; Hon. Prof., Faculty of Medicine, Sydney Univ., 1988–2002; Foundn Exec. Dir, Heart Res. Inst. Ltd, Sydney, Australia, 1988–2002; University of Canberra: Vice-Chancellor and Pres., and Prof., 2002–07; Founder, Sonic Communications Res. Gp, 2004. Founder and Artistic Dir, LYSIS and austraLYSIS, internat. sound and intermedia creative and perf. gp, 1970–. Hon. FAHA 2004. Musical and multimedia compositions, many included in compact disc pubns as creator and performer. Centenary Medal, Australia, 2003. *Publications:* include: (with Dr M. Davies) Protein Oxidation (monograph), 1997; Hyperimprovisation, 2003; contrib. learned jls in cell biol., music and humanities res. *Recreations:* film, visual arts. *Address:* MARCS Institute, University of Western Sydney, Locked Bag 1797, Penrith South, NSW 2751, Australia. *T:* (2) 97726902. *E:* roger.dean@uws.edu.au.

DEAN, Rosa Mary; Her Honour Judge Dean; a Circuit Judge, since 2011; *b* Cuckfield; *d* of Geoffrey and Una Dean; *m* 2000, Edward; four *s*. *Educ:* Brighton and Hove High Sch.; Westminster Sch.; Magdalen Coll., Oxford (BA). Called to the Bar, Gray's Inn, 1993, Bencher, 2015; a Dep. Dist Judge (Magistrates' Court), 2006–11; a Recorder, 2009–11. *Recreations:* cooking, gardening, football. *Address:* Wood Green Crown Court, Woodall House, Lordship Lane, N22 5LF.

DEAN, Roy; *see* Dean, C. R.

DEAN, Simon Dominic; Deputy Chief Executive, NHS Wales, since 2014; *b* Cheltenham, 28 March 1958; *s* of Denis and Margaret Dean; *m* 1988, Alison Downes; one *s* one *d*. *Educ:* Univ. of Warwick (BA Hons English and American Lit. 1980). MIHM 1986. Admin. Asst, NE Thames RHA, 1983; Hosp. Manager, Southend HA, 1984–90; Dir, Avon FHSA, 1990–94; Avon Health Authority: Dep. Dir, Contracting, 1994–96; Dir of Commng, 1996–2000; Dir, Planning and Organisational Develt, 2000–01; Chief Exec., 2001–02; Dir, Business Mgt, Avon, Glos and Wilts SHA, 2002–03; mgt consultant, 2004–05; Chief Exec., Health Commn Wales, 2006–07; Dir, Service Delivery, Dept of Health and Social Services, Welsh Govt, 2007–08; Transition Dir, Gwent (on secondment), 2008–09; Dir, Strategy, Dept of Health and Social Services, Welsh Govt, 2009–10; Chief Exec., Velindre NHS Trust, 2010–14; Interim Chief Exec., Betsi Cadwaladr Univ. Health Bd, 2015. *Recreations:* making and playing electric guitars, music, watching Rugby. *Address:* Department of Health and Social Services, Welsh Government, Cathays Park, Cardiff CF10 3NQ. *T:* (029) 2080 6305. *E:* simon.dean@wales.gsi.gov.uk.

DEAN, Tacita Charlotte, OBE 2013; RA 2008; artist; *b* Canterbury, 12 Nov. 1965; *d* of His Honour Joseph Jolyon Dean and of Hon. Jenefer Dean, *yr d* of 5th Baron Hillingdon, MC, TD; partner, Mathew Hale; one *s*. *Educ:* Kent Coll., Canterbury; Canterbury Coll. of Art (Art Foundn); Falmouth Sch. of Art (BA Hons Fine Art); Slade Sch. of Fine Arts (Higher Dip.). *Solo exhibitions:* Mus. für Gegenwartskunst, Basel, Museo de Arte Contemporáneo, Barcelona, Tate Britain, 2001; Kunstverein für die Rheinlande und Westfalen, Düsseldorf, 2002; ARC/Musée d'art moderne de la ville de Paris, 2003; De Pont, Tilburg, 2004; Tate St Ives, 2005; Nat. Mus. of Art, Architecture and Design, Oslo, Schaulager, Basel, 2006; Guggenheim, NY, Hugh Lane, Dublin, Miami Art Central, Miami, 2007; Dia:Beacon, NY, Fondazione Nicola Trussardi, Milan, Australian Centre for Contemporary Art, Melbourne, Sprengel Mus., Hanover, 2009; Museo Nacional Centre de Arte Reina Sofia, Madrid, 2010; MUMOK, Vienna, 2011; FILM (film), Tate Modern, 2011; JG (film), Arcadia Univ. Art Gall., Philadelphia, 2013; De Mar en Mar, Fundación Botín, Santander, The Measure of Things, Instituto Moreira Salles, Rio de Janeiro, Studio of Giorgio Morandi, MAMbo, Bologna, Fatigues, Marian Goodman Gall., NY, 2013. Mem., Akademie der Künste, 2007. *Publications:* Book with Leaves, 1995; Disappearance at Sea, 1997; Tacita Dean: missing narratives, 1997; Teignmouth Electron, 1999, 2nd edn 2009; (with Martyn Ridgewell) Floh, 2001; Tacita Dean: 12.10.02–21.12.02, 2002; Tacita Dean: the Green ray, 2003; Seven Books, 2003; Die Regimentstochter, 2005; An Aside, 2005; (with Jeremy Millar) Artworks: place, 2005; Darmstädter Werkblock, 2008; Fontainebleau is in France, 2008; (with W. G. Sebald and Joseph Beuys) Post-War Germany and 'Objective Chance', 2008; Film Works with Merce Cunningham, 2009; Seven Books Grey, 2011; The Friar's Doodle, 2011; Tacita Dean: FILM, 2011; Five Americans, 2012; artist's books: Clover Book, 2013; c/o Jolyon, 2013. *Recreation:* various collections. *Address:* Kurfürstenstrasse 13, 10785 Berlin, Germany. *Club:* Chelsea Arts.

DEAN, Victoria Glynis; HM Diplomatic Service; High Commissioner to Barbados and (non-resident) to Dominica, Grenada, Antigua, Barbuda, St Vincent and the Grenadines, St Lucia and St Christopher and Nevis, since 2013; *b* Chichester, W Sussex; *d* of Peter and Glynis Courtney; *m* 2006, Marcus Scott Dean; one *s* one *d*. *Educ:* Internat. Sch. of Geneva, Switzerland; Univ. of Kent (BSc Clin. Psychol. 1999). Entered FCO, 2000; Second, then First Sec., Paris, 2001–04; Head: of Communications, UK Perm. Repn, Brussels, 2004–08;

Political Team, Washington, 2009–10; of Strategic Finance, FCO, 2010–11; Dep. Dir, Europe, FCO, 2011–13. *Recreations:* travelling and exploring, reading, family, yoga, France, politics. *Address:* c/o Foreign and Commonwealth Office, King Charles Street, SW1A 2AH. *E:* victoria.dean@fco.gov.uk; British High Commission, Bridgetown, Barbados.

DEANE, family name of **Baron Muskerry**.

DEANE, Derek, OBE 2000; choreographer; Artistic Director, English National Ballet, 1993–2001; *b* 18 June 1953; *s* of William Gordon Shepherd and Margaret Shepherd; adopted Deane as stage name. *Educ:* Royal Ballet School. With Royal Ballet Co., 1972–89; Asst Dir, Rome Opera, 1990–92. Productions for English Nat. Ballet include: Alice in Wonderland, 1995; Swan Lake, 1997 and 2011; Strictly Gershwin, 2008 and 2011; Romeo and Juliet, 2014. *Recreations:* theatre, all performing arts, travelling, tennis.

DEANE, Robert Edward; HM Diplomatic Service; Head of Department, Foreign and Commonwealth Office, since 2013; *b* 28 Sept. 1962; *s* of Edward Stuart Deane and Jennifer Mary Deane; *m* 1993, Corinna Osmann; one *s* two *d*. *Educ:* London Sch. of Economics (BSc 1984); Univ. of Southampton (MSc 1985). HM Treasury, 1985–94; Bonn, 1994–99; First Sec., FCO, 1999–2005; Dep. Hd of Mission, Abu Dhabi, 2005–07; Counsellor, 2007–09, Dep. Hd of Mission, 2009–11, Rome; Counsellor, FCO, 2011–12; Dep. Hd of Mission, Baghdad, 2012–13. *Recreations:* photography, diving, travel, sailing. *Address:* c/o Foreign and Commonwealth Office, SW1A 2AH.

DEANE, Sir Roderick (Sheldon), KNZM 2012; PhD; Chairman: IHC Foundation (NZ), since 2006 (Vice President, 1982–88; President, 1988–94); Pataka Foundation, since 2014; *b* Birkenhead, Auckland, 8 April 1941; *s* of Reginald Roderick Deane and Jessie Margaret Deane; *m* 1964, Gillian Gibson; (one *d* decd). *Educ:* Pukekohe Primary and Mauku Primary Schs; Opunake and New Plymouth Boys High Schs; Victoria Univ. of Wellington (BCom 1st Cl. Hons; PhD). Union Steamship Co. of NZ Ltd, 1960–63; Reserve Bank of NZ, 1963–74; Alt. Exec. Dir, IMF, 1974–76; Dep. Governor, Reserve Bank of NZ, 1982–86; Chm., State Services Commn, 1986–87; Chief Executive Officer: Electricity Corp. of NZ, 1987–92; Telecom Corp. of NZ, 1992–99 (Chm., 1999–2006); Chairman: TransPower Ltd, 1987–2002; PowerDesignBuild Ltd, 1987–2002; Fletcher Bldg Ltd, 1999–2010; Pacific Road Gp, 2010–13; Director: Woolworths Ltd (Australia), 2000–13; ANZ Bank, 1994–2006; TransAlta Corpn, 2000–03. Part-time Lectr, 1964–78, Prof. of Econs, 2000–03, Victoria Univ. of Wellington. Chairman: Mus. of NZ (Te Papa), 2000–06; NZ Seed Fund, 2000–15. Trustee, Deane Endowment Trust, 1995–. FCIS 1987; FNZIM 1992. Fellow Associate Chartered Accountant, 1988. Hon. LLD Victoria Wellington, 1999. NZ Commemoration Medal, 1990. *Publications:* Foreign Investment in New Zealand Manufacturing, 1970; (ed with P. W. Nicholls and contrib.) Monetary Policy and the New Zealand Financial System, 1979, (ed jtly) 2nd edn 1983; (ed jtly and contrib.) External Economic Structure and Policy, 1981; (ed) Financial Policy Reform, 1986; research papers; contribs to jls incl. New Data for Econ. Res., Reserve Bank of NZ Bulletin, NZ Econ. Papers, NZ Economist. *Recreations:* being with friends, travelling, photography, wetland restoration. *Address:* Box 28049, Wellington 6150, New Zealand. *E:* roderick.deane@independenteconomics.com. *Club:* Wellington.

DEANE, Hon. Sir William (Patrick), AC 1988; KBE 1982; Governor General of the Commonwealth of Australia, 1996–2001; *b* 4 Jan. 1931; *s* of C. A. Deane, MC and Lillian Hussey; *m* 1965, Helen, *d* of Dr Gerald and Kathleen Russell; one *s* one *d*. *Educ:* St Christopher's Convent, Canberra; St Joseph's College, Sydney; Univ. of Sydney (BA, LLB); Trinity Coll., Dublin; Dip. Internat. Law, The Hague. Called to the Bar of NSW, 1957. Teaching Fellow in Equity, Univ. of Sydney, 1956–61 (Actg Lectr in Public Internat. Law, 1956–57); QC 1966; Judge, Supreme Court of NSW, 1977; Judge, Fed. Court of Australia, 1977–82; Pres., Trade Practices Tribunal, 1977–82; Justice of the High Court of Australia, 1982–95. Hon. LLD: Sydney, NSW, Griffith, Notre Dame, TCD, UTS, Melbourne, Queensland; DUniv: Southern Cross, Aust. Cath., Western Sydney, Qld Univ. of Technol.; Hon. Dr Sac. Theol. Melbourne Coll. of Divinity. KStJ 1996. *Address:* PO Box 4168, Manuka, ACT 2603, Australia.

DEANFIELD, Prof. John Eric, FRCP; Professor of Cardiology, since 1996, British Heart Foundation Vandervell Professor of Cardiology, since 2003, and Director, National Centre for Cardiovascular Disease Prevention and Outcomes, University College London, since 2012; Consultant Cardiologist, since 1984, and Academic Head, 1996–2012, Cardiothoracic Unit, Great Ormond Street Hospital; *b* 28 April 1952; *s* of Sigmund and Tina Deanfield; *m* 1983, Melanie Fulford; one *s* one *d*. *Educ:* Churchill Coll., Cambridge (BA 1972); Middlesex Hosp. Med. Sch. (MB BChir 1975). FRCP 1993. MRC Trng Fellow, RPMS, 1980–83; Sen. Registrar in Cardiol., Gt Ormond St Hosp., 1983–84. FACC; FESC. *Publications:* numerous peer reviewed contribs to med. jls. *Recreations:* fencing (represented GB in Fencing at Olympics, 1972, 1976, 1980), wine tasting, antique collecting (English porcelain lectr). *Address:* National Centre for Cardiovascular Disease Prevention and Outcomes, 170 Tottenham Court Road, W1T 7HA. *T:* (020) 3108 2356. *E:* j.deanfield@ich.ucl.ac.uk.

DEANS, Mungo Effingham; a Judge of the Upper Tribunal and Resident Judge, Immigration and Asylum Chamber, First-tier Tribunal, Glasgow, since 2010 (Resident Senior Immigration Judge, Glasgow, 2005–10); *b* Lytham St Anne's, Lancs, 25 May 1956; *s* of Effingham Fairnington Deans and (Agnes) Beryl (Hutchison) Deans (*née* Ramsey); *m* 1983, Kathryn Atkinson; three *s*. *Educ:* Fettes Coll., Edinburgh; London Sch. of Econs and Pol Sci. (BSc Econ 1977); Univ. of Edinburgh (LLB 1979). Admitted as solicitor, 1981; Lectr in Law, Univ. of Dundee, 1983–95; Regl Adjudicator, Immigration Appellate Authy, Glasgow, 1996–2005; Legal Mem., Immigration Appeal Tribunal, 2000–05. *Publications:* Scots Public Law, 1995. *Recreation:* tree planting. *Address:* First-tier Tribunal, Immigration and Asylum Chamber, 5th Floor, Eagle Building, 215 Bothwell Street, Glasgow G2 7EZ. *T:* 0300 123 1711. *Club:* Royal Over-Seas League.

DEAR, family name of **Baron Dear**.

DEAR, Baron *cr* 2006 (Life Peer), of Willersey in the County of Gloucestershire; **Geoffrey James Dear,** Kt 1997; QPM 1982; Vice Lord-Lieutenant, Worcestershire, 1998–2001; HM Inspector of Constabulary, 1990–97; *b* 20 Sept. 1937; *er s* of Cecil William Dear and Violet Mildred (*née* Mackney); *m* 1st, 1958, Judith Ann Stocker (*d* 1996); one *s* two *d*; 2nd, 1998, Alison Jean Martin Jones. *Educ:* Fletton Grammar Sch., Hunts; University Coll., London (LLB). Joined Peterborough Combined Police after cadet service, 1956; Mid-Anglia (now Cambridgeshire) Constab., 1965; Bramshill Scholarship, UCL, 1965–68 (Fellow, 1990); Asst Chief Constable (Ops), Notts (City and County), 1972–80; seconded as Dir of Comd Training, Bramshill, 1975–77; Metropolitan Police: Dep. Asst Comr, 1980–81; Asst Comr, 1981–85 (Personnel and Trng, 1981–84; Ops, 1984–85); Chief Constable, W Midlands Police, 1985–90. Member: Govt Adv. Cttee on Alcoholism, 1975–78; Glidewell Rev. into CPS, 1997–98; Council, RUSI, 1982–89 (Mem. Cttee, 1976–94). Lecture tour of Eastern USA univs, 1978; visited Memphis, Tenn, USA to advise on reorganisation of Police Dept, 1979. Non-executive Chairman: Image Metrics plc, 2001–03; Skyguard Technologies Ltd, 2001–11; Omniperception plc, 2005–12; Key Forensic Services Ltd, 2005–11; Forensic DNA Services Ltd, 2006–11; Blue Star Capital plc, 2008–13; Assoc. of Business Crime Partnerships Ltd, 2010–12; Blaythorne Gp Ltd, 2014–; non-executive Director: Reliance Security Services Ltd, 1997–2005; Reliance Custodial Services, subseq. Reliance Secure Task Management Ltd, 1999–2005; Mem. Adv. Bd, Pegasus Bridge Fund Mgt Ltd, 2006–08. Chm., Action against Business Crime, 2004–10. Vice Chm., London and SE Reg., Sports Council, 1984–85. Vice President: Warwickshire CCC, 1985–; W Midlands and Hereford & Worcester Grenadier Guards Assocs, 1992–2010. Trustee: Police Rehabilitation Trust, 1987–; World Horse Welfare, 2010–. Hon. Fellow, Birmingham City Univ. (formerly Univ. of Central England in Birmingham), 1991. Hon. Bencher, Gray's Inn, 2008. FRSA 1990. DL W Midlands, 1985, Hereford and Worcester, 1995. Freeman, City of London, 2003. CStJ 1996. Queen's Commendation for Bravery, 1979. *Publications:* (contrib.) The Police and the Community, 1975; articles in Police Jl and other pubns. *Recreations:* field sports, Rugby football (Pres., Met. Police RFC, 1983–85), fell-walking, literature, gardening, music, fine arts. *Address:* House of Lords, SW1A 0PW. *Clubs:* East India, Special Forces.

DEAR, Jeremy; General Secretary, National Union of Journalists, 2002–11; *b* 6 Dec. 1966; *s* of John and Jan Dear; *m* 1999, Paula Jolly. *Educ:* Coventry Polytech. (BA Hons Mod. Studies); UC Cardiff (Postgrad. Dip. Journalism). Journalist, freelance, and on staff of Essex Chronicle Series, and The Big Issue, 1989–94; Ed., Big Issue in the Midlands, 1994–97; Nat. Organiser, Newspapers, NUJ, 1997–2001.

DEARLOVE, Sir Richard (Billing), KCMG 2001; OBE 1984; Master of Pembroke College, Cambridge, 2004–15; Deputy Vice-Chancellor, University of Cambridge, 2005–10; *b* 23 Jan. 1945; *m* 1968, Rosalind McKenzie; two *s* one *d*. *Educ:* Monkton Combe Sch.; Kent Sch., Conn, USA; Queens' Coll., Cambridge (MA; Hon. Fellow, 2004). Entered FO, 1966; Nairobi, 1968–71; Prague, 1973–76; FCO, 1976–80; First Secretary: Paris, 1980–84; FCO, 1984–87; Counsellor: UKMIS Geneva, 1987–91; Washington, 1991–93; Secret Intelligence Service: Dir, Personnel and Admin, 1993–94; Dir, Ops, 1994–99; Asst Chief, 1998–99; Chief, 1999–2004. Chm., Ascot Underwriting Ltd, 2006–; Dir, Kosmos Energy, 2013–. Vis. Lectr, Fletcher Sch., Tufts Univ., Boston, USA, 2005–10. Advr, Monitor Gp, 2005–11; Mem. Adv. Bd, AIG, 2005–10. Chairman of Trustees: Cambridge Union Soc., 2007–15; Univ. of London, 2014–; Trustee, Kent Sch., Conn, USA, 2001–. Gov., ESU, 2008–10. Hon. LLD Exeter, 2007. *Address:* Pembroke College, Cambridge CB2 1RF.

DEARNLEY, Mark William, CEng; FIET, FBCS; Director General and Chief Digital and Information Officer, HM Revenue and Customs, since 2013; *b* Huddersfield, 12 April 1969; *s* of William and Margaret Dearnley; *m* 1991, Lorraine Michelle; two *c*. *Educ:* Dauntsey's Sch.; Brunel Univ. (BEng Hons Electrical and Electronic Engrg 1991). Prog. Dir, Boots Gp plc, 2002–04; Chief Information Officer: Cable & Wireless Internat. Gp, 2004–10; Vodafone UK, 2010–13. *Recreation:* tennis. *Address:* HM Revenue and Customs, 100 Parliament Street, SW1A 2BQ. *T:* 0300 058 4810. *E:* mark.dearnley@hmrc.gsi.gov.uk. *Club:* Morgan Sports Car.

DEARY, Prof. Ian John, PhD; FRCPE; FRCPsych; FBA 2003; FRSE; FMedSci; Professor of Differential Psychology, University of Edinburgh, since 1995; Director, University of Edinburgh Centre for Cognitive Ageing and Cognitive Epidemiology, since 2008; *b* 17 May 1954; *s* of Hugh McCulloch Deary and Isobelle Ferguson Deary; *m* 1978, Ann Marie Barclay; one *s* two *d*. *Educ:* Hamilton Acad.; Univ. of Edinburgh (BSc; MB ChB; PhD 1992). MRCPsych 1991, FRCPsych 2008; FRCPE 1995; FRSE 2003. Med. House Officer, 1983–84, Surgical House Officer, 1984, Royal Infirmary of Edinburgh; Sen. House Officer, Psychiatry, Bethlem Royal and Maudsley Hosps, 1984–85; Lectr, 1985–90, Sen. Lectr, 1990–92, Reader, 1992–95, in Psychology, Univ. of Edinburgh; Registrar, Psychiatry, Royal Edinburgh Hosp., 1989–90. FMedSci 2007. *Publications:* (with G. Matthews) Personality Traits, 1998, 3rd edn 2009; Looking Down on Human Intelligence: from psychometrics to the brain, 2000; Intelligence: a very short introduction, 2001; (with L. J. Whalley and J. M. Starr) A Lifetime of Intelligence, 2009; over 500 articles in learned jls on human mental abilities, personality, psychometrics and med. aspects of psychology. *Recreations:* cycling, lyric writing, saxophone, Motherwell FC, English Romantic composers, late Victorian English novelists. *Address:* Department of Psychology, University of Edinburgh, 7 George Square, Edinburgh EH8 9JZ. *T:* (0131) 650 3452, *Fax:* (0131) 651 1771. *E:* i.deary@ed.ac.uk.

DEATHRIDGE, Prof. John William, DPhil; FRCO; King Edward Professor of Music, King's College London, 1996–2013, now Emeritus; *b* 21 Oct. 1944; *s* of Leslie and Iris Deathridge; *m* 1985, Victoria L. Cooper; one *d*. *Educ:* King Edward's Sch., Birmingham; Lincoln Coll., Oxford (MA; DPhil 1974). FRCO 1967. Organist and Choirmaster, St Wolfgang, Munich, 1971–81; Ed., Richard Wagner-Gesamtausgabe, Munich, 1981–83; University of Cambridge: Fellow, and Dir, Studies in Music, King's Coll., 1983–96; Lectr in Music, 1983–95; Reader in Music, 1995–96. Pres., Royal Musical Assoc., 2005–08 (Vice-Pres., 2002–05). Corresp. Mem., Amer. Musicological Soc., 2002. *Publications:* Wagner's Rienzi: a reappraisal based on a study of the sketches and drafts, 1977; (with C. Dahlhaus) The New Grove Wagner, 1984; (jtly) Verzeichnis der musikalischen Werke Richard Wagners und ihrer Quellen, 1986; (ed) Family Letters of Richard Wagner, 1991; (ed jtly) Wagner Handbook, 1992; Wagner Beyond Good and Evil, 2008; edited with K. Döge: Richard Wagner: Lohengrin, 3 vols, 1996–2000; Dokumente und Texte zu "Lohengrin", 2003; contribs to Musical Times, 19th Century Music, Cambridge Opera Jl, Jl Royal Musical Assoc., Opera Quarterly. *Recreations:* keep fit, films, pond care. *Address:* 12 Cook Close, Cambridge CB4 1PH; Music Department, King's College London, Strand, WC2R 2LS. *E:* john.deathridge@kcl.ac.uk. *Club:* Athenæum.

DEAVE, John James; former barrister-at-law; *b* 1 April 1928; *s* of Charles John Deave and Gertrude Debrit Deave; *m* 1958, Gillian Mary, *d* of Adm. Sir Manley Power, KCB, CBE, DSO; one *s* one *d*. *Educ:* Charterhouse; Pembroke Coll., Oxford (MA). Served RA, 2nd Lieut, 1946–48; Pembroke Coll., 1948–51; called to the Bar, Gray's Inn, 1952; in practice at Nottingham, 1957–98; a Recorder, 1980–98. *Recreations:* history, gardening. *Address:* Greensmith Cottage, Stathern, Melton Mowbray, Leics LE14 4HE. *T:* (01949) 860340. *Club:* Nottinghamshire United Services.

DEAYTON, (Gordon) Angus; writer and presenter; *b* 6 Jan. 1956; *s* of Roger Davall Deayton and Susan Agnes Deayton (*née* Weir). *Educ:* Caterham Sch.; New Coll., Oxford (BA Modern Langs (French and German)). Dir, Oxford Revue, 1979. Writer and performer: *radio:* Radio Active, 1980–87 (Mem., Hee Bee Gee Bees pop parody band); It's Your Round, 2011–12; *stage:* Rowan Atkinson's Stage Show, 1986–90; *television:* Alexei Sayle's Stuff, 1987–90; KYTV, 1990–93; One Foot in the Grave, 1990–2000; Have I Got News For You?, 1990–2002; TV Hell, 1992; End of the Year Show, 1995–2000; Before They Were Famous, 1997–2004; Not Another Awards Show, 1999; Not Another Game Show, News Bulletin, Eurovision, 2002; University Challenge (for Comic Relief), 2002, 2004; Nighty Night, 2003; Absolute Power, 2004–07; Hell's Kitchen, 2004–07; Bognor or Bust, 2004; Heartless, New Year's Honours List, Marigold, Stick to What You Know, 2005; Help Yourself, Only Fools On Horses, 2006; Would I Lie to You?, 2007–08; Comedy Sketchbook, British Comedy Awards, 2008; Pete 'n Dud—The Lost Sketches, 2010; Pramface, 2011–14; Waterloo Road, 2013–15; World Cup Epic Fails, Christmas Epic Fails, 2014; *documentaries:* In Search of Happiness, 1995; The Lying Game, 1997; The Temptation Game, 1998; The History of Alternative Comedy, 1999; Posh 'n Becks: the Reign in Spain, 2003; *films:* Elizabeth, 1998: Swinging with the Finkels, 2011; The Great European Disaster Movie, 2015. *Publications:* Radio Active Times, 1986; The Uncyclopaedia of Rock, 1987; Have I Got News For You?, 1994; In Search of Happiness, 1995; Have I Got 1997 For You?, 1997. *Recreations:* soccer, tennis, ski-ing. *Address:* c/o Independent Talent Group Ltd, 40 Whitfield Street, W1T 2RH. *Clubs:* Garrick, Groucho, Soho House, Home House.

de BASTO, Gerald Arthur; Judge of the High Court of Hong Kong, 1982–89; *b* London, 31 Dec. 1924; *s* of Bernard de Basto and Lucie Marie, *d* of Raoul Melchior Pattard, Paris; *m* 1961, Diana, *d* of Dr Frederick Osborne Busby Wilkinson; two *s*. *Educ:* Riverview Coll., Sydney, Australia; Univ. of Sydney (LLB). Called to the Bar: Supreme Court of New South

Wales and High Court of Australia, 1952; Lincoln's Inn, 1955; admitted to the Hong Kong Bar, 1957; Chairman, Hong Kong Bar, 1968–70, 1973; QC 1968; Comr of High Court, Hong Kong, 1970–82; Judge of the District Court of Hong Kong, 1973–82; Pres., Deportation Tribunal, 1986–89. *Publications:* Life is Yours, 1949; An Indictment of Socialist Labour, 1950. *Recreations:* antiques, travel, reading. *Address:* 3 Roderick Way, Constantia, 7806, South Africa. *T:* (21) 7942778. *Clubs:* Hong Kong, Hong Kong Jockey (Hong Kong).

DEBBONAIRE, Thangam Rachel; MP (Lab) Bristol West, since 2015; *b* 3 Aug. 1966; *née* Singh. *Educ:* Bradford Girls' Grammar Sch.; Chetham's Music Sch.; ARCM 1986; Univ. of Oxford; St John's City Coll. of Technol., Manchester; Bristol Univ. (MSc 1995). Professional cellist in string quartets, chamber music and soloist, 1977–2006; cellist, Royal Liverpool Philharmonic Orch., 1990–91; House-parent, girls boarding, Chetham's Sch. of Music, Manchester, 1989–91; Nat. Children's Officer, Women's Aid Fedn, 1991–98; Dir and lead ind. practitioner, Domestic Violence Responses, 1997–; Accreditation Officer, 2006–08, Res. and Fundraising Manager, 2008–15, Respect. *Publications:* (contrib.) Children Living with Domestic Violence, 1994; (jtly) Health Professionals Responding to Men for Safety, 2014; Responding to Domestic Violence in Diverse Communities, 2015. *Address:* House of Commons, SW1A 0AA. *W:* www.debbonaire.co.uk.

DEBEN, Baron *cr* 2010 (Life Peer), of Winston in the County of Suffolk; **John Selwyn Gummer;** PC 1985; Chairman: Sancroft International Ltd, since 1997; Committee on Climate Change, since 2012; *b* 26 Nov. 1939; *s* of late Canon Selwyn Gummer and Sybille (*née* Mason); *m* 1977, Penelope Jane, *yr d* of John P. Gardner; two *s* two *d*. *Educ:* King's Sch., Rochester; Selwyn Coll., Cambridge (Exhibr). BA Hons History 1961; MA 1971; Chm., Cambridge Univ. Conservative Assoc., 1961; Pres., Cambridge Union, 1962; Chm., Fedn of Conservative Students, 1962. Editor, Business Publications, 1962–64; Editor-in-Chief, Max Parrish & Oldbourne Press, 1964–66; BPC Publishing: Special Asst to Chm., 1967; Publisher, Special Projects, 1967–69; Editorial Coordinator, 1969–70. Mem., ILEA Educn Cttee, 1967–70; Dir, Shandwick Publishing Co., 1966–81; Man. Dir, EP Gp of Cos, 1975–81; Chairman: Selwyn Shandwick Internat., 1976–81, Siemssen Hunter Ltd, 1979–80 (Dir, 1973–80). Contested (C) Greenwich, 1964 and 1966; MP (C) Lewisham W, 1970–Feb. 1974, Eye, Suffolk, 1979–83, Suffolk Coastal, 1983–2010. PPS to Minister of Agriculture, 1972; an additional Vice-Chm., Conservative Party, 1972–74; an Asst Govt Whip, 1981; a Lord Comr of HM Treasury, 1981–83; Parly Under-Sec. of State for Employment, Jan.–Oct. 1983; Minister of State, Dept of Employment, 1983–84; Paymaster-Gen., 1984–85; Chm., Cons. Party, 1983–85; Minister of State: MAFF, 1985–88; DoE, 1988–89; Minister of Agric., Fisheries and Food, 1989–93; Sec. of State for the Envmt, 1993–97. Chairman: Cons. Gp for Europe, 1997–2000; Marine Stewardship Council, 1998–2005; Quality of Life Commn, 2007–08. Chairman: Valpak Ltd, 1998–; Assoc. of Professional (formerly Ind.) Financial Advrs, 2003–; Veolia Water UK (formerly General Utilities Ltd), 2004–13 (Dir, 1997–2013); non-executive Director: Sovereign Reversions plc, 2004–10; Castle Trust Mgt Ltd, 2011–; Castle Trust Capital Mgt Ltd, 2011–; Sistema-Hals, 2007–09. Mem., Gen. Synod of the Church of England, 1979–92; joined Roman Catholic Church, 1993. *Publications:* (jtly) When the Coloured People Come, 1966; The Permissive Society, 1971; (with L. W. Cowie) The Christian Calendar, 1974; (contrib.) To Church with Enthusiasm, 1969; (contrib.) Faith In Politics, 1987; Christianity and Conservatism, 1990. *Address:* Sancroft International Ltd, 46 Queen Anne's Gate, SW1H 9AP.

See also Baron Chadlington, B. M. Gummer.

DE BENEDETTI, Carlo; Cavaliere del Lavoro, Italy, 1983; Chairman: Compagnie Industriali Riunite, 1995–2009, now Hon. Chairman (Vice-Chairman and Chief Executive, 1976–95); Compagnia Finanziaria De Benedetti, 1995–2009, now Hon. President (Chief Executive, 1991–95); Sogefi, 1981–2005, now Hon. Chairman; *b* 14 Nov. 1934; *m*; three *s*. *Educ:* Turin Polytechnic (degree in electrotech. engrg). Chm./Chief Exec., Gilardini, 1972–76; Chief Exec., Fiat, 1976; Olivetti SpA: Chief Exec., 1978–96; Chm., 1983–96; Hon. Chm., 1996–99. Director: Pirelli SpA; Valeo; l'Espresso SpA; Mem., European Adv. Cttee, NY Stock Exchange, 1985–2005; Chm., Cerus, 1986–99. Dir, Center for Strategic and Internat. Studies, Washington, 1978; Mem. Bd of Trustees, Solomon R. Guggenheim Foundn, NY, 1984; Vice Chm., Eur. Roundtable of Industrialists, Brussels, 1999–2004. Foreign Mem., Royal Swedish Acad. of Engrg Scis, Stockholm, 1987. Officier, Légion d'Honneur (France), 1987; Silver Medal of Merit (Austria), 2006. *Publications:* lectures and articles in business jls. *Address:* CIR SpA, Via Ciovassino 1, 20121 Milano, Italy. *T:* (2) 722701.

DEBENHAM, Sir Thomas Adam, 4th Bt *cr* 1931, of Bladen, co. Dorset; *b* 28 Feb. 1971; *s* of George Andrew Debenham and of Penelope Jane (*née* Carter); *S* grandfather, 2001; *m* 1998, Melanie Bargh. *Heir: uncle* William Michael Debenham [*b* 30 June 1940; *m* 1974, Gunnel Birgitta Holmgren; two *s*].

DEBENHAM TAYLOR, John, CMG 1967; OBE 1959; TD 1967; HM Diplomatic Service, retired; *b* 25 April 1920; *s* of John Francis Taylor and Harriett Beatrice (*née* Williams); *m* 1966, Gillian May James; one *d*. *Educ:* Aldenham School. Eastern Counties Farmers Assoc. Ltd, Ipswich and Great Yarmouth, 1936–39. Commnd in RA (TA), Feb. 1939; served War of 1939–46 in Finland, Middle East, UK and SE Asia (despatches, 1946). Foreign Office, 1946; Control Commn for Germany, 1947–49; 2nd Sec., Bangkok, 1950; Actg Consul, Songkhla, 1951–52; Vice-Consul, Hanoi, 1952–53; FO, 1953–54; 1st Sec., Bangkok, 1954–56; FO, 1956–58; Singapore, 1958–59; FO, 1960–64; Counsellor, 1964; Counsellor: Kuala Lumpur, 1964–66; FCO (formerly FO), 1966–69; Washington, 1969–72; Paris, 1972–73; FCO, 1973–77. *Recreations:* walking, reading, history. *Address:* Forest Grange Manor, Centre Wing, Colgate, Horsham, West Sussex RH12 4TG. *T:* (01293) 851812. *Club:* Naval and Military.

de BERNIÈRE-SMART, Louis Henry Piers; author, as Louis de Bernières; *b* 8 Dec. 1954; *s* of Major Reginald Piers Alexander de Bernière-Smart, *qv*; one *s* one *d*. *Educ:* Grenham House; Bradfield Coll.; Manchester Univ. (BA Hons Philosophy 1977); Leicester Poly. (PGCE 1981); Inst. of Educn, London Univ. (MA 1985). Landscape gardener, 1972–73; teacher and rancher, Colombia, 1974; philosophy tutor, 1977–79; car mechanic, 1980; English teacher, 1981–84; bookshop asst, 1985–86; supply teacher, 1986–93. Chancellor, Norfolk Children's Univ., 2010–. Patron: Families House, Norwich; Banjo, Mandolin and Guitar Fedn; Norfolk Youth Orch., 2009–; Families Need Fathers, 2010–. Mem., Antonius Players, 2002–10. FTCL 1999. *Publications:* The War of Don Emmanuel's Nether Parts, 1990; Señor Vivo and the Coca Lord, 1991; The Troublesome Offspring of Cardinal Guzman, 1992; Captain Corelli's Mandolin, 1994 (filmed, 2001); Red Dog, 2001 (filmed, 2012); Sunday Morning at the Centre of the World, 2001; Birds Without Wings, 2004; A Partisan's Daughter, 2008; Notwithstanding, 2009; Imagining Alexandria (poems in honour of Constantin Cavafis), 2013; The Dust That Falls From Dreams, 2015. *Recreations:* music, literature, golf, fishing, carpentry, gardening, cats, restoring and making musical instruments. *Address:* c/o Caroline Wood, Felicity Bryan Literary Agency, 2a North Parade Avenue, Oxford OX2 6LX. *T:* (01865) 513816.

de BERNIÈRE-SMART, Major Reginald Piers Alexander; Director, The Shaftesbury Homes and Arethusa, 1988–89, retired (General Secretary, 1971–88); general duties, Chichester Division, SSAFA/FHS, 1995–2000 (caseworker, 1990–94); *b* 3 March 1924; *s* of Kenneth de Bernière-Smart and Audrey (*née* Brown); *m* 1951, Jean Ashton Smithells (*d* 2010); one *s* two *d*. *Educ:* Bowden House, Seaford; Bradfield Coll. Commnd The Queen's Bays (2nd Dragoon Guards), 1943; Italian Campaign, 1944–45 (despatches); Staff, RAC OCTU and Mons OCS, 1948–49; GSO 3 7th Armd Bde, 1951; Adjt, The Queen's Bays, 1952–54; Adjt, RAC Centre, Bovington, 1956–58; retired from 1st The Queen's Dragoon Guards, 1959. Exec. Sec., British Diabetic Assoc., 1960–65; joined Shaftesbury Homes and Arethusa exec. staff, 1966. Dir, Wad (West Wittering) Management Co., 1992–94. Chm., Management Cttee, Bradfield Club, Peckham, 1990–92 (Mem. Council, 1992–2000). Member: IAM, 1959–; NCVCCO, 1971–89. West Wittering PCC, 1991–97; Foundn Gov., W Wittering Parochial C of E Sch., 1997–2000 (Chm. of Govs, 1998–2000). Hon. Fellow, Cancer Res. UK, 2003. *Publications:* (as Piers Alexander) Golden Apples (poetry), 2006. *Recreations:* open air activities, photography, steam and model railways, theatre, poetry, militaria. *Address:* 9 The Wad, West Wittering, Chichester, W Sussex PO20 8AH. *T:* (01243) 511072. *Clubs:* Cavalry and Guards, Victoria League for Commonwealth Friendship.

See also L. H. P. de Bernière-Smart.

de BERNIÈRES, Louis; *see* de Bernière-Smart, L. H. P.

de BERTODANO, Sylvia Philippa Theresa; Her Honour Judge de Bertodano; a Circuit Judge, since 2009; *b* Cirencester, 16 Oct. 1969; *d* of Martin de Bertodano and Tessa de Bertodano (*née* Avery); *m* 1995, Stuart Robert Alford, *qv*; two *s* two *d*. *Educ:* St Mary's Convent, Ascot; Marlborough Coll.; Christ Church, Oxford (BA Hons PPE). Called to the Bar, Middle Temple, 1993; in practice as a barrister specialising in internat. criminal law, 1994–2009. *Publications:* (contrib.) Internationalized Criminal Courts, 2004; (contrib.) Defense in International Criminal Proceedings, 2006; (contrib.) The Oxford Companion to International Criminal Justice, 2009; (jtly) Closing the Gap: the role of non-judicial mechanisms in addressing impunity, 2010. *Recreations:* opera, poetry, scuba diving, playing violin. *Address:* Warwickshire Justice Centre, 3 Newbold Terrace, Leamington Spa, Warwicks CV32 4EL. *T:* (01926) 682100.

de BLOCQ van KUFFELER, John Philip; Chairman: Non-Standard Finance plc, since 2014; Paratus AMC Ltd, since 2015; *b* 9 Jan. 1949; *s* of late Captain Frans de Blocq van Kuffeler and Stella de Blocq van Kuffeler (*née* Hall); *m* 1971, Lesley Callander (marr. diss. 2014); two *s* one *d*; *m* 2015, Eva Nijhof; one *d*. *Educ:* Atlantic Coll.; Clare Coll., Cambridge (MA). FCA 1975. Peat Marwick & Mitchell, 1970–77; Grindlays Bank: Manager, 1977–80; Head of Corporate Finance, 1980–82; Brown Shipley & Co.: Head: Corporate Finance, 1983–88; Investment Banking, UK and USA, 1986–88; Gp Chief Exec., 1988–91; Chief Exec., 1991–97, Chm., 1997–2014, Provident Financial plc; Chairman: Hyperion Insurance Gp Ltd, 2009–13; Marlin Financial Gp Ltd, 2010–14. Council Mem., CBI, 1997–99. Executive Chairman: Finsbury Smaller Quoted Companies Trust plc, 1992–2003; J. P. Morgan Fleming Technology Trust plc, 1998–2003; Huveaux plc, 2001–08; non-exec. Chm., Eidos plc, 2002–05; non-exec. Dir, Medical Defence Union, 2001–04. Mem. Council, Prince's Trust, 2001–08. *Recreations:* field sports, opera. *Address:* 5 Little Chester Street, SW1X 7AL. *Clubs:* City of London, Walbrook.

de BOIS, Geoffrey Nicholas, (Nick); *b* Ely, 23 Feb. 1959; *s* of Wing Comdr John de Bois and Paula de Bois; *m* Vanessa Coleman; one *s* three *d*; *m* 2009, Helen Seaman. *Educ:* Culford Sch.; Cambridge Coll. of Arts and Technol. (HND Business Studies 1981). Public Relns Exec., Advertising Standards Authy, 1982–84; Rapiergroup: Client Proj. Manager, 1984–86; Client Proj. Dir, 1986–88; Chm. and Man. Dir, 1989–2010. Contested (C): Stalybridge and Hyde, 1997; Enfield N, 2001, 2005. MP (C) Enfield N, 2010–15; contested (C) same seat, 2015. Mem., Justice Select Cttee, 2011–15; Vice Chm., All Party Parly Gp on Trade and Investment, 2012–15; Co-Chair, All Party Parly Gp on Public Health and Primary Care, 2012–15; Mem., Public Admin Cttee, 2010–11; Sec., 1922 Cttee, 2012–15. MInstD. *Recreations:* travel, writing, theatre, gym, armchair sports fan, dining out and entertaining, part-time broadcaster with LBC. *E:* nickdebois@gmail.com.

de BOISSIEU, Pierre; Secretary-General of the Council of the European Union, 2009–11 (Deputy Secretary-General, 1999–2009); *b* Paris, 14 June 1945; *s* of Michel and Françoise de Boissieu; *m* 1968, Béatrice; three *s* two *d*. *Educ:* École Nationale d'Administration. First Sec., French Embassy, Bonn, 1973–78; Hd, Cabinet of Vice-Pres., Eur. Commn, 1978–84; Dir for Econ. Affairs, Foreign Ministry, 1984–93; Perm. Rep. to EU, 1993–99. Commandeur de la Légion d'Honneur (France), 2010. *Address:* 29 avenue Bosquet, 75007 Paris, France.

de BONO, Dr Edward Francis Charles Publius; Lecturer in Medicine, Department of Medicine, University of Cambridge, 1976–83; Director of The Cognitive Research Trust, Cambridge, since 1971; Secretary-General, Supranational Independent Thinking Organisation (SITO), since 1983; *b* 19 May 1933; *s* of late Prof. Joseph de Bono, CBE and of Josephine de Bono (*née* O'Byrne); *m* 1971, Josephine (marr. diss.), *d* of Maj. Francis Hall-White, MBE; two *s*. *Educ:* St Edward's Coll., Malta; Royal Univ. of Malta; Christ Church, Oxford (Rhodes Scholar). BSc, MD Malta; DPhil Oxon; PhD Cantab. Research Asst, Dept of Regius Prof. of Medicine, Univ. of Oxford, 1958–60; Jun. Lectr in Med., Oxford, 1960–61; Asst Dir of Res., Dept of Investigative Medicine, Cambridge Univ., 1963–76. Research Associate: also Hon. Registrar, St Thomas' Hosp. Med. Sch., Univ. of London; Harvard Med. Sch., and Hon. Consultant, Boston City Hosp., 1965–66. Hon. Prof. of Thinking, Univ. of Pretoria, 2003; Da Vinci Prof. of Thinking, Univ. of Advancing Technol., Arizona, 2005–; Prof. of Constructive Thinking, Dublin City Univ., 2005–. EU Ambassador for Thinking, Year of Creativity, 2009. Chm. Council, Young Enterprise Europe, 1998–. Established World Centre for New Thinking, Malta, 2004. TV series: The Greatest Thinkers, 1981; de Bono's Thinking Course, 1982. Hon. LLD Dundee, 2005; Hon. DDes RMIT, 2003. Planet DE73 named edebono after him, 1997. Carl Sloans Award, Internat. Assoc. Mgt Consulting Firms, 2006. *Publications:* The Use of Lateral Thinking, 1967; The Five-Day Course in Thinking, 1968; The Mechanism of Mind, 1969; Lateral Thinking: a textbook of creativity, 1970; The Dog Exercising Machine, 1970; Technology Today, 1971; Practical Thinking, 1971; Lateral Thinking for Management, 1971; Beyond Yes and No, 1972; Children Solve Problems, 1972; Eureka!: an illustrated history of inventions from the wheel to the computer, 1974; Teaching Thinking, 1976; The Greatest Thinkers, 1976; Wordpower, 1977; The Happiness Purpose, 1977; The Case of the Disappearing Elephant, 1977; Opportunities: a handbook of business opportunity search, 1978; Future Positive, 1979; Atlas of Management Thinking, 1981; de Bono's Thinking Course, 1982; Tactics: the art and science of success, 1984; Conflicts: a better way to resolve them, 1985; Six Thinking Hats, 1985; Masterthinker's Handbook, 1985; Letters to Thinkers, 1987; I am Right, You are Wrong, 1990; Positive Revolution for Brazil, 1990; Handbook for a Positive Revolution, 1990; Six Action Shoes, 1992; Sur/Petition, 1992; Serious Creativity, 1992; Teach Your Child to Think, 1992; Water Logic, 1993; Parallel Thinking, 1994; Teach Yourself to Think, 1995; Mind Pack, 1995; Edward de Bono's Textbook of Wisdom, 1996; How To Be More Interesting, 1997; Simplicity, 1998; New Thinking for the New Millennium, 1999; Why I want to be King of Australia, 1999; The de Bono Code Book, 2000; Why So Stupid: how the human race has never really learned to think, 2003; How to have a Beautiful Mind, 2004; Six Value Medals, 2005; H+, 2006; How to have Creative Ideas, 2007; Free or Unfree?: are Americans really free?, 2007; Six Frames for Looking at Information, 2008; Think!: before it's too late, 2009; The Love of Two Cockroaches, 2009; contribs to Nature, Lancet, Clinical Science, Amer. Jl of Physiology, etc. *Recreations:* travel, toys, thinking. *Address:* L2 Albany, Piccadilly, W1J 0AZ. *Club:* Athenæum.

de BONO, John Hugh; QC 2014; *b* Cambridge, 6 Nov. 1972; *s* of Prof. David de Bono and Dr Anne de Bono; *m* 1998, Caroline Marshall; three *s* one *d*. *Educ:* Edinburgh Acad.; Downside Sch.; Oriel Coll., Oxford (MA 1st Cl. Philosophy and Theol. 1993); De Montfort

Univ. (CPE 1994). Called to the Bar, Gray's Inn, 1995; in practice as barrister, specialising in clinical negligence and police law. *Recreations:* sailing, walking. *Address:* Serjeants' Inn Chambers, 85 Fleet Street, EC4Y 1AE. *E:* jdebonoqc@serjeantsinn.com.

de BOTTON, Alain; author, since 1993; Creative Director, Living Architecture; *b* 20 Dec. 1969; *s* of late Gilbert de Botton and of Jacqueline (*née* Burgauer); *m* 2003, Charlotte Neser; two *s*. *Educ:* Gonville and Caius Coll., Cambridge (BA Hist. 1st Cl. Hons). Hon. FRIBA 2009. *Publications:* Essays in Love, 1993; The Romantic Movement, 1994; Kiss and Tell, 1995; How Proust Can Change Your Life, 1997; The Consolations of Philosophy, 2000; The Art of Travel, 2002; Status Anxiety, 2004; The Architecture of Happiness, 2006; The Pleasures and Sorrows of Work, 2009; A Week at the Airport: a Heathrow diary, 2009; Religion for Atheists: a non-believer's guide to the uses of religion, 2012; (jtly) Art as Therapy, 2013; The News: a user's manual, 2014. *Recreations:* French Cinema 1960–1970, nature, art. *Address:* c/o Caroline Dawnay, United Agents, 12–26 Lexington Street, W1F 0LE.

de BOTTON, Hon. Dame Janet (Frances Wolfson), DBE 2013 (CBE 2006); Trustee, since 1987, and Chairman, since 2010, Wolfson Foundation; *b* 31 March 1952; *d* of Baron Wolfson and Ruth, Lady Wolfson; *m* 1st, 1972, Michael Philip Green, *qv* (marr. diss. 1989); two *d*; 2nd, 1990, Gilbert de Botton (*d* 2000). *Educ:* St Paul's Girls' Sch. Dir, Christie's International, 1994–98. Trustee, Tate Gall., 1992–2002. *Address:* c/o Wolfson Foundation, 8 Queen Anne Street, W1G 9LD. *T:* (020) 7323 5730.

DEBRÉ, Jean Louis; President, Constitutional Council, France, since 2007; *b* Toulouse, 30 Sept. 1944; *s* of late Michel Jean-Pierre Debré; *m* 1971, Anne-Marie Engel; two *s* one *d*. *Educ:* Lycée Janson-de-Sailly; Institut d'Etudes Politiques, Paris; Faculté de Droit, Paris (DenD); Ecole Nationale de la Magistrature. Asst, Faculté de Droit, Paris, 1972–75; Technical Counsellor, then Chargé de Mission, office of Jacques Chirac, as Minister of Agric., 1973–74, Minister of the Interior, 1974, and Prime Minister, 1974–76; Dep. Public Prosecutor, High Court of Evry, 1976–78; Magistrate, Central Admin, Ministry of Justice, 1978; Chef de Cabinet to Minister of the Budget, 1978; Examng Magistrate, High Court of Paris, 1979. Dep. (RPR) for Eure, Nat. Assembly, 1986–95 and 1997–2007; Minister of the Interior, France, 1995–97; Pres., Nat. Assembly, 2002–07; Vice-Pres., 1990–95, Pres., 1997–2007, RPR Gp in Nat. Assembly. Councillor: Evreux, 1989–95; Paris, 1995–97; Conseiller Général, Canton de Nonancourt, 1992–; Mayor of Evreux, 2001–07. *Publications:* Les Idées constitutionnelles du Général de Gaulle, 1974; La Constitution de la Ve République, 1974; Le Pouvoir politique, 1977; Le Gaullisme, 1978; La Justice au XIXe, 1981; Les Républiques des Avocats, 1984; Le Curieux, 1986; En mon for intérieur, 1997; Pièges, 1998; Le Gaullisme n'est pas une nostalgie, 1999; Qu'est ce que l'Assemblée Nationale?, 2006; Quand les brochets font courir les carpes, 2008; Les oubliés de la République, 2008; Meutre à l'Assemblée, 2010; En tête-à-tête avec Charles de Gaulle, 2010; Regard de femme, 2010; Jeux de haine, 2011; En tête à tête avec les présidents de la République, 2012; Ces femmes qui ont réveillé la France, 2013. *Recreations:* horse-riding, tennis. *Address:* Conseil Constitutionnel, 2 rue de Montpensier, 75001 Paris, France.

de BROKE; *see* Willoughby de Broke.

de BRÚN, Bairbre; Member (SF) Northern Ireland, European Parliament, 2004–May 2012. *Educ:* University Coll., Dublin (BA Hons 1974); Queen's Univ., Belfast (PGCE 1980). Teacher, specialised in Irish Medium Educn, 1991–97. Mem. (SF) W Belfast, NI Assembly, 1998–2004; Minister of Health, Social Services and Public Safety, NI, 1999–2002. *Recreations:* hill-walking, theatre, cinema.

DEBY, John Bedford; QC 1980; a Recorder of the Crown Court, 1977–95; *b* 19 Dec. 1931; *s* of Reginald Bedford Deby and Irene (*née* Slater). *Educ:* Winchester Coll.; Trinity Coll., Cambridge (MA). Called to the Bar, Inner Temple, 1954, Bencher, 1986. *Address:* 11 Britannia Road, Fulham, SW6 2HJ. *T:* (020) 7736 4976. *Club:* Athenæum.

de CARDI, Beatrice Eileen, OBE 1973; FBA 2002; archaeologist; *b* 5 June 1914; *d* of Edwin Count de Cardi and Christine Berbette Wurfflein. *Educ:* St Paul's Girls' Sch.; University Coll. London (BA; Fellow, 1995). Secretary (later Asst), London Museum, 1936–44; Personal Asst to Representative of Allied Supplies Exec. of War Cabinet in China, 1944–45; Asst UK Trade Comr: Delhi, 1946; Karachi, 1947; Lahore, 1948–49; Asst Sec. (title changed to Sec.), Council for British Archæology, 1949–73. Archæological research: in Kalat, Pakistan Baluchistan, 1948; in Afghanistan, 1949; directed excavations: in Kalat, 1957; at Bampur, Persian Baluchistan, 1966; survey in Ras al-Khaimah (then Trucial States), 1968; Middle East lecture tour for British Council, 1970; survey with RGS's Musandam Expedn (Northern Oman), 1971–72; directed archæological research projects: in Qatar, 1973–74; in Central Oman, 1974–76, 1978; survey in Ras al-Khaimah, 1977, 1982, 1992. Winston Churchill Meml Trust Fellowship for work in Oman, 1973; Hon. Vis. Prof., UCL, 1998–2010. FSA 1950 (Vice-Pres., 1976–80; Dir, 1980–83). Al-Qasimi Medal (UAE), 1989 (for services to Ras al-Khaimah); Burton Meml Medal, RAS, 1993; Soc. of Antiquaries Medal, 2003, Gold Medal (for services to archaeol), 2014; presentations by Minister of Culture, UAE, for work in the Emirates, 2009, and by the Ruler in Ras al-Khaimah, 2011. *Publications:* Excavations at Bampur, a third millennium settlement in Persian Baluchistan, 1966 (Vol. 51, Pt 3, Anthropological Papers of the American Museum of Natural History), 1970; Archaeological Surveys in Baluchistan 1948 and 1957 (Inst. of Archaeology, Occasional Paper No 8), 1983; contribs to Antiquity, Iran, Pakistan Archæology, East and West, Jl of Oman Studies, Oriens Antiquus, Proc. Seminar for Arabian Studies. *Recreation:* keeping up with archaeological research. *Address:* 1a Douro Place, Victoria Road, W8 5PH. *T:* (020) 7937 9740.

de CARMOY, Hervé Pierre; Comte de Carmoy; Chairman, Supervisory Board: Grosshill Property, since 1993; Meridiam, since 2013; *b* 4 Jan. 1937; *s* of Guy de Carmoy and Marie de Gourcuff; *m* Roseline de Rohan Chabot; two *c*. *Educ:* Institut d'Etudes Politiques, Paris; Cornell Univ. Gen. Man., Western Europe, Chase Manhattan Bank, 1963–78; Chm., Exec. Bd, Midland Bank, Paris, 1978–79; Gen. Man., Europe, Midland Bank, London, 1979–84; Chief Exec., Internat. Midland Bank, London, 1984–86; Dir and Chief Exec., Global Banking Sector, Midland Bank, 1986–88; Chief Exec. Officer, Société Générale de Belgique, 1988–91; Chairman and Chief Executive: Union Minière, 1989–91; Banque Industrielle et Mobilière Privée, 1992–98; Man. Dir, Rhône Group LLC, New York, 1999–2003. Chairman: Cimenteries Belges Réunies, 1989–; Gechem, 1989–; Parvalind Gérance, 1991–; Almatis, 2003–07; Etam, 2009–13; Vice Chm., Générale de Banque, 1989–. Prof. of Internat. Strategy, Institut d'Etudes Politiques, Paris, 1996–2002. Chm., France, 1989–2004, Vice-Chm., Europe, 2004–, Trilateral Commn. Commandeur de la Légion d'Honneur (Côte d'Ivoire), 1978; Chevalier de l'Ordre du Mérite (France), 1987; Chevalier de la Légion d'Honneur (France), 1992. *Publications:* Third World Debt, 1987; Stratégie Bancaire: le refus de la dérive, 1988; La Banque du XXIe Siècle, 1996; L'entreprise, l'individu, l'Etat: conduire le changement, 1999; Euramérique, 2007; Où va l'Amérique d'Obama?, 2011. *Recreations:* tennis, music. *Address:* Chaussée de Waterloo, 965, Chelsea C 3.3, Uccle 1180, Belgium. *E:* herve@decarmoy.be.

de CHARETTE, Hervé; Deputy for Maine-et-Loire, 1988–93 and 1997–2012 (UDF, 1988–93 and 1997–2002; UMP, 2002–09; Nouveau Centre, 2009–12); Deputy President, Union pour la Démocratie Française, 1998–2002; *b* 30 July 1938; *s* of Hélion de Charette; *m* 1980, Michelle Delor; one *d*, and one *s* three *d* by former marriage. *Educ:* Institut d'Etudes Politiques; HEC; Ecole Nationale de l'Administration. Conseil d'Etat: Mem., 1966–; Auditor, 1966–73; Dep. Sec. Gen., 1969–73; Maître des Requêtes, 1973–; tech. advr to Minister of Social Affairs, 1973–74; Cabinet Director for: Sec. of State for Immigration, 1974–76; Minister of Employment, 1976–78; Chargé de Mission for Minister of Commerce, 1978–81; Conseil d'Etat, 1982–86; Asst to Prime Minister and Minister of Public Service, Planning and Social Econs, 1986–88; Minister of Housing, 1988–95; Minister for Foreign Affairs, 1995–97. Vice-Pres., UDF, 1989; Delegate-Gen., 1995–97, Pres., 1995–2002, PPDF. Vice-Pres., Pays-de-Loire Regl Council, 1992–2010; Mayor, St Florent-le-Vieil, 1989–2014. Pres., Franco-Arab Chamber of Commerce, 2008–. Pres., St Florent-le-Vieil Music and Dance Fest., 1989–2014. *Publications:* Whirlwind over the Republic, 1995; Lyautey, 1997.

de CHASSIRON, Charles Richard Lucien, CVO 2000; HM Diplomatic Service, retired; *b* 27 April 1948; *s* of Hugo and Deane de Chassiron; *m* 1974, Britt-Marie Medhammar; one *s* one *d*. *Educ:* Jesus Coll., Univ. of Cambridge (BA Hons 1969, MA 1973); Univ. of Harvard (MPA 1971). Joined Diplomatic Service, 1971; service in: Stockholm, 1972–75; Maputo, 1975–78; Mem., UK Delegn at Lancaster House Conf. on Rhodesia, 1979; FCO, 1980–82; service in Brasilia, 1982–85; Asst Hd, later Hd, S America Dept, FCO, 1985–89; Counsellor (Comm./Econ.), Rome, 1989–94; Ambassador to Estonia, 1994–97; Dir-Gen. for British Trade Develt in Italy, and Consul-Gen., Milan, 1997–2001; Vice-Marshal, Diplomatic Corps, and Hd, Protocol Div., FCO, 2002–06. Diplomatic Consultant, Royal Garden Hotel, London, 2006–11; Chm., Spencer House Ltd, 2006–11. Chm., British-Italian Soc., 2006–. Gov., British Inst. of Florence, 2007–. *Recreations:* art history, walking, Italian culture. *Address:* 47 College Road, Epsom, Surrey KT17 4HQ.

de CHASTELAIN, Gen. (Alfred) John (Gardyne Drummond), CC 2014 (OC 1993); CMM 1984; CH 1999; Chairman, Independent International Commission on Decommissioning, Northern Ireland, 1997–2011; *b* Bucharest, 30 July 1937; *s* of late Alfred George Gardyne de Chastelain, DSO, OBE, and Marion Elizabeth de Chastelain (*née* Walsh); *m* 1961, MaryAnn Laverty; one *s* one *d*. *Educ:* Fettes Coll., Edinburgh; Mount Royal Coll., Calgary, Alberta; Royal Mil. Coll. of Canada (BA Hons Hist. 1960); Army Staff Coll., Camberley. Commnd 2nd Lieut, 2nd Bn, PPCLI, 1960; Capt. 1962; Maj. 1967; Lt-Col 1970; CO, 2nd Bn, PPCLI 1970–72; Col 1974; Commander: Canadian Forces Base, Montreal, 1974–76; Canadian Contingent, UN Forces, Cyprus, 1976–77; Brig. Gen. 1977; Comdt, RMC of Canada, 1977–80; Comdr, 4th Canadian Mechanized Bde Gp, Germany, 1980–82; Dir Gen., Land Doctrine and Ops, Nat. Defence HQ, 1982–83; Maj.-Gen. 1983; Dep. Comdr, Mobile Comd, Quebec, 1983–86; Lt-Gen. 1986; Asst Dep. Minister (Personnel), NDHQ, 1986–88; Vice Chief, Defence Staff, 1988–89; Gen. 1989; Chief of Defence Staff, 1989–92; Ambassador for Canada to USA, 1993; Chief of Defence Staff, 1994–95; Mem., Internat. Body on Decommissioning of Arms in NI, 1995–96; Chm., Business Cttee and Co. Chm., Strand Two Talks, NI Peace Process, 1996–98. Col of Regt, PPCLI, 2000–03. Hon. Fellow, LMH, Oxford, 2006. Hon. DScMil RMC, Canada, 1996; Hon. LLD: Royal Roads, Canada, 2001; Carleton, Ontario, 2006; Queen's, Kingston, 2007; St Mary's, Halifax, NS, 2008; Brock, St Catharines, Ont, 2011; Concordia Univ., Montreal, 2012; Mt Allison, NB, 2014; Hon. DPhil (Educn) Nipissing, Ontario, 2006; Dr *hc* Edinburgh, 2014. CStJ 1991. CD (Canada), 1968; Medal of Merit and Honour (Greece), 1992; Comdr, Legion of Merit (USA), 1995. *Publications:* (contrib.) Canada on the Threshold of the 21st Century, 1992; (contrib.) Herding Cats: multiparty mediation in a complex world, 1999; (contrib.) From Political Violence to Negotiated Settlement, 2004; contrib. to Canadian Defence Qly. *Recreations:* painting, fishing, bagpipes. *Address:* 170 Acacia Avenue, Ottawa, ON K1M 0R3, Canada. *T:* (613) 7447300.

DECIE, Elizabeth Anne Scott P.; *see* Prescott-Decie.

DECIES, 7th Baron *cr* 1812 (Ire.); **Marcus Hugh Tristram de la Poer Beresford;** *b* 5 Aug. 1948; *o s* of 6th Baron Decies and of his 2nd wife, Diana, *d* of Wing Comdr George Turner-Cain and *widow* of Major David Galsworthy; *S* father, 1992; *m* 1st, 1970, Sarah Jane Gunnell (marr. diss. 1974); 2nd, 1981, Edel Jeannette, *d* of late Vincent Hendron; two *s* two *d*. *Educ:* St Columba's Coll.; Dublin Univ. (MLitt). FCIArb. *Heir:* *s* Hon. Robert Marcus Duncan de la Poer Beresford, *b* 14 July 1988.

de CLIFFORD, 27th Baron *cr* 1299; **John Edward Southwell Russell;** *b* 8 June 1928; *s* of 26th Baron de Clifford, OBE, TD, and Dorothy Evelyn (*d* 1987), *d* of late Ferdinand Richard Holmes Meyrick, MD; *S* father, 1982; *m* 1959, Bridget Jennifer, *yr d* of Duncan Robertson, Llangollen, Denbighshire. *Educ:* Eton; RAC Cirencester. *Heir:* *nephew* Miles Edward Southwell Russell [*b* 7 Aug. 1966; *m* 1995, Marion Elaine, *yr d* of D. W. Arkley; one *s* one *d*]. *Address:* Riggledown, Pennymoor, Tiverton, Devon EX16 8LR. *Club:* Naval and Military.

de COSSART, Linda Mary, CBE 2010; FRCS; Consultant Vascular and General Surgeon, 1988–2009, now Emeritus Consultant, and Director of Medical Education, 2010–14, Countess of Chester Hospital NHS Foundation Trust (formerly Countess of Chester Hospital); Director, Ed4MedPrac Ltd, since 2005; *b* Swansea, 9 Nov. 1947; *d* of Leonard and Elizabeth Jones; *m* 1977, Michael de Cossart (*d* 1989). *Educ:* Univ. of Liverpool Med. Sch. (MB ChB 1972; ChM 1983). FRCS 1977. Mersey Deanery: Associate Postgrad. Dean, 1993–2006; Prog. Dir, Gen. Surgery, 1993–2004. Jt Vice Pres., RCS, 2008–10 (Mem. Council, 1999–10). Hon. Sec., Vascular Soc. of GB and Ire., 1994–98. Member: Liverpool Medical Instn, 1977– (Pres., 2013–14); Travelling Surgical Soc., 1995–. Hon. Prof., Univ. of Chester, 2010–. FRSocMed 1985; FAcadMed 2012. *Publications:* Cultivating a Thinking Surgeon, 2005; Developing the Wise Doctor, 2007; articles in vascular and general surgery jls. *Recreations:* cooking, poetry, writing. *Address:* The Lodge, Cranham Corner, Cranham, Glos GL4 8HB. *T:* 07778 215801. *E:* decossart@btinternet.com. *Clubs:* Athenæum; Lister; Needles.

de COURCY, family name of **Baron Kingsale**.

de COURCY-IRELAND, Patrick Gault, CVO 1980; HM Diplomatic Service, retired; Director of Marketing, 1987–2013, Consultant, since 2013, Rezayat Group (formerly Alireza Group of Companies); Director, Rezayat Europe Ltd, 1988–2013; *b* 19 Aug. 1933; *e s* of late Lawrence Kilmaine de Courcy-Ireland and Elizabeth Pentland Gault; *m* 1957, Margaret Gallop; one *s* three *d*. *Educ:* St Paul's Sch.; Jesus Coll., Cambridge (MA). HM Forces (2nd Lieut), 1952–54. Joined Foreign Service, 1957; Student, ME Centre for Arab Studies, 1957–59; Third, later Second Sec., Baghdad, 1959–62; Private Sec. to HM Ambassador, Washington, 1963; Consul (Commercial), New York, 1963–67; UN (Polit.) Dept, 1967–69; Asst Head of Amer. Dept, 1969–71; First Sec. and Hd of Chancery, Kuwait, 1971–73; Asst Hd of SW Pacific Dept, 1973–76; Hd of Trng Dept and Dir, Diplomatic Serv. Language Centre, FCO, 1976–80; Consul-Gen., Casablanca, 1980–84; Consul-Gen., Jerusalem, 1984–87. Chm., British Sch. of Archaeology in Jerusalem, 1990–99; Member: Exec. Cttee, Palestine Exploration Fund, 1991–95; Council, Soc. for Moroccan Studies, 1992–99; Sec., MECAS Assoc., 2002–. Director: Napier Court Freehold Ltd, 2003–11; Napier Court Management Ltd, 2005–10. MEI (MInstPet 1992). Great Comdr, Order of KHS, 1985. *Recreations:* book collecting, opera. *Address:* 49 Napier Court, Ranelagh Gardens, SW6 3UU. *T:* (020) 7736 0622.

de DENEY, Sir Geoffrey Ivor, KCVO 1992 (CVO 1986); Clerk of the Privy Council, 1984–92; Chief Executive, Royal College of Anaesthetists, 1993–97; *b* 8 Oct. 1931; *s* of late Thomas Douglas and Violet Ivy de Deney; *m* 1959, Diana Elizabeth Winrow; two *s*. *Educ:* William Ellis Sch.; St Edmund Hall, Oxford (MA, BCL); Univ. of Michigan. Home Office: joined, 1956; Asst Principal, 1956–61 (Private Sec. to Parly Under Sec. of State, 1959–61); Principal, 1961–69; Sec. to Graham Hall Cttee on maintenance limits in magistrates' courts; Sec. to Brodrick Cttee on Death Certification and Coroners; Private Sec. to Sec. of State,

1968; Asst Sec., 1969–78; seconded to Cabinet Office, 1975; Asst Under Sec. of State, 1978–84; Community Programmes and Equal Opportunities Dept, 1978–80; General Dept (and Registrar of the Baronetage), 1980–84. Trustee, Gordon House Assoc., later Gordon Moody Assoc., 1990 (Chm., 2002–12). Hon. FRCA 1997. *Recreations:* books, walking. *Address:* 17 Ladbroke Terrace, W11 3PG.

DEDMAN, His Honour Peter George; Designated Civil Judge for Chelmsford South, 2007–10; a Circuit Judge, 2000–10; a Deputy Circuit Judge, 2010–12; *b* 22 May 1940; *s* of late George Stephen Henry Dedman and Jessie Maud Dedman (*née* Hanson); *m* 1965, Patricia Mary Gordon, JP, RGN, RHV; one *d. Educ:* Tottenham Grammar Sch. Magistrates' Courts Service, Brentford, Tottenham and Newham; Principal Asst to Clerk to the Justices, Newham, 1965–69; called to the Bar, Gray's Inn, 1968 (amongst first to qualify following removal of embargo on Justices' Clerks and their assts from reading for the Bar); in practice at the Bar, specialising in personal injury litigation; a Recorder, 1992–2000; South Eastern Circuit. Pres., Mental Health Tribunals, 2010–12. *Recreations:* music - playing the piano and trombone, plays in a number of jazz, dance and concert bands, theatre, film, attending concerts. *Address:* Adelaide House, 308 Roman Road, Mountnessing, Brentwood, Essex CM15 0TZ.

DEDRING, Isabel Margaret, JD; Deputy Mayor of London, Transport, since 2011; *b* Boston, Mass, 10 Aug. 1971; *d* of Jürgen and Elisabeth Dedring; *m* 2005, James Roland Sinker; one *s. Educ:* Hunter Collegiate High Sch., NY; Harvard Univ. (AB 1993 *magna cum laude*; JD 1998 *cum laude*). Mem., NY Bar. Mkt Entry Dir, Almaty, Kazakhstan, Ernst & Young, 1993–95; McKinsey & Co., London, 1998–2003; COS and Dir, Policy Unit, TfL, 2003–08; Mayor of London's Envmt Advr, GLA, 2008–11. Mem. Bd, Inst. for Sustainability, 2009–. *Recreations:* photography, hiking, swimming, cycling, playing piano. *Address:* 3 Agincourt Road, NW3 2PB. *T:* (office) (020) 7983 4026. *E:* isabel.dedring@london.gov.uk.

DEE, Christopher; *see* Evans, D. C.

DEE, Janie, (Mrs R. S. M. Wickham); actress; *b* 20 June 1962; *d* of John Henry Leonard Lewis and Ruth Winifred Lewis (*née* Miller); adopted stage name Janie Dee; *m* 1995, Rupert Stewart Makepeace Wickham; one *s* one *d. Educ:* Arts Educational Schs, London. *Theatre* includes: Carousel, RNT, 1992 (Best Supporting Performance in a Musical, Olivier awards, 1993); Comic Potential, Lyric, 1999, transf. NY, 2000 (Best Actress, Evening Standard, Critics' Circle, Olivier awards, 2000; Obie award, and Best Newcomer, Theater World Award, 2001); My One and Only, Chichester Fest. Th., 2001, transf. Piccadilly, 2002; Three Sisters, Chichester Fest. Th., 2001; Paradise Moscow, Opera North, UK tour, 2001; Women of Troy, NT, 2001; Divas at the Donmar, Donmar Warehouse, 2002; Much Ado About Nothing, Peter Hall Co., Bath, 2003; Mack and Mabel, Criterion, 2006; Old Times, UK tour, 2007; Shadowlands, Wyndham's, 2007; Woman in Mind, Vaudeville, 2009; The Apple Cart, Th. Royal, Bath, 2009; Calendar Girls, Noël Coward, 2009; The Little Hut, Yvonne Arnaud Th., 2010; A Month in the Country, Chichester, 2010; The King and I, The Curve, Leicester, 2010; All's Well That Ends Well, Shakespeare's Globe 2011; Private Lives, Nottingham Playhouse, 2011; Noises Off, Old Vic, 2011, transf. Novello Th., 2012; Janie Dee Show, Hippodrome, 2012; NSFW, Royal Court, 2012; Hello, Dolly!, Curve, Leicester, 2012 (Best Perf. in a Musical, UK Theatre Awards, 2013); Putting it Together, St James Th., 2014; Blithe Spirit, Gielgud Th., 2014; A Midsummer Night's Dream, Shakespeare's Globe on tour, Asia and Russia, 2014; 84 Charing Cross Road, Salisbury Playhouse, 2015; Ah, Wilderness!, Young Vic, 2015; The Seagull, Open Air Th., 2015; *television* includes: Death in Holy Orders, 2003; The Murder Room, 2004; Celebration, 2007; *films* include: Me and Orson Welles, 2009. Dir, Royal Theatrical Fund, 2002–. Trustee, Arts Educnl Schs, 2001–. *Recreations:* sailing, ballet, bell ringing.

DEE, Maurice Patrick, (Moz); Co-Founder and Director, Contented Digital Media, since 2013; *b* Coventry, 13 Sept. 1966; *s* of Maurice and Moira Dee; partner, Liane Charldwood; one *s* one *d. Educ:* Cardinal Newman Comprehensive Sch., Coventry. Actor and writer, 1983–91; presenter, BBC Coventry and Warwicks Radio, 1991–95; presenter, 1995–97, Hd of Sport, 1997–2000, Talk Radio; Editl Exec., Sports Rights and Programming, 2000–02; Commng Ed., 2002–05, Man. Ed., 2005–08, BBC Radio Five Live; Dir of Progs, talksport, 2008–13. Mem. Cttee, Radio Acad., 2005–. Radio Programmer of Year, Sony Radio Acad., 2011. *Recreations:* writing, cinema, fishing, golf. *Address:* Contented Digital Media, 2nd Floor, 1 Cavendish Place, W1G 0QF.

DEECH, family name of **Baroness Deech**.

DEECH, Baroness *cr* 2005 (Life Peer), of Cumnor in the County of Oxfordshire; **Ruth Lynn Deech,** DBE 2002; Chairman, Bar Standards Board, 2009–14; *b* 29 April 1943; *d* of Josef Fraenkel and Dora (*née* Rosenfeld); *m* 1967, Dr John Stewart Deech; one *d. Educ:* Christ's Hosp., Hertford; St Anne's Coll., Oxford (BA 1st Cl. 1965; MA 1969; Hon. Fellow, 2004); Brandeis Univ., USA (MA 1966). Called to the Bar, Inner Temple, 1967, Hon. Bencher, 1996. Legal Asst, Law Commn, 1966–67; Asst Prof., Faculty of Law, Univ. of Windsor, Canada, 1968–70; Oxford University: Fellow and Tutor in Law, 1970–91, Vice-Principal, 1988–91, Principal, 1991–2004, St Anne's Coll.; CUF Lectr in Law, 1971–91; Sen. Proctor, 1985–86; Mem., Hebdomadal Council, 1986–2000; Chm., Jt Undergrad. Admissions Cttee, 1993–97, Admissions Exec., 2000–03; Pro-Vice-Chancellor, 2001–04. Ind. Adjudicator for Higher Educn, 2004–08. Chm., HFEA, 1994–2002. Member: Cttee of Inquiry into Equal Opportunities on Bar Vocational Course, 1993–94; Human Genetics Commn, 2000–02; Chm., Nat. Working Gp on Women in Medicine, 2008–09. A Governor, BBC, 2002–06. Non-exec. Dir, Oxon HA, 1993–94. Mem., Exec. Council, Internat. Soc. on Family Law, 1988–2012. Visiting Professor: Osgoode Hall Law Sch., York Univ., Canada, 1978; Univ. of Florida, 2004; Santa Clara Univ., 2006; Gresham Prof. of Law, Gresham Coll., 2008–12. Governor: Carmel Coll., 1980–90; Oxford Centre for Hebrew and Jewish Studies, 1994–2000; UCS, 1997–2002. Rhodes Trustee, 1997–2006; Mandela Rhodes Foundn Trustee, 2003–06. Gov., United Jewish Israel Appeal, 1997–99. Freeman, City of London, 2003; Liveryman, Drapers' Co., 2008. FRSocMed 2001. Hon. Fellow, Soc. for Advanced Legal Studies, 1997. Hon. QC 2013. Hon. LLD: Strathclyde, 2003; Richmond American Internat. Univ. in London, 2006; Hon. PhD Ben Gurion, 2012. *Publications:* From IVF to Immortality, 2007; articles on family law and property law. *Recreations:* after-dinner speaking, music, entertaining. *Address:* House of Lords, SW1A 0PW. *E:* deechr@parliament.uk.

DEEDES, Hon. Jeremy (Wyndham); non-executive Chairman, Pelham Public Relations, 2007–10; *b* 24 Nov. 1943; *s* of Baron Deedes, KBE, MC, PC; *m* 1973, Anna Gray, *d* of late Maj. Elwin Gray; two *s. Educ:* Eton Coll. Reporter: Kent and Sussex Courier, 1963–66; Daily Sketch, 1966–69; Londoner's Diary, Evening Standard, 1969–76; Dep. Editor, Daily Express, 1976–79; Managing Editor: Evening Standard, 1979–85; Today, 1985–86; Editorial Dir, Daily Telegraph and Sunday Telegraph, 1986–96; Man. Dir, 1996–2003, Dep. Chm. and Chief Exec., 2004–05, Telegraph Gp Ltd; Chm., The Sportsman, 2005–06. Chm., Trafford Park Printers, 1998–2000; Dep. Chm., West Ferry Printers, 1998–2005; Director: Millbourne Productions (Watermill Theatre), 1985–; Horserace Totalisator Bd, 1992–98; Warwick Racecourse, 2005– (Chm., 2002–05). Chm., Nat. Publishers Assoc., 1998–99. *Recreations:* racing, cricket, golf, cabinet making. *Address:* Hamilton House, Compton, Newbury, Berks RG20 6QJ. *T:* (01635) 578695. *Clubs:* Boodle's, MCC; Sunningdale Golf, Huntercombe Golf; Royal Cape (Cape Town).

DEEKS, Rev. David Gerald; General Secretary of the Methodist Church, 2003–08; *b* 5 Jul 1942; *s* of Horace J. Deeks and Irene Deeks; *m* 1967, Jennifer Wakefield; one *s* two *d. Educ* Downing Coll., Cambridge (MA); Wesley House, Cambridge. Asst Tutor, Richmond Coll. Surrey, 1966–70; Ecumenical Lectr, Lincoln Theol Coll., 1970–74; Minister, Maidston Circuit, 1974–80; Tutor, Wesley House, Cambridge, 1980–88; Minister, Bristol (Clifton an Redland) Circuit, and Methodist Chaplain, Univ. of Bristol, 1988–92; Gen. Sec., Div. o Social Responsibility, 1992–96, Co-ordinating Sec., Church and Society, 1996–2003 Methodist Church. *Publications:* Calling, God?, 1976; Pastoral Theology: an inquiry, 1987 *Recreations:* walking, art, music. *Address:* 1 Shields Avenue, Bristol BS7 0RR. *E:* david.deeks@gmail.com.

DEELEY, Michael; film producer; *b* 6 Aug. 1932; *s* of John Hamilton-Deeley and Ann Deeley; *m* 1955, Teresa Harrison; one *s* two *d*; *m* 1970, Ruth Stone-Spencer. *Educ:* Stowe Entered film industry as film editor, 1952; Distributor, MCA TV, 1958–60; independen producer, 1961–63; Gen. Man., Woodfall Films, 1964–67; indep. prod., 1967–72; Man Director: British Lion Films Ltd, 1973–76; EMI Films Ltd, 1976–77; Pres., EMI Films Inc. 1977–79; Chief Exec. Officer, Consolidated Television Inc., 1984–90. Dep. Chm., Britis Screen Adv. Council, 1985 (Hon. Pres., 2015). Member: Prime Minister's Film Industr Working Party, 1975–76; Film Industry Interim Action Cttee, 1977–84. *Films* include Robbery; The Italian Job; The Knack; Murphy's War; Conduct Unbecoming; The Man wh fell to Earth; The Deer Hunter (Academy Award, Best Picture Producer, 1978); Convoy Blade Runner; many TV films and series. *Publications:* Blade Runners, Deer Hunters an Blowing the Bloody Doors Off, 2008. *Address:* 36 Elizabeth Court, SW10 0DA; 1010 Fairwa Road, Santa Barbara, CA 93108, USA. *Club:* Santa Barbara Polo and Racquet.

DEELY, Neil Matthew, RIBA; Director, Metropolitan Workshop, since 2005; *b* Harrow, Aug. 1972; *s* of Michael and Deirdre Deely; *m* 2005, Line Lund; two *s. Educ:* St Dominic' Coll., Harrow on the Hill; Univ. of Brighton (BA Hons; DipArch (Dist.)); Univ. of Arkansas RIBA 1998. Associate, 2000–02, Dir, 2002–05, MacCormac Jamieson Prichard Architects Built envmt expert, 2011–. Enabler, 2005–11, Mem., Nat. Design Rev. Panel, 2007–11 CABE; Member: Planning Cttee, London Thames Gateway Develt Corp., 2009–12; Desig Panel, American Embassy, London, 2010–12; Design Review Panel, London Bor. o Newham, 2011– (Chm., 2013–); London Legacy Quality Review Panel, 2012–; Cabe a Design Council Design Rev. Panel, London Bor. of Greenwich, 2014–; a Design Advr Urban Design London, 2009–. Major projects include: Jersey Archive, 2000; redevelt of BBC Broadcasting House, 2001–03; housing for Univ. of Cambridge, West Cambridge, 2004 Adamstown Dist Centre, Ire, 2005–07; Mus. of Conflict, Libya, 2009. Mem., Inst. o Norwegian Architects, 2007–. FRSA; FRGS 2012. *Recreations:* hill walking, expeditions t High Arctic, alpine sport, painting. *Address:* Metropolitan Workshop, Architecture & Urbanism, 14–16 Cowcross Street, EC1M 6DG. *T:* (020) 7566 0450. *E:* info@metwork.co.uk.

DEEM, Prof. Rosemary, OBE 2013; PhD; Vice Principal (Education), Royal Holloway University of London, since 2011; *b* 18 Jan. 1949; *d* of Leslie Thomas George Deem an Peggy Deem (*née* Stoyle); *m* 1985, Kevin Joseph Brehony (*d* 2013). *Educ:* Univ. of Leiceste (BA Hons Social Scis (Sociol.) 1970; MPhil Sociol. 1973); Open Univ. (PhD Sociol. o Leisure 1990). Lectr in Sociol., N Staffs Poly., 1975–79; Lectr in Sociol. of Educn, 1980–87 Sen Lectr in Educn, 1987–91, Open Univ.; Prof. of Educnl Res., 1991–2000, Dean of Socia Scis, 1994–97, Univ. of Lancaster; Founding Dir, Univ. of Lancaster Grad. Sch., 1998–2000 Prof. of Educn, 2001–09, Res. Dir, Faculty of Social Scis and Law, 2007–09, Univ. of Bristol Dean of Hist. and Social Scis, Royal Holloway, Univ. of London, 2009–11. Jt Man. Ed. Sociol. Rev., 2001–04. Dir, UK Subject Centre for Educn (ESCalate), Learning and Teaching Support Network, 2001–04. Chairman: British Sociol Assoc., 1986–87 and 1994–96 Publications Cttee, SRHE, 2004–; Develt Cttee, SRHE, 2007–09; Mem., UK Council fo Graduate Educn, 2012–. FAcSS (AcSS 2006); FSRHE 2010. *Publications:* Women an Schooling, 1978; (ed) Schooling for Women's Work, 1980; (ed) Co-education Reconsidered, 1984; All Work and No Play, 1986; Work, Unemployment and Leisure, 1988; (with K. J. Brehony and S. J. Heath) Active Citizenship and the Governing of Schools, 1995; (with S. Hillyard and M. Reed) Knowledge, Higher Education and the New Managerialism: the changing management of UK universities, 2007; contrib. numerous articles and chapters in social sci. jls and academic books. *Recreations:* walking, cycling (Mem., Cyclists Touring Club), photography, camping and caravanning (Mem., Camping and Caravanning Club), reading. *Address:* Principal's Office, Founders East, Royal Holloway, University of London, Egham Hill, Egham TW20 0EX. *T:* (01784) 443994. *E:* R.Deem@rhul.ac.uk.

DEENY, Hon. Sir Donnell (Justin Patrick), Kt 2004; **Hon. Mr Justice Deeny;** DL; a Judge of the High Court of Justice, Northern Ireland, since 2004; *b* 25 April 1950; *y s* of late Dr Donnell McLarnon Deeny, JP and Annie (*née* McGinley); *m* 1998, Alison Jane, *y d* of late Ian Scott and of Tressan Scott; one *s* two *d*, and two *d* by a previous marriage. *Educ:* Clongowes Wood Coll.; TCD (Auditor, The Hist.; MA); QUB. Called to the Bar: NI, 1974 (Bencher, 2001); Ireland, 1986; Middle Temple, 1987 (Bencher, 2006); one of Attorney Gen.'s Counsel, NI, 1985–2003; QC (NI) 1989; SC (Ireland) 1996. Mem., UK Spoliation Adv. Panel, 2001– (Chm., 2012–). Dir, Hearth Social Housing, 1999–2003. Mem. (APNI), Belfast CC, 1981–85. Mem., 1991–93, Chm., 1993–98, Arts Council of NI; Vice Chm., 1984–88, Chm., 1988–93, Opera NI. Trustee: Ulster Mus., 1983–85; Ireland Chair of Poetry Trust, 1997–2015 (Chm., 1997–2008); Dir, Tyrone Guthrie Centre, 2001–06; President: Ulster Architectural Heritage Soc., 2006–; Irish Legal Hist. Soc., 2015–. Pro Chancellor, Univ. of Dublin, 2014–. Hon. MRTPI 2012. High Sheriff 1983, DL 2003, Belfast; JP Co. Down, 1988. *Publications:* (ed) To the Millennium: a strategy for the arts in Northern Ireland, 1995. *Recreations:* books, the arts, ski-ing. *Address:* Royal Courts of Justice, Chichester Street, Belfast BT1 3JF.

See also M. F. A. Cook, M. E. McL. Deeny.

DEENY, Michael Eunan McLarnon, FCA; Chairman, Equitas Trust, since 2014 (Deputy Chairman, 1996–2014); *b* 12 Nov. 1944; *s* of late Dr Donnell McLarnon Deeny and Annie Deeny (*née* McGinley); *m* 1975, Dr Margaret Irene Vereker, *d* of late Dr Richard Vereker and Judy Vereker; one *s* two *d. Educ:* Clongowes Wood Coll., Ireland; Magdalen Coll., Oxford (MA). FCA 1974. Articled Clerk, Chalmers Impey, 1966–70; Chief Accountant, Peter Kennedy Ltd, 1970–71; Manager (Murray Head, Horslips, Noosha Fox, Barry McGuigan, etc), 1971–91; Concert Promoter (U2, Bruce Springsteen, Nirvana, The Eagles, Aerosmith, Luciano Pavarotti, etc), 1984–. Chairman: Gooda Walker Action Gp (obtained compensation for Lloyd's names), 1993–2008; Litigating Names' Cttee, 1994–; Assoc. of Lloyd's Members, 1998–2009 (Dir, 1995–). Director: GW Run-Off, 1995–97; Equitas Ltd, 1996–; non-exec. Dir, Randall and Quilter Underwriting Ltd, 2012–. Mem. Council, Lloyd's, 1996–97, 2009–. *Recreation:* taking risks and living to tell the tale. *Address:* Shepherds Close House, Upper Woodford, Salisbury SP4 6PA.

See also M. F. A. Cook, Hon. Sir D. J. P. Deeny.

de FERRANTI, Sebastian (Basil Joseph) Ziani; DL; Chairman, Ferranti plc, 1963–82 (Managing Director, 1958–75; Director 1954); Director, GEC plc, 1982–97; *b* 5 Oct. 1927; *er s* of Sir Vincent de Ferranti, MC, and late Dorothy H. C. Wilson; *m* 1st, 1953, Mona Helen (*d* 2008), *d* of T. E. Cunningham; one *s* two *d*; 2nd, 1983, Naomi Angela Rae, DL (*d* 2001); 3rd, 2011, Gillian Nadine Brown, *d* of John William France. *Educ:* Ampleforth. 4th/7th Dragoon Guards, 1947–49; Cheshire Yeo. Brown Boveri, Switzerland, and Alsthom, France, 1949–50. Director: British Airways Helicopters, 1982–84; Nat. Nuclear Corp., 1984–88. President: Electrical Research Assoc., 1968–69; BEAMA, 1969–70; Centre for Educn in

Science, Educn and Technology, Manchester and region, 1972–82. Chm., Internat. Electrical Assoc., 1970–72. Member: Nat. Defence Industries Council, 1969–77; Council, IEE, 1970–73. Trustee, Tate Gallery, 1971–78; Chm., Civic Trust for the North-West, 1978–83; Comr, Royal Commn for Exhibn of 1851, 1984–97. Pres., Hallé Concerts Soc., 1997– (Chm., 1988–96). Mem. Bd of Govs, RNCM, 1988–2000 (Hon. RNCM 1997). Chm. assessors, architect for Manchester City Art Gall extn, 1995–. FRSA 1972 (Vice-Pres., 1980–84). Lectures: Granada, Guildhall, 1966; Royal Instn, 1969; Louis Blériot, Paris, 1970; Faraday, 1970–71. High Sheriff of Cheshire, 1988–89; DL Cheshire, 1995. Hon. Fellow, UMIST. Hon. DSc: Salford Univ., 1967; Cranfield Inst. of Technology, 1973; Hon. LLD Manchester, 1998. *Address:* Henbury Hall, Macclesfield, Cheshire SK11 9PJ. *Clubs:* Cavalry and Guards, Pratt's.

DEFFEE, Leslie Ann; *see* Morphy, L. A.

de FONBLANQUE, John Robert, CMG 1993; HM Diplomatic Service, retired; Director, Office of High Commissioner on National Minorities, Organisation for Security and Co-operation in Europe, 2004–07; *b* 20 Dec. 1943; *s* of late Maj.-Gen. E. B. de Fonblanque, CB, CBE, DSO and of Elizabeth de Fonblanque; *m* 1984, Margaret Prest; one *s*. *Educ:* Ampleforth; King's College, Cambridge (MA); London School of Economics (MSc); Sch. of Oriental and African Studies, London Univ. (Dip. Asian Art 2009; MA 2012). FCO, 1968; Second Sec., Jakarta, 1969; Second, later First Sec., UK Representation to European Community, Brussels, 1972; Principal, HM Treasury, 1977; FCO, 1980; Asst Sec., Cabinet Office, 1983; Head of Chancery, New Delhi, 1986; Counsellor (Pol and Instnl), UK Repn to EC, Brussels, 1988; Vis. Fellow, RIIA, 1993; Asst Under-Sec. of State, Internat. Orgns, then Dir, Global Issues, FCO, 1994–98; Dir (Europe), FCO, 1998–99; Hd, UK Delegn to OSCE, Vienna (with rank of Ambassador), 1999–2003. Mem., PPARC, 1994–98. *Recreation:* mountain walking.

DE FREYNE, 8th Baron *cr* 1851, of Coolavin; **Fulke Charles Arthur John French;** valuation surveyor; *b* Dublin, 21 April 1957; *s* of 7th Baron De Freyne and of Shirley Ann, *d* of late D. R. Pobjoy; *S* father, 2009; *m* 1986, Julia Mary, *o d* of Dr James H. Wellard; two *s*. *Educ:* Downside; Poly. of South Bank (BA Hons 1986); London South Bank Univ. (MSc 2008). MRAC 1981. FRGS 1988. *Recreations:* photography, travel, tennis, sailing. *Heir: s* Hon. Alexander James Charles French, *b* 22 Sept. 1988. *Club:* Roehampton.

DEFRIEZ, Alistair Norman Campbell, FCA; financial consultant; Managing Director, UBS Investment Bank (formerly Warburg Dillon Read, then UBS Warburg), 1999–2007; *b* 2 Nov. 1951; *s* of late Norman William Defriez and Helen Catherine Defriez (*née* Maclean); *m* 1978, Linda Mavis Phillips, BSc, PGCE, ACA; two *s* one *d*. *Educ:* Dulwich Coll.; University Coll., Oxford (Open Gladstone Schol., MA). FCA 1981. With Coopers & Lybrand, 1973–78; joined S. G. Warburg & Co. Ltd, 1978, Dir, 1987; Dir-Gen., Panel on Takeovers and Mergers, 1996–99 (on secondment) (Mem., 2008–). *Recreations:* golf, Rugby, music, reading. *Clubs:* London Scottish; Royal Wimbledon Golf; Rye Golf; St George's Hill Golf.

DE FRUTOS, Javier; choreographer, director; *b* Caracas, 15 May 1963; *s* of Esteban De Frutos and Angela Fernandez. *Educ:* Caracas Sch. of Contemporary Dance; Merce Cunningham Sch., NY; London Sch. of Contemporary Dance. Dancer, Laura Dean Dancers and Musicians, NY, 1988–92; Choreographer in Residence, Movement Res., NYC, 1993; Founder and Artistic Dir, Javier De Frutos Dance Co., 1994–2000; Artistic Dir, Phoenix Dance Th., 2006–09. Fellow, Arts Council of England, 2000–02. *Choreographed:* for De Frutos Dance Co.: D, 1990; The Montana Affair, J, Trilogy + Country, Consecration, 1991; Almost Montana, Meeting, Hemisphere, Jota Dolce, 1993; Simone and the Jacaranda Tree, Dialogue Between Hemispheres, Frasquita, The Palace Does Not Forgive, Gota a Gota, 1994; Sweetie J, Meeting J, 1995; Carnal Glory, Out of J, Transatlantic, 1996; Grass, Weed, The Golden Impossibility, 1997; The Hypochondriac Bird, 1998; Mazatlan, 1999; Affliction of Loneliness, 2000; for Phoenix Dance Theatre: Nopalitos, 2006; Los Picadores, Paseillo, Blue Roses, 2007; Cattle Call, 2008; for Ricochet Dance Co.: E Muoio Disperato, 1995 (Bagnolet Prix d'Auteur, France, 1996); All visitors bring happiness, some by coming, some by going, 1995 (S Bank Award, 1997); for Rambert Dance Co.: The Celebrated Soubrette, 2000 (re-staged for Royal NZ Ballet, 2004); Elsa Canesta, 2003; Elysian Fields, 2011; for Royal NZ Ballet: Milagros, 2003; Banderillero, 2006; The Misty Frontier for Royal Ballet, 2001; for Sadler's Wells: The Most Incredible Thing (also dir), 2011 (London Evening Standard Beyond Th. award (jtly), 2011); *theatre:* Carousel, Chichester Fest., 2006; Cabaret, Lyric, 2006 (Olivier Award for Best Th. Choreographer, 2007); Macbeth, Shakespeare's Globe, 2010; London Road, NT, 2011; From Here to Eternity, Shaftesbury Th., 2013; Everyman, NT, 2015. Paul Hamlyn Foundn Award, 1995; Critics' Circle Nat. Dance Award for Best Choreog. (Contemp.), 2005. *Address:* 123 Lynton Road, SE1 5QX. *T:* 07582 841167. *E:* javierdefru@hotmail.com.

de GARR ROBINSON, Anthony John; QC 2006; *b* 4 July 1963; *s* of Peter de Garr Robinson and Audrey Robinson; *m* 1997, Miranda Wilson; one *s* one *d*. *Educ:* Brighton Coll.; University Coll., Oxford; Grad. Sch. of Arts and Scis, Harvard Univ.; Inns of Court Sch. of Law. Called to the Bar, Lincoln's Inn, 1987; in practice as barrister specialising in commercial and chancery law. Mem., Cttee, Chancery Bar Assoc., 2007–10. *Recreation:* winning at squash. *Address:* One Essex Court, Middle Temple, EC4Y 9AR. *T:* (020) 7583 2000.

de GIER, Johannes Antonie, (Hans); Chairman of the Board, GAM Holding AG, since 2009 (Chief Executive, 2009–13); *b* 24 Dec. 1944; *s* of W. G. de Gier and A. M. de Gier (*née* van Heijningen); *m* 1st, 1969, Anne-Marie Wintermans (marr. diss. 2006); one *s* one *d*; 2nd, 2006, Antonia Kathryn Adams; two *s* one *d*. *Educ:* Amsterdam Univ. (LLM). Legal counsel, ABN, 1970–73; Divl Man., Capital Markets, 1975–78, Dep. Gen. Man., Internat. Finance, 1978–79, AMRO; Dir, Corporate Finance, Orion Bank, 1979–80; Swiss Bank Corporation: Exec. Dir, Corporate Finance, 1980–87; Man. Dir and Chief Exec. Officer, 1987–96; Mem., Exec. Bd, and Hd, Global Corporate Finance, 1991–96; Mem., Gp Exec. Cttee, 1996; Chm. and Chief Exec., SBC Warburg, then Warburg Dillon Read, 1996–99; UBS AG: Mem., Gp Exec. Bd, 1998–99; Advr, 1999–2001; Vice Chm., 2001–03; Chm., SBC Wealth Mgt, 2003–05; Pres., Exec. Bd, Julius Baer Gp, 2005–08 and Gp CEO, Julius Baer Hldg Ltd, 2005–09. Vice-Chm., Banco di Lugano, 2003–06; Ehinger & Armand von Ernst, 2003–06 (latterly Chm.); Ferrier Lullin & Cie SA, 2003–06 (latterly Vice-Chm.); Member: Supervisory Bd, SHV Hldgs; Bd, Groupe Lhoist. Vice-Chm., Centre for Econ. Policy Res., 2000–02. Trustee, Fitzwilliam Mus., 2000–. *Recreations:* wildlife, music, art. *Clubs:* Turf, Boodles.

de GREY, family name of **Baron Walsingham**.

de GREY, Spencer Thomas, CBE 1997; RA 2008; RIBA; Senior Partner, since 1991, and Joint Head of Design, since 2007, Foster + Partners; *b* 7 June 1944; *s* of Sir Roger de Grey, KCVO, PPRA, and Flavia de Grey, RA; *m* 1977, Hon. (Amanda) Lucy, *d* of Baron Annan, OBE; one *s* one *d*. *Educ:* Eton Coll.; Churchill Coll., Cambridge (BA 1966; MA 1970; DipArch 1969). ARCUK 1969; RIBA 1993. Architect, Merton LBC, 1969–73; joined Foster Associates, later Foster & Partners, 1973–: estabd Hong Kong office, 1979; Dir, 1981– (responsible for Third London Airport, Stansted, 1991, and Sackler Galls, Royal Acad., 1991); *projects* include: Lycée Albert Camus, Fréjus, 1995; Law Faculty, Univ. of Cambridge, 1995; Commerzbank HQ, Frankfurt, 1997; Sir Alexander Fleming Med. Bldg, Imperial Coll., London, 1998; Nat. Botanical Gdns for Wales, 1999; Great Court, BM, 2000; Dresden Stn, 2002; World Squares for All, London, 2003; eight City Academies, 2003–08; HM Treasury, Whitehall, 2004; Sage Music Centre, Gateshead, 2005; Kogod Courtyard, Nat. Portrait Gall., Smithsonian Instn, 2007; Elephant House, Copenhagen, 2008; masterplan, Slussen, Stockholm, 2008–; Winspear Opera House, Dallas, 2009; Vieux Port, Marseille, 2010–; Mus. of Fine Art, Boston, USA, 2010; Mus. of Roman Antiquities, Narbonne, 2011–; masterplan, West Kowloon Cultural Dist, 2011–. Vis. Prof. of Design, Univ. of Cambridge, 2009–. Trustee, Royal Botanical Gardens, Kew, 1995–2003; Chm., Bldg Centre Trust, 2005–. FRSA 2006. *Recreations:* music, theatre, travel. *Address:* (office) Riverside Three, 22 Hester Road, SW11 4AN. *T:* (020) 7738 0455, *Fax:* (020) 7738 1107.

DE GROOT, Prof. Gerard Jan, PhD; Professor of History, University of St Andrews, since 2000; *b* 22 June 1955; *s* of Jan De Groot and Johanna Hendrika De Groot (*née* Jansen); *m* 1991, Sharon Lynn Roe; one *s* one *d*. *Educ:* Whitman Coll., USA (BA 1977); Edinburgh Univ. (PhD 1983). Beach lifeguard, San Diego, Calif, 1973–77; insce adjuster, Portland, Oregon, 1977–80; lollipop man, Edinburgh, 1980–81; pt-time Tutor, WEA and Edinburgh Univ., 1983–85; Lectr, Univ. of St Andrews, 1985–2000. Freelance journalist, 1988–. RUSI Westminster Medal for Mil. Lit., 2001; Ray and Pat Brown Award, Popular Culture Assoc./Amer. Culture Assoc., 2009. *Publications:* Douglas Haig 1861–1928, 1988; Liberal Crusader, 1993; Blighty, 1996; Military Miscellany, 1997; Student Protest, 1998; A Noble Cause, 1999; A Soldier and a Woman, 2000; The First World War, 2001; The Bomb: a life, 2004; Dark Side of the Moon, 2006; Sixties Unplugged, 2008; Seventies Unplugged, 2010; Back in Blighty, 2014; Selling Reagan, 2015. *Recreations:* cooking, carpentry, following baseball on the internet. *Address:* 11 Walker Place, St Andrews, Fife KY16 9NY. *T:* (01334) 473107. *E:* gjdg@st-andrews.ac.uk.

de GROOT, Lucy Manuela, CBE 2009; Chief Executive, Community Service Volunteers, 2011–14; *b* 7 June 1951. *Educ:* St Anne's Coll., Oxford (BA 1973); LSE (Dip Social Admin 1974). Prin. Employment Officer, Hackney BC, 1985–87; Employment Policy Advr, ALA, 1987–89; Hd of Policy, Lewisham BC, 1989–93; Hd of Policy, 1993–94, Acting Chief Exec., 1994–95, Chief Exec., 1995–2000, Bristol CC; Dir of Public Services, HM Treasury, 2000–03; Exec. Dir, Improvement and Devélt Agency, 2003–09. Independent Chair: Surrey Children's Services Improvement Bd, 2008–10; Cornwall Children's Services Improvement Bd, 2009–13. Vis. Prof., UWE, 2002–. Trustee: Common Purpose UK, 2000–09; Campaign for Learning, 2002–06; Coram (formerly Coram Family), 2005–12 (Gov., 2004–05); Join In Trust, 2012–; Baring Foundn Charitable Trust, 2013–; Gov., Working Men's Coll., 2007–. FRSA. *Address:* 8 Southcote Road, N19 5BJ.

de GRUBEN, Baron Thierry; Ambassador of Belgium to the Court of St James's, 2002–06, now Hon. Ambassador; *b* 17 Nov. 1941; *s* of Baron Guy de Gruben and Baroness Guy de Gruben (*née* Monique Dierckx de Casterlé); *m* 1980, Françoise Francq; one *s*. *Educ:* Namur; Univ. of Leuven (law degree). Joined diplomatic service, 1969; diplomatic trainee, NATO, Brussels, 1969–70; Press Service, Min. of Foreign Affairs, Brussels, 1970–71; Attaché, then Sec., Moscow, 1971–76; Sec., then First Sec., London, 1976–80; Consul General, Bombay, 1980–82; Private Office, Minister of External Relns, Brussels, 1982–85; Ambassador: Warsaw, 1985–90; Moscow, 1990–95; Dep. Pol Dir, Brussels, and Special Envoy for E Slavonia, Croatia, 1995–97; Ambassador and Perm. Rep. of Belgium to NATO, Brussels, 1997–2002. Commandeur, Ordre de Léopold (Belgium), 1996; Grand Officier: Ordre de Léopold II (Belgium), 2000; Ordre de la Couronne (Belgium), 2003. *Address:* 4 rue Descartes, 75005 Paris, France. *E:* dgrubt@hotmail.com.

de GRUCHY, Nigel Ronald Anthony; General Secretary, National Association of Schoolmasters Union of Women Teachers, 1990–2002; *b* 28 Jan. 1943; *s* of Robert Philip de Gruchy and Dorothy Louise de Gruchy (*née* Cullinane); *m* 1970, Judith Ann Berglund, USA; one *s*. *Educ:* De La Salle Coll., Jersey; Univ. of Reading (BA Hons (Econs and Philosophy) 1965); PGCE London Univ. 1969; Cert. Pratique de Langue Française, Paris Univ., 1968; Cert. de Français Parlé et du Diplôme de Langue Française, L'Alliance Française, 1968. TEFL, Berlitz Schs, Santander, 1965–66, Versailles, 1966–67; student of French/Tutor in English, Paris, 1967–68; Head of Econs Dept, St Joseph's Acad., ILEA, 1968–78; Asst Sec., 1978–82, Dep. Gen. Sec., 1982–89, NAS UWT. Sec., London Assoc., 1975–78, Mem., Nat. Exec., 1975–78, NAS UWT. Member: Gen. Council, TUC, 1989–2003 (Pres., 2002–03); Exec., The Educn Internat., 1993–2004; Accountancy Foundn, 2000–04. Sec., Orpington Lab. Party, 2007–. Contested (Lab) Orpington, 2015. *Publications:* History of the NASUWT 1919–2002: the story of a battling minority, 2013; contribs to Career Teacher. *Recreations:* sport, golf, literature, music, politics. *Address:* 26 Glentrammon Road, Green Street Green, Orpington, Kent BR6 6DE. *E:* nigel.degruchy1943@gmail.com.

DE GUCHT, Karel; Member, European Commission, 2009–14; *b* Overmere, Belgium, 27 Jan. 1954; *m* Mireille Schreurs; two *s*. *Educ:* Vrije Univ. Brussels (law degree). Lawyer, Dendermonde, 1976–2001; Prof. in Eur. Law, Vrije Univ. Brussels, 1991–2009. MEP, 1980–94; Alderman responsible for Finance, Lebbeke, 1983–88; Municipal Councillor, Berlare, 1989–2009 (Chm., 2006–09); Mayor, Berlare, 2006–09; Senator, 1994–95; Mem., Flemish Parlt, 1995–2003; Mem., House of Representatives, Belgium, 2003–09; Minister for Internat. Trade, 2007–09, for Foreign Affairs and Eur. Affairs, 2004–09; Dep. Prime Minister, 2008–09. Flemish Party for Freedom and Progress, later Flemish Liberal and Democratic Party: Mem., Bureau, 1977–; Vice Pres., 1985–88; Pres., 1999–2004. Pres., Brussels, 1974–75, Nat. Pres., 1975–77, Flemish Assoc. of Liberal Students; Pres., Young Flemish Liberal Movt, 1977–79. *Publications:* Time and Tide Wait for No Man: the changing European geopolitical landscape, 1991; (with Dirk Sterckx) Er zijn geen eilanden meer: over de democratie, vrijheid en de mensrechten, 1999; (with Johan Van Hecke) Het einde der pilaren: een Toscaans gesprek, 2001; De toekomst is vrij: over het liberalisme in de 21ste eeuw, 2002; Pluche—Over de banalisering van extreem rechts, 2007; Vrijheid: liberalisme in tijden van cholera, 2012.

de HAAN, Kevin Charles; QC 2000; a Recorder, since 2002; *b* 30 Oct. 1952; *s* of Michael James de Haan and Barbara Ada de Haan; *m* 1983, Katy Monica Foster. *Educ:* Davenant Foundn Grammar Sch.; Queen Mary Coll., Univ. of London (LLB); Vrije Univ., Brussels (LLM Internat. and Comparative Law). Called to the Bar, Inner Temple, 1976, Bencher, 1997. *Publications:* Food Safety Law and Practice, 1994; Pollution in the United Kingdom, 1994; (contrib.) Smith & Monckom, The Law of Betting, Gaming and Lotteries, 2nd edn 2000. *Recreations:* ski-ing, flying light aircraft, mountain bicycling, cooking. *Address:* Francis Taylor Building, Inner Temple, EC4Y 7BY. *Club:* Ski of GB.

DE HAAN, Sir Roger Michael, Kt 2014; CBE 2004; DL; philanthropist; Chairman, Saga Group, until 2004; *b* 1948; *s* of late Sidney De Haan. Co-Founder and Chm., Roger De Haan Charitable Trust, 1978– (incl. redevelt of Folkestone Harbour and Old Town); Chm., Creative Foundn. Trustee, NHMF, 2014–. DL Kent, 2003. Hon. DCL Kent, 2005.

de HAAS, Margaret Ruth, (Mrs I. S. Goldrein); QC 1998; **Her Honour Judge de Haas;** a Circuit Judge, since 2004; Designated Family Judge for Liverpool, since 2005, and for Cheshire and Merseyside, since 2010; a Senior Circuit Judge, since 2010; *b* 21 May 1954; *d* of Josef and Lilo de Haas; *m* 1980, Iain Saville Goldrein, *qv*; one *s* one *d*. *Educ:* Townsend Sch., Zimbabwe; Bristol Univ. (LLB Hons 1976). Called to the Bar, Middle Temple, 1977; in practice at the Bar, 1977–2004; a Recorder, 1999–2004. Mem., Criminal Injuries Compensation Bd, 1999–. *Publications:* (jtly) Butterworths Personal Injury Litigation Service, 1988–; (jtly) Property Distribution on Divorce, 1989; (jtly) Domestic Injunctions, 1997; (jtly) Medical Negligence: cost effective case management, 1997; (jtly) Structured Settlements, 1997. *Recreations:* family, swimming, reading, theatre. *Address:* c/o Liverpool Family and Civil Courts, 35 Vernon Street, Liverpool L2 2BX.

de HALPERT, Rear-Adm. Sir Jeremy (Michael), KCVO 2009; CB 2001; Deputy Master, Trinity House, 2002–11; *b* 9 July 1947; *s* of late Lt Comdr Michael Frances de Halpert and Eleanor Anne Love de Halpert; *m* 1972, Jane Fattorini, *d* of late Joseph Fattorini; two *s* one *d*. *Educ:* Canford Sch., Wimborne. Joined Royal Navy, 1966. BRNC, Dartmouth; served HM Ships Aurora, Chilcompton, London, Phoebe, Lowestoft, 1967–75; CO, HMS Sheraton, 1975–76; Specialised Principal Warfare Officer (Navigation): HMS Ajax and HMS Ariadne, 1978–80; HMS Bristol and Falklands Campaign, 1982–84; Comdr, 1984; CO, HMS Apollo, 1985–86; jsdc 1987; Directorate of Naval Staff Duties, MoD, 1987–89; USN War Coll., Newport, RI, 1989–90; Capt., 1990; CO, HMS Campbeltown, 1990–92; COS, Flag Officer Surface Flotilla, 1992–94; Dep. UK Mil. Rep., SHAPE, 1994–96; Cdre, 1996; Dir, Overseas Mil. Activity, MoD, 1996–98; Rear-Adm., 1998; Naval Sec., and Chief Exec., Naval Manning Agency, 1998–2002. Dir, Standard (London) P & I Club, 2002–11. Gov., Canford Sch., 2002–. Younger Brother, 1993, Elder Brother, 2001, Trinity House. Dir, World Wide Acad., 2012–; Trustee: Marine Soc. & Sea Cadets (formerly Marine Soc.), 2002–10; Royal Nat. Mission to Deep Sea Fishermen, 2012–; Rosemary Foundn, 2013–; Patron, Nat. Maritime Mus., 2012–. Pres., Veterans Outreach Support, 2014–. HM Lieut, City of London, 2006–. Liveryman, Shipwrights' Co., 2003– (Mem., Ct of Assts, 2008–; Renter Warden, 2015–April 2016). Mem., Tennis & Racquets Assoc. MRIN 1980, FRIN 2002, Hon. FRIN 2011; Hon. FNI 2011. Commandeur de Bordeaux à Londres, 2005. *Recreations:* Royal tennis, ski-ing, cricket, military history. *Address:* Carpenters Cottage, Froxfield Green, Petersfield, Hants GU32 1DH. *Clubs:* Boodle's, Royal Navy of 1765 and 1785, MCC.

de HAMEL, Christopher Francis Rivers, DPhil, PhD; FSA; FRHistS; Donnelley Librarian, and Fellow, Corpus Christi College, Cambridge, since 2000; *b* 20 Nov. 1950; *s* of Dr Francis Alexander de Hamel and Joan Littledale de Hamel (*née* Pollock); *m* 1st, 1978 (marr. diss. 1989); two *s*; 2nd, 1993, Mette Tang Simpson (*née* Svendsen) (*see* M. T. de Hamel). *Educ:* Otago Univ., NZ (BA Hons); Oxford Univ. (DPhil); PhD Cambridge 2005. FSA 1981; FRHistS 1986. Sotheby's: cataloguer of medieval manuscripts, 1975; Asst Dir, 1977; Dir, Western and Oriental, later Western, Manuscripts, 1982–2000. Vis. Fellow, All Souls Coll., Oxford, 1999–2000; Sandars Reader in Bibliography, Univ. of Cambridge, 2003–04; Lyell Reader in Bibliography, Univ. of Oxford, 2008–09. Chm., Assoc. for Manuscripts and Archives in Res. Collections, 2000–15. Hon. LittD St John's, Minn, 1994; Hon. DLitt Otago, 2002. *Publications:* include: Glossed Books of the Bible and the Origins of the Paris Booktrade, 1984; A History of Illuminated Manuscripts, 1986, 2nd edn 1994; (with M. Manion and V. Vines) Medieval and Renaissance Manuscripts in New Zealand Collections, 1989; Syon Abbey, The Library of the Bridgettine Nuns and their Peregrinations after the Reformation, 1991; Scribes and Illuminators, 1992; The British Library Guide to Manuscript Illumination, 2001; The Book: a history of the Bible, 2001; The Rothschilds and their Collections of Illuminated Manuscripts, 2004; Liber Bestiarum, 2008; Gilding the Lilly, 2010; Bibles: an illustrated history from papyrus to print, 2011. *Address:* Corpus Christi College, Trumpington Street, Cambridge CB2 1RH. *Clubs:* Athenæum, Roxburghe; Grolier (New York); Association Internationale de Bibliophilie (Paris).

de HAMEL, Mette Tang, FIIC; art historian and conservator in private practice, since 1999; *b* Copenhagen, 15 May 1945; *d* of late Axel Tang Svendsen and Grethe Svendsen (*née* Selchau); *m* 1st, 1965, David Melville Bromby Simpson (marr. diss.); two *s*; 2nd, 1993, Dr Christopher Francis Rivers de Hamel, *qv*. *Educ:* Newcastle upon Tyne Poly. (BA Hons History of Art 1979; Dip. in Conservation 1982). Conservator, Bowes Mus., 1979–80; Lectr, Newcastle upon Tyne Poly., 1982–86; Dir, Textile Conservation Centre, Hampton Court Palace, 1986–88; Sen. Conservator, Sotheby's, 1988–99. Mem., Conservation of Historic Interiors Cttee, Inst. of Conservation, 2007–. *Recreations:* painting, gardening, cooking, sewing. *Address:* 40 Lansdowne Gardens, SW8 2EF. *Club:* Sloane.

de HAVILLAND, Olivia Mary; actress; *b* Tokyo, Japan, 1 July 1916; *d* of Walter Augustus de Havilland and Lilian Augusta (*née* Ruse) (parents British subjects); *m* 1st, 1946, Marcus Aurelius Goodrich (marr. diss., 1953); one *s*; 2nd, 1955, Pierre Paul Galante (marr. diss. 1979); one *d*. *Educ:* in California; won scholarship to Mills Coll., 1934, but career prevented acceptance. *Theatre* (USA): Hermia in Max Reinhardt's stage production of Midsummer Night's Dream, 1934 (and in film version, 1935); Juliet in Romeo and Juliet, 1951; Candida, 1951 and 1952; A Gift of Time, 1962. *Films include:* The Adventures of Robin Hood, 1938; Gone With the Wind, 1939 (Acad. Award nomination); Hold Back the Dawn, 1941 (Acad. Award nomination); Princess O'Rourke, 1943; To Each His Own, 1946 (Acad. Award); The Dark Mirror, 1946; The Snake Pit, 1948 (Acad. Award nomination; NY and San Francisco Critics' Awards); The Heiress, 1949 (Acad. Award; NY and San Francisco Critics' Awards; Golden Globe Award; Venice Fest. Award); My Cousin Rachel, 1952; Not as a Stranger, 1955; The Ambassador's Daughter, 1956 (Belgian Prix Femina, 1957); Proud Rebel, 1958; Light in the Piazza, 1962; Lady in a Cage, 1964 (Films and Filming Award, UK, 1967); Hush … Hush, Sweet Charlotte, 1965; Airport '77, 1977. *Television includes:* Noon Wine, 1966; The Screaming Woman, 1972; Roots, The Next Generations, 1979; 3 ABC Cable-TV Cultural Documentaries, 1981; Murder is Easy, 1982; Charles & Diana, a Royal Romance, 1982; North and South, Book II, 1986; Anastasia, 1986 (Golden Globe Award); The Woman He Loved, 1988. US Lecture tours, 1971, 1972, 1973, 1974, 1975, 1976, 1978, 1979, 1980. First woman Pres. of Jury, Cannes Film Festival, 1965. Took part in narration of France's BiCentennial Gift to US, Son et Lumière, A Salute to George Washington, Mount Vernon, 19 May 1976; read excerpts from Thomas Jefferson at BiCentennial Service, American Cathedral in Paris, 4 July 1976. Special appearance, Acad. Awards, 2003, introducing 59 former winners; participated in Acad. tribute to Bette Davis, 2008. Hon. DHL Amer. Univ. of Paris, 1994; Hon. Dr Letters Univ. of Hertfordshire, 1998. Women's National Press Club Award, 1950; French Winged Victory Award, 1950; Filmex Tribute, 1978; Amer. Acad. of Achievement Award, 1978; Gold Medal, John F. Kennedy Center for Performing Arts, 2005; Amer. Acad. and Viennale Tributes, 2006. Amer. Legion Humanitarian Medal, 1967; Freedom Foundn American Exemplar Medal, 1980; Nat. Medal of Arts (USA), 2008. *Publications:* Every Frenchman Has One, 1961; (contrib.) Mother and Child, 1975.

DEHENNIN, Baron Herman; Hon. Grand Marshal of Belgian Royal Court; Hon. Belgian Ambassador; *b* 20 July 1929; created Baron, 1990; *s* of Alexander Dehennin and Flora Brehmen; *m* 1954, Margareta-Maria Donvil; two *s*. *Educ:* Catholic Univ. of Leuven. Dr in Law 1951. Lieut, Royal Belgian Artillery, 1951–53; entered Belgian Diplomatic Service, 1954; served The Hague, New Delhi, Madrid, the Congo; Ambassador to Rwanda, 1966–70; Economic Minister, Washington, 1970–74; Dir-Gen., Foreign Econ. Relations, Brussels, 1974–77; Ambassador to Japan, 1978–81; Grand Marshal, Belgian Royal Court, 1981–85; Ambassador: to USA, 1985–91; to UK, 1991–94. Pres., Special Olympics, Belgium, 1995. Chm., Club Chateau Ste Anne, Brussels, 1997, now Hon. Pres. Grand Cross, Order of Leopold, 1985; Grand Cross, Order of the Crown, 1983; foreign Orders: Comoros, France, Greece, Japan, Luxembourg, Mexico, Netherlands, Portugal, Rwanda, Sweden, Zaire. *Recreations:* hiking, reading (history, philosophy). *Clubs:* Royal Anglo-Belgian; Cercle Gaulois.

DEHMELT, Prof. Hans Georg; Professor of Physics, University of Washington, Seattle, 1961–2002; *b* 9 Sept. 1922; *s* of Georg Karl Dehmelt and Asta Ella Dehmelt (*née* Klemmt); US Citizen, 1961; *m* 1st; one *s*; 2nd, 1989, Diana Elaine Dundore. *Educ:* Graues Kloster, Berlin; Technische Hochschule, Breslau; Univ. of Göttingen (Dr rer. nat. 1950). Res. Fellow, Inst. Kopfermann, Göttingen, 1950–52; Res. Associate, Duke Univ., USA, 1952–55; Vis. Asst Prof., 1955, Associate Prof., 1957, Univ. of Washington. Consultant, Varian Associates, Palo Alto, Calif, 1956–70. Member: Amer. Acad. of Arts and Scis; Nat. Acad. of Scis; Fellow, Amer. Phys Soc.; FAAAS. Numerous awards and hon. degrees; Nobel Prize for Physics (jtly), 1989; Nat. Medal of Science, US, 1995. Leader of group which first saw with own eyes individual atom at rest in free space, 1979, reported 1980; isolated individual electron/positron at rest in empty space, 1973, 1981, and precisely measured its magnetism and size, 1976–87. *Publications:* papers on electron and atomic physics, charged atoms, proposed cosmonium world-atom hypothesis of big bang.

DEHN, Conrad Francis; QC 1968; Barrister; a Recorder of the Crown Court, 1974–98; a Deputy High Court Judge, 1988–96; *b* London, 24 Nov. 1926; *o s* of late C. G. Dehn, Solicitor and Cynthia Dehn (*née* Fuller) painter, musician and poet, as Francyn; *m* 1st, 1954, Sheila (*née* Magan) (marr. diss. 1978); two *s* one *d*; 2nd, 1978, Marilyn, *d* of late Peter and Constance Collyer. *Educ:* Charterhouse (Sen. Exhibnr); Christ Church, Oxford (Holford Schol. 1944; Slade Exhibnr 1948). Served RA, 1945–48, Best Cadet Mons Basic OCTU, 1946, 2nd Lieut 1947. 1st cl. hons PPE Oxon. 1950, MA 1952; Holt Schol. and Lord Justice Holker Sen. Exhibnr, Gray's Inn, 1951; Pres., Inns of Court Students Union, 1951–52. WEA Tutor, 1951–55. Called to Bar, Gray's Inn, 1952; Bencher, 1977; Chm., Management Cttee, 1987; Vice-Treas., 1995; Treas., 1996. Head, Fountain Court Chambers, 1984–89. Chairman: Bar Council Working Party on Liability for Defective Products, 1975–77; Planning Cttee, Senate of Inns of Court and Bar, 1980–83; London Univ. Disciplinary Appeals Cttee, 1986–90; Adv. Cttee, Gen. Comrs of Income Tax, Gray's Inn, 1994–2003. Dir, Bar Mutual Indemnity Fund Ltd, 1988–2010. Mem., Foster Cttee of Inquiry into Operators' Licensing, Dept of Transport, 1978. Member: Council of Legal Educn, 1981–86; London Legal Aid Cttee, 1965–92 (Vice-Chm., 1987–92); Hon. Advr, S London Psychotherapy Centre, 1982–2001; Hon. Legal Adviser: Age Concern London, 1987–2002 (Vice-Pres., 2001–02); Southwark Action for Voluntary Orgns, 2003–08. Pres., Camberwell Soc., 1996–2007. Member: Governing Body, United Westminster Schs, 1953–57; Adv. Bd, Inst. of Law, City Univ., 2002; Gov., Inns of Court Sch. of Law, 1996–2002. Appeared in film, The History Boys, 2007. Hon. Liberty, Camberwell, 2006. *Publications:* (contrib.) Ideas, 1954; (contrib.) Reform of Civil Procedure, 1996; (ed) Commercial Court Practice, 1999, 2nd edn 2000. *Recreations:* theatre, living in France. *Address:* 38 Camberwell Grove, SE5 8RE. *T:* (020) 7701 4758. *Club:* Reform.

De HOCHEPIED LARPENT, Lt Col Andrew Lionel Dudley, OBE 1992; Chief Executive, Southern Cross Care (South Australia and Northern Territory), since 2011; *b* 10 Feb. 1951; *s* of Douglas De Hochepied Larpent and Patience (*née* Johnson); *m* 1974, Anne Marion Knights; two *s* one *d*. *Educ:* Bradfield Coll.; RMA Sandhurst; Reading Univ. (BSc Hons Estate Mgt 1976). Royal Regt of Fusiliers, 1969–94, CO, 3rd Bn, 1990–92; Dir, Rehau Ltd, 1994–96; construction industry consultant, 1996–97; Chief Executive Officer: Cancer and Leukaemia in Childhood, 1997–2001; Somerset Care Gp, 2001–11. Chairman: Care Focus Somerset, 2005–07; Nat. Care Forum, 2006–11; Commonwealth Assoc. for the Ageing – CommonAge, 2012–; Dignity in Care Australia, 2014–; Mem. Bd, Internat. Assoc. of Homes and Services for the Ageing, 2006–12. *Recreations:* cycling, croquet.

de HOGHTON, Sir (Richard) Bernard (Cuthbert), 14th Bt *cr* 1611; KM; DL; landowner and investment manager; *b* 26 Jan. 1945; 3rd *s* of Sir Cuthbert de Hoghton, 12th Bt, and Philomena, *d* of late Herbert Simmons; *S* half-brother, 1978; *m* 1974, Rosanna Stella Virginia (*née* Buratti); one *s* one *d*. *Educ:* Ampleforth College, York; McGill Univ., Montreal (BA Hons); Birmingham Univ. (MA). Turner & Newall Ltd, 1967–70; international fund management, Vickers Da Costa & Co. Ltd, 1970–77; international institutional brokerage, de Zoete & Bevan & Co., 1977–86 (Partner, 1984–86); Dir, BZW Ltd (Europe), 1986–89; Asst Dir, Brown Shipley, 1989–94; Associate Dir, Teather & Greenwood, 1994–98; Dir, Tutton & Saunders Ltd, 1998–99. Pres., Royal Lancs Agricl Soc., 1995; Pres., Friends of Real Lancs, 2009–14; Nat. Vice-Pres., Internat. Tree Foundn, 1983–2013; Vice-Pres., Nat. Assoc. of Almshouses, 2012–. UN Special Ambassador, 1985. Patron: ACU (NW), 1980–2014; Internat. Spinal Res. Trust, 1984–2014. Chm., Hoghton Tower Preservation Trust, 1978–2015; Chm. and Dir, Hoghton Tower Ltd, 1991–2015. Founder Mem., HHA, 1973 (Mem., NW Reg. Exec. Cttee, 2006–). Hon. Lay Rector, The Minster, Preston, 1972–. FCSI. DL Lancs, 1988. Constantinian Order of S George (Naples), 1984; Kt SMO, Malta, 1980. *Recreations:* tennis, shooting, ski-ing, travelling, local historical research. *Heir: s* Thomas James Daniel Adam de Hoghton, *b* 11 April 1980. *Address:* South Wing, Hoghton Tower, Hoghton, Preston, Lancs PR5 0SH.

de HOOP SCHEFFER, Jakob Gijsbert, (Jaap), Hon. KCMG 2009; Secretary-General, NATO, 2004–09; Pieter Kooijmans Professor for Peace, Law and Security, Leiden University, since 2009; *b* 3 April 1948; *m* Jeannine van Oorschot; two *d*. *Educ:* Leiden Univ. (law degree 1974). Joined Foreign Service, Netherlands, 1976; Accra, 1976–78; Perm. Delegn, NATO, Brussels, 1978–80; i/c pvte office, Minister of Foreign Affairs, Netherlands, 1980–86. MP (Christian Democratic Alliance), Netherlands, 1986–2003; Minister of Foreign Affairs, 2002–03. Dep. Leader 1995–97, Leader, 1997–2001, Christian Democratic Alliance. Co-Pres., Security and Defence Agenda, 2010. *Address:* c/o NATO, Boulevard Leopold III, 1110 Brussels, Belgium.

DEIGHTON, family name of **Baron Deighton**.

DEIGHTON, Baron *cr* 2012 (Life Peer), of Carshalton in the County of Surrey; **Paul Clive Deighton,** KBE 2013; *b* 18 Jan. 1956; *s* of Walter Francis and Mabel Alice Deighton; *m* 1985, Alison Zoe Klebanoff; two *s*. *Educ:* Trinity Coll., Cambridge (BA 1978). Goldman Sachs International, 1983–2006: Investment Banking Div., 1983–93; Head of Controllers Dept, NY, 1993–96; Partner and Man. Dir, 1996–2000; Chief Operating Officer, Europe, 2000–06; Chief Exec., LOCOG, 2006–12. Commercial Sec., HM Treasury, 2013–15. *Address:* House of Lords, SW1 0PW.

DEIN, David; Vice Chairman, Arsenal Football Club, 1984–2007; former Vice Chairman, Football Association; *b* 7 Sept. 1943; *s* of Isidore and Sybil Dein; *m* 1972, Barbara Einhorn; two *s* one *d*. *Educ:* Orange Hill Grammar Sch., Edgware. Proprietor, sugar and commodity trading business, 1961–88; Dir, 1983–2007, full-time exec. role, 1988–2007, Arsenal FC. Mem. Bd, England 2018 FIFA World Cup Bid, 2009–10. Chm., Stage One (formerly Theatre Investment Fund), 2001. *Recreations:* theatre, films, tennis.

DEISENHOFER, Prof. Johann, PhD; Regental Professor and Professor in Biochemistry, University of Texas Southwestern Medical Center at Dallas, since 1988; Investigator, Howard Hughes Medical Institute, 1988–2010; *b* 30 Sept. 1943; *s* of Johann and Thekla Deisenhofer; *m* 1989, Kirsten Fischer-Lindahl, PhD. *Educ:* Technische Universität München (Physics Diploma 1971; PhD 1974). Max-Planck-Institut für Biochemie: graduate student, 1971–74; Postdoctoral Fellow, 1974–76; Staff Scientist, 1976–88. (Jtly) Biological Physics Prize, Amer. Physical Soc., 1986; (jtly) Otto Bayer Preis, 1988; (jtly) Nobel Prize in Chemistry, 1988. *Publications:* contribs to Acta Crystallographica, Biochemistry, Jl of Molecular Biology, Nature, Science, etc. *Recreations:* ski-ing, hiking, classical music. *Address:* University of Texas Southwestern Medical Center, 6001 Forest Park Road, Dallas, TX 75390–8816, USA. *T:* (214) 6455941.

DEJARDIN, Ian Alan Charles; Sackler Director (formerly Director), Dulwich Picture Gallery, since 2005; *b* 26 Aug. 1955; *s* of Alan A. Dejardin and Pamela B. Dejardin (*née* Wilcock); civil partnership 2007, *m* 2015, Eric Pearson. *Educ:* Daniel Stewart's Coll., Edinburgh; Univ. of Edinburgh (MA 1st Cl. Hons Hist. of Art 1977); Univ. of Manchester (Dip. Art Gall. and Mus. Studies 1987). Curatorial Asst, Royal Acad. of Arts, 1988–90; English Heritage: Curator of Paintings, London Historic Houses, 1990–94; Sen. Curator of

Collections, 1994–96, Hd, Historic Team, 1996–97, Historic Properties, London Reg.; Curator, Dulwich Picture Gall., 1998–2005. *Publications:* exhibition catalogues: Paintings from the Chantrey Bequest, 1989; Henry Moore at Dulwich Picture Gallery, 2004; Director's Choice, 2005; The Dutch Italianates: 17th Century masterpieces from Dulwich Picture Gallery, 2008; Painting Canada: Tom Thomson and the Group of Seven, 2011; From the Forest to the Sea: Emily Carr in British Columbia, 2014. *Recreations:* piano, knitting. *Address:* Dulwich Picture Gallery, Gallery Road, SE21 7AD. *T:* (020) 8299 8702, *Fax:* (020) 8299 8700.

de JERSEY, Hon. Paul, AC 2000; Governor of Queensland, since 2014; *b* 21 Sept. 1948; *s* of Ronald Claude and Moya Clarice de Jersey; *m* 1971, Kaye Brown; one *s* two *d. Educ:* C of E Grammar Sch., Brisbane; Univ. of Qld (BA, LLB Hons). Admitted to Qld Bar, 1971; QC (Qld) 1981; a Judge of the Supreme Court, Qld, 1985–2014; Chief Justice of Qld, 1998–2014. Chm., Qld Law Reform Commn, 1996–98; Pres., Industrial Court of Qld, 1996–98. Chm. Judicial Section, Law Assoc. for Asia and Pacific, 2006–. Chancellor, Anglican Dio. Brisbane, 1991–. Chm., Qld Cancer Fund, 1994–2001; Pres., Australian Cancer Soc., 1998–2001. Visitor, Univ. of South Pacific, 2006–09. Hon. LLD Qld, 2000; DUniv Southern Qld, 2008. *Recreations:* reading, music. *Address:* Government House, GPO Box 434, Brisbane, Qld 4001, Australia. *Clubs:* Queensland, United Service (Brisbane).

de JONGH, Nicholas Raymond; writer; Dramaturg, Bill Kenwright Ltd, 2013–14; *b* London; *s* of late Louis de Jongh and Vivian (*née* Creditor). *Educ:* Hall Sch., Hampstead; St Paul's Sch.; University Coll. London (BA Hons, MPhil 1983). Secker & Warburg, 1967; Scriptwriter, BBC External Services, 1968; The Guardian: Reporter, 1968; Theatre Reviewer, 1969; Dep. Theatre Critic, 1972–91; Arts Reporter, 1973–78; Arts Corresp., 1978–90; Theatre Critic: Mail on Sunday, 1983; Evening Standard, 1991–2009. Chm., Drama Section, Critics' Circle, 1984–86. Writer of plays: Plague Over England, Finborough Th., 2008, Duchess Th., 2009; To Keep the Ghost Awake, Finborough Th., 2010; There Goes My Future, Finborough Th., 2011; The Unquiet Grave of Garcia Lorca, Drayton Arms, 2014. *Publications:* (ed) Bedside Guardian, 1989, 1990; Not in Front of the Audience, 1992; (contrib.) Approaching the Millennium: essays on Angels in America, 2000; Politics, Prudery and Perversions (Theatre Book Prize, Soc. of Theatre Res.), 2000; (contrib.) British Theatre of the 1990s, 2007; Plague over England, 2009. *Recreation:* trying to make my dreams come true. *E:* nicholasdejongh@hotmail.co.uk. *Club:* Soho Athletic.

de KLERK, Frederik Willem; Leader of the Opposition, National Assembly of South Africa, 1996–97; Chairman: F W de Klerk Foundation; Global Leadership Foundation; *b* 18 March 1936; *s* of J. de Klerk; *m* 1st, 1959, Marike Willemse (marr. diss. 1998; she *d* 2001); two *s* one *d*; 2nd, 1998, Elita Georgiadis. *Educ:* Monument High School, Krugersdorp; Potchefstroom Univ. Law practice, 1961–72; MP (Nat. Party) Vereeniging, 1972–89; Information Officer, Transvaal, Nat. Party, 1975; Minister: of Posts and Telecommunications and Social Welfare and Pensions, 1978; of Posts and Telecommunications and of Sport and Recreation, 1978–79; of Mines, Energy and Environmental Planning, 1979–80; of Mineral and Energy Affairs, 1980–82; of Internal Affairs, 1982–85; of Nat. Educn and Planning, 1984–89; Leader, Nat. Party, 1989–97 (Transvaal Leader, 1982–89); Chm., Council of Ministers, 1985–89; State President, 1989–94, Dep. President, 1994–96, S Africa. Hon. LLD: Potchefstroom Univ., 1990; Bar-Ilan Univ., Tel Aviv; Hon. DPhil: Stellenbosch Univ., 1990; Nat. Chengchi Univ., Taipei, Taiwan. Prince of Asturias Prize, 1992, Nobel Peace Prize, 1993 (with N. R. Mandela). *Publications:* The Last Trek: a new beginning (autobiog.), 1999. *Address:* PO Box 15785, Panorama, 7506, Western Cape, South Africa.

de KRETSER, Prof. David Morritz, AC 2006 (AO 2000); MD; FRACP, FAA, FTSE; Sir John Monash Distinguished Professor, Monash University, since 2011; Governor of Victoria, Australia, 2006–11; *b* Colombo, Sri Lanka, 27 April 1939; *s* of Percival Shirley de Kretser and Iris Aileen de Kretser; *m* 1962, Janice Margaret Warren; four *s. Educ:* Camberwell Grammar Sch.; Univ. of Melbourne (MS BS 1962); Monash Univ. (MD 1969). FRACP 1976; FAA 1996; FTSE 2001. Lectr, 1966–68, Sen. Lectr, 1968, Dept of Anatomy, Monash Univ.; Sen. Fellow in Endocrinol., Dept of Medicine, Univ. of Washington, and USPHS Postdoctoral Fellow, 1969–71; Monash University: Sen. Lectr, Depts of Medicine and Anatomy, 1971–75; Reader in Anatomy, 1976–78; Prof. of Anatomy, 1978–2006, Emeritus Prof., 2006–11; Hd, Dept of Anatomy, 1978–91; Dir, Centre for Reproductive Biol., 1989–91; Dir, Inst. of Reproduction and Develt, subseq. Monash Inst. of Med. Res., 1991–2005; Associate Dean, Biotechnol. Develt, 2002–06; Prince Henry's Hospital: Asst Endocrinologist, 1971–85; Physician, 1973–74; Sen. Res. Fellow, 1974–78, Associate Dir, 1977–78, Med. Res. Centre; Consultant, Reproductive Medicine Clinic, Inst. of Med. Res., 1976–2006. Hon. LLD: Monash, 2011; Melbourne, 2012. Centenary Medal, Aust., 2003. *Publications:* The Pituitary and Testis: clinical and experimental studies, 1983; (Section Ed.) Endocrinology, 7th edn 2015; 496 papers in jls and 170 chapters in texts on endocrinology and infertility. *Recreations:* bushwalking, fishing, tennis, jazz. *Address:* Monash-Prince Henry's Institute of Medical Research, Monash University, PO Box 5418, Clayton, Vic 3168, Australia. *Clubs:* Athenæum, Royal Automobile (Melbourne); West Brighton (Vic).

de LA BARRE de NANTEUIL, Luc; Commandeur de l'Ordre National du Mérite; Officier de la Légion d'Honneur; Ambassadeur de France; Chairman, Les Echos Group, 1991–2003; *b* 21 Sept. 1925; *m* 1st, Philippa MacDonald; one *s*; 2nd, 1973, Hedwige Frerejean de Chavagneux; one *s* one *d. Educ:* school in Poitiers; BA, LLB Lyon and Paris; Dip. d'Etudes Supérieures (Econ); Graduate, Ecole Nat. d'Admin, 1949. French Ministry of Foreign Affairs: Economic Affairs Dept, 1950–51; Secrétariat Général, 1951–52; Pacts Service, 1952–53; Econ. Affairs Dept, 1954–59; First Sec., London, 1959–64; Asst Dir, Afr. and ME Affairs Dept, 1964–70; Hd of Econ. Co-operation Service, Directorate of Econ. Affairs, 1970–76; Ambassador to the Netherlands, 1976–77; French Permanent Representative: to EEC, Brussels, 1977–82 and 1985–86; to Security Council and to UN, New York, 1981–84; Diplomatic Adviser, 1986; Ambassador to UK, 1986–91. *Publications:* David (Jacques Louis), 1985. *Address:* 11 rue Parmentier, 92200 Neuilly-sur-Seine, France.

De la BÈRE, Sir Cameron, 2nd Bt *cr* 1953; jeweller, Geneva; *b* 12 Feb. 1933; *s* of Sir Rupert De la Bère, 1st Bt, KCVO, and Marguerite (*d* 1969), *e d* of late Sir John Humphery; *S* father, 1978; *m* 1964, Clairemonde (*d* 2004), *o d* of late Casimir Kaufmann, Geneva; one *d. Educ:* Tonbridge, and on the Continent. Translator's cert. in Russian. British Army Intelligence Corps, 1951–53. Company director of Continental Express Ltd (subsid. of Hay's Wharf), 1958–64. Engaged in promotion of luxury retail jewellery stores, Switzerland and France, 1965–. Liveryman, Skinners' Co. *Recreations:* riding, swimming, history. *Heir: b* Adrian De la Bère, *b* 17 Sept. 1939. *Clubs:* Hurlingham, Société Littéraire (Geneva).

de la BILLIÈRE, Gen. Sir Peter (Edgar de la Cour), KCB 1988; KBE 1991 (CBE 1983); DSO 1976; MC 1959 and Bar 1966; DL; Commander British Forces Middle East, 1990–91; *b* 29 April 1934; *s* of Surgeon Lieut Comdr Claude Dennis Delacour de Labillière (killed in action, HMS Fiji, 1941) and of Frances Christine Wright Lawley; *m* 1965, Bridget Constance Muriel Goode; one *s* two *d. Educ:* Harrow School; Staff College. Joined KSLI 1952; commissioned DLI; served Japan, Korea, Malaya (despatches 1958), Jordan, Borneo, Egypt, Aden, Gulf States, Sudan, Oman, Falkland Is; CO 22 SAS Regt, 1972–74; GSO1 (DS) Staff Coll., 1974–77; Comd British Army Training Team, Sudan, 1977–78; Dir SAS and Comd, SAS Group, 1978–82; rcds 1983; Comd, British Forces Falkland Is and Mil. Comr, 1984–85; GOC Wales, 1985–87; GOC SE Dist, and Perm. Peace Time Comdr, Jt Forces Operations Staff, 1987–90; ME Advr to MOD, 1991–92, retd. Col Comdt, Light Div., 1986–89. Chairman: ME Div., Robert Fleming Hldgs, 1998–99 (non-exec. Dir, 1992–98); Meadowland Meats Ltd, 1994–2002. Mem. Council, RUSI, 1975–77. Chm., FARM Africa, 1998–2001 (Mem. Bd, 1992–2001; Vice-Chm., 1995–98). Chm., Jt Services Hang Gliding, 1986–89; Cdre, Army Sailing Assoc., 1989–91. President: SAS Assoc., 1991–96; ACF, 1992–99. Vice-Pres., UK Falkland Is Assoc., 1993–. Comr, Duke of York's Mil. Sch., 1988–90. Presenter, TV series, Clash of the Generals, 2004. Trustee, Imperial War Mus., 1992–99; President: Imperial War Mus. Friends, 2001–08; Harrow Sch. Assoc., 2001–05; Herefordshire LI Mus. Friends, 2004–14. Special Advr to Vice Chancellor, Durham Univ., 2008–. Patron: Jt Educnl Trust, 1998–2009; Farm Africa, 2001–; Gallantry Medallists' League, 2005–07; Blind Veterans UK (formerly St Dunstan's), 2007–. Freeman, City of London, 1991; Hon. Freeman, Fishmongers' Co., 1991. Stowaway Mem., Southampton Master Mariners Assoc., 1992. Lord of the Manor of Garway, 1966–2010. DL Hereford and Worcester, 1993. Hon. DSc Cranfield Inst. of Technol., 1992; Hon. DCL Durham, 1993. Order of Bahrain, 1st Cl., 1991; Officer, 1991, Chief Comdr, 1992, Legion of Merit (USA); Meritorious Service Cross, (Canada), 1992; Order of Abdul Aziz, 2nd Cl. (Saudi Arabia), 1992; Kuwait Decoration, 1st Cl., 1992; Qatar Sash of Merit, 1992. *Publications:* Storm Command: a personal story, 1992; (autobiog.) Looking for Trouble, 1994; Supreme Courage: 150 years of the Victoria Cross, 2004. *Recreations:* family, squash, down market apiculture, tennis, farming, sailing. *Clubs:* Farmers, Naval and Military (Trustee, 1999–2003).

DELACOUR, Jean-Paul; Officer of Legion of Honour; Knight of National Order of Merit; Inspector General of Finance; Hon. Vice-Chairman, Société Générale, Paris (Chief Operating Officer, 1986–95; Vice-Chairman, 1992); *b* 7 Nov. 1930; *s* of Henri Delacour and Denise Brochet; *m* 1958, Claude Laurence; four *s* one *d. Educ:* Inst. of Political Studies, Paris (Dipl.); ENA (Nat. Sch. of Administration). Inspector of Finance, 1955–61; Dep. Dir, Crédit National, 1961–68; Dir, 1969, Dep. Gen. Manager, 1974, Bd Mem. and Man. Dir, 1986, Société Générale; Chm. and Chief Exec. Officer, Soc. Gén. Alsacienne de Banque, 1978–82; Chm., Sogebail, 1985–2000; senior functions in internat. banking and financial insts. Chm., Bd of Catholic Inst. Paris, 1984–2005. *Address:* Société Générale, 29 boulevard Haussmann, 75009 Paris, France. *T:* 42142336.

de LACY, Richard Michael; QC 2000; *b* 4 Dec. 1954; *e s* of Michael de Lacy, MN, and Barbara de Lacy (*née* Greene), Hobart, Tasmania; *m* 1980, Sybil del Strother (marr. diss. 2003); one *s* two *d. Educ:* Hymers Coll., Kingston upon Hull; Clare Coll., Cambridge (BA 1975; MA 1979). Called to the Bar, Middle Temple, 1976 (Harmsworth Schol.), Bencher, 2001; in practice at the Bar, England and Wales, 1978–2012; admitted to Cayman Bar, 2012; admitted to Bar of BVI, 2013; Partner and Hd of Litigation, Ogier, Cayman Is, 2012–15. Member: Practice Regulation Review Cttee, ICAEW, 1998–2004; Panel, FRC Disciplinary Tribunals, 2004–13. Jt Hon. Treas., Barristers' Benevolent Assoc., 1989–99; Chm., Endeavour Trng, 2005–11; Mem. Council, RBL Poppy Factory, 2006–11. Vis. Prof., QMUL, 2009–12. FCIArb 1991–2010. *Recreations:* music (Mem., Cayman Nat. Orch., 2012–), history. *Address:* 10 Market Street, #722, Camana Bay, Grand Cayman, KY1-9006, Cayman Islands. *Clubs:* Travellers', Garrick.

DELAHUNTY, Johanne Erica; QC 2006; barrister; a Recorder, since 2010; *b* 15 Sept. 1963; *d* of Pauline Delahunty; *m* 1990, Jonathan Light; one *s* two *d. Educ:* Copthall Comp. Sch., Mill Hill; St Anne's Coll., Oxford (BA Law Juris. 1983, MA). Called to the Bar, Middle Temple, 1986, Bencher, 2011; in practice, 1986–, specialist child abuse and family law practitioner; accredited specialist in family law and child protection. Accredited Family Mediator, 2011. Member: Family Law Bar Assoc.; Assoc. of Lawyers for Children; Assoc. of Women Barristers. Member: Amnesty; NSPCC; Barnardo's; Save the Children; Help the Aged. Patron, Assoc. for Multiple Endocrine Neoplasia Disorders. *Publications:* contribs to specialist child care and family law publications. *Recreations:* married to my partner of 34 years, Jonathan Light, with 3 children and 2 dogs to occupy a life outside the Bar, skilled at finding time to read Vogue, to indulge in a passion for modern British jewellery and retail therapy, guilt pangs alleviated by fine wine and good friends. *Address:* 4 Paper Buildings, Temple, EC4Y 7EX. *T:* (020) 7583 0816. *E:* jd@4pb.com.

de la MARTINEZ, Odaline, (Odaline de la Caridad Martinez), FRAM; Cuban American conductor and composer; *b* Matanzas, Cuba, 31 Oct. 1949; *d* of Julian J. Martinez and Odaline M. Martinez. *Educ:* schs in USA; Tulane Univ., New Orleans; Royal Acad. of Music, London; Surrey Univ. FRAM 1990. Jt Founder and Artistic Dir, Lontano (chamber ensemble), 1976–; first woman to conduct an entire Promenade Concert programme, Royal Albert Hall, 1984; Dir, European Women's Orchestra, 1990–; Principal Guest Cond., Camerata of the Americas, 1998. Founder, 1992, and Man. Dir, Lorelt recording co. Founder Mem., Women in Music, 1985; Founder, London Fest. of American Music, 2006. *Compositions include:* Litanies; Canciones; First String Quartet; *opera includes:* Sister Aimée: an American Legend, 1984; Imoinda, 2008; The Crossing, 2012; *choral works include:* Misa Breve Afro-Cubana; Two American Madrigals; A Las Cinco de la Tarde. *Publications:* Mendelssohn's Sister, 1999; Latin American Music, 1999; (ed) Dame Ethel Smyth: orchestral serenade, 2015. *Address:* c/o Lontano Trust Ltd, 458 Hoe Street, E17 9AH.

DELAMERE, 5th Baron *cr* 1821; **Hugh George Cholmondeley;** *b* 18 Jan. 1934; *s* of 4th Baron Delamere, and Phyllis Anne (*d* 1978), *e d* of late Lord George Scott, OBE; *S* father, 1979; *m* 1964, Mrs Ann Willoughby Tinne, *o d* of late Sir Patrick Renison, GCMG and Lady Renison, Mayfield, Sussex; one *s. Educ:* Eton; Magdalene Coll., Cambridge. MA Agric. *Heir: s* Hon. Thomas Patrick Gilbert Cholmondeley [*b* 19 June 1968; *m* 1998, Dr Sally Brewerton, *d* of Prof. and Mrs Derrick Brewerton; two *s*]. *Address:* Soysambu, Elmenteita, Kenya.

de la MORENA, Felipe, Hon. CBE 2001; Ambassador of Spain; President, British Hispanic Foundation, Madrid, since 1993; *b* 22 Oct. 1927; *s* of Felipe de la Morena and Luisa Calvet; *m* 1958, María Teresa Casado Bach; two *s* two *d. Educ:* Univ. Complutense de Madrid; Univs of Grenoble and Oxford; Diplomatic Sch., Madrid. Entered diplomatic service 1957; served Beirut, Berne, Washington and Min. of Foreign Affairs, Madrid; Dir, Technical Office, later Dir-Gen., Territorial Planning, Min. of Develt Planning, 1974–76; Minister Counsellor, Lisbon, 1976; Ambassador to People's Republic of China, 1978; Dir-Gen., Foreign Policy for Latin America, 1982; Ambassador to Syria and Cyprus (residence Damascus), 1983, to Tunisia, 1987, to UK, 1990–93; Permanent Rep. to WEU, 1990–93. Spanish Orders: Alfonso X el Sabio, 1965; Mérito Civil, 1973; Isabel la Católica, 1970; Carlos III, 1980; Gran Cruz del Mérito Naval, 1992; Sacra y Militar Orden Constantiniana de San Jorge, 1993; holds foreign decorations. *Recreation:* golf. *Address:* Fundación Hispano-Británica, Avda. Pío XII 92, 28036 Madrid, Spain. *Clubs:* Travellers; Puerta de Hierro, Real Automóvil de España, Gran Peña (Madrid).

DELANEY, Francis James Joseph, (Frank); writer and broadcaster, since 1972; *b* 24 Oct. 1942; 5th *s* of Edward Delaney and Elizabeth Josephine O'Sullivan; *m* 1st, 1966, Eilish (*née* Kelliher) (marr. diss. 1978); three *s*; 2nd, 1988, Susan Jane Collier (marr. diss. 1997; she *d* 2011); 3rd, 1999, Sally E. Vickers (marr. diss. 2000); 4th, 2002, Diane Meier. *Educ:* Abbey Schools, Tipperary, Ireland; Rosse Coll., Dublin. Bank of Ireland, 1961–72; journalism, 1972–: includes: broadcasting news with RTE, Dublin; current affairs and arts broadcasting with BBC Northern Ireland, BBC Radio Four, London, and BBC Television; weekly podcast Re:Joyce (deconstructing Ulysses), 2010–. Chm., NBL, 1984–86. Pres., Samuel Johnson Soc., 2001. Writer of TV screenplay, Goodbye, Mr Chips, 2002. *Publications:* James Joyce's Odyssey, 1981; Betjeman Country, 1983; The Celts, 1986; A Walk in the Dark Ages, 1988; A Walk to the Western Isles, 1993; Simple Courage, 2006; *fiction:* My Dark Rosaleen, 1989; The Sins of the Mothers, 1992; Telling the Pictures, 1993; A Stranger in their Midst, 1995; The Amethysts, 1997; Desire and Pursuit, 1998; Pearl, 1999; At Ruby's, 2001; Ireland: a novel, 2004; Tipperary: a novel, 2007; Shannon: a novel, 2009; Venetia Kelly's Travelling Show: a novel, 2010; The Matchmaker of Kenmare, 2011; The Last Storyteller: a novel, 2012; (as Francis Bryan) Jim Hawkins and the Curse of Treasure Island, 2002; sundry criticisms and introductions. *Recreations:* reading, conversation, walking, building. *E:* info@frankdelaney.com. *Clubs:* Athenæum, Chelsea Arts.

DELANEY, Ven. Peter Anthony, MBE 2001; Archdeacon of London, 1999–2009, now Emeritus; Priest-in-charge, St Stephen's Walbrook and St Swithun, City of London, 2005–14; *b* 20 June 1939; *s* of Anthony Mario Delaney and Ena Margaret Delaney. *Educ:* King's Coll., London (AKC); St Boniface Coll., Warminster. Ordained deacon, 1966, priest, 1967; Curate, St Marylebone Parish Church, 1966–70; Chaplain, London University Church of Christ the King, 1970–74; Canon Residentiary and Precentor, Southwark Cathedral, 1974–77; Vicar, All Hallows by the Tower, 1977–2004; Guild Vicar, St Katharine Cree, 1997–2002. Hon. Canon, St Paul's Cathedral, Nicosia, Dio. Cyprus and the Gulf, 1984–; Prebendary, St Paul's Cathedral, London, 1995–99. Director: City Churches Develt Gp, 1997–2000; London Internet Church, 2006. Trustee, Trust for London (formerly City Parochial Foundn), 2001–. Chm., Ind. Adv. Gp, City of London Police, 2006–. Gov., St Dunstan's Coll., Catford, 1977–2000; Master: Co. of World Traders of City of London, 1994–95; Gardeners' Co., 1999–2000. Kt Comdr, SMO of Knights Templars. *Publications:* The Artist and his Exploration into God, 1981; (contrib.) The Canon Law of the Church of England, 1975. *Recreations:* painting, theatre, gardening.

de LANGE, Prof. Nicholas Robert Michael, DPhil, PhD, DD; FBA 2011; Professor of Hebrew and Jewish Studies, University of Cambridge, 2001–11, now Emeritus; Fellow, Wolfson College, Cambridge, since 1985; *b* Nottingham, 7 Aug. 1944; *s* of late (George) David de Lange and Elaine de Lange (*née* Jacobus); *m* 1990, Patricia Touton-Victor (marr. diss. 1998); two *s* one *d*. *Educ:* Harrow Co. Sch.; Christ Church, Oxford (MA; DPhil 1970); Leo Baeck Coll. (Rabbinical Dip.); Univ. of Cambridge (PhD 1971; DD 2001). University of Cambridge: Lectr in Rabbinics, 1971–95; Reader in Hebrew and Jewish Studies, 1995–2001. MAE 2013. *Publications:* Origen and the Jews, 1976; Apocrypha: Jewish literature of the Hellenistic age, 1978; Atlas of the Jewish World, 1984; Judaism, 1986, 2nd edn 2003; Greek Jewish Texts from the Cairo Genizah, 1996; (ed) An Illustrated History of the Jewish People, 1997; An Introduction to Judaism, 2000, 2nd edn 2010; The Penguin Dictionary of Judaism, 2008; many articles and literary translations. *Recreations:* reading, conversation. *Address:* Wolfson College, Cambridge CB3 9BB. *T:* (01223) 740561. *E:* nrml1@cam.ac.uk.

DÉLANO ORTÚZAR, Juan Carlos; farmer; Director: Compañía de Seguros Generales Penta Security SA; Agrícola Gildemeister SA; *b* Santiago, 14 June 1941; *m* Maria Paz Valenzuela; three *s* one *d*. *Educ:* St George's Coll., Catholic Univ., Chile; OCD, Belgium. Private enterprise: Distribuidora Audicol SA, Commercial Magara Ltd; Pres., Trading Assoc. of Chile, Dir, Chamber of Commerce of Santiago, 1979–83; Pres., Chilean Nat. Chamber of Commerce and Advr to Confedn of Trade and Industry, 1983–85; Minister of Economy, Promotion and Reconstruction, 1985–87; Ambassador to UK, 1987–90. Chief Exec. Officer, Equs SA, 1990; Dir, Icare, 1990. Dir, Universidad Adolfo Ibáñez, 1998–2004. *Address:* Americo Vespucio Norte 1776, Dept 31, Vitacura, Santiago, Chile. *E:* juancdelano@yahoo.com. *Club:* Polo.

de LAROSIÈRE de CHAMPFEU, Jacques (Martin Henri Marie), Hon. KBE 1998; Grand Officier, Legion of Honour, 2013 (Commander, 1996); Chevalier, National Order of Merit, 1970; Inspector General of Finance, since 1981; Chairman, Eurofi, since 2011 (Co-Chairman, 2000–11); *b* 12 Nov. 1929; *s* of Robert de Larosière and Hugayte de Champfeu; *m* 1960, France du Bos; one *s* one *d*. *Educ:* Institut d'Etudes Politiques, Paris (L ès L, licencié en droit); Nat. Sch. of Administration, Paris. Inspecteur des Finances, 1958; appointments at: Inspectorate-General of Finance, 1961; External Finance Office, 1963; Treasury 1965; Asst Dir, Treasury, 1967; Dep. Dir then Head of Dept, Min. of Economics and Finance, 1971; Principal Private Sec. to Minister of Economics and Finance, 1974; Dir, Treasury, 1974–78; Man. Dir, IMF, 1978–87; Gov., Banque de France, 1987–93; Pres., EBRD, 1993–98. Prof., Sciences Po, Paris, 2013–. Advr, BNP Paribas, 1998–2008. Director: Renault, 1971–74; Banque Nat. de Paris, 1973–78; Air France and French Railways, 1974–78; Société nat. industrielle aérospatiale, 1976–78; Power Corp., 1998–2001; Alstom, 1998–2000; France Telecom, 1998–2009; Trustee, Reuters, 1999–2004. Director appointed by Treasury, General Council, Bank of France, 1974–78; Auditor: Crédit national, 1974–78; Comptoir des entrepreneurs, 1973–75; Crédit foncier de France, 1975–78. Vice Pres., Caisse nat. des télécommunications, 1974–78; Pres., Observatoire de l'Epargne Européenne, 1999–; Chm., Strategic Cttee, Agence France Trésor, 2000–; Mem., Conseil de Régulation Financière et du Risque Systematique, 2011–12. Member: Internat. Adv. Bd, AIG, 2002–09; Adv. Bd, China Develt Bank, 2005–08; Chm. Adv. Bd, Mid Europa Fund, 2006–. Chairman: OECD Econ. and Develt Review Cttee, 1967–71; Deputies Gp of Ten, 1976–78; Cttee of Gp of Ten, 1990–93. Institute of International Finance: Co-Chairman: Cttee on Crisis Mgt and Crisis Resolution in Emerging Markets, 2003–09; Mkt Monitoring Gp, 2009–; Principles for Stable Capital Flows, 2006–. Chm., Stichting NYSE Euronext (Dutch Foundn), 2007–14; Trustee, NYSE Gp Trust I (US Trust), 2007–14; Prés., Assoc. Internat. Cardinal Henri de Lubac, 1994–. Mem., Acad. of Moral and Pol Scis, 1993; Hon. Mem., Société des Cincinnati de France, 1992. Grand Cordon: Order of Sacred Treasure (Japan), 1993; Order of the Brilliant Star (Taipei), 1998; Grand Cross, Order of Merit: Argentina, 1992; Italy, 1993; Stana Platina (Bulgaria), 1993; Order of Aztec Eagle (Mexico), 1994; Cross, Order of Merit (Germany), 1996; Comdr, Order of Merit (Poland), 1997; Order of Friendship (Russia), 1997; Order of Merit (Hungary), 1998; Comdr, Order of Southern Cross (Brazil), 1999; Order of Cross of Terra Mariana (Estonia), 2001. *Address:* Eurofi, 66 Rue de Miromesnil, 75008 Paris, France.

de la RÚA, Fernando; President of Argentina, 1999–2001; *b* 15 Sept. 1937; *m* Inés Pertiné; three *c*. *Educ:* Liceo Militar General Paz, Córdoba Univ. (Dr of Laws). Mem., Unión Cívica Radical. Advr, Min. of the Interior, Argentina, 1963–66; Senator (UCR) for Buenos Aires, 1973–76 and 1989; Nat. Senator (UCR), 1983–89, 1992–99; Nat. Deputy (UCR), 1991; (Pres., UCR Gp); Mayor, City Buenos Aires, 1996. *Publications:* Operación Política: la causa del senado, 2006.

de la RUE, Sir Andrew (George Ilay), 4th Bt *cr* 1898, of Cadogan Square; company director; farmer; *b* 3 Feb. 1946; *s* of Sir Eric Vincent de la Rue, 3rd Bt and Cecilia (*d* 1963), *d* of late Maj. Walter Waring and Lady Clementine Waring, *d* of 10th Marquess of Tweedale; *S* father, 1989; *m* 1984, Tessa Ann, *er d* of David Dobson; two *s*. *Educ:* Millfield. With Lloyd's (Insurance), 1966; Dir, Private Company, 1976–. *Recreations:* shooting, coursing, tennis. *Heir:* *s* Edward Walter de la Rue, *b* 25 Nov. 1986. *Address:* Stragglethorpe Grange, Brant Broughton, Lincolnshire LN5 0RA. *T:* (01636) 626505.

de la TOUR, Frances; actress; *b* 30 July 1944; *d* of Charles de la Tour and Moyra (*née* Fessas); one *s* one *d*. *Educ:* Lycée français de Londres; Drama Centre, London. Royal Shakespeare Company, 1965–71: rôles include Audrey in As You Like It, 1967; Hoyden in The Relapse, 1969; Helena in A Midsummer Night's Dream (Peter Brooks's production), 1971 (also USA tour); Belinda in The Man of Mode, 1971; Violet in Small Craft Warnings, Comedy, 1973 (Best Supporting Actress, Plays and Players Award); Ruth Jones in The Banana Box, Apollo, 1973; Isabella in The White Devil, Old Vic, 1976; appearances at Hampstead Theatre, and Half Moon Theatre incl. title rôle in Hamlet, 1979; Stephanie in Duet for One, Bush Theatre and Duke of York's, 1980 (Best New Play, and Best Perf. by Actress, Drama Awards, Best Perf. by Actress in New Play, SWET Award, Best Actress, New Standard Award); Jean in Skirmishes, Hampstead, 1982 (also television, 1982); Sonya in Uncle Vanya, Haymarket, 1982; Josie in A Moon for the Misbegotten, Riverside, 1983 (SWET Best Actress award); title rôle in St Joan, NT, 1984; Dance of Death, Riverside, 1985; Sonya and Masha in Chekhov's Women, Lyric, 1985; Brighton Beach Memoirs, NT, 1986; Lillian, Lyric, 1986, Fortune, 1987; Façades, Lyric, Hammersmith, 1988; Regan in King Lear, Old Vic, 1989; Arkadina, Ranyevskaya and Olga Knipper in Chekhov's Women, Moscow Art Theatre, 1990; Miss Belzer in When She Danced, Globe, 1991 (Olivier Award); Witch in The Pope and the Witch, Comedy, 1992; Yoko Sitsuki in Greasepaint, Lyric, Hammersmith, 1993; Leonie in Les Parents Terribles, RNT, 1994; Three Tall Women, Wyndham's, 1994; Elinor in Blinded by the Sun, RNT, 1996; the woman in The Play about the Baby, Almeida, 1998; Raisa in The Forest, RNT, 1999; Cleopatra in Antony and Cleopatra, RSC, 1999; Jane in Fallen Angels, Apollo, 2000 (Variety Club Best Actress award); The Good Hope, 2001, Pinter Sketches, 2002, NT; Alice in Dance of Death, Lyric, 2003; Mrs Lintott in The History Boys, NT, 2004, NY, 2006 (Tony Award); Bertha in Boeing-Boeing, Comedy, 2007; The Habit of Art, NT, 2009–10; People, NT, 2012. *Films* include: Rising Damp, 1979 (Best Actress, New Standard British Film Award, 1980); The Cherry Orchard, 1998; Harry Potter and the Goblet of Fire, 2005; The History Boys, 2006; The Nutcracker, 2008; Book of Eli, Alice in Wonderland, Harry Potter and the Deathly Hallows, Pt 1, 2010; Hugo, 2011; Private Peaceful, 2012; Trap for Cinderella, Suspension of Disbelief, 2013; Into the Woods, Mr Holmes, Lady in the Van, 2015; Survivor, 2015. *Television* includes: Play for Today (twice), 1973–75; Rising Damp (series), 1974, 1976; Flickers, 1980; Duet for One, 1985; Cold Lazarus, 1995; Tom Jones, 1997; The Egg, 2002; Death on the Nile, 2003; Waking the Dead, 2004; Sensitive Skin, 2005; Vicious (series), 2013, 2015; Big School (series), 2013, 2014. *Address:* c/o Claire Maroussas, Independent Talent Group Ltd, 40 Whitfield Street, W1T 2RH. *T:* (020) 7636 6565.

DE LA WARR, 11th Earl *cr* 1761; **William Herbrand Sackville;** DL; Baron De La Warr, 1299 and 1572; Viscount Cantelupe 1761; Baron Buckhurst 1864; Director, Shore Capital Stockbrokers Ltd, 2004; Vice Chairman, Europe, Middle East and Africa, Shore Capital International Ltd, since 2010; farmer; *b* 10 April 1948; *s* of 10th Earl De La Warr and Anne Rachel, *d* of Geoffrey Devas, MC; *S* father, 1988; *m* 1978, Anne, Countess of Hopetoun, *e d* of Arthur Leveson; two *s* and two step *s*. *Educ:* Eton. Stockbroker, Credit Lyonnais Securities (formerly Laing & Cruickshank), 1980–2004. Dir, Shore Capital Stockbrokers Ltd, 2004–13. Non-exec. Dir, Cluff Natural Resources, 2012–. DL E Sussex, 2006. *Heir:* *s* Lord Buckhurst, *qv*. *Address:* Buckhurst Park, Withyham, E Sussex TN7 4BL; 21 Bourne Street, SW1W 8JR. *Clubs:* White's, Turf.

See also Hon. T. G. Sackville.

DELAY, Thomas Auguste Read, CEng; Chief Executive, Carbon Trust, since 2001; *b* London, 15 April 1959; *s* of late Francis and Jill Delay; *m* 1990, Valerie; two *s*. *Educ:* Univ. of Southampton (BSc Mech. Engrg 1981); INSEAD, Fontainebleau (MBA 1988). CEng, MIMechE 1985. Engrg/Ops Manager, Shell Djibouti, 1982–85; Project Engr, Shell UK, 1985–87; Sales/Mktg Manager, Shell Lubricants, 1988–90; Planning Manager, Shell UK, 1990–92; Gen. Manager, Pizo Shell, Gabon, 1992–96; Mgt Consultant, McKinsey & Co., 1996–98; Principal, A. T. Kearney, 1999–2001. *Recreations:* looking for powder snow, Surrey walks in my 1977 Fiat Spyder, cooking pasta, playing a reasonable game of tennis. *Address:* c/o The Carbon Trust, 4th Floor, Dorset House, 27–45 Stamford Street, SE1 9NT. *T:* (020) 7170 7000. *E:* tom.delay@carbontrust.com.

DELGADO, Ana Irene; Ambassador of Panama to the Court of St James's, and concurrently Ambassador to Iceland and the Republic of Ireland, 2011–14; Permanent Representative of Panama to International Maritime Organization, since 2011; *b* Panama, 18 April; *d* of Hernán Delgado and Irene de Delgado. *Educ:* French Inst., Panama; French Inst. Alliance Française, Paris; Colegio las Esclavas del Sagrado Corazón de Jesus; Beaver Coll., Pennsylvania; S Bend, Indiana Lang. Inst.; Univ. of Delaware; Florida State Univ. (BSc Internat. Affairs 2004); Santa Maria La Antigua Univ., Panama (BSc Law and Political Scis *summa cum laude* 2004); New York Univ. (Advanced Professional Cert. Law and Business 2006; Graduate of Yr, 2012); New York Univ. Sch. of Law (LLM 2006). Ed., Internat. Law and Policy Jl, Univ. of NY, 2005–06. Gen. Manager, Radio Emporium, Radio Gp integrated by Fabulosa Estero, Tropi Q, Power92 and Radio Ancon, 2003–05; Partner, Solis, Endara, Delgado and Guevara, 2006–. Member, Board of Directors: Latin America and Caribbean Friendship with People's Republic of China Fedn, 2009–; Panamanian Assoc. of Friendship with China, 2007–09 (Sec.; Vice Pres., 2011–); Panamanian Bar Assoc., 2007–09; (Counsel) Panama Chamber of Commerce and Industries, 2009–. Advr, Legal Affairs Cttee, Panamanian Assoc. of Business Execs, 2009–. Second Vice-Pres., IMO Assembly; Dir, Nat. and internat. cos related to trade and industry. Mem., Bd of Govs, World Maritime Univ., 2012–. *Publications:* contribs to Univ. mag., Cocuyo Child Mag., Panama. *Recreations:* golf, running, equestrian (jumping and cross-country; Equestrian Invitational Champion, Harroway, 2013; 6th in Europe, Coupe d'Europe, Naples, 2013), fencing (épée), flamenco dance (Grupo Alandaluz, City of Panama, 2001–), classical ballet (Ruffo Cholewa Acad., 1986–89, Teresa Mann Acad., 1990–97, City of Panama). *Address:* Calle 50 Edificio Solendeg, Panama. *T:* 81600828. *E:* anaidelgado@solendeg.com, anairene.delgado@gmail.com. *Clubs:* Royal Automobile, 5 Hertford Street, Lansdowne, HAC Saddle; Los Andes.

DELGADO, Prof. Maria Milagros, PhD; Professor and Director of Research, Royal Central School of Speech and Drama, University of London, since 2015; *b* London, 18 June 1965; *d* of Alfonso Delgado Alava and Severina Delgado (*née* González Pérez); *m* 1997, Henry Little; one *s*. *Educ:* St Peter's Comprehensive Sch., Huntingdon; University Coll. of Swansea (BA Spanish and Drama 1987); Univ. of Leeds (MA Theatre Studies 1988); Univ. of Newcastle upon Tyne (PhD 1994). Special Lectr in Drama, Univ. of Hull, 1988–89; Lectr, 1993–96, Sen. Lectr, 1996–97, in Drama, Manchester Metropolitan Univ.; Lectr, 1997–2000, Sen. Lectr, 2000–01, Reader, 2002–04, in Theatre Arts, Prof. of Theatre and Screen Arts, 2003–15, QMUL. George Watson Fellow, Univ. of Qld, 2013. Ed., Contemp. Th. Rev., 2003–; Member, Editorial Board: Theatre Forum, 1999–; Western Eur. Stages, 2004–12; Stychomythia, 2008–12; Don Galán, 2010–; Episkenion, 2012–; Eur. Stages, 2013–. Prog. Advr, BFI London Film Fest., 1997–; film programming and curatorial work for London Spanish Film Fest. and London Argentine Film Fest. Chair, Sub-panel 35 Music, Drama, Dance and Performing Arts, REF 2014, 2010–14. Arts and Humanities Research Council: Chm., Fellowships Panel, 2013; Member: Strategic Reviewers' Gp, 2011–13; Peer Rev. Coll., 2004–05, 2009–13; Res. Panel 7 (Music and Performing Arts), 2005–08); BGP2 Exp. of Interest Panel, 2012; BGP2 Panel, 2013; Mem., Expert Adv. Gp for REF 2009, Res. and Knowledge Exchange Strategic Adv. Cttee, 2015–, HEFCE. Artistic and Quality Assessor, Arts Council England, 2010–. Mem., Adv. Panel, Leverhulme Trust, 2010–. Chm. Bd, Actors Touring Co., 2009–; Mem., Bd of Dirs, People's Palace Projects, 1999–2004. Expert Mentor, Emerging Legacy Leaders East Prog., Legacy List, 2015. Mem., Res. Grants Panel, Portuguese Foundn for Sci. and Technol., 2010–11. Freelance critic and cultural commentator, BBC, Sight & Sound and other nat. and internat. media. Member, Jury: Nominating Panel, Rolex Mentor and Protegée Scheme, 2002; Buenos Aires Internat. Fest. of Ind. Cinema Comp., 2011. Founder Mem., Theatre and Performance Res. Assoc., 2003 (Life Mem. 2013). FRSA. Hon. Life Mem., Standing Conf. of Univ. Drama Depts, 2015. Premi Joan B. Cendrós, 2008; Excellence in Editing Award, Assoc. for Theatre in Higher Educn, 2013. Encomienda, Orden de Isabel la Católica (Spain), 2003. *Publications:* (trans.) Valle-Inclán: Plays One, 1993, rev. edn 1997; Other Spanish Theatres: erasure and inscription on the Twentieth-Century Spanish stage, 2003; Federico García Lorca, 2008; Otro teatro español: supresión e inscripción en la escena española de los siglos XX y XXI, 2015; edited jointly: In Contact with the Gods?: directors talk theatre, 1996; Teatro Contemporaneo d'autore: Peter Sellars, 1999; Diálogos no

Palco: 26 diretores falam sobre Teatro, 1999; Conducting a Life: reflections on the theatre of Maria Irene Fornes, 1999; The Paris Jigsaw: internationalism and the city's stages, 2002; Theatre in Crisis?: performance manifestos for a new century, 2002; Bernard-Marie Koltès: Plays Two, 2004; Contemporary European Theatre Directors, 2010; A History of Theatre in Spain, 2010; Spanish Cinema 1973–2010: auteurism, politics, landscape and memory, 2013; contrib. articles to learned jls. *Recreations:* theatre, cinema, reading, watching football, cooking, travel, Scandinavian crime drama, dinner table discussions, the family cat, music. *Address:* Royal Central School of Speech and Drama, University of London, Eton Avenue, NW3 3HY. *E:* maria.delgado@cssd.ac.uk.

DE L'ISLE, 2nd Viscount *cr* 1956; **Philip John Algernon Sidney,** MBE 1977; Baron De L'Isle and Dudley 1835; Bt of Castle Goring, 1806; Bt of Penshurst Place, 1818; Lord-Lieutenant of Kent, since 2011 (Vice Lord-Lieutenant, 2002–11); *b* 21 April 1945; *s* of 1st Viscount De L'Isle, VC, KG, GCMG, GCVO, PC and Hon. Jacqueline Vereker (*d* 1962), *o d* of Field-Marshal 6th Viscount Gort, VC, GCB, CBE, DSO, MVO, MC; *S* father, 1991; *m* 1980, Isobel Tresyllian, *y d* of Sir Edmund Compton, GCB, KBE; one *s* one *d*. *Educ:* Tabley House; Mons OCS; RMA Sandhurst. Commnd Grenadier Guards, 1966. Served BAOR, UKLF, NI, Belize and Sudan at Regtl Duty; GSO3 Ops/SD HQ 3 Inf. Bde, 1974–76; retired 1979. Landowner, 1979–. Member: H of L Adv. Panel on Works of Art, 1994–97; Lord Chancellor's Adv. Council on Nat. Records and Archives, 2004–09. Chm., Kent County Cttee, CLA, 1983–85. Chm., Canterbury Cathedral Trust Fund, 2007–. Vice-President: SE RFCA, 2011–; RE Mus. Foundn, 2011–; President: RBL Industries, 2011–; Assoc. of Men of Kent and Kentish Men, 2012–; St John's Kent Priory Gp, 2012–; Patron: Action with Communities in Rural Kent, 2011–; Kent Br., Army Benevolent Fund, 2011–; City of Canterbury Shrievalty Assoc., 2011–; Friends of Kent Churches, 2011–; Kent Community Foundn, 2011–; Kent People's Trust; RBL Kent, 2011–; St John's Ambulance Kent, 2011–12; SSAFA (formerly SSAFA Forces Help) Kent, 2011–; RE Mus. Foundn, 2011–13; Vice Patron, South of England Agricl Soc., 2007–; Trustee: Rochester Cathedral Trust, 2011–; Nat. Army Mus. Foundn, 2013–. Hon. Colonel: 5th (V) Bn, Princess of Wales's Royal Regt, 1992–99; Kent ACF, 2006–12. Freeman, City of London; Liveryman, Goldsmiths' Co. DL Kent, 1996. *Heir: s* Hon. Philip William Edmund Sidney, PhD, *b* 2 April 1985. *Address:* Penshurst Place, Penshurst, Tonbridge, Kent TN11 8DG. *T:* (01892) 870307, *Fax:* (01892) 870866. *E:* KentLL343@penshurstplace.com. *Clubs:* White's, Pratt's.

de LISLE, Timothy John March Phillipps; journalist, since 1979; *b* 25 June 1962; *s* of late Everard de Lisle and of Hon. Mary Rose de Lisle (*née* Peake); *m* 1991, Amanda Barford; one *s* one *d*. *Educ:* Sunningdale; Eton; Worcester Coll., Oxford (BA Hons). Freelance journalist, 1979–86, revs and features for LAM, Smash Hits, Harpers & Queen and The Observer; Founder, Undergraduate Tutors, 1982–86; The Daily Telegraph: diary reporter, 1986–87; chief rock critic, 1986–89; news reporter, 1987; feature writer, 1987–89; arts editor, The Times, 1989; Weekend editor, The Daily Telegraph, 1989–90; Independent on Sunday: cricket correspondent, 1990–91; arts editor, 1991–95; freelance, 1995–: features: Independent on Sunday and Daily Telegraph, 1995–98; The Guardian G2, 2004–07; cricket column: Independent, 1995–96; 1999–2003; Evening Standard, 1997–98; The Times, 2004–06; rock column, Mail on Sunday, 1999–; Wisden, 1996–2003: Editor: Wisden Cricket Monthly, 1996–2000 (Editor of the Year, Special Interest Mags, British Soc. of Mag. Editors, 1999); Wisden Online, 1999–2002; Wisden Cricketers' Almanack, 2003; Intelligent Life, 2008– (Dep. Ed., 2007–08) (Editor of the Year, Lifestyle Mags, British Soc. of Mag. Editors, 2010); founder and consultant editor, Wisden Asia Cricket mag., 2001–05; columnist, Cricinfo.com, 2006–09. *Publications:* (ed) Lives of the Great Songs, 1994, rev. edn 1995; Young Wisden, 2007, 2nd edn 2011. *Recreations:* watching football, opening emails. *Address:* c/o Mail on Sunday, 2 Derry Street, W8 5TS. *E:* tim.delisle@gmail.com. *Clubs:* Eton Ramblers; Cricket Writers'.

DELL, Prof. Anne, CBE 2009; PhD; FRS 2002; FMedSci; Professor of Carbohydrate Biochemistry, Imperial College London, since 1991; *b* 11 Sept. 1950; *d* of Edgar Dell and Elneth Dell; one *d*. *Educ:* Univ. of Western Australia (BSc); King's Coll., Cambridge (PhD 1975). Imperial College: Lectr, 1979–86; Reader, 1986–91; Hd, Dept of Biochemistry, 1999–2001. BBSRC Professorial Fellow, 2002–07. FMedSci 2008. *Recreations:* theatre, gardening, reading, walking. *Address:* Division of Molecular Biosciences, Imperial College London, SW7 2AZ. *T:* (020) 7594 5219, *Fax:* (020) 7225 0458. *E:* a.dell@imperial.ac.uk.

DELL, David Michael, CB 1986; Deputy Secretary, Department of Trade and Industry, 1983–91; *b* 30 April 1931; *s* of late Montague Roger Dell and Aimée Gabrielle Dell; partner, 1971, Eliseo Cabrejos (*d* 1995), Lima, Peru. *Educ:* Rugby Sch.; Balliol Coll., Oxford (MA). 2nd Lieut Royal Signals, Egypt and Cyprus, 1954–55. Admiralty, 1955; MoD, 1960; Min. of Technol., 1965; DTI, 1970; DoI, 1974, Under Sec., 1976; Regl Dir, Yorks and Humberside, DTI, 1976–78; Dir, EIB, 1984–87; Chief Exec., BOTB, 1987–91. Dir, Nesbit Evans Gp, 1991–93. Mem., British-Peruvian Trade & Investment Gp, 1997–2001. Mem., London Diocesan Conf., 1968–69. Chm., Christ Church Bentinck Sch., 1979–92. Sec., London Numismatic Club, 1995–97; Mem. Council, Oxford Soc., 1995–2001; Dep. Chm., Anglo-Peruvian Soc., 2005–07. *Clubs:* Oriental, Royal Automobile.

DELL, Michael S.; Chairman, since 1984, Chief Executive Officer, 1984–2004 and since 2007, Dell Inc. (formerly PCs Ltd, then Dell Computer Corporation); *b* Houston, Texas, 23 Feb. 1965; *s* of Alexander and Lorraine Dell; *m* 1989, Susan Lieberman; four *c* (incl. twins). *Educ:* Univ. of Texas. Founder, PCs Ltd, 1984; co. renamed Dell Computer Corp., 1987. Member: Computer Systems Policy Proj.; The Business Council; Member Board: US Chamber of Commerce; World Econ. Forum. *Publications:* Direct From Dell: strategies that revolutionized an industry, 1999. *Address:* Dell Inc., 1 Dell Way, Round Rock, TX 78682, USA.

DELL, Dame Miriam (Patricia), ONZ 1993; DBE 1980 (CBE 1975); JP (NZ); Hon. President, International Council of Women, 1986–88 (President, 1979–86; Vice-President, 1976–79); *b* 14 June 1924; *d* of Gerald Wilfred Matthews and Ruby Miriam Crawford; *m* 1946, Richard Kenneth Dell; four *d*. *Educ:* Epsom Girls Grammar Sch.; Univ. of Auckland (BA); Auckland Teachers' Coll. (Teachers' Cert. (Secondary Sch.)). Teaching, 1945–47, 1957–58 and 1961–71. Nat. Pres., Nat. Council of Women, 1970–74 (Vice-Pres., 1967–70); Chm., Cttee on Women, NZ, 1974–81; Chm., Envmt and Conservation Orgns of NZ, 1989–94; Chm., 1993 Suffrage Centennial Year Trust, 1991–94; Chair, Landmarks Project - Celebrating Women Trust, 1999–2010. Member: Nat. Develt Council, 1969–74; Cttee of Inquiry into Equal Pay, 1971–72; Nat. Commn for UNESCO, 1974–83; Social Security Appeal Authority, 1974–99; Anglican Provincial Commn on Ordination of Women, 1974; Project Develt Bd, Mus. of NZ, 1988–92; Dep. Chm., Wellington Conservation Bd, 1990–98; Nat. Convener, Internat. Women's Year, 1975; Co-ordinator, Internat. Council of Women Develt Prog., 1988–91; Sec., Inter-Church Council on Public Affairs, 1986–89 (Chm., 1982–86); Convener, Public Affairs Unit, Anglican Church of NZ, 1988–92. JP NZ 1975. Jubilee Medal, 1977; NZ Commemoration Medal, 1990; NZ Suffrage Centennial Medal, 1993. *Publications:* Role of Women in National Development, 1970; numerous articles in popular and house magazines, on role and status of women. *Recreations:* gardening, reading, handcrafts, beachcombing. *Address:* 137 Te Maire Road, Kahutara, Featherston 5771, New Zealand.

DELLER, Jeremy; artist; *b* London, 1966. *Educ:* Dulwich Coll.; Courtauld Inst. of Art (BA Art Hist. 1988); Sussex Univ. (MA Art Hist. 1992). Curator, producer and dir of projects, incl. orchestrated events, films and pubns. *Works include:* Acid Brass (collaboration with Williams Fairey Brass Band), 1997; (with A. Kane) Folk Archive, 2000; The Battle of Orgreave (filmed re-enactment), 2001; Social Parade (video), Five Memorials, This is US (CD), 2003; Memory Bucket (mixed-media installation), 2003 (Turner Prize, 2004); group exhibn, New British Art 2000: Intelligence, Tate Britain, 2000; Joy in People (retrospective), Hayward Gall., 2012; Sacrilege (inflatable Stonehenge), Glasgow, then UK tour, 2012; English Magic, Turner Contemporary, Margate, 2014. Trustee: Artangel, 2005– (Chm., 2015); Tate Gall., 2007–11 (Mem., Collection Cttee); Mem. Council, Tate Liverpool. *Address:* c/o Tate Britain, Millbank, SW1P 4RG.

DELLOW, Sir John (Albert), Kt 1990; CBE 1985 (OBE 1979); DL; Deputy Commissioner, Metropolitan Police, 1987–91; *b* 5 June 1931; *s* of Albert Reginald and Lily Dellow; *m* 1952, Heather Josephine Rowe; one *s* one *d*. *Educ:* William Ellis Sch., Highgate; Royal Grammar Sch., High Wycombe. Joined City of London Police, 1951; seconded Manchester City Police, 1966; Superintendent, Kent County Constabulary, 1966, Chief Supt, 1968; jssc 1969; Asst Chief Constable, Kent Co. Constabulary, 1969; Metropolitan Police: Deputy Assistant Commissioner: Traffic Planning, 1973; Personnel, 1975; No 2 Area, 1978; 'A' Dept Operations, 1979; Inspectorate, 1980; Assistant Commissioner: 'B' Dept, 1982; Crime, 1984; Asst Comr (Specialist Ops), 1985–87. Pres., ACPO, 1989–90 (Vice-Pres., 1988–89). Former Chairman: Metropolitan Police History Soc.; Metropolitan Police Climbing, Canoe, Rowing and Heavy Boat Sections; Cdre, Metropolitan Police Sailing Club. Member Council: London Dist, Order of St John of Jerusalem, 1988–96; RUSI, 1991–95. DL Greater London, 1991. *Publications:* contrib. RUSI Defence Studies series and other jls. *Recreations:* walking, history, listening to wireless, water colour painting.

DELORS, Jacques Lucien Jean; President, Council for Employment, Income and Social Cohesion, 2000–09; President, Commission of the European Economic Community, 1985–95; *b* Paris, 20 July 1925; *s* of Louis Delors and Jeanne (*née* Rigal); *m* 1948, Marie Lephaille; one *d* (one *s* decd). *Educ:* Paris Univ.; Dip., Centre for Higher Studies of Banking. Joined Banque de France, 1945; in office of Chief of Securities Dept, 1950–62, and in Sect. for the Plan and Investments, Conseil Economique et Social, 1959–61; Chief of Social Affairs, Gen. Commissariat of Plan Monnet, 1962–68; Gen. Sec. for Perm. Trng and Social Promotion, 1968; Gen. Sec., Interministerial Cttee for Professional Educn, 1969–73; Mem., Gen. Council, Banque de France, 1973–79, and Dir, on leave of absence, 1973. Special Advr on Social and Cultural Affairs to Prime Minister, 1969–72. Socialist Party Spokesman on internat. econ. matters, 1976–81; Minister of the Economy and Finance, 1981–83; Minister of Economy, Finance and Budget, 1983–84. Mem., European Parlt, 1979–81 (Pres., Econ. and Financial Cttee, 1979–81). Mayor of Clichy, 1983–84. Pres., Internat. Commn on Educn for the Twenty First Century, UNESCO, 1993–96. Associate Prof., Univ. of Paris-Dauphine, 1973–79. Dir, Work and Society Res. Centre, 1975–79; President: Bd of Admin, College of Europe, Bruges, 1996–2000; Notre Europe, 1996–2004. Founder, Club Echange et Projets, 1974–79. Hon. doctorates from 29 univs. Awards and honours from 15 countries. *Publications:* Les indicateurs sociaux, 1971; Changer, 1975; (jtly) En sortir ou pas, 1985; La France par L'Europe, 1988 (Our Europe: the community and national development, 1992); Le Nouveau Concert Européen, 1992; L'unité d'un homme, 1994; Combats pour l'Europe, 1996; Mémoires, 2004; L'Europe tragique et magnifique, 2006; Investir dans le social, 2009; essays and articles.

DELPY, Prof. David Thomas, CBE 2014; DSc; FMedSci; FRS 1999; FREng; Chair, Defence Scientific Advisory Council, Ministry of Defence, since 2014; Chief Executive, Engineering and Physical Sciences Research Council, 2007–14; *b* 11 Aug. 1948; *s* of R. M. Delpy and M. H. Delpy; *m* 1972, Margaret E. Kimber; two *s*. *Educ:* Heaton Grammar Sch., Newcastle upon Tyne; Brunel Univ. (BSc 1st Cl. Hons Applied Phys); UCL (DSc Med. Phys London). Technical Mgt Services, Darchem Ltd, Darlington, 1970–71; Non-clinical Lectr, UCL Med. Sch., 1971–76; University College Hospital, London: Sen. Physicist, 1976–82; Principal Physicist, 1982–86; University College London: Sen. Lectr, 1986–91; Hd, Dept of Med. Phys and Bioengrg, 1992–99; Hamamatsu Prof. of Med. Photonics, 1991–2007; Vice Provost, 1999–2007. Mem., BBSRC, 2004–07. FMedSci 2000; FREng 2002. *Publications:* numerous scientific papers. *Recreations:* work, classical music, gardening.

DELVIN, Lord; title borne by eldest son of Earl of Westmeath, *qv*; not at present used.

DELVIN, Dr David George; television and radio broadcaster, writer and doctor; Director, The Medical Information Service, since 1995; *b* 28 Jan. 1939; *s* of William Delvin, Ayrshire and Elizabeth Falvey, Co. Kerry; *m* 1st, Kathleen Sears, SRN, SCM; two *s* one *d*; 2nd, Christine Webber. *Educ:* St Dunstan's Coll.; King's Coll., Univ. of London; King's Coll. Hosp. (MB, BS 1962; psychol medicine, forensic medicine and public health prizes, 1962). LRCP, MRCS 1962; MRCGP 1974; DObstRCOG 1965; DCH 1966; DipVen, Soc. of Apothecaries, 1977; FPA Cert. 1972; FPA Instructing Cert. 1974. Dir, Hosp. Medicine Film Unit, 1968–69. Vice-Chm., 1982–87, Chm., 2007–10, Med. Journalists' Assoc.; General Medical Council: Elected Mem., 1979–94; Member: Health Cttee 1980–86; Professional Conduct Cttee, 1987–94; Standards & Ethics Cttee, 1992–94. Member: Educn Cttee, Back Pain Assoc., 1983–87; Faculty of Family Planning, RCOG, 1993–; Council, Section of Sexual Health, RSM, 2008–. Medical Consultant: FPA, 1981–90; Nat. Assoc. of Family Planning Doctors, 1990–93; Medical Advisor to: various BBC and ITV progs, 1974–; NetDoctor website, 1999–. Med. Editor, General Practitioner, 1972–90; Sen. Editor, The Lancet, 1996–98; Chm., Editorial Boards of Medeconomics, Monthly Index of Med. Specialities, and MIMS Magazine, 1988–91; Mem. Editorial Adv. Bd, British Jl of Family Planning, 1994–2002; Dr Jekyll Columnist in World Medicine, 1973–82; Columnist, BMA News Review, 1992–98; Med. Columnist, Glasgow Herald, 1995–97. Fellow, Faculty of Reproductive Health Care, RCOG, 2005. Cert. of Special Merit, Med. Journalists' Assoc., 1974 and (jtly) 1975. American Medical Writers' Assoc. Best Book Award, 1976; Consumer Columnist of the Year Award, 1986; Tony Thistlethwaite Book Award, MJA, 2010. Médaille de la Ville de Paris (échelon argent), 1983. Mem., Mastermind Club. *Publications:* The Good Sex Guide, 1994, and other books, articles, TV and radio scripts, short stories, humorous pieces, medical films and videos; papers on hypertension and contraception in BMJ etc. *Recreations:* athletics, opera, orienteering, scuba-diving, hang-gliding (retired hurt). *Address:* 10 Harley Street, W1G 9PF. *Club:* Royal Society of Medicine.

DEMACK, (James) David; a Judge of the Upper Tribunal (Tax and Chancery Chamber), 2009–14 (a Special Commissioner of Income Tax, 2000–09; Vice-President for England and Wales, VAT and Duties Tribunals, 2001–09); *b* 1 March 1942; *s* of James and Edith Annie Demack; *m* 1969, Ruth Cicely Hosker. *Educ:* Balshaw's Grammar Sch., Leyland, Lancs; Manchester Univ.; Manchester Poly.; Salford Poly. CTA (FTII 1982). Admitted solicitor, 1965; solicitor, private practice, 1965–93. Mem., 1986–92, pt-time Chm., 1990–93, full-time Chm., 1993–2001, VAT Tribunals, subseq. VAT and Duties Tribunals. Mem. UK Panel, Adv. Commn under EU Arbitration Convention, EU Jt Transfer Pricing Forum, 2002–14. Steward, York Minster, 1978–. Trustee, Cuerden Valley Park Trust, 1998–2007. *Recreations:* rehabilitation of injured and disabled wild birds of prey, walking, golf, classical music, railways, all things Swiss. *E:* jddemack@yahoo.co.uk. *Clubs:* Royal Over-Seas League; Leyland Golf.

de MAIZIÈRE, Dr Thomas; Member (CDU/CSU), Bundestag, since 2009; Federal Minister of the Interior, 2009–11 and since 2013; *b* Bonn, 21 Jan. 1954; *s* of Ulrich de Maizière and Eva de Maizière; *m* 1985, Martina Willeke; two *s* one *d*. *Educ:* Bonn; studied law and history, Albert-Ludwigs Univ., Freiburg and Wilhelms Univ., Münster (Dr Law 1986). Chief of Policy Br., Berlin Senate Chancellery, 1985–89; State Sec. of Educn, Mecklenburg-Western Pomerania, 1990–94; Hd, Mecklenburg-Western Pomerania State

Chancellery, 1994–98; State Minister and Hd, Saxon State Chancellery, 1999; State of Saxony: Minister of Finance, 2001–02, of Justice, 2002–04, of the Interior, 2004–05; Federal Minister and Hd, Federal Chancellery, 2005–09; Federal Minister of Defence, 2011–13. Hon. Prof., Univ. of Dresden, 2010. *Address:* Deutscher Bundestag, Platz der Republik 1, 11011 Berlin, Germany. *T:* (30) 22773625. *E:* thomas.demaiziere@bundestag.de.

de MARCHANT et d'ANSEMBOURG, Count Jan Mark Vladimir Anton; Ambassador of the Netherlands to the Court of St James's, 2003–06; *b* 9 Oct. 1941; *s* of Count François de Marchant et d'Ansembourg and Fernandine, Countess de Bombelles; *m* 1979, Countess Nicole de Marchant et d'Ansembourg-Rougé; (one *s* decd). *Educ:* Leyden Univ. (MA Law). Lieut, military service, 1961–63; diplomatic postings, Damascus, NY, The Hague, 1970–82; Counsellor, Paris, 1982; Dep. Hd of Delegation, CSCE Meeting, Vienna, 1986; Dir, UN Dept, Min. of Foreign Affairs, 1989; Dep. Permanent Rep., Permanent Mission to NY, 1990–94; Dir European Dept, Min. of Foreign Affairs, 1994–96; Ambassador at large, 1996; Dep. Political Dir, 1997; Ambassador to Spain, 1998–2003. Officer, Order of Orange Nassau (Netherlands), 1994; Commander: Cross of St Olav (Norway), 1996; Ordre du Mérite (France), 1997; Grand Cross, Isabella la Católica (Spain), 2001. *Address:* 9 rue Colbert, 7800 Versailles, France. *Club:* Haagsche (The Hague).

DEMARCO, Prof. Richard, CBE 2007 (OBE 1985); RSW; Professor of European Cultural Studies, Kingston University, 1993–2000, now Professor Emeritus; *b* 9 July 1930; *s* of Carmine Demarco and Elizabeth (*née* Fusco); *m* 1957, Anne Muckle. *Educ:* Holy Cross Academy, Edinburgh; Edinburgh College of Art. National Service, KOSB and RAEC, 1954–56. Art Master, Duns Scotus Academy, Edinburgh, 1956–67; Co-Founder, Traverse Theatre Club; Vice-Chm. and Director, Traverse Art Gall., 1963–67; Dir, Richard Demarco Gall., Melville Crescent, Edinburgh, 1966–92, appointed by co-founders John Martin, Andrew Elliott and James Walker; introduced contemporary visual arts into official Edinburgh Festival programme with Edinburgh Open 100 Exhibn, 1967; introduced work of 330 internat. artists to UK, mainly through Edinburgh Fest. exhibns, from Canada, 1968, W Germany, 1970, Romania, 1971, Poland, 1972 and 1979, France, 1973, Austria, 1973, Yugoslavia, 1975, Aust. and NZ, 1984, Netherlands, 1990; incl. Joseph Beuys, 1970, Gunther Uecker, 1991, and Tadeusz Kantor's Cricot Theatre, with prodns of The Water Hen, 1972, Lovelies and Dowdies, 1973, The Dead Class, 1976. Has presented, 1969–, annual programmes of theatre, music and dance prodns, incl. the Freehold Company's Antigone, 1970; Dublin Project Company's On Baille Strand, 1977; Mladen Materic's Obala Theatre from Sarajevo, 1988 and 1989; Teatro Settimo from Turin, and Grupa Chwilowa from Lublin, 1991; Yvette Bozsik Theatre from Budapest, 1993; prod Macbeth for Edinburgh Fest., on Inchcolm Is, 1988 and 1989. Director: Sean Connery's Scottish Internat. Educn Trust, 1972–74; Edinburgh Arts annual summer sch. and expedns, 1972–92; Artistic Advr, Eur. Youth Parlt, 1992–. Has directed annual exhibn prog. with Special Unit, HM Prison, Barlinnie, with partic. reference to sculpture of James Boyle, 1974–80; directed Edinburgh Fest. Internat. Confs, Towards the Housing of Art in the 21st Century, 1983, Art and the Human Environment, 1984 (also at Dublin Fest.). Was subject of film, Walkabout Edinburgh, dir. by Edward McConnell, 1970; acted in feature films: Long Shot, 1978; That Sinking Feeling, 1980; subject of TV film, The Demarco Dimension, 1987. Has broadcast regularly on television and radio, 1966–; has lectured in over 150 univs, art colls, schools, art galls; as water-colour painter and printmaker is represented in over 1600 public and private collections, incl. Nat. Gall. of Modern Art of Scotland, V&A Museum, Scottish Arts Council; retrospective exhibn, Richard Demarco at 80: a life in pictures, Royal Scottish Acad., 2010. Hon. Vis. Prof. of Fine Art, Dundee Univ., 2007. Trustee: Kingston Demarco European Art Foundn, 1993–; Green Cross (UK), 1999–; Edinburgh Coll. Develt Trust, 2014–; Vice-Pres., Kingston Th. Trust, 2001. Contributing Editor, Studio International, 1982–. SSA 1964; RWSScot 1966. Mem., AICA, 1992; FRSA 1998. Hon. FRIAS 1991; HRSA 2001; Hon. Fellow, Inst. of Contemp. Scotland, 2002; Hon. RWS 2006. Hon. Fellow: Edinburgh Coll. of Art, 2008; Rose Bruford Coll. of Th. and Performance, 2010; Southampton Solent Univ., 2011. Hon. DFA: Atlanta Coll. of Art, 1993; Wroclaw Acad. of Fine Art, 2006; DUniv Stirling, 2007. Gold Order of Merit, Polish People's Republic, 1976; Order of the Cavaliere della Repubblica d'Italia, 1987; Chevalier de l'Ordre des Arts et des Lettres (France), 1991; Gloria Artis Medal (Poland), 2007; Grand Cross, Order of Merit (Germany), 2010; Bene Merito Medal (Poland), 2010; Gloria Artis Medal (Poland), 2012; Order of Cultural Merit (Romania), 2012; Eur. Citizen of the Year, EP, 2013; Edinburgh Award, City of Edinburgh, 2013. *Publications:* The Artist as Explorer, 1978; The Road to Meikle Seggie, 1978; A Life in Pictures, 1994; (jtly) The Demarco Collection and Archive: an introduction, 2009. *Recreations:* exploring: the small and secret spaces in townscape; cathedrals, abbeys, parish churches; coastlines and islands and The Road to Meikle Seggie. *Address:* Demarco European Art Foundation, 11 Upper Cramond Court, Edinburgh EH4 6RQ; 23A Lennox Street EH4 1PY. *T:* (0131) 343 2124. *Club:* Scottish Arts (Hon. Mem.) (Edinburgh).

de MAULEY, 7th Baron *cr* 1838; **Rupert Charles Ponsonby,** TD 1988; *b* 30 June 1957; *s* of Hon. Thomas Maurice Ponsonby, TD and of Maxine Henrietta Ponsonby (*née* Thellusson); *S* uncle, 2002; *m* 2002, Hon. Lucinda Katherine Fanshawe Royle, *d* of Baron Fanshawe of Richmond, KCMG. *Educ:* Eton. FCA 1990 (ACA 1980). Director: Samuel Montagu & Co. Ltd, 1990–93; Standard Chartered Merchant Bank Asia Ltd, Singapore, 1994–99 (Man. Dir, 1996–99); FixIT Worldwide Ltd, 1999–2006. CO, The Royal Wessex Yeomanry (TA), 2003–04 (commnd, 1976). Elected Mem., H of L, March 2005; Opposition Whip and Opposition BERR (formerly DTI) spokesman, 2005–09; Opposition spokesman for Cabinet Office, 2006–08, DIUS, 2008–09; a Lord in Waiting (Govt Whip), 2010–12; govt spokesman for Home Office, 2010, for HM Treasury, BIS and DEFRA, 2010–12, for DWP, 2011–12; Parly Under-Sec. of State, DEFRA, 2012–15. *Heir: b* Hon. (Ashley) George Ponsonby [*b* 17 Nov. 1959; *m* 2006, Mrs Camilla Gordon Lennox (*née* Pilkington)].

DEMBRI, Mohamed-Salah; Ambassador of Algeria to the Court of St James's, and also to Ireland, 2005–10; *b* 30 Jan. 1938; *s* of Hardjem Dembri and Zelikha Dembri (*née* Bendaoud); *m* 1960, Monique Paule Alleaume; one *s* one *d*. *Educ:* Sorbonne Univ. (BA; Higher Educn Dip.). Secretary General: Min. of Higher Educn and Scientific Res., 1973–79; Min. of Foreign Affairs, 1979–82; Ambassador to Canada, 1982–84; Sec. Gen., Min. of Labour and Social Affairs, 1988–89; Official Rep. (Special Advr) to Hd of Govt on political and diplomatic issues, 1989–91; Ambassador to Hellenic Republic, 1991–93; Minister of Foreign Affairs, 1993–96; Ambassador to UN, Geneva, 1996–2004 and (non-resident), to Holy See, 1997–2004. Jubilee Medal (Bulgaria), 1979; Kt, Nat. Order of Chad, 1994; Gt Cross, Order of St Gregory the Gt (Vatican), 1999; Grand Officer, Nat. Order of Mono (Togo), 2002. *Publications:* contribs to Algerian Arts and Human Scis Rev., Algerian Notebooks of Comparative Lit., and publications of Algerian Inst. of Global Strategy and UN; papers on Euro-Mediterranean relations and on St Augustine. *Recreations:* reading, cinema, theatre, sight-seeing, tourism. *Address:* 9, 17[d] Ihabbēne Street, El-Biar, Algiers, Algeria.

DEMETRIOU, Marie-Eleni Eliza; QC 2012; *b* Brighton, 13 Feb. 1972; *d* of George and Doreen Demetriou; *m* 2009, Neil Richard Calver, *qv*; one *s* one *d*. *Educ:* St Hilda's Coll., Oxford (BA 1993; BCL 1994). Called to the Bar, Middle Temple, 1995, Bencher, 2013; in practice as barrister, 1995–; Référendaire, Eur. Court of Justice, 1999–2002. Mem., Attorney Gen.'s A Panel, 2009–12. Vis. Fellow, KCL, 2008–. *Publications:* (jtly) Sports Law, 1999, 2nd edn 2012; (with D. Anderson) References to the European Court, 2nd edn 2002. *Recreations:* family, wine, reading novels, opera, Tottenham Hotspur Football Club. *Address:* Brick Court Chambers, 7–8 Essex Street, WC2R 3LD. *T:* (020) 7379 3550.

De MEYER, Prof. Arnoud Cyriel Leo, PhD; President, Singapore Management University, since 2010; *b* 12 April 1954; *s* of Eugeen De Meyer and Emma (*née* De Winter). *Educ:* Univ. of Ghent (MSc Electrical Engrg; PhD Mgt 1983). Institut Européen d'Administration des Affaires (INSEAD): Prof. of Technol. Mgt, 1983–2006; Associate Dean for Exec. Educn, 1992–99; Dir Gen., Euro-Asia Centre, 1995–99; Akzo Nobel Fellow in Strategic Mgt, 1997–2006; Dean, Campus in Asia, 1999–2002; Dep. Dean, then Dean of Admin and Ext. Relns, 2001–06; Dir, Judge Business Sch., Univ. of Cambridge, 2006–10. Pt-time Prof., De Vlerick Leuven Gent Mgt Sch., Univ. of Ghent, 1988–2004. Vis. Prof., Grad. Sch. of Business Admin, Waseda Univ., Tokyo, 1999–2000. Board Member: Option Internat., NV, 1997; Dassault Systèmes, 2005–; Temasek Mgt Services Pte Ltd. *Publications:* (jtly) Benchmarking for Global Manufacturing, 1992; Creating Product Value: a strategic manufacturing perspective, 1992; (jtly) The Bright Stuff, 2001; Belgique On Line: 30 propositions pour la e-Belgique de demain, 2002; (jtly) Global Future, The Next Challenge for Asian Business, 2005; (with S. Garg) Inspire to Innovate, Management of Innovation in Asia, 2005; (jtly) Managing the Unknown: a new approach to managing high uncertainty and risk in projects, 2006; (jtly) The Information Society in an Enlarged Europe, 2006; contrib. articles to jls incl. R&D Mgt, IEEE Trans on Engrg Mgt, Sloan Mgt Rev., Strategic Mgt Jl. *Address:* Singapore Management University, Administration Building, 81 Victoria Street, Singapore 188065.

DEMIDENKO, Nikolai Anatolyevich; concert pianist; *b* 1 July 1955; *s* of Anatoli Antonovich Demidenko and Olga Mikhailovna Demidenko; granted British citizenship, 1995; *m* 1994, Julia B. Dovgiallo; one *s* by a previous marriage. *Educ:* Gnessin Music Sch., Moscow; Moscow State Conservatoire. Professional début, 1975; British début, 1985; NY début, 2001. Teacher: Moscow State Conservatoire, 1979–84; Yehudi Menuhin Sch. of Music, 1990–95; Vis. Prof., Univ. of Surrey. 2nd prize, Montreal Piano Competition, 1976; 3rd prize, Moscow Tchaikovsky Competition, 1978. Has made numerous recordings. Hon. Dr Surrey, 2014. Gramophone Award, 1992; Classic CD Award, 1995. *Recreations:* photography, computing. *Address:* International Classical Artists, Dunstan House, 14a St Cross Street, EC1N 8XA.

de MILLE, His Honour Peter Noël; a Circuit Judge, 1992–2010 (Midland and Oxford Circuit, 1992–2002; South Eastern Circuit, 2002–10); *b* 19 Nov. 1944; *s* of late Noël James de Mille and Ailsa Christine de Mille (*née* Ogilvie); *m* 1977, Angela Mary Cooper; one *d*. *Educ:* Fettes Coll.; Trinity Coll., Dublin (BA, LLB). Called to the Bar, Inner Temple, 1968; a Recorder, 1987–92. *Recreations:* sailing, music, theatre. *Club:* Aldeburgh Yacht.

de MOL, John H.; Owner and Chief Creative Director, Talpa Media Group, since 2004; *b* The Hague, 24 April 1955; one *s*. Founder: John de Mol Produkties, 1978; Endemol Entertainment, 1994; Talpa Media Gp, 2004; developed progs incl. Big Brother, Deal or No Deal and The Voice. *Recreation:* golf. *Address:* Talpa Media Group, PO Box 154, 1250 AD Laren, Netherlands. *T:* (35) 5333333.

de MOLEYNS; *see* Daubeny de Moleyns, family name of Baron Ventry.

de MOLLER, June Frances; DL; Managing Director, Carlton Communications plc, 1993–99; *b* 25 June 1947; *m* 1st, 1967 (marr. diss. 1980); 2nd, 1996, John Robert Giles Crisp. *Educ:* Roedean; Hastings Coll.; Sorbonne Univ., Paris. Exec. Dir, Carlton Communications, 1983–99. Non-executive Director: Anglian Water plc, 1992–2000; Riverside Mental Health NHS Trust, 1992–96; Lynx Gp plc, 1999–2002; Cookson Gp plc, 1999–2004; British Telecommunications plc, 1999–2002; J. Sainsbury plc, 1999–2005; Archant (formerly Eastern Counties Newspapers Gp) Ltd, 1999–2011; London Merchant Securities plc, subseq. Derwent London plc, 2002–; Temple Bar Investment Trust plc, 2006–. Mem., Listed Cos Adv. Cttee, Stock Exchange, 1998–99. Mem., Adv. Bd, Judge Inst. for Management Studies, Cambridge, 1996–2004. Member Council: Aldeburgh Music (formerly Productions), 2000–10; UEA, 2002–11. Mem. Cttee, Home of Rest for Horses, 1999–2005. DL Suffolk, 2009. *Recreations:* reading, travelling, breeding Red Poll cows.

de MONTEBELLO, (Guy) Philippe (Lannes); Director, 1978–2008, and Chief Executive Officer, 1999–2008, Metropolitan Museum of Art, now Director Emeritus; Fiske Kimball Professor in the History and Culture of Museums, Institute of Fine Arts, New York University, since 2009; *b* 16 May 1936; *s* of Roger Lannes de Montebello and Germaine (*née* Croisset); *m* 1961, Edith Bradford Myles; two *s* one *d*. *Educ:* Harvard Coll. (BA *magna cum laude*); New York Univ., Inst. of Fine Arts (MA). Curatorial Asst, European Paintings, Metropolitan Mus. of Art, 1963; Asst Curator, Associate Curator, MMA, until 1969; Director, Museum of Fine Arts, Houston, Texas, 1969–74; Vice-Director: for Curatorial Affairs, MMA, Jan.–June 1974; for Curatorial and Educnl Affairs, 1974–77; Actg Dir, MMA, 1977–78. Gallatin Fellow, New York Univ., 1981. Schol. in Residence, Prado Mus., Madrid, 2009. Mem., Bd of Trustees, Musée d'Orsay, 2009–. Hon. LLD: Lafayette Coll., East Pa, 1979; Bard Coll., Annandale-on-Hudson, NY, 1981; Dartmouth Coll., 2004; Hon. DFA Iona Coll., New Rochelle, NY, 1982; Hon. DArts: Harvard, 2006; New York, 2007. Alumni Achievement Award, New York Univ., 1978; Nat. Medal of Arts (USA), 2003; Amigos del Museo del Prado Prize, 2004. Officier, Ordre Nat. de la Légion d'Honneur (France), 2005. *Publications:* Peter Paul Rubens, 1968; (with Martin Gayford) Rendez-vous with Art, 2014. *Club:* Knickerbocker (New York).

DEMPSEY, Andrew; *see* Dempsey, J. A.

DEMPSEY, Dr Anthony Michael; Headmaster, Tiffin School, 1988–2004; *b* 12 June 1944; *s* of Michael and Bertha Laura Dempsey; *m* 1970, Sandra Lynn Atkins; one *s*. *Educ:* Tiffin Sch.; Bristol Univ. (BSc, PhD). Chemistry Teacher, King's College Sch., 1969–73; Heathland School, Hounslow: Head of Sci., 1973–75; Head, Maths and Sci. Faculty, 1975–79; Feltham Community School: Dep. Head, 1979–82; Sen. Dep. Head, 1982–88. *Publications:* Visual Chemistry, 1983; Science Master Pack, 1985; contrib. to Nuffield Chemistry books; papers in carbohydrate res. *Recreations:* walking, travel, sport, church, industrial archaeology. *Address:* 63 Gilpin Crescent, Twickenham TW2 7BP. *T:* (020) 8898 2860.

DEMPSEY, (James) Andrew; independent exhibition curator and organiser, since 1996; *b* 17 Nov. 1942; *s* of James Dempsey, Glasgow; *m* 1st, 1966, Grace (marr. diss. 1998), *d* of Dr Ian MacPhail, Dumbarton; one *s* one *d*; 2nd, 2006, Catherine Emily Lampert, *qv*. *Educ:* Ampleforth Coll.; Glasgow Univ. Whistler Research Asst, Fine Art Dept, Univ. of Glasgow, 1963–65; exhibn work for art dept of Arts Council, 1966–71; Keeper, Dept of Public Relations, V&A, 1971–75; Asst Dir of Exhibitions, Arts Council of GB, 1975–87; Asst Dir, 1987–94, Associate Curator, 1994–96, Hayward Gall., S Bank Centre.

DEMPSEY, Lisa; *see* Markwell, L.

DEMPSEY, Michael Bernard, RDI 1994; Founder, Studio Dempsey, since 2008; *b* 25 July 1944; *s* of John Patrick Dempsey and Britannia May (*née* Thompson); *m* 1st, 1967, Sonja Green (marr. diss. 1988); two *s* one *d*; 2nd, 1989, Charlotte Antonia Richardson (marr. diss. 2008); three *d*. *Educ:* St Vincent RC Primary Sch., Dagenham; Bishop Ward RC Secondary Mod. Sch., Dagenham. Asst designer, Cheveron Studio, 1963–64; in-house designer, Bryan Colmer Artist Agent, 1964–65; freelance designer, 1965–66; Designer, Cato Peters O'Brien, 1966–68; Art Director: William Heinemann Publishers, 1968–74; William Collins Publishers, 1974–79; Founder Partner, Carroll & Dempsey Ltd, 1979–85; Partner, 1985–2007, Chm. and Creative Dir, 1993–2007, Carroll, Dempsey Thirkell Ltd, later CDT Design Ltd. Feature film title designer: The Duellists, 1977; Wetherby, 1985; Comrades, 1986; Blackeyes, 1987; Paris By Night, 1989; Strapless, 1990; Call it Night, 1990; Heading Home, 1991; The Secret

Rapture, 1994; Look Me in the Eye, 1994; Beg, 1994; Blue Juice, 1995; Last Dance, 1996; The Designated Mourner, 1997; Consultant Art Dir to Royal Mail for 1999 Millennium stamps, 1997–99, designer: Mind and Matter stamps, 2000; Definitive stamps, 2006; Sounds of Britain stamps, 2006; Endangered Plants, 2009; Classic Album Covers stamps, 2010; identity and communications consultant, DCMS, 1997–99; Ext. Design Advr to Design Council, 2009–. Presenter and producer, RDInsights, RSA, 2006–. Art Dir and Mem., Editl Bd, RSA Jl, 1997–2002; feature writer: Design Week, 2001–; Blueprint, 2006–; Eye mag. Pres., British Design and Art Dirs Assoc., 1997–98. Master of Faculty, RDI, 2005–07. Member: AGI, 1998–2002, 2011–; BAFTA, 2003–. FRSA. Silver award, 1981, 1984, 1985, 1989, 1992, 2000, 2001, Gold award, 1985, Special Award for most awarded designer, 2012, D&AD (formerly Design and Art Dirs Assoc.); CSD Minerva Award, 1996; Reginald M. Phillips Medal, Royal Mail, 2010. *Publications:* Bubbles: early advertising art from A. & F. Pears, 1978; The Magical Paintings of Justin Todd, 1978; Pipe Dreams: early advertising art from the Imperial Tobacco Company, 1982. *Recreation:* living. *Address:* The Hayloft, Church Lane, Osmington, Dorset DT3 6EZ. *T:* (01305) 832520. *E:* mike@studiodempsey.co.uk. *W:* www.studiodempsey.co.uk. *Club:* Groucho.

DEMPSTER, John William Scott, CB 1994; Director, United Kingdom Major Ports Group Ltd, 1999–2007; *b* 10 May 1938; *m* 1965, Ailsa Newman (marr. diss. 1972). *Educ:* Plymouth Coll.; Oriel Coll., Oxford (MA PPE). HM Inspector of Taxes, Inland Revenue, 1961–65; Ministry of Transport: Asst Principal, 1965–67; Principal, 1967–73; Asst Sec., Property Services Agency, 1973–76; Principal Private Sec. to Sec. of State for the Environment, 1976–77; Asst Sec., Dept of Transport, 1977–80; Principal Estabt and Finance Officer, Lord Chancellor's Dept, 1980–84; Department of Transport: Head of Marine Directorate, 1984–89; Principal Establishment Officer, 1989–90; Principal Establishment and Finance Officer, 1990–91; Dir Gen. of Highways, 1991–94; Dep. Sec., Aviation and Shipping, 1994–96; Dir, Bahamas Maritime Authy, 1996–99. Chm., St John Ambulance Devon, 2008–12. *Publications:* The Rise and Fall of the Dock Labour Scheme, 2010. *Recreations:* mountaineering, sailing, bridge, Munro collecting. *Address:* 7 Willow Bridge Road, N1 2LB. *T:* (020) 7226 7553. *Clubs:* Alpine (Hon. Treas., 2014–), Fell and Rock; Swiss Alpine (Pres., Association of British Members, 2006–09).

DEMPSTER, Prof. Michael Alan Howarth, PhD; Professor Emeritus, Statistical Laboratory, Centre for Mathematical Sciences, since 2007, Professor of Management, Judge Institute of Management, 1996–2005, Emeritus, 2006, and Director, Centre for Financial Research, 1997–2008, University of Cambridge (Director of Research, 1997–2001; Director, PhD Programme, 1997–2002); Fellow, Hughes Hall, Cambridge, since 2002; *b* 10 April 1938; *s* of Cedric William Dempster and Honor Fitz Simmons Dempster (*née* Gowan); *m* 1st, 1963, Ann Laura Lazier (marr. diss. 1980); one *d*; 2nd, 1981, Elena Anatolievna Medova; one *d*. *Educ:* Univ. of Toronto (BA 1961); Carnegie Mellon Univ. (MS 1963; PhD 1965); Oxford Univ. (MA 1967); Cambridge Univ. (MA 2005). IBM Res. Fellow, Math. Inst., Oxford, 1965–66; Jun. Res. Fellow, Nuffield Coll., Oxford, 1966; Fellow, Tutor and Univ. Lectr in Maths, 1967–81, Lectr in Maths, 1982–87, Balliol Coll., Oxford; R. A. Jodrey Res. Prof. of Mgt and Inf. Scis, Sch. of Business Admin, and Prof. of Maths, Stats and Computing Science, Dalhousie Univ., 1981–93; Prof. of Maths, 1990–95, and Dir, Inst. for Studies in Finance, 1993–95, Univ. of Essex. Fellow, Center for Advanced Study in Behavioral Scis, Stanford, 1974–75; Sen. Res. Scholar, Internat. Inst. for Applied Systems Analysis, Laxenberg, Austria, 1979–81; Vis. Prof., Univ. of Rome, La Sapienza, 1988–89; Vis. Fellow, Princeton Univ., 1995. Chm., Oxford Systems Associates Ltd, 1974–79; Man. Dir, Cambridge Systems Associates Ltd, 1996–. Cons. to numerous cos and govts, 1965–. Mem., Res. Adv. Bd, Canadian Inst. for Advanced Res., 1986–2002. Foreign Mem., Academia Nazionale dei Lincei, 2013. FIMA 1974. Hon. FIA 2000. Editor: Quantitative Finance, 2000–; Oxford Handbooks in Finance, 2006–. *Publications:* (jtly) Introduction to Optimization Methods, 1974; (ed) Stochastic Programming, 1980; (ed jtly) Analysis and Optimization of Stochastic Systems, 1980; (ed jtly) Large-Scale Linear Programming, 1981; (ed jtly) Deterministic and Stochastic Scheduling, 1982; (ed jtly) Mathematical Models in Economics, 1994; (ed jtly) Mathematics of Derivative Securities, 1997; (ed) Risk Management: value at risk and beyond, 2002; (ed jtly) Quantitative Fund Management, 2009; (ed jtly) Stochastic Optimization Methods in Finance and Energy, 2011; (jtly) The Euro in Danger: reform and reset, 2012; (ed jtly) Commodities, 2015; *translations* from Russian: (jtly) Stochastic Models of Control and Economic Dynamics, 1987; (jtly) Sequential Control and Incomplete Information, 1990. *Recreations:* reading, gardening, tennis, sailing, ski-ing. *Address:* 1 Earl Street, Cambridge CB1 1JR; Statistical Laboratory, Centre for Mathematical Sciences, University of Cambridge, Wilberforce Road, Cambridge CB3 0WA.

DENARO, Maj.-Gen. Arthur George, CBE 1996 (OBE 1991); DL; Extra Equerry to the Prince of Wales, since 2000; *b* 23 March 1948; *s* of late Brig. George Tancred Denaro, CBE, DSO and of Francesca Violet Denaro (*née* Garnett); *m* 1980, Margaret Roney Acworth, *widow* of Major Michael Kealy, DSO; one *s* one *d*, and one step *s* two step *d*. *Educ:* Downside Sch.; RMA Sandhurst. Commissioned Queen's Royal Irish Hussars, 1968; Staff Coll., 1979–80; CO QRIH, 1989–91; Comdr 33 (later 20) Armd Bde, 1992–94; RCDS 1994; COS HQ UNPROFOR, former Yugoslavia, 1994–95; COS HQ British Forces, Cyprus, 1995–96; Chief, Combat Support, HQ ARRC, 1996–97; Comdt, RMA Sandhurst, 1997–2000; GOC 5th Div., 2000–03. Middle East Adviser: to Sec. of State for Defence, 1997–2002; to JCB, 2003–09; Advr to Ct of Crown Prince of Bahrain, 2003–07; Special Advr, Inspirational Develt Gp, 2007–; Sen. Advr to Qatar Nat. Food Security Prog., 2011–13; Advr to Conservative Middle East Council, 2011–. Col, Queen's Royal Hussars (Queen's Own and Royal Irish), 2004–09; Hon. Colonel: Royal Glos Hussars, 2003–13; Royal Wessex Yeomanry, 2003–09. Pres., Combined Irish Regts Assoc., 2003–. Chairman: Prince's Trust Team Prog., 2000–08; Army Benevolent Fund (Hereford), 2003–13. President: Army Rugby Union, 2001–03; Army Polo Assoc., 2002–09; Herefordshire Sector, St John Ambulance, 2011–. Chm. Govs, Moor Park Sch., 2011–. Trustee, Plant for Peace, 2012–. DL Herefordshire, 2008. *Recreations:* fieldsports, polo, ski-ing. *Clubs:* Cavalry and Guards, Pratt's.

de NAVARRO, Michael Antony; QC 1990; a Recorder, 1990–2014; *b* 1 May 1944; *s* of A. J. M. (Toty) de Navarro and Dorothy M. de Navarro; *m* 1975, Jill Margaret Walker (*d* 2013); one *s* two *d*. *Educ:* Downside School; Trinity College, Cambridge (BA Hons). Called to the Bar, Inner Temple, 1968, Bencher, 2000; pupil of Hon. Mr Justice Cazalet and Hon. Mr Justice Turner; Mem., Western Circuit. Chm., Personal Injuries Bar Assoc., 1997–99. Trustee: Longborough Fest. Opera, 2000–13; Broadway Arts Fest., 2010–. *Recreations:* opera, cricket, gardening, cooking. *Address:* 2 Temple Gardens, Temple, EC4Y 9AY. *T:* (020) 7822 1200.

DENBIGH, 12th Earl of, *cr* 1622, **AND DESMOND,** 11th Earl of, *cr* 1622; **Alexander Stephen Rudolph Feilding;** Baron Feilding 1620; Viscount Feilding 1620; Viscount Callan 1622; Baron St Liz 1663; *b* 4 Nov. 1970; *o s* of 11th Earl of Denbigh and Caroline Judith Vivienne, *o d* of Lt-Col Geoffrey Cooke; *S* father, 1995; *m* 1996, Suzanne Jane, *d* of Gregory R. Allen; two *s* one *d*. *Heir: s* Viscount Feilding, *qv*. *Address:* Newnham Paddox, Monks Kirby, Rugby CV23 0RX; 34 Keildon Road, Battersea, SW11 1XH.

DENCH, Dame Judith Olivia, (Dame Judi Dench), CH 2005; DBE 1988 (OBE 1970); actress (theatre, films and television); *b* 9 Dec. 1934; *d* of Reginald Arthur Dench and Eleanora Olave Dench (*née* Jones); *m* 1971, Michael Leonard Williams, actor (*d* 2001); one *d*. *Educ:* The Mount Sch., York; Central Sch. of Speech and Drama. *Theatre:* Old Vic seasons, 1957–61: parts incl.: Ophelia in Hamlet; Katherine in Henry V; Cecily in The Importance of Being Earnest; Juliet in Romeo and Juliet; also 1957–61: two Edinburgh Festivals; Paris-Belgium-Yugoslavia tour; America-Canada tour; Venice (all with Old Vic Co.). Subseq. appearances incl.: Royal Shakespeare Co., 1961–62: Anya in The Cherry Orchard; Titania in A Midsummer Night's Dream; Dorcas Bellboys in A Penny for a Song; Isabella in Measure for Measure; Nottingham Playhouse tour of W Africa, 1963; Oxford Playhouse, 1964–65: Irina in The Three Sisters; Doll Common in The Alchemist; Nottingham Playhouse, 1965: Saint Joan; The Astrakhan Coat (world première); Amanda in Private Lives; Variety London Critics' Best Actress of the Year Award for perf. as Lika in The Promise, Fortune, 1967; Sally Bowles in Cabaret, Palace, 1968; Associate Mem., RSC, 1969–; London Assurance, Aldwych, 1970, and New, 1972; Major Barbara, Aldwych, 1970; Bianca in Women Beware Women, Viola in Twelfth Night, doubling Hermione and Perdita in The Winter's Tale, Portia in The Merchant of Venice, the Duchess in The Duchess of Malfi, Beatrice in Much Ado About Nothing, Lady Macbeth in Macbeth, Adriana in The Comedy of Errors, Regan in King Lear, Imogen in Cymbeline; The Wolf, Oxford and London, 1973; The Good Companions, Her Majesty's, 1974; The Gay Lord Quex, Albery, 1975; Too True to be Good, Aldwych, 1975, Globe, 1976; Pillars of the Community, The Comedy of Errors, Aldwych, 1977; The Way of the World, 1978; Juno and the Paycock, Aldwych, 1980 (Best Actress award, SWET, Evening Standard, Variety Club, and Plays and Players); The Importance of Being Earnest, A Kind of Alaska, Nat. Theatre, 1982; Pack of Lies, Lyric, 1983 (SWET award); Mother Courage, Barbican, 1984; Waste, Barbican and Lyric, 1985; Mr and Mrs Nobody, Garrick, 1986; Antony and Cleopatra (Best Actress award, SWET, Evening Standard), Entertaining Strangers, Nat. Theatre, 1987; Hamlet, Royal Nat. Theatre, and Dubrovnik Theatre Fest., 1989; The Cherry Orchard, Aldwych, 1989; The Plough and the Stars, Young Vic, 1991; The Sea, Nat. Theatre, 1991; Coriolanus, Chichester, 1992; The Gift of the Gorgon, Barbican, 1992, transf. Wyndham's, 1993; The Seagull, RNT, 1994; Absolute Hell, RNT, 1995 (Best Actress, Olivier award, 1996); A Little Night Music, RNT, 1995 (Best Actress in a Musical, Olivier award, 1996); Amy's View, RNT, 1997, transf. Aldwych (Critics' Circle Drama Award), 1998, NY (Tony Award), 1999; Filumena, Piccadilly, 1998; The Royal Family, 2001, The Breath of Life, 2002, Theatre Royal, Haymarket; All's Well That Ends Well, RSC Stratford, transf. Gielgud, 2004; Hay Fever, Th. Royal, Haymarket, 2006; Merry Wives - The Musical, RSC Stratford, 2006; Madame de Sade, Wyndham's, 2009; Titania in A Midsummer Night's Dream, Rose Th., Kingston, 2010; Peter and Alice, Noël Coward Th., 2013; Director, for Renaissance Theatre Co.: Much Ado About Nothing, 1988; Look Back in Anger, 1989; Director: The Boys from Syracuse, Regent's Park, 1991; Romeo and Juliet, Regent's Park, 1993. Recital tour of W Africa, 1969; RSC tours: Japan and Australia, 1970; Japan, 1972. *Films:* He Who Rides a Tiger; A Study in Terror; Four in the Morning (Brit. Film Acad. Award for Most Promising Newcomer, 1965); A Midsummer Night's Dream, 1968; The Third Secret; Dead Cert; Saigon: Year of the Cat; Wetherby, 1984; A Room with a View, 1985 (Best Supporting Actress, BAFTA award, 1987); 84 Charing Cross Road, 1986; A Handful of Dust (Best Supporting Actress, BAFTA award), 1988; Henry V, 1990; Goldeneye, 1995; Mrs Brown (Best Actress awards: BAFTA Scotland, 1997; Golden Globe, London Film Critics, BAFTA, and Screen Actors' Guild, NY, 1998), Tomorrow Never Dies, 1997; Shakespeare in Love (Oscar and BAFTA Award for Best Supporting Actress), Tea with Mussolini, The World is Not Enough, 1999; Chocolat, 2001; Iris (Best Actress, BAFTA award), The Shipping News, The Importance of Being Earnest, Die Another Day, 2002; Ladies in Lavender, The Chronicles of Riddick, 2004; Pride and Prejudice, Mrs Henderson Presents, 2005; Casino Royale, 2006; Notes on a Scandal, 2007; Quantum of Solace, 2008; Nine, Rage, 2009; Jane Eyre, My Week with Marilyn, 2011; J. Edgar, The Best Exotic Marigold Hotel, Skyfall, 2012; Philomena, 2013; The Second Best Exotic Marigold Hotel, 2015. *Television* appearances include, 1957–: Talking to a Stranger (Best Actress of Year award, Guild of Television Dirs, 1967); Major Barbara; Hilda Lessways; Langrishe, Go Down; Macbeth; Comedy of Errors; On Giant's Shoulders; A Village Wooing; Love in a Cold Climate; Saigon; A Fine Romance (BAFTA Award, 1985); The Cherry Orchard; Going Gently; Mr and Mrs Edgehill (Best Actress, Amer. Cable Award, 1988); The Browning Version; Make or Break; Ghosts; Behaving Badly; Absolute Hell; Can You Hear Me Thinking?; As Time Goes By (8 series); Last of the Blonde Bombshells, 2000 (Best Actress, BAFTA TV Award, 2001); Cranford, 2007, 2009; Esio Trot, 2015. Member: Bd, Royal Nat. Theatre, 1988–; Council, Royal Theatrical Support (formerly Royal Shakespeare Theatre) Trust. Awards incl. British and foreign, for theatre, films and TV, incl. BAFTA award for best television actress, 1981, Rothermere Award for Lifetime Achievement, 1997, and Critics' Circle Award for Outstanding Achievement, 1998; William Shakespeare Award, Washington, DC, 2004; Evening Standard Lifetime Achievement Award, 2004; Sky Arts Award for Lifetime Achievement, 2011; Praemium Imperiale, 2011; Moscow Art Theatre's Golden Seagull, London Evening Standard Theatre Awards, 2012. Fellow BAFTA, 2001; Fellow BFI 2011. Hon. Fellow, Lucy Cavendish Coll., Cambridge, 2005. Hon. DLitt: Warwick, 1978; Birmingham, 1989; Loughborough, 1991; London, 1994; Oxford, 2000; Queen Margaret Univ. Coll., Edinburgh, 2000; UEA, 2000; Leeds, 2002; St Andrews, 2008; Nottingham Trent, 2010; DUniv: York, 1983; Open, 1992; RSAMD, 1995; Surrey, 1996; Hon. Dr: Wales, 2001; Mary Baldwin Coll., Staunton, 2004; Hull; Hon. Dr Fine Arts Juilliard Acad., 2004. *Publications:* *Films:* Scenes from My Life, 2005; And Furthermore, 2010. *Recreations:* sewing, drawing, catching up with letters.

DENDY, Prof. Richard Otwell, DPhil; FInstP; Professor of Physics, and Joint Director, Centre for Fusion, Space and Astrophysics, Warwick University, since 2006; Senior Research Staff, UK Atomic Energy Authority, since 2001; *b* Surrey, 31 May 1958; *s* of Dr Paul Dendy and Patricia Dendy; *m* 1989, Felicity Carr; one *s* one *d*. *Educ:* Magdalen Coll. Sch., Oxford; Merton Coll., Oxford (BA 1st Cl. Physics 1979); Peterhouse, Cambridge (Part III Mathematical Tripos 1980); Oxford Univ. (DPhil 1983). FInstP 1996. Physics res., Euratom/UKAEA, 1983– (Gp Leader for Theoretical Physics, 1995–2011); Jun. Res. Fellow, Wolfson Coll., Oxford, 1987–94. Hon. Professor: of Physics, Warwick Univ., 1997–2006; Res. Inst. for Applied Mechanics, Kyushu Univ., Japan, 2010–. Comr, Marshall Aid Commemoration Commn, 2010– (Chm., Educn Cttee, 2014–). Mem., Nuclear Res. Adv. Council, MoD, 2005–. Mem., Physical Scis Strategy Adv. Team, EPSRC, 2007–14. Mem., Physics Sub-Panel, REF 2014, 2012–14. Mem., Sci. Bd, Inst. of Physics, 2005–10. Vice Chm. Bd, Plasma Physics Div., Eur. Physical Soc., 2012–. Ed.-in-Chief, Plasma Physics and Controlled Fusion, 2005–. *Publications:* Plasma Dynamics, 1990; Plasma Physics: an introductory course, 1993; contrib. articles to jls on plasma physics and its applications. *Recreations:* running, gardening, cultivating my general knowledge (University Challenge, 1977). *Address:* Culham Science Centre, Abingdon, Oxon OX14 3DB. *T:* (01235) 466377. *E:* r.dendy@warwick.ac.uk.

DENEGRI, Simon; Chairman, INVOLVE, since 2011; National Director for Public Participation and Engagement in Research, National Institute for Health Research, since 2012; *b* 17 March 1967; *s* of Donald and Ann Denegri; *m* 2006, Nicola Margaret Bain; three *s* from former marr. *Educ:* Dean Row Jun. Sch., Handforth; New Beacon Sch., Sevenoaks; Judd Grammar Sch., Tonbridge; Univ. of Hull (BA Hons Politics and Legislative Studies). Hd, Public Affairs, Alzheimer's Soc., 1992–97; Corporate and Financial Media Relns Manager, Procter and Gamble, USA, 1997–2000; Dir, Communications, Sainsbury Centre for Mental Health, 2001–03; Asst Chief Exec., Alzheimer's Soc., 2003; Dir, Corporate Communications, RCP, 2003–06; Chief Executive: Assoc. of Medical Res. Charities, 2006–11; Ovarian Cancer Action, 2011. MCIPR 2003; MRSocMed 2010. *Recreations:* poetry, cinema, live music, gardening, supporting Crystal Palace Football Club. *Address:* c/o INVOLVE, Wessex House, Upper Market Street, Eastleigh, Hants SO50 9FD. *E:* sdenegri@invo.org.uk. *W:* http://simondenegri.com.

DENEUVE, Catherine; French film actress; *b* 22 Oct. 1943; *d* of Maurice Dorléac and Renée (*née* Deneuve); one *s* by Roger Vadim (*d* 2000); *m* 1967, David Bailey, *qv* (marr. diss.); one *d* by Marcello Mastroianni (*d* 1996). *Educ:* Lycée La Fontaine, Paris. Pres.-Dir Gen., Films de la Citrouille, 1971–79. Chm. Jury, Cannes Film Fest., 1994. *Films include:* Les petits chats, 1959; Les portes claquent, 1960; Le vice et la vertu, 1962; Les parapluies de Cherbourg, 1963; La Constanza della Ragione, 1964; Repulsion, 1964; Liebes Karusell, 1965; Belle de jour, 1967; Folies d'avril, 1969; Un flic, 1972; Le sauvage, 1975; Âmes perdues, 1976; Hustle, 1976; A nous deux, 1978; Le dernier métro, 1980 (César for best actress, 1981); Le choc, 1982; The Hunger, 1982; Le bon plaisir, 1984; Let's Hope It's A Girl, 1987; Drôle d'endroit pour une rencontre (Strange Place to Meet), 1989; Indochine, 1992; Ma Saison préférée, 1994; The Convent, 1995; Les voleurs, 1996; Généalogie d'un Crime, 1997; Place Vendôme, 1998; Pola X, Time Regained, Dancer in the Dark, East-West, 2000; The Musketeer, 8 Women, 2002; Les temps qui changent, 2005; Rois et Reine, 2005; Persepolis, 2008; Un Conte de Noël, 2009; Potiche, 2011; Beloved, 2012. *Publications:* A l'ombre de moi-même, 2004 (Close Up and Personal, 2005). *Address:* c/o Artmédia, 20 avenue Rapp, 75007 Paris, France.

DENHAM, 2nd Baron *cr* 1937, of Weston Underwood; **Bertram Stanley Mitford Bowyer,** KBE 1991; PC 1981; Bt 1660, of Denham; Bt 1933, of Weston Underwood; Captain of the Gentlemen at Arms (Government Chief Whip in the House of Lords), 1979–91; an Extra Lord-in-Waiting to the Queen, since 1998; *b* 3 Oct. 1927; *s* of 1st Baron and Hon. Daphne Freeman-Mitford (*d* 1996), 4th *d* of 1st Baron Redesdale; *S* father, 1948; *m* 1956, Jean, *o d* of Kenneth McCorquodale, Fambridge Hall, White Notley, Essex; three *s* one *d*. *Educ:* Eton; King's Coll., Cambridge. Mem. Westminster CC, 1959–61. A Lord-in-Waiting to the Queen, 1961–64 and 1970–71; Opposition Jun. Whip, 1964–70; Captain of the Yeomen of the Guard, 1971–74; Opposition Dep. Chief Whip, 1974–78; Opposition Chief Whip, 1978–79; elected Mem., H of L, 1999–. Countryside Comr, 1993–99. Dep. Pres., British Field Sports Soc., 1992–98. *Publications:* The Man who Lost his Shadow, 1979; Two Thyrdes, 1983; Foxhunt, 1988; Black Rod, 1997. *Recreation:* field sports. *Heir: s* Hon. Richard Grenville George Bowyer [*b* 8 Feb. 1959; *m* 1st, 1988, Eleanor (marr. diss. 1993), *o d* of A. Sharpe; 2nd, 1996, Dagmar, *o d* of Karel and Jaroslava Božek, Břeslaw, Czech Republic]. *Address:* The Laundry Cottage, Weston Underwood, Olney, Bucks MK46 5JZ. *T:* (020) 7219 6056. *Clubs:* Pratt's, Garrick.

DENHAM, Ernest William; Deputy Keeper of Public Records, Public Record Office, 1978–82; *b* 16 Sept. 1922; *s* of William and Beatrice Denham; *m* 1957, Penelope Agatha Gregory (*d* 2009); one *s* one *d*. *Educ:* City of London Sch.; Merton Coll., Oxford (Postmaster). MA 1948. Naval Intell., UK and SEAC, 1942–45. Asst Sec., Plant Protection Ltd, 1947–49; Asst Keeper 1949, Principal Asst Keeper 1967, Records Admin. Officer 1973, Public Record Office; Lectr in Palaeography and Diplomatic, UCL, 1957–73. *Recreation:* armchair criticism. *Address:* 4 The Ridge, 89 Green Lane, Northwood, Middx HA6 1AE. *T:* (01923) 827382.
See also J. M. G. Denham.

DENHAM, (John Martin) Giles, CBE 2004; Director of Workforce, Department of Health, since 2014; *b* 13 Feb. 1959; *s* of Ernest William Denham, *qv* and late Penelope Agatha Denham; *m* 1986, Heather Gillian Yarker; three *d*. *Educ:* Merchant Taylors' Sch., Northwood; Christ Church, Oxford (MA 1981). Various Civil Service appts, DHSS, HM Treasury and DoH, 1981–90; Gen. Manager, Eastman Dental Hosp., 1990–95; Branch Head, Dentistry, Community Pharmacy, Optometry and Community Care, 1995–2001, Hd of Policy, Children, Older People and Social Care, 2001–03, DoH; Dir, Civil Affairs, Coalition Provl Authy, Iraq, 2004; Dir of Policy, HSE, 2005–09; Dir of Medicines, Pharmacy and Industry Gp, DoH, 2009–14. Trustee: Marie Curie Cancer Care, 1991–2000; Kepplewray Trust, 2001–. *Address:* Department of Health, Richmond House, 79 Whitehall, SW1A 2NS. *T:* (020) 7210 5749. *Clubs:* Athenæum; Eastcote Lawn Tennis.

DENHAM, Rt Hon. John (Yorke); PC 2000; Chairman, Culture Southampton, since 2015; *b* 15 July 1953; *s* of Albert Edward Denham and Beryl Frances Ada Denham; *m* 1979, Ruth Eleanore Dixon (marr. diss.); one *s* one *d*; partner, Susan Jane Littlemore; one *s*. *Educ:* Woodroffe Comprehensive Sch., Lyme Regis; Univ. of Southampton (BSc Hons Chemistry; Pres., Students' Union, 1976–77). Advr, Energy Advice Service, Durham, 1977; Transport Campaigner, Friends of the Earth, 1977–79; Head, Youth Affairs, British Youth Council, 1979–82; Publications Sec., Clause IV Publications, 1982–84; Campaigns Officer, War on Want, 1984–88; Consultant to develt NGOs, 1988–92. Member (Lab): Hants CC, 1981–89; Southampton CC, 1989–93 (Chm., Housing Cttee, 1990–92). Contested (Lab) Southampton, Itchen, 1983, 1987. MP (Lab) Southampton, Itchen, 1992–2015. Parly Under-Sec. of State, DSS, 1997–98; Minister of State: DSS, 1998; Dept of Health, 1998–2001; Home Office, 2001–03; Secretary of State: for Innovation, Univs and Skills, 2007–09; for Communities and Local Govt, 2009–10; Shadow Sec. of State for Communities and Local Govt, 2010, for Business, Innovation and Skills, 2010–11; PPS to Leader of Opposition, 2011–13. Chm., Select Cttee on Home Affairs, 2003–07.

DENHAM, Pamela Anne, CB 1997; DL; PhD; management consultant, since 1998; Regional Director, Government Office for the North East, 1994–98; *b* 1 May 1943; *d* of late Matthew Gray Dobson and Jane (*née* Carter); *m* 1965, Paul Denham (marr. diss. 1980); partner, Brian Murray (*d* 1993). *Educ:* Central Newcastle High Sch.; King's Coll., Univ. of London (BSc 1964; PhD 1969). Asst Principal, Ministry of Technol., 1967–72; Department of Trade and Industry: Principal, 1972–79; Asst Sec., 1979–85; Under Sec., 1985–89; Under Sec., Cabinet Office (Office of Minister for CS), 1989–90; Regl Dir, DTI NE, 1990–94. Non-executive Director: Mono Pumps and Saunders Valve, 1982–85; Newcastle Primary Care Trust, 2001–13. Member: Governing Body, Sunderland Univ., 1993, 1998–2007; Local Governing Body, Central Newcastle High Sch., 1992–2006 (Chair, 2001–06); Trustee, Univ. of Sunderland Develt Trust, 1999–2008. Chair, Project North East, 1998–2009; Mem. Bd, Community Foundn serving Tyne & Wear and Northumberland, 2001–07. Trustee: Age UK (formerly Age Concern), Newcastle, 2000–15 (Chm., 2011–15); Age Concern England, 2002–05. FRSA. DL Tyne and Wear, 2000. Hon. LLD Sunderland, 1994. *Publications:* papers in scientific jls. *Recreations:* travel, reading, walking, cooking. *Address:* 43 Lindisfarne Close, Jesmond, Newcastle upon Tyne NE2 2HT. *T:* (0191) 212 0390.

DENHAM, Lt-Col Sir Seymour Vivian G.; *see* Gilbart-Denham.

DENHAM, Susan Gageby; Hon. Mrs Justice Denham; Chief Justice of Ireland, since 2011; *b* 22 Aug. 1945; *d* of late Douglas Gageby and Dorothy Mary Gageby (*née* Lester); *m* 1970, Brian Denham; three *s* one *d* (and one *s* decd). *Educ:* Trinity Coll. Dublin (BA (Mod.), LLB); Columbia Univ., NY (LLM); King's Inns, Dublin. Called to the Irish Bar, 1971, Bencher, King's Inns, 1991; in practice on Midland Circuit, 1971–87; SC, called to Inner Bar, 1987; Judge of High Court, 1991–92; Judge, Supreme Court of Ireland, 1992–2011. Chair: Working Gp on Courts Commn, 1995–98; Family Law Develt Cttee, 1999–2001; Finance Cttee, 2001–04; Cttee on Court Practice and Procedure, 2000–; Courts Service Bd, 2001–04, 2011– (Mem., Interim Bd and Courts Service Bd, 1999–2001; Chair, Interim Judicial Council, 2011–); Wkg Gp on a Court of Appeal, 2007–09; ISIS Steering Cttee to plan for system of inf. on sentencing, 2005–. Founding Mem., Eur. Network of Councils for the Judiciary, 2004 (Mem., Steering Cttee, 2004–07); Pres., Network of Presidents of Supreme Judicial Courts of EU, 2015– (Vice-Pres., 2011–15). MRIA 2013. Hon. Sec., Cttee on Judicial Conduct and Ethics, 1999–2002. Pro-Chancellor, Dublin Univ., 1996–2010. Gov., Marshall's Liby, Dublin, 2011–. Dist. Fellow, Griffith Coll. Dublin, 2013. Hon. Bencher, Middle Temple, 2005. Hon. LLD: QUB, 2002; Ulster, 2013; UCD, 2014; Hon. DPhil Dublin City, 2014. *Recreations:* gardens, horses, reading. *Address:* The Supreme Court, Four Courts, Dublin, Ireland. *T:* (1) 8886540.

DENHOLM, Allan; *see* Denholm, J. A.

DENHOLM, Sir Ian; *see* Denholm, Sir J. F.

DENHOLM, (James) Allan, CBE 1992; Chairman, East Kilbride Development Corporation, 1983–94 (Member, 1979–94); Director, William Grant & Sons Ltd, 1975–96 (Secretary, 1966–96); President, Institute of Chartered Accountants of Scotland, 1992–93; *b* 27 Sept. 1936; *s* of James Denholm and Florence Lily Keith (*née* Kennedy); *m* 1964, Elizabeth Avril McLachlan, CA; one *s* one *d*. *Educ:* Hutchesons' Boys' Sch., Glasgow. CA. Apprentice with McFarlane Hutton & Patrick, 1954–60; Chief Accountant, A. & W. Smith & Co. Ltd, 1960–66. Councillor, Eastwood DC, 1962–64. Mem., Council, Inst. of Chartered Accountants, Scotland, 1978–83 (Sen. Vice-Pres., 1991–92). Chm., Glasgow Jun. Chamber of Commerce, 1972–73. Director: Scottish Cremation Soc. Ltd, 1980–; Scottish Mutual Assurance PLC, 1987–2003 (Dep. Chm., 1992–2003); Abbey National PLC, 1992–97; Deputy Chairman: Abbey National Life PLC, 1997–2003; Scottish Provident Instn PLC, 2001–03 (Mem., Adv. Cttee, 2001–06). Visitor, Incorporation of Maltmen, Glasgow, 1980–81. Trustee: Scottish Cot Death Trust, 1985–96; Neurosciences Foundn, Glasgow, 2003–14; Dir, Assoc. for the Relief of Incurables in Glasgow and W of Scotland, 1999–. Mem., W of Scotland Adv. Bd, Salvation Army, 1996–. Elder, New Kilpatrick Parish Church, Bearsden, 1971–. Preses, Weavers' Soc., Anderston, 1994–95; President: 49 Wine & Spirit Club of Scotland, 1983–84; Assoc. of Deacons of the Fourteen Incorporated Trades, Glasgow, 1994–95; Deacon Convener, The Trades House, Glasgow, 1998–99; Deacon, Soc. of Deacons and Free Preseses, Glasgow, 1999–2000. Patron, Royal Incorp. of Hutchesons' Hosp., 1998–2009. FSAScot 1987. FRSA 1992. *Recreations:* golf, shooting. *Address:* Greencroft, 19 Colquhoun Drive, Bearsden, Glasgow G61 4NQ. *Club:* Western (Glasgow) (Chm., 2004–05).

DENHOLM, Sir John Ferguson, (Sir Ian), Kt 1989; CBE 1974; Chairman, J. & J. Denholm Ltd, 1974–98; *b* 8 May 1927; *s* of Sir William Lang Denholm, TD; *m* 1952, Elizabeth Murray Stephen (*d* 2015); two *s* two *d*. *Educ:* St Mary's Sch., Melrose; Loretto Sch., Musselburgh. Joined J. & J. Denholm Ltd, 1944. Chm., Murray Investment Trusts, 1985–93; Dep. Chm., P&O, 1980–85 (Dir, 1974–85); Director: Fleming Mercantile Investment Trust, 1985–94; Murray Trusts, 1973–93; Murray Johnstone, 1985–93; Member: London Bd, Bank of Scotland, 1988–91; West of Scotland Bd, Bank of Scotland, 1991–95. Member: Nat. Ports Council, 1974–77; Scottish Transport Gp, 1975–82. President: Chamber of Shipping of the UK, 1973–74; Gen. Council of British Shipping, 1988–89; British Internat. Freight Assoc., 1990–91; Baltic and Internat. Maritime Council, 1991–93. Hon. Norwegian Consul in Glasgow, 1975–97. DL 1980, JP 1984, Renfrewshire. *Recreations:* fishing, sailing. *Clubs:* Western (Glasgow); Royal Thames Yacht, Royal Northern and Clyde Yacht.

DE NIRO, Robert; actor and producer; *b* NYC, 17 Aug. 1943; *s* of late Robert De Niro and of Virginia Admiral; *m* 1st, 1976, Diahnne Abbott (marr. diss. 1988); one *s*, and one adopted *d*; 2nd, 1997, Grace Hightower (marr. diss. 1999; remarried 2004); one *s*; twin *s* by Toukie Smith. *Educ:* Rhodes Sch., NY; High Sch. of Music and Art, NY. Co-founder and Pres., Tribeca Prodns, 1989–. Chm. Jury, Cannes Film Fest., 2011. Co-creator, We Will Rock You (musical), 2002. *Films include:* The Wedding Party, 1969; Jennifer on my Mind, Bloody Mama, Born to Win, The Gang That Couldn't Shoot Straight, 1971; Bang the Drum Slowly, Mean Streets, 1973; The Godfather Part II, 1974 (Acad. Award for best supporting actor, 1975); The Last Tycoon, Taxi Driver, 1976; 1900, New York, New York, 1977; The Deer Hunter, 1978; Raging Bull (Acad. Award for best actor), 1980; True Confessions, 1981; The King of Comedy, 1983; Once Upon a Time in America, Falling in Love, 1984; Brazil, 1985; The Mission, 1986; Angel Heart, The Untouchables, 1987; Midnight Run, Letters Home from Vietnam, 1988; Jacknife, We're No Angels (also prod.), 1989; Stanley and Iris, Goodfellas, Awakenings, Fear No Evil, 1990; Guilty by Suspicion, Backdraft, Cape Fear, 1991; Mad Dog and Glory, Night and the City, Mistress (also co-prod.), 1992; This Boy's Life, A Bronx Tale (also dir and co-prod.), 1993; Mary Shelley's Frankenstein, 1994; Casino, Heat, 1995; The Fan, Sleepers, Marvin's Room (also prod.), 1996; Cop Land, Jackie Brown, Wag the Dog (also prod.), 1997; Great Expectations, Ronin, 1998; Analyse This, 1999; Flawless (also prod.), Meet the Parents (also prod.), 2000; The Adventures of Rocky and Bullwinkle (also prod.), Men of Honour, 15 Minutes (also prod.), The Score, 2001; Showtime, City By the Sea, 2002; Analyse That, Godsend, 2003; Meet the Fockers (also prod.), Hide and Seek, 2005; The Good Shepherd (also dir), Stardust, 2007; What Just Happened?, Righteous Kill, 2008; Everybody's Fine, Machete, Little Fockers (also prod.), 2010; Silver Linings Playbook, 2012; The Big Wedding, The Family, 2013; Grudge Match, 2014; *producer:* Thunderheart, 1992; Entropy, 1999; Conjugating Niki, 2000; Prison Song, About a Boy, 2001; Stage Beauty, 2004. Appearance in TV documentary, Remembering the Artist: Robert De Niro, Sr, 2014. Cecil B. DeMille Award for Lifetime Achievement, Golden Globe Awards, 2011. *Address:* c/o CAA, 2000 Avenue of the Stars, Los Angeles, CA 90067, USA; Tribeca Productions, 375 Greenwich Street, New York, NY 10013, USA.

DENISON, family name of **Baron Londesborough.**

DENISON, Prof. David Michael Benjamin, DPhil; FBA 2014; Smith Professor of English Language and Medieval Literature, University of Manchester, 2008–15, now Emeritus; *b* London, 6 Sept. 1950; *s* of William David Denison (formerly Wilhelm David Deutsch) and Celia Denison (*née* Cissie Shusman); *m* 1975, Elizabeth Ann Price; two *d*. *Educ:* Highgate Sch., London; St John's Coll., Cambridge (BA 1973); Lincoln Coll., Oxford (DPhil 1981). University of Manchester: Lectr, 1976–93; Sen. Lectr in English Lang., 1993–95; Prof. of English Linguistics, 1995–2008, now Emeritus. Vis. Lectr, Univ. of Amsterdam, 1985–86; Visiting Professor: Univ. of BC, 1992; Univ. of Santiago de Compostela, 1998; Univ. Sorbonne Nouvelle, Paris, 2006. Hon. PhD Uppsala, 2014. *Publications:* English Historical Syntax, 1993; Syntax 1776–1997, 1998; (ed jtly) Generative Theory and Corpus Studies, 2000; (ed jtly) Fuzzy Grammar, 2004; (ed jtly) A History of the English Language, 2006; (ed jtly) Analysing Older English, 2012; (ed jtly) Morphosyntactic Categories and the Expression of Possession, 2013; contrib. book chapters, jl articles and linguistic corpora. *Recreations:* cinema, music, being abroad. *Address:* School of Languages, Linguistics and Cultures, University of Manchester, Samuel Alexander Building, Oxford Road, Manchester M13 9PL. *E:* david.denison@manchester.ac.uk.

DENISON, Simon Neil; QC 2009; *b* Dar-es-Salaam, 28 Dec. 1961; *s* of His Honour (William) Neil Denison, QC and Philippa Jean Denison (*née* Wilkinson; later Napier); *m* 1991, Victoria Mary Wright; two *s* one *d*. *Educ:* St Catharine's Coll., Cambridge (BA Hons Law 1983). Called to the Bar, Lincoln's Inn, 1984; in practice as barrister, 1984–; Jun. Treasury Counsel, 2001–07; Sen. Treasury Counsel, 2007–14. *Recreations:* football, Rugby, ski-ing, golf, boating. *Address:* 21 College Hill, EC4R 2RP. *T:* (020) 3310 0910, *Fax:* (020) 3310 0911. *E:* simon.denison@6kbw.com. *Club:* Garrick.

DENISON-PENDER, family name of **Baron Pender.**

DENISON-SMITH, Lt-Gen. Sir Anthony (Arthur), KBE 1995 (MBE 1973); DL; Lieutenant, HM Tower of London, 1998–2001; *b* 24 Jan. 1942; *s* of late George Denison-Smith and Dorothy Gwendolin Phillips; *m* 1966, Julia Henrietta Scott; three *s*. *Educ:* Harrow; RMA, Sandhurst. Commissioned Grenadier Guards, 1962; Staff Coll., 1974; Brigade Major,

7th Armoured Brigade, 1977–79; Directing Staff, Staff Coll., 1979–81; CO 2nd Bn Grenadier Guards, 1981–83; Chief of Staff, 4th Armoured Div., 1983–85; Comdr, 22nd Armoured Brigade, 1985–87; Chief of Staff, 1 (BR) Corps, 1987–89; Dir Gen. Trng and Doctrine (Army), 1990–91; Comdr, 4th Armoured Div., 1991–93; Comdr, 1st (UK) Armoured Div., 1993–94; GOC Southern Dist, 1994–95; GOC 4th Div., 1995–96. Col, Princess of Wales's Royal Regt (Queen's and Royal Hampshires), 1992–99. Chm., ACFA, 1996–2001; President: Essex Br., Grenadier Guards Assoc., 1998–; Essex ABF The Soldiers' Charity (formerly Army Benevolent Fund), 2008–14. Hon. Col, Essex ACF, 2002–07. Consultant, Rave Technologies Ltd (formerly Karnataka Gp Ltd), 1996–. DL Essex, 2001. Comdr (1st cl.), Order of the Dannebrog (Denmark), 1996. *Recreation:* family and friends. *Address:* Cranford, Bran End, Stebbing, Dunmow, Essex CM6 3RX. *Clubs:* Cavalry and Guards; MCC; I Zingari, Free Foresters, Essex.

DENMAN, family name of **Baron Denman**.

DENMAN, 6th Baron *cr* 1834; **Richard Thomas Stewart Denman;** Bt 1945; *b* 4 Oct. 1946; *e s* of 5th Baron Denman, CBE, MC, TD and Sheila Anne (*née* Stewart); *S* father, 2012; *m* 1984, (Lesley) Jane, *d* of John Stevens; one *s* three *d*. *Educ:* Milton Abbey. *Heir:* *s* Hon. Robert Denman, *b* 19 Dec. 1995.

DENMAN, Sylvia Elaine, CBE 1994; Member, Housing Corporation, 1996–2002; Member, 1992–2000, Chairman, 1996–2000, Camden and Islington (formerly Bloomsbury and Islington) Health Authority; *b* Barbados; *d* of late Alexander Yarde and Euleen Yarde (*née* Alleyne), Barbados; *m* Hugh Frederick Denman (marr. diss.); one *d*. *Educ:* Queen's College, Barbados; LSE (LLM); called to the Bar, Lincoln's Inn, 1962. Lectr then Sen. Lectr, Oxford Polytechnic, 1965–76; Sen. Lectr and Tutor, Norman Manley Law Sch., Univ. of West Indies, Jamaica, 1977–82; Fulbright Fellow, New York Univ. Sch. of Law, 1982–83; Prin. Equal Opportunities Officer, ILEA, 1983–86; Pro Asst Dir, Polytechnic of South Bank, 1986–89; Dep. Dir of Educn, ILEA, 1989–90. Sole Ind. Chair, Ind. Internal Inquiry, CPS, 2000–02. Member: Oxford Cttee for Racial Integration, 1965–76; Oxford, Bucks and Berks Conciliation Cttee, Race Relations Bd, 1965–70; London Rent Assessment Panel, 1968–76 and 1984–2002; Race Relations Bd, 1970–76; Equal Opportunities Commission, 1975–76; Lord Chancellor's Adv. Cttee on Legal Aid, 1975–76; Criminal Justice Consultative Council, 1991–97; Council, NACRO, 1994–99; SSAC, 1998–2001. Trustee: Runnymede Trust, 1985–91; Windsor Fellowship, 1994–98; CAF, 1997–2001. Governor: Haverstock Sch., 1989–94; Oxford Brookes Univ., 1996–2000. *Recreations:* music, theatre, wandering about in the Caribbean.

DENNAY, Charles William, CEng; Consultant, Quantel Ltd, 1993–2001; *b* 13 May 1935; *s* of Charles Dennay and Elsie May Smith; *m* 1955, Shirley Patricia Johnston; one *s*. *Educ:* Humberston Foundation Sch.; Borough Polytechnic. DiPEE, MIERE. Scientific Asst (Govt), 1953; Technician, BBC, 1956; Transmitter Engineer, 1958; Asst Lectr/Lectr, 1961; Head of Ops Transmitters, 1973; Head of Engrg Transmitter Ops, 1976; Asst Chief Engineer, Transmitters, 1978; Chief Engineer, External Broadcasting, 1979; Controller, Ops and Engineering Radio, 1984; Asst Dir of Engineering, 1985; Dir of Engineering, 1987; Man. Dir, Resources Engrg and Services, 1993, retd. Director: Brighton Fest. Soc. Ltd, 1996–2000; Brighton Dome & Museum Develt Co. Ltd, 1999–2005. Mem., Steering Bd, Radio Communication Agency, 1996–2003. Vis. Prof., Internat. Acad. of Broadcasting, Montreux, 1994–98. President: IEEIE, 1994–98 (Vice-Pres., 1990–94); IIE, 2001–03. FRTS 1997 (a Vice-Pres., 1989–94); FIIE 1998, Hon. FIIE 2003. FRSA 1993. Hon. FIET; Hon. FBKS 1990. *Recreations:* photography, music, civil aviation. *Address:* Montmore Cottage, 1 Orchard Dean, Alresford, Hants SO24 9DE. *T:* (01962) 735103.

DENNE, Christopher James Alured, CMG 1991; HM Diplomatic Service, 1967–78 and 1983–98; *b* 20 Aug. 1945; *s* of late Lt Comdr John Richard Alured Denne, DSC, RN and Alison Patricia Denne; *m* 1968, Sarah Longman; two *s* one *d*. *Educ:* Wellington Coll.; Southampton Univ. (BSc Soc. Sci. 1967). Entered Diplomatic Service, 1967; New Delhi, 1969–72; Second Sec., FCO, 1972–74; First Sec. (Information), Lagos, 1974–77; FCO, 1977; resigned, 1978; BBC External Services, 1979–80; reinstated FCO, 1983; First Sec. and Dep. Permanent Rep., UK Mission to UN, Vienna, 1985–89; Head of Consular Dept, FCO, 1989–92; Dep. Hd of Mission, Athens, 1993–97. Mem., Nat. Council, European Movt, 2009–13 (Chm., Tamar Br., 2007–15). *Address:* 15 Plymouth Road, Tavistock, Devon PL19 8AU.

DENNEN, Ven. Lyle; Archdeacon of Hackney, 1999–2010; Vicar, St Andrew, Holborn, 1999–2014; *b* 8 Jan. 1942; *s* of Ernest and Rose Dennen; *m* 1977, Xenia Howard-Johnston, *d* of Rear Adm. C. D. Howard-Johnston, CB, DSO, DSC, and Lady Alexandra Haig (who *m* 1954, Hugh Trevor-Roper (later Lord Dacre of Glanton)); two *s*. *Educ:* Trinity Coll., Cambridge (BA 1970, MA 1975); Harvard Law Sch. (DJur); Harvard Univ. (PhD); Cuddesdon Coll., Oxford. Ordained deacon, 1972, priest, 1973; Curate, St Anne, S Lambeth, Southwark, 1972–75; Curate in charge, St Matthias, Richmond, 1975–78; Vicar, St John the Divine, Kennington, 1978–99; RD of Brixton, 1988–99; Permission to Officiate, Dio. London, 2014–. Hon. Canon, Southwark Cathedral, 1999. Chairman of Governors: St John the Divine Primary Sch., 1978–99; Charles Edward Brooke Secondary Sch., 1978–99; Chm., Lambeth WelCare, 1978–99. Chairman: London Cttee, Southwark & London Diocesan Housing Assoc., 1999–; Alexander Stafford Trust, 1999–; Trustee: St Gabriel's Coll. Trust, 1978–99; Bromfield Educnl Charity, 1999–2014; Lady Elizabeth Hatton Charity, 1999–2014; Lady Neville Charity, 1999–2014; St Andrew Holborn Ch Foundn, 1999–2014; St Andrew Holborn Parish Estates Charity, 1999–2014; St Andrew Holborn Charity, 2002–14. *Recreation:* sailing. *Address:* 5 St Andrew Street, EC4A 3AB. *T:* (020) 7353 3544, *Fax:* (020) 7583 2750. *Clubs:* Athenæum; Harlequins Supporters.

DENNER, Dr (William) Howard (Butler); freelance photographer, especially of pop, blues and jazz musicians, since 1996; *b* 14 May 1944; *s* of late William Ormonde Ralph Denner and Violet Evelyn Arscott; *m* 1966, Gwenda Williams (*d* 2008); two *d*; *m* 2014, Judith Dynes. *Educ:* Cyfarthfa Castle Grammar School, Merthyr Tydfil; UCW Cardiff (BSc, PhD Biochem.). Research Associate: Miami Univ., 1968; Cardiff Univ., 1969; Ministry of Agriculture, Fisheries and Food, 1972–96: Secretary: Food Additives and Contaminants Cttee, 1974–84; Cttee on Toxicity of Chemicals in Food, Consumer Products and the Environment, 1978–84; Mem., Jt FAO/WHO Expert Cttee on Food Additives, 1978–85; Head of Food Composition and Information Unit, 1984; Chm., Codex Cttee on Fats and Oils, 1987–92; Assessor, Adv. Cttees on Novel Foods and Processes and on Genetic Modification, 1985–92; Head of Food Sci. Div. II, 1989; Chief Scientist (Food), 1992–96. Lectr and Judge, E Anglia Fedn of Photographic Alliance of GB, 1978–88; Judge, Essex Internat. Salon of Photography, 1987–88. One-man exhibn of photographs, Half Moon Gallery, 1974; individual photographs in internat. exhibns, newspapers, jls and books. AFIAP 1972. *Publications:* papers on food safety in learned jls. *Recreations:* photography, golf. *Address:* 29 Pineheath Road, High Kelling, Holt, Norfolk NR25 6QF. *T:* (01263) 713495. *E:* howard@howarddenner.com.

DENNEY, Anna Louise; *see* Bancroft, A. L.

DENNEY, Stuart Henry MacDonald; QC 2008; *b* Welwyn, Herts, 15 June 1959; *s* of late Robert Waterson Denney and of Jane Denney (*née* Kemp); *m* 1988, Anna Louise Bancroft, *qv*; one *s*. *Educ:* Gonville & Caius Coll., Cambridge (BA 1980). Called to the Bar, Inner Temple, 1982; in practice as a barrister, specialising in criminal and regulatory law. *Recreation:* Rugby Union. *Address:* Deans Court Chambers, 24 St John Street, Manchester M3 4DF. *T:* (0161) 214 6000, *Fax:* (0161) 214 6001. *E:* clerks@deanscourt.co.uk; Thomas More Chambers, 7 Lincoln's Inn Fields, WC2A 3BP. *T:* (020) 7404 7000. *Club:* London Scottish Football.

DENNING, Prof. David Wemyss, FRCP, FRCPath; FMedSci; Professor of Infectious Disease in Global Health, University of Manchester, since 2013; *b* Gosport, 18 May 1957; *s* of Basil Wemyss Denning and Antoinette Carter Denning (*née* Gossett); *m* 1984, Merian Llewelyn Roberts; three *s*. *Educ:* St Paul's Sch., London; Guy's Hosp. Med. Sch., Univ. of London (LMSSA 1980; MB BS 1980; DCH 1984). FRCP 1995; FRCPath 1997. Postgrad. trng, London, Glasgow and Stanford Univ.; Clin. Res. Fellow, Infectious Diseases and Microbiol., Stanford Univ., 1987–90; Sen. Lectr in Infectious Disease, 1990–2005, Prof. of Medicine and Med. Mycology, 2005–13, Univ. of Manchester. Founder and Director: F2G Ltd, 1998, Consultant, 2004–12; Myconostica Ltd, 2006–11. Director: Nat. Aspergillosis Centre, 2009–; Leading Internat. Fungal Education, 2012–; Founder and Pres., Global Action Fund for Fungal Infections, 2013–. Ed., Aspergillus website, 1998–. Consultant to pharmaceutical cos incl. Pfizer, Merck, Gilead and Astellas. Scientific Advr, Fungal Infection Trust (formerly Fungal Res. Trust), 1991–. FMedSci 2010. *Publications:* (jtly) Medicine, 1997, 3rd edn 2008; (contrib.) Harrison's Principles of Internal Medicine, 18th edn 2011, 19th edn 2015; contribs to learned jls on infectious diseases, AIDS, fungal infections, asthma, fungal diagnostics and treatment of fungal disease. *Recreations:* ski-ing, drinking with friends, rough travelling. *Address:* Education and Research Centre, University Hospital of South Manchester, Southmoor Road, Manchester M23 9LT. *T:* (0161) 291 5811, *Fax:* (0161) 291 5806. *E:* ddenning@manchester.ac.uk.

DENNINGTON, Dudley, FREng; FICE; FIStructE; Partner, 1972–92, Senior Partner, 1989–92, Bullen and Partners; *b* 21 April 1927; *s* of John Dennington and Beryl Dennington (*née* Hagon); *m* 1951, Margaret Patricia Stewart; two *d*. *Educ:* Clifton Coll., Bristol; Imperial Coll., London Univ. (BSc). National Service, 2nd Lieut, RE, 1947–49; Sandford Fawcett and Partners, Consulting Engineers, 1949–51; D. & C. Wm Press, Contractors, 1951–52; AMICE 1953; Manager, Design Office, George Wimpey & Co., 1952–65; GLC 1965–72: Asst Chief Engineer, Highway Construction, 1965–67; Chief Engineer, Highway Construction, 1967–70; Traffic Comr and Dir of Development, 1970–72. Mem., Bd for Engineers' Registration, Engrg Council, 1983–85. Pres., British Sect., Conseil Nat. des Ingénieurs et des Scientifiques de France, 1992. Vis. Prof., King's Coll., London Univ., 1978–81. Chm., Blythe Sappers, 1997. FICE 1966 (Mem. Council, 1975–78 and 1981–84; Vice-Pres., 1990–92); FCGI 1984; FREng (FEng 1985). *Recreations:* mathematics, painting. *Address:* 25 Corkran Road, Surbiton, Surrey KT6 6PL.

DENNIS, Maj.-Gen. Alastair Wesley, CB 1985; OBE 1973; *b* 30 Aug. 1931; *s* of late Ralph Dennis and of Helen (*née* Henderson); *m* 1st, 1957, Susan Lindy Elgar (*d* 1998); one *s* two *d*; 2nd, 2000, Caroline Brenda Dowdall. *Educ:* Malvern Coll.; RMA, Sandhurst. Commanded 16th/5th The Queen's Royal Lancers, 1971–74; Col GS, Cabinet Office, 1974–75; Comd 20 Armoured Bde, 1976–77; Dep. Comdt, Staff Coll., 1978–80; Director of Defence Policy (B), MoD, Whitehall, 1980–82; Dir, Military Assistance Overseas, MoD, 1982–85. Sec., Imperial Cancer Res. Fund, 1985–91; Chm., Assoc. of Med. Res. Charities, 1987–91. Mem., Malvern Coll. Council, 1988–92. Col, 16th/5th The Queen's Royal Lancers, 1990–93, The Queen's Royal Lancers, 1993–95. *Recreations:* fishing, golf, gardening. *Address:* St Maur, Long Street, Sherborne, Dorset DT9 3BS.

DENNIS, Colin, CBE 2009; DL; PhD; Director-General, Campden BRI (formerly Campden Food and Drink Research Association, then Campden & Chorleywood Food Research Association), 1988–2009, now Hon. Member; adviser to UK government and food industry, since 2009; *b* Boston, Lincs, 10 May 1946; *s* of George Henry Dennis and Jane Dennis (*née* Simpson); *m* 1968, Susan Day; one *s* one *d*. *Educ:* Sheffield Univ. (BSc 1st Cl. Hons 1967; Boswell Meml Prize, Lindsey Educn Prize; PhD 1970). FIFST 1982; CSci 2004. Certified Food Scientist, 2013. Hd, Mycology Section, ARC Food Res. Inst., 1970–81; Hd, Food Technol. Div., Campden Food and Drink Res. Assoc., 1981–88. Hon. Lectr, UEA, 1971–76; Vis. Scientist, Norwegian Food Res. Inst., 1981; Unilever Vis. Prof., QUB, 1991–2006; Hon. Prof., Univ. of Birmingham, 1993–2009; Royal Agricultural University (formerly College): Vis. Prof., 2007–; Gov. (formerly Mem. Bd), 2009–; Pension Trustee, 2011–13. Non-exec. Dir, UK Accreditation Service, 1998–2009. Assessor, Knowledge Transfer Partnerships, Technol. Strategy Bd, 2001–; Member: Food Directorate Mgt Cttee, BBSRC, 1994–96; Food and Drink Foresight Panel, OST, 1994–98; Sustainable Food and Farming Res. Priorities Gp, DEFRA, 2003–06; Bioscis for Industry Panel, 2005–08, Modular Trng for Industry Panel, 2006–, BBSRC; Gen. Adv. Cttee on Sci., Food Standards Agency, 2012–; Chairman: Agric. Sector Adv. Gp, UK Trade and Investment, 2005–08; Industry Adv. Gp, Internat. Agri-Technology Centre, 2009–11; English Food and Drink Alliance, 2010–. Member Board: Glos Develt Agency, 2001–11 (Vice Chm., 2007–11); SW Food and Drink, 2002–10; Countryside and Community Res. Inst., 2007–; Nat. Skills Acad. for Food and Drink, 2008–; Internat. Food Information Service, 2009– (Chm., Bd of Trustees, 2013–); Inst. of Food Technologists, 2010–13; British Nutrition Foundn, 2012–; Pres., Inst. of Food Sci. and Technol., 2011–13. Member: Food Safety Adv. Council, Maple Leaf Foods Inc., 2010–; Adv. Bd, Internat. Food Network Inc., 2011–; Scientific Adv. Bd, Flanders Food, 2011– (Chm., 2012–). Mem. Bd, Friends of the Cotswolds, 2007–10. Mem. Court, Hon. Co. of Glos., 2012– (Warden, 2014–15). Fellow: Inst. of Food Sci. and Technol., 1982; Inst. of Food Technologists, 2001 (Pres., 2015–Sept. 2016); Internat. Acad. of Food Sci. and Technol., 2001; Hon. Mem., Soc. of Applied Microbiol., 2006 (Denver Meml Lectr, 2014). Hon. FRAgS 2010. FRSA 2000. DL Glos 2005. Myron Solberg Award, Inst. of Food Technol., USA, 2011. *Publications:* (ed jtly) Opportunities for Improving Crop Yields, 1980; (ed) Post-Harvest Pathology of Fruits and Vegetables, 1983; (ed jtly) Vegetable Processing, 1990; (ed jtly) Chilled Foods: a comprehensive guide, 1992, 2nd edn 2000. *Recreations:* gardening, golf, volunteer work, travel. *Address:* The Hill Farm, Hurdlers Lane, Ilmington, Warwickshire CV36 4PT. *T:* (01608) 682585, 07976 956468. *E:* cnsdennis@btinternet.com.

DENNIS, Geoffrey Adrian; Chief Executive Officer, Royal National Children's Foundation, since 2014; *b* 15 Aug. 1951; *s* of Clive Gardner Dennis and Audrey Joan Dennis; *m* 1998, Joanna Mary Snook; one *s*. *Educ:* Enfield Coll. (BA Hons); Univ. of Sussex (MA 1976). Main Bd Dir, Ewbank Preece Consultants, 1979–90; Man. Dir, Travers Morgan Consultants (Environmental), 1990–92; Internat. Dir, British Red Cross, and Hd of Delegn, Dem. People's Rep. of Korea, Internat. Fedn of the Red Cross, 1992–98; Hd of Regl Delegn, S Asia, Internat. Fedn of the Red Cross, 1998–2000; Chief Executive Officer: Friends of the Elderly, 2000–04; CARE Internat. UK, 2004–14. Mem. Global Bd, and Mem. Exec. Cttee, CARE Internat. Worldwide, 2006–14. Chm., Rocking Horse Appeal (volunteer), 2004–09. Badge of Honour, British Red Cross, 1998. *Recreations:* hockey (Sussex County 1st Eleven, Brighton Hockey Club), squash, travel. *Address:* Cuckfield, Sussex.

DENNIS, Hugh; *see* Dennis, P. H.

DENNIS, Rt Rev. John; Bishop of St Edmundsbury and Ipswich, 1986–96; an Hon. Assistant Bishop, Diocese of Winchester, since 1999; *b* 19 June 1931; *s* of late Hubert Ronald and Evelyn Dennis; *m* 1956, Dorothy Mary (*née* Hinnels); two *s*. *Educ:* Rutlish School, Merton; St Catharine's Coll., Cambridge (BA 1954; MA 1959); Cuddesdon Coll., Oxford (1954–56). RAF, 1950–51. Curate, St Bartholomew's, Armley, Leeds, 1956–60; Curate of Kettering, 1960–62; Vicar of the Isle of Dogs, 1962–71; Vicar of John Keble, Mill Hill, 1971–79; Area Dean of West Barnet, 1973–79; Prebendary of St Paul's Cathedral, 1977–79; Bishop Suffragan of Knaresborough, 1979–86; Diocesan Dir of Ordinands, Dio. Ripon, 1980–86; Asst Bp, Ely,

1996–99. Episcopal Guardian of Anglican Focolarini, 1981–96; Chaplain to Franciscan Third Order, 1988–94. Co-Chairman: English ARC, 1988–92; Anglican-Oriental Orthodox Dialogue, 1989–95. *Recreations:* walking, wood working. *Address:* 7 Conifer Close, Winchester, Hants SO22 6SH. *E:* 7johndennis@gmail.com.

See also J. D. Dennis, P. H. Dennis.

DENNIS, John David; HM Diplomatic Service; Ambassador to Angola and concurrently to São Tomé and Príncipe, since 2014; *b* 6 Aug. 1959; *s* of Rt Rev. John Dennis, *qv*; *m* 1989, Jillian Kemp; two *s*. *Educ:* Haberdashers' Aske's Sch., Elstree; St Catharine's Coll., Cambridge (BA Hons 1981). Entered FCO, 1981; Hong Kong, 1983–85; Peking, 1985–87; Hd, Political Section, Kuala Lumpur, 1992–96; on secondment to Standard Chartered Bank, 1997–98; Dir, Automotive, DTI, 1998–2001; Dir, Trade and Investment Promotion, New Delhi, 2001–03; Minister, Consul-Gen. and Dep. Head of Mission, Beijing, 2003–06; Additional Dir, Asia, FCO, 2006–08; Hd of Zimbabwe Unit, FCO, 2009–10; Hd of Africa Dept (South Central and Western), FCO, 2010–13. *Recreations:* my children, reading, creative writing. *Address:* Foreign and Commonwealth Office, King Charles Street, SW1A 2AH. *E:* jjdennis@btinternet.com.

See also P. H. Dennis.

DENNIS, Mark Jonathan; QC 2006; Senior Treasury Counsel, Central Criminal Court, 1998–2006; a Recorder, since 2000; *b* 15 March 1955; *s* of Edward John Dennis and Patricia Edna Dennis; *m* 1985, Christabel Birbeck; one *s* one *d*. *Educ:* Battersea Grammar Sch.; Peterhouse, Cambridge (BA Hons Law; MA). Called to the Bar, Middle Temple, 1977; Jun. Treasury Counsel, Central Criminal Court, 1993–98. *Address:* (chambers) 21 College Hill, EC4R 2RP. *T:* (020) 3301 0910. *Club:* Reform.

DENNIS, (Peter) Hugh; actor, comedian and writer; *b* Kettering, 13 Feb. 1962; *s* of Rt Rev. John Dennis, *qv*; *m* 1996, Kate Abbot Anderson; one *s* one *d*. *Educ:* University Coll. Sch., Hampstead; St John's Coll., Cambridge (BA 1984). Actor and comedian: *television:* Carrott Confidential, 1987–89; Canned Carrott, 1990–92; The Mary Whitehouse Experience, 1991–92; The Imaginatively Titled Punt & Dennis Show, 1994–95; My Hero, 2000–06; Mock the Week, 2005–; Outnumbered, 2007–14; The Great British Countryside, 2012; Ballot Monkeys, 2015; *radio:* The Now Show, 1998–; It's Been a Bad Week, 1999–2006. Punt and Dennis UK tour, 2011; Punt and Dennis: Ploughing on Regardless (UK tour), 2014. Mem., BAFTA. FRGS 2010. *Publications:* (jtly) The Mary Whitehouse Experience Encyclopedia, 1991; (with S. Punt) The Punt & Dennis Instant Library, 1993; The Now Show Book, 2010; Britty Britty Bang Bang, 2013. *Recreations:* running, cycling, reading, watching, being nice to my family. *Address:* c/o Independent Talent, 40 Whitfield Street, W1T 2RH. *T:* (020) 7636 6565.

See also J. D. Dennis.

DENNIS, Brig. Richard William, OBE 2004; Deputy Commander (Army), NATO Training Mission to Afghanistan, since 2012; *b* Chelmsford, 18 Aug. 1959; *s* of William Dennis and Elsie Dennis; *m* 1982, Suzannah Mott; four *s*. *Educ:* Portsmouth Grammar Sch.; RMA Sandhurst; Open Univ. (MBA); Cranfield Univ. Commnd Royal Hampshire Regt, 1978; COS 20 Armoured Bde, 1992–94; CO, 2nd Bn The Princess of Wales's Royal Regt, 1997–99; COS, HQ Theatre Troops, 2001–03; rcds 2004; Comdr 15 (NE) Bde, 2004–08; Dir, Infantry, 2008–11. Chair, Service Complaints Panel, 2013–. Col, The Princess of Wales's Royal Regt, 2010–. Comdr, 1st Cl., Order of the Dannebrog (Denmark), 2011. *Recreations:* family, ski-ing, sailing, golf, shooting, military history, cooking. *Address:* Regimental Headquarters, The Princess of Wales's Royal Regiment, HM Tower of London, EC3N 4AB. *T:* (020) 3166 6917. *E:* rhq@123pwrr.co.uk. *Club:* Naval and Military.

DENNIS, Ronald, CBE 2000; Chairman and Chief Executive, McLaren Group, 2000–09; Chairman, McLaren Automotive, since 2009; *b* 1 June 1947; *s* of late Norman Stanley Dennis and of Evelyn (*née* Reader); *m* 1985, Lisa Ann Shelton; one *s* two *d*. *Educ:* Guildford Technical Coll. (vehicle technology course). Mechanic, Cooper Racing Car Co.; Chief Mechanic, Brabham Racing Orgn; Founder, Rondel Racing; Owner/Manager, Project Four Racing, 1976–80 (winners: Procar Championship, 1979; Formula 3 Championship, 1979–80); merged with McLaren, 1980; McLaren Formula 1 Racing Team (winners: 8 Constructors' Championships; 11 Drivers' Championships). Co-Chm., Tommy's Campaign. Hon. DTech De Montfort, 1996; Hon. DSc City, 1997; DUniv Surrey, 2000; Hon. DEng Bath, 2013. Prince Philip Medal, RAEng 2008. *Recreations:* golf, snow and water ski-ing, diving, shooting. *Address:* McLaren Group, McLaren Technology Centre, Chertsey Road, Woking, Surrey GU21 4YH. *T:* (01483) 261002, *Fax:* (01483) 261261. *Club:* British Racing Drivers'.

DENNIS, Simon Richard; Principal, British International School, Jakarta, since 2013; *b* Epsom, 23 Dec. 1957; *s* of late Reginald Dennis and Patricia Dennis; *m* 1990, Kerry Bradshaw; four *s* two *d*. *Educ:* George Abbott Sch., Guildford; Coll. of St Mark and St John (BEd Hons); Birmingham Univ. (MEd); Nat. Coll. for Sch. Leadership (NPQH 1998). Hd of Geog., Granville Sch., Burton on Trent, 1983–89; Hd of Humanities, Antony Gell Sch., Wirksworth, 1989–94; Sen. Teacher, Blake High Sch., Hednesford, Staffs, 1994–96; Dep. Hd, Noel-Baker Community Sch., Derby, 1996–2001; Headteacher, S Wolds Community Sch., Keyworth, Notts, 2001–08; Principal, Hockerill Anglo-European Coll., Bishop's Stortford, 2008–13. *Recreations:* sailing badly!, walking, reading, listening to music. *Address:* British International School, Bintaro Campus, Bintaro Jaya Sektor IX, JL Raya Jombang, Ciledug, Pondok Aren, Tangerang 15227, Jakarta, Indonesia. *E:* simon.dennis57@gmail.com.

DENNIS, Toby Edward Drake; Lord-Lieutenant of Lincolnshire, since 2015; *b* Lincoln, 18 Sept. 1954; *s* of Richard and Mary Dennis; *m* 1982, Sarah Haggas; twin *s* one *d*. *Educ:* Heatherdown Prep. Sch.; Harrow Sch.; Royal Agricl Coll., Cirencester. Agriculture, 1976–. High Sheriff, Lincs, 2013–14. Hon. Col, Lincs ACF, 2014–. *Recreations:* shooting, conservation, oenology, Rugby, football, Elton John. *Address:* Rowston Manor, Lincoln LN4 3LT. *T:* 07730487901. *E:* toby.dennis@dennisestates.co.uk. *Clubs:* White's; Lincolnshire.

DENNISS, John Annear; His Honour Judge Denniss; a Circuit Judge, since 2009; *b* London, 7 Oct. 1951; *s* of Colin Denniss and Sheila Denniss; *m* 1980, Angela Frances Raisman; one *s* two *d*. *Educ:* Winchester Coll.; Bristol Univ. (LLB). Called to the Bar, Inner Temple, 1974; a Recorder, 2002–09. *Recreations:* music, reading, fishing, ski-ing, sailing, gardening. *Address:* Isleworth Crown Court, 36 Ridgeway Road, Isleworth TW7 5LP. *Clubs:* Lansdowne; Royal Cornwall Yacht.

DENNY, Sir Charles Alistair Maurice, 4th Bt *cr* 1913, of Dumbarton, co. Dunbarton; Associate Director, HSBC Global Markets, 2006–11 (Associate Director, HSBC Bank, 2004–06); *b* 7 Oct. 1950; *e s* of Sir Alistair Maurice Archibald Denny, 3rd Bt and of Elizabeth Hunt, *y d* of Major Sir Guy Lloyd, 1st Bt, DSO; *S* father, 1995; *m* 1st, 1981, Belinda (marr. diss. 2002), *yr d* of J. P. McDonald; one *s* one *d*; 2nd, 2011, Carolyn Hilton, *o d* of late Derek Davis and of Mrs Kathleen Redpath. *Educ:* Wellington Coll.; Edinburgh Univ. *Heir:* *s* Patrick Charles Alistair Denny, *b* 2 Jan. 1985. *Address:* Winston House, Standish Court, Stonehouse, Glos GL10 3DW. *E:* charlesdenny1950@msn.com.

DENNY, John Ingram, CMG 1997; RIBA; Managing Director, Property Consulting Ltd, 2001–05; *b* 28 May 1941; *s* of Thomas Ingram Denny, Macclesfield and Claire Dorothy Denny (*née* Lewis); *m* 1967, Carol Ann Frances, *d* of Walter James Hughes, St Leonards, Bournemouth; one *s* two *d*. *Educ:* Normain Coll., Chester; Northern Poly. (Dip. Arch. (Hons)); Univ. of Reading (MSc). RIBA 1967. Partner, 1970–90, Sen. Partner, 1990–95, Man. Dir, 1995–2001, Cecil Denny Highton, architects and project managers; Jt Man. Dir, HOK Internat., 1995–2001; Sen. Vice Pres., Hellmuth, Obata + Kassabaum Inc., 1995–2001. Involved in architecture, conservation and mgt; Consultant to FCO, Home Office, MoD, Parly Works Office, Royal Household, HM Treasury, Cabinet Office, PACE and Natural Hist. Mus. *Recreations:* golf, photography.

DENNY, Sir Piers Anthony de Waltham, 9th Bt *cr* 1782, of Tralee Castle, Co. Kerry, Ireland; *b* 14 March 1954; *s* of Sir Anthony Coningham de Waltham Denny, 8th Bt and Anne Catherine, *e d* of Samuel Beverley, FRIBA; *S* father, 2013, but his name does not appear on the Official Roll of the Baronetage; *m* 1987, Ella Jane, *o d* of Peter P. Huhne; two *d*. *Educ:* King Alfred Sch.; Westfield Coll., Univ. of London. *Heir:* *b* Thomas Francis Coningham Denny [*b* 12 May 1956; *m* 1985, Benita Jane Kevill-Davies; one *d*, and one adopted *s*].

DENNY, Ronald Maurice; Director, The Catalogue Co. Ltd (Malta), 1991–2004; *b* 11 Jan. 1927; *s* of Maurice Denny and Ada (*née* Bradley); *m* 1st, 1952, Dorothy Hamilton (*d* 2003); one *s* two *d*; 2nd, 2005, Audrey Halls. *Educ:* Gosport County Sch. CEng, FIET. BBC Engineering, 1943; served Royal Navy, 1946–49; BBC Engr (TV), 1949–55; ATV Ltd, 1955, Gen. Man., ATV, 1967; Rediffusion Ltd, 1970; Chief Exec., 1979–85, Chm., 1985–89, Rediffusion PLC; Director: (non-exec.) Thames Television, 1981–89; BET, 1983–89; Electrocomponents, 1984–95. Mem. of Trust, Philharmonia Orch., 1983–93. Hon. Mem., RCM, 1984–. FRSA 1985. *Recreation:* music. *Address:* 7 The Holt, Bishop's Cleeve, Cheltenham GL52 8NQ. *T:* (01242) 677151. *Club:* Arts.

DENNY, Ross Patrick; HM Diplomatic Service; Ambassador to Costa Rica and (non-resident) to Nicaragua, since 2015; *b* Southampton, 13 Sept. 1955; *s* of Clifford Charles and Doreen Agnes Denny; *m* 2000, Claudenise De Lima; two *s* two *d*. *Educ:* Eyre Tech. High Sch. Whyalla, SA; Bitterne Park Sch., Southampton. Served RN, 1972–79. Entered FCO, 1979; WI and Atlantic Dept, FCO, 1979–80; Santiago, 1980–83; Doha, 1983–85; Vice Consul, Warsaw, 1985–88; Personnel Dept, 1988–89, S Pacific Dept, 1989–92, FCO; Second Sec., Political and EU Affairs, The Hague, 1992–97; Vice Consul Commercial, São Paulo, 1998–2001; Dep. Hd of Mission, Luanda (and non-resident accredited to São Tomé e Príncipe), 2002–05; Res. Analysts Dept, FCO, 2005–08; Adminr, Ascension Is, 2008–11; Ambassador to Bolivia, 2011–15. Mem., Mensa Internat. *Recreations:* aviation, travel, languages. *Address:* c/o Foreign and Commonwealth Office, King Charles Street, SW1A 2AH; British Embassy, Edificio Centro Colón, Paseo Colón y Calles 38/40, San Jose, Costa Rica.

DENNY, William Eric, CBE 1984; QC 1975; barrister; a Recorder of the Crown Court, 1974–93; *b* 2 Nov. 1927; *s* of William John Denny and Elsie Denny; *m* 1960, Daphne Rose Southern-Reddin; one *s* two *d*. *Educ:* Ormskirk Grammar Sch.; Liverpool Univ. (Pres., Guild of Undergraduates, 1951–52; LLB). Served RAF, 1946–48. Called to the Bar, Gray's Inn, 1953, Bencher, 1985. Lectured at LSE, 1953–58. Chm., Home Secretary's Adv. Bd on Restricted Patients, 1980–85 (Mem., 1979). *Recreations:* music, sailing, gardening.

DENNYS, Nicholas Charles Jonathan; QC 1991; a Recorder, 2000–11; *b* 14 July 1951; *m* 1977, Frances Winifred Markham (marr. diss. 2001); four *d*. *Educ:* Eton; Brasenose Coll., Oxford (BA 1973). Admitted Middle Temple, 1973; called to the Bar, 1975, Bencher, 2001; Asst Recorder, 1996–2000. Chm. Trustees, China Oxford Scholarship Fund. *Publications:* (ed) Hudson's Building and Engineering Contracts, 12th edn 2011. *Recreations:* windsurfing, golf, music. *Address:* 26 Ansdell Terrace, W8 5BY.

DENT, Helen Anne, CBE 2010; Chief Executive, Family Action (formerly Family Welfare Association), 1996–2013; *b* 29 June 1951; *d* of Frederick and Muriel Dent. *Educ:* Lancaster Univ. (BEd 1977); South Bank Poly. (MSc 1987). London Bor. of Enfield, 1981–86; Cambs CC, 1986–90; NCH, 1990–96. Mem., ESRC, 2003–07. Non-exec. Dir, Gt Ormond St Hosp. for Children NHS Trust, 1998–2008. *Recreations:* music: choral and opera, theatre, cinema, reading, gardening.

DENT, Teresa Ogilvy, CBE 2015; Chief Executive Officer, Game and Wildlife Conservation Trust, since 2001; *b* London, 22 April 1959; *d* of Christopher John Neil Stanford and Jean Ethel Ogilvie Stanford; *m* 1991, Richard Goodwill Onslow Dent; one *d*. *Educ:* Salisbury Grammar Sch.; Reading Univ. (BSc Hons Agric.). FRASE. Partner, Strutt & Parker, 1981–2001. Non-exec. Bd Mem., Natural England, 2014–. Director: Game and Wildlife Trading Ltd, 2007–; Langholm Moor Demonstration Project, 2008–; Chm., Marlborough Downs Nature Enhancement Project, 2012–. Member: NFU; Countryside Alliance; CLA; British Assoc. of Shooting and Conservation; Hon. Mem., Gamekeepers' Assoc. *Recreations:* downhill ski-ing, dressmaking. *Clubs:* Ski of GB; Grasshoppers Farmers (Hon. Mem.).

DENTON, Dame Catherine Margaret Mary; *see* Scott, Dame M.

DENTON, Charles; Head of Drama, BBC Television, 1993–96; *b* 20 Dec. 1937; *s* of Alan Charles Denton and Mary Frances Royle; *m* 1961, Eleanor Mary Player; one *s* two *d*. *Educ:* Reading Sch.; Bristol Univ. BA History (Hons). Deckhand, 1960; advertising trainee, 1961–63; BBC TV, 1963–68; freelance television producer with Granada, ATV and Yorkshire TV, 1969–72; Dir, Tempest Films Ltd, 1969–71; Man. Dir, Black Lion Films, 1979–81; ATV: Head of Documentaries, 1974–77; Controller of Programmes, 1977–81; Dir of Progs, Central Ind. TV, 1981–84; Dir, Central Ind. Television plc, 1981–87; Chief Exec., Zenith Prodns, 1984–93. Chairman: Zenith North Ltd, 1988–93; Action Time Ltd, 1988–93; Producers Alliance for Cinema and TV, 1991–93; Cornwall Film, 2001–03. Mem., Arts Council of England, 1996–98. Chm., British Film and TV Producers Assoc., 1988–91. Governor, BFI, 1992–99; Mem. Bd, Film Council, 1999–2002; Chm., Nat. Film Trustee Co., 2001–08. FRSA 1988; FRTS 1988. *Recreations:* walking, music.

DENTON, Prof. Derek Ashworth, (Dick), AC 2005; FRACP, FRCP; FRS 1999; Founding Director, Howard Florey Institute of Experimental Physiology and Medicine, Melbourne, 1971–89, Emeritus Director and Consultant Scientist, since 1990; Honorary Professorial Fellow, Florey Neuroscience and Mental Health Institute, University of Melbourne, since 2004; *b* 27 May 1924; *s* of Arthur A. and Catherine Denton; *m* 1953, Catherine Margaret Mary Scott (*see* Dame Margaret Scott); two *s*. *Educ:* Launceston Grammar Sch.; Univ. of Melbourne (MB BS). FAA 1979; FRACP 1986; FRCP 1988. Haley Res. Fellow, Walter & Eliza Hall Inst., Melbourne, 1948; Med. Res. Fellow, then Sen. Med. Res. Fellow, 1948–62, Principal Res. Fellow, 1962–70, NH&MRC. Adjunct Scientist, Texas Biomed. Res. Inst. (formerly SW Foundn for Biomed. Res.), San Antonio, Texas, 1991–; Pres., Howard Florey Biomed. Foundn, Melbourne, 1997–2009. Dir, David Syme Ltd, 1984–93. First Vice-Pres., Internat. Union of Physiol. Sci., 1983–89 (Chm., Nominating Cttee, and Cttee on Commns, 1986–93). Mem. Jury, Albert and Mary Lasker Foundn Awards in Med. Sci., 1979–90. For. Med. Mem., Royal Swedish Acad. of Sci., 1974; Mem., Amer. Acad. Arts & Sci., 1986; Foreign Associate: NAS, 1995; French Acad. of Scis, 2000. Excellence in Hypertension Prevention through Dietary Salt Reduction at Popn Level Award, World Hypertension League, 2014. *Publications:* The Hunger for Salt, 1982; The Pinnacle of Life, 1994 (trans. French 1997, Japanese 1998); Les emotions primordiales et l'éveil de la conscience, 2005 (The Primordial Emotions: the dawning of consciousness, 2006). *Recreations:* wine, tennis, fly-fishing. *Address:* Office of the Dean, Faculty of Medicine, University of Melbourne, Parkville, Vic 3010, Australia; 816 Orrong Road, Toorak, Vic 3142, Australia. *Club:* Melbourne (Melbourne).

DENTON, Jane, CBE 2007; Director, Multiple Births Foundation, since 1999; *b* 30 June 1953; *d* of Ronald and Joan Gulliver; *m* 1987, Nigel Denton. *Educ:* Nottingham Bluecoat Sch.; St Bartholomew's Hosp., London (RGN 1974); Mill Rd Maternity Hosp., Cambridge

(RM 1976). Staff Nurse, St Bartholomew's Hosp., 1974–76; Midwife, Mill Road Maternity Hosp., 1977–78; Nursing Director: Hallam Med. Centre, 1978–91; Multiple Births Foundn, 1991–99. Mem., HFEA, 1992–2004 (Dep. Chm., 1997–2000). FRCN 2006. Hon. Mem., British Fertility Soc., 2008. *Publications:* (ed jtly) Infertility: nursing and caring, 1995; (jtly) Expecting Twins?: a complete guide to pregnancy, birth and your twins' first year, 2013; contrib. articles on multiple births. *Recreations:* music, walking. *Address:* Multiple Births Foundation, Queen Charlotte's and Chelsea Hospital, W12 0HS. *T:* (020) 3313 3519. *E:* jane.denton@imperial.nhs.uk.

DENTON, Prof. John Douglas, PhD; FRS 2000; FREng; Professor of Turbomachinery Aerodynamics, Cambridge University, 1991–2005; Fellow of Trinity Hall, Cambridge, 1977–2005, now Emeritus (Vice-Master, 2002–05); *b* 1 Dec. 1939; *s* of Donald and Mary Denton; *m* 1966, Maureen Hunt; three *d*. *Educ:* Trinity Hall, Cambridge (BA, PhD); Univ. of British Columbia (MASc). MIMechE, CEng, FREng (FEng 1993). Lectr, Univ. of East Africa, 1967–69; Res. Officer, later Section Head, CEGB, 1969–77; Lectr, Dept of Engrg, Cambridge, 1977–91. *Recreations:* travel, mountain walking, bee keeping.

DENTON, John Grant, AM 2005; OBE 1977; General Secretary, General Synod of Anglican Church of Australia, 1969–94 (part time until 1977); *b* 16 July 1929; *s* of Ernest Bengrey Denton and Gladys Leonard Stevenson; *m* 1956, Shirley Joan Wise; two *s* two *d*. *Educ:* Camberwell C of E Grammar School, Melbourne. Personnel and Industrial Relations Dept, Mobil Oil (Aust.), 1950–54; Administrative Sec., Dio. of Central Tanganyika, as CMS missionary, 1954–64; Dir of Information, Dio. of Sydney, 1964–69; Registrar, Dio. of Sydney, 1969–77. Mem., ACC, 1976–84 (Chm., 1980–84); Chm., Aust. Churches' Cttee for Seventh Assembly of WCC, Canberra, 1991. Mem., Central Coast Regl Council, Dio. of Newcastle, 1997–2005. Chm., Sydney Bethel Union Trust, 1986–2002. *Recreations:* model railway, photography. *Address:* 14A Torres Street, Killarney Vale, NSW 2261, Australia.

DENTON, Dame Margaret; *see* Scott, Dame M.

DENTON, Prof. Richard Michael, PhD, DSc; FMedSci; FRS 1998; Professor of Biochemistry, 1987–2011, now Emeritus, and Senior Research Fellow, since 2010, University of Bristol; *b* 16 Oct. 1941; *s* of Arthur Benjamin Denton and Eileen Mary Denton (*née* Evans); *m* 1965, Janet Mary Jones; one *s* two *d*. *Educ:* Wycliffe Coll.; Christ's Coll., Cambridge (MA, PhD 1967); Univ. of Bristol (DSc 1976). University of Bristol: Lectr in Biochemistry, 1967–78; Reader in Biochemistry, 1978–87; Hd, Dept of Biochemistry, 1995–2000; Chm., Med. Scis, 2000–04; Founder Dean, Med. and Vet. Scis, 2003–04. MRC Sen. Res. Leave Fellow, 1984–88. Mem., MRC, 1999–2004. Founder FMedSci 1998. *Publications:* more than 240 res. papers, mainly on molecular basis of effects of insulin on metabolism, and role of calcium ions in mitochondria, in internat. res. jls. *Recreations:* family, walking, keeping fit, cooking. *Address:* School of Biochemistry, Medical Sciences Building, University of Bristol, Bristol BS8 1TD. *T:* (0117) 331 2117.

DENTON, Zane William; Head, Commercial Litigation Team, since 2014, and Training Principal, since 2012, Government Legal Department (formerly Treasury Solicitor's Department); *b* Pembury, 20 Jan. 1967; *s* of William and Valerie; two *s* one *d*. *Educ:* Univ. of East Anglia (LLB Hons). Engr, 1983–93; admitted as solicitor, 1999; lawyer, Treasury Solicitor's Dept, then Govt Legal Dept, 1997–; Hd, Gen. Private Law and Tribunals Team, 2004–06; Asst Queen's Proctor, 2004–06; Hd, Gen. Public Law Team, 2006–09; Dir, Bona Vacantia Div., 2009–14. *Recreations:* cycling, motorcycling, photography, climbing, music, practical application. *Address:* Government Legal Department, One Kemble Street, WC2B 4TS. *T:* (020) 7210 3308.

DENYER, Caryn Dawn; *see* Franklin, C. D.

DENYER, Roderick Lawrence; QC 1990; **His Honour Judge Denyer;** a Circuit Judge, since 2002; Designated Civil Judge for Bristol, since 2010; *b* 1 March 1948; *s* of Oliver James Denyer and Olive Mabel Jones; *m* 1st, 1973, Pauline (*née* Vann) (marr. diss.); two *d*; 2nd, Yoko Ujile; two step *d*. *Educ:* Grove Park Grammar School for Boys, Wrexham; London School of Economics (LLM). Called to the Bar, Inner Temple, 1970, Bencher, 1996; Lectr in Law, Bristol Univ., 1971–73; in practice at Bar, 1973–2002; a Recorder, 1990–2002. Vis. Fellow, UWE, 1994–. Mem., Bar Council, 1992–95. *Publications:* Children and Personal Injury Litigation, 1993, 2nd edn 2002; Case Management in Criminal Trials, 2010, 2nd edn 2012; contrib. legal jls. *Recreations:* cricket, 19th century history, theatre, restaurants. *Address:* Bristol Civil Justice Centre, Redcliffe Street, Bristol BS1 6GK.

DENZA, Mrs Eileen, CMG 1984; Visiting Professor, University College London, 1997–2008 (Senior Research Fellow, 1996–97); Second Counsel to Chairman of Committees and Counsel to European Communities Committee, House of Lords, 1987–95; *b* 23 July 1937; *d* of Alexander L. Young and Mrs Young; *m* 1966, John Denza; two *s* one *d*. *Educ:* Aberdeen Univ. (MA); Somerville Coll., Oxford (MA); Harvard Univ. (LLM). Called to the Bar, Lincoln's Inn, 1963. Asst Lectr in Law, Bristol Univ., 1961–63; Asst Legal Adviser, FCO (formerly FO), 1963–74; Legal Counsellor, FCO, 1974–80; Counsellor (Legal Adviser), Office of UK Perm. Rep. to European Communities, 1980–83; Legal Counsellor, FCO, 1983–86. Pupillage and practice at the Bar, 1986–87. Member: EC Law Section of Adv. Bd, British Inst. of Internat. and Comparative Law, 1988–95; Adv. Bd, Inst. of European Public Law, 1992–96; Justice Expert Panel on Human Rights in the EU, 1997–2002. Vis. Lectr, QMUL, 2007–08, 2009–10. FRSA 1995. *Publications:* Diplomatic Law, 1976, 3rd edn 2008; The Intergovernmental Pillars of the European Union, 2002; contribs to: Satow's Guide to Diplomatic Practice, 5th edn 1976, 6th edn 2009; Essays in Air Law; Airline Mergers and Cooperation in the European Community; Lee's Consular Law and Practice, 2nd edn; Institutional Dynamics of European Integration; The European Union and World Trade Law; Legislative Drafting: a modern approach, 1998; Evans' International Law, 2003, 3rd edn 2010; EU Law for the 21st Century; The Harvard Research in Internat. Law; 1951 Convention Relating to the Status of Refugees and its 1967 Protocol: a commentary, 2010; The European Union after Lisbon, 2011; The International Responsibility of the European Union, 2013; Judging Europe's Judges, 2013; The Treaty on European Union, 2013; The EU Charter of Fundamental Rights, 2014; articles in British Yearbook of Internat. Law, Revue du Marché Commun, Internat. and Comparative Law Quarterly, Statute Law Rev., Common Market Law Rev., European Foreign Affairs Rev., European Law Rev.

DEPARDIEU, Gérard; actor; *b* 27 Dec. 1948; *m* 1970, Elisabeth Guignot (marr. diss. 1996); one *d* (one *s* decd). *Educ:* Ecole d'art dramatique de Jean Laurent Cochet. Pres., Cannes Film Fest. Jury, 1992. Fellow BFI, 1989. Chevalier, Ordre Nat. du Mérite (France), 1985; Chevalier, Légion d'Honneur (France), 1996. *Stage:* Les Garçons de la Bande, Th. Edouard VII, 1968; Une fille dans ma soupe, 1970, Galapagos, 1971, Th. de la Madeleine; Saved, Th. Nat. de Chaillot, 1972; Home, 1972, Isme, Isaac, 1973, La Chevauchée sur le Lac de Constance, 1974, Espace Pierre Cardin; Les Gens deraisonnables sont en voie de disparition, Nanterre, 1977; Tartuffe, Strasbourg, 1983; Lily Passion (musical), Zénith, 1986. *Films:* Le Tueur, 1971; L'affaire Dominici, Un peu de soleil dans l'eau froide, Au rendez-vous de la mort joyeuse, La Scoumoune, Deux hommes dans la ville, Le viager, 1972; Rude journée pour la reine, Stavisky, Les Gaspards, Les Valseuses, 1973; Vincent, François, Paul et les autres, Pas si méchant que ça, 1974; 1900, La dernière femme, Sept morts sur ordonnance, Maîtresse, 1975; Barocco, René la Canne, Baxter, Vera Baxter, 1976; Dites-lui que je l'aime, Le Camion, La nuit tous les chats sont gris, Préparez vos mouchoirs, Rêve de singe, 1977; Le Sucre, Les chiens, Le Grand embouteillage, 1978; Buffet froid, Rosy la bourrasque, Loulou, Mon oncle d'Amérique, 1979; Le dernier métro (Caesar best actor award, 1980), Inspecteur la Bavure, Je vous aime, 1980; Le Choix des armes, La Femme d'à côté, La Chèvre, Le Retour de Martin Guerre, Danton, 1981; Le Grand frère, La Lune dans le caniveau, 1982; Les Compères, Fort Saganne, 1983; Tartuffe (also dir), Rive droite, rive gauche, Police, 1984; Une femme ou deux, Tenue de soirée, Jean de Florette, 1985; Les Fugitifs, Sous le soleil de Satan, 1986; Camille Claudel, 1987; Drôle d'endroit pour une rencontre, Deux, Trop belle pour toi, I Want to go Home, 1988; Cyrano de Bergerac, 1989 (Best Actor, Cannes, 1990; Caesar and de Donatello best actor awards, 1991); Green Card (Golden Globe award, 1991), Uranus, Merci la vie, 1990; Mon Père ce héros, 1492: Columbus, Tous les matins du monde, 1991; Hélas pour moi, Germinal, 1992; Une pure formalité, Le Colonel Chabert, 1993; La Machine, Elisa, Les Cents et une nuits, Les anges gardiens, 1994; Unhook the Stars, 1995; Hamlet, 1997; The Man in the Iron Mask, 1998; Astérix et Obelix contre César, Un pont entre deux rives (dir), 1999; 102 Dalmatians, 2000; Astérix et Obelix: Mission Cléopatre, The Closet, 2002; Bon voyage, Nathalie, 2004; Les temps qui changent, 2005; Last Holiday, 36 Quai des Orfèvres, 2006; La Môme, La vie en rose, The Singer, 2007; Astérix aux Jeux Olympiques, Babylon A. D., 2008; Mesrine: Killer Instinct, 2009; My Afternoons with Margueritte, Potiche, Mammuth, 2011; Welcome to New York, 2014; has also appeared on TV. *Publications:* Lettres volées, 1988; Ca s'est fait comme ça (autobiog.), 2014. *Address:* c/o Artmédia, 20 avenue Rapp, 75007 Paris, France.

de PEAR, Ben; Editor, Channel 4 News, since 2012; *b* Hammersmith, 5 Dec. 1970; *s* of John Andrew de Pear and Susan Elizabeth Kerr de Pear; *m* 2003, Leila Amanpour; two *s* one *d*. *Educ:* St Gabriel's Sch., Bridgetown, Barbados; Oakham Sch., Oakham; Univ. of Leeds (BA Hons English Lit.). Trainee reporter, Staines & Ashford News, 1994; Sky News: runner, 1994–95; foreign producer (Kosovo, Turkey, Israel), 1996–2000; Africa Ed. (incl. fall of Baghdad, Afghanistan), 2000–05; Sen. Foreign Producer, 2005–08, Foreign Ed., 2008–12, Channel 4 News. *Recreations:* football, cricket, open water swimming, cycling, literature, theatre, film, TV drama. *Address:* c/o ITN, 200 Gray's Inn Road, WC1X 8XZ. *T:* (020) 7430 4601. *E:* Ben.depear@itn.co.uk. *Clubs:* Frontline, Serpentine Swimming; Queens Park Rangers Football, Wolverhampton Wanderers Football.

de PENCIER, Theo; Chief Executive, Freight Transport Association, since 2007; *b* Carlisle, 16 Feb. 1952; *s* of Edwin and Maria de Pencier; *m* 1976, Fiona Margaret Lyall; one *s* two *d*. *Educ:* Taunton Sch., Som; Univ. of Newcastle upon Tyne (BA Hons Econ 1974). Grad. trainee, Tube Investments Ltd, 1970–74; Mktg Exec., H. J. Heinz Ltd, 1974–79; Senior Manager: Grand Metropolitan plc, 1980–85; NFC plc, 1985–95; Managing Director: Danzas Ltd, 1995–99; Bibby Line Gp, 1999–2007. MInstD 2006. FCILT 2001. Liveryman, Co. of Carmen. *Recreations:* travel, Rugby, theatre. *Address:* Freight Transport Association Ltd, Hermes House, St John's Road, Tunbridge Wells, Kent TN4 9UZ. *T:* (01892) 526171, *Fax:* (01892) 552371. *E:* tdepencier@fta.co.uk.

de PEYER, David Charles; Director General, Cancer Research Campaign, 1984–96; *b* 25 April 1934; *s* of late Charles de Peyer, CMG and Flora (*née* Collins); *m* 1959, Ann Harbord. *Educ:* Rendcomb Coll., Cirencester; Magdalen Coll., Oxford (BA PPE). Asst Principal, Min. of Health, 1960; Sec., Royal Commn on NHS, 1976–79; Under Sec., DHSS, 1979–84. Vice-Chm., Suffolk HA, 1996–98. Mem., Criminal Injuries Compensation Appeals Panel, 1997–2006. Trustee: Disabled Living Foundn, 1988–2004; Res. into Ageing, 1996–2001. Chm., Friends of All Saints, Middleton, 2007–14. *Address:* 21 Southwood Park, N6 5SG.

de PEYER, Gervase; solo clarinettist; conductor; Founder and Conductor, Melos Sinfonia of Washington, 1992; Director, London Symphony Wind Ensemble; Founder Member and solo clarinettist, Chamber Music Society of Lincoln Center, New York, 1969–89; Co-founder and Artistic Director, Innisfree Music Festival, Pa, USA; *b* London, 11 April 1926; *m* 1980, Katia Perret Aubry; one step *d*; one *s* two *d* by a previous marriage. *Educ:* King Alfred Sch., London; Bedales; Royal College of Music. Served HM Forces, 1945 and 1946. Founder Mem., Melos Ensemble of London, 1950–69; Principal Clarinet, London Symphony Orchestra, 1955–72; formerly: Associate Conductor, Haydn Orch. of London; Resident Conductor, Victoria Internat. Fest., BC, Canada. ARCM; FRCM 1992; Hon. ARAM. Gold Medallist, Worshipful Co. of Musicians, 1948; Charles Gros Grand Prix du Disque, 1961, 1962; Plaque of Honour for recording, Acad. of Arts and Sciences of America, 1962. Most recorded solo clarinettist in world. *Recreations:* travel, cooking, kite-flying, sport, theatre. *Address:* 42 Tower Bridge Wharf, 86 St Katherine's Way, E1W 1UR. *T:* and *Fax:* (020) 7265 1110. *E:* kg.dp@fsmail.net. *W:* www.gervasedepeyer.com; La Source, 485 Chemin de La Hournère, 4770 Casteljaloux, France. *T:* (5) 53833154.

DE PIERO, Gloria; MP (Lab) Ashfield, since 2010; *b* Bradford, 21 Dec. 1972; *d* of Giorgio and Maddalena De Piero; *m* 2012, James Robinson. *Educ:* Yorkshire Martyrs Sch., Bradford; Bradford and Ilkley Coll.; Univ. of Westminster (BA Social Sci. 1996); Birkbeck Coll., Univ. of London (MSc Social and Political Theory 2001). Researcher, Jonathan Dimbleby prog., ITV, 1997–98; Producer/Reporter: On The Record, 1998–2002, Politics Show, 2002–03, BBC; Political Corresp., GMTV, 2003–10. Shadow Minister for Women and Equalities, 2013–15, for Young People and Voter Registration, 2015–. *Recreations:* karaoke, swimming. *Address:* House of Commons, SW1A 0AA. *T:* (020) 7219 7004, *Fax:* (020) 7219 0700. *E:* gloria.depiero.mp@parliament.uk.

DEPLEDGE, Prof. Michael Harold, PhD, DSc; FRSB; Professor of Environment and Human Health, since 2007, and Chairman, European Centre for Environment and Human Health, since 2010, University of Exeter Medical School (formerly Peninsula Medical School); *b* 8 Jan. 1954; *s* of Clifford and Edna Depledge; *m* 1977, Juliana Eileen Dearden; two *s*. *Educ:* Leeds Modern Grammar Sch.; Westfield Coll., Univ. of London (BSc 1st Cl. Hons Biol Scis 1975; PhD 1982; DSc 1996). Res. Fellow, Brompton Hosp., London, 1979; Clinical Scientist, Royal Marsden Hosp., Sutton, 1979–82; Lectr in Physiol., Med. Sch., Univ. of Hong Kong, 1983–87; Prof. of Ecotoxicol., Odense Univ., Denmark, 1987–94; Prof. of Ecotoxicol. and Dir, Plymouth Envmtl Res. Centre, Univ. of Plymouth, 1994–2002; Hd of Sci., 2002–05, Chief Scientific Advr, 2005–06, Envmt Agency. Sen. Scientific Advr, Plymouth Marine Lab., 2005–07. Keeley Vis. Fellow, Wadham Coll., Oxford, 2006; Vis. Prof. in Zool., Univ. of Oxford, 2008–; Hon. Visiting Professor: UCL, 2012–; Chiba Univ., Japan, 2013–. Member: NERC, 2003–06; Natural England, 2006–09; Royal Commn on Envmtl Pollution, 2006–11; Bd, Climate and Health Council, 2009–; Adv. Cttee on Hazardous Substances, 2012–; Global Health Cttee, Public Health England, 2014–; Sci. Adv. Cttee, UNEP, 2015; Vice-Chm., 2006–08, Chm., 2009–13, Sci. Adv. Cttee, DG Research, EC. Royal Soc. rep., Eur. Academies Sci. Adv. Council, 2008–15. Advr to various UN bodies, 1990–. Prod. and Narrator, The Blue Gym, 2010 (RTS award for best non-broadcast film, 2010). FRSA. Hon. DSc Westminster, 2011. Poulssen Medal of Honour, Norwegian Soc. of Pharmacology and Toxicology, 2009. *Publications:* contrib. numerous peer-reviewed scientific papers, book chapters and abstracts to internat. scientific literature and learned jls, incl. Lancet, Thorax, Envmtl Sci. and Technol., Envmtl Health Perspectives, Marine Biol., Aquatic Toxicol., Science, Nature Climate Change. *Recreations:* travel, guitar, football, sailing, reading. *Address:* European Centre for Environment and Human Health, University of Exeter, Medical School, Heavitree Road, Exeter EX1 2LU. *T:* (01393) 725585. *E:* m.depledge@exeter.ac.uk.

DEPP, John Christopher, (Johnny); actor; *b* 9 June 1963; *s* of John Christopher Depp and Betty Sue Depp (*née* Palmer); *m* 1983, Lori Anne Allison (marr. diss. 1985); one *s* one *d* by Vanessa Chantal Paradis; *m* 2015, Amber Heard. *Television series:* 21 Jump Street, 1987–90; United States of Poetry, 1995. *Films include:* A Nightmare on Elm Street, 1984; Private Resort, 1985; Platoon, 1986; Cry Baby, Edward Scissorhands, 1990; Freddy's Dead: The Final

Nightmare, 1991; Benny and Joon, What's Eating Gilbert Grape, Arizona Dream, 1993; Ed Wood, Don Juan DeMarco, 1994; Dead Man, Nick of Time, 1995; The Brave (also writer and dir), Donnie Brasco, 1997; Fear and Loathing in Las Vegas, 1998; The Astronaut's Wife, The Ninth Gate, Sleepy Hollow, 1999; The Man Who Cried, Before Night Falls, Chocolat, 2000; Blow, From Hell, 2001; Pirates of the Caribbean: The Curse of the Black Pearl, Once Upon a Time in Mexico, 2003; Secret Window, Finding Neverland, The Libertine, 2004; Charlie and the Chocolate Factory, 2005; Pirates of the Caribbean: Dead Man's Chest, 2006; Pirates of the Caribbean: At World's End, 2007; Sweeney Todd: The Demon Barber of Fleet Street, 2008 (Golden Globe for Best Actor in a Musical); Public Enemies, The Imaginarium of Dr Parnassus, 2009; Alice in Wonderland, When You're Strange, The Tourist, 2010; Pirates of the Caribbean: On Stranger Tides, The Rum Diary, 2011; Dark Shadows (also prod.), 2012; The Lone Ranger, 2013; Transcendence, 2014; Into the Woods, Mortdecai, Black Mass, 2015. *Address:* c/o United Talent Agency, 9336 Civic Center Drive, Beverly Hills, CA 90212, USA.

de PURY, Christopher Mark; Partner, since 2008, and Head of Real Estate, since 2013, Berwin Leighton Paisner LLP; *b* London, 11 Feb. 1968; *s* of Andrew and Lois de Pury; *m* 2000, Carolyn Sara Rice-Oxley; two *s* one *d. Educ:* Christ Church, Oxford (MA Hons Juris.). Admitted solicitor, 1992; Solicitor, Herbert Smith LLP, Partner, 1998–2008. Mem., Develt Bd, Old Vic. Chm., Sedos. Ind. Gov., Conservatoire of Drama and Dance. Ambassador, Children's Soc. *Recreations:* theatre, drama, the arts, family. *E:* chris.de.pury@blplaw.com.

de QUINCEY, Paul Morrison; Director, Russia, British Council, 2011–15; *b* 23 June 1954; *s* of Ronald Anthony and Margaret Claire de Quincey; *m* 1976, Theresa Elizabeth Patricia Casabayo; one *s* one *d. Educ:* Univ. of Leeds (BA Hons English 1975; PGCE English/Drama 1976; MA Linguistics 1979). Teacher: of English, Ubiaja, Nigeria, 1976–78; of English and Drama, Wakefield, 1979–81; British Council, 1981–2015: Asst Rep., S Korea, 1981–84; Consultant, ELSD, London, 1984–87; Deputy Director: Algeria, 1987–91; Czechoslovakia, 1991–93; Director: Venezuela, 1993–98; Americas, 1998–2000; UK, 2000–02; Grant Funded Services, 2002–04; Dir and Cultural Counsellor, France, 2004–09; Regl Dir, Russia and N Europe, 2009–11. FRSA. *Recreations:* fishing, shooting, the arts. *Address:* 167 Kennington Road, SE11 6SF.

DE RAMSEY, 4th Baron *cr* 1887, of Ramsey Abbey, Huntingdon; **John Ailwyn Fellowes;** DL; Chairman, Environment Agency, 1995–2000; *b* 27 Feb. 1942; *s* of 3rd Baron De Ramsey, KBE and Lilah Helen Suzanne (*d* 1987), *d* of Frank Labouchere; *S* father, 1993; *m* 1st, 1973, Phyllida Mary Forsyth; one *s*; 2nd, 1984, Alison Mary Birkmyre; one *s* two *d. Educ:* Winchester Coll.; Writtle Inst. of Agriculture. Dir, Cambridge Water Co., 1974–94 (Chm., 1983–89). Crown Estate Comr, 1994–2002. President: CLA, 1991–93; Assoc. of Drainage Authorities, 1993–94 and 2004–. FRAgS 1993 (Pres., 2001–02). DL Cambs, 1993. Hon. DSc Cranfield, 1997. *Recreations:* golf, fishing, fine arts. *Heir: s* Hon. Freddie John Fellowes, *b* 31 May 1978. *Address:* Abbots Ripton Hall, Huntingdon PE28 2PQ. *T:* (01487) 773555. *Club:* Boodle's.

DERBY, 19th Earl of, *cr* 1485; **Edward Richard William Stanley;** DL; Bt 1627; Baron Stanley 1832; Baron Stanley of Preston 1886; Chairman, FF&P Trustee Co. Ltd, since 2004; *b* 10 Oct. 1962; *er s* of Hon. Hugh Henry Montagu Stanley (*d* 1971), *g s* of 17th Earl, and of Mary Rose Stanley (*née* Birch); *S* uncle, 1994; *m* 1995, Hon. Caroline Emma Neville, *d* of 10th Baron Braybrooke, *qv*; two *s* one *d. Educ:* Ludgrove; Eton Coll.; RAC Cirencester. Commnd Grenadier Guards, 1982, resigned 1985. Merchant banker with Robert Fleming Hldgs Ltd, 1987–2001. Director: Fleming Private Fund Management Ltd, 1991–96; Fleming Private Asset Management Ltd, 1992–2000; The Haydock Park Racecourse Co. Ltd, 1994–; Robert Fleming & Co. Ltd, 1996–98; Robert Fleming Internat. Ltd, 1998–2001; Stonehage Fleming Family & Partners (formerly Fleming Family & Partners), 2001–. Trustee, Nat. Mus Liverpool (formerly Nat. Mus and Galls on Merseyside), 1995–2006 (Mem., Finance Cttee, 2006–). President: Liverpool Chamber of Commerce and Industry, 1995–; Knowsley Chamber of Commerce and Industry, 1995–; Sefton Chamber of Commerce and Industry, 1998; Liverpool Council of Social Service, 1996–. Aintree Trustee, 1995–. President: Royal Liverpool Philharmonic Soc., 1995–; Rugby Football League Assoc., 1997–; Vice Pres., PGA, 2001–. Mem. Council, Univ. of Liverpool, 1998–2004 and 2011– (Vice Pres., 2012–14; Pres., 2015–). Hon. LLD Liverpool, 2008; Hon. DBA Chester, 2009. DL Merseyside, 1999. *Publications:* Ouija Board: a mare in a million, 2007. *Recreations:* diving, shooting, ski-ing, food and wine. *Heir: s* Lord Stanley, *qv*. *Address:* Knowsley, Prescot, Merseyside L34 4AF. *T:* (0151) 489 6148. *E:* private.office@knowsley.com. *Clubs:* White's, Jockey Club Rooms (Newmarket).

See also Hon. P. H. C. Stanley.

DERBY, Bishop of, since 2005; **Rt Rev. Dr Alastair Llewellyn John Redfern;** *b* 1 Sept. 1948; *s* of Victor Redfern and Audrey Joan Redfern; *m* 1st, 1974, Jane Valerie Straw (*d* 2004); two *d*; 2nd, 2006, Caroline Elizabeth Boddington, *qv*. *Educ:* Christ Church, Oxford (MA Modern Hist.); Trinity Coll., Cambridge (MA Theol.); Westcott House, Cambridge; PhD Theol. Bristol. Curate, Tettenhall Regis, dio. Lichfield, 1976–79; Lectr in Church History, 1979–87, Vice Principal, 1985–87, Ripon Coll., Cuddesdon; Dir, Oxford Inst. for Church and Society, 1979–83; Curate, All Saints, Cuddesdon, 1983–87; Canon Theologian, Bristol Cathedral, 1987–97; Bishop Suffragan of Grantham, 1997–2005. Dean of Stamford, 1997–2005; Canon and Preb., Lincoln Cathedral, 2000–05. Mem., H of L, 2010. *Publications:* Ministry and Priesthood, 1999; Being Anglican, 2000; Growing the Kingdom, 2009; Public Space and Private Faith: a challenge to the churches, 2009; Thomas Hobbes and the Limits of Democracy, 2009; Community and Conflict, 2011; Out of the Depths, 2012; Leadership of the People of God, 2013; Discipleship: a call and commission, 2013; Mission in Action, 2014; Living in Love: mysticism in a material world, 2014; Sacrifice Remembered, 2014; The Word on the Street, 2015. *Recreations:* reading, walking. *Address:* The Bishop's House, 6 King Street, Duffield, Belper DE56 4EU. *T:* (office) (01332) 840132. *E:* bishop@bishopofderby.org.

DERBY, Dean of; *see* Davies, Very Rev. J. H.

DERBY, Archdeacon of; *see* Cunliffe, Ven. C. J.

DERBYSHIRE, Sir Andrew (George), Kt 1986; FRIBA; Chairman, Robert Matthew, Johnson-Marshall & Partners & RMJM Ltd, 1983–89; President, RMJM Group, 1989–98; *b* 7 Oct. 1923; *s* of late Samuel Reginald Derbyshire and late Helen Louise Puleston Derbyshire (*née* Clarke); *m* Lily Rhodes (*née* Binns), *widow* of late Norman Rhodes; three *s* one *d. Educ:* Chesterfield Grammar Sch.; Queens' Coll., Cambridge; Architectural Assoc. MA (Cantab), AA Dip. (Hons). Admty Signals Estabt and Bldg Research Station, 1943–46. Farmer & Dark, 1951–53 (Marchwood and Belvedere power stations); West Riding County Architect's Dept, 1953–55 (bldgs for educn and social welfare). Asst City Architect, Sheffield, 1955–61; responsible for central area redevelt and Castle Mkt. Mem. Research Team, RIBA Survey of Architects' Offices, 1960–62. Mem. RM, J-M & Partners, later RMJM Ltd, 1961–98, responsible for: develt of Univ. of York, 1961–98, Central Lancs New Town, NE Lancs Impact Study, Univ. of Cambridge, West Cambridge Develt and New Cavendish Laboratory, Preston Market and Guildhall, London Docklands Study, Hillingdon Civic Centre, Cabtrack and Minitram feasibility studies, Suez Master Plan Study; Castle Peak Power Stations, and Harbour Reclamation and Urban Growth Study, Hong Kong. Consultant on envmtl impact issues, listing of post-war bldgs and res. on feedback for construction industry, 1998–. Member: RIBA Council, 1950–72, 1975–81 (Senior Vice-Pres., 1980); NJCC, 1961–65; Bldg Industry Communications Res. Cttee, 1964–66 (Chm. Steering Cttee); DoE Planning and Transport Res. Adv. Council, 1971–76; Commn on Energy and the Environment, 1978–81. Pt-time Mem., CEGB, 1973–84; Board Member: Property Services Agency, 1975–79; London Docklands Develt Corp., 1984–88 (Chm., Planning Cttee, 1984–88); Construction Industry Sector Group, NEDC, 1988–92; Mem., Construction Industry Council, 1990–94. Trustee, Usable Buildings Trust, 2009–. Hoffman Wood Prof. of Architecture, Univ. of Leeds, 1978–80; External Prof., Dept of Civil Engineering, Univ. of Leeds, 1981–85; Gresham Prof. of Rhetoric, Gresham Coll., 1990–92; Hon. Fellow, Inst. of Advanced Architectural Studies, Univ. of York, 1994; Hon. FIStructE 1992. FRSA 1981 (Chm., Art for Architecture Project, 1994–98). DUniv York, 1972. *Publications:* The Architect and his Office, 1962; on professional consultancy, town planning, public transport, and energy conservation in construction; incl. papers on architecture, science and conservation of 20th century buildings, 1998–. *Recreations:* his family, the garden. *Address:* 4 Sunnyfield, Hatfield, Herts AL9 5DX. *T:* (01707) 265903. *E:* andrewderby@mailme.co.uk.

DERCON, Prof. Stefan Nicolaas Alfons Anna, DPhil; Chief Economist, Department for International Development, since 2011; Professor of Economic Policy, University of Oxford, since 2015; Fellow, Jesus College, Oxford, since 2015; *b* Ekeren, Belgium, 4 Dec. 1964; *s* of René Dercon and Maria Nelen; *m* 1996, Pramila Krishnan; one *s. Educ:* Katholieke Univ. Leuven, Belgium (BA Phil. 1985; License in Econs 1986); Queen's Coll., Oxford (MPhil Econs 1988; DPhil Econs 1993). Post-doctoral Res. Fellow, Nuffield Coll., Oxford, 1993–97; Prof. of Develt Econs, Katholieke Univ. Leuven, 1993–2000; University of Oxford: Lectr, 2001–04; Fellow and Tutor in Econs, Jesus Coll., 2001–04; Prof. of Develt Econs, 2004–15; Fellow, Wolfson Coll., 2004–15. Vis. Prof., Econs Dept, Addis Ababa Univ., 1992–93. *Publications:* Insurance Against Poverty, 2004; contribs to learned jls incl. Jl of Pol Econ., Rev. of Econs and Stats, Econ. Jl, Jl of Develt Econs, Demography. *Address:* Department of Economics, University of Oxford, Manor Road Building, Oxford OX1 3UQ.

DERHAM, Catherine Beatrice Margaret, (Katie), (Mrs J. Vincent); Presenter: BBC2 Proms, since 2009, and Proms Extra, since 2013; BBC Radio 3, since 2010; Managing Director, Peanut and Crumb Ltd, since 2015; *b* 18 June 1970; *d* of John and Margaret Derham; *m* 1999, John Vincent; two *d. Educ:* Cheadle Hulme Sch.; Magdalene Coll., Cambridge (BA Econ). Joined BBC, 1993: researcher, Money Box, Radio 4, 1993–94; Producer, Radio Business Progs, 1994–95; Presenter, Money Check, Radio 5 Live, 1995–96; Consumer Affairs Corresp., TV business progs, 1996–97; reporter, Film '96, '97; Media and Arts Corresp., 1998–2001, Media and Arts Editor, 2001–03, ITN; newscaster, ITV News, 1999–2010, and ITV Evening News, 2001–10; presenter: London Tonight, ITV, 2004–10; ITV lunchtime news, 2005–10; series for BBC Radio 4: Traveller's Tree, 2008–10; The Global Reach, 2012; documentaries for BBC Radio 4 include: Inside Fortress Bill, 2012; One Man's War, 2012; The Synchro Girls, 2012. Presenter: Classical Brit Awards, annually, 2001–04; Classic FM, 2002–09; LBC, 2003. Judge: Lost Booker Prize, 2010; Costa Book Prize, 2013. Contestant, Maestro, BBC TV, 2008; First Love, Sky Arts, 2010. *Recreations:* reading, travel, music - listening and playing, film, sailing. *Address:* c/o BBC Radio 3, Broadcasting House, W1A 1AA.

DERHAM, Patrick Sibley Jan, MA; Head Master, Westminster School, since 2014; *b* 23 Aug. 1959; *s* of John Joseph Sibley Derham and Helena Petronella Trimby (*née* Verhagen); *m* 1982, Alison Jane Sheardown; one *s* one *d. Educ:* Training Ship Arethusa; Pangbourne Coll. (Hd of Sch.); Pembroke Coll., Cambridge (Foundn Schol., 1st Cl. Hons Hist. 1982, MA 1985). Assistant Master: Cheam, 1982–84; Radley Coll., 1984–96 (Hd of Hist. and Tutor, 1990–96); Headmaster, Solihull Sch., 1996–2001; Head Master, Rugby Sch., 2001–14. Trustee: Solihull Community Foundn, 1998–2001; IntoUniversity, 2006– (Dep. Chm., 2008–); Gladstone Library, 2012–; Springboard Bursary Foundn, 2013–. *Publications:* The Irish Question 1868–1886: a collection of documents, 1988; (ed jtly) Liberating Learning: widening participation, 2010; Cultural Olympians, 2013; contrib. articles and reviews. *Recreations:* quizzes, collecting Tom Merry political cartoons, reading contemporary fiction, running, family. *Address:* Westminster School, Little Dean's Yard, Westminster, SW1P 3PF.

de RIVAZ, (Philippe) Vincent (Jacques Léon Marie), Hon. CBE 2012; Chief Executive, EDF Energy plc, since 2003; *b* Paris, 4 Oct. 1953; *s* of François de Rivaz and Isabelle de Rivaz (*née* de Buttet); *m* 1980, Anne de Valence de Minardière; three *s. Educ:* Ecole Nat. Supérieure d'hydraulique, Grenoble. Hydraulic engineer; Electricité de France: joined External Engrg Centre, 1977; Manager, Far East Div., 1985–91; Man. Dir, Hydropower Dept, 1991–94; Dep. Hd, Internat. Develt, i/c New Projects Develt, 1995–98; Corporate Finance and Treasury Dir, 1999–2001; Chief Exec., London Electricity, 2002–03; Mem., Exec. Cttee, EDF Gp, 2004–. Melchett Medal, Energy Inst., 2006. Chevalier de la Légion d'honneur (France), 2010. *Recreations:* photography, cycling. *Address:* EDF Energy plc, 40 Grosvenor Place, SW1X 7EN. *T:* (020) 7752 2101, *Fax:* (020) 7752 2104. *E:* vincent.de-rivaz@edfenergy.com.

DERMODY, Paul Bernard, OBE 2004; Director, 1997–2003, Chief Executive, 2000–03, De Vere Group plc (formerly Greenalls Group plc); *b* 1 Oct. 1945; *s* of Bernard and Jessie Dermody; *m* 1967, Margaret Eileen Horsfield; one *s* one *d. Educ:* De La Salle Coll., Salford; Salford Tech. Coll. ACMA 1971. Mgt accounting trainee, 1963–68, Asst Accountant, 1968–72, Groves & Whitnall; Mgt Accountant, Greenalls Brewery, 1972–77; Financial Controller, Greenalls Retail Div., 1977–84; Finance Dir and Dep. Man. Dir, 1984–89, Dep. Chm., 1989–95, De Vere Hotels; Chief Exec., Premier House & Village Leisure Hotels, 1995–97; Man. Dir, Greenalls Hotels & Leisure Ltd, 1997–2000. Non-exec. Chm., Conferma Ltd, 2008–; non-executive Director: Majestic Wine, 2004–13; Aga Rangemaster (formerly Foodservice) Gp plc, 2004–14. Chm., Nat. Football Mus., 2005–. School Governor. FIH (FHCIMA 1997); FBAHA 1985; FRSA 2000; CCMI 2001. *Recreations:* singing, swimming, reading, travel. *Address:* 6 Roe Green, Worsley, Manchester M28 2RF.

DERNIE, Prof. David James, RIBA; Dean, Faculty of Architecture and Built Environment, University of Westminster, since 2012; Principal, David Dernie Architects, since 2000; *b* 16 Dec. 1962; *s* of B. S. Broughton and M. J. Dernie; *m* 1997; one *s. Educ:* Lancaster Royal Grammar Sch.; Fitzwilliam Coll., Cambridge (BA 1985; DipArch 1988). RIBA 1990. Rome Scholar, British Sch. at Rome, 1991–93; Lectr in Architecture, Univ. of Cambridge, and Fellow, Fitzwilliam Coll., Cambridge, 1998–2005; Reader in Architecture, Univ. of Nottingham, 2005; Hd, Manchester Sch. of Architecture, 2005–09; Prof. of Architecture, Manchester Metropolitan Univ., 2005–09; Head, Leicester Sch. of Architecture, De Montfort Univ., 2009–12. Vis. Prof. of Architecture, Univ. of Lincoln, 2003–. *Publications:* Victor Horta, 1995; Villa D'Este at Tivoli, 1996; New Stone Architecture, 2003; Material Imagination, 2005; Exhibition Design, 2006; Architectural Drawings, 2010. *Recreations:* drawing, painting, music, travel. *Address:* 21 Highsett, Cambridge CB2 1NX. *T:* 07866 602574. *E:* daviddernie@icloud.com.

de ROS, 28th Baron *cr* 1264 (Premier Barony of England); **Peter Trevor Maxwell;** *b* 23 Dec. 1958; *s* of Comdr John David Maxwell, RN, and late Georgiana Angela Maxwell, 27th Baroness de Ros; *S* mother, 1983; *m* 1987, Siân Ross; one *s* two *d. Educ:* Headfort School, Kells, Co. Meath; Stowe School, Bucks; Down High School, Co. Down. Upholstered furniture maker. *Recreations:* gardening, travel and sailing. *Heir: s* Hon. Finbar James Maxwell, *b* 14 Nov. 1988.

de ROTHSCHILD; *see* Rothschild.

DERRICK, Peter; Chamberlain, City of London Corporation (formerly Corporation of London), 1999–2007; *b* 2 April 1948; *s* of John Moorhead Derrick and Lucy (*née* Norman); *m* 1972, Joyce Bainbridge; two *d. Educ:* Univ. of Lancaster (BA Hons Politics 1974). CPFA

1971. Gateshead CBC, 1965–71; Principal Accountant, Carlisle CC, 1974–77; Chief Tech. Asst, Knowsley MBC, 1977–79; Principal Accountant, Lothian Regl Council, 1979–81; Under Sec. (Finance), ADC, 1981–85; Director of Finance: London Bor. of Hounslow, 1985–88; London Bor. of Camden, 1988–91; Chief Exec., London Bor. of Hammersmith and Fulham, 1991–93; Dir, Finance and Corporate Services, Surrey CC, 1993–98. Actg Prin., GSMD, 2003–04. Chm., London Financial Adv. Cttee, CIPFA, 2000–06; Chm., Officer Adv. Gp, Local Govt Pension Scheme, Local Govt Employers Orgn, 1997–2006; Mem., Employer Task Force on Pensions, DWP, 2003–04. Council Mem., Nat. Assoc. of Pension Funds, 1997–2002; Pres., Soc. of London Treasurers, 2003–04. Order of the Dannebrog (Denmark), 2000. *Recreations:* football, golf, squash, film, opera. *Address:* 352 Wimbledon Central, Wimbledon, SW19 4BJ. *Clubs:* Wimbledon Racquets and Fitness; Wimbledon Park Golf; Sunderland AFC Supporters.

DERRY, Bishop of, (RC), since 2014; **Most Rev. Donal McKeown;** *b* Belfast, 12 April 1950; *s* of James McKeown and Rose McKeown (*née* McMeel). *Educ:* Mount St Michael's Primary Sch.; St MacNissi's Coll., Garron Tower; Queen's Univ. Belfast; Pontifical Gregorian Univ., Rome (LTh); Univ. of Leicester (MBA 2000). Teacher of English, Dieburg, Germany, 1970–71; NI Correspondent, Katholische Nachrichten Agentur, 1971–73; Teacher: St Patrick's Coll., Knock, 1978–83; St MacNissi's Coll., Garron Tower, 1983–87; Teacher, Dean of Seminary and Pres., St Malachy's Coll., Belfast; Titular Bishop of Cell Ausaille, and Auxiliary Bishop of Down and Connor, 2001–14. *Address:* Diocesan Offices, St Eugene's Cathedral, Francis Street, Derry BT48 9AP.

DERRY AND RAPHOE, Bishop of, since 2002; **Rt Rev. Kenneth Raymond Good;** *b* 1 Nov. 1952; *s* of (William Thomas) Raymond Good and Jean Beryl (*née* Hewson); *m* 1977, Mary Knox; two *s* one *d*. *Educ:* Dublin Univ. (BA 1974); Nottingham Univ. (BA Theol., 1976); NUI (HDipEd 1981, MEd 1984). Ordained deacon, 1977, priest, 1978; Curate, Willowfield Parish, Belfast, 1977–79; Chaplain and Hd of Religious Educn, Ashton Comprehensive Sch., Cork, 1979–84; Rector: Dunganstown Union, dio. Glendalough, 1984–90; Shankill Parish, Lurgan, 1990–2002; Archdeacon of Dromore, 1997–2002. *Publications:* A Heart for the Unchurched, 1996. *Recreations:* golf, swimming, opera. *Address:* The See House, 112 Culmore Road, Londonderry, Northern Ireland BT48 8JF. *E:* bishop@derry.anglican.org.

DERRY, Kim Daniel B.; *see* Bromley-Derry.

DERVAIRD, Hon. Lord; John Murray; Dickson Minto Professor of Company Law, Edinburgh University, 1990–99, now Professor Emeritus; a Senator of the College of Justice in Scotland, 1988–89; *b* 8 July 1935; *o s* of J. H. Murray, farmer, Stranraer; *m* 1960, Bridget Jane, *d* of Sir William Godfrey, 7th Bt, and of Lady Godfrey; three *s*. *Educ:* Stranraer schs; Edinburgh Academy; Corpus Christi Coll., Oxford (BA 1st cl. Lit. Hum., 1959); Edinburgh Univ. (LLB 1962). FCIArb 1991. Advocate, 1962; QC (Scot.) 1974. Dean, Faculty of Law, Edinburgh Univ., 1994–96. Mem., Scottish Law Commn, 1979–88. Chairman: Scottish Lawyers' European Gp, 1975–78; Scottish Council of Law Reporting, 1978–88; Scottish Cttee on Law of Arbitration, 1986–96; Scottish Council for Internat. Arbitration, 1989–2003; Panel of Professional Adjudicators, 2004–; Member: City Disputes Panel, 1994–; Panel of Arbitrators, Internat. Centre for Investment Disputes, 1998–2004; Adv. Bd, Internat. Arbitration Inst., Paris, 2000–; Academic Council, SICA-FICA, 2002–; Internat. Arbitration Club, 2009–; Vice-President: Centre of Conciliation and Arbitration for Advanced Techniques, Paris, 2000–; Scottish Arbitration Centre, 2011–. Vice-President: Agricultural Law Assoc., 1985–91 (Chm., 1979–85); Comité Européen de Droit Rural, 1989–91, 1995–96. Hon. Pres., Advocates' Business Law Group, 1988–. Dir and Chm., BT Scottish Ensemble, 1988–2000. Corresp. Mem., ICC Cttee on Business Law, Paris, 1994–. Trustee, David Hume Inst., 1994–2007. Grand Chaplain, Von Poser Soc. of Scotland, 1995; Knight, Order of Von Poser, 1996. *Publications:* contributed to: Festschrift für Dr Pikalo, 1979; Mélanges offerts à Jean Megret, 1985; Stair Encyclopedia of Scots Law, 1987, 1992, 1998, 2001; Scottish Legal Tradition, 1991; Corporate Law—the European Dimension, 1991; European Company Law, 1992; International Handbook on Commercial Arbitration, 1995; Essays in Honour of Lord Mackenzie-Stuart of Dean, 1996; Science and Law, 2000; The International Arbitration Review, 3rd edn 2013; articles in legal and ornithological jls. *Recreations:* farming, gardening, birdwatching, music, curling, field sports. *Address:* Auchenmalg House, Auchenmalg, Glenluce, Wigtownshire DG8 0JS. *T:* (01581) 500205, *Fax:* (0131) 220 0644; Wood of Dervaird Farm, Glenluce DG8 9JT. *T:* (01581) 300222. *E:* murraydervaird@talk21.com. *Clubs:* New (Edinburgh); Aberlady Curlers.

DERWENT, 5th Baron *cr* 1881; **Robin Evelyn Leo Vanden-Bempde-Johnstone,** LVO 1957; Bt 1795; DL; Deputy Chairman, Hutchison Whampoa (Europe) Ltd, 1998–2007 (Managing Director, 1985–97); *b* 30 Oct. 1930; *s* of 4th Baron Derwent, CBE and Marie-Louise (*d* 1985), *d* of Albert Picard, Paris; *S* father, 1986; *m* 1957, Sybille, *d* of late Vicomte de Simard de Pitray and Madame Jeanine Hennessy; one *s* three *d*. *Educ:* Winchester College; Clare Coll., Cambridge (Scholar, MA 1953). 2nd Lieut 1949, 60th Rifles; Lieut 1950, Queen Victoria's Rifles (TA). HM Diplomatic Service, 1954–69; served FO, Paris, Mexico City, Washington. Director, NM Rothschild & Sons, Merchant Bankers, 1969–85. Director: F&C (Pacific) Investment Trust Ltd, 1989–2001; Scarborough Building Soc., 1991–2001. Chm., London & Provincial Antique Dealers' Assoc., 1989–95. Mem., N York Moors Nat. Park Authy, 1997–99. Chm., Scarborough Mus Trust, 2004–08, Patron, 2008–. DL N Yorks, 1991. Hon. Freeman, Bor. of Scarborough, 2008. Chevalier de la Légion d'Honneur (France), 1957; Officier de l'Ordre National du Mérite (France), 1978. *Recreations:* shooting, fishing. *Heir:* *s* Hon. Francis Patrick Harcourt Vanden-Bempde-Johnstone [*b* 23 Sept. 1965; *m* 1990, Cressida, *o d* of late Christopher John Bourke; one *d*]. *Address:* Low Hall, Hackness, Scarborough YO13 0JN; Penthouse 6, Sovereign Court, 29 Wrights Lane, W8 5SH. *Club:* Boodle's.

DERWENT, Henry Clifford Sydney, CB 2006; climate change consultant, since 2012; Chief Executive, Climate Strategies, since 2011; *b* 19 Nov. 1951; *s* of late Clifford Sydney Derwent and Joan Kathleen (*née* Craft); *m* 1988, Rosemary Patricia Jesse Meaker; three *d*. *Educ:* Berkhamsted Sch.; Worcester Coll., Oxford. Department of the Environment, 1974–86: planning policy; PSA; London housing; commercial property; Rayner scrutiny; seconded to Midland Bank; inner cities; Department of Transport, subseq. DETR, now DEFRA, 1986–2008: private office; local finance; vehicle licensing; central finance; highways; Under Sec., then Dir, Nat. Roads Policy, 1992–97; (on secondment) Corporate Finance Div., SBC Warburg, later UBS Warburg, 1997–99; Dir, Envmt: Risks and Atmosphere, subseq. Climate, Energy and Envmtl Risk, then Internat. Climate Change Air and Analysis, 1999–2008; Pres. and CEO, Internat. Emissions Trading Assoc., 2008–12, now Hon. Vice Pres. *Recreations:* flutes, trombones, saxophones, riding, drawing, watercolours. *Address:* Climate Strategies, c/o UCL Energy Institute, Central House, 14 Upper Woburn Place, WC1H 0NN.

DERX, Donald John, CB 1975; non-executive Director, Glaxo Holdings, later Glaxo Wellcome plc, 1991–97; *b* 25 June 1928; *s* of John Derx and Violet Ivy Stroud; *m* 1956, Luisa Donzelli; two *s* two *d*. *Educ:* Tiffin Boys' Sch., Kingston-on-Thames; St Edmund Hall, Oxford (BA). Asst Principal, BoT, 1951; seconded to Cabinet Office, 1954–55; Principal, Colonial Office, 1957; Asst Sec., Industrial Policy Gp, DEA, 1965; Dir, Treasury Centre for Admin. Studies, 1968; Head of London Centre, Civil Service Coll., 1970; Under Sec., 1971–72, Dep. Sec., 1972–84, Dept of Employment; Dir, Policy Studies Inst., 1985–86; with Glaxo Holdings plc, 1986–90.

DESAI, family name of **Baron Desai**.

DESAI, Baron *cr* 1991 (Life Peer), of St Clement Danes in the City of Westminster; **Meghnad Jagdishchandra Desai,** PhD; Professor of Economics, 1983–2003, now Emeritus, Director, Centre for the Study of Global Governance, 1992–2003, and Hon. Fellow, 2005, London School of Economics and Political Science; *b* 10 July 1940; *s* of late Jagdishchandra and of Mandakini Desai; *m* 1st, 1970, Gail Graham Wilson (marr. diss. 2004); one *s* two *d*; 2nd, 2004, Kishwar Ahluwalia. *Educ:* Univ. of Bombay (BA Hons, MA); Univ. of Pennsylvania (PhD 1964). Associate Specialist, Dept of Agricultural Econs, Univ. of Calif, Berkeley, 1963–65; London School of Economics: Lectr, 1965–77, Sen. Lectr, 1977–80, Reader, 1980–83, Dept of Econs; Head, Develt Studies Inst., 1990–95. Pres., Assoc. of Univ. Teachers in Econs, 1987–90; Mem. Council, REconS, 1988. Life Pres., Islington South and Finsbury Constituency Labour Pty, 1993– (Chm., 1986–92). Hon. DSc Kingston, 1992; Hon. DSc (Econ) E London, 1994; DUniv Middlesex, 1993; Hon. DPhil London Guildhall, 1996; Hon. LLD Monash, 2005. Jewel of Ruia, Ruia Coll. Alumni Assoc., 2011. Pravasi Bharatiya Puraskar (India), 2004; Padma Bhushan (India) 2008. *Publications:* Marxian Economic Theory, 1974; Applied Econometrics, 1976; Marxian Economics, 1979; Testing Monetarism, 1981; (Asst Editor to Prof. Dharma Kumar) The Cambridge Economic History of India 1757–1970, 1983; (ed jtly) Agrarian Power and Agricultural Productivity in South Asia, 1984; (ed) Lenin on Economics, 1987; Macroeconomics and Monetary Theory: selected essays, vol. 1, 1995; Poverty, Famine and Economic Development: selected essays, vol. 2, 1995; (ed jtly) Global Governance, 1995; (ed) On Inequality, 1995; Marx's Revenge, 2002; Nehru's Hero: Dilip Kumar in the life of India, 2004; Development and Nationhood, 2005; Rethinking Islamism, 2006; The Route to All Evil: political economy of Ezra Pound, 2006; The Rediscovery of India, 2009; Dead on Time, 2009; Pakeeza: ode to a bygone age, 2013; Who Wrote the Bhagavad Gita?: a secular inquiry into a sacred text, 2014; contrib. Econometrica, Econ. Jl, Rev. of Econ. Studies, Economica, Econ. Hist. Rev. *Address:* House of Lords, SW1A 0PW.

DESAI, Anita, FRSL; novelist; *b* 24 June 1937; *d* of Toni Nimé and D. N. Mazumbar; *m* 1958, Ashvin Desai; two *s* two *d*. *Educ:* Queen Mary's Sch., Delhi; Miranda House, Univ. of Delhi (BA Hons). FRSL 1963. First story published 1946; novelist and book reviewer (freelance), 1963–. Helen Cam Vis. Fellow, 1986–87, Hon. Fellow, 1988, Girton Coll., Univ. of Cambridge; Elizabeth Drew Prof., Smith Coll., USA, 1987–88; Purington Prof. of English, Mount Holyoke Coll., USA, 1988–92; Prof. of Writing, 1993, John E. Burchard Emeritus Prof., 2003, MIT; Ashby Fellow, 1989, Hon. Fellow, 1991, Clare Hall, Univ. of Cambridge. Hon. Mem., Amer. Acad. of Arts and Letters, 1993. Neil Gunn Prize for Internat. Writers, Scotland, 1993; Alberto Moravia Prize for Internat. Writers, Italy, 1999. Padma Sri, 1990; Ca' Foscari Prize, Univ. of Venice, 2006; Giuseppe di Lampedusa Prize, Sicily, 2006. *Publications:* Cry, The Peacock, 1963; Voices in the City, 1965; Bye-Bye Blackbird, 1971; Where Shall We Go This Summer?, 1973; Fire on the Mountain, 1978 (Winifred Holtby Award, RSL, 1978); Games at Twilight, 1979; Clear Light of Day, 1980; The Village by the Sea, 1983 (Guardian Prize for Children's Fiction, 1983; filmed, 1992); In Custody, 1984 (screenplay, filmed 1994); Baumgartner's Bombay, 1988 (Hadassah Prize, Hadassah Magazine, NY, 1989); Journey to Ithaca, 1995; Fasting, Feasting, 1999; Diamond Dust and Other Stories, 2000; The Zigzag Way, 2004; The Artist of Disappearance, 2011. *Address:* c/o Rogers, Coleridge & White Ltd, 20 Powis Mews, W11 1JN.

de SAUMAREZ, 7th Baron *cr* 1831; **Eric Douglas Saumarez;** Bt 1801; farmer; *b* 13 Aug. 1956; *s* of 6th Baron de Saumarez and Joan Beryl, (Julia) (*d* 2004), *d* of late Douglas Raymond Charlton; *S* father, 1991; *m* 1st, 1982, Christine Elizabeth (marr. diss. 1990), *yr d* of B. N. Halliday; two *d*; 2nd, 1991, Susan M. Hearn. *Educ:* Milton Abbey; Nottingham Univ.; RAC, Cirencester. *Recreations:* flying, shooting, ski-ing, fishing. *Heir:* *twin b* Hon. Victor Thomas Saumarez, *b* 13 Aug. 1956. *Address:* Les Beaucamps de Bas, Castel, Guernsey GY5 7PE.

de SAVARY, Peter John; international entrepreneur; *b* 11 July 1944; *m* Marcia (marr. diss.; she *m* Maj. Hon. Sir John (Jacob) Astor, MBE, ERD); two *d*; *m* 1986, (Lucille) Lana Paton; three *d*. *Educ:* Charterhouse. Activities in the energy, property, finance, maritime and hospitality fields. Chm., Victory Syndicate, Admiral's Cup, 1981 and 1983 British Challenge for America's Cup. Founder of Clubs: Carnegie (Chm., 1994–2003); Carnegie Abbey; Cherokee Plantation; Abaco; London Outpost; St James's, NY, Antigua, London, Paris, LA. Diplomatic Ambassador for Inward Investment, Grenada. Contested (Referendum) Falmouth and Camborne, 1997. Patron, Teenage Cancer Trust, 1995–. Tourism Personality of the Year, English Tourist Bd, 1988. *Recreations:* sailing, riding, carriage driving, landscape gardening. *Clubs:* St James's, 5 Hertford Street, Royal Thames Yacht; Royal Burnham Yacht, Royal Torbay Yacht, Royal Corinthian Yacht, Royal Cornwall Yacht; New York Yacht.

de SILGUY, Count Yves-Thibault Christian Marie; Vice Chairman and Lead Director, VINCI, since 2010 (Chairman, 2006–10); Chairman, YTSeuropaconsultants, since 2010; *b* Rennes, 22 July 1948; *s* of Raymond de Silguy and Claude de Pompery; *m* 1976, Jacqueline de Montillet de Grenaud (decd); one *s* one *d*. *Educ:* Collège Saint-Martin; Univ. of Rennes (Law and Econ Scis); Sch. of Public Service, Institut d'Etudes Politiques, Paris (Dip.); Ecole Nationale d'Administration. Sec. for Foreign Affairs to Dir for Econ. and Financial Affairs, 1976–80; Advr, then Dep. Staff Dir for Vice-Pres. Ortoli, Comr for Econ. and Monetary Affairs, 1981–84; Advr i/c Econ. Affairs, French Embassy in Washington, 1985–86; Tech. Advr to Prime Minister i/c European Affairs and Internat. Econ. and Financial Affairs, 1986–88; Manager, Internat. Business Div. and Gp Internat. Business Dir, Usinor Sacilor, 1988–93; Sec. Gen., Interministerial Cttee for European Econ. Co-operation and Advr for European Affairs to Prime Minister, 1993–95; Mem., European Commn, i/c economic, monetary and financial affairs, 1995–99. Bd Mem., 2000–02, Sen. Exec. Vice-Pres., 2002–06, SUEZ. Gen. Deleg. of French Steel Fedn, 1990–93; Chm. Bd, Professional Center for Steel Stats, 1990–93; Chm., Finance Cttee, Eurofer, 1990–93; Trustee, Internat. Accounting Standards Cttee Foundn, 2010–13. Commandeur: Ordre des Arts et des Lettres (France), 2007 (Officier, 1994); du Mérite Agricole (France), 2010 (Officier, 1995); Légion d'Honneur (France), 2011; Officier, Ordre Nat. du Mérite (France), 2000. *Recreations:* tennis, yachting, hunting. *Address:* c/o VINCI, 1 cours Ferdinand de Lesseps, 92851 Rueil-Malmaison Cedex, France. *Clubs:* Polo, Cercle de l'Union Interalliée (Paris).

de SILVA, Rt Hon. Sir Desmond (George Lorenz), Kt 2007; PC 2011; QC 1984; international lawyer; Chief Prosecutor of UN-sponsored Special Court for Sierra Leone, 2005–06; *b* 13 Dec. 1939; *s* of late Edmund Frederick Lorenz de Silva, MBE, and Esme Gregg de Silva; *m* 1987, HRH Princess Katarina of Yugoslavia, *d* of HRH late Prince Tomislav of Yugoslavia and of HRH Princess Margarita of Baden; one *d*. *Educ:* Dulwich College Prep. Sch.; Trinity College, Ceylon. Served HM Forces. Called to the Bar: Middle Temple, 1964, Bencher, 2008; Sierra Leone, 1968; The Gambia, 1981; Gibraltar, 1992; a Dep. Circuit Judge, 1976–80; Dep. Prosecutor, Internat. War Crimes Court for Sierra Leone, 2002–05. UNDP Envoy to Belgrade, 2004; Mem., UN Human Rights Council Panel of experts apptd to report on Gaza flotilla incident, 2010; Chm., Finucane Review to report on state involvement in murder of Patrick Finucane, 1989, in NI, 2011–12. Chm., Inquiry into Torture and Executions of detainees in Syria, 2014. Chm., Adv. Council, Scipion Capital Ltd, 2015–. Vice-Chm., Westminster Community Relations Council, 1980–82; Councilman, City of London, 1980–95; Main Session Chm., First Internat. Conf. on Human Value, 1981. Member: Home Affairs Standing Cttee, Bow Gp, 1982; Editl Adv. Bd, Crossbow, 1984; Crime and Juvenile Delinquency Study Gp, Centre for Policy Studies, 1983–87. Sen. Associate Mem., St Antony's Coll., Oxford, 2005–. Member: Governing Council, Manorial Soc. of GB, 1982–; Nat. Cttee for 900th anniv. of Domesday; Internat. Assoc. of Prosecutors; Imperial Soc. of Kts Bachelor, 2007–. Mem., Racehorse Owners Assoc. Patron: Meml Gates

Trust, 1999–; PRESET, 2000–. Liveryman, Gunmakers' Co. Vice-Pres., St John Ambulance London (Prince of Wales's) Dist, 1984–; Mem., St John Council for London, 1986–; KStJ 1994. *Publications:* (ed) English Law and Ethnic Minority Customs, 1986. *Recreations:* politics, shooting, travel. *Address:* Goldsmith Chambers, Goldsmith Building, Temple, EC4Y 7BL; Taprobane Island, off Weligama, Sri Lanka. *Clubs:* Brooks's, Naval and Military, Carlton, Annabel's; Orient (Colombo).

de SILVA, Harendra (Aneurin Domingo); QC 1995; a Recorder, since 1991; *b* 29 Sept. 1945; *s* of Annesley de Silva and Maharani of Porbandar; *m* 1972, Indira Raj; one *s* one *d.* *Educ:* Doon Sch., Dehra Dun, India; Millfield Sch.; Queens' Coll., Cambridge (MA, LLM). Called to the Bar, Middle Temple, 1970, Bencher, 2003. *Recreations:* golf, bridge. *Address:* Goldsmith Chambers, Goldsmith Building, Temple, EC4Y 7BL. *T:* (020) 7353 6802. *Clubs:* Roehampton; Ooty (Ootacamund, S India).

DESLANDES, Ian Anthony; Chief Executive, Construction Confederation, 1997–99; *b* 17 July 1941; *s* of Albert Deslandes and Christine Veronica Deslandes (*née* Hale); *m* 1965, Mary Catherine Bowler; two *s.* *Educ:* Stonyhurst Coll.; St Catherine's Coll., Oxford. Conservative Res. Dept, 1965–70; PA to Conservative Party Chm., 1970–72; Dir, Housebuilders' Fedn, 1973–78; Dir, Manpower Services, 1978–86, Dep. Dir Gen., 1985–92, Dir Gen., 1992–97, Building Employers' Confedn. CBI: Chm., Trade Assoc. Council, 1999; Mem., Council and President's Cttee, 1999. *Recreations:* reading, jazz, gardening, walking. *Address:* Greystones, Downhouse Lane, Higher Eype, Bridport, Dorset DT6 6AH. *T:* (01308) 424498.

DESLONGCHAMPS, Prof. Pierre, OC 1989; OQ 1997; PhD; FRS 1983; FRSC 1974; FCIC; Professor of Organic Chemistry, Université de Sherbrooke, Canada, 1972–2006, now Emeritus; Executive Scientific Advisor, OmegaChem Inc., since 2008; Associate Professor, Laval University, Quebec, since 2008; *b* 8 May 1938; *s* of Rodolphe Deslongchamps and Madeleine Magnan; *m* 1st, 1960, Micheline Renaud (marr. diss. 1975); two *s*; 2nd, 1976, Shirley E. Thomas (marr. diss. 1983); 3rd, 1987, Marie-Marthe Leroux. *Educ:* Univ. de Montréal (BSc Chem., 1959); Univ. of New Brunswick (PhD Chem., 1964). FCIC 1980; FAAAS 1988. Post-doctoral Student with Dr R. B. Woodward, Harvard Univ., USA, 1965; Asst Prof., Univ. de Montréal, 1966; Asst Prof. 1967, Associate Prof. 1968, Univ. de Sherbrooke. A. P. Sloan Fellow, 1970–72; E. W. R. Steacie Fellow, 1971–74. Founder, NeoKimia, later Tranzyme Pharma Inc., 1998–2005. Member: Amer. Chem. Soc.; Ordre des Chemistes du Québec; Assoc. Canadienne-Française pour l'Avancement des Sciences; Fellow, World Innovation Foundn (UK), 2002; For. Asst Mem., Acad. des Scis de Paris, 1995. Dr *hc*: Univ. Pierre et Marie Curie, Paris, 1983; Bishop's Univ. and Univ. de Montréal, 1984; New Brunswick Univ., 1985; Univ. of Moncton, 1995. Scientific Prize of Québec, 1971; E. W. R. Steacie Prize (Nat. Scis), NRCC, 1974; Médaille Vincent, ACFAS, 1975; Merck, Sharp and Dohme Lectures Award, CIC, 1976; Canada Council Izaak Walton Killam Meml Scholarship, 1976–77; John Simon Guggenheim Meml Foundn Fellow, 1979; Médaille Pariseau, ACFAS, 1979; Marie-Victorin Médaille, Province of Quebec, 1987; Alfred Bader Award in Organic Chemistry, 1991, Lemieux Award, 1994, Bernard Belleau Award, 2011, Canadian Soc. for Chemistry; Canada Gold Medal for Science and Engrg, NSERCC, 1993. Holder of 21 patents. *Publications:* Stereoelectronic Effects in Organic Chemistry, 1983; over 240 contribs on organic chemistry in Tetrahedron, Jl Amer. Chem. Soc., Canadian Jl of Chem., Pure Applied Chem., Synth. Commun., Nouv. Jl Chim., Heterocycles, Jl Molecular Struct., Interface, Aldrichimica Acta, Angewandte Chemie, Internat. Edn, Jl Organic Chem., Organic Letters, Chem. - an Asian Jl, Bioorganic and Medical Chem. Letters, Eur. Jl of Chem., Bull. Soc. Chim., France, and Organic & Biomolecular Chem. *Recreations:* fishing, reading, walking. *Address:* 5607 St Louis Street, Apt 403, Lévis, QC G6V 4G2, Canada. *T:* (418) 6033753. *E:* pierre.deslongchamps@chm.ulaval.ca; OmegaChem Inc., 480 Perreault Street, St Romuald, QC G6W 7V6, Canada. *T:* (418) 8374444.

DESMET, Anne Julie, RA 2011; RWA 2008; RE 1988; artist-printmaker, since 1987; Editor, Printmaking Today magazine, 1998–2013; *b* Liverpool, 14 June 1964; *d* of late Louis Desmet and of Irene Desmet (*née* Irving); *m* 1994, Roy Willingham; one *s* one *d.* *Educ:* Seafield Grammar Sch., later Sacred Heart High Sch., Crosby, Liverpool; Worcester Coll./Ruskin Sch. of Drawing, Oxford (BFA 1986); Central Sch. of Art and Design (Postgrad. Dip. Printmaking 1988); British Sch. at Rome (Scholarship in Printmaking 1990); MA Fine Art Oxon 1991. Specialist in wood engraved prints and collages of architectural/metamorphosing subjects; *solo exhibitions* include: Duncan Campbell Fine Art, London, 1991, 1992, 1994, 1996, 1998, 2000, 2002; Royal Over-Seas League, 1992; Godfrey and Watt Gall., Harrogate, 1993, 1995, 2009; Ex Libris Mus., Moscow, 1995; Hart Gall., London, 2004, 2006, 2008, 2010, 2011, 2012; *retrospective exhibitions:* Towers and Transformations, Ashmolean Mus., Oxford and UK tour, 1998–99; Urban Evolution, Whitworth Art Gall., Manchester and UK tour, 2008–10; *group exhibitions* include: Royal Acad. Summer Exhibns, 1990–; Manhattan Graphics Centre, NY, 2001; Grafisch Mus., Groningen, 2001; Center for Contemp. Print, Connecticut, 2003; Nat. Art Club, New York, 2010; *work in public and private collections,* including: The Queen; V&A; RA; Nat. Art Liby; BM; BL; Ashmolean Mus.; Whitworth Art Gall.; Fitzwilliam Mus.; Bradford Mus. and Art Galls; Harrogate Mus.; Aberystwyth Univ. Mus.; Ex Libris Mus., Moscow; Contemp. Art Mus., Chamalières, France; Ostrobothnian Mus. and Lahti Art Mus., Finland; Mus. de Arte do Espirito Santo, Vitoria, Brazil; Lodz Mus., Poland, Mus. Civico, Cremona, Italy; *commissions* include: engravings for V&A, BM, Nat. Gall., BL, Sotheby's. Vis. lectr/tutor at instns incl. RA Schs, Middx Univ., Ruskin Sch. of Art, Oxford, 1989–. Arts Council funded artist-in-residence, Lauriston Primary Sch., Hackney, 2007–08. External examiner: Kingston Coll. of Art, 2010–13; Sch. of Art, Aberystwyth Univ., 2003–07. Hon. Fellow, Sch. of Art, Aberystwyth Univ., 2010–. Awards include: Pollock-Krasner Foundn Award, NY, 1998; Elizabeth Greenshields Foundn Award, Canada, 1989, 1996, 2007; RA Summer Exhibn Print Prize, 2010; V&A Purchase Prize, 2011. *Publications:* Anne Desmet: towers and transformations, 1998; (jtly) Handmade Prints, 2000, 4th edn 2012; (ed jtly) Printmakers: the directory, 2006; Primary Prints, 2010. *Recreations:* juggling work and family, vegetarian cuisine, Scandinavian and Italian TV dramas, sketching in Italy, book group. *Address:* Royal Academy of Arts, Burlington House, Piccadilly, W1J 0BD. *T:* (020) 7300 8000, *Fax:* (020) 7300 8001. *E:* anne.desmet@btinternet.com.

DESMOND, Denis Fitzgerald, CBE 1989; Lord-Lieutenant of Co. Londonderry, since 2000; Chairman, Desmond & Sons Ltd, 1970–95; *b* 11 May 1943; *s* of late Major James Fitzgerald Desmond, DL, JP and Harriet Ivy Desmond (*née* Evans); *m* 1965, Annick Marie Françoise Marguerite Faussemagne; one *d.* *Educ:* Trinity Coll., Glenalmond. 2nd Lieut, then Lieut RCT (TA), 1964–69. ADC to Governor of NI, 1967–69. Dir, Ulster Bank, 1990–97. Chm., Altnagelvin Hosps Health Trust, 1996–2004. Dir, Ulster Orchestra Soc. Ltd, 2008–12. Mem. Council, Prince's Trust, NI, 2008–12. Chm., Ulster Historical Foundn, 2008–. Pres., RFCA (NI), 2013–. Hon. Colonel: 1 Bn ACF (NI), 2005–10; 152 Transport Regt RLC (TA), 2010–13. High Sheriff 1973, DL 1992–2000, Co. Londonderry. Hon. DSc: QUB, 1987; Ulster, 1991. *Address:* Bellarena, Limavady, Co. Londonderry BT49 0HZ.

DESMOND, Michael John; Commercial Director, All England Lawn Tennis and Croquet Club, since 2010; Co-founder and Executive Chairman, IPCN, since 2007; *b* 10 March 1959; *s* of Frank and Eileen Desmond; *m* 1984, Christine; one *s* two *d.* *Educ:* Leeds Univ. Gp Sales Manager, Anglia TV, 1982–86; Sales Controller, HTV, London, 1986–88; Sales Controller, 1988–92, Sales Dir, 1992–94, Granada; Chief Executive Officer: Laser, 1994–98; Granada Media Sales, 1998; Granada Broadcasting and Enterprises; Jt Man. Dir, ITV, 2002–04; Chief Exec., ITV Broadcast, 2004–05; Internat. Advr, Hunan Broadcasting Co., 2006. *Recreations:* golf, tennis, watching most sports. *Address:* 5 Copse Hill, SW20 0NB. *Club:* Solus.

DESMOND, Richard Clive; Chairman, Northern & Shell Network, since 1974; Proprietor, Express Newspapers, since 2000; Owner, Channel 5 (formerly Five), 2010–14; Health Lottery, since 2011; *b* 8 Dec. 1951; *s* of late Cyril Desmond and of Millie Desmond; *m* 1983, Janet Robertson (marr. diss. 2010); one *s*; *m* 2012, Joy Canfield; one *s* one *d.* *Educ:* Christ's Coll., Finchley. Musician, 1967; Advertisement Exec., Thomson Gp, 1967–68; Group Advertisement Manager, Beat Pubns Ltd, 1968–74; launched International Musician, 1974 (separate editions in US, Europe, Australia and Japan); publr of numerous magazines in areas incl. leisure, music, hi tech, fitness, cooking, envmt, business, automotive, and men's and women's lifestyle; De Monde Advertising Ltd, 1976–89; OK! magazine, 1993– (separate editions in 20 countries); Fantasy Channel, 1995–; OK! TV, 1999–2011; owner: Portland TV, 1995–; Westferry Printers Ltd; Broughton Printers Ltd, 2000–; launched: Daily Star Sunday, 2002; New! mag., and Star mag., 2003. Pres., Norwood, 2006–; owner, Richard Desmond Crusaders Foundn, charitable trust. *Publications:* The Real Deal: the autobiography of Britain's most controversial media mogul, 2015. *Recreations:* music and drumming, fitness, family, philanthropy. *Address:* Northern & Shell Building, Number 10 Lower Thames Street, EC3R 6EN. *T:* (020) 8612 7000.

de SOUZA, Christopher Edward; freelance composer; broadcaster; Artistic Director, Southern Sinfonia, since 1998; *b* 6 June 1943; *s* of Denis Walter de Souza and Dorothy Edna (*née* Woodman); *m* 1971, Robyn Ann Williams (marr. diss. 1981); partner, Elinor Anne Kelly; two *s.* *Educ:* Prior Park Coll., Bath; Univ. of Bristol (BA Music 1966); Old Vic Theatre Sch. Head of Music, St Bernadette's RC Comp. Sch., Bristol, 1966–70; Producer, Sadlers Wells/ENO, 1971–75; Arts Producer, BBC Radio London, 1975–79; Producer, BBC Radio 3, 1980–95. Founder Dir, Liszt Fest. of London, 1977; (with J. Piper) music organiser, HM Silver Jubilee Fireworks, 1977. Director: UK stage premières: Don Sanche (Liszt), 1977; The Mother of Us All (Virgil Thompson), 1979; The Duenna (Prokofiev), 1980; Palestrina (Pfitzner), 1981; William Tell (Gretry), 1984; USA première: Don Sanche (Liszt), 1986. Founder (with Tristan de Souza and Sebastian de Souza), Artsplay.co.uk, 2009. *Compositions include:* music for TV, incl. Maharajahs, 1987; orch., chamber and choral works including The Ides of March, 1995, Bottom's Dream, 2009, Trombone Concerto, 2010, Loved and Unloved, 2011; (with Adrian Morris) Children of the Light (musical), 2001; Missa Douensis, 2003. *Publications:* A Child's Guide to Looking at Music, 1979; (ed jtly) Liszt: Don Sanche, 1985; Kingfisher Book of Music, 1996; contrib. to The Listener, Music and Musicians, Musical Times, Radio Times, Strad, The Times, British Music Year Book. *Recreations:* reading, travel, swimming, drawing. *Address:* 61 Westbrook, Boxford, Berks RG20 8DL. *Club:* Royal Over-Seas League.

DE SOUZA, Dame Rachel (Mary), DBE 2014; Chief Executive, Inspiration Trust, since 2012; *b* Scunthorpe, 12 Jan. 1968; *d* of David Kenny and Renate Kenny (*née* Fekete); *m* 1991, Christopher de Souza; one *s.* *Educ:* St Bede's RC Sch., Lincs; Heythrop Coll., Univ. of London (BA Hons Philosophy and Theol. 1989); King's Coll. London (PGCE; MA Educn). Teacher: Kidlington Sch., Oxford, 1991–93; Sir John Cass Sch., Tower Hamlets, 1993–96; Hd of Dept, Luton Sixth Form Coll., 1996–2003; Dep. Headteacher, Denbigh High Sch., Luton, 2004–06; Founding Principal, Barnfield W Acad., 2006–10; Exec. Principal, Ormiston Victory Acad., 2010–13. Trustee, Shakespeare's Globe Th., 2014–. *Address:* Inspiration Trust, Weights and Measures Building, Old Fire Station, Bethel Street, Norwich, Norfolk NR2 1NR. *T:* (01603) 280931. *E:* racheldesouza@inspirationtrust.org.

DESPONTIN, Dr Brenda; Principal, British School of Brussels, 2008–11; *b* 22 Oct. 1950; *d* of Telford and Nancy Betty Griffiths; *m* 1975, Robert Despontin; one *s.* *Educ:* University Coll., Cardiff (BA Hons Psychol.; MA English; PhD English - Children's Lit. 1996); Univ. of Bath (PGCE (Dist.)); Univ. of Hull (MBA); Cardiff Law Sch. (LLM Dist. 2013). Teacher, British Sch. of Brussels, 1973–77; residential social worker, 1977–78; teacher: Willlows Sch., Cardiff, 1978–85; New Coll., Cardiff, 1985–92; Principal, Girls' Div., King's Sch., Macclesfield, 1992–97; Headmistress, Haberdashers' Monmouth Sch. for Girls, 1997–2008. Pres., GSA, 2006. MCMI (MBIM 1995). FRSA. Teachers' Award for Sch. Leadership in Wales, 2003. *Publications:* (contrib. and ed jtly) Leading Schools in the 21st Century, 3 vols, 2008; contrib. Cardiff Law Sch. Jl, The Times, Daily Telegraph, FT, Independent, TES. *Recreations:* writing, reading, people-watching, following Fox's advice to 'walk cheerfully', travel, playing the piano (badly), pro bono work at Cardiff Law School.

DESPRÉS, Robert, OC 1978; GOQ 2003; President, DRM Holdings Inc., since 1987; Chairman, Cominar Real Estate Investment Trust, since 2006 (Director, since 1998); *b* 27 Sept. 1924; *s* of Adrien Després and Augustine Marmen; *m* 1949; two *s* two *d.* *Educ:* Académie de Québec (BA 1943); Laval Univ. (MCom 1947); (postgrad. studies) Western Univ. Comptroller, Québec Power Co., 1947–63; Reg. Manager, Administration & Trust Co., 1963–65; Dep. Minister, Québec Dept of Revenue, 1965–69; Pres. and Gen. Man., Québec Health Insurance Bd, 1969–73; Pres., Université du Québec, 1973–78; Pres. and Chief Exec. Officer, National Cablevision Ltd, 1978–80, and Netcom Inc., 1978–89; Chm. of the Bd, Atomic Energy of Canada Ltd, 1978–86. Chm., Domosys Corp.; Director: Sidbec Corp.; HRS Holdings Ltd; Infectio Diagnostic Inc.; GeneOhm Scis Inc.; Obzerv Technologies Inc. (Chm.). Director: Nat. Optics Inst.; Canadian Certified General Accountants' Res. Foundn; Council for Canadian Unity; la Soc. du Musée du Séminaire de Québec; Inst de cardiologie de Québec. *Publications:* contrib. Commerce, and Soc. of Management Accountants Revue. *Recreations:* golf, reading. *Clubs:* Rideau, Cercle Universitaire; Lorette Golf.

de SWIET, Eleanor Jane, MA; Headteacher, The Henrietta Barnett School, 1989–99, retired; *b* 18 Aug. 1942; *d* of Richard and Joan Hawkins; *m* 1964, Prof. Michael de Swiet; two *s* one *d.* *Educ:* Girton Coll., Cambridge (MA Classics); Inst. of Education (PGCE). Teacher of Classics: Francis Holland Sch., 1965–67; St Paul's Girls' Sch., 1967–70; Queen's Coll., London, 1975–84; City of London Sch., 1984–89. Pres., JACT, 1995–97; Chm., Assoc. of Maintained Girls' Schs, 1997–98. Mem. Council, Cheltenham Ladies' Coll., 1999–2008; Governor: Asmount Primary Sch., 2007–; Channing Sch., 2010–; Hornsey Girls' Sch., 2014–. Trustee: Open Door, 2000–09 (Chm., 2007–09); Toynbee Hall, 2001–08. *Recreations:* walking, reading, Yorkshire, travelling, opera. *Address:* 15 Wren View, 75 Hornsey Lane, N6 5LH. *T:* (020) 8347 9014. *E:* jdeswiet@gmail.com.

DETHRIDGE, Dame Kathleen, (Dame Kate), DBE 2015; Headteacher, Churchend Primary School, Reading, since 1998; *b* Barking, Essex, 1962; *d* of Frederick Caldon and Patricia Caldon; *m* 1986, Rod Dethridge; two *s.* *Educ:* Brentwood Ursuline Convent; Durham Univ. (BA Hons; PGCE). Class teacher, 1985–88; Dep. Headteacher, 1988–98; Exec. Headteacher, 2005–. Ofsted Inspector, 2000–; Mem., Headteacher Ref. Gp, Ofsted, 2011–; Vice Chm., Bureaucracy Ref. Gp, DfE, 2011–; Mem., Headteacher Bd, Regl Schs Comr for S Central England and NW London, 2014–. Sch. Improvement Advr, 2005–10. Associate Dir, Nat. Educn Trust, 2011–; Mem. Bd, Freedom and Autonomy for Schs - Nat. Assoc., 2014–. Nat. Leader of Educn, 2008. *Publications:* (contrib.) Taking Forward the National Curriculum, 2013. *Recreations:* cooking, riding, family, school governor, walking, cinema. *Address:* Heartwood, Water Street, Hampstead Norreys, Berks RG18 0RU. *T:* (01635) 202152. *E:* kate.dethridge@hotmail.co.uk.

DETMER, Prof. Don Eugene, MD; University Professor of Health Policy and Professor of Medical Education, University of Virginia, since 1999; *b* 3 Feb. 1939; *s* of Lawrence D. Detmer and Esther B. Detmer (*née* McCormick); *m* 1961, Mary Helen McFerson; two *d.* *Educ:* Univ. of Kansas (MD 1965); MA Cantab 2002. Asst Prof., 1973–77, Associate Prof., 1977–80, Prof., 1980–84, of Surgery and Preventive Medicine, Univ. of Wisconsin-Madison; Vice Pres. for Health Sci., and Prof. of Surgery and Med. Informatics, Univ. of Utah,

1984–88; University of Virginia: Vice Pres. for Health Sci., and Prof. of Surgery and Business Admin, 1988–92; Co-Dir, Virginia Health Policy Center, 1992–99; Vice Pres. and Provost for Health Sci., and Prof. of Health Policy and Surgery, 1993–96; Louis Nerancy Prof. of Health Scis Policy, Univ. Prof. and Sen. Vice Pres., 1996–99; Prof. Emeritus, 1999; Dennis Gillings Prof. of Health Mgt, Cambridge Univ., 1999–2003; Life Fellow, Clare Hall, Cambridge, 2000; Sen. Associate, Judge Inst. of Mgt, subseq. Judge Business Sch., Univ. of Cambridge, 2004–06; American Medical Informatics Association: Pres. and CEO, 2004–09; Sen. Advr, 2009–11; Dir, Advanced Interprofessional Informatics Certification, 2014; Med. Dir, Advocacy and Health Policy, Amer. Coll. of Surgeons, 2011–13. Vis. Prof., Centre for Health Informatics and Multiprofessional Educn, UCL, 2005–. *Publications:* (ed jtly and contrib.) The Computer-Based Patient Record: an essential technology for health care, 1991, rev. edn 1997; articles in jls and contribs to books. *Recreations:* fly-fishing, reading biographies, wilderness canoeing, handcrafts, tree farming. *Address:* Branch Point Farm, 5245 Brown's Gap Turnpike, Crozet, VA 22932, USA. *Club:* Colonnade (Charlottesville, Va) (Mem. Bd of Govs, 2014–).

de TRAFFORD, Sir John (Humphrey), 7th Bt *cr* 1841, of Trafford Park, Lancashire; MBE 2010; Chairman, National Savings and Investments, since 2012 (non-executive Director, since 2010); *b* London, 12 Sept. 1950; *e s* of Sir Dermot Humphrey de Trafford, 6th Bt and Patricia Mary Beeley; *S* father, 2010; *m* 1975, Anne, *d* of J. Faure de Pebeyre; one *s* one *d*. *Educ:* Ampleforth; Univ. of Bristol (BSc). Sales and Mktg Dir, Thistle Hotels, 1982–87; with American Express, 1987–2005 (Regl Pres., Northern Europe, 2000–04). Chm., Pension, Disability and Carers Service, 2008–10. *Recreation:* sailing. *Heir: s* Alexander Humphrey de Trafford [*b* 28 June 1978; *m* 2008, Imogen King; one *s* one *d*]. *Address:* Ground Floor, 17 Bolton Gardens, SW5 0AJ. *T:* (020) 7373 2669. *Clubs:* Royal Ocean Racing, Royal Cruising.

DETTMER, Ven. Douglas James; Archdeacon of Totnes, since 2015; *b* Kansas City, Missouri, 5 March 1964; *s* of Arlen and Peggy Dettmer; *m* 1998, Chloë Archer. *Educ:* Univ. of Kansas (BA 1986); Yale Univ. (MDiv 1990). Ordained deacon, 1990, priest, 1991; Asst Curate, Ilfracombe Team Ministry, 1990–94; Domestic Chaplain to Bishop of Exeter, 1994–98; Priest-in-charge: Raddon Team Ministry, 1998–2010; Stoke Canon Benefice, 2006–10; Rector, Netherexe Parishes, 2010–15. *Recreations:* reading, walking, gardening, music, museums. *Address:* Blue Hills, Bradley Road, Bovey Tracey, Newton Abbot, Devon TQ13 9EU. *T:* (01626) 832064. *E:* archdeacon.of.totnes@exeter.anglican.org.

DETTORI, Lanfranco, (Frankie), Hon. MBE 2000; flat race jockey; *b* Italy, 15 Dec. 1970; *s* of Gianfranco Dettori and Maria Dettori (*née* Nieman); *m* 1997, Catherine, *d* of W. R. Allen, *qv*; two *s* three *d*. Winner: Fillies' Mile, on Shamshir, 1990, on Glorosia, 1997, on Teggiano, 1999, on Crystal Music, 2000, on White Moonstone, 2010; World Young Jockey Championship, Japan, 1992, 1993; Ascot Gold Cup, on Drum Taps, 1992, 1993, on Papineau, 2004, on Colour Vision, 2012; French Derby; German Derby; Nonthorpe; Sussex Stakes; Prix de l'Abbaye, Longchamp, on Lochsong, 1993, 1994, on Var, 2004; Irish Derby, on Balanchine, 1994; Oaks, on Balanchine, 1994, on Moonshell, 1995, on Kazzia, 2002; Queen Elizabeth II, on Lammtarra, 1995, on Poet's Voice, 2010; St Leger, on Classic Cliché, 1995, on Shantou, 1996, on Scorpion, 2005, on Sixties Icon, 2006, on Conduit, 2008; Prix de l'Arc de Triomphe, on Lammtarra, 1995, on Sakhee, 2001, on Marienbard, 2002; Two Thousand Guineas, on Mark of Esteem, 1996, on Island Sands, 1999; Irish Champion Stakes, on Swain, 1998, on Daylami, 1999, on Fantastic Light, 2001, on Grandera, 2002, on Snow Fairy, 2012; One Thousand Guineas, on Cape Verdi, 1998; on Kazzia, 2002, on Blue Bunting, 2011; Breeders' Cup Turf, NY, on Daylami, 1999, on Fantastic Light, 2001, on Red Rocks, 2006, on Dangerous Midge, 2010; French Two Thousand Guineas, on Bachir, 2000, on Noverre, 2001, on Shamardal, 2005; Prix de Diane, on West Wind, 2007, on Star of Seville, 2015; Irish Oaks, on Lailani, 2001, on Vintage Tipple, 2003, on Blue Bunting, 2011; Epsom Derby, on Authorized, 2007, on Golden Horn, 2015; Goodwood Cup, on Schiaparelli, 2009, on Opinion Poll, 2011; Eclipse Stakes, on Golden Horn, 2015; all seven winners, Ascot, 28 Sept. 1996. Champion Jockey, 1994, 1995, 2004. Presenter, Channel 4 Racing, 2014. Jt Proprietor, Frankie's Italian Bar and Grill, London, Dublin and Dubai, 2004–. *Publications:* A Year in the Life of Frankie Dettori, 1996; (with Jonathan Powell) Frankie: the autobiography of Frankie Dettori, 2004. *Address:* c/o Peter Burrell, 5 Jubilee Place, SW3 3TD. *T:* (020) 7352 8899.

DEUCHAR, Rev. Andrew Gilchrist; independent consultant on international relations, sport and community development, since 2012; Director: BUILD, 2011–12; Football Clubs in Global Partnerships, since 2013; *b* 3 June 1955; *s* of late David and (Lucretia) Marian Deuchar; *m* 1977, Francesca Fowler; three *s* two *d*. *Educ:* Royal Hospital Sch., Ipswich; Southampton Univ. (BTh); Salisbury and Wells Theol Coll. HM Diplomatic Service, 1974–81; ordained deacon, 1984, priest, 1985; Asst Curate, Alnwick, Northumberland, 1984–88; Team Vicar, S Wye Team Ministry, Hereford, 1988–90; Social Responsibility Advr, Canterbury and Rochester dios, 1990–94; Archbp of Canterbury's Sec. for Anglican Communion Affairs, 1994–2000; Rector of St Peter and All Saints (formerly St Peter with St James), Nottingham, 2000–08; Priest-in-charge, St Mary the Virgin, Nottingham, 2004–08; a Chaplain to the Queen, 2004–08; Diocesan Audit Officer, Dio. of Moray, Ross and Caithness, 2008–10. Hon. Canon, Canterbury Cathedral, 1995–2000. Chaplain to High Sheriff of Notts, 2007–08. Mem. Bd of Trustees, USPG, 2003–06; Trustee: Swindon Town Football in the Community Trust, 2012–; Hay2Timbuktu Partnership, 2014–. Patron, Bishop Mubarak Scholarship Fund, 2004–08. *Publications:* (contrib.) Anglicanism: a global communion, 1998; (contrib.) An Introduction to the Anglican Communion, 1998; (ed) A Last Embrace: essays in honour of Nadir Dinshaw, 2003; (contrib.) Faith in Action: Njongonkulu Ndungane, Archbishop for the Church and the world, 2008. *Recreations:* music, travel, walking, football, the Isle of Skye, genealogy.

See also P. L. Deuchar.

DEUCHAR, Patrick Lindsay; *b* 27 March 1949; *s* of late David and of Marian Deuchar; *m* Gwyneth Miles (marr. diss.); one *s* one *d*; *m* 1997, Liz Robertson; one *d*. *Educ:* Christ's Hospital; Lackham Coll. of Agriculture. Farming, 1967–72; IPC Business Press, 1972–74; PR Manager, RASE, 1974–77; PR Manager, Earls Court and Olympia, 1977–80; European Dir, World Championship Tennis, 1981–89; Chief Exec., Royal Albert Hall, 1989–98; Chm., London Centre Mgt Co., 1998–99; Chief Exec., Rugby Hospitality for Rugby World Cup, 1998–99; Events Consultant: Somerset House Trust Ltd, 1998–99; 7th Regt Armory Conservancy, NY, 1998–99. Director: London First, 1996–99; TS2K (Trng and Skills 2000) (formerly Trafalgar Square 2000), 1996– (Dep. Chm.); Covent Gdn Fest., 1998–2001; (non-exec.) Cavendish Consultancy, 2000–. Chm., Sparks Charity, 1992–96; Member: Nat. Fundraising Cttee, Muscular Dystrophy Group, 1989–92; Nat. Music Day Cttee, 1993–97; London Visitor Council, 1994–97; Royal Concert Cttee, 1994–97; Mem. Council, 1995, Chm. Develt Cttee, 2000, RCM. Trustee: Albert Meml Trust, 1994–99; Cardiff Bay Opera House, 1994–96. Barker, Variety Club of GB, 1992; Mem., Inst. of Dirs. FRSA 1992. *Recreations:* music, theatre, art, cooking, wines, family life. *Address:* Flat 1, 27 Sloane Gardens, SW1W 8EB.

See also Rev. A. G. Deuchar.

DEUCHAR, Dr Stephen John, CBE 2010; Director, the Art Fund, since 2010; *b* 11 March 1957; *s* of late Rev. John Deuchar and of Nancy Dorothea Deuchar (*née* Jenkyns); *m* 1982, Prof. Katie Scott; one *s* three *d*. *Educ:* Dulwich Coll. (Schol.); Univ. of Southampton (BA 1st Cl. Hons Hist.); Westfield Coll., London (PhD Hist. of Art 1986). Curator of Paintings, then Exhibns Dir, National Maritime Museum, 1985–98; Dir, Tate Britain, 1998–2010. Andrew W. Mellon Fellow in British Art, Yale Univ., 1981–82. Member: Council, Southampton Univ., 2004–09; Adv. Cttee, Govt Art Collection, 2006–09. Trustee, Creative Foundn, 2008–. *Publications:* Noble Exercise: the sporting ideal in 18th century British art, 1982; Paintings, Politics and Porter: Samuel Whitbread and British art, 1984; (jtly) Concise Catalogue of Oil Paintings in the National Maritime Museum, 1988; Sporting Art in 18th Century England: a social and political history, 1988; (jtly) Nelson: an illustrated history, 1995; contrib. articles on British art. *Recreations:* motor sport, Middle Eastern travel. *Address:* the Art Fund, 2 Granary Square, King's Cross, N1C 4BH. *T:* (020) 7225 4800.

DEUTSCH, Anthony Frederick; Sheriff of Glasgow and Strathkelvin, since 2005; *b* 9 June 1952; *s* of Robert and Elizabeth Deutsch; *m* 1977, Barbara MacDonald; two *s* one *d*. *Educ:* Univ. of Edinburgh (MA, LLB). Admitted solicitor, 1978; Partner, Macdonalds Solicitors, Glasgow, 1980–2005. *Recreations:* reading (mostly history), walking (mostly Isle of Arran), cooking, wine. *Address:* Sheriff Court House, 1 Carlton Place, Glasgow G5 9DA. *E:* sheriffadeutsch@scotcourts.gov.uk.

DEUTSCH, Prof. David Elieser, DPhil; FRS 2008; Visiting Professor, Centre for Quantum Computation, Clarendon Laboratory, University of Oxford, since 1999; *b* Haifa, 18 May 1953; *s* of Oskar Deutsch and Tikva Deutsch. *Educ:* William Ellis Sch., London; Clare Coll., Cambridge (BA Natural Scis, Math. Tripos Pt III 1974); Wolfson Coll., Oxford (DPhil Theoretical Physics). *Publications:* The Fabric of Reality, 1997; The Beginning of Infinity, 2011. *Address:* Centre for Quantum Computation, Clarendon Laboratory, Parks Road, Oxford OX1 3PU. *E:* david.deutsch@qubit.org.

DEUTSCH, James Chobot, PhD; Vice President, Conservation Strategy, Wildlife Conservation Society, since 2014; *b* 28 Nov. 1963; *s* of late Harold Kauffman Deutsch and Barbara Chobot Deutsch. *Educ:* St George's Sch., Newport, RI; Harvard Coll. (AB 1987); King's Coll., Cambridge (MPhil 1988, PhD 1992). Temp. Lectr, UEA, 1992–93; Res. Fellow, Churchill Coll., Cambridge, 1993–95; Lectr, Imperial Coll., London, 1995–97; Chief Exec., Crusaid, 1997–2002; Africa Dir, Wildlife Conservation Soc., 2002–14. Chairman: Aidspan, 2002–11 (Bd Mem., 2002–); COMACO, 2010–; Member: Bd, AIDS Treatment Project, 1996–2000; Exec. Cttee, British HIV Assoc., 1999–2001; Council, Crusaid, 2002–10. *Publications:* (ed) Wild Rangelands, 2010; contrib. articles to Nature, Proc. Royal Soc., Evolution, HIV Medicine, Animal Behaviour, Conservation Biol., African Jl Ecol., and other jls. *Address:* Wildlife Conservation Society, 2300 Southern Boulevard, Bronx, NY 10460, USA. *T:* (646) 2291724.

DEVA, Niranjan Joseph Aditya, (Nirj); DL; Member (C) South East Region, England, European Parliament, since 1999; Director-General, Policy Research Centre for Business, since 1997; *b* Colombo, 11 May 1948; *s* of late Thakur Dr Kingsley de Silva Deva Aditya and of Zita Virginia Deva; *m* Indra Lavinia, *d* of Romy Govindia; one step *s*. *Educ:* St Joseph's Coll., Colombo; Loughborough Univ. of Technol. (BTech Hons Aero. Eng.). Company dir and adviser; Chm., Symphony Environmental Plastics Ltd; Director: Ceylon and Foreign Trades (Sri Lanka) Ltd; Distilleries Co. of Sri Lanka Ltd, 2006–; Aitken Spence Ltd, Sri Lanka, 2006–; Hotel Services (Sri Lanka) Ltd, 2009–. Pol Officer, 1979, Chm., 1981, Bow Gp. Organiser, Conf. on Overseas Develt and Brandt Report, 1979. Member: Governing Council, Royal Commonwealth Soc., 1979–83; Nat. Consumer Council, 1982–88; Dept of Employment Adv. Cttee, 1988–91; Chairman: DTI/NCC Cttee on De-regulation of European Air Transport, 1985–86; One Nation Forum Political Cttee, 1986–91. Pres., Bow Group Trade and Industry Cttee, 1996. Contested (C) Hammersmith, 1987; MP (C) Brentford and Isleworth, 1992–97; contested (C) same seat, 1997. PPS to Minister of State, Scottish Office, 1996–97. Mem., Select Cttee on Parly Admin (Ombudsman), 1992–96, on Educn, 1995–96; Vice-Chm., Cons. back bench Aviation Cttee, 1994–97 (Jt Sec., 1992); Member: Asylum Bill Cttee, 1992; Deregulation Bill Cttee, 1994–97; Caravans Rating Bill Cttee, 1996–97; Asylum and Immigration Bill Cttee, 1996–97; European Standing Cttee B, 1992–97; All-Party Manufacturing Gp, 1993–97; Hon. Sec., All-Party Uganda Gp, 1994–97. European Parliament: spokesman on overseas develt and co-operation, 1999, on internat. develt, 2009–; Member: Envmt Cttee, 1999–; EU-ACP Delegn, 1999–; Delegn to ASEAN countries, 2002–; Delegn to South Asian Assoc. for Regl Cooperation, 2004– (Vice Chm., 2007–); Foreign Affairs Cttee, 2004–09; Chm., Delegn to UN Commn on Sustainable Development, NY, 2005; Co-Leader, Delegn to World Summit and Gen. Assembly, 2006; Vice Chm., Internat. Develt Cttee, 2009–; Co-ordinator, Eur. Conservatives and Reformists Gp, 2009–; Rapporteur: WTO and Develt Issues of World Trade, 2000–; Aid to Uprooted People in Asia and Latin America, 2000–; Pacific Strategy, 2007–; Nation Building in Post-Conflict Situations, 2008–; Mem., Clinton Global Initiative, 2008–. Co-Chm., Burke's Club for Transatlantic Relns, 2009–. Chairman: Indonesia Gp, 2000–; Afghan Gp, 2000–; EU-India Chamber of Commerce, 2005–; EU-China Friendship Gp, 2006–; Wkg Gp 'A', Develt Cttee, 2006–; Vice Pres., India Gp, 2001–; EPP-ED Coordinator, Develt Commn, 2004–; Co-Chairman: Wkg Gp on Colombia, 2004–; Delegn to UN World Summit and Gen. Assembly, 2005; Tsunami Co-ordinator, 2005–; budget draftsman, Develt Budget, 2006. Pres., Internat. Cttee on Human Dignity. Hon. Advr to Prime Minister of Sri Lanka, 2002–. Editor, Crossbow, 1983–85. Presenter, Deva's Hour, Sunrise Radio, 1995, 1998–99. FRSA 1997. DL Greater London, 1986. Hon. Ambassador-at-Large for Sri Lanka, 2003–. Vishwa Kirthi Sri Lanka Ahbimani, 2007. Knight of Merit with Star, Sacred Military Constantinian Order of St George, 2011. MEP of the Year, Parlt Mag., 2012. *Publications:* Wealth of Nations Part II: Adam Smith revisited, 1998; various pamphlets and memoranda for Bow Group, 1980–85. *Recreations:* riding, reading, tennis. *Address:* (office) 96 Vine Lane, Hillingdon, Middx UB10 0BE. *T:* (01895) 470463, 07715 662226; European Parliament, 43–60 rue Wiertz, 1047 Brussels, Belgium. *T:* (22) 847245. *E:* office@nirjdeva.com. *W:* www.nirjdeva.com. *Clubs:* Carlton; Hounslow Conservative.

de VALLERA, João; Ambassador of Portugal to the Court of St James's, since 2011; *b* Malange, Angola, 1 June 1950; *s* of Manuel and Nolga de Vallera; *m* 1982, Margarida Azevedo; one *s*. *Educ:* Univ. of Lisbon (Dr in Econs). Joined Portuguese Diplomatic Service, 1974; Bonn, 1977–79; Perm. Mission to EC, Brussels, 1979–84; Hd, Eur. Integration Dept, 1986–89; Asst Dir Gen. for Eur. Communities, 1988; Minister, Madrid, 1989; Perm. Repn to EC, Brussels, 1990–98, Dep. Perm. Rep., 1993–98; Ambassador to Ireland, 1998–2001; Dir Gen., Eur. Affairs, 2001; Delegate to Convention on Future of Europe, 2002; Ambassador: to Germany, 2002–07; to USA, 2007–11. Officer, Order of Infante D. Henrique (Portugal), 1978; Grand Cross: Order of Merit (Portugal), 2002; Military Order of Christ (Portugal), 2005; Cross, Order of Merit 1st Cl. (Germany), 2006. *Recreations:* classical music, painting, photography. *Address:* Portuguese Embassy, 11 Belgrave Square, SW1X 8PP. *T:* (020) 7235 5331, *Fax:* (020) 7235 0739. *E:* londres@mne.pt. *Clubs:* Royal Automobile; Royal Mid-Surrey Golf; Grémio Literário (Lisbon).

DEVANE, Sir Ciarán Gearóid, Kt 2015; Chief Executive, British Council, since 2015; *b* 25 Oct. 1962; *s* of Micheal and Eibhlín Devane; *m* 1998, Katy Ashburner (*d* 2003). *Educ:* University Coll., Dublin (BEng); George Washington Univ. (Masters Internat. Policy and Practice). Process Engr, ICI, 1984–93; Mgt Consultant, Gemini Consulting, 1993–2003; Chm., Pavilion Housing Gp, 2004–05; Chief Exec., Macmillan Cancer Support, 2007–14. Trustee: Liver Gp, 2010–12; Makaton Charity, 2011–; NCVO, 2012–. Non-exec. Dir, NHS Commng Bd, 2012–. FRSA. *Recreations:* hill walking, theatre. *Address:* c/o British Council, 10 Spring Gardens, SW1A 2BN. *Club:* Royal Automobile.

DEVANEY, John Francis, CEng, FIET, FIMechE; Chairman: National Air Traffic Services, since 2005; Tersus Energy; Cobham plc, since 2010; *b* 25 June 1946; *s* of late George Devaney and Alice Ann Devaney; two *s* one *d*. *Educ:* St Mary's Coll., Blackburn; Sheffield Univ.

(BEng). FIMechE. Perkins Engines, 1968–89: manufacturing positions, Peterborough, 1968–76; Project Manager, Ohio, 1976–77; Director posts, UK, 1977–82; President, 1983–88; Group Vice-Pres., European Components Group, Peterborough, 1988 and Enterprises Group, Toronto, 1988–89; Chm. and Chief Exec. Officer and Group Vice-Pres., Kelsey-Hayes Corp., Michigan, 1989–92; Man. Dir, 1992, Chief Exec., 1993, Exec. Chm., 1995–98, Eastern Electricity plc, later Eastern Gp plc; Chairman: NFC, later Exel plc, 2000–02 (Dir, 1996–2002); Marconi, later telent plc, 2002–07; Nat. Express, 2009–13. Non-executive Director: HSBC (formerly Midland Bank), 1994–2000; British Steel, 1998–99; Northern Rock, 2007–10. President: Electricity Assoc., 1994–95; Inst. for Customer Services, 1997–2000. *Recreations:* ski-ing, golf, tennis, sailing. *Club:* Reform.

DEVAUX, John Edward; His Honour Judge Devaux; DL; a Circuit Judge, since 1993; *b* 1947; *s* of Henry Edward Devaux and Anne Elizabeth Devaux; *m* 1979, Fiona O'Conor; two *d. Educ:* Beaumont Coll.; Bristol Univ. (LLB). Called to the Bar, Lincoln's Inn, 1970; a Recorder, 1989–93; Resident Judge, Ipswich, 1998–2007. Hon. Recorder of Ipswich, 2000. DL Suffolk, 2013. *Address:* Ipswich Crown Court, The Courthouse, 1 Russell Road, Ipswich, Suffolk IP1 2AG. *T:* (01473) 228585.

de VERE WHITE, Hon. Mrs; *see* Glendinning, Hon. Victoria.

DEVEREAU, (George) Michael, CB 1997; Head of Government Information Service, 1990–97; Chief Executive (formerly Director General), Central Office of Information, 1989–96; *b* 10 Nov. 1937; *s* of George Alfred Devereau and Elspeth Mary Duff Devereau; *m* 1961, Sarah Poupart; four *s. Educ:* King William's Coll., Isle of Man; University Coll. London. Asst Ed., Architects' Jl, 1962; Information Officer, MPBW, BRE and DoE, 1967–75; Chief Information Officer: Price Commn, 1975; DoE, 1978; Dept of Transport, 1982; Gp Dir, 1985, Dep. Dir Gen., 1987, COI. Trustee, Manx Nat. Heritage, 2007–. *Publications:* Architects Working Details, 1964. *Recreations:* house restoration, travel. *Address:* 24 Fairway Drive, Ramsey, Isle of Man IM8 2BB.

DEVERELL, Gen. Sir John Freegard, (Sir Jack), KCB 1999; OBE 1986; DL; Commander-in-Chief, Allied Forces North, 2001–04; *b* 27 April 1945; *s* of Harold James Frank Deverell and Joan Beatrice Deverell (*née* Carter); *m* 1973, Jane Ellen Solomon; one *s* one *d. Educ:* King Edward's Sch., Bath; RMA Sandhurst. Commnd Somerset and Cornwall LI, 1965; RN Staff Coll., Greenwich, 1977; Comd 3rd Bn LI, 1984–86; Mil. Dir of Studies, RMCS, Shrivenham, 1988; Higher Command and Staff Course, Camberley, 1988; Comdr 1st Infantry Bde (UK Mobile Force), 1988–90; NDC, India, 1991; Dir, Army Recruiting, 1992–93; Dir Gen., Army Manning and Recruiting, 1993–95; Comdt, RMA Sandhurst, 1995–97; Dep. C-in-C, HQ Land Comd and Insp. Gen. TA, 1997–98 and 1999–2001; Dep. Comdr (Ops), HQ SFOR, Bosnia, 1998–99. Chm., Nat. Army Museum, 2005–14. Pres., ACFA, 2004–11. Pres., Free Foresters Cricket Club, 2013–. DL Wilts, 2015. *Recreations:* golf, cricket, horses. *Clubs:* Cavalry and Guards, Mounted Infantry.

DEVERELL, Richard George; Director, Royal Botanic Gardens, Kew, since 2012; *b* 4 Dec. 1965; *s* of Geoff and Pauline Deverell; *m* 1993, Sarah Ann Inigo-Jones; one *s* two *d. Educ:* St Mary's Coll., Southampton; Magdalene Coll., Cambridge (BA Nat. Scis 1987). Associate Consultant, LEK Partnership, 1990–92; joined BBC, 1992; Sen. Advr, Policy and Planning, 1992–96; Head: Strategy and Mktg, BBC News, 1996–2000; BBC News Interactive, 2000–05; Chief Operating Officer, 2005–06, Controller, 2006–09, BBC Children's; Chief Operating Officer, BBC North, 2009–11; Programme Dir, W12 Project, BBC, 2011–12; Dep. Gp Dir, Strategy, Ofcom, 2012. Trustee, Royal Botanic Gdns, Kew, 2003–09. *Recreations:* cooking, fly fishing. *Address:* Royal Botanic Gardens, Kew, Richmond, Surrey TW9 3AB.

DEVEREUX, family name of **Viscount Hereford**.

DEVEREUX, Alan Robert, CBE 1980; DL; Founder Director, Quality Scotland Foundation, since 1991; *b* 18 April 1933; *s* of Donald Charles and Doris Devereux; *m* 1st, 1959, Gloria Alma Hair (*d* 1985); one *s*; 2nd, 1987, Elizabeth Tormey Docherty. *Educ:* Colchester School; Clacton County High School; Mid-Essex Technical Coll. CEng, MIET, CIMgt. Marconi's Wireless Telegraph Co., 1950–56; Halex Div. of British Xylonite Co., 1956–58; Spa Div., Sanitas Trust, 1958–65; Gen. Man., Dobar Engineering, 1965–67; Norcros Ltd, 1967–69; Gp Man. Dir 1969–78, Dep. Chm. 1978–80, Scotcros Ltd; Dir-Gen., Scotcros Europe SA, 1976–79. Director: Scottish Mutual Assurance Soc., 1975; Walter Alexander PLC, 1980–90; Hambros Scotland Ltd, 1984–; Abbey National Life, 1999–2003; Scottish Advisor, Hambros Bank, 1984–90. Dep. Chm. 1975–77, Chm. 1977–79, CBI Scotland; CBI: Council Mem., 1972–; Mem. President's Adv. Cttee, 1979; UK Regional Chm., 1979; Mem., F and GP Cttee, 1982–84. Chairman: Small Industries Council for Rural Areas of Scotland, 1975–77; Scottish Tourist Bd, 1980–90; Scottish Ambulance Service NHS Trust, 1994–97; Member: Scottish Development Agency, 1977–82; BTA, 1980–90. Chairman: Mission Aviation Fellowship, 2004–; Police Dependants' Trust, Scotland. Scottish Free Enterprise Award, 1978. DL Renfrewshire, 1985. *Recreations:* clock restoration, walking, Christian charities. *Address:* South Fell, 24 Kirkhouse Road, Blanefield, Stirlingshire G63 9BX. *T:* (01360) 770464. *Club:* East India, Devonshire, Sports and Public Schools.

DEVEREUX, Prof. Michael Peter, PhD; Director, Oxford University Centre for Business Taxation, since 2006; Fellow, Oriel College, Oxford, since 2006; *b* Dover, 9 May 1959; *s* of Roy Devereux and Mary Margaret Devereux; *m* 1983, Katherine Mary Ronan; two *s* one *d. Educ:* St John's Coll., Oxford (BA 1980); London Sch. of Econs (MSc 1982); University Coll. London (PhD 1990). Institute of Fiscal Studies: Res. Officer, 1982–85; Sen. Res. Officer, 1985–86; Dir of Corporate Sector Prog., 1987–90; Prof. of Econs and Finance, 1990–98, and Chair, Econs Dept, 1993–96, Univ. of Keele; Prof. of Econs, 1998–2006, and Chair, Econs Dept, 2002–05, Univ. of Warwick. Res. Dir, Eur. Tax Policy Forum, 2004–; Pres., Internat. Inst. for Public Finance, 2012– (Vice Pres., 2009–12). Houblon-Norman Fellow, Bank of England, 1992–93; Research Fellow: IFS, 1990–; Centre for Econ. Policy Res., 2000–; CESifo, 2006–. *Publications:* (ed) The Economics of Tax Policy, 1996; (jtly) The Effective Levels of Company Taxation in the Member States of the EU, 2001; contrib. papers to jls incl. Econ. Jl, Econ. Policy, Jl Public Econs, Jl Econometrics, Internat. Tax and Public Finance, Jl Internat. Econs. *Recreations:* family, tennis, music. *Address:* Oxford University Centre for Business Taxation, Saïd Business School, Park End Street, Oxford OX1 1HP. *T:* (01865) 288507, *Fax:* (01865) 288805. *E:* michael.devereux@sbs.ox.ac.uk.
See also R. J. Devereux.

DEVEREUX, Robert Harold Ferrers; Chairman, New Forests Company Holding Ltd, since 2007; Founder and Director, African Arts Trust, since 2012; *b* Woking, 11 April 1955; *s* of Robert Humphrey Bouchier Devereux and Barbara Devereux (*née* Heywood); *m* 1983, Vanessa, *d* of late Edward James Branson; three *s* one *d. Educ:* Marlborough Coll.; Downing Coll., Cambridge (BA Hons 1978). Founding shareholder and Chm., Virgin Communications and Entertainment Gp, 1979–96; Chairman: Soho House, 1998–2008; Frieze Events Ltd, 2010–15; Frieze Publishing Ltd, 2010–15. Mem., DCMS Creative Industries Task Force; Mem. Supervisory Panel, Catalyst Partners LLP, 2011–. Trustee and Chm., Portobello Trust, 1993–2003; Chm., Trustees, Save the Rhino Internat., 1997–2006; Trustee, Westside Sch., Westminster, 2008–. Gov., South Bank Centre, 1997–2009; Chm., Tate Africa Acquisitions Cttee, 2011–; Mem. Adv. Bd, Cambridge Conservation Initiative, 2011–. *Recreations:* contemporary art, walking, tree planting, history, Africa, contemporary literature. *Address:* Flat 3, 128 Talbot Road, W11 1JA. *T:* 07768 270416. *E:* robert.hfd@virgin.net. *Club:* Soho House.
See also Sir R. C. N. Branson.

DEVEREUX, Robert John; Permanent Secretary, Department for Work and Pensions, since 2011; *b* 15 Jan. 1957; *s* of Roy Devereux and Mary Margaret Devereux; *m* 1980, Margaret Alexandra Johnson; two *d. Educ:* St John's Coll., Oxford (MA Maths); Edinburgh Univ. (MSc Stats). ODA, 1979–83; HM Treasury, 1984–94 (Hd, Defence Expenditure, 1992–94); Guinness Brewing Worldwide, 1995–96 (on secondment); Department for Social Security: Hd, Family Policy, 1996–98; Director: Fraud Strategy, 1998–2000; Working Age Strategy, 2000–01; Dir, Planning and Performance, DWP, 2001–02; Dir Gen., Roads, Regl and Local Transport, subseq. Road Transport, Aviation and Shipping, DfT, 2003–07; Permanent Sec., DfT, 2007–10. *Address:* Department for Work and Pensions, 4th Floor, Caxton House, 6–12 Tothill Street, SW1H 9NA.
See also M. P. Devereux.

de VESCI, 7th Viscount *cr* 1766; **Thomas Eustace Vesey;** Bt 1698; Baron Knapton, 1750; Managing Director, Horticultural Coir Ltd, since 1999; *b* 8 Oct. 1955; *s* of 6th Viscount de Vesci and Susan Anne (*d* 1986), *d* of late Ronald (Owen Lloyd) Armstrong-Jones, MBE, QC, DL, and of the Countess of Rosse; *S* father, 1983; *m* 1987, Sita-Maria, *oc* of late Brian de Breffny; two *s* one *d. Educ:* Eton; St Benet's Hall, Oxford. *Address:* Knapton, Abbeyleix, Co. Laois, Ireland.
See also Earl of Snowdon.

DE VILLE, Sir Harold Godfrey, (Sir Oscar), Kt 1990; CBE 1979; PhD; Chairman, Meyer International plc, 1987–91 (Deputy Chairman, 1985–87; Director, 1984–91); *b* Derbyshire, 11 April 1925; *s* of Harold De Ville and Anne De Ville (*née* Godfrey); *m* 1947, Pamela Fay Ellis; one *s. Educ:* Burton-on-Trent Grammar Sch.; Trinity Coll., Cambridge (MA); PhD London 1995. Served RNVR, 1943–46. Ford Motor Co. Ltd, 1949–65; BICC, 1965–84: Dir, 1971–84; Exec. Dep. Chm., 1978–84. Director: Balfour Beatty Ltd, 1971–78; Phillips Cables Ltd, Canada, 1982–84; Metal Manufacturers Ltd, Australia, 1983–84; Scottish Cables Ltd, S Africa, 1983–84. Mem., BRB, 1985–91. Chairman: Iron and Steel EDC, 1984–86; Govt Review of vocational qualifications, 1985–86; NCVQ, 1986–90; Nat. Jt Council for Engrg Construction Industry, 1985–87. Member: Commn on Industrial Relations, 1971–74; Central Arbitration Cttee, 1976–77; Council: ACAS, 1976–91; BIM, 1982–86; Confederation of British Industry, 1977–85 (Chm., Working Party on Employee Participation, 1975–78). Mem. Council, Reading Univ., 1985–91. *Recreation:* genealogy.

de VILLEPIN, Dominique Marie François René Galouzeau; Prime Minister of France, 2005–07; lawyer, since 2008; *b* Rabat, Morocco, 14 Nov. 1953; *s* of Xavier Galouzeau de Villepin and Yvonne (*née* Hétier); *m* 1985, Marie-Laure Le Guay; one *s* two *d. Educ:* Ecole Nat. d'Admin; Paris Inst. of Pol Scis (BA Arts and Law). Ministry of Foreign Affairs, France: Sec. of Foreign Affairs, Dept for African Affairs, 1980–81; Hd of Mission, Dept for African Affairs and Analysis and Forecasting Centre, 1981–84; First Sec., 1984–87, Press Officer and Spokesperson, 1987–89, Washington; Second Counsellor, 1989–90, First Counsellor, 1990–92, New Delhi; Dep. Hd, African Affairs, Min. of Foreign Affairs, 1992–93; COS to Minister of Foreign Affairs, 1993–95; Sec. Gen. of Presidency of Republic, 1995–2002; Minister of Foreign Affairs, 2002–04; Rep., Convention on Future of Europe, 2002; Minister of the Interior, Internal Security and Local Rights, 2004–05. Chm., Admin. Council, Nat. Forests Office, 1996–99. *Publications:* Les Cent Jours ou l'esprit de sacrifice, 2001; Le cri de la gargouille, 2002; Eloge des voleurs de feu, 2003; "Un autre monde": Cahiers de l'Herne, 2003; Le requin et la mouette, 2004; L'homme européen, 2005; Histoire de la diplomatie française, 2005; Le soleil noir de la puissance, 2007; Hôtel de l'insomnie, 2008; La chute ou l'Empire de la solitude, 2008; La cité des hommes, 2009; Le dernier témoin, 2009; De l'esprit de cour: la malédiction française, 2010; Notre vieux pays, 2011; Seul le devoir nous rendra libres, 2012; *poetry:* Parole d'exil, 1986; Le droit d'aînesse, 1988; Sécession, 1996; Elégies barbares, 1996. *Address:* 35 Rue Fortuny, 75017 Paris, France.

de VILLIERS, 4th Baron cr 1910; **Alexander Charles de Villiers;** *b* 29 Dec. 1940; *o s* of 3rd Baron de Villiers and Edna Alexis Lovett (*née* MacKinnon); *S* father, 2001; *m* 1966 (marr. diss.); *m* 1987, Christina Jacobsen.

de VILLIERS, Dawid Jacobus, DPhil; Advisor to the Secretary General of the United Nations World Tourism Organisation, since 2006 (Chairman, Strategic Committee and World Committee for Ethics in Tourism, since 2006); Deputy Secretary General, World Tourism Organisation, 1997–2005; *b* 10 July 1940; *m* 1964, Suzaan Mangold; one *s* three *d. Educ:* Univ. of Stellenbosch (BA Hons Philosophy; BTh, DPhil); Rand Afrikaans Univ. (MA Phil., 1972). Abe Bailey Scholar, 1963–64; Markotter Scholar, 1964. Part-time Lectr in Philosophy, Univ. of Western Cape, 1963–64; Minister of Dutch Reformed Church, Wellington, Cape, 1967–69; Lectr in Philosophy, 1969–72, and Pres. Convocation, 1973–96, Rand Afrikaans Univ.; MP for Johannesburg W, 1972–79, for Piketberg, 1981–94, list MP, 1994–97; Chm., Nat. Party's Foreign Affairs Cttee in Parlt; Ambassador of S Africa to London, 1979–80; Minister: of Trade and Industry (formerly Industries, Commerce and Tourism), SA, 1980–86; of Budget and Welfare, 1986–88; for Admin and Privatisation, 1988–90; for Public Enterprises, 1989–91; for Mineral and Energy Affairs, 1990–91; for Economic Co-ordination, 1991–92; for Public Enterprises, 1992–94; for the Envmt and Tourism, 1994–96; Leader, Houses of Parliament, 1989–92. Leader, Nat. Party, Cape Province, 1990–96. National Party Delegn Leader, Constitutional Conf., Convention for a Democratic S Africa, 1992. Visited: USA on US Leaders Exchange Prog., 1974; UK as guest of Brit. Govt, 1975; Israel as guest of Israeli Govt, 1977. Represented S Africa in internat. Rugby in S Africa, UK, Ireland, Australia, NZ, France and the Argentine, 1962–70 (Captain, 1965–70). State President's Award for Sport, 1968 and 1970; S African Sportsman of the Year, 1968; Jaycee's Outstanding Young Man of the Year Award, 1971; State President's Decoration for Meritorious Service, Gold, 1988. *Recreations:* sports, reading. *Address:* Koloniesland 8, Stellenbosch, 7600, South Africa.

de VILLIERS, Etienne Marquard; non-executive Chairman: BBC Worldwide, 2005–09; Virgin Racing, 2009–10; BrandsEye, since 2012; *b* Pretoria, SA, 19 Aug. 1949; *s* of Dr J. T. Marquard and Anita R. L. de Villiers; *m* 1973, Anita Du Plooy; one *s* one *d. Educ:* Pretoria Boys High Sch.; Univ. of Pretoria (BSc (Eng-Civil) *cum laude*; Galion Gold Medal 1970); Trinity Coll., Oxford (MA PPE). Rhodes Schol., 1971. Associate, McKinsey & Co., London, 1979–81; Exec. Dir, Solaglas Internat., 1981–84; CEO, Satbel, 1984–86; Walt Disney Co.: Man. Dir, 1986–2000; President: Buena Vista Internat., 1986–94; Walt Disney Internat. TV, 1994–99; Pres. and Man. Dir, Walt Disney Internat. EMEA, 1999–2000; Co-Founder, i-Gabriel, 2000–01; Mem. Bd, SLEC, 2001–02; Co-Founder, Englefield Capital, 2001–05; Exec. Chm. and Pres., ATP, 2005–08. Member, Board: Videonetworks, 2000–06; Carlton Communications, 2001–03; ITV plc, 2003–04; Jetix, 2005–07; non-exec. Dir, Pi Capital, 2002–. *Recreations:* football (Arsenal season ticket holder), passionate cyclist and tennis player, avid off piste ski-ing, despite the divorce threats; contemporary British figurative art collector thankfully curtailed by lack of wall space; music, film and TV fanatic; travelling with Anita and spending time in the Algarve; re-learning about life from my grandsons Leo, Elliot and Reuben who call me Oupie (the Afrikaans diminutive for Oupa (Grandpa)); also known by the name Oapil (Old Aged Pensioner in Lycra). *Address:* c/o Pi Capital, Berger House, 38 Berkeley Square, W1J 5AE. *T:* (020) 7529 5656. *E:* paula@boltongardens.co.uk. *Clubs:* Vincent's; Denham Golf; Quinta do Lago Golf, San Lorenzo Golf.

de VILLIERS, Fleur Olive Lourens, CMG 2011; Chairman of Trustees, International Institute for Strategic Studies, since 2002; *b* Port Elizabeth, South Africa, 1 Dec. 1937; *d* of late Frederick, (Dick) and Edna de Villiers (*née* Walker). *Educ:* Loreto Convent, Hillcrest; Univ. of Pretoria (BA); Harvard Univ. (Nieman Fellow 1981). Theatre critic, Econs Corresp., Political Reporter, then Leader writer, Pretoria News, 1961–73; Sunday Times, Johannesburg: Political Corresp. and travelling corresp., 1973–80; Asst Ed. and Opinion Page Ed., 1981–86; Leader Writer and consultant on S Africa for The Times, 1986–93. Public Affairs Consultant to: De Beers, 1988–2003; Anglo American Corp., 1988–98. Vis. Fellow, 1986–87, Vice Chm. Council, 2002–, IISS. Mem., Internat. Adv. Bd, 2004–, Global Ambassador, 2011–, SOAS. Mem. Council, Chelsea Soc., 2014–. *Publications:* Professional Secrecy in South Africa, 1983; Bridge or Barricade: a guide to South Africa's new constitution, 1983; Apartheid: Capitalism or Socialism?, 1986; articles in Strategic Survey, National Interest, TES, The Times, etc. *Recreations:* gardening, reading, music, theatre, talking politics. *Address:* International Insitute for Strategic Studies, Arundel House, 13–15 Arundel Street, Temple Place, WC2R 3DX. *T:* (020) 7379 7676.

DEVINE, Prof. Fiona, OBE 2010; PhD; FAcSS; Professor of Sociology, since 2001, and Head, Manchester Business School, since 2014 (Interim Head, 2013–14), University of Manchester; *b* 6 June 1962; *d* of Patrick Noel Devine and Martha (*née* Daly); *m* 2008, James B. Husband. *Educ:* Univ. of Essex (BA Sociol. and Govt 1983; MA Sociol.; PhD Sociol. 1990). Res. officer, PSI, 1988–89; Lectr in Sociol., Univ. of Liverpool, 1989–94; University of Manchester: Lectr, 1994–97; Sen. Lectr, 1997–99; Reader, 1999–2001; Hd of Sociol., 2004–07; Hd, Sch. of Social Scis, 2009–13. Mem. Council, ESRC, 2003–07 (Chm., Internat. Adv. Cttee, 2003–07). FAcSS (AcSS 2011); FRSA 2015. *Publications:* Affluent Workers Revisited, 1992; Social Class in America and Britain, 1997; (with S. Heath) Sociological Research Methods in Context, 1999; Class Practices, 2004; (with S. Heath) Doing Social Science, 2009. *Recreations:* walking in Spain, bird-watching, classical and world music, swimming, badminton. *Address:* Manchester Business School, University of Manchester, Booth Street West, Manchester M15 6PB. *T:* (0161) 275 2508. *E:* Fiona.Devine@manchester.ac.uk.

DEVINE, James; *b* 24 May 1953; *s* of James and Rose Devine; *m* 1974, Elizabeth (marr. diss.); one *s* one *d*. *Educ:* St Mary's Acad., W Lothian; Moray House Coll. Sch. of Nursing. Student teacher, 1970–72; student nurse, 1972–75; Staff Nurse, Bangour Hosp., 1975–77; Charge Nurse, psychiatric nursing team, Blackburn Health Centre, 1977–82; union official, COHSE, then Unison (Head of Health, Scotland), 1982–2005. MP (Lab) Livingston, Sept. 2005–2010. Hon. Lectr in Industrial Relns, Stirling Univ., 1985–2005. Agent, Rt Hon. Robin Cook, MP, 1982–2005. Mem., Scottish Exec., Labour Party, 1983–95; Chm., Scottish Labour Party, 1996–95. *Recreations:* reading, chess, football, horse racing. *Club:* Loganlea Miners.

DEVINE, Rt Rev. Joseph; Bishop of Motherwell, (RC), 1983–2013; *b* 7 Aug. 1937; *s* of Joseph Devine and Christina Murphy. *Educ:* Blairs Coll., Aberdeen; St Peter's Coll., Dumbarton; Scots Coll., Rome. Ordained priest in Glasgow, 1960; postgraduate work in Rome (PhD), 1960–64; Private Sec. to Archbishop of Glasgow, 1964–65; Assistant Priest in a Glasgow parish, 1965–67; Lecturer in Philosophy, St Peter's Coll., Dumbarton, 1967–74; a Chaplain to Catholic Students in Glasgow Univ., 1974–77; Titular Bishop of Voli and Auxiliary to Archbishop of Glasgow, 1977–83. Papal Bene Merenti Medal, 1962. *Recreations:* general reading, music, Association football. *Address:* 27 Smithycroft, Hamilton ML3 7UL.

DEVINE, Sir Thomas (Martin), Kt 2014; OBE 2005; PhD, DLitt; FBA 1994; FRSE; FRHistS; FSAScot; Sir William Fraser Professor of Scottish History and Palaeography, University of Edinburgh, 2005–11, Emeritus, 2014 (Head, School of History, Classics and Archaeology, 2008–10; Director, Scottish Centre for Diaspora Studies, 2008–14; Personal Senior Research Professor in History, 2012–14); *b* 30 July 1945; *s* of Michael Gerard Devine and Norah Martin; *m* 1971, Catherine Mary Lynas; two *s* three *d*. *Educ:* Strathclyde Univ. (BA; PhD 1972; DLitt 1992). FRHistS 1980; FRSE 1992. University of Strathclyde: Lectr in History, 1969–78; Sen. Lectr in History, 1978–83; Reader in Scottish History, 1983–88; Prof. of Scottish History, 1988–98; Dir, Res. Centre in Scottish History, 1993–98; Dean, Faculty of Arts and Social Studies, 1993–94; Dep. Principal, 1994–97; Aberdeen University: Univ. Res. Prof. in Scottish Hist. and Dir, Res. Inst. of Irish and Scottish Studies, 1998–2003; Dir, AHRB, subseq. AHRC Centre for Irish-Scottish Studies, 2001–06; Glucksman Res. Prof., 2004–06. Adjunct Professor in History: Univ. of Guelph, Canada, 1989–; Univ. of N Carolina, 1997–. Member: Sec. of State for Scotland's Adv. Cttee, 2001–04; Res. Awards Adv. Cttee, Leverhulme Trust, 2002–09; Adv. Cttee, ESRC Prog. on Devolution, 2002–06. Chm., Econ. and Social History Soc. of Scotland, 1984–88; Convenor of Council, Scottish Catholic Historical Assoc., 1990–95; Convener, Irish-Scottish Academic Initiative, 1998–2001; UK Rep., Internat. Commn for Hist. of Towns, 2000–06. Mem. Council, British Acad., 1998–2001. Mem., Adv. Cttee, Eur. Assoc. of History Educators, 2001–. Trustee, 1995–2002, Chair, 1999–2002, European Ethnol Res. Centre, Nat. Museums of Scotland. Gov., St Andrew's Coll. of Educn, 1990–94. Prothero Lectr, RHistS, 2005. FSAScot 2014. Hon. MRIA 2001. Hon. Fellow, Bell Coll., 2005. Hon. DLitt: QUB; Abertay Dundee; DUniv Strathclyde, 2006. Sen. Hume Brown Prize in Scottish Hist., 1976; Saltire Prize, 1992; Henry Duncan Prize, 1994, Royal Medal, 2001, RSE; John Aitkenhead Award and Medal, Inst. of Contemp. Scotland, 2006; RSE/Beltane Sen. Prize for Excellence in Public Engagement, 2012; Inaugural Sir Walter Scott Senior Prize for Excellence in Humanities and Creative Arts, RSE, 2012. *Publications:* The Tobacco Lords, 1975, 2nd edn 1990; (ed) Ireland and Scotland 1600–1850, 1983; (ed) Farm Servants and Labour in Lowland Scotland, 1984; A Scottish Firm in Virginia 1767–77, 1984; (ed) People and Society in Scotland, 1988; The Great Highland Famine, 1988; (ed) Improvement and Enlightenment, 1989; (ed) Conflict and Stability in Scottish Society 1700–1850, 1990; (ed) Irish Immigrants and Scottish Society in 18th and 19th Centuries, 1991; Scottish Emigration and Scottish Society, 1992; The Transformation of Rural Scotland 1660–1815, 1994; Clanship to Crofters' War, 1994; (ed) Scottish Elites, 1994; Glasgow, vol. I, 1995; Exploring The Scottish Past, 1995; (ed) Scotland in the Twentieth Century, 1996; (ed) Eighteenth Century Scotland: new perspectives, 1999; (ed) Celebrating Columba: Irish-Scottish connections 1597–1997, 1999; The Scottish Nation 1700–2000, 1999; (ed) Scotland's Shame?: bigotry and sectarianism in modern Scotland, 2000; (ed) Being Scottish: personal reflections on Scottish identity, 2002; Scotland's Empire 1600–1815, 2003; (ed jtly) The Transformation of Scotland, 2005; Clearance and Improvement: land, power and people in Scotland, 1660–1860, 2006; The Scottish Nation 1700–2007, 2006; (ed) Scotland and the Union, 1707 to 2007, 2008; To the Ends of the Earth: Scotland's global diaspora 1750–2010, 2011; (ed jtly) Scotland and the British Empire, 2011; (ed jtly) The Oxford Handbook of Modern Scottish History 1500–2010, 2012; numerous articles in learned jls. *Recreations:* grandchildren, walking and staying in the Hebrides, foreign travel, music, watching skilful soccer. *Address:* School of History, Classics and Archaeology, University of Edinburgh, William Robertson Wing, Teviot Place, Edinburgh EH8 9AG. *T:* (0131) 650 4029. *E:* t.m.devine@ed.ac.uk.

DEVITT, Sir James (Hugh Thomas), 3rd Bt *cr* 1916, of Chelsea, Co. London; hotel and leisure consultant; Managing Director, Herald Hotels Ltd, since 2013; *b* 18 Sept. 1956; *o s* of Sir Thomas Gordon Devitt, 2nd Bt and of Janet Lilian, *o d* of Col H. S. Ellis, CBE, MC; *S* father, 1995; *m* 1985, Susan Carol (*née* Duffus); two *s* one *d*. *Educ:* Corpus Christi Coll., Cambridge (MA). MRICS. Dir, CB Richard Ellis Hotels, 2003–12; Chartered Surveyor, Wivenhoe House Hotel Ltd, 2012–13. *Recreations:* family, football. *Heir:* *s* Jack Thomas Michael Devitt, *b* 29 July 1988. *Address:* The Old Rectory, Ford Lane, Alresford, Colchester, Essex CO7 8AX. *T:* (01206) 827315.

DEVLIN, Graham Thomas, CBE 2010; theatre writer and director, since 1973; arts consultant, since 1999; *b* London, 11 Nov. 1948; *s* of Alan Devlin and Eileen Devlin; *m* 2005, Susan Linda Hoyle, *qv*. *Educ:* Tonbridge Sch.; University Coll., Oxford (MA). Artistic Dir and Chief Exec., Major Road Theatre Co., 1973–97; Dep. Sec. Gen. and Acting Chief Exec., Arts Council of England, 1997–99. Fellow in Theatre, Bradford Univ., 1978–82; Dir, Wakefield Fest., 1981–82. Chairman: Phoenix Dance, 1989–97; Tipping Point, 2007–; Dep. Chm., Royal Court Th., 2005–; Exec. Chm., Dance Training and Accreditation Partnership, 2009–14. Vis. Prof., Queen Margaret University Coll., Edinburgh, 1998–2003. Dir of over 80 theatre and opera prodns. *Publications:* Stepping Forward, 1989; A Place to Think, 2010. *E:* graham_devlin@yahoo.co.uk.

DEVLIN, Hugh Gerard; Founding Partner, Delightful LLP, since 2008; *b* Lanark, 1 March 1962; *s* of Francis and Maureen Devlin; *m* 1998, Sarah Rebecca Polden. *Educ:* Our Lady's High Sch., Motherwell; Univ. of Glasgow (MA, LLB); Univ. of Edinburgh (DipLP). NP 1987. Solicitor, Drummond & Co., 1986–89; Manager, Corporate Finance, British Linen Bank, 1989–94; joined Withers LLP, 1994, Partner, 1995–2008, Consultant, 2008–. Mentor, Grad. Fashion Week, 2008–. Trustee, Design Mus., 2012–. *Recreations:* contemporary art and design, opera and ballet, Italy, fashion history, assisting creative talent. *Address:* 75 Aberdeen Park, N5 2AZ. *T:* (020) 7354 0233, 07879 465422. *E:* hugh@hughdevlin.com.

DEVLIN, (Josephine) Bernadette; *see* McAliskey, J. B.

DEVLIN, Stuart Leslie, AO 1988; CMG 1980; goldsmith, silversmith and designer in London since 1965; Goldsmith and Jeweller by appointment to HM the Queen, 1982; *b* 9 Oct. 1931; *m* 1986, Carole Hedley-Saunders. *Educ:* Gordon Inst. of Technology, Geelong; Royal Melbourne Inst. of Technology; Royal Coll. of Art. DesRCA (Silversmith), DesRCA (Industrial Design/Engrg). Art Teacher, Vic. Educn Dept, 1950–58; Royal Coll. of Art, 1958–60; Harkness Fellow, NY, 1960–62; Lectr, Prahran Techn. Coll., Melbourne, 1962; one-man shows of sculpture, NY and Sydney, 1961–64; Insp. Art in Techn. Schs, Vic. Educn Dept, 1964–65; exhibns of silver and gold in numerous cities USA, Australia, Bermuda, Middle East and UK, 1965–. Mem., Royal Mint Adv. Cttee, 1998–2007. Executed many commissions in gold and silver: designed coins for Australia, Singapore, Cayman Is, Gibraltar, IoM, Burundi, Botswana, Ethiopia and Bhutan; designed and made: cutlery for State Visit to Paris, 1972; Duke of Edinburgh trophy for World Driving Championship, 1973; silver to commemorate opening of Sydney Opera House, 1973; Grand National Trophy, 1975, 1976; Australian Bravery Awards, 1975; Regalia for the Order of Australia, 1975–76; Queen's Silver Jubilee Medal, 1977; Centrepiece for RE to commemorate their work in NI, 1984; Bas-relief portrait of Princess of Wales for Wedgwood, 1986; full set of Defence Awards for Australia, 1989; portraits of HM the Queen Mother, HRH the Princess of Wales, HRH the Princess Royal, HRH the Princess Margaret, 1991; British Athletics Fedn Badge and Chain of Office, 1992; 24 Sydney 2000 Olympic coins, 1997; Millennium commemorative dishes for Goldsmiths' Co. and Inf. Technologists' Co., 2000; four UK £1 coins representing London, Cardiff, Edinburgh and Belfast, 2010; silver flagon for Westminster Abbey, 2010. Developed strategy for use of champagne diamonds in jewellery for Argyle Diamond Mines, 1987. Computer presentations in USA and UK; Inaugural Chm., Engrg Modelling Systems Special Interest Gp, 1993; Vice Chm., Intergraph Graphics Users' Gp UK, 1996. Post-Grad. Dir, Goldsmiths' Inst., 2012–. Freeman, City of London, 1966; Liveryman, 1972, Mem. Ct of Assts, 1986–2007, Prime Warden, May 1996–97, Goldsmiths' Co. Hon. DocArts RMIT, 2000. Lifetime Achievement Award, Goldsmiths' Craft and Design Council, 2009; Australian of the Yr in the UK, Australia Day Foundn, 2011. *Recreations:* work, computer graphics. *Address:* 72 Shippam Street, Roman Quarter, Chichester, W Sussex PO19 1AG. *T:* (01243) 778007.

DEVLIN, Tim; Founder, Tim Devlin Enterprises, public relations consultancy, 1989–2013; *b* 28 July 1944; 3rd *s* of Rt Hon. Lord Devlin, PC, FBA, and Madeleine, *yr d* of Sir Bernard Oppenheimer, 1st Bt; *m* 1967, Angela Denise, *d* of late A. J. G. and Mrs Laramy; two *s* two *d*. *Educ:* Winchester Coll.; University Coll., Oxford (Hons degree, History). Feature Writer, Aberdeen Press & Journal, 1966; Reporter, Scotsman, 1967; Educn Reporter, Evening Echo, Watford, 1968–69; Reporter, later News Editor, The Times Educnl Supplement, 1969–71; Reporter, The Times, 1971–73, Educn Corresp., 1973–77; Nat. Dir, ISIS, 1977–84; Public Relations Dir, Inst. of Dirs, 1984–86; Assoc. Dir, Charles Barker Traverse-Healy, 1986–89. *Publications:* (with Mary Warnock) What Must We Teach?, 1977; Good Communications Guide, 1980; Independent Schools—The Facts, 1981; Choosing Your Independent School, 1984; (with Brian Knight) Public Relations and Marketing for Schools, 1990; (with Hywel Williams) Old School Ties, 1992; (with Angela Devlin) Anybody's Nightmare, 1998; Public Relations Manual for Schools, 1998. *Recreations:* writing, art, crochet, Italian life. *T:* (01424) 256352. *E:* tim.devlin.ostuni@gmail.com.

DEVLIN, Timothy Robert; barrister; *b* 13 June 1959; *e s* of late H. Brendan Devlin, CBE, FRCS and of Anne Elizabeth Devlin, MB BCh; *m* 1st, 1986 (marr. diss. 1989); 2nd, 1991 (marr. diss. 2002); 3rd, 2011, Donna Kusman. *Educ:* Dulwich Coll.; LSE; City Univ. Called to the Bar, Lincoln's Inn, 1985 (Hardwick and Thomas More Scholar; Mem., Finance Cttee, 2006–). Sen. Expert, Technical Assistance to CIS, EU, 1998–99; Consultant, Stanbrook & Hooper, Brussels, 1999–2000. Co. Sec., Furnival Ltd, 2008–. Dep. Chm., NHS Tribunal, 2001–. Mem., Cons. Research Dept, 1981; former Chm., LSE Conservatives; Chm., Islington North Cons. Assoc., 1986. MP (C) Stockton South, 1987–97; contested (C) same seat, 1997, 2001. PPS to Attorney Gen., 1992–94; PPS to Ministers of Trade and Industry, 1995–97. Mem., Select Cttee on Scottish Affairs, 1995–97; formerly Chm., Parly Panel on Charity Law; Chm., Northern Gp of Cons. MPs, 1992–97. Dep. Chm., Foreign Affairs Forum, 1990–92; Member: SE Circuit, Criminal Bar Assoc., 1998–; Bar Council, 2007–10, 2012–. Member: Soc. of Cons. Lawyers; European Bar Assoc.; Friends of the RA. Trustee, NSPCC, 1993–95; Gov., Yarm Sch., 1988–98. *Recreations:* sailing, opera, travel. *Address:* 32 Furnival Street, EC4A 1JQ. *Clubs:* Royal Ocean Racing, Bar Yacht (Rear Cdre); Island Sailing.

DEVON, 19th Earl of, *cr* 1553; **Charles Peregrine Courtenay;** Bt 1644; *b* 14 Aug. 1975; *o s* of 18th Earl of Devon and Diana Frances Courtenay (*née* Watherston); *S* father, 2015; *m* 2004, Allison Joy Langer; one *s* one *d*. *Educ:* St John's Coll., Cambridge (BA Hons History of Art, 1997; MA 2001; Rugby half-Blue 1996). Called to the Bar, Inner Temple, 1999; admitted to California Bar, 2004. Latham & Watkins LLP: Associate, Los Angeles, 2005–13; Counsel, 2014–, Hd of Intellectual Property Litigation, 2015–, London. London Scottish 1st XV Rugby, 1998–2003; Santa Monica 1st XV Rugby, 2003–05. Mem., Grocers' Co. *Heir:* *s* Lord Courtenay, *qv*. *Clubs:* Hawk's; St Moritz Tobogganing; Butterflies Cricket; Santa Monica Rugby.

DEVONPORT, 3rd Viscount *cr* 1917, of Wittington, Bucks; **Terence Kearley;** Bt 1908; Baron 1910; architect and landowner; Chairman: Peasmarsh Place (Country Care), since 1984; Millhouse Developments Ltd, since 1989; *b* 29 Aug. 1944; *s* of 2nd Viscount Devonport and Sheila Isabel, *e d* of Lt-Col C. Hope Murray; *S* father, 1973; *m* 1st, 1968, Elizabeth Rosemary (marr. diss. 1979), *d* of late John G. Hopton; two *d*; 2nd, 2000, Dr Meiyi Pu, *d* of Prof. Wan Jun Pu, Beijing; one *d*. *Educ:* Aiglon Coll., Switzerland; Selwyn Coll., Cambridge (BA, DipArch, MA); Newcastle Univ. (MPhil). Architect: Davis Brody, New York City, 1967–68; London Borough of Lambeth, 1971–72; Barnett Winskell, Newcastle-upon-Tyne, 1972–75; landscape architect, Ralph Erskine, Newcastle, 1977–78; in private practice, 1979–84 (RIBA, ALI); Forestry Manager, 1973–; farmer, 1978–. Chairman: Cape Acre Ltd; Devonport Farms Ltd; Devonport Estates; Man. Dir, Tweedswood Enterprises, 1979–2011, and dir various other cos, 1984–. Member: Lloyds, 1976–90; Internat. Dendrology Soc., 1978– (Council, 1995–); N Adv. Cttee, TGEW, 1978–94; N Adv. Cttee, CLA, 1980–85; Nat. Land Use and Envmt Cttee, TGUK, 1984–87. Pres., Arboricultural Assoc., 1995–2001; Forestry Commn Reference Panel, 1987–94. MInstD. Order of Mark Twain (USA), 1977. *Recreations:* nature, travel and good food; interests: trees, the arts, country sports. *Heir: cousin* Chester Dagley Hugh Kearley [*b* 29 April 1932; *m* 1974, Josefa Mesquida; one *s* one *d*]. *Address:* Ray Demesne, Kirkwhelpington, Newcastle upon Tyne NE19 2RG. *Clubs:* Royal Automobile, Beefsteak, Farmers, Royal Over-Seas League; Northern Counties (Newcastle upon Tyne).

DEVONSHIRE, 12th Duke of, *cr* 1694; **Peregrine Andrew Morny Cavendish,** KCVO 2009; CBE 1997; DL; Baron Cavendish, 1605; Earl of Devonshire, 1618; Marquess of Hartington, 1694; Earl of Burlington, 1831; Baron Cavendish (UK), 1831; Chairman, Chatsworth House Trust, since 2004; *b* 27 April 1944; *s* of 11th Duke of Devonshire, KG, MC, PC and Dowager Duchess of Devonshire, DCVO; *S* father, 2004; *m* 1967, Amanda Carmen, *d* of late Comdr E. G. Heywood-Lonsdale, RN, and of Mrs Heywood-Lonsdale; one *s* two *d*. *Educ:* Eton; Exeter Coll., Oxford. Sen. Steward, Jockey Club, 1989–94; Chm., British Horseracing Bd, 1993–96; HM's Rep., 1998–2011, and Chm., 1998–2008, Ascot Racecourse. Dep. Chm., Sotheby's Holdings Inc., 1996– (Dir, 1994–). Trustee: Wallace Collection, 2007–; Storm King Art Centre, New York, 2007–; Mus Sheffield (formerly Sheffield Galls and Mus) Trust, 2007–12; Derby Museums, 2012–. Mem. Shadow Bd, Derby, Derbyshire, Nottingham and Nottinghamshire Local Enterprise Partnership, 2010–12. DL Derbys, 2008. *Heir: s* Earl of Burlington, *qv*. *Address:* Chatsworth, Bakewell, Derbyshire DE45 1PP.

DEVONSHIRE, His Honour Michael Norman, TD 1969; a Circuit Judge, 1991–2000; *b* 23 May 1930; *s* of late Norman George Devonshire and late Edith Devonshire (*née* Skinner); *m* 1962, Jessie Margaret Roberts. *Educ:* King's Sch., Canterbury. Military Service, 2nd Lt, RA, served Korea, 1953–55; 4/5 Bn Queen's Own Royal West Kent Regt TA and 8 Bn Queen's Regt TA, 1955–69; retired in rank of Major, 1969. Admitted Solicitor, 1953; Partner, Doyle Devonshire Co., 1957–79; Master of the Supreme Court, Taxing Office, 1979–91; a Recorder, 1987–91; Dep. Circuit Judge, 2000–01. Chm., SE London Area Adv. Cttee on Magistracy, 1995–99. Pres., London Solicitors' Litigation Assoc., 1974–76; Mem., Law Soc. Family Law and Contentious Remuneration Cttees, 1969–79. Mem., Recreation and Conservation Cttee, Southern Water Authy, 1984–89. Mem., Council, Royal Yachting Assoc., 1978–92 and 1993–96 (Trustee, Seamanship Foundn, 1981–85; Chairman: Gen. Purposes Cttee, 1982–87; Regl Cttee, 1987–92; Internat. Affairs Cttee, 1990–2004; SE Region, 1993–98; Hon. Life Mem., 2000); Chm., Internat. Regs Cttee, ISAF (formerly IYRU), 1994–2004 (Mem., 1986–90; Vice Chm., 1991–94); Mem., Pleasure Navigation Commn, Union Internat. Motonautique, 1986–2000. FRIN 2004. Outstanding Service Award, Royal Norwegian Boating Fedn, 2004; Silver Medal for Outstanding Services, ISAF, 2005. *Recreations:* sailing, photography.

de VOS, Niels; Chief Executive Officer: UK Athletics, since 2007; World Athletics Championships London 2017, since 2013; *b* 27 March 1967; *s* of Leendert and Christine de Vos; *m* 1990, Kirsten Macleod; two *s* one *d*. *Educ:* Dorridge Jun. Sch.; King Edward's Sch., Edgbaston; Keble Coll., Oxford (BA Hons Modern Hist.). Hd, Corporate Relns, Barnardo's, 1994–97; Commercial Gen. Manager, Millennium Dome, 1997–99; Commercial Dir, Manchester 2002 Commonwealth Games, 1999–2002; CEO, Sale Sharks Rugby Club, 2002–07. Mem., Nat. Olympic Cttee, 2007–; Exec. Dir, British Olympic Assoc., 2009– (Chm., Audit Cttee, 2009–11). Founder and Trustee, Children's Promise, 1999–2004; non-exec. Dir, Birmingham Children's Hosp., 2010–11. *Recreations:* football, running, films, family holidays. *Address:* c/o UK Athletics, Athletics House, Back Straight Stand, Alexander Stadium, Walsall Road, Perry Barr, Birmingham B42 2LR.

DEVOY, Dame Susan (Elizabeth Anne), DNZM 1998; CBE 1993 (MBE 1986); professional squash rackets player, 1982–92, retired; formerly Chief Executive Officer, then Chairperson, Sport Bay of Plenty; *b* 4 Jan. 1964; *d* of John and Tui Devoy; *m* 1986, John Brandon Oakley; four *s*. *Educ:* McKillop Coll., Rotorua. Ranked no 1 internat. women's squash rackets player, 1984–92; winner: World Championships: Dublin, 1985; Auckland, 1987; Sydney, 1990; Vancouver, 1992; British Open Championships, 1984–90, 1992; 86 other internat. titles. Walked length of NZ in 53 days, raising NZ500,000 for Muscular Dystrophy, 1988. Trustee: Halberg Trust for Crippled Children (Chm., 1996–2005); Tauranga Energy Consumer Trust. Race Relations Comr, Human Rights Commn, NZ, 2013–. NZ Sportsperson of Year, Halberg Trust, 1985–87, 1990, 1992. *Publications:* Susan Devoy on Squash, 1988; Out on Top, 1993. *Recreation:* yoga.

DEW, John Anthony; HM Diplomatic Service, retired; consultant; illustrator and printmaker; *b* 3 May 1952; *s* of Roderick Dew and Katharina (*née* Kohlmeyer); *m* 1975, Marion, *d* of late Prof. Kenneth Kirkwood; three *d*. *Educ:* Hastings Grammar Sch.; Lincoln Coll., Oxford (Schol.); Ruskin Sch. of Drawing, Oxford. Joined HM Diplomatic Service, 1973; Third Sec., Caracas, 1975–79; FCO, 1979–83; First Sec., UK Delegn to OECD, Paris, 1983–87; Asst Hd, Falkland Is and Resource Mgt Depts, FCO, 1987–92; Counsellor, Dublin, 1992–96; Minister, Madrid, 1996–2000; Hd of Latin America and Caribbean Dept, FCO, 2000–03; on secondment to Lehman Brothers Internat., 2003–04; Ambassador: to Cuba, 2004–08; to Colombia, 2008–12. Printmaker, Taller Experimental de la Gráfica Havana and Taller Arte Dos, Bogotá. Solo exhibition: Galeria Arte Dos Bogotá, 2011. *Recreations:* books, pictures. *E:* johnanthonydew@gmail.com. *W:* www.johndew.co.uk. *Club:* Real Gran Pena (Madrid).

DEW, Most Rev. John Atcherley; *see* Wellington (NZ), Archbishop of, (RC).

DEW, Prof. Ronald Beresford; Professor of Management Sciences, University of Manchester Institute of Science and Technology, 1967–80, now Professor Emeritus, University of Manchester; *b* 19 May 1916; *s* of Edwyn Dew-Jones, FCA, and Jean Robertson Dew-Jones, BA, (*née* McInnes); *m* 1940, Sheila Mary Smith, BA; one *s* one *d*. *Educ:* Sedbergh; Manchester Univ. (LLB); Cambridge Univ. (MA). FCA 1947. Barrister-at-Law, Middle Temple, 1965. Lieut, RNVR, 1940–45. Asst Managing Dir, P-E Consulting Gp, 1952–62. Visiting Prof. of Industrial Administration, Manchester Univ., 1960–63; Head of Dept of Management Sciences, Univ. of Manchester Inst. of Science and Technology, 1963–70 and 1974–77; Prof. of Industrial Administration, Manchester Univ., 1963–67. Mem. Council, Internat. Univ. Contact for Management Educn, 1966–71; Dir, Centre for Business Research, 1965–69; Dir, European Assoc. of Management Training Centres, 1966–71; Dep. Chm., Manchester Polytechnic, 1970–72; Co-Chm., Conf. of Univ. Management Schools (CUMS), 1970–73. Member: Council of BIM, 1971–76 (Bd of NW Region, 1966–80); Council of Manchester Business School, 1967–76; Court of Manchester Univ., 1978–80; Trustee, European Foundation for Management Develt, 1975–77. *Recreations:* archaeology, ornithology, travel. *Address:* University of Manchester, School of Management, Sackville Street, Manchester M60 1QD.

de WAAL, Sir Constant Hendrik, (Sir Henry), KCB 1989 (CB 1977); QC 1988; First Parliamentary Counsel, 1987–91; *b* 1 May 1931; *s* of late Hendrik de Waal and Elizabeth von Ephrussi; *m* 1964, Julia Jessel (MBE 2008); two *s*. *Educ:* Tonbridge Sch. (scholar); Pembroke Coll., Cambridge (scholar; Hon. Fellow, 1992). 1st cl. Law Tripos, 1st cl. LLM. Called to the Bar, Lincoln's Inn, 1953, Bencher 1989; Buchanan Prize, Cassel Scholar. Fellow of Pembroke Coll., Cambridge, and Univ. Asst Lectr in Law, 1958–60. Entered Parliamentary Counsel Office, 1960; with Law Commission, 1969–71; Parly Counsel, 1971–81; Second Parly Counsel, 1981–86; Parly Counsel to Law Commn, 1991–96. *Recreation:* remaining (so far as possible) unaware of current events. *Address:* 21 Warwick Square, SW1V 2AB.

See also Rev. V. A. de Waal.

de WAAL, Edmund Arthur Lowndes, OBE 2011; artist and writer; *b* 10 Sept. 1964; *s* of Rev. Victor Alexander de Waal, *qv*; *m* 1997, Susan Chandler; two *s* one *d*. *Educ:* Trinity Hall, Cambridge (BA 1st cl. Hons (English Lit.) 1986; Hon. Fellow 2009); Sheffield Univ. (Postgrad. Dip. Japanese Lang. 1992). Apprenticeship with Geoffrey Whiting, 1981–83; Cwm Pottery, 1986–88; studios in: Sheffield, 1988–92; London, 1993–. Daiwa Anglo-Japanese Foundn Schol., 1991–93; University of Westminster: Leverhulme Special Res. Fellow, 1999–2001; Sen. Res. Fellow in Ceramics, 2000–02; Prof. of Ceramics, 2004–11. Trustee, Victoria and Albert Mus., 2011–. FRSA 1996; Sen. FRCA 2012. *Solo exhibitions* include: Galerie Besson, London, 1997; Garth Clark Gall., NY, 1998; High Cross House, Dartington Hall, 1999; Geffrye Mus., London, 2002; New Art Centre, Roche Court, Salisbury, 2004; Kunstindustrie Mus., Copenhagen, 2004; Mus. of Wales, 2005; Kettle's Yard, Cambridge, 2007; Middlesbrough Inst. of Modern Art, 2007; V&A Mus., 2009; Alan Cristea, London, 2010, 2012; Waddesdon Manor, 2012; Gagosian, NY, 2013; Fitzwilliam Mus., 2013–14; Turner Contemp., 2014. Hon. DPhil: Arts London, 2013; Sheffield, 2013; Nottingham, 2014; Hon. Dr Canterbury Christ Church, 2014. *Publications:* Bernard Leach, 1998, 3rd edn 2014; 20th Century Ceramics, 2003; The Hare with Amber Eyes, 2010; The Pot Book, 2011; The White Road, 2015. *Address:* Edmund de Waal Studio, Unit 3, 1–7 Ernest Avenue, SE27 0DQ. *T:* (020) 8761 1117. *E:* studio@edmunddewaal.com. *W:* www.edmunddewaal.com.

See also J. H. L. de Waal.

de WAAL, Sir Henry; *see* de Waal, Sir C. H.

de WAAL, John Henry Lowndes; QC 2013; *b* Cambridge, 7 Jan. 1962; *s* of Rev. Victor Alexander de Waal, *qv*; *m* 1994, Mandy Teresa O'Loughlin; one *s* one *d*. *Educ:* Pembroke Coll., Cambridge (BA 1983); Birmingham Univ. (Cert Ed); Birmingham Poly. (CPE); Inns of Court Sch. of Law. Teacher and lectr, 1983–90; called to the Bar, Middle Temple, 1992. *Recreations:* walking, camping. *Address:* Hardwicke Building, New Square, Lincoln's Inn, WC2A 3SB. *T:* (020) 7242 2523. *E:* john.dewaal@hardwicke.co.uk.

See also E. A. L. de Waal.

de WAAL, Judith Mary; *see* Slater, J. M.

de WAAL, Rev. Victor Alexander; Dean of Canterbury, 1976–86; *b* 2 Feb. 1929; *s* of late Hendrik de Waal and Elisabeth von Ephrussi; *m* 1960, Esther Aline Lowndes Moir, PhD; four *s*. *Educ:* Tonbridge School; Pembroke Coll., Cambridge (MA); Ely Theological College. With Phs van Ommeren (London) Ltd, 1949–50; Asst Curate, St Mary the Virgin, Isleworth, 1952–56; Chaplain, Ely Theological Coll., 1956–59; Chaplain and Succentor, King's Coll., Cambridge, 1959–63; Chaplain, Univ. of Nottingham, 1963–69; Chancellor of Lincoln Cathedral, 1969–76; Chaplain, SSC, Tymawr, 1990–2000. Hon. DD Nottingham, 1983. *Publications:* What is the Church?, 1969; The Politics of Reconciliation: Zimbabwe's first decade, 1990; Holy Wisdom: Father Augustine Baker (1575–1641), 2008; contrib.: Theology and Modern Education, 1965; Stages of Experience, 1965; The Committed Church, 1966; Liturgy Reshaped, 1982; Liturgie et Espace Liturgique, 1987; Vie Ecclesiale—communauté et communautés, 1989; Beyond Death, 1995; La Confession et les Confessions, 1995; Les Artisans de Paix, 1996; Travail et Repos, 2000; Loi et Transgression, 2002. *Address:* 6 St James Close, Bishop Street, N1 8PH. *T:* (020) 7354 2741.

See also Sir C. H. de Waal, E. A. L. de Waal, J. H. L. de Waal.

DEWAR, family name of **Baron Forteviot.**

DEWAR, Dame Alison Fettes; *see* Richard, Dame A. F.

DEWAR, David Alexander; an Assistant Auditor General, National Audit Office, 1984–94; *b* 28 Oct. 1934; *s* of James and Isabella Dewar; *m* 1959, Rosalind Mary Ellen Greenwood; one *s* one *d*. *Educ:* Leith Academy, Edinburgh. Entered Exchequer and Audit Dept, 1953; Chief Auditor, 1966; Deputy Director of Audit, 1973; Director of Audit, 1977; Dep. Sec. of Dept, 1981. *Recreations:* gardening, golf. *Address:* 14 Drovers Way, Barnham, Bognor Regis, W Sussex PO22 0DD. *T:* (01243) 553594.

DEWAR, Ian Stewart; JP; Member: South Glamorgan County Council, 1985–93 (Vice-Chairman, 1990–91; Finance Chairman, 1992–93); South Wales Valuation Tribunal, 1995–2001; *b* 29 Jan. 1929; *er s* of late William Stewart Dewar and Eileen Dewar (*née* Godfrey); *m* 1968, Nora Stephanie House; one *s* one *d*. *Educ:* Penarth County Sch.; UC Cardiff; Jesus Coll., Oxford (MA). RAF, 1947–49. Asst Archivist, Glamorgan County Council, 1952–53. Entered Min. of Labour, 1953; Asst Private Sec. to Minister, 1956–58; Principal, Min. of Labour and Civil Service Commn, 1958–65; Asst Sec., Min. of Labour, Dept of Employment and Commn on Industrial Relations, 1965–70; Asst Sec., 1970–73, and Under-Sec., 1973–83, Welsh Office. Member, Governing Body: Univ. of Wales, 1985–93; Nat. Mus. of Wales, 1985–93; Chm., Museum Schs Service Cttee, 1989–93. Mayor of Penarth, 1998–99. JP S Glam, 1985. *Address:* 59 Stanwell Road, Penarth, South Glamorgan CF64 3LR. *T:* (029) 2070 3255.

DEWAR, Robert Scott, CMG 2006; HM Diplomatic Service, retired; High Commissioner to Nigeria, and Permanent Representative to Economic Community of West African States, 2007–11; *b* 10 June 1949; *s* of Robert James Dewar, CMG, CBE and Christina Marianne Dewar (*née* Ljungberger); *m* 1979, Jennifer Mary Ward; one *s* one *d*. *Educ:* Loretto; Brasenose Coll., Oxford. VSO, Port Sudan, 1971–72; Scottish Office, 1972–73; FCO, 1973; served Colombo and FCO, to 1981, Asst Sec. Gen. to Lancaster House Conf. on Southern Rhodesia, 1979; Head of Chancery, Luanda, 1981–84; FCO, 1984–88; Dep. Head of Mission, Dakar, 1988–92; Dep. High Comr, Harare, 1992–96; Ambassador to Republic of Madagascar, 1996–99; FCO, 1999–2000; High Comr to Mozambique, 2000–03; Ambassador to Ethiopia, and Permanent Rep. to the African Union, 2004–07. Associate Fellow, Africa Prog., RIIA, 2011–. Mem., Assoc. of Oxfam, 2011–. Trustee: Durrell Wildlife Conservation Trust, 2012–; BRCS, 2013–. *Recreations:* sport, esp. squash, tennis and fly fishing.

DEWAR, Sally Marie; Managing Director, International Regulatory Risk, JP Morgan Chase & Co., since 2011; *b* Farnham, 25 Dec. 1968. *Educ:* Univ. of Manchester Inst. of Sci. and Technol. (BSc 1st Cl. Jt Hons Pure Maths and French). Corporate Finance Manager: KPMG Manchester, 1991–97; BOC, 1997–98; Associate, 1998–99, Manager, 1999–2000, Equity Mkts, UK Listing Authy, London Stock Exchange; Chief Financial Officer, LeisureHunt.com, 2000–01; Hd, Corporate Actions and Projects, London Stock Exchange, 2001–02; Financial Services Authority: Hd, UK Listing Authy, 2002–05; Dir of Mkts, 2005–07; Man. Dir, Wholesale and Instnl Mkts, 2008–09; Man. Dir, Risk, 2009–11. Mem., Business Develt Cttee, LPO, 2007–09. Mem., Bd of Trustees, Disability Challengers, 2007–. *Address:* JP Morgan Chase & Co., 25 Bank Street, Canary Wharf, E14 5JP.

DEWAR-DURIE, Andrew Maule, CBE 1999; DL; Chairman, Seafish Industry Authority, 2002–07 (Deputy Chairman, 2000–02); *b* 13 Nov. 1939; *s* of late Lt Col Raymond Varley Dewar-Durie and Frances St John Dewar-Durie (*née* Maule); *m* 1972, Marguerite Maria Jarmila Kottulinsky; two *s* one *d*. *Educ:* Cheam Sch.; Wellington Coll. Nat. Service, Argyll and Sutherland Highlanders, 1958–68, retd with rank of Captain. Export Rep. to Sen. Export Dir, White Horse Distillers, 1968–83; Internat. Sales Dir, Long John Distillers, 1983–87; Internat. Sales Dir, Man. Dir, then CEO, James Burrough Ltd, 1987–92; Man. Dir, 1992–97, Chm., 1997–99, Allied Distillers. Dir, Britannic Asset Mgt, 2001–04. Vice-Chm., 1996–97,

Chm., 1997–99, CBI Scotland. Dir, 2000–08, Vice Chm., 2008–10, Edinburgh Mil. Tattoo, later Royal Edinburgh Mil. Tattoo; Dir, St Andrews Links Ltd, 2012–. DL Dunbartonshire, 1996. *Publications:* The Scottish Sheep Industry: a way forward, 2000. *Recreations:* ski-ing, rough shooting. *Address:* Finnich Malise, Croftamie, W Stirlingshire G63 0HA. *T:* (01360) 660257, *Fax:* (01360) 660101. *E:* andrewdewardurie@gmail.com. *Club:* New (Edinburgh).

de WATERVLIET, Jean-Michel V.; *see* Veranneman de Watervliet.

DEWBERRY, David Albert; HM Diplomatic Service, retired; Deputy Head of Mission, the Holy See, Rome, 1996–2001; *b* 27 Sept. 1941; *s* of Albert Dewberry and Grace Dewberry (*née* Tarsey); *m* 1974, Catherine Mary (*née* Stabback); three *s* one *d*. *Educ:* Cray Valley Sch., Foots Cray, Kent. Joined CRO, 1958; Karachi, 1963; Kingston, 1966; Warsaw, 1970; Brussels, 1971; Second Sec. (Aid), Dhaka, 1972; FCO, 1974; Consul: Mexico City, 1977; Buenos Aires, 1980; FCO, 1982; Dep. High Comr, Dar es Salaam, 1987; FCO, 1991–96. *Recreations:* reading, walking. *E:* dadewberry@hotmail.com.

DEWE, Roderick Gorrie; Chairman: Dewe Rogerson Group Ltd, 1969–99; Roddy Dewe Consultants Ltd, 1997–2003; *b* 17 Oct. 1935; *s* of Douglas Percy Dewe and Rosanna Clements Gorrie (*née* Heggie); *m* 1964, Carol Anne Beach Thomas; one *s* one *d*. *Educ:* abroad and University Coll., Oxford (BA Hons). Treasury, Fedn of Rhodesia and Nyasaland Govt, 1957–58; Angel Court Consultants, 1960–68; founded Dewe Rogerson, 1969, Chm., 1969–95. Hon. FCIPR. *Recreations:* golf, flyfishing, travel. *Address:* Old Southill Station House, near Biggleswade, Beds SG18 9LP. *T:* (01462) 811274. *Clubs:* City of London, Beefsteak, Savile.

DEWEY, Sir Anthony Hugh, 3rd Bt *cr* 1917; JP; *b* 31 July 1921; *s* of late Major Hugh Grahame Dewey, MC (*e s* of 2nd Bt), and Marjorie Florence Isobel (who *m* 2nd, 1940, Sir Robert Bell, KCSI; she *d* 1988), *d* of Lieut-Col Alexander Hugh Dobbs; *S* grandfather, 1948; *m* 1949, Sylvia, *d* of late Dr J. R. MacMahon, Branksome Manor, Bournemouth; two *s* three *d*. JP Somerset, 1961. *Heir: s* Rupert Grahame Dewey [*b* 29 March 1953; *m* 1978, Suzanne Rosemary, *d* of late Andrew Lusk, Perthshire; two *s* one *d*]. *Address:* Rag, Galhampton, Yeovil, Som BA22 7AJ. *T:* (01963) 440213. *Club:* Army and Navy.

DEWEY, Prof. John Frederick, FRS 1985; FGS; FAA; Professor of Geology, University of Oxford, 1986–2001, now Emeritus; Fellow, since 1986 and Senior Research Fellow, since 2001, University College, Oxford; Professor of Geology, University of California, Davis, 2001–06, now Distinguished Professor Emeritus; *b* 22 May 1937; *s* of John Edward and Florence Nellie Mary Dewey; *m* 1961, Frances Mary Blackhurst, MA, DSc; one *s* one *d*. *Educ:* Bancroft's School; Queen Mary Coll. and Imperial Coll., Univ. of London (BSc, PhD, DIC); MA 1965, ScD 1988, Cantab; DSc Oxon 1989. CGeol 1990. Lecturer: Univ. of Manchester, 1960–64; Univ. of Cambridge, 1964–70; Prof., State Univ. of New York at Albany, 1970–82; Prof. of Geology, Durham Univ., 1982–86. Vis. Res. Fellow, British Geol Survey, 2001–; Vis. Res. Prof., Imperial Coll., Univ. of London, 2001–. MAE 1990; MNAS 1995. FAA 2011. Hon. MRIA 2008. Hon. DSc: Meml Univ. of Newfoundland, 1996; Rennes, 2012; Hon. LLD NUI, 1998. Numerous honours and awards, UK and overseas, incl. Penrose Medal, Geol Soc. of America, 1992; Arthur Holmes Medal, Eur. Union of Geoscis, 1993; Wollaston Medal, Geol Soc. of London, 1999; Fourmarier Medal, Royal Acad. of Scis, Belgium, 1999. *Publications:* 170 scientific papers; contribs to Geol Soc. of America Bulletin, Geol Soc. London Jl, Jl Geophysical Res. and other learned jls. *Recreations:* ski-ing, cricket, water colour and oil painting, English music 1850–1950, model railways. *Address:* Sherwood Lodge, 93 Bagley Wood Road, Kennington OX1 5NA. *T:* (01865) 735525.

DEWHURST, Neil Gordon, MD; FRCP, FRCPE, FRCPGlas; Consultant Cardiologist and General Physician, NHS Tayside, 1995–2013; President, Royal College of Physicians of Edinburgh, 2010–14; *b* Blackburn, Lancs, 8 Sept. 1952; *m* 1979, Elspeth Lucy Campbell. *Educ:* Hutton Grammar Sch.; Univ. of Edinburgh (BSc Hons 1st Cl. Bacteriol. 1974; MB ChB 1976; MD 1982). FRCPE 1991; FRCP 1995; FRCPGlas 2005. Lectr in Gen. Medicine, Univ. of Edinburgh, 1978–81; Registrar in Gen. Medicine with special interest in Cardiol., Edinburgh, 1981–83; Sen. Registrar in Gen. Medicine and Cardiol., Edinburgh, 1983–87; Consultant Cardiologist and GP, South Devon Healthcare Trust, 1987–95. Hon. Sen. Lectr in Medicine, Univ. of Dundee, 1995–2013. Hon. FACP 2010. *Recreations:* fishing, travel, music, gardening.

de WILDE, (Alan) Robin; QC 1993; *b* 12 July 1945; *s* of late Capt. Ronald Cedric de Wilde and of Dorothea Elizabeth Mary (*née* Fenningworth); *m* 1977, Patricia Teresa Bearcroft; three *s*. *Educ:* Dean Close Sch.; RAF Coll., Cranwell; Inns of Court Sch. of Law. Called to the Bar, Inner Temple, 1971, Bencher, 1996; a Recorder, 2000–04. Mem., Bar Council, 1985–90, 1998–99, 2002–04; Chm., Professional Negligence Bar Assoc., 1995–97 (Hon. Vice Pres., 1998–; Chm., Ogden Working Party, 2003–; Gen. Editor, Facts & Figures - Tables for the Calculation of Damages, annually 1996–); Mem. Council, Bodily Injury Claims Mgt Assoc., 2003–. FRSocMed 1997. *Address:* 218 Strand Chambers, 218 Strand, WC2R 1AT. *T:* 0845 083 3000.

DE WITT, Prof. Sir Ronald (Wayne), Kt 2002; international consultant, justice and health, since 2008; Chief Executive, HM Courts Service, 2004–07; *b* 31 March 1948; *s* of James Goldwyn De Witt and Una Doreen De Witt (*née* Lane). *Educ:* Sch. of Advanced Nursing, Wellington, NZ (RN; Dip. N 1978); Univ. of Humberside (BA Hons Business Studies, MA Health Mgt 1992; Hon. Fellow 1998). Registered Comprehensive Nurse 1970, NZ 1975, Canada 1970; SRN; Cert. of Burns and Plastic Surgery, 1971; Cert. of Mgt, 1976. Chief Nurse, Auckland Health Bd, 1988–89; Dist Manager, Central Auckland Health Services, 1989–90; Chief Executive: Auckland Hosp., 1990–91; Hull Acute Services, Hull HA, later Royal Hull Hosps NHS Trust, 1991–96; Leeds HA, 1996–99; KCH NHS Trust, 1999–2002; NW London Strategic HA, 2002–04. Chm., English Nat. Bd for Nursing, Midwifery and Health Visiting, 1996–2001. Patron, Foundn for Nursing Studies, 2010– (Trustee, 2005); Regency Patron, Royal Pavilion Brighton, 2013–; Trustee: Cancer BACUP, subseq. Cancerbackup, 2005–08; Gen. Nursing Council, 2005– (Mem., 1996–; Chair, 2008–); Chm., Lepra, 2011–15 (Trustee, 2007–10). Associate Mem. Bd, Bupa, 2011–. Hon. DCL Humberside, 2004. *Publications:* (contrib.) Public Health, 1999; Managing the Business of Health Care, 2001. *Recreations:* travel, reading, walking, books, antiques.

DEWS, Vivienne Margaret, (Mrs Alan Cogbill); Chief Executive, Office of Fair Trading, 2014 (Executive Director, 2008–14); *b* 29 Dec. 1952; *d* of late Albert Dews and of Eva Margaret Dews (*née* Hayman); *m* 1st, 1972, Stephen Ladner (marr. diss. 1977); 2nd, 1979, Alan Cogbill; one *s* one *d* (and two *d* decd). *Educ:* Northampton High Sch. for Girls; Newnham Coll., Cambridge (BA 1974). Joined Home Office, 1974, Private Sec. to Minister for Police and Prisons, 1979–80; Dep. Dir, Top Mgt Prog., Cabinet Office, 1987–89; Home Office: Head: Immigration Policy, 1989–91; After Entry Casework and Appeals, 1991–93; Consulting Efficiency and Market Testing, 1994–95; Dir, Finance and Services, Immigration and Nationality Directorate, 1995–99; Chief Exec., Police Inf. Technol. Orgn, 1999–2001; Dir, Modernising Corporate Support, Inland Revenue, 2002; Dir, Resources and Planning, HSE, 2002–08. Mem., CIPFA, 2007 (Mem., Wkg Gp on Corporate Governance in UK Public Services, 2014–). Member: Audit Cttee, Mencap, 2011–; Hon. Treas., Charity for Civil Servants, 2012–; Trustee: Henry Smith Charity, 2014–; Young Epilepsy, 2015–. Vice Chm., Governing Body, Fedn of St Elphege's and Regina Coeli Schs, 2014– (Mem., Interim Exec. Bd, Regina Coeli Catholic Prim. Sch., 2013–14); Mem., Governing Body, Winterbourne Nursery and Infants Sch., 2014– (Chm., 2015–). *Recreations:* family, home, garden, Italy. *Club:* Oxford and Cambridge.

DEXTER, Colin; *see* Dexter, N. C.

DEXTER, Edward Ralph, CBE 2001; Managing Director, Ted Dexter & Associates, 1978–2005; *b* 15 May 1935; *m* 1959, Susan Georgina Longfield; one *s* one *d*. *Educ:* Radley College; Jesus College, Cambridge (Captain of cricket and of golf). Served 11th Hussars, 1956–57 (Malaya Campaign Medal 1955). Cricketer, 1958–68; Captain of Sussex, 1960–65; Captain of England, 1962–65; freelance journalist, 1965–88; sports promotion consultant, 1978–. Chm., England (Cricket) Cttee, TCCB, 1989–93. Contested (C) Cardiff, 1965. *Publications:* Ted Dexter's Cricket Book, 1963; Ted Dexter Declares, 1966; (jtly) Test Kill, 1976; Deadly Putter, 1979; From Bradman to Boycott, 1981; My Golf, 1982; Ted Dexter's Little Cricket Book, 1996. *Recreations:* golf, reading. *Address:* 167 Tettenhall Road, Wolverhampton, W Midlands WV6 0BZ. *Clubs:* MCC (Chm., Cricket Cttee, 1998–2003; Pres., 2001–02), Sussex CC (Pres., 2007); Sunningdale Golf, Royal and Ancient Golf.

DEXTER, Michael; *see* Dexter, T. M.

DEXTER, (Norman) Colin, OBE 2000; author of crime novels; *b* 29 Sept. 1930; *s* of Alfred Dexter and Dorothy Dexter (*née* Towns); *m* 1956, Dorothy Cooper; one *s* one *d*. *Educ:* Stamford Sch.; Christ's Coll., Cambridge (MA). Assistant Classics Master: Wyggeston Boys' Sch., Leicester, 1954–57; Loughborough GS, 1957–59; Sen. Classics Master, Corby GS, 1959–66; Sen. Asst Sec., Oxford Delegacy of Local Exams, 1966–88. Member: CWA, 1978; Detection Club, 1980. Freedom, City of Oxford, 2001. Hon. Fellow, St Cross Coll., Oxford, 2005. Hon. MA Leicester, 1996; Hon. DLitt Oxford Brookes, 1998. Cartier Diamond Dagger, CWA, 1998; ITV3 Writer's Award for Classic TV Drama, 2008; CWA's Hall of Fame, 2009; John Logie Baird Medal, RTS Midlands, 2010. *Publications:* Last Bus to Woodstock, 1975; Last Seen Wearing, 1976; The Silent World of Nicholas Quinn, 1977; Service of All the Dead (Silver Dagger, CWA), 1979; The Dead of Jericho (Silver Dagger, CWA), 1981; The Riddle of the Third Mile, 1983; The Secret of Annexe 3, 1986; The Wench is Dead (Gold Dagger, CWA), 1989; The Jewel that was Ours, 1991; The Way Through the Woods (Gold Dagger, CWA), 1992; Morse's Greatest Mystery, 1993; The Daughters of Cain, 1994; Death is Now My Neighbour, 1996; The Remorseful Day, 1999; Morse Crosswords, 2006; Cracking Cryptic Crosswords, 2009. *Recreations:* poetry, crosswords, Wagner. *Address:* 456 Banbury Road, Oxford OX2 7RG.

DEXTER, Prof. (Thomas) Michael, PhD, DSc; FRS 1991; FMedSci; scientific consultant; Chairman, Stem Cell Sciences Ltd, 2003–06 (non-executive Director, 2003–09); *b* 15 May 1945; *s* of Thomas Richard Dexter and Agnes Gertrude Deplege; *m* 1966, Frances Ann Sutton (marr. diss. 1978); one *s* one *d* (twins); one *s* one *d* by Dr Elaine Spooncer; *m* 2009, Dr Clare Heyworth. *Educ:* Salford Univ. (BSc 1st class Hons 1970; DSc 1982); Manchester Univ. (PhD 1973). MRCPath 1987, FRCPath 1997; CBiol, FRSB (FIBiol 1997). Lady Tata Meml Scholar, 1970–73; Paterson Institute for Cancer Research: Res. Scientist, 1973; Prof. of Haematology and Hd of Dept of Exptl Haematol., 1982–98; Dep. Dir, 1994–97; Dir, 1997–98; Dir, Wellcome Trust, 1998–2003. Chairman: Centre for Life, Newcastle upon Tyne, 2003–07; Cockcroft Inst. for Accelerator Science, 2004–09. Internat. Scientific Advr, Rothschild Asset Mgt, 2003–08. Life Fellow, Cancer Res. Campaign, Manchester, 1978; Personal Chair, Univ. of Manchester, 1985, Emeritus Prof. of Hematol., 2013; Gibb Res. Fellow, CRC, 1992–97. Visiting Fellow: Sloan Kettering Inst., NY, 1976–77; Weizmann Inst., Israel, 1980. Lectures: Annual, Leukaemia Res. Fund, 1987; Michael Williams, RSM, 1990; Maximov, Leningrad, 1990; Almoth-Wright, St Mary's, London, 1992; Medawar, RPMS, 1994; Henry Hallett Dale, Nat. Inst. of Biol Standards of Control, 1997; Annual, British Soc. of Haematology, 1998; Inst. Distinguished, Inst. of Cancer Res., 1999; 5th Chamlong-Harinasuta, Bangkok, 1999; Lloyd Roberts, RCP, 2000. Member: MRC, 1993–96 (Chairman: Molecular and Cellular Medicine Bd, 1994–96; Human Genome Mapping Project Co-ordinating Cttee, 1996–98); Scientific Cttee, Leukaemia Res. Fund, 1983–86; Scientific Grants Cttee, CRC, 1987–93; Scientific Adv. Bd, Biomedical Res. Center, BC, 1987–91; Scientific Adv. Bd, Wellcome/CRC Inst., Cambridge, 1992–98; AFRC Grants Cttee, 1992–94; Cttee on Med. Aspects of Radiation in Envmt, 1994–98; Adv. Bd, EMF Trust, 1995–; NW Sci. Council, 2003–09; Adv. Bd, First London plc, 2008–09. Pres., Internat. Soc. for Exptl Hematology, 1988. Founder FMedSci 1998. Hon. MRCP 1995, Hon. FRCP 1998. Hon. DSc: Salford, 1998; UMIST, 1999; London, 2002; Lancaster, 2006; Manchester Metropolitan, 2014. *Publications:* author of 360 articles in scientific jls; editor of four books. *Recreations:* folk singing, gardening, poetry, dominoes.

DEY, Graeme James; Member (SNP) Scottish Parliament, since 2011; *b* Aberdeen, 29 Oct. 1962; *s* of Donald Dey and Marion Dey; *m* 1985, Linda Gatt; one *s* one *d*. *Educ:* Broomhill Primary Sch., Aberdeen; Springhill Primary Sch., Aberdeen; Harlaw Acad., Aberdeen. Sports Journalist, Aberdeen Office, DC Thomson, 1980–85; Sports Journalist, 1985–91, Sports Editor, 1991–2010, The Courier. Dep. Convenor, Rural Affairs Climate Change and Envmt Cttee, Scottish Parlt, 2012–. *Recreations:* golf, music, jogging, comedy. *Address:* Scottish Parliament, Holyrood, Edinburgh EH99 1SP. *T:* (0131) 348 6291. *E:* graeme.dey.msp@scottish.parliament.uk.

DEY, Rajeeb; Founder and Chief Executive Officer, Enternships.com, since 2009; Co-Founder, StartUp Britain, since 2011; *b* 6 Dec. 1985; *s* of Dr Krishna Ranjan Dey and Supriya Dey. *Educ:* King Edward VI Sch., Chelmsford; Jesus Coll., Oxford (BA 1st Cl. Hons Econs and Mgt; MA). Trustee: Phoenix Educn Trust, 2004–13; UnLtd, 2008–. Young Global Leader, WEF, 2012; Queen's Award for Enterprise Promotion, 2013. *Recreations:* travelling, fitness, ski-ing, eating out, cinema, theatres, voluntary work. *Address:* Enternships, 1st Floor, 35 Inverness Street, NW1 7HB.

d'EYNCOURT, Sir Mark Gervais T.; *see* Tennyson-d'Eyncourt, Sir M.

DHAMIJA, Dinesh; Chairman and Chief Executive, ebookers plc, 1999–2005; Chairman, Copper Beech Group, since 2006; *b* 28 March 1950; *s* of Jagan and Devika Dhamija; *m* 1977, Tani Malhotra; two *s*. *Educ:* King's Sch., Canterbury; Fitzwilliam Coll., Cambridge (BA 1974; MA). Founded first travel agency, Dabin Travel Ltd, 1980; estabd Flightbookers, 1983; Royal Nepal Airlines: Gen. Sales Agent, UK and Ireland, 1987–93; Regl Dir, Europe, 1993–96; established: Flightbookers.com, 1996; ebookers, 1999. Pres., The Indus Entrepreneurs UK, 2014–. *Recreations:* golf, tennis. *Address:* Cinnabar, Portnall Drive, Virginia Water, Surrey GU25 4NR. *Clubs:* Royal Automobile, Oxford and Cambridge; Wentworth, Queenwood; Delhi Golf, Delhi Gymkhana (Delhi).

DHANDA, Parmjit Singh; Parliamentary and Campaigns Officer, Prospect, since 2010; *b* 17 Sept. 1971; *s* of Balbir Singh Dhanda and Mrs Balbir Singh Dhanda; *m* 2003, Rupi Rai; one *s*. *Educ:* Mellow Lane Comprehensive, Hayes, Middx; Univ. of Nottingham (BEng (Hons) Elec Eng; MSc IT 1995). Labour Party Organiser, W London, 1996–98; Asst Nat. Organiser, Connect, 1998–2001. Mem. (Lab), Hillingdon BC, 1998–2002. Contested (Lab) SE Reg., England, EP elecn, 1999. MP (Lab) Gloucester, 2001–10; contested (Lab) same seat, 2010. An Asst Govt Whip, 2005–06; Parly Under-Sec. of State, DES, then Dept for Children, Schools and Families, 2006–07; Parly Under-Sec. of State, DCLG, 2007–08. Mem. Bd, Hanover Housing Assoc., 2010–. Member: Fabian Society; Co-operative Society; USDAW. *Recreations:* football, cricket, writing. *Address:* Prospect, New Prospect House, 8 Leake Street, SE1 7NN.

DHANOWA, Charles Pritam Singh, OBE 2007; Registrar, Competition Appeal Tribunal, since 2003; *b* Cardiff, 18 June 1961; *s* of Sumitar Singh Dhanowa and Eunice Dhanowa (*née* Lane); *m* 1990, Dara Ann Vexter; one *s* one *d*. *Educ:* Radyr Comp. Sch., Cardiff; Downing

Coll., Cambridge (MA); Coll. of Law, Christleton (Law Final); King's Coll. London (Dip. Competition Law). Admitted solicitor, 1986; commercial litigation, Linklaters & Paines, 1986–92; Mckenna & Co., 1993; corporate litigation, Treasury Solicitor's Dept, 1994–96; Asst Legal Advr, Monopolies and Mergers Commn, 1996–98; Competition Commission: Hd, Secretariat, 1999–2001; Registrar, Competition Commn Appeal Tribunals, 2000–03; Sec.-Gen., Assoc. of Eur. Competition Law Judges, 2002–. Hon. QC 2012. *Recreations:* gardening, reading, walking, painting. *Address:* Competition Appeal Tribunal, Victoria House, WC1A 2EB. *T:* (020) 7979 7979. *Club:* Athenæum.

DHARKER, Imtiaz; poet; *b* Lahore, 31 Jan. 1954; *d* of Kausar and Sher Mohd Mobarik; *m* 2006, Simon Powell (*d* 2009); one *d* by a previous marriage. *Educ:* Hutchesons' Grammar Sch.; Univ. of Glasgow (MA Eng. Lit. and Philos.). Artist (11 solo exhibns). Owner and Dir, Solo Films, 1980–. Dir, Poetry Live!, 2008–; Trustee and Editor, Poems on the Underground; Trustee, Poetry Archive; Mem. Bd, Poetry Trust. Queen's Gold Medal for Poetry, 2014. *Publications:* Purdah, 1989; Postcards From God (including Purdah), 1997; I Speak for the Devil, 2001; The Terrorist at my Table, 2006; Leaving Fingerprints, 2009; Over the Moon, 2014. *Address:* c/o Bloodaxe Books, UK, Eastburn, South Park, Hexham, Northumberland NE46 1BS. *T:* (01434) 611581. *E:* publicity@bloodaxebooks.com.

DHILLON, Jasbir Singh; QC 2013; *b* Taplow, 23 Feb. 1969; *s* of Karnail and Surjit Dhillon; *m* 2000, Ajneet Jassey; two *s*. *Educ:* Desborough Sch.; Keble Coll., Oxford (BA 1st cl. Hons 1991); Harvard Law Sch. (LLM 1992). Associate, Cravath, Swaine & Moore, NY, 1992–95; admitted to US Dist Court, Southern Dist of NY Bar, 1993; Attorney-at-Law, New York, 1993; Lectr and Tutor in Law, Exeter Coll., Oxford, 1995–96; called to the Bar, Gray's Inn, 1996; Pupil, Brick Court Chambers, 1996–97; in practice as barrister, specialising in commercial law, 1997–; admitted to US Supreme Court Bar, 1998. Mem., Attorney Gen.'s Panel on Counsel, 2002–11. Mem., Standards Cttee, Bar Standards Bd, 2006–11. Dir, Bar Mutual Indemnity Fund Ltd, 2013–. *Publications:* (contrib.) Paget's Law of Banking, 13th edn 2007; (contrib.) Competition Litigation, UK Practice and Procedure, 2010; (contrib.) SIAC Rules: an annotation, 2014. *Recreations:* basketball, history, music, football. *Address:* Brick Court Chambers, 7–8 Essex Street, WC2R 3LD. *T:* (020) 7379 3550. *E:* Jasbir.Dhillon@brickcourt.co.uk.

DHIR, Anuja Ravindra; QC 2010; **Her Honour Judge Dhir;** a Circuit Judge, since 2012; *b* Dundee, Scotland, 19 Jan. 1968; *d* of Prof. Ravindra Kumar Dhir, OBE and Bharti Dhir; *m* 2002, Nicholas Lavender, *qv*; two *s* one *d*. *Educ:* Harris Acad.; Dundee Univ. (LLB Hons). Called to the Bar, Gray's Inn, 1989, Bencher, 2009; a Recorder, 2009–12. *Recreations:* walking, cooking. *Address:* Woolwich Crown Court, 2 Belmarsh Road, SE28 0EY.

DHOLAKIA, family name of **Baron Dholakia**.

DHOLAKIA, Baron *cr* 1997 (Life Peer), of Waltham Brooks in the co. of West Sussex; **Navnit Dholakia,** OBE 1994; PC 2010; JP, DL; *b* 4 March 1937; *s* of Permananddas Mulji Dholakia and Shantabai Permananddas Dholakia; *m* 1967, Ann McLuskie; two *d*. *Educ:* Home Sch. and Inst. of Science, Bhavnagar, Gujarat; Brighton Tech. Coll. Medical Lab. Technician, Southlands Hosp., Shoreham-by-Sea, 1960–66; Develt Officer, Nat. Cttee for Commonwealth Immigrants, 1966–68; Sen. Develt Officer, 1968–74, Principal Officer and Sec., 1974–76, Community Relns Commn; Commission for Racial Equality: Principal Fieldwork, Admin and Liaison Officer, 1976–78; Principal Officer, Management, 1978–81; Head of Admin, Justice Section, 1984–94. Lib Dem spokesman on home affairs, 1997–; an Asst Lib Dem Whip, 1997–99, Dep. Leader of Lib Dems, 2004–, H of L. Member: Hunt Cttee on Immigration and Youth Service, 1967–69; Bd of Visitors, HM Prison, Lewes, 1978–95; Home Office Inter-Deptl Cttee on Racial Attacks and Harassment, 1987–92; Carlisle Cttee on Parole Systems Review, 1987–88; Sussex Police Authority, 1991–94; Ethnic Minority Adv. Cttee, Judicial Studies Bd, 1992–96; Council, Howard League for Penal Reform, 1992–94 (Mem. Editl Bd, Howard Jl of Criminology, 1993–); Police Complaints Authy, 1994–97. Mem., H of L Appts Commn, 1999–2010. Pres., NACRO, 2003– (Mem. Council, 1984–; Chm., Race Issues Adv. Cttee, 1989–; Vice-Chm., 1995–98; Chm., 1998–2003); Vice-Chm., Policy Res. Inst. on Ageing and Ethnicity, 1999–2014. Vice Pres., Mental Health Foundn, 2002– (Trustee, 1997–2002); Trustee: British Empire and Commonwealth Mus., Bristol, 1999–2005; Pallant House Gall., Chichester, 2000–09; Police Foundn, 2002–. Gov., Commonwealth Inst., 1998–2005. Chairman: Brighton Young Liberals, 1959–62; Brighton Liberal Assoc., 1962–64; Sec., Race and Community Relns Panel, Liberal Party, 1969–74; Liberal Democrats: Mem., Federal Policy and Federal Exec. Cttee, 1996–97; Pres., Lib Dem Party, 1999–2004; Trustee, 2005–. Mem. (L) Brighton CBC, 1961–64. Mem. Council, SCF, 1992– (Chm., Programme Adv. Cttee, 1992–). JP Mid Sussex, 1978; DL West Sussex, 1999. Hon. LLD: Hertfordshire, 2009; York, 2010; East London, 2010. *Publications:* articles on criminal justice. *Recreations:* photography, travel, gardening, cooking exotic dishes. *Address:* House of Lords, SW1A 0PW.

DIACK, Lamine; President, International Association of Athletics Federations (formerly International Amateur Athletics Federation), 1999–2015, now Honorary Life President; *b* 7 June 1933; *s* of Ibrahima Diack and Aissatou Cisse; *m* 1st, 1962, Tondut Fatoumata Bintou; four *s* seven *d* (and one *s* decd); 2nd, 1964, Gaye Ngoné Diaba (*d* 1981); one *s* three *d*; 3rd, 1988, Sy Aissatou (*d* 1994). *Educ:* Dakar Univ. (MA); Ecole Nationale des Impôts de Paris (Inspecteur des Impôts et Domaines). French long jump Champion, 1958; French Univ. long jump Champion, 1959; holder, French/W African long jump record, 1957–60; Member: Sengalese Volleyball team, 1953–59; Sengalese Football team, 1954–61. Football Coach, Foyer France Senegal, 1964–69; Tech. Dir, nat. football team, Senegal, 1966–69; Gen. Comr for State Sport, 1969–70; State Sec. for Youth and Sport, 1970–73; Pres., Assoc. Sportive et Culturelle Diarafs de Dakar, 1974–78 and 1994–; MP (Socialist Party) Senegal, 1978–93; Dep. Speaker, Nat. Assembly of Senegal, 1988–93; Chm., Nat. Water Co. of Senegal, 1995–2001. Member: Exec. Cttee, Supreme Council for Sport in Africa, 1973–87; Nat. Olympic Cttee of Senegal, 1974– (Pres., 1985–2002); IOC, 1999–2013 (Member: Olympic Games Study, 2002–03; Internat. Relns, 2004–09; Congress Commn, 2006–09; Hon. Mem., 2014–); Vice-Pres., 1976–91, Sen. Vice Pres., 1991–99, IAAF. Gen. Sec., 1963–64, Pres., 1974–78, Hon. Pres., 1978–, Senegalese Athletic Fedn; Pres., African Amateur Athletic Confedn, 1973–2003. Hon. Dr: Donetsk; Beijing Sports Univ.; Port Harcourt. Holds numerous decorations and orders, including: Olympic Order, 1994; Order of Merit, IAAF, 1997; Merit Award, Assoc. of Nat. Olympic Cttees, 2014; Chevalier: Ordre Nat. du Lion (Senegal), 1976; Légion d'Honneur (France), 1984; Ordre Nat. (Benin); Comdr, Order of Good Hope (RSA), 1999; Comdr of Distinction (Jamaica), 2002; Grand Cordon of Order of the Rising Sun (Japan), 2007; Order of Merit I Class (Ukraine), 2010; Order of Friendship (Russia); Officer, Nat. Order (Ivory Coast). *Recreations:* reading, family (grandchildren). *Address:* Route des Almadies, BP 16 641, Dakar-Yoff, Dakar-Fann, Senegal. *T:* 338202405, *Fax:* 338202406.

DIAMANTOPOULOU, Anna; President, Diktio Network for Reform in Greece and Europe; *b* Kozani, 1959; *m* Yannis Savalanos; one *s*. *Educ:* Aristotle Univ. of Thessaloniki (Civil Engrg); Panteion Univ. of Athens (Postgrad. Studies in Regl Develt). Civil engr, 1981–85; Lectr, Insts of Higher Technol Educn, 1983–85; Prefect of Kastoria, 1985–86; Sec. Gen. for Adult Educn, 1987–88, for Youth, 1988–89; Man. Dir, regl develt co., 1989–93; Sec. Gen. for Industry, 1994–96; MP for Kozani, 1996–99; Dep. Minister for Develt, Greece, 1996–99; Mem., European Commn, 1999–2004; MP (PASOK), 2004; Minister of Educn, Lifelong Learning and Religious Affairs, 2009–12, of Develt, Competitiveness and Shipping, 2012. Mem. Central Cttee, Panhellenic Socialist Movt, 1991–99. *Address:* Ath. Diakou 20 and Syggrou 1, 11743 Athens, Greece.

DIAMOND, His Honour Anthony Edward John; QC 1974; a Circuit Judge, 1990–98; international and maritime arbitrator; *b* 4 Sept. 1929; *s* of late Arthur Sigismund Diamond, former Master of the Supreme Court, and of Gladys Elkah Diamond (*née* Mocatta); *m* 1965, Joan Margaret Gee; two *d*. *Educ:* Rugby; Corpus Christi Coll., Cambridge (MA). Served RA, 1947–49. Called to the Bar, Gray's Inn, 1953 (Bencher, 1985); practised at Bar as a specialist in commercial law, 1958–90; Head of Chambers at 4 Essex Court, EC4, 1984–90; Dep. High Court Judge, 1982–90; a Recorder, 1985–90; Judge i/c of Central London County Court Business List, 1994–98. Chm., Banking Act Appeals, 1980; Mem., indep. review body under colliery review procedure, 1985. *Publications:* papers on maritime law and arbitration. *Recreation:* the visual arts. *Club:* Athenæum.

DIAMOND, Prof. Derek Robin; Professor of Geography with special reference to Urban and Regional Planning, London School of Economics and Political Science, 1982–95, now Emeritus Professor; *b* 18 May 1933; *s* of John Diamond (Baron Diamond, PC) and Sadie Diamond; *m* 1957, Esme Grace Passmore; one *s* one *d*. *Educ:* Oxford Univ. (MA); Northwestern Univ., Illinois (MSc). Lecturer: in Geography, 1957–65, in Town and Regional Planning, 1965–68, Glasgow Univ.; Reader in Geography, London School of Economics, 1968–82. Pres., IBG, 1994–95. Hon. MRTPI, 1989. Hon. Fellow LSE, 2006. Hon. Prof. of Human Geography, Inst. of Geography, Beijing, 1990. Editor: Progress in Planning, 1973–2003; Geoforum, 1974–93. *Publications:* Regional Policy Evaluation, 1983; Infrastructure and Industrial Costs in British Industry, 1989; Evaluating the Effectiveness of Land Use Planning, 1992; Metropolitan Governance: its contemporary transition, 1997; Managing the Metropolis in the Global Village, 2002; The 1898 Pictorial Issue of New Zealand, 2014. *Recreation:* philately. *Address:* 9 Ashley Drive, Walton-on-Thames, Surrey KT12 1JL. *T:* (01932) 223280. *Club:* Geographical.

DIAMOND, Prof. Sir Ian (David), Kt 2013; PhD; FBA 2005; FRSE; Principal and Vice Chancellor, University of Aberdeen, since 2010; *b* 14 March 1954; *s* of Harold and Sylvia Diamond; *m* 1997, Jane Harrison; one *s*, and one step *s* one step *d*. *Educ:* London Sch. of Econs and Pol Sci. (BSc (Econ.) 1975; MSc 1976); Univ. of St Andrews (PhD 1981). Lectr, Heriot-Watt Univ., 1979; University of Southampton: Lectr, 1980–88; Sen. Lectr, 1988–92; Prof. of Social Statistics, 1992–2002; Dep. Vice-Chancellor, 2001–02; Chief Exec., ESRC, 2003–10 (Mem., 2000–10). Chm., Lloyds TSB Foundn for England and Wales, 2009–. Trustee, WWF UK, 2008–14. FAcSS (AcSS 2000); FRSE 2009. *Publications:* (with J. Jefferies) Beginning Statistics in the Social Sciences, 2001; over 100 articles in acad. jls, incl. Jl of Royal Statistical Soc., Demography and Popn Studies. *Recreations:* family, swimming, running, football. *Address:* University of Aberdeen, King's College, Aberdeen AB24 3FX. *T:* (01224) 272135, *Fax:* (01224) 488605. *Club:* Bradford on Avon Swimming.

DIAMOND, Jane; *see* Hilsenrath, R. J.

DIAMOND, Michael; *see* Diamond, P. M.

DIAMOND, Prof. Peter A., PhD; Institute Professor and Professor of Economics, Massachusetts Institute of Technology, 1997–2011, now Emeritus; *b* New York, 29 April 1940; *m* 1966, Priscilla, (Kate), Myrick; two *s*. *Educ:* Yale Univ. (BA Maths 1960); Mass Inst. of Technol. (PhD Econs 1963). Asst Prof., 1963–65, Actg Associate Prof., 1965–66, Univ. of Calif, Berkeley; Massachusetts Institute of Technology: Associate Prof., 1966–70; Prof., 1970–88; John and Jennie S. MacDonald Prof., 1989–91; Paul A. Samuelson Prof., 1992–97. Fellow: Econometric Soc., 1968 (Pres., 1991); Amer. Acad. of Arts and Scis, 1978; MNAS 1984; Founder Mem., Nat. Acad. of Social Insce, 1988 (Pres., 1994–97; Chm., 1996–98; Mem. Bd, 1998–2001); Pres., AEA, 2003. (Jtly) Nobel Prize in Econs, 2010. Associate Ed., Jl of Econ. Theory, 1969–71; Adv. Ed., Jl of Public Econs, 1996– (Associate Ed., 1971–86; Co-Ed., 1986–95). *Publications:* (ed with M. Rothschild) Uncertainty in Economics: readings and exercises, 1978, rev. edn 1989; A Search Equilibrium Approach to the Micro Foundations of Macro-economics, 1984; (ed) Growth, Productivity, Unemployment: essays to celebrate Bob Solow's birthday, 1990; On Time: lectures on models of equilibrium, 1994; (ed jtly) Social Security: what role for the future?, 1996; Social Security Reform, 2002; Taxation, Incomplete Markets and Social Security, 2002; (with Peter R. Orszag) Saving Social Security: a balanced approach, 2004, rev. edn 2005; (ed with Hannu Vartiainen) Behavioral Economics and its Applications, 2007; (with Nicholas Barr) Reforming Pensions: principles and policy choices, 2008; (with Nicholas Barr) Pension Reform: a short guide, 2010; papers in jls. *Address:* Department of Economics, Massachusetts Institute of Technology, 50 Memorial Drive, Building E52, Room 344, Cambridge, MA 02142–1347, USA.

DIAMOND, (Peter) Michael, OBE 1996; MA, FMA; arts and heritage consultant, since 1995; Director, Birmingham City Museums and Art Gallery, 1980–95; *b* 5 Aug. 1942; *s* of late William Howard and Dorothy Gladys Diamond; *m* 1968, Anne Marie; one *s* one *d*. *Educ:* Bristol Grammar Sch.; Queens' Coll., Cambridge (BA Fine Art 1964, MA 1966). Dip. of Museums Assoc. 1968, FMA 1980. Sheffield City Art Galleries: Art Asst, 1965; Keeper, Mappin Art Gall., 1967; Dep. Dir, 1969; City Arts and Museums Officer, Bradford, 1976. Chairman: Gp of Dirs of Museums, 1985–89; Public Art Commns Agency, 1987–88. Chm., Avoncroft Mus. of Historic Buildings, 2005–; Member, Executive Committee: Yorks Arts Assoc., 1977–80; Yorks Sculpture Park, 1978–82 (Chm., 1978–82); Pres., Yorks Fedn of Museums, 1978–80; Member: Crafts Council, 1980–84; Council, Museums Assoc., 1987–90; Board, Museums Training Inst., 1990–93; Board, Worcester Porcelain Mus., 2001–; Fabric Adv. Cttee, Lichfield Cathedral, 2001–. Mem. Council, Aston Univ., 1983–92. Hon. DSc Aston, 1993. *Publications:* numerous exhibition catalogues incl. Victorian Paintings, 1968; Art and Industry in Sheffield 1850–75, 1975; Bike Art, 1994; (contrib.) Manual of Curatorship, 1984 and 1992; articles in Museums Jl and Internat. Jl of Arts Mgt. *Address:* 5 Anchorage Road, Sutton Coldfield, W Midlands B74 2PJ.

DIAMOND, Dr Philip John; Director General, SKA Organisation, since 2012; *b* Bude, 18 Feb. 1958; *s* of John Diamond and Denise Diamond; *m* 1985, Jill Hamblett; one *s* one *d*. *Educ:* Leeds Univ. (BSc Hons Physics with Astrophysics 1979); Manchester Univ. (Dip. Advanced Studies in Sci. 1980; PhD Radio Astronomy 1982). Royal Soc. Post-doctoral Res. Fellow, Onsala Space Observatory, Sweden, 1982–84; Staff Scientist, Max-Planck Inst. für Radioastronomie, Bonn, 1984–86; Asst Scientist, Computer Div., NRAO, Charlottesville, 1987–91; National Radio Astronomy Observatory, Socorro, USA: Asst Scientist, 1991–92, Associate Scientist, 1992–93, Scientist, 1994–95, Very Long Baseline Array Operations; Dep. Asst Dir for Very Large Array/Very Long Baseline Array Ops and Computing, 1995–99; Dir, Multi-Element Radio-Linked Interferometer Network and Very Long Baseline Interferometry Nat. Facility, Jodrell Bank Observatory, 1999–2006; Prof. of Radio Astronomy, 2002–10, Hd of Astronomy and Astrophysics and Dir, Jodrell Bank Centre for Astrophysics, 2006–10, Univ. of Manchester; Chief, CSIRO Astronomy and Space Science, 2012–12. Coordinator: RadioNet (EC-funded Integrated Infrastructure Initiative), 2003–; EC 7th Framework Prog. Preparatory Phase Proposal for Square Kilometre Array, 2007–10. *Publications:* contrib. numerous papers to jls incl. Nature and Science. *Recreations:* reading, playing squash, worldwide travel, Rugby Union, football.

DIAMOND, Yasmin, CB 2011; Senior Vice President Global Corporate Affairs, InterContinental Hotels Group, since 2012; *b* 27 Oct. 1967; *d* of Barkat Ali and Khurshid Begum; *m* 1999, Mark Diamond; one *s* one *d*. *Educ:* Univ. of Leeds (BA Hons Hist. with Business Mgt); Leeds Business Sch. (Postgrad. DipM). Sen. Communications Manager, NHS Exec., 1995–99; Publicity Comr, BBC Broadcast, 1999–2000; Head: Welfare to Work, DfEE, 2000–01; Strategic Mktg, DfES, 2001–05; Dir of Communications, DEFRA,

2005–07; Dir of Communication, Home Office, 2008–12. *Recreations:* spending leisure time with my family and friends, travelling, fashion and design. *Address:* c/o InterContinental Hotels Group, Broadwater Park, Denham, Bucks UB9 5HR. *Clubs:* Soho House, Ivy.

DIAS, His Eminence Cardinal Ivan Cornelius, DCnL; Prefect, Congregation for the Evangelisation of Peoples, 2006–11, now Emeritus; *b* 14 April 1936; *s* of late Carlos Nazario Dias and Maria Martins Dias. *Educ:* Pontifical Ecclesiastical Academy, Rome; DCnL Lateran Univ., Rome, 1964. Ordained priest, Bombay, 1958. Trained for Diplomatic Service, 1961–64; Foreign Service of Holy See, 1964–97; served Vatican Secretariat of State, preparing visit of HH the Pope to Bombay, Internat. Eucharistic Congress, 1964; Sec., Apostolic Nunciatures in Scandinavian countries, Indonesia and Madagascar, 1965–73; Chief of Desk at Vatican Secretariat of State for USSR, Baltic States, Byelorussia, Ukraine, Poland, Bulgaria, China, Vietnam, Laos, Cambodia, S Africa, Namibia, Lesotho, Swaziland, Zimbabwe, Ethiopia, Rwanda, Burundi, Uganda, Zambia, Kenya, Tanzania, 1973–82; Titular Archbishop of Rusubisir and Apostolic Pro-Nuncio to Ghana, Togo and Benin, 1982–87; Apostolic Pro-Nuncio: S Korea, 1987–91; Albania, 1991–97; Archbishop of Bombay, (RC), 1997–2006. Cardinal, 2001. Co-Pres., 10th Ordinary Gen. Assembly, Synod of Bishops, Rome, 2001. Special Papal Envoy to: Albania, 10th anniv. celebrations of Pope John Paul II's visit, 2003; Ghana, Centenary Celebrations of Evangelization in Northern Ghana, 2007. Member: Congregation for Doctrine of the Faith, 2001–; Congregation for Divine Worship and Discipline of the Sacraments, 2001–; Congregation for Catholic Educn, 2001–; Pontifical Council for Laity, 2001–; Pontifical Council for Culture, 2001–; Pontifical Commn for Cultural Heritage of Church, 2001–; Pontifical Council for Interreligious Dialogue, 2005–. *Address:* Palazzo di Propaganda Fide, Piazza di Spagna 48, 00187 Rome, Italy.

DIAS, Julia Amanda, (Mrs S. J. Orford); QC 2008; barrister; *b* Cambridge, 31 Jan. 1959; *d* of late Reginald Walter Michael Dias and Norah Hunter Dias (*née* Crabb); *m* 1983, Stuart John Orford; one *s* one *d. Educ:* Perse Sch. for Girls, Cambridge; Trinity Hall, Cambridge (BA 1981). MCIArb. Called to the Bar, Inner Temple, 1982. FRSA. Trustee, Magpie Dance, 2012–. *Recreations:* classical music, tennis, reading. *Address:* 7 King's Bench Walk, Temple, EC4Y 7DS. *T:* (020) 7910 8300, *Fax:* (020) 7910 8400. *E:* jdias@7kbw.co.uk.

DIBBEN, Michael Alan Charles; HM Diplomatic Service, retired; High Commissioner, Fiji, also accredited to Tuvalu, Kiribati and Nauru, 1997–2000; *b* 19 Sept. 1943; *s* of Lt-Col Alan Frank Dibben and late Eileen Beatrice Dibben (*née* Donoghue). *Educ:* Dulwich College. With Ottoman Bank, London, 1961–64; CRO 1964; Min. of Overseas Develt, 1965; Protocol Dept, FCO, 1966; served Montreal, Nassau, Stuttgart, Port of Spain, St Georges, Douala; First Sec., 1981; Nuclear Energy Dept, FCO, 1981–83; Munich and Hamburg, 1983–87; Inf. Dept, FCO, 1987–90; Ambassador to Paraguay, 1991–95; Head of Contracts, Travel and Related Services Gp, FCO, 1995–96. Mem., Horners' Co. *Recreations:* reading, walking, golf, classical music. *Address:* 4 Roman Street, Dalkeith, Midlothian EH22 2QZ.

DIBBLE, Roy Edwin, CEng, FBCS; HM Diplomatic Service, retired; Chief Executive Services, Foreign and Commonwealth Office, 2000–01; *b* 16 Dec. 1940; *s* of Edwin Dibble and Gwendoline Vera Dibble (*née* Nicholls); *m* 1967, Valerie Jean Denham Smith. *Educ:* Maidstone Tech. High Sch. DipEE; MIET. Central Computer Telecommunications Agency: Head of Div., HM Treasury, 1985–91, Cabinet Office, 1991–94; Dir, OPS, Cabinet Office, 1994–96; Dir, Gen. Services, FCO, 1996–2000. *Recreation:* sailing.

DICE, Brian Charles, OBE 1997; Chief Executive, British Waterways Board, 1986–96; *b* 2 Sept. 1936; *s* of late Frederic Charles Dice and Eileen Dice (*née* Rich); *m* 1965, Gwendoline Tazeena Harrison; two *d. Educ:* Clare College, Cambridge; Middle Temple. Cadbury Schweppes, 1960–86, Director, 1979; Managing Director, Schweppes, 1983.

DICK, Dennis John Nicoll, MBE 2014; Member: Scottish Biodiversity Committee, since 2008; Biodiversity and Land Use Communications Group, since 2013; *b* Dundee, 1 Oct. 1934; *s* of David Dick and Ella Dick (*née* Nicoll); *m* 1958, Mary Willis; one *s. Educ:* Gordonstoun Sch.; Stirling High Sch. Journalist and publicist, 1955–60; launched Grampian TV, 1961; writer and TV Ed., Radio Times, 1961–70; PR Officer, BBC S and W, 1970–78; TV producer and editor, TV Features, BBC West, 1978–84; Manager, BBC TV, Radio, Engrg, Aberdeen, 1984–88; Chm., Man. Dir and TV producer, Wildview Prodns Ltd, 1988–93. Chairman: Scottish Wildlife Trust, 2005–08; Aitken Arboretum, Perth, 2008–11; Tayside Biodiversity Partnership, 2010–14; Mem., Regl Forestry Forum, Forestry Commn Scotland Perth and Argyll, 2009–12. Burgess, City of Aberdeen, 1986. Trustee: Royal Botanic Gdn, Edinburgh, 2009–13; Botanics Foundn, 2011–13. Pres., St Andrews Probus Club, 2002. FRSA 2008. *Recreations:* trees, environment, photography, website development. *Address:* Flat 5, 8 New Cut Rigg, Edinburgh EH6 4QR. *E:* dennisdick@wildview.co.uk.

DICK, Sir Iain Charles M.; *see* Mackay-Dick.

DICK-LAUDER, Sir Piers Robert; *see* Lauder.

DICKENS, Frank; *see* Huline-Dickens, F. W.

DICKENSON, Alastair John; silver expert; Managing Director, Alastair Dickenson (formerly Alastair Dickenson Fine Silver) Ltd, since 1996; *b* Leatherhead, 27 Oct. 1950; *s* of Ronald William and Evelyn Marion Dickenson; *m* 1975, Julia Catherine Baguley (marr. diss. 2013); one *s* one *d*; partner, Hilary Morris. *Educ:* Epsom Coll.; Guildford Poly. (HND Business Studies). Cataloguer, valuer and auctioneer, Phillips Auctioneers, 1971–82; Sen. Buyer, ADC Heritage, 1982–83; Hd, Antique Silver and Dir, Antiques Dept, Asprey, 1983–95; Dir, Tessier, 1995–96. Expert, Antiques Roadshow, BBC, 1991–; Expert Advr to MLA; Advr to Metalwork Dept, West Dean Coll. Liveryman, Goldsmiths' Co., 2007; Founding Mem. and Freeman, Art Scholars' Co., 2006 (Liveryman; Mem. Court, 2007–11). *Recreations:* sailing, music, collecting guitars, golf, walking. *Address:* Alastair Dickenson Ltd, 102 High Street, Godalming, Surrey GU7 1DS. *T:* (01483) 425329. *E:* adickensonsilver@btconnect.com. *Clubs:* MCC; Bosham Sailing.

DICKENSON, Prof. Anthony Henry, PhD; Professor of Neuropharmacology, University College London, since 1995; *b* 5 Oct. 1952; *s* of Henry and Kathleen Dickenson; *m* 1975, Joanna Schepp; two *d. Educ:* St Mary's Coll., Southampton; Univ. of Reading (BSc 1974); PhD London 1977. MRC French Exchange Fellow, 1978–79; Scientific Staff, MRC, 1979–83; University College London: Lectr, 1983–90; Sen. Lectr, 1990–92; Reader, 1992–95. Mem. Council, Internat. Assoc. for Study of Pain, 1996–2002. Vis. Prof., Univ. of Calif, 1986; RSocMed Vis. Prof., USA, 1995; Medal and Lecture in Neuroscience, Univ. of Pavia, Italy, 1993. FMedSci 2007. Hon. Mem., British Pain Soc., 2009. *Publications:* (with M. M. Dale and D. G. Haylett) Companion to Pharmacology, 1993, 2nd edn 1995; (with J.-M. Besson) Pharmacology of Pain, 1997; contrib. chapters in books; numerous contribs to learned jls. *Recreations:* dubstep, friends, family, travel, tennis. *Address:* UCL Neuroscience, Physiology & Pharmacology, University College London, Gower Street, WC1E 6BT. *T:* (020) 7679 3742.

DICKENSON, Sir Aubrey Fiennes T.; *see* Trotman-Dickenson.

DICKEY, Prof. Eleanor, DPhil; FBA 2014; Professor of Classics, University of Reading, since 2013; *b* New Haven, Conn, 9 April 1967; *d* of Thomas Atherton Dickey and Barbara Dickey; civil partnership 2008, Philomen Probert. *Educ:* Bryn Mawr Coll., USA (AB 1989; MA 1989); Balliol Coll., Oxford (MPhil 1991); Merton Coll., Oxford (DPhil 1994). Asst Prof. of Classics, Univ. of Ottawa, Canada, 1995–99; Asst Prof., 1999–2005, Associate Prof. of Classics, 2005–07, Columbia Univ., NY; Associate Prof. of Classics, Univ. of Exeter, 2007–13. *Publications:* Greek Forms of Address, 1996; Latin Forms of Address, 2002; Ancient Greek Scholarship, 2007; The Colloquia of the Hermeneumata Pseudodositheana, vol. I, 2012, vol. II, 2015. *Recreations:* music, walking, admiring architecture. *Address:* Department of Classics, School of Humanities, University of Reading, Whiteknights, Reading RG6 6AA. *E:* E.Dickey@reading.ac.uk.

DICKIE, Brian James; General Director, Chicago Opera Theater, 1999–2012; Director of Auditions, Bertelsmann Stiftung, since 1999; *b* 23 July 1941; *s* of late Robert Kelso Dickie, OBE and Harriet Elizabeth (*née* Riddell); *m* 1st, 1968, Victoria Teresa Sheldon (*née* Price); two *s* one *d*; 2nd, 1989, Nancy Gustafson; 3rd, 2002, Elinor Rhys Williams; one *d. Educ:* Haileybury; Trinity Coll., Dublin. Admin. Asst, Glyndebourne Opera, 1962–66; Administrator, Glyndebourne Touring Opera, 1967–81; Glyndebourne Festival Opera: Opera Manager, 1970–81; Gen. Administrator, 1981–89. Artistic Dir, Wexford Fest., 1967–73; Artistic Advr, Théâtre Musical de Paris, 1981–87; Gen. Dir, Canadian Opera Co., 1989–93; Artistic Counsellor, Opéra de Nice, 1994–97; Gen. Dir, EU Opera, 1997–99. Member: Bd, Opera America, 1991–93, 2005–11; Bd, Chicago Coll. of the Performing Arts, 2003–12; Music Vis. Cttee, Univ. of Chicago, 2006–11. Chm., London Choral Soc., 1978–85; Vice-Chm., TNC, 1980–85 (Chm., TNC Opera Cttee, 1976–85); Vice-Pres., Theatrical Management Assoc., 1983–85. *Address:* 23 Primrose Mansions, Prince of Wales Drive, SW11 4EE. *Club:* Garrick.

DICKIE, John Kane; Director of Strategy and Policy, London First, since 2008; *b* 31 Aug. 1965; *s* of John Dickie and Gladys Dickie (*née* O'Neil); *m* 1991, Susan Grunstein; one *s* one *d. Educ:* Morecambe High Sch.; Worcester Coll., Oxford (BA Mod. Hist.); London Business Sch. (MBA). Grad. trainee, Swiss Bank Corp. Internat., 1987–89; Prima Europe, 1989–98 (Man. Dir, 1997–98); GPC International: Man. Dir, GPC London, 1998–99; Hd, Internat. Regulatory Practice, 1999–2000; Dir, Regulatory Affairs, European Competitive Telecommunications Assoc., 2000–03; Hd, Political and Parly Affairs, 2003–04, Public Affairs, 2004–06, Corporate Affairs, 2006–08, BBC. Mem., Camden LBC, 1994–2003 (Dep. Leader, 2000–03). *Recreations:* film, opera, reading, gym. *Address:* c/o London First, Middlesex House, 34–42 Cleveland Street, W1T 4JE. *T:* (020) 7665 1500. *E:* jdickie@London-first.co.uk. *Club:* Reform.

DICKINS, Janet Constance Elizabeth; *see* Watson, J. C. E.

DICKINS, Mark Frederick Hakon S.; *see* Scrase-Dickins.

DICKINS, Robert, CBE 2002; Chairman: Instant Karma Ltd, 1999–2007; Pop Art Ltd, since 1999; *b* 24 July 1950; *s* of late Percy Charles Dickins and Sylvia Marjorie Dickins; *m* 2000, Cherry Ann Gillespie. *Educ:* Ilford Co. High Sch. for Boys; Loughborough Univ. (BSc Politics, Sociol. and Russian 1971). Man. Dir, Warner Bros Music Ltd, 1974–79; Sen. Vice Pres., Warner Brothers Music Corp., 1979–83; Chairman: Warner Music Gp UK, 1983–98; Dharma Music Ltd, 1999–2011. Visiting Professor: Univ. of the Arts, London, 2008–14; London Metropolitan Univ., 2009–. Chm., British Phonographic Industry, 1986–88 and 1997–2002. Chairman: Nat. Mus. of Childhood, Bethnal Green, 2002–07; Theatres Trust, 2009–15; Trustee: BRIT Trust, 1997–; Nat. Foundn for Youth Music, 1999–2006; V&A Mus., 2000–07; Watts Gall., 2004–; Dimbola House, IoW, 2012–13; Handel House Mus., 2012–; Mem. Bd, V&A Enterprises, 2000–09. FRSA 2007. Hon. DLitt Loughborough, 2002; Hon. Dr Univ. of the Arts, London, 2014. *Recreations:* art, film, theatre, photography, music, design, travel. *E:* karmarob1@me.com. *Clubs:* Groucho, Ivy.

DICKINSON, family name of **Baron Dickinson**.

DICKINSON, 2nd Baron *cr* 1930, of Painswick; **Richard Clavering Hyett Dickinson;** *b* 2 March 1926; *s* of late Hon. Richard Sebastian Willoughby Dickinson, DSO (*o s* of 1st Baron) and May Southey, *d* of late Charles Lovemore, Melsetter, Cape Province, S Africa; *S* grandfather, 1943; *m* 1st, 1957, Margaret Ann (marr. diss. 1980), *e d* of late Brig. G. R. McMeekan, CB, DSO, OBE; two *s*; 2nd, 1980, Rita Doreen Moir. *Heir: s* Hon. Martin Hyett Dickinson, *b* 30 Jan. 1961. *Address:* The Stables, Gloucester Road, Painswick, Glos GL6 6TH. *T:* (01452) 813646.

See also Very Rev. H. G. Dickinson, Hon. P. M. de B. Dickinson.

DICKINSON, Maj. Gen. Alastair Scott, CBE 2015; FInstRE; Director General Army Basing and Infrastructure, Army Headquarters, since 2014; *b* Knutsford, 3 Aug. 1963; *s* of Arnold Dickinson and Eunice Dickinson; *m* 1992, Alice Mary McGee; two *s. Educ:* Rishworth Sch., Ripponden; Royal Military Acad. Sandhurst. Commnd Corps of RE, 1981; served with: 36 Engr Regt, 1983–85; Jun. Leaders Regt, 1985–86; 21 Engr Regt, 1986–88; Second i/c, 59 Ind. Cdo Sqn RE, 1989–91; Platoon Comdr, Rowallan Co., RMA Sandhurst, 1991–93; Jt Comd and Staff Course, Canadian Jt Service Staff Coll., Toronto, 1993–94; Officer Commanding: 59 Ind. Cdo Sqn RE, 1997–2000; 28 Engr Regt, Hameln, 2003–06; Col Army Plans, Army Resource and Plans, 2006–09; HCSC 2009; Comdr, 8 Force Engr Bde, 2009–11; Dir, Army Resource and Plans, 2011–13. FInstRE 2010. *Recreations:* ex water polo player (Combined Services), current parental sport supporter and taxi driver.

DICKINSON, Anne; *see* Dickinson, V. A.

DICKINSON, Prof. Anthony, DPhil; FRS 2003; Professor of Comparative Psychology, University of Cambridge, 1999–2011, now Emeritus; Fellow of Hughes Hall, Cambridge, since 1999; *b* 17 Feb. 1944; *m* 1977, Susan Caroline Melhuish; one *s* two *d. Educ:* Univ. of Manchester (BSc 1967); Univ. of Sussex (DPhil 1971); MA Cantab 2001. Postdoctoral Res. Fellow, Sussex Univ., 1971–77; Cambridge University: Demonstrator, 1977–78, Lectr, 1978–94, Dept of Exptl Psychol.; Reader in Comparative Psychol., 1994–99. *Address:* Department of Psychology, University of Cambridge, Downing Street, Cambridge CB2 3EB.

DICKINSON, Prof. (Christopher) John, DM, FRCP; ARCO; Professor of Medicine and Chairman, Department of Medicine, St Bartholomew's Hospital Medical College, 1975–92, now Professor Emeritus; *b* 1 Feb. 1927; *s* of Reginald Ernest Dickinson and Margaret Dickinson (*née* Petty); *m* 1953, Elizabeth Patricia Farrell; two *s* two *d. Educ:* Berkhamsted School; Oxford University (MA, MSc, DM); University College Hospital Medical College. FRCP 1968. Junior med. posts, UCH, 1953–54; RAMC (Junior Med. Specialist), 1955–56; Registrar and Research Fellow, Middlesex Hosp., 1957–60; Rockefeller Travelling Fellow, Cleveland Clinic, USA, 1960–61; Lectr, then Sen. Lectr and Consultant, UCH and Med. Sch., 1961–75. R. Samuel McLoughlin Vis. Prof., McMaster Univ., Canada, 1970; King Edward Fund Vis. Fellow, NZ, 1972. Examr in Medicine, UC Dublin and Univs of Oxford, Cambridge, London, Sheffield, Leeds, Southampton, Hong Kong, Singapore, Kuwait. Sec., European Soc. for Clinical Investigation, 1969–72; Censor, 1978–80, Senior Censor and Vice-Pres., 1982–83, Croonian Lectr, 1986, RCP; Pres., Sect. of Medicine, RSM, 1975–76. Chairman: Med. Research Soc., 1983–87; Assoc. of Professors of Medicine, 1983–87; Vice Chm. Council, BHF, 1995–2000; Mem., MRC, 1986–90. Medical Adviser: Jules Thorn Charitable Trust, 1994–98; St Thomas'/Guy's Hosps' Special Trustees, 1996–98; Trustee: St Bartholomew's Hosp. Foundn for Res., 1983–; BHF, 1995–2000; Chronic Disease Res. Foundn, 1996– (Chm., 1996–). ARCO 1987. FRSA 1995. *Publications:* Electrophysiological Technique, 1950; Clinical Pathology Data, 1951, 2nd edn 1957; (jtly) Clinical Physiology, 1959, 5th edn 1984; Neurogenic Hypertension, 1965, 2nd edn 1991; A Computer Model of Human Respiration, 1977; (jtly) Software for Educational Computing, 1980; 21 Medical Mysteries, 2000; Motorcycling in Towns and Cities, 2002; Medical Mysteries: the testament of a clinical scientist, 2005; Cardiovascular Hypertension, 2012; papers on hypertension, respiratory physiology, and general medicine. *Recreations:* theatre, opera, playing the organ, squash. *Address:* Wolfson Institute of Preventive Medicine, Charterhouse Square, EC1M 6BQ. *T:* (020) 7882 6219; Griffin Cottage, 57 Belsize Lane, NW3 5AU. *T:* (020) 7431 1845. *Club:* Garrick.

DICKINSON, David Roscoe; Partner, Simmons & Simmons, 1988–2011 (Managing Partner, 1999–2005; Senior Partner, 2006–11); *b* 13 Dec. 1950; *s* of John Roscoe Dickinson and Barbara Fleetwood Dickinson (*née* Thomas); *m* 1975, Linda Susan Voneshen; two *s* one *d*. Admitted solicitor: England and Wales, 1974; Hong Kong, 1998; Dir, Legal Services, UBS (Securities) Ltd, 1984–88. Trustee, SkillForce, 2013–. *Recreations:* family, garden, collecting. *Address:* Woldingham, Surrey.

DICKINSON, Gregory David Mark; QC 2002; **His Honour Judge Dickinson;** a Circuit Judge, since 2012; *b* 26 Aug. 1959; *s* of late David Dickinson and Ethel Dickinson; *m* 1989, Frances Judith Betts. *Educ:* Poole Grammar Sch.; Univ. of Leicester (LLB Hons 1980). Called to the Bar, Gray's Inn, 1981, Bencher, 2008; in practice, specialising in criminal law; Midland Circuit, 1982–2012; Asst Recorder, 1998–2000; a Recorder, 2000–12. Midland Circuit Rep., Bar Council, 2004–08. Mem. Court, Univ. of Leicester, 2011–. *Recreations:* gardening, walking, travelling, watching old movies with my wife. *Address:* Nottingham Crown Court, 60 Canal Street, Nottingham NG1 7EL.

DICKINSON, Prof. Harry Thomas, DLitt; FRHistS; FHA; FRSE; Richard Lodge Professor of British History, University of Edinburgh, 1980–2006, now Emeritus, and Hon. Professorial Fellow, since 2006; *b* 9 March 1939; *s* of Joseph Dickinson and Elizabeth Stearman Dickinson (*née* Warriner); *m* 1961, Jennifer Elizabeth Galtry; one *s* one *d*. *Educ:* Gateshead Grammar Sch.; Durham Univ. (BA 1960, DipEd 1961, MA 1963); Newcastle Univ. (PhD 1968); DLitt Edinburgh 1986. FRSE 1998. History Master, Washington Grammar Sch., 1961–64; Earl Grey Fellow, Newcastle Univ., 1964–66; Edinburgh University: Asst Lectr, Lectr and Reader, 1966–80; Associate Dean of Arts (Postgrad. Studies), 1992–95; Convener (Senatus, Postgrad. Studies), 1998–2001. Fulbright Award, 1973; Huntington Library Fellowship, 1973; Folger Shakespeare Library Sen. Fellowship, 1973; Winston Churchill Meml Trust Travelling Fellowship, 1980; Leverhulme Award, 1986–87; William Andrews Clark Library Fellow, 1987. Vis. Prof., Nanjing Univ., 1980, 1983, 1994, Concurrent Prof. of Hist., 1987–; Douglas Southall Freeman Prof., Univ. of Richmond, Va, 1997; Vis. Prof., Beijing Univ., 2004, 2011. Anstey Meml Lectr, Kent Univ., 1989; Vis. Lectr to USA, Japan, Taiwan, Canada, France, Czech Republic, Italy, Poland, Norway, Sweden, Estonia, Germany and China; Dean, Scottish Universities Summer School, 1979–85. Acad. Sponsor, Scotland's Cultural Heritage, 1984–91; Mem., Marshall Aid Commemoration Commn, 1986–98; Specialist Advr, CNAA, 1987–93 (Mem., Cttee on Humanities, 1990–93); Auditor, Quality Assurance Gp, Higher Educn Quality Council, 1992–2001; Mem., Hist. Panel, UFC RAE, 1992; Team Assessor (Hist.), Teaching Quality Assessment, SHEFC, 1995–96; Hist. Benchmarking Panel, 1998–99, Academic Reviewer, 1999–2001, QAA; Chm., Hist. Panel, AHRC (formerly AHRB), 2002–06 (Mem., 1999–2002); Mem., Lord Chancellor's Adv. Council on Nat. Records and Archives, 2002–14. Vice-Pres., RHistS, 1991–95 and 2003–06 (Mem., Council, 1986–90); Historical Association: Mem. Council, 1982–; Vice-Pres., 1995–96, 2005–07; Dep. Pres., 1996–98; Pres., 2002–05; Chm. of Publications, 1991–95; FHA 2007. FHEA 2007. Editor, History, 1993–2000; Mem. Editl Bds, Nineteenth Century Short Title Catalogue and Nineteenth Century Microfiche Series. *Publications:* (ed) The Correspondence of Sir James Clavering, 1967; Bolingbroke, 1970; Walpole and the Whig Supremacy, 1973; (ed) Politics and Literature in the Eighteenth Century, 1974; Liberty and Property, 1977; (ed) The Political Works of Thomas Spence, 1982; British Radicalism and the French Revolution 1789–1815, 1985; Caricatures and the Constitution 1760–1832, 1986; (ed) Britain and the French Revolution 1789–1815, 1989; The Politics of the People in Eighteenth Century Britain, 1995; (ed) Britain and the American Revolution, 1998; (ed jtly) The Challenge to Westminster, 2000; (ed) A Companion to Eighteenth-Century Britain, 2002; (ed) Constitutional Documents of the United Kingdom 1776–1849, 2005; (ed jtly) Reactions to Revolutions, 2007; (ed) British Pamphlets on the American Revolution, 8 vols, 2007–08; (ed) Ireland in the Age of the American Revolution, 3 vols, 2013; (ed) Ireland in the Age of the French Revolution, 3 vols, 2013; pubns trans. into French, German, Spanish, Polish, Romanian, Chinese and Japanese; pamphlets, essays, articles and reviews. *Recreations:* films, theatre, watching sports. *Address:* 44 Viewforth Terrace, Edinburgh EH10 4LJ. *T:* (0131) 229 1379.

DICKINSON, Very Rev. Hugh Geoffrey; Dean of Salisbury, 1986–96, now Emeritus; *b* 17 Nov. 1929; *s* of late Hon. Richard Sebastian Willoughby Dickinson, DSO (*o s* of 1st Baron Dickinson) and of May Southey, *d* of late Charles Lovemore; *m* 1963, Jean Marjorie Storey; one *s* one *d*. *Educ:* Westminster School (KS); Trinity Coll., Oxford (MA, DipTh); Cuddesdon Theol Coll. Deacon 1956, priest 1957; Curate of Melksham, Wilts, 1956–58; Chaplain: Trinity Coll., Cambridge, 1958–63; Winchester College, 1963–67; Bishop's Adviser for Adult Education, Diocese of Coventry, 1969–77; Vicar of St Michael's, St Albans, 1977–86. *Recreations:* woodturning, fishing, gardening. *Address:* 5 St Peter's Road, Cirencester, Glos GL7 1RE. *T:* (01285) 657710.

See also Hon. P. M. de B. Dickinson.

DICKINSON, Prof. Hugh Gordon; Sherardian Professor of Botany, Oxford, 1991–2009, now Emeritus Professor; Fellow of Magdalen College, Oxford, since 1991; *b* 5 Aug. 1944; *s* of Reginald Gordon Dickinson and Jean Hartley Dickinson; *m* 1980, Alana Gillian Fairbrother; one *s* one *d*. *Educ:* St Lawrence Coll., Ramsgate; Univ. of Birmingham (BSc, PhD, DSc). Postdoctoral Fellow, UCL, 1969–72; University of Reading: Lectr, 1972–79; Reader, 1979–85; Prof. of Plant Cell Genetics, 1985–91. Trustee, Royal Botanic Gardens, Kew, 1996–2001; Council Mem., John Innes Centre, 1999–. Chm., Annals of Botany Co., 2008–. *Publications:* (ed with C. W. Evans) Controlling Events in Meiosis, 1984; (ed with P. Goodhew) Proceedings of IXth European Congress for Electron Microscopy, 1988; (ed jtly) Post-Translational Modification in Plants, 1992; contribs to books and internat. jls, 1967–. *Recreations:* owning and restoring Lancia cars of the '50s and '60s, rock music 1955–75, Mozart operas. *Address:* Magdalen College, Oxford OX1 4AU.

DICKINSON, John; *see* Dickinson, C. J.

DICKINSON, Mark; *see* Dickinson, S. M. and Dickinson, W. M. L.

DICKINSON, Matthew John, (Matt); Chief Sports Correspondent, The Times, since 2007; *b* 16 Nov. 1968; *s* of Jimmy Gordon and Celia Dickinson; *m* 2000, Helen Willis; two *s*. *Educ:* Perse Sch., Cambridge; Robinson Coll., Cambridge (MA); NCTJ Postgrad. Dip in Journalism, Cardiff. Staff News Reporter, Cambridge Evening News, 1992–94; Sports Reporter: Daily Express, 1994–97; The Times, 1997–: Football Correspondent, 2000–02; Chief Football Correspondent, 2002–07. Young Sports Writer of the Year, Sports Council, 1992; Sports Journalist of the Year, British Press Awards, 2000; Specialist Correspondent of the Year, British Sports Journalism Awards, 2002, 2005. *Publications:* assisted with: David Beckham: My World, 2000; Gary Neville: Red, 2011; Bobby Moore: the man in full, 2014. *Recreations:* playing football, golf, film, travel. *Address:* c/o The Times, 1 London Bridge Street, SE1 9GF. *Clubs:* Roehampton; Cambridge University Lightweight Rowing.

DICKINSON, Patric Laurence, LVO 2006; Clarenceux King of Arms, since 2010; Secretary, Order of the Garter, since 2004; *b* 24 Nov. 1950; *s* of late John Laurence Dickinson and April Katherine, *d* of Robert Forgan, MC, MD, sometime MP. *Educ:* Marling Sch.; Exeter Coll., Oxford (Stapeldon Schol.; MA). Pres., Oxford Union Soc., 1972. Called to the Bar, Middle Temple, 1979, Bencher, 2015. Res. Asst, College of Arms, 1968–78; Rouge Dragon Pursuivant, 1978–89; Richmond Herald of Arms, 1989–2010; Norroy and Ulster King of Arms, 2010; Earl Marshal's Sec., 1996–2012. Hon. Treasurer: English Genealogical Congress, 1975–91; Bar Theatrical Soc., 1978–; Treas., Coll. of Arms, 1995–. Hon. Sec. and Registrar, British Record Soc., 1979–2010; Vice-Pres., 1988–2011, Pres., 2011–, Assoc. of Genealogists and Researchers in Archives (formerly Assoc. of Genealogists and Record Agents); Vice-Pres., 1997–2005, Pres., 2005–, Soc. of Genealogists; Pres., Bristol and Glos Archaeol Soc., 1998–99. Vice-Pres., Anthony Powell Soc., 2008– (Chm., 2003–07). FSG 2000. *Recreation:* exploding myths. *Address:* College of Arms, Queen Victoria Street, EC4V 4BT. *T:* (020) 7236 9612; 13 Old Square, Lincoln's Inn, WC2A 3UA. *Club:* Brooks's.

DICKINSON, Prof. Peter, DMus; composer, writer, pianist; Head of Music, Institute of United States Studies, University of London, 1997–2004; Professor of Music, Goldsmiths College, London University, 1991–97, now Emeritus; *b* 15 Nov. 1934; *s* of late Frank Dickinson, FBOA (Hons), FAAO, DOS, FRSH, contact lens specialist, and Muriel Porter; *m* 1964, Bridget Jane Tomkinson, *d* of late Lt-Comdr E. P. Tomkinson, DSO, RN; two *s*. *Educ:* The Leys Sch.; Queens' Coll., Cambridge (organ schol., Stewart of Rannoch schol.; MA); Juilliard Sch. of Music, New York (Rotary Foundn Fellow). DMus London 1992; LRAM, ARCM; FRCO. Teaching and freelance work in New York, 1958–61, London and Birmingham, 1962–74; first Prof. of Music, Keele Univ., 1974–84, subseq. Prof. Emeritus; founded Centre for American Music, Keele. Broadcasts and records as pianist (mostly with sister Meriel Dickinson, mezzo soprano, 1966–94). Member, Board: Trinity Coll. of Music, 1984–98; Inst. of US Studies, London Univ., 1994–2000. Trustee: Berners Trust, 1988–; Bernarr Rainbow Trust, 1996–. Contributor, Gramophone mag., 1989–. Hon. FTCL 1992. Hon. DMus Keele, 1999. *Publications: compositions include: orchestral:* Monologue for Strings, 1959; Five Diversions, 1969; Satie Transformations, 1970; Organ Concerto, 1971; Piano Concerto, 1984; Violin Concerto, 1986; Merseyside Echoes, 1988; *chamber:* String Quartet No 1, 1958; Juilliard Dances, 1959; Fanfares and Elegies, 1967; Translations, 1971; String Quartet No 2, 1975; American Trio, 1985; London Rags, 1986; Sonatas for piano and tape playback, 1987; Auden Studies, 1988; Swansongs, 1992; works for solo organ, piano, clavichord, recorder, flute, violin, guitar and baryton; *vocal:* Four Auden Songs, 1956; A Dylan Thomas Cycle, 1959; Elegy, 1966; Five Poems of Alan Porter, 1968; Extravaganzas, 1969; An E. E. Cummings Cycle, 1970; Winter Afternoons (Emily Dickinson), 1970; Three Comic Songs (Auden), 1972; Surrealist Landscape (Lord Berners), 1973; Lust (St Augustine), 1974; A Memory of David Munrow, 1977; Reminiscences (Byron), 1979; The Unicorns (John Heath-Stubbs), 1982; Stevie's Tunes (Stevie Smith), 1984; Larkin's Jazz (Philip Larkin), 1989; Summoned by Mother (Betjeman), 1991; *choral:* Martin of Tours (Thomas Blackburn), 1966; The Dry Heart (Alan Porter), 1967; Outcry, 1969; Late Afternoon in November, 1975; A Mass of the Apocalypse, 1984; Tiananmen 1989, 1990; *ballet:* Vitalitas, 1959; *musical drama:* The Judas Tree (Thomas Blackburn), 1965; various church music; (ed) Twenty British Composers, 1975; (ed) Songs and Piano Music by Lord Berners, 1982, 2nd edn 2000; The Music of Lennox Berkeley, 1989, 2nd edn 2003; Marigold: the music of Billy Mayerl, 1999; (ed) Copland Connotations, 2002; (ed) Collected Works for Solo Piano by Lennox Berkeley, 2003; (ed) CageTalk: dialogues with and about John Cage, 2006; Lord Berners: composer, writer, painter, 2008; (ed) Complete Piano Duets by Lord Berners, 2010; Samuel Barber Remembered: a centenary tribute, 2010; (ed) Lennox Berkeley and Friends: writings, letters and interviews, 2012; (ed) Music Education in Crisis: the Bernarr Rainbow Lectures and other assessments, 2013; contrib. to The New Grove, and various books and periodicals. *Recreation:* rare books. *Address:* c/o Novello & Co., 14–15 Berners Street, W1T 3LJ. *W:* www.foxborough.co.uk. *Club:* Garrick.

DICKINSON, Hon. Peter Malcolm de Brissac, OBE 2009; FRSL; author; *b* 16 Dec. 1927; *s* of late Hon. Richard Sebastian Willoughby Dickinson and of May Southey (Nancy) Lovemore; *m* 1st, 1953, Mary Rose Barnard (*d* 1988); two *d* two *s*; 2nd, 1992, Robin McKinley. *Educ:* Eton; King's Coll., Cambridge (BA). Asst Editor, Punch, 1952–69. Chm., Management Cttee, Soc. of Authors, 1978–80. FRSL 1999. *Publications: children's books:* The Weathermonger, 1968; Heartsease, 1969; The Devil's Children, 1970 (trilogy republished 1975 as The Changes); Emma Tupper's Diary, 1970; The Dancing Bear, 1972; The Gift, 1973; The Iron Lion, 1973; Chance, Luck and Destiny, 1975; The Blue Hawk, 1976 (Guardian Award); Annerton Pit, 1977; Hepzibah, 1978; Tulku, 1979 (Whitbread Prize; Carnegie Medal); The Flight of Dragons, 1979; City of Gold, 1980 (Carnegie Medal); The Seventh Raven, 1981; Healer, 1983; Giant Cold, 1984; (ed) Hundreds and Hundreds, 1984; A Box of Nothing, 1985; Mole Hole, 1987; Merlin Dreams, 1988; Eva, 1988; AK, 1990 (Whitbread Children's Award); A Bone from a Dry Sea, 1992; Time and the Clockmice etcetera, 1993; Shadow of a Hero, 1994; Chuck and Danielle, 1996; The Kin, 1998; Touch and Go, 1999; The Lion Tamer's Daughter, 1999; The Ropemaker, 2001; (with Robin McKinley) Elementals: Water, 2002; The Tears of the Salamander, 2003; The Gift Boat, 2004; Angel Isle, 2006; (with Robin McKinley) Fire: tales of elemental spirits, 2009; Tales of Elemental Creatures: Earth and Air, 2012; In the Palace of the Khans, 2012; *TV series,* Mandog (Mandog, by Lois Lamplugh, 1972, is based on the Changes series); *novels:* Skin Deep, 1968; A Pride of Heroes, 1969; The Seals, 1970; Sleep and His Brother, 1971; The Lizard in the Cup, 1972; The Green Gene, 1973; The Poison Oracle, 1974; The Lively Dead, 1975; King and Joker, 1976; Walking Dead, 1977; One Foot in the Grave, 1979; A Summer in the Twenties, 1981; The Last House-party, 1982; Hindsight, 1983; Death of a Unicorn, 1984; Tefuga, 1986; Perfect Gallows, 1988; Skeleton-in-Waiting, 1989; Play Dead, 1991; The Yellow Room Conspiracy, 1994; Some Deaths Before Dying, 2000; *poetry:* The Weir, 2008. *Recreation:* bridge. *Address:* 1 Arlebury Park Mews, Alresford, Hants SO24 9ER.

See also Baron Dickinson, Very Rev. H. G. Dickinson.

DICKINSON, Robert Henry, CBE 1998; DL; Senior Partner, Dickinson Dees, 1987–97; Chairman, Northern Rock PLC (formerly Northern Rock Building Society), 1992–99; *b* 12 May 1934; *s* of Robert Joicey Dickinson and Alice Penelope Dickinson (*née* Barnett); *m* 1963, Kyra Irina Boissevain; one *s* two *d*. *Educ:* Harrow; Christ Church, Oxford (MA). Admitted solicitor (Hons), 1960; Partner, Dickinson Dees, 1963–97. Chairman: Northern Investors PLC, 1984–2005; Grainger Trust PLC, 1992–2007; Director: Reg Vardy PLC, 1988–2002; Yorkshire Tyne Tees TV PLC, 1992–97. Chm., Univ. of Newcastle upon Tyne Devlt Trust, 2000–05. DL Northumberland, 1992. *Recreations:* shooting, fishing. *Address:* Styford Hall, Stocksfield, Northumberland NE43 7TY. *T:* (01434) 634452, *Fax:* (01434) 634634. *Clubs:* Boodle's, Pratt's; Northern Counties (Newcastle).

DICKINSON, Sally Jane; Policy Director, Magistrates' Association, 2010–12 (Secretary, 1994–2010); *b* 12 Sept. 1955; *d* of Colin James Rayner Godden and Margaret Godden (*née* Cowin); *m* 1987, James Anthony Dickinson. *Educ:* Chatham Grammar Sch. for Girls; Bristol Univ. (BA Theol); Bristol Poly. (BA Law). Clerical Officer, Inland Revenue Collection, 1978–81; Exec. Officer, Law Soc. (Legal Aid), 1981–85; Regl Dir, Apex Charitable Trust, 1985–92; Cttee Sec., Magistrates' Assoc., 1992–93. Trustee: Fair Trials Internat., 2011–14; Griffins Soc., 2013–. *Publications:* (Asst Ed.) The Magistracy at the Crossroads, 2012. *Recreations:* walking, sleeping. *Address:* 55 Noah's Ark, Kemsing, Kent TN15 6PA.

DICKINSON, Simon Clervaux; Chairman: Simon C. Dickinson Ltd, Agents and Dealers in Fine Art, since 1993; Dickinson Roundell Inc., since 1993; *b* 26 Oct. 1948; *s* of Peter Dickinson and Anne Dickinson (*née* Chayter); *m* 1983, Hon. Jessica, *d* of 2nd Baron Mancroft, KBE, TD; one *s* two *d*. *Educ:* Aysgarth Sch.; Harrow (art schol.; Mem., First cricket and football XIs). Christie's: joined 1968; Dir, 1974–93; Sen. Picture Dir, 1990–93. *Recreations:*

gardening, shooting, fishing, golf, tennis. *Address:* Simon C. Dickinson Ltd, 58 Jermyn Street, SW1Y 6LX. *T:* (020) 7493 0340, *Fax:* (020) 7493 0796. *E:* simon@simondickinson.com. *Clubs:* White's, Boodle's.

DICKINSON, (Stephen) Mark; Managing Director, Dickinson Communications, since 2012; Chairman, Prolific North Ltd, since 2013; *b* 20 Jan. 1951; *s* of Stanley Park Dickinson and Beatrice Joan Dickinson; *m* 1981, Pauline Patricia Mills; two *s* two *d*. *Educ:* Dame Alice Owen's Sch.; Univ. of Manchester (BA 2nd Cl. Hons Psychol). Publicity asst, Macmillan Jls, 1975–76; sub-editor, Daily Telegraph, Manchester, 1976–87; author, 1988–89; Chief Sub Editor: Tonight, Chester, 1990–91; Aberdeen Evening Express, 1991–92; Asst Ed., The Journal, Newcastle, 1992–93; Dep. Ed. in Chief, Chronicle Newspapers, Chester, 1993–96; Editor: The Journal, Newcastle, 1996–2000; Liverpool Echo, 2000–05; Ed.-in-Chief, Trinity Mirror NW and N Wales, 2002–05; Editl Dir, Trinity Mirror Midlands, 2005–07; Business Development Director: Trinity Mirror NW and Wales, 2007–10; Trinity Mirror Regionals, 2011–12. Dir and Gov., W Kirby Residential Sch., 2014–. *Publications:* The Manchester Book, 1984; To Break a Union, 1986; Goodbye Piccadilly: the history of abolition of Greater Manchester Council, 1990. *Recreations:* reading, gardening, football, Rugby, entertaining, my family.

DICKINSON, (Vivienne) Anne, (Mrs Basil Phillips); Chairman, Forexia UK, 1997–98; Director, Leedex Public Relations, 1993–96; *b* 27 Sept. 1931; *d* of F. Oswald Edward Dickinson and M. Ida Ismay Dickinson; *m* 1st, 1951, John Kerr Large (marr. diss.); one *s* decd; 2nd, 1979, David Hermas Phillips (*d* 1989); 3rd, 1993, Basil B. Phillips, OBE. *Educ:* Nottingham Girls' High School. Account Executive, W. S. Crawford, 1960–64; Promotions Editor: Good Housekeeping, 1964–65; Harpers Bazaar, 1965–67; Dir in charge of Promotions, Nat. Magazine Co., 1967–68; Dir, Benson PR (later Kingsway), 1968–69; Chm. and Chief Exec., Kingsway Public Relations Ltd (later Kingsway Rowland), 1969–89; Chairman: The Rowland Co., 1989–90; Graduate Appointments Ltd, 1993–94; Dir, Birkdale Group plc, 1991–96. Chm., PR Consultants' Assoc., 1989 (Chm., Professional Practices Cttee, 1989). Chm., Family Welfare Assoc., 1990–94. Member: Rye Town Council, 1995–99; Bd, Rye Health & Care Ltd, 1996–2004, 2009– (Vice Pres., 2004–08, Pres., 2008–). FCIPR (FIPR 1985); CCMI (CBIM 1986). PR Professional of the Year, PR Week, 1988–89. *Recreations:* friends, food, dogs. *Address:* St Mary's House, 62 Church Square, Rye TN31 7HF. *Club:* Sloane.

DICKINSON, William George Heneage; Head of Finance Audit, Global Internal Audit, HSBC Holdings plc, since 2013; *b* Bath, 11 Nov. 1966; *s* of Michael and Sonia Dickinson; *m* 1997, Nancy Zonana; one *s* one *d*. *Educ:* Marlborough Coll.; Durham Univ. (BSc Hons). FCA 1992. Accountant: KPMG Peat Marwick McLintock, subseq. KPMG Peat Marwick, Bristol, 1988–92; KPMG: Boston, 1992–94; London, 1994–99; Montvale, 1999–2001; Partner, 2001–09; Partner i/c UK Dept of Professional Practice for Audit, 2001–03; Audit Partner, Financial Services, 2003–09; UK Hd of Audit for Asset Mgt, 2007–08; on secondment as Dir Gen., Finance and Corporate Services, DIUS, later BIS, 2008–09; Financial Risk Dir, DWP, 2009–10; HM Treasury: Chief Financial and Operating Officer, 2010–11, Chief Exec., 2011–12, Asset Protection Agency; Dir, Financial Services Gp, 2012–13. *Recreations:* film, theatre, tennis, sailing, reading. *Address:* Top Maisonette, 6 Eccleston Square, SW1V 1NP. *T:* (020) 7931 7620. *E:* wghdickinson@gmail.com.

DICKS, Prof. Anthony Richard; QC (Hong Kong) 1994; Professor of Chinese Law, 1995–2002, now Emeritus, and Professorial Research Associate, since 2003, School of Oriental and African Studies, University of London; *b* 6 Jan. 1936; *s* of Henry Victor Dicks and Pretoria Maud Dicks (*née* Jeffery); *m* 1969, Victoria Frances Mayne. *Educ:* Westminster Sch.; Trinity Coll., Cambridge (Open and Westminster Exhibnr; BA Hist. and Law, LLB 1st Cl., MA). Called to the Bar, Inner Temple, 1961; admitted Hong Kong Bar, 1965, Brunei Bar, 1971. Nat. Service, 2nd Lieut, 3rd King's Own Hussars, 1954–56. Teaching Fellow, Univ. of Chicago Law Sch., 1960–61; Res. Fellow, Brit. Inst. Internat. and Comparative Law and Inst. Current World Affairs, London, Hong Kong and Japan, 1962–68; Fellow, Trinity Hall, and Univ. Asst Lectr in Law, Cambridge, 1968–70; Lectr in Oriental Laws, SOAS, 1970–74; in practice as barrister and arbitrator, Hong Kong, 1974–94. Vis. Prof., SOAS, 1987–94. Mem., various acad., professional and public cttees in Hong Kong, 1974–94. Advr, Foreign Compensation Commn on China Claims, 1987–88; Arbitrator in Internat. Chamber of Commerce, London Court of Internat. Arbitration, Hong Kong Internat. Arbitration Centre and China Internat. Econ. and Trade Arbitration Commn and other arbitrations. *Publications:* articles in China Qly and other jls. *Address:* School of Oriental and African Studies, Thornhaugh Street, Russell Square, WC1H 0XG. *Clubs:* Athenæum; Hong Kong (Hong Kong).

DICKS, Terence Patrick, (Terry); *b* 17 March 1937; *s* of Frank and Winifred Dicks; *m*; one *s* two *d*; *m* 1985, Janet Cross; one *d*. *Educ:* London Sch. of Econs and Pol Science (BScEcon); Oxford Univ. (DipEcon). Clerk: Imperial Tobacco Co. Ltd, 1952–59; Min. of Labour, 1959–66; Admin. Officer, GLC, 1971–86. Contested (C) Bristol South, 1979. MP (C) Hayes and Harlington, 1983–97. Mem., Select Cttee on Transport, 1986–92. Member: Council of Europe, 1993–97; WEU, 1993–97. Member (C): Surrey CC, 1999–2009; Runnymede BC, 2011–.

DICKSON, Brice; *see* Dickson, S. B.

DICKSON, George, CBE 1991 (OBE 1974); HM Diplomatic Service, retired; Consul General, Amsterdam, 1987–91; *b* 23 May 1931; *s* of late George James Stark Dickson and Isobel (*née* Brown). *Educ:* Aberdeen Acad. DSIR, 1952; CRO, 1952–54; Karachi, 1954–56; Penang, 1957–59; Nicosia, 1960–62; Kampala, 1962–66; FCO, 1966–68; Manila, 1968–71; Jakarta, 1971–75; Stuttgart, 1975–76; Beirut, 1976–79; Baghdad, 1979–81; Asst Dir, Internat. Affairs, Commonwealth Secretariat, 1981–85; Dep. High Comr, Kingston, Jamaica, 1985–87. *Address:* Flat 17, 12 Constitution Place, Edinburgh EH6 7DL. *T:* (0131) 237 2639. *Club:* Royal Northern and University (Aberdeen).

DICKSON, Jennifer (Joan), (Mrs R. A. Sweetman), CM 1995; RA 1976 (ARA 1970); RE 1965; graphic artist, photographer and lecturer on the history of gardens; *b* 17 Sept. 1936; 2nd *d* of late John Liston Dickson and Margaret Joan Turner, S Africa; *m* 1962, Ronald Andrew Sweetman; one *s*. *Educ:* Goldsmith's College Sch. of Art, Univ. of London; Atelier 17, Paris. Taught at Eastbourne Sch. of Art, 1959–62 (French Govt Schol., to work in Paris under S. W. Hayter). Directed and developed Printmaking Dept, Brighton Coll. of Art, 1962–68; developed and directed Graphics Atelier, Saidye Bronfman Centre, Montreal, 1970–72. Exhibitions: L'Ultimo Silenzio, Palazzo Te, Mantua, Italy, 1993; Romantic Idylls and Classical Dreams, Wallack Galls, Ottawa, 2011. Has held appointments of Vis. Artist at following Universities: Ball State Univ., Muncie, Indiana, 1967; Univ. of the West Indies, Kingston, Jamaica, 1968; Univ. of Wisconsin, Madison, 1972; Ohio State Univ., 1973; Western Illinois Univ., 1973; Haystack Mountain Sch. of Crafts, Maine, 1973; Vis. Artist, Queen's Univ., Kingston, Ont., 1977; part-time Instructor of Drawing, 1980–81, 1983, Sessional Instructor, 1980–85, Ottawa Univ.; Vis. Prof., 1987, Hon. LLD 1988, Univ. of Alberta. Founder Mem., Brit. Printmakers' Council. Prix des Jeunes Artistes (Gravure), Biennale de Paris, 1963; Major Prize, World Print Competition, San Francisco, 1974; Norwegian Print Biennale Prize, 1981. *Publications:* suites of original prints and photographs: Genesis, 1965; Alchemic Images, 1966; Aids to Meditation, 1967; Eclipse, 1968; Song of Songs, 1969; Out of Time, 1970; Fragments, 1971; Sweet Death and Other Pleasures, 1972; Homage to Don Juan, 1975; Body Perceptions, 1975; The Secret Garden, 1976; Openings, 1977; Three Mirrors to Narcissus, 1978; Il Paradiso Terrestre, 1980; Il Tempo Classico, 1981; Grecian Odes, 1983; Aphrodite Anadyomene, 1984; The Gardens of Paradise, part 1, 1984, part 2, 1985; Reflected Palaces, 1985; The Gilded Cage, 1986; Water Gardens, 1987; The Hospital for Wounded Angels, 1987; The Gardens of Desire, 1988; Pavane to Spring, 1989; Sonnet to Persephone, 1990; The Gardener's Journal, 1990; Cadence and Echo: the song of the garden, 1991; The Spirit of the Garden, 1992; The Haunted Heart, 1993; Sanctuaries and Paradeisos, 1994; Old and New Worlds, 1995; Quietude and Grace, 1996; Water Song, 1997; Sanctuary: a landscape of the mind, 2000; Nature and Artifice, 2003; Time is the Thief of Time, 2006; The Royal Academy Suites: passages and transitions, 2008; Romantic Idylls and Classical Dreams, 2011; Contemplative Moments, 2012; Water Games, 2013. *Address:* 20 Osborne Street, Ottawa, ON K1S 4Z9, Canada. *T:* (613) 7302083, *Fax:* (613) 7301818. *E:* jenniferdickson@kalixo.com.

DICKSON, Martin Charles Gregor; journalist; US Managing Editor, Financial Times, 2012–14; *b* London, 21 Aug. 1948; *s* of George and Stella Dickson; *m* 1973, Hilary Wilce; one *s* two *d*. *Educ:* Haileybury; Trinity Hall, Cambridge (BA Hist. 1970); Univ. of London (BSc Econ. ext.). VSO, Thailand, 1966–67; journalist, Reuters, UK, S Africa and Turkey, 1970–76; Financial Times: journalist, 1976–2014; Africa Ed., 1978–79; Energy Corresp., 1980–82; NY Bureau Chief, 1990–94; Financial Ed., 1994–2000; Lombard Columnist, 2001–05; Dep. Ed., 2005–12. Mem. Bd, British Library, 2015–. *Recreations:* singing, running, travel, wine, galleries, gardening. *E:* martincgdickson@hotmail.com.

DICKSON, Michael George Tufnell, CBE 2005; FREng; Founding Partner, 1976, Chairman, 1996–2005, and Consultant, since 2006, Buro Happold; *b* 22 Sept. 1944; *s* of late George Frederick Thomas Benson Dickson and Rosamond Mary (*née* Tufnell); *m* 1980, Euphemia Anne Galletly; two *d*. *Educ:* Trinity Coll., Cambridge (BA Mech. Scis Tripos); Cornell Univ., NY (MS Structural Engrg and Town Planning). CEng 1975; FREng 1999; FIStructE 1997; FICE 2000. Engineer, Ove Arup, 1968–76. Visiting Professor: of Engrg Design, Univ. of Bath, 1996–; Innsbruck, 2000, 2010. Mem., Lord Justice Taylor's Tech. Cttee on Safety of Sports Grounds, 1987; Chairman: Construction Industry Council, 2000–02; Construction Res. and Innovation Strategy Panel, 2002–04. Pres., IStructE, 2005–06 (Chm., Towards Sustainable Develt: construction without depletion, 1999; Vice Pres., 2002–05); Board Member: Creative Acads Trust, 2012–; BRE Trust, 2013– (Dep. Chm., Res. Cttee, 2013–). Dir, 1986–2010, Trustee, 2008–, Theatre Royal, Bath. FRSA 1992. Hon. FRIBA 2001. Hon. DEng Bath, 2007. *Publications:* (ed with Michael Barnes) Widespan Roof Structures, 2000; (with Dave Parker) Sustainable Timber Design, 2014. *Recreations:* reading, walking, tennis, cricket, engineering design. *Address:* 67 Carlisle Road, Hove BN3 4FQ. *T:* (01273) 239536, (office) (020) 927 9745. *E:* michael.dickson@burohappold.com. *Clubs:* Athenæum, MCC; Sussex County Cricket.

DICKSON, Niall Forbes Ross; Chief Executive and Registrar, General Medical Council, since 2010; *b* 5 Nov. 1953; *s* of late Sheriff Ian Anderson Dickson, WS and Margaret Forbes Ross or Dickson; *m* 1979, Elizabeth Selina Taggart, *d* of late James Mercer Taggart, Lisburn, Co. Antrim; one *s* two *d*. *Educ:* Glasgow Acad.; Edinburgh Acad.; Edinburgh Univ. (MA Hons; DipEd); Moray House Coll. of Educn (Cert Ed). Teacher, Broughton High Sch., Edinburgh, 1976–78; Publicity Officer, Nat. Corp. for Care of Old People, 1978; Press Officer, 1978–79, Hd of Publishing, 1979–81, Age Concern England; Editor: Therapy Weekly, 1981–83; Nursing Times, 1983–88; BBC News: Health Corresp., 1988–90; Chief Social Affairs Corresp., 1990–95; Social Affairs Editor, 1995–2004; Chief Exec., The King's Fund, 2004–09. Chairman: Direct Payments Steering Gp, DoH, 2004–06; Individual Budgets Reform Gp, 2006–08. Member: NHS Modernisation Bd, 2004–05; Nat. Leadership Network, DoH, 2005–07; CMO's Review of Med. Regulation and Related Matters, 2005–06; Wkg Party on Med. Professionalism, RCP, 2005–06; Health Honours Cttee, 2005–12; Ministerial Adv. Gp on social care reform, 2008–10; DoH Nat. Quality Bd, 2012–. Chm., Health Commn, LGA, 2007–08. Chair, Internat. Assoc. of Med. Regulatory Authorities, 2014–Sept. 2016. Mem. Council, Which?, 2006–10. Mem. Ct of Govs, LSHTM, 2005–10. Trustee, Leeds Castle Foundn, 2008–12 (Chm., 2012–). Hon. Fellow: Univ. of Cardiff, 2006; Inst. of Educn, Univ. of London, 2007; Queen's Nursing Inst., 2009. Hon. MRCP 2007; Hon. MRCGP 2008. DUniv Oxford Brookes, 2007. Charles Fletcher Med. Broadcaster of Year, BMA, 1997. *Publications:* contribs to newspapers, jls and specialist pubns on health and social issues. *Recreations:* golf, tennis, history, current affairs. *Address:* General Medical Council, Regent's Place, 350 Euston Road, NW1 3JN. *Clubs:* Reform; Golf House (Elie), Hever Castle Golf, Isle of Harris Golf.

See also R. H. Dickson.

DICKSON, Prof. Peter George Muir, DPhil, DLitt; FBA 1988; Professor of Early Modern History, University of Oxford, 1989–96; Fellow, St Catherine's College, Oxford, since 1960; *b* 26 April 1929; *s* of William Muir Dickson, and Regina Dowdall-Nicolls; *m* 1964, Ariane Faye; one *d*. *Educ:* St Paul's Sch.; Worcester Coll., Oxford (Schol.; BA (1st Cl. Hons), MA, DPhil); DLitt Oxon 1992. FRHistS. Research Fellow, Nuffield Coll., Oxford, 1954–56; Tutor, St Catherine's Soc., Oxford, 1956–60; Vice-Master, St Catherine's Coll., 1975–77; Reader in Modern Hist., Oxford Univ., 1978–89. *Publications:* The Sun Insurance Office 1710–1960, 1960; The Financial Revolution in England 1688–1756, 1967, rev. edn 1993; Finance and Government under Maria Theresia 1740–1780, 2 vols, 1987. *Recreations:* tennis, cinema, art. *Address:* Field House, Iffley, Oxford OX4 4EG. *T:* (01865) 779599.

DICKSON, Prof. Robert Andrew, DSc; FRCS, FRCSE; Professor and Head of Department of Orthopaedic Surgery, University of Leeds, 1981–2009; Consultant Surgeon, St James's University Hospital, Leeds, and Leeds General Infirmary, 1981–2009; *b* 13 April 1943; *s* of Robert Campbell Miller Dickson and late Maude Evelyn Dickson; *m* 1980, Ingrid Irene Sandberg; one *s*. *Educ:* Edinburgh Academy; Edinburgh Univ. (MB, ChB 1967, ChM 1973); MA 1979, DSc 1992, Oxon. FRCSE 1972; Moynihan Medal (Assoc. of Surgeons of GB and Ire.), 1977; FRCS *ad eund*, 1982. Lecturer, Nuffield Dept of Orthopaedic Surgery, Univ. of Oxford, 1972–75; Fellow in Spinal Surgery, Univ. of Louisville, Kentucky, 1975–76; Reader, Nuffield Dept of Orthopaedic Surgery, Univ. of Oxford, 1976–81. Chm., Professional Conduct Cttee, GMC, 2003–. Arris and Gale Lectr, and Hunterian Prof., RCS. Fellow, Brit. Orthopaedic Assoc. (Chm., Res. and Scholarship Cttee, 1999–); Member: Brit. Soc. for Surgery of the Hand; Brit. Orthopaedic Research Soc.; Brit. Scoliosis Soc. Treas., Council of Mgt, Jl of Bone and Jt Surgery, 2002–. *Publications:* Surgery of the Rheumatoid Hand, 1979; Musculo-skeletal disease, 1984; Management of spinal deformities, 1984; Management of spinal deformities, 1988; papers on scoliosis and spinal surgery. *Recreations:* squash, music. *Address:* 14A Park Avenue, Leeds LS8 2JH.

DICKSON, Robert Hamish, DL; WS; Sheriff of South Strathclyde, Dumfries and Galloway, at Airdrie, since 1988; *b* 19 Oct. 1945; *s* of late Sheriff Ian Anderson Dickson, WS, and Mrs Margaret Forbes Ross or Dickson; *m* 1976, Janet Laird (*d* 2004), *d* of late Alexander Campbell, Port of Menteith; one *s*. *Educ:* Glasgow Acad.; Drumtochty Castle; Glenalmond; Glasgow Univ. (LLB). WS 1969. Solicitor: Edinburgh, 1969–71; Glasgow, 1971–86 (Partner, Brown Mair Mackintosh, 1973–86); Sheriff of South Strathclyde, Dumfries and Galloway, at Hamilton, 1986–88 (floating). Pres., Sheriffs' Assoc., 2006–09; Mem., Sheriff Court Rules Council, 2011–. Pres., Scottish Medico Legal Soc., 2004–08. DL Lanarks, 2012. *Publications:* (jtly) Powers & Harris' Medical Negligence, 2nd edn 1994, 4th edn 2007; Medical and Dental Negligence, 1997; articles in medical legal jls. *Recreations:* golf, music, reading. *Address:* Airdrie Sheriff Court, Airdrie ML6 6EE. *T:* (01236) 751121. *Clubs:* Royal and Ancient Golf, Elie Golf House (Capt., 1997–99), Harris Golf.

See also N. F. R. Dickson.

DICKSON, Robert Maurice French C.; *see* Chatterton Dickson.

DICKSON, Sarah Margaret; HM Diplomatic Service; Director of Global Affairs, Scotch Whisky Association, since 2015; *b* London, 1972; *d* of Rowan Hill and Gabrielle Hill; *m* 2006, Philip Antony Dickson; two *d. Educ:* St John's Coll., Cambridge (BA Hons 1995). Joined FCO, 1995; Desk Officer, 1995–96; Third Sec., Belgrade, 1996–97; Second Sec. (Pol), Buenos Aires, 1997–2000; Hd, Internat. Security Section, Security Policy Dept, FCO, 2000–02; First Sec. (Pol/Mil.), Madrid, 2002–03; Hd, Migration and Justice and Home Affairs Section, EU-Internal, 2003–04, Hd, Consular and Africa Section, Press Office, 2004, FCO; Communications Dir and Internal Pol Officer, 2005–08, Manager for Embassy and Consulate Gen. relocation, 2008–09, COS, 2009–10, Madrid; Ambassador to Guatemala and (non-resident) to Honduras, 2012–15. *Address:* Scotch Whisky Association, 10 Greycoat Place, SW1P 1SB.

DICKSON, Prof. (Sidney) Brice; Professor of International and Comparative Law, Queen's University, Belfast, since 2005; *b* 5 Dec. 1953; *s* of Sidney Dickson and Mary Dickson (*née* Murray); *m* 1993, Patricia Mary Josephine Mallon; one step *d* (one step *s* decd). *Educ:* Wadham Coll., Oxford (BA, BCL); Univ. of Ulster (MPhil). Called to the Bar, NI, 1976; Lectr in Law, Univ. of Leicester, 1977–79; Lectr, 1979–89, Sen. Lectr, 1989–91, QUB; Prof. of Law, Univ. of Ulster, 1991–99; Chief Comr, NI Human Rights Commn, 1999–2005. Ind. Mem., Policing Bd of NI, 2012–. Leverhulme Eur. Student, 1976–77; Salzburg Fellow, 1985; Churchill Fellow, 1994; Leverhulme Res. Fellow, 1999, 2013–14. *Publications:* The Legal System of Northern Ireland, 1984, 5th edn 2005; Introduction to French Law, 1994; (ed) Human Rights and the European Convention, 1997; (ed) Civil Liberties in Northern Ireland: the CAJ handbook, 1990, 4th edn 2003; (ed with P. Carmichael) The House of Lords: its parliamentary and judicial roles, 1999; (ed) Judicial Activism in Common Law Supreme Courts, 2007; (ed jtly) The Judicial House of Lords 1876–2009, 2009; The European Convention on Human Rights and the Conflict in Northern Ireland, 2010; Law in Northern Ireland: an introduction, 2011, 2nd edn 2013; Human Rights and the UK Supreme Court, 2013; (ed jtly) Human Rights in Northern Ireland: the CAJ handbook, 2015. *Recreations:* fiction, classical music, philately, travel. *Address:* Maryville Park, Belfast BT9 6LP.

DICKSON, Stewart Clyde; Member (Alliance) East Antrim, Northern Ireland Assembly, since 2011; *b* Belfast, 8 Dec. 1950; *s* of Clyde Dickson and Evelyn Dickson; *m* 1978, Elizabeth Alexandra Millar. Sen. Employment Relns Officer, Labour Relations Agency, 1985–2011. Mem. (Alliance), Carrickfergus BC, 1977–81, 1985–2011. Chief Whip, Alliance Party (Chm., 2010–11). Contested (Alliance) E Antrim, 2015. Churchill Fellow, 1999. *Recreations:* reading, travel, Member of 1st Greenisland Boys' Brigade Company. *Address:* 6 Farm Lodge Park, Greenisland, Carrickfergus BT38 8BA. *E:* stewart.dickson@mla.niassembly.gov.uk. *Club:* Ulster Reform.

DICKSON, Susan Jane; HM Diplomatic Service; Legal Counsellor, Foreign and Commonwealth Office, since 2003; *b* 30 July 1964; *d* of John Morton Dickson and Marlene Linek Dickson (*née* Allan). *Educ:* Mearns Castle High Sch.; Univ. of Strathclyde (LLB Hons 1986; DipLP 1988); Europa Inst., Univ. of Amsterdam (Dip. in European Law 1987). Admitted solicitor (Scotland), 1990; Asst, then Sen. Asst, Legal Advr, FCO, 1990–97; First Sec. (Legal), UK Mission to UN, NY, 1997–2000; First Sec. (Legal Advr British Overseas Territories), British High Commn, Bridgetown, 2000–03. *Publications:* (with I. D. Hendry) British Overseas Territories Law, 2011. *Recreations:* yoga, tennis, reading, interior design, Caribbean beaches. *Address:* Legal Advisers, Foreign and Commonwealth Office, King Charles Street, SW1A 2AH. *T:* (020) 7008 3000. *E:* susan.dickson@fco.gov.uk.

DICKSON, William Andrew; HM Diplomatic Service, retired; Ambassador to Mongolia, 2009–11; Chief Executive Officer, Independent (UK) Exports Ltd, since 2012; Director of UK Operations, MongoliaNation Orgill-Dickson Associates, since 2011; Managing Partner, International Export Partners, since 2013; *b* Glasgow, 17 Dec. 1950; *s* of William Paul McBean Dickson and Isabella Dickson (*née* Goodwin); *m* 2007, Patricia Ann Daniels; two step *s. Educ:* Lenzie Acad.; Stirling Univ.; Willesden Coll.; Univ. of Northumbria (Law). Served RM; concrete engineer, construction industry; joined HM Diplomatic Service; Third Sec., Nairobi, 1980–82; Second Sec., Budapest, 1982–86; FCO spokesman, 1986–89; First Sec., Vienna, 1989–93; British Govt spokesman, Hong Kong, 1994–98; Administrator: Ascension, 2001; Tristan da Cunha, and Consul Gen., S Atlantic Ocean, 2001–04; Consul Gen., Erbil, Iraq, 2007–08. Mem., Navigation Cttee, Broads Authy, 2015–. Chm., Internat. Old Boys Assoc. UK, 2012–; Pres., Probus Club of Broadlands, 2014–. Gov., Stalham High Sch., 2012–. *Recreations:* boating on the Norfolk Broads, ocean racing, wooden sailing ship modelling Nelson's Navy, gardening in small spaces, thinking about getting fit. *Address:* 12 Trail Quay Cottages, Marsh Road, Hoveton, Norfolk NR12 8UH. *E:* shipwreckbt@hotmail.com. *Clubs:* Cape Town; Montagu Golf (Montagu, Western Cape); Foreign Correspondents' (Hong Kong).

DIEHL, His Honour John Bertram Stuart; QC 1987; a Circuit Judge, 1990–2011; Hon. Recorder of Swansea, 2001–11; *b* 18 April 1944; *s* of late E. H. S. Diehl and C. P. Diehl; *m* 1967, Patricia L. Charman; two *s. Educ:* Bishop Gore Grammar Sch., Swansea; University Coll. of Wales, Aberystwyth (LLB 1965). Called to the Bar, Lincoln's Inn, 1968, Bencher (Additional Bencher, 2007). Asst Lectr and Lectr in Law, Univ. of Sheffield, 1965–69; barrister, in practice on Wales and Chester Circuit, 1969–90; Asst Recorder, 1980–84; Recorder, 1984–90. *Address:* c/o Crown Court, St Helen's Road, Swansea SA1 4PF.

DIENES-WILLIAMS, Katherine Frances Maria, FRCO; Organist and Master of the Choristers, Guildford Cathedral, since 2008; Director, Southern Voices, since 2012; *b* Wellington, NZ, 10 Jan. 1970; *d* of Julius Joseph Eugene Dienes and Frances Armstrong Dienes; *m* 1996, Patrick Williams; one *d. Educ:* St Mark's Ch Sch., Wellington, NZ; Samuel Marsden Collegiate Sch., Wellington; Victoria Univ., Wellington (BA, BMus); Leeds Univ. (MA Music and Liturgy). LTCL (Piano 1986, Organ 1987); ARCO 1992, FRCO 1993. Richard Prothero Organ Schol., 1988–89, Asst Organist, 1990–91, Wellington Cathedral; Organ Schol., Winchester Cathedral, and Asst Organist, Winchester Coll., 1991–94; Organist and Asst Master of Choristers, Liverpool Metropolitan Cathedral, 1994–97; Asst Organist and Dir of Girls' Choir, Norwich Cathedral, 1997–2001; Dir of Music, St Mary's Collegiate Ch, Warwick, 2001–07. Mem. Council, RSCM, 2008–. Hon. ARSCM 2006. Knight: Order of Vitéz, 1994; Order of St László, 1995; Hon. GCM 2008. *Recreations:* classical music, travel, reading. *Address:* Cathedral Office, Stag Hill, Guildford, Surrey GU2 7UP. *T:* (01483) 547866. *E:* Katherine@guildford-cathedral.org.

DIEPPE, Prof. Paul Adrian, MD; FRCP; Chair, Health and Wellbeing, University of Exeter Medical School (formerly Peninsula Medical School), since 2012; Hon. Professor of Musculoskeletal Sciences, University of Oxford, since 2007; *b* 20 May 1946; *s* of late Richard Willan Dieppe and Muriel Grace Dieppe (*née* Gascoigne); *m* 1970, Elizabeth Anne Stadward; two *d. Educ:* Caterham Sch.; St Bartholomew's Hosp. Med. Coll. (BSc 1967; MB BS 1970; MD 1985). FRCP 1985. General medical trng posts in London and Southend, 1970–74; Rheumatology Registrar, Guy's Hosp., London, 1974–75; Res. Fellow and Sen. Registrar in Medicine and Rheumatology, St Bartholomew's Hosp., London, 1975–78; University of Bristol: Consultant Sen. Lectr, 1978–87; ARC Prof. of Rheumatology, 1987–97; Res. Dir, Clinical Medicine and Dentistry, 1993–95; Dean, Faculty of Medicine, 1995–97; Hon. Prof. of Health Services Res., 1997–2007; Dir, MRC Health Services Res. Collaboration, 1997–2007; Hon. Consultant Rheumatologist: to Bristol and Bath hosps, 1978–2007; United Bristol Healthcare NHS Trust, 1992–2007; N Avon Hosp. Trust, 1997–2007; Chair, Clinical Educn Res., Peninsula Med. Sch., 2009–12. *Publications:* Crystals and Joint Disease, 1983; Rheumatological Medicine, 1985; Atlas of Clinical Rheumatology, 1986; Arthritis: BMA Family Doctor Guide, 1988; Rheumatology, 1993, 2nd edn 1997; contrib. chapters in books and numerous papers in jls. *Recreations:* sailing, cycling, carving, reading, writing, resting.

DIFFLEY, Dr John Francis Xavier, FRS 2005; Principal Scientist, Cancer Research UK, London Research Institute, since 2002; *b* 4 March 1958; *s* of John and Joan Diffley. *Educ:* New York Univ. (BA 1978; PhD 1985). Postdoctoral Fellow, Cold Spring Harbor Lab., 1984–90; Imperial Cancer Research Fund, Clare Hall Laboratories: res. scientist, 1990–95; Sen. Scientist, 1995–99; Principal Scientist, 1999–2002. Mem., Eur. Acad. of Cancer Scis, 2011. FMedSci 2011. *Recreations:* playing the guitar, cycling. *Address:* Cancer Research UK, London Research Institute, Clare Hall Laboratories, Blanche Lane, South Mimms EN6 3LD.

DIGBY, family name of **Baron Digby**.

DIGBY, 12th Baron (Ire.) *cr* 1620, and 5th Baron (GB) *cr* 1765; **Edward Henry Kenelm Digby,** KCVO 1999; JP; DL; Lord-Lieutenant, Dorset, 1984–99 (Vice Lord-Lieutenant, 1965–84); Captain, late Coldstream Guards; *b* 24 July 1924; *o s* of 11th and 4th Baron Digby, KG, DSO, MC, and Hon. Pamela Bruce, OBE (*d* 1978), *y d* of 2nd Baron Aberdare; *S* father, 1964; *m* 1952, Dione Marian Sherbrooke (*see* Lady Digby); two *s* one *d. Educ:* Eton; Trinity Coll., Oxford; RMC. Served War of 1939–45. Capt. Coldstream Guards, 1947; Malaya, 1948–50; ADC to C-in-C: FARELF, 1950–51; BAOR, 1951–52. Director: Brooklyns Westbrick Ltd, 1970–83; Beazer plc, 1983–91; Kier Internat., 1986–91; Gifford-Hill Inc., 1986–91; PACCAR (UK) Ltd, 1990–97. Dep. Chm., SW Economic Planning Council, 1972–77. Mem. Council, Royal Agricultural Soc. of England, 1954; Chm., Royal Agricultural Soc. of Commonwealth, 1966–77, Hon. Fellow 1977. Pres., 1976, Vice Pres., 1977, Royal Bath and West Soc. Dorchester Rural District Councillor, 1962–68; Dorset County Councillor, 1966–81 (Vice Chm. CC, 1977–81). President: Wessex Br., Inst. of Dirs, 1980–97; Council, St John, Dorset, 1984–99; Patron, Dorset Br., British Red Cross Soc. Hon. Col, 4th Bn, Devonshire and Dorset Regt, 1992–96. DL 1957, JP 1959, Dorset. KStJ 1985. *Recreations:* ski-ing, shooting, tennis. *Heir: s* Hon. Henry Noel Kenelm Digby, ACA [*b* 6 Jan. 1954; *m* 1st, 1980, Susan (marr. diss. 2001), *er d* of Peter Watts; one *s* one *d*; 2nd, 2002, Sophie, *d* of Robin Malim; one *s* two *d* (of whom one *s* one *d* are twins)]. *Address:* West Wing, Minterne House, Minterne Magna, Dorchester, Dorset DT2 7AX. *T:* (01300) 341425. *Clubs:* Pratt's, Farmers.

DIGBY, Lady; Dione Marian Digby, DBE 1991; DL; Founder Chairman, 1963–2005, Artistic Director and Hon. Secretary, 1963–2012, Summer Music Society of Dorset; *b* 23 Feb. 1934; *d* of Rear-Adm. Robert St Vincent Sherbrooke, VC, CB, DSO, and of Rosemary Neville Sherbrooke (*née* Buckley), Oxton, Notts; *m* 1952, Baron Digby, *qv*; two *s* one *d. Educ:* Talindert State Sch., Victoria, Australia; Southover Manor Sch., Lewes, Sussex. Chairman: Dorset Assoc. of Youth Clubs, 1966–73; Dorset Community Council, 1977–79; Standing Conf. of Rural Community Councils and Councils of Voluntary Service SW Region, 1977–79. Councillor (Ind.) W Dorset DC, 1976–86; Mem. Dorset Small Industries Cttee, CoSIRA, 1977 (Chm. 1982–85); Mem., Wessex Water Authority, 1983–89; National Rivers Authority: Mem., 1989–96; Chm., Wessex Regl Adv. Bd, 1989–93; Co-Chm., S Western Adv. Bd, 1993–95; Chm., Southern Regl Adv. Bd, 1995–96. Dir, SW Regl Bd, then Western Adv. Bd, Nat. Westminster Bank, 1986–92. Member: BBC/IBA Central Appeals Adv. Cttee, 1975–80; Ethical Trust Adv. Bd, Scottish Widows Investment Partnership (formerly Abbey Life Investment Services), 1996–2003; Cttee of Reference, Premier Asset Mgt (formerly Credit Suisse Fellowship Trust), 1997–2011. Governor: Dorset Coll. of Agriculture, 1978–83; Sherborne Sch., 1986–2000; Chm. Adv. Bd, Jt Univ. Centre at Yeovil Coll., Bournemouth and Exeter Univs; Mem. Council, Exeter Univ., 1981–96; Chancellor, Bournemouth Univ., 2006–09 (Pro-Chancellor, 2001–06). Mem. Bath Festival Soc. Council of Management, 1971–81 (Chm. of the Society, 1976–81); Chm. Bath Fest. Friends Trust, 1982–87; Foundation Trustee, RAM, 1985–2000; Trustee, Tallis Scholars Trust, 1984–2004. Member: SW Arts Management Cttee, 1981–86; Arts Council of GB, 1982–86 (Chm., Trng Cttee; Vice-Chm., Dance Panel; Mem., Music Panel); South Bank Bd, 1985–88 (Gov., 1988–90); Bd of Mgt, Bournemouth Orchs, 1989–2000 (Mem. Bd of Mgt, Western Orchestral Soc., 1989–91); Chairman: S and W Concerts Bd, 1989–2001; Friends of Dorset Opera Trust, 2000–; President: Dorset Opera, 1975–2012, now Emeritus; Dorset Youth Assoc., 1994–2004. Mem., Council of Management, The Joseph Weld and Trimar (formerly Dorset Respite) Hospice Trust, 1990–2007 (Pres., 1993–2007). DL Dorset, 1983. Hon. DArts Bournemouth, 1997. *Recreations:* music and the arts, ski-ing; interest in local government, politics, history, people. *Address:* The West Wing, Minterne House, Dorchester, Dorset DT2 7AX. *T:* (01300) 341425.

DIGBY DAY, Richard; freelance director, since 1984; Director, London Dramatic Academy, 2003–12; *b* Wales, 27 Dec. 1940; *né* Richard Day; *s* of Donald Day and Doris Mary Day (*née* George). *Educ:* Rhiwbina Jun. Sch., Cardiff; Solihull Sch., Warks; Royal Acad. of Dramatic Art (Leverhulme Schol.; first student of direction). Thames TV trainee dir, Nottingham Playhouse, 1963–64; Artistic Director: Bournemouth Th. Co., 1966–68; New Shakespeare Co. Open Air Th., Regent's Park, 1967–85; Director: Welsh Th. Co., Cardiff, 1969–71; York Th. Royal, 1971–76; Northcott Th., Exeter, 1977–80; Nottingham Playhouse, 1980–84; freelance dir, prodns at Guildford, Colchester, Perth, West End and work in Canada, Denmark, Ireland and SA; Dir, National Th. Inst., O'Neill Centre, Waterford, Conn, 1990–98; Associate Prof., Connecticut Coll., 1993–; Founder, London Acad. of Theatre, Rutgers Univ., 1998–2003; teacher and lectr at univs in USA. Member: Regl Panel, Arts Council GB, 1980–83; Nat. Council for Drama Trng, 1981–90. Chm. of Associates, 2008–10, Mem. Council, 2008–13, RADA; Mem., Clarence Derwent Award Cttee, 1985–; Vice Pres., Shaw Soc., 1991–; Mem. Bd, Drama League of NY, 1991–99. *Recreations:* art (collecting watercolours and drawings), opera, ballet, sightseeing. *Address:* 14 Monkton House, Monkton Park, Chippenham, Wilts SN15 3PE. *E:* r.digbyday@btinternet.com.

DIGGLE, Prof. James, LittD; FBA 1985; Professor of Greek and Latin, University of Cambridge, 1995–2011, now Emeritus; Fellow of Queens' College, 1966–2011, now Life Fellow; *b* 29 March 1944; *m* 1973, Sedwell Mary Chapman; three *s. Educ:* Rochdale Grammar School; St John's College, Cambridge (Major Scholar; Classical Tripos Pt I, first cl., 1964, Pt II, first cl. with dist., 1965; Pitt Scholar, Browne Scholar, Hallam Prize, Members' Latin Essay Prize, 1963; Montagu Butler Prize, Browne Medals for Greek Elegy and Latin Epigram, 1964; Porson Prize, Chancellor's Classical Medal, Craven Student, Allen Scholar, 1965; BA 1965; MA 1969; PhD 1969; LittD 1985). Queens' College, Cambridge: Research Fellow, 1966–67; Official Fellow, 1967–2011; Sen. Fellow, 2007–11; Director of Studies in Classics, 1967–2011; Librarian, 1969–77; Praelector, 1971–73, 1978–2015; Cambridge University: Asst Lectr in Classics, 1970–75; Lectr, 1975–89; Reader in Greek and Latin, 1989–95; Chm., Faculty Bd of Classics, 1989–90; Orator, 1982–93. Jt Editor, Cambridge Classical Texts and Commentaries, 1977–. Corresponding Mem., Acad. of Athens, 2001. *Publications:* The Phaethon of Euripides, 1970; (jtly) Flavii Cresconii Corippi Iohannidos, Libri VIII, 1970; (ed jtly) The Classical Papers of A. E. Housman, 1972; (ed jtly) Dionysiaca: nine studies in Greek poetry, presented to Sir Denys Page, 1978; Studies on the Text of Euripides, 1981; Euripidis Fabulae (Oxford Classical Texts), vol. ii 1981, vol. i 1984, vol. iii 1994; (ed jtly) Studies in Latin Literature and its Tradition, in honour of C. O. Brink, 1989; The textual tradition of Euripides' Orestes, 1991; (ed jtly) F. R. D. Goodyear, Papers on Latin Literature, 1992; Euripidea: collected essays, 1994; Cambridge Orations 1982–1993: a selection, 1994; Tragicorum Graecorum Fragmenta Selecta, 1998; Theophrastus: Characters, 2004; (with R.

Bittlestone and J. Underhill) Odysseus Unbound: the search for Homer's Ithaca, 2005. *Recreations:* family life, Cambridge United FC. *Address:* Queens' College, Cambridge CB3 9ET. *E:* jd10000@cam.ac.uk.

DIGGLE, Judith Margaret, (Mrs P. J. Diggle); *see* Brown, Judith M.

DIGGORY, Dr Colin; Headmaster, Alleyn's School, 2002–10; Consultant, RSAcademics Ltd, since 2013; *b* 22 July 1954; *s* of late John Harold Diggory and Olga (*née* Midcalf); *m* 1976, Susan Janet Robinson; one *s* two *d*. *Educ:* Sir William Turner's Sch., Redcar; Univ. of Durham (BSc 1st cl. Hons Maths, PGCE); Open Univ. (MA 1999; EdD 2005 (Sir John Daniel Award, 2005)). CMath, FIMA 1994. Assistant Master: Manchester Grammar Sch., 1976–83; St Paul's Sch., Barnes, 1983–87; Head of Maths, Merchant Taylors' Sch., 1987–90; Second Master, 1990–91, Headmaster, 1991–2002, Latymer Upper Sch. Chief Examr, A Level Maths, Univ. of London, 1989–91. Sen. Educn Consultant, CfA Exec. Search and Selection, 2011–13. Chm., London Div., 1999, Jun. Schs Sub-Cttee, 1999–2001, HMC. Trustee, Dulwich Picture Gall., 2005–08; Vice Pres., Soc. of Schoolmasters and Schoolmistresses, 2011– (Trustee, 2004–08). Gov., Highgate Sch., 2003–08; Chm., Bd of Dirs, Radnor House Sch., Twickenham, 2010–. FRSA 1994. *Recreations:* walking, theatre. *Address:* c/o Alleyn's School, Dulwich, SE22 8SU. *Club:* East India, Devonshire, Sports and Public Schools.

DIGHT, Marc David; His Honour Judge Dight; a Senior Circuit Judge (Chancery), since 2007; Resident Judge, Central London Civil Justice Centre and Mayor's and City of London Court, since 2014; *b* 27 Feb. 1961; *s* of Harvey Dight and Gillian Dight (*née* Strauss); civil partnership 2009, Pierre Göran Folke Fredrik Andersson. *Educ:* Bancroft's Sch.; Univ. of Bristol (LLB Hons 1983). Called to the Bar, Inner Temple, 1984; admitted Lincoln's Inn *ad eundem*, 1986, Bencher, 2010; Recorder, 2002–07. Dep. Adjudicator, HM Land Registry, 2004–07; Lead Diversity and Community Relns Judge for England and Wales, 2010–. Trustee: Counsel and Care for the Elderly, 2003–11 (former Hon. Treas.; Chm., Fundraising Cttee); Independent Age, 2013–. Hon. Mem. Bd, UK Law Students' Assoc., 2011–. Freeman: City of London, 2009; Drapers' Co., 2009. *Recreations:* Swedish horticulture, Thai cuisine. *Address:* Royal Courts of Justice, Strand, WC2A 2LL. *Club:* Athenæum.

DILHORNE, 2nd Viscount *cr* 1964, of Green's Norton; **John Mervyn Manningham-Buller;** Bt 1866; Baron 1962; Barrister-at-Law; *b* 28 Feb. 1932; *s* of 1st Viscount Dilhorne, PC, and Lady Mary Lilian Lindsay, 4th *d* of 27th Earl of Crawford, KT, PC; *S* father, 1980; *m* 1st, 1955, Gillian Evelyn (marr. diss. 1973), *d* of Colonel George Stockwell; two *s* one *d*; 2nd, 1981, Prof. Susannah Jane Eykyn, MB BS, FRCS, FRCP, FRCPath. *Educ:* Eton; RMA Sandhurst. Called to the Bar, Inner Temple, 1979. Formerly Lieut, Coldstream Guards. Managing Director, Stewart Smith (LP&M) Ltd, 1970–74. Mem., Wilts County Council, 1967–70. Chm., VAT Tribunal, 1988–95; Member, Joint Parliamentary Committee: on Statutory Instruments, 1981–88; on Consolidation Bills, 1994–99; Mem., EC Select Cttee (Law and Instns), 1989–92. FTII (Mem. Council, 1967–74). *Heir:* *s* Hon. James Edward Manningham-Buller, formerly Captain Welsh Guards [*b* 20 Aug. 1956; *m* 1985, Nicola Marion, *e d* of Sven Mackie; one *s* one *d*. *Educ:* Harrow; Sandhurst]. *Address:* 382 Imperial Court, 225 Kennington Lane, SE11 5QN. *T:* (020) 7820 1660, *Fax:* (020) 7820 1418; The Dower House, Minterne Parva, Dorchester, Dorset DT2 7AP. *T:* (01300) 341392. *Clubs:* Pratt's, Buck's, Beefsteak; Swinley Forest Golf.

See also Baroness Manningham-Buller.

DILKE, Rev. Sir Charles (John Wentworth), 6th Bt *cr* 1862, of Sloane Street; FRAS; priest of the London Oratory, since 1966; *b* 21 Feb. 1937; *er s* of Sir John Dilke, 5th Bt and Sheila (*née* Seeds, later Knapp); *S* father, 1998. *Educ:* Ashdown House, Sussex; Winchester Coll.; King's Coll., Cambridge (BA). Joined the London Oratory, 1961; ordained priest, 1966; elected Provost (Superior), 1981–87. FRAS 2004. *Recreations:* painting, study of architecture, astronomy. *Heir:* *b* Dr Timothy Fisher Wentworth Dilke [*b* 1 Aug. 1938; *m* 1965, Caroline Sophia Dilke; one *s* one *d*]. *Address:* The Oratory, SW7 2RP. *T:* (020) 7808 0900. *Club:* Athenæum.

DILKE, Mary Stella F.; *see* Fetherston-Dilke.

DILKS, Prof. David Neville, FRHistS; FRSL; Vice-Chancellor, University of Hull, 1991–99; *b* Coventry, 17 March 1938; *s* of Neville Ernest Dilks and Phyllis Dilks; *m* 1963, Jill Medlicott; one *s*. *Educ:* Royal Grammar Sch., Worcester; Hertford Coll., Oxford (BA Modern Hist., Class II, 1959); St Antony's Coll., Oxford (Curzon Prizeman, 1960). Research Assistant to: Rt Hon. Sir Anthony Eden (later Earl of Avon), 1960–62; Marshal of the RAF Lord Tedder, 1963–65; Rt Hon. Harold Macmillan, 1964–67; Asst Lectr, then Lectr, in International History, LSE, 1962–70; University of Leeds: Prof. of Internat. History, 1970–91; Chm., Sch. of History, 1974–79; Dean, Faculty of Arts, 1975–77. Vis. Fellow, All Souls Coll., Oxford, 1973. Consultant, Sec.-Gen. of the Commonwealth, 1967–75; Chm., Commonwealth Youth Exchange Council, 1968–73. Member: Adv. Council on Public Records, 1977–85; Central Council, 1982–85, Library Cttee, 1982–91, Royal Commonwealth Soc.; British Nat. Cttee for History of Second World War, 1983–2006 (Pres., Internat. Cttee, 1992–2000); UFC, 1989–91; Adv. Council, Politeia, 1995–. Trustee: Edward Boyle Meml Trust, 1982–96 (Hon. Sec., 1981–82); Imperial War Museum, 1983–90; Lennox-Boyd Meml Trust, 1984–91; Nathaniel Trust, 1986–90. Pres., Worcester Old Elizabethans' Assoc., 1986–87. FRSL 1986; FCGI 1999. Liveryman, Goldsmiths' Co., 1984– (Freeman, 1979). Wrote and presented BBC TV series, The Loneliest Job, 1977; interviewer in BBC TV series, The Twentieth Century Remembered, 1982; historical consultant, TV films, The Gathering Storm, 2002, Winston Churchill at War, 2009. Hon. Dr of History, Russian Acad. of Scis, 1996. Médaille de Vermeil, Acad. Française, 1994. Emery Reves Award, Churchill Center, USA, 2006. *Publications:* Curzon in India, Vol. I, 1969, Vol. II, 1970; (ed) The Diaries of Sir Alexander Cadogan, 1971; (contrib.) The Conservatives (ed Lord Butler of Saffron Walden), 1977; (ed and contrib.) Retreat from Power, vol. 1, 1906–1939, Vol. 2, After 1939, 1981; (ed and contrib.) Britain and Canada (Commonwealth Foundn Paper), 1980; (ed and contrib.) The Missing Dimension: governments and intelligence communities in the twentieth century, 1984; Neville Chamberlain, Vol. I: Pioneering and Reform 1869–1929, 1984; (ed jtly and contrib.) Grossbritannien und der deutsche Widerstand, 1994; (ed jtly) Barbarossa: the axis and the allies, 1994; The Great Dominion: Winston Churchill in Canada 1900–1954, 2005; Churchill and Company, 2012; reviews and articles in English Historical Rev., Survey, History, Scandinavian Jl of History, etc. *Recreations:* ornithology, painting, railways, Bentley cars. *Address:* Wits End, Long Causeway, Leeds LS16 8EX. *T:* (0113) 267 3466. *Club:* Brooks's.

DILKS, John Morris Whitworth; Managing Director, Peribase Ltd, since 1999; Manager, Cranesbill Nursery, since 2012; *b* 10 Feb. 1950; *s* of John Amos Whitworth Dilks and Margaret (*née* Thraves); *m*; one *s* one *d*. *Educ:* Oakham Sch.; Sheffield Univ. (BA Hons). ACMA. Audit Manager, British Gas E Midlands, 1980–85; Asst Dir of Finance, British Gas, 1985–86; Regl Dir of Finance, British Gas NE, 1986–91; Regl Chm., British Gas Eastern, 1991–93; Dir, Transco, 1994–98; Chm., Britannia Movers International plc, 2004–12. Trustee, Hardy Plant Soc., 2013– (Chm.). *Recreations:* sailing, walking, gardening. *Address:* Greenhayes, Upper Westmancote, Tewkesbury, Glos GL20 7ES.

DILLAMORE, Ian Leslie, PhD, DSc; FREng; FIMMM; Chairman and Chief Executive, Doncasters plc, 1996–2000; *b* 22 Nov. 1938; *s* of Arthur Leslie Dillamore and Louise Mary Dillamore; *m* 1962, Maureen Birch; two *s*. *Educ:* Birmingham Univ. (BSc, MSc, PhD, DSc). ICI Research Fellow, Birmingham Univ., 1962–63, Lectr in Physical Metallurgy, 1963–69; Head of Phys. Metallurgy, BISRA, 1969–72; Head of Metals Technology Unit, British Steel Corp., 1972–76; Head of Metallurgy Dept, Aston Univ., 1976–81, Dean of Engineering, 1980–81; Director of Research and Development, INCO Europe, 1981–82; Dir of Technology, 1982–87, Gp Man. Dir, 1987–96, INCO Engineered Products Ltd. Hon. Professor of Metallurgy, Birmingham Univ., 1981–. Mem. Council: Metals Soc., 1980–84; Instn of Metallurgists, 1981–84; Vice-Pres., Inst. of Metals, 1985–88; Mem. SRC Metallurgy Cttee, 1972–75, Materials Cttee, 1977–82; Chm., Processing Sub-Cttee, SRC, later SERC, 1979–82; Mem., DTI Non Ferrous Metals Exec. Cttee, 1982–85; Pres. Birmingham Metallurgical Assoc., 1980–81. FREng (FEng 1985). Hon. DEng Birmingham, 1999. Sir Robert Hadfield Medal and Prize, Metals Soc., 1976; Platinum Medal, Inst. of Materials, 1999; Bunge Award, Internat. Conf. on Textures of Materials, 2008. *Publications:* An Industrial Evolution, 2014; numerous contribs to metallurgical and engrg jls. *Recreation:* industrial archaeology.

DILLEY, Sir Philip (Graham), Kt 2014; FICE; Chairman, Environment Agency, since 2014; *b* Portsmouth, 16 Feb. 1955; *s* of William Henry and Dorothy May Dilley; *m* 2003, June Donaldson; three *s*. *Educ:* Imperial Coll. of Sci., Technol. and Medicine, Univ. of London (BSc (Eng)). MIStructE 1982; FICE 2008. Joined Arup as grad. engr, 1976; Dir, Ove Arup Partners, 1993; Dir, Building Engrg Bd, 1998–2004; Hd, EMEA Reg., Arup, 2004–09; Exec. Chm., Arup Gp, 2009–14. Non-exec. Dir, Grosvenor Gp Ltd, 2014–. Chm., London First, 2012–. Mem. Council, Imperial Coll. London, 2011–. Trustee, Poppy Factory, 2013–. ACGI 1976. Hon. FRIBA 2013. *Recreations:* tennis, golf, opera, wine. *Address:* 13 Fitzroy Street, W1T 4BQ. *T:* (020) 7755 2029. *E:* sirphilip.dilley@gmail.com.

DILLON, family name of **Viscount Dillon**.

DILLON, 22nd Viscount *cr* 1622, of Castello Gallen, Co. Mayo, Ireland; **Henry Benedict Charles Dillon;** Count in France, 1711; *b* 6 Jan. 1973; *s* of 21st Viscount Dillon and of Mary Jane, *d* of late John Young, Castle Hill House, Birtle, Lancs; *S* father, 1982. *Heir:* *cousin* Thomas Arthur Lee Dillon, *b* 1 Oct. 1983].

DILLON, Sir Andrew (Patrick), Kt 2010; CBE 2003; Chief Executive, National Institute for Health and Care Excellence (formerly for Clinical Excellence, then for Health and Clinical Excellence), since 1999; *b* 9 May 1954; *m*; two *d*. *Educ:* Univ. of Manchester (BSc Hons Geog.). Dip. IHSM 1978. Asst Sector Adminr, Bolton Royal Infirmary, 1978–81; Unit Adminr, Queen Elizabeth Hosp. for Children, London, 1981–83; Dep., then Actg Unit Adminr, Royal London Hosp., 1983–86; Unit Gen. Manager, Royal Free Hosp., 1986–91; Chief Exec., St George's Gp, then St George's Healthcare NHS Trust, 1991–99. Non-exec. Dir, Health Technology Assessment Internat., 2003–05. Mem. Council, NHS Trust Fedn, 1995–97. Trustee, Centre for Mental Health, 2012–. *Recreation:* family. *Address:* National Institute for Health and Care Excellence, 10 Spring Gardens, SW1A 2BU. *T:* (020) 7045 2048.

DILLON, His Honour Thomas Michael; QC 1973; a Circuit Judge, 1985–2000; *b* 29 Nov. 1927; *yr s* of Thomas Bernard Joseph Dillon, Birmingham, and Ada Gladys Dillon (*née* Noyes); *m* 1956, Wendy Elizabeth Marshall Hurrell; two *s* one *d*. *Educ:* King Edward's Sch., Aston, Birmingham; Birmingham Univ. (LLB); Lincoln Coll., Oxford (BCL). Called to Bar, Middle Temple, 1952, Master of the Bench 1981. 2nd Lieut, RASC, 1953–54. In practice as barrister, 1954–85; a Recorder, 1972–85; Part-time Chm. of Industrial Tribunals, 1968–74. *Recreations:* reading, listening to music.

DILLWYN-VENABLES-LLEWELYN, Sir John Michael; *see* Venables-Llewelyn.

DILNOT, Sir Andrew (William), Kt 2013; CBE 2000; Warden, Nuffield College, Oxford, since 2012; *b* 19 June 1960; *s* of Anthony William John Dilnot and Patricia Josephine Dilnot; *m* 1984, Catherine Elizabeth Morrish; two *d*. *Educ:* Olchfa Comprehensive Sch.; St John's Coll., Oxford (BA Hons PPE; Hon. Fellow, 2002). Institute for Fiscal Studies: Res. Asst, 1981–83; Res. Officer, 1983–84; Sen. Res. Officer, 1984–86; Prog. Dir, 1986–90; Dep. Dir, 1990–91; Dir, 1991–2002; Principal, St Hugh's Coll., Oxford, 2002–12; Pro-Vice-Chancellor, Univ. of Oxford, 2005–12. Lectr (part-time) in Econs, Exeter Coll., Oxford, 1988–89. Vis. Fellow, ANU, 1986; Downing Meml Fellow, Melbourne Univ., 1989. Presenter, Radio 4: Analysis, 1994–2001; More or Less, 2001–07; A History of Britain in Numbers, 2013, 2015. Member: Social Security Adv. Cttee, 1992–2002; Retirement Income Inquiry, 1994–95; Foresight Panel on Aging Population, 1999–2001; Evidence Based Policy Panel, HM Treasury, 2001–03; Balance of Funding Inquiry, ODPM, 2002–04; Bd, NCC, 2003–08; OST Rev. of Use of Science in ODPM, 2005–06; Chairman: Commn on Funding of Care and Support, 2010–11 (report, Fairer Care Funding, 2011); UK Statistics Authy, 2012–. Member: Council, REconS, 1993–98; Chm., Statistics Users Forum, Royal Statistical Soc., 2009–12. Mem. Council, Westfield Coll., then QMW, Univ. of London, 1987–95. Mem. Bd, World Vision UK, 1991–97. Trustee: Relate, Oxon, 1999–2004; Our Right to Read, 2004–06; Nuffield Foundn, 2009–12. Patron, Oxford Youth Works, 2007–. FCGI 2014. Hon. FIA 2001. Hon. Fellow: Queen Mary, Univ. of London, 2004; Swansea Inst. of HE, 2004; St Hugh's Coll., Oxford, 2012. Hon. DSc City, 2002; DUniv Open, 2015. *Publications:* The Reform of Social Security, 1984; The Economics of Social Security, 1989; Pensions Policy in the UK: an economic analysis, 1994; The Tiger That Isn't: seeing through a world of numbers, 2007; contrib. articles on taxation, public spending and economics of public policy. *Address:* Nuffield College, Oxford OX1 1NF.

DILWORTH, Prof. Jonathan Robin, DPhil, DSc; FRSC; Professor of Chemistry, University of Oxford, 1998–2009, now Emeritus; Fellow of St Anne's College, Oxford, 1997–2009; *b* 20 Aug. 1944; *s* of Robert Arnold Dilworth and Jean Marion Dilworth; *m* 1971, Nicola Jane Still; two *d*. *Educ:* Jesus Coll., Oxford (BA 1967, MA 1972); Univ. of Sussex (DPhil 1970; DSc 1983). FRSC 1984. AFRC Unit of Nitrogen Fixation, 1967–85; Prof. of Chemistry, Univ. of Essex, 1985–97. *Publications:* some 300 papers and review articles in internat. chemistry jls. *Recreations:* tennis, badminton, golf. *Address:* The Croft, Newland Close, Eynsham, Oxon OX29 4LE. *T:* (01865) 884102.

di MAMBRO, Louise; Registrar of the Supreme Court of the United Kingdom, since 2009, and of the Privy Council, since 2011; *b* Trowbridge, Wilts, 14 Sept. 1953; *d* of Rolland Gaer and Joan Gaer; *m* 1978, David di Mambro; one *s*. *Educ:* Trowbridge Girls High Sch.; King's Coll. London (LLB Hons). Called to the Bar, Middle Temple, 1976; Treasury Solicitor's Dept, 1977–80; Lord Chancellor's Dept, 1980–98; a Dep. Master, Court of Appeal, 1998–2008; Dep. Hd, Judicial Office, H of L, 2008–09. *Publications:* (Gen. Ed.) The Civil Court Practice, 1999–; (Gen. Ed.) Butterworths Civil Court Precedents, 1999–; (contrib. ed.) Atkin's Court Forms, 2004–; (consulting and contrib. ed.) The Caribbean Civil Court Practice, 2008–; (contrib. ed.) Butterworths Costs Service, 2009–. *Recreations:* opera, shopping, avoiding gardening. *Address:* Judicial Committee of the Privy Council, Parliament Square, SW1P 3PD. *T:* (020) 7960 1985, *Fax:* (020) 7960 1901. *E:* louise.dimambro@supremecourt.uk.

DIMAS, Stavros; a Vice President, New Democracy Party, Greece, since 2010 (Secretary General, 1995–2000); *b* 30 April 1941. *Educ:* Univ. of Athens; NY Univ. (LLM). Sullivan & Cromwell, law firm, NY, 1969–70; lawyer, Internat. Finance Corp., World Bank, 1970–75; Dep. Gov., Hellenic Industrial Develt Bank, 1975–77. MP (New Democracy), Greece, 1977–2004; Dep. Minister of Econ. Co-ordination, 1977–80; Minister: of Trade, 1980–81; of Agriculture, 1989–90; of Industry, Energy and Technol., 1990–91; of Foreign Affairs, 2011–12. Mem., Eur. Commn, 2004–10. *Address:* c/o New Democracy Party, 340 Syggrou Avenue, Kalithea, 176 73 Athens, Greece.

DIMBLEBY, David; broadcaster; Chairman, Dimbleby & Sons Ltd, 1986–2001 (Managing Director, 1966–86); President, Dimbleby Cancer Care (formerly Richard Dimbleby Cancer Fund), since 2012 (Trustee and Chairman, 1966–2012); *b* 28 Oct. 1938; *e s* of (Frederick) Richard and Dilys Dimbleby; *m* 1st, 1967, Josceline Rose Gaskell (*see* J. R. Dimbleby) (marr. diss. 2000); one *s* two *d*; 2nd, 2000, Belinda Giles; one *s*. *Educ:* Glengorse Sch.; Charterhouse; Christ Church, Oxford (MA); Univs of Paris and Perugia. News Reporter, BBC Bristol, 1960–61; Presenter and Interviewer on network programmes on: religion (Quest), science for children (What's New?), politics (In My Opinion), Top of the Form, etc, 1961–63; Reporter, BBC2 (Enquiry), and Dir films, incl.: Ku-Klux-Klan, The Forgotten Million, Cyprus: Thin Blue Line, 1964–65; Special Correspondent CBS News, New York; documentary film (Texas-England) and film reports for '60 minutes', 1966–68; Reporter, BBC1 (Panorama), 1967–69; Presenter, BBC1 (24 Hours), 1969–72; Yesterday's Men, 1971; Chm., The Dimbleby Talk-In, 1971–74; films for Reporter at Large, 1973; Presenter: BBC 1 (Panorama), 1974–77, 1980–82, 1989–94; (People and Power), 1982–83; (This Week, Next Week), 1984–86; Chm., BBC Question Time, 1994–; Election Campaign Report, 1974; BBC Election and Results programmes, 1979, 1983, 1987, 1992, 1997, 2001, 2005, 2010, 2015; moderator for BBC Leaders' Debate, 2010 (Diamond Jubilee Broadcast Journalist Award, Political Studies Assoc.); Presenter, BBC 1 (US Presidential Elections), 1984, 1988, 1992, 1996, 2000, 2004, 2008, 2012; The People's Coronation, 2013; film series: The White Tribe of Africa, 1979 (RTS Supreme Documentary Award); An Ocean Apart, 1988; The Struggle for South Africa, 1990 (Emmy Award, 1991; Golden Nymph Award, 1991); David Dimbleby's India, 1997; Mandela: The Living Legend, 2003; A Picture of Britain, 2005 (TV Arts/Documentary Prog. Award, TRIC, 2006); How We Built Britain, 2007; Seven Ages of Britain, 2010; Britain and the Sea, 2013; live commentary on many public occasions including: State Opening of Parliament, Trooping the Colour, Remembrance Service at the Cenotaph; Lord Olivier Meml Service, 1989 (RTS Outside Broadcasts Award); funerals of Diana, Princess of Wales, 1997 (RTS Live Event Award) and of Her Majesty the Queen Mother, 2002; funeral of Baroness Thatcher, Coronation Anniv. Service, Westminster Abbey, funeral and meml progs in SA for Nelson Mandela, 2013; meml service for Nelson Mandela, Westminster Abbey, 2014. Richard Dimbleby Award, BAFTA, 1998; TRIC Special Award, 2006; Media Soc. Award, 2006; Lifetime Achievement Award, RTS, 2011. *Publications:* An Ocean Apart (with David Reynolds), 1988; A Picture of Britain, 2005; How We Built Britain, 2007; Seven Ages of Britain, 2010. *Address:* 3 Carlisle Place, SW1P 1NP.

See also J. Dimbleby.

DIMBLEBY, Jonathan; freelance broadcaster, journalist and author; *b* 31 July 1944; *s* of Richard and Dilys Dimbleby; *m* 1st, 1968, Bel Mooney, *qv* (marr. diss. 2006); one *s* one *d*; 2nd, 2007, Jessica Ray; two *d*. *Educ:* University Coll. London (BA Hons Philosophy). TV and Radio Reporter, BBC Bristol, 1969–70; BBC Radio, World at One, 1970–71; for Thames TV: This Week, 1972–78, 1986–88; TV Eye, 1979; Jonathan Dimbleby in South America, 1979; documentary series, Witness (Editor), 1986–88; for Yorkshire TV: series, Jonathan Dimbleby in Evidence: The Police, 1980; The Bomb, 1980; The Eagle and the Bear, 1981; The Cold War Game, 1982; The American Dream, 1984; Four Years On—The Bomb, 1984; First Tuesday (Associate Editor/Presenter), 1982–86; for TV-am: Jonathan Dimbleby on Sunday (Presenter/Editor), 1985–86; for BBC TV: On the Record, 1988–93; Election Call, 1992; documentary series, The Last Governor (presenter/producer), 1997; series, Russia: A Journey with Jonathan Dimbleby (writer/presenter), 2008; An African Journey (writer/presenter), 2010; A South American Journey (writer/presenter), 2011; The Road to El Alamein—Churchill's Desert Campaign (writer/presenter), 2012; for Central TV: Charles: the private man, the public role (documentary), 1994; for LWT: Jonathan Dimbleby, 1995–2005; for ITV: anchor, Gen. Election coverage, 1997, 2001, 2005; An Ethiopian Journey (writer/producer/dir), 1998; A Kosovo Journey (writer/presenter), 2000; Heseltine—A Life in the Political Jungle (writer/presenter), 2000; for Teachers TV: The Big Debate (series), 2006–08; Presenter, BBC Radio 4: Any Questions?, 1987–; Any Answers, 1989–2012; The Candidate, 1998. Pres., Soil Assoc., 1997–2008; Pres., CPRE, 1992–97; President: VSO, 1999–2012; RSPB, 2001–03; Bath Fests Trust, 2003–06 (Chm., 1996–2003); Chairman: Susan Chilcott Scholarship, 2007–09; Index on Censorship, 2008–13; Trustee: Dimbleby Cancer Care (formerly Richard Dimbleby Cancer Fund), 1966– (Chair, 2013–); Forum for the Future, 1995–2005. SFTA Richard Dimbleby Award, for most outstanding contribution to factual TV, 1974. *Publications:* Richard Dimbleby, 1975; The Palestinians, 1979; The Prince of Wales: a biography, 1994; The Last Governor, 1997; Russia: a journey to the heart of a land and its people, 2008; Destiny in the Desert: the road to El Alamein - the battle that turned the tide, 2012. *Recreations:* music, sailing, tennis. *Address:* c/o David Higham Associates Ltd, 7th Floor, Waverley House, 7–12 Noel Street, W1F 8GQ.

DIMBLEBY, Josceline Rose; writer; *b* 1 Feb. 1943; *d* of late Thomas Josceline Gaskell and Barbara Montagu-Pollock; *m* 1967, David Dimbleby, *qv* (marr. diss. 2000); one *s* two *d*. *Educ:* Cranborne Chase Sch., Dorset; Guildhall School of Music. Contributor, Daily Mail, 1976–78; cookery writer for Sainsbury's, 1978–98; Cookery Editor, Sunday Telegraph, 1982–97. Contributor: Food Prog., BBC Radio; Masterchef, BBC TV. André Simon Award, 1979; Glenfiddich Prize for Cookery Writer of Year, 1993. Talks at literary festivals and other events. *Publications:* A Taste of Dreams, 1976, 3rd edn 1984; Party Pieces, 1977; Josceline Dimbleby's Book of Puddings, Desserts and Savouries, 1979, 2nd edn 1983; Favourite Food, 1983, 2nd edn 1984; Josceline Dimbleby's Complete Cookbook, 1997; Josceline Dimbleby's Cooking Course, 1999; Josceline Dimbleby's Almost Vegetarian Cookbook, 1999; A Profound Secret: May Gaskell, her daughter Amy, and Edward Burne-Jones, 2004, US edn as May and Amy, 2005; Orchards in the Oasis: travels, food and memories, 2010 (Kate Whiteman Award, Guild of Food Writers, 2011); (for Sainsbury's): Cooking for Christmas, 1978; Family Meat and Fish Cookery, 1979; Cooking with Herbs and Spices, 1979; Curries and Oriental Cookery, 1980; Salads for all Seasons, 1981; Marvellous Meals with Mince, 1982, rev. edn 2012; Festive Food, 1982; Sweet Dreams, 1983; First Impressions, 1984; The Josceline Dimbleby Collection, 1984; Main Attractions, 1985; A Traveller's Tastes, 1986; The Josceline Dimbleby Christmas Book, 1987; The Josceline Dimbleby Book of Entertaining, 1988; The Essential Josceline Dimbleby, 1989; The Cook's Companion, 1991; The Almost Vegetarian Cookbook, 1994; The Christmas Book, 1994; contribs to magazines and newspapers. *Recreations:* singing, travel, photography. *Address:* c/o Lucas Alexander Whitley, 14 Vernon Street, W14 0RJ.

DIMERY, Bridget Maeve; *see* Phillipson, B. M.

DIMITROV, Konstantin Stefanov; Ambassador of Bulgaria to the Court of St James's, since 2012; *b* Sofia, Bulgaria, 28 Jan. 1957; *m* Nadya; one *d*. *Educ:* Univ. of Sofia (Masters degree in English and German Langs and Lit. 1984). Lectr in English Lang. and Anglo-American Studies, Technical Univ., Sofia, 1988–92; expert, Western Europe and N America Dept, Min. of Foreign Affairs, Bulgaria, 1992–94; Third Sec., Washington, 1994–95; expert, Information Dept, Min. of Foreign Affairs, 1995–97; Hd, Policy Planning and Coordination Dept, 1997, NATO, WEU and Security Issues Dept, 1997–98, Min. of Foreign Affairs; Dep. Minister of Foreign Affairs, 1998–2000; Hd, Mission to NATO and WEU and Ambassador to Belgium and Luxembourg, 2000–02; Dir, Inst. of Euro-Atlantic Security, Sofia, 2002–09. MP (Democrats for Strong Bulgaria), 2005–09; MEP, 2007; Dep. Foreign Minister for European Affairs, 2009–12. *Address:* Embassy of Bulgaria, 186–188 Queen's Gate, SW7 5HL. *T:* (020) 7584 9400, *Fax:* (020) 7584 4948. *E:* ambass.office@bulgarianembassy.org.uk. *Club:* Travellers.

DIMMOCK, Peter, CVO 1968; OBE 1961; Chairman, Zenith Entertainment (formerly Television Enterprise and Asset Management) plc, 1991–2000; *e s* of late Frederick Dimmock OBE, and Paula Dimmock (*née* Hudd); *m* 1st, 1960, Mary Freya, (Polly) (*d* 1987), *e d* of late Hon. Mr Justice Elwes, OBE, TD; three *d*; 2nd, 1990, Christabel Rosamund, *e d* of Sir John Bagge, 6th Bt, ED, DL and *widow* of James Hinton Scott. *Educ:* Dulwich Coll.; France. TA RAF pilot, instr, and Air Ministry Staff Officer, 1939–45. After demobilisation became Press Association correspondent; joined BBC as Television Outside Broadcasts Producer and commentator, 1946; produced both studio and outside broadcasts, ranging from documentaries to sporting, theatrical and public events; has produced or commentated on more than 500 television relays, including Olympic Games 1948, Boat Race 1949, first international television relay, from Calais, 1950, King George VI's Funeral, Windsor, 1952. Produced and directed television outside broadcast of the Coronation Service from Westminster Abbey, 1953; first TV State Opening of Parliament, 1958; first TV Grand National, 1960; TV for Princess Margaret's Wedding, 1960. Created BBC Sportsview Unit and introduced new television programme Sportsview, 1954, regular presenter of this live weekly network programme, 1954–64; Gen. Manager and Head of Outside Broadcasts, BBC TV, 1954–72; responsible for Liaison between BBC and Royal Family, 1963–77; Gen. Manager, BBC Enterprises, 1972–77; Vice-Pres., ABC Worldwide Sales and Marketing TV Sports, 1978–86; Vice-Pres. and Consultant, ABC Video Enterprises Div., Capital Cities. ABC Inc., NY, 1984–91; Dir, Entertainment and Sports Cable Network, 1984–90. Chm. Sports Cttee and Adviser, European Broadcasting Union, 1959–72. Mem., Greater London and SE Sports Council, 1972–77; Chm., Sports Develt Panel, 1976–77. FRTS 1978 (Hall of Fame, 1996). Freeman, City of London, 1977. *Publications:* Sportsview Annuals, 1954–65; Sports in View, 1964; (contrib.) The BBC Book of Royal Memories, 1990. *Recreations:* flying, winter sports, golf. *Address:* Exbury House, Upton Grey, Hants RG25 2SG. *Clubs:* Garrick, Boodle's, Royal Air Force; Berkshire Golf; St Enedoc Golf; New York Athletic.

DIMOND, Paul Stephen, CMG 2005; HM Diplomatic Service, retired; Outplacement Adviser, Foreign and Commonwealth Office, since 2006; Deputy Chairman, DAKS Simpson Group plc and DAKS Ltd, since 2007; *b* 30 Dec. 1944; *yr s* of late Cyril James Dimond and Dorothy Mabel Louisa Hobbs (*née* Knight); *m* 1965, Carolyn Susan Davis-Mees, *er d* of late Dennis Charles Mees and of Eileen Lilian (*née* Barratt); two *s*. *Educ:* St Olave's and St Saviour's Grammar Sch. for Boys, Bermondsey. British Bakeries Ltd, 1962–63; FO, 1963–65; Diplomatic Service Admin, 1965–66; Japanese lang. student, Tokyo, 1966–68; Vice-Consul (Commercial), 1968–70, Consul (Commercial), 1970–72, Osaka; Second Sec. (Commercial) Tokyo, 1972–73; seconded to Dept of Trade as assistant to Special Advr on Japanese Mkt BOTB, 1973–75; FCO, 1975–76; First Secretary: (Economic), Stockholm, 1977–80; FCO 1980–81; (Commercial), Tokyo, 1981–86; FCO, 1986–88; seconded to Smiths Industries plc as Strategic Marketing Advr, Smiths Industries Med. Systems, 1988–89; Commercial Counsellor, Tokyo, 1989–93; Dep. Hd of Mission, The Hague, 1994–97; Consul-Gen., Los Angeles, 1997–2001; Ambassador to the Philippines, 2002–04. Director: Intralink Ltd, 2005–; Baillie Gifford Japan Trust plc, 2006–; Westminster Gardens Ltd, 2006– (Chm., 2007–10) Man. Dir, H. O. Kammann GmbH, 2009–13. Fund Develt Officer, British Neurological Res Trust, 2005–11; Sen. Advr, Think London, 2005–10. Sec., First Anglo-Mongolian Round Table, Ulaan Baatar, 1987; Chm., FriendsPhilippines, 2006–. Member: BAFTA, 2002–; London Reg. Cttee, RSA, 2005–11; Central Council, ROSL, 2006–12. Mem. Council Japan Soc., 2005–11 (Vice Chm., 2008–11); Dir, Anglo-Netherlands Soc., 2010–. Governor British Sch. in the Netherlands, 1994–97; British Film Office, LA, 1998–2000. Chm., Torch Trophy Trust, 2013–; Bond Street Mgt Gp, 2014–. FRSA 1980; FCIL (FIL 1988); FCIM 1989–2015. *Recreations:* the arts, vintage Batsfords, city walking. *Clubs:* Travellers, Royal Over-Seas League.

di MONTEZEMOLO, Luca Cordero; Chairman, Alitalia, since 2015; *b* Bologna, 1947. *Educ:* Univ. of Rome (Law degree); Columbia Univ., NY (Internat. Commercial Law) Worked with Chiomenti law firm, Rome; with Bergreen & Bergreen, NY, until 1973; Asst to Enzo Ferrari and Team Manager, Maranello racing team, 1973–77 (won 2 Formula 1 world drivers' championships, 1975 and 1977); Sen. Vice Pres., Ext. Relns, Fiat Gp, 1977–81; Chief Executive Officer: ITEDI SpA (holding co. for Fiat Gp publishing activities), 1981–83 Cinzano Internat. SpA, 1984–86; Dir, Organizing Cttee, 1990 Italian World Cup Football Championship, 1986–90; CEO, RCS Video and Mem. Bd of Dirs, TFI, 1990–91; CEO 1991–2006, Chm., 1991–2014, Ferrari SpA; Chm. and CEO, Maserati SpA, 1997–2005 Chairman: Confindustria, 2004–08; Fiat SpA, 2004–10. Member Board: PPR; Tod's Merloni Elettrodomestici; Le Monde. Chm., Telethon, 2009–. Former President Industrialists of Modena; FIEG (Italian Newspaper Publishers Assoc.); President: Bologna Internat. Trade Fair; Libera Università Internazionale degli Studi Sociali, 2004–10; Vice Pres. UNICE. Hon. Dr Mech. Engrg Modena. Cavaliere del Lavoro (Italy); Legion d'Honneur (France), 2005. *Address:* Alitalia, Piazza Almerico da Schio 3, 00054 Fiumicino, Italy.

DINEEN, Peter Brodrick K.; *see* Kerr-Dineen.

DINENAGE, Caroline; MP (C) Gosport, since 2010; Parliamentary Under-Secretary of State, Department for Education and Ministry of Justice, since 2015; *b* Portsmouth, 28 Oct. 1971; *d* of Fred Dinenage, MBE and Beverley Dinenage; *m* 2014, (John) Mark Lancaster, *qv*; two *s* by a previous marriage. *Educ:* Univ. of Wales, Swansea (BA Hons English and Politics) Dir, Dinenage Ltd, 1996–. Mem. (C) Winchester CC, 1998–2003. Contested (C) Portsmouth S, 2005. PPS to Rt Hon. Nicola Morgan, 2014–15. Member: Sci. and Technol. Select Cttee 2012–13; BIS Select Cttee, 2012–15; Vice Chairman: (RN), All-Party Parly Gp for Armed Forces, 2010–14; Associate Parly Gp for Manufg, 2012–; Chairman: All-Party Parly Gp on Local Growth, 2012–14; All-Party Parly Gp on Maths and Numeracy, 2014–. *Address:* House of Commons, SW1A 0AA. *T:* (020) 7219 7078. *E:* caroline.dinenage.mp@parliament.uk.

DINES, Rev. Griff; *see* Dines, Rev. P. J. G.

DINES, Peter Munn, CBE 1991; Secretary, School Examinations and Assessment Council, 1988–91; *b* 29 Aug. 1929; *e s* of Victor Edward Dines and Muriel Eleanor Dines (*née* Turner); *m* 1952, Kathleen Elisabeth Jones (*d* 2008); two *s* one *d*. *Educ:* Palmer's Sch., Grays, Essex; Imperial Coll. London (ARCS; BSc 1st cl. 1949); Inst. of Education, London (PGCE 1950); Bristol Univ. (MEd 1968). RAF, 1950–53. Teaching maths, 1953–69; Headmaster, Cramlington High Sch., 1969–76; Jt Sec., Schools Council, 1976–78; Headmaster, Sir John Leman High Sch., Beccles, 1978–80; Examinations Officer, Schools Council, 1980–83; Dep. Chief Exec., 1983–87, Chief Exec., 1988, Secondary Examinations Council. Educn Consultant, British Council, Swaziland, 1993 and Pakistan, 1994. Mem., Schools Broadcasting Council, later Educn Broadcasting Council, 1982–91; occasional broadcaster on radio and TV. *Recreations:* sailing, esp. on W coast of Scotland; walking. *Address:* 39 Hollis Court, Castle Howard Road, Malton, N Yorks YO17 7AD.

See also Rev. P. J. G. Dines.

DINES, Rev. (Philip Joseph) Griff, PhD; Partner, McDougall Dines LLP, since 2005; Director, Barrio San Pedro Ltd, since 2008; *b* 22 June 1959; *s* of Peter Munn Dines, *qv* and Kathleen Elisabeth Dines; *m* 1st, 1987, Dr Margaret Owen (marr. diss. 2006); two *d*; 2nd, 2009, Rev. Sally-Anne McDougall. *Educ:* Royal Grammar Sch., Newcastle upon Tyne; University Coll. London (BScEng 1980); Clare Coll., Cambridge (PhD 1984); Westcott House, Cambridge; Univ. of Manchester (MA Theol 1993); City of Bath Coll. (Cert. English Lang. Teaching to Adults 2011); Bishop Grosseteste Univ. (PGCE 2013). Ordained deacon, 1986, priest, 1987; Curate: St Mary, Northolt, 1986–89; St Paul, Withington, 1989–91; Vicar, St Martin, Wythenshawe, 1991–98, and Priest-in-charge, St Francis, Newall Green, 1995–98;

Provost and Rector, St Mary's Cathedral, Glasgow, 1998–2005. Business Manager and Associate, Macdonald Associates Consultancy, 2005–09; Dir, Systems Leadership Consulting Ltd, 2009–11. Founder Mem., Unicorn Grocery Co-op., Manchester, 1996. Mem., Iona Community, 1999–2008. *Recreations:* travelling hopefully, exploring the boundaries, troglodytic living. *Address:* Flat 2, 13A Minster Yard, Lincoln LN2 1PW. *E:* griff@dines.org. *Club:* Castle Hill (Lincoln).

DINEVOR; *see* Dynevor.

DINGEMANS, Hon. Sir James (Michael), Kt 2013; **Hon. Mr Justice Dingemans;** a Judge of the High Court of Justice, Queen's Bench Division, since 2013; *b* 25 July 1964; *s* of Rear-Adm. Peter George Valentin Dingemans, *qv*; *m* 1991, Janet Griffiths; one *s* two *d*. *Educ:* Mansfield Coll., Oxford (Rugby Union blue, 1985; BA Jurisprudence 1986). Called to the Bar, Inner Temple, 1987; QC 2002; a Recorder, 2002–13; a Dep. High Ct Judge, 2010–13. Leading Counsel to Hutton Inquiry, 2003. Mem., Exec. Cttee, Commonwealth Lawyers' Assoc., 2002–13; Chm., Internat. Cttee, Bar Council, 2009–11 (Vice-Chm., Internat. Relations Cttee, 2006–08). Judicial Mem., Adv. Panel, Rugby Football League, 2005–10; Judicial Officer, RFU, 2013–. *Recreations:* Rugby, sailing, cricket. *Address:* Royal Courts of Justice, Strand, WC2A 2LL. *Clubs:* Broadhalfpenny Brigands Cricket; Bar Yacht.

DINGEMANS, Rear-Adm. Peter George Valentin, CB 1990; DSO 1982; Director, Sussex Innovation Centre Management Ltd, 2004–10; Governor, Queen Victoria Hospital Foundation Trust, 2005–10; *b* 31 July 1935; *s* of late Dr George Albert and Marjorie Dingemans; *m* 1961, Faith Vivien Bristow; three *s*. *Educ:* Brighton College. Entered RN 1953; served HM Ships Vanguard, Superb, Ark Royal, 1953–57; qualified Torpedo Anti Submarine specialist, 1961; Comd, HMS Maxton, 1967; RAF Staff Course, 1968; Directorate of Naval Plans, 1971–73; Comd, HMS Berwick, HMS Lowestoft, 1973–74; Staff Asst, Chief of Defence Staff, 1974–76; Captain, Fishery Protection, 1977–78; rcds, 1979; Comd HMS Intrepid, 1980–83 (incl. service South Atlantic, 1982); Commodore, Amphibious Warfare, 1983–85; Flag Officer Gibraltar, 1985–87; COS to C-in-C Fleet, 1987–90, retd. Director: Administration, Argosy Asset Management PLC, 1990–91; Ivory and Sime, 1991–92; Hd, Benefits Payroll and Insurances, Slaughter and May, 1992–2001; Strategic Advr, St Dunstan's, 2001–05. President: Royal Naval Assoc., Horsham, 1994–2011; British Legion, Cowfold, 1994–2011; Assoc. of Old Brightonians, 1995–97. Mem. Council, Sussex Univ., 1999–2005; Mem. Bd, Brighton Coll., 2001–06 (Mem. Council, 1998–2001). Trustee, Brighton Coll. Scholarship Trust Fund, 1999–2009. FCMI (FBIM 1990). Freeman, City of London, 1984; Liveryman, Coach Makers and Coach Harness Makers Co., 1984. *Recreation:* family and friends. *Address:* c/o Lloyds Bank, Steyning, Sussex BN44 3ZA. *Club:* Royal Naval of 1765 and 1785 (Trustee, 1995–2006, Chm. Trustees, 1996–2006).

See also Hon. Sir J. M. Dingemans.

DINGEMANS, Simon Paul; Executive Director and Chief Financial Officer, GlaxoSmithKline plc, since 2011; *b* Shoreham-by-Sea, 26 April 1963; *s* of Norman Dingemans and Patricia Dingemans; *m* 1994, Elizabeth, (Liz), Hawkins; one *s* two *d*. *Educ:* Kent Coll., Canterbury; Christ Church, Oxford (BA Hons Geog.; MA). S. G. Warburg & Co. Ltd, 1985–95; Goldman Sachs, 1995–2010; a Man. Dir, 1998–2010, Partner, 2000–10, Goldman Sachs Internat. *Recreations:* theatre, running, triathlon. *Address:* GlaxoSmithKline plc, 980 Great West Road, Brentford, Middx TW8 9GS. *Club:* Royal Automobile.

DINGLE, David Keith, CBE 2009; Chairman, Carnival UK, since 2014 (Chief Executive Officer, 2007–14); *b* Fareham, Hants, 11 Feb. 1957; *s* of Keith Dingle and Joy Dingle; *m* 1990, Lovie Tan; two *s*. *Educ:* Portsmouth Grammar Sch.; Jesus Coll., Cambridge (BA Classics 1978; MA 1981). Joined P&O, 1978; Mktg Dir, 1988–98, Commercial Dir, 1998–2000, P&O Cruises; Man. Dir, P&O Princess Cruises UK, later Carnival UK, 2000–07. Pres., UK Chamber of Shipping, 2007–08. Chm., Eur. Cruise Council, 2007–10. Younger Brother, Trinity House, 2008–. Hon. DBA Plymouth, 2012. *Recreations:* family, ski-ing, travel, opera, ballet, music, history. *Address:* Carnival UK, Carnival House, 100 Harbour Parade, Southampton, Hants SO15 1ST. *E:* david.dingle@carnivalukgroup.com. *Club:* Royal Automobile.

DINGLE, John Thomas, PhD, DSc; President, Hughes Hall, Cambridge, 1993–98 (Hon. Fellow, 1998); *b* 27 Oct. 1927; *s* of Thomas Henry and Violet Nora Dingle; *m* 1953, Dorothy Vernon Parsons; two *s*. *Educ:* King Edward Sch., Bath; London Univ. (BSc, DSc); Clare Coll., Cambridge (PhD). Royal National Hosp. for Rheumatic Diseases, Bath, 1951–59; Research Fellowship, Strangeways Research Laboratory, Cambridge, 1959–61; MRC External Staff, 1961–79; Strangeways Research Laboratory: Head of Tissue Physiology Dept, 1966; Dep. Dir, 1970–79; Dir, 1979–93; Fellow, Corpus Christi Coll., Cambridge, 1968–93 (Life Fellow, 1998); Bursar of Leckhampton, 1972–80, Warden, 1980–86. Co-Dir, Rheumatism Res. Unit, Addenbrooke's Hosp., 1997–2001. Visiting Professor: of Biochemistry, Royal Free Hosp. Med. Sch., 1975–78; of Rheumatology, New York Univ., 1977. Chm., British Connective Tissue Soc., 1980–87. Chm. Editorial Bd, Biochemical Jl, 1975–82. Pres., Cambridge Univ. RFC, 1990–2002 (Treas., 1982–90). Heberden Orator and Medalist, 1978; American Orthopaedic Assoc. Steindler Award, 1980. *Publications:* communications to learned jls. *Recreations:* Rugby football (playing member, Bath, Bristol, Somerset RFCs, 1943–57), sailing. *Address:* Hughes Hall, Cambridge CB1 2EW; Corpus Christi College, Cambridge CB2 1RH; Middle Watch, Mount Boone Hill, Dartmouth, Devon TQ6 9NZ. *Club:* Hawks (Cambridge).

See also T. T. Dingle.

DINGLE, Timothy Thomas; Chief Executive Officer, London School of Excellence, since 2011; *b* 9 June 1959; *s* of Dr John Thomas Dingle, *qv*. *Educ:* Perse Sch., Cambridge; UEA (BSc 1980; PGCE 1981); Univ. of Westminster (MBA 1998); London Sch. of Mediation (Mediator, 2007). Mill Hill School: Head of Biology Dept, 1985–90; Housemaster, 1990–95; Dep. Head, 1995–99; Headmaster, Royal Grammar Sch., High Wycombe, 1999–2006. Exec. Trng Consultant, Unitas, 2011–. Member: Cttee, Nat. Grammar Schs Assoc., 1999–2006; Conservative Party Task Force on Grammar Schs, 2000–06. Nat. Selector (Rugby), 1998; Member: Middlesex RFU, 1985–2001; London and SE RFU, 1990; Cttee, England Schs RFU, 2002 (Chm., 16 Gp, 2003). Governor: Highcrest Community Sch., 2001; Davenies Prep. Sch., 2001. Winston Churchill Fellow, 2002. Mem., BNI (Central London). MInstD. *Publications:* Cartilage Disc Degeneration, 1981; European Dimension in Schools, 1994; Hidden By Order, 2010; Revision and Learning, 2011; Pitch and Grow Rich, 2012; Want More Clients, 2013; multiple articles on digital learning, mobile learning and the highs of business. *Recreations:* Rugby, cricket, painting, sailing, travel, poetry, stand up comedy (comedy club owner, 2009–). *Address:* HMS President (1918), Victoria Embankment, EC4Y 0HJ. *Clubs:* MCC, National Liberal.

DINGWALL, Baron; *see* Lucas of Crudwell and Dingwall.

DINHAM, Martin John, CBE 1997; independent consultant, since 2010; Director General, International, Department for International Development, 2008–10; *b* 9 July 1950; *s* of late John A. Dinham and Gwenyth Dinham; *m* 1980, Jannie Sanderson; one *s* one *d*. *Educ:* Haberdashers' Aske's Sch., Elstree; Christ's Coll., Cambridge (BA Mod. Langs 1971). Joined ODM, later ODA, as exec. officer, 1974; Asst Private Sec. to successive Ministers for Overseas Develt, 1978–79; Desk Officer for Zambia and Malawi, ODA, 1979–81; on secondment to World Bank, Washington, as Asst to UK Exec. Dir, 1981–83; Hd, Personnel Br., ODA, 1983–85; Private Sec. to successive Ministers for Overseas Develt, 1985–87; Hd, SE Asia Develt Div., ODA, Bangkok, 1988–92; on secondment to Hong Kong Govt as Advr to Governor, 1992–97; Department for International Development: Hd of Personnel and Principal Estabt Officer, 1997–2000; Dir, Asia and the Pacific, then Asia, 2000–04; Dir, Europe, Middle E and Americas, subseq. Europe, Middle E, Americas, Central and E Asia, 2005–07; Dir, UN, Conflict and Humanitarian Div., 2007; Acting Dir Gen., Corporate Performance, 2007–08. Interim Chm. Bd, Global Fund to Fight AIDS, Tuberculosis and Malaria, 2011; Chairman: Sightsavers Internat., 2015– (Trustee, 2010–; Vice-Chm., 2012–15); Bd, Internat. HIV/AIDS Alliance, 2015– (Trustee, 2010–; Chm., Finance and Audit Cttee, 2010–15); Trustee, BBC Media Action, 2013–. *Recreations:* theatre, cinema, planning holidays, rock concerts for the over 50s. *E:* martin.dinham@btinternet.com.

DINKIN, Anthony David; QC 1991; barrister; a Recorder of the Crown Court, since 1989; *b* 2 Aug. 1944; *s* of late Hyman Dinkin and Mary (*née* Hine); *m* 1968, Derina Tanya (*née* Green), MBE. *Educ:* Henry Thornton Grammar Sch., Clapham; Coll. of Estate Management, London (BSc (Est. Man.)). Called to the Bar, Lincoln's Inn, 1968, Bencher, 2003. Legal Mem., Lands Tribunal, 1998–; Tribunal Judge (formerly Mem., Mental Health Review Tribunal), 2000–. Examr in Law, Reading Univ., 1985–93; Ext. Examr, City Univ., 2003–. Pres., Estate Mgt Club, 1998–99. *Recreations:* gardening, theatre, music, travel. *Address:* Cornerstone Barristers, 2–3 Gray's Inn Square, WC1R 5JH. *T:* (020) 7242 4986. *E:* ad.qc@cornerstonebarristers.com.

DINNAGE, Calista Jane; *see* Probyn, C. J.

DINSMORE, David; Chief Operating Officer, News UK, since 2015; *b* Glasgow, 2 Sept. 1968; *m* Jillian; one *s* one *d*. *Educ:* Strathallan Sch. Joined The Sun, 1990: Night Ed., 2004–06; Scottish Ed., 2006–10; Gen. Manager, News Internat. Scotland, 2010; Man. Ed., The Sun; Dir of Ops, News Internat., 2012–13; Ed., The Sun, 2013–15. *Recreation:* cycling. *Address:* News UK & Ireland Ltd, 1 London Bridge Street, SE1 9GF.

DINWIDDY, Bruce Harry, CMG 2003; HM Diplomatic Service, retired; Governor, Cayman Islands, 2002–05; *b* 1 Feb. 1946; *s* of late Thomas Lutwyche Dinwiddy and Ruth Dinwiddy (*née* Abbott); *m* 1974, Emma Victoria Llewellyn, *d* of Sir David Treharne Llewellyn and of Joan Anne Llewellyn (*née* Williams), OBE; one *s* one *d*. *Educ:* Winchester Coll.; New Coll., Oxford (MA). Economist, Govt of Swaziland (ODI Nuffield Fellow), 1967–70; Res. Officer, ODI, 1970–73; HM Diplomatic Service, 1973; First Sec., UK Deleg. to MBFR talks, Vienna, 1975–77; FCO, 1977–81; Head of Chancery, Cairo, 1981–83; FCO, 1983–86; Asst Sec., Cabinet Office, 1986–88; Counsellor, Bonn, 1989–91; Dep. High Comr, Ottawa, 1992–95; Head of African Dept (Southern), FCO, 1995–98; Comr (non-resident), British Indian Ocean Territory, 1996–98; High Comr, Tanzania, 1998–2001; on secondment to Standard Chartered Bank, 2001–02. Mem. Council, and Chm., Wider Caribbean Wkg Gp, UK Overseas Territories Conservation Forum, 2006–15; Consultant, UK Trade and Investment, 2007–09. *Publications:* Promoting African Enterprise, 1974. *Recreations:* golf (captained Oxford *v* Cambridge, 1967), swimming, music, theatre, travel. *Address:* 8 Connaught Avenue, East Sheen, SW14 7RH. *Clubs:* Vincent's (Oxford); Royal Wimbledon Golf.

DIOUF, Jacques, PhD; Director-General, 1994–2011, Special Envoy for the Sahel and the Horn of Africa, since 2014, United Nations Food and Agriculture Organization; *b* St Louis, Senegal, 1 Aug. 1938; *m* 1963, Aïssatou Seye; one *s* four *d*. *Educ:* Ecole nationale d'agriculture, Grignon-Paris (BSc Agric.); Ecole nationale d'application d'agronomie tropicale, Nogent-Paris, (MSc Trop. Agronomy); Panthéon-Sorbonne, Paris (PhD Agricl Econs). Dir, European Office and Agricl Prog. of Mkting Bd, Dakar/Paris, 1963–64; Executive Secretary: African Groundnut Council, Lagos, 1965–71; W Africa Rice Develt Assoc., Liberia, 1971–77; Sec. of State for Sci. and Technol., Senegal, 1978–83; MP Senegambian Confedn, 1983–84: Chm. and Elected Sec., Foreign Relns Cttee, 1983–84; Chm., Friendship Parly Gp, Senegal-UK, 1983–84; Advr to Pres. and Regl Dir, Internat. Develt Res. Centre, Ottawa, 1984–85; Central Bank for W African States, Dakar: Sec.-Gen., 1985–90; Special Advr to Governor, 1990–91; Ambassador, Senegal Perm. Mission to UN, 1991–93. Commander: Legion of Honour (France), 1998 (Officer 1978); Order of Agricl Merit (Canada), 1995; Grand Comdr, Order of Star of Africa (Liberia), 1977; Grand Cross: Order of Merit in Agric., Fisheries and Food (Spain), 1996; Order of May for Merit (Argentina), 1998; Order of Solidarity (Cuba), 1998. *Publications:* contrib. to learned jls.

DI ROLLO, Simon Ronald; QC (Scot.) 2002; *b* 28 Oct. 1961; *s* of late Rino Di Rollo and of Teresa Di Rollo (*née* de Marco); *m* 1990, Alison Margaret Lafferty (marr. diss. 2012); one *s* one *d*; *m* 2013, Kim Louise Leslie; one *s*. *Educ:* Holy Cross Acad., Edinburgh; Scotus Acad., Edinburgh; Univ. of Edinburgh (LLB Hons 1983; DLP 1984). Admitted: solicitor, 1986; to Faculty of Advocates, 1987; Advocate Depute, 1997. Lectr (pt-time) in Civil Procedure, Univ. of Edinburgh, 1999–2012. Mem., Sheriff Court Rules Council, 2002–11. Curator, Advocates Liby, 2009–13. *Recreations:* Italian, walking, food and drink. *Address:* Advocates' Library, Parliament House, Edinburgh EH1 1RF. *E:* sdirollo@advocates.org.uk; 2 West Savile Road, Edinburgh EH16 5NG. *Club:* Scottish Arts (Edinburgh).

DI RUPO, Elio; Prime Minister of Belgium, 2011–14; Mayor of Mons, since 2014; *b* Morlanwelz, Belgium, 18 July 1951. *Educ:* Univ. of Mons-Hainaut (DSc). Lectr, Univ. of Leeds. Mem., Mons Municipal Council, 1982–85, 1988–2000 (Alderman, 1986); Mayor of Mons, 2000–05, 2007. MP (Soc.) Mons-Borinage, 1987–89; MEP, 1989; Senator, 1991; Minister of Educn, 1992–94, of Audiovisual Policy, 1993–94; Dep. Prime Minister and Minister for Communications and Public Undertakings, 1994; Dep. Prime Minister and Minister for Economics and Telecommunications, and for Foreign Trade, 1998–99; Minister-Pres., Walloon Reg., 1999–2000, 2005–07; Minister of State, 2002–11; MP, 2003; Informateur, 2003; Préformateur, 2010–11; Formateur, 2011. Pres., Socialist Party, 1999–2011, 2014–; Vice Pres., Socialist Internat., 1999–. *Publications:* Le Progrès Partagé, 2003.

DISKI, Jenny, FRSL; writer, since 1984; *b* 8 July 1947; *d* of James Simmonds (*né* Israel Zimmerman) and Rene Simmonds (*née* Rachel Rayner); *m* 1st, 1976, Roger Diski (*né* Roger Marks) (marr. diss. 1993); 2nd, 2008, Ian Patterson. *Educ:* St Christopher's Sch., Letchworth (expelled); King Alfred Sch., London; Wandsworth Tech. Coll. (Cert. Proficiency for 16mm projection); UCL (BSc Anthropol. unfinished). Teacher: Freightliners Free Sch., 1972–73; Haggerston Comprehensive Sch., 1973–77; Islington 6th Form Centre, 1980–84. FRSL 1999. *Publications:* Nothing Natural, 1986; Rainforest, 1987; Like Mother, 1989; Then Again, 1990; Happily Ever After, 1991; Monkey's Uncle, 1994; The Vanishing Princess, 1995; The Dream Mistress, 1996; Skating to Antarctica, 1997; Don't, 1998; Only Human, 2000; Stranger on a Train, 2002; A View From the Bed, 2003; After These Things, 2004; On Trying to Keep Still, 2006; Apology for the Woman Writing, 2008; The Sixties, 2009; What I Don't Know About Animals, 2010. *Recreations:* taking baths, middle-distance staring, pain management. *Address:* c/o Peter Straus, Rogers, Coleridge and White, 20 Powis Mews, W11 1JN. *T:* (020) 7221 3717. *E:* peters@rcwlitagency.com. *W:* www.jennydiski.co.uk.

DISLEY, John Ivor, CBE 1979; Co-founder, and President, London Marathon Ltd, 1980–2011; President, London Marathon Charitable Trust, since 2011 (Chairman, 2006–11); *b* Corris, Merioneth, 20 Nov. 1928; *s* of Harold Disley and Marie Hughes; *m* 1957, Sylvia Cheeseman; two *d*. *Educ:* Oswestry High Sch.; Loughborough Coll. (Hon. DCL). Schoolmaster, Isleworth, 1951; Chief Instructor, CCPR Nat. Mountaineering Centre, 1955; Gen. Inspector of Educn, Surrey, 1958–71. Director: Ski Plan, 1971–75; Reebok, 1985–95. Member: Adv. Sports Council, 1964–71; Mountain Leadership Trng Bd, 1965–; Canal Adv. Bd, 1965–66; Internat. Orienteering Fedn, 1972–78; Countryside Commn, 1974–77; Water

Space Adv. Council, 1976–81; Royal Commn on Gambling, 1976–78. Vice-Chm., Sports Council, 1974–82; Chairman: Nat. Jogging Assoc., 1978–80; The Olympians, 1996–2002; President: Friends St Julitta's Church, 1990–; Snowdonia Soc., 2001–. Mem., British athletics team, 1950–59; Brit. record holder steeplechase, 1950–56; Welsh mile record holder, 1952–57; bronze medal, Olympics, Helsinki, 1952; Sportsman of the Year, 1955; Athlete of the Year, 1955; Welsh Sports Hall of Fame, 1998. Hon. Fellow, Bangor Univ., 2009. DUniv Loughborough, 2009. *Publications:* Tackle Climbing, 1959; Young Athletes Companion, 1961; Orienteering, 1966; Expedition Guide for Duke of Edinburgh's Award Scheme, 1965; Your Way with Map and Compass, 1971. *Recreations:* orienteering, mountain activities. *Address:* Hampton House, Upper Sunbury Road, Hampton, Middx TW12 2DW. *T:* (020) 8979 1707. *Clubs:* Alpine, Climbers'; Southern Navigators; London Athletic.

See also S. J. Cleobury.

DISMORE, Andrew; Member (Lab) Barnet and Camden, London Assembly, Greater London Authority, since 2012; *b* 2 Sept. 1954; *s* of late Ian and of Brenda Dismore. *Educ:* Warwick Univ. (LLB 1972); LSE, London Univ. (LLM 1976). Educn Asst, GMWU, 1976–78; Partner: Robin Thompson & Partners, Solicitors, 1978–95; Russell Jones & Walker, Solicitors, 1995–2003, consultant, 2003–09. Mem. (Lab), Westminster CC, 1982–97 (Leader, Labour Gp, 1990–97). MP (Lab) Hendon, 1997–2010; contested (Lab) same seat, 2010, 2015. Chm., Jt Cttee on Human Rights, H of C, 2005–10; Mem., Standards and Privileges Cttee, 2001–10. Chair, Economy Cttee, 2012–13, Mem., Econ., Envmt and Health Cttees, 2013–, London Assembly, GLA. Mem., London Fire and Emergency Planning Authy, 2012–13 and 2014–. *Recreations:* gardening, travel, Greece, Greek culture. *Address:* Greater London Authority, City Hall, Queen's Walk, SE1 2AA.

DISS, Eileen, (Mrs Raymond Everett), RDI 1978; freelance designer for theatre, film and television, since 1959; *b* 13 May 1931; *d* of Thomas and Winifred Diss; *m* 1953, Raymond Everett; two *s* one *d*. *Educ:* Ilford County High Sch. for Girls; Central Sch. of Art and Design. FRSA. BBC Television design, 1952–59. *Television* series and plays: Maigret, 1962–63; The Tea Party, 1964; Up the Junction, 1965; Somerset Maugham, 1969; Uncle Vanya, 1970; The Duchess of Malfi, and Candide, 1972; The Importance of Being Earnest, and Pygmalion, 1973; Caesar and Cleopatra, 1974; Moll Flanders, 1975; Ghosts, and The Winslow Boy, 1976; You Never Can Tell, 1977; The Rear Column, Hedda Gabler, 1980; The Potting Shed, 1981; Porterhouse Blue, 1987; Behaving Badly, 1989; Jeeves & Wooster, 1989, 1990, and 1992; Best of Friends, 1991; Head Over Heels, 1993; Love on a Branch Line, 1993; A Dance to the Music of Time, 1997; television opera: The Merry Widow, 1968; Tales of Hoffmann, 1969; Die Fledermaus, 1971; Falstaff, 1972; The Yeomen of the Guard, 1974; television films: Cider with Rosie, 1971; Robinson Crusoe, 1974; Longitude, 1999; Dead Gorgeous, 2002. *Theatre:* Exiles, 1969; Butley, 1971; The Caretaker, 1972, 1991, 2009 and 2010; Otherwise Engaged, 1975; The Apple-cart, 1977; The Rear Column, The Homecoming, 1978; The Hothouse, 1980; Translations, Quartermaine's Terms, Incident at Tulse Hill, 1981; Rocket to the Moon, 1982; The Communication Cord, 1983; The Common Pursuit, 1984; Other Places, The Seagull, Sweet Bird of Youth, 1985; Circe and Bravo, 1986; The Deep Blue Sea, 1988; Veterans Day, The Mikado, Steel Magnolias, 1989; Burn This, 1990; The Philanthropist, 1991; Private Lives, A Month in the Country, 1992; Oleanna, 1993; Pinter Fest., Dublin, 1994; Cell Mates, 1995; Taking Sides, The Hothouse, 1995; Twelve Angry Men, 1996; Ashes to Ashes, 1996; Life Support, 1997; A Letter of Resignation, 1997; The Heiress, 1997; Arcadia, 1999; The Late Middle Classes, 1999; The Room, and Celebration, 2000; Port Authority, and The Homecoming, 2001; The Dwarfs, 2002; The Old Masters, 2004; Endgame, 2006; National Theatre: Blithe Spirit, 1976; The Philanderer, 1978; Close of Play, When We Are Married, 1979; Watch on the Rhine, 1980; The Caretaker, 1980; Measure for Measure, 1981; The Trojan War Will Not Take Place, 1983; Landscape, 1994; No Man's Land, 2001. *Films:* Joseph Losey's A Doll's House, 1972; Sweet William, 1978; Harold Pinter's Betrayal, 1982; Secret Places, 1984; 84 Charing Cross Road, 1986; A Handful of Dust, 1988; August, 1994. Television Design Award, 1962, 1965, 1974, 1992 and 2000, Lifetime Achievement Award, 2006, BAFTA; RTS Lifetime Achievement award, 2002. *Recreations:* music, cinema. *Address:* 4 Gloucester Walk, W8 4HZ. *T:* (020) 7937 8794.

DISSANAIKE, Prof. Gishan Romesh, PhD; financial economist; Adam Smith Professor of Corporate Governance (formerly Robert Monks Professor of Corporate Governance), University of Cambridge, since 2010; *b* Colombo, Sri Lanka, 17 Feb. 1963; *s* of late Prof. George Alexander Dissanaike, PhD and of Vijayalakshmi Indranee Senanayake Atapattu; *m* 1988, Varnini Padmika; two *s*. *Educ:* Trinity Coll., Kandy; Univ. of Peradeniya (BA 1st Cl. Hons 1986); Trinity Coll., Cambridge (MPhil; PhD 1994). Exec. trainee, Banque Indosuez, 1987–88; Lectr in Econs, Univ. of Durham, 1993–94; University of Cambridge: Lectr in Financial Econs, 1994–99; Sen. Lectr in Finance, 1999–2004; Reader in Finance, 2004–09; Actg Dir, Studies for Mgt Studies, Queens' Coll., 1995–97, St John's Coll., 2006–07, Corpus Christi Coll., 2007–08, 2011; Director: Studies for Mgt Studies, Trinity Coll., 1996–; MPhil in Finance prog., 2001–12; Hd, Finance and Accounting Subject Gp, Judge Business Sch., 2010–11; Mem. Council, Sch. of Technol., 2014–; Member: Faculty Bd of Business and Mgt, 2000–02, 2005–; Univ. Finance Cttee, 2006–10; Bd, Cambridge Endowment for Res. in Finance, 2011–; Cambridge Finance, 2011–; Manager: Sir Evelyn De Rothschild Fund for Finance, 2010–; Pembroke Vis. Prof. of Internat. Finance Fund, 2010–; Keynes, J. M. Fellowships in Financial Economics, 2011. Mem., Investment Cttee, Comtrust Equity Fund, 2011–13; Member, Organising Committee: Corp. Governance: An Internat. Review Conf. on Nat. Governance Bundles, 2012; 40th Eur. Finance Assoc. Conf., 2013. Vis. Associate Prof., Cornell Univ., 2004. Ext. Res. Studentship, Trinity Coll., Cambridge, 1989–92; ORS Award, CVCP, 1989–92; ICAEW Acad. Fellow, 1995–2001; ESRC Res. Fellow, 1995–99; Finance Ed., Jl Asia Business Studies, 2007–10. Non-exec. Dir, Internat. Centre for Ethnic Studies, 2008–09. Co-chair, Eur. Financial Mgt Assoc. Symposium on Corporate Governance, 2009; Mem., Exec. Cttee, Emerging Mkts Finance and Econ. Conf., Istanbul, 2007. Ryde Gold Medal, Trinity Coll., Kandy, 1982; P. D. Khan Gold Medal and Arts Faculty Schol., Univ. of Peradeniya, 1986; Iddo Sarnat Prize, Jl Banking and Finance and Eur. Finance Assoc., 1995; Pilkington Prize, Univ. of Cambridge, 2002. *Publications:* contribs to learned jls and books on finance and econs. *Recreations:* travel, Ceylon history, genealogy. *Address:* Judge Business School, University of Cambridge, Trumpington Street, Cambridge CB2 1AG.

DITLHABI OLIPHANT, Tuelonyana Rosemary; High Commissioner of Botswana to Zambia, also accredited to Tanzania, Uganda and Democratic Republic of the Congo, since 2005; *b* 13 Sept. 1954; *d* of late Matlhape Ditlhabi and of Tsetsele Ditlhabi; *m* 1986, Clement S. Oliphant; one *s*. *Educ:* Univ. of Botswana (BA Admin 1977); Pennsylvania State Univ. (MPA 1981). Joined Public Service, Botswana, 1977: Asst, Sen. and Principal Admin. Officer, Min. of Mineral Resources and Water Affairs, 1977–85; transferred to Dept of Foreign Affairs, 1985: Counsellor: Washington, 1985–88; NY, 1988–90; High Comr, Namibia and Ambassador, Angola, 1990–96; Doyenne of Diplomatic Corps and African Gp, 1992–96; High Comr, UK, 1996–98; Dep. Perm. Sec., 1998–99, Perm. Sec. for Pol Affairs, 1999–2005; Dean of Diplomatic Corps and Africa Gp; Chair, Commonwealth Gp, Zambia. *Recreations:* music, reading, swimming, squash. *Address:* Botswana High Commission, PO Box 31910, Lusaka, Zambia. *E:* toliphant@gov.bw, tuelonyanaoliphant1@gmail.com, tuelonyana@yahoo.co.uk.

DITTNER, Patricia Ann; *see* Troop, P. A.

DIVALL, Prof. Colin Michael, PhD; Professor of Railway Studies, University of York, 1995–2015, now Emeritus; *b* 8 Nov. 1957; *s* of late (Ernest) Gordon Divall and Gwendoline Florence Divall; partner, Prof. Karen Hunt. *Educ:* Univ. of Bristol (BSc Physics and Phil. 1979); Victoria Univ. of Manchester (MSc Structure and Orgn of Sci. and Technol. 1980; PhD 1985). Ops mgt, BR, 1984–85; Res. Associate, Centre for Hist. of Sci., Technol. and Medicine, Univ. of Manchester, 1986–88; Sen. Lectr in Social Studies of Technol., Manchester Metropolitan Univ., 1989–94; Hd, Inst. Railway Studies and Transport Hist., Nat. Railway Mus. and Univ. of York, 1995–2014. Vice Pres., Internat. Assoc. for Hist. of Transport, Traffic and Mobility, 2008–13; Pres., Histl Model Railway Soc., 2015–. *Publications:* (with S. F. Johnston) Scaling Up: the Institution of Chemical Engineers and the rise of a new profession, 2000; (with A. Scott) Making Histories in Transport Museums, 2001; (ed with W. Bond) Suburbanizing the Masses: public transport and urban development in historical perspective, 2003; (ed with R. Roth) From Rail to Road and Back Again?: a century of transport competition and interdependency, 2015; (ed) Cultural Histories of Sociabilities, Spaces and Mobilities, 2015. *Recreations:* observing the feline world, listening to jazz, building Wimborne Station at 1/76th scale. *Address:* Department of History University of York, Heslington, York YO10 5DD. *T:* (01904) 322981. *E:* colin.divall@york.ac.uk.

DIX, Prof. Gerald Bennett, RIBA; Lever Professor of Civic Design, University of Liverpool, 1975–88; Professor Emeritus and Hon. Senior Fellow, Liverpool University, since 1988; Hon. Senior Research Fellow, Chinese Research Academy of Environmental Sciences, since 1989; *b* 12 Jan. 1926; *s* of late Cyril Dix and Mabel Winifred (*née* Bennett); *m* 1st, 1956 (marr. diss.); two *s*; 2nd, 1963, Lois Nichols; one *d*. *Educ:* Altrincham Grammar Sch.; Univ. of Manchester (BA (Hons Arch.), DipTP (dist.)); Harvard Univ. (MLA). Studio Asst, 1950–51, Asst Lectr in Town and Country Planning, 1951–53, Manchester Univ.; Asst Architect, 1954; Chief Architect-Planner, Addis Ababa, and chief asst to Sir Patrick Abercrombie, 1954–56; Planning Officer, Singapore, 1957–59; Acting Planning Adviser, 1959; Sen. Research Fellow, Univ. of Science and Technol., Ghana, 1959–63; UN Planning Mission to Ghana, 1962; Planner, later Sen. Planner, BRS/ODM, 1963–65 (adv. missions to W Indies, W Africa, Aden, Bechuanaland, Swaziland, Cyprus); Nottingham University: Lectr, 1966–68; Sen. Lectr, 1968–70; Prof. of Planning, and Dir, Inst. of Planning Studies, 1970–75; Liverpool University: Chm., Fac. of Social and Environmental Studies, 1983–84; Pro Vice-Chancellor, 1984–87. Dir, Cyprus Planning Project, 1967–71; adv. visits on planning educn, to Uganda 1971, Nigeria 1972, Sudan 1975, Mexico 1978, Egypt 1980; UK Mem., Adv. Panel on planning Canal towns, Egypt, 1974, and Western Desert, 1975; Jt Dir, Alexandria Comprehensive Master Plan Project, 1980–86. Member: Professional Literature Cttee, RIBA, 1966–80, 1981–88 (Chm. 1975–80); Library Management Cttee, 1969–72, 1975–80; Historic Areas Adv. Cttee, English Heritage, 1986–88. Vice-Pres., World Soc. for Ekistics, 1975–79, Pres., 1987–90. Mem., Editl Adv. Bd, Ekistics (journal), 1972–; Chm., Bd of Management, Town Planning Rev., 1976–88; (Founder) Editor, Third World Planning Rev., 1978–90. FRTPI (resigned 2001); FRSA 1977. Hon. DEng Dong-A Univ., Korea, 1995. *Publications:* ed, C. A. Doxiadis, Ecology and Ekistics, 1977, Boulder, Colo, 1978, Brisbane, 1978; numerous planning reports to govts in various parts of world; articles and reviews in Town Planning Rev., Third World Planning Rev., Ekistics, RIBA Jl, Arch. Rev. *Recreations:* photography, listening to music, travel, cooking, reading. *Address:* 49 Gaveston Gardens, Deddington, Banbury, Oxon OX15 0NX. *T:* (01869) 336215. *Club:* Athenæum.

DIX, (Walter) Malcolm (Hutton); President, Sport Newcastle (formerly Newcastle Sports Development Trust), since 2014 (Secretary, since 2000); *b* 10 May 1942; *s* of Charles Walter Dix and Rita May Dix; *m* 1964, Mary Johanne Nilsen; one *s* four *d*. *Educ:* Ascham House Sch., Gosforth; St Bees Sch., Cumbria; Coll. of Commerce, Newcastle upon Tyne (Business Studies). Drawing office, Walter Dix & Co., Newcastle, 1958–62; tech. sales rep., William Dickinson, Newcastle, 1962–68; Sales Manager, British Rototherm Ltd, London and S Wales, 1968–71; Chm. and Jt Man. Dir, Walter Dix & Co., Newcastle, 1971–97; Jt Founder, Magpie Gp, 1988. Chairman: Newcastle Sports Council, 1977–92; Tyne & Wear Sports Council, 1980–86. Executive Member: NE Fedn of Sport and Recreation, 2000–08 (Dir, 2008–); NE Sport, 2000–08. Chm., Beamish Develt Trust, 1995–99; Dir, Friends of Beamish Mus., 1999–. Chm., Tyne Th. and Opera Hse Preservation Trust, 2002–14 (Hon. Vice Pres., 2014). Trustee: McCrory Foundn, 2005–10; Newcastle Eagles Community Foundn, 2005–; NE Circus Develt Trust. Chm., NE Br., St Beghian Soc., 1992–2008 (Pres., 2006–08). Mem. Council for Northumbria, OStJ, 2004–10. Consultant, Special Events Cttee, Variety Club of GB, 2000–14. Chairman: Newcastle Supporters Assoc., 1978–82; Newcastle Gosforth Rugby Club, 1989–92 (Sen. Vice-Pres., 1992–95). Outstanding Contribution to Sport award, Newcastle upon Tyne Sports Council, 1992. *Recreations:* walking, reading and writing, music, all types (managed pop groups in the 1960s), driving, practically all sport. *Address:* 41 Ingram Drive, Chapel Park, Newcastle upon Tyne NE5 1TG. *T:* (0191) 267 6342. *E:* Dixysport5@aol.com. *Clubs:* Newcastle United Football (Hon. Life Vice-Pres., 1992); Newcastle Falcons Rugby; Jesmond Lawn Tennis.

DIXEY, John, OBE 1976; Development Co-ordinator, Evening Standard Company, 1987–91; *b* 29 March 1926; *s* of John Dixey and Muriel Doris Dixey; *m* 1948, Pauline Seaden; one *s* one *d*. *Educ:* Battersea Grammar Sch. Served Royal Marines and Royal Fusiliers, 1944–47. Press Telegraphist, Yorkshire Post and Glasgow Herald, 1948–59; Asst to Gen. Sec., Nat. Union of Press Telegraphists, 1959; Labour Officer, Newspaper Soc., 1959–63; Labour Adviser, Thomson Organisation Ltd, 1963–64; Asst Gen. Manager, Liverpool Daily Post & Echo, 1964–67; Executive Dir, Times Newspapers, 1967–74; Special Adviser to Man. Dir, Thomson Org., 1974; Dir, Newspaper Publishers Assoc. Ltd, 1975–76; Employment Affairs Advr, IPA, 1977–79; Sec., Assoc. of Midland Advertising Agencies, 1977–79; Production Dir and Bd Mem., The Guardian, 1979–84; Asst Man. Dir, Mirror Gp Newspapers, 1985; Newspaper Consultant, 1986. Chm., Advertising Assoc. Trade Union Liaison Group, 1975–84; Mem., TUC New Daily Newspaper Advisory Group, 1982–83. Ward-Perkins Vis. Fellow, Pembroke Coll., Oxford, 1978. Mem., Printing and Publishing Industry Trng Bd, 1975–76; Governor, London Coll. of Printing, 1975–76. *Recreations:* cooking, photography. *Address:* 1 Hornor Close, Norwich NR2 2LY. *T:* (01603) 505656.

DIXIT, Prof. Avinash Kamalakar; John J. F. Sherrerd '52 Professor of Economics, Princeton University, USA, 1989–2010, now Emeritus (Professor of Economics, 1981–89); *b* 8 June 1944; *s* of Kamalakar Ramchandra Dixit and Kusum Dixit. *Educ:* Bombay Univ. (BSc); Cambridge Univ. (BA, MA); Massachusetts Inst. of Technology (PhD). Acting Asst Professor, Univ. of California, Berkeley, 1968–69; Lord Thomson of Fleet Fellow and Tutor in Economics, Balliol Coll., Oxford, 1970–74; Professor of Economics, Univ. of Warwick, 1974–80. Guggenheim Fellowship, 1991–92. Pres., Amer. Economic Assoc., 2008 (Vice-Pres., 2002). Fellow: Econometric Society, 1977 (Pres., 2001); Amer. Acad. of Arts and Scis, 1992; US Nat. Acad. of Scis, 2005; Amer. Philosophical Soc., 2010. Corresp. FBA 2005. Co-Editor, Bell Journal of Economics, 1981–83. *Publications:* Optimization in Economic Theory, 1976; The Theory of Equilibrium Growth, 1976; (with Victor Norman) Theory of International Trade, 1980; (with Barry Nalebuff) Thinking Strategically, 1991; (with Robert S. Pindyck) Investment Under Uncertainty, 1994; The Making of Economic Policy: a transaction-cost politics perspective, 1996; (with Susan Skeath) Games of Strategy, 1999; Lawlessness and Economics, 2004; (with Barry Nalebuff) Art of Strategy, 2009; Microeconomics: a very short introduction, 2014; several articles in professional jls. *Recreations:* reading, listening to music, travel. *Address:* Department of Economics, Princeton University, Princeton, NJ 08544–1021, USA. *E:* dixitak@princeton.edu.

DIXON, family name of **Barons Dixon** and **Glentoran**.

DIXON, Baron *cr* 1997 (Life Peer), of Jarrow in the co. of Tyne and Wear; **Donald Dixon;** PC 1996; DL; *b* 6 March 1929; *s* of late Christopher Albert Dixon and Jane Dixon; *m* Doreen Morad; one *s* one *d*. *Educ:* Ellison Street Elementary School, Jarrow. Shipyard Worker, 1947–74; Branch Sec., GMWU, 1974–79. Councillor, South Tyneside MDC, 1963–81. MP (Lab) Jarrow, 1979–97. An Opposition Whip, 1984–96, Dep. Chief Opposition Whip, 1987–96. Mem. Select Cttee on H of C Services; Chm., PLP Shipbuilding Gp. Freeman of: Jarrow, 1972; S Tyneside, 1998. DL Tyne and Wear, 1997. *Recreations:* football, reading. *Address:* 1 Hillcrest, Jarrow NE32 4DP. *T:* (0191) 897635. *Clubs:* Jarrow Labour, Ex Servicemen's (Jarrow); Hastings (Hebburn).

DIXON, Prof. Adrian Kendal, MD; FRCP, FRCR, FRCS, FMedSci; Professor of Radiology, University of Cambridge, 1994–2009, now Emeritus; Master of Peterhouse, Cambridge, 2008–June 2016 (Fellow, since 1986); Hon. Consultant Radiologist, Addenbrooke's Hospital, Cambridge, 1979–2014; *b* 5 Feb. 1948; *s* of late Kendal Cartwright Dixon and Anne Sybil (*née* Darley); *m* 1979, Anne Hazel Lucas; two *s* one *d*. *Educ:* Uppingham; King's Coll., Cambridge; St Bartholomew's Hosp. Med. Coll., London; MD Cantab 1988. FRCR 1978; FRCP 1991; FRCS 2003. Medical posts in: St Bartholomew's Hosp., 1972–79; Gen. Hosp., Nottingham, 1973–75; Hosp. for Sick Children, Gt Ormond St, 1978; Lectr, Dept of Radiology, Univ. of Cambridge, 1979–94. Visiting Professor: Md and Washington, 1988; Dublin, 1991; Univ. of Otago, NZ, 1992; Stanford, 2002; Edmonton, 2007. Arnott Demonstrator, RCS, 1995; Skinner Lectr, RCR, 1996. Warden, RCR, 2002–06. FMedSci 1998. Hon. Fellow, Faculty of Radiology, RCSI, 1999 (Houghton Medal, 1999); Hon. FRANZCR 2001; Hon. FACR 2009; Hon. Member: Swedish Soc. of Radiology, 2001; Hungarian Soc. of Radiologists, 2002; Soc. Française de Radiologie, 2003; Swiss Radiology Soc., 2009; Spanish Radiol Soc., 2010; Radiol Soc. of N America, 2011; German Radiol Soc., 2015. Pres., Cambridge Univ. Golf Club, 2009–. Editor: Clinical Radiology, 1998–2002; European Radiology, 2007–13. Hon. MD: Cork, 2011; Ludwig Maximilians, Munich, 2013. Gold Medal, Eur. Soc. Radiol., 2014. *Publications:* Body CT, 1983; CT and MRI, Radiological Anatomy, 1991; Human Cross Sectional Anatomy, 1991, 2nd edn as Human Sectional Anatomy, 1999; (jtly) Diagnostic Radiology, 4th edn, 2002, 6th edn, 2014; papers on computed tomography, magnetic resonance imaging and radiological strategies. *Recreations:* family, golf. *Address:* Peterhouse, Cambridge CB2 1RD. *T:* (01223) 339066.

DIXON, Andrew; Director, Culture Creativity Place Ltd, since 2013; *b* Manchester; *s* of Geoff Dixon and Maureen Dixon; *m* 1988, Charlotte Kendall; one *s* one *d*. *Educ:* Univ. of Bradford (BSc Managerial Scis). Adminr and Youth Projects Dir, Major Road Theatre Co., 1981–84; County Arts Officer, Humberside CC, 1984–89; Northern Arts: Asst Dir, 1989–92; Dep. Dir, 1992–96; Chief Exec., 1997–2003; Exec. Dir, Arts Council England, 2003–05; Chief Executive: NewcastleGateshead Initiative, 2005–10; Creative Scotland, 2010–13. Prog. Dir, World Summit on Arts and Culture, 2006. Vis. Prof. in Cultural Policy, Univ. of Hull, 2014. Hon. DCL Northumbria, 2008. *Recreations:* ski-ing, vegetarian cooking, rock musician. *Address:* Culture Creativity Place Ltd, 12a Great Stuart Street, Edinburgh EH3 7TN.

DIXON, Andrew Michael G.; *see* Graham-Dixon.

DIXON, Barry, CBE 2007; QFSM 1999; DL; County Fire Officer and Chief Executive, Greater Manchester County Fire Service, 2002–09; *b* 5 Jan. 1951; *s* of Thomas Henry and Ruby Harriet Dixon; *m* 1976, Jill Ormrod; one *s* one *d*. *Educ:* Stand Grammar Sch. Joined Manchester City Fire Bde as jun. fireman, 1967; Gtr Manchester Fire Service, 1974; progressed through ranks; posts in Rochdale, Oldham and Bury; Asst Co. Fire Officer (Ops), 1995–2000; Dep. Co. Fire Officer, 2000–02. DL Gtr Manchester, 2008. *Recreations:* clay pigeon shooting, fishing, countryside in general.

DIXON, Dr Bernard, OBE 2000; science writer and consultant; *b* Darlington, 17 July 1938; *s* of late Ronald Dixon and Grace Peirson; *m* 1963, Margaret Helena Charlton (marr. diss. 1988); two *s* one *d*; partner, Kath Adams. *Educ:* Queen Elizabeth Grammar Sch., Darlington; King's Coll., Univ. of Durham; Univ. of Newcastle upon Tyne. BSc, PhD. Luccock Res. Fellow, 1961–64, Frank Schon Fellow, 1964–65, Univ. of Newcastle; Asst Editor, 1965–66, Dep. Editor, 1966–68, World Medicine; Editor, New Scientist, 1969–79; European Editor: The Scientist, 1986–89; Bio Technology, 1989–97; Amer. Soc. for Microbiol., 1997–; Member, Editorial Board: Biologist, 1988–2005; World Jl of Microbiology and Biotechnology, 1988–2002. Chm., Cttee, Assoc. of British Science Writers, 1971–72; Member: Soc. for General Microbiology, 1962–; Amer. Assoc. for Advancement of Sci., 1980–; CSS, 1982–91 (Vice-Chm., 1989–91); Soc. for Applied Microbiol. (formerly Applied Bacteriol.), 1989–; Amer. Soc. for Microbiol., 1995–; Council, BAAS, 1977–83 (Pres., Section X, 1979; Vice-Pres., Gen. Section, 1986–96); Bd, Edinburgh Internat. Science Fest., 1990–2003. Convenor, Eur. Fedn of Biotechnol. Task Gp on Public Perceptions of Biotechnol., 1996–. FRSB (FIBiol 1982); CBiol 1984. Hon. DSc Edinburgh, 1996. Charter Award, Inst. of Biol., 1999; Biochemical Soc. Award, 2002. *Publications:* (ed) Journeys in Belief, 1968; What is Science For?, 1973; Magnificent Microbes, 1976; Invisible Allies, 1976; Beyond the Magic Bullet, 1978; (with G. Holister) Ideas of Science, 1984; Health and the Human Body, 1986; Engineered Organisms in the Environment, 1986; Recombinant DNA: what's it all about, 1987; The Science of Science: changing the way we think, 1989; The Science of Science: changing the way we live, 1989; (ed) From Creation to Chaos: classic writings in science, 1989; (with A. L. W. F. Eddleston) Interferons in the Treatment of Chronic Virus Infections of the Liver, 1989; (with E. Millstone) Our Genetic Future: the science and ethics of genetic technology, 1992; Genetics and the Understanding of Life, 1993; Power Unseen: how microbes rule the world, 1994; Enzymes Make the World Go Round, 1994; Animalcules: the activities, impacts and investigators of microbes, 2009; *contributor to:* Animal Rights—A Symposium, 1979; The Book of Predictions, 1980; Development of Science Publishing in Europe, 1980; Medicine and Care, 1981; From Biology to Biotechnology, 1982; Encyclopædia Britannica, 15th edn, 1984; Encyclopædia Britannica Yearbook, 1986–2001; Inquiry into Life, 1986; The Domesday Project, 1986; Industrial Biotechnology in Europe: issues for public policy, 1986; Biotechnology Information, 1987; Future Earth, 1989; Harrap's Illustrated Dictionary of Science, 1989; Biotechnology—A Brave New World?, 1989; Soundings from BMJ columnists, 1993; Taking Sides: clashing views on controversial issues in health and society, 1993; Wider Application and Diffusion of Bioremediation Technologies, 1996; Biotechnology for Clean Industrial Products and Processes, 1998; numerous articles in scientific and general press on microbiology, and other scientific topics. *Recreations:* listening to Elgar, Mahler and Scottish traditional music, collecting old books. *Address:* 130 Cornwall Road, Ruislip Manor, Middlesex HA4 6AW. *T:* (01895) 632390.

DIXON, Catherine Helen; Chief Executive, Law Society of England and Wales, since 2015; *b* N Ferriby, 29 April 1966; *d* of late Kenneth Dixon and of Audrey Irene Dixon; *m* 2006, Sally Elizabeth Light, *qv*. *Educ:* Leeds Metropolitan Univ. (LLB Hons 1991); Coll. of Law; Open Univ. (MBA 2003). Admitted solicitor, 1994; Solicitor, Eversheds, 1997–99; Hd, Legal, 1999–2003, Commercial Dir, 2003–07, Bupa Care Services; Dir, Vancouver Coastal HA, 2007–08; Gen. Counsel and Co. Sec., NSPCC, 2009–12; Chief Exec., NHS Litigation Authy, 2012–15. Trustee, PDSA, 2010–. Army Officer, Royal Signals (TA), 1989–96, 2010–12, now RARO. *Recreation:* cycling. *Address:* Law Society of England and Wales, 113 Chancery Lane, WC2A 1PL. *T:* (020) 7320 5601. *E:* catherine.dixon@lawsociety.org.uk.

DIXON, Sir (David) Jeremy, Kt 2000; RIBA; architect in private practice; Principal, Dixon Jones Ltd (formerly Jeremy Dixon·Edward Jones), since 1991; *b* 31 May 1939; *s* of late Joseph Lawrence Dixon and Beryl Margaret Dixon (*née* Braund); *m* 1964, Fenella Mary Anne Clemens (separated 1990); one *s* two *d*; partner, Julia Somerville, *qv*. *Educ:* Merchant Taylors' School; Architectural Assoc. Sch. of Architecture (AA Dip. (Hons)). Principal: Jeremy Dixon, 1975–90 (with Fenella Dixon); Jeremy Dixon BDP, 1983–90. Work includes: international competitions, first prize: Northampton County Offices, 1973; Royal Opera House, 1983; Piazzale Roma, Venice, 1990; Chelsea Barracks, 2009; other competitions won: Tate Gallery Coffee Shop and Restaurant, 1984; Study Centre, Darwin Coll., Cambridge, 1988; Robert Gordon Univ. Residence, Aberdeen, 1991; Portsmouth Univ. Science Bldg, 1993; Nat. Portrait Gallery extension, 1994; Saïd Business Sch., Oxford, 1996; Magna Carta Building, Salisbury Cathedral, 2001; Panopticon, UCL, 2001; St Peter's Arcade, Liverpool, 2001; Kings Place Develt, 2002; Exhibition Road Project, 2004; other works: reconstruction of Tatlin Tower, 1971 and at RA, 2012; London housing, St Mark's Road, 1975; Compass Point, Docklands, 1989; Henry Moore Sculpture Inst., Leeds, 1988; Sainsbury's superstore, Plymouth, 1991; Regent Palace Development, 2005. Tutor: Architectural Assoc., 1974–83; RCA, 1979–81. Chm., RIBA Regl Awards Gp, 1991–. Exhibitions: Venice Biennale, 1980, 1991; Paris, 1981; Bordeaux Chateau, Paris, 1988. Trustee, Midsummer Music, 2012–; Patron, London Chamber Music Soc., 2012–. *Recreations:* walking in English landscape, contemporary sculpture and painting, music. *Address:* (office) 2–3 Hanover Yard, Noel Road, N1 8YA. *T:* (020) 7483 8888. *E:* jeremydixon@dixonjones.co.uk.

DIXON, Prof. Gordon Henry, OC 1993; PhD; FRS 1978; FRSC; Professor of Medical Biochemistry, 1974–94, now Emeritus, and Head of the Department, 1983–88, Faculty of Medicine, University of Calgary; *b* 25 March 1930; *s* of Walter James Dixon and Ruth Nightingale; *m* 1954, Sylvia Weir Gillen; three *s* one *d*. *Educ:* Cambs High Sch. for Boys; Trinity Coll., Cambridge (Open Schol. 1948; BA Hons, MA); Univ. of Toronto (PhD). FRSC 1970. Res. Asst Prof., Dept of Biochem., Univ. of Washington, Seattle, USA, 1954–58; Mem. staff, MRC Unit for res. in cell metabolism, Univ. of Oxford, 1958–59; Univ. of Toronto: Res. Associate, Connaught Med. Res. Lab., 1959–60; Associate Prof., Dept of Biochem., 1960–63; Prof., Dept of Biochem., Univ. of BC, Vancouver, 1963–72; Prof., Biochem. Group, Univ. of Sussex, 1972–74. Vis. Fellow Commoner, Trinity Coll., Cambridge, 1979–80. Mem. Exec., IUBMB (formerly IUB), 1988–94; President: Canadian Biochemical Soc., 1982–83; Pan-American Assoc. of Biochemical Socs, 1987–90 (Vice-Pres., 1984–87; Past Pres., 1990–93). Ayerst Award, Canadian Biochemistry Soc., 1966; Steacie Prize, 1966; Flavelle Medal, RSC, 1980; Izaak Walton Killam Meml Prize, 1991. Golden Jubilee Medal, 2002. *Publications:* over 200 pubns in learned jls, incl. Jl Biol Chem., Proc. Nat. Acad. Sci. (US), Nature, and Biochemistry. *Recreations:* hiking, reading, gardening. *Address:* 1866 St Anne Street, Victoria, BC V8R 5W1, Canada.

DIXON, (Henry) Joly, CMG 2004; Chairman: Fiscal Policy Panel, Jersey, since 2007; Fiscal Policy Panel, Guernsey, 2010–11; Special Adviser to Vice President of European Commission, attached to Task Force for Greece, since 2010; *b* 13 Jan. 1945; *s* of late Gervais Joly Dixon and Kay Dixon; *m* 1976, Mary Minch; three *s* two *d*. *Educ:* Shrewsbury Sch.; York Univ. Lecturer in: Econs and Stats, York Univ., 1970–72; Econs, Exeter Univ., 1972–74; European Commission, 1975–2003: Econ. Advr to Jacques Delors, 1987–92; Dir for Internat. Econ. and Financial Affairs, 1992–99; Dep. Special Rep. i/c econ. reconstruction and develt, UN Mission, Kosovo, on secondment, 1999–2001; Principal Advr, Directorate Gen. for Econ. and Financial Affairs, 2001–02; Special Advr to Pascal Lamy, EC, 2003–05; Statistics Comr, 2006–08; Sen. Advr, Office of Chief Economist, EBRD, 2007–; Special Advr to Olli Rehn, Vice Pres. of EC, 2011–. Associate, GPlus Europe, 2006–09. Chairman: Indirect Tax Policy Commn, Bosnia and Herzegovina, 2003–04; Governing Bd, Indirect Tax Policy Authority, Bosnia and Herzegovina, 2004–06; Strategic Adv. Bd for Intellectual Property Policy, 2008–10. Guest Scholar, Brookings Instn, Washington, 1980. Liveryman, Cordwainers' Co., 1969–. Fellow, Royal Statistical Soc., 2006. *Recreations:* gardening, photography. *Address:* 47 Clanricarde Gardens, W2 4JN. *E:* jdx@skynet.be.

DIXON, Dr Jennifer, CBE 2013; FFPH; Chief Executive, The Health Foundation, since 2013; Member, Board, Care Quality Commission, since 2013; *b* 25 April 1960; *m* 2002, John Simon Vorhaus; two *d*. *Educ:* Bristol Univ. (MB ChB); London Sch. of Hygiene and Tropical Medicine (MSc Public Health; PhD 2002). FFPH (FFPHM 1999). Harkness Fellow, Commonwealth Fund of NY, 1990–91; Sen. Registrar in Public Health and Hon. Lectr, LSHTM, 1991–95; Fellow, King's Fund Inst., 1995–98; Policy Advr to Chief Exec., NHS, 1998–2000; Dir of Policy, King's Fund, 2000–08; Chief Exec. (formerly Dir), Nuffield Trust, 2008–13. Member, Board: Audit Commn, 2004–12; Healthcare Commn, 2005–09. Visiting Professor: LSE, 2009–; Imperial Coll. Business Sch., 2009–; LSHTM, 2010–. Mem. Bd, Nat. Centre for Social Res., 2011–. Hon FRCP 2009. *Publications:* (with A. H. Harrison) The NHS: facing the future, 2000. *Recreations:* Russian literature, painting. *Address:* The Health Foundation, 90 Long Acre, WC2E 9RA.

DIXON, Sir Jeremy; *see* Dixon, Sir D. J.

DIXON, Joly; *see* Dixon, H. J.

DIXON, Jon Edmund, CMG 1975; Under Secretary, Ministry of Agriculture, Fisheries and Food, 1971–85; *b* 19 Nov. 1928; *e s* of Edmund Joseph Claude and Gwendoline Alice Dixon; *m* 1953, Betty Edith Stone; two *s* one *d* (and one *d* decd). *Educ:* St Paul's Sch., West Kensington; Peterhouse, Cambridge (Natural Sciences Tripos Part I and Part II (Physiology); MA). Asst Principal, Min. of Agric. and Fisheries, 1952; Private Sec. to successive Parliamentary Secretaries, 1955–58; Principal, 1958; Asst Sec., 1966; Under-Sec., 1971; Minister in UK Delegn, subseq. Office of Permanent Rep., to EEC, 1972–75. Founder, Music Publisher and Gen. Editor, JOED Music, 1988– (editing and publishing Renaissance polyphonic choral music). Recordings: Choral, Organ and String Music: a selection of works by Jon Dixon, 1970–85, 1986; Missa pro defunctis super Regina coeli à 8, 2001. *Publications:* Calico Pie (suite for vocal sextet), 1988; The Leuven Carols, 1988; The Pobble Who Has No Toes (4 part-songs), 1989; Missa pro defunctis super Regina coeli (for double choir), 1999; editions of Renaissance choral music by Aichinger, Animuccia, Arcadelt, Byrd, Clemens, Croce, Dering, Ferrabosco, Festa, A. Gabrieli, G. Gabrieli, Gombert, Guerrero, Hassler, Josquin, Lassus, de Monte, Morales, Mouton, Mundy, Palestrina, Philips, Hieronymus Praetorius, Schütz, Senfl, Sheppard, Taverner, Tallis, de Silva, Victoria (complete works), Walther, White and Willaert; contribs to Early Music News, Early Music Review, Musical Times. *Recreations:* singing, musical composition, oil painting, building harpsichords, gardening, walking.

DIXON, Sir Jonathan (Mark), 4th Bt *cr* 1919, of Astle, Chelford, Co. Chester; *b* 1 Sept. 1949; *s* of Captain Nigel Dixon, OBE, RN (*d* 1978), and of Margaret Josephine Dixon; *S* uncle, 1990; *m* 1978, Patricia Margaret, *d* of James Baird Smith; two *s* one *d*. *Educ:* Winchester Coll.; University Coll., Oxford (MA). *Recreation:* fishing. *Heir: s* Mark Edward Dixon, *b* 29 June 1982.

DIXON, Kenneth Herbert Morley, CBE 1996; DL; Chairman: Joseph Rowntree Foundation, 2001–04; Rowntree (formerly Rowntree Mackintosh) plc, 1981–89, retired; Vice-Chairman, Legal & General Group, 1986–94 (Director, 1984–94); Deputy Chairman, Bass, 1990–96 (Director, 1988–96); *b* 19 Aug. 1929; *yr s* of Arnold Morley Dixon and Mary Jolly; *m* 1955, Patricia Oldbury Whalley; two *s*. *Educ:* Cathedral Sch., Shanghai; Cranbrook Sch., Sydney, Australia; Manchester Univ. (BA(Econ) 1952); Harvard Business Sch. (AMP 1969). Lieut Royal Signals, 1947–49. Calico Printers Assoc., 1952–56; joined Rowntree &

Co. Ltd, 1956; Dir, 1970; Chm., UK Confectionery Div., 1973–78; Dep. Chm., 1978–81. Dir, Yorkshire-Tyne Tees (formerly Yorks) TV Hldgs, 1989–97; Mem., British Railways Bd, 1990–97. Member: Council, Incorporated Soc. of British Advertisers, 1971–79; Council, Cocoa, Chocolate and Confectionery Alliance, 1972–79; Council, Advertising Assoc., 1976–79; BIM Econ. and Social Affairs Cttee, 1980–84; Council, CBI, 1981–90 (Mem., Companies Cttee, 1979–84; Mem., Employment Policy Cttee, 1983–90); Governing Council, Business in the Community, 1983–90; Council, Food from Britain, 1986–89; Exec. Cttee, Food and Drink Fedn, 1986–89 (Mem. Council, 1986–87); Council for Industry and Higher Educn, 1986–97; Council, Nat. Forum for Management Educn & Develt, 1987–96; HEQC (Chm., Quality Audit Steering Council, 1993–97); Chm., Cttee of Univ. Chairmen, 1998–2000. Chm., Food Assoc., 1986. Trustee: York Civic Trust, 1996–2013; Joseph Rowntree Foundn, 1996–2004 (Dep. Chm., 1998); Nat. Centre for Early Music, 2010–. Treas., York Archaeol Trust, 1993–97. Mem. Council, York Univ., 1983–2001 (Chm., 1990–2001), Pro-Chancellor, 1987–2001; Mem. Adv. Gp, Business History Unit, LSE, 1981–2013 (Chm., 2000–10); Chm., Vis. Cttee, Open Univ., 1990–92. FRSA; CCMI. Member: Co. of Merchant Adventurers, 1981–; Co. of Merchant Taylors, 1981–. DL N Yorks, 1991. Morrell Fellow, Univ. of York, 2007. DUniv: York, 1993; Open, 1997. *Recreations:* reading, music, fell walking. *Address:* Joseph Rowntree Foundation, The Homestead, Water End, York YO30 6WP. *T:* (01904) 615901. *Club:* Reform.

DIXON, Sir Michael, Kt 2014; DPhil; Director, The Natural History Museum, since 2004; *b* 16 March 1956; *s* of late Walter Dixon and Sonia Ivy Dixon (*née* Doidge); *m* 1st, 1988, Richenda Milton-Thompson (marr. diss. 1999); one *s* one *d*; 2nd, 2001, Deborah Mary Reece (*née* McMahon); one *s*. *Educ:* Tiffin Boys' Sch., Kingston-upon-Thames; Imperial Coll., London (BSc; ARCS); Univ. of York (DPhil 1984). Sponsoring Ed., Pitman Publishing Ltd, 1980–83; Publisher, then Publishing Dir, John Wiley & Sons Ltd, 1983–96; Man. Dir, Thomson Sci. Europe, 1996–98; Gp Man. Dir, Sweet & Maxwell Ltd, 1998–99; Dir Gen., Zool Soc. of London, 2000–04. Chief Scientific Advr, 2006–07, Chm., Sci. and Res. Adv. Cttee, 2009–14, DCMS. Trustee: Internat. Trust for Zool Nomenclature, 2004–14 (Chm., 2008–14); WWF-UK, 2014–. Mem. Council, Royal Albert Hall, 2004–; Member of Court: Imperial Coll., London, 2005– (Chm., Res. Ethics Cttee, 2009–); Univ. of Reading, 2007–. Chm., Nat. Mus. Dirs Council (formerly Conf.), 2009–13. Gov., Powell-Cotton Mus., 2008–12. FCGI 2012. *Recreations:* natural history, photography, music. *Address:* The Natural History Museum, Cromwell Road, SW7 5BD. *Club:* Chelsea Arts.

DIXON, Michael David, OBE 2001; General Practitioner; Chairman, NHS Alliance, since 1998; *b* 12 May 1952; *s* of Anthony Neville Dixon and Hazel Dixon; *m* 1982, Joanna Withers-Lancashire; one *s* two *d*. *Educ:* Eton Coll.; Exeter Coll., Oxford (MA Hons 1973); Guy's Medical Sch. (MB BS 1979). LRCP 1979; DRCOG, MRCOG 1984; FRCGP 2001. House Surgeon, Royal Devon and Exeter Hosp., 1979; House Physician, Guy's Hosp., 1980; Exeter GP Vocational Trng Scheme, 1980–84; GP, College Surgery, Cullompton, 1984–. Chm. NHS Nat. Life Check Bd, 2007–10; Pres., 2012–14, Sen. Advr, 2014–, NHS Clinical Comrs. Med. Advr to the Prince of Wales, 2008–. Hon. Sen. Fellow, Sch. of Public Policy, Univ. of Birmingham, 2004–; Sen. Associate, 2005–, Sen. Advr, 2011–14, King's Fund; Hon. Sen. Lectr in Integrated Health, Peninsula Med. Sch., 2005–; Visiting Professor: Univ. of Westminster, 2006–; UCL, 2012–. Trustee, 2003–, Med. Dir, 2008–, Prince's Foundn for Integrated Health. Chm. Council, Coll. of Medicine, 2010–. Pres., Guild of Health Writers, 2010–13. *Publications:* (ed jtly) The Locality Commissioning Handbook, 1998; (ed with Kieran Sweeney) The Human Effect in Medicine, 2000; (ed with Kieran Sweeney) A Practical Guide to Primary Care Groups and Trusts, 2001; contrib. articles in all main med. jls. *Recreations:* fishing, gardening, writing, philosophy. *Address:* College Surgery Partnership, Culm Valley Integrated Centre for Health, Willand Road, Cullompton, Devon EX15 1FE. *T:* (01884) 831300. *Clubs:* Royal Society of Medicine, National Liberal.

DIXON, Sir Peter (John Bellett), Kt 2009; Chairman, Diabetes UK, since 2013; *b* 18 May 1945; *s* of Hugh and Mildred Dixon; *m* 1967, Judith Ann Duckworth; one *s* one *d* (and one *d* decd). *Educ:* Caterham Sch., Surrey; Corpus Christi Coll., Cambridge (MA); London Business Sch. (MSc). Asst Dir, Edward Bates & Sons Ltd, 1975–77; Managing Director: Metal Pretreatments Ltd, 1977–86; Turner Curzon Ltd, 1979–86; British Pepper & Spice Co. Ltd, 1981–83; Hd, Capital Markets, Den norske Bank, 1986–90; Chairman: Ketlon Ltd, 1991–93; Welpac PLC, 1994–95; Union Discount Ltd, 1997–2001; Manifest Voting Agency Ltd, 1998–2005. Chairman: Enfield and Haringey HA, 1998–2001; UCL Hosps NHS Foundn Trust (formerly NHS Trust), 2001–10; Office of Public Mgt, 2007–12; Colchester Hospital Univ. NHS Foundn Trust, 2009–10; Basildon and Thurrock Univ. Hosps, 2011–12; Pharmaceutical Services Negotiating Cttee, 2011–15; Barking, Havering and Redbridge Univ. Hosps, 2012–14; Anglia Ruskin Health Partnership, 2012–; Imperial Coll. Health Partners, 2014–. Lay Mem., Inf. Tribunal, 2003–12. Chm., Housing Corp., 2003–08; Dir, Quintain Estates and Develt plc, 2010–; Board Member: New Islington and Hackney Housing Assoc., 1976–98 (Chm., 1995–98); Focus Housing Gp, 1996–97; English Churches Housing Gp, 2000–01; London & Quadrant Housing Trust, 2001–03; Mem. Council, NHS Confedn, 1998–2008 (Trustee, 2002–08); Pres., English Rural Housing Assoc., 2009–. Mem., Broads Authy, 2010–. *Recreations:* sailing, mountains, music, theatre. *Address:* The Smea, Hickling, Norfolk NR12 0YL. *T:* (office) (020) 7226 2011. *E:* peterjbdixon@hotmail.com.

DIXON, Dr Philip Willis, FSA, FRHistS; Director, Philip Dixon Associates, archaeological consultancy, since 2003; Reader in Archaeology, University of Nottingham, 1996–2003; *b* 2 Jan. 1945; *s* of Dr C. Willis Dixon and Marjorie Dixon (*née* Harbron); *m* 1st, 1968, Doris Janet Davenport Sisson (marr. diss. 1973); 2nd, 1979, Patricia Borne (*d* 1987); 3rd, 2001, Jan White (*née* Greenwood). *Educ:* Tiffin Sch.; New Coll., Oxford (MA 1971; DPhil 1976). FSA 1977; FRHistS 1995. Lectr, 1972–81, Sen. Lectr, 1981–96, Nottingham Univ. Vis. Prof., Univ. of Aarhus, Denmark, 1997, 2006. Comr, Cathedrals Fabric Commn, 1996–2006. Sec., 1981–95, Pres., 1995–98, Council for British Archaeol.; Vice Pres., Royal Archaeol Inst., 2008–11. Director of excavations: Crickley Hill, Glos, 1969–96; Greenwich Palace, 1970–71; Richmond Palace, 1972, and other sites. Archaeologist: for Cathedrals of Ely, Lincoln, Southwell and Leicester; for Selby Abbey. *Publications:* Excavations at Greenwich Palace, 1972; Barbarian Europe, 1976; Crickley Hill: the Defences, 1994, the Hillfort Settlement, 2004; Knights and Castles, 2007; Lincoln Cathedral: the Romanesque frieze, 2010; (with Jane Kennedy): Mont Orgueil Castle: a review, 2001; Mont Orgueil Castle, 2002; contrib. numerous articles to learned jls. *Recreations:* visiting places, photographing them and consuming their food and drink. *Address:* Castle End, Dunstanburgh Road, Craster, Alnwick, Northumberland NE66 3TT. *T:* (01665) 576064; 24 Crown Street, Newark, Notts NG24 4UY. *T:* (01636) 659464.

DIXON, Piers; *b* 29 Dec. 1928; *s* of late Sir Pierson Dixon (British Ambassador in New York and Paris) and Lady (Ismene) Dixon; *m* 1st, 1960, Edwina (marr. diss. 1973), *d* of Rt Hon. Lord Duncan-Sandys, CH, PC; two *s*; 2nd, 1976, Janet (marr. diss. 1981), *d* of R. D. Aiyar, FRCS, and *widow* of 5th Earl Cowley; 3rd, 1984, Anne (marr. diss. 1985), *d* of John Cronin; one *s*; 4th, 1994, Ann Mavroleon, *d* of John Davenport. *Educ:* Eton (schol.); Magdalene Coll., Cambridge (exhibnr); Harvard Business Sch. Grenadier Guards, 1948. Merchant banking, London and New York, 1954–64; Sheppards and Chase, stockbrokers, 1964–81. Centre for Policy Studies, 1976–78. Contested (C) Brixton, 1966; MP (C) Truro, 1970–Sept. 1974; Sec., Cons. Backbenchers' Finance Cttee, 1970–71, Vice-Chm., 1972–74; sponsor of Rehabilitation of Offenders Act, 1974. *Publications:* Double Diploma, 1968; Cornish Names, 1973. *Recreations:* tennis, modern history. *Address:* 22 Ponsonby Terrace, SW1P 4QA. *T:* (020) 7828 6226. *Clubs:* Brooks's, Pratt's.

DIXON, Prof. Raymond Alan, DPhil; FRS 1999; Head, Department of Molecular Microbiology, John Innes Centre, 2010–12, Project Leader, since 2014 (Emeritus Fellow, 2012–13); *b* 1 Dec. 1947; *s* of late Henry George Dixon and Emily Dixon (*née* Emmins); *m* 1st, 1971, Ing-Britt Maj Wennerhag (marr. diss. 1980); one *d*; 2nd, 1985, Greta Margaret Dunne (marr. diss. 1995). *Educ:* Univ. of Reading (BSc 1st cl. Hons Microbiology 1969); Univ. of Sussex (DPhil Microbial Genetics 1972). University of Sussex: Postdoctoral Res. Fellow, 1973–75; Higher Scientific Officer, 1975–76, SSO, 1976–78, PSO, 1978–87, SPSO, 1987–95, Unit of Nitrogen Fixation; Res. Gp Leader, Nitrogen Fixation Lab. and Dept of Molecular Microbiol., John Innes Centre, 1995–2009. Hon. Prof., UEA, 1998–. Mem., EMBO, 1987. Fleming Medal, Soc. for Gen. Microbiology, 1984. *Publications:* numerous articles in learned jls. *Recreations:* music, various outdoor pursuits. *Address:* Department of Molecular Microbiology, John Innes Centre, Norwich NR4 7UH. *T:* (01603) 450747.

DIXON, Prof. Richard Newland, PhD, ScD; FRS 1986; CChem, FRSC; Senior Research Fellow, since 1996, and Alfred Capper Pass Professor of Chemistry, 1990–96, now Emeritus Professor, University of Bristol; *b* 25 Dec. 1930; *s* of late Robert Thomas Dixon and Lilian Dixon; *m* 1954, Alison Mary Birks; one *s* two *d*. *Educ:* The Judd Sch., Tonbridge; King's Coll., Univ. of London (BSc 1951); St Catharine's Coll., Univ. of Cambridge (PhD 1955; ScD 1976). FRSC 1976; CChem 1976. Scientific Officer, UKAEA, 1954–56; Res. Associate, Univ. of Western Ontario, 1956–57; Postdoctoral Fellow, NRCC, Ottawa, 1957–59; ICI Fellow, Univ. of Sheffield, 1959–60, Lectr in Chem., 1960–69; Bristol University: Prof. and Hd of Dept of Theoretical Chemistry, 1969–90; Dean, Faculty of Science, 1979–82; Pro-Vice-Chancellor, 1989–92. Sorby Res. Fellow, Royal Soc., 1964–69; Vis. Schol., Stanford Univ., 1982–83. Leverhulme Emeritus Fellow, 1996–99. Hallam Lectr, Univ. of Wales, 1988; Harkins Lectr, Univ. of Chicago, 1994. Mem. Council, Faraday Div., RSC, 1985–98, Vice-Pres., 1989–98; Mem., and Chm. sub-cttee, Laser Facility Cttee, 1987–90, and Mem., Physical Chem. Cttee, 1987–90, SERC. Non-exec. Dir, United Bristol Healthcare NHS Trust, 1994–2003 (Vice-Chm., 1995–2003). Trustee, Charitable Trusts for United Bristol Hosps, 2003–11 (Chm., 2006–11). Corday-Morgan Medal and Prize, Chemical Soc., 1968; Spectroscopy Medal, RSC, 1985; Liversidge Lectr and Medal, RSC, 1993–94; Rumford Medal, Royal Soc., 2004. *Publications:* Spectroscopy and Structure, 1965; Theoretical Chemistry: Vol. 1, 1974, Vol. 2, 1975, Vol. 3, 1978; numerous articles in res. jls of chemistry and physics. *Recreations:* mountain walking, travel, theatre, concerts. *Address:* 22 Westbury Lane, Bristol BS9 2PE. *T:* (0117) 968 1691; School of Chemistry, The University, Bristol BS8 1TS. *T:* (0117) 928 7661. *E:* r.n.dixon@bris.ac.uk.

DIXON, Maj.-Gen. Roy Laurence Cayley, CB 1977; CVO 1991; MC 1944; Chapter Clerk, College of St George, Windsor Castle, 1981–90; *b* 19 Sept. 1924; *s* of Lt-Col Sidney Frank Dixon, MC and Edith Mary (Sheena) (*née* Clark); *m* 1986, Anne Maureen Aspeslåen (marr. diss. 1988). *Educ:* Haileybury; Edinburgh Univ. Commnd Royal Tank Regt, 1944; served in armd units and on staff; psc 1956; BM 20 Armd Bde, 1957–59; Directing Staff, Staff Coll., 1961–64; comd 5th Royal Tank Regt, 1966–67; Mil. Asst to Chief of Gen. Staff, 1967–68; Comdr Royal Armd Corps, BAOR, 1968–70; Royal Coll. of Defence Studies, 1971; qual. helicopter pilot, 1973; Dir, Army Air Corps, 1974–76; Chief of Staff, Allied Forces Northern Europe, 1977–80. Col Comdt, RTR, 1978–83. Vice-Pres., Salisbury Civic Soc., 1998– (Chm., 1991–97). Freeman, City of London, 1990. *Address:* c/o Lloyds Bank, Cox's & Kings Branch, PO Box 1190, 7 Pall Mall, SW1Y 5NA. *Club:* Army and Navy.

DIXON, Dr Sarah Elizabeth Ann; Professor of Strategic Management and Dean, XJTLU Business School, Xi'an Jiaotong-Liverpool University, China, since 2013; *b* Stafford, 21 Nov. 1953; *d* of Aubrey Lacey Parsons and Kathleen Helen Parsons; one *s*. *Educ:* Univ. of Bradford (BA Hons Russian and German 1976); Chartered Inst. of Marketing (DipM 1983); Kingston Univ. (MBA Dist. 2002; PGCert Teaching and Learning in HE 2003); Henley Management Coll. (DBA 2006). Royal Dutch Shell Group: product mgt, mktg asst, translator and interpreter, 1976–86; Petrochemicals Manager, Austria, 1986–89; Area Manager, Petrochemicals, USSR and Poland, 1989–92; Chemicals Manager, Russia, 1992–96; Business Strategist, 1996–97; Mergers and Acquisitions Manager, 1998–2000; Vice Pres., DeWitt & Co. Inc., 2000–03; Dir, Postgrad. Progs, Principal Lectr, Sen. Lectr in Strategy, Faculty of Business and Law, Kingston Univ., 2002–08; Hd, MSc Progs and Sen. Lectr in Strategy, Univ. of Bath, 2008–10; Dean, Bradford Univ. Sch. of Mgt, 2010–12. Director: Albany Dixon Ltd, 2000–03; Kingston Strategy Consulting, 2006–11. *Publications:* Organisational Transformation in the Russian Oil Industry, 2008; contrib. Jl of Mgt Studies, Human Relations, Jl of Change Mgt, Leadership and Organisational Develt Jl. *Recreations:* walking, jogging, cycling, theatre, reading, travel. *Address:* XJTLU Business School, Xi'an Jiaotong-Liverpool University, 111 Ren Ai Road, Dushu Lake Higher Education Town, Suzhou Industrial Park, Suzhou, Jiangsu 215123, China.

DIXON-SMITH, family name of **Baron Dixon-Smith**.

DIXON-SMITH, Baron *cr* 1993 (Life Peer), of Bocking in Essex; **Robert William Dixon-Smith;** DL; farmer, since 1958; *b* 30 Sept. 1934; 2nd *s* of Dixon Smith, Braintree, Essex and Winifred Smith (*née* Stratton); Dixon Smith adopted by Deed Poll as surname, 1961; *m* 1960, Georgina Janet, *d* of George Cook, Halstead, Essex and Kathleen Cook; one *s* one *d*. *Educ:* Oundle; Writtle Coll. Nat. Service, 2nd Lt, King's Dragoon Guards, 1955–57. Member: Essex CC, 1965–93 (Chm., 1986–89); Association of County Councils, 1983–93 (Chm., 1992–93). Member: H of L EC Cttee sub-cttee C (Envmt), 1994–96; H of L Select Cttee on Sci. and Technol., 1994–98. Opposition spokesman, House of Lords: on local govt, 1998–2001, on home affairs, 2001–02, on envmtl affairs, 2003–07, on communities and local govt, 2007–09. Member: Local Govt Management Bd, 1991–93; Council, Essex Univ., 1991–94; Chm., Anglia Polytechnic Univ., 1992–93. Governor, Writtle Coll., 1967–94 (Chm., 1973–85; Fellow, 1993). Hon. Dr Anglia Poly. Univ., 1995. Freeman, City of London, 1988; Liveryman, Farmers' Co., 1991. DL Essex, 1986. *Recreations:* shooting, fishing, golf. *Address:* Sun House, Long Melford, Suffolk CO10 9HZ.

DIXSON, Maurice Christopher Scott, DPhil; FRAeS; Executive Chairman, Cranfield Aerospace Ltd, 2003–10; Chairman, Southside Thermal Sciences Ltd, 2004–12 (non-executive Director, since 2004); *b* 5 Nov. 1941; *s* of late Herbert George Muns Dixson and Elizabeth Eileen Dixson; *m* 1965, Anne Beverley Morris. *Educ:* Palmers Grammar Sch.; University Coll., Swansea (BA Jt Hons); Carleton Univ., Ottawa (MA); Pembroke Coll., Oxford (DPhil). Commercial Exec., Hawker Siddeley Aviation, 1969–74; Contracts Manager, Export, later Commercial Manager, Export, Mil. Aircraft Div., BAC, 1974–80; British Aerospace: Warton Division: Div. Commercial Manager, 1980–81; Exec. Dir, Contracts, 1981–83; Divl Commercial Dir, 1983–86; Military Aircraft Division: Dir-in-Charge, Saudi Arabian Ops, March–Aug. 1986; Commercial Dir and Dir-in-Charge, Saudi Arabian Ops, 1986–87; Chief Exec., Royal Ordnance PLC, 1987–88; Man. Dir, British Aerospace (Commercial Aircraft), 1988–90; Supervisory Man. Dir, Electronic Metrology and Components Groups, and Main Bd Dir, GEC, 1990–93; Chief Exec., Simon Engineering, then Simon Gp, 1993–2002; Dir, Higgs & Hill, then Swan Hill plc, 1994–2003. Chm., Kington Langley Parish Council, 2008–. Mem. Ct, Cranfield Univ., 2010–. *Recreations:* played representative soccer at school and university, supporter of Tottenham Hotspur Football Club, fishing, shooting, sport, fine arts, politics and current affairs. *Address:* The Poundhouse, Middle Common, Kington Langley, Chippenham, Wilts SN15 5NW. *Club:* Royal Automobile.

DJANOGLY, Sir Harry Ari Simon, Kt 1993; CBE 1983; Chairman, Coats plc (formerly Coats Viyella), 1999–2003; *b* 1 Aug. 1938. Former Man. Dir and Dep. Chm., Vantona Viyella; Dir, 1987–2003, Dep. Chm., 1999–2003, Singer & Friedlander; former Chm., Nottingham Manufacturing Co. Ltd. Non-exec. Dir, Carpetright plc, 1993–2005. Patron and Trustee, Djanogly City Acad., Nottingham; Patron, Djanogly Learning Resource Centre, Nottingham Univ.

DJANOGLY, Jonathan Simon; MP (C) Huntingdon, since 2001; *b* 3 June 1965; *s* of Sir Harry Djanogly, *qv* and Lady Djanogly; *m* 1991, Rebecca Silk; one *s* one *d*. *Educ:* University Coll. Sch.; Oxford Poly. (BA Hons); Guildford Law Sch. Admitted solicitor, 1990; Partner, S J Berwin LLP, 1998–2009. Chm., Pembroke VCT plc, 2012–; Consultant, King & Wood Mallesons LLP, 2012–. Mem. (C) Westminster LBC, 1994–2001. Contested (C) Oxford East, 1997. Shadow Minister, Constitutional, Legal and Home affairs, 2004–05; Shadow Solicitor Gen., and Shadow Trade and Industry Minister, 2005–10; Parly Under-Sec. of State, MoJ, 2010–12. Mem., Trade and Industry Select Cttee, 2001–05. *Recreations:* sports, arts. *Address:* House of Commons, SW1A 0AA. *T:* (020) 7219 2367.

DLHOPOLČEK, František, PhD; Ambassador of Slovakia to China, since 2010; *b* 13 Sept. 1953; *s* of Jozef Dlhopolček and Anna Pončková; *m* 1977, Dagmar Izraelova; one *s* one *d*. *Educ:* Sch. of Econs, Banská Bystrica, Czechoslovakia; Diplomatic Acad., Moscow (PhD History and Politology 1989). Univ. Asst Lectr, Sch. of Econs, Banská Bystrica, 1977–79; joined Federal Ministry of Foreign Affairs, Czechoslovakia, 1979: Nairobi, 1979–83; African Dept, 1983–84; Office of Minister of Foreign Affairs, 1984–87; Dept of Arab and Africa Countries, 1989–90; Dir, African Dept, 1990–91; Consul-Gen., Pretoria, 1991–92; Ambassador of Czech and Slovak Fed. Republic (subseq. of Slovak Republic) to RSA, 1992–93; Dir-Gen., Political Affairs, Min. of Foreign Affairs, 1993–94; Ambassador to Israel, 1994–98; Political Dir Gen., Min. of Foreign Affairs, 1998–2000; Ambassador to UK, 2000–05; Deputy Sec. Gen. and Dir of Human Resources, 2005–07, Dir, Dept of Central and N Europe, 2007–10, Min. of Foreign Affairs. *Address:* c/o Ministry of Foreign Affairs, Hlboká 2, 83336 Bratislava, Slovak Republic.

DOBBIE, Dr Robert Charles, CB 1996; public sector consultant; *b* 16 Jan. 1942; *s* of Scott U. Dobbie and Isobel M. Dobbie (*née* Jamieson); *m* 1st, 1964, Elizabeth Barbour (marr. diss. 2013); three *s*; 2nd, 2013, Susan Clayton (*née* Beale). *Educ:* Univ. of Edinburgh (BSc); Univ. of Cambridge (PhD). Res. Fellow, Univ. of Alberta, 1966–67; ICI Res. Fellow, Univ. of Bristol, 1967–68; Lectr in Inorganic Chemistry, Univ. of Newcastle upon Tyne, 1968–76; sabbatical, California State Univ., LA, 1974; Tutor, Open Univ., 1975–85; Principal, DTI, 1976–83; Asst Sec., Dept of Industry, 1983–90; Under Sec., DTI, 1990–97; Dir, Merseyside Task Force, 1990–92 (seconded to DoE); Head, Competitiveness Unit (formerly Industrial Competitiveness Div.), DTI, 1992–97; Regl Dir, Govt Office for NE, 1998–2001. Vis. Prof., Univ. of Newcastle upon Tyne, 2002–04. *Publications:* on inorganic and organometallic chemistry. *Recreations:* theatre, hill walking, malt whisky. *Address:* 1 Oak Hill Park, NW3 7LB.
See also S. J. Dobbie.

DOBBIE, Scott Jamieson, CBE 1998; Senior Advisor, Deutsche Bank AG, London, since 1999; Chairman, Securities and Investment Institute (formerly Securities Institute), 2000–09; *b* 24 July 1939; *s* of Scott U. Dobbie and Isobel M. Dobbie (*née* Jamieson); *m* 1962, Brenda M. Condie; two *d*. *Educ:* Dollar Acad.; Univ. of Edinburgh (BSc). Industrial mktg, Unilever, 1961–66, and ICI, 1966–72; Wood Mackenzie & Co., stockbrokers, 1972–88: Partner, 1975–82; Man. Partner, 1982–88; acquired by NatWest Securities, 1988: Man. Dir, 1988–93; Chm., 1993–98; acquired by Bankers Trust Internat., 1998–99 (Vice-Chm.). Chairman: CRESTCo Ltd, 1996–2001; Standard Life European Private Equity Trust, 2001–13; Edinburgh Investment Trust PLC, 2003–11 (non-exec. Dir, 1998–2002); non-executive Director: Murray VCT4 plc, 2000–03; Premier Oil plc, 2000–08; Scottish Financial Enterprise, 2001–05; FRESCO SICAV, 2001–03; QCA, later QCDA, 2009–12. Director: SFA, 1993–2001; Financial Services NTO, 2001–04; Comr, Jersey Financial Services Commn, 1999–2008; Mem., Regulatory Decisions Cttee, FSA, 2001–05. Ind. Mem., Standards Cttee, Corp. of London, 2001–09 (Chm., 2007–09). Liveryman, Clockmakers' Co., 2010. Hon. DSc City, 2009. *Recreations:* mechanical objects, books. *Address:* Deutsche Bank AG London, Winchester House, 1 Great Winchester Street, EC2N 2DB. *E:* scott.dobbie@db.com.
See also R. C. Dobbie.

DOBBIN, (Timothy) David, CBE 2005; Group Chief Executive, United Dairy Farmers Ltd, since 2000; Chairman, Belfast Harbour, since 2015 (Member, Board, since 2012); *b* 1 May 1955; *s* of George and Phoebe Dobbin; *m* 1977, Pauline Gregg; two *s*. *Educ:* Grosvenor Grammar Sch., Belfast; Queen's Univ., Belfast (BSc 1st cl. Hons Mech Engrg). Cert. of Professional Competence in Nat. Road Haulage Ops. CEng, MIMechE 1983. Manufg Manager, Rothmans Internat., 1977–83; Gen. Manager, Northern Publishing Office, 1983–85; Ops Dir, Cantrell & Cochrane, 1985–89; Regl Dir, Dalgety Agriculture, 1989–95; Gp Develt Dir, Boxmore Internat. plc, 1995–2000. Dir, Medevol, 2002–10. Non-executive Director: CBI, 2005–08 (Chm., CBI NI, 2003–05); Strategic Investment Bd, 2005–13 (Chm., 2009–13); Mem. Adv. Bd, BT Ireland, 2007–09; Mem. Bd, Invest NI, 2008–14. Vice Chm. and Dir, Belfast Port Employers Assoc., 1989–94; Pres. and Exec. Mem., NI Grain Trade Assoc., 1989–95; Director: Food and Drink Industry Trng Adv. Council NI, 1992–95; LEDU, 1998–2002; Investment Belfast, 1998–2002; Dairy UK and NI Dairy Council, 2002– (Vice Chm., 2013–); NI Food and Drink Assoc., 2002– (Chm., 2014–); Chairman: NI Quality Centre, 1995–97; NI Agricl Res. Council, 1997–2000; Intertrade Ireland, 2007–11; UK Internat. Dairy Fedn, 2007–09; Member: NI Water Council, 1986–92; Food from Britain Council, 2003–09. Chm., Sentinus, 1995–2003; Trustee, Prince's Trust, 2005–09 (Chm., Prince's Trust NI, 2005–09). Mem., Senate, QUB, 2007–14. FInstD 2009. Hon. DScEcon QUB, 2005. Hon. Chinese Citizenship, Kunshan City, 1998. Lunn's Award for Excellence, 2008, Large NI Company Dir of the Year, 2012, IoD. *Recreations:* Ulster Rugby (Chm., 2010–), golf, boating, gardening, music, Irish art. *Address:* Dale Farm House, 15 Dargan Road, Belfast BT3 9LS. *T:* (028) 9037 2237, *Fax:* (028) 9037 2206. *E:* david.dobbin@utdni.co.uk. *Clubs:* Farmers; Ulster Reform; Knock Golf.

DOBBIN, Rev. Dr Victor, CB 2000; MBE 1980; Chaplain General to the Forces, 1995–2000; *b* 12 March 1943; *s* of late Vincent Dobbin and Annie Dobbin (*née* Doherty); *m* 1967, Rosemary Gault; one *s* one *d*. *Educ:* Trinity Coll., Dublin (MA 1967); Queen's Univ., Belfast (MTh 1979; PhD 1984). Asst Minister, Rosemary Presbyterian Ch, Belfast, 1970–72; joined RAChD, 1972; Dep. Warden, RAChD Centre, 1982–86; Sen. Chaplain, 3rd Armd Div., 1986–89; Staff Chaplain, HQ BAOR, 1989–91; Sen. Chaplain, SE Dist, 1991–93; Asst Chaplain Gen., Southern Dist, 1993–94. QHC 1993–2000. Mem., Council of Reference, Barnabas Fund, 1998–. Hon. DD Presbyterian Theol Faculty, Ireland, 1995. *Recreations:* golf, walking, cycling, reading. *Address:* Glenview, 20 Cushendall Road, Bonamargy, Ballycastle, Co. Antrim, N Ireland BT54 6QR.

DOBBS, family name of **Baron Dobbs**.

DOBBS, Baron *cr* 2010 (Life Peer), of Wylye in the County of Wiltshire; **Michael John Dobbs;** novelist, dramatist and parliamentarian; *b* Nov. 1948; *s* of Eric William Dobbs and Eileen Dobbs; *m*; four *s*. *Educ:* Christ Church, Oxford (MA); Fletcher School of Law and Diplomacy, USA (PhD, MALD, MA). Govt Special Adviser, 1981–87; Chief of Staff, Conservative Party, 1986–87; Dep. Chm., Saatchi & Saatchi, 1983–86, 1988–91; Jt Dep. Chm., Cons. Party, 1994–95. Presenter, Despatch Box, BBC, 1999–2001; Exec. Producer, TV series, House of Cards, 2013. Lifetime Achievement Award: Political Book Awards, 2014; Tufts Univ., 2014; P. T. Barnum Excellence in Entertainment Award, 2014. *Publications:* House of Cards, 1989 (televised, 1990, US version, 2013); Wall Games, 1990; Last Man to Die, 1991; To Play the King, 1992 (televised, 1993); The Touch of Innocents, 1994; The Final Cut, 1995 (televised, 1995); Goodfellowe MP, 1996; The Buddha of Brewer Street, 1998; Whispers of Betrayal, 2000; Winston's War, 2002; Never Surrender, 2003 (Benjamin Franklin Award, 2008); Churchill's Hour, 2004; Churchill's Triumph, 2005; First Lady, 2006; The Lord's Day, 2007; The Edge of Madness, 2008; The Turning Point (play), 2009; A Family Affair (play), 2009; The Reluctant Hero, 2010; Old Enemies, 2011; A Sentimental Traitor, 2012; A Ghost at the Door, 2013. *Recreations:* genealogy, walking. *Address:* House of Lords, SW1A 0PW. *W:* www.michaeldobbs.com. *Club:* Royal Automobile.

DOBBS, Prof. (Edwin) Roland, PhD, DSc; Hildred Carlile Professor of Physics, University of London, 1973–90, and Head of Department of Physics, Royal Holloway and Bedford New College, 1985–90; Emeritus Professor of Physics, University of London, 1990; *b* 2 Dec. 1924; *s* of late A. Edwin Dobbs, AMIMechE, and Harriet Dobbs (*née* Wright); *m* 1947, Dorothy Helena (*d* 2004), *o d* of late Alderman A. F. T. Jeeves, Stamford, Lincs; two *s* one *d*. *Educ:* Ilford County High Sch.; Queen Elizabeth's Sch., Barnet; University College London. BSc (1st cl. Physics) 1943, PhD 1949; DSc London 1977; FInstP 1964; FIOA 1977. Radar research, Admiralty, 1943–46; DSIR Res. Student, UCL, 1946–49; Lectr in Physics, QMC, Univ. of London, 1949–58; Fulbright Scholar, Applied Maths, 1958–59, Associate Prof. of Physics, 1959–60, Brown Univ., USA; AEI Fellow, Cavendish Lab., Univ. of Cambridge, 1960–64; Prof. and Head of Dept of Physics, Univ. of Lancaster, 1964–73; Bedford College, London University: Head of Dept of Physics, 1973–85; Vice-Principal, 1981–82; Dean, Faculty of Science, 1980–82; Chm., Bd of Studies in Physics, Univ. of London, 1982–85; Vice-Dean, 1986–88, Dean, 1988–90, Faculty of Science, Univ. of London. Member: Physics Cttee, SRC, 1970–73, SERC, 1983–86; Nuclear Physics Bd, SRC, 1974–77; Paul Instrument Fund Cttee, 1984–2002. Visiting Professor: Brown Univ., 1966; Wayne State Univ., 1969; Univ. of Tokyo, 1977; Univ. of Delhi, 1983; Cornell Univ., 1984; Univ. of Florida, 1989; Univ. of Sussex, 1989–2003. Pres., Inst. of Acoustics, 1976–78; Hon. Sec., Inst. of Physics, 1976–84. Convenor, Standing Conf. of Profs of Physics of GB, 1985–88. Member: Caius Coll. Club; Physical Soc. Club. Hon. Fellow: Indian Cryogenics Council, 1977; Inst. of Acoustics, 2007. Freeman, City of London, 2005. *Publications:* Electricity and Magnetism, 1984 (trans. Chinese 1990); Electromagnetic Waves, 1985 (trans. Chinese 1992); Basic Electromagnetism, 1993; Solid Helium Three, 1994; Helium Three, 2001; research papers on metals and superconductors in Procs of Royal Soc., on solid state physics and acoustics in Jl of Physics, Physical Rev. Letters, Physical Acoustics, and on superfluid helium 3 in Jl Low Temperature Physics, etc. *Recreations:* travel, opera, gardening. *Address:* Merryfield, Best Beech Hill, Wadhurst, E Sussex TN5 6JT.
See also M. A. Jeeves.

DOBBS, Hon. Dame Linda (Penelope), DBE 2004; legal consultant, since 2013; a Judge of the High Court of Justice, Queen's Bench Division, 2004–13; *b* 3 Jan. 1951; *m* (marr. diss.). *Educ:* Univ. of Surrey (BSc 1976); London School of Economics and Political Science (LLM 1977; PhD 1980). Called to the Bar, Gray's Inn, 1981, Bencher, 2002; QC 1998; in practice at the Bar, 1982–2004. Chm., Criminal Bar Assoc., 2003–04. Interim Pres., Internat. Lawyers for Africa, 2014– (Mem., Adv. Bd, 2010); Member, Advisory Board: Protimos, 2011–; I-ProBono, 2014–. Trustee: Oxford Sch. of Drama, 2006–; Internat. Law Book Facility, 2009–14 (Patron, 2015–); Patron: African Prisons Proj., 2008–; Lotte Bette-Priddy Educn Trust, 2008–; Masiphumele Trust, 2010–; BLD Foundn, 2012–; Pinotage Youth Devlt Acad., 2013–; Alison Wetherfield Foundn, 2013–14; Make it Happen in Sierra Leone, 2013–. Mem., Ct of Govs, 2006–, Chm., Ethics Policy Cttee, 2012–, LSE. DUniv: Sheffield Hallam, 2006; Surrey, 2010; Hon. LLD: City, 2008; Coll. of Law, 2009; BPP University Coll., 2010. *Publications:* (with M. Lucraft) Road Traffic Law and Practice, 1993, 3rd edn 1995; (Consultant Ed.) Fraud: law, practice and procedure, 2004–. *Recreations:* reading, music, theatre, travel, food and wine.

DOBBS, Mattiwilda; Order of North Star (Sweden), 1954; opera singer (coloratura soprano); *b* Atlanta, Ga, USA, 11 July 1925; *d* of John Wesley and Irene Dobbs; *m* 1957, Bengt Janzon (*d* 1997), retired Dir of Information, Nat. Ministry of Health and Welfare, Sweden; no *c*. *Educ:* Spelman Coll., USA (BA 1946); Columbia Univ., USA (MA 1948). Studied voice in NY with Lotte Leonard, 1946–50; special coaching Paris with Pierre Bernac, 1950–52. Marian Anderson Schol., 1948; John Hay Whitney Schol., 1950; 1st prize in singing, Internat. Comp., Geneva Conservatory of Music, 1951. Appeared Royal Dutch Opera, Holland Festival, 1952. Recitals, Sweden, Paris, Holland, 1952; appeared in opera at La Scala, Milan, 1953; Concerts, England and Continent, 1953; Glyndebourne Opera, 1953–54, 1956, 1961; Covent Garden Opera, 1953, 1954, 1956, 1958; command performance, Covent Garden, 1954. Annual concert tours: US, 1954–90; Australia, New Zealand, 1955, 1959, 1968; Australia, 1972, 1977; Israel, 1957 and 1959; USSR concerts and opera (Bolshoi Theater), 1959; San Francisco Opera, 1955; début Metropolitan Opera, 1956; there annually, 1956–64. Appearances Hamburg State Opera, 1961–63; Royal Swedish Opera, 1957 and there annually, 1957–73; Norwegian and Finnish Operas, 1957–64. Vis. Prof., Univ. of Texas at Austin, 1973–74; Professor: Univ. of Illinois, 1975–76; Univ. of Georgia, 1976–77; Howard Univ., Washington, 1977–91. Hon. Dr of Music: Spelman Coll., Atlanta, 1979; Emory Univ., Atlanta, 1980.

DOBBS, Roland; *see* Dobbs, E. R.

DOBKIN, His Honour Ian James; a Circuit Judge, 1995–2010; *b* 8 June 1948; *s* of Morris Dobkin, dental surgeon, Leeds, and Rhoda Dobkin; *m* 1980, Andrea, *d* of Jack and Rose Dante; two *s*. *Educ:* Leeds Grammar Sch.; Queen's Coll., Oxford (Hastings Exhibnr in Classics; BA Jurisp. 1970; MA 1974). Called to the Bar, Gray's Inn, 1971; barrister, North Eastern Circuit, 1971–95; Asst Recorder, 1986–90; Recorder, 1990–95; Liaison Judge, Leeds Area Magistrates' Courts, 2002–07. Judicial Mem., W Yorks Probation Bd, 2002–08. Mem., Adv. Cttee, Centre for Criminal Justice Studies, Univ. of Leeds, 1987–. United Hebrew Congregation, Leeds: Vice-Pres., 1981–84 and 1992–96; Pres., 1984–88, 1996–99 and 2005–06; Hon. Life Vice-Pres., 2003; Vice-Chm., Leeds Hillel Foundn, 1989–2009. Contested (C) Penistone, July 1978, gen. election, 1979. *Recreations:* crosswords, reading, music. *Clubs:* Moor Allerton Golf (Leeds); Yorkshire County Cricket.

DOBLE, Denis Henry; HM Diplomatic Service, retired; Consul-General, Amsterdam, 1991–96; *b* 2 Oct. 1936; *s* of Percy Claud Doble and Dorothy Grace (*née* Petley); *m* 1975, Patricia Ann Robinson; one *d* one *s*. *Educ:* Dover Grammar School; New College, Oxford (MA Modern Hist.). RAF, 1955–57. Colonial Office, 1960–64; Asst Private Sec. to Commonwealth and Colonial Sec., 1963–64; HM Diplomatic Service, 1965; First Sec., Brussels, 1966–68, Lagos, 1968–72; S Asian and Defence Depts, FCO, 1972–75; First Sec. (Economic), Islamabad, 1975–78; Head of Chancery, Lima, 1978–82; E African Dept, FCO, 1982–84; Actg Dep. High Comr, Bombay, 1985; Deputy High Commissioner: Calcutta, 1985–87; Kingston, 1987–91. Mem. Council, Anglo-Netherlands Soc., 1996–; Member, Committee: BACSA, 1998–; London Br., Oxford Univ. Soc., 2002–. Mem. Cttee, Oxford Mission, 2001–; Mem., London Br., Prayer Book Soc., 2001– (Mem. Cttee, 2002–11). Member: Battersea Pk Rotary Club, 1998– (Pres., 2003–04); Anglo-Peruvian Soc., 1998–; Anglo-Belgian Soc., 1999–; Britain-Nigeria Educnl Trust, 1999–; Pakistan Soc., 2000–; P. G. Wodehouse Soc., 2006–; Life Mem., RAFA 1990. Mem., Royal Soc. for Asian Affairs, 1997–. Mem., Friends of Georgian Soc. of Jamaica, 1999– (Trustee, 2007–11). Freeman, City of London, 2009. SBStJ 1972. *Recreations:* cricket, tennis, long rail and road journeys, British colonial history, English cathedrals, quizzes, walking in France. *Address:* 38 Eglantine Road, Wandsworth, SW18 2DD. *Clubs:* Pilgrims, MCC (Life Mem.); Lord's Taverners.

DOBLE, John Frederick, OBE 1981; HM Diplomatic Service, retired; High Commissioner to Swaziland, 1996–99; *b* 30 June 1941; *s* of Comdr Douglas Doble, RN and Marcella (*née* Cowan); *m* 1st, 1975, Isabella (marr. diss. 1992), *d* of late Col W. H. Whitbread, TD; one *d*; 2nd, 2009, Susan Maria, *d* of Sir Henry Francis Colden Farrington, 7th Bt. *Educ:* Sunningdale; Eton (Scholar); RMA Sandhurst; Hertford College, Oxford. 17th/21st Lancers, 1959–69 (Captain); attached Lord Strathcona's Horse (Royal Canadians), 1967–69; joined HM Diplomatic Service, 1969; Arabian Dept, FCO, 1969–72; Beirut, 1972–73; UK Delegn to NATO, Brussels, 1973–77; Commonwealth Dept, FCO, 1977–78; Maputo, 1978–81; Inf. Dept, FCO, 1981–83; attached Barclays Bank International, 1983–85; Consul General, Edmonton, 1985–89; Consul General, Johannesburg, 1990–94. *Recreations:* mountaineering, history, manual labour. *Address:* Hole Farm, Hockworthy, Devon TA21 0NQ.

See also Sir H. W. Farrington, Bt.

DOBROSIELSKI, Marian, PhD; Banner of Labour, 1st Class 1975 (2nd Class 1973); Knight Cross of the Order of Polonia Restituta, 1964; Professor of Philosophy, Warsaw University, 1974–88; Ambassador *ad personam*, since 1973; *b* 25 March 1923; *s* of Stanislaw and Stefania Dobrosielski; *m* 1950; one *d*. *Educ:* Univ. of Zürich (PhD); Univ. of Warsaw. Served in Polish Army in France, War of 1939–45. With Min. of Foreign Affairs, 1948–81; Polish Legation, Bern, 1948–50; Head of Section, Min. of Foreign Affairs, 1950–54; Asst Prof., Warsaw Univ. and Polish Acad. of Sciences, 1954–57; Mem. Polish delegn to UN Gen. Assembly, 1952, 1953, 1958, 1966, 1972, 1976. First Sec., Counsellor, Polish Embassy in Washington, 1958–64; Min. of Foreign Affairs: Counsellor to Minister, 1964–69; Acting Dir, Research Office, 1968–69; Polish Ambassador to London, 1969–71; Dir, Polish Inst. of Internat. Affairs, 1971–80; Dep. Minister of Foreign Affairs, 1978–81. Univ. of Warsaw: Associate Prof., 1966; Vice-Dean of Faculty of Philosophy, 1966–68; Dir, Inst. of Philosophy, 1971–73 (Chm. Scientific Council, 1969). Chair of Diplomacy, Private Coll. of Business and Admin, Warsaw, 1999–2008; Prof. of European Studies, Univ. of Ateneum, Gdansk, 2007–12. Chm., Editorial Bd of Studia Filozoficzne, 1968–69; Sec., Polish Philos. Soc., 1955–57 and 1965–69. Chm., Polish Cttee for European Security and Co-operation, 1973–79 (Vice-Chm., 1971–73); Vice-Chm., Cttee on Peace Research, Polish Acad. of Scis, 1984–91; Chm., Scientific Council, Inst. of Peace Res. and Security Policy, Univ. of Hamburg, 1987–97. Hon. Vice-Pres., Scottish-Polish Cultural Assoc., Glasgow, 1969–71; Chm., Polish delegn to: 2nd stage Conf. on Security and Co-operation in Europe, 1973–75; CSCE Belgrade Meeting, 1977–78; CSCE Meeting, Madrid, 1980–81. Chm., Polish Nat. Interest Club, 1991–98. Hon. Mem., World Innovation Foundn, 1999. *Publications:* A Basic Epistemological Principle of Logical Positivism, 1947; The Philosophical Pragmatism of C. S. Peirce, 1967; On some contemporary problems: Philosophy, Ideology, Politics, 1970; (trans. and introd) Selection of Aphorisms of G. C. Lichtenberg, Oscar Wilde, Karl Kraus, M. von Ebner-Eschenbach, Mark Twain, C. Norwid, 1970–85; On the Theory and Practice of Peaceful Coexistence, 1976; Belgrad 77, 1978; Chances and Dilemmas, 1980; The Crisis in Poland, 1984; On Politics and Philosophy, 1988; Philosophy of Reason, 1988; Karl R. Popper's Philosophy of History and Politics, 1991; (jtly) Next Europe, 1993; (jtly) Prominent Diplomats of the XX Century, 1996; Rationalism and Irrationalism, 1999; On History, Myths and Facts - Politico-philosophical Essays, 2004; Poland-Germany-Europe, 2007; numerous articles on philosophy and internat. problems in professional jls. *Address:* Kozia Street 9–14, 00–070 Warszawa, Poland.

DOBRY, His Honour George Leon Severyn, CBE 1977; QC 1969; a Circuit Judge, 1980–92; arbitrator, 1993–2008; *b* 1 Nov. 1918; *m* 1948, Margaret Headley Smith (*d* 1978); two *d*; *m* 1982, Rosemary Anne Alexander, *qv*. *Educ:* Warsaw Univ.; Edinburgh Univ. (MA). Served War of 1939–45: Army, 1939–42 (despatches); Air Force, 1942–46. Called to Bar, Inner Temple, 1946; Bencher 1977. A Recorder of the Crown Court, 1977–80. Legal Sec., Internat. Commn of Jurists, 1955–57. Founder Member, Justice, 1956–, Mem., Council on Law Reporting, 1984–94. Adviser to Sec. of State for Environment and Sec. of State for Wales on Develt Control, 1973–75; Mem., Docklands Jt Cttee, 1974–76; Inspector, Inquiry into M25, 1978–79; Review of Internat. Legal Relns for Lord Chancellor, 2000. Founder, British Centre for English Legal Studies, Warsaw Univ., 1991. Founder, and Chm. Trustees, Lord Slynn of Hadley European Law Foundn, 1997–2004. Trustee, Roy Jenkins Meml Foundn, 2005–. Founder, British-Polish Legal Assoc. Hon. Dr Juris Warsaw, 1994. Comdr, Starred Cross of Merit (Poland), 1999 (Order of Merit, 1993). Gold Medal, Polish Bar, 1999. *Publications:* Woodfall's Law of Landlord and Tenant, 25th edition (one of the Editors), 1952; Blundell and Dobry, Town and Country Planning, 1962; Blundell and Dobry, Planning Appeals and Inquiries, 1962, 5th edn, as Planning, 1996; Review of the Development Control System (Interim Report), 1972 (Final Report), 1975; (ed jtly) Development Gains Tax, 1975; Hill and Redman, Landlord and Tenant (Cons. Editor), 16th edn, 1976; (Gen. Editor) Encyclopedia of Development Law, 1976; articles on town planning and internat. law. *Address:* 105 Whitelands House, Cheltenham Terrace, SW3 4RA. *T:* (07786) 012259. *E:* george@georgedobry.com. *Clubs:* Garrick, Beefsteak, Buck's, Essex.

DOBRY, Rosemary Anne; *see* Alexander, R. A.

DOBSON, Prof. Christopher Martin, DPhil; ScD; FRS 1996; FRSC; FMedSci; John Humphrey Plummer Professor of Chemical and Structural Biology, University of Cambridge, since 2001; Master, St John's College, Cambridge, since 2007 (Fellow, since 2001); *b* 8 Oct. 1949; *s* of Arthur Dobson and Mabel Dobson (*née* Pollard); *m* 1977, Dr Mary Janet Schove (*see* M. J. Dobson); two *s*. *Educ:* Abingdon Sch.; Keble Coll., Oxford (BSc, MA; Hon. Fellow 2009); Merton Coll., Oxford (DPhil; Hon. Fellow 2009); ScD Cambridge, 2007. FRSC 1996. Jun. Res. Fellow, Merton Coll., Oxford, 1974–76; IBM Res. Fellow, Linacre Coll., Oxford, 1976–77; Asst Prof. of Chemistry, Harvard Univ., 1977–80; Vis. Scientist, MIT, 1977–80; University of Oxford: Lectr in Chemistry, 1980–95; Reader in Chemistry, 1995–96; Aldrichian Praelector, 1995–2001; Prof. of Chemistry, 1996–2001; Dir, Oxford Centre for Molecular Scis, 1998–2001; Fellow, LMH, 1980–2001, Emeritus Fellow, 2002, Hon. Fellow, 2008; Lectr, Brasenose Coll., Oxford, 1980–2001. Howard Hughes Med. Inst. Internat. Res. Scholar, 1992–97; Royal Soc. Leverhulme Trust Sen. Res. Fellow, 1993–94; Presidential Vis. Prof., Univ. of Calif at San Francisco, 2001–02; Vis. Prof., Univ. of Florence, 2002–; Dist. Vis. Prof., Rutgers Univ., 2007; Sammet Guest Prof., J. W. Goethe Univ., Frankfurt, 2007; Vallee Foundn Vis. Fellow, 2014. Lectures: National, Biophysical Soc., USA, 1998; John S. Colter, Univ. of Alberta, 1998; Frederic M. Richards, Yale Univ., 1999; Cynthia Ann Chan Meml, Univ. of Calif, Berkeley, 1999; A. D. Little, MIT, 2001; Sackler, Univ. of Cambridge, 2002; Royal Soc. Bakerian, 2003; Wills, Univ. of London, 2003; Bayer Dist., Univ. of Washington, St Louis, 2003; Anfinsen Meml, Johns Hopkins Univ., 2003; Joseph Black, Glasgow Univ., 2003; Centenary, Strathclyde Univ., 2004; Presidential, Scripps Res. Inst., La Jolla, 2005; Burroughs Wellcome, Univ. of E Carolina, 2005; 50th Anniv., IUBMB, 2005; Sir John Kendrew, Weizmann Inst., 2005; William H. Stein Meml, Rockefeller Univ., 2006; John D. Ferry, Madison Univ., 2006; Linus Pauling, Stanford Univ., 2006; James B. Sumner, Cornell Univ., 2008; Ada Doisy Meml, Illinois Univ., 2008; Weaver Meml, Univ. of Calif, Davis, 2008; Linus Pauling, CIT, 2008; Roy E. Moon, Angelo State Univ., 2009; Hans Neurath, Univ. of Washington, 2009; Brian Bent Meml, Columbia Univ., 2010; Alumni, Univ. of Qld, 2010; G. N. Ramachandran Meml, Indian Biophysical Soc., 2012; T. Y. Shen, MIT, 2012; Evans, Ohio State Univ., 2012; Antonini Meml, Univ. of Rome, 2013; Searle Dist., Northwestern Univ., 2014; Philippe Wiener, Fondation Wiener Anspach, Brussels, 2014. Mem., EMBO, 1999. Pres., Protein Soc., 1999–2001. Fellow, Eton Coll., 2001–. FMedSci 2005. MAE 2011. Hon. Fellow: Linacre Coll., Oxford, 2008; Darwin Coll., Cambridge, 2014. Hon. Fellow: Indian Chemical Council, 2010; British Biophysical Soc., 2010; Indian Biophysical Soc., 2012. For. Hon. Mem., American Acad. of Arts and Scis, 2007; For. Associate, NAS, 2013. Dr *hc*: Leuven, 2001; Liege, 2007; Hon. DM: Umea, Sweden, 2005; Florence, 2006; Hon. DSc KCL, 2012. Corday Morgan Medal and Prize, 1983, Interdisciplinary Award, 1999, Khorana Prize, 2010, RSocChem; Dewey and Kelly Award, Univ. of Nebraska, 1997; Bijvoet Medal, Univ. of Utrecht, 2002; Silver Medal, Italian Soc. of Biochemistry, 2002; Stein and Moore Award, 2003, Hans Neurath Award, 2006, Protein Soc.; Davy Medal, 2005, Royal Medal, 2009, Royal Soc.; Heineken Prize for Biophys and Biochem., Royal Netherlands Acad. of Arts and Scis, 2014; Feltrinelli Internat. Prize for Medicine, Accademia Nazionale dei Lincei, Rome, 2014. *Publications:* numerous contribs to learned jls. *Recreations:* family, friends, travel. *Address:* Department of Chemistry, University of Cambridge, Lensfield Road, Cambridge CB2 1EW. *T:* (01223) 763070. *E:* cmd44@cam.ac.uk; Master's Lodge, St John's College, Cambridge CB2 1TP. *T:* (01233) 338635. *E:* c.m.dobson@joh.cam.ac.uk.

DOBSON, Vice-Adm. Sir David (Stuart), KBE 1992; Secretary-General, Institute of Investment Management and Research, later Chief Executive, UK Society of Investment Professionals, 1995–2002; *b* 4 Dec. 1938; *s* of Walter and Ethel Dobson; *m* 1962, Joanna Mary Counter; two *s* one *d*. *Educ:* English School, Nicosia, Cyprus; RN College, Dartmouth. Joined RN 1956; qualified Observer, 1961; served HM Ships Ark Royal, Protector, Eagle; BRNC Dartmouth, 1968–70; Flight Comdr, HMS Norfolk, 1970–72; Staff of FO Naval Air Comd, 1972–74; CO HMS Amazon, 1975–76; Naval Sec's Dept, MoD, 1976–78; Naval and Air Attaché, Athens, 1980–82; Senior Naval Officer, Falklands, 1982–83; Captain 5th Destroyer Sqdn (HMS Southampton), 1983–85; Captain of the Fleet, 1985–88; Naval Sec., 1988–90; Chief of Staff to Comdr Allied Naval Forces Southern Europe, 1991–94. Chm. of Trustees, Hands Around the World, charity, 1995–2009. Vice-Pres., Royal Star and Garter Home, Richmond, 2004– (Gov., 1996–2003; Chm. Govs, 1999–2003). Pres., FAA Field Gun Assoc., 1998–. Pres., RN Bird Watching Soc., 1992– (Ed., Sea Swallow jl, 2012–); Ed., Steep and Stroud Newsletter, 1997–. *Recreations:* hill walking, bird watching, choral singing. *Address:* c/o Lloyds Bank, The Square, Petersfield, Hants GU32 3HL. *Clubs:* Royal Navy of 1765 and 1785 (Chm., 1995–98), Union Jack (Pres., 2001–11).

DOBSON, Rt Hon. Frank (Gordon); PC 1997; *b* 15 March 1940; *s* of late James William and Irene Shortland Dobson, York; *m* 1967, Janet Mary, *d* of Henry and Edith Alker; three *c*. *Educ:* Dunnington County Primary Sch., York; Archbishop Holgate's Grammar Sch., York; London School of Economics (BScEcon). Administrative jobs with Central Electricity Generating Bd, 1962–70, and Electricity Council, 1970–75; Asst Sec., Commn for Local Administration (local Ombudsman's office), 1975–79. Member, Camden Borough Council, 1971–76 (Leader of Council, 1973–75); Chm., Coram's Fields and Harmsworth Meml Playground, 1977–. MP (Lab) Holborn and St Pancras S, 1979–83, Holborn and St Pancras, 1983–2015. Front bench spokesman on educn, 1981–83, on health, 1983–87; Shadow Leader of the Commons and Party Campaign Co-ordinator, 1987–89; opposition front bench spokesman on energy, 1989–92, on employment, 1992–93, on transport, 1993–94, on London, 1993–97, and on the envmt, 1994–97; Sec. of State for Health, 1997–99. Chm., NHS Unlimited, 1981–89. Gov., Coram, 2008–. Governor: LSE, 1986–2001; Inst. of Child Health, 1987–92; RVC, 2002–. Member, Court: Univ. of York, 2001–; LSHTM, 2008–. Fellow, Birkbeck, Univ. of London, 2010; Hon. FRCP 2010. *Address:* 22 Great Russell Mansions, Great Russell Street, WC1B 3BE. *T:* (020) 7242 5760. *Club:* Covent Garden Community Centre.

DOBSON, Jo-Anne Elizabeth; Member (UU) Upper Bann, Northern Ireland Assembly, since 2011; *b* Banbridge, Co. Down; *d* of Eric Elliott and Joan Elliott; *m* 1986, John Ernest Dobson; two *s*. *Educ:* Abercorn Prim. Sch., Banbridge; Banbridge Acad. Mem. (UU), Craigavon BC, 2010–. Sec., All Party Parly Gp on Learning Disabilities, NI Assembly, 2011–; Chm., All Party Parly Gp on Organ Donation, NI Assembly, 2013–. Mem., NI Assembly Br., Commonwealth Parly Assoc., 2011–. Contested (UU) Upper Bann, 2015. Mem., NI Kidney Patients' Assoc., 2008–. *Recreations:* reading, gym. *Address:* (office) 18 Rathfriland Street, Banbridge BT32 3LA. *T:* (028) 4066 9004. *E:* jo-anne.dobson@mla.niassembly.gov.uk. *Club:* Waringstown Cricket.

DOBSON, Very Rev. John Richard; Dean of Ripon, since 2014; *b* Swillington, Leeds, 16 Nov. 1964; *s* of Sidney Dobson and Barbara Dobson; *m* 1989, Nicola Jane Hollinshead; one *s* one *d*. *Educ:* Garforth Comprehensive; Van Mildert Coll., Univ. of Durham (BA Hons Dunelm 1997); Ripon Coll., Cuddesdon (PGCTh Oxon 1989). Ordained deacon, 1989, priest, 1990; Assistant Curate: Benfieldside, Durham, 1989–92; St Cuthbert, Darlington, 1992–96; Curate-in-charge, Blackwell Conventional District, 1996–98; Vicar of Blackwell, 1998–2014; Area Dean of Darlington, 2001–14; Priest-in-charge, Coniscliffe, 2004–14. Mem. Bd, Darlington Strategic Partnership, 2003–14. Trustee: Darlington Abbeyfield Soc., 2003–14; Darlington CVS, 2003–14. Gov. of several Darlington schs, 2000–14. *Recreations:* walking, bell ringing, golf, music, wine tasting, rotarian, charities trustee. *Address:* The Minster House, Bedern Bank, Ripon, N Yorks HG4 1PE. *T:* (01765) 602609; The Cathedral Office, Liberty Court House, Minster Road, Ripon, N Yorks HG4 1QS. *T:* (01765) 603462. *E:* deanjohn@riponcathedral.org.uk.

DOBSON, Keith; *see* Dobson, W. K.

DOBSON, Dr Mary Janet; author; Director, Wellcome Unit for History of Medicine, and Reader in the History of Medicine, University of Oxford, 1999–2001; Fellow, Green College, Oxford, 1997–2001; *b* 27 Dec. 1954; *d* of late Derek Justin Schove and Vera Florence Schove; *m* 1977, Christopher Martin Dobson, *qv*; two *s*. *Educ:* Sydenham High Sch. (GPDST); St Hugh's Coll., Oxford (BA 1st Cl. Hons Geog. 1976); Harvard Univ. (AM 1980); Nuffield Coll., Oxford (DPhil 1982). Harkness Fellow, Harvard Univ., 1978–80; University of Oxford: E. P. Abraham and Prize Res. Fellow, Nuffield Coll., 1981–84; Deptl Demonstrator, Sch. of Geog., 1983–89; Lectr in Human Geog., Keble Coll., 1985–88; Res. Fellow, Wolfson Coll., 1987–94; Wellcome Fellow in Health Services Res., Dept of Community Medicine and Gen. Practice, 1989–90; Wellcome Unit for History of Medicine: Wellcome Res. Fellow in Historical Epidemiol., 1990–93; Sen. Res. Officer, 1993–98; Actg Dir and Wellcome Trust Unit Fellow, 1998–99. Affiliated Res. Scholar, Dept of Hist. and Philos. of Sci., Univ. of Cambridge, 2005–11; Res. Associate, Wellcome Centre for Hist. of Medicine, UCL, 2005–11. Radcliffe Sen. Common Room Mem., Green Templeton Coll., Oxford, 2011–. FRSTM&H 1997. Member: Soc. of Authors, 1996–; Historical Novel Soc., 1997–. *Publications:* Contours of Death and Disease in Early Modern England, 1997; Tudor Odours, 1997; Roman Aromas, 1997; Victorian Vapours, 1997; Reeking Royals, 1998; Vile Vikings, 1998; Wartime Whiffs, 1998; Greek Grime, 1998; Mouldy Mummies, 1998; Medieval Muck, 1998; Messy Medicine, 1999; Disease: the extraordinary stories behind history's deadliest killers, 2007, US edn 2014 (trans. Japanese, Chinese, German); The Story of Medicine: from bloodletting to biotechnology, 2013 (trans. German); Murderous Contagion: a human history of disease, 2015. *Address:* The Master's Lodge, St John's College, Cambridge CB2 1TP.

DOBSON, Prof. Michael, DPhil; FEA; Director, Shakespeare Institute, Stratford-upon-Avon, and Professor of Shakespeare Studies, University of Birmingham, since 2011; *b* Bournemouth, 28 Sept. 1960; *s* of Derek and June Dobson; *m* 1987, Prof. Nicola Watson; two *d*. *Educ:* Bournemouth Grammar Sch.; Christ Church, Oxford (BA English Lang. and Lit.

1982; MA 1984; DPhil 1990). Lectr in English, Christ Ch, Oxford, 1987; Vis. Fellow and Tutor, Harvard Univ., 1987–89; Asst Prof., Indiana Univ., Bloomington, 1989–93; Associate Prof., Univ. of Illinois at Chicago, 1993–95; Prof. of Renaissance Drama, Roehampton Inst., London, 1996–2005; Prof. of Shakespeare Studies, Birkbeck, Univ. of London, 2005–11. Vis. Asst Prof., Northwestern Univ., 1991–92; Vis. Fellow, Peking Univ., 1999; Vis. Prof., Lund Univ., 2010. Hon. Gov., RSC, 2011–; Exec. Trustee, Shakespeare Birthplace Trust, 2011–. Hon. Patron, Brownsea Open-Air Th., 2013–. FEA 2012. Hon. Dr Craiova. *Publications:* The Making of the National Poet, 1992; (with S. Wells) The Oxford Companion to Shakespeare, 2001, rev. edn 2016; (with N. Watson) England's Elizabeth: an afterlife in fame and fantasy, 2002; Performing Shakespeare's Tragedies Today, 2006; Great Shakespeareans: John Philip Kemble, 2010; Shakespeare and Amateur Performance, 2011; contrib. essays, reviews and articles to London Rev. of Books, Shakespeare Survey, Shakespeare Qly, Shakespeare Bull., Around the Globe, The Guardian. *Recreations:* theatre-going, writing programme notes at short notice, playing in rock 'n' roll bands, walking. *Address:* c/o Shakespeare Institute, Mason Croft, Church Street, Stratford-upon-Avon, Warks CV37 6HP. *T:* (0121) 414 9500. *E:* m.dobson@bham.ac.uk.

DOBSON, Captain Michael F.; *see* Fulford-Dobson.

DOBSON, Michael William Romsey; Chief Executive, Schroders plc, since 2001; *b* 13 May 1952; *s* of Sir Denis (William) Dobson, KCB, OBE, QC; *m* 1998, Frances, *d* of Count Charles de Salis; two *d.* *Educ:* Eton; Trinity Coll., Cambridge. Joined Morgan Grenfell, 1973: Morgan Grenfell NY, 1978–80, Man. Dir, 1984–85; Hd, Investment Div., 1987–88; Dep. Chief Exec., 1988–89; Gp Chief Exec., Morgan Grenfell, then Deutsche Morgan Grenfell, 1989–97; Mem., Bd of Man. Dirs, Deutsche Bank AG, 1996–2000; Chm., Beaumont Capital Mgt, 2001. *Address:* Schroders plc, 31 Gresham Street, EC2V 7QA.

DOBSON, Prof. Peter James, OBE 2013; PhD; FInstP; FRSC; Professor of Engineering Science, 1996–2013, now Emeritus, and Academic Director, Begbroke Science Park, 2002–13, University of Oxford; Fellow, Queen's College, Oxford, since 1988; *b* Liskeard, Cornwall, 24 Oct. 1942; *s* of Cyril and Mary Dobson; *m* 1965, Catherine Roberts; two *d.* *Educ:* Newquay Grammar Sch.; Southampton Univ. (BSc Physics 1965; PhD 1968). FInstP 2003; FRSC 2011. Lectr, Imperial Coll., London, 1968–84; Sen. Principal Scientist, Philips Res. Labs, 1984–88; Lectr in Engrg Sci., Univ. of Oxford, 1988–94. Co-founder: Oxonica, 1999; Oxford Biosensors, 2000; Oxford NanoSystems, 2012. Strategic Advr on Nanotechnol. to Res. Councils UK, 2009–13. Mem., ACS, 1999. Principal Fellow, Warwick Manufg Gp, 2013. *Recreations:* gardening, cooking, surfing. *Address:* Queen's College, Oxford OX1 4AW. *T:* (01865) 515436. *E:* peter.dobson@queens.ox.ac.uk; 92 Lonsdale Road, Oxford OX2 7ER. *T:* (01865) 515436.

DOBSON, Roger Swinburne, OBE 1987; FREng, FICE; Chairman, Hill Farm Orchards Ltd, since 2008 (Managing Director, 2000–14); *b* 24 June 1936; *s* of Sir Denis William Dobson, KCB, OBE, QC and Thelma Swinburne; *m* 2nd, Deborah Elizabeth Sancroft Burrough; one *s* one *d.* *Educ:* Bryanston Sch.; Trinity Coll., Cambridge (MA); Stanford Univ., Calif (DEng). FICE 1990; FREng 1993. Qualified pilot, RN, 1955. Binnie & Partners, 1959–69; Bechtel Ltd, 1969–90: Gen. Manager, PMB Systems Engrg, 1984–86; Man. Dir, Laing-Bechtel Petroleum Develt, 1986–90; Dir-Gen. and Sec., ICE, 1990–99. Deputy Chairman: Thomas Telford (Holdings) Ltd, 1990–99; Thomas Telford Ltd (formerly Thomas Telford Services Ltd), 1991–99; Director: Yearco Ltd, 1996–98; Quinco: campaign to promote engineering, 1997–2002 (Founding Chm., 1997–98; Trustee, 1997–2002; Hon. Treas., 1998–2002). Chairman: Computer Aided Design Computer Aided Manufacturing Gp, NEDC, 1981–85; Energy Industries Council, 1987–90; Mem., Construction Industry Sector Gp, NEDC, 1988–92. Dir, Pathfinder Fund Internat., 1997–2002. *Publications:* Applications of Digital Computers to Hydraulic Engineering, 1967; contrib. Procs of ICE and IMechE. *Recreations:* croquet, gardening. *Address:* Etchilhampton House, Etchilhampton, Devizes, Wilts SN10 3JH. *Club:* Royal Ocean Racing.

See also M. W. R. Dobson.

DOBSON, Ronald James, CBE 2011; QFSM 2005; Commissioner for Fire and Emergency Planning, London Fire Brigade, 2007–15; *b* Lambeth, 9 March 1959; *s* of Ronald and Patricia Dobson; *m* 1979, Jacqueline Joy Willson; two *s* one *d.* MIFireE 1996. Joined London Fire Bde, 1979; Asst Divl Officer, 1988–92, Divl Officer, 1992–96, Southwark Trng Centre; Divl Comdr, Ops, Eastern Comd, 1996–2000; Asst Comr, 2000–07. Dir, Chief Fire Officers Assoc., 2007–. Pres., London Fire Bde Retd Mems' Assoc., 2008–. *Recreations:* golf, music, walking. *Club:* Sunridge Park Golf (Bromley).

DOBSON, Sue; freelance travel writer and editor; Travel Editor, Choice, 2002–05 (Editor-in-Chief, 1994–2002); *m* 1966, Michael Dobson (marr. diss. 1974). *Educ:* convent schs; DipHE; BA Hons CNAA. From 1964, worked for a collection of women's magazines, including Femina and Fair Lady in S Africa, variously as fashion, cookery, beauty, home and contributing editor, editor at SA Institute of Race Relations and editor of Wedding Day and Successful Slimming in London, with breaks somewhere in between in PR and doing research into the language and learning of children; Editor, Woman and Home, 1982–94. Mem. Bd, Plan Internat., 1993–2004. *Publications:* The Wedding Day Book, 1981, 2nd edn 1989; Travellers Cape Verde, 2008, 2nd edn 2010; Travellers Namibia, 2008, 2nd edn 2010. *Recreations:* travelling, photography, reading, exploring.

DOBSON, (William) Keith, OBE 1988; Director, Interstate Programmes Ltd, 2005–11; *b* 20 Sept. 1945; *s* of Raymond Griffin Dobson and Margaret (*née* Wylie); *m* 1972, Valerie Guest; two *d.* *Educ:* King Edward's Grammar School, Camp Hill, Birmingham; Univ. of Keele (BA Internat. Relns 1968); Univ. of Essex (DipSoc 1972). With Clarks Ltd, Shoemakers, 1968–71; British Council, 1972–2000: Lagos, 1972–75; London, 1975–77; Ankara, 1977–80; Caracas, 1980–84; Budapest, 1984–87; London, 1987–90; Europe Div., 1990–93; Dir, Germany, 1993–2000; Sec.-Gen., Anglo-German Foundn, 2000–05. Gov., ESU, 2002–. *Recreations:* music, cinema, bridge, woodworking. *Address:* 18C Church Green, Witney, Oxon OX28 4AW. *E:* keithdobson20@googlemail.com.

DOCHERTY, Dr David; Chairman, Digital Television Group, since 2009; Chief Executive Officer, National Centre for Universities and Business (formerly Council for Industry and Higher Education), since 2009; *b* Glasgow, 10 Dec. 1956; *s* of David Docherty and Anna Docherty (*née* Graham); *m* 1992, Kate, *d* of Sir Murray Stuart-Smith, *qv*; two *d.* *Educ:* St Mungo's Acad.; Univ. of Strathclyde (BA 1st Cl. Hons 1979); London Sch. of Econs and Pol Sci. (PhD 1983; MSc 1985). Dir of Res., Broadcasting Standards Council, 1988–89; Head: Broadcasting Analysis, BBC TV, 1990–92; Television Planning and Strategy, BBC Network TV, 1992–96; Dir of Strategy and Channel Develt, 1996–97, Dep. Dir of Television, 1997–99, BBC Broadcast; former Dir, New Media, BBC; Chief Exec., YooMedia, 2003–05. Former Chm., Bd of Govs, Univ. of Bedfordshire. Former Chair, Broadcasting Cttee, Soc. of Authors. Hon. Fellow, Univ. of Bedfordshire. *Publications: non-fiction:* The Last Picture Show?, 1987; Keeping Faith, Channel 4 and its Audience, 1988; Running the Show, 1990; Violence in Television Fiction, 1990; *fiction:* The Spirit Death, 2000; The Killing Jar, 2002; The Fifth Season, 2003. *Recreations:* writing, running. *Address:* Serge Hill, Serge Hill Lane, Bedmond, Herts WD5 0RY. *T:* (01923) 291167.

DOCHERTY, Dame Jacqueline, DBE 2004; Chief Executive, West Middlesex University Hospital, since 2009; *b* 19 Feb. 1950; *d* of William Docherty and Elizabeth Barrie Docherty. *Educ:* Hairmyres Hosp. (RGN; Gold Medallist); Caledonian Univ. (MBA Dist.; DMS Dist.). Sen. Sister, Royal Free Hosp., London, 1973–79; Nursing Officer, Inverclyde Royal Infirmary, Greenock, 1979–80; Sen. Nurse, Royal Infirmary, Glasgow, 1980–90; Dep. Dir of Nursing, St John's Hosp., W Lothian, 1990–92; Nursing Officer, Scottish Office, DoH, 1992–96; Exec. Dir of Nursing and Ops, 1996–2009, Dep. Chief Exec., 2007–09, King's Coll. Hosp. Ind. Consultant, Evidence-based Medicine Prog., Mexican Dept of Health, 1997–2000. Visiting Prof., S Bank Univ., 2004–; KCL, 2006–. Trustee: GNC Trust, 2007– (Chm., 2010–13); King's Fund, 2007–13 (Mem., Commn on Leadership and Mgt in the NHS, 2010). *Publications:* (contrib.) A Critical Guide to the UKCC's Code of Conduct, 1999; contribs to DoH (Scotland) clinical pubns, and various articles in professional jls. *Recreations:* country walks, antiques, music, socialising with friends. *Address:* West Middlesex University Hospital, Twickenham Road, Isleworth, Middx TW7 6AF.

DOCHERTY, Joseph Paul; Chief Executive, NCG (formerly Newcastle College Group), since 2013; *b* Helensburgh, 7 Sept. 1969; *s* of Patrick Docherty and Mary Docherty; partner, Marcelo Digap; one *s.* *Educ:* St Mary's Prim. Sch., Alexandria; St Joseph's Prim. Sch., Milngavie; St Ninians High Sch., Kirkintilloch; Univ. of Strathclyde (BEng Hons Civil Engrg 1992; MPhil Construction Mgt 1994); Harvard Business Sch. (Ralph James Scholar; AMP 2011). Barclays plc: Grad. Trainee, Business Analyst, 1994–96; Asst to Chm., 1996–97; Special Policy Advr, Northern Develt Co., 1997–98 (on secondment); Asst Dir, 1998–2000, Dir, 2000–02, Corporate Banking Div.; Chief Exec., Tees Valley Regeneration, 2002–09; Exec. Dir, Enterprise and Develt, 2009–12, Dep. Chief Exec., 2012–13, Home Gp. Mem., Commn on Public Services in N of England, IPPR, 2006. Arts Council England: Trustee and Mem. Council, 2011–; Chm., NE Bd, 2011–14; Chm., Museums and Libraries Accreditation Scheme, 2011–; Chm., Area Council North, 2014–. Chm., Govt Office London Objective 2 Implementation Cttee, 2000–02; Member: HM Govt Urban Sounding Bd, 1998–2004; London Develt Agency Private Investment Commn, 2000–01; British Urban Regeneration Assoc. Steering and Development Forum, 2004–10. Trustee: Baltic Centre for Contemporary Art, 1999–2007 (Chm., Finance and Gen. Purpose Cttee, 2001–07); and Mem. Council, Univ. of Durham, 2007– (Chm., George Stephenson Coll., 2007–12; Chm., Finance and Gen. Purposes Cttee, 2012–); Esmée Fairbairn Foundn, 2013–. FRSA 2008. Mem., Editl Bd, Jl for Urban Regeneration and Renewal, 2007–13. *Recreations:* art, architecture, current affairs and history, travel. *Address:* NCG, Rye Hill House, Scotswood Road, Newcastle upon Tyne NE4 7SA. *Club:* Reform.

DOCHERTY, Martin John; MP (SNP) West Dunbartonshire, since 2015; *b* 1971. *Educ:* Glasgow Coll. of Food Technol. (HND Business Admin 1997); Univ. of Essex (BA Politics); Glasgow Sch. of Art (MA 2004). W Dunbartonshire Community and Volunteering Services. Member (SNP): Clydebank DC, 1992; Glasgow CC, 2012–15. *Address:* House of Commons, SW1A 0AA.

DOCHERTY, Michael, FCCA, CPFA; Chief Executive, South Lanarkshire Council, 1999–2006; *b* 12 Jan. 1952; *s* of Michael and Susan Docherty; *m* 1972, Linda Thorpe; two *s* one *d.* *Educ:* St Mungo's Acad., Glasgow. FCCA 1978; CPFA 1986. Accountancy trainee, S of Scotland Electricity Bd, 1970–74; Accounts Asst, Coatbridge Burgh Council, 1974–75; Accountant: Monklands DC, 1975–77; Stirling DC, 1977–79; Sen. Accountant, 1979–80, Principal Accountant, 1980–82, Monklands DC; Principal Accountant, Renfrew DC, 1982–84; Depute Dir of Finance, Motherwell DC, 1984–92; Dir of Finance, 1992–94, Chief Exec., 1994–95, Hamilton DC; Depute Chief Exec. and Exec. Dir, Corporate Resources, 1995–97, Depute Chief Exec. and Exec. Dir, Enterprise Resources, 1997–99, S Lanarkshire Council. *Recreations:* music, reading, running, golf.

DOCHERTY, Paul Francis; Director, France, British Council, since 2014; *b* 17 Sept. 1951; *s* of Joseph Docherty and Elizabeth Eileen Docherty (*née* Waters); *m* 1987, Karen Leithead (marr. diss. 2007); three *s.* *Educ:* Queen Victoria Sch., Dunblane; Univ. of Strathclyde (BA Hons 1977; MLitt 1985). English teacher, Spain, 1977–83; Lectr in English, Moscow State Univ., 1983–84; joined British Council, 1985: Helsinki, 1986–89; English Language Div., 1989–93; Moscow, 1993–96; Corporate Affairs, 1996–97; Sec., 1997–2000; Dir, Czech Republic, and Cultural Counsellor, Prague, 2000–03; Director: Italy, 2003–09; Scotland, 2009–11; UK 2012, 2011–12; UK Major Events, 2013–14. Gov., British Inst., Florence, 2003–09. FRSA 2008. *Recreations:* listening to opera, playing blues/rock guitar, film and television. *Address:* c/o British Council, 10 Spring Gardens, SW1A 2BN. *T:* (020) 7930 8466.

DOCHERTY, Sadie; Lord Provost and Lord Lieutenant of Glasgow, since 2012; *b* Glasgow, 6 June 1956; *d* of Patrick and Margaret Boyle; *m* 1978, William Docherty; one *s* one *d.* *Educ:* Daigsie Terrace Primary Sch.; St Margaret Mary's Secondary Sch.; Strathclyde Univ. (Scottish Local Authy Mgt 1999). Neighbourhood Housing Manager, Glasgow CC, 1996–2007. Mem. (Lab) Glasgow CC, 2007–. *Recreations:* reading, gardening. *Address:* Glasgow City Council, City Chambers, George Square, Glasgow G2 1DU. *T:* (0141) 287 4171.

DOCHERTY, Thomas; *b* 28 Jan. 1975; *s* of Robert and Margarita Docherty; *m* 2004, Katie McCulloch; one *s.* *Educ:* Open Univ. Res. Asst to Scott Barrie, MSP, 1999–2002; Public Affairs Officer, BNFL, 2002–05; Communications Manager, Network Rail, 2006–07; Account Dir, communications consultancy, 2007–10. MP (Lab) Dunfermline and W Fife, 2010–15; contested (Lab) same seat, 2015. PPS: to Shadow Chief Sec. to the Treasury, 2010–11; to Shadow Leader of H of C, 2011–15. Member: Envmt, Food and Rural Affairs Select Cttee, 2010–15; Defence Select Cttee, 2010–15; Admin Select Cttee, 2010–15; Procedure Cttee, 2011–15. Contested (Lab): Tayside N, 2001; S of Scotland, Scottish Parlt, 2003.

DOCKRAY, Prof. Graham John, PhD; FRS 2004; FMedSci; Professor of Physiology, University of Liverpool, 1982–2013, now Emeritus; *b* 19 July 1946; *s* of Ben and Elsie Dockray; *m* 1985, Andrea Varro; one *s* one *d.* *Educ:* Univ. of Nottingham (BSc 1st cl. Hons (Zool.) 1967; PhD 1971). University of Liverpool: Lectr in Physiol., 1970–78; Sen. Lectr, 1978–80; Reader, 1980–82; Pro-Vice-Chancellor, 2004–06; Dep. Vice-Chancellor, 2006–08. Fogarty Internat. Fellow, UCLA/Veterans Hosp., LA, 1973–74. FMedSci 1998. Hon. FRCP 2001. *Publications:* Cholecystokinin (CCK) in the Nervous System: current developments in neuropeptide research, 1987; The Neuropeptide Cholecystokinin (CCK), 1989; Gut Peptides: physiology and biochemistry, 1994; numerous papers in peer-reviewed jls. *Recreation:* gardening. *Address:* Cell and Molecular Physiology, Institute of Translational Medicine, University of Liverpool, Crown Street, Liverpool L69 3BX. *T:* (0151) 794 5324, *Fax:* (0151) 794 5315. *E:* g.j.dockray@liverpool.ac.uk.

DOCTOR, Brian Ernest; QC 1999; *b* 8 Dec. 1949; *s* of Hans and Daphne Doctor; *m* 1973, Estelle Ann Lewin; three *s.* *Educ:* Balliol Coll., Oxford (BCL); Univ. of Witwatersrand (BA, LLB). Solicitor, 1978–80; Advocate, S Africa, 1980–92; SC S Africa 1990; called to the Bar, Lincoln's Inn, 1991, Bencher, 2009; in practice at the Bar, 1992–. *Recreations:* reading, theatre, opera, cycling. *Address:* Fountain Court Chambers, Temple, EC4Y 9DH. *T:* (020) 7583 3335.

DOCTOROW, Cory Efram; writer; *b* Toronto, 17 July 1971; *s* of Gordon and Roslyn Doctorow; *m* 2008, Alice Jane Taylor; one *d.* Canadian Fulbright Chair in Public Diplomacy, UCLA, 2006–07; Vis. Sen. Lectr, Open Univ., 2009; Schol. in Virtual Residence, Univ. of Waterloo, Ont, 2009. FRSA. *Publications:* Down and Out in the Magic Kingdom, 2003; Eastern Standard Tribe, 2003; A Place so Foreign and Eight More (short stories), 2003; Someone Comes to Town, Someone Leaves Town, 2004; Overclocked (short stories), 2007; Cory Doctorow's Futuristic Tales of the Here and Now, 2008; Content, 2008; Little Brother, 2008; Makers, 2009; For the Win, 2010. *Address:* Unit 306, 456–458 Strand, WC2R 0DZ. *E:* doctorow@craphound.com. *Club:* Shoreditch House.

DODD, Dominic; Chairman, Royal Free London NHS Foundation Trust, since 2009; Director, UCL Partners, since 2009; *b* Ely, 16 Aug. 1967; *s* of Charles Gordon Dodd and Jennifer Anne Dodd; *m* 1999, Catherine Apap Bologna; two *s*. *Educ:* Lincoln Coll., Oxford (BA Hons PPE). Marakon Associates: Consultant, 1989–97; Partner and UK Br. Manager, 1997–2000; Man. Partner, 2000–03; Sen. Advr, 2004–07; Exec. Dir, Children's Investment Fund Foundn, 2008–09. Non-executive Director: Royal Free Hampstead NHS Trust, 2006–09; Permanent TSB plc, 2012–. *Publications:* (jtly) The Three Tensions, 2007; contrib. Harvard Business Rev. *Recreations:* sea, garden, guitar, walking, wood, magic. *Address:* Royal Free London NHS Foundation Trust, Royal Free Hospital, Pond Street, NW3 2QG.

DODD, John Stanislaus; QC 2006; **His Honour Judge Dodd;** a Circuit Judge, since 2012; *b* 3 April 1957; *s* of James and Mary Dodd; *m* 1990, Margaret Ann Roberts; two *s*. *Educ:* St Aloysius' Coll.; Univ. of Leicester (LLB Hons 1978); London Sch. of Economics. Called to the Bar, Gray's Inn, 1979, Bencher, 2011; barrister, specialist in criminal law; a Recorder, 2000–12. Standing Counsel to HM Customs and Excise, subseq. HMRC, 2002–06. Member: Cttee, SE Circuit, 1995–; Bar Council, 1998–2006; Magistrates' Courts Rules Cttee; Sec., Criminal Bar Assoc., 2002–03. *Recreations:* long-distance cycling, squash, playing violin. *Address:* Chelmsford Crown Court, New Street, Chelmsford, Essex CM1 1EL.

DODD, Kenneth Arthur, (Ken Dodd), OBE 1982; comedian, singer and actor; *b* 8 Nov. 1927; *s* of late Arthur and Sarah Dodd; unmarried. *Educ:* Holt High School, Liverpool. Made professional début at Empire Theatre, Nottingham, 1954; created record on London Palladium début, 1965, by starring in his own 42 week season; his record, Tears, topped British charts for six weeks; awarded numerous Gold, Platinum, and Silver Discs (Love Is Like A Violin, Happiness, etc); has starred in numerous pantomimes (holds box office record at Birmingham Hippodrome), summer seasons and Royal Variety Performances, and travels widely with his Happiness Show; starred in own TV and radio series. Shakespearean stage début as Malvolio in Twelfth Night, Playhouse Th., Liverpool, 1971; film début as Yorick in Hamlet, 1997; Mr Mouse in Alice in Wonderland, C4 TV, 1999. Freeman, City of Liverpool, 2001. Hon. Fellow, Liverpool John Moores Univ., 1997. Hon. DLitt: Chester, 2009; Liverpool Hope, 2010. First member, TV Times Hall of Fame, 2002; Living Legend Award, Brit. Comedy Soc., 2003; Lifetime Achievement Award, Brit. Comedy Awards, 1993; voted Greatest Merseysider of All Time by people of Merseyside, 2003. *Relevant publication:* How Tickled I Am: Ken Dodd, by Michael Billington, 1977. *Recreations:* reading, relaxing. *Address:* 76 Thomas Lane, Knotty Ash, Liverpool L14 5NX.

DODD, Nicholas Henry; Chief Executive, Museums Sheffield, 2002–12; *b* Broxbourne, Herts, 9 Dec. 1959; *s* of Mark Wilson Dodd and Shirley Mary Elizabeth Dodd; *m* 1984, Catherine Clare; one *s* one *d*. *Educ:* Univ. of Sussex (BA Hons 1981); Univ. of Leicester (Dip. Museums Studies 1983); Univ. of Warwick (MA Cultural Policy and Admin 1994). AMA 1987. Exhibn Officer, Nat. Postal Mus., 1982–84; Educn and Interpretation Officer, Kent CC, 1984–88; Sen. Curator and Proj. Dir, Coventry CC, 1988–94; Hd, Arts and Mus, Wolverhampton CC, 1994–2002. Trustee, NHMF and HLF, 2000–06; Mem. Bd, MLA, 2006–11. Mem. Bd, Craftspace Touring, 1994–2002. Mem. Court, Univ. of Sheffield, 2006–10. Guardian, Assay Office of Sheffield, 2011. FRSA. *Recreations:* making marmalade, gardening, taking busman's holidays, walking around. *Address:* The Old Hall, 2 Stoney Lane, Chapelthorpe, Wakefield WF4 3JN. *T:* (01924) 254387, 07711 400079. *E:* nick.dodd1@gmail.com.

DODD, Philip; Founder, Made in China, consultancy, 2004; *b* Grimethorpe, 25 Oct. 1949; *s* of Ernest and Mavis Dodd; *m* 1976, Kathryn; two *s*. *Educ:* UC, Swansea (BA Hons); Univ. of Leicester (MA). Lectr in English Literature, Univ. of Leicester, 1976–89; Dep. Editor, New Statesman and Society, 1989–90; Editor, Sight and Sound, BFI, 1990–97; Dir, ICA, 1997–2004. Visiting Professor: KCL, 2000–03; Univ. of the Arts London, 2004–. Consultant, Music and Arts: BBC, 1986–91; Wall to Wall TV, 1991–97. Presenter, Night Waves, BBC Radio 3, 2000–. Chief Internat. Advr, Shanghai eArts Festival, 2007–; Advr, Beijing Internat. Cultural and Creative Industry Expo, 2008. Small Publisher of the Year, PPA, 1993; Sony Radio Award, 1996. *Publications:* (ed jtly) Englishness: politics and culture 1880–1920, 1986; (jtly) Relative Values: what's art worth, 1991; The Battle over Britain, 1995; (ed jtly) Spellbound, Art and Film, 1996.

DODD, Philip Kevin, OBE 1987; a District Judge (Magistrates' Courts) (formerly Stipendiary Magistrate), Cheshire, 1991–2004; *b* 2 April 1938; *s* of Thomas and Mary Dodd; *m* 1962, Kathleen Scott; one *s* one *d*. *Educ:* St Joseph's Coll., Dumfries; Leeds Univ. (BA, LLB). Admitted Solicitor, 1966. Articled Clerk, Ashton-under-Lyne Magistrates' Court, 1961–63; Dep. Justices' Clerk, 1963–67; Justices' Clerk: Houghton-le-Spring and Seaham, 1967–70; Wolverhampton, 1970–76; Manchester, 1976–91. Council Member: Justices' Clerks' Soc., 1974–89 (Pres., 1985–86); Manchester Law Soc., 1978–91 (Pres., 1987–88). Sec., Standing Conf., Clerks to Magistrates' Courts Cttees, 1974–82 (Chm., 1983–84). *Recreation:* planning holidays.

DODDS, Dr Anneliese Jane; Member (Lab) South East Region, European Parliament, since 2014; *b* Aberdeen, 16 March 1978; partner, Edward Turner; one *s*. *Educ:* St Hilda's Coll., Oxford (BA 1st Cl. Hons PPE 2001); Univ. of Edinburgh (MRes Dist. 2002); London Sch. of Econs and Pol Sci. (PhD Govt 2006). ESRC Postdoctoral Fellow, LSE, 2006; Lectr in Public Policy, 2007–10, and Actg Dir, NIHR Patient Safety and Service Quality Res. Centre, 2009–10, KCL; Sen. Lectr in Public Policy, Aston Univ., 2010–14. Vis. Prof., Univ. of Prishtina, 2010. Contested (Lab): Billericay, 2005; Reading E, 2010. *Publications:* Comparative Public Policy, 2013; contribs to books and peer-reviewed articles. *Address:* European Parliament, 60 Rue Wiertz, 1047 Brussels, Belgium; (office) Unit A, Bishops Mews, Transport Way, Oxford OX4 6HD.

DODDS, Diane Jean; Member (DemU) Northern Ireland, European Parliament, since 2009; *b* 16 Aug. 1958; *m* 1985, Nigel Alexander Dodds (*see* Rt Hon. N. A. Dodds); two *s* one *d*. *Educ:* Banbridge Acad.; Queen's Univ., Belfast (BA Hist. and English); Stranmillis Coll. (PGCE). Teacher of History and English, Laurelhill High Sch., Lisburn. Mem. (DemU) W Belfast, NI Assembly, 2003–07. Mem. (DemU), Belfast CC, 2005–10. *Address:* European Parliament, Rue Wiertz, 1047 Brussels, Belgium.

DODDS, John Charles; Director, Transformation, Department for Business, Innovation and Skills, since 2013; *b* Darlington, 15 Feb. 1961; *s* of John Dodds and Jean Dodds; *m* 2008, Clare Alexander. *Educ:* Hummersknott Sch., Darlington; Queen Elizabeth Sixth Form Coll., Darlington; Christ's Coll., Cambridge (BA Maths 1982); Manchester Univ. (MSc Stats 1983). Statistician, Inland Revenue, 1983–87; HM Treasury: Policy Advr, 1987–94; Hd, Budget Coordination, 1994–97; Dir, Inf. Services, 1997–2002; Hd, Defence, Diplomacy and Intelligence, 2002–06; Dir, Regulatory Reform, Better Regulation Exec., Cabinet Office, 2006–07, BERR, subseq. BIS, 2007–11; Dir, Innovation, BIS, 2011–13. Mem., London Library. *Recreations:* collecting books, exploring the history of technology and food, following equestrian sport. *Address:* Department for Business, Innovation and Skills, 1 Victoria Street, SW1H 0ET. *T:* (020) 7215 0283. *E:* john.dodds@bis.gsi.gov.uk. *Club:* Durham County Cricket.

DODDS, Rt Hon. Nigel (Alexander), OBE 1997; PC 2010; MP (DemU) Belfast North, since 2001; barrister; *b* 20 Aug. 1958; *s* of Joseph Alexander and Doreen Elizabeth Dodds; *m* 1985, Diana Jean Harris (*see* D. J. Dodds); two *s* one *d*. *Educ:* Portora Royal Sch., Enniskillen; St John's Coll., Cambridge (MA); Inst. of Professional Legal Studies, Belfast (Cert. of Professional Legal Studies). Called to the Bar, NI, 1981. Mem., Belfast City Council, 1985–2010 (Chairman: F and GP Cttee, 1985–87; Develt Cttee, 1997–99); Lord Mayor of Belfast, 1988–89 and 1991–92; Alderman, Castle Area, 1989–97. Mem., NI Forum, 1996–98. Mem. (DemU) Belfast N, NI Assembly, 1998–2010; Minister: for Social Develt, NI, 1999–2000 and 2001–02; of Enterprise, Trade and Investment, NI, 2007–08; for Finance and Personnel, NI, 2008–09. Vice Pres., Assoc. of Local Authorities of NI, 1988–89. Mem., Senate, QUB, 1987–93. *Address:* House of Commons, SW1A 0AA.

DODDS, (Robert) Stephen; His Honour Judge Dodds; a Circuit Judge, since 2007; *b* Blackburn, 6 Nov. 1952; *s* of George Dodds and Edith Mary Dodds; *m* 1980, Kathryn Hadley (separated 2010); one *s* one *d*. *Educ:* Queen Elizabeth's Grammar Sch., Blackburn; Leeds Poly. (LLB); Coll. of Law. Called to the Bar, Gray's Inn, 1976; Asst Recorder, 1995–99; Recorder, 1999–2007. Asst Parly Boundary Comr, 2003–07. Chm., Old Blackburnians' Assoc., Queen Elizabeth's Grammar Sch., Blackburn, 2011–14. *Recreations:* watching Blackburn Rovers FC, collecting football programmes, collecting malt whisky, reading, cricket (Lancashire CCC). *Address:* Liverpool Civil and Family Court, 35 Vernon Street, Liverpool L2 2BX. *Club:* District and Union (Blackburn).

DODGE, Ian James; National Director, Commissioning Strategy, NHS England, since 2014; *b* Tunbridge Wells, 20 Aug. 1971; *s* of Ron Dodge and Jean Dodge; *m* 2001, Elizabeth Woodeson (CBE 2012). *Educ:* Kent Coll., Canterbury; Lincoln Coll., Oxford (BA Hons Mod. Hist. 1993); Imperial Coll. London (MBA 2000). Department of Health, 1993–2014: Hd, Primary Care, 2001–04; Dep. Dir, NHS Performance, 2004–05; (on secondment) Sen. Policy Advr to the Prime Minister, 2005–06; Dir, Policy Unit, DoH, 2006–12; Hd, Policy Profession, 2010–14; Dir, NHS Policy and Outcomes Group, 2012–14. Adjunct Prof., Inst. of Global Health Innovation, Imperial Coll. London, 2012–. *Recreations:* Greek islands, new music, running, tennis, clematis. *Address:* 22 Alma Street, NW5 3DJ. *T:* (020) 7267 6008. *E:* iandodge@gmail.com.

DODGSHON, Prof. Robert Andrew, PhD; FBA 2002; FLSW; Gregynog Professor of Human Geography, 2001–07, now Emeritus Professor, and Director, 1998–2003, Institute of Geography and Earth Sciences, University of Wales, Aberystwyth; *b* 8 Dec. 1941; *s* of Robert and Dorothy Dodgshon; *m* 1969, Katherine Simmonds; two *d*. *Educ:* Liverpool Univ. (BA 1963, PhD 1969). Asst Keeper, Mus. of English Rural Life, Univ. of Reading, 1966–70; Lectr, 1970–80, Sen. Lectr, 1980–84, Reader, 1984–88, Prof., 1988–2001, UCW Aberystwyth, subseq. Univ. of Wales, Aberystwyth. Council Member: Countryside Council for Wales, 1997–2004; NT, 2001–08; Mem., JNCC, 2003–04. Pres., Soc. for Landscape Studies, 1997–2008. Founding FLSW 2010. Murchison Award, RGS, 1996; Scottish Geographical Medal, RSGS, 2003. *Publications:* (ed jtly) An Historical Geography of England and Wales, 1978, 2nd edn 1990; The Origin of British Field Systems, 1980; Land and Society in Early Scotland, 1980; The European Past, 1987; From Chiefs to Landlords, 1998; Society in Time and Space, 1998; (ed jtly) An Historical Geography of Europe, 1998; The Age of the Clans, 2002; No Stone Unturned, 2015. *Recreations:* travel, music, historic landscapes, arts and crafts movement. *Address:* 4 Stratton Audley Manor, Mill Road, Stratton Audley, Oxon OX27 9AR. *T:* (01869) 278258. *E:* rad@aber.ac.uk.

DODGSON, Clare; External Complaints Reviewer, Parliamentary and Health Service Ombudsman, since 2011; *b* 10 Sept. 1962; *d* of William Baxter and Ann Baxter (*née* Mattimoe); *m* 1988, Gerard Dodgson. *Educ:* St Robert of Newminster Sch., Washington; Newcastle Business Sch. (MBA). Dir of Planning and Service Develt, S Tyneside FHSA, 1990–92; Chief Executive: Newcastle FHSA, 1992–93; Sunderland HA, 1993–99; Dir, Jobcentre Services, subseq. Chief Operating Officer, Employment Services Agency, DfEE, 1999–2002; Chief Operating Officer, DWP, Jobcentre Plus, 2002–03; Chief Exec., Legal Services Commn, 2003–06; Public Appts Ambassador, Govt Equalities Office, then Home Office, 2009–12. Chm., Strategic Adv. Bd, Bar Tribunals and Adjudication Service, 2014–. Non-executive Director: NW London Strategic HA, 2002–06; HMRC Prosecution Office, 2008–; Ind. Dir, Agric. and Hort. Develt Bd, 2007–12; Seafish Authy, 2012–, DEFRA; Ind. Panel Mem., Judicial Conduct Investigation Office (formerly Office for Judicial Complaints), 2012–; Ind. Mem., Service Complaints Panels, MoD, 2013–. Mem., Healthcare Commn, 2007–09. Public Interest Mem., Regulation and Compliance Bd, ICAS, 2011–. *Recreations:* travel, Ariel Atom 3-300bhp, good food with friends, felines. *Address:* Parliamentary and Health Service Ombudsman, Millbank Tower, Millbank, SW1P 4QP.

DODGSON, Paul; His Honour Judge Dodgson; a Circuit Judge, since 2001; *b* 14 Aug. 1951; *s* of late Reginald Dodgson and of Kathleen Dodgson; *m* 1982, Jan Hemingway; one *s* two *d*. *Educ:* Tiffin Sch.; Univ. of Birmingham (LLB Hons). Called to the Bar, Inner Temple, 1975; Asst Recorder, 1992–96; a Recorder, 1996–2001. Mem., Parole Bd of Eng. and Wales, 2003–. Treas., Criminal Bar Assoc., 1992–94. *Recreations:* ski-ing, sailing, golf, socialising.

DODS, Roanne Watson; Artistic Director, PAL Labs, since 2013; Director, Jerwood Charitable Foundation, 1998–2009; *b* 16 Sept. 1965; *m* 1999, Paul Harkin (*d* 2013); one *s*. *Educ:* St Andrews Univ. (MA); Edinburgh Univ. (LLB; DipLP); Laban Centre, London (MA). Solicitor: Loudons WS, 1990–94; Erskine McAskill, 1994–96; Balfour & Manson, 1996–97; Consultant to Lottery Project, Laban Centre, London, 1998. Vice-Chm., Scottish Ballet, 2007–10; Chairman: Innovative Craft, 2008–11; Battersea Arts Centre, 2009–; Performing Arts Labs, 2010–; Co-Dir, Mission Models Money, 2008–11; Dir, Rose Orange, 2008–; Dep. Dir, Dovecot Studios (formerly Dovecot Foundn), 2011–; Producer, Internat. Futures Forum, 2011– (Mem., 2008–11)); Member: Bd, Sistema Scotland, 2007–10; Bd, Cove Park. Chair, The Work Room, Glasgow. Producer, Small is Beautiful conf., Glasgow, 2014. *Recreations:* windsurfing, swimming, contemporary dance, contemporary fiction, photography. *Address:* 11 Glencairn Drive, Glasgow G41 4QP. *T:* (0141) 423 7516. *E:* roanne@roseorange.com.

DODSON, family name of **Baron Monk Bretton**.

DODSON, Prof. Eleanor Joy, FRS 2003; Research Fellow, University of York, since 1976; *b* 6 Dec. 1936; *d* of Arthur McPherson and Alice Power; *m* 1965, (George) Guy Dodson, FRS (*d* 2012); three *s* one *d*. *Educ:* Univ. of Melbourne (BA Hons). Res. Asst, Lab. of Dorothy Hodgkin, Univ. of Oxford, 1961–76. *Recreations:* family, theatre, opera. *Address:* 101 East Parade, York YO31 7YD. *T:* (01904) 424449. *E:* E.Dodson@ysbl.york.ac.uk.

DODSON, Joanna; QC 1993; *b* 5 Sept. 1945; *d* of late Jack Herbert Dodson and Joan Muriel (*née* Webb); *m* 1974 (marr. diss. 1981). *Educ:* James Allen's Girls' Sch.; Newnham Coll., Cambridge (entrance exhibnr; BA 1967; MA 1971). Called to the Bar, Middle Temple, 1971, Bencher, 2000. Gov., James Allen's Girls' Sch., 1999–2009.

DODSON, Robert North; *see* North, R.

DODSWORTH, Sir David John S.; *see* Smith-Dodsworth.

DODSWORTH, Geoffrey Hugh; JP; FCA; Chairman, Dodsworth & Co. Ltd, since 1988; *b* 7 June 1928; *s* of late Walter J. J. Dodsworth and Doris M. Baxter; *m* 1st, 1949, Isabel Neale (decd); one *d*; 2nd, 1971, Elizabeth Ann Beeston; one *s* one *d*. *Educ:* St Peter's Sch., York. MP (C) Herts SW, Feb. 1974–Oct. 1979, resigned. Mem. York City Council, 1959–65; JP York 1961, later JP Herts. Dir, Grindlays Bank Ltd, 1976–80; Chief Exec., Grindlay Brandts Ltd, 1977–80; Pres. and Chief Exec., Oceanic Finance Corp., 1980–85, Dep. Chm., 1985–86; Chm., Oceanic Financial Services, 1985–86; Director: County Properties Group, 1987–88;

First Internat. Leasing Corp., 1990–94. *Recreation:* riding. *Address:* Up Yonder, Well Bank, Well, Bedale, N Yorks DL8 2QQ. *T:* (01677) 470712, *Fax:* (01677) 470903. *E:* dodsworth1971@googlemail.com. *Club:* Carlton.

DODSWORTH, Prof. (James) Martin; Professor of English, Royal Holloway (formerly Royal Holloway and Bedford New College), University of London, 1987–2001, now Emeritus; *b* 10 Nov. 1935; *s* of Walter Edward and Kathleen Ida Dodsworth; *m* 1967, Joanna Rybicka; one *s*. *Educ:* St George's Coll., Weybridge; Univ. of Fribourg, Switzerland; Wadham Coll., Oxford (MA). Asst Lectr and Lectr in English, Birkbeck Coll., London, 1961–67; Lectr and Sen. Lectr, Royal Holloway Coll., later Royal Holloway and Bedford New Coll., London, 1967–87. Vis. Lectr, Swarthmore Coll., Pa, 1966. Chairman: English Assoc., 1987–92 (Centenary Hon. Fellow, 2006); Cttee for University English, 1988–90; Mem., Common English Forum, 2001–05. Editor, English, 1976–87; Advr, Agenda, 2004–11. *Publications:* (ed) The Survival of Poetry, 1970; Hamlet Closely Observed, 1985; (ed) English Economis'd, 1989; (ed) The Penguin History of Literature, vol. 7: The Twentieth Century, 1994; (with J. B. Bamborough) Commentary to Robert Burton, the Anatomy of Melancholy, vol. 1, 1998, vols 2 and 3, 2000; Assessing Research Assessment in English, 2006; contribs to The Guardian, Essays in Criticism, The Review, etc. *Recreations:* reading, eating and drinking, short walks. *Address:* 59 Temple Street, Brill, Bucks HP18 9SU. *T:* (01844) 237106.

DODWELL, Christina; writer and explorer; Chairman, Dodwell Trust, since 1996; Senior Attaché, Madagascar Consulate, since 1990; *b* Nigeria, 1 Feb. 1951; *d* of Christopher Bradford Dodwell and Evelyn Dodwell (*née* Beddow); *m* 1991, Stephen Hobbs (*d* 2013). *Educ:* Southover Manor, Lewes; Beechlawn Coll., Oxford. Journeys through Africa by horse, 1975–78, and through Papua New Guinea by horse and canoe, 1980–81; presenter, BBC films: River Journey-Waghi, 1984 (BAFTA award); Black Pearls of Polynesia, 1991; African Footsteps—Madagascar, 1996; over 40 documentary progs for BBC Radio 4. FRGS 1982. Mungo Park Medal, RSGS, 1989; Internat. Medal, Spanish Geographical Soc., 2014. *Publications:* Travels with Fortune, 1979; In Papua New Guinea, 1982; An Explorer's Handbook, 1984; A Traveller in China, 1986; A Traveller on Horseback, 1987; Travels with Pegasus, 1989; Beyond Siberia, 1993; Madagascar Travels, 1995. *Address:* c/o Madagascar House, 16 Lanark Mansions, Pennard Road, W12 8DT.

DODWORTH, Air Vice-Marshal Peter, CB 1994; OBE 1982; AFC 1971; DL; Royal Air Force, retired; Military Adviser to Vosper Thornycroft (formerly Bombardier Aerospace Defence Services), 1996–2003; *b* 12 Sept. 1940; *e s* of Eric and Edna Dodworth; *m* 1963, Kay Parry; three *s* (and one twin *s* decd). *Educ:* Southport Grammar Sch.; Leeds Univ. (BSc Physics, 1961). Served: 54 Sqn Hunters, 1963–65; 4 FTS Gnats, 1965–67; Central Flying Sch., 1967–68; Harrier Conversion Team, 1969–72; Air Staff RAF Germany, 1972–76; OC Ops, RAF Wittering, 1976–79; ndc 1980; Air Comdr, Belize, 1980–82; staff, RAF Staff Coll., 1982–83; Stn comdr, RAF Wittering, 1983–85; Command Group Exec., HQ AAFCE, Ramstein, 1985–87; RCDS, 1987; Dir of Personnel, MoD, 1988–91; Defence Attaché and Hd, British Defence Staff (Washington), 1991–94; Sen. DS (A), RCDS, 1995–96. FRAeS 1997–2011. DL Lincs, 2004. Vice Chm., Burma Star Assoc., 2006–12. Chm. of Govs, Stamford Endowed Sch., 2005–10. Liveryman, Hon. Co. of Air Pilots (formerly GAPAN), 2004–. *Recreations:* golf, DIY, reading. *Club:* Royal Air Force (Chm., 1994–96).

DOE, Rt Rev. Michael David; an Hon. Assistant Bishop, Diocese of Southwark, since 2004; Preacher to Gray's Inn, since 2011; *b* Lymington, Hants, 24 Dec. 1947; *s* of late Albert Henry Doe and Violet Nellie Doe (*née* Curtis). *Educ:* Brockenhurst Grammar Sch.; Durham Univ. (BA 1969); Ripon Hall Theol Coll., Oxford. Ordained deacon, 1972, priest, 1973; Asst Curate, 1972–76, Hon. Curate, 1976–81, St Peter, St Helier, Morden; Youth Sec., BCC, 1976–81; Priest-Missioner, 1981–88, Vicar, 1988–89, Blackbird Leys LEP, Oxford; RD, Cowley, 1986–89; Social Responsibility Advr, dio. of Portsmouth, and Canon Residentiary, Portsmouth Cathedral, 1989–94; Suffragan Bp of Swindon, 1994–2004; Gen. Sec., USPG: Anglicans in World Mission (formerly Utd Soc. for the Propagation of the Gospel), 2004–11. Hon. LLD Bath, 2002. *Publications:* Seeking the Truth in Love, 2000; Today! The Mission of Jesus in the Gospel of Luke, 2009; Saving Power: the mission of God and the Anglican Communion, 2011. *Recreations:* theatre, radio, English fiction. *Address:* 405 West Carriage House, Royal Carriage Mews, Royal Arsenal, Woolwich, SE18 6GA.

DOE, Prof. William Fairbank, FRCP, FRACP, FMedSci; Provost, Aga Khan University, 2008–11; Professor and Head of Medical School, University of Birmingham, 1998–2007, now Professor Emeritus of Medicine (Dean of Medicine, Dentistry and Health Sciences, 1998–2002; Dean of Medicine, 2002–07); *b* 6 May 1941; *s* of Asa Garfield Doe and Hazel Thelma Doe; *m* 1982, Dallas Elizabeth Edith Ariotti; two *s*. *Educ:* Newington Coll., Sydney; Univ. of Sydney (MB BS); Chelsea Coll., Univ. of London (MSc). FRACP 1978; FRCP 1982. MRC Fellow, 1970–71, Lectr, 1973–74, RPMS; Consultant, Hammersmith Hosp., 1973–74; Lilly Internat. Fellow, 1974–75, Postdoctoral Fellow, 1975–77, Scripps Clinic and Res. Foundn, Calif; Associate Prof., Univ. of Sydney, and Hon. Physician, Royal N Shore Hosp., 1978–81; Prof. of Medicine and Clin. Scis, 1982–88, Head of Div. of Molecular Medicine, 1988–98, John Curtin Sch. of Med. Res., ANU; Dir of Gastroenterology, Canberra Hosp., 1991–97; Prof. of Medicine, Univ. of Sydney, 1995–98. WHO Cons., Beijing, 1987; Dist. Vis. Fellow, Christ's Coll., Cambridge, 1988–89. Dep. Chm., Council of Hds of Med. Schs, 2002–06. Non-executive Director: Birmingham HA, 1998–2003; Birmingham and Black County Strategic HA, 2003–06. Pres., Gastroenterological Soc. of Australia, 1989–91 (Dist. Res. Medal, 1997); Member: NH&MRC Social Psychiatry Adv. Cttee, 1982–92; Council, Nat. Centre for Epidemiology Population Health, 1987–98; Aust. Drug Evaluation Cttee, 1988–95; Council, RACP, 1993–98 (Censor, 1980–87); NH&MRC Res. Strategy Cttee, 1997–98; Workforce Develt Confedn, 2002–06; Wkg Party, Defining and Maintaining Professional Values in Medicine, RCP, 2004–07. Mem. Council, Univ. of Birmingham, 2004–06; Gov., Univ. of Worcester (formerly UC Worcester), 2004–07. Mem., Lunar Soc., 1999–2008. FMedSci 1999. Sen. Editor, Jl Gastroenterology and Hepatology, 1993–2001. *Publications:* numerous scientific papers on molecular cell biology of mucosal inflammation and colon cancer. *Recreations:* opera, reading, wine, tennis. *E:* williamfdoe@gmail.com. *Club:* Athenæum.

DOEL, Air Cdre Martin Terry, OBE 1998; FRAeS; Chief Executive, Association of Colleges, since 2008; *b* Romsey, Hants, 21 Nov. 1956; *s* of Terry and Brenda Doel; *m* 1980, Angela; two *s*. *Educ:* Totton Grammar Sch.; Totton Sixth Form Coll.; King Alfred's Coll., Winchester (BEd 1st Cl. Hons); King's Coll. London (MA War Studies (Dist.)); RAF Staff Coll., Cranwell. FRAeS 2002. Served RAF, 1980–2008: RAF Staff Coll., 1994; Mem., Directing Staff, JSCSC, 1998–2000; Station Comdr, RAF Wyton, Brampton and Henlow, 2000–03; Director: RAF Div., JSCSC, 2003–04; Personnel and Trng Strategy, RAF, 2004–06; Trng and Educn, MoD, 2006–08. Member: UK Council of Colls, 2010–; Adv. Bd, Skills Funding Agency, 2010–; Bd, Skills Show (UK), 2011–13; Owner's Bd, QAA, 2013–; Further Educn Learning Technol. Action Gp, 2013–; Owners' Bd, JISC, 2014–; Internat. Educn Adv. Forum, British Council, 2014–; Bd, UK/India Educn and Res. Initiative, 2015–. Treas., World Fedn of Colls and Polys, 2009–. Trustee, Aspire and Achieve Foundn, 2008–14. FRSA 2008. *Publications:* contrib. articles on military assistance in humanitarian aid ops, apprenticeships and enterprise educn. *Recreations:* soccer (Life Vice-Pres., RAF FA), cinema, modern art, military history and theory. *Address:* Association of Colleges, 1–3 Stedham Place, WC1A 1HU. *T:* (020) 7034 9900. *E:* martin_doel@aoc.co.uk. *Club:* Royal Air Force.

DOERR, Michael Frank, FIA; Group Chief Executive, Friends Provident Life Office, 1992–97; *b* 25 May 1935; *s* of Frank and May Doerr; *m* 1958, Jill Garrett; one *s* one *d*. *Educ:* Rutlish Sch. FIA 1959. Friends Provident Life Office, 1954–97: Pensions Actuary, 1960–66; Life Manager, 1966–73; Gen. Manager, Marketing, 1973–80; Gen. Manager, Ops, and Dir, 1980–87; Dep. Man. Dir, 1987–92. Director: Endsleigh Insce Services Ltd, 1980–94; Seaboard Life Insce Co. (Canada), 1987–92; Friends Provident Life Assce Co. (Australia), 1990–92; Friends Provident Life Assce Co. (Ireland), 1990–92; Friends Vilas-Fischer Trust Co. (US), 1996–98. Chairman: Preferred Direct Insce, 1992–97; FP Asset Mgt, 1996–97. *Recreations:* golf, tennis, chess, theatre, sailing. *Clubs:* Royal Automobile; Royal Southern Yacht.

DOERRIES, Chantal-Aimée Renée Amelia Annemarie; QC 2008; *b* 26 Aug. 1968; *d* of Dr Reinhard R. Doerries and Elaine L. Doerries (*née* Sulli). *Educ:* Roedean Sch.; Univ. of Pennsylvania; New Hall, Cambridge (BA 1990). Pres., Cambridge Union Soc., 1989. Called to the Bar, Middle Temple, 1992 (Maj. Harmsworth Entrance Exhibn and Diplock Schol.), Bencher, 2010. Chm., Technol. and Construction Bar Assoc., 2010–13 (Vice-Chm., 2007–10); Vice Chm., Bar Council of England and Wales, 2015 (Chm., Internat. Cttee, 2011–14); Co-Chair, Forum for Barristers and Advocates, Internat. Bar Assoc., 2009–11. Fellow, Amer. Bar Foundn, 2010. Jt Ed., Building Law Reports, 1999–; Co-Ed. in Chief, Internat. Construction Law Rev., 2015–. Gertrude de Gallaix Achievement Award, Fedn of Amer. Women's Clubs Overseas, 1990. *Publications:* (contrib. ed) Hudson's Building and Engineering Contracts, 12th edn, 2010. *Address:* 1 Atkin Building, Gray's Inn, WC1R 5AT. *T:* (020) 7404 0102. *E:* clerks@atkinchambers.com.

DOGANIS, Sally Elizabeth; freelance executive television producer, broadcaster, journalist and media consultant; Executive Producer, Brook Lapping, since 2005; *b* London, 16 Jan. 1942; *d* of Joe and Freda Davis; *m* 1968, Prof. Rigas Doganis; one *s* one *d*. *Educ:* Woodhouse Grammar Sch.; Sorbonne, Paris (Dip. Civilisation Français); London Sch. of Econs (Leverhulme Schol.; BA Hons); Univ. of Calif, Berkeley (Fulbright Schol.; MA). W African corresp., BBC Africa Service and Sunday Times, 1967–68; Producer Director: Money Prog., 1968–71; Current Affairs Special Projects, BBC World Service, 1972–73; Dir, two films for English learners, BBC External Service, 1975–76; sen. producer and exec. producer, Nationwide, 1978–80, Money Prog., 1980 (Shell Award for best financial film, 1980), Newsnight, 1982, Panorama (Best Journalism Awards, RTS, 1982, 1983), Everyman and documentary series, BBC TV; producer, 1978–94: The Marketing of Margaret; The Falklands and the Media; Jasmine a Death too Many; A Bitter Pill; Family Secrets; TV and No. 10; Out of the Doll's House; The People's Century; Legendary Trails; On Trial; Just Deserts; Series Ed., Hard Luck Stories, 1981–82; Exec. Producer, Mentorn, 1995–96; Consultant, Channel One, on trng video journalists, 1995–97; Mental Health Manager: Tower Hamlets, 1997–99; Royal Free Hosp., 2000–04; Exec. Producer and Controller, Factual Progs, Carlton TV, 1998–2003: producer: Churchill's Secret Army; Ancient Greek Olympics; Britain at War in Colour; The Facts of Life; Kelly and her Sisters (BAFTA, RTS, Broadcast and Grierson Awards for Best Documentary, 2002); Hd of Documentaries, Target, 2004–05. Vis. Course Leader in Media Mgt, London Business Sch., 1985–88. Member: AHRC, 2007–13 (Chm., Stakeholders Cttee, 2012–13); Adv. Bds, Res. Councils UK, 2008–; Ethics Cttee, NHS, 2011–. Mem. Council, RTS, 1996–2003. Trustee: MA Media Mgt Course, LSE, 1997–2001; Catch 22 (charity), 2003–10; Fundraising Cttee, Central Ballet Sch., 2004–07; Mem. Council, Friends of Kenwood, 2004–; Chm., Corporate Benefactors Cttee, Kenwood, 2010–; Mem., Develt Cttee, Tricycle Th., 2010–. Member Board: Forum UK, 2010–; Internat. Women's Fedn UK, 2011–. Jury mem. for awards from RTS, BAFTA, Grierson, One World Trust and Emmy Awards, 1997–. FRTS 1997. Golden Jury USA Award, Worldfest Houston, 1998; Gemini Canada Award, Canadian Acad. of Film and TV, 1998. *Publications:* (with Margaret Jay) Battered: the abuse of children, 1986; for children: Three Bags Full, 1976; The Milk Run, 1976; Bricks and Mortar, 1977; Fish and Ships, 1977; contrib. articles to The Guardian, Sunday Times, The Listener, History Today. *Recreations:* tennis, swimming, ballet, learning Greek, relaxing in Antiparos, grandmothering. *E:* sally@doganisassociates.co.uk. *Club:* Globe Tennis.

DOGGART, George Hubert Graham, OBE 1993; Headmaster, King's School, Bruton, 1972–85; *b* 18 July 1925; *e s* of late Alexander Graham Doggart and Grace Carlisle Hannan; *m* 1960, Susan Mary, *d* of R. I. Beattie, Eastbourne; one *s* one *d* (and one *d* decd). *Educ:* Winchester; King's Coll., Cambridge. BA History, 1950; MA 1955. Army, 1943–47 (Sword of Honour, 161 OCTU, Mons, 1944); Coldstream Guards. On staff at Winchester, 1950–72 (exchange at Melbourne C of E Grammar Sch., 1963); Housemaster, 1964–72. HMC Schools rep. on Nat. Cricket Assoc., 1964–75; President: English Schools Cricket Assoc., 1965–2000; Quidnuncs, 1983–88; Cricket Soc., 1983–98; Member: Cricket Council, 1968–71, 1972, 1983–92; MCC Cttee, 1975–78, 1979–81, 1982–92 (Pres., 1981–82; Treas., 1987–92; Hon. Life Vice-Pres., 1992). Captain, Butterflies CC, 1986–97. Chm., Friends of Arundel Castle CC, 1992–2003. *Publications:* (ed) The Heart of Cricket: memoir of H. S. Altham, 1967; (jtly) Lord Be Praised: the story of MCC's bicentenary celebrations, 1988; (jtly) Oxford and Cambridge Cricket, 1989; (ed) Reflections in a Family Mirror, 2002; (contrib.) A Breathless Hush: the MCC anthology of cricket verse, 2004; Cricket's Bounty, 2014. *Recreation:* literary and sporting (captained Cambridge v Oxford at cricket, Association football, rackets and squash, 1949–50; played in Rugby fives, 1950; played for England v W Indies, two tests, 1950; captained Sussex, 1954). *Address:* Georgian Priory, 3B Westgate, Chichester, West Sussex PO19 3ES. *Clubs:* MCC, Lord's Taverners; Hawks (Cambridge).

DOHERTY, Hon. Lord; (Joseph) Raymond Doherty; a Senator of the College of Justice in Scotland, since 2010; *b* 30 Jan. 1958; *s* of James Doherty and Mary Doherty; *m* 1994, Arlene Donaghy; one *s* two *d*. *Educ:* St Mungo's Primary Sch., Alloa; St Joseph's Coll., Dumfries; Univ. of Edinburgh (LLB 1st Cl. Hons 1980); Hertford Coll., Oxford (BCL 1982); Harvard Law Sch. (LLM 1983). Lord Reid Schol., 1983–85; admitted Faculty of Advocates, 1984; QC (Scot.) 1997. Standing Junior Counsel: MoD (Army), Scotland, 1990–91; Scottish Office Industry Dept, 1992–97; Advocate Depute, 1998–2001; Mem., Lands Valuation Appeal Court, 2011–; Judge, Upper Tribunal (Tax and Chancery Chamber), 2014–; Commercial Judge, 2014–; Exchequer Judge, 2014–; Competition Appeal Tribunal, 2015–. Clerk of the Faculty of Advocates, 1990–95. *Publications:* (ed jtly) Armour on Valuation for Rating, 1990–; (contrib.) Stair Memorial Encyclopaedia of the Laws of Scotland. *Address:* Supreme Courts, Parliament House, Parliament Square, Edinburgh EH1 1RQ.

DOHERTY, Berlie; author, playwright and librettist, since 1982; *b* 6 Nov. 1943; *d* of Walter and Margaret Hollingsworth; *m* 1st, 1966, Gerard Doherty (marr. diss. 1996); one *s* two *d*; 2nd, 2013, Alan James Brown. *Educ:* Upton Hall Convent; Durham Univ. (BA Hons English); Liverpool Univ. (Postgrad. Cert. Social Studies); Sheffield Univ. (Postgrad. Cert Ed). Social worker, Leics Social Services, 1966–67; English teacher, Sheffield, 1979–82; on secondment to BBC Radio Sheffield Schools Progs, 1980–82. Various writing workshops for WEA, Sheffield Univ. and Arvon Foundn, 1978–90. Hon. Dr Derby, 2002. *Publications:* How Green You Are!, 1982; The Making of Fingers Finnigan, 1983; Tilly Mint Tales, 1984; White Peak Farm, 1984; Children of Winter, 1985; Granny Was a Buffer Girl, 1986; Tilly Mint and the Dodo, 1988; Tough Luck, 1988; Paddiwak and Cosy, 1988; Spellhorn, 1989; Dear Nobody, 1991; Requiem, 1991; Snowy, 1993; Walking on Air, 1993; Big Bulgy Fat Black Slugs, 1993; Old Father Christmas, 1993; Street Child, 1993; The Vinegar Jar, 1994; Willa and Old Miss Annie, 1994; The Magical Bicycle, 1995; The Golden Bird, 1995; The Snake-Stone, 1995; Our Field, 1996; Daughter of the Sea, 1996; Running on Ice (collected stories), 1997; Bella's Den, 1997; Tales of Wonder and Magic, 1997; Midnight Man, 1998; The

Forsaken Merman, 1998; The Sailing Ship Tree, 1998; The Snow Queen, 1998; Fairy Tales, 2000; The Famous Adventures of Jack, 2000; Zzaap and the Wordmaster, 2000; Holly Starcross, 2001; The Nutcracker, 2002; Blue John, 2003; Coconut Comes to School, 2003; Deep Secret, 2003; Tricky Nelly's Birthday Treat, 2003; The Starburster, 2004; Jinnie Ghost, 2005; Jeannie of White Peak Farm, 2005; The Humming Machine, 2006; Abela: the girl who saw lions, 2007; The Oxford Book of Bible Stories, 2007; The Windspinner, 2008; A Beautiful Place for a Murder, 2008; A Calf called Valentine, 2009; Valentine's Day, 2009; Nightmare, 2009; Treason, 2011; The Three Princes, 2011; Wild Cat, 2012; The Company of Ghosts, 2013; The Starburster Stories, 2013; Snowy, 2014; Far From Home, 2015; *playscripts include:* Sacrifice, 1985; Return to the Ebro, 1986; Dear Nobody, 1995; Morgan's Field, 1995; Heidi, 1996; The Water Babies, 1998; Lorna Doone, 2001; Granny Was a Buffer Girl, 2002; Street Child, 2005; The Snake-stone, 2006; Thin Air, 2012; *operas include:* The Magician's Cat, 2004; Daughter of the Sea, 2004; Wild Cat, 2007. *Recreations:* walking, music, reading, theatre and opera going. *Address:* c/o David Higham Associates Ltd, 7th Floor, Waverley House, 7–12 Noel Street, W1F 8GQ.

DOHERTY, Michael Eunan; Chairman, Epsom and St Helier NHS Trust, 2002–07; *b* 21 Sept. 1939; *s* of Michael Joseph Doherty and Grace Doherty (*née* Gallagher); *m* 1st, 1965, Judy Battams (marr. diss 2008); two *s* two *d*; 2nd, 2009, Marion Eames. *Educ:* St Bernard's RC Sch., London. FCA 1977. Partner, Turquands Barton Mayhew, 1960–72; Man. Dir, Anglo-Thai Gp, 1973–82; Chief Exec., Cope Allman Internat. plc, 1982–88; Chairman: Henlys plc, 1985–88, 1991–97; Norcros plc, 1988–97. Chm., King's Healthcare, then King's Coll. Hosp., NHS Trust, 1996–2002; Trustee, KCH Charitable Trust, 1999–2004. Chm. Govs, St John's Sch., Leatherhead, 1997–2006. CCMI (CIMgt 1985). *Recreations:* golf, music, reading, politics. *Address:* Walnut Tree House, 10 Sycamore Close, Fetcham, Surrey KT22 9EX. *T:* (01372) 375212. *Club:* Royal Automobile.

DOHERTY, Pat; MP (SF) West Tyrone, since 2001; *b* Glasgow, 18 July 1945; *m* Mary; two *s* three *d*. Sinn Féin: Dir of Elections, 1984–85; Nat. Organiser, 1985–88; Vice-Pres., 1988–2009; Leader of delegn to Forum for Peace and Reconciliation, Dublin, 1994–96. Northern Ireland Assembly: Mem. (SF) W Tyrone, 1998–June 2012; Chm., Enterprise, Trade and Investment Cttee, 1999–2002. Contested (SF) West Tyrone, 1997. *Address:* (office) 1A Melvin Road, Strabane, Co. Tyrone BT82 9PP; c/o House of Commons, SW1A 0AA.

DOHERTY, Prof. Peter Charles, AC 1997; FRS 1987; FAA 1983; Laureate Professor, Department of Microbiology and Immunology, University of Melbourne, since 2002; *b* 15 Oct. 1940; *s* of Eric C. and Linda M. Doherty; *m* 1965, Penelope Stephens; two *s*. *Educ:* Univ. of Queensland (BVSc, MVSc); Univ. of Edinburgh (PhD). Veterinary Officer, Queensland Dept of Primary Industries, 1962–67; Scientific Officer, Moredun Research Inst., Edinburgh, 1967–71; Research Fellow, Dept of Microbiology, John Curtin Sch. of Med. Research, Canberra, 1972–75; Associate Prof., later Prof., Wistar Inst., Philadelphia, 1975–82; Prof. of Experimental Pathology, John Curtin Sch. of Medical Res., ANU, 1982–88; Michael F. Tamer Chair of Biomed. Res., 1988–, Chm., Dept of Immunology, 1988–2002, St Jude Children's Res. Hosp., Memphis. Bd Mem., Internat. Lab. for Res. on Animal Disease, Nairobi, 1987–92. Mem., US Nat. Acad. of Sci., 1998. Hon. doctorates from 23 univs. Paul Ehrlich Prize and Medal for Immunology, 1983; Gairdner Internat. Award for Med. Research, 1987; Alumnus of Year, Univ. of Queensland, 1993; Lasker Award for Basic Med. Res., 1995; (jtly) Nobel Prize in Physiology or Medicine, 1996. *Publications:* The Beginner's Guide to Winning the Nobel Prize, 2005; A Light History of Hot Air, 2007; Sentinel Chickens: what birds tell us about our health and the world, 2012, new edn as Their Fate is Our Fate: how birds foretell threats to our health and our world, 2013; Pandemics: what everyone needs to know, 2013; papers in scientific jls. *Recreations:* walking, reading, listening to music. *Address:* Department of Microbiology and Immunology, Peter Doherty Institute, University of Melbourne, Vic 3010, Australia. *T:* (3) 83447968.

DOHERTY, Raymond; *see* Doherty, Hon. Lord.

DOHMANN, Barbara; QC 1987; *b* Berlin; *d* of Paul Dohmann and Dora Dohmann (*née* Thiele). *Educ:* schools in Germany and USA; Univs of Erlangen, Mainz and Paris. Called to the Bar, Gray's Inn, 1971, Bencher, 2007; a Recorder, 1990–2002; a Dep. High Court Judge, 1994–2003. Judge (part-time) of Civil and Commercial Court, Qatar Financial Centre, Doha, 2007–. Arbitrator: ICC; London Court of Internat. Arbitration; Mediator, CEDR, 2010. Member: BVI Bar; Learned Soc. for Internat. Civil Procedure Law, 1991–; London Ct of Internat. Arbitration, 2012–; Chm., Commercial Bar Assoc., 1999–2001 (Treas., 1997–99; Mem. Cttee, 2001–); Member: Gen. Council of the Bar, 1999–2001, 2014–; Legal Services Cttee, 2000–01; German Bar Assoc., 2012–; Bar Eur. Gp, 2000– (Leader, Eur. Circuit, 2014–); Lord Chancellor's Standing Cttee of Internat. Law, 2007–; London Metal Exchange: Special Cttee, 2007–; Appeal Panel; Arbitration Panel, 2014–. Member: Bd of Govs, London Inst. Higher Educn Corp., 1993–2000; Chancellor's Forum, Univ. of the Arts, London (formerly London Inst. Higher Educn Corp.), 2000–. *Recreations:* gardening, mountain walking, opera, art. *Address:* Blackstone Chambers, Blackstone House, Temple, EC4Y 9BW. *T:* (020) 7583 1770. *Club:* Athenæum.

DOHNÁNYI, Christoph v.; *see* von Dohnányi.

DOIG, David William Neal; Clerk of Bills, House of Commons, 2006–08; *b* 15 Jan. 1950; *s* of William Doig and Audrey Doig; *m* 1977, Alison Dorothy Farrar; one *s* three *d*. *Educ:* Perse Sch., Cambridge; Jesus Coll., Cambridge (BA Mod. and Mediaeval Langs 1972); City of London Poly. (Dip. Tech. and Specialist Translation 1973). House of Commons: Asst Clerk, 1973–77; Sen. Clerk, 1977–85; Dep. Principal Clerk, 1985–2000; Registrar of Members' Interests, 2000; Principal Clerk of Select Cttees, 2001–06. Advr, Inquiry into MPs' expenses, Cttee on Standards in Public Life, 2009. *Recreations:* gardening, cricket, meccano. *Address:* Quayham, Foots Lane, Burwash Weald, E Sussex TN19 7LE.

DOIMI DE FRANKOPAN, Peter; *see* Frankopan, P. D. de.

DOLAN, Dorothy Elizabeth; *see* Porter, D. E.

DOLAN, Prof. Liam, PhD; FRS 2014; Sherardian Professor of Botany, University of Oxford, since 2009; Fellow, Magdalen College, Oxford, since 2009. *Educ:* University Coll. Dublin (BSc, MSc); Univ. of Pennsylvania (PhD). Project Leader, Cell Patterning, Morphogenesis and Evolution in Plants, John Innes Centre, Norwich, until 2009. Hon. Prof. of Biol., UEA, until 2009. Mem. EMBO, 2009. *Publications:* (jtly) Plant Biology, 2009; articles in jls. *Address:* Department of Plant Sciences, University of Oxford, South Parks Road, Oxford OX1 3RB.

DOLAN, Prof. Paul, DPhil; Professor of Behavioural Science, London School of Economics and Political Science, since 2010. *Educ:* University Coll. of Swansea (BSc (Econ) 1989); Univ. of York (MSc (Econ) 1991; DPhil (Econ) 1997). Res. Fellow, Centre for Health Scis, Univ. of York, 1991–94; Lectr in Econs, Univs of Newcastle upon Tyne and York, 1994–98; University of Sheffield: Sen. Lectr in Health Econs, 1998–2000; Prof. of Health Econs, 2000–06; Dir, Centre for Well-being in Public Policy, 2004–06; Prof. of Econs, Imperial Coll. London, 2006–09; on secondment as Mem., Behavioural Insights Team, Cabinet Office, 2010–11. Vis. Res. Schol., Princeton Univ., 2004–05. Philip Leverhulme Prize for Econs, Leverhulme Trust, 2002. *Publications:* (with J. Olsen) Distributing Health Care: economic and ethical issues, 2002; Happiness by Design, 2014. *Address:* Department of Social Policy, 2nd Floor, Old Building, London School of Economics and Political Science, Houghton Street, WC2A 2AE. *E:* p.h.dolan@lse.ac.uk.

DOLAN, Prof. Raymond Joseph, MD; FRCP, FRCPsych, FMedSci; FRS 2010; Kinross Professor of Neuropsychiatry, since 2001, and Director, Wellcome Trust Centre for Neuroimaging, since 2006, University College London; *b* 21 Jan. 1954; *s* of John Dolan and Julia Dolan (*née* Coppenger); *m* 1996, Sheela Kulaveerasingam; three *s*. *Educ:* St Jarlath's Coll., Tuam; University Coll. Galway Medical Sch. (MB BCh BAO Hons 1977; MD 1987). FRCPsych 1995; FRCP 2002. Psychiatry trng, Royal Free and Maudsley Hosps; Sen. Lectr, Royal Free Hosp. Sch. of Medicine, 1987–94; Reader, Inst. of Neurology, 1995–96; Prof., Inst. of Neurology, UCL, 1996–2001. Einstein Vis. Fellow, 2010. Ext. Scientific Mem., Max Planck Soc., 2012–. FMedSci 2000. Hon. MRIA 2011. Klaus Joachim Zülch Prize, Gertrud Reemtsma Foundn, 2013. *Publications:* Human Brain Function, 1997, 2nd edn 2004; over 400 papers in jls incl. Nature, Science, Neuron, Jl of Neuroscience, Nature Neuroscience, Brain. *Recreations:* walking, reading, music, fly-fishing, midnight rambling. *Address:* Wellcome Trust Centre for Neuroimaging, 12 Queen Square, WC1N 3BG. *T:* (020) 3448 4346. *E:* r.dolan@ucl.ac.uk. *Clubs:* Groucho, Soho House; Country Half-Life.

DOLBY, Elizabeth Grace; *see* Cassidy, E. G.

DOLCE, Domenico; Chief Executive Officer, Dolce & Gabbana; *b* 13 Sept. 1958; *s* of Saverio Dolce. Worked in father's clothing factory, Sicily; Asst in design studio, Milan; with Stefano Gabbana opened fashion consulting studio, 1982; Co-founder, Dolce & Gabbana, 1985; first major women's collection, 1986; knitwear, 1987; beachwear, lingerie, 1989; men's collection, 1990; women's fragrance, 1992; D&G line, men's fragrance, 1994; eyewear, 1995; opened boutiques in major cities in Europe, America and Asia. *Publications:* (with Stefano Gabbana): 10 Years Dolce & Gabbana, 1996; Wildness, 1997; Mémoires de la Mode, 1998; Animal, 1998; Calcio, 2004; Music, 2005; 20 Years Dolce & Gabbana, 2005; (with Eve Claxton and Stefano Gabbana) Hollywood, 2003. *Address:* Dolce & Gabbana, Via Santa Cecilia 7, 20122 Milan, Italy.

DOLE, Robert Joseph, (Bob); Purple Heart; Special Counsel, Alston & Bird, since 2003; Founder and President, Bob Dole Enterprises Inc.; *b* Russell, Kansas, 22 July 1923; *s* of Doran and Bina Dole; *m* 1975, Elizabeth Hanford; one *d*. *Educ:* Univ. of Kansas (AB); Washburn Municipal Univ. (LLB). Served US Army, 1943–48; Platoon Ldr, 10th Mountain Div., Italy; wounded and decorated twice for heroic achievement. Captain. Kansas Legislature, 1951–53; Russell County Attorney, Kansas, 1953–61; US House of Reps, 1960–68; US Senator, 1968–96; Republican Leader, 1985–96, Leader, 1995–96, US Senate; Leader, Republican Party, US, 1992–96; Republican Nominee for President, 1996. Special Counsel, Verner, Liipfert, Bernhard, McPherson and Hand, 1999–2003. Chairman: Internat. Commn on Missing Persons, 1997–; Nat. World War II Meml. US Presidential Medal of Freedom, 1997. *Publications:* (ed) Great Political Wit, 1998; (ed) Great Presidential Wit; One Soldier's Story (autobiog.), 2005. *Address:* c/o Alston & Bird LLP, 10th Floor, The Atlantic Building, 950 F Street NW, Washington, DC 20004–1404, USA.

DOLLERY, Sir Colin (Terence), Kt 1987; FRCP, FMedSci; Senior Consultant, Research and Development, GlaxoSmithKline (formerly Smithkline Beecham) plc, since 1996; Dean, Royal Postgraduate Medical School, 1991–96, Pro-Vice-Chancellor for Medicine (formerly Medicine and Dentistry), 1992–96, University of London; *b* 14 March 1931; *s* of Cyril Robert and Thelma Mary Dollery; *m* 1958, Diana Myra (*née* Stedman); one *s* one *d*. *Educ:* Lincoln Sch.; Birmingham Univ. (BSc, MB, ChB); FRCP 1968. House officer: Queen Elizabeth Hosp., Birmingham; Hammersmith Hosp., and Brompton Hosp., 1956–58; Hammersmith Hospital: Med. Registrar, 1958–60; Sen. Registrar and Tutor in Medicine, 1960–62; Consultant Physician, 1962–; Lectr in Medicine, 1962–65, Prof. of Clinical Pharmacology, 1965–87, Prof. of Medicine, 1987–91, Royal Postgrad. Med. Sch. Member: MRC, 1982–84; UGC, subseq. UFC, 1984–91. Founder FMedSci 1998; FIC 2003. Hon. Mem., Assoc. of Amer. Physicians, 1982. Wellcome Gold Medal, British Pharmacol Soc., 2008; Oscar B. Hunter Award in Therapeutics, American Soc. of Clinical Pharmacol. and Therapeutics, 2009. Chevalier de l'Ordre National du Mérite (France), 1976. *Publications:* The Retinal Circulation, 1971 (New York); Therapeutic Drugs, 1991, 2nd edn 1998; numerous papers in scientific jls concerned with high blood pressure and drug action. *Recreations:* travel, amateur radio, work. *Address:* 101 Corringham Road, NW11 7DL. *T:* (020) 8458 2616. *Club:* Athenæum.

DOLMAN, Edward James; Chairman and Chief Executive Officer, Phillips, since 2014; *b* 24 Feb. 1960; *s* of James William Dolman and Jean Dolman; *m* 1987, Clare Callaghan (marr. diss.); one *s* one *d*. *Educ:* Dulwich Coll.; Southampton Univ. (BA Hons History). Joined Christie's, 1984; Dir and Head of Furniture Dept, Christie's S Kensington, 1990–95; Man. Dir, Christie's Amsterdam, 1995–97; Commercial Dir, 1997, Man. Dir, 1998–99, Christie's Europe; Dir, Christie, Manson & Woods Ltd, 1997; Man. Dir, Christie's America, 1999–2000; CEO, 2000–10, Chm., 2010–11, Christie's International plc; Exec. Dir, 2011–14, Acting Chief Exec., 2012–14, Qatar Museums Authy. Officier, Légion d'Honneur (France), 2012 (Chevalier, 2007). *Recreations:* art history, Rugby, cricket, sailing. *Clubs:* Royal Automobile, Royal Thames Yacht, Old Alleynian (Vice Pres., 1998–); New York Yacht.

DOLMAN, Rev. Dr William Frederick Gerrit; JP; HM Assistant Coroner (formerly Assistant Deputy Coroner), Inner West London, since 2007, South London, since 2008, and Inner North London, since 2012; *b* 14 Nov. 1942; *s* of Dr Gerrit Arnold Dolman and Madeline Joan Dolman. *Educ:* Whitgift Sch., Croydon; KCH Med. Sch., Univ. of London (MB BS 1965); LLB Hons London (ext.) 1987; SE Inst. of Theol Educn (DipTh Univ. of Kent 2007). MRCS 1965; LRCP 1965; FFFLM 2005. Principal in Gen. Practice, 1967–74; Asst Dep. Coroner, 1974–86, Dep. Coroner, 1986–93, S London; Medical Referee, Croydon Crematorium, 1986–; Asst Dep. Coroner, 1988–89, Dep. Coroner, 1989–93, Inner W London; Coroner, N London, 1993–2007; Dep. Coroner, E London, 2007–12. Associate Dermatology Specialist, St Helier Hosp., Carshalton, 1992–2000. BBC Radio Doctor, Jimmy Young Show, Radio 2, 1977–2002. FRSocMed 1967 (Mem. Council, Forensic and Legal Medicine Section, 1996–2000); Pres., Croydon Medical Soc., 2002; Med. Sec., Coroners' Soc., 2004–08. Examiner, Soc. of Apothecaries, 2002–04 and 2007–10. Med. Editor, Modern Medicine, 1976–80; Editor: Coroner sect., Atkin's Court Forms, 2003–08; The Coroner, 2003–07. Founder and benefactor, Dolman Travel Book Award, 2006–. Ordained deacon, 2006, priest, 2007. JP Croydon, 1975 (Chm. Bench, 2007–08). *Publications:* Can I Speak to the Doctor?, 1981; Doctor on Call, 1987. *Recreations:* classical music, good food, fine wine, real ale, sitting in the garden looking at work that ought to be done. *Address:* Coroner's Court, Barclay Road, Croydon CR9 3NE. *Clubs:* Authors' (Chm., 2000–04), Savile, National Liberal.

DOLPHIN, Prof. Annette Catherine, PhD; FMedSci; FRS 2015; Professor of Pharmacology, University College London, since 1997; *b* Maidenhead, 3 April 1951; *d* of Geoffrey William Dolphin and Yvonne Mary Dolphin (*née* Dowsett); *m* 2010, William James Frith. *Educ:* Alwyn Sch., Maidenhead; Hooker Sch., New Haven, Conn; Courthouse Sch., Maidenhead; Sch. of St Helen and St Katherine, Abingdon; St Hugh's Coll., Oxford (BA 1st Cl. Biochem. 1973); Inst. of Psychiatry, London (PhD 1977). MRC French Exchange Fellow, Collège de France, Paris, 1977–78; Fellowship, Yale Univ., 1978–80; Scientist, NIMR, 1980–83; Lectr, St George's Hosp. Med. Sch., 1983–89; Prof. of Pharmacol. and Chair of Dept, Royal Free Hosp. Sch. of Medicine, 1990–97. FMedSci 1999. *Publications:* over 200 primary res. papers, reviews and book chapters. *Recreation:* extreme trekking. *Address:* Department of Neuroscience, Physiology and Pharmacology, University College London, Gower Street, WC1E 6BT. *E:* a.dolphin@ucl.ac.uk.

DOLPHIN, Prof. David Henry, OC 2006; PhD; FRS 2002; FRS(Can); FRSC, FCIC; QLT/NSERC Industrial Research Professor of Photodynamic Technology, University of British Columbia, since 2005 (Professor of Chemistry, 1979–2005, now Emeritus). *Educ:* Univ. of Nottingham (BSc 1962; PhD 1965; DSc 1982). FRS(Can) 2001; FCIC 1981. Joined Harvard Univ. as Res. Fellow, 1965, subseq. Associate Prof. of Chemistry, until 1974; Associate Prof. of Chemistry, Univ. of BC, 1974. Vice-Pres., Technol. Develt, Quadra Logic Technologies, Vancouver, 1992. Guggenheim Fellow, 1980; Univ. Killam Prof., 2004. Gold Medal in Health Scis, Sci. Council of BC, 1990; Syntex Award, CIC, 1993; Bell Canada Forum Award, 1993; Izaak Walton Killam Res. Prize, Canada Council, 1996; Prix Galien Award, 2002; Friesen-Rygiel Prize, 2002; Award of Leadership in Canadian Pharmaceutical Scis, Canadian Soc. for Pharmaceutical Scis, 2002; Academic of the Year, Confedn of Univ. Faculty Assocs of BC, 2003; Hero of Chemistry, Amer. Chem. Soc., 2004; Award of Excellence, 2004, Herzberg Award, 2006, NSERC. *Publications:* (jtly) Tabulation of Infrared Spectral Data, 1977; (ed jtly) Biological Aspects of Inorganic Chemistry, 1977; (ed jtly) The Porphyrins, vol. I–VII, 1978–79; (ed jtly) Biomimetic Chemistry, 1980; Murakami and I. Tabushi, 1980; (ed) B12, 2 vols, 1982; (ed jtly) Biological Chemistry of Iron, 1982; (ed jtly) Coenzymes and Cofactors, vol. 1, 1986, vol. 2, 1987, vol. 3, 1989; articles in jls. *Address:* Department of Chemistry, University of British Columbia, 2036 Main Mall, Vancouver, BC V6T 1Z1, Canada.

DOMBROVSKIS, Valdis; Member and a Vice-President, European Commission, since 2014; *b* Riga, 5 Aug. 1971. *Educ:* Univ. of Latvia (BSc Physics 1993); Riga Tech. Univ. (BA Econs 1995; Professional Master's degree in customs and tax admin 2007); Univ. of Latvia and Univ. of Meinz (MSc Physics 1996); Univ. of Maryland (PhD 1998). Laboratory assistant: Inst. of Solid State Physics, Univ. of Latvia, 1991–93; Faculty of Physics and Maths, Dept of Semi-conductor Physics, Univ. of Latvia, 1993–95; Inst. of Physics, Meinz Univ., Germany, 1995–96; researcher, Inst. of Solid State Physics, Univ. of Latvia, 1997; lab. asst, Dept of Electrical Engrg, Univ. of Maryland, 1997–98; Monetary Policy Board, Bank of Latvia: specialist in macroecons, 1998–99; Sen. Economist, 1999–2001; Chief Economist, 2001–02; MP (New Era) Saeima, 2002–04; Minister for Finance, 2002–03; Advr to Minister of Econs, 2004–06; MEP (New Era) and Hd, Latvian delegn in ETP-ED gp, 2004–09; Minister for Children, Family and Integration Affairs, March–July 2009; Prime Minister of Latvia, 2009–13; MP (Unity), 2010–14. *Publications:* (jtly) Aufgelöste J2 Spektren mit Breitbandigen LasernÄ, 1997; (contrib.) The Role of Tax Administration and Customs in National Economy, 2003; contribs on econs and politics to periodicals, jls and electronic media. *Address:* European Commission, Rue de La Loi, 1049 Brussels, Belgium.

DOMINGO, Placido, Hon. KBE 2002; tenor singer, conductor; General Director: Washington Opera, 1996–2011; Los Angeles Opera, since 2000; *b* Madrid, 21 Jan. 1941; *s* of Placido Domingo and Pepita (*née* Embil), professional singers; *m* 1962, Marta Ornelas, lyric soprano; two *s* (and one *s* by former marriage). *Educ:* Instituto, Mexico City; Nat. Conservatory of Music, Mexico City. Operatic début, Monterrey, as Alfredo in La Traviata, 1961; with opera houses at Dallas, Fort Worth, Israel, to 1965; débuts: NY City Opera, 1965; at NY Metropolitan Opera, as Maurizio in Adriana Lecouvreur, 1968; at La Scala, title rôle in Ernani, 1969; at Covent Garden, Cavaradossi in Tosca, 1971; has sung record 130 tenor rôles, 1961–2009; title rôle in Simon Boccanegra, State Opera, Berlin, 2009, Covent Garden, 2010. Has conducted in Vienna, Barcelona, NY and Frankfurt; début as conductor in UK, Covent Garden, 1983. *Films:* La Traviata, 1983; Carmen, 1984; Otello, 1986; appears on TV, makes recordings, throughout USA and Europe. Founder, Operalia competition, 1993. FRCM; FRNCM. Hon. doctorates include: RNCM, 1982; Philadelphia Coll. of Performing Arts, 1982; Complutense, Madrid, 1989; Anáhuac, Mexico, 2001; Hon. DMus Oxon, 2003. Birgit Nilsson Prize, Birgit Nilsson Foundn, 2009. Medal of City of Madrid; Orden de Isabel la Católica (Spain), 1986; Gran Cruz, Orden del Mérito Civil (Spain), 2002; foreign orders include: Chevalier, Legion of Honour (France), 2002 (Officer, 1983); US Medal of Freedom, 2002; Comdr, Ordre des Arts et des Lettres (France); Grande Ufficiale, Ordine al Merito della Repubblica Italiana; Grand Cross, Order of Infante Dom Henrique (Portugal); Order of Aztec Eagle (Mexico). *Publications:* My First Forty Years (autobiog.), 1983. *Recreations:* piano, swimming, football (Real Madrid), tennis, Formula 1. *Address:* c/o Petra Weiss, PO Box 2018, 68710 Schwetzingen, Germany. *W:* www.placidodomingo.com.

DOMINICZAK, Prof. Anna Felicja, OBE 2005; MD; FRCPGlas; FMedSci; FRSE; Vice Principal and Head, College of Medical, Veterinary and Life Sciences, since 2010, and Regius Professor of Medicine and Therapeutics, since 2009, University of Glasgow; *b* 26 Aug. 1954; *d* of Jacob Penson and Joanna Muszkowska; *m* 1976, Marek Dominiczak; one *s*. *Educ:* Medical Sch., Gdansk, Poland (MD Hons); Univ. of Glasgow (MD); MRCPGlas 1986, FRCPGlas 1995. Jun. House Officer, Glasgow Royal Infirmary, 1982; Sen. House Officer and Registrar, Royal Alexandra Hosp., Paisley, 1983–86; MRC Clin. Scientist and Sen. Registrar, Western Infirmary, Glasgow, 1986–89; Res. Fellow and Associate Prof., Univ. of Michigan, Ann Arbor, 1990–91; Clin. Lectr and Hon. Sen. Registrar, Univ. of Glasgow, 1992–93; University of Glasgow and Western Infirmary, Glasgow: BHF Sen. Res. Fellow, 1993–97; Sen. Lectr, 1993–96; and Reader in Medicine, 1996–97; BHF Prof. of Cardiovascular Medicine, 1998–2010; Hon. Consultant Physician and Endocrinologist, 1993–. Pres., European Soc. of Hypertension, 2013–15. Ed.-in-Chief, Hypertension, 2012–. Vice Pres., Life Scis, RSE, 2012–. FAHA 1996; FMedSci 2001; FRSE 2003. *Publications:* (ed) Genetics of Essential Hypertension, 1999; (ed) Genetics of Hypertension, 2007. *Recreation:* modern literature. *Address:* College of Medical, Veterinary and Life Sciences, University of Glasgow, Wolfson Medical School Building, University Avenue, Glasgow G12 8QQ. *T:* (0141) 330 2738, *Fax:* (0141) 330 5339. *E:* Anna.Dominiczak@glasgow.ac.uk.

DOMOKOS, Dr Mátyás; Ambassador, retired; General Director, CD Hungary (formerly Diplomatic Service Directorate, Ministry of Foreign Affairs, Hungary), 1989–95; *b* 28 Oct. 1930; *m* 1956, Irén Beretyán; one *d*. *Educ:* Karl Marx Univ. of Econs, Budapest. Foreign trading enterprises, 1954–57; Commercial Sec., Damascus and Trade Comr, Khartoum, 1958–61; various posts in Ministry for Foreign Trade, Hungary, 1961–74; Ambassador to UN, Geneva, 1974–79; Head of Dept of Internat. Organisations, Ministry of Foreign Affairs, 1979–84; Ambassador to UK, 1984–89. *Recreations:* gardening, chess. *Address:* 32 Str. Árnyas, 1121 Budapest, Hungary.

DON, Montagu Denis Wyatt, (Monty); writer and broadcaster; *b* 8 July 1955; *s* of late Denis Don and Janet Wyatt; *m* 1983, Sarah; two *s* one *d*. *Educ:* Magdalene Coll., Cambridge (MA Eng. 1979). Jt Founder, Monty Don Ltd (costume jewellery co.), 1981–91; freelance gardening journalist, 1988–; TV broadcaster, 1989–; presenter: Gardeners' World, 2002–08 and 2011–; Chelsea Flower Show, 2014–. Gardening Editor, The Observer, 1994–2006. Pres., Soil Assoc., 2008–. *Publications:* The Prickotty Bush, 1990; The Weekend Gardener, 1995; The Sensuous Garden, 1997; Gardening Mad, 1997; Urban Jungle, 1998; Fork to Fork, 1999; The Complete Gardener, 2003; (with Sarah Don) The Jewel Garden, 2004; Gardening from Berryfield, 2005; My Roots, 2005; Growing out of Trouble, 2006; Around the World in 80 Gardens, 2008; The Ivington Diaries, 2009; Gardening at Longmeadow, 2012; The Road to Tholonet: a French garden journey, 2013. *Recreations:* gardening, farming.

DON, Nigel Anderson; Member (SNP) Angus North and Mearns, Scottish Parliament, since 2011 (Scotland North East, 2007–11); *b* 16 April 1954; *s* of late Derek Don and Margaret Don; *m* 1977, Wendy Wrieden; one *s* one *d*. *Educ:* King's College Sch., Wimbledon; Pembroke Coll., Cambridge (BA 1975; MA 1979; MEng 2001); Univ. of London (LLB (ext.) 1982). CEng, MIChemE 1982. Chemical engr, Unilever plc, 1976–89; self-employed musician, 1989–2007. Mem. (SNP), Dundee CC, 2003–07. *Recreations:* music, walking. *Address:* Scottish Parliament, Edinburgh EH99 1SP. *T:* (0131) 348 5996, *Fax:* (0131) 348 6998. *E:* nigel.don@scottish.parliament.uk.

DON-WAUCHOPE, Sir Roger (Hamilton), 11th Bt *cr* 1667 (NS), of Newton Don and of Edmonstone; chartered accountant, retired, South Africa; Partner, Deloitte & Touche, 1972–98; *b* 16 Oct. 1938; *s* of Sir Patrick George Don-Wauchope, 10th Bt and Ismay Lilian Ursula (who later *m* George William Shipman), *d* of Sidney Richard Hodges; *S* father, 1989; *m* 1963, Sallee, *yr d* of Lt-Col Harold Mill-Colman, OBE, AMICE, Durban; two *s* one *d*. *Educ:* Hilton Coll., Natal; Univ. of Natal, Durban; Univ. of Natal, Pietermaritzburg (Higher Diploma in Taxation). Past Chm., Midlands Branch, KZN Inst. of Chartered Accountants. Former Gov. and Dep. Chm., Hiltonian Soc. Former Trustee, Tembaletu Educn Trust; Trustee, Emuseni Centre for the Aged. Mem. Cttee, Senior Golfers' Soc. of KwaZulu-Natal (Capt., 2011; Pres., 2013). *Heir: s* Dr Andrew Craig Don-Wauchope [*b* 18 May 1966; *m* 1990, Louise Sylvia, *d* of John Crawford Johnstone-Dougall; one *s* two *d*]. *Address:* Newton, 53 Montrose Drive, Pietermaritzburg 3201, KwaZulu-Natal, South Africa. *T:* (033) 3471107. *E:* don-wauchope@intekom.co.za. *Clubs:* Victoria Country (Chm., 1993–95), Fleur-de-Lys (Treas.) (Pietermaritzburg); Durban Country (Durban); Old Hiltonian (Chm., 1992–97; Vice Pres., 1998–); Prince's Grant Golf (Stanger).

DONAGHY, Baroness *cr* 2010 (Life Peer), of Peckham in the London Borough of Southwark; **Rita Margaret Donaghy,** CBE 2005 (OBE 1998); FCIPD; Chair, Advisory, Conciliation and Arbitration Service, 2000–07; *b* 9 Oct. 1944; *d* of late William Scott Willis and Margaret Brenda Willis (*née* Howard, later Bryan); *m* 1968, James Columba Donaghy (*d* 1986); *m* 2000, Ted Easen-Thomas. *Educ:* Leamington Coll. for Girls; Durham Univ. (BA 1967). FCIPD 2002. Tech. asst, NUT, 1967–68; Asst Registrar, 1968–84, Perm. Sec., Students' Union, 1984–2000, Inst. of Educn, Univ. of London. Member: Low Pay Commn, 1997–2000; Cttee on Standards in Public Life, 2001–07 (Interim Chm., 2007); Select Cttee on Personal Services, 2014; Chair, H of L Inf. Cttee, 2014–. Member: Nat. Exec. Council, NALGO/UNISON, 1973–2000; TUC Gen. Council, 1987–2000; President: NALGO, 1989–90; TUC, 2000; Mem. Exec., Eur. TUC, 1992–2000. Non-exec. Dir, KCH NHS Trust, 2005–09. Chm., DWP Inquiry into Fatal Construction Accidents, 2009. Member: Business Adv. Bd, Birmingham Univ., 2006–; Adv. Bd, Modern Records Centre, Warwick Univ., 2007–. DUniv: Open, 2002; Keele, 2004; Hon. DBA Greenwich, 2005. *Recreations:* theatre, gardening, photography, watching cricket, eating out, reading. *Address:* House of Lords, SW1A 0PW. *Club:* Surrey County Cricket.

DONAHOE, Arthur Richard; QC (Can.) 1982; Secretary-General, Commonwealth Parliamentary Association, 1993–2001; *b* 7 April 1940; *s* of Richard A. Donahoe and Eileen (*née* Boyd); *m* 1972, Carolyn Elizabeth MacCormack. *Educ:* public schools in Halifax, NS; St Mary's Univ. (BComm 1959); Dalhousie Univ. (LLB 1965). Admitted to Bar of Nova Scotia, 1966; Exec. Asst to Leader of Opposition, Senate of Canada, 1967; barrister and solicitor, 1968–81; Lectr in Commercial Law, St Mary's Univ., 1972–75; MLA (PC), Nova Scotia, 1978–92, Speaker, 1981–91. Canadian Regl Rep., CPA Exec. Cttee, 1983–86. Hon. LLD St Mary's, 2008. *Publications:* contrib. articles to Parliamentarian, Canadian Parly Rev., and Round Table. *Recreations:* golf, reading, bridge. *Address:* Unit 13, 6770 Jubilee Road, Halifax, NS B3H 2H8, Canada. *T:* (902) 4227937. *Clubs:* Ashburn Golf (Pres., 1982–83), Halifax (Halifax, NS).

DONALD, Sir Alan (Ewen), KCMG 1988 (CMG 1979); HM Diplomatic Service, retired; Ambassador to People's Republic of China, 1988–91; *b* 5 May 1931; 2nd *s* of Robert Thomson Donald and Louise Turner; *m* 1958, Janet Hilary Therese Blood; four *s*. *Educ:* Aberdeen Grammar Sch.; Fettes Coll., Edinburgh; Trinity Hall, Cambridge. BA, LLM. HM Forces, RA (L Battery, 2nd Regt RHA), 1949–50. Joined HM Foreign Service, 1954: Third Sec., Peking, 1955–57; FO, 1958–61: Private Sec. to Parly Under-Sec., FO, 1959–61; Second, later First Sec., UK Delegn to NATO, Paris, 1961–64; First Sec., Peking, 1964–66; Personnel Dept, Diplomatic Service Admin Office, later FCO, 1967–71; Counsellor (Commercial), Athens, 1971–73; Political Advr to Governor of Hong Kong, 1974–77; Ambassador to: Republics of Zaire, Burundi, Rwanda and Congo Brazzaville, 1977–80; Asst Under-Sec. of State (Asia and the Pacific), FCO, 1980–84; Ambassador to Republic of Indonesia, 1984–88. Director: China Fund Inc. (NY), 1992–2003; HSBC China Fund Ltd, 1994–2004; J. P. Morgan Fleming Asian Investment Trust Ltd (formerly Fleming Asian Investment Trust), 1997–2001 (Fleming Far Eastern Investment Trust, 1991–97). Pres., China Assoc., 2003–08. Hon. LLD Aberdeen, 1991. *Recreations:* music, military history, water colour sketching. *Address:* Applebys, Chiddingstone Causeway, Kent TN11 8JH.

DONALD, Prof. Dame Athene Margaret, DBE 2010; PhD; FRS 1999; Professor of Experimental Physics, University of Cambridge, since 1998; Master, Churchill College, Cambridge, since 2014; *b* 15 May 1953; *d* of Walter Griffith and Annette Marian (*née* Tylor); *m* 1976, Matthew J. Donald; one *s* one *d*. *Educ:* Camden Sch. for Girls; Girton Coll., Cambridge (BA, MA; PhD 1977). Postdoctoral researcher, Cornell Univ., 1977–81; University of Cambridge: SERC Res. Fellow, 1981–83; Royal Soc. Univ. Res. Fellow, 1983–85; Lectr, 1985–95; Reader, 1995–98; Dir, Women in Sci., Engrg and Technol. Initiative, 2007–14, and Gender Equality Champion, 2010–14; Fellow, Robinson Coll., Cambridge, 1981–2014. Member: Council, Royal Soc., 2004–06 and 2013–; Scientific Council, Eur. Res. Council, 2013; Pres., British Sci. Assoc., 2015–Sept. 2016. Mem., Governing Council, Inst. Food Res., 1999–2003. Mem. Cttee, Longitude Prize, 2014–. Trustee, Nat. Mus. of Sci. and Industry, 2011–. Hon. DSc: Exeter, 2012; UEA, 2012; Sheffield, 2013; Swansea, 2014; UCL, 2014. Bakerian Prize Lect., Royal Soc., 2006; Samuel Locker Award in Physics, Birmingham Univ., 1989; Charles Vernon Boys Prize, 1989, Mott Prize, 2005, Faraday Medal, 2010, Inst. of Physics; Rosenhain Medal and Prize, Inst. Materials, 1995; William Hopkins Prize, Cambridge Philosophical Soc., 2003; For Women in Science Award, L'Oréal-UNESCO, 2009; Women of Outstanding Achievement Lifetime Achievement Award, UKRC, 2011. *Publications:* (with A. H. Windle) Liquid Crystalline Polymers, 1992, 2nd edn (with S. Hanna and A. H. Windle) 2006; (jtly) Starch: structure and function, 1997; Starch: advances in structure and function, 2001; articles on polymer, biopolymer, proteins, colloid and food physics and cellular biophysics in learned jls. *Address:* Cavendish Laboratory, University of Cambridge, J. J. Thomson Avenue, Cambridge CB3 0HE; Churchill College, Storey's Way, Cambridge CB3 0DS.

DONALD, George Malcolm, RSA 1992 (ARSA 1975); RSW 1976; SSA 1976; Keeper, Royal Scottish Academy, 2003–09 and since 2013; *b* 12 Sept. 1943; *s* of George Donald and Margaret (*née* Tait); *m* 1966 (marr. diss.); one *s* one *d*. *Educ:* Edinburgh Coll. of Art (DA 1966; Post Grad. Dip. 1967); Hornsey Coll. of Art, London Univ. (ATC 1969); Edinburgh Univ. (MEd 1980). ILTM 2002. Edinburgh College of Art: Lectr, Sch. of Drawing and Painting, 1972–96; Tutor and Asst to Vice Principal (Art and Design), 1984–87; Director: Summer Sch., 1991–2004; Centre for Continuing Studies, 1996–2001. Printmaker in Residence, Soulisquoy Print Workshop, Orkney Is, 1988; Visiting Artist: Szechuan Fine Art Inst., China, 1989; Silpakorn Univ., Thailand, 1989; Chulalongkorn Univ., Thailand, 1989; Visiting Professor: Zhejiang Acad. Fine Art, China, 1994–; Univ. of Sharja, 2003–; British Council Vis. Prof., Kyoto, 1999, 2002, Korea, 2000; Adjunct Prof., Univ. of Central Florida, 2002–; Hon. Prof., Al Maktoum Inst., Dundee, 2009–; Vis. Lectr, Prince's Drawing Sch., London, 2008–. Solo exhibitions include: Art Dept Gall., Univ. of Central Florida, 1985, 2002, 2003; Dept of Fine Art, Univ. of Georgia, 1987; Open Eye Gall., Edinburgh, 1987, 1990, 1993, 1995, 1998, 2002, 2003, 2005, 2007, 2012, 2013, 2015; Galerija Fakulteta Likovnih Umetnosti, Belgrade, 1987; Bohun Gall., Henley-on-Thames, 2009, 2011, 2013; Scottish

Arts Club, Edinburgh, 2012, 2015; touring exhibn, UK and France, 1990; Christopher Hull Gall., London, 1992; World Trade Centre, Dubai, 1994; Art Connection, Dubai, 2003, 2007, 2009; commissions: portrait, Glasgow Univ., Univ. of Edinburgh and Scottish Arts Council, 1985; window design, New Scottish Nat. Library, Edinburgh, 1986; portrait: Edinburgh Chamber of Commerce, 1986; St John's Hosp., Livingston, 1994; public collections include: Scottish Arts Council; Edinburgh, Aberdeen and Leeds CCs; Hunterian Mus., Glasgow Univ.; Heriot-Watt Univ.; Edinburgh Univ.; Victoria and Albert Mus.; IBM; BBC; Nat. Library of Scotland; private collections in UK, Europe, Canada and USA, Asia and Australia. Latimer Award 1970, Guthrie Award 1973, Royal Scottish Acad.; Scottish Arts Council Bursary, 1973; Gillies Bequest Travel Award to India, Royal Scottish Acad., 1978, 2003. *Publications:* The New Maths, 1969; An Account of Travels in Turkey, Iran, Afghanistan, Pakistan, India, Kashmir and Nepal, 1969; An Indian Diary, 1980; Aims and Objectives in Teaching Drawing and Painting, 1980; The Day Book, 1987; Anatomia: an artists' book, 2004. *Recreations:* music, travelling. *Address:* c/o Royal Scottish Academy, Edinburgh EH2 2EL. *W:* www.georgedonald.com.

DONALD, James Graham, FRICS; Consultant, Strutt & Parker, since 2004 (Chairman 1996–2003); *b* 4 April 1944; *s* of William Graham Donald and Jean (Bubbles) Donald; *m* 1976, Jennifer Seaman; one *s* two *d*. *Educ:* Cranleigh Sch.; Coll. of Estate Mgt (BSc Estate Mgt). FRICS 1981. Savills, 1966–72; joined Strutt & Parker, 1972, Partner, 1978–2004. *Recreations:* cycling, travel, supporting the children, sport, reading. *Address:* c/o Strutt & Parker, 13 Hill Street, W1J 5LQ. *T:* (020) 7318 5020. *Clubs:* Boodle's; Richmond FC; Old Cranleighans.

DONALD, Rob, CEng, FCILT; Director General, Centro (West Midlands Passenger Transport Executive), 1995–2006; *b* 25 March 1949; *s* of John Donald and Mary Donald (*née* Gardiner); *m* 1st, 1972, Yvonne Dyer (marr. diss.); two *d*; 2nd, 1991, Marilyn Downie. *Educ:* George Heriot's Sch., Edinburgh; Univ. of Edinburgh (BSc Hons); Imperial Coll., Univ. of London (MSc). MICE 1976; CEng 1976; FCILT (FCIT 1996). Graduate Asst, Brian Colquhoun and Partners, Consultants, London, 1971–73; Sen. Asst Officer, SIA Transport Consultants, London, 1973–75; Project Leader, County Surveyor's Dept, Kent CC, 1975–79; Chief Transportation Officer, Jt Transportation Unit, Merseyside CC, 1979–86; Merseytravel: Section Leader, then Manager, 1986–91; Passenger Services Dir, 1991–95. *Recreations:* travelling, reading, computing. *Address:* Norton Lodge, 32 Greyhound Lane, Stourbridge, W Midlands DY8 3AG. *T:* (01384) 838735.

DONALDSON, Dr Alexander Ivan, OBE 2003; Visiting Professor, Royal Veterinary College, University of London, since 2008; *b* 1 July 1942; *s* of Basil Ivan Donaldson and Dorothy Cunningham Donaldson; *m* 1966, Margaret Ruth Elizabeth Swan; one *d* one *s*. *Educ:* High Sch., Dublin; Trinity Coll., Univ. of Dublin (BA 1965; MVB 1965; MA 1968; ScD 1983); Ontario Veterinary Coll., Univ. of Guelph (PhD 1969). MRCVS 1965. Post-doctoral research, 1969–71, Vet. Res. Officer, 1973–76, Principal Vet. Res. Officer, 1976–89, Animal Virus Res. Inst., subseq. AFRC. Inst. for Animal Health, Pirbright Lab.; Head: World Ref. Lab. for Foot-and-Mouth Disease, 1985–89; Pirbright Lab., Inst. for Animal Health, 1989–2002. Vis. Prof., Ontario Vet. Coll., Univ. of Guelph, 1972–73. Hon. FRCVS 2003. Hon. DVM&S Edinburgh, 2002. Research Medal, RASE, 1988; Gold Medal, World Orgn for Animal Health, 2004. *Publications:* numerous articles on animal virology in learned jls. *Recreations:* reading, listening to music, travelling, walking, photography. *Address:* 290 London Road, Burpham, Guildford, Surrey GU4 7LB.

DONALDSON, Brian; HM Diplomatic Service, retired; Ambassador to Republic of Madagascar and concurrently to The Comoros, 2002–05; *b* 6 April 1946; *s* of late William Donaldson and Elsie Josephine Donaldson; *m* 1st, 1969, Elizabeth Claire Sumner (marr. diss. 2011); three *s*; 2nd, 2012, Nicole Rasoamiaramanana. Assistant, Establishments Office, Min. of Civil Aviation, 1963–65; joined HM Diplomatic Service, 1965: Mgt Officer, Algiers, 1968–71; Archivist, La Paz, 1971–73; Communications Ops Dept, FCO, 1974–75; Entry Clearance Officer, Lagos, 1975–79; Vice Consul, Luxembourg, 1979–82; Second Sec., Trade Relns and Exports Dept, FCO, 1982–83; Asst Private Sec. to Minister of State, FCO, 1983–85; Second, later First Sec., Port Louis, Mauritius, 1985–89; Dep. Hd of Mission, Yaoundé, Cameroon, 1989–92; First Sec., Dhaka, 1992–96; Personnel Mgt Dept, FCO, 1996–97; Dep. Hd, Information Dept, FCO, 1997–99; High Comr, Republic of Namibia, 1999–2002. Dir Gen., President of Madagascar's Small Grants Scheme, 2005–08. Political Advisor: Fuelstock, 2008–11; Madagascar Development Partners, 2010–. Patron, Madagascar Development Fund, 2008–; Trustee, Equitrade Foundn, 2006–08. Council Mem., Assoc. of Business Execs, 2006–11; Mem., Adv. Bd, Africa Res. Inst., 2009–. Chm., Grants Cttee, Kitchen Table Charities Trust, 2006–. *Recreations:* family, work, people watching. *Address:* Villa Mahatamana, Lot II M 88 E, Antsakaviro, Boite Postale 13056 67 Ha, Antananarivo 101, Madagascar; 2 The Crescent, St Austell, Cornwall, PL25 4TA.

DONALDSON, Prof. (Charles) Ian (Edward), FBA 1993; Foundation Director, 1974–90, Director, 2004–07, Humanities Research Centre, Australian National University, now Emeritus Professor; Hon. Professorial Fellow, School of Culture and Communication, University of Melbourne, since 2007; Fellow, Trinity College, Melbourne, since 2012; *b* 6 May 1935; *s* of Dr William Edward Donaldson and Elizabeth Donaldson (*née* Weigall); *m* 1st, 1962, Tamsin Jane Procter (marr. diss. 1990); one *s* one *d*; 2nd, 1991, Grazia Maria Therese Gunn. *Educ:* Melbourne Grammar Sch.; Melbourne Univ. (BA 1957); Magdalen Coll., Oxford (BA 1960; MA 1964). Sen. Tutor in English, Univ. of Melbourne, 1958; Oxford University: Harmsworth Sen. Scholar, Merton Coll., 1960–62; Fellow and Lectr in English, Wadham Coll., 1962–69; CUF Lectr in English, 1963–69; Prof. of English, ANU Canberra, 1969–91; Regius Prof. of Rhetoric and English Lit., Univ. of Edinburgh, 1991–95; University of Cambridge: Grace I Prof. of English, 1995–2002; Fellow, King's College, 1995–2005; Dir, Centre for Res. in the Arts, Social Scis and Humanities, 2001–03. Vis. appts, Univ. of California Santa Barbara, Gonville and Caius Coll., Cambridge, Cornell Univ., Melbourne Univ. Syndic, CUP, 1997–2001. President: Australian Acad. of Humanities, 2008–09; Nat. Academies Forum, 2009. FAHA 1975; Corresp. FBA 1987; FRSE 1993. Hon. DLitt Melbourne, 2014. *Publications:* The World Upside-Down: comedy from Jonson to Fielding, 1970; (ed) Ben Jonson Poems, 1975; The Rapes of Lucretia, 1982; (ed) Jonson and Shakespeare, 1983; (ed) Transformations in Modern European Drama, 1983; (ed with Tamsin Donaldson) Seeing the First Australians, 1985; (ed) Ben Jonson, 1985; (ed jtly) Shaping Lives: reflections on biography, 1992; (ed) Ben Jonson: Selected Poems, 1995; Jonson's Magic Houses, 1997; Ben Jonson: a life, 2011; (gen. ed. with David Bevington and Martin Butler) The Cambridge Edition of the Works of Ben Jonson, 7 vols, 2012; (ed jtly) Taking Stock: the humanities in Australian life since 1968, 2012. *Address:* School of Culture and Communication, University of Melbourne, Vic 3010, Australia.

DONALDSON, David Torrance; QC 1984; a Recorder, since 1994; *b* 30 Sept. 1943; *s* of Alexander Walls Donaldson and Margaret Merry Bryce. *Educ:* Glasgow Academy; Gonville and Caius College, Cambridge (Maj. Schol.; MA); University of Freiburg i. Br., West Germany (Dr jur). Fellow, Gonville and Caius College, Cambridge, 1965–69. Called to the Bar, Gray's Inn, 1968, Bencher, 1995. *Address:* Blackstone Chambers, Blackstone House, Temple, EC4Y 9BW. *T:* (020) 7583 1770.

DONALDSON, Graham Hunter Carley, CB 2009; Hon. Professor, School of Education, University of Glasgow, since 2011; *b* 11 Dec. 1946; *s* of Matthew and Margaret Donaldson; *m* 1972, Dilys Lloyd; two *s* one *d*. *Educ:* High Sch. of Glasgow; Univ. of Glasgow (MA, DipEd, MEd). Teacher, Glasgow, 1970–73; Hd of Dept, Dumbartonshire, 1973–75; Lectr, Jordanhill Coll. of Educn, 1975–83; Inspector of Schs, 1983–90; Chief Inspector, 1990–96; Depute Sen. Chief Inspector, 1996–2002; Sen. Chief Inspector of Educn in Scotland, 2002–10. Leader: Rev. of Teacher Educn in Scotland, 2010–11 (report published, 2011); Rev. of Curriculum and Assessment in Wales, 2014–15. Pres., Standing Internat. Conf. of Inspectorates, 2007–12. Nat. Curriculum Evaluator, 1975–83. FRSA 2003. *Publications:* James IV: a Renaissance King, 1975; Industry and Scottish Schools, 1981; Teaching Scotland's Future, 2011; (jtly) Work-Based Learning in Teacher Education, 2013. *Recreations:* golf, supporting Motherwell FC, reading, particularly history and biographies. *Address:* School of Education, University of Glasgow, St Andrew's Building, 11 Eldon Street, Glasgow G3 6NH. *E:* Graham.Donaldson@gla.ac.uk.

DONALDSON, Hamish, MBE 2013; DL; Chairman, Haslemere Festival, since 2003; *b* 13 June 1936; *s* of late James Donaldson and Marie Christine Cormack; *m* 1965, Linda, *d* of late Dr Leslie Challis Bousfield; three *d*. *Educ:* Oundle School; Christ's College, Cambridge (MA). Nat. Service, 2nd Lieut, Seaforth Highlanders, 1955–57. De La Rue Bull, 1960–66; Urwick, Orr & Partners, 1966–73; Hill Samuel & Co., 1973–91; Man. Dir, Hill Samuel Merchant Bank (SA), 1985–86; Chief Exec., Hill Samuel Bank, 1987–91. Director: TSB Bank, 1988–91; TSB Group, 1990–91; Macquarie Bank, 1989–91; RSH Trading Ltd, 1994–. Chm., Guildford DAC for the Care of Churches and Churchyards, 1992–2011; Founder Chm., Surrey Churches Preservation Trust, 1997–. Lay Canon, Guildford Cathedral, 2012–. Gov., Royal Sch., Haslemere, 1994– (Chm., 2009–13). Freeman, City of London, 1988; Liveryman, Information Technologists' Co., 1992–. DL Surrey, 2004. *Publications:* A Guide to the Successful Management of Computer Projects, 1978; Mantrap: avoiding the pitfalls of project management, 2006. *Recreation:* amateur operatics. *Address:* Edgecombe, Hill Road, Haslemere, Surrey GU27 2JN. *T:* (01428) 644473.

DONALDSON, Ian; *see* Donaldson, C. I. E.

DONALDSON, Rt Hon. Jeffrey (Mark); PC 2007; MP Lagan Valley, since 1997 (UU, 1997–2003, DUP, since 2004); *b* 7 Dec. 1962; *s* of James Alexander Donaldson and Sarah Anne Donaldson; *m* 1987, Eleanor Mary Elizabeth Cousins; two *d*. *Educ:* Castlereagh Coll. (DipEE); Chartered Insurance Inst. (Financial Planning Cert.). Agent to Rt Hon. J. Enoch Powell, MP, 1983–85; Mem., NI Assembly, 1985–86; Partner in financial services/estate agency practice, 1986–97. Mem., NI Forum, 1996–98. Mem., Lagan Valley, NI Assembly, 2003–10 (UU, 2003–04, DUP, 2004–10). Jun. Minister, Office of the First Minister and Dep. First Minister, NI, 2008–09. Alderman, Lisburn CC, 2005–10. Hon. Sec., 1988–2000, Vice-Pres., 2000–03, UU Council. Chm., Causeway Inst. for Peace Building and Conflict Resolution, 2011–. *Recreations:* travelling, walking, reading, war graves and battlefield heritage. *Address:* House of Commons, SW1A 0AA. *T:* (020) 7219 3407; Old Town Hall, 29 Castle Street, Lisburn, Co. Antrim BT27 4DH. *T:* (028) 9266 8001.

DONALDSON, Joanna Mary, FCIPD; Director, Human Resources, 2010–13, Acting Director General, Corporate Effectiveness, 2012, Department for Business, Innovation and Skills; *b* 11 Oct. 1955; *d* of Norman Donaldson and Caryl Donaldson; *m* 1979, Crispin Southgate; two *s* one *d*. *Educ:* St Anne's Coll., Oxford (BA Hons PPE). Fast stream, DTI, 1977; Private Sec. to Minister for Industry, 1981–83; policy, then HR roles: DTI; Oftel, 1985–87; OST, 1998–99; BERR, subseq. BIS. Trustee, St Christopher's Hospice, 2013–. *Recreations:* family, walking, sailing, reading, bridge. *Address:* Department for Business, Innovation and Skills, 1 Victoria Street, SW1H 0ET.

DONALDSON, Julia Catherine, MBE 2011; writer of books, songs and plays for children; Children's Laureate, 2011–13; *b* 16 Sept. 1948; *d* of James Shields and Elizabeth Shields (*née* Ede); *m* 1972, Malcolm Donaldson; two *s* (and one *s* decd). *Educ:* Camden Sch. for Girls; Univ. of Bristol (BA Drama and French 1970); Falmer Coll. of Educn (PGCE English 1976). Editl Asst, Michael Joseph, 1971–72; Short-Story Editor, BBC Radio Bristol, 1973–74; Editor, Robert Tyndall, 1974–75; English Teacher, St Mary's Hall, Brighton, 1976–78; freelance contrib. of songs to BBC television progs, 1974–. Writer in Residence, Easterhouse, Glasgow, 1998–2001. Chm., Assoc. of Children's Writers and Illustrators in Scotland, 2001–03. Volunteer, CAB, Glasgow, 1993–97. Hon. DLitt Bristol, 2011. *Publications:* A Squash and a Squeeze, 1993; The Gruffalo, 1999; Monkey Puzzle, Follow the Swallow, Tales from Acorn Wood: Fox's Socks, Rabbit's Nap, Postman Bear, Hide and Seek Pig, 2000; Room on the Broom, 2001; The Dinosaur's Diary, Night Monkey Day Monkey, 2002; The Smartest Giant in Town, Spinderella, The Head in the Sand, Bombs and Blackberries, The Magic Paintbrush, Conjuror Cow, Princess Mirror-Belle, The Snail and the Whale, Brick-A-Breck, 2003; The Wrong Kind of Bark, Wriggle and Roar, Sharing a Shell, The Giants and the Joneses, The Gruffalo's Child, One Ted Falls out of Bed, Crazy Mayonnaisy Mum, 2004; The Gruffalo Song and other Songs, Princess Mirror-Belle and the Magic Shoes, Chocolate Mousse for Greedy Goose, Rosie's Hat, The Jungle House, The Quick Brown Fox Cub, Charlie Cook's Favourite Book, 2005; Hippo Has a Hat, Princess Mirror-Belle and the Flying Horse, Play Time!, The Princess and the Wizard, (with John Henderson) Fly Pigeon Fly, 2006; Room on the Broom and other Songs, Tyrannosaurus Drip, Tiddler, 2007; One Mole Digging a Hole, Stick Man, 2008; Running on the Cracks, What the Ladybird Heard, Toddle Waddle, Tabby McTat, 2009; Cave Baby, Zog, Freddie and the Fairy, 2010; The Rhyming Rabbit, Jack and the Flumflum Tree, Zog, The Highway Rat, 2011; Sugarlump and the Unicorn, 2013; The Scarecrows' Wedding, 2014; Princess Mirror-belle and the Dragon Pox, 2014; also various educnl pubns incl. Songbirds (series of 60 phonic reading books), part of Oxford Reading Tree, 2006–09. *Recreations:* piano playing, singing, walking, study of flowers and fungi. *Address:* c/o Macmillan Children's Books, 20 New Wharf Road, N1 9RR.

DONALDSON, Sir Liam (Joseph), Kt 2002; MD; FRCP, FRCPE, FRCSE, FFPH, FRCGP, FMedSci; Professor of Health Policy, Imperial College London, since 2011; Chief Medical Officer, Department of Health, 1998–2010; *b* 3 May 1949. *Educ:* Univ. of Bristol (MB, ChB 1972); Univ. of Birmingham (MSc 1976); Univ. of Leicester (MD 1982). FRCSE 1977; FFPH (FFCM 1987; FFPHM 1990); FRCP 1997; FRCGP 1999; FRCPE 1999. House Officer, United Bristol Hosps, 1972–73; Lectr in Anatomy, Univ. of Birmingham, 1973–75; Surgical Registrar, United Birmingham Hosps, 1975–77; Lectr in Anatomy, then Sen. Lectr in Epidemiol., Univ. of Leicester, 1977–86; Regl Med. Officer and Head of Clinical Policy, then Director of Public Health, Northern RHA, 1986–92; Regl Gen. Manager and Dir of Public Health, Northern and Yorks RHA, later Regl Dir and Dir of Public Health, Northern and Yorks NHS Exec., 1994–98. Hon. Prof. of Applied Epidemiol., 1989–, Chancellor, 2009–, Univ. of Newcastle upon Tyne. Patient Safety Envoy to Dir Gen. (formerly Chm., World Alliance for Patient Safety), WHO, 2010–; Chairman: Ind. Monitoring Bd on Global Polio Eradication, 2011–; Nat. Patient Safety Agency, 2010–12. QHP 1996–99. FMedSci 1999. Hon. doctorates from univs of Bristol, Leicester, Cranfield, Huddersfield, Portsmouth, York, Sheffield, Teesside, Birmingham, De Montfort, Nottingham, Hull, East Anglia, Sunderland and Imperial Coll. London. Gold Medal, RCSE, 2000. *Publications:* (with R. J. Donaldson) Essential Community Medicine, 1983, 3rd edn (with G. Scally) as Donaldsons' Essential Public Health, 2009; (ed with B. R. McAvoy) Health Care for Asians, 1990; (with S. Sheard) The Nation's Doctor, 2005; over 190 papers on various aspects of health services research. *Address:* Institute of Global Health Innovation, Department of Surgery and Cancer, Imperial College London, 10th Floor, QEQM, St Mary's Hospital, Praed Street, Paddington, W2 1NY.

DONALDSON, Maureen; *see* Watt, M.

DONALDSON, Air Vice-Marshal Michael Phillips, MBE 1973; FRAeS; Chief Executive and Principal, Yorkshire Coast College, 1996–2003; *b* 22 July 1943; *s* of George Millar Donaldson and Mabel Donaldson (*née* Phillips); *m* 1970, Mavis Cornish; one *s* one *d*. *Educ:*

Chislehurst and Sidcup Grammar Sch. for Boys. RAF Gen. Duties; Pilot and Weapons Instructor; No 23 Sqn (Lightning), 1965–68; No 226 OCU, 1969; USAF Florida (F106), 1970–73; No 29 Sqn (Phantom), 1974–76; No 228 OCU, 1977; Army Staff Coll., 1978; PSO to Dep. Comdr in Chief AFCENT, Brunssum, 1979–80; MoD, 1980–83; OC 19 Sqn, 1983–85; OC 23 Sqn (Falkland Is), 1985; Dep. PSO to CDS, 1986–87; OC RAF Wattisham, 1987–89; RCDS 1990; SASO, 11 Group, 1990–93; Comdt, RAF Staff Coll., 1993–96. Life Vice-Pres., RAF Squash Rackets Assoc., 1996. MInstD; FRAeS 1997; FRSA 1999. *Recreations:* music, history, squash, tennis, golf. *Club:* Royal Air Force.

DONALDSON, Dame Patricia Anne; *see* Hodgson, Dame P. A.

DONALDSON, Sir Simon (Kirwan), Kt 2012; DPhil; FRS 1986; Professor of Pure Mathematics, Imperial College London, since 1998; *b* 20 Aug. 1957; *m* 1986, Ana Nora Hurtado; two *s* one *d*. *Educ:* Sevenoaks Sch., Kent; Pembroke Coll., Cambridge (BA 1979; Hon. Fellow, 1992); Worcester Coll., Oxford (DPhil 1983). Jun. Res. Fellow, All Souls Coll., Oxford, 1983–85; Wallis Prof. of Maths, and Fellow, St Anne's Coll., Univ. of Oxford, 1985–98, Hon. Fellow, 1998. Fields Medal, IMU, 1986; Frederic Esser Nemmers Prize, Northwestern Univ., 2008; Shaw Prize in Math. Scis, 2009. *Publications:* (with P. B. Kronheimer) The Geometry of Four-manifolds, 1990; papers in mathematical jls. *Recreation:* sailing. *Address:* Department of Mathematics, South Kensington Campus, Imperial College London, SW7 2AZ.

DONALDSON, Stuart Blair; MP (SNP) West Aberdeenshire and Kincardine, since 2015; *s* of Bruce Donaldson and Maureen Donaldson (*see* Maureen Watt). *Educ:* Banchory Acad.; Univ. of Glasgow (MA 2013). Formerly Parly Asst to Christian Allard, MSP. *Address:* House of Commons, SW1A 0AA.

DONCASTER, Bishop Suffragan of, since 2012; **Rt Rev. Peter Burrows;** *b* 27 May 1955; *s* of Alfred and Eileen Burrows; *m* 1975, Jane Susan Allsop; one *s* one *d*. *Educ:* Salisbury and Wells Theol Coll.; BTh Southampton (ext.) 1980. Nursing Asst, Derbyshire Royal Infirmary, 1973–76; Clerical Officer, DHSS, 1976–80. Ordained deacon, 1983, priest, 1984; Curate, Baildon, 1983–87; Rector: Broughton Astley, 1987–93; Broughton Astley and Croft with Stoney Stanton, 1993–2000; RD, Guthlaxton First Deanery, 1994–2000; Diocese of Leicester: Dir of Ordinands and Parish Develt Officer, 2000–03; Dep. Dir of Ministry, 2002–03, Dir of Ministry, 2003–05; Archdeacon of Leeds, 2005–12. Mem., Gen. Synod of C of E, 2009–11. MInstD 2008. *Recreations:* cooking Indian food, entertaining and hospitality, theatre, cinema, amateur dramatics, reading, motor sport, travel. *Address:* Doncaster House, Church Lane, Fishlake, Doncaster DN7 5JW. *T:* (01302) 846610.

DONCASTER, Archdeacon of; *see* Wilcockson, Ven. S. A.

DONE, Frances Winifred, CBE 2003; FCA; Chair, Youth Justice Board, 2008–14; *b* 6 May 1950; *d* of Rt Hon. Lord Bishopston, PC and Winifred Mary (*née* Bryant); *m* 1981, James Hancock; two *s*. *Educ:* Manchester Univ. (BA Econ.). FCA 1976. Chm., Finance Cttee, Manchester CC, 1984–88; Treas., 1991–98, Chief Exec. and Treas., 1998–2000, Rochdale MBC; Chief Exec., Manchester 2002 Ltd, XVII Commonwealth Games Org. Cttee, 2000–03; Man. Dir, Local Govt, Housing and Criminal Justice, subseq. Local Govt and Housing, Audit Commn, 2003–06; Interim Dir Gen., RBL, 2007. Trustee: Waterways Trust, 2003–12; Canal and River Trust, 2013–. *Recreations:* canals, walking, family.

DONEGALL, 8th Marquess of, *cr* 1791 (Ire.); **Arthur Patrick Chichester;** Viscount Chichester and Baron Chichester of Belfast, 1625; Earl of Donegall, 1647; Earl of Belfast, 1791; Baron Fisherwick (GB), 1790; Baron Templemore (UK), 1831; Hereditary Lord High Admiral of Lough Neagh; Governor of Carrickfergus Castle; farmer; *b* 9 May 1952; *s* of 7th Marquess of Donegall, LVO and Lady Josceline Gabrielle Legge, *y d* of 7th Earl of Dartmouth, GCVO, TD; *S* father, 2007; *m* 1989, Caroline, *er d* of Major Christopher Philipson; one *s* one *d*. *Educ:* Harrow; Royal Agricl Coll., Cirencester. Coldstream Guards. *Recreations:* hunting, shooting, fishing. *Heir:* *s* Earl of Belfast, *qv*. *Address:* Dunbrody Park, Arthurstown, Co. Wexford, Eire; Howthill, Jedburgh, Roxburghshire TD8 6QR.

DONELAN, Michelle; MP (C) Chippenham, since 2015; *b* Whitley, Cheshire, 8 April 1984; *d* of Michael and Kathryn Donelan. *Educ:* Univ. of York (BA Hons Hist. and Politics). Mktg asst on Marie Claire mag. and That's Life mag., Pacific Magazines, 2006–07; Mktg Exec., then Sen. Mktg Exec., Hist. Channel, AETN UK, 2007–10; Internat. Mktg Manager, World Wrestling Entertainment, 2010–14; mktg freelancer, Wilts, 2014–15. Contested (C) Wentworth and Dearne, 2010. *Recreations:* cycling, swimming, walking, cooking. *Address:* House of Commons, SW1A 0AA. *T:* 07794 040334. *E:* michelle.donelan.mp@parliament.uk.

DONERAILE, 10th Viscount *cr* 1785 (Ire.); **Richard Allen St Leger;** Baron Doneraile, 1776; *b* 17 Aug. 1946; *s* of 9th Viscount Doneraile and of Melva, Viscountess Doneraile; *S* father, 1983; *m* 1970, Kathleen Mary Simcox, Churchtown, Mallow, Co. Cork; one *s* one *d*. *Educ:* Orange Coast College, California; Mississippi Univ. Served US Army. Air Traffic Control specialist; antiquarian book appraiser, 1970–73; food marketing analyst, 1974. *Recreations:* outdoor sports, ski-ing, golf, sailing. *Heir:* *s* Hon. Nathaniel Warham Robert St John St Leger, *b* 13 Sept. 1971. *Club:* Yorba Linda Country (California).

DONLEAVY, James Patrick; author and artist; *b* 23 April 1926; *m* Valerie Heron (marr. diss.); one *s* one *d*; *m* Mary Wilson Price (marr. diss.); one *s* one *d*. *Educ:* schs in USA; Trinity Coll., Dublin. Evening Standard Drama Critics' Award, 1961; Brandeis Univ. Creative Arts Award, 1962; AAAL Grantee, 1975; Worldfest Houston Gold Award, 1992. *Art exhibitions:* Painter's Gall., Dublin, 1950, 1951; Bronxville, NY, 1959; Langton Galls, London, 1975; Caldwell Galls, Belfast, 1987; Anna Mei Chadwick Gall., London, 1989, 1991; Alba Fine Art Gall., London, 1991; The Front Lounge, Dublin, 1995; Walton Gall., London, 2002; Molesworth Gall., Dublin, 2006, 2008, 2010; National Arts Club, NY, 2007; Mullingar, 2008. *Publications:* The Ginger Man (novel), 1955; Fairy Tales of New York (play), 1960; What They Did In Dublin With The Ginger Man (introd. and play), 1961; A Singular Man (novel), 1963 (play, 1964); Meet My Maker The Mad Molecule (short stories), 1964; The Saddest Summer of Samuel S (novella), 1966 (play, 1967); The Beastly Beatitudes of Balthazar B (novel), 1968 (play, 1981); The Onion Eaters (novel), 1971; The Plays of J. P. Donleavy, 1972; A Fairy Tale of New York (novel), 1973; The Unexpurgated Code: a complete manual of survival and manners, 1975; The Destinies of Darcy Dancer, Gentleman (novel), 1977; Schultz (novel), 1980; Leila (novel), 1983; De Alfonce Tennis: the superlative game of eccentric champions, its history, accoutrements, rules, conduct and regimen (sports manual), 1984; J. P. Donleavy's Ireland, in all her Sins and in some of her Graces, 1986 (Cine Golden Eagle Award, 1993, for television prodn (writer and narrator)); Are You Listening Rabbi Low (novel), 1987; A Singular Country, 1989; That Darcy, That Dancer, That Gentleman (novel), 1990; The History of the Ginger Man (autobiog.), 1994; The Lady Who Liked Clean Rest Rooms (novella), 1996; An Author and His Image: the collected short pieces, 1997; Wrong Information Is Being Given Out at Princeton (novel), 1998; contribs to jls etc, incl. The Observer, The Times (London), New York Times, Washington Post, Daily Telegraph, Daily Mail, Irish Ind., Esquire, Envoy, Punch, Guardian, Saturday Evening Post, Holiday, Atlantic Monthly, Saturday Review, The New Yorker, Queen, Vogue, Penthouse, Playboy, Architectural Digest, Vanity Fair, Rolling Stone, Liberation (Paris). *Address:* Levington Park, Mullingar, Co. Westmeath, Ireland.

DONLEY, Dr Anita Jane, OBE 2007; FRCP; Consultant Physician in Acute Medicine, Plymouth Hospitals NHS Trust, since 1990; Clinical Vice President, Royal College of Physicians, since 2013; *b* Warwick, 13 Aug. 1952; *d* of Charles Edwin Robert Donley and Daisy Phyllis Grant Donley; *m* (marr. diss.); one *s* one *d*. *Educ:* King's High School for Girls, Warwick; Univ. of Bristol Med. Sch. (MB ChB; PhD 1991); Univ. of Wales Coll. of Medicine (DipMedEd 1992). FRCP 1992. MRC/AFRC Fellow in Nutrition, 1986–88; Sen. Lectr and Consultant Physician, Univ. of Southampton, 1988–90; BAAS Media Fellow, 1989. Head Assessor, Professional Performance Procedures, GMC, 2000–11; Nat. Clin. Dir, Venous Thromboembolism Prevention, 2007–10; Med. Dir, Revalidation, DoH, 2011–13. Member: Lowermoor Subgp, Cttee on Toxicity, 2001–11; Scientific Adv. Cttee on Nutrition, FSA, 2001–11; Postgrad. Med. Educn and Trng Bd, 2002–09 (Chair, Trng Cttee, 2002–09); UK Panel for Res. Integrity in Health and Biomedical Sci., 2005–08; Human Genetics Commn, 2007–12. INSEAD Eur. Health Leadership Alumnus, 2010. Hon. MRCGP 2005; Hon. MFPH 2014. *Publications:* contrib. to learned publications on nutrition and care of older people; ind. reports on venous thromboembolism and medical care of suspected internal drugs traffickers. *Recreations:* theatre, literature, drama, trekking. *Address:* Morvah, Landrake with St Erney, Saltash, Cornwall PL12 5AB. *E:* anitadonley@me.com. *Club:* Royal Automobile.

DONN, Mary Cecilia; *see* Spinks, M. C.

DONNACHIE, Prof. Alexander, FInstP; Professor of Physics, 1969–2001, now Emeritus, and Hon. Professor of Physics and Astronomy, 2001, University of Manchester; *b* 25 May 1936; *s* of John Donnachie and Mary Ramsey Donnachie (*née* Adams); *m* 1960, Dorothy Paterson; two *d*. *Educ:* Kilmarnock Acad.; Glasgow Univ. (BSc, PhD). DSIR Res. Fellow 1961–63, Lectr 1963–65, UCL; Res. Associate, CERN, Geneva, 1965–67; Sen. Lectr, Univ. of Glasgow, 1967–69; University of Manchester: Hd of Theoretical Physics 1975–85; Dean of Faculty of Science, 1985–87; Chm., Dept of Physics, 1988–94; Dir of Physical Labs, 1989–94; Dean, Faculty of Science and Engrg, 1994–97. Mem., SERC, 1989–94 (Chm., Nuclear Phys Bd, 1989–93); CERN: Chairman: Super Proton Synchrotron Cttee, 1988–90; Super Proton Synchrotron and LEAR Cttee, 1991–93; Member: Res. Bd, 1988–95; Sci. Policy Cttee, 1988–93; Council, 1989–94; Particle, Space and Astronomy Bd, 1993–94; Sec., C11 Commn, IUPAP, 1989–91. *Publications:* Electromagnetic Interactions of Hadrons, vols I and II, 1978; Pomeron Physics and QCD, 2002; Electromagnetic Interactions and Hadronic Structure, 2007; nearly 200 articles in learned jls of Particle Physics. *Recreations:* sailing, walking. *Address:* c/o School of Physics and Astronomy, University of Manchester, Manchester M13 9PL.

DONNAI, Prof. Dian, CBE 2005; FRCP, FRCOG, FMedSci; Professor of Medical Genetics, University of Manchester, 2001–10, now Emerita (Hon. Professor, 1994–2001); Consultant Clinical Geneticist, Regional Genetics Service, St Mary's Hospital, Manchester, since 1980; *b* 15 Feb. 1945; *d* of Arnold Sydney Aughton and May Aughton; *m* 1968, Paul Donnai; one *s* one *d*. *Educ:* Whitchurch Girls' High Sch., Shropshire; St Mary's Hosp. Med. Sch., London Univ. (MB BS 1968). FRCP 1984; FRCOG *ad eundem* 1995; FMedSci 2001. Consultant Advr in Genetics to CMO, DoH, 1998–2003. President: Med Scis Section, BAAS, 2007; European Soc. of Human Genetics, 2009–10. *Publications:* (ed jtly) Congenital Malformation Syndromes, 1996; (ed jtly) Antenatal Diagnosis of Fetal Abnormalities, 1991; (ed jtly) Early Fetal Growth and Development, 1994; (with A. Read) New Clinical Genetics, 2007, 2nd edn 2010; numerous articles on genetic disorders and syndromes. *Recreation:* learning French. *Address:* Manchester Centre for Genomic Medicine, 6th Floor, Manchester Academic Health Sciences Centre, St Mary's Hospital, Central Manchester University Hospitals NHS Foundation Trust, Oxford Road, Manchester M13 9WL. *T:* (0161) 276 6002, *Fax:* (0161) 276 6145. *E:* Dian.Donnai@cmft.nhs.uk.

DONNAN, Prof. Hastings Samuel Charles, DPhil; FBA 2013; Professor of Anthropology, since 1997, and Director, Institute for Study of Conflict Transformation and Social Justice, since 2012, Queen's University Belfast; *b* Portadown, 12 March 1953; *s* of Robert J. and Noreen C. Donnan; *m* 1985, Katharine Marshall; three *d*. *Educ:* Bangor Grammar Sch.; Queen's Univ. Belfast (BA Hons 1975); Univ. of Sussex (DPhil 1981). Lectr in Anthropol., QUB, 1979–97. Panel Chair: RAE, 2005–08; REF, 2010–14. MRIA 2001. FAcSS (AcSS 1999). *Publications:* Marriage Among Muslims: preference and choice in Northern Pakistan, 1988; (ed with G. McFarlane) Social Anthropology and Public Policy in Northern Ireland, 1989; (ed with P. Werbner) Economy and Culture in Pakistan: migrants and cities in a Muslim society, 1991; (ed jtly) Irish Urban Cultures, 1993; (ed with A. S. Ahmed) Islam, Globalization and Postmodernity, 1994; (ed with F. Selier) Family and Gender in Pakistan: domestic organization in a Muslim society, 1997; (ed with G. McFarlane) Culture and Policy in Northern Ireland: anthropology in the public arena, 1997; (ed) Interpreting Islam, 2002; (ed with F. Magowan) Transgressive Sex: subversion and control in erotic encounters, 2009; (with F. Magowan) The Anthropology of Sex, 2010; *with T. M. Wilson:* (ed) Border Approaches: anthropological perspectives on frontiers, 1994; (ed) Border Identities: nation and state at international frontiers, 1998; Borders: frontiers of identity, nation and state, 1999 (Turkish edn 2005; Polish edn 2007); (ed) Culture and Power at the Edges of the State: national support and subversion in European borderlands, 2005; The Anthropology of Ireland, 2006; (ed) Borderlands: ethnographic approaches to security, power and identity, 2010; (ed) A Companion to Border Studies, 2012. *Recreations:* equestrian. *Address:* Institute for the Study of Conflict Transformation and Social Justice, Queen's University Belfast, Belfast, Northern Ireland BT7 1NN. *T:* (028) 9097 3284. *E:* h.donnan@qub.ac.uk.

DONNE, Jeremy Nigel, RD 1992; QC 2003; **His Honour Judge Donne;** a Circuit Judge, since 2012; *b* 22 Jan. 1954; *s* of Tom and Shirley Donne; *m* 1984, Caroline Susan O'Brien-Gore; two *d*. *Educ:* County Grammar Sch., Merthyr Tydfil; Cyfarthfa High Sch., Merthyr Tydfil; Inns of Court Sch. of Law. Called to the Bar, Middle Temple, 1978, Bencher, 2011; specialised in criminal, regulatory and disciplinary law; Asst Recorder, 1998–2000; Recorder, 2000–12. Mem., S Eastern Circuit. Chm., British Equestrian Fedn Disciplinary Appeals Panel, 2011–12; Member: Justice, 2005–; Exec. Council, British Acad. of Forensic Sci., 2013– (Treas., 2015–); former Mem., Criminal Bar Assoc. Mem., RNSA, 1980–. Chm., Govs, All Saints C of E Sch., Putney, 2006–09. *Recreations:* sailing, ski-ing, cycling. *Address:* Inner London Crown Court, Sessions House, Newington Causeway, SE1 6AZ. *Clubs:* Royal Naval Volunteer Reserve Yacht (Cdre, 2007–08), Royal Thames Yacht, Bar Yacht.

DONNE, Sir John (Christopher), Kt 1976; Chairman, National Health Service Training Authority, 1983–86; *b* 19 Aug. 1921; *s* of late Leslie Victor Donne, solicitor, Hove, and Mabel Laetitia Richards (*née* Pike); *m* 1945, Mary Stuart (*née* Seaton) (*d* 2009); three *d*. *Educ:* Charterhouse. Royal Artillery, 1940–46 (Captain); served Europe and India. Solicitor, 1949; Notary Public; Consultant, Donne Mileham & Haddock, 1985–92; Pres., Sussex Law Soc., 1969–70. Chairman: SE (Metropolitan) Regional Hosp. Bd, 1971–74; SE Thames RHA, 1973–83. Governor, Guy's Hosp., 1971–74, Guy's Hosp. Med. Sch., 1974–82; Dep. Chm., RHA Chairmen, 1976–78 (Chm., 1974–76); Mem., Gen. Council, King Edward's Hosp. Fund for London, 1972–91 (Mem., Management Cttee, 1978–84); a Governing Trustee, Nuffield Provincial Hosp. Trust, 1975–98; Dir, Nuffield Health and Soc. Services Fund, 1976–98. Member: Council, Internat. Hosp. Fedn, 1979–85; Council, Inst. for Med. Ethics (formerly Soc. for Study of Medical Ethics), 1980–86; Court of Univ. of Sussex, 1979–87. FRSA 1985–92; FRSocMed 1985. Mem. Ct of Assts, Hon. Company of Broderers, 1979– (Master, 1983–84). Mem., Editorial Bd, Jl Medical Ethics, 1977–79. *Recreations:* genealogy, gardening, photography, listening to music. *Address:* The Old School House, Acton Burnell, Shrewsbury SY5 7PG. *T:* (01694) 731647. *Clubs:* Pilgrims, MCC; Butterflies, Sussex Martlets.

DONNELLAN, Declan Michael Martin; Joint Artistic Director, Cheek By Jowl, since 1981; Associate Director, Royal National Theatre, 1989–97; *b* 4 Aug. 1953; *s* of Thomas Patrick John Donnellan and Margaret Josephine Donnellan. *Educ:* Queens' Coll., Cambridge (MA). Called to the Bar, Middle Temple, 1978. Associate Dir, Russian Th. Confedn, 1999–. Productions: Cheek By Jowl: The Country Wife, 1981; Othello, 1982; Vanity Fair, 1983; Pericles, 1984; Andromache, 1985; A Midsummer Night's Dream, 1985; The Man of Mode, 1985; The Cid, 1986; Twelfth Night, 1986; Macbeth, 1987; A Family Affair, 1988; Philoctetes, 1988; The Tempest, 1988; Lady Betty, 1989; The Doctor of Honour, 1989; Sara, 1990; Hamlet, 1991; As You Like It, 1992, 1995; Don't Fool with Love, 1993; The Blind Man, 1993; Measure for Measure, 1994, 2015; The Duchess of Malfi, 1996; Out Cry, 1997; Much Ado About Nothing, 1998; Othello, 2004; The Changeling, 2006; Cymbeline, 2007; Troilus and Cressida, 2008; Macbeth, 2010; 'Tis Pity She's a Whore, 2012; Ubu Roi, 2013; Royal National Theatre: Fuente Ovejuna, 1989; Peer Gynt, 1990; Angels in America: part 1, Millennium, 1991, part 2, Perestroika, 1993; Sweeney Todd, 1992; The Mandate, 2004; Royal Shakespeare Company: The School for Scandal, 1998; King Lear, 2002; Great Expectations, 2005; Russian Theatre Confederation: Boris Godunov, 2000; Twelfth Night, 2003; Three Sisters, 2005; The Tempest, 2011; The Winter's Tale, Maly Drama Theatre, St Petersburg, 1997; Le Cid, Avignon Fest., 1998; Homebody/Kabul, NY, 2001; Falstaff, Salzburg Fest., 2001; Romeo and Juliet, Bolshoi Ballet, Moscow, 2003; Shakespeare in Love, Noël Coward Th., 2014. Dir, Bel Ami (film), 2012. Several internat. awards incl. Observer Award for Outstanding Achievement. Chevalier, Ordre des Arts et des Lettres (France). *Publications:* The Actor and the Target, 2002 (trans. 13 languages). *Address:* c/o Cheek By Jowl, Barbican Centre, Silk Street, EC2Y 8DS.

DONNELLY, Alan John; Executive Chairman: Sovereign Strategy, since 2000; International Management Partners, since 2012; Secretary, Co-operative Commission, since 2000; *b* 16 July 1957; *s* of John and Josephine Donnelly; *m* 1979 (marr. diss. 1982); one *s*. *Educ:* Valley View Primary School and Springfield Comprehensive School, Jarrow; Sunderland Poly. (Hon. Fellow, Sunderland Univ., 1993). GMBATU Northern Region: Health and Safety Officer, 1978–80; Education Officer, 1980–84; Finance and Admin Officer, 1984–87; GMB Central Finance Manager, 1987–89. European Parliament: Member (Lab): Tyne and Wear, 1989–99; NE Reg., England, 1999–Jan. 2000; Pres., Delegn, Relations with USA, 1992–98; Leader, Lab. Party, 1998–2000; a Vice Pres., Socialist Gp. Mem., S Tyneside MBC, 1979–82. B Director, Unity Trust Bank, 1987–89. Kt Comdr, Order of Merit (Germany), 1991. *Recreations:* tennis, swimming, reading.

DONNELLY, Brendan Patrick; Director, Federal Trust, since 2003; Secretary, Federal Union, since 2010 (Chairman, 2003–10); *b* 25 Aug. 1950; *s* of Patrick Aloysius Donnelly and late Mary Josephine Donnelly (*née* Barrett). *Educ:* Christ Church, Oxford (BA Classics 1972; MA 1976). Theodor Heuss Travelling Scholar, Munich, 1974–76; FCO, 1976–82; Private Sec. to Sir Henry Plumb, 1983–86; on staff of Lord Cockfield, a Vice-Pres. of CEC, 1986–87; Political Consultant on EC, 1987–90; Special Advr to Leader of Conservatives in EP, 1990–94. MEP (C) Sussex S and Crawley, 1994–99. Sen. Res. Fellow, Global Policy Inst., 2011–. Contested (4 Freedoms) London, EP, 2014. *Publications:* (jtly) Not in Our Name, 2005; (with Hugh Dykes) On the Edge: Britain and Europe, 2012; numerous articles on European Union. *Recreations:* watching cricket, modern languages, modern history. *Address:* 61 Leopold Road, N2 8BG. *T:* (020) 8444 0154.

DONNELLY, Sir Brian; *see* Donnelly, Sir J. B.

DONNELLY, Prof. Christl Ann, ScD; Professor of Statistical Epidemiology, Imperial College London, since 2002; *b* 19 June 1967; *d* of Rett F. Donnelly and Lou Ellen Donnelly (*née* Hartke); *m* 2000, Ben Hambly; two *s*. *Educ:* Oberlin Coll., Ohio (BA 1988); Harvard Univ. (MSc 1990; ScD 1992). Lectr, Univ. of Edinburgh, 1992–95; Hd, Statistics Unit, Wellcome Trust Centre for Epidemiol. of Infectious Disease, Univ. of Oxford, 1995–2000; Lectr, St Catherine's Coll., Oxford, 1998–2000; Reader, Imperial Coll., London, 2000–02. Dep. Chm., Ind. Scientific Gp on Cattle TB, 1998–2007; Member: Scientific Cttee on Health and Wellbeing in Changing Urban Envmt, ICSU, 2012–; WHO Ebola Response Team, 2014–. Mem. Council, Royal Statistical Soc., 2001–05. Associate Editor: Applied Statistics, 2001–04; Jl of Applied Ecology, 2007–10; Member, Editorial Board: Internat. Jl of Biostatistics, 2004–12; Procs of Royal Soc. B, 2011–13; founding Co-Ed., Statistical Communications in Infectious Diseases, 2009–12. Franco-British Prize, Acad. des Scis, Paris, 2002; Dist. Alum Award, Dept of Biostats, Harvard Univ., 2005. *Publications:* (with N. M. Ferguson) Statistical Aspects of BSE and vCJD: models for epidemics, 2000; (with D. R. Cox) Principles of Applied Statistics, 2011; many contribs to learned jls, incl. Nature, Science, New England Jl of Medicine and Lancet. *Recreations:* travel, running, being a soccer/football mom, theatre. *Address:* Department of Infectious Disease Epidemiology, Faculty of Medicine, Imperial College London, St Mary's Campus, Norfolk Place, W2 1PG. *T:* (020) 7594 3394. *E:* c.donnelly@imperial.ac.uk.

DONNELLY, Christopher Nigel, CMG 2004; TD 1982; Director, Institute for Statecraft (formerly for Statecraft and Governance), since 2005; *b* 10 Nov. 1946; *s* of Anthony Donnelly and Dorothy Mary Donnelly (*née* Morris); *m* 1971, Jill Norris; one *s* one *d*. *Educ:* Cardinal Langley Sch., Middleton, Lancs; Manchester Univ. (BA Hons (Russian Studies) 1969). Royal Military Academy Sandhurst: Instructor, 1969–72; Sen. Lectr, 1972–79, Dir, 1979–89, Soviet Studies Res. Centre; Special Advr for Central and E European affairs to Sec. Gen. of NATO, 1989–2003; Sen. Fellow, Defence Acad. of UK, 2005–11; Dir, Atlantic Council of UK, 2008–11. Adjunct Professor: Carnegie Mellon Univ., 1985–89; Georgia Inst. of Technol., 1989–93. TA Officer (Intelligence Corps), 1970–93. *Publications:* Red Banner, 1988, 2nd edn 1989; War and the Soviet Union, 1990; Gorbachev's Revolution, 1991; Nations, Alliances and Security, 2004; (jtly) Defence Acquisition for the Twenty-First Century, 2015. *Recreations:* shooting, fishing. *Address:* Institute for Statecraft, 2 Temple Place, WC2R 3BD. *T:* (020) 3273 1006, *Fax:* (01539) 722707. *E:* cdonnelly@statecraft.org.uk. *Club:* Army and Navy.

DONNELLY, Declan Joseph Oliver; actor and presenter; *b* Newcastle upon Tyne, 25 Sept. 1975; *s* of Alphonsus and Anne Donnelly. Music career, 1993–97 (14 Top 20 hits; UK, European and world tours); *television:* actor: Byker Grove, 1989–93; A Tribute to the Likely Lads, 2002; presenter of series with Anthony McPartlin, *qv* as Ant and Dec: The Ant and Dec Show, 1995; Ant and Dec Unzipped, 1997; SM:TV Live, 1998–2001 (British Comedy Award, 2000; RTS Award, 2001); CD:UK, 1998–2001; Ant and Dec's Secret Camera Show, 2000; Friends Like These, 2000; Slap Bang with Ant and Dec, 2001; Pop Idol, 2001–03; Ant and Dec's Saturday Night Takeaway, 2002– (British Comedy Awards, 2003, 2004, 2005; Nat. TV Awards, 2007, 2010; British Acad. TV Award, 2014); I'm a Celebrity… Get Me Out of Here!, 2002– (British Comedy Award, 2004; Best Entertainment Perf., BAFTA, 2010; Nat. TV Awards, 2011–15; TRIC Special Award, 2013; RTS Award, 2013); Gameshow Marathon, 2005; Pokerface, 2006–07; Britain's Got Talent, 2007–; Wanna Bet? (USA), 2008; Push the Button, 2010–11; Red or Black?, 2011–; host (with Anthony McPartlin) Brit Awards, 2013; *film:* Alien Autopsy, 2006. Awards with Anthony McPartlin include: Most Popular Entertainment Presenter, annually, 2001–08 and 2010–15, Landmark Award, 2014, Nat. TV Awards; Best Entertainment Personality, British Comedy Awards, 2003, 2004; Best Entertainment Performers, RTS Awards, 2011; Personality of the Year, Freesat Free TV Awards, 2014; TV Personality of the Year, TRIC Awards, 2013, 2014. *Publications:* (with A. McPartlin) Ooh! What a Lovely Pair: our story, 2009. *Address:* c/o James Grant Media Ltd, 94 Strand on the Green, Chiswick, W4 3NN. *T:* (020) 8742 4950.

DONNELLY, Jane Caroline; *see* Owen, J. C.

DONNELLY, Sir (Joseph) Brian, KBE 2003; CMG 1998; HM Diplomatic Service, retired; Ambassador (formerly High Commissioner) to Zimbabwe, 2001–04; *b* 24 April 1945; *s* of Joseph Donnelly and Ada Agnes (*née* Bowness); *m* 1st, 1966, Susanne Gibb (marr. diss. 1994); one *d*; 2nd, 1997, Julia Mary Newsome; one step *s* one step *d*. *Educ:* Workington Grammar Sch.; Queen's Coll., Oxford (Wyndham Scholar, MA; Hon. Fellow, 2015); Univ. of Wisconsin (MA). Admin. trainee, GCHQ, 1970; joined HM Diplomatic Service, 1973; 2nd Sec., FCO, 1973; 1st Sec., UK Mission to UN, NY, 1975–79; Head of Chancery, Singapore, 1979–82; Asst Head, Personnel Policy Dept, FCO, 1982–84; Dep. to Chief Scientific Adviser, Cabinet Office, 1984–87; Counsellor and Consul General, Athens, 1988–91; RCDS, 1991; Head of Non-Proliferation Dept, FCO, 1992–95; Minister and Dep. Perm. Rep., UK Delegn to NATO and WEU, Brussels, 1995–97; Ambassador to Yugoslavia, 1997–99; Dir and Special Rep. for SE Europe, FCO, 1999–2000, on secondment to BP Amoco, 2000–01. Special Advr to Sec. of State for Foreign and Commonwealth Affairs, 2005–06; Vis. Directing Staff, RCDS, 2007–09. Mem., Commonwealth Scholarships Commn, 2006–12; Trustee: Senhouse Museum Trust, 2007–08; Cumbria Community Foundn, 2010–13; Dir, Roman Maryport Ltd, 2011–13. *Recreations:* MG cars, flying kites, reading, golf. *E:* donnewjb@yahoo.co.uk. *Clubs:* MG Owners'; Maryport Golf.

DONNELLY, Martin Eugene, CMG 2002; Permanent Secretary, Department for Business, Innovation and Skills, since 2010; *b* 4 June 1958; *s* of Eugene Lawrence Donnelly and Mary Jane Ormsby; *m* 1985, Carol Jean Heald (*d* 1996); three *d*. *Educ:* Campion Hall, Oxford (MA); Coll. of Europe (Dip. European Studies 1980). Joined HM Treasury, 1980; Private Sec. to Financial Sec., 1982–83; Ecole Nationale d'Admin, Paris, 1983–84; Principal, HM Treasury, 1984–87; Private Sec. to Sec. of State for NI, 1988; Mem., cabinet of Sir Leon Brittan, EC, 1989–92; Asst Sec., Defence Team, HM Treasury, 1993–95; chargé de mission, Direction du Trésor, Finance Min., France, 1995–96; Dep. Hd, European Secretariat, Cabinet Office, 1997–2003; Dep. Dir Gen., Immigration and Nationality Directorate, Home Office, 2003–04; Dir Gen. (Econ.), subseq. (Europe and Globalisation), FCO, 2004–08; Sen. Partner, Office of Communications, 2008–09 (on secondment); Leader, Smarter Govt Review, Cabinet Office, 2009; Acting Perm. Under-Sec., FCO, 2010. *Publications:* articles on G-8, European Commission and cabinet system. *Recreations:* reading, music, walking. *Address:* Department for Business, Innovation and Skills, 1 Victoria Street, SW1H 0ET.

DONNELLY, Prof. Peter Duncan, MD; FRCP, FRCPE, FFPH; President and Chief Executive Officer, Public Health Ontario, since 2014; Professor, Dalla Lana School of Public Health, University of Toronto, since 2015; *b* 27 Jan. 1963; *s* of Dr James Donnelly and Gwyneth Donnelly; *m* 1988, Joan Dymock; three *s*. *Educ:* Univ. of Edinburgh (MB ChB; MD 1999); Univ. of Stirling (MBA 1989, NHS Mgt Develt Gp scholar); Univ. of Wales Coll. of Medicine (MPH); Harvard Univ. (PMD). FFPH 1997; FRCP 2000; FRCPE 2001. Junior hosp. doctor appts, 1985–88; South Glamorgan Health Authority: Registrar, 1989–90; Sen. Registrar, 1990–92; Consultant in Public Health Medicine, 1992–93; Actg Dir, Planning and Procurement, 1993–94; Dep. Chief Admin. MO/Dep. Dir of Public Health Medicine, 1994–96; Dir of Public Health and Exec. Mem. Bd, Morgannwg HA, 1996–2000; Dir, Public Health and Health Policy, Lothian Health Bd, 2000–04; Dep. Chief Medical Officer to Scottish Exec., later Scottish Govt, 2004–08; Prof. of Public Health Medicine, Bute Med. Sch., later Sch. of Med. and Biol Scis, Univ. of St Andrews, 2008–14 (Hon. Prof., 2014–). Lectr, 1989–92, Sen. Lectr, 1992–96, Hon. Sen. Lectr, 1996–2000, in Public Health Medicine, UWCM; Hon. Sen. Lectr in Public Health Medicine, Univ. of Wales, Swansea, 1996–2000; Hon. Prof. of Public Health, Univ. of Edinburgh, 2002–11. Pres., Assoc. of Dirs of Public Health, 1999–2001; Vice Pres., Faculty of Public Health Medicine, RCP, 2001–04 (Treas., 1999–2001). Hon. DSc Napier, 2003. *Publications:* articles in scientific and professional press on public health and resuscitation. *Recreations:* running, ski-ing, golf. *Address:* Public Health Ontario, Suite 300, 480 University Avenue, Toronto, ON M5G 1V2, Canada.

DONNELLY, Prof. Peter James, DPhil; FRS 2006; FMedSci; Professor of Statistical Science, since 1996, and Director, Wellcome Trust Centre for Human Genetics, since 2007, University of Oxford; Fellow of St Anne's College, Oxford, since 1996; *b* 15 May 1959; *s* of late Augustine Stanislaus Donnelly and Sheila Bernadette Donnelly (*née* O'Hagan); *m* 1986, Dr Sarah Helen Harper (marr. diss. 2006); one *s* two *d*; one *d* by Kerstin Sallows. *Educ:* St Joseph's Coll., Brisbane; Univ. of Queensland (BSc 1979; Univ. Medal 1980); Balliol Coll., Oxford (Rhodes Schol., DPhil 1983; Hon. Fellow, 2014). FMedSci 2008. Vis. Asst Prof., Michigan Univ., 1983–84; Res. Fellow, UC Swansea, 1984–85; Lectr, UCL, 1985–88; Prof. of Math. Stats and Operational Res., QMW, 1988–94; Prof. of Stats and Ecology and Evolution, Chicago Univ., 1994–96. Medallion Lectr, Inst. of Math. Stats, 2007. Mem., EMBO, 2014–. Hon. FIA 1999. Mitchell Prize, Amer. Statistical Soc., 2002; Guy Medal, Silver, Royal Statistical Soc., 2004; Weldon Meml Prize, Univ. of Oxford, 2008. *Publications:* (ed jtly) Progress in Population Genetics and Human Evolution, 1997; (ed jtly) Genes, Fossils and Behaviour, 2001; contrib. to learned jls. *Recreations:* sport, music, children. *Address:* Wellcome Trust Centre for Human Genetics, Roosevelt Drive, Oxford OX3 7BN. *T:* (01865) 287725.

DONNISON, David Vernon; Hon. Research Fellow, Glasgow University, since 1991; *b* 19 Jan. 1926; *s* of late Frank Siegfried Vernon Donnison, CBE and Ruth Seruya Singer, MBE, JP; *m* 1st, Jean Kidger; two *s* two *d*; 2nd, 1987, Catherine McIntosh, (Kay), Carmichael (*d* 2009). *Educ:* Marlborough Coll., Wiltshire; Magdalen Coll., Oxford. Asst Lectr and Lectr, Manchester Univ., 1950–53; Lectr, Toronto Univ., 1953–55; Reader, 1956–61, Prof. of Social Administration, 1961–69, LSE (Hon. Fellow, 1981); Dir, Centre for Environmental Studies, 1969–75; Chm., Supplementary Benefits Commn, 1975–80; Prof. of Town and Regl Planning, Glasgow Univ., 1980–91, now Emeritus. Chm., Public Schs Commn, 1968–70. Hon. doctorates: Bradford, 1973; Hull, 1980; Leeds, Southampton, 1981. *Publications:* The Neglected Child and the Social Services, 1954; Welfare Services in a Canadian Community, 1958; Housing since the Rent Act, 1961; The Government of Housing, 1967; An Approach to Social Policy, 1975; Social Policy and Administration Revisited, 1975; (with Paul Soto) The Good City, 1980; The Politics of Poverty, 1982; (with Clare Ungerson) Housing Policy, 1982; (ed with Alan Middleton) Regenerating the Inner City: Glasgow's Experience, 1987; (ed with D. Maclennan) The Housing Service of the Future, 1991; A Radical Agenda, 1991; Long-term Unemployment in Northern Ireland, 1996; Policies for a Just Society, 1998; Last of the Guardians, 2005; Speaking to Power, 2009; Requiem, 2010. *Address:* Flat 0/1, 17 Cranworth Street, Glasgow G12 8BZ. *T:* (0141) 334 5817.

DONOGHUE, Barbara Joan, (Mrs S. Vavalidis); Director, Manzanita Capital, since 2007; *b* 16 July 1951; *d* of Hubert Graham Donoghue and Marjorie Larlham Donoghue; *m* 1976, Stefanos Vavalidis; two *s*. *Educ:* McGill Univ., Montreal (BCom 1972; Schol.; Transportation Develt Agency Fellow, 1974; MBA 1974). Canadian Pacific Ltd, 1973–77; Bank of Nova Scotia, 1977–79; Vice Pres., Bankers Trust Co., 1979–93; Man. Dir, NatWest Markets/Hawkpoint Partners, 1994–98; Teaching Fellow, London Business Sch., 2000–04; Dir, Noventus Partners, 2004–06. Non-exec. Dir, Eniro AB, 2003–11. Member: ITC, 1999–2003; Competition Commn, 2005–14. Trustee, Refuge, 2009–. *Recreation:* learning Greek. *E:* barbara.donoghue@btinternet.com. *Club:* Hurlingham.

DONOGHUE, Bernard; Director, Association of Leading Visitor Attractions, since 2011; *b* Aylesbury, Bucks, 22 March 1969; *s* of late Michael Donoghue and Carmel Donoghue; civil partnership 2007, Nigel Campbell. *Educ:* Aylesbury Grammar Sch.; Goldsmiths Coll., Univ. of London (BA Hons). Chm., British Youth Council, 1991–93; Parly and Campaigns

Manager, SENSE, 1992–96; Sen. Parly and Policy Manager, Nat. Aids Trust, 1996–97; Hd of Govt and Public Affairs, VisitBritain, 1997–2010. Chm., Visit Manchester, 2008–10. Chairman: Young@Now UK and USA, 1996–2005; London Internat. Fest. of Theatre, 2010– (Trustee, 2005–); Council of Ambassadors, WWF-UK, 2012– (Trustee, 2004–10); Dep. Chm., Tourism Alliance, 2014–. Mem., Cathedral Council, St Paul's Cathedral, 2009–. Trustee: Centrepoint, 1995–2012; Tourism Soc., 2001–13; Kaleidoscope Trust, 2011–13; Geffrye Mus. of the Home, 2012–; Kids in Museums, 2012– (Dep. Chm., 2014–); Heritage Alliance, 2012–; Nat. Funding Scheme, 2013–; Prince's Regeneration Trust Enterprise Bd, 2015–. MCIPR 2002. FTS 2007; FRSA. *Recreations:* theatre, travel, collecting contemporary art, museums and galleries, indulgent uncle and godfather. *Address:* c/o Association of Leading Visitor Attractions, Somerset House, New Wing, WC2R 1LA. *E:* bernarddonoghue@alva.org.uk.

DONOGHUE, Prof. Denis, MA, PhD, LittD; literary critic; Henry James Professor of Letters, New York University, since 1979; *b* 1 Dec. 1928. *Educ:* University College, Dublin. BA 1949, MA 1952, PhD 1957; MA Cantab 1965. Admin. Office, Dept of Finance, Irish Civil Service, 1951–54. Asst Lectr, Univ. Coll., Dublin, 1954–57; Coll. Lectr, 1957–62; Visiting Schol., Univ. of Pennsylvania, 1962–63; Coll. Lectr, Univ. Coll., Dublin, 1963–64; University Lectr, Cambridge Univ., 1964–65; Fellow, King's Coll., Cambridge, 1964–65; Prof. of Modern English and American Literature, University Coll., Dublin, 1965–79. Mem. Internat. Cttee of Assoc. of University Profs of English. Mem. BBC Commn to monitor the quality of spoken English on BBC Radio, 1979. Reith Lectr, BBC, 1982. *Publications:* The Third Voice, 1959; Connoisseurs of Chaos, 1965; (ed jtly) An Honoured Guest, 1965; The Ordinary Universe, 1968; Emily Dickinson, 1968; Jonathan Swift, 1969; (ed) Swift, 1970; Yeats, 1971; Thieves of Fire, 1974; (ed) W. B. Yeats, Memoirs, 1973; Sovereign Ghost: studies in Imagination, 1978; Ferocious Alphabets, 1981; The Arts without Mystery, 1983; We Irish (selected essays), 1987; Pure Good of Theory, 1992; Walter Pater: lover of strange souls, 1995; The Practice of Reading, 1998; Words Alone: the poet T. S. Eliot, 2001; Adam's Curse, 2001; Speaking of Beauty, 2003; The American Classics: a personal essay, 2005; On Eloquence, 2008; Irish Essays, 2011; contribs to reviews and journals. *Address:* New York University, English Department, 19 University Place (5th Floor), New York, NY 10003, USA; Gaybrook, North Avenue, Mount Merrion, Dublin, Ireland.

DONOGHUE, Prof. Philip Conrad James, PhD; FRS 2015; Professor of Palaeobiology, University of Bristol, since 2010; *b* Morriston, 5 April 1971; *s* of Terrence and Margaret Donoghue; *m* 1998, Mandy Howells; two *s*. *Educ:* Univ. of Leicester (BSc Geol. 1992; PhD Palaeontol. 1997); Univ. of Sheffield (MSc Palynology 1994). 1851 Res. Fellow, Univ. of Birmingham, 1997–98; NERC Res. Fellow, Univ. of Leicester, then Univ. of Birmingham, 1998–2002; Lectr in Palaeobiol., Univ. of Birmingham, 1999–2003; Lectr, 2003–07, Sen. Lectr, 2007–08, Reader in Geol., 2008–10, Univ. of Bristol. President's Award, 1996, Hudson Prize Fund, 2005, Palaeontol Assoc.; Murchison Prize, 2002, Bigsby Medal, 2007, Geol Soc.; Philip Leverhulme Prize, Leverhulme Trust, 2004; Charles Schuchert Award, Paleontol Soc., 2010; Wolfson Merit Award, Royal Soc., 2013. *Publications:* Telling the Evolutionary Time: molecular clocks and the fossil record, 2003; contrib. papers to internat. peer-reviewed jls, incl. Nature, Science, Proc. NAS. *Recreation:* running. *Address:* School of Earth Sciences, University of Bristol, Life Sciences Building, 24 Tyndall Avenue, Bristol BS8 1TQ. *T:* (0117) 394 1209. *E:* phil.donoghue@bristol.ac.uk.

DONOHOE, Brian Harold; *b* 10 Sept. 1948; *s* of late George Joseph Donohoe and Catherine Sillars Donohoe (*née* Ashworth); *m* 1973, Christine Pawson; two *s*. *Educ:* Irvine Royal Academy; Kilmarnock Technical Coll. Apprentice fitter-turner, 1965–69; draughtsman, 1969–81; Trade Union Official, NALGO, 1981–92. MP (Lab) Cunninghame S, 1992–2005, Central Ayrshire, 2005–15; contested (Lab) same seat, 2015. PPS to Minister of Transport, 2008–09, to Sec. of State for Transport, 2009–10. Member, Select Committee: on transport, 1993–97 and 2002–05; on environment, transport and the regions, 1997–2001; on transport, local govt and the regions, 2001–02; Admin, 2005–10. Jt Chm., All Party Parly Gp against Fluoridation, 2005–15; Chm., All Parly Aviation Gp, 2009–15; Secretary: All Party Parly Gardening and Horticl Gp, 1994–2015; All Party Parly Scotch Whisky and Spirits Gp (formerly Scotch Whisky Gp), 1996–15; Jt Treas., 2002–09, Hon. Sec., 2009–15, British-American Parly Gp; Chm., PLP Transport Cttee, 2004–15. Chm., Parliamentary Contributory Pension Fund, 2011–15. Trustee, Thrive, 2003– (Chm., 2011–). *Recreations:* gardening, cycling, flying model helicopters.

DONOHOE, Peter Howard, CBE 2010; pianist; *b* 18 June 1953; *s* of Harold Donohoe and Marjorie Donohoe (*née* Travis); *m* 1980, Elaine Margaret Burns; one *d*. *Educ:* Chetham's School of Music, Manchester; Leeds Univ.; Royal Northern Coll. of Music; Paris Conservatoire. BMus; GRNCM, ARCM; Hon. FRNCM 1983. Professional solo pianist, 1974–; London début, 1978; concert tours in Europe, USA, Canada, Australia, Asia, USSR; regular appearances at Royal Festival Hall, Barbican Hall, Queen Elizabeth Hall, Henry Wood Promenade concerts, 1979–; numerous TV and radio broadcasts, UK and overseas; recordings include music by Rachmaninov, Stravinsky, Prokofiev, Britten, Messiaen, Muldowney, Tchaikovsky; British piano concertos. Competition finalist: British Liszt, London, 1976; Liszt-Bartok, Budapest, 1976; Leeds International Piano, 1981; winner, Internat. Tchaikovsky competition, Moscow, 1982. Concerto Recording Award, Gramophone, 1988; Grand Prix Internat. du Disque Liszt. *Recreations:* jazz, golf, helping young musicians, clock collecting. *Address:* c/o Ikon Arts Management, 114 Business Design Centre, 52 Upper Street, N1 0QH.

DONOHOE, Prof. Timothy James, DPhil; Professor of Chemistry, University of Oxford, since 2004; Fellow, Magdalen College, Oxford, since 2001; *b* Darwen, Lancs, 28 Jan. 1967; *s* of William Thomas and Christine Ruth Donohoe; *m* 1991, Ann Louise Budge; two *s*. *Educ:* Tarleton High Sch.; Hutton Grammar Sch.; Univ. of Bath (BSc Hons); Univ. of Oxford (DPhil 1992). Post-doctoral researcher, Univ. of Texas at Austin, 1993–94; Lectr in Chem., 1994–2000, Reader in Chem., 2000–01, Univ. of Manchester; University of Oxford: Lectr, 2001–04; Hd of Organic Chem., 2006–11. Established Career Fellow, EPSRC, 2014. Ed., Tetrahedron Letters, 2015. Corday Morgan Medal, RSC, 2006; Synthetic Organic Chemistry Award, RSC, 2011; UK Prize for Process Chemistry Res., SCI, 2012; Charles Rees Award, RSC, 2014. *Publications:* Oxidation and Reduction in Organic Synthesis, 2000; contrib. papers to learned jls. *Recreations:* squash, golf. *Address:* Chemistry Research Laboratory, Department of Chemistry, University of Oxford, Mansfield Road, Oxford OX1 3TA.

DONOUGHMORE, 8th Earl of, *cr* 1800; **Richard Michael John Hely-Hutchinson;** Baron Donoughmore, 1783; Viscount Hutchinson (UK), 1821; Chairman, Hodder Headline (formerly Headline Book Publishing) PLC, 1986–97; *b* 8 Aug. 1927; *er s* of 7th Earl of Donoughmore and Dorothy Jean (MBE 1947) (*d* 1995), *d* of late J. B. Hotham; *S* father, 1981; *m* 1st, 1951, Sheila (*d* 1999), *oc* of late Frank Frederick Parsons and Mrs Learmond Perkins; four *s*; 2nd, 2001, Margaret, *widow* of Comdr J. M. W. Morgan, RN and *d* of late E. C. Stonehouse. *Educ:* Winchester; Groton Sch., USA; New College, Oxford (MA; BM, BCh). *Heir:* *s* Viscount Suirdale, *qv*. *Address:* Frogwell, 14 Bushey Row, Bampton, Oxon OX18 2JU.

See also Hon. T. M. Hely Hutchinson.

DONOUGHUE, family name of **Baron Donoughue**.

DONOUGHUE, Baron *cr* 1985 (Life Peer), of Ashton in the County of Northamptonshire; **Bernard Donoughue;** *b* 8 Sept. 1934; *s* of late Thomas Joseph Donoughue and of Maud Violet Andrews; *m* 1st, 1959, Carol Ruth Goodman (marr. diss. 1989); two *s* two *d*; 2nd, 2009, Sarah Anne Berry, (Hon. Lady Berry). *Educ:* Secondary Modern Sch. and Grammar Sch., Northampton; Lincoln Coll. and Nuffield Coll., Oxford (BA (1st class hons), MA, DPhil). Henry Fellow, Harvard, USA. Mem., Editorial Staff: The Economist, Sunday Times, Sunday Telegraph. Sen. Res. Officer, PEP, 1960–63; Lectr, Sen. Lectr, Reader, LSE, 1963–74; Sen. Policy Advr to the Prime Minister, 1974–79; Development Dir, Economist Intelligence Unit, 1979–81; Asst Editor, The Times, 1981–82; Partner, 1983–86, Head of Res. and Investment Policy, 1984–86, Grieveson, Grant & Co.; Dir, 1986–88, Head of Res., 1986–87, of Internat. Res. and Investment Policy, 1987–88, Kleinwort Grieveson Securities; Exec. Vice-Chm., London and Bishopsgate Internat. Investment Holdings, 1988–91. Opposition spokesman on Treasury, 1991–92, on Energy, 1991–93, on Nat. Heritage, 1992–97; Parly Under-Sec. of State, MAFF, 1997–99; Mem., H of L Select Cttee on Stem Cell Res., 2001–02; Treas., All Party Parly Gp on Integrated Educn in NI; Sec., All Party Racing and Bloodstock Cttee, 2001–; Mem., All Party Jt Scrutiny Cttee on Gambling, 2003–04. Chairman: British Horseracing Bd Commn Inquiry into stable staff, 2003–04; Starting Price Regulatory Bd, 2003–; Future Funding of Racing Gp, 2005–06; Inquiry into Regulation of British Greyhound Industry, 2007–08. Dir, Towcester Racecourse Ltd, 1992–97. Vis. Prof., LSE, 2000–02. Member: Sports Council, 1965–71; Commn of Enquiry into Association Football, 1966–68; Ct of Governors, LSE, 1968–74, 1982–97; Civil Service Coll. Adv. Council, 1976–79; Adv. Bd, Wissenschaftzentrum, Berlin, 1978–91; Bd, Centre for European Policy Studies, Brussels, 1982–87; London Arts Bd, 1991–97. Trustee, Inst. for Policy Res., 1990–. Consultant, British Horse Industry Confedn, 1999–2005. Chm. Exec. Cttee, London Symphony Orch., 1978–93 (Patron, 1989–). Associate Mem., Nuffield Coll., Oxford, 1982–87; Mem., Sen. Common Room, Lincoln Coll., Oxford, 1985– (Hon. Fellow, 1986); Patron: Inst. of Contemporary British History, 1988–; Hansard Soc., 2001–; Vice Pres., Assoc. of Comprehensive Schs, 2000–08. Pres., Gambling Care, 1997; Trustee: Dorneywood Trust, 1997–; Internat. League for Protection of Horses, 2002–08; World Horse Welfare, 2008–10. Hon. Fellow: LSE, 1989; Northampton Univ., 2006. Hon. LLD Leicester, 1990. *Publications:* (ed jtly) Oxford Poetry, 1956; Wage Policies in the Public Sector, 1962; Trade Unions in a Changing Society, 1963; British Politics and the American Revolution, 1964; (with W. T. Rodgers) The People into Parliament, 1966; (with G. W. Jones) Herbert Morrison: portrait of a politician, 1973; Prime Minister, 1987; The Heat of the Kitchen (memoirs), 2003; Downing Street Diary: with Harold Wilson in Number 10, 2005; Downing Street Diary Volume Two: with James Callaghan in Number 10, 2008. *Recreations:* politics, sport, economics, music. *Address:* House of Lords, SW1A 0PW. *Club:* Pratt's.

DONOVAN, Prof. Desmond Thomas; Yates-Goldsmid Professor of Geology and Head of Department of Geology, University College, London, 1966–82; Hon. Curator, Wells Museum, Somerset, 1982–85; *b* 16 June 1921; *s* of T. B. Donovan and M. A. Donovan (*née* Benker); *m* 1959, Shirley Louise Saward (*d* 2007); two *s* one *d*. *Educ:* Epsom Coll.; University of Bristol (BSc 1942; PhD 1951; DSc 1960). FGS 1942, CGeol 1991; FLS 1960. Asst Lectr in Geology, University of Bristol, 1947–50; Lectr in Geology, Bristol, 1950–62; Prof. of Geology, University of Hull, 1962–66. Geologist on Lauge Koch's Danish expeditions to E Greenland, 1947–57. Pres., Palaeontographical Soc., 1979–84. *Publications:* Stratigraphy: An Introduction to Principles, 1966; (ed) Geology of Shelf Seas, 1968; Wells Cathedral: conservation of figure sculpture 1977–1986, 2011; papers on fossil cephalopods, Jurassic stratigraphy, Quaternary deposits, marine geology. *Recreations:* opera, geology. *Address:* 4 North Grove, Wells, Somerset BA5 2TD. *T:* (01749) 677981.

DONOVAN, Ian Edward, FRAeS; FCMA; Director, Aeronautical Trusts Ltd, 2002–10; Chairman of Trustees, Royal Aeronautical Society Pension and Assurance Scheme, 2007–10; *b* 2 March 1940; *s* of late John Walter Donovan and Ethel Molyneux; *m* 1969, Susan Betty Harris; two *s*. *Educ:* Leighton Park, Reading. FCMA 1985. Gen. Factory Manager, Lucas CAV, 1969–72; Finance Man., Lucas Girling, 1972–78; Finance Director: Lucas Girling, Koblenz, 1978–81; Lucas Electrical Ltd, 1982–84; Mem., 1985–88, Gp Dir, Finance and Central Services, 1986–88, CAA; Dir and Gp Controller, 1988–98, Gp Dir, Aerospace, 1998–2000, Smiths Industries Aerospace & Defence Ltd; Chm., Chart Co. Ltd, 1998–2000; Dir, Cranfield Aerospace Ltd, 2002–07; Pres., Lambda Advanced Analog Inc., 2000. Dir, English Symphony Orch., 2000–02. Mem. Council, SBAC, 1994–97; Hon. Treasurer: Air League, 1995–2000 and 2002–05; Homeless Network, 1999–2002; Trustee, Air League Educnl Trust, 1995–2000 and 2002–05. FRAeS 2001. *Recreations:* fly fishing, sailing, gardening, music, golf. *Address:* Lawn Farm, Church Lane, Tibberton, Droitwich, Worcs WR9 7NW. *Club:* Royal Air Force.

DONOVAN, Joël; QC 2011; *b* Paris, 20 Sept. 1963; *s* of John Donovan and Françoise Donovan; *m* 2002, Clare Gambling; one *d*. *Educ:* Diss High Sch.; Norwich City Coll.; Durham Univ. (BA Law 1986); Coll. of Law, Chester. Admitted Solicitor, 1989; called to the Bar, Lincoln's Inn, 1991; in practice as a barrister, specialising in complex clinical negligence and personal injury, New Court Chambers, 1992–2000, Cloisters, 2000–. *Recreations:* visual arts, tennis, family. *Address:* Cloisters, 1 Pump Court, Temple, EC4Y 7AA. *T:* (020) 7827 4080. *E:* jd@cloisters.com. *Club:* Hartswood Lawn Tennis.

DONOVAN, Judith, CBE 1997; Chairman, DIY Direct Marketing, since 2000; *b* 5 July 1951; *d* of late Ernest and Joyce Nicholson; *m* 1977, John Patrick Donovan. *Educ:* Univ. of Hull (BA Hons English 1973); DipCAM 1979. Mktg Asst, Ford Motor Co., 1973–75; Account Handler, J. Walter Thomson, 1975–77; Advertising Manager, Grattan, 1977–82; Chm., JDA, 1982–2000. Dir, British Direct Marketing Assoc., 1987–91; Chm., Direct Marketing Assoc., 1999–2001 (Dir, 1991–2001); Pres., Bradford Chamber of Commerce, 1999–2001 (Dir, 1988–2003); Director: Bradford City Challenge, 1988–89; Business Link West Yorks, 2001–03; Dep. Chm., Bradford Breakthrough, 1988–90; Chairman: Bradford & Dist TEC, 1989–98; Postwatch, N of England (formerly Northern Region), 2000–08 (Vice Chair, Postwatch Nat. Council, 2007–08); Chair, Keep Me Posted Campaign, 2012–. Member: Millennium Commn, 2000–06; Health and Safety Commn, 2000–10; UK Bd, Big Lottery Fund, 2007–11; British Wool Marketing Bd, 2009–; Lord Chancellor's Adv. Cttee, N Yorks, 2009–; DEFRA Task Force on Farming Regulation, 2009–10; Public Mem., Network Rail, 2012–. Diversity in Public Appts Ambassador, Cabinet Office, 2010–11. Chairman: Yorks Tourist Bd, 2005–08; Ripon City Partnership, 2009–13; Eden Project Ltd, 2013–Feb. 2016; Director: Yorks Dales Nat. Park Authy, 2012–March 2016; York Mailing Gp, 2013–. Mem. Adv. Bd, York Minster, 2008–09; Chm., Project Bd, York Minster Revealed, 2010–12. Dir, Northern Ballet Theatre, 1991–2008. Mem., Alumni Adv. Bd, 2011–, Trustee, Univ. Union, 2012–, Hull Univ. Freeman: City of London, 1999; Guild of Entrepreneurs, 2014– (Middle Warden); Liveryman: Co. of Woolmen, 2010; Co. of Marketors, 1999. Gov., Margaret McMillan Sch., 1985–87. Gov., Legacy Trust, 2007–13. FRSA 1996; FCAM 1996; FCIM 1998; FInstD 2000; CCMI (CIMgt 2000); FIDM 2001. Hon. Dr Leeds Metropolitan, 2003; Hon. DLitt Hull, 2009. *Recreations:* after dinner speaking, the Western Front, pets. *Address:* DIY Direct Marketing, Biggin Barns, Ringbeck, Kirkby Malzeard, Ripon, N Yorks HG4 3TT. *T:* (01765) 650000, *Fax:* (01765) 650153. *E:* judith@diydirectmarketing.co.uk. *Club:* Reform.

DONOVAN, Justin; Director of Education, Sport and Culture, States of Jersey, since 2014; *b* Cardiff, 1 June 1957; *s* of John and Frances Donovan; *m* 1981, Yvette Chandler; two *s* two *d*. *Educ:* Shoreditch Coll., Univ. of London (BEd; CertEd); Univ. of E London (MEd Policy Studies). Teacher, Angering Sch., Littlehampton, W Sussex, 1979–81; Hd of Dept, Brentside High Sch., Ealing, 1981–83; Hd of Faculty, Grey Court Sch., Richmond, 1983–86; Sen. Advr and Ofsted Inspector, Barking and Dagenham, 1986–2004; Dep. Dir, 2004–10, Dir of Educn, 2010–11, Dir of Educn and Early Intervention, 2011–14, Herts CC. *Recreation:* wreck diving (BSAC advanced diver). *Address:* Department of Education, Sport and Culture, PO Box 142, St Saviour, Jersey JE3 8QJ. *T:* (01534) 449437. *E:* j.donovan@gov.je.

DONOVAN, Dame Katharine Mary; *see* Barker, Dame K. M.

DONOVAN, Mgr Paul Anthony; Parish Priest, St Aidan's Church, Northampton, since 2012; *b* London, 13 Dec. 1956; *s* of James Donovan and Edith Donovan. *Educ:* Slough Grammar Sch.; Venerable English Coll., Rome; Pontifical Gregorian Univ. (Licence in Sacred Theology 1982); Open Univ. (MBA 2002). Ordained priest, 1981; Asst Priest, Kettering, 1982–85; Chaplain, RN, 1985–2007; Principal RC Chaplain (Naval) and Vicar Gen. to Bishop of the Forces, 2007–11. QHC 2007–11. *Recreation:* Italiana. *Address:* Manor House, 10 Manor Road, Northampton NN2 6QJ. *T:* (01604) 715661.

DONOVAN, Stephen Kenneth, PhD, DSc; Researcher (formerly Curator) of Palaeozoic and Mesozoic Macroinvertebrates, Naturalis Biodiversity Center (formerly Nationaal Natuurhistorisch Museum, then Nederlands Centrum voor Biodiversiteit - Naturalis), Netherlands, since 2001; *b* 3 June 1954; *s* of Alfred Haig Donovan and Beatrice Georgina Donovan (*née* Nichols); *m* 1st, 1997, Catriona Margaret Isobel MacGillivray, PhD (*d* 2003); one *s* one *d*; 2nd, 2005, Fiona Elizabeth Fearnhead (marr. diss. 2009). *Educ:* Univ. of Manchester (BSc 1980); Univ. of Liverpool (PhD 1983; DSc 1994). Royal Soc. Res. Fellow, TCD, 1983–84; Higher Scientific Officer, NERC, 1985–86; University of West Indies, Jamaica: Lectr, 1986–89; Sen. Lectr, 1989–92; Reader in Palaeozoology, 1992–96; Prof. of Palaeozoology, 1996–98; Keeper of Palaeontology, Natural Hist. Mus., 1998–2001. Sen. Res. Fellow, Nat. Mus. of Natural History, Smithsonian Instn, Washington, 1994–95; Visiting Professor: Univ. of Portsmouth, 1996–2004; UCL, 2000–01; Univ. of Liverpool, 2001–02; Adjunct Prof., Univ. of New Brunswick, 2000–. Sec., Palaeontographical Soc., 2011–. Ed., Scripta Geologica, 2002–; Book Rev. Ed., Geological Jl, 2009–; Exec. Ed., GeoResJ, 2013–. FLS 2004; Fellow, Geol Soc. of America, 2013. Linnean Medal for Zoology, 2008. *Publications:* (ed) Mass Extinctions: processes and evidence, 1989; (ed) The Processes of Fossilization, 1991; (ed) The Palaeobiology of Trace Fossils, 1994; (ed jtly) Caribbean Geology: an introduction, 1994; (ed jtly) The Adequacy of the Fossil Record, 1998; (ed) The Pliocene Bowden Shell Bed, Southeast Jamaica, 1998; (ed) The Mid-Cainozoic White Limestone Group of Jamaica, 2004; (ed) Palaeontological Papers in Honour of Chris Paul, 2005; (ed) Trace Fossils in the Museum, 2006; (ed) Crustal and Biotic Evolution of the Caribbean Plate, 2008; (jtly) British Silurian Crinoidea, 3 vols, 2009–12; (ed) Jamaican Rock Stars 1823–1971: the geologists who discovered Jamaica, 2010; (ed jtly) Early Palaeozoic Ecosystems, Environments and Evolution, 2011; How Not to Alienate your Editor: some everyday aspects of academic publishing, 2014; (jtly) British Devonian Crinoidea, Pt 1, 2014; numerous res. papers and reviews, particularly on palaeontology and Caribbean geology. *Recreations:* reading, writing, walking, cricket, tramway and railway history. *Address:* Naturalis Biodiversity Center, Postbus 9517, 2300 RA Leiden, Netherlands. *T:* (71) 5687642.

DOOCEY, family name of **Baroness Doocey**.

DOOCEY, Baroness *cr* 2010 (Life Peer), of Hampton in the London Borough of Richmond upon Thames; **Elizabeth, (Dee), Doocey,** OBE 1993; Member (Lib Dem), 2004–12, and Deputy Chairman, 2011–12, London Assembly, Greater London Authority (Chair, 2010–11); *m* James Doocey; one *s*. Finance Dir, Lib Dem Party; Financial Advr, Lib Dem Parly Party; Gp Man. Dir, internat. fashion co.; mgt consultant. Mem. (Lib Dem) Richmond-upon-Thames BC, 1986–94. Chm., Economy, Culture and Sport (formerly Econ. Devalt, Culture, Sport and Tourism) Cttee, GLA. Mem., Metropolitan Police Authy, 2006–12; Govt Rep., Criminal Justice Bd, 2010–. *Address:* House of Lords, SW1A 0PW.

DOOLEY, Michael Matthew Patrick, FRCOG; Consultant Gynaecologist, since 1992; Surgeon Gynaecologist to the Duchess of Cornwall, since 2007; *b* London, 30 March 1957; *s* of late Denis Dooley and of Eileen Dooley; *m* 1981, Barbara Thompson; two *s* one *d*. *Educ:* King's Coll. Sch., Wimbledon; Charing Cross Hosp., Univ. of London (MB BS 1980); Univ. of Galway (Master Med. Sci. 1985). FRCOG 1998. Res. Fellow, King's Coll. Hosp., 1988–89; Sen. Registrar, St Thomas' Hosp., 1989–91; Consultant Gynaecologist: Dorset Co. Hosp., 1992–; King Edward VII Hosp., London, 1998–; Lister Hosp., 2002–; Med. Dir, 1994–, Consultant Gynaecologist, 2004–, Poundbury Clinic. Dir, Sport Sci. and Medicine, BEF, 1995–2002; Sport Gynaecologist, Olympic Med. Inst., 1998–. Mem., Med. Soc. of London. *Publications:* (ed jtly) Understanding Common Disorders in Reproductive Endocrinology, 1994; (jtly) DRCOG Practice Exams, 2004; (jtly) Your Change Your Choice, 2006; Fit for Fertility, 2007. *Recreations:* walking, gardening, opera, ballet. *Address:* 132 Harley Street, W1G 7JX; Poundbury Clinic, Middlemarsh Street, Poundbury, Dorchester, Dorset DT1 3FD. *T:* (01305) 262626. *E:* mdooley@mdooley.co.uk. *Club:* Royal Society of Medicine.

DORAN, Frank; *b* 13 April 1949; *s* of Francis Anthony Doran and Betty Hedges or Doran; *m* 1st, 1967, Patricia Ann Govan or Doran (marr. diss.); two *s*; 2nd, 2010, Rt Hon. Joan Mary Ruddock (*see* Rt Hon. Dame J. M. Ruddock). *Educ:* Ainslie Park Secondary Sch.; Leith Acad.; Dundee Univ. (LLB Hons). Admitted Solicitor, 1977. Eur. Parly Cand. (Lab) NE Scotland, 1984. MP (Lab) Aberdeen S, 1987–92; contested (Lab) same seat, 1992; MP (Lab) Aberdeen Central, 1997–2005, Aberdeen N, 2005–15. Chm., Admin Select Cttee, H of C, 2005–10; Secretary: All Party Parly Fisheries Gp, 1997–2015; All Party Parly Dance Gp, 2007–15; Trade Union Gp of Lab. MPs, 2001–15; Chm., Speaker's Adv. Cttee on Works of Art, 2010–15; Mem., H of C Commn, 2010–15. Asst Editor, Scottish Legal Action Group Bulletin, 1975–78. *Recreations:* cinema, art, sports. *Club:* Aberdeen Trades Council.

DORAN, Gregory; Artistic Director, Royal Shakespeare Company, since 2012 (Associate Director, 1996–2005; Chief Associate Director, 2005–12); *b* 24 Nov. 1958; *s* of John Doran and Margaret Freeman; civil partnership 2005, Sir Antony Sher, *qv*. *Educ:* Bristol Univ. (BA Hons); Bristol Old Vic Theatre Sch. Joined RSC 1987; *RSC productions include:* The Odyssey, 1992; Henry VIII, 1996; Cyrano de Bergerac, 1997; The Merchant of Venice, The Winter's Tale, 1998; Oroonoko, Timon of Athens, Macbeth, 1999; As You Like It, 2000; King John, Jubilee, 2001; Much Ado About Nothing, The Island Princess, 2002; The Taming of the Shrew, The Tamer Tamed, All's Well That Ends Well, 2003; Othello, Venus and Adonis, 2004; A Midsummer Night's Dream, Sejanus, Canterbury Tales, 2005; Antony and Cleopatra, Merry Wives (musical), 2006; Coriolanus, 2007; Hamlet, Love's Labour's Lost, A Midsummer Night's Dream, 2008; Twelfth Night, 2009; Morte D'Arthur, 2010; Cardenio (Shakespeare's 'lost play' re-imagined), 2011; Written on the Heart, 2011; Julius Caesar, The Orphan of Zhao, 2012; Richard II, 2013; Henry IV Parts I & II, The Witch of Edmonton, 2014; Death of a Salesman, Henry V, 2015; *other productions include:* Long Day's Journey into Night, Waiting for Godot, Nottingham Playhouse, 1982–83; Titus Andronicus, Market Th., Johannesburg, and RNT, 1995 (TMA Award for Best Production); Black Comedy, and The Real Inspector Hound, Comedy Th., 1998; York Millennium Mystery Plays, York Minster, 2000; Mahler's Conversion, Aldwych, 2001; The Merchant of Venice, Japan, 2007; The Giant, Hampstead Th., 2007; Anjin: The English Samurai, Tokyo, 2009, Sadler's Wells, 2013; *films:* Macbeth, 1999; Hamlet, 2009; Julius Caesar, 2012; Richard II, 2013; Henry IV, Parts I and II, 2014. Humanitas Vis. Prof. in Drama, Oxford Univ., 2012–13. Hon. Fellow, Shakespeare Birthplace Trust, 2010; Hon. Sen. Res. Fellow, Shakespeare Inst., 2013. Hon. DLitt: Huddersfield, 2004; Bristol, 2011; Nottingham, 2011; Warwick, 2013. Olivier Award for Outstanding Achievement of the Year, 2003; Sam Wanamaker Award, Globe Th., 2012. *Publications:* (with Sir Antony Sher) Woza Shakespeare!, 1996; The Shakespeare Almanac, 2009; Shakespeare's Lost Play: in search of Cardenio, 2012. *Address:* c/o Royal Shakespeare Theatre, Stratford-upon-Avon, Warwicks CV37 6BB.

DORBER, Very Rev. Adrian John; Dean of Lichfield, since 2005; *b* 23 Sept. 1952; *s* of John and Thelma Dorber; *m* 1984, Caroline Perry; three *s* two *d*. *Educ:* St John's Coll., Durham (BA 1974); King's Coll. London (MTh 1991); Westcott House, Cambridge. Ordained deacon, 1979, priest, 1980; Curate, St Michael and St Mary Magdalene, Easthampstead, 1979–85; Priest-in-charge, St Barnabas, Emmer Green, 1985–88; Chaplain, Portsmouth Poly., 1988–92; Lectr, 1991–97, Sen. Chaplain and Public Orator, 1992–97, Portsmouth Univ.; Priest-in-charge, Brancepeth, 1997–2000; Dir, Ministries and Trng, Dio. Durham, 1997–2005. Hon. Chaplain, Portsmouth Cathedral, 1992–97; Hon. Canon, Durham Cathedral, 1997–2005. *Recreations:* gardening, modern fiction, cinema, good food. *Address:* The Deanery, 16 The Close, Lichfield, Staffs WS13 7LD. *T:* (01543) 306250. *E:* adrian.dorber@lichfield-cathedral.org.

DORCHESTER, Area Bishop of, since 2000; **Rt Rev. Colin William Fletcher,** OBE 2000; *b* 17 Nov. 1950; *s* of Alan Philip Fletcher, QC; *m* 1980, Sarah Elizabeth Webster; one *s* two *d*. *Educ:* Marlborough Coll.; Trinity Coll., Oxford (MA 1976). Ordained deacon, 1975, priest, 1976; Asst Curate, St Peter, Shipley, 1975–79; Tutor, Wycliffe Hall, Oxford and Asst Curate, St Andrew, N Oxford, 1979–84; Vicar, Holy Trinity, Margate, 1984–93; Rural Dean of Thanet, 1988–93; Chaplain to the Archbishop of Canterbury, 1993–2000. Cross of St Augustine, 2008. *Recreations:* ornithology, walking, sport. *Address:* Arran House, Sandy Lane, Yarnton, Oxford OX5 1PB. *T:* (01865) 208218.

See also P. J. Fletcher.

DORCHESTER, Archdeacon of; *see* French, Ven. J. K.

DORE, Prof. Ronald Philip, CBE 1989; FBA 1975; Senior Research Fellow, then Associate, Centre for Economic Performance, London School of Economics and Political Science, 1991–2000; *b* 1 Feb. 1925; *s* of Philip Brine Dore and Elsie Constance Dore; *m* 1957, Nancy Macdonald; one *s* one *d*; one *s* with Maria Paisley. *Educ:* Poole Grammar Sch.; SOAS, Univ. of London (BA). Lectr in Japanese Instns, SOAS, London, 1951; Prof. of Asian Studies, Univ. of BC, 1956; Reader, later Prof. of Sociol., LSE, 1961–69 (Hon. Fellow, 1980); Fellow, IDS, Univ. of Sussex, 1969–82; Asst Dir, Technical Change Centre, 1982–86; Dir, Japan-Europe Industry Res. Centre, ICSTM, 1986–91. Vis. Prof. of Sociol., Harvard Univ., 1986–89; Adjunct Prof., MIT, 1989–94. Mem., Academia Europaea, 1989. Hon. Foreign Mem., Amer. Acad. of Arts and Scis, 1978; Hon. Foreign Fellow, Japan Acad., 1986–. Order of the Rising Sun (Third Class), Japan, 1988. *Publications:* City Life in Japan, 1958, 2nd edn 1999; Land Reform in Japan, 1959, 2nd edn 1984; Education in Tokugawa Japan, 1963, 2nd edn 1983; (ed) Aspects of Social Change in Modern Japan, 1967; British Factory, Japanese Factory, 1973, 2nd edn 1990; The Diploma Disease, 1976, 2nd edn 1997; Shinohata: portrait of a Japanese village, 1978, 2nd edn 1992; (ed with Zoe Mars) Community Development, Comparative Case Studies in India, The Republic of Korea, Mexico and Tanzania, 1981; Energy Conservation in Japanese Industry, 1982; Flexible Rigidities: structural adjustment in Japan, 1986; Taking Japan Seriously: a Confucian perspective on leading economic issues, 1987; (ed jtly) Japan and World Depression, Then and Now: essays in memory of E. F. Penrose, 1987; (with Mari Sako) How the Japanese Learn to Work, 1988, rev. edn 1998; (ed jtly) Corporatism and Accountability: organized interests in British public life, 1990; Will the 21st Century be the Age of Individualism?, 1991; (ed with Masahiko Aoki) The Japanese Firm: the source of competitive strength, 1994; Japan, Internationalism and the UN, 1997; Stockmarket Capitalism, Welfare Capitalism: Japan and Germany *vs* the Anglo Saxons, 2000; Social Evolution, Economic Development and Culture, 2001; Collected writing of Ronald Dore, 2002; Whose interests should corporations be made to serve?, 2006; Finance takes all, 2009; The Finance Industry Hijacks the World Economy, 2011; Turning Point for Japan: how to survive between the two giants, US and China, 2012; Disillusion: the musings of a former Japanophile, 2014; Cantankerous Essays, 2015. *Address:* 157 Surrenden Road, Brighton, East Sussex BN1 6ZA. *T:* (01273) 501370.

DOREY, Gregory John, CVO 1997; HM Diplomatic Service; Ambassador to the Federal Democratic Republic of Ethiopia, Djibouti and the African Union, since 2011; *b* 1 May 1956; *s* of Michael John Dorey and Avril Dorey (*née* Gregory); *m* 1981, Alison Patricia Taylor; two *s* one *d*. *Educ:* Painswick Co. Primary Sch.; Rendcomb Coll., Cirencester; Exeter Coll., Oxford (MA Modern Hist.); Open Univ. (Post Grad. Cert. in Business Admin). Nat. Westminster Bank, 1973–74; Supply and Transport Service, RN, 1977–78; Army Dept, 1978–79, Defence Secretariat, 1979–81, MoD; UK Delegn to NATO, 1982–84; MoD PE, 1984–86; Soviet Dept, FCO, 1986; Asst Hd, CSCE Dept, FCO, 1986–89; First Sec., Budapest, 1989–92; Private Sec., Minister of State, FCO, 1992–94; Asst Hd, ME Dept, FCO, 1994–96; Counsellor, then Dep. Head of Mission, Islamabad, 1996–99; on secondment to HSBC plc, 2000; Dep. Hd of Mission, Hong Kong, 2000–04; Asst Dir (Ops), HR Directorate, FCO, 2005–07; Ambassador to Republic of Hungary, 2007–11. *Recreations:* literature, theatre, cinema, tennis, gardening, travel. *Address:* c/o Foreign and Commonwealth Office, King Charles Street, SW1A 2AH.

DORFMAN, Prof. Ariel; Walter Hines Page Professor of Literature and Latin American Studies, Duke University, since 1984; author, poet, playwright, journalist, academic and human rights activist; *b* Buenos Aires, 6 May 1942; *s* of Adolfo Dorfman and Fanny Zelicovich; naturalized Chilean citizen; *m* 1966, Angélica Malinarich; two *s*. *Educ:* Univ. of Chile. Univ. of Chile, Santiago, 1963–73; Univ. of Calif, Berkeley, 1968–69; Friedrich Ebert Stiftung Res. Fellow, Bonn, 1974–76; Sorbonne, Paris IV, 1975–76; Univ. of Amsterdam, 1976–80; Woodrow Wilson Internat. Centre for Scholars at the Smithsonian, Washington, DC, 1980–81; Inst. for Policy Studies, Washington, DC, 1981–84; Univ. of Maryland, Coll. Park, 1983. Member: Acad. Adv. Bd, NPR Contemp. Latino-American Novel Series, 1981–82; American Stories Project, Radio Smithsonian, 1982–83; Adv. Cttee, Nat. Public Radio Latin-America Writers and Their Times Project, Annenburg, 1985–87; Acad. Universelle des Cultures, Paris, 1993–; Amer. Acad. Arts and Scis, 2001–; Internat. PEN; Nat. Writers' Union; Drama Guild; Sociedad de Escritores Chilenos; Academic Freedom Cttee, America Watch; Member, Editorial Advisory Board: Readers Internat.; New Press, New York; Revista de Crítica Literaria Latinoamericana; Editl Advr, Internat. Encyclopedia of Communications. Hon. DHL: Illinois Wesleyan Univ., 1989; Bradford Coll., 1993; American Univ., 2001; Franklin and Marshall Coll., 2011; Hon. LitD Wooster Coll., 1991. *Publications: fiction:* Hard Rain, 1973, 1991; My House is on Fire, 1979, 2nd edn 1991; Widows, 1983, 4th edn 2002; The Last Song of Manuel Sendero, 1987; Mascara, 1988, 3rd edn 2004; Konfidenz, 1995, 3rd edn 2003; The Nanny and the Iceberg, 1999, 2nd edn 2003; Blake's Therapy, 2001; The Rabbit's Rebellion, 2001; (with J. Dorfman) The Burning City, 2003, 2nd edn 2005; *poetry:* Missing, 1982; Last Waltz in Santiago and Other Poems of Exile and Disappearance, 1988; In Case of Fire in a Foreign Land, 2002; *plays:* (adaptation, with Tony Kushner) Widows, 1988, 2008; Death and the Maiden, 1991, 2nd edn 1992; Reader, 1995, 2008; (with R. Dorfman) Who's Who, 1997; (adaptation, with R. Dorfman) Mascara, 1998; The Resistance Trilogy, 1998; Purgatorio, 1999, 3rd edn 2006; Speak Truth to Power: voices from beyond the dark, 2000; Manifesto for Another World: voices from beyond the dark, 2004; The Other Side, 2004, 2008; Picasso's Closet, 2006; Dancing Shadows, 2007; *non-fiction:* (with A. Mattelart) How to Read Donald Duck, 1971, 2nd edn 1975; The Empire's Old Clothes, 1983, 3rd edn 1996; Some Write to the Future, 1991, 2nd edn 1992; Heading South, Looking North: a bilingual journey (memoir, vol. 1), 1998, 3rd edn 2011; Exorcising Terror: the incredible unending trial of Gen. Augusto Pinochet, 2002; Desert Memories: journeys through the Chilean North, 2004; Other Septembers, Many Americas: selected provocations 1980–2004, 2004; Writing the Deep South: the Mandela lecture and other mirrors for South Africa, 2011; Feeding on Dreams: confessions of an unrepentant exile (memoir, vol. 2), 2011. *Address:* 101 Friedl Building, PO Box 90670, 1316 Campus Drive, Duke University, Durham, NC 27708, USA.

DORFMAN, Lloyd Marshall, CBE 2008; Founder and President, Travelex Group (Chairman and Chief Executive, 1977–2005; Chairman, 2005–15); Chairman: Office Group, since 2010; Doddle, since 2014; Esselco, since 2007; *b* 25 Aug. 1952; *s* of Harold and Anita Dorfman; *m* 1974, Sarah (*née* Matthews); one *s* two *d*. *Educ:* St Paul's Sch. Non-exec. Dir, M & C Saatchi plc, 2004–; Dep. Chm., QTec (formerly Quest Ltd, subseq. Monitor Quest Ltd, then Quest Global Hldgs Ltd), 2007–14. Chm., Roundhouse, 2007–10. Chm., Prince's Trust, 2015– (Trustee, 2007–; Chm., Develt Cttee, 2007–); Trustee: Community Security Trust, 1997– (Dep. Chm., 2005–); Royal Nat. Theatre, 2007–15; Royal Opera House, 2015– (Mem. Hon. Bd, 2012–); Royal Acad. Trust, 2014–; JW3. Gov., St Paul's Sch., London, 2005–. Hon. Fellow, St Peter's Coll., Oxford, 2003. Hon. Bencher, Lincoln's Inn, 2013. FRSA 2006. *Recreations:* travel, theatre, sailing. *Address:* 22 Manchester Square, W1U 3PT. *T:* (020) 7725 1234. *E:* chairman@esselco.org. *Clubs:* Garrick; Royal Southern Yacht.

DORGAN, John Christopher, FRCS; Consultant Orthopaedic and Spinal Surgeon, Royal Liverpool Children's Hospital Alder Hey, 1984–2009; *b* 26 Nov. 1948; *s* of William Leonard Dorgan and Mary Ellen Dorgan (*née* Gorringe); *m* 1978, Ann Mary Gargan (*d* 2003); three *d*. *Educ:* Thornleigh Salesian Coll., Bolton; Liverpool Univ. (MB ChB 1973; MChOrth 1979). FRCS 1977. House Officer, Walton Hosp., Liverpool, 1973–74; Sen. House Officer, Royal Southern Hosp., Liverpool, 1974–75; Registrar, Whiston and St Helens Hosps, 1975–77; Research Fellow, Univ. of Liverpool, 1977–78; Registrar, Broadgreen Hosp. and Royal Liverpool Children's Hosp., 1978–80; Lectr, Dept of Orthopaedic Surgery, Univ. of Liverpool, 1981–84; Consultant Orthopaedic Surgeon, Royal Liverpool Univ. Hosp., 1984–96. Ext. Examr, MChOrth course, Univ. of Dundee, 2010–13. Pres., British Scoliosis Soc., 2005–06 (Hon. Sec. and Treas., 1999–2002; Mem., Exec. Cttee, 2002–03). *Publications:* articles on orthopaedic and spinal surgery in med. jls. *Recreations:* member of two trad jazz bands, watching Bolton Wanderers FC and Waterloo RUFC. *Address:* 23 Elton Avenue, Blundellsands, Liverpool L23 8UW. *T:* (0151) 924 1818. *Club:* Stamps (Crosby).

DORIN, Bernard Jean Robert, Hon. GCVO; Commandeur de la Légion d'Honneur; Officier de l'Ordre National du Mérite; Ambassadeur de France; Conseiller d'Etat, 1993–97, now honorary; *b* 25 Aug. 1929; *s* of Robert Dorin and Jacqueline Dorin (*née* Goumard); *m* 1971, Christine du Bois de Meyrignac; two *s* two *d*. *Educ:* Inst. d'Etudes Politiques, Paris; Ecole Nat. d'Administration. Attaché, French Embassy, Ottawa, 1957–59; Min. of Foreign Affairs, 1959–64; technical adviser: for sci. research, nuclear and space, 1966–67; to Minister of Nat. Educn, 1967–68; to Minister for sci. research, 1968–69; Harvard Univ., 1969–70; Min. of Foreign Affairs, 1970–71; Ambassador in Port-au-Prince, 1972–75; Head of Francophone Affairs Dept, 1975–78; Ambassador in Pretoria, 1978–81; Dir for America, Min. of Foreign Affairs, 1981–84; Ambassador, Brazil, 1984–87, Japan, 1987–90, UK, 1990–93. Hon. Pres., Avenir de la langue française (Pres., 1998); President: Les Amitiés francophones, 1998–; Les Amitiés Acadiennes, 1998–. Mem., Acad. des scis d'outre mer. *Recreation:* collections of naïve paintings. *Address:* 59 rue Michel Ange, 75016 Paris, France.

DORIS, Robert Joseph; Member (SNP) Glasgow, Scottish Parliament, since 2007; *b* 11 May 1973; *s* of Robert Doris and Mary Drummond Doris; *m* 2011, Janet Tyson. *Educ:* Univ. of Glasgow (MA Soc. Sci. with Distn 1994); St Andrew's Coll. (PGCE (secondary) Hist. and Mod. Studies 1995). Teacher, Hist. and Mod. Studies, 1995–2007. Mem., Local Govt and Communities Cttee, 2007–11, Dep. Convener, Health and Sport Cttee, Scottish Parlt. *Address:* Parliamentary Constituency Office, Empire House, 131 West Nile Street, Glasgow G1 2RX; Scottish Parliament, Edinburgh EH99 1SP. *E:* bob.doris.msp@scottish.parliament.uk.

DORKEN, (Anthony) John; Chief Executive, British Tyre Manufacturers' Association, 2006–09; Secretary, Tyre Industry Federation, 2005–09; *b* 24 April 1944; *s* of late Oscar Roy Dorken, OBE and Margaret Dorken; *m* 1972, Satanay Mufti; one *s* one *d*. *Educ:* Mill Hill Sch.; King's Coll., Cambridge (BA Classics 1965; MA 1969). VSO, Libya, 1965–66; Asst Principal, BoT, 1967–71; Private Sec. to Parly Under Sec. of State for Industry, 1971–72; Principal, DTI, later Dept of Energy, 1972–77; seconded to Cabinet Office, 1977–79; Asst Sec., Dept of Energy, 1980–86; seconded to Shell UK Exploration and Prodn, 1986–89; Dir of Resource Management, Dept of Energy, 1989–92; Dep. Dir Gen., Office of Gas Supply, 1992–93; Head of Consumer Affairs Div., DTI, 1993–96; Dep. Dir, 1996–97, Dir, 1997–2005, British Rubber Manufacturers' Assoc. Sec., British Rubber and Polyurethane Products Assoc., 2006–. Sec. and Treas., Medical Aid and Relief for Children of Chechnya, 2001–. *Publications:* articles on gas regulation and tyre issues in specialist jls. *Recreations:* reading, walking, music, squash. *Address:* 10 Connaught Gardens, N10 3LB. *T:* (020) 8372 6213.

DORKING, Bishop Suffragan of; *no new appointment at time of going to press.*

DORKING, Archdeacon of; *see* Bryer, Ven. P. D.

DORLING, Prof. Danny, PhD; Halford Mackinder Professor of Geography, University of Oxford, since 2013; Fellow, St Peter's College, Oxford, since 2013; *b* Oxford, 16 Jan. 1968; *s* of David and Bronwen Dorling; *m* 1999, Alison Briggs; two *s* one *d*. *Educ:* Cheney Comprehensive Secondary Sch.; Univ. of Newcastle upon Tyne (BSc 1st Cl. Jt Hons Geog., Maths and Stats 1989; PhD Visualization of Social Spatial Structure 1991). Teacher and pt-time researcher, 1987–91; University of Newcastle upon Tyne: Joseph Rowntree Foundn Fellow, 1991–93; British Acad. Res. Fellow, 1993–96; Lectr in Geographical Scis, 1996–99, Reader in Geog., 1999–2000, Univ. of Bristol; Professor: of Quantitative Human Geog., Univ. of Leeds, 2000–03; of Human Geog., 2003–12, for Public Understanding of Social Sci., 2013, Univ. of Sheffield. Visiting Professor: Dept of Social Medicine, Univ. of Bristol, 2002–; Dept of Sociol., Goldsmiths, Univ. of London, 2013–Sept. 2016; Adjunct Prof., Dept of Geog., Univ. of Canterbury, NZ, 2007–; Vis. Fellow, IPPR, 2012–. Advr, UN World Econ. and Social Survey, 2014. Comr, London Fairness Commn, 2015–. Mem., Editl Adv. Bd, 2002–, Graphics Ed., 2009–, Envmt and Planning A; Member, Editorial Board: Local Economy, 2008–; Jl Social and Cultural Geog., 2010–15. Hon. Pres., Soc. of Cartographers, 2008–. Patron, RoadPeace, 2011–. FAcSS (AcSS 2003). FRSA 2010. Hon. FFPH 2014. Award for Excellence in Leading Geography, Geographical Assoc., 2007, 2013; Back Award (1882), RGS, 2009; Political Studies Communicator Award for Explaining Complexity, Political Studies Assoc., 2013. *Publications:* A New Social Atlas of Britain, 1995; (jtly) The Population of Britain in the 1990s: a social and economic atlas, 1996; (with D. Fairbairn) Mapping Ways of Representing the World, 1997; (jtly) The Widening Gap: health inequalities and policy in Britain, 1999; (ed with S. Simpson) Statistics in Society: the arithmetic of politics, 1999 (trans. Japanese, 2003); (ed jtly) Inequalities in Health: the evidence, 1999; (jtly) Inequalities in Life and Death: what if Britain were more equal?, 2000; (ed jtly) Poverty, Inequality and Health: 1800–2000: a reader, 2001; (jtly) Health, Place and Society, 2002; (with B. Thomas) People and Places: a census atlas of the UK, 2004; (jtly) Geography Matters: simulating the local impacts of national social policies, 2004; Human Geography of the UK, 2005; (jtly) Life in Britain: using Millennial Census data to understand poverty, 2005; (jtly) The Great Divide: an analysis of housing inequality, 2005; (jtly) Poverty, Wealth and Place in Britain, 1968 to 2005, 2007; (with B. Thomas) Identity in Britain: a cradle-to-grave atlas, 2007; (jtly) The Real World Atlas, 2008, 2nd edn 2010 (Gold Prize, Geographical Assoc., 2009) (trans. German, Dutch, French, Italian, Japanese, Korean, 2010); (jtly) The Grim Reaper's Road Map: an atlas of mortality in Britain, 2008; (jtly) Criminal Obsessions: why harm matters more than crime, 2008; Injustice: why social inequality persists, 2010 (trans. Korean 2012); So You Think You Know About Britain?, 2011; (with B. Thomas) Bankrupt Britain: an atlas of social change, 2011; (jtly) Introduction to Maps and Cartographic Methods, 2011; The No-nonsense Guide to Equality, 2012; The Visualization of Social Spatial Structure, 2012; The Population of the UK, 2012; Fair Play: a reader on social justice, 2012; Unequal Health: the scandal of our times, 2013; The 32 Stops: lives on London's Central Line, 2013; Population 10 Billion: the coming demographic crisis and how to survive it, 2013; All That Is Solid: the great housing disaster, 2014; (jtly) The Social Atlas of Europe, 2014; Inequality and the 1%, 2014. *Recreations:* sandcastles and hydrological sand sculpture (dams) on beaches, preferably somewhere warm. *Address:* School of Geography and the Environment, University of Oxford, South Parks Road, Oxford OX1 3QY. *T:* (01865) 275986. *E:* danny.dorling@ouce.ox.ac.uk.

DORMAN, Sir Philip (Henry Keppel), 4th Bt *cr* 1923, of Nunthorpe, co. York; tax accountant; *b* 19 May 1954; *s* of Richard Dorman (*d* 1976) and of Diana Keppel (*née* Barrett); *S* cousin, 1996; *m* 1982 (marr. diss. 1992); one *d*; *m* 1996 (marr. diss. 2004); *m* 2011, Sally Crawford. *Educ:* Marlborough; Univ. of St Andrews. Life Protector, Dorman Mus., Middlesbrough, 1996–. *Recreation:* golf. *E:* pd@philipdorman.co.uk. *Clubs:* MCC; Lewes Golf.

DORMAN, Richard Bostock, CBE 1984; HM Diplomatic Service, retired; High Commissioner to Vanuatu, 1982–85; Chairman, British Friends of Vanuatu, 1990–99 (Co-ordinator, 1986–90); *b* 8 Aug. 1925; *s* of late John Ehrenfried and Madeleine Louise Dorman; *m* 1950, Anna Illingworth; one *s* two *d*. *Educ:* Sedbergh Sch.; St John's Coll., Cambridge. Army Service (Lieut, S Staffs Regt), 1944–48; Asst Principal, War Office, 1951; Principal, 1955; transferred to Commonwealth Relations Office, 1958; First Sec., British High Commission, Nicosia, 1960–64; Dep. High Commissioner, Freetown, 1964–66; SE Asia Dept, FO, 1967–69; Counsellor, Addis Ababa, 1969–73; Commercial Counsellor, Bucharest, 1974–77; Counsellor, Pretoria, 1977–82. Order of Merit (Vanuatu), 1999. *Address:* 67 Beresford Road, Cheam, Surrey SM2 6ER. *T:* (020) 8642 9627.

DORMANN, Jürgen; Chairman, V-Zug AG, since 2007; *b* Heidelberg, 12 Jan. 1940. *Educ:* Univ. of Heidelberg (MEc). Joined Hoechst AG as mgt trainee, 1963; Fiber Sales Dept, 1965–72; Corporate Staff Dept, 1973–84 (Head of Dept, 1980–84); Dep. Mem., Bd of Mgt, 1984–87; Chief Financial Officer, 1987–94; Chm., 1994–99; Hoechst merged with Rhône-Poulenc to form Aventis, 1999; Chm., Bd of Mgt, 1999–2002, Chm., Supervisory Bd, 2002–04, Aventis; Dir, 1998–2007, Chm., 2001–07, CEO, 2002–04, ABB; Vice-Chm., Sanofi-aventis, 2004–07; Dir, 2004–08, Chm., 2007–08, Adecco; Chairman: Sulzer AG, 2009–13; Metall Zug AG, 2008–13. Non-executive Director: IBM, 1999; Allianz AG, 1999; BG Gp, 2005–10. Sen. Advr, Internat. Adv. Bd, Blackstone Gp. *Address:* V-Zug AG, Industriestrasse 66, 6300 Zug, Switzerland.

DORMENT, Richard, CBE 2014; FSA; PhD; Art Critic, Daily Telegraph, 1986–2015; *b* 15 Nov. 1946; *s* of James Dorment and Marguerite Dorment (*née* O'Callaghan); *m* 1st, 1970, Kate S. Ganz (marr. diss. 1981); one *s* one *d*; 2nd, 1985, Harriet Mary Waugh. *Educ:* Georgetown Prep. Sch.; Princeton Univ. (BA 1968); Columbia Univ. (MA 1969, MPhil, PhD 1975). Faculty Fellow, Columbia Univ., 1968–72; Asst Curator, European Painting, Philadelphia Mus. of Art, 1973–76; Curator, Alfred Gilbert: Sculptor and Goldsmith, RA, 1985–86; Art Critic, Country Life, 1986; Co-curator, James McNeill Whistler, Tate Gall., 1994–95. Member: Judging Panel, Turner Prize, 1989; Adv. Cttee, Govt Art Collection, 1996–2005; Reviewing Cttee on the Export of Works of Art, 1996–2002; British Council Visual Arts Adv. Cttee, 1997–2006. Trustee: Watts Gallery, 1996–2014 (Chm., Collections Cttee, 2006–14); Wallace Collection, 2003–13 (Chm., Internat. Council, 2008–13); Wallace Collection Foundn, 2014–. Hawthornden Prize for art criticism in Britain, 1992; Critic of the Year, British Press Awards, 2000. FSA 2014. *Publications:* Alfred Gilbert, 1985; British Painting 1750–1900: A Catalogue of the British Paintings in the Philadelphia Museum of Art, 1986; Alfred Gilbert Sculptor and Goldsmith, 1986; (with Margaret McDonald) James McNeill Whistler, 1994; Oscar Wilde in Context, 2013; contributor to exhibition catalogues: Victorian High Renaissance, 1978; Pre-Raphaelite and Other Masters: the Andrew Lloyd Webber Collection, 2003; Manet and the Sea, 2003; reviews for NY Rev. of Books; contrib. to Burlington Magazine, TLS, Literary Rev. *Address:* Flat 1, 63 Montagu Square, W1H 2LU. *Club:* Brooks's.

DORMER, family name of **Baron Dormer**.

DORMER, 17th Baron *cr* 1615, of Wenge, co. Buckingham; **Geoffrey Henry Dormer;** Bt 1615; *b* 13 May 1920; *s* of Captain Edward Henry Dormer (*d* 1943) and Hon. Vanessa Margaret Dormer (*d* 1962), *d* of 1st Baron Borwick; *S* cousin, 1995, but does not use the title; *m* 1st, 1947, Janet Readman (marr. diss. 1957); two *d*; 2nd, 1958, Pamela Simpson; two *s*. *Educ:* Eton; Trinity Coll., Cambridge. RNVR Officer, 1939–46; RNR Officer, 1960–70 (Lt-Comdr 1968); RNVR Officer, 1970–81. Farmer until 1958; small-holder; gardener. *Recreations:* sailing, gardening. *Heir:* *s* Hon. William Robert Dormer [*b* 8 Nov. 1960; *m* 1st, 1985, Paula (marr. diss. 2011), *d* of Peter Robinson; one *s* one *d*; 2nd, 2013, Susan Viney (*née* Rivière)]. *Address:* Dittisham, Devon.

DORMER, Ian Gareth; Managing Director, Rosh Engineering Ltd, since 1989; *b* Loughborough, 30 March 1964; *s* of Roy Leonard and Sheila Ann Dormer; *m* 1996, Prof. Julia Lindsey Newton; one *s* one *d*. *Educ:* Essex Univ. (BA Hons Govt 1986); Georgetown Univ., Washington. Reporter, Flight Internat., 1986–89. Dir, ING Ltd, 2008–11. Chairman: Business Link Tyne & Wear, 2002–04; Enterprise Develt NE Ltd, 2008–11; Mem. Bd, One North East, 2007–12. Dir, NE Says No, 2004. Dir, 1999–2010, Chm., 2012–15, Inst. of Dirs; CDir 2013. *Recreations:* ski-ing, family, travel. *Address:* Rosh Engineering Ltd, Durham Road, Birtley, Co. Durham DH3 2QW. *T:* (0191) 410 6300. *E:* ian@rosh.co.uk.

DORMER, Robin James; Parliamentary Counsel, 2005–11; on secondment to Law Commission, 2006–11; *b* 30 May 1951; *s* of late Dudley James Dormer and Jean Mary (*née* Brimacombe). *Educ:* Internat. Sch. of Geneva, Switzerland; University Coll. of Wales, Aberystwyth (LLB). Admitted solicitor, 1980; articled clerk and asst solicitor, Messrs Coward Chance, 1976–80; Mem. Staff, Law Commn, 1980–87; Asst Parly Counsel, Office of Parly Counsel, 1987–90; Solicitor's Office, DoH, 1990–99, Grade 5 (Sen. CS), 1992–99; Office of the Parliamentary Counsel, 1999–2011: Prin. Asst Parly Counsel, 1999–2000; Dep. Parly Counsel, 2000–05. Mem., Legal Services Gp, Terrence Higgins Trust, 1987–99 (Gp Leader, 1992–95). Co. Sec., Food Chain, 2003–06.

DORNAN, Prof. James Connor, MD; FRCOG, FRCPI; Consultant, Royal Maternity Hospital, Belfast, 1986–2013; Senior Vice President, Royal College of Obstetricians and Gynaecologists, 2004–07; *b* 5 Feb. 1948; *s* of James Dornan and Clare Elizabeth Dornan (*née* Dunn); *m* 1st, 1970, Lorna Jordan (*d* 1998); one *s* two *d*; 2nd, 2002, Samina Mahsud. *Educ:* Bangor Grammar Sch.; Queen's Univ. of Belfast (MB BCh, BAO; MD 1981). MRCOG 1978, FRCOG 1991; FRCPI 2003. Queen's University of Belfast: Sen. Lectr and Consultant, Sch. of Clinical Medicine, 1986–92; Hon. Clinical Lectr, 1993–98; Hon. Sen. Clinical Lectr, 1998–2002; Hon. Reader, 2002–06; Hon. Prof. of Fetal Medicine, 2006–. Hon. Prof. of Health and Life Scis, Univ. of Ulster, 2003–. Mem. Council, RCOG, 1999–2004 and 2008–14. Pres., Tinylife (formerly NI Mother and Baby Action), 2006– (Chm., 1996–2006). *Publications:* contrib. chapters to med. textbooks; contrib. numerous papers to learned jls on biophysical assessment of fetal well-being and fetal behaviour; many contribs to med. jls. *Recreations:* tennis, golf, good conversation. *Address:* Shigar, Ballymullan Road,

Crawfordsburn, Co. Down BT19 1JG. *T:* (028) 9185 3375. *E:* JimDornan@me.com. *Clubs:* Royal Society of Medicine; Gynaecological Travellers; Royal Belfast Golf; Royal Northern Ireland Yacht.

DORNAN, Prof. Peter John, DSc; FRS 2003; FInstP; Professor of Physics, Imperial College London, 1991–2012, now Emeritus (Head, High Energy Physics Group, 1991–2007); *b* 5 Sept. 1939; *s* of Philip James and Edith Mary Dornan; *m* 1963, Mary Gwendoline Clarke; one *s* one *d. Educ:* Lancaster Royal Grammar Sch.; Emmanuel Coll., Cambridge (BA 1961; PhD 1965). FInstP 1992. Res. Associate, Brookhaven Nat. Lab., NY, 1965–68; Lectr, ICSTM, 1968–91. Scientific Associate, CERN, Geneva, 1989–91 and 1997–2000 (Spokesman, Aleph Experiment, 1997–2000). Hon. DSc Lancaster, 2000. *Publications:* contribs to Physics Letters, Physical Rev. Letters, Physics Reports, Jl European Physics, Nuclear Instruments and Methods. *Recreations:* travel, photography, walking, food, wine. *Address:* Blackett Laboratory, Imperial College London, SW7 2BW. *T:* (020) 7594 7822, *Fax:* (020) 7823 8830. *E:* p.dornan@imperial.ac.uk.

DORRANCE, Dr Richard Christopher; Company Secretary, Brilliant Publications Ltd, since 2000 (Partner, 1996–2013); *b* 25 Feb. 1948; *s* of Eric and Joan Dorrance; *m* 1996, Priscilla Hannaford; one *s* one *d. Educ:* Wolverhampton GS; Aylesbury GS; Univ. of East Anglia (BSc Chem. 1969; PhD 1973); London Univ. (PGCE 1974 ext.). FRSC. Res. into properties of detergents, Unilever and UEA, 1969–72; taught chemistry and geology, Royal GS, High Wycombe (and i/c stage lighting), 1972–80; Head of Science, Monks Walk Sch., Welwyn Garden City, 1980–83; Gen. Advr, Berks CC, 1983–88; Asst Chief Exec., Nat. Curriculum Council, 1989–91; Dep. Chief Exec., Sch. Exams and Assessment Council, 1991–93 (acting Chief Exec., 1991–92); Chief Exec., Early Years NTO, 1998–2005. Chief Exec., Council for Awards in Care, Health and Educn (formerly Children's Care and Educn), 1994–2013. Mem. UK Cttee, Organisation Mondiale pour l'Education Préscolaire, 1996–99 (Treas., 1998–99). Member, Board: Fedn of Awarding Bodies, 2010–; Open Schs Trust, 2013–; Training Qualifications UK, 2014–; Mem., Adv. Bd, Gordon Associates, 2013–. Gov., West Herts Coll., 1997–2001. Advr, Nursery World magazine, 1997–2007. Trustee, Northall Village Hall Mgt Cttee, 2007–. *Publications:* Eye (computer prog.), 1983; GAS 81, 1982; papers in professional jls. *Recreations:* walking, foreign travel, natural history, bowling, gardening, model making, photography. *Address:* The Old School Yard, Leighton Road, Northall, Dunstable, Beds LU6 2HA. *T:* (01525) 221273.

DORRELL, Rt Hon. Stephen (James); PC 1994; *b* 25 March 1952; *s* of Philip Dorrell; *m* 1980, Penelope Anne Wears, *y d* of Mr and Mrs James Taylor, Windsor; three *s* one *d. Educ:* Uppingham; Brasenose Coll., Oxford (BA 1973). Personal asst to Rt Hon. Peter Walker, MBE, MP, Feb. 1974; contested (C) Kingston-upon-Hull East, Oct. 1974. MP (C) Loughborough, 1979–97, Charnwood, 1997–2015. PPS to the Secretary of State for Energy, 1983–87; Asst Govt Whip, 1987–88; a Lord Comr of HM Treasury (Govt Whip), 1988–90; Parly Under-Sec. of State, DoH, 1990–92; Financial Sec. to HM Treasury, 1992–94; Secretary of State: for Nat. Heritage, 1994–95; for Health, 1995–97; Shadow Sec. of State for Educn, 1997–98. Chm., Health Select Cttee, H of C, 2010–14. *Recreations:* walking, reading.

DORRIAN, Rt Hon. Lady; Leeona June Dorrian; PC 2013; a Senator of the College of Justice in Scotland, since 2005; *b* 16 June 1957; *d* of Thomas and June Dorrian. *Educ:* Cranley Sch.; Univ. of Aberdeen (LLB 1977). Admitted to Faculty of Advocates, 1981; QC (Scot.) 1994; Standing Jun. Counsel, Health and Safety Exec. and Commn, 1987–94; Advocate Depute, 1988–91; Standing Jun. Counsel, Dept of Energy, 1991–94; a Temp. Judge, Court of Session, 2002–05. Mem., English Bar, Inner Temple, 1991–. Mem., CICB, 1998–2002. Pres., Franco-British Lawyers Soc., 2008–11. Hon. LLD Aberdeen, 2012. *Address:* Court of Session, Parliament House, Parliament Square, Edinburgh EH1 1RF. *Clubs:* Royal Automobile; Scottish Arts (Edinburgh); Royal Forth Yacht, Royal Highland Yacht.

DORRIES, Nadine; MP (C) Mid Bedfordshire, since 2005; *b* 21 May 1957; *d* of George and Sylvia Bargery; *m* 1984, Paul Dorries (marr. diss.); three *d. Educ:* Halewood Grange Comprehensive Sch., Liverpool; Warrington Dist Sch. of Nursing. Former nurse and businesswoman. Dir, BUPA. Advr to Oliver Letwin, MP. Contested (C) Hazel Grove, 2001. *Publications:* The Four Streets, 2014 (novel). *Address:* House of Commons, SW1A 0AA. *E:* dorriesn@parliament.uk. *Club:* Carlton.

DORSET, Archdeacon of; *see* MacRow-Wood, Ven. A. C.

DORWARD, David Keay; Chief Executive, Dundee City Council, 2009–14 (Director of Finance, 1995–2009); *b* 24 May 1954; *s* of David Dorward and Christina Dorward (*née* Keay); *m* 1977, Gail Elizabeth Bruce; three *d. Educ:* Kinross High Sch.; Perth High Sch.; Glasgow Coll. of Technology. CPFA 1982. Trainee Accountant, Perth and Kinross Jt CC, 1971–75; Tayside Regional Council: Trainee Accountant, 1975–82; Sen. Accountant, 1982–83; Principal Accountant, 1983–84; Financial Planning Officer, 1984–86; Chief Financial Planning Officer, 1986–93; Depute Dir of Finance, 1993–95. *Recreations:* golf, supporting Dundee United, bowls, going to the theatre. *Address:* 4 Norrie Street, Broughty Ferry, Dundee DD5 2SD. *T:* (01382) 739006. *Clubs:* Dundee United Businessmen's (Dundee); Broughty Bowling; Abertay Golf.

DOSANJH, Hon. Ujjal; PC (Can.) 2004; QC (BC) 1995; *b* India, 9 Sept. 1947; *s* of Giani Pritam Singh Dosanjh and Surjit Kaur Dosanjh; *m* Raminder; three *s. Educ:* Simon Fraser Univ. (BA); Univ. of BC (LLB). Called to Canadian Bar, 1977; opened law practice, Dosanjh & Pirani, 1979, subseq. Dosanjh Woolley, now Vertlieb Dosanjh. MLA (NDP) Vancouver-Kensington, 1991–2001; Attorney Gen., BC, 1995–2000; Premier, BC, 2000–01. Leader, NDP, 2000–01. MP (L) Vancouver S, 2004–11; contested (L) same seat, 2011. Minister of Health, Canada, 2004–06; Official Opposition Critic: for Nat. Defence, 2006–07, 2008–09; for Foreign Affairs, 2007; for Public Safety, 2007–08. Hon. LLD Guru Nanak Dev Univ., Amritsar, 2001. *Recreations:* jogging, reading. *Address:* 2520 SW Marine Drive, Vancouver, BC V6P 6C2, Canada.

DOSS, Alan Claude, CMG 2011; Executive Director, Kofi Annan Foundation, Geneva, since 2014 (Senior Political Adviser, 2011–14); *b* 7 Jan. 1945; *m* Soheir; three *d. Educ:* London Sch. of Econs and Pol Sci. UN Resident Coordinator and UNDP Resident Rep., Benin, Zaire and Vietnam, 1977–79; Dep. Resident Rep., UNDP, China, 1979; Resident Coordinator and UNDP Regl Rep., Bangkok and Dir, UN Border Relief Gp, Thai-Cambodian border; Director: UNDP Eur. Office, Geneva; UN Develt Gp; Dep. Special Rep. of UN Sec.-Gen. for Sierra Leone and UN Resident Coordinator, Humanitarian Coordinator and UNDP Resident Rep., until 2004; Principal Dep. Special Rep. of UN Sec.-Gen. for Côte d'Ivoire, 2004–05; Special Rep. for Liberia, 2005–07; Special Rep. and Hd, UN Mission in Democratic Republic of Congo, 2007–10. Vis. Fellow, Geneva Centre for Security Policy, 2010. *Address:* c/o Kofi Annan Foundation, PO Box 157, 1211 Geneva 20, Switzerland.

DOSSETT, David Patrick, MBE 2011; Executive Chairman, BEAMA (formerly British Electrotechnical and Allied Manufacturers' Association) Ltd, 2008–10, Adviser to President and Chief Executive Officer, 2010–12 (Director General, 1998–2001; Chief Executive, 2001–08); Chief Executive, BEAMA Installation Ltd, 1999–2010; *b* 20 Oct. 1943; *s* of John Dossett and Elizabeth Dossett (*née* Walsh); *m* 1964, Teresa Richards; four *s* two *d. Educ:* City Univ., London (BSc (Electrical and Electronic Engrg)). MIET (MIEE 1990). Distribn engr, London Electricity Bd, 1967–71; Tech. Officer, BSI, 1971–77; Hd of Standards, Kala (Iranian oil co.), 1977–84; Sen. Tech. Officer, AMDEA, 1984–91; Dir, EIEMA, 1991–98. Director: ASTA BEAB (formerly Asta) Certification Services, 1991–2007; Electrical Safety Council (formerly NICEIC), 2001– (Vice-Chm., 2005–07, Chm., 2007–09); Pres., CENELEC, 2010–12 (Vice Pres., 2008–09). Chm., Orgalime, 2005–07. Gov., St Bede's Sch., Romford, 1978–88 (Chm., 1984–88). *Recreations:* West Ham United, real ale, 14 grandchildren. *Address:* 12A Marlborough Drive, Sudbury CO10 2PS. *T:* 07768 045211. *E:* dpd1@hotmail.co.uk.

DOTRICE, Roy, OBE 2008; actor (stage, films and television); *b* 26 May 1925; *m* 1946, Kay Newman (*d* 2007), actress; three *d. Educ:* Dayton and Intermediate Schs, Guernsey, CI. Served War of 1939–45: Air Gunner, RAF, 1940; PoW, 1942–45. Acted in Repertory, 1945–55; formed and directed Guernsey Theatre Co., 1955; Royal Shakespeare Co., 1957–65 (Caliban, Julius Caesar, Hotspur, Firs, Puntila, Edward IV, etc); World War 2½, New Theatre, London, 1966; Brief Lives, Golden Theatre, New York, 1967; Latent Heterosexual and God Bless, Royal Shakespeare Co., Aldwych, 1968; Brief Lives (one-man play), Criterion, 1969 (over 400 perfs, world record for longest-running solo perf.), toured England, Canada, USA, 1973, Mayfair, 1974 (over 150 perfs), Broadway season, and world tour (over 1,700 perfs), 1974, Australian tour, 1975, UK revival, 2008; Peer Gynt, Chichester Festival, 1970; One At Night, Royal Court, 1971; The Hero, Edinburgh, 1970; Mother Adam, Arts, 1971; Tom Brown's Schooldays, Cambridge, 1972; The Hollow Crown, seasons in USA 1973 and 1975, Sweden 1975; Gomes, Queen's, 1973; The Dragon Variation, Duke of York's, 1977; Othello, The Apple Cart, Australian tour with Chichester Festival, 1978; Passion of Dracula, Queen's, 1978; Oliver!, Albery, 1979; Mister Lincoln (one-man play on Abraham Lincoln), Washington, NY and TV special, 1980, Fortune, 1981; A Life, NY, 1980–81; Henry V, and Falstaff in Henry IV, American Shakespeare Theatre, Stratford, Conn, 1981; Murder in Mind, Strand, 1982; Winston Churchill (one-man play), USA 1982 (also CBS TV); Kingdoms, NY, 1982; The Genius, Los Angeles, 1984 (Dramalogue Best Perf. Award); Down an Alley, Dallas, 1984; Great Expectations, Old Vic, 1985; Enemy of the People, NY, 1985; Hay Fever, NY and Washington, 1986; The Homecoming, NY, 1991; The Best of Friends, NY, 1993, Hampstead Th., London, 2006; The Woman in Black, USA, 1995, A Moon for the Misbegotten, NY, 2000 (Tony, Critics' Circle, Drama Desk and Jefferson Awards for best actor); The Islander, Theatre Royal, Lincoln, 2002; Carousel, Chichester, 2006; Brief Lives, UK tour, 2008; *films include:* Heroes of Telemark, Twist of Sand, Lock up Your Daughters, Buttercup Chain, Tomorrow, One of Those Things, Nicholas and Alexandra, Amadeus, Corsican Brothers, The Eliminators, Camilla, L-Dopa, The Lady Forgets, Lounge People, The Cutting Edge, The Scarlet Letter, Swimming with Sharks, The Beacon, La Femme Musketeer, Go Go Tales, Hellboy II. *Television:* appearances in: Dear Liar, Brief Lives, The Caretaker (Emmy award), Imperial Palace, Misleading Cases, Clochemerle, Dickens of London, Stargazy on Zummerdown, Strange Luck, Babylon 5, Earth 2, Mr and Mrs Smith (series), Murder She Wrote, Picket Fences (series), Children of the Dark, Family Reunion (USA), Tales of the Gold Monkey (USA), The Wizard (USA), A Team (USA), Tales from the Dark-Side (USA), Beauty and the Beast (USA), Going to Extremes (series) (USA), The Good Policeman (USA), Madigan Men (series) (USA), Heartbeat, Doctors, Are You Jim's Wife?; Game of Thrones. Various radio productions and book recordings. TV Actor of the Year Award, 1968; Tony Nomination for A Life, 1981. *Recreations:* fishing, soccer. *Address:* c/o Eric Glass Ltd, 25 Ladbroke Crescent, W11 1PS. *Club:* Garrick.

DOUBLE, Paul Robert Edgar, LVO 2012; Remembrancer, since 2003, and Parliamentary Agent, since 2004, City of London; Parliamentary Agent, The Honourable The Irish Society, since 2004; *b* 4 Oct. 1951; *s* of Edgar Harold Double and Iris Joan Double; *m* 1986, Glynis Mycock (Dr Glynis Double, MB, ChB, MSc, FRCPath, FFPHM); one *s* three *d. Educ:* Univ. of Bristol (BSc); University Coll. London (LLM). MRSC 1984. Called to the Bar, Middle Temple, 1981; joined Civil Service, 1974; seconded to Univ. of Aston, 1975; Sec., Printing Industry Adv. Cttee, Dept of Employment, 1976; Mem., Legislation Review Unit, 1981; apptd Counsel to City Remembrancer, following pupillage in chambers of Hon. Sir Michael Turner and as prosecutor for HM Factory Inspectorate, 1985; Asst Remembrancer, 1994–98; Dir, 1998–2003. City Corporation's Patron, Financial Markets Law Cttee, 2009–. Dir, Lord Mayor's Show Ltd, 2004–; Hon. Sec., Lord Mayor and Sheriffs' Cttee, 2003–. Dir, Global Law Summit, 2013–; Mem., 2014–, Trustee, 2015–, Agincourt 600 Organising Cttee. Trustee, Magna Carta Trust, 2011–. Gov., Sutton's Hosp. in Charterhouse, 2007–. Vis. Lectr in Law, Univ. of London, 1983–98. Freeman, City of London, 1985. Consulting Ed., London Govt, Halsbury's Laws of England, 2011–. *Recreations:* sailing, leisure cycling. *Address:* Guildhall, EC2P 2EJ. *T:* (020) 7332 1200, *Fax:* (020) 7710 8579. *Club:* Guildhall.

DOUBLE, Stephen Daniel; MP (C) St Austell and Newquay, since 2015; *b* St Austell, 19 Dec. 1966; *m* 1986, Anne Bird; three *s. Educ:* Poltair Sch., St Austell. Barclays Bank, 1983–92; church pastor, 1992–2002. Director: Bay Direct Media Ltd, 2001–15; Phoenix Corporate Ltd, 2011–15. Mem. (C), Cornwall Council, 2009–15. *Address:* House of Commons, SW1A 0AA.

DOUBLEDAY, John Vincent; sculptor, since 1968; *b* 9 Oct. 1947; *s* of late Gordon V. and Margaret E. V. Doubleday; *m* 1969, Isobel J. C. Durie; two *s* (and one *s* decd). *Educ:* Stowe; Goldsmiths' College School of Art. *Exhibitions include:* Waterhouse Gallery, 1968, 1969, 1970, 1971; Galerie Sothmann, Amsterdam, 1969, 1971, 1979; Richard Demarco Gallery, Edinburgh, 1973; Laing Art Gallery, Newcastle, Bowes Museum, Barnard Castle, 1974; Pandion Gallery, NY, Aldeburgh Festival, 1983; Ujjain Internat. Fest., 2010; *works include:* Baron Ramsey of Canterbury, 1974; King Olav of Norway, 1975; Prince Philip, Duke of Edinburgh, Earl Mountbatten of Burma, Golda Meir, 1976; Charlie Chaplin (Leicester Square), 1982; Beatles (Liverpool), Dylan Thomas, 1984; Royal Marines Commando Meml, Lympstone, Devon, 1986; Sherlock Holmes (Meiringen), 1991; Dorothy L. Sayers (Witham), 1994; J. B. Pflug (Biberach), 1994; Nelson Mandela (Mbabane and London), 1997; Gerald Durrell (Jersey Zoo), Sherlock Holmes (Baker Street Stn, London), 1999; The Dorset Shepherd, Dorchester, 2000; Col Jabara (USAF ACAD., Colorado Springs), 2004; Nelson (Gibraltar), 2005; Battle of Maldon Monument (Blackwater Estuary, Essex), 2006; Guruji Chinchalkar (Indore), 2010; Municipal Mus., Meiringen, Switzerland, 2012; HM The Queen, Gibraltar and Southend-on-Sea, 2013; Herbert Columbine VC (Walton-on-the-Naze), 2014; *works in public collections:* Ashmolean Mus., British Mus., Herbert F. Johnson Mus., USA, Tate Gall., V & A, Nat. Mus. of Wales. *Recreation:* enthusiasm for the unnecessary. *Address:* Goat Lodge, Goat Lodge Road, Great Totham, Maldon, Essex CM9 8BX. *T:* (01621) 891329.

DOUCE, Prof. John Leonard, FREng; FIEE; Professor of Electrical Science, Warwick University, 1965–94 (part-time 1989–94), now Emeritus; *b* 15 Aug. 1932; *s* of John William and Florrie Douce; *m* 1959, Jean Shanks; one *s* one *d. Educ:* Manchester Grammar Sch.; Manchester Univ. (BSc, MSc, PhD, DSc). Lectr, Sen. Lectr, Reader, Queen's Univ., Belfast, 1958–65. Member: Technology Sub-Cttee, UGC, 1980–89; Engrg Bd, 1987–91, Science Bd, 1989–91, SERC; Contract Assessor, HEFCE, 1993–94. FIEE 1970; FREng 1991. Sir Harold Hartley Silver Medal, Inst. of Measurement and Control, 1989. *Publications:* Introduction to Mathematics of Servomechanisms, 1963, 2nd edn 1972; papers on control engineering. *Recreations:* bridge, boating, home-brewing. *Address:* 259 Station Road, Balsall Common, Coventry CV7 7EG. *T:* (01676) 532070. *E:* jdouce@iee.org.

DOUCET, Lyse Marie, OBE 2014; presenter and correspondent, since 1999, and Chief International Correspondent, since 2012, BBC World News TV and BBC World Service Radio; *b* Bathurst, NB, Canada, 24 Dec. 1958; *d* of Clarence and Norma Doucet. *Educ:* Queen's Univ., Kingston, Ont (BA Hons 1980); Univ. of Toronto (MA Internat. Relns 1982). Joined BBC, 1983; W Africa reporter, 1983–88; Kabul corresp., 1988–89; Pakistan corresp., 1989–94; Jordan corresp., 1994–95; ME corresp., 1995–99. Member, Council:

Chatham House, 2004–10; Internat. Council on Human Rights Policy, 2005–12. Hon. Patron, Canadian Crossroads Internat., 2006. Mem., Friends of Aschiana, 2006–. Hon. DCL King's Coll., Halifax, 2003; Hon. DLitt: New Brunswick, 2006; Moncton, 2010; Hon. DLaws: Toronto, 2009; St Andrews, 2014; Hon. Dr York, 2012; Hon. DHL Liverpool Hope, 2015. Silver Sony Radio News Broadcaster of Year, 2003; TV Personality of Year, Assoc. for Internat. Broadcasting, 2007; News and Factual Award, Women in Film and TV, 2007; David Bloom Award for Excellence in Enterprise Reporting, Radio and Television Correspondents Assoc., 2010; Gold Sony News Journalist of the Year, 2010; Peabody Award, Univ. of Georgia, 2010, 2013; Edward R. Murrow Award, Radio TV Digital News Assoc., 2012; James Cameron Prize, 2013; Women in Film and TV - ITV Studios Achievement of the Year, 2014. *E:* lyse.doucet@bbc.co.uk. *Club:* Frontline.

DOUEK, Ellis Elliot, FRCS; Consultant Otologist, 1970–99, now Emeritus, and Chairman, Hearing Research Group, 1974–99, Guy's Hospital; author; *b* 25 April 1934; *s* of Cesar Douek and Nelly Sassoon; *m* 1993, Gill Green; two *s* by former marriage. *Educ:* English School, Cairo; Westminster Medical School. MRCS, LRCP 1958; FRCS 1967. House appts, St Helier Hosp., 1959, and Whittington Hosp., 1963; nat. service, RAMC, 1960–62; ENT Registrar, Royal Free Hosp., 1966; Sen. Registrar, King's College Hosp., 1968. Mem., MRC working party on Hearing Research, 1975; MRC Rep. to Eur. Communities on Hearing Res., 1980; UK Rep. to Eur. Communities on Indust. Deafness, 1983; Mem., Scientific Cttee, Inst. de Recherche sur la surdité, Paris, 1989–. Littman Meml Lect., UCL, 2005. Dalby Prize for hearing research, RSM, 1978. *Publications:* Sense of Smell—Its Abnormalities, 1974; Eighth Nerve, in Peripheral Neuropathy, 1975; Olfaction, in Scientific Basis of Otolaryngology, 1976; Cochlear Implant, in Textbook of ENT, 1980; A Middle Eastern Affair (autobiog.), 2004; Overcoming Deafness; the story of hearing and language, 2014; papers on hearing and smell; contrib. online jl, The Fickle Grey Beast. *Recreations:* drawing and painting, studying history. *Address:* (home) 14 Heathcroft, Hampstead Way, NW11 7HH. *T:* (020) 8455 6427; Consulting Rooms, Princess Grace Hospital, 42–52 Nottingham Place, W1U 5NY. *E:* elgildouek@aol.com. *Club:* Athenæum.

DOUETIL, Dane Jonathan, CBE 2007; Group Chief Executive Officer: Minova Insurance Holdings (formerly BMS Associates) Ltd, since 2013; Brit Insurance Holdings N.V. (formerly PLC), 2005–11 (Director, 1999–2011); Chief Executive, Brit Syndicates Ltd, 2002–11; Head, Brit Group Underwriting, 2002–11; *b* 28 July 1960; *s* of late Dane Peter Douetil and of Fleur Caroline Douetil; *m* 1986, Antonia Clare Williamson; three *d. Educ:* Birmingham Univ. (BA Hons Commerce 1982). Willis Faber Gp, 1982–89 (Dir, Political and Financial Risk Div., 1988–89); Founding Shareholder and Dir, Special Risk Services Ltd, 1989–94; Consultant, Benfield Gp, 1997; Dir and Chief Exec., Brit Insce Ltd, 1998–2011. Mem., and Chm., London Mkt Reform Gp, 2006–07; Dir, ABI, 2010–11. *Recreations:* fishing, shooting, wine, cricket. *Club:* Boodle's.

DOUGAL, Andrew James Harrower; non-executive Director and Chairman, Audit Committee, Carillion plc, since 2011; *b* 2 Sept. 1951; *s* of Andrew James Harrower Dougal and Muriel Mary Dougal (*née* MacDonald); *m* 1978, Margaret Mairi MacDonald; two *s* one *d. Educ:* Greenock Acad.; Paisley GS; Glasgow Univ. (BAcc 1972). CA 1975. Articled Clerk, then Asst Manager, Arthur Young Glasgow, 1972–77; Gp Chief Accountant, Scottish & Universal Investments Ltd, 1977–86; Hanson plc, 1986–2002: Finance Comptroller, 1986–89; Finance Dir, ARC Ltd, 1989–92; Man. Dir, ARC Southern, 1992–93; Dep. Finance Dir, 1993–95; Finance Dir, 1995–97; Chief Exec., 1997–2002. Non-executive Director: Taylor Woodrow plc, 2002–07 (Chm., Audit Cttee, 2003–07); BPB, 2003–05; Celtel Internat. BV, 2004–05; Premier Farnell, 2006–15; Creston, 2006–; Taylor Wimpey plc, 2007–11 (Chm., Audit Cttee, 2007–09); Victrex plc, 2015–. Institute of Chartered Accountants of Scotland: Mem. Council and Oversight Bd, 2012–; Mem., Qualification Bd, 2000–05; Convenor, Business Policy Cttee, 2010–12; Mem., Tech. Policy Bd, 2010– (Chm., 2012–). CCMI (CIMgt 1999); FRSA 2005. *Recreations:* family, sports, travel, history. *Address:* Gameswood, Crawley Drive, Camberley, Surrey GU15 2AA. *E:* ajhdougal@gmail.com.

DOUGAL, Malcolm Gordon; HM Diplomatic Service, retired; *b* 20 Jan. 1938; *s* of late Eric Gordon Dougal and Marie (*née* Wildermuth); *m* 1st, 1964, Elke (marr. diss.); one *s*; 2nd, 1995, Brigid Pritchard (*née* Turner) (*d* 2000); two step *s*; 3rd, 2003, Diana Blade (*née* Price); two step *s. Educ:* Ampleforth Coll., Yorkshire; The Queen's Coll., Oxford (MA Mod. History). National Service in Korea and Gibraltar with Royal Sussex Regt, 1956–58; Oxford, 1958–61; Contracts Asst, De Havilland Aircraft, Hatfield, 1961–64; Asst to Export Manager, Ticket Equipment Ltd (Plessey), 1964–66; Export Manager, Harris Lebus Ltd, 1967–69; entered HM Diplomatic Service, 1969; Foreign Office, 1969–72; 1st Secretary (Commercial): Paris, 1972–76; Cairo, 1976–79; Foreign Office, 1979–81; Consul Gen., Lille, 1981–85; Dep. High Comr and Head of Chancery, Canberra, 1986–89; RCDS, 1990; Dir, Jt FCO/DTI Directorate of Overseas Trade Services, FCO, 1991–94; Consul Gen., San Francisco, 1994–98. Warden, John Spedan Lewis Trust for the Advancement of the Natural Scis, 1998–2005. *Publications:* (contrib.) The Third Battle of Ypres (Seaford House Papers), 1990. *Recreations:* natural history, history, walking, books, sport, horse racing, wine. *Address:* Eglesfield Cottage, Monk Sherborne, Tadley, Hants RG26 5HH.

DOUGAN, Dr David John; County Arts Officer, Essex County Council, 1989–97; *b* 26 Sept. 1936; *s* of William John Dougan and Blanche May; *m* 1st, 1959, Eileen Ludbrook (marr. diss. 1985); one *s*; 2nd, 1986, Barbara Taylor; one *s* one *d. Educ:* Durham Univ. (BA, MA); City Univ. (PhD 1982); BA Open Univ. 2002. Reporter, Tyne Tees Television, 1963; presenter, BBC, 1966; Director, Northern Arts, 1970; Dir, Crafts Council, 1984–88. Chairman: Nat. Youth Dance Trust, 1985–91; Dance East, 1999–2003; Suffolk Univs of the Third Age, 2005–. Special Advr, H of C Educn, Sci. and Arts Cttee, 1981–82; Mem., Calouste Gulbenkian Foundn Enquiry into the Arts in Schs, 1982. *Publications:* History of North East Shipbuilding, 1966; Great Gunmaker, 1968; Shipwrights Trade Union, 1971; The Jarrow March, 1976; To Return a King, 2006. *Recreations:* theatre, music, tennis. *Address:* Grovelands, 1 Grove Road, Bury St Edmunds, Suffolk IP33 3BE. *T:* (01284) 752588.

DOUGAN, Prof. Gordon, PhD; FRS 2012; FMedSci; Principal Research Scientist, Head of Pathogen Research and Member, Board of Management, Wellcome Trust Sanger Institute; Fellow, Wolfson College, Cambridge. *Educ:* Univ. of Sussex (BSc Biochem.; PhD). Postdoctoral studies, Univ. of Washington, Seattle; Lectr, Moyne Inst., TCD; Wellcome Foundn, until 1992; Rank Prof. of Physiological Biochem., and Dir, Centre for Molecular Microbiol. and Infection, Imperial Coll. London, now Vis. Prof. Hon. Prof., Veterinary Sch., Univ. of Cambridge; Visiting Professor: LSHTM; Univ. of Nottingham. Chm., New Vaccines Steering Cttee, WHO. Chair, Scientific Adv. Bd, Novartis Vaccines and Diagnostics; Mem., Scientific Adv. Bd, GlycoVaxyn, AG. Mem., EMBO. FMedSci 2002. *Publications:* contribs to jls. *Address:* Wellcome Trust Sanger Institute, Wellcome Trust Genome Campus, Hinxton, Cambridge CB10 1SA.

DOUGHERTY, Charles Egmont; QC 2013; *b* Stockholm, 27 July 1972; *s* of Peter Dougherty and Wanja Dougherty (*née* Tornberg). *Educ:* Winchester Coll.; Magdalen Coll., Oxford (BA; BCL). Law tutor and researcher, Freie Univ., Berlin, 1994–95; Mgt Consultant, Arkwright Ltd, 1995–96; called to the Bar, Middle Temple, 1997; in practice as barrister, specialising in commercial law, 1997–. *Publications:* (asst ed.) European Civil Practice, 2nd edn 2004. *Recreations:* theatre, art, wine travel, walking. *Address:* 2 Temple Gardens, Temple, EC4Y 9AY. *T:* (020) 7822 1200, *Fax:* (020) 7822 1300. *E:* cd@2tg.co.uk.

DOUGHERTY, Prof. Michele Karen, PhD; FRS 2012; FRAS; Professor of Space Physics, Blackett Laboratory, Imperial College London; *b* 1962. *Educ:* Univ. of Natal (PhD 1988). Postdoctoral Fellow, Germany; Imperial College London: PPARC Advanced Fellow in Space Physics; Lectr, 2000; Reader in Space Physics; Mem., Team for Jupiter analysis of Ulysses Mission, 1991–; Eur. Hd, NASA-ESA Europa Jupiter system mission to Jupiter; Guest Investigator, NASA Jupiter System Data Analysis Prog.; Principal Investigator, Internat. NASA-ESA-ASI Cassini Huygens mission to Saturn and its moons. Associate Ed., Jl Geophysical Res. - Space Physics. Chair, Scientific Prog. Adv. Cttee, UK Space Agency, 2013–. Fellow, Amer. Geophysical Union. Zeldovich Medal, Russian Acad. Scis and Cttee on Space Res., 1996; Hughes Medal, Royal Soc., 2008. *Publications:* contribs to learned jls, incl. Jl Geophysical Res. - Space Physics, Planetary and Space Sci. *Address:* Department of Physics, Imperial College London, South Kensington Campus, SW7 2AZ.

DOUGHERTY, Air Vice-Marshal Simon Robert Charles, FRCP; FFOM; Chief of Staff Health HQ Air Command and Director-General Medical Services, Royal Air Force, 2006–08 (Director-General Medical Services (RAF), 2004–06); *b* 26 Feb. 1949; *s* of late Patrick Cecil George Dougherty and Valerie June Dougherty (*née* Appleby); *m* 1971, Margaret Snape; two *s* one *d. Educ:* Framlingham Coll.; London Hosp. Med. Coll. (MB BS 1971); LSHTM (MSc Occupational Medicine 1986). DObstRCOG 1976; DAvMed (Stewart Meml Prize) 1979; AFOM 1980, MFOM 1984, FFOM 1993; FRCP 2009. Commnd RAF Med. Br., 1969; MO, RAF Binbrook, 1974–75; UK Delegn & Support Unit HQ AFCENT, 1975–77; Sen. MO, UK Support Unit, HQ AAFCE, 1977–78; DAvMed course, RAF Inst. of Aviation Medicine, 1979; Chief Instructor, RAF Aviation Medicine Trng Centre, 1979–82; Sen. MO, TriNat. Tornado Trng Est., RAF Cottesmore, 1982–85; Deputy Principal Medical Officer: (Occupational Health and Safety) HQ RAF Support Comd, 1986–87; HQ RAF Germany, 1987–91; jsdc, Greenwich, 1991–92; Officer Commanding: RAF Inst. of Health and Med. Trng, 1992–94; Princess Mary's Hosp., RAF Halton, 1994; Dep. Dir, Med. Policy and Plans (RAF), HQ PTC, 1994–96; CO, The Princess Mary's Hosp., RAF Akrotiri and Comd Med. Advr, HQ British Forces Cyprus, 1996–99; Dir Health Services (RAF), HQ PTC, 1999–2001; Dir Med. Personnel, Policy and Plans (RAF), HQ PTC, 2001–02; Dir Med. Policy, Defence Med. Services Dept, MoD, 2002–04. QHP 2002–09. Taylor Prof. of Occupational Medicine, Jt RAF and RCP, 1990–96; Consultant Advr, Occupational Medicine, RAF, 1997–2002. Hon. Air Cdre, 4626 Aeronautical Evacuation Sqdn, RAuxAF, 2009–. Member: Ct of Govs, LSHTM, 2004–; Fellowship Cttee, Faculty of Occupational Medicine, 2006–08. Chm. of Trustees, Stewart Meml Trust, 2004–08; Trustee: Headley Court Charity, 2010–13; RAF Benevolent Fund, 2012– (Chm., Main Grants Cttee, 2012–; Chm., Welfare Cttee, 2012–); Governor: Royal Star and Garter Homes, 2004–; Framlingham Coll., 2008–. Mem. SOM, 1980; MRAeS 1982, FRAeS 2000; FRSocMed 1994 (United Services Section Council, 2002–08; Vice Pres., 2004–08); FCMI (FIMgt 1999). Freeman, City of London, 2008. Member: Soc. of Apothecaries, 2006–; Hon. Co. of Air Pilots (formerly GAPAN), 2007–. Pres., Soc. of Old Framlinghamians, 2011–13 (Vice Pres., 2003–11). Parish Councillor, Abberton and Langenhoe, 2010–. OStJ 1991. *Recreations:* travelling, ski-ing, computers, gardening, cruising the East Coast. *Clubs:* Royal Air Force; West Mersea Yacht.

DOUGHTY, Louise; author, since 1990; *b* Melton Mowbray, 4 Sept. 1963; *d* of Kenneth Herbert George Doughty and Avis Doughty; two *c. Educ:* Leeds Univ. (BA Hons English Lit. 1984); Univ. of E Anglia (MA Creative Writing 1987). Ian St James Award, 1990; Radio Times Drama Award, 1990; K. Blundell Trust Award, 1999; Writers' Award, Arts Council, 2001. *Publications:* Crazy Paving, 1995; Dance With Me, 1996; Honey-Dew, 1998; Fires in the Dark, 2003; Stone Cradle, 2006; A Novel in a Year, 2007; Whatever You Love, 2010; Apple Tree Yard, 2013. *Recreations:* playing the piano badly, singing badly, sleeping very well. *Address:* c/o Antony Harwood, Antony Harwood Literary Agency Ltd, 103 Walton Street, Oxford OX2 6EB.

DOUGHTY, Stephen John; MP (Lab) Cardiff South and Penarth, since Nov. 2012; *b* Cardiff, 1980; *s* of Barry and Eileen Doughty. *Educ:* Llantwit Major Comprehensive Sch.; Lester B. Pearson United World Coll.; Corpus Christi Coll., Oxford (BA Hons 2001); St Andrews Univ. (MLitt 2003). Campaigns Coordinator, World Vision UK, 2004–06; Hd, Govt Relns, Oxfam GB, 2006–09; Special Advr, DFID, 2009–10; Hd, Oxfam Cymru/Wales, 2011–12. PPS to Shadow Chief Sec. to HM Treasury, 2013; an Opposition Whip, 2013–. *Recreations:* walking, music, travel, singing, outdoor pursuits. *Address:* House of Commons, SW1A 0AA. *T:* (020) 7219 5348. *E:* stephen.doughty.mp@parliament.uk.

DOUGHTY, Stuart John, CMG 2005; CEng, FICE, FCIHT; Chief Executive, Costain Group plc, 2001–05; Chairman, Silverdell plc, 2006–13; *b* 13 Sept. 1943; *s* of late Henry John Doughty and of Marie Louise Doughty; *m* Penelope Ann; one *d* (one *s* decd). *Educ:* UC, Cardiff (BSc). CEng; FICE; FIHT. John Laing Construction: grad. trainee, 1965; Regl Manager, 1974–84; Man. Dir, Civil Engrg Div., 1984–86; Exec. Dir, Tarmac Construction, 1986–91; Chm. and Man. Dir, Construction Div., Alfred McAlpine, 1991–94; Dir, Hyder Plc, 1994–97; Chm., Alstec Ltd, Beck & Pollitzer, and Kennedy Construction, 1997–2001. Non-exec. Dir, Viborant plc, 1997–2001; Sen. non-exec. Dir, Scott Wilson plc, 2005–11; non-exec. Chm., Somero plc, 2006–09. Chm., UK Trade Internat. (Sectors), DTI, 1997–. Mem. Council, ECGD, 1997–2001. Lt Col, Engr and Logistics Staff Corps, 1998–. Gov., King's Sch., Worcester, 1999–2012; Mem. Council, Aston Univ., 2012–. *Recreations:* classic and historic motor sport and houses. *Address:* Bradley Farm House, Kinlet, Bewdley, Worcs DY12 3BU. *T:* (01299) 841327.

DOUGHTY, Susan Kathleen, (Mrs D. Orchard); Director, Corporate Climate Ltd, 2006–10; independent advisor on environment and government, since 2006; *b* 13 April 1948; *d* of Ronald and Olive Powell; *m* 1st, 1974, John Doughty (marr. diss.); two *s*; 2nd, 1995, David Orchard; two step *d. Educ:* Northumberland Coll. of Educn (CertEd); holds various business qualifications. Primary sch. teacher, 1969–70; Work Study Analyst, Northern Gas Mgt Services, 1970–73; Work Study Officer, CEBG Mgt Services, 1974–75; Orgn and Method Analyst, Wilkinson Match Mgt Services, 1976–77; career break (charity work), 1977–83; Ind. Mgt Consultant, 1984–89, 1999–2001; Project Manager, Thames Water, 1989–98. MP (Lib Dem) Guildford, 2001–05; contested (Lib Dem) same seat, 2005, 2010. Lib Dem spokesman on envmt, 2001–03, front bench spokesman on envmt, 2003–05. Mem., Envmtl Audit Select Cttee, 2001–05. Chm., Thatcham Children's Centre, 1982–84. *Recreations:* gardening, cricket, walking, theatre, opera, Arsenal, the arts. *Address:* 3 Wharf Cottages, Stonebridge Wharf, Shalford, Surrey GU4 8EH.

DOUGILL, John Wilson, FREng, FICE, FIStructE, FASCE; Chief Executive and Secretary, Institution of Structural Engineers, 1994–99 (Director of Engineering, 1987–94); *b* 18 Nov. 1934; *s* of William John Dougill and Emily Firmstone Wilson; *m* 1959, Daphne Maude Weeks (*d* 2008); one *s* one *d. Educ:* Trinity Sch. of John Whitgift, Croydon; King's Coll., London; Imperial Coll. of Science and Technology. MScEng, DIC, PhD; FREng 1990. Engineer with George Wimpey, 1956–58 and 1960–61; Research Asst to Prof. A. L. L. Baker, Imperial Coll., 1961–64; King's College London: Lectr in Civil Engrg, 1964–73; Reader in Engrg Science, 1973–76; Prof. of Engrg Science, 1976–81; Prof. of Concrete Structures and Technology, Imperial Coll., 1981–87. Vis. Res. Engineer, Univ. of California, Berkeley, 1967–68; Visiting Professor: Dept of Civil Engrg, Imperial Coll., 1991–97; Sch. of Engrg, Univ. of Surrey, 2000–06; South China Univ. of Technol., 2001–. Chm., SERC Civil Engrg Sub-Cttee, 1982–83; Mem., NEDO Res. Strategy Cttee, 1983–85. Sec. Gen., Fedn Internat. de la Précontrainte, 1992–98. Mem. Court of Governors, Whitgift Foundn, 1981–2007. FCGI 1997. *Publications:* papers in jls of engrg mech., materials and struct. engrg. *Recreations:*

coarse gardening, travel, good food, walking, continuing interest in structural mechanics and particularly human structure interaction. *Address:* Ashcroft, 4 Larch Close, Kingswood, Tadworth, Surrey KT20 6JF. *T:* (01737) 833283.

DOUGLAS, family name of **Marquess of Queensberry**, **Earl of Morton**, and **Viscount Chilston**.

DOUGLAS AND CLYDESDALE, Marquess of; Douglas Charles Douglas-Hamilton; *b* 9 July 2012; *s* and *heir* of Duke of Hamilton, *qv*.

DOUGLAS, Anthony Gordon, CBE 2008; Chief Executive, Children and Family Court Advisory and Support Service, since 2004; *b* 4 July 1949; *s* of late Gordon Louis Albert Douglas and Lily Douglas (*née* Graves); *m* 1975, Margaret Olga Jean Friedlander; two *d*. *Educ:* St Nicholas Grammar Sch., Northwood; St Peter's Coll., Oxford (Pt I PPE); N London Poly. (CQSW 1980); Open Univ. (BSc 1984). Social worker, Hackney Social Services, 1976–83; various mgt posts in Southwark, Barnet and Newham Councils, London, 1983–91; Asst Dir of Social Services, Hackney, 1991–96; Havering Council: Dir, Social Services, 1996–98; Exec. Dir, Community Services, 1998–2002; Dir, Social Care and Health, Suffolk CC, 2002–04. Visiting Fellow: UEA, 2003–; Univ. of Plymouth, 2012–. Chair: London Assoc. of Dirs of Social Services, 1997–2000; British Assoc. for Adoption and Fostering, 2003–. *Publications:* (with T. Philpot) Caring and Coping, 1998; (with A. Weir) Child Protection and Adult Mental Health: conflicts of interest, 1999; Is Anyone Out There?, 2002; (with T. Philpot) Adoption: changing families, changing times, 2003; Partnership Working, 2009. *Recreations:* cricket, opera. *Address:* CAFCASS, 3rd Floor, 21 Bloomsbury Street, WC1B 3HF. *T:* (0300) 456 4000. *E:* anthony.douglas@cafcass.gsi.gov.uk. *Clubs:* Middlesex CC, Arsenal Football.

DOUGLAS, Barry; *see* Douglas, W. B.

DOUGLAS, Boyd; farmer; Member (U) Limavady Borough Council, since 1997; *b* 13 July 1950; *s* of William Douglas and late May Douglas; *m* 1972, Kathleen Semple; two *s* two *d*. *Educ:* Burnfoot Primary Sch.; Dungiven Secondary Sch.; Strabane Agriculture Coll. Farmer, 1970–. Mem. (U) E Londonderry, NI Assembly, 1998–2003. *Address:* 279 Drumrane Road, Dungiven, Co. Londonderry BT47 4NL.

DOUGLAS, Caroline; Director, Contemporary Art Society, since 2013; *b* London, 25 June 1961; *d* of John and Elizabeth Douglas; *m* 2001, Guy Morey; one *s*. *Educ:* Leeds Univ. (BA Jt Hons French and Spanish 1983); Courtauld Inst. of Art (MA Hist. of Art 1994). Exhibns Coordinator, Momart Ltd, 1987–92; Asst Gall. Manager, Whitechapel Art Gall., 1993–94; Curator, Visual Arts Dept, British Council, 1994–2006; Hd, Arts Council Collection, 2006–13. Member: Fine Art Faculty, British Sch. at Rome, 2006–; AICA (UK), 2007–. Trustee: Space Studios, London, 2006–; Charles Wallace (India) Trust, 2006–. Hon. Dr Norwich Univ. of Arts, 2014. *Recreations:* theatre, opera, reading, cinema, gardening. *Address:* Contemporary Art Society, 59 Central Street, EC1V 3AF. *T:* (020) 7017 8400. *E:* caroline@contemporaryartsociety.org.

DOUGLAS, Colin Antony; Director, Southside Communications Ltd, since 2013; *b* 10 Sept. 1963; *s* of Kendric Manasseh Douglas and Adassa Beatrice Douglas; *m* 1992, Petrina Hall; two *s*. *Educ:* Tulse Hill Comprehensive Sch., S London; Keble Coll., Oxford (BA Hons PPE); Oxford Brookes Univ. (MBA). Dip. Mktg, CIM. Dir, Citigate Public Relns, 1994–99; Dir of Communications, Sport England, 1999–2001; Dir of Public Affairs, Transport for London, 2001–02; Director of Communications: Audit Commn, 2002–04; HSE, 2004–08; Dir of NHS Communications, DoH, 2008–13. Non-exec. Dir, London Ambulance Service, 1996–2006. *Publications:* West Indian Women at War: British racism in World War II, 1991. *Recreations:* photography, family.

DOUGLAS, Derek Jack, CBE 2006; CA; Founder, Chairman and Chief Executive Officer, Adam Smith Ltd, since 1988; *b* 17 Oct. 1953. *Educ:* Heriot-Watt Univ. (BSc); Aberdeen Univ. CA 1982. Chartered accountant: Coopers & Lybrand, 1978–81; Arthur Young, 1981–83; Gen. Manager, NZ United Corp., 1983–85; Barclays de Zoete Wedd, 1985–88. Chairman: Digital Animations Gp plc, 1996–2001; Kymata Ltd, 1998–99; Acuid Corp. Ltd, 2001–06; Carlton Bingo Plc, 2001–08; NGenTec Ltd, 2009–; Dir, Bremner plc, 1990–91. Chm. and Trustee, Maggie Keswick Jencks Cancer Caring Centres Trust, 1996–2003; Dir and Trustee, Macmillan Cancer Support, 2006–12. FRSA 2003. Hon. DBA Abertay, 2003. *Publications:* contribs to Jl ICAS. *Recreations:* sailing, golf. *Address:* Adam Smith Ltd, Adam Smith House, Melville Castle Estate, Lasswade, Edinburgh EH18 1AW. *T:* (0131) 654 7000. *Club:* Bruntsfield Links Golfing Society.

DOUGLAS, Prof. (Felicity) Gillian, LLD; FLSW; Professor of Law, Cardiff University, since 1998; *b* London, 11 Nov. 1955; *d* of Jack and Doris Douglas; *m* 1981, Hugh Fenton Rawlings, *qv*; one *s* one *d*. *Educ:* City of London Sch. for Girls; Univ. of Manchester (LLB 1977); London Sch. of Econs and Pol Sci. (LLM 1978); Cardiff Univ. (LLD 2011). Lectr in Law, Univ. of Bristol, 1978–89; Cardiff University: Lectr in Law, 1989–92; Sen. Lectr, 1992–95; Reader, 1995–98; Dep. Hd, 2000–05, Hd, 2005–10, Cardiff Law Sch. Vis. Teaching Fellow, NUS, 1983–84; Leverhulme Major Res. Fellow, 2015–. Chair, Law Sub-panel, REF, 2010–14. Trustee, Family Mediation Cardiff, 2002–12. FHEA 2007; FLSW 2012. *Publications:* Law, Fertility and Reproduction, 1991; (with C. Barton) Law and Parenthood, 1995; (with N. Lowe) Bromley's Family Law, 9th edn 1998 to 11th edn 2014; An Introduction to Family Law, 2001, 2nd edn 2004. *Recreations:* reading, theatre, cinema, following Arsenal FC. *Address:* Cardiff Law School, Cardiff University, Museum Avenue, Cardiff CF10 3AX. *T:* (029) 2087 5447. *E:* douglasg@cardiff.ac.uk.

DOUGLAS, Henry Russell, FCIJ; journalist; Legal Manager, News Group Newspapers, 1976–89; *b* Bishopbriggs, Lanarkshire, 11 Feb. 1925; 2nd *s* of late Russell Douglas and Jeanie Douglas Douglas (*née* Drysdale); *m* 1951, Elizabeth Mary, *d* of late Ralph Nowell, CB; two *s* three *d*. *Educ:* various Scottish and English Grammar Schools; Lincoln Coll., Oxford (MA Hons). Served RNVR, 1943–46 (Sub-Lt, submarines). Merchant Navy, 1946–47; Oxford Univ., 1947–50; Liverpool Daily Post, 1950–69; The Sun, 1969–76. Inst. of Journalists, 1956: Fellow, 1969; Pres., 1972–73; Chm. of Executive, 1973–76; Member: Press Council, 1972–80; Council, Newspaper Press Fund, 1972–76, 1986–2004 (Chm., 1990–91); Founder Mem., Media Society, 1973 (Treas., 1973–86, Vice-Pres., 1987–89); Founder, Soc. of Fleet Street Lawyers, 1989. *Recreations:* chess, painting, history. *Address:* Flat 44, Mayford Grange, 99 Westfield Road, Woking, Surrey GU22 9AX. *T:* (01483) 763853. *Club:* Naval.

DOUGLAS, Hilary Kay, CB 2002; Executive Coach, Praesta Partners, since 2010; *b* 27 July 1950; *d* of late James Robert Keith Black and Joan Margaret Black (*née* Boxall); *m* 1972, Robert Harold Douglas, *qv*; two *s*. *Educ:* Wimbledon High Sch.; New Hall, Cambridge (BA Hons History 1971). Press Librarian, RIIA, 1971–73; joined DES, 1973: Sec. of State's Private Office, 1975–76; appts in teacher trng, educnl disadvantage and local authy finance, 1977–84; Head: Teacher Supply Div., 1985–87; School Govt Div., 1987–89; freelance consultancy and teaching, Netherlands, 1989–91; Sec., FEFC, 1991–92; set up SCAA, 1992–93; Hd of Personnel, DFE, 1993–94; Dir of Admin, Office for Standards in Educn, 1994–96; Dir, Civil Service Employer Gp, Cabinet Office, 1996–97; Dir, Personnel and Support Services, DfEE, 1997–2000; Man. Dir, Corporate Services and Develt, HM Treasury, 2000–04; Chief Operating Officer, ONS, 2004–06; Chief Operating Officer, later Dir Gen., Ops and Change, DTI, then BERR, later BIS, 2006–09. Trustee, British Red Cross, 2013–. *Recreations:* travel, European languages, singing. *Address:* Praesta Partners, Berger House, 38 Berkeley Square, W1J 5AH.

DOUGLAS, Janet Elizabeth, CMG 2008; HM Diplomatic Service; Deputy Head of Mission, Ankara, since 2011; *b* Deal, Kent, 6 Jan. 1960; *d* of late Duncan and of Mary Douglas; *m* 2012, George Anthony Furlong. *Educ:* Cheltenham Ladies' Coll.; St Catharine's Coll., Cambridge (BA Hons Archaeol. and Anthropol. 1982). Joined FCO, 1985; Second, later First Sec., Ankara, 1988–92; UN Dept, FCO, 1992–94; on secondment to ODA, 1994–96; First Sec. (EU), Stockholm, 1996–2000; Dep. Hd, Africa Dept (Southern), FCO, 2000–02; Head: Personnel Mgt Unit, HR Directorate, 2002–04; Consular Assistance Gp, Consular Directorate, 2004–07; Africa Dept (Southern, later Southern, Central and Western), FCO, 2007–10; Asst Dir, HR Directorate, FCO, 2010–11. *Recreations:* ski-ing, sailing (fair weather only), visiting art galleries and museums, reading crime fiction. *Address:* c/o Foreign and Commonwealth Office, King Charles Street, SW1A 2AH.

DOUGLAS, Jonathan David; Director, National Literacy Trust, since 2007; *b* Birmingham, 16 Jan. 1970; *s* of John and Margaret Douglas; partner, Gary Mack. *Educ:* Handsworth Grammar Sch.; Durham Univ. (BA Hons Theol. 1991); London Metropolitan Univ. (Postgrad. Dip. IS 1996). MCLIP 1998. Librarian, Westminster Libraries, 1992–99; Professional Advr, Youth and Sch. Libraries, CLIP/Liby Assoc., 1999–2003; Hd, Policy Develt, Mus, Libraries and Archives Council, 2003–07. Non-exec. Dir, Money Advice Service, 2011–. Mem., Adv. Gp, Man Booker Prize, 2009–. Hon. Life Mem., Youth Libraries Gp, 2003. Chm., Govs, St William of York Primary Sch., 2012–. Hon. DLitt Oxford Brookes, 2014. *Publications:* The CILIP Guidelines for Secondary School Libraries, 2004. *Recreations:* opera, concerts, food, wine and friends, contemporary fiction. *Address:* National Literacy Trust, 68 South Lambeth Rioad, SW8 1RL. *E:* jonathan.douglas@literacytrust.org.uk.

DOUGLAS, Kenneth George, ONZ 1999; President, New Zealand Council of Trade Unions, 1987–99; *b* 15 Nov. 1935; *s* of John Atholwood Douglas and Marjorie Alice (*née* Farrow); *m* 1956, Lesley Barbara Winter (marr. diss. 1986); two *s* two *d*; partner, Marilyn Gay Tucker. *Educ:* Wellington Coll. President: Wellington Section, Drivers Union, 1958–79; NZ Drivers Fedn, 1972–79; Treas., Nat. Sect., NZ Fedn of Labour, 1979–87. Mem., Exec. Bd, ICFTU, 1987–99; Pres., ICFTU-Asia Pacific Regl Orgn, 1990–99. Mem., Prime Minister's Enterprise Council, 1990–99. Mem. (Ind.), Porirua CC, 1998–. JP Porirua, 1999. Hon. LLD Victoria Univ. of Wellington, 1999. *Publications:* contrib. articles on industrial relns and Labour movement to jls. *Recreation:* golf. *Address:* 8 View Road, Titahi Bay, Porirua, New Zealand. *T:* (4) 2368857. *Clubs:* Porirua, Titahi Golf (NZ).

DOUGLAS, Lesley; Founder, Lonesome Pine Productions, since 2013; *b* 7 June 1963; *d* of William and Sarah Douglas; *m* Nick Scripps; one *s* one *d*. *Educ:* Manchester Univ. (BA English). Joined BBC, 1986: prodn asst, res. dept, then David Jacobs Show, 1986–87; Promotions Asst, 1987–88; Producer: Music Dept, 1988–90; Promotions, 1990–93; Ed., Presentation and Planning, Radio 2, 1993–97; Managing Ed., 1997–2000, Hd of Progs, 2000–04, Radio 2; Controller, Radio 2 and 6 Music, 2004–08; Dir of Programming and Business Develt, Universal Music UK, 2008–12; Chief Exec., Lime Pictures, 2012–13. Chm., Steering Cttee, Radio Fest. Mem. Bd, Sage, Gateshead. Fellow, Radio Acad. Hon. Fellow, Univ. of Sunderland. Woman of Year Award, Music Industry, 2004.

DOUGLAS, Michael John; QC 1997; a Recorder, since 2000; *b* 7 Aug. 1952; *s* of late James Murray Douglas, CBE. *Educ:* Westminster Sch.; Balliol Coll., Oxford (BA Hons Jurisprudence). Called to the Bar, Gray's Inn, 1974. *Recreations:* theatre, cinema, eating out, football, travel. *Address:* 4 Pump Court, Temple, EC4Y 7AN. *T:* (020) 7842 5555.

DOUGLAS, Michael Kirk; actor and producer; *b* 25 Sept. 1944; *s* of Kirk Douglas, actor and late Diana Douglas; *m* 1977, Diandra Morrell Luker (marr. diss.); one *s*; *m* 2000, Catherine Zeta-Jones (CBE 2010); one *s* one *d*. *Educ:* Univ. of Calif at Santa Barbara (BA 1967). *Films* include: *actor:* Hail Hero, 1969; Napoleon and Samantha, 1972; Star Chamber, 1983; A Chorus Line, 1985; Black Rain, 1990; The War of the Roses, 1990; Shining Through, 1992; Basic Instinct, 1992; Falling Down, 1993; Disclosure, 1994; The American President, 1995; The Game, 1997; Traffic, 2001; Don't Say a Word, 2002; The In-Laws, 2003; You, Me and Dupree, 2006; The Sentinel, 2006; King of California, 2007; Beyond a Reasonable Doubt, 2009; Ghosts of Girlfriends Past, 2009; Solitary Man, 2009; Behind the Candelabra, 2013 (Best Actor in a Mini-Series or TV Movie, Golden Globe Awards, 2014); Last Vegas, 2014; And So It Goes, 2014; The Reach, 2014; *producer:* One Flew Over the Cuckoo's Nest, 1975; Flatliners, 1990; (jtly) Made in America, 1993; The Rainmaker, 1997; A Song for David, 2000; Ant-Man, 2015; *actor and producer:* The China Syndrome, 1979; Romancing the Stone, 1984; The Jewel of the Nile, 1985; Fatal Attraction, 1987; Wall Street, 1988 (Academy Award for best actor); A Perfect Murder, 1998; Wonder Boys, 1999; Still Life, 1999; One Night at McCool's, 2001; It Runs in the Family, 2003; The Sentinel, 2006; narrator, One Day in September (documentary), 2000; Wall Street: Money Never Sleeps, 2010; *television* includes: Streets of San Francisco, 1972–76. UN Messenger of Peace, 1998; UN Ambassador for Nuclear Disarmament, 2000. Genesis Foundn Prize, Israel, 2015. *Address:* c/o William Morris Endeavor, 9601 Wilshire Boulevard, Beverly Hills, CA 90210, USA.

DOUGLAS, Neil; Sheriff of North Strathclyde at Paisley, 1996–2014; *b* 15 Oct. 1945; *s* of Dr Neil Douglas and Doreen Douglas; *m* 1971, Morag Isles; two *d*. *Educ:* Glasgow Acad.; Glasgow Univ. (LLB). Solicitor, 1968; Notary Public, 1972. Trainee solicitor, Brechin Welsh & Risk, Glasgow, 1968–70; Asst Solicitor, Ross Harper & Murphy, Glasgow, 1970–72; Partner, Brechin Robb, Glasgow, 1972–95; Floating Sheriff, All Scotland, 1995–96. *Recreations:* hill-walking, ski-ing, Scottish country dancing.

DOUGLAS, Prof. Sir Neil (James), Kt 2009; MD, DSc; FRCP, FRCPE; Professor of Respiratory and Sleep Medicine, University of Edinburgh, 1995–2012, now Emeritus; President, Royal College of Physicians of Edinburgh, 2004–10 (Dean, 1995–2000; Vice-President, 2000–03); Chairman, Faculty of Medical Leadership and Management, since 2011; *b* 28 May 1949; *s* of Sir Donald Macleod Douglas, MBE and of (Margaret) Diana Douglas; *m* 1977, Susan McLaren Galloway; one *s* one *d*. *Educ:* Glenalmond Coll.; St Andrews Univ. (Schol.); Univ. of Edinburgh (MB ChB 1973; MD 1983; DSc 2003). FRCPE 1985; FRCP 1998. University of Edinburgh: Lectr in Medicine, 1975–83; Sen. Lectr, 1983–91; Reader in Medicine, 1991–95. MRC Fellow, Univ. of Colorado, 1980–81; Dir, Scottish Nat. Sleep Centre, Royal Infirmary, Edinburgh, 1983–2004. Chm., Acad. of Med. Royal Colls, 2009–12. Hon. Sec., British Thoracic Soc., 1988–90. Ed.-in-Chief, Clinical Science, 1990–92. Hon. MD St Andrews, 2007. *Publications:* Clinicians' Guide to Sleep Medicine, 2002; over 300 papers in jls, mainly on breathing during sleep. *Recreations:* hill-walking, fishing, ski-ing, sailing. *E:* n.j.douglas@ed.ac.uk.

DOUGLAS, Richard Philip, CB 2006; Director General, Finance and NHS (formerly Director of Finance, then Director General Finance and Chief Operating Officer, later Director General, Policy, Strategy and Finance), Department of Health, since 2001; *b* 20 Nov. 1956; *s* of William Ronald Douglas and Margery Alice Douglas; *m* 1978, Carole Elizabeth Hodgson; two *s* one *d*. *Educ:* Archbishop Holgate's Grammar Sch., York; Hull Univ. (BA Hons). HM Customs and Excise, 1978–80; Exchequer and Audit Dept, later Nat. Audit Office, 1980–96 (Dir, 1994–96); Dep. Dir of Finance, NHS Exec., 1996–99; Dir of Finance, Nat. Savings, 1999–2001; Hd, Govt Finance Profession, HM Treasury, 2011–14. Mem., CIPFA, 1983. *Recreations:* reading, gardening, walking. *Address:* Department of Health, Richmond House, 79 Whitehall, SW1A 2NS.

DOUGLAS, Robert Harold, CBE 2005; DL; Director, Douglas Associates Ltd, since 2000; Chairman, UK Space Agency Steering Board, since 2011; *b* Gosforth, Northumberland, 27 July 1948; *s* of Robert Francis Douglas and Cecily Isabel Douglas (*née* Mills); *m* 1972, Hilary Kay Black (*see* H. K. Douglas); two *s*. *Educ:* Fettes Coll., Edinburgh; Churchill Coll., Cambridge (BA Anglo-Saxon and Old Norse 1971; MA); Univ. of Liverpool (Dip. Study of Records and Admin of Archives 1972). Assistant archivist: Hudson's Bay Co., 1972–73; Guildhall Liby, London, 1973–74; HM Inspector of Taxes, Inland Revenue, 1974–80; Royal Dutch Shell: Tax Advr, 1980–85; Shell UK Tax Manager, 1985–88; Hd, Internat. Tax, 1989–91; Area Co-ordinator, Far East, 1992–95; Chief Executive: Belgian Shell, 1995–96; Shell Italia, 1997; Vice-Pres., Mergers, Acquisitions and Competitive Intelligence, Global Exploration and Prodn, 1997–99. Chm., Iceni Oil and Gas Ltd, 2007. Member: Energy Gp Adv. Bd, DTI, 2004–06; Bd, Small Business Service, 2006–07; Fair Mkts Gp Adv. Bd, BERR, later BIS, 2007–10. Chm., Surrey, 2000–07, Mem., SE Regl Council, 2007–10, LSC; Member: Bd, SEEDA, 2001–07 and 2009–12 (Dep. Chm., 2003–07; Chm., 2009–12); Bd, HEFCE, 2008–13. Gov. and Trustee, Nat. Centre for Langs, CILT, 2007–10. Chm., Queen Elizabeth's Foundn for Disabled People, 2011–. Trustee: Walton Charity, 2011–; The Lightbox, Woking, 2012. High Sheriff, 2010–11, DL, 2012, Surrey. FRSA. *Recreations:* walking, bird watching, opera, foreign travel, languages. *Address:* c/o Queen Elizabeth's Foundation for Disabled People, Leatherhead Court, Woodlands Road, Leatherhead, Surrey KT22 0BN. *Clubs:* Reform, Lansdowne.

DOUGLAS, Hon. Sir Roger (Owen), Kt 1991; MP (ACT NZ) New Zealand, 2008–11; *b* 5 Dec. 1937; *s* of Norman and Jennie Douglas; *m* 1961, Glennis June Anderson; one *s* one *d*. *Educ:* Auckland Grammar Sch.; Auckland Univ. (Accountancy Degree). Company Sec. and Acct. MP (Lab) Manurewa, 1969–90; Cabinet Minister, NZ, 1972–75; Minister in Charge of Inland Revenue Dept and Minister in Charge of Friendly Societies, 1984; Minister of Finance, 1984–88; Minister of Immigration and Minister of Police, 1989–90. Director: Brierley Investments Ltd, 1990–99 (Chm., 1998); Aetna Health NZ Ltd, 1995–99; John Fairfax Hldgs, 1997–98. Finance Minister of the Year, Euromoney Mag., 1985; Freedom Prize, Max Schmidheiny Foundn, 1996; Ludwig Erhard Prize for Economic Journalism, 1997; Friedrich von Hayek Medal, 2001. *Publications:* There's Got to be a Better Way, 1981; papers on NZ economy: An Alternative Budget, 1980; Proposal for Taxation, 1981; Toward Prosperity, 1987; Unfinished Business, 1993; Completing the Circle, 1996. *Recreations:* cricket, Rugby League, reading. *Address:* 411 Redoubt Road, Totara Park, Auckland 2016, New Zealand. *T:* (9) 2639596.

DOUGLAS, Rowan Malcolm; Chief Executive Officer, Global Analytics, Willis Re, since 2010; *b* Woking, 12 Dec. 1968; *s* of David and Marlene Douglas; *m* 2005, Dr Ana Gonzalez Pelaez; one *s* one *d*. *Educ:* Shebbear Coll., N Devon; Univ. of Durham (BA Hons Geog.); Bristol Univ. (MPhil Geog.). Asst underwriter, M. W. Petzold and others, Lloyd's, 1992–94; Founder and Man. Dir, WIRE Ltd, 1994–2000; with Willis Gp, 2000–; Chm., Willis Res. Network, 2006–. Member: Investment and Innovation Cttee, NESTA, 2005–06; NERC, 2008– (Mem., Audit Cttee, 2011–). Member: External Adv. Cttee, Sch. of Engrg, Computing and Maths, Univ. of Exeter, 2008–11; Adv. Council, Inst. of Hazard, Risk and Resilience, Durham Univ., 2008–11; Adv. Cttee, Earth Systems Lab., Nat. Center for Atmospheric Res., Boulder, Colo, 2010–; Co-Chair, Willis Res. Network Capital Forum, Georgia State Univ., 2011–. Mem., Governing Bd, Global Earthquake Model Foundn, 2009–. Member: Private Sector Adv. Gp, UN Internat. Strategy for Disaster Reduction, Geneva, 2010–; Insce Commn, UN Envmt Prog. Finance Initiative, Geneva, 2010–; Prime Minister's Council for Sci. and Technol., 2011–. Hon. Vis. Res. Fellow, Sci. and Technol. Policy Res. Unit, Univ. of Sussex, 1995–2000. *Recreation:* anything with Ana. *Address:* Willis Building, 51 Lime Street, EC3M 7DQ. *E:* rowan.douglas@willis.com. *Club:* Athenæum.

DOUGLAS, Steven Franklyn; Partner, Altair Consultancy & Advisory Services Ltd (formerly Director, DouglasWood Ltd (housing, regeneration and development consultants)), since 2009; *b* Hackney, 1964; *s* of Baldwin Douglas and Pamela Douglas (*née* Rodney); four *s*. *Educ:* Sedgehill Comprehensive Sch.; Corpus Christi Coll., Oxford (BA PPE 1985). Sen. Valuation Surveyor, London & Quadrant Housing Trust, 1986–89; Hd of Develt, London & Quadrant Housing Trust, 1989–94; Chief Executive: Spitalfields Housing Assoc., 1994–96; ASRA Housing Assoc., 1996–2001; Housing Corporation: Dir, Investment and Regeneration, 2001–04; Dir (London), 2004–05; Dep. Chief Exec., 2005–06; Chief Exec., 2007–08. Member: Callcutt rev. gp into house bldg delivery, 2006–07; Commn on Integration and Cohesion, 2006–07. Vice Chm., Williams Commn into Design and Quality in Thames Gateway, 2006–07. Chairman: London Housing Fedn Develt Gp, 1994–97; Greenwich Jt Commng Forum, 1994–99; London Develt Conf., 1997–99; Vice-Chm., AmicusHorizon Housing Gp, 2009–; Member: Housing Mgt and Maintenance Cttee, Nat. Housing Fedn, 1994–99; Bd, Hexagon Housing Assoc., 1994–99. Trustee: Richmix, 2010–; Commonweal Social Justice Charity. *Recreations:* football, watching and playing, particularly with my boys, Aaron, Ethan, Freddie and Theo, Arsenal, R&B music, Mary J. Blige, dancing. *Address:* Altair Consultancy & Advisory Services Ltd, Tempus Wharf, 29a Bermondsey Wall West, SE16 4SA.

DOUGLAS, Susan Margaret; media consultant, since 2009; Co-founder, Phoenix Newspaper Publishing Ltd, 2012; New Business Director, The Tab, since 2015; *b* 29 Jan. 1957; *d* of Kenneth Frank Douglas and Vivienne Mary Douglas; *m* 1994, Niall Campbell Ferguson, *qv* (marr. diss. 2011); two *s* one *d*. *Educ:* Tiffin Girls' Sch., Kingston; Southampton Univ. (BSc Hons Biochem.). Management consultant, Arthur Andersen & Co., 1978–79; Haymarket Publishing, 1979; reporter, writer, Sunday Express, Johannesburg, 1979–80; Mail on Sunday: medical corresp., 1980–81; Features Editor and Associate Editor, 1981–86; Asst Editor, Daily Mail, 1986–91; Sunday Times: Associate Editor, 1991–94; Dep. Editor, 1995; Editor, Sunday Express, 1996; Consultant Editor, Scotsman, Scotland on Sunday, Edinburgh Evening News, Sunday Business, and Gear magazine (NY), 1997–2001; Exec. Consultant, Sunday Business, 1998–2001; Dir, 1999–2001, Pres., 2001–07, New Business, Condé Nast; New Business Dir, Peters Fraser and Dunlop, 2008–09; Publisher, Sunday brands, Trinity Mirror, 2013–14. Media consultant: HarperCollins, 2009; Future Publishing, 2009–10; LuxeTV, 2010–; New Business Dir, Barefoot Books, 2010–; Dir, Lingospot Media Software, 2010–. Member: Develt Bd and Med. Develt Bd, Univ. of Oxford, 2008–; Develt Cttee, Globe Th., 2008–10; Media Bd, Prince's Foundn for Children and the Arts, 2008–; K. T. Wong Foundn for Cultural Exchange with China, 2011. *Recreations:* riding, shooting. *Address:* Middle Park Farm, Beckley, Oxon OX3 9SX. *E:* susandouglas@aol.com. *Clubs:* Arts, Chelsea Arts, Ivy, Royal Automobile, Soho House.

DOUGLAS, (William) Barry, OBE 2002; concert pianist; *b* 23 April 1960; *m* Deirdre O'Hara; two *s* one *d*. *Educ:* Royal College of Music; private study with Maria Curcio. Gold Medal, Tchaikovsky International Piano Competition, Moscow, 1986; Berlin Philharmonic début, 1987; engagements incl. regular appearances in major European, US and Far East cities; European première, Penderecki piano concerto Resurrection, 2002. Artistic Founder Dir, Camerata Ireland, 1999– (first all-Ireland orch.; concerts in Ireland and abroad; début USA tour, 2001). Prince Consort Prof. of Piano, Royal Coll. of Music, 1998–. Recordings incl. Tchaikovsky Concerto No 1 and Sonata in G, Mussorgsky Pictures at an Exhibition, Brahms Piano Quintet in F minor and Piano Concerto No 1, Liszt Concertos Nos 1 and 2, Beethoven Sonata Op 106, Prokofiev Sonatas 2 and 7, Rachmaninov Concerto No 2, Reger Concerto, Strauss Burleske, Britten Concerto, Debussy Fantaisie, Brahms: works for solo piano vol. 1, vol. 2, vol. 3, Schubert: works for solo piano vol. 1, Celtic Reflections. Vis. Fellow, Oriel Coll., Oxford, 1992–93. Hon. DMus QUB, 1986. *Recreations:* driving, reading, food and wine. *Address:* c/o IMG Artists, The Light Box, 111 Power Road, Chiswick, W4 5PY.

DOUGLAS, Dr Zachary; QC 2015; Associate Professor of International Law, Graduate Institute, Geneva, since 2011; *b* Melbourne, Australia, 23 Oct. 1974; *s* of Ronald and Susan Douglas; *m* 2007, Marion Colombani; one *s* two *d*. *Educ:* Univ. of Melbourne (BA, LLB Hons); Univ. of Oxford (BCL Hons); Univ. of Cambridge (MA, PhD). Solicitor-Advocate, Freshfields, Paris, 2001–05; called to the Bar, Gray's Inn, 2006; Lecturer: UCL, 2005–07; Univ. of Cambridge, 2007–11. *Publications:* The International Law of Investment Claims, 2009; contrib. British Yearbook of Internat. Law; contribs to jls incl. Internat. and Comparative Law Qly. *Recreations:* sailing, ski-ing, jazz. *Address:* Matrix Chambers, Griffin Building, Gray's Inn, WC1R 5LN. *T:* (020) 7407 3447. *E:* zacharydouglas@matrixlaw.co.uk. *Clubs:* Royal Ocean Racing; Société Nautique de Genève.

DOUGLAS-HAMILTON, family name of **Duke of Hamilton and Brandon, Earldom of Selkirk** and **Baron Selkirk of Douglas**.

DOUGLAS-HOME, family name of **Earl of Home** and **Baroness Dacre**.

DOUGLAS-HOME, Jessica Violet, (Lady Leach of Fairford); painter; freelance theatre set and costume designer, since 1968; *b* 7 Feb. 1944; *d* of John Gwynne and Patricia (*née* Morrison-Bell); *m* 1st, 1966, Charles Cospatrick Douglas-Home (*d* 1985), Editor, The Times; two *s*; 2nd, 1993, (Charles Guy) Rodney Leach (*see* Baron Leach of Fairford). *Educ:* Cranborne Chase Sch.; Chelsea Sch. of Art; Slade Sch. of Fine Art. Productions include: When We Are Married, RNT, 1979; Watch on the Rhine, 1980; Anyone for Dennis, Whitehall, 1981; The Mikado, Savoy, 1989. Solo exhibns of paintings and etchings in London, Brussels, Washington and Princeton, USA, 1977–85. Worked with dissidents behind the Iron Curtain, 1983–90. Trustee: Jan Hus Foundn and Jagiellonian Trust, 1983–; Butrint Foundn, 2002–12; Founder and Chm., Mihai Eminescu Trust, 1987–. Europa Nostra Cultural Heritage Award, 2007. Officer, National Order for Faithful Service (Romania), 2007; Knight, Order of the Crown (Romania), 2014. *Publications:* Violet: the life and loves of Violet Gordon Woodhouse, 1996; Once Upon Another Time, 2000; A Glimpse of Empire, 2011; contributed drawings: Book on Dinosaurs, 1975; Love Life, 1979; The English Taste, 1991. *Recreations:* reading, riding. *Address:* Knights Mill, Quenington, Cirencester, Glos GL7 5BN.

DOUGLAS HOME, Mark; author; Editor, The Herald, 2000–05; *b* 31 Aug. 1951; *s* of late Edward Charles Douglas Home and Nancy Rose Douglas Home; *m* 1976, Colette O'Reilly; one *s* one *d*. *Educ:* Eton Coll.; Univ. of Witwatersrand. Scottish corresp., The Independent, 1986–90; News Ed., 1990–93, Asst Ed., 1993–94, The Scotsman; Deputy Editor: Scotland on Sunday, 1994–98; Sunday Times Scotland, 1998–99; Scotland Editor, Sunday Times, 1999–2000. *Publications:* The Sea Detective (novel), 2011; The Woman Who Walked into the Sea (novel), 2013; The Malice of Waves, 2015. *Recreation:* gardening.

DOUGLAS MILLER, Robert Alexander Gavin; Director, Edinburgh Worldwide Investment Trust, 1988–2008; *b* 11 Feb. 1937; *s* of late F. G. Douglas Miller and Mora Kennedy; *m* 1963, Judith Madeleine Smith; three *s* one *d*. *Educ:* Harrow; Oxford Univ. (MA). 9th Lancers, 1955–57; Oxford, 1958–61. Treasurer, Queen's Body Guard for Scotland (Royal Company of Archers), 1977–88. Chm., Jenners (Princes St Edinburgh) Ltd, 1975–2005; Director: Kennington Leasing Ltd, 1977–2005; Dunedin Income Growth Trust, 1988–2006. Pres., Edinburgh Chamber of Commerce & Manufactures, 1985–87. Mem., Kyle & Sutherland Fishery Bd, 1980–2007; Member, Council: Assoc. of Scottish Salmon Fishery Bds, 1984–90; Atlantic Salmon Trust, 1989–90; Chm., Game Conservancy (Scotland), 1990–94. Chm., Outreach Trust, 1976–94. Pres., Royal Warrant Holders, 1987–88. *Recreations:* shooting, fishing. *Address:* Bavelaw Castle, Balerno, Midlothian EH14 7JS. *T:* (0131) 449 3972; Forneth Estate, Blairgowrie, Perthshire PH10 6SN. *T:* (01250) 884255. *Club:* New (Edinburgh).

DOUGLAS-PENNANT, family name of **Baron Penrhyn**.

DOUGLAS-SCOTT, Prof. Sionaidh; Professor of European and Human Rights Law, University of Oxford, since 2008; Fellow, Lady Margaret Hall, Oxford; *b* Edinburgh, 1959; *m* 1st, 1984, Michael Douglas-Scott; 2nd, 2009, Peter Winship; two *s* one *d*. *Educ:* St Denis Sch., Edinburgh; Edinburgh Acad.; University Coll. London (BA Hons); London Sch. of Econs and Pol Sci. (LLM); City Univ. (DipLaw); MA Oxon. Called to the Bar, Inner Temple; Lectr, Reader, then Prof., KCL, 1991–2007. Vis. Prof., Univ. of Bonn, 1994. *Publications:* (ed with O. Tadros) Faith in Law, 2000; Constitutional Law of the European Union, 2002, 2nd edn 2013; Law After Modernity, 2013; contrib. articles on EU law, public law and legal theory. *Address:* Lady Margaret Hall, Oxford OX2 6QA.

DOUGLAS-SCOTT-MONTAGU, family name of **Baron Montagu of Beaulieu**.

DOULTON, John Hubert Farre; Principal, Elizabeth College, Guernsey, 1988–98; *b* 2 Jan. 1942; *s* of late Alfred John Farre, CBE, TD; *m* 1986, Margaret Anne (*née* Ball); two step *d*. *Educ:* Rugby School; Keble College, Oxford (1st Mods, 2nd Greats). Teacher: Rugby, 1965–66; Radley, 1966–88. *Recreations:* music, walking, boats, foreign travel, carpentry. *Address:* 15 Hungerford Hill, Lambourn, Berks RG17 8NP.

DOUNE, Lord; Jack Alexander Stuart; *b* 30 Nov. 2002; *s* and *heir* of Earl of Moray, *qv*.

DOURO, Marquess of, courtesy title of Duke of Wellington, not used by current heir; *see* Earl of Mornington.

DOVE, Arthur Allan, CBE 1998; CEng, CStat; Chairman, Council for Registered Gas Installers, 1994–2000; *b* 20 May 1933; *s* of William Joseph Dove and Lucy Frances Dove; *m* 1958, Nancy Iris Powell; two *s* one *d*. *Educ:* Taunton's Sch., Southampton; King's Coll. and London Sch. of Econs and Pol Science, Univ. of London (BSc; AKC 1954). CEng, FIGEM (FIGasE 1974); MIS 1962. Asst Statistician, 1958, Marketing Officer, 1961, Southern Gas; Controller of Sales and Marketing, Scottish Gas, 1965; Commercial Sales Manager, Gas Council, 1969; Dep. Chm., South Eastern Gas, 1973; Regl Chm., British Gas plc, S Eastern, 1982–87, N Thames, 1988–91; Managing Director: Regions, 1991–92; Regl Services, 1992–93. Chm., Parkside Housing Gp, 1998–2002. *Recreation:* sailing. *Address:* 19 Sunning Avenue, Ascot, Berks SL5 9PN.

DOVE, Claire, OBE 2013 (MBE 1993); DL; Chief Executive, Blackburne House Group (formerly Women's Technology and Education Centre), since 1985; *b* Liverpool, 29 Aug. 1952; *d* of B. L. Dove and Frances Murnane; *m* 2004, Colin V. F. Henfrey; three *s* one *d*. *Educ:* Univ. of Liverpool (BA Hons). Chairman: Social Enterprise UK (formerly Social Enterprise Coalition), 2007–; Liverpool Fairness Commn. Mem. Bd, Charity Commn, 2013–. Former Dep. Chm., Liverpool Community Coll.; former Mem. Bd, Liverpool John Moores Univ. DL Merseyside, 2005. FRSA. Queen's Lifetime Achievement Award for Enterprise Promotion, 2013. *Address:* Blackburne House Group, Blackburne House, Blackburne Place, off Hope Street, Liverpool L8 7PE. *T:* (0151) 708 3932. *E:* clairedove@blackburnehouse.co.uk.

DOVE, Hon. Sir Ian William, Kt 2014; **Hon. Mr Justice Dove;** a Judge of the High Court, Queen's Bench Division, since 2014; *b* 31 Dec. 1963; *s* of Jack Richard Dove and Janet Yvonne Dove; *m* 1988, Juliet Caroline Gladston; two *s*. *Educ:* Northampton Sch. for Boys; St Catherine's Coll., Oxford (MA); Inns of Court Sch. of Law. Called to the Bar, Inner Temple,

1986, Bencher, 2010; QC 2003; a Recorder, 2003–14; a Dep. High Ct Judge, 2008–14. Immigration Adjudicator (pt-time), 2001–04; Mem., Immigration Appeal Tribunal, 2004–05; an Immigration Judge, 2005–14. *Recreations:* supporting Northampton Saints and Aston Villa FC, walking, poetry, the visual arts, good food, music, bell ringing. *Address:* Royal Courts of Justice, Rolls Building, Fetter Lane, EC4A 1NL.

DOVE, Jonathan; composer; National Theatre Associate, since 2003; *b* 18 July 1959; *s* of Myles Harrison Dove and Deirdre Cecily Dove. *Educ:* St Joseph's Acad., Blackheath; ILEA Centre for Young Musicians; Trinity Coll., Cambridge (MA); Goldsmiths' Coll., London (MMus). Asst Chorus Master, Glyndebourne, 1987–88; Music Advr, Almeida Th., 1990–2009; Artistic Director, Spitalfields Fest., 2001–06. Composer of scores for 30 plays (Almeida, NT, RSC) and of music for film and television. Trustee: Stephen Oliver Trust, 1997–2006; Michael Tippett Foundn, 1999–. Patron: London Fest. of Contemp. Church Music, 2007–; Durham Opera Ensemble, 2007–. Hon. RAM, 2013. Hon. DMus East London, 2006. *Compositions* include: Figures in the Garden, 1991; Seaside Postcards, Tuning In, 1995; The Ringing Isle, 1997; The Magic Flute Dances, 1999; The Passing of the Year, 2000; Stargazer, Out of Time, 2001; Moonlight Revels, Koethener Messe, 2002; The Middleham Jewel, The Far Theatricals of Day, Run to the Edge, The Crocodiamond, 2003; Out of Winter, 2003; Across the Walls, 2004; All the Future Days, 2004; On Spital Fields, Work in Progress: Fourteen Site-Visits for Piano and Orch. with Film, 2004; Airport Scenes, 2005; Hojoki, 2006; It sounded as if the Streets were running, 2007; Minterne, 2007; There Was a Child, 2008; Missa Brevis, Piano Quintet, 2009; River Songs, A Song of Joys, Innocence, 2010; Cut My Shadow, Three Tennyson Songs, 2011; Two Sonnets, The Pied Piper, 2011; The Immortal Ship, The Wells Service, A Portrait of Aung San Suu Kyi, Diana and Actaeon (ballet), 2012; The Portsmouth Service, Out of the Whirlwind, Who Wrote the Book of Love?, 2013; Gaia Theory, Psalms for Leo, 2014; For an Unknown Soldier, The Dancing Pipes, Te Deum, 2014; *operas:* Pig, 1992; L'Augellino Belverde, Siren Song, 1994; Flight, 1998; Tobias and the Angel, 1999; The Palace in the Sky, 2000; The Hackney Chronicles, L'Altra Euridice, 2001; When She Died: Death of a Princess, 2002; La Dama ed il Pulitore di Damasco, Le Porte di Bagdad, 2003; Kwasi & Kwame (formerly The Two Hearts of Kwasi Boachi), 2005; The Enchanted Pig, Man on the Moon, An Old Way to Pay New Debts, 2006; The Adventures of Pinocchio, 2007; Swanhunter, Seven Angels, 2009; Mansfield Park, 2010; Life is a Dream, The Walk from the Garden, 2012; The Day After, The Monster in the Maze, 2015. *Recreation:* photography. *Address:* c/o Peters Edition Ltd, 2-6 Baches Street, N1 6DN. *T:* (020) 7553 4000.

DOVER, Bishop Suffragan of, since 2010; **Rt Rev. Trevor Willmott;** *b* 29 March 1950; *s* of Frederick and Phyllis Willmott; *m* 1973, Margaret Anne Hawkins; one *d*. *Educ:* St Peter's Coll., Oxford (MA); Fitzwilliam Coll., Cambridge (DipTh); Westcott House, Cambridge. Ordained deacon, 1974, priest, 1975; Asst Curate, St George's, Norton, 1974–78; Asst Chaplain, Oslo with Trondheim, 1978–79; Chaplain of Naples with Capri, Bari and Sorrento, 1979–83; Rector of Ecton, 1983–89; Diocesan Dir of Ordinands and Post Ordination Training, Peterborough, 1986–97; Canon Residentiary of Peterborough Cathedral, 1989–97; Archdeacon of Durham, 1997–2002; Bishop Suffragan of Basingstoke, 2002–09. *Recreations:* travel, cooking, the appreciation of good wine, sport, music. *Address:* The Bishop's Office, Old Palace, The Precincts, Canterbury CT1 2EE. *T:* (01227) 459382. *E:* trevor.willmott@bishcant.org.

DOVER, Den; Member, North West Region, England, European Parliament, 1999–2009 (C, 1999–2008; Ind, 2008–09); *b* 4 April 1938; *s* of Albert and Emmie Dover; *m* 1st, 1959, Anne Marina Wright (marr. diss. 1986); one *s* one *d*; 2nd, 1989, Kathleen Edna Fisher. *Educ:* Manchester Grammar Sch.; Manchester Univ. BSc Hons. CEng, MICE. John Laing & Son Ltd, 1959–68; National Building Agency: Dep. Chief Executive, 1969–70; Chief Exec., 1971–72; Projects Dir, Capital and Counties Property Co. Ltd, 1972–75; Contracts Manager, Wimpey Laing Iran, 1975–77. Director of Housing Construction, GLC, 1977–79. Member, London Borough of Barnet Council, 1968–71. MP (C) Chorley, 1979–97; contested (C) same seat, 1997. Mem., Commons Select Cttee on Transport, 1979–87, on Envmt, 1995–97. European Parliament: Budgets Spokesman, 2000–05; Regl Develt Spokesman, 2005; Chief Whip (C), 2007–08. *Recreations:* cricket, hockey, golf; Methodist. *Address:* 166 Furzehill Road, Boreham Wood, Herts WD6 2DS. *T:* (020) 8953 5945.

DOW, Carol, CMG 2003; Chief Medical Adviser, Foreign and Commonwealth Office, 1998–2003; Consultant in Occupational Health, Guy's and St Thomas' Hospital NHS Trust, London, 1989–2003; *b* 3 April 1951; *d* of John Dickson Dow and Catherine Dow (*née* Robertson). *Educ:* St Bartholomew's Hospital Medical Sch., London Univ. (MB BS 1976; DTM&H 1988); Univ. of Glasgow (Dip. Travel Medicine 1996). MRCP 1981; AFOM 1992. Registrar, St George's Hosp., 1982–86; Malaria Emergency Unit and Air Evacuation Service, African Med. and Res. Foundn, Nairobi, 1983–84; Registrar, Hosp. for Tropical Diseases, London, 1986–88; Med. Registrar, Middlesex Hosp., 1988–89; Principal Med. Advr, FCO, 1989–98. *Publications:* (contrib.) Health Information for Overseas Travel, 1995, 2nd edn 2001; (contrib.) Dawood's Travellers' Health: how to stay healthy abroad, 4th edn 2002. *Recreations:* travel, fishing, hill-walking, medicine. *Address:* Upper Camerory, Ballieward, Grantown-on-Spey, Moray PH26 3PR. *T:* (01479) 872548. *E:* carol.dow146@btinternet.com.

DOW, Rear-Adm. Douglas Morrison, CB 1991; DL; Director, National Trust for Scotland, 1992–97; *b* 1 July 1935; *s* of George Torrance Dow and Grace Morrison MacFarlane; *m* 1959, Felicity Margaret Mona Napier, *d* of John Watson Napier and Beatrix Mary Carson; two *s*. *Educ:* George Heriot's School; BRNC Dartmouth. Joined RN, 1952; served HMS Sheffield, 1957–59; Staff of C-in-C Plymouth, 1959–61; HMS Plymouth, 1961–63; RN Supply Sch., 1963–65; Staff of Comdr FEF, 1965–67; HMS Endurance, 1968–70; BRNC Dartmouth, 1970–72; Asst Dir, Officer Appointments (S), 1972–74; Sec. to Comdr British Navy Staff, Washington, 1974–76; HMS Tiger, 1977–78; NDC Latimer, 1978–79; CSO(A) to Flag Officer Portsmouth, 1979; Sec. to Controller of the Navy, 1981; Captain, HMS Cochrane, 1983; Commodore, HMS Centurion, 1985; RCDS 1988; Dir Gen., Naval Personal Services, 1989–92. Hon. ADC to the Queen, 1986–89. President: South Queensferry Sea Cadets, 1994–2009; Royal Naval Assoc., Edin., 1996–. Gov., George Heriot's Sch., 1993–2009 (Vice Chm., 1997–2009). DL Edinburgh, 1996. *Recreations:* Royal Navy Rugby Union (Chairman, 1985–91), fly fishing, shooting, golf, gardening.

DOW, Rt Rev. Geoffrey Graham; Bishop of Carlisle, 2000–09; an Honorary Assistant Bishop: Diocese of Chester, since 2009; Diocese of Manchester, since 2011; *b* 4 July 1942; *s* of Ronald Graham Dow and Dorothy May Dow (*née* Christie); *m* 1966, Molly Patricia (*née* Sturges); three *s* one *d*. *Educ:* St Albans Sch.; Queen's Coll., Oxford (BA 1963; BSc 1965; MA 1968; MSc 1981); Clifton Theol Coll.; Birmingham Univ. (Dip. Pastoral Studies 1974); Nottingham Univ. (MPhil 1982). Ordained deacon, 1967, priest, 1968; Asst Curate, Tonbridge Parish Church, 1967–72; Chaplain-Student, St John's Coll., Oxford, 1972–75; Lectr in Christian Doctrine, St John's Coll., Nottingham, 1975–81; Vicar, Holy Trinity, Coventry, 1981–92; Canon Theologian, Coventry Cathedral, 1988–92; Area Bp of Willesden, 1992–2000. Chairman: Govs, St Martin's Coll., 2002–08; Council, Ridley Hall, 2003–10; Mem., Gov. Body, Univ. of Cumbria, 2007–09. Trustee, Settle and Carlisle Railway Trust, 2009–. *Publications:* Dark Satanic Mills? Shaftesbury Project, 1979; The Local Church's Political Responsibility, 1980; St John's College Extension Studies B1—God and the World, 1980; Whose Hand on the Tiller?, 1983; Those Tiresome Intruders, 1990; Explaining Deliverance, 1991; Christian Renewal in Europe, 1992; A Christian Understanding of Daily Work, 1994; Pathways of Prayer, 1996; Reader Upbeat!, 2008; When He Comes, 2010; Leading Rural Churches for Growth, 2015. *Recreations:* steam and narrow gauge railways, model railways, travel, music, political biographies. *Address:* 34 Kimberley Avenue, Romiley, Stockport SK6 4AB.

DOW, Simon Charles; Chief Executive, The Guinness Partnership (formerly Guinness Trust Group), since 2001; *b* 21 Sept. 1950; *s* of Alan Dow and Rosamund Dow; *m* 1984, Virginia Anne, *d* of late Arthur Charles William Crook; one *s* one *d*. *Educ:* King's Sch., Chester; United World Coll. of the Atlantic (Internat. Bacc.; RNLI coxswain); SOAS, London Univ. (BA Hons); Brunel Univ. (MA Public Admin). Notting Hill Housing Trust, 1974–78; Dep. Dir, New Islington and Hackney Housing Assoc., 1978–87; Sen. Regulation Manager, Housing Corp., 1985–87 (on secondment); Gp Chief Exec., Samuel Lewis Housing Trust, subseq. Southern Housing Gp, 1987–95; Housing Corporation: Dep. Chief Exec., 1995–97; Chief Ops Officer, 1997–2000; Actg Chief Exec. and Accounting Officer, 2000. Dir, ARHAG Housing Assoc., 2006–08. Chm., 1991–2006 and 2013–, Mem. Bd, 1991–, London Housing Foundn; Dir, Housing Forum, 2000–02 (Chm., Off-site Manufg Gp, 2001–03); Member: Nat. Council, 2002–06, Bd of Dirs, 2003–06, Nat. Housing Fedn; Dep. Prime Minister's Home Ownership Task Force, 2003; Ministerial Adv. Gp on Planning Obligations, 2004–05; ODPM Ministerial Task Force on Planning Obligations, 2004–06; Ind. Ext. Chm., Audit Cttee, Ind. Police Complaints Commn, 2005–09; Cave Review of Social Housing Regulation, 2006–07; Chair, Homeless Internat., 2011– (Mem., Financial Services Gp, 2010–; Mem. Council, 2010–). MInstD 2003; FRSA 2009. Nat. Private Pilot's Licence, 2009. *Recreations:* sailing, flying, being outdoors. *Address:* The Guinness Partnership, 17 Mendy Street, High Wycombe, Bucks HP11 2NZ. *T:* (01494) 535823. *E:* simon.dow@guinness.org.uk.

DOWD, James Patrick; MP (Lab) Lewisham West and Penge, since 2010 (Lewisham West, 1992–2010); *b* Germany, 5 March 1951; *s* of late James Patrick Dowd and Elfriede Anna Dowd (*née* Janocha). *Educ:* Dalmain JM&I Sch., London; Sedgehill Comprehensive, London; London Nautical School. Apprentice telephone engineer, GPO, 1967–72; Station Manager, Heron petrol stations, 1972–73; Telecomms Engineer, Plessey Co., later GPT, 1973–92. Group Rep. and Br. Cttee, PO Engrg Union, 1967–72; Sen. Negotiator, ASTMS, then MSF. Lewisham Council: Councillor, 1974–94: Chief Whip; Chm. of Cttees; Dep. Leader; Dep. Mayor, 1987, 1991; Mayor, 1992. Former Mem., Lewisham and Southwark DHA. Contested (Lab): Beckenham, 1983; Lewisham W, 1987. An Opposition Whip, 1993–95; opposition front-bench spokesman on Northern Ireland, 1995–97; a Lord Comr of HM Treasury (Govt Whip), 1997–2001. Member: Select Cttee on Health, 2001–10; Select Cttee on Sci. and Technol., 2012–. Former school governor. *Recreations:* music, reading, theatre, Cornwall, being with friends. *Address:* House of Commons, SW1A 0AA. *T:* (020) 7219 4617. *Club:* Bromley Labour.

DOWD, Peter; MP (Lab) Bootle, since 2015; *b* Bootle, 20 June 1957. *Educ:* Liverpool Univ.; Lancaster Univ. CQSW. Health and social care worker, Merseyside. Member (Lab): Merseyside CC, 1981–86; Sefton BC, 1991– (Leader, Labour Gp, 2008–15; Leader of Council, 2011–15). *Address:* House of Commons, SW1A 0AA.

DOWDALL, John Michael, CB 2003; Comptroller and Auditor-General for Northern Ireland, 1994–2009; *b* 6 Sept. 1944; *s* of late Lt-Col W. Dowdall, MBE, and E. Dowdall; *m* 1964, Aylerie (*née* Houston); three *s* one *d*. *Educ:* King Edward's Sch., Witley, Surrey; Queen's Univ., Belfast (BScEcon). CPFA 2001. Lectr in Economics, Royal Univ. of Malta, 1966–69; Lectr in Political Econ., King's Coll., Univ. of Aberdeen, 1969–72; Economic Advr, Dept of Commerce, N Ireland, 1972–78, Principal, Dept of Commerce, 1978–82; Asst Sec., Dept of Finance and Personnel, N Ireland, 1982–85; Dep. Chief Exec., Industrial Develt Bd, NI, 1986–89; Under Sec., Dept of Finance and Personnel, NI, 1989–94. Vis. Prof., Faculty of Business and Mgt, Univ. of Ulster, 2002–.

DOWDALLS, Catherine; QC (Scot.) 2013; *b* Hamilton, Scotland, 18 Sept. 1962; *d* of Hugh Kentigern Dowdalls and Mary Dowdalls. *Educ:* Holy Cross High Sch., Hamilton; Univ. of Strathclyde (LLB Hons; DipLP). Admitted as solicitor, 1985; Solicitor, 1985–99; Called to the Bar, 2000; Advocate, specialising in family law, 2000–. *Address:* Advocates Library, Parliament House, Edinburgh EH1 1RF. *T:* (0131) 226 5071. *E:* katedowdalls@amadvocates.co.uk.

DOWDEN, Oliver James, CBE 2015; MP (C) Hertsmere, since 2015; *b* Park St, Herts; *m* Blythe; one *s* one *d*. *Educ:* Parmiters' Sch., Watford; Trinity Hall, Cambridge (BA). Teacher, Japan; lawyer, London; Account Dir, LLM; Dep. Campaigns Dir, Cons. Party; Man. Consultant, Hill and Knowlton Strategies, 2007; Dep. Dir, Political Ops, Cons. Party; Dep. COS and Advr to Prime Minister on policy and political issues, 2012–14. *Address:* House of Commons, SW1A 0AA.

DOWDEN, Penny; *see* Mansfield, P.

DOWDEN, Richard George; Africa analyst and writer; Executive Director, Royal African Society, since 2002; *b* 20 March 1949; *s* of late Peter Dowden and Eleanor Dowden; *m* 1976, Penny Mansfield, *qv*; two *d*. *Educ:* St George's Coll., Weybridge, Surrey; London Univ. (BA History). Volunteer Teacher, Uganda, 1971–72; Asst Sec., Justice and Peace Commn, 1973–76; Editor, Catholic Herald, 1976–79; journalist, The Times, 1980–86; Africa Editor, 1986–94, Diplomatic Editor, 1994–95, The Independent; Africa Editor, The Economist, 1995–2001. Mem. Bd, Nation Media Gp, 2010–. *Publications:* Africa: altered states, ordinary miracles, 2008. *Address:* 7 Highbury Grange, N5 2QB.

DOWDESWELL, Prof. Julian Andrew, PhD; Professor of Physical Geography, since 2001, and Director, Scott Polar Research Institute, since 2002, University of Cambridge; Fellow, Jesus College, Cambridge, since 2002; *b* 18 Nov. 1957; *s* of Robert Dowdeswell and Joan Marion Dowdeswell (*née* Longshaw); *m* 1983, Evelyn Kae Lind; one *s* one *d*. *Educ:* Magdalen Coll. Sch., Oxford; Jesus Coll., Cambridge (BA 1980; schol., 1980; PhD 1985); Univ. of Colorado (MA 1982). Research Associate, Scott Polar Res. Inst., Univ. of Cambridge, 1985; Lectr, Univ. of Wales, Aberystwyth, 1986–89; University of Cambridge: Sen. Asst in Research, 1989–92; Asst Dir of Res., Scott Polar Res. Inst., 1992–94; Dir, Centre for Glaciology, 1994–98, and Dir, Inst. of Geog. and Earth Scis, 1997–98, Univ. of Wales, Aberystwyth; Prof. of Physical Geog. and Dir, Bristol Glaciology Centre, Bristol Univ., 1998–2001. Natural Environment Research Council: Member: Polar Science and Technol. Bd, 1995–97; Earth Scis Res. Grants and Training Awards Cttee, 1996–2000; Polar Scis Expert Gp, 1997–99; Earth Scis Bd, 1997–2000; Peer Review Coll., 2003–06, 2012–. Hd of Glaciers and Ice Sheets Div., Internat. Commn for Snow and Ice, 1999–2011. Chm., UK Nat. Cttee on Antarctic Res., 2002–06; UK Alternate Deleg. to Council, Scientific Cttee on Antarctic Res., 2002–06; UK Deleg. to Council, Internat. Arctic Science Cttee, 2002–10; UK Mem., Arctic Ocean Scis Bd, 2006–10. Mem. Council, Internat. Glaciol Soc., 1993–96. Trustee: Fuchs Foundn, 2008–; Oates Mus., 2010–. Gov., Plascrug Sch., Aberystwyth, 1996–98. FRGS 1985. Polar Medal, 1995; Gill Meml Award, 1998, Founder's Medal, 2008, RGS; Louis Agassiz Medal, Eur. Geoscis Union, 2011; IASC Medal, Internat. Arctic Sci. Cttee, 2014. *Publications:* (ed jtly) Glacimarine Environments: processes and sediments, 1990; (ed jtly) The Arctic and Environmental Change, 1996; (ed jtly) Glacial and Oceanic History of the Polar North Atlantic Margins, 1998; Islands of the Arctic, 2002; (ed jtly) Glacier-influenced sedimentation on high-latitude continental margins, 2002; The Antarctic Paintings of Edward Seago, 2006; papers in learned jls on glaciology, glacier-marine interactions, cryosphere and climate change, and satellite remote sensing of ice. *Recreations:* hill-walking, ski-ing, watching Oxford United FC. *Address:* Jesus College, Cambridge CB5 8BL.

DOWDING, family name of **Baron Dowding**.

DOWDING, 3rd Baron *cr* 1943, of Bentley Priory, Middlesex; **Piers Hugh Tremenheere Dowding;** Professor of English, Okayama Shoka University, Japan, 1999–2013, now Emeritus (Associate Professor, 1977–99); *b* 18 Feb. 1948; *s* of 2nd Baron Dowding and of his 2nd wife, Alison Margaret, *d* of Dr James Bannerman and *widow* of Major R. W. H. Peebles; *S* father, 1992; *m* Noriko Shiho; two *d*. *Educ:* Fettes Coll.; Amherst Coll., Mass (BA 1971). LTCL. Patron, Assoc. of RAF Fighter Control Officers. Life Pres., Dumfries and Galloway Aircrew Assoc., 1996–. *Heir: b* Hon. Mark Denis James Dowding [*b* 11 July 1949; *m* 1982, Heather Arter; one *s*].

DOWDING, Nicholas Alan Tatham; QC 1997; *b* 24 Feb. 1956; *s* of Alan Lorimer Dowding and Jennifer Mary Dowding (*née* Hughes); *m*; three *d*. *Educ:* Radley Coll.; St Catharine's Coll., Cambridge (BA 1978; MA 1982). Called to the Bar, Inner Temple, 1979. Chm., Property Bar Assoc., 2006–08. Hon. RICS 2007. *Publications:* (ed jtly) Handbook of Rent Review, 1980–85; (ed jtly) Woodfall on Landlord and Tenant, 1994–; (jtly) Dilapidations: the modern law and practice, 1995, 5th edn 2013; (ed) Landlord and Tenant Reports, 1998–. *Recreations:* sailing, riding, music, juggling, limericks. *Address:* Falcon Chambers, Falcon Court, EC4Y 1AA. *T:* (020) 7353 2484, *Fax:* (020) 7353 1261. *E:* dowding@falcon-chambers.com.

DOWDING, Hon. Peter M'Callum; SC 2002; barrister; *b* 6 Oct. 1943; *m*; five *c*. *Educ:* Hale School, Perth; Univ. of Western Australia (LLB 1964). Churchill Fellowship, 1974, UK and Canada. In practice as solicitor and barrister until 1983 and as barrister, 1990–; Partner, Briggs Paul Dowding, 1992–94; Man. Partner, DCH Legal Gp, 1994–96. Dir, Biotech Internat. Ltd, 1998–2001. MLC North Province, WA, 1980–86; MLA (ALP) Maylands, 1986–90; Cabinet Member, 1983–90; Minister for: Mines, Fuel and Energy, 1983; Planning, and Employment and Training, 1983–84; Consumer Affairs, 1983–86; Minister assisting the Minister for Public Sector Management, 1984–88; Minister for Works and Services, Labour, Productivity and Employment, and assisting the Treasurer, 1987–88; Treasurer, and Minister for Productivity, 1988–89; Leader, WA Parly Lab. Party, 1987–90; Premier, WA, 1988–90; Minister, Public Sector Management, and Women's Interests, 1989–90. *Recreations:* sailing, bushwalking, reading. *Address:* PO Box 1262, Fremantle, WA 6959, Australia. *T:* (8) 94304411, *Fax:* (8) 94304417. *E:* pdowding@peterdowding.com.au.

DOWDING, Sally; Her Honour Judge Dowding; a Circuit Judge, since 2013; *b* Hereford; *d* of late Edward Charles Wisnom Dowding and Grace Evelyn Dowding (*née* Ridley); *m* 1976; two *d*. *Educ:* Stratford upon Avon Grammar Sch. for Girls; Univ. of Manchester (LLB); Keele Univ. (MA). Admitted as solicitor, 1979; Solicitor, Elwyn Jones and Co., Bangor, 1987–2007; Dep. Dist Judge, 2000–07; Dist Judge, 2007–13. Pres., Gwynedd Law Soc., 2005–06. *Address:* Wolverhampton Combined Court Centre, Pipers Row, Wolverhampton WV1 3LQ.

DOWELL, Sir Anthony (James), Kt 1995; CBE 1973; Senior Principal, 1967–2001, Director, 1986–2001, Royal Ballet, Covent Garden (Assistant to Director, 1984–85; Associate Director, 1985–86); *b* 16 Feb. 1943; *s* of late Catherine Ethel and Arthur Henry Dowell; unmarried. *Educ:* Hampshire Sch., St Saviour's Hall, Knightsbridge; Royal Ballet Sch., White Lodge, Richmond, Surrey; Royal Ballet Sch., Barons Court. Joined Opera Ballet, 1960, Royal Ballet, for Russian Tour, 1961; promoted Principal Dancer, 1966. *Principal roles with Royal Ballet include:* La Fête Etrange, 1963; Napoli, 1965; Romeo and Juliet, 1965; Song of the Earth, 1966; Card Game, Giselle, Swan Lake, 1967; The Nutcracker, Cinderella, Monotones, Symphonic Variations, new version of Sleeping Beauty, Enigma Variations, Lilac Garden, 1968; Raymonda Act III, Daphnis and Chloe, La Fille Mal Gardée, 1969; Dances at a Gathering, 1970; La Bayadère, Meditation from Thaïs, Afternoon of a Faun, Anastasia, 1971; Triad, Le Spectre de la Rose, Giselle, 1972; Agon, Firebird, 1973; Manon, 1974; Four Schumann Pieces, Les Sylphides, 1975; Four Seasons, 1975; Scarlet Pastorale, 1976; Rhapsody, 1981; A Month in the Country, The Tempest, Varii Capricci, 1983; Sons of Horus, Frankenstein: the modern Prometheus, 1986; Ondine, 1988. Guest Artist with Amer. Ballet Theater, 1977–79; *performed in:* The Nutcracker; Don Quixote; Other Dances; *created:* The Dream, 1964; Shadow Play, 1967; Pavane, 1973; Manon, 1974; Contredanses; Solor in Makarova's La Bayadère; Fisherman in Le Rossignol (Ashton's choreography), NY Metropolitan Opera, 1981; Winter Dreams, 1991. Narrator in A Wedding Bouquet (first speaking role), Joffrey Ballet, 1977; guest appearances with Nat. Ballet of Canada (The Dream, Four Schumann Pieces), 1979 and 1981; Anthony Dowell Ballet Gala, Palladium, 1980 (for charity); narrated Oedipus Rex, NY Metropolitan Opera, 1981. *Television performances:* La Bayadère (USA); Swan Lake, Cinderella, Sleeping Beauty, A Month in the Country, The Dream, Les Noces (all BBC); Winter Dreams; All the Superlatives (personal profile), Omnibus, BBC. Dance Magazine award, NY, 1972. *Recreations:* painting, paper sculpture, theatrical costume design. *Address:* c/o Royal Opera House, Covent Garden, WC2E 9DD.

DOWELL, Ian Malcolm, MBE 1999; Editor, Birmingham Evening Mail, 1987–2001; *b* 15 Nov. 1940; *s* of late James Mardlin and Lilian Dowell; *m* 1st, 1967, Maureen Kane; two *d*; 2nd, 1980, Pauline Bridget Haughian. *Educ:* Exmouth Grammar Sch., Devon. Reporter, Exmouth and East Devon Journal, 1958; Sub-Editor, Woodrow Wyatt Newspapers, 1960; Editor, Wallingford News, Berks, 1962; Dep. Editor, Birmingham Planet, 1964–66; Birmingham Evening Mail: Sub-Editor, 1966; Dep. Features Editor, 1972; Chief Sub-Editor, 1976; Asst Editor, 1981; Dep. Editor, 1985. Bd Mem., Birmingham Post & Mail Ltd, 1992–2001. Chm., W Midlands Reg. Guild of Editors, 1994; Mem., Code of Practice Cttee, Newspaper and Magazine Publishing in the UK, 1996–2001. Pres., Black Country Olympics Cttee, 1985–94; Mem. Foundn Bd, Solihull Coll., 1994–98. Chm., Birmingham Mail Christmas Tree Fund, 1992–2001; Member: Bd, Birmingham Jazz Festival, 1996–2001; Birmingham Town Hall Adv. Panel, 1999–2001. Fellow, RSPB, 1987. *Recreations:* the countryside, gardening. *Address:* 3 Cutters Wharf, Exmouth Quay, Exmouth, Devon EX8 1XS.

DOWELL, Prof. John Derek, FRS 1986; CPhys, FInstP; Poynting Professor of Physics, University of Birmingham, 1997–2002, now Emeritus; *b* 6 Jan. 1935; *s* of William Ernest Dowell and Elsie Dorothy Dowell (*née* Jarvis); *m* 1959, Patricia Clarkson; one *s* one *d*. *Educ:* Coalville Grammar Sch., Leics; Univ. of Birmingham (BSc, PhD) CPhys, FInstP 1987. Research Fellow, Univ. of Birmingham, 1958–60; Res. Associate, CERN, Geneva, 1960–62; University of Birmingham: Lectr, 1962–70; Sen. Lectr, 1970–75; Reader, 1975–80; Prof. of Elementary Particle Physics, 1980–97. Vis. Scientist, Argonne Nat. Lab., USA, 1968–69. CERN, Geneva: Scientific Associate, 1973–74, 1985–87; Mem., Scientific Policy Cttee, 1982–90, 1993–96; Co-spokesman, UA1 Experiment (discovery of W and Z particles), 1985–88; Mem., Res. Bd, 1993–96; Chairman: Large Electron Positron Collider Cttee, 1993–96; ATLAS Collaboration Bd, 1996–97. Mem., Nuclear Physics Bd, 1974–77, 1981–85, Chm., Particle Physics Cttee, 1981–85, SERC; Member: Eur. Cttee for Future Accelerators, 1989–93; BBC Science Consultative Gp, 1992–94; Deutsches Elektronen Synchrotron Extended Scientific Council, 1992–98; PPARC, 1994–97. Mem., Panel for Physics, 2001 RAE, HEFCE. Vice Pres. and Mem. Council, Royal Soc., 1997–98. Lay Chm., Birmingham Children's Hosp. NHS Trust, 2004–. Mem. Court, Univ. of Warwick, 1992–2001. Fellow, APS, 2004. Rutherford Prize and Medal, InstP, 1988. *Publications:* numerous, in Phys. Letters, Nuovo Cimento, Nuclear Phys., Phys. Rev., Proc. Royal Soc., and related literature. *Recreations:* piano, amateur theatre, golf. *Address:* 57 Oxford Road, Moseley, Birmingham B13 9ES; School of Physics and Astronomy, University of Birmingham, Birmingham B15 2TT.

DOWER, Michael Shillito Trevelyan, CBE 1996; Director-General, Countryside Commission, 1992–96; *b* 15 Nov. 1933; *s* of late John Gordon Dower and Pauline Dower; *m* 1960, Agnes Done; three *s*. *Educ:* Leys Sch., Cambridge; St John's Coll., Cambridge (MA); University Coll. London (DipTP). MRTPI, MRICS. Town Planner: LCC, 1957–59; Civic Trust, 1960–65; Amenity and Tourism Planner, UN Develt Prog., Ireland, 1965–67; Dir, Dartington Amenity Res. Trust and Dartington Inst., Devon, 1967–85; Nat. Park Officer, Peak Park Jt Planning Bd, 1985–92. Vis. Prof., Univ. of Glos (formerly Cheltenham and Gloucester Coll. of HE), 1996–. Co-ordinator, PREPARE Partnership for Rural Europe, 2000–06, 2014–. Chm., Public Inquiry into Foot and Mouth Disease in Northumberland, 2002. Member: Sports Council, 1965–72; English Tourist Bd, 1969–76; Founder Chm., Rural Voice, 1980; European Council for Village and Small Town: Pres., 1986–90; Sec.-Gen., 1995–2000; Vice-Pres., 2000–04. Vice-President: YHA, 1996–; TCV (formerly BTCV), 1996–; Scottish Campaign for Nat. Parks, 2009–; Hon. Councillor, Rural Buildings Preservation Trust, 1996–2000; Patron: Landscape Design Trust, 1997–; Acad. for Sci. of Acting, 2004–. Mem. Exec. Cttee, S Dorset (formerly Chalk and Cheese) Local Action Gp (Dorset), 2013–. Ambassador, Nat. Forest Co., 2011–. Trustee, Afghanaid, 2002–03. Hon. FLI 1995. Hon. DSc Plymouth, 1994. *Publications:* Fourth Wave, 1965; Hadrian's Wall, 1976; (jtly) Leisure Provision and People's Needs, 1981; (jtly) Community Spirit Wins, 2013; Rubbish! A history of refuse disposal in the Beaminster area, 2014; Empowering Rural Stakeholders in the Western Balkans, 2014; research and consultancy reports. *Recreations:* walking, landscape painting, sculpture, travel, woodland management. *Address:* 6 Newtown, Beauminster, Dorset DT8 3EW.

DOWLEY, Dominic Myles; QC 2002; *b* 25 March 1958; *s* of Laurence Edward Dowley and Audrey Virginia Dowley (*née* Jorgensen); *m* 1985, Emma Sîan Elizabeth (*née* Lewis); five *d*. *Educ:* Ampleforth Coll., Yorks; New Coll., Oxford (MA Hons). Called to the Bar, Gray's Inn, 1983. *Address:* 6 New Square, Lincoln's Inn, WC2A 3QS. *Clubs:* Garrick, MCC; Royal West Norfolk Golf.

See also L. J. Dowley.

DOWLEY, (Laurence) Justin, FCA; Chairman, Intermediate Capital Group plc, since 2010 (non-executive Director, 2006–10); *b* Leicester, 9 June 1955; *s* of Laurence Edward Dowley and Audrey Virginia Dowley (*née* Jorgensen); *m* 1st, 1980, Sarah Hamilton-Fairley (marr. diss. 1984); 2nd, 1986, Emma Louise Lampard; two *s* two *d*. *Educ:* Ampleforth; Balliol Coll., Oxford (BA Mod. Hist.; MA). Price Waterhouse, 1977–80; Morgan Grenfell & Co., 1981–96, Dir, 1988–96; Merrill Lynch, 1996–2001, Co-Hd, Investment Banking, Europe, 1999–2001; Founder Partner, Tricorn Partners, 2003–09; Vice Chm., Nomura Internat. plc, 2010–11. Non-executive Director: Wyevale Garden Centres plc, 2001–06; Bridgewell Gp plc, 2001–07; Sporting Exchange Ltd, 2005–06; Ascot Authy (Hldgs) Ltd, 2008–15; Ind. Port Handling Ltd, 2009–; Melrose plc, 2011–; Scottish Mortgage Investment Trust plc, 2015–; Chm., Greenhouse Sports, 2014–15. Non-exec. Dir, Nat. Crime Agency, 2013–. Adv. Bd, Open Europe, 2008–. Chm., Lord Mayor of London's Appeal, 2011–12. Gov., St Francis of Assisi Sch., Notting Hill, 1986–2003; Mem., Develt Council, RNT, 1993–2006; Endowment Trustee, Balliol Coll., Oxford, 2008–; Trustee, New Schools Network, 2012–. Mem., Gunmakers' Co. *Address:* 8 Norland Square, W11 4PX. *E:* justin@dowley.me. *Clubs:* Boodle's, Garrick, Jockey, MCC (Treas., 2006–12); Royal West Norfolk Golf; Aldeburgh Golf; Royal St George's (Sandwich).

See also D. M. Dowley.

DOWLING, Prof. Dame Ann Patricia, (Dame Ann Hynes), DBE 2007 (CBE 2002); PhD, ScD; FRS 2003; FREng; FIMechE; FRAeS; Professor of Mechanical Engineering, University of Cambridge, since 1993 (Head, Department of Engineering, 2009–14; Deputy Vice-Chancellor, 2013–14); Fellow, Sidney Sussex College, Cambridge, since 1979; President, Royal Academy of Engineering, since 2014; *b* 15 July 1952; *d* of Mortimer Joseph Patrick Dowling and Joyce Dowling (*née* Barnes); *m* 1974, Dr Thomas Paul Hynes. *Educ:* Ursuline Convent Sch., Westgate, Kent; Girton Coll., Cambridge (BA 1973; MA 1977; PhD 1978; ScD 2006). CEng, FIMechE 1990 (Hon. FIMechE 2011); FREng (FEng 1996); FRAeS 1997; Fellow, Inst. Acoustics, 1989. Cambridge University: Res. Fellow, 1977–78, Dir of Studies in Engrg, 1979–90, Sidney Sussex Coll.; Asst Lectr in Engrg, 1979–82; Lectr, 1982–86; Reader in Acoustics, 1986–93; Dep. Hd, Engrg Dept, 1990–93, 1996–99. Jerome C. Hunsaker Vis. Prof., MIT, 1999–2000; Moore Dist. Schol., CIT, 2001–02. Member: AIAA, 1990; Defence and Aerospace Technology Foresight Panel, 1994–97; Defence Sci. Adv. Council, 1998–2001; EPSRC, 2001–06 (Mem., 1998–2002, Chm., 2003–06, Technical Opportunities Panel). Non-executive Director: DRA, 1995–97; BP plc, 2012–; BIS, 2014–. Mem. Scientific Adv. Bd, DERA, 1997–2001. Member, Council: Royal Acad. of Engrg, 1998–2002 (Vice-Pres., 1999–2002); Royal Soc., 2009–10. Trustee: Ford of Britain Trust, 1993–2002; Cambridge European Trust, 1994–2014; Nat. Mus. of Sci. and Industry, 1999–2008; Foundn of Queen Elizabeth II Prize for Engrg, 2014–; Trustee and Council Mem., Royal Foundn for Sci. and Technology, 2014–. Gov., Felsted Sch., 1994–99. Foreign Associate: French Acad. of Scis, 2002; US NAE, 2008; MAE 2009; Fellow, AIAA, 2011. Hon. ScD: TCD, 2008; Kent, 2013; KTH Royal Inst. of Technol., Stockholm, 2013. A. B. Wood Medal, Inst. of Acoustics, 1990; Sugden Prize, Combustion Inst., 2012; Kate Gleason Award, Amer. Soc. of Mech. Engrs, 2013; Inst. of Acoustics Engrg Medal, 2014. *Publications:* (with J. E. Ffowcs Williams) Sound and Sources of Sound, 1983; (with D. G. Crighton *et al.*) Modern Methods in Analytical Acoustics, 1992; contribs to scientific and engrg jls, mainly on fluid mechanics, combustion, vibration and acoustics. *Recreations:* opera, walking. *Address:* Engineering Department, Cambridge University, Trumpington Street, Cambridge CB2 1PZ. *T:* (01223) 332739.

DOWLING, Prof. Patrick Joseph, CBE 2001; DL; PhD; FRS 1996; FREng; Chairman, British Science Association (formerly British Association for the Advancement of Science), 2005–09; Vice President, Community Foundation for Surrey, since 2015 (Founder Chairman, 2005–14); *b* 23 March 1939; *s* of John Dowling and Margaret McKittrick, Dublin; *m* 1966, Grace Carmine Victoria Lobo, *d* of Palladius Lobo and Marcilia Moniz, Zanzibar; one *s* one *d*. *Educ:* Christian Brothers Sch., Dublin; University Coll., Dublin (BE NUI 1960); Imperial Coll. of Science and Technol., London (DIC 1961; PhD 1968; FIC 1997). FRINA 1985; FIStructE 1978; FICE 1979; FREng (FEng 1981); FCGI 1989; FIAE 2000. Demonstr in Civil Engrg, UC Dublin, 1960–61; Post-grad. studies, Imperial Coll., London, 1961–65; Bridge Engr, British Constructional Steelwork Assoc., 1965–68; Imperial Coll., London: Res. Fellow, 1968–74; Reader in Structural Steelwork, 1974–79; British Steel Prof. of Steel Structures, 1979–94; Hd of Civil Engrg Dept, 1985–94; Vice Chancellor and Chief Exec., Univ. of Surrey, 1994–2005. Partner, Chapman and Dowling, Consulting Engineers, 1981–94. Chm., Eurocode 3 (Steel Structures) Drafting Cttee, 1981–94. Mem. UK Bd, UUK, 2000–05. Member: Council, RHBNC, 1990–95; Governing Authy, University Coll., Dublin, 2009–13. Pres., IStructE, 1994–95; Chairman: Steel Construction Inst., 1998–2002; Engrg Council, 2002–03 (Senator, 1996–2002); Mem., Engrg Technology Bd, 2002–08. Foreign Member: Nat. Acad. of Engrg, Korea, 1997; Yugoslav Acad. of Engrg, 2003; Corresponding Member: Nat. Acad. of Engrg of Argentina, 2001; Nat. Acad. of Exact, Physical and Natural Scis, Argentina, 2001. Non-executive Director: DSTL, 2005–08; Ploughshare Innovations Ltd, 2006–08. Patron, Yvonne Arnaud Th., 2007– (Mem. Bd of Trustees, 2002–07). Editor, Jl of Constructional Steel Research, 1980–2005. DL Surrey, 1999. Hon. Mem., RIA, 2007. Hon. LLD: NUI, 1995; Roehampton, 2005; Hon. DSc: Vilnius Tech. Univ., 1996; Ulster, 1998; Hon. PhD Kuopio, 2005; DUniv Surrey, 2006. Institution of Structural Engineers: Oscar Faber Award, 1971; Henry Adams Medal, 1976; Guthrie Brown Medal, 1979; Oscar Faber Medal, 1985, 1996; Telford Premium, ICE, 1976; Gustave

Trasenster Medal, Assoc. des Ingénieurs sortis de l'Univ. de Liège, 1984; Silver Medal, RINA, 1993; Curtin Medal, ICE, 1993; James Alfred Ewing Medal, ICE, 2006. *Publications:* Steel Plated Structures, 1977; Buckling of Shells in Offshore Structures, 1982; Structural Steel Design, 1988; Constructional Steel Design, 1992; technical papers on elastic and inelastic behaviour and design of steel and composite land-based and offshore structures. *Recreations:* travelling, theatre, reading, the enjoyment of good company. *Address:* A4 Trinity Gate, Epsom Road, Guildford, Surrey GU1 3PJ. *Clubs:* Athenæum, Chelsea Arts; Guildford County; National Yacht of Ireland.

DOWLING, Sir Robert, Kt 2002; Chairman, Board of Trustees and Education Committee, St George's School, Edgbaston, Birmingham (Headmaster, 2009); *s* of Nicholas and Elizabeth Dowling; *m* 1967, Helen Bernadette Ryan; two *s* one *d. Educ:* St Mary's Univ. Coll., Twickenham (qualified teacher, London Univ.); Cambridge Inst. of Educn (Dip Exp. Psychology); Univ. of Nottingham (MEd); University Coll. Northampton (Dip SPLD). Headmaster: Collingwood Sch., Birmingham, 1976–90; Selly Oak Special Sch., Birmingham, 1990–96; Uffculme Sch., Birmingham, 1996–98; George Dixon Internat. Sch., Birmingham, 1998–2008. Sen. Educn Advr, Birmingham LEA, 1988–92. Non-exec. Chm., Care Through the Millennium, 2010– (CEO, 2009). Member: Catenian Assoc.; Birmingham and Edgbaston Debating Soc. *Recreations:* golf, theatre, music, reading, debating. *Address:* St George's School, 31 Calthorpe Road, Edgbaston, Birmingham B15 1RX. *Club:* Edgbaston Golf.

DOWN AND CONNOR, Bishop of, (RC), since 2008; **Most Rev. Noel Treanor;** *b* Silverstream, Co. Monaghan, 25 Dec. 1950. *Educ:* St Patrick's Coll., Maynooth; Pontifical Gregorian Univ., Rome. Ordained priest, 1976; Asst Priest, Dio. of Clogher, 1980; Dir of Studies, Pontifical Irish Coll. in Rome, 1981–85; Dir of Adult Educn, Dio. of Clogher, 1985; Sec. Gen., Commn of Bishops' Conferences of European Community, 1993–2008. *Address:* Lisbreen, 73 Somerton Road, Belfast BT15 4DE. *T:* (028) 9077 6185.

DOWN AND DROMORE, Bishop of, since 1997; **Rt Rev. Harold Creeth Miller;** *b* 23 Feb. 1950; *s* of Harold Miller and Violet (*née* McGinley); *m* 1978, Elizabeth Adelaide Harper; two *s* two *d. Educ:* Trinity Coll., Dublin (MA); Nottingham Univ. (BA Hons Theol.); St John's Theol Coll., Nottingham (DPS). Ordained deacon, 1976, priest, 1977; Asst Curate, St Nicholas, Carrickfergus, 1976–79; Dir of Extension Studies and Chaplain, St John's Coll., Nottingham, 1979–84; Chaplain, QUB, 1984–89; Rector of Carrigrohane Union of Parishes, Cork, 1989–97. *Publications:* Anglican Worship Today, 1980; Whose Office? daily prayer for the people of God, 1982; Finding a Personal Rule of Life, 1984, 2nd edn 1987; New Ways in Worship, 1986; Making an Occasion of It, 1994; Outreach in the Local Church, 2000; The Desire of our Soul, 2004; (contrib.) The Oxford Guide to the Book of Common Prayer, 2006; Week of All Weeks, 2015; articles in Search. *Recreations:* music, travel, phillumeny. *Address:* The See House, 32 Knockdene Park South, Belfast BT5 7AB. *T:* (028) 9023 7602. *E:* bishop@down.anglican.org.

DOWN, Ven. Philip Roy; Archdeacon of Ashford, since 2011; *b* 28 March 1953; *s* of Keith Phillip Down and Ivy Olive Down; *m* 1972, Christine Mary Oakley; one *s* three *d. Educ:* Royal Melbourne Inst. of Technol. (Dip. Applied Sci. 1976); Melbourne Coll. of Divinity (BTh 1982, MTh 1988); Hull Univ. (MA 1993). Medical scientist: Dept of Pathology, Austin Hosp., Melbourne, 1971–76; Macleod Pathology Services, Melbourne, 1976–78; Siddons Fellow (postgrad. teaching fellowship), Melbourne Coll. of Divinity, 1982; Minister, Brighton Parish, Uniting Ch in Aust., 1983–86; Associate Minister, British Methodist Conf., Scunthorpe Circuit and Westcliffe LEP, and Chaplain (part-time), Scunthorpe Gen. Hosp., 1986–89; ordained deacon and priest, 1989; Curate, 1989–91, Team Vicar, 1991–95, Grimsby; Rector, St Stephen's, Canterbury, 1995–2002; Area Dean of Canterbury, 1999–2002; Archdeacon of Maidstone, 2002–11. *Recreations:* opera, poetry, music, natural history, travel, theatre, cinema, dogs. *Address:* The Archdeaconry, Pett Lane, Charing, Ashford, Kent TN27 0DL. *T:* and *Fax:* (01233) 712649. *E:* pdown@archdeacashford.org.

DOWN, Rt Rev. William John Denbigh; Assistant Bishop of Leicester and Priest-in-charge, St Mary, Humberstone, 1995–2001; Hon. Assistant Bishop, Diocese of Oxford, since 2001; *b* 15 July 1934; *s* of late William Leonard Frederick Down and Beryl Mary Down (*née* Collett); *m* 1960, Sylvia Mary Aves; two *s* two *d. Educ:* Farnham Grammar School; St John's Coll., Cambridge (BA 1957; MA 1961); Ridley Hall, Cambridge. Deacon 1959, priest 1960, Salisbury; Asst Curate, St Paul's Church, Salisbury, 1959–63; Chaplain, Missions to Seamen, 1963–74: South Shields, 1963–65; Hull, 1965–71; Fremantle, WA, 1971–74; Dep. Gen. Secretary, Missions to Seamen, 1975, Gen. Sec. 1976–90; Chaplain, St Michael Paternoster Royal, 1976–90; Hon. Asst Curate, St John's, Stanmore, 1975–90; Bishop of Bermuda, 1990–95. Hon. Canon of Gibraltar, 1985–90, of Kobe, 1987–. Chaplain RANR, 1972–74. Hon. Chaplain, Worshipful Co. of Carmen, 1977–90 (Hon. Chaplain Emeritus, 1990), of Farriers, 1983–90 (Hon. Chaplain Emeritus, 1990), of Innholders, 1983–90. Freeman, City of London, 1981. Hon. FNI 1991. *Publications:* On Course Together, 1989; (contrib.) Chaplaincy, 1999; Down to the Sea (autobiog.), 2004; The Bishop's Bill of Fare, 2005; contrib. to Internat. Christian Maritime Assoc. Bulletin. *Recreations:* sport (keen follower of soccer, cricket, golf), ships and the sea, travel, walking. *Address:* 54 Dark Lane, Witney, Oxon OX28 6LX. *T:* (01993) 706615. *E:* Bishbill@aol.com. *Club:* MCC.

DOWNE, 12th Viscount *cr* 1680; **Richard Henry Dawnay;** Bt 1642; Baron Dawnay of Danby (UK) 1897; *b* 9 April 1967; *o s* of 11th Viscount Downe and of Alison Diana (*née* Sconce); *S* father, 2002. *Educ:* Eton; Durham Univ. FCA 1992. *Heir: cousin* Thomas Payan Dawnay, *b* 24 July 1978.

DOWNER, Hon. Alexander John Gosse, AC 2013; High Commissioner for Australia in the United Kingdom, since 2014; *b* 9 Sept. 1951; *s* of Hon. Sir Alexander Downer, KBE and of Mary Downer (*née* Gosse); *m* 1978, Nicola Robinson; one *s* three *d. Educ:* Geelong GS, Vic; Radley Coll., Oxford; Univ. of Newcastle upon Tyne (BA Hons Pol. and Econs). Economist, Bank of NSW, Sydney, 1975–76; Australian Diplomatic Service, 1976–82: Mission to EEC, Representation to NATO, and Belgium and Luxembourg, 1977–80; Sen. Foreign Affairs Rep., S Australia, 1981; political advr to Prime Minister and Federal Leader of Opposition, 1982–83; Exec. Dir, Australian Chamber of Commerce, 1983–84. MP (L) Mayo, SA, 1984–July 2008; Shadow Minister: for Arts, Heritage and Envmt, 1987; for Housing, Small Business and Customs, 1988–89; for Trade and Trade Negotiations, 1990–92; for Defence, 1992–93; Shadow Treas., 1993–94; Leader of Opposition, 1994–95; Shadow Minister for Foreign Affairs, 1995–96; Minister for Foreign Affairs, 1996–2007; UN Special Advr on Cyprus, 2008–14. Mem. Bd, Adelaide SO, 2009–10. *Recreations:* reading, music, tennis, golf. *Address:* Australian High Commission, Strand, WC2B 4LA. *Club:* Adelaide.

DOWNER, Dame Jocelyn Anita; *see* Barrow, Dame J. A.

DOWNER, Prof. Martin Craig; Emeritus Professor, University College London, since 2009 (Hon. Professor, University of London, 1996–2009); Hon. Professor, University of Manchester, since 1996; writer and independent oral health consultant; *b* 9 March 1931; *s* of Dr Reginald Lionel Ernest Downer and Mrs Eileen Maud Downer (*née* Craig); *m* 1961, Anne Catherine (*née* Evans); four *d. Educ:* Shrewsbury Sch.; Univ. of Liverpool; Univ. of Manchester (PhD 1974; DDS 1989); Univ. of London; Bath Spa Univ. (MA 2010). LDSRCS 1958; DDPH RCS 1969. Dental Officer, St Helens Local Authority, 1958–59; gen. dental practice, 1959–64; Dental Officer, Bor. of Haringey, 1964–67; Principal Dental Officer, Royal Bor. of Kensington and Chelsea, 1967–70; Res. Fellow in Dental Health, Univ. of Manchester, 1970–74; Area Dental Officer, Salford HA (also Hon. Lectr, Univ. of Manchester), 1974–79; Chief Dental Officer, SHHD (also Hon. Sen. Lectr, Univs of Edinburgh and Dundee), 1979–83; Chief Dental Officer (Under Sec.), Dept of Health (formerly DHSS), 1983–90; Prof. and Head of Dept, Dental Health Policy, and Hon. Consultant in Dental Public Health, Eastman Dental Inst., London Univ., 1990–96; Dir, Oral Health Consultancy Services, 1996–2010. Distinguished Scientist Award for Behavioural, Epidemiologic and Health Services Res., Internat. Assoc. for Dental Res., 2010. *Publications:* contribs to books and papers in learned jls in gen. field of dental public health, incl. epidemiology and biostatistics, clin. trials and trial methodology, inf. systems, health services res., and econs of dental care. *Recreations:* creative writing, music, reading, cookery, natural history, vintage aviation, walking. *Address:* 1 Middle Croft, Stapleton, Shrewsbury SY5 7EA. *T:* (01743) 719413.

DOWNES, Sir (Charles) Peter, Kt 2015; OBE 2004; PhD; FMedSci, FRSE, FRSB; Principal and Vice Chancellor, since 2009, and Professor of Biochemistry, since 1989, University of Dundee; *b* Manchester, 15 Oct. 1953; *s* of George Downes and Ada Downes; *m* 1983, Elizabeth Naomi Hodgson; one *d* (one *s* decd). *Educ:* King's Sch., Macclesfield; Stockport Coll. of Technol. (HNC Applied Biol. 1975; MIBiol 1978); Univ. of Birmingham (PhD 1981). Scientific Officer, ICI Pharmaceuticals, 1973–78; MRC Trng Fellow, Univ. of Cambridge, 1981–83; Biosci. Gp Leader, ICI Pharmaceuticals, 1983–85; Cellular Pharmacologist, Smith Kline and French, then SmithKline Beecham, 1985–89; University of Dundee: Dean, Life Scis, 2000–06; Hd, Coll. of Life Scis, 2006–09. FRSE 1990; FRSB (FSB 2009); FMedSci 2010. *Publications:* over 200 biochem. and cell biol. articles in jls. *Recreations:* football (past player, current supporter), golf, running. *Address:* University of Dundee, Dundee DD1 4HN. *T:* (01382) 355555, *Fax:* (01382) 229948. *E:* c.p.downes@dundee.ac.uk.

DOWNES, Prof. David Malcolm; Professor of Social Administration, London School of Economics, 1987–2003, now Emeritus; *b* 26 Aug. 1938; *s* of Bernice Marion Downes and Herman Leslie Downes; *m* 1961, Susan Onaway Correa-Hunt; one *s* two *d. Educ:* King Edward VII Grammar Sch., Sheffield; Keble Coll., Oxford (BA Hons Mod. Hist. 1959); LSE (PhD Criminology 1964). London School of Economics: Asst Lectr, Lectr, Sen. Lectr in Social Admin, 1963–82; Reader, 1982–87; Dir, Mannheim Centre for Criminology and Criminal Justice, 1998–2003; Vice-Chm., Academic Bd, 1996–99. Sen. Res. Fellow, Nuffield Coll., Oxford, 1970–72. Visiting Professor/Academic Visitor: Univ. of California at Berkeley, 1975; Univ. of Toronto, 1977; Free Univ. of Amsterdam, 1981; Univ. of Bologna, 1991. British Mem., Harvard Internat. Seminar, 1966. Member, Council: Centre for Crime and Justice Studies, KCL, 1998–2008; Liberty, 2003–09. Mem., Family Commn, Nat. Family and Parenting Inst., 2004–05. Mem., BFI. Editor, British Jl of Criminology, 1985–90. Jt Official Historian, Criminal Justice System, 2009–. *Publications:* The Delinquent Solution, 1966, 3rd edn 1973; Gambling, Work and Leisure, 1976; (ed with Paul Rock) Deviant Interpretations, 1979; (with Paul Rock) Understanding Deviance, 1982, 6th edn 2011; Contrasts in Tolerance: postwar penal policy in the Netherlands and England and Wales, 1988; (ed) Crime and the City: essays in memory of John Mays, 1989; (ed) Unravelling Criminal Justice, 1992; (ed jtly) Crime, Social Control and Human Rights: from moral panics to states of denial - essays in honour of Stanley Cohen, 2007; (ed jtly) The Eternal Recurrence of Crime and Control: essays in honour of Paul Rock, 2010; Working Out of Crime, 2012. *Recreations:* modern literature, cinema, theatre. *Address:* 140 Poplar Road South, Merton Park, SW19 3JY. *T:* (020) 8715 2212.

DOWNES, Giles Patrick Stretton, CVO 1998; Partner, Sidell Gibson Partnership, 1988–2011, consultant architect and sculptor, since 2011; *b* 11 Nov. 1947; *s* of late George Stretton Downes, CBE; *m* 1989, Jessica Jane Harness; one *d. Educ:* Wimbledon Coll.; Kingston Coll. of Art (DipArch 1972). ARCUK 1973; RIBA 1989. Foster Associates, 1969–73; Farrell Grimshaw Partnership, 1973–74; joined Sidell Gibson Partnership, 1974: Associate in charge of Housing Projects, 1980; Equity Partner, 1988–2011. *Projects* include: Sheltered Housing Schemes for English Courtyard Assoc., 1978– (Housing Design Awards, 1983 (2), 1987 (3), 1989, 1991, 1993 (2)); Redevelt of Winchester Peninsula Barracks, 1988; Prince of Wales Sch., Dorchester, 1992; Thomas Hardye Sch., Dorchester, 1993; New Design Areas for Fire Restoration of Windsor Castle, 1994 (Bldg of the Year award, Royal Fine Art Commn, for Lantern Lobby, RIBA Award, RICS Conservation Award, 1998; Carpenters Special Award, 1999; Europa Nostra Conservation Award, 2000); 3 Sheldon Square, Paddington (British Council for Offices Award, 2003); 7–10 Old Bailey, 2009 ((jtly) Best New Global Design, Chicago Athenaeum Internat. Architecture Awards, 2010). Exhibitions of sculpture: Artshow, France, 2014; Parallax, London, 2014. Mem., Fabric Cttee, Royal Albert Hall, 2007–. Mem., IWSc: Wood Technol. Soc., Inst. of Materials, Minerals and Mining (formerly Inst. of Wood Science), 2008–. Gov., Building Crafts Coll., 2002– (Chm., 2011–). Liveryman, Carpenters' Co., 2001– (Master, 2010–11); Brother, Art Workers Guild, 2012. *Publications:* (jtly) Timber in Contemporary Architecture: a designer's guide, 2009. *Recreations:* sculpture, ceramics, building craft skills, sketching.

See also Dame J. S. Higgins.

DOWNES, Prof. Kerry John, OBE 1994; FSA; Professor of History of Art, University of Reading, 1978–91, now Emeritus; *b* 8 Dec. 1930; *s* of late Ralph William Downes, CBE and Agnes Mary Downes (*née* Rix); *m* 1962, Margaret Walton (*d* 2003). *Educ:* St Benedict's, Ealing; Courtauld Institute of Art. BA, PhD London. Library, Courtauld Inst. of Art, 1954–58; Librarian, Barber Inst. of Fine Arts, Univ. of Birmingham, 1958–66; Lectr in Fine Art, Univ. of Reading, 1966–71, Reader, 1971–78. Vis. Lectr, Yale Univ., 1968; Hon. Vis. Prof., Univ. of York, 1994–. Mem., Royal Commission on Historical Monuments of England, 1981–93; Pres., Soc. of Architectural Historians of GB, 1984–88. Consultant for Trophy Room, St Paul's Cathedral, 1995–97. Hon. DLitt Birmingham, 1995. *Publications:* Hawksmoor, 1959, 2nd edn 1979; English Baroque Architecture, 1966; Hawksmoor, 1969; Christopher Wren, 1971; Whitehall Palace, in Colvin and others, History of the King's Works, V, 1660–1782, 1976; Vanbrugh, 1977; The Georgian Cities of Britain, 1979; Rubens, 1980; The Architecture of Wren, 1982, 2nd edn 1988; Sir John Vanbrugh, a Biography, 1987; Sir Christopher Wren: Design for St Paul's Cathedral, 1988; St Paul's and its Architecture, 1998; Christopher Wren, 2007; Borromini's Book, 2009; contribs to Oxford DNB, Burlington Magazine, Architectural History, Architectural Rev., TLS, Alexander Jl, etc. *Recreations:* drawing, making music, baking, procrastination. *Address:* c/o History of Art, Department of History, University of Reading, Whiteknights, PO Box 218, Reading RG6 6AA. *T:* (0118) 378 8890.

DOWNES, His Honour Paul Henry; a Circuit Judge, 1995–2011; *b* 23 Nov. 1941; *s* of Eric and Lavinia Downes; *m* 1st; two *s* one *d*; 2nd, 1986, Beverley Jill Rogers; one *s. Educ:* Ducie High Sch., Manchester; Coll. of Commerce, UMIST; Coll. of Law, London (Bar degree 1967); Cardiff (LLM Canon Law 2003). Deputy Magistrates' Clerk: Manchester Co. Magistrates' Court, 1960–63; Sheffield City Magistrates' Court, 1963–67; Nottingham City Magistrates' Court, 1967; County Prosecuting Service, Suffolk, 1967–71; in private practice at Norwich Bar, 1971–95; Asst Recorder, 1991–94; Recorder, 1994–95. Pres., Mental Health Review Tribunals, 2008–. Vice Chancellor, Dio. St Edmundsbury and Ipswich, 2001–; Chancellor: Dio. of Wakefield, 2007–12; Dio. of Norwich, 2007–12. Chm., Norwich Cathedral Choir Endowment Trust, 2013–. Hon. LLD UEA, 2008. *Recreations:* music, singing, chamber choir, instrumental playing, reading, walking, solo baritone singing. *Address:* The Old Chapel, Chapel Road, Sea Spalling, N Norfolk NR12 0UQ.

DOWNES, Sir Peter; *see* Downes, Sir C. P.

DOWNEY, Aileen Patricia; Her Honour Judge Downey; a Circuit Judge, since 2014; *b* Ballycastle, NI, 26 Sept. 1969. *Educ:* Rye St Antony Sch., Oxford; King's Coll., London (LLB Hons). Called to the Bar, Lincoln's Inn, 1991; barrister, 1991–2014; a Recorder, 2009–14. *Address:* c/o Croydon County Court, The Law Courts, Altyre Road, Croydon, Surrey CR9 5AB.

DOWNEY, Sir Gordon (Stanley), KCB 1984 (CB 1980); Parliamentary Commissioner for Standards, 1995–98; Comptroller and Auditor General, 1981–87; *b* 26 April 1928; *s* of Stanley William and Winifred Downey; *m* 1952, Jacqueline Goldsmith; two *d. Educ:* Tiffin Sch.; London Sch. of Economics (BSc(Econ)). Served RA, 1946–48. Ministry of Works, 1951; entered HM Treasury, 1952; Asst Private Sec. to successive Chancellors of the Exchequer, 1955–57; on loan to Ministry of Health, 1961–62; Asst Sec., 1965, Under-Sec., 1972, Head of Central Unit, 1975; Dep. Sec., 1976–81; on loan as Dep. Head, Central Policy Review Staff, Cabinet Office, 1978–81. Special Advr, Ernst & Young (formerly Ernst & Whinney), 1988–90; Complaints Comr, The Securities Assoc., 1989–90; Chairman: FIMBRA, 1990–93; PIA, 1993. Readers' Rep., The Independent, 1990–95. Chm., Delegacy, King's College Med. and Dental Sch., 1989–91; Mem. Council, KCL, 1989–91; FKC 2002. *Recreations:* reading, visual arts. *Address:* 137 Whitehall Court, SW1A 2EP. *T:* (020) 7321 0914. *Club:* Athenæum.

DOWNEY, Michael Shaun; Chief Executive, Lawn Tennis Association, since 2014; *b* Toronto, 12 June 1957; *s* of Ross and Ruth Downey; *m* 2013, Jinder Chalmers; two *s. Educ:* Univ. of Western Ontario (HBA). Molson Canada: Sen. Vice Pres., Mktg, 2000–02; Regl Pres., 2002–04; Pres., Molson Sports and Entertainment, 2001–03; CEO, Tennis Canada, 2004–13. Pres., Toronto Humane Soc., 2010–11. *E:* michael.downey@lta.org.uk.

DOWNIE, Caren; Brand Director and Founder, Finery London, since 2014; *b* Enfield, 24 Dec. 1960; *d* of Roger and Margaret Wheaton; *m* 1988, Charles Downie. *Educ:* London Sch. of Econs (BSc Hons Internat. Trade and Develt). Began career at Warehouse, 1983, subseq. progressed via many High St names incl. French Connection, Wallis, Framework and Pilot; Buying Dir, Topshop, 2003–08; Buying Dir, Womenswear, ASOS plc, 2008–12. Mem. Panel, New Generation, British Fashion Council, 2000–; Ext. Examr, Univ. of the Arts, London (formerly London Inst.), 2000–. *Publications:* articles in Elle mag. and Daily Telegraph. *Recreations:* shopping the world, collecting expensive shoes.

DOWNIE, Prof. Robert Silcock, (Robin), FRSE 1986; Professor of Moral Philosophy, 1969–2002, now Emeritus, Hon. and Professorial Research Fellow, since 2002, Glasgow University; *b* 19 April 1933; *s* of late Robert Mackie Downie and late Margaret Barlas Downie; *m* 1958, Eileen Dorothea Flynn; three *d. Educ:* The High Sch. of Glasgow; Glasgow Univ. (MA, first cl. hons, Philosophy and Eng. Lit., 1955); The Queen's Coll., Oxford (Ferguson Schol., 1958; BPhil 1959). Russian linguist, Intelligence Corps, 1955–57; Glasgow University: Lectr in Moral Philosophy, 1959; Sen. Lectr in Moral Philosophy, 1968; Stevenson Lectr in Med. Ethics, 1985–88. Visiting Professor: of Philosophy, Syracuse Univ., NY, USA, 1963–64; Univ. of BC, 1997; Univ. of Sydney, 1997; Hong Kong Health Authy, 1999; Univ. of Durham, 1999–2002. FRSA 1997. *Publications:* Government Action and Morality, 1964; (jtly) Respect for Persons, 1969; Roles and Values, 1971; (jtly) Education and Personal Relationships, 1974; (jtly) Values in Social Work, 1976; (jtly) Caring and Curing, 1980; Healthy Respect, 1987; (jtly) Health Promotion: models and values, 1990; (jtly) The Making of a Doctor, 1992; (ed) Francis Hutcheson: selected writings, 1994; (ed) The Healing Arts: an Oxford anthology, 1994; Palliative Care Ethics, 1996; (ed) Medical Ethics, 1996; Clinical Judgement: evidence in practice, 2000; (jtly) The Philosophy of Palliative Care, 2006; Bioethics and the Humanities, 2007; End of Life Choices: consensus and controversy, 2009; contribs to: Mind, Philosophy, Analysis, Aristotelian Society, Political Studies, Scottish Rev. *Recreations:* music (especially composition), assorted public performances. *Address:* Department of Moral Philosophy, University of Glasgow G12 8QQ. *T:* (0141) 339 1345.

DOWNING, Anne Elizabeth; *see* Fleming, A. E.

DOWNING, Carolyn Louise; freelance sound designer, since 2003; *b* Salford, 3 May 1980; *d* of Peter Downing and Angela Gabrielle Downing; partner, David Holmes; one *d. Educ:* Moorside High Sch., Salford; Eccles Coll., Salford; Royal Central Sch. of Speech and Drama, London (BA 1st Cl. Hons Theatre Practice (Sound Design)). Sound designer in theatre, museum and gallery exhibns, fashion shows and film (live action and animation); theatre includes: Royal Shakespeare Co.: The Winter's Tale, Pericles, 2007; The Gods Weep; King John, 2012; Donmar Warehouse: Absurdia, 2008; Dimetos, 2009; Fathers and Sons, 2014; Frantic Assembly: Beautiful Burnout, 2010; Lovesong, The Believers, 2014; National Theatre: Double Feature, 2011; Dara, As You Like It, Our Country's Good, The Mother F***er with the Hat, 2015; Royal Court: Choir Boy, 2012; The Low Road, 2013; The Pass, Hope, 2014; other productions: All My Sons, NY, 2007; Chimerica, Almeida and West End, 2013 (Olivier Award for Best Sound Design (jtly), 2014); exhibitions include: Collider, Sci. Mus., London, 2012. *Recreations:* books, art installation and galleries, sound art installation and performance, theatre, travelling and exploring, playing jigsaws with my daughter, enjoying life of the city and open beauty space of the countryside.

DOWNPATRICK, Lord; Edward Edmund Maximilian George Windsor; Analyst, J P Morgan Private Bank, since 2012; *b* 2 Dec. 1988; *s* and *heir* of Earl of St Andrews, *qv. Educ:* King's Coll. Sch., Cambridge; Dragon Sch., Oxford; Eton Coll.; Keble Coll., Oxford. *Clubs:* Turf; Kandahar Ski; Royal West Norfolk Golf (Jun. Captain, 2005–06).

DOWNS, Carolyn Grace, CB 2011; Chief Executive, Local Government Association, since 2011; *b* 25 Feb. 1960; *d* of Eric and Mildred Downs; *m* 1988, Prof. Jonathan Michie, *qv*; two *s. Educ:* Kingston Univ. (BA Hons French and Politics); UCL (Postgrad. DipLib, MA Liby and Inf. Studies). Asst Dir of Leisure Services, Stevenage BC, 1994–96; Dir of Leisure Services, Calderdale MBC, 1996–99; Corporate Dir, 1999–2003, Chief Exec., 2003–09, Shropshire CC; Dep. Perm. Sec. and Dir Gen., Corporate Perf., MoJ, 2009–10; Chief Exec., Legal Services Commn, 2010–11. *Recreations:* tennis, ski-ing, watching Manchester United. *Address:* Local Government Association, Local Government House, Smith Square, SW1P 3HZ.

DOWNSHIRE, 9th Marquess of, *cr* 1789 (Ire.); **Arthur Francis Nicholas Wills Hill;** Viscount Hillsborough, Baron Hill, 1717; Earl of Hillsborough, Viscount Kilwarlin, 1751; Baron Harwich (GB), 1756; Earl of Hillsborough, Viscount Fairford (GB), 1772; Baron Sandys 1802; Hereditary Constable of Hillsborough Fort; company director and landowner; *b* 4 Feb. 1959; *e s* of 8th Marquess of Downshire and Hon. Juliet Mary (*d* 1986), *d* of 7th Baron Forester; *S* father, 2003; *m* 1990, Janey, *d* of Gerald Bunting; one *s* three *d. Educ:* Eton College; Royal Agricultural Coll., Cirencester; Central London Polytechnic. ACA 1985. Touche Ross & Co., 1981–87; Finance Controller, 1988–89, Finance Dir, 1989–2001, Scheduling Technol. Gp Ltd; Chm., Identify UK Ltd, 2001–12; Director: Animalcare Group plc (formerly Ritchey Tagg Ltd, then Ritchey plc), 1998–; base2stay (formerly Western Heritable Apartco) Ltd, 2004–12; Farmway Ltd, 2007–14; MFB Ltd, 2010–; STL Ltd, 2011–. Chm., Yorks Br., CLA, 2014–. Trustee, Game and Wildlife Conservation Trust. *Recreations:* country pursuits, sport. *Heir: s* Earl of Hillsborough, *qv*.

DOWNSIDE, Abbot of; *no new appointment at time of going to press.*

DOWNWARD, Prof. Julian, PhD; FRS 2005; FMedSci; Associate Research Director, Francis Crick Institute, since 2015; *b* 25 Oct. 1960; *s* of Maj.-Gen. Sir Peter Aldcroft Downward, KCVO, CB, DSO, DFC; *m* 1997, Tanya Basu; three *d. Educ:* Eton Coll.; Clare Coll., Cambridge (BA 1982); ICRF/Imperial Coll. London (PhD 1986). Res. Fellow, MIT, 1986–89; Hd, Signal Transduction Lab., 1989–2015, Associate Dir, 2005–15, CRUK, London Res. Inst. (formerly ICRF Lab.). Hon. Professor: Biochem. Dept, UCL, 1997–; Barts and the London, Queen Mary Sch. of Medicine and Dentistry, 2004–. FMedSci 2009. Hon. FRCP 2012. *Publications:* contrib. papers on molecular biol. of cancer to scientific jls. *Recreations:* ski-ing, theatre, scuba diving, music. *Address:* Francis Crick Institute, Brill Place, Ossulston Street, NW1 1HG. *E:* julian.downward@crick.ac.uk.

DOWSE, John; His Honour Judge Dowse; a Circuit Judge, since 2001; *b* 12 Nov. 1946; *s* of Douglas Richard Maurice Dowse and Lilian Maude Dowse (*née* Cade); *m* 2000, Elaine Winstanley (*née* McLean); two step *s* one step *d*, and one *s* two *d* from former marriage. *Educ:* Univ. of Leeds (LLB Hons 1972); Univ. of Wales, Cardiff (LLM 1996). Called to the Bar, Lincoln's Inn, 1973; Asst Recorder, 1990–94; Recorder, 1994–2001; Magistrates' Court Liaison Judge, N Bank of Humberside, 2002. *Recreations:* cooking, eating out, tennis, snooker, chess. *Address:* Hull Combined Court Centre, Lowgate, Hull HU1 2EZ. *T:* (01482) 586161.

DOWSE, Vivien Frances; *see* Life, V. F.

DOWSON, Prof. Duncan, CBE 1989; FRS 1987; FREng; Professor of Engineering Fluid Mechanics and Tribology, 1966–93, now Professor Emeritus, Hon. Fellow, since 1993, and Research Professor, since 1995, Leeds University; *b* 31 Aug. 1928; *o s* of Wilfrid and Hannah Dowson, Kirkbymoorside, York; *m* 1951, Mabel, *d* of Mary Jane and Herbert Strickland; one *s* (and one *s* decd). *Educ:* Lady Lumley's Grammar Sch., Pickering, Yorks; Leeds Univ. (BSc Mech Eng. 1950; PhD 1952; DSc 1971) FIMechE; Fellow ASME 1973 (Life Fellow); FREng (FEng 1982); Fellow ASLE 1983. Research Engineer, Sir W. G. Armstrong Whitworth Aircraft Co., 1953–54; Univ. of Leeds: Lecturer in Mechanical Engineering, 1954; Sen. Lecturer, 1963; Reader, 1965; Dir, Inst. of Tribology, Dept of Mech. Engrg, 1967–87; Pro-Vice-Chancellor, 1983–85; Head of Dept of Mech. Engrg, 1987–92; Dean for Internat. Relns, 1987–93. Hon. Professor: Hong Kong Univ., 1992–2004; Bradford Univ., 1996–2003; External Prof., Loughborough Univ., 2001–; Dist. Res. Prof., Univ. of Cardiff, 2004–13. Hinton Lectr, Royal Acad. of Engrg, 1990. Pres., IMechE, 1992–93 (Chm., Tribology Group Cttee, 1967–69). Chm., Yorks Region, RSA, 1992–97. Mem., EPSRC Peer Rev. Coll., 2003–05. Hon. Citizen, Kirkbymoorside, 2008. Editor: Pt H (Engrg in Medicine), 1981–90, Pt C, Jl Mech. Engrg Sci., 1990–2008, IMechE Proceedings; WEAR, 1983–98, now Emeritus; Engrg Res. Bk Series, 1999–2003. Foreign Mem., Royal Swedish Acad. of Engrg Sciences, 1986. FCGI 1997. Hon. FIPEM 1998; Hon. Fellow, Soc. of Tribologists and Lubrication Engrs; Hon. FIMechE 2001; Hon. FRSE 2011. Hon. DTech Chalmers Univ. of Technology, Göteborg, 1979; Hon. DSc: Institut Nat. des Sciences Appliquées de Lyon, 1991; Loughborough, 2005; Dr *hc* Liège, 1996; DEng *hc*: Waterloo, Canada, 2001; Bradford, 2003; Leeds, 2004. Institution of Mechanical Engineers: James Clayton Fund Prize (jtly), 1963; Thomas Hawksley Gold Medal, 1966; James Clayton Prize, 1978; Tribology Gold Medal, 1979; James Clayton Meml Lectr, 2000; James Watt Internat. Gold Medal, 2001; (jtly) Water Arbitration Prize, 2004; Gold Medal, British Soc. of Rheology, 1969; Nat. Award, ASLE, 1974; American Society of Mechanical Engineers: Lubrication Div. Best Paper Awards (jt), 1975, 1976, 1999; Melville Medal (jt), 1976; Mayo D. Hersey Award, 1979; Engr Historian Award, 1995; first Robert Henry Thurston Award, 2000; (jtly) Tribology Best Paper Award, 1999; Kelvin Medal, ICE, 1998; Sarton Medal, Univ. of Gent, 1998. *Publications:* Elastohydrodynamic Lubrication—the fundamentals of roller and gear lubrication (jtly), 1966, 2nd edn 1977; History of Tribology, 1979, 2nd edn 1998; (jtly) An Introduction to the Biomechanics of Joints and Joint Replacement, 1981; (jtly) Ball Bearing Lubrication: The Elastohydrodynamics of Elliptical Contacts, 1981; papers on tribology and bio-medical engrg, published by: Royal Society; Instn of Mech. Engineers; Amer. Soc. of Mech. Engineers; Amer. Soc. of Lubrication Engineers. *Recreations:* genealogy, calligraphy. *Address:* Ryedale, 23 Church Lane, Adel, Leeds LS16 8DQ. *T:* (0113) 267 8933.

DOWTON, Prof. (Stephen) Bruce, MD; FRACP; Vice-Chancellor and President, Macquarie University, Sydney, since 2012; *b* Ivanhoe, NSW, 23 April 1956; *s* of Cecil and Ailsa V. Dowton; two *s* one *d. Educ:* Dubbo High Sch., NSW; Univ. of Sydney (MB BS Hons 1980; MD 1994). FRACP 1999. Internship and residency in paediatrics and Fellow of Cell Biol., Children's Hosp., Boston and Harvard Med. Sch., 1985–86; Dir, Div. of Med. Genetics, St Louis Children's Hosp., 1986–97; Washington University School of Medicine: Associate Dean for Med. Educn, 1993–96; Associate Vice-Chancellor, 1996–98; Dean, Sch. of Medicine and Prof. of Paediatrics, Univ. of NSW, 1998–2005; Vice-Pres. and Chief Operating Officer, Harvard Med. Internat., 2008–12; Clin. Prof. of Paediatrics, Harvard Med. Sch., 2009–12; CEO, Dowton Consulting Internat., 2012–. Independent Consultant: in Higher Educn and Health Care Systems, Office of the Pres., Univ. of Calif, 2006–07; in Health System and Academic Develt, Edith Cowan Univ., 2006; Sen. Consultant, 2007, Sen. Vice-Pres., 2007–08, Exec. Vice-Pres., 2008, Vice-Pres. and Chief Operating Officer, 2008–11, Harvard Medical Internat.; Pediatrician, Mass Gen. Hosp., 2008–12. Chair: Med. Educn and Trng Council, Australia, 2001–04; Cttee of Deans of Australian Med. Schs, 2002–04. Mem. Bd, Maggie Beer Foundn, 2013–. *Publications:* contrib. articles to jls incl. Science, Med. Jl Australia, Blood, Scandinavian Jl Immunol., Biochem., Jl Biol Chem., Amer. Jl Genetics. *Recreations:* photography, cooking. *Address:* Office of the Vice-Chancellor, Macquarie University, NSW 2109, Australia. *T:* 98507440, *Fax:* 98509950. *E:* vc@mq.edu.au.

DOYLE, Most Rev. Adrian Leo; *see* Hobart (Australia), Archbishop of, (RC).

DOYLE, Dr Amanda Mary, OBE 2014; General Practitioner Partner, Bloomfield Medical Centre, Blackpool, since 1995; Chief Clinical Officer, NHS Blackpool Clinical Commissioning Group, since 2012; Co-Chair, NHS Clinical Commissioners, since 2013; *b* Liverpool, 22 Sept. 1964; *d* of John Doyle and Mary Doyle; *m* 1992, William Morrison; four *s. Educ:* Notre Dame High Sch.; Univ. of Manchester (MB ChB 1988). Jun. med. posts, 1988–95; Med. Dir, Blackpool PCT, 2006–12. *Recreations:* reading, family, cooking. *Address:* NHS Clinical Commissioners, 50 Broadway, SW1H 0DB; NHS Blackpool Clinical Commissioning Group, The Stadium, Seasiders Way, Blackpool FY1 6JX. *T:* (01253) 951227. *E:* amanda.doyle@blackpool.nhs.uk.

DOYLE, Dr Anthony Ian, FBA 1992; Hon. Reader in Bibliography, Durham University, since 1985; *b* 24 Oct. 1925; *s* of Edward Doyle and Norah Keating. *Educ:* St Mary's Coll., Great Crosby, Liverpool; Downing Coll., Cambridge (BA 1945; MA 1949; PhD 1953). Durham University: Asst Librarian, 1950–59; Keeper of Rare Books, 1959–82; Reader in Bibliography, 1972–85. Pres., Assoc. for Manuscripts and Archives in Res. Collections, 2000–. Mem., Comité Internat. de Paléographie Latine, 1979. Corresp. Fellow, Mediaeval Academy of America, 1991. Hon. Fellow, UC, Durham, 2004. Israel Gollancz Prize, British Academy, 1983; Chancellor's Medal, Durham Univ., 2010; Gold Medal, Bibliographical Soc., 2015. *Publications:* Palaeographical introductions to facsimiles of the Hengwrt Manuscript, 1979, Vernon Manuscript, 1987, and Ellesmere Manuscript, 1995, and of Hoccleve's autograph poems, 2003; articles on medieval MSS, early printed books and collectors. *Address:* University Library, Palace Green, Durham DH1 3RN. *T:* (0191) 334 1219.

DOYLE, Bernard; *see* Doyle, F. B.

DOYLE, Dr Brian John; President, Employment Tribunals (England and Wales), since 2014; *b* 12 Jan. 1955; *s* of late Jude Doyle and Mary Doyle (*née* Clancy); *m* 1st, 1986, Antoinette Cecile Chang (marr. diss. 2006); one *d*; 2nd, 2007, Helen Rippon Wile (*née* Glover); one *d. Educ:* St Joseph's Primary Sch., Crayford; St Joseph's Acad., Blackheath; Queen Mary Coll.,

Univ. of London (LLB Hons 1976, LLM 1978); Coll. of Law, London; PhD Salford 1993. Called to the Bar, Inner Temple, 1977; Res. Asst in Law, Poly of N London, 1978–80; Lectr in Law, 1980–88, Sen. Lectr in Law, 1988–95, Univ. of Salford; Prof. of Law, and Dean, Faculty of Law, Univ. of Liverpool, 1995–2000; Chm., Employment Tribunals, 2000–03; Regl Employment Judge (formerly Regl Chm. of Employment Tribunals), Manchester and Liverpool, 2003–14. *Publications:* New Directions Towards Disabled Workers' Rights, 1994; Disability Discrimination and Equal Opportunities, 1994; Disability Discrimination: the new law, 1995; Disability Discrimination Law and Practice, 1996, 6th edn 2008; Employment Tribunals: the new law, 1998; Equality and Discrimination: the new law, 2010; (contrib.) Tolley's Employment Law, 1994–; (contrib.) Jordans Employment Law Service, 1998–; contrib. articles to Industrial Law Jl, Modern Law Rev. *Recreations:* walking, travel, literature, computing, theatre. *Address:* Employment Tribunals (England and Wales), Victory House, 30–34 Kingsway, WC2B 6EX.

DOYLE, David Charles; His Honour Deemster Doyle; HM First Deemster and Clerk of the Rolls, Isle of Man, since 2010; a Judge of Appeal, Courts of Jersey and Guernsey, since 2015; *b* 26 April 1960; *s* of late David Gordon Doyle and Beatrice Lilian Doyle (*née* Cain); *m* 1991, Barbara, *d* of late John Denton and Doreen Holgate; three *s*. *Educ:* King William's Coll., I of M; Univ. of Newcastle upon Tyne (LLB 1981). Called to the Bar, Gray's Inn, 1982, Bencher, 2011; admitted to the Manx Bar, 1984; partner, Dickinson Cruickshank & Co., Advocates, 1985–2003; HM Second Deemster, I of M, 2003–10. Deputy High Bailiff and Coroner of Inquests, 2002–03. Isle of Man Law Society: Mem. Council, 1997–2003; Chm., Educn Cttee, 1997–2003; Chm., Human Rights Cttee, 2001–03; Vice Pres., 2003. Mem. Council, I of M Chamber of Commerce, 1997–2003; Mem., Corporate Services Review Cttee, 2001–03. Parent Governor, Peel Clothworkers' Sch., 2001. *Publications:* Manx Criminal Law and Procedure, 2010; *contributions to:* Solly's Government and Law in the Isle of Man, 1994; Solly's Isle of Man Partnership Law, 1996; International Tracing of Assets, 1998; Offshore Cases and Materials, 1999; Offshore Financing: security and insolvency, 1998; various articles on legal topics in professional jls. *Recreations:* family, Manx law past, present and future, running, walking. *Address:* Isle of Man Courts of Justice, Deemsters Walk, Bucks Road, Douglas, Isle of Man IM1 3AR. *T:* (01624) 685248, *Fax:* (01624) 685236.

DOYLE, Elaine Mary; *see* Griffiths, E. M.

DOYLE, (Frederick) Bernard; Partner, Gatenby Sanderson, 2005–09; *b* 17 July 1940; *s* of James Hopkinson Doyle and Hilda Mary Doyle (*née* Spotsworth); *m* 1963, Ann Weston; two *s* one *d*. *Educ:* St Bede's Coll.; Univ. of Manchester (BSc Hons); Harvard Business Sch., 1965–67 (MBA). CEng 1965; FICE 1980; FIWEM (FIWES 1986). Resident Civil Engineer with British Rail, 1961–65; Management Consultant with Arthur D. Little Inc., 1967–72; Booker McConnell Ltd: Secretary to Executive Cttee, 1973; Director, Engineering Div., 1973–76; Chairman, General Engineering Div., 1976–78; Chm. and Chief Exec., Booker McConnell Engineering, and Director, Booker McConnell, 1978–81; Chief Executive: SDP, 1981–83; Welsh Water Authy, 1983–87; MSL International, then MSL Search and Selection: Dir, Public Sector Ops, 1988–90; Dir, 1994–97; Man. Dir, 1997–99; Man. Dir, Hamptons, 1990–92; Gen. Manager, Bristol & West Building Soc., 1992–94; Dir, MSL Gp, 1996–99; Hd of Public Sector Practice, Hoggett Bowers Exec. Search and Selection, 1999–2000; Dir, KPMG Search and Selection, 2001–05. Chairman: Sustainability W Midlands, 2003–07; Wolverhampton Sangat Educn Trust, 2013–. Vice-Chm., NE Worcester Coll., 1998–2002, 2003–07; Gov., Warwicks Coll., 2009– (Chm., 2011–13). CCMI (CBIM 1987); FRSA 1987. *Recreations:* sailing (Times Clipper 2000 Round the World Yacht Race), theatre, reading, walking, bird watching. *Address:* 38A West Road, Bromsgrove, Worcs B60 2NQ. *T:* (01527) 873565.

DOYLE, Gemma; *b* Vale of Leven, 1981. *Educ:* Our Lady and St Patrick's High Sch., Dumbarton; Univ. of Glasgow (MA Eur. Civilisation). Conf. Develt Manager, 2006–07; Conf. Producer, ICE, 2007–08; Political Officer, Parly Lab Party, 2008–10. MP (Lab) W Dunbartonshire, 2010–15; contested (Lab) same seat, 2015. Shadow Minister for Defence Personnel, Welfare and Veterans, 2010–15. Contested (Lab) Scotland, EP, 2004. Member: Unite; Community Union; Co-op Party.

DOYLE, John Howard, MBE 1995; PPRWS (RWS 1968); landscape painter; President, Royal Watercolour Society, 1996–2000; *b* 15 Feb. 1928; *s* of Eric Howard Doyle and Frances Doyle (*née* Maclean); *m* 1st, 1956, Caroline Knapp-Fisher (marr. diss.); one *s* one *d*; 2nd, 1968, Elizabeth Rickatson-Hatt; one *s* one *d*. *Educ:* Sherborne Sch. Dir, C. F. Doyle Ltd, 1961–96; Chm., Thomas Seager Ltd, 1968–86. Mem., Canterbury DAC, 1975–85 (Advr, 1985–). Founder Mem. and Chm., Romney Marsh Historic Churches Trust, 1980–90 (Pres., 1986–). Exhibitions: Chapter House, Canterbury Cathedral, 1973–76, 1997, 2008 and 2009; Spink & Sons, 1981–84, 1991, 1997; Catto Gall., 1988; Sanders of Oxford, 1999; Chris Beetles Gall., 2002; Nat. Trust, Sissinghurst Castle, 2010; Paintings of Mount Athos, Hellenic Centre, Paddington, 2014; exhibitor, RA, 1982–90. Hon. RE 1996; Hon. RI 1996. *Publications:* An Artist's Journey down the Thames, 1993. *Recreations:* golf, gardening. *Address:* Church Farm, Warehorne, Ashford, Kent TN26 2LP. *Club:* Garrick.

DOYLE, Hon. John Jeremy, AC 2002; Chief Justice, Supreme Court of South Australia, 1995–2012; *b* 4 Jan. 1945; *s* of John Malcolm Doyle and Mary Margaret Doyle; *m* 1969, Marie McLoughlin; two *s* three *d*. *Educ:* St Ignatius Coll., Norwood; Univ. of Adelaide (LLB); Magdalen Coll., Oxford (BCL). Partner, Kelly & Co., 1970–77; called to the Bar, SA, 1970; Barrister, Hanson Chambers, 1977–86; QC (SA) 1981; Solicitor-General for S Australia, 1986–95. Pro-Chancellor, Flinders Univ. of S Australia, 1988–2001. Chm., Nat. Judicial Coll. of Australia, 2002–07. Hon. LLD Flinders, 2002; DUniv Adelaide, 2008. *Address:* c/o Chief Justice's Chambers, Supreme Court, 1 Gouger Street, Adelaide, SA 5000, Australia. *T:* (8) 82040390, *Fax:* (8) 82040442.

DOYLE, John Michael; freelance theatre director and writer; *b* 9 Nov. 1952; *s* of John Martin Doyle and Mary Christina Doyle; one *d*; partner, Robert Wilson. *Educ:* RSAMD (DSD); Univ. of Glasgow (CertDS). Jun. Artist-in-Residence, Univ. of Georgia, 1973–74; Dir, Tie-up Th. Co., 1975–78; Dir of Prodns, Eden Court Th., Inverness, 1979–80; Artistic Director: Swan Th., Worcester, 1982–85; Everyman Th., Cheltenham, 1985–89; Everyman Th., Liverpool, 1989–93; Theatre Royal, York, 1993–97; Associate Director: Watermill Th., Newbury, 1997–2005; Classic Stage Co., NY. Productions in NY include: Sweeney Todd (Tony Award for Best Dir of a Musical, 2006); Company; A Catered Affair; Road Show; engagements with Scottish Opera, NY Metropolitan Opera, LA Opera, American Conservatory Th., Stratford Ontario, Houston Grand Opera, Cincinnati Playhouse in the Park, Opera Australia, Royal Danish Opera. Visiting Artist: Univ. of Western Kentucky, 1997, 2000, 2003; Oregon State Univ., 2002; Artist in Residence, Pace Univ., NY, 2013–14; Prof. in Theatre, Princeton Univ. Fellow, Rose Bruford Coll., 2004. FRSA 2001. *Publications:* (with R. Lischner) Shakespeare for Dummies, 1999; contribs to acad. textbooks. *Recreations:* music, tennis, being in Italy. *Address:* Creative Artists Agency, 405 Lexington Avenue, 19th Floor, New York, NY 10174, USA.

DOYLE, (Michael) Leo (Haygarth), CB 2004; Director for Policy and Resources, Government Communications Headquarters, 2003–04; *b* 14 March 1944; *s* of late James Harold Doyle and Florence Doyle (*née* Brown); *m* 1967, Barbara Sillence; two *d*. *Educ:* St John's Coll., Cambridge (Maths Tripos; BA 1965, MA 1969). Joined GCHQ, 1965; on secondment to Diplomatic Service, Washington, 1986–89. Non-exec. Dir, Great Western Ambulance Service NHS Trust, 2006–13. *Recreations:* bell-ringing, gardening. *E:* Leo.Doyle@doylehome.org.uk.

DOYLE, Patrick; composer of film and television scores; *b* 6 April 1953; *s* of Patrick and Sarah Doyle; *m* 1978, Lesley Howard; two *s* two *d*. *Educ:* Royal Scottish Acad. of Music and Drama (FRSAMD 2004). Composer and musical dir, Renaissance Th. Co., 1987–92; *compositions* include: The Thistle and the Rose (song cycle for soprano and mixed choir) to commemorate 90th birthday of the Queen Mother, 1990; *TV scores include:* Look Back in Anger; Twelfth Night; *film scores* include: Henry V, 1989 (Ivor Novello Award for Best Film Theme); Shipwrecked, 1990; Dead Again, 1991; Indochine, Into the West, 1992; Much Ado About Nothing, Carlito's Way, 1993; Frankenstein, 1994; A Little Princess (LA Critics Best Film Score), Une Femme Française, Sense and Sensibility, 1995; Mrs Winterbourne, Hamlet, 1996; Donnie Brasco, 1997; (and songs) Great Expectations, 1998; East West, 1999; Love's Labour's Lost, 2000; Bridget Jones's Diary, Gosford Park, 2001; Killing Me Softly, 2002; Calendar Girls, 2003; Nouvelle France, 2004; Man to Man, Jekyll & Hyde, Nanny McPhee, Harry Potter and the Goblet of Fire, 2005; Wah Wah, 2006; As You Like It, Pars Vite et Reviens Tard, Eragon, The Last Legion, Sleuth, 2007; Nim's Island, Igor, 2008; Jig, La Ligne Droite, Thor, Rise of the Planet of the Apes, 2011; Brave, 2012; The Enchanted Kingdom, 2013; Jack Ryan, 2014; Cinderella, 2015. *Recreations:* swimming, tennis. *Address:* c/o Air-Edel, 18 Rodmarton Street, W1U 8BJ. *T:* (020) 7486 6466, *Fax:* (020) 7224 0344. *E:* air-edel@air-edel.co.uk. *Club:* Glasgow Arts.

DOYLE, Dr Peter, CBE 1992; FRSE; Chairman, Biotechnology and Biological Sciences Research Council, 1998–2003; *b* 6 Sept. 1938; *s* of late Peter and Joan Penman Doyle; *m* 1962, Anita McCulloch; one *s* one *d*. *Educ:* Univ. of Glasgow (BSc Hons 1st class 1960; PhD 1963). FRSE 1993. Research Chemist, ICI Pharmaceuticals, 1963; Manager, Quality Control Dept, 1973–75; Manager, Chemistry Dept, 1975–77; Research Dir, ICI Plant Protection, 1977–86; Business Dir, ICI Seeds, 1985–86; Dep. Chm. and Technical Dir, ICI Pharmaceuticals, 1986–88; Res. and Technol. Dir, ICI Gp, 1989–93; Dir, Zeneca Gp, 1993–99. Dir, AFRC Rothamsted Experimental Station, 1991–98; non-exec. Dir, Oxford Molecular Group PLC, 1997–2000. Member: ACOST, 1989–93; MRC, 1990–94; Royal Commn on Envmtl Pollution, 1994–98; Central R&D Cttee for NHS, 1995–98; UK Round Table on Sustainable Develt, 1998–2000. Trustee, Nuffield Foundn, 1998–2011. Foreign Mem., Royal Swedish Acad. of Engineering Scis, 1990. Liveryman, Salters' Co., 1983 (Master, 2003–04). Hon. DSc: Glasgow, 1992; Nottingham, 1993; Dundee, 1995; Sussex, 1996. *Publications:* contribs to Chemical Communications and Jl Chem. Soc. *Recreation:* golf.

DOYLE, Peter John; QC 2002; *b* 29 Dec. 1951; *s* of Kenneth Charles Doyle and Margaret Doyle (*née* Porter); *m* 1977, Gail Patricia Horspool; one *s* two *d*. *Educ:* Portchester Sch.; Southampton Univ. (LLB Hons). Called to the Bar, Middle Temple, 1975; in practice in criminal law, particularly in serious and complex fraud and related cases; appeared in Public Inquiries incl. Stephen Lawrence, Marchioness, Victoria Climbié. Instructed on behalf of mems of Sen. Police Officers' Assoc. (ACPO ranks). Member: Assoc. of Regulatory and Disciplinary Lawyers; Financial Services Lawyers Assoc. Founder Chair and Trustee, Kalisher Scholarship Trust. Volunteer speaker for Inspiring the Future, Educn and Employers Taskforce. *Recreations:* book collecting, music, gardens. *Address:* 25 Bedford Row, WC1R 4HD. *T:* (020) 7067 1500, *Fax:* (020) 7067 1507. *E:* peterdoyle9@aol.com.

DOYLE, Rt Rev. Peter John Haworth; *see* Northampton, Bishop of, (RC).

DOYLE, Sir Reginald (Derek Henry), Kt 1989; CBE 1980; HM Chief Inspector of Fire Services, 1987–94; *b* 13 June 1929; *s* of John Henry and Elsie Doyle; *m* 1953, June Margretta (*née* Stringer) (*d* 2006); two *d*. *Educ:* Aston Commercial College. RN 1947–54. Fire Brigades, 1954–84; Chief Fire Officer: Worcester City and County, 1973; Hereford and Worcester County, 1974; Kent County, 1977; Home Office Fire Service Inspector, 1984–87. Warden, Guild of Fire Fighters. OStJ 1990. *Recreations:* shooting, swimming, badminton, horses. *Club:* Rotary (Weald of Kent).

DOYLE, Prof. William, DPhil; FBA 1998; FRHistS; Professor of History, 1986–2008, now Emeritus, and Senior Research Fellow, since 2008, University of Bristol; *b* 4 March 1942; *s* of Stanley Joseph Doyle and Mary Alice Bielby; *m* 1968, Christine Thomas. *Educ:* Bridlington Sch.; Oriel Coll., Oxford (BA 1964; MA, DPhil 1968). FRHistS 1976. University of York: Asst Lectr, 1967; Lectr, 1969; Sen. Lectr, 1978; Prof. of Modern History, Univ. of Nottingham, 1981–85. Visiting Professor: Univ. of S Carolina, 1969–70; Univ. de Bordeaux III, 1976; Ecole des Hautes Etudes en Sciences Sociales, Paris, 1988; Vis. Fellow, All Souls Coll., Oxford, 1991–92; Hans Kohn Mem., IAS, Princeton, 2004; Douglas Southall Freeman Prof. of History, Univ. of Richmond, Va, 2010. Dr *hc* Bordeaux, 1987. *Publications:* The Parlement of Bordeaux, 1974; The Old European Order 1660–1800, 1978; Origins of the French Revolution, 1980; The Ancien Régime, 1986; (ed jtly) The Blackwell Dictionary of Historians, 1988; The Oxford History of the French Revolution, 1989; Officers, Nobles and Revolutionaries, 1995; Venality: the sale of offices in eighteenth century France, 1996; (ed jtly) Robespierre, 1999; Jansenism, 1999; La Vénalité, 2000; (ed) Old Regime France, 2001; The French Revolution: a very short introduction, 2001; Aristocracy and its Enemies in the Age of Revolution, 2009; Aristocracy: a very short introduction, 2010; (ed) The Oxford Handbook of the Ancien Regime, 2011; France and the Age of Revolution: regimes old and new from Louis XIV to Napoleon Bonaparte, 2013; Napoleon Bonaparte, 2015; contribs to Past and Present, Historical Jl, French Historical Studies, Studies on Voltaire, Trans RHistS. *Recreations:* books, decorating, travelling about, historical memorabilia. *Address:* (home) Linden House, College Road, Lansdown, Bath BA1 5RR. *T:* (01225) 314341. *Clubs:* Athenæum, Oxford and Cambridge.

DOYLE, William Patrick, PhD; President/Proprietor, Middle East-Asia Consultants, since 1997; President, Texaco Middle East/Far East, 1991–96; *b* 15 Feb. 1932; *s* of James W. Doyle and Lillian I. Doyle (*née* Kime); *m* 1957, Judith A. Gosha; two *s* one *d* (and one *s* decd). *Educ:* Seattle Univ. (BS 1955); Oregon State Univ. (PhD 1959). Texaco, USA: Chemist, 1959; Res. Supervisor, 1966; Asst to Vice Pres. of Petrochemicals, 1968; Asst to Sen. Vice Pres. of Supply and Distribn, 1971; Asst Manager, Producing, 1972; Asst Regional Man., Marketing, 1974; Texaco Ltd: Dep. Man. Dir, 1977; Man. Dir, Exploration and Production, 1981; Vice President: Texaco Europe, 1987; Texaco Latin America and Africa, 1989. Pres., UK Offshore Operators Assoc., 1985 (Vice Pres., 1984). Mem. Council, Amer. Geographic Soc., 1994–2002 (Pres., 2000–02); Vice Chm., Forum of World Affairs, 1998. CCMI (FBIM 1980); MInstD 1982. *Publications:* contrib. Jl of Amer. Chem. Soc. *Recreations:* tennis, music, theatre. *Address:* PO Box 246, Williamsburg, VA 23187–0246, USA.

DOYLE-PRICE, Jackie; MP (C) Thurrock, since 2010; an Assistant Government Whip, since 2015; *b* Sheffield, 5 Aug. 1969; *d* of Brian and Kathleen Doyle-Price. *Educ:* Notre Dame RC Sch., Sheffield; Univ. of Durham (BA Hons Econs/Politics). Asst Parly Officer, City of London, 1993–2000; Asst Private Sec. to Lord Mayor of City of London, 2000–05; Associate, FSA, 2005–10. Mem., Grays RAFA. *Recreations:* reading, theatre, music. *Address:* House of Commons, SW1A 0AA. *T:* (020) 7219 7171. *E:* jackie.doyleprice.mp@parliament.uk. *Club:* Grays Conservative.

D'OYLY, Sir Hadley Gregory, 15th Bt *cr* 1663, of Shottisham, Norfolk; *b* 29 May 1956; *o s* of Sir Nigel D'Oyly, 14th Bt and Dolores, *d* of R. H. Gregory; *S* father, 2000; *m* 1st, 1978, Margaret May Dent (marr. diss. 1982); 2nd, 1991, Annette Frances Elizabeth (*née* White); two *d*. *Educ:* Milton Abbey.

DRABBLE, Jane; *see* Drabble, M. J.

DRABBLE, Dame Margaret, (Dame Margaret Holroyd), DBE 2008 (CBE 1980); author; *b* 5 June 1939; 2nd *d* of His Honour J. F. Drabble, QC and late Kathleen Marie Bloor; *m* 1st, 1960, Clive Walter Swift, *qv* (marr. diss. 1975); two *s* one *d*; 2nd, 1982, Michael (de Courcy Fraser) Holroyd (*see* Sir Michael Holroyd). *Educ:* The Mount Sch., York; Newnham Coll., Cambridge. Lives in London and W Somerset. Chm., Nat. Book League, 1980–82 (Dep. Chm., 1978–80). E. M. Forster Award, 1973, Hon. Mem., 2002, Amer. Acad. of Arts and Letters; Hon. Fellow, Sheffield City Polytechnic, 1989. Hon. DLitt: Sheffield, 1976; Manchester, 1987; Keele, 1988; Bradford, 1988; Hull, 1992; UEA, 1994; York, 1995; Cambridge, 2006. St Louis Literary Award, St Louis Univ. Liby Associates, 2003; Golden Pen Award, 2011. *Publications:* A Summer Birdcage, 1963; The Garrick Year, 1964; The Millstone (John Llewellyn Rhys Prize), 1966 (filmed, as A Touch of Love, 1969); Jerusalem the Golden (James Tait Black Meml Prize), 1967; The Waterfall, 1969; The Needle's Eye, 1972; (ed with B. S. Johnson) London Consequences, 1972; The Realms of Gold, 1975; The Ice Age, 1977; The Middle Ground, 1980; The Radiant Way, 1987; A Natural Curiosity, 1989; The Gates of Ivory, 1991; The Witch of Exmoor, 1996; The Peppered Moth, 2001; The Seven Sisters, 2002; The Red Queen, 2004; The Sea Lady, 2006; A Day in the Life of a Smiling Woman: complete short stories, 2011; The Pure Gold Baby, 2013; *non-fiction:* Wordsworth, 1966; Arnold Bennett, a biography, 1974; (ed) The Genius of Thomas Hardy, 1976; (ed jtly) New Stories 1, 1976; For Queen and Country, 1978; A Writer's Britain, 1979; (ed) The Oxford Companion to English Literature, 5th edn, 1985, 6th edn 2000; (ed with Jenny Stringer) The Concise Oxford Companion to English Literature, 1987; Safe as Houses, 1989; Angus Wilson: a biography, 1995; The Pattern in the Carpet: a personal history with jigsaws, 2009. *Recreations:* walking, dreaming. *Address:* c/o United Agents Ltd, 12–26 Lexington Street, W1F 0LE.

See also R. J. B. Drabble.

DRABBLE, (Mary) Jane, OBE 2000; Director of Education, BBC, 1994–99; Chair, Bath Festivals, 2009–14; *b* 15 Jan. 1947; *d* of late Walter Drabble and of Molly (*née* Boreham). *Educ:* Bristol Univ. (BA Hons 1968). BBC: Studio Manager, 1968–72; Producer, Radio Current Affairs, 1972–75; Asst Producer, then Producer, TV Current Affairs, 1975–87; Editor, Everyman, 1987–91; Head of Factual Progs, 1993–94, Asst Man. Dir, 1991–94, Network TV. Comr for Judicial Appts, 2001–06; Mem., Capability Reviews Team, Cabinet Office, 2006–09. Mem., LSC, 2000–06; Vice-Chm., Basic Skills Agency, 2001–04. Chair: Mental Health Media, 2002–06; Nat. Skills Academies Panel, 2005–08; Arts Award Partnership Bd, 2005–10. Mem., SW Regl Arts Council, 2012–13. Director: Birmingham Royal Ballet, 2002–10; Bournemouth SO, 2013–. Gov., 2002–, Bd Mem., 2003–12, RSC.

DRABBLE, Richard John Bloor; QC 1995; *b* 23 May 1950; *s* of His Honour John Frederick Drabble, QC and late Kathleen Marie Drabble; *m* 1980, Sarah Madeleine Hope Lewis; two *s* (and one *s* decd). *Educ:* Leighton Park Sch., Reading; Downing Coll., Cambridge (BA Hons). Called to the Bar, Inner Temple, 1975, Bencher, 2002; Junior Counsel to the Crown, Common Law, 1992. Chm., Administrative Law Bar Assoc., 1999–2001; Mem., Law Reform Cttee, Bar Council. *Publications:* (contrib.) Judicial Review, ed Supperstone and Goudie, 1992, 5th edn 2006; (ed) Local Authorities and Human Rights, 2004; (consultant ed.) Halsbury's Law: welfare benefits and state pensions, 2014; various articles. *Recreations:* reading, walking. *Address:* Landmark Chambers, 180 Fleet Street, EC4A 2HG. *T:* (020) 7430 1221.

See also Dame A. S. Byatt, Dame M. Drabble.

DRABU, Khurshid Hassan, CBE 2010; a Senior Immigration Judge, Asylum and Immigration Tribunal (formerly a Vice President, Immigration Appeal Tribunal), 2000–08; a First-tier Fee Paid Tribunal Judge, since 2009; a Deputy Judge of the Upper Tribunal, Immigration and Asylum Chamber, since 2010; *b* Srinagar, Kashmir, 8 March 1946; *o s* of late Ghulam Nabi and Zarifa Nabi Drabu; *m* 1972, Reefat Khurshid Drabu, GP; one *s* three *d*. *Educ:* Univ. of Jammu and Kashmir (BA Hons 1967); Aligarh Muslim Univ., India (LLB 1st Cl., Gold Medal, 1969). Called to the Bar, Inner Temple, 1977; Counsellor, 1977–84, Dep. Dir, 1984–89, UKIAS; Dep. Legal Dir and Hd of Litigation, CRE, 1990–97; Special Adjudicator, Immigration Appeals, 1997–2000. Part-time Legal Mem., Mental Health Rev. Tribunal, 1987–2000. Muslim Council of Britain: Advr on Constitutional Affairs, 1996–; Convenor, Bd of Counsellors, 2006–; Chm., Friends, 2006–. Muslim Advr to MoD, 2002–. Project Dir, Nat. Adv. Bd, Mosques and Imams, 2007–09 (Special Advr, 2009–). Founder Trustee, Kashmir Med. Relief Trust UK, 1982–; Chm., Kashmiri Assoc. of GB, 1997–2005; Chm., Art Asia Trust Ltd, 1996–2002. Mem., Editl Bd, Immigration and Nationality, Law and Practice, 1985–89. Chm., Southampton Medina Mosque Trust Ltd, 2010–. Trustee, Joseph Interfaith Foundn, 2013–. JP Eastleigh, 1985–98. Lifetime Achievement Award: Global Peace and Unity, 2007; Assoc. of Muslim Lawyers UK, 2007; 'Good Citizenship' Alija Izetbegović Prize, Muslim News Awards for Excellence, 2007. *Publications:* Mandatory Visas, 1991. *Recreations:* cricket, gardening, photography, travel.

DRACE-FRANCIS, Charles David Stephen, CMG 1987; *b* 15 March 1943; *m* 1967, Griselda Hyacinthe Waldegrave; two *s* one *d*. *Educ:* Magdalen Coll., Oxford. HM Diplomatic Service, 1965–2001: Third Sec., FO, 1965; Tehran, 1967; Second, later First Sec., FCO, 1971; Asst Political Advr, Hong Kong, 1974; First Sec., Office of UK Rep. to EEC, Brussels, 1978; FCO, 1980; All Souls Coll., Oxford, 1983; Chargé d'affaires, Kabul, 1984; Counsellor, Lisbon, 1987; Govt Affairs Dir, BAe, 1991 (on secondment); Head, West Indian and Atlantic Dept, FCO, 1994–97; High Comr, PNG, 1997–2000.

DRAGO RODRÍGUEZ, Rolando; Ambassador of Chile to the Court of St James's, since 2014; *b* Santiago, Chile, 27 May 1953; *s* of Angel Drago and Elsa Rodríguez; *m* Edith Gallardo; one *s* one *d*. *Educ:* Technol. Inst. of Chile (BA 1974); Univ. Católica de Chile (MA Internat. Relns 1977); Diplomatic Acad. of Chile. Ambassador and Dir of HR, Min. of Foreign Affairs, Chile, 2005; Ambassador to Indonesia and E Timor, 2006–07; to Venezuela, 2007–09; Ambassador and Dir of Protocol, Min. of Foreign Affairs, 2009–10; Ambassador to Cuba, 2010–14. *Recreations:* scuba diving, squash. *Address:* Embassy of Chile, 37–41 Old Queen Street, SW1H 9JA. *T:* (020) 7222 2361. *E:* rdragoster@gmail.com. *Club:* Canning.

DRAINEY, Rt Rev. Terence Patrick; *see* Middlesbrough, Bishop of, (RC).

DRAINVILLE, Rt Rev. Dennis Paul; *see* Quebec, Bishop of.

DRAKE, Baroness *cr* 2010 (Life Peer), of Shene in the County of Surrey; **Jeannie Lesley Patricia Drake,** CBE 2006 (OBE 2002); a Deputy Secretary General, Communication Workers Union, 1995–2008; *b* 16 Jan. 1948. *Educ:* Brunel Univ. (BSc); London Sch. of Econs and Pol Sci. (MSc). Res. Officer, NUPE; Gp Sec., CPSA Post and Telecom Gp, 1976–85; Dep. Gen. Sec., Nat. Communication Union, 1985–95. Pres., TUC, 2004–05. Comr, Equal Opportunities Commn, 2000–07; Member: Pensions Commn, 2002–06; Equality and Human Rights Commn, 2006–09; Chm., Rly Pensions Commn, 2006–08. Member: Employment Tribunal, 1988–2001; Employment Appeal Tribunal, 2001–; Bd, Sector Skills Develt Agency, 2001–08; Personal Accounts Delivery Authority, 2007–08 (actg Chm., 2008–10); Ind. Mem., Walker Guidelines Monitoring Gp (Private Equity), 2008–. Non-exec. Dir, Pension Protection Fund, 2004–10. Mem., Supervisory Bd, Union Moderation Fund, BIS (formerly BERR), 2005–11. Trustee: Alliance & Leicester Pension Scheme, 1992–; O2 Pension Scheme, 2003–. Gov., Pensions Policy Inst. *Address:* House of Lords, SW1A 0PW.

DRAKE, David Paul, FRCS, FRCPCH; Consultant Paediatric Surgeon, Evelina London Children's Hospital, 2012–15; *b* 9 Feb. 1945; *s* of late Ronald Ingram Drake and of Diana Louisa Drake (*née* Markham); *m* 1976, Linda Ann Callear; two *s*. *Educ:* Blundell's Sch., Tiverton; Clare Coll., Cambridge (MA; MB BChir). FRCS 1974; FRCPCH 1997. Consultant Paediatric Surgeon: Guy's Hosp., London, 1979–88; Gt Ormond St Hosp. for Children, 1988–2010 (Med. Dir, 2002–05). Hon. Sen. Lectr, Inst. of Child Health, Univ. of London, subseq. UCL, 1988–2012. Hon. Paediatric Surgeon, St Luke's Hosp. for the Clergy, 1989–2004; Vis. Paediatric Surgeon, Kilimanjaro Christian Med. Coll., Tanzania, 2011–12. Pres., British Assoc. of Paediatric Surgeons, 2008–10. Mem., Christian Med. Fellowship. *Publications:* contrib. chapter on neonatal surgery to The New Aird's Companion in Surgical Studies, ed K. Burnand and A. Young, 1992, 2nd edn 1998; contrib. papers to surgical and paediatric jls on neonatal surgical and paediatric surgical topics. *Recreations:* travelling, reading, cycling. *Address:* 14 College Gardens, Dulwich, SE21 7BE. *T:* (020) 8693 3220. *Club:* Royal Society of Medicine.

DRAKE, Howard Ronald, OBE 2002; HM Diplomatic Service; High Commissioner to Canada, since 2013; *b* 13 Aug. 1956; *s* of late Ronald Henry Drake and Marie Kathleen Drake; *m* 1988, Gillian Summerfield; one *s* one *d*. *Educ:* Churcher's Coll., Petersfield. Joined Foreign and Commonwealth Office, 1975; Vice-Consul (Commercial), Los Angeles, 1981–83; Second Sec. (Political), Santiago, 1985–88; First Sec., FCO, 1988–92; First Sec. and Head of Chancery, Singapore, 1992–95; Dep. Head, Non-Proliferation Dept, FCO, 1995–97; Dir, Invest in Britain Bureau USA, subseq. Invest UK-USA, and Dep. Consul-Gen., NY, 1997–2002; Asst Dir, Human Resources, FCO, 2002–05; Ambassador to Chile, 2005–09; High Comr to Jamaica and the Commonwealth of the Bahamas, 2010–13. *Recreations:* cricket, tennis, golf, squash, ski-ing, music. *Address:* c/o Foreign and Commonwealth Office, King Charles Street, SW1A 2AH.

DRAKE, James Frederick; QC 2011; barrister and arbitrator; *b* Adelaide, SA, 13 March 1959; *s* of Frederick George Drake and Palmira Rose Drake; *m* 1993, Karen Falcocchio; one *s* two *d*. *Educ:* Sacred Heart Coll., Adelaide; Univ. of South Australia (BA 1980); Univ. of Adelaide (LLB Hons 1985); Columbia Univ., NY (LLM 1992). Chartered Arbitrator 2004; FCIArb 2004; Fellow, Australian Centre for Internat. Commercial Arbitration, 2012. Admitted: Barrister and Solicitor, SA, 1985; Solicitor, NSW, 1987; Attorney, NY, 1991; called to the Bar, Lincoln's Inn, 1998. Accountant, KPMG Adelaide, 1980–81; solicitor, Reilly Ahern and Kerin, Adelaide, 1985–86; Sen. Associate, Baker & McKenzie, Sydney and NY, 1987–93; Attorney and Partner, Owen & Davis, NY, 1994–98; barrister, 7 King's Bench Walk, 1999–. Chair, Anglo-Australasian Lawyers Soc., 2012–. *Recreations:* family, vineyard, wine, golf, travel, reading. *Address:* 7 King's Bench Walk, Temple, EC4Y 7DS. *T:* (020) 7910 8300, *Fax:* (020) 7910 8400. *E:* jdrake@7kbw.co.uk. *Clubs:* Roehampton; Wentworth.

DRAKE, John Gair; Chief Registrar and Chief Accountant, Bank of England, 1983–90; *b* 11 July 1930; *s* of John Nutter Drake and Anne Drake; *m* 1957, Jean Pamela Bishop; one *s* one *d*. *Educ:* University College School; The Queen's College, Oxford. MA. Joined Bank of England, 1953; editor, Quarterly Bulletin, 1971; Asst Chief Cashier, 1973; Management Development Manager, 1974; Dep. Chief, Economic Intell. Dept, 1977; Dep. Chief Cashier and Dep. Chief, Banking Dept, 1980. Governor, South Bank Univ. (formerly Poly.), 1987–96 (Hon. Fellow, 1997). *Address:* 42B Manor Avenue, Caterham, Surrey CR3 6AN. *T:* (01883) 346130. *Clubs:* MCC; Chaldon Cricket; Bletchingly Golf.

DRAKE, Julius Michael; pianist; Artistic Director, Machynlleth Festival, since 2009; *b* 5 April 1959; *s* of Michael Drake and late Jean Drake (known professionally as Jean Meikle); *m* 1987, Belinda, *d* of Gen. Sir (James) Michael Gow, GCB; two *d*. *Educ:* Purcell Sch.; Royal Coll. of Music (ARCM). Débuts: Wigmore Hall, with Nicholas Daniel, 1983; Paris, with Sally Burgess, 1990; New York, with Derek Lee Ragin, 1991; Tokyo, with Emma Johnson, 1993; since 1983 has appeared regularly at all major concert halls in Europe and USA, with Victoria de los Angeles, Simon Keenlyside, Sir Thomas Allen, Olaf Bär, Ian Bostridge, Wolfgang Holzmair, Thomas Quasthoff, Angelika Kirchschlager, Dorothea Röschman, Alice Coote, Gerald Finley, Christopher Maltman, etc; has also performed in vocal and instrumental recitals in Amsterdam, Cologne, Salzburg Fest., Edinburgh Fest., Frankfurt, London, NY, Chicago, Paris, San Francisco, Vienna and Zurich; has taken masterclasses in Amsterdam, Oxford, Vienna, Brussels, Porto, Toronto and Cleveland, Ohio. Director: Perth Internat. Chamber Music Fest., Australia, 2001–03; Leeds Lieder, 2009. Professor: Royal Acad. of Music, 1992–; Kunstuniversität, Graz, 2010–. Devised song recital series: Schumann, S Bank, 1990; Britten, 1995–96, Nineties, 1997–98, Vaughan Williams, 2008–09, Schumann, 2010; Wolf Songbooks 2011–12: Wigmore Hall; Brahms, Concertgebouw Amsterdam, 2002–03; Julius Drake and Friends, Middle Temple Hall, 2005–06, 2007–08, 2008–09, 2009–10, 2011–12, 2013. Broadcasts include: presenting and performing Complete Songs of Gabriel Fauré (radio), 1994; with Ian Bostridge, Schubert's Winterreise (TV film and documentary), 1997. Recordings with world's leading singers incl. Schumann Myrten op. 25, Howells Complete Songs, Schumann Dichterliebe, Schubert Lieder (2 vols), Schumann Lieder, The English Songbook, Sibelius Songs, Gurney Songs, Britten Canticles, Ives Songs, Spanish Songs, Barber Songs, Mahler Songs, Schumann Frauenliebe und Leben, Grieg Songs, Schumann Heine Songs, Tchaikovsky Songs, Ravel Songs, Britten Songs, French Sonatas (oboe and piano), Kodaly Sonata (cello and piano), Songs with Words (solo piano). Hon. FRAM. Hon. Bencher, Middle Temple, 2013. Gramophone Award, 1998, 2007, 2009, 2011; Edison Award, 2002; BBC Music Mag. Award, 2010, 2012; Juno Award, 2015. *Recreations:* tennis, walking, novels. *Address:* c/o IMG Artists, The Light Box, 111 Power Road, Chiswick, W4 5PY. *T:* (020) 7957 5800, *Fax:* (020) 8742 8758. *E:* aianni@imgartists.com. *W:* www.juliusdrake.com.

DRAKE, Madeline Mary; consultant and writer; Chief Executive, Richmond Fellowship, 1995–2001; *b* 5 Oct. 1945; *d* of Ernest and Olive Drake; *m* 1st, 1971, Anthony Gerald Biebuyck (marr. diss.); 2nd, 1983, Prof. Stephen Bernard Torrance; one *s* one *d*. *Educ:* Birmingham Univ. (BA Hons Russian/French; DipSocSc); Middlesex Univ. (BSc Herbal Medicine 2009). Home Office researcher, 1972–73; researcher, Centre for Envmtl Studies, 1973–80; Founder and Dir, Housing and Social Policy Res., 1980–95. Member, Board: Circle Thirty Three Gp, 1976–2005 (Vice-Chm., 1987–94); Shelter, 1987–2005 (Mem., Audit and Finance Cttee, 2007–); Dir, Turnstone Support, 2009–; Mem. Council, Internat. Year for Shelter for Homeless, 1987. Lectures, broadcasts. Mem., IPSM. FRSA. *Publications:* Single and Homeless, 1981; Homelessness: a capital problem, 1984; Managing Hostels, 1986; Housing Associations and 1992, 1992; Europe and 1992, 1992; numerous articles on housing, Europe and the Soviet Union in nat. and internat. jls. *Recreations:* violin, walking, riding, gardening. *Address:* 13 Quernmore Road, N4 4QT.

DRAKEFORD, Mark; Member (Lab) Cardiff West, National Assembly for Wales, since 2011; Minister for Health and Social Services, since 2013; *m*; three *c*. Probation Officer, then Sen. Probation Officer, S Glam Probation Service, 1979–89; Project Leader, Ely Community Shop, Barnardo's, 1989–91; Lectr in Applied Social Studies, Univ. of Wales, Swansea, 1991–95; Cardiff University: Lectr, Sch. of Social and Admin. Studies, 1995–99; Sen. Lectr, 1999–2003; Prof. of Social Policy and Applied Social Scis, 2003–. Health and Social Policy Advr and Hd, First Minister's Political Office, Welsh Assembly Govt, 2000–10. Mem. (Lab) S Glamorgan CC, 1985–93. *Publications:* (with Ian Butler) Scandal, Social Policy and Social Welfare, 2003, 2nd edn 2005; (with Ian Butler) Social Work on Trial: the Maria Colwell Inquiry and the state of welfare, 2011; (with Bill Jordan) Social Policy and Social Work, 2012; articles in jls and chapters in books. *Address:* National Assembly for Wales, Cardiff Bay, Cardiff CF99 1NA.

DRAPER, Alan Gregory; Director, Defence Procurement Management Group, Royal Military College of Science, 1988–91; *b* 11 June 1926; *e s* of late William Gregory Draper and Ada Gertrude (*née* Davies); *m* 1st, 1953, Muriel Sylvia Cuss, FRSA (marr. diss.); three *s*; 2nd,

1977, Jacqueline Gubel (*d* 2006); one step *d. Educ:* Leeds Grammar Sch.; The Queen's Coll., Oxford (Scholar 1944; MA 1951). RNVR, 1945; Sub-Lt, 1946–47. Admiralty: Asst Principal, 1950; Private Sec. to Civil Lord of the Admiralty, 1953–55; MoD, 1957–60; Head of Pol Sect., Admiralty, 1960–64; First Sec., UK Delegn to NATO, 1964–66; Asst Sec., MoD, 1966; Counsellor, UK Delegn to NATO, 1974–77; Chm., NATO Budget Cttees, 1977–81; Royal Ordnance Factories: Personnel Dir, 1982–84; Dir Gen., Personnel, 1984; Dir, Management/Career Develt, Royal Ordnance plc, 1985; Sen. Lectr, Defence Procurement, RMCS, 1986–91. MIPM 1985. *Publications:* British Involvement in Major European Collaborative Defence Projects 1957–87, 1990. *Recreations:* reading, music, watching international Rugby Union on television. *Address:* 63 Homelawn House, Bexhill on Sea, E Sussex TN40 1PN.

DRAPER, Gerald Carter, OBE 1974; Chairman: G. Draper Consultancy, since 1988; Draper Associates Ltd, 1982–88; *b* 24 Nov. 1926; *s* of Alfred Henderson Draper and Mona Violanta (*née* Johnson); *m* 1951, Winifred Lilian Howe; one *s* three *d. Educ:* Univ. of Dublin, Trinity Coll. (MA). FCIM, FCIT. Joined Aer Lingus, 1947; Advertising and PR Manager, 1950; Commercial Man., Central Afr. Airways, 1959; British European Airways: Advertising Man., 1964; Asst Gen. Man. (Market Develt), 1966; Gen. Man. and Dir, Travel Sales Div., 1970; British Airways: Dir, Travel Div., 1973; Marketing Dir, 1977; Dir, Commercial Ops, 1978; Mem. Bd, 1978–82; Man. Dir, Intercontinental Services Div., 1982. Chairman: British Air Tours Ltd, 1978–82; Silver Wing Surface Arrangements Ltd, 1971–82; Deputy Chairman: Trust Houses Forte Travel Ltd, 1974–82; ALTA Ltd, 1977–82; Hoverspeed, 1984–87; Member Board: Internat. Aeradio Ltd, 1971–82; British Airways Associated Cos Ltd, 1972–82; British Intercontinental Hotels Ltd, 1976–82; Communications Strategy Ltd, 1984–86; AGB Travel Research Internat. Ltd, 1984–86; Centre for Airline and Travel Marketing Ltd, 1986–; BR (Southern Region), 1990–92; British Travel Educnl Trust, 1990–2005. Chm., Outdoor Advertising Assoc., 1985–92. Master, Co. of Marketors, 1990; Mem., Guild of Freemen, 1991. FRSA 1979. Chevalier de l'Ordre du Tastevin, 1980; Chambellan de l'Ordre des Coteaux de Champagne, 1982. *Recreation:* shooting. *Address:* Old Chestnut, Onslow Road, Burwood Park, Walton-on-Thames, Surrey KT12 5AY. *Club:* National Clay Shooting Centre (Bisley).

DRAPER, Very Rev. Dr Jonathan Lee; Dean of Exeter, since 2012; *b* Boston, Mass, 27 Feb. 1952; *s* of Robert and Lois Draper; *m* 1979, Maggie Barham; one *s* two *d. Educ:* Plainfield High Sch., NJ; Gordon Coll., USA (BA 1976); Univ. of Durham (BA Hons 1978; PhD 1984); Univ. of Oxford (CTh 1983). Ordained deacon, 1983, priest, 1984; Asst Curate, St John the Divine, Manchester, 1983–85; Lectr in Theology, and Dir of Studies, Ripon Coll., Cuddesdon, Oxford, 1985–92; Vicar of Putney, 1992–2000; Canon Theologian, York Minster, 2000–12. Trustee, BasicNeeds, 1999–. *Publications:* (ed) Communion and Episcopacy, 1988; To Love and Serve, 2003; (ed jtly) Liberating Texts?, 2008; (ed jtly) Christianity and the renewal of Nature, 2011; articles and reviews in jls incl. Modern Believing, Cross Currents, Modern Theology, Jl of Theol. Studies, Jl of Coll. of Preachers. *Recreations:* walking in wild places, entertaining, cinema, sport, reading, running. *Address:* The Cathedral Offices, 1 The Cloisters, Exeter EX1 1HS. *T:* (01392) 255573. *E:* dean@exeter-cathedral.org.uk.

DRAPER, Michael William; Under Secretary, Department of Health and Social Security, 1976–78, retired; *b* 26 Sept. 1928; *s* of late John Godfrey Beresford Draper and Aileen Frances Agatha Draper (*née* Masefield); *m* 1952, Theodora Mary Frampton, *o d* of late Henry James Frampton, CSI, CIE; one *s* two *d. Educ:* St Edward's Sch., Oxford. FCA. Chartered Accountant, 1953; various posts in England, Ireland, Burma, Nigeria, Unilever Ltd, 1953–64; joined Civil Service, 1964; Principal, Min. of Power, 1964; Asst Sec., DHSS, 1972–76. Sec., Diocese of Bath and Wells, 1978–88; mem. of staff team, Lamplugh House, Christian Renewal Conf. Centre, 1988–89; working with Anglican Church in Zambia, 1991; associated with Sharing of Ministries Abroad, 1992–2000. *Recreations:* philately, church affairs. *Address:* 25 Clift House, 14 Langley Road, Chippenham, Wilts SN15 1DS.

DRAPER, Prof. Paul Richard, PhD; Professor of Finance, 2002–08, now Emeritus, and Head of School of Business and Economics, 2002–08, University of Exeter; Professor of Finance (part-time), University of Leeds, 2009–14; *b* 28 Dec. 1946; *s* of James Krishen Draper and Dorothy Jean Draper; *m* 1972, Janet Margaret Grant; one *s* one *d. Educ:* Univ. of Exeter (BA Econs 1968); Univ. of Reading (MA Econs 1969); Univ. of Stirling (PhD Finance 1973). Esmée Fairbairn Lectr, Univ. of St Andrews, 1973–75; Lectr, Univ. of Edinburgh, 1976–78; University of Strathclyde: Esmée Fairbairn Sen. Lectr, 1976–86, Prof., 1986–95; Hd, Dept of Accounting and Finance, 1990–95; Vice Dean, Business Sch., 1993–97; University of Edinburgh: Walter Scott and Partners Prof. of Finance, 1997–2001; Hd, Sch. of Business and Econs, 2000–01. Hon. Prof., Heriot-Watt Univ., 2011–; Vis. Prof., Portsmouth Business Sch., Univ. of Portsmouth, 2013–. Director: Thomas Hall Estates, 2005–08; China Eagle Hedge Fund, 2013–. Member: Panel for Accounting and Finance, 2001 and 2008 RAEs; Acad. Bd, Inst. of Financial Services, 2005–08. *Publications:* The Scottish Financial Sector (jtly), 1988; Investment Trust Industry in the UK, 1989; articles in Jl of Derivatives, Jl of Futures Markets, Jl of Financial Res., Jl of Business Finance and Accounting, European Financial Mgt, Financial Analysts Jl, etc. *Recreations:* travel, urban walking, houses. *Address:* 58 Lynch Road, Farnham, Surrey GU9 8BX. *T:* (01252) 710175. *E:* P.R.Draper@ex.ac.uk.

DRAPER, Peter Sydney, CB 1994; Principal Establishment and Finance Officer, Property Services Agency, 1993–95; *b* 18 May 1935; *s* of late Sydney George Draper and Norah Draper; *m* 1959, Elizabeth Ann (*née* French); two *s* (and one *s* decd). *Educ:* Haberdashers' Aske's; Regent Polytechnic Sch. of Management (Dip. in Management Studies). Joined GCHQ, Cheltenham, 1953; Min. of Transport, 1956–70; Principal, 1969; Department of the Environment, 1970–95: Directorate of Estate Management Overseas, PSA, 1970; Asst Sec., 1975; Head of Staff Resources Div., 1975–78; Asst Dir, Home Regional Services, 1978–80; RCDS, 1981; Dir, Eastern Reg., 1982–84, Under Sec., Dir of Defence Services II, 1985–87, Principal Establishment Officer, 1987–93, PSA. Mem., CSAB, 1996–2002. Dir, City of Cambridge Brewery Co. Ltd, 2002–12. *Recreations:* gardening, golf. *Address:* Langdale, 22 Brewery Road, Pampisford, Cambs CB22 3EN. *Club:* Saffron Walden Golf.

DRAPER, Roger James; Chief Executive, Warrington Wolves, since 2015; *b* 19 Jan. 1970; *s* of Eric Draper and Marjorie Draper; *m* 1994, Nicola Entract; two *s. Educ:* Bolton Sch.; Winstanley Coll.; Loughborough Univ. (BSc Hons (PE, Sports Sci. and Recreation Mgt)). Dir of Develt, LTA, 1998–2002; Sport England: Chief Operating Officer, 2002–03; Chief Exec., 2003–06; Chief Exec., LTA, 2006–13. MInstD 1999; Mem., Inst. of Leisure and Amenity Mgt, 2000–. *Recreations:* Rugby League (professional player, GB Students Rugby League, 1988–94), tennis (winner, British Univs Tennis Championship, 1989–92; senior county player; Captain, Lancs and Surrey, 1996–). *Club:* International Club of GB.

DRAPER, Prof. Ronald Philip, PhD; Regius Chalmers Professor of English, University of Aberdeen, 1986–94, now Professor Emeritus; *b* 3 Oct. 1928; *s* of Albert William and Elsie Draper; *m* 1950, Irene Margaret Aldridge; three *d. Educ:* Univ. of Nottingham (BA, PhD). Educn Officer, RAF, 1953–55. Lectr in English, Univ. of Adelaide, 1955–56; Lectr, Univ. of Leicester, 1957–68, Sen. Lectr, 1968–73; Prof., Univ. of Aberdeen, 1973–86. *Dramatic scripts:* (with P. A. W. Collins) The Canker and the Rose, Mermaid Theatre, 1964; (with Richard Hoggart) D. H. L., A Portrait of D. H. Lawrence, Nottingham Playhouse, 1967 (televised 1980). *Publications:* D. H. Lawrence, 1964, 3rd edn 1984; (ed) D. H. Lawrence, The Critical Heritage, 1970, 3rd edn 1986; (ed) Hardy, The Tragic Novels, 1975, rev. edn 1991; (ed) George Eliot, The Mill on the Floss and Silas Marner, 1977, 3rd edn 1984; (ed) Tragedy, Developments in Criticism, 1980; Lyric Tragedy, 1985; The Winter's Tale, Text and Performance, 1985; (ed) Hardy, Three Pastoral Novels, 1987; (ed) The Literature of Region and Nation, 1989; (with Martin Ray) An Annotated Critical Bibliography of Thomas Hardy, 1989; (ed) The Epic: developments in criticism, 1990; (ed with P. Mallett) A Spacious Vision: essays on Hardy, 1994; An Introduction to Twentieth-Century Poetry in English, 1999; Shakespeare: the comedies, 2000; contrib. Oxford DNB; articles and reviews in Archiv für das Studium der Neueren Sprachen und Literaturen, Critical Qly, Essays in Criticism, Etudes Anglaises, English Studies, Jl of D. H. Lawrence Soc., Lit. of Region and Nation, Longman Critical Essays, MLR, New Lit. Hist., Notes and Queries, Revue des Langues Vivantes, Rev. of English Studies, Shakespeare Qly, Studies in Short Fiction, THES, Thomas Hardy Annual, Thomas Hardy Jl. *Recreations:* reading, listening to music. *Address:* Eldon House, Wootton Village, Boars Hill, Oxford OX1 5HP. *T:* (01865) 682158.

See also I. F. Hudson.

DRAX, Richard Grosvenor; MP (C) South Dorset, since 2010; farmer; *b* 29 Jan. 1958; *s* of (Henry) Walter Plunkett-Ernle-Erle-Drax and Hon. Pamela Rose (*née* Weeks); *m* 1st, 1985, Zara Victoria Legge-Bourke (marr. diss. 1997); two *s* two *d*; 2nd, 1998, Eliza Sarah Dugdale; 3rd, 2009, Elsebet Bødtker. *Educ:* Harrow Sch.; Royal Agricl Coll., Cirencester (Dip. Rural Land Mgt 1990); Dip. Journalism 1995. Served Coldstream Guards, 1978–87. Journalist: Yorks Evening Press, 1991–96; Tyne Tees TV, Daily Express and Daily Telegraph, 1996–97; and reporter, BBC Radio Solent and BBC South Today, 1997–2006. *Address:* House of Commons, SW1A 0AA.

DRAYSON, family name of **Baron Drayson**.

DRAYSON, Baron *cr* 2004 (Life Peer), of Kensington in the Royal Borough of Kensington and Chelsea; **Paul Rudd Drayson;** PC 2008; PhD; FREng; Chairman and Chief Executive Officer, Drayson Technologies; Managing Director, Drayson Racing Technologies (formerly Drayson Motor Racing) LLP; *b* 5 March 1960; *s* of Michael Rudd Drayson and Ruth Irene Drayson; *m* 1994, Elspeth Jane Bellhouse; three *s* two *d. Educ:* St Dunstan's Coll., London; Aston Univ. (BSc Hons; PhD); FREng 2011. Man. Dir, Lambourn Food Co., 1986–91; founder and Dir, Genysys Develt Ltd, 1991–95; co-founder, 1993 and Chief Exec., 1993–2003, PowderJect Pharmaceuticals; Entrepreneur in Residence, Saïd Business Sch., Oxford Univ., 2003–05. Parly Under-Sec. of State, MoD, 2005–07; Minister of State: MoD and BERR, 2007; DIUS, later BIS, 2008–10; MoD, 2009–10. Chm., BioIndustry Assoc., 2001–02. Non-exec. Dir, Royal Navy Bd. Mem. Council, Univ. of Oxford. Chm., Oxford Children's Hosp. Campaign, 2002–05. Hon. Pres., Motorsport Industry Assoc. *Recreations:* sword fencing, motor racing. *Address:* House of Lords, SW1A 0PW. *Clubs:* British Racing Drivers, Royal Automobile.

DRECHSLER, Paul Joseph, Hon. CBE 2015; Chairman, Bibby Line Group, since 2015; President, Confederation of British Industry, since 2015; *b* 16 April 1956; *s* of Frank Stephen Drechsler and Marie Winifred Drechsler (*née* Clancy); *m* 1981, Wendy Isobel Hackett; two *s* one *d. Educ:* Trinity Coll., Dublin (BA); INSEAD (IEP). Chief Executive Officer: ICI Brasil SA, 1992; ICI Acrylics Inc., 1993–96; ICI Polyester, 1996–98; Quest Internat., 1998–2003; Exec. Dir, ICI plc, 1999–2003; Chief Exec., 2004–13, Chm., 2006–13, Wates Gp Ltd. Sen. Ind. Dir, Essentra (formerly Filtrona) plc, 2005–. Chm., Teach First, 2013–. Dir, BITC, 2011–; Mem., Main Bd, CBI, 2012–. Mem., Adv. Bd, Business Sch., TCD, 2005–. *Recreations:* Blues music, ski-ing, golf, family vacations, music of Eric Clapton.

DREHER, Derek; Consultant, Northern Ireland Office, since 1997; *b* 12 Jan. 1938; *s* of Frederick Charles Dreher and Mary Emily Dreher (*née* Rutherford); *m* 1961, Patricia Audrey Dowsett; one *s* one *d. Educ:* Roan Grammar Sch., Greenwich. Joined War Office as Exec. Officer, 1956; Nat. Service, RAF, 1956–58 (trained as Russian linguist); with War Office, 1958–64, then MoD: postings include: Cyprus, 1962–65; NI, 1969–71; on secondment to Treasury, 1976–79; Asst Sec., 1980; Asst Under Sec. of State, 1992–97. *Recreations:* all forms of sport, but particularly tennis, theatre, foreign travel, reading, particularly political works. *Address:* Kantara, Church Road, Hartley, Kent DA3 8DL. *Club:* Hartley Country.

DREW, David Elliott; *b* 13 April 1952; *s* of Ronald Montague Drew and late Maisie Joan Drew; *m* 1990, Anne Baker, *d* of Brian and Sheila Baker; two *s* two *d. Educ:* Kingsfield Sch., Glos; Nottingham Univ. (BA Hons 1974); Birmingham Univ. (PGCE 1976); Bristol Poly., later UWE (MA 1988; MEd 1994). Teacher: Princethorpe Coll., Warwicks, 1976–78; St Michael's Sch., Stevenage, 1978–82; Maidenhill Sch., Glos, 1982–85; Dene Magna Sch., Glos, 1985–86; Sen. Lectr, Bristol Poly., later UWE, 1986–97. Member: Stevenage BC, 1981–82; Stroud DC, 1987–95; Stonehouse Town Council, 1987–; Glos CC, 1993–97. Contested (Lab) Stroud, 1992. MP (Lab and Co-op) Stroud, 1997–2010; contested (Lab and Co-op) same seat, 2010, 2015.

DREW, David Ernest, MBE 2006; Character Principal Dancer, Royal Ballet, since 1974; choreographer; Founder, Ballet Scenarios, 2007; *b* London, 12 March 1938; *s* of Thomas Ernest Drew and Phyllis Adelaide (*née* Talbot-Tindale); *m* 1st, 1962, Avril Bergen (marr. diss. 1973); one *s*; 2nd, 1985, June Ritchie; one step *d. Educ:* Bristol Grammar Sch.; Westbury Sch. of Dancing, Bristol; Royal Ballet Upper Sch. Nat. Service, commnd RCS, 1958–60. Joined Royal Ballet at Royal Opera House, Covent Gdn, 1955: Soloist, 1961; Prin. Dancer, 1974; *created rôles* with Royal Ballet include: Bay Middleton, Mayerling; Demetrius, The Dream; Max Merx, Isadora; Celestial, Shadow-Play; Gaoler, Manon; The Master, Rituals; The Captain, Different Drummer; Leading Baboon, Prince of the Pagodas; G. B. Shaw, Grand Tour; Giles, The Crucible; *major rôles* include: Von Rothbart, Swan Lake; Monsieur G. M., Manon; Hilarion and Duke of Courtland, Giselle; Thomas, La Fille Mal Gardée; Catalabutte and King, Sleeping Beauty; Mercutio, Lord Capulet and Tybalt, Romeo and Juliet; Step Sister, Cinderella; Ivan and Kostchei, The Firebird; Mrs Pettitoes, Tales of Beatrix Potter; Armand's Father, Marguerite and Armand; Rajah and Brahmin, La Bayadère; *choreographic work* includes: five ballets for Sadler's Wells Royal Ballet: Intrusion, 1969; From Waking Sleep, 1970; St Thomas' Wake, 1971; Sacred Circles, 1972; Sword of Alsace, 1973; *musicals* include: Canterbury Tales, 1968; His Monkey Wife, 1970; *operas* include: Dido and Aeneas; Macbeth; Die Fledermaus; writer of scenario, The Three Musketeers, Northern Ballet Th., 2006, Estonian Nat. Ballet, 2009; also contribs to theatre and TV. Teacher, Royal Ballet Upper Sch., Pas de Deux at all levels, incl. Grad. Class, 1976–99; assisted in Direction of Choreographic Composition Course, 1986–99. Founder Pres., Ballet Assoc., 1975. Gold Medal, Royal Acad. of Dancing, 1954. *Recreations:* writing, theatre, inventing non-computer games and composing brainteasers. *Address:* c/o Royal Opera House, Covent Garden, WC2E 9DD.

DREW, Dorothy Joan; a Vice President, Immigration Appeal Tribunal, 2000–01; *b* 31 March 1938; *d* of late Francis Marshall Gant and Wilhelmina Frederica Gant (*née* Dunster); *m* 1959, Patrick K. Drew; two *s* one *d. Educ:* Sch. of St Helen and St Katharine; Univ. of London (LLB ext.). Called to the Bar, Gray's Inn, 1981; Chm. (pt-time), Social Security Appeal Tribunal, 1986–92; Adjudicator, Immigration Appeal Tribunal, 1989–93 (Special Adjudicator, 1993–2000); Regl Adjudicator, Hatton Cross, 1998–2000; Chm., Child Support Appeal Tribunal, 1993–94. JP Reading, 1975–95. *Recreations:* music, theatre, family and friends.

DREW, John Sydney Neville; Chancellor, since 2013, and Director, Institute of Contemporary European Studies, since 2011, and Jean Monnet Visiting Professor of European Business and Government, since 2007, European Business School, Regent's University London (formerly Regent's College, London); *b* 7 Oct. 1936; *s* of late John William Henry Drew and Kathleen Marjorie (*née* Wright); *m* 1962, Rebecca Margaret Amanda (*née* Usher); two *s* one *d. Educ:* King Edward's Sch., Birmingham; St John's Coll.,

Oxford (MA); Fletcher School of Law and Diplomacy, Tufts Univ. (AM). 2nd Lieut, Somerset LI, 1955–57. HM Diplomatic Service, 1960–73: Third Sec., Paris, 1962; MECAS, 1964; Second Sec., Kuwait, 1965; First Sec., Bucharest, 1968; FCO, 1970; Sloan Fellow, 1971, Dir of Marketing and Exec. Programmes, 1973–79, London Business Sch.; Dir of Internat. Corporate Affairs, Rank Xerox, 1979–84; Dir of European Affairs, Touche Ross Internat., 1984–86; Head of UK Offices, EEC, 1987–93; Dir, Europa Times, 1993–94; Dep. Chm., ESG, 1993–95; Dir, Change Gp Internat., 1996–2003. Associate Fellow, Templeton Coll., Oxford, 1982–86; Visiting Professor of European Management: Imperial Coll. of Science and Technology, 1987–91; Open Univ., 1993–99. Durham University: Special Advr, Howlands Trust, 1994–95; Dir, Res. Inst. for the Study of Change, subseq. Chm., Durham Res. Inst., later Durham Inst., 1996–2003; Vis. Prof. of European Business, 1995–2004. Chm., DSL Ltd, 1995–97. President: Inst. of Linguists, 1993–99 (Hon. FIL 1993); European Transpersonal Assoc., 1998–2003. Trustee, Thomson Foundn, 1996–2007. Hon. Editor, European Business Jl, 1987–2002. Hon. MBA Univ. of Northumbria, 1991. *Publications:* Doing Business in the European Community, 1979, 3rd edn 1991 (trans. Spanish and Portuguese 1987); Networking in Organisations, 1986; (ed) Readings in International Enterprise, 1995, 2nd edn 1999; (ed) Ways Through the Wall, 2005; (ed jtly) UK and Europe: costs, benefits, options, 2013; articles on European integration and management development. *Recreations:* writing, travelling, meditating, golf. *Address:* 49 The Ridgeway, NW11 8QP. *Club:* Oxford and Cambridge.

DREW, Jonathan Iqbal, MBE 2009; HM Diplomatic Service; High Commissioner to Mauritius, since 2014; *b* Toronto, 5 Feb. 1970; *s* of John and Rani Drew; civil partnership 2012, Grant Suckling. *Educ:* Hills Rd Sixth Form Coll., Cambridge; London Sch. of Econs and Pol Sci. (BSc (Econ) 1991); Sch. of Oriental and African Studies, Univ. of London (MA 1993). Entered FCO, 1993; Producer, TV Unit, FCO, 1993–97; on secondment to British Antarctic Survey, 1997–98; Desk Officer (Australia), 1998–2000; Dep. Rep. to E Timor, 2000–01; Dep. High Comr, PNG, 2001–04; Consul (Commercial), Toronto, 2004; Dep. Hd, Counter Terrorist Assistance Section, FCO, 2004–06; Head: W Africa Team, FCO, 2007–09; Political-Mil. Team, Kabul, 2009–10; Dep. Hd, Africa Dept - Central and Southern, FCO, 2012–14. Afghanistan Civil Service Medal, 2011. *Recreations:* tennis, walking, sailing, diving. *Address:* c/o Foreign and Commonwealth Office, King Charles Street, SW1A 2AH. *E:* jonathan.drew@fco.gov.uk.

DREW, Philippa Catherine, CB 2001; Vice-Chairman, Coalition for International Court for the Environment, since 2011 (Trustee, since 2009); *b* 11 May 1946; *d* of Sir Arthur Charles Walter Drew, KCB and Rachel Anna Drew (*née* Lambert). *Educ:* St Paul's Girls' Sch.; St Anne's Coll., Oxford (MA Hons 1968 PPE); Univ. of Pennsylvania (MA Hons 1969 Internat. Relations). Foreign and Commonwealth Office: Central and Southern Africa Dept, 1969; New Delhi, 1970–74; First Sec., S Asia Dept, 1974–75; Home Office: EEC Referendum Count Unit, 1975; Criminal Dept, 1975–78; Police Dept, 1978–81; Gen. Dept, 1981–84; Prison Dept, 1984–85; Field Dir, SCF, Nepal, 1985–87; Head, Probation Service Div., 1987–91; Dir of Custody, HM Prison Service, 1992–95; Dir, Personnel and Office Services, then Corporate Resources, Home Office, 1995–99; Dir for Educn, Trng, Arts and Sport, DCMS, 1999–2002; Dir, Global Issues, FCO, 2002–06. Chm., Diplomatic Service Appeal Bd, 2006–11; Member: London Probation Bd, 2007–08; Bd, Oxford Research Gp, 2007–10. Trustee: Stakeholder Forum, 2011–15; Human Dignity Trust, 2014–; Kaleidoscope Trust, 2014–. *Recreations:* opera, travel, talk. *Address:* 12 Thorney Hedge Road, Chiswick, W4 5SD. *T:* (020) 8747 0836.

See also J. R. Bretherton.

DREW, Simon Patrick; QC 2011; **His Honour Judge Drew;** a Circuit Judge, since 2012. *Educ:* Leeds Univ. (LLB Hons). Called to the Bar, Lincoln's Inn, 1987; in practice as barrister, Birmingham, London and Bristol, specialising in criminal law and licensing law; Recorder, 2005–12. *Address:* Birmingham Crown Court, Queen Elizabeth II Law Courts, 1 Newton Street, Birmingham B4 7NA.

DREW, Thomas, CMG 2015; HM Diplomatic Service; Visiting Fellow, McKinsey Global Institute (on secondment), 2015; *b* Haslemere, Surrey, 26 Sept. 1970; *s* of Peter John Drew and Rosemary Jane Beverley Drew (*née* Sach). *Educ:* Charterhouse; Trinity Coll., Oxford (BA Hons Lit.Hum. (Classics) 1993). McKinsey and Co., London, 1993–95; entered FCO, 1995; Second Sec., FCO, 1995–97; Russian lang. trng, 1997–98; Second, then First Sec., Moscow, 1998–2002; Head: EU Intergovtl Conf. Unit, FCO, 2002–04; EU Enlargement and SE Europe Gp, FCO, 2004–06; Political Counsellor, Islamabad, 2006–08; on loan to Home Office as Dir, Office for Security and Counter-Terrorism, 2008–11; Dir for Nat. Security, FCO, 2011–12; Principal Pte Sec. to Sec. of State for Foreign Affairs, 2012–14. *Recreations:* cycling, triathlon, opera, food. *Address:* c/o Foreign and Commonwealth Office, King Charles Street, SW1A 2AH.

DREWIENKIEWICZ, Maj.-Gen. Karol John, CB 1998; CMG 2000; Consultant, Security Sector Reform (formerly Peace Support Operations), 2001, 2003 and since 2006; Chairman, Lest We Forget Ltd, since 2014; *b* 2 Jan. 1946; *s* of late Wojciech Drewienkiewicz and of Barbara Drewienkiewicz; *m* 1970, Christine Elizabeth Bailey; two *s*. *Educ:* Stamford Sch.; RMA, Sandhurst; Sidney Sussex Coll., Cambridge (BA 1970; MA 1974; Hon. Fellow, 2007). Commnd RE, 1966; Staff Coll., Camberley, 1978 and 1985; CO, 22 Engr Regt, 1985–88; Sec. to UK Chiefs of Staff, MoD, 1988–90; Comdr, RE Trng Bde, 1990–91; RCDS 1992; Dir of Manning, Army, 1993–94; Engr-in-Chief, Army, 1994–95; Dir of Support, HQ Allied Land Forces, Central Europe, 1995–96; COS HQ IFOR/SFOR (Sarajevo), 1996–97; Comdg Gen., SFOR Support Comd (Zagreb), May–Aug. 1997; Dir of Support, HQ Allied Land Forces, Central Europe, Sept.–Dec. 1997; Mil. Advr to High Representative, Sarajevo, 1998; Dep. Hd of Mission, OSCE Kosovo Verification Mission, 1998–99; Sen. Army Mem., RCDS, 1999–2000; retd 2001; Chief, Plans, 2002, Dir and Mil. Advr to High Representative, Sarajevo, 2004–05, Dept for Security Co-operation, OSCE Mission to Bosnia and Herzegovina. Vis. Fellow, Dept of Internat. Studies, Univ. of Cambridge, 2002–03. Trustee, Haig Homes, 2004–14. Pres., Cambridge Univ. Engrs Alumni, 2006–12. *Publications:* Training the Territorial Army in 1939 and 1940, 1992; (contrib.) The Battle for France and Flanders Sixty Years On, 2001; Budgets as Arms Control, 2003; (contrib.) The New Protectorates, 2012; (with A. Poole) Wargaming in History: Gettysburg 1863, 2011; (with A. Poole) Wargaming in History: the first Bull Run campaign, 2012; (with A. Brentnall) Wargaming in History: Austro-Prussian War of 1866: opening battles, 2013; (with A. Poole) Jackson in the Shenandoah 1862, 2014. *Recreations:* military history, wargaming, gardening. *Address:* c/o Cox's & Kings, 7 Pall Mall, SW1Y 5NA.

DREWRY, Prof. David John; Vice-President and Board Member, European University Association, since 2009; Vice-Chancellor, 1999–2009, and Professor, 1999–2009, now Emeritus, University of Hull; *b* 22 Sept. 1947; *s* of late Norman Tidman Drewry and Mary Edwina Drewry (*née* Wray); *m* 1971, Gillian Elizabeth (*née* Holbrook). *Educ:* Havelock School, Grimsby; Queen Mary Coll., Univ. of London (BSc 1st cl. hons 1969; Hon. Fellow, QMW, 1992); Emmanuel College, Cambridge (PhD 1973; Hon. Fellow, 2007). FRGS 1972, CGeog 2002. UK-US Antarctic Expdns, 1969–70 and 1971–72; Sir Henry Strakosh Fellow, 1974; UK-US Antarctic Expdns, 1974–75, 1977–78 (leader), 1978–79 (leader); Sen. Asst in Research, Univ. of Cambridge, 1978–83; leader, UK-Norwegian Svalbard Expdns, 1980, 1983, 1985, 1986; Asst Dir of Research, Univ. of Cambridge, 1983; Director: Scott Polar Res. Inst., Univ. of Cambridge, 1984–87; British Antarctic Survey, 1987–94 (Emeritus Fellow, 2009); Sci. and Technol., NERC, 1994–98; Dir Gen., British Council, 1998. Vis. Fellow, Green Coll., Oxford, 1995; Vis. Prof., QMUL (formerly QMW), 1996–2001, 2008–; Vis. Scholar, Univ. of Cambridge, 1999; Guest Prof., Xiamen Univ., China, 2006–; Hon. Prof., Krakow Acad., 2010–. Vice-President: Council, RGS, 1990–93 (Mem., 1986–93 and 1995–96); Council, Internat. Glaciological Soc., 1990–96 (Mem., 1980–82); Member: Council of Managers, Nat. Antarctic Programmes, 1988–95 (Chm., 1988–91); Royal Soc. Interdisciplinary Scientific Cttee on Antarctic Res., 1990–98; Internat. Arctic Sci. Cttee, 1994–2002 (Pres., 1997–2002); Exec. Council, ESF, 1996–98 (Mem., Eur. Polar Bd); Trustee, Antarctic Heritage Trust, 1993–2005; UK alternate deleg., Sci. Cttee on Antarctic Res., 1985–97. Chm., S Georgia Assoc., 2010–. Trustee, Nat. History Mus., 2008–; Chm., Univ. of Hull Maritime History Trust, 2014–. Chm., Yorkshire Univs, 2002–04; Mem., Yorkshire Innovation (formerly Yorkshire Science), 2005–09. Non-executive Director: Hull Urban Regeneration Co., 2003–09; The Deep, 2006–09. CCMI (Pres., Humberside Br., 2002–04). Hon. DSc: Robert Gordon, 1993; Humberside, 1994; Anglia Poly. Univ., 1998; Hull, 2010. US Antarctic Service Medal, 1979; Cuthbert Peek Award, 1979, Patron's Medal, 1998, RGS; Polar Medal, 1986; Prix de la Belgica Gold Medal, Royal Acad. of Belgium, 1995. *Publications:* Antarctica: glaciological and geophysical folio, 1983; Glacial Geologic Processes, 1986; papers on polar glaciology, geophysics, remote sensing, science policy in learned jls. *Recreations:* music, ski-ing, walking, gastronomy. *Address:* University of Hull, Hull HU6 7RX. *T:* (01482) 465131. *Clubs:* Athenæum, Geographical.

DREYFUS, Prof. Laurence, PhD; FBA 2002; Professor of Music, University of Oxford, since 2006 (Lecturer, 2005–06); Fellow of Magdalen College, Oxford, since 2005; *b* Boston, Mass, 28 July 1952; naturalised British citizen, 2002. *Educ:* studied 'cello with Leonard Rose, Juilliard Sch.; Yeshiva Univ. (BA Pol Sci. 1973); Columbia Univ. (MA 1975, MPhil 1976, PhD 1980, in Musicology); studied viola da gamba with Wieland Kuijken, Royal Conservatory, Brussels, 1979–81 (Premier Prix, 1980; Diplôme supérieur, 1981); DLitt Oxon 2013. Lectr, Univ. of Wisconsin-Madison, 1979; Mellon Fellow in Humanities, Columbia Univ., 1979–81; Asst Prof., Washington Univ. in St Louis, 1981–82; Asst Prof., 1982–88, Associate Prof. of History of Music and Sen. Faculty Fellow, 1988–89, Yale Univ.; Associate Professor of Music: Univ. of Chicago, 1989–90; Stanford Univ., 1990–93; King's College, London: Prof. of Perf. Studies in Music, with the RAM, 1992–96; Thurston Dart Prof. of Perf. Studies in Music, 1996–2005; Hd, Dept of Music, 1995–99. *Appearances* include: Bergen Fest., Norway, 1990; Early Music Network tour of GB, 1990; Utrecht Early Music Fest., 1991; San Francisco SO, 1992; Skálholt Music Fest., Iceland, 1992–95; London Bach Fest., 1993, 1994; Three Choirs Fest., 2006; Edinburgh Fest., 2007. Dir-at-Large, Amer. Musicol Soc., 1989–91 (Otto Kinkeldey Prize, 1997); Vice-Pres., Amer. Bach Soc., 1992–94; Mem. Council, RMA, 1994–98. Hon. RAM 1995. First Prize, Bodky Competition in Early Music, Boston, 1978. Several solo and chamber recordings, incl. Purcell's Complete Fantasies for Viols (Gramophone award for best baroque instrumental recording, 1997) and Orlando Gibbons' Consorts for Viols (Gramophone award, 2004). Jt Gen. Ed., Musical Performance and Reception (formerly Cambridge Musical Texts and Monographs), 1994–. *Publications:* Bach's Continuo Group: players and practices in his vocal works, 1987; Bach and the Patterns of Invention, 1996; (contrib.) The Cambridge Companion to Bach, 1997; Wagner and the Erotic Impulse, 2010; papers, and articles in jls. *Address:* Magdalen College, Oxford OX1 4AU. *E:* laurence.dreyfus@magd.ox.ac.uk.

DRIELSMA, Sir Claude Dunbar H.; *see* Hankes-Drielsma.

DRIFE, Prof. James Owen, MD; FRCOG, FRCSE, FRCPE; Professor of Obstetrics and Gynaecology, University of Leeds, 1990–2009, now Emeritus; *b* 8 Sept. 1947; *s* of late Thomas Drife and Rachel Drife (*née* Jones); *m* 1973, Diana Elizabeth, *d* of late Ronald Haxton Girdwood, CBE; one *s* one *d*. *Educ:* Cumnock Acad.; Univ. of Edinburgh (BSc Hons; MB ChB 1971; MD 1982). FRCPE 1998. Hosp. appts, Edinburgh, 1971–79; MRC Res. Fellow in Reproductive Biology, Edinburgh, 1974–76; Lectr in Obst. and Gyn., Univ. of Bristol, 1979–82; Dept of Surgery, Frenchay Hosp., Bristol, 1980–81; Sen. Lectr, Obst. and Gyn., Univ. of Leicester, 1982–90. Non-exec. Dir, United Leeds Teaching Hosps NHS Trust, 1991–98. Mem., Cases Cttee, Medical Protection Soc., 1985–94; Assessor for England, Enquiries into Maternal Deaths, 1992–2011; Mem., Midwifery Cttee, UKCC, 1993–99; Mem. Council, RCOG, 1993–2008 (Convenor of Study Gp, 1989–92; Chm., Liby Cttee, 1994–97; Jun. Vice-Pres., 1998–2001); Mem., GMC, 1994–2005; Chairman: Assoc. of Profs of Obstetrics and Gynaecology, 2002–06; Academic Assoc. of Obstetrics and Gynaecology, 2006–07; Pres., N of England Obstetric and Gynaecol Soc., 2007–08. FRSA 1997. Hon. FASPOG, 1988; Hon. Fellow, Amer. Gynecol and Obstetrical Soc., 1998; Hon. FCOG(SA) 2002; Hon. FFSRH 2009; Hon. Mem., Jordanian Soc. of Obstetricians and Gynaecologists, 2000. Editor or co-editor, obst. and gyn. jls, 1985–; Editor-in-Chief, Eur. Jl of Obstetrics and Gynaecology, 2010–14 (Co-Editor-in-Chief, 2003–09). *Publications:* Dysfunctional Uterine Bleeding and Menorrhagia, 1989; (jtly) Micturition, 1990; (with J. Studd) HRT and Osteoporosis, 1990; (with D. Donnai) Antenatal Diagnosis of Fetal Abnormalities, 1991; (with A. Calder) Prostaglandins and the Uterus, 1992; (with A. Templeton) Infertility, 1992; (with D. Baird) Contraception, 1993; The Benefits and Risks of Oral Contraceptives, 1994; (with J. J. Walker) Caesarean Section, 2001; (with B. Magowan) Clinical Obstetrics and Gynaecology, 2004, 3rd edn 2013; (jtly) Obstetrics and Gynaecology for the MRCOG, 2004, 3rd edn 2015; contribs to BMJ. *Recreations:* songwriting (founder Mem., Abracadabarets; perf. at Edinburgh Fringe Fest., 1974, 1979, 1982, 1989, 1997, 2000, 2002, 2007, 2009, 2010, 2012), theatre going, opera, walking. *Address:* School of Medicine, Clarendon Wing, Belmont Grove, Leeds LS2 9NS. *T:* (0113) 292 3888. *Clubs:* Athenæum, National Liberal, Royal Society of Medicine.

DRINKWATER, Surgeon Rear-Adm. John Brian, FRCS; Clinical Medical Officer, Community Child Health, Mid Argyll, Kintyre, Islay and Jura, 1989–97; *b* 5 June 1931; *s* of Ellis Drinkwater and Hilda May Drinkwater; *m* 1958, Rosalind Joy Taylor; two *d*; *m* 1986, Carole Anne Coutts; two *d*. *Educ:* Henry Mellish Grammar Sch., Nottingham; Sheffield Univ. Med. Sch. (MB, ChB). FRCS 1961. House appts, 1954–55; joined RN 1955: SMO, 6th FS (Cyprus, Suez), 1955–57; RN Hosp., Haslar, 1957; Hammersmith Hosp., 1961; HMS Ganges, 1962; RN Hosps, Malta, Gibraltar, Plymouth, Haslar, 1962–67; Gt Ormond St Hosp., 1967; Consultant Surgeon, RN Hosps, 1968–82; Advr in Surgery, 1981–82; Dir of Medical Orgn, 1982–83; MO i/c RN Hosp., Haslar, 1983–84; QHS 1983–87; Dep. Med. Dir Gen. (Naval), 1984; Surgeon Rear-Adm. (Operational Med. Services), 1985–87; Dir of Support Services, Muscular Dystrophy Gp, 1987–88. Member: British Soc. for Digestive Endoscopy, 1972; British Soc. of Gastroenterology, 1980–83. FRSocMed 1961; Fellow, Assoc. of Surgeons, 1974. OStJ 1983. *Recreations:* music, bridge. *Address:* c/o HSBC, 593–599 Fulham Road, SW6 1EX.

DRINKWATER, Sir John (Muir), Kt 1988; QC 1972; a Commissioner of Income Tax, 1983–2000; *b* 16 March 1925; *s* of late Comdr John Drinkwater, OBE, RN (retd); *m* 1st, 1952, Jennifer Marion (*d* 1990), *d* of Edward Fitzwalter Wright, Morley Manor, Derbs; one *s* three *d* (and one *d* decd); 2nd, 1998, Deirdre, *d* of Derek Curtis-Bennett, QC and *widow* of James Boscawen. *Educ:* RNC Dartmouth. HM Submarines, 1943–47; Flag Lieut to C-in-C Portsmouth and First Sea Lord, 1947–50; Lt-Comdr 1952; invalided 1953. Called to Bar, Inner Temple, 1957, Bencher, 1979; a Recorder, 1972–90. Mem., Parly Boundary Commn for England, 1977–80. Mem. Bd, British Airports Authy, 1985–87, Dir, BAA plc, 1987–94. Life Mem. Council, SPAB, 1982. Pres., Cotswold Cons. Assoc., 1999–2006 (Chm., 1995–99). Governor, St Mary's Hosp., 1960–64. *Recreations:* gardening, reading, travel. *Address:* Glebe Court, Park Street, Fairford, Glos GL7 4JL. *T:* (01285) 712305; Lohitzun, 64120 St Palais, France. *Clubs:* Garrick, Pratt's.

DRISCOLL, Daphne Jane; *see* Todd, D. J.

DRISCOLL, Dr James Philip, CEng; independent management consultant; Partner, PricewaterhouseCoopers (formerly Coopers & Lybrand, then Coopers & Lybrand Deloitte), 1990–99, retired; *b* 29 March 1943; *s* of Reginald Driscoll and Janetta Bridget Driscoll; *m* 1969, Josephine Klapper, BA; two *s* two *d*. *Educ:* St Illtyd's Coll., Cardiff; Birmingham Univ. (BSc 1964; PhD 1972); Manchester Business Sch. MIChemE 1975; MIGEM (MIGasE 1975); MInstF 1975. Taught at St Illtyd's Coll., Cardiff, 1964; res. posts with Joseph Lucas, Solihull, 1968–69; British Steel Corporation: res. posts, 1969–70; commercial posts, 1971–79, incl. Manager, Divl Supplies, 1973; Reg. Manager, BSC (Industry), 1979–82; Dir, S Wales Workshops, 1980–82; Industrial Dir, Welsh Office, 1982–85; Associate Dir, 1985–87, Dir, 1987–90, Coopers & Lybrand Associates. Non-exec. Dir of a number of companies. Mem., Glas Cymru. *Publications:* various technical papers. *Recreations:* family, sport. *Address:* 6 Cory Crescent, Wyndham Park, Peterston-super-Ely, Cardiff CF5 6LS. *T:* (01446) 760372. *Club:* Peterston Football (Cardiff).

DRISCOLL, Lindsay Jane; Consultant, Bates Wells & Braithwaite, since 2008; *b* 17 April 1947; *d* of Clement Milligan Woodburn and Evelyn Miriam Woodburn; *m* 1978, Rev. Canon David Driscoll; two *s*. *Educ:* Queen's Sch., Chester; St Hugh's Coll., Oxford (MA Hons Jurisp.). Admitted Solicitor, 1971; Asst Solicitor, Biddle & Co., 1971–73; Asst Public Trustee of Kenya, 1973–78; Lectr, Kenya Sch. of Law, 1973–78; charity law consultant, 1982–87; Consultant, Bowling & Co., 1985; Asst Legal Advr, 1987–90, Legal Advr, 1990–95, NCVO; Partner, 1995–2000, Consultant, 2000–03, Sinclair Taylor & Martin. Chair, Bd, Internat. Center for Not for Profit Law, US, 2011–13 (non-exec. Dir, 1996–2003 and 2007–11). Mem., Exec. Cttee, Charity Law Assoc., 1997–2003; Charity Comr, 2003–08. Chm., Steering Gp, Code of Governance for Voluntary and Community Sector, 2009–. Trustee: Newham Community Renewal Prog., 1981–87; Friends of Internat. Centre of Insect Physiology and Ecology Trust, 1997–2005; Assoc. of Church Accountants and Treasurers, 1998–2000; Womankind Worldwide, 1998–2006; ICNL Charitable Trust, 1998–2003; Widows Rights Internat. (formerly Empowering Widows in Develt), 2000–05; Balkans Community Initiatives Fund, 2002–06; Historia Theatre Co., 2003–; St Katherine and Shadwell Trust, 2005–10; Dance United, 2006–11; Journey of a Lifetime Trust, 2008–11; Rosa, 2010–; Sangahta Global, 2011–12. Mem. Bd, Pemsel Case Foundn, 2012–. Governor: Davenant Foundn Sch., 1990–97; St Laurence Sch. Acad., Bradford on Avon, 2014–. *Publications:* (with Bridget Phelps) The Charities Act 1992: a guide for charities and other voluntary organisations, 1992, 2nd edn as The Charities Acts 1992 and 1993, 1993, 4th edn 1995; (contrib.) Modernising Charity Law, 2010; articles on charity law in charity and legal press. *Recreations:* travel, walking, theatre. *Address:* 24 Baileys Barn, Bradford on Avon BA15 1BX.

DRISCOLL, Michael John; QC 1992; *b* 22 Feb. 1947; *s* of John and Gladys Mary Driscoll; *m* 1970, Heather Edyvean Nichols (marr. diss. 1986); one *s* two *d* (and one *s* decd); *m* 2010, Mary-Anne Cooke (*née* Bowles); two step *s* one step *d*. *Educ:* Rugby Sch.; St John's Coll., Cambridge (BA, LLB). Asst Lectr, Manchester Univ., 1969–70; called to the Bar, Middle Temple, 1970; Bencher, Lincoln's Inn, 2000. *Recreation:* family. *Address:* Maitland Chambers, 7 Stone Buildings, Lincoln's Inn, WC2A 3SZ.

DRISCOLL, Prof. Michael John; Professor of Economics, since 1989, and Vice-Chancellor, since 1996, Middlesex University (formerly Middlesex Polytechnic); *b* 27 Oct. 1950; *s* of late Michael Driscoll and of Catherine Driscoll; one *s* one *d*. *Educ:* Boteler GS, Warrington; Trent Poly. (BA 1973). Res. Asst, Sheffield Univ., 1973–77; Lectr, Birmingham Univ., 1977–89; Economist, OECD, Paris, 1986–89; Middlesex Polytechnic, later University: Hd of Sch. of Econs, 1989–91; Dean of Business Sch., 1991–95; Pro Vice-Chancellor, 1993–95; Dep. Vice-Chancellor, 1995–96. Visiting Professor: Indian Statistics Inst., 1978; Centre for Econs and Maths Inst., Moscow, 1981; Limoges Univ. (annually), 1981–89; Univ. of the S Pacific, 1984. Chair, Lee Valley Business and Innovation Centre, 1996; Member: Ealing Tertiary Coll. Corp., 1995–96; Weald Coll. Corp., 1996–98; Coll. of NE London Corp., 1997–2005. Member: Council, London Playing Fields Soc., 1998–2000; Steering Cttee, London Higher (formerly London Higher Educn Consortium), 2000–06; N London LSC, 2001–04; Bd, UUK, 2001–; Chairman: Higher Educn Partnership for Sustainability, 2000–04; CMU, 2003–07. Patron, N London Hospice, 2002–. MInstD 1997; CCMI (FIMgt 1995); FRSA 1995. *Publications:* (jtly) Risk and Uncertainty in Economics, 1994; (jtly) The Effects of Monetary Policy on the Real Sector, 1994; numerous articles in academic jls. *Recreations:* following Aston Villa FC, the arts, water sports, walking, mountain biking, food and wine. *Address:* Middlesex University, The Burroughs, NW4 4BT. *T:* (020) 8411 5606, *Fax:* (020) 8411 5465. *E:* m.driscoll@mdx.ac.uk.

DRIVER, Alastair James; National Conservation Manager, Environment Agency, since 2002; *b* Gloucester, 9 Oct. 1956; *s* of Dr Peter Driver and Margaret Driver; *m* 1980, Belinda Christina Anderson-Dixon; three *s*. *Educ:* Randwick Primary Sch.; Marling Grammar Sch., Stroud; Lancaster Univ. (BSc Hons Ecol.). Regl Conservation Officer, Thames Water Authy, 1984–89; Regional Conservation Manager, Thames Region: Nat. Rivers Authy, 1989–96; Envmt Agency, 1996–2002. Biodiversity Advr, Commonwealth Secretariat, 2005–. Ambassador, Internat. Riverfoundn, 2007–; Member: Council, RSNC, 2000–02; Council, Wildfowl and Wetlands Trust, 2010–; Natural Envmt Adv. Panel, NT, 2010–. Chm., Sonning Cricket Club, 2006–13 (Hon. Life Vice-Pres., 2014); Dictator of Rugby, Reading Rhinos Rugby team, 2010–12; Vice-Pres., Reading Rugby Club, 2010–. Creator and voluntary warden, Ali's Pond Local Nature Reserve, Sonning, 1997–; Founder Mem., Sonning and Sonning Eye Soc., 2004–; Hon. Mem. and Expert Adviser, Vole Club, 2000–. FCIEEM (FIEEM 2012). Co-founder and Judge, European River Prize, Internat. RiverFoundation, 2013–. *Publications:* (contrib.) River Projects and Conservation, 1991; (contrib.) The New Rivers and Wildlife Handbook, 1994; scientific papers in Regulated Rivers: res. and mgt, Jl of Inst. of Water and Envmtl Mgt, British Wildlife. *Recreations:* former first class Rugby player and honours tie winner for London Irish, also played Rugby for Cainscross, Slough and Reading; club cricketer for Sonning Cricket Club; keen naturalist and moth botherer. *Address:* Environment Agency, Kings Meadow House, Kings Meadow Road, Reading, Berks RG1 8DQ. *T:* 07836 600868, *Fax:* (0118) 969 7035. *E:* alastair.driver@environment-agency.gov.uk. *W:* www.twitter.com/AliDriverEA.

DRIVER, Anne; *see* Phillips, Anne.

DRIVER, Bryan; Chairman, Rail Access Disputes (formerly Rail Access Disputes Resolution) Committee, 1996–2002 (Vice Chairman, 2002–10); *b* 26 Aug. 1932; *s* of Fred and Edith Driver; *m* 1955, Pamela Anne (*née* Nelson); two *d*. *Educ:* Wath-upon-Dearne Grammar School. Joined British Railways (Junior Clerk), 1948; Royal Air Force, 1950–52; management training with BR, 1958–59; posts in London, Doncaster, Newcastle, 1959–69; Divisional Operating Manager, Norwich, 1969–71, Liverpool Street, 1971–72; Divisional Manager, West of England, 1972–75, South Wales, 1975–77; Dep. Gen. Manager, Eastern Region, 1977–82; Man. Dir, 1982–87, Chm., 1985–87, Freightliners Ltd; Bryan Driver Associates, 1987–96; Consultant Advr, 1987–88, Ops Dir, then Dir, Ops and Rolling Stock, 1988–93, Transmanche-Link (Channel Tunnel Contractors). *Recreations:* cricket, Rugby football. *Address:* Riverds Lea, 4 Shilton Garth Close, Earswick, York YO32 9SQ. *T:* (01904) 762848. *Clubs:* MCC; York Golf (Social Mem.).

DRIVER, Charles Jonathan, MPhil; writer; Master of Wellington College, 1989–2000; *b* 19 Aug. 1939; *s* of Rev. Kingsley Ernest Driver and Phyllis Edith Mary (*née* Gould); *m* 1967, Ann Elizabeth Hoogewerf; two *s* one *d*. *Educ:* St Andrew's Coll., Grahamstown; Univ. of Cape Town (BA Hons, BEd, STD); Trinity Coll., Oxford (MPhil). Pres., National Union of S African Students, 1963–64; Asst Teacher, Sevenoaks Sch., 1964–65 and 1967–68; Housemaster, Internat. Sixth Form Centre, Sevenoaks Sch., 1968–73; Dir of Sixth Form Studies, Matthew Humberstone Sch., 1973–78; Res. Fellow, Univ. of York, 1976; Principal, Island Sch., Hong Kong, 1978–83; Headmaster, Berkhamsted Sch., 1983–89. Hon. Sen. Lectr, Sch. of Lit. and Creative Writing, UEA, 2007–. Biogliasco Fellow, 2008; MacDowell Fellow, 2010; Hawthornden Fellow, 2012. FRSA. Trustee: Lomans Trust, 1986–; Beit Trust, 1998–; Governor: Benenden Sch., 1987–2005 (Advr, 2006–10); Eagle House Prep. Sch., 1989–2000; Milton Abbey Sch., 1998–2005 (Visitor, 2005–09); Farlington Sch., 1999–2004 (Chm. Governors, 2000–04); Millfield, 2001–10; Frewen Coll., 2002–. Editor, Conference and Common Room, 1993–2000. *Publications: novels:* Elegy for a Revolutionary, 1968 (reissued, 2010); Send War in Our Time, O Lord, 1969 (reissued, 2010); Death of Fathers, 1972 (reissued, 2010); A Messiah of the Last Days, 1974 (reissued, 2010); Shades of Darkness, 2004; *poetry:* I Live Here Now, 1979; (with Jack Cope) Occasional Light, 1979; Hong Kong Portraits, 1986; In the Water-Margins, 1994; Holiday Haiku, 1997; Requiem, 1998; So Far: selected poems 1960–2004, 2005; Rhymes for the Grandchildren: Moose, Mouse and other rhymes, 2011; Citizen of Elsewhere: selected poems, 2013; *biography:* Patrick Duncan, 1980, 2nd edn 2000; My Brother and I, 2013. *Recreations:* keeping fit, reading, Rugby. *Address:* Apple Yard Cottage, Mill Lane, Mill Corner, Northiam, Rye, E Sussex TN31 6JU. *E:* jontydriver@hotmail.com. *W:* www.jontydriver.co.uk.

DRIVER, Daniel Amir, (Danny); concert pianist, since 2001; *b* London, 1977; *m* 1999, Rebecca Miller; one *d*. *Educ:* Clare Coll., Cambridge (BA Hons); Royal Coll. of Music (Postgrad. Dip.). Concerts in UK, USA, Australia, Hong Kong, Germany and Canada, including: Wigmore Hall, 2001, 2006, 2008, 2011, 2012, 2014; BBC Proms, 2011. Artistic Dir, Hampstead and Highgate Fest., 2010. Several recordings. *Address:* c/o Mark Kendall Artists Management Ltd, 56 St Anselm's Road, Worthing, West Sussex BN14 7EN. *T:* (01903) 233229.

DRIVER, Prof. Felix, PhD; FBA 2011; Professor of Human Geography, Royal Holloway, University of London, since 1999; *b* Wednesbury, 23 Aug. 1961. *Educ:* Westminster City Sch., London; Emmanuel Coll., Cambridge (BA 1982; PhD 1987). FRHistS 1999; FRGS. Lectr, Univ. of Exeter, 1986–88; Lectr, 1988–96, Reader, 1996–99, Royal Holloway, Univ. of London. FAcSS (AcSS 2007). *Publications:* Geography Militant, 2001; Imperial Cities, 2003; Tropical Visions, 2005; Power and Pauperism, 2004; Hidden Histories of Exploration, 2009. *Address:* Department of Geography, Royal Holloway, University of London, Egham, Surrey TW20 0EX.

DRIVER, Most Rev. Jeffrey William; *see* Adelaide, Archbishop of.

DRIVER, Olga Lindholm; *see* Aikin, O. L.

DRIVER, Paul William; writer and critic; *b* 14 Aug. 1954; *s* of Thomas Driver and Thelma Driver (*née* Tavernor). *Educ:* Salford Grammar Sch.; St Edmund Hall, Oxford (MA Hons English Lit.). Contrib. music reviews, later book and theatre reviews to FT, 1979–95; Music Critic: Daily Telegraph, 1982–83; Boston Globe, 1983–84; Sunday Times, 1984–; contributor to: The Listener, Tempo, Musical Times, TLS, London Rev. of Books, Guardian, NY Times and numerous other pubns; frequent broadcasts on Radio 3, Radio 4, BBC 2, Channel 4, etc; has lectured on music in Britain and USA. Mem. Bd, Contemporary Music Rev., 1981–. Patron, Manchester Musical Heritage Trust, 2000–. *Publications:* (ed) A Diversity of Creatures, by Rudyard Kipling, 1987; (ed jtly) Music and Text, 1989; (ed) Penguin English Verse, 1995; (ed) Penguin Popular Poetry, 6 vols, 1996; Manchester Pieces, 1996; (contrib.) Sing, Ariel, 2003; Four Elegies (verse), 2009; A Metropolitan Recluse (novel), 2010; A Verlaine Dozen (verse), 2013. *Recreations:* walking, swimming, travel. *Address:* 15 Victoria Road, NW6 6SX. *T:* (020) 7624 4501. *Club:* Critics' Circle.

DRIVER, Ven. Penelope May; Archdeacon of Westmorland and Furness, since 2012; *b* 20 Feb. 1952; *d* of Arthur Anderson Glover and Bessie Glover. *Educ:* All Saints' Coll., London (Teaching Cert.); Northern Ordination Course (DipTh 1983); Manchester Univ. (MEd Adult Educn 1992). Ordained deacon, 1987, priest, 1994; Diocesan Youth Advr, dio. Newcastle, 1986–88; Curate of Cullercoats, Newcastle, 1987–88; Youth Chaplain, Ripon, 1988–96; Diocese of Ripon and Leeds: Asst Dir of Ordinands, 1996–98, Diocesan Dir of Ordinands, 1998–2006; Bishop's Advr in Women's Ministry, 1991–2006; Minor Canon, 1996–2006, Hon. Canon, 1998–2006, Ripon Cathedral; Archdeacon of Exeter, 2006–12. Mem., Gen. Synod, 2010–. *Recreations:* entertaining, singing, fell walking. *Address:* The Vicarage, Windermere Road, Lindale, Grange-over-Sands LA11 6LB.

DRIVER, Sheila Elizabeth; a District Judge (Magistrates' Courts) (formerly Stipendiary Magistrate), South Yorkshire, since 1995; *b* 7 Oct. 1950; *d* of Alfred Derek Robinson and Joan Elizabeth Robinson; *m* 1974, John Graham Driver; one *s* two *d*. *Educ:* Bradford Girls' GS; Leeds Univ. (BA Hons Hist.); London School of Economics (MA Internat. Hist.). Admitted Solicitor, 1978; Solicitor: City of Bradford MDC, 1978–79; County Prosecuting Office, W Yorks, 1979–80; in private practice, 1981–95. *Recreations:* amateur dramatics, reading.

DROGHEDA, 12th Earl of, *cr* 1661 (Ireland); **Henry Dermot Ponsonby Moore;** Baron Moore of Mellifont, 1616; Viscount Moore, 1621; Baron Moore of Cobham (UK), 1954; photographer, professional name Derry Moore; *b* 14 Jan. 1937; *o s* of 11th Earl of Drogheda, KG, KBE and of Joan *o d* of late William Henry Carr; *S* father, 1989; *m* 1st, 1968, Eliza Lloyd (marr. diss. 1972), *d* of Stacy Barcroft Lloyd, Jr, and Mrs Paul Mellon; 2nd, 1978, Alexandra, *d* of Sir (John) Nicholas Henderson, GCMG, KCVO; two *s* one *d*. *Educ:* Eton; Trinity College, Cambridge. *Publications:* (as Derry Moore): (with Brendan Gill) The Dream Come True, Great Houses of Los Angeles, 1980; (with George Plumptre) Royal Gardens, 1981; (with Sybila Jane Flower) Stately Homes of Britain, 1982; (with Henry Mitchell) Washington, Houses of the Capital, 1982; (with Michael Pick) The English Room, 1984; (with Alvilde Lees-Milne) The Englishwoman's House, 1984; (with Alvilde Lees-Milne) The Englishman's Room, 1986; (with the Marchioness of Salisbury) The Gardens of Queen Elizabeth the Queen Mother, 1988; (with Sarah Hollis) The Shell Guide to the Gardens of England and Wales, 1989; Evening Ragas, 1997; (with Clive Aslet) The House of Lords, 1998; Rooms, 2006; Notting Hill, 2007; (with The Dowager Marchioness of Salisbury) A Gardener's Life, 2008; (with Tim Knox) Sir John Soane's Museum, London, 2009; In House, 2009; (with Monty Don) Great Gardens of Italy, 2011; An English Room, 2013. *Heir: s* Viscount Moore, *qv*. *Address:* 40 Ledbury Road, W11 2AB. *E:* moorederry@aol.com. *Clubs:* Brooks's, Garrick.

DROMER, Alain Henri Pierre; Chief Executive Officer, Aviva Investors, 2007–12; *b* France, 16 May 1954; *s* of Jean Dromer and Eliane Dromer (*née* Dhombres); partner, Bénédicte Massiet; one *s* one *d*. *Educ:* Ecole Polytéchnique, Paris; Ecole Nat. de la Statistique et de l'Admin Economique. Nat. Inst. for Stats and Econ. Studies and Treasury Dept, Min. of Finance, France, 1978–87; Dir, Capital Mkts, Compagnie Financiére Edmond de Rothschild, Paris, 1987–91; Chief Executive Officer: Asset Mgt and Insce, Crédit Commercial de France, Paris, 1991–2000; Global Asset Management, HSBC, London, 2001–07. Independent non-executive Director: Santander UK, 2013–; Moody's Investors Service Eur. Business, 2013–; Majid Al Futtaim Trust (Dubai), 2013–; Henderson Eur. Focus Trust plc (London), 2014–. Chm., Investment Cttee, Assoc. of British Insurers, 2010–12. *Recreations:* piano, mandolin, learning Mandarin Chinese. *Address:* Rue du Mail 88, 1050 Brussels, Belgium. *T:* 25440469, 0477954682. *E:* alain.dromer@gmail.com. *Club:* Reform.

DROMEY, Jack; MP (Lab) Birmingham Erdington, since 2010; *b* 29 Sept. 1948; *m* 1982, Harriet Harman (*see* Rt Hon. H. Harman); two *s* one *d*. *Educ:* Cardinal Vaughan Grammar Sch. Sec., Brent Trades Council, 1976–78; Transport and General Workers' Union, later Unite: various posts from dist officer to nat. organiser, 1978–2003; Dep. Gen. Sec., 2003–10. Treas., Labour Party, 2004–10. Shadow Minister for Housing, 2010–13, for Home Affairs, 2013–15. Member, Select Committee: Business, Innovation and Skills, 2010; Regulatory Reform, 2010–15. *Address:* House of Commons, SW1A 0AA.

DROMGOOLE, Dominic Charles Fleming; Artistic Director, Shakespeare's Globe Theatre, 2006–April 2016; *b* 25 Oct. 1963; *s* of Patrick Shirley Brookes Fleming Dromgoole, *qv*; partner, Sasha Hails; three *d*. *Educ:* Millfield Sch.; St Catharine's Coll., Cambridge (BA (English Lit.) 1985). Artistic Dir, Bush Th., 1990–96; New Plays Dir, Old Vic Th., 1997; Artistic Dir, Oxford Stage Co., 1999–2005. Director: Shadow of a Gunman, Tricycle, 2004; Someone Who'll Watch Over Me, New Ambassadors, 2005. Producer, Saltwater (film), 2000. Essayist, Sunday Times and others, 2001–. *Publications:* The Full Room, 2001; Will and Me: how Shakespeare took over my life, 2006. *Recreations:* walking, drinking. *Address:* 5 Newick Road, E5 0RP.

DROMGOOLE, Jolyon; Director (Council Secretariat), Institution of Civil Engineers, 1985–91; Deputy Under-Secretary of State (Army), Ministry of Defence, 1984–85; *b* 27 March 1926; 2nd *s* of late Nicholas and Violet Dromgoole; *m* 1956, Anthea, *e d* of Sir Anthony Bowlby, 2nd Bt; five *d* (incl. triplets). *Educ:* Christ's Hospital; Dulwich Coll.; University Coll., Oxford (matric. 1944; BA 2nd Cl. Hons (History) 1950; MA). Entered HM Forces, 1944; commissioned 14/20 King's Hussars, 1946. Entered Administrative Cl., Civil Service; assigned to War Office, 1950; Private Sec. to Permanent Under-Sec., 1953; Principal, 1955; Private Sec. to Sec. of State, 1964–65; Asst Sec., 1965; Command Sec., HQ FARELF, Singapore, 1968–71; Royal Coll. of Defence Studies, 1972; Under-Sec., Broadcasting Dept, Home Office, 1973–76; Asst Under-Sec. of State, Gen. Staff, 1976–79, Personnel and Logistics, 1979–84, MoD. FRSA 2000. Trustee and Gov., Royal Sch., Hampstead, 1985–99. Mem., Samuel Pepys Club, 1993–; Chm., Samuel Pepys Award Trust, 2002–07. *Recreations:* literature, publisher. *Address:* Montreal House, Barnsley, Glos GL7 5EL. *T:* (01285) 740331. *Club:* Athenæum.

See also P. S. B. F. Dromgoole.

DROMGOOLE, Patrick Shirley Brookes Fleming; Chairman, PDP Ltd, since 1992; *b* 30 Aug. 1930; *s* of late Nicholas and Violet Dromgoole; *m* 1st, 1960, Jennifer Veronica Jill Davis (marr. diss. 1991); two *s* one *d*; 2nd, 1991, June Kell Morrow. *Educ:* Dulwich Coll.; University Coll., Oxford (MA). Actor and various employments in London and Paris, 1947–51; BBC Drama Producer/Dir, 1954–63; freelance theatre, film and television dir (directed first plays in West End of Orton, Wood, Welland, Halliwell and others), 1963–69; directed regularly Armchair Theatre for ABC TV and Thames TV; made number of films for cinema; joined HTV Ltd as Programme Controller, 1969; Asst Man. Dir, 1981; Man. Dir, HTV, 1987; Chief Exec., HTV Gp, 1988–91. Various awards incl. Pye Oscar, RTS, for Thick as Thieves, 1971; Best Play of the Year, for Machinegunner, 1973; Amer. Emmy, for D. P., 1985. FRTS 1978; FRSA 1989. *Recreations:* travel, œnophilia, pre-Raphaelite art, reading. *Address:* Penkill Castle, Girvan, Ayrshire KA26 9TQ. *Clubs:* Garrick, Groucho.

See also D. C. F. Dromgoole, J. Dromgoole.

DROMORE, Bishop of, (RC), since 1999; **Most Rev. John McAreavey;** *b* Banbridge, Ireland, 2 Feb. 1949. *Educ:* St Colman's Coll., Newry; Maynooth Coll.; Pontifical Univ., Maynooth; Pontifical Gregorian Univ., Rome. Ordained priest, 1973; Teacher, St Colman's Coll., Newry, 1978–79; Vice Judicial Vicar, 1979–83, Judicial Vicar, 1983–88, Armagh Regl Marriage Tribunal; Prof. of Canon Law, St Patrick's Coll., Maynooth, 1988–99. *Address:* Bishop's House, 44 Armagh Road, Newry, Co. Down BT35 6PN.

DRONKE, Prof. (Ernst) Peter (Michael), FBA 1984; Fellow of Clare Hall, 1964–2001, now Emeritus, and Professor of Medieval Latin Literature, 1989–2001, now Emeritus, University of Cambridge; *b* 30 May 1934; *s* of Senatspräsident A. H. R. Dronke and M. M. Dronke (*née* Kronfeld); *m* 1960, Ursula Miriam (*née* Brown) (*d* 2012); one *d*. *Educ:* Victoria University, NZ (MA 1st Cl. Hons 1954); Magdalen College, Oxford (BA 1st Cl. Hons 1957; MA 1961); MA Cantab 1961. Research Fellow, Merton Coll., Oxford, 1958–61; Lectr in Medieval Latin, 1961–79, Reader, 1979–89, Univ. of Cambridge. Guest Lectr, Univ. of Munich, 1960; Guest Prof., Centre d'Etudes Médiévales, Poitiers, 1969; Leverhulme Fellow, 1973; Guest Prof., Univ. Autónoma, Barcelona, 1977; Vis. Fellow, Humanities Res. Centre, Canberra, 1978; Vis. Prof. of Medieval Studies, Westfield Coll., 1981–86. Lectures: W. P. Ker, Univ. of Glasgow, 1976; Matthews, Birkbeck Coll., 1983; Jackson, Harvard Univ., 1992; O'Donnell, Univ. of Toronto, 1993; Barlow, UCL, 1995. Corresp. Fellow: Real Academia de Buenas Letras, 1976; Royal Dutch Acad., 1997; Medieval Acad. of America, 1999; Austrian Acad. of Scis, 2001; Fondazione Lorenzo Valla, 2006; Istituto Lombardo Acad. of Scis and Letters, 2007. Hon. Pres., Internat. Courtly Literature Soc., 1974. Co-Editor, Mittellateinisches Jahrbuch, 1977–2002. Premio Internazionale Ascoli Piceno, 1988; Premio Bettarini, 2014. *Publications:* Medieval Latin and the Rise of European Love-Lyric, 2 vols, 1965–66; The Medieval Lyric, 1968; Poetic Individuality in the Middle Ages, 1970; Fabula, 1974; Abelard and Heloise in Medieval Testimonies, 1976; (with Ursula Dronke) Barbara et antiquissima carmina, 1977; (ed) Bernardus Silvestris, Cosmographia, 1978; Introduction to Francesco Colonna, Hypnerotomachia, 1981; Women Writers of the Middle Ages, 1984; The Medieval Poet and his World, 1984; Dante and Medieval Latin Traditions, 1986; Introduction to Rosvita, Dialoghi drammatici, 1986; (ed) A History of Twelfth-Century Western Philosophy, 1988; Hermes and the Sibyls, 1990; Latin and Vernacular Poets of the Middle Ages, 1991; Intellectuals and Poets in Medieval Europe, 1992; Verse with Prose: from Petronius to Dante, 1994; Nine Medieval Latin Plays, 1994; (ed with A. Derolez) Hildegard of Bingen, *Liber divinorum operum*, 1996; Sources of Inspiration, 1997; Dante's Second Love, 1997; Introduction to Alessandro nel medioevo occidentale, 1997; (with Ursula Dronke) Growth of Literature: the sea and the God of the sea, 1998; (ed) Etienne Gilson's Letters to Bruno Nardi, 1998; (ed with Charles Burnett) Hildegard of Bingen: the context of her thought and art, 1998; Imagination in the late Pagan and Early Christian World, 2003; Forms and Imaginings, 2007; The Spell of Calcidius, 2008; (ed) Giovanni Scoto Eriugena, Periphyseon I, 2012, II, 2013, III, 2014, IV, 2016; essays in learned jls and symposia. *Recreations:* music, film, Brittany. *Address:* 6 Parker Street, Cambridge CB1 1JL.

DROWN, Julia Kate; *b* 23 Aug. 1962; *d* of David Christopher Robert Drown and Audrey Marion Harris; *m* 1999, Bill Child; one *s* one *d* (and one *d* decd). *Educ:* Hampstead Comprehensive Sch.; University Coll., Oxford (BA); CIPFA Educn and Trng Coll., Croydon. Unit Accountant, Oxfordshire Unit for People with Learning Difficulties, 1988–90; Dir of Finance, Radcliffe Infirmary, Oxford, 1990–96. Mem. (Lab) Oxfordshire CC, 1989–96. MP (Lab) Swindon South, 1997–2005. Mem., Select Cttee on Health, 1997–99 and 2001–03; Chair, Select Sub-cttee on Maternity Services, 2003; All Party Groups: Chair: on Maternity, 2000–05; on Heavily Indebted Poor Countries (formerly Third World Debt), 2001–05; Co-Chair, on Illegal Camping and Traveller Mgt, 2002–05; Vice Chair: on Further Educn, 1998–99; Voice, 1998–2004. Hon. Secretary: on Osteoporosis, 1999–2005; on Rwanda, the Great Lakes Region and the Prevention of Genocide, 2001–05. Member: Health Professions Council, 2009–13; Appeals Cttee, HFEA, 2009–; Chair, Veterinary Medicines Directorate Mgt Bd, 2014–; Nursing and Midwifery Council: Pension Trustee, 2009–; Partner Mem., Business Planning and Governance Cttee, 2009–10; Mem., Audit Cttee, 2011–13 (Chair, 2011–12). Patron, Advocacy after Fatal Domestic Abuse, 2009–14. Mem., CIPFA, 1989–2005. *Recreations:* family, dance, music.

DRU DRURY, Martin; *see* Drury.

DRUCKER, Prof. Daniel Joshua, OC 2015; MD; FRCPC; FRSC 2012; FRS 2015; Professor of Medicine, University of Toronto, since 1987; Senior Scientist, Lunenfeld-Tanenbaum Research Institute (formerly Samuel Lunenfeld Research Institute), Mount Sinai Hospital, Toronto, since 2006; *b* Montreal, Quebec, 23 June 1956; *s* of Ernest Drucker and Cila Bernstein. *Educ:* Univ. of Toronto (MD 1980). FRCPC 1984. Intern in Medicine, Johns Hopkins Hosp., Baltimore, 1980–81; Toronto General Hospital: Resident in Medicine, 1981–82; Fellow in Endocrinol., 1982–83; Chief Med. Resident, 1983–84; Centennial Res. Fellow, Med. Res. Council of Canada, 1984–87; Res. Fellow in Medicine, Massachusetts Gen. Hosp., Harvard Univ., 1984–87; Staff Physician: Endocrinol., Toronto Gen. Hosp., 1987–2006; Mount Sinai Hosp., Toronto, 2006–; University of Toronto: Dir, Div. of Endocrinol., Dept of Medicine, 1992–2001; Dir, Banting and Best Diabetes Centre, until 2011. *Publications:* articles in learned jls. *Recreations:* golf, water sports, biking. *Address:* Mount Sinai Hospital, 600 University Avenue, TCP5-1004, Toronto, ON M5G 1X5, Canada. *T:* (416) 3612661, *Fax:* (416) 3612669.

DRUCKMAN, Paul Bryan, FCA; Chief Executive Officer, International Integrated Reporting Council, since 2011 (Chairman, Working Group, 2009–11); Chairman, Clear Group, since 2005; *b* 23 Dec. 1954; *s* of Leonard and Phoebe Druckman; *m* 1983, Angela Samuel; one *s* one *d*. *Educ:* King's Coll. Sch., Wimbledon; Warwick Univ. (PGCE 1981); Dip. Envmtl Mgt, British Safety Council, 2002. FCA 1979. Sales Dir, Orchard Business Systems Ltd, 1986–90; Managing Director: Dit Ltd, 1990–99; Aston IT Gp, 1999–2001; Chairman: IT Faculty, 2001–02; SME Forum, 2001–03; Director: Business Link for London Ltd, 2004–06; Access UK (formerly Access Accounts, then Access Technol. Gp), 2004–11 (Chm., 2009–11). Pres., ICAEW, 2004–05. Mem., Takeover Panel, 2004–05; Dir, Financial Reporting Council, 2004–07; Chairman: CCAB, 2004–05; M Institute, 2006–. Chairman: Corporate Responsibility Adv. Gp, ICAEW, 2006–11; Sustainability Policy Gp, FEE, 2007–11; Prince of Wales's Accounting for Sustainability Forum (formerly Ext. Reporting Wkg Party), 2007–11; Mem., Eminent Persons Adv. Gp on Human Rights Standards, 2013–. Freeman, City of London, 2003; Mem., Ct of Assts, Chartered Accountants' Co., 2004–05. *Recreations:* golf, tennis. *Address:* c/o International Integrated Reporting Council, 29 Lincoln's Inn Fields, WC2A 3EE. *E:* paul@druckman.co.uk. *Clubs:* Royal Wimbledon Golf, Westside Lawn Tennis (Wimbledon).

DRUICK, Dr Douglas; President and Eloise W. Martin Director, Art Institute of Chicago, since 2011. *Educ:* McGill Univ., Montreal (BA Hons English and Philosophy 1966); Univ. of Toronto (MA English 1967); Oberlin Coll., Ohio (MA Hist. of Art 1970); Yale Univ. (MPhil Hist. of Art 1972; PhD Hist. of Art 1979). Asst to Curator of Prints and Drawings, Yale Univ. Art Gall., 1971–72; Curator, Eur. and American Prints, Nat. Gall. of Canada, Ottawa, 1973–84; Art Institute of Chicago: Chair and Prince Trust Curator of Prints and Drawings, 1985–89; Searle Curator of Eur. Painting, 1989–2004; Searle Curator of Medieval through Modern Eur. Painting and Modern Eur. Sculpture, 2004–06; Chair and Searle Curator of Medieval to Modern Eur. Painting and Sculpture, 2006–11. Chm., Arts and Artifacts Indemnity Adv. Panel, Nat. Endowment for the Arts, 2002–04; Founding Bd Mem., Assoc. of Art Mus. Curators, 2002–08; Member: Nat. Cttee for the Hist. of Art, 2003–09; Bd of Dirs, After Sch. Matters, 2011–; Assoc. of Art Mus. Dirs, 2011–; Internat. Gp of Organizers of Large-scale Exhibns (Bizot Gp), 2011–. Mem., Editl Adv. Bd, Master Drawings, Master Drawings Assoc. Inc., 2002–. *Address:* Art Institute of Chicago, 111 South Michigan Avenue, Chicago, IL 60603–6404, USA.

DRUMLANRIG, Viscount; Sholto Francis Guy Douglas; *b* 1 June 1967; *s* and *heir* of 12th Marquess of Queensberry, *qv*.

DRUMM, Rev. Mgr Walter Gregory; Rector, Pontifical Beda College, Rome, 1987–91; *b* 2 March 1940; *s* of Owen and Kathleen Drumm. *Educ:* St Joseph's Sch. and St Aloysius' Coll., Highgate; Balliol Coll., Oxford (MA). Tutor, The Grange, Warlingham, 1962–66; studied at Beda Coll., 1966–70; ordained, Westminster Dio., 1970; Asst Priest, Wood Green, 1970–73; Chaplain, Oxford Univ., 1973–83; Parish Priest, Our Lady of Victories, Kensington, 1983–87. Prelate of Honour to the Pope, 1988. *Address:* Nazareth House, 162 East End Road, N2 0RU.

DRUMMOND, family name of **Earl of Perth** and **Baron Strange**.

DRUMMOND, Caroline Jane, (Mrs Philip Ward), MBE 2009; CEnv; FRSB; Chief Executive, LEAF (Linking Environment and Farming), since 1991; Director, LEAF Marque, since 2004; *b* Hill Head, Fareham, Hants, 24 June 1963; *d* of Lt Comdr (Geoffrey) Mortimer Heneage Drummond and Sarah Drummond; *m* 1998, Philip Ward; one *d*. *Educ:* Rookesbury Park, Wickham; St Swithun's, Winchester; Seale Hayne Agricultural Coll. (BSc Hons Agric.). CEnv 2009. Agronomy Lectr, Shuttleworth Agric. Coll., 1989–91. Dir, Oxford Farming Conf., 2003–05 (Chm., 2005). Governor: Inst. of Envmt and Grassland Res., 2005–08; Royal Agricultural Univ., 2006–14; Rothamsted Res. (formerly Rothamsted Experimental Station), 2007–; British Nutrition Foundn, 2009–; Trustee, CPRE, 2008–11. Mem., DEFRA Civil Soc. Adv. Bd, 2009–14. Hon. DSc Harper Adams, 2013. FRAgS 1998; FIAgrM 2008; CEnv 2008; FRSA 2010; FRSB (FSB 2012). Hon. FSE 2014. Frank Arden Nuffield Scholarship, 2013. Pioneer to Life of the Nation, 2003; Ecological Engagement Award, British Ecol Soc., 2009. *Publications:* numerous scientific and farming articles, papers and comments. *Recreations:* singing, countryside matters, scientific kitchen experiments and art projects with my daughter. *Address:* LEAF, National Agricultural Centre, Stoneleigh, Warwicks CV8 2LG. *T:* (024) 7641 3911. *E:* caroline.drummond@leafuk.org; Butterwell, Horningtops, Liskeard, Cornwall PL14 3QD. *Club:* Farmers.

DRUMMOND, Colin Irwin John Hamilton, OBE 2012; Chairman, Taunton and Somerset NHS Foundation Trust, since 2014; *b* 22 Feb. 1951; *s* of Rev. William Balfour Drummond, MA and Annie Rebecca Drummond (*née* Roy); *m* 1975, Georgina Lloyd; two *s*. *Educ:* Wadham Coll., Oxford (BA (double 1st Cl. Hons Classics), MA 1978); Harvard Graduate Sch. of Business Admin (Harkness Fellow; MBA 1977). LTCL 1969 (Colman Prize). Asst Superintendent, Economic Intelligence Dept, Bank of England, 1973–78; Consultant, Boston Consulting Gp, 1978–84; Dir for Corporate Develt, Renold plc, 1984–86; Chief Exec., Yarns Div., Coats Viyella plc, 1986–92; Exec. Dir, Pennon Gp plc, 1992–2013; Chief Executive: Viridor Ltd, 1998–2002; Viridor Waste Mgt Ltd, 2002–13; Chm., Viridor Ltd, 2013–14. Non-exec. Dir, Vymura plc, 1998–99. Member: Adv. Cttee on Business and the Envmt, 2001–03; Council, SW Reg., CBI, 1997–2003. Dir, Sustainability SW, 2005–12. Chairman: Envmt and Water Sector Adv. Gp (formerly Envmt Sector Adv. Gp), 2005–12; Envmtl Knowledge Transfer Network, 2007–09; Envmtl Sustainability Knowledge Transfer Network, 2009–13; Business Adv. Bd, Living with Envmtl Change, 2010–15. Vis. Sen. Fellow, Earth Scis, Oxford Univ., 2007–13. CCMI 2002. Hon. FSE 2013. Freeman, City of London, 1999; Liveryman, 1999–, Mem., Ct of Assts, and Master, 2007–08, Water Conservators' Co.; Chm., Water Related Livery Cos, 2009–13; Liveryman: Gardeners' Co., 2010–; Musicians' Co., 2011–. Gov., Corp. of the Sons of the Clergy, 2008–. Organist and choirmaster, parish church of St John the Baptist, Wellington, Somerset, 1993–2006. Appearance in Undercover Boss, TV prog., 2010. Hon. DBA Edge Hill, 2014. *Recreations:* sport, music, vegetable gardening. *Address:* Taunton and Somerset NHS Foundation Trust, Musgrove Park Hospital, Taunton, Somerset TA1 5DA. *T:* (01823) 342512. *Club:* Oxford and Cambridge.

DRUMMOND, David Classon, FRSB; Deputy Director, Research and Development Service, Agricultural Development Advisory Service, Ministry of Agriculture, Fisheries and Food, 1987–88, retired; *b* 25 July 1928; *s* of Roger Hamilton Drummond and Marjorie Holt Drummond; *m* 1952, Barbara Anne, *d* of late Prof. Alfred Cobban; three *d*. *Educ:* St Peter's Sch., York; University Coll., London (BSc 1952); Pennsylvania State Univ., USA (Kellogg Fellow; MS 1962). FRSB (FIBiol 1975). Project Manager, FAO, UN, Karachi, 1971–72; Agricultural Science Service, MAFF: Head of Rodent Res. Dept, and Officer i/c Tolworth Lab., 1974–82; Head of Biol. Div., and Officer i/c Slough Lab., 1982–85; Sen. Agricl Scientist with special responsibilities for R&D, 1985–87. Mem., WHO Expert Adv. Panel on Vector Biology and Control, 1980–97. *Publications:* William C. Hooker's Great American Mouse Trap, 2002, 2nd edn 2013; Nineteenth Century Mouse Traps Patented in the USA, 2004; Mouse Traps: a quick scamper through their long history, 2005; McGill Mouse Traps and the Stilson Brothers, 2006; Twentieth Century Mouse Traps Patented in the USA, 1900–1924, 2007; British Mouse Traps and their Makers, 2008; Twentieth Century Mouse Traps Patented in the USA, 1925–1949, 2008; Twentieth Century Mouse Traps Patented in the USA the Last Fifty Years, 2009; Norway Rat, Erie Canal and Little Giant, 2009; Neroth Mouse Traps and their Makers, 2010; German Mouse Traps and their Makers, 2011; French Mouse Traps and their Makers, 2012; Rats, Mice and Religion, 2012; A Book of Old Rat Catchers, 2012; Cat and Mouse, 2012; A Celebration of Mice, 2013; Twenty First Century Mouse Traps, 2013; Ceramic Mice, 2014; scientific papers and reviews mainly concerned with rodent biology and control and develt of agricl and urban rat control programmes. *Recreations:* travel, gardening, history of mouse traps and rat catching. *Address:* 22 Knoll Road, Dorking, Surrey RH4 3EP. *W:* www.mousetrapbooks.com.

DRUMMOND, Felicia Jane Beatrix; MP (C) Portsmouth South, since 2015; *b* 16 June 1962; *d* of (George) Anthony Shepherd and Sarah Shepherd; *m* 1987, Hereward John Heneage Drummond; two *s* two *d*. *Educ:* Hull Univ. (BA SE Asian Studies 1983); Southampton Univ. (MA Global Politics and Internat. Relns 2007). Insce broker, 1983–87; Ofsted lay sch. inspector, 1994–99; Dir, Corporate Affairs, Cons. Middle East Council, 2010–11; Dep. Chm., Political, Portsmouth S Cons. Assoc., 2011–13. Member: Healthwatch; Community Health Council. Mem. (C) Winchester CC, 1996–99. Contested (C): Southampton Itchen, 2005; Portsmouth S, 2010. Trustee: Portsmouth CAB; Internat. Traditional Boatbuilding Coll., Portsmouth Historic Dockyard; ANA. Mem., Intelligence Corps, TA. *Address:* House of Commons, SW1A 0AA.

DRUMMOND, Gillian Vera, OBE 2008; DL; Commissioner, English Heritage, 2002–10; *b* 15 Sept. 1939; *d* of Gavin and Vera Clark; *m* 1st, 1958, Graham Turner Laing (marr. diss. 1978; he *d* 2007); three *d* (and one *s* decd); 2nd, 1978, Maldwin Andrew Cyril Drummond, *qv*; one *s*. *Educ:* Roedean Sch.; Poggio Imperiale, Florence. Founder Chm., Hampshire Gardens Trust, 1984–96 (Pres., 2011–); Mem., Council of Mgt, 1989–2010, Adv. Cttee, 2011–, Sir Harold Hillier Gardens & Arboretum; Chairman: Wessex Region, Historic Houses Assoc., 2000–05; Historic Parks and Gardens Panel (formerly Adv. Cttee), English Heritage, 2001–06 (Mem., 1985–2001); Adv. Gp, Capability Brown Birthday Celebrations and Festival 2016, 2012–; Mem., Urban Green Spaces Taskforce, ODPM, 2001–03 (Chm., Wkg Gp); President: Waterside Charities, 1981–95; Blackfield Gardening Soc., 1993–; Assoc. of Gardens Trusts, 1995– (Founder Chm., 1992–95); Vice-Pres., Royal Southampton Soc., 1986–. Trustee: Solent Rescue, 1988–98; Learning Through Landscape Trust, 1991–2010; Gilbert White's House and The Oates Collection (formerly Oates Meml Mus.), 1992–2013; Chawton House Library, 1993–; Countryside Educn Trust, 1999–2013; Nat. Maritime Mus., 2005–13; Chiswick House and Gardens Trust (formerly Chiswick House and Park Trust), 2006–12; Llanthony Secunda Priory Trust, 2007–10. Patron: Folly Fellowship, 2001–; Green Space, 2002–. Sen. Judge, Southern Region In Bloom, 1986–2001. County Pres., St John Ambulance Bde, Hants, 1990–2003. Gov., Millbrook Sch., Southampton, 1988–2005. DL Hants, 1994. Gold Veitch Meml Medal, RHS, 1996. *Recreations:* gardening, sailing, art, architecture. *Address:* Stanswood Farm House, Fawley, Southampton SO45 1AB. *T:* (023) 8089 1543; Wester Kames Castle, Port Bannatyne, Isle of Bute PA20 0QW. *T:* (01700) 503983. *E:* gilly@cadland.co.uk. *Clubs:* Royal Cruising (Assoc. Mem.); Royal Yacht Squadron (Lady Assoc. Mem.).

See also S. H. Turner Laing.

DRUMMOND, James Robert, CBE 2009; international development consultant, since 2012; Director, Western and Southern Africa, Department for International Development, 2010–12; *b* 12 July 1953; *s* of Brian and Isobel Drummond; *m* 1988, Glynis Joan Fell; two *s* one *d*. *Educ:* Trinity Coll., Cambridge (MA Hist. 1979). Head: Develt Sect., British High Commn, New Delhi, 1989–92; Central and Southern Africa Dept, 1992–95, Personnel, 1995–97, ODA; Central Africa, Harare, DFID, 1997–2000; Asst Hd, Defence and Overseas Secretariat, Cabinet Office, 2000–03; Dir, Iraq, 2003–04, UN Conflict and Humanitarian Div., 2005–07, S Asia Div., 2007–10, DFID. Trustee, Orchid Project, Acid Survivors Trust Internat., 2012–. FRGS 2012. *Recreations:* village cricket, birds, African history. *Club:* Shamley Green Cricket (Pres., 2009–14).

DRUMMOND, Jamie; Co-founder and Executive Director, ONE. *Educ:* Univ. of Bristol (BA Eng. and Philos. 1991); Sch. of Oriental and African Studies, London (MA Develt 1992). Christian Aid, 1992–98; Jubilee 2000 Drop the Debt, 1998–2001; Co-founder and Executive Director, Debt, AIDS, Trade, Africa, 2002, ONE: the Campaign to Make Poverty History, 2004, merged as ONE, 2008. *Recreation:* adventure.

DRUMMOND, Kevin; *see* Drummond, T. A. K.

DRUMMOND, Lorna Allison; QC (Scot.) 2011; Sheriff of Tayside, Central and Fife at Dundee, since 2014; *b* Edinburgh, 19 Dec. 1967; *d* of Iain P. Drummond and Dorothy J. Drummond; *m* 2001, Derrick Guild; two *d*. *Educ:* Hutchesons' Grammar Sch.; Glasgow Univ. (LLB Hons 1989); Sidney Sussex Coll., Cambridge (MPhil 1990); Edinburgh Univ. (DipLP 1991). Admitted to Faculty of Advocates, 1998; Asst Scottish Parly Counsel and Asst Legal Sec. to Scottish Law Officers, 1994–97; Standing Junior: to Home Office, 2002–07; to Scottish Govt, 2009–11; pt-time Sheriff, 2009–14. *Recreations:* running, yoga, sailing. *E:* lornadrummond@aol.com.

DRUMMOND, Maldwin Andrew Cyril, OBE 1990; DL; farmer and author; *b* 30 April 1932; *s* of late Maj. Cyril Drummond, JP, DL, and Mildred Joan Quinnell; *m* 1st, 1955, Susan Dorothy Cayley (marr. diss. 1977); two *d*; 2nd, 1978, Gillian Vera Turner Laing (*see* G. V. Drummond); one *s*. *Educ:* Eton Coll.; Royal Agricl Coll., Cirencester; Univ. of Southampton (Cert. in Environmental Sci., 1972). 2nd Lieut, Rifle Bde, 1950–52; Captain, Queen Victoria's, later Queen's, Royal Rifles (TA), retd 1967. Official Verderer of the New Forest, 1999–2002 (Verderer of New Forest, 1961–90); Chairman: Heritage Coast Forum, 1989–95; New Forest Cttee, 1990–98 (Chm., Consultative Panel, 1982–98); Mem., Countryside Commn, 1980–86. Member: Southampton Harbour Bd, 1967; British Transport Docks Bd, Southampton, 1968–74; Southern Water Authority, 1984–87. Chairman: Sail Training Assoc., 1967–72; Maritime Trust, 1979–89; Cutty Sark Soc., 1979–89; Warrior (formerly Ships) Preservation Trust, 1979–91; Assoc. of Yachting Historians, 2005–12; Pres., Shellfish Assoc. of GB, 1987–2008; Vice-Pres., 1983–, and Chm. Boat Cttee, 1983–92, RNLI; Trustee, World Ship Trust, 1980–91; Chairman: Hampshire Bldgs Preservation Trust, 1986–92; Hampshire and Wight Trust for Maritime Archaeology, 2003–09. Younger Brother of Trinity House, 1991–. Prime Warden, Fishmongers' Co., 1996–97. Mem., New Forest RDC, 1957–66; Hampshire: County Councillor, 1967–75; JP 1964–98 (Chm., New Forest Bench, 1992–97); DL 1975; High Sheriff, 1980–81. FRGS 1978; FRSA 1987; FSA 2003. Hon. DSc: Bournemouth, 1994; Southampton Inst., 1996. *Publications:* Conflicts in an Estuary, 1973; Tall Ships, 1976; Salt-Water Palaces, 1979; (with Paul Rodhouse) Yachtsman's Naturalist, 1980; (with Philip Allison) The New Forest, 1980; The Riddle, 1985; West Highland Shores, 1990; (ed) Lord Bute, 1996; (with Robin MacInnes) The Book of the Solent, 2001; After You Mr Lear, 2007. *Recreation:* cruising under sail and wondering about the sea. *Address:* Stanswood Farmhouse, Stanswood Road, Fawley, Southampton SO45 1AB. *T:* (office) (023) 8089 2039, (home) (023) 8089 1543; Wester Kames Castle, Port Bannatyne, Isle of Bute PA20 0QW. *T:* (01700) 503983. *Clubs:* White's, Pratt's, Royal Cruising; Royal Yacht Squadron (Cdre, 1991–96) (Cowes); Leander (Henley).

DRUMMOND, Rev. Norman Walker, CBE 2014; MA, BD; FRSE; Founder and Chairman: Drummond International, since 1999; Columba 1400, Community and International Leadership Centre, Isle of Skye, since 1997; Visiting Professor of Leadership in Education, University of Edinburgh, since 2009; *b* 1 April 1952; *s* of late Edwin Payne Drummond and Jean (*née* Walker); *m* 1976, Lady Elizabeth Helen Kennedy, *d* of 7th Marquess of Ailsa, OBE; three *s* two *d*. *Educ:* Merchiston Castle Sch.; Fitzwilliam Coll., Cambridge (MA Law); New Coll., Univ. of Edinburgh (BD). FRSE 2008. Ordained as Minister of the Church of Scotland, and commnd to serve as Chaplain to HM Forces in the Army, 1976; Chaplain: Depot, Parachute Regt and Airborne Forces, 1977–78; 1st Bn The Black Watch (Royal Highland Regt), 1978–82; to the Moderator of the Gen. Assembly of the Church of Scotland, 1980; Fettes Coll., 1982–84; Headmaster, Loretto Sch., 1984–95; Minister of Kilmuir and Stenscholl, Isle of Skye, 1996–98. Chaplain to Gov. of Edinburgh Castle, 1991–93; Chaplain to the Queen in Scotland, 1993–. BBC Nat. Gov., and Chm., Broadcasting Council for Scotland, 1994–99; Mem., Scottish Broadcasting Commn, 2007–08. Chair, Scottish Commemorations Panel, 2012–; Special Rep. for Scotland, UK Adv. Gp, World War I Commemorations, 2012–. Chm., BBC Children in Need, 1997–99. Chairman: Musselburgh and Dist Council of Social Service, 1984–94; Community Action Network, Scotland, 2001–03; Lloyds TSB Foundn for Scotland, 2003–09; Founder and non-exec. Chm., The Change Partnership Scotland, 1999–2003. Non-exec. Dir, J. & J. Denholm Ltd, 2002–. Mem., Queen's Bodyguard for Scotland (Royal Co. of Archers), 1990–. Mem. Court, Heriot-Watt Univ., 1986–92; Gov., Gordonstoun Sch., 1995–2000; Chm. Govs, Aiglon Coll., Switzerland, 1999–2005. Former Trustee: Arthur Smith Meml Trust; Foundn for Skin Res. President: Edinburgh Bn, Boys' Bde, 1993–98; Victoria League in Scotland, 1995–98. Cambridge Univ. Rugby Blue, 1971; Captain: Scottish Univs XV, 1974; Army XV and Combined Services XV, 1976–77. DUniv Glasgow Caledonian, 2010. *Publications:* The First Twenty-five Years: official history of The Black Watch Kirk Session, 1979; Mother's Hands (collection of short stories for children, parents and teachers), 1992; The Spirit of Success: how to connect your heart to your head in work and life, 2004; The Power of Three: discovering what really matters in life, 2010; Step Back: finding the way forward in life, 2015. *Recreations:* Rugby football, cricket, golf, curling, traditional jazz, Isle of Skye. *Address:* 35 Drummond Place, Edinburgh EH3 6PW. *Clubs:* MCC; New (Edinburgh); Hawks (Cambridge).

DRUMMOND, Peter; Director, since 1991, and Chairman, BDP South, since 2014, Building Design Partnership (Chief Executive, 2004–13); *b* Essex, 12 Nov. 1953; *s* of Ian and Eileen Drummond; *m* 1977, Susan Jane Barrows; two *s*. *Educ:* Univ. of Manchester (BA Hons Town Planning). MRTPI 1978. Planner, Building Design Partnership, 1976–79; Sen. Planner, Bolton MBC, 1979–80; Building Design Partnership: Sen. Planner, 1980–84; Associate, 1984–87; Associate Dir, 1987–91. FRSA. Mem., Acad. of Urbanism, 2009–; Pres., BCSC, 2012. *Publications:* Urban Design for Retail Environments, 2002. *Recreations:* ski-ing, offshore ocean racing, Arsenal FC. *Address:* Building Design Partnership, 16 Brewhouse Yard, Clerkenwell, EC1V 4LJ. *T:* (020) 7812 8032. *E:* peter.drummond@bdp.com.

DRUMMOND, Roderick Ian; HM Diplomatic Service; High Commissioner to Fiji, and Head, South Pacific Network, since 2013; *b* 7 Sept. 1962; *s* of Ian Drummond and Sarah (*née* Laird); *m* Yasmin Sudabe; one *s* two *d* by former marriage. *Educ:* Edinburgh Univ. (MA Hons Hist.). Entered FCO, 1985; lang. trng, SOAS, 1986, Univ. of Jordan, 1987; Second Sec. (Pol/Econ.), Algiers, 1988–92; First Sec., FCO, 1992–96; Dep. Consul-Gen., Johannesburg, 1996–98; UK Rep. to EU, Brussels, 1998–2002; Deputy Head of Mission: Amman, 2002–04; Damascus, 2004–07; Hd of Mission, Doha, 2007–08; FCO, London, 2008–09; Dep. Hd of Mission, Riyadh, 2009–13. *Recreations:* Rugby, golf, food, wine, jazz, exploring, scuba diving, Scrabble, tennis. *Address:* c/o Foreign and Commonwealth Office, King Charles Street, SW1A 2AH. *Club:* Royal Over-Seas League.

DRUMMOND, (Thomas Anthony) Kevin; QC (Scot.) 1987; Sheriff of Lothian and Borders at Jedburgh, Selkirk and Duns, 2000–13, and at Peebles, 2011–13; *b* 3 Nov. 1943; *s* of Thomas Drummond, BSc, and Mary (*née* Hughes); *m* 1966, Margaret Evelyn Broadley; one *d* (and one *d* decd). *Educ:* Blairs Coll., Aberdeen; St Mirin's Acad., Paisley; Edinburgh Univ. (LLB). Estate Duty Office, CS, 1963–70; Solicitor, 1970; admitted Faculty of Advocates, 1974; Advocate-Depute, 1985–90, Home Advocate-Depute, 1996–97, Crown Office, Edinburgh; Sheriff of Glasgow and Strathkelvin, 1997–2000. Member: Criminal Injuries Compensation Bd, 1990–96; Firearms Consultative Cttee, 1990–97; Criminal Injuries Compensation Authy, 1996. Chm., Discipline Tribunal, Inst. of Chartered Accts of Scotland, 1994–. Chm., Legislation, Regulation and Guidance Cttee, Partnership for Action against Wildlife Crime (Scotland), 2009–. Cartoonist, Scots Law Times, 1981–. Hon. US Dep. Marshal, 1998. *Publications:* legal cartoons under name of TAK: The Law at Work, 1982; The Law at Play, 1983; Great Defences of Our Time, 1995. *Recreations:* shooting, hill-walking, fishing, underwater hang-gliding. *Address:* Pomathorn House, Howgate, Midlothian EH26 8PJ. *T:* (01968) 74046.

DRUMMOND YOUNG, Rt Hon. Lord; James Edward Drummond Young; PC 2013; a Senator of the College of Justice in Scotland, since 2001; Chairman, Scottish Law Commission, 2007–12; *b* 17 Feb. 1950; *s* of late Duncan Drummond Young, MBE, DL, Edinburgh, and Annette (*née* Mackay); *m* 1991, Elizabeth Mary, *d* of John Campbell-Kease; one *d*. *Educ:* John Watson's Sch.; Sidney Sussex Coll., Cambridge (BA 1971); Harvard Univ. (Joseph Hodges Choate Meml Fellow, 1971–72; LLM 1972); Edinburgh Univ. (LLB 1974). Admitted to Faculty of Advocates, 1976. Standing Jun. Counsel in Scotland to Bd of Inland Revenue, 1986–88; QC (Scot.) 1988; Advocate-Depute, 1999–2001. *Publications:* (with J. B. St Clair) The Law of Corporate Insolvency in Scotland, 1988, 3rd edn 2004; (contrib.) Stair Memorial Encyclopaedia of Scots Law, 1989. *Recreations:* music, travel.

DRUMMOND YOUNG, James Edward; *see* Drummond Young, Rt Hon. Lord.

DRURY, Caroline Mary; *see* Elam, C. M.

DRURY, Very Rev. John Henry; Chaplain and Fellow, All Souls College, Oxford, since 2003; *b* 23 May 1936; *s* of Henry and Barbara Drury; *m* 1st, 1972, (Frances) Clare Nineham (*d* 2004), *d* of Rev. Prof. D. E. Nineham, *qv*; two *d*; 2nd, 2009, Caroline Mary Elam *qv*. *Educ:* Bradfield; Trinity Hall, Cambridge (MA (Hist. Pt 1, Cl. 1; Theol. Pt 2, Cl. 2/1); Hon. Fellow, 1997); Westcott House, Cambridge. Curate, St John's Wood Church, 1963; Chaplain of Downing Coll., Cambridge, 1966; Chaplain and Fellow of Exeter Coll., Oxford, 1969 (Hon. Fellow, 1991); Res. Canon of Norwich Cathedral and Examining Chaplain to Bp of Norwich, 1973–79; Vice-Dean of Norwich, 1978; Fleck Resident in Religion, Bryn Mawr Coll., USA, 1978; Lectr in Religious Studies, Sussex Univ., 1979–81; Dean, 1981–91, Fellow, 1982–91, King's College, Cambridge; Dean, Christ Church, Oxford, 1991–2003 (Hon. Student, 2003). Syndic, Fitzwilliam Museum, Cambridge, 1988–91. Examining Chaplain to Bp of Chichester, 1980–82. Mem., Doctrine Commn for C of E, 1978–82. Hussey Lectr, Univ. of Oxford, 1997. Jt Editor, Theology, 1976–86. *Publications:* Angels and

Dirt, 1972; Luke, 1973; Tradition and Design in Luke's Gospel, 1976; The Pot and The Knife, 1979; The Parables in the Gospels, 1985; Critics of the Bible 1724–1873, 1989; The Burning Bush, 1990; Painting the Word, 1999; Music at Midnight: the life and poetry of George Herbert, 2013; articles and reviews in Jl of Theol. Studies, Theology, Expository Times, TLS. *Recreations:* drawing, carpentry, reading. *Address:* All Souls College, Oxford OX1 4AL.

DRURY, Martin Dru, CBE 2001; FSA; Director-General, National Trust, 1996–2001 (Deputy Director-General, 1992–95); *b* 22 April 1938; *s* of late Walter Neville Dru Drury, TD; *m* 1971, Elizabeth Caroline, *d* of Hon. Sir Maurice Bridgeman, KBE; two *s* one *d. Educ:* Rugby. Commissioned, 3rd Hussars, 1957. Insurance Broker at Lloyd's, 1959–65; Mallett & Son Ltd, 1965–73; joined National Trust as Historic Buildings Rep., SE, and Furniture Advr, 1973; Historic Buildings Sec., 1981–95. Comr, Royal Hosp. Chelsea, 2002–08. Trustee: Attingham Trust, 1982– (Vice-Chm., 1982–13); Landmark Trust, 1988–2011 (Chm., 1992–95, 2001–11); Heritage of London Trust, 1996–2008 (Chm., 2007–08; Vice-Pres., 2008–); Wallace Collection, 2001–11. Chairman: Stowe Adv. Panel, 2005–12; Goldsmiths' Centre Trust, 2007–12 (Trustee, 2007–13); Strawberry Hill Conservation Steering Cttee, 2008–; Project Hougoumont UK Appeal Cttee, 2011–. Member: Council, Georgian Group, 1994– (Mem. Exec. Cttee, 1976–94); Fabric Adv. Cttee, St Paul's Cathedral, 1991–; Exec. Cttee, SPAB, 2006–14. Mem. Council, UK Overseas Territories Conservation Forum, 2000–05. Vice-Pres., Nat. Assoc. of Decorative and Fine Arts Socs, 2008–. FSA 1992. Mem., Court of Assts, Goldsmiths' Co., 1994– (Prime Warden, 2005–06). Hon. DArts Greenwich, 2000. Esher Award, for services to SPAB, 2002; EU Prize and Europa Nostra Award, for dedicated service to Cultural Heritage of Europe, 2013. *Address:* 3 Victoria Rise, SW4 0PB; 18 The Street, Stedham, West Sussex GU29 0NQ. *Clubs:* Brooks's, Pratt's; Seaview Yacht.

DRURY, Michael John, CMG 2011; Partner, BCL Burton Copeland, Solicitors, since 2010; *b* Camberwell, 22 May 1959; *s* of Kenneth and Joan Drury; *m* 1983, Elizabeth Greenhill; two *d. Educ:* Queen Mary Coll., Univ. of London (LLB Hons 1980; LLM 1981). Called to the Bar, Middle Temple, 1982; Legal Asst, HM Customs and Excise, 1985–88; Case Controller, Serious Fraud Office, 1988–96; admitted solicitor, 1996; Legal Advr, 1996–2002, Dir for Legal Affairs, 2002–10, GCHQ. *Recreations:* rowing, opera, Oxford United FC. *Address:* BCL Burton Copeland, 51 Lincoln's Inn Fields, WC2A 3LZ. *T:* (020) 7430 2277. *E:* mdrury@bcl.com. *Club:* Wallingford Rowing.

DRURY, Raymond Michael; Under Secretary and Executive Director (Personnel), NHS Executive, Department of Health, 1993–95; *b* 28 Sept. 1935; *s* of late James Joseph Drury and Annie Drury (*née* Greenwood); *m* 1959, Joyce Mary (*née* Clare); two *s* two *d. Educ:* Manchester Grammar Sch.; University Coll. London (BA Hons Classics (Latin and Greek)). Exec. Officer, Nat. Assistance Bd, 1958–64; HEO and Manager, Legal Aid Assessment Office, N Western Reg., 1964–70; Principal, DHSS, 1970–77; Asst Sec. and Dir (Exports), DHSS, 1977–79; Sec. of State's Rep. on Mgt Sides of Whitley Councils for Health Services (GB) responsible for NHS pay and conditions of service, 1979–88; Hd, Industrial Relns and Negotiations, DoH, 1988–93. *Recreations:* family, gardening, walking, DIY. *Address:* Penlan, Main Street, Clopton, Kettering, Northants NN14 3DZ. *T:* (01832) 720129.

DRY, Philip John Seaton; Partner, Biggart Baillie, 1971–2007; President, Law Society of Scotland, 1998–99 (Vice-President, 1997–98); *b* 21 April 1945; *s* of William Good Dry and Georgina Wilson Macpherson or Dry; *m* 1970, Joyce Christine Hall; one *s* one *d. Educ:* George Watson's Coll.; Greenock Acad.; Glasgow Univ. (LLB). Apprenticeship, 1966–68, Asst Solicitor, 1968–70, with Biggart Lumsden & Co. Dir, Fyfe Chambers (Glasgow) Ltd, 1990–98. Mem., Disciplinary Appeal Bd, Faculty of Actuaries, 1999–2005. Dir, Westcot Homes plc and Westcot Homes II plc, 1989–2000. Mem., PO Users' Council for Scotland, 1994–98. Director: Scots Law Trust, 1998–99; Scottish Council of Law Reporting, 1998–99. Dir, Glasgow Renfrewshire Soc. *Recreations:* sailing, the garden, opera, swimming, travel. *Address:* 107 Octavia Terrace, Greenock, Renfrewshire PA16 7PY. *Club:* Royal Gourock Yacht.

DRYDEN, Sir John (Stephen Gyles), 8th and 11th Bt *cr* 1795 and 1733; *b* 26 Sept. 1943; *s* of Sir Noel Percy Hugh Dryden, 7th and 10th Bt, and Rosamund Mary (*d* 1994), *e d* of late Stephen Scrope; *S* father, 1970; *m* 1970, Diana Constance, *o d* of late Cyril Tomlinson, Highland Park, Wellington, NZ; one *s* one *d. Educ:* Oratory School. *Heir: s* John Frederick Simon Dryden [*b* 26 May 1976; *m* 2005, Fiona Louise Marsh; one *s* one *d*]. *Address:* Spinners, Fairwarp, East Sussex TN22 3BE.

DRYSDALE, Laura, (Mrs John Tipler); consultant to museums and heritage organisations; Founder and Chief Executive, The Restoration Trust; *b* 28 April 1958; *d* of late Andrew Drysdale and of Merida Drysdale; *m* 1989, John Tipler; one *s* one *d*, and one step *s* one step *d. Educ:* Charterhouse; St Andrews Univ. (MA 1979); City Univ. (C&G MA 1987). Textile Conservator: Dalmeny House, 1979–81; V&A Mus., 1981–83; Textile Conservation Studio, 1983–86; Conservation Projects, 1986–92; Partner, Drysdale and Halahan, 1992–96; Head of Collections Conservation, English Heritage, 1996–99; Head of Adv. Services, Mus and Galls Commn, 1999–2000; Dir, Sector and Professional Services, Resource: Council for Mus, Archives and Libraries, 2000. FIIC 1996. *Publications:* articles in learned jls, conf. proceedings. *Recreation:* treading grapes. *Address:* 49 The Close, Norwich NR1 4EG.

DRYSDALE, Lynda; *see* McMullan, L.

DRYSDALE, Thomas Henry, WS; solicitor, retired; *b* 23 Nov. 1942; *s* of late Ian Drysdale and Rosalind Marion Drysdale; *m* 1967, Caroline, *d* of late Dr Gavin B. Shaw, CBE; one *s* two *d. Educ:* Cargilfield; Glenalmond; Edinburgh Univ. (LLB). Partner, Shepherd & Wedderburn WS, 1967–99 (Man. Partner, 1988–94); Dep. Keeper of HM Signet, 1991–98; Partner, Olivers WS, 1999–2004. Dir, Edinburgh Solicitors' Property Centre, 1976–89 (Chm., 1981–88). Legal Chm., Tribunals Service, later part time First-tier Tribunal Judge, 2003–13. Mem., Gullane Area Community Council, 2012– (Vice Chm., 2013–). Hon. Consul in Scotland, Republic of Hungary, 2001–13. Sec. and Treas., Stair Soc., 1999–. *Recreations:* ski-ing, walking, gardening, reading. *Address:* 6 The Glebe, Manse Road, Dirleton, East Lothian EH39 5FB. *Club:* New (Edinburgh).

D'SOUZA, family name of **Baroness D'Souza**.

D'SOUZA, Baroness *cr* 2004 (Life Peer), of Wychwood in the County of Oxfordshire; **Frances Gertrude Claire D'Souza,** CMG 1999; PC 2009; DPhil; Lord Speaker, House of Lords, since 2011; *b* 18 April 1944; *d* of Robert Anthony Gilbert Russell and Pauline Mary Russell (*née* Parmet); *m* 1st, 1959, Stanislaus D'Souza (marr. diss. 1974); two *d*; 2nd, 1985, Martin Griffiths (marr. diss. 1994); remarried 2003, Stanislaus D'Souza (*d* 2011). *Educ:* St Mary's, Princethorpe; UCL (BSc 1970); Lady Margaret Hall, Oxford (DPhil 1976). Ford Foundn Res. Fellow in Comparative Physiology, Nuffield Inst. of Comparative Medicine, 1973–77; pt-time adult educn lectr, Morley Coll. and City Lit., 1973–78; pt-time Lectr on Race and Culture, LSE, 1974–80; Sen. Lectr, Dept of Humanities, Oxford Poly., 1977–80; Founder Dir and Res. Dir, Internat. Relief and Develt Inst., 1977–85; Ind. Res. Cons. for UN, SCF, Ford Foundn, carrying out field work in Africa, Asia, S Europe, Pacific Region, 1985–88; ODA Res. Fellow, 1988–89; Exec. Dir, Article 19, Internat. Centre against Censorship, 1989–98; Fellow, Open Soc. Inst. (Soros Inst.), 1998–99. Dir, 2002–04, Consultant, 2004–06, Redress Trust. Mem., RGS expedn to the Karakorums, 1980. Convenor of crossbench peers, 2007–11. Regular broadcasts, 1989–98. Editor, Internat. Jl of Disaster Studies and Practice, 1978–82. *Publications:* (ed) Striking a Balance: hate speech, freedom of expression and non-discrimination, 1992; (jtly) The Right to Know: human rights and access to reproductive health information, 1995; numerous reports, scientific papers, contribs to books and articles in jls, incl. Nature, Scientific American, Third World Qly. *Recreations:* music (opera and string quartets), serious walking. *Address:* Lord Speaker's Office, House of Lords, SW1A 0PW.

D'SOUZA, Most Rev. Henry Sebastian; Archbishop of Calcutta, (RC), 1986–2002, now Emeritus; *b* 20 Jan. 1926; *s* of George William and Aurelia Clotilde D'Souza. *Educ:* Papal Atheneum, Kandy (LPH, LD); Urban Univ., Rome (DCL). Ordained priest, 1948; Bishop of Cuttack-Bhubaneswar, 1974–85; Coadjutor Archbishop, Calcutta, 1985–86. Secretary General: Catholic Bishops' Conference of India, 1979–82; Federation of Asian Bishops' Confs, 1983–93. Pres., Conf. of Catholic Bishops of India (Latin Rite), 1988–94, 1998–2002. *Address:* The Presbytery, 9/3 Middleton Row, Kolkata 700071, India.

DUBE, Alfred Uyapo Majaye; President, American Chamber of Commerce, Botswana, since 2012; *b* 8 June 1949; *s* of Mbangwa Edison Majaye and Phakela Majaye (*née* Mongwa); *m* 1977, Elvyn Jones (*d* 2012); three *s. Educ:* Poly. of North London; Univ. of Essex (BA Hons Govt). Librarian, Nat. Liby Service, 1971–74; Foreign Service Officer, Dept of Ext. Affairs, Botswana, 1977–79; First Sec., Botswana Embassy and Mission to EC, Brussels, 1979–80; Counsellor, London, 1980–81; Under-Sec., Min. of Mineral Resources and Water Affairs, 1981–83; Minister Counsellor, Brussels, 1983–87; Under-Sec., Dept of Ext. Affairs, 1987–89; Ambassador to Sweden, all Nordic countries and USSR/Russia, 1989–93; High Comr, UK, 1993–96; Ambassador to Japan, 1996–98, to People's Republic of China, Republic of Korea, and Democratic People's Republic of Korea, and concurrently High Comr to Malaysia and Singapore, 1996–2002; Special Envoy on Diamonds, 2001–02; Perm. Rep. to UN, 2002–05; High Comr to Jamaica and Guyana, and Ambassador to Cuba, 2002–05. Man. Dir, Lazare Kaplan Botswana (Pty) Ltd, 2006–13. Non-exec. Dir, Barclays Bank Botswana, 2009–. *Recreations:* reading, jazz, wine, golf.

DUBENS, Peter Adam Daiches; Managing Partner, Oakley Capital Ltd, since 1999; *b* London, 24 Sept. 1966; *s* of Stanley Maurice Dubens and Rachel Helen Dubens; *m* 1996, Joanna Penelope Cowan; three *d. Educ:* Sussex Hse Prep. Sch. Chairman: 365 Media plc, 2001–06; Pipex Communications plc, 2002–07; Daisy Gp plc, 2007–. Co-Founder and Director: KX Gym UK; Palmer Capital LLP; Global Licensing Ltd; Co-Founder: James Perse UK Ltd; Latitude Brands Ltd (Penfield); Humyo.com Ltd; Global Accessories Ltd (Vans & Eastpack). Entrepreneur of Year, Aim Market, London Stock Exchange, 2004. *Recreations:* golf, tennis, sailing, contemporary art, antiques. *Address:* Oakley Capital Ltd, 3 Cadogan Gate, SW1X 0AS. *T:* (020) 7766 6909. *E:* peter.dubens@oakleycapital.com. *Clubs:* Royal Automobile, Queen's; Royal Thames Yacht; Sunningdale Golf, Morfontaine Golf (France); Lyford Cay (Bahamas); Deepdale Golf (USA).

DUBERLY, Sir (Archibald) Hugh, KCVO 2015; CBE 1996; Lord-Lieutenant for Cambridgeshire, since 2003; *b* 4 April 1942; *s* of late Commander Archibald Gray, DSO, RN, and Grey Cunliffe Gray (*née* Duberly); adopted surname Duberly, 1963; *m* 1967, Sarah Elizabeth Robertson; two *s* one *d. Educ:* Winchester Coll. Pres., Country Landowners' Assoc., 1993–95; Dir, Agricultural Mortgage Corp. Plc, 1995–2002. Crown Estate Comr, 2002–09. Chm., Ely Diocesan Bd of Finance, 1992–. Chairman: Papworth Trust, 1995–2012; Shuttleworth Trust, 2001–13. Chm., Kimbolton Sch., 1992–2000; Gov., Writtle Coll., 1997–2009. DL 1989, High Sheriff, 1991–92, Cambs. *Address:* Place House, Great Staughton, Huntingdon PE19 5BB. *T:* (01480) 860305. *Club:* Boodle's.

DUBLIN, Archbishop of, and Primate of Ireland, since 2011; **Most Rev. Michael Geoffrey St Aubyn Jackson,** PhD, DPhil; Bishop of Glendalough, since 2011; *b* 24 May 1956; *s* of late Robert Stewart Jackson and of Margaret Jane Frances Jackson (*née* Sloan); *m* 1987, Inez Elizabeth (*née* Cooke); one *d. Educ:* Trinity Coll. Dublin (BA Classics 1979, MA 1982); St John's Coll., Cambridge (BA Theol. and Religious Studies 1981, MA 1985; PhD 1986); C of I Theol Coll.; Christ Church, Oxford (MA, DPhil 1989, by incorporation). Ordained deacon, 1986, priest, 1987; Curate-asst, Zion Parish, Rathgar, 1986–89; Minor Canon, Treasurer's Vicar and Chancellor's Vicar, St Patrick's Cathedral, Dublin, 1987–89; Asst Lectr, Dept of Hebrew, Biblical and Theol Studies, TCD, and in C of I Theol Coll., 1987–89; Chaplain, Christ Church, Oxford, 1989–97; Asst Lectr, Theology Faculty, Oxford Univ., 1991–97; Dir of Studies in Theol., St Anne's Coll., Oxford, 1995–97; Incumbent, St Fin Barre's Union, Cork and Dean of Cork, 1997–2002; Chaplain to UC, Cork and Cork Inst. of Technol., and Asst Lectr, Sch. of Classics and Sch. of Educn, UC, Cork, 1997–2002; Bishop of Clogher, 2002–11. Examining Chaplain to Bp of Cork, Cloyne and Ross, 1999–2002. Chm., Network of Inter-Faith Concerns of Anglican Communion, 2004–; Mem., Anglican/Oriental Orthodox Internat. Commn, 2002–. Chm., St Fin Barre's Beyond 2000, 1998–2002. *Publications:* A History of the Vaughan Charity (with Claire Jackson), 1980; articles, papers and reviews. *Address:* Church of Ireland House, Church Avenue, Rathmines, Dublin 6, Republic of Ireland. *T:* (1) 4125663. *E:* archbishop@dublin.anglican.org.

DUBLIN, Archbishop of, and Primate of Ireland, (RC), since 2004; **Most Rev. Diarmuid Martin;** *b* Dublin, 8 April 1945. *Educ:* UC Dublin; Dublin Diocesan Seminary; Pontifical Univ. of St Thomas Aquinas (Angelicum), Rome. Ordained priest, 1969; Curate, St Brigid, Cabinteely, 1973–74; respons. for pastoral care of Dublin pilgrims in Rome, 1975; entered service of Holy See, 1976, Pontifical Council for the Family; Under-Sec., 1986, Sec., 1994, Pontifical Council for Justice and Peace; Titular Bp of Glendalough, 1999–2003; Archbishop, 2001, Permanent Observer of Holy See at UN, Geneva, 2001–03; Coadjutor Archbishop of Dublin, 2003–04. *Address:* Archbishop's House, Drumcondra, Dublin 9, Ireland.

DUBLIN, (Christ Church), Dean of; *see* Dunne, Very Rev. D. P. M.

DUBLIN, (St Patrick's), Dean of; *see* Stacey, Very Rev. V. G.

DUBOIS, Edward George, FRINA, FREng; Chairman and Managing Director, Dubois Naval Architects Ltd, since 1980; Chairman, Dubois Yachts Ltd, since 2001; *b* Croydon, 18 April 1952; *s* of Robin Hermon and Doreen Marjorie Dubois; *m* 1996, Honor Alexandra Sharpe; two *s* two *d. Educ:* Whitgift Sch.; Southampton Inst. (Coll. Dip. Yacht and Boat Design 1974). FRINA 2005; FREng 2010. Chm., Exec. Cttee, Superyacht Racing Assoc., 2011–. Hon. DDes Nottingham Trent, 2004. *Recreations:* sailing, music. *Address:* Dubois Naval Architects Ltd, Beck Farm, Sowley, Lymington, Hants SO41 5SR. *T:* (01590) 626666, *Fax:* (01590) 626696. *E:* eddubois@duboisyachts.com. *Clubs:* Royal Thames Yacht, Royal Yacht Squadron, Royal Ocean Racing, Beaulieu River Sailing; Yacht Costa Smeralda.

du BOULAY, Sir Roger William H.; *see* Houssemayne du Boulay.

DUBOWITZ, Prof. Victor, MD, PhD; FRCP, FRCPCH; Professor of Paediatrics, University of London, at the Royal Postgraduate Medical School, 1972–96, now Emeritus; Consultant Paediatrician, Hammersmith Hospital, 1972–96; Director, Muscle Research Centre, Royal Postgraduate Medical School, 1975–96; *b* 6 Aug. 1931; *s* of late Charley and Olga Dubowitz (*née* Schattel); *m* 1960, Dr Lilly Magdalena Suzanne Sebok; four *s. Educ:* Beaufort West Central High Sch., S Africa; Univ. of Cape Town (BSc, MB, ChB, 1954; MD 1960). PhD Sheffield, 1965; DCH 1958; FRCP 1972; FRCPCH 1997. Intern, Groote Schuur Hosp., Cape Town, 1955; Sen. House Officer, Queen Mary's Hosp. for Children, Carshalton, 1957–59; Res. Associate in Histochem., Royal Postgrad. Med. Sch., 1958–59; Lectr in Clin. Path., National Hosp. for Nervous Diseases, Queen Square, London, 1960; Lectr in Child Health, 1961–65, Sen. Lectr, 1965–67, and Reader, 1967–72, Univ. of

Sheffield; Res. Associate, Inst. for Muscle Diseases, and Asst Paediatrician, Cornell Med. Coll., New York, 1965–66; Dir of Therapeutic Studies, European Neuro Muscular Centre, 1999–2003. Several lectureships and overseas vis. professorships. President: British Paediatric Neurol. Assoc., 1992–94; European Paediatric Neurology Soc., 1994–97; World Muscle Soc., 1995–; Medical Art Soc., 1996–2000. Curator of Art, RCPCH, 1997–. Founding Editor: Neuromuscular Disorders, 1990–; European Jl of Paediatric Neurology, 1996–2003. Hon. FRCPCH 1997. Arvo Ylppö Gold Medal, Finland, 1982; Baron ver Heyden de Lancey Prize, Med. Art Soc., 1980, 1982, 2002; Jean Hunter Prize, RCP, 1987; Gaetano Conte Medal, Italy, 1991; Cornelia de Lange Medal, Netherlands, 1997; Duchenne Erb Prize, German Speaking Muscular Dystrophy Assocs, 1999; James Spence Medal, RCPCH, 2007. Peter Emil Becker Prize, German-speaking Neuropediatric Soc., 2011. Comdr, Order of Constantine the Great, 1980. *Publications:* Developing and Diseased Muscle: a histochemical study, 1968; The Floppy Infant, 1969, 2nd edn 1980; (with M. H. Brooke) Muscle Biopsy: a modern approach, 1973, 4th edn (with C. Sewry and A. Oldfors) 2012; (with L. M. S. Dubowitz) Gestational Age of the Newborn: a clinical manual, 1977; Muscle Disorders in Childhood, 1978, 2nd edn 1995; (with L. M. S. Dubowitz) The Neurological Assessment of the Preterm and Full-term Newborn Infant, 1981, 2nd edn 2000; Colour Atlas of Muscle Disorders in Childhood, 1989; (jtly) A Colour Atlas of Brain Lesions in the Newborn, 1990; Ramblings of a Peripatetic Paediatrician, 2005; chapters in books and articles in learned jls on paediatric topics, partic. muscle disorders and newborn neurology. *Recreations:* sculpting, photography. *Address:* 25 Middleton Road, Golders Green, NW11 7NR. *T:* (020) 8455 9352.

DUBS, family name of **Baron Dubs**.

DUBS, Baron *cr* 1994 (Life Peer), of Battersea in the London Borough of Wandsworth; **Alfred Dubs;** Chairman, Broadcasting Standards Commission, 2001–03 (Joint Deputy Chairman, 1997); *b* Prague, Czechoslovakia, Dec. 1932; *m*; one *s* one *d*. *Educ:* LSE. BSc (Econs). Local govt officer. Mem., Westminster CC, 1971–78; Chm., Westminster Community Relns Council, 1972–77; Mem., Kensington, Chelsea and Westminster AHA, 1975–78. Dir, British Refugee Council, 1988–95. Member: TGWU; Co-operative Party. Contested (Lab): Cities of London and Westminster, 1970; Hertfordshire South, Feb. and Oct. 1974; Battersea, 1987 and 1992. MP (Lab): Wandsworth, Battersea S, 1979–83; Battersea, 1983–87. Mem., Home Affairs Select Cttee, 1981–83 (Mem., Race Relations and Immigration Sub-Cttee, 1981–83); opposition front bench spokesman on home affairs, 1983–87. House of Lords: an Opposition Whip, 1994–97; opposition front bench spokesman on energy, 1995–97, on health and safety, 1996–97; Parly Under-Sec. of State, NI Office, 1997–99; Member: Select Cttee on European Communities, 1995–97; Sub-Cttee F, European Select Cttee, 2003–07. Chairman: All Pty Parly Gp on Eur. Enlargement, 2000–, on Moldova, 2006–, on Portugal, 2008–; Lab Party in H of L, 2000–06; Mem., Jt Cttee on Human Rights, 2007–12. Mem., 1988–94, Dep. Chm., 1995–97, Broadcasting Standards Council; Vice-Chm., ITC, 2000–01; Chairman: Road Safety Foundn, 2007–; Eastern Alliance Safe and Sustainable Transport, 2009–. Chm., Ind. Code Panel, Assoc. of Energy Suppliers, 2004–. *Recreation:* walking in the Lake District. *Address:* c/o House of Lords, SW1A 0PW.

du CANN, Col Rt Hon. Sir Edward (Dillon Lott), KBE 1985; PC 1964; Chairman, Lonrho Plc, 1984–91 (Director, 1972–91; Joint Deputy Chairman, 1983–84); *b* 28 May 1924; *er s* of late C. G. L. du Cann, Barrister-at-Law, and Janet (*née* Murchie); *m* 1st, 1962, Sallie Innes (marr. diss. 1990; she *d* 2007), *e d* of late James Henry Murchie, Caldy, Cheshire; one *s* two *d*; 2nd, 1990, Jenifer Patricia Evelyn (*d* 1995), *yr d* of late Evelyn Mansfield King, and *widow* of Sir Robert Cooke. *Educ:* Colet Court; Woodbridge Sch.; St John's Coll., Oxford (MA, Law). Served with RNVR, 1943–46 (CO, HMMTB 5010). Vice-Pres., Somerset and Wilts Trustee Savings Bank, 1956–75; Founder, Unicorn Group of Unit Trusts, 1957 (pioneered modern British unit trust industry and equity linked life assurance); Chairman: Barclays Unicorn Ltd and associated cos, 1957–72; Keyser Ullman Holdings Ltd, 1970–75; Cannon Assurance Ltd, 1972–80. Founder Mem. and Chm., Association of Unit Trust Managers, 1961. Contested (C): West Walthamstow Div., 1951; Barrow-in-Furness Div., 1955. MP (C) Taunton Div. of Somerset, Feb. 1956–1987. Economic Sec. to the Treasury, 1962–63; Minister of State, Board of Trade, 1963–64. Mem., Lord Chancellor's Adv. Cttee on Public Records, 1960–62; Joint Hon. Sec.: UN Parly Group, 1961–62; Conservative Parly Finance Group, 1961–62; Mem., Select Cttee on House of Lords Reform, 1962; Founder Chairman: Select Cttee on Public Expenditure, 1971–73; All-Party Maritime Affairs Parly Gp, 1984–87; Mem., Select Cttee on Privilege, 1972–87; Chairman: Select Cttee on Public Accounts, 1974–79; 1922 Cttee, 1972–84; Liaison Cttee of Select Cttee Chairmen, 1974–83; (founder) Select Cttee on Treasury and Civil Service Affairs, 1979–83; (first) Public Accounts Commn, 1984–87; Cons. Party Organisation, 1965–67; Burke Club, 1968–79. President: (founder) Anglo-Polish Cons. Soc., 1972–74; Nat. Union of Conservative and Unionist Assocs, 1981–82; Cons. Parly European Community Reform Gp, 1985–87; Vice-Chm., British American Parly Gp, 1978–81. Jt Leader, British-American Parly Gp delegns to USA, 1978, 1980; Leader, British Parly Gp delegn to China, IPU, 1982. Dir, James Beattie Ltd, 1965–79. Pres., Inst. of Freight Forwarders Ltd, 1988–89; Vice-Pres., British Insurance Brokers Assoc., 1978; Patron, Assoc. of Insurance Brokers, 1974–77. Visiting Fellow, Univ. of Lancaster Business School, 1970–82. Member: Panel of Judges, Templeton Foundn, 1984; Management Council, GB-Sasakawa Foundn, 1984–91. Patron, Human Ecology Foundn, 1987–2007. Mem. Governing Council, Taunton Sch., 1972–93; Governor, Hatfield Coll., Durham Univ., 1988–92. Vice Pres., Limassol Hospice, 2002–07; Pres., Somerset Macmillan Cancer Appeal, 1985. Commodore, 1962, Admiral, 1974–87, House of Commons Yacht Club; President, Cyprus Branch: RN Assoc., 2003–13; Oxford Univ. Soc., 2005–. Hon. Col, 155 (Wessex) Regt, RCT (Volunteers), 1972–82; Hon. Life Member: Instn of RCT, 1983; Taunton Racecourse, 1991 (Dir, 1984–91). Sen. Pres., Oxford Univ. Rugby League FC, 2004–12. Lecturer, broadcaster. Mem. Court of Assts, Fruiterers' Co. (Master, 1990); elected first Freeman of Taunton Deane Borough, 1977. FRSA 1986. *Publications:* Investing Simplified, 1959; Two Lives: the political and business careers of Edward du Cann, 1995; Wellington Caricatures, 2000; (jtly) Dog Stories, 2010; pamphlets, and articles on financial and international affairs (incl. The Case for a Bill of Rights, How to Bring Government Expenditure within Parliamentary Control, A New Competition Policy, Hoist the Red Ensign, The Progress of the New Departmental Select Committees). *Recreations:* travel, gardening, sailing. *Address:* Lemona, 8545 Pafos, Cyprus; Flat 7, 42 Great Smith Street, SW1P 3BU. *Clubs:* Army and Navy, Carlton (Hon. Mem.); Royal Western Yacht.

DUCAT, Rt Hon. Dame Dawn; *see* Primarolo, Rt Hon. Dame D.

duCHARME, Gillian Drusilla Brown; educational consultant, since 2000; Headmistress, Benenden School, 1985–2000; *b* 23 Jan. 1938; *d* of Alfred Henry Brown and Alice Drusilla Grant; *m* 1969, Jean Louis duCharme (marr. diss.). *Educ:* Girton College, Cambridge. BA 1960, MA 1964. British Council, 1964–66; Chm., French Dept and Head of Upper Sch., Park Sch., Brookline, Mass, 1969–77; Registrar, Concord Acad., Concord, Mass, 1977–80; Headmistress, The Town Sch., New York City, 1980–85. Governor: Marlborough House Sch., 1987–; Wellington Coll., Crowthorne, 1996–2006; Blackheath Prep. (formerly Nursery and Prep.) Sch., 2009–. Mem., Adv. Bd, Westminster Acad., 2009–13. Consultant, Beeline Solutions, 2013–. Member: Council, Friends of Nat. Maritime Mus., 2001–07 (Chm., 2004–07); Bd, Internat. Rescue Cttee, UK, 2004–11. Hon. DEd Greenwich, 2005. *Recreations:* hill-walking, art, design and architecture, film, birdwatching, travel, books. *Address:* 3 Saint Alfege Passage, Greenwich, SE10 9JS. *T:* (020) 8858 8186. *E:* gillianducharme@hotmail.com.

DUCIE, 7th Earl of, *cr* 1837; **David Leslie Moreton;** Baron Ducie, 1763; Baron Moreton, 1837; Chairman, Tortworth Estate Company; *b* 20 Sept. 1951; *e s* of 6th Earl of Ducie and Alison May, *d* of L. A. Bates; *S* father, 1991; *m* 1975, Helen, *er d* of M. L. Duchesne; one *s* one *d*. *Educ:* Cheltenham College; Wye Coll., London Univ. (BSc 1973). *Heir: s* Lord Moreton, *qv*. *Address:* Talbots End Farm, Cromhall, Glos GL12 8AJ.

DUCK, Michael Charles; QC 2011; *b* Solihull, 6 June 1965; *s* of Peter Duck and Valerie Duck; *m* 1990, Dawn Marie Job; two *d*. *Educ:* Solihull Sch.; Univ. of Warwick; Staffordshire Univ. (LLB Hons). Called to the Bar, Gray's Inn, 1988; in practice as a barrister, specialising in crime. *Recreations:* golf, water ski-ing, cinema. *Address:* No 5 Chambers, Steelhouse Lane, Birmingham B4 6DR. *T:* (0121) 606 0500. *E:* mcd@no5.com.

DUCKWORTH, Cecil, CBE 2013 (OBE 2004); Chairman, Worcester Warriors Rugby Club, since 1993; *b* Macclesfield, 1937; *s* of Charles Duckworth and Jean Duckworth; *m* 1962, Beatrice Elizabeth Lee; one *s* one *d*. *Educ:* Worcester and Cheltenham Coll. CEng 1967. Founder, CEO and Chm., Worcester Engineering Ltd, subseq. Worcester Heat Systems Ltd, 1962–92; co. sold to Bosch, 1992; Hd, Thermotechnol. Div., Bosch, 1992–96. Founder, Duckworth Worcestershire Trust, 1998. Mem., 2000–, High Master, 2009–, Clothiers' Co., Worcester. *Publications:* Worcester Warrior, 2012. *Recreations:* golf, following Rugby, live theatre. *Address:* Worcestershire.

DUCKWORTH, Sir James (Edward Dyce), 5th Bt *cr* 1909, of Grosvenor Place, City of Westminster; *b* 20 Dec. 1984; *s* of Sir Edward Richard Dyce Duckworth, 4th Bt and of Patricia, *o d* of Thomas Cahill; *S* father, 2005; *m* 2012, Suzanne, *d* of Nicholas Law. *Heir: uncle* Antony George Dyce Duckworth [*b* 20 Nov. 1946; *m* 1974, Geraldine Broderick; one *s*].

DUCKWORTH, John Alan, (Joe); Chief Executive, League Against Cruel Sports, since 2011; *b* St Helens, 18 May 1955; *s* of George and Alice Duckworth; *m* 1990, Julie Ratty; two *s* one *d*. *Educ:* Bristol Univ. (BSc Hons Econs); Manchester Univ. (MA Econs). National Research Officer: USDAW, 1980–83; Instn of Professionals, Managers and Specialists, 1983–91; Dir of Personnel, York CC, 1991–95; County Personnel Officer, Surrey CC, 1995–97; Exec. Dir, London Bor. of Hackney, 1997–2000; Dir, Envmt and Leisure, 2000–04, Dep. Chief Exec., 2004–06, Westminster CC; Chief Executive: Isle of Wight Council, 2006–08; Newham LBC, 2008–10. *Recreation:* cycling.

DUCKWORTH, Rt Rev. Justin Charles Hopkins; *see* Wellington (NZ), Bishop of.

DUCKWORTH, Prof. Roy, CBE 1987; MD; FRCS, FDSRCS, FRCPath; Emeritus Professor of Oral Medicine, University of London; Dean, The London Hospital Medical College, 1986–94; *b* Bolton, 19 July 1929; *s* of Stanley Duckworth and Hilda Evelyn Moores; *m* 1953, Marjorie Jean Bowness, Flimby; two *s* one *d*. *Educ:* King George V Sch., Southport; Univ. of Liverpool (BDS; MD 1964). FDSRCS 1957; FRCPath 1973; FRCS 1986. Served RAF Dental Br., 1953–55. Nuffield Fellow, RPMS and Guy's Hosp. Dental Sch., 1959–61; The London Hospital Medical College: Sen. Lectr in Oral Medicine, 1961; Reader in Oral Medicine, 1965; Dean of Dental Studies, 1969–75; Prof. and Head, Dept of Oral Medicine, 1968–90. Consultant in Oral Medicine, The London Hosp., 1965–90. Dean, Faculty of Dental Surgery, RCS, 1983–86. Civil Consultant: in Dental Surg., to Army, 1977–90; in Oral Medicine and Oral Path., to RN, 1982–90; Temp. Consultant, WHO, 1973; British Council Visitor, 1977. Vis. Prof. in many countries. President: British Soc. of Periodontology, 1972–73; British Soc. for Oral Medicine, 1986–87; BDA, 1990–91. Chm., Standing Dental Adv. Cttee, Dept of Health, 1988–92 (Mem., 1984–88); Member: Adv. Council on Misuse of Drugs, 1977–85; Medicines Commn, 1980–83; Council, Fédération Dentaire Internationale, 1981–90 (Mem., List of Honour, 1993); GDC, 1984–89. Hon. Fellow, QMW, 1997. Scientific Adviser, British Dental Jl, 1975–82; Editor, Internat. Dental Jl, 1981–90. *Publications:* contrib. professional jls. *Recreation:* sailing.

du CROS, Sir Julian Claude Arthur Mallet, 4th Bt *cr* 1916, of Canons, Middlesex; *b* 23 April 1955; *o s* of Sir Claude Philip Arthur Mallet du Cros, 3rd Bt and Christine Nancy du Cros (*née* Bennett); *S* father, 2014, but his name does not yet appear on the Official Roll of the Baronetage; *m* 1984, Patricia Mary Wyatt (marr. diss. 2003); one *s* two *d*. *Educ:* Eton. *Heir: s* Alexander Julian Mallet du Cros, *b* 25 Aug. 1990.

DUDBRIDGE, Prof. Glen, PhD; FBA 1984; Shaw Professor of Chinese, University of Oxford, 1989–2005; Fellow of University College, Oxford, 1989–2005, now Emeritus; *b* 2 July 1938; *s* of George Victor Dudbridge and Edna Kathleen Dudbridge (*née* Cockle); *m* 1965, Sylvia Lo (Lo Fung-young); one *s* one *d*. *Educ:* Bristol Grammar School; Magdalene College, Cambridge (MA, PhD); New Asia Institute of Advanced Chinese Studies, Hong Kong. MA Oxon. Nat. Service, RAF, 1957–59. Research Fellow, Magdalene College, Cambridge, 1965; Lectr in Modern Chinese, 1965–85 and Fellow, Wolfson Coll., 1966–85 (now Emeritus Fellow), Univ. of Oxford; Prof. of Chinese and Fellow, Magdalene Coll., Univ. of Cambridge, 1985–89. Visiting Professor: Yale Univ., 1972–73; Univ. of California, Berkeley, 1980, 1998. Hon. Mem., Chinese Acad. of Social Scis, 1996. *Publications:* The Hsi-yu chi, 1970; The Legend of Miao-shan, 1978, 2nd edn 2004 (Chinese edn, 1990); The Tale of Li Wa, 1983; Religious experience and lay society in T'ang China, 1995; Lost Books of Medieval China, 2000; Books, Tales and Vernacular Culture, 2005; A Portrait of Five Dynasties China, 2013. *Address:* University College, Oxford OX1 4BH.

DUDDING, Richard Scarbrough; freelance public policy consultant, since 2002; *b* 29 Nov. 1950; *s* of Sir John Scarbrough Dudding and Lady (Enid Grace) Dudding; *m* 1987, Priscilla Diana Russell; two *s*. *Educ:* Cheltenham Coll.; Jesus Coll., Cambridge (MA 1st Cl. Hons History). Joined DoE, 1972; Private Sec. to John Smith, MP, 1976–78; Principal, 1977; Asst Sec., 1984; Sec., Cttee of Inquiry into Conduct of Local Govt Business, 1985–86; Under Sec., 1990; Finance Dir, 1990–93; Director: Pollution Control and Wastes, 1993–96; Personnel and Central Support Services, 1996–97; Dir Gen., Strategy and Corporate Services, DETR, then DTLR, 1997–2002; Dir for Envmt and Economy, Oxfordshire CC, 2003–08. *Recreations:* gardening, local history, running, golf.

DUDDRIDGE, James Philip; MP (C) Rochford and Southend East, since 2005; *b* 26 Aug. 1971; *s* of Philip and Jennifer Duddridge; *m* 2004, Kathryn Brigid Thompson; two *s* one *d*. *Educ:* Univ. of Essex (BA Politics). With Barclays Bank, 1993–2002: Sales Dir, Ivory Coast, 1997–98; Sales Manager for unit trust business, UK, 1998–2001; Service Delivery Dir, Botswana, 2001–02; Account Dir, YouGov, 2001–05; Dir, Okavango Ltd, 2002–05. An Opposition Whip, 2008–10; a Lord Comr of HM Treasury (Govt Whip), 2010–12; Parly Under Sec. of State for Foreign and Commonwealth Affairs, 2014–15. Chm., Regulatory Reform Select Cttee, 2013–. *Recreations:* running, cycling, real ale. *Address:* House of Commons, SW1A 0AA. *T:* (020) 7219 4830, *Fax:* (020) 7219 3888. *E:* james@jamesduddridge.com. *Clubs:* Southend United Football, Southampton Football.

DUDGEON, Alexander Stewart, (Sandy); Managing Director, Cazenove Capital Management Asia Ltd, since 2013; *b* Edinburgh, 16 Oct. 1957; *s* of John Dudgeon and late Sheila Dudgeon (*née* Stein); *m* 1985, Jennifer Waddell; two *s* one *d*. *Educ:* Glenalmond Coll.; Univ. of Aberdeen (MA). CA 1982. Trainee, Arthur Young McClelland Moores & Co., 1979–83; Co. Sec., 1983–87, Dep. Man. Dir, 1991–94, Adam & Co. plc; Dir, Martin Currie Investment Mgt Ltd, 1994–2003; Man. Dir, Thornhill Hldgs Ltd, 2003–10; Dir, Private Wealth Mgt, Cazenove Capital Mgt Ltd, 2010–13. Director: Dunedin Investment Trust plc, 1998–2006; Man Alternative Investments Ltd, 2001–04. Steward, Jockey Club, 2009–12. Mem., High Constables and Guard of Honour of Holyroodhouse, 1988–. *Recreations:* racing, golf, shooting. *Address:* Flat 1–01, 150 Kennedy Road, Hong Kong. *E:* sandy.dudgeon@cazenovecapital.com. *Clubs:* Jockey; New (Edinburgh); Hon. Company of Edinburgh Golfers; Jockey (Hong Kong).

DUDGEON, Wing Comdr Michael Greville, OBE 1996; Vice Lord-Lieutenant of Greater London, since 2011; *b* Northampton, 6 Nov. 1943; *s* of Air Vice-Marshal Antony Greville Dudgeon, CBE, DFC and Phyllis Dudgeon; *m* 1973, Gillian Mary Kathrine de Chazal; two *d.* *Educ:* Eton; RAF Coll. Cranwell. RAF Officer and Pilot, 1966–2000: qualified Flying Instructor, 1971; sqdn service in various overseas and home appts; Chinook Proj. Pilot, Philadelphia, 1978–80; psc 1984; OC 78 Sqdn, Falklands, 1991; Staff HQ ARRC, 1993–95; Airpower Liaison Officer, Army Directorate of Land Warfare, 1996–2000. Chm., Action for Blind People, 2010–11. Vice Chm., Gresham Coll., 2009–12. Master, Mercers' Co., 2002–03. DL Hammersmith and Fulham, 2009–11. *Recreations:* family, travel, photography, history, City of London guide, bell ringing. *Clubs:* Royal Air Force, Hurlingham.

DUDLEY, 5th Earl of, *cr* 1860; **William Humble David Jeremy Ward;** Baron Ward, 1644; Viscount Ednam, 1860; *b* 27 March 1947; *s* of 4th Earl of Dudley and of Stella Viscountess Ednam, *d* of M. A. Carcano, KCMG, KBE; *S* father, 2013; *m* 1st, 1972, Sarah (marr. diss. 1976), *o d* of Sir Alastair Coats, Bt, *qv*; 2nd, 1976, Debra Louise (marr. diss. 1980), *d* of George Robert and Marjorie Elvera Pinney; one *d.* *Educ:* Eton; Christ Church, Oxford. *Heir: half-b* Hon. Leander Grenville Dudley Ward, *b* 30 Oct. 1971.

DUDLEY, 15th Baron *cr* 1439 (called out of abeyance, 1916); **Jim Anthony Hill Wallace;** *b* 9 Nov. 1930; *e s* of Baroness Dudley (14th in line) and Guy Raymond Hill Wallace; *S* mother, 2002; *m* 1962, Nicola Jane, *d* of Lt-Col P. W. E. L. Dunsterville; two *s.* *Educ:* Lancing. *Recreations:* photography, listening to classical music, model engineering, restoring vintage vehicles and old machinery. *Heir: s* Hon. Jeremy William Guilford Wallace, *b* 12 Sept. 1964.

DUDLEY, Bishop Suffragan of, since 2014; **Rt Rev. Graham Barham Usher;** *b* York, 11 Sept. 1970; *s* of Michael Usher and Fionna Usher; *m* 1996, Rachel Margaret Sarah Thomson; one *s* one *d.* *Educ:* Univ. of Edinburgh (BSc); Corpus Christi Coll., Cambridge (MA). Ordained deacon, 1996, priest, 1997; Asst Curate, St Mary's, Nunthorpe, Middlesbrough, 1996–99; Vicar, Holy Trinity, N Ormesby, Middlesbrough, 1999–2004; Rector and Lectr, Hexham Abbey, 2004–14; Area Dean of Hexham, 2006–11. Hon. Canon, St Cyprian's Cathedral, Kumasi, Ghana, 2007–14. Sec. of State appointee, Northumberland Nat. Park Authy, 2009–13; Chm., Adv. Cttee, NE Region, Forestry Commn, 2009–14. Lay Mem., Access and Governance Cttee, Newcastle Biomedicine Biobank, 2012–14. *Publications:* Places of Enchantment: meeting God in landscapes, 2012. *Recreations:* wild lonely places, painting and drawing, reading, the company of friends. *Address:* The Bishop's House, 60 Bishop's Walk, Cradley Heath, W Midlands B64 7RH. *T:* (0121) 550 3407. *E:* bishop.dudley@cofe-worcester.org.uk.

DUDLEY, Archdeacon of; *see* Groarke, Ven. N. J.

DUDLEY, Anthony Edward; Hon. Mr Justice Dudley; Chief Justice, Gibraltar, since 2010; *b* Gibraltar, 18 Jan. 1967; *s* of George Dudley and Maria Dudley (*née* del Carmen Arrellano); *m* 1992, Lesley Curran; two *d.* *Educ:* Bayside Comp. Sch., Gibraltar; Univ. of Hull (LLB); Inns of Court Sch. of Law. Called to the Bar: England and Wales, 1989; Gibraltar, 1989; a Stipendiary Magistrate, 2004; Puisne Judge, Supreme Court, Gibraltar, 2010. *Recreations:* rowing, running, reading, eating. *Address:* Supreme Court, 277 Main Street, Gibraltar. *T:* 20078808, *Fax:* 20077118. *E:* jackiespiteri@supremecourt.gov.gi.

DUDLEY, Rev. Martin Raymond, PhD; Rector, Priory Church of St Bartholomew the Great, London, since 1995; Priest-in-charge, St Bartholomew the Less, Smithfield Gate, since 2012; *b* 31 May 1953; *s* of Ronald Frank Dudley and Joyce Mary (*née* Gardiner); *m* 1976, Paula Jones; two *s.* *Educ:* King Edward's Sch., Birmingham; RMA Sandhurst; KCL (BD, AKC 1977, MTh 1978); St Michael's Coll., Llandaff; PhD London 1994; Cass Business Sch., City Univ. (MSc 2006); Univ. of Helsinki. Ordained deacon, 1979, priest, 1980; Curate, Whitchurch, 1979–83; Vicar, Weston, 1983–88; Priest i/c, Ardeley, 1986–88; Vicar, Owlsmoor, 1988–95. Chaplain: Imperial Soc. of Kts Bach., 1995–2005; Butchers' Co., 1995–2009, 2013–14, 2015–16; Co. of Chartered Secretaries and Administrators, 1995–2000; Hackney Carriage Drivers' Co., 1998–; Master, Farmers' Co., 1999–2000, 2002–03; Co. of Inf. Technologists, 2001–; Master, Fletchers' Co., 2001–02, 2004–09, 2010–11; Tax Advisers' Co., 2002–; Aldermanic Sheriff, City of London, 2003–04; City of London Br., Royal Soc. of St George, 2003– (Vice Chm., 2014–15; Chm., 2015–); Public Relations Practitioners' Co., 2003–11, 2014–. Mem., London Dio. Synod, 2003–06 (Mem., Bp's Council, 2003–06). Common Councilman (Aldersgate Ward), Corp. of London, 2002– (Master, Aldersgate Ward Club, 2015–). Member, Professional Conduct and Complaints Committee: Bar Council, 2000–07; CIArb, 2005–; Mem., Professional Standards Panel, CIPR, 2014–. Member: Hampstead Heath Mgt Cttee, 2003–04, 2010–; Audit and Risk Mgt Cttee, City of London Corp., 2011–; Court, Bridewell Royal Foundn, 2003–14; Licensing Cttee, 2004–, Planning & Transportation Cttee, 2005–, Community and Children's Services Cttee, 2006– (Chm., 2011–14), City Bridge Trust, 2007–11, Standards Cttee, 2007–11 and 2012–14, City of London Corp. (formerly Corp. of London); City of London Health and Well-Being Bd, 2012– (Chm., 2013–). Chm., Resource Centre (London) Ltd, 2007–11. Governor: City Lit. Inst., 2001–03; City of London Sch. for Girls, 2002–14; City of London Acad., Southwark, 2003–13; Gatehouse Sch., 2009–12; Mus. of London, 2007–14 (Chm., Audit Cttee, 2009–14). Mem. Ct, City Univ., 2009–; Mem. Bd, Assoc. of Governing Bodies of Ind. Schs, 2007–13; City of London Acad., Islington, 2014–. Trustee: Butchers' and Drovers' Charitable Instn, 1996–2004; London Liby, 2003–07; Trust for London (formerly City Parochial Foundn), 2005–15. Liveryman, Farriers' Co., 2000; Hon. Liveryman, Hackney Carriage Drivers' Co., 2014; Hon. Freeman: Farmers' Co., 2000; Guild of Public Relns Practitioners, 2005 (Master, 2012–13); Pres., Farringdon Ward Club, 2008–09 (Sen. Vice-Pres., 2007–08). Hon. MCGI 2011. FRHistS 1995; FSA 1997; FRSA 2006–14. SBStJ 1998. Hon. DArts City, 2014. *Publications:* The Collect in Anglican Liturgy, 1994; (ed) Like a Two-edged Sword, 1995; A Manual of Ministry to the Sick, 1997; Humanity and Healing, 1998; Ashes to Glory, 1999; A Herald Voice, 2000; Risen, Ascended, Glorified, 2001; Crowning the Year, 2003; with Virginia Rounding: Churchwardens: a survival guide, 2003, 2nd edn 2009; The Parish Survival Guide, 2004; Serving the Parish, 2006. *Recreations:* learning Finnish, Dudley genealogy. *Address:* St Bartholomew the Great Parish Office, Church House, Cloth Fair, EC1A 7JQ. *T:* (020) 7600 0440. *E:* rector@greatstbarts.com; martin.dudley@cityoflondon.gov.uk. *Clubs:* Athenæum, Guildhall.

DUDLEY, His Honour Michael John; a Circuit Judge, 2003–15; *b* 24 Jan. 1947; *s* of John Kenneth and Ruby Marguerite Dudley; *m* 1968, Barbara; one *s* one *d.* *Educ:* Magdalen Coll. Sch., Brackley; Univ. of Birmingham (LLB); Univ. of Leeds (PGCE). Called to the Bar, Lincoln's Inn, 1972; specialised in crime and general common law; Dep. Stipendiary Magistrate, 1984–90; Asst Recorder, 1993–99, Recorder, 1999–2003. *Recreations:* walking, golf, photography, music, watching Rugby. *Clubs:* Sutton Coldfield Rugby Football; Sutton Coldfield Golf.

DUDLEY, William Stuart, RDI 1989; Associate Designer, Royal National Theatre, since 1981; *b* 4 March 1947; *s* of William Dudley and Dorothy Stacey. *Educ:* Highbury Sch., London; St Martin's School of Art; Slade School of Art. DipAD, BA Fine Art; UCL Postgrad. Dip. Fine Art. First production, Hamlet, Nottingham Playhouse, 1970; subseq. prodns include: The Duchess of Malfi and Man is Man, Royal Court, 1971; *National Theatre,* 1971–: Tyger, 1974; The Good-Natured Man, 1974; The Passion, 1977; Lavender Blue, 1977; The World Turned Upside Down, Has Washington Legs?, 1978; Dispatches, Lost Worlds, Lark Rise to Candleford, Undiscovered Country (SWET award, Designer of the Year, 1980), 1979; Good Soldier Schweyk, 1982; Cinderella, 1983; The Mysteries, Real Inspector Hound/The Critic, 1985 (Laurence Olivier (formerly SWET) Award, Designer of the Year, 1985); Futurists, 1986; Waiting for Godot, 1987; Cat on a Hot Tin Roof, The Shaughraun, and The Changeling, 1988; Bartholomew Fair, 1988; The Crucible, 1990; The Coup, 1991; Pygmalion, 1992; On the Ledge, 1993; Under Milk Wood, 1995; Mary Stuart, 1996; The Homecoming, 1997; The London Cuckolds, 1998; All My Sons, 2000 (Laurence Olivier Awards, Best Set Designer, 2001); The Coast of Utopia, 2002; Honour, 2003; The Permanent Way, Cyrano de Bergerac, 2004; *Royal Court:* Live Like Pigs, 1972; Merry-Go-Round, 1973; Magnificence, 1975; The Fool, 1975; Small Change, 1976; Hamlet, 1980; Kafka's Dick, 1986; Etta Jenks, 1990; I Licked a Slag's Deodorant, 1996; Hitchcock Blonde, 2003, transf. Lyric, 2003; *RSC:* Twelfth Night, 1974; Ivanov, 1976; That Good Between Us, 1977; Richard III, The Party, Today, 1984; Merry Wives of Windsor, 1985, 1992; A Midsummer Night's Dream, Richard II, 1986; Kiss Me Kate, 1987; The Winter's Tale, 2013; *West End:* Mutiny, Piccadilly, 1985; Heartbreak House, Haymarket, 1992; A Streetcar Named Desire, Haymarket, 1996; The Breath of Life, Haymarket, 2002; Woman in White, Palace, 2004; Carousel, Savoy, 2008; All My Sons, Apollo, 2010; *other productions:* The Ship, Glasgow, 1990; The Deep Blue Sea, Almeida, 1993; The Big Picnic, Glasgow, 1994; Some Sunny Day, Hampstead, 1996; The Alchemist, Birmingham, 1996; Titus Andronicus, Shakespeare's Globe, 2006 and 2014; Betrayal, Donmar Warehouse, 2007; Peter Pan, Kensington Gdns, 2009; The Beggar's Opera, Regent's Park, 2011; King Lear, Th. Royal, Bath, 2013; Fings Ain't Wot They Used T'be, Th. Royal, Stratford East, 2014; For Services Rendered, Minerva, Chichester, 2015; *opera:* WNO: Il barbiere di Siviglia, 1976; Idomeneo, 1991; Metropolitan, NY: Billy Budd, 1978; Glyndebourne: Die Entführung aus dem Serail, 1980; Il barbiere di Siviglia, 1981; Royal Opera: Les Contes d'Hoffman (sets), 1980; Don Giovanni, 1981; The Cunning Little Vixen, 1990, revived 2003; Bayreuth: Der Ring des Nibelungen, 1983; Der Rosenkavalier, 1984; Salzburg Festival: Un ballo in maschera, 1989; *television film:* Persuasion, 1994 (BAFTA and RTS Awards for set design). Designer of the Year, Laurence Olivier Awards, 1980, 1985, 1986, 1993. *Recreation:* playing the concertina. *Address:* 11 Halstow Road, SE10 0LD.

DUDLEY-SMITH, Rt Rev. Timothy, OBE 2003; Bishop Suffragan of Thetford, 1981–92; *b* 26 Dec. 1926; *o s* of Arthur and Phyllis Dudley Smith, Buxton, Derbyshire; *m* 1959, June Arlette MacDonald (*d* 2007); one *s* two *d.* *Educ:* Tonbridge Sch.; Pembroke Coll., and Ridley Hall, Cambridge. BA 1947, MA 1951; Certif. in Educn 1948. Deacon, 1950; priest, 1951; Asst Curate, St Paul, Northumberland Heath, 1950–53; Head of Cambridge Univ. Mission in Bermondsey, 1953–55, Hon. Chaplain, 1955–60; Hon. Chaplain to Bp of Rochester, 1953–60; Editor, Crusade, and Editorial Sec. of Evangelical Alliance, 1955–59; Asst Sec. of Church Pastoral-Aid Soc., 1959–65, Sec., 1965–73; Archdeacon of Norwich, 1973–81; Commissary to Archbp of Sydney, 1971–92; Exam. Chap. to Bp of Norwich, 1971–85. President: Evangelical Alliance, 1987–91; C of E Evangelical Council, 1990–93; Vice-Pres., UCCF, 1992–. Chm. of Govs, 1992–96, Patron, 1996–, Monkton Combe Sch. Fellow, Hymn Soc. in the US and Canada, 1997; Hon. Vice-Pres., Hymn Soc. of GB and Ireland, 2003. FRSCM 2011. MLitt Lambeth, 1991; Hon. DD Durham, 2009. *Publications:* Christian Literature and the Church Bookstall, 1963; What Makes a Man a Christian?, 1966; A Man Named Jesus, 1971; Someone who Beckons, 1978; Lift Every Heart, 1984; A Flame of Love, 1987; Songs of Deliverance, 1988; Praying with the English Hymn Writers, 1989; A Voice of Singing, 1992; John Stott: a comprehensive bibliography, 1995; (compiled) Authentic Christianity, 1995; Great is the Glory, 1997; John Stott: the making of a leader, 1999; John Stott: a global ministry, 2001; (jtly) Beneath a Travelling Star, 2001; A House of Praise, 2003, Pt 2 2015; A Door for the Word, 2006; (jtly) A Calendar of Praise, 2006; (jtly) High Days and Holy Days, 2007; (jtly) The Voice of Faith, 2008; (jtly) Above Every Name, 2009; Praise to the Name, 2009; (jtly) Draw Near to God, 2010; Beyond our Dreaming, 2012; (jtly) A Mirror to the Soul, 2013; contributor to hymn books. *Recreations:* reading, writing, verse, family and friends. *Address:* 9 Ashlands, Ford, Salisbury, Wilts SP4 6DY. *T:* (01722) 326417.

DUDLEY-WILLIAMS, Sir Alastair (Edgcumbe James), 2nd Bt *cr* 1964, of Exeter; Director, Wildcat Consultants, 1986–2010; *b* 26 Nov. 1943; *s* of Sir Rolf Dudley Dudley-Williams, 1st Bt and Margaret Helen, *er d* of F. E. Robinson, OBE; *S* father, 1987; *m* 1972, Diana Elizabeth Jane, twin *d* of R. H. C. Duncan; three *d.* *Educ:* Pangbourne College. Hughes Tool Co. (Texas), 1962–64; Bay Drilling Corp. (Louisiana), 1964–65; Bristol Siddeley Whittle Tools Ltd, 1965–67; Santa Fe Drilling Co., 1967–72; Inchcape plc, 1972–86. *Recreations:* shooting, fishing, cultivating vegetables. *Heir: b* Malcolm Philip Edgcumbe Dudley-Williams [*b* 10 Aug. 1947; *m* 1973, Caroline Anne Colina, twin *d* of R. H. C. Duncan; two *s* one *d*]. *Address:* Fairfield House, 17 The Green, East Meon, Petersfield, Hants GU32 1QT.

DUDSON, Ian James, CBE 2002; Lord-Lieutenant of Staffordshire, since 2012; non-executive Chairman, Dudson (Holdings) Ltd, since 2009; *b* Congleton, Cheshire, 15 July 1950; *s* of late Derek Hubert Dudson and Audrey Margaret Dudson (*née* Hamilton); *m* 1975, Jane, *d* of late Ralph and Marjorie Bassett; two *d.* *Educ:* Shrewsbury Sch.; Dundee Univ. (BSc); Staffordshire Univ. Dudson (Holdings) Ltd: Trainee Manager, 1973–75; Works Manager, 1975–82; Works Dir, 1982–88; Chief Exec., 1988–2009. Pro-Chancellor and Chm. Council, Keele Univ., 2005–12. Chm., Staffs Magistrates' Adv. Cttee, 2012–. President: Eur. Fedn of Porcelaine and Faience, 2005–08; British Ceramic Confedn, 2007–09. Chm. Trustees, Dudson Centre, 1998–. Vice Pres., RFCA W Midlands, 2012–. President: Tennis Staffs, 1999–; Staffs Co. Scouts, 2012–; St John Staffs, 2012–. Hon. Pres., Douglas Macmillan Hospice, 2005–; Jt Patron, Friends of Lichfield Cathedral, 2012–. DL, 2001, High Sheriff, 2010–11, Staffs. CStJ 2013. *Recreations:* gardening, walking, travel, dining out. *Address:* Lieutenancy Office, Martin Street, Stafford ST16 2LH. *T:* (01785) 276805, *Fax:* (01785) 276115. *E:* officer.lieutenancy@staffordshire.gov.uk.

DUERDEN, Prof. Brian Ion, CBE 2008; MD; FRCPath, FRCPE; Inspector of Microbiology and Infection Control (formerly of Microbiology), Department of Health, 2004–10; Professor of Medical Microbiology, Cardiff University (formerly University of Wales College of Medicine), 1991–2008, now Emeritus; *b* 21 June 1948; *s* of Cyril Duerden and Mildred (*née* Ion); *m* 1972, Marjorie Hudson. *Educ:* Nelson Grammar Sch., Nelson, Lancs; Edinburgh Univ. (BSc Hons Med. Sci. Bacteriol. 1970; MB ChB 1972; MD 1979). MRCPath 1978, FRCPath 1990; FRCPE 2005. House Officer, Thoracic Surgery, 1972–73, and Infectious Diseases, 1973, City Hosp., Edinburgh; Lectr in Bacteriol., Univ. of Edinburgh Med. Sch., 1973–76; University of Sheffield Medical School: Lectr in Med. Microbiol., 1976–79; Sen. Lectr, 1979–83; Prof. of Med. Microbiol., 1983–90; Hon. Consultant in Med. Microbiol., Sheffield Children's Hosp., 1979–90; Dir, Cardiff Public Health Lab., and Hd, S Glamorgan Microbiol. Services, 1991–95; Dep. Dir, 1995–2002 and Med. Dir, 1999–2002, Dir, 2002–03, PHLS; Dir, Clinical Quality, HPA, 2003. Ed. in Chief, Jl Med. Microbiol., 1983–2002. *Publications:* (contrib. and vol. ed.) Topley and Wilson's Principles of Bacteriology, Virology and Immunology, 7th edn 1980 to 9th edn 1997; Textbook of Microbial and Parasitic Infection, 1987, 2nd edn 1993; Anaerobes in Human Disease, 1991; contrib. numerous scientific articles to professional jls. *Recreations:* travel, photography, music, cricket. *Address:* Pendle, Welsh Street, Chepstow, Monmouthshire NP16 5LU. *E:* bduerden@doctors.org.uk.

DUFF, Andrew Nicholas, OBE 1997; Member (Lib Dem) Eastern England, European Parliament, 1999–2014; *b* 25 Dec. 1950; *s* of late Norman Bruce Duff and Diana (*née* Wilcoxson). *Educ:* Sherborne Sch.; St John's Coll., Cambridge (MA; MLitt 1978); Université Libre de Bruxelles. Res. Officer, Hansard Soc. for Parly Govt, 1974–76; consultant and researcher on EC affairs, 1977–88; Res. Fellow, Joseph Rowntree Reform Trust, 1989–92; Dir, Federal Trust for Educn and Res., 1993–99. Mem. (L), 1982–87, (Lib Dem), 1987–90, Cambridge CC. Contested: (L) Cambridge and N Beds, 1984, (Lib Dem) Cambridgeshire, 1989, 1994, EP elecns; (Lib Dem) Huntingdon, Parly elecns, 1992; (Lib Dem) Eastern England, 2014. Vice Pres., Liberal Democrats, 1994–97. European Parliament: Constitutional Affairs spokesman, Alliance of Liberals and Democrats for Europe (formerly Eur. Lib Dem Gp), 1999–2014; Leader, UK Lib Dems, 2007–09; Vice-Pres., delegn to Convention on Future of Europe, 2002–03; Pres., Union of Eur. Federalists, 2008–13. *Publications:* include: (ed jtly) Maastricht and Beyond: building the European Union, 1994; Reforming the European Union, 1997; (ed) The Treaty of Amsterdam, 1997; The Struggle for Europe's Constitution, 2005; Saving the European Union: the logic of the Lisbon Treaty, 2009; (ed) Making the Difference, 2010; On Governing Europe, 2012; A Fundamental Law of the EU, 2013; Pandora, Penelope, Polity: how to change the European Union, 2015. *Recreation:* music. *Club:* National Liberal.

DUFF, Anthony Michael; communications strategist and executive coach, since 1999; *b* 7 Aug. 1946; *s* of Anthony Duff and Alice Mary Duff (*née* Conway); *m* 1997, Marisol de Lafuente. *Educ:* St Conleth's Coll., Dublin; University Coll., Dublin (BA Hons). LGSM (Drama) 1968; LRAM (Drama) 1970; RSA Dip. TEFLA 1972. Dir, Teacher Trng and Foundn Dir, Café Théâtre Anglais, Internat. House, Paris, 1971–74; Vis. Lectr in Drama, Thomond Coll., Co. Limerick, 1975–76; Pedagogic Advr to Longman Italia, 1977–79; International House, London: Dir of Educn, 1979–83; Dir, 1984–89; Dir-Gen., 1990–99. FRSA 1993. *Publications:* English For You, 2 vols, 1979, 1981; (ed) Explorations in Teacher Training, 1989. *Recreations:* music, reading, the theatre, walking, being solitary. *Address:* Villa della Luna, Località La Calandrina, 01015 Sutri (VT), Italy.

DUFF, Antony; *see* Duff, R. A.

DUFF, Sir Gordon (William), Kt 2007; PhD; FRCP, FRCPE, FMedSci, FRSE; Principal, St Hilda's College, Oxford, since 2014; Chairman, Biotechnology and Biological Sciences Research Council, since 2015; *b* 27 Dec. 1947; *s* of William Munro Duff and Marion Gertrude Duff; *m* 1969, Naida Margaret, *d* of Air Cdre Charles Clarke, OBE and Eileen Clarke; two *d*. *Educ:* Perth Acad.; Hipperholme GS, Yorks; St Peter's Coll., Oxford (BA 1969, MA 1975; BM BCh 1975; Hon. Fellow, 2006); St Thomas's Hosp. Med. Sch., Univ. of London (PhD 1980); Saybrook Coll., Yale Univ. FRCPE 1989; FRCP 1998. House Officer in Medicine, St Thomas's Hosp., London, and in Surgery, Stracathro Hosp., Brechin, 1975–76; Senior House Officer in Medicine: RAF Unit, King Edward VII Hosp., Midhurst, 1976–77; (Clinical Pharmacol.) Hammersmith Hosp. and RPMS, 1977–78; Med. Registrar posts, 1978–80; Yale University School of Medicine: Res. Associate, Internal Medicine (Infectious Diseases) and Pathol. (Immunol.), 1980–83; Associate Investigator, Howard Hughes Inst. of Cellular and Molecular Immunol., 1981–83; Clin. Lectr in Rheumatol., 1984–86, Clin. Sen. Lectr, Dept of Medicine, 1986–90, Univ. of Edinburgh; Hon. Consultant Physician, Lothian Health Bd, 1986–90; University of Sheffield: Lord Florey Prof. of Molecular Medicine, 1991–2014; Res. Dean, Sheffield Med. Sch., 1997–2002; Director: Div. of Molecular and Genetic Medicine, 1997–2000; of Res., Faculty of Medicine, 1999–2002; Div. of Genomic Medicine, 2000–06; Hon. Consultant Physician, Sheffield Teaching Hosps NHS Trust, 1991–. RSocMed Vis. Prof. to USA (Yale, NIH, Pfizer Res.), 1995; Lectures: Honyman-Gillespie, Univ. of Edinburgh, 1991; Harry Bostrom, Swedish Soc. Med., 1996; Faculty, Univ. of Geneva, 2001. Founding Ed., Cytokine, 1988–. Committee on Safety of Medicines: Mem., 1995–2005, Chm., 2003–05; Chairman: Biol Sub-cttee, 1998–2003 (Mem., 1995–2005); vCJD and Blood Products Expert Gp, 1998–2005; vCJD and Vaccines Expert Gp, 2000–05; Tissue Engrg Expert Gp, 2001–05; Mem., Safety and Efficacy Sub-cttee, 1992–95. Chairman: Foresight Internat. Health Gp, DTI (OST), 1998–2000; Nat. Biol Standards Bd, 2002–09; Gene Therapy Commissioning Gp, DoH, 2004; Commn on Human Medicines, 2005–12; Scientific Pandemic Influenza Adv. Cttee, 2008; Medicines and Healthcare Products Regulatory Agency, 2013–14; Member: Health and Life Scis Foresight Panel, DTI, 1997–99; Genomic Medicine Gp, Foresight Healthcare, 1999–2000; Adv. Gp on Genetics Res., DoH, 2003–07. Member: Adv. Bd, MRC, 1997–2005; Health Metrology Panel, EPSRC, 2000. Expert Advr (Biol Medicines), EMEA, 2001–. Clin. Trials Monitor, WHO, 1995–97. Member: R&D Exec., Central Sheffield Univ. Hosp. NHS Trust, 1996–99 (Chm., Res. Mgt Cttee, 1996–98); R&D Strategy Gp, Trent RHA, 2000–04. Mem., Internat. Scientific Adv. Bd, Medical Solutions plc, 1999–2005. Member: Council, Internat. Cytokine Soc., USA, 1992– (Pres., 1997–98); Council, Eur. Cytokine Soc., Paris, 1997–; International Scientific Advisory Board: Deutsches Rheuma-Forschungzentrum, Berlin, 1996–99; Dublin Molecular Medicine Centre, 2000–. Mem., Clin. Interest Gp, Wellcome Trust, 1994–97. Member: Res. Cttee, Arthritis and Rheumatism Council, 1993–97; Scientific Cttee, DEBRA (Fragile Skin Diseases), 1996–99; Scientific Cttee, GDBA, 1996–99. Mem. Council, Univ. of Sheffield, 2000–04. FMedSci 1999; FRSE 2008. Mem., Assoc. of Physicians of GB and Ireland, 1986–. MD (hc) Edinburgh, 2008. (Jtly) Sir Hiram Maxim Award for Res. in Immunol., 1987; Medal, Swedish Soc. Med., 1996. *Publications:* contribs to res. jls in fields of inflammation, immunology and genetics; thirty patents in field of genetic diagnostics for common diseases. *Recreations:* ski-ing, hill-walking, botany, carpentry. *Address:* St Hilda's College, Cowley Place, Oxford OX4 1DY. *Clubs:* Athenæum, Royal Over-Seas League.

DUFF, Graham, CB 1999; barrister; Consultant, Jacqueline Duff & Co., Solicitors, since 2008; *b* 7 Jan. 1947; *s* of Norman Alexander Duff and Doris Duff; *m* 1987, Jacqueline Tremble; one *s* one *d*. *Educ:* Newcastle Royal Grammar Sch.; Univ. of Durham (BA (Hons) Law); Univ. of Newcastle upon Tyne (Grad. Cert Ed). Called to the Bar, Lincoln's Inn, 1976. Asst Dir of Public Prosecutions, 1986; Br. Crown Prosecutor, Inner London, 1986; Chief Crown Prosecutor, Northumbria and Durham, 1987; a Dir, CPS, 1990–98; Mem., Trinity Chambers, Newcastle upon Tyne, 1999–2008. Mem., Cartington Parish Council, 2002–. *Recreations:* old Riley motor cars, Northumbrian countryside. *Address:* Jacqueline Duff & Co., Lynnholm, Thropton, Northumberland NE65 7JE. *T:* (01669) 621987.

DUFF, Prof. Michael James, PhD; FRS 2009; FInstP; Abdus Salam Professor of Theoretical Physics, Imperial College London, since 2006; *b* Manchester, 28 Jan. 1949; *s* of Edward Duff and Elizabeth Duff (*née* Kaylor); *m* 1984, Lesley Yearling; one *s* one *d*. *Educ:* De La Salle Coll., Salford; Queen Mary Coll., London (BSc 1969); Imperial Coll. London (DIC, PhD 1972). FInstP 2004. Post-doctoral Fellowships at Internat. Centre for Theoretical Physics, Trieste, Univ. of Oxford, KCL, QMC and Brandeis Univ., 1972–79; Faculty Mem., Imperial Coll., London, 1979–88; Sen. Physicist, CERN, Geneva, 1984–87; Prof. of Physics, 1988–92, Dist. Prof. of Physics, 1992–99, Texas A & M Univ.; Oscar Klein Prof. of Physics, Univ. of Michigan, 1999–2005; Dir, Michigan Center for Theoretical Physics, 2000–05; Prof. of Physics and Principal, Faculty of Physical Scis, Imperial Coll. London, 2005–06. Fellow, APS, 1994. FRSA. Meeting Gold Medal, El Colegio Nacional, Mexico, 2004. *Publications:* The World in Eleven Dimensions, 1999; numerous articles on unified theory of elementary particles. *Recreations:* watercolours, golf. *Address:* Physics Department, Imperial College London, Prince Consort Road, SW7 2BZ. *T:* (020) 7594 8571, *Fax:* (020) 7594 7844. *E:* m.duff@imperial.ac.uk.

DUFF, Prof. (Robin) Antony, FBA 2004; FRSE; Professor, Department of Philosophy, University of Stirling, 1990–2009, now Emeritus; Professor, School of Law, University of Minnesota, since 2010; *b* 9 March 1945; *s* of Rt Hon. Sir (Arthur) Antony Duff, GCMG, CVO, DSO, DSC, PC and of Pauline Marion Duff; partner, Sandra Marshall. *Educ:* St Peter's Sch., Seaford; Sedbergh Sch.; Christ Church, Oxford (BA). Vis. Lectr, Dept of Philos., Univ. of Washington, Seattle, 1968–69; University of Stirling: Lectr, Dept of Philos., 1970–80; Sen. Lectr, 1980–90; Reader, 1990. FRSE 1996. *Publications:* Trials and Punishments, 1986; Intention, Agency and Criminal Liability, 1990; Criminal Attempts, 1996; Punishment, Communication and Community, 2001; Answering for Crime, 2007; The Trial on Trial, 2007. *Address:* Department of Philosophy, University of Stirling, Stirling FK9 4LA. *E:* r.a.duff@stir.ac.uk.

DUFF GORDON, Sir Andrew (Cosmo Lewis), 8th Bt *cr* 1813; *b* 17 Oct. 1933; *o s* of Sir Douglas Duff Gordon, 7th Bt and Gladys Rosemary (*d* 1933), *e d* of late Col Vivien Henry, CB; *S* father, 1964; *m* 1st, 1967, Grania Mary (marr. diss. 1975; she *d* 2012), *d* of Fitzgerald Villiers-Stuart, Ireland; one *s*; 2nd, 1975, Eveline Virginia, BA, *d* of S. Soames, Newbury; three *s*. *Educ:* Repton. Served with Worcs Regiment and 1st Bn Ches Regt, 1952–54. Mem. of Lloyd's, 1962–91. Jt Hon. Pres., Nomadic Preservation Soc., 2006–. *Publications:* (with R. W. D. Fenn) The Life and Times of Sir George Cornewall Lewis, Bt, 2005; contrib. to Tarmac Papers. *Recreations:* golf, shooting, ski-ing. *Heir:* *s* Cosmo Henry Villiers Duff Gordon [*b* 18 June 1968; *m* 2006, Araminta de Clermont; one *s*]. *Address:* Downton House, Walton, Presteigne, Powys LD8 2RD. *T:* (01544) 350223; 27 Cathcart Road, SW10 9JG. *T:* (020) 7351 1170. *Club:* Kington Golf.

DUFFELL, Lt-Gen. Sir Peter Royson, KCB 1992; CBE 1988 (OBE 1981); MC 1966; Consultant, Special Projects, Dechert LLP (formerly Titmuss Sainer Dechert), 2006–14 (Chief Executive, 1995–2006); *b* 19 June 1939; *s* of late Roy John Duffell, Lenham, Kent, and Ruth Doris (*née* Gustaffson); *m* 1982, Ann Murray, *d* of late Col Basil Bethune Neville Woodd, Rolvenden, Kent; one *s* one *d*. *Educ:* Dulwich Coll. psc, rcds. FRGS 1975; FRAS 1992. Commnd 2nd KEO Gurkha Rifles, 1960; Staff Coll., Camberley, 1971; Bde Major 5 Bde, 1972–74; MA to C-in-C UKLF, 1976–78; Comdt 1st Bn 2nd KEO Gurkha Rifles, 1978–81; Col GS, MoD, 1981–83; Comdr Gurkha Field Force, 1984–85; COS 1 (BR) Corps, 1986–87; RCDS, 1988; Cabinet Office Efficiency Unit, 1989; Comdr, British Forces Hong Kong, and Maj.-Gen. Brigade of Gurkhas, 1989–92; Inspector Gen. Doctrine and Trng, MoD, 1992–95. Col, Royal Gurkha Rifles, 1994–99. Mem., Internat. Adv. Bd, SOAS, 2006–. Trustee, Foyle Foundn, 2006–. Gov., Sandroyd Sch., 1995–2009. Pres., Sirmoor Rifles Assoc., 2006–. Freeman, City of London, 2001. *Recreations:* collecting beautiful things, watching cricket, my family. *Clubs:* Travellers, Pratt's, MCC.

DUFFERIN AND CLANDEBOYE, 11th Baron *cr* 1800 (Ire.); **John Francis Blackwood;** Bt (Ire.) 1763; Bt (UK) 1814; architect; *b* 18 Oct. 1944; *s* of 10th Baron and of Margaret Alice, *d* of Hector Kirkpatrick; *S* father, 1991 (claim to peerage not yet established); *m* 1971, Annette Kay, *d* of Harold Greenhill; one *s* one *d*. *Educ:* Barker Coll., Hornsby; Univ. of NSW (BArch). AAIA (ARAIA 1970). *Recreations:* organic farming, fishing. *Heir:* *s* Hon. Francis Senden Blackwood, *b* 6 Jan. 1979. *Address:* PO Box 1815, Orange, NSW 2800, Australia. *T:* (2) 63625608.

DUFFETT, Roger Hugh Edward; Secretary, Royal College of Surgeons of England, 1988–97; *b* 20 Jan. 1936; *s* of Dr Edward Cecil Duffett and Cicely Duffett (*née* Haw); *m* 1959, Angela Julie Olden; one *d* (one *s* decd). *Educ:* Sherborne Sch. (Scholar); Peterhouse, Cambridge (Scholar; MA). Commissioned RA (Nat. Service), 1954–56; British Petroleum Co.: joined 1956; refinery process foreman, 1959–60; research, molecular sieve properties of synthetic zeolites and reactions of frozen free radicals, 1960–64; creation of computerised manpower planning models, 1964–68; creation and operation of computerised linear programming models for integrated oil ops, 1968–71; application of mathematical models to corporate planning, 1971–73; planning, internat. ops for lubricants, 1973–78; negotiation and op., crude oil contracts, 1978–79; consultancy for analysis and resolution of orgnl problems: in shipping, research, engrg, marketing and personnel; for management of secondary schools, Cambs; Unicef (UK); employment of secondees to Enterprise Bds, 1979–87; orgn and systems consultant for BP Oil Internat., for Riding for Disabled, 1987–88. Gov., Basingstoke NHS Foundn Trust, 2006–08. Member, Management Committee, Clare Park, 1979–83; Riding for Disabled, 1990–2004 (Trustee, 1999–2004; Hon. Life Vice Pres., 2007); Dir, Quinta Nursing Home, Farnham, 1983–88. Freeman, Barbers' Co., 1998. Hon. FRCS 1997; Hon. DGDP 1998. Mem., Editl Bd, Primary Dental Care, 2010–. *Publications:* contribs to learned jls. *Recreations:* golf, servicing golf club website magazine, coarse gardening, creating brain teasers, writing, reading. *Address:* Tavistock Cottage, Bentley, Farnham, Surrey GU10 5JA. *T:* and *Fax:* (01420) 520283. *E:* r.duffett@btinternet.com. *Club:* Liphook Golf.

DUFFIELD, Christopher Paul; Town Clerk and Chief Executive, City of London Corporation (formerly Corporation of London), 2003–12; *b* 20 May 1952; *s* of late Jack and Irene Duffield; *m* 1st, 1971 (marr. diss. 1979); one *s*; 2nd, 1987, Tricia Jackson; two *s*. *Educ:* St Albans Sch.; Univ. of Newcastle-upon-Tyne (BA Hons 1973). CPFA 1978. Asst Dir of Finance, GLC, 1983–85; Dep. Dir of Finance, London Bor. of Redbridge, 1985–87; Dep. County Treas., Essex CC, 1988–91; London Borough of Bexley: Dir of Finance, 1991–95; Chief Exec., 1995–2003. Mem., London Regl Risk and Audit Cttee, HM Courts Service, 2006–10. Member: London Resilience Partnership (formerly Regl Resilience Forum), 2004–12 (Chm., Local Authy Panel, 2008–12; Dep. Chm., 2011–12); Exec. Task Force, Film London, 2008–12; London Charter Bd, 2009–11; London Finance Commn, 2012–13; Chm., Central London Resilience Forum, 2006–10. Dep. Chm., Bexley PCT, 2001–03. Trustee, Hackney Quest, 2009–12.

DUFFIELD, Linda Joy, CMG 2002; HM Diplomatic Service, retired; Chief Executive, Westminster Foundation for Democracy, 2009–14; *b* 18 April 1953; *d* of Bryan Charles Duffield and Joyce Eileen Duffield (*née* Barr). *Educ:* St Mary's Sch., Northwood, Middx; Exeter Univ. (BA Hons 1975). DHSS, 1976–85; Ecole Nat. d'Admin, Paris, 1985–86; joined FCO, 1987; First Sec., Moscow, 1989–92; First Sec., later Counsellor, FCO, 1993–95; Dep. High Comr, Ottawa, 1995–99; High Comr, Sri Lanka, 1999–2002; Dir, Wider Europe, FCO, 2002–04; Ambassador to the Czech Republic, 2004–09. *Recreations:* music, ski-ing, gardening.

DUFFIELD, Dame Vivien (Louise), DBE 2000 (CBE 1989); Chairman, Clore Duffield Foundation, since 2000; *b* 26 March 1946; *d* of Sir Charles Clore and Mrs Francine Clore (*née* Halphen); *m* 1969, John Duffield (marr. diss. 1976); one *s* one *d*. *Educ:* Cours Victor Hugo, Paris; Lycée Français de Londres; Heathfield Sch.; Lady Margaret Hall, Oxford (MA). Chairman: Clore Foundn, 1979–2000; Vivien Duffield Foundn, 1987–2000. Member: NSPCC Centenary Appeal Cttee, 1983; NSPCC Financial Develt Cttee, 1985; Vice-Chairman: Great Ormond Street Hosp. Wishing Well Appeal, 1987; Royal Marsden Hosp. Cancer Appeal, 1990; Campaign Chm., Univ. of Oxford, 2007–10; Director: Royal Opera House Trust, 1985–2001 (Dep. Chm., 1988–2001); Royal Opera House, 1990–2001 and 2014– (Chm., Royal Opera House Endowment Fund, 2005–); South Bank Bd, 2002–; Mem., Royal Ballet Bd, 1990–; Gov., Royal Ballet, 2002–; Trustee: Dulwich Coll. Picture Gall., 1993–2002; Jewish Community Centre for London, 2004–. Mem. Bd, Clore Leadership Prog., 2004–. Hon. DLitt Buckingham, 1990; Hon. DPhil Weizmann Inst., 1985; Hon. RCM, 1987. *Recreations:* ski-ing, opera, ballet, shooting. *Address:* c/o Clore Duffield Foundation, 3 Chelsea Manor Studios, Flood Street, SW3 5SR; 79 Grubenstrasse, Gruben, Gstaad 3780, Switzerland.

DUFFY, Sir (Albert Edward) Patrick, Kt 1991; PhD; *b* 17 June 1920. *Educ:* London Sch. of Economics (BSc (Econ.), PhD); Columbia Univ., Morningside Heights, New York, USA. Served War of 1939–45, Royal Navy, incl. flying duties with FAA. Lecturer, University of Leeds, 1950–63, 1967–70. Visiting Professor: Drew Univ., Madison, NJ, 1966–70; Amer. Grad. Sch. of Internat. Business, 1982–93; Internat. Business Inst., Wheaton, Ill, 1992–; Associate, Centre of Defence Studies, Univs of Hull and Lancaster, 1997–. Contested (Lab) Tiverton Division of Devon, 1950, 1951, 1955. MP (Lab): Colne Valley Division of Yorks, 1963–66; Sheffield, Attercliffe, 1970–92. PPS to Sec. of State for Defence, 1974–76; Parly Under-Sec. of State for Defence (Navy), MoD, 1976–79; opposition spokesman on defence, 1979–80, 1983–84. Chairman: PLP Economic and Finance Gp, 1965–66, 1974–76; Trade and Industry Sub-Cttee of Select Cttee on Expenditure, 1972–74; PLP Defence Cttee, 1979–84; Vice-Chm., Anglo-Irish Gp, 1979–92. Pres., N Atlantic Assembly, 1988–90 (Mem., 1979–92; Chm., Defence Co-op. sub-cttee, 1983–87); Dep. Chm., Atlantic Council of UK, 1994–97. Co-Chm., Carrier Conclave Gp, 1997–2012. President: Lower Don Valley Community Develt Trust, 1997–2005; The Labour Life Gp, 2001–; Doncaster Mayo Assoc., 2001–. Mem., Catholic Club, Doncaster. Hon. DHL Dominican Univ., Illinois, 1993. *Publications:* Growing up Irish in Britain and British in Ireland: and in Washington, Moscow, Rome and Sydney, 2013; contrib. to Economic History Review, Victorian Studies, Manchester School, Annals of Amer. Acad. of Pol. and Soc. Sci., etc. *Recreations:* annual pilgrimages on foot, incl. Walsingham, Croagh Patrick, Co. Mayo and Santiago de Compostela. *Address:* 153 Bennetthorpe, Doncaster, South Yorks DN2 6AH. *Club:* Naval.

DUFFY, Dame Antonia Susan; *see* Byatt, Dame A. S.

DUFFY, Bernadette Marie, OBE 2005; Head Teacher, Thomas Coram Centre, since 1998; *b* St Albans, 28 June 1958; *d* of James Edward Duffy and Mary Teresa Duffy; *m* (marr. diss.). *Educ:* Mater Dei Sch. for Girls, Welwyn Garden City; W London Inst. of Higher Educn (Cert Ed); Roehampton Inst. of Higher Educn (MA Primary and Early Educn). Teacher: Kilburn and Brondesbury High Sch., Brent, 1979; Wood End Lane Infants Sch., Hillingdon, 1980; St Mary's Infants Sch., Kensington and Chelsea, 1980–84; Rylston Day Nursery, Hammersmith, 1984–86; Dep. Hd, 1986–88, Head Teacher, 1988–98, Dorothy Gardner Centre; Foundn Stage Advr, QCA (on secondment), 2005–07. Member: Steering Gp for Effective Provision of Pre-sch. Educn Project, DFES, 1997–2003; Expert Gp for Early Years Foundn Stage, DFE, 2010–11. Member: Adv. Cttee for Cambridge Rev. of Primary Educn, 2007–09; Nat. Council for Educnl Excellence, 2008–10. Chm., British Assoc. for Early Childhood Educn, 2006–09. Trustee, Froebel Trust, 2009–. *Publications:* Supporting Creativity and Imagination in Early Years, 1998, 2nd edn 2006; Contemporary Issues in the Early Years, 2013. *Recreations:* drawing, painting, godchildren, family. *Address:* Thomas Coram Centre, 49 Mecklenburgh Square, WC1N 2NY. *T:* (020) 7520 0385, *Fax:* (020) 7520 0386. *E:* head@Thomascoram.camden.sch.uk.

DUFFY, Dame Carol Ann, DBE 2015 (CBE 2002; OBE 1995); FRSL; poet and freelance writer; Poet Laureate, since 2009; Professor of Contemporary Poetry, Manchester Metropolitan University, since 2004; *b* 23 Dec. 1955; *d* of Frank Duffy and May Black; one *d*. *Educ:* St Joseph's Convent, Stafford; Stafford Girls' High Sch.; Univ. of Liverpool (BA Hons Philosophy 1977). FRSL 1999; FRSA 2001. Hon. FBA 2015. Hon. DLitt: Hull, 2001; Warwick, 2001. *Awards:* Eric Gregory, 1983; Somerset Maugham, 1987; Dylan Thomas, 1990; Cholmondeley, 1992; Lannan, USA, 1995; Signal Poetry, 1997; PEN/Pinter, 2012. *Plays:* Take My Husband, 1982; Cavern of Dreams, 1984; Little Women, Big Boys, 1986; Loss (radio), 1986; Grimm Tales, 1994, More Grimm Tales, 1996, Young Vic; Beasts and Beauties, Bristol Old Vic, 2004; Casanova, W Yorks Playhouse, 2007; Rapunzel (ballet), Durham Gala Th., 2012; Rat's Tales, Royal Exchange, Manchester, 2012; Everyman, NT, 2015. *Publications:* Standing Female Nude, 1985; Selling Manhattan, 1987, 4th edn 1994; (ed) Home and Away, 1988; The Other Country, 1990; (ed) I Wouldn't Thank You for a Valentine, 1992; Mean Time, 1993 (Whitbread Prize, Forward Prize, 1993); Selected Poems, 1994; (ed) Anvil New Poets, 1995; (ed) Stopping for Death, 1996; The Pamphlet, 1998; The World's Wife (poetry), 1999; Meeting Midnight (for children), 1999; Rumpelstiltskin and other Grimm Tales (for children), 1999; (ed) Time's Tidings (poetry), 1999; The Oldest Girl in the World (for children), 2000; (ed) Signal Poetry, 2000; (ed) E. M. Forster, 2001; (ed) Hand in Hand, 2001; Feminine Gospels (poetry), 2002; Underwater Farmyard (for children), 2002; Queen Munch and Queen Nibble (for children), 2002; (ed) Overheard on a Saltmarsh, 2003; (ed) Out of Fashion: an anthology of poems, 2004; Doris the Giant (for children), 2004; Rapture (poetry), 2005 (T. S. Eliot Prize, 2006); The Hat (poetry), 2007; New and Collected Poems for Children, 2009; To the Moon (anthology), 2009; Love Poems, 2010; The Gift (for children), 2010; The Bees (poetry), 2011 (Costa Poetry Award, 2011); (ed) Jubilee Lines (poetry), 2012; (ed) Sylvia Plath: poems, 2012. *Address:* c/o Picador Books, 20 New Wharf Road, N1 9RR.

DUFFY, Prof. Eamon, PhD, DD; FBA 2004; FSA; Professor of the History of Christianity, University of Cambridge, 2003, now Emeritus; Fellow, Magdalene College, Cambridge, since 1979 (President (Senior Fellow and Vice-Master), 2001–06, 2008); *b* Dundalk, Eire, 9 Feb. 1947; *s* of Patrick Duffy and Lillian Frances Duffy (*née* Todd); *m* 1968, Jennifer Elizabeth Browning; one *s* two *d*. *Educ:* Univ. of Hull (BA 1968); Selwyn Coll., Cambridge (PhD 1972); Magdalene Coll., Cambridge (DD 1994). Res. Fellow in Arts, Dept of Hist., Univ. of Durham, 1971–74; Lectr in Ecclesiastical Hist., KCL, 1974–79; Lectr in Divinity, 1979–94, Reader in Church Hist., 1994–2003, Univ. of Cambridge. Hon. Prof., Univ. of Durham, 2011–. Mem., Pontifical Historical Commn, 2001–07. President: Ecclesiastical Hist. Soc., 2004–05 (Hon. Fellow 2011); Catholic Theol Assoc. of GB, 2004–06. Hon. (Etheldreda) Canon, Ely Cathedral, 2014–. Chm. Editl Bd, Calendar of Papal Registers, 1999–. FSA 2011. Hon. MRIA 2012. Hon. DD: Hull, 2004; Durham, 2013; Hon. DLitt KCL, 2009; Hon. Dr Medieval Studies, Pontifical Inst. for Medieval Studies, Toronto, 2013. Hawthornden Prize for Lit., 2002. *Publications:* (ed and contrib.) Challoner and His Church: a Catholic bishop in Georgian England, 1981; (ed and contrib. with B. Bradshaw) Humanism, Reform and Reformation: the career of Bishop John Fisher, 1988; The Stripping of the Altars, 1992; (jtly) A History of Magdalene College, Cambridge 1428–1988, 1994; The Creed in the Catechism: the life of God for us, 1996; Saints and Sinners: a history of the Popes, 1997, 2nd edn 2001 (trans. several langs); Catholicism and Its Pasts, 2000; The Voices of Morebath: Reformation and rebellion in an English village, 2001; Faith of Our Fathers: reflections on Catholic tradition, 2004; (ed jtly) The Church of Mary Tudor, 2006; Walking to Emmaus, 2006; Marking the Hours: English people and their prayers 1240–1570, 2006; Fires of Faith: Catholic England under Mary Tudor, 2009; Ten Popes who Shook the World, 2011; Saints, Sacrilege, Sedition: religion and conflict in the Tudor Reformations, 2012; The Heart in Pilgrimage: a prayerbook for Catholic Christians, 2014. *Recreations:* early music, landscape painting, dog-walking. *Address:* Magdalene College, Cambridge CB3 0AG. *E:* ed10000@cam.ac.uk.

DUFFY, Most Rev. Francis; *see* Ardagh and Clonmacnoise, Bishop of, (RC).

DUFFY, Dr Francis Cuthbert, CBE 1997; PPRIBA; with DEGW, 1974–2011 (Founder, 1974); with DEGW North America, 2001–04; independent consultant, since 2012; *b* 3 Sept. 1940; *s* of late John Austin Duffy and Annie Margaret Duffy (*née* Reed); *m* 1965, Jessica Bear; three *d*. *Educ:* Architectural Assoc. Sch. (AA Dip Hons); Univ. of California at Berkeley (MArch); Princeton Univ. (MA, PhD). Asst Architect, Nat. Building Agency, 1964–67; Commonwealth Fund Harkness Fellow, Berkeley and Princeton, 1967–70; established London office, JFN Associates (of NY), 1971. Member: Council, RIBA, 1989–97 (Pres., 1993–95); Architects Registration Bd, 1997–2003; UKTI Construction Sector Adv. Gp, 2008–; Pres., Architects' Council of Europe, 1994; Vice Pres., Architl Assoc., 2013–. Chairman: Architecture, Design and Workplace Cttee, BBC, 2006–09; Stratford City Design Rev. Panel, 2006–. Trustee, Architecture Foundn, 1999–2009. Visiting Professor: MIT, 2001–04; Reading Univ., 2007–; Univ. of Lancaster, 2009–. Mem., Adv. Council, Sch. of Architecture, Princeton Univ., 2009–11. Editor, AA Jl, 1965–67; founder Editor, Facilities, 1985–90. President's Award for Lifetime Achievement in Workplace Design, British Council of Offices, 2004; Lifetime Achievement Award, British Inst. of Facilities Mgt, 2013. *Publications:* Office Landscaping, 1966; (jtly) Planning Office Space, 1976; (jtly) The Changing City, 1989; The Changing Workplace, 1992; (jtly) The Responsible Workplace, 1993; The New Office, 1997; Architectural Knowledge, 1998; (jtly) New Environments for Working, 1998; Work and the City, 2008. *Recreations:* walking, talking, reading. *Address:* Threeways, The Street, Walberswick, Suffolk IP18 6UE. *T:* (01502) 723814. *Club:* Reform.

DUFFY, Most Rev. Joseph, DD; Bishop of Clogher, (RC), 1979–2010; *b* 3 Feb. 1934; *s* of Edward Duffy and Brigid MacEntee. *Educ:* St Macartan's College, Monaghan; Maynooth College. MA, BD, HDipEd. Ordained priest, 1958; Teacher, 1960–72; Curate, 1972–79. *Publications:* Patrick in his own words, 1972, 2nd edn 2000; Lough Derg Guide, 1980; Monaghan Cathedral, 1992. *Recreations:* local history, travel. *Address:* Doire na gCraobh, Monaghan, Ireland. *T:* (47) 62725.

DUFFY, Maureen Patricia, FRSL 1985; FEA; author; *b* 1933; *oc* of Grace Rose Wright. *Educ:* Trowbridge High Sch. for Girls; Sarah Bonnell High Sch. for Girls; King's College, London (BA; FKC 2002). Chairman: Greater London Arts Literature Panel, 1979–81; Authors Lending and Copyright Soc., 1982–94 (Pres. of Honour, 2002–); British Copyright Council, 1989–98 (Vice Chm., 1981–86; Vice-Pres., 1998–2003; Hon. Pres., 2003); Copyright Licensing Agency, 1996–99 (Vice-Chm., 1994–96). Pres., Writers' Guild of GB, 1985–88 (Jt Chm., 1977–78); Co-founder, Writers' Action Group, 1972–79; Pres., European Writers Congress, 2003–05 (Vice-Pres., 1992–2003). FEA 2015. Hon. DLitt: Loughborough, 2011; Kent, 2013. Gold Medal for Lit., CISAC, 2002; Benson Silver Medal for Lit., RSL, 2004; Medal of Honour, Portuguese Soc. of Authors, 2009. *Publications:* That's How It Was, 1962; The Single Eye, 1964; The Microcosm, 1966; The Paradox Players, 1967; Lyrics for the Dog Hour (poetry), 1968; Wounds, 1969; Rites (play), 1969; Love Child, 1971; The Venus Touch, 1971; The Erotic World of Faery, 1972; I want to Go to Moscow, 1973; A Nightingale in Bloomsbury Square (play), 1974; Capital, 1975; Evesong (poetry), 1975; The Passionate Shepherdess, 1977; Housespy, 1978; Memorials of the Quick and the Dead (poetry), 1979; Inherit the Earth, 1980; Gorsaga, 1981 (televised as First Born, 1988); Londoners: an elegy, 1983; Men and Beasts, 1984; Collected Poems 1949–84, 1985; Change (novel), 1987; A Thousand Capricious Chances: Methuen 1889–1989, 1989; Illuminations (novel), 1991; Occam's Razor (novel), 1993; Henry Purcell (biog.), 1994; Restitution (novel), 1998; England: The Making of the Myth, 2001; Alchemy (novel), 2004; Family Values (poetry), 2008; The Orpheus Trail (novel), 2009; Sappho Singing (play), 2010; Environmental Studies (poetry), 2013; In Times Like These (novel), 2013; *visual art:* Prop art exhibn (with Brigid Brophy), 1969. *Address:* 18 Fabian Road, SW6 7TZ. *T:* (020) 7385 3598.

DUFFY, Sir Patrick; *see* Duffy, Sir A. E. P.

DUFFY, Philip James; Chief Operating Officer, Border Force, Home Office, since 2014; *b* Ascot, Berks, 5 May 1979; *s* of Henry Philip and Linda Gaye Duffy; partner, Robert Young. *Educ:* St Bernard's Convent Grammar Sch., Slough; Trinity Coll., Cambridge (MA Japanese Studies 2001); French Nat. Sch. of Govt. Dep. Dir, Strategy, 2007–08, Housing Mkts, 2008–09, DCLG; Hd, Strategy Team, UK Border Agency, 2009–11; Dir, Immigration and Border Policy, Home Office, 2011–14. *Recreations:* playing the clarinet, gardening, running, complicated travel. *Address:* Home Office, 2 Marsham Street, SW1P 4DF. *T:* (020) 7035 3337. *E:* philip.duffy4@homeoffice.gsi.gov.uk.

DUFFY, Sean Richard Gerard, MD; FRCSGlas, FRCOG; Senior Lecturer, University of Leeds, since 1994; Consultant Gynaecologist, St James's Hospital, Leeds, since 1994; National Clinical Director for Cancer, NHS England, since 2013; *b* Limerick, Ireland, 10 April 1959; *s* of Peter and Peggie Duffy; *m* 1984, Wendy Peard; two *s*. *Educ:* St Clement's Coll., Limerick; University Coll., Cork (MB BCh BAO 1993; MD 1993). FRCSGlas 1987; FRCOG 2001. Res. Registrar and Registrar (Obstetrics and Gynaecol.), then Lectr and Sen. Registrar (Obstetrics and Gynaecol.), Northern Gen. Hosp., Sheffield, 1988–94; Clin. Dir, Leeds Teaching Hosps NHS Trust, 2000–05; Med. Dir, 2005–13, Dir, 2009–13, Yorks Cancer Network. *Publications:* contrib. book chapters and to peer reviewed jls. *Recreation:* gardening. *Address:* The Hawthorns, Milner Lane, Thorner, Leeds LS14 3AG. *E:* s.r.duffy@leeds.ac.uk.

DUFFY, Simon Patrick; Chairman, YouView TV Ltd, since 2014; *b* 27 Nov. 1949; *s* of Patrick and Eileen Duffy; *m* 1978, Katherine Haney; two *s*. *Educ:* Brasenose Coll., Oxford (BA (PPE)); Harvard Business Sch. (MBA; Harkness Fellow). Analyst: N. M. Rothschild & Sons, 1973–76; Shell, 1978–80; Consultant, Bain & Co., 1980–82; Gen. Manager, Planning and Treasury, Consolidated Gold Fields, 1982–86; Dir, Corporate Finance, Guinness, 1986–89; Ops Dir, United Distillers, 1989–92; Group Finance Director: Thorn EMI, 1992–96; EMI Gp, 1996–99 (also Dep. Chm.); Dep. Chm. and CEO, World Online Internat., 1999–2001; CEO, End2End, 2001–02; Chief Financial Officer, Orange SA, 2002–03; CEO, 2003–06, Exec. Vice-Chm., 2006–07, ntl; Exec. Chm., QXL Ricardo, later Tradus plc, 2007–08. Chairman: Cadogan Petroleum plc, 2008–11; mBlox Inc.; Symbiotic Technologies Pty Ltd; bwin.party digital entertainment plc, 2011–14; non-executive Director: Oger Telecom Ltd; Modern Times Gp AB, 2008–. FRSA 1995. *Recreations:* music, literature, science, politics. *Club:* Brooks's.

DUFFY, Timothy David; Chief Executive Officer, M & C Saatchi UK, since 2004 (Chairman, 2005–14); *b* 13 June 1963; *s* of Michael Duffy and Pauline Duffy; *m* 2006, Georgie Eyre; one *s* one *d*. *Educ:* Cheltenham Grammar Sch.; King's Coll., Cambridge (BA 1985). Saatchi & Saatchi: graduate trainee, 1986–87; Strategic Planner, 1987–92; Gp Account Dir, 1992–95; M & C Saatchi: Gp Account Dir, 1995–97; Man. Dir, 1997–2004. Mem., Mktg Gp of GB. Chm. Trustees, Free Word, 2012–. *Recreations:* history, ski-ing, US dramas, literature. *Address:* c/o M & C Saatchi, 36 Golden Square, W1F 9EE. *T:* (020) 7544 3609. *E:* Timd@mcsaatchi.com. *Club:* Century.

DUFTON, Robert; Director of Campaigns, University of Sheffield, since 2014; *b* Nairobi, 20 March 1962; *s* of Maj. Felix Dufton and Rosemary Dufton. *Educ:* Sevenoaks Sch., Kent; Univ. of Bristol (LLB); Coll. of Law; City Univ. (Postgrad. Dip. Gen. Mgt). Articled clerk and solicitor, Lovells, 1984–90; admitted solicitor, 1986; Consultant, Adrian Ellis Associates, 1991; Prog. Dir, Arts & Business, 1992–94; Dep. Dir Ops, Heritage Lottery Fund, 1995–2002; Director: Rayne Foundn, 2002–04; Paul Hamlyn Foundn, 2004–13; Hon. Sen. Vis. Fellow, Cass Business Sch., 2013–14. Member: Bd, Arts Council London, 2012–14; AHRC, 2014–. Trustee, 2012–14, Patron, 2014–, Nat. Funding Scheme. Mem. Council, 2002–08, Dep. Chm., Alumni, 2010–14, Univ. of Bristol. Gov., Mus. of London, 2004–13. Hon. LLD Bristol, 2014. *Recreations:* climbing, singing. *Address:* University of Sheffield, 40 Victoria Street, Sheffield S10 2TN. *E:* robert.dufton@sheffield.ac.uk.

DUGDALE, family name of **Baron Crathorne**.

DUGDALE, Paul Damian Norwood; His Honour Judge Dugdale; a Circuit Judge, since 2011; *b* W Sussex, 24 June 1967; *s* of late Peter Robin Dugdale, CBE and of (Esmé) Cyraine Dugdale (*née* Norwood Brown); *m* 1993, Alison, *d* of Frederick Elms and Rosemary Elms (*née* Groves); one *s*. *Educ:* Canford Sch.; King's Coll. London (LLB). Called to the Bar, Gray's Inn,

1990; barrister, 2 King's Bench Walk, 1991–2011; a Recorder, 2005–11. Mem., Western Circuit, 1991–. Chm. Govs, St Faith's Sch., Winchester, 1997–2011. *Recreations:* English choral music, music festivals and gigs, evenings spent with friends, Digby Dog. *Address:* Isleworth Crown Court, 36 Ridgeway Road, Isleworth, Middx TW7 5LP. *Clubs:* Noblemen and Gentlemen's Catch; Wykeham (Winchester).

DUGDALE, Sir (William) Matthew (Stratford), 3rd Bt *cr* 1936, of Merevale and Blyth, co. Warwick; DL; farmer and landowner; *b* Birmingham, 22 Feb. 1959; *s* of Sir William Stratford Dugdale, 2nd Bt, CBE, MC and Lady Belinda Dugdale, *d* of 6th Earl of Radnor; *S* father, 2014, but his name does not appear on the Official Roll of the Baronetage; *m* 1990, Paige Perkins Sullivan; two *s* two *d*. *Educ:* Eton Coll. Former Chm., Warwicks CLA. Governor: Foundn of Lady Katherine Leveson; Kingsbury Sch.; Lady Katherine Leveson Primary Sch. High Sheriff 2002, DL 2012, Warwickshire. *Recreations:* golf, cycling. *Heir: s* William Stratford Dugdale, *b* 15 Aug. 1992. *Address:* Merevale Hall, Atherstone, Warwickshire CV9 2HG. *T:* (home) (01827) 711653, (office) (01827) 712181, 07768 520601, *Fax:* (01827) 718090. *E:* matthew9595@me.com. *Club:* White's.

DUGGAN, Gregory Alan R.; *see* Ripley-Duggan.

DUGGAN, (James) Ross; His Honour Judge Duggan; a Circuit Judge, since 2006; a Deputy High Court Judge, since 2007; a Family Court Judge, since 2014; *b* 14 July 1956; *s* of late Leonard Heaton Duggan and Dr Mona Leslie Duggan; *m* 1983, Fiona Elspeth Robb Fowlie. *Educ:* Merchant Taylors' Sch., Crosby; Univ. of Liverpool (LLB Hons 1977). Called to the Bar, Middle Temple, 1978; barrister, Northern Circuit (Liverpool), 1979–2006; Circuit Junior, 1981; Asst Recorder, 1993–97; Recorder, 1997–2006. Designated Family Judge, Stoke-on-Trent, 2007–14. Dir, Local Solutions (formerly Merseyside CVS), 1990–2008. *Recreations:* cricket, countryside, theatre, music. *Address:* Sessions House, Lancaster Road, Preston PR1 2PD. *Club:* Lancashire County Cricket.

DUGGAN, Michael; QC 2014; Director, Duggan Press Ltd, since 2012; *b* Durham, 27 April 1960; *s* of Francis Sidney Duggan and Kathleen Duggan; *m* 1988, Michelle Jane; three *s*. *Educ:* Keele Univ. (BA); Durham Univ. (BCL); Sidney Sussex Coll., Cambridge (LLM 1985). Called to the Bar, Gray's Inn, 1984. Accredited Mediator, ADR, 2005. Mem., Bar Council, 2015– (Mem., Equality and Diversity Cttee, 2015–). *Publications:* The Modern Law of Strikes, 1987; Business Reorganisations and Employment Law, 1992; Unfair Dismissal, 2000, 2nd edn 2015; Wrongful Dismissal, 3rd edn 2015; Duggan on Employment Contracts, 4th edn 2014; (jtly) The Law of Industrial Action and Trade Union Recognition, 2nd edn 2011; The Equality Act 2010, 2010. *Recreations:* guitar, guitarviol, violin, mandolin, driving my Morgan, music, walking, renovating waterwheel in Norfolk cottage, watching Chelsea FC. *Address:* Littleton Chambers, 3 Kings Bench Walk, Temple, EC4Y 7HR. *T:* (020) 7797 8600, *Fax:* (020) 7797 8699. *E:* md@littletonchambers.co.uk.

DUGGAN, Patrick Gerald; actor (as **Patrick Malahide**) and writer; *b* 24 March 1945; *s* of John Cuthbert Duggan and Mary Clementine Duggan (*née* Andrews); *m* 1st, 1970, Rosemary Wright (marr. diss. 1990); one *s* one *d*; 2nd, 1993, Jo Ryan. *Educ:* Douai Sch.; Edinburgh Univ. Stage Manager, 1969, Dir of Prodns, 1970–72, Byre Th., St Andrews; joined Royal Lyceum Th., Edinburgh, as actor, 1972–76; *plays* include: The Android Circuit, Traverse and ICA, 1978; Judgement (one man show), Liverpool Playhouse, and subseq. at Edinburgh, Dublin and Amsterdam Fests, 1979; The Tempest, 1980, King Lear, 1981, Bristol Old Vic; Operation Bad Apple, Royal Court, 1982; Cock-ups, Manchester Royal Exchange, 1983; Bristol Old Vic: The Cherry Orchard, 1987; In The Ruins (one man show), transf. Royal Court, 1989–90; Clandestine Marriage, Uncle Vanya, 1990; Map of the Heart, Globe, 1991; Mutabilitie, RNT, 1998; Hinterland, RNT, 2002; Embers, Duke of York's, 2006; Hamlet, RNT, 2010; *television* series and serials include: Minder, 1979–87; Charlie, The Pickwick Papers, 1984; The Singing Detective, 1986; The One Game, The Franchise Affair, 1988; Children of the North, 1990; The Secret Agent, 1991; The Blackheath Poisonings, 1992; The Inspector Alleyn Mysteries, 1993–94; Middlemarch, 1994; In Search of the Brontës, 2003; Elizabeth I, 2005; Five Days, 2007; plays: Miss Julie, 1987; A Doll's House, 1991; All the King's Men, 1999; Victoria and Albert, 2001; Goodbye Mr Chips, 2002; Friends and Crocodiles, 2005; A Short Stay in Switzerland, 2009; Game of Thrones, 2012; Hunted, 2012; The Paradise, 2012; Indian Summers, 2015; *films* include: The Killing Fields, Comfort and Joy, 1984; A Month in the Country, 1987; December Bride, 1990; A Man of No Importance, 1994; Two Deaths, Cutthroat Island, 1995; The Long Kiss Goodnight, 1996; US Marshals, 1998; The World is not Enough, 1999; Billy Elliot, Quills, 2000; Captain Corelli's Mandolin, 2001; Sahara, 2005; Brideshead Revisited, 2008. Dir, Bristol Old Vic Trust, 2008–14. *Publications:* screenplays as P. G. Duggan: Reasonable Force, 1988; The Writing on the Wall, 1996; Pleas and Directions, 2002. *Recreations:* sailing, walking. *Address:* c/o Independent Talent Group Ltd, 40 Whitfield Street, W1T 2RH. *Club:* Royal Fowey Yacht.

DUGGAN, Ross; *see* Duggan, J. R.

DUGGIN, Sir Thomas (Joseph), Kt 2004; HM Diplomatic Service, retired; Ambassador to Colombia, 2001–05; *b* 15 Sept. 1947; *s* of late Joseph Duggin and Alice Lilian (*née* Mansfield); *m* 1st, 1968 (marr. diss.); two *s*; 2nd, 1983 (marr. diss.); 3rd, 1999, Janette Mortimer (*née* David). *Educ:* Thornleigh Salesian Coll. Joined HM Diplomatic Service, 1967; Third Sec., Oslo, 1969–73; Third, later Second Sec. (Commercial), Bucharest, 1973–75; FCO, 1976–79; Second Sec., Bangkok, 1979–82; FCO, 1982–85; Head of Chancery and HM Consul, La Paz, 1985–88; Head of Chancery, Mexico City, 1989–91; High Comr, Vanuatu, 1992–95; Hd of Security Dept, then Asst Dir for Security, subseq. Hd of Security Comd, then Hd of Security Strategy Unit, FCO, 1995–2001. Bd Mem., British and Colombian Chamber of Commerce, 2005–. MSM, Order of Vanuatu, 1992. *Recreations:* walking, tennis, reading, music. *Address:* Oak Tree, 3 Woodside, North Walsham, Norfolk NR28 9XA.

DUGGLEBY, (Charles) Vincent (Anstey), MBE 2005; freelance broadcaster and financial journalist, since 1989; *b* 23 Jan. 1939; *s* of late Bernard Waldby Duggleby and Vivien Duggleby (*née* Hawkins); *m* 1964, Elizabeth Nora Frost; two *d*. *Educ:* Blundell's Sch.; Worcester Coll., Oxford (BA 1962, MA 2005). FRPSL 1979. Reporter, Bristol Evening Post, 1957–59; Sub-editor, Daily Express, 1960; BBC, 1963–89: sub-editor and sports presenter, 1963–67; Asst Sports Editor, 1967–70; Asst Editor, Current Affairs, 1970–80; Financial Editor, 1980–89. Mem., Royal Mint Adv. Cttee, 1987–94. Royal Philatelic Society: Mem. Council, 1979–2002; Hon. Treas., 1988–93; Vice-Pres., 1994–99. Numerous awards, including: Broadcasting Financial Journalist of Year, Harold Wincott Foundn, 1992; Best Personal Finance Broadcaster, ABI, 1997. *Publications:* Highlights from 21 Years of Sports Report, 1969; English Paper Money, 1975, 8th edn 2011; (with Louise Botting) Making the Most of Your Money, 1984, 2nd edn 1985; Days Beyond Recall: a brief history of the Duggleby family, 2005. *Recreations:* philately, genealogy, classic jazz.

DUGHER, Michael Vincent; MP (Lab) Barnsley East, since 2010; *b* Doncaster, 26 April 1975; *s* of Robert Dugher and Isobel Dugher (*née* Archer); *m* 2004, Joanna Nunney; one *s* two *d*. *Educ:* St Mary's RC Sch., Edlington; McAuley RC Sch., Doncaster; Univ. of Nottingham (BA Hons Politics). Convenor, Notts and Derbys NUS, 1995–96; Nat. Chair, Labour Students, Lab. Party, 1997–98; Res. Officer, 1998–2000, Hd of Policy, 2000–01, AEEU; Special Adviser: to Minister for Transport, 2001–02; to Sec. of State for Defence, 2002–05; to Leader of H of C, 2005–06; UK Dir, Govt Relns, EDS, 2006–07; Special Advr to Govt Chief Whip, 2007–08; Chief Political Spokesman to Prime Minister, 2008–10. Shadow Minister for Defence Equipment, Support and Technol., 2010–11; PPS to Leader of the Opposition, 2011; Shadow Minister without Portfolio, Cabinet Office, 2011–13; Shadow Minister for Cabinet Office, 2013–14, for Transport, 2014–15, for Culture, Media and Sport, 2015–. Vice-Chair, Labour Party, 2012–13. *Publications:* (with J. Spellar) Fools Gold: dispelling the myth of the Tory economic legacy, 1999; (contrib.) Dictionary of Labour Biography, 2001. *Recreations:* football (watching), music (playing and listening), history. *Address:* House of Commons, SW1A 0AA; (office) West Bank House, West Street, Hoyland, Barnsley S74 9EE. *T:* (01226) 743483. *E:* michael.dugher.mp@parliament.uk.

DUGUID, Andrew Alexander; Integration, Marketing & Planning Executive, Global Aerospace, 2001–04; *b* 22 June 1944; *s* of Wing Comdr (retd) Alexander Gordon Duguid and Dorothy Duguid (*née* Duder); *m* 1967, Janet Hughes; two *s* one *d*. *Educ:* Whitby Dist High Sch.; Ashbury Coll., Ottawa; Sidcot Sch.; LSE (BSc Econs); Univ. of Lancaster (MA Marketing). Res. Assistant, Brunel Univ., 1967–69; Marketing Executive: Interscan Ltd, 1969–72; Ogilvy Benson and Mather, 1972–73; joined DTI as Principal, 1973; Prin. Pvte Sec. to Sec. of State for Industry, 1977–79; Asst Sec., seconded to Prime Minister's Policy Unit, 1979; returned to set up Policy Planning Unit, Dept of Industry, later DTI, 1982; Under Sec., DTI, 1985–86; Lloyd's of London: Head of Regulatory Services, 1986–88; Head of Market Services, 1988–92; Dir, Marketing Services, 1993–94; Dir, Policy and Planning, and Sec. to Council of Lloyd's, 1995–99; Dir, Develt, 1999–2000. Non-executive Director: Kingsway Public Relations, 1982–85; Hammersmith and Fulham NHS PCT, 2005–11; Central London Community Healthcare, 2008–10 (Chm., 2008–09). *Publications:* (with Elliott Jaques) Case Studies in Export Organisation, 1971; On the Brink: how a crisis transformed Lloyd's of London, 2014. *Recreations:* tennis, ski-ing, walking, canoeing, photography. *Address:* 1 Binden Road, W12 9RJ. *T:* (020) 8743 7435. *Clubs:* Reform; Hartswood Lawn Tennis (Pres., 2006–).

DUIGAN, Catherine Anne, PhD; FLS, FRSB; Evidence Analysis Manager, Evidence, Knowledge and Advice Department, Natural Resources Wales, since 2014; *b* Dublin, 21 April 1962; *d* of Patrick Joseph Duigan and Christina Anne Duigan (*née* Phelan); *m* 1988, Dr Warren Kovach; one *s*. *Educ:* Sacred Heart Secondary Sch., Tullamore; University Coll. Dublin (BSc 1983; PhD 1989). FLS 1992; FRSB (FSB 2010). Vis. Res. Associate, Indiana Univ., Bloomington, 1984, 1986–87; Biologist (pt-time), Marine Studies Ltd, Aberdeen Univ., 1987–88; Scientific Officer, Freshwater Loch Survey - Isle of Skye and Kyle of Lochalsh, Nature Conservancy Council for Scotland, 1989; Post-doctoral Researcher, Inst. of Earth Studies, Univ. of Wales, Aberystwyth, 1989–91; Res. Fellow, Univ. of Wales, 1991–92; Countryside Council for Wales, later Natural Resources Wales: Freshwater Ecologist, 1992–2005; Head: Marine and Freshwater Scis, 2005–11; Marine and Freshwater Ecosystems Gp, Evidence, Knowledge and Advice Dept (formerly Evidence and Advice Directorate), Bangor, 2011–14. Mem., Editl Bd, The Biologist, Soc. of Biol., 2011–. Member: Fisheries, Ecol. and Recreation Adv. Cttee, Envmt Agency, 2001–04; Sci. and Innovation Strategy Bd, NERC, 2010–13. Mem., Council, Freshwater Biol Assoc., 2001–05. Hon. Lectr, Bangor Univ., 2011–. Contrib. to UK National Ecosystem Assessment, 2011. *Publications:* (jtly) Vegetation Communities of British Lakes: a revised classification, 2006; (ed jtly) The Rivers of Wales: a natural resource of international and historical significance, 2009. *Recreations:* walking coastal paths, social media, Anglesey art, all things Irish, my garden. *Address:* Natural Resources Wales, Maes-Y-Ffynnon, Penrhosgarnedd, Bangor, Gwynedd LL57 2DW.

DUKAKIS, Michael Stanley; Distinguished Professor of Political Science, Northeastern University, since 1991; Governor, Commonwealth of Massachusetts, 1975–79, and 1983–90; *b* 3 Nov. 1933; *s* of Panos Dukakis and Euterpe Boukis-Dukakis; *m* 1963, Katharine Dickson; one *s* two *d*. *Educ:* Brookline High Sch. (Dip. 1951); Swarthmore Coll., Pa (BA 1955); Harvard Law Sch. (JD 1960). Attorney, Hill & Barlow, Boston, Mass, 1960–74; Lectr and Dir, Intergovtl Studies, John F. Kennedy Sch. of Govt, Harvard Univ., 1979–82. Visiting Professor: Univ. of Hawaii, 1991; UCLA, 1991–. Dir, Amtrack, 1998–2003. Moderator of public television's The Advocates, 1971–73. State Representative, Brookline, Mass, 1963–71; Democratic Candidate for the Presidency of the USA, 1988. *Publications:* (with Rosabeth Moss Kanter) Creating the Future: Massachusetts comeback and its promise for America, 1988; (jtly) How to Get Into Politics - And Why, 2000; (jtly) The Crisis Strikes, 2001; (jtly) Leader-Managers in the Public Sector, 2010. *Recreations:* walking, playing tennis, gardening. *Address:* 85 Perry Street, Brookline, MA 02446–6935, USA.

DUKE, family name of **Baron Merrivale**.

DUKE, Guy Roderick John; independent consultant, ecosystem markets, policy, research and knowledge exchange, since 2008; Director, Europe and Research (formerly Director, Europe), Environment Bank Ltd, since 2010; *b* Claygate, Surrey, 13 Dec. 1962; *s* of John Duke and Diane Duke (*née* Marks); *m* 1994, Paola Movalli; one *d*. *Educ:* Dorking Grammar Sch.; Ashcombe Comp. Sch., Dorking; Collingwood Coll., Durham Univ. (BSc Hons Botany and Geog.); Wye Coll., Univ. of London (MSc Landscape Ecol., Design and Maintenance). Ind. ecologist and explorer, 1985–91; Coordinator and Chief Tech. Advr, Palas Conservation and Develt Project, NWFP, Pakistan, BirdLife Internat., 1991–97; Tech. Dir, Biodiversity and Natural Resources, Internat. Develt Services, Envmtl Resources Mgt Ltd, 1998–2002; Principal Administrator, Biodiversity Policy, Directorate Gen. Envmt, EC, 2002–07. Ind. Mem., 2009–, Dep. Chm., 2015–, JNCC (Chm., Audit and Risk Mgt Cttee, 2012–). Sen. Vis. Res. Associate, Sch. of Geog. and Envmt, Envmtl Change Inst., Univ. of Oxford, 2011–. FRGS 1986. *Publications:* white papers, consulting reports; contrib. articles in Ambio, Public Service Review EU, Geographical Mag. *Recreations:* being with family and dog, woodland walks, playing piano, music (jazz, classical), reading, swimming. *E:* guy.duke@skynet.be.

DUKE, Timothy Hugh Stewart; Norroy and Ulster King of Arms, since 2014; *b* 12 June 1953; *s* of William Falcon Duke and Mary Cecile Duke (*née* Jackson). *Educ:* Uppingham; Fitzwilliam Coll., Cambridge (MA). Peat, Marwick, Mitchell & Co., 1974–81; Research Asst, Coll. of Arms, 1981–89; Rouge Dragon Pursuivant, 1989–95; Chester Herald of Arms, 1995–2014; Registrar, Coll. of Arms, 2000–07. Hon. Sec., Harleian Soc., 1994–. *Address:* College of Arms, Queen Victoria Street, EC4V 4BT. *T:* (020) 7236 7728. *Club:* Travellers.

DUKES, Alan M.; Public Affairs Consultant, Wilson Hartnell Public Relations, since 2003 (Director, 2008–12); Chairman, Irish Bank Resolution Corporation (formerly Anglo Irish Bank), 2010–13 (non-executive Director, 2008–13); *b* 22 April 1945; *s* of James and Rita Dukes; *m* 1968, Fionnuala Corcoran; two *d*. *Educ:* Coláiste Mhuire, Dublin; University College Dublin (MA). Chief Economist, Irish Farmers' Assoc., 1967–72; Dir, Irish Farmers' Assoc., Brussels, 1973–76; Personal Advr to Comr of European Communities, 1977–80. TD (FG) Kildare, 1981–2002; Minister for Agriculture, 1981–82; opposition spokesman on agric., March–Dec. 1982; Minister: for Finance, 1982–86; for Justice, 1986–87; for Transport, Energy and Communications, 1996–97; opposition spokesman on envmt and local govt, then on agriculture, marine and natural resources, 1977–2002. Leader, 1987–90, President, 1987–92, Fine Gael Party. Chm., Jt Oireachtas Cttee on Foreign Affairs, 1995–96. Vice-President: Internat. European Movt, 1991–96 (Pres., 1987–91, Chm., 1997–2000, Irish Council); European People's Party, 1987–96; Mem., Council of State, 1988–90. Adjunct Prof. of Public Admin/Management, Univ. of Limerick, 1991–2000. Dir Gen., Inst. of Eur. Affairs, Dublin, 2003–07. Governor: EIB, 1982–86; IMF. Officier, Légion d'Honneur (France), 2004; Comdr's Cross, OM (Poland), 2004. *Address:* Tully West, Kildare, Co. Kildare, Eire.

DUKES, Philip Timothy, FGS; international viola soloist and conductor; *b* 7 Jan. 1968; *s* of Ronald and Enid Dukes; *m* 2002, Caroline Lefilliatre; two *s*. *Educ:* Wells Cathedral Sch.; Guildhall Sch. of Music and Drama (FGS (FGSM 2006)). Artist-in-Residence, Queen's

Univ., Belfast, 2000–09; Prof. of Viola, Royal Acad. of Music, 2003–; Hd of Strings, Wells Cathedral Sch., 2005–08; Artistic Director: Fest. International de Musique de la Hague, 2005–; Marlborough Coll., 2008–. Guest Prof. of Viola and Chamber Music, McGill Univ., 2009–. Hon. ARAM 2007. *Recreations:* cricket, fine wines, food, obsession with Birmingham City Football Club, Jaguar cars. *Address:* Hamelin, Bath Road, Marlborough, Wilts SN8 1NN. *Club:* Royal Over-Seas League.

DULEY, Giles Angus Guy; freelance documentary photographer, specialising in photography of humanitarian issues and the consequences of conflict, since 1996; *b* Wimbledon, 15 Sept. 1971; *s* of Ray Duley and Flora Duley (*née* Stewart). *Educ:* Perrott Hill Sch.; Canford Sch. Photographer for Select, Q, Esquire, GQ, Elle, Vogue, Sunday Times, Observer, Sunday Telegraph; has worked with charities incl. Médecins sans Frontières, UNHCR. Ambassador, Find a Better Way, 2014–. Trustee, Emergency UK, 2013–. Hon. FRPS 2013. *Publications:* Afghanistan: 2012, 2013. *Recreations:* Yeovil Town supporter, bee keeping, gardening. *E:* info@gilesduley.com. *Clubs:* Chelsea Arts, Frontline.

DULIEU, Nicola Joy; non-executive Director: Hobbs Ltd, since 2014 (Chief Executive, 2008–14); Adnams plc, since 2014; *b* Chingford, 26 Dec. 1963; *d* of Ronald and Phyllis Dulieu; *m* Adam Brace. *Educ:* Chingford Sen. High Sch. FCCA; Order of Merit, Assoc. of Accounting Technicians. Joined Marks and Spencer plc, 1982, Property, Retail and HR Finance Dir, 2000–03, Food Gp Finance Dir, 2003–06; Finance Dir, Hobbs Ltd, 2006–08. *Recreation:* garden design and development. *Address:* Yaxham Park, Station Road, Yaxham, Norfolk NR19 1RD. *T:* 07795 664998.

DULVERTON, 3rd Baron *cr* 1929, of Batsford; **Gilbert Michael Hamilton Wills;** Bt 1897; farmer, forester and industrialist; *b* 2 May 1944; *s* of 2nd Baron and his 1st wife, Judith Betty (*d* 1983), *d* of Lt-Col Hon. Ian Leslie Melville, TD; *S* father, 1992; *m* 1st, 1980, Rosalind van der Velde-Oliver (marr. diss. 1999); one *s* one *d*; 2nd, 2000, Mrs Mary Vicary. *Educ:* Gordonstoun; RAC, Cirencester. Chm., Thwaites Ltd; Director: W Highland Woodlands Ltd; Batsford Estates (1983) Co. Ltd. Trustee, Dulverton Trust. *Heir: s* Hon. Robert Anthony Hamilton Wills, *b* 20 Oct. 1983.

DUMAS, Roland; Officier de la Légion d'Honneur; Croix de Guerre (1939–45); Croix du Combattant Volontaire; Minister of Foreign Affairs, France, 1988–93; *b* Limoges, Haute-Vienne, 23 Aug. 1922; *s* of Georges Dumas and Elisabeth (*née* Lecanuet); *m* 1964, Anne-Marie Lillet; two *s* one *d*. *Educ:* Lycée de Limoges; Faculté de Droit, Paris; Ecole des Sciences Politiques, Paris; Univ. of London; Ecole de langues orientales, Paris. LLL; Diplomas: in Advanced Studies in Laws; in Political Science, Paris, and London School of Economics. Counsel, Court of Appeal, Paris, 1950–; journalist; Sen. Political Dir, Journal Socialiste Limousin; Political Dir of weekly, La Corrèze Républicaine et Socialiste, 1967–; Deputy: UDSR, Haute Vienne, 1956–58; FGDS, Corrèze, 1967–68; Socialiste de la Dordogne, 1981–83, 1986–88; Minister for European Affairs, 1983–84; Govt spokesman, 1984; Minister for External Relations, 1984–86; Pres. Commn for Foreign Affairs, Nat. Assembly, 1986–87. Pres., Conseil Constitutionel, 1995–99. Grand Cross, Order of Isabel (Spain), 1982. *Publications:* J'ai vu vivre la Chine, 1960; Les Avocats, 1970; Le Droit de l'Information et de la Presse, 1981; Plaidoyer pour Roger Gilbert Lecomte, 1985; Le droit de la propriété littéraire et artistique, 1986; Le Peuple Assemblé, 1989; Le Fil et la Pelote (memoirs), 1996; L'Epreuve, 2003; Diplomatie: les nœuds de l'histoire, 2007; (with J. Vergès) Crimes et fraudes en Côte d'Ivoire, 2011; (with J. Vergès) Sarko sous BHL, 2011; Coups et blessures, 2011. *Address:* 19 quai de Bourbon, 75004 Paris, France.

DUMBELL, Dr Keith Rodney; Senior Specialist in Microbiology, Medical School, University of Cape Town, 1982–90, retired; *b* 2 Oct. 1922; *s* of late Stanley Dumbell and Dorothy Ellen (*née* Hewitt); *m* 1st, 1950, Brenda Margaret (*née* Heathcote) (*d* 1971); two *d*; 2nd, 1972, Susan (*née* Herd); two *s*. *Educ:* Wirral Gram. Sch.; University of Liverpool, MB, ChB 1944; MD (Liverpool), 1950; DSc (Med) Cape Town, 2001. FRCPath 1975. Asst Lecturer, Dept of Bacteriology, University of Liverpool, 1945–47; Mem. of Scientific Staff, MRC, 1947–50; Junior Pathologist, RAF, 1950–52; Asst in Pathology and Microbiology, Rockefeller Inst. for Medical Research (Dr Peyton Rous' laboratory), 1952–53; Lecturer in Bacteriology, University of Liverpool, 1952–58; Senior Lecturer, 1958–64; Prof. of Virology, Univ. of London at St Mary's Hosp. Med. Sch., 1964–81. Vis. Prof., Univ. of Florida, 1994. Dir, WHO Collaborative Centre for Poxvirus Res., London, 1969–82; Mem., Global Commn for Certification of Smallpox Eradication, 1977–79. *Publications:* articles in various medical and scientific journals. *Address:* PO Box 22522, Fish Hoek, Western Cape 7974, South Africa.

See also Bishop Suffragan of Hull.

DUMBRECK, Nicholas John, FIA, FSA; Principal and Consulting Actuary, Milliman LLP, since 2009; *b* Woking, 12 Nov. 1954; *s* of late Alan Edwin Dumbreck and Sibyll Elisabeth Dumbreck; *m* 1978, Lesley Ann Devlin; one *s* two *d*. *Educ:* Royal Grammar Sch., Guildford; Jesus Coll., Cambridge (BA Maths 1976). FIA 1982; FSA 2008; CERA 2008. Various posts incl. Corporate Actuary, Imperial Life Assce Co. of Canada, 1976–86; Consulting Actuary, R. Watson & Sons, later Watson Wyatt Partners, then Watson Wyatt LLP, subseq. Watson Wyatt Ltd, 1986–2009 (Partner, 1987–2005). Actuarial Function: Omnilife Insce Co., 2005–; St James's Place UK, 2010–; With-Profits Actuary: Ecclesiastical Life, 2005–09; Cooperative Insce Soc., 2010–14; Liverpool Victoria Friendly Soc., 2012–14; Ind. Expert for transfers of life assce business, 1995–; Mem., With Profits Cttee, Royal London Mutual, 2015–. Dir, Milliman Inc., 2014–. Institute of Actuaries: Mem. Council, 1993–98 and 1999–2010; Hon. Sec., 1996–98; Vice Pres., 2003–05; Pres., 2006–08. Chm., Staple Inn Actuarial Soc., 2002–04; Mem. Council, 2008–10, Mem. Exec. Cttee, 2010–13, Internat. Actuarial Assoc.; Mem., Ct of Assts, Actuaries' Co., 2006–08 and 2009–. FRSA. *Recreations:* opera, watching cricket, wine, travel, art. *Address:* Meadow Barn, Priorsfield Road, Hurtmore, Godalming, Surrey GU7 2RQ. *T:* (01483) 415258. *E:* nick.dumbreck@btinternet.com.

DUMFRIES, Earl of; John Bryson Crichton-Stuart; *b* 21 Dec. 1989; *s* and *heir* of Marquess of Bute, *qv*.

DUMONT, Dame Ivy (Leona), DCMG 1995; DPA; Governor-General of the Bahamas, 2001–05; *b* 2 Oct. 1930; *d* of Alphonso Tennyson Turnquest and Cecilia Elizabeth Turnquest; *m* 1951, Reginald Deane Dumont (*d* 2011); one *s* one *d*. *Educ:* Univ. of Miami (BEd 1970); Nova Univ., USA (DPA 1978). Teacher, later Dep. Dir of Educn, Min. of Educn and Culture, Bahamas, 1945–75; Dep. Permanent Sec., Min. of Works and Utilities, 1975–78; Trng Officer, Personnel Manager then Gp Relations Manager, Natwest Trust Corp. (Bahamas) Ltd, then Coutts & Co., 1978–91; Minister of Health and Envmt, 1992–94; Minister of Education, 1995–2001. Mem. (FNM), Senate, 1992–2001 (Govt Leader, 1992–2001). *Publications:* Rose's to Mount Fitzwilliam (memoir), 2009. *Recreations:* dressmaking and design, horticulture (roses), public speaking, family. *Address:* c/o Government House, Government Hill, PO Box N8301, Nassau, Bahamas. *T:* 3221875; PO Box SS-5316, Nassau, Bahamas. *T:* 3234188.

DUMVILLE, Prof. David Norman, PhD; FRHistS; FRSAI, FSA, FSAScot; Professor of History, Palaeography and Celtic, since 2005, and Associate Director, Research Institute of Irish and Scottish Studies, since 2006, University of Aberdeen; Fellow, Girton College, Cambridge, since 1978; *b* 5 May 1949; *s* of late Norman Dumville and Eileen Florence Lillie Dumville (*née* Gibbs); *m* 1974, Sally Lois Hannay (*d* 1989); one *s*. *Educ:* Emmanuel Coll., Cambridge (BA Hons, MA); Ludwig-Maximilian Universität, Munich; Univ. of Edinburgh (PhD 1976). FRHistS 1976; FRSAI 1989; FSAScot 1999. Fellow, Univ. of Wales, Swansea, 1975–77; Asst Prof. of English, Univ. of Pennsylvania, 1977–78; O'Donnell Lectr in Celtic Studies, Univ. of Oxford, 1977–78; Lectr in Anglo-Saxon, Norse and Celtic, Univ. of Cambridge, 1977–91; British Acad. Res. Reader in Humanities, 1985–87; Reader in Early Mediaeval History and Culture of British Isles, 1991–95, Prof. of Palaeography and Cultural History, 1995–2004, Univ. of Cambridge. Res. Associate, Sch. of Celtic Studies, Dublin Inst. for Advanced Studies, 1989– (Vis. Prof., 1996–97); Visiting Professor of Mediaeval Studies: UCLA, 1995; Univ. of Calif, Berkeley, 1997. Vice-Pres., Centre International de Recherche et de Documentation sur le Monachisme Celtique, 1986–. Hon. MA Pennsylvania, 1979. *Publications:* (with Kathryn Grabowski) Chronicles and Annals of Mediaeval Ireland & Wales, 1984; (with Michael Lapidge) The Annals of St Neots, 1985; The Historia Brittonum, 1985; (ed jtly) The Anglo-Saxon Chronicle, 1985, 1995, 2007; Histories and Pseudo-Histories of the Insular Middle Ages, 1990; Wessex and England from Alfred to Edgar, 1992; Liturgy and the Ecclesiastical History of Late Anglo-Saxon England, 1992; Britons and Anglo-Saxons in the Early Middle Ages, 1993; English Caroline Script and Monastic History, 1993; Saint Patrick, 1993; The Churches of North Britain in the First Viking-Age, 1997; Three Men in a Boat (inaugural lect.), 1997, 2nd edn 2004; Councils and Synods of the Gaelic Early and Central Middle Ages, 1997; A Palaeographer's Review, vol. 1 1999, vol. 2 2004; Saint David of Wales, 2001; Annales Cambriae, 2002–; The Annals of Iona, 2002; (with Pádraig Ó Néill) Cáin Adomnáin and Canones Adomnani, 2003; The Early Mediaeval Insular Churches and the Preservation of Roman Literature, 2004; Abbreviations used in Insular Script before AD 850, 2004; Brenhinoedd y Saeson, 2005–. *Recreations:* travelling in North America, politics and other arguments. *Address:* School of Divinity, History and Philosophy, University of Aberdeen, G11 Crombie Annexe, Meston Walk, Old Aberdeen AB24 3FX. *T:* (01224) 272199.

DUN, Peter John; HM Diplomatic Service; Foreign Policy Adviser to President and Member, President's Bureau of European Policy Advisers, European Commission, 2008–12; *b* 6 July 1947; *s* of late Herbert Ernest Dun and Joyce Hannah Dun (*née* Tozer); *m* 1984, Cheng Kiak Pang; two *s*. *Educ:* Bristol Grammar Sch.; Univ. of Birmingham (BA); Univ. of Cologne; Univ. of Freiburg; Univ. of Strasbourg. British High Commn, Kuala Lumpur, 1972–76; FCO, 1976–80; UK Repn to EU, 1980–83; UK Mission to UN, 1983–87; Dep. Hd, Disarmament Dept, FCO, 1987–89; rcds, 1989; Counsellor, British High Commission, Islamabad, 1990–93; Foreign Policy Advr and Advr on Balkans Affairs to Ext. Affairs Comr, EC, Brussels, 1993–96; Hd of Information Dept, FCO, 1996–2000; Counsellor, Berlin, 2000–02; Asst to EU Special Rep. for Afghanistan, 2002; Advr, Dir-Gen. for Ext. Relns, EC, Brussels, 2002–08. Vis. Fellow, Stiftung Wissenschaft und Politik, Berlin, 2000–. *Recreations:* music, travel, maps. *Address:* 43 Boulevard Charlemagne, 1000 Brussels, Belgium.

DUNALLEY, 7th Baron *cr* 1800 (Ire.), of Kilboy, Tipperary; **Henry Francis Cornelius Prittie;** Social Worker, Shetland Islands Council, 2003–13; *b* 30 May 1948; *s* of 6th Baron Dunalley and Mary Philippa, *oc* of late Hon. Philip Cary; *S* father, 1992; *m* 1978, Sally Louise, *er d* of Ronald Vere; one *s* three *d*. *Educ:* Gordonstoun Sch.; Trinity Coll., Dublin (BA); Bedford Coll., Univ. of London (CQSW). Probation Officer: Inner London Probation Service, 1977–80; Buckinghamshire Probation Service, 1980–83; Oxfordshire and Bucks Probation Service, 1983–2001; Thames Valley Probation Service, 2001–03. *Heir: s* Hon. Joel Henry Prittie, *b* 29 April 1981. *Address:* 97 Lower Seedley Road, Salford, Greater Manchester M6 5NG.

DUNANT, Sarah; novelist and broadcaster; *b* 8 Aug. 1950; *d* of David Dunant and Estelle (*née* Joseph); two *d* by Ian Willox. *Educ:* Godolphin and Latymer Girls' Sch.; Newnham Coll., Cambridge (BA Hons 1972). Actress, 1972–73; producer, Radio 4, 1974–76; freelance writer, TV and radio broadcaster and journalist, 1977–; The Late Show, BBC2, 1989–95. Lectr in Renaissance Studies, Univ. of Washington in St Louis, Missouri, 2009, 2011, 2014. Creative Writing Fellow, Oxford Brookes Univ., 2010–. Teacher, Faber Acad., 2011–. *Publications:* as Peter Dunant, (with Peter Busby): Exterminating Angels, 1983; Intensive Care, 1986; as Sarah Dunant: Snow Storms in a Hot Climate, 1988; Birth Marks, 1991; Fatlands, 1993 (Silver Dagger Award); (ed) The War of the Words, 1994; Under my Skin, 1995; (ed jtly) Age of Anxiety, 1996; Transgressions, 1997; Mapping the Edge, 1999; The Birth of Venus, 2003; In the Company of the Courtesan, 2006; Sacred Hearts, 2009; Blood and Beauty: the Borgias (novel), 2013. *Recreations:* movies, travel, nosing out renaissance frescos in churches all over Italy. *Address:* c/o Clare Alexander, Aitken Alexander Associates, 291 Gray's Inn Road, WC1X 8EB. *T:* (020) 7373 8672.

DUNBABIN, Dr Jean Hymers, FBA 2009; Senior Research Fellow, St Anne's College, Oxford, since 2004 (Fellow and Tutor, 1973–2004); Reader in Medieval History, University of Oxford, 1997–2004; *b* 12 May 1939; *d* of David Mackay and Peggy Mackay (*née* Stewart); *m* 1962, John Dunbabin; two *d*. *Educ:* St Leonard's Sch., St Andrews; St Hilda's Coll., Oxford (MA, DPhil 1965). Jun. Research Fellow, Somerville Coll., Oxford, 1961–63; Vice-Principal, St Anne's Coll., Oxford, 1994–97 (Hon. Fellow, 2011). Mem., IAS, Princeton, 1989. Ed., English Historical Rev., 2000–03. *Publications:* France in the Making 843–1180, 1985, 2nd edn 2000; A Hound of God: Pierre de la Palud and the Fourteenth Century Church, 1991; Charles I of Anjou: power, kingship and state-making in thirteenth-century Europe, 1998; Captivity and Imprisonment in Medieval Europe 1000–1300, 2002; The French in the Kingdom of Sicily, 1266–c.1305, 2011; contributions to: The Cambridge History of Later Medieval Philosophy, 1982; The Cambridge History of Medieval Political Thought, 1988; The New Cambridge Medieval History, vol. III, 1999; contrib. various jls. *Recreations:* walking, travelling. *Address:* St Anne's College, Oxford OX2 6HS. *T:* (01865) 274872.

DUNBAR of Northfield, Sir Archibald (Ranulph), 11th Bt *cr* 1700; *b* 8 Aug. 1927; *er s* of Sir (Archibald) Edward Dunbar, 9th Bt (by some reckonings 10th Bt) and Olivia Douglas Sinclair (*d* 1964), *d* of Maj.-Gen. Sir Edward May, KCB, CMG; *S* father, 1969; *m* 1974, Amelia Millar Sommerville, *d* of Horace Davidson; one *s* two *d*. *Educ:* Wellington Coll.; Pembroke Coll., Cambridge; Imperial Coll. of Tropical Agriculture, Trinidad. Mil. Service, 2nd Lt, Cameron (att. Gordon) Highlanders, 1945–48. Entered Colonial Agricultural Service, Uganda, as Agricultural Officer, 1953; retired, 1970. Hon. Sheriff, Sheriff Court District of Moray, 1989–. Kt of Honour and Devotion, SMO Malta, 1989. *Publications:* A History of Bunyoro-Kitara, 1965; Omukama Chwa II Kabarega, 1965; The Annual Crops of Uganda, 1969; various articles in Uganda Jl. *Heir: s* Edward Horace Dunbar, Younger of Northfield, *b* 18 March 1977. *Address:* The Old Manse, Duffus, Elgin, Scotland IV30 5QD. *T:* (01343) 830270.

DUNBAR, David; architect; Managing Director, ADF Architects Ltd, Glasgow, since 1998 (Director, since 1991); *b* Glasgow, 19 March 1959; *s* of John Dunbar and Mary Dunbar; *m* 1981, Carol Mary Shaw; three *d*. *Educ:* Hillhead High Sch.; Univ. of Strathclyde (BSc Architectural Studies 1981; BArch 1983; LLM Construction Law 2004). RIBA 1984; MCIArb 2005. Partner, Dunbar and Stewart Architects, 1988–91. President: Glasgow Inst. of Architects, 2006–08; RIAS, 2009–11. Dir, Scottish Building Contracts Cttee, 2011– (Vice Chm., 2012–). Deacon, Incorporation of Cordiners in Glasgow, 1999–2000. Dep. Convenor, Court, Univ. of Strathclyde, 2007–11. *Recreations:* music, theatre, Partick Thistle FC. *Address:* ADF Architects Ltd, 23 Blythswood Square, Glasgow G2 4BG. *T:* (0141) 226 8010, *Fax:* (0141) 226 8011. *E:* d.dunbar@adf.co.uk.

DUNBAR, Sir David H.; *see* Hope-Dunbar.

DUNBAR, Ian Duncan; Sheriff of Tayside Central and Fife at Dunfermline, 2005–12; *b* 31 Oct. 1948; *s* of John Duncan Dunbar and Mary Golden; *m* 1973, Sue Young. *Educ:* Lawside Acad., Dundee; Queen's Coll., Dundee (St Andrews Univ., subseq. Dundee Univ.) (LLB

1969). Apprentice Solicitor, Soutar Reid & Mill, Dundee, 1969–71; Sneddon Campbell & Munro, Perth, later Miller Sneddon, then Miller Hendry, Perth and Dundee: Asst Solicitor, 1971–72; Partner, 1972–98; Chm., 1994–98; Floating Sheriff, 1998–2000; Sheriff of Tayside Central and Fife at Dundee, 2000–05. Pres., Law Soc. of Scotland, 1993–94 (Vice Pres., 1992–93). Trustee, Perth Coll. Develt Trust, 1995–98. *Recreations:* golf, Rugby, cooking, food, wine. *Address:* 2 New Dunbarney Gait, Bridge of Earn, Perth PH2 9FA. *Clubs:* Blairgowrie Golf (Capt., 2005–06); Royal Perth Golfing Society.

DUNBAR, Jacqueline; *see* Hayden, J.

DUNBAR of Mochrum, Colonel Sir James Michael, 14th Bt *cr* 1694 (NS), of Mochrum, Wigtownshire; *b* 17 Jan. 1950; *s* of Sir Jean Ivor Dunbar, 13th Bt and of Rose Jeanne, *d* of Henry William Hertsch; *S* father, 1993; *m* 1st, 1978, Margaret Jacobs (marr diss. 1989; she *d* 1991); two *s* one *d*; 2nd, 1989, Margaret, *d* of Roger Gordon Talbot; one *d*. Colonel, USAF. *Heir: s* Michael Joseph Dunbar, *b* 5 July 1980.

DUNBAR, John Greenwell, OBE 1999; architectural historian; Secretary, Royal Commission on the Ancient and Historical Monuments of Scotland, 1978–90; *b* 1 March 1930; *o s* of John Dunbar and Marie Alton; *m* 1974, Elizabeth Mill Blyth. *Educ:* University College Sch., London; Balliol Coll., Oxford (MA). FSA. Joined staff of Royal Commission on the Ancient and Historical Monuments of Scotland, 1953; Member: Ancient Monuments Board for Scotland, 1978–90; Regl Adv. Cttee, Forestry Commn, 1997–2000. Vice-President: Soc. for Medieval Archaeology, 1981–86; Soc. of Antiquaries of Scotland, 1983–86. Lectures: Lindsay-Fischer, Oslo, 1985; Rhind, Edinburgh, 1998. Hon. FRIAS; Hon. FSA Scot. *Publications:* The Historic Architecture of Scotland, 1966, rev. edn 1978; (contrib.) The Cilician Kingdom of Armenia, 1978; (ed with John Imrie) Accounts of the Masters of Works 1616–1649, 1982; Sir William Burrell's Northern Tour 1758, 1997; Scottish Royal Palaces, 1999; (jtly) The Buildings of Scotland: Borders, 2006; numerous articles in archaeological jls, etc. *Address:* Patie's Mill, Carlops, By Penicuik, Midlothian EH26 9NF. *T:* (01968) 660250. *Club:* New (Edinburgh).

DUNBAR of Hempriggs, Sir Richard (Francis), 9th Bt *cr* 1706 (NS); *b* 8 Jan. 1945; *s* of Lady Dunbar of Hempriggs, Btss (8th in line) and Leonard James Blake (*d* 1989); assumed the name of Dunbar, 1965; *S* to mother's Btcy, 1997; *m* 1969, Elizabeth Margaret Jane Lister; two *d*. *Educ:* Charterhouse. Businessman. *Heir:* (to father's Btcy) *d* Emma Katherine Dunbar of Hempriggs, *b* 9 Nov. 1977.

DUNBAR of Durn, Sir Robert (Drummond Cospatrick), 10th Bt *cr* 1698 (NS); *b* 17 June 1958; *o s* of Sir Drummond Cospatrick Ninian Dunbar, 9th Bt, MC and Sheila Barbara Mary, *d* of John B. de Fonblanque; *S* father, 2000; *m* 1994, Sarah Margaret, *yr d* of Robert Anthony Brooks; one *s* one *d*. *Educ:* Harrow; Christ Church, Oxford (MA). Associate, Soc. of Investment Professionals. Allen & Overy (Private Client Dept), 1982–86; Merrill Lynch Investment Managers, 1986–2003. *Heir: s* Alexander William Drummond Dunbar, Younger of Durn, *b* 1 March 1995.

DUNBAR, Prof. Robin Ian MacDonald, PhD; FBA 1998; FRAI; Professor of Evolutionary Psychology, University of Oxford, since 2012; Fellow, Magdalen College, Oxford, since 2007; *b* 28 June 1947; *s* of George MacDonald Dunbar and Betty Lilian (*née* Toon); *m* 1971, Eva Patricia Melvin; two *s* one *d*. *Educ:* Magdalen Coll. Sch., Brackley; Magdalen Coll., Oxford (BA 1969); Univ. of Bristol (PhD 1974). FRAI 1992. SERC Advanced Res. Fellow, King's Coll., Cambridge, 1977–80; Res. Fellow, Zool. Dept, Univ. of Cambridge, 1980–82; docent, Zool Inst., Univ. of Stockholm, 1983; Res. Fellow, Zool. Dept, Liverpool Univ., 1985–87; University College London: Lectr, Anthropol. Dept, 1987–92; Prof. of Biol Anthropol., 1992–94; Prof. of Evolutionary Psychol., 1994–2007, British Acad. Res. Prof., Sch. of Biol Scis, 2003–07, Univ. of Liverpool; Prof. of Evolutionary Anthropol., Univ. of Oxford, 2007–12. Vis. Prof., Sch. of Biomed. Engrg and Computational Sci., Aaltu Univ., Finland, 2012–. Monro Lect., Univ. of Edinburgh, 1994, 2009; Dr van Hofsten Meml Lect., Uppsala Univ., Sweden, 1997; British Assoc./BPsS Annual lect., 2007; Stirling Lect., Univ. of Kent, 2009. Co-Dir, British Acad. Centenary Res. Project, 2003–07. Member: Animal Procedures Cttee, Home Office, 1997–2004; Internat. Adv. Cttee, Jean-Marie Delwart Foundn, Brussels, 2000–; Isle of Rum Ecol Mgt Cttee, 2000–07; Scientific Adv. Cttee, Courant Res. Centre, Univ. of Göttingen, 2007–. Member: Assoc. for Study of Animal Behaviour, 1970–; Primate Soc., 1973– (Pres., 1990–92); British Ecol. Soc., 1979–2005; Galton Inst., 1988– (Galton Lect., 2006); Fauna and Flora Internat., 1995–; BACSA, 1998–; Chester Caledonian Assoc., 2001–. Hon. DSc Aaltu, 2012. Osman Hill Medal, Primate Soc. of GB, 1994. Co-editor: Animal Behaviour, 1994–95; Jl Cultural and Evolutionary Psychol., 2003–08; Member, Editorial Board: Proc. B of Royal Soc., London; Biol. Letters; Behaviour; Internat. Jl of Primatol.; Evolutionary Psychol.; Jl of Evolutionary Psychol.; Human Nature; Primates; Jl of Ethology; Behavioral Ecol. and Sociobiol. *Publications:* Social Dynamics of Galada Baboons, 1975; Reproductive Decisions, 1984; Primate Social Systems, 1988; World of Nature, 1988; The Trouble with Science, 1995; (ed) Human Reproductive Decisions, 1995; Grooming, Gossip and the Evolution of Language, 1996; (ed) The Evolution of Culture, 1999; Primate Conservation Biology, 2000; Cousins, 2000; Human Evolutionary Psychology, 2002; The Human Story, 2004; Evolutionary Psychology: a beginner's guide, 2005; Oxford Handbook of Evolutionary Psychology, 2007; (ed) Social Brain, Distributed Mind, 2009; How Many Friends Does One Person Need?, 2010; The Science of Love and Betrayal, 2012; Thinking Big, 2014; Human Evolution, 2014; Lucy to Language, 2014. *Recreations:* poetry, Medieval and Renaissance music, hill-walking. *Address:* Department of Experimental Psychology, University of Oxford, Oxford OX1 3UD.

DUNBAR-NASMITH, Sir James (Duncan), Kt 1996; CBE 1976; RIBA; PPRIAS; FRSA, FRSE; Partner, Law & Dunbar-Nasmith, architects, Edinburgh, Forres, 1957–99; Professor Emeritus, Heriot-Watt University, since 1988; *b* 15 March 1927; *y s* of late Adm. Sir Martin Dunbar-Nasmith, VC, KCB, KCMG, DL and Justina Dunbar-Nasmith, CBE, DStJ. *Educ:* Lockers Park; Winchester; Trinity Coll., Cambridge (BA); Edinburgh Coll. of Art (DA; Hon. Fellow 2007). ARIBA 1954. Architekten Kammer Hessen, 1994. Lieut, Scots Guards, 1945–48. Prof. and Hd of Dept of Architecture, Heriot-Watt Univ. and Edinburgh Coll. of Art, 1978–88. President: Royal Incorporation of Architects in Scotland, 1971–73; Edinburgh Architectural Assoc., 1967–69. Member: Council, RIBA, 1967–73 (a Vice-Pres., 1972–73; Chm., Bd of Educn, 1972–73); Council, ARCUK, 1976–84 (Vice-Chm., Bd of Educn, 1977); Royal Commn on Ancient and Historical Monuments of Scotland, 1972–96; Ancient Monuments Bd for Scotland, 1969–83 (interim Chm., 1972–73); Historic Buildings Council for Scotland, 1966–93; Edinburgh New Town Conservation Cttee/Edinburgh World Heritage Trust, 1972–2004; Council, Europa Nostra, 1986–2004 (Vice-Pres., 1997–2004; Hon. Life Mem., 2005); Dep. Chm., Edinburgh Internat. Festival, 1981–85; Pres., Scottish Civic Trust, 2003– (Chm., 1995–2003); Trustee, Architectural Heritage Fund, 1976–97; Theatres Trust, 1983–95. Lifetime Achievement Award, RIAS, 2012. *Recreations:* music, theatre, ski-ing, sailing. *Address:* Sandbank, Findhorn, Moray IV36 3YY. *T:* (01309) 690445. *Clubs:* Royal Ocean Racing; New (Edinburgh).

DUNBOYNE, 30th Baron by Prescription, 1324, 20th Baron by Patent *cr* 1541 (Ire.); **Richard Pierce Theobald Butler;** *b* 5 July 1983; *o s* of 29th/19th Baron Dunboyne and of Diana Caroline (*née* Williams); *S* father, 2013; *m* 2012, Anneka Eileen, *d* of A. Anketell-Jones; one *d*. *Educ:* Winchester; Bristol Univ. *Heir: cousin* Michael James Butler [*b* 7 July 1944; *m* 1981, Jennifer Williams; one *d*].

DUNCAN, Agnes Lawrie Addie, (Laura); Sheriff of Glasgow and Strathkelvin, 1982–2006; *b* 17 June 1947; *d* of late William Smith, District Clerk, and Mary Marshall Smith McClure; *m* 1990, David Cecil Duncan, farmer, cricket coach, *y s* of late Dr and Mrs H. C. Duncan, Edinburgh; one *s*. *Educ:* Hamilton Acad.; Glasgow Univ. (LLB 1967). Admitted Solicitor, 1969; called to the Scottish Bar, 1976. Solicitor, private practice, 1969–71; Procurator Fiscal Depute, 1971–75; Standing Junior Counsel to Dept of Employment, 1982. Winner, Scottish Ladies Single handed Dinghy Championship, 1990. *Recreations:* sailing, walking.

DUNCAN, Rt Hon. Sir Alan (James Carter), KCMG 2014; PC 2010; MP (C) Rutland and Melton, since 1992; *b* 31 March 1957; 2nd *s* of late Wing Comdr J. G. Duncan, OBE and Anne Duncan (*née* Carter); civil partnership 2008, James Dunseath. *Educ:* Merchant Taylors' Sch.; St John's Coll., Oxford. Pres., Oxford Union, 1979. With Shell Internat. Petroleum, 1979–81; Kennedy Schol., Harvard Univ., 1981–82; oil trader, Marc Rich & Co., 1982–88; self-employed oil broker, 1988–92. PPS to Min. of State, DoH, 1993–94, to Chm. of Cons. Party, 1995–97; a Vice Chm. of Cons. Party, 1997–98; Parly Political Sec. to Leader of the Opposition, 1997; Opposition spokesman on health, 1998–99, on trade and industry, 1999–2001, on foreign affairs, 2001–03; Shadow Sec. of State for Constitutional Affairs, 2003–04, for Internat. Develt, 2004–05, for Transport, 2005, for Trade and Industry, 2005–07, for Business, Enterprise and Regulatory Reform, 2007–09; Shadow Leader, H of C, 2009; Shadow Jun. Justice Minister for Prisons, 2009–10; Minister of State, DFID, 2010–14; Special Envoy to Yemen and to Oman, 2014–. Member: Select Cttee on Social Security, 1993–95; Intelligence and Security Cttee, 2015–. Contested (C) Barnsley W and Penistone, 1987. Vis. Parly Fellow, St Antony's Coll., Oxford, 2002–03. Freeman, City of London, 1980; Liveryman, Merchant Taylors' Co., 1987. *Publications:* An End to Illusions, 1993; (with D. Hobson) Saturn's Children: how the state devours liberty, prosperity and virtue, 1995. *Address:* House of Commons, SW1A 0AA. *Club:* Beefsteak.

DUNCAN, Alastair James; QC (Scot.) 2012; Standing Junior Counsel to Scottish Government, since 2006; *b* Edinburgh, 3 Feb. 1969; *s* of Alan and Mary Duncan; *m* 2004, Esther Thackrey; one *d*. *Educ:* Newton Mearns Primary Sch.; Hutcheson's Grammar Sch.; Univ. of Glasgow (LLB Hons 1991; LLM 1994). Admitted Faculty of Advocates, 1999; in practice as Advocate specialising in commercial litigation. *Address:* Advocates Library, Parliament House, Edinburgh EH1 1RF. *E:* alastair.duncan@advocates.org.uk.

DUNCAN, Dr Allan George; environmental consultant, since 2000; *b* 17 Oct. 1940; *s* of Donald Allan Duncan and Annabella Duncan (*née* Thom); *m* 1972, Alison Patricia Reid; two *s* one *d*. *Educ:* Robert Gordon's Coll., Aberdeen; Aberdeen Univ. (BSc Hons 1963); New Coll., Oxford, (DPhil 1966). CEnv 2006. Research Engineer: California Univ., 1966–67; US Nat. Bureau of Standards, 1967–69; UKAEA, Harwell, 1969–79; Radiochemical Inspectorate, DoE, 1979–87 (Dep. Chief Inspector, 1984–87); HM Inspectorate of Pollution, 1987–96 (Chief Inspector, 1995–96); Hd, Radioactive Substances Regulation, EA, 1996–2000. Member: EC Network of Envmtl Regulators, 1993–2000; Euratom Scientific and Tech. Cttee, 1994–2013; Envmtl Assessment Panel, UK Accreditation Service, 1994–99. MIEMA; FRSA. *Publications:* various contribs to scientific literature. *Recreations:* sailing, walking, North American history. *Address:* 14 Rawlings Grove, Abingdon, Oxon OX14 1SH. *T:* (01235) 529096.

DUNCAN, Amanda Louise Elliot; *see* Evans, A. L. E.

DUNCAN, Andy; Chief Executive, Camelot UK Lotteries Ltd, since 2014 (Managing Director, 2011–14); *b* 31 July 1962. *Educ:* Univ. of Manchester Inst. of Sci. and Technol. (BSc). Joined Unilever, 1984; Chm., Business Unit and Mktg Controller for spreads and margarines, 1995–97, Mktg Dir, 1997–99, Van Den Bergh Foods; Eur. Gen. Man., Food and Beverages Div., 1999–2001; Dir, Marketing and Communications, subseq. Marketing, Communications and Audiences, BBC, 2001–04; Chief Executive: Channel Four, 2004–09; HR Owen plc, 2010–11. Founding Chm., Freeview, 2002–04. Non-executive Director: HMV plc, 2009–13; Oasis Trust, 2009–. Chm., Media Trust, 2006–.

DUNCAN, Prof. Archibald Alexander McBeth, FBA 1985; FRSE; Professor of Scottish History and Literature, Glasgow University, 1962–93; *b* 17 Oct. 1926; *s* of Charles George Duncan and Christina Helen McBeth; *m* 1954, Ann Hayes Sawyer, *d* of W. E. H. Sawyer, Oxford; two *s* one *d*. *Educ:* George Heriot's Sch.; Edinburgh Univ.; Balliol Coll., Oxford. Lecturer in History, Queen's Univ., Belfast, 1951–53; Lecturer in History, Edinburgh Univ., 1953–61; Leverhulme Research Fellow, 1961–62. Glasgow University: Clerk of Senate, 1978–83; Dean of Faculties, 1998–2000. Mem., Royal Commn on the Ancient and Historical Monuments of Scotland, 1969–92. FRSE 1979. DUniv Glasgow, 2001. *Publications:* Scotland: The Making of the Kingdom, 1975; (ed and revised) W. Croft Dickinson's Scotland from the Earliest Times to 1603, 3rd edn 1977; Regesta Regum Scottorum, vol. v, The Acts of Robert I, 1306–29, 1988; (ed, with trans. and notes), John Barbour, The Bruce, 1997; The Kingship of the Scots 842–1292, 2002. *Address:* 45 Norwood Park, Bearsden, Glasgow G61 2RZ.

DUNCAN, Bob; Lord Provost and Lord-Lieutenant, Dundee, since 2012; *b* Dundee, 1946; *m* Brenda. *Educ:* Rockwell Secondary Sch.; Duncan of Jordanstone Coll., Dundee; Stow Coll., Glasgow. Valentines of Dundee, subseq. part of Hallmark Cards: joined as apprentice; latterly Print and Graphics Manager. Mem. (SNP), Dundee CC, 2003–. Mem. Court, Univ. of Dundee, 2012–. *Address:* Dundee City Council, 21 City Square, Dundee DD1 3BY.

DUNCAN, Rev. Canon Bruce, MBE 1993; Principal, Sarum College, and Canon and Prebendary of Salisbury Cathedral, 1995–2002, now Canon Emeritus; *b* 28 Jan. 1938; *s* of late Andrew Allan Duncan and of Dora Duncan (*née* Young); *m* 1966, Margaret Holmes Smith; three *d*. *Educ:* St Albans Sch.; Univ. of Leeds (BA 1960); Cuddesdon Coll., Oxford. Founder/Director: Children's Relief Internat., 1960–62; Northorpe Hall Trust, 1962–65; ordained deacon, 1967, priest, 1968; Curate, St Bartholomew, Armley, Leeds and Curate in charge, St Mary of Bethany, Leeds, 1967–69; Hon. Curate, St Mary the Less, Cambridge, 1969–70; Chaplain, Order of Holy Paraclete, Whitby, 1970–71; Chaplain to HM Ambassadors in Austria, Hungary and Czechoslovakia, based in Vienna, 1971–75; Vicar, Collegiate Church of Holy Cross and the Mother of Him Who Hung Thereon, Crediton, Devon, 1976–82; Rural Dean of Cadbury, 1976–81; Rector, Crediton and Shobrooke, 1982–86; Residentiary Canon, Manchester Cathedral and Fellow, Coll. of Christ in Manchester, 1986–95. Commissary in UK for Bp of N Eastern Caribbean and Aruba, 2006–. Internat. Consultant, Trinity Inst. for Christianity and Culture, later Awareness Foundn, 2004–11; Development Consultant: Scargill Movt Council, 2009–14; Lee Abbey Movt, 2011–. Lazenby and St Luke's Chaplain, Exeter Univ., 2003–04; Theologian in Residence, Episcopal Ch of St Michael and All Angels, Sanibel, Fla, 2006–. Chm. of Trustees, St Luke's Coll. Foundn, 2006–09; Trustee, Families for Children Adoption Agency, 2006–10 (Chm., 2006–10); Hon. Pres., Northorpe Hall Child and Family Trust, 1997–. FRSA 1989. Hon. Fellow, Sarum Coll., 2006. Hon. DD Graduate Theol. Foundn, Indiana, 2002. Cross of St Augustine, 2004. *Publications:* Children at Risk (ed A. H. Denney), 1968; Sich Selbst Verstehen, 1993; Pray Your Way, Your Personality and God, 1993. *Recreations:* travel, walking, bookbinding. *Address:* 92 Harnham Road, Salisbury, Wilts SP2 8JW. *E:* churchpath1@ntlworld.com. *Club:* Athenæum.

DUNCAN, Craig; Director of External Affairs, Royal College of Surgeons of England, 2008–10; *b* 1 May 1951; *s* of William Sneddon Duncan and of Jessie Clark Sloan Duncan (*née* Mackie); *m* 1st, 1975, Janet Elizabeth Gillespie (marr. diss. 1988); one *s* one *d*; 2nd, 1998, Jane Alison Pavitt. *Educ:* Allan Glen's Sch., Glasgow; Univ. of Strathclyde (BA 1st Cl. Hons Geog.). Administrative Assistant: Univ. of Durham, 1973–76; Univ. of Southampton, 1976–82; Royal College of Surgeons of England, 1982–2010: Admin. Asst and Asst Sec.,

1982–88; Asst Sec., Inst. Basic Med. Scis, 1982–86; Secretary: Hunterian Inst., 1986–88; for Ext. Affairs, 1989–97; Senate of Surgery of GB and Ireland, 1993–97; Coll. Secretary, 1997–2001; Chief Exec., 2001–05; Advr to the Pres., 2005–08. Hon. FRCS 2010. McNeill Love Medal, RCS, 2007. *Recreations:* music, opera, reading, water-colour painting, golf. *Address:* 35 Wood End Way, Chandlers Ford, Eastleigh, Hants SO53 4LN. *T:* (023) 8027 5161. *Club:* Bramshaw Golf.

DUNCAN, Geoffrey Stuart, OBE 1998; General Secretary, General Synod Board of Education and National Society for Promoting Religious Education, 1990–98; *b* 10 April 1938; *s* of Alexander Sidney Duncan and Gertude Ruth (*née* Page); *m* 1962, Shirley Bernice Matilda Vanderput; one *d* (one *s* decd). *Educ:* Hemel Hempstead Grammar Sch.; Univ. of London (BScEcon); Univ. of Exeter (MA). Served RAEC, 1960–64. School and technical coll. teaching, 1964–72; LEA Advr and Officer, 1972–82; Schs Sec. and Dep. Sec., Gen. Synod Bd of Educn and Nat. Soc. for Promoting Religious Educn, 1982–90. Part-time WEA Tutor, 1966–70; part-time Open Univ. Counsellor, 1971–72. Dir, Urban Learning Foundn, 1990–98; Company Sec., Inst. of Consumer Scis, 2000–01. Trustee: St Gabriel's Educnl Trust, 1990–98; St Christopher's Educnl Trust, 1990–98; Winchester Shoei Coll. Foundn, 1990–. Governor, Coll. of St Mark & St John, Plymouth, 1990–2005. MUniv Surrey, 1998. *Publications:* contributor to: Faith for the Future, 1986; Schools for Tomorrow, 1988; various educn jls. *Recreations:* campanology, travel. *Address:* 14 Compton Lodge, Compton Place Road, Eastbourne BN21 1EQ. *T:* (01323) 416746.

DUNCAN, George; Chairman, Laporte plc, 1995–2001 (Director, 1987–95); *b* 9 Nov. 1933; *s* of William Duncan and Catherine Gray Murray; *m* 1965, Frauke Ulrike Schnuhr (marr. diss.); one *d*. *Educ:* Holloway County Grammar Sch.; London Sch. of Economics (BSc(Econ)); Wharton Sch.; Univ. of Pennsylvania (MBA). Mem., Inst. of Chartered Accountants (FCA). Chief Executive, Truman Hanbury Buxton and Co. Ltd, 1967–71; Chief Executive, Watney Mann Ltd, 1971–72; Vice-Chm., Internat. Distillers and Vintners Ltd, 1972; Chm., Lloyds Bowmaker Finance Ltd (formerly Lloyds and Scottish plc), 1976–86; Dir, Lloyds Bank Plc, 1982–87. Chairman: Allied Steel and Wire (Hldgs) Ltd, subseq. ASW Hldgs plc, 1986–2002; Household Mortgage Corp., 1986–94; Humberclyde Finance Gp, 1987–89; Whessoe PLC, 1987–97; Rubicon Group plc, 1992–95; Higgs and Hill plc, subseq. Swan Hill Gp, 1993–2003; Alldays plc, 1999–2001; Hurlingham School Ltd, 2000–; Director: Pauls & Whites, 1974–86; Haden plc, 1974–85 (Dep. Chm., 1984–85); Fitch Lovell plc, 1976–86; City of London Investment Trust (formerly TR City of London Trust PLC), 1977–2000; BET plc, 1981–96; Associated British Ports PLC, 1986–2003 (Dep. Chm., 1998–2003); Newspaper Publishing plc, 1986–93; Crown House PLC, 1987; Dewe Rogerson Gp Ltd, 1987–95; Calor Gp, 1990–97. Chm., CBI Companies Cttee, 1980–83; Mem., CBI President's Cttee, 1980–83. Mem., Eur. Adv. Bd, Wharton Sch., 1995–99. Freeman, City of London, 1971. *Recreations:* opera, golf. *Address:* 16 Belgrave Mews West, SW1X 8HT.

DUNCAN, Rt Rev. Dr Gregor Duthie; *see* Glasgow and Galloway, Bishop of.

DUNCAN, Ian James; Member (C) Scotland, European Parliament, since 2014; *b* Alyth, Perthshire, 13 Feb. 1973; *s* of late Robert Duncan and Audrey Duncan (*née* Doig); civil partnership, 2012, Benjamin Neal Brust. *Educ:* Alyth High Sch.; St Andrews Univ. (BSc 1st Cl. Hons Geol. 1994); Bristol Univ. (PhD Palaeontol. 1997). FGS. Intern: Smithsonian Instn, Washington, 1995; Mus. of Comparative Zool., Harvard Univ., 1996; Teaching Fellow, Bristol Univ., 1997–98; Policy Analyst, BP, 1998–99; Dep. Chief Exec., Scottish Fishermen's Fedn, 1999–2003; Hd, Policy and Communication, Scottish Refugee Council, 2004–05; Hd, Scottish Parlt's Office, Brussels, 2005–11; Clerk, Eur. and Ext. Relns Cttee and EU Advr, Scottish Parlt, 2011–13; Speech and Debates Officer, ESU, 2013–14. Contested (C) Aberdeen S, Scottish Parlt, 2003. European Parliament: Spokesman on fisheries, 2014–, on energy and climate change, 2014–; Chief Whip, Cons. Delegn, 2014–; Sen. Vice-Pres., Delegn for Relns with S Asia; Vice-President: Wine and Spirits Intergp; LGBTI Intergp. Sec. Gen., New Direction - Foundn for Eur. Reform, 2014–; Mem. Bd, Eur. Forum for Renewable Energy Sources, 2015–. Chm., ESU Scotland, 2014–. *Recreations:* geology, US politics, oil painting, carpentry. *Address:* European Parliament, 60 Rue Wiertz, 1047 Brussels, Belgium. *Club:* New (Edinburgh).

DUNCAN, Jacqueline Ann, OBE 2013; FIIDA; Founder and Principal of Inchbald School of Interior Design and Garden Design (formerly Inchbald Schools of Design and Fine Arts), since 1960; *b* 16 Dec. 1931; *d* of Mrs Donald Whitaker; *m* 1st, 1955, Michael John Chantrey Inchbald (marr. diss. 1964; he *d* 2013); one *s* one *d*; 2nd, 1974, Brig. Peter Trevenen Thwaites (*d* 1991); 3rd, 1994, Col Andrew Tobin Warwick Duncan, LVO, OBE. *Educ:* Convent of the Sacred Heart, Brighton; House of Citizenship, London. MBIID (FIDDA 1991); FIIDA 1994. Founded: Inchbald Sch. of Design, 1960; Inchbald Sch. of Fine Arts, 1970; Inchbald Sch. of Garden Design, 1972; Inchbald Online, 2008. Member: Monopolies Commn, 1972–75; Whitfield Cttee on Copyright and Design, 1974–76; London Electricity Cons. Council, 1973–76; Westminster City Council (Warwick Ward), 1974–78. Mem., Vis. Cttee, RCA, 1986–90; International Society of Interior Designers: Acting Pres., London Chapter, 1987–90; Chm., 1990–92. Trustee, St Peter's Research Trust, 1987–90. JP South Westminster, 1976–2001. Outstanding Contribution Award, BIDA, 2006. *Publications:* Directory of Interior Designers, 1966; Bedrooms, 1968; Design and Decoration, 1971. *Recreations:* fishing, travel. *Address:* Lime Tree House, Fifehead Magdalen, Gillingham, Dorset SP8 5RT; (office) 32 Eccleston Square, SW1V 1PB.

DUNCAN, Sir James (Blair), Kt 1981; Chairman: Transport Development Group, 1975–92; Boalloy Industries Ltd, 1992–2005; *b* 24 Aug. 1927; *s* of late John Duncan and Emily MacFarlane Duncan; *m* 1974, Dr Betty Psaltis (*d* 2005), San Francisco. *Educ:* Whitehill Sch., Glasgow. Qualified as Scottish Chartered Accountant. Joined Transport Development Group, 1953; Dir, 1960; Chief Exec., 1970–90; retd, 1992. Mem., LTE (part-time), 1979–82. Scottish Council: Mem. 1976–2002, and Chm. 1982–99, London Exec. Cttee; Vice Pres., 1983–99, Pres., 1999–2002. Confedn of British Industry: Mem. Council, 1980–82; Mem. 1979–90, and Chm. 1983–88, London Region Roads and Transportation Cttee; Mem., Transport Policy Cttee, 1983–92. London Chamber of Commerce: Mem. Council, 1982–; Mem., Gen. Purposes Cttee, 1983–90; Dep. Chm., 1984–86; Chm., 1986–88; Chm., Commercial Educn Trust, 1992–98. Pres., IRTE, 1984–87. FCILT (Pres., CIT, 1980–81; Spurrier Meml Lectr, 1972; Award of Merit, 1973; Herbert Crow Medal, 1978); CCMI; FRSA 1977. Liveryman, Co. of Carmen, 1983– (Award of Merit, 1992); Freeman, Co. of Watermen & Lightermen of the River Thames, 1982. *Publications:* papers on transport matters. *Recreations:* travel, reading, walking, swimming, theatre, golf. *Address:* 17 Kingston House South, Ennismore Gardens, SW7 1NF. *T:* (020) 7589 3545. *Clubs:* Hurlingham, Caledonian, Royal Automobile; Wisley Golf.

DUNCAN, John, FRS 2008; FBA 2009; Programme Leader, MRC Cognition and Brain Sciences Unit, Cambridge. Hon. Professor of Cognitive Neuroscience: Univ. of Cambridge; Univ. of Bangor; Professorial Res. Fellow, Univ. of Oxford. Heineken Award for Cognitive Sci., Royal Netherlands Acad. of Arts and Scis, 2012. *Publications:* (with N. Kanwisher) Attention and Performance XX, 2004; (ed jtly) Measuring the Mind, 2005; How Intelligence Happens, 2010; contribs to jls incl. Jl Exptl Psychol., Psychol. Rev., Perception and Psychophysics, Cognition, Ergonomics, Nature, Science, Cognitive Psychol. *Address:* MRC Cognition and Brain Sciences Unit, 15 Chaucer Road, Cambridge CB2 7EF.

DUNCAN, Ven. John Finch, MBE 1991; Archdeacon of Birmingham, 1985–2001; *b* 9 Sept. 1933; *s* of John and Helen Maud Duncan; *m* 1st, 1965, Diana Margaret Dewes (*d* 2001); one *s* two *d*; 2nd, 2011, Caroline Jane Fordham. *Educ:* Queen Elizabeth Grammar School, Wakefield; University Coll., Oxford; Cuddesdon Coll. MA (Oxon). Curate, St John, South Bank, Middlesbrough, 1959–61; Novice, Society of St Francis, 1961–62; Curate, St Peter, Birmingham, 1962–65; Chaplain, Univ. of Birmingham, 1965–76; Vicar of All Saints, Kings Heath, Birmingham, 1976–85. Chairman: Copec Housing Trust, 1970–91; Focus Housing Assoc., 1991–96. *Recreations:* golf, theatre, convivial gatherings. *Address:* 66 Glebe Rise, Kings Sutton, Banbury, Oxon OX17 3PH. *T:* (01295) 812641.

DUNCAN, John Lawrence, QPM 1999; Lord Lieutenant for Ayrshire and Arran, since 2006; *b* 15 Oct. 1942; *s* of John Duncan and Emily Gordon Duncan (*née* Legge); *m* 1st, 1964, Margaret Thomson Clark (*d* 1993); one *s* one *d*; 2nd, 2005, Jess Young; one step *d*. *Educ:* Buckie High Sch. Renfrew and Bute Constabulary, 1959–75 (Cadet, 1959–61); Strathclyde Police, 1975–2001: Head, Complaints and Discipline Br., 1989–92; Divl Comdr, Ayr, 1992–95; Head: of Force Inspectorate, 1995–96; of Force Personnel, 1996; Asst Chief Constable, 1996–99; Dep. Chief Constable, 1999–2001. Chm., Ayr United FC, 2003–04. OStJ 2011. *Recreations:* football, reading, music, art, church, Rotary. *Address:* Braeside, Stewarton, Kilmarnock KA3 5LL. *T:* (01560) 484050. *E:* johnlduncan@btinternet.com. *Club:* Glasgow Art.

DUNCAN, Prof. John Sidney, DM; FRCP, FMedSci; Professor of Neurology, UCL Institute of Neurology, University College London, since 1998; Clinical Director, National Hospital for Neurology and Neurosurgery, since 2012; *b* 12 Dec. 1955; *s* of John Graham Duncan and Elizabeth Mabella Duncan; *m* 1983, Elizabeth Hills; one *s* one *d*. *Educ:* Westminster Sch.; Worcester Coll., Oxford (BM BCh 1979; MA 1980; DM 1988). FRCP 1994. Sen. Lectr in Neurology and Consultant Neurologist, Nat. Hosp. for Neurology and Neurosurgery, 1989–98. Med. Dir, Nat. Soc. for Epilepsy, 1998–2012. FMedSci 2005. *Publications:* Clinical Epilepsy, 1995; MRI Neuroanatomy, 1996; Functional Imaging of the Epilepsies, 2000; contrib. original papers on treatment of epilepsy and brain imaging applied to epilepsy. *Recreations:* opera, horse riding. *Address:* Box 29, National Hospital for Neurology and Neurosurgery, Queen Square, WC1N 3BG. *T:* and *Fax:* (020) 3448 8612. *E:* j.duncan@ucl.ac.uk.

DUNCAN, John Stewart, OBE 1993; HM Diplomatic Service; Governor, British Virgin Islands, since 2014; *b* 17 April 1958; *s* of late Ernest Stewart Duncan and Joyce Fenner Duncan (*née* Austin); *m* 1984, Anne Marie Jacq; one *s* one *d*. *Educ:* Wycliffe Coll.; Univ. de Paris-Sorbonne (dip. langue et civilisation); Keele Univ. (BA Hons); NATO Defence Coll. Entered FCO, 1980; Scandinavia Desk, FCO, 1980–82; Chancery, Paris, 1982–84; Overseas Aid Admin, Khartoum, 1984–88; Head of Section: Defence Sales and Policy, FCO, 1988–89; Non-Proliferation, FCO, 1989–91; Asst Private Sec. to Minister for Overseas Aid and Africa, 1991–92; Chargé d'Affaires, Tirana, 1992–93; Mem., UK Delegn, NATO, 1993–96; Deputy Head: S Atlantic Dependent Territories Dept, FCO, 1996–97; Security Policy Dept, FCO, 1998; UK Pol Advr to SACEUR and Dep. SACEUR, 1998–2001; Dir, Trade and Investment, Paris, 2002–06; Ambassador for Multilateral Arms Control and Disarmament and UK Perm. Rep. to Conf. on Disarmament, Geneva, 2006–11; Special Rep. to London Conf. on Cyberspace, 2011; Dir of Engagement and Communications, FCO, 2012–13; Additional Dir, Overseas Territory Directorate, FCO, 2013–14. NATO Kosovo Medal, 2011. *Publications:* Rethinking NATO, 2002. *Recreations:* military history, gardening, jazz. *Address:* Government House, Tortola, British Virgin Islands.

DUNCAN, Laura; *see* Duncan, A. L. A.

DUNCAN, Lindsay Vere, CBE 2009; actress; *b* 7 Nov. 1950; *m* Hilton McRae, actor; one *s*. *Educ:* Central Sch. of Speech and Drama. *Television:* series: Dead Head, 1985; Traffik, 1989; GBH, 1991; A Year in Provence, 1993; Get Real, 1998; Dirty Tricks, 2000; Rome, 2005; Spooks, 2005–06; serials: The Rector's Wife, 1994; Oliver Twist, 1999; Shooting the Past, 1999; Perfect Strangers, 2001; Criminal Justice, 2008; Lost in Austen, 2008; Margaret, 2009; Dr Who, 2009; The Sinking of the Laconia, 2010; Christopher and His Kind, 2010; White Heat, 2012; Richard II, 2012; Black Mirror, 2012; Spy, 2012; You, Me & Them, 2013; *theatre:* Les Liaisons Dangereuses, RSC, 1986 (Olivier Award); Hedda Gabler, Hampstead, 1988; Cat on a Hot Tin Roof, NT, 1988 (Evening Standard Award); A Midsummer Night's Dream, RSC; Berenice, NT, 1990; Three Hotels, Tricycle, 1993; The Cryptogram, Ambassadors, 1994; Ashes to Ashes, Royal Court Upstairs, 1996; The Homecoming, RNT, 1997; Celebration, and The Room, Almeida, 2000; Mouth to Mouth, Royal Court (Critics' Circle Award) and Albery, 2001; Private Lives, Albery, 2001, NY, 2002 (Critics' Circle, Olivier, Tony, NY Drama Desk and Variety Club Awards, 2002); That Face, Royal Court, 2007, transf. Duke of York's, 2008; John Gabriel Borkman, Abbey Th., Dublin, 2010, NY, 2011; Hay Fever, Noël Coward Th., 2012; A Delicate Balance, NY, 2014; *films:* Prick Up Your Ears, 1987; Manifesto, 1988; The Reflecting Skin, 1990; City Hall, 1995; A Midsummer Night's Dream, 1996; Mansfield Park, 2000; An Ideal Husband, 2000; Under the Tuscan Sun, 2003; Afterlife, 2004 (Bowmore Scottish Screen Award, Best Actress, Bratislava Film Fest.); Starter for Ten, 2006; (for TV) Longford, 2006; Alice in Wonderland, 2010; About Time, 2013; Le Weekend, 2013 (Best Actress, British Independent Film Awards, 2013); The Last Passenger, 2013; Birdman, 2014. *Address:* c/o Dalzell & Beresford, Paddock Suite, The Courtyard, 55 Charterhouse Street, EC1M 6HA.

DUNCAN, Martin David Anson; freelance opera and theatre director; Joint Artistic Director, Chichester Festival Theatre, 2002–05; Artistic Adviser, Olympics Culture Festival 2012, 2009–12; *b* 12 July 1948; *s* of Ronald Francis Hamilton Anson Duncan and Margaret Elizabeth (*née* Thurlow). *Educ:* Durston House Sch., Ealing; Westminster Sch.; London Acad. of Music and Dramatic Art (Stage Mgt). Actor in rep., West End, television and film, 1968–89; composer of musical scores for over 50 theatre prodns; Associate Artist, Crucible Theatre, Sheffield, 1988; Artistic Dir, Nottingham Playhouse, 1994–99. *Theatre productions include:* Rocky Horror Show, Munich and Milan, 1985; School for Clowns, Lilian Baylis Th., 1988; Performance, Pet Shop Boys' tour (Associate Dir), 1991; The Nutcracker, Opera North (Dir and co-writer), 1992; The Comedy of Errors, Berlin, 2001; The Blacks, Johannesburg and Stockholm, 2001; *Royal Lyceum Edinburgh:* Man of La Mancha, 2007; Private Lives, 2014; *National Theatre of Brent:* The Greatest Story Ever Told, 1987; The French Revolution, 1989; All the World's a Globe, 1990; Love upon the Throne, 1998; Massive Landmarks of the 20th Century, 1999; The Wonder of Sex, 2001; The Arts and How They Was Done, 2006; *Nottingham Playhouse:* The Nose, 1995, The Adventures of Pinocchio, 1995; Happy End, Time and the Room, 1996; Le Bourgeois Gentilhomme, 1998; Endgame, and Krapp's Last Tape, 1999; *Chichester:* The Gondoliers, 2003; Out of this World, Seven Doors, 2004; How to Succeed in Business Without Really Trying, The Government Inspector, 2005; *opera productions:* Opera North: L'heure Espagnole, Gianni Schicchi, 1990; The Thieving Magpie, 1992, 2005; Iolanta, Orpheus in the Underworld, 1992; The Adventures of Pinocchio, 2007; A Midsummer Night's Dream, 2008; Bavarian State Opera, Munich: Xerxes, 1996; La Clemenza di Tito, 1999; The Rake's Progress, 2002; Die Entführung aus dem Serail, 2003; Albert Herring, Canadian Opera Co., 1991; The Magic Flute, Scottish Opera, 1993; HMS Pinafore, Die Fledermaus, D'Oyly Carte Opera Co., 1994; Ariadne auf Naxos, Scottish Opera, 1997, Garsington Opera, 2007, Norwegian Opera, 2010; The Last Supper, Berlin State Opera, 2000; The Love of Three Oranges, Cologne Opera, 2001; The Last Supper, Glyndebourne, 2001; Pagliacci/Cavalleria Rusticana, Royal Albert Hall, 2002; La Traviata, Flanders Opera, 2003; The Gondoliers, ENO, 2006; The Original Chinese Conjuror, Aldeburgh Fest., 2006; The Adventures of Pinocchio, Chemnitz Opera 2008, Minnesota Opera, 2009, Moscow, 2011; Artaxerxes, Royal Opera House, 2009; Armida, Garsington Opera, 2010; La Forza del Destino, Holland Park, 2010; Betrothal in a Monastery, Théâtre du Capitole Toulouse, Opéra Comique Paris, 2011; Il Turco in Italia, Garsington Opera, 2011; Moses, Theater St Gallen, 2013; BBC Proms: Sondheim at 80, 2010; The Yeoman of the Guard, 2012.

DUNCAN, Peter; actor, presenter, theatre director and documentary maker, since 1969; Chief Scout, 2004–09; *b* 3 May 1954; *s* of Alan Gale and Patricia Kaye; *m* 1985, Annie Francis; one *s* three *d*. *Educ:* Hawes Down Sec. Mod. Sch.; Italia Conti Stage Sch.; Open Univ. Actor: NT, Old Vic, 1970–72; *films* include: Stardust, 1974; The Lifetaker, 1975; Flash Gordon, 1980; *television* includes: Space: 1999, Survivors, Warship, 1976; King Cinder, 1977; The Flockton Flyer, 1977–78; Tumble, 2014; presenter: Blue Peter, 1980–84, 1985–86 (Gold Blue Peter Badge 2007); Duncan Dares, 1984–86; Peter Duncan's Family Travels (documentary), 2002–07; Demolition Dad, 2005–07; *theatre* includes: Pump Boy and Dinettes, Piccadilly Th.; Funny Peculiar, UK tour; The Card, Regent's Park Th., 1993; Me and My Girl, UK tour, 1995; title rôle in Barnum, UK tour, 1999; Macbeth, Fantastic Mr Fox, Regent's Park Th., 2007; Birdsong, UK tour, 2014. Pantomime writer and dir, Oxford Playhouse, 2006–14. Patron: Action for Children's Arts, 2010–; Youth Music Th., 2011–; Pohwer Advocacy, 2013–; Neighbourhood Midwives, 2013–. *Recreations:* gardening, singing, football, yoga. *Address:* 24 Wimbledon Park Road, SW18 1LT. *E:* heres.one@which.net. *W:* www.heresoneimadeearlier.com.

DUNCAN, Peter John; politician and strategic communications consultant; Managing Director, Message Matters Ltd, since 2012; *b* 10 July 1965; *s* of late Ronald Duncan and Aureen Duncan (*née* Anderson); *m* 1994, Lorna Forbes; one *s* one *d*. *Educ:* Univ. of Birmingham (BCom Hons); Manchester Business Sch. (MBA). Project Manager, Mackays Stores Ltd, 1985–88; Man. Dir, John Duncan & Son, 1988–2000; freelance business consultant, 1998–2000. MP (C) Galloway and Upper Nithsdale, 2001–05; contested (C) Dumfries and Galloway, 2005, 2010. Shadow Sec. of State for Scotland, 2003–05. Mem. (C) Dumfries and Galloway Council, 2007–12 (Chm. of Resources, 2007–12). Chm., Scottish Conservative and Unionist Party, 2004–07. *Recreations:* Scottish Rugby, English Test and county cricket. *Address:* Birkhill House, Earlston, Berwickshire TD4 6AR.

DUNCAN, His Honour Sean Bruce; a Circuit Judge, 1988–2009; *b* 21 Dec. 1942; *s* of late Joseph Alexander Duncan and Patricia Pauline Duncan; *m* 1974, Dr Diana Bowyer Courtney; three *s* one *d*. *Educ:* Shrewsbury Sch.; St Edmund Hall, Oxford (MA). Called to the Bar, Inner Temple, 1966; Northern Circuit (Hon. Sec., Circuit Cttee, 1985–88); a Recorder, 1984–88. Pres., Council of HM Circuit Judges, 2002 (Hon. Sec., 1996–99). Served with Cheshire Yeomanry (TA), 1963–68. Chairman: Old Swan Boys Club, Liverpool, 1974–79; Liverpool Youth Organisations Cttee, 1977–83; Vice-Chm., Liverpool Council of Voluntary Service, 1982–88. *Recreations:* theatre, sport, music. *Clubs:* Royal Liverpool Golf (Capt., 2003); Liverpool Ramblers AFC (Pres., 2000–02).

DUNCAN, Stanley Frederick St Clair, CMG 1983; HM Diplomatic Service, retired; *b* 13 Nov. 1927; *yr s* of late Stanley Gilbert Scott and Louisa Elizabeth Duncan; *m* 1967, Jennifer Jane Bennett; two *d*. *Educ:* Latymer Upper Sch.; Open Univ. (Dip. European Humanities 1999; BA Hons 2002). FRGS. India Office, 1946; CRO, 1947; Private Sec. to Parly Under-Sec. of State, 1954; Second Sec., Ottawa, 1954–55; Brit. Govt Information Officer, Toronto, 1955–57; Second Sec., Wellington, 1958–60; First Sec., CRO, 1960; seconded to Central African Office, 1962–64; Mem., Brit. Delegn to Victoria Falls Conf. on Dissolution of Fedn of Rhodesia and Nyasaland, 1963; First Sec., Nicosia, 1964–67; FCO, 1967–70; FCO Adviser, Brit. Gp, Inter-Parly Union, 1968–70; Head of Chancery and First Sec., Lisbon, 1970–73; Consul-General and subsequently Chargé d'Affaires in Mozambique, 1973–75; Counsellor (Political), Brasilia, 1976–77; Head of Consular Dept, FCO, 1977–80; Canadian Nat. Defence Coll., 1980–81; Ambassador to Bolivia, 1981–85; High Comr in Malta, 1985–87. Mem., UN Observer Mission to S African elections, 1994. Officer, Military Order of Christ (Portugal), 1973. *Address:* Tucksmead, Longworth, Oxon OX13 5ET.

DUNCAN-JONES, Prof. Katherine Dorothea, FRSL; Fellow, and Tutor in English Literature, Somerville College, Oxford, 1966–2001; Professor of English Literature, University of Oxford, 1998–2001; Senior Research Fellow, Somerville College, and Faculty of English, University of Oxford, since 2001; *b* 13 May 1941; *d* of late Prof. Austin Ernest Duncan-Jones and Elsie Elizabeth Duncan-Jones (*née* Phare); *m* 1971, Andrew N. Wilson, *qv* (marr. diss. 1990); two *d*. *Educ:* King Edward VI High Sch. for Girls, Birmingham; St Hilda's Coll., Oxford (BLitt, MA). Mary Ewart Res. Fellow, Somerville Coll., Oxford, 1963–65; Fellow, New Hall, Cambridge, 1965–66. Hon. Res. Fellow, UCL, 2000–. FRSL 1992; FEA 2000. Ben Jonson Discoveries Prize, 1996. *Publications:* (ed jtly) Miscellaneous Prose of Sir Philip Sidney, 1977; (ed) Sir Philip Sidney, 1989; Sir Philip Sidney: courtier poet (biog.), 1991; (ed) Shakespeare's Sonnets, 1997, 2nd edn 2010; Ungentle Shakespeare (biog.), 2001; Shakespeare's Life and Work, 2004; (ed jtly) Shakespeare's Poems, 2007; Shakespeare: Upstart Crow to Sweet Swan 1592–1623, 2011; contrib. numerous articles in Rev. of English Studies, TLS, and other jls. *Recreations:* swimming, theatre-going. *Address:* Somerville College, Oxford OX2 6HD. *T:* (01865) 281267.

See also R. P. Duncan-Jones, Viscount Runciman of Doxford.

DUNCAN-JONES, Richard Phare, PhD; FBA 1992; Fellow, Gonville and Caius College, Cambridge, since 1963; *b* 14 Sept. 1937; *s* of late Austin Ernest Duncan-Jones and Elsie Elizabeth Duncan-Jones; *m* 1986, Julia Elizabeth Poole. *Educ:* King Edward's Sch., Birmingham; King's Coll., Cambridge (MA, PhD). Gonville and Caius College, Cambridge: W. M. Tapp Res. Fellow, 1963–67; Domestic Bursar, 1967–84; Official Fellow, 1967–; College Lectr and Dir of Studies in Classics, 1984–2004. Mem., Inst. for Advanced Study, Princeton, 1971–72. *Publications:* The Economy of the Roman Empire, 1974, 2nd edn 1982; Structure and Scale in the Roman Economy, 1990; Money and Government in the Roman Empire, 1994; articles in learned jls. *Recreations:* wine tasting, continental cinema. *Address:* Gonville and Caius College, Cambridge CB2 1TA. *T:* (01223) 332394.

See also K. D. Duncan-Jones.

DUNCAN SMITH, Rt Hon. (George) Iain; PC 2001; MP (C) Chingford and Woodford Green, since 1997 (Chingford, 1992–97); Secretary of State for Work and Pensions, since 2010; *b* 9 April 1954; *s* of late Group Captain W. G. G. Duncan Smith, DSO (Bar), DFC (2 Bars) and Pamela Mary Duncan Smith (*née* Summers); *m* 1982, Hon. Elizabeth Wynne Fremantle, *er d* of Baron Cottesloe, *qv*; two *s* two *d*. *Educ:* HMS Conway (Cadet School); RMA Sandhurst; Dunchurch Coll. of Management. Scots Guards, 1975–81; ADC to Gen. Sir John Acland, 1979–81; GEC, 1981–88; Dir, Bellwinch (Property), 1988; Dir, Jane's Inf. Group, 1989–92. Vice-Chm., Fulham Cons. Assoc., 1991. Contested (C) Bradford West, 1987. Shadow Sec. of State for social security, 1997–99, for defence, 1999–2001; Leader, Cons. Party and Leader of the Opposition, 2001–03. Member, Select Committee: on Health, 1994–95; on Nolan, 1995; on Standards and Privileges, 1996–97. Sec., Cons. Backbench Cttee on Foreign and Commonwealth Affairs, 1992–97; Vice Chm., Cons. European Affairs Cttee, 1996–97; Mem., Cons. Party Adv. Council, 2003–. Chm. and Founder, Centre for Social Justice, 2004–10 (Patron, 2010–). Trustee: Lygon Alms-house, 1985–91; Whitefield Develt Trust. Freeman, City of London. *Publications:* The Devil's Tune (novel), 2003; Breakdown Britain, 2006; Breakthrough Britain, 2007; (jtly) Early Intervention: good parents, great kids, better citizens, 2009; various pamphlets on social security, European and defence issues; occasional journalism. *Recreations:* family, painting, fishing, cricket, tennis, shooting, opera, reading. *Address:* House of Commons, SW1A 0AA. *T:* (020) 7219 2667 and 3000.

DUNCANNON, Viscount; Frederick Arthur William Ponsonby; *b* 9 Aug. 1974; *e s* and *heir* of Earl of Bessborough, *qv*; *m* 2005, Emily, *d* of Dr Peter D. Mott, Pittsford, NY; one *s* one *d*. *Educ:* Harrow; UEA. *Heir:* *s* Hon. William Ponsonby, *b* 6 May 2008.

DUNCOMBE, family name of **Baron Feversham.**

DUNCOMBE, Sir David Philip Henry P.; *see* Pauncefort-Duncombe.

DUNCUMB, Dr Peter, FRS 1977; consultant in materials analysis by X-rays and ultrasonics, since 1997; Director and General Manager, Tube Investments, later TI Group, Research Laboratories, 1979–87; *b* 26 Jan. 1931; *s* of late William Duncumb and of Hilda Grace (*née* Coleman); *m* 1955, Anne Leslie Taylor; two *s* one *d*. *Educ:* Oundle Sch.; Clare Coll., Cambridge (BA 1953, MA 1956, PhD 1957). Commnd GD Br., RAF, qualif. Pilot, 1949–50; No 22RFS Cambridge, RAFVR, 1950–54; DSIR Res. Fellow, Cambridge Univ., 1957–59; Tube Investments, subseq. TI Group, Research Laboratories: Res. Scientist and Gp Leader, 1959–67, Head, Physics Dept, 1967–72; Asst Dir, 1972–79. Hon. Prof., Warwick Univ., 1990–2000. FInstP 1969. Hon. Member: Microbeam Analysis Soc. of America, 1973; European Microbeam Analysis Soc., 1997. C. V. Boys Prize, Inst. of Physics, 1966; Henry Clifton Sorby Award, Internat. Metallographic Soc., 1996. *Publications:* numerous on electron microscopy and analysis in various jls. *Recreations:* photography, ballet, family history. *Address:* 5A Woollards Lane, Great Shelford, Cambridge CB22 5LZ. *T:* (01223) 843064.

DUNDAS, family name of **Marquess of Zetland,** and **Viscount Melville.**

DUNDAS, James Frederick Trevor; Chairman, Jupiter Fund Management plc, 2008–14; *b* 4 Nov. 1950; *s* of Sir Hugh Dundas, CBE, DSO, DFC, and of Hon. Lady Dundas; *m* 1979, Jennifer Daukes; one *s* two *d*. *Educ:* Eton; New Coll., Oxford (BA Hons Jurisp.). Called to the Bar, Inner Temple, 1972; Morgan Grenfell & Co. Ltd, 1972–91: Dir, 1981–91; Head, Corporate and Internat. Banking, 1987–91; Mem., Mgt Cttee, Morgan Grenfell Gp plc, 1989–91; Finance Dir, Hong Kong Airport Authy, 1992–96; Finance Dir, 1997–99, Chief Exec., 1999–2003, MEPC plc. Non-executive Director: J. Sainsbury plc, 2000–07; Standard Chartered PLC, 2004–; Drax Gp plc, 2005–10; Francis Crick Inst., 2011–. Dep. Pres., Macmillan Cancer Support, 2010– (Chm., 2001–10).

DUNDAS-BEKKER, Althea Enid Philippa; DL; owner and administrator, Arniston House, Midlothian; *b* 4 Nov. 1939; *d* of Sir Philip Dundas, 4th Bt and Jean Marion Dundas; *m* 1972, Aedrian Ruprecht Bekker (*d* 1990); two *d*. *Educ:* Inverleny, Callander; Oakfield Sch., Kirkby Lonsdale. Inherited Arniston House, 1970. Mem., Royal Commn on Historical MSS, 1994–2003. DL Midlothian, 1991. *Recreations:* Scottish history and songs, walking dogs. *Address:* Arniston House, Gorebridge, Midlothian EH23 4RY. *T:* (01875) 830238, *Fax:* (01875) 830573.

DUNDEE, 12th Earl of, *cr* 1660 (Scotland); **Alexander Henry Scrymgeour;** DL; Viscount Dudhope and Lord Scrymgeour, 1641 (Scotland); Lord Inverkeithing, 1660 (Scotland); Lord Glassary (UK), 1954; Hereditary Royal Standard-Bearer for Scotland; *b* 5 June 1949; *s* of 11th Earl of Dundee, PC, and Patricia Katherine, *d* of late Col Lord Herbert Montagu Douglas Scott; *S* father, 1983; *m* 1979, Siobhan Mary, *d* of David Llewellyn, Gt Somerford, Wilts; one *s* three *d*. *Educ:* Eton; St Andrews Univ. Contested (C) Hamilton, by-election May 1978. A Lord in Waiting (Govt Whip), 1986–89; elected Mem., H of L, 1999. DL Fife, 2003. *Heir:* *s* Lord Scrymgeour, *qv*. *Address:* Farm Office, Birkhill, Cupar, Fife KY15 4QP. *Clubs:* White's; New (Edinburgh).

DUNDONALD, 15th Earl of, *cr* 1669; **Iain Alexander Douglas Blair Cochrane;** Lord Cochrane of Dundonald, 1647; Lord Cochrane of Paisley and Ochiltree, 1669; Chairman, Duneth Securities and associated companies, 1986; Director, Anglo Scientific (formerly Anglo Digital) and associated companies, since 2001; *b* 17 Feb. 1961; *s* of 14th Earl of Dundonald and Aphra Farquhar (*d* 1972), *d* of late Comdr George Fetherstonhaugh; *S* father, 1986; *m* 1987, Beatrice (marr. diss. 2011), *d* of Adolphus Russo; two *s* one *d*. *Educ:* Wellington College; RAC Cirencester. DipREM. Dir, Anglo Pacific Gp, 1995–98. Mem. Council, PITCOM, subseq. PICTFOR, 1994–. Hon. Consul in Scotland for Chile, 1993–. *Recreations:* rural affairs, sailing, innovation. *Heir:* *s* Lord Cochrane, *qv*. *Address:* Lochnell Castle, Benderloch, Argyll PA37 1QT.

DUNEDIN, Bishop of, since 2010; **Rt Rev. Kelvin Wright;** *b* Timaru, NZ, 14 April 1952; *s* of Norman Trevor Wright and Patricia Wright; *m* 1976, Clemency Underhill; one *s* two *d*. *Educ:* Aranui High Sch.; Univ. of Canterbury (BA 1973); Univ. of Otago (BD 1978); San Francisco Theol Seminary (DMin 1988). Vicar: Waihao Downs, 1982–85; Hillcrest, Hamilton, 1985–91; Sumner, Christchurch, 1991–93; Bishop's Chaplain for Ministry, Dio. of Waikato, 1994–98; Vicar, St John's, Roslyn, 1999–2010; Vicar Gen., Dio. of Dunedin, 2003–09. *Recreations:* photography, sailing. *Address:* 1 Glenfinnan Place, Anderson's Bay, Dunedin, New Zealand. *T:* (3) 4544073. *Club:* Dunedin.

DUNFORD, Sir John (Ernest), Kt 2014; OBE 1994; PhD; education consultant; General Secretary, Association of School and College Leaders, 1998–2010; *b* Burnham-on-Sea, Som, 10 Nov. 1946; *s* of Leslie Donald Dunford and Mary Dunford; *m* 2001, Sue Rust D'Eye; one *s* one *d* and two step *d*. *Educ:* Cheltenham Coll.; Univ. of Nottingham (BSc Jt Hons Maths and Econs; PGCE); Univ. of Durham (MEd 1976; PhD 1992; Hon. Fellow, 2007). Pres. of Union, Univ. of Nottingham, 1968–69. Teacher of Maths: Mundella Sch., Nottingham, 1970–72; Hylton Red House Sch., Sunderland, 1972–73; Framwellgate Moor Comp. Sch., Durham, 1973–78 (Sen. Teacher, 1974–78); Dep. Head, Bede Sch., Sunderland, 1979–82; Hd, Durham Johnston Comprehensive Sch., 1982–98. Trustee: Worldwide Volunteering, 1995– (Chm., 2010–); Teach First, 2003–11; Education for All, 2009–; Chartered Inst. of Educl Assessors, 2010–14 (Chm., 2010–14); Board Member: Specialist Schs and Acads Trust, 2005–09; Future Leaders, 2006–11; Chm., Whole Educn, 2010–. Mem. Governing Council, Nat. Coll. for Leadership of Schs and Children's Services, 2010–12. Nat. Pupil Premium Champion, 2013–. Gov., St Andrew's C of E Primary Sch., N Kilworth, 2004–. Conducted Review of Office of the Children's Commissioner (England), 2010. Hon. LLD Nottingham, 2013. *Publications:* Her Majesty's Inspectorate of Schools 1860–1870, 1980; Her Majesty's Inspectorate of Schools since 1944, 1998; (ed) State Schools: New Labour and the Conservative legacy, 1999; School Leadership: national and international perspectives, 2000; The Growth of Academy Chains: implications for leaders and leadership, 2012; Establishing and Leading New Types of School: challenges and opportunities for leaders and leadership, 2013. *Recreations:* cooking, birdwatching, opera, gardening, golf, walking. *Address:* Cobblestones, Church Street, North Kilworth, Leics LE17 6EZ. *E:* johndunford@easynet.co.uk.

DUNGARVAN, Viscount; Rory Jonathan Courtenay Boyle; naval architect (yachts); *b* 10 Dec. 1978; *o s* and *heir* of Earl of Cork and Orrery, *qv*. *Educ:* Harrow; Newcastle Univ. (BEng Hons). CEng 2008; MRINA 2008. *Recreations:* sailing, ski-ing, design, technology, country sports, reeling. *Address:* 86 Archel Road, W14 9QP.

DUNGAVELL, Ian Robert, PhD; FSA; Chief Executive, Highgate Cemetery, since 2012; *b* 4 Sept. 1966; *s* of Robert Charles Dungavell and Barbara Marie Dungavell. *Educ:* ANU (BA Hons Art Hist. 1989); Royal Holloway, London (PhD Architectl Hist. 1999); Univ. of Reading (MSc Conservation of Historic Envmt 2010). FSA 2007. Assoc. Lectr, ANU, 1992–93; Lectr, Sotheby's Inst., 1998–2000; Dir, The Victorian Soc., 2000–12 (Dir, Summer Sch., 1998–99). Member: Exec. Cttee, Soc. of Architectl Historians of GB, 1996–99; Places of Worship Forum, English Heritage, 2006–10; Conservation Working Gp, Churches

Conservation Trust, 2007–12. Hon. Sec., Jt Cttee of Nat. Amenity Socs, 2005–10. Winston Churchill Travelling Fellow, 2005. Banister Fletcher Lect., London Soc., 2008. Trustee, Cremation Soc. GB, 2015–. *Publications:* (contrib.) Birmingham (Pevsner City Guide), 2005; (ed with D. Crellin) Architecture and Englishness 1880–1914, 2006; (contrib.) Building Conservation Directory, 2007; contrib. Oxford DNB; contribs to Jl of Decorative Arts Soc., Crafts Mag., Studies in Victorian Architecture and Design. *Recreations:* architecture, swimming, eating. *Address:* Highgate Cemetery, Swain's Lane, Highgate, N6 6PJ. *T:* (020) 8340 1834. *E:* ian@dungavell.net.

DUNGER, Prof. David Brian, MD; FRCP, FRCPCH; FMedSci; Professor of Paediatrics, University of Cambridge, since 2000; *b* Rochford, 28 March 1948; *s* of Brian and Jean Dunger; one *d*; *m* 2005, Dame Jane Elisabeth Roberts, *qv*; one *s*. *Educ:* Charing Cross Hosp. Med. Sch., Univ. of London (MB BS 1971; MD 1983). FRCP 1993; FRCPCH 1997. Sen. Registrar in Paediatrics, Gt Ormond St Hosp., London, 1980–86; Consultant Paediatric Endocrinologist, John Radcliffe Hosp., Oxford, 1986–2000; Prof. of Paediatric Endocrinol., Univ. of Oxford, 1999–2000. FMedSci 2012. Andrea Prader Prize, Eur. Soc. for Paediatric Endocrinol., 2012. *Publications:* peer-reviewed pubns and reviews. *Address:* Church Barn, Butchers Hill, Ickleton, Saffron Walden, Essex CB10 1SR. *E:* dbd25@cam.ac.uk.

DUNGER, Dame Jane (Elisabeth); *see* Roberts, Dame J. E.

DUNGEY, Prof. James Wynne, PhD; Professor of Physics, Imperial College, University of London, 1965–84; *b* 30 Jan. 1923; *s* of Ernest Dungey and Alice Dungey; *m* 1950, Christine Scotland (*née* Brown); one *s* one *d*. *Educ:* Bradfield; Magdalene Coll., Cambridge (MA, PhD). Res. Fellow, Univ. of Sydney, 1950–53; Vis. Asst Prof., Penn State Coll., 1953–54; ICI Fellow, Cambridge, 1954–57; Lectr, King's Coll., Newcastle upon Tyne, 1957–59; Sen. Principal Scientific Officer, AWRE, Aldermaston, 1959–63; Res. Fellow, Imperial Coll., London, 1963–65. Fellow, Amer. Geophysical Union, 1973. Hon. Mem., European Geophysical Soc., 1994. Chapman Medal, RAS, 1982; Gold Medal for Geophysics, RAS, 1990; Fleming Medal, Amer. Geophysical Union, 1991. *Publications:* Cosmic Electrodynamics, 1958; papers on related topics. *Address:* 20 Walkers Court, 101 Southdown Road, Harpenden, Herts AL5 1QL.

DUNGLASS, Lord; Michael David Alexander Douglas-Home; *b* 30 Nov. 1987; *s* and *heir* of Earl of Home, *qv*. A Page of Honour to the Queen, 1998–2000. *Address:* The Hirsel, Coldstream, Berwickshire TD12 4LP.

DUNHILL, Rosemary Carole, OBE 2003; FSA; County Archivist, Hampshire Record Office, 1982–2001, retired; *b* 21 June 1944; *d* of Harold John Dunhill and Freda Dunhill (*née* Best); *m* 2007, David Lloyd. *Educ:* Palmer's Girls' Sch., Grays; Cheadle Grammar Sch.; Methodist Coll., Belfast; Somerville Coll., Oxford (BA Modern Hist. 1965, MA). Archivist: Harrowby MSS Trust, 1969–71; Devon Record Office, 1972–76; Northants Record Office, 1976–82; (pt-time) Jesus Coll., Oxford, 2002–07. Member: Royal Commn on Historical MSS, 1999–2003; Lord Chancellor's Adv. Council on Public Records, 1999–2001; Adv. Council on Nat. Records and Archives, 2003–05. Chm., Assoc. of Chief Archivists in Local Govt, 1997–99. FSA 1996. Hon. DLitt King Alfred's Coll., Winchester, 2000. Ellis Prize, Soc. of Archivists, 1996. *Publications:* (with D. Burrows) Music and Theatre in Handel's World: the family papers of James Harris 1735–1780, 2002. *Recreations:* nephews and nieces, archives, fair trade. *Address:* 27 Sunnydown Road, Winchester, Hants SO22 4LD. *T:* (01962) 869007. *E:* rcdunhill@gmail.com.

DUNION, Kevin Harry, OBE 1999; Executive Director, Centre for Freedom of Information, since 2012; *b* 20 Dec. 1955; *s* of late Harry Dunion and of Mary Leckie Bertolini; *m* 1st, 1978, Christine Elizabeth Hannam (marr. diss. 1997); two *s*; 2nd, 1997, Linda Gray. *Educ:* St Andrew's High Sch., Kirkcaldy; St Andrews Univ. (MA Hons); Edinburgh Univ. (MSc Dist.). HM Inspector of Taxes, 1978–80; Administrator, Edinburgh Univ. Students' Assoc., 1980–84; Scottish Campaign Manager, OXFAM, 1984–91; Dir, Friends of the Earth Scotland, 1991–2003; Chm., Friends of the Earth Internat., 1996–99; Scottish Information Comr, 2003–12; Lord Rector, Univ. of St Andrews, 2008–11. Vis. Prof., Univ. of Northumbria, 2011–; Hon. Prof., Univ. of Dundee, 2012–. Member: Cabinet sub-cttee on Sustainable Scotland, Scottish Exec., 2000–03; Bd, Scottish Natural Heritage, 2000–03; Scottish Legal Complaints Commn, 2013–. Co-dir, Centre for Freedom of Information, 2009–; Mem. Bd, Access to Information Appeals Bd, World Bank, 2012–. Chair, Students' Assoc. Bd, Univ. of St Andrews, 2011–14. Hon. Sen. Res. Fellow, Univ. of Strathclyde, 2000–03. Editor, Radical Scotland mag., 1981–85. FRSA 1997. Hon. LLD St Andrews, 2011. *Publications:* Living in the Real World: the international role for Scotland's Parliament, 1995; Troublemakers: the struggle for environmental justice in Scotland, 2003; The Democracy of War, 2007; Freedom of Information in Scotland in Practice, 2011. *Recreations:* Scottish local history, curling. *Address:* Third Acre, 2 Fairies Road, Perth PH1 1NB.

DUNITZ, Prof. Jack David, FRS 1974; Professor of Chemical Crystallography at the Swiss Federal Institute of Technology (ETH), Zürich, 1957–90; *b* 29 March 1923; *s* of William Dunitz and Mildred (*née* Gossman); *m* 1953, Barbara Steuer; two *d*. *Educ:* Hillhead High Sch., Glasgow; Hutchesons' Grammar Sch., Glasgow; Glasgow Univ. (BSc, PhD). Post-doctoral Fellow, Oxford Univ., 1946–48, 1951–53; California Inst. of Technology, 1948–51, 1953–54; Vis. Scientist, US Nat. Insts of Health, 1954–55; Sen. Res. Fellow, Davy Faraday Res. Lab., Royal Instn, London, 1956–57. Overseas Fellow, Churchill Coll., Cambridge, 1968; Vis. Professor: Iowa State Univ., 1965; Tokyo Univ., 1967; Technion, Haifa, 1970; Hill Vis. Prof., Univ. of Minnesota, 1983; Fairchild Distinguished Scholar, CIT, 1985; Hooker Distinguished Vis. Prof., McMaster Univ., 1987; Alexander Todd Vis. Prof., Cambridge Univ., 1990; Oscar K. Rice Vis. Prof., Univ. of N Carolina, Chapel Hill, 1991; Robert B. Woodward Vis. Prof., Harvard Univ., 1992. Lectures: British Council, 1965; Treat B. Johnson Meml, Yale Univ., 1965; 3M Univ. of Minnesota, 1966; Reilly, Univ. Notre Dame, US, 1971; Kelly, Purdue Univ., 1971; Gerhard Schmidt Meml, Weizmann Inst. of Sci., 1973; George Fisher Baker, Cornell Univ., 1976; Centenary, Chem. Soc., 1977; Appleton, Brown Univ., 1979; H. J. Backer, Gröningen Univ., 1980; Havinga, Leiden Univ., 1980; Karl Folkers, Wisconsin Univ., 1981; A. L. Patterson Meml, Inst. for Cancer Res., Philadelphia, 1983; C. S. Marvel, Illinois Univ., 1987; Birch, Canberra, 1989; Dwyer, Sydney, 1989; Bijvoet, Utrecht Univ., 1989; Bragg, British Crystallographic Assoc., 1999. Mem., Bd of Govs, Cambridge Crystallographic Data Centre, 1987–99. Foreign Member: Royal Netherlands Acad. of Arts and Sciences, 1979; Amer. Phil Soc., 1997; Member: Leopoldina Acad., 1979; European Acad. of Scis and Arts, 1991; Foreign Associate, US Nat. Acad. of Scis, 1988; Mem., Academia Europaea, 1989; Hon. Member: Swiss Soc. of Crystallography, 1990; Swiss Chem. Soc., 2004; British Crystallographic Assoc., 2012; For. Hon. Mem., Amer. Acad. of Arts and Scis, 1997; Fellow AAAS, 1981. Hon. FRSC 2000. Hon. DSc: Technion, Haifa, 1990; Weizmann Inst. of Sci., 1992; Glasgow Univ., 1999. Tishler Award, Harvard Univ., 1985; Paracelsus Prize, Swiss Chem. Soc., 1986; Gregori Aminoff Prize, Swedish Royal Acad., 1990; Martin Buerger Award, Amer. Crystallographic Assoc., 1991; Arthur C. Cope Scholar Award, ACS, 1997. Jt Editor, Perspectives in Structural Chemistry, 1967–71; Mem. Editorial Bd: Helvetica Chimica Acta, 1971–85; Structure and Bonding, 1971–81. *Publications:* X-ray Analysis and the Structure of Organic Molecules, 1979; (with E. Heilbronner) Reflections on Symmetry in Chemistry… and Elsewhere, 1993; papers on various aspects of crystal and molecular structure in Acta Crystallographica, Helvetica Chimica Acta, Jl Chem. Soc., Jl Amer. Chem. Soc., etc. *Recreation:* walking. *Address:* Obere Heslibachstrasse 77, 8700 Küsnacht, Switzerland. *T:* (44) 9101723; (office) Chemistry Department, ETH-Zürich, 8093 Zürich, Switzerland. *T:* (44) 6322892.

DUNKELD, Bishop of, (RC), since 2014; **Rt Rev. Mgr Stephen Robson;** *b* Carlisle, 1 April 1951; *s* of Leslie and Margery Robson. *Educ:* Caldey Grange Sch., Wirral; Carlisle and Lanark Grammar Schs; Edinburgh Univ. (BSc 1974; MTh 1988); St Andrew's Coll., Drygrange; Pontifical Gregorian Univ., Rome (STL 2000; STD 2003; JCL 2006). CBiol 1985. Ordained priest, 1979; Assistant Priest: St Mary's Cathedral, Edinburgh, 1979; Our Lady of the Perpetual Succour, Kircaldy, 1979–81; teacher training in-service, 1981; Prof., St Mary's Coll., Blairs, 1981–86; Sec. to Archbishop O'Brien, 1986–88; Asst, Holy Cross, Edinburgh, 1986–88; Parish Priest, Duns, 1988–89; Novice, Ampleforth Abbey, 1989–90; Parish Priest, Dunbar, 1990–93; Asst Episcopal Vicar for Educn, 1990–93, Vicar Episcopal for Educn, 1993–98; Parish Priest: St John Vianney, Edinburgh, 1993–97; St Theresa's, East Calder, 1997–98; Spiritual Dir, Pontifical Scots Coll., Rome, 1998–2006; Prof., Pontifical Beda Coll., Rome, 1999–2001; Parish Priest, North Berwick, 2006–12; Chancellor, Archdiocese of St Andrews and Edinburgh, 2007–13; Parish Priest, SS John Cantius and Nicholas, 2012; Titular Bishop of Tunnuna, and Auxiliary Bishop, Archdiocese of St Andrews and Edinburgh, 2012–13. Chaplain to His Holiness, 2008. Judge, Scottish Nat. Tribunal, 2006–; Mem., Canon Law Soc. of GB and Ireland, 2006–. Bishop Promoter for Scotland, Apostleship of the Sea. President: Priests for Scotland, 2013; Scottish Bps Conference Commn for the Permanent Diaconate; Member: Scottish Catholic Internat. Aid Fund, 2013–; Scottish Catholic Heritage Collections Trust, 2013–; Charles Trotter Trust, 2013–. *Publications:* With the Spirit and Power of Elijah, 2004. *Recreations:* music, reading, cinema, theatre. *Address:* Diocese of Dunkeld, 24–28 Lawside Road, Dundee DD3 6XY.

DUNKERLEY, Susan Margaret; Head, Wheathampstead House (formerly Head, Juniors), St Albans High School for Girls, 1998–2009; *b* Howden, E Yorks, 18 June 1954; *d* of George Donald Whitaker and Muriel Whitaker; *m* 1977, Colin Dunkerley; two *d*. *Educ:* Goole Grammar Sch.; Homerton Coll., Cambridge (BEd Hons Newnham Coll.); Inst. of Educn, London Univ. (MA Geog. and Educn). Hd of Yr and Hd of Geog., Furzehill Middle Sch., Borehamwood, 1976–83; various posts teaching geog. with additional subjects, Beaumont Sec. Sch., St Albans, 1984–89; Haberdashers' Aske's Sch. for Girls, Elstree, 1986, 1990, 1991, 1992–98: Dir, Curriculum Studies, 1993–98; Dep. Hd, Lower Sch., 1995–98. Tutoring, 1983–91. Inspector, ISI, 2003–08. Member: Primary and Middle Sch. Cttee, Geographical Assoc., 1994–99; IAPS, 2007–. Gov., Northwood Coll., 2010–14. *Publications:* contrib. article and book reviews of geographical books for Primary Geog. mag. *Recreations:* textile art, scrapbooking, choral singing, watching Manchester United, card making, reading, travel. *E:* sue@dunkerley.com.

DUNKLEY, Christopher; freelance journalist and broadcaster; *b* 22 Jan. 1944; 2nd *s* of late Robert Dunkley and Joyce Mary Dunkley (*née* Turner); *m* 1967, Carolyn Elizabeth (marr. diss. 2004), *e d* of Col A. P. C. Lyons; one *s* one *d*. *Educ:* Haberdashers' Aske's (expelled). Various jobs, incl. theatre flyman, cook, hospital porter, 1961–63; general reporter, then cinema and theatre critic, Slough Observer, 1963–65; feature writer and news editor, UK Press Gazette, 1965–68; night news reporter, then mass media correspondent and TV critic, The Times, 1968–73; TV Critic, Financial Times, 1973–2002; feature writer, Daily Mail, 2002–03. Frequent radio broadcaster, 1963–; Presenter, Feedback, Radio 4, 1986–98; occasional television presenter/script writer/chairman. Critic of the Year, British Press Awards, 1976, 1986; Broadcast Journalist of the Year, TV-am Awards, 1989; Best Individual Contrib. to Radio, Voice of the Listener and Viewer Awards, 1998. *Publications:* Television Today and Tomorrow: Wall to Wall Dallas?, 1985. *Recreations:* motorcycling, collecting almost everything, especially dictionaries, tin toys, Victorian boys' books. *Address:* May Villas, 20 Byfield Road, Isleworth, Middx TW7 7AF.

DUNLEATH, 6th Baron *cr* 1892, of Ballywalter, co. Down; **Brian Henry Mulholland;** Bt 1945; DL; *b* 25 Sept. 1950; *o s* of 5th Baron Dunleath and Elizabeth (*d* 1989), twin *d* of Laurence B. Hyde; *S* father, 1997; *m* 1st, 1976, Mary Joan (marr. diss. 2005), *y d* of Major R. J. F. Whistler; two *s* one *d*; 2nd, 2006, Vibeke, *yr d* of late Col Jens Christian Lunn, Denmark. *Educ:* Eton; Royal Agricl Coll. Director: Dunleath Estates Ltd, 1994– (Chm., 1998–); Downpatrick Race Club Ltd, 1999–. DL County Down, 2009. *Recreations:* shooting, fishing, gardening. *Heir: s* Hon. Andrew Henry Mulholland, *b* 15 Dec. 1981. *Address:* (office) The Estate Office, Ballywalter Park, Newtownards, Northern Ireland BT22 2PA. *T:* (028) 4275 8264, *Fax:* (028) 4275 8818; (home) Ballywalter Park, Newtownards, Northern Ireland BT22 2PP. *E:* bd@dunleath-estates.co.uk. *Club:* MCC.

DUNLEAVY, Prof. Patrick John, DPhil; FAcSS; Professor of Political Science and Public Policy (formerly of Government), London School of Economics and Political Science, since 1989; Centenary Research Professor, Institute for Governance and Policy Analysis, University of Canberra, since 2015; *b* 21 June 1952; *s* of Vincent Dunleavy and Kathleen Mary Dunleavy; *m* 1974, Sheila Dorothea Squire; two *s* one *d*. *Educ:* St Mary's Grammar Sch., Sidcup; Corpus Christi Coll., Oxford (MA 1973); Nuffield Coll., Oxford (DPhil 1978). Research Fellow, Nuffield Coll., Oxford, 1976–78; Lectr in Urban Studies, Open Univ., 1978–79; London School of Economics and Political Science: Lectr in Govt, 1979–86; Reader, 1986–89; Chair, Public Policy Gp, 1992–; Dir, MPA Prog., 2003–09. Co-Dir, Democratic Audit UK, 2013–. Mem. Exec., UK Political Studies Assoc., 1980–83, 1993–94 and 1999–2005. Councillor, Bucks CC, 1981–85. Mem., Milton Keynes CHC, 1982–90. FAcSS (AcSS 1999). Special Recognition Award, Pol Studies Assoc., 2013. Founding Editor: Politics, 1980–82; (jtly) Global Policy, 2009–; Editor: Political Studies, 1999–2005; Political Studies Review, 2003–05; mem. editl bd, various jls. *Publications:* Urban Political Analysis, 1980; The Politics of Mass Housing in Britain, 1981; (ed jtly) Developments in British Politics, vol. 1, 1983, vol. 2, 1986, vol. 3, 1990, vol. 4, 1993, vol. 5, 1997, vol. 6, 2000; (with C. T. Husbands) British Democracy at the Crossroads, 1985; Studying for a Degree, 1987; (with B. O'Leary) Theories of the State, 1987; Democracy, Bureaucracy and Public Choice, 1991; (ed with R. A. W. Rhodes) Prime Minister, Cabinet and Core Executive, 1995; (jtly) Making Votes Count, 1997; (with H. Margetts) Government on the Web, 1999; (ed jtly) British Political Science, 2000; (with H. Margetts) Government on the Web 2, 2002; Authoring a PhD, 2002; (with H. Margetts) Difficult Forms, 2003; (jtly) Citizen Redress, 2005; (jtly) Digital-Era Governance, 2006; (jtly) Government on the Internet, 2007; (with J. Dryzek) Theories of the Democratic State, 2009; (with A. White) Making and Breaking Whitehall Departments, 2010; (with L. Carrera) Growing the Productivity of Government Services, 2013; (with S. Bastow and J. Tinkler) The Impact of the Social Sciences, 2014; articles in learned jls. *Recreations:* family, travel, undermining the (old) constitution, advancing social media in academia, Twitter @PJDunleavy and @Write4Research. *Address:* Department of Government, London School of Economics, Houghton Street, WC2A 2AE. *T:* (020) 7955 7178. *E:* p.dunleavy@lse.ac.uk.

DUNLOP, family name of **Baron Dunlop**.

DUNLOP, Baron *cr* 2015 (Life Peer), of Helensburgh in the County of Dunbarton; **Andrew James Dunlop;** Parliamentary Under-Secretary of State, Scotland Office, since 2015; *b* Helensburgh, 21 June 1959; *s* of Robert Jack Dunlop and Dorothy Shirley Dunlop; *m* 1991, Lucia Mary Elizabeth Campbell; three *d*. *Educ:* Trinity Coll., Glenalmond; Glasgow Acad.; Edinburgh Univ. (MA Hons Politics and Modern Hist.); King's Coll., London (Postgrad. Dip. European Competition Law). Midland Bank Internat., 1981–82; Hd of Policy and Res., Scottish Cons. Party, 1982–84; Cons. Res. Dept, 1984–86; Special Advr, Sec. of State for Defence, 1986–88; Prime Minister's Policy Unit, 1988–90; founder and Man. Dir, Politics Internat. Ltd, 1991–2008; Man. Dir, 2008–10, Exec. Chm., 2010–11, Interel Consulting UK; Mem. Mgt Bd, Interel Gp, Brussels, 2008–11; Special Advr to Prime Minister on Scotland and Devolution, 2012–15. Mem. Mgt Cttee, Sussex County, 2009–11, SE Region, 2011–12,

Amateur Swimming Assoc. *Recreations:* swimming, tennis, sailing, gardening, ski-ing, following football. *Address:* House of Lords, SW1A 0PW. *Clubs:* Reform; Atlantis Horsham Swimming (Chm., 2008–12).

DUNLOP, Elizabeth Sarah Ann, (Mrs C. C. H. Dunlop); *see* Craig-McFeely, E. S. A.

DUNLOP, Frank, CBE 1977; theatre director; Director, Edinburgh International Festival, 1983–91; *b* 15 Feb. 1927; *s* of Charles Norman Dunlop and Mary Aaron. *Educ:* Kibworth Beauchamp Grammar Sch.; University Coll., London (Fellow, 1979). BA Hons, English. Postgrad. Sch. in Shakespeare, at Shakespeare Inst., Stratford-upon-Avon; Old Vic Sch., London. Served with RAF before going to University. Director: (own young theatre co.) Piccolo Theatre, Manchester, 1954; Arts Council Midland Theatre Co., 1955; Associate Dir, Bristol Old Vic, 1956; Dir, Théâtre de Poche, Brussels, 1959–60; Founder and Dir, Pop Theatre, 1960; Dir, Nottingham Playhouse, 1961–63; New Nottingham Playhouse, 1963–64; (dir.) The Enchanted, Bristol Old Vic Co., 1955; (wrote and dir.) Les Frères Jaques, Adelphi, 1960; Director: London Première, The Bishop's Bonfire, Mermaid, 1960; Schweyk, Mermaid, 1963; The Taming of the Shrew, Univ. Arts Centre, Oklahoma, 1965; Any Wednesday, Apollo, 1965; Too True to be Good, Edinburgh Fest., also Strand and Garrick, 1965; Saturday Night and Sunday Morning, Prince of Wales, 1966; The Winter's Tale and The Trojan Women, Edin. and Venice Festivals, also Cambridge Theatre, London, 1966; The Burglar, Vaudeville, 1967; Getting Married, Strand, 1967; A Midsummer Night's Dream and The Tricks of Scapin, Edin. Fest. and Saville Theatre, London, 1967; A Sense of Detachment, Royal Court, 1972; Sherlock Holmes, Aldwych, 1974, NY 1974; Habeas Corpus, NY 1975; The New York Idea, The Three Sisters, NY 1977; The Devil's Disciple, LA and NY, 1978; The Play's the Thing, Julius Caesar, NY, 1978; The Last of Mrs Cheyney, USA, 1978; Rookery Nook, Birmingham and Her Majesty's, 1979; Camelot, USA, 1980, London, 1996; Sherlock Holmes, Norwegian Nat. Th., Oslo, 1980; Lolita, NY, 1981; Oberon (Weber), Edinburgh, Frankfurt, 1986 (filmed); L'Elisir d'Amore, Opéra de Lyon, 1992 (filmed 1996); My Fair Lady, European tour, 1994; Carmen, Royal Albert Hall, 1997; Ecole des Femmes, Belgium, 1998; The Invisible Man, USA, 1998–99; Scapino, Tel Aviv, 1999; Napoleon at St Helena, Waterloo, 2000, Monte Carlo, 2001; Turn of the Screw, Belgium, 2001; (adapted and dir.) Address Unknown, NY, 2004; Oscar and the Pink Lady, San Diego, 2007, NY, 2008, 2009; *National Theatre:* Assoc. Dir, 1967–74 and Admin. Dir, 1968–73; productions: *Nat. Theatre:* Edward II (Brecht and Marlowe); Home and Beauty; Macrune's Guevara; The White Devil; Captain of Köpenick; *Young Vic:* Founder, 1969; Mem. Bd, 1969–92; Dir, 1969–78 and 1980–83; Consultant, 1978–80; productions: (author and Dir) Scapino 1970, 1977, NY 1974, LA 1975, Australia 1975, Oslo 1975; The Taming of the Shrew, 1970, 1977; The Comedy of Errors, 1971; The Maids, Deathwatch, 1972; The Alchemist, 1972; Bible One, 1972; French Without Tears, 1973; Joseph and the Amazing Technicolor Dreamcoat (Roundhouse and Albery Theatre), 1973, NY 1976; Much Ado About Nothing, 1973; Macbeth, 1975; Antony and Cleopatra, 1976; King Lear, 1980; Childe Byron, 1981; Masquerade, 1982; *for Théâtre National de Belgique:* Pantagleize, 1970; Antony and Cleopatra, 1971; Pericles, 1972. Mem., Arts Council Young People's Panel, 1968. Governor, Central School of Arts and Crafts, 1970. Hon. Fellow of Shakespeare Inst. Hon. Dr of Theatre, Philadelphia Coll. of Performing Arts, 1978; DUniv Heriot-Watt, 1989; Dr *hc* Edinburgh, 1990. Chevalier, Order of Arts and Literature (France), 1987. *Recreation:* reading and looking. *Address:* c/o J. Nives, Miracle Management, 250 West 57th Street, Suite 1332, New York, NY 10019, USA. *T:* (212) 2658787.

DUNLOP, Very Rev. John, CBE 2004; Minister, Presbyterian Church in Ireland, 1966–2004; *b* 19 Sept. 1939; *s* of Joseph and Annie Dunlop; *m* 1965, Rosemary Willis; one *s* one *d*. *Educ:* QUB (BA); Univ. of Edinburgh (BD). Ordained 1966; Minister: Fitzroy Avenue Presbyterian Ch, Belfast, 1966–68; United Ch of Jamaica and Grand Cayman, 1968–78; Rosemary Presbyterian Ch, Belfast, 1978–2004; Moderator, Gen. Assembly of Presbyterian Ch in Ireland, 1992–93. Hon. DD: Presbyterian Theol Faculty of Ireland, 1992; TCD, 1993; Hon. LLD: Ulster, 2001; QUB, 2001. *Publications:* A Precarious Belonging: Presbyterians and the conflict in Ireland, 1995. *Address:* 98 Whitehouse Park, Newtownabbey BT37 9SH.

DUNLOP, John Leeper, OBE 1996; racehorse trainer, 1965–2012; *b* 10 July 1939; *s* of Dr John Leeper Dunlop, MC, FRCS and Margaret Frances Mary Dunlop; *m* 1965, Susan Jennifer Page; two *s* (and one *s* decd). *Educ:* Marlborough Coll. Royal Ulster Rifles, 1959–61. Leading trainer, 1984; champion trainer, 1995; wins include: Shirley Heights, Derby, 1978; Circus Plume, Oaks, 1984; Salsabil, Oaks, 1990; Erhaab, Derby, 1994; One Thousand Guineas: Quick as Lightning, 1980; Salsabil, 1990; Shadayid, 1991; St Leger: Moon Madness, 1986; Silver Patriarch, 1997; Millenary, 2000. Flat Trainer of the Year, Derby Awards, 1995. *Recreations:* breeding race horses and (formerly) show horses, gardening. *Address:* House on the Hill, Arundel, West Sussex BN18 9LJ. *T:* (01903) 882106. *Club:* Turf.

DUNLOP, Robert Alastair; QC (Scot.) 1990; Sheriff Principal of Tayside Central and Fife, 2000–14; *b* 30 June 1951; *s* of Robert Jack Dunlop and Dorothy Shirley Dixon or Dunlop; *m* 1st, 1975, Jane Christian Rankin (marr. diss. 1998); one *s* two *d*; 2nd, 1999, Evelyn Templeton Mackenzie. *Educ:* Trinity Coll., Glenalmond; Univ. of Dundee (LLB). Admitted solicitor, Scotland, 1976; admitted to Faculty of Advocates and called to Scottish Bar, 1978; Advocate Depute, 1985–88; Standing Jun. Counsel, Dept of Transport, 1988–90; part-time Chairman: Pensions Appeal Tribunal, 1991–2000; Employment Tribunals, 1998–2000; Mem., Scottish Court Service Bd, 2010–. Procurator to Gen. Assembly of Ch of Scotland, 1991–2000. Comr, Northern Lighthouses, 2000– (Chm., 2011–13). *Recreations:* sailing, golf, music, ski-ing. *Address:* 5 Temple Village, Gorebridge, Midlothian EH23 4SQ. *T:* (01875) 830344. *Clubs:* New (Edinburgh); Royal Northern and Clyde Yacht.

DUNLOP, Robert Daubeny, (Robin) B.; *see* Buchanan-Dunlop.

DUNLOP, Roderick William; QC (Scot.) 2010; *b* Glasgow, 10 June 1970; *s* of William Dunlop, *qv*; *m* 2001, Kate Elizabeth Stirling; one *s* one *d*. *Educ:* High Sch. of Glasgow; Univ. of Edinburgh (LLB Hons 1992; DipLP 1993). Admitted Faculty of Advocates, 1998. *Recreations:* Rugby, rock music. *Address:* Advocates Library, Parliament House, Edinburgh EH1 1RF. *T:* (0131) 226 5071. *E:* roddy@parliamenthouse.co.uk.

DUNLOP, Sir Thomas, 4th Bt *cr* 1916, of Woodbourne, co. Renfrew; *b* 22 April 1951; *o s* of Sir Thomas Dunlop, 3rd Bt and of Adda Mary Alison Dunlop (*née* Smith); *S* father, 1999; *m* 1984, Eileen, *er d* of A. H. Stevenson; one *s* one *d*. *Educ:* Rugby; Aberdeen Univ. (BScFor). MICFor. *Heir:* *s* Thomas Dunlop, *b* 11 March 1990. *Address:* Bredon Croft, Bredon's Norton, Tewkesbury, Glos GL20 7HB.

DUNLOP, William; QC (Scot.) 2011; Sheriff of North Strathclyde, 1995–2014; Temporary Judge, Court of Session and High Court, since 2009; *b* 7 March 1944; *s* of William Dunlop and Catherine (*née* McKenzie); *m* 1st, 1968, Katherine Frances Howden (marr. diss. 1976); one *s* one *d*; 2nd, 1979, Janina Marthe Merecki; one *d*. *Educ:* High Sch. of Glasgow; Univ. of Glasgow (LLB 1965). Solicitor in family firm, 1968; called to the Scottish Bar, 1985; in practice at the Bar, 1985–95. Mem. Council, Sheriffs' Assoc., 2001–04. Six Nations Match Comr, 2000–13, Chm., Championship Appeals Panel, 2005–, Scottish Rugby Union. Governor, High Sch. of Glasgow, 1999–2011. *Recreations:* watching Rugby football, playing bad golf, enjoying good food and wine. *Address:* High Court of Justiciary, 1 Mart Street, Glasgow G1 5JT. *Clubs:* Western (Glasgow); Glasgow Golf.

See also R. W. Dunlop.

DUNLOP, Prof. William, CBE 2005; PhD; FRCSE, FRCOG; Professor of Obstetrics and Gynaecology, University of Newcastle upon Tyne, 1982–2006, now Emeritus; President, Royal College of Obstetricians and Gynaecologists, 2001–04; *b* 18 Aug. 1944; *s* of Alexander Morton Dunlop and Annie Denham Rennie (*née* Ingram); *m* 1968, Sylvia Louise Krauthamer; one *s* one *d*. *Educ:* Kilmarnock Acad.; Glasgow Univ. (MB ChB 1967); Univ. of Newcastle upon Tyne (PhD 1982). FRCSE 1971; MRCOG 1971, FRCOG 1984. Various junior posts in obstetrics and gynaecol., Glasgow Univ., 1969–74; seconded as Lectr, Univ. of Nairobi, 1972–73; on MRC scientific staff, 1974–75; University of Newcastle upon Tyne: Sen. Lectr, 1975–82; Hd, Dept of Obstetrics and Gynaecology, 1982–99; Hd, Sch. of Surgical and Reproductive Scis, 1999–2001. Vis. Associate Prof., Medical Univ. of S Carolina, 1980. Royal College of Obstetricians and Gynaecologists: Hon. Sec., 1992–98; Chm., Exam. Cttee, 1990–92; Chm., Specialist Trng Cttee, 1999–2001; Hon. Treasurer: European Bd and Coll. of Obstetrics and Gynaecology, 1999–2005 (Pres., 2005–08); UEMS Sect. of Obstetrics and Gynaecology, 2002–05 (Pres., 2006–10); Chm., UEMS Gp 2 (Surgical) Specialities, 2008–10. Chairman: Professional Adv. Panel, NHS Litigation Authority, 2002–04; Jt Consultants Cttee, 2003–07; Vice-Chairman: Acad. of Medical Royal Colls, 2002–04; Specialist Trng Authority, 2002–04. Chm., Assoc. of Profs of Obstetrics and Gynaecology, 1999–2002. Chm., Blair-Bell Research Soc., 1989–92. Mem. Council, GMC, 2006–08. Chm., Scientific Prog. Cttee, 20th FIGO World Congress of Gynaecology and Obstetrics, 2009–12. Hon. Member: S African Soc. of Obstetricians and Gynaecologists, 2003; Soc. of Obstetricians and Gynaecologists of Canada, 2003; Soc. of Gynaecol. and Obstetrics of Nigeria, 2003; Hon. Fellow: Acad. of Medicine, Singapore, 2002; FFPRHC 2005; Hon. Fellow *qua* Surgeon RCPSG, 2003; FRCP 2003; Hon. FACOG 2003; Hon. FRCPI 2003; Hon. FCPS (Pak) 2004; Hon. FSLCOG 2004. Dr *hc* Athens, 2006. Editor-in-Chief, Fetal and Maternal Medicine Rev., 1989–99. *Publications:* (ed jtly) High Risk Pregnancy, 1992; Recent Advances in Obstetrics and Gynaecology 22, 2003, 23, 2005, 24, 2008. *Recreations:* music, drama, literature. *Address:* 30 Eslington Terrace, Newcastle upon Tyne NE2 4RN. *T:* (0191) 281 4697.

DUNLUCE, Viscount; Randal Alexander St John McDonnell; DL; Partner, Sarasin & Partners (formerly Sarasin Chiswell), since 2008 (Director, 2004–08); *b* 2 July 1967; *o s* and heir of Earl of Antrim, *qv*; *m* 2004, Aurora, *d* of David Gunn; one *s* one *d*. *Educ:* Gresham's Sch., Holt; Worcester Coll., Oxford (MA Hons). Fund Manager: NCL Investments Ltd, 1992–97; Sarasin Investment Mgt Ltd, 1998–2004. Dir, Aberdeen Asian Smaller Companies Investment Trust, 2013–. Director: Game Conservancy Trust, 2003–06; Irish Landmark Trust, 2004–08; Glenarm Bldgs Preservation Trust, 2005–10; Northern Salmon Co., 2006– (Chm., 2009–); Irish Grouse Conservation Trust, 2006–. DL Co. Antrim, 2013. *Heir:* *s* Hon. Alexander David Somerled McDonnell, *b* 30 June 2006. *Address:* Glenarm Castle, Glenarm, Ballymena, Co. Antrim BT44 0AL. *Clubs:* Pratt's, White's.

DUNMORE, 12th Earl of, *cr* 1686 (Scot.); **Malcolm Kenneth Murray;** Viscount of Fincastle, Lord Murray of Blair, Moulin and Tillimet, 1686; Electrical Technical Officer, Air Services Australia, now retired; *b* 17 Sept. 1946; *er s* of 11th Earl of Dunmore and Margaret Joy (*d* 1976), *d* of P. D. Cousins; *S* father, 1995; *m* 1970, Joy Anne, *d* of A. Partridge; one *s* one *d* (both adopted). *Educ:* Launceston Technical High School (Board A Certificate and various tech. qualifs). Patron: Tasmanian Caledonian Council; Launceston Caledonian Soc.; Armorial and Heraldry Soc. of Australasia Inc.; Scottish Australian Heritage Council; Sunnybank Br., RSL; Murray Clan Soc. of NZ; Murray Clan Edinburgh; Co. of Armigers, Australia; Lodge Amalthea No 914, A. F. & A. Masons of Victoria (Master, 2011–13); St Andrew's First Aid Australia, 2009–; Tullibardine Pipe Band NSW, 2010–; Crown Internat. Dance Assoc., 2011–; Patron and Member: St Andrew Soc., Tas; Murray Clan Soc. of Vic and Qld; Co-Patron: Australia Day Council (Victoria) Inc., 2009–. High Comr for Clan Murray in Australia and NZ, 2006–. Past Master, Concord Masonic Lodge, No. 10 Tasmanian Constitution. KStJ 2008. Knight, Imperial and Royal Order of St Stanislaw (Russia), 2012. *Recreations:* flying (retired Tow Master for Soaring Club of Tasmania), astronomy, fly-fishing, music (saxophone and piano). *Heir:* *b* Hon. Geoffrey Charles Murray [*b* 31 July 1949; *m* 1974, Margaret Irene, *d* of H. Bulloch]. *Address:* PO Box 100E, East Devonport, Tas 7310, Australia. *E:* malc5@bigpond.com. *Clubs:* Devonport Fly Fishing, Soaring Club of Tasmania, Burns Club of Launceston (Tasmania).

DUNMORE, Helen, FRSL; poet and novelist; *b* 12 Dec. 1952; *d* of Maurice Dunmore and Betty (*née* Smith); *m* 1980, Francis Charnley; one *s* one *d* and one step *s*. *Educ:* Univ. of York (BA Hons). FRSL 1997. Hon. DLitt: Glamorgan, 1998; Exeter, 2001. *Publications: poetry:* The Apple Fall, 1983; The Sea Skater, 1986 (Alice Hunt Bartlett Prize, Poetry Soc., 1987); The Raw Garden, 1988; Short Days, Long Nights: new and selected poems, 1991; Recovering a Body, 1994; Bestiary, 1997; Out of the Blue: new and selected poems, 2001; Glad of These Times, 2007; The Malarkey, 2012; *fiction:* Zennor in Darkness, 1993 (McKitterick Prize, Soc. of Authors, 1994); Burning Bright, 1994; A Spell of Winter, 1995 (Orange Prize for Fiction, 1996); Talking to the Dead, 1996; Love of Fat Men, 1997; Your Blue-eyed Boy, 1998; With Your Crooked Heart, 1999; Ice Cream, 2000 (short stories); The Siege, 2001; Mourning Ruby, 2003; Rose, 1944 (short stories), 2005; House of Orphans, 2006; Counting the Stars, 2008; The Betrayal, 2010; The Greatcoat, 2012; The Lie, 2014; *for children:* Going to Egypt, 1994; Secrets (Signal Poetry for Children Award), 1994; In the Money, 1995; Amina's Blanket, 1996; Go Fox, 1996; Fatal Error, 1996; Allie's Apples, 1997; Great-grandma's Dancing Dress, 1998; Clyde's Leopard, 1998; Brother Brother, Sister Sister, 1999; Allie's Rabbit, 1999; Zillah and Me, 2000; The Zillah Rebellion, 2001; Snollygoster, 2001; Ingo, 2005; The Tide Knot, 2006; The Deep, 2007; The Crossing of Ingo, 2008; The Ferry Birds, 2010; The Islanders, 2011; Stormswept, 2012. *Address:* A. P. Watt at United Agents, 12–26 Lexington Street, W1F 0LE. *T:* (020) 3214 0800. *W:* www.helendunmore.com.

DUNMORE, Stephen Lloyd, OBE 2011; Interim Chief Executive, Family and Childcare Trust, since 2015; *b* 4 Dec. 1948; *s* of Leslie Alfred Dunmore and Josephine Mary Dunmore (*née* Bettles); *m* 1987, Isabel Mary Robertson; one *d*. *Educ:* Kettering Grammar Sch.; King's Coll. London (BA Hons Hist.). Urban Archaeol Officer, Ipswich BC, 1974–76; Department of the Environment: Inspector of Ancient Monuments, 1976–84; Principal, Housing, Construction Industry, Inner Cities, 1984–90; on secondment as Actg Chief Exec., Liverpool HAT, 1990–91; Principal, Citizen's Charter Unit, Cabinet Office, 1991; Regl Controller, Urban and Economic Affairs, Merseyside Task Force, 1991–94; Dir, Regeneration, Transport and Planning, Govt Office for Merseyside, 1994–98; Chief Executive: New Opportunities Fund, 1998–2004; Community Fund, 2003–04; Big Lottery Fund, 2004–08; Interim Chief Executive: Responsible Gambling Fund and Responsible Gambling Strategy Bd, 2009–10; Diana, Princess of Wales Meml Fund, 2009 and 2011; Lumos, 2010–11; Chm., Capacitybuilders, 2009–11 (non-exec. Dir, 2008–09); Interim Dir, Transition, Consumer Focus, 2012–13; Chief Exec., Consumer Focus, 2014. Mem., Adv. Body, Office for Civil Society (formerly Office of the Third Sector), 2008–11. Chairman: Nat. Family Mediation, 2007–11; BBC Charity Appeals Adv. Cttee, 2008–13. Trustee, The Prince's Countryside Fund, 2010–. *Recreations:* cricket, books, walking, theatre. *Address:* 37 Pages Hill, N10 1EH. *T:* (020) 8883 3905.

DUNN, Baroness *cr* 1990 (Life Peer), of Hong Kong Island in Hong Kong and of Knightsbridge in the Royal Borough of Kensington and Chelsea; **Lydia Selina Dunn,** DBE 1989 (CBE 1983; OBE 1978); Executive Director, John Swire & Sons Ltd, since 1996; *b* 29 Feb. 1940; *d* of Yencheun Yeh Dunn and Chen Yin Chu; *m* 1988, Michael David Thomas, *qv*. *Educ:* St Paul's Convent Sch., Hong Kong; Univ. of Calif, Berkeley. MLC, Hong Kong, 1976–88 (Sen. Mem., 1985–88); MEC, 1982–95 (Sen. Mem., 1988–95). Director: John Swire & Sons

(HK) Ltd, 1978–2003; Swire Pacific Ltd, 1981–2015; Hongkong and Shanghai Banking Corp., 1981–96 (Dep. Chm., 1992–96); HSBC Hldgs plc, 1990–2008 (Dep. Chm., 1992–2008); Volvo AB, 1991–93 (Mem. Internat. Adv. Bd, 1985–91); Christie's Internat. plc, 1996–98; Christie's Fine Art Ltd, 1998–2000; Marconi (formerly GEC) plc, 1997–2002; Advr to Bd, Cathay Pacific Airways Ltd, 1997–2002 (Dir, 1985–97); Mem., Adv. Bd, Christie's Greater China, 2009–. Chairman: Hong Kong/Japan Business Co-operation Cttee, 1988–95 (Mem., 1983–88); Hong Kong Trade Develt Council, 1983–91; Mem., Hong Kong/US Econ. Co-op. Cttee, 1984–93. Mem., Adv. Council, Confucius Inst. for Business, 2006–. Chm., Lord Wilson Heritage Trust, 1993–95; Pres., Hong Kong LEP Trust, 1993–. Mem., H of L, 1990–2010. Hon. Fellow, London Business Sch., 2000. Hon. LLD: Chinese Univ. of Hong Kong, 1984; Univ. of Hong Kong, 1991; Univ. of British Columbia, 1991; Leeds Univ., 1994; Hon. DSc Univ. of Buckingham, 1995. Prime Minister of Japan's Trade Award, 1987; USA Sec. of Commerce's To Peace and Commerce Award, 1988. *Publications:* In the Kingdom of the Blind, 1983. *Recreations:* art and antiquities, music, ballet, opera. *Address:* John Swire & Sons Ltd, Swire House, 59 Buckingham Gate, SW1E 6AJ.

DUNN, Anderson; Assistant Commissioner, Metropolitan Police, 1994–2001; *b* 6 May 1944; adopted *s* of William Rennie and Wilma Rennie (*née* Turner); *m* 1967, Margaret Docherty; one *s* one *d*. *Educ:* Queen Mary Coll., London (LLB Hons; Hon. Fellow, QMW, 1998). Joined Metropolitan Police, 1963; transf. to Thames Valley Police as Chief Supt, 1987; Asst Chief Constable, Operations, 1988–93; Dep. Chief Constable, Northants, 1993–94. Former Mem. Bd, Northants Probation Service. *Recreations:* walking, reading, most sports.

DUNN, David Hedley; HM Diplomatic Service, retired; Director, New Business, Policy and External Affairs, Arwon Capital, since 2012; *b* 21 Sept. 1968; *s* of Francis Hedley Dunn and Jean Mary Dunn (*née* Osborne). *Educ:* Penrice Comp. Sch.; St Austell Coll. Joined HM Diplomatic Service, 1991; Political Attaché: Oslo, 1992–94; Suva, 1996–97; Third, later Second, Sec., NY, 1997–98; on secondment to UN, 1998–2000; First Sec., Stockholm, 2000–01; Private Sec. to the Minister for Europe, FCO, 2001–03; Dep. High Comr, Freetown, 2004–06; High Comr, Papua New Guinea, 2007–10; Counsellor (Political), FCO, 2011–12. *Recreations:* Cornish Rugby Union, squash, running, euchre, sea fishing. *E:* daviddunn10000@gmail.com.

DUNN, Prof. Douglas Eaglesham, OBE 2003; FRSL; poet and short-story writer; Professor of English, 1991–2008, now Emeritus, and Director, St Andrews Scottish Studies Institute, 1992–2008, St Andrews University; *b* 23 Oct. 1942; *s* of William Douglas Dunn and Margaret McGowan; *m* 1st, 1964, Lesley Balfour Wallace (*d* 1981); 2nd, 1985, Lesley Jane Bathgate; one *s* one *d*. *Educ:* Univ. of Hull (BA). Became full-time writer, 1971. St Andrews University: Fellow in Creative Writing, 1989–91; Hd, Sch. of English, 1994–99. Hon. Vis. Prof., Dundee Univ., 1987–89. Mem., Scottish Arts Council, 1992–94. FRSL 1981. Hon. Fellow, Humberside Coll., 1987. Hon. LLD Dundee, 1987; Hon. DLitt Hull, 1995. Cholmondeley Award, 1989; Queen's Gold Medal for Poetry, 2013. *Publications:* Terry Street, 1969 (Somerset Maugham Award, 1972); The Happier Life, 1972; (ed) New Poems, 1972–73, 1973; Love or Nothing, 1974 (Geoffrey Faber Meml Prize, 1976); (ed) A Choice of Byron's Verse, 1974; (ed) Two Decades of Irish Writing, 1975 (criticism); (ed) The Poetry of Scotland, 1979; Barbarians, 1979; St Kilda's Parliament, 1981 (Hawthornden Prize, 1982); Europa's Lover, 1982; (ed) A Rumoured City: new poets from Hull, 1982; (ed) To Build a Bridge: celebration of Humberside in verse, 1982; Elegies, 1985 (Whitbread Poetry Prize, 1985; Whitbread Book of the Year Award, 1986); Secret Villages, 1985 (short stories); Selected Poems 1964–1983, 1986; Northlight, 1988 (poetry); New and Selected Poems 1966–1988, 1989; Andromache, 1990; (ed) The Essential Browning, 1990; (ed) Scotland: an anthology, 1991; (ed) Faber Book of 20th Century Scottish Poetry, 1992; Dante's Drum-Kit, 1993; Boyfriends and Girlfriends, 1995 (short stories); Oxford Book of Scottish Short Stories, 1995; The Donkey's Ears, 2000 (poetry); The Year's Afternoon, 2000 (poetry); New Selected Poems, 2003; contrib. to Counterblast pamphlet series, Glasgow Herald, New Yorker, TLS, etc. *Recreations:* playing the clarinet and saxophone, listening to jazz music, philately, gardening. *Address:* School of English, St Andrews University, St Andrews, Fife KY16 9AL.

DUNN, Hubert; *see* Dunn, His Honour W. H.

DUNN, Inga Margaret Amy; *see* Grimsey, I. M. A.

DUNN, Prof. James Douglas Grant, PhD, DD; FBA 2006; Lightfoot Professor of Divinity, University of Durham, 1990–2003, now Professor Emeritus; *b* 21 Oct. 1939; *s* of David and Agnes Dunn; *m* 1963, Meta Russell; one *s* two *d*. *Educ:* Hutchesons' Boys' Grammar Sch., Glasgow; Univ. of Glasgow (MA 1961, BD 1964); Clare Coll., Cambridge (PhD 1968; BD 1976; DD 1991). Chaplain to Overseas Students, Edinburgh, 1968–70; Lectr, 1970–79, Reader, 1979–82, Univ. of Nottingham; Prof. of Divinity, 1982–90, Chm., Dept of Theol., 1984–86 and 1996–99, Univ. of Durham. Sir Derman Christopherson Foundn Fellow, 1999–2000. Numerous invited (named) and vis. lectureships. Ed., New Testament Theol. series (16 vols), 1991–2003. Pres., UK New Testament Conf., 1980–82 and 1992–96. Founder and Chm., Assoc. of Univ. Depts of Theol. and Religious Studies, 1985–92. Vice-Pres. Council, St John's Coll., Durham, 1995–2005 (Hon. Life Fellow, 2007). Pres., SNTS, 2002–03. *Publications:* Baptism in the Holy Spirit, 1970 (trans. Spanish 1977), 2nd edn 2010; Jesus and the Spirit, 1975 (trans. Spanish 1981); Unity and Diversity in the New Testament, 1977, 3rd edn 2006 (trans. Russian 1997, 2009); Christology in the Making, 1980, 2nd rev. edn 1989; The Evidence for Jesus, 1985 (trans. Dutch 1987); The Living Word, 1987, 2nd edn 2009; (with J. P. Mackey) New Testament Theology in Dialogue, 1987; Word Biblical Commentary, Vol. 38, Romans, 2 vols, 1988; Jesus, Paul and the Law, 1990; The Partings of the Ways between Christianity and Judaism and their Significance for the Character of Christianity, 1991, 2nd edn 2006 (trans. Chinese 2014); Jesus' Call to Discipleship, 1992 (Japanese edn 1996, Spanish edn 2001); Christian Liberty, 1993; A Commentary on the Epistle to the Galatians, 1993 (Japanese edn 1998); (with A. M. Suggate) The Justice of God, 1993; Epistles to the Colossians and to Philemon, 1996; The Acts of the Apostles, 1996; The Theology of Paul the Apostle, 1998 (trans. Italian 1999, Korean edn 2003); Christianity in the Making, Vol. 1: Jesus Remembered, 2003 (trans. Italian 2006, Spanish 2009, Korean 2010); (ed) The Cambridge Companion to St Paul, 2003; (Gen. Ed.) Eerdmans Commentary on the Bible, 2003; A New Perspective on Jesus, 2005 (trans. Spanish 2006, Chinese 2007, Russian 2009, Korean 2010, Italian 2011, Portuguese 2013); The New Perspective on Paul: collected essays, 2005, rev. edn 2008 (Portuguese edn 2011, Italian edn 2014); (ed with S. McKnight) The Historical Jesus in Recent Research, 2005; Christianity in the Making, Vol. 2: Beginning from Jerusalem, 2009 (trans. Spanish 2012, Italian 2012); New Testament Theology: an introduction, 2009 (Chinese edn 2012); Did the First Christians Worship Jesus?, 2010 (Spanish edn 2011); Jesus, Paul and the Gospels, 2011 (Italian edn 2012, Spanish and Hungarian edns 2014); The Oral Gospel Tradition, 2013; contrib. numerous articles to jls, Festschriften, symposia and dictionaries. *Recreations:* choral singing, local preaching, fell walking, writing and reading, sudoku, visiting new places, checking out The Good Pub Guide. *Address:* 65 Maplehurst Road, Chichester, W Sussex PO19 6RP. *T:* (01243) 527857. *E:* j.d.g.dunn@btopenworld.com.

DUNN, Prof. John Montfort, FBA 1989; Professor of Political Theory, University of Cambridge, 1987–2007, now Emeritus; Fellow of King's College, Cambridge, since 1966; *b* 9 Sept. 1940; *s* of Col. Henry George Montfort Dunn and Catherine Mary Dunn; *m* 1st, 1965, Susan Deborah Fyvel (marr. diss. 1971); 2nd, 1973, Judith Frances Bernal (*see* J. F. Dunn) (marr. diss. 1987); one *s* (and one *s* decd) by Prof. Heather Joan Glen; 3rd, 1997, Ruth Ginette Scurr (marr. diss. 2013); two *d*. *Educ:* Winchester Coll.; King's Coll., Cambridge (BA 1962). Harkness Fellow, Graduate Sch. of Arts and Sciences, Harvard Univ., 1964–65; Official Fellow in History, Jesus Coll., Cambridge, 1965–66; Dir of Studies in History, King's Coll., Cambridge, 1966–72; Lectr in Pol Science, 1972–77, Reader in Politics, 1977–87, Cambridge Univ. Vis. Lectr, Dept of Pol Science, Univ. of Ghana, 1968–69; Visiting Professor: Dept of Civics and Politics, Univ. of Bombay, 1979–80; Faculty of Law, Tokyo Metropolitan Univ., 1983–84; Chiba Univ., Japan, 2007–09; Distinguished Vis. Prof., Murphy Inst. of Pol Economy, Tulane Univ., New Orleans, 1986; Benjamin Evans Lippincott Dist. Prof., Minnesota Univ., 1990; Olmsted Vis. Prof., 1991, Leitner Vis. Prof. in Political Sci. and Internat. Affairs, 2008, Henry L. Stimson Lectr and Vis. Prof., 2011, Yale Univ. Foreign Hon. Mem., Amer. Acad. of Arts and Scis, 1991. Mem., Bd of Consultants, Kim Dae-Jung Peace Foundn for the Asia-Pacific Region, 1994–. Mem. Council, British Acad., 2004–07. FAcSS (AcSS 2009). FRSA 1993. Sir Isaiah Berlin Prize, British Political Studies Assoc., 2007. *Publications:* The Political Thought of John Locke, 1969; Modern Revolutions, 1972; Dependence and Opportunity: political change in Ahafo, 1973; (ed) West African States: failure and promise, 1978; Western Political Theory in the Face of the Future, 1979; Political Obligation in its Historical Context, 1980; Locke, 1984, rev. edn as Locke: A Very Short Introduction, 2003; The Politics of Socialism, 1984; Rethinking Modern Political Theory, 1985; (ed) The Economic Limits to Modern Politics, 1989; (ed) Contemporary West African States, 1989; Interpreting Political Responsibility, 1990; (ed) Democracy: the unfinished journey, 1992; Contemporary Crisis of the Nation State?, 1995; The History of Political Theory, 1995; (ed with Ian Harris) Great Political Thinkers, 20 vols, 1997; The Cunning of Unreason: making sense of politics, 2000; Pensare la politica, 2002; Setting the People Free: the story of democracy, 2005; (jtly) Exploring Utopian Futures of Politics, 2008; Breaking Democracy's Spell, 2014. *Address:* King's College, Cambridge CB2 1ST. *T:* (01223) 529223.

DUNN, Prof. Judith Frances, PhD; FBA 1996; FMedSci; Research Professor, Social, Genetic and Developmental Psychiatry Research Centre, Institute of Psychiatry, Psychology and Neuroscience (formerly Institute of Psychiatry), King's College London, since 1995; *d* of James Pace and Jean Stewart; *m* 1st, 1961, Martin Gardiner Bernal (marr. diss.); 2nd, 1973, John Montfort Dunn, *qv* (marr. diss. 1987); 3rd, 1987, Robert Plomin, *qv*. *Educ:* New Hall, Cambridge (BA 1962; MA 1968); King's Coll., Cambridge (PhD 1982). MRC Develt and Integration of Behaviour Unit, and Fellow, King's Coll., Cambridge, 1978–86; Evan Pugh Professor of Human Develt, Pennsylvania State Univ., 1986–95. FMedSci 2000. *Publications:* (jtly) First Year of Life: psychological and medical implications of early experience, 1979; (jtly) Siblings: love, envy and understanding, 1982; Sisters and Brothers, 1984; (ed with R. Plomin) Study of Temperament: changes, continuities and challenges, 1986; Beginnings of Social Understanding, 1988; (jtly) Separate Lives, 1990; (ed jtly) Children's Sibling Relationships, 1992; Young Children's Close Relationships, 1993; (ed jtly) Stepfamilies, 1994; (ed) Connections between Emotion and Understanding in Development, 1995; From One Child to Two, 1995; Children's Friendships, 2004; (ed with R. Layard) A Good Childhood, 2009. *Address:* Social, Genetic and Developmental Psychiatry Research Centre, Institute of Psychiatry, Psychology and Neuroscience, King's College London, De Crespigny Park, Denmark Hill, SE5 8AF.

DUNN, Martin; Founder and Chief Executive Officer, StreetSmartVideo.com, since 2011; *b* 26 Jan. 1955. *Educ:* Dudley Grammar Sch., Worcs. Dudley Herald, 1974–77; Birmingham Evening Mail, 1977; Birmingham Post, 1978; Daily Mail, 1978–79; freelance journalist, 1979–83; New York Correspondent, The Sun, 1983–84; The Sun, London, 1984–88; Deputy Editor: News of the World, 1988–89; The Sun, 1989–91; Editor: Today, 1991–93; The Boston Herald, 1993; Editor-in-Chief, The New York Daily News, 1993–96; Editor, Channel One Television, 1996–98; Managing Director: DMG New Media, 1998–2000; DMG Front of Mind Ltd, 2000–03. *Recreations:* running, golf.

DUNN, Nicola Ann, (Nicky); Managing Director, IMD Group, since 2011; Director, London Legacy Development Corporation, since 2012; *b* Liverpool, 23 Jan. 1957; *d* of William Scott Dunn and Joan Phyllis Dunn. *Educ:* Fareham Girls' Grammar Sch.; Dorset House Coll., Oxford. Occupational therapist: Knowle Hosp., 1978–79; Torrance Meml Hosp., Calif, 1979–82; London Hosp., 1982–84; Founder and Owner, Yard Fitness Centre, 1984–88; London Arena: Event Coordinator, 1988–90; Ops Dir, 1990–91; Arena Dir, 1991–94; Commercial Dir, 1994–2000; Chief Exec., Odyssey Arena, Belfast, 2000–10. Member, Board: Ticket ABC, 2013–; E20 Stadium LLP, 2013–. Chair, Titanic Foundn, 2012–; Mem. Bd, Princes Trust (NI), 2007–11; Trustee, Lyric Th., Belfast, 2009–. *Recreations:* running, yoga, gardening, friends, nieces, walking Sprout the dog. *Address:* 5 Fairlawn Grove, W4 5EL. *E:* enquiries@imdgroup.co.uk. *Club:* Soho House.

DUNN, Most Rev. Patrick James; *see* Auckland (NZ), Bishop of, (RC).

DUNN, Rosamund Mary; Chief Executive, Thames Gateway London Partnership, 2008–12; *b* 10 June 1952; *d* of Stelio Democratis and Grace Matchette; *m* 1st, 1975, Patrick Dunn (marr. diss. 2007); three *d*; 2nd, 2008, David Simon Lunts. *Educ:* Univ. of Hull (BA Hons Philosophy). HM Treasury: Head: Resource Accounting and Budgeting Team, 1995–2000; Devolved Countries and Regions Team, 2000–04; Dir, Strategy and Corporate Planning, London Develt Agency, 2004–06; Department for Communities and Local Government: Dir, Thames Gateway Strategy, 2006; Dir, Local Develt and Renewal, 2007–08; Mem., Homes and Communities Agency Set Up Team, 2008. Chair, S Kilburn Neighbourhood Trust, 2012–. *Recreations:* theatre, cinema, socialising, holidays in (mainly) France. *Address:* Flat 20, The Old Fire Station, 46 Renfrew Road, SE11 4NA. *E:* ros.dunn@lundunn.com.

DUNN, Shona Hunter; Director General, Education Standards, Department for Education, since 2013; *b* Catterick, 15 Oct. 1969; *d* of William James and Patricia Nielson Dunn; *m* 2009, Simon Gerald Lamb; two *s* one *d*. *Educ:* Birmingham Univ. (BSc Biol.); Durham Univ. (MSc Ecol.). Policy advr, DoE, 1995–98; Asst Private Sec. to Dep. Prime Minister, DETR, 1998–2000; Head: Internat. and Central Policy, ODPM, 2002–04; of Policy, Westminster CC, 2005–06 (on secondment); Department for Communities and Local Government: Dep. Dir, Sustainable Buildings, 2007–08; Dir, Fire and Resilience, 2008–11; Dir, Planning, 2011–13. Dir, Skills for Justice, 2009–11. *Recreations:* travel, reading, music (listening and playing), spending time with friends and family. *Address:* Department for Education, Sanctuary Buildings, 20 Great Smith Street, SW1P 3BT. *T:* 0370 000 2288. *E:* shona.dunn@education.gsi.gov.uk.

DUNN, William Francis N.; *see* Newton Dunn.

DUNN, His Honour (William) Hubert; QC 1982; a Circuit Judge, 1993–2005, a Senior Circuit Judge, 1998–2005; Chief Immigration Adjudicator, 1998–2001; *b* 8 July 1933; *s* of William Patrick Millar Dunn and Isabel (*née* Thompson); *m* 1971, Maria Henriqueta Theresa d'Arouje Perestrello de Moser; one *s* one *d*. *Educ:* Rockport, Co. Down, N Ireland; Winchester Coll.; New Coll., Oxford (Hons degree PPE) (Half-Blue fencing 1954–55). 2nd Lieut, Life Guards, 1956–57; Household Cavalry Reserve of Officers, 1957–64. Cholmondeley Scholar, Lincoln's Inn, 1958, called to Bar, 1958; Bencher, Lincoln's Inn, 1990. A Recorder, 1980–93. Fellow, Soc. for Advanced Legal Studies, 1998. *Recreations:* travel, literature. *Address:* 207 Ashley Gardens, Emery Hill Street, SW1P 1PA. *Club:* Boodle's.

DUNNE, Very Rev. Dermot Patrick Martin; Dean of Christ Church Cathedral, Dublin, since 2008; *b* Portarlington, Co. Laois, 25 March 1959; *s* of late Michael Dunne and of Brigid Dunne (*née* Whelan); *m* 1996, Celia Dorothy, *d* of late James Burl and Dorothy Burl (*née* Smith). *Educ:* Pontifical Univ., Maynooth (Dip. Phil. 1980; DipTh 1983); Church of Ireland

Theol Coll.; Chiron Centre for Integrative Psychotherapy (Cert. Psychotherapy 1995); Dublin City Univ. (BA 2004; MA 2014). Ordained deacon, 1983, priest, 1984, Church of Ireland priest, 1998; various posts in RC Church, 1983–95; Dean's Vicar, Christ Church Cathedral, Dublin, 1999–2001; Rector, Crosspatrick Gp of Parishes, Dio. of Ferns, 2001–08; Precentor, Ferns Cathedral, 2004–08; Archdeacon of Ferns, 2007–08. Warden, Cashel and Ossory Guild of Lay Readers, 2007–. *Address:* The Deanery, Werburgh Street, Dublin 8, Ireland. *T:* (office) (1) 6778099, *Fax:* (office) (1) 6798991. *E:* dean@christchurch.ie.

DUNNE, Sir Martin, KCVO 2013; Lord-Lieutenant of Warwickshire, 1997–2013; *b* 30 March 1938; *s* of Philip Dunne, MC and Margaret Dunne (*née* Walker); *m* 1964, Alicia Juliet Barclay; three *d. Educ:* Eton; Christ Church, Oxford. High Sheriff, 1982–83, JP 1984, DL 1993, Warwicks.
See also Sir T. R. Dunne.

DUNNE, Nicholas Cosmo Edward; Executive Chairman, G. Heywood Hill Ltd, since 2011; *b* Oxford, 21 June 1970; *s* of Sir Thomas (Raymond) Dunne, *qv*; *m* 2003, Lady Jasmine Cavendish, *d* of Duke of Devonshire, *qv*; three *s. Educ:* Eton Coll.; Univ. of Manchester (BSocSci 1992). Shipbroker, Clarkson, 1993–96; Consultant, Batey Burn, 1996–97; Asst, Enigma Productions, 2002–03; Communications Consultant, Quiller Consultants, 2003–11. Non-exec. Dir, G. Heywood Hill Ltd, 2003–11. *Recreations:* old books, new music. *Address:* G. Heywood Hill Ltd, 10 Curzon Street, W1J 5HH. *T:* (020) 7493 3742. *E:* enquiries@heywoodhill.com. *Club:* Pratt's.

DUNNE, Philip Martin; MP (C) Ludlow, since 2005; Minister of State, Ministry of Defence, since 2015; *b* 14 Aug. 1958; *s* of Sir Thomas Raymond Dunne, *qv*; *m* 1989, Domenica Margaret Anne Fraser; two *s* two *d. Educ:* Eton Coll.; Keble Coll., Oxford (BA 1980; MA 2006). S. G. Warburg & Co. Ltd, 1980–88; Dir, Corp. Develt, James Gulliver Associates, 1988–90; Partner, Phoenix Securities, 1991–97; a Man. Dir, Donaldson, Lufkin & Jenrette, 1997–2001; Dir, Business Develt, 2002–05, non-exec. Dir, 2006–09, Ruffer LLP. Co-founder, Dir, 1987–97, non-exec. Chm., 1997–2006, Ottakar's plc; non-exec. Chm., Baronsmead VCT 4 plc, 2001–10. Partner, Gatley Farms, 1987–. Mem. (C), S Shropshire DC, 2001–07. Asst Opposition Whip, 2008–10; Asst Govt Whip, 2010–12; Parly Under-Sec. of State, MoD, 2012–15. Member: Work and Pensions Select Cttee, 2005–06; Public Accounts Cttee, 2006–08; Treasury Select Cttee, 2007–08. Dep. Chm., Internat. Office, Cons. Party, 2008–10; Gov. (C) Westminster Foundn for Democracy, 2008–10. Dir, Juvenile Diabetes Res. Foundn, 1999–2005. *Address:* (office) 54 Broad Street, Ludlow, Shropshire SY8 1GP; House of Commons, SW1A 0AA.
See also N. C. E. Dunne.

DUNNE, Sir Thomas (Raymond), KG 2008; KCVO 1995; JP; Lord-Lieutenant for Herefordshire, 1998–2008, and for Worcestershire, 1998–2001 (Lord-Lieutenant, County of Hereford and Worcester, 1977–98); *b* 24 Oct. 1933; *s* of Philip Dunne, MC, and Margaret Walker; *m* 1957, Henrietta Crawley; two *s* two *d. Educ:* Eton; RMA Sandhurst. Served Army, 1951–59: Royal Horse Guards. Herefordshire CC, 1962–68. President: 3 Counties Agric. Soc., 1977; W Midlands TA Assoc., 1988–98; National Vice Pres., Royal British Legion, 1982–89. Mem., West Mercia Police Authy, 1980–99; Dir, West Regional Bd, Central TV, 1981–92. Chm., Lord-Lieutenants' Assoc., 2001–08. Chm., Hereford Cathedral Council, 2001–. Trustee: Dyson Perrins Mus. Trust, 1980–; Worcester Mus. of Porcelain, 1980–2007 (Chm., 1984–2000). Hon. Colonel: 4th Worcester and Sherwood Foresters (formerly 2nd Mercian Volunteers), 1987–93; 5th Bn LI, 1993–98. High Sheriff 1970, DL 1973, Herefordshire; JP Hereford and Worcester, 1977. Hon. Fellow, Univ. of Worcester, 2008. KStJ 1978. *E:* goathollow@trippleton.com.
See also Sir M. Dunne, N. C. E. Dunne, P. M. Dunne.

DUNNELL, Dame Karen (Hope), DCB 2009; National Statistician and Chief Executive, Office for National Statistics, 2005–09; *b* 16 June 1946; *d* of Richard Henry Williamson and Winifred May Beeching; *m* 1st, 1969, Keith Malvern Dunnell (marr. diss. 1976); 2nd, 1979, Prof. Michael William Adler, *qv* (marr. diss. 1994); two *d. Educ:* Bedford Coll., London (BSc Sociology 1967); MA Oxon, 1987. Res. Officer, Inst. of Community Studies, 1967–71; Lectr, St Thomas's Hosp. Med. Sch., 1971–74; Office of Population Censuses and Surveys, then Office for National Statistics, 1974–2009: Dep. Dir, 2000–02, Actg Dir, 2001–02, of Social Stats; Exec. Dir of Surveys and Admin. Sources, 2002–05; Registrar Gen. for England and Wales, 2005–08. Non-exec. Mem., Public Interest Body, PricewaterhouseCoopers, 2010–. Vis. Fellow, Nuffield Coll., Oxford, 1987–95 and 2008–; Vis. Prof., LSHTM, 1999–. Trustee, Nat. Heart Forum, 2009–14. Gov., Univ. of Westminster, 2012–. *Publications:* (with Ann Cartwright) Medicine Takers, Prescribers and Hoarders, 1972; Family Formation 1976, 1979; Nurses Working in the Community, 1982. *Recreations:* yoga, reading modern novels and biography, small house in South of France. *Address:* 53 Woodsome Road, NW5 1SA. *E:* karen.dunnell@btinternet.com.

DUNNETT, Anthony Gordon, CBE 2004; President: International Health Partners (UK) Ltd, since 2004; International Health Partners Inc., since 2009 (Director, since 2007); Chairman, Esteem Resource Network, 2012–14 (Member of Board, since 2011); *b* 17 June 1953; *s* of Peter Sydney Dunnett and Margaret Eileen (*née* Johnson); *m* 1975, Ruth Elizabeth Barker; one *s* two *d. Educ:* St Dunstan's Coll.; McGill Univ. (BComm, DipCS); Exeter Univ. (MA Econs). FCIB 1981. Nat. Westminster Bank, 1975–77; Royal Bank of Canada, Montreal, 1977–80 and 1982–86, Curaçao, 1980–82; Midland Bank: Corporate Banking Dir, 1986–88; Corporate Banking Dir, Samuel Montagu, 1988–89; Corporate Dir, 1990–91; Finance Dir, Corporate and Instnl Banking, 1991–94; Dir, Industrial Develt Unit, DTI, 1994–96; Chief Executive: English Partnerships, 1996–98; SEEDA, 1999–2003. Chm., Two-Five-Four-0 LLP, 2004–07. Member: Steering Bd, Insolvency Service, 1994–96; Urban Task Force, 1998–2005; Adv. Bd, Relationships Foundn, 2000–09; Bd, Berks Learning and Skills Council, 2001–05. Director: Countryside Maritime, 1997–2004; Citylife Ltd, 2001–06; Mem. Bd of Trustees and Mems, Internat. Health Partners (UK) Ltd, 2004–; Member, Board: Health Partners Internat. of Canada, 2010–; Mercy Ships, 2012–. Mem., Mgt Bd, Kingsmead Homes, 1997–99. Mem., Wadhurst Parish Council, 2012– (Chm., Highways, Transport and Lighting Cttee). Mem., PCC for St Peter and St Paul's Ch, Wadhurst, 1990–. FRSA 1997; MInstD 1999. Hon. FRCOG 2012. *Recreations:* local church, gardening, theatre, opera, sports. *Address:* The Fold, Beech Hill, Wadhurst, E Sussex TN5 6JR. *T:* (01483) 484118, *Fax:* (01483) 484696.

DUNNETT, Denzil Inglis, CMG 1967; OBE 1962; HM Diplomatic Service, retired; *b* 21 Oct. 1917; *s* of late Sir James Dunnett, KCIE and late Annie (*née* Sangster); *m* 1946, Ruth Rawcliffe (*d* 1974); two *s* (one *d* decd). *Educ:* Edinburgh Acad.; Corpus Christi Coll., Oxford. Served with RA, 1939–45. Diplomatic Service: Foreign Office, 1947–48; Sofia, 1948–50; Foreign Office, 1950–53; UK Delegn to OEEC, Paris, 1953–56; Commercial Sec., Buenos Aires, 1956–60; Consul, Elisabethville, 1961–62; Commercial Counsellor, Madrid, 1962–67; seconded to BoT, 1967–70; Counsellor, Mexico City, 1970–73; Ambassador to Senegal, Mauritania, Mali and Guinea, 1973–76, and to Guinea-Bissau, 1975–76; Diplomatic Service Chm., CS Selection Bd, 1976–77. London Rep., Scottish Develt Agency, 1978–82. *Publications:* Bird Poems, 1989; The Weight of Shadows: poems descriptive and religious, 2001; Wounds (poems), 2007. *Recreations:* chess, music. *Address:* St Wilfrid's, 29 Tite Street, SW3 4JX.

DUNNETT, Maj. Graham Thomas, TD 1964; JP; Lord-Lieutenant of Caithness, 1995–2004; *b* 8 March 1929; *s* of late Daniel Dunnett and Elizabeth E. Macadie, Wick; *m* 1963, Catherine Elizabeth Sinclair, Westerdale; three *s. Educ:* Wick High Sch.; Archbishop Holgate's Grammar Sch., York. 1st Seaforth Highlanders, Malaya, 1948–51; 11th Seaforth Highlanders, Caithness, 1951–71; Major and Company Comdr, 1964. DL 1975, Vice Lord-Lieutenant 1986, JP 1996, Caithness. *Recreations:* gardening, walking, country dancing. *Address:* Cathel Sheiling, Loch Calder, Thurso, Caithness KW14 7YH. *T:* (01847) 871220.

DUNNETT, John Jacob, (Jack); President, Football League, 1981–86 and 1988–89 (Member, Management Committee, 1977–89); *b* 24 June 1922; *m* 1951; two *s* three *d. Educ:* Whitgift Middle Sch., Croydon; Downing Coll., Cambridge (BA 1947; LLB 1949; MA 1950; LLM 1989). Served with Cheshire Regt, 1941–46 (Capt.). Admitted Solicitor, 1949. Middlesex CC, 1958–61; Councillor, Enfield Borough Council, 1958–61; Alderman, Enfield Borough Council, 1961–63; Councillor, Greater London Council, 1964–67. MP (Lab) Central Nottingham, 1964–74, Nottingham East, 1974–83; former PPS to: Minister of State, FCO; Minister of Transport. Mem. FA Council, 1977–89, Vice-Pres., 1981–86, 1988–89; Mem., Football Trust, 1982–89; Chm., Notts County FC, 1968–87; Vice-Chm., Portsmouth FC, 1989–90. *Recreation:* watching professional football.

DUNNETT, Stephen Bruce, DSc; Professor, School of Biosciences, Cardiff University, since 2005 (Cardiff Professorial Research Fellow, 2000–05); *b* 28 Jan. 1950; *s* of Peter Sidney Dunnett and Margaret Eileen Dunnett (*née* Johnson); *m* 1984, Dr Sarah-Jane Richards. *Educ:* Eltham Coll.; Churchill Coll., Cambridge (BA Hons 1972; MA 1976; PhD 1981; DSc 1999); Poly. of N London (Dip in Social Work, CQSW 1976); Birkbeck Coll., Univ. of London (BSc Hons 1978). Social worker, London Borough of Southwark, 1972–78; research student, Churchill Coll., Cambridge, 1978–81; Fellow, Clare Coll., Cambridge, 1981–99; Department of Experimental Psychology, University of Cambridge: Wellcome Trust Mental Health Res. Fellow, 1982–83; Demonstrator, 1983–86; Lectr, 1986–95; Reader in Neurobiology, 1995–99; Dir, Scientific Progs, MRC Cambridge Centre for Brain Repair, 1992–99. Vis. Scientist, Univ. of Lund, Sweden, 1981–82. FMedSci 2003 (Mem. Council, 2014–); FLSW 2011. Spearman Medal, BPsS, 1988; Alfred Meyer Medal, British Neuropathol Soc., 1998. *Publications:* (ed with S.-J. Richards) Neural Transplantation: from molecular basis to clinical application, 1990; (ed with A. Björklund): Neural Transplantation: a practical approach, 1992; Functional Neural Transplantation, 1994, Functional Neural Transplantation II, 2000, Functional Neural Transplantation III (Pts 1 and 2), 2012; (with R. A. Barker) Neural Repair, Transplantation and Rehabilitation, 1999; (ed jtly) Neural Transplantation Methods, 2000; (jtly) Brain Damage, Brain Repair, 2001; Dopamine, 2005; Dopamine Handbook, 2010; Animal Models of Movement Disorders (2 vols), 2011; over 650 research papers on topics of brain function, animal models of neurodegenerative disease and neural transplantation. *Recreations:* flying, food and wine, France. *Address:* School of Biosciences, Cardiff University, Museum Avenue, Cardiff CF10 3AX. *Club:* Royal Society of Medicine.

DUNNING, Geoffrey William; Director, Geoff Dunning Ltd, since 2014; *b* Pannal, 28 Nov. 1950; *s* of Oswald Dunning and May Dunning; *m* 1980, Sandra June King; two *d. Educ:* Harrogate Grammar Sch. Sales Rep., Ringways Garages, Leeds, 1972–75; Asst Regl Sec., Freight Transport Assoc., 1975–87; Road Haulage Association Ltd: Dist Manager, 1987–94; Regl Dir, 1994–2009; Chief Exec., 2009–14. *Recreations:* failing to stay out of trouble, manufacture of invisibility cloaks, being as good a friend, father and husband as possible, collecting mild versions of what can be serious illnesses. *T:* 07979 531470. *E:* geoff@geoffdunning.co.uk.

DUNNING, Graham; QC 2001; *b* 13 March 1958; *s* of late Maj. James E. Dunning and of Jane P. Dunning (*née* Hunt); *m* 1986, Claire Abigael Williams; three *s* one *d. Educ:* King Edward VI Sch., Southampton; Emmanuel Coll., Cambridge (MA); Harvard Law Sch. (LLM). Called to the Bar, Lincoln's Inn, 1982, Bencher, 2009; joined Essex Court Chambers, 1983; in practice at commercial bar and as internat. arbitrator, 1983–. *Recreations:* travel, skiing, golf. *Address:* Essex Court Chambers, 24 Lincoln's Inn Fields, WC2A 3EG. *T:* (020) 7813 8000. *Clubs:* Woking Golf; Rye Golf.

DUNNING, Sir Simon (William Patrick), 3rd Bt *cr* 1930; *b* 14 Dec. 1939; *s* of Sir William Leonard Dunning, 2nd Bt, and Kathleen Lawrie (*d* 1992), *d* of J. P. Cuthbert, MC; *S* father, 1961; *m* 1975, Frances Deirdre Morton, *d* of Major Patrick Lancaster; one *d. Educ:* Eton. *Address:* Low Auchengillan, Blanefield, by Glasgow G63 9AU. *T:* (01360) 770323. *Club:* Turf.

DUNNINGTON-JEFFERSON, Sir John Alexander, 3rd Bt *cr* 1958, of Thorganby Hall, East Riding of Yorks; *b* 23 March 1980; *o s* of Sir Mervyn Stewart Dunnington-Jefferson, 2nd Bt and of Caroline Anna Dunnington-Jefferson (*née* Bayley); *S* father 2014; *m* 2011, Joanna Margaret Rothwell Lee; one *s* one *d. Heir: s* James Mervyn Rothwell Dunnington-Jefferson, *b* 13 May 2015.

DUNROSSIL, 3rd Viscount *cr* 1959; **Andrew William Reginald Morrison;** Director, Brundage Management Company, San Antonio, Texas, since 1990; *b* 15 Dec. 1953; *e s* of 2nd Viscount Dunrossil, CMG and of Mavis Dawn (*née* Spencer-Payne); *S* father, 2000; *m* 1st, 1986, Carla Marie Brundage (marr. diss. 2010); one *s* three *d*; 2nd, 2012, Mary Shell Conoly Koontz Somoza. *Educ:* Eton (KS); University Coll., Oxford (BA Lit Hum). FCO, 1978–79; Kleinwort Benson Ltd, 1979–89. Chairman: Amer. Financial Services Assoc., 2007–08; Nat. Inst. of Consumer Credit Mgt. Hon. British Consul, San Antonio, Texas, 2004–. Chm., Soc. of Scottish Armigers, 2012– (Vice Chm., 2011). Mem., Standing Council of Scottish Chiefs, 2012–. Dist. Service Award, Amer. Financial Services Assoc., 2005. *Recreations:* clan history, theology, poetry, sports. *Heir: s* Hon. Callum Alasdair Brundage Morrison, *b* 12 July 1994. *Address:* 410 Patterson Avenue, San Antonio, TX 78209, USA. *T:* (office) (210) 7359393. *Clubs:* Argyle (San Antonio); Withington Cricket (Glos).

DUNSANY, 21st Baron of, *cr* 1439; **Randal Plunkett;** *b* 9 March 1983; *er s* of 20th Baron of Dunsany and of Maria Alice Villela de Carvalho; *S* father, 2011. *Heir: b* Hon. Oliver Plunkett, *b* 26 Sept. 1985.

DUNSMORE, Rev. Barry William; Minister, Cathedral Church of St Machar, Aberdeen, since 2015; *b* 27 Jan. 1954; *s* of late William Dunsmore and of Mildred Dunsmore (*née* Laing); *m* 1978, Dr Hilda Burns; one *s* one *d. Educ:* Hillhead High Sch., Glasgow; Univ. of Glasgow (MA, BD). Post-grad. res., Univ. of Nairobi, 1980–81; ordained and inducted, Erskine Ch, Saltcoats, 1982; inducted: St Columba's Ch, Stirling, 1988; Presbytery Clerk, Presbytery of Stirling, 1994–2000; Minister: St Columba's Ch of Scotland, Pont Street, London, linked with St Andrew's, Newcastle, 2000–09; Christ Ch, Warwick, Bermuda, 2009–15; Vice-Convener, Ch of Scotland Bd of Ministry, 2003–05. *Publications:* Challenge, Comfort, Forgiveness and Welcome (book of sermons), 2007. *Recreations:* golf, music, travel. *Address:* 39 Woodstock Road, Aberdeen AB15 5EX.

DUNSTAN, (Andrew Harold) Bernard, RA 1968 (ARA 1959); painter; *b* 19 Jan. 1920; *s* of late Dr A. E. Dunstan; *m* 1949, Diana Maxwell Armfield, *qv*; two *s* (and one *s* decd). *Educ:* St Paul's; Byam Shaw Sch.; Slade Sch. Has exhibited at RA since 1945. Many one-man exhibitions. Pictures in public collections include Royal Collection, London Museum, Bristol Art Gall., Nat. Gall. of NZ, Arts Council, Nat. Portrait Gall., many in private collections. Member: NEAC; RWA (Pres., 1980–84); Pastel Soc. Chm., Artists' General Benevolent Instn, 1987–91. Trustee, RA, 1989–95. *Publications:* Learning to Paint, 1970; Painting in Progress, 1976; Painting Methods of the Impressionists, 1976; (ed) Ruskin, Elements of Drawing, 1991; The Paintings of Bernard Dunstan, 1993. *Recreation:* music. *Address:* 10 High Park Road, Kew, Richmond, Surrey TW9 4BH. *T:* (020) 8876 6633. *Club:* Arts.

DUNSTAN, Very Rev. Gregory John Orchard; Dean of Armagh, and Keeper of Armagh Public Library, since 2011; *b* Abingdon, 17 Oct. 1950; *s* of Gordon Dunstan and Ruby, (Ruth), Dunstan. *Educ:* Westminster Sch.; Clare Coll., Cambridge (BA 1972); Univ. of Newcastle upon Tyne (Dip. Landscape Design 1974); Trinity Coll., Dublin (BTh 1990). Asst Landscape Architect to Mary Mitchell, 1974–77; Landscape Architect, Brady Shipman Martin, Dublin, 1977–87; ordained deacon, 1990, priest, 1991; Curate, St Patrick's, Ballymena, 1990–93; Rector, St Matthew's, Shankill, Belfast, 1993–2011. *Recreations:* cycling, walking, music, gardening. *Address:* Library House, 43 Abbey Street, Armagh BT61 7DY. *T:* (028) 3752 3142, (home) (028) 3751 8447. *E:* dean@armagh.anglican.org.

DUNSTAN, Tessa Jane; Director, Legal Services A, Department of Trade and Industry, 2001–04; retired; Appeal Officer for community interest companies, 2006–11; *b* 18 July 1944; *d* of Alfred Thomas Fripp and Kathleen Jennie (*née* Kimpton); *m* 1973, Richard James Rowley Dunstan; two *s* two *d*. *Educ:* Convent of the Sacred Heart, Woldingham, Surrey; Lady Margaret Hall, Oxford (MA). Called to the Bar, Middle Temple, 1967; Legal Asst, Solicitor's Office, BoT, 1968; Sen. Legal Asst, Solicitor's Office, DTI, 1973–84; Legal Advr, Office of Telecommunications; 1984–87; Solicitor's Office/Legal Department, Department of Trade and Industry, 1987–2004: Investigations Div., 1989–98; Grade 3, Dir Legal Services D, 1998–2001; Legal Project Dir (Co. Law Review), Legal Services, DTI, 2001. *Recreations:* opera, travel, gardening. *Address:* Shalesbrook, Forest Row, Sussex RH18 5LS. *T:* (01342) 823079.

DUNSTONE, Sir Charles, Kt 2012; CVO 2015; Chairman: Dixons Carphone (formerly The Carphone Warehouse Group), since 2010; TalkTalk Telecoms Group, since 2010 (Founder, 1989, Chief Executive Officer, 1989–2010, The Carphone Warehouse); *b* 21 Nov. 1964; *s* of Denis and Anne Dunstone; *m* 2009, Celia Gordon Shute; one *s* one *d*. *Educ:* Uppingham Sch. Sales Manager, Communications Div., NEC, 1985–89. Non-executive Director: Halifax, 2000–01; HBOS, 2001–08; Daily Mail & Gen. Trust. Chairman: Prince's Trust, 2009–; Trustees, Royal Museums Greenwich, 2013–. *Recreation:* sailing. *Address:* TalkTalk Telecoms Group, 11 Evesham Street, W11 4AR. *Clubs:* Royal Ocean Racing, Royal Thames Yacht; Royal Yacht Squadron (Cowes).

DUNT, Vice Adm. Sir John (Hugh), KCB 1998; CEng, FIET; Chief of Fleet Support and Member, Admiralty Board, 1997–2000; *b* 14 Aug. 1944; *s* of Harris Hugh Dunt and Margaret Rea Dunt (*née* Morgan); *m* 1972, Alynne Margaret Wood; two *d*. *Educ:* Duke of York Sch., Nairobi; RNEC Manadon (BScEng). Joined RN at BRNC Dartmouth, 1963; served in HM Ships Kent, Ajax, Dundas, Collingwood, Nubian; MoD (PE); Staff, C-in-C Fleet, 1980; Naval Operational Requirements, 1980–82; HMS Invincible, 1982–84; Staff Weapon Engr Officer to FO Sea Training, 1984; Naval Staff Duties, 1985–87; RCDS 1988; Higher Command and Staff Course, Camberley, 1989; Captain, HMS Defiance, 1989–90; Dir, Defence Systems, MoD, 1991–93; Dir, Gen. Fleet Support (Ops and Plans), 1993–95; DCDS (Systems), MoD, 1995–97. Defence Advr, Cap Gemini Ernst & Young, 2001–03. Chm. Trustees, Armed Forces Memorial Trust, 2003–. Chm. Govs, Royal Star and Garter Home, Richmond, 2003–. Patron, Portsmouth Sail Trng Trust. *Publications:* articles in naval and professional jls. *Recreations:* sport (golf, squash), gardening, travel. *Address:* Woodley House, Hill Brow, Liss, Hants GU33 7QG. *Clubs:* MCC; Royal Navy Cricket; Liphook Golf.

See also Vice-Adm. P. A. Dunt.

DUNT, Vice Adm. Peter Arthur, CB 2002; DL; Chairman, Royal Surrey County Hospital NHS Foundation Trust, since 2010; *b* 23 June 1947; *s* of Harris Hugh Dunt and Margaret Rae Dunt; *m* 1974, Lesley Gilchrist; two *d*. *Educ:* Duke of York Sch., Nairobi; Merchant Taylors' Sch., Liverpool; BRNC, Dartmouth. Midshipman, HMS Arethusa, 1966; Sub Lieut courses, 1967–69; Captain's Sec., HMS Charybdis, 1969–71; Flag Lieut to Flag Officer, Medway, 1971–74; Dep. Supply Officer, HMS Kent, 1974; Supply Officer, HMS Aurora, 1975–77; Officer's Trng Officer, HMS Pembroke, 1977–79; Asst Sec. to Vice Chief of Naval Staff, 1979–82; Comdr, 1982; Sec. to Flag Officer, 1st Flotilla, 1982–84 (Gp Logistics Officer, HMS Hermes, Falklands Conflict); Supply Officer, BRNC, Dartmouth, 1984–86; Sec. to Dir Gen. Naval Manpower and Trng, 1986–88; Captain, 1988; Dep. Dir Naval Staff Duties, 1988; Sec. to 2nd Sea Lord, 1989–92; Captain, HMS Raleigh, 1992–94; Dir Naval Personnel Corporate Programming, 1994–97; rcds 1997; Rear Adm., 1998; COS to Second Sea Lord and C-in-C Naval Home Command, 1998–2000; Sen. Naval Directing Staff, RCDS and Chief Naval Supply Officer, 2000–02; Vice Adm., 2002; Chief Exec., Defence Estates, 2002–07. Dir, Pollen Estate, 2007–14; Non-exec. Dir, Enterprise Managed Services, 2009–11. Chm., ABTA Appeal Bd, 2010–. Mem. Council, White Ensign Assoc., 2007–. Chm. Govs, Queen Anne's Sch., Caversham, 2007–. FCIPD 2000. DL Surrey, 2011. *Recreations:* golf, walking, gardening, DIY. *Address:* The Lodge, Great Tangley, Guildford, Surrey GU5 0PT. *Club:* Army and Navy.

See also Vice-Adm. Sir J. H. Dunt.

DUNTZE, Sir Daniel Evans, 9th Bt *cr* 1774, of Tiverton, Devon; *b* 11 Aug. 1960; *o s* of Sir Daniel Evans Duntze, 8th Bt and Marietta Duntze (*née* Welsh); *S* father, 1997, but his name does not appear on the Official Roll of the Baronetage.

DUNWICH, Viscount; Robert Keith Rous; *b* 17 Nov. 1961; *s* and *heir* of Earl of Stradbroke, *qv*.

DUNWICH, Bishop Suffragan of; *no new appointment at time of going to press.*

DUNWOODY, Richard; *see* Dunwoody, T. R.

DUNWOODY, Tamsin; Managing Director, TeeDem Ltd, since 2011; *b* 3 Sept. 1958; *d* of late Dr John Elliott Orr Dunwoody, CBE and Gwyneth Patricia Dunwoody, MP (Lab) Crewe and Nantwich; *m* 1992 (marr. diss. 2006); two *s* three *d*. *Educ:* Univ. of Kent (BA); Univ. of South Bank (AHSM 1982). NHS Manager, St Mary's, Whittington, Royal Northern and Royal Free Hosps, London, 1979–91; Co. Sec., St David's Care in the Community, 1992–97; small business advr/commercial tutor, 1997–2003. Mem. (Lab) Preseli Pembrokeshire, Nat. Assembly for Wales, 2003–07. Deputy Minister: for Econ. Devlt and Transport, 2005–07; for Envmt Planning and the Countryside, 2005–07. Chair, Wales Adv. Gp, Coed Cymru, 2007–. Contested (Lab): Preseli Pembrokeshire, Nat. Assembly for Wales, 2007; Crewe and Nantwich, May 2008. Mem., Labour Party, 1973–. Mem., RHS, 1993–. *Recreations:* smallholder, embroidery, reading. *T:* (01348) 881510. *E:* tamsindunwoody@gmail.com.

DUNWOODY, (Thomas) Richard, MBE 1993; National Hunt jockey, 1982–99; *b* 18 Jan. 1964; *s* of George Rutherford and Gillian Mary Dunwoody; *m* 1988, Carol Ann Abraham (marr. diss. 2000). *Educ:* Rendcomb Coll., Glos. Wins include: Grand National, on West Tip, 1986, on Miinnehoma, 1994; Cheltenham Gold Cup, on Charter Party, 1988; King George VI Chase, on Desert Orchid, 1989 and 1990, on One Man, 1995 and 1996; Champion Hurdle, on Kribensis, 1990; Breeders' Cup Steeplechase, on Highland Bud, 1989 and 1992; Champion National Hunt Jockey, 1992–93, 1993–94 and 1994–95. 1699 National Hunt wins, incl. ten consecutive centuries, 1999. Jt Pres., Jockeys' Assoc., 1993–99. Completed 680 mile Shackleton South Pole expedn, 2008. *Publications:* (with Marcus Armytage) Hell for Leather, 1993; (with S. Magee) Duel, 1994; (with Marcus Armytage) Hands and Heels, 1997; (with David Walsh) Obsessed: the autobiography, 2000; Horses of My Life, 2005; Method in my Madness, 2009. *Recreations:* sport, travel. *Address:* Hewins Wood House, Bradfield, Berks RG7 6DH.

DUNWORTH, John Vernon, CB 1969; CBE 1955; President, International Committee of Weights and Measures, Sèvres, France, 1975–85 (Vice President, 1968–75); *b* 24 Feb. 1917; *oc* of late John Dunworth and Susan Ida (*née* Warburton); *m* 1967, Patricia Noel Boston; one *d*. *Educ:* Manchester Grammar Sch.; Clare Coll., Cambridge (Denman Baynes Research Studentship, 1937, Robins Prize, 1937); Trinity Coll., Cambridge (Twisden Studentship and Fellowship, MA, PhD 1941). War Service: Ministry of Supply on Radar Development, 1939–44; National Research Council of Canada, on Atomic Energy Development, 1944–45. Univ. Demonstrator in Physics, Cambridge, 1945. Joined Atomic Energy Research Establishment, Harwell, 1947; Dir, NPL, 1964–76. Alternate United Kingdom Member on Organising Cttee of UN Atoms for Peace Confs in Geneva, 1955 and 1958. Fellow Amer. Nuclear Soc. 1960. Chm., British Nuclear Energy Soc., 1964–70; Vice-President, Institute of Physics: Physical Soc., 1966–70. CEng 1966. Comdr (with Star), Order of Alfonso X el Sabio, Spain, 1960. *Address:* Apartment 902, Kings Court, Ramsey, Isle of Man IM8 1LP. *T:* (01624) 813003. *Club:* Athenæum.

DUPAS, Gabrielle Teresa S.; *see* Solti-Dupas.

Du PLESSIS, Jan Petrus; Chairman: Rio Tinto plc and Rio Tinto Ltd, since 2009; SABMiller, since 2015; *b* 22 Jan. 1954; *m* 1978, Magdalena, (Leni), Nel; two *s* one *d*. *Educ:* Univ. of Stellenbosch (BCom Law 1973, LLB 1977). CA 1980 (SA). Internat. Financial Manager, Rembrandt Gp Ltd, 1981–87; Group Finance Director: Co. Financière Richemont, SA, 1988–2004; Rothmans International plc, 1990–96; Chairman: British American Tobacco plc, 2004–09; RHM, 2005–07. Non-executive Director: Lloyds Banking (formerly Lloyds TSB) Gp plc, 2005–09; Marks and Spencer Gp plc, 2008–15. *Recreations:* golf, ski-ing, scuba diving, walking. *Address:* Rio Tinto plc, 2 Eastbourne Terrace, W2 6LG. *Club:* Beaconsfield Golf.

DUPPLIN, Viscount; William Charles Thomas Hay; *b* 24 June 2011; *s* and *heir* of Earl of Kinnoull, *qv*.

Du QUESNAY, Heather Le Mercier, CBE 1996; Chief Executive, English Schools Foundation, Hong Kong, 2005–13; *b* 10 Nov. 1947; *d* of Eric William and Agnes Elizabeth Openshaw; *m* 1969, Ian Mark Le Mercier Du Quesnay; two *d*. *Educ:* Univ. of Birmingham (BA, Cert Ed). Teacher, 1972–78, Dep. Head, 1978–83, Bartley Green Girls' Sch., Birmingham; Educn Officer, Cambs CC, 1983–89; Dep. Co. Educn Officer, Essex CC, 1989–90; Dir of Educn, Herts CC, 1991–96; Exec. Dir of Educn, 1996–2000, Interim Chief Exec., 2000, Lambeth BC; Chief Exec., Nat. Coll. for Sch. Leadership, 2000–05. FRSA 1994. Hon. DEd de Montfort, 1997; DUniv UCE, 2002. *Publications:* essays and articles in educ. jls and newspapers. *Recreations:* walking, food, wine, family.

DURAND, Sir Edward (Alan Christopher David Percy), 5th Bt *cr* 1892, of Ruckley Grange, Salop; English teacher and writer; *b* 21 Feb. 1974; *s* of Rev. Sir (Henry Mortimer) Dickon (Marion St George) Durand, 4th Bt and of Stella Evelyn Durand (*née* L'Estrange); *S* father, 1993; *m* 1st, 2004, Rachel King (separated 2007; marr. diss. 2013); one *d*; 2nd, 2013, Amanda Anara Ashwood (*née* Amanda Clare Melbourne); one *d*. *Educ:* St Columba's Coll., Dublin; Milltown Inst., Dublin (Nat. Cert. in Philosophy); Univ. of Ulster at Coleraine (BA Phil.); Nat. Trng Authy dips in herbalism and parapsychology. *Recreations:* mysticism, metaphysics, ecology. *Heir: b* David Michael Dickon Percy Durand, *b* 6 June 1978. *Address:* Montpellier, France.

DURAND, (Julia) Alison; *see* Noble, J. A.

DURANT, Sir Anthony; *see* Durant, Sir R. A. B.

DURANT, Ian Charles; Chairman: Capital & Counties Properties plc, since 2010; Greggs plc, since 2013 (non-executive Director, since 2011); *b* Lusaka, 5 July 1958; *s* of John Durant and Jean Durant; *m* 1984, Sally Sharpe; one *s* two *d*. *Educ:* Gordonstoun; Univ. of Kent (BA). FCA 1994; FCT 1994. Trainee chartered acct, Joliffe Cork, later Thornton Baker/Joliffe Cork, 1980–84; Financial Controller, Allders, Hanson plc, 1984–89; Exec. Asst to Man. Dir, Jardine Matheson, 1989–90; Finance Dir, Dairy Farm, Asia, 1990–93; Finance Director: Hongkong Land, 1993–98; Dairy Farm Internat., 1998–2001; Thistle Hotels, 2001–03; Chief Financial Officer, SeaContainers, 2005–07; Finance Dir, Liberty Internat. plc, 2008–10. Non-executive Director: Westbury plc, 2003–06; Greene King, 2007–; Home Retail Gp plc, 2011–; Mem., Adv. Bd, Eurosite Power Inc., 2011–. Chm., Ealing Swimming Club, 2009–12. Trustee, Richmond Parish Lands Charity, 2012–. *Recreations:* literary pursuits, golf, jazz music of Abdullah Ibrahim. *Address:* Capital & Counties Properties plc, 15 Grosvenor Street, W1K 4QZ. *T:* (020) 3214 9150. *E:* ian.durant@capitalandcounties.com.

DURANT, Prof. John Robert, PhD; Director, MIT Museum, since 2005; Adjunct Professor, Science, Technology and Society Program, Massachusetts Institute of Technology, since 2005; *b* 8 July 1950; *s* of Kenneth Albert James Durant and Edna Kathleen Durant (*née* Norman); *m* 1st, 1977, Nirmala Naidoo (marr. diss. 1996); two *s* one *d*; 2nd, 2000, Prof. Anne Harrington; one *s*. *Educ:* Queens' College, Cambridge (MA Nat. Scis; PhD Hist. of Sci.). Staff Tutor in Biological Scis, Dept of Extramural Studies, UC Swansea, 1976–82; Staff Tutor in Biol Scis, Dept of External Studies, Univ. of Oxford, 1983–89; Hd, then Dir, Sci. Communication, Sci. Mus., 1989–2000; Chief Exec., At-Bristol, 2000–05. Imperial College London: Vis. Prof. of Hist. and Public Understanding of Sci., 1989–93; Prof., 1993–2002, Vis. Prof., 2002–05, of Public Understanding of Sci.; Vis. Prof., UWE, 2001–05. Exec. Dir, Cambridge Sci. Festival, 2007–. *Publications:* (ed) Darwinism and Divinity, 1985; (with P. Klopfer and S. Oyama) Aggression: conflict in animals and humans reconsidered, 1988; (ed) Museums and Public Understanding of Science, 1992; (ed) Public Participation in Science, 1995; (ed) Biotechnology in the Public Sphere: a European sourcebook, 1998; articles in professional jls. *Recreations:* family, the art of surviving. *Address:* MIT Museum, Building N51–201, 265 Massachusetts Avenue, Cambridge, MA 02139, USA. *T:* (617) 2535653. *E:* jdurant@mit.edu.

DURANT, Louise; *see* Charlton, L.

DURANT, Sir (Robert) Anthony (Bevis), Kt 1991; *b* 9 Jan. 1928; *s* of Captain Robert Michael Durant and Mrs Violet Dorothy Durant (*née* Bevis); *m* 1958, Audrey Stoddart; two *s* one *d*. *Educ:* Dane Court Prep. Sch., Pyrford, Woking; Bryanston Sch., Blandford, Dorset. Royal Navy, 1945–47. Coutts Bank, Strand, 1947–52; Cons. Party Organisation, 1952–67 (Young Cons. Organiser, Yorks; Cons. Agent, Clapham; Nat. Organiser, Young Conservatives). MP (C): Reading N, Feb. 1974–1983; Reading W, 1983–97. PPS to Sec. of State for Transport and to Sec. of State for Employment, 1983–84; Asst Govt Whip, 1984–86; a Lord Comr of HM Treasury, 1986–88; Vice-Chamberlain of HM Household, 1988–90. Member: Select Cttee Parly Comr (Ombudsman), 1973–83, 1990–93; Select Cttee on Members' Interests, 1993–95; Chm., Select Cttee on Channel Tunnel Rail Link Bill, 1995–96; Mem., Exec., 1922 Cttee, 1990–97; Chairman: All Party Gp on Widows and One Parent Families, 1977–85; All Party Gp on Inland Waterways, 1992–97; Cons. Nat. Local Govt Adv. Cttee, 1981–84; Backbench Envmt Cttee, 1991–97; All Party Gp on Film Industry, 1991–97; Vice-Chm., Parly Gp for World Govt, 1979–84. Leader, UK delegn to Council of Europe, 1996–97 (Mem., 1992–96); Chm., British Br., CPA, 1988–90; Mem., Council of Europe, 1981–83, 1990–97 (Ldr, UK Delegn, 1996–97). Dir, Southern Demolition Co. Ltd, 1998–2012; former Consultant: The Film Production Association of Great Britain Ltd; Delta Electrical Div. of Delta Metal Co. Ltd; Allied Industrial Designers. Dir, British Industrial Scientific Film Assoc., 1967–70; Mem. Bd of Govs, BFI, 1992–98. Member: Inland Waterways Adv. Council, 1975–84; Kennet and Avon Canal Trust (Pres.,

1996–2010); River Thames Soc. (Pres., 1996–2010). Freeman: City of London, 1997; Watermen and Lightermen's Co., 1998–. *Recreations:* boating, golf. *Address:* Hill House, Surley Row, Caversham, Reading RG4 8ND.

DURANTE, Viviana Paola; Principal Guest Artist: Royal Ballet Company; K-Ballet Tokyo, since 2003; Founder, Viviana Durante Company, 2010; *b* Italy, 8 May 1967; *d* of Giulio and Anna Maria Durante; *m* 2009, Nigel Cliff; one *s*. *Educ:* Royal Ballet School. Came to England in 1977; joined Royal Ballet Co., 1984; soloist, 1987; Principal Dancer, 1989; Guest Artist, 1999; first major rôle, Swan Lake, Covent Garden, 1988; rôles include Manon, Ondine, La Bayadère, Giselle, Kitri (in Don Quixote), Aurora, Cinderella, Juliet, Carmen, Coppelia. Principal Dancer, American Ballet Theater, 1999; *film:* Ogni 27 Agosto, 2005; *theatre:* Escaping Hamlet, Edinburgh Fest., 2007; Fram, NT, 2009. Time Out Award, 1989; Evening Standard Ballet Award, 1989; Laurence Olivier Award, 1997.

DURÃO BARROSO, José Manuel; President, European Commission, 2004–14; *b* 23 March 1956; *s* of Luís Barroso and Marie Elisabete Durão; *m* 1980, Maria Margarida Pinto Ribeiro de Sousa Uva Barroso; three *s*. *Educ:* Univ. of Lisbon (LLD Hons 1978); Univ. of Geneva (Master in Pol Sci. 1981); European Univ. Inst., Univ. of Geneva (Dip.). Lecturer: Faculty of Law, Lisbon Univ., 1978–81; Pol Sci. Dept, Geneva Univ., 1981–85; Prof. of Internat. Relns, Universidade Lusíada (Hd of Dept, 1995–99). Vis. Scholar, 1985, Vis. Prof., 1996–98, Univ. of Georgetown, Washington. Ed., Revista de Ciência Política. MP (PSD): Lisbon, 1985–87, 1995–2004; Viseu, 1987–95; Secretary of State for: Home Affairs, 1985–87; Foreign Affairs and Co-operation, 1987–92; Minister for Foreign Affairs, Portugal, 1992–95; Prime Minister of Portugal, 2002–04. Chm., Commn for For. Affairs, Portuguese Parlt, 1995–99. Leader, PSD, 1999–2004 (Mem., Nat. Council, 1984–2004; Chm., Dept for Internat. Relns). Leader, Internat. Inst. for Democracy and Electoral Assistance mission to Bosnia Hercegovina, 1996; UN Advr, Project for Peace Process in Africa, Tanzania, 1997. Vice President: EPP, 1999–2002; Center Democrats Internat., 2001–05. Scholarship Fellow: Swiss Confedn; CEC; Volkswagenwerk Foundn; NATO; Swiss Nat. Fund for Scientific Res. *Publications:* (jtly) Governmental System and Party System, 1980; Le Système Politique Portugais face à l'Intégration Européenne, 1983; Política de Cooperação, 1990; Uma Certa Idéia de Europa, 1999; Uma Idéia para Portugal, 2000; Mudar de Modelo, 2001; Reformar: dois anos de governo, 2004; contrib. to collective works, encyclopaedias and internat. scientific jls.

DURBIN, Richard Michael, PhD; FRS 2004; Senior Group Leader (formerly Principal Investigator), Genome Informatics Group, since 1992, and Acting Head, Computational Genomics, since 2014, The Wellcome Trust Sanger Institute (formerly Sanger Centre), Hinxton, Cambridge (Joint Head, Human Genetics Division, 2011–14); *b* 30 Dec. 1960; *s* of Prof. James Durbin, FBA; *m* 1996, Dr Julie Ahringer; one *s* one *d*. *Educ:* Highgate Sch.; St John's Coll., Cambridge (BA Maths 1982; PhD Biology 1987). Res. Fellow, King's Coll., Cambridge, 1986–88; Vis. Fellow, Stanford Univ., 1988–90; Staff Scientist, MRC Lab. of Molecular Biology, 1990–96; Sanger Centre, later The Wellcome Trust Sanger Institute, Hinxton, Cambridge: Jt Hd, 1992–94, Hd, 1994–2006, Informatics Div.; Dep. Dir, 1997–2006. Hon. Prof., Univ. of Cambridge, 2008–. Member: Human Genome Org., 1994–; Sci. Cttee, UK BioBank, 2003–05; EMBO, 2009–. FSS 2003; Fellow, Internat. Soc. for Computational Biology, 2011 (Mem., 2000). Mullard Medal, Royal Soc., 1994; Lord Lloyd of Kilgerran Award, 2004. *Publications:* (jtly) Biological Sequence Analysis, 1998; papers in jls on genomic and computational biology. *Recreation:* walking in wild places. *Address:* The Wellcome Trust Sanger Institute, The Wellcome Trust Genome Campus, Hinxton, Cambs CB10 1SA. *E:* rd@sanger.ac.uk.

DURELL, Prof. John Leonard, PhD; CPhys, FInstP; Professor of Nuclear Physics, University of Manchester, 1998–2008, now Emeritus (Head, School of Physics and Astronomy, 2004–08); *b* 26 Oct. 1945; *s* of Leonard Joseph John Durell and Hilda Durell; *m* 1968, Susan Rolfe; two *d*. *Educ:* Beckenham Grammar Sch.; Univ. of Liverpool (BSc Hons; PhD 1970). CPhys, FInstP 1995. Royal Soc. Fellow, Max-Planck Inst., Heidelberg, 1970–71; University of Manchester: Lectr in Physics, 1971–82; Sen. Lectr, 1982–95; Reader in Physics, 1995–98; Hd, Dept of Physics and Astronomy, 2000–02; Dean, Faculty of Sci. and Engrg, 2002–04. Mem. Council, CCLRC, 2002–05. *Publications:* numerous papers in acad. jls. *Recreation:* birdwatching. *Address:* 6 Elf Meadow, Poulton, Cirencester, Glos GL7 5HQ. *E:* john.durell@manchester.ac.uk.

DURHAM, 7th Earl of, *cr* 1833; **Edward Richard Lambton;** Baron Durham 1828; Viscount Lambton 1833; *b* 19 Oct. 1961; *o s* of Antony Claud Frederick Lambton, (Viscount Lambton), who disclaimed his peerages for life, and Belinda Bridget (*née* Blew-Jones); *S* father, 2006; *m* 1st, 1983, Christabel McEwen (marr. diss. 1995); one *s*; 2nd, 1995, Catherine (marr. diss. 2002), *e d* of late Desmond John Villiers Fitz-Gerald; 3rd, 2011, Marina Hanbury; one *d*. *Heir:* *s* Viscount Lambton, *qv*.

DURHAM, Bishop of, since 2014; **Rt Rev. Paul Roger Butler;** *b* 18 Sept. 1955; *s* of Denys Michael Butler and Jean Florence Butler; *m* 1982, Rosemary Jean Johnson; two *s* two *d*. *Educ:* Nottingham Univ. (BA Hons (English and History) 1977); Wycliffe Hall, Oxford (BA (Theol.) 1982; Cert. Theol. 1983). Ordained deacon, 1983, priest, 1984; Curate, Holy Trinity, Wandsworth, 1983–87; Inner London Evangelist, 1987–92, Dep. Hd of Missions, 1992–94, Scripture Union; NSM, St Paul, East Ham, 1988–94; Priest-in-charge: St Mary with St Stephen, and St Luke, Walthamstow, 1994–97; St Gabriel, Walthamstow, 1997; Team Rector, Parish of Walthamstow, 1997–2004; Area Dean, Waltham Forest, 2000–04; Bishop Suffragan of Southampton, 2004–09; Bishop of Southwell and Nottingham, 2009–14. Hon. Canon, St Paul's Cathedral, Byumba, Rwanda, 2001–. Entered H of L, 2014. Bishops' Advocate for Children, 2004–. Chairman: Church Mission Soc., 2007–10; Churches Nat. Safeguarding Cttee, 2011–. Pres., Scripture Union, 2011–. *Publications:* Reaching Children, 1992; Reaching Families, 1994; God's Friends, 1994; Following Jesus, 1994; Want to be in God's Family?, 1998; Growing Up in God's Family, 1998; Temptation and Testing, 2007; (contrib.) Through the Eyes of a Child, 2009; Offering the Best Children's Ministry, 2011; (jtly) Living your Confirmation, 2012; (contrib.) Being a Curate, 2014. *E:* bishop.of.durham@durham.anglican.org.

DURHAM, Dean of; *no new appointment at time of going to press.*

DURHAM, Archdeacon of; *see* Jagger, Ven. I.

DURHAM, John Clive; HM Diplomatic Service, retired; Ambassador to Mongolia, 1997–99; *b* 12 July 1939; *s* of Fred Durham and Eva Lucy (*née* Sykes); *m* 1962, Sandra Kay, (Shan), Beaumont; one *s* one *d*. *Educ:* Castleford Grammar Sch.; Leeds Coll. of Commerce. Min. of Pensions and Nat. Insce, 1955–67; joined HM Diplomatic Service, 1967: FCO, 1967–69; 3rd Sec., Wellington, NZ, 1969–72; Vice-Consul, Mogadishu, 1972–74; seconded to DTI, 1974–77; 2nd, later 1st Sec. (Commercial), Khartoum, 1977–81; Consul (Commercial), Frankfurt, 1981–86; FCO, 1986–93; Consul-Gen., Brisbane, 1993–97. *Recreations:* fell walking, travel, genealogy, steam locomotion. *Address:* 31 Crescent Wood Road, SE26 6SA. *Club:* Royal Over-Seas League.

DURHAM, Kenneth John; Headmaster, University College School, 1996–2013; *b* 23 Oct. 1953; *s* of John Clifford Durham and Geraldine Mary Durham (*née* Trinder); *m* 1984, Vivienne Mary Johnson (*see* V. M. Durham). *Educ:* St John's Sch., Leatherhead; Brasenose Coll., Oxford. St Albans Sch., 1975–87, Head of Econs, 1984–87; Head of Econs, 1987–92, Dir of Studies, 1991–96, King's Coll. Sch., Wimbledon. Chm., HMC, 2011–12. Chm., Professional Develt Sub-Cttee, HMC/GSA, 2004–10. Mem. Adv. Bd, Westminster Acad. Governor: Arnold Hse Sch., New Coll. Sch., The Perse Sch. Chautauqua Bell Tower Scholarship to USA, ESU, 1989. *Publications:* The New City, 1992. *Recreations:* reading, theatre, music, film, walking, history of Polar exploration. *Address:* 5 Redington Road, Hampstead, NW3 7QX.

DURHAM, Vivienne Mary; educational consultant, since 2016; Headmistress, Francis Holland School, Regent's Park, London, 2004–15; *b* Rustington, 12 July 1961; *m* 1984, Kenneth John Durham, *qv*. *Educ:* St Hilda's Coll., Oxford (MA). Dep. Hd, South Hampstead High Sch., 1997–2004. *Recreations:* reading, travel, theatre, music, ski-ing, riding. *Clubs:* Lansdowne, University Women's.

DURHAM HALL, Jonathan David; QC 1995; **His Honour Judge Durham Hall;** a Circuit Judge, since 2003; *b* 2 June 1952; *s* of Peter David Hall and Muriel Ann Hall, Sheffield; *m* 1973, Patricia Helen Bychowski (marr. diss. 1995), *d* of Stefan Bychowski, Whitehaven; one *s* one *d*; *m* 1996, J. Hilary Hart, GRSM, LRAM, *d* of late Edgar Alfred Hart, Hants. *Educ:* King Edward VII Sch., Sheffield; Nottingham Univ. (LLB Hons). Called to the Bar, Gray's Inn, 1975; joined North Eastern Circuit, 1976: Junior, 1982; Cryer, 1990–95; an Asst Recorder, 1991–95; a Recorder, 1995–2003; Resident Judge, Doncaster Crown Court, 2009–10. Head of Chambers, 1993–2003. Part-time Chm., Mental Health Review Tribunal, 2001–. Mem., Bar Council, 1994–95. Legal Assessor, GMC Professional Conduct Cttee, 2002–. *Recreations:* the creation and preservation of woodland, the plays of Shakespeare, all things Portuguese. *Address:* Bradford Crown Court, Bradford BD1 1JA.

DURIE, Andrew Maule D.; *see* Dewar-Durie.

DURIE, Sir David Robert Campbell, KCMG 2003 (CMG 1995); Governor and Commander-in-Chief, Gibraltar, 2000–03; *b* 21 Aug. 1944; *s* of late Frederick Robert Edwin Durie and Joan Elizabeth Campbell Durie (*née* Learoyd); *m* 1966, Susan Frances Weller; three *d*. *Educ:* Fettes Coll., Edinburgh; Christ Church, Oxford (MA Physics). Asst Principal, 1966, Pvte Sec. to Perm. Sec., 1970, Min. of Technology; Principal, DTI, 1971; First Sec., UK Delegn to OECD, 1974; Dept of Prices and Consumer Protection, 1977; Asst Sec., 1978; Dept of Trade, 1979; Cabinet Office, 1982; DTI, 1984; Under Sec., 1985–91; Dep. Sec., 1991; Minister and Dep. UK Perm. Rep. to EC/EU, Brussels, 1991–95; Dir Gen. (formerly Dep. Sec.), Enterprise and Regions, DTI, 1995–2000. Chm., Responsibility in Gambling Trust, 2004–06. Mem., Lord Chancellor's Adv. Panel on Nat. Records and Archives, 2005–14; Ind. Mem., Standards Cttee, GLA, 2008–12. CCMI (CIMgt 2000). FRSA 1996. KStJ 2000. Kt Comdr, Royal Order of Francis I, 2003. *Recreations:* moderately strenuous outdoor exercise, theatre, admiring my grandchildren. *Address:* 62 Burlington Avenue, Kew Gardens, Richmond, Surrey TW9 4DH.

DURKAN, (John) Mark; MP (SDLP) Foyle, since 2005; Leader, Social Democratic and Labour Party, 2001–10; *b* 26 June 1960; *s* of Brendan Durkan and Isobel Durkan (*née* Tinney); *m* 1993, Jackie Green; one *d*. *Educ:* St Columb's Coll., Derry; Queen's Univ., Belfast. Asst to John Hume, 1984–98. Mem. (SDLP) Derry CC, 1993–2000. Member: Forum for Peace and Reconciliation, Dublin, 1994–96; NI Forum (Talks Negotiator), 1996–98. Northern Ireland Assembly: Mem. (SDLP) Foyle, 1998–2010; Minister for Finance and Personnel, 1999–2001; Dep. First Minister, 2001–02; Chm., Cttee for Enterprise, Trade and Investment, 2007–09. Chairperson, SDLP, 1990–95. *Address:* (office) 23 Bishop Street, Derry BT48 6PR. *T:* (028) 7136 0700, *Fax:* (028) 7136 0808.

DURKIN, Claire; consultant, since 2014; Head, Global Knowledge and Innovation, Department for Business, Innovation and Skills, since 2015; *b* 18 May 1956; *d* of Richard Durkin and Mollie (*née* Frazer); *m* 1990, Stephen Morgan. *Educ:* Liverpool Univ. (BA 1st cl. Hons); Univ. of Victoria, BC (MA); Wolverhampton Poly. (PGCE). Lectr, Further and Higher Educn, Vauxhall Coll., South Bank Polytech., 1982–88; Department of Employment: Principal, 1988–89; Private Secretary: to Minister for Employment, 1989–90; to Minister for Educn, 1990–91; Asst Dir, Labour Mkt Policies, 1991–95; Asst Dir Deregulation, Central Policy Unit, DTI, 1995–97; Asst Sec., 1997–98, Sec., 1998–2000, Low Pay Commn; Dir, Consumer and Competition Policies, 2000–02, Energy Innovation and Businesses, 2003–05, Energy Markets, 2005–08, DTI, subseq. BERR; Dir, Europe and Internat. Trade Policy, then Europe, Internat. Trade and Develt Policy, later Internat. Trade, Investment and Develt, BERR, subseq. BIS, 2008–10; Vice Pres. and Regl Exec., Europe, URS Corp. Ltd, 2010–14. *Recreations:* history, politics, exploring the Welsh Marches.

DURLACHER, Nicholas John, CBE 1995; Chairman, Xoserve Ltd, since 2011; *b* 20 March 1946; *s* of late John Sidney Durlacher, MC and of Alma Gabrielle (*née* Adams); *m* 1971, Mary Caroline Mclaren; one *s*. *Educ:* Stowe; Magdalene Coll., Cambridge (BA Econs). Mem., Stock Exchange, 1970–86; Partner, Wedd Durlacher, 1972–86; Director: BZW Ltd, 1986–98; BZW Futures, 1986–96; U.F.J. Internat., 2002–04; Chairman: Ennismore Smaller Cos Fund, 1999–; EMX, 2000–07; BSC Co. Ltd, 2000–10; Ffastfill, 2000–02; Elexon Ltd, 2000–10. Dir, 1984–96, Chm., 1992–95, LIFFE; Dir, 1987–95, Chm., 1995–2001, SFA; Dir, Investor's Compensation Scheme, 1992–2001; Chm., Balancing and Settlement Code Panel, 2000–10. Chm., Allied Schs, 2008–. Trustee and Dir, Brain and Spine Foundn, 1994–2011. *Recreations:* ski-ing, golf, tennis. *Address:* 10 Rutland Street, SW7 1EH. *Clubs:* White's, Hawks.

DURMAN, David John; Editor-in-Chief, IPC Magazines, 1994–99; *b* 10 July 1948; *s* of late John Durman and Joan Durman; *m* 1973, Hilary Pamela Aldrick. *Educ:* Leeds Univ. (BA). Dep. Editor, Woman's Own, 1986–88; Editor, Woman, 1988–94. Chm., BSME, 1996. *Recreations:* reading, theatre, life. *Address:* c/o IPC Media, Blue Fin Building, 110 Southwark Street, SE1 0SU.

DURNING, Josephine Marie; freelance translator, French to English, since 2013; Co-Director, Europe and World Trade, Department of Trade and Industry, 2003–05; *b* 27 Aug. 1952; *d* of late Cecil and of Isobel M. Durning; *m* 1984, Paul Stephen Capella (*d* 2004); one *s* one *d*. *Educ:* Loreto Coll., St Albans; Univ. of Keele (BA Hons Eng. and Politics 1974). Entered CS as admin trainee, 1974; Private Sec. to Parly Under-Sec. of State, Dept of Employment, 1978–79; Sec. to HSE, 1982–85; Labour Attaché, Paris, 1985–89; Head of Sen. Mgt Support Unit, Dept of Employment, 1990–91; Head of Internat. and Gen. Policy, HSE, 1991–96; with Econ. and Domestic Secretariat, Cabinet Office, 1996–98; Dir, Transdeptl Gp, OST, 1998–2002, Head, Community Interest Company Team, 2002–03, DTI; ind. consultant, 2005–12. Vis. Lectr (Dip. Trans.), Univ. of Westminster, 2015–. FRSA 2000. *Recreations:* reading, riding. *Address:* 29 Gold Street, Saffron Walden, Essex CB10 1EJ.

DURR, Kent Diederich Skelton; consultant, and trustee of family trusts, since 2005; *b* 28 March 1941; *s* of Dr John Michael Durr and Diana (*née* Skelton); *m* 1st, 1966, Suzanne Wiese (*d* 2010); one *s* two *d*; 2nd, 2011, Melanie Catherine Williamson; two *s*. *Educ:* South African Coll. Schs; Cape Town Univ. Dir, family publishing co., 1966–68; Founder and later Man. Dir, Durr Estates, 1968–84. Elected to Provincial Council of Cape, 1974; MP for Maitland, SA, 1977–91; Dep. Minister, Trade and Industry, 1984–86, Finance, 1984–88; Minister of Budget and Public Works in Ministers' Council, 1988–89; Cabinet Minister of Trade and Industry and Tourism, 1989–91; S African Ambassador to UK, 1991–94; High Comr for S Africa in London, 1994–95; Chairman: Fuel-Tech NV, 1995–97; Clean Diesel Technologies, Inc., 1995–97; Commonwealth Investment Guarantee Agency Ltd, 1997–99; MP (African Christian Democratic Party) Western Cape Province, 1999–2005. Mem., SA Nat. Foundn for Conservation of Coastal Birds, 1985 (Award of Honour, 1987). Freeman: City of London,

1995; Vintners' Co., 1995. *Publications:* numerous articles in newspapers and jls on econs, foreign affairs, constitutional affairs, urban renewal, conservation and business. *Recreations:* history, field sports, conservation. *Address:* 7 Bosch Heuvel, Violet Road, Upper Claremont 7708, Cape Town, South Africa. *Clubs:* Royal Over-Seas League; Kelvin Grove (Cape Town, SA).

DURRAN, Alexia Grainne; Her Honour Judge Durran; a Circuit Judge, since 2014; *b* London, 10 July 1971; *d* of Richard and Lesley Durran; *m* 2004, Rupert Pardoe. *Educ:* Lady Manners Sch., Bakewell, Derbys; St Catharine's Coll., Cambridge (BA Hons 1992; MA 1996); Univ. of Westminster (CPE); Inns of Court Sch. of Law. Called to the Bar, Middle Temple, 1995; in practice as criminal barrister, 1995–2014; a Recorder, 2009–14. *Recreations:* reading, cinema, family, theatre. *Address:* Reading Crown Court, The Old Shire Hall, The Forbury, Reading, Berks RG1 3EH. *T:* (0118) 967 4400. *E:* hhjudge.durran@judiciary.gsi.gov.uk.

DURRANDS, Prof. Kenneth James, CBE 1992; DGS (Birm), MSc, CEng, FIMechE, FIET; Vice-Chancellor and Rector, University of Huddersfield, 1992–95 (Rector, The Polytechnic, Huddersfield, 1970–92; Professor, 1985); *b* 24 June 1929; *s* of A. I. Durrands, Croxton Kerrial; *m* 1956 (marr. diss. 1971); one *s*; *m* 1983, Jennifer Jones; one *s*. *Educ:* King's Sch., Grantham; Nottingham Technical Coll.; Birmingham Univ. Min. of Supply Engrg Apprentice, ROF, Nottingham, 1947–52; Techn. Engr, UKAEA, Risley, 1954–58; Lecturer in Mechanical and Nuclear Engrg, Univ. of Birmingham, 1958–61; Head of Gen. Engrg Dept, Reactor Engrg Lab., UKAEA, Risley, 1961–67; Technical Dir, Vickers Ltd, Barrow Engrg Works, 1967–70. Vis. Lectr, Manchester Univ., 1962–68. Member: DoI Educn and Training Cttee, 1973–75 (Chm., 1975–80); DoI Garment & Allied Industries Requirements Bd, 1975–79 (Chm. Computer Cttee, 1975–79); BEC Educn Cttee, 1975–79; BEC Business Studies Bd, 1976–79; Inter-Univ. and Polytech. Council, 1978–81; Yorks Consumers' Cttee, Office of Electricity Regulation, 1990–94; British Council: Higher Educn Cttee, 1981–91; Engrg and Technology Adv. Cttee, 1981–90; Cttee, CICHE, 1985–95; Council for the Accreditation of Teacher Educn, 1991–92; Hon. Sec./Treas., Cttee of Dirs of Polytechnics, 1970–79. Educn Comr, MSC, subseq. Training Commn, 1986–89. Mem. Council, IMechE, 1963–66. Preliminary Judge, Prince of Wales Award for Industrial Innovation and Production, 1982–95. Member, Court: Leeds Univ., 1970–95; Bradford Univ., 1973–95; Mem. Council, Barnsley Coll., 1996–2000; Governor, King's Sch., Grantham, 1999– (Vice-Chm., 2004–). Founder Chm., Assoc. of Lincs Sch. Governing Bodies, 2005–07 (Mem. Exec. Cttee, 2005–11); Mem., Lincs Schs' Forum, 2007–. *Publications:* technical and policy papers. *Recreations:* gardening, reading, walking. *Address:* Church Cottage, Croxton Kerrial, Grantham, Lincolnshire NG32 1PY. *Club:* Athenæum.

DURRANI, Prof. Tariq Salim, OBE 2003; PhD; FRSE; FIET, FIEEE, FREng; Research Professor, Electronic and Electrical Engineering, University of Strathclyde, since 2009; *b* Amraoti, India, 27 Oct. 1943; *s* of Mohammed Salim Khan Durrani and Bilquis Jamal; *m* 1972, Clare Elizabeth Kellas; one *s* two *d*. *Educ:* E Pakistan Univ. of Engrg and Technol., Dacca (BEng Hons 1965); Univ. of Southampton (MSc 1967; PhD 1970). FIET (FIEE 1982); FIEEE 1989; FREng 1996. Res. Fellow, Univ. of Southampton, 1970–76; University of Strathclyde: Lectr, 1976–79; Sen. Lectr, 1979–82; Prof. of Signal Processing, 1982–2009; Hd, Signal Processing Div., 1982–2006; Chair, Electrical and Electronic Engrg, 1986–90; Special Advr (IT) to Principal, 1991–94; Dep. Principal, 2000–06; Special Advr to Principal, 2007–08. Fellow, Third World Acad. Scis, 1998; Vis. Professorial Fellow, 1996–98, Vis. Res. Collaborator, 2012–15, Princeton Univ.; Vis. Prof., USC, 2012–13; Hon. Prof., Univ. of Stirling, 2011–15. Director: Scottish Electronics Technol. Gp, 1986–2004; NATO Advanced Study Inst., Les Houches, 1987; UK Inst. for Systems Level Integration, 1999–2010; Scottish Inst. for Enterprise, 2001–05; Glasgow Chamber of Commerce, 2003–14; Leadership Foundn for UK Higher Educn, 2003–09; Kelvin Inst., 2004–05; SFC, 2005–09; UK Equality Challenge Unit, 2009–12; UK Nat. Commn for UNESCO, 2011–. Mem., Parly and Scientific Cttee, Houses of Parlt, 1991–94. Member: Council, Scottish Electronics Forum, 1993–95; Coll. of Peers on IT-Communications, EPSRC, 1997–2009; Scottish Sci. Adv. Bd, 2002–04. Mem., Complaints Cttee, Law Soc. of Scotland, 1999–2004. Member: Res. Rev. Bd, Govt of Netherlands, 1999; Internat. Rev. Cttee, Min. of Educn and Industry, Carnegie Mellon-Portugal Prog., 2006–13. Member: Internat. Adv. Bd, Etisalat Coll. of Technol., Sharjah, 1996–99; Bd of Councillors, US NSF Centre of Excellence in Immersive Multimedia Systems, USC, 2000–05; Adv. Bd, Centre for Multimedia Signal Processing, Hong Kong Poly. Univ., 2002–06; Great Master, III Project, Univ. of Electronic Sci. and Technol. of China, Chengdu, 2011–15. Royal Society of Edinburgh: Mem. Council, 2003–06; Vice Pres. (Natural Scis), 2007–10; Vice Pres. (Internat.), 2012–15. Institute of Electrical and Electronics Engineers: Pres., Signal Processing Soc., 1994–95; Chair: Periodicals Council, 1996–97; Periodicals Rev. Cttee, 1998–99; Vice-Chair, Tech. Activities Reg. 8, 2004–06; Pres., Engrg Mgt Soc., 2006–07; Dir, EMEA Reg., Communications Soc., 2009–11; Vice Pres., Educnl Activities Bd, 2010–11. FRSE 1994. Mem., Eta Kappa Nu, 2010. Aerospace and Electronic Systems M. Barry Carlton Honourable Mention Award, Signal Processing Soc., 1974; Meritorious Service Award, 2000, Third Millennium Medal, 2001, IEEE. *Publications:* (with C. Greated) Laser Systems in Flow Measurements, 1977; (with E. Robinson) Geophysical Signal Processing, 1986; (ed jtly) Signal Processing, 1987; (ed) Mathematics and Signal Processing, 1987; (ed) Transputer Applications 3, 1991; 350 contribs to archival jls and internat. confs. *Recreation:* occasional golf. *Address:* Department of Electronic and Electrical Engineering, University of Strathclyde, 204 George Street, Glasgow G1 1XW. *T:* (0141) 548 2540, *Fax:* (0141) 552 2487. *E:* durrani@strath.ac.uk. *Clubs:* Western (Glasgow); Ross Priory (Loch Lomond).

DURRANT, His Honour Anthony Harrisson; a Circuit Judge, 1991–99; *b* 3 Jan. 1931; *s* of Frank Baston Durrant and Irene Maud Durrant; *m* 1956, Jacqueline Ostroumoff; one *s* two *d*. *Educ:* Sir Joseph Williamson's Mathematical Sch., Rochester. Admitted Solicitor, 1956; Partner, 1960, Sen. Partner, 1976–91, Horwood & James, Aylesbury; a Recorder, 1987–91. Dep. Chm., Agricl Land Tribunal, 1987–91. Pres., Berks, Bucks and Oxon Incorp. Law Soc., 1977–78; Chm., Berks, Bucks and Oxon Jt Consultative Cttee of Barristers and Solicitors, 1985–91.

See also A. J. Trace.

DURRANT, Anthony Richard Charles; Chief Executive Officer, Premier Oil, since 2015 (Finance Director, 2005–14); *b* Luton, Beds, 7 Aug. 1958; *s* of Geoffrey and Margaret Durrant; *m* 1985, Jan Rennie; one *s* one *d*. *Educ:* King's Sch., Canterbury; Corpus Christi Coll., Oxford (Schol.; BA PPE 1980). With Arthur Andersen & Co., 1980–86; Audit Senior, 1983–84; Senior, Mgt Consulting, 1985–86; Lehman Brothers, 1986–2005 (Man. Dir and Hd, Eur. Natural Resources Gp, 1997–2005). Non-executive Director: Clipper Windpower plc, 2005–; Greenenergy Fuels Hldgs Ltd, 2012–. *Recreations:* golf, Rugby, cricket, travel. *Address:* 1 Woodborough Road, Putney, SW15 6PX. *T:* (020) 8788 6437. *E:* tdurrant@premieroil.com.

DURRANT, Jennifer Ann, RA 1994; painter; began living and working in Umbria, 2000; *b* 17 June 1942; *d* of Caleb John Durrant and Winifred May (*née* Wright); *m* 1964, William Alistair Herriot Henderson (marr. diss. 1976); *m* 2000, Richard Alban Howard Oxby. *Educ:* Varndean Grammar Sch. for Girls, Brighton; Brighton Coll. of Art; Slade Sch. of Fine Art; University Coll. London (Dip. Fine Art). FRCA 1993. Postgrad. Scholar, Slade Sch. of Fine Art, 1965–66. Artist in Residence, Somerville Coll., Oxford, 1979–80. Part-time Lecturer: RCA, 1979–2000; Royal Acad. Schs, 1990–98. External Assessor: Reading Univ. MA Fine Art, 1980s; Duncan of Jordanstone Coll. of Art, Univ. of Dundee, 1993–97; Limerick and Cork Colls of Art, 1998–2001; Falmouth Coll. of Art, 1998–2002. *Solo exhibitions* include: Arnolfini Gall., Bristol, 1979; Mus. of Modern Art, Oxford, 1980; Nicola Jacobs Gall., London, 1982 and 1983; Serpentine Gall., 1987; Newlyn Orion Gall., Penzance, 1988; Concourse Gall., Barbican, 1992; Salander-O'Reilly Galls, NY, 1993 and 2000; Francis Graham-Dixon Gall., London, 1996; Friends' Room, Royal Acad., 1996 and 2005; Art First Contemporary Art, Cork St, 2005; Richmond Hill Gall., London, 2011; *group exhibitions* include: Hayward Gall., 1976, 1979, 1980 and 1990; Mus. of Fine Art, Boston, Mass and Royal Acad., 1977; Salander-O'Reilly Galls, NY, 1981; Tate Gall. and Carnegie Inst., Pittsburgh, 1982; Serpentine Gall., 1983 and 1984; Royal Acad., 1985; Mall Galls, London, 1990–92; also in provincial galls in UK, and in Europe; has exhibited at Royal Acad. Summer Exhibn, 1986, 1987 and annually, 1989–; *works in public collections* including: Arts Council, British Council; Contemporary Art Soc.; Mus. of Fine Arts, Boston, Mass; Tate Gall.; Govt Art Collection; Neue Galerie, Aachen; Trinity Coll., Cambridge; *commissions:* Newham Hosp.; R. P. Scherer 50th Anniv., Swindon, 1987; Thomas Neal, Covent Gdn, 1992; Glaxo UK, Stevenage, 1994. Arts Council Award, 1976; Arts Council Major Award, 1978; Gtr London Arts Assoc. Award, 1980; Athena Art Award, 1988; Artist of the Year, Independent on Sunday, 1996. *Recreations:* classical music, opera, archaeology, museums, painting and sculpture, the natural world. *Address:* La Vigna, Via Bondi 14, 06069 Tuoro-sul-Trasimeno (PG), Italy. *T:* and *Fax:* (075) 829010.

DURRANT, Sir William (Alexander Estridge), 8th Bt *cr* 1784, of Scottow, Norfolk; *b* 26 Nov. 1929; *o s* of Sir William Henry Estridge Durrant, 7th Bt and Georgina Beryl Gwendoline (*d* 1968), *d* of Alexander Purse; *S* father, 1994; *m* 1953, Dorothy (*d* 2012), *d* of Ronal Croker, Quirindi, NSW; one *s* one *d*. *Heir: s* David Alexander Durrant [*b* 1 July 1960; *m* 1st, 1989, Maria Lucia Leonard (marr. diss. 2002); three *s*; 2nd, 2006, Mary Josephine Renehan]. *Address:* Red Hill, Nundle Road, Nemingha, NSW 2340, Australia.

DURRANT-WHYTE, Prof. Hugh Francis, PhD; FRS 2010; FTSE, FIEEE; FAA; Chief Executive Officer, NICTA, since 2010; *b* London, 6 Feb. 1961; *s* of Hugh and Dorothy Durrant-Whyte; *m* 1986, Daphne Adie; two *s* two *d*. *Educ:* Richard Hale Sch., Hertford; Queen Mary Coll., Univ. of London (BSc 1st Cl. Hons Engrg 1983); Univ. of Pennsylvania (MSE Systems Engrg 1985; PhD Systems Engrg 1986). University of Oxford: BP Res. Fellow, Dept of Engrg Sci., and Fellow, St Cross Coll., 1986–87; Univ. Lectr in Engrg Sci., and Fellow, Oriel Coll., 1987–95; Prof. of Mechatronic Engrg, Dept of Aerospace, Univ. of Sydney, 1995–2010; Dir, Aust. Res. Council Centre of Excellence for Autonomous Systems, 2003–10. Aust. Res. Council Fedn Fellow, 2002–. FTSE 2002; FIEEE 2005; FAA 2009. *Publications:* five books; over 350 academic articles. *Recreations:* geology, opera, running. *Address:* NICTA, Australian Technology Park, Level 5, 13 Garden Street, Eveleigh, NSW 2015, Australia.

DURRINGTON, Prof. Paul Nelson, MD; FRCP, FRCPath, FMedSci; Professor of Medicine, University of Manchester, since 1995; Hon. Consultant Physician, Manchester Royal Infirmary, 1982–2012; *b* 24 July 1947; *s* of Alec Edward Durrington and May Ena Durrington (*née* Nelson); *m* 1969, Patricia Joyce Gibbs; one *s* two *d*. *Educ:* Chislehurst and Sidcup Grammar Sch. for Boys; Univ. of Bristol (BSc Hons Physiol. 1969; MB ChB 1972; MD 1978). MRCP 1975, FRCP 1987; MRCPath 1982, FRCPath 1994. Hse Officer and SHO appts in medicine, paediatrics and surgery, Bristol, 1972–76; Lectr, 1976–82, Sen. Lectr, 1982–92, Reader, 1992–95, in Medicine, Univ. of Manchester. Travelling Fellow, BHF and Amer. Heart Assoc. (Vis. Prof., Div. of Metabolism, Dept of Medicine, UCSD), 1979–80. Dir, R&D, Central Manchester Healthcare NHS Trust, 1997–2001. Med. Dir, Family Heart Assoc., 1995–. Chm., British Hyperlipidaemia Assoc., 1992–95. Mem., Assoc. of Physicians of GB and Ireland, 1992. FMedSci 2001; Fellow, Amer. Heart Assoc. 2001; FACP 2010. *Publications:* Hyperlipidaemia, Diagnosis and Treatment, 1989, 3rd edn 2007; Pocketbook of Preventative Cardiology, 1993, 2nd edn 2001; (with A. Sniderman) Hyperlipidaemia, 2000, 5th edn 2010; contrib. articles on lipid metabolism, diabetes and coronary heart disease to learned jls. *Recreations:* angling (Mem., Prince Albert Angling Soc.), hill-walking (Mem., Ramblers' Assoc.), oenology (Mem., Commanderie de Bordeaux à Manchester). *Address:* Cardiovascular Research Group, School of Biomedicine, Core Technology Facility (3rd Floor), University of Manchester, 46 Grafton Street, Manchester M13 9NT. *T:* (0161) 275 1201, *Fax:* (0161) 275 1183. *E:* pdurrington@manchester.ac.uk.

du SAUTOY, Prof. Marcus Peter Francis, OBE 2010; DPhil; Professor of Mathematics, since 2002, and Charles Simonyi Professor for the Public Understanding of Science, since 2008, University of Oxford; Fellow, New College, Oxford, since 2008; *b* 26 Aug. 1965; *s* of Bernard and Jennifer du Sautoy; *m* 1994, Shani Ram; one *s* twin *d* (and one *s* decd). *Educ:* Gillotts Comprehensive Sch., Henley-on-Thames; King James Sixth Form Coll., Henley-on-Thames; Wadham Coll., Oxford (BA Hons Maths 1986); DPhil Oxon 1989. SERC Postdoctoral Res. Fellow, QMW, Univ. of London, 1989–90; Postdoctoral Res. Fellow, All Souls Coll., Oxford, 1990–95; Royal Society University Research Fellow: Univ. of Cambridge, 1995–2001; Univ. of Oxford, 2001–05; Fellow, Wadham College, Oxford, 2005–08. Pres., Math. Assoc., 2012–13. Christmas Lectr, Royal Instn, 2006. BBC presenter: Mindgames, 2004–05; Music of the Primes, 2005; The Story of Maths, 2008; Horizon, 2009–12; The Code, 2011; Maestro at the Opera, 2012; Precision: The Measure of All Things, 2013; co-presenter, Dara Ó Briain's Sch. of Hard Sums, 2012–13. Berwick Prize, LMS, 2001; Michael Faraday Prize, Royal Soc., 2009. *Publications:* The Music of the Primes, 2003, 6th edn 2007; Finding Moonshine: a mathematician's journey through symmetry, 2008; The Number Mysteries, 2011. *Recreations:* No 17 for Recreativo Hackney FC, playing the trumpet, theatre. *Address:* New College, Oxford OX1 3BN.

DUTHIE, Sir Robert Grieve, (Sir Robin), Kt 1987; CBE 1978; CA; Vice Chairman, Advisory Board for Scotland, BP, 1990–2002; *b* 2 Oct. 1928; *s* of George Duthie and Mary (*née* Lyle); *m* 1955, Violetta Noel Maclean; two *s* one *d*. *Educ:* Greenock Academy. Apprentice Chartered Accountant with Thomson Jackson Gourlay & Taylor, CA, 1946–51 (CA 1952); joined Blacks of Greenock, 1952: Man. Dir, 1962; Chairman: Black & Edgington Ltd, 1972–83; Insight Internat. Tours Ltd, 1979–84; Bruntons (Musselburgh), 1984–86; Britoil, 1988–90; Tay Residential Investment Ltd, 1989–96; Neill Clerk Gp plc, 1994–98; Director: British Assets Trust, 1977–98; Royal Bank of Scotland, 1978–99; Investors Capital Trust, 1985–94; Carclo Engineering Gp, 1986–98; British Polythene Industries (formerly Scott & Robertson), 1989–99; Devol Engineering Ltd, 1994–2004. Chm., Greenock Provident Bank, 1974; Dir, Greenock Chamber of Commerce, 1967–68; Tax Liaison Officer for Scotland, CBI, 1976–79. Chm., SDA, 1979–88; Member: Scottish Telecommunications Bd, 1972–77; E Kilbride Devel Corp., 1976–78; Clyde Port Authority, 1971–83 (Chm., 1977–80); Council, Inst. of Chartered Accountants of Scotland, 1973–78; Scottish Econ. Council, 1980–95; Council, Strathclyde Business Sch., 1986–94; Governing Council, Scottish Business in the Community, 1987–95. Chm., Made Up Textiles Assoc. of GB, 1972; Pres., Inverkip Soc., 1966; Mem. of Council, Royal Caledonian Curling Club, 1985–88. Commissioner: Queen Victoria Sch., Dunblane, 1972–89; Scottish Congregational Ministers Pension Fund, 1973–2003; Treasurer, Greenock W URC, 1970–. Fellow, Scottish Vocational Council, 1988. CCMI (CBIM 1976); FRSA 1983. Hon. FRIAS, 1989. Hon. Fellow, Paisley Coll., 1990. Hon. LLD Strathclyde, 1984; Hon. DTech Napier Coll., 1989. *Recreation:* golf. *Address:* Fairhaven, Finnart Street, Greenock PA16 8JA. *T:* (01475) 722642.

DUTTON, Maj.-Gen. Bryan Hawkins, CB 1997; CBE 1990 (OBE 1984; MBE 1978); Director-General, Leonard Cheshire Disability (formerly Leonard Cheshire Foundation), 1998–2008; *b* 1 March 1943; *s* of late Ralph Dutton and Honor Badcoe (formerly Dutton, *née* Morris); *m* 1972, Angela Margaret Wilson; one *s* one *d*. *Educ:* Lord Weymouth Sch.; RMA

Sandhurst. Commissioned, Devonshire and Dorset Regt, 1963; served NI, British Guiana, Libya, Belize, Germany, UK; Instructor, Sch. of Infantry, 1969–71; RMCS and Staff Coll., 1974–75; C-in-C's Mission to Soviet Forces in Germany, 1976–78; Co. Comdr, 1st Devonshire and Dorset, 1978–79 (despatches 1979); Planning Staff, NI Office, 1979–81; Instructor, Staff Coll., 1981–82; MA to Adjutant-Gen., 1982–84; CO 1st Bn Devonshire and Dorset Regt, 1984–87; Ops Staff, UKLF, 1987; Comdr 39 Infantry Brigade, 1987–89; Dir, Public Relations (Army), 1990–92; Dir of Infantry, 1992–94; Comdr British Forces, Hong Kong, 1994–97. Col Comdt, POW Div., 1996–99; Col, Devonshire and Dorset Regt, 1998–2003. Chairman: Voluntary Orgns Disability Gp, 2004–08; The Keep Military Mus. of Devon and Dorset, 2008–; Action for Stammering Children (formerly Assoc. for Res. into Stammering in Childhood), 2009–14. Gov., 1999–, Trustee, 2011–, Hayes Dashwood Foundn. FRSA; CCMI. *Recreations:* golf, fishing, wild-life, Rugby spectator, history, classical music. *Address:* Highwood, East Grimstead, Wilts SP5 3SA.

DUTTON, Lt-Gen. Sir James Benjamin, KCB 2010; CBE 2003; Governor and Commander-in-Chief, Gibraltar, 2013–15; *b* 21 Feb. 1954; *s* of Edgar and Aileen Dutton; *m* 1978, Elizabeth Waddell; one *s* one *d*. *Educ:* King's Sch., Chester; City Univ., London (BSc Hons (Systems and Mgt)); RCDS. Joined RM, 1972; COS, 3 Commando Bde, 1991–93; Comdr, RM Officers' Trng, 1993; Asst Dir, Jt Warfare, MoD, 1996; CO, 40 Commando, 1996–98; Dir, NATO Policy, MoD, 1998–2000; seconded to Jt Staff, Pentagon, 2001–02; Comdr, 3 Commando Bde, 2002–04; Comdr Multinat. Div. SE and GOC British Forces Iraq, 2005; Comdt Gen., Royal Marines, and Comdr, UK Amphibious Forces, 2004–06; COS (Capability) to C-in-C Fleet, 2006–07; Dep. Chief of Jt Ops (Ops), later COS (Ops), MoD, 2007–08; Dep. Comdr, ISAF, 2008–09. Infrastructure and Ops Manager, Bechtel Corp., 2010–11; Prog. Dir, Gabon Infrastructure Project, Bechtel Internat., Libreville, Gabon, 2011–13; Dir-Gen., Agence Nat. des Grands Travaux, Gabon (on secondment), 2012–13. US Legion of Merit, 2010. *Recreation:* sailing.

DUTTON, Prof. P(eter) Leslie, FRS 1990; Professor of Biochemistry and Biophysics, since 1981 (Chairman, Department of Biochemistry and Biophysics, 1994–2008), and Director, Johnson Foundation for Molecular Biophysics, since 1991, University of Pennsylvania; *b* 12 March 1941; *s* of Arthur Bramwell Dutton and Mary Dutton; *m* 1965, Dr Julia R. Dwyer; two *s* one *d*. *Educ:* Univ. of Wales (BSc Hons Chem.; PhD Biochem.). PD Fellow, Dept of Biochem. and Soil Science, Univ. of Wales, 1967–68; University of Pennsylvania: PD Fellow, 1968–71, Asst Prof., 1971–76, Johnson Res. Foundn; Associate Prof., Dept of Biochem. and Biophysics, 1976–81; Hon. MA 1976. *Recreations:* painting (several one-man and group shows in Wales and USA), sailing. *Address:* Department of Biochemistry and Biophysics, University of Pennsylvania, Stellar-Chance Building, Suite 1005, 422 Curie Boulevard, Philadelphia, PA 19104–6059, USA. *T:* (215) 8980991, *Fax:* (215) 5732235; 654 West Rose Tree Road, Media, PA 19063, USA. *Clubs:* Mantoloking Yacht (NJ); Corinthian Yacht (Philadelphia).

DUTTON, Roger Thomas; His Honour Judge Dutton; DL; a Circuit Judge, since 1996; *b* 24 March 1952; *s* of late Donald Roger Dutton and Doreen May Dutton (*née* Ankers); *m* 1977, Elaine Alison Dixon (*d* 2014); one *s* two *d*. *Educ:* Acton Sch., Wrexham; Grove Park Grammar Sch., Wrexham; Univ. of Kent (BA Hons Law 1973); Inns of Court Sch. of Law. Called to the Bar, Middle Temple, 1974; in practice at the Bar, 1974–96; Mem., Wales and Chester Circuit. Asst Recorder, 1988–92; Recorder, 1992–96; Liaison Judge, N Wales Magistrates, 1998–2007, Macclesfield, Crewe and Nantwich Magistrates, 2007–; Disciplinary Investigating Judge, 2007–; Interviewing Judge for Lord Chancellor's Dept, 2002–06, for Judicial Appts Commn, 2006–. Mem., Judges' Council for England and Wales, 2014. Circuit Rep., Cttee of Council of HM's Circuit Judges, 2004–05 (Hon. Treas., 2005–12; Jun. Vice-Pres., 2012; Sen. Vice-Pres., 2013; Pres., 2014). Mem., Tutor Judge Panel, Judicial Coll. (formerly Judicial Studies Bd), 2007–. North Wales Institute of Higher Education, later Glyndŵr University: Mem. Bd Govs, 2002–07; Mem. Nominations Cttee, 2008–14; Hon. Fellow, 2009. Vicar Gen., Principal and Pres. of Consistory Court, and Chancellor, Dio. of St Asaph, 2010–. DL Clwyd, 2008. *Recreations:* golf, walking, travel, gardening, watching cricket, soccer, Rugby Union. *Address:* The Crown Court, The Castle, Chester CH1 2AN. *T:* (01244) 317606. *Clubs:* Lansdowne; Chester City (Pres., 2011–12), Cheshire Pitt; Wrexham Golf.

DUTTON, Timothy Christopher; QC 2013; *b* Essex, 1962; *s* of John Arthur and Patricia Dutton. *Educ:* Godalming Co. Grammar Sch.; Univ. of Durham (BA). Called to the Bar, Inner Temple, 1985; in practice as barrister, 1985–. *Recreations:* Association Croquet, music (performing and listening), opera. *Address:* Maitland Chambers, 7 Stone Buildings, Lincoln's Inn, WC2A 3SZ. *T:* (020) 7406 1200, *Fax:* (020) 7406 1300. *Club:* Hurlingham.

DUTTON, Timothy James; QC 1998; a Recorder, since 2000; a Deputy High Court Judge; *b* 25 Feb. 1957; *s* of late J. D. Dutton, MA, JP and of J. R. Dutton (*née* Parsons); *m* 1987, Sappho Raschid-Dias; one *d*. *Educ:* Repton Sch.; Keble Coll., Oxford (BA Jurisp. 1978). Called to the Bar, Middle Temple, 1979, Bencher, 2003; an Asst Recorder, 1998–2000. Leader, SE Circuit, 2004–06. Hd, Fountain Court Chambers, 2008–13. Chm., Bench Selection Adv. Cttee, Middle Temple, 2012–14. Advocacy teaching for Nat. Inst. for Trial Advocacy and the Bar, UK and USA, 1987–; Founder and Dir, Keble Advanced Advocacy Course, 1994–2004. Chm., Inns of Court Advocacy Trng Cttee, 2000–04; Bar Council: Vice-Chm., 2007; Chm., 2008; Vice-Chm., Direct Access Cttee, 2001–03; Chm., Wkg Party into Advocacy Trng, 2002–04; Vice-Chm., Educn and Trng Cttee, 2003–. Founder Mem., Burma Justice Cttee, 2007–. Chm., Assoc. of Regulatory and Disciplinary Lawyers, 2009–. Member: Admin. Law Bar Assoc.; Commercial Bar Assoc. Lectured widely on professional negligence, regulation and legal services. Gov., Legal Educn Foundn (formerly Coll. of Law), 2011–. Founder and Chm., Bar Choral Soc. *Publications:* (contrib.) Guide to the Legal Services Act 2007, 2008; contribs to Lloyds List, Financial Times, (on insce law) World Policy Review Guide. *Recreations:* music (French Horn, baritone, choral), sailing, gardening. *Address:* Fountain Court Chambers, Temple, EC4Y 9DH. *T:* (020) 7583 3335.

DUTTON, Prof. William Harold, PhD; Quello Chair, Department of Media and Information, and Director, Quello Center, College of Communication Arts and Sciences, Michigan State University, since 2014; *b* 23 Aug. 1947; *s* of Paul V. Dutton and Rosa Lee Dutton; *m* 1981, Diana; two *d*. *Educ:* Univ. of Missouri, Columbia (BA Hons Pol Sci. 1969); State Univ. of NY, Buffalo (MA 1971; PhD Pol Sci. 1974); MA Oxon 2002. Instructor, Dept of Pol Sci., SUNY, Buffalo, 1972–73; Asst Prof., Dept of Pol Sci., Univ. of S Florida, 1973–74; Asst Res. Pol Scientist, Public Policy Res. Orgn, Univ. of Calif, Irvine, 1974–78; Associate Prof., Sch. of Public Admin and Urban Studies, San Diego State Univ., 1978–80; Annenberg School for Communication, University of Southern California: Associate Prof., 1980–82; Associate Prof. (with tenure), 1983–89; Prof., 1990–2002; Prof. of Internet Studies, 2002–14, Founding Dir, Oxford Internet Inst., 2002–11, Univ. of Oxford; Fellow, Balliol Coll., Oxford, 2002–14. Vis. Res. Pol Scientist, Univ. of Calif, Irvine, 1979–82; Brunel University: Fulbright Schol. and Vis. Prof., Dept of Human Scis, 1986–87; Nat. Dir, Prog. on Inf. and Communication Technol., ESRC and Vis. Prof., Dept of Human Scis, 1993–95. Chm., Adv. Cttee for England, 2009, Mem. for SE, 2009, Ofcom. *Publications:* (jtly) The Management of Information Systems, 1981; (jtly) Computers and Politics: high technology in American local governments, 1982; (with K. L. Kraemer) Modeling as Negotiating: the political dynamics of computer models in the policy process, 1985; (ed jtly) Information and Communication Technologies: visions and realities, 1996; (ed jtly) The Social Shaping of the Information Superhighway: European and American roads to the information society, 1997; Society on the Line: information politics in the digital age, 1999; (ed jtly) Digital Academe, 2002; Social Transformation in the Information Society, 2004; (ed jtly) Transforming Enterprise, 2005; (ed jtly) World Wide Research, 2010; (jtly) Freedom of Connection—Freedom of Expression, 2011; The Oxford Handbook of Internet Studies, 2013; (ed jtly) Society and the Internet, 2014; contrib. chapters in books; contrib. articles to professional jls incl. Prometheus, Information, Communication & Society. *Recreations:* walking, blogging, learning to play the piano. *Address:* Quello Center, 406 Communication Arts Building, Michigan State University, East Lansing, MI 48824–1212, USA. *T:* (517) 4328001, *Fax:* (517) 4328065. *E:* quello@msu.edu.

DUVAL, Robin Arthur Philip, CBE 2005; Director, British Board of Film Classification, 1999–2004; *b* 28 April 1941; *s* of Arthur and Jane Duval; *m* 1968, Lorna Eileen Watson; four *d* (one *s* decd). *Educ:* King Edward's Sch., Birmingham; University Coll. London (BA); Univ. of Michigan (Fulbright Schol.). Studio manager, BBC, 1964–65; TV producer, J. Walter Thompson, 1965–68; documentary and film producer, COI, 1968–78; Hd, Overseas Prodn, COI, 1978–81; Principal, Home Office, 1981–83; Hd, UK Prodn, COI, 1983–85; Chief Asst, Television, IBA, 1985–90; Dep. Dir, Programmes, ITC, 1991–98. *Publications: novels:* Bear in the Woods, 2010; Below the Thunder, 2013; Not Single Spies, 2015; articles in jls. *Recreations:* music, food, Aston Villa. *Address:* 35 Castlebar Park, Ealing, W5 1DA.

DUVALL, Leonard, OBE 1998; Member (Lab) Greenwich and Lewisham, since 2000, and Leader, Labour Group, since 2004, London Assembly, Greater London Authority; *b* 26 Sept. 1961; *m* (marr. diss.); two *s*. *Educ:* Hawthorn Sch., London. Mem., Greenwich LBC, 1990–2000 (Leader of Council, 1992–2000). Chairman: London Thames Gateway Partnership, 1997–2000; Local Govt Improvement and Develt Agency, 1998–2000; Dep. Chm., Assoc. of London Govt, 1996–2000; Chm., Commonwealth Local Govt Forum, 2000–05 (Vice-Chm., 1998–2000). Vice-Chm., London Develt Agency, 2000–03; Chairman: London Health Commn, 2002–04; Metropolitan Police Authy, 2004–08. Chm., Gtr London Lab. Party, 2002–. Non-exec. Dir, Tilfen Land, 2001–14. Chm., Greenwich Heritage Trust, 2014–; Trustee, Greenwich Foundn for Old Royal Naval Coll., 1997–2002; non-exec. Dir, Royal Artillery Museums Trust, 1998–2009. *Address:* Greater London Authority, City Hall, Queen's Walk, SE1 2AA. *T:* (020) 7983 4408/4517.

DUXFIELD, Julian; Human Resources Director, University of Oxford, since 2013; Fellow, Somerville College, Oxford, since 2013; *b* 9 Sept. 1962; *s* of John and Wendy Duxfield; partner Lucie Carrington; two *s* one *d*. *Educ:* Corpus Christi Coll., Oxford (BA PPE); London Sch. of Econs (MSc HR Mgt). HR rôles in Unilever, 1988–2000; HR Dir, Carlsberg UK, 2000–03; Dir, Human Resources, DfT, 2003–07; HR Dir, G4S Cash Solutions (formerly Cash Services UK, Gp 4 Securicor), 2007–11; UK HR Dir, G4S, 2011–12. Ext. Mem., Remuneration Cttee, Care Quality Commn, 2009–13. Member: Climbers' Club; Fell and Rock Climbing Club; Oxford Alpine Club. *Recreation:* mountaineering. *Address:* University of Oxford, Wellington Square, Oxford OX1 2JD. *E:* Julian.duxfield@admin.ox.ac.uk.

DWEK, Prof. Raymond Allen, CBE 2013; DPhil, DSc; FRS 1998; CChem, FRSC; CBiol, FRSB; Professor of Glycobiology, and Director of Glycobiology Institute (formerly Unit), University of Oxford, since 1988; Professorial Fellow, Exeter College, Oxford, 1988–2009, now Emeritus (Fellow, 1974–88); *b* 10 Nov. 1941; *s* of Victor Joe Dwek and Alice Liniado; *m* 1964, Sandra (*née* Livingstone); two *s* two *d*. *Educ:* Carmel Coll.; Manchester Univ. (BSc 1st Cl. Hons Chemistry and Mercer Scholar, 1963; MSc 1964); Lincoln Coll., Oxford (DPhil 1966; Hon. Fellow 2004); Exeter Coll., Oxford (DSc 1985). CChem, FRSC 1993; CBiol, FRSB (FIBiol 1999). Oxford University: Deptl Demonstrator, 1969–74; Lectr, 1976–88; Associate Hd, 1996–2000, Head, 2000–06, Biochem. Dept; Royal Soc. Locke Res. Fellow, 1974–76; Christ Church: Res. Lectr in Physical Chemistry, 1966–68, in Biochem., 1975–76; Lectr in Inorganic Chem., 1968–75; Lectr in Biochem., Trinity Coll., 1976–84. Vis. Royal Soc. Res. Fellow, Weizmann Inst., Rehovot, Israel, 1969; Kluge Chair of Technol. and Soc., Liby of Congress, Washington, 2007; Visiting Professor: Duke Univ., NC, seconded to Inst. of Exploratory Res., Fort Monmouth, NJ, 1968; Univ. of Trieste, Italy, 1974; Univ. of Lund, Sweden, 1977; Inst. of Enzymology, Budapest, 1980. Boyce Thompson Dist. Lectr in Glycobiology, Cornell Univ., USA, 1997; Sir Douglas Hague Lectr, Oxford Business Sch., 2010. Dir and Founding Scientist, Oxford GlycoScience (formerly Oxford GlycoSystems) Ltd, 1988–2003; Chm., Oxford University Consulting Ltd, 2000–02; Director: United Therapeutics, 2002–; Isis Innovation, 2003–08. Co-Chm., British Israel Academic Exchange Regenerative Medicine Initiative, 2012–. Member: Oxford Enzyme Gp, 1971–88; MRC AIDS Antiviral Steering Cttee, 1987–89; Founder Mem., Oxford Oligosaccharide Gp, 1983. Mem., Bd of Scientific Governors, 2003–, and Inst. Prof., Scripps Res. Inst., La Jolla, 2008–; Special Advr on Biotechnol. to Pres., Ben Gurion Univ. of the Negev, 2001–. Pres., Inst. of Biol., 2007–09. Hon. FRCP 2007. Internat. Mem. (formerly Foreign Mem.), Amer. Philosophical Soc., 2007. Mem., editl bds. Wellcome Trust Award, for research in biochemistry related to medicine, 1994. Hon. Dr: Leuven, 1996; Univ. Coll. Dublin, 2010; Hon. PhD Ben Gurion Univ. of Negev, 2001; Hon. DSc Scripps Res. Inst., USA, 2004; Dr *hc* Causa Cluj, Romania, 2006; Dip. *hc* Romanian Acad., 2010. First Scientific Leadership Award, Hepatitis B Foundn, Philadelphia, 1997; Centennial Award, Delaware Valley Coll., Penn, 1997; Huxley Medal, Inst. Biol., 2007; K. T. Wang Prize, Taiwan, 2010. Comdr, Nat. Order for Merit (Romania), 2000. *Publications:* Nuclear Magnetic Resonance (NMR) in Biochemistry, 1973; (jtly) Physical Chemistry Principles and Problems for Biochemists, 1975, 3rd edn 1983; (jtly) NMR in Biology, 1977; (jtly) Biological Spectroscopy, 1984; articles in books and jls on physical chemistry, biochemistry and medicine; various patents. *Recreations:* family, Patent Law, sport, listening to music. *Address:* Exeter College, Oxford OX1 3DP. *T:* (01865) 275344; Glycobiology Institute, Department of Biochemistry, University of Oxford, South Parks Road, Oxford OX1 3QU.

DWESAR, Sandeep, FCA; Chief Operating and Financial Officer, Barbican Centre and Guildhall School of Music and Drama, since 2010 (Finance Director, 2007–10); *b* New Delhi, India, 7 Jan. 1960; *s* of Mahendra and Asha Dwesar; *m* 1987, Kiran Bala Makkar; one *s* one *d*. *Educ:* Bristol Poly. (BA Hons). ACA 1989, FCA 2011. Lawrence Fink & Co., 1982–86; Fraser Limebeer, 1986–87; Financial Controller, Tiphook Rail Ltd, 1988–91; Eur. Treasury Manager, J. I. Case, Tenneco Inc., 1991–92; Hd of Finance, Lewisham Directeam, 1992–95; Consultant, London Bor. of Haringey, 1995–98; Finance Dir, Barbican Centre, 1999–2007. Non-exec. Dir, Cavendish Publishing Ltd, 1999–2005. Vis. Lectr, Artthink S Asia, 2009–. Trustee: Friends of Baale Mane (shelter for homeless girls in Bangalore), 2007–; Punchdrunk (immersive th. co.), 2010–; Design Council, 2011–. *Recreations:* history, travel, golf, debating. *Address:* Barbican Centre, Silk Street, EC2Y 8DS. *T:* (020) 7382 7075. *E:* sandeep.dwesar@barbican.org.uk. *Club:* Purley Downs Golf.

DWIGHT, Reginald Kenneth; *see* John, Sir E. H.

DWORKIN, Prof. Gerald; Herbert Smith Professor of European Law and Director, Centre of European Law, King's College, University of London, 1993–97, now Professor Emeritus; Director, Intellectual Property Academy, Singapore, 2003–05; *b* 8 July 1933; *s* of Louis and Rose Dworkin; *m* 1960, Celia Sharon Levin; two *s* one *d*. *Educ:* Raine's Grammar Sch., London; Univ. of Nottingham (LLB 1954). Admitted solicitor of Supreme Court, 1957; Asst Lectr, Lectr, then Reader, LSE, 1958–67; Prof. of Law, Univ. of Southampton, 1968–86; Herchel Smith Prof. of Intellectual Property Law, QMW, Univ. of London, 1986–92. Visiting Professor: Univ. of Monash, 1965–67, 1980, 1987; Univ. of NSW, 1975; Nat. Univ. of Singapore, 1985, 1991, 1997; Arizona State Univ., 1985. Mem., EC Cttee, Academic Experts on Copyright Law. Member: Council, Intellectual Property Inst. (formerly Common Law Inst. of Intellectual Property); Brit. Literary and Artistic Copyright Soc.; Law Soc. Sub-cttee on Intellectual Property. Chm., British Copyright Council. FRSA 1993. Member of

Board: Mod. Law Rev.; European Intellectual Property Law Rev.; Intellectual Property Jl. *Publications:* (with R. Taylor) Guide to Copyright Law, 1989. *Address:* 30 Keverstone Court, 97 Manor Road, Bournemouth BH1 3EX. *T:* (01202) 392256.

DWYER, Aileen Margaret; *see* Keel, A. M.

DWYER, Glenn N.; *see* Neil-Dwyer.

DWYER, Sir Joseph (Anthony), Kt 2001; FREng; DL; Group Chairman, George Wimpey PLC, 1996–99 (Director, 1988; Group Chief Executive Officer, 1991–98); *b* 20 June 1939. CEng, FREng (FEng 1997); FICE, FCIOB. President: CIOB, 1998–99; ICE, 2000–01. Dir, ETB, 2001–02. Chairman: Liverpool Vision (Urban Regeneration Co.), 1999–2008; Construction for Merseyside Ltd, 2004–08. DL Merseyside, 2008. Hon. Fellow, Liverpool John Moores Univ., 2003. Hon. LLD Liverpool, 2002; Hon. DSc Nottingham, 2004. Citizen of Honour Award, Liverpool City, 2009.

DYCHE, Dame Rachael (Mary), DBE 1997 (CBE 1992); Regional Director, Midlands, Conservative Party, 1993–98; *b* 29 Nov. 1945; *d* of late George Henry Dyche and Doreen Mary Dyche (*née* Rudgard). *Educ:* Burton upon Trent Tech. High Sch. Conservative Party: Agent: Burton, 1968–72; Harwich, 1972–75; Deputy Central Office Agent: Wales, 1975–76; W Midlands, 1976–85; Wessex, 1985–88; Central Office Agent, E Midlands, 1988–93. Mem., Nat. Soc. Cons. and Unionist Agents, 1968–. Member: PCC, All Saints, Lubenham, 2003– (Asst Church Warden, 2004–07; Church Warden, 2007–); Village Hall Cttee, Lubenham, 1999–; Heritage Gp, Lubenham, 2001–. *Recreations:* golf, gardening, music, horse riding. *Address:* 11 Acorn Close, Lubenham, Market Harborough, Leics LE16 9SP. *T:* (01858) 432379.

DYCKHOFF, Thomas Charles; writer, architectural historian and broadcaster; *b* St Albans, 27 Feb. 1971; *s* of Brian and Helen Dyckhoff; *m* 2009, Claire Barrett; one *s*. *Educ:* Aylesbury Grammar Sch.; Royal Grammar Sch., Worcester; Christ Church, Oxford (MA Hons Geog.); University Coll. London (MSc Hons Architectural Hist.). Asst Ed., Perspectives on Architecture, 1995–98; Dep. Ed., Space, 1998–2001, Prodn Ed., Weekend, 2001–03, The Guardian; Architecture Critic, The Times, 2003–11. TV presenter, BBC, Channel 4, 2004–. Hon. Sen. Res. Associate, UCL, 2011–. Mem., Stirling Prize Jury, RIBA, 2008–11. Hon. FRIBA 2011. Ed., Sir Banister Fletcher's A History of Architecture, 2014–. *Recreations:* gluttony, staring out of the window, butchery and pie-making. *E:* tom@tomdyckhoff.com.

DYE, Dr Christopher, FMedSci; FRS 2012; FRSB; Director of Strategy, Office of Director General, World Health Organization, Geneva, since 2014; *b* Belfast, 15 April 1956; *s* of Albert Edward Dye and Shirley Helen Dye (*née* Wooldridge); *m* 1988, Enricke Bouma; three *s*. *Educ:* De La Salle Coll., Sheffield; Vyners Sch., Ickenham, Middx; Univ. of York (BA 1st Cl. Hons Biol. 1978); Wolfson Coll., Oxford (DPhil Zool. 1982). FRSB (FSB 2008). Postgrad. Res. Asst (desert ecol.), New Mexico State Univ., 1978–79; NERC Postdoctoral Fellow (ecol. of insect vectors of disease), Imperial Coll. London, 1982–84; London School of Hygiene and Tropical Medicine: MRC Postdoctoral Res. Fellow, 1984–85; Lectr, Sen. Lectr, then Reader in Population Biol., 1985–96; Hd, Vector Biol. and Epidemiol. Unit, 1990–96; World Health Organization, Geneva: Coordinator, Tuberculosis Monitoring and Evaluation, Tuberculosis Dept, 1996–2008; Dir, Office of Health Information, HIV/AIDS, Tuberculosis, Malaria and Neglected Tropical Diseases, 2008–14. Gresham Prof. of Physic (and other Biol Scis), Gresham Coll., London, 2006–09; Vis. Prof. in Zool., Univ. of Oxford, 2009–. Member: British Ecol Soc., 1980; British Soc. for Parasitol., 1986. FRSTM&H 1985; Scientific FZS 1994; FMedSci 2008. *Publications:* Global Tuberculosis Control, 12 vols, 1997–2008; World Malaria Report 2008, 2008; World Health Report 2013, 2013; The Population Biology of Tuberculosis, 2015; contrib. 300 articles to scientific jls and books. *Recreations:* cycling, mountain biking, especially in the Jura. *Address:* Office of the Director General, World Health Organization, Avenue Appia, 1211 Geneva 27, Switzerland. *T:* 795090621. *E:* dyec@who.int.

DYE, Air Vice-Marshal Peter John, OBE 1992; DPhil, CEng; Director General, RAF Museum, 2009–14 (Deputy Director General and Director, Collections Division, 2008–09); historian and museum consultant; *b* 17 Aug. 1953; *s* of Roy Mackenzie Dye and Margaret Mary Dye (*née* Chauffourier); *m* 1985, Anne Catherine Waine; two *d*. *Educ:* Sevenoaks Sch.; Imperial Coll., Univ. of London (BSc Eng 1975); RAF Coll., Cranwell; Univ. of Birmingham (DPhil 2014). CEng 1989; MRAeS 1989. Commnd RAF, 1972; served UK, Germany and Canada; Sen. Engrg Officer, No IX Sqdn, 1986–88; OC Engrg and Supply Wing, RAF Coltishall, 1990–91; PSO AOC-in-C, RAF Support Comd, 1991–94 and AOC-in-C, Logistics Comd, 1994; Dir, Dept of Specialist Ground Trng, 1994–96; rcds 1997; AO Wales, 1999–2001; Air Cdre Ground Trng, 2001–05; Dep. C-in-C, Personnel and Trng Comd, and COS to Air Mem. for Personnel, 2005–07; Head: RAF Process and Orgn Rev., 2006–07; Collocated HQ, 2006–08; RAF Transformation, 2007–08. Hon. Res. Fellow, Coll. of Arts and Law, Univ. of Birmingham. ACGI 1975. Pres., Cross and Cockade, First World War Aviation Histl Soc. *Publications:* The Bridge to Air Power, 2015; articles and reviews. *Recreations:* aviation history, archaeology. *Club:* Royal Air Force.

DYER, Alexander Patrick; Chief Executive and Deputy Chairman, BOC Group plc, 1993–96; Deputy Chairman, Bunzl plc, 1996–2005 (Chairman 1993–96); *b* 30 Aug. 1932; *m* 1954, Shirley Shine; one *s* (and one *s* decd). *Educ:* US Military Acad. (BSc Engrg); Harvard Business Sch. (MBA). US Army, 1954–57; Esso Corp., 1959–63; Air Products, 1963–89; Gp Vice Pres., Gases, 1978–87; Exec. Vice Pres., Gas and Equipment, 1987–89; Bd Dir, 1988–89; Man. Dir, Gases, BOC Gp, 1989–93. *Recreations:* golf, skeet. *Address:* 2117 Kirkland Village Circle, Bethlehem, PA 18017, USA. *Clubs:* University (New York); Saucon Valley Country; Weyhill Skeet; Blooming Grove Hunting and Fishing.

DYER, Charles; playwright and novelist; actor-director (as Raymond Dyer); *b* 7 July 1928; *s* of James Sidney Dyer and Florence (*née* Stretton); *m* 1959, Fiona Thomson, actress; three *s*. *Educ:* Queen Elizabeth's Sch., Barnet. *Plays:* Clubs Are Sometimes Trumps, 1948; Who On Earth!, 1951; Turtle in the Soup, 1953; The Jovial Parasite, 1954; Single Ticket Mars, 1955; Time, Murderer, Please, and Poison In Jest, 1956; Wanted—One Body!, 1958; Prelude to Fury, 1959 (also wrote theme music); Rattle of A Simple Man, 1962 (also in Berlin, Paris, NY, Rome and London), 1981, 2004, USA, 1985, 1990, Netherlands, 1988, Germany, 1993, Scandinavia, 1993, 1995; Staircase, 1966 (for RSC; also in NY, Paris (1968, 1982, 1986, 1992), Amsterdam, Berlin, Rome, 1988, 1992, Vienna, Brazil, 1992, trans-Germany, 1992–95); Mother Adam, Paris, Berlin, 1970, London, 1971, 1973, NY, 1974; The Loving Allelujah, 1974; Circling Dancers, 1979; Lovers Dancing, 1981, 1983; Futility Rites, 1981; as R. Kraselchik: Red Cabbage and Kings, 1960 (also wrote theme music); *screenplays:* Rattle, 1964; Insurance Italian Style, 1967; Staircase, 1968; Brother Sun and Sister Moon, 1970. Also directed plays for the stage and television. *Acted* in 230 plays and films; London début as Duke in Worm's Eye View, Whitehall, 1948; *films* include: Cuptie Honeymoon, 1947; Britannia Mews, 1949; Road Sense, 1950; Off The Record, 1952; Pickwick Papers, 1952; Dockland Case, 1953; Strange Case of Blondie, 1953; Naval Patrol, 1959; Loneliness of the Long Distance Runner, 1962; Mouse On The Moon, 1962; Knack, 1964; Rattle of A Simple Man, 1964; How I Won The War, 1967; Staircase, 1968; *television:* Charlie in Staircase, BBC, 1986; *television series:* Hugh and I, 1964. *Publications:* (as Charles Dyer): plays: Wanted—One Body!, 1961; Time, Murderer, Please, 1962; Rattle Of A Simple Man, (Fr.) 1963; Staircase, 1966; Mother Adam, 1970; The Loneliness Trilogy, 1972; Hot Godly Wind, 1973; Red Plush and Trombones: the lonely trilogy, 2011; novels: Rattle Of A Simple Man, 1964; Charlie Always Told Harry Almost Everything, 1969 (USA and Europe, 1970); The Rising of our Herbert, 1972; Wilderness of Monkeys (autobiog.), 2005. *Recreations:* amateur music and carpentry. *Address:* Old Wob, Austenwood Common, Gerrards Cross, Bucks SL9 8SF.

DYER, Prof. Christopher Charles, CBE 2008; PhD; FBA 1995; FSA; Professor of Regional and Local History, and Director, Centre for English Local History, University of Leicester, 2001–10, now Emeritus, and Leverhulme Emeritus Fellow, 2011–12; Honorary Senior Research Fellow, Institute of Historical Research, University of London, 2013–July 2016; *b* 24 Dec. 1944; *s* of Charles James Dyer and Doris Mary Dyer; *m* 1967, Jenifer Ann Dent; one *s* one *d*. *Educ:* Univ. of Birmingham (BA, PhD). Asst Lectr in History, Univ. of Edinburgh, 1967–70; Lectr, Sen. Lectr, then Reader, 1970–90, Prof. of Medieval Social History, 1991–2001, Univ. of Birmingham. Ford Lectr in Hist., Oxford Univ., 2000–01. Leverhulme Emeritus Fellow, 2011–12; Sen. Res. Fellow, Univ. of Birmingham, 2013–14. President: Soc. for Medieval Archaeology, 1998–2001 (Vice-Pres., 2011–); Bristol and Glos Archaeol Soc., 2001–02; British Agricl Hist. Soc., 2004–07 (Vice-Pres., 2009–); Worcs Histl Soc., 2012–; Vice-President: Medieval Settlement Res. Gp, 2010– (Pres., 1997–99); English Place-Name Soc., 2014–. Chairman: Victoria County History Cttee, 1997–2004; Dugdale Soc., 2003–; Records of Social and Economic History Cttee, British Acad., 2004–10. FSA 1994; AcSS 2006–08. *Publications:* Lords and Peasants in a Changing Society, 1980; Standards of Living in the later Middle Ages, 1989; Everyday Life in Medieval England, 1994; Making a Living in the Middle Ages 850–1520, 2002; An Age of Transition, 2005; A Country Merchant 1495–1520: trading and farming at the end of the Middle Ages, 2012. *Address:* Centre for English Local History, University of Leicester, Marc Fitch House, 5 Salisbury Road, Leicester LE1 7QR. *T:* (0116) 252 2765.

DYER, Sir Henry Peter Francis S.; *see* Swinnerton-Dyer.

DYER, James Archibald Thomson, OBE 2003; FRCPsych; Scottish Parliamentary Standards Commissioner, 2003–09; Medical Member, Mental Health Tribunal for Scotland, since 2005; *b* 31 Dec. 1946; *s* of Rev. Thomas James Dyer, MA and Mary Watt Dyer; *m* 1969 (marr. diss. 1994); two *s* one *d*; *m* 1994, Suzanne Paula Whitaker (marr. diss. 2012); two step *d* (one step *s* decd). *Educ:* Bo'ness Acad.; Robert Gordon's Coll., Aberdeen; Univ. of Aberdeen (MB ChB Hons 1970). FRCPsych 1992. Various trng posts in psychiatry, Royal Edinburgh Hosp., 1972–77; SO, MRC Unit for Epidemiological Studies in Psychiatry, 1977–81; Consultant Psychiatrist, Royal Edinburgh Hosp. and Hon. Sen. Lectr in Psychiatry, Univ. of Edinburgh, 1981–91; Medical Comr, 1991–2003, and Dir, 1993–2003, Mental Welfare Commn for Scotland. Mem., Registration and Conduct Sub-Cttees, Scottish Social Services Council, 2010–13. FRSA 2000. *Publications:* contrib. book chapters; contrib. articles and res. papers on parasuicide and suicide, schizophrenia, mental health services, mental health law and psychological aspects of nuclear war. *Recreations:* reading, photography, Radio 4, swimming, learning French.

DYER, Lois Edith, OBE 1984; FCSP; international physiotherapy consultant; *b* 18 March 1925; *d* of Richard Morgan Dyer and Emmeline Agnes (*née* Wells). *Educ:* Middlesex Hospital. FCSP 1986. Variety of posts as physiotherapist in Britain, Southern, Central and North Africa, 1948–71; extensive travel world wide, visiting and lecturing at national and internat. conferences. First Physiotherapist Member, NHS Health Adv. Service, 1971; first Advr in Physiotherapy, DHSS, 1976–85. Mem., Camden (formerly Hampstead) CHC, 1996–2001. First non-medical Chm., Chartered Society of Physiotherapy, 1972–75; Founder Mem., Soc. for Res. in Rehabilitation, 1978–; Hon. Life Vice-Pres., S African Soc. of Physiotherapy. Editor-in-Chief, Physiotherapy Practice, 1985–90. CMLJ 2001. *Publications:* Care of the Orthopaedic Patient (jtly), 1977; numerous papers in professional jls. *Recreations:* music, country pursuits, bird watching, bridge, ecology, wildlife, conservation. *Address:* Garden Flat, 6 Belsize Grove, NW3 4UN. *T:* (020) 7722 1794.

DYER, Nigel Ingram John; QC 2006; *b* 21 Sept. 1957; *s* of late Derek Ingram Dyer and Elizabeth Dyer; *m* 1986, Victoria Duckham; one *s* one *d*. *Educ:* St Mary's Sch., Nairobi; Oratory Sch.; Durham Univ. (BA Jt Hons Law and Politics). Called to the Bar: Inner Temple, 1982; BVI, 2011; Mem., Western Circuit. Member: President's Ancillary Relief Adv. Gp, Family Div., 2000–05; Money and Property Cttee, Family Justice Council, 2005–11. *Publications:* (ed jtly) Rayden and Jackson on Divorce and Family Matters, 18th edn 2005; (ed jtly) Detection and Preservation of Assets in Financial Remedy Claims, 2014. *Recreations:* gardening, opera, theatre, running. *Address:* 1 Hare Court, Temple, EC4Y 7BE. *T:* (020) 7797 7070, *Fax:* (020) 7797 7435. *E:* dyer@1hc.com. *Clubs:* Hurlingham, MCC; Rye Tennis.

DYER, Penelope Jane, (Penny), (Mrs N. C. J. Day); freelance voice and dialect specialist, since 1983; *b* St Leonards-on-Sea, Sussex, 30 May 1957; *d* of Paul M. C. Dyer and June D. Dyer (*née* Guy); *m* 1996, Nicholas C. J. Day. *Educ:* Barton Sch. Kindergarten, St Leonards-on-Sea; St Mary's Sch., St Leonards-on-Sea; Central Sch. of Speech and Drama (BEd and Advanced Dip. Voice Studies). Speech, drama and English teacher, Bodiam Manor, Bedgebury, Cranbrook, St Mary's and Ancaster Hse schs, E Sussex and Kent, 1979–83; peripatetic teacher, Rose Bruford Coll. of Speech and Drama, Drama and Musical Depts of Arts Educnl Schs, Italia Conti Stage Sch. and Questors Th. Drama Course, 1984–87; Main Voice and Dialect Tutor, Actg Course and Voice Dip., Central Sch. of Speech and Drama, 1987–90; Speech and Dialect Tutor, RADA, 1991–95; Voice and Dialect Tutor, The Poor Sch., 1991–95. Work in theatre, TV and film, 1986–: *theatre* includes: Another Time, 1989; Shadowlands, Wyndhams, 1990; Cyrano de Bergerac, 1992; Mojo, Royal Court; The Blue Room, Donmar; My Fair Lady; The Crucible, RSC; Frost Nixon, Gielgud; Parade, Donmar; Fiddler on the Roof, Savoy; Boeing, Boeing, Comedy; Speed the Plow, Old Vic; Piaf, Donmar; *television* includes: A Small Dance (screenplay), 1990; Band of Gold; Longford; The Deal, 2003; Blackpool, 2004; A Short Stay in Switzerland, 2009; *films* include: Bhaji on the Beach, 1993; Elizabeth, 1998; The War Zone, 1999; The Importance of Being Earnest, 2002; Dirty Pretty Things, 2003; Ladies in Lavender, 2004; Mrs Henderson Presents, 2005; The Da Vinci Code, 2006; Infamous, 2006; The Queen, 2006; Elizabeth: the Golden Age, 2007. *Publications:* Access Accents, 2007; booklets on British and American dialects. *Recreations:* swimming, walking, reading, poetry, yoga, food, all music, maps, art, all while talking in funny voices! *E:* sarah.upson@voicecoach.tv. *Clubs:* Union, Ronnie Scott's.

DYER, Dr Richard George, OBE 2007; Chief Executive, Biosciences Federation, 2006–09; *b* 18 July 1943; *s* of late Comdr Charles William Dyer, RN and Dorothy Patricia Victoria Vaughan-Hogan; *m* 1st, 1967, Shirley James Foulsham (marr. diss. 1995); two *s* one *d*; 2nd, 2000, Dr Caroline Edmonds (*née* Porter); one *d*. *Educ:* Churcher's Coll., Petersfield; Univ. of London (BSc 1967); Univ. of Birmingham (MSc 1968); Univ. of Bristol (PhD 1972). Research, Dept of Anatomy, Bristol Med. Sch., 1968–74; ARC Institute of Animal Physiology, subseq. AFRC Institute of Animal Physiology and Genetics Research, then Babraham Institute: Head, Dept of Neuroendocrinology, 1985–90; Head, Cambridge Station, 1989–90; Associate Dir of Inst., 1991–93; Exec. Dir, 1993–94; Dir, 1994–2005. Teacher of Physiol., Jesus Coll., Cambridge, 1977–90; Res. Fellowships, Germany and France; Consultant for WHO, Shanghai, 1983–86. Member: AFRC Animals Res. Bd, 1992–93; AFRC Strategy Bd, 1993; various BBSRC cttees and panels, 1993–2012, incl. Animal Sci. and Psych. Cttee, 1994–96; Cttee, R&D Soc., 1998–2000; European Science Foundation: Member: Life and Envmtl Scis Standing Cttee, 1995–2000; Eur. Medical Res. Councils, 1996–2000; Exec. Bd, 1999–2007; Chm., Finance and Audit Cttee, 2004–07; Vice-Pres., 2004–07. Member, Board: Babraham Bioscience Technologies Ltd, 1998–2008 (Chm., 2000–05); Univ. of Cambridge Challenge, then Venture, Fund, 1999–2004. Medal, Soc. for Endocrinology, 1986; Medal, Polish Physiol. Soc., 1987. Former Member, Editorial Board:

Exptl Brain Res.; Jl of Endocrinology. *Publications:* (ed with R. J. Bicknell) Brain Opioid Systems in Reproduction, 1989; numerous papers on neuroendocrine topics in learned jls. *Recreations:* finding bargains, escaping to mountains and sea, lively dinners.

DYER, Prof. Richard William, PhD; FBA 2012; Professor of Film Studies, King's College London, since 2006; Professorial Fellow in Film Studies, St Andrews University, since 2011 (Wardlaw Professor, 2013); *b* Leeds, 1 June 1945; *s* of Gilbert and Kathleen Dyer. *Educ:* St Andrews Univ. (MA French 1968); Centre for Contemp. Cultural Studies, Birmingham Univ. (PhD 1973). Lectr, Univ. of Keele, 1974–77; Lectr, 1979–88, Sen. Lectr, 1988–93, Prof., 1993–2006, Univ. of Warwick, 1979–2006. Dist. Adjunct Prof., UCD, 2010; Visiting Professor: Univ. of Pennsylvania, Annenberg Sch. of Communications, 1985; Univ. of Stockholm (Cinema Studies), 1996, 2006, 2010; New York Univ. (Cinema Studies), 2003; Bauhaus Univ., Weimar, 2009; Univ. of Indiana Bloomington, 2015. Lifetime Hon. Mem., Soc. for Cinema and Media Studies, 2007. Hon. DH Turku, 2009. Lifetime Achievement Award, British Assoc. of Film, TV and Screen Studies, 2014. *Publications:* Stars, 1979, new edn 1998; Heavenly Bodies, 1987, new edn 2004; Now You See It, 1990, new edn 2003; Only Entertainment, 1992, new edn 2002; The Matter of Images, 1993, new edn 2003; Brief Encounter, 1993; White, 1997; Seven, 1999; The Culture of Queers, 2002; Pastiche, 2006; Nino Rota, 2010; In the Space of a Song, 2011. *Recreations:* talking with friends, theatre, film, dance, art, novels. *Address:* Film Studies, King's College London, Strand, WC2R 2LS. *T:* (020) 7898 1158.

DYET, Fergus John C.; *see* Cochrane-Dyet.

DYKE; *see* Hart Dyke.

DYKE, Gregory; Chairman: British Film Institute, since 2008; Ambassador Theatre Group Ltd, since 2009; Football Association, since 2013; *b* 20 May 1947; *s* of Joseph and Denise Dyke; *m* 2009, Sue Howes; one *s* one *d*; one step *s* one step *d*. *Educ:* Hayes Grammar Sch.; York Univ. (BA Politics). Varied career, 1965–83; Editor in Chief, TV-am, 1983–84; Dir of Programmes, TVS, 1984–87; London Weekend Television: Dir of Progs, 1987–91; Dep. Man. Dir, 1989–90; Man. Dir, subseq. Gp Chief Exec., 1990–94; Chm., GMTV, 1993–94; Director: Channel Four Television, 1988–92; BSkyB, 1995; Chm. and Chief Exec., Pearson Television, 1995–99; Exec. Dir, Pearson plc, 1996–99; Chm., Channel 5 Broadcasting, 1997–99; Dir-Gen., BBC, 2000–04. Chairman: HIT Entertainment Ltd, 2005–12; Brentford FC, 2006–13. Non-executive Director: ITN, 1990–92; Manchester United FC, 1997–99; ProSiebenSat.1 Media AG, 2004–. Chm., ITV Council, 1992–94. Chancellor, York Univ., 2004–15. Trustee: Science Museum, 1996–2005; English Nat. Stadium Trust, 1997–99. *Publications:* Inside Story (memoirs), 2004. *Recreations:* football, ski-ing, horse-riding, movies, theatre. *Address:* Football Association, PO Box 1966, London, SW1P 9EQ.

DYKES, family name of **Baron Dykes**.

DYKES, Baron *cr* 2004 (Life Peer), of Harrow Weald in the London Borough of Harrow; **Hugh John Maxwell Dykes;** *b* 17 May 1939; *s* of Richard Dykes and Doreen Ismay Maxwell Dykes; *m* 1965, Susan Margaret Dykes (*née* Smith) (marr. diss. 2000); two *s* (and one *s* decd). *Educ:* Weston super Mare Grammar Sch.; Pembroke Coll., Cambridge. Partner, Simon & Coates, Stockbrokers, 1968–78; Associate Mem., Quilter, Hilton, Goodison, Stockbrokers, 1978. MCSI (MSI 1993). Dir, Dixons Stores Far East Ltd, 1985. Contested (C) Tottenham, 1966. MP (C) Harrow East, 1970–97; contested (C) same seat, 1997; joined Lib Dem party, 1997; contested (Lib Dem) London Region, Eur. Parly elecns, 1999. PPS: to three Parly Under-Secs of State for Defence, 1970; to Parly Under-Sec. of State in Civil Service Dept attached to Cabinet Office, 1973; Mem., H of C EEC Select Cttee, 1983–97. Mem., European Parlt, Strasbourg, 1974–77; Chairman: Cons. Parly European Cttee, 1979–80 (Vice-Chm., 1974–79); Commons Euro-Gp, 1988–97; Vice-Pres., Cons. Gp for EEC, 1982–86 (Chm., 1978–81). Chm., European Movement, 1990–97 (Jt Hon. Sec., 1982–87); Chm., 2005–07, Pres., 2007–09, European-Atlantic Gp. Mem., Lib Dem Team on EU, Foreign Affairs and Defence Policy, 1997–2004; Lib Dem spokesman on EU, 2005–10, on Envmt, Food and Rural Affairs, 2006–10, H of L. Research Sec., Bow Gp, 1965; Chm., Coningsby Club, 1969. Governor: Royal Nat. Orthopaedic Hosp., 1975–82; N London Collegiate Sch., 1982. Order of Merit (Germany), 1993; Médaille pour l'Europe (Luxembourg), 1993; Chevalier: Ordre National du Mérite (France), 1994; Légion d'Honneur (France), 2003. *Publications:* (ed) Westropp's "Invest £100", 1964, and Westropp's "Start Your Own Business", 1965; (jtly) On the Edge: Britain and Europe, 2012; many articles and pamphlets on political and financial subjects. *Recreations:* music, theatre, swimming, travel, gardening. *Address:* House of Lords, SW1A 0PW. *Clubs:* Garrick, Beefsteak.

DYKES, David Wilmer, MA, PhD; Director, National Museum of Wales, 1986–89; *b* 18 Dec. 1933; *s* of late Captain David Dykes, OBE and Jenny Dykes; *m* 1967, Margaret Anne George; two *d*. *Educ:* Swansea Grammar Sch.; Corpus Christi Coll., Oxford (MA); PhD (Wales). FRNS 1958 (Parkes-Weber Prize, 1954); FRSAI 1963; FRHistS 1965; FSA 1973. Commnd RN and RNR, 1955–62. Civil Servant, Bd of Inland Revenue, 1958–59; administrative appts, Univ. of Bristol and Univ. Coll. of Swansea, 1959–63; Dep. Registrar, Univ. Coll. of Swansea, 1963–69; Registrar, Univ. of Warwick, 1969–72; Sec., Nat. Museum of Wales, 1972–86, Acting Dir, 1985–86. Mem., Treasure Valuation Cttee, DCMS, 2010–14. Hon. Lectr in History, University Coll., Cardiff, later Univ. of Wales Coll. of Cardiff, 1975–95. Pres., 1999–2003, Vice-Pres., 2009–, British Numismatic Soc. (Mem. Council, 1966–70 and 1997–). Trustee, UK Numismatic Trust, 1999–. Liveryman: Worshipful Co. of Tin Plate Workers, 1985; Livery Co. of Wales (formerly Welsh Livery Guild), 1993; Freeman, City of London, 1985. KStJ 1993 (CStJ 1991; Chancellor, Priory for Wales, 1991–98; Bailiff of St Davids, 1999–2002). *Publications:* Anglo-Saxon Coins in the National Museum of Wales, 1977; (ed and contrib.) Alan Sorrell: Early Wales Re-created, 1980; Wales in Vanity Fair, 1989; The University College of Swansea: an illustrated history, 1992; Coinage and Currency in Eighteenth-Century Britain: the provincial coinage, 2011 (North Book Prize, British Numismatic Soc., 2012); articles and reviews in numismatic, historical and other jls. *Recreations:* numismatics, writing. *E:* davwd@btinternet.com. *Clubs:* Athenæum; Cardiff and County (Cardiff).

DYKES, Richard Thornton Booth; Chairman, Carrenza Ltd, since 2001; *b* 7 April 1945; *s* of Alan Thornton Dykes and Myra McFie Dykes (*née* Booth); *m* 1970, Janet Rosemary Cundall (marr. diss. 1995); one *s*. *Educ:* Rossall Sch. Articled clerk, Dehn & Lauderdale, solicitors, 1965–67; EO, later HEO, Min. of Labour, 1967–73; Private Sec. to Sec. of State for Employment, 1974–76; Principal, Econ. Policy Div., Dept of Employment, 1976–77; Dir, Industrial Relns, British Shipbuilders, 1977–80; Non-exec. Dir, Austin & Pickersgill Ltd, Sunderland, 1979–80; Principal Private Sec. to Sec. of State for Employment, 1980–82; Department of Employment: Hd, Unemployment Benefit Service, 1982–85; Sec., Sen. Mgt Gp, 1985–86; Hd, Inner Cities Central Unit, 1986; Post Office Counters Ltd: Gen. Manager for Gtr London, 1986–87; Dir of Ops, 1987–92; Man. Dir, 1993–96; Gp Man. Dir, Royal Mail, and Exec. Bd Mem., The Post Office, later Consignia plc, 1996–2001. Non-exec. Dir, Employment Service, 1998–2002. Member: Forensic Sci. Service Adv. Bd, Home Office, 1991–98; EDC, BITC, 1994–2003; Design Council, 1994–2001; Chm., HSC and DTLR Work-related Road Safety Task Gp, 2000–01. *Recreations:* travel, hill-walking. *Address:* The Old Rectory, Upper Slaughter, Glos GL54 2JB.

DYKSTRA, Ronald Gerrit Malcolm; Senior Partner, Addleshaw Sons & Latham, solicitors, 1987–94, retired; *b* 4 March 1934; *s* of Gerrit Abe Dykstra and Margaret Kirk Dykstra (*née* McDonald); *m* 1st, 1960, Jennifer Mary Cramer (marr. diss. 1985); three *s*; 2nd, 1986, Sonia Hoole. *Educ:* Edinburgh Academy. Admitted Solicitor, 1957; Asst Solicitor, 1957, Partner, 1961, Addleshaw Sons & Latham, Manchester. Pres., Wilmslow Green Room Soc., 2011–. *Recreations:* swimming, cycling, amateur drama, walking, sailing. *Address:* 7 Racecourse Road, Wilmslow, Cheshire SK9 5LF. *T:* (01625) 525856.

DYLAN, Bob; *see* Zimmerman, R. A.

DYMOCK, Vice Adm. Sir Anthony (Knox), KBE 2008; CB 2003; consultant on maritime security, European Union 2009–14; Director, Wise Pens International Maritime Security Consultancy, 2011–14; Senior Mentor, UK Defence Academy, 2010–14; consultant on international maritime security policy; *b* 18 July 1949; *s* of Richard Challis Dymock and Irene Mary Dymock (*née* Knox); *m* 1977, Elizabeth Mary Frewer (*d* 2015); one *s* one *d*. *Educ:* Brighton, Hove and Sussex Grammar Sch.; Univ. of E Anglia (BA Hons Russian and Philosophy); Kennedy Sch. of Govt, Harvard Univ. MNI 1992. BRNC, 1969–70; served: HMS Yarmouth, 1972–74; HMS Brighton, 1974; HMS Antrim, 1981–83 (Falklands War); i/c HMS Plymouth, 1985–88; MoD, Whitehall, 1989–91; HMS London, 1991–92 (Gulf War); i/c HMS Campbeltown, 1992–93; MoD Naval Staff, 1993–96; i/c 2nd Frigate Sqdn, HMS Cornwall, 1996–98; Dep. Comdr, UK Task Gp (HMS Invincible), Gulf and Kosovo, 1998–99; Dep. Comdr, Striking and Support Forces Southern Region, 2000–02; Defence Attaché and Hd of British Defence Staff, Washington, 2002–05; UK Mil. Rep. to NATO, 2006–08. Member: RYA; RNSA. *Publications:* (jtly) Military Capability Development in the EU, 2012. *Recreations:* sailing, ski-ing. *Clubs:* Royal Cruising, Royal Yacht Squadron.

DYMOND, Duncan Simon, MD; FRCP; Consultant Cardiologist, Barts Health NHS Trust (formerly Barts and The London NHS Trust), since 1987; *b* North Cheam, Surrey, 25 Feb. 1950; *s* of late Sydney Dymond and Adele Dymond; partner, Christine Baldwin; one *s* one *d*. *Educ:* St Paul's Sch., London; St Bartholomew's Hosp. Med. Sch., London (MB BS 1972; MD 1980). MRCP 1974, FRCP 1991. House Physician, 1973, Registrar in Cardiol., 1975–80, St Bartholomew's Hosp.; Asst Prof. and Dir, Nuclear Cardiol., Mount Sinai Hosp. and Univ. of Wisconsin, 1980–81; Sen. Registrar in Cardiol., St Bartholomew's Hosp., 1981–86. Lead Clinician for Clinical Standards, and Co-Chm., Clinical Governance Bd, Wellington Hosp., London, 2001–. Chm., London Consultants' Assoc., 2009–. Chm., Wkg Gp on Nuclear Cardiol., Eur. Soc. of Cardiol., 1984–88; Hon. Sec., 1990–94, Mem., Finance Cttee, 2009–, British Cardiovascular Soc. (formerly British Cardiac Soc.). Patron, Forces Children Trust, 2009–. FACC 1983; FESC 1991. *Publications:* Atlas of Myocardial Infarction, 1994; Plain English Guide to Heart Diseases, 1996; How to Cope Successfully with High Blood Pressure, 2003; approx. 100 articles. *Recreations:* football, tennis, cricket, ski-ing, classical piano, cinema, theatre, travel. *Address:* 84 Harley Street, W1G 7HW. *T:* (020) 7079 4260, *Fax:* (020) 7079 4269. *E:* dymondheart@hotmail.co.uk. *Clubs:* MCC, Lord's Taverners.

DYNEVOR, 10th Baron *cr* 1780; **Hugo Griffith Uryan Rhys;** *b* 19 Nov. 1966; *o s* of 9th Baron Dynevor and of Lucy Catherine King, *o d* of Sir John Rothenstein, CBE; *S* father, 2008. *Educ:* Bryanston.

DYSART, 13th Earl of, *cr* 1643; **John Peter Grant of Rothiemurchus;** DL; Lord Huntingtower, 1643; *b* 22 Oct. 1946; *o s* of Colonel John Peter Grant of Rothiemurchus, MBE (*d* 1987) and Countess of Dysart (12th in line); *S* mother, 2011; *m* 1971, Wendy Philippa Chance; one *s* two *d*. *Educ:* Gordonstoun. DL Inverness-shire, 1986. *Heir:* *s* Lord Huntingtower, *qv*.

DYSON, Rt Hon. Lord; John Anthony Dyson, Kt 1993; PC 2001; Master of the Rolls and Head of Civil Justice, since 2012; *b* 31 July 1943; *s* of late Richard Dyson and Gisella Dyson; *m* 1970, Jacqueline Carmel Levy; one *s* one *d*. *Educ:* Leeds Grammar Sch.; Wadham Coll., Oxford (Open Classics Scholar; MA; Hon. Fellow, 2001). Harmsworth Law Scholar, 1968, called to Bar, Middle Temple, 1968, Bencher, 1990; QC 1982; a Recorder, 1986–93; a Judge of the High Court of Justice, QBD, 1993–2001; Presiding Judge, Technology and Construction Court, 1998–2001; a Lord Justice of Appeal, 2001–10; Dep. Hd of Civil Justice, 2003–06; a Justice of the Supreme Court of the UK, 2010–12. Dep. Chm., 2003–06, Chm., 2012–, Civil Justice Council. Chm., Civil Procedure Rule Cttee, 2012– (Mem., 2002–06). Chairman: Adv. Council on Nat. Records and Archives, 2012–; Magna Carta Trust, 2012–. Member: Council of Legal Educn, 1992–96; Judicial Studies Bd, 1994–98. Vis. Prof., Queen Mary, Univ. of London, 2007–. Hon. Freeman, Drapers' Co., 2014. Hon. Fellow: Soc. of Advanced Legal Studies, 1998–; Hebrew Univ. of Jerusalem, 2004. Hon. LLD: UCL, 2013; Essex, 2013; Leeds, 2014. *Recreations:* piano playing, singing, walking. *Address:* Royal Courts of Justice, Strand, WC2A 2LL.

DYSON, Prof. Freeman John, FRS 1952; Professor, School of Natural Sciences, Institute for Advanced Study, Princeton, New Jersey, 1953–94, Professor Emeritus since 1994; *b* 15 Dec. 1923; *s* of late Sir George Dyson, KCVO; *m* 1st, 1950, Verena Esther (*née* Huber) (marr. diss. 1958); one *s* one *d*; 2nd, 1958, Imme (*née* Jung); four *d*. *Educ:* Winchester; Cambridge; Cornell University. Operational research for RAF Bomber Command, 1943–45. Fellow of Trinity Coll., Cambridge, 1946–50, Hon. Fellow, 1989; Commonwealth Fund Fellow at Cornell and Princeton, USA, 1947–49; Mem. of Institute for Advanced Study, Princeton, USA, 1949–50; Professor of Physics, Cornell Univ., Ithaca, NY, USA, 1951–53. Mem. of National Academy of Sciences (USA), 1964; For. Associate, Acad. des Scis, Paris, 1989. Gifford Lectr, Aberdeen, 1985; Radcliffe Lectr, Oxford, 1990. Lorentz Medal, Royal Netherlands Acad. of Sciences, 1966; Hughes Medal, Royal Soc., 1968; Max Planck Medal, German Physical Soc., 1969; Templeton Prize, 2000; Henri Poincaré Prize, Internat. Assoc. of Math. Physics, 2012. *Publications:* Disturbing the Universe, 1979; Values at War, 1983; Weapons and Hope, 1984; Origins of Life, 1986, 2nd edn 1999; Infinite in All Directions, 1988; From Eros to Gaia, 1991; Imagined Worlds, 1997; Technology and Social Justice, 1998; The Sun, the Genome and the Internet, 1999; The Scientist as Rebel, 2006; A Many-Colored Glass, 2007; Advanced Quantum Mechanics, 2007; Birds and Frogs: selected papers, 1990–2014, 2015; contrib. to The Physical Review, Annals of Mathematics, etc. *Address:* School of Natural Sciences, Institute for Advanced Study, Einstein Drive, Princeton, NJ 08540, USA.

DYSON, Sir James, Kt 2007; CBE 1998; RDI 2005; FRS 2015; FREng; FCSD; Founder, 1992, and Chairman, 1992–2010, Dyson Ltd (formerly Prototypes Ltd, then Dyson Research); Founder and Trustee, James Dyson Foundation, since 2002; *b* 2 May 1947; *s* of late Alec Dyson and Mary (*née* Bolton); *m* 1967, Deirdre Hindmarsh; two *s* one *d*. *Educ:* Gresham's Sch.; Royal Coll. of Art (MDes). FCSD 1996; FREng 2005. Dir, Rotork Marine, 1970–74 (design and manufacture of Sea Truck high speed landing craft); Man. Dir, Kirk-Dyson, 1974–79 (design and manufacture of Ballbarrow wheelbarrow); developed and designed Dyson Dual Cyclone vacuum cleaner, 1979–93, Dyson Contrarotator washing machine, 2000, Dyson Digital Motor, 2004, Dyson Airblade Hand Dryer, 2006, Dyson Air Multiplier Fan, 2009, Dyson Hot Fan Heater, 2011; Dyson Airblade Tap, 2013; Dyson 360 Eye Robot, 2014; Dyson Humidifier, 2014. Mem., Design Council, 1997–; Chairman: Design Mus., 1999–2004; Adv. Bd, Design London, 2007–. Mem., Prime Minister's Business Adv. Gp, 2010–. Provost, RCA, 2011– (Ext. Examr, 1993–96; Mem. Council, 1998–). Patron: Design and Technol. Assoc., 2010–; Royal United Hosp. Bath Cancer Care Campaign, 2013–. Trustee, Roundhouse Th., London. Dyson vacuum cleaners on permanent display in museums: Sci. Mus., V&A and Design Mus., London; MOMA, NY; Boymans Mus., Rotterdam; Powerhouse Mus., Sydney; San Francisco Mus. of Modern Art; Mus. of Scotland; Design Mus., Zurich; Mus. für angewandte Kunst, Germany; Centre Georges Pompidou, Paris; Cité des Scis et de l'Industrie, Paris. Hon. FRIBA 2006. Hon. doctorates: Oxford Brookes, 1997; Brunel, 1999; RCA, Bath, 2000; Imperial Coll. London,

2001. Awards incl.: Design and Innovation Award for Ballbarrow, Building Design, 1976; Internat. Design Fair Prize, Japan, 1991; Minerva Award, CSD, 1995; Gerald Frewer Trophy, Inst. Engrg Designers, 1996; Industrial Design Prize of America, 1996; Eversheds Grand Prix Trophy, Design Council, 1996; European Design Prize, EC, 1997; Prince Philip's Designers Prize; European Design Prize, 1997; French Oscar, Livre Mondial des Inventions, 1997; Gold Award, Industrial Design Promotion Orgn, Japan, 1999; Gal. Lafayette Prix Innovation-Design, France, 1999; Mingay Most Innovative Product Award, Australia, 2000; Lord Kilgerran Prize, Royal Soc., 2000; Queen's Award for Innovation, 2003; Giant of Design, USA, 2004; Queen's Award for Export, 2006; Lifetime Achievement Award, Plus X Awards, 2007; Le Janus de l'Industrie, Inst Français du Design, 2007. *Publications:* Doing a Dyson, 1996; Against the Odds (autobiog.), 1997; History of Great Inventions, 2001; Genius of Britain, 2010; Ingenious Britain, 2010. *Recreations:* running, garden design, bassoon, opera, tennis. *Address:* c/o Tetbury Hill, Malmesbury, Wilts SN16 0RP. *T:* (01666) 828282. *Club:* Chelsea Arts.

DYSON, John Anthony; *see* Dyson, Rt Hon. Lord.

DYSON, John Michael; Chief Master of the Supreme Court of Judicature (Chancery Division), 1992–98 (a Master, 1973–98); a Recorder, 1994–98; *b* 9 Feb. 1929; *s* of late Eric Dyson, Gainsborough and Hope Patison (*née* Kirkland). *Educ:* Bradfield Coll.; Corpus Christi Coll., Oxford. 2nd Lieut, Royal Tank Regt, 1948. Admitted Solicitor, 1956; Partner, Field Roscoe & Co., 1957 (subseq. Field Fisher & Co. and Field Fisher & Martineau). *Address:* 20 Keats Grove, NW3 2RS. *T:* (020) 7794 3389. *Club:* Oxford and Cambridge.

DYSON, Prof. Kenneth Herbert Fewster, PhD; FRHistS; FBA 1997; FLSW; FAcSS; Distinguished Research Professor, School of Law and Politics (formerly School of European Studies, then School of Politics and International Relations), Cardiff University, since 2003; Visiting Professor of European Politics, University of Bradford, since 2002; *b* 10 Nov. 1946; *s* of Arthur Dyson and Freda Dyson; *m* 1971, Patricia Ann Holmes; two *s*. *Educ:* Scarborough Grammar Sch.; London Sch. of Econs (BSc Econs, MSc Econs); Univ. of Liverpool (PhD 1980). FRHistS 1981. Lectr in Politics, 1969–79, Sen. Lectr, 1979–81, Univ. of Liverpool; Prof. of European Studies, 1982–2002, and Co-Dir, European Briefing Unit, 1987–2002, Univ. of Bradford. Visiting Professor: in Politics, Univ. of Konstanz, Germany, 1981–82; Inst d'Etudes Politiques de Lille, 2004. Chairman: Assoc. for Study of German Politics, 1978–81; Standing Conf. of Heads of European Studies, 1990–93; HEFCE Panel for European Studies, RAEs 1996 and 2001; British Academy: Grants Officer, Politics Section, 1999–; Mem., Overseas Policy Cttee, and Res. Grants Cttee, 2003–. FRSA 1993; FAcSS (AcSS 2000); Founding FLSW 2010 (Mem. Council, 2010–). Hon. DLitt Aston, 2003. Federal Service Cross (1st Cl.) (Germany), 1990. *Publications:* Party, State and Bureaucracy in Germany, 1978; The State Tradition in Western Europe, 1980; (with S. Wilks) Industrial Crisis, 1983; European Detente, 1986; The Politics of the Communications Revolution in Western Europe, 1986; Local Authorities and New Technologies, 1987; Broadcasting and New Media Policies in Western Europe, 1988; Combatting Long-Term Unemployment, 1989; Political Economy of Communications, 1990; Politics of German Regulation, 1992; Elusive Union, 1994; Culture First, 1996; (with K. Featherstone) The Road to Maastricht, 1999; The Politics of the Euro-Zone, 2000; European States and the Euro, 2002; (with K. Goetz) Germany, Europe and the Politics of Constraint, 2003; Enlarging the Euro Area: external empowerment and domestic transformation in East Central Europe, 2006; The Euro at Ten, 2008; (with M. Marcussen) Central Banking in the Age of the Euro, 2009; (with A. Sepos) Which Europe?: the politics of differentiated integration, 2010; (with L. Quaglia) European Economic Governance and Policies, Vol. I: history and institutions, Vol. II: policies, 2010; States, Debt and Power, 2014. *Recreations:* Renaissance Florence, classical music, charity work for the disabled, walking, swimming. *Address:* School of Law and Politics, Cardiff University, Cardiff CF10 3YQ.

DYSON, Nicholas Graham; olive farmer, since 2010; permaculture designer, practitioner and blogger, since 2011; *b* 29 Nov. 1945; *s* of Hugh Norman Dyson and Joyce Dyson; *m* 2010, Sharon Lynda (*née* Jones); one *s* two *d* by previous marriages. *Educ:* Brunel Univ. (BSc Maths). Work in private sector, 1967–74; Statistician, Dept of Industry, 1974–82; Consultant, European Stats Office, 1982–85; Course Dir, CS Coll., 1985–88; Nat. Statistician, Solomon Is, 1988–91; Advr to OFT, 1991–94; Dir and Chief Statistician, Information Centre, DSS, later DWP, 1994–2002; Dir of Inf. and Analysis, DWP, 2002–05; Dir of Knowledge, Analysis and Intelligence, 2005–07, Dir, Data Integration for Govt, 2007–08, HMRC. Ind. information consultant, 2008–10. *Recreations:* sustainable house design, off-grid living, photography.

DYSON, Richard George, FCA; Partner, Ernst & Young LLP (formerly Ernst & Whinney), 1983–2008; *b* Huddersfield, 6 April 1949; *s* of George Hirst Dyson and Margaret Esther Dyson; *m* 1st, 1986, Valerie Anne Conlen (marr. diss. 1997); two *d*; 2nd, 1998, Jane Veronica Kay. *Educ:* Clifton Coll.; Queens' Coll., Cambridge (BA 1971). ACA 1974. Articles with Whinney Murray & Co., London, 1971; Ernst & Whinney, subsequently Ernst & Young: Head: Due Diligence Services in NW, 1983–97; Forensic Accounting Services, N of England, 1997–2001; Nat. Risk Mgt Partner, 2001–06. Mem. Council, ICAEW, 2001–10 (Pres., 2006–08). Chm., Wythenshawe Hosp. Transplant Fund, 2008–. Trustee: Charity Service Ltd, 2009– (Chm., 2009–); David Lewis Centre, 2009– (Chm.); Dir, Gtr Manchester Centre for Voluntary Orgn, 2014–. Gov., Bell Concord Educnl Trust, 2010–. Mem. Ct, Chartered Accountants' Co., 2009–. *Recreations:* golf, opera, travel. *Address:* Portinscale, 45 Arthog Road, Hale, Cheshire WA15 0LU. *T:* (0161) 980 5552. *E:* richard@portinscale.com. *Clubs:* Hawks (Cambridge); St James' (Manchester) (Hon. Treas., 2010–13); Denham Golf, Formby Golf, Stockport Golf.

DYSON, Stephen John; journalist, media analyst and consultant; Director, Dyson Media Ltd, since 2010; *b* 5 March 1968; *s* of Rev. Colin Dyson and Frances Dyson (*née* Ward); *m* 1992, Ruth Emma Lillywhite; three *s*. *Educ:* Primrose Hill Secondary Sch.; Matthew Boulton Coll., Birmingham; Lancaster Univ. (BA 1990). Trainee journalist, Caters News Agency, 1991; reporter: Birmingham Metro News, 1992; Sunday Mercury, Birmingham, 1993; Birmingham Evening Mail: industrial corresp., 1994–96; Dep. News Ed., 1996–98; Features Ed., 1998–99; Hd of News, 1999–2001; Dep. Ed., 2001–02; Ed., Evening Gazette, Teesside, 2002–05; Ed., Birmingham Mail, 2005–09, Sunday Mercury, Birmingham, 2008–09; Ed., BQ W Midlands, 2013–. Presenter, Hardtalk (series), 2010–11, Special Correspondent, 2010–, BBC WM Radio; Columnist, www.holdthefrontpage.co.uk, 2010–. Chm., Birmingham Mail Charity Trust, 2005–09. Non-exec. Bd Mem., Waterloo Housing Gp, 2012–. Midland Business Journalist of Year, BT Regl Awards, 1995; Ed., Newspaper of Year, NE Press Awards, 2003; Ed., Newspaper of the Year, Midland Press Awards, 2008; Ed., Regl Newspaper of the Year, Campaign for Plain English, 2009. *Publications:* (jtly) We Ain't Going Away!: the battle for Longbridge, 2000. *Recreations:* family, travelling, walking, reading, meeting folk, drinking real ale, eating pork scratchings, learning from mistakes. *Address:* 29 Goldieslie Road, Sutton Coldfield, W Midlands B73 5PE. *T:* 07818 004575. *E:* steve.dysonmedia@gmail.com. *Club:* Birmingham Press.

DYSON, Prof. Timothy Peter Geoffrey, FBA 2001; Professor of Population Studies, London School of Economics, since 1993; *b* 1 Aug. 1949; *s* of Geoffrey Dyson and Maureen (*née* Gardner); *m* 1979, Susan Ann Borman; two *s*. *Educ:* Queen's Univ., Kingston, Ont.; London Sch. of Econs (BSc Sociol. 1971, MSc Demography 1973). Res. Officer, Inst. of Develt Studies, Univ. of Sussex, 1973–75; Res. Fellow, Centre for Population Studies, LSHTM, 1975–80; Lectr in Population Studies, 1980–88, Reader, 1988–93, LSE. *Publications:* (ed) India's Historical Demography, 1989; (ed) Sexual Behaviour and Networking, 1992; Population and Food: global trends and future prospects, 1996; (ed jtly) Twenty-first Century India, 2005; Population and Development: the demographic transition, 2010. *Recreation:* gardening. *Address:* Department of International Development, London School of Economics, Houghton Street, WC2A 2AE. *T:* (020) 7955 7662.

DYTOR, Clive Idris, MC 1982; Head Master, Oratory School, 2000–15; *b* 29 Oct. 1956; *s* of (Cecil) Frederick Dytor and Maureen (Margaret) Dytor (*née* Owen); *m* 1985, Sarah Louise Payler; one *s* one *d*. *Educ:* Trinity Coll., Cambridge (MA Hons Oriental Studies); Wycliffe Hall, Oxford (MA Hons Theology). Served Royal Marines, 1980–86: officer trng, 1980–81; Troop Officer, 45 Cdo, 1981–82; Instructor, Officers' Training Wing, 1982–83; 2nd i/c Trng Team in Persian Gulf, 1983–84; Officer Recruiting Liaison Officer, 1984–86; ordained deacon 1989, priest 1990; Curate, Rushall (Dio. of Lichfield), 1989–92; Chaplain, Tonbridge Boys' Sch., 1992–94; received into RC Church, 1994; Housemaster, St Edward's Sch., Oxford, 1994–2000. Public Sch. Headmaster of Year, Tatler, 2013. *Recreations:* sport, music, Hispanic studies. *Clubs:* East India, Lansdowne; Pitt (Cambridge); Leander.

DYVIG, Peter; Comdr (1st cl.), Order of the Dannebrog, 1986; Chamberlain to Her Majesty Queen Margrethe II of Denmark, 1999; *b* 23 Feb. 1934; *m* 1959, Karen Dyvig (*née* Møller); one *s* one *d*. *Educ:* Copenhagen Univ. (grad. in Law). Entered Danish For. Service, 1959; bursary at Sch. of Advanced Internat. Studies, Washington, 1963–64; First Secretary: Danish Delegn to NATO, Paris, 1965–67; Brussels, 1967–69; Min. of For. Affairs, Copenhagen, 1969–74; Minister Counsellor, Washington, 1974–76; Ambassador, Asst Under-Sec. of State, Min. of For. Affairs, Copenhagen, 1976–79; Under-Sec. for Pol Affairs, 1980; State Sec., 1983–86; Ambassador: to UK, 1986–89; to USA, 1989–95; to France, 1995–99. Chairman: Exec. Bd, European Center for Minority Issues, Flensburg, Germany, 1999–2005; Exec. Bd, La Maison du Danemark, Paris, 2000–04; British Import Union, Copenhagen, 2000–06; Rohde Nielsen Holding A/S, 2006–11. Dir, various Danish cos. *Address:* Christiansgave 56, 2960 Rungsted Kyst, Denmark.

E

EACOTT, Rt Rev. Leonard Sidney, AM 2007; Anglican Bishop to the Australian Defence Force, 2007–12; *b* Toowoomba, Qld, 14 June 1947; *s* of Sidney Stephen Eacott and Ivy Jane McMurray Eacott (*née* Geizer); *m* 1971, Sandra Carol Danson; one *s* one *d* (and one *s* decd). *Educ:* Queensland Agricultural Coll. (Cert. in Rural Technol. (Soil Conservation) 1971); Univ. of Queensland (BA Religion and Sociol. 1983); Univ. of South Australia (Grad. Dip. in Religious Educn 1998). Soil Conservation Advr, Queensland Dept of Primary Industries, 1969–80; Officer, Royal Australian Infantry (Reserve), 1972–84; ordained deacon and priest, 1983; Parish Priest, Dio. of Brisbane, 1983–89; Chaplain, Royal Australian Army Chaplains' Dept, 1984–2007; Regular Army Chaplain, 1990–2007; Archdeacon to Army and Principal Chaplain, Army, 2002–07. Locum Bp, Western Reg., Dio. Brisbane, 2014. Mem., Religious Adv. Cttee to Services, 2007–. Chaplain, UN Transitional Authy in Cambodia, 1993; Sen. Chaplain, Internat. Force for E Timor, 1999–2000. Chaplain, Scouts Aust., 1996–2000. KStJ 2012. *Recreations:* bushwalking, off-road cycling, genealogical research, reading (adventure novels in preference to theology). *Address:* 6 Springwood Avenue, Pacific Pines, Qld 4211, Australia. *Clubs:* United Service (Brisbane); Australian (Sydney).

EADES, Robert Mark; His Honour Judge Eades; a Circuit Judge, since 2001; *b* 6 May 1951; *s* of John Robert Eades and Margaret Ursula Eades; *m* 1982, Afsaneh, (Sunny), Atri; two *d*. *Educ:* Moffats Sch., Bewdley, Worcs; Leighton Park Sch., Reading; Bristol Univ. (LLB). Called to the Bar, Middle Temple, 1974; in practice as barrister, specialising in criminal law, 1974–2001. *Recreations:* gardening, watching cricket, current affairs, English domestic architecture, local history. *Address:* Stafford Combined Court Centre, Victoria Square, Stafford ST16 2QQ.

EADIE, Roland Rennie Alistair, FRICS; Vice Lord-Lieutenant of Fermanagh, since 2014; *b* Enniskillen, Co. Fermanagh, NI, 21 Aug. 1944; *s* of Ian Chapman Eadie and Nancy Dawson Eadie; *m* 1976, Lois Cecily Sullivan. *Educ:* Gloucester House Prep. Sch., Enniskillen; Portora Royal Sch., Enniskillen. FRICS 1978. With Osborne King & Megran, Chartered Surveyors, Belfast, 1962–71; qualified as Chartered Surveyor, 1968; Sen. Partner, 1971–96, Consultant, 1996–, Eadie, McFarland & Co., Enniskillen. Member: Black Inquiry into Inland Fisheries in NI, 1978–80; NI Milk Quota Tribunal, 1982–84; Lord Chancellor's Adv. Cttee, Fermanagh, 1985–97. Member: Ulster Countryside Commn for NI, 1980–86; Historic Bldgs Council for NI, 1987–90. Chm., Enniskillen Yacht Club Charitable Trust, 1987–; Hon. Sec., Fermanagh Harriers Hunt Club, 1972–92. Gov., Portora Royal Sch., Enniskillen, 1994–. DL 1978, High Sheriff, 1984, Fermanagh. *Recreations:* gardening, breeding race horses, farming, forestry. *Address:* Aghavea Glebe, 125 Boyhill Road, Brookeborough, Co. Fermanagh BT94 4LP. *T:* (028) 8953 1310, *Fax:* (028) 8953 1847. *E:* rolandeadie@gmail.com. *Clubs:* Royal Over-Seas League; Kildare Street and University (Dublin).

EADY, family name of **Baron Swinfen**.

EADY, Sir David, Kt 1997; a Judge of the High Court of Justice, Queen's Bench Division, 1997–2013; *b* 24 March 1943; *s* of late Thomas William Eady and Kate Eady; *m* 1974, Catherine, *yr d* of J. T. Wiltshire; one *s* one *d*. *Educ:* Brentwood Sch.; Trinity Coll., Cambridge (Exhibnr; Pt I Moral Science Tripos, Pt II Law Tripos; MA, LLB). Called to the Bar, Middle Temple, 1966, Bencher, 1991; QC 1983; a Recorder, 1986–97. Mem., Cttee on Privacy and Related Matters (Calcutt Cttee), 1989–90. *Publications:* The Law of Contempt (with A. J. Arlidge), 1982, 4th edn (ed with A. T. H. Smith), 2011.

EADY, Jennifer Jane; QC 2006; **Her Honour Judge Eady;** a Circuit Judge, since 2013; *b* 31 May 1965; *d* of Gordon James Eady and Theresa Alice Eady; *m* 2006, Paul Noordhof; one *s*. *Educ:* High Sch., Boston, Lincs; St Hugh's Coll., Oxford (BA Hons PPE 1986); Poly. of Central London (Dip. Law 1988). Called to the Bar, Inner Temple, 1989; in practice, specialising in employment law; a Recorder, 2003–13. Chm., Employment Tribunals, later Employment Judge (pt-time), 2001–08; Mem. Council, ACAS, 2008–. Trustee: Free Representation Unit, 2006–; Wallace Collection, 2013–. *Recreation:* my family. *Address:* Employment Appeal Tribunal, Fleetbank House, 2–6 Salisbury Square, EC4Y 8AE.

EAGAR, (Edward) Patrick; freelance photographer, since 1965; *b* 9 March 1944; *s* of late Desmond Eagar and Marjorie Eagar; *m* 1968, Annabel Trench (*d* 1996); one *s* one *d*. *Educ:* Magdalene Coll., Cambridge (BA 1965). Retrospective exhibn, Lord's Cricket Ground, 2005, 2006. *Publications:* (with John Arlott) An Eye for Cricket, 1979; (with Alan Ross) A Summer to Remember, 1981; Test Decade, 1982; Summer of the All Rounder, 1982; Summer of Speed, 1983; Kiwis and Indians, 1983; Botham, 1985; An Australian Summer, 1985; Summer of Suspense, 1986; West Indian Summer, 1988; Tour of Tours, 1989; (with Richard Wilson) Caught in the Frame, 1992; The Ashes in Focus, 2005. *Recreations:* wine, golf, gardening. *Address:* Queensberry Place, Richmond, Surrey TW9 1NW. *T:* (020) 8940 9269. *Clubs:* MCC; Royal Mid-Surrey Golf.

EAGLAND, (Ralph) Martin; Managing Director, Eagland Planning Associates (formerly Director, Martin Eagland Economic Development Consultancy), since 1995; *b* 1 May 1942; *s* of Norman Albert Eagland and Jessie Eagland; *m* 1963, Patricia Anne Norton; one *s* one *d*. *Educ:* Hipperholme Grammar Sch.; Leeds Sch. of Town Planning; Univ. of Bradford (MSc); Univ. of Birmingham. FRTPI. Jun. planning posts, Huddersfield, Dewsbury and Halifax, 1959–67; Principal Planning Officer, City of Gloucester, 1967–72; Asst Co. Planning Officer, Northants CC, 1972–74; Chief Planner (Envmt), W Yorks CC, 1974–79, Head of Econ. Develt Unit, 1979–84; Chief Exec., Kettering Borough Council, 1984–88; Chief Exec. and Accounting Officer, Leeds Develt Corp., 1988–95. Director: Urban Regeneration Partnership, 1996–98; BURA, 2001– (Mem. Panel, 1995; Vice-Chm., 2002–04). Mem., W Yorks Cttee, CoSIRA, 1985–88; Sec., Kettering Enterprise Agency, 1986–88; Mem., Electricity Consumers' Cttee, Yorks Reg., 1997. Hon. Public Relns Officer, RTPI (Yorks Br. Exec. Cttee), 1990–92. Vice-Chm., Colne and Holme Valley Jt Cttee for the Blind, 1994–99; Mem., Rotary Club of Leeds, 1992–95. *Publications:* contribs to RTPI Jl, Instn of Highways and Transportation Jl and various property jls and publications. *Recreations:* environmental studies, music, history, gardening. *T:* (office) (01723) 866033. *Club:* Yorkshire Society (Leeds).

EAGLE, Angela; MP (Lab) Wallasey, since 1992; *b* 17 Feb. 1961; twin *d* of André and late Shirley Eagle; civil partnership 2008, Maria Exall. *Educ:* Formby High Sch.; St John's Coll., Oxford (BA PPE). Economic Directorate, CBI, 1984; Confederation of Health Service Employees: Researcher, 1984; Press Officer, 1986; Parly Officer, 1987–92. Parly Under-Sec. of State, DETR, 1997–98, DSS, 1998–2001, Home Office, 2001–02; Exchequer Sec. to HM Treasury, 2007–09; Minister of State (Minister for Pensions and Ageing Society), DWP, 2009–10; Shadow Chief Sec. to the Treasury, 2010–11; Shadow Leader, H of C, 2011–15; Shadow First Sec. of State and Shadow Sec. of State for Business, Innovation and Skills, 2015–. Mem., Nat. Women's Cttee, 1989–, Nat. Exec. Cttee, 2006–, Labour Party. Chair, Nat. Policy Forum, 2012–. Mem., BFI. *Recreations:* chess (Jun. Internat. Hons), cricket, cinema. *Address:* House of Commons, SW1A 0AA. *T:* (020) 7219 4074.
See also M. Eagle.

EAGLE, Maria; MP (Lab) Garston and Halewood, since 2010 (Liverpool, Garston, 1997–2010); *b* 17 Feb. 1961; twin *d* of André Eagle and late Shirley Eagle. *Educ:* Formby High Sch.; Pembroke Coll., Oxford (BA Hons); Coll. of Law, Lancaster Gate. Articles, Brian Thompson & Partners, Liverpool, 1990–92; Goldsmith Williams, Liverpool, 1992–95; Sen. Solicitor, Steven Irving & Co., Liverpool, 1994–97. Contested (Lab) Crosby, 1992. Parliamentary Under-Secretary of State: DWP, 2001–05; DfES, 2005–06; NI Office, 2006–07; MoJ, 2007–09; Govt Equalities Office, 2008–09; Minister of State, MoJ and Govt Equalities Office, 2009–10; Shadow Sec. of State for Transport, 2010–13, for Envmt, Food and Rural Affairs, 2013–15, for Defence, 2015–. *Address:* House of Commons, SW1A 0AA.
See also A. Eagle.

EAGLEN, Jane; international opera singer (soprano); *d* of late Ronald Arthur Eaglen and of Kathleen Eaglen; *m* 2000, Brian Lyson. *Educ:* Royal Northern Coll. of Music (vocal studies with Joseph Ward). Principal Soprano, ENO, 1983–91; major house débuts include: Donna Anna in Don Giovanni, Vienna State Opera, 1993; Brunnhilde in Die Walküre, La Scala, Milan, 1994; Norma, Seattle Opera, 1994; Amelia in Un Ballo in Maschera, Opéra National de Paris-Bastille, 1995; Brunnhilde in Ring Cycle, Lyric Opera, Chicago, 1996, Seattle, 2000–01, Metropolitan Opera, NY, 2000; Brunnhilde in Die Walküre, San Francisco Opera, 1995; Donna Anna, Metropolitan Opera, NY, 1996; Lady Macbeth, Macbeth, Vancouver Opera, 2006; Senta, Der Fliegende Holländer, Seattle Opera, 2007; other appearances include: La Gioconda, Chicago, 1999; Isolde, in Tristan and Isolde, Seattle and Chicago, 1999, Metropolitan Opera, NY, 2000; Julia, in La Vestale, ENO, 2002; Seattle Opera: Fidelio, 2003, Ariadne, in Ariadne auf Naxos, 2004 and 2005, Ortrud in Lohengrin, 2004, Brunnhilde in Ring Cycle, 2005, Rosalinda in Die Fledermaus, 2006; Brunnhilde in Ring Cycle, Chicago, 2005; Ariadne, Pittsburgh Opera, 2005. Recordings include Tosca, Norma, Tannhäuser (Grammy Award, 2002) and five solo discs of opera arias and song cycles. Prof. of Voice, Baldwin Wallace Coll., Ohio, 2010–13; Glasham Internat. Chair in Voice, RSAMD, later Royal Conservatoire of Scotland, 2011–; Prof. of Voice, New England Conservatory, 2013–. Hon. Dr: McGill Univ., 2005; Lincoln Bp Grosseteste, 2008. Lifetime Achievement Award, Licia Albanese-Puccini Foundn, 2008. *Recreations:* computing, sport spectator. *E:* jane.eaglen@necmusic.edu. *Club:* Rainier (Seattle).

EAGLES, Ven. Peter Andrew, QHC 2013; Archdeacon for the Army, since 2011; Deputy Chaplain-General, HM Land Forces, since 2014; *b* 6 July 1959; *s* of Peter Frank Eagles and Elizabeth Howie Eagles; *m* 1992, Gail Seager; one *s*. *Educ:* Royal Grammar Sch., Guildford; King's Coll., London (BA 1st cl. Hons German and Russian 1982); Univ. of Heidelberg (Deutsche Akademische Austauschdienst Scholarship); St Stephen's House, Oxford (BA Hons Theol. 1988; MTh Theol. 2004). Asst Master, Tonbridge Sch., 1982–86; freelance translator, 1982–86; ordained deacon, 1989, priest, 1990; Asst Priest, St Martin's, Ruislip, 1989–92; Chaplain to the Forces, Royal Army Chaplains' Dept, 1992–; Asst Chaplain-Gen., 2008–; Mem., RCDS, 2013–14. Mem., Gen. Synod, 2011–. *Recreations:* hills and mountains, languages and literature, European history, piano and oboe. *Address:* Ministry of Defence Chaplains (Army), Army Headquarters, Marlborough Lines, Monxton Road, Andover, Hants SP11 8HJ. *T:* (01264) 383452, *Fax:* (01264) 381418. *E:* peter.eagles330@mod.uk.

EAGLESTONE, Her Honour Diana Barbara; a Circuit Judge, 1995–2015; *b* 24 May 1949; *d* of Frank Nelson Eaglestone and Irene Eaglestone; three *d*. *Educ:* Manchester Univ. (LLB). Called to the Bar, Gray's Inn, 1971; a Recorder, 1986–95.

EAGLETON, Prof. Terence Francis, PhD; FBA 2003; Professor of English Literature, University of Lancaster, since 2008; *b* 22 Feb. 1943; *s* of Francis Paul Eagleton and Rosaleen (*née* Riley); *m* 1st, 1966, Elizabeth Rosemary Galpin (marr. diss. 1976); two *s*; 2nd, 1997, Willa Murphy; two *s* one *d*. *Educ:* Trinity Coll., Cambridge (MA, PhD). Fellow in English, Jesus Coll., Cambridge, 1964–69, Hon. Fellow, 2009; Oxford University: Tutorial Fellow, Wadham Coll., 1969–89; Lectr in Critical Theory, 1989–92; Fellow, Linacre Coll., 1989–92; Thomas Warton Prof. of English Lit., 1992–2001; Fellow, St Catherine's Coll., 1992–2001; Prof. of Cultural Theory and John Rylands Fellow, 2001–06, John Edward Taylor Prof. of English Lit., 2006–08, Univ. of Manchester. Adjunct Prof. of Cultural Theory, Nat. Univ. of Ireland, Galway, 2008–; Dist. Visitor, Univ. of Notre Dame, 2009–. Hon. DLitt: Salford, 1993; NUI, 1997; Santiago di Compostela, 1999; Central Lancs, 2005; Durham, 2008; Halifax, NS, 2010; E Anglia, 2010. *Publications:* Criticism and Ideology, 1976; Marxism and Literary Criticism, 1976; Literary Theory: an introduction, 1983; The Function of Criticism, 1984; The Ideology of the Aesthetic, 1990; Ideology: an introduction, 1993; Heathcliff and the Great Hunger: studies in Irish culture, 1995; Crazy John and the Bishop, and other Essays on Irish Culture, 1998; The Truth about the Irish, 1999; The Idea of Culture, 2000; The Gatekeeper: a memoir, 2002; Sweet Violence: a study of the tragic, 2002; After Theory, 2003; The English Novel: an introduction, 2004; Holy Terror, 2005; How to Read a Poem, 2006; The Meaning of Life, 2007; Trouble with Strangers, 2008; Reason, Faith and Revolution: reflections on the God debate, 2009; On Evil, 2010; Why Marx was Right, 2011; The Event of Literature, 2012; How to Read Literature, 2013; Across the Pond, 2013; Culture and the Death of God, 2014. *Recreation:* Irish music. *Clubs:* Irish; United Arts (Dublin).

EAGLING, Wayne John; dancer and choreographer; Artistic Director, English National Ballet, 2005–12; *s* of Eddie and Thelma Eagling. *Educ:* P. Ramsey Studio of Dance Arts; Royal Ballet Sch. Sen. Principal, Royal Ballet, 1975–91; Artistic Dir, Dutch Nat. Ballet, 1991–2003. Has danced lead rôles in major classics including Sleeping Beauty, Swan Lake, Cinderella; first rôle created for him was Young Boy in Triad, 1972; subsequent created rôles include: Solo Boy in Gloria; Ariel in The Tempest; Woyzeck in Different Drummer. Choreographed: The Hunting of the Snark by Michael Batt; (for Royal Ballet) Frankenstein, The Modern Prometheus, 1985; Beauty and the Beast, 1986; The Wall, Berlin, 1990; (for Dutch Nat. Ballet) Ruins of Time, 1993, Symphony in Waves, 1994, Duet, 1995, Lost Touch, 1995, Holding a Balance (for opening of Vermeer exhibn in Mauritshuis), 1996, (with Toer van Schayk) Nutcracker and Mouseking, 1996, Magic Flute, 1999, Le sacré du printemps, 2000, Frozen, 2001; (for La Scala, Milan) Alma Mahler, 1994; (for English Nat. Ballet) Resolution, 2008; Sleeping Beauty (for Nat. Ballet of Japan), 2014; choreographed, produced and directed various galas. *Publications:* (with Ross MacGibbon and Robert Jude) The Company We Keep, 1981. *Recreations:* golf, scuba diving, tennis, antique cars.

EAMES, family name of **Baron Eames**.

EAMES, Baron *cr* 1995 (Life Peer), of Armagh, in the County of Armagh; **Rt Rev. Robert Henry Alexander Eames,** OM 2007; PhD; Archbishop of Armagh and Primate of All Ireland, 1986–2006; *b* 27 April 1937; *s* of William Edward and Mary Eleanor Thompson Eames; *m* 1966 Ann Christine Daly (*see* Lady Eames); two *s*. *Educ:* Belfast Royal Acad.; Methodist Coll., Belfast; Queen's Univ., Belfast (LLB (hons), PhD); Trinity Coll., Dublin. Research Scholar and Tutor, Faculty of Laws, QUB, 1960–63; Curate Assistant, Bangor Parish Church, 1963–66; Rector of St Dorothea's, Belfast, 1966–74; Examining Chaplain to Bishop of Down, 1973; Rector of St Mark's, Dundela, 1974–75; Bishop of Derry and Raphoe, 1975–80; Bishop of Down and Dromore, 1980–86. Select Preacher, Oxford Univ., 1987. Irish Rep., 1984, Mem. Standing Cttee, 1985, ACC; Chairman: Commn on Communion and Women in the Episcopate, 1988–90; Commn on Inter-Anglican Relations, 1988–91; Lambeth Commn on Communion, 2004 (Windsor Report). Co-Chm., Consultative Panel on the Past, NI, 2007–08. Mem., Ind. Police Commn for England and Wales, 2012–. Governor, Church Army, 1985–90. Chairman: Armagh Observatory and Planetarium, 1986–2006; Bd, Royal Sch., Armagh, 1986–2006; Mem. Bd, St George's House, Windsor, 2008–. Hon. Bencher, Lincoln's Inn, 1998. Hon. LLD: QUB, 1989; TCD, 1992; Lancaster, 1994; Hon. DD Cambridge, 1994 and other hon. degrees from UK, Irish and US univs. *Publications:* A Form of Worship for Teenagers, 1965; The Quiet Revolution—Irish Disestablishment, 1970; Through Suffering, 1973; Thinking through Lent, 1978; Through Lent, 1984; Chains to be Broken, 1992; *relevant publication:* Nobody's Fool: the life of Archbishop Robin Eames, by Alf McCreary, 2004; contribs to New Divinity, Irish Legal Quarterly, Criminal Law Review, The Furrow. *Address:* House of Lords, SW1A 0PW.

EAMES, Lady; Ann Christine Eames, OBE 2006; Member, Northern Ireland Human Rights Commission, 2001–07; Lay Member, General Medical Council, since 2013; *b* 21 Jan. 1943; *d* of Captain William Adrian Reynolds Daly and Olive Margaret Daly; *m* 1966, Rt Rev. Robert Henry Alexander Eames (*see* Baron Eames); two *s*. *Educ:* Ashleigh House Sch., Belfast; Queen's Univ., Belfast (LLB Hons, MPhil). World-Wide Pres., Mothers' Union, 1995–2000. Mem. Bd, Hunterhouse Sch., Belfast, 2008–. Trustee: Leonard Cheshire Disability, 2009–; Christian Aid (Ireland), 2009–. *Recreations:* sailing, reading. *Address:* 3 Downshire Crescent, Hillsborough, Co. Down BT26 6DD. *Club:* Hillsborough Tennis.

EARDLEY-WILMOT, Sir Benjamin John, 7th Bt *cr* 1821, of Berkswell Hall, Warwickshire; *b* 24 Jan. 1974; *er s* of Sir Michael John Assheton Eardley-Wilmot, 6th Bt and Wendy Eardley-Wilmot (*née* Wolstenholme); *S* father, 2014, but his name does not appear on the Official Roll of the Baronetage; *m* 2009, Clementine Daisy Langton; one *s*. *Heir: s* Arlo Timothy Eardley-Wilmot, *b* 28 May 2012.

EARL, Belinda Jane; Style Director, Marks & Spencer, since 2012; *b* 20 Dec. 1961; *d* of late Colin Lee and of Diana Lee; *m* 1985, David Mark Earl; two *s*. *Educ:* UCW, Aberystwyth (BScEcon (Econs and Business); Hon. Fellow, 2003). Controller, Fashion Div., Harrods, 1983–85; Debenhams Retail Plc: Merchandiser (Menswear), 1985–88; Controller (Children's), 1988–92; Dir (accessories, women's), 1992–97; Trading Dir, 1997–2000; Debenhams Plc: Dir, 1999–2003; Chief Exec., 2000–03. Chm., Skillsmart, 2002–04; Chief Exec., Jaeger, 2004–12; Chm., AlexandAlexa.com, 2009–12. FCGI 2006.

EARL, Eric Stafford; Clerk to the Worshipful Company of Fishmongers, 1974–88, retired; *b* 8 July 1928; *s* of late Alfred Henry Earl and Mary Elizabeth Earl; *m* 1951, Clara Alice Alston (*d* 2010). *Educ:* SE Essex Technical Coll.; City of London Coll. Served with RA, 1946–48. Joined Fishmongers' Co. 1948: Accountant, 1961–68; Asst Clerk, 1969–73; Actg Clerk, 1973–74; Liveryman, 1977. Clerk to Governors of Gresham's Sch., 1974–88; formerly: Sec., City and Guilds of London Art School Ltd; Sec., Atlantic Salmon Res. Trust Ltd; Mem. Exec. and Mem. Council, Salmon and Trout Assoc.; Mem., Nat. Anglers' Council (Chm., 1983–85). Hon. Sec., Shellfish Assoc. of GB, 1974–88; Jt Hon. Sec., Central Council for Rivers Protection, 1974–88; Hon. Asst River Keeper of River Thames, 1968–88; Mem. Council, Anglers' Co-operative Assoc., 1974– (Vice Chm., 1988–). Director: Hulbert Property Co. Ltd, 1975–88; Hulbert Property Holdings Ltd, 1975–88. FZS 1988. Hon. Freeman, Watermen's Co., 1984. *Recreations:* fishing, gardening, tennis, cricket. *Address:* Dolphins, Watling Lane, Thaxted, Essex CM6 2RA. *T:* (01371) 830758.

EARL, John, FSA; Consultant, Theatres Trust, since 1996 (Director, 1986–95); *b* 11 April 1928; *s* of Philip Haywood Earl and May Florence (*née* Walsh); *m* 1952, Valerie Atkins; one *s* (one *d* decd). *Educ:* Roan Sch.; Brixton Sch. of Building. MRICS (ARICS 1952); FSA 1978. Nat. Service, RE, 1947–49. London County Council: Architect's Dept, 1954–56; Historic Bldgs Section, 1956–61; MPBW (Special Services), 1961–65; Section Leader, GLC Historic Bldgs Div., 1965–86. Private consultancy, 1986–. Lectr, various bldg conservation courses, 1970–2004; External Examiner for conservation courses at: Heriot-Watt Univ., 1982–84; Architectl Assoc., 1984–86; RICS Coll. of Estate Mgt, 1990–95 (Chm., Adv. Bd, 1996–2000); Tutor for SPAB William Morris Craft Fellows, 1987–90. Pres., Frank Matcham Soc., 1999–2015. Trustee: Talawa Theatre Co., 1996–2000; Raymond Mander and Joe Mitchenson Theatre Collection, 1996–2004. FRSA 1992; IHBC 1998. Hon. Fellow, Coll. of Estate Mgt, 2001. *Publications:* (with J. Stanton) Canterbury Hall and Theatre of Varieties, 1982; Philosophy of Building Conservation, 1996, 3rd edn 2003; Dr Langdon-Down and the Normansfield Theatre, 1997, 2nd enlarged edn 2010 as Dr Langdon Down's Normansfield Theatre; (architectural ed.) Theatres Trust Guide to British Theatres, 2000; British Theatres and Music Halls, 2005, 2nd edn 2011; conservation plans and historical reviews for a number of listed theatres; contrib. numerous books and jls on building conservation and theatre buildings. *Recreation:* avoiding organised sport and religion.

EARL, Prof. Michael John, FBCS; Professor of Information Management, University of Oxford, 2002–07, now Emeritus; Dean, Templeton College, Oxford, 2002–08, now Hon. Fellow, Green Templeton College; Acting Pro-Vice-Chancellor, Development and External Affairs, University of Oxford, 2008–10; *b* 11 Jan. 1944; *s* of late Vincent and Marjorie Earl; *m* 1969, Alison Jennifer Eades; one *s* one *d*. *Educ:* Univ. of Newcastle-upon-Tyne (BA 1966); Univ. of Warwick (MSc 1971). FBCS 1992. Systems Analyst, United Steel Cos, 1966–68; Sen. Systems Analyst, Bowater Paper Corp., 1968–69; Gp Systems Manager, GEC Telecommunications Ltd, 1969–74; Lectr in Mgt Control, Manchester Business Sch., 1974–76; Fellow in Information Mgt, Templeton Coll., Univ. of Oxford, 1976–90; London Business School: Prof. of Information Mgt, 1991–2002; Dep. Principal, 1996–98; Actg Principal, 1998. Chm., First Residential Properties PLC, 2011–12; Founding Consultant, Formicio Ltd, 2011–. Non-executive Director: Shell Information Services BV, 1997–98; Institut V, Stockholm Sch. of Economics, 2000–. Trustee, and Chm., Finance Cttee, Oxford Philomusica, 2004–. Hon. Fellow, Harris Manchester Coll., Oxford, 2008. *Publications:* (with A. M. McCosh) Accounting Control and Financial Strategy, 1978; (jtly) Developing Managerial Information Systems, 1979; (jtly) Information Society: for richer, for poorer, 1982; Perspectives on Management, 1983; Information Management: the strategic dimension, 1989; Management Strategies for Information Technology, 1989; Information Management: the organizational dimension, 1996; articles in learned and professional jls. *Recreations:* golf, music, tennis, travel. *Address:* Green Templeton College, University of Oxford, Oxford OX2 6HG. *T:* (01865) 274797, *Fax:* (01865) 284598. *E:* Michael.Earl@gtc.ox.ac.uk. *Clubs:* Oxford and Cambridge; Frewen (Oxford); Frilford Heath Golf; Burford Golf.

EARL, Stephen, TD 1992; a District Judge (Magistrates' Courts), since 2004; *b* 16 April 1958; *s* of Leslie Earl and Anne Earl; *m* 2002, Gillian Douglass; one *s* one *d*, and two step *s* four step *d*. *Educ:* Beverley Grammar Sch.; Manchester Polytech. (BA Hons Law); Guildford Coll. of Law. Articled clerk, Hart Scales & Hodges, 1980–82; admitted solicitor, 1982; Asst Solicitor, Gibson & Co., 1983–90; sole practitioner, Earl Galpin, 1990–2004. A Dep. Dist Judge, 2000–04. VRSM 2001. *Recreations:* family, travel, reading, watching football. *Address:* Newcastle Magistrates' Court, Market Street, Newcastle upon Tyne NE99 1AU. *T:* (0191) 232 7326, *Fax:* (0191) 221 0025.

EARL, Col Timothy James, OBE 2000; Private Secretary to HRH the Princess Royal, 1999–2002; *b* 2 July 1943; *s* of Rowland William Earl and Elizabeth Sylvia Earl; *m* 1968, Elizabeth Mary Ghislaine de Pelet; two *s* one *d*. *Educ:* Brentwood Sch.; RMA Sandhurst. Commnd 1st Bn King's Own Royal Border Regt, 1964; served British Guyana, Gulf States, Cyprus, Gibraltar and Germany; transf. to Life Guards, 1974; served Germany, Norway, Belize; CO, 1983–85; RCDS, 1985–87; MoD, 1987–90; HQ UKLF, 1990–93; Sec., Govt Hospitality Fund, 1993–99. Hon. Sec., Piscatorial Soc., 2008–. *Recreations:* field sports, planting trees. *Address:* Haddon Lodge, Stourton Caundle, Dorset DT10 2LB. *T:* (01963) 362241. *Club:* Flyfishers'.

EARLE, Arthur Frederick; management and economic consultant, since 1983; *b* Toronto, 13 Sept. 1921; *s* of Frederick C. Earle and Hilda M. Earle (*née* Brown); *m* 1946, Vera Domini Lithgow; two *s* one *d*. *Educ:* Toronto; London Sch. of Economics (BSc (Econ.), PhD; Hon. Fellow 1980). Royal Canadian Navy (Rating to Lieut Comdr), 1939–46. Canada Packers Ltd, 1946–48; Aluminium Ltd cos in British Guiana, West Indies and Canada, 1948–53; Treas., Alumina Jamaica Ltd, 1953–55; Aluminium Union, London, 1955–58; Vice-Pres., Aluminium Ltd Sales Inc., New York, 1958–61; Dir, 1961–74, Dep. Chm., 1961–65, Man. Dir, 1963–65, Hoover Ltd; Founding Principal, London Graduate Sch. of Business Studies, 1965–72. Pres., Internat. Investment Corp. for Yugoslavia, 1972–74; Pres., Boyden Consulting Group Ltd, 1974–82; Associate, 1974–82, Vice-Pres., 1975–82, Boyden Associates, Inc.; Advisor to the Pres., Canada Develt Investment Corp., 1983–86; Director: Rio Algom Ltd, 1983–92; National Sea Products Ltd, 1984–86; Bathpaul Ltd, UK, 1984–86; Monkwells Ltd, UK, 1984. Sen. Res. Fellow, Nat. Centre for Management R & D, Univ. of Western Ontario, 1987–90. Member: Commn of Enquiry, Jamaican Match Industry, 1953; Consumer Council, 1963–68; NEDC Cttee on Management Educn, Training and Develt, 1967–69; NEDC for Electrical Engineering Industry. Chm., Canadian Assoc. of Friends of LSE, 1975–96. Dir, Nat. Ballet of Canada, 1982–85. Governor: Ashridge Management Coll., 1962–65; LSE, 1968–95; NIESR, 1968–74; Governor and Mem. Council, Ditchley Foundn, 1967. Fellow, London Business Sch., 1988. Thomas Hawksley Lecture, IMechE, 1968. *Publications:* numerous, on economics and management. *Recreations:* hill climbing, model ship building. *Address:* 901–1230 Marlborough Court, Oakville, ON L6H 3K6, Canada. *T:* (905) 8429547.

EARLE, Sir George; *see* Earle, Sir H. G. A.

EARLE, Glenn Peter Jonathan; Managing Director and Chief Operating Officer, Europe, Middle East and Africa, Goldman Sachs, 2006–11; *b* Douglas, I of M, 12 Jan. 1958; *s* of Brian Peter Earle and Elsie Florence Earle; *m* 1983, Phyllida Charlotte Gerrard; one *s* two *d*. *Educ:* Millfield Sch.; Emmanuel Coll., Cambridge (BA Hons 1979); Harvard Business Sch. (MBA with High Dist.). With Grindlays Bank, subseq. ANZ Grindlays, 1979–85; with Goldman Sachs, incl. roles in NY, Frankfurt and London, 1987–2011 (Partner, 1996; Co-hd, Eur. M&A Adv. Gp, 1999–2003). Non-executive Director: Fiat Chrysler Automobiles, NV; Affiliated Managers Gp, Inc.; Rothesay Life Gp. Chm., Adv. Bd, Judge Business Sch., Cambridge Univ., 2010–; Mem., Adv. Bd, Sutton Trust, 2013–. Trustee: RNT, 2009–; Teach First, 2012–. *Recreations:* theatre, sport, the outdoors. *Clubs:* MCC; Queen's; Royal Ashdown Golf, Queenwood Golf; Bath and Racquets.

EARLE, Sir (Hardman) George (Algernon), 6th Bt *cr* 1869; *b* 4 Feb. 1932; *S* father, 1979; *m* 1967, Diana Gillian Bligh, *d* of Col F. F. B. St George, CVO; one *s* one *d*. *Heir: s* Robert George Bligh Earle [*b* 24 Jan. 1970; *m* 2007, Nico Germaine Erzsebet, *d* of Miklōs Kōs; one *s*].

EARLE, Joel Vincent, (Joe); Senior Consultant for Japanese Works of Art, Bonhams, since 2012; *b* 1 Sept. 1952; *s* of late James Basil Foster Earle and Mary Isabel Jessie Weeks; *m* 1980, Sophia Charlotte Knox; two *s*. *Educ:* Westminster Sch.; New Coll., Oxford (BA 1st Cl. Hons Chinese). Far Eastern Department, Victoria & Albert Museum: Res. Asst, 1974–77; Asst Keeper, 1977–82; Keeper, 1982–87; Head of Public Services, V&A Mus., 1987–89; independent curator, 1990–2003; Chair, Dept of Art of Asia, Oceania and Africa, Mus. of Fine Arts, Boston, 2003–07; Vice-Pres. and Dir, Japan Soc. Gall., NY, 2007–12. Consultant, Christie's, 1998–2003. Exhibns Co-ordinator, Japan Fest. 1991, 1990–91; *other exhibitions include:* Japan Style, V&A, 1980; Japanese Lacquer, V&A, 1980; Great Japan Exhibition, RA, 1981; The Toshiba Gall. of Japanese Art, V&A, 1986; British Design, South Coast Plaza, 1990; Visions of Japan, V&A, 1991–92; London Transport Posters, 1994; Da un antico castello inglese, Milan, 1994; Shibata Zeshin, Nat. Mus. of Scotland, 1997; Splendors of Meiji, USA, 1999; Netsuke, Mus. of Fine Arts, Boston, 2001; Serizawa: Master of Japanese Textile Design, Nat. Mus of Scotland, 2001; New Bamboo: contemporary Japanese masters, Japan Soc., 2008; Buriki: Japanese tin toys from the golden age of the American automobile, Japan Soc., 2009; Fiber Futures: Japan's Textile Pioneers, Japan Soc., 2011; Silver Wind: the arts of Sakai Hoitsu (1761–1828), Japan Soc., 2012. *Publications:* An Introduction to Netsuke, 1980, 2nd edn 1982; An Introduction to Japanese Prints, 1980; (contrib.) Japan Style, 1980; (contrib.) The Great Japan Exhibition, 1981; (trans.) The Japanese Sword, 1983; The Toshiba Gallery: Japanese art and design, 1986; Flower Bronzes of Japan, 1995; (ed) Treasures of Imperial Japan: Lacquer, 1995; (ed) The Index of Inro Artists, 1995; Shibata Zeshin, 1996; Shadows and Reflections: Japanese lacquer art, 1996; Flowers of the Chisel, 1997; R. S. Huthart Collection of Netsuke, 1998; Splendors of Meiji, 1999; Infinite Spaces: the art and wisdom of the Japanese garden, 2000; Netsuke of Iwami Province, 2000; Japanese Lacquer: The Denys Eyre Bower Collection, 2000; Netsuke: fantasy and reality in Japanese miniature sculpture, 2001; Splendors of Imperial Japan, 2002; Lethal Elegance: the art of Samurai sword fittings, 2004; Contemporary Clay: Japanese ceramics for the new century, 2005; Serizawa: master of Japanese textile design, 2009; (trans.) Melk's Golden Acres, 2011; (trans.) A White Camellia in a Vase, 2012; (contrib.) In the Moment: Japanese art from the Larry Ellison collection, 2013; Inro from a Private European Collection, 2013; (contrib. and ed) Grace Tsumugi Fine Art: Japanese works of art, 2014; (contrib. and ed) Erik Thomsen: Japanese paintings and works of art, 2014; (contrib. and ed) Erik Thomsen: Inoue Yuichi, 2014; (contrib. and ed) Bonhams 1793: the Misumi Collection of imported works of lacquer art and paintings, Part I,

2014; articles in learned jls. *Recreation:* reading Japanese fiction. *Address:* 123 Middleton Road, E8 4LL. *T:* (020) 7254 5178, 07880 313351. *E:* joevearle@gmail.com.
See also T. F. Earle.

EARLE, Prof. Thomas Foster, DPhil; King John II Professor of Portuguese Studies, University of Oxford, 1996–2013; Fellow, St Peter's College, Oxford, 1996–2013, now Emeritus; *b* 5 April 1946; *s* of late James Basil Foster Earle and Mary Earle (*née* Weeks); *m* 1970, Gisèle Hilary Wilson; one *s* one *d. Educ:* Westminster Sch.; Wadham Coll., Oxford (BA 1967; DPhil 1976). University of Oxford: Lectr in Portuguese Studies, 1968–96; Fellow, Linacre Coll., 1968–96; Dir, Portuguese Studies, 1976–96; Chm., Centre for Study of Portuguese Discoveries, Linacre Coll., 1989–. Founder Mem., Associação Internacional de Lusitanistas, 1984; Corresp. Fellow, Acad. das Ciências de Lisboa, 2010. Pres., Assoc. of British and Irish Lusitanists, 2006–09. Grande oficial, Ordem do Infante D. Henrique (Portugal), 1995. *Publications:* Theme and Image in the Poetry of Sá de Miranda, 1980 (trans. Portuguese 1985); The Muse Reborn: the poetry of António Ferreira, 1988 (trans. Portuguese 1990); (ed) Castro de António Ferreira, 1990; (with J. Villiers) Albuquerque: Caesar of the East, 1990; (ed) Poemas Lusitanos de António Ferreira, 2000, 2nd edn 2008; O Livro de Eclesiastes, 2002; Portuguese Writers and English Readers: books by Portuguese writers published before 1640 in the libraries of Oxford and Cambridge, 2009 (trans. Portuguese, 2014); Estudos sobre literatura e cultura portuguesa do Renascimento, 2013; (ed with J. Camões) Comédias de Sá de Miranda, 2013; articles in collections, learned jls, etc. *Recreations:* music, gardening, walking. *Address:* c/o St Peter's College, New Inn Hall Street, Oxford OX1 2DL.
See also J. V. Earle.

EARLES, Prof. Stanley William Edward, PhD, DScEng; FREng, FIMechE; Professor of Mechanical Engineering, King's College, University of London, 1976–94, Emeritus since 1994; *b* 18 Jan. 1929; *s* of late William Edward Earles and Winnifred Anne Cook; *m* 1955, Margaret Isabella Brown; two *d. Educ:* King's Coll., Univ. of London (BScEng, PhD, DScEng; AKC; FKC 1993). FIMechE 1976; FREng (FEng 1992). Nuffield Apprentice, Birmingham, 1944–50; King's Coll., Univ. of London, 1950–53; Scientific Officer, Royal Naval Scientific Service, 1953–55; University of London: Queen Mary College: Lectr in Mech. Engrg, 1955–69; Reader in Mech. Engrg, 1969–75; Prof. of Mech. Engrg, 1975–76; King's College: Head, Dept of Mech. Engrg, 1976–90, 1991–94; Dean of Engrg, 1986–90; Hd of Sch. of Phys. Scis and Engrg, 1990–91. James Clayton Fund prize, IMechE, 1967; Engineering Applied to Agriculture Award, IMechE, 1980. *Publications:* papers and articles in Proc. IMechE, Jl of Mech. Engrg Science, Jl of Sound and Vibration, Wear, Proc. ASME and ASLE, and Eng. *Recreations:* Real tennis, gardening, fell walking. *Address:* Woodbury, Church Lane, Wormley, Broxbourne, Herts EN10 7QF. *T:* (01992) 464616.

EARLY, Fergus, OBE 2009; dancer and choreographer; Founder and Artistic Director, Green Candle Dance Company, since 1987; *b* Worthing, 4 Aug. 1946; *s* of Dr Noel Early and Hilda Early (*née* West); *m* 2005, Jacky Lansley; one *d. Educ:* Royal Ballet Sch.; RAD major exams. Founder Mem., Balletmakers Ltd, 1962–69; dancer, Royal Ballet, 1964–68; Ballet Master and Resident Choreographer, Ballet for All company, Royal Ballet, 1965–70; Sen. Teacher, London Sch. of Contemp. Dance, 1971–74; Founder Member: Dance Organisation, 1975–76; X6 Dance Space, 1976–80; Chisenhale Dance Space, 1981–88. Co-Founder and Co-Ed., New Dance Mag., 1977–82. Chm., Gtr London Arts Dance Panel, 1979–84; Trustee: Scarabeus Theatre Co., 1999–2012 (Chm., 2006–11); Oxford House, Bethnal Green, 2004– (Vice Chm., 2009–). Churchill Fellow, 2010. Hon. DA De Montfort, 2011. *Publications:* Growing Bolder: a start-up guide to creating dance with older people, 1996; The Wise Body: conversations with experienced dancers, 2011; articles in dance and arts jls. *Recreations:* playing cricket, walking. *Address:* Green Candle Dance Company, Oxford House, Derbyshire Street, E2 6HG. *T:* (020) 7739 7722, *Fax:* (020) 7739 7731. *E:* fergus@greencandledance.com.

EARNSHAW, Prof. William Charles, PhD; FMedSci; FRS 2013; FRSE; Professor of Chromosome Dynamics, Institute of Cell Biology, University of Edinburgh. *Educ:* Lenox Sch., Lenox, Mass; Colby Coll. (BA Biol. and Art 1972); Massachusetts Inst. of Technol. (PhD Microbiol. 1977). Postdoctoral Fellow: MRC Molecular Biol. Lab., Cambridge, 1977–81; Univ. of Geneva, 1981–82; Prof., Sch. of Medicine, Johns Hopkins Univ., 1982–95; Wellcome Trust Principal Res. Fellow, Univ. of Edinburgh, 1996–. FRSE 2002; FMedSci 2009; FAAAS; Mem. EMBO. *Publications:* Cell Biology (with Thomas Pollard), 2nd edn 2007. *Address:* Wellcome Trust Centre for Cell Biology, University of Edinburgh, Michael Swann Building, Max Born Crescent, Edinburgh EH9 3BF.

EARWICKER, Martin John, FREng; Vice Chancellor and Chief Executive, and Personal Chair, London South Bank University, 2009–13; *b* 11 May 1948; *s* of George Allen Earwicker and Joan Mary Earwicker (*née* West); *m* 1970, Pauline Ann Josey; two *s. Educ:* Farnborough Grammar Sch.; Univ. of Surrey (BSc Hons Physics 1970). FREng 2000. Various research posts, ARE, 1970–86; Dir, Science (Sea), MoD, 1986–89; Hd, Attack Weapons Dept, 1989–90, Hd, Flight Systems Dept, 1990–92, RAE; Dir, Operational Studies, 1992–93, Dir, Air Systems Sector, 1993–96, DRA; Dep. Chief Scientist (Scrutiny and Analysis), 1996–98, Dir Gen. (Scrutiny and Analysis), 1998–99, MoD; Man. Dir, Analysis, DERA, 1998–99; Hd of Science and Engrg Base Gp, OST, DTI, 1999–2001; Chief Exec., Defence Sci. and Technol. Lab., MoD, 2001–06; Dir, NMSI, 2006–09. Vis. Prof., Faculty of Engrg, Imperial Coll., London, 2005–09. Chairman: Farnborough Coll. of Technol., 2004–10; Tower Hamlets Coll., 2010–. Non-exec. Dir and Chm. Audit Cttee, Dorset County Hosp. NHS Foundn Trust, 2013–. Trustee: Hart CAB, 2013–; Regent's Univ., London, 2014–. Pres., Assoc. for Sci. Educn, 2008. Vice Pres., RAEng, 2009–12. DUniv Surrey, 2010. A. B. Wood Medal and Prize, Inst. of Acoustics, 1984. *Recreations:* cycling, woodwork, music. *Address:* 21 Basingbourne Road, Fleet, Hants GU52 6TE.

EASMON, Prof. Charles Syrett Farrell, CBE 2000; MD, PhD; Professor of Health Policy, University of West London (formerly Thames Valley University), 2003–10, now Emeritus; *b* 20 Aug. 1946; *s* of Dr McCormack Charles Farrell Easmon and Enid Winifred Easmon; *m* 1977, Susan Lynn (*née* Peach). *Educ:* Epsom Coll.; St Mary's Hospital Med. Sch. (Open Schol.; MB BS; MD); PhD London. MRCP; FRCPath. Pathology trng, St Bartholomew's Hosp., 1970–71; St Mary's Hospital Medical School: Research Asst, 1971; Lectr, 1973; Sen. Lectr, 1976; Reader and Actg Head of Dept, 1980; Personal Chair, 1983; Fleming Prof. of Med. Microbiol., 1984–92; Dean of Postgrad. Med. for NW Thames, BPMF, Univ. of London, 1992–95; Dir of Educn and Trng, N Thames, then London, Reg., NHS Exec., 1994–2002; Clin. Dir, Directorate of Health and Social Care for London, DoH, 2002–03. Dep. Chm., HPA, 2003–13. Non-exec. Dir, SW London Strategic HA, 2003–06. Founder FMedSci 1998. *Publications:* (ed) Medical Microbiology, vol. 1 1982, vols 2 and 3 1983, vol. 4 1984; (ed) Infections in the Immunocompromised Host, 1983; (ed) Staphylococci and Staphylococcal Infections, 1983; numerous papers in learned jls. *Recreations:* music, history, fishing. *Address:* 21 Cranes Park Avenue, Surbiton, Surrey KT5 8BS. *Club:* Athenæum.

EASSIE, Rt Hon. Lord; Ronald David Mackay; PC 2006; a Senator of the College of Justice in Scotland, since 1997; Chairman, Scottish Law Commission, 2002–06; *b* 1945; *s* of Robert Ostler Mackay and Dorothy Lilian Johnson or Mackay; *m* 1988, Annette Frenkel; one *s. Educ:* Berwickshire High Sch.; Univ. of St Andrews (MA Hons); Univ. of Edinburgh (LLB). Admitted to Faculty of Advocates, 1972; Official of Court of Justice of European Communities, Luxembourg, 1979–82; QC (Scot.) 1986; Advocate Depute, 1986–90. *Publications:* (ed with H. L. MacQueen) Gloag & Henderson, The Law of Scotland, 13th edn 2012. *Recreations:* walking, ski-ing. *Address:* Parliament House, Parliament Square, Edinburgh EH1 1RQ. *Club:* New (Edinburgh).

EASSON, Gillian; Chairman, Stockport NHS Foundation Trust, since 2012 (Deputy Chairman, 2007–12); *b* Stockport, 2 Dec. 1950; *d* of late Stanley and Joan Oakley; *m* 1972, Malcolm Cameron Greig Easson (*d* 2010); one *s* one *d. Educ:* Marple Hall Sch. for Girls; Girton Coll., Cambridge (BA 1972; MA 1976). Admitted as solicitor, 1975; Solicitor, Gtr Manchester Council, prosecuting for NW Prosecuting Solicitors' Dept, 1977–86; Crown Prosecutor, 1986–87; sole practitioner, 1987–2000. Mem. Bd, Ofqual, 2010–12 (Chair: Ext. Equality Adv. Gp, 2010–12; 2010 GCSE, AS and A Level Exam. Marking Inquiry, 2010–12). Chair, Manchester Univ. Press., 2010–13; non-executive Director: Christie Hosp. NHS Trust, 2000–06 (Chair: Charitable Funds Cttee, 2001–02; Audit Cttee, 2001–03; Finance Cttee, 2003–06); Project Unity Ltd, 2004; UMIP Ltd, 2005–07 (Chair, Audit Cttee, 2006–07). Mem. Council and Court, UMIST, 2001–04; University of Manchester: Mem., 2004–08, Dep. Chm., 2008–12, Bd of Govs; Chm., Risk Cttee, 2004–09; Pro-Chancellor, 2012–; Chair, Nominations Cttee, 2012–; Mem., Global Leadership Bd, 2012–. Trustee and Mem. Bd, NHS Providers, 2014–. *Recreation:* light aviation. *Address:* Trust Headquarters, Stockport NHS Foundation Trust, Stepping Hill Hospital, Poplar Grove, Hazel Grove, Stockport SK10 7JE. *T:* (0161) 419 5030. *E:* gillian.easson@stockport.nhs.uk.

EAST, John Anthony, CBE 1996 (OBE 1982); Chairman: Continuum Group (formerly Heritage Projects Ltd), since 1997; Greenway LLP, since 2007; Kent Life, since 2009; Sustainable Villages Ltd, since 2010; E-Riser Ltd, since 2014; *b* 25 May 1930; *s* of John East and Jessie Mary East; *m* 1st, 1957, Barbara Collins (marr. diss. 1980); two *s* one *d*; 2nd, 1982, Susan Finch (marr. diss. 1996); two *d. Educ:* Bromley Grammar School. Reuter's, 1954–58; Notley Advertising, 1958–60; Director: French Government Tourist Office, 1960–70; English Tourist Bd, 1970–95 (Chief Exec., 1985–95). Chm., Watermark, 1995–97. *Publications:* History of French Architecture, 1968; Gascony and the Pyrenees, 1969; articles on France and French architecture. *Recreations:* walking, gardening, studying things French. *Address:* Continuum Group, St Edmunds House, Margaret Street, York YO10 4UX.

EAST, Rt Hon. Paul Clayton, CNZM 2005; PC 1998; QC (NZ) 1995; High Commissioner for New Zealand in the United Kingdom, 1999–2002; *b* 4 Aug. 1946; *s* of Edwin Cuthbert East and Edith Pauline Addison East; *m* 1972, Marilyn Kottman; three *d. Educ:* King's Coll., Auckland; Auckland Univ. (LLB 1970); Univ. of Virginia, USA (LLM 1972). Barrister and solicitor, Auckland, 1971; Graduate Fellow, Univ. of Va Sch. of Law, 1971–72; Partner, 1974–78, Consultant, 1978–90, East Brewster, Solicitors, Rotorua. City Councillor, and Dep. Mayor of Rotorua, 1974–79 (Chm., Finance Cttee, 1977–79). MP (N) New Zealand, 1978–99 (for Rotorua, 1978–96). Opposition Spokesman, NZ Parliament: for Commerce and Customs, 1984; on Justice, Attorney-Gen. and Constitutional Affairs, 1985–90; on Health, 1986; Attorney-Gen., 1990–97; Minister: for Crown Health Enterprises, 1991–96; of State Services, 1993–97; of Defence, and of Corrections, 1996–97. Leader of House of Representatives, 1990–93. Chm., Parly Select Cttee on Official Information, 1982; Member: Nat. Exec., NZ Nat. Party, 1985–87; NZ Delegn, Council of Europe and Eur. Parlt, 1985; Dep. Chm., Commonwealth Eminent Persons Observer Gp, Kenya Elections, 2008; Chm., Commonwealth Eminent Persons Gp, Tanzania Elections, 2010. Chm., Rotorua Airport Cttee, 1977–79; Mem. Exec., Airport Authorities of NZ, 1974–79. Chm., Perpetual Capital Mgt Ltd, 2006–; Director: Taylors Gp Ltd, 2002–; Benfield Gp (formerly Grieg) (NZ) Ltd, 2002–; Agriquality Ltd. Chm., Charity Gaming Assoc., 2002–. Trustee: NZ Antarctic Heritage Trust, 2002– (Chm., 2005–); Rotorua Energy Charitable Trust, 2004–. Fellow, Australia/NZ Foundn, 1983. *Publications:* numerous articles. *Recreations:* ski-ing, fishing, golf. *Address:* PO Box 608, Rotorua, New Zealand. *Club:* Northern (Auckland).

EAST, Ronald Joseph; Director, Kleinwort Charter Investment Trust PLC, 1987–97; formerly Director, Kleinwort Development Fund PLC; *b* 17 Dec. 1931; *s* of Joseph William and Marion Elizabeth Emma East; *m* 1955, Iris Joyce Beckwith; two *d. Educ:* Clare Coll., Cambridge Univ. (MA). Engineering Apprenticeship, Ford Trade Sch., Ford Motor Co. Ltd, 1945–52. Troop Comdr, RA (Lieut), 1953–55. Managerial posts in economics, product planning, finance, and engineering areas of Ford Motor Co. Ltd, 1959–65; Guest, Keen & Nettlefolds Ltd: Corporate Staff Dir of Planning, 1965–70; Planning Exec., Automotive and Allied Products Sector, 1972–73; Chairman: GKN Castings Ltd, 1974–77; GKN Kent Alloys Ltd, 1974–77; GKN Shotton Ltd, 1974–77; Dir, GKN (UK) Ltd, 1974–77; Corporate Staff Dir, Group Supplies, GKN Ltd, 1976–77. Dir, Programme Analysis and Review (PAR) and Special Advisor to Chief Sec. to the Treasury, 1971–72. Chairman: Hale Hamilton Hldgs, 1981–89; Hale Hamilton (Valves), 1981–89. *Recreation:* walking. *Address:* 12 Rutland Gate, SW7 1BB.

EAST, Trevor James; Chairman, Pitch International LLP, since 2005; *b* Derby, 22 Oct. 1950; *s* of Ralph James and Hazel Jean East; *m* 1st, 1975, Penelope Anne McLean (marr. diss. 1987); two *s* one *d*; 2nd, 1995, Katharine Judith Brown; two *s* one *d. Educ:* Bemrose Grammar Sch., Derby. Trainee journalist, then journalist, Raymonds News Agency, 1967–72; Producer and Presenter, ATV Sport, 1972–78; Presenter, Tiswas, 1973–78; Sports Ed., Central TV, 1978–84; Exec. Producer, 1984–92, Dep. Hd, 1992–94, Hd, 1994–95, ITV Sport; Dep. Man. Dir, Sky Sports, 1995–2005; Dir of Sport, Setanta, 2005–09. Dir, Cleanevent Gp Ltd, 2012–. *Recreations:* sport, music, food, wine. *Address:* Pitch International LLP, 27 Brewhouse Lane, Putney, SW15 2JX.

EAST ANGLIA, Bishop of, (RC), since 2013; **Rt Rev. Alan Stephen Hopes;** *b* 17 March 1944; *s* of William Stephen and Ivy Beatrice Hopes. *Educ:* Enfield Grammar Sch.; King's Coll., London (BD, AKC 1966). Ordained deacon, 1967, priest, 1968; Assistant Curate: All Saints, E Finchley, 1967–72; St Alphage, Burnt Oak (in charge of Grahame Park Estate), 1972–78; Vicar, St Paul, Tottenham, 1978–94; Area Dean, E Haringey, 1982–88; Preb., St Paul's Cathedral, 1987–94; ordained priest in the Roman Catholic Church, 1995; Asst Priest, Our Lady of Victories, Kensington, 1995–97; Parish Priest, Holy Redeemer, Chelsea, 1997–2001; VG, Westminster Archdiocese, 2001–03; Auxiliary Bishop of Westminster, (RC), 2003–13; Titular Bishop of Cuncacestre, 2003–13. *Recreations:* books, art, films, classical music, opera, travel. *Address:* The White House, 21 Upgate, Poringland, Norwich NR14 7SH.

EAST RIDING, Archdeacon of; *see* Broom, Ven. A. C.

EASTELL, Prof. Richard, MD; FRCP, FRCPE, FRCPath, FMedSci; Professor of Bone Metabolism, since 1995, and Director, Mellanby Centre for Bone Research, since 2008, University of Sheffield; Hon. Consultant Physician, Sheffield Teaching Hospitals NHS Trust (formerly Northern General Hospital, Royal Hallamshire Hospital and Nether Edge Hospital), since 1989; *b* 12 Feb. 1953; *s* of Kenneth Eastell and Betty Eastell (*née* Hoare); *m* 1974, Joyce Rachel Noble; two *s* one *d. Educ:* Univ. of Edinburgh (BSc Hons 1974; MB ChB 1977; MD 1984). FRCP 1996; FRCPE 2000; FRCPath 2000. House Officer, Royal Infirmary and Western Gen. Hosp., Edinburgh, 1977–78; MRC Res. Fellow, 1978–80, Registrar, 1980–82, Western Gen. Hosp., Edinburgh; Registrar, Northwick Park Hosp., Harrow, 1982–84; Res. Associate and Sen. Clinical Fellow, Mayo Clinic, Rochester, Minn., 1984–89; University of Sheffield: Sen. Res. Fellow, 1989–92, Sen. Lectr, 1992–95, Dept of Human Metabolism and Clinical Biochemistry; Res. Dean, Sch. of Medicine and Biomed. Scis, 2002–05; Dir, Bone Biomedical Res. Unit, 2008–12. Director: Div. of Clinical Scis (North), 1999–2003; R&D for Sheffield Teaching Hosps Trust, 2003–05. Sen. Investigator, NIHR, 2009–. Visiting Professor in Endocrinology: Mayo Clinic, Rochester, USA, 1999;

Univ. of Pittsburgh, 2002; Path West Vis. Lectr, Perth, Australia, 2005. Member: ARC Res. Cttee, 1998–2004; Res. Adv. Council, Res. into Ageing, 2001–04; MRC Physiological Systems and Clinical Scis Bd, 2003–06; MRC and NIHR Efficacy and Mechanism Evaluation Bd, 2009–. President: Bone and Tooth Soc., 2002–05; Eur. Calcified Tissue Soc., 2005–08; Chm., Nat. Osteoporosis Soc., 2007–08. FMedSci 2000. Hon. FRCPI 1998. Randall G. Sprague Award, Mayo Clinic, 1989; Corrigan Medal, RCPI, 1998; Queen's Anniversary Award for Higher Educn, 2002; Kohn Award, Nat. Osteoporosis Soc., 2004; Soc. for Endocrinol. Medal, 2004; Sen. Investigator Award, NIHR, 2009; Philippe Bordier Award for Clinical Investigation, Eur. Calcified Tissue Soc., 2012; Frederic C. Bartter Award, Amer. Soc. of Bone and Mineral Res., 2014. *Publications:* (ed jtly) Bone Markers: biochemical and clinical perspectives, 2001; over 300 articles in med. literature. *Recreations:* golf, hill walking. *Address:* 289 Ringinglow Road, Bents Green, Sheffield, South Yorks S11 7PZ. *T:* (0114) 271 4705. *E:* r.eastell@sheffield.ac.uk.

EASTER, Rev. Canon Ann Rosemarie; Chief Executive Officer, Renewal Programme, 1995–2015; Chaplain to the Queen, since 2007; Associate Priest, East Ham Team, since 2011; *b* Upton Park, 9 Sept.; *d* of Harry Easter and Audrey Easter (*née* Boater); *m* 1987, Rev. Christopher Owens; two *s* one *d*. *Educ:* George Green's Grammar Sch.; Queen's Coll., Birmingham (Dip. in Religious Studies 1979); Univ. of East London (Dip. in Mgt Studies 1994). Ordained deaconess, 1980, deacon, 1987, priest, 1994; Parish Minister, St John, St James and Christchurch, London, 1980–89; Manager, Newham Crossroads, 1990–95; Area Dean, Newham, 1996–2007. Hon. Canon, Chelmsford Cathedral, 2000–; Hon. Curate (part-time), All Saints, West Ham, 2008–10. Regular contribs to Good Morning Sunday and Pause for Thought, BBC Radio 2. *Publications:* This Month We Celebrate, 1990. *Recreations:* playing the piano, entertaining and being entertained. *Address:* 67 Disraeli Road, E7 9JU. *T:* (020) 8555 6337.

EASTERLING, Prof. Patricia Elizabeth, FBA 1998; Regius Professor of Greek, Cambridge University, 1994–2001, and Fellow of Newnham College, Cambridge, 1994–2001 (Hon. Fellow, 1987–94 and since 2001); *b* 11 March 1934; *d* of Edward Wilson Fairfax and Annie Smith; *m* 1956, Henry John Easterling; one *s*. *Educ:* Blackburn High School for Girls; Newnham College, Cambridge (BA 1955, MA 1959). Asst Lectr, Univ. of Manchester, 1957–58; University of Cambridge: Asst Lectr, 1968; Lectr, 1969–87; Newnham College, Cambridge: Asst Lectr, 1958–60; Fellow and Lectr, 1960–87; Dir of Studies in Classics, 1979–87; Vice-Principal, 1981–86; Prof. of Greek, UCL, 1987–94. Townsend Lectr, Cornell Univ., 1990. Chm., Council of Univ. Classical Depts, 1990–93. President: Classical Assoc., 1988–89; Hellenic Soc., 1996–99. Mem., Academia Europaea, 1995. Corresp. étranger, 2004, Associé étranger, 2013, Acad. des Inscriptions et Belles-Lettres, Inst de France. Hon. Mem., Hungarian Acad. of Scis, 2013. Hon. Fellow, UCL, 1997. Hon. DPhil: Athens, 1996; Uppsala, 2000; Ioannina, 2002; Hon. DLitt Bristol, 1999; Hon. DLit London, 1999. *Publications:* (with E. J. Kenney) Ovidiana Graeca, 1965; (ed) Sophocles, Trachiniae, 1982; (with B. M. W. Knox, ed and contrib.) Cambridge History of Classical Literature, vol. I, 1985; (ed with J. V. Muir) Greek Religion and Society, 1985; (ed) Cambridge Companion to Greek Tragedy, 1997; (ed with C. M. Handley) Greek Scripts, 2001; (ed with E. M. Hall) Greek and Roman Actors, 2002. *Address:* Newnham College, Cambridge CB3 9DF. *T:* (01223) 335700.

EASTHAM, Kenneth; *b* 11 Aug. 1927; *s* of late James Eastham; *m* 1951, Doris, *d* of Albert Howarth; one *d*. Planning engr, GEC, Trafford Park. Mem., Manchester CC, 1962–80 (Dep. Leader 1975–79; Chairman: Planning Cttee, 1971–74; Educn Cttee, 1978–79); Mem., NW Econ. Planning Council, 1975–79. MP (Lab) Manchester, Blackley, 1979–97. An Opposition Whip, 1987–92. *Address:* 12 Nan Nook Road, Manchester M23 9BZ.

EASTMAN, Roger; a Master, Senior (formerly Supreme) Court, Queen's Bench Division, since 2009; *b* Maidstone, 23 May 1953; *s* of late Maurice George Eastman and Marian Eastman (*née* Pettman); *m* 1994, Ruth Denton Farnsworth; one step *s* one step *d*. *Educ:* Maidstone Grammar Sch.; St John's Coll., Durham (BA 1975). Called to the Bar, Gray's Inn, 1978, Bencher 2001; in practice at the Bar, specialising in common law, 1980–2009. Dean of Chapel, Gray's Inn, 2010–. FRSA. *Publications:* (Jt Ed.) Civil Procedure (formerly Supreme Court Practice), 2009–; (ed) Pleadings Without Tears, 8th edn 2012; (Jt Gen. Ed.) Rev. Roger Holloway, OBE, MA: a collection of favourite sermons preached in the Chapel of Gray's Inn 1997–2010, 2012; (contrib.) Atkin's Court Forms, 2014–. *Recreations:* music (active and passive), art, cooking, gardening, enthusiastic but flawed tennis and ski-ing. *Address:* Royal Courts of Justice, Strand, WC2A 2LL. *Club:* Clapham Common All Weather Tennis.

EASTON, Carole, PhD; Chief Executive, Young Women's Trust (formerly Platform 51), since 2013; *b* 13 July 1954; *d* of Laszlo Easton and late Naomi Easton. *Educ:* Brunel Univ. (BSc; PhD); Tavistock Clinic (Child and Adolescent Psychotherapist). Child Psychotherapist, NHS, 1984–91. Counselling Manager, ChildLine, 1992–96; Hd, Clinical Services, The Place to Be, 1996–98; Chief Executive: Cruse Bereavement Care, 1998–2001; ChildLine, 2001–06; CLIC Sargent, 2006–09; Dep. Chief Exec., Changing Faces, 2010–13. *E:* eastoncarole@gmail.com.

EASTON, David John; HM Diplomatic Service, retired; consultant on Arab and South Asian matters; *b* 27 March 1941; *o s* of Air Cdre Sir James Easton, KCMG, CB, CBE, and Anna, *d* of Lt-Col J. A. McKenna, Ottawa; *m* 1964, Alexandra Julie, *er d* of Kenneth W. Clark (MBE 2000), London, W8; two *s* two *d*. *Educ:* Stone House, Broadstairs; Stowe (Exhbnr); Balliol Coll., Oxford (Trevelyan Schol.; BA Hons Jurisprudence 1963, MA 1973). Apprentice, United Steel Cos, Workington, 1960. TA, 1959–65; 2nd Lieut, Oxford Univ. OTC, 1962; Lieut, Inns of Court and City Yeo., 1964. Entered Foreign Office, 1963; Third Sec., Nairobi, 1965–66; Second Sec., UK Mission to UN, Geneva, 1967–70; MECAS, Lebanon, 1970–72; First Sec., FCO, 1972–73; First Sec. (Information), Tripoli, 1973–77; Defence Dept, FCO, 1977–80; First Sec. (Chancery), later Political Counsellor, Amman, 1980–83; Counsellor, FCO, 1984–86; Counsellor (Political), New Delhi, 1986–89; FCO, 1990–94; Gen. Manager, Network Security Mgt Ltd, 1994–95; Dir (Internat. Affairs), ICAEW, 1995–97; Sec., RSAA, 1997–2001. Director, Internat. Community Sch. (Jordan) Ltd, 1980–83 (Chm. 1981–83). Pres., Delhi Diplomatic Assoc., 1988–89; Chm., Lansdowne Residents' Assoc., 1990–96. FRSA 1996; FRGS 1998. *Recreations:* swimming, travel, antiques and antiquities.

EASTON, James, OBE 1986; HM Diplomatic Service, retired; Feature Writer, Accordion Times, since 1992; *b* 1 Sept. 1931; *s* of John Easton and Helen Easton (*née* Whitney); *m* 1960, Rosemary Hobbin (*d* 2006); one *s* two *d*. *Educ:* St John Cantius Catholic Sch., Broxburn. Served 3rd Hussars, 1952–55. Admiralty, 1957–60; FO, 1960; Prague, 1960–62; Paris, 1963–65; FO, 1965–68; Vice-Consul: Belgrade, 1968–71; La Paz, 1971–74; Second Sec. (Commercial), New York, 1974–78; FCO, 1978–83; First Sec., Rome, 1983–87; Counsellor (Admin) and Consul-Gen., Brussels, 1987–89. *Recreation:* music. *Address:* 6 Cedar Gardens, Sutton, Surrey SM2 5DD. *T:* (020) 8643 2432.

EASTON, Karen Elisabeth Dind; *see* Jones, K. E. D.

EASTON, Mark Richard Erskine; Home Editor, BBC News, since 2004; *b* 12 March 1959; *s* of Stephen and Fiona Easton; *m* 1987, Antonia Higgs; one *s* three *d*. *Educ:* Peter Symonds Grammar Sch., Winchester. Southern Evening Echo, 1978–80; Radio Victory, 1980–81; Radio Aire, 1981–82; LBC Radio, 1982–86; Corresp., BBC, 1986–96; Political Ed., Channel 5, 1996–98; Home and Social Affairs Ed., Channel 4, 1998–2004. FRSA 2007. *Publications:* Britain etc, 2012. *Recreations:* piano blues, Arsenal FC. *E:* mark.easton@bbc.co.uk.

EASTON, Robert Alexander, PhD; Chief Executive, Delta plc, 1989–96; *b* 24 Oct. 1948; *s* of Malcolm Edward George Easton and Violet May Liddell Easton (*née* Taylor); *m* 1983, Lynden Anne Welch; two *d*. *Educ:* St Lawrence Coll.; Univ. of Manchester (BSc Hons); Univ. of Aston (PhD). Delta plc, 1974–96: Dir of Planning, 1980–83; Man. Dir, Industrial Services Div., 1984–87; Dep. Chief Exec., 1988–89. Director: G. E. Crane (Holdings), 1986–91; Elementis (formerly Harrisons & Crosfield) plc, 1991–2001. *Recreations:* golf, travel, medieval art and architecture.

EASTWOOD, Basil Stephen Talbot, CMG 1999; HM Diplomatic Service, retired; *b* 4 March 1944; *s* of late Christopher Gilbert Eastwood, CMG and Catherine Emma (*née* Peel); *m* 1970, Alison Faith Hutchings; three *d* (and one *d* decd). *Educ:* Eton (KS); Merton College, Oxford. Entered Diplomatic Service, 1966; Middle East Centre for Arab Studies, 1967–68; Jedda, 1968–69; Colombo, 1969–72; Cairo, 1972–76; Cabinet Office, 1976–78; FCO, 1978–80; Bonn, 1980–84; Khartoum, 1984–87; Athens, 1987–91; Dir of Res. and Analysis, FCO, 1991–96; Ambassador to Syria, 1996–2000; Project Dir, Middle East Inst., 2000–01; Ambassador to Switzerland, 2001–04. Chairman: Cecily's Fund, 1998–2009; Oxfordshire Historic Churches Trust, 2013–. *Address:* Church End, Church Street, Somerton, Oxon OX25 6NB.

EASTWOOD, Clinton, (Clint); actor, film director and producer; *b* San Francisco, 31 May 1930; *s* of Clinton and Ruth Eastwood; *m* 1st, 1953, Maggie Johnson (marr. diss. 1978); one *s* one *d*; 2nd, 1996, Dina Ruiz; one *d*; one *d* with Frances Fisher; one *d* with Roxanne Tunis; one *s* one *d* with Jacelyn Reeves. *Educ:* Oakland Tech. High Sch.; LA City Coll. Actor, TV series, Rawhide, 1959–66. *Films include: actor:* A Fistful of Dollars, 1964; For a Few Dollars More, 1965; The Good, The Bad and The Ugly, 1966; Hang 'Em High, 1968; Where Eagles Dare, Coogan's Bluff, 1968; Paint Your Wagon, 1969; Kelly's Heroes, 1970; The Beguiled, Dirty Harry, 1971; Joe Kidd, 1972; Magnum Force, 1973; Thunderbolt and Lightfoot, 1974; The Enforcer, 1976; Every Which Way But Loose, 1978; Escape from Alcatraz, 1979; Tightrope (and prod.), City Heat, 1984; The Dead Pool, 1988; Pink Cadillac, 1989; In the Line of Fire, 1993; Trouble with the Curve, 2012; *actor and director:* Play Misty for Me, 1971; High Plains Drifter, 1973; The Eiger Sanction, 1975; The Outlaw Josey Wales, 1976; Bronco Billy, 1980; The Rookie, 1990; *actor, director and producer:* Firefox, Honkytonk Man, 1982; Sudden Impact, 1983; Pale Rider, 1985; Heartbreak Ridge, 1986; White Hunter Black Heart, 1990; Unforgiven, 1992 (Academy Awards for Best Dir and Best Picture, 1993); A Perfect World, 1993; The Bridges of Madison County, 1995; Absolute Power, 1997; True Crime, 1999; Space Cowboys, 2000; Blood Work, 2002; Million Dollar Baby (Golden Globe Award for Best Dir; Academy Awards for Best Dir and Best Picture), 2005; Gran Torino, 2009; *director and producer:* Bird, 1988 (Golden Globe Award for Best Dir, 1989); Midnight in the Garden of Good and Evil, 1997; Mystic River, 2003; Flags of Our Fathers, 2006; Letters From Iwo Jima, 2007; Changeling, 2008 (Special Prize, Cannes Film Fest., 2008); Invictus, 2010; Hereafter, 2011; J. Edgar, 2012; Jersey Boys, 2014; American Sniper, 2015. Founder and owner, Malpaso Prodns, 1969–. Proprietor: Mission Ranch, Carmel, Calif; Tehama Golf Club, Carmel Valley, Calif; co-founder, Tehama, clothing co., 1997. Mayor of Carmel, Calif, 1986–88. Commandeur, Légion d'Honneur (France), 2009.

EASTWOOD, Sir David (Stephen), Kt 2014; DL; DPhil; FRHistS; Vice-Chancellor and Principal, University of Birmingham, since 2009; *b* 5 Jan. 1959; *s* of Colin Eastwood and Elaine Clara Eastwood; *m* 1980, Jan Page; one *s* two *d*. *Educ:* Sandbach Sch., Cheshire; St Peter's Coll., Oxford (BA 1st Cl. Hons Modern Hist.; MA 1985; DPhil 1985; Hon. Fellow 2003). FRHistS 1991. Jun. Res. Fellow, Keble Coll., Oxford, 1983–87; Fellow and Tutor in Modern Hist., 1988–95, Sen. Tutor, 1992–95, Pembroke Coll., Oxford; Dep. Chair, Bd of Faculty of Modern Hist., Univ. of Oxford, 1994–95; University of Wales, Swansea: Prof. of Social Hist., 1995–2000; Hd, Dept of Hist., 1996–2000; Actg Hd, Dept of Philosophy, 1998–99; Dean, Faculty of Arts and Social Studies, 1997–99; Pro-Vice-Chancellor, 1999–2000; Chief Exec., AHRB, 2000–02; Vice-Chancellor, UEA, 2002–06, Emeritus Prof. of Hist., 2006; Chief Exec., HEFCE, 2006–09. British Acad. Post-Doctoral Fellow, 1986–87. Literary Dir, RHistS, 1994–2000; Chm. Edit Bd, RHistS Studies in History series, 2000–04. Chair of Examrs, A Level Hist., UODLE, O&C, OCR, 1991–2000. Chair: Adv. Gp on Benchmarking, QAA, 2003–06; Assoc. of Univs in E of England, 2003–06; City of Westminster Educn Commn, 2009; Supporting Professionalism in Admissions Prog., 2009–11; Russell Gp; Member: RAE Review Gp, HEFCE, 2002–03; Res. Support Libraries Gp, 2002–03; 14–19 Wkg Gp, DfES, 2003–04; Res. Strategic Cttee, HEFCE, 2003–06; Bd, QAA, 2004–06; Bd, UUK; Bd, UCAS, 2009– (Chm., 2010–); Govt Rev. Panel on Funding and Student Finance; Ind. Rev. of Higher Educn Funding and Student Finance, 2009–11; AHRC, 2011–; Dir, Univs Superannuation Scheme. Mem. Bd, Mktg Birmingham, 2011–14. Co-founder and non-exec. Chair, Nat. Centre for Public Policy, 1998–2000. Mem. Bd, Gtr Birmingham and Solihull LEP, 2012–13. Member: Gov. Council, John Innes Centre, 2003–06 (Dep. Chm., 2004–06); Council, Sainsbury Lab., 2003–06; Adv. Bd, Higher Educn Policy Inst., 2003–; Grants Cttee, Hong Kong Univ., 2011–. Mem., Marshall Aid Meml Commn, 2003–10 (Dep. Chair, 2006–). FRSA. DL W Midlands, 2012. Hon. Fellow, Swansea Univ., 2010. Hon. DLitt: UWE, 2003; UEA, 2006. *Publications:* Governing Rural England: tradition and transformation in local government 1780–1840, 1994; Government and Community in the English Provinces 1700–1870, 1997; (ed with L. Brockliss) A Union of Multiple Identities: the British Isles *c* 1750–*c* 1850, 1997; (ed with N. Thompson) The Social and Political Writings of William Cobbett, 16 vols, 1998; numerous papers in scholarly jls, edited vols, etc. *Recreations:* music, collecting CDs, current affairs, walking, wine, watching sport. *Address:* Vice-Chancellor's Office, University of Birmingham, Birmingham B15 2TT. *T:* (0121) 414 4536, *Fax:* (0121) 414 4534. *Club:* Athenæum.

EASTWOOD, Noel Anthony Michael, MA; CEng, MRAeS; Chairman, InterData Group, 1981–93; *b* 7 Dec. 1932; *s* of Edward Norman Eastwood and Irene Dawson; *m* 1965, Elizabeth Tania Gresham Boyd, *d* of Comdr Thomas Wilson Boyd, CBE, DSO, DL and Irene Barbara Gresham; three *s*. *Educ:* The Leys School, Cambridge; Christ's College, Cambridge. Lieut RA, 1951–54; Pilot Officer, RAFVR, 1954–57; de Havilland Aircraft Co., 1956–60; Rio Tinto, 1960–61; AEI Group, 1961–64; Director: Charterhouse Development, 1964–69; Charterhouse Japhet, 1969–79 (Pres., Charterhouse Japhet Texas, 1974–77); Charterhouse Middle East, 1975–79; Burnett & Rolfe Ltd, 1964–69 (Chm.); Wharton Crane & Hoist, 1967–70 (Chm.); Daniel Doncaster & Son (International Nickel), 1971–81; The Barden Corp., 1971–82; Hawk Publishing (UAE), 1981–87; Oryx Publishing (Qatar), 1981–87; Falcon Publishing (Bahrain), 1981–84; Caribbean Publishing, 1981–84; IDP InterData (Australia), 1984–92 and 1995–96; European Public Policy Advisers Gp, 1987–97; Spearhead Communications, 1988–99; Founder, Seafish Falklands Ltd (Port Stanley), 1990–95. Sec., RAeS, 1983. Member: London Cttee, Yorkshire & Humberside Development Assoc., 1975–94; Management Cttee, Offshore Europe Conf. and Exhibn, 1990–2000; S Atlantic Council, 1991– (Hon. Treas., 1998–). Member: Much Hadham PCC, 1989–2007; Much Hadham Parish Council, 1995–97; St Albans Diocesan Synod, 1997–2006. Hon. Treas., 1992–99, Vice Chm., 2004–08, Vice Pres., 2008–, Herts Soc.; Mem. Exec. Cttee, CPRE, 1995–98 (Chm., SE Reg., 1995–2000; Vice-Chm., E of England Cttee, 1999–2005); Chm., Thames NE Area Envmt Gp, 1997–2000; Mem. Exec. Cttee, E England Envmtl Forum, 1999–2006 (Founding Chm., 1999); Mem., Thames and Chilterns Regl Cttee, 2001–02, E of England (formerly E Anglia) Regl Cttee, 2002–11 (Chm., Projects and Acquisitions Gp, 2006–11), Nat. Trust. Mem., Friends Council, Firepower - Royal Artillery Mus., 2009–. Founder, Royal Artillery Heritage Campaign, 1991. *Recreations:* ski-ing, sailing, vintage sportscars, family picnics, desert travel, trekking the Grand Canyon. *Address:* Palace House, Much Hadham, Herts SG10 6HW. *T:* (01279) 842409. *Club:* Royal Thames Yacht.

EASTY, Prof. David Leonello, MD; FRCS, FRCOphth; Professor of Ophthalmology and Head of Department of Ophthalmology, University of Bristol, 1982–99, now Professor Emeritus; *b* 6 Aug. 1933; *s* of Arthur Victor Easty and Florence Margaret (*née* Kennedy); *m* 1963, Božana Martinović; three *d. Educ:* King's Sch., Canterbury; Univ. of Manchester. MD 1963; FRCS 1969; FRCOphth (FCOphth 1988). Capt., RAMC, 1959; Med. Officer, British Antarctic Survey, 1960. Moorfield's Eye Hospital: Resident, 1966–69; Lectr, 1969–72; Consultant, Bristol Eye Hosp., 1972–82. Dir, Corneal Transplant Service Eye Bank, 1986–99. Lectures: Lang, RSocMed, 1998; Doyne, Oxford Congress of Ophthalmol., 1999; Bowman, RCOphth, 2000; Castroviejo, Amer. Acad. of Ophthalmol., 2002. Nettleship Medal for Research, Ophthalmol Soc., 1999. Member: BMA; RSocMed (Pres., Sect. of Ophthalmol., 1998–2000). Member: Antarctic Club; Piscatorial Soc. *Publications:* Virus Disease of the Eye, 1985; (with G. Smolim) External Eye Disease, 1985; (ed) Current Ophthalmic Surgery, 1990; (with N. Ragge) Immediate Eye Care, 1990; Oxford Textbook of Ophthalmology, 1999. *Recreations:* fishing, running, opera, lawn tennis, Real tennis. *Address:* The Barn, Grove Place, Upton Lane, Nursling, Southampton SO16 0XY. *Clubs:* Army and Navy; Clifton (Bristol).

EATOCK TAYLOR, Prof. (William) Rodney, FREng; Professor of Mechanical Engineering, University of Oxford, 1989–2009, now Emeritus (Head of Department of Engineering Science, 1999–2004); Fellow of St Hugh's College, Oxford, 1989–2009, now Emeritus; *b* 10 Jan. 1944; *s* of late William Taylor, Hadley Wood, Herts and Norah O'Brien Taylor (*née* Ridgeway); *m* 1971, Jacqueline Lorraine Cannon, *d* of late Desmond Cannon Brookes; two *s. Educ:* Rugby Sch.; King's Coll., Cambridge (BA, MA); Stanford Univ. (MS, PhD). FRINA 1986; FIMechE 1989; FREng (FEng 1990). Engineer, Ove Arup and Partners, 1968–70; University College London: Res. Asst, 1970; Lectr, 1972; Reader, 1980; Prof. of Ocean Engineering, 1984–89; Dean, Faculty of Engineering, 1988–89. Hon. Prof., Harbin Engrg Univ., China, 2008; Vis. Prof., Nat. Univ. of Singapore, 2010–; Adjunct Prof., Univ. of WA, 2015–. Dir, Marine Technology Directorate Ltd, 1990–95; Chm., Marine Technology Trust, 1991–. Mem., Marine Technology Foresight Panel, OST, 1995–97. Mem. Council, 2003–07, Vice Pres., 2004–07, Royal Acad. of Engrg. Gov., Queenswood Sch., 1990–2003. Associate Ed., Jl Fluids and Structures, 1990–2011; Member, Editorial Boards: Engineering Structures, 1978–2008; Applied Ocean Research, 1984–2012; Ocean Engineering, 2008–; series: Ocean Technology, 1986–2001; Engineering Science, 1990–98. Hon. Fellow, UCL, 2008. *Publications:* numerous contribs to learned jls of structural dynamics and marine hydrodynamics. *Recreations:* walking, music. *Address:* Department of Engineering Science, Parks Road, Oxford OX1 3PJ. *Club:* Athenæum.

EATON, family name of **Baroness Eaton**.

EATON, Baroness *cr* 2010 (Life Peer), of Cottingley in the County of West Yorkshire; **(Ellen) Margaret Eaton,** DBE 2010 (OBE 2003); DL; Chairman, Local Government Association, 2008–11 (Vice President, 2011–12); *b* Bradford; *d* of John and Evelyn Midgley; *m* 1969, John Eaton; one *s* one *d. Educ:* Hanson Grammar Sch.; Balls Park Teacher Trng Coll. (Cert Ed). Former teacher. Mem. (C), Bradford MDC, 1986– (Leader, 2000–06). Chm., Bd of Trustees, Near Neighbours (Trustee, 2011–). Pres., Bradford Choral Soc., 2010–13. Guardian, Holy Shrine of Walsingham, 2014–. Fellow, Bradford Coll., 2012. Hon. DEd Bradford, 2012. DL W Yorks 2008. *Recreations:* music, theatre, cooking, Germany and the German language. *Address:* House of Lords, SW1A 0PW. *E:* eatonm@parliament.uk. *Clubs:* United and Cecil; Bradford (Bradford).

EATON, Deborah Ann; QC 2008; a Recorder, since 2004; a Deputy High Court Judge, since 2011; *b* Nottingham, 28 March 1962; *d* of Stanley Eaton and Margaret Ann Eaton. *Educ:* Univ. of Keele (BSocSci Hons 1983); City Univ., London (Dip. Law 1984). Called to the Bar, Inner Temple, 1983; in practice as a barrister, specialising in family law; Midland Circuit, 1985–. *Publications:* (author, and ed with Stephen Wildblood) Financial Provision in Family Matters, 1998. *Address:* 1 King's Bench Walk, Temple, EC4Y 7DB. *T:* (020) 7936 1500, *Fax:* (020) 7936 1590. *E:* deatonqc@1kbw.co.uk.

EATON, Rt Rev. Derek Lionel, QSM 1985; Bishop of Nelson, New Zealand, 1990–2006; *b* 10 Sept. 1941; *s* of Henry Jackson Eaton and Ella Barbara (*née* McDouall); *m* 1964, Alice Janice Maslin; two *s* one *d. Educ:* Christchurch Boys' High Sch. (NZ); AG Graduate Sch., Missouri (MA *cum laude*); Christchurch Teachers' Coll. (Teacher Trng Cert); Switzerland (Cert. Française); Univ. of Tunis (Cert. Arabic and Islamics); Missionary Training Coll., Australia (DipTheol); Trinity Theol Coll., Bristol. School teacher, 1964. Missionary with Worldwide Evangelisation Crusade, Tunisia, 1968–78; ordained deacon and priest, 1971; Curate, St Luke's, Bristol, 1971–72; Vicar of Tunis, 1972–78; Hon. Chaplain, British Embassy, Tunis, 1972–78; Provost, Cairo Cathedral, Egypt, 1978–83 (Emeritus, 1984); Hon. Chaplain, British Embassy, Egypt, 1978–83; with Church Missionary Society, 1980–84; Associate Vicar, Papanui, Bishopdale, NZ, 1984–85; Vicar, Sumner, Redcliffs, NZ, 1985–90; Asst Anglican Bp of Egypt with N Africa and the Horn of Africa, 2007–09; Dean, All Saint's Cathedral, Cairo, 2007–09. Hon. Canon, 1985, Episcopal Canon, 1992, Cairo Cathedral. Chaplain to staff and students, Bishopdale Theol Coll., Nelson, NZ, 2009–. *Publications:* What awaits us there: between reality and illusion (Arabic), 2002; Life After Death: welcome to the future, 2004; contrib. theol and missiological jls. *Recreations:* swimming (Competitive Ocean Swimming and Masters Swimming), reading, walking and hiking. *Address:* 67 Grove Street, The Wood, Nelson 7010, New Zealand.

EATON, Duncan; *see* Eaton, N. D.

EATON, Fredrik Stefan, OC 1990; OOnt 2001; Chairman, White Raven Capital Corporation; *b* 26 June 1938; *s* of late John David Eaton and Signy Hildur Eaton (*née* Stephenson); *m* 1962, Catherine Howard (Nicky) Martin; one *s* one *d. Educ:* Univ. of New Brunswick (BA). T. Eaton Co. Ltd: joined 1962; positions in Victoria, London, England and Toronto, 1962–67; Dir, 1967–99; Pres. and CEO, 1979–88; Dir, Eaton's of Canada, 1969–; Chm., 1988–91; High Comr for Canada in the UK, 1991–94. Former Director: Masonite (formerly Premdor); Abitibi Consolidated; Norcen Energy; Maple Leaf Foods; Toronto-Dominion Bank; Bata Shoe Museum. Trustee: The Catherine and Fredrik Eaton Charitable Foundn; Canadian Mus. of Civilization (Chm., Bd of Trustees, 2007–11); Hon. Trustee, Univ. Health Network (Chair, Bd of Trustees, 1994–2000); Member: ICBP Rare Bird Club; Polite Soc. Patron, ESU of Canada. FRSA. Chancellor, Univ. of New Brunswick, 1993–2003. Internat. Retailer of the Year Award, Nat. Retail Merchants Assoc., NY, 1978; McGill Univ. Management Award, 1987. Hon. LLD: New Brunswick, 1983; QUB, 1995. *Recreations:* sailing, fishing. *Address:* (office) 55 St Clair Avenue West, Suite 260, Toronto, ON M4V 2Y7, Canada.

EATON, James Thompson, CBE 1992; TD 1963; Lord-Lieutenant, County Borough of Londonderry, 1986–2002; *b* 11 Aug. 1927; *s* of late J. C. Eaton, DL, and Mrs E. A. F. Eaton, MBE; *m* 1954, Lucy Edith Smeeton (OBE 1986); one *s* one *d. Educ:* Campbell Coll., Belfast; Royal Technical Coll., Glasgow. Man. Dir, Eaton & Co. Ltd, 1965–80. Mem., Londonderry Develt Commn, 1969–73 (Chm., Educn Cttee, 1969–73); Chm., Londonderry Port and Harbour Comrs, 1989–95 (Mem., 1977–95; Vice Chm., 1985). Served North Irish Horse (TA), 1950–67 (Major, 1961). Hon. Col, 1st (NI) Bn, ACF, 1992–98. High Sheriff, Co. Londonderry, 1982. *Recreations:* military history, gardening. *Address:* Cherryvale Park, Limavady, Co. Londonderry, Northern Ireland BT49 9AH.

EATON, Keith John, PhD; FIStructE; Chief Executive, Institution of Structural Engineers, 1999–2008; *b* 4 May 1945; *s* of John Ernest Eaton and Phyllis Marguerite (*née* Groom); *m* 1967, Janet Marion, *d* of Geoffrey and Winifred Allanson Walker; two *d. Educ:* Bishopshalt Grammar Sch., Hillingdon, Middx; Univ. of Birmingham (BSc Civil Engrg 1966); UCL (PhD Structural Engrg 1971). FRMetS 1971; CEng 1975; FIStructE 1986. Joined BRE, 1966; Head: Wind Loading Section, 1971–77; Overseas Develt Res. Unit, 1977–84; Structural Design Div., 1984–89; European Manager, 1989–91, Dep. Dir, 1991–99, Steel Construction Inst. Mem. Council, Hon. Sec. and Hon. Treas., IStructE, 1986–92. FCGI 2004. MASCE 1991–2009. Freeman, City of London, 2003; Liveryman, Engineers' Co., 2003–09. *Publications:* Wind Loading Handbook, 1971; Wind Effects on Buildings and Structures, 1977; Buildings and Tropical Windstorms, 1981; A Comparative Environmental Life Cycle Assessment of Modern Office Buildings, 1998; technical papers on wind loading, earthquake engrg, sustainability and envmtl issues in learned jls. *Recreations:* playing bridge, gardening, walking, being a grandfather. *Address:* 18 Sandpit Lane, St Albans AL1 4HN. *T:* (01727) 853915.

EATON, Adm. Sir Kenneth (John), GBE 1994; KCB 1990; FREng, FIET; Rear Admiral of the United Kingdom, 2001–07; Chairman, Society for Nautical Research, since 2011; *b* 12 Aug. 1934; *s* of John and May Eaton; *m* 1959, Sheena Buttle; two *s* one *d. Educ:* Borden Grammar Sch.; Fitzwilliam Coll., Cambridge (BA). FIET (FIEE 1989); FREng (FEng 1994). HMS Victorious, 1959–61; ASWE, 1961–65; HM Ships Eagle, Collingwood and Bristol, 1965–71; Defence Communications Network, 1971–72; ASWE, 1972–76; HMS Ark Royal, 1976–78; MoD, 1978–81; ASWE, 1981–83; Dir Torpedoes, 1983–85; Dir-Gen. Underwater Weapons (Navy), 1985–87; Flag Officer, Portsmouth, and Naval Base Comdr, Portsmouth, 1987–89; Controller of the Navy, 1989–94. Chm., UKAEA, 1996–2002. Chairman: Guy's and St Thomas' NHS Trust, 1995–99; National Remote Sensing Centre (Infoterra Ltd), 1995–2001. Chm., Mary Rose Trust, 2001–07. Hon. DSc Aston, 2006. *Recreations:* art, countryside, theatre, opera, classical music. *Address:* c/o Naval Secretary, Fleet Headquarters, Whale Island, Portsmouth PO2 8BY.

EATON, Martin Roger, CMG 1993; HM Diplomatic Service, retired; Deputy Legal Adviser, Foreign and Commonwealth Office, 1991–2000; *b* 10 Nov. 1940; *m* 1972, Sylvia White; two *s* one *d*. Admitted Solicitor, 1968; FCO, 1970; Bonn, 1977; FCO, 1981; Legal Counsellor: FCO, 1982; UKREP Brussels, 1987; FCO, 1991. Chm., Council of Europe Steering Cttee on Human Rights, 2003–04. *Recreations:* choral singing, gardening.

EATON, (Neil) Duncan, FCIPS; adviser, government and commercial sector; Chairman, Kimal Holdings Ltd, since 2008; *b* 28 May 1946; *s* of John and Bessie Eaton; *m* 1st, 1969, Ainsley Elizabeth Isles (marr. diss. 2006); two *d*; 2nd, 2010, Karen (*née* Fielding). *Educ:* King's Sch., Macclesfield; Manchester Coll. of Commerce (HND Business Studies); Dip. Inst. Healthcare Mgt; Dip. Chartered Inst. Purchasing and Supply. FCIPS (FInstPS 1985); MIHM 1972. Hosp. mgt and supply mgt posts, Manchester, Swindon and Wolverhampton, 1966–74; Area Supplies Officer: Tameside AHA, 1974–78; Northants AHA, 1978–83; Dir of Ops, NW Thames RHA, 1983–90; Chief Executive: Bedfordshire HA, 1990–2000; NHS Purchasing and Supply Agency, 2000–06. Non-executive Director: Policy Connect, 2008–; BCAS Biomed, 2012–. Strategic Advr, BiP Solutions, 2009–; Exec. Advr, All Party Parly Health Gp, 2008–. President: Chartered Inst. Purchasing and Supply, 1992–93; Health Care Supplies Assoc., 1996–2001. Hon. Prof., Univ. of Bath, 2013–. *Recreations:* amateur dramatics, Rugby, football. *Address:* 14 Knights Court, Linen Street, Warwick CV34 4DJ.

EATON, Robert James; Director, Chevron (formerly Texaco, then ChevronTexaco) Inc., 2000–12; Chairman, Daimler Chrysler (formerly Chairman and Chief Executive, Chrysler Corporation), 1993–2000; *b* 13 Feb. 1940; *s* of Gene and Mildred Eaton; *m* 1964, Cornelia Cae Drake; two *s. Educ:* Univ. of Kansas (BS Mech Eng). Joined General Motors, 1963, transf. to English staff, 1971; Chevrolet Div., 1975; Oldsmobile, 1979; Vice-Pres. in charge of Tech. Staffs, 1986; Pres., General Motors Europe, 1988–92; Mem., Bd of Dirs, Lotus Group, 1986–2000; Chm., Saab Auto, 1990–2000. Member: Industrial Adv. Board, Stanford Univ.; Business Roundtable and Business Council. Mem. Bd, Dama. Former Chm., Nat. Acad. of Engrg; FSAE.

EATON, Sara Elizabeth; *see* Cockerill, S. E.

EATWELL, family name of **Baron Eatwell**.

EATWELL, Baron *cr* 1992 (Life Peer), of Stratton St Margaret in the County of Wiltshire; **John Leonard Eatwell;** President, Queens' College, Cambridge, since 1997; Professor of Financial Policy, Judge Business School (formerly Judge Institute of Management Studies), University of Cambridge, 2002–12, now Emeritus; *b* 2 Feb. 1945; *s* of Harold Jack and Mary Eatwell; *m* 1970, Hélène Seppain (marr. diss. 2002); two *s* one *d*; *m* 2006, Hon. Mrs Susan Elizabeth Digby (OBE 2007). *Educ:* Headlands Grammar Sch., Swindon; Queens' Coll., Cambridge (BA 1967; MA 1971); Harvard Univ. (PhD 1975). Teaching Fellow, Grad. Sch. of Arts and Scis, Harvard Univ., 1968–69; Res. Fellow, Queens' Coll., Cambridge, 1969–70; Fellow, Trinity Coll., Cambridge, 1970–96; University of Cambridge: Asst Lectr, 1975–77, Lectr, 1977–2002, Faculty of Econs and Politics; Dir, Cambridge Endowment for Res. in Finance, Judge Business Sch. (formerly Judge Inst. of Mgt Studies), 2002–12. Visiting Professor of Economics: New Sch. for Social Res., NY, 1982–96; USC, 2012–; Vis. Fellow, St Antony's Coll., Oxford, 2011. Econ. Advr to Rt Hon. Neil Kinnock, MP, Leader of the Labour Party, 1985–92. Opposition spokesman on Treasury affairs, and on trade and industry, H of L, 1992–93; Principal Opposition spokesman on Treasury and econ. affairs, H of L, 1993–97 and 2010–13. Mem., Jersey Financial Services Commn, 2010– (Chm., 2014–). Adviser: to E. M. Warburg Pincus & Co. Internat. Ltd, 1996–; to Palamon Capital Partners LLP, 2000–; Chief Econ. Advr to Chartered Mgt Inst., 2009–10. Chm., British Screen Finance Ltd, 1997–2000; Dir, SFA, 1997–2002; Mem., Regulatory Decisions Cttee, FSA, 2001–06. Trustee, Inst. for Public Policy Res., 1988– (Sec., 1988–97; Chm., 1997–2000). Non-executive Director: Anglia Television Gp, 1994–2000; Cambridge Econometrics Ltd, 1996–2006; Rontech Ltd, 2003–08; SAV Credit Ltd, 2007–; Chm., Deutsche Wealth and Asset Mgt Global Financial Inst., 2012–. Chairman: Commercial Radio Cos Assoc., 2000–04; Consumer Panel, Classic fm, 2007–11. Chm., Crusaid, 1993–98. Chm., Extemporary Dance Theatre, 1990; Governor: Contemporary Dance Trust, 1991–95; Royal Ballet Sch., 2003–06; Dir, Arts Theatre Trust, Cambridge, 1991–98; Mem. Bd, Royal Opera House, 1998–2006; Chm., British Library Bd, 2001–06. Chm. Trustees, Royal Opera Hse Pension Fund, 2007–. *Publications:* (with Joan Robinson) An Introduction to Modern Economics, 1973; Whatever Happened to Britain?, 1982; (ed with Murray Milgate) Keynes's Economics and the Theory of Value and Distribution, 1983; (ed with Murray Milgate and Peter Newman): The New Palgrave: A Dictionary of Economics, 4 vols, 1987; The New Palgrave Dictionary of Money and Finance, 3 vols, 1992; Transformation and Integration: shaping the future of central and eastern Europe, 1995; (ed) Global Unemployment: loss of jobs in the '90s, 1996; Not "Just Another Accession": the political economy of EU enlargement to the East, 1997; (with L. Taylor) Global Finance at Risk: the case for international regulation, 2000; Hard Budgets, Soft States, 2000; Social Policy Choices in Central and Eastern Europe, 2002; (with L. Taylor) International Capital Markets, 2002; (jtly) Global Governance of Financial Systems: the legal and economic regulation of systemic risk, 2006; (jtly) Financial Supervision and Risk Management in the EU, 2007; (ed with P. Arestis) Issues in Finance and Industry: essays in honour of Ajit Singh, 2008; (jtly) Clearing and Settlements in the EU, 2009; (jtly) Crisis Management, Burden Sharing and Solidarity Mechanisms in the EU, 2010; (with M. Milgate) The Fall and Rise of Keynesian Economics, 2011; articles in sci. jls and other collected works. *Recreations:* classical and contemporary dance, Rugby Union football. *Address:* Queens' College, Cambridge CB3 9ET. *T:* (01223) 335532, *Fax:* (01223) 335555. *E:* president@queens.cam.ac.uk. *Clubs:* Harvard (New York), Bohemian (San Francisco).

EAVES, Prof. Laurence, CBE 2003; FRS 1997; Research Professor, School of Physics and Astronomy, University of Nottingham, since 2011; Professor of Physics, University of Manchester, since 2012; *b* 13 May 1948; *s* of Raymond Eaves and late Margaret Eaves (*née* Howells); *m* 1985, Dr Ffiona Helen Gilmore. *Educ:* Rhondda Co. Grammar Sch.; Corpus Christi Coll., Oxford (BA 1st Cl. Hons Physics 1969; MA 1973; DPhil 1973; Hon. Fellow, 2013). FInstP 1996. Res. Fellow, Clarendon Lab., Univ. of Oxford, 1972–74; Res. Lectr, Christ Church, Oxford, 1972–75; Miller Fellow, Univ. of Calif, Berkeley, 1974–75; University of Nottingham: Lectr, 1976–84, Reader, 1984–86, Dept of Physics; Prof. of Physics, 1986–2000; Lancashire-Spencer Prof. of Physics, 2000–11. Vis. Prof., Inst. for Solid State Physics, Univ. of Tokyo, 1995. Royal Soc. Leverhulme Sen. Res. Fellow, 1993–94; EPSRC Sen. Res. Fellow, 1994–99. Chm., Condensed Matter Div., Inst. of Physics, 1998–99; Member: Council, Royal Soc., 2002–04 (Mem., Sectional Cttee 2, 1999–2001, 2008–10, 2014–); HEFCE RAE Physics sub-panel, 2004–08; Leverhulme Trust Res. Awards Adv. Cttee, 2008–; HEFCE REF 2014 Physics sub-panel, 2011–14. FLSW 2011. Mott Lectr, Inst. of Physics, 1988; European Physical Soc. Lectr, 1991. Guthrie Medal and Prize, Inst. of Physics, 2001. *Publications:* (jtly) numerous res. articles in jls incl. Physical Rev., Physical Rev. Letters, Nature, Science, Applied Physics Letters. *Address:* School of Physics and Astronomy, University of Nottingham, Nottingham NG7 2RD. *T:* (0115) 951 5136.

EBADI, Dr Shirin; lawyer in private practice in Iran, specialising in human rights, since 1992; *b* 21 June 1947; *d* of late Mohammad Ali Ebadi; *m*; two *d. Educ:* Univ. of Tehran. Judge, 1969–79, Pres., 1975–79, Tehran City Court. Lectr in Law, Univ. of Tehran. Co-founder and President: Assoc. for Support of Children's Rights, 1995–2000; Human Rights Defence Centre, 2001–. Nobel Peace Prize, 2003. *Publications:* Criminal Laws, 1972; The Rights of the Child, 1987 (trans. English 1993); Medical Laws, 1988; Young Workers, 1989; Copyright Laws, 1989; Architectural Laws, 1991; The Rights of Refugees, 1993; History and Documentation of Human Rights in Iran, 1993; (jtly) Tradition and Modernity, 1995; Children's Comparative Law, 1997 (trans. English 1998); The Rights of Women, 2002; Iran Awakening: a memoir of revolution and hope, 2006; Refugee Rights in Iran, 2008; The Golden Cage: three brothers, three choices, one destiny, 2011; articles in learned jls. *Address:* No 19 Street 57, Seied Jamal eldin Asad Abadi Avenue, Tehran 14349, Iran.

EBAN, Anna Maeve; *see* Guggenheim, A. M.

EBBSFLEET, Bishop Suffragan of, since 2013; **Rt Rev. Jonathan Michael Goodall,** SSC; Provincial Episcopal Visitor, Province of Canterbury, since 2013; *b* 1961; *m* Sarah; one *s* one *d. Educ:* Royal Holloway Coll., Univ. of London (BMus 1983); Wycliffe Hall, Oxford. Macmillan Publishers; ordained deacon, 1989, priest, 1990; Asst Curate, Bicester with Bucknell, Caversfield and Launton, 1989–92; Asst Chaplain, HM Prison Bullingdon, 1990–92; Minor Canon, Chaplain and Sacrist, Westminster Abbey, 1992–98; Bishop's Chaplain and Res. Asst, Dio. of Europe, 1998–2005; Archbishop's Chaplain and Ecumenical Officer, 2005–09; Archbishop's Personal Chaplain and Ecumenical Sec., 2009–13. Priest-Vicar, Westminster Abbey, 2004–; Canon, Gibraltar Cath., 2005–. Hon. Curate, St Matthew, Westminster, 1999–2003. *Address:* Hill House, The Mount, Caversham, Reading, Berks RG4 7RE. *T:* (0118) 948 1038.

EBDON, Prof. Leslie Colin, CBE 2009; DL; PhD; CChem, FRSC; Vice-Chancellor and Chief Executive, University of Bedfordshire (formerly University of Luton), 2003–12; Director of Fair Access to Higher Education, since 2012; *b* 26 Jan. 1947; *s* of Harold and Doris Ebdon; *m* 1970, Judith Margaret Thomas; two *s* one *d* (and one *s* decd). *Educ:* Hemel Hempstead Grammar Sch.; Imperial Coll., Univ. of London (BSc, PhD; ARCS, DIC). MCIWEM. Lectr in Chem., Makerere Univ., Uganda, 1971–73; Sen. Lectr, Sheffield City Poly., 1973–80; Plymouth Polytechnic, later Polytechnic SouthWest, then Plymouth University: Reader in Analytical Chem., 1981–89; Hd, Dept of Envmtl Scis, 1989; Prof. of Analytical Chem., 1986–2003; Dep. Dir, 1989–92; Dep. Vice-Chancellor, 1992–2003. Schs Lectr, Analytical Div., RSC, 1986. Chair, Editorial Board: Jl Analytical Atomic Spectroscopy, 1987–91; Chemistry World, 2003–08. Member: Nat. Council of Educn Excellence, 2007–10; Further Educn and Skills Ministerial Adv. Panel, 2010–. Member: Measurement Bd, BIS (formerly Measurement Adv. Cttee, DTI), 1999–; East of England Regl Economic Forum, 2009–10; Bd, SE Midlands Local Enterprise Partnership, 2012–. Chairman: Assoc. of Universities in East of England, 2006–11; Student Experience Policy Cttee, Universities UK, 2007–12; Million+, 2007–12. Mem. Council, RSC, 1996–2008 (Chm., Pubns Bd, 1996–2000, Strategy and Resources Bd, 2003–05); Trustee: Luton Christian Educn Trust, 2010–; RSC Pension Fund, 2010–; Bletchley Park Trust, 2011–. Pres., Luton UNA, 2009–; Vice Pres., Bedford Hosps Charity, 2010–. DL Beds, 2011. FRSA. Hon. DSc Plymouth, 2008. 13th Soc. for Analytical Chem. Silver Medal for Analytical Chem., RSC, 1986; Benedetti-Pichler Meml Award, Amer. Microchem. Soc., 1995. *Publications:* An Introduction to Analytical Atomic Spectroscopy, 1982, 2nd edn 1998; 270 contribs to refereed jls. *Recreations:* vegetable gardening, Baptist lay preacher. *Address:* Office for Fair Access to Higher Education, Northavon House, Coldharbour Lane, Bristol BS16 1QD.

EBERLE, Adm. Sir James (Henry Fuller), GCB 1981 (KCB 1979); Vice Admiral of the United Kingdom, 1994–97; President, Association of Masters of Harriers and Beagles (Chairman, 1998); writer on international affairs and security; *b* 31 May 1927; *s* of late Victor Fuller Eberle and of Joyce Mary Eberle, Bristol; *m* 1950, Ann Patricia Thompson (*d* 1988), Hong Kong; one *s* two *d. Educ:* Clifton Coll.; RNC Dartmouth and Greenwich. Served War of 1939–45 in MTBs, HMS Renown, HMS Belfast; subseq. in Far East; qual. Gunnery Specialist 1951; Guided Missile Develt and trials in UK and USA, 1953–57; Naval Staff, 1960–62; Exec. Officer, HMS Eagle, 1963–65; comd HMS Intrepid, 1968–70; Asst Chief of Fleet Support, MoD (RN), 1971–74; Flag Officer Sea Training, 1974–75; Flag Officer Carriers and Amphibious Ships, 1975–77; Chief of Fleet Support, 1977–79; C-in-C, Fleet, and Allied C-in-C, Channel and Eastern Atlantic, 1979–81; C-in-C, Naval Home Comd, 1981–82, retired 1983. Rear Adm. of the UK, 1990–94. UK-Japan 2000 Gp, 1983–98. Vice-Pres., RUSI, 1979; Dir, RIIA, 1984–90. Dir, Countryside Alliance, 2000–07. Chm. Council, Clifton Coll., 1984–94; Chm., Devon Rural Skills Trust, 1992–93. President: HMS Cossack Assoc., 2004–; HMS Belfast Assoc., 2009–. Freeman: Bristol, 1946; London, 1982. Hon. LLD: Bristol, 1989; Sussex, 1992. *Publications:* Management in the Armed Forces, 1972; Jim, First of the Pack, 1982; Britain's Future in Space, 1988; Admiral Jim: a trilogy: Wider Horizons, From Greenland's Icy Shore, Life on the Ocean Wave, 2007. *Recreations:* hunting (Master of Britannia Beagles), tennis. *Clubs:* Society of Merchant Venturers (Bristol); All England Lawn Tennis.

EBERS, Prof. George Cornell, MD; FRCP, FRCPC, FMedSci; Professor of Clinical Neurology, University of Oxford, 1999–2011, now Emeritus (Head, Department of Clinical Neurology, 1999–2004); Fellow, St Edmund Hall, Oxford, since 1999; *b* Budapest, 24 July 1946; *s* of Cornell George Ebers and Leontine Amant Ebers; *m* 1997, Sharon Vitali; one *s* one *d. Educ:* De La Salle Coll.; Univ. of Toronto (MD 1970); MA Oxon. FRCPC 1977. University of Western Ontario: Asst Prof., 1977–82; Associate Prof., 1982–87; Prof., Dept of Clinical Neurol Scis, 1987–99. Numerous vis. professorships and named lectures. Member, Editorial Board: Jl Neuroimm., 1983–2011; Canadian Jl Neuro. Sci., 1985–2011; MS Res. Reports, 1987–2011; Jl Tropical Geog. Neurol., 1990–94; Neuroepidemiol., 1992–2011; Multiple Sclerosis, 1994–2011. FMedSci 2001. John Dystel Award for MS Res., Amer. Acad. of Neurol., 2013. Mem., Bayfield Histl Soc. *Publications:* The Diagnosis of MS, 1984; Multiple Sclerosis, 1998; sole or jt author of over 400 peer reviewed pubns. *Recreations:* book collecting, ornithology, history of medicine, windmill restoration. *Address:* Department of Neurology, Level 3, West Wing, John Radcliffe Hospital, Oxford OX3 9DU. *T:* (01865) 231903. *Club:* Osler.

EBRAHIM, Sir (Mahomed) Currimbhoy, (Sir Mohamed Currimbhoy), 4th Bt *cr* 1910; BA, LLB; Advocate, Pakistan; Member, Standing Council of the Baronetage, 1961; *b* 24 June 1935; *o s* of Sir (Huseinali) Currimbhoy Ebrahim, 3rd Bt, and Alhaja Lady Amina Khanum, *d* of Alhaj Cassumali Jairajbhoy; *S* father, 1952; *m* 1958, Dur-e-Mariam, *d* of Minuchehir Ahmud Ghulamaly Nana; three *s* one *d. Recreations:* tennis (Karachi University No 1, 1957, No 2, 1958), cricket, table-tennis, squash, reading (literary), art, poetry writing, debate, quotation writing. *Heir: s* Zulfiqar Ali Currimbhoy Ebrahim [*b* 5 Aug. 1960; *m* 1984, Adila, *d* of Akhtar Halipota; one *s* one *d*].

EBRAHIM, Prof. Shaheen Brian John, FRCP, FFPH; Professor of Public Health, London School of Hygiene & Tropical Medicine, 2005–14, now Hon. Professor; *b* 19 July 1952; *s* of Dr Donald William Ebrahim and Marjorie Sybil (*née* Evans); *m* 1st, 1984, Julia Lesley Shaw (marr. diss. 2002); 2nd, 2004, Fiona Clair Taylor. *Educ:* King Henry VIII Sch., Coventry; Nottingham Univ. Med. Sch. (BMed Sci; BM BS 1975; DM 1985). FRCP 1993; FFPH (FFPHM 1993). Wellcome Trust Clinical Epidemiology Trng Fellow, Nottingham Univ. Med. Sch., 1981–83; Lectr in Geriatric Medicine, Univ. of Nottingham, 1983–85; Wellcome Trust Lectr in Epidemiology, Dept of Social Medicine and Gen. Practice, St George's Hosp. Med. Sch., London, 1985–86; Cons. Physician and Sen. Lectr, Dept of Geriatric Medicine, Royal Free Hosp. Sch. of Medicine, 1987–89; Prof. of Geriatric Medicine, London Hosp. Med. Coll. and St Bartholomew's Hosp. Med. Coll., 1989–92; Prof. of Clinical Epidemiology, Royal Free Hosp. Sch. of Med., 1992–98; Prof. of Epidemiology of Ageing, Univ. of Bristol, 1998–2005. Vis. Prof., Christchurch Med. Sch., NZ, 1990; Nat. Heart Foundn of NZ Vis. Prof. in Stroke, 1991; Australian Veterans Vis. Prof., 1995; Visiting Professor: McMaster Univ., Canada, 1996; Sydney Univ., Australia, 2003; Univ. of Bristol, 2013–; Hon. Professor: UCL 2003–; Public Health Foundn of India, 2009–; Adjunct Prof., Internat. Inst. of Diarrheal Disease Res., Bangladesh, 2009–. *Publications:* Clinical Epidemiology of Stroke, 1990, 2nd edn 1999; (ed jtly) The Health of Older Women, 1992; (with G. Bennett) Essentials of Health Care in Old Age, 1992, 2nd edn 1995; (ed jtly) Epidemiology in Old Age, 1996; (ed jtly) Handbook of Health Research Methods, 2005; scientific papers on public health, clinical epidemiology and geriatric medicine. *Recreations:* coarse fishing, music of Velvet Underground and Don Van Vliet. *Address:* Faculty of Epidemiology and Population Health, London School of Hygiene & Tropical Medicine, Keppel Street, WC1E 7HT. *Club:* Royal Society of Medicine.

EBRINGER, Prof. Alan Martin, MD; FRACP, FRCP, FRCPath; Professor of Immunology, King's College, London, 1995, now Emeritus; *b* 12 Feb. 1936; *s* of late Bernard Ebringer and Maria Ebringer; *m* 1960, Eva Marie Ernest; two *s* one *d. Educ:* Melbourne High Sch.; Univ. of Melbourne (BSc Maths 1961; MB BS 1962; MD 1971). FRACP 1967; MRCP 1970, FRCP 1987; FRCPath 1997. Prosector in Anatomy, Univ. of Melbourne, 1958–; Pathology Registrar, Geelong Hosp., 1964; Research Fellow: Walter and Eliza Hall Inst., Royal Melbourne Hosp., 1965–66; Austin Hosp., 1967–69; RACP Overseas Travelling Schol., Dept of Immunol., Middx Hosp., 1970; Berkeley Fellow, Middx Hosp. and Gonville and Caius Coll., Cambridge, 1971; King's College, London: Lectr, 1972–77; Sen. Lectr, 1977–82; Reader, 1982–95; Hon. Consultant Rheumatologist, UCL Hosps (formerly Middx Hosp.), i/c of Ankylosing Spondylitis Res. Clinic, 1980–2002. Appeared before Phillips Inquiry into BSE, 1998. Member: British Soc. Immunol., 1970; British Soc. Rheum., 1972; Amer. Coll. Rheumatol., 1996. Vis. Lectr, Melbourne, Edinburgh, Glasgow, Sheffield, Paris, Marseille, Brest, Madrid, Helsinki, Turku, Bratislava, Moscow, Suzdal, Innsbruck, San Antonio, Dallas, Uppsala. Life Mem., RSocMed, 2008. Hon. FRSPH (Hon. FRSH 2001). Donaldson Gold Medal, RSH, 2003. *Publications:* Rheumatoid Arthritis and Proteus, 2011; Ankylosing Spondylitis and Klebsiella, 2012; Multiple Sclerosis, Mad Cow Disease and Acinetobacter, 2014; contrib. numerous papers dealing with autoimmune diseases produced by molecular mimicry to ext. agents, esp. ankylosing spondylitis (klebsiella), rheumatoid arthritis (proteus), bovine spongiform encephalopathy (acinetobacter), multiple sclerosis (acinetobacter) and Crohn's disease (Klebsiella). *Recreations:* languages, Karl Popper, walking. *Address:* 76 Gordon Road, W5 2AR.

ECCLES, family name of **Viscount Eccles** and **Baroness Eccles of Moulton**.

ECCLES, 2nd Viscount *cr* 1964, of Chute, co. Wilts; **John Dawson Eccles,** CBE 1985; Baron 1962; Chairman, The Bowes Museum, County Durham, 2000–08; *b* 20 April 1931; *er s* of 1st Viscount Eccles, CH, KCVO, PC and Sybil (*d* 1977), *d* of 1st Viscount Dawson of Penn, GCVO, KCB, KCMG, PC; *S* father, 1999; *m* 1955, Diana Catherine Sturge (*see* Baroness Eccles of Moulton); one *s* three *d. Educ:* Winchester Coll.; Magdalen Coll., Oxford (BA). Commnd 1st 60th KRRC, 1950. Director: Glynwed International plc, 1972–96; Investors in Industry plc, 1974–88; Chairman: Head Wrightson & Co. Ltd, 1976–77 (Man. Dir, 1968); Chamberlin & Hill plc, 1982–2004; Acker Deboeck, corporate psychologists, 1994–2006; Courtaulds Textiles plc, 1995–2000 (Dir, 1992–2000); Director: The Nuclear Power Gp Ltd, 1968–74; Davy Internat. Ltd, 1977–81; Govett Strategic Investment Trust plc, 1996–2004. Member: Monopolies and Mergers Commn, 1976–85 (Dep. Chm., 1981–85); Industrial Develt Adv. Bd, 1989–93; Gen. Manager, subseq. Chief Exec., Commonwealth Develt Corp., 1985–94 (Mem., 1982–85). Chm., Bd of Trustees, Royal Botanic Gardens, Kew, 1983–91. Mem. Council, Eccles Centre for American Studies, BL, 2003–. Chm., Hosp. for Tropical Diseases Foundn, 2000–. Elected Mem., H of L, March 2005. Hon. DSc Cranfield Inst. of Technology, 1989. *Recreations:* gardening, theatre. *Heir: s* Hon. William David Eccles [*b* 9 June 1960; *m* 1984, Claire Margaret Alison Seddon (*d* 2001); two *s* one *d*]. *Address:* 5 St John's House, 30 Smith Square, SW1P 3HF. *T:* (020) 7222 4040; Moulton Hall, Richmond, N Yorks DL10 6QH. *T:* (01325) 377227. *Club:* Brooks's.

ECCLES OF MOULTON, Baroness *cr* 1990 (Life Peer), of Moulton in the County of North Yorkshire; **Diana Catherine Eccles, (Viscountess Eccles);** DL; Chairman, Ealing, Hammersmith and Hounslow Health Authority, 1993–2000 (Chairman, Ealing District Health Authority, 1988–93); *b* 4 Oct. 1933; *d* of late Raymond Sturge and Margaret Sturge; *m* 1955, John Dawson Eccles (*see* Viscount Eccles); one *s* three *d. Educ:* St James's Sch., West Malvern; Open Univ. (BA). Voluntary work, Middlesbrough Community Council, 1955–58; Partner, Gray Design Associates, 1963–77. Director: Tyne Tees Television, 1986–94; J. Sainsbury, 1986–95; Yorkshire Electricity Gp, 1990–97; National & Provincial Building Soc., 1991–96; Opera North, 1998–2011; Ind. Nat. Dir, Times Newspapers Holdings Ltd, 1998–. Member: North Eastern Electricity Bd, 1974–85; British Railways Eastern Bd, 1986–92; Teesside Urban Develt Corp., 1987–98; Yorkshire Electricity Bd, 1989–90. Member: Adv. Council for Energy Conservation, 1982–84; Widdicombe Inquiry into Local Govt, 1985–86; Unrelated Live Transplant Regulatory Authority, 1990–99. Vice Chairman: Nat. Council for Voluntary Orgns, 1981–87; Durham Univ. Council, 1985–2004 (Lay Mem., 1981–85). Trustee: Charities Aid Foundn, 1982–89; York Minster Fund, 1989–99 and 2006–09; London Clinic, 2003–08. DL N Yorks, 1998. Hon. DCL Durham, 1995. *Address:* Moulton Hall, Richmond, N Yorks DL10 6QH. *T:* (01325) 377227; 5/30 Smith Square, SW1P 3HF. *T:* (020) 7222 4040.

ECCLES, (Hugh William) Patrick; QC 1990; **His Honour Judge Eccles;** a Circuit Judge, since 2000; *b* 25 April 1946; *s* of late Gp Captain (retd) Hugh Haslett Eccles and Mary Eccles; *m* 1972, Rhoda Ann Eccles (*née* Moroney); three *d. Educ:* Stonyhurst Coll.; Exeter Coll., Oxford (MA). Called to the Bar, Middle Temple, 1968, Bencher, 1998; practising barrister, head of chambers, 1985–2000; a Recorder, 1987–2000; approved to sit as Dep. High Court Judge, QBD, 1997–2015, Chancery and Family Divs, 2002–15. Asst Parly Boundary Comr, 1992; Legal Mem., First-tier Tribunal (Health, Educn and Social Care Chamber) (formerly Mental Health Review Tribunal (Restricted Patients)), 2000–. Mem., County Court Rule Cttee, 1986–91. Trustee and Sec., Friends of Church of St Birinus, 2001–14. Gov., Sch. of St Helen and St Katharine, Abingdon, 1992–2013. *Recreations:* playing tennis, watching Rugby and football, enjoying opera, theatre, reading, travel, mowing the lawn. *Address:* c/o Oxford Combined Court Centre, St Aldate's, Oxford OX1 1TL.

ECCLESHARE, (Christopher) William; Chief Executive Officer, Clear Channel Outdoor Holdings Inc., since 2012 (President and Chief Executive Officer, Clear Channel International, 2009–12); *b* 26 Oct. 1955; *s* of late Colin Forster Eccleshare and Elizabeth Eccleshare; *m* 1980, Carol Ann Seigel; two *s* one *d. Educ:* Fitzjohns Primary Sch.; William Ellis Sch.; Trinity Coll., Cambridge (BA Hist. 1978). Account Exec., 1978–89, Man. Dir, 1990–92, J. Walter Thompson; Chief Exec., PPGH/JWT Amsterdam, 1993–95; Global Strategy Dir, J. Walter Thompson, 1995–96; Chief Exec., Ammirati Puris Lintas, London, 1996–99; Partner, Leader Eur. Branding Practice, McKinsey & Co., 2000–02; Chairman and Chief Executive Officer: Young & Rubicam, Europe, 2002–05; BBDO EMEA, 2005–09. Non-exec. Dir, Hays plc, 2004–14. Mem., Mktg Gp of GB, 2006–. Mem. Council, University Coll. Sch., 2002–12. Mem. Bd and Trustee, Donmar Warehouse Th., 2013–. FIPA 1998 (Mem. Council, 1998–2000; Judge, IPA Effectiveness Awards, 2002). *Publications:* (contrib.) The Timeless Works of Stephen King, ed J. Lannon, 2007; contribs to Campaign, Admap, Market Leader. *Recreations:* American and European politics, theatre, running, music of Bruce Springsteen. *Address:* Clear Channel Outdoor, 33 Golden Square, W1F 9JT. *T:* (020) 7478 2334. *E:* williameccleshare@clearchannel.com; 9 The Mount, NW3 6SZ. *Club:* Thirty.
See also J. J. Eccleshare.

ECCLESHARE, Julia Jessica, MBE 2014; journalist and broadcaster; *b* 14 Dec. 1951; *d* of late Colin Forster Eccleshare and of Elizabeth Eccleshare; *m* 1977, John Lemprière Hammond, *s* of Prof. Nicholas Geoffrey Lemprière Hammond, CBE, DSO, FBA; three *s* one *d. Educ:* Camden Sch. for Girls; Girton Coll., Cambridge. Editorial assistant: TLS, 1973–78; Puffin Books, 1978–79; Fiction editor, Hamish Hamilton Children's Books, 1979–82; selector of Children's Books of Year for Book Trust, 1982–92; Children's Book corresp., Bookseller, 1993–97; Children's Books Editor, Guardian, 1997–. Co-dir, Centre for Literacy in Primary Educn, 2004–13; Hd of Advocacy and Policy, Public Lending Right, 2014–. Chm. Judges, Smarties Award, 1994–; Member: Adv. Body, Reading is Fundamental (UK), 1996–; Poetry Book Soc., 2012–15; Trustee: Listening Books, 2000–; Volunteer Reading Help, 2003–06; Siobhan Dowd Trust, 2014–. Contributor to BBC Treasure Islands, Night Waves, Kaleidoscope, Woman's Hour and Open Book, 1985–. Hon. DLitt Worcester, 2014. Eleanor Farjeon Award, 2000. *Publications:* The Woman's Hour Guide to Children's Books, 1987; A Guide to the Harry Potter Novels, 2002; Beatrix Potter to Harry Potter, 2002; The Rough Guide to Teenage Reading, 2003; The Rough Guide to Picture Books, 2008; 1001 Children's Books You Must Read Before You Grow Up, 2009; ed numerous anthologies. *Recreations:* theatre, walking. *Address:* 21 Tanza Road, NW3 2UA. *T:* (020) 7431 1295. *E:* julia.eccleshare@blueyonder.co.uk.
See also C. W. Eccleshare.

ECCLESHARE, William; *see* Eccleshare, C. W.

ECCLESTON, Christopher; actor; *b* 16 Feb. 1964; *s* of Joseph Ronald Eccleston and Elsie Lavinia Eccleston. *Educ:* Central Sch. of Speech and Drama. *Films include:* Let Him Have It, 1991; Shallow Grave, 1994; Jude, 1996; Elizabeth, A Price Above Rubies, 1998; Heart, Old New Borrowed Blue, eXistenZ, 1999; Gone in 60 Seconds, 2000; The Invisible Circus, The Others, 2001; I Am Dina, 28 Days Later, 2002; A Revenger's Tragedy, 2003; Song for Marion, Thor: The Dark World, 2013; Legend, 2015. *Television includes:* Cracker (series), 1993–94; Hearts and Minds, 1995; Our Friends in the North (series), Hillsborough, 1996; Strumpet, 2001; Flesh and Blood, Othello, Sunday, 2002; The Second Coming, 2003; Doctor Who (series), 2005; Perfect Parents, 2006; Lennon Naked, 2010; The Shadow Line, The Borrowers, 2011; Blackout, 2012; Lucan, 2013; Fortitude, Safe House, 2015. *Theatre includes:* Miss Julie, Haymarket, 2000; Hamlet, 2002, Electricity, 2004, W Yorks Playhouse; Antigone, NT, 2012. *Address:* c/o Independent Talent Group Ltd, 40 Whitfield Street, W1T 2RH.

ECCLESTONE, Bernard, (Bernie); Chief Executive Officer: Formula One Administration Ltd; Formula One Management Ltd; *b* Suffolk, 27 Oct. 1930; *m* 1st; one *d*; 2nd, Slavica (marr. diss. 2009); two *d*; 3rd, 2012, Fabiana Flosi. *Educ:* Woolwich Polytechnic (BSc). Est. car and motorbike dealership, Midweek Car Auctions; racing car driver, F3; owner, Connaught racing team, 1957; Manager, Jochen Rindt; owner, Brabham racing team, 1970–90. Vice-Pres., Fed. Internat. de l'Automobile. Person of the Year, Motorsport Industry Assoc., Business Achievement Awards; inaugural Gold Medal, British Racing Drivers' Club. Keys to Cities of São Paulo and Rio de Janeiro. Medal (1st degree), Bahrain; Silver Medals, Monaco; Bandeirante Medal, Brazil. Grand Officer, Equestrian Order of St Agata, San Marino; Grand Decoration of Honour, Austria; Order of Merit, Hungary; Grand Officer, Order of Merit, Italy. *Address:* Formula One Administration Ltd, 6 Prince's Gate, SW7 1QJ. *T:* (020) 7584 6668, *Fax:* (020) 7589 0311. *E:* lhibberd@fomltd.com, emarenghi@fomltd.com, ckai@fomltd.com.

ECCLESTONE, Jacob Andrew; Assistant General Secretary, Writers' Guild, 1999–2001; *b* 10 April 1939; *s* of late Rev. Alan Ecclestone and Delia Reynolds Abraham; *m* 1966, Margaret Joan Bassett; two *s* one *d. Educ:* High Storrs Grammar Sch., Sheffield; Open Univ. (BA). Journalism: South Yorkshire Times, 1957–61; Yorkshire Evening News, 1961–62; The Times, 1962–66, 1967–81; Dep. Gen. Sec., NUJ, 1981–97 (Mem., 1977, Vice-Pres. 1978, Pres., 1979, Nat. Exec.). Member: Press Council, 1977–80; Exec., NCCL, 1982–86. *Recreations:* gardening, walking, music. *Address:* North House, 50 Mount Street, Diss, Norfolk IP22 4QG. *T:* (01379) 644949. *E:* ecclestones@btinternet.com.

ECE; *see* Hussein-Ece.

ECHENIQUE, Prof. Marcial Hernan, OBE 2009; DArch; Professor of Land Use and Transport Studies, University of Cambridge, 1993–2013, now Emeritus (Head, Department of Architecture, 2004–08); Fellow, Churchill College, Cambridge, since 1972; *b* 23 Feb. 1943; *s* of Marcial Echenique and Rosa de Echenique (*née* Talavera); *m* 1963, Maria Luisa Holzmann; two *s* one *d. Educ:* Catholic Univ. of Chile; Univ. of Barcelona (DArch). MA Cantab 1972. MRTPI 1990; ARIBA 1997. Asst Lectr, Univ. of Barcelona, 1964–65; University of Cambridge: Research Officer, 1967–70; Lectr, 1970–80; Reader in Architecture and Urban Studies, 1980–93. Founder and Mem., Bd of Applied Res., Cambridge, 1969–83. Advr to Public Works and Transport Ministers, Chilean Govt, 1991–2014. Chm., Marcial Echenique & Partners Ltd, England, 1978–2001; Pres., Marcial Echenique y Compañía SA, Spain, 1988–2007; Member Board: Trasporti e Territorio SRL, Italy, 1992–2007; Autopista Vasco-Aragonesa SA, Spain, 1994–99; Tecnologica SA, Spain, 1994–96; Ferrovial-Agroman, Construcciones, Spain, 1995–2000; Dockways Ltd, Jersey, 1996–2000. Bank of Bilbao-Vizcaya of Spain: Mem. Bd, 1988–94; Trustee of Foundn, 1990–94. *Publications:* (ed jtly) La Estructura del Espacio Urbano, 1975; (ed jtly) Urban Development Models, 1975; (ed) Modelos Matemáticos de la Estructura Espacial Urbana: aplicaciones en America Latina, 1975; (with L. Piemontese) Un Modello per lo Sviluppo del Sistema Grecia-Italia Meridionale, 1984; (jtly) Cambridge Futures, 1999; (ed jtly) Cities for the New Millennium, 2001; (jtly) Cities of Innovation: shaping places for high-tech, 2003. *Recreations:* music, reading, gardening. *Address:* Farm Hall, Godmanchester, Cambs PE29 2HQ.

ECKERBERG, (Carl) Lennart, Hon. KCMG 1983; Officer of Royal Northern Star 1970; Swedish Ambassador to the Court of St James's, 1991–94; *b* 2 July 1928; *s* of late Enar Lars Eckerberg and of Dagmar Liljedahl; *m* 1965, Willia Fales; two *s* one *d. Educ:* Univ. of Stockholm (law degree 1953). Swedish Foreign Service in Stockholm, London, Warsaw and Washington, 1954–71; Disarmament Ambassador, Geneva, 1971; Minister Plenipotentiary, Washington, 1975; Ambassador, Dar es Salaam, 1977; Under Sec., Political Affairs, Stockholm, 1979; Ambassador, Bonn, 1983–91. Orders from Finland, Germany, Iceland, Spain and Mexico. *Recreations:* golf, tennis, bridge. *Address:* (summer) Martornsvägen 3, 23940 Falsterbo, Sweden. *Clubs:* Chevy Chase (Washington); Falsterbo (Sweden).

ECKERSLEY-MASLIN, Rear Adm. David Michael, CB 1984; retired, RN; *b* Karachi, 27 Sept. 1929; *e s* of late Comdr C. E. Eckersley-Maslin, OBE, RN, Tasmania, and Mrs L. M. Lightfoot, Bedford; *m* 1955, Shirley Ann, *d* of late Captain H. A. Martin; one *s* one *d. Educ:* Britannia Royal Naval Coll. Qual. Navigation Direction Officer, 1954; rcds 1977. Navigating Officer, HMS Michael, Far East Malayan Campaign, 1950–53; Australian Navy, 1954–56; BRNC Dartmouth, 1959–61; commanded HM Ships Eastbourne, Euryalus, Fife and Blake, 1966–76; Captain RN Presentation Team, 1974; Dir, Naval Operational Requirements, 1977–80; Flag Officer Sea Training, 1980–82; ACNS (Operational Planning) (Falklands), 1982; ACDS (CIS), 1982–84; Asst Dir (CIS), IMS, NATO, Brussels, 1984–86; Dir Gen., NATO Communications and Inf. Systems Agency, 1986–91. ADC to the Queen, 1980. Vice Pres., AFCEA, 1987–90 (Gold Medal, 1991). Pres., Algerines Assoc., 1997–2000. Mem. Council, Shipwrecked Mariners Soc., 1992–97. Naval Gen. Service Decoration, Palestine, 1948, and Malaya, 1951. *Recreations:* tennis, cricket. *Address:* 8 First Avenue, Denvilles, Havant, Hants PO9 2QN. *T:* (023) 9311 4618. *Club:* MCC.

ECKERT, Neil David; Chairman, Aggregated Micro Power Holdings plc, since 2012 (Chief Executive Officer, Aggregated Micro Power Ltd, 2010–12); *b* 20 May 1962; *s* of Clive and Mary Eckert; *m* 1986, Nicola Lindsay; three *d. Educ:* Merchant Taylors' Sch., Northwood, Middx. Reinsurance broker, 1980; joined Benfield Lovick & Rees & Co. Ltd, 1986; Mem. Bd, Benfield Gp plc, 1991–2000; Brit Insurance plc: Dir, 1995–2005; CEO, 1999–2005; non-exec. Dir, 2006–08; Chief Exec., Climate Exchange plc, 2005–10. Non-exec. Chm., Design Technology and Innovations Ltd; non-executive Director: Titan (Southwest) Ltd; Arthur J. Gallagher (UK) Ltd, 2013–; Ebix Inc.; Evofem LLC; Cosmederm Bioscience Inc. *Recreations:* golf, sailing, tennis, other watersports in general, going to concerts, all types of music. *Address:* Aggregated Micro Power Holdings plc, 5 Clifford Street, W1S 2LG. *T:* (020) 7382 7800, *Fax:* (020) 7382 7810. *Clubs:* Royal Automobile, Hurlingham, City of London; St Enodoc Golf.

ECONOMIDES, Alain Giorgio Maria; Ambassador of Italy to the Court of St James's, 2010–13; *b* Rome, 6 March 1948; *s* of Alessandro Economides and Elena Economides (*née* Potsios); *m* 1975, Franca Giannini; one *s* one *d. Educ:* Univ. of Rome (law degree 1973). Entered Diplomatic Service, Italy, 1975; Political Directorate, Min. of For. Affairs, 1976–79; First Sec., Perm. Repn to UN, NY, 1979–83; Counsellor: (Commercial) Harare, 1983–85; Human Resources Directorate, Min. of For. Affairs, 1985; Cabinet of Sec. of State for For. Affairs, 1986–89; First Counsellor, Perm. Repn to EEC, Brussels, 1989–93; Hd, Secretariat Unit, Political Directorate, 1993, Advr to Sec. Gen., 1994–96, Min. of For. Affairs; Minister Plenipotentiary, Perm. Repn to EU, Brussels, 1996–2001; Ambassador to Dakar, and concurrently to Mauritania, Gambia, Cape Verde, Mali, Guinea and Guinea Bissau, 2001–03; Dep. Dir Gen., Internat. Develt Directorate, Min. of For. Affairs, 2003; Dep. Chef de Cabinet to Sec. of State for For. Affairs, 2004–06; Dir Gen., Internat. Develt Directorate, Min. of For. Affairs, 2006–08; Chef de Cabinet to Sec. of State for For. Affairs, 2008–10. Medaglia al Merito Croce Rossa Italiana (Italy), 2004; Gran Croce dell'Ordine al Merito Melitense; Grande Ufficiale, Ordine al Merito della Repubblica Italiana. *Publications:* articles on the law of the sea. *Recreations:* tennis, swimming, golf.

EDBROOKE, Rowan Clare; Headmistress, St Helen & St Katharine, Abingdon, 2008–14; *b* Belize City, 27 Oct. 1961; *d* of Dr Donald Edbrooke and Vicky Edbrooke; partner, Bill Gott. *Educ:* St Catherine's Sch., Surrey; Godalming Sixth Form Coll.; Bedford Coll. of Higher Educn (BEd Hons). Teacher, Queen Elizabeth's Girls Sch., Barnet, 1984–86; South Hampstead High School: PE Teacher, 1986–88; Hd, PE Dept, 1988–93; Hd of Middle Sch., 1989–95; Sen. Teacher, 1995–98; Hd of Sixth Form, 1998–2001, Dep. Hd, 2001–04, Haberdashers' Aske's Sch. for Girls, Elstree; Headmistress, St Margaret's Sch., Exeter, 2004–08. *Recreations:* England netball (21 caps, 1981–84); currently tennis, golf, sailing, literature, choral music. *Address:* 9 Moorlands Road, Budleigh Salterton, Devon EX9 6AG. *T:* (01395) 442379.

EDDERY, Patrick James John, Hon. OBE 2005; trainer; founder, Pat Eddery Racing, 2003; *b* 18 March 1952; *s* of Jimmy and Josephine Eddery; *m* (marr. diss.); one *s* two *d*. Rode for Peter Walwyn, 1972–80; Champion Jockey, 1974, 1975, 1976, 1977, 1986, 1988, 1989, 1990, 1991, 1993, 1996; Champion Jockey in Ireland, 1982; retired as jockey, 2003. Winner: Oaks, on Polygamy, 1974, on Scintillate, 1979, on Lady Carla, 1996; Derby, on Grundy, 1975, on Golden Fleece, 1982, on Quest for Fame, 1990; Prix de l'Arc de Triomphe, on Detroit, 1980, on Rainbow Quest, 1985, on Dancing Brave, 1986, on Trempolino, 1987; St Leger, on Moon Madness, 1986, on Toulon, 1991, on Moonax, 1994, on Silver Patriarch, 1997 (his 4,000th win in GB). *Recreations:* watching tennis, snooker. *Address:* Musk Hill Farm, Nether Winchendon, Aylesbury, Bucks HP18 0EB. *T:* (01844) 296153, *Fax:* (01844) 290282.

EDDINGTON, Sir Roderick Ian, (Sir Rod), Kt 2005; AO 2012; DPhil; non-executive Chairman: Australia and New Zealand, JPMorgan, since 2006; Lion, since 2012; Chairman, Advisory Council, Infrastructure Australia, 2008–14; *b* 2 Jan. 1950; *s* of Gil and April Eddington; *m* 1994, Young Sook Park; one *s* one *d. Educ:* Univ. of WA (BEng Hons; MEng Sci.); Lincoln Coll., Oxford (DPhil 1979). Res. Lectr, Pembroke Coll., Oxford, 1978–79; John Swire & Sons, 1979–96 (on secondment to Cathay Pacific Airways as Man. Dir, 1992–96); Director: Swire Pacific, 1992–96; John Swire & Sons Pty Ltd, 1997–; Exec. Chm., Ansett Australia, 1997–2000; Dir, News Ltd, 1997–2000; CEO, British Airways plc, 2000–05. Non-executive Director: News Corp., 2000–13; Rio Tinto plc, 2005–11; CLP Holdings, 2006–; 20th Century Fox, 2013–; Chm., Victoria Major Events Co., 2006–; Allco Finance Gp Ltd, 2006–09. Mem., Asia-Pacific Econ. Cooperation Business Adv. Council, 2014–. Commnd by HM Treasury and DFT to provide long-term strategy for UK's transport infrastructure, 2005 (report, Eddington Transport Study, 2006). *Recreations:* cricket, bridge. *Address:* JPMorgan, Level 31, 101 Collins Street, Melbourne, Vic 3000, Australia. *Clubs:* Vincent's (Oxford); Melbourne; Hong Kong, Shek O (Hong Kong).

EDDLESTON, Prof. Adrian Leonard William Francis, DM; FRCP; Professor of Liver Immunology, London University, 1982–2000, now Emeritus, and Dean, Guy's, King's College and St Thomas' School of Medicine of King's College London, 1998–2000; *b* 2 Feb. 1940; *s* of late Rev. William Eddleston and Kathleen Brenda (*née* Jarman); *m* 1966, Hilary Kay Radford; three *s* one *d. Educ:* St Peter's Coll., Oxford (BA 1961; MB BCh, MA 1964; DM 1972); Guy's Hosp. Med. Sch., London. MRCS 1965; LRCP 1965, MRCP 1967, FRCP 1979. House Surgeon, Casualty Officer, House Physician, Sen. House Officer and Jun. Med. Registrar, Guy's Hosp., 1965–67; Med. Registrar, KCH, 1967–68; King's College School of Medicine and Dentistry: Res. Fellow and Hon. Lectr in Med., 1968–70, Hon. Sen. Lectr, 1972–78, Liver Unit; Dean, Faculty of Clinical Med., 1992–97; Dean, 1997–98; Hon.

Consultant Physician, KCH, 1982–2000. Mem., London Health Commn, 2000–04. MRC Vis. Res. Fellow, Clin. Immunol. Lab., Minnesota Univ., 1970–72. Non-exec. Dir, King's Healthcare NHS Trust, 1990–2000; Chm., Bromley Primary Care Trust, 2001–05. Vice-Chm., King's Fund Mgt Cttee, 2002–07 (Mem., 2000–07). Mem., Gen. Osteopathic Council, 2002–12 (Chm., 2008–12). Trustee: St Christopher's Hospice, 2000–01; Keswick Choral Soc., 2008– (Sec., 2010–). Dir, Threlkeld Community Coffee Shop CIC, 2011–. FKC 1996. Founder FMedSci 1998. *Publications:* Immune Reactions in Liver Disease, 1979; Interferons in the Treatment of Chronic Virus Infection of the Liver, 1990; contrib. learned publications on immunology of auto-immune and virus-induced liver diseases. *Recreations:* choral singing, HF electronics, computing. *Address:* Bridge End Farm, Threlkeld, Keswick, Cumbria CA12 4SX.

EDDY, Prof. Alfred Alan; Professor of Biochemistry, 1959–94, now Emeritus, and Honorary Visiting Scientist, since 1995, University of Manchester (formerly University of Manchester Institute of Science and Technology); *b* 4 Nov. 1926; Cornish parentage; *s* of late Alfred and Ellen Eddy; *m* 1954, Susan Ruth Slade-Jones; two *s*. *Educ:* Devonport High Sch.; Open scholarship Exeter Coll., Oxford, 1944; BA 1st Class Hons, 1949. ICI Research Fellow, 1950; DPhil 1951. Joined Brewing Industry Research Foundation, Nutfield, 1953. *Publications:* various scientific papers. *Recreations:* walking, talking, wining and dining. *Address:* Larchfield, Buxton Road, Disley, Cheshire SK12 2LH.

EDDY, Thomas Edward Dacombe, CBE 2002; Secretary, Royal Commission on Environmental Pollution, 2004–09; *b* 4 Aug. 1949; *s* of Thomas Charles Eddy and Myrtle Constance Eddy (*née* Dacombe); *m* 1980, Cherry Eva; two *s*. *Educ:* Queen Elizabeth Grammar Sch., Wimborne; Pembroke Coll., Cambridge (BA Natural Scis 1970, MA 1973). Joined MAFF, 1973; Head of: Countryside Div., 1990–93, Animal Health Div., 1993–96, BSE Div., 1996–99, EU Div., 1999–2004, MAFF, subseq. DEFRA. Mem., World Ship Soc. *Recreations:* commercial shipping history, reading, croquet. *Address:* 46 Grove Way, Esher, Surrey KT10 8HL. *E:* the4eddys@hotmail.com.

EDE, Anthony Roger; a District Judge (Magistrates' Courts), since 2006; *b* 20 Dec. 1945; *s* of Hugh Geoffrey Ede and Rosalie Ede; *m* 1st (marr. diss.); 2nd, Jill Frances Drower (marr. diss.); one *s* one *d*; 3rd, 2006, Akiyo Yamamoto; one *d* (one *s* decd). *Educ:* Hull Univ. (LLB Hons 1968). Admitted as solicitor, 1971; Partner, Dundon, Ede & Studdert, solicitors, Lavender Hill, 1975–88; Lectr in Law, Coll. of Law, Guildford, 1988–90; Dir, Practical Legal Trng, London, 1990–91; Law Society: Sec., Criminal Law Cttee, 1991–2000; Internat. Projects Manager, 2000–06. Mem., Governing Council, Council for Registration of Forensic Practitioners, 1998–2005. *Publications:* (with E. Shepherd) Active Defence, 1997, 2nd edn 2000; (with A. Edwards) Criminal Defence, 2000, 3rd edn 2008; (with L. Townley) Forensic Practice in Criminal Cases, 2003. *Recreations:* world travel, food, cinema, music. *Address:* Bromley Magistrates' Court, The Court House, London Road, Bromley BR1 1RA. *T:* (020) 8437 3503, (020) 8736 3619.

EDE, Ven. Dennis; Archdeacon of Stoke-upon-Trent, 1989–97, now Emeritus; permission to officiate, Dioceses of Lichfield and Southwark, since 2002; *b* 8 June 1931; *m* 1956, Angela Horsman; one *s* two *d*. *Educ:* Prebendal Choir Sch., Chichester; Ardingly Coll.; Portsmouth Tech. Coll.; Univ. of Nottingham (BA Theology 1955); Barnett House, Oxford (Cert. of Social Studies); Ripon Hall, Oxford; MSocSc Birmingham, 1972. Nat. Service, RAF, 1950–52; Pilot Officer, Admin. Branch. Asst Curate, St Giles, Sheldon, dio. Birmingham, 1957–60; Asst Curate-in-charge, St Philip and St James, Hodge Hill, Birmingham, 1960–64, Priest-in-charge 1964–70, Team Rector 1970–76; part-time Chaplain, East Birmingham Hosp., 1961–76; Vicar of All Saints Parish Church, West Bromwich, dio. Lichfield, 1976–89; Rural Dean, W Bromwich, 1976–89; Hon. Priest i/c, All Saints, Tilford, dio. Guildford, 1997–2002; permission to officiate, Dio. of Guildford, 2002. Mem., Gen. Synod of C of E, 1975–76, 1980–90. Diocese of Lichfield: Chm. House of Clergy, 1985–90; Chm. of Communications, 1983–97; Prebendary of Lichfield Cathedral, 1983–89; Hon. Canon, 1989–97. Chairman: Sandwell Volunteer, 1980–86; Faith in Sandwell, 1986–89; Shallowford House, 1990–97; Diocesan Clergy Retirement Cttee, 1990–97; Widows (Diocesan) Officers Cttee, 1990–97; Surrey and Sussex Churches Broadcasting Cttee, 1997–2002. Co-ordinator for religious bodies in Staffs in major disasters, 1990–97. Broadcaster, local radio, 1960–97; epilogian, ATV, 1961–73. *Recreation:* walking. *Address:* Tilford, 13 Park Close, Carshalton, Surrey SM5 3EU. *T:* (020) 8647 5891. *E:* dennisangelaede@aol.com.

EDELKOORT, Lidewij de Gerarda Hillegonda; design forecaster, strategist and educator; Founder and Chief Executive Officer, Trend Union, since 1986; *b* Wageningen, The Netherlands, 29 Aug. 1950; *d* of Jan Edelkoort and Hillegonda van der Spek; partner, Anthon Beeke. *Educ:* Acad. of Fine Arts, Arnhem (Bachelor in Fashion 1972). Stylist, De Bijenkorf, Amsterdam, 1972–75; collection developer, Exporters India Ltd and India Handicraft, Inc., 1975–79; freelancer, Comité de Coordination des Industries de la Mode, Paris, 1976–86; Founder and Forecaster, Studio Edelkoort, Paris, 1991–; Founder and Director: Edelkoort INC, 1999–; Edelkoort EAST, 2008–. In-house trend forecaster, Première Vision, 1986–93. Design Academy, Eindhoven: Hd, Man and Leisure Dept, 1991–98; Chairwoman, 1998–2008; Co-Founder and Art Dir, Sch. of Form, Poznan, 2010–; Dean, Hybrid Design Studies, Parsons Sch. of Design, The New Sch., New York and Paris, 2015–. Founder and Dir, Heartwear, 1993–; Founder and Artistic Dir, Designhuis Eindhoven, 2006; Founder and creator, Laurier, restaurant, 2007, Mem. Bd, Fondation d'entreprise, 2013–, Galeries Lafayette, Paris. Founder and creator, magazines: View on Colour, 1992–; Bloom, a Horticultural View, 1997–. Curator, exhibitions, incl. Oracles du Design, La Gaîté Lyrique, Paris, 2015. Hon. DArt Nottingham Trent, 2008. Grand Seigneur Prize, Netherlands, 2004; Prins Bernhard Cultuurfonds Prijs, Netherlands, 2012; Hon. RDI, 2014. Knight, Order of Oranje Nassau (Netherlands), 2008; Officier des Arts et des Lettres (France), 2014 (Chevalier, 2008). *Publications:* Fetishism in Fashion, 2013. *Recreations:* design, fashion, education, art, craft, trend forecasting, curating. *Address:* Trend Union, 30 Boulevard Saint Jacques, 75014 Paris, France. *T:* (1) 44086880. *E:* li@edelkoort.com.

EDELL, Stephen Bristow; ombudsman, 1987–2005; *b* 1 Dec. 1932; *s* of late Ivan James Edell and late Hilda Pamela Edell; *m* 1958, Shirley Ross Collins; two *s* one *d*. *Educ:* St Andrew's Sch., Eastbourne; Uppingham; LLB London. Commnd RA, 1951. Articled to father, 1953; qual. Solicitor 1958; Partner, Knapp-Fishers (Westminster), 1959–75; Law Comr, 1975–83; Partner, Crossman Block and Keith (Solicitors), 1983–87; Building Societies Ombudsman, 1987–94; PIA Ombudsman, 1994–97; Waterways Ombudsman, 1997–2005. Chm., Ind. Monitoring Bd, Tinsley House Immigration Removal Centre, Gatwick, 2010–11 (Mem., 2007–11). Legal Mem., RTPI, 1971–92. Mem. Cttee, 1973–85, Vice-Pres., 1980–82, Pres., 1982–83, City of Westminster Law Soc. Oxfam: Mem., Retailing and Property Cttee, 1984–93 (Chm., 1989–93); Mem. Council, 1985–93; Mem., Exec., 1987–93. Dir, Catholic Bldg Soc., 1998–2003. Chm. Council, Hurstpierpoint Coll., 1997–2002; Donation Gov., Christ's Hosp., 2010–. Makers of Playing Cards' Company: Liveryman, 1955–2012; Mem., Ct of Assts, 1978–2000; Sen. Warden, 1980–81; Master, 1981–82; Sen. Freeman, 2012–; Tallow Chandlers' Company: Freeman, 2002–; Liveryman, 2006–. *Publications:* Inside Information on the Family and the Law, 1969; The Family's Guide to the Law, 1974; articles in Conveyancer, Jl of Planning and Environmental Law, and newspapers. *Recreations:* family life; music, opera, theatre; early astronomical instruments; avoiding gardening; interested in problems of developing countries. *Address:* The Old Farmhouse, Twineham, Haywards Heath, Sussex RH17 5NP. *T:* (01273) 832058.

EDELMAN, Colin Neil; QC 1995; barrister and arbitrator; a Recorder, since 1996; Deputy High Court Judge, since 2008; *b* 2 March 1954; *s* of late Gerald Bertram Edelman and of Lynn Queenie Edelman (*née* Tropp); *m* 1978, Jacqueline Claire Seidel; one *s* one *d*. *Educ:* Haberdashers' Aske's Sch., Elstree; Clare Coll., Cambridge (MA). Called to the Bar, Middle Temple, 1977, Bencher, 2003; Asst Recorder, 1993–96; Head of Chambers, 2002–11. Dir, Bar Mutual Indemnity Fund Ltd, 2007– (Dep. Chm., 2009–13; Chm., 2013–). *Publications:* (contrib.) Insurance Disputes, 1999, 3rd edn 2011; (ed) The Law of Reinsurance, 2005, 2nd edn 2013. *Recreations:* badminton, ski-ing, walking, Luton Town FC. *Address:* Devereux Chambers, Queen Elizabeth Building, Temple, EC4Y 9BS. *T:* (020) 7353 7534, *Fax:* (020) 7583 5150.

EDELMAN, Keith Graeme; Managing Director, Arsenal Football Club, 2000–08; *b* 10 July 1950; *m* 1974, Susan Brown; two *s*. *Educ:* Haberdashers' Aske's Sch.; UMIST (BSc). IBM, 1971–73; Rank Xerox, 1973–78; Bank of America, 1978–83; Grand Metropolitan, 1983–84; Corporate Planning Dir and Chm., Texas Homecare, Ladbroke Group, 1984–91; Man. Dir, Carlton Communications, 1991–93; Chief Exec., Storehouse and BHS, 1993–99. Non-exec. Chm., Glenmorangie, 2002–05; non-executive Director: Eurotunnel plc, 1995–2004; Eurotunnel SA, 1995–2004; Channel Tunnel Gp Ltd, 1995–2004; France-Manche SA, 1995–2004; Qualceram Shires plc, 2005–09; Nirah, 2006–; Beale plc, 2008–; Olympic Park Legacy Co., later London Legacy Develt Corp., 2009–; Supergroup plc, 2009–; Arnotts Hldgs, 2009–10; Safestore, 2009–; Argentium, 2010–; Thorntons plc, 2012–. *Recreations:* tennis, ski-ing. *Address:* Laurimar, 7 Linksway, Northwood, Middx HA6 2XA. *T:* (01923) 823990.

EDELSTEIN, Victor Arnold; painter of portraits and interiors; *b* 10 July 1945; *s* of late Israel and Rebecca Edelstein; *m* 1973, Anna Maria Succi. Trainee Designer, Alexon, 1962–66; Asst Designer, Biba, 1966–68; formed own small dress designing co., 1968–72; Salvador, 1972–76; Designer, Christian Dior, 1976–78; founded Victor Edelstein Ltd, 1978, closed 1993. Ballet design, Rhapsody in Blue, 1989. One-man exhibitions: Sotheby's, 1996; Hopkins Thomas, Paris, 1999; Hazlitt, Gooden & Fox Gall., 2001; Didier Aaron, NY, 2004, 2015 (Gilded Interiors); (portraits) The Studio, Glebe Place, London, 2005; (pastels) Derek Johns Gall., Duke Street, London, 2011; Didier Aaron, Paris (Gilded Interiors), 2015. *Recreations:* walking, music, gardening. *Address:* Gloucestershire.

EDEN, family name of **Barons Auckland, Eden of Winton** and **Henley**.

EDEN OF WINTON, Baron *cr* 1983 (Life Peer), of Rushyford in the County of Durham; **John Benedict Eden;** PC 1972; Bt (E) 1672 and Bt (GB) 1776; Chairman, Lady Eden's Schools Ltd, 1974–2001 (Director, 1949–70); *b* 15 Sept. 1925; *s* of Sir Timothy Calvert Eden, 8th and 6th Bt and Patricia (*d* 1990), *d* of Arthur Prendergast; *S* father, 1963; *m* 1st, 1958, Belinda Jane (marr. diss. 1974), *o d* of late Sir John Pascoe; two *s* two *d*; 2nd, 1977, Margaret Ann, Viscountess Strathallan. Lieut Rifle Bde, seconded to 2nd KEO Goorkha Rifles and Gilgit Scouts, 1943–47. Contested (C) Paddington North, 1953; MP (C) Bournemouth West, Feb. 1954–1983. Mem. House of Commons Select Cttee on Estimates, 1962–64; Vice-Chm., Conservative Parly Defence Cttee, 1963–66 (formerly: Chm., Defence Air Sub-Cttee; Hon. Sec., Space Sub-Cttee); Vice-Chm., Aviation Cttee, 1963–64; Additional Opposition Front Bench Spokesman for Defence, 1964–66; Jt Vice-Chm., Cons. Parly Trade and Power Cttee, 1966–68; Opposition Front Bench Spokesman for Power, 1968–70; Minister of State, Min. of Technology, June–Oct. 1970; Minister for Industry, DTI, 1970–72; Minister of Posts and Telecommunications, 1972–74; Mem., Expenditure Cttee, 1974–76; Chairman: House of Commons Select Cttee on European Legislation, 1976–79; Home Affairs Cttee, 1981–83. Mem., H of L, 1983–2015. Vice-Chm., Assoc. of Conservative Clubs Ltd, 1964–67, Hon. Life Vice-Pres., 1970–; President: Wessex Area Council, Nat. Union of Conservative and Unionist Assocs, 1974–77; Wessex Area Young Conservatives, 1978–80. UK Deleg. to Council of Europe and to Western European Union, 1960–62; Mem., NATO Parliamentarians' Conf., 1962–66. Chm., Royal Armouries, 1986–94. Chairman: WonderWorld plc, 1982–98; Gamlestaden plc, 1987–92; Bricom Gp, 1990–93. Pres., Independent Schs Assoc., 1969–71; a Vice-Pres., Nat. Chamber of Trade, 1974–86; Vice-Pres., Internat. Tree Foundn (formerly The Men of the Trees), 1953–98. Hon. Vice-Pres., Nat. Assoc. of Master Bakers, Confectioners & Caterers, 1978–82. Chm., British Lebanese Assoc., 1990–98. *Heir* (to baronetcies only): *s* Hon. Robert Frederick Calvert Eden, *b* 30 April 1964. *Clubs:* Boodle's, Pratt's.

EDEN, Prof. Colin L., PhD; Professor of Management Science and Strategic Management, Associate Dean and Director, International Division, Strathclyde Business School, University of Strathclyde, since 2006; *b* 24 Dec. 1943; *s* of John and Connie Eden; *m* 1967, Christine. *Educ:* Univ. of Leicester (BSc); Univ. of Southampton (PhD). Operational Researcher, then Operational Res. Manager, then Mgt Cons., 1967–73; Lectr, then Sen. Lectr, then Reader, Sch. of Mgt, Univ. of Bath, 1974–87; Prof., Business Sch., 1988–99, Dir, Grad. Sch. of Business, 1999–2006, Univ. of Strathclyde. Advr, SHEFC; Mem., Mgt Bd, Scottish Exams Bd and Scottish Qualifications Authy. *Publications:* Management Decision and Decision Analysis, 1976; Thinking in Organizations, 1979; Messing About in Problems, 1983; Tackling Strategic Problems, 1990; Managerial and Organizational Cognition, 1998; Making Strategy, 1998; Visible Thinking, 2004; Practice of Making Strategy, 2005; over 170 papers in learned jls. *Recreations:* sailing, ski-ing, walking. *Address:* (office) 199 Cathedral Street, Glasgow G4 0QU. *Club:* Clyde Cruising.

EDEN, (Geoffrey) Philip, FRMetS; Trustee and Director, Chilterns Observatory Trust, since 2007; *b* 14 July 1951; *s* of late Edmund Benham Eden and Céline Eden (*née* Malpeyre). *Educ:* Luton Grammar Sch.; Luton Sixth Form Coll.; Univ. of Birmingham (BA 1972; MSc 1973). FRMetS 1980. Meteorologist, Univ. of Birmingham, 1973–76; Forecaster, IMCOS Marine Ltd, 1976–81; Principal Meteorologist, Noble Denton and Associates, 1981–86; Proprietor, Philip Eden Weather Consultancy, 1983–; Weather Presenter: LBC, 1983–93; BBC Radio 5 Live, 1994–; Weather Correspondent: Sunday Telegraph, 1986–; Daily Telegraph, 1998–2012; Wisden Cricketers' Almanack, 1999–. Mem., Cttee to Review Weather Extremes, World Meteorological Orgn, 2011–12. Royal Meteorological Society: Life Mem., 1993; Council Mem., 1987–90 and 2007–09; Hon. Press Officer, 1990–2007; Vice-Pres., 2007–09; Michael Hunt Award, 1993; Gordon Manley Weather Prize, 2001 and 2010. Council Mem. and Hon. Meteorology Sec., Hampstead Scientific Soc., 1983–. *Publications:* Weatherwise, 1995; Weather Facts, 1995; The Secrets of the Weather, 1997; Flood, 2000; Daily Telegraph Book of the Weather, 2003; Change in the Weather, 2005; Great British Weather Disasters, 2008; contrib. meteorological jls. *Recreations:* cricket, classical music, musicals, France, cutting down trees. *Address:* Observatory Lodge, The Green, Whipsnade, Dunstable LU6 2LG. *T:* (01582) 872226. *E:* philip@weather-uk.com. *Clubs:* Warwickshire County Cricket; MG Owners'.

EDEN, Prof. Osborn Bryan, (Tim), FRCPE, FRCP, FRCPath, FRCPCH, FRCR; CRUK (formerly CRC) Professor of Paediatric Oncology, 1994–2005, Teenage Cancer Trust Professor of Teenage and Young Adult Cancer, 2005–08, Hon. Professor, 2008–10, now Professor Emeritus of Paediatric and Adolescent Oncology, University of Manchester; Medical Adviser: Teenage Cancer Trust UK, 2005–10; Teenage Cancer Trust in Scotland, 2010–12; *b* 2 April 1947; *s* of late Eric Victor Eden and Gwendoline Eden (*née* Hambly); *m* 1970, Randi Forsgren; one *s* one *d*. *Educ:* University Coll. London (MB BS 1970). DRCOG 1972; FRCPE 1983; FRCP 1992 (MRCP 1974); FRCPath 1995; FRCPCH 1997; FRCR 2007. House physician, UCH, 1970–71; house surgeon, Portsmouth, 1971; Sen. House Officer appts, IoW, UCH, Simpson Meml Pavilion and Royal Hosp. for Sick Children,

Edinburgh, 1971–73; Registrar, Paediatrics and Haematology, Royal Hosp. for Sick Children, Edinburgh, 1974–76; Fellow, Stanford Univ., Calif., 1976–77; Leukaemia Res. Fellow, Edinburgh, 1977–78; Lectr, Edinburgh Univ., 1978–79; Consultant Clinical Haematologist, Bristol Children's Hosp., 1979–82; Consultant Paediatric Haematologist and Oncologist, Royal Hosp. for Sick Children, Edinburgh, 1982–91; Prof. of Paediatric Oncology, St Bartholomew's Hosp., 1991–94; Lead Clinician, Paediatric Oncology, Royal Manchester Children's Hosp., 1994–2007; Lead Clinician, Teenage Cancer Trust Young Oncology Unit, Christie Hosp. NHS Trust, 1994–2007; Hon. Consultant, Central Manchester and Manchester Children's Univ. Hosps NHS Trust, 1994–2007. Chm., UK Children's Cancer Study Gp, 1989–92 (Chm., Haematology Oncology Div., 2000–06); Member: MRC Childhood Leukaemia Working Party, 1978–2008 (Chm., 1991–2000); MRC Leukaemia Steering Cttee, 1991–2002; Cttee on Med. Effects of Radiation in the Envmt, 1991–2003; Clin. Trials Cttee, CRC, 1998–2002; Med. and Scientific Panel and Clin. Trials Cttee, Leukaemia Res. Fund, 2000–04; Clinical Trials Adv. and Awards Cttee, MRC/CRUK, 2002–04; Clinical and Translational Res. Cttee, CRUK, 2007–10; Scottish Ministerial Steering Gp on Chronic Pain, 2015–. Pres., Internat. Soc. of Paediatric Oncology, 2004–07 (Chm., Scientific Cttee, 1996–99); Hon. Treas., Genetics Section, RSocMed, 2003–04 (Hon. Sec., 2001–03). Non-exec. Dir, Manchester Children's Hosps NHS Trust, 1996–2001. Med. Advr and Founding Mem., Over the Wall Gang Camp, 2001–08. Trustee, Malcolm Sargent Cancer Fund, 1985–95; Founding Medic, World Child Cancer (formerly World Child Cancer Foundn), 2007– (Trustee, 2007–12; Med. Patron, 2012–; Volunteer Advr and Mentor, 2012–); Chm., World Child Cancer Global, 2013–14. Paediatric Advr, AfrOx, 2008–. Faculty Associate, Brooks Poverty Inst., Univ. of Manchester, 2008–. Hon. Mem., Burma Med. Assoc., 1985. *Publications:* over 300 scientific papers, editorials and chapters on paediatric and adolescent haematology and oncology. *Recreations:* development of overseas aid projects, my family, writing, travelling, reading. *Address:* 5 South Gillsland Road, Edinburgh EH10 5DE.

EDEN, Philip; *see* Eden, G. P.

EDEN, Prof. Richard John, OBE 1978; Professor of Energy Studies, Cavendish Laboratory, University of Cambridge, 1982–89, now Emeritus; Fellow of Clare Hall, Cambridge, 1966–89, now Emeritus (Vice-President, 1987–89; Hon. Fellow, 1993); *b* 2 July 1922; *s* of James A. Eden and Dora M. Eden; *m* 1949, Elsie Jane Greaves; one *s* one *d* and one step *d*. *Educ:* Hertford Grammar Sch.; Peterhouse, Cambridge (BA 1943, MA 1948, PhD 1951). War service, 1942–46, Captain REME, Airborne Forces. Cambridge University: Bye-Fellow, Peterhouse, 1949–50; Stokes Student, Pembroke Coll., 1950–51; Clare College: Research Fellow, 1951–55; Official Fellow, 1957–66; Dir of Studies in Maths, 1951–53, 1957–62; Royal Soc. Smithson Res. Fellow, 1952–55; Sen. Lectr in Physics, Univ. of Manchester, 1955–57; Cambridge University: Lectr in Maths, 1957–64 (Stokes Lectr, 1962); Reader in Theoretical Physics, 1964–82; Head of High Energy Theoretical Physics Gp, 1964–74, Hd of Energy Res. Gp, 1974–89, Cavendish Lab. Mem., Princeton Inst. for Advanced Study, 1954, 1959, 1973, 1989; Visiting Scientist: Indiana Univ., 1954–55; Univ. of California, Berkeley, 1960, 1967; Visiting Professor: Univ. of Maryland, 1961, 1965; Columbia Univ., 1962; Scuola Normale Superiore, Pisa, 1964; Univ. of Marseilles, 1968; Univ. of California, 1969. Member: UK Adv. Council on Energy Conservation, 1974–83; Eastern Electricity Bd, 1985–93; Energy Adviser to UK NEDO, 1974–75. Syndic, CUP, 1984–95. Chm., Cambridge Energy Res. Ltd, subseq. Caminus Energy Ltd, 1985–91. Companion, Inst. of Energy, 1985. Smiths Prize, Univ. of Cambridge, 1949; Maxwell Prize and Medal, Inst. of Physics, 1970; Open Award for Distinction in Energy Economics, BIEE, 1989. *Publications:* (jtly) The Analytic S Matrix, 1966; High Energy Collisions of Elementary Particles, 1967; Energy Conservation in the United Kingdom (NEDO report), 1975; Energy Prospects (Dept of Energy report), 1976; World Energy Demand to 2020 (World Energy Conf. report), 1977; (jtly) Energy Economics, 1981; (jtly) Electricity's Contribution to UK Energy Self Sufficiency, 1984; (jtly) UK Energy, 1984; Clare College and the Founding of Clare Hall, 1998; (jtly) Clare Hall 40, 2006; Clare Hall, 2009; Sometimes in Cambridge (memoirs), 2012; papers and review articles on nuclear physics and theory of elementary particles. *Recreations:* writing, painting, reading, gardening, travel. *Address:* Clare Hall, Cambridge CB3 9AL. *T:* (01223) 332360.

EDEN, Tim; *see* Eden, O. B.

EDENBOROUGH, Dr Michael Simon; QC 2010; barrister. *Educ:* Sidney Sussex Coll., Cambridge (MA Natural Scis); Exeter Coll., Oxford (MSc Bio-organic Chem.; DPhil Biophysics). Called to the Bar, Middle Temple, 1992; in practice as barrister, specialising in intellectual property law, 1994–. *Publications:* Organic Reaction Mechanisms: a step by step approach, 1994, 2nd edn 1999; Lecture Notes on Intellectual Property Law, 1995. *Address:* Serle Court, Lincoln's Inn, WC2A 3QS.

EDER, Prof. Andrew Howard Eric, FDS RCSE; Professor of Restorative Dentistry and Dental Education, UCL Eastman Dental Institute, since 2008, and Pro-Vice-Provost (Life Learning), since 2013, University College London; Hon. Consultant in Restorative Dentistry, UCLH Foundation Trust, since 2002; Clinical Director, Specialist Dental Care and London Tooth Wear Centre, since 1998; *b* London, 21 April 1964; *s* of Hans and Helga Eder; *m* 1988, Rosina Jayne Saideman; two *s* one *d*. *Educ:* St Paul's Sch.; King's Coll. Sch. of Medicine and Dentistry (BDS 1986); LDS RCS 1987; Eastman Dental Inst., Univ. of London (MSc 1990). MFGDP 1993; MRD RCS RCPSG 1994; FDS RCSE 2003. KCH School of Medicine and Dentistry: Hse Officer, Paediatric, Orthodontic and Restorative Dentistry, 1987–88; Clin. Asst in Restorative Dentistry, 1988–89; Eastman Dental Hospital: Registrar in Restorative Dentistry, 1990–91; Associate Specialist in Restorative Dentistry, 1998–2002; Eastman Dental Institute, subseq. UCL Eastman Dental Institute: Clin. Lectr, 1991–94, Sen. Clin. Lectr, 1995–2002, in Restorative Dentistry; Dir, Continuing Professional Develt, 2002–12; Dir, Educn, 2005–12; Associate Dean for Continuing Educn, Sch. of Life and Med. Scis, UCL, 2008–12. Specialist in Restorative Dentistry and Prosthodontics, 1998–. Member, Editorial Advisory Board: Eur. Jl Restorative Dentistry and Prosthodontics, 1995–; Private Dentistry, 1997–; British Dental Jl, 2005–13 (Academic Lead for CPD, 2014–); Premium Practice Dentistry, 2011–14 (Chm., 2011–14); Dental Tribune, 2011–. President: Alpha Omega, 1994–95 (Chm. Trustees, 2003–); Dental Section, RSocMed, 2001–02; British Soc. for Restorative Dentistry, 2005–06. FHEA 2002. *Publications:* (ed jtly) Tooth Surface Loss, 2000; contrib. chapters in textbooks and articles to academic jls. *Recreations:* tennis, swimming, ski-ing. *Address:* UCL Life Learning, The Network Building, 97 Tottenham Court Road, W1T 4TP. *T:* (020) 7679 9358, 9353. *E:* a.eder@ucl.ac.uk; 57A Wimpole Street, W1G 8YP. *T:* (020) 7486 7180. *E:* andreweder@restorative-dentistry.co.uk.

See also Hon. Sir H. B. Eder.

EDER, Hon. Sir (Henry) Bernard, Kt 2011; a Judge of the High Court, Queen's Bench Division, 2011–15; *b* 16 Oct. 1952; *s* of Hans and Helga Eder; *m* 2008, Claire Green; four *s* one *d* by a former marriage. *Educ:* Haberdashers' Aske's School, Elstree; Downing College, Cambridge (BA 1974). Called to the Bar, Inner Temple, 1975, Bencher, 2007; QC 1990; an Asst Recorder, 1996–2000; a Recorder, 2000–01. Vis. Prof., UCL, 1999–2003. *Publications:* Jt Ed., Scrutton on Charterparties, 22nd edn, 2011. *Recreations:* tennis, ski-ing.

See also A. H. E. Eder.

EDES, (John) Michael, CMG 1981; HM Diplomatic Service, retired; Ambassador and Head, UK Delegation to Conventional Arms Control Negotiations, Vienna, 1989–90; *b* 19 April 1930; *s* of late Lt-Col N. H. Edes and Mrs Louise Edes; *m* 1978, Angela Mermagen; two *s*. *Educ:* Blundell's Sch.; Clare Coll., Cambridge (Scholar; BA); Yale Univ. (MA). HM Forces, 1948–49; Mellon Fellow, Yale Univ., 1952–54; FO, 1954; MECAS, 1955; Dubai, 1956–57; FO, 1957–59 (Moscow, 1959); Rome, 1959–61; FO, 1961–62; UK Delegn to Conf. on Disarmament, Geneva, 1962–65 (UK Mission to UN, NY, 1963); FO, 1965–68; Cabinet Office, 1968–69; FCO, 1969–71; Ambassador to Yemen Arab Republic, 1971–73; Mem., UK Delegn to CSCE, Geneva, 1973–74; FCO, 1974–77; RIIA, 1977–78; Paris, 1978–79; Ambassador to Libya, 1980–83; Hd, UK Delegn to Conf. on Confidence and Security Building Measures and Disarmament in Europe, Stockholm, 1983–86; Hd, UK team at conventional arms control mandate talks, 1987–89. Vis. Fellow, IISS, 1987. *Recreations:* listening to music, gardening. *Address:* c/o Lloyds Bank, Cox's & King's Branch, 8–10 Waterloo Place, SW1Y 4BE. *Clubs:* Athenæum; Hawks (Cambridge).

EDEY, Philip David; QC 2009; *b* Johannesburg, SA, 23 Feb. 1971; *s* of Russell and Celia Edey; *m* 1999, Alison Baxter; three *s*. *Educ:* Eton Coll.; Lady Margaret Hall, Oxford (BA 1st Cl. Juris. 1993; MA). Called to the Bar, Gray's Inn, 1994. Chm. of Govs, Ludgrove Sch., 2013–. *Recreations:* Real Tennis, lawn tennis, golf, wine. *Address:* 20 Essex Street, WC2R 3AL. *T:* (020) 7842 1200. *Clubs:* Queen's, Garrick, Jesters; Vincents (Oxford).

EDGAR, (Christopher) George, OBE 2011; HM Diplomatic Service; Ambassador to Uzbekistan, 2012–15; *b* 21 April 1960; *s* of Dr William Macreadie Edgar and Dr Freda Elizabeth Edgar; *m* 1994, Elena Ryurikovna Nagornichnykh; two *d*. *Educ:* Trinity Coll., Cambridge Univ. (MA Philosophy); Open Univ. (MA Envmt, Policy and Society). FCO, 1981–83; Moscow, 1984–85; Lagos, 1986–88; FCO, 1988–92; resigned 1992, reinstated 1995; FCO, 1995–97; Ambassador to Cambodia, 1997–2000; Ambassador to Macedonia, 2001–04; Consul Gen., St Petersburg, 2004–06; Envoy for Climate Security in Africa, FCO, 2006–07; Head: Consular Assistance Gp, FCO, 2007–10; Papal Visit Team, FCO, 2010; Chargé d'Affaires, Holy See, 2011; Additional Dir, Protocol Directorate, FCO, 2011–12. *Recreation:* music. *Address:* c/o Foreign and Commonwealth Office, King Charles Street, SW1A 2AH.

EDGAR, David Burman; author and playwright; Chair, MA in Playwriting Studies, 1989–99, Hon. Professor, since 1992, University of Birmingham; *b* 26 Feb. 1948; *s* of late Barrie Edgar and Joan (*née* Burman); *m* 1st, 1979, Eve Brook (*d* 1998); two *s*; 2nd, 2012, Stephanie Dale. *Educ:* Oundle Sch.; Univ. of Manchester (BA 1969). FRSL. Fellow in Creative Writing, Leeds Polytechnic, 1972–74; Resident Playwright, Birmingham Rep. Theatre, 1974–75, Board Mem., 1985–; UK/US Bicentennial Arts Fellow, USA, 1978–79; Literary Consultant, 1984–88, Hon. Associate Artist, 1989, RSC; Hon. Sen. Res. Fellow, 1988–92, Prof. of Playwriting Studies, 1995–99, Birmingham Univ.; Humanitas Vis. Prof. of Playwriting, Univ. of Oxford, 2014–15. Hon. Fellow, Birmingham Polytechnic, 1991; Judith E. Wilson Fellow, Clare Hall, Cambridge, 1996. Hon. MA Bradford, 1984; DUniv Surrey, 1993; Hon. DLitt: Birmingham, 2002; Warwick, 2012. *Plays:* The National Interest, 1971; Excuses Excuses, Coventry, 1972; Death Story, Birmingham Rep., 1972; Baby Love, 1973; The Dunkirk Spirit, 1974; Dick Deterred, Bush Theatre, 1974; O Fair Jerusalem, Birmingham Rep., 1975; Saigon Rose, Edinburgh, 1976; Blood Sports, incl. Ball Boys, Bush Theatre, 1976; Destiny, Other Place, 1976, Aldwych, 1977; Wreckers, 1977; Our Own People, 1977; (adaptation) The Jail Diary of Albie Sachs, Warehouse Theatre, 1978; (adaptation) Mary Barnes, Birmingham Rep., then Royal Court, 1978–79; (with Susan Todd) Teendreams, 1979; (adaptation) Nicholas Nickleby, Aldwych, 1980, Plymouth Theatre, NY, 1981; Maydays, Barbican, 1983; Entertaining Strangers, 1985, Nat. Theatre, 1987; That Summer, Hampstead, 1987; (with Stephen Bill and Anne Devlin) Heartlanders, Birmingham Rep., 1989; The Shape of the Table, NT, 1990; (adaptation) Dr Jekyll and Mr Hyde, Barbican, 1991; Pentecost, Other Place, 1994, Young Vic, 1995; (adaptation) Albert Speer, NT, 2000; The Prisoner's Dilemma, RSC, 2001; Continental Divide (2 play cycle, Daughters of the Revolution, and Mothers Against), Oregon Shakespeare Fest./Berkeley Rep., 2003, Barbican, 2004; (trans.) The Life of Galileo, Birmingham Rep.; Playing with Fire, NT, 2005; Testing the Echo, Out of Joint (tour), 2008; Black Tulips (part of The Great Game), Tricycle Th., 2009–10; (adaptation) Arthur & George, Birmingham Rep., 2010; (translation) The Master Builder, Chichester Th., 2010; Written on the Heart, RSC, 2011, transf. Duchess, 2012; Concerning Faith (part of Sixty-Six Books), Bush Th., 2011; If Only, Minerva, Chichester, 2013; *TV and radio:* The Eagle has Landed, 1973; Sanctuary, 1973; I know what I meant, 1974; Ecclesiastes, 1977; (with Neil Grant) Vote for Them, 1989; A Movie Starring Me, 1991; Buying a Landslide, 1992; Citizen Locke, 1994; Talking to Mars, 1996; (adaptation) The Secret Parts, 2000; Brave Faces, 2006; Something Wrong about the Mouth, 2007; *film:* Lady Jane, 1986. *Publications:* Destiny, 1976; Wreckers, 1977; The Jail Diary of Albie Sachs, 1978; Teendreams, 1979; Mary Barnes, 1979; Nicholas Nickleby, 1982; Maydays, 1983; Entertaining Strangers, 1985; Plays One, 1987; That Summer, 1987; The Second Time as Farce, 1988; Vote for Them, 1989; Heartlanders, 1989; Edgar Shorts, 1990; Plays Two, 1990; The Shape of the Table, 1990; Plays Three, 1991; Dr Jekyll and Mr Hyde, 1992; Pentecost, 1995; (ed) State of Play, 1999; Albert Speer, 2000; The Prisoner's Dilemma, 2001; Continental Divide, 2004; Playing with Fire, 2005; (with Stephanie Dale) A Time to Keep, 2007; Testing the Echo, 2008; How Plays Work: a practical guide to playwriting, 2009; contrib. Black Tulips, in The Great Game, 2009; Arthur & George, 2010; The Master Builder, 2010; contrib. Concerning Faith, in Sixty-Six Books, 2011; Written on the Heart, 2011; If Only, 2012. *Recreation:* correspondence. *Address:* c/o Alan Brodie Representation, Paddock Suite, The Courtyard, 55 Charterhouse Street, EC1M 6HA. *T:* (020) 7253 6226.

EDGAR, George; *see* Edgar, C. G.

EDGAR, Pauline Claire; Principal, Queenswood School, since 2006; *b* Birmingham, 13 March 1956; *d* of Peter Brown and Christine Brown; *m* 1982, Hamish Edgar; two *s* one *d*. *Educ:* Dudley Girls' High Sch.; Bedford Coll., Univ. of London (BA Hons); Inst. of Educn, Univ. of London (PGCE). Hd, Sixth Form and Hd, History and Politics, Francis Holland Sch., NW1, 1988–2006. *Recreations:* travel, reading, galleries, swimming. *Address:* Queenswood, Shepherd's Way, Brookmans Park, Hatfield AL9 6NS. *T:* (01707) 602500. *E:* pauline.edgar@queenswood.org. *Clubs:* University Women's, Lansdowne.

EDGAR, William, CBE 2004; FREng, FIMechE; FRSE; Group Director, John Wood Group plc, 1995–2004; Chairman and Chief Executive, Wood Group Engineering Ltd, 1995–2004; Chairman, J. P. Kenny Engineering Ltd, 1995–2004; *b* 16 Jan. 1938; *s* of William Edgar and Alice Anderson McKerrell; *m* 1961, June Gilmour; two *s*. *Educ:* Royal Coll. of Science and Technology (Strathclyde Univ.); ARCST 1961; Birmingham Univ. (MSc 1962). CEng, FIMechE 1979. Develt Engr, BSC, Motherwell and Glasgow, 1954–62; Principal Aeromech. Engr, BAC, Warton, 1963–67; Chief Develt Engr, Gen. Manager Sales and Service, Gen. Works Manager, Weir Pumps, Glasgow, 1967–73; Chief Exec., Seaforth Engineering and Corporate Develt Dir, Seaforth Maritime, Aberdeen, 1973–86; Business Develt Dir, Vickers Marine Engineering, Edinburgh, 1986–88; Exec. Chm., Cochrane Shipbuilders, Yorks, 1988–90; Chief Exec., Nat. Engrg Lab., 1990–95. Chairman: European Marine Energy Centre, 2005–14; Subsea UK Ltd, 2005–; Nat. Subsea Res. Inst., 2009–14; non-exec. Dir, Online Electronics Ltd, 2008–. Vis. Prof., Strathclyde Univ., 2001–14. Chm., Offshore Contractors Assoc., 2000–03; Pres., IMechE, 2004–05 (Dep. Pres., 2002–04; Chm., Scottish Br., 1996–98). FREng 1999; FRSE 2003. Hon. FIMechE 2009. Liveryman, Engineers' Co., 2006–. Hon. DSc Aberdeen, 2009. *Recreations:* golf, walking, reading, soccer. *Club:* Sloane.

EDGAR-JONES, Philip; Director, Sky Arts, since 2014; *b* Leeds, 13 July 1966; *s* of Edward Jones and Isabella Jones (*née* Macpherson); *m* 1990, Wendy Edgar; one *d*. *Educ:* Royal High Sch., Edinburgh; Queen Margaret Coll., Edinburgh (BA Hons Communication Studies). Journalist, Sky Mag., 1988–90; freelance sub-editor, 1990–92; presenter, Moviewatch, 1992; Series Editor: The Big Breakfast, 1993–96; Jack Docherty Show, 1996–97; The Priory, 1998–2000; Exec. Producer, Big Brother, 2000–11; Hd of Entertainment, BSkyB, 2012–14. *Recreations:* drums, guitar, piano, composition, reading, theatre, ballet, rock 'n' roll, gardening, chuckling, eating, walking, writing, cooking. *Address:* BSkyB, Grant Way, Isleworth, Middx TW7 5QD. *T:* 07725 235644. *E:* philip.edgar-jones@sky.uk.

EDGAR-WILSON, Jennifer Chase; *see* Barnes, J. C.

EDGCUMBE, family name of **Earl of Mount Edgcumbe**.

EDGE, Geoffrey; Managing Director, Geonomics Ltd, since 2007; *b* 26 May 1943; single. *Educ:* London Sch. of Econs (BA); Birmingham Univ. Asst Lectr in Geography, Univ. of Leicester, 1967–70; Lectr in Geog., Open Univ., 1970–74. Member: Bletchley UDC, 1972–74 (Chm. Planning Sub-cttee 1973–74); Milton Keynes DC, 1973–76 (Vice-Chm. Planning Cttee, 1973–75); Bucks Water Bd, 1973–74; W Midlands CC, 1981–86 (Chm., Econ. Develt Cttee); Walsall MBC, 1983–90 (Leader, 1988–90). MP (Lab) Aldridge-Brownhills, Feb. 1974–1979; PPS to Minister of State for Educn, Feb.–Oct. 1974, 1976–77, to Minister of State, Privy Council Office, Oct. 1974–1976. Research Fellow, Dept of Planning Landscape, Birmingham Polytechnic, 1979–80; Senior Research Fellow: Preston Polytechnic, 1980–81; NE London Polytechnic, 1982–84; Hon. Res. Fellow, Birmingham Polytechnic, 1980–81; New Initiatives Co-ordinator, COPEC Housing Trust, 1984–87; Sen. Associate, P-E Inbucon, then P-E Internat., 1987–97. Chm., West Midlands Enterprise Ltd, 1982–2007; Associate Dir, W. S. Atkins plc, 1997–99; Dir, Winning Pitch plc, 2007–09. *Publications:* (ed jtly) Regional Analysis and Development, 1973; Open Univ. booklets on industrial location and urban development. *Recreations:* music, reading, touring. *Address:* 5 Sedgefield Close, Dudley DY1 2UU.

EDGE, Prof. Kevin Anthony, PhD, DSc; CEng, FREng, FIMechE; Professor of Mechanical Engineering, 1991–2015, now Emeritus, and Deputy Vice-Chancellor, 2008–15, University of Bath; *b* 1 July 1949; *s* of George and Marion Edge; *m* 2008, Delyth Ann Davies. *Educ:* Univ. of Bath (BSc 1971; PhD 1975; DSc 1995). CEng 1982; FIMechE 1990. Sen. Control Systems Engr, Rolls Royce Ltd, 1974–76; University of Bath: Res. Officer, 1976; Lectr, 1976–87; Sen. Lectr, 1987–91; Reader, 1991; Dep. Dir, Centre for Power Transmission and Motion Control, 1993–2008; Hd, Mech. Engrg, 1997–2003; Pro-Vice-Chancellor (Research), 2003–08. FREng 2003. *Publications:* papers in professional jls. *Recreations:* classical music, photography. *Address:* University of Bath, Claverton Down, Bath BA2 7AY. *E:* k.a.edge@bath.ac.uk.

EDGE, Captain Sir (Philip) Malcolm, KCVO 1995; FNI; Deputy Master and Chairman, Board of Trinity House, 1988–96; *b* 15 July 1931; *s* of Stanley Weston Edge and Edith Edge (*née* Liddell); *m* 1st, 1967, (Kathleen) Anne Greenwood (*d* 1994); one *s* one *d*; 2nd, 2003, Carol Mann. *Educ:* Rock Ferry High School; HMS Conway. Master Mariner. Apprenticed to Shipping subsidiary of British Petroleum, 1949, and served in all ranks; in command, world wide, 1969–78. Elder Brother and Mem. Board, Trinity House, 1978; Mem., PLA, 1980–97. Dir, Standard Steamship Owners' Protection & Indemnity Assoc. Ltd, 1988–97 (Chm., 1992–97). Mem. Council, Internat. Assoc. of Lighthouse Authies, 1988–96 (Pres., 1988–90). Freeman, City of London, 1980; Liveryman: Hon. Co. of Master Mariners, 1980–; Shipwrights' Co., 1990–2006; Master, Watermen and Lightermen's Co., 1996–97. *Recreations:* sailing, family. *Address:* c/o Trinity House, Tower Hill, EC3N 4DH. *T:* (020) 7481 6900. *Clubs:* Royal Yacht Squadron (Hon.); Royal Lymington Yacht; The Cachalots (Hon.) (Southampton).

EDGE, Stephen Martin; Corporate Tax Partner, Slaughter and May, since 1982; *b* Farnworth, Lancs, 29 Nov. 1950; *s* of late Harry Edge and Mary Edge; *m* 1975, Melanie Lawler; two *d*. *Educ:* Canon Slade Grammar Sch., Bolton; Exeter Univ. (LLB Hons). Admitted solicitor, 1975; joined Slaughter and May, 1973 (Mem., Partnership Bd, 1986–2011). Mem., Practice Council, Internat. Tax Adv. Prog., Sch. of Law, New York Univ., 2011–. Non-exec. Dir, Bournemouth SO, 2013–. Mem., Alumni Network Gp (formerly Alumni and Develt Bd), Exeter Univ., 2004– (Chm., 2014–). Vice President: Lancs Cricket Fedn, 1995–; Lancs CCC, 2011–; Pres., Amberley CC, 2000–. Hon. LLD Exeter, 2012. *Publications:* contrib. to tax pubns. *Recreations:* walking, golf, theatre, watching cricket and soccer. *Address:* Slaughter and May, 1 Bunhill Row, EC1Y 8YY. *T:* (020) 7600 1200, *Fax:* (020) 7090 5000. *E:* steve.edge@slaughterandmay.com. *Club:* MCC.

EDGE, William, (3rd Bt *cr* 1937); *S* father, 1984, but does not use the title and his name does not appear on the Official Roll of the Baronetage. *Heir:* *s* Edward Knowles Edge.

EDGINGTON, Prof. Dorothy Margaret Doig, FBA 2005; Senior Research Fellow, Department (formerly School) of Philosophy, Birkbeck, University of London, since 2006; *b* 29 April 1941; *d* of late Edward Milne and of Rhoda Milne (*née* Blair); *m* 1965, John Edgington; one *s* (one *d* decd). *Educ:* St Leonards Sch., St Andrews; St Hilda's Coll., Oxford (BA 1964; Hon. Fellow, 2004); Nuffield Coll., Oxford (BPhil 1967). Lectr in Philosophy, 1968–90, Sen. Lectr, 1990–96, Birkbeck Coll., London Univ.; Prof. of Philosophy, Oxford Univ., and Fellow of UC, Oxford, 1996–2001; Prof. of Philosophy, Birkbeck Coll., London Univ., 2001–03; Waynflete Prof. of Metaphysical Philosophy, Univ. of Oxford, 2003–06, now Emeritus, and Fellow of Magdalen Coll., Oxford, 2003–06. British Acad. Res. Reader in the Humanities, 1992–94; visiting posts: Univ. of British Columbia, 1974–75, 1990, 1992; Univ. Nacional Autónoma de México, 1985, 1988, 1990, 1995; Princeton Univ., 1986; Univ. of Calif, Berkeley, 1993. Pres., Mind Assoc., 2004–05. Hon. Sec., 1986–92, Pres., 2007–08, Aristotelian Soc. (Ed., Proc. of Aristotelian Soc., 1986–90). *Publications:* contrib. anthologies, and learned jls incl. Analysis, British Jl for Philos. of Sci., Crítica, Mind, Proc. of Aristotelian Soc., Revista Latinoamericana de Filosofía. *Address:* Department of Philosophy, Birkbeck, University of London, Malet Street, WC1E 7HX.

EDINBURGH, Bishop of, since 2012; **Rt Rev. Dr John Andrew Armes;** *b* London, 10 Sept. 1955; *m* 1983, Clare; one *s* three *d*. *Educ:* Sidney Sussex Coll., Cambridge (BA 1977; MA 1981); Manchester Univ. (PhD 1996); Sarum and Wells Theol Coll. Ordained deacon, 1979, priest, 1980; Asst Curate, St Mary the Virgin, Walney Island, 1979–82; Chaplain to Agriculture, Dio. of Carlisle, 1982–86; Chaplain, Manchester Univ., 1986–94; Priest-in-charge, St Mary and All Saints, Goodshaw and St John's Crawshawbooth, 1994–98; Area Dean, Rossendale, 1994–98; Rector, St John the Evangelist, Edinburgh, 1998–2012; Dean of Edinburgh, 2010–12. *Recreations:* cinema, theatre, travel, watching sport, walking, writing unpublishable novels. *Address:* Diocesan Office, 21a Grosvenor Crescent, Edinburgh EH12 5EL. *T:* (0131) 538 7044.

EDINBURGH, Dean of; *see* Macdonald, Very Rev. S. E.

EDINBURGH, (St Mary's Cathedral), Provost of; *see* Forbes, Very Rev. G. J. T.

EDINGTON, (George) Gordon, CBE 2007; FRICS; an Ambassador (formerly Vice-President), Action for Children (formerly NCH, the Children's Charity), since 1998 (Chair of Trustees, 2001–07); *b* 7 Sept. 1945; *s* of George Adam Edington and Phyllis Mary (*née* Allan); *m* 1st, 1973, Jane Mary Adie (marr. diss. 2007); four *s*; 2nd, 2013, Paula Carrington Edmunds. *Educ:* St Mary's Sch., Kenya; St Lawrence Coll., Kent. FRICS 1970. Man. Dir, Lynton plc, 1981–94; Director: BAA plc, 1991–99; Lend Lease Corp., 1999–2013; Chm., Earls Court and Olympia Gp Ltd, 2000–01. Pres., British Property Fedn, 1998–99. Chairman: Michael Stuckey Trust, 1988–98; Public Art Develt Trust, 1992–98. Trustee: Tennis First Charitable Trust, 1999– (Chm., 2007–); Fulham Palace Trust, 2011– (Dep. Chm., 2011–); Dir and Trustee, Sponsoring Bd, Chobham Acad., Stratford, 2013–. Gov., Wilson Centre, Cambridge Internat. Land Inst., 1993–98. FRSA 1992; Mem., Henley Royal Regatta. Freeman, City of London, 1994; Liveryman, Chartered Surveyors' Co., 1994–. *Publications:* The Clowes Family of Chester Sporting Artists, 1985; Property Management: a customer focused approach, 1997; Gordon McLean Allan 1912–1942, 2014. *Recreations:* four sons, tennis, golf, fly fishing, hill walking, historic Thames rivercraft. *Address:* 78 Hotham Road, SW15 1QP. *E:* gordonedington@snowshill.co.uk. *Clubs:* Royal Wimbledon Golf; Riverside Racquets; Leander (Henley).

EDINGTON, Martin George Ritchie; Sheriff of Lothian and Borders at Livingston, since 2009 (at Linlithgow, 2007–09); *b* 28 Oct. 1955; *s* of George and Eva Edington; *m* 1979, Susan Jane Phillips; two *s*. *Educ:* Fettes Coll.; Dundee Univ. (LLB). NP 1981; WS 1985; Partner, Turnbull, Simson & Sturrock, WS, 1983–2001; Temp. Sheriff, 1999–2000; All-Scotland Floating Sheriff, 2001–03; Floating Sheriff at Linlithgow, 2003–07. *Recreations:* fine wines and whiskies, eating, travelling, curling, Rugby, cricket, making decisions. *Address:* Sheriff Court, Howden South Road, Livingston EH54 6FF. *T:* (01506) 402400, *Fax:* (01506) 415262.

EDIS, Hon. Sir Andrew (Jeremy Coulter), Kt 2014; **Hon. Mr Justice Edis;** a Judge of the High Court of Justice, Queen's Bench Division, since 2014; *b* 9 June 1957; *s* of late Dr Peter Marcus Edis and Barbara Louise Edis; *m* 1984, Sandy Wilkinson; one *s* two *d*. *Educ:* Liverpool Coll.; University Coll., Oxford (MA). Called to the Bar, Middle Temple, 1980, Bencher, 2004; Junior, Northern Circuit, 1983–84; Asst Recorder, 1994–99; QC 1997; Recorder, 1999–2014; Sen. Treasury Counsel, 2009–14; Dep. High Court Judge, 2001–14. Hd of Atlantic Chambers, 2000–06. *Recreations:* cricket, travel. *Address:* Royal Courts of Justice, Strand, WC2A 2LL. *Club:* Oxford and Cambridge.

See also A. W. B. Edis.

EDIS, (Angus) William (Butler); QC 2008; a Recorder, since 2003; *b* Liverpool, 15 June 1961; *s* of late Dr Peter Marcus Edis and Barbara Louise Edis; *m* 1996, Mary Elizabeth Pinder; two *s*. *Educ:* Liverpool Coll.; Trinity Coll., Oxford (BA Lit.Hum.; MA); City Univ. (Dip. Law). Called to the Bar, Lincoln's Inn, 1985; in practice, specialising in healthcare and disciplinary law. *Publications:* contribs to medico-legal jls. *Recreations:* family, football, bridge. *Address:* (chambers) 1 Crown Office Row, Temple, EC4Y 7HH. *T:* (020) 7797 7500, *Fax:* (020) 7797 7550. *Club:* Everton Football.

See also Hon. Sir A. J. C. Edis.

EDKINS, Dr Antony; Chief Executive, Landau Forte Charitable Trust, since 2014; *b* Hillingdon, 15 April 1969; *s* of Daisy Veronica Small, thereafter adopted and fostered; *m* 2007, Annette Mary Frances Rand; one *d* and one step *s* one step *d*. *Educ:* Univ. of Exeter (BA Hons); Ridley Hall, Cambridge (PGCE); Brunel Univ. (MEd; Postgrad. Dip.); Univ. of Leicester (MBA); Univ. of Sussex (EdD 2006); Coll. of Preceptors, London (ACP). Hd of RE, Westgate Sch., Slough, 1991–93; Hd of RE, Charters Sch., Sunningdale, 1993–96; Hd of Year and of Curriculum Develt, Longford Sch., Feltham, 1996–98; Dep. Headteacher, then Headteacher, Falmer High Sch., Brighton, 1998–2003; Hd, Secondary Sch. Improvement, E Sussex, 2003–04; Exec. Headteacher, Harrop Fold High Sch., Salford, 2004–10; Regl Exec., Exec. Principal and Sen. Partner, United Learning Trust, 2010–14. Hon. Asst Lectr, Univ. of Brighton and Brunel Univ., 1998–2004. Hon. Mem., Grenadier Guards Assoc., 2013. FCollP 1997; FRSA. *Publications:* contrib. articles on educnl leadership and on factors that cause educnl failure; book reviews for British Educnl Res. Jl and Educnl Mgt and Leadership Jl. *Recreations:* opera, gym. *Address:* Landau Forte Charitable Trust, Fox Street, Derby DE1 2LF. *T:* 07717 703944, (01332) 386766. *E:* aedkins@lfct.org.uk.

EDLESTON, Rear Adm. Hugh Anthony Harold Greswell; defence consultant to International Defence and Non-Governmental Organisations, since 2004; *b* 24 Jan. 1949; *s* of late Tony Edleston and of Dorothy Edleston; *m* 1973, Lynne Taylor; one *s* one *d*. *Educ:* Wellington Coll.; BRNC, Dartmouth. Qualified Advanced Warfare Officer (A), 1980; Ops Officer, HMS Glamorgan, Falklands War, 1981–83; pce 1983; CO, HMS Glasgow, 1986–88; Asst Dir, ME, MoD, 1992–95; jsdc 1993; Commanding Officer: HMS Exeter, 1996; HMS Cardiff, and Capt., Fifth Destroyer Sqdn, 1996–98; Dir, Corporate Communications (RN), MoD, 1998–2001; hcsc 2001; Comdr, UK Task Gp, 2001. Mil. Advr to High Rep., Sarajevo, 2002–04. Accredited OGC High Risk Review Team Leader, 2007–. MNI 1991; ACMI (AMBIM 1991); AIPR 2000. Freeman, City of London, 2000; Liveryman, Co. of Carmen, 1998–2008. *Recreations:* blues and jazz music, classic cars, crosswords. *E:* huedles@hotmail.com. *Club:* Liberal.

EDMISTON, family name of **Baron Edmiston**.

EDMISTON, Baron *cr* 2011 (Life Peer), of Lapworth in the County of Warwickshire; **Robert Norman Edmiston;** Chairman, IM Group Ltd, since 1988; *b* New Delhi, India, 6 Oct. 1946; *s* of Vivian Edmiston and Norma Margaret Mary Edmiston (*née* Grostate); *m* 1998, Tracie Jacqueline Spicer; one *s* two *d* by a former marriage. *Educ:* Abbs Cross Technical High Sch., Hornchurch; Barking Regl Coll. of Technol. ACMA 1974, FCMA 1991. Bank Clerk, English, Scottish and Australian Bank, 1964–66; Treasury Clerk, Chrysler International SA Treasury, 1966–67; Financial Analyst, Ford Motor Co., 1967–70; Chrysler (UK) Ltd: Sen. Analyst, 1970–71; Capital Planning Manager, 1971–72; Economic Res. Analyst, 1972; Manager, Financial Analysis and Admin, 1972–74; Financial Controller and Co. Sec., 1974–75, Dir of Finance, 1975–76, Jensen Motors Ltd; Man. Dir, Jenson Parts and Service Ltd, 1976–80; Chm., International Motors Ltd, 1980–88. Mem., H of L, 2011–15. Chm., Midlands Industrial Council, 2002–10. Founder and Trustee, Christian Vision, 1988–; Founder, Grace Foundn, 2003–; Sponsor and Gov., Grace Academies, 2003–. *Recreations:* playing guitar, golf, ski-ing, tennis, scuba.

EDMONDS, David Albert, CBE 2003; Chairman, NHS Shared Business Services, since 2005; *b* 6 March 1944; *s* of Albert and Gladys Edmonds; *m* 1966, Ruth Beech; two *s* two *d*. *Educ:* Helsby County Grammar School; University of Keele. BA Hons Political Institutions and History. Asst Principal, Min. of Housing and Local Govt, 1966–69; Private Sec. to Parly Sec., MHLG and DoE, 1969–71; Principal, DoE, 1971–73; Observer, CSSB, 1973–74; Vis. Fellow, Centre for Metropolitan Planning and Research, Johns Hopkins Univ., 1974–75; Private Sec. to Perm. Sec., DoE, 1975–77; Asst Sec., DoE, 1977–79; Principal Private Sec. to Sec. of State, DoE, 1979–83; Under Sec., Inner Cities Directorate, DoE, 1983–84; Chief Exec., Housing Corporation, 1984–91; Gen. Manager, then Man. Dir, Central Services, NatWest Gp, 1991–97; Dir Gen. of Telecommns, 1998–2003. Dir, Housing Finance Corp., 1988–91; Member: Bd, English Partnerships, 2000–03; Steering Bd, Radiocommunications Agency, 1998–2003; OFCOM, 2002–05; Bd, Legal Services Commn, 2004–08; Chairman: NHS Direct, 2004–08; Legal Services Bd, 2008–14. Non-executive Director: Hammerson PLC, 2003–11 (Chm., Pension Trustees, 2005–14); Wincanton plc, 2003–11 (Chm., 2008–11); William Hill plc, 2005–14; Olympic Park Legacy Co., later London Legacy Develt Corp., 2009–; Barchester Healthcare Ltd, 2012–; Chairman: Swanton Care and Community Ltd, 2012–14; E20 LLP, 2014–. Pres., Internat. New Town Assoc., 1987–91; Mem. Cttee, Notting Hill Housing Trust, 1991–94. Dep. Chm., New Statesman and Society, 1988–90 (Chm., New Society, 1986–88). Mem. Bd, Social Market Foundn, 2001–09. Chair of Trustees, Crisis, 1996–2002. Mem. Council, Chm., Finance Cttee, and Univ. Treas., Keele Univ., 1997–2003; Chm. Governing Bd, Kingston Univ., 2012–. Hon. DLitt Keele, 2004.

Recreations: cycling, opera, walking, golf. *Address:* 61 Cottenham Park Road, West Wimbledon, SW20 0DR. *T:* (020) 8946 3729. *Clubs:* Savile, MCC; Wimbledon Park Golf (Captain, 1997–98; Vice Pres., 2012–).

EDMONDS, John Christopher Paul, CBE 1993; Chief Executive, Railtrack, 1993–97; *b* 22 April 1936; *s* of late Frank Winston Edmonds and Phyllis Mary Edmonds; *m* 1962, Christine Elizabeth Seago; one *s* one *d. Educ:* Lowestoft Grammar School; Trinity College, Cambridge. Nat. Service Commission, RAF, 1955–57. Joined British Rail, 1960; Chief Freight Manager, London Midland Region, 1981; Nat. Business Manager, Coal, 1982; Dir, Provincial, 1984; Gen. Manager, Anglia Region, 1987; Bd Mem., and Man. Dir, Gp Services, 1989–93. *Recreations:* theatre, music, gardening.

EDMONDS, John Walter; General Secretary, GMB (formerly General, Municipal, Boilermakers and Allied Trades Union), 1986–2003; *b* 28 Jan. 1944; *s* of Walter and Rose Edmonds; *m* 1967, Linden (*née* Callaby); two *d. Educ:* Brunswick Park Primary; Christ's Hosp.; Oriel Coll., Oxford (BA 1965, MA 1968). General and Municipal Workers' Union: Res. Asst, 1966; Dep. Res. Officer, 1967; Reg. Officer, 1968; Nat. Industrial Officer, 1972. Mem. Council, ACAS, 1992–2000. Pres., TUC, 1997–98. Chm., TU Adv. Cttee on Sustainable Develt, 1998–2003. Director: National Building Agency, 1978–82; Unity Trust Bank, 1986–2003 (Pres., 2001–03). Mem., Royal Commn on Environmental Pollution, 1979–89; a Forestry Comr, 1995–2001; Director: EA, 2002–09; Carbon Trust, 2002–13; Chair: Inland Waterways Adv. Council, 2006–12; River Thames Alliance, 2012–. Dir, Salix Finance, 2004–. Vis. Fellow, Nuffield Coll., Oxford, 1986–94; Res. Fellow, KCL, 2003–; Vis. Prof., Durham Univ. Business Sch., 2014–. Mem. Council, Consumers' Assoc., 1991–96. Trustee: Inst. of Public Policy Research, 1988–2002; NSPCC, 1995–2002. Gov., LSE, 1986–95. Hon. LLD Sussex, 1994. *Recreations:* cricket, carpentry. *Address:* 50 Graham Road, Mitcham, Surrey CR4 2HA. *T:* (020) 8648 9991.

EDMONDS, Prof. Michael Edwin, MD; FRCP; Consultant Physician, King's College Hospital, London, since 1986; *b* Wareham, Dorset, 28 Aug. 1948; *s* of Arthur Percy Edmonds and Freda Joan Edmonds; *m* 1982; one *s. Educ:* Swanage Grammar Sch.; King's Coll. Hosp. Med. Sch. (BSc 1969; AKC 1969; MB BS 1972; MD 1985). MRCP 1977, FRCP 1991. Jun. appts, KCH and Poole and Weymouth Hosps, 1973–77; Med. Registrar, St Stephen's Hosp., Fulham, 1977–79; Res. Fellow and Lectr, Diabetic Dept, KCH, 1979–86; Hon. Sen. Lectr, Diabetic Dept, 1986–2007, Hon. Prof. of Diabetic Foot Medicine, 2007–, KCL. Karel Bakker Internat. Foot Award, 2011; Edward James Olmos Award for Advocacy in Amputation Prevention, 2014. *Publications:* (with A. V. M. Foster) Managing the Diabetic Foot, 2000 (trans. Spanish, 2004), 2nd edn 2005 (trans. Japanese, 2006); (jtly) A Practical Manual of Diabetic Foot Care, 2004 (Med. Book of Year, BMA, 2004) (trans. Chinese 2006), 2nd edn 2008; (with A. V. M. Foster) A Colour Atlas of the Foot and Ankle, 2008; (with A. V. M. Foster) Diabetic Foot Care: case studies in clinical management, 2010. *Address:* Diabetic Foot Clinic, King's College Hospital, Denmark Hill, SE5 9RS. *T:* (020) 3299 3223, *Fax:* (020) 3299 4536. *E:* michael.edmonds@nhs.net.

EDMONDS, Noel E.; DL; television presenter; *b* 22 Dec. 1948; *s* of Dudley Edmonds and Lydia Edmonds; *m* 1st, 1971, Gillian Slater (marr. diss.); 2nd, 1986, Helen Soby (marr. diss.); four *d*; 3rd, 2009, Liz Davies. *Educ:* Brentwood Sch. Newsreader, Radio Luxembourg, 1968–69; presenter, BBC Radio, 1969–2000, incl. Breakfast Show, 1973–78; BBC TV, 1970–2000; presenter, BBC TV series: Z Shed, 1975; Multicoloured Swap Shop, 1976–81; Lucky Numbers, 1978; The Late Late Breakfast Show, 1982–86; Time of Your Life, 1983; Telly Addicts, 1985–98; Saturday Roadshow, 1987; Noel's House Party, 1991–99; presenter: Channel 4 TV series, Deal or No Deal, 2005–; Sky One series, Are You Smarter Than a 10 Year Old?, 2007–. Chm., Unique Group, 1985. DL Devon, 2004.

EDMONDS-BROWN, (Cedric Wilfred) George; HM Diplomatic Service, retired; Executive Secretary, Canada-UK Council (formerly Colloquia), since 2001; *b* 24 April 1939; *s* of late Maj. W. R. E. Edmonds-Brown and E. M. Edmonds-Brown; *m* 1st, 1964, Everild A. V. Hardman (*d* 1988); one *s* two *d*; 2nd, 1990, Teiko Watanabe; one *s* one *d. Educ:* Dame Allan's Boys' Sch., Newcastle; King's Coll., Durham Univ. Joined CRO, 1962; Lagos, 1963; Karachi, 1964–68; Third Sec., Buenos Aires, 1968–73; FCO, 1973–76; Second Sec., Bucharest, 1976–80; First Sec. and HM Consul, Caracas, 1980–85; ODA, 1985–88; Head of Chancery, Ottawa, 1988; Dep. High Comr, Barbados, 1989–91; First Sec., Rome, 1991–95, Geneva, 1995–97; Consul, Geneva, 1997–99. *Recreations:* writing, art, travel, cricket. *Address:* 4 The Willows, Wootton, Oxon OX1 5LD.

EDMONDSON, family name of **Baron Sandford**.

EDMONDSON, Alex; *see* Crawford, A. C.

EDMONDSON, Rt Rev. Christopher Paul; *see* Bolton, Bishop Suffragan of.

EDMONSTONE, Sir Archibald (Bruce Charles), 7th Bt *cr* 1774; *b* 3 Aug. 1934; *o* surv. *s* of Sir Charles Edmonstone, 6th Bt, and Gwendolyn Mary (*d* 1989), *d* of late Marshall Field and Mrs Maldwin Drummond; *S* father, 1954; *m* 1st, 1957, Jane (marr. diss. 1967), *er d* of Maj.-Gen. E. C. Colville, CB, DSO; two *s* one *d*; 2nd, 1969, Juliet Elizabeth, *d* of Maj.-Gen. C. M. F. Deakin, CB, CBE; one *s* one *d. Educ:* St Peter's Court; Stowe Sch. *Heir: s* Archibald Edward Charles Edmonstone [*b* 4 Feb. 1961; *m* 1988, Ursula (marr. diss. 1994), *e d* of late Benjamin Worthington]. *Address:* Duntreath Castle, Blanefield, Stirlingshire G63 9AJ.

EDMONTON, Area Bishop of, since 2015; **Rt Rev. Robert James Wickham;** *b* 3 May 1972; *s* of John and Christine Wickham; *m* 2000, Helen Parker; two *s* one *d. Educ:* Grey Coll., Durham (BA 1994); Ridley Hall, Cambridge; King's Coll. London (MA 2012). Ordained deacon, 1998, priest, 1999; Curate: St Mary, Willesden, 1998–2001; St Mary the Virgin, Somers Town, 2001–03; Team Vicar, Old Church, St Pancras, 2003–07; Rector, St John-at-Hackney, 2007–15; Area Dean, Hackney, 2014–15. *Publications:* (contrib.) Anglican Church School Education, 2012. *Address:* 27 Thurlow Road, NW3 5PP. *E:* bishop.edmonton@london.anglican.org.

EDMUNDS, Alan Geoffrey; Editor, Western Mail, since 2002; Editor-in-Chief, Media Wales Ltd and Deputy Editorial Director, Trinity Mirror Regionals, since 2012; *b* 2 Aug. 1963; *s* of Geoffrey and Carol Edmunds; *m* 1988, Susanne; three *d. Educ:* Bristol Univ. (LLB Hons 1984); UC Cardiff (Postgrad. Dip. Journalism 1986). Ed., Wales on Sunday, 1997–2002; Man. Dir, Media Wales Ltd, 2011–12. *Recreations:* football, tennis, Rugby Union, reading, coin collecting, children's TV trivia from the 1970s. *Address:* 10 Duffryn Avenue, Lakeside, Cardiff CF23 6LF. *T:* (029) 2024 4747. *E:* alan.edmunds@mediawales.co.uk.

EDMUNDS, Martin James Simpson; QC 2006; **His Honour Judge Edmunds;** a Circuit Judge, since 2009; *b* 4 Dec. 1959; *s* of Brian Edmunds and Moira Edmunds. *Educ:* Brentwood Sch., Essex; Corpus Christi Coll., Cambridge (BA 1982). Called to the Bar, Middle Temple, 1983, Bencher, 2014; barrister, Walnut House, Exeter, and 33 Chancery Lane, London; a Recorder, 1999–2009.

EDMUNDS, Prof. Michael Geoffrey, PhD; Professor of Astrophysics, Cardiff University, 1997–2007, now Emeritus; *b* 18 June 1949; *s* of Geoffrey and Joyce Edmunds; *m* 1987, Margaret Morris; one *d*, and one step *d. Educ:* Woking Co. Grammar Sch.; Downing Coll., Cambridge (BA Natural Scis 1971; PhD 1976). FRAS 1975; FInstP, CPhys 2003. Bye-Fellow, Downing Coll., Cambridge, 1973–74; Cardiff University: Res. Fellow, 1974–76; Lectr, 1976–88; Sen. Lectr, 1988–96; Reader, 1996–97; Hd, Sch. of Physics and Astronomy, 2003–06. Chm., Antikythera Mechanism Res. Project, 2005–. Royal Astronomical Society: Darwin Lectr, 2004; Mem. Council, 2007–10; Chm., Astronomical Heritage Cttee, 2009–; Vice-Pres., 2014–16; Chm., Curriculum Cttee, Inst. of Physics, 2013–. Member: PPARC, 2004–07 (Chm., Sci. and Soc. Adv. Panel, 2004–11); Sci. and Technol. Facilities Council, 2007–10. *Publications:* res. papers in Nature, Monthly Notices of RAS, Astrophysical Jl, etc. *Recreations:* walking, sailing, music, old railways. *Address:* School of Physics and Astronomy, Cardiff University, Queens Buildings, The Parade, Cardiff CF24 3AA. *T:* (029) 2087 4458, *Fax:* (029) 2087 4056. *E:* mge@astro.cf.ac.uk; 3 Tyrwhitt Crescent, Roath Park, Cardiff CF23 5QP.

EDNEY, James David; public sector consultant and pension fund independent adviser, since 2007; *b* 22 April 1953; *s* of late James William John Edney and of Alma Mary Edney; *m* 1974, Heather Anita Sayer; one *s* two *d. Educ:* Dr Morgan's Grammar Sch., Bridgwater; Univ. of Newcastle upon Tyne (BA Hons (Hist.)); New Coll., Durham (CPFA 1979). Asst Dir, Finance and Admin, Cambridgeshire CC, 1985–89; Deputy County Treasurer: Lincolnshire CC, 1989–91; Essex CC, 1991–2002; Chief Financial Officer, Essex CC, 2002–03; Dep. Chief Exec. and Exec. Dir of Resources, Lancashire CC, 2003–06. Non-exec. Dir, Blackpool NHS Foundn Trust, 2013–. Mem. Bd, Univ. of Central Lancashire, 2012–. Treas., St Annes on the Sea URC, 2012–. *T:* 07805 322721. *E:* jim@edneyj.wanadoo.co.uk.

EDSON, Ven. Michael; Archdeacon of Leicester, 1994–2002, now Archdeacon Emeritus; Acting Archdeacon of Barnstaple, 2014–15; *b* 2 Sept. 1942; *s* of Joseph Pratt and Elsie (*née* Edson); name changed to Edson, 1989; *m* 1968, (Ann) Frances Tuffley; three *s* one *d. Educ:* Univ. of Birmingham (BSc Hons 1964); Univ. of Leeds (BA Hons 1971); College of the Resurrection, Mirfield. Management Consultant, 1966–68. Ordained deacon, 1972, priest, 1973; Curate, Barnstaple, Devon, 1972–77; Team Vicar, Barnstaple, 1977–82; Chaplain, N Devon Dist Hosp., 1976–82; Vicar, Roxbourne, Harrow, 1982–89; Area Dean of Harrow, 1985–89; Warden of Lee Abbey Fellowship, Devon, 1989–94. Leicester Diocesan Evangelist, 1997–2002; Team Rector, Torridge Estuary Team Ministry, 2002–09. *Publications:* The Renewal of the Mind, 1988; Loved into Life, 1993. *Recreations:* hill-walking, people, writing, spirituality, art, upholstery. *Address:* 11 Belmont Road, Ilkley, Yorks LS29 8PE.

EDUR, Agnes; *see* Oaks, A.

EDUR, Thomas, CBE 2010; former ballet dancer; teacher; choreographer, since 2000; Artistic Director, Estonian National Ballet, since 2009; *b* 20 Jan. 1969; *s* of Enn and Ludmilla Edur; *m* 1990, Agnes Oaks, *qv*; one *d. Educ:* Estonian State Ballet Sch. Principal Dancer: Estonian Nat. Opera, 1988–90; English Nat. Ballet, 1990–96; Birmingham Royal Ballet, 1996–97; internat. freelance dancer, and with English Nat. Ballet, 1997–2009, with Zurich Ballet, 2000–01. Guest Artist: La Scala, Milan, 1994–2001; Finnish Nat. Opera, 1999–2004; Berlin Staatsoper, 2000–02; Cape Town City Ballet, 2001–07. Choreographed: one-act ballets: Serenade de Florence, and Mozart, Estonian Th., Vanemuine, 2005; Anima, 2006; full length ballets: Modigliani, 2012; Labayadere, 2013, The Sleeping Beauty, 2014; *other works:* Forever, 2000; Fete Polonaise, 2008; Confessions, St Paul's Cathedral, 2009; other appearances include: Concert for Diana, 2007; Royal Variety Performance, 2007. Patron: British Ballet Orgn, 2004; English Nat. Ballet Sch., 2008–. Evening Standard Award, 1994; Best Dancer Award and Unique Partnership Award (with Agnes Oaks), Critics Circle, 2003; Laurence Olivier Award for Outstanding Achievement in Dance (with Agnes Oaks), 2004. Order of White Star, 3rd Cl. (Estonia), 2001. *Recreations:* Formula 1, nature, reading, photography. *Address:* Estonian National Ballet, National Opera and Ballet Theatre, Estonia av. 4, Tallinn 10148, Estonia. *E:* t.edur@ballet.ee.

EDWARD, Rt Hon. Sir David (Alexander Ogilvy), KCMG 2004 (CMG 1981); PC 2005; QC (Scotland) 1974; FRSE; Judge of the Court of Justice of the European Communities, 1992–2004 (Judge of the Court of First Instance, 1989–92); Temporary Judge, Court of Session, Scotland, 2004–09; *b* 14 Nov. 1934; *s* of J. O. C. Edward, Travel Agent, Perth; *m* 1962, Elizabeth Young McSherry; two *s* two *d. Educ:* Sedbergh Sch.; University Coll., Oxford (Hon. Fellow, 1995); Edinburgh Univ. Sub-Lt RNVR (Nat. Service); HMS Hornet, 1956–57. Admitted Advocate, 1962; Clerk of Faculty of Advocates, 1967–70, Treasurer, 1970–77. Pres., Consultative Cttee of Bars and Law Societies, EC, 1978–80; Salvesen Prof. of European Instns, 1985–89, Hon. Prof., 1990, Prof. Emeritus, 2008, Univ. of Edinburgh. Mem. Law Adv. Cttee, British Council, 1974–88; Specialist Advr, H of L Select Cttee on EC, 1985, 1986 and 1987. Mem., Panel of Arbitrators, Internat. Centre for Settlement of Investment Disputes, 1981–89 and 2004–. Director: Continental Assets Trust plc, 1985–89 (Chm.); Adam & Co. Group plc, 1983–89; Harris Tweed Association Ltd, 1984–89. Member: Foundation Senate, Europa Universität Viadrina, Frankfurt/Oder, 1991–93; Bd of Trustees, Acad. of European Law, Trier, 1993–. Trustee: Nat. Library of Scotland, 1966–95; Industry and Parlt Trust, 1995–2013 (Vice Pres., 2013–); Carnegie Trust for Univs of Scotland, 1996–2015 (Chm., 2003–15); Council for the Defence of British Univs, 2013–. Chm., Scottish Council of Ind. Schs, 2005–10; Member: Scotland Cttee, British Council, 2008–14; Commn on Scottish Devolution, 2008–09; Commn on a Bill of Rights, 2011–12. Vice-Pres., British Inst. Internat. and Comparative Law, 2002–. Patron, Scottish European Educn Trust, 2014–. President: Johnson Soc., Lichfield, 1995; Franco-Scottish Soc., 1996–2015; Edinburgh Sir Walter Scott Club, 2001–02. FRSE 1990 (Royal Medal, 2005). Hon. Bencher, Gray's Inn, 1992. Hon. LLD: Edinburgh, 1993; Aberdeen, 1997; Napier, 1998; Glasgow, 2003; DUniv Surrey, 2003; Dr (*hc*): Saarbrücken, 2001; Münster, 2001. Distinguished Cross, First Class, Order of St Raymond of Penafort (Spain), 1979; Officier de la Légion d'Honneur (France), 2012; Chevalier de l'Ordre des Arts et des Lettres (France), 2012. *Publications:* The Professional Secret, Confidentiality and Legal Professional Privilege in the EEC, 1976; (with R. C. Lane) European Community Law: an introduction, 1991, 2nd edn 1995; European Union Law, 2013; articles in legal jls, etc. *Address:* 32 Heriot Row, Edinburgh EH3 6ES. *Clubs:* Athenæum; New (Edinburgh).

EDWARDES, family name of **Baron Kensington**.

EDWARDES, Sir Michael (Owen), Kt 1979; Director: Flying Pictures Ltd, 1987–2012; Jet Press Holdings BV, since 1990; President, Strand Partners Ltd, 2009–13; *b* 11 Oct. 1930; *s* of Denys Owen Edwardes and Audrey Noel (*née* Copeland); *m* 1st, 1958, Mary Margaret (*née* Finlay) (marr. diss.; she *d* 1999); three *d*; 2nd, 1988, Sheila Ann (*née* Guy). *Educ:* St Andrew's Coll., Grahamstown, S Africa; Rhodes Univ., Grahamstown (BA; Hon. LLD). Chairman: Chloride Gp PLC, 1969–77 and 1986; BL Ltd (formerly British Leyland), 1977–82; Mercury Communications Ltd, 1982–83; ICL PLC, 1984; Dunlop Hldgs plc, 1984–85; Tryhorn Investments Ltd, 1987–2007; Charter PLC, 1988–96; Porth Gp, 1991–95; ARC Internat. Ltd (BVI), 1991–98; Strand Partners, 1994–2007; Syndicated Services Co. Inc., 1995–2007; Dep. Chm., R K Carvill (Internat. Hldgs) Ltd, 1988–2010; Director: Hill Samuel Gp, 1980–87; Minorco SA, 1984–93; Standard Securities PLC, 1985–87; Delta Motor Corp. (Pty) Ltd, 1986–99; Lansing Bagnall, 1987–88. Dir, Internat. Management Develt Inst., Washington, 1978–94. CCMI (Vice-Chm., BIM, 1977–80); Hon. FIMechE, 1981. President: Squash Rackets Assoc., 1991–95; Veterans Squash Club of GB, 1981–94. Trustee, Thrombosis Res. Inst., 1991–2001. *Publications:* Back From the Brink, 1983. *Recreations:* sailing, squash, water ski-ing, tennis. *Clubs:* Royal Automobile; Jesters; Rand and Country (Johannesburg).

EDWARDS, family name of **Baron Crickhowell**.

EDWARDS, Alan Francis; publicist, since 1976; Chief Executive Officer, Outside Organisation, since 1994; *b* London, 19 July 1955; *s* of Harrington and Elizabeth Edwards; four *d.* Journalist, Sounds, Record Mirror, 1973; with Keith Altham Publicity, 1974–77; formed Modern Publicity, 1977, Grant Edwards Mgt, 1980; Entertainment Dir, Rogers &

Cowan, 1989; Poole Edwards PR, 1990. Contributing Ed., GQ mag., 2005–. *Recreations:* reading, watching Arsenal FC. *Address:* The Outside Organisation, Butler House, 177–178 Tottenham Court Road, W1T 7NY. *T:* (020) 7436 3633, *Fax:* (020) 7462 2920. *Club:* Ivy.

EDWARDS, Rev. Canon Aled, OBE 2006; Chief Executive, CYTÛN Churches Together in Wales, since 2006; *b* 4 Oct. 1955; *s* of David Samuel Edwards and Katie Olwen Edwards; *m* 1976, Susan Marie Ball; two *s* one *d*. *Educ:* St David's UC, Lampeter (BA Jt Hons Hist. and Theol. Wales 1977); Trinity Coll., Bristol. Ordained deacon, 1979, priest, 1980; Asst Curate, Glanogwen, 1979–82; Vicar: Llandinorwig with Penisa'rwaun, 1982–85; Botwnnog, 1985–93; Dewi Sant, Cardiff, 1993–99; CYTÛN Nat. Assembly Liaison Officer, 1999–2006. Metropolitical Canon, Llandaff Cathedral, 2014–. Wales Comr, Commn for Racial Equality, 2006–07; Mem., Wales Cttee, Equality and Human Rights Commn, 2007–. Dir, Millennium Stadium plc, 2013–. Mem., Gorsedd of Bards, 2008. Recognising Achievement Award, Welsh Assembly Govt, 2010. *Publications:* Transforming Power: a Christian reflection on Welsh devolution, 2001; From Protest to Process: stories from the National Assembly for Wales, 2003; West Wing Wales - Obama for America: a Welsh campaign experience, 2009. *Recreations:* supporting Llanelli Scarlets, watching West Wing, running ultra marathons. *Address:* CYTÛN, 58 Richmond Road, Cardiff CF24 3UR. *T:* (029) 2046 4378, *Fax:* (029) 2046 4371. *E:* aled@cytun.org.uk.

EDWARDS, (Alfred) Kenneth, CBE 1989 (MBE 1963); Deputy Director-General, Confederation of British Industry, 1982–88; Director: Reliance Bank Ltd, 1992–2008; Salvation Army Trustee Co., 1996–2006; SATCOL Ltd, 2003–10; *b* 24 March 1926; *s* of late Ernest Edwards and Florence Edwards (*née* Branch); *m* 1st, 1949, Jeannette Lilian (*d* 2002), *d* of David Speeks, MBE; one *s* two *d*; 2nd, 2004, Jenefer, *d* of John Nicholas. *Educ:* Latymer Upper Sch.; Magdalene Coll., Cambridge; University Coll. London. Served RAF, 1944–47; RAF Coll., Cranwell, 1945, FO (Pilot). Entered HMOCS, Nigeria, 1952; Provincial Administration, Warri and Benin, 1952–54; Lagos Secretariat, 1954; Sen. Asst Sec., Nigerian Min. of Communications and Aviation, 1959; retired, 1962. Secretary, British Radio Equipment Manufrs' Assoc., 1962; Gp Marketing Manager, Thorn Elec. Industries Ltd, 1965; Internat. Dir, Brookhirst Igranic Ltd (Thorn Gp), 1967; Gp Marketing Dir, Cutler Hammer Europa, 1972; Dep. Chm., BEAMA Overseas Trade Cttee, 1973; Chief Exec., BEAMA, 1976–82. CBI: Member: Council, 1974, 1976–82; Finance and Gen. Purposes Cttee, 1977–82; Vice-Chm., Eastern Reg. Council, 1974; Chm., Working Party on Liability for Defective Products, 1978–82; Mem., President's Cttee, 1979–82. Chm., Facilities & Properties Management Plc, 1989–91; Dir, Polar Electronics PLC, 1984–96. Member: Elec. Engrg EDC, 1976; Council, Elec. Res. Assoc. Ltd, 1976–82; Exec. Cttee, ORGALIME, 1976–82; Management Bd, Eur. Cttee for Develt of Vocational Training, 1988–; BSI Bd, 1978–82, 1984–89 (Chm., British Electrotechnical Cttee and Electrotechnical Divisional Council, 1981–82; Chm., Quality Policy Cttee, 1988–); BOTB, 1982–88; BTEC, 1983–89; BBC Consultative Gp on Indust. and Business Affairs, 1983–88; Bd and Exec. Cttee, Business in the Community, 1987–88; President: CENELEC, 1977–79; Liaison Cttee for Electrical and Electronic Industries, ORGALIME, 1979–82 (Chm., 1980–82); Mem. Exec. Cttee, 1982–89, and Chm. Finance Cttee, 1983–89, UNICE. Dep. Chm., Salvation Army Adv. Bd, 1995–2000 (Mem., 1982). Mem. Court, Cranfield Inst. of Technol., 1970–75. *Publications:* contrib. technical jls; lectures and broadcasts on industrial subjects. *Recreations:* music, books, walking. *Address:* Greenfield House, Bedford Road, Rushden, Northants NN10 0ND. *Club:* Royal Air Force.

EDWARDS, Andrew John Cumming, CB 1994; composer and conductor; Deputy Secretary, HM Treasury, 1990–95; public sector consultant, 1995; *b* 3 Nov. 1940; *s* of John Edwards and Norah Hope Edwards (*née* Bevan); *m* 1st, 1969, Charlotte Anne Chilcot (marr. diss. 1987); one *s* two *d*; 2nd, 1994, Ursula Mary Richardson; one *s*. *Educ:* Fettes Coll., Edinburgh; St John's Coll., Oxford (MA); Harvard Univ. (AM, MPA). Asst master, Malvern Coll., 1962–63; HM Treasury: Asst Principal, 1963–67; Pvte Sec. to Jt Perm. Sec., 1966–67; Principal, 1967–75; Harkness Fellow, Harvard Univ., 1971–73; Asst Sec., 1975–83; RCDS, 1979; Asst Sec., DES, 1983–85; Under Sec., HM Treasury, 1985–89. Professional advr to Greenbury Cttee, 1995; conducted reviews of BM, 1996, Financial Regulation in Crown Dependencies, 1998, Finance Ministries of Bulgaria, 1999, Slovakia, 2000, Greece, 2002, and HM Land Registry, 2000–01; Mem., Financial Issues Adv. Gp for Scottish Parliament, 1998; Chm., Acacia Prog., 2002–05; Leader, OGC Gateway Reviews, 2003–14. Chm., Bishop Gilpin Sch. Appeal, 2001–02. Gov., British Inst. of Recorded Sound, 1974–79; Sec., Bd of Dirs, Royal Opera House, 1988–2006 (Sec., Develt Bd, 1984–87); Chm. Trustees, Wimbledon Music Fest., 2009–14. Conductor, Academy Choir and Orchs, Wimbledon, 1980–. *Publications:* Nuclear Weapons, the balance of terror, the quest for peace, 1986; reports; *music:* Missa Brevis, 2007; The Easter Story (oratorio), 2010; The Christmas Story (oratorio), 2015. *Recreations:* reading, walking. *Address:* 15 Highbury Road, SW19 7PR.

EDWARDS, (Ann) Mererid; Her Honour Judge Mererid Edwards; a Circuit Judge, since 2013; *b* Wrexham, 10 March 1968; *d* of William Henry Edwards and Dr Ann Eleri Edwards; *m* 1996, Adrian Philip Jackson; one *s* two *d*. *Educ:* Ysgol-Y-Berwyn, Y Bala; Yale Sixth Form Coll.; Univ. of Wales, Aberystwyth (LLB Hons). Called to the Bar, Gray's Inn, 1991; lawyer, S4C, 1990–91; in practice as barrister, Paradise Chambers, Sheffield, 1992–2013; a Recorder, 2008–13. *Recreation:* keeping up with the kids and ironing. *Address:* Cardiff Civil and Family Justice Centre, 2 Park Street, Cardiff CF10 1ET.

EDWARDS, Prof. Anne, PhD; Professor of Education, University of Oxford, 2005, now Emerita (Director, Department of Education, 2010–12); Fellow, St Hilda's College, Oxford; *b* Swansea, 31 Oct. 1946; *d* of Owen Terence Davies and Glory Marie Louise, (Jackie), Davies (*née* Jacobsen); *m* 1991, David Christopher Webb; two *d*, and one step *s* one step *d*. *Educ:* Grammar Sch. for Girls, Pontypool; Univ. of Wales, Cardiff (BA 1968; MEd 1977; PhD 1984). ESRC Postdoctoral Fellow, Dept of Psychology, University Coll. Cardiff, 1983–85; Sen. Lectr, then Principal Lectr in Postgrad. Educnl Studies, West Glamorgan Inst. of HE, 1985–87; Principal Lectr, then Prof., St Martin's Coll., Lancaster, 1987–95; Prof. of Primary Educn, Sch. of Educn, Univ. of Leeds, 1996–99; Prof. of Pedagogic Practices, Sch. of Educn, Univ. of Birmingham, 1999–2005. Visiting Professor: Faculty of Educn, Univ. of Oslo, 2006–; Centre for Human Activity Theory, Kansai Univ., 2006–. AFBPsS 1985; FAcSS (AcSS 2004). Hon. PhD: Helsinki, 2010; Oslo, 2012. *Publications:* (with D. Galloway) Primary School Teaching and Educational Psychology, 1991; (with D. Galloway) Secondary School Teaching and Educational Psychology, 1992; (with R. Talbot) The Hard-Pressed Researcher: a handbook for practitioner researchers in the caring professions, 1994, 2nd edn 1999; (with P. Knight) Effective Education in the Early Years, 1994; (ed with P. Knight) The Assessment of Competences in Higher Education, 1995; (with J. Collison) Mentoring and Developing Practice in Primary Schools, 1996; (with A. Anning) Promoting Learning from Birth to Five: developing professional practice in the pre-school, 1999, 2nd edn 2006; (jtly) Rethinking Teacher Education: an interdisciplinary analysis, 2002; (ed with H. Daniels) RoutledgeFalmer Reader: the psychology of Education, 2003; (jtly) Improving Inter-professional Collaborations: multi-agency working for children's wellbeing, 2009; (ed jtly) Activity Theory in Practice: promoting learning across boundaries and agencies, 2009; (ed jtly) Learning Teaching: cultural historical perspectives on teacher education and development, 2010; Being an Expert Professional Practitioner: a relational turn, 2010; (jtly) Improving User-engagement in Educational Research, 2011; (ed jtly) Motives, Emotions and Values in the Development of Children and Young People, 2012; (ed jtly) Pedagogy in Higher Education, 2013; contribs in ed collections and acad. jls. *Recreations:* family, theatre, walking. *Address:* Department of Education, University of Oxford, 15 Norham Gardens, Oxford OX2 6PY. *T:* (01865) 242669, *Fax:* (01865) 274027. *E:* anne.edwards@education.ox.ac.uk.

EDWARDS, Prof. (Anthony) David, DSc; FRCP, FRCPCH, FMedSci; Professor of Paediatrics and Neonatal Medicine, King's College London, since 2012; Director, Centre for the Developing Brain, King's College London (formerly at Imperial College London), since 2008; Consultant Neonatologist, Guy's and St Thomas' Hospitals NHS Trust, since 2012; *b* 26 Nov. 1954; *s* of Raymond Edwards and Nora Edwards; *m* 1978, Catherine James; one *s* one *d*. *Educ:* St Peter's Coll., Oxford (MA; Univ. Boat Race winning crew, 1976); Harvard Univ.; Guy's Hosp. Med. Sch., Univ. of London (MB BS); Imperial Coll. London (DSc 2010). FRCP 1993; FRCPCH 1997; FMedSci 2002. Sen. Lectr in Paediatrics, UCL, 1992–93; Imperial College London: Weston Prof. of Neonatal Medicine, 1993–2012; Chm., Div. of Paediatrics, Obstetrics and Gynaecol., 1998–2005; Lead for Imaging Res., 2006–08; Hd, Neonatal Medicine Gp, MRC Clin. Scis Centre, Hammersmith Hosp., 1999–2012. Assoc. Dir, UK Medicines for Children Res. Network, 2006–12. Visiting Professor: UCL, 1994; Univ. of Hong Kong, 2000. Member: Sci. Adv. Bd, Liggins Inst., Auckland, NZ, 2001; INSERM, 2004–; MRC, 2004–05; Nat. Centre for Growth and Develt, NZ, 2005–. Hon. Mem., RCR, 2010. Arvo Ylppö Medal, Foundn for Paediatric Res., Finland, 2007. *Publications:* contrib. numerous papers to scientific jls. *Recreations:* Manouche jazz, the renaissance lute, sailing. *Address:* Centre for the Developing Brain, King's College London, St Thomas' Hospital, Westminster Bridge Road, Lambeth, SE1 7HY. *T:* (020) 7188 9158. *E:* ad.edwards@kcl.ac.uk. *Clubs:* Athenæum; Royal Solent Yacht.

EDWARDS, Prof. Anthony William Fairbank, FRS 2015; Professor of Biometry, University of Cambridge, 2000–03; Fellow, Gonville and Caius College, Cambridge, since 1970; *b* London, 4 Oct. 1935; *s* of late Harold Clifford Edwards and Ida Margaret Atkinson Edwards (*née* Phillips); *m* 1958, (Elsa Helny) Catharina Edlund; one *s* two *d*. *Educ:* Uppingham Sch.; Trinity Hall, Cambridge (BA 1957; PhD 1961; ScD 1972; LittD 2005). Res. Fellow, Dept of Genetics, Univ. of Cambridge, 1960; Res. Assoc., Univ. of Pavia, 1961–64; Actg Asst Prof., Depts of Genetics and Maths, Stanford Univ., 1964–65; Sen. Lectr in Statistics, Univ. of Aberdeen, 1965–68; University of Cambridge: Bye Fellow, Gonville and Caius Coll., 1968–70; Reader in Biometry, 1978–2000; Asst Dir of Res., 1970–78; Sen. Proctor, 1978–79. Hon. Prof., Univ. of Pavia, 1999. *Publications:* Likelihood, 1972, 2nd edn 1992; Foundations of Mathematical Genetics, 1977, 2nd edn 2000; Pascal's Arithmetical Triangle, 1987, 2nd edn 2002; (with H. A. David) Annotated Readings in the History of Statistics, 2001; Cogwheels of the Mind, 2004; (jtly) Ending the Mendel-Fisher Controversy, 2008. *Recreation:* gliding. *Address:* Nickersons, 104 High Street, Barton, Cambridge CB23 7BG. *T:* (01223) 262367. *E:* awfe@cam.ac.uk.

EDWARDS, Prof. Brian, CBE 1988; FHSM; Professor of Health Care Development, University of Sheffield, 1996–2002, now Emeritus (Foundation Dean, School of Health and Related Research, 1996–99); *b* 19 Feb. 1942; *s* of John Albert Edwards and Ethel Edwards; *m* 1964, Jean (*née* Cannon); two *s* two *d*. *Educ:* Wirral Grammar Sch. FHSM 1983. Jun. Administrator, Clatterbridge Hosp., 1958–62; Dep. Hosp. Sec., Cleaver Hosp., 1962–64; National Trainee, Nuffield Centre, Leeds, 1964–66; Administrator, Gen. Infirmary, Leeds, 1966–67; Hosp. Sec., Keighley Victoria Hosp., 1967–68; Administrator, Mansfield HMC, 1969–70; Lectr, Univ. of Leeds, 1970–72; Dep. Gp Sec., Hull A HMC, 1972–74; Nuffield Travelling Fellow, USA, 1973; Dist Administrator, Leeds AHA(T), 1974–76; Area Administrator, Cheshire AHA, 1976–81; Regional Administrator, 1981–84, Regl Gen. Man., 1984–93, Trent RHA; Chief Exec., W Midlands RHA, 1993–96; Regl Dir, NHS Exec., 1994–96. Chm., Clinical Pathology Accreditation Ltd, 1992–2000. Vis. Lectr, Health Care Studies, 1973–93, and Associate Fellow, Nuffield Inst., 1987–93, Univ. of Leeds; Vis. Prof., Health Care Studies, Univ. of Keele, 1989; Queen Elizabeth Nuffield Fellow, Nuffield Provincial Hosps Trust, 1991; Hon. Prof., Univ. of Keele, 1993. Adviser to WHO, 1982–; Chairman: NHS Manpower Planning Adv. Gp, 1983–86; Regional Gen. Managers Gp, 1986–87, 1991–94; NHS Patient Empowerment Gp, 1991–94; Patient's Charter Team, 1992; Council for the Professions Supplementary to Medicine, 1997–2002; Notts Health NHS Trust, 2001–07; Member: Steering Cttee on Future of Nursing, 1988; Standing Cttee on Medical Audit, RCP, 1989–94; Ashworth Inquiry, 1997–98; Leader: Sec. of State's Task Force on Quality in NHS, 1993; UK Delegn, Hosp. Cttee for Europe, 1994–2005 (Pres., 2005–08). Chairman: ATM Consulting, 2007–09; Pain Management Solutions, 2009–10; Referrals Direct Ltd, 2010–; Director: Shirehall Gp, 1996–99; Health on the Box Ltd, 1999–2001. Institute of Health Service Administrators: Mem., 1964–; Pres., 1982–83; Mem. Editorial Cttee, Health Care in the UK: its organisation and management, 1982–83; Pres., Assoc. of Health Service Supplies Officers, 2001–04. Patron, NHS Retirement Fellowship, 2002–07. Trustee: Marie Curie Trust, 1996–2000; Pharmacy Practice Res. Trust, 2006–. Jt Editor, Health Services Manpower Review, 1970–91; Editor, Euro Hospital Yearbook, 1998–2005. CCMI (CBIM 1988); Hon. FRCPath 1996; Professorial FRSPH 2013. DUniv UCE, 1998. *Publications:* Si Vis Pacem—preparations for change in the NHS, 1973; Profile for Change, 1973; Bridging in Health, Planning the Child Health Services, 1975; Industrial Relations in the NHS: managers and industrial relations, 1979; Manpower Planning in the NHS, 1984; Employment Policies for Health Care, 1985; Distinction Awards for Doctors, 1987; (contrib.) Doctors' Contracts, 1992; (contrib.) Public Sector Managers' Handbook, 1992; The NHS: a manager's tale, 1993, 2nd edn 1995; (contrib.) Management for Doctors, 1994; (contrib.) Managed Healthcare, 1998; (ed) NHS 50th Anniversary Lectures, 1999; The Executive Year of the NHS, 2005; An Independent NHS, 2007; A History of the NHS in the South West, 2010; A Collapse in the Culture of Care: the Stafford Inquiries, 2013; papers presented at numerous nat. and internat. confs; contrib. prof. jls. *Recreation:* golf. *Address:* 3 Royal Croft Drive, Baslow, Derbyshire DE45 1SN. *T:* (01246) 583459. *Clubs:* Athenæum; Bakewell Golf (Captain, 1991; Pres., 2015); La Manga (Spain).

EDWARDS, His Honour (Charles) Marcus; a Circuit Judge, 1986–2008; *b* 10 Aug. 1937; *s* of late John Basil Edwards, CBE; *m* 1st, 1963, Anne Louise Stockdale (*d* 1970), *d* of Sir Edmund Stockdale, 1st Bt; 2nd, 1975, Sandra Wates (*née* Mouroutsos); one *d* and three step *d*. *Educ:* Dragon Sch., Oxford; Rugby Sch.; Brasenose Coll., Oxford (scholar; BA Jurisprudence). Trooper, RAC, 1955; 2nd Lieut, Intelligence Corps, Cyprus, 1956–57. HM Diplomatic Service, 1960–65; Third Sec., 1960, Spain, 1961, FO, 1961–62, South Africa and High Commn Territories, 1962–63, Laos, 1964; Second Sec., FO, 1965, resigned. Called to the Bar, Middle Temple, 1962; practised, London, 1966–86; Mem., Midland and Oxford Circuit; a Recorder, 1985–86. Chm., Pavilion Opera, 1987–. *Recreations:* gardening, walking, talking, food and drink. *Address:* Mathon Lodge, Mathon, Herefordshire WR14 4DW. *T:* (01684) 564592; Menginolle, 32730 Malabat, France. *Clubs:* Beefsteak, Vincent's.

EDWARDS, Sir Christopher (John Churchill), 5th Bt *cr* 1866; Adjunct Professor, University College, University of Denver, and Affiliate Professor, Regis University, Denver, Colorado since 1999; President, Rocky Mountain Information Specialists, Westminster, Colorado, since 2007; *b* 16 Aug. 1941; *s* of Sir (Henry) Charles (Serrell Priestley) Edwards, 4th Bt and of Lady (Daphne) Edwards (*née* Birt); *S* father, 1963; *m* 1972, Gladys Irene Vogelgesang (*d* 2005); two *s*. *Educ:* Frensham Heights, Surrey; Loughborough Univ., Leics (DLC Hons; BSc); Regis Univ., Denver, USA (MSc). Gen. Manager, Kelsar Inc., American Home Products, San Diego, Calif, 1979–84; Vice-Pres., Valleylab Inc., Boulder, Colo, 1981–89; Dir, Ohmeda BOC Group, Louisville, 1989–92; Pres., Intermed Consultants, Westminster, Colo, 1992–99; Exec. Vice-Pres. and Gen. Manager, RAM Electronics Corp., Fort Collins, Colo, 1995–97. Affiliate Prof. of MSc in Mgt, Regis Univ., Denver, 1999–;

Adjunct Prof. of MSc in Inf. Technol. and Organization Leadership, Univ. of Denver, 1999–. Ruth Murray Underhill Teaching Award, Univ. of Denver, 2006. *Heir:* s David Charles Priestley Edwards, b 22 Feb. 1974. *Address:* 11637 Country Club Drive, Westminster, CO 80234–2649, USA. *T:* (303) 4693156.

EDWARDS, Sir Christopher (Richard Watkin), Kt 2008; MD; FRCP, FRCPE, FMedSci; FRSE; Chairman: Council, British Heart Foundation, since 2009; Cluff Geothermal, since 2014; Icappic Ltd, since 2015; *b* 12 Feb. 1942; *s* of Thomas Archibald Watkin Edwards and Beatrice Elizabeth Ruby Watkin Edwards; *m* 1968, Sally Amanda Kidd; two *s* one *d*. *Educ:* Marlborough Coll.; Christ's Coll., Cambridge (BA, MB, BChir, MA, MD). St Bartholomew's Hospital: Lectr in Medicine, 1969–75; Sen. Lectr in Medicine and MRC Sen. Res. Fellow, 1975–80; Hon. Consultant Physician, 1975–80; University of Edinburgh: Moncrieff Arnott Prof. of Clinical Medicine, 1980–95; Dean, Faculty of Medicine, 1991–95; Provost, Faculty Group of Medicine and Veterinary Medicine, 1992–95; Principal and Prof. of Medicine, ICSM, Univ. of London, 1995–2000; Vice-Chancellor, Univ. of Newcastle upon Tyne, 2001–07. Chairman: Chelsea and Westminster NHS Foundn Trust, 2007–14; NHS Medical Educn England, 2008–12. Non-executive Director: Celltech, 1997–2004; Argenta Discovery, 2000–04; One NorthEast, 2001–07. Mem., MRC, 1991–95. Gov., Wellcome Trust, 1994–2005. Trustee, Planet Earth Inst., 2012–. Founder FMedSci 1998; FIC 2003. Hon. DSc Aberdeen, 2000. *Publications:* (ed) Clinical Physiology, 5th edn, 1984; (ed) Essential Hypertension as an Endocrine Disease, 1985; Endocrinology, 1986; (ed) Recent Advances in Endocrinology Metabolism, vol. 3, 1989; (ed) Davidson's Principles and Practice of Medicine, 17th edn, 1995; 421 scientific papers and communications. *Recreations:* running, reading, golf, ski-ing. *Address:* 4 Thames Walk, SW11 3BG. *Club:* Athenæum.

EDWARDS, Rev. Canon Clare; *see* Edwards, Rev. Canon D. C.

EDWARDS, David; *see* Edwards, Anthony D.

EDWARDS, (David) Elgan (Hugh); His Honour Judge Elgan Edwards; DL; a Circuit Judge, since 1989, a Senior Circuit Judge, since 2002; *b* 6 Dec. 1943; *s* of Howell and Dilys Edwards; *m* 1982, Carol Anne Smalls; two *s* two *d*. *Educ:* Rhyl Grammar Sch.; University Coll. of Wales, Aberystwyth (LLB Hons 1966; Pres., Students Union, 1967; Hon. Fellow, 2005). Called to the Bar, Gray's Inn, 1967 (Bencher, 2004); a Recorder, Wales and Chester Circuit, 1983–89; Hon. Recorder, Chester, 1997; Resident Judge for Cheshire, 2006–. Contested (C): Merioneth, 1970; Stockport South, Feb. 1974. President: Cheshire Br., Magistrates' Assoc., 2010–; Cheshire Br., Red Cross. Freeman, City of London, 2002. Sheriff, City of Chester, 1977–78; DL Cheshire, 2000. *Recreations:* Manchester United FC, Chester Races. *Address:* The Crown Court, Chester Castle, Chester CH1 2AN. *T:* (01244) 317606. *Club:* Chester City (Chester).

EDWARDS, Very Rev. David Lawrence, OBE 1995; Provost of Southwark Cathedral, 1983–94, Emeritus since 1994; *b* 20 Jan. 1929; *s* of late Lawrence Wright and Phyllis Boardman Edwards; *m* 1st, 1960, Hilary Mary (*née* Phillips) (marr. diss. 1984); one *s* three *d*; 2nd, 1984, Sybil (*d* 2015), *d* of Michael and Kathleen Falcon. *Educ:* King's Sch., Canterbury; Magdalen Coll., Oxford. Lothian Prize, 1951; 1st cl. hons Mod. Hist., BA 1952; MA 1956. Fellow, All Souls Coll., Oxford, 1952–59. Deacon, 1954; Priest, 1955. On HQ staff of Student Christian Movement of Gt Brit. and Ireland, 1955–66; Editor and Man. Dir, SCM Press Ltd, 1959–66; Gen. Sec. of Movt, 1965–66. Curate of: St John's, Hampstead, 1955–58; St Martin-in-the-Fields, 1958–66; Fellow and Dean of King's College, Cambridge, 1966–70; Asst Lectr in Divinity, Univ. of Cambridge, 1967–70; Rector of St Margaret's, Westminster, 1970–78; Canon of Westminster, 1970–78; Sub-Dean, 1974–78; Speaker's Chaplain, 1972–78; Dean of Norwich, 1978–82. Exam. Chaplain: to Bp of Manchester, 1965–73; to Bp of Durham, 1968–72; to Bp of Bradford, 1972–78; to Bp of London, 1974–78; to Archbishop of Canterbury, 1975–78. Hulsean Lectr, 1967; Six Preacher, Canterbury Cathedral, 1969–76. Chairman: Churches' Council on Gambling, 1970–78; Christian Aid, 1971–78. Hon. Prof., King Alfred's Coll., Winchester, 1999–2003. Hon. Fellow, South Bank Univ. (formerly Poly.), 1990. DD Lambeth, 1990. *Publications:* A History of the King's School, Canterbury, 1957; Not Angels But Anglicans, 1958; This Church of England, 1962; God's Cross in Our World, 1963; Religion and Change, 1969; F. J. Shirley: An Extraordinary Headmaster, 1969; The Last Things Now, 1969; Leaders of the Church of England, 1971; What is Real in Christianity?, 1972; St Margaret's, Westminster, 1972; The British Churches Turn to the Future, 1973; Ian Ramsey, Bishop of Durham, 1973; Good News in Acts, 1974; What Anglicans Believe, 1974; Jesus for Modern Man, 1975; A Key to the Old Testament, 1976; Today's Story of Jesus, 1976; The State of the Nation, 1976; A Reason to Hope, 1978; Christian England: vol. 1, Its story to the Reformation, 1981; vol. 2, From the Reformation to the Eighteenth Century, 1983; vol. 3, From the Eighteenth Century to the First World War, 1984; The Futures of Christianity, 1987; Essentials: a Liberal-Evangelical dialogue with John Stott, 1988; The Cathedrals of Britain, 1989; Tradition and Truth, 1989; Christians in a New Europe, 1990; The Real Jesus, 1992; What is Catholicism?, 1994; Christianity: the first two thousand years, 1997; A Concise History of English Christianity, 1998; After Death?: past beliefs and real possibilities, 1999; John Donne: a man of flesh and spirit, 2001; The Church That Could Be, 2002; What Anglicans Believe in the 21st Century, 2002; Poets and God, 2005; Yes: a positive faith, 2006; *edited:* The Honest to God Debate, 1963; Collins Children's Bible, 1978; Christianity and Conservatism, 1990; Robert Runcie: a portrait by his friends, 1990. *Address:* 4 Morley College, Market Street, Winchester, Hants SO23 9LF. *Club:* Athenæum.

EDWARDS, David Leslie; QC 2006; *b* 8 Nov. 1966; *s* of Leslie Joseph Edwards and Angela Mary Edwards; *m* 1994, Caroline May Evans; three *s*. *Educ:* King's Sch., Chester; Peterhouse, Cambridge (BA 1988, MA 1991). Called to the Bar, Lincoln's Inn, 1989; in practice as barrister, 1990–, specialising in commercial law, incl. insurance, reinsurance, banking, internat. trade and professional negligence. Mem., Standards Cttee, Bar Standards Bd, 2011–. Chm. Council, Friends of Peterhouse, 2010–. *Recreations:* football, wine, classical music, reading. *Address:* 7 King's Bench Walk, Temple, EC4Y 7DS. *T:* (020) 7910 8300.

EDWARDS, David Michael, CMG 1990; international commercial mediator; Adjunct Professor, Singapore Management University, since 2007; Program Director, Chief Legal Officers' Council and Emerging Markets Risk and Compliance Council (Asia Pacific), The Conference Board, since 2011; *b* 28 Feb. 1940; *s* of late Ernest William Edwards and Thelma Irene Edwards; *m* 1st, 1966, Veronica Margaret Postgate (marr. diss. 1996); one *s* one *d*; 2nd, 1996, Rain Ren; one *s* one *d*. *Educ:* The King's Sch., Canterbury; Univ. of Bristol (LLB Hons). Admitted to Roll of Solicitors, 1964. Solicitor of Supreme Court, 1964–67; Asst Legal Adviser, Foreign Office, 1967; Legal Adviser: British Military Govt, Berlin, 1972; British Embassy, Bonn, 1974; Legal Counsellor, 1977; Gen. Counsel and Dir, Legal Div., IAEA, Vienna, 1977–79; Legal Counsellor, FCO, 1979; Agent of the UK Govt in cases before European Commn and Court of Human Rights, 1979–82; Counsellor (Legal Adviser), UK Mission to UN, New York, and HM Embassy, Washington, 1985–88; Legal Counsellor, 1988–89, Dep. Legal Advr, 1989–90, FCO; Sen. Counsel, Bechtel Ltd, 1990; Law Officer (Internat. Law), Hong Kong Govt, 1990–95; Sen. Counsel, Bechtel Ltd, London, 1995–97; Asia Pacific Chief Counsel and Vice-Pres., Bechtel Internat. Inc., Singapore, 1997–2002; Chief Legal Counsel, Shell/CNOOC Nanhai Petrochemical Complex, Guangdong Province, China, 2002–05. *Recreations:* reading, travel, antique clocks. *Club:* Tanglin (Singapore).

EDWARDS, Prof. David Olaf, DPhil; FRS 1988; University Professor of Physics, Ohio State University, 1988–95, now Distinguished Professor Emeritus; *b* 27 April 1932; *s* of Robert Edwards and Margaret Edwina (*née* Larsen); *m* 1967, Wendy Lou Townsend (*d* 2009); one *s* one *d*. *Educ:* Holt High Sch., Liverpool; Brasenose Coll., Oxford (BA 1st cl. Hons, 1953; Sen. Hulme Schol., 1953–56; MA; DPhil 1957). FAPS. Pressed Steel Co. Res. Fellow, Clarendon Lab., Oxford Univ., 1957–58; Ohio State University: Vis. Asst Prof., 1958–60; Asst Prof., 1960–62; Associate Prof., 1962–65; Prof., 1965–88. Visiting Professor: Imperial Coll., London, 1964; Sussex Univ., 1964, 1968; Technion, Israel, 1971–72; Ecole Normale Supérieure, Paris, 1978, 1982, 1986; Vis. Scientist, Brookhaven Nat. Lab., 1975. Consultant: Brookhaven Nat. Lab., 1975–77; Los Alamos Scientific Lab., 1979–81. Sir Francis Simon Prize, British Inst. of Physics, 1983; Dist. Schol. Award, Ohio State Univ., 1984; Special Creativity Awards, US Nat. Sci. Foundn, 1981, 1986; Oliver E. Buckley Condensed Matter Physics Prize, APS, 1990. Mem. Editl Bd, Jl of Low Temperature Physics, 1990–2004. *Publications:* (ed jtly) Proceedings of the Ninth International Conference on Low Temperature Physics (LT9), 1966; numerous articles on low temp. physics in scientific jls. *Recreations:* beagling (Master, Rocky Fork Beagles, 1975–90), snorkeling (Grand Cayman), crossword puzzles, reading detective stories. *Address:* 2345 Dorset Road, Columbus, OH 43221, USA. *T:* (614) 4864553; Department of Physics, Ohio State University, 191 West Woodruff Avenue, Columbus, OH 43210–1117, USA. *Fax:* (614) 2927557.

EDWARDS, David Stanley, OBE 2005; Chief Executive, Cardiff and Vale NHS Trust, 1999–2004; Chairman, Cambridgeshire and Peterborough NHS Foundation Trust, since 2012; *b* 5 Oct. 1943; *s* of Stanley and May Edwards; partner, Christine Baxter; two *s*. *Educ:* Coll. of Advanced Technol., Birmingham (HND Prodn and Mech. Engrg 1966); Coll. of Commerce, Birmingham (Dip. Mgt Studies 1969). DipHSM 1981. Tech. engr, then industrial engr, British Steel, Wednesbury (Tube Prodn), 1960–67; Sen. Industrial Engr, GKN (Birwelco) Ltd, Halesowen (Engrg), 1967–68; West Midlands Regional Health Authority: Orgn and Methods Assignment Officer, 1968–70; Mgt by Objectives Advr, 1970–72; Asst Regl Orgn and Methods Work Study Manager, 1972–74; West Birmingham Health Authority: Dist Support Services Manager, 1974–77; Dist Gen. Adminr (Planning), 1977–79; Central Birmingham Health Authority: Sector Adminr, Gen., Dental and Jaffray Hosp. and Community Services, 1979–82; Dep. Dist Adminr, 1982–85; Dir, Admin and Planning, 1985–86; Dist Gen. Manager, 1986–91; Chief Exec., Queen's Med. Centre, Nottingham Univ. Hosp. NHS Trust, 1991–99. Chm., NHS Great Yarmouth and Waveney, 2009–12; non-exec. Dir, James Paget Univ. Hosps NHS Foundn Trust, 2007–. Vice Chm., Council, UEA, 2011– (Mem. Council, 2005–; Chm., Audit Cttee, 2006–10; Mem. Bd, Univ. Campus Suffolk, 2010–). Fellow, Univ. of Nottingham, 1994. Companion IHM 2002; CCMI 2003. Hon. DCL UEA, 2014. *Recreations:* two sons, two granddaughters, antique clocks and Victorian relief moulded jugs, classic cars, scuba diving (in warm water!), squash, running and all sport, foreign travel, walking, reading for pleasure, music and playing the piano in private. *Address:* The Grove, Smee Lane, Great Plumstead, Norwich, Norfolk NR13 5AU. *T:* (01603) 717310.

EDWARDS, Rev. Canon (Diana) Clare; Canon Pastor, Canterbury Cathedral, since 2004; *b* 14 Feb. 1956; *d* of Bryan Reginald Edwards and Vivienne Edwards. *Educ:* London Hosp., Whitechapel (SRN 1977); Hosp. for Sick Children, Gt Ormond St (RSCN 1981); London Univ. (DipN 1983); Nottingham Univ. (BTh 1986). Staff Nurse, London Hosp., Whitechapel, 1977–79; Community Mem., Scargill House, Yorks, 1979–80; Post Registration Student, Hosp. for Sick Children, Gt Ormond St, 1980–81; Staff Nurse, Mayday Hosp., Croydon, 1981–83; ordained deaconess, 1986, deacon, 1987, priest, 1994; Deaconess, 1986–87, Deacon, 1987–90, Holy Trinity & St Peter, S Wimbledon; Curate, St Peter & St Paul with St George, Crowhurst, and Chaplain, Lingfield Hosp. Sch., 1990–95; Rector, St Mary the Virgin, Bletchingley, 1995–2004; Rural Dean, Godstone, 1997–2004; Hon. Canon, 2001–04, Dean of Women's Ministry, 2003–04, dio. of Southwark. *Publications:* Human Rites (contrib.), 1995; Isabella Gilmore: forerunner of today's women parish priests, 2009. *Recreations:* swimming, windsurfing, embroidery, arts and crafts. *Address:* 22 The Precincts, Canterbury CT1 2EP. *T:* (01227) 865227. *E:* canonclare@canterbury-cathedral.org.

EDWARDS, Prof. Dianne, CBE 1999; ScD; FRS 1996; FRSE; FLSW; Distinguished Research Professor in Palaeobotany, Cardiff University (formerly University of Wales, Cardiff), since 1996; President, Linnean Society of London, 2012–15; *b* 23 Feb. 1942; *d* of William John Edwards and Enid Edwards; *m* 1965, Thomas Geoffrey Morgan (*d* 1997); one *s*. *Educ:* Girton Coll., Cambridge (BA, MA; PhD 1968; ScD 1989). Res. Fellow, Girton Coll., Cambridge, 1967–70; Fellow, Univ. of Wales, 1970–72; University College, Cardiff: Lectr in Botany, 1972–82; Sen. Lectr, 1982–86; Reader in Plant Sci., 1986–92; Prof. of Palaeobotany, 1992–96. Royal Soc. Leverhulme Trust Sen. Res. Fellow, 1994–95. Mem., Countryside Council for Wales, 2001–07. Corresp. Mem., Botanical Soc. of America, 1994. Trustee: Nat. Botanic Garden of Wales, 1997–2006; Royal Botanic Garden, Edinburgh, 1999–2006; Natural Hist. Mus., 2003–11. Founder Fellow and Vice Pres., Learned Soc. of Wales, 2010–. FRSE 2001. Hon. Fellow, Univ. of Wales, Swansea, 1997. Hon. ScD TCD, 2005; Hon. Dr Uppsala, 2014. Ed., Botanical Jl of Linnean Soc., 1993–2006. Linnean Medal for Botany, 2010; Lapworth Medal, Palaeontological Soc., 2013. *Publications:* contrib. to jls incl. Palaeontology, Rev. of Palaeobotany and Palynology, Botanical Jl Linnean Soc., Nature. *Recreations:* gardening, Mozart, opera. *Address:* School of Earth and Ocean Sciences, Cardiff University, Cardiff CF10 3AT. *T:* (029) 2087 4264.

EDWARDS, Douglas; *see* Edwards, P. D.

EDWARDS, Duncan; *see* Edwards, John D.

EDWARDS, Elgan; *see* Edwards, D. E. H.

EDWARDS, Elizabeth Alice; *see* Wilson, E. A.

EDWARDS, Prof. Elizabeth Jane Mary, FBA 2015; Research Professor in Photographic History and Director, Photographic History Research Centre, De Montfort University, 2011–Jan. 2016, now Emerita; *b* Carlisle, 24 Feb. 1952; *d* of Dennis and Sheila Edwards; *m* 1977, Simon Edwards; one *d*. *Educ:* Univ. of Reading (BA); Univ. of Leicester (MA). Curator of Photographs, Pitt Rivers Mus., 1977–2005, Lectr in Visual Anthropol., 1990–2005, Univ. of Oxford; Professorial Res. Fellow, Univ. of Arts, London, 2005–11. Vis. Schol., Max Planck Inst. für Wissenschaftsgeschichte, 2008; Fellow, Inst. of Advanced Studies, Univ. of Durham, 2012. Mem. Adv. Bd, Nat. Media Mus. (Science Mus.), 2015–. Vice-Pres., RAI, 2009–12. *Publications:* Anthropology and Photography 1865–1920, 1992; Raw Histories: photographs, anthropology and museums, 2001; (ed jtly) Photographs Objects Histories, 2004; (ed jtly) Sensible Objects: colonialism, material culture and the senses, 2006; (with P. James) A Record of England, 2006; (ed jtly) Photography, Anthropology and History, 2009; Camera as Historian: amateur photographers and historical imagination 1885–1918, 2012; (ed jtly) Uncertain Images: museums and the work of photographs, 2014; (ed jtly) Photographs, Museums, Collections: between art and information, 2015; contrib. articles to Hist. and Theory, Hist. and Anthropol., Hist. of Photography. *Recreations:* chamber music, growing vegetables. *Address:* Photographic History Research Centre, Portland School of Humanities, De Montfort University, Leicester LE1 9BH. *E:* eedwards@dmu.ac.uk.

EDWARDS, Gareth Huw; Principal, George Watson's College, Edinburgh, 2001–14; *b* Swansea, 9 April 1958; *s* of Roy and Gwyneth Edwards; *m* 1981, Jane Rees; one *d*. *Educ:* Tudor Grange Grammar Sch.; Solihull Sixth Form Coll.; Exeter Coll., Oxford (BA Hons Lit.Hum.); Univ. of Bristol (PGCE). Asst Classics Master, King Edward's Sch., Birmingham,

1981–85; Hd of Classics, Boys' Div., Bolton Sch., 1985–90; Vice-Principal, Newcastle-under-Lyme Sch., 1990–96; Rector, Morrison's Acad., Crieff, 1996–2001. *Recreations:* choral singing, Welsh Rugby fan, Hellenophile.

EDWARDS, His Honour Gareth Owen; QC 1985; a Circuit Judge, 1991–2006; *b* 26 Feb. 1940; *s* of Arthur Wyn Edwards and Mair Eluned Edwards; *m* 1967, Katharine Pek Har Goh; two *s* one *d.* *Educ:* Herbert Strutt Grammar Sch., Belper; Trinity Coll., Oxford (BA, BCL). Called to the Bar, Inner Temple, 1963; Army Legal Service, 1963–65; Commonwealth Office, 1965–67. Practised, Wales and Chester Circuit, 1967–91; Recorder, Crown Court, 1978–91. *Recreations:* climbing, chess. *Address:* 58 Lache Lane, Chester CH4 7LS. *T:* (01244) 677795. *Clubs:* Army and Navy; Athenæum (Liverpool).

EDWARDS, Sir Gareth (Owen), Kt 2015; CBE 2007 (MBE 1975); retired 1978 as Welsh Rugby footballer; chairman of leisure company in S Wales; *b* 12 July 1947; *s* of Granville and Anne Edwards; *m* 1972, Maureen Edwards; two *s.* *Educ:* Pontardawe Tech. Sch.; Millfield Sch.; Cardiff College of Educn. Rugby Football: 1st cap for Wales, 1967 (*v* France); Captain of Wales on 13 occasions; youngest Captain of Wales (at 20 years), 1968; British Lions Tours: 1968, 1971, 1974; Barbarians, 1967–78. Member of Cardiff RFC, 1966–; a record 53 consecutive caps, to 1978. *Publications:* Gareth: an autobiography, 1978; (jtly) Rugby Skills, 1979; Rugby Skills for Forwards, 1980; Gareth Edwards on Fishing, 1984; Rugby, 1986; Gareth Edwards' 100 Great Rugby Players, 1987; (with Peter Bills) Gareth Edwards: the autobiography, 1999; (with Peter Bills) Tackling Rugby: the changing world of professional Rugby, 2002. *Recreations:* fishing, golf. *Address:* 211 West Road, Nottage, Porthcawl, Mid-Glamorgan CF36 3RT. *T:* (01656) 785669.

EDWARDS, Graham, FRICS; Chief Executive, TelerealTrillium, since 2001; *b* London, 4 Jan. 1964; partner, Georgina Black; one *d*, and one *s* one *d* by a previous marriage. *Educ:* Fitzwilliam Coll., Cambridge (BA Econs 1987). ACA 1990. Investment Mgt Cert. Level 3 1997. Associate Mem., ACT, 1995; Associate, UK Soc. of Investment Professionals, 1998. Auditor, 1987–90, Corporate Finance Exec., 1990–91, Stoy Hayward; Hd, Property Finance, 1991–94, Corporate Finance Manager, 1994–97, BT plc; Fund Manager, Merrill Lynch Mercury Asset Mgt, 1997–99; Chief Investment Officer, 1999–2004, Dir, 2004–12, Talisman Global Asset Mgt. Trustee: MDA, 2006–; Pennies Foundn, 2010–. FRICS 2012. *Recreations:* bridge, tennis, ski-ing, investing. *Address:* (office) Clive House, 2 Old Brewery Mews, Hampstead, NW3 1PZ. *T:* (020) 7433 0667. *E:* gedwards@telerealtrillium.com.

EDWARDS, Helen, CB 2012; CBE 2001; Director General, Localism, Department for Communities and Local Government, since 2013; *b* 2 Aug. 1953; *d* of Charlton and Isobel Edwards; *m* 1987, David John Rounds; three *s.* *Educ:* Univ. of Sussex (BA Hons 1975); Univ. of Warwick (MA 1977; CQSW 1977). Social Worker, E Sussex CC, 1975–80; Dep. Project Dir, Save the Children Fund, 1980–83; National Association for Care and Resettlement of Offenders: Policy Develt Officer, 1983–85; Principal Officer, 1985–88; Asst Dir, 1988–93; Dir of Policy, Res. and Develt, 1993–96; Chief Exec., 1997–2001; Dir, Active Community Unit, 2002–04, Dir Gen., Communities Gp, 2004–05, Home Office; Chief Exec., Nat. Offender Mgt Service, Home Office, subseq. at MoJ, 2005–08; Dir Gen., Justice Policy (formerly Criminal Justice) Gp, MoJ, 2008–13. Member: New Deal Adv. Task Force, 1997–2001; Working Gp reviewing prison Bds of Visitors, 2000–01; Learning and Skills Council, 2000–02. Non-exec. Dir, Central and NW London NHS Foundn Trust, 2009–. Trustee, Lloyds Bank Foundn, 2011–. FRSA 1997. DUniv Middlesex, 2004. *Publications:* articles in jls on crime, social exclusion and criminal justice. *Recreation:* family and friends. *Address:* Department for Communities and Local Government, 2 Marsham Street, SW1P 4DF.

EDWARDS, Huw; Presenter: BBC News at Ten (formerly Ten O'Clock News), since 2003; BBC News at Five, since 2006; The Wales Report, since 2012; *b* 18 Aug. 1961; *s* of late Prof. Hywel Teifi Edwards and of Aerona Edwards (*née* Protheroe); *m*; five *c.* *Educ:* Llanelli Boys' Grammar Sch.; UWCC (BA French). Joined BBC as trainee journalist, 1984; Parly Corresp., BBC Wales, 1986–88; Political Corresp., then Chief Political Corresp., BBC TV News and BBC News 24, 1988–99; Presenter, BBC Six O'Clock News, 1999–2002. Presenter of BBC TV and radio progs incl. Trooping the Colour, Festival of Remembrance, State Opening of Parliament, D-Day 60, The Story of Welsh, Songs of Praise, Lloyd George, Gladstone and Disraeli, The Royal Wedding, The Story of Wales, The Diamond Jubilee, Opening and Closing Ceremonies of London 2012 Olympic Games, and progs on classical music; newsreader cameo role, Skyfall (film), 2012. Hon. Prof. of Journalism, 2006, Pro-Chancellor, 2012–, Cardiff Univ. Hon. Fellow: Cardiff Univ., 2003; Univ. of Wales, Lampeter, 2006; Univ. of Wales, Swansea, 2007; Univ. of Wales, Newport, 2007; Swansea Inst. of Higher Educn, 2007. Ambassador, Prince's Trust. Patron: Cancer Research, Wales; Nat. Coll. of Music; George Thomas Hospice, 2007–; Bridgend Male Choir, 2008–; Trinity Hospice, London, 2010–; Ty Bryngwyn Hospice, Llanelli, 2012–; President: Gwalia Male Voice Choir, 2006–; Llanelli Community Heritage, 2006–; London Welsh Trust, 2008–; London Welsh Male Voice Choir, 2012– (Vice Pres., 2005–12). DUniv Glamorgan, 2007. Presenter of the Year, BAFTA Cymru/Wales, 2001, 2002, 2003, 2004, 2009, 2012. *Publications:* Capeli Llanelli: our rich heritage, 2009; City Mission: the story of London's Welsh chapels, 2014. *Clubs:* Garrick, London Welsh (Pres., 2008–).

EDWARDS, Huw William Edmund; independent training consultant on democratic governance; Training Director, Your Legal Eyes; *b* 12 April 1953; *s* of late Rev. Dr Ifor M. Edwards and Esme Edwards; *m* 2005, Tess Cooling; one step *s* one step *d.* *Educ:* Eastfields High Sch., Mitcham; Manchester Polytechnic; Univ. of York (BA, MA, MPhil). Lecturer in Social Policy: Coventry (Lanchester) Poly., 1980–81; Univ. of Sheffield, 1983–84; Poly. of the South Bank, 1984–85; Manchester Poly., 1985–88. Res. Associate, Low Pay Unit, 1985–97; Tutor with Open Univ., 1987–95; Sen. Lectr in Social Policy, Brighton Poly., later Univ. of Brighton, 1988–91, 1992–97; Res. Student, Constitution Unit, UCL, 2007–11; former Associate Lectr, Nat. Sch. of Govt. MP (Lab) Monmouth, May 1991–1992, 1997–2005; contested (Lab) same seat, 1992, 2005. Member: Select Cttee on Welsh Affairs, 1991–92, 1998–2001, and 2002–05; Modernisation Cttee, H of C, 1997–98. Chm., Welsh Parly Labour Gp, 2000–01; Sec., All Party Commons and Lords Rugby Club. Member: Labour campaign for Electoral Reform; Fabian Soc., 1992–. Internat. Expert, EU funded project on governance and parly reform in Libya, 2012–14. Pres., Chepstow Mencap, 1992–; Mem. Exec., Shelter Cymru, 1988–91; Mem. Monmouth Gp, Amnesty Internat., 1969–. Patron, Gwent ME Soc., 1997–. Mem., Boro' Welsh Congregational Chapel, London. Vice-Pres., Monmouth Rugby Club, 1997–. *Publications:* reports on low pay in Wales and a fair electoral system for the Welsh Assembly; articles in professional jls. *Recreations:* sport, football, Rugby, cricket, Welsh choral music (Member, Gwalia Male Voice Choir; Chairman, Monmouth Male Voice Choir). *Address:* Wyefield House, The Paddocks, Monmouth NP25 3NP. *W:* www.huwedwardstraining.com. *Club:* London Welsh Association.

EDWARDS, Ian Anthony; Regional Chairman of Industrial, subsequently Employment, Tribunals, Southampton, 1996–2003, a part-time Chairman, 2004–06; *b* 18 June 1940; *s* of Gordon Burrows Edwards and Florence Hilda Edwards; *m* 1976, Susan Joy Rooth; one *s* one *d.* *Educ:* Liverpool Inst.; Liverpool Univ. (LLB 1961); Southampton Univ. (LLM 1962). Admitted as solicitor, 1965; Partner, Paris Smith & Randall, Southampton, 1970–87; Chm., part-time, 1985–87, full-time, 1987–96, Industrial Tribunals, Southampton. *Publications:* (ed jtly) Mead's Unfair Dismissal, 5th edn, 1994. *Recreations:* leader of Urban Saints (formerly Crusaders), walking, music, railways.

EDWARDS, (Ifan) Prys; Director, Prys Edwards Consultancy, since 1986; *b* 11 Feb. 1942; *m* 1966, Catherine Williams; one *s* one *d.* *Educ:* Leighton Park Sch., Reading; Welsh Sch. of Architecture, Cardiff (DipArch). RIBA 1965. Principal Partner, Prys Edwards Partnership, 1966–86. Member: Wales and the Marches Postal Bd, 1974–76; Develt Bd for Rural Wales, 1976–84; BTA, 1984–92; Chairman: Wales Tourist Bd, 1984–92; Welsh Fourth Channel Authy, 1992–98. Dir, Wales Millennium Centre, 1997–2006 (Life Vice-Pres., 2008). Hon. Pres., Urdd Gobaith Cymru (Welsh League of Youth), 1981–. *Recreations:* sailing, watching Rugby, golf. *Address:* Bryn Aberoedd, Caemelyn, Aberystwyth SY23 2HA. *T:* (01970) 623001.

EDWARDS, Jennifer Fitzgerald, CBE 2011; Chief Executive Officer, Mental Health Foundation, since 2013; *b* Bristol, 26 Dec. 1954; *d* of William Terence Chalmers Edwards and Cora Marion Edwards; *m* 1994, Jean Pierre Ferraroli (marr. diss. 2014); one *s.* *Educ:* Torquay Girls' Grammar Sch.; Girton Coll., Cambridge (BA 1976; MA 1981). Fast Stream Civil Servant, MAFF, 1976–81; Nat. Organiser, CND, 1981–83; various posts, London Bor. of Camden, 1983–89; Nat. Coordinator, Ministry for Women Initiative, 1990–92; Sen. Policy Advr to Leader, Camden Council, 1992–93; Dir/CEO, Nat. Campaign for the Arts, 1993–98; London Dir, Ext. Relns and Develt, Arts England, 1998–2004; Chief Exec., Homeless Link, 2004–11; Interim Exec. Dir, Interights, 2012–13. Dir, Taproot Consultancy, 2011–13. Mem. (Lab), Westminster CC, 1990–93. Chair, Ashford Place, 2012–14. FRSA 1995. *Publications:* (contrib. with P. Farmer) Hidden Loneliness, 2014. *Recreations:* gardening, opera, creative digital work. *Address:* Mental Health Foundation, Colechurch House, 1 London Bridge Walk, SE1 2SX. *T:* (020) 7803 1134, *Fax:* (020) 7803 1111. *E:* mlawrence@mentalhealth.org.uk.

EDWARDS, Jeremy John Cary; Group Managing Director, Henderson Administration Group, 1989–95; *b* 2 Jan. 1937; *s* of late William Philip Neville Edwards, CBE, and Hon. Mrs Sheila Edwards (*née* Cary); *m* 1st, 1963, Jenifer Graham (*née* Mould) (decd); one *s* one *d*; 2nd, 1974, April Philippa Harding (marr. diss. 1993); one *s*; 3rd, 1994, Mrs Amanda Barber. *Educ:* Ridley Coll., Ontario; Vinehall Sch., Sussex; Haileybury and Imperial Service Coll. Unilever, 1955–57; Hobson Bates & Co., 1957–59; Overseas Marketing and Advertising, 1959–61; Courtaulds, 1961–63; Vine Products, 1963–66; Loewe SA, 1966–68; Jessel Securities, 1968–70; Man. Dir, Vavasseur Unit Trust Management, 1970–74; Henderson Admin Gp, 1974–95; Jt Man. Dir, 1983–89. Non-executive Director: College Hill Associates, 1996–2002; Tribune Trust, 1997–2006; Liontrust First UK Investment Trust, 1999–2004. Hon. Treas., WWF (UK), 1984–2002; Children's Society (formerly C of E Children's Society): Mem. Council, 1987–2002; Vice-Chm., 1996–2002; Chm., Jewson Associates (formerly E. Jewson Services to Charities) Ltd, 2000–06; Trustee, Breast Cancer Haven (formerly Haven Trust), 1998–2008. *Address:* 59 Dorothy Road, SW11 2JJ. *T:* (020) 7228 6055. *Club:* Boodle's.

EDWARDS, Rev. Joel; International Director, Micah Challenge, 2009–14; *b* 15 Oct. 1951; *m* 1976, Carol Munroe-Edwards; one *s* one *d.* *Educ:* London Bible Coll. (BA Theology 1975). Probation Officer, 1978–88; Gen. Sec., African and Caribbean Evangelical Alliance, 1988–92; UK Dir, Evangelical Alliance, 1992–97; Gen. Dir, Evangelical Alliance UK, 1997–2008. Pastor, 1985–95, Associate Pastor, 1996–2003, Mile End New Testament Church of God. Hon. Canon, St Paul's Cathedral, 2002. Comr, Equality and Human Rights Commn, 2007–10. Advr, Tony Blair Faith Foundn, 2008; Mem., Human Rights Adv. Gp, FCO, 2010–. Fellow, St John's Coll., Durham, 2009. Hon. DD: Caribbean Grad. Sch. of Theol., Jamaica, 2006; St Andrews, 2007. Prime Minister's Award (Jamaica), 2003. *Publications:* Lord Make Us One—But Not All the Same!, 1999; The Cradle, The Cross and The Empty Tomb, 2000; Hope, Respect and Trust: valuing these three, 2004; Falling Back on God: a Lent group study on trust, 2006; (with D. Killingray) Black Voices: the shaping of our Christian experience, 2007; Advent Hope: a spiritual focus for personal or group use, 2007; An Agenda for Change: a global call for spiritual and social transformation, 2008. *Recreations:* gym, reading.

EDWARDS, John Charles; JP; Lord Mayor of Cardiff, 1980–81; *b* 3 April 1925; *s* of John Robert Edwards and Elsie Florence Edwards; *m* 1946, Cynthia Lorraine Bushell; one *s* two *d.* *Educ:* Lansdowne Road Sch., Cardiff. Served War of 1939–45, RM (1939–45 Star, France and Germany Star, War Medal 1939–45); TA, 1948–62, RASC (TEM). Postal Exec. Officer, GPO. Member: Cardiff CC, 1962–83 (Dep. Lord Mayor, 1978–79); S Glam CC, 1974–78; Associate Mem., Inst. of Transport Admin, 1982. Freeman of City of London, 1981. JP S Glam, 1979. Mem., St John's Council for S Glam; CStJ 1997 (OStJ 1980). *Recreations:* athletics, football. *Address:* 61 Cosmeston Street, Cathays, Cardiff CF24 4LQ. *T:* (029) 2040 7977. *Club:* Civil Service.

EDWARDS, John Coates, CMG 1989; HM Diplomatic Service, retired; Head of UK Delegation, EC Monitoring Mission in former Yugoslavia, April–Sept. 1995, April–Aug. 1996, May–Sept. 1997, April–July 1998 and March–June 1999; *b* 25 Nov. 1934; *s* of late Herbert John and Doris May Edwards; *m* 1959, Mary Harris (*d* 2006); one *s* one *d.* *Educ:* Skinners' Co. Sch., Tunbridge Wells, Kent; Brasenose Coll., Oxford (MA). Military Service, 1953–55: Lieut, RA. Asst Principal: Min. of Supply, 1958; Colonial Office, 1960; Private Sec. to Parly Under Sec. of State for the Colonies, 1961; Principal: Nature Conservancy, 1962; Min. of Overseas Develt, 1965; First Sec. (Develt), and UK Perm. Rep. to ECAFE, Bangkok, Thailand, 1968; Asst Sec., Min. of Overseas Develt, 1971; Head of E Africa Develt Div., Nairobi, Kenya, 1972; Asst Sec., Min. of Overseas Develt, 1976; Head of British Develt Div. in the Caribbean, Barbados, and UK Dir, Caribbean Develt Bank, 1978; Hd, West Indian and Atlantic Dept, FCO, 1981–84; Dep. High Comr, Kenya, 1984–88; High Commissioner: Lesotho, 1988–91; Botswana, 1991–94. Chm., Kenya Soc., 1997–2012. JP Kent, 2000. *Address:* Fairways, Back Lane, Ightham, Sevenoaks, Kent TN15 9AU. *Clubs:* Royal Over-Seas League (Mem. Central Council, 2003–); Muthaiga Country (Life Mem.) (Nairobi).

EDWARDS, (John) Duncan; President and Chief Executive, Hearst Magazines International, since 2009; Vice Chairman, Hearst Magazines UK, since 2009; *b* 28 March 1964; *s* of Dr Vernon A. Edwards, OBE, JP and Jean Edwards; *m* 1993, Sarah Kennedy; two *s.* *Educ:* Merchant Taylors' Sch., Northwood; Univ. of Sheffield (BA Hons Geog. and Politics 1985). With Media Week Ltd, 1985–89; Publisher, Company mag., 1989–93; National Magazine Co. Ltd: Business Develt Dir, 1993–98; Dep. Man. Dir, 1998–2002; Man. Dir, later Chief Exec., 2002–09; Chm., Comag Ltd, 2002; Mem., Bd of Dirs, Hearst Corp., 2011–. Mem. Adv. Bd, British Amer. Business Assoc., 2010–; Dir, Foreign Policy Assoc., 2012–. Dir, St George's Soc. of NY, 2014–. *Recreations:* running, leading a full life! *Address:* Hearst Corporation, 300 West 57th Street, New York, NY 10024, USA. *E:* dedwards@hearst.com. *Clubs:* Soho House, George; Old Merchant Taylors' Rugby Football.

EDWARDS, John Reid, JD; attorney; Partner, Edwards Kirby, since 2013; US Senator from North Carolina, 1999–2005; *b* 10 June 1953; *s* of Wallace R. Edwards and Catherine Edwards; *m* 1977, (Mary) Elizabeth Anania (*d* 2010); one *s* two *d* (and one *s* decd). *Educ:* NC State Univ. (BS 1974); Univ. of NC at Chapel Hill (JD 1977). Called to the Bar: NC, 1977; Tenn, 1978; Associate, Dearborn and Ewing, Nashville, Tenn, 1978–81; trial lawyer, 1981; Associate, 1981–83, Partner, 1984–92, Tharrington Smith and Hargrove, Raleigh, NC; Partner, Edwards and Kirby, Raleigh, NC, 1993–99. Dir, Center on Poverty, Work and Opportunity, Univ. of N Carolina at Chapel Hill, 2005–06. Vice-Presidential cand. (Democrat), 2004, Presidential cand. (Democrat), 2008, US elections.

EDWARDS, Jonathan; MP (Plaid Cymru) Carmarthen East and Dinefwr, since 2010; *b* Capel Hendre, Carmarthenshire, 26 April 1976. *Educ:* Ysgol Gyfun Maes yr Yrfa; Univ. of Wales, Aberystwyth (BA Hist. and Politics; postgrad. degree in Internat. Hist.). COS to

Rhodri Glyn Thomas, Mem., Nat. Assembly for Wales and Adam Price, MP; with Nat. Campaigns Directorate, Plaid Cymru, 2005–07; with Citizens Advice Cymru, 2007–. Plaid Cymru spokesman for: Business, Innovation and Skills, 2010–; Communities and Local Government, 2010–15; Culture, Olympics, Media and Sport, 2010–15; Transport, 2010–; Treasury, 2010–; Foreign Intervention, 2015–. Mem., Welsh Affairs Select Cttee, 2010–15. *Address:* House of Commons, SW1A 0AA.

EDWARDS, Jonathan David, CBE 2001 (MBE 1996); athlete, retired 2003; broadcaster, BBC Sport; *b* 10 May 1966; *s* of Andrew David Edwards and Jill Edwards (*née* Caulfield); *m* 1990, Alison Joy Briggs; two *s*. *Educ:* Durham Univ. (BSc Hons). Triple jump athlete: English Schs Champion, 1984; Gold Medallist: World Cup, 1992, 2002; World Championships, Gothenburg, 1995 (estabd world record, 18.29m), Edmonton, 2001; Eur. Indoor Championships, Valencia, 1998; Eur. Championships, Budapest, 1998; Olympic Games, Sydney, 2000; Commonwealth Games, Manchester, 2002. Mem. Bd, London Organising Cttee, 2012 Olympic Games, 2005–13. Mem. for England, Content Bd, Ofcom, 2003–06. Sports Personality of Year Award, BBC, 1995. *Publications:* A Time to Jump, 2000. *Address:* c/o MTC (UK) Ltd, 71 Gloucester Place, W1U 8JW. *T:* (020) 7935 8000.

EDWARDS, Rev. Jonathan Page; Executive Ambassador, Prospects, since 2013; *b* Westcliff-on-Sea, Essex, 23 Feb. 1956; *s* of Linley Gordon Edwards and Barbara Elizabeth Hindley Edwards (*née* Baker); *m* 1984, Susan Lesley Stevens; one *s* two *d*. *Educ:* Westcliff High Sch. for Boys; St John's Coll. and Regent's Park Coll., Oxford (MA). Ordained minister, 1982; Minister, Southgate Church, Bury St Edmunds, 1983–91; Sen. Minister, Orpington Baptist Church, 1991–98; Gen. Superintendent, SW Area, Baptist Union of GB, 1998–2001; Sen. Regl Minister, SW Baptist Assoc., 2001–06; Gen. Sec., Baptist Union of GB, 2006–13. Sec., Baptist Ministers' Fellowship, 1994–99. Chm., Membership Cttee, Baptist World Alliance, 2010–. *Recreations:* family, music, postcard collecting.

EDWARDS, Dame Julie Andrews; *see* Andrews, Dame J. E.

EDWARDS, Kenneth; *see* Edwards, A. K.

EDWARDS, Dr Kenneth John Richard; Vice-Chancellor, University of Leicester, 1987–99; *b* 12 Feb. 1934; *s* of John and Elizabeth May Edwards; *m* 1958, Janet Mary Gray; two *s* one *d*. *Educ:* Market Drayton Grammar Sch.; Univ. of Reading (BSc 1st class 1958); University Coll. of Wales, Aberystwyth (PhD 1961; Hon. Fellow). Nat. Service, RAF, 1952–54. Fellow, Univ. of California, 1961–62; ARC Fellow, Welsh Plant Breeding Station, Aberystwyth, 1962–63, Sen. Sci. Officer, 1963–66; Cambridge University: Lectr in Genetics, 1966–84; Head of Dept of Genetics, 1981–84; Sec. Gen. of Faculties, 1984–87; St John's College: Fellow, 1971–87; Lectr, 1971–84; Tutor, 1980–84. Vis. Lectr in Genetics, Univ. of Birmingham, 1965; Vis. Prof., INTA, Buenos Aires, 1973; Leverhulme Res. Fellow, Univ. of California, 1973. Chm., CVCP, 1993–95; Member: Marshall Aid Commemoration Commn, 1991–98; Council, ACU, 1994–99; Bd, CRE, 1994–2001 (Pres., 1998–2001). Mem. Bd, USS Ltd, 1994–97. Chm. Governing Body, Inst. of Grassland and Envmtl Res., 1994–99. Chm. Council, CRAC, 2001–08; Chm. Govs, Perse Sch., Cambridge, 2002–09. Hon. LLD: QUB, 1995; Leicester, 1999; Hon. DSc: Reading, 1995; Loughborough, 1995; Warwick, 2000; Hon. MA Nene Coll., 1997; Dr (*hc*) Babeş-Bolyai, Romania, 1998; Maribor, Slovenia, 2001; Olomouc, Czech Republic, 2002. *Publications:* Evolution in Modern Biology, 1977; articles on genetics in sci. jls. *Recreations:* music, gardening. *Address:* 10 Sedley Taylor Road, Cambridge CB2 8PW. *T:* (01223) 245680.

EDWARDS, Lionel Antony, (Tony), CEng, FRAeS; Head, Defence Export Services Organisation, 1998–2002; *b* 4 Nov. 1944; *s* of Lionel Victor and Marjorie Edwards. *Educ:* Abingdon Sch.; Univ. of Birmingham (BSc Hons 1966); Harvard Business Sch. (MBA 1972). CEng 1991; FRAeS 1991. Apprentice Engr, Rolls-Royce, Derby, 1962–68; Mfg Engr, General Electric, Lynn, Mass, 1968–71; Lectr, Harvard Univ., 1972–73; Manager/Dir, General Electric, Lynn and Cincinatti, Ohio, 1973–82; Gen. Manager, Storno A/S, Copenhagen, 1983–86; Corporate Vice-Pres., Motorola, Copenhagen, 1986–88; President: Challenger Exec. Jet Div., Montreal, 1988–89; Canadair Aerospace Gp, Montreal, 1989; Man. Dir, Lucas Aerospace Ltd, Solihull, 1989–92; Gp Man. Dir, Lucas Industries, 1992; Chief Exec., Dowty, and Main Bd Dir, TI Gp PLC, 1992–98; Chm. and Chief Exec., Messier-Dowty, 1994–98. Chm., Defence and Aerospace Sector Panel, OST Technology Foresight Prog., 1995–97. Member: Council, SBAC, 1989–98 (Vice-Pres. 1990–91, Pres. 1991–92, Dep. Pres. 1992–93); DTI Aviation Cttee, 1992–98; Council, Air League, 1992; Council, RAeS, 1992 (Pres., 1999–2000); NDIC, 1992–2001. Trustee: RAF Mus.; Swordfish Heritage Trust, subseq. Fly Navy Heritage Trust. *Recreations:* preservation of historic aircraft, shooting, classic cars, farming. *Address:* Wincott Hill Farm, Long Compton Road, Whichford, Warwickshire CV36 5PQ.

EDWARDS, Hon. Sir Llewellyn (Roy), AC 1989; Kt 1984; FRACMA; Consultant, Jones Lang La Salle (formerly Jones Lang Wootton), Brisbane, 1989–2009; *b* 2 Aug. 1935; *s* of Roy Thomas Edwards and Agnes Dulcie Gwendoline Edwards; *m* 1st, 1958, Leone Sylvia Burley (decd); two *s* one *d*; 2nd, 1989, Jane Anne Brumfield, AM. *Educ:* Raceview State Sch.; Silkstone State Sch.; Ipswich Grammar Sch.; Univ. of Queensland (MB, BS 1965). Qualified Electrician, 1955. RMO and Registrar in Surgery, Ipswich Hosp., 1965–67; gen. practice, Ipswich, 1967–74. MLA (L) Ipswich, Qld Parlt, 1972–83; Minister for Health, Qld, 1974–78; Dep. Premier and Treasurer, Qld, 1978–83; Dep. Med. Supt, Ipswich Hosp., 1983–85. Chairman: Ansvar Australia Insurance Ltd, 1984–94; World Expo 88 Authority, 1984–89; Australian Coachline Holdings Ltd, 1992–96; Micromedical Industries, 1993–96; Multi-Function Polis Develt Corp., SA, 1995–98; UQ Hldgs Pty Ltd, 1998–2009; Director: Westpac Banking Corp., 1988–2004; James Hardie Industries Pty Ltd, 1989–2001; Uniseed Pty Ltd, 2001–09. Chm., Pacific Film and Television Commn, 1991–2008; Mem., Australia Japan Foundn Bd, 1992–2006. Chancellor, Univ. of Queensland, 1993–2009 (Mem. Senate, 1984–2009). FRACMA 1984. Hon. FAIM 1988. Hon. LLD Queensland, 1988; DUniv: Griffith, 1998; Qld Univ. of Technol., 1999. *Recreations:* tennis, walking, cricket, Rugby Union. *Address:* 8 Ascot Street, Ascot, Qld 4007, Australia. *Clubs:* Brisbane, Tattersall's (Brisbane, Qld); United Services (Qld); Brisbane Polo.

EDWARDS, Malcolm John, CBE 1985; Chairman, Coal Investments Plc, 1993–96; founded Edwards Energy Ltd, 1992; Commercial Director, British Coal (formerly National Coal Board), 1985–92; Member of the Board, British Coal, 1986–92; *b* 25 May 1934; *s* of John J. Edwards and Edith (*née* Riley); *m* 1967, Yvonne, *d* of Mr and Mrs J. A. W. Daniels, Port Lincoln, S Australia; two *s*. *Educ:* Alleyn's Sch., Dulwich; Jesus Coll., Cambridge (MA). Joined NCB as trainee, 1956; Industrial Sales Manager, 1962; Dir of Domestic and Industrial Sales, 1969; Dir Gen. of Marketing, 1973; responsible for coal utilisation R & D, 1984–92; Chm., British Fuels Gp, 1988–92; Dep. Chm., Inter Continental Fuels, 1989–92. Chm., Finance Cttee, Southwark Diocesan Bd of Educn, 1992–. *Publications:* (with J. J. Edwards) Medical Museum Technology, 1959. *Recreations:* book collecting, arts and crafts movement, music, gardening. *Address:* 80 Waller Road, SE14 5LY.

EDWARDS, Marcus; *see* Edwards, His Honour C. M.

EDWARDS, Margaret Elizabeth; Vice President, UK Commissioning, McKesson, since 2011; *b* 21 May 1962; *d* of Bertie Arthur John Edwards and Christine Edwards (*née* Hamilton-Bell); partner, Michael Ramsden. *Educ:* UEA (BA Hons (Econs) 1983); Univ. of Plymouth (MBA 1993); Royal Soc. of Apothecaries (DPhilMed 1996); INSEAD (top mgt prog. 1998). Planning and Inf. Manager, Norwich HA, 1983–85; various mgt posts, Plymouth HA, 1985–94; Dir of Clin. Services, 1995–98, Chief Exec., 1998–2001, Heatherwood and Wexham Park NHS Trust; Dir of Performance, 2001–02, Dir of Access, 2002–06, DoH Chief Exec., Yorks and the Humber Strategic HA, 2006–09; Nat. Dir, NHS Productivity and Efficiency Unit, 2009; Interim Chief Exec., Wales Probation Service, 2010; Special Advr to Lord Carter, McKesson Health Solutions, 2010–11. Mem., Sen. Salaries Review Body 2012–. *Recreations:* reading, travel, philosophy and ethics.

EDWARDS, Mererid; *see* Edwards, A. M.

EDWARDS, Sir Michael, Kt 2014; OBE 2006; PhD; poet; Professor of Literary Creation in the English Language, Collège de France, since 2002; Member, Académie française, since 2013; *b* Barnes, 29 April 1938; *s* of Frank Edwards and Irene Edwards (*née* Dalliston); *m* 1964 Danielle Bourdin; one *s* one *d*. *Educ:* Kingston Grammar Sch.; Christ's Coll., Cambridge (BA 1960; MA 1964; PhD 1965; Hon. Fellow 2013). Lectr in French, Univ. of Warwick 1965–73; Reader in Literature, Univ. of Essex, 1973–87; Prof. of English, Univ. of Warwick 1987–2002; Eur. Chair, Collège de France, 2000–01. Commandeur des Arts et des Lettres (France), 2013. *Publications:* La Tragédie racinienne, 1972; Eliot/Language, 1975; Towards a Christian Poetics, 1984; Poetry and Possibility, 1988; Of Making Many Books, 1990 Raymond Mason, 1994; Éloge de l'attente, 1996; De Poetica Christiana, 1997; Beckett ou le don des langues, 1998; Leçons de poésie, 2001; Sur un vers d'Hamlet, 2001; Ombres de lune 2001; Un monde même et autre, 2002; Shakespeare et la comédie de l'émerveillement, 2003 Terre de poésie, 2003; Étude de la création littéraire en langue anglaise, 2004; Racine et Shakespeare, 2004; Shakespeare et l'œuvre de la tragédie, 2005; Le Génie de la poésie anglaise 2006, 2nd edn 2014; De l'émerveillement, 2008; Shakespeare: le poète au théâtre, 2009 L'Étrangèreté, 2010; Le Bonheur d'être ici, 2011; Le Rire de Molière, 2012; Discours de Réception à l'Académie française, 2015; *poetry:* To Kindle the Starling, 1972; Where, 1975 The Ballad of Mobb Conroy, 1977; The Magic, Unquiet Body, 1985; Poèmes, 1989; Rivage mobile, 2003; Paris demeure, 2008; At the Root of Fire/À la racine du feu, 2009; Ce que dit la lumière, 2010; Paris aubaine, 2012. *Recreations:* theatre, music, art, conversation. *Address:* 22 rue de Rivoli, 75004 Paris, France. *T:* (01) 40299579. *E:* michael.edwards@college-de-france.fr. *Club:* Cambridge Union.

EDWARDS, Dr Michael Frederick, OBE 1993; FREng, FIChemE; Principal Engineer Unilever, 1987–2001; *b* 27 April 1941; *s* of H. S. Edwards and J. Edwards (*née* Wallwork); *m* 1964, Margaret Roberta Thorne; one *s* one *d*. *Educ:* University Coll., Swansea (BSc, PhD). FIChemE 1980; FREng (FEng 1992). Lectr in Engrg Scis, Univ. of Warwick, 1966–69; Lectr, Sen. Lectr in Chem. Engrg, 1969–81, Prof. of Chemical Engrg, 1981–87, Bradford Univ. Mem., various research council bds and cttees. *Publications:* Mixing in the Process Industries, 1985, 2nd edn 1992; papers on process engrg in learned jls. *Recreations:* hill-walking, classical music, golf. *Address:* 44 Long Meadow, Gayton, Wirral CH60 8QQ. *T:* (0151) 342 5602.

EDWARDS, Prof. Michael Martin; JP; Joint Chairman, 2002–07, Chairman, 2007–08, Association of Governing Bodies of Independent Schools (Chairman, Governing Bodies Association, 1998–2002); *b* 19 July 1934; *s* of Charles Samuel and Lilian Edwards; *m* 1956, Dorothy Mildred Mayall; two *s*. *Educ:* London Sch. of Economics (BSc (Econ), PhD); London Univ. Inst. of Education (PGCE); Univ. of Maryland (Fulbright Schol.). Hd of Econs Sch., Woolwich Poly., 1959–67; Hd of Dept of Mgt and Business Studies, Hendon Coll. of Technology, 1967–71; Asst Dir, Poly. of South Bank, 1971–73; Academic Dir and Dep. Chief Exec., Middlesex Poly., 1973–91. Lectured at summer schs and confs, Univs of Bremen, Cologne, Hamburg, Heidelberg, Munich, Poznan, Trondheim and Warsaw, 1975–92; leader of educn missions to Hong Kong, Malaysia and Singapore, 1990–94. Dir, ISC, 1998– (Mem., 1998–). Non-exec. Dir, Harrow Community NHS Trust, 1991–94. Chairman: Bishop of London's Industrial Adv. Council, 1970–84; Higher and Further Educn Cttee, London Dio., 1973–80; Fulbright Awards Selection Cttee, 1984–96 (Mem., Fulbright Commn, 1986–96); John Lyon Charity, 1993–; St Mark's Hosp. Academic Inst., 1995–2001; St Mark's Res. Foundn, 1998–2011. Mem., Wkg Gp, RNT Trust, 2002–14; Hon. Mem. Council, RNT. Chairman of Governors: Harrow Coll. of Higher Educn, 1981–85; John Lyon Sch., 1982–2002; Mem. Governing Council, Oak Hill Theol Coll., 1981–91; Governor: Harrow Sch., 1982–2004; Lancing Coll., 2004–09; Mem., Council, Royal Alexandra and Albert Sch., 2008–11. Fellow, Woodard Corp., 2004–09. FRSocMed 1999. JP Harrow, 1991. *Publications:* The Growth of the British Cotton Trade 1780–1815, 1967; Aspects of Capital Investment, 1971; N. J. Smelser and the Cotton Factory Family, 1971. *Recreations:* music, Victorian literature, theatre, golf.

See also N. C. M. Edwards.

EDWARDS, Nigel Charles Michael; Chief Executive, Nuffield Trust, since 2014; *b* Lambeth, 1961; *s* of Prof. Michael Martin Edwards, *qv*; *m* 1993, Virginia Burns; three *d*. *Educ:* University Coll., Oxford (BA PPE); Westminster Univ. (MBA). Ops Dir, Central Middx Hosp., 1985–90; Reform Manager, Oxford RHA, 1990–92; Dir, London Health Econs Consortium, LSHTM, 1992–99; Dir of Policy, 1999–2010, Actg Chief Exec., 2010–11, NHS Confederation; Sen. Fellow, King's Fund, 2011–14. Expert, KPMG Global Centre of Excellence on Health, 2011–14. Hon. Vis. Prof., LSHTM, 2000–. *Publications:* The Triumph of Hope over Experience: lessons from NHS reorganisation, 2010. *Address:* Nuffield Trust, 59 New Cavendish Street, W1G 7LP. *T:* (020) 7631 8450. *E:* nicole.phillips@nuffieldtrust.org.uk.

EDWARDS, Norman L.; *see* Lloyd-Edwards.

EDWARDS, Patricia Anne, (Mrs Roger Cox); Legal Director, Office of Fair Trading, 1996–2004; *b* 29 May 1944; *d* of late Maurice James Edwards and of Marion Edwards (*née* Lewis); *m* 1970, His Honour Roger Charles Cox (*d* 2009). *Educ:* Barry and Purley County Grammar Schools; King's College London (LLB). Called to the Bar, Middle Temple, 1967, Bencher, 2003; Criminal Appeal Office, 1965–74; Law Officers' Dept, 1974–77; Home Office: Sen. Legal Asst, 1977–80; Asst Legal Adviser, 1980–88; Principal Asst Legal Advr, 1988–94; Dep. Parly Comr for Admin, 1994–96. *Recreations:* music, travel, reading, domestic pursuits.

EDWARDS, Sir Paul; *see* Edwards, Sir R. P.

EDWARDS, Prof. Paul Kerr, DPhil; FBA 1998; FAcSS; Professor of Employment Relations, Birmingham Business School, Birmingham University, since 2011 (Head, Department of Management, 2011–13); *b* 18 March 1952; *s* of Ernest Edwards and Ida Vivienne Edwards (*née* Kerr); *m* 1975, Susan Jane Martin; one *s* one *d*. *Educ:* Magdalene Coll., Cambridge (BA 1973); Nuffield Coll., Oxford (BPhil 1975; DPhil 1977). Warwick University: Res. posts, 1977–88, Dep. Dir, 1988–98, Dir, 1998–2002, Indust. Relns Res. Unit; Prof. of Industrial Relns, 1992–2010; Associate Dean, Warwick Business Sch., 2007–10. Chm., Social Scis Gp, British Acad., 2006–10. Mem., Business and Mgt sub-panel, RAE 2008, 2005–08, REF 2014, 2011–14. Fellow, AIM, 2004–07. FAcSS (AcSS 2008). Ed., Work, Employment and Society, 1996–98; Associate Ed., 2006–11, Ed.-in-Chief, 2012–, Human Relations. *Publications:* Strikes in the United States, 1981; (jtly) The Social Organization of Industrial Conflict, 1982; Conflict at Work, 1986; Managing the Factory, 1987; (jtly) Attending to Work, 1993; (ed) Industrial Relations, 1995, 2nd edn 2003; (jtly) Managers in the Making, 1997; (ed jtly) The Global Economy, National States and the Regulation of Labour, 1999; (jtly) The Politics of Working Life, 2005; (ed jtly) Social Theory at Work, 2006; (ed jtly) Studying Organizations using Critical Realism, 2014. *Recreation:* cycling.

EDWARDS, Prof. Peter Philip, PhD; FRS 1996; Professor of Inorganic Chemistry, University of Oxford, since 2003 (Head of Inorganic Chemistry, 2003–13); Fellow of St Catherine's College, Oxford, since 2003; *b* 30 June 1949; *s* of late Ronald Goodlass and of Ethel Mary, who later *m* Arthur Edwards; *m* 1970, Patricia Anne Clancy; two *s* one *d*. *Educ:* Univ. of Salford (BSc; PhD 1974). Fulbright Scholar and NSF Fellow, Baker Lab. of Chem., Cornell Univ., 1975–77; SERC/NATO Fellow and Ramsay Meml Fellow, Inorganic Chem. Lab., Oxford Univ., 1977–79; Cambridge University: Demonstrator in Inorganic Chem., 1979–81, Lectr, 1981–91, Univ. Chem. Labs; Dir of Studies in Chem., Jesus Coll., 1979–91; Co-Founder and Co-Dir, IRC in Superconductivity, 1988; Nuffield Sci. Res. Fellow, 1986–87; BP Venture Res. Fellow, 1988–90; Birmingham University: Prof. of Inorganic Chem., 1991–2003, of Chem. and of Materials, 1999–2003; Hd, Sch. of Chem., 1996–99; Royal Soc. Leverhulme Sen. Res. Fellow, 1996–97. Vis. Prof., Cornell Univ., 1983–86. Mem., HEFCE Res. Assessment Panel, RAE for 1996 and 2001. FRSC 1988 (Vice-Pres., Dalton Div., 1995; Corday-Morgan Medal, 1985; Tilden Medal, 1992; Liversidge Medal, 1999). Mem., German Acad. Scis, 2009. Hughes Medal, Royal Soc., 2003. *Publications:* (with C. N. R. Rao): The Metallic and Non-Metallic States of Matter, 1985; Metal-Insulator Transitions Revisited, 1995; contrib. Angewandte Chemie Internat. Edn. *Address:* St Catherine's College, Oxford OX1 3UJ.

EDWARDS, Peter Robert; Director, Personal Investment Authority, 1992–2001; *b* 30 Oct. 1937; *s* of Robert and Doris Edith Edwards; *m* 1st, 1967, Jennifer Ann Boys; one *s*; 2nd, 1970, Elizabeth Janet Barrett; one *d*; 3rd, 2000, Marjorie Ann Edworthy. *Educ:* Christ's Hospital. Chartered Accountant. Ernst & Young (and predecessor firms), 1955–90; Chief Exec., Secretan, 1990–92. Ind. Mem. Council, FIMBRA, 1990–94. Dir, Blackwall Green Ltd, 1992–96. *Recreations:* ornithology, gardening. *Address:* Quince Cottage, The Street, Bury, Pulborough, West Sussex RH20 1PA.

EDWARDS, (Philip) Douglas; QC 2010; *b* Blaina, S Wales, 10 June 1970; *s* of John Edwards and Leslie Edwards (*née* Silk). *Educ:* Nantyglo Comp. Sch.; Univ. of Birmingham (LLB Hons 1991). Called to the Bar, Lincoln's Inn, 1992; in practice as barrister specialising in planning, envmt and public law. Asst Parly Boundary Comr, 2011–; Lead Asst Comr for E Midlands Region, 2011–. Mem., Bar Representation Cttee, Hon. Soc. of Lincoln's Inn, 2012–. *Recreations:* ski-ing, walking, reading, natural history, Rugby. *Address:* Francis Taylor Building, Temple, EC4Y 9DB. *T:* (020) 7353 8415. *E:* douglas.edwardsqc@ftb.eu.com.

EDWARDS, Prof. Philip Walter, PhD; FBA 1986; King Alfred Professor of English Literature, University of Liverpool, 1974–90, now Emeritus; *b* 7 Feb. 1923; *er s* of late R. H. Edwards, MC, and late Mrs B. Edwards; *m* 1st, 1947, Hazel Margaret (*d* 1950), *d* of late Prof. C. W. and late Mrs E. R. Valentine; 2nd, 1952, Sheila Mary, *d* of late R. S. and late Mrs A. M. Wilkes, Bloxwich, Staffs; three *s* one *d*. *Educ:* King Edward's High Sch., Birmingham; Univ. of Birmingham. MA, PhD Birmingham; MA Dublin. Royal Navy, 1942–45 (Sub-Lieut RNVR). Lectr in English, Univ. of Birmingham, 1946–60; Commonwealth Fund Fellow, Harvard Univ., 1954–55; Prof. of English Lit., TCD, 1960–66; Fellow of TCD, 1962–66; Prof. of Lit., Univ. of Essex, 1966–74; Pro-Vice-Chancellor, Liverpool Univ., 1980–83. Visiting Professor: Univ. of Michigan, 1964–65; Williams Coll., Mass, 1969; Otago Univ., NZ, 1980; Internat. Christian Univ., Tokyo, 1989; Visiting Fellow: All Souls Coll., Oxford, 1970–71; Huntington Liby, Calif., 1977, 1983. *Publications:* Sir Walter Ralegh, 1953; (ed) Kyd, The Spanish Tragedy, 1959; Shakespeare and the Confines of Art, 1968; (ed) Pericles Prince of Tyre, 1976; (ed with C. Gibson) Massinger, Plays and Poems, 1976; Threshold of a Nation, 1979; (ed jtly) Shakespeare's Styles, 1980; (ed) Hamlet Prince of Denmark, 1985; Shakespeare: a writer's progress, 1986; Last Voyages, 1988; The Story of the Voyage, 1994; Sea-Mark, 1997; Pilgrimage and Literary Tradition, 2005; numerous articles on Shakespeare and literature of his time in Shakespeare Survey, Proc. British Acad., etc. *Recreations:* gardening, calligraphy. *Address:* High Gillinggrove, Gillinggate, Kendal, Cumbria LA9 4JB.

EDWARDS, Prys; *see* Edwards, I. P.

EDWARDS, Richard, PhD; Member (Lab) Preseli Pembrokeshire, National Assembly for Wales, 1999–2003; Member, Carmarthen Town Council, since 2008; *b* 1956. *Educ:* Queen Elizabeth Grammar Sch., Carmarthen; Univ. of Swansea; Univ. of Birmingham. Posts in local govt and political res. Mem., Carmarthen Town Council, 1991–99; Mayor of Carmarthen, 1997. Chair, Envmt, Planning and Transport Cttee, Nat. Assembly for Wales, 2000–03. Mem., ICSA. *Address:* c/o Carmarthen Town Council, St Peter's Civic Hall, 1 Nott Square, Carmarthen SA31 1PG.

EDWARDS, Prof. Robert; PhD; FRSC. Professor of Crop Protection and Head, School of Agriculture, Food and Rural Development, Newcastle University, since 2014; *b* Watford, 28 Dec. 1957; *s* of Dennis and Sheila Edwards; *m* 1988, Lesley Davies; one *s* one *d*. *Educ:* Mill Hill Sch., London; Univ. of Bath (BSc Hons Biochem. 1981); St Mary's Med. Sch., Univ. of London (PhD Biochem. 1984). FRSC 2011. Postdoctoral researcher, Royal Holloway, Univ. of London, 1984–86; Team Leader, Schering Agrochemicals, 1986–88; Section Hd, Noble Foundn, Oklahoma, 1988–90; University of Durham: Lectr, 1990–98; Reader, 1998–2003; Prof., 2003–10; Hd of Sch., Biol. Dept, 2008–10; Prof. of Crop Protection, Univ. of York, 2010–14; Chief Scientist, Food and Envmt Res. Agency, 2010–14. Res. Develt Fellow, BBSRC, 2003–08. *Publications:* contribs to peer-reviewed jls. *Recreations:* historic car restoration, yacht sailing, designing and installing bathrooms. *Address:* 48 Ancroft Garth, Durham DH1 2UD. *T:* (0191) 384 9541. *E:* robert.edwards@ncl.ac.uk.

EDWARDS, Sir (Robert) Paul, Kt 2009; Chief Executive, School Partnership Trust Academies, since 2007; *b* Doncaster, 25 July 1957; *s* of Richard Edwards and Edna Edwards; *m* 1984, Christine; two *d*. *Educ:* Univ. of Warwick (BA Hons Eng. and Philos. 1978); Univ. of Sheffield (MA Educn Mgt 1985; PGCE Eng. (Dist.) and Drama 1985; Adv. Dip. Educn Studies 1985). Teacher of English, Stanley High Sch., Southport, 1980–83; Hd of Drama, Mexborough Sch., Doncaster, 1983–86; Dep. Hd of English, Baysgarth Sch., Barton upon Humber, 1986–88; Hd of English, Hartland Sch., Worksop, 1988–90; Dep. Hd, Garibaldi Sch., Mansfield, 1990–95; Headteacher, Knottingley High Sch., 1995–2000; Principal, Garforth Academy (formerly Community College), 2000–11; Executive Headteacher: John Smeaton, 2001–11; Agnes Stewart, 2003–11. Advr, DCSF, later DFE Academies Unit, 2004–. *Recreations:* art, keen sportsman. *Address:* School Partnership Trust Academies, Unit 2 Carolina Court, Wisconsin Drive, Lakeside, Doncaster DN4 5RA. *T:* (01302) 379240.

EDWARDS, Robin Anthony, CBE 1981; Partner with Dundas & Wilson, CS (formerly Davidson & Syme, WS), 1965–96; *b* 7 April 1939; *s* of Alfred Walton Edwards and Ena Annie Ruffell; *m* 1963, Elizabeth Alexandra Mackay (marr. diss.); one *s* one *d*; *m* 1986, Janet Cant Pow. *Educ:* Daniel Stewart's Coll., Edinburgh; Edinburgh Univ. (MA, LLB (distinction), Cl. Medallist). Former Lectr in Conveyancing, Edinburgh Univ.; Admitted Member, WS Society, 1964; Mem. Council, Law Society of Scotland, 1969–84, Vice-Pres., 1978–79, Pres., 1979–80 (youngest Pres. ever, at that time). Mem., Lands Tribunal for Scotland, 1991–2001. *Recreation:* French travel and cuisine.

EDWARDS, Sara Elinor; Vice Lord-Lieutenant of Dyfed, since 2011; *b* Cardiff, 8 Feb.; *d* of John Morris Edwards, MS, FRCS, FACNM and Gwenyth Petty, actress and broadcaster; *m* 2009, Lt-Gen. Jonathon Peter Riley, *qv*; one *d*. *Educ:* James Allen's Girls Sch.; Greenacre Girls Sch.; Epsom Coll.; Bedford Coll., Univ. of London (BA Hons Medieval and Modern Hist.). Dip. de la Petite Cuisine, Richmond. Broadcaster and writer: freelance work for BBC Wales, incl. news and current affairs, countryside documentaries, interviews; outside broadcasting for agric., the arts and hist., incl. Royal Welsh Show, Nat. Eisteddfod of Wales and Llangollen Internat. Musical Eisteddfod. Pres., Cardiff NSPCC, 2000–, Mem., Wales Regl Forum, NSPCC, 2011–; Vice Pres., Nat. Parks of England and Wales. Sister, St John Cymru. Patron, Hijinx Th. Co. *Recreations:* cooking, gardening, fishing, the countryside, reading, music, visiting museums and art galleries. *W:* www.saraedwards.co.uk.

EDWARDS, Sian; freelance conductor; Music Director, English National Opera, 1993–95; Head of Conducting, Royal Academy of Music, since 2013; *b* 27 Aug. 1959; *m* 1992, Ian Kemp (*d* 2011); one *s*. *Educ:* Royal Northern Coll. of Music; Leningrad Conservatoire. Since 1985 has conducted many orchestras incl. LPO, RPO, Royal Scottish Orch., City of Birmingham SO, Hallé, English Chamber Orch. and Docklands Sinfonietta; conducted Orchestre de Paris and Philharmonique de Lille in France, and Pittsburgh Symphony, Philadelphia Orch., San Francisco Symphony, Los Angeles Philharmonic, Nat. Symphony, Atlanta Symphony, Minnesota Orch. in USA, and Ensemble Modern, Südwest funk Orchester, ND Radiofunkorchester in Germany; has also conducted orchestras in Canada, Belgium, Austria, Russia and Australia. Operatic début with Mahagonny (Weill), then Carmen, Scottish Opera, 1986; world première of Greek (Turnage), Munich Biennale and Edinburgh Fest., 1988; Glyndebourne: La Traviata, 1987; Katya Kabanova, 1988; New Year (Tippett), 1990; Royal Opera, Covent Garden: The Knot Garden (Tippett), 1988; Rigoletto, 1989; Il Trovatore, 1991; Madam Butterfly, 1992; English National Opera: The Gambler (Prokofiev), 1992; The Queen of Spades, 1993; La Bohème, Marriage of Figaro, Jenufa, The Mikado, Khovanshchina, 1995; Mahagonny, Carmen, Eugene Onegin, 1998; Peter Grimes, 2001; La Clemenza di Tito, Bordeaux, 1996; Clara (Gefors), Opéra Comique, Paris, 1997; Don Giovanni, Danish Royal Opera, 2001; The Death of Klinghoffer (John Adams), La Damnation de Faust, Finnish Nat. Opera, 2001; A Streetcar Named Desire (Previn), 2007, Dead Man Walking (Heggie), 2008, Rape of Lucretia (Britten), 2011, La Traviata (Verdi), 2014, Theater an der Wien; A Night at the Chinese Opera (Weir), 2008, Rake's Progress, 2012, Scottish Opera; Jenufa, WNO, 2008; Hansel and Gretel, Royal Acad. of Music, 2008. Recordings incl. orchestral works by Tchaikovsky, Prokofiev, Ravel, Britten, John Adams, and opera by Judith Weir. *Address:* c/o Ingpen & Williams Ltd, 7 St George's Court, 131 Putney Bridge Road, SW15 2PA. *T:* (020) 8874 3222.

EDWARDS, Dr Steven, CBE 2009; MRCVS; Consultant Editor, World Organisation for Animal Health, since 2009; Chief Executive, Veterinary Laboratories Agency, 2000–08, on secondment as interim Chief Executive, Animal Health, 2008, Department for Environment, Food and Rural Affairs (formerly Ministry of Agriculture, Fisheries and Food); *b* 9 March 1948; *s* of late William Edward Edwards and Daisy May Edwards (*née* Candelent); *m* 1976, Virginia Elizabeth Marian Lynch Evans; two *s*. *Educ:* Wolverhampton Grammar Sch.; Trinity Hall, Cambridge (MA, VetMB); Edinburgh Univ. (MSc, DVMS). MRCVS 1972. General veterinary practice, Montgomery, Powys, 1972–76; Univ. of Edinburgh, 1976–77; MAFF Veterinary Investigation Centre, Aberystwyth, 1977–78; Tech. Co-op. Officer, ODM, El Salvador, 1978–80, Bolivia, 1980; MAFF Central Veterinary Laboratory: Vet. Research Officer, 1980–92; Head of Virology Dept, 1992–98; MAFF Veterinary Laboratories Agency: Dir of Lab. Services, 1998–99; Dir of Surveillance and Lab. Services, 1999–2000. Visiting Professor: Farm Animal Studies, Univ. of Liverpool, 2001–10; Veterinary Infectious Diseases, RVC, London, 2002–09. Sec. General, 1991–2000, Vice Pres., 2000–03, Pres., 2003–09, Biological Standards Commn (formerly Standards Commn), World Orgn for Animal Health (formerly Office Internat. des Epizooties, Paris). Chm., World Orgn for Animal Health (formerly Office Internat. des Epizooties)/FAO Network on Avian Influenza, 2005–13. Founder Mem., European Soc. for Vet. Virology, 1987 (Sec., 1988–94; Hon. Mem., 1997); Pres., Vet. Res. Club, London, 1995–96. Co-founder, Sec. and Ed., Foundn for Medieval Genealogy, 2002–; Asst Sec., Harleian Soc., 2011–. Chm., St Lawrence Chobham Handbell Ringers, 2004–06. Churchwarden, St Bartholomew's, Vowchurch, 2012–. Gold Medal, World Orgn for Animal Health, 2009. *Publications:* contribs and editl for veterinary jls, text books and conf. proceedings, and for genealogy jls. *Recreations:* genealogy, railway preservation, local history.

EDWARDS, Susan; Director, Enforcement, Insolvency and Corporate Law, Department for Business, Innovation and Skills, 2009–12; *b* Preston, 17 Feb. 1949; *d* of Maurice Wilkinson and Nora Wilkinson; *m* 1993, Peter Edwards; one *s* one *d*, and two step *s*. *Educ:* Queen Mary Sch., Lytham; Queen Mary Coll., London (LLB). Called to the Bar, Gray's Inn, 1972; barrister, 1972–75; Prosecutor, HM Customs and Excise, 1975–77; Lectr in Law, Suffolk Coll. of Higher and Further Educn, 1980–81; Magistrate, Stow PSD, 1981; HM Customs and Excise: Prosecutor, 1982; Criminal Law Advr, 1982–88, Tax Adv. Lawyer, 1989–92; Sen. Prosecutor, 1992–93; Hd, Criminal Adv. Team, 1993–96; Hd, Civil Litigation, 1996–99, Hd, Prosecutions, 1999–2003, DoH and DSS, later DWP; Hd, Legal, Assets Recovery Agency, 2003–07; Dir, Litigation and Ops, Solicitor's Office, HMRC, 2007. *Recreations:* reading, country walks, listening to music, truffling in charity shops, massacre of noxious weeds.

EDWARDS, Thomas Mowbray C.; *see* Charles-Edwards.

EDWARDS, Tony; *see* Edwards, L. A.

EDWARDS, Tracy Karen, MBE 1990; consultant on team-building, personal insolvency, leadership and management; Director, Safer World Training Ltd, since 2013; Managing Director and Trustee, Maiden Rescue Ltd, since 2014; *b* 5 Sept. 1962; *d* of Antony Herbert Edwards and Patricia Edwards; one *d*; *m* twice (both marrs diss.). *Educ:* Highlands Primary Sch., Berks; Arts Educnl, Tring; Gowerton Comprehensive Sch., Swansea; Roehampton Univ. (BSc Psychol. and Criminol. 2012). Assembled first all-female crew to compete in 1989 Whitbread Round the World Race (Maiden Project), 1987; set world fastest ocean record, 1997. Man. Dir, Tracy Edwards Associates Ltd, 1990–2002; CEO, Quest Series Ltd, 2003–05; managed Oryx Quest yacht race, Qatar, 2005; Project Manager, Child Exploitation and Online Protection Centre, 2007–08. Presenter/Commentator, TV broadcasts, incl. 1993–94 Whitbread Race; Science of Sailing, 2001; On the Crest of a Wave, 2002. Patron: Just a Drop, 2009–; Regenerate, 2009–; Ambassador: Prince's Trust, 1990–; Duke of Edinburgh Award Scheme, 1998–; Gingerbread, 2007–. *Publications:* Maiden, 1990; Living Every Second (autobiog.), 2001. *Recreations:* riding, theatre, travel, reading, music, shooting, ski-ing. *Address:* c/o Lucas Alexander Whitley, 14 Vernon Street, W14 0RJ. *W:* www.tracyedwards.com. *Clubs:* Royal Ocean Racing, Mosimann's, Home House; Royal Yachting Association.

EDWARDS, Dr Victoria Mary, (Mrs R. M. Taylor), OBE 2004; FRICS; FAAV; CEnv; Partner, Taylor-Edwards Environmental Communications, since 2010; Associate Professor in Real Estate and Planning, Henley Business School, University of Reading, since 2011; *b* 14 Aug. 1963; *d* of George Wade Brown Edwards and Betty Kathleen Edwards (*née* Mack); *m* 1999, Richard Michael Taylor; one step *s* one step *d*. *Educ:* Birkenhead High Sch.; Univ. of Reading (BSc; PhD 1995); Univ. of Canterbury, NZ (MSc Hons). FAAV 1985; FRICS 1986; CEnv 2008. Chartered Surveyor, Dreweatt-Neate, 1984–87; Commonwealth Schol., Univ. of Canterbury, NZ, 1987–89; Consultant (pt-time), QEII Nat. Trust, Wellington, NZ, 1988–89; University of Portsmouth: Sen. Lectr, 1989–94, Principal Lectr, 1994–2006, Head, 2006–07, Faculty of Envmt; Res. Dir, Sch. of Envmtl Design and Mgt, 2007–10. Winston Churchill Travelling Fellow, 1991; Carthage Fellow, Pol Econ. Res. Center, Montana, 1991. Member: Countryside Commn, 1998–99; Bd, Countryside Agency, 1999–2004; Forestry Commn, 1999–2006. Mem., Burns Cttee for Inquiry into Hunting with Dogs, 1999–2000. Mem., Adv. Cttee, Sch. of Rural Econ. and Land Mgt, RAC, Cirencester, 1996–2001; Gov., Macaulay Land Res. Inst., 2001–03. Mem., Surveying Courses Bd, 1991–96, Educn and Membership Cttee, 1992–96, RICS. Trustee: Countryside Educn Trust, Beaulieu, Hants,

1998–2001; Habitat Res. Trust, 2003–09; Ernest Cook Trust, 2007–. *Publications:* Dealing in Diversity: America's market for nature conservation, 1995; Corporate Property Management: aligning real estate with business strategy, 2004; contrib. articles to envmtl jls. *Recreations:* golf, ski-ing, riding, travel, cooking for friends, walking, West Highland Terriers, the New Forest. *E:* v.m.edwards@reading.ac.uk.

EDWARDS-MOSS, (Sir) David John, (5th Bt *cr* 1868); *S* father, 1988, but does not use the title and his name does not appear on the Official Roll of the Baronetage.

EDWARDS-STUART, Hon. Sir Antony James Cobham, Kt 2009; **Hon. Mr Justice Edwards-Stuart;** a Judge of the High Court of Justice, Queen's Bench Division, since 2009; Judge in charge, Technology and Construction Court, since 2013; *b* 2 Nov. 1946; *s* of late Lt-Col Ivor Arthur James Edwards-Stuart and Elizabeth Aileen Le Mesurier Edwards-Stuart (*née* Deck); *m* 1973, Fiona Ann, *d* of late Paul Weaver, OBE; two *s* two *d*. *Educ:* Sherborne Sch.; RMA Sandhurst; St Catharine's Coll., Cambridge. MCIArb. Called to the Bar, Gray's Inn, 1976, Bencher, 2009; QC 1991; an Asst Recorder, 1991–97; a Recorder, 1997–2009; a Deputy High Ct Judge, 2003–09. Head of Chambers, 2005–09. Chm., Home Office Adv. Cttee on Service Candidates, 1995–98. Commnd 1st RTR, 1966; Adjutant: 1st RTR, 1973–75; Kent and Sharpshooters Sqn, Royal Yeomanry, 1976–77. *Recreations:* woodwork, restoring property in France. *Address:* Royal Courts of Justice, Strand, WC2A 2LL. *T:* (020) 7947 7205.

EDWARDSON, Prof. James Alexander, PhD; Professor of Neuroendocrinology, Newcastle University, 1982–2013, now Emeritus; Director, Institute for Ageing and Health (formerly Institute for the Health of the Elderly), Newcastle University, 1994–2006; *b* 18 March 1942; *s* of James Thompson Hewson Edwardson and Isabel Ann Edwardson; *m* 1965, Caroline Hunter; one *s* two *d*. *Educ:* South Shields Grammar-Technical Sch. for Boys; Univ. of Nottingham (BSc Hons Zoology 1963); Inst. of Psychiatry, Univ. of London (PhD 1966). MRC Junior Res. Fellow, Inst. of Psychiatry, 1966–67; Lectr in Physiology, Aberdeen Univ., 1967–69; MRC Scientist and Lectr in Biochem., Imperial Coll., London, 1970–75; Sen. Lectr, then Reader, in Physiology, St George's Hosp. Med. Sch., 1975–79; Director: MRC Neurochem. Pathology Unit, 1979–2000; MRC-Newcastle Univ. Centre Develt for Clinical Brain Ageing, 2000–04. Chairman: Years Ahead - NE Regl Forum on Ageing, 2005–09; VOICE North, 2011–. Vice-President: Alzheimer's Disease Soc., 1989–; Age Concern Newcastle, 2007–. Mem. Council, Natural Hist. Soc. of Northumbria, 2004–; Vice Chm., Northumbria Reg., U3A, 2012–. *Publications:* numerous papers on brain biochem., physiology and behaviour and on Alzheimer's Disease and related neurodegenerative disorders. *Recreations:* allotment, bird watching, Labour Party, poetry. *Address:* 18 Leslie Crescent, Newcastle upon Tyne NE3 4AN. *T:* (0191) 285 0159.

EDZARD, Christine; film director; Managing Director, Sands Film Studios, since 1975; *b* 15 Feb. 1945; *d* of Dietz Edzard and Susanne Eisendieck, painters; *m* 1968, Richard Goodwin; one *d*, and one step *s* one step *d*. *Educ:* Ecole Nationale de Science Politique, Paris (Econ degree). Asst designer to Lila de Nobili and Rostislav Doboujinsky, Paris; asst on Zeffirelli's Romeo and Juliet, 1966; designer for Hamburg Opera, WNO and Camden Town Fest.; designer, costumes and sets and wrote (with Richard Goodwin) script of film, Tales of Beatrix Potter, 1971; directed short films, The Little Match Girl, The Kitchen and Little Ida, released as Tales from a Flying Trunk; dir, The Nightingale, 1979; wrote and directed: Biddy, 1981 (first feature film); Little Dorrit, 1987 (BAFTA Award, Best Screenplay; LA Critics Award, Best Film; Orson Welles Award, Best Director); The Fool, 1991; directed and produced, As You Like It, 1992; designed and directed, Menotti's Amahl and the Night Visitors, Spoleto Fest., 1996; wrote, designed and directed: The Nutcracker, 1997; The Children's Midsummer Night's Dream, 2000. *Address:* Sands Films Costumes Ltd, 82 Saint Marychurch Street, SE16 4HZ. *T:* (020) 7231 2209, *Fax:* (020) 7231 2209. *E:* CE@sandsfilms.co.uk.

EEKELAAR, John Michael, FBA 2001; Reader in Family Law, University of Oxford, 1990–2005; Academic Director, Pembroke College, Oxford, 2005–09, now Emeritus Fellow (Tutorial Fellow, 1965–2005); *b* Johannesburg, 2 July 1942; *s* of John (Jan) Eekelaar and Delphine Eekelaar (*née* Stoughton); *m* 1978, Pia Nicole Lewis; two *d*. *Educ:* King's Coll., London (LLB); University Coll., Oxford (BCL). Rhodes Schol., 1963–65; Vinerian Schol., 1965. University of Oxford: Lectr in Law, 1966–90; Res. Fellow, Centre for Socio-Legal Studies, 1976–2000; Co-Dir, Oxford Centre for Family Law and Policy, 2000–. Dist. Vis. Fellow, NZ Law Foundn, 2005. Pres., Internat. Soc. of Family Law, 1985–88. Gen. Ed., Oxford Jl Legal Studies, 1993–; Founding Co-ed., Internat. Jl Law Policy and the Family, 1987–. *Publications:* Family Security and Family Breakdown, 1971; Family Law and Social Policy, 1978, 2nd edn 1984 (trans. German 1983); (ed jtly) Family Violence: an international and interdisciplinary study, 1978; (ed jtly) Marriage and Cohabitation in Contemporary Societies, 1982; (jtly) The Protection of Children: state intervention and family life, 1983; (ed jtly) The Resolution of Family Conflict: comparative legal perspectives, 1984; (jtly) Maintenance after Divorce, 1986; (ed jtly) Family, State and Individual Economic Security, 1988; (ed jtly) Divorce Mediation and the Legal Process, 1988; (ed jtly) An Aging World: dilemmas and challenges for law and social policy, 1989; (jtly) The Reform of Child Care Law, 1990; Regulating Divorce, 1991; (ed jtly) Parenthood in Modern Society: social and legal issues for the Twenty-First century, 1993; (ed jtly) A Reader on Family Law, 1994; (jtly) The Parental Obligation: a study of parenthood across households, 1997; (ed jtly) The Changing Family: family law and family forms in international perspective, 1998; (jtly) Family Lawyers: the divorce work of solicitors, 2000; (ed jtly) Cross Currents: family law and policy in the US and England, 2000; Family Law and Personal Life, 2006, enlarged edn 2007; (jtly) Family Law Advocacy 2009; (ed jtly) Managing Family Justice in Diverse Societies, 2013; (jtly) Family Justice, 2013; contrib. articles to jls and chapters in books. *Recreation:* music. *Address:* Ridgeway Cottage, The Ridgeway, Boars Hill, Oxford OX1 5EX. *T:* (01865) 735485.

EELES, Maj. Gen. Nicholas Henry, CBE 2014; General Officer Commanding, 2nd Division, Scotland, and Governor, Edinburgh Castle, 2012–15; *b* Lyndhurst, 24 April 1961; *s* of Maj. Anthony Thomas Eeles, MC, RA and Valerie Mildred Eeles (*née* Hayes); *m* 1990, Carolyn, (Wob), Stirling Smith; one *s* two *d*. *Educ:* Homefield Coll.; Brockenhurst Coll.; Bristol Univ. (BSc Biochem. 1982); RMA Sandhurst. Commnd RA, 1983; psc 1993; Battery Comdr, C Battery, RHA, 1996–98; CO, 26 Regt RA, 2001–03; Col Manning (A), 2003–05; hcsc 2005; CRA 3 (UK) Div., 2005–07; Brig., Gen. Staff, 2007–10; Dir, RA, 2010–11. Hon. Regt Col, 26 Regt RA, 2011–. Col Comdt, RA, 2012–. Chairman: RA Centre for Personal Develt, 2010–; RA Historical Trust, 2012–. *Recreations:* tennis, modern poetry, World War I history, ornithology.

EFFINGHAM, 7th Earl of, *cr* 1837; **David Mowbray Algernon Howard;** DL; Baron Howard of Effingham 1554; Commander RN, retd; National President, The Royal British Legion, 2003–06; *b* 29 April 1939; *s* of Hon. John Algernon Frederick Charles Howard (*d* 1971), *yr s* of 5th Earl, and his 1st wife, Suzanne Patricia (*née* Macassey); *S* uncle, 1996; *m* 1st, 1964, Anne Mary Sayer (marr. diss. 1975); one *s*; 2nd, 1992, Mrs Elizabeth Jane Turner; two step *s*. *Educ:* Fettes Coll., Edinburgh; Royal Naval Coll., Dartmouth. Royal Navy, 1961–91. DL Essex, 2006. *Recreations:* horse racing, fishing. *Heir:* *s* Lord Howard of Effingham, *qv*. *Address:* (home) Readings, Blackmore End, Essex CM7 4DH. *T:* (office) (01787) 461182. *Clubs:* Royal Navy, Army and Navy; Essex.

See also C. A. F. Howard.

EFFORD, Clive Stanley; MP (Lab) Eltham, since 1997; *b* 10 July 1958; *s* of Stanley Charles Efford and Mary Agnes Elizabeth Christina Caldwell; *m* 1981, Gillian Vallins; three *d*. *Educ:* Walworth Comprehensive Sch. Sen. Adventure Playground Leader; Asst to Warden, Pembroke Coll. Mission; former London taxi driver. Mem. (Lab) Greenwich LBC, 1986–98 (former Gp Sec.; Chief Whip; Chm., Social Services Cttee, Health and Envmt Cttee). Contested (Lab) Eltham, 1992. Shadow Minister for the Home Office, 2010–11, for Sports, Tourism and Gambling, 2011–15; PPS to successive Ministers for Housing, DCLG, 2008–10. Mem., Procedure Select Cttee, 1997–2000, Transport Select Cttee, 2002–09, H of C. Prelim. FA Coach's Badge. *Recreations:* sports, reading, cinema. *Address:* (office) 132 Westmount Road, Eltham, SE9 1UT. *T:* (020) 8850 5744. *Clubs:* Eltham Hill Working Man's, Woolwich Catholic.

EFSTATHIOU, Prof. George Petros, FRS 1994; Professor of Astrophysics, since 1997, and Director, Kavli Institute for Cosmology, since 2008, University of Cambridge; Fellow, King's College, Cambridge, since 1997; *b* 2 Sept. 1955; *s* of Petros Efstathiou and Christina (*née* Parperi); *m* 1st, 1976, Helena Jane (*née* Smart) (marr. diss. 1997); one *s* one *d*; 2nd, 1998, Yvonne Nobis; two *s*. *Educ:* Somerset Comprehensive Sch.; Keble Coll., Oxford (BA); Univ. of Durham (Dept of Physics) (PhD). Res. Asst, Astronomy Dept, Univ. of California, Berkeley, 1979–80; SERC Res. Asst, Inst. of Astronomy, Univ. of Cambridge, 1980–83; Jun. Res. Fellow, 1980–84, Sen. Res. Fellow, 1984–88, King's Coll., Cambridge; Institute of Astronomy, Cambridge: Sen. Asst in Res., 1984–87; Asst Dir of Res., 1987–88; Head of Astrophysics, 1988–94; Savilian Prof. of Astronomy, and Fellow, New Coll., Oxford, 1988–97; PPARC Sen. Fellow, 1994–99; Dir, 2004–08. Mem., PPARC, 2001–04. Maxwell Medal and Prize, Inst. of Physics, 1990; Bodossaki Foundn Academic and Cultural Prize for Astrophysics, 1994; Robinson Prize in Cosmology, Univ. of Newcastle, 1997; Heineman Prize for Astrophysics, Amer. Inst. of Physics, 2005; Gruber Cosmol. Prize, Peter and Patricia Gruber Foundn, 2011. *Publications:* articles in astronomical jls. *Recreations:* running, playing the guitar. *Address:* Institute of Astronomy, Madingley Road, Cambridge CB3 0HA. *T:* (01223) 337548.

EFUNSHILE, Althea; Deputy Chief Executive, Arts Council England, since 2013 (Executive Director, Arts Planning and Investment, 2007; Chief Operating Officer, 2009–13); *b* 20 Aug. 1956; *d* of Chas L. Barrett and Ena Louise Barrett; partner, David Reardon; one *s* one *d*. *Educ:* Univ. of Essex (BA Hons Sociol.); Goldsmiths' Coll., London (PGCE); Buckinghamshire Coll. (DMS). Teacher, Brent, 1980–83; Dir, Elimu Community Educn Centre, 1983–85; detached youth worker, 1987, Area Youth Worker, 1987–89, Bucks CC; Educn Officer, Harrow, 1989–93; Asst Dir of Educn, Merton, 1993–96; Exec. Dir, Educn and Culture, Lewisham, 1996–2001; Dir, Children and Young People's Unit, then Safeguarding Children Gp, subseq. Vulnerable Children Gp, DFES, 2001–06. *Recreations:* travel, reading, cinema. *Address:* Arts Council England, 21 Bloomsbury Street, WC1B 3HF.

EGAN, Sir John (Leopold), Kt 1986; DL; Chairman, Severn Trent plc, 2005–10; Chancellor, Coventry University, since 2007; *b* 7 Nov. 1939; *m* 1963, Julia Emily Treble; two *d*. *Educ:* Bablake Sch., Coventry; Imperial Coll., London Univ., 1958–61 (BSc Hons; FIC 1985); London Business Sch., London Univ., 1966–68 (MScEcon). Petroleum Engineer, Shell International, 1962–66; General Manager, AC-Delco Replacement Parts Operation, General Motors Ltd, 1968–71; Managing Director, Leyland Cars Parts Div., Parts and Service Director, Leyland Cars, BLMC, 1971–76; Corporate Parts Director, Massey Ferguson, 1976–80; Chm. and Chief Exec., Jaguar Cars Ltd, 1980–85, Jaguar plc, 1985–90; Chief Exec., BAA plc, 1990–99; Chairman: MEPC plc, 1998–2000; Inchcape plc, 2000–05; Harrison Lovegrove Ltd, 2000–05; QinetiQ, 2001–02. Director: Foreign and Colonial Investment Trust, 1985–97; Legal & General Group, 1987–97 (Dep. Chm., 1993–97). Chm., 1993–97, Pres., 1998–, London Tourist Bd; Dir, BTA, 1994–97. Dep. Pres., 2001–02, Pres., 2002–04, CBI. Hon. Professor: Dept of Engrg, Warwick Univ., 1990; Aston Univ., 1990. DL Warwicks, 1988. Sen. Fellow, RCA, 1987; FCIPS 1993; FRAeS 1994; FCIT 1994. Hon. FCIM 1989. Hon. Fellow: London Business Sch., 1988; Wolverhampton Poly., 1989. Dr *hc* Cranfield Inst. of Technology, 1986; Hon. DTech: Loughborough, 1987; Brunel, 1997; Hon. DBA Internat. Business Sch., 1988; Hon. LLD Bath, 1988; Hon. DSc Aston, 1992. Hon. Insignia for Technology, CGLI, 1987. Internat. Distinguished Entrepreneur Award, Univ. of Manitoba, 1989. MBA Award of the Year, 1988. *Recreations:* music, ski-ing, tennis. *Clubs:* Royal Automobile, MCC; Warwick Boat.

EGAN, Michael Flynn John; QC 2006; Queen's Coroner and Attorney, Master of the Crown Office and Registrar of Criminal Appeals, since 2011, and Registrar of the Court Martial Appeal Court, since 2012; *b* Dungarvan, Co. Waterford, 14 March 1952; *s* of late Maurice Egan and of Joan Egan (*née* Flynn); *m* 1976, Shelagh Patricia Terry; one *s* one *d*. *Educ:* Coll. of Law, Lancaster Gate. Articled clerk, Turberville Smith & Co., 1971–76; admitted as solicitor, 1976; Kingsley Napley & Co., 1977–81; called to the Bar, Gray's Inn, 1981 (Bencher, 2012); Asst Recorder, 1998–2000; Recorder, 2000–; Special Counsel, 2004; Special Advocate, 2009. *Recreations:* Rugby, football, horology, 2CVs. *Address:* Room C220, Royal Courts of Justice, Strand, WC2A 2LL. *T:* (020) 7947 6103. *E:* master.eganqc@hmcts.x.gsi.gov.uk.

EGAN, Penelope Jane, CBE 2013; Executive Director, Fulbright Commission, since 2007; *b* 18 July 1951; *d* of late Derek A. Morris and of June E. Morris; *m* 1975, David Anthony Egan; two *s*. *Educ:* St Paul's Girls' Sch.; Leicester Univ. (BA 1971). Mus. Asst, 1971–73, Press Officer, 1973–75, Victoria & Albert Mus.; Press Officer, Prime Minister's Office, 1975–77; Press and Publicity Officer, Crafts Council, 1977–82; Lecture Sec., 1986–95, Programme Develt Dir, 1995–97, Exec. Dir, 1998–2006, RSA. Mem., Design Council, 1999–2008. Trustee: Geffrye Mus., 2006–14 (Chm. Trustees, 2010–14); Demos, 2009–13; RSA Academies, 2014–. Mem. Council, Warwick Univ., 2007–12 and 2013–. Hon. FRCA 2006. Hon. FRSA 2006. *Recreations:* tennis, cooking, cinema. *Address:* Fulbright Commission, Battersea Power Station, 188 Kirtling Street, SW8 5BN. *T:* 07885 398050. *E:* penny@pennyegan.com. *Club:* Roehampton.

EGAN, Rt Rev. Dr Philip; *see* Portsmouth, Bishop of, (RC).

EGAN, Rt Rev. Mgr Canon Thomas; Parish Priest of Our Lady of Lourdes, New Southgate, since 2001; *b* 15 Feb. 1942; *s* of Frank and Mary Egan. *Educ:* St Joseph's Primary Sch., Macklin St, Holborn; Challoner Sec. Sch., Finchley; St Edmund's Coll., Ware; Inst. of Educn, London Univ. (BEd). Asst priest, Our Lady and St Joseph, Hanwell, 1967–72; Home Mission Team, 1972–73; asst priest, St Joan of Arc, Highbury, 1973–78; Parish Priest, St Pius X, St Charles Square, 1978–86; Pastoral Dir, Allen Hall Seminary, 1986–90; Parish Priest, Our Lady of Hal, Camden Town, 1990–93; VG, Archdio. Westminster, 1993–2001. Mem., Westminster Cath. Chapter of Canons, 2005–. *Recreations:* fishing, swimming, football. *Address:* 373 Bowes Road, New Southgate, N11 1AA.

EGDELL, Dr John Duncan; Consultant in Public Health Medicine (formerly Community Physician), Clwyd Health Authority, 1986–92, now Hon. Consultant, North Wales Health Authority; *b* 5 March 1938; *s* of late John William Egdell and Nellie (*née* Thompson); *m* 1963, Dr Linda Mary Flint; two *s* one *d*. *Educ:* Clifton Coll.; Univ. of Bristol. MB, ChB (Bristol) 1961; DipSocMed (Edin.) 1967; FFPH (FFPHM 1990; MFCM 1973; FFCM 1979). Ho. Phys. and Ho. Surg., Bristol Gen. Hosp., 1961–62; gen. practice, 1962–65; Med. Administration: with Newcastle Regional Hosp. Bd, 1966–69; with South Western Regional Hosp. Bd, 1969–74; Regional Specialist in Community Med., South Western Regional Health Authority, 1974–76; Regional Medical Postgrad. Co-ordinator, Univ. of Bristol,

1973–76; Regl MO, Mersey RHA, 1977–86; Hon. Lectr in Community Health, Univ. of Liverpool, 1980–86. *Recreations:* delving into the past, nature conservation. *Address:* Ravenswood, Glen Auldyn, Lezayre, Isle of Man IM7 2AQ. *T:* (01624) 818012.

EGERTON, family name of **Duke of Sutherland**.

EGERTON, Keith Robert, FRICS; non-executive Director, Rowlandson Organisation, 2002–12; Chairman, Native Land Ltd, 2003–07; *b* 26 June 1942; *s* of Harold and Doris Egerton; *m* 1968, Pauline Steele; one *s* one *d*. FRICS 1988 (ARICS 1966). Development Surveyor, Laing Properties, 1970–73; Commercial Union Properties: S Area Develt Manager, 1973–75; Dir, Belgian and Dutch projects, 1975–77; Dir, 1978–82; Dir, 1977–82, Chief Exec., 1978–82, Commercial Union Property Develts Ltd; Costain plc, 1982–91: Man. Dir, 1982–85, Chief Exec., 1985–91, County & District Properties; Director: resp. for Property, 1986–90; resp. for UK, Spanish and Calif Housing Ops and Property, 1990–91; joined Taylor Woodrow plc, 1991; Dir, 1992–2002; Gp Chief Exec., 1998–2002; Man. Dir, 1991–98, and Chm., 1992–99, Taylor Woodrow Property Co. Ltd; Director: Taywood Homes, 1996–98; Monarch Develt Corp., 1998–2002. *Recreations:* cycling, gardening, hill walking, country pursuits, motorbikes, vintage and other interesting cars. *Address:* The White House, Run Common, Shamley Green, Guildford, Surrey GU5 0SY. *T:* (01483) 272944.

EGERTON, Sir William (de Malpas), 17th Bt *cr* 1617, of Egerton and Oulton, Cheshire; *b* Bromley, 27 April 1949; *o s* of Maj.-Gen. (Sir) David Boswell Egerton, (16th Bt), CB, OBE, MC and Margaret Gillian, ARCM (*d* 2004), *d* of Canon C. C. Inge; *S* father, 2010; *m* 1971, Ruth, *d* of late Rev. George Watson; two *s*. *Educ:* St John's Coll., Cambridge (BA 1970; MA). Technical Manager, QinetiQ plc, 2005–09. *Recreation:* local history. *Heir: s* Matthew Robert Egerton, *b* 19 May 1977. *Address:* Northdown Farmhouse, 106 Sutton Road, Sutton Poyntz, Weymouth, Dorset DT3 6LW. *T:* (01305) 832872.

EGGAR, Rt Hon. Tim(othy John Crommelin); PC 1995; Chairman: Cape plc, since 2011; MyCelx Technologies Corporation, since 2011; Haulfryn Group, since 2012; *b* 19 Dec. 1951; *s* of late John Drennan Eggar and of Pamela Rosemary Eggar; *m* 1977, Charmian Diana Minoprio; one *s* one *d*. *Educ:* Winchester Coll.; Magdalene Coll., Cambridge (MA). Called to the Bar, Inner Temple, 1976. European Banking Co., 1975–83; Director: Charterhouse Petroleum, 1984–85; LASMO plc, 1999–2000; Chairman: M W Kellogg, 1996–98; AGIP (UK) Ltd, 1997–98; Nitol Solar plc, 2007–12. Chm., Cambridge Univ. Cons. Assoc., 1972; Vice-Chm., Fedn of Cons. Students, 1973–74. MP (C) Enfield N, 1979–97. PPS to Minister for Overseas Develt, 1982–85; Parly Under-Sec. of State, FCO, 1985–89; Minister of State: Dept of Employment, 1989–90; DES, 1990–92; DTI (Minister for Energy, 1992–96, also for Industry, 1994–96). Chief Exec., Monument Oil and Gas PLC, 1998–99 (Dir, 1997–98); Vice-Chm., ABN AMRO Corporate Finance, 2000–05; Chairman: Harrison Lovegrove & Co. Ltd, 2005–08; Indago Petroleum plc, 2005–09; 3Legs Resources, 2010–15; Dir, Anglo-Asian Mining plc, 2005–08. Pres., Russo-British Chamber of Commerce, 2004–13. Chm. Govs, Shiplake Coll., 2009–. *Recreations:* ski-ing, shooting, Rugby. *Address:* Nettlebed House, Nettlebed, Oxon RG9 5DD. *T:* (01491) 642833. *Club:* Carlton.

EGGINGTON, Dr William Robert Owen; Chief Medical Adviser, Department of Health and Social Security, later Department of Social Security, 1986–92; part-time Medical Adviser, Nestor Disability Alliance, 1999–2002; *b* 24 Feb. 1932; *s* of Alfred Thomas Eggington and Phyllis Eggington (*née* Wynne); *m* 1961, Patricia Mary Elizabeth, *d* of Henry David and Elizabeth Grant; one *s* one *d*. *Educ:* Kingswood School, Bath; Guy's Hosp. MB, BS 1955, DTM&H 1960, DPH 1962, DIH 1963; MFCM 1970. House Surgeon, Guy's Hosp., 1955; House Physician, St John's Hosp., Lewisham, 1956. RAMC, 1957–73, retired as Lt-Col, Senior Specialist Army Health. DHSS, later DSS, 1973–92. Medical Adviser: War Pensions Agency, 1994–98; Benefits Agency, 1998. *Recreations:* Goss heraldic china, military history, football spectator. *Address:* 33 Chestnut Road, Farnborough, Hants GU14 8LD.

EGGINTON, Anthony Joseph, CBE 1991; consultant; *b* 18 July 1930; *s* of Arthur Reginald Egginton and Margaret Anne (*née* Emslie); *m* 1957, Janet Leta, *d* of late Albert and Florence Herring; two *d*. *Educ:* Selhurst Grammar Sch., Croydon; University Coll., London (BSc 1951; Fellow, 1992). Res. Assoc., UCL, 1951–56; AERE Harwell (Gen. Physics Div.), 1956–61; Head of Beams Physics Gp, NIRNS Rutherford High Energy Lab., 1961–65; DCSO and Head of Machine Gp, SRC Daresbury Nuclear Physics Lab., 1965–72; Head of Engrg Div., 1972–74, Under Sec. and Dir of Engineering and Nuclear Physics, 1974–78, Dir of Science and Engrg Divs, 1978–83, SRC; Science and Engineering Research Council: Dir of Engrg, 1983–88; Dir Progs, and Dep. Chm., 1988–91. Vis. Prof., UCL, 1993–99. Head, UK Delegn, 1978–83, Chm., 1982–83, Steering Cttee, Inst. Laue-Langevin, Grenoble. *Publications:* papers and articles in jls and conf. proceedings on particle accelerators and beams. *Recreations:* sport, cinema, music. *Address:* 2 Millers Mews, Witney, Oxon OX28 1QT. *T:* (01993) 706738.

EGGLESTON, Anthony Francis, OBE 1968; Headmaster, Campion School, Athens, 1983–88, retired; *b* 26 Jan. 1928; *s* of late J. F. Eggleston and late Mrs J. M. Barnard, Harrow, Middx; *m* 1957, Jane Morison Buxton, JP (*d* 2009), *d* of late W. L. Buxton, MBE and Mrs F. M. M. Buxton, Stanmore, Middx; one *s* two *d*. *Educ:* Merchant Taylors' Sch., Northwood (Schol.); St John's Coll., Oxford (Sir Thomas White Schol.; BA 1949, MA 1953; 2nd cl. hons Chemistry). National Service, 1950–52; 2nd Lieut, RA, Suez Canal Zone. Asst Master, Cheltenham Coll., 1952–54; Sen. Science Master, English High Sch., Istanbul, 1954–56; Asst Master, Merchant Taylors' Sch., Northwood, 1956–62; Principal, English Sch., Nicosia, 1962–68; Headmaster, Felsted Sch., 1968–82. *Recreation:* looking at and talking about buildings of all periods. *Address:* Garden House, Chester Place, Norwich NR2 3DG. *T:* (01603) 616025.

See also H. M. M. Baldwin.

EGGLESTON, Prof. James Frederick; Professor of Education, University of Nottingham, 1972–84, now Emeritus; *b* 30 July 1927; *s* of Frederick James and Anne Margaret Eggleston; *m* 1956, Margaret Snowden; three *s* two *d*. *Educ:* Appleby Grammar Sch.; Durham Univ. (King's Coll., Newcastle upon Tyne). BSc Hons Zoology; DipEd; FRSB (FIBiol 1975). School teacher, 1953–64, Head of Biol., later Head of Sci., Hinckley Grammar Sch.; Res. Fellow, Res. Unit for Assessment and Curriculum Studies, Leicester Univ. Sch. of Educn, 1964; team leader, later consultant, Nuffield Sci. Teaching Project, 1964–68; Lectr in Educn, Leicester Univ. Sch. of Educn, 1966; apptd to Colls and Curriculum Chair of Educn, Nottingham Univ., 1973, Dean of Educn, 1975–81. *Publications:* A Critical Review of Assessment Procedures in Secondary School Science, 1965; Problems in Quantitative Biology, 1968; (with J. F. Kerr) Studies in Assessment, 1970; (jtly) A Science Teaching Observation Schedule, 1975; (jtly) Processes and Products of Science Teaching, 1976; contributions to: The Disciplines of the Curriculum, 1971; The Art of the Science Teacher, 1974; Frontiers of Classroom Research, 1975; Techniques and Problems of Assessment, 1976; (with Trevor Kerry) Topic Work in the Primary School, 1988; articles in professional jls. *Recreations:* fell walking, golf, photography. *Address:* The Old Chapel, Church Street, Fritchley, Derbys DE56 2FQ. *T:* (01773) 850255.

EGGLETON, Anthony, AO 1991; CVO 1970; Director, since 1996, Member of Advisory Council, since 2007, CARE Australia (National Director, 1995–96; Vice-Chairman, 2001–04; Chairman, 2004–07); Chairman, CARE International Strategy and Governance Committees, 2003–07; *b* 30 April 1932; *s* of Tom and Winifred Eggleton; *m* 1953, Mary Walker, Melbourne; two *s* one *d*. *Educ:* King Alfred's Sch., Wantage. Journalist, Westminster Press Group, 1948–50; Editorial Staff, Bendigo Advertiser, Vic, 1950–51; Australian Broadcasting Commn, 1951–60 (Dir of ABC-TV News Coverage, 1956–60); Dir of Public Relations, Royal Australian Navy, 1960–65; Press Sec. to Prime Ministers of Australia, 1965–71 (Prime Ministers Menzies, Holt, Gorton, McMahon); Commonwealth Dir of Information, London, 1971–74; Special Advr to Leader of Opposition, and Dir of Communications, Federal Liberal Party, 1974–75; Federal Dir, Liberal Party of Australia, 1975–90; Campaign Dir, Federal Elections, 1975, 1977, 1980, 1983, 1984, 1987, 1990. Sec.-Gen., 1991–95, Bd Mem., 2001–07, CARE Internat., Brussels; CEO, Centenary of Federation Council, 1997–2002. Chairman: Asia Pacific Democrat Union, 1998–2005 (Exec. Sec., 1982–84, 1985–87, Dep. Chm., 1987–90, Pacific Democrat Union); Australian Centre for Democratic Instns, 2007–10. Mem., Australian Govt Aid Adv. Council, 2002–08. Mem. Bd, Nat. Stroke Foundn, 1997–2002. Chm., C. E. W. Bean (War Correspondents) Assoc., 2002–; Chair, Commonwealth Day Cttee, Canberra, 2006–. Mem., Editl Adv. Bd, Australian Dept of Foreign Affairs, 1999–. Australian Public Relations Inst.'s 1st Award of Honour, 1968; Outstanding Service Award, Liberal Party of Australia, 1990; Centenary Medal, Australia, 2003. *Address:* 87 Buxton Street, Deakin, ACT 2600, Australia. *Clubs:* (Foundn Pres.) National Press (Canberra), Commonwealth (Canberra).

EGGLETON, Hon. Arthur C.; PC (Can.) 1993; Senator of Canada, since 2005; *b* 29 Sept. 1943; *m*; one *d*. Former accountant; consultant, urban mgt and policy issues. Toronto City Council: Mem., 1969–93; Budget Chief, 1973–80; Pres., 1975–76, 1978–80; Mayor of Toronto, 1980–91; former Member: Metropolitan Police Commn; Bd, Canadian Nat. Exhibn. MP (L) York Centre, Toronto, 1993–2004; Pres., Treasury Bd, and Minister responsible for Infrastructure, 1993–96; Minister: for Internat. Trade, 1996–97; of Nat. Defence, 1997–2002; Vice-Chm., Cabinet Cttee on Economic Policy, 1997–2002. Mem. Adv. Bd Dirs, Skylink Gp of Cos Inc. Chm., Rebuilding Lives Campaign, St John's Rehabilitation Hosp. Civic Award of Merit, Toronto, 1992. *Address:* Senate of Canada, Room 804, Victoria Building, Ottawa, ON K1A 0A4, Canada.

EGILSSON, Ólafur; attorney and diplomat; *b* 20 Aug. 1936; *s* of Egill Kristjánsson and Anna Margrjet Thuríður Ólafsdóttir Briem; *m* 1960, Ragna Sverrisdóttir Ragnars; one *s* one *d*. *Educ:* Commercial College, Iceland (grad. 1956); Univ. of Iceland, Faculty of Law (grad. 1963). Reporter on Vísir, 1956–58, Morgunblaðið, 1959–62; publishing Exec., Almenna bókafélagið, 1963–64; Head, NATO Regional Inf. Office, Iceland, 1964–66, and Gen. Sec., Icelandic Assoc. for Western Co-operation and Atlantic Assoc. of Young Political Leaders of Iceland; Icelandic Foreign Service, 1966; Foreign Ministry, 1966–69; First Sec., later Counsellor, Icelandic Embassy, Paris, and Dep. Perm. Rep. to OECD, UNESCO, 1969–71, and Council of Europe, Strasbourg, 1969–70; Dep. Perm. Rep., NATO and Dep. Head, Icelandic Delegn to EEC, Brussels, 1971–74; Counsellor, later Minister Counsellor, Political Div., Min. of Foreign Affairs, 1974–80; Chief of Protocol, with rank of Ambassador, 1980–83; Acting Principal Private Sec. to President of Iceland, Oct. 1981–June 1982; Dep. Perm. Under Sec. and Dir Gen. for Political Affairs, Min. of Foreign Affairs, 1983–87; Ambassador: to UK, 1986–89, and concurrently to the Netherlands, Ireland and Nigeria; to USSR, later Russia, 1990–94, and concurrently to Bulgaria, Japan, Romania and Ukraine; to Denmark, 1994–96, and also to Italy, Israel, Japan, Lithuania and Turkey; in charge of Arctic co-operation, 1996–98, also accredited to the Holy See, Turkey, Australia and NZ; Ambassador to China, and concurrently to Australia, Indonesia, Japan, Korea, Mongolia, New Zealand, Thailand and Vietnam, 1998–2002; Ambassador to Thailand, Singapore, Malaysia, Indonesia and Cambodia, 2003–06. Chm., Governing Bd, Icelandic Internat. Develt Agency, 1982–87; Sec., Commn revising Foreign Service Act, 1968–69. President: Nat. Youth Council of Iceland, 1963–64; Acad. Assoc. of Reykjavík, 1967–68; Executive Member: Bible Soc., 1977–87 and 1996–2013; History Soc., 1982–88. Commander, Icelandic Order of the Falcon, 1981 (Mem. Council, 2007–); holds numerous foreign orders. *Publications:* (jtly) Iceland and Jan Mayen, 1980; (ed) Bjarni Benediktsson: Contemporaries' views, 1983; (jtly) NATO's Anxious Birth: the prophetic vision of the 1940s, 1985; (ed) Shaping Culture, 2012. *Recreations:* walking, music (opera), history. *Address:* Valhusabraut 35, 170 Seltjarnarnes, Iceland. *T:* 6151121, *Fax:* 5515411. *E:* olegice@simnet.is.

EGLIN, Philip Michael; ceramic artist; Senior Lecturer, Staffordshire University (formerly Staffordshire Polytechnic), 1987–2011; *b* Gibraltar, 29 Nov. 1959; *s* of Jack and Mary Eglin; *m* 1987, Jennet Walters; two *s*. *Educ:* Harlow Tech. Coll.; Staffordshire Poly. (BA 1982); Royal Coll. of Art (MA Ceramics 1986). Mem., Selected Index Cttee, Crafts Council, 1997–2000. Fellow, Arts Foundn, 1993. *Solo exhibitions* include: Stafford Art Gall., 1990; Oxford Gall., 1991; New Work, Scottish Gall., Edinburgh, 2004; Franklin Parrasch Gall., NY; Barrett Marsden Gall., London, 2001, 2003, 2006 and Hands Off Berbatov (ceramics), 2008; Borrowings, Nottingham Mus. and Art Gall., 2007; Dean Proj., Sculpture Objects and Functional Art Fair, NY, 2007; Spiritual Heroes (ceramics), Glynn Vivian Art Gall., Swansea, 2008; Popes, Pin-ups and Pooches, Scottish Gall., Edinburgh, 2009; Mixed Marriage(s), Blackwell Hse, Cumbria, 2011; Nice Pair of Jugs, Marsden Woo Gall., London, 2013; Aberystwyth Arts Centre, 2015; *group exhibitions* include: Contemporary Applied Arts, London, 1986, 1988, 1989, 1992; Crafts Council, London, 1991, 1996, 1999; One From the Heart, Aberystwyth Arts Centre, 1995; The Nude in Clay, Chicago, 1995; Hell Fire, Stedelijk Mus. in De Nieuwe Kerk, Amsterdam, 2008; Galerie Handwerk, Munich, 2009; Inscription, Jerwood Space, London, 2010; Modern British Potters, Goldmark Gall., Uppingham, 2010; Double Take, Marsden Woo Gall., London, 2010; Taiwan Ceramics Biennale, Taipei Ceramics Mus., 2010; Contemp. British Studio Ceramics, Graine Collection, Charlotte, NC, 2010; British Ceramics Biennial, Stoke-on-Trent, 2011; RA Summer Show, 2012; Gp Jug Show, 2013, Motifs, Places, Figures Libres, 2014, Helene Azziza Gall., Paris; Positions of Design, 2014, Meister der Moderne, 2014, Galerie Handwerk, Munich; Taste Contemp. Craft, Art Genève, 2015; Nat. Mus. of Wales, Cardiff, 2015; work in public collections, including: V&A Mus.; Brighton Mus.; Crafts Council, London; Portsmouth City Mus. and Art Gall.; Fitzwilliam Mus., Cambridge; York Mus.; Middlesbrough Inst. Modern Art; Stedelijk Mus., Amsterdam; Gardiner Mus., Toronto; Mint Mus., N Carolina; Sèvres Mus., Paris; La Piscine Mus., Roubaix. Jerwood Prize for Applied Arts, Jerwood Foundn, 1996. *Publications:* Philip Eglin, 1997; (with Tony Hayward) Eglin's Etchings, 2008; *catalogues*: Borrowings, 2007; Popes, Pin-ups and Pooches, 2009; Mixed Marriage(s), 2011. *Recreations:* manager of football teams, Westpoint Wanderers (mini-soccer league, under 11s) and Shamblers FC (Potteries jun. youth league, under 13s).

EGLINGTON, Charles Richard John; Director, 1986–95, Vice-Chairman, 1990–95, S. G. Warburg Securities; *b* 12 Aug. 1938; *s* of late Richard Eglington and Treena Margaret Joyce Eglington. *Educ:* Sherborne. Dir, Akroyd & Smithers, 1978–86. Mem. Council, Stock Exchange, 1975–86, Dep. Chm., 1981–84. Governor: Sherborne Sch., 1979–2008; Twyford Sch., 1984–2013. *Recreations:* golf, cricket. *Address:* 2 Rectory Orchard, Church Road, Wimbledon, SW19 5AS. *Clubs:* MCC; Royal and Ancient Golf (St Andrews); Rye Golf.

EGLINTON and WINTON, 18th Earl of, *cr* 1507; **Archibald George Montgomerie;** Lord Montgomerie, 1448; Baron Seton and Tranent, 1859; Baron Kilwinning, 1615; Baron Ardrossan (UK), 1806; Earl of Winton (UK), 1859; Hereditary Sheriff of Renfrewshire; *b* 27 Aug. 1939; *s* of 17th Earl of Eglinton and Winton and Ursula (*d* 1987), *er d* of Hon. Ronald Watson, Edinburgh; *S* father, 1966; *m* 1964, Marion Carolina, *o d* of John Dunn-Yarker; four *s*. *Educ:* Eton. Man. Dir, Gerrard & National Hldgs, 1972–92 (Dep. Chm., 1992); Chairman: Gerrard Vivian Gray Ltd, 1992–94; Edinburgh Investment Trust plc, 1992–2003; Charities Investment Managers, 2000–09. Asst Grand Master, United Grand Lodge of England, 1989–95. *Heir: s* Lord Montgomerie, *qv*. *Address:* Balhomie House, Cargill, Perth PH2 6DS.

EGLINTON, Prof. Geoffrey, PhD, DSc; FRS 1976; Professor of Organic Geochemistry, 1973–93, now Emeritus, and Senior Research Fellow, Biogeochemistry Research Centre, since 1995 (Director, 1991–96), University of Bristol; Adjunct Scientist: Woods Hole Oceanographic Institution, Massachusetts, since 1991; Dartmouth College, Hanover, New Hampshire, since 2003; *b* 1 Nov. 1927; *s* of Alfred Edward Eglinton and Lilian Blackham; *m* 1955, Pamela Joan Coupland; two *s* (one *d* decd). *Educ:* Sale Grammar Sch.; Manchester Univ. (BSc, PhD, DSc). Post-Doctoral Fellow, Ohio State Univ., 1951–52; ICI Fellow, Liverpool Univ., 1952–54; Lectr, subseq. Sen. Lectr and Reader, Glasgow Univ., 1954–67; Sen. Lectr, subseq. Reader, Bristol Univ., 1967–73. Mem., NERC, 1984–90. Hon. Fellow, Plymouth Polytechnic, 1981. Gold Medal for Exceptional Scientific Achievement, NASA, 1973; Hugo Müller Silver Medal, Chemical Soc., 1974; Alfred Treibs Gold Medal, Geochem. Soc., 1981; Coke Medal, 1985, Wollaston Medal, 2004, Geol Soc. of London; H. C. Urey Award, European Assoc. of Geochem., 1997; Royal Medal, Royal Soc., 1997; Martin Gold Medal, Chromatographic Soc., 1999; Goldschmidt Medal, Geochemical Soc., 2000; (jtly) Dan David Prize for Geoscis, 2008. *Publications:* Applications of Spectroscopy to Organic Chemistry, 1965; Organic Geochemistry: methods and results, 1969; 'Chemsyn', 1972, 2nd edn 1975; (with S. M. Gaines and J. Rullkötter) Echoes of Life, 2009; contrib. Nature, Geochim. Cosmochim. Acta, Phytochem., Chem. Geol., Sci. American. *Recreations:* gardening, walking, sailing. *Club:* Rucksack (Manchester).

EGREMONT, 2nd Baron *cr* 1963, **AND LECONFIELD,** 7th Baron *cr* 1859; **John Max Henry Scawen Wyndham;** DL; FRSL, FSA; *b* 21 April 1948; *s* of John Edward Reginald Wyndham, MBE, 1st Baron Egremont and 6th Baron Leconfield, and Pamela, *d* of late Captain the Hon. Valentine Wyndham-Quin, RN; *S* father, 1972; *m* 1978, Caroline, *er d* of A. R. Nelson, Muckairn, Taynuilt, Argyll, and Hon. Lady Musker; one *s* three *d*. *Educ:* Eton; Christ Church, Oxford (MA Modern History). Mem., Royal Commn on Historical MSS, 1989–2001. Chm., Friends of the Nat. Libraries, 1985–; Trustee: Wallace Collection, 1988–2000; British Museum, 1990–2000; Nat. Manuscripts Conservation Trust, 1995– (Chm., 2000–). President: ACRE, 1993–99; Sussex Heritage Trust, 2009–. DL W Sussex, 1988. FRSL 2001; FSA 2005. *Publications:* (as Max Egremont) The Cousins: a biographical study of Wilfrid Scawen Blunt and George Wyndham, 1977 (Yorkshire Post First Book Award); Balfour: a life of Arthur James Balfour, 1980; Under Two Flags: the life of Major-General Sir Edward Spears, 1997; Siegfried Sassoon, 2005: Forgotten Land: journeys among the ghosts of East Prussia, 2011; Some Desperate Glory: the First World War the poets knew, 2014; *novels:* The Ladies' Man, 1983; Dear Shadows, 1986; Painted Lives, 1989; Second Spring, 1993. *Heir: s* Hon. George Ronan Valentine Wyndham, *b* 31 July 1983. *Address:* Petworth House, Petworth, West Sussex GU28 0AE. *T:* (01798) 342447. *E:* egremont@leconfield.net.

EHLERS, Prof. Anke, PhD; FBA 2010; FMedSci; Professor of Experimental Psychopathology, and Wellcome Principal Research Fellow, University of Oxford, since 2012; *b* Kiel, Germany, 11 Jan. 1957; *d* of Hans Werner and Hella Ehlers; *m* 1994, Prof. David Millar Clark, *qv*; two *s*. *Educ:* Eberhard-Karls-Univ. Tübingen (Dip. Psychol. 1983; PhD 1985); Philipps-Univ. Marburg (Dr rer. nat. habil. 1990). Res. Scholar, Stanford Univ., 1983–85; Asst Prof., Philipps-Univ. Marburg, 1985–90; Associate Prof., Free Univ. of Berlin, 1990; Prof., Georg-August-Univ. Göttingen, 1991–93; Wellcome Principal Res. Fellow, Univ. of Oxford, 1993–2000; Prof. of Experimental Psychopathology, and Wellcome Principal Res. Fellow, KCL, 2000–11. MAE 2012. Fellow, German Acad. of Scis Leopoldina, 2005. FMedSci 2014. German Psychology Prize, Eur. Fedn of Psychologists' Assoc., 2013; Oswald Külpe Prize, Univ. of Würzburg, 2013; Award for Distinguished Scientific Contribs to Clinical Psychol., Amer. Psychol Assoc., 2014. *Publications:* (ed jtly) Perspectives and Promises of Clinical Psychology, 1992; numerous articles in scientific jls. *Recreations:* theatre, art, cinema, travel. *Address:* Department of Experimental Psychology, University of Oxford, South Parks Road, Oxford OX1 3UD. *T:* (01865) 618602. *E:* anke.ehlers@psy.ox.ac.uk.

EHRMAN, Sir William (Geoffrey), KCMG 2007 (CMG 1998); HM Diplomatic Service, retired; Ambassador to the People's Republic of China, 2006–10; *b* 28 Aug. 1950; *s* of John Patrick William Ehrman, FBA and of Susan (*née* Blake); *m* 1977, Penelope Anne, *d* of late Brig. H. W. Le Patourel, VC and of Babette Le Patourel; one *s* three *d*. *Educ:* Eton; Trinity Coll., Cambridge (MA); Royal Agricultural Coll. (DipAgr 2011). Joined Diplomatic Service, 1973; language student, Hong Kong, 1975–76; Third/Second Sec., Peking, 1976–78; First Secretary, UK Mission to UN, NY, 1979–83, Peking, 1983–84, FCO, 1985–89; Pol Advr, Hong Kong, 1989–93; Head, Near East and N Africa Dept, FCO, 1993–94; UK Mem., Bosnia Contact Gp, 1994–95; Prin. Pvte Sec. to Sec. of State for Foreign and Commonwealth Affairs, 1995–97; seconded to Unilever (China) Ltd, 1997–98; Ambassador to Luxembourg, 1998–2000; Dir, Internat. Security, 2000–02, Dir Gen., Defence and Intelligence, 2002–04, FCO; Chm., Jt Intelligence Cttee, and Hd, Intelligence and Security Secretariat, Cabinet Office, 2004–05. *Recreations:* sailing, walking, ski-ing. *Club:* Royal Cruising.

EICHEL, Hans; Member (SPD), Bundestag, 2002–09; Minister of Finance, Germany, 1999–2005; *b* Kassel, 24 Dec. 1941; *m*; two *c*. Secondary sch. teacher, Kassel, 1970–75. Mem., Kassel City Council, 1968–75; Mayor, Kassel, 1975–91; Mem. (SPD), Assembly, and Premier, Hesse Land, 1991–99. German Convention of Municipal Authorities: Mem., Presidium, 1981–91; Pres., 1985–87 and 1989–91. Joined SPD, 1964: Mem., Exec. Cttee, 1984–2005; Chm., Hesse, 1989–2005.

EICHELBAUM, Rt Hon. Sir (Johann) Thomas, GBE 1989; PC 1989; Chief Justice of New Zealand, 1989–99; Judge of Appeal, Fiji, 1999–2007; non-permanent Judge, Court of Final Appeal, Hong Kong, 2000–09; *b* 17 May 1931; *s* of Dr Walter and Frida Eichelbaum; *m* 1956, Vida Beryl Franz (decd); three *s*. *Educ:* Hutt Valley High School; Victoria University College (LLB). Partner, Chapman Tripp & Co., Wellington, 1958–78; QC 1978; Judge of High Court of NZ, 1982–88. Pres., NZ Law Soc., 1980–82. Chm., Royal Commn on Genetic Modification, 2000–01. *Publications:* (Editor in Chief) Mauet's Fundamentals of Trial Techniques, NZ edn, 1989; (Consulting Editor) Advocacy in New Zealand, 2000. *Recreations:* reading, music, bridge. *Address:* Raumati Beach, Kapiti Coast. *Club:* Wellington (Wellington).

EICKE, Tim; QC 2011; *b* Hannover, Germany, 27 July 1966; *s* of Reinhard Eicke and Gerda Adeline Eicke (*née* Loescher); *m* 1993, Andrea Elisabeth Hielscher; two *s*. *Educ:* Ulrichsgymnasium Norden; Passau Universität; Univ. of Dundee (LLB Hons English Law 1992). Called to the Bar, Middle Temple, 1993; Jun. Counsel to the Crown, 1999–2011; Bencher, Lincoln's Inn, 2014. Ed., European Human Rights Reports, 1999–. *Publications:* (ed jtly) The Strasbourg Case Law: leading cases from the European Court of Human Rights, 2001; (jtly) Human Rights Damages: principles and practice, 2001. *Recreations:* family, cycling, cooking, bread making. *Address:* Essex Court Chambers, 24 Lincoln's Inn Fields, WC2A 3EG. *T:* (020) 7813 8000, *Fax:* (020) 7813 8080. *E:* teicke@essexcourt.net.

EIGEN, Manfred; physicist, at Max-Planck-Institut für biophysikalische Chemie, Göttingen, since 1953 (Director, 1964); *b* 9 May 1927; *s* of Ernst and Hedwig Eigen (*née* Feld); *m* 1952, Elfriede Müller; one *s* one *d*. *Educ:* Göttingen Univ. Dr rer. nat. (Phys. Chem.) 1951. Research Asst, Inst. für physikal. Chemie, Göttingen Univ., 1951–53; Asst, Max-Planck-Institut für physikal. Chemie, 1953; Research Fellow, Max-Planck-Ges., 1958; Head of separate dept of biochemical kinetics, Max-Planck-Inst., 1962. Andrew D. White Prof. at Large, Cornell Univ., 1965; Hon. Prof., Technische Hochschule Braunschweig, 1965. For. Hon. Mem., Amer. Acad. of Arts and Sciences, 1964; Mem. Leopoldina, Deutsche Akad. der Naturforscher, Halle, 1964; Mem., Akad. der Wissenschaften, Göttingen, 1965; Hon. Mem., Amer. Assoc. Biol Chemists, 1966; For. Assoc., Nat. Acad. of Scis, Washington, 1966; For. Mem., Royal Soc., 1973. Dr of Science *hc* Washington, Harvard and Chicago Univs, 1966. Has won prizes, medals and awards including: Nobel Prize for Chemistry (jointly), 1967; Paul Ehrlich Award, 1996. *Publications:* numerous papers in learned jls on mechanics of biochemical reactions, molecular self-organisation and evolutionary biotechnology. *Address:* Max-Planck-Institut für biophysikalische Chemie, Am Fassberg 11, 37077 Göttingen, Germany.

EILLEDGE, Elwyn Owen Morris, CBE 2001; FCA; Chairman, Financial Reporting Advisory Board to HM Treasury, 1996–2010; Senior Partner, Ernst & Young, Chartered Accountants, 1989–95; *b* 20 July 1935; *s* of Owen and Mary Elizabeth Eilledge; *m* 1962, Audrey Ann Faulkner Ellis; one *s* one *d*. *Educ:* Merton College, Oxford (BA, MA). FCA 1968. Articled with Farrow, Bersey, Gain, Vincent & Co., later Binder Hamlyn, 1959–66; Whinney Murray & Co. subseq. Ernst & Whinney, now Ernst & Young, Liberia, 1966–68; Ernst & Whinney: Audit Manager, Hamburg, 1968–71; Partner, London, 1972; Managing Partner, London office, 1983–86; Dep. Sen. Partner, 1985; Sen Partner, 1986–89; Chairman: Ernst & Whinney Internat., 1988–89; Ernst & Young Internat., 1989–95. Chm., BTR, 1996–98; Dir, BG Group plc, 1997–2005. Member: Accounting Standards Bd, 1989–91; Financial Reporting Council, 1989–95. *Recreations:* gardening, swimming, tennis, listening to classical music. *Address:* Whitethorn House, Long Grove, Seer Green, Beaconsfield, Bucks HP9 2QH. *Club:* Brooks's.

EILON, Prof. Samuel, FREng; Professor of Management Science, Imperial College of Science, Technology and Medicine, University of London, 1963–89, Professor Emeritus, since 1989 (Senior Research Fellow, 1989–2002); industrial consultant on corporate performance and strategy; *b* 13 Oct. 1923; *s* of Abraham and Rachel Eilon; *m* 1946, Hannah Ruth (*née* Samuel); two *s* two *d*. *Educ:* Reali Sch., Haifa; Technion, Israel Inst. of Technology, Haifa; Imperial Coll., London. PhD London, 1955; DSc(Eng) London, 1963. FREng (Founder FEng 1976); FIMechE; FIET. Engr, Palestine Electric Co. Ltd, Haifa, 1946–48; Officer, Israel Defence Forces, 1948–52; CO of an Ordnance and workshop base depot (Major); Res. Asst, Imperial Coll., 1952–55; Lectr in Production Engrg, Imperial Coll., 1955–57; Associate Prof. in Industrial Engrg, Technion, Haifa, 1957–59; Imperial College: Head of Section, 1955–57; Reader, 1959–63; Head of Dept, 1959–87. Consultant and Lectr, European Productivity Agency, Paris, 1960–62. Professorial Research Fellow, Case Western Reserve Univ., Cleveland, Ohio, 1967–68. Vis. Fellow, University Coll., Cambridge, 1970–71. Mem., Monopolies and Mergers Commn, 1990–97. Past Mem. of several cttees of IProdE and DES; Member: Council, Operational Res. Soc., 1965–67; Council, Inst. of Management Scis, 1970–72, 1980–82; Exec. Cttee, British Acad. of Management, 1985–89. Adviser, P-E Consulting Gp, 1961–71; Principal and Dir, Spencer Stuart and Associates, 1971–74; Director: Amey Roadstone Corp., subseq. ARC, 1974–88; Campari Internat., 1978–80. Chief Editor, OMEGA, Internat. Jl of Management Science, 1972–94; Deptl Editor, Management Science, 1969–77. Hon. FCGI 1978. Two Joseph Whitworth Prizes for papers, IMechE, 1960; Silver Medal, ORS, 1982. *Publications:* Elements of Production Planning and Control, 1962; Industrial Engineering Tables, 1962; (jtly) Exercises in Industrial Management, 1966; (jtly) Industrial Scheduling Abstracts, 1967; (jtly) Inventory Control Abstracts, 1968; (jtly) Distribution Management, 1971; Management Control, 1971, 2nd edn 1979; (jtly) Applications of Management Science in Banking and Finance, 1972; (jtly) Applied Productivity Analysis for Industry, 1976; Aspects of Management, 1977, 2nd edn 1979; The Art of Reckoning: analysis of performance criteria, 1984; Management Assertions and Aversions, 1985; (jtly) The Global Challenge of Innovation, 1991; Management Practice and Mispractice, 1992; Management Science: an anthology, 1995; Management Strategies: a critique of theories and practices, 1999; some 300 papers and articles in the field of management. *Recreations:* theatre, walking. *Address:* 1 Meadway Close, NW11 7BA. *T:* (020) 8458 6650.

EIRUG, Aled; Member, S4C Authority, 2012–Nov. 2016; Chair, Wales Committee, British Council, since 2012; *b* London, 1 July 1955; *s* of Dewi Aled Eirug Davies and Emily Maud Davies; surname changed to Eirug by deed poll, 1974; *m* 2003, Margaret Anne Russell; one *s* and one step *s* one step *d*. *Educ:* Penlan Sch., Swansea; University Coll. of Wales, Aberystwyth (BA Hons Hist. 1977); London Sch. of Econs and Pol Sci. (MSc Hons Urban and Regl Planning 1982). Parly researcher, 1979–82; current affairs researcher and prog. ed., ITV Wales, 1982–91; BBC Wales: Hd, News, 1992–2003; Hd, Corporate Social Responsibility, 2003–06; Constitnl Advr to Presiding Officer, Nat. Assembly for Wales, 2007–11; Lang. Policy Advr to Welsh Govt, 2012–13; Strategic Policy Advr, Univ. of Swansea, 2013–; Mem., Nominet Adv. Cttee for Wales, 2014–. Chair, Welsh Refugee Council, 2006–12. Mem. Bd, Linc Housing Assoc., 2005–09. Member: Llafur, 1974–; Inst. Welsh Affairs, 2000–; Bevan Foundn, 2009–. Part-time PhD student, Univ. of Cardiff, 2013–. *Recreations:* football, Rugby, cricket, Welsh history, theatre. *Address:* 14 Denbigh Street, Cardiff CF11 9JQ. *E:* aled.eirug@mac.com. *Clubs:* Civil Service; Cardiff City Football; Glamorgan CC.

EISEN, Prof. Timothy George Quentin, PhD; FRCP; Professor of Medical Oncology, University of Cambridge, since 2006; Fellow, Homerton College, Cambridge, since 2014; Vice President, Clinical Discovery, AstraZeneca, since 2014; *b* London, 13 Dec. 1963; *s* of Vuk and Phyl Eisen; *m* 2003, Julia Hardiman; one *s* one *d*. *Educ:* Arnold House Sch., London; Westminster Sch.; Middlesex Hosp. Med. Sch. (BSc); Gonville and Caius Coll., Cambridge (BChir 1986, MB 1987); Marie Curie Res. Inst., Surrey (PhD 1996). FRCP 2002. Clin. Res. Fellow, Marie Curie Res. Inst., 1990–94; Sen. Registrar, Royal Marsden Hosp., 1994–98; Senior Lecturer in Medical Oncology: UCL, 1998–2001; Inst. of Cancer Res., 2001–06. Chair: Lung Clin. Studies Gp, NCRI, 2004–10; Macmillan Clinical Adv. Bd (formerly Med. Adv. Cttee, Macmillan Cancer Backup), 2006–. Trustee and Med. Advr, Balkans Relief, 1996–98; Trustee: Kidney Cancer UK, 2004–; Macmillan Cancer Support, 2012–. *Publications:* (ed) Clinical Progress in Renal Cancer, 2007; contribs on kidney cancer, lung cancer and melanoma. *Recreations:* hill-bagging in Cambridgeshire (and beyond), tennis, trying to find a balance between unbridled optimism and pessimism. *Address:* Department of Oncology, Box 193, Addenbrooke's Hospital, Cambridge CB2 0QQ. *T:* (01223) 769312, *Fax:* (01223) 769313. *E:* tgqe2@cam.ac.uk. *Club:* Athenæum.

EISENBERG, Neville; Senior Partner, Berwin Leighton Paisner LLP, Solicitors, since 2015 (Partner, 1996–99; Managing Partner, 1999–2015); *b* 12 April 1962; *s* of late Benjamin Elieser Eisenberg and of Masha Eisenberg. *Educ:* Paul Roos Primary Sch.; Paul Roos Gymnasium; Pretoria Boys High Sch.; Univ. of Witwatersrand (BCom 1982; LLB 1984); London Sch. of Econs and Pol Sci. (LLM 1988). Articled clerk, Werksmans Attorneys, 1985–87; solicitor, Berwin Leighton Paisner, 1989–95; admitted solicitor, England and Wales, 1991. Mem., London Council, CBI, 2002–08, 2011–. Chm., Lawyers on Demand Ltd, 2012–. Chm., British Israel Law Assoc., 1996–. Nat. Chm., South African Union of Jewish Students, 1982–84; Comptroller, World Union of Jewish Students, 1986–89. Assoc. Gov., Hebrew Univ. of Jerusalem, 2004–. *Recreations:* current affairs, theatre, music, travel. *Address:* Berwin Leighton Paisner LLP, Adelaide House, London Bridge, EC4R 9HA. *T:* (020) 3400 1000, *Fax:* (020) 3400 1111. *E:* neville.eisenberg@blplaw.com. *Club:* Home House.

EISENSTADT, Naomi, CB 2005; Senior Research Fellow, Oxford University, since 2010; *b* 10 Feb. 1950; *d* of Berthold and Cecilia Leidner; *m* Prof. Marc Eisenstadt (marr. diss.); one *s*; *m* Michael Moutrie. *Educ:* Univ. of Calif, San Diego (BA; Post-grad. Dip. Early Childhood Educn); Cranfield Univ. (MSc Social Policy). Centre Leader, Moorlands Children's Centre, Milton Keynes, 1978–83; Lectr, Sch. of Educn, Open Univ., 1983–86; SCF, 1986–92; NCVO, 1992–96; Chief Exec., Family Service Units, 1996–99; Dir, Sure Start and Extended Schs, DfES, 1999–2006; Chief Advr on Children's Services to Sec. of State for Children, Schs and Families (formerly for Educn and Skills), 2006–07; Dir, Social Exclusion Task Force,

Cabinet Office, 2007–09. Mem., Editl Bd, Children and Society, 2002–13. DUniv Open, 2002. Philanthropy Champions Award, Milton Keynes Community Foundn. *Recreations:* cooking, movies.

EISNER, Prof. David Alfred, DPhil; FMedSci; BHF Professor of Cardiac Physiology, University of Manchester, since 2000 (Professor of Cardiac Physiology, 1999–2000); *b* Manchester, 3 Jan. 1955; *s* of Herbert Eisner and Gisela Eisner (*née* Spanglet); *m* 1983, Susan Wray; two *s* one *d*. *Educ:* Manchester Grammar Sch.; King's Coll., Cambridge (BA 1976); Balliol Coll., Oxford (DPhil 1979). Lectr in Physiol., 1980–86, Wellcome Trust Sen. Lectr, 1986–90, UCL; Prof. of Veterinary Biol., Univ. of Liverpool, 1990–99. Lectures: Q. R. Murphy, Univ. of Wisconsin, 1992; Reimer, Internat. Soc. for Heart Res., 2008; Carmeliet-Coraboeuf-Weidmann, Eur. Soc. of Cardiol., 2013; G. L. Brown, Physiol Soc., 2014. FMedSci 1999; Fellow, Internat. Soc. for Heart Res., 2000. Hon. FRCP 2010. Pfizer Prize for Res. in Biol., 1985; Wellcome Prize in Physiol., 1988. *Publications:* articles in physiol and cardiovascular jls. *Recreations:* photography, walking. *Address:* Institute of Cardiovascular Sciences, University of Manchester, 3.18 Core Technology Facility, 46 Grafton Street, Manchester M13 9NT. *T:* (0161) 275 2702. *E:* eisner@manchester.ac.uk.

EISNER, Prof. Manuel Peter, PhD; Professor of Comparative and Developmental Criminology, since 2009, and Director, Violence Research Centre, since 2013, Institute of Criminology, and Director, Social Science Research Methods Programme, since 2009, University of Cambridge; *b* Berne, 7 May 1959; *s* of Gerhard Eisner and Marlies Eisner-Odenbreit; *m* 1991, Ruth Schmid; one *s* two *d*. *Educ:* Univ. of Zurich (MA Hist., Sociol. and Social Psychol. 1985; PhD Sociol. 1991; Habilitation (venia legendi-private docent) 1997). Res. Associate, Inst. of Sociol., Univ. of Zurich, 1985–93; Asst Prof., 1993–96, Associate Prof., 1996–2001, Dept of Sociol., Swiss Federal Inst. of Technol.; Lectr, 2000–01, Reader in Sociological Criminol., 2002–09, Inst. of Criminol., Univ. of Cambridge. *Publications:* contrib. articles to peer-reviewed jls and ed vols. *Address:* Institute of Criminology, University of Cambridge, Sidgwick Site, Cambridge CB3 9DA.

EISNER, Michael D(ammann); Founder and Chief Executive Officer, Tornante Company, since 2005; Chief Executive Officer, 1984–2005, Director, 1984–2006, Walt Disney Co. (Chairman, 1984–2004); *b* 7 March 1942; *s* of Lester Eisner and Margaret Eisner (*née* Dammann); *m* 1967, Jane Breckenridge; three *s*. *Educ:* Lawrenceville Sch.; Denison Univ. (BA English Lit. and Theatre 1964). ABC Entertainment Corporation: Dir of Program Develt, East Coast, 1968–71; Vice President: Daytime Programming, 1971–75; Program Planning and Develt, 1975–76; Sen. Vice Pres., Prime-Time Production and Develt, 1976; Pres. and Chief Operating Officer, Paramount Pictures Corp., 1976–84. Jt Founder, Eisner Foundn, 1996. Host, TV show, Conversations with Michael Eisner, 2006–. Member of Board: California Inst. of the Arts; American Film Inst. Chevalier, Légion d'Honneur (France). *Publications:* Work in Progress (autobiog.), 1998; Camp (autobiog.), 2005. *Address:* c/o Eisner Foundation, 9401 Wilshire Boulevard, Suite 735, Beverly Hills, CA 90212, USA.

EKANEY, Nkumbe; QC 2011; *b* London, 4 Aug. 1967; *s* of Thomas Kolle Ekaney and Lydia Ndolo Ekaney; *m* 1994, Lucy Monjoa; four *d*. *Educ:* Oratory Sch., Woodcote; Univ. of Bristol (LLB Hons). Called to the Bar, Gray's Inn, 1990; in practice as a barrister, specialising in family law. *Recreations:* travel, African art and music, socialising. *Address:* Albion Chambers, Broad, Street, Bristol BS1 1DR. *T:* (0117) 927 2144, *Fax:* (0117) 926 2569. *E:* nkumbe.ekaneyqc@albionchambers.co.uk.

EKERS, Prof. Ronald David, PhD; FRS 2005; FAA; CSIRO Fellow, Australia Telescope National Facility, since 2008 (Director, 1988–2003; ARC Federation Fellow, 2003–08); *b* 18 Sept. 1941. *Educ:* Univ. of Adelaide (BSc 1963); Australian Nat. Univ. (PhD 1967). FAA 1993. Calif Inst. of Technol., 1967–70; Inst. of Theoretical Astronomy, Univ. of Cambridge, 1970–71; Kapteyn Lab., Groningen, 1971–80; Asst Dir, and Dir for Very Large Array Ops, Nat. Radio Astronomy Observatory, Socorro, USA, 1980–88. Pres., IAU, 2003–06. Mem., Amer. Philosophical Soc., 2003. Flinders Medal, Aust. Acad. of Sci., 2005; Grote Reber Medal, Grote Reber Foundn, 2014. Centenary Medal, Australia, 2003. *Publications:* 498 articles in learned jls. *Address:* Australia Telescope National Facility, CSIRO Astronomy and Space Science, PO Box 76, Epping, NSW 1710, Australia.

EKERT, Prof. Artur Konrad, DPhil; FInstP; Professor of Quantum Physics, Oxford University, since 2007; Fellow of Merton College, Oxford, since 2007; Director, Centre for Quantum Technologies, Singapore, since 2007; *b* 19 Sept. 1961; *s* of Kazimierz and Janina Ekert; *m* 1990, Beata Wijowska. *Educ:* Jagiellonian Univ., Kraków, Poland (MSc); Wolfson Coll., Oxford (DPhil). FInstP 2004. Oxford University: Jun. Research Fellow, 1991–94, Res. Fellow, 1994–98, Merton Coll.; Prof. of Physics, 1998–2002; Fellow and Tutor, Keble Coll., 1998–2002; Leigh Trapnell Prof. of Quantum Physics, Cambridge Univ., 2002–07; Fellow, King's Coll., Cambridge, 2002–07. Howe Res. Fellow, Royal Soc., 1994–2000; Temasek Prof., Univ. of Singapore, 2002–05; Lee Kong Chian Centennial Prof., Nat. Univ. of Singapore, 2006–. Visiting Professor: Univ. of Innsbruck, 1994, 1998; Nat. Univ. of Singapore, 2001. Maxwell Medal and Prize, Inst. of Physics, 1995; (jtly) Descartes Prize, EU, 2004; Hughes Medal, Royal Soc., 2007. *Publications:* articles in scientific jls. *Recreations:* scuba diving, water sports, ski-ing, general aviation. *Address:* Mathematical Institute, University of Oxford, Andrew Wiles Building, Radcliffe Observatory Quarter, Woodstock Road, Oxford OX2 6GG. *E:* artur.ekert@qubit.org.

EKINS, Prof. Paul Whitfield, OBE 2015; PhD; Professor of Resources and Environmental Policy (formerly of Energy and Environment Policy), since 2009, and Director, UCL Institute for Sustainable Resources, since 2012, University College London; *b* 24 July 1950; *s* of John Robert Ekins and Lydia Mary Ekins (*née* Daukes); *m* 1979, Susan Anne Lofthouse; one *s*. *Educ:* Imperial Coll., London (BSc Eng); Univ. of Bradford (MPhil); Birkbeck Coll., London (MSc Econ; PhD 1996). Res. Fellow, Birkbeck Coll., London, 1990–96; Sen. Lectr, then Reader, 1996–2000, Prof. of Sustainable Develt, 2000–02, Keele Univ.; Prof. of Sustainable Develt and Hd, Envmt Gp, Policy Studies Inst., Univ. of Westminster, 2002–07; Prof. of Energy and Envmt Policy, KCL, 2008–09. Mem., Royal Commn on Envmtl Pollution, 2002–08. Mem. Bd, NCC, 1996–2002. *Publications:* A New World Order, 1992; (ed jtly) Global Warming and Energy Demand, 1995; Economic Growth and Environmental Sustainability, 2000; (ed jtly) Understanding the Costs of Environmental Regulation in Europe, 2009; Trade, Globalization, and Sustainability Impact Assessment: a critical look at methods and outcomes, 2009; Carbon-Energy Taxation: lessons from Europe, 2009; (ed) Hydrogen Energy: economic and social challenges, 2010; (ed jtly) Energy 2050: the transition to a secure, low-carbon energy system for the UK, 2011; Environmental Tax Reform: a policy for green growth, 2011; contrib. numerous jl papers and articles. *Recreations:* music, theatre. *Address:* UCL Institute for Sustainable Resources, Central House, 14 Upper Woburn Place, WC1H 0NN. *T:* (020) 3108 5990. *E:* p.ekins@ucl.ac.uk.

EKINS, Prof. Roger Philip, PhD, DSc; FRS 2001; Professor of Biophysics, University of London, 1972–88, now Emeritus Professor; former Head, Department of Molecular Endocrinology, University College London Medical School (formerly at Middlesex Hospital Medical School); *b* 22 Sept. 1926; *s* of William Norman and Mathilde Therese Ekins; *m* 1st, 1947, Jane Woodger (marr. diss. 1963); two *d*; one *s* two *d*; 2nd, 1990, Marisa Antonietta Sgherzi. *Educ:* Westminster City Sch.; Emmanuel Coll., Cambridge (MA); Middx Hosp. Med. Sch. (PhD 1963; DSc 1990). Middlesex Hospital Medical School: Lectr in Physics Applied to Medicine, 1949–61; Lectr, then Sen. Lectr, 1961–68, Reader and Dep. Dir, 1968–72, Inst. of Nuclear Medicine; Dir, UK Supraregl Assay Service Centre, 1972–93 (Chm., SAS Dirs' Cttee, UK Supraregl Assay Service, 1974–77). Hon. Fellow, UCL, 2010. Dr *hc* Univ. Claude Bernard, Lyons, 1993. Georg von Hevesy Medal, von Hevesy Foundn, Switzerland, 1984; Dist. Clin. Chemist Award, Internat. Fedn Clin. Chem., 1993; Inaugural Edwin F. Ullman Award, Amer. Assoc. Clin. Chem., 1998; Lifetime Achievement Award, DoH, 2006; Enterprise Lifetime Achievement Award, UCL, 2012. *Publications:* contrib. numerous res. papers and book chapters relating to effects of maternal hormones on fetal brain develt, and develt of microarray and other microanalytical methods for sensitive measurement of substances of biol importance (e.g. hormones, DNA and RNA). *Recreations:* weaving rya rugs, potting, sailing, building houses, tasting fine wines, gardening, talking to attractive women. *Address:* Wolfson House, University College London, 4 Stephenson Way, NW1 2HE; Pondweed Place, Friday Street, Abinger Common, Dorking, Surrey RH5 6JR.

EKLUND, Graham Nicholas; QC 2002; barrister; *b* 23 Dec. 1950; *s* of Alan Nicholas Eklund and Mollie Jean (*née* Talbot); *m* 1987, Deborah Anne Bartley; one *s* one *d* (and one *s* decd). *Educ:* Auckland Univ. (BA; LLB Hons). Barrister and solicitor, Agar Keesing McLeod & Co., NZ, 1975–78; solicitor, Herbert Smith, 1981–84; called to the Bar, Inner Temple, 1984; in practice as a barrister, 1984–. *Recreations:* wine, sport, song. *Address:* 4 New Square, Lincoln's Inn, WC2A 3RJ. *T:* (020) 7822 2000, *Fax:* (020) 7822 2001. *E:* g.eklund@4newsquare.com.

EKSERDJIAN, Prof. David Patrick Martin, PhD; Professor of History of Art and Film, University of Leicester, since 2004; *b* 28 Oct. 1955; *s* of late Nubar Martin Ekserdjian and Mabel Brown Ekserdjian (*née* Angus); *m* 1990, Susan Moore; one *s* one *d*. *Educ:* Westminster Sch.; Trinity Coll., Cambridge (BA Modern and Medieval Langs 1977); Courtauld Inst. of Art, Univ. of London (MA 1979; PhD 1988). Christie's Jun. Res. Fellow, Balliol Coll., Oxford, 1983–86; Lectr, Courtauld Inst. of Art, 1986–87; Slade Fellow, Corpus Christi Coll., Oxford, 1987–91; with Christie, Manson & Woods, 1991–97; Editor, Apollo, 1997–2004 (Mem., Editl Adv. Panel, 2012–); Leverhulme Trust Major Res. Fellow, 2008–11. Guest Scholar, J. Paul Getty Mus., 2006. Member: Bd, Courtauld Inst. of Art, 1998–2002; Comitato Scientifico, Fondazione il Correggio, 2002–; Reviewing Cttee on Export of Works of Art, 2002–12; Bd, MA course in history of design, V&A/RCA, 2003–13; Adv. Bd, Bampton Opera, 2003–06. Trustee: Nat. Gall., 2005–13; Tate Gall., 2008–13; Public Catalogue Foundn, 2012–. Hon. Citizen, Correggio, 2004. *Publications:* (introd. and notes) Vasari, Lives of the Artists, 1996; Correggio, 1997; Parmigianino, 2006; Alle origini della natura morta, 2007; (notes) Benvenuto Cellini: autobiography, 2010; *exhibition catalogues:* (with D. Mahon) Guercino Drawings, 1986; Old Master Paintings from the Thyssen-Bornemisza Collection, 1987; Mantegna, 1992; Treasures from Budapest, 2010; Bronze, 2012; contrib. to Macmillan Dictionary of Art, Saurs Allgemeine Künstlerlexicon, etc. *Recreations:* wine, Real tennis, opera, moths. *Address:* Department of History of Art and Film, University of Leicester, University Road, Leicester LE1 7RH. *T:* (0116) 252 2905. *Club:* Beefsteak.

ELAM, Caroline Mary, (Mrs J. H. Drury); Senior Research Fellow, Warburg Institute, University of London, since 2012; *b* 12 March 1945; *d* of John Frederick Elam and Joan Barrington Elam (*née* Lloyd); *m* 2009, Very Rev. John Henry Drury *qv*. *Educ:* Colchester County High Sch.; Lady Margaret Hall, Oxford (BA); Courtauld Inst. of Art, Univ. of London. MA London and Cantab. Lectr, Fine Art Dept, Univ. of Glasgow, 1970–72; Jun. Res. Fellow, King's Coll., Cambridge, 1972–76 (Hon. Fellow, 1992); Lectr, History of Art Dept, Westfield Coll., Univ. of London, 1976–87; Editor, Burlington Mag., 1987–2002; Andrew W. Mellon Prof., Center for Advanced Study in the Visual Arts, Nat. Gall. of Art, Washington, 2002–04; Ruth and Clarence Kennedy Prof. in Renaissance Studies, Smith Coll., Northampton, Mass, 2008. Villa I Tatti, Florence: Fellow, Harvard Univ. Center for Renaissance Studies, 1981–82, 2002; Vis. Prof., 2005; Accademica, Accademia Raffaello, Urbino, 2005–. Chair, SH5 Panel, Starting Grants, Eur. Res. Council, 2012. Member: Exec. Cttee, NACF, 1988–2002; Bd, Warburg Inst., 1992–97; Bd, Courtauld Inst. of Art, 1993–98; Syndic, Fitzwilliam Mus., Cambridge, 1993–2002; Trustee, Friends of Courtauld Inst., 2009–. Hon. DArts Oxford Brookes, 2005. Agnes and Elizabeth Mongan Prize, 2004. Exec. Ed., I Tatti Studies, 2004–12. *Publications:* Roger Fry and the Re-evaluation of Piero della Francesca, 2005; Roger Fry: Mantegna, 2006; Roger Fry: Giovanni Bellini, 2007; Roger Fry's Journey: from the primitives to the post-impressionists, 2008; articles in Art History, Burlington Magazine, I Tatti Studies, Mitteilungen des Kunsthistorischen Insts in Florenz, Renaissance Quarterly, Renaissance Studies, Jl of RSA, etc.

See also J. N. Elam.

ELAM, (John) Nicholas, CMG 1994; HM Diplomatic Service, retired; *b* 2 July 1939; *s* of John Frederick Elam, OBE and Joan Barrington Elam (*née* Lloyd); *m* 1967, Florence Helen, *d* of P. Lentz; two *s* one *d*. *Educ:* Colchester Royal Grammar Sch.; New Coll., Oxford (schol.). Frank Knox Fellow, Harvard Univ., 1961–62. Entered HM Diplomatic Service, 1962; served: Pretoria and Cape Town, 1964–68; Bahrain, 1971; Brussels, 1972–76; FCO, 1976–79, Dep. Head of News Dept, 1978–79; Counsellor and Dep. British Govt Rep., Salisbury, 1979; Dep. High Comr, Salisbury (later Harare), 1980–83; Consul-General, Montreal, 1984–87; Hd of Cultural Relations Dept, FCO, 1987–94; Ambassador to Luxembourg, 1994–98. Chm., Cultural Co-operation Council, Council of Europe, 1993–94. Administrator, Caine Prize for African Writing, 1999–2011; Co. Sec., Africa 95, 1999–; Dir, Dance Umbrella, 1999–2004; Consultant, Serious Internat. Music Producers, 1999–2002; Trustee, Triangle Arts Trust, 1998–2010; Chairman: Henri Oguike Dance Co., 2002–10; Friends of UCL Art Collections, 2003–. Mem., British Council, 1994. Hon. Sen. Res. Fellow, Dept of History of Art, UCL, 2003–04. *Recreations:* travel, the arts. *Address:* 86 Camberwell Church Street, SE5 8QZ. *Club:* Chelsea Arts.

See also C. M. Elam.

ELAND, Prof. John Hugh David, DPhil; FRS 2006; FRCS; Professor of Physical Chemistry, University of Oxford, 1997–2006; Fellow and Tutor in Chemistry, Worcester College, Oxford, 1983–2006, now Emeritus Fellow; *b* 6 Aug. 1941; *s* of Rev. Thomas Eland and Verna Prosser Eland (*née* Reynolds); *m* 1967, Ieva Antonovics; three *s*. *Educ:* St John's Sch., Leatherhead; University Coll., Oxford (BA 1963; MA, DPhil, 1966). FRCS 2005. Physicist, Argonne Nat. Lab., USA, 1976–80; Lectr, Queen's Coll., Oxford, 1980–83. Visiting Professor: Univ. of Paris, 1981, 1995; Inst. Molecular Sci., Japan, 1989; Uppsala Univ., 1995; Tohoku Univ., Japan, 2002; Guest Prof. in Physics and Astronomy, Uppsala Univ., 2010–14; Guest Prof. in Physics, Gothenburg Univ., 2014–. *Publications:* Photoelectron Spectroscopy, 1972, 2nd edn 1984; contrib. numerous articles to learned jls. *Recreations:* astronomy, linguistics, walking. *Address:* Physical and Theoretical Chemistry Laboratory, University of Oxford, South Parks Road, Oxford OX1 3QZ. *T:* (01865) 275400, *Fax:* (01865) 275410. *E:* john.eland@chem.ox.ac.uk.

ELAND, Michael John, CB 2006; Commissioner, 2000–12, and Director General, Enforcement and Compliance, 2005–12, HM Revenue and Customs (formerly Customs and Excise); *b* 26 Sept. 1952; *s* of George and Betty Eland; *m* 1981, Luned Rhiannon Wynn Jones; one *s* one *d*. *Educ:* Worksop Coll.; Trinity Coll., Oxford (BA Jurisp, MA). Called to the Bar, Middle Temple, 1975. Administration Trainee, HM Customs and Excise, 1975; Private Sec. to Chm., 1979–81; Cabinet Office, 1982–87; Private Sec. to Lord President of the Council (Viscount Whitelaw), 1987–88; Asst Sec., 1988–92, Comr, 1992–97, HM Customs and Excise; Dep. Dir-Gen., Policy, Immigration and Nationality Directorate, Home Office, 1997–2000; HM Customs and Excise, later Revenue and Customs: Dir Gen., Business Services and Taxes, 2000–03; Actg Chm., 2003–04; Dir Gen., Law Enforcement, 2004–05. *Recreations:* walking, theatre.

ElBARADEI, Dr Mohamed Mostafa; Director General, International Atomic Energy Agency, 1997–2009, now Emeritus; *b* Egypt, 17 June 1942; *s* of Mostafa and Aida ElBaradei; *m* 1975, Aida ElKachef; one *s* one *d*. *Educ:* Cairo Univ. Sch. of Law (Licence en droit 1962; Dip. Advanced Studies, Admin. Law, 1964); NY Univ. Sch. of Law (LLM 1971; JSD Internat. Law 1974). Dept of Internat. Orgns, Min. of Foreign Affairs, Egypt, 1964–67; Perm. Mission of Egypt to UN, NY, 1967–71; Sen. Fellow, Center for Internat. Studies, NY Univ., 1973–74; Special Asst to Foreign Minister, Min. of Foreign Affairs, Egypt, 1974–78; Perm. Mission of Egypt to UN, Geneva, and Alternate Rep., Cttee on Disarmament, 1978–80; Sen. Fellow and Dir, Internat. Law and Orgns Prog., UN Inst. for Trng and Res., NY, 1980–84; International Atomic Energy Agency: Rep. of Dir Gen. to UN, NY, 1984–87; Dir, Legal Div. and Legal Advr, Vienna, 1987–91; Dir, Ext. Relns, Vienna, 1991–93; Asst Dir Gen. for Ext Relns, 1993–97. Adjunct Prof. of Internat. Law, NY Univ. Sch. of Law, 1981–87. Rep. of Egypt or IAEA, to UN Gen. Assembly, UN Security Council, Cttee on Disarmament, Rev. Confs of Treaty on Non-Proliferation of Nuclear Weapons, OAU, UNDP, ILO and WHO. Has lectured widely on internat. law and orgns, arms control and non-proliferation and peaceful uses of nuclear energy. Nobel-Laureate-in-Residence, Fletcher Sch. of Law and Diplomacy, Tufts Univ., USA, 2014. Nobel Peace Prize (jtly), 2005. *Publications:* The Right of Innocent Passage through Straits, 1974; (jtly) The International Law Commission: the need for a new direction, 1981; (jtly) Crowded Agendas, Crowded Rooms, 1981; Model Rules for Disaster Relief Operations, 1982; (jtly) The International Law of Nuclear Energy, 1993; The Age of Deception, 2011; contribs to NY Univ. Jl of Internat. Law and Politics, Leiden Jl of Internat. Law, etc.

ELBORN, Peter Leonard, OBE 1990; Regional Director, East and Central Africa, and Director, Kenya, British Council, 2000–04; *b* 11 June 1945; *s* of Leonard and Joyce Elborn; *m* 1997, Sue Unsworth; three *s*. *Educ:* UC, Swansea (BA). British Council: Mexico, 1970–74; Croatia/Slovenia, 1977–82; Iraq, 1987–91; Zimbabwe, 1991–94; Kenya, 2000–04. Mem. Bd, Acad. of Live and Recorded Arts, 2009–. Sec., British-Croatian Soc., 2010–. Trustee, Charles Wallace Pakistan Trust, 2008–. *Recreations:* walking, swimming, reading. *Address:* 5 Well Road, NW3 1LH. *T:* (020) 7431 3179. *E:* peterelborn@hotmail.co.uk.

ELCHO, Lord; Francis Richard Percy Charteris; *b* 15 Sept. 1984; *s* and *heir* of Earl of Wemyss and March, *qv*. *Educ:* Eton Coll.; Edinburgh Univ. (MA History). Student, Inner Temple. Volunteer, Free Representation Unit. Interest in industrial law and legal, political and military history. *Recreations:* hunting, shooting, football, boxing, hill-walking.

ELCOAT, Dame Catherine Elizabeth, DBE 2002; independent healthcare adviser, 2010; Director of Nursing and Patient Care, East Midlands Strategic Health Authority, 2006–10; *b* 26 Feb. 1954; *d* of Derrick and Johanna Goulding; *m* 1975, Richard Thomas Elcoat. *Educ:* Birmingham Univ. (MScSoc); Darlington Meml Hosp. (RGN); Univ. of Teesside (DipHV). Student Nurse, 1972–75; North Tees Hospital: Staff Nurse, 1975–77; Ward Sister, 1977–82; Clinical Nurse Specialist, 1982–87; Health Visitor, 1987–90; Quality Manager, Darlington Meml Hosp., 1990–93; Exec. Dir of Nursing and Quality, S Durham Healthcare NHS Trust, 1993–96; Nursing Officer, NHS Exec., Leeds, 1996–97; Exec. Nurse Dir, City Hosp., Birmingham, 1997–99; Dep. Hd, NHS Clinical Governance Team, 1999–2001; Exec. Chief Nurse, Univ. Hosp. Birmingham NHS Trust, 2001–06. Nat. Clinical Advr, Health Care Commn, 2005–07. Mem., NHS Reconfiguration Panel, 2004–05. Special Prof., Univ. of Nottingham, 2007–13; Adjunct Prof. of Nursing, Univ. of Tasmania, 2009–13. Hon. DSc De Montfort, 2008. *Publications:* Stoma Care Nursing, 1986, rev. edn 2003; contribs to various nursing, medical and professional jls. *Recreations:* embroidery, quilting, sewing, craft work. *Address:* Basford Hill Farm, Ashby Road, Ticknall, Derbyshire DE73 7JJ. *T:* (01332) 862816.

ELDEN, Prof. Stuart Robert, PhD; FBA 2013; Professor of Political Theory and Geography, University of Warwick, since 2013; *b* Ipswich, 8 Dec. 1971; *s* of Colin Richard Elden and Rosemary Jill Elden; *m* 2002, Susan Renee Rizor. *Educ:* Brunel Univ. (BSc Hons 1994; PhD 1999); Durham Univ. (DLitt 2013). Lectr in Politics, Univ. of Warwick, 1999–2002; Prof. of Political Geog., Durham Univ., 2002–13. Ed., Envmt and Planning D: Society and Space, 2006–. Globe Book Award, 2010, Meridian Book Award, 2014, Assoc. American Geographers; Murchison Award, RGS, 2011. *Publications:* Mapping the Present: Heidegger, Foucault and the project of a spatial history, 2001; Understanding Henri Lefebvre: theory and the possible, 2004; Speaking Against Number: Heidegger, language and the politics of calculation, 2006; Terror and Territory: the spatial extent of sovereignty, 2009; The Birth of Territory, 2013. *Recreations:* cycling, watching cricket, music. *Address:* Department of Politics and International Studies, University of Warwick, Coventry CV4 7AL. *E:* stuart.elden@warwick.ac.uk.

ELDER, Baron *cr* 1999 (Life Peer), of Kirkcaldy in Fife; **Thomas Murray Elder;** Chancellor, Al-Maktoum College of Further Education (formerly Institute for Arabic and Islamic Studies), Dundee, since 2003; *b* 9 May 1950. *Educ:* Kirkcaldy High Sch.; Edinburgh Univ. (MA). Bank of England, 1972–80; Res. Asst to Shadow Trade and Industry Sec., 1980–84; Gen. Sec., Scottish Labour Party, 1988–92; Chief of Staff to Leader of Labour Party, 1992–94; Political Advr to Leader of Labour Party, 1994; Special Advr, Scottish Office, 1997–99. Contested (Lab) Ross, Cromarty & Skye, 1983. Chm. Trustees, Smith Inst. *Address:* House of Lords, SW1A 0PW.

ELDER, Dorothy-Grace; freelance journalist and commentator; political columnist, Scottish Daily Express, 2002–13; *m* George Welsh; one *s* two *d*. Journalist; former campaigning columnist, Scotland on Sunday. MSP, Glasgow, 1999–2003 (SNP 1999–2002, Ind. 2002–03). Hon. Prof., Robert Gordon Univ., Aberdeen, 2006–, lectrg (pt-time) on investigative journalism. Oliver Brown Award, Scots Independent, 1995; UK Reporter of the Year, UK Press Awards, 1996; London Award for campaigning for chronic pain patients, British Medical Journalists' Assoc., 2014. *E:* dg.elder@ntlworld.com.

ELDER, Sir Mark (Philip), Kt 2008; CBE 1989; conductor; Music Director, Hallé Orchestra, since 2000; *b* 2 June 1947; *s* of late John and Helen Elder; *m* 1980, Amanda Jane Stein; one *d*. *Educ:* Bryanston Sch.; Corpus Christi Coll., Cambridge (Music Scholar, Choral Scholar; BA, MA). Music staff, Wexford Festival, 1969–70; Chorus Master and Asst Conductor, Glyndebourne, 1970–71; music staff, Covent Garden, 1970–72; Staff Conductor, Australian Opera, 1972–74; Staff Conductor, ENO, 1974, Associate Conductor, 1977, Music Dir, 1979–93; Music Dir, Rochester Philharmonic Orch., USA, 1989–94. Principal Guest Conductor: London Mozart Players, 1980–83; BBC Symphony Orchestra, 1982–85; CBSO, 1992–95. *Address:* c/o Ingpen and Williams Ltd, 7 St George's Court, 131 Putney Bridge Road, SW15 2PA.

ELDER, Prof. Murdoch George, MD, DSc; FRCS, FRCOG; Professor of Obstetrics and Gynaecology, University of London, at Institute of Obstetrics and Gynaecology, Royal Postgraduate Medical School, 1978–98, now Professor Emeritus, and Hon. Fellow, since 2001, Imperial College School of Medicine; Chairman, Division of Paediatrics, Obstetrics and Gynaecology, Imperial College School of Medicine, 1996–98; *b* 4 Jan. 1938; *s* of late Archibald James and Lotta Annie Elder; *m* 1964, Margaret Adelaide McVicker; two *s*. *Educ:* Edinburgh Acad.; Edinburgh Univ. (MB ChB 1961, MD 1973). DSc London, 1994. FRCS 1968; FRCOG 1978. Junior posts, Edinburgh and Bristol, 1961–68; Lectr, Inst. of Obst. and Gyn. and Royal Univ. of Malta, 1968–71; Sen. Lectr and Reader, Charing Cross Hosp. Med. Sch., Univ. of London, 1971–78; Dean, Institute of Obstetrics and Gynaecology, RPMS, 1985–95. Green Armytage Scholarship, RCOG, 1976; WHO Travelling Scholarship, 1977; Dir, Clinical Res. Centre, WHO, 1980–94; Member: Steering Cttee on Contraception, WHO, 1980–86; WHO Scientific Ethics Res. Cttee, 1996–2005. Mem., Hammersmith and Queen Charlotte's Special Health Authy, 1982–90. Mem. Council, RPMS, 1979–97. Visiting Professor: UCLA, 1984, 1986 and 1997; Singapore Univ., 1987; Natal Univ., 1988. Ext Examr for DSc, PhD, Masters and MB, BS degrees of 19 univs in several countries. Silver Medal, Hellenic Obstetrical Soc., 1983; Bronze Medal, Helsinki Univ., 1996. Mem., Editl Bds, Jl of Obst. and Gyn. and Clinical Reproduction, 1985–98. *Publications:* Human Fertility Control, 1979; (ed) Preterm Labour, 1980; (ed) Reproduction, Obstetrics and Gynaecology, 1988; Preterm Labour, 1997; Obstetrics and Gynaecology, 2001; chapters in books and learned articles on biochemistry in reproduction and pre term labour, clinical obstetrics, gynaecology and contraception. *Recreations:* travel, golf, curling. *Address:* Burnholm, Broughton, Biggar ML12 6HQ. *T:* (01899) 830359. *Club:* 1942.

ELDER, Air Vice-Marshal Ronald David, CBE 1991; Managing Director, RED Partners LLP, since 2007; *b* 27 May 1946; *m* Sue; one *s* one *d*. *Educ:* RAF Coll., Cranwell. Commissioned RAF pilot, 1968; jun. appts and RAF Staff Coll., to 1981; Central Tactics and Trials Orgn, 1981–86; Comdr No 20 Sqdn, Laarbruch, 1986–88; Stn Comdr, Tri-National Tornado Trng Estabt, RAF Cottesmore, 1988–90; RAF Comdr, Tabuk, Saudi Arabia, 1990–91; RCDS 1991; Policy Area, Central Staff, MoD, 1991–93; Dir of Airspace Policy, CAA, 1993–98; RAF retd, 1999. Civil Aviation Authority: Hd, Gen. Aviation, 1999–2000; Hd, Personnel Licensing, 2000–03; Hd, Licensing Standards Div., 2003–07. FRAeS 1997. *Recreations:* Real tennis, golf. *Club:* Royal Air Force.

ELDERFIELD, Prof. Henry, PhD, ScD; FRS 2001; Director of Research, Department of Earth Sciences, University of Cambridge, since 2011; Fellow, St Catharine's College, Cambridge, 1984–2010, now Emeritus; *b* 25 April 1943; *s* of late Henry Elderfield and Rhoda May Elderfield (*née* Risbrough); *m* 1st, 1965, Brenda Pauline Holliday (marr. diss.); two *d*; 2nd, 1992, Marlene Wrankle. *Educ:* Sir William Turner's Sch., Coatham; Eston Grammar Sch.; Liverpool Univ. (BSc; PhD 1970); MA, ScD 1989, Cantab. Res. Fellow, Imperial Coll., London, 1968–69; Lectr, Univ. of Leeds, 1969–82; Asst Dir in Res., 1982–89, Reader, 1989–99, Prof. of Ocean Geochem. and Palaeochem., 1999–2010, Univ. of Cambridge. Visiting Professor: Univ. of RI, 1977–78; MIT, 1988–89 (Fulbright Schol., 1988); Lady Davis Vis. Prof., Hebrew Univ., Jerusalem, 1992; Vis. Schol., Woods Hole Oceanographic Instn, 1982; Vis. Scientist, Columbia Univ., 2004. Fellow: Geochem. Soc., 2000; Eur. Assoc. for Geochem., 2000; Amer. Geophysical Union, 2001; Hon. Fellow, Eur. Union of Geoscis, 2001. Prestwich Medal, 1993, Lyall Medal, 2003, Geol Soc.; Plymouth Medal, 1998; Patterson Medal, 2002, V. M. Goldschmidt Award, 2013, Geochem. Soc.; Urey Medal, Eur. Assoc. for Geochem., 2007. *Publications:* numerous contribs to scientific jls. *Recreations:* walking, running, cinema. *Address:* Department of Earth Sciences, University of Cambridge, Downing Street, Cambridge CB2 3EQ. *T:* (01223) 333400; St Catharine's College, Cambridge CB2 1RL. *T:* (01223) 338300.

See also J. Elderfield.

ELDERFIELD, John, PhD; Chief Curator of Painting and Sculpture, Museum of Modern Art, New York, 2003–08, now Emeritus; Senior Advisor, Art.sy, since 2012; Consultant, Gagosian Gallery, since 2012; Allen R. Adler, Class of 1967, Distinguished Curator and Lecturer, Princeton University Art Museum, since 2015; *b* 25 April 1943; *s* of late Henry Elderfield and Rhoda May Elderfield (*née* Risbrough); *m* 1st, 1965, Joyce Davey (marr. diss.); two *s*; 2nd, 1989, Jill Elizabeth Moser (marr. diss.); 3rd, 2005, Jeanne Collins. *Educ:* Univ. of Manchester; Univ. of Leeds (BA 1966; MPhil 1970); Univ. of London (PhD 1975). Lectr in Hist. of Art, Winchester Sch. of Art, 1966–70; Harkness Fellow, Yale Univ., 1970–72; John Simon Guggenheim Meml Fellow, 1972–73; Lectr in Hist. of Art, Univ. of Leeds, 1973–75; Museum of Modern Art, New York: Curator of Painting and Sculpture, 1975–93; Dir, Dept of Drawings, 1980–93; Chief Curator at Large, 1993–2003; Dep. Dir for Curatorial Affairs, 1996–99. Adjunct Prof. of Fine Arts, Inst. of Fine Arts, NY Univ., 1994. Vis. Scholar, Getty Res. Inst., Calif, 2001; Vis. Fellow, Amer. Acad. at Rome, 2006. Editor, Studies in Modern Art, 1991–2008. Member, Board of Directors: Dedalus Foundn, NY, 1996–; Master Drawings Assoc., 2000–09; Members Bd, Phillips Collection, Washington, 2000–; Member: Adv. Bd, Kate Weare Dance Co., 2010–; Art Adv. Council, Internat. Foundn for Art Res., 2012–. Member: Assoc. of Literary Scholars, Critics, and Writers, 2011–; Internat. Assoc. of Art Critics, 2012–. Hon. Mem., Proyecto Armando Reverón, Caracas, 2007–. Hon. DLit Leeds, 2006. Officier des Arts et Lettres (France), 2006 (Chevalier, 1989). *Publications:* Hugo Ball: the flight out of time, 1974, 2nd edn 1996; The Wild Beasts: Fauvism and its affinities, 1976; European Master Paintings from Swiss Collections: Post Impressionism to World War II, 1976; The Cut-outs of Henri Matisse, 1978; Matisse in the Collection of the Museum of Modern Art, 1978; The Modern Drawing, 1983; The Drawings of Henri Matisse, 1984; Kurt Schwitters, 1985; Morris Louis, 1986; The Drawings of Richard Diebenkorn, 1988; Helen Frankenthaler, 1988; (jtly) Matisse in Morocco, 1990; Henri Matisse: a retrospective, 1992; Pleasuring Painting: Matisse's feminine representations, 1995; (jtly) Howard Hodgkin: paintings, 1995; The Language of the Body: drawings by Pierre-Paul Prud'hon, 1996; (jtly) The Art of Richard Diebenkorn, 1997; (jtly) Bonnard, 1998; (jtly) Modern Starts, 1999; (jtly) Bridget Riley: reconnaissance, 2001; (jtly) Matisse-Picasso, 2002; Modern Painting and Sculpture: 1880 to the present, 2004; (jtly) Against the Grain, 2006; Manet's "The Execution of the Emperor Maximilian", 2006; Armando Reverón, 2007; Martin Puryear, 2007; (jtly) Matisse: radical invention, 1913–17, 2010; (jtly) Bob Dylan: the Brazil series, 2010; (jtly) Bob Dylan: the Asia series, 2011; De Kooning: a retrospective, 2011; Painted on 21st Street: Helen Frankenthaler from 1950 to 1959, 2013; (jtly) Willem de Kooning: ten paintings 1983–85, 2013; (jtly) Bob Dylan: face value, 2013; In the Studio: paintings, 2015. *Address:* 175 East 62 Street, #16A, New York, NY 10065, USA. *T:* (917) 2074041. *Club:* Century (New York).

See also H. Elderfield.

ELDERFIELD, Maurice; Chairman and Chief Executive, Berfield Associates Ltd, 1980–92; Chairman: Midland Industrial Leasing Ltd, 1979–90; Saga Ltd, 1979–90; Sheldon & Partners Ltd, 1981–91; *b* 10 April 1926; *s* of Henry Elderfield and Kathleen Maud Elderfield; *m* 1953, Audrey June (*née* Knight); one *s* three *d*. *Educ:* Southgate Grammar Sch. FCA. Fleet Air Arm, 1944–47. Thomson, Kingdom & Co., Chartered Accountants (qual. 1949), 1947–49; Personal Asst to Man. Dir, Forrestell, Land, Timber & Railway Co., 1949–57; Group Chief Accountant, Stephens Group, 1957–60; various posts, Segas, culminating in Board Mem. and Dir for Finance, 1960–73; Dir of Finance, Southern Water Authority, 1973–75; PO Board Mem. for Finance and Corporate Planning, 1975–76; Dir of Finance, Ferranti Ltd, 1977; Finance Mem., British Shipbuilders, 1977–80. Director: S. P. International Ltd, Hong Kong, 1987–90; PV Ltd, 1987–90. Chairman: Throgmorton Trust, 1972–84; Throgmorton Investment Management, 1981–84; Capital for Industry Ltd, 1980–84.

ELDON, 5th Earl of, *cr* 1821; **John Joseph Nicholas Scott;** Baron Eldon 1799; Viscount Encombe 1821; *b* 24 April 1937; *s* of 4th Earl of Eldon, GCVO, and Hon. Magdalen Fraser, OBE (*d* 1969), *d* of 16th Baron Lovat; *S* father, 1976; *m* 1961, Comtesse Claudine de Montjoye-Vaufrey et de la Roche, Vienna; one *s* two *d*. *Educ:* Ampleforth; Trinity Coll., Oxford. 2nd Lieut Scots Guards (National Service). Lieut AER. *Heir:* *s* Viscount Encombe, *qv*.

ELDON, David Gordon, GBS 2004; CBE 2005; JP; Senior Adviser, PricewaterhouseCoopers, 2005–14; Chairman: Hongkong and Shanghai Banking Corporation Ltd, 1999–2005; HSBC Bank Middle East Ltd, since 2011; Director, HSBC Holdings plc, 1999–2005; *b* Inverness, 14 Oct. 1945; *s* of late Leslie Gordon Eldon and Mary Forbes Eldon (*née* Smith); *m* 1975, Maria Margarita Gaus; two *s* one *d*. *Educ:* Duke of York's Royal Mil. Sch. Union Internat. Co., 1963–64; Commercial Banking Co. of Sydney, 1964–67; with British Bank of the Middle East, later HSBC Group, 1968–2005: Dist

Manager, Mongkok, 1982–84; Dep. Man. Dir, Saudi British Bank, 1984–87; CEO, Malaysia, 1988–92; Exec. Dir, Internat., 1993–95; CEO, Hongkong and Shanghai Banking Corp., 1996–98. Chm., Hang Seng Bank Ltd, 1996–2005; Director: Swire Pacific Ltd, 1996–2005; MTR Corp. Ltd, 1999–2008; Eagle Asset Management Ltd, 2006–11; China Central Properties Ltd, 2007–09; Shui On Construction and Materials, 2010–12; Cassis International Pte Ltd, 2010–12; Dubai Internat. Financial Centre Higher Bd, 2011–; New Lily Internat., 2013–; KC Maritime Ltd, 2014–; Lead Ind. Dir, Noble Gp, 2010– (Chm., 2007–09). Non-executive Chairman: Hong Kong Gen. Chamber of Commerce, 2005–07; Dubai Internat. Financial Centre Authy, 2006–11; HSBC Bank Oman SAOG, 2013–; Founding Mem., Seoul Internat. Business Adv. Council, 2001–07 (Chm., 2002–05); Special Advr, Korea Nat. Competitiveness Council, Office of the President, 2008–12. Member: Council, Hong Kong Trade Develt Council, 1996–2007; Internat. Council, Bretton Woods Cttee, 2006–10; Adv. Bd, Unisys, 2006–10; Capital Adequacy Review Tribunal, 2007–12; Adv. Bd, Chartis Asia Pacific, 2011–13; Chairman, Advisory Board: Asiya Investments, 2010–; HSBC Global Commercial Bank Risk Cttee, 2012–; Alexander Proudfoot, 2014–; Advr, Southern Capital Gp, 2007–. Vice Patron, Community Chest. JP Hong Kong, 2000. FCIB 1986; FCIB (Hong Kong) 1995. Hon. DBA Hong Kong City Univ., 2003; Hon. Dr Hong Kong Acad. of Performing Arts, 2011. Businessman of the Year, DHL and S China Morning Post, 2003. *Recreations:* sports, music, reading, travel. *Address:* 18th Floor, Mass Mutual Tower, 38 Gloucester Road, Hong Kong. *Clubs:* Hong Kong, Hong Kong Jockey (Steward, 1996–2008; Dep. Chm., 2006–08; Hon. Steward, 2008–), China.

ELDON, Sir Stewart (Graham), KCMG 2009 (CMG 1999); OBE 1991; HM Diplomatic Service, retired; Senior Adviser on defence and security issues, Transparency International, since 2010; *b* 18 Sept. 1953; *s* of late John Hodgson Eldon and of Rose Helen (*née* Stinton); *m* 1978, Christine Mary Mason; one *s* one *d*. *Educ:* Pocklington Sch.; Christ's Coll., Cambridge (BA Electrical Scis 1974; MSc 1976; MA 1977). MIET (MIEE 2002). Joined HM Diplomatic Service, 1976: UK Mission to UN, NY, 1976; FCO, 1977; Third, later Second Sec., Bonn, 1978–82; First Sec., FCO, 1982; Private Sec. to Minister of State, 1983–86; First Sec., UK Mission to UN, NY, 1986–90; Asst Hd, ME Dept, FCO (also Dep. Crisis Manager, Gulf War), 1990–91; Counsellor, Eur. Secretariat, Cabinet Office, 1991–93; Fellow, Center for Internat. Affairs, Harvard Univ., 1993–94; Counsellor (Political), UK Delegn to NATO, Brussels, 1994–97; Dir (Confs), FCO, 1997–98; Ambassador and Dep. Perm. Rep., UK Mission to UN, NY, 1998–2002; Ambassador to Ireland, 2003–06; UK Perm. Rep., UK Delegn to NATO, 2006–10; NATO Subject Matter Expert on Building Integrity, 2010–. Ind. Mem., Parole Bd for England and Wales, 2010–; Mem., Investigating Cttee, GDC, 2014–. Civil Advr, HCSC, UK Defence Acad., 2011–. Vis. Fellow, Yale Univ., 2002. Ambassador Partnership accredited mediator. *Publications:* contrib. RIIA paper, to RIIA jl and to Internat. Peace Acad. pubns. *Recreations:* music, travel, science fiction, breaking computers. *W:* www.stewarteldon.com. *Club:* Athenæum.

ELEY, Prof. Daniel Douglas, OBE 1961; ScD, PhD Cantab; MSc, PhD Manchester; FRS 1964; CChem, FRSC; Professor of Physical Chemistry, University of Nottingham, 1954–80, now Emeritus; Dean of Faculty of Pure Science, 1959–62; *b* 1 Oct. 1914; *s* of Daniel Eley and Fanny Allen Eley (*née* Ross); *m* 1942, Brenda May Williams, MA, MB, BChir (Cantab) (*d* 1992), 2nd *d* of Benjamin and Sarah Williams, Skewen, Glam; one *s*. *Educ:* Christ's Coll., Finchley; Manchester Univ.; St John's Coll., Cambridge; Manchester Univ. (Woodiwiss Schol. 1933, Mercer Schol. 1934, Darbishire Fellow 1936, DSIR Sen. Award 1937; PhD 1937); PhD 1940, ScD 1954, Cambridge. Bristol University: Lectr in Colloid Chemistry, 1945; Reader in Biophysical Chemistry, 1951. Leverhulme Emeritus Fellow, 1981. Lectures: Reilly, Univ. of Notre Dame (USA), 1950; Royal Aust. Chem. Inst., 1967; Sir Jesse Boot Foundn, Nottingham Univ., 1955, 1981; Sir Eric Rideal, Soc. of Chem. Industry, 1975. Mem. Council of Faraday Soc., 1951–54, 1960–63; Vice-Pres., 1963–66. Corresp. Mem., Bavarian Acad. of Sciences, 1971. Meetings Sec., British Biophysical Soc., 1961–63, Hon. Sec., 1963–65, Hon. Mem., 1983. Scientific Assessor to Sub-Cttee on Coastal Pollutions, House of Commons Select Cttee on Science and Technology, 1967–68. Medal of Liège Univ., 1950. *Publications:* (ed) Adhesion, 1961; papers in Trans Faraday Soc., Proc. Royal Soc., Jl Chem. Soc., Biochem. Jl, etc. *Recreations:* hill walking, gardening, reading. *Address:* Brooklands, 35 Brookland Drive, Chilwell, Nottingham NG9 4BD; Chemistry Department, Nottingham University, University Park, Nottingham NG7 2RD.

ELFER, His Honour David Francis; QC 1981; a Circuit Judge, 1996–2000; *b* 15 July 1941; *s* of George and Joy Elfer; *m* 1968, Karin Ursula Strub; two *s*; *m* 1988, Alexandra Smith-Hughes; one *s*. *Educ:* St Bede's Coll., Manchester; Emmanuel Coll., Cambridge (MA). Called to the Bar, Inner Temple, 1964, Bencher, 1989; a Recorder, 1978–96. Bar Col rep. for W Circuit, 1987–89. *Recreation:* music. *Address:* c/o Circuit Office, Rose Court, 2 Southwark Bridge, SE1 9HS.

ELGIN, 11th Earl of, *cr* 1633, **AND KINCARDINE,** 15th Earl of, *cr* 1647; **Andrew Douglas Alexander Thomas Bruce,** KT 1981; CD 1981; JP; Lord Bruce of Kinloss, 1604, Lord Bruce of Torry, 1647; Baron Elgin (UK), 1849; 37th Chief of the Name of Bruce; Lord-Lieutenant of Fife, 1987–99; late Scots Guards; Captain; Royal Company of Archers, HM Body Guard for Scotland; Hon. Colonel, 31 Combat Engrs (The Elgins), Canada; *b* 17 Feb. 1924; *e s* of 10th Earl of Elgin, KT, CMG, TD and Hon. Katherine Elizabeth Cochrane (DBE 1938) (*d* 1989), *er d* of 1st Baron Cochrane of Cults; *S* father, 1968; *m* 1959, Victoria Mary, *o d* of Dudley Usher, MBE and Mrs Usher of Larach Bhan, Kilchrennan, Argyll; three *s* two *d*. *Educ:* Eton; Balliol College, Oxford (BA Hons, MA Hons). Served War of 1939–45 (wounded). Dir, Royal Highland and Agricultural Soc., 1973–75; Pres., Scottish Amicable Life Assurance Soc., 1975–94. Chm., Nat. Savings Cttee for Scotland, 1972–78; Mem., Scottish Post Office Bd (formerly Scottish Postal Bd), 1980–96. Chm., Scottish Money Management Assoc., 1981–95. Lord High Comr, Gen. Assembly of Church of Scotland, 1980–81. Regent, RCSE, 1997–. County Cadet Commandant, Fife, 1952–65. Hon. Col, 153(H) Regt RCT(V), TAVR, 1976–86. JP 1951, DL 1955, Fife. Grand Master Mason of Scotland, 1961–65. Brigade Pres. of the Boys' Brigade, 1966–85; Pres., Royal Caledonian Curling Club, 1968–69. Hon. LLD: Dundee, 1977; Glasgow, 1983; Hon. DLitt St Mary's, Halifax, NS. Freeman: Bridgetown, Barbados; Regina; Port Elgin; Winnipeg; St Thomas, Ont; Moose Jaw. Order of Merit (Norway), 1994; Chevalier, Légion d'Honneur (France), 2014. *Heir: s* Lord Bruce, *qv*. *Address:* Broomhall, Dunfermline KY11 3DU. *T:* (01383) 872222, *Fax:* (01383) 872904. *Clubs:* Beefsteak, Caledonian, Pratt's; New (Edinburgh).

See also Hon. A. R. Bruce.

ELIAS, Gerard; QC 1984; a Recorder of the Crown Court, since 1984; a Deputy High Court Judge, since 1997; *b* 19 Nov. 1944; *s* of late Leonard Elias and Patricia Elias, JP; *m* 1970, Elisabeth Kenyon; three *s*. *Educ:* Cardiff High School; Exeter University (LLB). Barrister; called to the Bar, Inner Temple, 1968, Bencher, 1993; Wales and Chester Circuit (Circuit Treasurer, 1990–92; Leader, 1993–95); Asst Comr, Boundary Commission for Wales, 1981–83, 1985–; Chancellor, dio. of Swansea and Brecon, 1999–. Mem., Bar Council, 1985–89, 1993–95; Dir, Bar Mutual Insurance Fund, 1987–97. Governor and Mem. Council, Malvern Coll., 1988–96. Mem. Governing Body, Ch in Wales, 2000–05. Chairman: Disciplinary Commn, ECB (formerly TCCB), 1996–; Glam CCC, 1998–2003 (Mem. Exec. Cttee, 1986–93; Dep. Chm., 1993–98); Sport Resolutions UK, 2007–. Pres., Disciplinary Tribunal, Church in Wales, 2007–. *Recreations:* music, cricket. *Address:* 13 The Cathedral Green, Llandaff, Cardiff, South Glamorgan CF5 2EB. *T:* (029) 2057 8857. *Club:* Cardiff and County.

See also Rt Hon. Sir P. Elias.

ELIAS, Rt Hon. Sir Patrick, Kt 1999; PC 2009; **Rt Hon. Lord Justice Elias;** a Lord Justice of Appeal, since 2009; *b* 28 March 1947; *s* of late Leonard and Patricia Mary Elias; *m* 1970, Wendy Kinnersley-Haddock; three *s* one *d*. *Educ:* Cardiff High Sch.; Univ. of Exeter (LLB 1969); King's Coll., Cambridge (MA; PhD 1973). Called to the Bar, Inner Temple, 1973, Bencher, 1995; QC 1990; a Judge of the High Court, QBD, 1999–2009; Pres., Employment Appeal Tribunal, 2006–08. Fellow of Pembroke Coll., Cambridge, 1973–84, Hon. Fellow, 2010; Lectr, Univ. of Cambridge, 1975–84. Hon. LLD: Exeter, 2001; City, 2003. *Publications:* (ed) Harvey on Industrial Relations and Employment Law, 1976; (jtly) Labour Law: cases and materials, 1979; (with Keith Ewing) Trade Union Democracy, Members' Rights and the Law, 1987. *Recreations:* reading, music, painting, cricket, Rugby. *Address:* Royal Courts of Justice, Strand, WC2A 2LL.

See also G. Elias.

ELIAS, Rt Hon. Dame Sian, GNZM 1999; PC 1999; Chief Justice of New Zealand, since 1999; *b* 12 March 1949; *m* 1970, Hugh Alasdair Fletcher, *qv*; two *s*. *Educ:* Diocesan High Sch. for Girls; Auckland Univ. (LLB Hons 1972); Stanford Univ., Calif (JSM 1972). Admitted to Bar of NZ, 1970; Tutor, Law Sch., Univ. of Auckland, 1970; solicitor, 1972–75; Barrister, 1975–95; QC 1988; Judge of the High Court of NZ, 1995. Mem., NZ Law Commn, 1985–89. Commemoration Medal (NZ), 1990. *Recreations:* chess, piano. *Address:* Chief Justice's Chambers, High Court, DX SX 10084, Wellington, New Zealand. *T:* (4) 9188399. *Clubs:* Northern (Auckland); Wellington (Wellington).

ELIASSEN, Kjell, Hon. GCMG 1981; Commander with Star, Royal Order of Saint Olav, 1982; Norwegian Ambassador to Germany, 1994–98; *b* 18 Aug. 1929; *s* of Carl August Eliassen and Bergljot (*née* Store); *m* 1953, Vesla Skretting; one *s* one *d*. *Educ:* Oslo Univ. (law degree). Entered Norwegian Foreign Service 1953; served Belgrade, Moscow, London; Counsellor, Min. of Foreign Affairs, 1963–67; Moscow, 1967–70; Dep. Dir-Gen., Min. of Foreign Affairs, 1970–72; Dir-Gen., 1972–77; Ambassador to Yugoslavia, 1977–80; Perm. Under-Sec., Min. of Foreign Affairs, 1980–84; Ambassador: to USA, 1984–89; to UK, 1989–94. Numerous foreign decorations. *Address:* Generallunden 21, 0381 Oslo, Norway.

ELIASSON, Jan; President, UN General Assembly, 2005–06; Deputy Secretary-General, United Nations, since 2012; *b* Göteborg, 1940; *m* 1967, Kerstin Englesson; one *s* two *d*. *Educ:* Swedish Naval Acad.; Sch. of Econs, Göteborg (MEcons 1965). Harare, 1980; Diplomatic Advr to Swedish Prime Minister, 1982–83; Dir Gen. for Pol Affairs, Min. for For. Affairs, 1983–87; Swedish Ambassador to the UN, NY, 1988–92; UN Under-Sec.-Gen. for Humanitarian Affairs, 1992; State Sec. for For. Affairs, 1994–2000; Swedish Ambassador to the USA, 2000–05; Foreign Minister, Sweden, 2006. Chm., UN Trust Fund for S Africa, 1988–92; Chm., working gp on emergency relief, UN Gen. Assembly, 1991; Vice Pres., ECOSOC, 1991–92; Special Envoy of UN Sec.-Gen. for Darfur, 2007–08. Visiting Professor: Uppsala Univ., 2006–; Göteborgs Univ., 2007–. Chairman: Anna Lindh Meml Fund, 2007–11; WaterAid Sweden, 2009–12. Hon. Dr: American Univ., Washington, 1994; Göteborgs, 2001; Bethany Coll., Kansas, 2005; Uppsala, 2006. *Address:* Stockbyvägen 15, SE 18278 Stocksund, Sweden.

ELIBANK, 14th Lord *cr* 1643 (Scotland); **Alan D'Ardis Erskine-Murray;** Bt (Nova Scotia) 1628; personnel consultant; Deminex UK Oil and Gas, 1981–86; *b* 31 Dec. 1923; *s* of Robert Alan Erskine-Murray (*d* 1939) and Eileen Mary (*d* 1970), *d* of late John Percy MacManus; *S* cousin, 1973; *m* 1962, Valerie Sylvia (*d* 1997), *d* of late Herbert William Dennis; two *s*. *Educ:* Bedford Sch.; Peterhouse, Cambridge (MA Law). Barrister-at-Law. RE, 1942–47; Cambridge Univ., 1947–49; Practising Barrister, 1949–55; Shell International Petroleum Co., 1955–80. *Heir: s* Master of Elibank, *qv*. *Clubs:* Sloane, MCC.

ELIBANK, Master of; Hon. Robert Francis Alan Erskine-Murray; *b* 10 Oct. 1964; *s* and *heir* of 14th Lord Elibank, *qv*; *m* 1996, Antonia, *yr d* of Roger Carrington; two *d*. *Educ:* The Grove, Harrow School; Reading Univ. (BA (Hons) History and Politics, 1987). *Recreations:* golf, tennis.

ELINGER, John; *see* Ball, Sir C. J. E.

ELIOT, family name of **Earl of St Germans**.

ELIOT, Lord; Albert Charger Eliot; *b* 2 Nov. 2004; *s* of Jago Nicholas Aldo Eliot, (Lord Eliot) (*d* 2006) and of Bianca Eliot (*née* Ciambriello); *g s* and *heir* of Earl of St Germans, *qv*.

ELIOT, Simon Flowerdew, MA; Headmaster, Sherborne School, 2000–10; *b* 20 July 1952; *s* of late Geoffrey Philip Eliot and Margery Hope Eliot-Sutton; *m* 1983, Olivia Margaret Cicely Roberts; one *s* one *d*. *Educ:* Radley Coll.; Queens' Coll., Cambridge (MA). Sedgwick Forbes (Marine), 1974–75; Asst Master, Radley Coll., 1975–76; Winchester College: Asst Master, 1976–2000; Housemaster, 1988–2000. *Recreations:* history, theatre, music, horse racing. *Address:* 28 Daniel Street, Bath BA2 6ND. *T:* (01225) 462156.

ELIOTT of Stobs, Sir Charles (Joseph Alexander), 12th Bt *cr* 1666 (NS); *b* 9 Jan. 1937; *s* of Charles Rawdon Heathfield Eliott (*d* 1972) and Emma Elizabeth Harris (*d* 1999); *S* cousin, 1989; *m* 1959 (marr. diss. 1996); one *s* four *d* (and one *s* decd). *Educ:* St Joseph's Christian Brothers' College, Rockhampton. *Heir: s* Rodney Gilbert Charles Eliott [*b* 15 July 1966; *m* 1988 (marr. diss. 1998); one *s* two *d*]. *Address:* PO Box 402, Longreach, Qld 4730, Australia.

ELIS-THOMAS, family name of **Baron Elis-Thomas**.

ELIS-THOMAS, Baron *cr* 1992 (Life Peer), of Nant Conwy in the County of Gwynedd; **Dafydd Elis Elis-Thomas,** PC 2004; Member (Plaid Cymru) Dwyfor Meirionnydd, National Assembly for Wales, since 2007 (Meirionnydd Nant Conwy, 1999–2007); *b* 18 Oct. 1946; name changed from Thomas to Elis-Thomas by deed poll, 1992; *m* 1st, 1970, Elen M. Williams (marr. diss.); three *s*; 2nd, 1993, Mair Parry Jones. *Educ:* Ysgol Dyffryn Conwy; UC North Wales. Research worker, Bd of Celtic Studies, 1970; Tutor in Welsh Studies, Coleg Harlech, 1971; Lectr, Dept of English, UC North Wales, 1974. MP (Plaid Cymru) Merioneth, Feb. 1974–1983, Merionnydd Nant Conwy, 1983–92. National Assembly for Wales: Presiding Officer, 1999–2011; Chair, Envmt and Sustainability Cttee, 2011–14. Pres., Plaid Cymru, 1984–91. Mem., Arts Council for Wales; Chairman: Welsh Lang. Bd, 1993–99; Screen Wales; a Gov., BFI, 1997–2000. Part-time freelance broadcaster, BBC Wales, HTV, 1970–73; has also broadcast on S4C and Radio Wales. Chancellor (formerly Pres.), Bangor Univ. (formerly Univ. of Wales, Bangor), 2001–. Mem., Church in Wales. *Recreations:* hill walking, running, arts, Welsh literature. *Address:* 7 Bank Place, Porthmadog, Gwynedd LL49 9AA. *T:* (01766) 515028.

ELKAN, Prof. Walter; Professor of Economics, and Head of Economics Department, Brunel University, 1978–88, now Emeritus Professor; *b* Hamburg, 1 March 1923; *s* of Hans Septimus Elkan and Maud Emily (*née* Barden); *m* Susan Dorothea (*née* Jacobs) (marr. diss. 1982); one *s* two *d*. *Educ:* Frensham Heights; London Sch. of Economics (BScEcon, PhD). Army, 1942–47; Research Asst, LSE, 1950–53; Sen. Res. Fellow, E African Inst. of Social Research, 1954–58; Vis. Res. Assoc., MIT and Lectr, N Western Univ., 1958; Lectr in Econs, Makerere UC, 1958–60; Lectr in Econs, Durham Univ., 1960; Prof. of Econs, 1966–78, and rotating Head of Dept, 1968–78, Durham Univ. Vis. Res. Prof., Nairobi Univ., 1972–73. Member: Council, Overseas Develt Inst., 1978–2001; Econ. and Social Cttee, EEC, 1982–86; Bd of Management, Sch. of Hygiene and Trop. Med., 1982–86; Econ. and Social Cttee for Overseas Res., 1977–92; Associate, Inst. of Development Studies. Former Pres., African Studies Assoc.; former Member: Northern Economic Planning Council; REconS. Sometime consultant to Govts of Basutoland, Mauritius, Solomon Is, Fiji, Kenya and others. *Publications:* An African

Labour Force, 1956; Migrants and Proletarians, 1960; Economic Development of Uganda, 1961; Introduction to Development Economics, 1973, 2nd edn 1995; articles mainly on contemp. African econ. history in econ. and other social science jls; ILO, UNESCO, IBRD and British Govt reports. *Recreation:* music. *Address:* 98 Boundary Road, NW8 0RH. *T:* (020) 7624 5102.

ELKES, Prof. Joel, MD, ChB; FACP, FAPA; psychiatrist and pharmacologist; Distinguished Service Professor Emeritus, The Johns Hopkins University, since 1975; Distinguished University Professor Emeritus, University of Louisville; Founding Fellow, 1989 and Senior Scholar-in-Residence, since 1993, Fetzer Institute, Kalamazoo; *b* 12 Nov. 1913; *s* of Dr Elchanan Elkes and Miriam (*née* Malbin); *m* 1st, 1943, Dr Charmian Bourne (marr. diss.); one *d*; 2nd, 1975, Josephine Rhodes (*d* 1999), MA; 3rd, 2001, Sally Ruth Lucke. *Educ:* private schools; Lithuania and Switzerland; St Mary's Hosp., London; Univ. of Birmingham Med. Sch. (MB, ChB 1947; MD Hons 1949). University of Birmingham: Sir Halley Stewart Research Fellow, 1942–45; Lectr, Dept of Pharmacology, 1945–48; Senior Lectr and Actg Head of Dept, 1948–50; Prof. and Chm., Dept of Experimental Psychiatry, 1951–57 (first dept of its kind in the world); Clinical Professor of Psychiatry, George Washington Univ. Med. Sch., Washington, 1957–63; Chief of Clinical Neuropharmacology Research Center, Nat. Inst. of Mental Health, Washington, 1957–63; Dir, Behavioral and Clinical Studies Center St Elizabeth's Hosp., Washington, 1957–63; Henry Phipps Prof. and Dir, Dept of Psychiatry and Behavioural Scis, Johns Hopkins Univ. Sch. of Medicine, and Psychiatrist-in-Chief, Johns Hopkins Hosp., 1963–74; Samuel McLaughlin Prof.-in-residence, McMaster Univ., 1975; Professor of Psychiatry: McMaster Univ., 1976–80; Univ. of Louisville, 1980–84 (Director: Div. of Behavioral Medicine, 1982; Arts in Medicine Prog.). Dir, Foundns Fund for Research in Psychiatry, 1964–68; Consultant, WHO, 1957. Vis. Fellow, New York Univ. and New England Med. Center, Boston, 1950; Benjamin Franklin Fellow, RSA, 1974. Lectures: Harvey, 1962; Salmon, 1963; Jacob Bronowski Meml, 1978, etc. President: (first) Amer. Coll. of Neuropsychopharmacology, 1962; Amer. Psychopathological Assoc., 1968; Chairman: Bd, Israel Inst. of Psychobiol., 1961–2004; Foundns Fund Prize Bd for Res. in Psychiatry, 1977–81; Board Member: Inst. for Advancement of Health, 1982; Govs, Hebrew Univ. of Jerusalem; Govs, Haifa Univ. Formerly Member: Council, Collegium Internationale Neuro-psychopharmacologicum; Central Council, Internat. Brain Research Organisation, UNESCO (Chm., Sub-Cttee on Educn); RSM. Life Fellow, Amer. Psych. Assoc.; Charter Fellow, RCPsych, GB; Fellow: Amer. Acad. of Arts and Scis; Amer. Coll. of Psychiatry; Amer. Coll. of Neuropsychopharmacol. (Joel Elkes Internat. Award estab. 1986); Amer. Acad. of Behavioral Medicine Res. and Soc. of Behavioral Medicine; Fetzer Inst., 1990; Fellow and Mem. Exec. Cttee, World Acad. of Art and Sci., 1985; Former Member: Physiological Soc., GB; Pharmacological Soc., GB; Amer. Soc. for Pharmacology and Experimental Therapeutics; Sigma Xi; Scientific Assoc.; Acad. of Psychoanalysis. Hon. DPhil Hebrew Univ. of Jerusalem, 1989. Hans Selye Internat. Award, 1994; (jtly) First Internat. Pioneer Award in Psychopharmacology, Glasgow Congress, 1998; Lifetime-Achievement Award, Louisville Cathedral Heritage Foundn, 2000. Two internat. symposia in his honour, 1984, 1985; Joel Elkes Res. Labs, Dept of Psychiatry, Johns Hopkins Univ., dedicated 1989; Elkes Cottage, Fetzer Inst., dedicated 1998. One man show, In Praise of Trees, Selby Gardens, Sarasota, 2008. *Publications:* papers to various jls and symposia. *Recreation:* painting. *Address:* Fetzer Institute, 9292 WKL Avenue, Kalamazoo, MI 49009, USA. *Club:* Cosmos (Washington).

ELKIN, Sonia Irene Linda, OBE 1981 (MBE 1966); Director for Regions and Smaller Firms, Confederation of British Industry, 1985–92; *b* 15 May 1932; *d* of Godfrey Albert Elkin and Irene Jessamine Archibald. *Educ:* Beresford House Sch., Eastbourne. Association of British Chambers of Commerce, 1950–66; Lloyds Bank Overseas Dept, 1966–67; Confederation of British Industry, 1967–92. Commissioner, Manpower Services Commission, 1982–85. Non-executive Director: Greggs plc, 1992–2004; Kall Kwik Printing (UK), 1993–95. Chm. Trustees, Greggs Pension Fund, 1999–2009. *Publications:* What about Europe?, 1967; What about Europe Now?, 1971. *Club:* Oxford and Cambridge (Lady Associate).

ELKINGTON, Ven. Dr Audrey Anne; Archdeacon of Bodmin, since 2011; *b* 1 Nov. 1957; *d* of Henry and Alexandra King; *m* 1986, David Elkington. *Educ:* St Catherine's Coll., Oxford (BA 1980); UEA (PhD 1983); St John's, Nottingham; East Anglian Ministerial Trng Course; Durham Univ. (MA 1999). Ordained deaconess, 1988, deacon, 1992, priest, 1994; Parish Deacon, St Mary the Virgin, Ponteland, 1992–93; Asst Curate, St Mary Magdalene, Prudhoe, 1993–2002; Rural Dean, Corbridge, 1999–2002; Dir of Ordinands and Bishop's Domestic Chaplain, Dio. of Newcastle, 2002–11. Bishop's Advr for Women in Ministry, Dio. of Newcastle, 2001–11; Hon. Canon, Newcastle Cathedral, 2006–11. *Address:* 4 Park Drive, Bodmin PL31 2QF.

ELKINGTON, Benjamin Michael Gordon; QC 2012; *b* London, 2 Aug. 1971; *s* of Prof. Andrew Robert Elkington, CBE; *m* 1998, Annabel, *d* of Robin Francis Leigh Oakley, *qv*; one *s* three *d*. *Educ:* Winchester Coll.; Trinity Coll., Cambridge (Univ. Schol.; Jun. and Sen. Schol.; BA 1st Cl. Hons 1993; MA); Univ. of Virginia (LLM 1994); Inns of Ct Sch. of Law (Scarman Schol. 1996). Associate, Sullivan & Cromwell, NY, 1994–95; admitted to NY Bar, 1995; called to the Bar, Gray's Inn, 1996 (Gray's Inn Schol., 1995); in practice as barrister, specialising in commercial law, 1996–. *Publications:* (jtly) Professional Liability Precedents, 2000; (ed jtly) Jackson & Powell Professional Liability, 2011. *Recreations:* family, walking and fishing on the Isle of Mull, lighting fires in the rain. *Address:* 4 New Square, Lincoln's Inn, WC2A 3RJ. *T:* (020) 7822 2000, *Fax:* (020) 7822 2001. *E:* b.elkington@4newsquare.com.

ELKINGTON, John Brett; environmentalist, entrepreneur, consultant, author, speaker; Co-Founder and Director, SustainAbility Ltd, since 1987 (Chairman, 1996–2006; Chief Entrepreneur, 2006–08; Honorary Life Chairman, 2014); Founding Partner and Executive Chairman, Volans Ventures Ltd, since 2008; Acting Chair, Board of Trustees, Ecological Sequestration Trust, since 2011; *b* Padworth, Berks, 23 June 1949; *s* of John Francis Durham, (Tim), Elkington and Patricia Elkington; *m* 1973, Elaine Waite; two *d*. *Educ:* various schs in England, NI and Cyprus; Glencot Prep. Sch., Wookey Hole; Bryanston Sch.; Univ. of Essex (BA Hons 1970); University Coll. London (MPhil 1974). Associate and Sen. Planner, Transport and Envmt Studies, 1974–78; Environmental Data Services Ltd, 1978–83, Man. Dir, 1981–83, Editor, ENDS Report, 1978–83; Editor, Biotechnology Bulletin, 1983–98; Founder Dir, John Elkington Associates, 1983–. Chairman: Envmt Foundn, later Foundn for Democracy and Sustainable Develt, 1995–2012; Adv. Council, Export Credits Guarantee Dept, 2005–07; Member: EU Consultative Forum on the Envmt and Sustainable Develt, 1994–2001; Faculty, World Econ. Forum, 2002–08; WWF-UK Council of Ambassadors, 2006–. Visiting Professor: Doughty Centre for Corporate Responsibility, Sch. of Mgt, Cranfield Univ., 2007–; Imperial Coll. London, 2013–; UCL, 2013–. Chm. Bd, Envmt Faculty, Herning Inst. of Business Admin and Technol., Denmark, 1995–98. Mem. Bd, Global Reporting Initiative, Netherlands, 2009–13; Mem., Internat. Integrated Reporting Council (formerly Cttee), 2010–; Member, Advisory Board: Instituto Ethos, Brazil, 2007–; Zouk Ventures, 2008–; EcoVadis, France, 2008–; Nestlé Creating Shared Value, 2009–; Carbon War Room Gigaton awards, 2010–11; Friends Life Cttee of Ref. (formerly F&C Investment Cttee of Ref.), 2010–; Recyclebank, 2011–; Clean Revolution Campaign, Cleantech Gp; Member: Bd, Biomimicry 3.8 Inst., 2013–; SunRise Adv. Bd, Bayer MaterialScience, 2013–. Hon. Fellow, The Hub, 2008. Hon. Dr Essex, 2014. FRSA. *Publications:* The Ecology of Tomorrow's World, 1980; Sun Traps: the renewable energy forecast, 1984; The Gene Factory, 1985; The Poisoned Womb, 1985; (with T. Burke) The Green Capitalists, 1987; (with J. Hailes and T. Burke) Green Pages: the business of saving the world, 1988; A Year in the Greenhouse, 1990; (with J. Hailes and P. Knight) The Green Business Guide: how to take up – and profit from – the environmental challenge, 1991; Cannibals with Forks: the triple bottom line of 21st century business, 1997; The Chrysalis Economy: how citizen CEOs and corporations can fuse values and value creation, 2001; (with P. Hartigan) The Power of Unreasonable People: how social entrepreneurs create markets that change the world, 2008; The Zeronauts: breaking the sustainability barrier, 2012; (with J. Zeitz) The Breakthrough Challenge: 10 ways to connect today's profits with tomorrow's bottom line, 2014; with Julia Hailes: The Green Consumer Guide: from shampoo to champagne, 1988; The Green Consumer's Supermarket Shopping Guide, 1989; The Young Green Consumer's Guide, 1990; Holidays That Don't Cost the Earth, 1992; Manual 2000: life choices for the future you want, 1998; The New Foods Guide: what's here, what's coming, what it means for us, 1999; author or jt author of over 40 reports; columnist and/or blogger for various pubns incl. China Dialogue, Director Mag., Época Negócios, GreenBiz, Eco-Business, Nikkei Ecology, CSR Wire, FastCompany.com, Monday Morning and The Guardian. *Recreations:* playing with ideas, thinking around corners, conversations with unreasonable people, reading an Alpine range of books (history to science fiction) and US business and science magazines, risking life and limb as a London cyclist, catch-it-as-you-can photography, art and design, writing all hours, sleeping, pre-1944 aircraft, New World wines, 20th century popular music—and Johann Strauss II. *E:* johnelkington@mac.com, john@volans.com. *W:* www.johnelkington.com.

ELLAM, Michael James, CB 2014; Managing Director, Public Sector Banking Team, Financial Institutions Group, HSBC, since 2013; *b* London, 4 Oct. 1968; *s* of Brian and Kathleen Ellam; *m* 1995, Karina Saroukhanian; one *s* one *d*. *Educ:* Forest Hill Sch. for Boys; Peterhouse, Cambridge (BA 1990); London Sch. of Econs (MSc Econ 1991). Economist: Credit Suisse First Boston, 1992–93; HM Treasury, 1993–94; Pvte Sec. to Chancellor of the Exchequer, 1994–96; First Sec. (Econ.), Beijing, 1996–98; HM Treasury: Economist, EMU Policy Team, 1998–2000; Head: Debt and Reserves Mgt Team, 2000; Communications, 2000–03; Perf. and Efficiency Team, Public Services Directorate, 2004; Dir of Policy and Planning, 2004–07; Dir of Communications and Prime Minister's Spokesman, Prime Minister's Office, 2007–09; Man. Dir, Internat. and Europe, then Dir Gen., Internat. Finance, HM Treasury, 2009–13. *Recreations:* family, cinema, golf, watching football. *Address:* HSBC Holdings plc, 8 Canada Square, E14 5HQ. *Club:* West Ham United.

ELLAM, Prof. Robert Mark, PhD; FRSE; Professor of Isotope Geochemistry, University of Glasgow, since 2007, and Director, Scottish Universities Environmental Research Centre, since 2012 (Director of Research, 2007–12); *b* Shipley, W Yorks, 15 April 1962; *s* of late Derek Ellam and of Margaret Ellam (*née* Thomas); *m* 1985, Elspeth Rowena Wood; one *s* one *d*. *Educ:* Imperial Coll. London (BSc 1983); Open Univ. (PhD 1987). ARSM 1983. Post Doctoral Res. Asst, Univ. of Oxford, 1987–89; Lectr, 1990–2000, Reader, 2000–06, Univ. of Glasgow. FRSE 2010. *Publications:* more than 140 articles in learned jls. *Recreations:* 5-string banjo, listening to the radio, 1973 pinball restoration project. *Address:* Scottish Universities Environmental Research Centre, Rankine Avenue, East Kilbride G75 0QF. *T:* (01355) 270130, *Fax:* (01355) 229898. *E:* r.ellam@suerc.gla.ac.uk, rob.m.ellam@gmail.com.

ELLEN, Eric Frank, QPM 1980; LLB; Chairman and Director, First Approach Ltd, since 1999; Board Member, International Chamber of Commerce Commercial Crime Services, 1999–2001 (Executive Director, 1994–99; First Director: International Maritime Bureau, 1981–99; Counterfeiting Intelligence Bureau, 1985–99; Commercial Crime Bureau, 1992–99; Regional Piracy Centre, Kuala Lumpur, 1992–99); Consultant, ICC, 1999–2002; *b* London, 30 Aug. 1930; *s* of late Robert Frank Ellen and of Jane Lydia Ellen; *m* 1st, 1949, Gwendoline Dorothy Perkins (marr. diss. 2010); one *s* one *d*; 2nd, 2010, S. Lin Kuo-Ellen; one *d*. *Educ:* Wakefield Central Sch., East Ham; Holborn Coll. of Law, Univ. of London (LLB Hons, London Univ. Certificate in Criminology). CCMI (FBIM 1978). Joined PLA Police, 1951; Sgt 1956; Inspector 1961; Chief Insp. 1972; Supt and Chief Supt 1973; attended 11th Sen. Comd Course, Bramshill Police Coll., 1974; Dep. Chief Constable 1975; Chief Constable, 1975–80. Adviser on security to Ports Div. of Dept of Environment; advised Barbados Govt on formation of Barbados Port Authy Police Force, 1983; reviewed port security at Jeddah and Dammam. Sec., Internat. Assoc. of Airport and Seaport Police, 1980–88 (Pres., 1977–78 and 1978–79); Founder, Chm. and Life Mem., EEC Assoc. of Airport and Seaport Police, 1975–78; Chm., Panel on Maritime Fraud, Commonwealth Secretariat, 1982–90; Consultant, Commercial Crime Unit. Member: Internat. Assoc. of Ports and Harbours Standing Cttee on Legal Protection of Port Interests, 1977–79 (Chm., Sub-Cttee on Protection of Ports against Sabotage and Terrorism, 1977–79); Cttee of Conservative Lawyers, 1985–; Shipbrokers Cttee on Maritime Fraud; British Acad. of Forensic Sciences; Hon. Soc. of Middle Temple. Police Long Service and Good Conduct Medal, 1974. Freeman of the City of London, 1978. Police Medal Republic of China, 1979. *Publications:* (co-author) International Maritime Fraud, 1981; (ed) Violence at Sea, 2nd edn, 1987; (ed) Piracy at Sea, 1989; (ed) Ports at Risk, 1993; (ed) Shipping at Risk: the rising tide of organised crime, 1998; A Guide to the Prevention of Money Laundering, 1998; professional articles on marine fraud and counterfeiting, terrorism, piracy and port policing, money laundering and fraud in commerce (has lectured on these topics at seminars in over 50 countries). *Recreations:* golf, swimming, yoga. *Address:* 38 Tyle Green, Hornchurch, Essex RM11 2TB.

ELLEN, Prof. Roy Frank, PhD; FBA 2003; FLS; Professor of Anthropology and Human Ecology, 1988–2012, now Emeritus, and Director, Centre for Biocultural Diversity, 2007–12, University of Kent; *b* 30 Jan. 1947; *s* of Gerald Frank Ellen and Nancy Eileen (*née* Childs); *m* 1978, Nicola Jane Goward; two *d*. *Educ:* LSE (BSc; PhD); Univ. of Leiden. Lectr, LSE, 1972–73; Lectr, 1973–80, Sen. Lectr, 1980–86, Reader, 1986–88, Univ. of Kent, Canterbury. Visiting Fellow: ANU, 1981; Netherlands Inst. for Adv. Study, 1984; Vis. Prof., Univ. of Leiden, 1994. President: Anthropol. and Archaeol. Section, BAAS, 2004–05; RAI, 2007–11. Mem. Council, British Acad., 2010–13. Lectures: Curl, RAI, 1987; Munro, Univ. of Edinburgh, 1994; Stirling, Univ. of Kent, 2007; Layton, Univ. of Durham, 2013. FLS 2001. *Publications:* Nuaulu Settlement and Ecology, 1978; (ed with P. H. Burnham) Social and Ecological Systems, 1979; (ed with D. Reason) Classifications in Their Social Context, 1979; (ed) Environment, Subsistence and System, 1982, 2nd edn 2002; (ed) Ethnographic Research, 1984; (ed jtly) Malinowski Between Two Worlds, 1988; The Cultural Relations of Classification, 1993; Nuaulu Ethnozoology, 1993; (ed with C. W. Watson) Understanding Witchcraft and Sorcery in Southeast Asia, 1993; (ed with K Fukui) Redefining Nature, 1996, 2nd edn 2002; (ed jtly) Indigenous Environmental Knowledge and its Transformations, 2002; On the Edge of the Banda Zone, 2003; The Categorical Impulse, 2006; (ed) Ethnobiology and the Science of Humankind, 2006; (ed) Modern Crises and Traditional Strategies: local ecological knowledge in Island Southeast Asia, 2007; Nuaulu Religious Practices: the frequency and reproduction of rituals in a Moluccan society, 2012; (ed jtly) Understanding Cultural Transmission in Anthropology, 2013. *Address:* School of Anthropology and Conservation, University of Kent, Canterbury, Kent CT2 7NR. *T:* (01227) 720464, *Fax:* (01227) 827289. *E:* R.F.Ellen@kent.ac.uk.

ELLEN, Susan Caroline; Chairman, West Middlesex University Hospital NHS Trust, 2002–10; *b* 15 Dec. 1948; *d* of late Albert John Davies and of (Winnifred) Ivy (Caroline) (*née* Emberton); *m* 1974, Simon Tudor Ellen; two *d*. *Educ:* Cardiff High Sch.; Malvern Girls' Coll.; Bristol Univ. (BSc Politics and Sociol.); Dip HSM. With NHS, 1970–77; joined BUPA, 1977: Dir, 1990–95; Man. Dir, BUPA Health Services, 1990–95; Man. Dir, United Racecourses (Hldgs) Ltd, 1996–2002; Non-executive Director: Asda Gp plc, 1992–98; Birmingham Midshires Building Soc., 1996–2000; Portman Building Soc., 2001–07;

PruHealth (formerly Prudential Health), 2006–; Nationwide Bldg Soc., 2007–09. Member: Financial Reporting Rev. Panel, 1992–98; Financial Reporting Council, 1995–96. Trustee, St John Ambulance, 2006–. *Recreations:* family, racing, the arts.

ELLENA, Rt Rev. Richard; *see* Nelson (NZ), Bishop of.

ELLENBOGEN, Naomi Lisa, (Mrs M. S. Barklem); QC 2010; *b* Liverpool, 20 March 1970; *d* of late Dr Wilfred Ellenbogen and of Margaret Rose Ellenbogen (*née* Ognall, later Unger) and step *d* of late Dr Philip Carl Unger; *m* 2008, Martyn Stephen Barklem, *qv*; two step *s*. *Educ:* King David Primary Sch., Liverpool; King David High Sch., Liverpool; New Coll., Oxford (BA Juris. 1991; MA 1996). Called to the Bar, Gray's Inn, 1992, Bencher, 2014; in practice at the Bar, specialising in employment, commercial and professional negligence law, 1993–. Jt Hd, Littleton Chambers, 2014–. Mem., 2005–10, Vice Chm., 2011–, Professional Conduct Cttee, Bar Standards Bd (formerly Professional Complaints and Conduct Cttee, Bar Council, then Complaints Cttee, Bar Standards Bd). *Publications:* (Gen. Ed.) Butterworths Employment Law: Practice, Procedure and Precedents, 5th edn 2007. *Recreations:* sailing, travel, theatre, music, enjoying her husband's culinary delights. *Address:* Littleton Chambers, 3 King's Bench Walk North, Temple, EC4Y 7HR. *T:* (020) 7797 8600. *E:* nellenbogen@littletonchambers.co.uk. *Clubs:* Bar Yacht; Hong Kong Cricket.

ELLENBOROUGH, 9th Baron *cr* 1802; **Rupert Edward Henry Law;** Senior Investment Director, Investec Wealth & Investment, since 2012; *b* London, 28 March 1955; *s* of 8th Baron Ellenborough and Rachel Mary (*née* Hedley); *S* father, 2013; *m* 1981, Hon. Grania Janet Gray, *d* of Baron Boardman, MC, TD; two *s* one *d*. *Educ:* Eton Coll. Major, Coldstream Guards, retd. *Heir:* *s* Hon. James Rupert Thomas Law [*b* 8 March 1983; *m* Sophie]. *Address:* Bridge House, Kelmarsh Road, Clipston, Market Harborough LE16 9RX. *Club:* Cavalry and Guards.

ELLERAY, Anthony John; QC 1993; a Recorder, since 1999; *b* 19 Aug. 1954; *s* of late Alexander John Elleray and of Sheila Mary Elleray (*née* Perkins); *m* 1982, Alison Elizabeth Potter; one *s* one *d*. *Educ:* Bishop's Stortford Coll.; Trinity Coll., Cambridge (MA). Called to the Bar, Inner Temple, 1977. *Recreations:* pictures, garden, wine. *Address:* 201 Deansgate, West Riverside, Manchester M3 3NW. *T:* (0161) 833 2722. *Clubs:* Oxford and Cambridge; Manchester Tennis and Racquet.

ELLES, James Edmund Moncrieff; Member (C) South East Region, England, European Parliament, 1999–2014 (Oxford and Buckinghamshire, 1984–94; Buckinghamshire and Oxfordshire East, 1994–99); *b* 3 Sept. 1949; *s* of late N. P. M. Elles and Baroness Elles; *m* 1977, Françoise Le Bail (marr. diss. 1997); one *s* one *d*. *Educ:* Ashdown House; Eton College; Edinburgh University. External Relations Div., EEC, 1976–80; Asst to Dep. Dir Gen. of Agriculture, EEC, 1980–83. European Parliament: EPP spokesman on the Budget, 1994–99; Vice-Pres., EPP-ED Gp, 1999–2004 (Chm., Wkg Party C); Mem., Budget Cttee; Substitute Mem., US Delegn. Founder: Transatlantic Policy Network, 1992 (Chm., 1992–99, 2009–); Founder, European Ideas Network, 2002 (Chm., 2002–08). Co-founder, European Internet Foundn, 2002. Co-founder, EU Baroque Orch. *Clubs:* Carlton; Royal and Ancient Golf (St Andrews).

ELLETSON, Harold Daniel Hope, PhD; Director, New Security Foundation, since 2006; *b* 8 Dec. 1960; *m* 1987, Fiona Margaret Ferguson; two *s*. *Educ:* Eton Coll.; Exeter Univ.; Voronezh Univ., USSR; Poly. of Central London; Bradford Univ. (PhD). Mem. (C) Lancashire CC, 1984–88; worked in journalism and public affairs, 1984–88; CBI and Illingworth Morris plc, 1988–90; public affairs adviser and consultant to cos trading in Eastern Europe, 1990–. Contested (C) Burnley, 1987. MP (C) Blackpool North, 1992–97; contested (C) Blackpool North and Fleetwood, 1997. Joined Liberal Democrats, 2002; Mem., Lib Dem foreign affairs team, 2003 (Chm.). Dir, NATO Forum on Business and Security, 2004. Associate, Centre for Defence and Internat. Security Studies. *Publications:* The General Against the Kremlin—Alexander Lebed: power and illusion, 1998.

ELLICOTT, Russel; Headteacher, Pate's Grammar School, since 2012 (Deputy Headteacher, 2008–12); *b* Newmarket, Suffolk, 26 Oct. 1970; *s* of Bryan and Jennifer Ellicott; *m* 2001, Catherine Rees; one *s* one *d*. *Educ:* Castle Manor Upper Sch., Haverhill; Royal Holloway and Bedford New Coll., Univ. of London (BA Hons); Univ. of Hull (PGCE; MEd). Teacher of History, Crypt Sch., Glos, 1994–2004; Asst Head Teacher, Marling Sch., Stroud, 2004–08. *Recreations:* enjoying all sports, travelling and time with my family, a VW Campervan enables us to enjoy time together and explore new places. *Address:* Pate's Grammar School, Princess Elizabeth Way, Cheltenham, Glos GL51 0HG. *T:* (01242) 523169. *E:* head@patesgs.org.

ELLINGTON, Prof. Charles Porter, PhD; FRS 1998; Professor of Animal Mechanics, University of Cambridge, 1999–2010, now Emeritus; Fellow of Downing College, Cambridge, 1979–2010, now Emeritus; *b* 31 Dec. 1952; *s* of Dr Charles Porter Ellington and Margaret Moselle Ellington; *m* 1977, Dr Stephanie Katharine Lindsay Buckley; two *s*. *Educ:* Duke Univ. (BA 1973); Downing Coll., Cambridge (MA 1979; PhD 1982). Cambridge University: Demonstrator and Lectr in Zoology, 1979–97; Reader in Animal Mechanics, 1997–99. Editor, Jl of Experimental Biology, 1990–94. Scientific Medal, Zoological Soc., 1990. *Publications:* (ed with T. J. Pedley) Biological Fluid Dynamics, 1995; (ed with J. D. Altringham) Designs for Life: the science of biomechanics, 1999; (ed with D. Floreano, J.-C. Zufferey and M. V. Srinivasan) Flying Insects and Robots, 2009; papers on mechanics and physiology of insect flight. *Recreations:* cooking, gardening, wood- and metal-working. *Address:* Department of Zoology, University of Cambridge, Downing Street, Cambridge CB2 3EJ. *T:* (01223) 336668, 336600.

ELLINGTON, Marc Floyd, FSA; DL; communications and heritage consultant; *b* 16 Dec. 1945; *s* of late Homer Frank Ellington, Memsie, Aberdeenshire, and of Harriette Hannah Ellington (*née* Kellas); *m* 1967, Karen Leigh, *d* of Capt. Warren Sidney Streater; two *d*. Chm., Heritage Press (Scot.); Board Member: Soundcraft Audio Guides, 1979–; Aberdeen Univ. Res. Ltd, 1980–85; Gardenstown Estates Ltd, 1983–; Grampian Enterprises Ltd, 1992–96; Partner, Heritage Sound Recordings, 1981–. Composer and recording artiste; producer of documentary films and TV progs. Chm., Grampian Reg. Tourism Task Force, 1991–. Trustee, Nat. Galls of Scotland, 2002–10; non-exec. Dir, Historic Scotland, 2005–11; Member: Historic Bldg Council for Scotland, 1980–98; Cttee for Scotland, Heritage Lottery Fund, 1998–. Member: British Heritage Cttee, 1992–; HHA; PRS. FSA 1987; Hon. FRIAS. DL Aberdeenshire, 1984. Vice-Pres., Buchan Heritage Soc., 1986; Mem., Convention of Baronetage of Scotland. Patron, Banffshire Wildlife Rehabilitation Trust. Baron of Towie Barclay; Laird of Gardenstown and Crovie. OStJ 2004. Saltire Award, 1973; Eur. Architectural Heritage Award, 1975; Civic Trust Award, 1975, 1993. *Publications:* contribs to architectural and historic jls and periodicals. *Recreations:* sailing, historic architecture, art collecting, music. *Address:* Towie Barclay Castle, Auchterless, Turriff, Aberdeenshire AB53 8EP. *T:* (01888) 511347, *Fax:* (01888) 511522. *E:* soundcraft@towiebarclay.co.uk.

ELLIOT; *see* Elliot-Murray-Kynynmound, family name of Earl of Minto.

ELLIOT, Dr Alison Janet, OBE 2003; Associate Director, Centre for Theology and Public Issues, Edinburgh University, since 2001; Convener, Scottish Council for Voluntary Organisations, 2007–13; *b* 27 Nov. 1948; *d* of Kenneth and Janet Macrae; *m* 1979, John Christian Elliot; one *s* one *d*. *Educ:* Bathgate Acad.; Edinburgh Univ. (MA 1970; PhD 1976); Sussex Univ. (MSc 1971). FRSE 2008. Lecturer in Psychology: Lancaster Univ., 1974–76; Edinburgh Univ., 1977–85. Elder, 1984, and Session Clerk, 2000–07, Greyfriars, Tolbooth and Highland Kirk, Edinburgh. Moderator of the Gen. Assembly, Church of Scotland, 2004–05; Convener: Church and Nation Cttee, Church of Scotland, 1996–2000; Action of Churches Together in Scotland, 2002–06; Mem., Central Cttee, Conf. of European Churches, 1997–2009. Chair, Land Reform Rev. Gp, Scottish Govt, 2012–14. Hon. FRCPE 2007. Hon. LLD TCD, 2004; Hon. DD: St Andrews, Edinburgh, Knox Coll., Toronto, 2005. *Publications:* Child Language, 1981; Scottish Churches and the Political Process Today, 1987; The Miraculous Everyday, 2005; Growing Citizens, 2009. *Recreations:* friends, family, food. *Address:* New College, Mound Place, Edinburgh EH1 2LX. *E:* Alison.Elliot@ed.ac.uk.

ELLIOT, Benjamin William; Co-Founder and Co-Chairman, Quintessentially Group, since 1999; *b* London, 11 Aug. 1975; *s* of Simon and Annabel Elliot; *m* 2011, Mary Clare Winwood; one *s*. *Educ:* Eton Coll.; Bristol Univ. (BSc Politics). Non-exec. Dir, YouGov plc, 2009–. Exec. Producer, documentary, Fire in Babylon, 2011. Chm., Quintessentially Foundn, 2008–. *Recreations:* cricket, cycling, gardening. *Address:* Quintessentially, 29 Portland Place, W1B 1QB. *T:* (020) 3073 6600. *E:* ben@quintessentially.com. *Clubs:* 5 Hertford Street, MCC (Associate Mem.).

ELLIOT, Caroline Margaret, (Carma), CMG 2011; OBE 2004; Regional Director, China, British Council, since 2013; *b* 24 Aug. 1964; two adopted *d*. *Educ:* Fudan Univ., Shanghai. Entered FCO, 1987; Peking, 1989–91; Brussels, 1991–94; EC Presidency Liaison Officer, Bonn, Paris and Madrid, 1994–96; Second, later First Sec., FCO, 1996–2000; Consul General: Chongqing, 2000–04; Jeddah, 2004–06; Shanghai, 2006–10; Exec. Dir, China, Half the Sky Foundn, 2011–13. *Address:* British Council, 4/f Landmark Building Tower 1, 8 North Dongsanhuan Road, Chaoyang District, Beijing 100004, China.

ELLIOT, Sir Gerald (Henry), Kt 1986; FRSE; Chairman, Christian Salvesen plc, 1981–88; *b* 24 Dec. 1923; *s* of late Surg. Captain J. S. Elliot, RN, and Magda Salvesen; *m* 1950, Margaret Ruth Whale (MBE 1993), *d* of Rev. J. S. Whale; two *s* one *d*. *Educ:* Marlborough Coll.; New Coll., Oxford (BA PPE 1948; Hon. Fellow 2002). FRSE 1978. Captain FF Rifles, Indian Army, 1942–46. Christian Salvesen Ltd, 1948–88, Dep. Chm. and Man. Dir, 1973–81. Dir, Scottish Provident Instn, 1971–89, Chm., 1983–89; Chairman: Chambers and Fargus, 1975–79; Scottish Br., RIIA, 1973–77 (Sec., 1963–73); FAO Fishery Industries Develt Gp, 1971–76; Forth Ports Authority, 1973–79; Scottish Arts Council, 1980–86. Chairman: Scottish Unit Managers Ltd, 1984–88; Martin Currie Unit Trusts, 1988–90; Biotal, 1987–90. Sec., National Whaling Bd, 1953–62; Mem., Nat. Ports Council, 1978–81. Chm., Scottish Div., Inst. of Dirs, 1989–92; Vice-Chm., Scottish Business in the Community, 1987–89. Chairman: Prince's Scottish Youth Business Trust, 1987–94; Scottish Opera, 1987–92 (Vice-Pres., 1994–99). A Vice-Pres., RSE, 1988–91. Pres., UN 50 Scotland, 1993–95. Trustee: David Hume Inst., 1985–98 (Chm., 1985–95); Nat. Museums of Scotland, 1987–91; The Prince's Trust, 1992–94; Edinburgh Fest. Th., 1995–98; Pres., Edinburgh Univ. Develt Trust, 1990–94. Member Court: Edinburgh Univ., 1984–93; Regents, RCSE, 1990–99. Dr *hc* Edinburgh, 1989; Hon. LLD Aberdeen, 1991. Consul for Finland in Edinburgh, 1957–89; Dean, Consular Corps in Edinburgh-Leith, 1986–88. Prince of Wales Medal for Arts Philanthropy, 2012. Kt 1st Cl., Order of White Rose of Finland, 1975. *Publications:* A Whaling Enterprise, 1998; A Memoir of India 1942–46, 2014; papers on control of whaling and fishing, arts administration and economic management. *Address:* 39 Inverleith Place, Edinburgh EH3 5QD. *T:* (0131) 552 3005.

ELLIOT, Iain Fleming, OBE 2000; PhD; Director, East-West Insight, since 2000; *b* 24 May 1943; *s* of John Darling Elliot and Isabel Elliot (*née* MacLean); *m* 1970, Dr Elisabeth Mary Robson; one *s* one *d*. *Educ:* Univ. of Glasgow (MA); Univ. of Sussex (MA); Univ. of Bradford (PhD 1974). Res. student, Univ. of Leningrad, 1967–68; res. asst and Lectr, Univ. of Bradford, 1969–70; Sen. Lectr, Univ. of Brighton, 1971–88; leader writer and specialist on Soviet affairs, The Times, 1982–86; Associate Dir, with responsibility for Russian broadcasting, Radio Liberty, subseq. also Chief Ed. and Dir, analytic research, RFE/RL Research Inst., Munich, 1987–93; Dir, Britain-Russia Centre, and British East-West Centre, 1993–2000. Ed., Soviet Analyst, 1972–88. *Publications:* The Soviet Energy Balance, 1974; (ed jtly) Demise of the USSR, 1995; contrib. books, jls and newspapers on Soviet and Russian affairs. *Address:* 42 Preston Park Avenue, Brighton, Sussex BN1 6HG. *T:* (01273) 556156. *Club:* Athenæum.

ELLIOT, (Robert) John, WS; Deputy Keeper of HM Signet, 1999–2008; *b* 18 Jan. 1947; *s* of Robert Thomas Elliot and Barbara Elliot; *m* 1971, Christine Anne Glencross; one *s* one *d*. *Educ:* Craigflower Prep. Sch., Dunfermline; Loretto Sch., Musselburgh; Edinburgh Univ. (LLB). WS 1971; Admitted solicitor, 1971; with Lindsays WS, Edinburgh, 1969–2011: Partner, 1973–2011; Man. Partner, 1988–94; Chm., 1994–2010; Chm., William Simpsons, 2010–. Pres., Law Soc. of Scotland, 1997–98 (Mem. Council, 1990–99). Chm., Age Concern Edinburgh IT, 1995–. *Recreations:* golf, politics, argument, wine, literature. *Address:* 1 Lauder Loan, Edinburgh EH9 2RB. *T:* (0131) 667 9339.

ELLIOT, Virginia Helen Antoinette, MBE 1986; trainer of National Hunt jockeys and horses; former equestrian event rider; Eventing High Performance Coach, Horse Sport Ireland, 2008–13; *b* 1 Feb. 1955; *d* of late Col Ronald Morris Holgate, RM and of Heather Holgate; *m* 1st, 1985, Hamish Julian Peter Leng (marr. diss. 1989), *s* of Gen. Sir Peter Leng, KCB, MBE, MC; 2nd, 1993, Michael Elliot. *Educ:* Bedgebury Park, Goudhurst, Kent. Three day event equestrian team trainer, 1996 Olympic Games. Three day event wins: Junior European Champion, 1973 (Dubonnet); Mini Olympics, 1975 (Jason); Burghley, 1983 (Priceless), 1984 (Nightcap), 1985 (Priceless), 1986 (Murphy Himself), 1989 (Master Craftsman); Badminton, 1985 (Priceless), 1989 (Master Craftsman), 1993 (Houdini); European Championship, 1985 (Priceless), 1987 (Nightcap), 1989 (Master Craftsman); World Championship, 1986 (Priceless); Team Silver Olympic Medal, 1984 and 1988; Bronze Individual Olympic Medal, 1984 (Priceless), and 1988 (Master Craftsman). *Publications:* (with Genevieve Murphy) Ginny, 1986; (with Nancy Roberts) Priceless, 1987; (with Genevieve Murphy) Ginny and Her Horses, 1987; (with Genevieve Murphy) Training the Event Horse, 1990; *novels for children:* Winning, 1995; Race against Time, 1996; High Hurdle, 1997. *Recreations:* ski-ing, cooking, art, theatre. *Address:* Holliers House, Worton Road, Chipping Norton, Oxon OX7 7DU.

ELLIOT MAJOR, Dr Lee; Chief Executive, Sutton Trust, since 2014; *b* 20 Aug. 1968; *s* of Terry William Major and Dianne Margaret Major; partner, Siobhan Scannell; one *s* one *d*. *Educ:* Isleworth and Syon Sch. for Boys; Richmond upon Thames Coll.; Univ. of Sheffield (BSc Phys; PhD Theoretical Phys 1993); Imperial Coll. London (MSc Sci. Communication). Reporter, 1995–97, Dep. Editor, 1997–99, Research Fortnight; Educn reporter, Guardian News and Media, 2000–02; Dir, Policy, Wellcome Trust, 2002–04; News Editor, THES, 2004–06; Dir of Res., 2006–12, Dir of Develt and Policy, 2012–14, Sutton Trust. Member: Adv. Gp, Office for Fair Access; Social Mobility Transparency Bd. Trustee, Educn Endowment Foundn (Chm., Evaluation Adv. Bd); Mem., Res. Adv. Panel, Great Ormond Street Hosp. Children's Charity. Foundn Gov., William Ellis Sch. (Chm., Sch. Improvement Cttee). *Recreations:* playing EP Dad's football, playing guitar for the Spontaneous Emissions, compiling the educational backgrounds of people in Who's Who, yoga. *Address:* Sutton Trust, 9th Floor, Millbank Tower, 21–24 Millbank, SW1P 4QP. *T:* (020) 7802 1660. *E:* lee.elliotmajor@suttontrust.com.

ELLIOT-MURRAY-KYNYNMOUND, family name of **Earl of Minto**.

ELLIOTT, Anthony Michael Manton, (Tony Elliott); Founder, 1968 and Chairman, Time Out Group; *b* 7 Jan. 1947; *s* of late Katherine and Alan Elliott; *m* 1st, 1976, Janet Street-Porter, *qv* (marr. diss. 1978); 2nd, 1989, Jane L. Coke; three *s* (incl. twins). *Educ:* Stowe Sch.;

Keele Univ. Time Out Group publishing activities include: Time Out London; Time Out New York; Time Out Chicago; timeout.com; licensed local edns of Time Out worldwide, annual guides. Time Out Trust formed 1989. Director: Roundhouse Trust, 1998–; Somerset House Trust, 1999–; Photographers' Gall., 1999–2004; Soho Th. Co., 2000–03; Film London, 2003–09. Gov., BFI, 1997–2003 (Chm., Production Bd, 1998–2000). Dir, Human Rights Watch, 2006– (Chm., London Cttee, 2003–). *Recreations:* travel, watching television, cinema going, eating out with friends, reading newspapers and magazines, being with family. *Address:* Time Out Group, Universal House, 251 Tottenham Court Road, W1T 7AB. *T:* (020) 7813 3000, *Fax:* (020) 7813 6001.

ELLIOTT, Prof. (Barbara) Jane, PhD; Chief Executive, Economic and Social Research Council, since 2014; *b* Mancot, Flint, 25 Jan. 1966; *d* of late Keith Elliott and of Barbara Joy Elliott; *m* 2001, Jon Lawrence; one *s*. *Educ:* Sharnbrook Upper Sch.; Bedford Coll. of Higher Educn; King's Coll., Cambridge (BA 1987); Univ. of Manchester (PhD Sociol. 2001). Res. Associate, Univ. of Cambridge, 1987–92; Res. Fellow, Univ. of Manchester, 1994–99; Lectr, Univ. of Liverpool, 1999–2004; Institute of Education, University of London: Principal Investigator, 1970 and 1958 British Birth Cohort Studies, 2004–11; Prof. of Sociol., 2009–; Dir, Centre for Longitudinal Studies, 2010–14. Vis. Lectr, Harvard Univ., 2002–03. *Publications:* Using Narrative in Social Research: qualitative and quantitative approaches, 2005; (with C. Marsh) Exploring Data, 2nd edn 2008; articles in major jls incl. Sociology, Eur. Sociol Rev., Soc. Sci. and Medicine, Internat. Jl of Epidemiol. *Recreations:* a cappella singing, growing vegetables, hiking, birdwatching. *Address:* Economic and Social Research Council, Polaris House, North Star Avenue, Swindon SN2 1UJ. *E:* esrc.ceo@esrc.ac.uk.

ELLIOTT, Brent; *see* Elliott, W. B.

ELLIOTT, Rev. Dr Charles Middleton; Fellow, Dean and Chaplain of Trinity Hall, 1990–2001, Affiliated Lecturer in Theology, 1991–2001, in Social and Political Sciences, 1993–2001, University of Cambridge; *b* 9 Jan. 1939; *s* of Joseph William Elliott and Mary Evelyn Elliott; *m* 1962, Hilary Margaret Hambling; three *s* (one *d* decd). *Educ:* Repton; Lincoln and Nuffield Colls, Oxford (MA, DPhil). Deacon, 1964; priest, 1965. Lectr in Econs, Univ. of Nottingham, 1963–65; Reader in Econs, Univ. of Zambia, 1965–69; Asst Sec., Cttee on Society, Develt and Peace, Vatican and World Council of Churches, 1969–72; Sen. Lectr in Develt Econs, Univ. of E Anglia, 1972–73; Dir, Overseas Develt Gp, UEA, 1973–77; Minor Canon, Norwich Cathedral, 1974–77; Prof. of Develt Policy and Planning, and Dir, Centre of Develt Studies, Univ. of Wales, 1977–82; Director of Christian Aid, 1982–84; Asst Gen. Sec., BCC, 1982–84; Benjamin Meaker Prof., Bristol Univ., 1985–86; Sen. Consultant, ODI, 1986–87. G. E. M. Scott Fellow, Univ. of Melbourne, 1984–85; Hon. Vis. Prof. of Christian Ethics, Univ. of Edinburgh, 1985–87; Vis. Prof. in Theology, KCL, 1986–88. Chm., Ind. Gp on British Aid, 1981–89. Prebendary of Lichfield Cathedral, 1987–95. *Publications:* The Development Debate, 1972; Inflation and the Compromised Church, 1973; Patterns of Poverty in the Third World, 1975; Praying the Kingdom: an introduction to political spirituality, 1985 (Biennial Collins Prize for Religious Lit., 1985); Comfortable Compassion, 1987; Praying through Paradox, 1987; Signs of Our Times, 1988; Sword and Spirit, 1989; Memory and Salvation, 1995; Strategic Planning for Churches: an appreciative approach, 1997; Locating the Energy for Change: an introduction to appreciative inquiry, 1999; articles in Jl of Develt Studies, Econ. Hist. Rev., Theology, World Health Forum, World Develt, Lancet, BMJ and in Proc. Royal Soc. *Recreations:* sailing, fly-fishing, walking, chatting to rural craftsmen.

ELLIOTT, (Charles) Thomas, CBE 1994; PhD; FRS 1988; Tom Elliott Consultancy Ltd, 1999–2006; *b* 16 Jan. 1939; *s* of Charles Thomas and Mary Jane Elliott; *m* 1962, Brenda Waistell; one *s* two *d*. *Educ:* Washington Grammar Sch.; Manchester Univ. (BSc 1960; PhD 1965). Univ. of Manchester: Research student, 1960–63; Asst Lectr/Lectr, 1963–67 (research on dielectric breakdown); joined RSRE 1967, to study electrical transport in semiconductors; SSO, 1967–73; Vis. Scientist, MIT, Lincoln Lab., USA, 1970–71; research into infrared detectors, infrared emitters, novel and ultra-high-speed semiconductor devices, 1972–2006; PSO, 1973–79, SPSO, 1979–86, DCSO, 1986–91, RSRE; CSO (Individual Merit), DRA, Electronics Sector, 1991–99; Chief Scientist, Electronics Sector, DERA, 1996–99. Part-time Prof. of Physics, 1999–2005, Hon. Prof. of Physics, 2005–, Heriot-Watt Univ. Hon. FRPS 2001. Rank Prize for optoelectronics and IEE Electronics Div. Premium Award, 1982; Churchill Medal, Soc. of Engineers, 1986; MacRobert Award for Engineering, 1991; Paterson Medal, Inst. of Physics, 1997; J. J. Thomson Medal, IEE, 1998; Progress Medal, RPS, 2001. *Publications:* numerous papers and patents. *Recreations:* reading, golf, music, motor caravanning. *Address:* Weardale, 8 Hall Green, Malvern, Worcs WR14 3QX. *T:* (01684) 562474.

ELLIOTT, Christine Anne; Chief Executive and Director, Institute for Turnaround (formerly Society of Turnaround Professionals), since 2007; *b* 10 Oct. 1954; *d* of Charles Archbold Elliott and Geneviève Suzanne Marie Thérèse Elliott (*née* Colombé); marr. diss.; two *d*. *Educ:* Blyth Grammar Sch., Northumberland; Sheffield Univ. (BA Hons Law); Chambre de Commerce et d'Industrie, Paris (DS). Thomson Regl Press, 1977–78; NFWI, 1978–80; mkting and PR consultancy, 1980–93; Wiggins Gp plc and Hayklan Industries, 1994–97; Dir, Bletchley Park, 1998–2006; Chief Exec., Ramblers Assoc., 2006. Non-exec. Dir, Coll. of Policing, 2015–; non-exec. Advr, Lyonsdown Ltd, 2014–. Vis. Lectr, Univ. of Westminster, 1989–91; Expert Panellist, Cass Business Sch., 2005–; speaker, London Business Sch., 2010–; speaker and mentor, Inspiring the Future, 2013– (Chm., IFT Awards, 2014). Mem., Leadership Gp, Inst. for Turnaround Foundn, 2011–; Hon. Mem., Inst. for Turnaround, 2011. Lay Mem., Editors' Code of Practice Cttee, 2015–. Mem., Marketors' Co. Member: Poetry Soc.; Oxford-Perm Assoc. *Publications:* Bye Bye Belle (illustrated story book), 1996; Hijacking Enigma, 2003; Can You Keep a Secret?: children's codebreaking, 2004. *Recreations:* saxophone, piano, creative writing. *Address:* Institute for Turnaround, Juxon House, 100 St Paul's Churchyard, EC4M 8BU.

ELLIOTT, Maj.-Gen. Christopher Haslett, CVO 2004; CBE 1994; Director, Army Sport Control Board, 2005–15; *b* 26 May 1947; *s* of late Lt-Col Blethyn Elliott and of Zara Elliott; *m* 1970, Annabel Melanie Emerson; four *d*. *Educ:* Kelly Coll., Tavistock; Mons Officer Cadet Sch.; Staff Coll., Camberley (psc). Commnd into S Wales Borderers, 1966: regtl duty appts, 1966–80 (despatches, NI, 1975); Army Staff Coll., Camberley, 1980; COS, Berlin Inf. Bde, 1981–83; Mem., Directing Staff, Army Staff Coll., Camberley, 1985–87; CO, 1st Bn, Royal Regt of Wales, 1987–90; Comdr, British Forces Belize, 1990–93; Dir, Army Recruiting, MoD, 1993–94; Comdr, Brit. Mil. Adv. and Trng Team, S Africa, 1994–97; GOC UKSC (Germany), 1997–2001; Defence Services Sec. and Dir Gen., Reserve Forces and Cadets, 2001–04. Col Comdt POW Div., 1999–2009; Col, Royal Regt of Wales, 1999–2004. Chief Exec., Army Sport Control Bd Charitable Fund, 2005–15; Chm., Army Sports Lottery Grants Cttee, 2005–15; Member: Combined Services Sports Bd, 2005–15 (Chm., 2006–09 and 2013–15); Army Grants Planning Forum, 2007–15; Army Welfare Grants Cttee, 2010–15. Mem. Council for S Africa, Royal Commonwealth Ex-Services League, 2006–. *Recreations:* fly-fishing, rough shooting, walking, watersports. *Club:* Army and Navy.

See also N. B. Elliott.

ELLIOTT, Maj. Gen. Christopher Leslie, CB 1999; MBE 1969; Director, Doctrine and Strategic Analysis, General Dynamics UK Ltd, 2002–10; Director General, Dynamics UK Research Foundation, 2002–12; *b* 18 March 1947; *s* of Peter Archibald Elliott and Evelyn Sarah (*née* Wallace); *m* 1970, Margaret Bennett; two *d*. *Educ:* Pocklington Sch., York; RMA, Royal Mil. Coll. of Sci. (BSc Hons Eng); Cranfield Inst. of Technol. (MPhil). Commnd RE, 1967 (MBE for Gallantry); OC 48 Field Sqn RE, 1980; CO, 21 Engr Regt, 1986–88; ACOS 1 (BR) Corps, 1988–90; Comdr, 6th Armd Bde, 1990–91; Dir of Studies, Staff Coll., Camberley, 1991–92; Dir, Mil. Ops, 1993–95; UK Mil. Advr to Chm., Internat. Conf. on former Yugoslavia, 1995–96; Dir Gen. Army Trng and Recruiting, and Chief Exec., Army Trng and Recruiting Agency, 1996–99; COS, HQ QMG, 1999–2000; Dir-Gen. Develt and Doctrine, MoD, 2000–02. Comr, Royal Hosp., Chelsea, 1996–2002. Trustee, Army Central Fund, 1998–2000. Col Comdt, RE, 2000–08. Consultant, Ove Arup and Partners, 2002–. Chm., Purple Secure Systems Ltd, 2007–09. Vis. Prof., Cranfield Univ., 2002–; Research Fellow: Changing Character of War Prog., Faculty of History, Pembroke Coll., Oxford, 2012–; Reading Univ., 2012–; Associate Fellow, RUSI, 2012–. Mem. Senate, Cranfield Univ., 1996–99; Mem. Adv. Council, RMCS, 2000–02; Pres., Instn of RE, 2002–07 (Fellow, 2007). Pres., Jt Services Paragliding and Hang-gliding Assoc., 1993–2002; Cdre, Army Sailing Assoc., 2001–02 (Vice-Cdre, 1993–94). Pres., Victim Support, Wilts, 2003–09. Mem., Easton Royal Parish Council, 2003–. *Publications:* (contrib.) Blast Damage to Buildings, 1995, repr. 2010; High Command: British military leadership in the Iraq and Afghanistan wars, 2014. *Recreations:* sailing, paragliding, reading. *E:* cle@clelliott24.freeserve.co.uk. *Clubs:* Royal Ocean Racing, Royal Cruising (Mem. Cttee, 2000–); Royal Engineer Yacht (Chatham) (Cdre, 1995–96); Royal Lymington Yacht.

ELLIOTT, Sir Clive (Christopher Hugh), 4th Bt *cr* 1917, of Limpsfield, Surrey; independent consultant on migratory pests in agriculture, since 2006; *b* Moshi, Tanganyika, 12 Aug. 1945; *s* of Sir Hugh Elliott, 3rd Bt, OBE and Elizabeth Margaret (*d* 2007), *d* of A. G. Phillipson; *S* father, 1989; *m* 1975, Marie-Thérèse, *d* of H. Rüttimann; two *s*. *Educ:* Dragon Sch., Oxford; Bryanston Sch., Dorset; University Coll., Oxford (BA Hons Zoology); Univ. of Cape Town, S Africa (PhD Zoology 1973). University of Cape Town: Research Officer, FitzPatrick Inst. of Ornithology, 1968–71; first Officer i/c National Unit for Bird-ringing Admin, 1972–75; Food and Agriculture Organization of the UN: ornithologist/ecologist, crop protectionist/project manager: Chad, 1975–78; Tanzania, 1978–86; Kenya, 1986–89; Country Projects Officer, Eastern and Southern Africa, 1989–95; Sen. Officer, Migratory Pests, 1995–2004; Sen. Officer, i/c Locust and Other Migratory Pests Gp, Plant Protection Service, 2004–06. Mem., Field Staff Assoc. of FAO (Chm., 1992). *Publications:* (ed jtly with R. L. Bruggers) Quelea Quelea: Africa's Bird Pest, 1989; (ed) Desert Locust Control Organization for East Africa: celebrating 50 years of service to member countries, 2012; (ed with K. Cressman) FAO South-West Asia Desert Locust Commission: a celebration of 50 years, 2014; contrib. to books and jls on ornithology. *Recreations:* tennis, fishing, birdwatching, wildlife conservation. *Heir: s* Dr Ivo Antony Moritz Elliott, BSc(MedSci) St Andrews, MB ChB Manchester, MRCP, FRCPath [*b* 9 May 1978; *m* 2008, Catriona, *d* of Dr R. Wootton; one *d*]. *Address:* Blue Barn House, South Leigh, Oxon OX29 6XH. *Clubs:* British Ornithologists' Union; Oxford Ornithological Soc. (Pres., 2013–); Tristan da Cunha Assoc. (Mem. Cttee); N Oxford Lawn Tennis.

ELLIOTT, Sir David (Murray), KCMG 1995; CB 1987; Director General (Internal Market), General Secretariat of Council of European Union, 1991–95; *b* 8 Feb. 1930; *s* of late Alfred Elliott, ISM, and Mabel Kathleen Emily Elliott (*née* Murray); *m* 1956, Ruth Marjorie Ingram; one *d* (one *s* decd). *Educ:* Bishopshalt Grammar Sch.; London Sch. of Economics and Political Science (BScEcon); Kitchener Scholar. National Service, RAF, 1951–54; Gen. Post Office, 1954–57; seconded to Federal Ministry of Communications, Enugu, Nigeria, 1958–62; GPO, 1962–69 (Principal, 1964; Clerk in Waiting, 1964–69); Asst Secretary: Min. of Posts and Telecommunications, 1969–74 (Dep. Leader, UK Delegn to Centenary Congress, UPU, Lausanne, 1974); Dept of Industry, 1974–75; Counsellor at UK Representation to the European Communities, Brussels, 1975–78; Under Sec., European Secretariat, Cabinet Office, 1978–82; Minister and Dep. UK Perm. Rep. to the Eur. Communities, Brussels, 1982–91. Advr on EU affairs under UK Know-How Fund and EU PHARE progs, 1995–98. Mem., Sen. European Experts Gp, 2000–. Member Board: CARE UK, 1995–2001; CARE Internat., 1998–2001. *Address:* 31 Ailsa Road, Twickenham, Middlesex TW1 1QJ. *Club:* Travellers.

ELLIOTT, David Stewart Innes; Honorary Treasurer, The Baring Foundation (Trustee, since 2011); *b* 6 April 1945; *s* of late John Innes Elliott, CBE and Edith Agnes Elliott; *m* 1978, Patricia Nicholson; two *s*. *Educ:* Whitgift Sch.; Oriel Coll., Oxford (MA). Commercial Evaluation Dept, 1966–68, Market and Commercial Analyst, 1969–70, Vickers Ltd; Corporate Finance Dept, Baring Brothers & Co. Ltd, 1970–80 (Asst Dir, 1978); Exec. Vice-Pres., Baring Brothers Inc., NY, 1981–84; Finance Dir, ENO, 1985–90; Dir of Finance and Admin, 1991–93, Dep. Chief Exec., 1994–97, Chief Exec., 1998–2009, Royal Albert Hall. Chm., English Touring Opera, 2009–15 (Mem. Bd, 2007–15). Chm., Benesh Inst. of Choreology, 1997–2007; Mem. Exec. Cttee, Royal Acad. Dancing, 1997–2007. Hon. Treas., Lyric Th. Hammersmith, 1999–2006. *Recreations:* opera, theatre, realising my shortcomings as a painter, sailing.

ELLIOTT, David Stuart; independent curator, writer, teacher and museum consultant, since 2008; Artistic Director: Sydney 17th Biennale of Art, 2008–10; Kiev First Biennale of Contemporary Art, 2011–12; 4th International Biennale of work by young artists, Moscow, 2012–14; Director, Istanbul Museum of Modern Art, 2007–08; *b* 29 April 1949; *s* of Arthur Elliott and May Elliott; *m* 1974, Julia Alison (marr. diss. 2006); two *d*. *Educ:* Loughborough Grammar Sch.; Durham Univ. (BA Hons Mod. Hist.); Univ. of London (MA Hist. of Art, Courtauld Inst.). Asst Stage Manager, Phoenix Theatre, Leicester, 1966; Asst, City Art Gallery, Leicester, 1971; Regional Art Officer, Arts Council, 1973–76; Director: Mus. of Modern Art, Oxford, 1976–96; Moderna Museet, Stockholm, 1996–2001; Mori Art Mus., Tokyo, 2001–06. Visitor, Ashmolean Mus., Oxford, 1992–2000. Rudolf Arnheim Guest Prof. of Art History, Humboldt Univ., Berlin, 2008; Vis. Prof., Dept of Mus. Studies, Chinese Univ., Hong Kong, 2008–15. Art Advr for revitalisation of Central Police Stn site in Hong Kong into centre for contemp. art and heritage, 2010–12. Chm. Bd, Triangle Arts Network, London, 2009–. Pres., Internat. Cttee for Museums and Collections of Modern Art, ICOM, 1998–2004. President of Jury: La Biennale des Arts, Dakar, 2000; Internat. Architectural Competition for Tsunami Meml, Thailand, 2005. Contribs to radio and TV. Hon. DA Oxford Brookes, 1998. NACF Award, 1988. Orden de Mayo (Argentina), 2001. *Publications:* Alexander Rodchenko, 1979; José Clemente Orozco, 1980; New Worlds: Russian Art and Society 1900–1937, 1986; (ed jtly) Eisenstein at 90, 1988; (ed jtly) 100 Years of Russian Art 1889–1989, 1989; (ed jtly) Alexander Rodchenko: Works on Paper, 1991; (ed jtly) Engineers of the Human Soul: Soviet Socialist Realism, 1992; Photography in Russia 1840–1940, 1992; (ed) Art from Argentina 1920–1994, 1994; (ed jtly) Wounds: between democracy and redemption in contemporary art, 1998; (ed jtly) After the Wall: art and culture in post-Communist Europe, 1999; Organising Freedom: Nordic art of the '90s, 2000; (ed jtly) Happiness: a survival guide for art and life, 2003; (ed jtly) Hiroshi Sugimoto, 2005; (ed) The Beauty of Distance: songs of survival in a precarious age, 2010; Bye, Bye Kitty!!!: between heaven and hell in contemporary Japanese art, 2011; Between Heaven & Earth: contemporary art from the centre of Asia, 2011; The Best of Times, The Worst of Times: rebirth and apocalypse in contemporary art, 2012; Art from Elsewhere, 2014; contribs to arts catalogues and magazines. *Recreations:* keeping fit, travelling. *E:* david@elliott.as.

ELLIOTT, Edward Charles; Head, The Perse School, Cambridge, since 2008; *b* Worcester, 27 May 1970; *s* of (Charles) Richard Elliott and Janet Elizabeth Elliott; *m* 2002, Dr Susan Broster; one *s* two *d*. *Educ:* Royal Grammar Sch., Worcester; St Anne's Coll., Oxford (BA 1991). Asst Hd, Sixth Form, Whitgift Sch., Croydon, 1995–97; Hd, Sixth Form, 1997–2004, Dep. Hd, 2004–08, The Perse Sch., Cambridge. *Publications:* University Applications (with

Michael Punt), 2004; (contrib.) Leading Schools in the 21st Century: heads of department, 2008. *Recreations:* cricket, horticulture, reading political biographies. *Address:* The Perse School, Hills Road, Cambridge CB2 8QF. *T:* (01223) 403800, *Fax:* (01223) 403810. *E:* ecelliott@perse.co.uk.

ELLIOTT, Eric Alan; QC 2006; a Recorder, 1993; *b* West Hartlepool, 12 July 1951; *s* of Alan and Sheila Elliott; *m* 1st (marr. diss.) one *s* one *d*; 2nd, 2010, Sally Bradley (*d* 2014). *Educ:* West Hartlepool Grammar Sch.; Liverpool Univ. (LLB). Called to the Bar, Gray's Inn, 1974; in practice as a barrister, until 2013, specialising in criminal law and regulatory and disciplinary law, particularly relating to equine matters; Asst Recorder, 1989–93. *Recreations:* most sports, but particularly horse racing (licensed trainer, 1995–2006) and football (especially following Hartlepool United FC), French culture, fine food and wine.

ELLIOTT, Rt Rev. George; *see* Elliott, Rt Rev. M. G. H.

ELLIOTT, George, FRICS; Senior Partner, Edmond Shipway and Partners, 1985–93; *b* 20 Aug. 1932; *s* of Harry Elliott and Nellie Elizabeth Elliott; *m* 1st, 1958, Winifred Joan (marr. diss. 1990); one *s* one *d*; 2nd, 1992, Hazel Ann Willis. *Educ:* Sir George Monoux Grammar Sch.; SW Essex Technical Coll. FRICS 1966. Founder Partner, Edmond Shipway, 1963; Chief Exec., British Urban Develt Services Unit, 1975–78. Pres., Western Australian Chapter, Naval Hist. Soc. of Australia, 2003–09. *Recreations:* travel, naval history, croquet. *Address:* 4 Langtry View, Mount Claremont, WA 6010, Australia. *T:* (8) 93842147.

ELLIOTT, Prof. (James) Keith, DPhil, DD; Professor of New Testament Textual Criticism, University of Leeds, 1997–2007, now Emeritus; *b* 19 March 1943; *s* of James and Lillian Elliott; *m* 1971, Carolyn Tull; one *d*. *Educ:* Liverpool Inst. High Sch.; University Coll. of N Wales, Bangor (BA 1st Cl. Hebrew and Biblical Studies 1964); St Peter's Coll., Oxford (DPhil 1967); DD Wales 1988. Leeds University: Lectr in New Testament Lang. and Lit., 1967–89; Sen. Lectr, 1989–93, Reader, 1993–97, Dept of Theol.; Warden, Charles Morris Hall, 1971–83. Ed., 1977–87, Sec., 1987–2010, Internat. Greek New Testament Project; Asst Sec., Studiorum Novi Testamenti Societas, 1983–93; Book Rev. Ed., 1990–, Pres., Editl Bd, 2008–, Novum Testamentum (Leiden). Mem. Cttee, Vacation Term for Biblical Study, Oxford, 2003– (Vice-Chm., 2005–14; Chm., 2014–). Gov., Harrogate Grammar Sch., 1989–93, 1996–2000. *Publications:* The Greek Text of the Epistles to Timothy and Titus, 1968; Questioning Christian Origins, 1982; Codex Sinaiticus and the Simonides Affair, 1982; A Survey of Manuscripts used in Editions of the Greek New Testament, 1987; A Bibliography of Greek New Testament Manuscripts, 1989, 3rd edn 2015; Essays and Studies in New Testament Textual Criticism, 1992; The Apocryphal New Testament, 1993; The Apocryphal Jesus: legends of the Early Church, 1996; (with D. R. Cartlidge) Art and the Christian Apocrypha, 2001; A Synopsis of the Apocryphal Nativity and Infancy Narratives, 2006; New Testament Textual Criticism: the application of thoroughgoing principles, 2010; (ed jtly) Textual Research on the Psalms and Gospels, 2012. *Recreations:* walking in the Yorkshire Dales, cycling in Austria, music (big bands, grand opera, especially Wagner). *Address:* 11 Cundall Way, Harrogate HG2 0DY. *E:* j.k.elliott@leeds.ac.uk. *Club:* Army and Navy.

ELLIOTT, Jane; *see* Elliott, B. J.

ELLIOTT, Prof. John, DLitt; Professor of Education, University of East Anglia, 1987–2002, Emeritus Professor, 2004 (Professorial Fellow, 2002–04); Chief Editor, Journal for Lesson and Learning Studies, since 2011; *b* 20 June 1938; *s* of Alfred George Lewis Elliott and Mary Doris Elliott (*née* Greason); *m* 1st, 1967, Jean Marion Walford (marr. diss. 1993); three *d*; 2nd, 1998, Anne Christine O'Hanlon. *Educ:* Ashford Grammar Sch.; City of Portsmouth Trng Coll.; Bishop Otter Coll., Chichester; London Univ. Inst. of Educn (Dip. Phil. Ed. 1970; MPhil 1980); DLitt E Anglia, 2003. Horticultural researcher, E Malling Res. Stn, 1956–59; sch. teacher, 1962–67; Educnl Researcher, Schs Council, 1967–72; Lectr in Applied Educnl Res., UEA, 1972–76; Tutor in Curriculum Studies, Cambridge Inst. of Educn, 1976–84; University of East Anglia: Reader, 1984–87; Dean, Sch. of Educn and Professional Develt, 1992–95; Dir, Centre for Applied Res. In Educn, 1996–99. Adv. Prof., Hong Kong Inst. of Educn, 2000–06. R and D Advr, Curriculum Develt, Inst. of Hong Kong, 2000–07; Associate, Centre for Educnl R and D, von Hügel Inst., St Edmund's Coll., Cambridge, 2004–08. Ind. Acad. Advr, Home Office, 2003–04. Mem., Fellowship Council, RSA, 2009–14. Visiting Professor: Manchester Metropolitan Univ., 2004–; Sheffield Univ., 2004–; University Campus Suffolk, 2013–. Member: Norfolk Learning and Skills Council, 2001–08; Norfolk 14–19 Strategy Gp, 2006–09. Pres., World Assoc. of Lesson Studies, 2009–10. Gov., Sewell Park Coll. and Kett Sixth Form Coll., Norwich, 2009–12. FRSA 1992; FAcSS (AcSS 2011). Hon. DEd Hong Kong Inst. of Educn, 2002; Hon. Dr: Autonomous Univ. of Barcelona, 2003; Jönköping Univ., 2014. *Publications:* Action Research for Educational Change, 1991; The Curriculum Experiment, 1999; (ed with H. Altrichter) Images of Educational Change, 2000; Reflecting Where the Action Is: selected works, 2007; (ed with N. Norris) Curriculum, Pedagogy and Educational Research, 2012; contrib. numerous papers to learned jls. *Recreations:* golf, countryside, reading, cinema and theatre. *Address:* Centre for Applied Research in Education, University of East Anglia, Norwich NR4 7TJ. *T:* (01603) 592859. *Clubs:* Royal Norwich Golf; Narin and Portnoo Golf (Co. Donegal).

ELLIOTT, John Dorman; Chairman, Australian Product Traders Pty Ltd, 1992; Deputy Chairman, Foster's Brewing Group (formerly Elders IXL Ltd), 1990–92 (Chairman and Chief Executive, 1985–90); *b* 3 Oct. 1941; *s* of Frank Faithful Elliott and Anita Caroline Elliott; *m* 1st, 1965, Lorraine Clare (*née* Golder) (marr. diss. 1986); two *s* one *d*; 2nd, 1987, Amanda Mary Drummond Moray (*née* Bayles); one *d*. *Educ:* Carey Baptist Grammar School, Melbourne; BCom (Hons) 1962, MBA Melbourne 1965. With BHP, Melbourne, 1963–65; McKinsey & Co., 1966–72; formed consortium and raised 30 million to acquire Henry Jones (IXL), and became Man. Dir, 1972; Elder Smith Goldsbrough Mort merged with Henry Jones (IXL) to form Elders IXL, 1981; Elders IXL acquired Carlton & United Breweries, 1983, largest takeover in Aust. history. Pres., Liberal Party of Australia, 1987–90. Pres., Carlton FC, 1983–2002. *Publications:* Big Jack: my sporting life, 2003. *Recreations:* football, tennis, Royal tennis. *Address:* 44/108 Elgin Street, Carlton, Vic 3053, Australia. *T:* (3) 96060711. *Club:* Savage (Melbourne).

ELLIOTT, Sir John (Huxtable), Kt 1994; FBA 1972; Regius Professor of Modern History, and Fellow of Oriel College, Oxford, 1990–97 (Hon. Fellow, Oriel College, 1997); *b* 23 June 1930; *s* of late Thomas Charles Elliott and Janet Mary Payne; *m* 1958, Oonah Sophia Butler. *Educ:* Eton College; Trinity College, Cambridge (MA, PhD). Fellow of Trinity Coll., Cambridge, 1954–67, Hon. Fellow, 1991; Asst Lectr in History, Cambridge Univ., 1957–62; Lectr in History, Cambridge Univ., 1962–67; Prof. of History: KCL, 1968–73; Inst. for Advanced Study, Princeton, NJ, 1973–90. Mem., Scientific Cttee, Prado Mus., 1996 (Hon. Trustee, 2015). Chm., Adv. Council, Inst. for the Study of the Americas, Univ. of London, 2004–11. King Juan Carlos Vis. Prof., New York Univ., 1988; Vis. Hon. Prof., Univ. of Warwick, 2003–07. Wiles Lectr, QUB, 1969; Trevelyan Lectr, Cambridge Univ., 1982–83. Chm., Council, Omohundro Inst. of Early American Hist. and Culture, Williamsburg, 2007–10. FKC 1998. Corresp. Fellow, Real Academia de la Historia, Madrid, 1965; Fellow, Amer. Acad. Arts and Scis, 1977; Mem., Amer. Philosophical Soc., 1982; Corresponding Member: Hispanic Soc. of America, 1975 (Hon. Fellow, 1997); Real Academia Sevillana de Buenas Letras, 1976 (Hon. Mem., 2008); Royal Acad. of Letters, Barcelona, 1992; Nat. Acad. of History, Venezuela, 1992; Accademia delle Scienze di Torino, 2009; Foreign Mem., Accademia Nazionale dei Lincei, 2003. Hon. Fellow, Lady Margaret Hall, Oxford, 2013. Dr *hc*: Universidad Autónoma de Madrid, 1983; Genoa, 1992; Barcelona, 1994; Valencia, 1998; Lleida, 1999; Complutense, Madrid, 2003; Seville, 2011; Alcalá, 2012; Cantabria, 2015; Hon. DLitt: Portsmouth, 1993; Warwick, 1995; London, 2007; Carlos III, Madrid, 2008; Hon. DHL: Brown, 1996; Coll. of William and Mary, 2005; Hon. LittD Cambridge, 2013. Medal of Honour, Universidad Internacional Menéndez y Pelayo, 1987; Medalla de Oro al Mérito en las Bellas Artes, Spain, 1990; Premio Antonio de Nebrija, Univ. of Salamanca, 1993; Prince of Asturias Prize for Social Scis, 1996; Gold Medal, Spanish Inst., NY, 1997; Balzan Prize for History 1500–1800, Internat. Balzan Foundn, 1999. Visitante Ilustre de Madrid, 1983; Comdr, 1984, Grand Cross, 1988, Order of Alfonso X El Sabio; Comdr, 1987, Grand Cross, 1996, Order of Isabel la Católica; Cross of St George (Catalonia), 1999. *Publications:* The Revolt of the Catalans, 1963; Imperial Spain, 1469–1716, 1963; Europe Divided, 1559–1598, 1968; The Old World and the New, 1492–1650, 1970; (ed with H. G. Koenigsberger) The Diversity of History, 1970; (with J. F. de la Peña) Memoriales y Cartas del Conde Duque de Olivares, 2 vols, 1978–80, 2nd edn 2013; (with Jonathan Brown) A Palace for a King, 1980, 2nd edn 2003; Richelieu and Olivares, 1984 (Leo Gershoy Award, Amer. Hist. Assoc., 1985); The Count-Duke of Olivares, 1986 (Wolfson History Prize, 1986); Spain and its World 1500–1700, 1989; (ed) The Hispanic World, 1991; (ed with Laurence Brockliss) The World of the Favourite, 1999; (ed with Jonathan Brown) The Sale of the Century, 2002; Empires of the Atlantic World (Francis Parkman Prize, Soc. of American Historians), 2006; Spain, Europe and the Wider World, 1500–1800, 2009; History in the Making, 2012. *Recreation:* looking at paintings. *Address:* Oriel College, Oxford OX1 4EW; 122 Church Way, Iffley, Oxford OX4 4EG. *T:* (01865) 716703.

ELLIOTT, John Stanley; teacher of mathematics; Chief Economist, 2007–11, and Director for Social Science, 2010–11, Home Office; *b* 26 March 1959; *s* of late Stanley Elliott and Betty Elliott (*née* Cornish); partner, Shirley Ann McClune; (one *s* decd). *Educ:* Bemrose Sch., Derby; Jesus Coll., Oxford (MA PPE 1980; MPhil Econ. 1982); Sheffield Hallam Univ. (PGCE 2014); Open Univ. (Cert. Maths). Econ. Asst, MSC, 1982–83; Sen. Econ. Asst, DES, 1983–86; Econ. Advr, MoD, 1986–89; Econ. Advr, 1989–92, Sen. Econ. Advr, 1992–95, Dept of Employment; Sen. Econ. Advr, DFEE, then DFES, 1995–2004; Chief Economist, DFES, then DCSF, 2004–07. Mem. Council, Inst. for Employment Studies, 2005–12. Gov., Firth Park Acad. (formerly Firth Park Community Arts Coll.), 2006–10 and 2013– (Chm., 2008–09; Associate Gov., 2010–13). *Recreations:* crosswords, rowing. *Club:* City of Sheffield Rowing.

ELLIOTT, Prof. Julian George, PhD; CPsychol; Professor of Education, since 2004, and Principal, Collingwood College, since 2011, Durham University; *b* Epsom, 27 July 1955; *s* of George and Helen Elliott; *m* 1977, Ruth White; one *s* one *d*. *Educ:* Wimbledon Coll.; Durham Univ. (BEd; BA; MA; MSc; PhD 1994). CPsychol 1988; AFBPsS 1988. Teacher (SEN), Seaham Community Home, Co. Durham, 1977–80, Ryhope Sch., Sunderland, 1980–84; educnl psychologist, 1984–90; School of Education and Lifelong Learning, Sunderland Polytechnic, later Sunderland University: Sen. Lectr, 1990–92; Principal Lectr, 1992–96; Reader, 1996–97; Prof., 1997–2004; Associate Dean (Res.), 1999–2003; Actg Dean, 2003–04. FAcSS (AcSS 2010). *Publications:* Children in Difficulty: a guide to understanding and helping, 1998, 3rd edn 2012; Frameworks for Thinking, 2005; Motivation, Engagement and Educational Performance, 2005; The Sage Handbook of Emotional and Behavioural Difficulties, 2014; The Dyslexia Debate, 2014. *Recreations:* racquetball, table tennis, walking, theatre. *Address:* Collingwood College, Durham University, South Road, Durham DH1 3LT. *E:* joe.elliott@durham.ac.uk.

ELLIOTT, Julie; MP (Lab) Sunderland Central, since 2010; *b* Whitburn, Sunderland, 1963; one *s* three *d*. *Educ:* Seaham Northlea Comprehensive Sch.; Newcastle Poly. (BA Govt and Public Policy). Regl Organiser, Labour Party, 1993–98; Agent, gen. election, Tynemouth, 1997; Regl Officer, Nat. Asthma Campaign, 1998–99; Regl Organiser, GMB, 1999–2010. Shadow Minister for Energy and Climate Change, 2013–15. Member: Eur. Scrutiny Select Cttee, 2010–15; Business, Innovation and Skills Select Cttee, 2011–13. *Address:* House of Commons, SW1A 0AA.

ELLIOTT, Keith; *see* Elliott, J. K.

ELLIOTT, Lawrence Brian; JP; Economics Editor, The Guardian, since 1995; *b* 29 Aug. 1955; *s* of Brian and Peggy Elliott; *m* 1980, Carol Ann Lelliott; two *d*. *Educ:* St Albans Sch.; Fitzwilliam Coll., Cambridge (BA Hist. 1977). Evening Post-Echo, Hemel Hempstead, 1978–83; Economics Correspondent: Press Assoc., 1983–88; The Guardian, 1988–95. Sen. Res. Fellow, Univ. of Herts. Council Mem., ODI. Mem., Scott Trust, 2001–11. JP Central Herts, 1992. *Publications:* with Dan Atkinson: The Age of Insecurity, 1998; Fantasy Island, 2007; The Gods that Failed, 2008; Going South, 2012; (ed jtly) Crisis and Recovery, 2010. *Recreations:* soccer, golf, music, cooking, walking. *Address:* The Guardian, Kings Place, 90 York Way, N1 9AG. *E:* larry.elliott@guardian.co.uk.

ELLIOTT, Margaret, CBE 1999; solicitor in private practice, since 1976; *b* 20 March 1951; *d* of Malachy and Kathleen Trainor; *m* 1973, Acheson Elliott; two *s* (twins) one *d*. *Educ:* Our Lady's Grammar Sch., Newry; Queen's Univ., Belfast (LLB Hons). Pres., Law Soc. of NI, 1989–90; Chm., Legal Aid NI, 1990–91. Non-executive Director: Ulsterbus/Citybus, 1990–95; Northern Bank Ltd, 1992–2005; National Irish Bank, 2001–05; Oaklee Housing Assoc. Ltd, 2009–; Irish Times Ltd, 2012–. Fair Employment Comr, 1993–96; Civil Service Comr, 1995–2006. Chm., Bd of Trustees, Nat. Mus and Galls NI, 1998–2008. Gov., Irish Times Trust, 2008–. Mem., Disciplinary Tribunal, ICAI, 2008–. Hon. LLD, 2002. *Recreations:* reading, cooking, travelling. *Address:* c/o The Elliott-Trainor Partnership, 3 Downshire Road, Newry, Co. Down BT34 1ED. *T:* (028) 3026 8116, *Fax:* (028) 3026 9208. *E:* margaret.elliott@etpsolicitors.com.

ELLIOTT, Margaret Anne; *see* O'Brien, M. A.

ELLIOTT, Prof. Marianne, OBE 2000; DPhil; FBA 2002; Andrew Geddes and John Rankin Professor of Modern History, 1993–2009, Director, Institute of Irish Studies, 1997–2014, and Blair Chair of Irish Studies, 2008–14, University of Liverpool; *b* 25 May 1948; *d* of Terry Burns and Sheila Burns (*née* O'Neill); *m* 1975, Trevor Elliott; one *s*. *Educ:* Queen's University, Belfast (BA Hons History); Lady Margaret Hall, Oxford (DPhil 1975). Lectr II, W London Inst. of Higher Educn, 1975–77; Univ. Res. Fellow, 1977–79, Temp. Lectr, 1981–82, UC, Swansea; Univ. Res. Fellow, 1984–87, Hon. Fellow, 1987–93, Dept of History, Univ. of Liverpool; Simon Sen. Res. Fellow, Univ. of Manchester, 1988–89; Lectr in History, Birkbeck Coll., Univ. of London, 1991–93. Visiting Professor: Iowa State Univ., 1983; Univ. of S Carolina, 1984. Part-time Tutor: Balliol Coll., Oxford, 1974–75; Westminster Tutors, 1974–75; Dept of History and WEA/Dept of Educn, Univ. of Reading, 1974–75; Course Tutor, Open Univ., 1979–85; Tutor, Univ. of Warwick, 1980–81. Ford Lectr, Oxford, 2005. Mem., 1995–98, Chm., 1998, AHRB res. panel (hist. and archaeol.); Mem., Res. Cttee, 2002–05, Council, 2006–09, British Acad. Mem., Opsahl Commn on NI, 1992–93. *Publications:* Partners in Revolution: the United Irishmen and France, 1982; Watchmen in Sion: the Protestant idea of Liberty, 1985; (trans.) The People's Armies, 1987; Wolfe Tone: prophet of Irish independence, 1989; (jtly) A Citizens' Inquiry: the report of the Opsahl Commission on Northern Ireland, 1993; The Catholics of Ulster: a history, 2000; (ed) The Long Road to Peace in Northern Ireland, 2002; Robert Emmet: the making of a legend, 2003; When God Took Sides: religion and identity in Ireland - unfinished history, 2009; contribs to books and learned jls. *Recreations:* running, cycling, reading. *Address:* Institute of Irish Studies, University of Liverpool, Liverpool L69 7WY. *T:* (0151) 794 3831, *Fax:* (0151) 794 3836. *E:* melliott@liv.ac.uk.

ELLIOTT, Marianne; Associate Director, National Theatre, since 2006; *b* London, 27 Dec. 1966; *d* of Michael Elliott and Rosalind Elliott (*née* Knight); *m* 2000, Nick Sidi; one *d*. *Educ:* St Hilary's Sch., Alderley Edge; Stockport Grammar Sch.; Hull Univ. (BA). An Artistic Dir, Manchester Royal Exchange Th.; Associate Dir, Royal Court Th. Productions include: Much Ado About Nothing, RSC, 2006; Sweet Bird of Youth, Old Vic, 2013; National Theatre: Pillars of the Community, 2005 (Evening Standard Award); Therese Raquin, 2006; St Joan, 2007 (Best Revival, Olivier Awards; South Bank Show Award); Warhorse, 2007, transf. NY, 2011 (Outer Critics' Circle Award for Outstanding Dir, 2011; Tony Award for Best Dir, 2011); All's Well That Ends Well, 2009; Women Beware Women, 2010; Season's Greetings, 2010; The Curious Incident of the Dog in the Night-Time, 2012 (Olivier Award for Best Dir, 2013), transf. NY, 2014 (Tony Award for Best Dir, 2015); Port, 2013; The Light Princess, 2013; Rules for Living, 2015. *Address:* National Theatre, Upper Ground, South Bank, SE1 9PX. *T:* (020) 7452 3347.

ELLIOTT, Mark, CMG 1988; HM Diplomatic Service, retired; *b* 16 May 1939; *s* of William Rowcliffe Elliott, CB, and Karin Tess Elliott (*née* Classen); *m* 1964, Julian Richardson; two *s*. *Educ:* Eton Coll. (King's Scholar); New Coll., Oxford. HM Forces (Intell. Corps), 1957–59. FO, 1963; Tokyo, 1965; FCO, 1970; Private Sec. to Perm. Under-Sec. of State, 1973–74; First Sec. and Head of Chancery, Nicosia, 1975–77; Counsellor, 1977–81, Head of Chancery, 1978–81, Tokyo; Hd of Far Eastern Dept, FCO, 1981–85; Under-Sec. on secondment to N Ireland Office, 1985–88; Ambassador to Israel, 1988–92; Dep. Under-Sec. of State, FCO, 1992–94; Ambassador to Norway, 1994–98. Grand Cross, Order of Merit (Norway), 1994. *Recreations:* fell walking, nature, music, photography.

ELLIOTT, Prof. Martin John, MD; FRCS; Professor of Cardiothoracic Surgery, University College London, since 2004; Consultant Paediatric Cardiothoracic Surgeon, since 1985, and Medical Director, since 2010, Great Ormond Street Hospital for Children; Director, National Service for Severe Tracheal Disease in Children, since 2001; *b* Sheffield, 8 March 1951; *s* of John Elliott and Muriel Elliott; *m* 1977, Lesley Rickard; one *s* (and one *s* decd). *Educ:* King Edward VII Grammar Sch., Sheffield; Univ. of Newcastle upon Tyne (MB BS 1973; MD 1983). FRCS 1978. Postgrad. surgical trng, Newcastle and Southampton, 1973–78; First Asst in Cardiothoracic Surgery, Univ. of Newcastle Upon Tyne, 1978–84; Sen. Registrar in Paediatric Cardiothoracic Surgery, 1984–85, Chm., Cardiorespiratory Services, 2006–10, Great Ormond Street Hosp. for Children. Dir, Eur. Congenital Heart Defects Database, 1990–99. Gresham Prof. of Physic, Gresham Coll., London, 2014–. Visiting Professor: Warsaw; Univ. of Calif at San Francisco; Vanderbilt Univ.; Medical Univ. of S Carolina. Founder Mem., Eur. Congenital Heart Surgeons Assoc., 1991; Pres. Internat. Soc. for Nomenclature in Congenital Heart Disease, 2000–12; active in Eur. and US professional socs; over 350 invited lectures. *Publications:* (with R. A. Jonas) Cardiopulmonary Bypass in Neonates, Infants and Young Children, 1994; (with M. Kanani) Applied Surgical Vivas, 2004; 38 chapters in books; over 280 articles in jls relating to pathophysiol. of cardiopulmonary bypass, outcomes of surgery for congenital heart defects, teamwork and tracheal problems in children. *Recreations:* reading, cycling, cinema, music, London Library. *Address:* Medical Director's Office, Great Ormond Street Hospital for Children NHS Trust, WC1N 3JH. *T:* (020) 7405 9200. *E:* martin.elliott@gosh.nhs.uk, martin.elliott@icloud.com.

ELLIOTT, Rt Rev. (Matthew) George (Holden); a Suffragan Bishop of Toronto (Area Bishop of York-Simcoe), 2001–13; *b* 17 Feb. 1949; *s* of George and Phyllis Elliott; *m* 1977, Linda Ann Martinez; one *s* one *d*. *Educ:* Univ. of Toronto (BA 1972); George Brown Coll. (Dip. Food Services Mgt 1973); Wycliffe Coll. (MDiv 1979; Hon. DD 2002). Asst Curate, St Thomas à Becket, Toronto, 1979–80; Incumbent: Parish of Minden, 1981–88; All Saints', King City, 1989–2001. Regional Dean: Victoria/Haliburton, 1985–88; Holland, 1993–2000. Director: Toronto Parish Trng Prog., 1988–91; Wycliffe Coll. Internship Prog., 1992–94. Member: Communications Inf. Resources Cttee, Nat. Church, 2007–13; Inf. and Communications Standards Develt Cttee, Ont Disability Council, 2007–09. Pres. Bd, Anglican Jl, 2008–13. *Recreations:* golf, cooking, gardening, reading. *Address:* 28 Charles Street, King City, ON L7B 1J7, Canada. *T:* (905) 8334988. *E:* bishopgeorge@sympatico.ca.

ELLIOTT, Matthew Jim; Co-Founder, TaxPayers' Alliance, 2004; Founder, Big Brother Watch, 2009; Founder and Chief Executive, Business for Britain, since 2013; *b* Leeds, 12 Feb. 1978; *s* of Geoffrey Edward Elliott and Kathryn Georgiana Elliott (*née* Collins); *m* 1st, 2005, Florence Liselotte Sarah Heath (marr. diss. 2012); 2nd, 2014, Sarah Brunson Smith. *Educ:* Leeds Grammar Sch.; London Sch. of Econs and Pol Sci. (BSc Govt). Press Officer, Eur. Foundn, 2000–01; Pol Sec. to Timothy Kirkhope, MEP, 2001–04; Chief Executive: TaxPayers' Alliance, 2004–12; Big Brother Watch, 2009–12. Campaign Dir, NO to AV, 2010–11. Non-exec. Dir, Wess Digital Ltd, 2013–14. Trustee, Social Affairs Unit, 2014–. MInstD. FRSA 2008. *Publications:* (jtly) The Bumper Book of Government Waste, 2006; (jtly) The Bumper Book of Government Waste 2008, 2007; (jtly) The Great European Rip-Off, 2009; (jtly) Fleeced!, 2009. *Recreations:* playing pool and the organ, visiting America. *Address:* 55 Tufton Street, SW1P 3QL. *T:* (020) 7340 6023. *E:* matthew@businessforbritain.org. *Clubs:* Arts; Cheshire Pitt (Hon. Mem.).

ELLIOTT, Michael Alwyn; actor, writer, producer and director; *b* 15 July 1936; *s* of W. A. Edwards and Mrs J. B. Elliott (assumed stepfather's name); *m* Caroline Margaret McCarthy (MBE 2011); two *s* one *d*. *Educ:* Raynes Park Grammar School. AMP INSEAD, 1976. Journalist, 1955–59; Public Relations, Avon Rubber Co. Ltd, 1959–63; Marketing, CPC International, 1963–68; Kimberly-Clark Ltd: Product Manager, 1968; Marketing Manager, 1969; Marketing and Development Manager, 1975; General Manager, 1976; Director, 1977; Gen. Administrator, Nat. Theatre, 1979–85 (Associate, 1983–85); Dir of Admin, Denton, Hall, Solicitors, 1985–88; Head, Theatres Div., Bill Kenwright Ltd, 1992–93. Theatre Consultant: Gardner Arts Centre, 1988–99; Thorndike Th., 1992–95; Liverpool Playhouse, 1992–93; Yvonne Arnaud Th., 1994–97. Founder, Bitesize Lunchtime Theatre Co., 2002. Member: Executive Council, SWET, 1980–85; Council, The Actors Charitable Trust, 2003–07. Trustee, Trinity Th. and Arts Centre Ltd, 2009–12. Stage appearances incl: Anagnos in The Miracle Worker, Comedy, then Wyndhams, 1994; Dr Grimwig in Oliver, London Palladium, 1996; Corin in As You Like It, Shakespeare's Globe, 1997; O'Hara in Maddie, Lyric, 1997; television: The Bill, 1999; The Tenth Kingdom, 2000; Dogma, 2000; Baddiel Syndrome, 2001; Tales from the Tower, 2001; My Hero, 2003, 2005; Little Britain, 2004; Big Top, 2009; EastEnders, 2012. Writer and narrator, The Weald at War, portrait of life of Siegfried Sassoon in words, poems, music and song, Finchcocks Muscial Mus. and UK tour, 2014. *Recreations:* golfing, walking, ski-ing. *Address:* The Coach House, 51A Frant Road, Tunbridge Wells, Kent TN2 5LE. *T:* (01892) 530615.

ELLIOTT, Michael Norman; Mayor of Ealing, 2005–06; *b* 3 June 1932; *m* 1979, Julia Perry. *Educ:* Brunel College of Technology. Formerly res. chemist in food industry. Mem., Ealing Borough Council, 1964–86 and 2002–10 (former Leader of Council and Chm., Educn Cttee). MEP (Lab) London W, 1984–99; contested (Lab) London Region, 1999. Formerly: Member: Civil Liberties Parly Cttee (Lab party spokesperson); Parly Cttee of Inquiry into Racism and Xenophobia; Parly Jt Cttees with Poland and with Malta; Substitute Mem., Econ. and Monetary Cttee; Pres., Parly Intergroup for Animal Welfare and Conservation. Chm., Ealing Aircraft Noise Action Gp. Member: CND, 1961–; Friends of the Earth, 1985–. Hon. Fellow, Ealing Coll. of Higher Educn, 1988. Hon. Freeman, London Bor. of Ealing, 2011. *Address:* 4 Fern Dene, Ealing, W13 8AN.

ELLIOTT, Michele Irmiter, OBE 2008; Founder and Director, Kidscape Children's Charity, 1984–2009; *b* 7 Jan. 1946; *d* of James Irmiter and Ivy (*née* Dashwood); *m* 1968, Edward Elliott; two *s*. *Educ:* Univ. of S Florida (MA *summa cum laude* 1967); Univ. of Florida (MA *cum laude* 1969). Educational Psychologist: Booker Washington Sch., Fla, 1969–71; Amer. Sch. in London, 1971–84. Winston Churchill Fellow, 1991. Chairman: Home Office Working Gp on prevention of sexual abuse, 1988; WHO Cttee on prevention of sexual abuse, 1989. Mem., Video Consultative Council, BBFC, 1992–99. Member: Hon. Adv. Bd, NSPCC, 1994–; Nat. Toy Council, 1996–; Bd, Internet Watch Foundn, 2003–08. Mem., Soc. of Authors, 1990–. Hon. PhD Post Univ., Conn, 1993; Hon. DSc Birmingham, 2003. Children and Young People's Champion, Children & Young People Now, 2009. *Publications:* Preventing Child Sexual Assault: a practical guide to talking with children, 1985, 2nd edn 1987 (trans. Norwegian); Kidscape Primary Kit, 1986, 3rd edn 2001; Under Fives Programme, 1987, 4th edn 1999; Keeping Safe, 1988, 2nd edn 1995 (trans. German, French, Chinese, Czech, Norwegian, Polish, Slovenian, Russian); The Willow Street Kids, 1986, 2nd edn 1997; Dealing with Child Abuse, 1989; Teenscape, 1990, 3rd edn 2002; Feeling Happy Feeling Safe, 1991, 2nd edn 1999; Bullying: a practical guide to coping for schools, 1991, 3rd edn 2002 (trans. Spanish 2010); Protecting Children: a training package, 1992; Bullies Meet the Willow Street Kids, 1993, 2nd edn 1997; (ed) Female Sexual Abuse of Children: the ultimate taboo, 1993, 2nd edn 1997; (with J. Kilpatrick) How to Stop Bullying: a Kidscape training guide, 1994, 3rd edn 2002 (trans. Japanese); 501 Ways to be a Good Parent, 1996 (trans. Russian, Estonian, Chinese, Polish, German); 101 Ways to Deal with Bullying: a guide for parents, 1997 (trans. Japanese, Chinese); Bullying: wise guide, 1998; Bully Free, 1999; 601 Ways to be a Good Parent, 1999; Stop Bullying Pocketbook, 2005, 2nd edn 2010; Tackling Bullying: the essential guide, 2011; Bullies, Cyberbullies and Frenemies, 2013 (Children's Literary Gold Award, Children's Literary Classics, USA, 2013); numerous contribs to learned jls. *Recreations:* piano, cycling, walking, dancing, swimming. *Address:* Kidscape, 2 Grosvenor Gardens, SW1W 0DH. *T:* (020) 7730 3300.

ELLIOTT, Nicholas Blethyn; QC 1995; *b* 11 Dec. 1949; *s* of late Col Blethyn William Treharne Elliott, late South Wales Borderers, and of Zara Elliott; *m* 1976, Penelope, (Nemmy), Margaret Longbourne Browne; two *s*. *Educ:* Kelly Coll.; Bristol Univ. (LLB Hons). Called to the Bar, Gray's Inn, 1972, Bencher, 2003. Asst Boundary Comr, 2000–. *Publications:* (ed jtly) Banking Litigation, 1999, 3rd edn 2011; (ed) Byles on Bills of Exchange and Cheques, 28th edn 2007; (contrib.) Money Laundering and Financial Services, 2003. *Recreations:* tennis, cycling, swimming, bridge, rock and roll dancing. *Address:* Old Whistley Farmhouse, Potterne, Devizes, Wilts SN10 5TD.

See also Maj. Gen. C. H. Elliott.

ELLIOTT, Oliver Douglas; British Council Representative in Yugoslavia, 1979–85; *b* 13 Oct. 1925; *y s* of Walter Elliott and Margherita Elliott, Bedford; *m* 1954, Patience Rosalie Joan Orpen; one *s*. *Educ:* Bedford Modern Sch.; Wadham Coll., Oxford (MA); Fitzwilliam House, Cambridge. Served RNVR (Sub-Lt), 1944–47. Colonial Educn Service, Cyprus, 1953–59; joined British Council, 1959; served Lebanon, 1960–63; Dep. Rep., Ghana, 1963; Dir, Commonwealth I Dept, 1966; Dir, Service Conditions Dept, 1970; Dep. Educn Advr, India, 1973; Representative in Nigeria, 1976–79. *Recreation:* golf.

ELLIOTT, Paul; Finance Director, Hanover Foundations, 2007–12; *b* 27 Oct. 1949; *s* of John and Winifred Elliott; *m* 1995, Sharon Amanda Jordan; one *s* one *d*. *Educ:* Clare Coll., Cambridge (Hons Modern Langs). Joined MAFF, 1971; Private Secretary: to Perm. Sec., 1974–75; to Minister, 1975–76; First Sec. (Agriculture), Bonn, 1984–89; Head, Milk Div., 1989–94; Rural White Paper Team, 1994–95; Prin. Finance Officer, MAFF, then DEFRA, 1996–2001; Dir, Rural Economies and Communities Directorate, DEFRA, 2001–03; Strategic Projects Officer, London Bor. of Camden, 2003–04. Clerk, Scriveners' Co., 2007–11. *Recreations:* music, photography, cricket, ICT, travel.

ELLIOTT, Prof. Paul, PhD; FRCP, FFPH, FMedSci; Professor of Epidemiology and Public Health Medicine, since 1995 and Head, Department of Epidemiology & Biostatistics, School of Public Health (formerly Division of Primary Care and Population Health Sciences, Faculty of Medicine), since 1998, Imperial College London; *b* 21 April 1954; *s* of Dr Arnold Elliott, OBE and Esther Elliott; *m* Nina Gay; one *s* two *d*. *Educ:* Brentwood Sch., Essex; Christ's Coll., Cambridge (BA, MA Maths and Med. Scis); UCL (MB BS 1978); LSHTM (MSc 1983; PhD 1991). FFPH (FFPHM 1995); FRCP 1998; FMedSci 2000. Med. Registrar, Edgware Gen. Hosp., Middlesex, 1981–82; Wellcome Res. Fellow, St Mary's Hosp. Med. Sch. and LSHTM, 1982–87; Lectr, 1987–88, Sen. Lectr, 1988–93, Reader, 1993–95, in Epidemiology, LSHTM. Hon. Consultant Physician, Dept of Medicine, Hammersmith Hosp., London, 1990–; Hon. Consultant: in Public Health Medicine, Kensington and Chelsea PCT (formerly Kensington, Chelsea and Westminster HA), 1995–2013; Imperial College Healthcare NHS Trust (formerly St Mary's Hosp. NHS Trust, London), 1998–. Director: UK Small Area Health Stats Unit, 1991–; MRC-PHE (formerly MRC-HPA) Centre for Envmt and Health, 2009–. *Publications:* (ed jtly) Geographical and Environmental Epidemiology: methods for small-area studies, 1992; (ed jtly) Coronary Heart Disease Epidemiology: from aetiology to public health, 1992, 2nd edn 2005; (ed jtly) Spatial Epidemiology: methods and applications, 2000; (ed jtly) Oxford Handbook of Epidemiology for Clinicians, 2012; articles in learned jls on diet and blood pressure, epidemiology, small-area health statistics and methodology. *Recreations:* family, swimming. *Address:* Department of Epidemiology & Biostatistics, School of Public Health, Imperial College London, St Mary's Campus, Norfolk Place, W2 1PG. *T:* (020) 7594 3328, *Fax:* (020) 7594 3456. *E:* p.elliott@imperial.ac.uk.

ELLIOTT, Paul Richard; theatrical producer, director, writer; Managing Director, Paul Elliott Ltd, since 1999; Joint Director, Triumph Entertainment Ltd, since 2000; Managing Director, E&B Productions, 1964–2000; *b* 9 Dec. 1941; *s* of late Lewis Arthur Elliott and Sybil Elliott; *m* 1st, 1971, Jenny Logan (marr. diss. 1986); one *s*; 2nd, 1987, Linda Hayden; one *s* one *d*. *Educ:* Bournemouth Sch. Actor, 1958–63; appeared in Dixon of Dock Green, 1961–62. *London productions* include: When We Are Married, Strand, 1970; The King and I, Adelphi, 1973; Grease, New London, 1973; The Pleasure of His Company, and I Do, I Do, Phoenix, 1974; Hedda Gabler, Aldwych, 1975; Hello Dolly, Theatre Royal, 1979; Run for Your Wife, Criterion, Whitehall, Aldwych, 1983–92; Buddy, Victoria Palace, Strand, 1989–2002; The Pirates of Penzance, Palladium, 1990; Jolson, Victoria Palace, 1996 (Olivier Award, Best Musical, 1996); The Goodbye Girl, Albery, 1997; Kat and the Kings, Vaudeville, 1998 (Olivier Award, Best Musical, 1999); Annie, Victoria Palace, 1998; Stones in His Pockets (Olivier and Evening Standard Awards, Best Comedy), Duke of York's, 2000, transf. NY, 2001; The Tempest, Old Vic, 2003; Thoroughly Modern Millie, Shaftesbury, 2004; The Philadelphia Story, Old Vic, 2005; As You Desire Me, Playhouse, 2006; The Last Confession, Haymarket, 2007; Macbeth, Gielgud, 2007, transf. NY, 2008; Waiting for Godot, Th. Royal, Haymarket, 2010; Private Lives, Vaudeville, 2010; Pygmalion, Garrick, 2011; Blithe Spirit, Apollo, 2011; Rosencrantz and Guildenstern are Dead, The Tempest, Haymarket, 2011; David Suchet in The Last Confession, world tour, 2014; numerous pantomime prodns throughout UK; London *pantomimes* include: Aladdin, Shaftesbury, 1983; Snow White and the Seven Dwarfs, Strand, 1990; Jack and the Beanstalk, Piccadilly, 1991; Babes in the Wood, Sadler's Wells; Snow White and the Seven Dwarfs, Victoria Palace, 2004–05; *New York productions:* The Hollow Crown; Brief Lives; Run for Your Wife, 1989; Buddy, 1990; Private Lives (Tony Award), 2002 and 2011 (also Toronto); touring prodns in UK and overseas incl. USA, Canada, Australia, NZ, Japan, Hong Kong, Zimbabwe, India and Europe; co-producer and writer of play, There's No Place Like a Home, 2006. Dir, SOLT, 1996–. Hon. Fellow,

Bournemouth Univ., 2012. Award for Contribution to Provincial Theatre, Theatre Managers Assoc., 1996. *Recreation:* watching sport! *Address:* 1 Wardour Street, WC1D 6PA. *T:* (020) 7379 4870.

ELLIOTT, Ven. Peter; Archdeacon of Northumberland, 1993–2005; *b* 14 June 1941; *s* of James Reginald and Hilda Elliott; *m* 1967, Evelyn Embleton; one *d*. *Educ:* Queen Elizabeth Grammar Sch., Horncastle; Hertford Coll., Oxford (MA Mod. History); Lincoln Theological Coll. Assistant Curate: All Saints, Gosforth, 1965–68; St Peter, Balkwell, 1968–72; Vicar: St Philip, High Elswick, 1972–80; North Gosforth, 1980–87; Embleton with Rennington and Rock, 1987–93. RD of Alnwick, 1989–93; Hon. Canon, 1990–93, Residentiary Canon, 1993–2005, Newcastle Cathedral. English Heritage: Member: Cathedrals and Churches Adv. Cttee, 1998–2001; Historic Built Envmt Cttee, 2001–03; Places of Worship Panel, 2001–05; Adv. Cttee, 2003–05. *Recreations:* genealogy, travel, railway timetables, food, wine, gardening. *Address:* 56 King Street, Seahouses, Northumberland NE68 7XS. *T:* (01665) 721133.

ELLIOTT, Robert Anthony K.; *see* Keable-Elliott.

ELLIOTT, Prof. Robert Francis, FRSE; Professor of Health Economics (part-time), Health Economics Research Unit, University of Aberdeen, since 2012 (Professor of Economics, since 1990); *b* Thurlow, Suffolk, 15 June 1947; *s* of Francis Percy Elliott and Margaret Elliott (*née* Hunter); *m* 1970, Susan Gutheridge; one *s*. *Educ:* Haverhill Sec. Mod. Sch.; Ruskin Coll., Oxford (Special Dip. Soc. Studies 1970); Balliol Coll., Oxford (BA PPE 1972); Univ. of Leeds (MA Labour Econs 1973). University of Aberdeen: Res. Fellow, 1973–78; Lectr, 1978–82; Sen. Lectr, 1982–89; Dir, Health Econs Res. Unit, 2002–12. Dir, Scottish Doctoral Prog. in Econs, 1989–99; Chm., Rev. of Area Cost Adjustment (Elliott Rev.), 1995–96; Mem., McCrone Cttee of Inq. into Professional Conditions of Service for Teachers, 1999–2000; Ind. Mem., Low Pay Commn, 2007–. Econ. Advr, Police Fedn of England and Wales, 1986–; Consultant to: HM Treasury, 1992–98; OECD, 1992–99; EC, 1994–2005. Pres., Scottish Econ. Soc., 2003–05. Visiting Professor: New York Univ., 1978–80; Stanford Univ., 1981, 1986; Cornell Univ., 1985–86; Paris II, 1995, 1997–99, 2001–02; Indiana Univ. - Purdue Univ. at Indianapolis, 1996; Univ. of Wisconsin, 2001; Università Cattolica, Milan, 2001–05; Univ. of Melbourne, 2011, 2012. FRSE 2001. *Publications:* (ed with J. L. Fallick) Incomes Policy, Inflation and Relative Pay, 1981 (trans. Spanish, 1983); (ed jtly) Incomes Policy, 1981; (jtly) Macmillan Dictionary of Modern Economics, 1981, 4th edn 1992 (trans. 14 langs); (ed with A. E. H. Speight) Unemployment and Labour Market Efficiency: a study of the Aberdeen and Grampian labour markets, 1989; (with J. L. Fallick) Pay in the Public Sector, 1991; Labor Economics: a comparative text, 1991 (trans. Turkish, 1997); (ed jtly) Public Sector Pay Determination in the European Union, 1999; (ed jtly) Advances in Health Economics, 2002; (with K. Bender) Decentralised Pay Setting: a study of collective bargaining reform in the civil service in Australia, Sweden and the UK, 2003; (jtly) Public Sector Remuneration in Scotland, 2012; articles in econs jls. *Recreations:* hillwalking, opera, jazz, all classical music, wine discovery, reading, golf. *Address:* Health Economics Research Unit, University of Aberdeen, Polwarth Building, Foresterhill, Aberdeen AB25 2ZD. *T:* (01224) 437197. *E:* pec016@abdn.ac.uk.

ELLIOTT, Sir Roger (James), Kt 1987; FRS 1976; FInstP; Secretary to the Delegates and Chief Executive of Oxford University Press, 1988–93; Professor of Physics, Oxford University, 1989–96, now Emeritus; Fellow of New College, Oxford, 1974–96, now Emeritus; *b* Chesterfield, 8 Dec. 1928; *s* of James Elliott and Gladys Elliott (*née* Hill); *m* 1952, Olga Lucy Atkinson (*d* 2007); one *s* two *d*. *Educ:* Swanwick Hall Sch., Derbyshire; New Coll., Oxford (MA, DPhil; Hon. Fellow, 1999). FInstP (FPhysS 1960). Research Fellow, Univ. of California, Berkeley, 1952–53; Research Fellow, UKAEA, Harwell, 1953–55; Lectr, Reading Univ., 1955–57; Fellow of St John's College, Oxford, 1957–74, Hon. Fellow, 1988; University Reader, Oxford, 1964–74; Wykeham Prof. of Physics, 1974–89; Senior Proctor, 1969; Delegate, Oxford Univ. Press, 1971–88. Chm., Computer Bd for Univs and Research Councils, 1983–87; Vice-Chm., Parly Office of Sci. and Technol., 1990–93; Member: Adv. Bd for Res. Councils, 1987–90; (part-time) UKAEA, 1988–94; British Council Bd, 1990–98. Non-exec. Dir, Blackwell Ltd, 1996–2002 (Chm., 1999–2002); Chm., ICSU Press, 1997–2002. Chm., Disability Information Trust, 1998–2002. Physical Sec. and Vice-Pres., Royal Soc., 1984–88; Treas., ICSU, 2002–08. Pres., Publishers Assoc., 1993–94 (Treas., 1990–92). Visiting Prof., Univ. of California, Berkeley, 1961; Miller Vis. Prof., Univ. of Illinois, Urbana, 1966; Vis. Dist. Prof., Florida State Univ., 1981; Vis. Dist. Prof., Michigan State Univ., 1997–2000. Mem., Mexican Acad. of Scis, 2003; MAE 2008. Hon. DSc: Paris, 1983; Bath, 1991; Essex, 1993. Maxwell Medal, 1968, Guthrie Medal, 1990, Inst. of Physics. *Publications:* Magnetic Properties of Rare Earth Metals, 1973; Solid State Physics and its Applications (with A. F. Gibson), 1973; papers in Proc. Royal Soc., Jl Phys., Phys. Rev., etc. *Address:* 11 Crick Road, Oxford OX2 6QL. *T:* (01865) 273997. *Club:* Athenæum.

See also R. C. Wilkin.

ELLIOTT, Thomas; *see* Elliott, C. T.

ELLIOTT, Thomas; MP (UU) Fermanagh and South Tyrone, since 2015; *b* 11 Dec. 1963; *s* of late John Elliott and of Noreen Elliott; *m* 1989, Anne; one *s* one *d*. *Educ:* Ballinamallard Primary Sch.; Duke of Westminster High Sch., Ballinamallard; Enniskillen Coll. of Agric. Self-employed farmer, 1981–. Mem. (pt-time), UDR/Royal Irish Regt, 1982–99. Mem. (UU), Fermanagh DC, 2001–10. Mem. (UU) Fermanagh and S Tyrone, NI Assembly, 2003–June 2015. Leader, Ulster Unionist Party, 2010–12. *Recreations:* community activity, sport, church. *Address:* 1 Regal Pass, Enniskillen, Co. Fermanagh BT74 7NT. *T:* (028) 6632 2028, *Fax:* (028) 6634 2846; House of Commons, SW1A 0AA. *E:* t.elliott6@btopenworld.com.

ELLIOTT, Prof. Timothy John, PhD; FMedSci; FRSB; Professor of Experimental Oncology, University of Southampton, since 2000; *b* Sheffield, 5 July 1961; *s* of Colin and Myra Elliott; *m* 1996, Prof. Anneke Lucassen; two *d*. *Educ:* Balliol Coll., Oxford (BA Biochem.); Univ. of Southampton (PhD Immunol.). Res. Associate, MIT, 1986–89; Lectr, Balliol Coll., Oxford, 1989–93; Sen. Res. Fellow, Inst. for Molecular Medicine, Univ. of Oxford, 1993–99; Res. Dean, Faculty of Medicine, Univ. of Southampton, 2006–15. FRSB (FSB 2012); FMedSci 2014. *Publications:* contrib. articles to learned jls incl. Nature, Cell, Science, Immunity, Proc. NAS. *Recreations:* cooking, cycling, hillwalking, thinking at the interface between art and science, contemporary art. *Address:* Somers Cancer Research Building, University Hospital Southampton, Mailpoint 824, Tremona Road, Southampton SO16 6YD. *T:* (023) 8120 6196, *Fax:* (023) 8120 6186. *E:* tje@soton.ac.uk.

ELLIOTT, Timothy Stanley; QC 1992; *b* 2 April 1950; *s* of John Edwin Elliott and Annie Elizabeth Stanley (*née* Lowe); *m* 1973, Katharine Barbara Lawrance (*d* 2008); one *s* one *d*. *Educ:* Marlborough Coll.; Trinity Coll., Oxford (Exhibnr, MA Lit. Hum. 1973). Called to the Bar, Middle Temple, 1975. *Address:* 15 Essex Street, WC2R 3AA. *T:* (020) 7544 2600.

ELLIOTT, Tobin David, (Toby), OBE 2007; Vice Lord-Lieutenant of Gwent, since 2012; *b* Farnham, 22 April 1944; *s* of James Newenham Elliott, RN and Joanne Elliott; *m* 1971, Imogen Margaret Pugh; two *s* one *d*. *Educ:* Cranbrook Sch.; BRNC Dartmouth. Served RN, 1963–97; Commanding Officer: HMS Otter, 1974–76; HMS Resolution, 1980–82; HMS Trafalgar, 1986–88; Captain, 10th Submarine Sqdn, 1989–91; CO HMS Brilliant and Captain, 2nd Frigate Sqdn, 1991–93; Chief Exec., Ex-Services Mental Welfare Soc. (Combat Stress), 1999–2010. Dir, Highland Power Ltd, 2012–. Trustee, Headley Court Trust, 2005–. President: Monmouth Br., RNA; Welsh Br., Submariners Assoc.; Monmouth Br., RBL; Ross and Monmouth Sea Cadet Unit. Younger Brother, Trinity House, 1997. High Sheriff 2005, DL 2009, Gwent. *Recreations:* country pursuits, gardening, family and friends. *Address:* Cwm Cae, Maypole, Monmouth, Gwent NP25 5QH. *T:* (01600) 713558. *E:* toby.elliott@btopenworld.com.

ELLIOTT, Trudi Margaret, CBE 2010; Chief Executive, Royal Town Planning Institute, since 2011; *b* Croydon, 19 Sept. 1957; *d* of Patrick James Gerald Job and Sheila Mary Job; *m* 1986, Prof. Geoffrey Clifford Elliott; two *s*. *Educ:* Crown Woods Sch., London; University Coll. of Wales, Aberystwyth (BSc Econ (Law and Econs) 1980); Coll. of Law, Chester. Admitted as solicitor, 1983; Solicitor and Partner, Lickfold Wiley and Powles, Solicitors, London, 1981–89; youth worker (pt-time), ILEA, 1983–85; Interview Panellist and Local Conciliator (pt-time), Solicitors Complaints Bureau, 1990–92; Planning Solicitor, Wyre Forest DC, 1992–93; Solicitor to Council, 1993–95, Chief Exec., 1995–2003, Bridgnorth DC; Dir, Local Govt Practice (W Midlands), ODPM, 2003–04; Lead Official, Walsall MBC, 2003–04; Chief Exec., W Midlands Regl Assembly and W Midlands Local Govt Authy, 2004–06; Dir, Govt Office for W Midlands, 2006–11. Internat. Observer, first elections in Czech Republic, 2002. Chair: Bridgnorth Community Safety Partnership, 1998–2000; W Midlands Regl Bd, 2006–10; Member, Board: Shropshire Regeneration Partnership, 1998–2000; W Midlands Regl Skills Partnership, 2004–06; Business in the Community (W Midlands), 2007–09; Birmingham and Solihull Employment and Skills, 2007–09; Member: Birmingham Strategic Partnership, 2007–10; W Midlands Econ. Task Force, 2009–10. Chair: Shropshire Active Sports Partnership, 1999–2003; W Midlands 2012 Olympics Steering Gp, 2004–06; Vice Chair, 2003–08, Actg Chair, 2004–05, W Midlands Regl Sports Bd, Sport England. Mem., editl team, Jl Planning Theory & Practice, 2012–. Mem. Council, Univ. of Warwick, 2008–. Gov., Shrewsbury Coll. of Arts and Technol., 1995–2000. *Recreations:* tennis, The Arsenal. *Address:* Royal Town Planning Institute, 41 Botolph Lane, EC3R 8DL. *T:* (020) 7929 9494, *Fax:* (020) 7929 9490. *E:* trudi.elliott@rtpi.org.uk. *Club:* Bewdley Tennis.

ELLIOTT, William, OBE 2003; Director, Cormont Ltd, since 2011; *b* Boston, Lincs, 16 March 1968; *s* of Roger Elliott and Rebecca Short (*née* Fernandez); *m* 2003, Daria Chrin; one *s* three *d*. *Educ:* Alderman Peel High Sch., Wells, Norfolk; Wymondham Coll.; Univ. of York (BA Eng. and Related Lit.). Lectr in English, Lodz and Tbilisi, 1991–92; entered HM Diplomatic Service, 1993; Second Sec., Warsaw, 1995–98; First Secretary: FCO, 1998; Kabul, 2001–02; Dep. Hd of Mission, Tallinn, 2002–06; Consul-Gen., St Petersburg, 2006–10. *Recreations:* history and literature of Europe and S Asia, cricket, food and drink. *Club:* English (St Petersburg).

ELLIOTT, (William) Brent, PhD; Historian, Royal Horticultural Society, since 2007; *b* 10 Jan. 1952; *s* of William Alfred and Annie Irene Elliott; *m* 1981, Dr Frances Margaret Clegg; one *s*. *Educ:* Univ. of BC (BA 1973; MA 1974); King's Coll., London (PhD 1978). Asst Librarian, 1977–82, Librarian and Archivist, 1982–2007, RHS. Ed., Garden Hist. (Jl Garden Hist. Soc.), 1984–88. English Heritage: Member: Gardens Cttee, 1985–89; Historic Landscapes Panel, 1989–93; Historic Parks and Gardens Adv. Cttee, 1994–2011. Member: Council, Garden Hist. Soc., 1979–89; Main Cttee, Victorian Soc., 1983–93 (Chm., Cemeteries Sub-cttee, 1980–89). Ed., Occasional Papers from RHS Lindley Liby, 2009–. FLS 1995. Veitch Meml Medal, RHS, 1994. Greensfelder Medal, Missouri Botanical Garden, 2008. *Publications:* Victorian Gardens, 1986; (with A. Clayton-Payne) Victorian Flower Gardens, 1988; (with C. Brooks) Mortal Remains, 1989; Waddesdon Manor: the gardens, 1994; Treasures of the Royal Horticultural Society, 1994; The Country House Garden, 1995; Flora: an illustrated history of the garden flower, 2001; The Royal Horticultural Society 1804–2004: a history, 2004; (with V. Buchan) Garden People, 2007; (vol. ed.) Flora: the Erbario Miniato and other drawings, in The Paper Museum of Cassiano dal Pozzo, 2007; RHS Chelsea Flower Show, 2013; Federico Cesi's Botanical Manuscripts, 2015. *Recreations:* visiting parks, gardens and cemeteries, gardening, reading. *Address:* c/o Royal Horticultural Society, 80 Vincent Square, SW1P 2PE. *T:* (020) 7821 3050.

ELLIS, family name of **Baron Seaford**.

ELLIS, Dr Adrian Foss, CB 2004; FREng; Director of Field Operations, Health and Safety Executive, 1996–2003; *b* 15 Feb. 1944; *s* of Henry James Ellis and Marjorie Foss Ellis (*née* Smith); *m* 1st, 1968, Lesley Maxted Smith (*d* 1970); 2nd, 1973, Hilary Jean Miles; two *d* one *s*. *Educ:* Dean Close Sch., Cheltenham; Univ. of London (1st cl. Hons Chem. Eng.); Loughborough Univ. of Technology (PhD). FIChemE 1977; FInstE 1977; FREng (FEng 1995). Student Apprentice, Richard Thomas & Baldwins, 1962–66; British Steel Corp., 1966–71; DoE (Alkali and Clean Air), 1971–83; Health and Safety Executive: Major Hazards Assessment Unit, 1983–86; Dep. Chief Inspector (Chemicals), 1986; Regl Dir, 1990; Dir of Technology and Dir of Hazardous Installations Policy, 1990; Dir of Technology and Health Scis Div., 1991–96. ILO Consultant on major hazards control in India, Pakistan, Thailand, Indonesia. Vis. Prof., Dept of Applied Energy, Cranfield Univ. (formerly Inst. of Technology), 1992–99. Pres., Internat. Assoc. of Labour Inspection, 2002–05 (Vice-Pres. and Sec. Gen., 1999–2002). Mem. Council, IChemE, 1993–97. *Publications:* papers on risk assessment and major hazards control. *Recreations:* bridge, Swindon Town FC, exploring car boot sales. *Address:* 1 Wootton Oast, Garlinge Green Road, Petham, Canterbury, Kent CT4 5RJ. *T:* (01227) 700137. *Club:* Kent County Cricket.

ELLIS, Alexander Wykeham, CMG 2013; HM Diplomatic Service; Ambassador to Brazil, since 2013; *b* London, 5 June 1967; *s* of Roger Wykeham Ellis, *qv*; *m* 1996, Teresa Adegas; one *s*. *Educ:* Dragon Sch., Oxford; Winchester Coll.; Magdalene Coll., Cambridge (BA Hons Mod. Hist. 1989). Teacher, St Edward's Sch., Oxford, 1989–90; FCO, 1990–92; Third, then Second Sec., Lisbon, 1992–96; First Sec. (Econ.), UK Repn to EU, Brussels, 1996–2001; FCO, 2001–03; Counsellor, EU, Madrid, 2003–05; Advr to Pres. of EC, 2005–07; Ambassador to Portugal, 2007–10; Dir of Strategy, FCO, 2011–13. *Recreations:* most ball games, music, theatre, history. *Address:* c/o Foreign and Commonwealth Office, King Charles Street, SW1A 2AH. *Clubs:* MCC; Estoril; Denham Golf.

ELLIS, Andrew Steven, OBE 1984; international consultant on elections, constitutions, democracy building and governance issues, since 1989; *b* 19 May 1952; *s* of late Peter Vernon Ellis and Kathleen Dawe; *m* 1st, 1975, Patricia Ann Stevens (marr. diss. 1987); 2nd, 1990, Helen Prudence Drummond. *Educ:* Trinity Coll., Cambridge (BA Mathematics); Univ. of Newcastle upon Tyne (MSc Statistics); Newcastle upon Tyne Polytechnic (BA Law). Proprietor, Andrew Ellis (Printing and Duplicating), Newcastle upon Tyne, 1973–81; freelance Election Agent/Organizer, 1981–84; Sec.-Gen., Liberal Party, 1985–88; Chief Exec., Social and Liberal Democrats, 1988–89; freelance political consultant, 1989–93; Dir, GJW Hldgs Ltd, 1993–99; Associate Dir, GJW, subseq. GJW-BSMG Worldwide, then GJW Europe-Weber Shandwick Worldwide, 1999–2002; International Institute for Democracy and Electoral Assistance: Head of Electoral Progs, 2003–06; Dir of Ops, 2006–09; Asia and Pacific Dir, 2009–14. Consultant Nat. Agent, Welsh Liberal Party, 1984–88. Contested (L): Newcastle upon Tyne Central, Oct. 1974, Nov. 1976, 1979; Boothferry, 1983; Leader, Liberal Gp, Tyne & Wear CC, 1977–81; Vice-Chm., Liberal Party, 1980–86. Tech. Advr to Chm., Palestine Central Election Commn, 1994–96; Co-ordinator, OSCE Observation Mission for Registration of Voters, Bosnia and Hercegovina, 1997; designer of Eur. Commn electoral assistance to Cambodia, 1997–98; Sen. Advr on constitutional, electoral and decentralisation issues, Nat. Democratic Inst., Indonesia, 1998–2003. *Publications:* Algebraic Structure (with Terence Treeby), 1971; Let Every Englishman's Home Be His Castle, 1978; (contrib.) Indonesia Matters, 2003; (contrib.) International Handbook of Electoral Systems, 2004; (jtly) Electoral System Design: the New International IDEA Handbook, 2006; (jtly)

Electoral Management Design, 2006; (jtly) Voting Abroad, 2007; (jtly) Direct Democracy, 2008; (jtly) Electoral Justice, 2010; (jtly) The Integrity of Elections: the role of regional organizations, 2012; Citizen-led Assessment of Democracy: local and regional contexts in Pakistan, 2015. *Recreation:* travel. *Address:* 28 Kimberley Park Road, Falmouth, Cornwall TR11 2DB. *Club:* National Liberal.

ELLIS, Arthur John, CBE 1986; Chairman, Fyffes Group Ltd, 1984–2008 (Chief Executive Officer, 1969–95); *b* 22 Aug. 1932; *s* of Arthur Ellis and Freda Jane Ellis; *m* 1956, Rita Patricia Blake; two *s* one *d*. *Educ:* Chingford Jun. High Sch.; South West Essex Technical Coll. FCCA; FCMA; FCIS; MBCS. Joined Fyffes Gp Ltd, Finance and Admin Dept, 1954; Chief Financial Officer, 1965; Financial Dir, 1967; Dir, Fyffes plc, 1991–2001. Chm., Nat. Seed Develt Organisation Ltd, 1982–87. Chm., Intervention Bd for Agricl Produce, later Intervention Bd Exec. Agency, 1986–95. *Recreations:* golf, reading, gardening. *Club:* Farmers.

ELLIS, Bryan James; Under-Secretary, Department of Health and Social Security, later Department of Social Security, 1977–93; *b* 11 June 1934; *s* of late Frank and Renée Ellis; *m* 1960, Barbara Muriel Whiteley; one *s* one *d*. *Educ:* Merchant Taylors' Sch.; St John's Coll., Oxford (BA Lit.Hum. 1957; MA 1960); Open Univ. (BA Hist. 1998). Sec., Oxford Union Soc., 1956. Joined Min. of Pensions and National Insurance as Asst Principal, 1958; Principal, 1963; Asst Sec., DHSS, 1971; served in CSSB as Chm., 1986, and in OPCS as Dep. Dir, 1987–90. Chm., Assoc. of First Div. Civil Servants, 1983–85. Chm., Trustees of Leopardstown Park Hosp., Dublin, 1979–84. *Publications:* Pensions in Britain 1955–75, 1989; Walton Past, 2002. *Address:* 8 The Chestnuts, Walton-on-Thames KT12 1EE.

ELLIS, David Charles; Chief Executive, National Star College, since 2010; *b* 29 Dec. 1960; *s* of Oswald David Ellis and Joyce Mary Ellis; *m* 1990, Yvonne (*née* Pauline); two *s*. *Educ:* Exeter Univ. (BSc Hons Physics). Overseas aid worker, Southern Sudan, 1984–87; with various UK disability charities, 1987–92; Regl Dir, British Red Cross, 1992–98; Dir of Services, Guide Dogs for the Blind, 1998–2001; Chief Exec., Cancer and Leukaemia in Childhood, then CLIC Sargent, 2001–05; Dir of Business Improvement, National Trust, 2006–10. *Recreations:* photography, gardening, reading. *Address:* National Star College, Ullenwood, Cheltenham GL53 9QU. *T:* (01242) 527631.

ELLIS, His Honour David Raymond; a Circuit Judge, 1995–2014; *b* 4 Sept. 1946; *s* of Raymond Ellis and Ethel Ellis (*née* Gordon); *m* 1974, Cathleen Margaret Hawe; one *s* one *d*. *Educ:* St Edward's Sch., Oxford; Christ Church, Oxford (MA Jurisprudence). Called to the Bar, Inner Temple, 1970; barrister, 1970–95; a Recorder, 1991–95. Chm., Lord Chancellor's SE London Adv. Cttee, 2000–05. *Recreations:* travel, theatre, boating, the garden. *Club:* Leander (Henley).

ELLIS, Diana; QC 2001; a Recorder, since 1998; *d* of Evan Henry Ellis and Irene Sarah Jeanette Ellis (*née* Behrens); *m* 2001, Geoffrey Keith Watts. *Educ:* London Sch. of Econs (Dip. Social Admin); LLB Hons London. Teacher, Italia Conti Stage Sch., 1971–74; called to the Bar, Inner Temple, 1978; in practice as barrister, SE Circuit, 1978–, specialising in criminal and internat. law and human rights. *Recreations:* reading, theatre, walking and relaxing in Italy. *Address:* 25 Bedford Row, WC1R 4HD.

ELLIS, Dame Diana (Margaret), DBE 2013 (CBE 2004); Chairman, British Rowing (formerly Amateur Rowing Association Ltd), 1989–2013, now Hon. President; *b* 11 April 1938; *d* of Robert and Mabel Helen Hall; *m* 1966, John David Ellis; one *d*. *Educ:* Guildford Coll. of Technol. MRSPH (MRSH 1994). Accounts manager, 1958–68; Dist Manager, Surrey CC, 1987–97. Steward, Henley Royal Regatta, 1997– (1st Lady Steward); Mem. Exec. Bd, British Olympic Assoc., 1997–2013 (Life Vice Pres., 2013); Director: Confedn of British Sport, 1999–2014; CCPR 2000–13 (Dep. Chm., 2005–09); Sport Resolutions Panel (formerly Sports Dispute Resolution Panel), 2001–; Skills Active, 2004–07; Vice Pres., Sport and Recreation Alliance, 2013–. Trustee: British Olympic Med. Trust, 2000–08; River and Rowing Mus., 2006–15; British Olympic Foundn, 2013–. FRSA. *Recreation:* rowing. *Clubs:* Leander (Henley), Twickenham Rowing.

ELLIS, (Dorothy) June; Headmistress, The Mount School, York, 1977–86; Clerk to Central Committee, Quaker Social Responsibility and Education, 1987–90; *b* 30 May 1926; *d* of Robert Edwin and Dora Ellis. *Educ:* La Sagesse, Newcastle upon Tyne; BSc Pure Science, Durham; DipEd Newcastle upon Tyne. Assistant Mistress: Darlington High Sch., 1947–49; Rutherford High Sch., 1949–50; La Sagesse High Sch., 1950–53; Housemistress, 1953–61, Sen. Mistress, 1961–64, St Monica's Sch.; Dep. Head, Sibford Sch., 1964–77. Clerk, 1986–90, Mem., 1990–98, Swerford Parish Council; Mem., Milcombe PCC, 1999–2006, 2008–. Mem. Cttee, Bray d'Oyley Housing Assoc., 1993–96. Mem. Council, Woodbrooke Coll., 1987–93; Governor: Ellerslie Sch., Malvern, 1987–92; Friends' Sch., Saffron Walden, 1990–93; St Mary's Primary Sch., Bloxham, 2000–04. *Recreations:* gardening, home-making.

ELLIS, Sir Doug; *see* Ellis, Sir H. D.

ELLIS, Eileen Mary, RDI 1984; freelance woven textile designer, retired; *b* 1 March 1933; *m* 1954, Julian Ellis; one *s* two *d*. *Educ:* Leicester, Central and Royal Colleges of Art. Des RCA 1957; FCSD (FSIAD 1976). Designer of contract and decorative woven furnishing fabrics, carpets and woven wall coverings; designed for Ascher & Co., 1957–59; Partner, Orbit Design Group, 1960–73; formed Weaveplan, to provide design and consultancy services, 1973–2005. Lecturer: Hornsey Coll. of Art/Middx Polytechnic, 1965–74; RCA, 1974–82. Director: Jamasque Ltd, 1982–96; Curragh Tintawn Carpets Ltd, 1987–95. Hon. Pres., Textile Soc., 2003–08. Textile Inst. Design Medal, 1985; Silver Medal, Weavers' Co., 2002. *Recreations:* country life, bird ringing for British Trust for Ornithology. *Address:* Weaveplan, The Granary Studio, Holbeam Road, Stalisfield, Faversham, Kent ME13 0HS. *T:* (01795) 890602.

ELLIS, Prof. George Francis Rayner, PhD; FRS 2007; FRSSAf; Professor of Applied Mathematics, University of Cape Town, 1973–87 and 1989–2005, now Emeritus; President, Royal Society of South Africa, 1992–96; *b* 11 Aug. 1939; *s* of George Rayner Ellis and Gwendoline Hilda Ellis (*née* MacRobert); *m* 1st, 1963, Jane Mary Sue Parkes; one *s* one *d*; 2nd, 1978, Mary MacDonald Wheeldon (*d* 2008); 3rd, 2009, Carole Bloch. *Educ:* Univ. of Cape Town (BSc Hons 1960; Fellow, 1982); St John's Coll., Cambridge (PhD 1964). FRSSAf 1983 (Hon. FRSSAf, 2008). Lectr, Cambridge Univ., 1968–73; Prof., Scuola Internazionale Superiore di Studi Avanzati Trieste, 1987–89. Vis. Prof., Univs of Texas, Hamburg, Chicago, Alberta, and QMC London. Pres., Internat. Soc. of General Relativity and Gravitation, 1987–91. Clerk, S Africa Yearly Meeting of Quakers, 1982–86; Chairman: Quaker Service, W Cape, 1978–86; Quaker Peace Work Cttee, W Cape, 1989–. Fellow, Third World Acad. of Sci., 2006. Hon. DSc: Haverford Coll., 1995; Natal Univ., 1998; London, 2001; Cape Town, 2009. Herschel Medal, Royal Soc. of S Africa, 1978; Medal, SA Assoc. for Advancement of Science, 1993; Gold Medal, SA Math. Soc., 2001; Templeton Prize, 2004; De Beers Gold Medal, SA Inst. of Physics, 2010. Star of S Africa Medal, 1999; Order of Mapungubwe, 2005. *Publications:* (with S. W. Hawking) The Large Scale Structure of Space-Time, 1973; (with D. Dewar) Low Income Housing Policy, 1979; Before the Beginning, 1993; (with N. Murphy) On the Moral Nature of the Universe, 1996; The Far Future Universe, 2001; (jtly) Relativistic Cosmology, 2010. *Recreations:* mountain climbing, gliding. *Address:* Department of Applied Mathematics, University of Cape Town, Rondebosch 7701, Cape Town, South Africa; 10 Brabant Court, Marina da Gama 7945, Cape Town, South Africa. *T:* (21) 7888387. *Club:* Mountain of South Africa (Cape Town).

ELLIS, Prof. Harold, CBE 1987; MA, MCh, DM; FRCS; FRCOG; Clinical Anatomist, University of London, at Guy's campus, since 1993; *b* 13 Jan. 1926; *s* of Samuel and Ada Ellis; *m* 1958, Wendy Mae Levine; one *s* one *d*. *Educ:* Queen's Coll. (State Scholar and Open Scholar in Natural Sciences), Oxford; Radcliffe Infirmary, Oxford. BM, BCh, 1948; FRCS, MA, 1951; MCh 1956; DM 1962; FRCOG *ad eundem*, 1987. House Surgeon, Radcliffe Infirmary, 1948–49; Hallett Prize, RCS, 1949. RAMC, 1950–52. Res. Surgical Officer, Sheffield Royal Infirm., 1953–54; Registrar, Westminster Hosp., 1955; Sen. Registrar and Surgical Tutor, Radcliffe Infirm., Oxford, 1956–60; Sen. Lectr in Surgery, 1960–62, Hon. Consultant Surgeon, 1960–89, Westminster Hosp.; Prof. of Surgery, Univ. of London, 1962–89; Clinical Anatomist, Univ. of Cambridge and Fellow, Churchill Coll., Cambridge, 1989–93. Hon. Consultant Surgeon to the Army, 1978–89. Mem. Council, RCS, 1974–86. Member: Association of Surgeons; British Soc. of Gastroenterol.; Surgical Research Soc.; Council: RSocMed; British Assoc. of Surgical Oncology; Associé étranger, L'Academie de Chirurgie, Paris, 1983. Hon. FACS 1989; Hon. FRCP 2004. *Publications:* Clinical Anatomy, 1960; Anatomy for Anaesthetists, 1963; Lecture Notes on General Surgery, 1965; Principles of Resuscitation, 1967; History of the Bladder Stone, 1970; General Surgery for Nurses, 1976; Intestinal Obstruction, 1982; Notable Names in Medicine and Surgery, 1983; Famous Operations, 1984; Wound Healing for Surgeons, 1984; Maingot's Abdominal Operations, 1985; Research in Medicine, 1990; Cross-sectional Anatomy, 1991; Surgical Case-Histories from the Past, 1994; (ed) French's Index of Differential Diagnosis, 1996; A History of Surgery, 2000; numerous articles on surgical topics in medical journals. *Recreation:* medical history. *Address:* 16 Bancroft Avenue, N2 0AS. *T:* (020) 8348 2720.

ELLIS, Sir Herbert Douglas, (Sir Doug), Kt 2012; OBE 2005; Chairman, Aston Villa Football Club, 1968–75 and 1982–2006, now Hon. Life President; *b* Cheshire, 3 Jan. 1924; *s* of Herbert Ellis; *m* 1963, Heidi Marie Kroeger; three *s*. *Educ:* Chester Secondary Sch. Served RN, 1942–46. With Frames Tours, Preston, 1946–48; started travel agency, Birmingham, 1948; founder, package tour co., 1955; Chm. and owner, travel cos, incl. Mato, Global, Sunflight, Jetway and Ellis Travel, until 1976; Chairman: Ellis Gp of Cos (Ellmanton Construction Co. Ltd, Ellmanton Investments Ltd); Aston Manor Brewery Co., 1985. Hon. Dr Aston, 2007.

ELLIS, Ian David; non-executive Chairman: Arcus Services Ltd, since 2011; Mill Residential Reit plc, since 2014; non-executive Director, Telereal Trillium, since 2015 (Chairman, 2009–14); *b* Colchester, 4 Dec. 1955; *s* of John Douglas Vernon and Heather Ellis; *m* 1997, Clare Poyner; three *s* two *d*. FRICS 1991. District Valuer and Valuation Officer, Ipswich, 1974–83; Richard Ellis City Team, 1983–94; Shareholding Partner, Richard Ellis, 1994–98; Hd of Corporate Real Estate, Trillium, 1998–2002; Chief Exec., Land Securities Trillium, 2002–09; Dir, Land Securities Gp plc, 2002–09. Dir, Portman Settled Estates, 2007–. Member: Estates Bd, KCL, 2010–; Estates Cttee, Nat. Hist. Mus., 2013–. *Recreations:* family, cricket, World War II, books. *Address:* Telereal Trillium, 140 London Wall, EC2Y 5DN.

ELLIS, Dr Jeffrey Graham, FRS 2009; FAA; Research Scientist and Programme Leader, Genetic Engineering for Plant Improvement, Commonwealth Scientific and Industrial Research Organisation Plant Industry, Canberra. *Educ:* Univ. of Adelaide (BAgrSc Hons 1976; PhD 1980). Joined CSIRO Plant Industry, 1982; CSIRO Fellow, 2008. FAA 2005. *Publications:* (contrib.) Infectious Disease: innate immunity, 2003; articles in learned jls. *Address:* CSIRO Plant Industry, Black Mountain Laboratories, Clunies Ross Street, Canberra, ACT 2601, Australia.

ELLIS, Jennifer; *see* Rowe, J.

ELLIS, John; Member, Local Government Planning Executive, 2000–03; Steel Worker, British Steel plc, Scunthorpe, 1980–89; *b* Hexthorpe, Doncaster, 22 Oct. 1930; *s* of George and Hilda Ellis; *m* 1953, Rita Butters; two *s* two *d*. *Educ:* Rastrick Gram. Sch., Brighouse. Laboratory technician, Meteorological Office, 1947–63; Vice-Chm., Staff side, Air Min. Whitley Council, 1961–63; Member Relations Officer, Co-op. Retail Services, Bristol/Bath Region, 1971–74. Member: Easthampstead RDC, 1962–66; Bristol City Council, 1971–74; Humberside County Council, 1987–96; N Lincs Council, 1995–2003 (Vice Chm., Housing Cttee, 1998–99; Chm., Planning Cttee, 1999–2003). Chairman: Humberside Social Service Council, 1992–94 (Vice-Chm., 1990–92); Social Services Children's Cttee, 1991–94; Member: Scunthorpe HA, 1988–91 (Chm., Jt Consultative Cttee, 1988–2000); NRA (formerly Lincs Land Drainage Cttee), 1988–96 (Member: Anglian Regl Flood Defence cttee; Lincs Flood Defence cttee). Contested (Lab) Wokingham, 1964; MP (Lab) Bristol North-West, 1966–70, Brigg and Scunthorpe, Feb. 1974–1979; PPS to Minister of State for Transport, 1968–70; an Asst Govt Whip, 1974–76. Formerly Mem., Select Cttee on Nationalised Industries. Chm., 1985–2002, Sec./Treas., 2002–05, Co-op. Party. JP North Riding Yorks, 1960–61. *Publications:* (jtly) Fabian pamphlet on MPs from Unions, 1974. *Recreations:* gardening, watching cricket. *Address:* 102 Glover Road, Scunthorpe DN17 1AS.

ELLIS, John; *see* Ellis, Jonathan R.

ELLIS, John Russell, FCILT; transport consultant, since 1997; Chairman, Cotswold Line Promotion Group, since 2009; *b* 21 May 1938; *s* of Percy Macdonald Ellis and Winifred Maud (*née* Bunker); *m* 1962, Jean Eileen Taylor; two *d*. *Educ:* Rendcomb Coll., Cirencester; Pembroke Coll., Oxford (BA Hons PPE). FCILT 1997. Joined BR as Grad. Management Trainee, 1962; various posts, 1963–80; Chief Freight Manager, 1980–83, Divl Manager, 1983–84, Asst Gen. Manager, 1984–85, Eastern Region; Dep. Gen. Manager, Southern Region, 1985–87; Gen. Manager, ScotRail, 1987–90; Gen. Manager, Southern Region, 1990–91; Dep. Man. Dir, InterCity, 1992–93; Dir, Production, Railtrack, 1993–95; Man. Dir, ScotRail, 1995–97. Director: GB Railfreight, 2001–10; Rail Estate Consultancy, 2002–. Trustee, Campaign for Better Transport Trust (formerly Transport 2000 Trust), 2001–13. Chairman: Nat. Railway Heritage Awards, 2001–; Campden and District Peelers Trust, 2001–; Dir, Glos Market Towns Forum, 2004–13. *Recreations:* walking, gardening, music. *Address:* St Anne's, High Street, Chipping Campden, Glos GL55 6AL. *T:* (01386) 841253.

ELLIS, Prof. Jonathan Richard, (John), CBE 2012; PhD; FRS 1985; Senior Staff Physicist, Theoretical Studies Division, CERN, Geneva, 1994–2011 (Leader, 1988–94); Clerk Maxwell Professor of Theoretical Physics, King's College London, since 2010; *b* 1946; *s* of Richard Ellis and Beryl Lilian Ellis (*née* Ranger); *m* 1985, Maria Mercedes Martinez Rengifo; one *s* one *d*. *Educ:* Highgate Sch.; King's Coll., Cambridge (BA, PhD; Hon. Fellow, 2006). Postdoctoral research, SLAC, Stanford, 1971–72; Richard Chase Tolman Fellow, CIT, 1972–73; Staff Mem., CERN, Geneva, 1973–2011, Advr to Dir-Gen. for relns with non-member States. Member: PPARC, 2004–07; Sci. Bd, STFC, 2007. FInstP. Maxwell Medal, Royal Soc., 1982. *Recreations:* movies, reading, travel, hiking in the mountains.

ELLIS, June; *see* Ellis, D. J.

ELLIS, Prof. Katharine, DPhil; FBA 2013; Stanley Hugh Badock Professor of Music, University of Bristol, since 2013. *Educ:* University Coll., Oxford (BA, DPhil); Guildhall Sch. of Music. Jun. Res. Fellow, French Studies, St Anne's Coll., Oxford; Open Univ., 1991–94; Royal Holloway, Univ. of London, 1994–2013; Dir, Inst. of Musical Res., Sch. of Advanced Study, Univ. of London, 2006–09. MAE 2010. *Publications:* Music Criticism in Nineteenth-Century France, 1995; Interpreting the Musical Past, 2005; The Politics of Plainchant in fin-de-siècle France, 2013; (ed jtly) Words and Notes in the Long Nineteenth Century, 2013. *Address:* Department of Music, University of Bristol, Victoria Rooms, Queens Road, Bristol BS8 1SA.

ELLIS, Keith; *see* Ellis, R. K.

ELLIS, Laurence Edward, MA; Rector, The Edinburgh Academy, 1977–92; *b* 21 April 1932; *s* of Dr and Mrs E. A. Ellis; *m* 1961, Elizabeth Ogilvie; two *s* one *d*. *Educ:* Winchester Coll.; Trinity Coll., Cambridge (MA). 2/Lieut Rifle Bde, 1950–52. Marlborough Coll., 1955–77 (Housemaster, 1968). Reader, Salisbury, 1960–2010. *Publications:* (part-author) texts on school maths, statistics, computing, and calculating; articles in jls. *Recreations:* writing, music. *Address:* Glendene, Wick Lane, Devizes, Wilts SN10 5DW.

ELLIS, Martin Arthur; Taxing Master of the Supreme Court, 1990–2000, Costs Judge, 1999–2000; *b* 10 Jan. 1933; *s* of Walter Ellis and Phoebe Alicia Ellis; *m* 1961, Moira Herbert; one *s* (and one *s* decd). *Educ:* Beckenham Grammar School. Solicitor, admitted 1956; 2nd Lieut, 4th Regt, Royal Horse Artillery, 1957–58; Partner, Simmons & Simmons, 1973–90. *Recreations:* sport, golf, cricket. *Address:* Field House, North Road, Sandwich Bay, Kent CT13 9PJ. *T:* and *Fax:* (01304) 619375. *Clubs:* MCC; Royal St George's Golf.

ELLIS, Michael Henry, OBE 2007; Chairman, Skipton Building Society, since 2011; *b* 4 Aug. 1951; *s* of late John Ellis and Joan (*née* Lawton); *m* 1973, Jeanette Booth; two *d*. *Educ:* Open Univ. (BA). CIPFA 1973. Various posts in local govt sector, 1967–87; Halifax Building Society, later Halifax plc: Gp Treas., 1987–92; Gen. Manager, Treasury and Eur. Ops, 1992–95; Man. Dir, Treasury and Overseas Ops, 1995–96; Banking and Savings Dir, 1996–99; Financial Services Dir, 1999; Chief Operating Officer, 1999–2001; Gp Finance Dir, HBOS plc, 2001–04, 2008–09. Fund Comr and Chm., Fund Distribution Ltd, 2005–06. Non-exec. Dir, W H Smith plc, 2005–13. *Recreations:* travel, football, music, reading. *Club:* Royal Automobile.

ELLIS, Michael Tyrone; MP (C) Northampton North, since 2010; *b* Northampton, 13 Oct. 1967; *s* of Jack Ellis and Margaret Ellis (*née* Surgenor). *Educ:* Wellingborough Sch.; Univ. of Buckingham (LLB); Inns of Court Sch. of Law (BVC). Called to the Bar, Middle Temple, 1993; in practice as barrister, 1993–2010. Mem. (C) Northants CC, 1997–2001. Member: Home Affairs Select Cttee, 2011–15; Jt Cttee on Statutory Instruments, 2010–; Chm., All-Party Parly Gp on the Queen's Diamond Jubilee, 2010–13. Pres., Commonwealth Jewish Council, 2012–14. *Recreations:* theatre, British Royal history. *Address:* House of Commons, SW1A 0AA. *T:* (020) 7219 7220, *Fax:* (020) 7219 6375. *E:* michael.ellis.mp@parliament.uk. *Club:* Carlton.

ELLIS, Morag; *see* Ellis, Rosalind M.

ELLIS, Nicholas St John; QC (Scot.) 2002; *b* 11 Nov. 1958; *s* of Anthony Brian Ellis and Pauline Ellis; *m* 1997, Victoria Craig; one *s* one *d*. *Educ:* Edinburgh Univ. (LLB). Admitted solicitor, 1981; WS 1985; called to the Scottish Bar, 1990. *Recreations:* hill-walking, fine wine. *Address:* Norham House, Norham, Berwick-upon-Tweed TD15 2LF. *T:* (01289) 382658. *E:* Nstje@aol.com.

ELLIS, Dr Norman David; Under Secretary, British Medical Association, 1980–2000 (Senior Industrial Relations Officer, 1978–82); *b* 23 Nov. 1943; *s* of late George Edward Ellis and late Annie Elsie Scarfe; *m* 1966, Valerie Ann Fenn, PhD; one *s*. *Educ:* Minchenden Sch.; Univ. of Leeds (BA); MA (Oxon), PhD. Research Officer, Dept of Employment, 1969–71; Leverhulme Fellowship in Industrial Relations, Nuffield Coll., Oxford, 1971–74; Gen. Sec., Assoc. of First Division Civil Servants, 1974–78. *Publications:* (with W. E. J. McCarthy) Management by Agreement, 1973; Employing Staff, 1984; (with J. Chisholm) Making sense of the Red Book, 1993, 3rd edn 1997; (ed with T. Stanton) Making sense of Partnerships, 1994; Making sense of General Practice, 1994; (with J. Lindsay) Making sense of Pensions and Retirement, 1995; General Practitioners' Handbook, 1997, 2nd edn (with D. Grantham), 2000; GP Employment Handbook, 1998; (with J. Lindsay) Staff Pensions in General Practice, 1998; various contribs to industrial relations literature. *Recreations:* maritime history, reading, travel, swimming. *Address:* 7 South Row, SE3 0RY. *T:* (020) 8852 6244.

ELLIS, Osian Gwynn, CBE 1971; harpist; Professor of Harp, Royal Academy of Music, London, 1959–89; *b* Ffynnongroew, Flints, 8 Feb. 1928; *s* of Rev. T. G. Ellis, Methodist Minister; *m* 1951, Rene Ellis Jones (*d* 2012), Pwllheli; one *s* (and one *s* decd). *Educ:* Denbigh Grammar Sch.; Royal Academy of Music. Has broadcast and televised extensively. Has given recitals/concertos all over the world; shared poetry and music recitals with Dame Peggy Ashcroft, Paul Robeson, Burton, C. Day-Lewis, etc. Mem., Melos Ensemble; solo harpist with LSO, 1961–94. Former Mem., Music and Welsh Adv. Cttees, British Council. Works written for him include Harp Concertos by Hoddinott, 1957 and by Mathias, 1970, Jersild, 1972, Robin Holloway, 1985; chamber works by Gian Carlo Menotti, 1977; William Schuman, 1978; from 1960 worked with Benjamin Britten who wrote for him Harp Suite in C (Op. 83) and (for perf. with Sir Peter Pears) Canticle V, Birthday Hansel, and folk songs; from 1974 accompanied Sir Peter Pears on recital tours, Europe and USA; records concertos, recitals, folk songs, etc. Film, The Harp, won a Paris award; other awards include Grand Prix du Disque and French Radio Critics' Award. FRAM 1960. Hon. DMus Wales, 1970. *Publications:* Story of the Harp in Wales, 1991. *Address:* Arfryn, Ala Road, Pwllheli, Gwynedd LL53 5BN. *T:* (01758) 612501.

ELLIS, Prof. Reginald John, PhD; FRS 1983; Professor of Biological Sciences, University of Warwick, 1976–96, now Emeritus; *b* 12 Feb. 1935; *s* of Francis Gilbert Ellis and Evangeline Gratton Ellis; *m* 1963, Diana Margaret Warren; one *d*. *Educ:* Highbury County Sch.; King's Coll., London (BSc, PhD). ARC Fellow, Univ. of Oxford, 1961–64; Lectr in Botany and Biochemistry, Univ. of Aberdeen, 1964–70; Sen. Lectr, 1970–73, Reader, 1973–76, Dept of Biol Sciences, Univ. of Warwick; SERC Senior Res. Fellow, 1983–88. Sen. Vis. Fellow, St John's Coll., Oxford, 1992–93; Vis. Prof., Oxford Centre for Molecular Scis, 1997–2001. Mem. EMBO, 1986. LRPS 1987. Tate & Lyle Award (for contribs to plant biochem.), 1980; Internat. Gairdner Foundn Award, 2004; Internat. Medal, Cell Stress Soc., 2007; Croonian Lect. Prize, Royal Soc., 2011. Research interests include chloroplast biogenesis, protein aggregation, and molecular chaperones. *Publications:* How Science Works: evolution, 2010, 2016; 170 papers in biochem. jls. *Recreations:* photography, hill walking.

ELLIS, Dr (Richard) Keith, FRS 2009; Scientist, Fermi National Accelerator Laboratory, USA, since 1984 (Head, Theory Department, 1992–2004); *b* Aberdeen, 17 Nov. 1949; *s* of Richard Tunstall Ellis and Jean Bruce Maitland Ellis; *m* 1990, Theresa Pedemonte; one *s* two *d*. *Educ:* Fettes Coll., Edinburgh; New Coll., Oxford (MA); Wadham Coll., Oxford (DPhil 1974). Royal Soc. Res. Fellow, Rome, 1974–76; Research Fellow: Imperial Coll., London, 1977; MIT, 1978–79; Calif Inst. of Technol., 1980; CERN, 1980–82; Rome, 1982–84. Fellow, Amer. Physical Soc., 1988. *Publications:* (jtly) QCD and Collider Physics, 1996; contribs to Physical Rev., Nuclear Physics, Jl of High Energy Physics, Physics Rev. Letters. *Address:* MS 106, Fermi National Accelerator Laboratory, PO Box 500, Batavia, IL 60510–0500, USA. *T:* (630) 8403749, *Fax:* (630) 8405435. *E:* ellis@fnal.gov.

ELLIS, Richard Marriott; Chairman, The Original Cottage Company, since 2010; *b* 23 Jan. 1955; *s* of late Martin Beazor Ellis and Janet Pamela Ellis (*née* Morgan); *m* 1987, Lesley Anne Smith; three *s* two *d*. *Educ:* Shene Grammar Sch.; Norwich City Coll. ACMA 1979. Financial Dir, Tucker Foods Ltd, 1984–92; Man. Dir, Norfolk Country Cottages, 1992–; Chief Exec., Kettle Foods Ltd, 1994–2000. Chairman: Arts and Business East, 2000–03; East of England Sustainable Develt Round Table, 2001–03; East of England Develt Agency, 2003–10; Norfolk Tourism, 2010–12. Dir, Heart Mercers Ltd, 2009–14. Chairman: Earlham Early Years Centre, 2000–04; Sheringham Little Theatre, 2010–; Visit East Anglia Ltd, 2011–; Trustee: Norwich Th. Royal, 1999–; The Forum Trust, 2002–; Norwich Heritage and Econ. Regeneration Trust, 2004–11; Rothamsted Research, 2005–08; Holt Fest., 2012–. Gov., Norwich Univ. (formerly Norwich Univ. Coll.) of the Arts, 2011–. FRSA. *Recreations:* travel, ski-ing badly, seeking adrenaline (bungee jumping, sky diving, etc.), finding things which aren't there, avoiding Who Was Who! *Address:* The Original Cottage Company, Bank House, Market Place, Reepham, Norfolk NR10 4JJ. *T:* (01603) 876214, *Fax:* (01603) 870304. *E:* r.ellis@tocc.co.uk. *Club:* Norfolk.

ELLIS, Prof. Richard Salisbury, CBE 2008; FRS 1995; Steele Professor, California Institute of Technology, since 2002 (Professor of Astronomy, since 1999); *b* 25 May 1950; *s* of late Capt. Arthur Ellis, MBE and of Marion Ellis (*née* Davies); *m* 1972, Barbara Williams; one *s* one *d*. *Educ:* Abergele GS; University Coll. London (BSc Hons 1971; Fellow, 1998); Wolfson Coll., Oxford (DPhil 1974) FRAS 1974; FInstP 1998. Durham University: Sen. Demonstrator in Physics, 1974–77; Res. Asst, 1977–81; Lectr in Astronomy, 1981–83; Principal Res. Fellow, Royal Greenwich Observatory, 1983–85; Prof. of Astronomy, Durham Univ., 1985–93; SERC Sen. Res. Fellow, 1989–94; Cambridge University: Plumian Prof. of Astronomy and Exptl Philosophy, 1993–99; Dir, Inst. of Astronomy, 1994–99; Professorial Fellow, Magdalene Coll., 1994–99; Director: Palomar Observatory, 2000–02; Caltech Optical Observatories, 2002–05; Royal Soc. Prof., Dept of Astrophysics, Univ. of Oxford, 2008–09; Fellow, Merton Coll., Oxford, 2008–09. Chm., SERC Large Telescope Panel, 1986–90; Mem., Anglo-Australian Telescope Bd, 1991–95. Associate, Canadian Inst. of Advanced Res., 1993–; Member: Space Telescope Science Inst. Council, 1995–2001; Gemini Telescopes Bd, 1996–98; Bd, W. M. Keck Observatory, 2000–05; Bd, Thirty Meter Telescope Proj., 2003–. Visiting Professor: Space Telescope Science Inst., 1985, 2006; Anglo-Australian Observatory, 1991; CIT, 1991, 1997; Princeton, 1992; Carnegie Observatory, 1998; UCL, 2005; Toronto, 2006; Oxford, 2007; Tokyo, 2011; Carnegie Centennial Prof., Edinburgh, 2015–; Hon. Prof., Observational Astrophysics, Univ. of Cambridge, 2000–03. Lectures: J. L. Bishop, Princeton, 1992; Halley, Oxford, 1993; Cormack, RSE, 1996; Lockyer, RAS, 1997; Sackler, Harvard, 1998; Bakerian, Royal Soc., 1998; Poynting, Birmingham, 1998; Grubb Parsons, Durham, 1999; Rosenblum, Jerusalem, 1999; Lansdowne, Victoria, 2001; Allison-Levick, Astronomical Soc., Australia, 2004; J. Bahcall, NASA, 2006; J. L. Bishop, NY, 2007; E. Spreadbury, UCL, 2008; Neils Bohr, Copenhagen, 2009; Schopp, San Diego, 2010; Oort, Leiden, 2010; Rittenhouse, Pennsylvania, 2012; J. Bahcall, Israel, 2012; Watson, Caltech, 2013; Fundación BBVA, Madrid, 2013; Darwin, Cambridge. FAAAS 2001. Hon. DSc Durham, 2002. Gold Medal, RAS, 2011. *Publications:* Epoch of Galaxy Formation, 1988; Observational Tests of Cosmological Inflation, 1991; Large Scale Structure in the Universe, 1999; numerous articles in astronomical jls. *Recreations:* exploration, photography, music, ski-ing. *Address:* Astronomy Department, Mailstop 249–17, California Institute of Technology, Pasadena, CA 91125, USA. *T:* (626) 3952598.

ELLIS, Rev. Dr Robert Anthony; Principal, Regent's Park College, Oxford, since 2007; *b* Cardiff, 24 Aug. 1956; *s* of John and Joyce Ellis; *m* 1977, Susan Winters; three *s* one *d*. *Educ:* Cathays High Sch., Cardiff; Regent's Park Coll., Oxford (MA; DPhil 1984); Colgate Rochester Divinity Sch., NY. Minister: Spurgeon Baptist Ch, Bletchley, 1981–87; Tyndale Baptist Ch, Bristol, 1987–2001; Tutor, Bristol Baptist Coll., 1995–2001; Tutorial Fellow in Pastoral Studies, Regent's Park Coll., 2001–07. Mem. Council, Baptist Union of GB, 1990–; Moderator, Baptist Union Ministry Exec., 2003–09. Chm., Religious Adv. Panel, BBC Bristol, 1993–2000. Mem. Bd, Bristol Churches Housing Assoc., 1987–96. *Publications:* Answering God: towards a theology of intercession, 2005; The Games People Play: theology, religion and sport, 2014; contrib. articles to jls incl. Jl Religion, Religious Studies, Baptist Qly, Epworth Rev. *Recreations:* sports spectating, especially Rugby Union, walking the dog, reading, music, caravanning, family chilling. *Address:* Regent's Park College, Pusey Street, Oxford OX1 3LU. *T:* (01865) 288120, *Fax:* (01865) 288121. *E:* robert.ellis@regents.ox.ac.uk.

ELLIS, Ven. Robin Gareth; Archdeacon of Plymouth, 1982–2000; *b* 8 Dec. 1935; *s* of Walter and Morva Ellis; *m* 1964, Anne Ellis (*née* Landers); three *s*. *Educ:* Worksop Coll., Notts; Pembroke Coll., Oxford (BCL, MA). Curate of Swinton, 1960–63; Asst Chaplain, Worksop Coll., 1963–66; Vicar of Swaffham Prior and Reach, and Asst Director of Religious Education, Diocese of Ely, 1966–74; Vicar of St Augustine, Wisbech, 1974–82; Vicar of St Paul's, Yelverton, 1982–86. *Recreations:* cricket, theatre, prison reform. *Address:* 24 Lyndhurst Road, Exmouth, Devon EX8 3DT. *T:* (01395) 272891.

ELLIS, Roger Wykeham, CBE 1984; Master of Marlborough College, 1972–86; *b* 3 Oct. 1929; *s* of Cecil Ellis, solicitor, and Pamela Unwin; *m* 1964, Margaret Jean, *d* of William Hugh Stevenson; one *s* two *d*. *Educ:* St Peter's Sch., Seaford; Winchester Coll.; Trinity Coll., Oxford (Schol., MA). Royal Navy, 1947–49. Asst Master, Harrow Sch., 1952–67, and Housemaster of the Head Master's House, 1961–67; Headmaster of Rossall Sch., 1967–72. Graduate Recruitment Manager, Barclays Bank, 1986–91. Chm., HMC, 1983. Member: Harrow Borough Educn Cttee, 1956–60; Wilts County Educn Cttee, 1975–86. Governor: Campion Sch., Athens, 1981–2003; Cheam Sch., 1975–93 (Chm., 1987–93); Hawtreys Sch., 1975–86; Sandroyd Sch., 1982–86; Fettes Coll., 1983–94; St Edward's Sch., Oxford, 1985–2006 (Chm., 1992–99); Harrow Sch., 1987–97. Dir, Asquith Ct Schs Ltd, 1992–2000. Trustee, Hanover Foundn, 2001–05. *Publications:* Who's Who in Victorian Britain, 1997; (with Geoffrey Treasure) Britain's Prime Ministers, 2005. *Recreations:* golf, fishing, bridge. *Address:* 32 Hillcroft Crescent, Ealing, W5 2SQ. *Clubs:* East India, MCC; Denham Golf.

See also A. W. Ellis, Dame E. A. Griffiths, Sir H. A. Stevenson.

ELLIS, (Rosalind) Morag, (Mrs A. Bushell); QC 2006; *b* 5 June 1962; *d* of Ivor and Pamela Ellis; *m* 1985, Rev. Anthony Bushell; two *s* one *d*. *Educ:* Penrhos Coll., Colwyn Bay; St Catharine's Coll., Cambridge (BA 1983); Inns of Court Sch. of Law. Called to the Bar, Gray's Inn, 1984; in practice, specialising in law of planning, local government and village greens. Chm., Planning and Envmt Bar Assoc., 2012– (Vice-Chm., 2007–12). Mem. Council, Wescott House, Cambridge, 2010–. Commissary Gen., Dio. of Canterbury, 2011–; Dep. Chancellor, Dio. of Southwark, 2012–. Church of England Reader. *Publications:* (contrib.) Halsbury's Laws of England, 4th edn, 1998 reissue; (contrib.) Gambling for Local Authorities, 2nd edn 2010; articles in Jl Planning and Envmt Law. *Recreations:* music: Member, Bach Choir, violin, viola. *Address:* Francis Taylor Building, Temple, EC4Y 7BY. *T:* (020) 7353 8415, *Fax:* (020) 7353 7622. *E:* morag.ellis@ftb.eu.com.

ELLIS, Timothy David; Chief Executive, Keeper, and Registrar General, National Records of Scotland, since 2013; *b* London, 14 April 1971; *m* 2003, Catriona Brown; three *d*. Dept of Transport, 1989–98; Scottish Office, 1998–2003; Hd, Freedom of Information Unit, Scottish Exec., 2003–06; Sen. Manager, Communities Scotland, 2006–08; Dep. Dir, Housing Investment, 2008–10, Hd, Cabinet and Corporate Secretariat, 2011–13, Scottish Govt. *Address:* HM General Register House, Edinburgh EH1 3YY. *T:* (0131) 535 1314. *E:* rg-keeper@scotland.gsi.gov.uk.

ELLIS, Rt Rev. Timothy William, DPhil; Bishop Suffragan of Grantham, 2006–13; an Honorary Assistant Bishop: Diocese of Lincoln, since 2013; Diocese of Sheffield, since 2014; *b* 26 Aug. 1953; *s* of Albert and Betty Ellis; *m* 1976, Susan Weston; two *s* one *d*. *Educ:* King's Coll., London (AKC 1975); York Univ. (DPhil 1998). Ordained deacon, 1976, priest, 1977; Asst Curate, St John, Old Trafford, 1976–80; Vicar, St Thomas, Pendleton and Chaplain to Salford Coll. of Technol., 1980–87; Vicar, St Leonard, Norwood, 1987–2001; Priest i/c, St Hilda, Shiregreen, 1994–97; RD Ecclesfield, 1994–99; Archdeacon of Stow and Lindsey, 2001–06. Sec., 1988–94, Chm., 1999–2001, Sheffield DAC; Member, Fabric Advisory Committee: York Minster, 2000–; Sheffield Cathedral, 2000–; Lincoln Minster, 2005–07.

Hon. Canon, Sheffield Cathedral, 2000–01. Pres., Lincs Rural Housing Assoc., 2006–. Chairman: Living Stones Consortium, 2011–; Lincolnshire Community Land Trust, 2012–; Sheffield Faiths Together Exec., 2015–. *Recreations:* Sheffield Wednesday FC, wine, foreign travel, golf, gardening, DIY, hen husbandry. *Address:* 8 Mason Grove, Sheffield S13 8LL.

ELLIS, Sir Vernon (James), Kt 2011; Chairman, British Council, since 2010; *b* 1 July 1947; *s* of Norman and Phyllis Ellis; *m* 1972, Hazel Marilyn Lucas; one *s* one *d*. *Educ:* Magdalen Coll. Sch., Oxford; Magdalen Coll., Oxford (MA Hons PPE 1969). FCA 1982. Andersen Consulting, later Accenture, 1969–2010: Partner, 1979; Man. Partner, UK, 1986–89; Man. Partner, Europe, ME, Africa and India, 1989–99; Internat. Chm., 1999–2008; Sen. Advr, 2008–10. Chm., Arts and Media Hons Cttee, 2013–. Chairman: Martin Randall Travel, 2008–; Country Greenhouses Ltd, 2008–11; Passionato Ltd, 2009–11; OneMedicare LLP, 2010–14; OneMedical Gp, 2014–. Dir, World-Links, Washington, 2002–06. Member: Bd, Prince of Wales Business Leaders Forum, 1997–2006 (Chm. Bd, 2001–05); Adv. Bd, Centre for European Reform, 1998–2010; Council, World Economic Forum, 1999–2001; Mem., 2001–04, Dep. Chm., 2002–04, Mayor of Seoul's Internat. Adv. Council. UK private sector delegate, G8 Digital Opportunities Task Force, 2000–02. Member: Develt Cttee, Magdalen Coll., Oxford, 1999–2010; Adv. Council, Saïd Business Sch., Univ. of Oxford, 1996–2006; Foundn Bd, Internat. Inst. of Mgt Develt, Lausanne, 1996–2004; Internat. Council, INSEAD, 2001–04; Bd, Arts & Business, 2003–06; Adv. Bd, Bridges Ventures, 2008–10. Chairman: Classical Opera, 1996–2009 (Pres., 2009–); ENO, 2006–12 (Mem., 2001–12; Pres., 2012–); Sacconi Trust, 2007–10; Nat. Opera Studio, 2012–; Appeal Bd, Stop MS, 2015–; Trustee: Florestan Trio, 2003–11; Royal Coll. of Music, 2004–10; Kathleen Ferrier Prize, 2004–; Young Singers Welfare Foundn, 2008–10; Leopold Trust, 2009–13; London Music Masters, 2015–. Mem., Philanthrophy Rev., 2011. Barclay Fellow, Templeton Coll., Oxford, 2002–06. FRCM 2012. Hon. Fellow, Trinity Laban Conservatoire, 2012. Hon. DLit Goldsmiths, Univ. of London, 2011; Hon. DSc QUB, 2012; Hon. LLD Warwick, 2014. Beacon Fellow for Cultural Philanthropy, 2013. Assoc. of British Orchestra's Award, 2014. *Recreations:* music, opera, theatre, gardening, wine, cooking, photography. *Address:* British Council, 10 Spring Gardens, SW1A 2BN. *E:* vernon.ellis@britishcouncil.org. *Clubs:* Athenæum, Garrick.

ELLIS-REES, Hugh Francis, CB 1986; Regional Director, West Midlands, Departments of the Environment and Transport, 1981–89; *b* 5 March 1929; *s* of late Sir Hugh Ellis-Rees, KCMG, CB and Lady (Eileen Frances Anne) Ellis-Rees; *m* 1956, Elisabeth de Mestre Gray; three *s* one *d*. *Educ:* Ampleforth Coll.; Balliol Coll., Oxford. Served Grenadier Guards, 1948–49. Joined War Office, 1954; DoE, 1970; Cabinet Office, 1972–74; Under Sec., DoE, 1974. Mem., Black Country Develt Corp., 1990–98. Chm., Burford and Dist Soc., 2005–10; Trustee, Burford Fest., 2007–13 (Chm., 2007).

ELLISON, Jane; MP (C) Battersea, since 2010; Parliamentary Under-Secretary of State, Department of Health, since 2013; *b* Bradford, 15 Aug. 1964; *m* John Samiotis. *Educ:* St Hilda's Coll., Oxford (BA PPE). With John Lewis Partnership, London, 1986–2010: grad. trainee; Manager, Customer Direct Mktg; Sen. Manager, Edition, customer mag.; on secondment with music charity, Sing for Pleasure, 2004. Mem. (C) Barnet LBC, 1991–94, 2006–08. Contested (C): Barnsley E, Dec. 1996; Barnsley E and Mexborough, 1997; Tottenham, June 2000; Pendle, 2005. Member: Works and Pensions Select Cttee, 2012–13; Backbench Business Cttee, 2010–13. Trustee, Sing for Pleasure, 2008–. *Address:* House of Commons, SW1A 0AA.

ELLISON, Dame Jillian Paula Anne, (Dame Jill), DBE 2001; Director of Nursing, Heart of England Foundation Trust (formerly East Birmingham Hospital, then Birmingham Heartlands and Solihull NHS Trust), 1990–2007; *b* 31 Jan. 1955; *d* of Joseph Ellison and Mollie Yvonne Ellison (*née* North). *Educ:* St Margaret's Sch., Bushey; Birmingham Poly. (HVCert 1980); MA UCE, 2001. Trained at Middx Hosp. Sch. of Nursing, 1973–76 (SRN); Staff Nurse: Middx Hosp., London, 1976–77; Hadassah Hosp., Israel, 1978–79; (Intensive Care) Charing Cross Hosp., 1979–80; Sandwell Health Authority: Health Visitor, 1980–85; Nurse Manager, 1985–87; Dist Sen. Nurse, 1987–90. Chm., Nurse Directors Assoc., 2005–07. *Recreations:* walking, cycling. *Address:* 4 The Badgers, Barnt Green, Birmingham B45 8QR.

ELLISON, Rt Rev. John Alexander; Bishop of Paraguay, 1988–2007; an Hon. Assistant Bishop, Diocese of Winchester, since 2008; *b* 24 Dec. 1940; *s* of Alexander and Catherine Ellison; *m* 1964, Judith Mary Cox; one *s* two *d*. *Educ:* London College of Divinity (ALCD); Borough Road College (Teacher's Cert.). Secondary school teacher, 1961–64. Deacon 1967, priest 1968; Curate, St Paul, Woking, 1967–71; missionary, church planter, evangelist; Bible school/Bible institute lecturer, 1971–79; Asst to Archdeacon, St Saviour, Belgrano, Dio. Argentina, 1979–82; Rector, Aldridge, Dio. Lichfield, 1983–88. *Recreations:* walking, gardening, family, dining out. *Address:* The Furrow, Evingar Road, Whitchurch, Hants RG28 7EU. *T:* (01256) 892126. *E:* jyjellison@btinternet.com.

ELLISON, Lawrence J., (Larry); Executive Chairman and Chief Technology Officer, Oracle Corporation, since 2014 (Chief Executive Officer, 1977–2014; President, 1977–96; Chairman, 1996–2004); *b* New York City, 1944; *s* of Florence Spellman; adopted by Louis and Lillian Ellison; *m* 2003, Melanie Craft. *Educ:* High Sch., Chicago; Univ. of Illinois. Formerly computer programmer, Calif; posts with Amdahl Inc., 1967–71, and Ampex Corp., 1972–77; Founder (with Bob Miner), Oracle, 1977. Dir, Apple Computer Inc., 1997–2002. *Address:* Oracle Corporation, 500 Oracle Parkway, Redwood Shores, CA 94065, USA.

ELLISON, Mark Christopher; QC 2008; a Recorder, since 2000; a Deputy High Court Judge, since 2010; *b* 8 Oct. 1957; *s* of late Anthony Ellison and of Arlette Maguire Ellison (*née* Blundell); *m* 1981, Kate Augusta (*née* Middleton); two *s* two *d*. *Educ:* Pocklington Sch.; Skinners' Sch.; UWIST (LLB). Called to the Bar, Gray's Inn, 1979, Bencher, 2012; in practice at the Bar, 1980–; Treasury Counsel at CCC, 1994; Sen. Treasury Counsel, 2000–08; First Sen. Treasury Counsel, 2006–08. Member: Criminal Justice Council, 2008–12; Professional Practice Cttee, Bar Council, 2009–12. *Recreations:* my children, dinghy sailing. *Address:* 1–2 Laurence Pountney Hill, EC4R 0EU. *T:* (020) 7933 8855. *E:* barristers@qebholliswhiteman.co.uk.

ELLISON, Robin Charles; Partner, Pinsent Masons, since 2002; *b* 3 Feb. 1949; *s* of Cecil Ellison and Vera Ellison (*née* Glicher); *m* 1986, Micheline Harris; two *s*. *Educ:* Manchester Grammar Sch. Cecil Ellison & Co., Manchester, 1973–75; Res. Fellow, Wolfson Coll., Cambridge, 1976–81; admitted Solicitor, 1979; Sen. Partner, Ellison Westhorp, Solicitors, 1981–94; Consultant, Hammond Suddards, 1994–97; Nat. Hd of Pensions, Eversheds, 1997–2002. Visiting Professor: Pensions Law and Econs, Cass Business Sch., City Univ., 2006; Pensions Law, Birmingham City Univ., 2008–11. Chairman: Nat. Assoc. of Pension Funds, 2005–07; Instnl Investors Tort Recovery Assoc., 2012–. Chairman: Trustee Guild, 2000–; London & Colonial Assurance Gp, 2003–; Carillion Trustees, 2011–. Chairman: Magen David Adom UK, 2003–; Lung Cancer Res., 2004–. Chm., U Party, 2010–. FPMI 1997; FRSA; FRSocMed 2007. Freeman, City of London, 2013. *Publications:* Pensions for Partners, 1978, 4th edn 1984; Private Occupational Pension Schemes, 1979; Pension Schemes for Controlling Directors, 1980, 3rd edn 1984; Pensions for Partners, 4th edn 1984; Pension Problems on Mergers and Acquisitions, 1984; Pensions Law and Practice (looseleaf), 1987–; (ed) Pensions Benefits Law Reports, 1989–; Pensions and Divorce, 1991; Pensions: Europe and equality, 1993, 2nd edn 1995; Pension Disputes, 1995; Pension Trustees Handbook, 1995, 4th edn 2006; (jtly) Family Breakdown and Pensions, 1997, 3rd edn 2006; (jtly) Pensions and Insolvency, 1997; The Pocket Pensions Guide, 1998; Pensions and Investments, 2006; Pension Fund Investment Law, 2008; (jtly) Pensions and Divorce, 2010; Pensions for You and Your Business, 2013. *Recreations:* walking, sailing, brutalist architecture. *Address:* 110 Frognal, NW3 6XU. *T:* (020) 7435 7330. *E:* robin@pensionslaw.net. *Club:* Royal Society of Medicine.

ELLMAN, Louise Joyce; MP (Lab and Co-op) Liverpool Riverside, since 1997; *b* 14 Nov. 1945; *d* of late Harold and Annie Rosenberg; *m* 1967, Geoffrey David Ellman; one *s* one *d*. *Educ:* Manchester High Sch. for Girls; Hull Univ. (BA Hons); York Univ. (MPhil). Worked in further educn and on Open Univ., 1970–76. Member: Lancs CC, 1970–97 (Leader, Lab Gp, 1977–97; Leader, Council, 1981–97; Chm., 1981–85; Hon. Alderman, 1998–); W Lancs DC, 1974–87; Local Govt Adv. Cttee, Labour Party NEC, 1977–90; Regl Exec., NW Labour Party, 1985– (Chm., 1993–98). A Vice Pres., LGA, 1997, 2011–. Contested (Lab) Darwen, 1979. Member: Select Cttee on Envmt, Transport and Regl Affairs, 1997–2001; Select Cttee on Transport, 2002– (Chm., 2008–); Vice Pres., All Pty Parly Cttee against Anti-semitism, 2007–; Jt Sec., All Pty Gp against Trafficking, 2007–11; Treas., All Pty Parly Friends of the Bahá'ís Gp. Chm., PLP Regl Govt Gp, 1999. Chair: Jewish Labour Movement, 2004–; Labour-Regeneration Gp, 2005–10; Vice Chair: Labour Friends of Israel, 2004–; Parly Liverpool Capital of Culture Gp, 2006–. Mem., Bd of Deputies of British Jews, 2007–. Vice-Chm., Lancashire Enterprises, 1982–97; Founder Mem., Co-operative Enterprises NW, 1979–; Founder Chm., NW Regl Assoc., 1992–93; Mem., NW Partnership, 1993–97. Youngest mem., Lancs CC, 1970; youngest mem. and first woman to be Chm., 1981. *Address:* House of Commons, SW1A 0AA.

ELLORY, Prof. (John) Clive, PhD; Professor of Physiology, University of Oxford, 1996, now Emeritus; Fellow of Corpus Christi College, Oxford, 1985, now Emeritus; *b* 16 April 1944; *s* of Ronald and Muriel Ellory; *m* 1969, Jane Metcalfe; one *s* one *d*. *Educ:* Latymer Upper Sch.; Univ. of Bristol (BSc Biochemistry 1964; PhD Zoology 1967); MA 1975, ScD 1995, Cantab; MA 1985, DSc 1996, Oxon. SO, 1967–71, SSO, 1971–75, PSO, 1975, Inst. of Animal Physiology, Babraham; Lectr, Dept of Physiology, Univ. of Cambridge, 1975–84; Fellow, Queens' Coll., Cambridge, 1975–84; Reader in Human Physiology, 1985–96, Hd of Physiology Dept, 1994–2006, Univ. of Oxford. Vis. Associate Prof., Yale, and Guest Fellow, Silliman Coll., 1971; Vis. Associate Prof., 1975, Vis. Prof., 1982, Univ. of Illinois; Investigator, US Antarctic Res. Program, McMurdo, Antarctica, 1980; Vis. Prof., Univ. of Nice, 1985, 1993; Royal Soc. Israel Res. Prof., Technion, Haifa, 1994. FMedSci 1999. *Publications:* jointly: Membrane Transport in Red Cells, 1977; Red Cell Membranes: a methodological approach, 1982; The Binding and Transport of Anions in Living Tissues, 1982; The Sodium Pump, 1985; Patronage and Plate at Corpus Christi College, Oxford, 1999; Red Cell Membrane Transport in Health & Disease, 2003. *Recreations:* food, antique silver, hill walking. *Address:* Corpus Christi College, Merton Street, Oxford OX1 4JF. *T:* (01865) 276760.

ELLWOOD, Sir Peter (Brian), Kt 2011; CBE 2001; DL; Director, St Andrew's Healthcare, since 2010; *b* 15 May 1943; *s* of Isaac and Edith Ellwood; *m* 1968, Judy Ann Windsor; one *s* two *d*. *Educ:* King's Sch., Macclesfield. FCIB. Barclays Bank, 1961–89; Chief Exec., Barclaycard, 1985–89; Chief Exec., Retail Banking, TSB, 1989–92; Gp Chief Exec., TSB Gp, 1992–95; Chm., Visa International, 1994–99; Dep. Gp Chief Exec., 1995–97, Gp Chief Exec., 1997–2003, Lloyds TSB Gp plc. Dep. Chm., 2003, Chm., 2004–08, ICI PLC; Chm., Rexam PLC, 2008–12. Dir, Supervisory Bd, Akzo Nobel, 2008–14. Non-exec. Dir, Royal Philharmonic Orchestra Ltd, 1996–2007. Chairman: The Work Foundn, 2001–07; Royal Parks Adv. Bd, 2003–07; Royal Parks Foundn, 2003–08. Pres., Northampton Bach Choir, 2005–. Trustee, Royal Theatre, Northampton, 1982–99. Mem. Court, Univ. of Northampton (formerly Nene Coll., later UC Northampton), 1989–. FRSA. Hon. LLD Leicester, 1994; DUniv Central England, 1995. DL 2005, High Sheriff 2008, Northants. *Recreations:* theatre, music. *Address:* Wyndham House, Main Street, Church Stowe, Northampton NN7 4SG.

ELLWOOD, Peter David Roger, OBE 2002; Regional Director, Americas (formerly Latin America and Caribbean), British Council, 2009–12; consultant on international partnerships, University of Sussex, 2013–14; *b* 17 Oct. 1948; *s* of John and Eileen Ellwood; *m* 1976; one *s* two *d*; *m* 2010, Maria Karutina. *Educ:* Trinity Hall, Cambridge (BA Hons English 1970, MA). Shell-Mex and BP, 1970–75; British Council, 1975–2012: Asst Rep., Nepal, 1975–79; Regl Officer, Middle East (based in London), 1979–81; Pvte Sec. to Dir Gen., 1981–83; Dep. Rep., Indonesia, 1983–86; Dir, Cameroon, 1986–89; Dep. Dir, France, 1989–94; Director: Sri Lanka, 1994–98; Pakistan, 1998–2002; Regional Director: Middle East, UAE, 2002–04; N and Central Europe, Sweden, 2004–07; Russia and N Europe, Prague, 2007–09. *Recreations:* travel, birdwatching, theatre, opera. *Address:* 25 Queens Park Road, Brighton BN2 0GJ.

ELLWOOD, Tobias; MP (C) Bournemouth East, since 2005; Parliamentary Under-Secretary of State, Foreign and Commonwealth Office, since 2014; *b* 12 Aug. 1966; *s* of Peter Ellwood and Dr Caroline Ellwood; *m* 2005, Hannah Ryan. *Educ:* Vienna Internat. Sch.; Loughborough Univ. (BA Hons Design and Technol.); City Univ. Business Sch. (MBA); Kennedy Sch. of Govt, Harvard Univ. (Exec. Course on Nat. and Internat. Security). Served Army, RGJ, 1991–96. Researcher for Rt Hon. Tom King, 1996–97; Senior Business Develt Manager: London Stock Exchange, 1998–2002; Allen & Overy, 2002–04. Shadow Minister for culture, media and sport, 2007–10; PPS to Sec. of State for Defence, 2010–11, to Minister for Europe, 2011–13, to Sec. of State for Health, 2013–14. Mem., Parly Delegn to NATO, 2014–; Parly Advr to Prime Minister for NATO Summit, 2014. *Recreations:* private pilot, wind-surfing, travel, diving, landscape gardening, military history. *Address:* House of Commons, SW1A 0AA. *T:* (020) 7219 3000. *E:* tobias.ellwood.mp@parliament.uk.

ELLY, His Honour (Richard) Charles; DL; a Circuit Judge, 1998–2012; Partner, Reynolds, Parry-Jones & Crawford, solicitors, 1968–98; *b* 20 March 1942; *s* of Harold Elly and Dora Ellen Elly (*née* Luing); *m* 1967, Marion Rose Blackwell; one *s* one *d*. *Educ:* Sir William Borlase's Sch., Marlow; Hertford Coll., Oxford (MA); Coll. of Law, London. Admitted solicitor, 1966. Secretary: Southern Assoc. of Law Socs, 1975–82; Berks, Bucks and Oxon Law Soc., 1975–82 (Pres., 1988–89); Law Society: Mem. Council, 1981–97; Dep. Vice-Pres., 1992–93; Vice-Pres., 1993–94; Pres., 1994–95. Mem., Lord Chancellor's Adv. Cttee on Legal Educn and Conduct, 1997–98. Mem., Berks CC, 1980–81. Chairman: Maidenhead Deanery Synod, 1972–79; High Wycombe and Dist CAB, 1983–88; Maidenhead Contact Centre, 2012–; Dir, Diocesan Trustees (Oxford) Ltd, 2012–. President: Cookham Soc., 1987–97; Hertford Coll. Lawyers Assoc., 1995–98; Criminal Law Solicitors Assoc., 1995–98. Gov., Coll. of Law, 1984–2000; Gov., 1995–2011 (Chm. Govs, 1996–2001), Chm. Trustees, 2001–, Sir William Borlase's Sch. Chm., Berks Gardens Trust, 2013–. FRSA 1995. DL Berks, 2011. Hon. LLD Kingston, 1994. *Recreations:* bird-watching, theatre, walking, gardening. *Address:* Court Cottage, Dean Lane, Cookham Dean, Maidenhead, Berks SL6 9AF. *Club:* Oxford and Cambridge.

ELMES, Caroline Myfanwy Tonge, CMG 2001; HM Diplomatic Service, retired; *b* 20 Sept. 1948. Second Sec., FCO, 1975; First Secretary: Czechoslovakia, 1978–81; FCO, 1981–85; (Econ.), Rome, 1985–89; Dep. High Comr and Head of Chancery, Sri Lanka, 1989–92; Dep. Head of Mission, Czechoslovakia, 1992–95; Head of S Asia Dept, FCO, 1995–98; language trng, 1998; Ambassador to Angola, 1998–2002.

ELMS, Marsha Marilyn, (Marsha Carey-Elms), OBE 2012; JP; MA; Executive Head Teacher, Kendrick School and Reading Girls' School, 2007–12; Education Adviser, Department for Education, 2012; *b* 11 June 1946; *d* of James F. Carey and Carolyn M. Carey;

m (marr. diss.); one *s* one *d*. *Educ:* Tottenham County Grammar Sch.; Bedford Coll., London Univ. (BA); Brunel Univ. (PGCE 1969); Reading Univ. (MA 1988). Featherstone High School, Southall: teacher, 1969–90; Head, Liberal Studies Faculty, 1973–75; Dep. Head, 1990; Dep. Headteacher, Magna Carta Sch., Staines, 1990–93; acting Headteacher, Ashmead Sch., Reading, Summer term 1998; Headteacher, Kendrick Girls' Sch., 1993–2007. Mem., ASCL (formerly SHA), 1994–2012; Pres., Assoc. of Girls' Maintained Schs, 2002–03; Chm., Berkshire Assoc. of Heads, 2009–12; Mem., Graduation Bd, Nat. Professional Qualification for Headship, 2011–. Nat. Leader of Educn, 2007–12. Exec. Hd, Kendrick Fedn, 2006–12. Governor: Reading Girls' Sch., 2007–; Shiplake Coll., Henley; Altwood Sch., Maidenhead; Trustee, Kendrick Sch., 2012–. JP Middx 1982 (Mem., W London Adv. Cttee, 2012–). *Publications:* articles for ASCL and in educnl jls. *Recreations:* family, holidays, Spurs supporter, food, painting. *Address:* Roseneath, Altwood Bailey, Maidenhead, Berks SL6 4PQ. *T:* (01628) 620085. *Clubs:* Lansdowne; Phyllis Court (Henley-on-Thames).

ELPHICK, Dr Clive Harry; Independent Director: National Grid Gas plc, since 2014; National Grid Electricity Transmission plc, since 2014; Member, Competition Appeal Tribunal, since 2011; Board Member, Environment Agency, since 2011; *b* Eastbourne, 24 Nov. 1956; *s* of late Leonard Harry Elphick and of Pamela Joan Elphick (*née* Reed); *m* 1st, 1979, Kathryn Heasman (marr. diss. 1986); 2nd, 2003, Jane Harris (*née* Adams). *Educ:* Eastbourne Grammar Sch.; Queens' Coll., Cambridge (BA 1978; MA); Univ. of Birmingham (MSc; PhD 1981). FCMA 1990. United Utilities Group plc: Gp Financial Controller, 1991–92; Econ. Regulation Dir, 1992–94; Gp Strategic Planning Dir, 1995–2005; Chief Operating Officer, Transformation, 2006–07; Man. Dir, Asset Mgt and Regulation, 2007–09. Board Member: DCMS, 2003–07; NI Authy for Utility Regulation, 2006–12; Northwest RDA, 2010–11. Chm., NW CBI, 2008–09. Mem., England Cttee, Wildlife Trusts, 2012–. Trustee: Lancs Wildlife Trust, 2010–; Nat. Museums and Galleries of Liverpool, 2012–. Liveryman, Water Conservators' Co., 2009–. FRSA. *Publications:* contrib. papers on econ. regulation, maths and graph theory. *Recreations:* hiking, mountain biking, classical music, New Zealand. *E:* clive.elphick@gmail.com.

ELPHICKE, Charles; MP (C) Dover, since 2010; a Lord Commissioner of HM Treasury (Government Whip), since 2015; *b* Huntingdon, 14 March 1971; *m* 1996, Natalie Ross (OBE 2015); one *s* one *d*. *Educ:* Felsted Sch.; Nottingham Univ. (LLB Hons). Called to the Bar, Middle Temple, 1994; admitted solicitor, 1998; Partner and Hd of Tax, Reed Smith, solicitors, 2001–05; Partner and Hd of Eur. Tax, Hunton & Williams, solicitors, 2006–10. Mem. (C) Lambeth LBC, 1994–98. Contested (C) St Albans, 2001. *Publications:* papers for Centre for Policy Studies. *Recreations:* sailing, making Britain a richer, more exciting place to be. *Address:* House of Commons, SW1A 0AA. *T:* (020) 7219 3000. *E:* charlie.elphicke.mp@parliament.uk. *Club:* Royal Cinque Ports Yacht.

ELPHINSTON of Glack, Sir Alexander, 12th Bt *cr* 1701, of Logie Elphinstone and Nova Scotia; Senior Associate Solicitor, Anthony Collins Solicitors, since 2005; *b* Gloucester, 6 June 1955; *s* of Sir John Elphinston of Glack, 11th Bt and of Margaret Doreen Elphinston (*née* Tasker); *S* father 2015, but his name does not appear on the Official Roll of the Baronetage; *m* 1986, Ruth Mary Dunnett; three *s* one *d*. *Educ:* Repton; Durham Univ. (BA Gen. Arts 1977). Admitted solicitor, 1980; in practice, 1980–; Partner, Foot Anstey, 1991–2001. Chm., STEP, England and Wales, 2014– (Mem., Birmingham Cttee, 2001–; Mem., Mental Capacity Gp, 2013–); Member: Solicitors for the Elderly, 2001– (Mem., Birmingham Cttee, 2001–); Court of Protection User Gp, 2013–. *Publications:* articles in STEP Jl. *Recreations:* walking, jazz, theatre, jigsaws. *Heir: s* Daniel John Elphinston, *b* 24 Sept, 1989. *Address:* 43 Lonsdale Road, Harborne, Birmingham B17 9QX.

ELPHINSTONE, family name of **Lord Elphinstone**.

ELPHINSTONE, 19th Lord *cr* 1509; **Alexander Mountstuart Elphinstone;** Baron (UK) 1885; *b* 15 April 1980; *e s* of 18th Lord Elphinstone and of Willa Mary Gabriel, 4th *d* of Major David Chetwode; *S* father, 1994; *m* 2007, Nicola Jane, *yr d* of Michael Hall, Beaconsfield; two *s* one *d*. *Educ:* Belhaven Hill Sch.; Eton Coll.; Univ. of Newcastle upon Tyne (MSc 2002); Sch. of Oriental and African Studies, London (MA Develt Studies 2005). *Heir: s* Hon. Jago Alexander Elphinstone, Master of Elphinstone, *b* 19 Aug. 2011.

ELPHINSTONE, Sir John (Howard Main), 6th Bt *cr* 1816, of Sowerby, Cumberland; *b* 25 Feb. 1949; *o s* of Sir Douglas Elphinstone, 5th Bt and of Helen Barbara Elphinstone (*née* Main); *S* father, 1995; *m* 1990, Diane Barbara Quilliam, *d* of Dr B. Q. Callow. *Educ:* Loretto Sch., Midlothian. *Heir: cousin* Henry Charles Elphinstone, *b* 7 July 1958. *Address:* Crooklands, Clapham, Lancaster LA2 8HY.

ELS, Theodore Ernest, (Ernie); South African golfer; *b* 17 Oct. 1969; *s* of Cornelius, (Nils), and Hester Els; *m* 1998, Liezl Wehmeyer; one *s* one *d*. *Educ:* Delville Sch.; Jan de Klerk Tech. Coll. Professional golfer, 1989–; winner: Jun. World Championship, USA, 1984; South African Open, 1992, 1996, 1998, 2006, 2010; US Open, 1994, 1997; World Match Play Championship, 1994, 1995, 1996, 2002, 2003, 2004, 2007; European Order of Merit, 1995; South African PGA Championship, 1995; Million Dollar Challenge, Sun City, 1999; Nedbank Golf Challenge, Sun City, 2000, 2002; Open, Muirfield, 2002; Open, Royal Lytham and St Annes, 2012.

ELSE, Jean, MA; Headteacher, Whalley Range High School, Manchester, 1994–2006. Teacher: Counthill Sch., Oldham; various schs in Rochdale and Trafford. Co-ordinator for Manchester, DFES Excellence in the Cities, 1999. Trustee, Imperial War Mus., 2003–07.

ELSE, Martin Thomas; Chief Executive, Royal College of Physicians, 2005–13; *b* 21 May 1953; *s* of late Richard Else and of Lilian Margaret Else (*née* Stickells); *m* 1978, Jennifer Louise Bridges; one *s* one *d*. *Educ:* Farnborough Grammar Sch.; Univ. of Salford (BSc Econ); Southampton Coll. of Technol.; London Business Sch. (Sloan Fellowship with Dist.). CPFA (IPFA 1979). Finance trainee, City and Hackney HA, 1975–79; Principal Finance Planning Manager, 1979–82, Principal Asst Treas., 1982–83, NE Thames RHA; Dep. Treas., 1983–86, Dir of Finance, 1986–90, Hampstead HA; Royal Free Hampstead NHS Trust: Dir of Finance and Dep. Chief Exec., 1990–94; Chief Exec., 1994–2005. Policy Advr, DoH, 2005; Dir, RCP Regent's Park Ltd, 2005–13. Treas., Alzheimer's Disease Internat., 2005–13; Mem., Independent Age, 2010–. Royal Free Hospital: Hon. Sec. and Treas. to Special Trustees, 1986–2005; Trustee, Appeal Trust, 1988–92; Chm., Cancerkin Mgt Cttee, 1990–94; Trustee: Hampstead Wells and Campden Trust, 1996–2005; CORESS, 2006–. Health Comr, Liverpool, 2013–14. FRSocMed 2007–13. Hon. FRCP 2013. *Recreations:* football, cricket, golf, horseracing. *E:* martin.else@hotmail.co.uk.

ELSEY, Roger William; a District Judge (Magistrates' Courts), since 2004; *b* 12 June 1954; *s* of William Gattie Elsey and Rita Alillian Elsey; *m* 1985, Susan Coull; three *d*. *Educ:* Bede Sch.; Univ. of Newcastle upon Tyne (LLB Hons); Open Univ. (MA 2008). Called to the Bar, Gray's Inn, 1977; practised in criminal law, N Eastern Circuit. Actg Stipendiary Magistrate, 1999–2004. Jt Ed., Signpost mag., 2000–. Mem., Durham Diocesan Synod, 2003–08. *Recreations:* cycling, theatre, walking, Anglican affairs. *Address:* Sunderland Magistrates' Court, Gillbridge Avenue, Sunderland SR1 3AP. *T:* (01915) 141621.

ELSON, Anthony Kenneth; independent consultant, since 2004; *b* 15 June 1948; *s* of William and Elsie Elson; *m* 1971, Joy Waterworth. *Educ:* Birmingham Univ. (BSc 1st cl. Hons Exptl Physics 1969); Liverpool Univ. (BPhil Applied Social Studies 1972); CQSW. Social Worker, 1972–76; Principal Lectr in Social Work, Worcester Coll. of Further Educn, 1976–78; Social Services, Birmingham City Council: Team Manager, 1978–81; Area Manager, 1981–83; Asst Dir, 1983–88; Kirklees Metropolitan Borough Council: Dir of Social Services, 1988–89; Exec. Dir (Housing and Social Services), 1989–97; Exec. Dir (Social Services and Educn), 1997–98; Chief Exec., 1998–2004. Local Govt Advr, DoH, 2004. *E:* tony.elson@broomstileconsultants.co.uk.

ELSON, Prof. Diane Rosemary, PhD; Professor of Sociology, University of Essex, 2000–12, now Emeritus; *b* Bedworth, Warwickshire, 20 April 1946; *d* of Edwin and Vera Elson; one *s*. *Educ:* St Hilda's Coll., Oxford (BA Hons PPE 1968); Univ. of Manchester (PhD Econs 1994). Res. Asst, Inst. of Commonwealth Studies and St Antony's Coll., Oxford, 1968–71; Teaching Fellow, Dept of Economics, Univ. of York, 1971–75; Res. Officer, Inst. of Develt Studies, Univ. of Sussex, 1975–77; Temp. Lectr, Univ. of Manchester, 1978–79; part-time consultant and occasional lectr, 1979–84; University of Manchester: Hon. Res. Fellow, Internat. Develt Centre and Dept of Sociol., 1984–85; Lectr, 1985–91, Reader, 1992–95, in Develt Econs; Prof. of Develt Studies, 1995–98; Special Advr, UN Develt Fund for Women, 1998–2000; Advr, UN Women, 2012–. Member: UN Taskforce on Millennium Develt Goals, 1998–2000; Strategic Res. Bd, ESRC, 2008–10; UN Cttee on Develt Policy, 2013–. *Publications:* Male Bias in the Development Process, 1991, 2nd edn 1995; Progress of World's Women, 2000; Budgeting for Women's Rights, 2006; (ed jtly) Economic Policy and Human Rights Obligations, 2011; (ed jtly) Harvesting Feminist Knowledge for Public Policy, 2011; (ed jtly) Financial Governance from a Feminist Perspective, 2011; (ed jtly) Human Rights and the Capabilities Approach: an interdisciplinary dialogue, 2012. *Recreations:* gardening, bird watching, campaigning for women's rights. *Address:* c/o Department of Sociology, University of Essex, Wivenhoe Park, Colchester CO4 3SQ. *T:* (01206) 873539, *Fax:* (01206) 873410. *E:* drelson@essex.ac.uk.

ELSON, Graham Peel; Chief Executive, South West One, political and public affairs company, since 1998; *b* 21 Aug. 1949; *s* of George Ernest Elson and Rhoda (*née* Atkinson); *m* 1975, Jane Rosamunde Isaac. *Educ:* Palmers Endowed Sch. for Boys, Grays, Essex; NE London Polytechnic (BA Business Studies). Brand Manager, Rank Hovis McDougall Foods, 1972–74; Gen. Manager, Wilkinson Sword Gp, 1974–85. Councillor (Lib Dem) and Leader, Oxfordshire CC, 1985–89; Councillor (Lib Dem), Mid Devon DC, 1999–2003. Gen. Sec., Liberal Democrats, 1989–97. *Recreations:* boating, gardening, supporting West Ham United FC. *Address:* 3 The Halt, Alphington, Exeter EX2 8FX.

ELSTEIN, David Keith; Chairman, Open Democracy, since 2010; *b* 14 Nov. 1944; *s* of late Albert Elstein and Millie Cohen; *m*; one *s*. *Educ:* Haberdashers' Aske's; Gonville and Caius Coll., Cambridge (BA, MA). BBC, 1964–68; ITV, 1968–82; founded Brook Prodns, 1982; Man. Dir, Primetime Television, 1983–86; Dir of Programmes, Thames Television, 1986–92; Hd of Programmes, BSkyB, 1993–96; Chief Exec., Channel 5 Broadcasting, 1996–2000. Visiting Professor: Univ. of Oxford, 1999; Univ. of Westminster, 2001–04; Univ. of Stirling, 2002–07. Beesley Lectr, 2009. Chairman: Nat. Film and Television Sch., 1996–2002; British Screen Adv. Council, 1997–2008; Really Useful Theatres, 2001–06; Screen Digest Ltd, 2004–; Commercial Radio Companies Assoc., 2004–06; Sparrowhawk Investments Ltd, 2004–07; DCD Media (formerly Digital Classics), 2005–10; Luther Pendragon Hldgs, 2006–10; Vice-Chm., Kingsbridge Capital Ltd (formerly Hardt Gp (UK)), 2003–; non-executive Director: Virgin Media (formerly NTL), 2003–08; Orion Holdings, 2006–09; Primacom AG, 2008–10. Chm., Broadcasting Policy Gp, 2003–. *Recreations:* film, theatre, bridge, reading.

ELSTON, Christopher David; Chief Executive, London Bullion Market Association, 1995–99; *b* 1 Aug. 1938; *s* of Herbert Cecil Elston and Ada Louisa (*née* Paige); *m* 1964, Jennifer Isabel Rampling; one *s* two *d*. *Educ:* University Coll. Sch., Hampstead; King's Coll., Cambridge (BA Classics, 1960, MA 1980); Yale Univ. (MA Econs, 1967). Bank of England, 1960–95: seconded to Bank for Internat. Settlements, Basle, Switzerland, 1969–71; Private Sec. to Governor of Bank of England, 1974–76; Asst to Chief Cashier, 1976–79; seconded to HM Diplomatic Service, as Counsellor (Financial), British Embassy, Tokyo, 1979–83; Advr, later Sen. Advr (Asia and Australasia), 1983–94. Advr, KorAm Bank London Br., 1995–2000. Ordinary Mem. Council and Chm. Business Gp, Japan Soc., 1997–2000. *Recreations:* music, garden, photography. *Address:* 23 Grasmere Avenue, Harpenden, Herts AL5 5PT. *T:* (01582) 760147.

ELTIS, Walter Alfred, DLitt; Emeritus Fellow of Exeter College, Oxford, since 1988; *b* 23 May 1933; *s* of Rev. Martin Eltis and Mary (*née* Schnitzer); *m* 1959, Shelagh Mary, *d* of Rev. Preb. Douglas Owen; one *s* two *d*. *Educ:* Wycliffe Coll.; Emmanuel Coll., Cambridge (BA Econs 1956); Nuffield Coll., Oxford. MA Oxon 1960; DLitt Oxon 1990. Nat. Service, Navigator, RAF, 1951–53. Res. Fellow, Exeter Coll., Oxford, 1958–60; Lectr in Econs, Exeter and Keble Colls, Oxford, 1960–63; Fellow and Tutor in Econs, Exeter Coll., Oxford, 1963–88; National Economic Development Office: Econ. Dir, 1986–88; Dir Gen., 1988–92; Chief Economic Advr to Pres., BoT, 1992–95. Vis. Reader in Econs, Univ. of WA, 1970; Visiting Professor: Univ. of Toronto, 1976–77; European Univ., Florence, 1979; Reading Univ., 1992–2004; Gresham Prof. of Commerce, Gresham Coll., 1993–96. Mem. Council, 1987–93, Chm., Social Scis Cttee, 1987–88, CNAA; Member Council: European Policy Forum, 1992–; Foundn for Manufacturing and Industry, 1993–96. Vice-Pres., European Soc. of Hist. of Econ. Thought, 2000–04. Gov., Wycliffe Coll., 1972–88. Gen. Ed., Oxford Economic Papers, 1975–81. *Publications:* Economic Growth: analysis and policy, 1966; Growth and Distribution, 1973; (with R. Bacon) The Age of US and UK Machinery, 1974; (with R. Bacon) Britain's Economic Problem: too few producers, 1976, 3rd edn (as Britain's Economic Problem Revisited), 1996; The Classical Theory of Economic Growth, 1984, 2nd edn 2000; (with P. Sinclair) Keynes and Economic Policy, 1988; Classical Economics, Public Expenditure and Growth, 1993; (ed with S. M. Eltis) Condillac, Commerce and Government, 1997; Britain, Europe and EMU, 2000; contribs to econ. jls. *Recreations:* chess, music. *Address:* Danesway, Jarn Way, Boars Hill, Oxford OX1 5JF. *T:* (01865) 735440. *Club:* Reform (Chm., 1994–95).

ELTOM, Mohammed Abdalla Ali; Ambassador of the Republic of Sudan to the Court of St James's, since 2014; *b* Annuhoud, Sudan, 10 Nov. 1963; *s* of Abdalla Ali Eltom and Aysha Mukhtar Abuaagla; *m* 1994, Amani Abuaagla; four *s*. *Educ:* Univ. of Khartoum (BSc Econs, Econ. and Pol Sci.; Post Grad. Dip. Internat. Relns); Juba Univ. (MSc Peace and Develt Studies). Entered Min. of Foreign Affairs, Sudan, 1988; Second Secretary: Abu Dhabi, 1990–92; Amman, 1993–95; First Sec., Damascus, 1995–97; Counsellor i/c Congressional Affairs, Washington, 2001–05; Minister Plenipotentiary, 2008–10, Dep. Hd of Mission, 2010–12, UK. *Recreations:* reading, walking, watching football. *Address:* Embassy of the Republic of Sudan, 3 Cleveland Row, SW1A 1DD. *T:* (020) 7839 8080. *E:* info@sudan-embassy.co.uk.

ELTON, family name of **Baron Elton**.

ELTON, 2nd Baron *cr* 1934, of Headington; **Rodney Elton,** TD 1970; a Deputy Speaker, House of Lords, 1999–2008; *b* 2 March 1930; *s* of 1st Baron Elton and of Dedi (*d* 1977), *d* of Gustav Hartmann, Oslo; *S* father, 1973; *m* 1st, 1958, Anne Frances (separated 1973; marr. diss. 1979), *e d* of late Brig. R. A. G. Tilney, CBE, DSO, TD; one *s* three *d*; 2nd, 1979, (Susan) Richenda (DCVO 2010), *y d* of late Sir Hugh Gurney, KCMG, MVO, and Lady Gurney. *Educ:* Dragon Sch., Oxford; Eton; New Coll., Oxford (MA). Farming, 1954–64. Assistant Master: Loughborough Grammar Sch., 1964–67; Fairham Comprehensive School for Boys, Nottingham, 1967–69; Lectr, Bishop Lonsdale College of Education, 1969–72. Contested (C) Leics, Loughborough, 1966, 1970. Cons. Whip, House of Lords, Feb. 1974–76, an Opposition spokesman, 1976–79; Parly Under Sec. of State, NI Office, 1979–81, DHSS,

1981–82, Home Office, 1982–84; Minister of State: Home Office, 1984–85; DoE, 1985–86. House of Lords: Mem., Delegated Powers Scrutiny Cttee, 1993–96; a Dep. Chm. of Cttees, 1997–2008; elected Mem., 1999; Member: Lord Privy Seal's Cttee on Neill Report, 2001; Offices Select Cttee, 2001–02; Select Cttee on the Constitution, 2002–07; Jt Ecclesiastical Cttee, H of L and H of C, 2002–. Mem. Exec. Cttee, Assoc. of Cons. Peers, 1986–93, 1994–97, 2001–03 (Dep. Chm., 1991–93). Chm., FIMBRA, 1987–90; Mem., Panel on Takeovers and Mergers, 1987–90. Formerly Director: Overseas Exhibition Services Ltd; Building Trades Exhibition Ltd. Dep. Chm., Andry Montgomery Ltd, 1978–79 and 1986–2001. Dep. Sec., Cttee on Internat. Affairs, Synod of C of E, 1976–78. Licensed Lay Minister, Oxford dio., C of E, 1998–. Mem. Boyd Commn to evaluate elections in Rhodesia, 1979; Chm., Cttee of Enquiry into discipline in schools, 1988. Chm., Intermediate Treatment Fund, 1990–93; Vice-Pres., Inst. of Trading Standards Administrators, 1990–; Member of Council: CGLI, 1987–91 (Chm., Quality and Standards Cttee, 1999–2005; Hon. FCGI 2005); Rainer Foundn, 1990–96; Founding Chm., DIVERT Trust, 1993–2001; Pres., Building Conservation Trust, 1990–95; Trustee: City Parochial Foundn, 1990–97; Trust for London, 1990–97. Late Captain, Queen's Own Warwickshire and Worcs Yeo.; late Major, Leics and Derbys (PAO) Yeo. Lord of the Manor of Adderbury, Oxon, 1973. *Heir: s* Hon. Edward Paget Elton [*b* 28 May 1966; *m* 2004, Claire Helen Pauline, *y d* of Sir Morgan O'Connell, 6th Bt; one *s*]. *Address:* House of Lords, SW1A 0PW. *Clubs:* Pratt's, Beefsteak, Cavalry and Guards.

See also Lord Gray.

ELTON, Sir Arnold, Kt 1987; CBE 1982; FRCS; Consultant Surgeon, Northwick Park Hospital and Clinical Research Centre, 1970–85; *b* 14 Feb. 1920; *s* of late Max Elton and of Ada Elton; *m* 1952, Billie Pamela Briggs; one *s*. *Educ:* University Coll. London (exhibnr; MB BS 1943); UCH Med. Sch. (MS 1951); Jun. and Sen. Gold Medal in Surgery. LRCP 1943; MRCS 1943, FRCS 1946. House Surg., House Physician and Casualty Officer, UCH, 1943–45; Sen. Surgical Registrar, Charing Cross Hosp., 1947–51 (Gosse Res. Schol.); Consultant Surgeon: Harrow Hosp., 1951–70; Mount Vernon Hosp., 1960–70; British Airways, 1981–95. First Chm., Med. Staff Cttee, Chm., Surgical Div. and Theatre Cttee, Mem., Ethical Cttee, Northwick Park Hosp. Mem., Govt Wkg Party on Breast Screening for Cancer, 1985–. Mem., Tricare Europe Preferred Provider Network, 1997–. Med. Dir, 1997–2003, Dep. Chm., 2000–03, Medical Marketing Internat. Gp (formerly Management of Medical Innovation) plc; Chairman and Executive Director: Healthy Living (UK) Ltd, 1997–; Healthy Living (Durham) Ltd, 1998–; Universal Lifestyle Ltd, 1999–; Health Executive: Bovis Lend Lease, 2001–; BDL plc, 2009–; Chm., Medical Consulting Services Ltd, 1991–. Examiner: GNC; RCS, 1971–83; Surgical Tutor, RCS, 1970–82. Pres., Cons. Med. Soc., 1992–97, now President Emeritus (Nat. Chm., 1975–92; Eur. Rep., 1994–; Chm., Eur. Gp; Ed., Eur. Bull., 1994–); Mem., Cons. Central Council and Nat. Exec. Cttee, 1976–93. Chm., Internat. Med. and Science Fundraising Cttee, BRCS, 1998–. Founder Officer, British Assoc. of Surgical Oncology, 1972–; Member: Eur. Soc. of Surgical Oncology, 1994–; World Fedn Surgical Oncology Socs, 1994–; Ct of Patrons, RCS, 1986–; Dir and Co-ordinator, RCS Exchange of Surgeons with China, 1994–. Mem. and UK Chm., Internat. Med. Parliamentarians Orgn, 1996–. Chairman: Med. and Sci. Div., World Fellowship Duke of Edinburgh's Award, 1997–; Events Cttee, Duke of Edinburgh's Award, 2008–; Internat. Benefactor, Duke of Edinburgh's Award, 2009–. International Advisor: World Fedn Surgical Oncology Socs, 1998–; PPP/Colombia, subseq. HCA, Gp of Hosps, 1998–; Med. Advr, Virgin Active (Healthy Living Centres), 1997–; Health Consultant and Advr, Keltbray Ltd, 2003–. Fellow, Assoc. of Surgeons of GB; FRSocMed; FICS; Fellow, European Fedn of Surgeons. Freeman, City of London; Liveryman: Apothecaries' Soc.; Carmen's Co. Jubilee Medal, 1977. *Publications:* contribs to med. jls. *Recreations:* tennis, music, cricket. *Address:* 58 Stockleigh Hall, Prince Albert Road, NW8 7LB; The Consulting Rooms, Wellington Hospital, Wellington Place, NW8 9LE. *T:* (020) 7483 5275. *Clubs:* Carlton, Royal Automobile, MCC.

ELTON, Benjamin Charles; author and performer; *b* 3 May 1959; *s* of Prof. Lewis Richard Benjamin Elton, *qv* and (Kathleen) Mary Elton (*née* Foster); *m* 1994, Sophie Gare; two *s* one *d* (of whom one *s* one *d* are twins). *Educ:* Godalming Grammar Sch.; S Warwicks Coll. of Further Educn; Manchester Univ. (BA Drama). First professional appearance, Comic Strip Club, 1981; writer for television: Happy Families, 1985; Filthy Rich and Catflap, 1986; The Thin Blue Line, 1995, 1996; jointly: The Young Ones, 1982, 1984; Blackadder II, 1987; Blackadder the Third, 1988; Blackadder goes Forth, 1989; writer and performer: Friday Live, 1987–88; Saturday Live, 1986–87, 1988; The Man from Auntie, 1990, 1994; Stark, 1993; The Ben Elton Show, 1998; Get A Grip, 2007; writer and director: Silly Cow, Theatre Royal, Haymarket, 1991; Maybe Baby (film), 2000; We Will Rock You (musical), 2002; Tonight's the Night (musical), Victoria Palace, 2003; Blessed (TV), 2005; writer: Gasping, Theatre Royal, Haymarket, 1990; Popcorn, Apollo, 1997; The Beautiful Game (musical), 2000; (jtly) Love Never Dies (book of musical), 2010; actor: Much Ado About Nothing (film), 1993; numerous tours as a stand-up comic, 1986, 1987, 1989, 1993, 1996–97, 2005–06. Hon. Dr Manchester. *Publications: novels:* Stark, 1989; Gridlock, 1991; This Other Eden, 1993; Popcorn, 1996; Blast from the Past, 1998; Inconceivable, 1999; Dead Famous, 2001; High Society, 2002; Past Mortem, 2004; The First Casualty, 2005; Chart Throb, 2006; Blind Faith, 2007; Meltdown, 2009; Two Brothers, 2012; Time And Time Again, 2014; *plays:* Gasping, 1990; Silly Cow, 1991; Popcorn, 1996; Blast from the Past, 1998. *Recreations:* walking, reading, drinking, cutting firewood, Sunday lunch. *Address:* c/o Phil McIntyre, 3rd Floor, 85 Newman Street, W1T 3EU. *Club:* Groucho.

ELTON, Sir Charles (Abraham Grierson), 11th Bt *cr* 1717; film and television producer; *b* 23 May 1953; *s* of Sir Arthur Hallam Rice Elton, 10th Bt, and Margaret Ann (*d* 1995), *d* of Olafur Bjornson; *S* father, 1973; *m* 1990, Lucy Lauris (*see* L. L. Heller) (marr. diss. 2007), *d* of late Lukas Heller; one *s* one *d*. *Educ:* Eton Coll.; Reading Univ. Publishing, 1976–79; BBC, 1979–84; Director: Curtis Brown, 1984–91; First Choice Productions, 1991–2000; Exec. Producer, Carlton Television, subseq. ITV Productions, 2000–08. *Publications:* Mr Toppitt, 2009. *Heir: s* Abraham William Elton, *b* 27 Sept. 1995. *Address:* Clevedon Court, Somerset BS21 6QU; 25 Dartmouth Park Hill, NW5 1HP. *Club:* Garrick.

ELTON, Dr George Alfred Hugh, CB 1983; consultant in biochemistry, since 1985; *b* 27 Feb. 1925; *s* of Horace and Violet Elton; *m* 1951, Theodora Rose Edith Kingham; two *d*. *Educ:* Sutton County Sch.; London Univ. (evening student). BSc 1944, PhD 1948, DSc 1956; FRSC (FRIC 1951); CChem 1974; EurChem 1993; FIFST 1968; FRSB (FIBiol 1976); CBiol 1984. Mem. Faculty of Science, and Univ. Examr in Chemistry, Univ. of London, 1951–58; Dir, Fog Res. Unit, Min. of Supply, 1954–58; Reader in Applied Phys. Chemistry, Battersea Polytechnic, 1956–58; Dir, British Baking Industries Res. Assoc., 1958–66; Dir, Flour Milling and Baking Res. Assoc., 1967–70; Ministry of Agriculture, Fisheries and Food: Chief Sci. Adviser (Food), 1971–85; Head of Food Science Div., 1972–73; Dep. Chief Scientist, 1972; Under-Sec. 1974; Chief Scientist (Fisheries and Food), 1981–85. Vis. Prof., Surrey Univ., 1982–97; Vis. Lectr, various overseas univs, 1952–92. Consultant: FAO, 1992; Internat. Life Scis Inst., USA, 1997–2001. Chairman: National Food Survey Cttee, 1978–85; Adv. Bd, Inst. of Food Res. (Bristol), 1985–88; Scientific Advr, BFMIRA, 1986–92; Scientific Governor: British Nutrition Foundn, 1971–2000; Internat. Life Scis Inst. (Europe), 1987–97; Vice-Chm., EEC Scientific Cttee for Food, 1987–92; Member: Cttee on Medical Aspects of Food Policy, 1971–85; UK Delegn, Tripartite Meetings on Food and Drugs, 1971–85; AFRC (formerly ARC), 1981–85; NERC, 1981–85; Fisheries Res. and Develt Bd, 1982–85; Adv. Bd for Research Councils, 1981–84; Council: Chemical Soc., 1972–75; BIBRA, 1990–2000 (Chm., 1993–95; Vice-Pres., 1996–2000). Co-inventor, Chorleywood Bread Process (Queen's Award to Industry 1966); Silver Medallist, Royal Soc. of Arts, 1969. Hon. DSc Reading, 1984; DUniv Surrey, 1991. *Publications:* research papers in jls of various learned societies. *Recreation:* golf. *Address:* Green Nook, Bridle Lane, Loudwater, Rickmansworth, Herts WD3 4JH. *Clubs:* MCC; Beaconsfield Golf.

ELTON, Prof. Lewis Richard Benjamin, MA, DSc; CPhys; FSRHE; Visiting Distinguished Scholar, SCEPTrE, University of Surrey, since 2006; Hon. College Professor of Higher Education, University College London, since 2003 (Professor of London University, 1994–99, College Professor, 1999–2003); *b* 25 March 1923; *yr s* of late Prof. Victor Leopold Ehrenberg, PhD, and Eva Dorothea (*née* Sommer); *m* 1950, (Kathleen) Mary, *d* of late Harold William Foster and Kathleen (*née* Meakin); three *s* one *d*. *Educ:* Stepanska Gymnasium, Prague; Rydal Sch., Colwyn Bay; Christ's Coll., Cambridge (Exhibr; BA 1945, MA 1948); Univ. Correspondence Coll., Cambridge, and Regent Street Polytechnic (Cert Ed Cantab 1945; BSc (External) 1st Cl. Hons Maths 1947); University Coll. London (Univ. Research Studentship; PhD 1950). Asst Master, St Bees Sch., 1944–46; Asst Lectr, then Lectr, King's Coll., London, 1950–57; Head of Physics Dept, Battersea Coll. of Technology, 1958–66; University of Surrey: Prof. of Physics, 1964–71; Head of Physics Dept, 1966–69; Prof. of Sci. Educn, 1971–86; Hd, Inst. of Educnl Develt (formerly Educnl Technol.), 1967–84; Associate Head, Dept of Educnl Studies, 1983–86; Prof. of Higher Educn, 1987–90, now Emeritus. Sen. Fulbright Award, 1955–56; Research Associate: MIT, 1955–56; Stanford Univ., 1956; Niels Bohr Inst., Copenhagen, 1962; Visiting Professor: Univ. of Washington, Seattle, 1965; UCL, 1970–77; Univ. of Sydney, 1971; Univ. of Sao Paulo, 1975; Univ. of Science, Malaysia, 1978, 1979; Univ. of Malaya, 1982, 1983; Asian Inst. of Technology, 1985, 1986; Fundação Armando Alvares Penteado, São Paulo, 1985–89; Univ. of Manchester, 2005–07; of Higher Educn, Univ. of Gloucestershire, 2008–09. Higher Educn Advr, DfEE (formerly DoE), 1989–96. Member: Governing Body, Battersea Coll. of Technology, 1962–66; Council, Univ. of Surrey, 1966–67, 1981–83; Council for Educational Technology of UK, 1975–81; Army Educn Adv. Bd, 1976–80; Convener, Standing Conf. of Physics Profs, 1971–74; Chairman: Governing Council, Soc. for Research into Higher Educn, 1976–78 (Fellow, 1987). Vice-Pres., Assoc. for Educnl and Trng Technology, 1976–95. Fellow, Amer. Physical Soc., 1978. AcSS 2009. FRSA. Hon. Life Mem., Staff and Educnl Develt Assoc., 1994. Hon. LittD Kent, 1997; Hon. PhD Glos, 2003; Hon. DLitt London (ext), 2008. The Times Higher Lifetime Achievement Award, 2005. Univ. of Surrey Art Gall. named Lewis Elton Gall., 1997. *Publications:* Introductory Nuclear Theory, 1959, 2nd edn 1965 (Spanish edn 1964); Nuclear Sizes, 1961 (Russian edn 1962); Concepts in Classical Mechanics, 1971; (with H. Messel) Time and Man, 1978; Teaching in Higher Education: appraisal and training, 1987 (Japanese edn 1989); (with E. Timms) Eva Ehrenberg, 2008; contribs to sci. jls on nuclear physics, higher education, science educn, med. educn, and educnl technology. Festschrift: (ed) P. Ashwin, Changing Higher Education: the development of learning and teaching, 2006. *Recreation:* words. *Address:* Flat 22 West Court, Burpham Lane, Guildford GU4 7LJ. *T:* (01483) 576548.

See also B. C. Elton.

ELTON, Michael Anthony; Director General, National Association of Pension Funds, 1987–95; *b* 20 May 1932; *s* of late Francis Herbert Norris Elton and Margaret Helen Elton (*née* Gray); *m* 1955, Isabel Clare, *d* of late Thomas Gurney Ryott and Clare Isabel Ryott; two *s* two *d*. *Educ:* Peter Symonds Sch.; Brasenose Coll., Oxford (Class. Mods 1952, BA 1st cl. Jurisp. 1954; MA, BCL 1955). Articled to Sir Andrew Wheatley, Clerk of Hants County Council, 1954; solicitor; Cumberland CC, 1958–61; Surrey CC, 1961–65; Asst Clerk, Bucks CC, 1965–70, Dep. Clerk of the Peace, 1967–70; Chief Exec., Assoc. of British Travel Agents, 1970–86; Dir Gen., European Fedn for Retirement Provision, 1987–91. FRSA. *Publications:* (with Gyles Brandreth) Future Perfect: how to profit from your pension planning, 1988; Travelling to Retirement: plus ça change, plus c'est la même chose, 1989; Memories of Many Minds (autobiog.), 2005; articles in professional jls. *Recreations:* tennis, music, oil painting, bridge. *Address:* 6 Royal Winchester Mews, Chilbolton Avenue, Winchester, Hants SO22 5HX. *T:* (01962) 868470.

ELVEDEN, Viscount; Arthur Benjamin Jeffrey Guinness; *b* 6 Jan. 2003; *s* and *heir* of Earl of Iveagh, *qv*.

ELVERY, Nathan Dominic; Chief Executive, London Borough of Croydon, since 2014 (Interim Chief Executive, 2013–14); *b* 2 June 1969; *s* of Patricia Anne Bennett and adopted *s* of Richard William Foote; *m* 2003, Silke Anette Benneckenstein; one *s* two *d*. *Educ:* Thomas Bennett Community Coll., Sussex; NE Surrey Coll. of Technol.; Lewes Tertiary Coll.; Brighton Coll.; CIPFA Educn Trng and Employment Centre. MAAT 1991; CIPFA 1995, CPD 2000. Principal consultant, Crawley BC, 1995–2000; Dep. Hd of Core Finance, GLA, 2000–02; Asst Dir, Finance and Business Mgt, Westminster CC, 2002–04; London Borough of Croydon: Dir of Finance, 2004–05; Dir of Finance and Resources, 2005–07; Exec. Dir of Resources and Customer Services, 2008–11; Dep. Chief Exec. and Exec. Dir of Corporate Resources and Customer Services, 2011–13. Chief Exec., London Councils, 2013–; Chairman: London Authorities Mutual Ltd, 2007–09; Croydon Enterprise Loans Fund Ltd, 2008–13; S London Partnership Chief Exec. Gp, 2014–; Croydon Strategic Metropolitan Bd, 2014–; Dep. Chm., Capital Ambition Efficiency Bd, 2008; Member, Board: London Finance Adv. Cttee, 2005–13; CCURV Ltd, 2008–12; Assoc. of Local Authorities Treasurers, 2011–13 (Pres., 2012–13); Mem., Local Govt Reference Panel, 2013–. Local Government Association: Mem., Chief Exec. Sounding Bd, 2013–; Mem., Rotherham Improvement Bd, 2014–; Chief Exec. Advr, Safer and Stronger Communities Bd, 2015–. Member: Soc. of London Treasurers, 2004–13 (Pres., 2011–12); Soc. of Municipal Treasurers, 2004–13; Soc. of Local Authy Chief Execs, 2007–. Dir of Finance of the Year for Public and Vol. Sector, Accountancy Age, 2005. *Publications:* articles in Public Finance, Local Govt Chronicle, Municipal Jl, Accountancy Age, PQ Mag., Public Servant, Insurance Times, Daily Mail and The Times. *Recreations:* my family, travelling, running, golf, cycling, charity fund raising. *Address:* Resources Department, London Borough of Croydon, Bernard Weatherill House, Floor 9, Zone B, 8 Mint Walk, Croydon CR0 1EA. *E:* nathan.elvery@croydon.gov.uk.

ELVIDGE, Gillian; *see* Matthews, G.

ELVIDGE, John Cowie; QC 2010; *b* Perth, Scotland, 27 Nov. 1964; *s* of late John Elvidge and of Flora Elvidge (*née* Cowie, now Taylor); *m* 1993, Gillian Matthews, *qv*; two *d*. *Educ:* King Edward VII Sch., Sheffield; Univ. of Newcastle Upon Tyne (LLB). Called to the Bar, Gray's Inn, 1988, Bencher, 2014. Head: York Chambers, 2011; Dere Street Barristers Chambers, 2011–. Leader, NE Circuit, 2014–. *Recreations:* sport, cinema, genealogy. *Address:* Dere Street Barristers Chambers, 14 Toft Green, York YO1 6JT. *T:* 0844 3351551; Dere Street Barristers Chambers, 33 Broad Chare, Newcastle upon Tyne NE1 3DQ.

ELVIDGE, Sir John (William), KCB 2006; FRSE; Chairman, Edinburgh Airport, since 2012; *b* 9 Feb. 1951; *s* of Herbert William Elvidge and Irene Teresa Elvidge; *m* 2003, Maureen Margaret Ann McGinn. *Educ:* Sir George Monoux Sch., Walthamstow; St Catherine's Coll., Oxford (BA English Lang. and Lit.). Joined Scottish Office, 1973: Principal, 1978–84; Asst Sec., 1984–88; Dir, Scottish Homes, 1988–89 (on secondment); Asst Sec., 1989–93; Under Sec., 1993–98; Dep. Hd, Econ. and Domestic Secretariat, Cabinet Office, 1998–99 (on secondment); Hd, Educn Dept, 1999–2002, Finance and Central Services Dept, 2002–03, Scottish Exec.; Perm. Sec., Scottish Govt (formerly Scottish Exec.), 2003–10. *Recreations:* painting, film, theatre, music, modern novels, food and wine. *Address:* 6 Sciennes Gardens, Edinburgh EH9 1NR.

ELVIN, David John; QC 2000; a Recorder, since 2002; a Deputy High Court Judge, since 2008; *b* 30 April 1960; *s* of Walter and Margaret Elvin; *m* 1985, Helen Julia Shilling. *Educ:* A. J. Dawson Grammar Sch.; Hertford Coll., Oxford (BA 1st Cl. Hons Jurisprudence 1981, BCL 1982). Called to the Bar: Middle Temple, 1983, Bencher 2015; NI, 2009. Asst Comr, 2000–09, Mem., 2009–, Boundary Commn. Mem. Council, RSCM, 2004–08. Accredited Mediator, 2010. *Publications:* Unlawful Interference with Land, 1995, 2nd edn 2002; (ed jtly) The Planning Encyclopaedia (loose-leaf); contrib. articles to Law Qly Rev., Judicial Rev., Jl of Planning and Envmt Law. *Recreations:* music (playing, singing, listening), opera, history. *Address:* Landmark Chambers, 180 Fleet Street, EC4A 2HG. *T:* (020) 7430 1221.

ELVIN, Joanne; Editor, Glamour magazine, since 2000; *b* Sydney, 21 Feb. 1970; *d* of Harry Elvin and Leonie Elvin; *m* 2000, Ross Jones; one *d*. *Educ:* Univ. of Western Sydney. Publicist, TV series, Neighbours, 1992; Dep. Editor, TV Hits mag., 1993–94; Editor: Sugar mag., 1994–96; B mag., 1996–98; New Woman mag., 1998–2000. *Address:* Glamour, Condé Nast Publications Ltd, Vogue House, Hanover Square, W1S 1JU. *T:* (020) 7499 9080. *Clubs:* Groucho, Soho House.

ELVIN, Violetta, (Violetta Prokhorova), (Signora Fernando Savarese); ballerina; a prima ballerina of Sadler's Wells Ballet, Royal Opera House, London (now The Royal Ballet), 1951–56; Director, Ballet Company, San Carlo Opera, Naples, 1985–87; *b* Moscow, 3 Nov. 1925; *d* of Vassilie Prokhorov, engineer, and Irena Grimouzinskaya, former actress; *m* 1st, 1944, Harold Elvin (divorced 1952), of British Embassy, Moscow; 2nd, 1953, Siegbert J. Weinberger, New York; 3rd, 1959, Fernando Savarese, lawyer; one *s*. *Educ:* Bolshoi Theatre Sch., Moscow. Trained for ballet since age of 8 by: E. P. Gerdt, A. Vaganova, M. A. Kojuchova. Grad, 1942, as soloist; made mem. Bolshoi Theatre Ballet; evacuated to Tashkent, 1943; ballerina Tashkent State Theatre; rejoined Bolshoi Theatre at Kuibishev again as soloist, 1944; left for London, 1945. Joined Sadler's Wells Ballet at Covent Garden as guest-soloist, 1946; later became regular mem. Has danced all principal rôles, notably, Le Lac des Cygnes, Sleeping Beauty, Giselle, Cinderella, Sylvia, Ballet Imperial, etc. Danced four-act Le Lac des Cygnes, first time, 1943; guest-artist Stanislavsky Theatre, Moscow, 1944, Sadler's Wells Theatre, 1947; guest-prima ballerina, La Scala, Milan, Nov. 1952–Feb. 1953 (Macbeth, La Gioconda, Swan Lake, Petrouchka); guest artist, Cannes, July 1954; Copenhagen, Dec. 1954; Teatro Municipal, Rio de Janeiro, May 1955 (Giselle, Swan Lake, Les Sylphides, Nutcracker, Don Quixote and The Dying Swan); Festival Ballet, Festival Hall, 1955; guest-prima ballerina in Giselle, Royal Opera House, Stockholm (Anna Pavlova Memorial), 1956; concluded stage career when appeared in Sleeping Beauty, Royal Opera House, Covent Garden, June 1956. *Appeared in films:* The Queen of Spades, Twice Upon a Time, Melba. Television appearances in Russia and England. Has toured with Sadler's Wells Ballet, France, Italy, Portugal, United States and Canada. *Recreations:* reading, painting, swimming. *Address:* Hotel Le Axidie, Via Marina di Equa, 80069 Vico Equense, Napoli, Italy.

ELWEN, His Honour Christopher; a Circuit Judge, 1995–2011; Resident Judge, Truro Combined Courts, 2008–11; *b* 14 Sept. 1944; *s* of Kenneth Spence Elwen and Joan Marie Elwen; *m* 1967, Susan Elizabeth Allan; one *s* one *d*. *Educ:* Quarry Bank High Sch., Liverpool; Univ. of Liverpool (LLB). Called to the Bar, Gray's Inn, 1969; Wm Brandts Sons & Co. Ltd, 1970–72; Cripps Warburg Ltd, 1972–75; Holman Fenwick & Willan, 1975–89; admitted solicitor, 1976; Stephenson Harwood, 1989–95; a Recorder, 1993–95. *Recreations:* painting, golf, mediaeval history, walking. *Address:* Daymer Dunes, Trebetherick, Cornwall PL27 6SF. *T:* (01208) 862315. *Club:* Garrick.

ELWES, Sir Henry (William George), KCVO 2009; JP; Lord-Lieutenant of Gloucestershire, 1992–2010; *b* 24 Oct. 1935; *s* of John Hargreaves Elwes, MC, Major, Scots Guards (killed in action, N Africa, 1943) and late Isabel Pamela Ivy Beckwith, *g d* of 7th Duke of Richmond and Gordon, KG, GCVO, CB; *m* 1962, Carolyn Dawn Cripps; two *s* (and one *s* decd). *Educ:* Eton; RAC, Cirencester (Hon. Fellow, 2009). FRAC 2010. Served Army, Lieut, Scots Guards, 1953–56. Member: Cirencester RDC, 1959–74; Glos CC, 1970–91 (Vice-Chm., 1976–83 and 1991; Chm., 1983–85). Regl Dir, Lloyds Bank, 1985–91. Mem., Nat. Jt Council for Fire Brigades, 1979–91; Director: Colesbourne Estate Co., 1969–; Cirencester Friendly Soc. (formerly Cirencester Benefit Soc. Trustee Co.) Ltd, 1974–2000. Pres., Western Woodland Owners Ltd, 1986–2003 (Chm., 1972–86). Pro Chancellor, Univ. of Gloucestershire, 2012–. Patron, Pres. and Mem. of many Glos trusts and societies. Gloucestershire: High Sheriff, 1979–80; DL 1982; JP 1992; Hon. Alderman, 1992. Liveryman, Gardeners' Co., 2004–. Hon. Lay Canon, Gloucester Cathedral, 2001–. Hon. DPhil Gloucestershire, 2002; Hon. LLD UWE, 2006. Confrérie des Chevaliers du Tastevin. KStJ 1992. *Address:* Colesbourne Park, near Cheltenham, Glos GL53 9NP.

ELWES, Sir Jeremy (Vernon), Kt 1994; CBE 1984; Chairman, St Helier NHS Trust, 1990–99; *b* 29 May 1937; *s* of late Eric Vincent Elwes and Dorothea Elwes, OBE (*née* Bilton); *m* 1963, Phyllis Marion Relf, 2nd *d* of late George Herbert Harding Relf and Rose Jane Relf (*née* Luery); one *s*. *Educ:* Wirral Grammar Sch.; Bromley Grammar Sch.; City of London Coll. ACIS 1963. Technical Journalist, Heywood & Co., 1958–62; Accountant and Co. Sec., Agricultural Press, 1962–70; Sec. and Dir, East Brackland Hill Farming Development Co., 1967–70; IPC Business Press: Pensions Officer, 1966–70; Divl Personnel Manager, 1970–73; Manpower Planning Manager, 1973–78; Exec. Dir (Manpower), 1978–82; Personnel Dir, Business Press Internat., then Reed Business Publishing, 1982–93; Human Resources Dir, Reed Publishing Europe, 1993–94. Director: Periodicals Trng Council, 1986–92; Sutton Enterprise Agency Ltd, 1987–94 (Chm., 1987–90). Chairman: Cons. Political Centre Nat. Adv. Cttee, 1981–84; Cons. SE Area, 1986–90; Mem., Nat. Union Exec. Cttee, 1972–94; Co-ordinator, Specialist Gps, Cons. Pty, 2000–13; Hon. Sec., Cons. Med. Soc., 1996–2000; Pres., Sevenoaks Cons. Assoc., 2007–09. Mem. Exec. Cttee, GBGSA, 1996–99, 2000–03; Dir and Trustee, Eur. Sch. of Osteopathy, 1999–2007. Pres., Sevenoaks Div., 2000–13, Dep. County Pres., Kent, 2001–, St John Ambulance. Chm. of Governors, Walthamstow Hall, 1984–2003, now Gov. Emeritus, 2003. FRSA 1994. Liveryman: Stationers' and Newspapermakers' Co., 1991– (Master and Wardens Cttee, 1999–2002; Chm., Livery Cttee, 2000–02; Livery Rep., 2005–07; Mem. Ct Assts, 2007–10; Chm., Hall and Heritage Cttee, 2008–10); Chartered Secretaries' and Administrators' Co., 2003–12 (Sec., 2005–06, Chm., 2006–11, Livery Liaison Gp). Member Council: Imperial Soc. of Kts Bachelor, 2002– (Treas., 2012–); Printers' Charitable Corp., 2002–08 (Pres., 2004; Dep. Chm., 2005–06, Chm., 2006–08; Pres. Emeritus, 2009); Hospice in the Weald, 2003–11; Foundn for Liver Res., 2005–. OStJ 2009. Chevalier, Ordre des Chevaliers Bretvins (Chancelier to 1992). *Recreations:* wine and food, reading, walking, golf, cruise ship lecturing. *Address:* Crispian Cottage, Weald Road, Sevenoaks, Kent TN13 1QQ. *T:* (01732) 454208. *Clubs:* City Livery; Knole; Nizels Golf and Leisure (Captain, Veterans, 1998–99).

ELWOOD, Sir Brian (George Conway), Kt 1990; CBE 1985; Chairman, Kiwifruit New Zealand, since 2004; Chief Ombudsman of New Zealand, 1994–2003; *b* 5 April 1933; *s* of Jack Philip Elwood and Enid Mary Elwood; *m* 1956, Dawn Barbara Elwood (*née* Ward); one *s* two *d*. *Educ:* Victoria Univ., Wellington (LLB); Trinity Coll., London (ATCL). Barrister and Solicitor, 1957. Ombudsman, 1992–94. Chairman: Local Govt Commn, NZ, 1985–92; Survey Industry Review Commn, 1990–92; Comr, Wellington Area Health Bd, 1990–92. Mayor, Palmerston North City, 1971–85. Life Mem., Internat. Ombudsman Inst., 2002 (Regl Vice Pres., 1996–98; Internat. Pres., 1999–2002). Mem., Wellington Harbour Bd, 1968–74. Chairman: Age Concern (Wellington) Charitable Trust, 2004–; Central Energy Trust, 2012– (Trustee, 2006–). Hon. Mem., NZ Inst. of Surveyors. Hon. DLitt Massey, 1994. Medal for Distinguished Public Service, Lions Club Internat., 1985. *Recreations:* golf, fishing, gardening. *Address:* Box 170, Waikanae, Kapiti Coast, New Zealand. *T:* (4) 2938113. *Club:* Wellington.

ELWORTHY, Air Cdre Hon. Sir Timothy (Charles), KCVO 2001 (CVO 1995); CBE 1986; Her Majesty's Senior Air Equerry, 1995–2001; Director of Royal Travel, 1997–2001; Extra Equerry to the Queen, since 1991; *b* 27 Jan. 1938; *e s* of Marshal of the RAF Baron Elworthy, KG, GCB, CBE, DSO, LVO, DFC, AFC and late Audrey Elworthy; *m* 1st, 1961, Victoria Ann (marr. diss.), *d* of Lt Col H. C. W. Bowring; two *d*; 2nd, 1971, Anabel, *d* of late Reginald Harding, OBE; one *s*. *Educ:* Radley; RAF Coll., Cranwell. CO 29 (Fighter) Sqn, 1975 (Wing Comdr); PSO to AO Commanding-in-Chief, Strike Comd, 1979; CO RAF Stn Leuchars, 1983 (Gp Capt.); RCDS, 1986; Dir, Operational Requirements, (Air), MoD, 1987 (Air Cdre); Captain of The Queen's Flight, 1989–95. Liveryman, GAPAN, 1995. QCVSA 1968. *Recreations:* country pursuits, wine, travel. *Address:* Coates House, Swyncombe, Henley-on-Thames, Oxon RG9 6EG. *Club:* Boodle's.

ELY, 9th Marquess of, *cr* 1801; **Charles John Tottenham;** Bt 1780; Baron Loftus 1785; Viscount Loftus 1789; Earl of Ely 1794; Baron Loftus (UK) 1801; Director of Admissions (formerly Head of French Department), Strathcona-Tweedsmuir School, Calgary, until 2004; *b* 2 Feb. 1943; *e s* of 8th Marquess of Ely and Katherine Elizabeth (*née* Craig); *S* father, 2006; *m* 1969, Judith Marvelle, *d* of Dr J. J. Porter, FRS, Calgary, Alberta; one *s* one *d*. *Educ:* Trinity Coll. Sch., Port Hope, Ont; Ecole Internationale de Genève; Univ. of Toronto (MA). *Heir:* *b* Lord Timothy Craig Tottenham [*b* 17 Jan.1948; *m* 1973, Elizabeth Jane McAllister; two *s*]. *Address:* 153 Chaparral Circle, Calgary, AB T2X 3M2, Canada.

ELY, Bishop of, since 2010; **Rt Rev. Stephen David Conway;** *b* 22 Dec. 1957; *s* of late David Conway and of Dorothy Isabella (*née* Jarman, now Lambert). *Educ:* Archbishop Tenison's Grammar Sch., London; Keble Coll., Oxford (BA Mod. Hist. 1980, MA 1984; PGCE 1981); Selwyn Coll., Cambridge (BA Theol. 1985; MA 2005); Westcott House, Cambridge. Asst Master, Glenalmond Coll., 1981–83; ordained deacon, 1986, priest, 1987; Curate: Heworth, 1986–89; Bishopwearmouth, 1989–90; St Margaret, Durham, 1990–94; Diocesan Dir of Ordinands, Durham, 1989–94; Priest i/c, subseq. Vicar, Cockerton, 1994–98; Sen. Chaplain to Bishop of Durham and Diocesan Communications Officer, 1998–2002; Archdeacon of Durham, and Canon Residentiary, Durham Cathedral, 2002–06; Area Bishop of Ramsbury, 2006–10. Entered H of L, 2014. Mem., Gen. Synod of C of E, 1995–2000. Visitor: Jesus Coll., Cambridge, 2010–; Peterhouse, Cambridge, 2010–; St John's Coll., Cambridge, 2010–; Soc. of Sacred Mission, 2014–. Chairman: Develt and Appts, Gp of Hse of Bishops, 2013–; C of E Bd of Educn, 2014–; Nat. Soc. of C of E, 2014–. Trustee, Affirming Catholicism, 2001–08 (Chm., Exec., 1997–2003; Vice Pres., 2008–). Chm., Bd of Trustees, Mental Health Matters, 2004–10. Mem., Internat. Ch Leaders Gp, L'Arche Community, 2013–; C of E Rep., Faith and Order Commn, World Council of Churches, 2014. Episcopal Visitor, Co. of Servers 2010–. Warden, Guild of St Raphael, 2013. Mem. Council, Radley Coll., 2014–. *Publications:* (ed) Living the Eucharist, 2001; (contrib.) This is Our Calling, 2004; (contrib.) The Vicar's Guide, 2005; (ed) Generous Ecclesiology: towards a generous ecclesiology, 2013. *Recreations:* walking, cinema, wine, travel, books. *Address:* Bishop's House, Ely, Cambs CB7 4DW. *T:* (01353) 662749. *E:* Bishop@ely.anglican.org. *Clubs:* Athenæum, Nobody's Friends, Nikaean; Cambridge County.

ELY, Dean of; *see* Bonney, Very Rev. M. P. J.

ELY, Archdeacon of; *see* Beer, Ven. J. S., Archdeacon of Cambridge.

ELY, Keith; *see* Ely, S. K.

ELY, Philip Thomas, OBE 2003; Chairman, Legal Services Commission, 2003–04; *b* 22 March 1936; *s* of Eric Stanley Ely and Rose Josephine Ely; *m* 1966, Diana Mary (*née* Gellibrand); two *s* three *d*. *Educ:* Douai Sch.; LLB (external) London Univ. Admitted Solicitor, 1958. National Service, RN, 1958–60 (commnd, 1959). Articled Hepherd Winstanley & Pugh, Southampton, 1953–58; joined Paris Smith & Randall, Southampton, as Asst Solicitor, 1960; Partner, 1961–98, Sen. Partner, 1981–98. Law Society: Mem. Council, 1979–93; Vice-Pres., 1990–91; Pres., 1991–92; Hampshire Incorporated Law Society: Asst Hon. Sec., 1961–66; Hon. Sec., 1966–74; Hon. Treasurer, 1974–79; Pres., 1979. Appointed by HM Treasury to conduct enquiry into powers of Inland Revenue to call for papers of tax accountants, 1994. Mem., Legal Services Commn (formerly Legal Aid Bd), 1996–2004 (Chm., Regl Legal Services Cttees, Reading, 1998–2002, London, 1998–2003); Chm., Police Disciplinary Appeals Tribunal, 1996–2003. Hon. LLD Southampton, 1992. *Recreations:* fly-fishing, gardening, music, reading. *Address:* Orchard Cottage, Crawley, Winchester, Hants SO21 2PR. *T:* (01962) 776379.

ELY, (Sydney) Keith; writer; *b* 17 April 1949; *s* of Charles Rodenhurst Ely and Dorothy Mary Ely (*née* Rowlands); *m* 1st, 1970, Patricia Davies (marr. diss. 1994); three *d*; 2nd, 1994, Jo Ann Beroiz. *Educ:* Maghull Grammar Sch.; Open Univ. (BA). Journalist: Liverpool Daily Post & Echo, 1968–78; Reuters, 1978–80; Daily Post, Liverpool: Business Editor, 1980–84; Acting Asst Editor, 1984; Systems Develt, 1985–86; Features Editor, 1987; Dep. Editor, 1987; Editor, 1989–95; Man. Dir, Trinity Weekly Newspapers Ltd, 1995–96; Editor and Gen. Manager, Channel One TV, Liverpool, 1996–97; Regl Ops Dir, Liverpool Daily Post & Echo Ltd, 1998–2000 (Dir, 1989–95 and 1998–2000); Man. Dir, Corporate Culture Plc, 2000–01 (Dir, 1988, 2000). Owner, Keith Ely Media Services, 2002–. *Recreations:* music, computing. *Address:* Medford, OR 97504, USA.

ELYSTAN-MORGAN, family name of **Baron Elystan-Morgan**.

ELYSTAN-MORGAN, Baron *cr* 1981 (Life Peer), of Aberteifi in the County of Dyfed; **His Honour Dafydd Elystan Elystan-Morgan;** a Circuit Judge, 1988–2003; *b* 7 Dec. 1932; *s* of late Dewi Morgan and late Mrs Olwen Morgan; *m* 1959, Alwen (*d* 2006), *d* of William E. Roberts; one *s* one *d*. *Educ:* Ardwyn Grammar Sch., Aberystwyth; UCW, Aberystwyth. LLB Hons Aberystwyth, 1953. Research at Aberystwyth and Solicitor's Articles, 1953–57; admitted a Solicitor, 1957; Partner in N Wales (Wrexham) Firm of Solicitors, 1958–68; Barrister-at-law, Gray's Inn, 1971; a Recorder, 1983–87. MP (Lab) Cardiganshire, 1966–Feb. 1974; Chm., Welsh Parly Party, 1967–68, 1971–74; Parly Under-Secretary of State, Home Office, 1968–70; front-bench spokesman on Home Affairs, 1970–72, on Welsh Affairs, 1972–74, on Legal and Home Affairs, House of Lords, 1981–85. Contested (Lab): Cardigan, Oct. 1974; Anglesey, 1979. President: Welsh Local Authorities Assoc., 1967–73; Parlt for Wales Campaign, 1979. President: Univ. Coll. of Wales, Aberystwyth, subseq. Aberystwyth Univ., 1997–2007; Welsh Sch. of Legal Studies, 1998–. Hon. Fellow, Univ. of Wales, Aberystwyth, 1992. Elder, Presbyterian Church of Wales, 1971–. *Address:* Carreg Afon, Dolau, Bow Street, Dyfed SY24 5AE.

EMANUEL, David, FCSD; fashion designer; *b* 17 Nov. 1952; *s* of John Lawrence Morris Emanuel and late Elizabeth Emanuel; *m* 1975, Elizabeth Florence Weiner (*see* E. F. Emanuel) (separated 1990; marr. diss. 2008); one *s* one *d*. *Educ:* Cardiff Coll. of Art (Diploma); Harrow Sch. of Art (Diploma); Royal College of Art (MA). Final Degree show at RCA, 1977. Emanuel (couture business) commenced in Mayfair, W1, 1977, Jt Partner/Dir, 1977–90; The Emanuel Shop (retail), London, SW3, 1986–90; ready-to-wear business partnership in USA, 1988; formed David Emanuel Couture, 1990. Designed: wedding gown for the Princess of Wales, 1981; ballet productions, incl. Frankenstein, the Modern Prometheus, Royal Opera House, Covent Garden, 1985 and La Scala, Milan, 1987; uniforms for Virgin Atlantic Airways, 1990; prodns for theatre, film, TV and operatic recitals. Television presenter, fashion shows, 1994–. FCSD (FSIAD 1984). Hon. FRWCMD (Hon. FWCMD 2000). *Publications:* (with Elizabeth Emanuel): Style for All Seasons, 1983; A Dress for Diana, 2006. *Recreations:*

horse-riding, jet-ski-ing, tennis, opera. *Address:* David Emanuel Couture, c/o Lanesborough Hotel, Lanesborough Place, SW1X 7TA. *T:* (020) 7482 6486, *Fax:* (020) 7267 6627. *Clubs:* White Elephant; Royal Ascot Tennis (Berks).

EMANUEL, Elizabeth Florence, FCSD; fashion designer; *b* 5 July 1953; *d* of Samuel Charles Weiner and Brahna Betty Weiner; *m* 1975, David Emanuel, *qv* (separated 1990; marr. diss. 2008); one *s* one *d*. *Educ:* City of London Sch. for Girls; Harrow Sch. of Art (Diploma with Hons); Royal Coll. of Art (MA 1977; DesRCA 1977). FCSD 1984. Emanuel (couture) commenced in Mayfair, W1, 1977; The Emanuel Shop (retail), London, SW3, 1986–90; launched internat. fashion label, Elizabeth Emanuel, 1991; set up Elizabeth Emanuel Enterprises, 1999; designer, Luxury Brand Gp, 2001–02; started new label: Art of Being, Little Venice, 2005–; Eva Ave, 2013–; Art of Being Ltd, 2013–. Designed: wedding gown for the Princess of Wales, 1981; advertisement campaigns for Estee Lauder with Elizabeth Hurley, 1997 and 1998; range of wedding dresses for: Berkertex, 1995; BHS, 2008; Takami Bridal, Japan, 2014–; Little Black Dress Collection, 2010; Chocolate Couture Collection, 2013; ballet productions, incl. Frankenstein, the Modern Prometheus, Royal Opera House, Covent Garden, 1985 and La Scala, Milan, 1987; costumes for films: The Changeling, 1995; RosBeef, 2004; Metamorphosis, 2006; uniforms for: Virgin Atlantic Airways, 1990; Britannia Airways, 1995; prodns for theatre and operatic recitals. *Publications:* (with David Emanuel): Style for All Seasons, 1983; A Dress for Diana, 2006. *Recreations:* ballet, films, writing children's books, supporting animal charities. *Address:* Garden Studio, 51 Maida Vale, Little Venice, W9 1SD. *T:* (020) 7289 4545.

EMBLEY, Lloyd William; Editor-in-Chief, Daily Mirror and Sunday Mirror, since 2012; *b* Birmingham, 16 March 1966; *s* of David Embley and Elizabeth Jennings; *m* 1998, Soraya Khan; one *s* one *d*. *Educ:* Malvern Coll. Daily Mirror: Associate Night Ed., 1999–2001; Night Ed., 2001–04; Asst Ed., 2004–08; Ed., The People, 2008–12. *Recreations:* golf, ski-ing, wine and wine books, cooking and cook books. *Address:* Mirror, 1 Canada Square, Canary Wharf, E14 5AP. *Clubs:* Royal Cinque Ports Golf, Press Golfing Society; Ski of GB.

EMBREY, Derek Morris, OBE 1986; CEng, FIMechE; Technical Director, Streamwatch Ltd, 2004–10; Chairman, Turnock Ltd (formerly George Turnock Ltd), 1998–2000; Group Technical Director, AB Electronic Products Group PLC, 1973–91; *b* 11 March 1928; *s* of Frederick and Ethel Embrey; *m* 1st, 1951, Frances Margaret Stephens (marr. diss. 1995); one *s* one *d*; 2nd, 1999, Jean McKay Stevens, *d* of late Norman McKay Fairgrieve. *Educ:* Wolverhampton Polytechnic (Hon. Fellow, 1987). Chief Designer (Electronics), Electric Construction Co. Ltd, 1960–65, Asst Manager Static Plant, 1965–69; Chief Engineer, Abergas Ltd, 1969–73. Member: Engineering Council, 1982–87; Welsh Industrial Develt Adv. Bd, 1982–85; NACCB, 1985–87; Council, IERE, 1984–88 (Vice Pres., 1985–88); National Electronics Council, 1985–99; Welsh Adv. Bd, 1986–90 (Chm., 1987–90). Vis. Prof., Univ. of Technology, Loughborough, 1978–84 (External Examr, Dept of Mechanical Engrg, 1984–88); Visiting Lecturer: Loughborough Univ., 1988–97; Birmingham Univ., 1989–2000. Member: Council, UWIST, Cardiff, 1984–88; Bd, Inst. of Transducer Technol., Southampton Univ., 1986–2000; Council, IEE, 1992–95 (Chm., Management and Design Divl Bd, 1993–94); Air Cadet Council, 1988–95; Regl Civilian Chm., ATC, Wales, 1988–95; Dir and Mem. Council, BTEC, 1993–96. Freeman, City of London, 1986; Liveryman, Scientific Instrument Makers' Co., 1986–; founder Liveryman, Livery Co. of Wales (formerly Welsh Livery Guild), 1994–. Hon. Fellow UWIC, 1992. *Recreations:* fondly remembering flying and navigating powered aircraft and gliders; music, English history, archaeology, amateur radio communication (MW0 GTN), family history research. *Address:* 21 Rockfield Glade, Penhow, Caldicot, Monmouthshire NP26 3JF. *T:* (01633) 400995. *Club:* Royal Air Force.

EMBUREY, John Ernest; Director of Cricket, Middlesex County Cricket Club, 2006–08 (Director of Coaching, 2001–06); *b* 20 Aug. 1952; *s* of John Alfred Emburey and Rose Alice Emburey (*née* Roff); *m* 1980, Susan Elizabeth Anne Booth; two *d*. *Educ:* Peckham Manor. Professional cricketer: Middx CCC, 1971–95; England Test cricketer, 1978–95; 64 Test matches (Captain, 1988); 63 one-day internationals; Manager, England A Team tour to Pakistan, 1995; Chief Coach and Manager, Northants CCC, 1996–98; coach, England A Team tour, Zimbabwe and S Africa, 1999; player/coach, Berks CCC, 2000. *Publications:* Emburey (autobiog.), 1986; Spinning in a Fast World, 1989. *Recreations:* golf, reading. *Club:* MCC.

EMECHETA, Buchi, OBE 2004; writer and lecturer, since 1972; *b* 21 July 1944; *d* of Alice and Jeremy Emecheta; *m* 1960, Sylvester Onwordi; two *s* three *d*. *Educ:* Methodist Girls' High Sch., Lagos, Nigeria; London Univ. (BSc Hons Sociol.). Librarian, 1960–69; Student, 1970–74; Youth Worker and Res. Student, Race, 1974–76; Community Worker, Camden, 1976–78. Visiting Prof., 11 Amer. univs, incl. Penn. State, Pittsburgh, UCLA, Illinois at Urbana-Champaign, 1979; Sen. Res. Fellow and Vis. Prof. of English, Univ. of Calabar, Nigeria, 1980–81; lectured: Yale, Spring 1982; London Univ., 1982. Proprietor, Ogwugwn Afo Publishing Co. Included in twenty 'Best of Young British', 1983. Member: Arts Council of GB, 1982–83; Home Sec's Adv. Council on Race, 1979. Hon. DLitt Fairleigh Dickinson Univ., NJ, 1992. *Publications:* In the Ditch, 1972; Second Class Citizen, 1975; The Bride Price, 1976; The Slave Girl, 1977; The Joys of Motherhood, 1979; Destination Biafra, 1982; Naira Power, 1982; Double Yoke, 1982; The Rape of Shavi, 1983; Head Above Water (autobiog.), 1984; Gwendolen, 1989; Kehinde, 1994; The New Tribe, 2000; *for children:* Titch the Cat, 1979; Nowhere to Play, 1980; The Moonlight Bride, 1981; The Wrestling Match, 1981; contribs to New Statesman, TLS, The Guardian, etc. *Recreations:* gardening, going to the theatre, listening to music, reading. *Clubs:* Africa Centre, PEN, International PEN (Trustee, 1993–98).

EMERSON, David; *see* Emerson, J. D.

EMERSON, Joanna; *see* Hardy, J.

EMERSON, (John) David, CBE 2015; Chief Executive, Association of Charitable Foundations, since 2003; *b* Pembury, Kent, 7 April 1951; *s* of John Raine Emerson and Evelyn Ethel Emerson (*née* Hedge); *m* 2008, Baroness Pitkeathley, *qv*; one step *s* one step *d*. *Educ:* East Grinstead County Grammar Sch.; University Coll. London (BSc Geog. 1972); Wye Coll., Univ. of London (MSc Landscape Ecol., Design and Maintenance 1973); Webber Douglas Acad. (Postgrad. Dip. Drama 1983). Rural Officer, Cheshire Community Council, 1973–78; Dep. Hd, Rural Dept, NCVO, 1978–82; actor, West End and internat. tours, 1983–89; freelance theatre prodn and stage mgt, 1989–96; Sen. Exec., TMA, 1996–2003. Pt-time tutor, Extra Mural Studies, Univ. of Liverpool, 1975–78. Chair: Nitro Theatre Co., 2009–15; ACRE, 2014–. FRGS 1973. *Publications:* (with Jill Pitkeathley) The Only Child, 1992 (trans. 8 foreign langs); (with Jill Pitkeathley) Age Gap Relationships, 1994. *Recreations:* British orchids and managing a wild flower meadow, walking, music, theatre and tap dance, directing the village pantomime. *Address:* Association of Charitable Foundations, Acorn House, 314–320 Gray's Inn Road, WC1X 8DP. *T:* (020) 7255 4499. *E:* demerson@acf.org.uk.

EMERSON, Michael Ronald, MA; FCA; Associate Senior Research Fellow, Centre for European Policy Studies, Brussels, since 1998; *b* 12 May 1940; *s* of late James Emerson and Priscilla Emerson; *m* 1st, 1966, Barbara Brierley; one *s* two *d*; 2nd, 2000, Elena Prokhorova. *Educ:* Hurstpierpoint Coll.; Balliol Coll., Oxford (MA (PPE)). Price Waterhouse & Co., London, 1962–65; Organisation for Economic Cooperation and Development, Paris: several posts in Develt and Economics Depts, finally as Head of General Economics Div., 1966–73; EEC, Brussels: Head of Division for Budgetary Policy, Directorate-General II, 1973–76; Economic Adviser to President of the Commission, 1977; Dir for Nat. Economies and Economic Trends, 1978–81; Dir for Macroecon. Analyses and Policies, 1981–86; Dir, Economic Evaluation of Community Policies, Directorate-General II, 1987–90; Ambassador and Head of EC Delegn to USSR, subseq. Russia, 1991–96. Fellow, Centre for Internat. Affairs, Harvard Univ., 1985–86; Sen. Res. Fellow, LSE, 1996–98. Hon. DLitt Keele, 1993; Hon. DCL Kent, 1993. *Publications:* (ed) Europe's Stagflation, 1984; What Model for Europe, 1987; The Economics of 1992, 1988; One Market, One Money, 1991; Redrawing the Map of Europe, 1998; Wider Europe Matrix, 2004; (ed) Britain's Future in Europe, 2015; contribs to various economic jls and edited volumes on internat. and European economics. *Address:* CEPS, 1 Place du Congrès, 1000 Brussels, Belgium.

EMERSON, Dr Peter Albert, MD; FRCP; Hon. Consultant Physician, Chelsea and Westminster Hospital (formerly Westminster and Charing Cross Hospitals), since 1988; *b* 7 Feb. 1923; *s* of Albert Emerson and Gwendoline (*née* Davy); *m* 1947, Ceris Hood Price; one *s* one *d*. *Educ:* The Leys Sch., Cambridge; Clare Coll., Univ. of Cambridge (MA); St George's Hosp., Univ. of London (MB, BChir 1947; MD 1954). FRCP 1964; Hon. FACP 1975. House Physician, St George's Hosp., 1947; RAF Med. Bd, 1948–52 (Sqdn Leader); Registrar, later Sen. Registrar, St George's Hosp. and Brompton Hosp., London, 1952–57; Asst Prof. of Medicine, Coll. of Medicine, State Univ. of New York, Brooklyn, USA, 1957–58; Consultant Phys., Westminster Hosp., 1959–88; Civilian Consultant Phys. in Chest Diseases to RN, 1974–88; Dean, Westminster Medical Sch., London, 1981–84. Hon. Consultant Phys., King Edward VII Hosp., Midhurst, 1969–88. Royal Coll. of Physicians: Asst Registrar, 1965–71; Procensor and Censor, 1978–80; Vice-Pres. and Sen. Censor, 1985–86; Mitchell Lectr, 1969. *Publications:* Thoracic Medicine, 1981; articles in med. jls and chapters in books on thoracic medicine and the application of decision theory and expert systems to clinical medicine. *Address:* 3 Halkin Street, SW1X 7DJ. *T:* (020) 7235 8529. *Clubs:* Royal Air Force, Royal Society of Medicine, Caledonian.

EMERSON, Richard Martyn; writer; Chief Inspector of Historic Buildings, Historic Scotland, 1999–2004; *b* 19 Dec. 1949; *s* of late Maj. Hugh Emerson and Keyna Emerson (*née* Parson); *m* 1st, 1971, Vanessa Leadam Andrews (marr. diss. 1990); two *s* one *d*; 2nd, 1991, Anne Grenfell Macdonald; one *s* one *d*. *Educ:* Wellington Coll.; Courtauld Inst. of Art, London Univ. (BA Hons). Dep. Conway Librarian, Courtauld Inst. of Art, 1971–73; Res. Asst, Nat. Monuments Record for Scotland, Royal Commn on Ancient and Historical Monuments of Scotland, 1973–78; Principal Inspector of Historic Bldgs, Historic Scotland, 1978–99. Hon. FRIAS 2006. *Publications:* contribs to architectural history jls and books. *Recreation:* practising contentment by the Mediterranean. *Address:* 4 rue de la Casette, 06570 Saint-Paul, France; 15/6 Tron Square, Edinburgh EH1 1RT. *E:* palazzo-lilo@hotmail.fr.

EMERSON, Ronald Victor; Chairman, British Business Bank plc, since 2013; *b* Hartlepool, 22 Feb. 1947; *s* of Albert Victor Emerson and Doris Emerson; *m* 1996, Angela Jane Stephenson; four *s*. *Educ:* West Hartlepool Grammar Sch.; Manchester Univ. (BSc); Durham Univ. (MSc); Templeton Coll. Oxford (MLitt); Green Templeton Coll., Oxford (MA). De La Rue, 1970–75; Bank of America, 1975–89; Nomura, 1989–90; Gp Hd, Corporate Banking, Standard Chartered Bank, 1990–96. Senior Advisor: Bank of England, 1997–2000; FSA, 1997–2000. Chm., Fairfield Energy, 2010–; non-executive Director: Premier Oil plc, 2001–08; Ace Eur. Gp Ltd, 2004–12; Specialist Energy Gp plc, 2010–12. Associate Fellow, Said Business Sch., Univ. of Oxford, 1997–; Barclay Fellow, Green Templeton Coll., Oxford, 2014–. FInstD 2012; FRSA. *Recreations:* reading, flying (PPL). *Address:* The Reeds, Remenham Lane, Henley on Thames RG9 3DA. *E:* ronemerson@btinternet.com. *Club:* Oxford and Cambridge.

EMERTON, Baroness *cr* 1997 (Life Peer), of Tunbridge Wells in the co. of Kent and of Clerkenwell in the London Borough of Islington; **Audrey Caroline Emerton,** DBE 1989; RGN, RM, RNT; Chief Commander, St John Ambulance, 1998–2002; Chairman, Brighton Health Care NHS Trust, 1994–2000 (Vice Chairman, 1993–94); *b* 10 Sept. 1935; *d* of late George Emerton and Lily (*née* Squirrell). *Educ:* Tunbridge Wells GS; St George's Hosp.; Battersea Coll. of Technol. Sen. Tutor, Experimental 2 year and 1 year Course, St George's Hosp., SW1, 1965–68; Principal Nursing Officer, Educn, Bromley HMC, 1968–70; Chief Nursing Officer, Tunbridge Wells and Leybourne HMC, 1970–73; Regl Nursing Officer, SE Thames RHA, 1973–91. St John Ambulance, Kent: Co. Nursing Officer, 1967–85; Co. Comr, 1985–88; St John Ambulance: Chief Nursing Officer, 1988–98; Chm. of Med. Bd, 1993–96; Chief Officer, Care in the Community, 1996–97; Chief Officer, Nursing and Social Care, 1997–98. Lay Mem., GMC, 1996–2001. Mem., Prime Minister's Commn on the Future of Nursing and Midwifery, 2009–10. Pres., Assoc. of Nurse Administrators, 1979–82; Hon. Vice Pres., RCN, 1994–99. Chairman: English Nat. Bd for Nursing, Midwifery and Health Visiting, 1983–85; UKCC, 1985–93; Vice-Pres., Attend (formerly Assoc. of Hosp. and Community Friends), 2008– (Chm., 2003–07); Pres., Florence Nightingale Foundn, 2004–. Trustee: Kent Community Housing Trust, 1993–99; Defence Med. Welfare Service, 2001–12 (Patron, 2012–). DL Kent, 1992–2010. Hon. Fellow: Christ Church UC, Canterbury, 2003; KCL, 2009. Hon. FRCN 2009. Hon. DCL Kent, 1989; Hon. DSc Brighton, 1997; DUniv Central England, 1997; Hon. Dr of Science Kingston, 2001. GCStJ 2004. *Address:* House of Lords, SW1A 0PW.

EMERY, Prof. Alan Eglin Heathcote, MD, PhD, DSc; FRSE, FRCP, FRCPE; FLS; Chief Scientific Advisor, European Neuromuscular Center, Baarn, The Netherlands, since 1999 (Research Director, and Chairman, Research Committee, 1989–99); Professor of Human Genetics, University of Edinburgh and Hon. Consultant Physician, Lothian Health Board, 1968–83, now Emeritus Professor and Hon. Fellow; Hon. Fellow, Green College, later Green Templeton College, Oxford, 2006 (Hon. Visiting Fellow, 1986–2006); *b* 21 Aug. 1928; *s* of Harold Heathcote Emery and Alice Eglin; *m* 1988, Marcia Lynn (*née* Miller); three *s* three *d* from a previous marriage. *Educ:* Manchester Univ. (BSc (double 1st cl. Hons), MD, DSc; John Dalton Prize); Johns Hopkins Univ., Baltimore (PhD). FRSPH (FRIPHH 1965); FRCPE 1970; MFCM 1974; FRSE 1972; FLS 1985; FRCP 1985. Formerly Resident in Medicine and Surgery, Manchester Royal Infirmary; Fellow in Medicine, Johns Hopkins Hosp., Baltimore, 1961–64; Reader in Medical Genetics, Univ. of Manchester, 1964–68 and Hon. Consultant in Medical Genetics, United Manchester Hosps; Sen. Res. Fellow, Green Coll., Oxford, 1985–86. Hon. Vis. Prof., Peninsular Med. Sch., 2006–. Pres., British Clinical Genetics Soc., 1980–83; Council Mem., British Genetic Soc. (Mem. cttees on trng in genetics, 1976, 1979 and 1983 and NHS services, 1978, 1980, 1983 and 1989); Vice Pres., Muscular Dystrophy UK (formerly Muscular Dystrophy Campaign), 1999–; Pres., Med. Genetics Sect., RSocMed, 2002–04 (Trustee, 2007–08). Hon. Member: Assoc. of British Neurologists, 1999; Netherlands Genetic Soc., 1999. FRSA 2002. Hon. FRSSAf 1989; Hon. FACMG 1993; Hon. FRSocMed 2006. Hon. MD: Naples, 1993; Würzburg, 1995; Athens, 2008; Hon. DSc Chester, 2014. Nat. Foundn (USA) Internat. Award for Research, 1980; Gaetano Conte Award and Medal, Gaetano Conte Acad., Italy, 2000; Pro Finlandiae Gold Medal, Univ. of Helsinki, 2000; Elsevier Sci. Award, 2001; Assoc. Française Contre Les Myopathies Prize, 2001; Life-time Achievement Award, World Fedn of Neurology, 2002; Cockcroft Medal and Alumnus of the Year Award, Manchester Univ., 2006; Doubleday Medal in Medicine, Doubleday Foundn, 2007; Internat. Honoree, Internat. Congress on Neuromuscular Disorders, 2010; Internat. Award in Genetic Educn, Amer. Soc. of Human Genetics, 2012; Lifetime Achievement Award, Muscular Dystrophy Campaign, 2012. Exec. Editor, Procs B, RSE, 1986–90. *Publications:* Elements of Medical Genetics, 1968, 14th edn as Emery's Elements of Medical Genetics (ed P. Turnpenny and S. Ellard), 2011; Methodology in Medical Genetics, 1976, 2nd edn 1986; Recombinant DNA—an introduction, 1984, 2nd edn (with S. Malcolm) 1995; Duchenne Muscular Dystrophy, 1987, 3rd edn 2003; Muscular Dystrophy: the facts, 1994, 3rd edn 2008; The History of a Genetic Disease, 1995, 2nd edn 2010; with M. Emery: Medicine and Art, 2002; Surgical and Medical Treatment in Art, 2005; Mother and Childcare in Art, 2007; editor: Modern Trends in Human Genetics, vol. 1, 1970, vol. 2, 1975; Antenatal Diagnosis of Genetic Disease, 1973; Registers for the Detection and Prevention of Genetic Disease, 1976; Principles and Practice of Medical Genetics, 1983, 5th edn as Emery & Rimoin's Principles and Practice of Medical Genetics, 2007; Psychological Aspects of Genetic Counselling, 1984; Diagnostic Criteria for Neuromuscular Disorders, 1994, 2nd edn 1997; Neuromuscular Disorders: clinical and molecular genetics, 1998; The Muscular Dystrophies, 2002; numerous scientific papers. *Recreations:* oil painting, medical and art history, writing poetry (4 published books). *Address:* c/o Green Templeton College, Oxford OX2 6HG.

EMERY, Fred; author and broadcaster; Presenter, Panorama, BBC TV, 1978–80 and 1982–92; *b* 19 Oct. 1933; *s* of Frederick G. L. Emery and Alice May (*née* Wright); *m* 1958, E. Marianne Nyberg; two *s*. *Educ:* Bancroft's Sch.; St John's Coll., Cantab (MA). RAF fighter pilot, 266 & 234 Squadrons, National Service, 1953. Radio Bremen, 1955–56; joined The Times, 1958, Foreign Correspondent, 1961; served in Paris, Algeria, Tokyo, Indonesia, Vietnam, Cambodia, Malaysia and Singapore until 1970; Chief Washington Corresp., 1970–77; Political Editor, 1977–81; Home Editor, 1981–82; Exec. Editor (Home and Foreign), and Actg Editor, 1982. Reporter, Watergate (TV series), 1994 (Emmy Award, 1995). Press Officer, Crystal Palace Campaign, 1999–2008. *Publications:* Watergate: the corruption and fall of Richard Nixon, 1994. *Recreations:* ski-ing, hill walking. *Address:* 5 Woodsyre, SE26 6SS. *T:* (020) 8761 0076. *Club:* Garrick.

EMERY, Joyce Margaret; *see* Zachariah, J. M.

EMERY, Nicola Susan; *see* Clayton, N. S.

EMERY, Prof. Paul, MD; FRCP; Arthritis Research UK (formerly ARC) Professor of Rheumatology, and Head, Leeds Institute of Rheumatic and Musculoskeletal Medicine (formerly Division of Musculoskeletal Disease), University of Leeds, since 1995; Director, Leeds Musculoskeletal Biomedical Research Unit, Leeds Teaching Hospitals Trust, since 1995; *b* 30 Nov. 1952; *s* of late Leonard Leslie Emery and Beryl Emery; *m* 1980, Shirley; two *d*. *Educ:* Cardiff High Sch.; Churchill Coll., Cambridge (BA, MA 1976); Guy's Hosp. Med. Sch.; MB BChir 1977, MD 1985 Cantab. MRCP 1979, FRCP 1992. Accredited Rheumatol. and Gen. (Internal) Medicine, JCHMT, 1985. Hse Officer and SHO rotation, Guy's Hosp., 1979; SHO, Brompton Hosp., 1980; Registrar, then Sen. Registrar in Gen. Medicine and Rheumatol., 1980–85; Hd of Rheumatol., Walter and Eliza Hall Inst., Melbourne and Hon. Consultant, Royal Melbourne Hosp., 1985–87; Sen. Lectr, Univ. of Birmingham, 1987–95. Licentiate Mem., Western Acad. Acupuncture, 1982. Treas., Eur. League Against Rheumatism, 2003. Roche Biennial Award for Clinical Rheumatol., 1991; Hosp. Dr of the Year (Rheumatol.), 1999; Outstanding contrib. to rheumatol., Eur. League against Rheumatism, 2002; Carol Nachman Award, 2012. *Publications:* Visual Diagnosis Self-tests in Rheumatology, 1996, 2nd edn 2001; Clinician's Manual on COX-2 Inhibition, 1999, 2nd edn 2002; Adalimumab and Rheumatoid Arthritis, 2003; New Treatments in Arthritis, 2003; Early Rheumatoid Arthritis: rheumatic disease clinics of North America, 2006; 73 book chapters and over 950 peer-reviewed pubns. *Recreations:* golf, walking, music. *Address:* Leeds Institute of Rheumatic and Musculoskeletal Medicine, Chapel Allerton Hospital, Chapeltown Road, Leeds LS7 4SA. *T:* (0113) 392 4884, *Fax:* (0113) 392 4991. *E:* p.emery@leeds.ac.uk. *Clubs:* Oakdale Golf, Newport Golf, Harrogate Academy Sports.

EMERY, Richard James, OBE 2009; Chairman: CSC Media Group Ltd, 2008–14; Wildscreen Charitable Trust, since 2008; *b* 21 July 1946; *s* of Frederick Harold Emery and Hilda Emery (*née* Newson); *m* 1st, 1978, Patricia Moore (marr. diss. 1993); one *s*, and one step *s*; 2nd, 1995, Hazel Susan Challis; one step *s* two step *d*. *Educ:* Reading Blue Coat Sch. Sales Controller: Anglia Television, 1976; TVS Ltd, 1982; Sales Dir, Central Independent Television Ltd, 1984; Jt Man. Dir and Founder, TSMS Ltd, 1989; Commercial Dir, ITN Ltd, 1991; Dir, Market Strategy, ITV Network Centre, 1993; Man. Dir, BBC Worldwide TV, 1994; Chief Operating Officer, BBC Worldwide Ltd, 1997; Chief Exec., UKTV Ltd, 1998–2008. *Recreations:* Rugby, walking, reading, boating. *Address:* New Oak, Mill Road, Shiplake, Henley-on-Thames RG9 3LW. *T:* (0118) 940 6503.

EMERY, William Hubert, PhD; JP; Chair: Northern Ireland Authority for Utility Regulation, since 2012; Centre on Regulation in Europe, since 2012; *b* 28 June 1951; *s* of Prof. John Lewis and Marjorie Rose Emery (*née* Mytton); *m* 1975, Celia Joan Abbott, PhD; one *s* one *d*. *Educ:* Univ. of Sheffield (BEng 1972; PhD 1976); Univ. of Bradford (MBA 1981). CEng, MICE 1978. Various posts, Yorkshire Water Authy, 1975–90; Office of Water Services: Hd, Engrg Intelligence, 1990–94; Asst Dir, 1994–98; Chief Engr and Dir of Costs and Performance, 1998–2005; Chief Exec., Office of Rail Regulation, 2005–11. JP S Yorks, 1981.

EMERY-WALLIS, Frederick Alfred John, FSA; Member (C), 1973–2001, Chairman, 1999–2001, Hampshire County Council; Vice-President, Southern Tourist Board, 1988–2001 (Chairman, 1976–88); *b* 11 May 1927; *o s* of Frederick Henry Wallis and Lillian Grace Emery Coles; *m* 1960, Solange, *o d* of William Victor Randall, London, and Albertine Beaupère, La Guerche-sur-l'Aubois; two *d*. *Educ:* Blake's Academy, Portsmouth. Royal Signals SCU4 (Middle East Radio Security), 1945–48. Portsmouth City Council, 1961–74; Lord Mayor, 1968–69; Alderman, 1969–74; Vice-Chm., 1975–76, Leader, 1976–93 and 1997–99, Hants CC. Chm., Recreation Cttee, 1982–85, Mem., Exec. and Policy Cttees, ACC, 1974–93; Mem., LGA, 1997–2000. Chairman: Portsmouth Develt and Estates Cttee, 1965–74; Portsmouth Papers Editorial Bd, 1966–82; S Hampshire Plan Adv. Cttee, 1969–74; Portsmouth South Cons. and Unionist Assoc., 1971–79, 1982–85; Portsmouth Record Series Adv. Panel, 1982–2002; Hampshire Archives Trust, 1986–2001; Exec. Cttee, Hampshire Sculpture Trust, 1988–2001; Director: Warrior Preservation Trust, 1988–91; WNO, 1990–99; Learning Through Landscapes Trust, 1991–2001; Member: Economic Planning Council for the South East, 1969–74; SE Regl Cultural Consortium; British Library Adv. Council, 1979–84, 1986–91; Council, British Records Assoc., 1979–2004 (Vice-Pres., 1996–2004); Library and Information Services Council, 1980–83; Mary Rose Develt Trust, 1980–90; Arts Council of GB Reg. Adv. Bd, 1984–88; Hampshire Gardens Trust, 1984–99; Nat. Council on Archives, 1992–94; English Heritage Archives, Libraries and Information Adv. Cttee, 1999–2001; Victoria County History Cttee, 1993–2002. President: Hampshire Field Club, 1971–74; Hatrics, the Southern Information Network, 1978–2001. Gov., Univ. of Portsmouth, 1991–96 (Mem., 1961–92, Vice-Chm., 1967–75, Portsmouth Polytechnic); Chm. of Govs, Portsmouth High Sch. for Girls, 1982–92. Trustee: New Theatre Royal, Portsmouth, 1982–92; Royal Naval Mus., Portsmouth, 1987–2002; Royal Marines Mus., Portsmouth, 1993–94. Pres., Portsmouth YMCA, 1978–88. DL Hants 1988. Hon. Fellow, Portsmouth Polytechnic, 1972. FSA 1980. Hon. FRIBA 1985; Hon. FCLIP (Hon. FLA 1996). *Publications:* various publications concerning history and develt of Portsmouth and Hampshire. *Recreations:* book collecting, music. *Address:* Sussex House, 19 Sussex Road, Portsmouth PO5 3EX.

EMIN, Tracey, CBE 2013; RA 2007; artist; *b* 1963. *Educ:* Maidstone Coll. of Art (BA 1986); Royal Coll. of Art (MA 1989). Solo exhibitions include: White Cube, London, 1993, 2001, 2005, 2009, 2014, São Paulo, 2012; S London Gall., 1997; Galerie Gebauer, Berlin, 2000; Stedelijk Mus., Amsterdam, 2002; Haus der Kunst, Munich, 2002; Modern Art Oxford, 2002; Art Gall. of NSW, 2003; Platform Garanti Contemp. Art Centre, Istanbul, 2004; Venice Biennale, 2007; (retrospective) Scottish Nat. Gall. of Modern Art, 2008 (toured Malaga, 2008, Bern, 2009); (retrospective) Love is What You Want, Hayward Gall., 2011; Turner Contemporary, Margate, 2012. Group exhibns incl. Sensation, RA, 1997; Tracey Emin-Egon Schiele: where I want to go, Leopold Mus., Vienna, 2015. Set designer, Les Parents Terribles, Jermyn Street Th., 2004. Film, Top Spot, 2004. Founder, Tracey Emin Museum, London, 1995–98. Eranda Prof. of Drawing, Royal Acad. Schs, 2011–13. *Publications:* Strangeland, 2005; Tracey Emin: my life in a column, 2011. *Address:* c/o White Cube, 144–152 Bermondsey Street, SE1 3TQ.

EMLEY, Miles Lovelace Brereton; Chairman, St Ives plc, 1993–2011; *b* 23 July 1949; *s* of late Col Derek Emley, OBE and Mary Georgina Emley (*née* Lovelace); *m* 1976, Tessa Marcia Radclyffe Powell; two *s* one *d*. *Educ:* St Edward's Sch., Oxford; Balliol Coll., Oxford (MA). N. M. Rothschild & Sons Ltd, 1972–89 (Dir, 1982–89); Man. Dir, UBS Phillips & Drew, 1989–92. Non-exec. Dir, Marston's plc (formerly Wolverhampton & Dudley Breweries plc), 1998–2012. Master, Leathersellers' Co., 2011–12. *Club:* White's.

EMLYN, Viscount; James Chester Campbell; *b* 7 July 1998; *s* and *heir* of Earl Cawdor, *qv*.

EMMERSON, David, CBE 1989; AFC 1982; Chair, ARK Cancer Centre (North Hampshire) Charity Appeal (formerly North Hampshire Cancer Centre Appeal), 2012–14; *b* 6 Sept. 1939; *s* of late Alfred Robert and Sarah Helen Emmerson; *m* 1961, Martha (Marie) Katherine Stuart. *Educ:* Colchester Royal Grammar Sch. Operational and instructional flying, 1959–73; Canadian Staff Coll. and Air Staff Ottawa, 1974–76; Policy Staff, MoD, 1976–77; Air Staff, Washington, 1978–80; OC 206 Sqn, 1981–82; Gp Capt. Ops, Northwood, 1983; Stn Comdr, RAF Kinloss, 1984–85; RCDS, 1986; Principal Staff Officer to CDS, 1987–88; Chief of Staff, HQ 18 Gp, Northwood, 1989–90; retired in rank of Air Vice-Marshal. Chief Executive, Elizabeth FitzRoy Homes, 1991–2000; Chairman: Assoc. for Residential Care, 1995–2000; N Hants Hosp. NHS Trust, 2002–05. *Recreations:* travel, world politics, all sports. *Clubs:* Royal Air Force; Chichester Yacht.

EMMETT, Bryan David; Chairman, EAGA Group, 1998–2000 (Director, EAGA Ltd, 1991–2000); *b* 15 Feb. 1941; *m* 1960, Moira Miller (marr. diss. 1994); one *s*. *Educ:* Tadcaster Grammar Sch. Clerical Officer, Min. of Labour, and National Service, 1958–59; Exec. Officer, War Dept, 1959–64; Asst Principal, MOP, 1965–69 (Asst Private Sec. to Ministers of Power, 1968–69); Principal, Electricity Div., DTI, 1969–74; Department of Energy: Principal, and Private Sec. to Minister of State, 1974–75; Asst Sec., and Principal Private Sec. to Sec. of State for Energy, 1975–76; Asst Sec., Petroleum Engrg Div., 1977–80; Under Sec., and Principal Estab. Officer, 1980–81; Principal Estab. and Finance Officer, 1981–82; Chief Exec., Employment Div., MSC, 1982–85; Department of Energy: Head, Energy Policy Div., 1985–86; Head of Oil Div., 1986–87; Dir Gen., Energy Efficiency Office, 1987–88; seconded as Chief Exec., Educn Assets Bd, Leeds, 1988–90; compulsorily retired, 1991. Subpostmaster, Greenham Court PO and Store, Newbury, 1995–98. Adminr, EAGA Charitable Trust, 1993–95. Mem. (Lib Dem, 1997–2000, C, 2000), Newbury DC, later West Berks Council (Chm., Lib Dem Gp, May–Sept. 1998). *Recreations:* National Hunt racing, horseriding, golf. *Address:* Cedar Lea, Staples Barn Lane, Henfield, W Sussex BN5 9PR.

EMMOTT, Linda Mary; *see* Mulcahy, L.-A. M.

EMMOTT, Stephen, PhD; Head of Computational Science, Microsoft Research, since 2004; *b* Keighley, W Yorks, 3 June 1960; *s* of James Emmott and Sandra Emmott. *Educ:* Univ. of York (BSc 1st Cl. Experimental Psychol. 1987); Univ. of Stirling (PhD Computational Neurosci. 1993). Post-doctoral Scientist, AT&T Bell Laboratories, USA, 1993–96; Dir and Chief Scientist, Advanced Res. Lab., NCR Corp., 1997–2001; Hd, Intelligent Media Initiative, UCL, 2002–03. Vis. Prof., UCL, 2003–; Vis. Prof. of Computational Sci., Univ. of Oxford, 2005–. Trustee, NESTA, 2009–12. *Publications:* Towards 2020 Science, 2005; Ten Billion, 2013. *Recreations:* cooking, reading, music, travel. *Address:* Microsoft Research, 21 Station Road, Cambridge CB1 2FB. *T:* (01223) 479854. *E:* semmott@microsoft.com.

EMMOTT, William John, (Bill); author and consultant; *b* 6 Aug. 1956; *s* of Richard Anthony Emmott and Audrey Mary Emmott; *m* 1st, 1982, Charlotte Crowther (marr. diss.); 2nd, 1992, Carol Barbara Mawer. *Educ:* Latymer Upper Sch., Hammersmith; Magdalen Coll., Oxford (BA Hons PPE; Hon. Fellow, 2002); Nuffield Coll., Oxford. The Economist: Brussels corresp., 1980–82; Economics corresp., 1982–83; Tokyo corresp., 1983–86; Finance Editor, 1986–88; Business Affairs Editor, 1989–93; Editor-in-chief, 1993–2006; Editorial Dir, Economist Intelligence Unit, May–Dec. 1992. Member: European Exec. Cttee, Trilateral Commn, 1999–2009; BBC World Service Governors' Consultative Gp, 2000–06; Swiss Re Chairman's Adv. Panel, 2006–; Univ. of Tokyo President's Council, 2006–; Co-Chm., Canada-Europe Roundtable for Business, 2006–13; Econ. Advr, Stonehage Fleming Family and Partners (formerly Fleming Family & Partners), 2011–. Non-executive Director: Development Consultants International, 2006–09; eAccess Ltd, 2009–10; Lo Stellone Ltd, 2012–; Chm., Peer Index (formerly Viewsflow) plc, 2009–14. Dir, Salzburg Global Seminar, 2008–11. Chm., London Library, 2009–15; Chm. and Founder, Wake Up Foundn, 2013–. Trustee, Internat. Inst. for Strategic Studies, 2009–15. Columnist: The Times, 2010–12; La Stampa, 2010–; Nikkei Business, 2014–. Co-writer, Girlfriend in a Coma (documentary film), 2012; Exec. Producer, The Great European Disaster Movie (documentary film), 2015. Hon. LLD Warwick, 1999; Hon. DLitt: City, 2001; Northwestern, 2008. *Publications:* The Pocket Economist (with Rupert Pennant-Rea), 1983; The Sun Also Sets, 1989; Japan's Global Reach, 1992; Kanryo no Taizai, 1996; 20:21 Vision, 2003; The Sun Also Rises, 2006; Nihon no Sentaku, 2007; Rivals: how the power struggle between China, India and Japan will shape our next decade, 2008; Sekai Choryu no Yomikata, 2008; Kawaru Sekai, Tachiokureru Nihon, 2010; Forza, Italia: come ripartire dopo Berlusconi, 2010; Good Italy, Bad Italy, 2012. *Recreations:* cricket, dogwalking, journalism. *Address:* PO Box 23, Dulverton, Somerset TA22 9WW. *W:* www.billemmott.com. *Clubs:* Arts, Frontline.

EMMS, David Acfield, OBE 1995; MA; Director, The London Goodenough Trust (formerly London House) for Overseas Graduates, 1987–95; *b* 16 Feb. 1925; *s* of late Archibald George Emms and Winifred Gladys (*née* Richards); *m* 1950, Pamela Baker Speed; two *s* one *d* (and one *s* decd). *Educ:* Tonbridge Sch.; Brasenose Coll., Oxford. BA Hons Mod. Langs Oxford, 1950, Diploma in Education, 1951; MA 1954. Served War of 1939–45, RA, 1943–47. Undergraduate, 1947–50; Asst Master, Uppingham Sch. (Head of Mod. Languages Dept, CO, CCF Contingent), 1951–60; Headmaster of: Cranleigh School, 1960–70; Sherborne School, 1970–74; Master, Dulwich Coll., 1975–86. Chm., HMC, 1984; Pres., ISCO, 2001–06. Dep. Chm., E-SU, 1984–89; Chm., Jt Educnl Trust, 1987–90; Mem. Cttee, GBA, 1989–92. Vice-Chm. Council and Dep. Pro-Chancellor, City Univ., 1989–91; Governor: Bickley Park, 1978–81; Feltonfleet, 1967–86; Brambletye, 1982–88; St Felix Sch., Southwold, 1981–88; Portsmouth Grammar Sch., 1987–98; Tonbridge, 1988–2000; St George's, Montreux, 1989–2000; St Dunstan's Coll., 1992–97. President: Alleyn Club, 1985; Brasenose Soc., 1987. Mem. Council, Fairbridge Soc., 1984–96. FRSA 1988. Freeman, City of London; Master, Skinners' Co., 1987–88. Hon. Col, 39th (City of London) Signal Regt (Special Communications) (Volunteers), 1988–91. Chm., RNLI, Chichester, 1997–2005. Cdre, Alleynian Sailing Soc., 2008–14. Played Rugby football: Oxford *v* Cambridge, 1949, 1950; Northampton, 1951–56; Eastern Counties, 1951–57 (Capt. 1957); Barbarians, 1953. *Publications:* HMC Schools and British Industry, 1981. *Recreation:* putting names to faces. *Clubs:* East India, Devonshire, Sports and Public Schools, Pilgrims; Vincent's (Oxford).

EMMS, Peter Fawcett; public administration consultant in former communist countries, since 1995; *b* 25 April 1935; *s* of late Reginald Emms and Hetty Emms; *m* 1960, Carola Wayne; three *d*. *Educ:* Derby Sch., Derby; Magdalen Coll., Oxford, 1956–59 (Open Schol. in Mod. Langs; MA French and German). National Service, Jt Services Russian Course, 1954–56. Assistant Master: Abingdon Sch., 1959–62; Rugby Sch., 1962–74; Vis. Master, Groton Sch., Mass, 1967–68; Hd of Mod. Langs 1969–71, Housemaster of Town House 1971–74, Rugby Sch.; joined DoE as Principal, 1974, with posts in Road Safety, Construction Industries and Housing; Asst Sec., 1979; Hd of Greater London Housing, 1979–81; seconded to DES, Further and Higher Educn Br., 1981–83; Hd of Housing Management Div., and of Estate Action Unit, DoE, 1983–87; Nuffield Leverhulme Travelling Fellowship, 1987–88; Hd, Dept of Transport Internat. Transport Div., Mem., Central Rhine Commn, 1988–89; Under Sec., 1989; Regl Dir, Eastern Reg., DoE and Dept of Transport, 1989–94; Leader, Know How Fund adv. team to Ukrainian govt, 1994–95. *Publications:* Social Housing: a European dilemma?, 1990; (contrib.) Changing Housing Finance Systems, 1991. *Recreation:* travel. *Address:* 28 Sherard Court, 3 Manor Gardens, N7 6FA; 71800 Vauban, France.

EMPEY, family name of **Baron Empey**.

EMPEY, Baron *cr* 2011 (Life Peer), of Shandon in the City and County Borough of Belfast; **Reginald Norman Morgan Empey,** Kt 1999; OBE 1994; Member (UU), Belfast City Council, 1985–2010; Chairman, Ulster Unionist Party, since 2012 (Leader, 2005–10); *b* 26 Oct. 1947; *s* of Samuel Frederick Empey and Emily Winifred (*née* Morgan); *m* 1977, Stella Ethna Donnan (MBE 2007); one *s* one *d*. *Educ:* The Royal Sch., Armagh; Queen's Univ., Belfast (BSc (Econ)). Cons. & Unionist Assoc., QUB, 1967; Publicity Officer, 1967–68, Vice-Chm., 1968–72, Ulster Young Unionist Council; Chm., Vanguard Unionist Party, 1974–75; Mem., E Belfast, NI Constitutional Convention, 1975–76. Dep. Lord Mayor, 1988–89, Lord Mayor of Belfast, 1989–90 and 1993–94. Northern Ireland Assembly: Mem. (UU) Belfast E, 1998–2011; Minister of Enterprise, Trade and Investment, 1999–2002, for Employment and Learning, 2007–10. Member: Belfast Harbour Comrs, 1985–89; Eastern Health and Social Services Bd, 1985–86; Ulster Unionist Council, 1987– (Hon. Sec., 1990–96; Vice-Pres., 1996–2004); Bd, Laganside Corp., 1992–98; Police Authy for NI, 1992–2001; European Cttee of the Regions for NI, Brussels, 1994–2002; Standing Adv. Commn on Human Rights, 1994–96. Contested: (UU) Belfast East, 2005; (UCUNF) South Antrim, 2010. *Recreations:* walking, gardening. *Address:* Knockvale House, 205 Sandown Road, Belfast BT5 6GX. *T:* (028) 9046 3900.

EMPEY, Prof. Duncan William, FRCP; Responsible Officer, BMI Healthcare (formerly General Healthcare Group), since 2011 (Group Medical Director, 2008–12); Consultant Physician, London Chest Hospital and Royal London Hospital, 1979–2004; *b* 9 Sept. 1946; *s* of Henry Gordon Empey and Katherine Isobel (*née* Hooper); *m* 1972, Gillian Mary Charlesworth; three *d*. *Educ:* Christ's Coll., Finchley; University Coll. London; Westminster Hosp. Med. Sch. (MB, BS). MRCS 1969; FRCP 1983 (LRCP 1969). NIH Fogarty Internat. Res. Fellow, Cardiovascular Res. Inst., San Francisco, 1974–75; Hon. Lectr, London Hosp. Med. Coll., 1975–79; Hon. Sen. Registrar, London Hosp., 1975–79; Hon. Sen. Lectr, St Bartholomew's and Royal London Sch. of Medicine and Dentistry, 1995–2004; Hon. Consultant Physician, King Edward VII Hosp. for Officers, 1995–2015; Hon. Prof., Univ. of Keele Centre for Health Planning and Mgt, 2002–05; Foundn Prof. and Dean, Beds and Herts Postgrad. Med. Sch., 2005–09. Medical Director: Royal Hosps, then Barts and the London, NHS Trust, 1994–2001; NHS Executive (N Thames) Trust Unit, 1997–98; Associate Dir, Rapid Response Unit, subseq. Performance Develt Team, NHS Modernisation Agency, 2002–04. Pres., Section of Respiratory Medicine, RSocMed, 2013–14. Trustee, British Lung Foundn, 2009–14. Ed., British Jl of Diseases of the Chest, 1984–88. Sec.-Gen., European Soc. for Clinical Respiratory Physiol., 1979–84; Mem. Council, British Thoracic Soc., 2003–06. *Publications:* (jtly) Lung Function for the Clinician, 1981; papers on medical management, asthma, chronic bronchitis, pulmonary circulation, tuberculosis and cystic fibrosis. *Recreation:* equestrianism. *Address:* BMI The London Independent Hospital, 1 Beaumont Square, E1 4NL. *T:* (020) 7780 2585, 07985 513067. *Clubs:* Savage, Groucho.

EMPEY, Rt Rev. Walton Newcombe Francis; Archbishop of Dublin and Primate of Ireland, 1996–2002; Bishop of Glendalough, 1996–2002; *b* 26 Oct. 1934; *m* 1960, Louise E. Hall; three *s* one *d*. *Educ:* Portora Royal School and Trinity College, Dublin. Curate Assistant, Glenageary, Dublin, 1958–60; Priest-in-charge, Grand Falls, NB, Canada, 1960–63; Parish Priest, Edmundston, NB, 1963–66; Incumbent, Stradbally, Co. Laois, Ireland, 1966–71; Dean of St Mary's Cathedral and Rector, Limerick City Parish, 1971–81; Bishop of Limerick and Killaloe, 1981–85; Bishop of Meath and Kildare, 1985–96. *Recreations:* reading, fishing, walking. *Address:* Rathmore Lodge, Rathmore, Tullow, Co. Carlow, Republic of Ireland.

EMSLEY, Dr John, FRSC; writer and broadcaster; *s* of Charles and Mary Emsley; *m* 1963, Joan Feather; one *s* one *d*. *Educ:* Manchester Univ. (BSc, MSc; PhD 1963); DSc London 1983. FRSC 1983. Lectr, 1966–84, Reader, 1984–90, KCL; Science Writer in Residence: Imperial Coll., London, 1990–97; Dept of Chem., Univ. of Cambridge, 1997–2002. Consultant, Broadcast Advertising Clearance Centre, 1996–2007. Columnist: Molecule of the Month, Independent, 1990–96; Wired mag., 2009–13. *Publications:* (with C. D. Hall) The Chemistry of Phosphorus, 1976; The Elements, 1989, 3rd edn 1998; The Consumer's Good Chemical Guide, 1994; Molecules at an Exhibition, 1998 (Chinese edn 2012); (with P. Fell) Was it something you ate?, 1999; The Shocking History of Phosphorus, 2000; Nature's Building Blocks, 2001, 2nd edn 2011; Vanity, Vitality & Virility, 2004; Elements of Murder, 2005 (Korean edn 2012); Better Looking, Better Living, Better Loving, 2007; Molecules of Murder, 2008 (trans. Hungarian 2013); A Healthy, Wealthy, Sustainable World, 2010; Islington Green, 2012; The Newsletter, 2013; Sweet Dreams, 2013; Chemystery, 2013; popular sci. books trans. into foreign langs, incl. German, French, Italian, Spanish, Portuguese, Polish, Finnish, Chinese and Japanese; original res. papers on phosphorus chem. and strong hydrogen-bonded systems; contrib. numerous sci. articles and features to jls incl. New Scientist, Independent, Guardian, Chem. in Britain, ChemMatters, Focus, Sci. Watch. *Recreation:* walking. *Address:* Alameda Lodge, 23A Alameda Road, Ampthill MK45 2LA. *T:* (01525) 404718. *E:* JohnEmsley38@aol.com.

EMSLIE, Rt Hon. Lord; Hon. George Nigel Hannington Emslie; PC 2011; a Senator of the College of Justice in Scotland, 2001–12; *b* 17 April 1947; *s* of Rt Hon. Lord Emslie, PC, MBE; *m* 1973, Heather Ann Davis; one *s* two *d*. *Educ:* Edinburgh Acad.; Trinity Coll., Glenalmond; Gonville and Caius Coll., Cambridge (BA); Edinburgh Univ. (LLB). Admitted to Faculty of Advocates, 1972; Standing Junior Counsel: to Forestry Commn in Scotland and to Dept of Agric. and Fisheries for Scotland, 1981–82; to Inland Revenue in Scotland, 1982–86; QC (Scot.) 1986. Part-time Chm., Med. Appeal Tribunals, 1988–97. Dean, Faculty of Advocates, 1997–2001. *Address:* c/o Court of Session, Parliament House, Edinburgh EH1 1RQ. *T:* (0131) 225 2595. *Clubs:* Hawks (Cambridge); New (Edinburgh).

See also Rt Hon. Lord Kingarth.

EMSLIE, Hon. Derek Robert Alexander; *see* Kingarth, Rt Hon. Lord.

EMSLIE, Donald Gordon; Chairman: Royal Lyceum Theatre Co., 2004–12; Thorpe Hall Leisure Ltd, since 2012; *b* 8 May 1957; *s* of Francis G. Emslie and Margaret Evelyn (*née* Campbell); *m* 1998, Sarah, *d* of Peter Gardner; two *d*. *Educ:* Jordanhill Coll., Glasgow (BEd Physical Educn). Teacher, Kingussie High Sch., 1979–82; with Bochringer Ingelheim Pharmaceuticals, 1982–85; sales, 1985–94, Commercial Dir, 1994–97, Scottish TV; Man. Dir, Broadcasting, SMG plc, 1997–99; Chief Executive: SMG Television, 1999–2006; SMG plc, 2006–07. Chairman: GMTV Ltd, 2002–04; Queuebay Ltd, 2008–11. Chairman: ITV Council, 2002–07; Scottish Industry Skills Panel, 2004–09; RZSScot, 2008–11. Chm., Castle Hotel Mgt Co., 2009–; non-executive Director: Scottish Water, 2008–; SRU plc, 2008–11. Member, Board: Scottish Screen, 2000–07; Skillset, 2004–09; Screen Acad. Scotland, 2006–11 (Chm., Adv. Bd, 2006–11); Jt Bd, Scottish Screen and Scottish Arts Council, 2007–10. Jt Hon. Chm., BAFTA Scotland, 2004–07. FRTS; FRSA. Hon. DBA Robert Gordon, 2010. *Recreations:* golf, tennis, theatre. *Address:* 32 Drumsheugh Gardens, Edinburgh EH3 7RN. *T:* (0131) 226 3938.

EMSLIE, Rt Hon. George Nigel Hannington; *see* Emslie, Rt Hon. Lord.

ENCOMBE, Viscount; John Francis, (Jock), Scott; independent business and organisational psychologist; Chairman, Mercy Corps; *b* 9 July 1962; *s* and *heir* of 5th Earl of Eldon, *qv*; *m* 1993, Charlotte, *d* of Robert de Vlaming; one *s* one *d*, and one *s* one step *d*. *Educ:* Oxford Univ. (MA); UKCP (DipCAT). FRSA.

ENDERBY, Charles; *see* Enderby, S. C.

ENDERBY, Sir John (Edwin), Kt 2004; CBE 1997; FRS 1985; H. O. Wills Professor of Physics, 1981–96, now Emeritus, and Senior Research Fellow, since 1996, University of Bristol; *b* 16 Jan. 1931; *s* of late Thomas Edwin Enderby and Rheita Rebecca Hollinshead (*née* Stather); *m* Susan, *yr d* of late Harold Vincent Bowles, OBE and Colleen Bessie Bowles; one *s* two *d*, and one *d* (one *s* decd) of previous marriage. *Educ:* Chester Grammar Sch.; London Univ. (BSc, PhD). Lecturer in Physics: Coll. of Technology, Huddersfield, 1957–60; Univ. of Sheffield, 1960–67; Reader in Physics, Univ. of Sheffield, 1967–69; Prof. in Physics and Head of the Dept, Univ. of Leicester, 1969–76; Prof. of Physics, Bristol Univ., 1976–81; Head of Dept of Physics, and Dir, H. H. Wills Physics Lab., Bristol Univ., 1981–94; Directeur-Adjoint, Institut Laue-Langevin, Grenoble, 1985–88. Fellow, Argonne Nat. Lab., Ill., USA, 1989–91; Visiting Fellow, Battelle Inst., 1968–69; Visiting Professor: Univ. of Guelph, Ont., 1978; Univ. of Leiden, 1989. Humphrey Davy Lectr, Royal Soc., 1997. Member: Physics Cttee, SRC, 1974–77; Neutron Beam Res. Cttee, SRC, 1974–80 and 1988–91 (Chm., 1977–80 and 1988–91); PPARC, 1994–98. Chm., Physics Panel, 2001 RAE, HEFCE, 1999–2001. Chm., Liquids Bd, Eur. Physical Soc., 1991–96. Member: Council, Institut Laue-Langevin, Grenoble, 1973–80; Council, Royal Soc., 1990–92 (Physical Sec. and Vice-Pres., 1999–2004). Chm., Melys Diagnostics Ltd, 2004–. MAE 1989. FInstP 1970 (Chm., SW Br., 1979–83; Guthrie Medal, 1995; Pres., 2004–06). Associate Editor, Philosophical Magazine, 1975–81; Editor, Proc. Royal Soc. A, 1989–94; Editor in Chief, Jl of Physics Condensed Matter, 1997–2002; Chief Sci. Advr, Inst. of Physics Publishing, 2002–11. Hon. Fellow, Birkbeck Coll., London, 1991. Hon. FInstP 2010. Hon. DSc: Loughborough, 1996; Leicester, 2006; Bristol, 2006; Sheffield, 2006; UEA, 2007; Kent, 2008; Huddersfield, 2011; Chester, 2013. *Publications:* (jointly): Physics of Simple Liquids, 1968; Amorphous and Liquid Semiconductors, 1974; many publications on the structure and properties of liquids in: Phil. Mag. Adv. Phys, Jl Phys, Proc. Royal Soc., etc. *Recreations:* gardening, woodwork, watching Association football. *Address:* H. H. Wills Physics Laboratory, Tyndall Avenue, Bristol BS8 1TL. *T:* (0117) 928 8737; 7 Cotham Lawn Road, Bristol BS6 6DU. *T:* (0117) 973 3411.

ENDERBY, Major (Samuel) Charles, LVO 2010; JP; Lieutenant, Queen's Body Guard of the Yeoman of the Guard, 2006–09; *b* 18 Sept. 1939; *s* of late Col Samuel Enderby, CVO, DSO, MC and of Pamela Enderby (*née* Hornby); *m* 1973, Mary Justina Compton; two *d*. *Educ:* Wellington Coll.; RMA, Sandhurst. Commnd 12th Royal Lancers, 1959; retd 1985, in rank of Major. Queen's Body Guard of Yeoman of the Guard: Exon, 1987–2002; Ensign, 2002–04; Clerk of the Cheque, 2004–06. Chm., Hexham Steeplechase Co. Ltd, 1991–. JP Tynedale, 1991. *Recreations:* gardening, reading, bird ringing, shooting. *Address:* The Riding, Hexham, Northumberland NE46 4PF. *Clubs:* Army and Navy, Pratt's.

ENDICOTT, Grattan, OBE 1998; Chief Executive and Secretary to the Trustees, Foundation for Sport and the Arts, 1991–2004; *b* 12 Jan. 1924; *s* of late Cecil George Endicott and Annette Rose Endicott; *m* 1st, 1944, Paolina Cicoria (marr. diss. 1955); two *s*; 2nd, 1961, Jean Thurgeson (marr. diss. 1981). *Educ:* Rhyl Co. Grammar Sch. Served RN, 1941–46; Principal Linguist, Navy Sub-Commn, Allied Commn, Rome, 1944–46. Personnel Asst, ICI, 1946–57; Littlewoods Pools: Asst Permutation Manager, 1957–66; Hd, Permutation Services, 1966–89. European Bridge League: Member: Exec. Cttee, 1989–93; Appeals Cttee (Standing), 1999–2011; Laws Cttee, 1999–2011; Systems Cttee, 1999–2011; Tournament Dirs Cttee, 1999–2001 and 2003–07; World Bridge Federation: Member: Systems Cttee, 1990–95; Rules and Regulations Cttee, 1992–95 and 2000–10; Appeals Cttee (Standing), 1993–95 and 2000–10; Convention Card Cttee, 1987–89; Laws Cttee, 1987 (Vice-Chm., 1988–95; Sec., 1998–2013; Hon. Life Sec., 2013); Laws Drafting Subcttee, 2001–10. Vice Pres., English Bridge Union; Pres., Merseyside and Cheshire Contract Bridge Assoc. FRSA. Gold Medal, World Bridge Fedn, 2005; Gold Medal, English Bridge Union, 2013. *Publications:* European Bridge League Commentary on the Laws of Duplicate Contract Bridge 1987, 1992; (jtly) Draft Laws of Duplicate Bridge, 2006; (jtly) Laws of Duplicate Bridge, 2007. *Recreation:* competition (duplicate) bridge. *Address:* 14 Elmswood Court, Palmerston Road, Mossley Hill, Liverpool L18 8DJ. *T:* (0151) 724 1484. *Club:* Liverpool Bridge.

ENDICOTT, Prof. Timothy Andrew Orville, DPhil; Professor of Legal Philosophy, since 2006, and Dean, Faculty of Law, since 2007, University of Oxford; Fellow, Balliol College, Oxford, since 1999; *b* Golden, BC, 9 July 1960; *s* of Orville and Julianne Endicott; one *s* one *d*. *Educ:* Harvard Univ. (AB 1983); Univ. of Oxford (MPhil 1985; DPhil 1997); Univ. of Toronto (LLB 1988). Barrister and solicitor, Oslers, Toronto, 1988–91; Lectr in Law, Jesus Coll., 1994–95, St Anne's Coll., 1995–96, St Catherine's Coll., 1996–99 (Fellow, 1998–99), Oxford. Bencher, Inner Temple, 2011. *Publications:* Vagueness in Law, 2000; Administrative Law, 2009, 2nd edn 2011; articles in law and philos. jls. *Address:* Balliol College, Oxford OX1 3BJ. *T:* (01865) 271564, *Fax:* (01865) 271493.

ENFIELD, Viscount; William Robert Byng; computer systems developer, CCP York, since 2002; *b* 10 May 1964; *s* and *heir* of 8th Earl of Strafford, *qv*; *m* 1994, Karen Elizabeth, *d* of S. Graham Lord, Leyland, Preston; twin *s* three *d*. *Educ:* Winchester Coll.; Durham Univ. *Heir:* *s* Hon. Samuel Peter Byng, *b* 17 July 1998. *Address:* 7 Church Street Villas, Durham DH1 3DW.

See also Hon. J. E. Byng.

ENFIELD, Harry; comedy actor and writer; *b* 30 May 1961; *m* 1997, Lucy Lyster; one *s* one *d*. *Educ:* York Univ. (BA Hons Politics). TV programmes include: Sir Norbert Smith: a life, 1989 (Silver Rose of Montreux, Emmy Award); Smashie and Nicey: the end of an era, 1994 (Silver Rose of Montreux); Norman Ormal, 1998; Kevin's Guide to Being a Teenager, 1999; Skins, 2007, 2008; series: Harry Enfield's Television Programme, 1990, 1992; Harry Enfield's Guide to the Opera, 1993; Harry Enfield and Chums, 1994 (Writers Guild Award) and 1997 (Silver Rose of Montreux); St Albion Parish Council, 1998, 1999; Harry Enfield's Brand Spanking New Show, 2000; Celeb, 2002; Ruddy Hell! It's Harry and Paul, 2007; Harry and Paul, 2008, 2010, 2012; Skins, 2009; (narrator) Crackanory, 2013; Bad Education, 2013–14; Blandings, 2014; An Evening with Harry Enfield and Paul Whitehouse, 2015; also appeared regularly in: Saturday Night Live, 1986; Friday Night Live, 1988; Gone to the Dogs, 1991; Men Behaving Badly, 1992; films: Kevin and Perry Go Large, 2000; Churchill: the Hollywood Years, 2003; Tooth, 2004. Top BBC 1 Comedy Personality, British Comedy Awards, 1998. *Publications:* Harry Enfield and his Humorous Chums, 1997. *Address:* c/o Curtis Brown Group Ltd, Haymarket House, 28–29 Haymarket, SW1Y 4SP.

ENGEL, Matthew Lewis; columnist, Financial Times, since 2004; Editor, Wisden Cricketers' Almanack, 1992–2000 and 2003–07; *b* 11 June 1951; *s* of late Max David and Betty Ruth Engel; *m* 1990, Hilary Davies; one *d* (one *s* decd). *Educ:* Carmel Coll.; Manchester Univ. (BA Econ). Reporter, Chronicle and Echo, Northampton, 1972–75; Reuters, 1977–79; The Guardian: journalist, 1979–2004; cricket corresp., 1982–87; feature writer, sports columnist, occasional war, political and foreign corresp., 1987–2001; columnist, 1998–2004; Washington corresp., 2001–03. Vis. Prof. of Media, Oxford Univ., 2010–11. Co-Founder, Laurie Engel Fund, 2005. Sports Writer of the Year, What the Papers Say, 1985; Sports Journalist of the Year, British Press Awards, 1991. *Publications:* Ashes '85, 1985; (ed) Guardian Book of Cricket, 1986; (ed) Sportswriter's Eye, 1989; (ed) Sportspages Almanac, 1990, 1991, 1992; (with A. Radd) History of Northamptonshire CCC, 1993; Tickle the Public, 1996; Extracts from the Red Notebooks, 2007; Eleven Minutes Late, 2009; Engel's England, 2014. *Recreation:* wishful thinking. *Address:* Fair Oak, near Bacton, Herefordshire HR2 0AT. *Clubs:* Garrick; Northamptonshire CC (Vice-Pres.).

ENGEL, Natascha; MP (Lab) North East Derbyshire, since 2005; Second Deputy Speaker of Ways and Means, and a Deputy Speaker, since 2015; *b* 9 April 1967; *d* of Achaz and Christina Engel; *m* 2001, David Salisbury Jones (marr. diss. 2012); three *s*. *Educ:* King's Coll., London (BA 1st Cl. Hons Mod. Langs); Westminster Press Dip. Journalism; Westminster Univ. (MA Tech. and Specialist Translation). Journalist, Dover Express, 1990; English and German teacher, Spain, 1990–92; teletext subtitler, 1992–97; GPMU Organiser, TUC Organising Acad., 1997–98; TU Liaison, Labour Party, 1998–2001; Prog. Dir, John Smith Inst., 2001–02; Co-ordinator, TU Political Fund Ballots, 2002–03. *Address:* House of Commons, SW1A 0AA. *T:* (020) 7219 3000. *E:* natascha.engel.mp@parliament.uk.

ENGEL, Dame Sister Pauline Frances, DBE 1995 (CBE 1986); Vicar for Education, Diocese of Auckland (RC), New Zealand, 1994–2003; *b* 10 Sept. 1930; *d* of John Edmond Engel and Eileen Frances Engel (*née* McDavitt). *Educ:* St Mary's Coll., Wellington; Univ. of Auckland (MA Hons). Registered Teacher. Entered Sisters of Mercy Congregation, 1960; Dep. Principal, McAuley High Sch., 1978–79; Principal, Carmel Coll., 1983–91. Gen. Exec. Sec. to Major Superiors Conference, NZ, 1992–93. Sisters of Mercy Leadership Council, 1995–2000. *Publications:* The Abolition of Capital Punishment in New Zealand 1935–61, 1976. *Recreations:* classical music, reading. *Address:* Mount Carmel Convent, Box 31142, Milford, Auckland 0741, New Zealand; Sisters of Mercy Auckland Ltd, PO Box 6015, Wellesley Street, Auckland 1141, New Zealand.

ENGESET, Jetmund, Hon. LVO 2004; FRCSE; FRCSG; Consultant Surgeon, Grampian Health Board, 1987–2004; Surgeon to the Queen in Scotland, 1985–2004; *b* 22 July 1938; *s* of Arne K. Engeset and Marta Engeset; *m* 1966, Anne Graeme (*née* Robertson); two *d*. *Educ:* Slemdal and Ris Skole, Oslo, Norway; Oslo University; Aberdeen University (MB ChB, ChM Hons). House Officer (Surgical and Medical), Aberdeen Royal Infirmary, 1964–65; Aberdeen University: Res. Assistant, Dept of Surgery, 1965–67; Surgical Registrar, 1967–70; Lectr in Surgery, 1970–74; Sen. Lectr in Surgery, 1974–87; Head of Dept of Surgery, 1982–85 (seconded to Salgrenska Hosp. Surgical Unit, Gothenburg, Sweden, 1972–74). Golden Jubilee Medal, 2002. *Publications:* papers on microcirculation, vascular surgery, organ preservation and tissue transplantation. *Recreations:* ski-ing, angling, squash, gardening. *Address:* 66 Greystoke Park, Gosforth, Newcastle-upon-Tyne NE3 2DZ. *T:* (0191) 236 3223.

ENGLAND, Angela Catherine; *see* Finnerty, A. C.

ENGLAND, Prof. George Leslie, DScEng; CEng, FICE, FNucI; Professor of Mechanics and Structures, Imperial College, London, 1989–2000; *b* 9 Oct. 1935; *s* of John Edward Philip England and Rose Gladys England; *m* 1968, W. Margaret Landon. *Educ:* East Barnet Grammar Sch.; King's Coll., London (Sambrooke Schol.; BScEng 1st Cl. Hons; Jameson Prize (Eng); Eng. Soc. Centenary Prize, Tennant Medal (Geol); PhD 1961; DScEng 1974). King's College, London: Lectr, 1961; Reader in Engrg Mechanics, 1975; Dean, 1983–85; Vice-Dean, 1985–86; Prof. of Mechanics and Structures, 1986–89. Consultant to: HSE, NII, 1971; UN Develt Project, Central Soils and Materials Res. Station, India, 1992. MASCE. Patent holder for the design of long-span integral bridges with improved performance. *Publications:* contribs to learned jls on time-dependent service-life performance of concrete structures, behaviour of structures at high temperatures and cyclic soil-structure interaction problems. *Recreations:* landscape gardening, mountain walking. *Address:* Department of Civil and Environmental Engineering, Imperial College of Science, Technology and Medicine, SW7 2BU.

ENGLAND, Prof. Philip Christopher, FRS 1999; Professor of Geology, Oxford University, since 2000; Fellow, University College, Oxford, since 2000; *b* 30 April 1951; *s* of Anthony Christopher England and Margaret Jean England; *m* 1978, Pamela Anne Shreeve; one *s* two *d*. *Educ:* Bristol Univ. (BSc Physics 1972); DPhil Geophysics, Oxford, 1976. NERC Research Fellow, 1977–79, IBM Res. Fellow, 1979–81, Dept Geodesy and Geophysics, Univ. of Cambridge; Asst, then Associate Prof., Harvard Univ., 1981–86; Lectr in Geophysics, Oxford Univ., 1986–99; Fellow, Exeter Coll., Oxford, 1986–2000. Fellow, Amer. Geophysical Union, 1996. *Publications:* contribs to earth science jls. *Recreations:* family, music.

ENGLAND, Rear-Adm. Timothy John, FIET; maritime and transport consultant, since 1997; Chief Staff Officer (Support) to Commander-in-Chief Fleet, 1992–94; *b* Llandudno, 6 Feb. 1942; *s* of late Wilfred James England and Kathleen Helen England (*née* Stacey); *m* 1966, Margaret Ann Cullen; one *s* one *d*. *Educ:* Trinity Sch. of John Whitgift, Croydon; RNEC Manadon. BScEng ext. London Univ. CEng. Joined RN at BRNC Dartmouth as Weapon Engineering specialist, 1960; served HM Ships Alert, Collingwood, London, Salisbury; Staff of DG Ships; HM Dockyard, Devonport; HMS Bristol; Staff of C-in-C Fleet; Directorate of Naval Operational Requirements, 1978–80; Weapon Engineer Officer, HMS Invincible, incl. Falklands Campaign, 1981–82; Staff Weapon Engineer Officer to FO Sea Training, 1982–84; Defence Operational Requirements, 1984–86; RCDS 1987; Fleet Weapon Engineer Officer, 1988–89; WRNS Sea Service Implementation Team Leader, 1990; Captain, RNEC, Manadon, 1990–92. Harbour Master, River Hamble, 1995–96. MInstD. *Publications:* articles in Naval and professional jls. *Recreations:* sailing/cruising, photography, information technology. *Address:* 14 East Hill Close, Fareham, Hants PO16 8SE.

ENGLE, Sir George (Lawrence Jose), KCB 1983 (CB 1976); QC 1983; First Parliamentary Counsel, 1981–86; *b* 13 Sept. 1926; *m* 1956, Irene, *d* of late Heinz Lachmann; three *d*. *Educ:* Charterhouse (scholar); Christ Church, Oxford (Marjoribanks and Dixon schols, MA). Served RA, 1945–48 (2nd Lt, 1947). Firsts in Mods and Greats; Cholmeley Schol., Lincoln's Inn, 1952. Called to Bar, Lincoln's Inn, 1953, Bencher, 1984. Joined Parly Counsel Office, 1957; seconded as First Parly Counsel, Fedn of Nigeria, 1965–67; Parly Counsel, 1970–80; with Law Commn, 1971–73; Second Parly Counsel, 1980–81. Pres., Commonwealth Assoc. of Legislative Counsel, 1983–86. Mem., Hansard Soc. Commn on the Legislative Process, 1992–93. Pres., Kipling Soc., 2001–08. *Publications:* Law for Landladies, 1955; (ed jtly) Cross on Statutory Interpretation, 2nd edn 1987, 3rd edn 1995; contributor to: Ideas, 1954; O Rare Hoffnung, 1960; The Oxford Companion to English Literature, 1985; articles in Kipling Jl. *Recreations:* books, theatre. *Address:* 32 Wood Lane, Highgate, N6 5UB. *T:* (020) 8340 9750.

ENGLE, Prof. Robert Fry, PhD; Professor of Finance, 1999, and Michael Armellino Professor in the Management of Financial Services, since 2000, Leonard N. Stern School of Business, New York University; *b* Nov. 1942; *m* 1969, Marianne Eger; one *s* one *d*. *Educ:* Williams Coll. (BS highest Hons (Physics) 1964); Cornell Univ. (MS (Physics) 1966; PhD (Econs) 1969). Asst Prof., 1969–74, Associate Prof., 1975, MIT; University of California, San Diego: Associate Prof., 1975–77; Prof., 1977; Chair, 1990–94; Chancellors' Associates Prof. of Econs, 1993–; Prof. Emeritus and Dist. Res. Prof., 2003; New York University: Co-Founding Pres., Soc. for Financial Econometrics, 2007–11; Founder and Dir, Volatility Inst., 2009–. Fellow, Wharton Financial Instns Center, Philadelphia, 2009–10; Dist. Vis. Scholar, Kenan-Flagler Business Sch., Univ. of N Carolina Chapel Hill, 2010; Dist. Vis. Scholar, McDonough Sch. of Business, Georgetown Univ., 2012; T. C. Liu Vis. Scholar, Becker Friedman Inst., Univ. of Chicago, 2013. Principal, Robert F. Engle Econometric Services. Mem. Econ. Panel, NSF, 1979–81; Res. Associate, Nat. Bureau of Econ. Res., 1987–. Fellow: Econometric Soc., 1981 (Mem. Council, 1994; Mem., Nominating Cttee for Council, 1995); Amer. Acad. of Arts and Scis, 1995; Amer. Statistical Assoc., 2000; Amer. Finance Assoc., 2004; Inst. for Quantitative Res. in Finance, 2006. Associate Editor: Econometrica, 1975–81; Jl of Regl Sci., 1978–; Jl of Forecasting, 1985–; Jl of Applied Econometrics, 1988– (Co-Ed., 1985–89); Rev. of Econs and Stats, 1992; Adv. Ed., Empirical Finance, 1992. Hon Dr: Southern Switzerland, 2003; Savoie, 2005; HEC Paris, 2005; Williams Coll., 2007. Roger F. Murray Prize, Inst. for Quantitative Res. in Finance, 1991; (jtly) Nobel Prize for Econs, 2003. *Publications:* (ed jtly) Long Run Economic Relations: readings in cointegration, 1991; (ed jtly) Handbook of Econometrics, vol. IV, 1994; (ed jtly) ARCH: selected readings, 1995; (ed jtly) Cointegration, Causality, and Forecasting: a festschrift in honor of Clive W. J. Granger, 1999; Anticipating Correlations, 2008; contribs to Econometrica, Jl of Business and Econ. Stats, Jl of Econometrics, Jl of Finance, Review of Financial Studies, Jl of Financial Economics, etc. *Address:* Leonard N. Stern School of Business, New York University, Salomon Center, 44 West Fourth Street, Suite 9–62, New York, NY 10012, USA. *T:* (212) 9980710, *Fax:* (212) 9954220. *E:* rengle@stern.nyu.edu.

ENGLEHART, Robert Michael; QC 1986; a Recorder, since 1987; a Deputy High Court Judge, since 1994; *b* 1 Oct. 1943; *s* of G. A. F. and K. P. Englehart; *m* 1971, Rosalind Mary Foster; one *s* two *d*. *Educ:* St Edward's Sch., Oxford; Trinity Coll., Oxford (MA); Harvard Law School (LLM); Bologna Centre (Dip. in Internat. Relns). Assistente, Univ. of Florence, 1968. Called to the Bar, Middle Temple, 1969 (Astbury Scholar; Bencher, 1995); practising barrister, 1969–. Chm., London Common Law and Commercial Bar Assoc., 1990–91. Trustee, Free Representation Unit, 1991–. *Publications:* (contrib.) Il Controllo Giudiziario: a comparative study of civil procedure, 1968. *Recreations:* shooting, cricket. *Address:* Blackstone Chambers, Blackstone House, Temple, EC4Y 9BW. *T:* (020) 7583 1770. *Clubs:* Garrick, MCC.

ENGLISH, Hon. Bill; *see* English, Hon. S. W.

ENGLISH, Gerald; Australian Artists Creative Fellow, 1994–99; *b* 6 Nov. 1925; *m* 1954, Jennifer Ryan; two *s* two *d*; *m* 1974, Linda Jacoby; one *s*. *Educ:* King's Sch., Rochester. After War service studied at Royal College of Music and then began career as lyric tenor; subsequently travelled in USA and Europe, appeared at Sadler's Wells, Covent Garden and Glyndebourne and recorded for major gramophone companies; Professor, Royal Coll. of Music, 1960–77; Director, Opera Studio, Victorian Coll. for the Arts, Melbourne, 1977–89; Lectr, Music Dept, Newcastle Univ., 1990–94. Recorded all vocal music of Peggy Glanville-Hicks and all music written for him by Andrew Ford, 1994–99; retired from singing, 2004. Hon. DMus Sydney, 1989.

ENGLISH, Judith Frances, (Lady English); Principal, St Hilda's College, Oxford, 2001–07; Dean of Scholars, Oxford Centre for Islamic Studies, since 2010; *b* 1 March 1940; *d* of Dr Kenneth James Grant Milne and Dr Constance Nellie Milne; *m* 1st, 1973, Ralph Talbot (marr. diss. 2001); two *d*; 2nd, 2002, Sir Terence English, *qv*. *Educ:* Notre Dame High Sch., Sheffield (State Schol.); Girton Coll., Cambridge (Crewdson Prize; MA 1963; Hon. Fellow 2004); University Coll. Hosp. Med. Sch., London (MB BChir 1965). MRCP 1968; MRCPsych 1973, FRCPsych 2002. Medical house staff posts, Whittington Hosp., Brompton Hosp. and UCH, 1965–67; Lectr in Clinical Immunology, Inst. of Chest Diseases, London Univ., 1967–70; Registrar in Psychiatry, Maudsley Hosp., 1970–74; Fellow in Consultation-Liaison Psychiatry, then Staff Psychiatrist, UCLA, 1974–79; Director, Psychiatric Consultation Service: Boston Veterans' Affairs Med. Center, 1980–95; New England Med. Center, 1986–93; Chief of Staff, Boston Veterans' Affairs Med. Center, 1996–2000; Asst Prof. of Psychiatry, Tufts Univ., 1986–2000; Associate Clinical Prof. of Psychiatry, Boston Univ. Sch. of Medicine, 1998–2000. *Publications:* contribs to med. and psychiatric jls. *Recreations:* reading, poetry, dance, textile collage. *Address:* 28 Tree Lane, Iffley Village, Oxford OX4 4EY.

ENGLISH, Michael; Chairman, London Local Involvement Network, 2010–11; *b* 24 Dec. 1930; *s* of late William Agnew English; *m* 1976, Carol Christine Owen; one *s* one *d*. *Educ:* King George V Grammar Sch., Southport; Liverpool Univ. (LLB). Employed until 1964 as Asst Manager of department concerned with management services in subsidiary of large public company. Joined Labour Party, 1949 (Hon. Life Mem.); Member: Rochdale County Borough Council, 1953–65 (Chairman Finance Cttee until 1964); Lambeth BC, 1990–2002. Mem., London Fire and Civil Defence Authy, 1992–2000; Chm., Lambeth CHC, 1993–94. Chm., London Network of NHS Patients' Forums, 2006–08. Pres., SE London Valuation Panel, 1996–2002. Contested (Lab) Shipley Div., WR Yorks, 1959; MP (Lab) Nottingham West, 1964–83. Parly Private Sec., BoT, 1966–67. Chm., Gen. Sub-Cttee of H of C Expenditure Cttee, 1974–79; formerly Mem., Chairmen's Panel, Treasury and Civil Service, Procedure (Finance) and Sound Broadcasting Cttees. Chairman: Parly Affairs Gp, PLP, 1970–76; E Midlands Gp, PLP, 1976–78; E Midlands Regl Lab. Party, 1979–80. *Recreation:* reading history. *Address:* 12 Denny Crescent, Kennington, SE11 4UY. *T:* (020) 7582 9970.

ENGLISH, Prof. Richard Ludlow, PhD; FBA 2009; FRHistS; FRSE; Wardlaw Professor of Politics, and Director of the Centre for the Study of Terrorism and Political Violence, University of St Andrews, since 2011; *b* Belfast, 16 Dec. 1963; *s* of Donald English and Bertha English (*née* Ludlow); *m* 1989, Maxine Cresswell; two *d*. *Educ:* Keble Coll., Oxford (BA Modern Hist.; Hon. Fellow, 2014); Keele Univ. (PhD Hist. 1990). Lectr in Politics, 1990–95, Reader in Politics, 1995–99, Prof. of Politics, 1999–2011, QUB. MRIA 2009. FRHistS 1996; FRSE 2015. *Publications:* Radicals and the Republic: socialist republicanism in the Irish Free State 1925–37, 1994; Ernie O'Malley: IRA intellectual, 1998; Armed Struggle: the history of the IRA, 2003; Irish Freedom: the history of nationalism in Ireland, 2006; Terrorism: how to respond, 2009; Modern War: a very short introduction, 2013. *Recreations:* Handel, Wagner, the Arsenal. *Address:* Centre for the Study of Terrorism and Political Violence, School of International Relations, The Scores, University of St Andrews, St Andrews KY16 9AX. *T:* (01334) 462988. *E:* rle2@st-andrews.ac.uk.

ENGLISH, Hon. Simon William, (Bill); MP (Nat.) Clutha-Southland, New Zealand, since 1996; Deputy Prime Minister, since 2008; Minister of Finance, since 2008, and for Regulatory Reform, since 2013; *b* 30 Dec. 1961; *s* of Mervyn English and Norah (*née* O'Brien); *m* 1987, Dr Mary Scanlon; five *s* one *d*. *Educ:* St Patrick's Coll., Silverstream; Otago Univ. (BCom); Victoria Univ. of Wellington (BA Hons English Lit.). Sheep farmer, Dipton, until 1987; Policy Analyst, NZ Treasury, 1987–89; MP (Nat.) Wallace, 1990–96; Parly Under-Sec. for Health and Crown Health Enterprises, 1993–96; Minister for Crown Health Enterprises, Associate Minister of Educn and Mem., Cabinet, Feb.–Dec. 1996; Minister of Health, 1996–99; Associate Minister of Revenue, 1997–99; Associate Treas., 1998–99; Minister of Finance and Minister of Revenue, 1999; Opposition spokesman for educn, 2003–06, on finance, 2006–08; Minister for Infrastructure, 2008–11. Dep. Leader, 2001–02 and 2006–, Leader, 2002–03, Nat. Party. *Recreations:* Rugby, running. *Address:* Parliament Buildings, Wellington, New Zealand. *T:* (4) 4719999.

ENGLISH, Sir Terence (Alexander Hawthorne), KBE 1991; FRCS; FRCP; Master of St Catharine's College, Cambridge, 1993–2000; Consultant Cardiothoracic Surgeon, Papworth and Addenbrooke's Hospitals, Cambridge, 1973–95; *b* 3 Oct. 1932; *s* of late Arthur Alexander English and Mavis Eleanor (*née* Lund); *m* 1st, 1963, Ann Dicey (marr. diss. 2002); two *s* two *d*; 2nd, 2002, Judith Frances Milne (*see* J. F. English). *Educ:* Hilton Coll., Natal; Witwatersrand Univ. (Transvaal Chamber of Mines Scholarship, 1951–54; BSc(Eng) 1954); Guy's Hosp. Med. Sch. (MB, BS 1962); MA Cantab 1977. FRCSE 1967; FRCS 1967; FRCP 1990. House appointments, Guy's Hosp., 1962–63; Demonstrator, Anatomy Dept, Guy's Hosp., 1964–65; Surgical Registrar: Bolingbroke Hosp., 1966; Brompton Hosp., 1967–68; Res. Fellow, Dept of Surgery, Univ. of Alabama, 1969; Sen. Registrar, Brompton, National Heart and London Chest Hosps, 1968–72; Dir, Papworth Heart Transplant Res. Unit, 1980–88 (performed Britain's 1st successful heart transplant, 1979); non-exec. Dir, Papworth Hosp. NHS Trust, 1997–2001. Chief Med. Advr, BUPA, 1991–99. Mem., Audit Commn, 1993–98. Chm., Asia Healthcare plc, 1995–98. Member: British Cardiac Soc., 1973–; British Transplantation Soc., 1980–; Soc. of Thoracic and Cardiovascular Surgeons, 1972– (Exec. Council, 1975–77); Thoracic Soc., 1971– (Exec. Council, 1978–81). Member: Specialists Adv. Cttee in Cardiothoracic Surgery, 1980–87; Council, BHF, 1983–87; GMC, 1983–89; Standing Med. Adv. Cttee, 1989–92; Jt Consultants Cttee, 1989–92; Supraregional Services Adv. Gp, 1990–92; Clinical Standards Adv. Gp, 1991–94; Steering Cttee, Healthcare Professionals for Assisted Dying, 2010–15. President: Internat. Soc. of Heart Transplantation, 1984–85; Soc. of Perfusionists of GB and Ireland, 1985–86; RCS, 1989–92 (Mem. Council, 1981–93; Court of Patrons, 1994; Trustee, Hunterian Mus., 1996–); Cardiothoracic Sect., RSM, 1992–93; BMA, 1995–96; Vice Pres., British Lung Foundn, 2002–15. Upjohn Lectr, Royal Soc., 1988. Capt., Guy's Hosp. RFC, 1959–60. Gov., Leys Sch., Cambridge, 1993–2001. Trustee: Northwick Park Inst. for Med. Res., 1996–2006; Comparative Clinical Science Foundn, 2003–; Med. Aid for Palestinians, 2010–. Member Council: Winston Churchill Meml Trust, 1995–2009; Univ. of Cambridge, 1998. Patron: Primary Trauma Care Foundn, 2006–; Emthonjeni Trust, 2006–; Dignity in Dying, 2009–. Hon. Freeman, Barbers' Co., 1993. DL Cambs, 1996–2001. FACC 1986. Hon. FRCSCan 1990; Hon. FRACS 1991; Hon. FCSSA 1991; Hon. FRCS (Thailand) 1991; Hon. FCP&S (Pakistan), 1991; Hon. FRCAnaes, 1991; Hon. FDSRCS 1992; Hon. FACS 1992; Hon. FRCSI 1992; Hon. FRCSGlas 1992; Hon. FCOphth 1993; Hon. FRSocMed 2007; Hon. Fellow: St Catharine's Coll., Cambridge, 1992; Hughes Hall, Cambridge, 1993; UMDS, Guy's and St Thomas' Hosps (now KCL), 1993; Worcester Coll., Oxford, 2003. Hon. DSc: Sussex, 1992; Hull, 1996; Oxford Brookes, 2013; Hon. MD: Nantes, 1992; Mahidol, Thailand, 1993; Witwatersrand, 2008. Man of the Year, RADAR, 1980; Clement Price Thomas Award, RCS, 1986; Lifetime Achievement Award, Soc. for Cardiothoracic Surgery in GB and Ireland, 2009; Lifetime Achievement Award, Internat. Soc. of Heart and Lung Transplantation, 2014; Ray C. Fish Award for Scientific Achievement in Cardiovascular Disease, Texas Heart Inst., 2014. *Publications:* (jtly) Principles of Cardiac Diagnosis and Treatment: a surgeons' guide, 1992; Follow Your Star: from mining to heart transplants - a surgeon's story, 2011; chapter on Surgery of the Thorax and Heart in Bailey and Love's Short Practice of Thoracic Surgery, 1980; numerous articles in medical jls on matters relating to the practice of heart transplantation and cardiothoracic surgery. *Recreations:* reading, 4 x 4 rallies, travel, classic cars. *Address:* 28 Tree Lane, Iffley Village, Oxford OX4 4EY. *E:* tenglish@doctors.org.uk. *Clubs:* Athenæum; Hawks (Cambridge).

ENGLISH, Terence Michael; a District Judge (Magistrates' Courts) (formerly Metropolitan Stipendiary Magistrate), 1986–2009; *b* 3 Feb. 1944; *s* of John Robert English and Elsie Letitia English; *m* 1st, 1966, Ivy Joan Weatherley (*d* 1997); one *s* one *d*; 2nd, 2001, Clare Joanne Evans. *Educ:* St Ignatius Coll., London N15; London Univ. (external LLB 1967). Admitted Solicitor of the Supreme Court, 1970. Assistant, Edmonton PSD, 1962–71; Dep. Clerk to Justices, Bullingdon, Bampton E, Henley and Watlington PSDs, 1972–76; Clerk to the Justices: Newbury and Hungerford and Lambourn PSDs, 1977–85; Slough and Windsor PSDs, 1985–86. A Recorder, 1994–97. Chairman: Family Panel, 1991–92; Inner London Juvenile Ct Panel, 1989–2002. *Recreations:* philately, music, travel, arts. *Address:* c/o Chief Magistrate's Office, Westminster Magistrates' Court, 181 Marylebone Road, NW1 5BR.

ENNALS, Sir Paul (Martin), Kt 2009; CBE 2002; Chief Executive, National Children's Bureau, 1998–2011; *b* 7 Nov. 1956; *s* of Baron Ennals, PC, and of Eleanor Maud Ennals (*née* Caddick); *m* 1996, Christine Reid. *Educ:* King's Coll. Sch., Wimbledon; New Coll., Oxford (BA Psychology). Director: Services, SENSE, 1983–89; Educn and Employment, RNIB, 1989–98. Chairman: Council for Disabled Children, 1991–98; Special Educnl Consortium, 1992–97; Independent Rev. of Pre-Schools, 1999; Children's Workforce Develt Council, 2009– (Shadow Chm., 2004–05); Children's Workforce Network, 2006–09; Strategic Reference Gp, Changing Lives, 2014–; Local Safeguarding Children Bd, Haringey, 2014–; Vice-Chairman: Nat. Adv. Gp on Special Educnl Needs, 1997–2001; Children's Inter-agency Gp, 2008–11; Member: Children's Task Force, 2001–04; Children's Workforce Expert Gp, 2008–09; Child Health Adv. Gp, DoH, 2008–10; DFE (formerly DCSF) Prog. Bd for Children in Care, 2008–10; Stakeholder's Bd, DFE (formerly DCSF), 2008–10. Trustee: Sightsavers, 1995–2007; Wave Trust, 2011–. *E:* paulennals@yahoo.co.uk.

ENNIS, Catherine Mary, (Mrs J. A. Higham); concert organist; Organist, St Lawrence Jewry-next-Guildhall, EC2, since 1985; *b* 20 Jan. 1955; *d* of Séamus and Margaret Ennis; *m* 1988, John Arthur Higham, *qv*; two *s* one *d*, and one step *s* two step *d*. *Educ:* Christ's Hosp., Hertford; Kingsway Further Educn Coll.; St Hugh's Coll., Oxford (MA). Recitals, Europe and USA, 1977–; Dir of Music, St Marylebone Parish Church, 1978–90; Asst Organist, Christ Church Cathedral, Oxford, 1984–86; Professor: RAM, 1982–90; GSM, 1985–86; Mem. staff, Trinity Coll. of Music, 2001–08. Dir, John Hill Meml Recitals, 2006–. Estabd and Editor-in-Chief, London Organ Concerts Guide, 1995–. President: IAO, 2005–07; RCO, 2013–15 (Mem. Council, 2006–08). Trustee, Nicholas Danby Trust, 1999–. Presenter, recitalist, concerto soloist and conductor on radio and TV; has made several commercial recordings. Prizewinner: GSM, 1973; Manchester Internat. Organ Comp., 1981 and 1983. *Publications:* contribs to organ jls. *Recreations:* family, reading, gardening, opera. *Address:* c/o The Vestry, St Lawrence Jewry-next-Guildhall, EC2V 5AA. *E:* cmennis@aol.com.

ENNIS, Jeffrey; *b* 13 Nov. 1952; *s* of William Ennis and Jean Ennis; *m* 1980, Margaret Angela Knight; three *s*. *Educ:* Redland Coll.; Univ. of Bristol (BEd Hons). Teacher: Elston Hall Jun. Sch., Fordhouses, Wolverhampton, 1976–78; Burngreave Middle Sch., Sheffield, 1978–79; Hillsborough Primary Sch., Sheffield, 1979–96. Barnsley Metropolitan Borough Council: Councillor (Lab), 1980–97; Dep. Leader, 1988–95; Leader, 1995–96. MP (Lab) Barnsley E, Dec. 1996–1997, Barnsley E and Mexborough, 1997–2010. PPS to Minister for Public Health, DoH, 1997–99, to Minister for Employment, 1999–2001, to Chancellor of Duchy of Lancaster and Cabinet Sec., 2007–08; Dep. Minister for Yorks and Humberside, 2008–10. Mem., Educn and Skills Select Cttee, 2001–10. Mem., British-Irish Inter-Parly Body, 1998–2010; Jt Chair, All Party Racing and Bloodstock Gp, 2001–10; Treas., All Party China Gp, 2005–10; Sec., Lab back-bench Gp on Regeneration, 2005–10; Founder Mem. and Chm., All Party Brass Band Gp, 2008–10. Member: Co-op Party; TGWU; Chm., Brierley Lab. Pty Br., 1998–2010. *Recreations:* most sports, especially swimming, hill-walking, caravanning.

ENNIS, Richard; Executive Director of Finance and Corporate Services, Homes and Communities Agency, since 2009; *b* 9 Oct. 1965; *s* of Thomas and Wendy Ennis; *m* 1990, Theresa Dawn Jones; three *s*; partner, Alison Siggs. *Educ:* W London Poly.; Harrow College (Finance and Business Studies degree 1989); Middlesex Poly. (Dip. Mgt Studies 1991); Thames Valley Univ. (ACMA 1995). Mgt Accountant, PO Ltd, 1986–90; Accountant, Slough BC, 1990–96; Finance and Systems Manager, Guildford Spectrum Leisure, 1996–98; Assistant Director, Finance: Slough Unitary Council, 1998–2000; Westminster CC, 2000–03; Exec. Dir of Finance, Lambeth LBC, 2003–05; Exec. Dir of Corporate Resources (formerly of Finance and Business Support), Ealing LBC, 2005–09. *Recreation:* football coach. *Address:* Homes and Communities Agency, Fry Building, 2 Marsham Street, SW1P 4DF.

ENNIS-HILL, Jessica, CBE 2013 (MBE 2011); athlete; *b* Sheffield, 28 Jan. 1986; *d* of Vinnie Ennis and Alison Powell; *m* 2013, Andrew Hill; one *s*. *Educ:* King Ecgbert Secondary Sch., Sheffield; Univ. of Sheffield (BSc Psychol. 2007). Heptathlon wins include: Commonwealth Games: Bronze Medal, 2006; World Championships: Gold Medal, 2009, 2015; Silver Medal, 2011; European Championships: Gold Medal, 2010; Olympic Games: Gold Medal, 2012; pentathlon wins include: World Indoor Championships: Gold Medal, 2010; Silver Medal, 2012. Hon. LittD Sheffield, 2010. Freedom of Sheffield, 2013. *Publications:* Unbelievable (autobiog.), 2013. *Address:* c/o JCCM Ltd, 12 Whiteladies Road, Bristol BS8 1PD.

ENNISKILLEN, 7th Earl of, *cr* 1789 (Ire.); **Andrew John Galbraith Cole;** Baron Mountflorence 1760; Viscount Enniskillen 1776; Baron Grinstead (UK) 1815; company director; *b* 28 April 1942; *s* of 6th Earl of Enniskillen, MBE and Sonia (*d* 1982), *d* of Major Thomas Syers, RA; *S* father, 1989; *m* 1964, Sarah, *o d* of Maj.-Gen. J. Keith-Edwards, CBE, DSO, MC, Nairobi; three *d*. *Educ:* Eton. Captain, Irish Guards, 1965. Airline pilot; Man. Dir, Kenya Airways, 1979–81; CEO and Chm., AAR Health Services, 1991–2006. Mem., Nat. Envmt Council, Kenya, 2010–. *Heir: cousin* Berkeley Arthur Cole [*b* 17 Dec. 1949; *m* 1978, Hon. Cecilia Anne Ridley (marr. diss. 2002), *e d* of 4th Viscount Ridley; two *s*].

ENO, Brian Peter George St John Baptiste de la Salle, RDI 2012; musician and artist; *b* 15 May 1948; *s* of William Arnold Eno and Maria Alphonsine Eno (*née* Buslot); *m* 1st, 1967, Sarah Grenville; one *d*; 2nd, 1988, Anthea Norman-Taylor; two *d*. *Educ:* Ipswich Sch. of Art; Winchester Coll. of Art. With Roxy Music, 1971–73. Vis. Prof., RCA, 1995–; Hon. Prof. of New Media, Berlin Univ. of Art, 1998–; Founder, Long Now Foundn, 1996–. Hon. DTech Plymouth, 1995. Brit Award, Best Producer, 1994. *Music:* solo recordings: Here Come the Warm Jets, 1974; Taking Tiger Mountain (By Strategy), 1974; Another Green World, 1975; Discreet Music, 1975; Before and After Science, 1977; Music for Films, 1978; Music for Airports, 1978; On Land, 1981; Thursday Afternoon, 1984; Nerve Net, 1992; The Shutov Assembly, 1992; Neroli, 1993; The Drop, 1997; Another Day on Earth, 2005; collaborative recordings: (with David Bowie) Low, 1977, Heroes, 1977, Lodger, 1979; (with David Byrne) My Life in the Bush of Ghosts, 1980; (with Daniel Lanois and Roger Eno) Apollo, 1983; (with J. Peter Schwalm) Drawn from Life, 2001; (with Paul Simon) Surprise, 2006; (with David Byrne) Everything that Happens Will Happen Today, 2008; *productions:* Talking Heads: More Songs about Buildings and Food, Fear of Music, Remain in Light, 1978–80; U2: Unforgettable Fire, The Joshua Tree, Rattle and Hum, Achtung Baby, Zooropa, All That You Can't Leave Behind (Grammy Award, Record of the Year: for track Beautiful Day, 2000, for track Walk On, 2001), 1984–2001; David Bowie: Outside, 1995; *visual:* over 80 exhibns of video artworks and audio-visual installations in museums and galleries worldwide, incl. Stedelijk Mus., Amsterdam, 1984; Venice Biennale, 1986; Marble Palace, St Petersburg, 1997; Hayward Gall., London, 2000; San Francisco Mus. of Modern Art, 2001; Lyon Biennial, 2005; Mus. für Abgüsse Klassischer Bildwerke, Munich, 2005. *Publications:* (with Peter Schmidt) Oblique Strategies (set of cards), 1975, 5th edn 2001; A Year with Swollen Appendices, 1996. *Recreation:* perfumery. *Address:* c/o Opal Ltd, 1 Pratt Mews, NW1 0AD.

ENOCH, Dafydd Huw; QC 2008; a Recorder, since 2004; *b* Chelmsford, 24 April 1961; *s* of Dr Morgan David Enoch and late Margaret Joyce Enoch; *m* 1997, Naomi Jane Hartridge; one *s* two *d*. *Educ:* Univ. of Buckingham (LLB 1984); Univ. d'Aix-Marseille III (Diplôme d'Etudes Juridiques). Called to the Bar, Gray's Inn, 1985; in practice as barrister specialising in criminal and disciplinary law. *Recreations:* playing the guitar and drums, travelling, sport of all types. *Address:* 23 Essex Street, WC2R 3AA. *T:* (020) 7413 0353, *Fax:* (020) 7413 0374. *E:* dafyddenoch@23es.com.

ENRIGHT, Neil James, MA; Headmaster, Queen Elizabeth's School, Barnet, since 2011; *b* London, 5 Sept. 1977. *Educ:* John Lyon Sch., Harrow; St John's Coll., Oxford (BA Geog. 1999); Nat. Coll. for Sch. Leadership (NPQH 2007); Inst. of Educn, Univ. of London (MBA 2010). Gifted and Talented Co-ordinator and Teacher of Geog., St Gregory's RC Sci. Coll., 2000–02; Hd of Geog., 2002–07, Hd of Year, 2007–08, Asst Hd, 2008–10, Dep. Headmaster, 2010–11, Queen Elizabeth's Sch., Barnet. Gov., Longfield Primary Sch., Harrow, 2009–; Chm., Mgt Cttee, Northgate Sch., Edgware, 2011–. *Recreations:* family, friends, education, geography, music (clarinettist), art, cinema, theatre, travel, food and wine, watching sports, club level football (especially Luton Town FC), international cricket and Rugby. *Address:* Queen Elizabeth's School, Queen's Road, Barnet, Herts EN5 4DQ. *T:* (020) 8441 4646. *E:* hmoffice@qebarnet.co.uk.

ENRIGHT, Seán; His Honour Judge Enright; a Circuit Judge, since 2008; *m* Lorna. In practice as a barrister, 1982–2008. Chm., Discipline Panel, RFU. Consultant Ed., Halsbury's Laws. *Publications:* Taking Liberties: criminal jury in the 1990s (with James Morton), 1990; The Trial of Civilians by Military Courts: Ireland 1921, 2012; Easter Rising 1916: the trials, 2013. *Club:* Market Deeping Rugby.

ENRIQUES, Prof. Luca, PhD; Allen & Overy Professor of Corporate Law, University of Oxford, since 2014; Fellow, Jesus College, Oxford, since 2014; *b* Bologna, 17 Feb. 1970; *s* of Federico Enriques and Raffaella Tommasi; *m* 1997, Claudia Barbara; two *s* one *d*. *Educ:* Liceo Ginnasio Statale L. Galvani, Bologna (Dip.); Univ. of Bologna (degree in law *cum laude*); Harvard Law Sch. (LLM); Univ. Commerciale L. Bocconi, Milan (PhD 1999). Lawyer, Banking Supervision Dept, Legislation Div., Bank of Italy, 1996–99; Faculty of Law, University of Bologna: Asst Prof. of Business Law, 1999–2001; Associate Prof. of Business Law, 2001–04; Prof. of Business Law, 2004–12; on leave as Comr, Consob (Italian Stock Exchange), 2007–12; Prof. of Business Law, LUISS Guido Carli Univ., Rome, 2012–13. Nomura Vis. Prof. of Internat. Financial Systems, Harvard Law Sch., 2012–13. Ind. Consultant, Cleary Gottlieb, Steen & Hamilton, Rome and Milan, 2003–07. Advr on corporate, banking and financial mkts law, Min. of Econ. and Finance, Italy, 2000–06 and 2014–. Mem., Adv. Bd, Yale Prog. on Financial Stability, 2013–. Ed., Law Wkg Paper Series, Eur. Corporate Governance Inst., 2013–. *Publications:* Il conflitto d'interessi degli amministratori di società per azioni, 2000; Mercato del controllo societario e tutela degli investitori, 2002; (with Renzo Costi) Il mercato mobiliare, 2004; (contrib.) Commentario del codice civile Scialoja-Branca, 2007; (jtly) The Anatomy of Corporate Law, 2nd edn 2009; contrib. to jls incl. Univ. of Pennsylvania Jl Internat. Law, Harvard Business Law Rev., Eur. Co. and Financial Law Rev., Jl Corporate Law Studies, Cambridge Law Jl, Jl Econ. Perspectives, Tulane Law Rev., Cornell Law Rev. *Address:* Jesus College, Oxford OX1 3DW.

ENSOR, Anthony; *see* Ensor, His Honour G. A.

ENSOR, David, OBE 1986; Managing Director, Croydon Advertiser Ltd, 1979–85; *b* 2 April 1924; *s* of Rev. William Walters and Constance Eva Ensor; *m* 1947, Gertrude Kathleen Brown (*d* 2015); two *s*. *Educ:* Kingswood Sch., Bath; London Coll. of Printing. Served Royal

Signals, 1942–46, Captain; ADC to GOC Bengal Dist. Managing Director: George Reveirs, 1947–59; Charles Skipper & East, 1959–69; Knapp Drewett & Sons, 1969–79; Chairman: Methodist Newspaper Co., 1975–94; Methodist Publishing House, 1981–96. A Vice-Chm., Press Council, 1987–90 (Mem., 1982–90); Mem. Council, Newspaper Soc., 1979–94. Pres., London Printing Industries Assoc., 1976. Vice-Pres., Methodist Conf., 1981. *Address:* Sunrise, 6 Upper Kings Drive, Eastbourne, E Sussex BN20 9AN. *T:* (01323) 525000.

ENSOR, His Honour (George) Anthony; a Circuit Judge, 1995–2008; *b* 4 Nov. 1936; *s* of George and Phyllis Ensor; *m* 1968, Jennifer Margaret Caile, MB, ChB; two *d. Educ:* Malvern College; Liverpool University (LLB). Solicitor, 1961 (Atkinson Conveyancing Medal, 1962; Rupert Bremner Medal, 1962); Partner, 1962–92, Sen. Partner, 1992–95, Rutherfords, later Weightman Rutherfords, Solicitors, Liverpool; a Recorder, 1983–95; Dep. Sen. Judge, Sovereign Base Area, Cyprus, 2005. Deputy Coroner, City of Liverpool, 1966–95; part-time Chairman, Industrial Tribunals, 1975–95; Asst Parly Boundary Comr, 1992–95. Mem., Judicial Studies Bd, 1987–89; President, Liverpool Law Society, 1982. Trustee, Empire Theatre (Merseyside) Trust, Ltd, 1986–. Dir, Liverpool FC, 1985–93. *Recreations:* golf, theatre. *Clubs:* Artists (Liverpool); Formby Golf; Waterloo Rugby Union.

ENTWISTLE, George; Director General, BBC, 2012; *b* 8 July 1962; *s* of Philip and Wendy Entwistle; *m* 1992, Jane Porter; one *s* one *d. Educ:* Durham Univ. (BA Hons Philosophy and Politics 1983). Sub-ed. and Ed., Haymarket Magazines, 1984–89; joined BBC, 1989; broadcast journalism trainee, 1989–90; Asst Producer, Panorama, 1990–92; Producer, On The Record, 1993–94; Producer, 1994–97, Asst Ed., 1997–99, Newsnight; Dep. Ed., Tomorrow's World, 1999–2000; Dep. Ed., 2000–01, Ed., 2001–04, Newsnight; Ed., The Culture Show, 2004–05; Hd of TV Current Affairs, 2005–07; Actg Controller, BBC Four, 2007; Controller, Knowledge Commissioning, BBC TV, 2008–11; Dir, BBC Vision, 2011–12. Mem., Exec. Cttee, Edinburgh Internat. TV Fest., 2011– (Chair, Adv. Cttee, 2011). Trustee: Comic Relief, 2011–12; Public Catalogue Foundn, 2013–. *Recreations:* design history, reading novels, listening to music, fell walking, armchair Rugby Union. *E:* george.e.entwistle@gmail.com. *Club:* Battersea Ironsides Rugby Football.

ENTWISTLE, John Nicholas McAlpine, OBE 2005; Consultant Solicitor, Davies Wallis Foyster, 1992–2004; President, British Chambers of Commerce, 1998–2000; *b* 16 June 1941; *s* of Sir (John Nuttall) Maxwell Entwistle and Lady (Jean Cunliffe McAlpine) Entwistle; *m* 1968, Phillida Gail Sinclair Burgess; one *s* one *d. Educ:* Uppingham Sch. Admitted Solicitor, 1963. Asst Attorney, Shearman & Sterling, NY, 1963–64; Partner, Maxwell Entwistle & Byrne, Solicitors, 1966–91. Regl Dir, Midshires Building Soc., 1977–87; non-exec. Dir, Rathbone Brothers plc, 1992–98. Founder Dir, Merseyside TEC, 1990–91; Dep. Dist Chm., Appeals Service, 1999–2006 (pt-time Chm., Social Security Appeals Tribunal, 1992–99); pt-time Immigration Judge, 2000–10. Member: Parole Bd, 1994–2000; Criminal Injuries Compensation Tribunal (formerly Appeals Panel), 2000–12; Disciplinary Cttee, Mortgage Code Compliance Bd, 1999–2004; Chancellor of Exchequer's Standing Cttee on Preparation for EMU, 1998–2000; Adv. Council, Migration Watch UK, 2010–. Trustee: Nat. Museums and Galls on Merseyside, 1990–97 (Chm., Develt Trust, 1991–95); RA Trust, 2006–11, now Emeritus; Friends of the Lake District, 2014–. Gen. Comr for Income Tax, 1978–83. Mem. (C), Liverpool CC, 1968–71. Contested (C) Huyton, 1970. DL Merseyside, 1992–2002. Hon. Fellow, Liverpool John Moores Univ., 2010. *Recreations:* collecting and painting pictures, gardening. *Address:* Low Crag, Crook, Cumbria LA8 8LE. *T:* (015395) 68268. *E:* entwistlej@mail.com. *Clubs:* Carlton (Mem., Political Cttee, 2004–08), Lansdowne.

ENTWISTLE, Prof. Kenneth Mercer; Professor of Metallurgy and Materials Science, University of Manchester Institute of Science and Technology, 1962–90, now Emeritus; *b* 3 Jan. 1925; *s* of William Charles and Maude Elizabeth Entwistle; *m* 1949, Alice Patricia Mary Johnson; two *s* two *d. Educ:* Urmston Grammar Sch.; Univ. of Manchester (BSc Elect. Eng. 1945, MSc 1946, PhD 1948). FIMMM, CEng. University of Manchester: Lectr in Metallurgy, 1948; Sen. Lectr, 1954; Reader, 1960; Dean, Faculty of Technology, 1976–77; Pro-Vice-Chancellor, 1982–85; Vice-Principal, UMIST, 1972–74. Adjunct Prof., Univ. of Canterbury, NZ, 2001–. Chairman: Materials Cttee, CNAA, 1972–74; Educn Cttee, Instn of Metallurgists, 1977–79; Metallics Sub-Cttee, SRC, 1979–81; Mem., UGC, 1985–89 (Chm., Technology Sub-Cttee, 1985–89); Engrg Advr to Chief Exec. of UFC, 1989–92. Comp. UMIST, 1991. Hon. Fellow, Sheffield Polytechnic, 1971. *Publications:* numerous papers in scientific jls. *Recreations:* Scottish dancing, choral singing. *Address:* Heronswood, 22 Castlegate, Prestbury, Macclesfield, Cheshire SK10 4AZ. *T:* (01625) 829269. *E:* ken.entwistle@manchester.ac.uk. *Club:* Athenæum.

EÖTVÖS, Peter; composer and conductor; *m* 1st, 1968, Piroska Molnar (marr. diss. 1975); one *s*; 2nd, 1976, Pi-Hsien Chen (marr. diss. 1994); one *d*; 3rd, 1995, Maria Mezei. *Educ:* Acad. of Music, Budapest; Musik Hochschule, Cologne. Composer, chamber music, electronic music, opera and orchestral music; conductor and musical director, Ensemble Intercontemporain, Paris, 1979–91; principal guest conductor, BBC Symphony Orchestra, 1985–88; first Guest Conductor, Budapest Fest. Orch., 1992–95; Chief Conductor, Radio Chamber Orch. Hilversum, 1994–2005; first Guest Conductor, Radio Symphony Orchestra Vienna, 2009–12. Professor: Musikhochschule Karlsruhe, 1992–2007; Musikhochschule Köln, 1998–2001; Founder: Internat. Eötvös Inst., for young conductors and composers, 1991; Peter Eötvös Contemporary Music Foundn, 2004. *Recreations:* walking, pipe smoking, jazz. *W:* www.eotvospeter.com.

EPHRAUMS, Maj.-Gen. Roderick Jarvis, CB 1977; OBE 1965; Major-General Royal Marines, Commando Forces, 1976–78, retired; *b* 12 May 1927; *s* of Hugh Cyril Ephraums and Elsie Caroline (*née* Rowden); *m* 1955, Adela Mary (*née* Forster); two *s* one *d. Educ:* Tonbridge. Commnd 2nd Lieut, RM, 1945; HMS Mauritius, 1946–48; 42 Commando, RM, 1952–54; RMFVR Merseyside, 1954–57; 42 Commando, RM, 1957–59, 1966–67; Staff Coll., Camberley, 1960; Bde Major, 3 Commando Bde, 1962–64; CO, 45 Commando RM, 1969–71; Royal Coll. of Defence Studies, 1972; Comdr, 3 Commando Bde, 1973–74; ADC to the Queen, 1974–76; NATO Defense Coll., Rome, 1975. A Col Comdt, RM, 1985–, Rep. Col Comdt, 1987 and 1988. DL Angus, 1985–98. Silver Medal, RNLI, 1989. CStJ 1993. *Recreations:* painting, gardening. *Club:* Army and Navy.

EPSTEIN, Sir Anthony; *see* Epstein, Sir M. A.

EPSTEIN, Prof. David Bernard Alper, PhD; FRS 2004; Professor, Mathematics Institute, University of Warwick, 1969–2005, now Professor Emeritus; *b* 16 May 1937; *s* of Dr Ben Epstein and Pauline Alper Epstein; *m* 1958, Rona; one *s* two *d. Educ:* Univ. of Witwatersrand (BSc Hons 1955); Trinity Coll., Cambridge (BA 1957); PhD Cantab 1960. Instructor, Princeton Univ., 1960–61; Princeton Inst. for Advanced Study, 1961–62; Cambridge University: Fellow, Trinity Coll., 1960–62; Lectr, 1962–64; Dir, Studies in Maths, Churchill Coll., 1962–64; Reader in Maths, Univ. of Warwick, 1964–69. Scientific Dir, NSF Geometry Center, Minneapolis, 1990–91. Vis. Prof., Univ. of Paris, Orsay, 1974–75; Ordway Dist. Vis. Prof., Minnesota, 1986. *Publications:* (with N. E. Steenrod) Cohomology Operations, 1963; (jtly) Word Processing in Groups, 1992. *Recreations:* gardening, friends. *Address:* Mathematics Institute, University of Warwick, Zeeman Building, Coventry CV4 7AL. *T:* (024) 7652 2677. *E:* David.Epstein@warwick.ac.uk.

EPSTEIN, Sir (Michael) Anthony, Kt 1991; CBE 1985; FRS 1979; Fellow, 1986–2001, Hon. Fellow, since 2001, Wolfson College, Oxford; Professor of Pathology, 1968–85 (now Emeritus), and Head of Department, 1968–82, University of Bristol; Hon. Consultant Pathologist, Bristol Health District (Teaching), 1968–82; *b* 18 May 1921; *yr s* of Mortimer and Olga Epstein; *m* 1950, Lisbeth Knight (separated 1965; she *d* 2015); two *s* one *d. Educ:* St Paul's Sch., London; Trinity Coll., Cambridge (Perry Exhibr, 1940); Middlesex Hosp. Medical Sch. MA, MD, DSc, PhD; FRCPath. Ho. Surg., Middlesex Hosp., London, and Addenbrooke's Hosp., Cambridge, 1944; Lieut and Captain, RAMC, 1945–47; Asst Pathologist, Bland Sutton Inst., Middx Hosp. Med. Sch., 1948–65, with leave as: Berkeley Travelling Fellow, 1952–53; French Govt Exchange Scholar at Institut Pasteur, Paris, 1952–53; Vis. Investigator, Rockefeller Inst., NY, 1956; Reader in Experimental Pathology, Middx Hosp. Med. Sch., 1965–68; Hon. Consultant in Experimental Virology, Middx Hosp., 1965–68. Member: Cttee, Pathological Soc. of GB and Ire., 1969–72 (Hon. Mem., 1987); Council, and Vice-Pres., Pathology Section of RSM, 1966–72 (Hon. Mem., 1988); Study Gp on Classification of Herpes Viruses, of Internat. Commn for Nomenclature of Viruses, 1971–81; Scientific Adv. Bd, Harvard Med. Sch.'s New England Regional Primate Center, 1972–96; Cancer Research Campaign MRC Jt Cttee, 1973–77, 1982–87 (Chm. 1983–87); Cttee, British Soc. for Cell Biology, 1974–77; MRC, 1982–86 (Mem., 1979–84, Chm., 1982–84, Cell Bd; Mem., 1984–85, Chm., 1985–88, Tropical Medicine Res. Bd); Council, Royal Soc., 1983–85, 1986–91 (Foreign Sec. and a Vice-Pres., 1986–91; Assessor on MRC, 1987–91); Medical and Scientific Panel, Leukaemia Research Fund, 1982–85; Scientific Adv. Cttee, Lister Inst., 1984–87; Expert Working Party on Bovine Spongiform Encephalopathy, DoH, 1988; Exec. Bd, ICSU, 1990–93 (Chm., Cttee on Sci. in Central and Eastern Europe, 1992–95); Exec. Council, ESF, 1990–93; Program Adv. Gp, World Bank China Key Studies Project, 1992–97; Special Rep. of Dir Gen. UNESCO for Sci. in Russia, 1992. Discovered in 1964 a new human herpes virus, now known as Epstein-Barr virus, which causes infectious mononucleosis and is also causally implicated in some forms of human cancer (esp. Burkitt's lymphoma, nasopharyngeal carcinoma and post-transplant lymphomas). Fellow, 1992, Hon. Fellow, 2010, UCL. Founder FMedSci 1998. Mem., Academia Europaea, 1988. Mem. d'honneur, Belgian Soc. for Cancer Res., 1979. Hon. Professor: Sun Yat-Sen Med. Univ., Guangzhou, 1981; Chinese Acad. of Preventive Medicine, Beijing, 1988. Hon. Fellow: Queensland Inst. of Med. Research, 1983; CRUK, 2004; Bristol Univ., 2006; Hon. FRCP 1986; Hon. FRSE 1991; Hon. FRCPA 1995. Hon. MD: Edinburgh, 1986; Charles Univ., Prague, 1998; Hon. DSc Birmingham, 1996. Paul Ehrlich and Ludwig Darmstaedter Prize and Medal, Paul Ehrlich Foundn, W Germany, 1973; Markham Skerrit Prize, 1977; (jtly) Bristol-Myers Award, NY, 1982; Leeuwenhoek Prize Lectr, Royal Soc., 1983; Prix Griffuel, Assoc. pour la recherche sur le cancer, Paris, 1986; David Henderson Medal, PHLS, 1986; Samuel Weiner Distinguished Visitor Award, Univ. of Manitoba, 1988; John H. Lattimer Award, Amer. Urol Assoc., 1988; Internat. Award, Gairdner Foundn, Toronto, 1988; Jenner Medal, St George's Hosp. Med. Sch., 1989; Royal Medal, Royal Soc., 1992; Gold Medal, Charles Univ., Prague, 1998. *Publications:* over 250 scientific papers in internat. jls on tumour cell structure, viruses, tumour viruses, Burkitt's lymphoma, and the EB virus. Jt Founder Editor, The Internat. Review of Experimental Pathology (vols 1–28, 1962–86); (ed jtly) The Epstein-Barr Virus, 1979; (ed jtly) The Epstein-Barr Virus: recent advances, 1986; (ed jtly) Oncogenic γ-herpesviruses: an expanding family, 2001. *Address:* Wolfson College, University of Oxford, Linton Road, Oxford OX2 6UD. *T:* (01865) 250885.

EPSTEIN, Paul Jeremy; QC 2006; *b* London, 9 Aug. 1963; *s* of Maurice and late Jill Epstein; partner, Laura Binns; two *d. Educ:* Balliol Coll., Oxford (BA Hist. and Mod. Langs); City Univ., London (Dip. Law). Called to the Bar, Middle Temple, 1988, Bencher, 2013; barrister, Cloisters chambers, 1990–. *Recreation:* enthusiastic cyclist. *Address:* Cloisters, 1 Pump Court, Temple, EC4Y 7AA. *T:* (020) 7827 4000, *Fax:* (020) 7827 4100. *E:* clerks@cloisters.com.

EPSTEIN, Sophie Lysandra; *see* Thomas, S. L.

ERAUT, Prof. Michael Ruarc, PhD; Professor of Education, University of Sussex, 1986–2006, now Emeritus; *b* 15 Nov. 1940; *s* of Lt-Col Ruarc Bertrand Sorel Eraut and Frances Mary (*née* Hurst); *m* 1964, (Mary) Cynthia Wynne; two *s. Educ:* Winchester Coll. (Scholar); Trinity Hall, Cambridge (Scholar; BA Nat. Sci.; PhD Chem.). Fulbright Scholar, 1965–67; Res. Assistant, 1965–66, Vis. Asst Prof., 1966–67, Univ. of Illinois, Chicago; University of Sussex: Fellow, 1967–71; Sen. Fellow, 1971–73; Dir, Centre for Educnl Technol., 1973–76; Reader in Educn, 1976–86; Dir, Inst. of Continuing and Professional Educn, 1986–91. Chm. of Corporation, Lewes Tertiary Coll., 1992–97. Ed.-in-Chief, Learning in Health and Social Care, 2002–06. *Publications:* (with N. Mackenzie and H. C. Jones) Teaching and Learning: new methods and resources in higher education, 1970, 3rd edn 1976 (trans. French, German, Spanish and Portuguese); In-Service Education for Innovation, 1972; The Analysis of Curriculum Materials, 1975 (trans. German 1976); Accountability in the Middle Years of Schooling, 1980; (with B. Connors and E. Hewton) Training in Curriculum Development and Educational Technology in Higher Education, 1980; (with T. Becher and J. Knight) Policies for Educational Accountability, 1981; Curriculum Development in Further Education, 1985; (with J. Burke) Improving the Quality of YTS, 1986; Local Evaluation of INSET, 1988; (ed) International Encyclopaedia of Educational Technology, 1989; (with G. Cole) Business Education: a handbook for schools, 1990; Education and the Information Society, 1991; (with C. Nash and M. Fielding) Flexible Learning in Schools, 1991; (with G. Cole) Assessing Competence in the Professions, 1993; Developing Professional Knowledge and Competence, 1994; Learning to Use Scientific Knowledge in Education and Practice Settings, 1995; Assessment of NVQs, 1996; Development of Knowledge and Skills in Employment, 1998; Evaluation of Vocational Training of Science Graduates in the NHS, 1998; (with B. Du Boulay) Developing the Attributes of Medical Professional Judgement and Competence, 1999; (with S. Steadman and J. James) Evaluation of Higher Level S/NVQs, 2001; (with W. Hirsch) The Significance of Workplace Learning for Individuals, Groups and Organisations, 2007; (ed with Anne McKee and contrib.) Learning Trajectories, Innovation and Identity for Professional Development (Div. 1 - Educn in the Professions - Outstanding Pubn Award, American Educnl Res. Association, 2013), 2011; (contrib.) Workplace Learning in Teacher Education: international practice and policy, 2014; chapters in books and numerous conference papers. *Recreations:* music, travel. *Address:* 49 St Anne's Crescent, Lewes, E Sussex BN7 1SD. *T:* (01273) 475955.

ERECIŃSKA, Barbara; *see* Tuge-Erecińska.

EREMIN, Prof. Oleg, MD; FRCSE, FRACS, FMedSci; Honorary Professor (formerly Special Professor) in Surgery, University of Nottingham, at Queen's Medical Centre, Nottingham, since 1998; Honorary Senior Research Fellow, United Lincolnshire Hospitals (formerly Lincoln) NHS Trust, since 2014 (Director of Research and Development, 2001–14); *b* 12 Nov. 1938; *s* of Theodor and Maria Eremin; *m* 1963, Jennifer Mary Ching; two *s* one *d. Educ:* Christian Brothers' Coll., St Kilda, Melbourne; Univ. of Melbourne. MB BS 1964; MD 1985. FRACS 1971; FRCSE 1983. Clinical posts: Royal Melbourne Hosp., 1965–72; Norfolk and Norwich Hosps, 1972–74; Research Asst-Associate, Dept of Pathology, Univ. of Cambridge, 1974–80; Sen. Lectr, Dept Clinical Surgery, Univ. of Edinburgh, 1981–85; Regius Prof. of Surgery, Univ. of Aberdeen, 1985–98. Consultant Breast Surgeon and Lead Clinician, United Lincs Hosps (formerly Lincoln) NHS Trust, 1999–2011; Clinical Dir, Trent Comp. Local Res. Network, 2007–14. Hon. Professorial Fellow, Rowett Res. Inst., 1992; Vis. Prof., Univ. of Lincoln, 2003–. Founder FMedSci 1998; Hon. FRCST 2003. Hon. DSc Lincoln. *Publications:* articles in surgical, oncological and immunological jls and textbooks. *Recreations:* music, sport, reading. *Address:* Orchard House, 51A Washdyke Lane, Nettleham, Lincoln LN2 2PX. *T:* (01522) 750669.

ERIKSSON, Peter Eskil; Head Coach, Athletics Canada, since 2013; *b* Stockholm, 19 Nov. 1952; *s* of Eskil and Ellen Eriksson; *m* 1992, Rhonda Nishio; four *d. Educ:* Univ. of Stockholm (Special Educn degree 1983; MSc Physical Educn 1984). Speed skating competitor for

Sweden, 1963–80; coach for speed skating, ice hockey, then athletics, 1980–87; coach, Canadian Paralympic athletes, 1987–2008; High Performance Dir, Speed Skating Canada, 1992–95; Sales Manager, Corel Corp., 1995–97; Manager, Distribn and Corporate Resellers, JetForm Corp., 1997–99; Exec. Vice-Pres., Business and Develt and Strategic Alliances, Runaware Inc., 1999–2005; Hd Coach, Athletics, US Paralympics, 2005; High Performance Advr, Own the Podium 2010 (Olympic and Paralympic Sports), 2005–08; Hd Coach and Performance Dir, Paralympic Progs, UK Athletics, 2008–12; Head Coach, UK Athletics, 2012–13. Coach of Year, Manitoba Wheelchair Sports Assoc., 1989; Coaching Association of Canada: Wittenauer Coaching Excellence Award, 1993, 1995, 1996, 1998, 2000; Petro-Canada Coaching Excellence Award, 2004, 2006, 2008; Coach of Year: Canadian Wheelchair Sports Assoc., 2004, 2008; Ontario Sports Awards, 2005; Canadian Sports Awards, 2005; Athletics Canada, 2008; UK Coaching Awards: UK Coach, 2012; High Performance Coach of Year, 2012; Order of Ikkos, US Olympic Cttee, 2008. *Publications:* Wheel into Fitness: management of spinal cord injuries, 1991; contribs to jls and conf. procs incl. Skridskonytt, Svenskidrott, Medicine and Sci. in Sports and Exercise, New England Jl Medicine, Archives of Physical Medicine and Rehabilitation, Paraplegia, Adapted Physical Activity Qly, Canadian Jl Applied Physiol. *E:* coachesforum@hotmail.com.

ERIKSSON, Sven-Göran; Head Coach, Shanghai East Asia, since 2014; *b* Torsby, Sweden, 5 Feb. 1948; *s* of Sven and Ulla Eriksson; *m* Ann-Kristin (marr. diss.); one *s* one *d.* Former footballer (defender); clubs include Torsby IF, Sifhalla and KB Karlskoga (all Sweden); managerial posts: Asst Manager, 1976, Manager, 1977–78, Degerfors, Sweden; Manager: IFK Gothenburg, Sweden, 1979–82; Benfica, Portugal, 1982–84; AS Roma, Italy, 1984–87; AC Fiorentina, Italy, 1987–89; Benfica, 1989–92; Sampdoria, Italy, 1992–97; SS Lazio, Italy, 1997–2000 (winners: Italian Cup, 1998; Italian Super Cup, 1998; UEFA Cup Winners Cup, 1999; UEFA Super Cup, 1999; Italian Championship, 2000); Hd Coach, England Football Team, 2001–06; Manager, Manchester City FC, 2007–08; Hd Coach, Mexico Football Team, 2008–09; Dir of Football, Notts County FC, 2009–10 (Hon. Pres., 2010); Manager: Ivory Coast Team, World Cup, 2010; Leicester City FC, 2010–11; Technical Director: Bec Tero Sasana, Thailand, 2012–13; Al-Nasr Sports Club, UAE, 2013; Chief Coach, Guangzhou R&F FC, China, 2013–14. *Publications:* Sven: my story (autobiog.), 2013. *Address:* c/o Athole Still Ltd, Foresters Hall, 25 Westow Street, SE19 3RY. *E:* athole@atholestill.co.uk.

ERLEIGH, Viscount; Julian Michael Rufus Isaacs; Corporate Financier, Cantor Fitzgerald (Europe); *b* 26 May 1986; *s* and *heir* of Marquess of Reading, *qv. Educ:* Cheltenham Coll.; Univ. of the West of England Business School, Bristol (BA 2009). *Recreations:* motorsport, tennis, Reading FC. *Address:* 7 Cecily Hill, Cirencester, Glos GL7 2EF.

ERMISCH, Prof. John Francis, FBA 1995; Professor of Family Demography, University of Oxford, since 2011; *b* 1 July 1947; *s* of Elmer and Frances Ermisch; *m* 1977, Dianne M. Monti. *Educ:* Univ. of Wisconsin (BSc); Univ. of Kansas (MA, PhD 1973). Res. Economist, US Dept of Housing and Urban Develt, 1974–76; Res. Fellow, Centres for Environmental Studies and for the Study of Social Policy, London, 1976–78; Sen. Res. Fellow, PSI, 1978–86; Sen. Res. Officer, NIESR, 1986–91; Bonar-Macfie Prof., Univ. of Glasgow, 1991–94; Prof. of Econs, ESRC Res. Centre on Micro-Social Change, later Inst. for Social and Econ. Res., Univ. of Essex, 1994–2011. *Publications:* The Political Economy of Demographic Change, 1983; Lone Parenthood: an economic analysis, 1991; An Economic Analysis of the Family, 2003; contribs to economic and demographic jls. *Recreations:* films, music. *Address:* Department of Sociology, University of Oxford, Manor Road Building, Manor Road, Oxford OX1 3UQ.

ERNE, 6th Earl of, *cr* 1789; **Henry George Victor John Crichton,** KCVO 2012; JP; Baron Erne 1768; Viscount Erne (Ireland), 1781; Baron Fermanagh (UK), 1876; Lord Lieutenant of Co. Fermanagh, Northern Ireland, 1986–2012; *b* 9 July 1937; *s* of 5th Earl and Lady Katharine Cynthia Mary Millicent (Davina) Lytton (who *m* 1945, Hon. C. M. Woodhouse, later 5th Baron Terrington, DSO, OBE; she *d* 1995), *yr d* of 2nd Earl of Lytton, KG, PC, GCSI, GCIE; *S* father, 1940; *m* 1958, Camilla Marguerite (marr. diss. 1980), *er d* of late Wing-Comdr Owen G. E. Roberts and Mrs Roberts; one *s* four *d*; *m* 1980, Mrs Anna Carin Hitchcock (*née* Bjork). *Educ:* Eton. Page of Honour to the Queen, 1952–54 (to King George VI, 1952). Lieut, North Irish Horse, 1959–66. Member: Royal Ulster Agricultural Society; Royal Forestry Society. JP Co. Fermanagh. *Recreations:* sailing, fishing, shooting. *Heir: s* Viscount Crichton, *qv. Address:* Crom Castle, Newtownbutler, Co. Fermanagh BT92 8AP. *T:* (028) 6773 8208. *Clubs:* White's; Lough Erne Yacht.

ERNEST, Most Rev. (Gerald James) Ian; *see* Indian Ocean, Archbishop of the.

ERNST, Prof. Edzard, MD, PhD; FMedSci, FRSB, FRCP, FRCPE; Professor of Complementary Medicine, Peninsula Medical School, Universities of Exeter and Plymouth, 2000–12 (Professor of Complementary Medicine at University of Exeter, 1993–2012, now Emeritus); *b* 30 Jan. 1948; *s* of Wolfgang Ernst and Erika (*née* Tillwichs); *m* 1983, Danielle Johnson (*née* Le Mignon). *Educ:* Maximilian Ludwig Univ., Munich (MD 1978; PhD 1985). FRCPE 1997; FRCP 2003. University of Munich: Sen. House Officer, 1977–79; Registrar, then Sen. Registrar, 1981–89; Res. Assistant, St George's Hosp., London, 1979–81; Prof. of Physical Medicine and Rehabilitation, Univ. of Hanover, 1989; Prof. of Physical Medicine and Rehabilitation, Univ. of Vienna, 1990–93. Visiting Professor: RCPS, Canada, 1999; UCLA, 2005. Member: Medicines Commn, British Medicines and Healthcare Products Regulatory Agency (formerly British Medicines Control Agency), 1993–2005; Scientific Cttee on Herbal Medicinal Products, Irish Medicines Bd. Editor-in-Chief: Perfusion, 1987–; Focus on Alternative and Complementary Therapies, 1996–. FMedSci 2009; FRSB (FSB 2010). HealthWatch Award, 2005, Amer. Botanical Council Annual Award, 2006, In Praise of Reason Award, Cttee for Skeptical Inquiry, 2012, and 10 other scientific awards. *Publications:* Meyler's Side Effects of Drugs, 2000; Desk Top Guide to Complementary and Alternative Medicine, 2001, 2nd edn 2006; (contrib.) Oxford Textbook of Medicine, 4th edn 2003; Oxford Handbook of Complementary Medicine, 2008; (with S. Singh) Trick or Treatment? Alternative Medicine on Trial, 2008; A Scientist in Wonderland: a memoir of searching for truth and finding trouble, 2015; numerous articles in med. jls. *Recreations:* music, writing. *Address:* (office) Veysey Building, Salmon Pool Lane, Exeter EX2 4SG. *T:* (01392) 726029.

ERNST, Prof. Richard Robert; Professor of Physical Chemistry, Swiss Federal Institute of Technology (ETH-Z), 1976–98, now Emeritus; *b* 14 Aug. 1933; *s* of Prof. Robert Ernst, architect, and Irma Ernst (*née* Brunner); *m* 1963, Magdalena Kielholz; one *s* two *d. Educ:* Winterthur schools; ETH-Zentrum (DipChemEng 1956; PhD 1962). Mil. Service, 1956–57. Scientist, Instrument Div., Varian Associates, Calif., 1963–68; Swiss Federal Institute of Technology (ETH-Z): Lectr in Phys. Chem., 1968–70 (Group Leader in Magnetic Resonance Spectroscopy); Asst Prof., 1970; Associate Prof., 1972–76; Pres., Research Council, 1990. Mem. Bd, Spectrospin AG (Vice-Pres., 1989). Fellow, Amer. Phys. Soc.; For. Mem., Royal Soc., 1993; Member: internat. scientific bodies; editl bds of learned jls. Hon. doctorates: ETH Lausanne; Technical Univ., Munich; Zürich; Antwerp; Cluj-Napoca; Montpellier. Numerous medals and prizes, Swiss and foreign; Nobel Prize in Chemistry, 1991; Wolf Prize, 1991; Louisa Gross Horwitz Prize, 1991. *Address:* Laboratorium für Physikalische Chemie, Wolfgang Pauli Strasse 10, ETH Hönggerberg, HCI D 217, 8093 Zürich, Switzerland. *T:* (44) 6324368. *E:* richard.ernst@nmr.phys.chem.ethz.ch; Kurlistrasse 24, 8404 Winterthur, Switzerland. *T:* (52) 2427807.

ERNST, Prof. Wolfgang, DIur; Regius Professor of Civil Law, University of Oxford, since 2015; Fellow, All Souls College, Oxford, since 2015; *b* Bonn, Germany, 28 June 1956; *s* of Dr Hermann Ernst and Anna Elisabeth Ernst; *m* 1985, Dr Katharina von Zglinitzki; one *s* three *d. Educ:* Arndt Gymnasium, Bonn; Bonn Univ. (DIur 1981); Yale Law Sch. (LLM 1982). Stagiaire, Cologne Ct of Appeal, 1982–85; Res. Asst, Inst. for Roman Law, Bonn Univ., 1986–89; Prof. of Private and Roman Law, Tübingen Univ., 1990–2000; Prof. of Private Law and Dir, Inst. for Roman Law, Bonn Univ., 2000–04; Arthur Goodhart Prof. in Legal Sci., Cambridge Univ. and Fellow, Magdalene Coll., Cambridge, 2002–03; Prof. of Roman Law and Private Law, Univ. of Zurich, 2004–15. *Publications:* (with D. Fox) Money in the Western Legal Tradition, 2015; contrib. articles to law and legal history jls. *Recreations:* hiking, Abraham Lincoln studies. *Address:* All Souls College, Oxford OX1 4AL. *T:* (01865) 279379. *E:* ernst.wolfgang@gmail.com.

ERRERA, Gérard, Hon. CVO 2004; Officier de la Légion d'Honneur, 2009 (Chevalier, 1992); Chairman (France), Blackstone Group, since 2012 (Special Adviser, since 2009); Senior Adviser for International Affairs, August et Debouzy, since 2009; Director, International Advisory Council, Huawei, since 2010; *b* 30 Oct. 1943; *s* of Paul and Bella Errera; *m* Virginie Bedoya; two *s* one *d. Educ:* Institut d'Etudes Politiques, Paris; Ecole Nationale d'Administration. Joined Min. of Foreign Affairs, 1969; First Sec., Washington, 1971–75; Special Advr to Minister of Foreign Affairs, 1975–77; Political Counsellor, Madrid, 1977–80; Special Advr to Minister of Foreign Affairs, 1980–81; Consul General, San Francisco, 1982–85; Dir for Internat. Relns, French Atomic Energy Commn, and Governor for France, IAEA, 1985–90; Ambassador, Conf. on Disarmament, Geneva, 1991–95; Ambassador to NATO, Brussels, 1995–98; Political Dir, Min. of Foreign Affairs, 1998–2002; Ambassador to the Court of St James's, 2002–07; Sec. Gen., Min. of Foreign Affairs, France, 2007–09. Dir, EDF/Areva, 2007–09. Dir, Musée des Arts Décoratifs, Paris, 2012–. Officier de l'Ordre National du Mérite (France), 1999; Officer: Order of the White Rose (Finland), 1976; Order of Civil Merit (Spain), 1980. *Recreations:* ski-ing, music, guitar.

ERRINGTON, Viscount; Alexander Rowland Harmsworth Baring; *b* 5 Jan. 1994; *s* and *heir* of Earl of Cromer, *qv*.

ERRINGTON, Col Sir Geoffrey (Frederick), 2nd Bt *cr* 1963; OBE 1998; Chairman, Harefield Hospital NHS Trust, 1991–98; *b* 15 Feb. 1926; *er s* of Sir Eric Errington, 1st Bt, JP, and Marjorie (*d* 1973), *d* of A. Grant Bennett; *S* father, 1973; *m* 1955, Diana Kathleen Forbes, *o d* of late E. Barry Davenport, Edgbaston, Birmingham; three *s. Educ:* Rugby Sch.; New Coll., Oxford. psc 1958. GSO 3 (Int.), HQ 11 Armd Div., 1950–52; GSO 3, MI3 (b), War Office, 1955–57; Bde Major 146 Inf. Bde, 1959–61; Coy Comdr, RMA Sandhurst, 1963–65; Military Assistant to Adjutant-General, 1965–67; CO 1st Bn, The King's Regt, 1967–69; GSO 1, HQ 1st British Corps, 1969–71; Col. GS, HQ NW District, 1971–74; AAG MI (Army), MoD, 1974–75; retired 1975. Col, The King's Regt, 1975–86; Chm., The King's and Manchester Regts Assoc., 1971–86. Director: Personnel Services, British Shipbuilders, 1977–78; Executive Appointments, 1979–90 (Chm., 1982–90). Employer Bd Mem., Shipbuilding ITB, 1977–78. Chm., Assoc. for Prevention of Addiction, Community Drug and Alcohol Initiatives, 1994–98 (Vice-Chm., 1991–94); Mem. Gen. Cttee, Not Forgotten Assoc., 1991–. Chm., Standing Council of the Baronetage, 2001–06 (Vice-Pres., 2006–). Vice-Pres., Britain-Australia Soc., 2009– (Hon. Dir, 1998–2006; Dir-Gen., 2006–09). Chm., Woodroffe's Club, 1988–94. Freeman, City of London, 1980; Liveryman: Broderers' Co.; Coachmakers' and Coach Harness Makers' Co. FRSA 1994. *Recreations:* music, travelling, gardening. *Heir: s* Robin Davenport Errington [*b* 1 July 1957; *m* 2001, Margerita Dudek; two *s*]. *Address:* Stone Hill Farm, Sellindge, Ashford, Kent TN25 6AJ; 203A Gloucester Place, NW1 6BU. *Clubs:* Boodle's, Oxford and Cambridge.

See also S. G. Errington.

ERRINGTON, Prof. Jeffery, PhD; FRS 2003; Professor of Cell and Molecular Biosciences, since 2005, and Director, Centre for Bacterial Cell Biology, since 2012, Newcastle University (Director, Institute of Cell and Molecular Biosciences, 2005–12); *b* 3 May 1956; *s* of Sidney Errington and Elizabeth Errington (*née* Wright); *m* 1982, Veronica Mary Geoghegan; two *d. Educ:* Blaydon Secondary Sch.; Univ. of Newcastle upon Tyne (BSc Hons Genetics/Zoology 1977); Thames Poly. (PhD 1981); MA Oxon 1989. Oxford University: Royal Soc. Univ. Res. Fellow, 1985–89; Lectr in Chemical Pathology, 1989–2000, Prof. of Microbiology, 2000–05, Sir William Dunn Sch. of Pathology; Fellow: Magdalen Coll., 1989–2001; Wadham Coll., 2001–06; BBSRC Sen. Res. Fellow, 1997–2002. Lectures: Kluyver, Dutch Microbiology Soc., 2009; Fred Griffiths Prize Rev., Soc. for Gen. Microbiol., 2009. Scientific Founder and Dir, Prolysis Ltd, 1998–2009; Founder and Dir, Demuris Ltd, 2007–; Dir, BIOTA Pharmaceuticals Inc. (formerly BIOTA Hldgs Ltd), 2010–13. Mem., EMBO, 2004; FMedSci 2007; Fellow, Amer. Acad. of Microbiol., 2007. Trustee, EPA Cephalosporin Res. Fund, 1999–. BBSRC Anniversary Medal, 2014; Novartis Medal and Prize, Biochem. Soc., 2014; Leeuwenhoek Medal and Prize, Royal Soc., 2015. *Publications:* over 150 peer-reviewed scientific papers; six patents. *Recreations:* soccer, snorkelling, ski-ing, walking, gardening. *Address:* Centre for Bacterial Cell Biology, Baddiley-Clark Building, Newcastle University, Richardson Road, Newcastle upon Tyne NE2 4AX. *T:* (0191) 208 3232, *Fax:* (0191) 208 3205.

ERRINGTON, Stuart Grant, CBE 1994; JP; DL; Chairman, National Association of Citizens' Advice Bureaux, 1989–94; *b* 23 June 1929; *yr s* of Sir Eric Errington, 1st Bt and late Marjorie Lady Errington; *m* 1954, Anne (*d* 2006), *d* of late Eric and Eileen Baedeker; two *s* one *d. Educ:* Rugby; Trinity College, Oxford (MA). National Service, 2nd Lieut Royal Artillery, 1947–49. Ellerman Lines, 1952–59; Astley Industrial Trust, 1959–70; Exec Dir, 1970, Man. Dir, 1977, Chm., 1985, Mercantile Credit Co., Chm. and Chief Exec., Mercantile Gp, 1988–89. Chairman: Equipment Leasing Assoc., 1976–78; European Fedn of Leasing Assocs, 1978–80; Finance Houses Assoc., 1982–84; Director: Barclays Merchant Bank, Barclays Bank UK, 1979–86; Kleinwort Overseas Investment Trust, 1982–98; Municipal Mutual Insurance, 1989–; Northern Electric, 1989–96; Nationwide Building Soc., 1989–97; Associated Property Owners Ltd, 1998–2002; Associated Property Hldgs Ltd, 2002–. Mem., 1989–, Vice-Chm., 1995–2005, Council, Royal Holloway (formerly RHBNC), London Univ. Chm., Sportsmatch England Award Panel, Dept of Culture, Media and Sport (formerly Dept of Heritage), 1992–2005. Chm., Berks and Oxfordshire Magistrates' Courts Cttee, 1999–2000. Hon. Fellow, RHUL, 2007. JP Windsor Forest, 1970; DL Berks, 2000. *Recreations:* fishing, golf, opera, travel. *Address:* Earleywood Lodge, Ascot SL5 9JP. *T:* (01344) 621977. *Club:* Boodle's.

ERROLL, 24th Earl of, *cr* 1452; **Merlin Sereld Victor Gilbert Hay;** Lord Hay, 1429; Baron of Slains, 1452; Bt 1685; 28th Hereditary Lord High Constable of Scotland, *cr* 1314; Celtic title, Mac Garadh Mor; 33rd Chief of the Hays (from 1171); Senior Great Officer, Royal Household in Scotland; computer consultant; *b* 20 April 1948; *er s* of 23rd Countess of Erroll and Sir Iain Moncreiffe of that Ilk, 11th Bt, CVO, QC; *S* mother, 1978 (and to baronetcy of father, 1985); *m* 1982, Isabelle Astell, *o d* of late T. S. Astell Hohler, MC; two *s* two *d. Educ:* Eton; Trinity College, Cambridge. Page to the Lord Lyon, 1956. Lieut, Atholl Highlanders, 1974. Chm., Cost Reduction Consultants Ltd, 1995–. Elected Mem., H of L, 1999; Member: Library and Computers Sub-Cttee, 1999–2001; Bd, POST, 2000–; Council, PITCOM, subseq. PICTFOR, 2000–; Council, European Inf. Soc. Gp, 2000–; H of L Inf. Cttee, 2001–. Prime Warden, Fishmongers' Co., 2000–01. Hon. Col, RMP TA, 1992–97. OStJ 1977. Member, Queen's Body Guard for Scotland, Royal Company of Archers, 1978. Patron, Keepers of the Quaich. *Recreation:* country pursuits. *Heir: s* Lord Hay, *qv. Address:* Woodbury Hall, Sandy, Beds SG19 2HR. *E:* errollm@parliament.uk. *Clubs:* White's, Pratt's; Puffin's (Edinburgh).

ERSHAD, Lt-Gen. Hussain Muhammad; Leader, Jatiya Party, Bangladesh; *b* 1 Feb. 1930; *s* of late Makbul Hussain, Advocate, and of Mojida Begum; *m* 1956, Begum Raushad Ershad; one *s* one adopted *d*. *Educ:* Carmichael Coll., Rangpur; Dhaka Univ. (BA 1st Div.). Staff Course, Defence Service Command and Staff Coll., Quetta, Pakistan, 1966; War Course, National Defence Coll., New Delhi, India, 1975. Infantry Regimental Service, 1953–58; Adjt, E Bengal Regimental Centre (Basic Inf. Trng Centre), 1960–62; E Pakistan Rifles, 1962–65; Bde Major/Dep. Asst Adjt and Quarter Master General, 1967–68; CO, Inf. Bn, 1969–71; Adjt General, Bangladesh Army, 1973–74; Dep. Chief of Army Staff, Bangladesh Army, Chm., Coordination and Control Cell for National Security, 1975–78; Chief of Army Staff, Bangladesh Army, 1978–86; C-in-C, Bangladesh Armed Forces, 1982; Chief Martial Law Administrator, Bangladesh, 1982–86; President: Council of Ministers, 1982–90; Bangladesh, 1983–90; Minister of Defence, Estabt, Health and Population Control, 1986–90. Elected MP, Bangladesh, 1991, 1996. Chm., National Sports Control Bd. *Publications:* poems in Bengali contributed occasionally to literary jls. *Address:* Jatiya Dal, c/o Jatiya Sangsad, Dhaka, Bangladesh. *Club:* Kurmitola Golf (Dhaka).

ERSKINE; *see* St Clair-Erskine.

ERSKINE, family name of **Earls of Buchan** and **Mar and Kellie**.

ERSKINE, Gerald David; Deputy Head, Strategic Assessments, Ministry of Defence, 2011–12; greyhound owner, since 2013; *b* Woking, 15 Nov. 1956; *s* of late Robert Gordon Erskine, MRCVS and Nona Erskine; *m* 1987, Patricia Cumisky; one *s* one *d*. *Educ:* Ranelagh Sch., Bracknell; Oxford Poly. (BA Geog./Hist. 1978). Sales Exec., construction engrg, 1978–79; civil staff, Metropolitan Police, 1980–83; served Army (short service volunteer commn), 1984–86 (Captain); Civil Servant, MoD, 1986–2005; Enforcement and Compliance, HMRC (on attachment), 2005–08; Chief, PHIA and Strategic Horizons, Cabinet Office (on attachment), 2008–10; Civilian Mem., Overseas Basing Study Team, 2010–11, Dep. Head, Global Combat Ship Export Team, 2011, MoD. Served TA, 2 Wessex Regt and Intelligence Corps, 1974–84 and 1986–87. Gov., Ashburton Community Sch., Croydon, 2000–09 (Chm., 2008–09); Trustee, Ashburton Develt Trust, 2008–13. *Recreations:* dog walking, shooting, travelling, railways, horse racing. *Address:* c/o 29–31 Abercromby Place, Edinburgh EH3 6QE. *Club:* Royal Scots (Edinburgh).

ERSKINE, Sir Peter; *see* Erskine, Sir T. P. N.

ERSKINE, Peter Anthony; Chairman, Ladbrokes plc, 2009–15; *b* 10 Nov. 1951; *s* of Stanley and Winifred Erskine; *m* 1975, Jan Green; three *s* one *d*. *Educ:* Bancroft's Sch., Woodford Green; Liverpool Univ. (BA Hons Psychology 1973). Various appointments at Polycell, Colgate and Palmolive; Sen. Vice-Pres. Sales and Marketing, Unitel, 1990–93; British Telecommunications: Man. Dir, BT Mobile, 1993–95; Pres. and CEO, Concert, USA, 1995–98; CEO, BT Cellnet, 1998–2000; CEO, 2001–08 and Chm., 2006–08, BT Wireless, subseq. mmO_2, then O_2, later Telefónica O_2 Europe plc; Dir, 2006–08, non-exec. Dir, 2008–, Telefónica SA. Adv. Bd, Univ. of Reading Bus. Sch., 2003. Hon. LLD Reading, 2008. *Recreations:* football, family, cinema, curry.

ERSKINE, Ralph; *see* Erskine, T. R.

ERSKINE, Sir (Thomas) Peter (Neil), 6th Bt *cr* 1821, of Cambo, Fife; DL; laird, Cambo Estate, since 1976; *b* 28 March 1950; *s* of Sir (Thomas) David Erskine, 5th Bt and Ann Erskine (*née* Fraser-Tytler); *S* father, 2007; *m* 1972, Catherine Hewlett; two *s* two *d*. *Educ:* Birmingham Univ. (BSc Psychol.); Edinburgh Univ. (DipRuralAg). LBIPP. Cambo Estate: opened farm park, 1982, photo studio, 1990; gardens opened to public and holiday accommodation in mansion, 1993; opened Kingsbarns Golf Links, 2000. Founder, Scottish Organic Producers Assoc., 1986. *Recreations:* blues guitarist and singer, garden photography, cycling, reading, theatre and arts. *Heir: s* Thomas Struan Erskine, *b* 6 Feb. 1977. *Address:* Cambo House, Kingsbarns, St Andrews, Fife KY16 8QD. *T:* (01333) 450054, *Fax:* (01333) 450987. *E:* peter@camboestate.com. *W:* www.camboestate.com. *Clubs:* New (Edinburgh); Royal & Ancient (St Andrews).

ERSKINE, (Thomas) Ralph, CB 1986; First Legislative Counsel, Northern Ireland, 1979–93; *b* 14 Oct. 1933; *m* 1966, Patricia Joan Palmer; one *s* one *d*. *Educ:* Campbell College; Queen's University, Belfast. Called to the Bar, Gray's Inn, 1962. *Publications:* (with Arthur Bauer and Klaus Herold) Funkpeilung als alliierte Waffe gegen deutsche U-Boote 1939–1945, 1997; (ed with Michael Smith) Action This Day: Bletchley Park from the breaking of the Enigma code to the birth of the modern computer, 2001; (ed with Michael Smith) The Bletchley Park Codebreakers: how ultra shortened the war and led to the birth of the computer, 2011; contrib. Oxford DNB; contribs to Cryptologia, Annals of the History of Computing, legal jls, etc. *Recreations:* researching subjects relating to Bletchley Park, writing. *Address:* c/o Office of the Legislative Counsel, Parliament Buildings, Belfast BT4 3SW.

ERSKINE CRUM, Douglas Vernon, CBE 1994 (OBE 1990); Chief Executive, Juddmonte Group, since 2013; *b* 31 May 1949; *s* of late Lt-Gen. Vernon Forbes Erskine Crum, CIE, MC and Rosemary (*née* Dawson); *m* 1980, Jacqueline Margaret Wilson; one *s* two *d*. *Educ:* Eton; RMA Sandhurst. Commissioned Scots Guards 1970; operational and intelligence roles; Staff Coll., Camberley, 1982; Brigade Major, Household Div., 1987–89; CO 2 SG, 1989–91; ACOS Ops, HQ N Ireland, 1991–92; Comdr 3 Inf. Brigade, 1992–94; Chief Executive: Ascot Racecourse, 1994–2007; Horserace Betting Levy Bd, 2008–13. Dir, EFC & Partners Ltd, 2006–. *Recreations:* most sports, books, travel, military history.

ERSKINE-HILL, Sir (Alexander) Roger, 3rd Bt *cr* 1945, of Quothquhan, Co. Lanark; *b* 15 Aug. 1949; *s* of Sir Robert Erskine-Hill, 2nd Bt and of Christine Alison, *o d* of late Capt. (A) Henry James Johnstone of Alva, RN; *S* father, 1989; *m* 1st 1984, Sarah Anne Sydenham (marr. diss. 1994), *er d* of late Dr R. J. Sydenham Clarke and of Mrs Charles Clarke; one *s* one *d*; 2nd, 2000, Gillian Elizabeth Borlase Mitchell, *d* of David and Sheila Surgey. *Educ:* Eton; Aberdeen Univ. (LLB). Director: Map Marketing Ltd, 1986–2002 and 2008–; The Hillbrooke Partnership Ltd, 2002–. *Heir: s* Robert Benjamin Erskine-Hill, *b* 6 Aug. 1986. *Address:* The Old Malthouse, Briton Street, Bampton, Devon EX16 9LN.

ERSKINE-HILL, Sir Roger; *see* Erskine-Hill, Sir A. R.

ERSKINE-MURRAY, family name of **Lord Elibank**.

ERTL, Prof. Gerhard; Director, Department of Physical Chemistry, Fritz-Haber-Institut der Max-Planck-Gesellschaft, 1986–2004, now Professor Emeritus; *b* Stuttgart, 10 Oct. 1936; *s* of Ludwig and Johanna Ertl; *m* 1964, Barbara Maschek; one *s* one *d*. *Educ:* Technical Univ., Stuttgart (Dip. Phys. 1961); Technical Univ., Munich (Dr rer. nat. 1964). Asst and Lectr, Technical Univ., Munich, 1965–68; Professor of Physical Chemistry: Technical Univ., Hanover, 1968–73; Ludwig Maximilians Univ., Munich, 1973–86. Nobel Prize in Chemistry, 2007; many other awards and prizes. *Publications:* three books; over 600 articles in jls. *Address:* Fritz-Haber-Institute, Faradayweg 4, 14195 Berlin, Germany. *T:* (30) 84135100, *Fax:* (30) 84135106. *E:* ertl@fhi-berlin.mpg.de.

ESAKI, Leo; Chairman, Science and Technology Promotion Foundation of Ibaraki, Japan, since 1998; President, Yokohama College of Pharmacy, since 2006; *b* 12 March 1925; *s* of Soichiro Esaki and Niyoko Ito; *m* 1986, Masako Kondo; one *s* two *d* by previous *m*. *Educ:* Univ. of Tokyo. MS 1947, PhD 1959. Sony Corp., Japan, 1956–60; IBM Research, 1960–92; IBM Fellow, 1967–92. Dir, IBM-Japan, 1976–92. President: Univ. of Tsukuba, Japan, 1992–98; Shibaura Inst. of Technol., 2000–05; Dir-Gen., Tsukuba Internat. Congress Centre, 1998. Research in tunnelling in semiconductor junctions which led to the discovery of the Esaki tunnel diode; subsequently research on man-made semiconductor superlattice in search of predicted quantum mechanical effect. Sir John Cass sen. vis. res. fellow, London Poly., 1982. Councillor-at-Large, Amer. Phys. Soc., 1971–75; Dir, Amer. Vacuum Soc., 1972–76; Member: Japan Academy, 1975; Max-Planck-Ges., 1989; For. Associate, Nat. Acad. of Sciences, USA, 1976; For. Associate, Nat. Acad. of Engineering, USA, 1977; Corresp. Mem., Academia Nacional De Ingenieria, Mexico, 1978; Hon. Academician, Academia Sinica, Taiwan, 2008. Nishina Meml Award, 1959; Asahi Press Award, 1960; Toyo Rayon Foundn Award, 1961; Morris N. Liebmann Meml Prize, 1961; Stuart Ballantine Medal, Franklin Inst., 1961; Japan Academy Award, 1965; (jtly) Nobel Prize for Physics, 1973; Science Achievement Award, US-Asia Inst., 1983; Centennial Medal, IEEE, 1984; Internat. Prize for New Materials, Amer. Physical Soc., 1985; Distinguished Foreign-born Individual Award, Internat. Center, NY, 1986; IEEE Medal of Honor, 1991; Japan Prize, 1998. Order of Culture (Japan), 1974; Grand Order of Rising Sun, First Class (Japan), 1998. *Publications:* numerous papers in learned jls. *Address:* Yokohama College of Pharmacy, Totsuka-ku, Yokohama, Kanagawa 245–0066, Japan.

ESCHENBACH, Christoph; conductor and pianist; Music Director, National Symphony Orchestra and John F. Kennedy Center for Performing Arts, Washington, since 2010; *b* 20 Feb. 1940. *Educ:* Hamburg Conservatory; State Music Conservatory, Cologne. Chief Conductor, Tonhalle Orch., Zürich, and Artistic Dir, Tonhalle-Gesellschaft, Zürich, 1982–86; Music Director: Houston SO, 1988–99, now Conductor Laureate; Ravinia Fest., 1994–2003; NDR SO, 1998–2004; Orch. de Paris, 2000–10; Philadelphia Orch., 2003–08; Artistic Dir, Schleswig-Holstein Music Fest., 1999–2002; Co-Artistic Dir, Pacific Music Fest., 1992–98. *As conductor:* studied with W. Bruckner Ruggeberg, George Szell; guest appearances include: NY Philharmonic, Boston Symphony, Chicago Symphony, Cleveland Orch., Pittsburgh Symphony, Los Angeles Philharmonic, London Symphony, BBC Philharmonia, Berlin Philharmonic, Bavarian Radio Symphony Munich, Munich Philharmonic, Vienna Philharmonic, Czech Philharmonic, New Japan Philharmonic, Houston Grand Opera, Metropolitan Opera, and Vienna State Opera. *As pianist:* studied with Eliza Hansen; winner: Internat. Piano Competition, Munich, 1962; Concours Clara Haskil, 1965; Canadian début, Montreal Expo, 1967; US début, Cleveland Orch., 1969; has toured Europe, N and S America, USSR, Israel, Japan, China, Australia; and has performed as pianist with leading orchs incl. Concertgebouw Amsterdam, Orch. de Paris, London Symphony, Berlin Philharmonic, and Cleveland Orch.; festivals incl. Salzburg, Lucerne, Bonn, Aix-en-Provence, and BBC Proms. (Jtly) Best Classical Compendium, Grammy Awards, 2014. Officer's Cross with Ribbon, 1990, Commander's Cross, 1993, Order of Merit (Germany). *Address:* John F. Kennedy Center for Performing Arts, 2700 F Street NW, Washington, DC 20566, USA.

ESCOTT COX, Brian Robert; *see* Cox.

ESCUDIER, Prof. Marcel Paul, PhD, DSc(Eng); FREng, FIMechE, FCGI; Harrison Professor of Mechanical Engineering, University of Liverpool, 1989–2008, now Emeritus Professor; *b* 17 July 1942; *s* of late Isabel Kate Escudier; *m* 1st, 1966, Sonja Kennedy Allen (marr. diss. 1973); 2nd, 1973, Agnes Margaret Simko; one *s*. *Educ:* Sir Walter St John's Grammar Sch., London; Imperial Coll., London Univ. (BScEng; DIC; PhD 1967); DSc(Eng) 1990. ACGI 1963; FIMechE 1995; FREng 2000; FCGI 2003. Res. Associate, MIT, 1967–69; Asst Prof., Univ. of Southern Calif, 1969–73; Mem., Plasmaphysics Res. Gp, 1973–74, Leader, Fluid Mechanics Res. Gp, 1974–86, Brown Boveri Res. Centre, Switzerland; Hd, Fluid Mechanics Res. Dept, Schlumberger Cambridge Res. Ltd, Cambridge, 1986–88; Hd, Dept of Mech. Engrg, Univ. of Liverpool, 1990–97. *Publications:* The Essence of Engineering Fluid Mechanics, 1998; (with A. G. Atkins) A Dictionary of Mechanical Engineering, 2013; contrib. papers on vortex flows, non-Newtonian fluid flow, etc, to scientific jls. *Recreations:* gardening, cooking, erotic art, motor racing (non participatory), digital photography. *Address:* Silverburn, Park Road, Willaston, Neston CH64 1TJ. *T:* (0151) 327 2949.

ESDALE, Patricia Joyce, (Mrs G. P. R. Esdale); *see* Lindop, P. J.

ESHER, 5th Viscount *cr* 1897; **Christopher Lionel Baliol Brett;** Baron 1885; *b* 23 Dec. 1936; *s* of 4th Viscount Esher and Christian (*née* Pike); *S* father, 2004; *m* 1st, 1962, Camilla Charlotte (marr. diss. 1970), *d* of Sir (Horace) Anthony Rumbold, 10th Bt, KCMG, KCVO, CB; one *s* two *d*; 2nd, 1971, Valerie Harrington; two *s* twin *d*. *Educ:* Eton; Magdalen Coll., Oxford. *Heir: s* Hon. Matthew Christopher Anthony Brett [*b* 2 Jan. 1963; *m* 1992, Hon. Emma Charlotte Denison-Pender, *e d* of Baron Pender, *qv*; one *s* two *d*]. *Address:* Beauforest House, Newington, Wallingford, Oxon OX10 7AG.

See also M. N. C. Thomas.

ESIRI, Prof. Margaret Miriam, DM; FRCPath; Professor of Neuropathology, Departments of Neuropathology and Neurology, Oxford University, 1996–2007, now Emeritus; Professorial Fellow, St Hugh's College, Oxford, 1988–2007, now Emeritus; *b* 5 Oct. 1941; *d* of William Alfred Evans and Doreen Mary (*née* Bates); *m* 1963, Frederick Obukowho Uruemuowho Esiri; two *s* one *d*. *Educ:* Croydon High Sch. (GPDST); St Hugh's Coll., Oxford (BSc, MA, DM). FRCPath 1988. University of Oxford: preregistration med. and surgical posts and scholarship for trng in research methods, 1967–69; Jun. Res. Fellow in Neuropathology, 1970–72; trng posts in Histopathology, 1973–79; MRC Sen. Clinical Fellow in Neuropathology, 1980–85; Consultant Neuropathologist, Radcliffe Infirmary, 1986–88; Clinical Reader in Neuropathology, 1988–96. *Publications:* (with J. Booss) Viral Encephalitis, 1986; (with D. R. Oppenheimer) Diagnostic Neuropathology, 1989, 2nd edn 1996, 3rd edn (with D. Perl) 2006; (ed with J. H. Morris) The Neuropathology of Dementia, 1997, 2nd edn (ed with V. M.-Y. Lee and J. Q. Trojanowski) 2004; (with J. Booss) Human Viral Encephalitis, 2003; over 300 original pubns. *Recreation:* grandchildren. *Address:* Neuropathology Department, Level 1, West Wing, John Radcliffe Hospital, Headington, Oxford OX3 9DU. *T:* (01865) 234403. *E:* margaret.esiri@ndcn.ox.ac.uk.

ESKENAZI, Giuseppe, (J. E. Eskenazi); Managing Director, Eskenazi Ltd, since 1969; *b* 8 July 1939; *s* of late Isaac Eskenazi and of Lea Eskenazi; *m* 1963, Laura (*née* Bandini); one *s* one *d*. *Educ:* King's School, Sherborne; The Polytechnic, Regent Street; University College London. Art dealer, primarily Chinese and Japanese, 1962–; Eskenazi Ltd founded by father in 1960. Mem., steering cttee to estab. Asian Art in London, 1997–98, Chm., 2002, 2003; Member: Exec. Cttee, Asia House, 1993–2007; Council, Oriental Ceramic Soc., 1998–2002, 2004–07; Adv. Bd, Bard Grad. Center for Studies in the Decorative Arts, NY, 2000–15. Trustee, Asia House Trust (London), 2000–07. Adviser to Royal Academy for exhibitions: 100 Masterpieces of Imperial Chinese Ceramics from the Au Bak Ling Collection, 1998; Return of the Buddha, The Qingzhou Discoveries, 2002. Chevalier, Légion d'Honneur (France), 2006. *Publications:* A Dealer's Hand: the Chinese art world through the eyes of Giuseppe Eskenazi, 2012, Chinese edn 2015; over 80 exhibition catalogues. *Recreations:* sailing, opera. *Address:* Eskenazi, 10 Clifford Street, W1S 2LJ. *T:* (020) 7493 5464.

ESLER, Gavin William James; presenter: BBC World, since 1998; BBC Radio Four, since 2000; *b* 27 Feb. 1953; *s* of William John Esler and Georgena Esler; *m* 1979, Patricia Margaret Warner (marr. diss.); one *s* one *d*. *Educ:* George Heriot's Sch., Edinburgh; Kent Univ. (BA English and American Lit); Leeds Univ. (MA Anglo-Irish Lit. (Dist.)). Reporter, Belfast Telegraph, 1975–76; BBC: Reporter and Presenter, Northern Ireland, 1977–82; Reporter, Newsnight, 1982–88; Washington Corresp., 1989; Chief N America Corresp., 1989–97; presenter: Newsnight, 1997, 2003–14; BBC News 24, 1997–2002. Columnist, The Scotsman, 1998–2005. Chancellor, Univ. of Kent, 2014–. Hon. MA, 1995, Hon. DCL, 2005,

Kent. RTS Award, 1989; Sony Gold Award, 2007. FRSA 2000. *Publications:* The United States of Anger: the people and the American dream, 1997; Lessons from the Top: how leaders succeed through telling stories, 2012; novels: Loyalties, 1990; Deep Blue, 1992; The Blood Brother, 1995; A Scandalous Man, 2008; Powerplay, 2009. *Recreations:* hiking, ski-ing, camping, especially in the American West. *Address:* BBC News Centre, Broadcasting House, Portland Place, W1A 1AA.

ESLER, Prof. Philip Francis, DPhil, DD; FRSE; Principal and Professor of Biblical Interpretation, St Mary's University College, Twickenham, 2010–13, now Emeritus Professor; Portland Chair in New Testament Studies, University of Gloucestershire, since 2013; *b* 27 Aug. 1952; *s* of Patrick Joseph Esler and Evelyn Elizabeth Esler; *m* 1983, Patricia Kathryn Curran; two *s* one *d*. *Educ:* Sydney Univ. (BA Hons LLB, LLM); Magdalen Coll., Oxford (DPhil 1984); DD Oxford 2008. Associate to Justice W. H. Collins of NSW Supreme Court, 1977; articled clerk, then solicitor, Allen, Allen & Hemsley, Sydney, 1978–81 and 1984–86; barrister, NSW Supreme Court, 1986–92; University of St Andrews: Reader in New Testament, 1992–95; Prof. of Biblical Criticism, 1995–2010; Vice-Principal for Res., and Provost, St Leonard's Coll., 1998–2001; Chief Exec., AHRC, 2005–09. Mem. Bd, Scottish Enterprise Fife, 1999–2003. FRSE 2009. *Publications:* Community and Gospel in Luke - Acts, 1987; The First Christians in their Social Worlds, 1994; Galatians, 1998; Conflict and Identity in Romans, 2003; (with J. Boyd) Velázquez and Biblical Text, 2004; New Testament Theology, 2005; (with R. A. Piper) Lazarus, Martha and Mary, 2006; Sex, Wives and Warriors: reading biblical narrative with its ancient audience, 2011. *Recreations:* swimming, walking, tennis. *Address:* 27 Rosehill Street, Cheltenham GL52 6SQ.

ESMONDE, Sir Thomas (Francis Grattan), 17th Bt *cr* 1629 (Ire.), of Ballynastragh, Wexford; MD; Consultant Neurologist, Antrim Area Hospital, since 2007; *b* 14 Oct. 1960; *s* of Sir John Henry Grattan Esmonde, 16th Bt and of Pamela Mary, *d* of late Francis Stephen Bourke, FRCPI; *S* father, 1987; *m* 1986, Pauline Loretto Kearns; one *s* two *d*. *Educ:* Sandford Park Secondary School, Ranelagh, Dublin; Medical School, Trinity College, Dublin (MB, BCh, BAO 1984; MD 1995). MRCPI, MRCP (UK) 1987. Junior House Officer, Whiteabbey Hosp., 1984–85; SHO, Royal Victoria, Musgrave Park and Whiteabbey Hosps, 1985–87, Altnagelvin Hosp., Londonderry, 1987–88; Med. Registrar, Royal Gwent Hosp., Newport, 1988–89; Registrar in Neurology, Univ. Hosp. of Wales, 1989–90; Clinical Res. Fellow, Dept of Neurosci., Western General Hosp., Edinburgh, 1990–92; Sen. Registrar, 1992–96, Consultant Neurologist, 1996–2007, Royal Victoria Hosp., Belfast. *Recreations:* chess, fishing. *Heir: s* Sean Vincent Grattan Esmonde, *b* 8 Jan. 1989.

ESOM, Steven Derek; Chairman: Advantage Travel Partnership, since 2013; British Amateur Boxing Association, since 2013; *b* 13 Nov. 1960; *s* of Derek Esom and Shirley Esom (*née* Beldom); *m* 1994, Fiona; one *s* one *d*. *Educ:* St Edward's Sch., Romford; Univ. of Wales, Swansea (BSc Hons Geog.). Sen. Manager, Buying, J. Sainsbury plc, 1982–93; with US subsidiary, Shaws, Boston, 1991–99; Buying and Merchandising Dir, Texas Homecare, Ladbroke Gp, 1994–95; Vice-Pres., Global Merchandising, Hilton Internat., 1995–96; Dir of Buying, 1996–2002, Man. Dir, 2002–07, Waitrose; Dir of Food, Marks and Spencer, 2007–08; Operating Partner, Langholm Capital, 2009–13. Dir, CIES, 2004–07; Chairman: Bart Spices, 2010–13; British Retail Consortium Trading, 2011–; Ice Orgn, 2011–. Non-executive Director: Carphone Warehouse Gp plc, 2005–09; Cranswick Foods, 2009–; Tyrrells Potato Chips, 2009–. FRSA; FIGD. *Recreations:* food & wine, ski-ing, fitness. *Address:* c/o Product Chain Ltd, 4 City Limits, Reading RG6 4UP.

ESPEJO, Genefer D.; Headmistress, Nonsuch High School for Girls, Cheam, 1995–2009; *b* 17 July 1949; *d* of late Rev. D. G. Larkinson and of Mrs S. Larkinson; *m* 1972, Dr L. G. Espejo; one *s*. *Educ:* Queen's Univ., Belfast (BA Hons); Univ. of Sussex (PGCE). Dep. Hd, Kings' Sch., Winchester, 1985–92; Headmistress, Reading Girls' Sch., 1992–95. FRSA. *Recreations:* walking, visiting art galleries, theatre, contemporary fiction.

ESPLEN, (Sir) John Graham, 3rd Bt *cr* 1921, of Hardres Court, Canterbury, but does not use the title; *b* 4 Aug. 1932; *s* of Sir William Graham Esplen, 2nd Bt and Aline Octavia, *d* of late A. Octavius Hedley; *S* father, 1989; *m*; one *s* three *d*. *Educ:* Harrow; St Catharine's Coll., Cambridge. *Heir: s* William John Harry Esplen [*b* 24 Feb. 1967; *m* 1996, Helen Chesser; one *s* two *d*].

ESQUIVEL, Rt Hon. Sir Manuel, KCMG 2010; PC 1986; Prime Minister of Belize, 1984–89 and 1993–98; Member, House of Representatives, Belize, 1984–98; Leader, United Democratic Party, 1982–98; *b* 2 May 1940; *s* of John and Laura Esquivel; *m* 1971, Kathleen Levy; one *s* two *d*. *Educ:* Loyola Univ., New Orleans (BSc Physics); Bristol Univ. (Cert Ed.). Instructor in Physics, St John's Coll., Belize City, 1967–82. Member: Belize City Council, 1974–80; Nat. Senate, 1979–84; Leader of the Opposition, Belize, 1989–93. Chm., Utd Democratic Party, 1976–82. Hon. DHL Loyola Univ., 1986. *Recreation:* electronics. *Address:* PO Box 1344, Belize City, Belize.

ESSAAFI, M'hamed; Grand Officier, Order of Tunisian Republic, 1963; Disaster Relief Co-ordinator and Under Secretary General, United Nations, 1982–92; *b* 26 May 1930; *m* 1956, Hedwige Klat; one *s* one *d*. *Educ:* Sadiki Coll., Tunis; Sorbonne, Paris. Secretariat of State for For. Affairs, 1956; 1st Sec., Tunisian Embassy, London, 1956; 1st Sec., Tunisian Embassy, Washington, 1957; Secretariat of State for For. Affairs, Tunis: Dir of Amer. Dept, 1960; America and Internat. Confs Dept, 1962; Ambassador to London, 1964–69; Ambassador to Moscow, 1970–74; Ambassador to Bonn, 1974–76; Sec.-Gen., Ministry of Foreign Affairs, Tunis, 1969–70 and 1976–78; Ambassador to Belgium and EEC, 1978–79; Permanent Rep. of Tunisia to the UN, and Special Rep. of the Sec.-Gen., 1980–81, Chef de Cabinet 1982. *Address:* rue de la Mosquée BH20, La Marsa, Tunis, Tunisia; 41 Chemin Moïse-Duboule, 1209 Geneva, Switzerland.

ESSER, Robin Charles; Executive Managing Editor, Daily Mail, since 1998; editorial and media consultant, since 1990; *b* 6 May 1935; *s* of late Charles and Winifred Eileen Esser; *m* 1959, Irene Shirley Clough (decd); two *s* two *d*; *m* 1981, Tui (*née* France); two *s*. *Educ:* Wheelwright Grammar School, Dewsbury; Wadham College, Oxford (BA Hons, MA). Edited Oxford Univ. newspaper, Cherwell, 1954. Commissioned, King's Own Yorkshire Light Infantry, 1956. Freelance reporter, 1957–60; Daily Express: Staff Reporter, 1960; Editor, William Hickey Column, 1963; Features Editor, 1965; New York Bureau, 1969; Northern Editor, 1970; Exec. Editor, 1985; Consultant Editor, Evening News, 1977; Editor, Sunday Express, 1986–89; Gp Editl Consultant, Express Newspapers, 1989–90. Pres., Soc. of Editors, 2011 (Fellow, 2013). Freeman, Stationers' and Newspaper Makers' Co., 2014; Freeman, City of London, 2015. *Publications:* The Hot Potato, 1969; The Paper Chase, 1971. *Recreations:* lunching, shooting, tennis, reading. *Clubs:* Garrick, Hurlingham.

ESSERY, David James, CB 1997; Under Secretary, Scottish Office Home (formerly Home and Health) Department, 1991–97; *b* 10 May 1938; *s* of Lawrence and Edna Essery; *m* 1963, Nora Sim; two *s* one *d*. *Educ:* Royal High Sch., Edinburgh. Entered Dept of Health for Scotland, 1956; Private Sec. to Minister of State, Scottish Office, 1968; Principal, Scottish Develt Dept, 1969; Assistant Secretary: Scottish Economic Planning Dept, 1976; Scottish Develt Dept, 1981–85; Under Sec., Scottish Office Agric. and Fisheries Dept, 1985–91. Mem. Mgt Cttee, Hanover (Scotland) Housing Assoc., 2005–12. *Recreations:* reading, music, golf. *Address:* 110 Grange Loan, Edinburgh EH9 2EF.

ESSEX, 11th Earl of, *cr* 1661; **Frederick Paul de Vere Capell;** Baron Capell 1641; Viscount Malden 1661; Deputy Head Teacher, Skerton County Primary School, Lancaster, 1990–95 (Acting Head, 1992–93); *b* 29 May 1944; *s* of 10th Earl of Essex, and of Doris Margaret, *d* of George Frederick Tomlinson; *S* father, 2005. *Educ:* Skerton Boys' School; Lancaster Royal Grammar School; Didsbury College of Education, Manchester; Northern School of Music. ACP, LLCM(TD), ALCM. Assistant teacher, Marsh County Junior School, 1966–72; Deputy Head, 1972–75; Acting Head, 1975–77; Deputy Head Teacher, Marsh County Primary School, 1977–78; Head Teacher, Cockerham Parochial CE School, Cockerham, Lancaster, 1979–80; in charge of Pastoral Care, Curriculum Develt and Music, Skerton County Primary School, Lancaster, 1981–90. Patron, Friends of Cassiobury Park, Watford, 1998–. FRSA. *Recreations:* music, gardening, gym. *Heir: kinsman* William Jennings Capell [*b* 9 Aug. 1952; *m* 1971, Sandra Elaine Matson; one *s* one *d*].

ESSEX, David Albert, OBE 1999; singer, actor and composer; *b* 23 July 1947; *s* of Albert Cook and Doris Cook (*née* Kemp); *m* 1971, Maureen Annette Neal; one *s* one *d*; *m* 2010, Susan Hallam-Wright; one *s*. *Educ:* Shipman Secondary Sch., E London. Music industry début, 1965; acting début, touring repertory co.; Jesus, in Godspell, Wyndhams, 1972 (Most Promising Newcomer Award, Variety Club of GB); Che Guevara, in Evita, Prince Edward, 1978; Byron, in Childe Byron, Young Vic, 1981; Fletcher Christian, in Mutiny, Piccadilly, 1985 (also wrote score); She Stoops to Conquer, Queen's, 1993; All the Fun of the Fair, UK tour and Garrick, 2008–10 (also wrote score); annual Christmas appearances in own musical version of Robinson Crusoe. Films include: That'll Be the Day, 1973; Stardust, 1974; Silver Dream Racer (also wrote score), 1979; Shogun Mayeda, 1991; Traveller, 2013. Many best-selling singles and albums; first concert tour of UK, 1974; tours, 1975–, incl. Europe, USA, Australia, and a world tour; TV and radio appearances, incl. BBC TV series, The River, 1988; Eastenders, 2011. Mem. Council, VSO (Ambassador, 1990–92). *Publications:* (autobiography) A Charmed Life, 2002; Over the Moon: my autobiography, 2012; Travelling Tinker Man and Other Rhymes, 2015. *Address:* c/o David Essex Management, PO Box 390, Billingshurst, W Sussex RH14 0BE.

ESSEX, Susan Linda, (Sue); Member (Lab) Cardiff North, National Assembly for Wales, 1999–2007; Minister for Finance, Local Government and Public Services, 2003–07; *b* 29 Aug. 1945; *m* 1967, Richard Essex; one *s* one *d*. *Educ:* Leicester Univ. (BA). MRTPI. Lectr in Planning, Univ. of Wales, Cardiff, 1992–99. Member (Lab): Cardiff City Council, 1983–96 (former Leader); Cardiff County Council, 1995–99. Sec., then Minister, for the Envmt, Nat. Assembly for Wales, 2000–03. Member: Countryside Council for Wales, 1994–99; Commn on Devolution in Wales, 2011–. *Address:* 29 Lon-y-Dail, Rhiwbina, Cardiff CF14 6DZ.

ESSIG, Philippe Louis Charles Marie; Officier de l'Ordre National du Mérite, 1984; Commandeur de la Légion d'Honneur, 1994; international consultant, since 1991; Chairman, Board of Transmanche-Link, 1988–91; *b* 19 July 1933; *s* of Jean Essig and Germaine Olivier; *m* 1960, Isabelle Lanier; one *s* three *d*. *Educ:* Lycée Janson-de-Sailly; Ecole Polytechnique; Engineer, Ponts et Chaussées. Engr, Dakar-Niger railway, 1957–59; Asst Dir, Régie du chemin de fer Abidjan-Niger, 1960–61; Dir, Régie des chemins de fer du Cameroun, 1961–66; Régie autonome des transports parisiens (RATP): Chief Engr, Research Dept, 1966–71; Chief Op. Officer, Ops Dept, 1971–73; Man. Dir, Railways, Paris, 1973–81; Gen. Manager, 1982–85; Pres., SNCF, 1985–88. Sec. of State for Housing, 1988. Officier de l'Ordre de la Valeur Camerounaise, 1966. *Recreations:* walking, ski-ing, shooting. *Address:* 5 Avenue Fourcault de Pavant, 78000 Versailles, France. *E:* essigph@wanadoo.fr.

ESSWOOD, Paul Lawrence Vincent; singer (counter-tenor); conductor; Professor of Baroque Vocal Interpretation, Royal Academy of Music, 1985; Principal Conductor, Polish Orchestra of the XVIII Century; *b* West Bridgford, Nottingham, 6 June 1942; *s* of Alfred Walter Esswood and Freda Garratt; *m* 1st, 1966, Mary Lillian Cantrill, ARCM (marr. diss.); two *s*; 2nd, 1990, Aimée Désirée Blattmann; one *s* one *d*. *Educ:* West Bridgford Grammar Sch.; Royal Coll. of Music (ARCM). Lay-Vicar, Westminster Abbey, 1964–71. Prof., RCM, 1973–85; Specialist in baroque performance; first broadcast, BBC, 1965; co-founder: Pro Cantione Antiqua; A Cappella Male Voice Ensemble for Performance of Old Music, 1967; joined The Musicke Companye, 1998; operatic début in Cavalli's L'Erismena, Univ. of California, Berkeley, 1968; début at La Scala, Milan with Zurich Opera in L'Incoronazione di Poppea and Il Ritorno d'Ulisse, 1978; Scottish Opera début in Dido and Aeneas, 1978; world premières: Penderecki's Paradise Lost, Chicago Lyric Opera, 1979; Philip Glass's Echnaton, Stuttgart Opera, 1984; Herbert Willi's Schlafes Bruder, Zurich Opera, 1996; performed in major festivals: Edinburgh, Leeds Triennial, English Bach, Vienna, Salzburg, Zurich, Hamburg, Berlin, Naples, Israel, Lucerne, Flanders, Wexford, Holland. Has made over 150 recordings for major cos, incl. solo recitals of Purcell, Schumann, English lute songs, Benjamin Britten folk songs and Canticle II (Abraham and Isaac). Début as conductor, Chichester Fest., 2000, conducted Purcell's The Fairy Queen, King Arthur, Dido and Aeneas, Handel's Messiah and Bach's B Minor Mass; conducted modern world première, Cavalli's Pompeo Magno, Varazdin Fest., Croatia, 2002; conducted Capella Cracoviensis in Purcell's The Fairy Queen and Handel's Israel in Egypt, Cracow. Hon. RAM 1990. *Recreations:* gardening (organic), apiculture. *Address:* Jasmine Cottage, 42 Ferring Lane, Ferring, West Sussex BN12 6QT. *T:* and *Fax:* (01903) 504480.

ESTERSON, William; MP (Lab) Sefton Central, since 2010; *b* 27 Oct. 1966; *s* of Derek and Joyce Esterson; *m* 1998, Caroline Herbert; one *s* one *d*. *Educ:* Rochester Mathematical Sch.; Leeds Univ. (BSc Maths and Phil. 1990). Accountancy trng; Dir, Leaps and Bounds (Trng) Ltd. Mem. (Lab) Medway Council, 1995–2010. Member: Envmt, Food and Rural Affairs Select Cttee, 2010–11; Educn Select Cttee, 2010–15; Communities and Local Govt Select Cttee, 2011–13; Treasury Select Cttee, 2015–. *Address:* House of Commons, SW1A 0AA.

ESTEVE-COLL, Dame Elizabeth Anne Loosemore, DBE 1995; Vice-Chancellor, University of East Anglia, 1995–97; Chancellor, University of Lincoln, 2001–08; *b* 14 Oct. 1938; *o d* of P. W. and Nora Kingdon; *m* 1960, José Alexander Timothy Esteve-Coll (*d* 1980). *Educ:* Darlington Girls High Sch.; Birkbeck Coll., London Univ. (BA 1976). Head of Learning Resources, Kingston Polytechnic, 1977; University Librarian, Univ. of Surrey, 1982; Keeper, National Art Library, 1985, Dir, 1988–95, V&A Museum. *Recreations:* reading, music, foreign travel. *Address:* The Tabernacle, Millgate, Aylsham, Norfolk NR11 6HR.

ESTRIN, Prof. Saul, DPhil; Professor of Management, London School of Economics and Political Science, since 2006; *b* 7 June 1952; *s* of Maurice Estrin and Irene Estrin (*née* Redhouse); *m* 1985, Jennifer Ann Lockwood; one *s* three *d*. *Educ:* St John's Coll., Cambridge (BA 1974; MA 1977); Univ. of Sussex (DPhil 1979). Lectr, Southampton Univ., 1977–84; Lectr, 1984–89, Sen. Lectr, 1989–90, in Econs, LSE, 1984–90; London Business School: Associate Prof. of Econs, 1990–94; Prof. of Economics, 1994–2006; Dir, CIS Middle Europe Centre, 1997–2000; Dep. Dean (Faculty and Academic Planning), 1998–2006; Res. Dir, Centre for New and Emerging Markets, 2000–06; Acting Dean, 2002; Founding Hd, Dept of Mgt, LSE, 2006–13. *Publications:* Self-Management: economic theory and Yugoslav practice, 1984; (jtly) Introduction to Microeconomics, 4th edn, 1993; (ed jtly) Competition and Competition Policy, 1993; Privatisation in Central and Eastern Europe, 1994; (ed jtly) Essential Readings in Economics, 1995; Foreign Direct Investment in Central and Eastern Europe, 1997; numerous academic papers. *Recreation:* family. *Address:* Department of Management, London School of Economics and Political Science, New Academic Building, 54 Lincoln's Inn Fields, WC2A 3LJ. *T:* (020) 7955 6629. *E:* s.estrin@lse.ac.uk.

ETCHINGHAM, Julie Anne; Presenter, News at Ten, ITV News, since 2008; *b* Leicester, 21 Aug. 1969; *d* of James and Sheila Etchingham; *m* 1997, Nicholas Gardner; two *s*. *Educ:* English Martyrs RC Comprehensive Sch., Leicester; Newnham Coll., Cambridge (BA Hons English 1991). Reporter, BBC, 1992–94; presenter and reporter, BBC Newsround, 1994–97; reporter, BBC News, 1997–2001; presenter, Sky News, 2002–08. Hon. DLaws Leicester, 2012. Presenter of Year, RTS, 2010. *Recreations:* reading, raising small boys. *Address:* ITV News, 200 Grays Inn Road, WC1X 8XZ. *E:* julie.etchingham@itn.co.uk.

ETHERIDGE, Prof. Alison Mary, (Mrs Lionel Mason), DPhil; FRS 2015; Professor of Probability, University of Oxford, since 2003; Fellow, Magdalen College, Oxford, since 1997; *b* Wolverhampton, 27 April 1964; *d* of Arnold and Catherine Etheridge; *m* 1997, Lionel Mason; one *s* one *d*. *Educ:* Smeston Comprehensive Sch., Wolverhampton; New Coll., Oxford (MA; DPhil Maths). Sir Christopher Cox Jun. Res. Fellow, New Coll., Oxford, 1987–90; SERC Postdoctoral Fellow, Univ. of Cambridge, 1990–91; Lectr in Pure Maths, Univ. of Edinburgh, 1990–96; Neyman Asst Prof., Univ. of Calif, Berkeley, 1992; Reader in Probability and Stats, QMW, 1996–97; Lectr in Applied Maths, Oxford Univ., 1997–2002. EPSRC Advanced Fellow, 1997–2005. *Publications:* Introduction to Super Processes, 2000; A Course in Financial Calculus, 2002; (with M. Davis) Louis Bachelier's Theory of Speculation: the origins of modern finance, 2006; Some Mathematical Models from Population Genetics, 2012. *Recreations:* hill walking, theatre. *Address:* Mathematical Institute, University of Oxford, Andrew Wiles Building, Radcliffe Observatory Quarter, Woodstock Road, Oxford OX2 6GG.

ETHERIDGE, Brian Ernest, CBE 2010; Director of Integrated Delivery, Rail Executive, Department for Transport, since 2015; *b* Basingstoke, 12 May 1959; *s* of Cyril and Kathleen Etheridge; *m* 1988, Julia Brant; two *s*. *Educ:* Aston Univ. (BSc Hons Envmtl Health); Brunel Univ. (MSc Envmtl Pollution Sci.). Envmtl Health Officer, London Bor. of Brent, 1981–85; Dist Envmtl Health Officer, Basingstoke and Deane BC, 1985–87; Prin. Policy Officer, 1987–89, Asst Sec., 1989–95, Assoc. of Dist Councils; Hd, Local Envmt Mgt, DoE, 1995–97; Health and Safety Executive: Hd, Local Authy Unit, 1997–2001; Hd, Gas and Transport Safety, 2001–02; Dir of Strategy, 2002–04; Dir, London Reg., 2004–06; Dep. Dir, Prime Minister's Delivery Unit, 2006–08; Dir, Civil Service Capability, later Civil Service Capability and HR Ops, Cabinet Office, 2008–11; Man. Dir, Motoring Services, DfT, 2011–15. Ind. Mem. Bd, Sentinel Housing Assoc., 2005– (Vice Chm., 2010–). *Publications:* (contrib.) Clay's Handbook of Environmental Health, 19th edn 2004. *Recreations:* cycling, golf, gardening. *Address:* Department for Transport, Great Minster House, 33 Horseferry Road, SW1P 4DR.

ETHERIDGE, William; Member (UK Ind) West Midlands, European Parliament, since 2014; *b* Wolverhampton, 18 March 1970; *s* of Alan and Valerie Etheridge; *m* 2008, Star; three step *c*. *Educ:* Parkfield Sch., Wolverhampton; Wolverhampton Poly. Purchasing/sales, British Steel Stainless, 1990–94; selling stainless steel for cos incl. Thyssen, 1994–2014. Campaign Exec., Dudley Conservatives, 2010; Regl Organiser, UKIP, W Midlands, 2013. Mem. (UK Ind) Dudley MBC. Prospective Parly Candidate (UK Ind), Dudley North. *Publications:* Black Country Revolutionary, 2011; The Rise of UKIP, 2014. *Recreations:* cricket, football, Wolves season ticket. *Address:* 11 Tipton Street, Sedgeley, Dudley, W Midlands DY3 1HE. *T:* (01902) 664670. *E:* bill@mepukip.com. *Clubs:* Claverley Cricket; Sedgeley Working Men's.

ETHERIDGE, Zina Ruth; Deputy Chief Executive, Haringey Council, since 2013; *b* Cheltenham, 9 Nov. 1971; *d* of Colin Etheridge and Jackie Etheridge; *m* 2005, Chris Megainey; two *s* one *d*. *Educ:* Keble Coll., Oxford (BA Hons); Univ. of Wales, Aberystwyth (MSc Econ). Joined Dept of Transport, later DETR, 1996: various appts, then Hd, Transport and Envmt Team, 1999–2001; in-house policy consultant, 2001–04; Hd, Reform Strategy, Cabinet Office, 2004–07; Dir of Strategy and Communications, DIUS, 2007–09; Asst Chief Exec., London Bor. of Barnet, 2009–11; Exec. Dir, Civil Service Reform, Cabinet Office, 2011–12; Dir, Transformation and Strategy, Home Office, 2012–13. *T:* 07763 487900. *E:* zinaetheridge@gmail.com.

ETHERINGTON, David Charles Lynch; QC 1998; a Recorder, since 2000; *b* 14 March 1953; *s* of late Charles Henry Etherington and Beryl Etherington (*née* Croft). *Educ:* Keble Coll., Oxford (BA 1976, MA 2001; Special DPSA (Distinction) 1977). Called to the Bar, Middle Temple, 1979, Bencher, 2005; Asst Recorder, 1997–2000. Hd of Chambers, 2005–12. Bar Council: Chm., Professional Conduct Cttee, 2003–04; Chm., Professional Practice Cttee, 2006–08. Legal Advr, GDC, 2004–. Deputy Chancellor: Dio. of Norwich, 2005–07; Dio. of Ely, 2012–; Dep. Chancellor, 2007–09, Chancellor, 2009–, Dio. of St Edmundsbury and Ipswich. *Address:* 18 Red Lion Court, EC4A 3EB. *T:* (020) 7520 6000. *Club:* Garrick.

ETHERINGTON, Sir Stuart (James), Kt 2010; Chief Executive, National Council for Voluntary Organisations, since 1994; *b* 26 Feb. 1955; *s* of late Ronald Etherington and Dorothy Etherington (*née* West). *Educ:* Sondes Place Sch., Dorking; Brunel Univ. (BSc Politics 1977); Essex Univ. (MA Soc. Sci. Planning 1981); London Business Sch. (MBA 1992); SOAS (MA Internat. Relns and Diplomacy 1999). Social Worker, London Borough of Hillingdon, 1977–79; Sen. Res. Officer, Joseph Rowntree Meml Trust, Circle 33, 1980–82; Policy Advr, BASW, 1982–84; Dir, Good Practices in Mental Health, 1984–87; Dir, Public Affairs, 1987–91, Chief Exec., 1991–94, RNID. Mem. Council, ESRC, 1998–2003. Mem., Econ. and Social Cttee, EU, 2010–. Trustee: CAF, 1995–2004; BITC, 1995–2008; Civicus, 2001–07 (Treas., 2004–07); Chm., GuideStar UK, 2008–09. Member: RIIA, 1997; IISS. Mem. Council, Open Univ., 2002–07; Mem. Court, 2004–13, Pro Chancellor, 2008–13, Greenwich Univ. Visiting Professor: London South Bank Univ., 2002–; City Univ., 2003–. FRSA 1995. Hon. DSocSc Brunel, 2000. *Publications:* Mental Health and Housing, 1984; Emergency Duty Teams, 1985; The Sensitive Bureaucracy, 1986; Social Work and Citizenship, 1987. *Recreations:* reading biographies, theatre, opera, watching cricket and Charlton Athletic. *Address:* National Council for Voluntary Organisations, Regents Wharf, 8 All Saints Street, N1 9RL. *T:* (020) 7713 6161; 49 King George Street, Greenwich, SE10 8QB. *T:* (020) 8305 1379. *Clubs:* Reform; Surrey CC.

ETHERINGTON, William; *b* 17 July 1941; *m* 1963, Irene; two *d*. *Educ:* Monkwearmouth Grammar Sch.; Durham Univ. Apprentice fitter, Austin & Pickersgill shipyard, 1957–63; fitter, Dawdon Colliery, 1963–83; full-time NUM official, 1983–92. Mem., NUM, 1963– (Vice-Pres., NE Area, 1988–92). MP (Lab) Sunderland N, 1992–2010. Mem., 1997–2010, Dep. Leader, 2002–10, UK delegn to Council of Europe and WEU. Secretary: Miners' Parly Gp, 1994–2010; All-Party Against Fluoridation Gp, 1998–2006.

ETHERTON, Gillian Felicity Amanda; QC 2011; *b* Wimbledon, London, 2 Aug. 1965; *d* of Alan Kenneth Etherton and Elaine Myrtle Etherton (*née* Maccoby); civil partnership 2012, *m* 2015, Cindy Irvine. *Educ:* Stanway Sch.; Rosemead Sch.; Lancashire Poly. (LLB Hons). Called to the Bar, Middle Temple, 1988; in practice as a barrister, specialising in serious sex crime, serious cases of child cruelty and murder. *Recreations:* reading, swimming, playing the piano, tennis, art. *Address:* Atkinson Bevan Chambers, 2 Harcourt Buildings, Temple, EC4Y 9DB. *T:* (020) 7353 2112. *E:* clerks@2hb.co.uk. *Club:* Groucho.

See also Rt Hon. Sir T. M. E. B. Etherton.

ETHERTON, Rt Hon. Sir Terence (Michael Elkan Barnet), Kt 2001; PC 2008; Chancellor of the High Court, since 2013; *b* 21 June 1951; *s* of Alan Kenneth Etherton and Elaine Myrtle (*née* Maccoby); civil partnership 2006, *m* 2014, Andrew Howard Stone. *Educ:* Holmewood House Sch., Tunbridge Wells; St Paul's Sch., London (Sen. Foundn Schol.); Corpus Christi Coll., Cambridge (Open Exhibnr; MA (History and Law); LLM; Hon. Fellow, 2007). FCIArb 1993. Called to the Bar, Gray's Inn, 1974 (Uthwatt Schol., 1972; Holker Sen. Award, 1974; Arden Atkin and Mould Prize, 1975; Bencher 1998); in practice, 1975–2000; QC 1990; a Dep. High Court Judge, 2000; a Judge of the High Court, Chancery Div., 2001–08; a Lord Justice of Appeal, 2008–13. Chm., Law Commn, 2006–09. Mem., Bar Council, 1978–81; Chm., Young Barristers' Cttee of Bar Council, 1980–81; Mem., Lord Rawlinson's Cttee on the Constitution of the Senate of the Inns of Court and the Bar, 1985–86; Vice Chm., Chancery Bar Assoc., 1999–2001; Pres., Council of the Inns of Court, 2009–12. Mem., Mental Health Review Tribunal, 1994–99; Chairman: Broadmoor Hosp. Authy, 1999–2001; West London Mental Health NHS Trust, 2000–01; Dir (non-exec.), Riverside Mental Health NHS Trust, 1992–99 (Chm., Ethics Forum, 1994–99). Claims Adjudicator, Savings and Investment Bank (IOM) Depositors' Compensation Scheme, 1993–94. Chm., DoE/MAFF Ind. Review Panel on designation of nitrate vulnerable zones under EC Nitrate Directive, 1995 (report published, 1995). Mem. Council, RHBNC, 1992–2002 (Hon. Fellow, Royal Holloway, London Univ., 2005); Chm., City Law Sch. Adv. Bd, City Univ., 2006–08. Vis. Prof., Birkbeck, Univ. of London, 2010–14; Hon. Prof., Kent Univ., 2011–14. Blundell Meml Lect., 1996. FRSA 2000. Hon. LLD City, 2009. Captain, Cambridge Univ. Fencing Team, 1971–72; Mem., GB Sen. Internat. Fencing Team (Sabre), 1977–80 (World Championships, 1977, 1978, 1979); England Sabre Team Gold Medal, Commonwealth Fencing Championships, 1978; selected for Moscow Olympics, GB Fencing Team, 1980. *Publications:* articles in various legal jls. *Address:* Royal Courts of Justice, Strand, WC2A 2LL. *Club:* Hawks (Cambridge).

See also G. F. A. Etherton.

ETIANG, Paul Orono, BA London; Chairman: Rock FM Radio Ltd, since 2002; Uganda Railways Corporation, 2003–06; *b* 15 Aug. 1938; *s* of late Kezironi Orono and Mirabu Achom Orono; *m* 1967, Zahra Ali Foum; two *s* two *d*. *Educ:* Makerere Univ. Coll. Uganda Admin Officer, 1962–64; Asst Sec., Foreign Affairs, 1964–65; 3rd Sec., 1965–66, 2nd Sec., 1966–67, Uganda Embassy, Moscow; 1st Sec., Uganda Mission to UN, New York, 1968; Counsellor, 1968–69, High Commissioner, 1969–71, Uganda High Commission, London; Chief of Protocol and Marshal of the Diplomatic Corps, Uganda, 1971; Permanent Sec., Uganda Min. of Foreign Affairs, 1971–73; Minister of State for Foreign Affairs, 1973; Minister of State in the President's office, 1974; Minister of Transport and Communications, July 1976, of Transport, Communications and Works, Mar. 1977, of Transport and Works, 1978; an Asst Sec.-Gen., OAU, Addis Ababa, 1978–87; Minister for Regl Co-operation, March–Dec. 1988; Minister: of Commerce, 1989–91; of Information, 1991–96; Third Dep. Prime Minister, 1996–98; Minister: of Labour and Social Services, 1996–98; for Disaster Preparedness and Refugees, 1998–99. *Recreations:* chess, classical music, billiards. *Address:* Kampala, Uganda.

EUROPE, Suffragan Bishop in; *see* Gibraltar in Europe, Suffragan Bishop of.

EUROPE, Archdeacon in; *see* Williams, Ven. C. H.

EUSTACE, Dudley Graham, FCA; Chairman, Smith & Nephew plc, 2000–06; *b* 3 July 1936; *s* of Albert and Mary Eustace; *m* 1964, Carol Diane Zakrajsek; two *d*. *Educ:* Cathedral Sch., Bristol; Univ. of Bristol (BA Econ). FCA 1972. John Barritt & Son, Hamilton, Bermuda, 1962; Internat. Resort Facilities, Ont, 1963; Aluminium Securities Ltd, Montreal, 1964–65; Aluminium Co. of Canada Ltd, Vancouver, 1966–69, Montreal, 1969–73; Alcan Aluminio America Latina, Buenos Aires, 1973–76, Rio de Janeiro, 1976–79; Empresa Nacional del Aluminio, Madrid, 1979–83; Alcan Aluminium Ltd, Montreal, 1983–84; British Alcan Aluminium PLC, Gerrards Cross, Bucks, 1984–87; BAe, 1987–92 (Finance Dir, 1988–92); Chief Financial Officer, 1992–97, Vice Pres., 1992, Exec. Vice Pres. and Dep. Chm., 1992–99, Philips Electronics NV, Eindhoven. Chm., Sendo Hldgs PLC, 2000–05; Chief Financial Officer, Royal Ahold NV, 2003; Member, Advisory Council: Bayerische Landesbank, Munich, 1995–99; Rothschilds, 2005–12; Member, Supervisory Board: Aegon NV, 1997–2010 (Chm. Bd, 2005–10); Hagemeyer NV, 1999–2006; KLM Royal Dutch Airlines, 1999–2004; Charterhouse Vermogensbeheer BV, 1999–2014; KPN NV, 2000–08; Stork NV, 2007–08; Mem., Adv. Bd, Vallstein NV, 2009–11; Member, Board: sonae.com SGPS, 1999–2003; Providence Capital NV, 2008–. Chm., Nielsen Co., 2005–09. Member: Council, ECGD, 1988–92; Bd, Assoc. for Monetary Union in Europe, 1992–99; Bd, Amsterdam Inst. of Finance, 2001–05. Mem. Council, Univ. of Surrey, 2005–14 (Vice Chm., 2007–14). Liveryman, Chartered Accountants' Co., 1991. Officier, Order of Oranje-Nassau (Netherlands), 2013. *Recreations:* gardening, reading, fishing. *Address:* Avalon, Old Barn Lane, Churt, Surrey GU10 2NA.

EUSTICE, (Charles) George; MP (C) Camborne and Redruth, since 2010; Minister of State, Department for Environment, Food and Rural Affairs, since 2015; *b* Penzance, 1971; *s* of Paul Eustice and Adele Eustice. *Educ:* Truro Cathedral Sch.; Truro Sch.; Cornwall Coll.; Writtle Coll. Dir, Trevaskis Farm Ltd, 1996–99; Campaign Dir, No Campaign Against the Euro, 1999–2003; Hd of Press, Conservative Party, 2003–05; Press Sec. to Rt Hon. David Cameron, MP, 2005–07; Hd, External Relns, Conservative Party, 2008–09; Associate Dir, Portland PR, 2009–10. Parly Under-Sec. of State, DEFRA, 2013–15. *Recreation:* running. *Address:* House of Commons, SW1A 0AA. *T:* (020) 7219 7032. *E:* george.eustice.mp@parliament.uk.

EUSTON, Earl of; Alfred James Charles FitzRoy; *b* 26 Dec. 2012; *s* and *heir* of Duke of Grafton, *qv*.

EVAIN, Christophe; Chief Executive Officer, Intermediate Capital Group plc, since 2010; *b* Paris 14, 14 June 1962; *m* 1988, Priscille Jeanne Genevieve; two *s* one *d*. *Educ:* Dauphine Univ., Paris (Master of Strategic Mgt 1987). Credit Analyst, Corporate Treasury and Ops, Credit Lyonnais, USA, 1987–88; Asst Accounts Exec., National Westminster Bank, Paris, 1988–91; Asst Dir, Strategic Finance Unit, Banque de Gestion Privée, Paris, 1991–94; Intermediate Capital Group plc, 1994–, a Man. Dir, 2005–. *Recreations:* music and film, reading about history, Rugby, good quality wine. *Address:* Intermediate Capital Group plc, Juxon House, 100 St Paul's Churchyard, EC4M 8BU. *T:* (020) 3201 7700.

EVAN, Prof. Gerard Ian, PhD; FRS 2004; FMedSci; Sir William Dunn Professor of Biochemistry, and Head, Department of Biochemistry, University of Cambridge, since 2009; *b* 17 Aug. 1955; *s* of Robert Evan (*née* Ekstein) and Gwendoline Evan; one *s* one *d*. *Educ:* St Peter's Coll., Oxford (BA, MA); King's Coll., Cambridge (PhD 1982). Asst Mem., Ludwig Inst. for Cancer Res., Cambridge, 1984–88; Principal Scientist, ICRF, London, 1988–99; Royal Soc. Napier Res. Prof., UCL, 1996–99; Gerson and Barbara Bass Bakar Distinguished Prof. of Cancer Biol., UCSF, 1999–2009. Mem., EMBO, 1996. FMedSci 1999. Joseph Steiner Prize in Cancer Res., 1996. *Publications:* contrib. numerous res. pubns to learned jls. *Recreations:* hiking, music, mountain biking. *Address:* Department of Biochemistry, University of Cambridge, Tennis Court Road, Cambridge CB2 1GA. *E:* gie20@cam.ac.uk.

EVANS; *see* Parry-Evans and Parry Evans.

EVANS, family name of **Baroness Blackstone** and **Barons Evans of Parkside, Evans of Temple Guiting, Evans of Watford** and **Mountevans**.

EVANS OF BOWES PARK, Baroness *cr* 2014 (Life Peer), of Bowes Park in the London Borough of Haringey; **Natalie Jessica Evans;** a Baroness in Waiting (Government Whip), since 2015; *b* London, 29 Nov. 1975; *d* of Nicholas David Evans and Ann Elizabeth Evans; *m* 2010, James Oliver Wild. *Educ:* Henrietta Barnett Sch.; New Hall, Cambridge (BA Social and

Political Sci. 1998). Hd of Policy, British Chambers of Commerce, 2006–08; Dep. Dir, Policy Exchange, 2008–11; Chief Operating Officer, 2011–12, Dir, 2012–15, New Schools Network. *Recreations:* cricket, football, theatre, travel, fine wine. *Address:* House of Lords, SW1A 0PW.

EVANS OF PARKSIDE, Baron *cr* 1997 (Life Peer), of St Helens, in the co. of Merseyside; **John Evans;** Chairman of Labour Party, 1991–92; *b* 19 Oct. 1930; *s* of late James Evans, miner and Margaret (*née* Robson); *m* 1959, Joan Slater; two *s* one *d. Educ:* Jarrow Central School. Apprentice Marine Fitter, 1946–49 and 1950–52; Nat. Service, Royal Engrs, 1949–50; Engr, Merchant Navy, 1952–55; joined AUEW (later AEU), 1952; joined Labour Party, 1955; worked in various industries as fitter, ship-building and repairing, steel, engineering, 1955–65, 1968–74. Mem. Hebburn UDC, 1962, Leader 1969, Chm. 1972; Sec./Agent Jarrow CLP, 1965–68. MP (Lab) Newton, Feb. 1974–1983, St Helens, North, 1983–97. An Asst Govt Whip, 1978–79; Opposition Whip, 1979–80; PPS to Leader of Labour Party, 1980–83; opposition spokesman on employment, 1983–87. Mem., European Parlt, 1975–78; Chm., Regional Policy, Planning and Transport Cttee, European Parlt, 1976–78. Mem., Lab Party NEC, 1982–96. Mem., H of L, 1997–2015. *Recreations:* watching football, reading, gardening. *Address:* 6 Kirkby Road, Culcheth, Warrington, Cheshire WA3 4BS. *Clubs:* Labour (Earlestown); Daten (Culcheth).

EVANS OF TEMPLE GUITING, Baron *cr* 2000 (Life Peer), of Temple Guiting in the co. of Gloucestershire; **Matthew Evans,** CBE 1998; Chairman, EFG Private Bank Ltd, 2008–14 (Adviser to Chief Executive Officer, 2007–08); a Lord in Waiting (Government Whip), 2002–07; Chairman, Faber & Faber Ltd, 1981–2002 (Managing Director, 1972–93); *b* 7 Aug. 1941; *s* of late George Ewart Evans, and Florence Ellen Evans; *m* 1st, 1966, Elizabeth Amanda (*née* Mead) (marr. diss. 1991); two *s*; 2nd, 1991, Caroline Jayne Michel, *qv*; two *s* one *d. Educ:* Friends' Sch., Saffron Walden; LSE (BScEcon). Bookselling, 1963–64; Faber & Faber, 1964–2002. Chairman: National Book League, 1982–84; English Stage Company, 1984–90; Library and Information Commn, 1995–99 (Chm. Working Gp on New Library: The People's Network, 1997); Re:source (Museums, Libraries and Archives Council), 2000–02. Shadow Minister for the Arts, H of L, 2010–12. Dir, Which? Ltd, 1997–2000. Member: Council, Publishers Assoc., 1978–84; Literary Adv. Panel, British Council, 1986–97; DCMS Adv. Panel for Public Appts, 1996–2002; Arts Council Nat. Lottery Adv. Panel, 1997–99; Univ. for Industry Adv. Gp, 1997; Sir Richard Eyre's Working Gp on Royal Opera House, 1997; Arts and Humanities Res. Bd, 1998–2002. Pres., British Antique Dealers Assoc., 2013–. Mem., Franco-British Soc., 1981–95. Governor, BFI, 1982–97 (Vice Chm., 1996–97). FRSA 1990; Hon. FRCA 1999; Hon. FCLIP (Hon. FLA 1999). *Recreation:* cricket. *Address:* House of Lords, SW1A 0PW. *Club:* Groucho (Founder Mem., and Dir, 1982–97).

EVANS OF TEMPLE GUITING, Lady; *see* Michel, C. J.

EVANS OF WATFORD, Baron *cr* 1998 (Life Peer), of Chipperfield in the co. of Hertfordshire; **David Charles Evans;** Director, Newsdesk Media Ltd, since 2012 (Chairman, 2013–14); Chairman, Senate Consulting Ltd, since 2002; *b* 30 Nov. 1942; *s* of Arthur and Phyllis Evans; *m* 1966, June Scaldwell (marr. diss. 2008); one *s* one *d*; one *s* by Jeanne Pieplenbosch. *Educ:* Hampden Secondary Sch.; Watford Coll. of Technology. Apprentice printer, Stone and Cox Ltd, 1957. Founded: Centurion Press Ltd, 1971; (with Susanne Lawrence) Personnel Publications Ltd, 1975; Centurion Press bv, 1975; Chairman: Centurion Press Gp, 1971–2002; Senate Media (formerly Centurion Media) Gp bv, 1974–2002; Personnel Publications Ltd, 1981–2011; Redactive Publishing (formerly Centurion Publishing) Ltd, 1995–2011; Inst. for Collaborative Working (formerly Partnership Sourcing Ltd), 2002–; TU Ink Ltd, 2005–; Kennedy Scott Ltd, 2014–; Indigo Publishing Ltd; Evans Mitchell Books; One Gold Radio; Advanced Oncotherapy plc; Ace Consortium Ltd; Ace Funding Ltd; Forum Print Mgt Ltd. Non-exec. Dir, Care Capital plc. Director: RAF; Watford Community Events; Dep. Chm., Internat. Medical Educn Trust; former Dir, KISS 100 FM; former Mem. Develt Bd, UCL Hosp. Charitable Trust. Mem., H of L Select Cttee for Small and Medium Enterprises, 2012–13. Former Trustee, RAF Mus. Hon. Fellow, Cancer Research UK. Patron: Watford Peace Hospice; VITAL; Alma Hosp. Trust; Eliminating Domestic Violence. Freeman, Marketors' Co., 1991. FCIM 1991; FCGI 2001. *Publications:* articles on marketing, print management and purchasing. *Recreations:* theatre, art, reading, travel. *Address:* Newsdesk Media Ltd, 184–192 Drummond Street, NW1 3HP. *T:* (020) 7650 1639. *E:* lordevans@senateconsulting.co.uk.

EVANS OF WEARDALE, Baron *cr* 2014 (Life Peer), of Toys Hill in the County of Kent; **Jonathan Douglas Evans,** KCB 2013; DL; Director-General, Security Service, 2007–13; *b* 1958. *Educ:* Sevenoaks Sch.; Bristol Univ. (BA Classical Studies). Security Service, 1980–2013; Dep. Dir-Gen., 2005–07. Non-exec. Dir, HSBC, 2013–. Sen. Associate Fellow, RUSI, 2013– (Mem. Council, 2007–10). Hon. Prof., Univ. of St Andrews, 2013–. Mem., Adv. Bd, Darktrace, 2013–. Patron: Sevenoaks Sch., 2012–; W Kent YMCA, 2013–. Freeman, City of London, 2011; Liveryman, Skinners' Co., 2013–. DL Kent, 2015. Hon. LLD Bristol, 2008. *Recreations:* classic cars, town and country walks. *Address:* House of Lords, SW1A 0PW.

EVANS, Alan; *see* Evans, D. A.

EVANS, Dr Alison Margaret; Chief Commissioner, Independent Commission for Aid Impact, since 2015; *b* Sutton Coldfield, 7 July 1962; *d* of Geoffrey Morris Evans and Margaret Evans; civil partnership 2007, Jan Mathew; one *s* two *d. Educ:* Univ. of Sussex (BA Hons 1st Cl. Econs 1983; DPhil Develt Studies 1997); Queens' Coll., Cambridge (MPhil Econs and Politics of Develt 1984). University of Sussex: Res. Officer, Inst. of Develt Studies, 1983–89; Lectr in Econs, 1990–94; Sen. Economist, 1994–97, Sen. Evaluation Officer, 1997–2000, World Bank; Dir, Progs, 2006–09, Dir, 2009–13, ODI. Non-exec. Dir, Oxford Policy Mgt, 2013–15. Mem., Adv. Council, Queen Elizabeth House, Oxford, 2009–13. Trustee: BBC Media Action (formerly BBC World Service Trust), 2010–; Social Finance, 2014–. *Recreations:* film, literature, walking, theatre.

EVANS, Alun; *see* Evans, T. A.

EVANS, Alun Trevor Bernard; Chief Executive and Secretary, British Academy, since 2015; *b* 8 Dec. 1958; *s* of late Thomas Francis Evans and Marjorie Gladys Evans (*née* Macken); *m* 1986, Ingrid Elisabeth Dammers; two *d. Educ:* County Sch., Ashford, Middx; Essex Univ. (BA Hons); Birmingham Univ. (MPhil 1983). Civil Servant, Dept of Employment, subseq. DfEE, 1983–98: Private Sec. to Paymaster Gen. and Minister for Employment, 1986; Asst Regl Dir, Eastern Reg., 1992–93; Hd, Nuclear Safety Policy Div., HSE, 1993–94; Principal Private Sec. to Sec. of State for Employment, 1994–95, to Sec. of State for Educn and Employment, 1995–98; Hd, Strategic Communications Unit, Prime Minister's Office, 1998–2000; Dir of Communications, DETR, then DTLR, 2000–01; Sec. to Inquiry into lessons to be learned from foot and mouth disease outbreak, 2001–02; Cabinet Office, 2002–03; Dir of Civil Resilience, ODPM, subseq. of Fire and Resilience, DCLG, 2003–06; Director General: Transformation, DCLG, 2006–08; Sci. and Res., DIUS, 2008; Dir, Policy and Analysis Profession, DIUS, 2008–09; Dir, Delivery and Implementation, later Strategy, BIS, 2009–10; Sec., Detainee Inquiry, 2010–12; Dir, Scotland Office, 2012–15. Sen. Fellow (pt-time), Inst. for Government, 2011–; Gwilym Gibbon Fellow, Nuffield Coll., Oxford, 2014–. *Recreations:* political history, family, cricket, running, art, opera. *Address:* British Academy, 10–11 Carlton House Terrace, SW1Y 5AH. *Clubs:* Occasionals, Mandarins Cricket.

See also R. J. E. Evans.

EVANS, Amanda Louise Elliot, (Mrs A. S. Duncan); freelance writer, editor and editorial consultant, since 1997; reflexologist specialising in fertility, pregnancy and babies, since 2009; *b* 19 May 1958; *d* of late Brian Royston Elliot Evans and of June Annabella (*née* Gilderdale); *m* 1989, Andrew Sinclair Duncan; one *s* two *d. Educ:* Tonbridge Girls' Grammar Sch. Editorial writer, Interiors magazine, 1981–83; Consultant Editor, Mitchell Beazley Publishers, 1983–84; freelance writer and stylist on A la carte, Tatler, Country Homes & Interiors, Sunday Times, 1984–86; Dep. Editor, April–Oct. 1986, Editor, 1986–96, Homes & Gardens. *Publications:* Homes and Gardens Bedrooms, 1997; Making the Most of Living Rooms, 1998. *Recreations:* mountain walking, opera, camping. *Address:* 98 Addison Gardens, W14 0DR. *T:* (020) 7603 1574.

EVANS, Anne Celia; *see* Segall, A. C.

EVANS, Dame Anne (Elizabeth Jane), DBE 2000; soprano; *b* 20 Aug. 1941; *d* of late David and Eleanor, (Nellie), Evans; *m* 1st, 1962, John Heulyn Jones (marr. diss. 1981); 2nd, 1981, John Philip Lucas. *Educ:* Royal Coll. of Music; Conservatoire de Genève. Début, Annina in La Traviata, Grand Théâtre, Geneva, 1967; UK début, Mimi in La Bohème, Coliseum, 1968; Principal soprano, ENO, 1968–78; subseq. major rôles at Metropolitan Opera House, NY, San Francisco Opera, Deutsche Oper, Berlin, Dresden State Opera, Vienna State Opera, Paris Opéra, Rome Opera, Théâtre de la Monnaie, Brussels, Teatro Colón, Buenos Aires, Royal Opera House, Covent Garden, WNO, Scottish Opera; rôles include: Brünnhilde in Der Ring des Nibelungen (incl. Bayreuth Fest., 1989–92), Isolde in Tristan und Isolde, Sieglinde in Die Walküre, Elsa in Lohengrin, Elisabeth in Tannhäuser, Senta in Der fliegende Holländer, Leonore in Fidelio, Cassandre in Les Troyens, Chrysothemis in Elektra, Marschallin in Der Rosenkavalier, Ariadne in Ariadne auf Naxos; recitals incl. Edinburgh Fest., Wigmore Hall; Last Night of the Proms, 1997. Trustee, Countess of Munster Musical Scholarships, 2009–. FRWCMD (FWCMD 1996). Hon. DMus Kent, 2005. *Recreations:* cooking, gardening. *Address:* c/o Ingpen & Williams Ltd, 7 St George's Court, 131 Putney Bridge Road, SW15 2PA.

EVANS, Anthony; *see* Evans, D. A.

EVANS, Sir Anthony (Adney), 2nd Bt *cr* 1920; *b* 5 Aug. 1922; *s* of Sir Walter Harry Evans, 1st Bt, and Margaret Mary, *y d* of late Thomas Adney Dickens; *S* father, 1954; *m*; two *s* one *d. Educ:* Shrewsbury; Merton Coll., Oxford.

EVANS, Anthony Clive Varteg, FCIL; Head Master, King's College School, Wimbledon, 1997–2008; *b* 11 Oct. 1945; *s* of Edward Varteg Evans and Doris Lilian Evans; *m* 1968, Danielle Jacqueline Nicole Bégasse (*d* 1997); two *s. Educ:* De la Salle Grammar Sch., London; St Peter's Coll., Oxford (MA); University Coll. London (MPhil); Inst. of Educn, London Univ. (Advanced DipEd). FCIL (FIL 1975). Assistant Master: Eastbourne Coll., 1967–72; Winchester Coll., 1972–77; Hd of Mod. Langs and Hd of Humanities, Dulwich Coll., 1977–83; Headmaster, Portsmouth Grammar Sch., 1983–97. Headmasters' and Headmistresses' Conference: Chm., 1996; Mem., 1985–94, Chm., 1990–94, Acad. Policy Cttee; Mem., Common Entrance Cttee, 1988–90; Mem., Cttee, 1989–97; Mem., HMC/GSA Univ. Cttee, 1993–2002 (Co-Chm., 1993–95). Member: Admiralty Interview Bd, 1985–97; Nat. Curriculum Council, 1989–91; ISC Council, 1996–2000; HEFCE, 1999–2002; Bd, Assoc. of Governing Bodies of Ind. Schs, 2008–14; Chm., ISC Adv. Council, 1997–99; Co-Chm., ISC Unity Cttee, 1997–99; Chm., Large Ind. Day Schs Gp, 2002–06. Fellow, Winchester Coll., Hants, 1997–2006; Governor: Mall Sch., Twickenham, 1997–2007; Sevenoaks Sch., 2000–13 (Chm., 2008–13); Ecole Saint-Georges, Montreux, 2000–07; Perse Sch., Cambridge, 2003–05; Lancing Coll., 2008–15; Marlborough Coll., 2008–; British Sch. of Paris, 2010–. FKC 2008. *Publications:* Souvenirs de la Grande Guerre, 1985. *Recreations:* France, theatre, Southampton FC, avoiding dinner parties. *Address:* 15 Castelnau Mansions, Castelnau, Barnes, SW13 9QX; 15 Route de Saint Hubert, 33450 St Sulpice et Cameyrac, France. *Club:* East India.

EVANS, Rt Hon. Sir Anthony (Howell Meurig), Kt 1985; RD 1968; PC 1992; arbitrator; a Justice of the Court of Appeal, Bermuda, 2003–15; Chief Justice, DIFC Court, Dubai, 2005–10; Chairman, Dubai World Special Tribunal, since 2009; *b* 11 June 1934; *s* of late His Honour David Meurig Evans and Joy Diedericke (*née* Sander); *m* 1963, Caroline Mary Fyffe Mackie, *d* of late Edwin Gordon Mackie; one *s* two *d. Educ:* Bassaleg Sec. Grammar Sch., Mon; Shrewsbury Sch.; St John's Coll., Cambridge (BA 1957; LLB 1958). Nat. Service, RNVR, 1952–54 (Lt-Comdr RNR). Called to Bar, Gray's Inn, 1958 (Arden Scholar and Birkenhead Scholar; Bencher, 1979; Treas., 2000); QC 1971; a Recorder, 1972–84; a Presiding Judge, Wales and Chester Circuit, 1986–88; a Judge of the High Court of Justice, QBD, 1984–92; Judge in charge of the Commercial Court, 1991–92; a Lord Justice of Appeal, 1992–2000. Dep. Chm., Inf. Tribunal (Pres., Nat. Security Appeals), 2000–04; Vice-Pres., Internat. Cttee on Holocaust Era Insurance Claims Appeal Tribunal, 2000–06. Mem., Melbourne, Vic, Bar, 1975–84, Hon. Mem., 1985. Dep. Chm., Boundary Commn for Wales, 1989–92. Visitor: Cardiff Univ., 1999–2013; SOAS, 2002–07. Pres., Bar Musical Soc., 1998–2008. Hon. Fellow, Internat. Acad. of Trial Lawyers, 1985; FCIArb 1986 (Patron, Wales Br., 1988–98; Hon. Pres., 1998–2001; Companion, 2007). A Vice President: British Maritime Law Assoc., 1992–; Assoc. of Average Adjusters, 1997–. Freeman, 2000, Liveryman, 2001, Shipwrights' Co. *Publications:* (Jt Editor) The Law of the Air (Lord McNair), 1964. *Recreations:* sailing, music. *Address:* Essex Court Chambers, 24 Lincoln's Inn Fields, WC2A 3EG. *Clubs:* Royal Yacht Squadron; Royal Welsh Yacht.

EVANS, Prof. Anthony John, PhD; Professor in Department of Information and Library Studies (formerly Library and Information Studies), 1973–95, now Emeritus Professor, and Director, Alumni Office, 1992–95, Loughborough University of Technology, now Loughborough University; *b* 1 April 1930; *s* of William John and Marian Audrey (*née* Young); *m* 1954, Anne (*née* Horwell); two *d. Educ:* Queen Elizabeth's Hosp., Bristol (Pres., Old Boys' Soc., 1999); Sch. of Pharmacy and University College, Univ. of London. BPharm, PhD. Lectr in Pharm. Eng. Sci., Sch. of Pharmacy, Univ. of London, 1954–58; Librarian, Sch. of Pharmacy, Univ. of London, 1958–63; University Librarian, 1964–91, and Dean, Sch. of Educnl Studies, 1973–76, Loughborough Univ. of Technology. Pres., IATUL, 1970–75 (Bd Mem. and Treasurer, 1968–70; Hon. Life Mem., 1976–); Mem. Exec. Bd, IFLA, 1983–89 (Treas., 1985–89; Consultative Cttee, 1968–76; Standing Cttee on Sci. and Tech. Libraries, 1977–87; Standing Cttee on Univ. Libraries, 1989–93; Chm., Cttee on Access to Information and Freedom of Expression, 1995–97); Pres., Commonwealth Library Assoc., 1994–96; ASLIB: Vice-Pres., 1985–88; Mem. Council, 1970–80, 1985–88; Internat. Relations Cttee, 1974–85; Annual Lecture, 1985; BSI: Mem. Bd, 1984–86; Chm., Documentation Standards Cttee, 1980–86 (Mem., 1976–86); Member: Inf. Systems Council, 1980–86. Member: Adv. Cttee, Sci. Ref. Library, 1975–83; Vice-Chancellors and Principals Cttee on Libraries, 1972–77; Jt UNESCO/ICSU Cttee for establishment of UNISIST, 1968–71; Internat. Cttee, LA, 1985–96; Adv. Council to Bd of Dirs of Engineering Information Inc., USA, 1986–91; Chm., Adv. Gp on Documentation Standards, ISO, 1983–85; consultancy work for British Council, ODA, UNESCO, UNIDO, World Bank in Africa, Asia and Latin America, especially China, Kenya and Mexico. Pres., Jaguars Wheelchair Basketball Club, 1997–2004. Hon. FCLIP (Hon. FLA 1990). Medal IFLA, 1989. *Publications:* (with D. Train) Bibliography of the tabletting of medicinal substances, 1964, suppl. 1965; (with R. G. Rhodes and S. Keenan) Education and training of users of scientific and technical information, 1977; articles in librarianship and documentation. *Recreations:* genealogy, sport, especially wheelchair basketball. *Address:* The Moorings, Mackleys Lane, North Muskham, Newark, Notts NG23 6EY. *T:* (01636) 700174. *E:* ajevans54@btinternet.com.

EVANS, Anthony Thomas; a District Judge (Magistrates' Courts) (formerly Metropolitan Stipendiary Magistrate), 1990–2008; *b* 29 Sept. 1943; *s* of late Emlyn Roger Evans and Dorothy Evans; *m* 1st, 1965, Gillian Celia Mather (*d* 1988); one *s*; 2nd, 1991, Margaret Elizabeth Ryles (*née* Howorth); one step *s* one step *d*. *Educ:* Bishop Gore Grammar Sch., Swansea; Univ. of Manchester (LLB 1965; LLM 1968). Asst Lectr, Univ. of Manchester, 1965–68; admitted Solicitor, 1971; Partner: Haye & Reid, 1971–85; Evans & Co., 1985–89; sole practitioner, 1989–90. Chairman: Inner London Family Courts, 1991–2006; Inner London Youth Courts, 1993–2006. Mem., Criminal Procedure Rules Cttee, 2004–07. Mem., British Acad. of Forensic Scis, 1994. *Recreations:* reading, music, theatre.

EVANS, Bethan; Senior Partner, Bevan Brittan LLP, since 2012; *b* Wednesbury, W Midlands, 22 Jan. 1958; *d* of Dennis Evans and Sybil Evans; partner, Steve Evans. *Educ:* Queen Mary's High Sch. for Girls, Walsall; Univ. of Bristol (LLB Hons 1980); Guildford Law Sch. (Law Soc. Finals 1981). Trainee solicitor, Veale Benson Solicitors, Bristol, 1981–83; admitted as solicitor, 1983; Solicitor: Wansdyke DC, 1983–85; Bristol CC, 1985–88; Asst County Solicitor, Avon CC, 1988–96; Dir, Corporate Services, S Gloucestershire Council, 1996–99; Dir, Syniad, Cardiff, 1999–2002; Partner, Bevan Brittan LLP, 2002–. *Recreation:* living long enough to see any football team I support do anything decent (Walsall FC and England). *Address:* Bevan Brittan LLP, Kings Orchard, 1 Queen Street, Bristol BS2 0HQ. *T:* 0870 194 8993. *E:* bethan.evans@bevanbrittan.com.

EVANS, Carole Denise M.; *see* Mills-Evans.

EVANS, Charles A. W.; *see* Wynn-Evans.

EVANS, Christina Hambley, (Lady Evans); *see* Brown, Tina.

EVANS, Christopher; radio and television presenter; Executive Producer and Writer, UMTV, since 2002; *b* 1 April 1966; *m* 1991, Carol McGiffin (marr. diss.); *m* 2001, Billie Piper (marr. diss. 2007); *m* 2007, Natasha Shishmanian; two *s*; one *d* from a previous relationship. Started broadcasting career with Piccadilly Radio, Manchester; *radio:* producer and presenter, GLR; presenter: Radio One Breakfast Show, BBC, 1995–97; Virgin Radio Breakfast Show, 1997–2001; The Chris Evans Show, 2005–06, Drive Time Show, 2006–09, The Chris Evans Breakfast Show, 2010–, BBC Radio 2; *television:* presenter, Power Station, BSB Channel; Channel 4: co-presenter: The Big Breakfast, 1992–93; Top Gear, 2015–; devised, wrote and presented, Don't Forget Your Toothbrush, 1993 (BAFTA Award, 1995); TFI Friday, 1997–2000, 2015. Chairman: Ginger Prodns, 1993–2000; Ginger Media Gp, 1997–2000; Virgin Radio, 1997–2001. Radio Personality of the Year, TRIC, 1997, 2012; Sony Radio Awards for Entertainment Personality and Music Radio Personality, 2007. *Publications:* It's Not What You Think (autobiog.), 2009; Memoirs of a Fruitcake, 2010. *Address:* Zimple Ltd, Second Floor, Aldwych House, 81 Aldwych, WC2B 4HN.

EVANS, Christopher Charles, MD; FRCP, FRCPI; Consultant Physician, Cardiothoracic Centre and Royal Liverpool University Hospital, 1974–2003, now Emeritus; President and Chairman, Medical Defence Union, 2006–12 (Vice President and Vice Chairman, 2001–06); *b* 2 Oct. 1941; *s* of Robert Percy Evans and Nora Carson Evans; *m* 1966, Dr Susan Fuld; one *s* two *d*. *Educ:* Wade Deacon Grammar Sch., Widnes; Univ. of Liverpool Med. Sch. (MB ChB 1964; MD 1973). MRCP 1968, FRCP 1979; FRCPI 1997. Hon. Sen. Lectr, Univ. of Liverpool, 1974–2003. Consulting Medical Officer: Royal Sun Alliance, 1977–2005; Swiss Life, 1990–2005. Pres., Liverpool Med. Instn, 1991–92. Academic Vice Pres., RCP, 2001–03. Chm., NW Reg., British Lung Foundn, 1993–2000. *Publications:* (ed jtly) Symptoms and Signs in Clinical Medicine, 12th edn 1997; contrib. on general med. and thoracic topics, Thorax, BMJ, Lancet. *Recreations:* tennis, ski-ing, fell-walking, watching Liverpool FC, theatre, birdwatching. *Address:* Lagom, Glendyke Road, Liverpool L18 6JR. *T:* (0151) 724 5386. *E:* christoffe58@hotmail.com. *Clubs:* Reform; XX (Pres., 1993–94), Artists (Liverpool) (Pres., 2010–11); Liverpool Cricket (Pres., 2014–16).

EVANS, Christopher James; MP (Lab Co-op) Islwyn, since 2010; *b* Llwynipia, Rhondda; *s* of Michael Alan Evans and Lynne Evans; *m* 2013, Julia Teresa Ockenden. *Educ:* Porth Co. Comp. Sch.; Pontypridd Coll.; Trinity Coll., Carmarthen (BA Hist.). Office Manager, Jack Brown Bookmakers Ltd, 1998–2001; Personal Account Manager, Lloyds TSB Bank plc, 2001–03; Marketing Exec., Univ. of Glamorgan, 2003–04; Area Sec., Union of Finance Staff, 2004–06; Parly Researcher, Don Touhig, MP, 2006–10. Contested (Lab) Cheltenham, 2005. *Recreations:* running, reading, watching most sports. *Address:* (office) 6 Woodfieldside Business Park, Penmaen Road, Pontllanfraith, Blackwood NP12 2DG. *T:* (01495) 231990.

EVANS, Dr (Christopher) Paul; regeneration consultant, since 2008; Strategic Director of Regeneration and Neighbourhoods, London Borough of Southwark, 2001–07; *b* 25 Dec. 1948; *s* of Colwyn and late Margery Evans; *m* 1971, Margaret Beckett; two *d*. *Educ:* St Julian's High Sch., Newport; Trinity Coll., Cambridge (MA, DipArch, PhD). Department of the Environment, subseq. of the Environment, Transport and the Regions, then Department for Transport, Local Government and the Regions, later Office of the Deputy Prime Minister, 1975–2001: Private Sec. to Permanent Sec., 1978–80; Principal, 1980; Asst Sec., 1985; Under Sec., 1993; Dir, Urban Policy Unit, 1997–2001. Vice Chm., British Urban Regeneration Assoc., 2007–10; Dir, UK Regeneration, 2010–13; Dir, Catalyst Housing, 2010– (Vice Chm., 2014–).

EVANS, Air Marshal (Christopher) Paul (Anthony), CB 2014; QHP 2005; FRAeS; Surgeon General, since 2012; *b* 1954. *Educ:* MB BCh 1978; DAvMed 1987; MSc 1999. FRAeS 2009. Joined RAF as Med. Cadet, 1975; Jun. MO, RAF Wyton and RAF Hosps at Ely, Nocton Hall and Halton, 1979–83; SMO, RAF Leeming, Coltishall and Valley, 1983–90; Comd Flight MO, RAF Support Comd, 1990–92; OC Med. Wing, RAF Hosp. Wegberg, 1992–95; Medico-Legal Advr to DGMS(RAF), 1995–96; Course Leader, RAF Staff Coll., 1996; MO responsible for clin. policy, Surgeon Gen.'s Dept, 1997–99; Dir responsible for med. policy and plans, Directorate of DGMS(RAF), 1999–2002; MO lead on Surgeon Gen.'s Change Mgt Team, 2002–03; Dir Healthcare, Surgeon Gen.'s Dept, 2003–08; COS Health and DGMS, RAF, 2008–09; Comdr, Jt Med. Comd, 2009–12. *Address:* HQ SG, Coltman House, Defence Medical Services (Whittington), Coltman House, Lichfield, Staffs WS14 9PY.

EVANS, Sir Christopher (Thomas), Kt 2001; OBE 1995; PhD; CBiol, FRSB; CChem, FRSC; Founder and Chairman: Excalibur Fund Managers (formerly Merlin Biosciences Ltd), since 1996; Excalibur Group, since 2008; *b* 29 Nov. 1957; *s* of Cyril and Jean Evans; *m* 1985, Judith Anne; twin *s* two *d*. *Educ:* Imperial Coll., London (BSc 1979; ARCS 1979); Univ. of Hull (PhD). CBiol 1994, FRSB (FIBiol 1994); CChem 1995; FRSC 1995. Postdoctoral Res., Univ. of Michigan, 1983; Alleix Inc., Toronto, 1984–86; Genzyme Biochemicals Ltd, Maidstone, 1986–87; Founder and Director: Enzymatix Ltd, 1987–; Chiroscience plc, 1992–; Celsis Internat. plc, 1992– (Chm., 1998–); Cerebrus Ltd, 1995–; Founder, Director and Chairman: Toad Innovations plc, 1993–; Merlin Scientific Services Ltd, 1995–; Enviros Ltd, 1995–; Cyclacel Ltd, 1996–; Dir, Microscience Ltd, 1997. Founder: Merlin Fund, 1996; Merlin Biosciences Fund. Mem., Prime Minister's Council for Sci. and Technol. FRSA 1995; FMedSci 2003; Fellow: Bath Univ.; Univ. of Wales, Aberystwyth. Hon. Prof., Univs of Manchester, Liverpool, Exeter and Bath, and Imperial Coll., London; Hon. Fellow: UWCC, 1996; Univ. of Wales Swansea, 1996; Hon. FREng 2005. Hon. DSc: Hull, 1995; Nottingham, 1995; East Anglia, 1998; Cranfield, 1998; Bath, 2000. Henderson Meml Medal, Porton Down, 1997; SCI Centenary Medal, 1998; RSC Interdisciplinary Medal, 1999. *Publications:* numerous scientific papers and patents. *Recreations:* wife, Rugby, gym, fly-fishing, electric guitar. *Address:* Excalibur Fund Managers, Berkeley Square House, Berkeley Square, Mayfair, W1J 6BD. *T:* (020) 7887 7644.

EVANS, Air Vice-Marshal Clive Ernest, CBE 1982; DL; Senior Directing Staff (Air), Royal College of Defence Studies, 1988–91, retired; *b* 21 April 1937; *s* of Leslie Roberts Evans and Mary Kathleen Butcher; *m* 1963, Therese Goodrich (*d* 2013); one *s* one *d*. *Educ:* St Dunstan's Coll., Catford. Flying training, RAF, 1955–56; graduated as pilot, 1956, as qualified flying instr, 1960; served on Vampires, Jet Provosts, Canberras, Lightnings and F111s (exchange tour with USAF), 1960–72; RAF Staff Coll., 1972; PSO to Controller Aircraft, 1973; OC No 24 Sqn (Hercules), 1974–76; Nat. Defence Coll., 1976–77; DS RAF Staff Coll., 1977–79; Head of RAF Presentation Team, 1979–81; OC RAF Lyneham, 1981–83; RCDS, 1984; COS and Dep. Comdr, British Forces Falkland Is, 1985; Dep. Air Sec., 1985–88. Pres., Surrey Wing, ATC. DL Greater London, 1997. *Recreations:* reading, cricket, golf, gardening. *Address:* 43 Purley Bury Close, Purley, Surrey CR8 1HW. *T:* (020) 8660 8115. *Club:* Royal Air Force.

EVANS, Colin Rodney; Director, Weapon Systems Research Laboratory, Defence Science and Technology Organisation, Adelaide, 1989–91; *b* 5 June 1935; *s* of John Evans and Annie (*née* Lawes); *m* 1963, Jennifer MacIntosh; two *d*. *Educ:* Bridlington Sch.; Woolwich Polytechnic; Imperial Coll., London. BSc(Eng); HND; MIMechE. Scientific Officer, ARDE (now RARDE), 1959–60; Lectr, RNC, Greenwich, 1960–61; Scientific Officer, then Sen. Scientific Officer and PSO, ARDE, 1961–69; SO to Chief Scientist (Army), MoD, 1969–71; British Defence Staff, Washington, 1971–73; SPSO, RARDE, 1973–79; Dep. Dir, Scientific and Technical Intell., MoD, 1979–81; seconded to Sir Derek Rayner's study team on efficiency in govt, 1981; RCDS, 1982; Dep. Dir (1), RARDE, 1983–84; Asst Under Sec. of State, MoD, Dep. Dir (Vehicles) and Hd of RARDE (Chertsey), 1985–89. President: Kent Squash Rackets Assoc., 1992–2010; Maudslay Soc., 1993–99. *Recreations:* travel, tennis, bird watching, stamp collecting. *Address:* c/o HSBC, 105 Mount Pleasant, Tunbridge Wells TN1 1QP.

EVANS, Daniel Gwyn; Artistic Director, Sheffield Theatres, since 2009; *b* Rhondda, S Wales, 31 July 1973; *s* of Gwyn and Val Evans. *Educ:* Guildhall Sch. of Music and Drama (BA Acting). *Theatre* includes: *as actor:* A Midsummer Night's Dream, RSC and NY tour, 1994; Cardiff East, Peter Pan, RNT, 1997; Cleansed, Royal Court, 1998; Merchant of Venice, Troilus and Cressida, Candide, 1999, RNT; Merrily We Roll Along, Donmar Warehouse, 2000 (Olivier Award for Best Actor in a Musical, 2001); Other People, 2000, 4:48 Psychosis, 2001, Where Do We Live, 2002, Royal Court; Ghosts, English Touring Th., 2002; The Tempest, Crucible, Old Vic, 2002; Measure for Measure, Cymbeline, RSC, 2003; Cloud Nine, Crucible, 2004; Grand Hotel, Donmar Warehouse, 2004; Sunday in the Park with George, Menier Chocolate Factory, transf. Wyndhams, 2006, NY 2008 (Olivier Award for Best Actor in a Musical, 2007); Total Eclipse, Menier Chocolate Factory, 2007; Sweeney Todd, Southbank Centre, 2007; The Pride, Company, Crucible, 2011; *as director:* Crucible Theatre: Othello, Company, 2011; Macbeth, My Fair Lady (Best Regl Prodn, Whatsonstage Awards, 2014), 2012; This is My Family (Best Musical Prodn, UK Th. Awards, 2013), Oliver!, 2013 (Best Regl Prodn, Whatsonstage Awards, 2015); The Full Monty, 2013, transf. Noel Coward Th., 2014; Anything Goes, 2014; The Effect, 2015; American Buffalo, Wyndham's Th., 2015. Actor: *television* includes: Great Expectations, 1999; Love in a Cold Climate, 2001; The Vice, 2001; Daniel Deronda, 2002; To the Ends of the Earth, 2005; The Passion, 2008; *films* include: A Midsummer Night's Dream, 1996; Tomorrow La Scala!, 2002; Les Misérables, 2012; Gov. GSMD, 2012–14. DUniv Sheffield Hallam, 2012. *Recreations:* marathon running, cinema. *Address:* Crucible Theatre, 55 Norfolk Street, Sheffield S1 1DA. *E:* d.evans@sheffieldtheatres.co.uk.

EVANS, Dr (Daniel) John (Owen); President and General Director, Oregon Bach Festival, 2007–14; *b* 17 Nov. 1953; *s* of John Leslie Evans and Avis Evans (*née* Jones). *Educ:* Gowerton Boys' Grammar Sch.; University Coll., Cardiff (ATCL 1974; BMus 1975; MA 1976; PhD 1984). First Res. Schol., Britten-Pears Liby and Archive, Aldeburgh, Suffolk, 1980–84; Music Producer, BBC Radio 3, 1985–89; Sen. Producer, BBC Singers, 1989–92; Chief Producer, Series, BBC Radio 3, 1992–93; Head of Music Dept, BBC Radio 3, 1993–97; Head of Classical Music, BBC Radio, 1997–2000; Head of Music Programming, BBC Radio 3, 2000–06. Artistic Director: Volte Face Opera, 1986–89; Covent Garden Chamber Orch., 1990–94; Mem., South Bank Music Adv. Panel, 1994–96. Chm., IMZ Audio Gp, 1996–2000. Dir, The Britten Estate, 1999–2010; Chairman: Concentric Circles Theatre Co., 1999–2005; DreamArts, 2005–07; Member, Board: Chorus America, 2011–14; All Classical FM, Portland, Oregon, 2011–14. Chairman: Opera Jury for Royal Phil. Soc. Awards, 2000–05; Radio Music Jury, Prix Italia, 2005; BBC Choir of the Year, 2005; Mem., Opera Jury, Laurence Olivier Awards, 2000–02; Juror: BBC Singer of the World, Cardiff, 2003 and 2005; Music Broadcaster of the Year, Sony Radio Acad. Awards, 2006. Exec. Trustee, Peter Pears Award, 1989–92; Trustee: Masterprize Composing Competition, 1996–2001; Britten-Pears Foundn, 1999–2007; Britten-Pears Will Trust, 2006–; Britten Family and Charitable Settlement, 2006–. Vice Pres., Welsh Music Guild, 2005–. Prix Italia Award and Charles Heidsieck Award, 1989; Royal Philharmonic Soc. Award, 1994; Sony Radio Award, 1997. *Publications:* (with D. Mitchell) Benjamin Britten: pictures from a life 1913–1976, 1978; (ed) Benjamin Britten: his life and operas, by Eric Walter White, rev. edn 1982; (ed) Journeying Boy: the diaries of the young Benjamin Britten 1928–1938, 2009; contributions to: A Britten Companion, 1984; A Britten Source Book, 1987; ENO, Royal Opera Hse and Cambridge Opera guides on Britten's Peter Grimes, Gloriana, The Turn of the Screw and Death in Venice. *Recreations:* theatre, musicals, cooking, fine wines, entertaining, travel. *Address:* 7 Kingfisher House, Juniper Drive, Battersea Reach, SW18 1TX. *E:* djoevans@mac.com.
See also D. C. Evans.

EVANS, Dr David; *see* Evans, Dr W. D.

EVANS, David, CBE 1992; Director-General, National Farmers' Union, 1985–96 (Deputy Director-General, 1984–85); Director, Federation of Agricultural Co-operatives UK, 1995–2001; *b* 7 Dec. 1935; *yr s* of late William Price Evans and Ella Mary Evans; *m* 1960, Susan Carter Connal, *yr d* of late Dr John Connal and Antoinette Connal; one *s* (one *d* decd). *Educ:* Welwyn Garden City Grammar Sch.; University Coll. London (BScEcon). Joined Min. of Agriculture, Fisheries and Food, 1959; Private Sec. to Parliamentary Sec. (Lords), 1962–64; Principal, 1964; Principal Private Sec. to Ministers, 1970–71; Asst Sec., 1971; seconded to Cabinet Office, 1972–74; Under-Sec., MAFF, 1976–80; joined NFU as Chief Economic and Policy Adviser, 1981. Mem., EU Econ. and Social Cttee, 1998–2002. Director: ACT Ltd, 1996–2004; Drew Associates Ltd, 1997–2003. *Address:* 6 Orchard Rise, Kingston upon Thames, Surrey KT2 7EY. *T:* (020) 8336 5868.

EVANS, Rev. Canon David; Rector of Heyford with Stowe-Nine-Churches, 1989–2001, of Flore, 1996–2001, and Brockhall, 1997–2001; *b* Llanglydwen, Carmarthenshire, 15 Feb. 1937; *o s* of late Rev. W. Noel Evans, JP, and Frances M. Evans; *m* 1962, Jenifer Margaret (*née* Cross); three *s*. *Educ:* Sherborne; Keble Coll., Oxford (MA); Wells Theological Coll. (BD London). 2nd Lieut, Royal Signals, 1956–57. Minor Canon, Brecon Cath., and Asst Curate, Brecon St Mary with Battle, 1964–68; Bishop's Chaplain to Students, UC, Swansea, and Asst Curate, Swansea St Mary with Holy Trinity, 1968–71; Bishop of Birmingham's Chaplain for Samaritan and Social Work, 1971–75; Dir, Samaritans of Swansea, 1969–71, of Birmingham, 1971–75; Jt Gen. Sec., 1975–84, Gen. Sec., 1984–89, The Samaritans; Licensed Priest, Dio. of Oxford, 1975–89; RD of Daventry, 1995–2000. Chaplain, Northamptonshire Police,

1990–2001. Non-Residentiary Canon, Peterborough Cath., 1997–2001. Mem., Church in Wales Liturgical Commn, 1969–75. *Recreations:* music, railways, bird-watching. *Address:* Curlew River, The Strand, Starcross, Exeter EX6 8PA. *T:* (01626) 891712.

EVANS, (David) Alan; Director, Legal Services, Department for Business, Innovation and Skills, since 2012; *b* 21 Oct. 1965; *s* of David Lynn Evans and Sarah Eleanor Elvira Evans (*née* Rees). *Educ:* Olchfa, Swansea; London Sch. of Econs and Pol Sci. (BSc (Econ) Govt 1987). Macfarlanes, 1990–92; admitted as solicitor, 1992; Wilde Sapte, 1992–95; Taylor Joynson-Garrett, 1995–97; DWP, 1997–2000; Eur. Commn, 2000–02; Cabinet Office Legal Advrs, 2002–05; Director: DTI, 2005–09; HMRC, 2009–12. *Address:* Department for Business, Innovation and Skills, 1 Victoria Street, SW1H 0ET.

EVANS, Prof. David Alan Price, FRCP; Senior Consultant Physician (formerly Director of Medicine), Department of Medicine, Riyadh Armed Forces Hospital, Saudi Arabia, 1983–2007; Emeritus Professor of Medicine, Liverpool University, since 1994; *b* 6 March 1927; *s* of Owen Evans and Ellen (*née* Jones). *Educ:* Univ. of Liverpool (MD, PhD, DSc); Johns Hopkins Univ. RAMC, Jun. Med. Specialist, BMH Kure, Field Hosp. Korea, BMH Singapore and BMH Kinrara, Malaysia, 1953–55; Capt. RAMC, 1954–55. House Physician and House Surg. 1951–52, and Med. Registrar, 1956–58 and 1959–60, United Liverpool Hosps; Res. Fellow, Div. of Med. Genetics, Dept of Medicine, Johns Hopkins Hosp., 1958–59; Lectr 1960–62, Sen. Lectr 1962–68, Personal Chair, 1968–72, Dept of Medicine, Univ. of Liverpool; Prof. and Chm., Dept of Medicine and Dir, Nuffield Unit Medical Genetics, Univ. of Liverpool, 1972–83; Cons. Physician, Royal Liverpool Hosp. (formerly Royal Liverpool Infirmary) and Broadgreen Hosp., Liverpool, 1965–83. Visiting Professor: Karolinska Univ., Stockholm, 1968; Johns Hopkins Univ., 1972; Univ. Michigan at Ann Arbor, 1981. Lectures: Poulson Meml, Oslo Univ., 1972; first Sir Henry Dale, and Medallist, Johns Hopkins Univ., 1972; first Walter Idris Jones, Univ. of Wales, 1974; Watson Smith, RCP, 1976. Member: BMA, 1951; Assoc. of Physicians of GB and Ireland, 1964. Hon. LLD Liverpool, 2008. University of Liverpool: Roberts Prize, 1959; Samuels Prize, 1965; Thornton Prize, Eastern Psychiatric Assoc., 1964. Life Mem., Johns Hopkins Soc. of Scholars, 1972. Scientific Ed., Saudi Med. Jl, 1983–93; Member, Editorial Board: Internat. Jl of Clinical Pharmacology Res., 1980–; Jl of Saudi Heart Assoc., 1988–2005; Pharmacogenetics, 1995–2001. *Publications:* Genetic Factors in Drug Therapy, 1993; medical and scientific, principally concerned with genetic factors determining responses to drugs. *Address:* 28 Montclair Drive, Liverpool L18 0HA. *T:* (0151) 722 3112.

EVANS, (David) Anthony; QC 1983; a Recorder of the Crown Court, 1980–2003; *b* 15 March 1939; *s* of Thomas John Evans, MD and May Evans; *m* 1974, Angela Bewley, *d* of John Clive Bewley, JP and Cynthia Bewley; two *d. Educ:* Clifton Coll., Bristol; Corpus Christi Coll., Cambridge (BA). Called to the Bar, Gray's Inn, 1965, Bencher, 2004; in practice at the Bar, Swansea, 1965–84, London, 1984–2013; Hd of Chambers, 9–12 Bell Yard, 1996–2003. DTI Inspector, 1988–92. Chm., Jt Disciplinary Scheme Tribunals, 2000–05; Mem., Accountancy Investigation and Disciplinary Bd Tribunal, 2005–13. *Recreation:* sport of all kinds. *Address:* Carey Hall, Neath, W Glamorgan SA10 7AU. *T:* (01639) 643859; Flat 3, 115 Ifield Road, SW10 9AS. *T:* (020) 7370 1025. *Clubs:* Turf, MCC; Cardiff and County (Cardiff).

EVANS, David Christopher, (Christopher Dee); tenor; Founder, Director and Chorus Master, Maida Vale Singers, since 1999; *b* Morriston, Wales, 13 Dec. 1960; *s* of John Leslie Evans and Avis Evans (*née* Jones). *Educ:* Royal Welsh Coll. of Music and Drama (LWCMD); Guildhall Sch. of Music and Drama. Vocal contractor: Peacock Theatre: Side by Side by Jerome Kern, 1999; Man of La Mancha, 2000; A Funny Thing Happened…, 2001; Royal Albert Hall: Spirit of Fire, 2003; Strictly Gershwin, 2008, 2011; Danny Elfman's Music from the Films of Tim Burton, 2013, 2014; Alice in Wonderland, 2015; Festival Hall: A Salute to New York, 2003; Candide, 2005; Sweeney Todd, 2007; BBC Proms: Oklahoma!, 2002; HMS Pinafore, 2005; 60 Years of British Film Music, 2007; 75 Years of MGM Film Musicals, 2009; A Celebration of Rodgers and Hammerstein, 2010; Hooray for Hollywood, 2011; The Broadway Sound, 2012; Sondheim Inside Out, Queen Elizabeth Hall, 2013; *television*: Victoria Wood Christmas Show, 2001; Never Mind the Buzzcocks, 2003; *radio*: Der Kuhhandel, 2000; On Your Toes, 2002; Pal Joey, 2002; A Bernstein Celebration, 2004; Sondheim at 75, 2005; Friday Night is Music Night, 2005, 2010; Menna, 2008; A Tribute to Charles Strauss, 2008; Good Companions, 2009. Several recordings. *Recreations:* musical theatre, opera, theatre, bridge, fine wines, fine dining, board and card games. *Address:* 7b Lanhill Road, Maida Vale, W9 2BP. *T:* (020) 7266 1358. *E:* maidavalesingers@cdtenor.freeserve.co.uk.

See also D. J. O. Evans.

EVANS, Air Chief Marshal Sir David (George), GCB 1979 (KCB 1977); CBE 1967 (OBE 1962); Bath King of Arms, 1985–99; Deputy Chairman, NAAFI, 1991–2001 (Director, 1984–2001; President of Council, 1981–83); *b* Windsor, Ont, Canada, 14 July 1924; *s* of William Stanley Evans, Clive Vale, Hastings, Sussex; *m* 1949, Denise Marson Williamson-Noble (*d* 2009), *d* of late Gordon Till, Hampstead, London; two *d*, and two step *s. Educ:* Hodgson Sch., Toronto, Canada; North Toronto Collegiate. Served War, as Pilot, in Italy and NW Europe, 1944–45. Sqdn Pilot, Tactics Officer, Instructor, 1946–52; Sqdn Comdr, Central Flying Sch., 1953–55; RAF Staff Coll. course, 1955; OC No 11 (F) Sqdn, in Germany, 1956–57; Personal Staff Officer to C-in-C, 2nd Allied TAF, 1958–59; OC Flying, RAF, Coltishall, 1959–61; Coll. of Air Warfare course, 1961; Air Plans Staff Officer, Min. of Defence (Air), 1962–63; OC, RAF Station, Gutersloh, Germany, 1964–66; IDC, 1967; AOC, RAF Central Tactics and Trials Organisation, 1968–70; ACAS (Ops), 1970–73; AOC No 1 (Bomber) Group, RAF, 1973–76; Vice-Chief of Air Staff, 1976–77; C-in-C, RAF Strike Command, and UK NATO Air Forces, 1977–80; VCDS (Personnel and Logistics), 1981–83. Mil. Advr and Dir, BAe, 1983–92, and dir several BAe subsids; Chairman: BAe Canada Ltd, 1987–92; Arabian Gold, later Finngold Resources, plc, 1989–99; Dir, Intermin Resource Corp. Ltd, 1986 (Chm., 1989–93); Chairman: Officers Pensions Soc. Ltd; OPS Investment Co. Ltd; Trustees, OPS Widows' Fund; Dir, Airshow Canada. Queen's Commendation for Valuable Service in the Air (QCVSA), 1955. CCMI (CBIM 1978; Mem. Bd of Companions, 1983–; Dep. Chm., 1989–). *Recreations:* rep. RAF at Rugby football and winter sports (President: RAF Winter Sports Assoc.; Combined Services Winter Sports Assoc.); has rep. Gt Brit. at Bobsleigh in World Championships, Commonwealth Games and, in 1964, Olympic Games. *Address:* Royal Bank of Canada Europe Ltd, 71A Queen Victoria Street, EC4V 4DE. *Clubs:* Royal Air Force; Phyllis Court (Henley-on-Thames).

EVANS, David Howard; QC 1991; a Recorder of the Crown Court, 1992–2010; *b* 27 July 1944; *s* of David Hopkin Evans and Phoebe Dora Evans (*née* Reading); *m* 1973, Anne Celia Segall, *qv*; two *s. Educ:* London Sch. of Economics (BSc Econ 1965; MSc 1967); Wadham Coll., Oxford (BA 1970; MA 2002). Asst Economic Adviser, HM Treasury, 1967–68; called to the Bar, Middle Temple, 1972, Bencher, 2004; Asst Recorder of the Crown Court, 1987. *Recreations:* tennis, swimming, listening to music. *Address:* 33 Chancery Lane, WC2A 1EN. *T:* (020) 7440 9950.

EVANS, (David) Hugh; HM Diplomatic Service; Ambassador to Lao People's Democratic Republic, since 2015; *b* Santa Elena, Ecuador; *s* of David Evans and Mary Evans; *m* 1988, Nirmala Vinodhini; two *d. Educ:* St Joseph's Coll., Dumfries; Univ. of London (BA Hons 1st Mod. Hist., Econ. Hist. and Politics 1980); Univ. of Chicago (MA Pol Sci. 1982). Joined FCO, 1985; Res. Analyst, FCO, 1985–94; officer on loan to US State Dept, 1995–99; First Sec. (Pol), Nairobi, 2001–05; Dep. Hd of Mission, Khartoum, 2006–08; Mgt Counsellor, Moscow, 2008–12; Consul Gen., Erbil, 2012–14. Chm., Bd of Govs, Anglo-American Sch., Moscow, 2010–11. *Recreations:* travel, reading, theatre. *Address:* c/o Foreign and Commonwealth Office, King Charles Street, SW1A 2AH.

EVANS, David Julian; Director, Eastern India, British Council, 1999–2002; *b* 12 May 1942; *s* of David Thomas Evans and Brenda Muriel Evans (*née* Bennett); *m* 1967, Lorna Madeleine Jacques; three *s. Educ:* Fosters Sch., Sherborne; Queen Mary Coll., London Univ. (BA Hist. 1963). Teacher, Rajasthan, VSO, 1963–64; Mgt Trainee, J. Sainsbury Ltd, 1964–65; British Council: seconded to VSO, 1965–67; Sierra Leone, 1967–70; Dep. Rep., Wales, 1970–72; educn trng course, UC, Cardiff, 1972–73; Enugu, Nigeria, 1973–76; Dir, Istanbul, 1976–80; Dir Gen's Dept, 1980–81; Dep. Dir, Germany, 1981–85; Dir, Youth Exchange Centre, 1985–88; Dir, Drama and Dance, 1988–89; Dep. Dir, Arts Div., and Head, Arts Projects, 1989–94; Dir, USA, and Cultural Counsellor, British Embassy, Washington, 1994–98; Hd of Global Advice, Facilities Gp, 1999. Ind. Mem., Gen. Council, BUNAC, 2006–12. *Recreations:* the arts, history, travel, walking. *Address:* The Garret, Old Probate House, 5 Duncombe Place, York YO1 7ED. *T:* (01904) 621125.

EVANS, David Lewis; QC 2012; *b* Wegberg BMH, 4 Sept. 1963; *s* of Alan Evans and Janet Evans; *m* 1993, Caroline Lewis; one *s* one *d. Educ:* Monmouth Sch.; Christ's Coll., Cambridge (BA 1987). Called to the Bar, Middle Temple, 1988; in practice as a barrister, specialising in clinical negligence and regulatory, govt work, gp actions, public inquiries, inquests, 1988–; Mem., Attorney Gen.'s Panel of Counsel to the Crown (Common Law), 2004–12. *Recreations:* history, hill-walking, gardening, bee-keeping, lobster-potting. *Address:* 1 Crown Office Row, Temple, EC4Y 7HH. *T:* (020) 7797 7500. *E:* david.evans@1cor.com.

EVANS, David Lloyd C.; *see* Carey Evans.

EVANS, His Honour David Marshall; QC 1981; a Circuit Judge, 1987–2002, a Senior Circuit Judge, 2002–03; Designated Civil Judge, Liverpool Group, 1998–2003; *b* 21 July 1937; *s* of Robert Trevor and Bessie Estelle Evans; *m* 1961, Alice Joyce Rogers; two *s. Educ:* Liverpool Coll.; Trinity Hall, Cambridge (MA, LLM); Law Sch., Univ. of Chicago (JD). Called to the Bar, Gray's Inn, 1964. Teaching Fellow, Stanford University Law Sch., 1961–62; Asst Professor, Univ. of Chicago Law Sch., 1962–63; Lectr in Law, University Coll. of Wales, Aberystwyth, 1963–65; joined Northern Circuit, 1965; a Recorder, 1984–87. Mem., Vis. Cttee, Univ. of Chicago Law Sch., 1995–98. *Recreations:* walking, photography, visual arts, bird-watching, motorsport. *Address:* c/o Queen Elizabeth II Law Courts, Derby Square, Liverpool L2 1XA. *T:* (0151) 473 7373.

EVANS, David Morgan, FSA; General Secretary, Society of Antiquaries of London, 1992–2004; *b* 1 March 1944; *s* of David Morgan Evans and Elizabeth Margaret Evans (*née* Massey); *m* 1973, Sheena Gilfillan (*née* Milne); three *d. Educ:* King's Sch., Chester; UC Cardiff (BA 1966). MIFA 1983 (Hon. MIFA 2002); FSA 1987. Insp. of Ancient Monuments, Wales, 1969–77, England, 1977–92, DoE and English Heritage. Vis. Prof., Univ. of Chester, 2006–; Hon. Lectr, UCL, 2003–. Chm., Butser Ancient Farm Trust, 2003–11. Hon. Sec., All-Party Parly Archaeology Gp, 2004–08. *Publications:* Rebuilding the Past: a Roman villa, 2003; articles on heritage and law, heritage management, 18th century antiquarianism, early medieval western Britain. *Recreations:* walking, gardening, Montgomeryshire, opera.

EVANS, Rt Rev. David Richard John; an Assistant Bishop, Diocese of Coventry, since 2003; *b* 5 June 1938; *s* of William Henry Reginald Evans and Beatrix Catherine Mottram; *m* 1964, Dorothy Evelyn Parsons; one *s* two *d. Educ:* Caius College, Cambridge (Hons degree in Mod. Langs and Theology, 1963; MA 1966). Curate, Christ Church, Cockfosters, 1965–68; Missionary Pastor and Gen. Sec., Argentine Inter-Varsity Christian Fellowship, in Buenos Aires, Argentina, 1969–77; Chaplain, Good Shepherd Church, Lima, Peru, 1977–82; Bishop of Peru, 1978–88 (with delegated jurisdiction of Bolivia from 1980); Assistant Bishop: dio. of Bradford, 1988–93; dios of Chichester, Canterbury and Rochester, 1994–97; dio. of Birmingham, 1997–2003; Associate Priest, Stourdene Gp of Parishes, 2003–10. Gen. Sec., S Amer. Mission Soc., 1993–2003. Internat. Co-ordinator, Evangelical Fellowship of the Anglican Communion, 1989–2003. Pres., Church's Ministry among Jewish People, 2010– (Vice-Pres., 2009–10). *Publications:* En Diálogo con Dios, 1976; Have Stick: Will Travel… Mainly South American Journeys, 2012. *Recreations:* golf, philately. *Address:* 30 Charles Street, Warwick CV34 5LQ. *T:* (01926) 258791. *E:* bishopdrjevans@talktalk.net.

EVANS, Hon. Sir (David) Roderick, Kt 2001; a Judge of the High Court, Queen's Bench Division, 2001–13; Pro-Chancellor, Swansea University, since 2013; *b* 22 Oct. 1946; *s* of Thomas James and Dorothy Evans; *m* 1971, Kathryn Rebecca Lewis; three *s* one *d. Educ:* Bishop Gore Grammar School, Swansea; University College London (LLB 1967; LLM 1968). Called to the Bar, Gray's Inn, 1970 (Bencher, 2001), Lincoln's Inn *ad eund*, 2001; a Recorder, 1987–92; QC 1989; a Circuit Judge, 1992–2001; Resident Judge: Merthyr Tydfil Crown Ct, 1994–98; Swansea Crown Ct, 1998–99; Cardiff Crown Court, 1999–2001; Recorder of Cardiff, 1999–2001; Presiding Judge: Wales and Chester Circuit, 2004–07; Wales, 2007. Member: Criminal Cttee, Judicial Studies Bd, 1998–2001; Parole Bd, 2011–. Sec., Assoc. of Judges of Wales, 2008–12. Trustee, Aberglasney Restoration Trust, 2013–. Hon. Mem., Gorsedd of Bards, 2002. Visitor, Aberystwyth Univ., 2014–. Fellow: Univ. of Wales, Aberystwyth, 2003; Univ. of Wales, Swansea, 2007; Univ. of Wales, Bangor, 2010. *Recreations:* reading, walking, Welsh ceramics.

EVANS, Delyth; Executive Director, Dress for Success London, 2010–14; Chief Executive, Smart Works Charity, 2010–14; *b* 17 March 1958; *d* of David Gwynne Evans and Jean Margaret Evans; partner, Edward Charles Richards, *qv*; one *s* one *d. Educ:* Ysgol Gyfun Rhydfelen, Pontypridd; University Coll. of Wales, Aberystwyth (BA Hons French); Centre for Journalism Studies, Cardiff. Journalist, HTV Wales and BBC Radio 4, 1985–91; policy advr and speechwriter to John Smith, MP, Leader of Labour Party, 1992–94; Mgt Consultant, Adrian Ellis Associates, 1995–98; Special Advr to First Sec., Nat. Assembly for Wales, 1999–2000. Mem. (Lab) Mid and W Wales, Nat. Assembly for Wales, 2000–03. Contested (Lab) Carmarthen W and Pembrokeshire S, 2015. Policy and communications consultant, 2005–09. Mem. Bd, Film Agency for Wales, 2009–13. *Recreations:* keeping fit, reading, the arts, family activities.

EVANS, Derek; *see* Evans, J. D.

EVANS, Dylan J.; *see* Jones-Evans, D.

EVANS, (Elizabeth Gwendoline) Nerys; Director, Deryn Consulting, since 2012; *b* 22 March 1980; *d* of Glanmor and Wendy Evans. *Educ:* Univ. of Manchester (BA Hons Govt and Pol Theory 2001); Cardiff Univ. (MSc Hons Welsh Politics 2004). Plaid Cymru: Organiser and Press Officer, Carmarthenshire CC, 2002–03; Pol Officer, Nat. Assembly for Wales, 2003–07; Dir of Policy, 2008–12; Educn Comr for Welsh Govt, 2011–12. Mem. (Plaid Cymru) Wales Mid and West, Nat. Assembly for Wales, 2007–11. Contested (Plaid Cymru) Carmarthen W and Pembrokeshire S, Nat. Assembly for Wales, 2011. Mem., Williams Commn, 2012.

EVANS, Ena Winifred; Headmistress, King Edward VI High School for Girls, Birmingham, 1977–96; *b* 19 June 1938; *d* of Frank and Leonora Evans. *Educ:* The Queen's Sch., Chester; Royal Holloway Coll., Univ. of London (BSc); Hughes Hall, Cambridge (CertEd). Asst Mistress, Bolton Sch. (Girls' Div.), 1961–65; Bath High School (GPDST): Head of Mathematics Dept, 1965–72; Second Mistress, 1970–72; Dep. Head, Friends' Sch., Saffron Walden, 1972–77. Pres., GSA, 1987–88. Mem., Central Birmingham DHA, 1988–90. Mem.

Council: Aston Univ., 1989–98; Queen's Coll., Birmingham, 1996–2010; Birmingham Univ., 2000–05. FRSA 1986. Hon. DSc Aston, 1996. *Recreation:* music. *Address:* 26 Weoley Hill, Selly Oak, Birmingham B29 4AD.

EVANS, His Honour Fabyan Peter Leaf; a Circuit Judge, 1988–2005; *b* 10 May 1943; *s* of late Peter Fabyan Evans and Catherine Elise Evans; *m* 1967, Karen Myrtle (*née* Balfour), *gd* of 1st Earl Jellicoe; two *s* one *d*. *Educ:* Clifton College. Called to the Bar, Inner Temple, 1969. A Recorder, 1985–88. Resident Judge, Middx Guildhall Crown Court, 1995–2005. Chairman: Area Criminal Justice Liaison Cttee, London and Surrey, 1997–2000; London Area Criminal Justice Strategy Cttee, 2000–03. Mem., Parole Bd for England and Wales, 2005–15. *Recreations:* golf, sailing, singing (Chm., London Concert Choir, 2012–). *Clubs:* Brooks's; New Zealand Golf.

EVANS, Hon. Gareth (John), AC 2012 (AO 2001); QC (Vic and ACT) 1983; Chancellor, since 2010, and Honorary Professorial Fellow, since 2012, Australian National University; Professorial Fellow, University of Melbourne, 2011–12 (Hon. Professorial Fellow, 2009–10); *b* 5 Sept. 1944; *m* 1969, Merran Anderson; one *s* one *d*. *Educ:* Melbourne High Sch.; Melbourne Univ. (law and arts); Oxford Univ. (PPE). Lectr in Law, 1971–74, Sen. Lectr, 1974–76, Melbourne Univ.; practising Barrister, 1977–78. Senator (Lab) for Victoria, 1978–96; Shadow Attorney-General, 1980–83; Attorney-General, 1983–84; Minister for Resources and Energy, 1984–87, for Transport and Communications, 1987–88, for Foreign Affairs, 1988–96; Dep. Leader of Govt in Senate, 1987–93, Leader, 1993–96; MP (ALP) Holt, Vic, 1996–99; Dep. Leader of Opposition and Shadow Treasurer, Australia, 1996–98. Co-Chm., Internat. Commn on Intervention and State Sovereignty, 1999–2001; Pres. and Chief Exec., Internat. Crisis Gp, 2000–09, now Pres. Emeritus; Chm., World Economic Forum Peace and Security Expert Gp, 2003–06; Co-Chm., Internat. Commn on Nuclear Non-Proliferation and Disarmament, 2008–10; Member: Internat. Task Force on Global Public Goods, 2003–06; UN Sec.-Gen.'s High Level Panel on Threats, Challenges and Change, 2003–04; Commn on Weapons of Mass Destruction, 2004–06; Bd of Sponsors, Bulletin of Atomic Scientists, 2015–. Humanitas Vis. Prof. of Statecraft and Diplomacy, Univ. of Cambridge, 2013; Vis. Prof., Central European Univ., Budapest, 2014; Vis. Distinguished Diplomat in Residence, Indiana Univ., 2015. Hon. Fellow: Magdalen Coll., Oxford, 2004; Acad. of Social Scis in Australia, 2012; Australian Inst. of Internat. Affairs, 2012. Hon. LLD: Melbourne, 2002; Carleton, Canada, 2005; Sydney, 2008; Queen's, Canada, 2010. Franklin D. Roosevelt Four Freedoms Award for Freedom from Fear, 2010. *Publications:* (ed) Labor and the Constitution, 1972; (ed) Law, Politics and the Labor Movement, 1980; (ed) Labor Essays, 1980, 1981, 1982; (jtly) Australia's Constitution, 1983; (jtly) Australia's Foreign Relations, 1991, 2nd edn 1995; Co-operating for Peace, 1993; The Responsibility to Protect: ending mass atrocity crimes once and for all, 2008; (ed jtly) Nuclear Weapons: the state of play, 2013, 2nd edn 2015; Inside the Hawke-Keating Government: a cabinet diary, 2014. *Recreations:* reading, writing, travel. *Address:* Melbourne, Australia. *E:* ge@gevans.org.

EVANS, Gareth Robert William; QC 1994; a Recorder, since 1993; *b* 19 Jan. 1947; *s* of late David M. J. Evans and Megan Evans; *m* 1971, Marion Green; one *s* one *d*. *Educ:* Caerphilly Grammar Tech. Sch.; Birmingham Poly.; LLB Hons London. Called to the Bar, Gray's Inn, 1973, Bencher, 2007. Head of No 5 Chambers (Birmingham, London, Bristol), 2002–07; Leader, Midland Circuit, 2008–11. *Recreations:* watching Rugby, reading poetry, sailing, cooking, attempting to play golf. *Address:* No 5 Chambers, Fountain Court, Steelhouse Lane, Birmingham B4 6DR. *T:* 0870 203 5555, *Fax:* (0121) 606 1501. *E:* ge@no5.com.

EVANS, Gay Jeanette H.; *see* Huey Evans, G. J.

EVANS, George James; Sheriff of Tayside, Central and Fife at Cupar, 1997–2009; *b* 16 July 1944; *s* of Colin Evans and Caroline Catherine Kennedy MacPherson Harris; *m* 1973, Lesley Jean Keir Cowie; two *d*. *Educ:* Ardrossan Acad.; Glasgow Univ. (MA Hons); Edinburgh Univ. (LLB). Advocate, 1973; Standing Jun. Counsel, Dept of Energy, Scotland, 1982; Sheriff of Glasgow and Strathkelvin at Glasgow, 1983–97. *Publications:* contribs to legal periodicals. *Recreations:* art, literature, history, choral and individual singing, visiting English cathedrals. *Address:* Catherine Bank, Bridgend, Ceres KY15 5LS. *T:* (01334) 652121.

EVANS, Georgina Mary; *see* Mace, G. M.

EVANS, Prof. Gillian Rosemary, FRHistS; Professor of Medieval Theology and Intellectual History, University of Cambridge, 2002–05, now Emeritus; *b* Birmingham, 26 Oct. 1944; *d* of late Arthur Raymond Evans and Gertrude Elizabeth (*née* Goodfellow). *Educ:* King Edward VI High Sch. for Girls, Birmingham; St Anne's Coll., Oxford (MA 1966; DipEd 1967); Grad. Centre for Medieval Studies, Univ. of Reading (PhD 1974); DLitt Oxon 1983; LittD Cantab 1983. FRHistS 1978. Asst Mistress, Queen Anne's Sch., Caversham, 1967–72; Res. Asst, Univ. of Reading, 1974–78; Lectr in Theol., Univ. of Bristol, 1978–80; Lectr in Hist., Univ. of Cambridge, 1980–2002; British Acad. Res. Reader, 1986–88. Mem. Council, Univ. of Cambridge, 1997–2001. Called to the Bar, Gray's Inn, 2002. Vis. lectureships in USA and Canada and various European countries. Consulting Editor: Dictionary of Biblical Interpretation in English; Encyclopaedia of Medieval, Renaissance and Reformation Christian Thought; Jl Hist. of Biblical Interpretation; Jl of ADR, Mediation and Negotiation; Series Ed., I. B. Taurus History of the Christian Church, 2005–. Mem., Civil Mediation Council, 2005–. Member: Faith and Order Adv. Gp, Gen. Synod of C of E, 1986–96; Archbp's Gp on Episcopate, 1987–90; English Anglican-Roman Catholic Cttee, 1997–2002. Officer, Council for Acad. Freedom and Acad. Standards, 1994–2003; Mem., Cttee for Auctores Britannici Medii Aevi, Brit. Acad., 1980–2001. Co-Founder, Oxcheps Higher Educn Mediation Service, 2004; Project Leader, HEFCE-funded project on dispute resolution in higher educn, 2007–10; Founder Mem. and Chief Exec., Improving Dispute Resolution Adv. Service, 2010–. Freeman, Co. of Educators (formerly Guild of Educators), 2004 (Liveryman, 2014–). Hon. DLitt: Nottingham Trent, Southampton Inst. of Higher Educn, 2001. FRSA 1996. *Publications:* include: Anselm and Talking About God, 1978; Anselm and a New Generation, 1980; Old Arts and New Theology, 1980; The Mind of St Bernard of Clairvaux, 1983; Alan of Lille, 1983; Augustine on Evil, 1983; The Anselm Concordance, 1984; The Logic and Language of the Bible, 2 vols, 1984–85; The Thought of Gregory the Great, 1986; (ed) Christian Authority, 1988; Problems of Authority in the Reformation Debates, 1992; Philosophy and Theology in the Middle Ages, 1994; The Church and the Churches, 1994; Method in Ecumenical Theology, 1996; The Reception of the Faith, 1997; Calling Academia to Account, 1998; The Medieval Epistemology of Error, 1998; Discipline and Justice in the Church of England, 1999; Bernard of Clairvaux, 2000; (ed) Managing the Church, 2000; (ed) A History of Pastoral Care, 2000; (ed) The Medieval Theologians, 2001; (jtly) Universities and Students, 2001; Law and Theology in the Middle Ages, 2002; Academics and the Real World, 2002; Faith in the Medieval World, 2002; A Brief History of Heresy, 2002; (ed) The First Christian Theologians, 2004; Inside the University of Cambridge in the Modern World, 2004; Wyclif, a Biography, 2005; Belief, 2006; The Church in the Early Middle Ages, 2007; The Good, the Bad and the Moral Dilemma, 2007; A History of Christian Europe, 2008; The Effort to Create a National System of Higher Education in Great Britain 1850–2010, 2009; The University of Cambridge: a new history, 2009; The University of Oxford: a new history, 2010; Roots of the Reformation: tradition, emergence and rupture, 2012; First Light: a history of Creation myths from Gilgamesh to the God-Particle, 2013; Edward Hicks: a pacifist bishop at war, 2014; A History of Western Monasticism, 2015; Medieval Christianity, 2016; contribs to jls, etc on medieval intellectual history, ecumenical theology, higher educn law and policy issues. *Recreation:* painting. *E:* gre1001@cam.ac.uk. *Clubs:* Nikaean, Royal Over-Seas League.

EVANS, Dame Glynne; *see* Evans, Dame M. G. D.

EVANS, Graham; MP (C) Weaver Vale, since 2010; *b* Poynton, Cheshire, 10 Nov. 1963; *s* of Gordon Evans and Violet Evans; *m* 1995, Cheryl Browne; two *s* one *d*. *Educ:* Poynton High Sch.; Manchester Metropolitan Univ. (BA Hons Business Studies 2000); Postgrad. Dip. Mktg Mgt 2001. BAE Systems, 1982; sales mgt, Sun Chemical, 1988–99; sales mgt, Hewlett Packard, 1999–2004. Mem., Macclesfield BC, 2000–09. Contested (C) Worsley, 2005. MInstD. *Recreations:* cricket, football, Rugby, running, 5-a-side, British history (military, social and economic; specialist First World War historian). *Address:* House of Commons, SW1A 0AA. *T:* (020) 7219 7183. *E:* mail@grahamevansmp.com.

EVANS, Sir Harold (Matthew), Kt 2004; author and editor; Editor at Large: The Week, 2001–12; Thomson Reuters, since 2011; *b* 28 June 1928; *s* of late Frederick and late Mary Evans; *m* 1st, 1953, Enid (marr. diss. 1978), *d* of late John Parker and of Susan Parker; one *s* two *d*; 2nd, 1981, Christina Hambley Brown (*see* Tina Brown); one *s* one *d*. *Educ:* St Mary's Road Central Sch., Manchester; Durham Univ. BA 1952, MA Dunelm 1966. Ashton-under-Lyne, Lancs, Reporter Newspapers, 1944–46 and 1949; RAF, 1946–49; Durham Univ., 1949–52; Manchester Evening News, 1952; Commonwealth Fund Fellow in Journalism, Chicago and Stanford Univs, USA, 1956–57; Asst Ed., Manchester Evening News, 1958–61; Ed., Northern Echo, 1961–66; Editor-in-Chief, North of England Newspaper Co., 1963–66; Sunday Times: Chief Asst to Editor, 1966; Managing Editor, 1966; Editor, 1967–81; Editor, The Times, 1981–82; Editor-in-Chief, Atlantic Monthly Press, NY, 1984–86; Founding Editor, Condé-Nast Traveler Magazine, 1986–90; Editl Dir, 1984–86, Contributing Editor, 1986–, US News and World Report, Washington; Vice-Pres. and Sen. Editor, Weidenfeld & Nicolson, NY, 1986–87; Pres. and Publisher, Random House Trade Gp, 1990–97; Editl Dir and Vice-Chm., NY Daily News Inc., US News & World Report, Atlantic Monthly, and Fast Company, 1998–99. Member, Executive Board: Times Newspapers Ltd, 1968–82 (Mem. Main Bd, 1978); International Press Inst., 1974–80; Director: The Sunday Times Ltd, 1968–82; Times Newspapers Ltd, 1978–82. Writer and presenter: Evans on Newspapers, BBC TV, 1981; A Point of View, BBC Radio 4, 2005. Hon. Vis. Prof. of Journalism, City Univ., 1978; Vis. Prof., Inst. of Public Affairs, Duke Univ., N Carolina, 1984. Fellow, Freedom Forum. Hon. FSIAD. Internat. Editor of the Year, 1975; Gold Medal Award, Inst. of Journalists, 1979; Hood Medal, RPS, 1981; Editor of the Year, 1982; President Award, D&AD, 1983; Lotos Club Medal, NY, 1993; Ortega y Gasset Prize, 2012. DUniv Stirling, 1982; Hon. DCL Durham, 1998. *Publications:* The Active Newsroom, 1961; Editing and Design (five volumes): vol. 1, Newsman's English, 1972; vol. 5, Newspaper Design, 1973; vol. 2, Newspaper Text, 1974; vol. 3, Newspaper Headlines, 1974; vol. 4, Pictures on a Page, 1977; Good Times, Bad Times, 1983, 4th edn 2011; (jointly): We Learned To Ski, 1974; The Story of Thalidomide, 1978; (ed) Eye Witness, 1981; How We Learned to Ski, 1983; Front Page History, 1984; The American Century, 1998; They Made America, 2004; My Paper Chase: true stories of vanished times (autobiog.), 2009. *Recreations:* swimming, music, chess, Sunday in the park with George and Isabel. *Clubs:* Garrick, Royal Automobile; Century, Yale (New York).

EVANS, (Henry) Nicholas; a District Judge (Magistrates' Courts) (formerly Metropolitan Stipendiary Magistrate), 1994–2014; *b* 7 Nov. 1945; 3rd *s* of Gilbert Arthur Evans and Muriel Elaine Evans (*née* Oxford); *m* 1980, Diana Claire Smith; one *s* one *d*. *Educ:* Highgate Sch. Called to the Bar, Middle Temple, 1971, Lincoln's Inn, *ad eundem*, 1975. *Clubs:* Garrick, Bar Yacht.

EVANS, Prof. (Hubert) Roy, CBE 2002; PhD; FREng; FICE, FIStructE; Vice-Chancellor, University of Wales, Bangor, 1995–2004; *b* 27 May 1942; *s* of David James Evans and Sarah Ann Evans; *m* 1966, Eira John; two *s* two *d*. *Educ:* Llandysul Grammar Sch.; University Coll. of Swansea (BSc, MSc; PhD 1967). Res. Fellow, University Coll. of Swansea, 1966–67; Asst Engr, Freeman Fox & Partners, 1967–69; University College, Cardiff, later University of Wales College of Cardiff: Lectr, 1969–75; Sen. Lectr, 1975–79; Reader, 1979–83; Prof. of Civil and Structural Engrg, 1983–95; Hd of Dept, 1984–95; Dean, 1987–88; Dep. Principal, 1990–93 and 1994–95. Vis. Prof., Univ. of W Virginia, 1983. FREng (FEng 1992); Founding FLSW 2010. Hon. Fellow: UC, Swansea, 1995; Univ. of Wales, Cardiff, 1998. Telford Premium, 1976, 1979 and 1987, George Stephenson Medal, 1980, ICE; Henry Adams Bronze Medal, IStructE, 1976; Medal, Acad. of Scis, Czech Republic, 1995. *Publications:* numerous contribs in field of structural engrg and plate structures. *Recreations:* hill-walking, gardening, cricket, soccer. *Address:* Pwllcorn, Moylegrove, Cardigan, Pembrokeshire SA43 3BS. *T:* (01239) 881274.

EVANS, Hugh; *see* Evans, D. H.

EVANS, Huw David; Director General, Policy, Association of British Insurers, since 2015 (Deputy Director General, and Director, Policy, 2013–15); *b* Banbury, 27 Aug. 1971; *s* of Anthony Evans and Geraldine Evans; *m* 2005, Katharine Mahoney; one *s* one *d*. *Educ:* Kingsfield Sch., Bristol; St Brendan's VIth Form Coll., Bristol; Lady Margaret Hall, Oxford (BA Hons 1993). Journalist, Newbury Weekly News, 1993–96; Press Officer, Labour Party, 1996–99; Dir, Communications, Welsh Labour Party, 1999–2001; Special Advisor: to Home Sec., 2001–04; to the Prime Minister, 2005–06; Sen. Manager, Gp Strategy, RBS, 2006–08; Dir, Ops, ABI, 2008–13. *Recreations:* family, Welsh Rugby, history, reading. *Address:* Association of British Insurers, 51 Gresham Street, EC2V 7HQ. *T:* (020) 7216 7401. *E:* huw.evans@abi.org.uk.

EVANS, Iain Richard, CBE 2013; FCA; Chairman, LEK Consulting (formerly L/E/K Partnership), 1991–2015; *b* 17 May 1951; *s* of late Alan Caradog Crawshay Evans and Barr Hargreave Bell (*née* Dalglish); *m* 1st, 1973, Zoe Dorothy Valentine (*d* 2002); two *s*; 2nd, 1988, Jayne Doreen Almond; one *d*. *Educ:* John Lyon Sch.; Rotherham Sixth Form Coll.; Bristol Univ. (BSc Hons 1972); Harvard Univ. Grad. Sch. of Business Admin (MBA with High Distinction, Baker Scholar, Loeb Rhoades Fellow, 1978). ACA 1975, FCA 1977. Arthur Young McClelland Moores & Co., 1972–76; Bain & Co., 1978–83, Partner 1982; Founding Partner, L/E/K Partnership, subseq. LEK Consulting, 1983. Non-exec. Dir, Hyder (formerly Welsh Water Authy, then Welsh Water) plc, 1989–98 (Dep. Chm., 1992–93; Chm., 1993–98). *Recreations:* tennis, golf, fishing, marine paintings. *Address:* c/o LEK Consulting LLP, 40 Grosvenor Place, SW1X 7JL.

EVANS, Dr (Ian) Philip, OBE 1999; FRSC; Head Master, Bedford School, 1990–2008; *b* 2 May 1948; *s* of Joseph Emlyn Evans and late Beryl Evans; *m* 1972, Sandra Veronica Waggett; two *s*. *Educ:* Ruabon Boys' Grammar Sch.; Churchill College, Cambridge (BA 1970; MA 1973; 1st cl. hons Nat. Scis Tripos); Imperial College of Science and Technology (PhD, DIC). CChem, FRSC 1997. Post-Doctoral Fellow, Res. Sch. of Chemistry, ANU, 1973–75; Asst Master, St Paul's Sch., 1975–90 (Head of Chemistry Dept, 1984–90). Member: Schs Exams and Assessment Council, 1991–93; SCAA, 1993–97; Qualifications and Curriculum Authority, 1997–99. Chief Examr, A-level Chem., Univ. of London Schs Exam. Bd, 1987–90. Member Council: Nat. Trust, 1999–2001; RSC, 2007–11 (Trustee, 2007–11; Chm., Educn Policy Bd, 2007–10; Mem., Sci., Educn and Industry Bd, 2011–14). *Publications:* (with S. V. Evans) Anyone for Science?, 1994; contribs to books; papers in learned jls. *Recreations:* music, cricket, poetry, wine. *Address:* Rue du Chagnot, Monthélie, Côte d'Or, 21190, France. *Club:* East India.

EVANS, James, CBE 1995; Chairman, Bristol United Press, 1997–2000; *b* 27 Nov. 1932; *s* of late Rex Powis Evans and Louise Evans; *m* 1961, Jette Holmboe; two *d*. *Educ:* Aldenham School; St Catharine's College, Cambridge (MA). Called to the Bar, Gray's Inn, 1959;

admitted Solicitor, 1972; recalled to the Bar, Gray's Inn, 1991, Bencher, 1993. Commissioned 26th Field Regt RA, 1951–53. Legal Dept, Kemsley Newspapers Ltd, 1956–59; practised at Bar, 1959–65; Legal Adviser: Thomson Newspapers Ltd, 1965–73; Times Newspapers Ltd, 1967–73; Sec. and Mem. Exec. Bd, 1973–78, Dir, 1978–86, Thomson Organisation Ltd; Dir, 1977–81, Chm., 1980–81, Times Newspapers Ltd; Chm., Thomson Withy Grove Ltd, 1979–84; International Thomson Organisation plc: Dir, 1978; Jt Dep. Man. Dir, 1982–84; Man. Dir and Chief Exec., 1985–86; Chm., 1986; Chm. and Chief Exec., 1982–84, Dir, 1982–96, Thomson Regional Newspapers Ltd; Dir, Liverpool Daily Post and Echo Ltd, 1996–97. Dir, 1983–90, Chm., 1987–89, Press Assoc.; Dir, Reuters Holdings, 1984–92. Mem., Monopolies and Mergers Commn, 1989–97. Dir, Press Standards Bd of Finance, 1990–2000. Trustee, Visnews, 1985–95. Member: Council, Newspaper Soc., 1984–2001 (Vice-Pres., 1998–99; Pres., 1999–2000); Press Council, 1987–90; Council of Legal Educn, 1992–94. Mem., Home Office Deptl Cttee on Official Secrets Act (Franks Cttee), 1971. *Recreation:* various. *Address:* 6 Fishpool Street, St Albans, Herts AL3 4RT. *T:* (01727) 853064. *Club:* Garrick.

EVANS, James Humphrey R.; *see* Roose-Evans.

EVANS, Jane Elizabeth; *see* Collins, Jane E.

EVANS, Jeremy David Agard; Director, Public Affairs, British Rail, 1990–97; *b* 20 June 1936; *s* of Arthur Burke Agard Evans and Dorothy (*née* Osborne); *m* 1964, Alison Mary (*née* White); one *s* two *d*. *Educ:* Whitgift Sch.; Christ's Coll., Cambridge (BA Hons). Ministry of Power, 1960–69; Sloan Fellow, London Business Sch., 1969–70; DTI, 1970–73; Asst Sec., DTI, 1973, Dept of Energy, 1974 (Offshore Supplies Office, 1973); seconded as Sec. to BNOC on its foundn, 1976–78; a Man. Dir, 1978; Man. Dir Corporate Develt, and Sec., 1980–82, Mem. Bd, 1981–82; Dir, Britoil plc, 1982–88. Mem., GDC, 1989–94. Gov., St Piers Sch., subseq. NCYPE, 1998–2001. *Recreations:* opera, ski-ing, walking, golf. *Address:* Dormans House West, Dormans Park, East Grinstead, West Sussex RH19 2LY. *T:* (01342) 870518.

EVANS, (Jeremy) Roger; Member (C) Havering and Redbridge, since 2000, and Deputy Mayor, since 2015, London Assembly, Greater London Authority; *b* 23 June 1964; *s* of Ronald Evans and Doris Valentine Evans. *Educ:* Univ. of Sheffield (BSc Hons 1985); Westminster Univ. (CPE); Inns of Court School of Law. Various managerial rôles, Royal Mail, 1985–95; law student, 1995–98; called to Bar, Middle Temple, 1997; legal advr, Spring Gp, 1998–2000. Member (C): Waltham Forest LBC, 1990 (Leader, Cons. Gp, 1994–98); Havering LBC, 2006–. *Recreations:* badminton, swimming, public speaking. *Address:* Greater London Authority, City Hall, Queen's Walk, SE1 2AA.

EVANS, Jillian; Member (Plaid Cymru) Wales, European Parliament, since 1999; President, Plaid Cymru, 2010–13; *b* 8 May 1959; *d* of Horace Burge and Valma Burge; *m* 1992, Syd Morgan. *Educ:* UCW, Aberystwyth (BA Hons Welsh); MPhil CNAA, 1986. Res. Asst, Poly. of Wales, Trefforest, 1980–85; self-employed administrator, 1986–89; Admin./Public Affairs Officer, 1989–93, Project Officer, 1994–97, NFWI Wales; Wales Regl Organiser, Child, Infertility Support Network, 1997–99. *Address:* 45 Gelligaled Road, Ystrad, Rhondda Cynon Taf, Wales CF41 7RQ.

EVANS, John; *see* Evans, D. J. O.

EVANS, Dr John; *see* Evans, Dr N. J. B.

EVANS, Prof. John, PhD; Professor of Chemistry, University of Southampton, since 1990; *b* 2 June 1949; *s* of Leslie and Eleanor Evans; *m* 1972, Hilary Jane Fulcher; two *d*. *Educ:* Rutherford Grammar Sch., Newcastle upon Tyne; Imperial Coll. London (BSc 1970; ARCS); Sidney Sussex Coll., Cambridge (PhD 1973). Research Fellow, Princeton Univ., 1973–74; Cambridge University: ICI Res. Fellow, 1974–75; Royal Soc. Pickering Res. Fellow, 1975–76; Southampton University: Res. Fellow, 1976–78; Lectr, 1978–84; Sen. Lectr, 1984–87; Reader, 1987–90; Dean of Science, 1997–2000; Hd of School, 2007–10. Science and Engineering Research Council: Chm., Synchrotron Radiation Cttee, 1991–94; UK Deleg. to Council of European Synchrotron Radiation Facility, 1991–94 (Mem., Scientific Adv. Cttee, 1995–98); Mem., Facilities Commn, 1993–94. Sci. Prog. Advr, Diamond Light Source Ltd, 2002–07 (Vice-Chm., Diamond Scientific Adv. Cttee, 2000–02). Member: Photon Sci. Adv. Cttee, Paul Scherrer Inst., 2009–13; ALBA Panel for Sci. Review, Barcelona, 2012–14; Diamond Peer Rev. Panel, 2012–15. Royal Society of Chemistry: Sec. and Treas., Dalton Div., 1993–96; Council Mem., 1994–97. Tilden Lectr, RSC, 1994. Editor, Inorganic Chemistry Series, Oxford Chemistry Primers Text Book Series, 1991–2000. Meldola Medal, RSC, 1978. *Publications:* contrib. scientific jls, incl. Jl RSC. *Recreations:* garden work, travel. *Address:* School of Chemistry, University of Southampton, Southampton SO17 1BJ. *T:* (023) 8059 3307.

EVANS, John; *see* Evans, M. J.

EVANS, John Alfred Eaton; Headmaster, Brentwood School, 1981–93; *b* 30 July 1933; *s* of John Eaton Evans and Millicent Jane Evans (*née* Righton); *m* 1958, Vyvyan Margaret Mainstone; two *s* one *d*. *Educ:* Bristol Grammar Sch.; Worcester Coll., Oxford. MA (Lit. Hum.). Nat. Service, 1952–54, commnd RAOC. Assistant Master: Blundell's Sch., 1958–63; Rugby Sch., 1963–73; Housemaster: Phillips Acad., Andover, Mass, USA, 1968–69; Rugby Sch., 1973–81. Chm., London Div., HMC, 1993. Member selection panels: CMS, 1983–91; Admiralty, 1985–96; Army Scholarship Bd, 1990–2002; ABM, 1992–2002. Chm. Trustees, Crescent Sch., Rugby, 1968–78; Governor: Colfe's Sch., 1993–2002; Prior Park Coll., 1998–2004; Mem. Adv. Bd, St Christopher's Sch., Burnham-on-Sea, 1994–97. FRSA 1983. *Publications:* various articles on community service in education. *Recreations:* cricket, Rugby fives, piano, singing, drama, walking. *Address:* Manor Farm House, Easton, near Wells, Somerset BA5 1EB. *Clubs:* Vincent's (Oxford); Savage (Bristol); Jesters; Cryptics Cricket.

EVANS, (John) Derek, CBE 2001; Chief Conciliator, Advisory, Conciliation and Arbitration Service, 1992–2001; *b* 11 Sept. 1942; *s* of late Leslie and Mary Evans; *m* 1964, Betty Wiseman; two *d*. *Educ:* Roundhay Sch., Leeds. FCIPD. Dept of Employment, 1962–74; Advisory, Conciliation and Arbitration Service: Midlands, 1974–78; Head Office, 1978–82; Dir, Wales, 1982–88; Dir, Adv. Services, 1988–91; Dir, Conciliation and Arbitration, 1991–92. Mem., Employment Appeal Tribunal, 2003–12; Chm., Agricl Wages Bd, 2003–13. Chm., URC (Wales) Trust, 2009–12 (Dir, 2007–09). Industrial Fellow, Kingston Univ., 1994–2013. Ind. Chm., Standards Cttee, Wokingham DC, 2002–04. *Recreations:* golf, driving, music. *Address:* 23 Ty-Gwyn Road, Rhiwbina, Cardiff CF14 6NF. *T:* (029) 2115 2077. *Club:* Whitchurch Golf (Cardiff).

EVANS, Sir John G.; *see* Grimley Evans.

EVANS, John Kerry Q.; *see* Quarren Evans.

EVANS, John Roger W.; *see* Warren Evans.

EVANS, Sir John (Stanley), Kt 2000; QPM 1990; DL; consultant in security and counter terrorism; Special Security Advisor: to the Football Association, 2004–09; to the England and Wales Cricket Board, since 2008; *b* 6 Aug. 1943; *s* of late William Stanley and Doris Evans; *m* 1965, Beryl Smith; one *s* one *d*. *Educ:* Wade Deacon Grammar Sch., Widnes; Liverpool Univ. (LLB Hons 1972). Liverpool City, then Merseyside Police, 1960–80; Asst Chief Constable, Greater Manchester Police, 1980–84; Dep. Chief Constable, Surrey Constabulary, 1984–88; Chief Constable, Devon and Cornwall Constabulary, 1989–2002. Pres., ACPO, 1999–2000. Chm., Police Athletic Assoc., 1996–2002 (Life Vice Pres., 2002). Chm., Your Radio Ltd, 2003–06. Prince's Trust: Chm., SW England, 2001–08; Mem., Nat. Trustees Council, 2005–07; Vice Chm., English Regions Council, 2005–07. Member: Public Inquiry into alleged sectarian murder of Robert Hamill, NI; several Police Appeal Tribunals. President: Devon and Cornwall Victim Support Schemes, 2002–07; Combined Community Watch Assoc., 2002–; Life Educn Wessex, 2010–; Ind. Chm., Wakeley Stakeholders Reference Gp, NHS Northern, Eastern and Western Devon, 2015–. Patron: Dream Away, 1990–; Wooden Spoon (Devon Co.), 2002–; Vice Patron, Exeter Leukaemia Fund, 2003–. Mem., Otter Valley Rotary Club, 2003– (Pres., 2012–13). DL Devon, 2000. *Recreations:* most sports (ran London Marathon, 1988, 1989), service and charitable activities. *Address:* c/o Woodbury Park Hotel, Golf & Country Club Ltd, Woodbury Castle, Woodbury, Exeter, Devon EX5 1JJ. *Club:* Woodbury Park Golf and Country (Pres., 2001–).

EVANS, Very Rev. (John) Wyn; *see* St Davids, Bishop of.

EVANS, (John) Wynford, CBE 1995; Chairman: Bank of Wales, 1995–2002; South Wales Electricity plc (formerly South Wales Electricity Board), 1984–95; *b* 3 Nov. 1934; *s* of late Gwilym Everton and Margaret Mary Elfreda Evans; *m* 1957, Sigrun Brethfeld; two *s* (and one *s* decd). *Educ:* Llanelli Grammar Sch.; St John's Coll., Cambridge (MA). FBCS. Served RAF (Flying Officer), 1955–57. IBM, 1957–58; NAAFI, W Germany, 1959–62; Kayser Bondor, 1962–63; various posts, inc. Computer and Management Services Manager, S Wales Electricity Bd, 1963–76; ASC, Henley, 1968; Dep. Chm., London Electricity Bd, 1977–84. Dir, 1992 Nat. Garden Festival Ltd, 1987–88. Member: Milton Keynes IT Adv. Panel, 1982–84; Welsh Regional Council, CBI, 1984–99 (Chm., 1991–93); Council, CBI, 1988–97. Chm., SE Wales Cttee, Industry Year 1986. Dep. Chm., Prince of Wales Cttee, 1989–96. Mem., 1985–90, Dep. Chm., 1995–2001, Nat. Trust Cttee for Wales; Member: Hon. Soc. of Cymmrodorion, 1978–; Civic Trust Bd for Wales, 1984–88; Welsh Language Bd, 1988–89; Council, Nat. Mus. and Galls of Wales, 2000–07 (Chm., Pension Fund, 2000–06). Dir, Welsh Nat. Opera Ltd, 1988–93; Trustee and Dep. Chm., Cardiff Bay Opera House Trust, 1994–97; Trustee: Nat. Botanic Garden of Wales, 1998–2001; Gateway Gardens Trust, 2004–06. Mem. Council, Europa Nostra, 1996–2008 (Chm., Heritage Awards Panel, 2001–05). Mem. Court, Cranfield Inst. of Technol., 1980–88; Governor, Polytechnic of Wales, 1987–88. Liveryman: Tin Plate Workers alias Wireworkers' Co.; Livery Co. of Wales (formerly Welsh Livery Guild). High Sheriff, S Glamorgan, 1995–96. Hon. Druid, Gorsedd of Bards of Island of Britain, 1999–. FInstD 1988. *Recreations:* fishing, opera, walking, reading. *Club:* Cardiff and County (Cardiff).

EVANS, Jonathan, OBE 2005; Company Secretary of Royal Mail Group (formerly Secretary to the Post Office, then Consignia), 1999–2010; *b* 21 April 1952; *s* of Alec H. Evans and Beryl Evans; *m* 1978, Gillian Eileen Blundell; one *s* two *d*. *Educ:* King Edward VI Sch., Nuneaton; Durham Univ. (BSc Maths 1974). Joined Post Office, 1974; mgt trainee, 1974–76; Ops Exec., Midlands Postal Bd, 1976–82; Personal Asst to Chm., 1982–84; Asst Head Postmaster, Leicester, 1984–86; Asst Personnel Dir, PO Counters Ltd, 1986–92; Dir of Orgn, 1992–93; Gen. Manager, Midlands Region, 1993–95; Network Dir, 1995–99. Trustee Dir, Royal Mail Pension Plan, 2005–13; Chm., Royal Mail Sen. Exec. Pension Plan, 2007–13. Mem., Audit Cttee, Archbps' Council, 2011–. Chm., Claverdon Community Shop Ltd, 2011–15. Trustee: Rowland Hill Fund, 2007–14 (Chm., 2010–14); Postal Heritage Trust, 2010– (Vice Chm., 2010–); Gov., Foundn of Lady Katherine Leveson, 2008–. Mem. Chapter, 2013–, Chair, Finance Cttee, 2013–, Coventry Cathedral. *Recreations:* music, campanology, cricket. *E:* jonathan.evans3@btinternet.com.

EVANS, Jonathan Edward; QC 2014; *b* Maidstone, 9 Aug. 1969; *s* of Clive Mortimer Evans and Belinda Jane Evans; *m* 1996, Harriet Alice Tatton Brown; two *s* two *d*. *Educ:* Maidstone Grammar Sch.; Oriel Coll., Oxford (BA). Called to the Bar, Middle Temple, 1994; barrister, Wilberforce Chambers, 1994–. *Recreations:* cycling the 'Cent Cols Challenge' courtesy of the incomparable P. Deeker, Esq. *Address:* Wilberforce Chambers, 8 New Square, Lincoln's Inn, WC2A 3QP.

EVANS, Jonathan Peter; solicitor; *b* 2 June 1950; *s* of late David John Evans and Harriet Mary Drury; *m* 1975, Margaret Thomas; one *s* two *d*. *Educ:* Lewis Sch., Pengam; Howardian High Sch., Cardiff; Coll. of Law, Guildford and London. Admitted Solicitor of Supreme Court, 1974; Leo Abse & Cohen, Cardiff: Partner, 1974–92; Man. Partner, 1987–92; Dir of Insce, Eversheds, 1997–99, consultant, 1999–2009; Dir, NFU Mutual Insce Gp, 2000–10; Chairman: Pearl Gp Ltd, 2005–09; Phoenix Life Ltd, 2009–; Allied World Managing Agency, 2015–. Dep. Chm., Tai Cymru (Welsh Housing Corp.), 1988–92. Contested (C): Ebbw Vale, Feb. and Oct., 1974; Wolverhampton NE, 1979; Brecon and Radnor, 1987. MP (C) Brecon and Radnor, 1992–97; contested (C) Brecon and Radnorshire, 1997; MP (C) Cardiff N, 2010–15. PPS to Minister of State, NI Office, 1992–94; Parly Under-Sec. of State, DTI, 1994–95 (Minister for Corporate Affairs, 1994–95, for Competition and Consumer Affairs, 1995); Parly Sec., Lord Chancellor's Dept, 1995–96; Parly Under-Sec. of State, Welsh Office, 1996–97; Chief Cons. Party Spokesman for Wales, 1997–98. MEP (C) Wales, 1999–2009; Leader, Conservatives, EP, 2001–05; Pres., EP Delegn for Relns with US Congress, 2004–09; Mem. Adv. Bd, Transatlantic Economic Council, 2007–09. Chm., All Party Parly Gp on Insurance and Financial Services, 2010–15; Co-Chm., All Party Parly Gp on Building Socs and Financial Mutuals, 2010–15; Chm., Associate Parly Gp on Wholesale Financial Mkts and Services, 2012–15. Mem. Bd, Cons. Party, 2002–05; Chairman: Assoc. of Cons. Clubs, 2007–15 (Pres., 2004–05); Welsh Cons. Party, 2014–. Vice Pres., Catholic Union of GB, 2001–. Hon. Consultant on law and policy, NSPCC, 1991–94; Dep. Chm., Welsh NSPCC Council, 1991–94; Pres., Cardiff and Dist NSPCC, 1992–94. FRSA 1995. *Recreations:* watching Rugby Union and cricket, reading. *Clubs:* Farmers, Carlton (Chm., Political Cttee, 2013–15); Cardiff and County (Cardiff).

EVANS, Julian Ascott; HM Diplomatic Service; Director of Protocol and Vice-Marshal of the Diplomatic Corps, since 2015; *b* 5 July 1957; s of Frederick Evans and late Glenys Evans (*née* Williams); *m* 1991, Gayle Evelyn Louise (*née* Sperring); two *d*. *Educ:* Llanelli Grammar Sch.; Price's Coll., Fareham; University Coll. London (BA Hons Geog.). Joined HM Diplomatic Service, 1978; Russian lang. trng, RAEC, Beaconsfield, 1981; Third Secretary: (Scientific), Moscow, 1982–84; (Commercial), Zurich, 1985–86; Asst Private Sec. to Minister of State, FCO, 1987–89; FCO, 1989–91; Second, later First, Sec., UKMIS to UN, NY, 1991–95; FCO, 1996–2002; Deputy High Commissioner: Islamabad, 2002–03; Ottawa, 2003–07; Consul Gen., San Francisco, 2007–11; Dep. High Comr to India, 2011–15. *Recreations:* travel, military history. *Address:* c/o Foreign and Commonwealth Office, King Charles Street, SW1A 2AH.

EVANS, Kim, OBE 2007; arts consultant, since 2006; Chair, Clean Break Theatre Company, since 2012; Member, Parole Board for England and Wales, since 2006; *b* 3 Jan. 1951; *d* of Jon Evans and Gwendolen (*née* McLeod); *m* 2001, David Hucker. *Educ:* Putney High Sch.; Our Lady of Sion Convent; Warwick Univ. (BA Hons Eng. and Amer. Lit.); Leicester Univ. (MA Hons Victorian Lit. and Society). Press Asst, Design Council, 1973–74; Asst Editor, Crafts mag., 1974–76; Chief Sub-Editor, Harpers & Queen, 1976–78; South Bank Show, LWT: researcher, 1978–82; Producer/Dir, 1982–89; BBC Television: Producer, Omnibus, 1989–92; Asst Hd, Music and Arts, 1992–93; Head of Music and Arts, subseq. of Arts, BBC TV, then of BBC Arts and Classical Music, 1993–99; Exec. Dir, Arts, Arts Council of England, later Arts Council England, 1999–2006. Trustee: Chelsea and Westminster Health Charity, 2008–12; Nat. Heritage Meml Fund, 2008–14; Nat. Portrait Gall., 2010–; Dance

United, 2010–. FRTS 1999. Hon. FRCA 2006. Huw Wheldon Award for Best Arts Prog., BAFTA, 1993. *Recreations:* travelling (particularly in Africa), dreaming, reading. *Address:* c/o Clean Break Theatre Company, 2 Patshull Road, NW5 2LB.

EVANS, Leslie Elizabeth; Permanent Secretary, Scottish Government, since 2015; *b* 11 Dec. 1958; *d* of Philip Charles Evans and Mary Elizabeth Nora Evans (*née* Else); *m* 1990, Derek George McVay; one *s*. *Educ:* Liverpool Univ. (BA Hons Music). Asst to Dir, Greenwich Fest., 1981; Entertainments Officer, London Bor. of Greenwich, 1981–83; Arts Co-ordinator, Sheffield CC, 1983–85; Sen. Arts Officer, Edinburgh DC, 1985–87; Principal Officer, Stirling CC, 1987–89; Asst Dir of Recreation, 1989–99, Strategic Projects Manager, 1999–2000, City of Edinburgh Council; Scottish Executive, later Scottish Government: Head: Local Govt, Constitution and Governance, 2000–03; Public Service Reform, 2003–05; Tourism, Culture and Sport, Scottish Exec. Educn Dept, 2006–07; Dir, Culture, Ext. Affairs and Tourism (formerly Europe, Ext. Affairs and Culture), 2007–09; Dir Gen., Educn, 2009–11; Dir Gen., Learning and Justice, 2011–15. Mem., Scotch Malt Whisky Soc. *Recreations:* the arts, Pilates and keeping fit, handbags. *Address:* Scottish Government, St Andrews House, Edinburgh EH1 3DG. *E:* leslie.evans@scotland.gsi.gov.uk.
See also T. W. Evans.

EVANS, Lewis Jones; Chairman, Post Office Board, Wales and the Marches, 1997–2000; *b* 14 Feb. 1938; *s* of Evan Jones Evans and Jane Jones Evans (*née* Morgans); *m* 1961, Siân, *e d* of Rev. Harri Hughes and Blodwen Hughes, Penclawdd; two *s* one *d*. *Educ:* Tregaron County Sch.; Trinity Coll., Carmarthen (DipEd; Hon. Fellow, 2006). FCIB 1986. Schoolmaster, 1960–62; Lloyds Bank plc, 1962–90: branch and head office appts incl. Manager, Llanelli Br., 1970–73; Sen. Manager, Newcastle upon Tyne, 1982–84; Regl Dir and gen. mgt, 1984–90; Dir, Lloyds Develt Capital Ltd, Alex Lawrie Factors Ltd, and Internat. Factors Ltd, 1989–90; Dep. Man. Dir, 1990–91, Man. Dir, 1991–96, Girobank; Dir, Alliance and Leicester Building Soc., 1991–96. Mem. Council, British Bankers' Assoc., 1992–96. Member: Wales Tourist Bd, 1996–2004; Wales Adv. Bd, BITC, 1996–2000 (Chairman: Professional Firms Gp, Cardiff, 1996–99; Community Loan Fund for Wales, 1997–2000; Mem. Council, UK Local Investment Fund, 1997–2000); Wales Adv. Bd, Barclays Wealth (formerly Gerrard Ltd), 2000–08; Panel of Ind. Assessors for Public Appts, 2000–04; Chairman: Cwlwm Busnes, Caerdydd, 1998–2006; GSL Farm and Pet Place Ltd, 2000–02. Member: Council, Royal Nat. Eisteddfod of Wales, 1999–2006 (Chm., Resources and Finance Cttee, 1999–2006); Council, CBI for Wales, 1997–2000; Dir, Cardiff Bay Opera Trust Ltd, 1994–97. Jt Chm., Action Res. Project on the Underachievement of Boys, 1996–98; Dep. Chm., NPFA, 2004–07 (Chm., NPFA Cymru, 2000–07). Hon. Vice-Pres., London Welsh Trust and Assoc., 1994–2000. Hon. Treas. and Mem. Council, Univ. of Wales, Lampeter, 1993–99; University of Wales: Member: Court, 1996–2002; Audit Cttee, 1997–2000; Council, 2004–07; Bd, Univ. of Wales Press, 2004–07. Governor: Univ. of Glamorgan, 1999–2002; Trinity Univ. Coll. (formerly Trinity Coll.), Carmarthen, 2006–10; Univ. of Wales Trinity St David, 2010–14; Swansea Metropolitan Univ., 2011–14. CCMI (CIMgt 1994); FRSA 1994. Hon. Druid, Gorsedd of Bards, Isle of Britain, 1994. Hon. DSc Econs Wales, 2014. *Recreations:* family, music, sport. *Clubs:* Cardiff and County (Cardiff); Crawshays Rugby Football; Royal Porthcawl Golf.

EVANS, Lindsay; *see* Evans, W. L.

EVANS, Lyndon Rees, CBE 2001; PhD; FRS 2010; Project Leader, Large Hadron Collider, Organisation Européenne pour la Recherche Nucléaire (CERN), 1994–2010; *b* Aberdare, 24 July 1945; *m* 1967, Lynda Mear; one *s* one *d*. *Educ:* Aberdare Boys' Grammar Sch.; Univ. of Wales, Swansea (BSc 1st Cl. Hons Physics 1966; PhD Physics 1970; Hon. Fellow 2002). CERN: Fellow, Linac Gp, 1969; Res. Fellow, Proton Synchrotron Div., 1970–71; joined 300 GeV project, 1971; Dep. Leader, Super Proton Synchrotron Div., 1988–89; Leader, Super Proton Synchrotron—Large Electron Positron Div., 1990–93; Associate Dir, Future Accelerators, 1994. Fellow, APS, 1991. Robert R. Wilson Prize, APS, 2008; Glazebrook Medal, Inst. of Physics, 2013. *Address:* c/o CERN, 1211 Geneva 23, Switzerland.

EVANS, Dame (Madelaine) Glynne (Dervel), DBE 2000; CMG 1992; PhD; HM Diplomatic Service, retired; Senior Adviser: Olive Group Ltd, since 2006; Restrata Ltd, since 2013; *b* 23 Aug. 1944. *Educ:* Univ. of St Andrews (MA Hons 1st cl. Mediaeval and Modern Hist. 1966); University Coll. London (PhD 1971). Res. Fellow, Centre for Latin American Studies, Univ. of Liverpool, 1969–70; Vis. Lectr, Coll. of William and Mary, Williamsburg, 1970–71; Second Sec., FCO, 1971; Buenos Aires, 1972; First Sec., FCO, 1975; Pte Sec. to Parly Under-Sec. of State, 1977; on loan to UN Secretariat, NY, 1978; First Sec., UKMIS NY, 1979; First Sec., subseq. Counsellor, FCO, 1982; Counsellor and Dep. Hd of Mission, Brussels, 1987; Head of UN Dept, FCO, 1990–96; Res. Associate, IISS, 1996–97; Ambassador to Chile, 1997–2000; Dist. Vis. Scholar, NATO Defense Coll., Rome, 2000–01; Ambassador to Portugal, 2001–04. Advr to Dir, Defence Acad. of the UK, 2006–07. Associate Fellow, RUSI, 2004–09. Advr, CAB, 2005–06. *Publications:* Responding to Crises in the African Great Lakes, 1997; articles on internat. peacekeeping and conflict management. *Address:* c/o Olive Group Ltd, 23 Buckingham Gate, SW1E 6LB. *E:* gevans@olivegroup.com.

EVANS, His Honour (Maldwyn) John; a Circuit Judge, 2005–15; *b* 11 July 1950; *s* of late Comdr David Anthony Evans and of Margaret Evans; *m* 1998, Miriam Dorothy Swaddle (*née* Beaumont); one step *s* two step *d*, and two *s* one *d* from former marriage. *Educ:* Royal Hospital Sch., Holbrook; Newcastle upon Tyne Polytechnic (BA Hons 1972). Called to the Bar, Gray's Inn, 1973; a Recorder of the Crown Court, 1989; Hd, New Court Chambers, Newcastle, 1999–2005. Gov., King's Sch., Tynemouth, 2000–; Fellow, Woodard Corp., 2002. *Recreations:* sport, ski-ing, sailing, cricket, Rugby in particular, holidays, walking, contemporary cinema.

EVANS, Prof. Margaret, PhD; Pro Vice-Chancellor, De Montfort University, 2000–02; *b* 29 April 1946; *d* of late Roderick McKay Campbell McCaskill and Gladys May McCaskill (*née* Ireland); *m* 1st, 1967, Anthony Howell (marr. diss.); two *d*; 2nd, 1978, Alan Fearn (marr. diss.); 3rd, 1985, Herbert Kinnell (marr. diss.); 4th, 1989, Gwynne Evans (marr. diss.). *Educ:* Nottingham Poly. (BA CNAA); Leicester Poly. (MBA CNAA); Loughborough Univ. (PhD); Nottingham Univ. (PGCE). FCLIP (FLA 1994; FIInfSc 1995). Librarian: Nottingham City Libraries, 1964–65; Notts Co. Libraries, 1967–69; Sutton in Ashfield Libraries, 1971–73; antiquarian bookseller, 1973–75; Loughborough University: Lectr, 1979–88; Sen. Lectr, 1988–94; Prof. of Information Studies, 1994–2000; Hd of Dept of Information and Liby Studies, 1994–98; Dean, Sci. Faculty, 1998–2000. *Publications:* (jtly) Book acquisition and use by young people: a review of recent research initiatives, 1988; (ed) Planned Public Relations for Libraries, 1989; (ed) The Learning Experiences of Overseas Students, 1990; (ed) Managing Fiction in Libraries, 1991; All Change?: public library management strategies for the 1990s, 1991; (jtly) Managing Library Resources in Schools, 1994; (jtly) Meeting the marketing challenge: strategies for public libraries and leisure services, 1994; (jtly) Continuity and Innovation in the Public Library, 1996; (jtly) Marketing in the Not-for-profit Sector, 1997; (jtly) Learning support for special educational needs: potential for progress, 1997; (jtly) Adult reading promotion in UK public libraries, 1998; Northern Working Lives from the 18th to 20th centuries, 2013; numerous other books, reports and articles. *Recreations:* Jamie, Lizzie, Flossie, Tom, animals.

EVANS, Mark; QC 1995; a Recorder, 1996–2009; a Deputy High Court Judge; *b* 21 March 1946; *s* of Rev. Clifford Evans and Mary (*née* Jones); *m* 1971, Dr Barbara Skew (marr. diss. 1995); one *s* one *d*; *m* 2001, Carolyn Poots, barrister. *Educ:* Christ Coll., Brecon; King's Coll., London (LLB Hons). Called to the Bar, Gray's Inn, 1971; practice in Bristol, 1973; founded St John's Chambers, 1978. *Recreations:* music, vintage cars. *Club:* Savages (Bristol).

EVANS, Mark Armstrong, CVO 1994; Director, British Council, Austria, 1996–2000; *b* 5 Aug. 1940; *s* of late Charles Tunstall Evans, CMG, Birmingham, and Kathleen Armstrong, Newcastle; *m* 1965, Katharine, *d* of Alfred Bastable, Brecon; one *s* one *d*. *Educ:* Marlborough Coll.; Clare Coll., Cambridge (BA 1962; MA 1966); Moscow State Univ.; Bristol Univ. (PGCE 1964). Head, Russian and German, Chichester High Sch. for Boys, 1964–69; apptd to British Council, 1969; Bahrain, 1969–71; Frankfurt, 1971–73; MECAS, Lebanon, 1973–74; Dir, UAE in Dubai, 1974–77; temp. posting, Kabul, 1977; Asst Dir, Educnl Contracts, 1977–79; Dep. Rep. and Cultural Attaché, France, 1979–85; Head, Office Services, 1985–88; Dir, Canada, and Cultural Counsellor, Ottawa, 1988–92; Dir, and Cultural Counsellor, Russia, 1992–96. Chm., Chailey Parish Council, 2005–09. Mem., E Sussex Valuation Tribunal, 2002–12. Member: RSAA, 1972; Adv. Bd, Österreich Institut, 1999–2008. Gov., RNLI, 1995. Gov., Chailey Sch., 2004–. Mem., Bluebell Railway Preservation Soc., 1997–. *Recreations:* building models, gardening, household chores. *Address:* High Field, North Chailey, Sussex BN8 4JD. *Club:* Union (Cambridge).

EVANS, Sir Martin (John), Kt 2004; PhD, ScD; FMedSci; FRS 1993; Chancellor, Cardiff University, since 2012 (President, 2009–12; Director, Cardiff School of Biosciences, and Professor of Mammalian Genetics, 1999–2009); Founder, Chairman and Chief Scientific Officer, Cell Therapy Ltd, since 2009; *b* 1 Jan. 1941; *s* of Leonard Wilfred Evans and Hilary Joyce (*née* Redman); *m* 1966, Judith Clare Williams, MBE; two *s* one *d*. *Educ:* St Dunstan's Coll., Catford; Christ's Coll., Cambridge (BA Pt II in Biochem., MA; Hon. Fellow 2004); PhD London 1969; ScD Cambridge 1996. University College London: Res. Assistant, Dept of Anatomy and Embryology, 1963–66; Asst Lectr, 1966–69; Lectr, 1969–78; Cambridge University: Lectr, Dept of Genetics, 1978–91; Reader, 1991–94; Prof. of Mammalian Genetics, 1994–99; Fellow, St Edmund's Coll., Cambridge, 1998–99; Vice Provost, Sch. of Medicine, Biol., Health and Life Scis, Cardiff Univ., 2004–06. Discovered embryonic stem cells, 1981. Member: CMO's expert gp on Therapeutic Cloning, 1999–2000; Steering Cttee, UK Stem Cell Bank and for Use of Stem Cell Lines, 2002–07; UK Nat. Stem Cell Network Steering Cttee, 2006–09. Trustee, Breakthrough Breast Cancer, 2004–15; Pres., Techniquest, 2009. Mem., EMBO, 1990; Founder FMedSci 1998 (Hon. FMedSci 2008). Hon. Mem. Biochem. Soc., 2008. Liveryman, Livery Co. of Wales (formerly Welsh Livery Guild), 2005; Hon. Freeman, Soc. of Apothecaries of London, 2008. Hon. Fellow, St Edmund's Coll., Cambridge, 2002. Hon. DSc: Mount Sinai Sch. of Medicine, 2002; Bath, 2005; Buckingham, 2009; Hon. DSc (Med) UCL, 2008; Hon. Dr: Athens, 2008; Univ. of Wales, 2008. March of Dimes Prize in Develtl Biol., 1999; Albert Lasker Award for Basic Medical Research, 2001; Special Achievement Award, Miami Nature Biotechnol. Winter Symposium, 2003; (jtly) Nobel Prize for Medicine, 2007; Morgan Stanley Great Britons Award for Sci. and Innovation, 2007; Gold Medal, RSocMed, 2008; Copley Medal, Royal Soc., 2009. *Publications:* numerous contribs to scientific works. *Recreations:* family, walking, golf. *Address:* Cardiff University, Park Place, Cardiff CF10 3AT.

EVANS, Martyn Robert Rowlinson; Chief Executive, Carnegie UK Trust, since 2009; *b* Hamilton, Bermuda, 11 July 1952; *s* of Lt Col John Evans and Connie Evans; *m* 2004, Angela Morton; two *s*. *Educ:* City of Birmingham Poly. (BA Hons); Univ. of Manchester (MA Econs). Housing Aid Officer, Thamesside Housing Aid Centre, 1977–79; Housing Aid Worker, Glasgow Shelter Housing Aid Centre, 1980–84; Dep. Dir, 1984–87, Dir, 1987–92, Shelter (Scotland); CEO, Citizens Advice Scotland, 1992–97; Dir, Scottish Consumer Council, 1998–2008; Sen. Dir, Consumer Focus, 2008–09. Vis. Prof. of Law, Univ. of Strathclyde, 1996–2003. Chair, Quality Improvement Scotland, 2009–10 (Vice Chair, 2004–09). FRSA 2011. *Address:* Carnegie UK Trust, Andrew Carnegie House, Pittencrieff Street, Dunfermline, Fife KY12 8AW. *T:* (01383) 721445. *E:* martyn@carnegieuk.org.
See also R. E. R. Evans.

EVANS, Michael; *see* Evans, His Honour T. M.

EVANS, Michael Stephen James; freelance defence writer, The Times, since 2013; *b* 5 Jan. 1945; *s* of Reginald and Beatrix Evans; *m* 1971, Robyn Nicola Coles; three *s*. *Educ:* Christ's Hosp.; QMC, London Univ. (BA Hons English). Reporter, 1968–69, News Editor, Loughton office, 1969–70, Express and Independent; Daily Express: Reporter, Action Line consumer column, 1970–72; Reporter, 1972–77; Home Affairs Correspondent, 1977–82; Defence and Diplomatic Correspondent, 1982–86; The Times: Whitehall Correspondent, 1986–87; Defence Correspondent, 1987–98; Defence Editor, 1998–2010; Pentagon Correspondent in Washington, 2010–13. *Publications: fiction:* A Crack in the Dam, 1978; False Arrest, 1979; Double Lives, 2011; *non-fiction:* Great Disasters, 1981; South Africa, 1987; The Gulf Crisis, 1988. *Recreations:* cricket, golf, tennis, playing piano. *Address:* c/o The Times, 1 London Bridge Street, SE1 9GF. *T:* 07768 081797.

EVANS, Nerys; *see* Evans, E. G. N.

EVANS, Nicholas; *see* Evans, H. N.

EVANS, Nicholas Henry Robert; Command Secretary, Land Forces, Ministry of Defence, 2006–10; *b* 21 July 1950; *s* of Ivor Robert Evans and Esther Jane Evans; *m* Sally Vera Carter; two *s*. *Educ:* Reading Sch.; St John's Coll., Oxford (MA Hons Modern History). Joined MoD, 1971; posts in RN, Army and Air Force policy, planning and finance, incl. Private Sec. to Under-Sec. of State for the Army, 1974–75, and Civil Advr to GOC NI, 1975–77; Asst Private Sec. to Sec. of State, 1981–84; Head: Naval Manpower and Trng, 1985–87; Mgt Services Div., 1987–90; Next Steps Implementation Team, 1990–92; Resources and Progs (Air), 1992–95; Asst Under-Sec. of State (Quartermaster), 1995–99; Exec. Dir (Finance), Defence Procurement Agency, 1999–2000; Dir Gen., Defence Logistics (Finance and Business Planning), then Resources, Defence Logistics Orgn, 2000–02; Dir Gen., Mgt and Orgn, 2003–06. *Recreations:* walking, gardening, house maintenance, reading history.

EVANS, Nigel Martin; MP (C) Ribble Valley, since 1992; *b* 10 Nov. 1957; *s* of late Albert Evans and Betty Evans. *Educ:* Swansea Univ. (BA Hons). Retail Newsagent, family business, 1979–90. West Glamorgan County Council: Councillor (C), 1985–91; Dep. Leader, 1989. Chm., Welsh Cons. Candidates Policy Gp, 1990; Pres., Cons. NW Parly Gp, 1991. Contested (C): Swansea West, 1987; Pontypridd, Feb. 1989; Ribble Valley, March 1991. PPS to Sec. of State for Employment, 1993–94, to Chancellor of Duchy of Lancaster, 1994–95; Opposition front bench spokesman on Welsh and constitutional affairs, 1997–2001; Shadow Welsh Sec., 2001–03; First Dep. Chm. of Ways and Means and a Dep. Speaker, H of C, 2010–13. Mem., Select Cttee on Transport, 1993, on Envmt, 1996–97, on Public Service, 1996–97, on Trade and Industry, 2003–05, on Culture, Media and Sport, 2005–09, on Internat. Devel t, 2009–10; Sec., 1992–97, Chm., 2010–12, NW Gp of Cons. MPs; Secretary: Manufacturing Cttee; All-Party Tourism Cttee; Chairman: All-Party Music Gp, 1996–97 (Vice-Chm., 2002–10); All-Party Identity Fraud Gp, 2006–10; All-Party Egypt Gp, 2007–10; Co-Chm., All-Party Drugs Gp, 1997–2010; Pres., All-Party Beer Gp, 2010–; Patron, Parly Space Cttee, 2010–. Vice-Chm., Cons. Party (Wales), 1999–2001. Director: Made in the UK Ltd; Small Business Bureau. *Recreations:* tennis, swimming, theatre, tourism, new technology, defence, broadcasting. *Address:* Brooklyn Cottage, Main Street, Pendleton, Clitheroe, Lancs BB7 1PT. *T:* (01200) 443875; House of Commons, SW1A 0AA. *Clubs:* Carlton, Royal Automobile, Lansdowne, Groucho.

EVANS, Dr (Noel) John (Bebbington), CB 1980; Deputy Secretary, Department of Health and Social Security, 1977–84; *b* 26 Dec. 1933; *s* of William John Evans and Gladys Ellen (*née* Bebbington); *m* 1st, 1960, Elizabeth Mary Garbutt (marr. diss.); two *s* one *d*; 2nd, 1974, Eileen Jane McMullan. *Educ:* Hymers Coll., Hull (State scholar); Christ's Coll., Cambridge (scholar; 1st cl., Nat. Sci. Tripos); Westminster Medical Sch., London; London Sch. of Hygiene and Tropical Med. (Newsholme prize, Chadwick Trust medal and prize). MA, MB, BChir; FRCP, DPH (Dist.), FFPH. Called to Bar, Gray's Inn, 1965. House officer posts at: Westminster, Westminster Children's, Hammersmith, Central Middlesex and Brompton Hosps, 1958–60; Medical Registrar and Tutor, Westminster Hosp., 1960–61; Asst MoH, Warwickshire CC, 1961–65; Dept of Health and Social Security (formerly Min. of Health), 1965–84, DCMO 1977–82; Sir Wilson Jameson Travelling Fellowship, 1966. Chairman: Welsh Cttee on Drug Misuse, 1986–91; Nat. Biological Standards Bd, 1988–2002 (Mem., 1975–2002); UK Transplant Support Service Authority, 1991–98; Member: Welsh Cttee, Countryside Commn, 1985–89; Welsh Health Promotion Authority, 1987–89. Conducted Review of External Advice to DoH, reported 1995. Privy Council Mem., Council of Royal Pharmaceutical Soc., 1988–2003 (Hon. MRPharmS 2003). *Publications:* The Organisation and Planning of Health Services in Yugoslavia, 1967; Health and Personal Social Service Research in Wales, 1986; (with P. Benner) Isle of Man Health Services Inquiry, 1986; (with P. Cunliffe) Study of Control of Medicines, 1987; Postgraduate Medical and Dental Education in Wales, 1991; contribs to med. jls. *Recreations:* canals, photography. *Address:* Apartment 27, Holyshute Lodge, Honiton, Devon EX14 1NU. *T:* (01404) 41604.

EVANS, Dame Oremi, DBE 2015; Headteacher, Brookfield School, Hereford, since 2001; Executive Headteacher, Behaviour, Herefordshire Council, since 2011; *b* Lagos, Nigeria, 7 Oct. 1956; *d* of Sir Mobolaji Bank-Anthony, KBE and Mrs Suzy Iseli (*née* Gray); *m* 1979, Clifford Evans; two *d*. *Educ:* Queen's Coll., Lagos; Avery Hill Higher Educn Coll. (BEd Hons); Univ. of Worcester (MSc). Teacher of Sci., 1979–89, Special Educnl Needs Coordinator, 1989–94, Whitecross High Sch., Hereford; Dep. Hd, 1994–99, Headteacher, 1999–2001, John Venn Unit, Hereford. *Recreations:* music, theatre, ballet, opera, travelling. *Address:* 58 Three Elms Road, Hereford HR4 0RH. *T:* (01432) 354142. *E:* evans@hr4orh.freeserve.co.uk.

EVANS, Ven. Patrick Alexander Sidney; Archdeacon of Canterbury, and a Canon Residentiary, Canterbury Cathedral, 2002–07, now Archdeacon Emeritus; *b* 28 Jan. 1943; *m* 1969, Jane Kemp; two *s* one *d*. *Educ:* Clifton College, Bristol; Lincoln Theological Coll. Curate: Holy Trinity, Lyonsdown, Barnet, 1973–76; Royston, 1976–78; Vicar: Gt Gaddesden, 1978–82; Tenterden, 1982–89; RD of West Charing, 1988–89; Archdeacon of Maidstone, 1989–2002; Diocesan Dir of Ordinands, Canterbury, 1989–94. Selector, ABM, 1992–95. Mem., Gen. Synod, 1996–2005; Chairman: Bd of Mission, 1994–95, and Pastoral Cttee, 1994–2002, dio. of Canterbury; Canterbury & Rochester Church in Society (formerly Council for Social Responsibility), 1997–2007. Trustee, Dorset Historic Churches Trust, 2008–12. *Address:* Wills Tenement, Trehan, Trematon, Cornwall PL12 4QN. *E:* patrickevans120@hotmail.co.uk.

EVANS, Paul; *see* Evans, Christopher P.

EVANS, Air Marshal Paul; *see* Evans, Air Marshal C. P. A.

EVANS, Paul Anthony; Clerk of the Journals, House of Commons, since 2014; *b* 15 Oct. 1955; *s* of late John Evans and Cecilia Evans (*née* Monks); *m* 1991, Katharine; one *s* one *d*. *Educ:* St Peter's RC Primary Sch., Winchester; Peter Symonds, Winchester; Sevenoaks Sch.; King's Coll., Cambridge (BA 1977). Vis. Schol., Univ. of Siena, 1976; Vis. Fellow, Univ. of Heidelberg, 1980; Jun. Res. Fellow, St Edmund's House, Cambridge, 1980–81; Clerk, House of Commons, 1981–: Health Cttee, 1991–93; Defence Cttee, 1997–2001; Human Rights Cttee, 2001–04; Principal Clerk: Delegated Legislation, 2005–06; Select Cttees, 2006–11; Table Office, 2011–14. Presidential Advr, Parly Assembly of Council of Europe, 2003–06. Chair, Study of Parlt Gp, 2005–07; Trustee, Industry and Parlt Trust, 2010–15. Associate, Inst. for Govt, 2011–. FAcSS 2012; FRSA 2012. *Publications:* (contrib.) Parliamentary Accountability, 1995; Dod's Handbook of House of Commons Procedure, 1997, 8th edn 2011; (contrib.) The Future of Parliament, 2005; (with Paul Silk) Parliamentary Assembly of the Council of Europe: practice and procedure, 10th edn 2008, 11th edn 2013; The Growth of Many Centuries: Thomas Erskine May and the history of parliamentary procedure, 2015; articles in jls on parly matters. *Recreations:* British Constitution, Victorian and 20th century architecture, walking, silence and empty places, Wales. *Address:* Department of Chamber and Committee Services, House of Commons, SW1A 0AA. *T:* (020) 7219 3315. *E:* evansp@parliament.uk.

EVANS, Paul Gareth; Lecturer, Leadership and Management Development, Manchester Business School, since 2012; *b* 9 Sept. 1963; *s* of Thomas Neville Evans and Rosamund Sheila Evans; *m* 1998, Barbara Shih Wen Chan; one *s* two *d*. *Educ:* Chilwell Comprehensive Sch.; Univ. of Surrey (BSc Hons); Univ. of Manchester (MBA; PhD). Project Manager, Kirin Beer, Tokyo, 1993; Area Manager, Whitbread Inns, 1994–98; Regl Ops Dir, Rank Holidays Div., Rank Orgn plc, 1998–2000; Chief Operating Officer, 2000–03, Master and Chief Exec., 2003–08, Royal Armouries. *Recreation:* fly fishing.

EVANS, Paul William; Headteacher, Colyton Grammar School, since 2008; *b* Plymouth, 10 April 1960; *s* of William and Eileen Evans; *m* 1983, Serena Pratt; one *d*. *Educ:* Coll. of St Mark and St John, Plymouth (BEd Hons 1983); Bulmershe Coll. of Higher Educn, Reading (MEd 1988). NPQH 2001. Sci. Teacher, Park House Sch., Newbury, 1983–86; Hd of Biol., 1986–89, Hd of Maths and Sci., 1989–97, Theale Green Sch., Reading; Dep. Headteacher, Colyton Grammar Sch., 1997–2008. FCollT 2007; FRSA 2012. *Recreations:* walking, photography, listening to classical music, theatre. *Address:* Colyton Grammar School, Colyford, Colyton, Devon EX24 6HN. *T:* (01297) 552327, *Fax:* (01297) 553853. *E:* pevans.education@gmail.com. *Club:* Lansdowne.

EVANS, Peter, CBE 1986; National Secretary, General Workers' Trade Group, Transport & General Workers' Union, 1974–90; *b* 8 Nov. 1929; *m* 1st, 1957, Christine Pamela (marr. diss.); one *d*; 2nd, 1975, Gillian Rosemary (decd); two *s* one *d*; 3rd, 1980, Joy Elizabeth (decd); 4th, 2009, Eileen Rose. *Educ:* Culvert Road Secondary School, Tottenham. London bus driver, 1955–62; District Officer, TGWU, 1962–66; Regional Trade Group Sec., Public Services, 1966–74. *Recreations:* talking, swimming in deep water, golf. *Address:* Margaret House, Church End, Barley, Royston, Herts RG8 8JS. *T:* (01763) 848372. *Clubs:* Victoria, Players' Theatre.

EVANS, Prof. Peter Angus, DMus; FRCO; Professor of Music, University of Southampton, 1961–90; *b* 7 Nov. 1929; *y s* of Rev. James Mackie Evans and Elizabeth Mary Fraser; *m* 1953, June Margaret Vickery. *Educ:* West Hartlepool Grammar Sch.; St Cuthbert's Soc., University of Durham. BA (1st cl. hons Music), 1950; BMus, MA 1953; DMus 1958; FRCO 1952. Music Master, Bishop Wordsworth's Sch., Salisbury, 1951–52; Lecturer in Music, University of Durham, 1953–61. Conductor: Palatine Opera Group, 1956–61; Southampton Philharmonic Soc., 1965–90. Hon. GSM 1998. *Publications:* Sonata for Oboe and Piano, 1953; Three Preludes for Organ, 1955; Edns of 17th Century Chamber Music, 1956–58; The Music of Benjamin Britten, 1979, 3rd edn 1996; contributor to: Die Musik in Geschichte und Gegenwart; A Concise Encyclopædia of Music, 1958; New Oxford History of Music, 1974; New Grove Dictionary of Music, 1981; Blackwell History of Music in Britain, 1995; writer and reviewer, especially on twentieth-century music. *Address:* Pye's Nest Cottage. Parkway, Ledbury, Herefordshire HR8 2JD. *T:* (01531) 633256.

EVANS, Philip; *see* Evans, I. P.

EVANS, Dr Philip Richard, FRS 2005; Member of Scientific Staff, Medical Research Council Laboratory of Molecular Biology, Cambridge, since 1976; *b* 25 May 1946; *s* of Maurice Lionel Evans and Janette Marjorie (*née* Burridge); *m* 1969, Carol Ann Watkins; two *s* one *d*. *Educ:* Christ's Hosp.; Wadham Coll., Oxford (MA, DPhil 1974). IBM Res. Fellow, Oxford Univ., 1974. *Publications:* contrib. res. papers to scientific jls. *Recreations:* playing bassoon, walking. *Address:* MRC Laboratory of Molecular Biology, Francis Crick Avenue, Cambridge CB2 0QH. *T:* (01223) 267000. *E:* pre@mrc-lmb.cam.ac.uk.

EVANS, Rebecca Mary; Member (Lab) Wales Mid and West, National Assembly for Wales, since 2011; *b* Bridgend, 2 Aug. 1976; *d* of Ven. Alun Wyn Evans and Evelyn Evans; *m* 2010, Paul Michael Evans. *Educ:* Univ. of Leeds (BA Hons Hist. 1997); Sidney Sussex Coll., Cambridge (MPhil Histl Studies 1998); Sheffield Hallam Univ. (Postgrad. Cert. Asperger Syndrome, 2011). Mid and W Wales Organiser, Welsh Labour, 2004–06; Sen. Researcher and Communications Officer for Carl Sargeant, Mem., Nat. Assembly for Wales, 2006–09; Policy and Public Affairs Officer, Nat. Autistic Soc., Cymru, 2009–11. Dep. Minister for Farming and Food, Welsh Govt, 2014–. *Recreations:* reading, the arts, walking, travel. *Address:* National Assembly for Wales, Cardiff Bay CF99 1NA. *T:* 0300 200 7160. *E:* rebecca.evans@assembly.wales.

EVANS, Sir Richard (Harry), Kt 1996; CBE 1986; Independent Director, SWF Samruk-Kazyna JSC, Kazakhstan; *b* 1942; *m*; three *d*. *Educ:* Royal Masonic Sch. Joined Civil Aviation section, Min. of Transport, 1960; Min. of Technology, 1961; Govt Contracts Officer, Ferranti, 1967; British Aerospace (formerly British Aircraft Corporation): Contracts Officer, 1969, Commercial Dir, 1978, Asst Man. Dir, 1981, Dep. Man. Dir, 1983, Warton Div.; Mktg Dir, 1987; Chairman: British Aerospace (Dynamics), 1988; BAe (Military Aircraft), 1988; Chief Exec., 1990–98, Chm., 1998–2004, BAe plc, then BAE SYSTEMS. Former Chm., Royal Ordnance; Dir, Panavia, 1981; Chm., United Utilities, 2001–08 (non-exec. Dir, 1997–2008). Chancellor, Univ. of Central Lancs, 2001–15.

EVANS, Richard Jeremy; *b* 28 June 1953; *s* of late George Evans and Helen Maud Evans; *m* 1976, Alison Mary Thom. *Educ:* Ipswich Sch., Suffolk. Journalist: East Anglian Daily Times, 1974–78; Cambridge Evening News, 1978–79; with The Times, 1979–99 (Racing Correspondent, 1991–99); Racing Correspondent, Daily Telegraph, 1999–2005. Racing Journalist of the Year, Horserace Writers' Assoc., 1995. *Recreations:* golf, bridge. *Address:* Old Village Hall, Stansfield, Suffolk CO10 8LP. *T:* (01284) 789478. *E:* richardevans53@me.com.

EVANS, Sir Richard (John), Kt 2012; FBA 1993; FRHistS, FRSL, FLSW; Regius Professor of History (formerly Regius Professor of Modern History), University of Cambridge, 2008–14, now Emeritus; President, Wolfson College, Cambridge, since 2010; Provost, Gresham College, London, since 2014; *b* 29 Sept. 1947; *s* of late Ieuan Trefor Evans and Evelyn Evans (*née* Jones); *m* 1st, 1976, Elín Hjaltadóttir (marr. diss. 1993); 2nd, 2004, Christine L. Corton; two *s*. *Educ:* Forest Sch., London; Jesus Coll., Oxford (Open Schol.; 1st Cl. Hons Mod. Hist. 1969; Stanhope Hist. Essay Prize 1969; Hon. Fellow, 1998); St Antony's Coll., Oxford (MA, DPhil 1973); Hamburg Univ. (Hanseatic Schol.); LittD East Anglia, 1990. Lectr in History, Univ. of Stirling, 1972–76; University of East Anglia: Lectr, 1976; Prof. of European History, 1983–89; Birkbeck College, London: Prof. of History, 1989–98; Vice-Master, 1993–97; Acting Master, 1997; Prof. of Modern History, Univ. of Cambridge, 1998–2008; Fellow, Gonville and Caius Coll., Cambridge, 1998–2010 (Hon. Fellow, 2011). Vis. Associate Prof. of European History, Columbia Univ., 1980; Vis. Fellow, Humanities Res. Centre, ANU, Canberra, 1986; Alexander von Humboldt Fellow, Free Univ. of Berlin, 1981, 1985, 1989. FRHistS 1978; FRSL 2000; Founding FLSW 2010. Hon. DLit London, 2012. Wolfson Literary Award for History, 1987; William H. Welch Medal, Amer. Assoc. for Hist. of Medicine, 1989; Medaille für Kunst und Wissenschaft der Hansestadt Hamburg, 1993; Fraenkel Prize in Contemporary History, Inst. of Contemp. Hist., 1994; Norton Medlicott Medal, Histl Association, 2014. *Publications:* The Feminist Movement in Germany 1894–1933, 1976; The Feminists, 1977; (ed) Society and Politics in Wilhelmine Germany, 1978; Sozialdemokratie und Frauenemanzipation im deutschen Kaiserreich, 1979; (ed jtly) The German Family, 1981; (ed) The German Working Class, 1982; (ed jtly) The German Peasantry, 1986; (ed jtly) The German Unemployed, 1987; Comrades and Sisters, 1987; Rethinking German History, 1987; Death in Hamburg, 1987; (ed) The German Underworld, 1988; (ed) Kneipengespräche im Kaiserreich, 1989; In Hitler's Shadow, 1989; Proletarians and Politics, 1990; (ed jtly) The German Bourgeoisie, 1992; Rituals of Retribution, 1996; Rereading German History, 1997; In Defence of History, 1997; Tales from the German Underworld, 1998; Telling Lies About Hitler, 2002; The Coming of the Third Reich, 2003; The Third Reich in Power, 2005; The Third Reich at War, 2008; Cosmopolitan Islanders, 2009; Altered Pasts, 2014; (essays) Third Reich in History and Memory, 2015. *Recreations:* playing the piano, opera, reading, cooking for friends. *Address:* Wolfson College, Barton Road, Cambridge CB3 9BB.

EVANS, Richard Llewellyn; JP; Director of Social Services, Birmingham City Council, 1994–99; *b* 1 June 1949; *s* of Robert Ellis Evans and Sarah Christine (*née* Cassidy); *m*; one *s* one *d*. *Educ:* Chiswick Poly.; Dundee Univ. (Dip. Social Work; CQSW; Dip. TMHA). Aircraft engr, BAC, 1964–69; Surrey County Council: Instructor, 1969–72; Dep. Manager, 1972–73; Trng Officer, Lothian Regl Council, 1973–77; Manager, Emergency Duty Team, Wilts CC, 1977–79; Principal Officer, Lothian Regl Council, 1979–81; Develt Officer, London Boroughs' Regl Children's Planning Cttee, 1981–83; Avon County Council: Asst Dir of Social Services, 1983–90; Dir, Social Services, 1990–94. Chm., BBC Children in Need Appeal for South and West, 2004–06. JP Bristol and North Avon, 2006. *Recreations:* music, cinema, entertaining.

EVANS, Sir Robert, Kt 1994; CBE 1987; FREng; FIMechE, FInstE; Chairman, British Gas plc, 1989–93 (Chief Executive, 1983–92 and Member of the Board, 1983–89); *b* 28 May 1927; *s* of Gwilym Evans and Florence May Evans; *m* 1950, Lilian May (*née* Ward) (*d* 2009); one *s* one *d*. *Educ:* Old Swan Coll., Liverpool; Blackburn Coll.; City of Liverpool Coll. (Tech.). FREng (FEng 1991). D. Napier & Son Ltd, 1943–49; North Western Gas Bd, 1950–56; Burmah Oil Co., 1956–62; Dir of Engrg, Southern Gas Bd, 1962–70; Dep. Dir (Ops), Gas Council, 1972; Dir of Operations, British Gas, 1972–75; Dep. Chm., North Thames Gas, 1975–77; Chm., E Midlands Gas Region, 1977–82; Man. Dir, Supplies, British Gas Corp., 1982–83. President: Instn of Gas Engrs, 1981–82; Inst. of Energy, 1991–92; Pipeline Industries Guild, 1990–94. Founder Chm., Indo British Partnership, 1991–97. Founder Chm., Nat. Council for Hospice and Specialist Palliative Care Services. FInstE (MInstE 1988); Hon. FIGasE 1961; CCMI (CBIM 1983); Hon. FCGI. Freeman, City of London, 1974; Mem., Engineers' Co., 1984. *Recreations:* reading, golf.

EVANS, Prof. Robert, PhD; FRS 2005; FInstP; H. O. Wills Professor of Physics, University of Bristol, 2005–11, now Emeritus; *b* 7 April 1946; *s* of John David Evans and Mary Evans; *m* 1967, Margaret Hume; one *s*. *Educ:* A. J. Dawson Grammar Sch., Wingate; Univ. of Birmingham (BSc); Univ. of Bristol (PhD 1970). FInstP 1981. University of Bristol: Lectr, 1978–84; Reader, 1984–92; Prof. of Physics, 1992–2005; Hd, Dept of Physics, 2005–11. Res. Prof., Univ. of Wuppertal, 1997–98; A. von Humboldt Res. Prof., Max Planck Institut,

Stuttgart, 2002–05; Kramers Prof. of Theoretical Physics, Univ. of Utrecht, 2011. *Publications:* contrib. numerous articles to learned jls. *Address:* H. H. Wills Physics Laboratory, University of Bristol, Tyndall Avenue, Bristol BS8 1TL.

EVANS, Robert John Emlyn; independent consultant, lecturer, trainer and freelance journalist, specialising in South Asia; *b* 23 Oct. 1956; *s* of late T. F. Evans and Marjorie Evans. *Educ:* County Sch., Ashford, Middlesex; Shoreditch Coll. of Educn; Inst. of Educn, London Univ. (BEd 1978; MA 1993). Teacher: Thames Ditton Middle Sch., 1978–83; Woodville Middle Sch., Leatherhead, 1983–85; Dep. Headteacher, Town Farm Middle Sch., 1985–89; Headteacher, Crane Jun. Sch., Hanworth, Hounslow, 1990–94. MEP (Lab): London NW, 1994–99, London Region, 1999–2009; European Parliament: Member: Youth, Culture, Educn and Media Cttee, 1994–2001; Rules of Procedure Cttee, 1994–99 (Vice Pres., 1997–99); Cttee on Citizens' Freedoms and Rights, Justice and Home Affairs, 1999–2004 (Vice Pres., 1999–2004); Cttee on Transport and Tourism, 2004–09; Mem. Delegn for Relns with Countries of S Asia, 1994–09 (Chm., 2007–09), with Romania, 1997–2006, with Georgia, Armenia and Azerbaijan, 2004–09, with Moldova, 2005–09, with Afghanistan, 2007–09; Chief EU Observer, Cambodian Elections, 2003; Rapporteur: mobility for students, volunteers, teachers and trainers, 2001; prevention of trafficking in human organs, 2003; certification of seafarers, 2004; access to aircraft for disabled people and passengers of reduced mobility, 2005. Contested (Lab): Berkshire East, 1987; Uxbridge, 1992; Brent E, Sept. 2003; London South and Surrey, European Parly election, 1989. Mem. (Lab), Surrey CC, 2013–. Member: NUT (Pres., Leatherhead Br., 1984–85); GMB; Nat. Exec., Socialist Educnl Assoc., 1989–98; League Against Cruel Sports, 1976– (Hon. EP Consultant, 1997–2009). Trustee: Interact Worldwide, 2003–07; BRAC (UK), 2009–; NGO Shipbreaking Platform, 2013–. Mem. Corp., Coll. of NW London, 2004–. DUniv Brunel, 1998. *Recreations:* cricket, hockey, swimming, cycling, ski-ing, cinema, psephology, mowing the lawn, theatre, travel, history of education. *E:* rjeevans@globalnet.co.uk. *Clubs:* MCC; Ruskin House Labour (Croydon); Ashford Hockey, Ashford Cricket (Middlesex); Middlesex County Cricket, Incogniti Cricket.

See also A. T. B. Evans.

EVANS, Prof. Robert John Weston, PhD; FBA 1984; Regius Professor of History (formerly Modern History), University of Oxford, 1997–2011; Fellow, Oriel College, Oxford, 1997–2011, now Hon. Fellow; *b* 7 Oct. 1943; *s* of Thomas Frederic and Margery Evans (*née* Weston), Cheltenham; *m* 1969, Kati Róbert; one *s* (one *d* decd). *Educ:* Dean Close School; Jesus College, Cambridge (BA 1st Cl. with distinction 1965, PhD 1968). Oxford University: Fellow, Brasenose Coll., 1968–97, Emeritus Fellow, 2010; Lectr, 1969–90; Reader in Modern History of E Central Europe, 1990–92; Prof. of European History, 1992–97. Mem., Inst. for Advanced Study, Princeton, 1981–82. Fellow: Hungarian Acad. of Scis, 1995; Austrian Acad. of Scis, 1997; Learned Soc. of Czech Republic, 2004; Founding FLSW 2010. Hon. DPhil Charles Univ., Prague, 2005. František Palacký Medal, Czechoslovakia, 1991; Ehrenkreuz für Wissenschaft und Kunst, Austria, 2009. Jt Editor, English Historical Review, 1985–95. *Publications:* Rudolf II and his World, 1973; The Wechel Presses, 1975; The Making of the Habsburg Monarchy, 1979 (Wolfson Literary Award for History, 1980; Anton Gindely Preis, Austria, 1986); (ed with H. Pogge von Strandmann) The Coming of the First World War, 1988; (ed with T. V. Thomas) Crown, Church and Estates: Central European politics, 1991; (ed with H. Pogge von Strandmann) The Revolutions in Europe, 1848–9, 2000; Austria, Hungary and the Habsburgs: essays on Central Europe *c* 1683–1867, 2006; (ed with M. Cornwall) Czechoslovakia in a Nationalist and Fascist Europe 1918–48, 2007; (ed with T. Charles-Edwards) Wales and the Wider World, 2010; (ed with G. Marchal) The Uses of the Middle Ages in Modern European States: history, nationhood, and the search for origins, 2011; (ed jtly) The Holy Roman Empire 1495–1806, 2011; (ed jtly) The Holy Roman Empire 1495–1806: a European perspective, 2012. *Recreations:* music, walking, natural (and unnatural) history. *Address:* Oriel College, Oxford OX1 4EW; Rowan Cottage, 45 Sunningwell, Abingdon, Oxon OX13 6RD.

EVANS, Maj.-Gen. Robert Noel, CB 1981; Postgraduate Dean and Commandant, Royal Army Medical College, 1979–81; *b* 22 Dec. 1922; *s* of William Evans and Norah Moynihan; *m* 1950, Mary Elizabeth O'Brien (*d* 2007); four *s* one *d*. *Educ:* Christian Brothers Sch., Tralee, Co. Kerry; National University of Ireland (MB, BCh, BAO 1947). DTM&H 1961; FFARCS 1963. Commnd RAMC 1951; Consultant Anaesthetist, 1963; CO BMH Rinteln, 1969–71; ADMS 4th Div., 1971–73; DDMS HQ BAOR, 1973–75; Comdt, RAMC Trng Centre, 1975–77; DMS, HQ BAOR, 1977–79; QHP 1976–81. Col Comdt, RAMC, 1981–86. MFCM 1978. OStJ 1978. *Recreations:* gardening, walking, music. *Address:* 32 Folly Hill, Farnham, Surrey GU9 0BH. *T:* (01252) 726938.

EVANS, Robin Edward Rowlinson, FRICS; Chief Executive, Canal and River Trust (formerly British Waterways), 2002–13; *b* 24 March 1954; *s* of Lt Col John and Connie Evans; *m* 1978, Hilary; two *s* one *d*. *Educ:* Reading Univ. (BSc Estate Mgt). FRICS 1990. Land Agent, NT, 1979–87; Dir, Landmark Trust, 1987–95; Palaces Dir, Historic Royal Palaces, 1995–99; Commercial Dir, British Waterways, 1999–2002. Mem. Bd, Valuation Tribunal Service, 2014–. Trustee, Volunteer England, 2012–13. Mem. Council, Univ. of Reading, 2009– (Chm., Investments Cttee, 2011–). CCMI 2007. *Recreations:* family, walking, tennis. *T:* (01494) 863482.

See also M. R. R. Evans.

EVANS, Hon. Sir Roderick; *see* Evans, Hon. Sir D. R.

EVANS, Roger; *see* Evans, Jeremy R.

EVANS, Roger Kenneth; barrister; a Recorder, since 2000; *b* 18 March 1947; *s* of late G. R. Evans and Dr A. M. Evans; *m* 1973, June Rodgers, MA, barrister; two *s*. *Educ:* The Grammar Sch., Bristol; Trinity Hall, Cambridge (MA). President: Cambridge Union, 1970; Cambridge Georgian Gp, 1969; Chm., Cambridge Univ. Conservative Assoc., 1969. Called to the Bar: Middle Temple, 1970 (Astbury Schol.); Inner Temple, *ad eundem*, 1979; in practice, 1970–94, 1997–; an Asst Recorder, 1998–2000. Contested (C): Warley West, Oct. 1974, 1979; Ynys Môn, 1987; Monmouth, May 1991. MP (C) Monmouth, 1992–97; contested (C) same seat, 1997, 2001. Parly Under-Sec. of State, DSS, 1994–97. Member: Welsh Affairs Select Cttee, 1992–94; Ecclesiastical Cttee of Parlt, 1992–97. Chairman: Friends of Friendless Churches, 1998–; Prayer Book Soc., 2001–06 (Vice-Pres., 1995–2001); Mem., Ecclesiastical Law Soc., 1988–. Freeman, City of London, 1976. *Recreations:* architectural and gardening history, building, gardening. *Address:* 2 Harcourt Buildings, Temple, EC4Y 9DB. *E:* revans@harcourtchambers.co.uk. *Clubs:* Carlton, Coningsby (Chm., 1976–77; Treas., 1983–87).

EVANS, Roger W.; *see* Warren Evans.

EVANS, Roy; *see* Evans, H. R.

EVANS, Roy Lyon, OBE 1993; General Secretary, Iron and Steel Trades Confederation, 1985–93; *b* 13 Aug. 1931; *s* of David Evans and Sarah (*née* Lyon); *m* 1960, Brenda Jones; one *s* two *d*. *Educ:* Gowerton Grammar Sch., Swansea. Employed in Tinplate Section of Steel Industry, 1948. Iron and Steel Trades Confederation: Divl Organiser, NW Area, 1964–69; Divl Organiser, W Wales Area, 1969–73; Asst Gen. Sec., 1973–85. Mem., Gen. Council, TUC, 1985–93. Jt Sec., Jt Industrial Council for the Slag Industry, 1975–85; Mem., ECSC Consultative Cttee, 1985–93 (Pres., 1986–88); Hon. Sec., British Section, IMF, 1985–93 (Pres., Iron and Steel Dept (World), 1986). Member: Jt Accident Prevention Adv. Cttee, 1974–93 (Chm., 1983); NEC of Labour Party, 1981–84. Bd Mem., British Steel (Industry) Ltd, 1986–94. *Recreations:* reading, walking.

EVANS, Russell Wilmot, MC 1945; Chairman, Rank Organisation, 1982–83; *b* 4 Nov. 1922; *s* of William Henry Evans and Ethel Williams Wilmot; *m* 1956, Pamela Muriel Hayward (*d* 1989); two *s* one *d*. *Educ:* King Edward's Sch., Birmingham; Birmingham Univ. LLB Hons. Served HM Forces, 1942–47; commnd Durham LI, 1942, Major, 1945. Admitted Solicitor, Birmingham, 1949; Solicitor with Shakespeare & Vernon, Birmingham, 1949–50; Asst Sec., Harry Ferguson, 1951; Sec., Massey-Ferguson (Hldgs) and UK subsids, 1955–62; Dir, gp of private cos in construction industry, 1962–67; joined Rank Organisation, 1967: Dep. Sec., 1967–68; Sec., 1968–72; Dir, 1972–83; Man. Dir, 1975–82; Dep. Chm., 1981; Dir, principal subsid. and associated cos incl. Rank Xerox, 1975–83; Fuji Xerox, 1976–83; Chm., Rank City Wall, 1976–83. Director: Eagle Star Holdings, 1982–87; Oxford Economic Forecasting Ltd, 1986–96; Medical Cyclotron Ltd, 1988–2011. *Recreations:* formerly tennis, golf and photography. *Address:* Walnut Tree, Roehampton Gate, SW15 5JR. *T:* (020) 8876 2433. *Clubs:* English-Speaking Union, Roehampton (Dir 1971–87, Chm., 1984–87, Pres., 1991–).

EVANS, Ruth Elizabeth; Chair, Association of Television on Demand, since 2010; *b* 12 Oct. 1957; *d* of Peter Evans and Dr Anne Evans; one *d*. *Educ:* Girton Coll., Cambridge (MA Hist.). Dir, Maternity Alliance, 1981–86; Dep. Dir, then Actg Dir, Nat. Assoc. for Mental Health (MIND), 1986–90; Gen. Sec., War On Want, 1990; Mgt Consultant, 1990–91; Dir, Nat. Consumer Council, 1992–98; Chairman: Inquiry into Paediatric Cardiac Services, Royal Brompton and Harefield NHS Trust, 1999–2001; Ind. Inquiry into Drug Testing at Work, 2002–04. Non-executive Director: Financial Ombudsman Service, 1999–2002; Liverpool Victoria Gp, 1999–2002; Nationwide Bldg Soc., 2002–05; PhonePay Plus, 2008–; Nat. Audit Office, 2010–12 (Chair, Remuneration Bd, 2010–12); Alacrity Entrepreneurship Foundn, 2011– (Founding Trustee, 2010–); CPP Gp plc, 2013– (Chair, Remuneration Cttee, 2013–); Serious Fraud Office, 2015–; Mem. Adv. Bd, ING Direct, UK, 2007–10. Mem., Central R&D Cttee, NHS, 1995–99; Chm., Standing Adv. Gp on Consumer Involvement, NHS R&D Prog., 1995–99; Dep. Chm., Ofcom Consumer Panel, 2002–; Member: Ind. Rev. Panel for advertising of medicines for human use, 1999–2003; Human Genetics Commn, 1999–2002; Medicines Commn, 2002–03; Law Soc. Governance Review Gp, 2003–04. Lay Mem., 1999–2007, and Chm., Standards and Ethics Cttee, 2004–06, GMC. Chm., Bar Standards Bd, 2006–08. Member: UK Round Table on Sustainable Develt, 1995–99; Expert Panel on Sustainable Develt, DETR, 1998–99; Commn on Taxation and Citizenship, Fabian Soc., 1999–2000; BBC Licence Fee Review Panel, DCMS, 1999; Bd, Financial Services Ombudsman Scheme, subseq. Financial Ombudsman Service, 1999–2002; Panel of Ind. Assessors, Office of Comr for Public Appts, 1999–2005; Council, Britain in Europe, 1999–2004; Ind. Complaints Panel, Audit Commn, 2004–06; Queen's Counsel Selection Panel, 2005–08; Customer Impact Panel, ABI, 2006–09; Ind. Police Complaints Commn, 2009– (Chair, Remuneration Bd, 2009–). Trustee, Money Advice Trust, 1994–2000 (Chm., Adv. Gp of UK money advice agencies, 1994–2000). *Recreations:* daughter, writing, music, swimming. *Address:* 24 Falkland Road, NW5 2PX. *T:* (020) 7482 0420, 07973 370677. *E:* ruth@ruthevans.org.

EVANS, Sally Anne; Deputy Legal Adviser, Home Office, 1995–2000; *b* 20 March 1948; *d* of late Arthur Francis Gardiner Austin and Joy Austin (*née* Ravenor); *m* 1977, Richard Maurice Evans. *Educ:* High Sch. for Girls, Darlington; Univ. of Manchester (LLB Hons 1970). Called to the Bar, Gray's Inn, 1971; Barclays Bank DCO, then Barclays Bank Internat. Ltd, 1970–72; Western American Bank Ltd, 1972–73; Legal Adviser's Br., Home Office, 1974–2000. Vice Chm., Friends of The Royal Marsden, 2006–08. *Recreations:* theatre, cooking, summer gardening.

EVANS, Sarah Hauldys, OBE 2014; educational consultant, since 2013; Principal (formerly Headmistress), King Edward VI High School for Girls, 1996–2013; *b* 4 March 1953; *d* of Nancy and Wyndham Evans; *m* 1989, Andrew Romanis Fowler; one *s*. *Educ:* King James' Grammar Sch., Knaresborough; Univ. of Sussex (BA Hons English); Univ. of Leicester (MA Victorian Studies); Univ. of Leeds (PGCE). English Teacher, Leeds Girls' High Sch., 1976–84; Dep. Head, Fulneck Girls' Sch., 1984–89; Head, Friends' Sch., Saffron Walden, 1989–96. *Recreation:* the arts.

EVANS, Stephen Nicholas, CMG 2002; OBE 1994; HM Diplomatic Service; Assistant Secretary General for Operations, NATO, since 2011 (on secondment); *b* 29 June 1950; *s* of late Vincent Morris Evans and Doris Mary Evans (*née* Braham); *m* 1975, Sharon Ann Holdcroft; one *s* two *d*. *Educ:* King's Coll., Taunton; Bristol Univ. (BA); Corpus Christi Coll., Cambridge (MPhil). Royal Tank Regt (Lieut), 1971–74; FCO, 1974; language student (Vietnamese), SOAS, 1975; FCO, 1976; First Sec., Hanoi, 1978–80; FCO, 1980–82; language training (Thai), Bangkok, 1982–83; First Sec., Bangkok, 1983–86; FCO, 1986–90; First Sec. (Political), Ankara, 1990; Counsellor (Econ., Commercial, Aid), Islamabad, 1993–96; seconded to UN Special Mission to Afghanistan, 1996–97; Counsellor and Head: OSCE and Council of Europe Dept, FCO, 1997–98; S Asian Dept, FCO, 1998–2002; Chargé d'Affaires, Kabul, 2002; High Comr, Sri Lanka, 2002–06; Ambassador to Afghanistan, 2006–07; Dir, Afghanistan Inf. Strategy, FCO, 2007–08; High Comr, Bangladesh, 2008–11. *Recreations:* military and naval history, golf, cycling. *Address:* NATO, Boulevard Leopold III, 1110 Brussels, Belgium. *Club:* Athenæum.

EVANS, Susan Louise Carr; QC 2010; **Her Honour Judge Susan Evans;** a Circuit Judge, since 2011; *b* Arbroath, 16 June 1966; *d* of Anthony Evans and Jeanette Carr; *m* 2000, John Pemberton. Called to the Bar, Gray's Inn, 1989; Recorder, 2005–11. *Address:* Winchester Combined Court, High Street, Winchester SO23 9EL. *E:* HHJudgeSusan.EvansQC@judiciary.gsi.gov.uk.

EVANS, (Thomas) Alun, CMG 1994; HM Diplomatic Service, retired; *b* 8 June 1937; *s* of late Thomas Evans and Mabel Elizabeth (*née* Griffiths); *m* 1964, Bridget Elisabeth, *d* of late Peter Lloyd, CBE and of Nora Kathleen Williams (*née* Patten); three *s*. *Educ:* Shrewsbury Sch.; University Coll., Oxford (MA). Army, 1956–58, commd KOYLI. Entered HM Foreign Service, 1961; Third Sec., Rangoon, 1962–64; Second Sec., Singapore, 1964–66; FO, 1966–70; First Sec., Geneva, 1970–74; FCO, 1974–79; Counsellor: Pretoria, 1979–82; FCO, 1983–95. Internat. Risk and Internat. Affairs Advr, British Airways, 1995–2002; Internat. Affairs Advr, Cathay Pacific Airways, 2002–08; Director: Fleming, subseq. J. P. Morgan, Asian Investment Trust, 2001–12; Sigma Internat. Ltd, 2002–04; Advr, Nimbus Trng, 2003–06; Chairman: Lexicon Data Ltd, 2007–; Oceanfoil Ltd, 2012–. Dir, British Iranian and Central Asian Assoc., 2000–01; Vice-Chairman: British Iranian Chamber of Commerce, 2001–; Thames Concerts, 2008–11. Trustee, Pimpernel Trust, 1997–2005. *Recreations:* France, music, travel. *Club:* Travellers.

EVANS, His Honour (Thomas) Michael; QC 1973; a Circuit Judge, 1979–98; *b* 7 Sept. 1930; *s* of late David Morgan Evans, Barrister, and of Mary Gwynydd Lloyd; *m* 1957, Margaret Valerie Booker; one *s* four *d*. *Educ:* Brightlands Prep. Sch., Newnham, Glos; Marlborough Coll., Wilts; Jesus Coll., Oxford (MA (Juris.)). Called to the Bar, Gray's Inn, 1954; Wales and Chester Circuit, 1955; a Recorder of the Crown Court, 1972–79. Legal Chm., Mental Health Review Tribunal for Wales, 1970. Chancellor, Diocese of St Davids, 1986–2005; Pres., Provincial Court, Church in Wales, 1997–2007. Gov., Christ Coll., Brecon, 1992–2009 (Chm. of Govs, 1999–2003). *Recreations:* walking, fishing, genealogy. *Address:* 31 Saxon Road, Manor Park, Tavistock, Devon PL19 8JS.

EVANS, Timothy Hugh David; Apothecary to the Queen and to the Royal Households of London, since 2003; Private General Practitioner, since 1990; *b* 3 May 1955; *s* of late David Lawrence Evans and Betty Joan Evans; *m* 2000, Annabel Clare Blake (*d* 2008); one *s* one *d*. *Educ:* Marlborough Coll.; Westminster Hosp. Med. Sch. (MB BS). MRCS 1979, LRCP 1979; DRCOG 1984; MRCGP 1985; DA 1987. House Officer, Westminster Hosp., 1979–80; SHO, Andrew Fleming Hosp., Harare, 1980–81; Dist MO, Kariba Hosp., Zimbabwe, 1981–83; SHO, Obstetrics, Cheltenham Gen. Hosp., 1984; GP Registrar, Tewkesbury, 1985; SHO, Anaesthetics, Cheltenham Gen. Hosp., 1986; RMO, London Clinic, Portland Hosp. for Women and Children, 1987–89. Founder and Med. Dir, Grace Belgravia, 2012–. Mem., Chelsea Clinical Soc., 1993–. *Recreations:* golf, tennis, sailing, music, theatre. *Address:* Bazeley House, Bazeley Copse Lane, Micheldever, Hants SO21 3AA. *Club:* Royal Wimbledon Golf.

EVANS, Lt Gen. Timothy Paul, CBE 2012 (MBE 2000); DSO 2008; Commander Allied Rapid Reaction Corps, since 2013; *b* Iserlöhn, Germany, 21 Sept. 1962; *s* of Col Peter Benwell Evans and Ray Evans; *m* 1987, Helen Mary O'Reilly; two *d*. *Educ:* Monkton Combe Jun. Sch.; Monkton Combe Sen. Sch.; Royal Military Acad., Sandhurst. Commnd 1982; Platoon Comdr, 1st Bn LI, then Trng Platoon Comdr, Light Div. Depot, 1984–86; ADC to GOC Wales, 1986–87; Ops Officer, 3rd Bn LI, 1988–89; Troop Comdr, Special Forces, 1990–93; Staff Coll., 1994; Ops Officer, HQ DSF, 1995–96; Co. Comdr, 1st Bn LI, 1997; Sqdn Comdr, Special Forces, 1998–2000; Jt Doctrine and Concept Centre, 2000–01; CO, 1st Bn LI, 2001–02; COS, 3(UK) Div., 2002–05; Bde Comdr, 19 Light Bde, 2006–08; Comdr, Jt Force Ops, PJHQ, 2008–09; COS ISAF Jt Comd HQ, Afghanistan, 2010–11; COS HQ ARRC, 2009–12; Comdt, RMA, 2012–13. *Recreations:* running, hill walking, water ski-ing, ski-ing, bridge.

EVANS, Prof. Timothy William, MD, PhD, DSc; FRCP, FRCA; FMedSci; Professor of Intensive Care Medicine, Imperial College of Science, Technology and Medicine, University of London, since 1996; Head, Unit of Critical Care, National Heart and Lung Institute, since 1993; Consultant in Intensive Care and Thoracic Medicine, Royal Brompton Hospital, since 1987; Medical Director, since 2005, Responsible Officer, since 2011, Deputy Chief Executive Officer, since 2006 and Director of Research, since 2008, Royal Brompton and Harefield Hospitals NHS Trust; *b* 29 May 1954; *s* of Philip Charles Evans and Mary Elizabeth Norah Evans (*née* Else); *m* 1987, Josephine Emer MacSweeney, Consultant in Neuroradiology, *d* of Prof. James MacSweeney; three *s* one *d*. *Educ:* High Storrs Grammar Sch., Sheffield; Univ. of Manchester (BSc Hons 1976; MB ChB Hons 1979; MD 1990); Univ. of Sheffield (PhD 1985; DSc 1997). MRCP 1982, FRCP 1993; FRCA 2000. House Officer, Univ. Dept of Neurosurgery, 1979–80, Renal and Gen. Medicine Dept, 1980, Manchester Royal Infirmary; Senior House Officer: Professorial Med. Unit, Royal Hallamshire Hosp., Univ. of Sheffield, 1980–81; in Gen. Medicine and Gastroenterology, Hammersmith Hosp./RPMS, 1981–82; in Thoracic Medicine, Brompton Hosp., 1982; Trent RHA Res. Fellow, and Hon. Med. Registrar, Acad. Div. of Medicine, Univ. of Sheffield, 1982–84; MRC Travelling Fellow, Cardiovascular Res. Inst., Univ. of Calif, San Francisco, 1984–85; Sen. Registrar in Thoracic and Gen. Medicine, Brompton and King's Coll. Hosps, 1985–86; Doverdale Fellow in Intensive Care and Hon. Sen. Registrar, Brompton Hosp., 1986–87; Cons. Physician, Chelsea and Westminster Hosp., 1988–. Hon. Consultant: in Intensive Care Medicine, HM Forces, 1998–; The Royal Hosp., Chelsea, 2004–. Member: Adv. Gp on Intensive Care Services, Nat. Audit Commn, 1998–99; Nat. Expert Gp, Adult Critical Care Services, NHS Exec., 1999–2000. Member: BMA Grants Cttee, 1989–94; British Lung Foundn Grants Cttee, 1992–95; BHF Grants Cttee, 2002–05; Council, British Thoracic Soc., 1993–96; Council, European Intensive Care Soc., 1997–2005; Royal College of Physicians: Member: Thoracic Medicine Cttee, 1994–98; Gen. Medicine Cttee, 1996–2005; Censor, 2003; Academic Registrar, 2005–; Academic Vice-Pres., 2009–12; Vice Dean, Faculty of Intensive Care, 2010–13. Trustee and Board Member: Faculty of Pharmaceutical Medicine, 2013–; Nuffield Trust, 2014–. FMedSci 1999. Member, Editorial Board: Thorax, 1991–94; Intensive Care Medicine, 1996–99; Amer. Jl of Respiratory and Critical Care Medicine, 1997–2006; Amer. Jl of Physiology, 2000–03. *Publications:* jointly: Slide Interpretation for MRCP, 1988; Respiratory Medicine, 1989; The Drug Treatment of Respiratory Disease, 1994; Acute Respiratory Distress in Adults, 1996; Recent Advances in Critical Care 5, 1996; (ed jtly) Acute Lung Injury, 1997; (ed jtly) Tissue Oxygenation in Sepsis, 2001; more than 250 articles on scientific and clinical aspects of intensive care medicine. *Recreations:* flying, housework. *Address:* Department of Anaesthetics and Intensive Care Medicine, Royal Brompton Hospital, Sydney Street, SW3 6NP. *T:* (020) 7351 8523, *Fax:* (020) 7351 8524. *E:* t.evans@rbht.nhs.uk.

See also L. E. Evans.

EVANS, Dr Trevor John; consultant in governance and change management; *b* 14 Feb. 1947; *o s* of late Evan Alban Evans and Margaret Alice Evans (*née* Hilton); *m* 1973, Margaret Elizabeth (*née* Whitham); three *s* one *d*. *Educ:* King's Sch., Rochester; University Coll., London (BSc (Eng) 1968, PhD 1972; Fellow, 1997; Hon. Fellow, 2010); Univ. of Liverpool (MA Dist. 2013). CEng, FIChemE (Hon. FIChemE 2006). Res. Officer, CSIR, Pretoria, 1968–69; Ford Motor Co., Aveley, Essex, 1972–73; Institution of Chemical Engineers: Asst Sec., Technical, 1973–75; Dep. Sec., 1975–76; Gen. Sec., 1976–94; Chief Exec., 1994–2006; Chief Exec., Ergonomics Soc., 2007; Chief Exec., AATSE, 2007–08. Member: Bd, Council of Science and Technology Institutes, 1976–87; Exec. Cttee, Commonwealth Engineers Council, 1976–2004; Steering Cttee, DTI Action for Engrg Prog., 1995–96, Bd, Science Council, 2001–06; Bd, Engrg Council (UK), 2002–06 (Dep. Chm., 2005–06); Engrg and Technology Bd, 2005–07; Chm. Exec. Cttee, World Chem. Engrg Council, 2006. Vis. Prof., UCL, 2011–14. Jt Hon. Sec., 1976–2006, Hon. Mem., 2008, European Fedn of Chem. Engrg. Mem. Ct, Imperial Coll., London, 1998–2006. FRSA. Hon. Mem., Czech Soc. of Chemical Engrg, 2006. Kurnakov Meml Medal, USSR Acad. of Scis, 1991; Titanium Achema Plaque, 1997. *Publications:* scientific and historical papers and general articles in Chemical Engrg Science, The Chem. Engr, etc. *Recreations:* study of slavery, 18th, 19th century and WW1 history. *Address:* Welsh Row House, 50 Welsh Row, Nantwich, Cheshire CW5 5EJ.

EVANS, Very Rev. Trevor Owen; Dean of Bangor, 1998–2003; *b* 10 July 1937; *s* of John James Pierce Evans and Elizabeth Jane Evans; *m* 1962, Ann Christine Stephens; one *s* one *d*. *Educ:* Dolgellau Boys' Grammar Sch.; UCW, Aberystwyth (BSc); Coll. of the Resurrection, Mirfield. Ordained deacon, 1961, priest, 1962; Diocese of Bangor: Curate, Barmouth, 1961–64; Curate, 1964–70, Vicar, 1970–75, Llandudno; Vicar, Llanidloes, 1975–89; RD, Arwystli, 1976–89; Preb. and Canon of Bangor Cathedral, 1982–98; Rector of Trefdraeth, 1989–90; Dir of Ministry, 1989–98; Rector of Llanfair PG with Penmynydd, 1990–98, also with Llanddaniel-Fab and with Llanedwen, 1997–98; Surrogate, 1978–98. *Recreations:* hill-walking, wood-turning, ornithology, geology, geomorphology. *Address:* Hafan, 3 Coed y Castell, Bangor LL57 1PH.

EVANS, Maj.-Gen. William Andrew, CB 1993; DL; Secretary, Council of TAVRAs, 1993–2001; *b* 5 Aug. 1939; *s* of late Maj.-Gen. Roger Evans, CB, MC and Eileen Evans; *m* 1964, Virginia Susan (*d* 2014), *e d* of late William Robert Tomkinson and Helen Mary Tomkinson, MBE; two *d*. *Educ:* Sherborne; RMA Sandhurst; Christ Church, Oxford (MA). Commnd 5th Royal Inniskilling Dragoon Guards, 1959; served in BAOR, Middle East, Cyprus, Libya, N Ireland; Staff Coll., Bracknell, 1971; Army Instructor, RAF Cranwell, 1974–75; Instructor, Army Staff Coll., 1978–80; CO 5th Royal Inniskilling Dragoon Guards, 1980–82 (despatches, 1981); Col, Asst Dir (Policy), Defence Policy Staff, 1982–83; Comdr 4 Armd Bde, 1983–85; RCDS 1986; DCS, HQ BAOR, 1987–89; GOC Eastern Dist, 1989–92, retired. Pres., Essex, Army Benevolent Fund, 1997–2008; Vice Chm., Royal Dragoon Guards Regtl Assoc., 1992–2002; Member Council: ACFA, 1993–2001; Union Jack Club, 1995–2009. Pres., Army Cricket Assoc., 1989–91; Chm., Combined Services Cricket Assoc., 1990. Trustee, Daws Hall Trust, 2000–08. Mem., Court, Essex Univ., 1994–2009. Liveryman, Broderers' Co., 1992–2014. DL Essex, 1998. *Recreations:* fishing, birdwatching, golf, grandchildren. *Club:* Essex.

EVANS, Dr (William) David; Director, Innovation and International, Department for Business, Innovation and Skills (formerly Department for Innovation, Universities and Skills), 2008–09; *b* 20 April 1949; *s* of late Harold Evans and Gladys Evans (*née* Webber); *m* 1980, Elizabeth Crowe; three *s* one *d*. *Educ:* Haberdashers' Aske's School, Elstree; St Catherine's College, Oxford (BA 1971; DPhil 1974; Senior Scholar). FRAS 1975. Dept of Energy, 1974–80; First Sec., Science and Technology, British Embassy, Bonn, 1980–83; Asst Sec., 1984–89, Chief Scientist, 1989–92, Dept of Energy; Department of Trade and Industry: Hd of Envmt Div., 1992–94; Hd of Technology and Innovation Div., 1994–96; Director: Technol. and Standards, later Technol. and Standards Directorate, 1996–98; Competitiveness, 1998–2001; Dep. Chief Exec., Small Business Service, 2001–03; Dir, Finance and Resource Mgt, 2003–05; Acting Dir Gen., Services Gp, 2005–06; Dir, Technol. and Innovation, DTI, later Dir, Innovation, DIUS, 2006–08. Member: NERC, 1989–92; EPSRC, 1994–98; PPARC, 1994–98; Assessor, SERC, ACORD, 1989–92. Interim Chief Exec., 2007, Sen. Govt Advr, 2009–13, Technol. Strategy Bd. Institution of Engineering and Technology: Chm., Standards Cttee, 2013–; Chm., Knowledge Services Bd, 2014–; Vice Pres. and Trustee, 2014–. Senator, Engrg Council, 1996–98; Hon. Treas., Science Council, 2009–13. Adjunct Prof., Imperial Coll. Business Sch., 2010–. *Publications:* scientific papers in professional jls. *Recreations:* music, reading, history of technology.

EVANS, (William) Lindsay; DL; freelance lecturer, television actor and presenter; Trustee, National Heritage Memorial Fund, 1992–99; Chairman, Committee for Wales, Heritage Lottery Fund, 1998–99; *b* 22 March 1933; *o s* of John Evans and Nellie (*née* Davies). *Educ:* Swansea GS; Univ. of Wales (BA, MA, DipEd); Jesus Coll., Oxford (MLitt 1961). School teacher, Middlesex CC, 1958–60; freelance newsreader, BBC, 1960–61; Asst Master, Llandovery Coll., 1961–65; Lectr in Drama, Bangor Normal Coll., 1965–67; Prin. Lectr and Hd of Drama Dept, Cartrefle Coll., Wrexham, 1967–91. Lectr, summer schools, Extra-Mural Dept, UCNW, Bangor, 1967–70; Standish Barry Lectr, Irish Georgian Soc., 2005. Member: Exec. Cttee, N Wales Arts Assoc., 1973–76; Welsh Arts Council, 1982–88; Historic Bldgs Council for Wales, 1977–99; Welsh Cttee, NT, 1984–90. Trustee, Patti Theatre Preservation Trust, 2004–. Hon. Fellow, Glyndŵr Univ., 2012. DL Clwyd, 1999. Author of numerous radio and television plays and documentaries in English and Welsh. *Publications:* Y Gelltydd (novel), 1980; The Castles of Wales, 1998; *contributed to:* Everyman's Guide to England & Wales, 2000; Treasures of Britain, 2002; The Twentieth Century Great House, 2002; Art and Industry, 2012; articles on aspects of built envmt. *Recreations:* friends, music, discovering places and buildings. *Address:* 100 Erddig Road, Wrexham LL13 7DR.

EVANS, Very Rev. Wyn; *see* St Davids, Bishop of.

EVANS, Wynford; *see* Evans, J. W.

EVANS-ANFOM, Emmanuel, FRCSE 1955; Commissioner for Education and Culture, Ghana, 1978–88; Member, Council of State, 1979; Chairman, National Education Commission, since 1984; *b* 7 Oct. 1919; *m* 1952, Leonora Francetta Evans (*d* 1980); three *s* one *d*; *m* 1984, Elise Henkel. *Educ:* Achimota School; Edinburgh University (MB ChB 1947; DTM&H; Alumnus of the Year Award, 1996). House Surgeon, Dewsbury Infirmary, 1948–49; Medical Officer, Gold Coast Medical Service, 1950–56, Specialist Surgeon, 1956–67; Senior Lecturer, Ghana Medical School, 1966–67; Vice-Chancellor, Univ. of Science and Technology, Kumasi, 1967–74. Mem., WHO Expert Panel on Med. and Paramed. Educn, 1972–; Chairman: Nat. Council for Higher Educn, 1974–78; W African Exams Council, 1991–94; Chairman: Med. and Dental Council; Akrofi-Christaller Centre for Mission Res. and Applied Theology, 1986–; Inter-church and Ecumenical Relations Cttee, Presbyterian Church of Ghana, 1990–. Titular Mem., Internat. Assoc. Surgeons; Past President: Ghana Medical Assoc.; Assoc. of Surgeons of W Africa; FICS. Fellow: Ghana Acad. Arts and Sciences, 1971 (Pres., 1987–91); African Acad. of Scis, 1986. Chm., Ghana Hockey Assoc. Pres., Ghana Boys' Brigade Council, 1987–. Hon. DSc: Salford, 1974; Kwame Nkrumah Univ. of Sci. and Technol., 2003; Hon. DLitt Akrofi-Christaller Inst., 2012. Millennium Excellence Award of Ghana, 2000; Life Achievement Award, Ghana Med. and Dental Council, 2004. Mem., Order of the Star of Ghana, 2006. *Publications:* Aetiology and Management of Intestinal Perforations, Ghana Med. Jl, 1963; Traditional Medicine in Ghana: practice problems and prospects, 1986; To the Thirsty Land: autobiography of a patriot, 2003. *Recreations:* hockey, music, art. *Address:* PO Box M135, Accra, Ghana.

EVANS-BEVAN, Sir Martyn Evan, 2nd Bt *cr* 1958; *b* 1 April 1932; *s* of Sir David Martyn Evans-Bevan, 1st Bt, and Eira Winifred, *d* of late Sidney Archibald Lloyd Glanley; *S* father, 1973; *m* 1957, Jennifer Jane Marion, *d* of Robert Hugh Stevens; four *s*. *Educ:* Uppingham. Entered family business of Evan Evans Bevan and Evans Bevan Ltd, 1953. High Sheriff of Breconshire, 1967; Liveryman, Worshipful Co. of Farmers; Freeman, City of London. *Recreations:* shooting, fishing. *Heir:* *s* David Gawain Evans-Bevan [*b* 16 Sept. 1961; *m* 1987, Philippa, *y d* of Patrick Sweeney; two *s* one *d*]. *Address:* Spring Box, Rue de Creux, Baillot St Ouen, Jersey, CI JE3 2DR. *Club:* Carlton.

EVANS-FREKE, family name of **Baron Carbery**.

EVANS-GORDON, Jane-Anne Mary; Her Honour Judge Evans-Gordon; a Circuit Judge, since 2014; *b* Northampton; *d* of Dr J. G. O'Hagan and P. J. O'Hagan; *m* 1982, Alastair Kenmure Evans-Gordon; one *s*. *Educ:* Univ. of Reading (LLB 1st Cl. Hons 1991). Called to the Bar, Inner Temple, 1992; in practice as a barrister, New Square Chambers, 1993–2014; Recorder, 2009–14. Guardian, Staffs Hoard, Birmingham Mus. *Publications:* (contrib.) Cohabitation: law and precedents, 1999–; (contrib.) Williams, Mortimer and Sunnucks, Executors, Administrators and Probate, 20th edn 2013; (contrib.) Theobald on Wills, 18th edn, 2015.

EVANS-LOMBE, Hon. Sir Edward (Christopher), Kt 1993; a Judge of the High Court of Justice, Chancery Division, 1993–2008; *b* 10 April 1937; *s* of Vice-Adm. Sir Edward Evans-Lombe, KCB, and Lady Evans-Lombe; *m* 1964, Frances Marilyn MacKenzie, DL; one *s* three *d*. *Educ:* Eton; Trinity Coll., Cambridge (MA). National Service, 1955–57: 2nd Lieut Royal Norfolk Regt. Called to the Bar, Inner Temple, 1963, Bencher, 1985. Standing Counsel to Dept of Trade in Bankruptcy matters, 1971; QC 1978; a Recorder, 1982–93. Chm., Agricultural Land Tribunal, S Eastern Region, 1983–93. *Recreations:* fishing, ornithology, amateur archaeology. *Address:* c/o Royal Courts of Justice, Strand, WC2A 2LL. *Club:* Norfolk (Norwich).

EVANS-TIPPING, (Sir) David Gwynne, (5th Bt *cr* 1913, of Oaklands Park, Awre, Co. Gloucester); *b* 25 Nov. 1943; *e s* of Sir Francis Loring Gwynne-Evans, 4th Bt (who assumed name of Evans-Tipping, 1943–58), and his 1st wife, Elisabeth Fforde, *d* of J. Fforde-Tipping; *S* father, 1993, but does not use the title, and his name does not appear on the Official Roll of the Baronetage; *m* 2003, Françoise Lucie Saldes. *Educ:* Trinity Coll., Dublin (BAgrSc). *Heir:* *b* Christopher Evan Evans-Tipping [*b* 27 Feb. 1946; *m* 1974, Fenella Catherine Morrison; one *s* one *d*].

EVATT, Hon. Elizabeth Andreas, AC 1995 (AO 1982); Member: World Bank Administrative Tribunal, 1998–2006; International Commission of Jurists, since 2003; *b* 11 Nov. 1933; *d* of Clive Raleigh Evatt, QC and Marjorie Hannah (*née* Andreas); *m* 1960, Robert J. Southan, *qv*; one *d* (one *s* decd). *Educ:* Sydney Univ. (LLB); Harvard Univ. (LLM). Called to the Bar: NSW, 1955; Inner Temple, 1958. Chief Judge, Family Court of Australia, 1976–88. Dep. Pres., Australian Conciliation and Arbitration Commn, 1973–89; Chairperson, Royal Commn on Human Relationships, 1974–77; Dep. Pres., Australian Ind. Relns Commn, 1989–94; Pres., Australian Law Reform Commission, 1988–93 (Mem., 1993–94). Member: UN Cttee on Elimination of Discrimination against Women, 1984–92 (Chairperson, 1989–91); UN Human Rights Cttee, 1993–2000; Human Rights and Equal Opportunity Commn, Australia, 1995–98. Chancellor, Univ. of Newcastle, 1988–94. Fellow, Aust. Inst. of Internat. Affairs, 2010. Hon. LLD: Sydney, 1985; Macquarie, 1989; Queensland, 1992; Flinders, 1994; Univ. of NSW, 1996; Hon. Dr Newcastle, 1988. *Publications:* Guide to Family Law, 1986, 2nd edn 1991. *Recreation:* music. *Address:* Unit 2003, 184 Forbes Street, Darlinghurst, NSW 2010, Australia. *Club:* Royal Corinthian Yacht.

EVE, family name of **Baron Silsoe**.

EVE, Judith Mary, CBE 2005 (OBE 1998); Legal Chairman (part-time) for the Appeals Service, since 1984; *b* 13 April 1949; *d* of Edward Steele and Adele Steele (*née* Barnes); *m* 1st, 1971, Richard Eve (marr. diss. 1987); one *s*; 2nd, 1992, John McQuoid (*d* 2013). *Educ:* Queen's Univ. of Belfast (LLB 1971). Called to the Bar, NI, 1973; Queen's University of Belfast: Lectr in Law, 1971–82; Sen. Lectr, 1982–92; Dean, Faculty of Law, 1986–89; Internat. Liaison Officer, 1989–2002. Member: Rent Assessment Panel for NI, 1985–91 and 1994–97; Mental Health Commn for NI, 1986–90; EOC for NI, 1992–98; Bd, Public Appts Service (Ireland), 2011– (Chm., 2014–); Mem., 1993–2006, Chair, 1998–2006, CS Comrs for NI. Non-exec. Dir, N and W Belfast HSS Trust, 1993–2000. Mem., NI Council for Postgrad. Med. and Dental Educn, 2002–04; Mem. and Dep. Chm., NI Med. and Dental Trng Agency, 2004–13. Ind. Assessor, OCPA (NI), 2004–13. Mem., Bd of Visitors, Maghaberry Prison, 1990–92. Dir, Helm Housing (formerly BIH Housing Assoc.), 1984–2012 (Chm., 1985–87). Member, Board: Odyssey Trust Co., 2008–; Northern Regl Coll. (NI), 2013–. *Recreation:* travel.

EVE, Trevor John; actor, since 1974; producer, since 1997; *b* 1 July 1951; *s* of Stewart Frederick Eve and Elsie (*née* Hamer); *m* 1980, Sharon Maughan; two *s* one *d*. *Educ:* Bromsgrove Sch.; Kingston Sch. of Architecture; Royal Acad. of Dramatic Art (Bancroft Gold Medal). *Theatre* includes: John, Paul, George, Ringo and Bert, 1975, Filumena, 1977, Lyric; A Bit of Rough, Soho Poly, 1977; Children of a Lesser God, Albery (Best Actor, Olivier Awards and Variety Club of GB), 1981; The Genius, Royal Court, 1983; High Society, Victoria Palace, 1986; Man Beast and Virtue, RNT, 1989; A Winter's Tale, Young Vic, 1991; Inadmissible Evidence, RNT, 1993; Uncle Vanya, Albery (Best Actor in Supporting Role, Olivier Awards and British Regl Th. Awards), 1997; *films* include: Dracula, 1979; Scandal, 1989; Aspen Extreme, 1993; The Tribe, Appetite, 1998; Possession, 2002; Troy, 2004; She's Out of My League, 2008; Death of a Farmer, 2014; *television* includes: Shoestring, 1979–81 (Best TV Actor, Variety Club of GB, 1980); Jamaica Inn, 1983; A Wreath of Roses, 1986; Shadow of the Sun, 1987; A Sense of Guilt, 1988; Parnell and the Englishwoman, 1990; A Doll's House, 1992; Murder in Mind, Black Easter, The Politician's Wife, 1994; Heat of the Sun, 1997; An Evil Streak, 1998; David Copperfield, 1999; Waking the Dead, 2000–10; Lawless, 2004; The Family Man, 2006; Hughie Green, Most Sincerely, 2008; Framed, 2009; Bouquet of Barbed Wire, 2010; Death Comes to Pemberley, 2013; The Interceptor, 2015; Unforgotten, 2015. CEO and Exec. Prod. for Projector Pictures: Alice Through the Looking Glass, 1998; Cinderella, 2000; Twelfth Night, 2003; Kidnap and Ransom (and actor), 2011, 2012. Patron: Childhope Internat., 1998–. Hon. DLitt Newman Univ., Birmingham, 2014. *Recreations:* tennis, golf, painting, architecture. *Address:* c/o Projector Pictures, 75 Dean Street, W1D 3PU. *T:* (020) 7432 3808. *E:* film@projector.co.uk. *Clubs:* Chelsea Arts, Hurlingham, Queen's; Wentworth.

EVENNETT, Rt Hon. David (Anthony); PC 2015; MP (C) Bexleyheath and Crayford, since 2005; a Lord Commissioner of HM Treasury (Government Whip), since 2012; *b* 3 June 1949; *s* of late Norman Thomas Evennett and Irene Evennett; *m* 1975, Marilyn Anne Smith; two *s*. *Educ:* Buckhurst Hill County High School for Boys; London School of Economics and Political Science (BSc (Econ) Upper Second Hons, MSc (Econ)). School Master, Ilford County High School for Boys, 1972–74; Marine Insurance Broker, Lloyd's, 1974–81; Mem., Lloyd's, 1976–92; Dir, Lloyd's Underwriting Agency, 1982–91; Commercial Liaison Manager, Bexley Coll., 1997–2001; mgt lectr and consultant, 2001–05. Consultant, J & H Marsh and McLennan (UK), then Marsh (UK), Ltd, 1998–2000. Redbridge Borough Councillor, 1974–78. Contested (C) Hackney South and Shoreditch, 1979; MP (C) Erith and Crayford, 1983–97; contested (C) Bexleyheath and Crayford, 1997, 2001. PPS to Minister of State, Dept of Educn, 1992–93, to Sec. of State for Wales, 1993–95, to Minister of State, Home Office, 1995–96, to Sec. of State for Educn and Employment, 1996–97, to Sec. of State for Educn, 2010–12; an Opposition Whip, 2005–09; Shadow Minister for Univs and Skills (formerly Innovation, Univs and Skills), 2009–10. Member, Select Committee: on Educn, Science and the Arts, 1986–92; for Educn and Skills, 2005. *Recreations:* my family, reading, history, music, cinema. *Address:* House of Commons, SW1A 0AA. *Club:* Bexleyheath Conservative.

EVENS, Rt Rev. Robert John Scott; Bishop Suffragan of Crediton, 2004–12; an Honorary Assistant Bishop: Diocese of Gloucester, since 2013; Diocese of Bristol, since 2013; *b* 29 May 1947; *s* of Reginald Evens and Sheila (*née* Scott); *m* 1972, Sue Hayes; one *s* one *d*. *Educ:* Maidstone Grammar Sch.; Trinity Coll., Bristol (DipTh); ACIB. Nat. Westminster Bank, 1964–74; ordained deacon, 1977, priest, 1978; Assistant Curate: St Simon's, Southsea, 1977–79; St Mary's, Portchester, 1979–83; Vicar, St John's, Locks Heath, 1983–96; RD of Fareham, 1993–96; Archdeacon of Bath, 1996–2004. *Recreations:* caravanning in France, gardening, walking with Sue. *Address:* 30 Highland Road, Charlton Kings, Cheltenham GL53 9LT.

EVERALL, Mark Andrew; QC 1994; **His Honour Judge Everall;** a Circuit Judge, since 2006; *b* 30 June 1950; *s* of late John Everall, FRCP and Pamela Everall; *m* 1978, Anne Perkins; two *d*. *Educ:* Ampleforth Coll., York; Lincoln Coll., Oxford (MA). Called to the Bar, Inner Temple, 1975, Bencher, 1998; Asst Recorder, 1993–96; a Recorder, 1996–2006. *Publications:* (ed jtly) Rayden and Jackson on Divorce and Family Matters, 17th edn 1997 to 18th edn 2005; (jtly) International Movement of Children, 2004. *Recreations:* walking, music, architecture. *Address:* 1 Hare Court, Temple, EC4Y 7BE.

EVERARD, Sir Henry Peter Charles, (Sir Harry), 5th Bt *cr* 1911, of Randlestown, co. Meath; *b* 6 Aug. 1970; *s* of Sir Robin Charles Everard, 4th Bt and of Ariel Ingrid (*née* Cleasby-Thompson); *S* father, 2010; *m* 2003, Nicola Anne de Poher, *y d* of late Geoffrey de la Poer Wilkinson; two *s* one *d*. *Educ:* Gresham's Sch., Holt; RMA Sandhurst. Late Queen's Royal Lancers. Hd of Ops, Massive Ltd; Proj. Manager, Castlecomer Discovery Park; Estate Manager, Mount Congreve; Rural Recreation Officer. *Heir:* *s* Benjamin Richard Nugent Everard, *b* 1 Jan. 2005.

EVERARD, Lt Gen. James Rupert, CBE 2005 (OBE 2000); Commander Land Forces, since 2014; *b* Tilton-on-the-Hill, Leics, 23 Sept. 1962; *s* of late Simon Everard and Jo Everard (*née* Holt); *m* 1992, Caroline Mary Simpson; two *s* one *d*. *Educ:* Uppingham Sch.; RMAS. Commnd 17th/21st Lancers, 1983; acsc 1994; COS 4th Armoured Bde, 1994–95; CO Queen's Royal Lancers, 2000–02; DACOS J5(B) PJHQ, 2002–04; HCSC 2005; CDS Liaison Officer to Chm. Jt Chiefs of Staff, 2005; Comdr 20th Armoured Bde, 2006–07; Dir Commitments HQ Land Forces, 2008–09; GOC 3rd (UK) Div., 2009–11; Asst Chief of Gen. Staff, 2011–13; DCDS Mil. Strategy and Ops, 2013–14. Colonel Commandant: RAC, 2012–; RAVC, 2012–; POW Div., 2013–; Hon. Col, FANY, 2014–. Army Champion, LGBT Forum, 2011–. QCVS 1996 and 2007. *Recreations:* walking, travel, shooting. *Address:* Home Headquarters, Queen's Royal Lancers, Lancer House, Prince William of Gloucester Barracks, Grantham, Lincs NG31 7TJ. *T:* (0115) 957 3195. *E:* james.everard882@mod.uk. *Clubs:* Cavalry and Guards, Army and Navy.

EVERARD, John Vivian; HM Diplomatic Service, retired; Ambassador to the Democratic People's Republic of Korea, 2006–08; independent media commentator, since 2013; *b* 24 Nov. 1956; *s* of William Ralph Everard and Margaret Nora Jennifer Everard (*née* Massey); *m* 1990, Heather Ann Starkey. *Educ:* King's Sch., Chester; King Edward VI Sch., Lichfield; Emmanuel Coll., Cambridge (BA 1978; MA 1986); Peking Univ.; Manchester Business Sch. (MBA 1986); London Film Acad. (Cert. 2013). Joined HM Diplomatic Service, 1979: FCO, 1979–81; Third (later Second) Sec., Peking, 1981–83; Second Sec., Vienna, 1983–84; Manchester Business Sch., 1984–86; Metapraxis Ltd, 1986–87; FCO, 1987–90; First Sec., Santiago, 1990–93; Chargé d'Affaires, Minsk, 1993; Ambassador, Belarus, 1993–95; OSCE Mission to Bosnia and Hercegovina, 1995–96; Dep. Hd, Africa (Equatorial) Dept, FCO, 1996–98; Counsellor (Political, Econ. and Develt), Peking, 1998–2000; Ambassador, Uruguay, 2001–05. Co-Ordinator, UN Panel of Experts on Sanctions on the Democratic People's Republic of Korea, 2011–12. Vis. Fellow, Stanford Univ., 2010–11. Trustee: YHA, 2009–10; London Cycling Campaign, 2009–10. Patron, UK Defence Forum, 2014–. *Publications:* Only Beautiful Please: a British diplomat in North Korea, 2012. *Recreations:* reading, travel, cats, cycling.

EVERARD, Richard Anthony Spencer, OBE 2011; DL; Chairman, Everards Brewery Ltd, since 1988 (Director, since 1983); Vice Lord-Lieutenant of Leicestershire, 2003–13; *b* 31 March 1954; *s* of late Maj. Richard Peter Michael Spencer and Bettyne Ione (*née* Everard; formerly Lady Newtown-Butler); name changed to Everard by deed poll, 1971; *m* 1981, Caroline Anne Hill; one *s* one *d*. *Educ:* Eton; RMA Sandhurst. Commnd 1973, Lieut 1975, Royal Horse Guards 1st Dragoons, 1973–77. Pres., Age Concern Leics, 1992–; Trustee: Leics Police Charitable Trust, 1998–; County Air Ambulance, 1999–. Hon. Col, Leics, Northants and Rutland ACF, 2007–. Master, Co. of Brewers, 2004. DL 1997, High Sheriff, 2002–03, Leics. Hon. DLaws Leicester, 2009. *Recreations:* shooting, ski-ing, motorcycling, tennis, golf. *Address:* East Farndon Hall, Market Harborough, Leics LE16 9SE; Everards Brewery Ltd, Castle Acres, Narborough, Leics LE19 1BY. *T:* (0116) 201 4307, *Fax:* (0116) 281 4198. *Clubs:* MCC; Eton Ramblers; Luffenham Heath Golf.

EVERARD, Timothy John, CMG 1978; HM Diplomatic Service, retired; Secretary General, Order of St John, 1988–93; *b* 22 Oct. 1929; *s* of late Charles M. Everard and Monica M. Everard (*née* Barford); *m* 1955, Josiane Romano; two *s* two *d*. *Educ:* Uppingham Sch.; Magdalen Coll., Oxford. BA (Mod. Langs). Banking: Barclays Bank DCO, 1952–62, in Egypt, Sudan, Kenya, Zaire. Entered Foreign (later Diplomatic) Service: First Sec., FO, 1962–63; First Sec., Commercial, Bangkok, 1964–66; resigned to take up directorship in Ellis & Everard Ltd, 1966–67. Rejoined Foreign and Commonwealth Office, Oct. 1967: First Sec., FO, 1967–68; Bahrain, 1969–72 (First Sec. and Head of Chancery, HM Political Residency); seconded to Northern Ireland Office, FCO, April–Aug. 1972; Consul-Gen., then Chargé d'Affaires, Hanoi, 1972–73; Economic and Commercial Counsellor, Athens, 1974–78; Commercial Counsellor, Paris, 1978–81; Minister, Lagos, 1981–84; Ambassador to GDR, 1984–88. Trustee, Dresden Trust, 1994–2005. Freeman, City of London, 1991. KStJ 1988. *Address:* 10 The Dene, Sevenoaks, Kent TN13 1PB. *Club:* Reform.

EVERED, David Charles; Special Adviser, International Agency for Research on Cancer, World Health Organisation, 2001–03; *b* 21 Jan. 1940; *s* of late Thomas Charles Evered and Enid Christian Evered; *m* 1st, 1964, Anne Elizabeth Massey Lings, (Kit) (*d* 1998), *d* of John Massey Lings, Manchester; one *s* two *d*; 2nd, 2000, Sheila May Pusinelli, *d* of Charles Cecil Lennox Pusinelli and Margaret Chaloner Pusinelli, Thornton-le-Dale, Yorks. *Educ:* Cranleigh Sch., Surrey; Middlesex Hosp. Med. Sch. (BSc 1961, MB 1964, MD 1971). MRCP 1967, FRCP 1978; FRSB (FIBiol 1979). Junior hospital appointments, London and Leeds, 1964–70; First Asst in Medicine, Wellcome Sen. Res. Fellow and Consultant Physician, Univ. of Newcastle upon Tyne and Royal Victoria Infirmary, 1970–78; Dir, Ciba Foundn, 1978–88; Second Sec., MRC, 1988–96. Member: British Library Medical Information Review Panel, 1978–80; Council, St George's Hosp. Med. Sch. 1983–91; Cttee, Assoc. of Med. Res. Charities, 1981–84, 1987–88 (Vice-Chm., 1987–88); COPUS, Royal Soc., 1986–88; Media Resource Service Adv. Cttee, NY, 1986–88; NW Thames RHA, 1988–90; Hammersmith & Queen Charlotte's SHA, 1989–94; Bd, Hammersmith Hosps NHS Trust, 1995–96; Council, Internat. Agency for Res. into Cancer (Lyon), 1988–96; Council, RPMS, 1994–96; Vice-Pres., Science Cttee, Louis Jeantet Fondation de Médecine, 1984–91; Chairman: Anglia & Oxford Res. Ethics Cttee, 1997–99; Nuffield Orthopaedic Centre NHS Trust, 1998–2001. FRSocMed; Scientific Fellow, Zool Soc. of London (Mem. Council, 1985–89). Member: Soc. for Endocrinology; Eur. Thyroid Assoc. (Mem. Exec. Cttee, 1977–81, Sec.-Treas., 1983–89). *Publications:* Diseases of the Thyroid, 1976; (with R. Hall and R. Greene) Atlas of Clinical Endocrinology, 1979, 2nd edn 1990; (with M. O'Connor) Collaboration in Medical Research in Europe, 1981; numerous papers on medicine, education and science policy. *Recreations:* reading, history, tennis, Real tennis, gardening. *Address:* Old Rectory Farm, Rectory Road, Padworth Common, Berkshire RG7 4JD.

EVEREST, Anne Christine; Head, St George's School for Girls, Edinburgh, since 2010; *b* E Riding of Yorks, 23 Sept. 1956; *d* of Charles Vincent and Bessie Flanagan; *m* 1977, Paul Andrew Everest; two *s* one *d*. *Educ:* Univ. of Hull (BA 1st Cl. Hons; PGCE Classics); Univ. of Aberdeen (PGCE Guidance and Pupil Support). Lectr in Classics (pt-time), Univ. of Hull, 1980–81 and 1988–90; Robert Gordon's College, Aberdeen: teacher of Classics, 1992–2007; Principal Teacher of Guidance (Careers), 2001–02; Deputy Hd, 2002–07; Hd, St Margaret's Sch. for Girls, Aberdeen, 2007–10. *Recreations:* reading, walking. *Address:* St George's School for Girls, Garscube Terrace, Edinburgh EH12 6BG. *T:* (0131) 311 8000.

EVEREST, Prof. Kelvin Douglas, PhD; FEA; Andrew Cecil Bradley Professor of Modern Literature, since 1991, Director, Academic Affairs for China, since 2008, and Pro-Vice-Chancellor, since 2010, University of Liverpool; *b* 9 Sept. 1950; *s* of Les and Catherine Everest; *m* 1971, Faith Mary Rissen; three *d*. *Educ:* Reading Univ. (BA 1972; PhD 1977). Lectr, St David's UC Lampeter, 1975–79; Lectr, then Reader, Leicester Univ., 1979–91; Sen. Pro-Vice-Chancellor, Univ. of Liverpool, 2001–07. Mem., NW Regl Bd, NT, 2006–11. Mem. Bd of Govs, RNCM, 2006–11. An Associate Ed., Oxford DNB, 1997–. Foundn FEA 1999. *Publications:* Coleridge's Secret Ministry, 1979; (ed) Shelley Revalued, 1983; (ed) The Poems of Shelley, vol. 1 1989, vol. 2 2000, vol. 3 2011, vol. 4 2013; English Romantic Poetry, 1990; (ed) Revolution in Writing, 1991; (ed) Bicentenary Essays on Shelley, 1992; (ed with A. Yarrington) Reflections of Revolution, 1993; Keats, 2002; contrib. numerous articles and chapters. *Recreations:* cricket, Liverpool FC, jazz guitar, wildlife, cooking, drinking. *Address:* University of Liverpool, The Foundation Building, 765 Brownlow Hill L69 7ZX. *T:* (0151) 794 2220, *Fax:* (0151) 794 2929. *E:* k.d.everest@liverpool.ac.uk.

EVERETT, Bernard Jonathan, CVO 1999; HM Diplomatic Service, retired; Chairman, Goddard Consultants CIC, since 2009; *b* 17 Sept. 1943; *s* of late Arnold Edwin Everett and Helene May Everett (*née* Heine); *m* 1970, Maria Olinda, *d* of late Raul Correia de Albuquerque and of Maria de Lourdes Gonçalves de Albuquerque; two *s* one *d* (and one *d* decd). *Educ:* King's Coll. Sch., Wimbledon; Lincoln Coll., Oxford (BA 1965). Researcher, Reader's Digest, 1965; entered HM Diplomatic Service, 1966; Third, later Second Sec., Lisbon, 1967; FCO, 1971; Consul, Luanda, 1975; FCO, 1976; Head of Chancery, Lusaka, 1978; Consul (Commercial), Rio de Janeiro, 1980; Asst Head, Information Dept, FCO, 1983; on secondment as Head, Sub-Saharan Africa Br., DTI, 1984; Ambassador to Guatemala, 1987–91; Consul-Gen., Houston, 1991–95; High Comr, Mozambique, 1996–2000; Consul-Gen., São Paulo and Dir of Trade and Investment for Brazil, 2000–03. Member: Public Liaison Cttee, British Thoracic Soc., 2013–; Governor Policy Bd, NHS Providers, 2014–15. Public Governor, Chesterfield Royal Hospital Foundn Trust, 2007–15. Vice-Chair, Foundn Trust Governors' Assoc., 2011–14. *Recreations:* sport, performing arts, walking, gardening, family history, local issues.

EVERETT, Charles William Vogt; Vice-Chair, Hastings and Rother Clinical Commissioning Group, since 2013; *b* 15 Oct. 1949; *s* of Dr Thomas Everett and Ingeborg Everett (*née* Vogt); *m* 1978, Elizabeth Vanessa Ellis; three *s*. *Educ:* Bryanston Sch.; Reading Univ. Admin. trainee, Lord Chancellor's Dept, 1971; Asst Private Sec. to Lord Chancellor, 1974–76; Dept of Transport, 1982–84; Lord Chancellor's Department: Asst Sec., 1984; Under Sec., 1991; Head of Policy and Legal Services Gp, 1991–94; Dir, Resource and Support Services, The Court Service, 1994–99; Home Office, 1999–2006: Director: Fire and Emergency Planning, 1999–2002; Corporate Develt and Services, 2002–06. Chair, Hastings and Rother PCT, 2007–11; Vice-Chair, NHS Sussex, 2011–13. Member: Sussex Probation Bd, 2007–10; Surrey and Sussex Probation Trust Bd, 2010–14. Trustee, St Michael's Hospice, Hastings, 2012–. *Address:* Hastings and Rother Clinical Commissioning Group, Bexhill Hospital, Holliers Hill, Bexhill-on-Sea, E Sussex TN40 2DZ.

EVERETT, Christopher Harris Doyle, CBE 1988; MA; Director General and Secretary, Daiwa Anglo-Japanese Foundation, 1990–2000; *b* 20 June 1933; *s* of late Alan Doyle Everett, MBE, MS, FRCS, and Annabel Dorothy Joan Everett (*née* Harris); *m* 1955, Hilary (Billy) Anne (*née* Robertson); two *s* two *d*. *Educ:* Winchester College; New College, Oxford (MA 1st cl. Class. Mods and 1st cl. Lit. Hum.). Nat. Service, 2nd Lieut, Grenadier Guards, 1951–53. HM Diplomatic Service, 1957–70: posts included MECAS, Lebanon, Embassies in Beirut and Washington, and Foreign Office (Personnel Dept and Planning Staff); Headmaster: Worksop Coll., 1970–75; Tonbridge Sch., 1975–89. Chm., 1986, Vice-Chm., 1987, HMC. Pt-time Chm., CSSB, 1972–92; Mem., Extended Interview Bd for Police Service, 1975–2013, for Prison Service, 1998–2011; pt-time assessor, Home Office Promotion and Selection Bds, 2002–13. Trustee: Guild of Aid (formerly for Gentlefolk), 1995– (Chm., Cttee of Mgt, 1995–2007); Professional Classes Aid Council, 1995– (Pres., 2007–; Chm., Exec. Cttee, 2007–); Daiwa Anglo-Japanese Foundation, 2005–13. Non-exec. Dir, The Learning Trust, Hackney, 2007–12. Hon. Liveryman, Skinners' Co., 1993– (Mem., Ct of Assts, 1997–; Master, 2002–03; Chm., Skinners' Co. Sch. for Girls, 2001–10; Chm., Friends of Skinners' Kent Acad., 2011–). JP Worksop, 1971–75, Tonbridge and W Malling, 1976–89. FRSA 1988. Hon. FCP 1988. *Recreations:* family, reading, walking, current affairs. *Address:* Lavender House, 12 Madeira Park, Tunbridge Wells, Kent TN2 5SX. *T:* (01892) 525624. *E:* christopher@twells.freeuk.com.

EVERETT, Eileen, (Mrs Raymond Everett); *see* Diss, E.

EVERETT, Prof. Martin George, DPhil; Professor of Social Network Analysis, University of Manchester, since 2009; *b* 25 May 1955; *s* of late Reginald Douglas Walter Everett and Joan Gladys Everett; *m* 1981, Vanessa Ann Kendrick; two *s*. *Educ:* Loughborough Univ. (BSc Maths 1976); Trinity Coll., Oxford (MSc Maths 1977; DPhil 1980). Thames Polytechnic, then University of Greenwich: Lectr, 1980–83; Sen. Lectr, 1983–86; Prin. Lectr, 1986–88; Reader, 1988–89; Prof., 1990–2003; Hd of Computing and Maths, 1991–2003; Campus Provost and Pro Vice-Chancellor, Univ. of Westminster, 2003–07; Vice-Chancellor, UEL, 2007–09. Vis. Hon. Fellow, Dept of Sociol., Univ. of Surrey, 1989–92. Treas., UK Heads of Depts of Mathematical Scis, 1999–2003. Mem., London Higher Bd, 2007–09. Mem. Bd, Internat. Network of Social Network Analysts, 1994–2010 (Pres., 2000–03). FAcSS (AcSS 2004). *Publications:* (jtly) Ucinet for Windows: software for social network analysis, 2002; papers on methods for social network analysis. *Recreations:* wine, theatre, Charlton Athletic FC. *Address:* School of Social Sciences, University of Manchester, Oxford Road, Manchester M13 9PL.

EVERETT, Oliver William, CVO 1991 (LVO 1980); Librarian, Windsor Castle and Assistant Keeper of The Queen's Archives, 1985–2002, Librarian Emeritus, since 2002; lecturer, since 2005; *b* 28 Feb. 1943; *s* of Charles Everett, DSO, MC and Judy Rothwell; *m* 1965, Theffania Vesey Stoney (separated 2003); two *s* two *d*; partner, 2003, Diana Jervis-Read. *Educ:* Felsted Sch.; Western Reserve Acad., Ohio, USA; Christ's Coll., Cambridge; Fletcher Sch. of Law and Diplomacy, Mass, USA. HM Diplomatic Service, 1967–81: First Sec., New Delhi, 1969–73; Head of Chancery, Madrid, 1980–81; Asst Private Sec. to HRH The Prince of Wales, 1978–80; Private Sec. to HRH The Princess of Wales, 1981–83. *Recreations:* lecturing, film, baseball. *Address:* 49 Queen's Gate Mews, SW7 5QN. *T:* (020) 3674 0069. *E:* o.everett05@tiscali.co.uk. *Clubs:* Roxburghe, Chelsea Arts.

EVERETT, Rupert; actor; *s* of Major Anthony Everett and Sara Everett. *Educ:* Ampleforth Coll.; Central Sch. of Speech and Drama. Trained with Glasgow Citizens' Theatre, 1979–82; *stage* includes: Glasgow Citizens' Theatre: Waste of Time; Don Juan; Heartbreak House; The Vortex, 1988, transf. Garrick, 1989; The Picture of Dorian Gray, 1993; The Milk Train Doesn't Stop Here Anymore, 1994, transf. Lyric, Hammersmith, 1997; Another Country, Greenwich, transf. Queen's, 1982; Mass Appeal, Lyric, Hammersmith; L'importance d'être Constant, Théâtre de Chaillot, Paris, 1996; Some Sunny Day, Hampstead, 1996; Blithe Spirit, Broadway, NY, 2009; Pygmalion, Chichester Festival Th., 2010; Six Actors in Search of a Director, Charing Cross Th., 2012; The Judas Kiss, Hampstead Th., transf. Duke of York's, 2012; Amadeus, Chichester Fest. Th., 2014; *films* include: A Shocking Accident, 1982; Another Country, 1984; Dance with a Stranger, 1985; Duet for One, 1986; The Comfort of Strangers, 1990; Inside Monkey Zetterland, 1992; Prêt-à-Porter, 1994; The Madness of King George, 1995; My Best Friend's Wedding, 1997; B Monkey, 1998; An Ideal Husband, Shakespeare in Love, A Midsummer Night's Dream, 1999; The Next Best Thing, 2000; Unconditional Love, The Importance of Being Earnest, 2002; To Kill a King, 2003; Stage Beauty, 2004; Separate Lies, 2005; St Trinian's, 2007; St Trinian's 2: the Legend of Fritton's Gold, 2009; Wild Target, 2010; Hysteria, 2011; A Royal Night Out, 2015; *television* includes: The Far Pavilions, 1982. *Publications:* Hello Darling, Are You Working?, 1992; The Hairdressers of St Tropez, 1995; Red Carpets and Other Banana Skins (autobiog.), 2006; Vanished Years (autobiog.), 2012. *Address:* c/o Ed Victor Ltd, 6 Bayley Street, WC1B 3HE.

EVERETT, Steven George; His Honour Judge Everett; a Circuit Judge, since 2007; *b* 21 July 1956; *s* of George and Jean Everett; *m* 1985, Melinda Birch; two *s*. *Educ:* Newport High Sch.; Lanchester Poly., Coventry (BA Business Law 1978). Admitted as solicitor, 1981; called to the Bar, Gray's Inn, 1989; criminal defence solicitor, 1981–83; prosecuting solicitor, 1983–86; Crown Prosecutor, 1986–89; barrister, Wales and Chester Circuit, 1989–2007; Asst Recorder, 1999–2000, Recorder, 2000–07. Bar Council: Member: Panel, Complaints Adv. Service, 1995–2007; Professional Conduct Cttee, 2005–07. A Panel Chm., Parole Bd, 2010–12. Tutor Judge, Judicial Coll., 2012–. Mem. Cttee, Council of Circuit Judges, 2015–. *Recreations:* campanology, circuit training (i.e. keeping fit - not training advocates), cycling (only in fine weather and not too far), visiting places of interest (especially NT properties), watching most sport (especially following Everton FC, Newport County and Welsh Rugby), eating out with my family, watching decent TV, trying to keep up with the latest films at the cinema (could do better), reading. *Address:* Queen Elizabeth II Law Courts, Derby Square, Liverpool, Merseyside L2 1XA.

EVERETT, Thomas Henry Kemp; Deputy Special Commissioner of Income Tax, 2000–03 (Special Commissioner of Income Tax, 1983–2000); *b* 28 Jan. 1932; *s* of late Thomas Kemp Everett and Katharine Ida Everett (*née* Woodward); *m* 1st, 1954, June (*née* Partridge) (*d* 2012); three *s*; 2nd, 2015, Jocelyn Heather Payne (*née* Trease). *Educ:* Queen Elizabeth Hospital, Bristol; Univ. of Bristol (LLB Hons 1957). Solicitor (Hons), admitted 1960; Partner, Meade-King & Co., 1963–83. Clerk to General Commissioners, Bedminster Div., 1965–83. Chairman: Service 9, 1972–75; Bristol Council of Voluntary Service, 1975–80; St Christopher's Young Persons' Residential Trust, 1976–83; Mem., Governing Council, St Christopher's School, Bristol, 1983–89; Gov., Queen Elizabeth Hosp., 1974–92 (Vice-Chm. Govs, 1980–91); Pres., Queen Elizabeth Hosp. Old Boys' Soc., 1990–91. *Recreations:* music, motoring, gardening. *Address:* Aries, 26a Sidcot Lane, Winscombe, Som BS25 1LP. *T:* (01934) 842380.

EVERHART, Prof. Thomas Eugene, PhD; President, and Professor of Electrical Engineering and Applied Physics, California Institute of Technology, 1987–97, now President Emeritus and Professor Emeritus; *b* 15 Feb. 1932; *s* of William E. Everhart and Elizabeth A. Everhart (*née* West); *m* 1953, Doris A. Wentz; two *s* two *d*. *Educ:* Harvard Coll. (AB 1953); Univ. of California (MSc 1955); Clare Coll., Cambridge (PhD 1958). Department of Electrical Engineering and Computer Science, University of California, Berkeley: Asst Prof., 1958–62; Associate Prof., 1962–67; Prof., 1967–78; Dept Chm., 1972–77; Dean, Coll. of Engrg, Cornell Univ., 1979–84; Chancellor, Univ. of Illinois, Urbana-Champaign, 1984–87; Pro-Vice-Chancellor, Cambridge Univ., 1998. Director: General Motors Corp., 1989–2002; Hewlett-Packard Co., 1991–99; Reveo Inc., 1994–2003; Saint Gobain, 1996–2008; Raytheon Co., 1998–2006; Hughes Electronics Corp., 1999–2002; Agilent Technologies, 1999–2002. Trustee: CIT, 1998–; Harvard Bd of Overseers, 1999–2005 (Pres., 2004–05). Mem., NAE (USA), 1978; Foreign Mem., Royal Acad. of Engrg, 1990. Hon. LLD: Ill Wesleyan, 1990; Pepperdine, 1990; Hon. DEng Colo Sch. of Mines, 1990. Centennial Medal, 1984, Founders Medal, 2002, IEEE; Benjamin Garver Lamme Award, 1989, Centennial Medal, 1993, ASEE; Clark Kerr Award, Univ. of Calif., Berkeley, 1992; Okawa Prize, Okawa Foundn, 2002. *Publications:* Microwave Communications, 1968; over 90 articles in jls, book chapters, etc, 1955–96. *Recreations:* hiking, fishing, ski-ing. *Address:* President Emeritus, Mail Code 202–31, California Institute of Technology, Pasadena, CA 91125, USA. *T:* (818) 3956303. *Clubs:* Athenæum (CIT), California (LA); Channel City (Santa Barbara).

EVERITT, Anthony Michael; writer; Secretary-General, Arts Council of Great Britain, 1990–94 (Deputy Secretary-General, 1985–90); *b* 31 Jan. 1940; *s* of late Michael Anthony Hamill Everitt and Simone Dolores Cathérine (*née* Vergriette; she *m* 2nd, John Brunel Cohen). *Educ:* Cheltenham Coll.; Corpus Christi Coll., Cambridge (BA Hons English, 1962). Lectured variously at National Univ. of Iran, Teheran, SE London Coll. of Further Educn, Birmingham Coll. of Art, and Trent Polytechnic, 1963–72; The Birmingham Post: Art Critic, 1970–75; Drama Critic, 1974–79; Features Editor, 1976–79; Director: Midland Gp Arts Centre, Nottingham, 1979–80; E Midlands Arts Assoc., 1980–85. Vis. Prof., Performing and Visual Arts, Nottingham Trent Univ., 1996–2010. Lead Reviewer, HK Arts Develt Council, 1998; Reviewer of Arts Councils: of NI, 2000; of Wales, 2001; of Ireland, 2001; of I of M, 2005. Chairman: Ikon Gall., Birmingham, 1976–79; Birmingham Arts Lab., 1977–79; Vice-Chm., Council of Regional Arts Assocs, 1984–85; Member: Drama Panel, 1974–78, and Regional Cttee, 1979–80, Arts Council of GB; Cttee for Arts and Humanities, 1986–87, Performing Arts Cttee, 1987–92, CNAA; General Adv. Council, IBA, 1987–90. Gov., Liverpool Inst. of Performing Arts, 2006–11 (Companion, 2003). Hon. Fellow, Dartington Coll. of Arts, 1995. *Publications:* Abstract Expressionism, 1974; In from the Margins, 1996; Joining In, 1997; The Governance of Culture, 1997; The Creative Imperative, 2000; Cicero: a turbulent life, 2001; New Voices, 2003; New Voices: an update, 2004; The First Emperor, Caesar Augustus and the Triumph of Rome, 2006; Hadrian, 2009; Rise of Rome, 2012; SPQR: a Roman miscellany, 2014; contribs to The Independent, The Guardian, Financial Times, Studio Internat., Country Life, etc. *Address:* Westerlies, Anchor Hill, Wivenhoe, Essex CO7 9BL.

EVERITT, Prof. Barry John, PhD, ScD; FRS 2007; FMedSci; Master, Downing College, Cambridge, 2003–13 (Fellow, 1976–2003; Hon. Fellow, 2013); Professor of Behavioural Neuroscience, Department of Experimental Psychology, University of Cambridge, since 1997; Provost, Gates Cambridge Trust, since 2013; *b* 19 Feb. 1946; *s* of Frederick John Everitt and Winifred Everitt; *m* 1st, 1966, Valerie Sowter (marr. diss. 1978); one *s*; 2nd, 1979, Dr Jane Carolyn Sterling; one *d*. *Educ:* Univ. of Hull (BSc Zool. 1967); Univ. of Birmingham (PhD 1970); MA, ScD 2004, Cantab. MRC Res. Fellow, Univ. of Birmingham Med. Sch., 1970–73; MRC Travelling Res. Fellow, Karolinska Inst., Sweden, 1973–74; Department of Anatomy, University of Cambridge: Demonstrator, 1974–79; Lectr, 1979–91; Reader in Neurosci., 1991–97; Dir of Studies in Medicine, Downing Coll., Cambridge, 1978–98. Ciba-Geigy Sen. Res. Fellow, Karolinska Inst., 1982–83; Vis. Prof., Univ. of Calif, San Francisco, 2000; Sterling Vis. Prof., Univ. of Albany, NY, 2005; Internat. Dist. Scientist, Riken Inst., Tokyo, 2006; Lectures: EBBS Review, Madrid, 1993; Maudsley Bequest, 1997; Grass, Texas, 1997; Swammerdam, Amsterdam, 1999; Swedish Neurosci. Review, 1999; Hillarp, Miami, 1999; Soc. for Neurosci., Orlando, 2002; NIH Dir's, Washington, 2004; Internat. Narcotics, Kyoto, 2004; Spanish Psychobiol. Soc., 2004; Matarazzo, Univ. of Portland, Oregon, 2005; Dalbir Bindra, McGill, Canada, 2006; Grass Internat., UCLA, 2006; Johns Hopkins Univ., 2007; BMI Lausanne, 2007; Wallenberg, Stockholm, 2007; Elsevier, EBBS, Trieste, 2008; Internat. Basal Ganglia Soc., Amsterdam, 2008; President's, Fedn of Eur. Neurosci. Socs, 2008; Stephan von Apáthy, Hungarian Acad. of Sci., 2009; Nat. Inst. on Drug Abuse, Baltimore, 2009; Karolinska Res., Stockholm, 2009; John P. Flynn Meml, Yale Univ., 2010; Bryan Kolb, Univ. of Calgary, 2011; French Neurosci. Soc., 2013. Editor-in-Chief: Physiol. and Behavior, 1994–99; European Jl Neurosci., 1997–; Reviewing Ed., Science, 2003–; Mem. Editl Bd, Philos. Trans of Royal Soc. B, 2014–. Scientific Counsellor, Nat. Inst. on Drug Abuse, USA, 2002–06. Chairman: MRC Res. Studentships and Trng Awards Panel, 1995–97; Human Sci. Frontier Prog. Fellowships Cttee, 1994–96; Scientific Adv. Bd, Astra Arcus, Sweden, 1998–2001, Astra-Zeneca, 2001–04; Neurogenetics and Behavior Center, Johns Hopkins Univ., 2002–10; Ecole des Neurosciences de Paris, 2008–13; Prog. Cttee, Soc. for Neurosci., 2011–13 (Mem., 2005–08); Member: Helsinki Neurosci. Centre, 2000–10; MRC Neurosci. and Mental Health Bd, 2001–05; Cttee on Cttees, Soc. for Neurosci., 2010–12; Ind. Sci. Cttee on Drugs, 2010–; Video Standards Council Appeals Cttee, 2012–; EMBO, 2014–. Member, Scientific Advisory Board: Brain-Mind Inst., Lausanne, 2008–10; Centre for Research on Sex Differences, Univ. of Michigan, 2011–14; Portland Alcohol Research Center, Univ. of Portland, Oregon, 2012–; Wellcome Trust Centre for Neuroimaging, UCL, 2012–; Inst. of Experimental Medicine, Hungarian Acad. of Scis, 2013–16; Brain Mind Inst., École Fédéral de Lausanne, 2013–16. President: Brit. Assoc. Psychopharmacology, 1992–94; Eur. Brain and Behaviour Soc., 1998–2000; Eur. Behavioural Pharmacology Soc., 2003–05; Fedn of Eur. Neurosci. Socs, 2016–. Fellow, Amer. Coll. of Neuropsychopharmacology, 1999 (Mem. Council, 2013–); FMedSci 2008. Highly Cited Neurosci. Researcher, Inst. Scientific Information, 2002–. Hon. DSc: Hull, 2009; Birmingham, 2010; Hon. MD Karolinska Inst., Stockholm, 2015. Dist. Sci. Contribn Award, Amer. Psychol Assoc., 2011; Dist. Achievement Award, Eur. Behavioural Pharmacol. Soc., 2011; Fed. of Eur. Neurosci. Socs-Eur. Jl of Neurosci. Award, 2012; Lifetime Achievement Award, British Assoc. of Psychopharmacol., 2012; Fondation Ipsen Neuronal Plasticity Prize,

2014. *Publications:* Essential Reproduction, 1980, 5th edn 1999; over 400 papers in scientific jls. *Recreations:* opera, wine, cricket. *Address:* Department of Psychology, Downing Street, Cambridge CB2 3EB.

EVERITT, Father (Charles) Gabriel, OSB; Headmaster, Ampleforth College, 2004–14; *b* 7 Jan. 1956; *s* of Prof. William Norrie Everitt and Katharine Elisabeth Everitt (*née* Gibson). *Educ:* Dundee High Sch.; Edinburgh Univ. (MA History 1978); Balliol Coll., Oxford (MA Theol. 1985; DPhil History 1986); St Stephen's House, Oxford. Asst Curate, St Aidan and St Columba, Hartlepool, 1986–89; recd into RC Church, 1989; entered Ampleforth Abbey, 1990, professed, 1991; ordained priest, 1994; Ampleforth College: Asst Master, 1992–97, Head, 1997–2003, Dept of Christian Theol.; Housemaster: St Aidan's, 1997–98; St Oswald's, 1998–2003; Third Master, 2000–03. *Recreations:* reading, cinema. *Address:* Ampleforth Abbey, York YO62 4EN.

EVERITT, Ven. Michael John; Archdeacon of Lancaster, since 2011; *b* Banbury, 26 Aug. 1968; *s* of Raymond Edward Everitt and Edna Dorothy Everitt (*née* Scotford); *m* 1992, Ruth Anne, *d* of Rev. Canon Rex Anthony Chapman, *qv*; one *s* one *d*. *Educ:* Warriner Sch., Bloxham; Banbury Sch.; King's Coll., London (BD Hons 1990; AKC 1990); Queen's Coll., Birmingham (DipTh 1992); Venerable English Coll., Rome. Office clerk, Zoffany Ltd, 1988–90; lay worker, St Paul's, Covent Garden, 1988–90; ordained deacon, 1992, priest, 1993; Asst Curate, St Andrew's, Cleveleys, 1992–95; Succentor, 1995, Precentor, 1996–98, Bloemfontein Cathedral; Anglican Chaplain, Nat. Hosp., Bloemfontein, 1995–98; Anglican Chaplain and Asst Lectr, Univ. of Orange Free State, 1996–98; Sen. Coll. Chaplain, St Martin's Coll., Lancaster, 1998–2002; Asst Dir, Ordinands, Blackburn dio., 2000–02; Rector, Standish, 2002–11; Priest in Charge, Appley Bridge, 2006–10; Area Dean, Chorley, 2004–11; Hon. Canon, Blackburn, 2010–11. Member: Blackburn Diocesan Synod, 1994–95, 2002–; Bloemfontein Diocesan Synod, 1995–98; Bishop's Panel, 1999–2010; Gen. Synod, 2013–; Church Bldg Council, 2014–. Chm., Lancaster City Council of Churches, 1999–2001; Bishops' Advr, Ministry Div., C of E, 2013–. Mem., Panel, Blackburn Diocesan Adoption Agency, 2003–07; Dir, Blackburn Diocesan Bd of Finance, 2011–, of Educn, 2013– (Chm., 2014–). Tutor, Carlisle and Blackburn Diocesan Trng Inst., 2002–10. Mem., Cidari Multi Acad. Trust, 2013–. Governor: St Wilfrid's C of E Prim. Sch., Standish, 2002–11 (Vice Chm., 2002–06, 2007–11; Chm., 2006–07); Standish Community High Sch., 2002–11; All Saints Appley Bridge Prim. Sch., 2006–10; St Aidan's C of E Technol. Coll., Preesall, 2011–13; St Hilda's C of E Primary Sch., Carleton, 2012–14 (Chm., 2012–14). President: Standish Arts Fest., 2002–11; St Wilfrid's Bowling Club, 2002–11. *Publications:* (contrib.) The Bible Uncovered, 1993. *Recreations:* drawing, watercolour painting, photography, travel. *Address:* 6 Eton Park, Preston PR2 9NL. *T:* (01772) 700337. *E:* michael.everitt@blackburn.anglican.org. *Club:* Nikaean.

EVERITT, Richard Leslie, CBE 2014; Chief Executive, Port of London Authority, 2004–14; *b* 22 Dec. 1948. Admitted solicitor; five yrs in private practice; joined legal dept, BAA, 1978, Head of Legal, 1984–90; Dir, Planning and Regulatory Affairs, 1990; Chief Exec., NATS Ltd, 2001–04. Non-exec. Dir, Air Partner plc, 2004– (Chm., 2012–).

EVERITT, William Howard, FREng; FIMechE, FIET; Group Managing Director, Technology, T & N plc, 1995–96; *b* 27 Feb. 1940; *s* of H. G. H. Everitt and J. S. Everitt; *m* Antha Cecilia; two *s*. *Educ:* Leeds Univ. (BSc). Director of Operations, IBM Europe, 1974; Managing Director: Wellworthy, AE, 1975–76; Bearings, AE, 1977–79; AE plc, 1983–86 (Dir, 1978); Dir, T & N plc, 1987–96; Man. Dir, Automotive, T & N, 1990–93. Non-exec. Dir, Domino Printing Services plc, 1997–2008. FREng (FEng 1988). *Recreation:* golf. *Address:* Horley House, Hornton Lane, Horley, near Banbury, Oxon OX15 6BL. *T:* (01295) 730603.

EVERITT-MATTHIAS, David Richard; Co-proprietor and chef, Le Champignon Sauvage, Cheltenham, since 1987; *b* 29 Oct. 1960; *m* 1985, Helen. *Educ:* Sir Walter St John's Grammar Sch., London; Ealing Coll. of Higher Educn (C&G). Chef, Inn on the Park, London, 1978–83; Head Chef: Grand Café, 1983–85; Steamer's Fish Restaurant, 1985–86; Fingal's Restaurant, Putney, 1986–87. Member: Acad. Culinaire de France; Sir Walter St John's Old Boys' Assoc. Hon. PhD Glos, 2009. Awards include: Acorn Award, Midland Chef of Year, 1995, 1996; Egon Ronay Dessert Chef of Year, 1996; Nat. Chef of Year, 1996, 1997; Chef of Year: Cotswold Life, 2005; Catey Awards, 2007; Good Food Guide, 2014; Observer Outstanding Contribn Award, 2013. Restaurant awards: Michelin Star, 1995–99, 2 Michelin Stars, 2000–15; 4 Rosettes, AA Guide, 1997–2015; 2 Egon Ronay Stars, 2005; Restaurant of Year, Good Food Guide, 2005. *Publications:* Essence: recipes from Le Champignon Sauvage, 2006; Dessert: dessert recipes from Le Champignon Sauvage, 2009; Beyond Essence, 2013. *Recreations:* cricket, squash, art, jazz, reading. *Address:* Le Champignon Sauvage, Suffolk Road, Cheltenham, Glos GL50 2AQ.

EVERSHED, Prof. Richard Peter, PhD; FRS 2010; Professor of Biogeochemistry and Director, Biogeochemistry Research Centre, University of Bristol, since 2000; *b* 25 July 1956. *Educ:* Trent Poly., Nottingham (BSc Applied Chem. 1978); Univ. of Keele (PhD 1982). FRSC 2011. Postdoctoral res., Sch. of Chem., Univ. of Bristol, 1981–84; Dept of Biochem., Univ. of Liverpool, 1984–93; Lectr, 1993–96, Reader, 1996–2000, Sch. of Chem., Univ. of Bristol. Dir, Bristol node, NERC Life Scis Mass Spectrometry Facility; Mem., NERC Peer Review Coll. *Address:* Biogeochemistry Research Centre, University of Bristol, Senate House, Tyndall Avenue, Bristol BS8 1TH. *T:* (0117) 928 7671, *Fax:* (0117) 925 1295. *E:* r.p.evershed@bristol.ac.uk.

EVERSON, John Andrew; *b* 26 Oct. 1933; *s* of Harold Leslie Everson and Florence Jane Stone; *m* 1961, Gilda Ramsden; two *s*. *Educ:* Tiffin Boys' Sch., Kingston-upon-Thames; Christ's Coll., Cambridge (MA); King's Coll., London (PGCE). Teacher: Haberdashers' Aske's Sch., Elstree, 1958–65; City of London Sch., 1965–68; Schools Inspectorate, DES, later Dept for Educn, 1968–92; Chief Inspector for Secondary Educn, 1981–89; seconded to Peat Marwick McLintock, 1989; Chief Inspector for Teacher Training, 1990–92. *Publications:* (with B. P. FitzGerald) Settlement Patterns, 1968; (with B. P. FitzGerald) Inside the City, 1972. *Recreations:* opera, walking, theatre, chess. *Address:* 74 Longdown Lane North, Epsom, Surrey KT17 3JF. *T:* (01372) 721556. *Club:* Athenæum.

EVERSON, Simon John; Headmaster, Merchant Taylors' School, Northwood, since 2013; *b* 31 Oct. 1965; *s* of John and Gilda Everson; *m* 2001, Virginia Murphy. *Educ:* St Alphege Jun. Sch.; Solihull Sch.; Fitzwilliam Coll., Cambridge (BA 1987; PGCE 1990; MA 2004); Nottingham Univ. (MA 1999). NPQH 2006. English teacher: Bretton Woods Community Coll., 1990–92 and 1993–94; Myokokogen Jun. High Sch., Japan, 1992–93; Nottingham High Sch. for Boys, 1994–99; Hd of English, Arnold Sch., 1999–2003; Dep. Headmaster, Westcliff High Sch. for Boys, 2003–06; Headmaster, The Skinners' Sch., Tunbridge Wells, 2006–13. Chm., Grammar Sch. Heads Assoc., 2010. *Recreations:* reading, running, music, philosophy, wine, prehistory. *Address:* Merchant Taylors' School, Sandy Lodge, Moor Park, Middx HA6 2HT.

EVERT, Christine Marie; American tennis player, retired 1989; founder, Chris Evert Charities Inc., 1989; *b* 21 Dec. 1954; *d* of late James and of Colette Evert; *m* 1st, 1979, John Lloyd (marr. diss. 1987); 2nd, 1988, Andy Mill (marr. diss.); three *s*; 3rd, 2008, Gregory John Norman, *qv* (marr. diss. 2009). *Educ:* St Thomas Aquinas High Sch., Fort Lauderdale. Amateur tennis player, 1970–72, professional player, 1972–89. Semi-finalist in US Open at age of 16; won numerous titles, including: Wimbledon: 1974, 1976, 1981 (doubles, 1976); French Open: 1974–75, 1979–80, 1983, 1985–86; US Open: 1975–78, 1980, 1982; Australian Open: 1982, 1984. Represented USA in Wightman Cup, 1971–73, 1975–82, and in Federation Cup, 1977–82. Pres., Women's Tennis Assoc., 1982–91. *Address:* c/o IMG, 1360 East 9th Street, Suite 100, Cleveland, OH 44114, USA; 7200 West Camino Real, Suite 310, Boca Raton, FL 33433, USA.

EVERY, Sir Henry (John Michael), 13th Bt *cr* 1641, of Egginton, Derbyshire; DL; Chairman of Governors, Repton School, since 2012 (Governor, since 2003); Chairman, Tala PR, 2010–13; *b* 6 April 1947; *s* of Sir John Simon Every, 12th Bt and Janet Marion, *d* of John Page; *S* father, 1988; *m* 1974, Susan Mary, *er d* of Kenneth Beaton, JP, Eastshotte, Hartford, Cambs; three *s*. *Educ:* Malvern College. FCA. Qualified as Chartered Accountant, 1970; worked in South Africa, 1970–74; Partner, Josolyne Layton-Bennett, Birmingham, 1979–81; merged with BDO Binder Hamlyn, 1982, then with Touche Ross, 1994, to form Deloitte & Touche; retired as Partner, 2001. Chairman: Burton Hosps NHS Trust, 2003–04; Derby Cathedral Council, 2003–12. Pres., Birmingham and West Midlands Dist Soc. of Chartered Accountants, 1995–96 (Chm., Dist Trng Bd, 1991–93). Mem., Egginton Parish Council, 1987–2006 and 2012–. Mem. Cttee, Lunar Soc., 1993–2003. Trustee, Repton Foundn, 2002–04, 2006–; Consultant to Nat. Meml Arboretum, 2003–13 (Trustee, 1996–2003); Chm., Derbys Crimebeat, 2009–13; Patron, Derbys Children's Holiday Centre, 2012–. Mem., Adv. Panel, McCarthy & Stone, 2012–15. FRSA 1996. DL, 2006, High Sheriff, 2009–10, Derbys. *Recreations:* travel, National Trust, gardening; supporter of Nottingham Forest FC. *Heir:* *s* Edward James Henry Every [*b* 3 July 1975; *m* 2007, Sosennah Mary, *e d* of David Siviter; one *s* one *d*]. *Address:* Cothay, Egginton, Derby DE65 6HJ.

EVES, David Charles Thomas, CB 1993; Associate Director, Sancroft International Ltd, since 2002; Deputy Director General, 1989–2002 and HM Chief Inspector of Factories, 1985–88 and 1992–2002, Health and Safety Executive; *b* 10 Jan. 1942; *s* of Harold Thomas Eves and Violet Eves (*née* Edwards); *m* 1964, Valerie Ann Carter; one *d*. *Educ:* King's Sch., Rochester; University Coll., Durham (BA Hons). Teacher, Kent CC, 1963–64; HM Inspector of Factories, Min. of Labour, 1964–74; Health and Safety Executive, 1974–2002: Under Sec., 1985–89, Dep. Sec., and Dep. Dir Gen., 1989–2002; Dir, Resources and Planning Div., 1988–89. International Association of Labour Inspection: Vice Pres., 1993–99; Sec. Gen., 1996–99; Technical Advr, 1999–2005; Ambassador, Nat. Exam. Bd for Occupational Safety and Health, 2006–. Ext. Examiner, Sch. of Law, Univ. of Warwick, 2007–12. Hon. Vice Pres., Safety Gps UK (formerly Nat. Health and Safety Gps Council), 2004–12. FIOSH (Hon. Vice Pres., 1992–). Hon. Fellow, IIRSM, 2009. *Publications:* (jtly) Questioning Performance: the Director's essential guide to health, safety and the environment, 2005; Disasters: learning the lessons for a safer world, 2010; Two Steps Forward, One Step Back: a brief history of health and safety law in the United Kingdom, 2014. *Recreations:* music, reading, painting, gardening, wood turner.

EVES, Ernest (Larry); Chairman, Jacob Securities Inc., 2007; *b* Windsor, Ont, 17 June 1946; *s* of Harry Eves and Julie Eves (*née* Hawrylechko); *m*; one *d* (one *s* decd). *Educ:* Vincent Massey High Sch.; Univ. of Toronto; Osgoode Law Sch. (LLB 1970). Called to the Bar, Ont, 1972; QC (Ont) 1983. MPP (PC) Parry Sound, 1981–99, Parry Sound-Muskoka, 1999–2001, Dufferin-Peel-Wellington-Grey, Ontario, 2002–05. Government of Ontario: Parly Asst to Minister of Educn and Minister of Colls and Univs, 1983; Minister: of Skills Develt, 1985; of Resource Develt and Provincial Sec. for Resources, 1985; of Community and Social Services, 1985; PC Party Chief Whip, 1985–90, House Leader, 1990; Govt House Leader, 1995–96; Dep. Premier and Minister of Finance, 1995–2001; Vice-Chm., Policy and Priorities Bd, and Mgt Bd, Cabinet, 1995–2000; Premier of Ontario, Pres. of the Council, and Minister of Intergovtl Affairs, 2002–03; Leader of Opposition, 2003–04. Leader, PC Party, Ont, 2002–04. Partner, Green and Eves, 1972–81; Vice Chm. and Sen. Advr, Credit Suisse First Boston (Toronto), 2000–02; Lawyer, Borden, Ladner, Gervaise LLP, 2001–02. Chairman: Gilla Inc., 2012–; Gravitas Financial Inc., 2013–; PACE Securities Corp., 2014–; Director: Medifocus, 2011–; Canada Lithium Corp., 2013–; Nighthawk Gold Corp., 2013–; RB Energy, 2013–14. Chm., Ont Olympic Sports and Waterfront Develt Agency, 2000–01; Chm. and Special Advr, Ontario Trade and Investment Adv. Council, 2006–; Dir, CB Richard Ellis Ltd (Canada), 2006–. Founder and Chm., Justin Eves Foundn, 2005–.

EVISON, Raymond John, OBE 2000; VMH 1995; nurseryman and breeder, horticultural exhibitor and judge, lecturer, author and photographer; Founder and Chairman: Guernsey Clematis Nursery Ltd, since 1984; Raymond J. Evison Ltd, since 1997; *b* Shrewsbury, 9 March 1944; *s* of Eric John William Evison and Edith Annie Evison (*née* Trow); three *d*. *Educ:* Diddlebury and Burford Primary Schs; Ludlow Secondary Mod. Sch. Man. Dir and Jun. Partner, Treasures of Tenbury Ltd, 1969–87. Chm., Mont Rose of Guernsey Ltd, 2008–. Exhibitor at RHS Shows, incl. Chelsea Flower Show (numerous Gold medals, 6 Williams Meml Medals, 2 Lawrence Medals). Judge: garden exhibits, Chelsea Flower Show, 1985–; leading flower shows in USA, 1994–. Lectured in UK, Europe, USA, Canada, China, Japan and NZ. Designer of stamps: Guernsey postage stamps, 2004; Wild Flora Guernsey stamps, issue 1, 2008, issue 2, 2009. Royal Horticultural Society: Mem. Council, 1985–96; Chm., Shows Cttee, 1988–95; Vice Pres., 2005–; Trustee and Mem. Council, 2007–12; Chm., Woody Plant Cttee, 2009–14; Chm., Plants Adv. Cttee, 2010–12; Mem., Awards Cttee, 2010–. Member: Nat. Council for Conservation of Plants and Gardens, 1980–88 (Chm., Guernsey Gp, 1999–2011); Horticultural Bd, 2012–14. Founder, Internat. Clematis Soc., 1984 (Pres., 1989–91); International Plant Propagators' Society: Vice-Pres., 1976, Pres., 1977, GB and NI Reg.; Internat. Vice-Pres., 1981, Internat. Pres. 1982. Pres., Guernsey Botanical Trust, 2007–. FCIHort (FIHort 1993). Trustee, Caritas, Guernsey, 2007–. Rose Bowl Award, Plant Propagators' Soc., 1979; Reginald Cory Meml Cup, RHS, 2004; Achievement in Horticulture Award, Inst. of Horticulture, 2012; Contributor Award, Perennial Plant Assoc., USA, 2014. *Publications:* Making the Most of Clematis, 1979, 2nd edn 1991 (Dutch edn 1987); The Gardener's Guide to Growing Clematis, 1997 (Dutch edn 1998); Clematis for Everyone, 2000; Clematis du 3e millénaire, 2002; Clematis for Small Spaces, 2007. *Recreations:* hockey, swimming, tennis, gardening, conservation work with native and cultivated plants, wildlife. *Address:* Guernsey Clematis Nursery Ltd, Domarie Vineries, Les Sauvagees, St Sampson's, Guernsey GY2 4FD. *T:* (01481) 245942, *Fax:* (01481) 248987. *E:* raymondjevison@guernsey-clematis.com. *Club:* Sloane.

EWAN, Pamela Wilson, CBE 2007; FRCP, FRCPath; Consultant Allergist, Addenbrooke's Hospital, Cambridge, since 1997; *b* Forfar, 23 Sept. 1945; *d* of Norman Ewan and Frances Ewan; *m* 1979, Sir (David) Keith Peters, *qv*; two *s* one *d*. *Educ:* Forfar Acad., Angus; Royal Free Hosp. Med. Sch., London (MA, MB BS 1969). FRCP 1986; FRCPath 1997. Jun. hosp. posts, Royal Free, Guy's and Hammersmith Hosps, London, 1969–80; Sen. Lectr and Hon. Consultant, St Mary Hosp. Med. Sch., London, 1980–88; MRC Clinical Scientist and Hon. Consultant Allergist, Addenbrooke's Hosp., Cambridge, 1988–97. Pres., British Soc. for Allergy and Clin. Immunol., 1999–2002; Chm., Nat. Allergy Strategy Gp, 2005–. William Frankland Award, British Soc. for Allergy and Clin. Immunol., 2000; Silver Medal, Chelsea Flower Show, 2003, 2004; Lifetime Achievement Award, Allergy UK, 2011. *Publications:* scientific papers and chapters on allergy, esp. nut allergy and anaphylaxis. *Recreations:* cats, art. *Address:* 7 Chaucer Road, Cambridge CB2 7EB. *T:* (01223) 217777, *Fax:* (01223) 216953. *E:* pamela.ewan@addenbrookes.nhs.uk.

EWART, David Scott; QC 2006; barrister; *b* 29 April 1964; *s* of David and Christina Ewart; *m* 2011, Sarah Dunn; one *s* two *d*, and one *s* one *d* from a previous marriage. *Educ:* Hamilton Grammar Sch.; Trinity Coll., Oxford (BA 1986). Called to the Bar, Gray's Inn, 1988. *Recreation:* bridge. *Address:* Pump Court Tax Chambers, 16 Bedford Row, WC1R 4EF. *T:* (020) 7414 8080. *Club:* Young Chelsea Bridge.

EWART, Dr Michael; Director, Scottish International Education Trust, since 2009; *b* 9 Sept. 1952; *s* of late James Ewart and Joyce Goulden; *m* 2010, Dr Sally Anderson; one *s* one *d*. *Educ:* Jesus Coll., Cambridge (BA Hons 1974); York Univ. (DPhil 1977). Scottish Office, 1977–81; Asst Private Sec. to Sec. of State for Scotland, 1981–82; CS Fellow in Politics, Univ. of Glasgow, 1982–83; Health Service Mgt Reform, 1983–86; Hd, Schs Div., Scottish Educn Dept, 1986–91; Dep. Dir, Scottish Courts Admin, 1991–93; Chief Exec., Scottish Court Service, 1993–99; Hd, Schs Gp, 1999–2002, Hd of Dept, 2002–06, Scottish Exec. Educn Dept; Chief Exec., Scottish Prison Service, 2007–09. Member: Bd, Scottish Ballet, 2007–13; Bd, Quality Scotland, 2007–09; Bd, Phoenix Futures, 2012–; Mgt Adv. Bd, Education Scotland, 2012–; Chm., Phoenix Futures Scotland, 2013–. Lay Mem., Judicial Appts Bd for Scotland, 2010–. *Recreations:* music, books, military history, running, climbing (ice and rock), ski-ing, geocaching. *Address:* Scottish International Education Trust, Turcan Connell, Princes Exchange, 1 Earl Grey Street, Edinburgh EH3 9EE.

EWART, Sir Michael; *see* Ewart, Sir W. M.

EWART, Penelope Jane Clucas; *see* Marshall, P. J. C.

EWART, Sir (William) Michael, 7th Bt *cr* 1887, of Glenmachen, Co. Down and of Glenbank, Co. Antrim; *b* 10 June 1953; *o s* of Sir (William) Ivan (Cecil) Ewart, 6th Bt and Pauline Preston (*d* 1964); *S* father, 1995. *Educ:* Radley. *Recreations:* racing, ski-ing, travel. *Heir:* none. *Address:* Hill House, Hillsborough, Co. Down BT26 6AE. *Club:* Naval.

EWEN, Air Vice-Marshal Peter Ronald, CB 2015; CEng; FRAeS; Director Air Support, Defence Equipment and Support, Ministry of Defence, since 2013; *b* London, 1959; *s* of Ronald and Marion Ewen; one *d* (and one *d* decd). *Educ:* Campion Sch.; BSc 1st Cl. Hons Engrg; Postgrad. Dip Mgt Studies; Postgrad. Dip. Mgt Consultancy; DPhil 2008. FRAes 2004; CEng 2005. Head: Nimrod, 2009–11; Air, Intelligence, Surveillance, Target Acquisition and Reconnaissance, 2011–12; COS, Support and Exec. Officer, RAF, 2012–13.

EWENS, Prof. Warren John, PhD; FRS 2000; Professor of Genetics, University of Pennsylvania (Professor of Biology, 1972, now Emeritus); *b* 23 Jan. 1937; *s* of John and Gwendoline Ewens; *m* 1st, 1961, Helen Wiley (marr. diss.); one *s* one *d*; 2nd, 1981, Kathryn Gogolin. *Educ:* Trinity Coll., Melbourne Univ. (MA); Australian Nat. Univ. (PhD 1964). Professor, Department of Mathematics: La Trobe Univ., 1967–72; Monash Univ., 1977–96. *Publications:* Population Genetics, 1969; Mathematical Population Genetics, 1979; Probability and Statistics in Bioinformatics, 2000. *Recreations:* tennis, bridge, reading. *Address:* 324 Leidy Laboratories, University of Pennsylvania, PA 19104, USA. *T:* (215) 8987109.

EWER, Graham Anderson, CB 1999; CBE 1991; President, 2004–06, Vice President, 2006–08, Hon. Member, since 2009, European Logistics Association; *b* 22 Sept. 1944; *s* of late Robert and Maud Ewer; *m* 1969, Mary Caroline Grant; two *d*. *Educ:* Truro Cathedral Sch.; RMA, Sandhurst. FCILT (FILT 1999; FCIT 1999). Commnd RCT, 1965; served Germany, UK and ME, 1966–75; Army Staff Coll., 1976; Lt Col, Directing Staff, Army Staff Coll., 1984; CO, 8 Regt RCT, Munster, 1985–87; Col, DCS, G1/4 HQ 1st Armd Div., Verden, Germany and Gulf War, 1988–91; Comdt, Army Sch. of Transportation, 1991; Col, Logistic Support Policy Secretariat, 1992; Brig. 1993; Comd, Combat Service Support Gp, Germany and Guetersloh Garrison, 1993–94; Dir, Logistic Planning (Army), 1995; Maj. Gen. 1996; ACDS (Logistics), 1996–99; Chief Exec., Chartered Inst. of Logistics and Transport (UK), 1999–2004. Col Comdt, RLC, 1999–2009. *Publications:* (contrib.) Blackadder's War, ed M. S. White, 1995; (contrib.) Sustainable Supply Chain Management: the bestLog textbook, 2010; contrib. to various jls. *Recreations:* sailing, military history, motorcycling, caravanning. *Address:* c/o HSBC, 17 Boscawen Street, Truro, Cornwall TR1 2QZ.

EWING; *see* Orr-Ewing and Orr Ewing.

EWING, Rt Rev. Allan; *see* Bunbury, Bishop of.

EWING, Annabelle Janet; solicitor; Member (SNP) Scotland Mid and Fife, Scottish Parliament, since 2011; Minister for Youth and Women's Employment, since 2014; *b* 20 Aug. 1960; *d* of late Stewart Martin Ewing and of Winifred Margaret Ewing, *qv*. *Educ:* Craigholme Sch., Glasgow; Univ. of Glasgow (LLB Hons); Bologna Center, Johns Hopkins Univ.; Europa Inst., Amsterdam Univ. Apprentice lawyer, Ruth Anderson and Co., 1984–86; admitted solicitor, 1986; Legal Service, DG XIV, CEC, 1987; Associate, Lebrun de Smedt and Dassesse, Brussels, 1987–89; Associate, 1989–92, Partner, 1993–96, Akin Gump, Brussels; Special Counsel, McKenna and Cuneo, Brussels, 1996; EC lawyer, 1997; Associate, 1998–99, Partner, 1999–2001, Ewing & Co., solicitors, Glasgow; Consultant, Leslie Wolfson & Co., solicitors, Glasgow, 2001–03. MP (SNP) Perth, 2001–05; contested (SNP) Ochil and South Perthshire, 2005, 2010. *Address:* Scottish Parliament, Edinburgh EH99 1SP.

EWING, Bernadette Mary; *see* Kelly, B. M.

EWING, Maria Louise; soprano; *b* Detroit, 27 March 1950; *y d* of Norman Ewing and Hermina Ewing (*née* Veraar); *m* 1982, Sir Peter Reginald Frederick Hall, *qv* (marr. diss. 1990); one *d*. *Educ:* High School; Cleveland Inst. of Music. Studied with Marjorie Gordon, Eleanor Steber, Jennie Tourel, Otto Guth. First public performance, Meadowbrook, 1968 (Rigoletto); débuts Metropolitan Opera and La Scala, 1976; sings at Covent Garden, Glyndebourne, Salzburg, Paris, Metropolitan Opera, LA Opera, La Scala and other major venues; rôles include Begbick, Blanche, Carmen, Geschwitz, Jezibaba, Klythaemnestra, Lucretia, Lady Macbeth, Mélisande, La Périchole, Poppea; concerts and recitals.

EWING, Mrs Winifred Margaret; Member (SNP) Highlands and Islands, Scottish Parliament, 1999–2003; *b* 10 July 1929; *d* of George Woodburn and Christina Bell Anderson; *m* 1956, Stewart Martin Ewing, CA (*d* 2003); two *s* one *d*. *Educ:* Queen's Park Sen. Sec. Sch.; University of Glasgow (MA, LLB). Qual. as Solicitor, 1952. Lectr in Law, 1954–56; Solicitor, practising on own account, 1956–. Sec., Glasgow Bar Assoc., 1961–67, Pres., 1970–71. MP (SNP): Hamilton, Nov. 1967–1970; Moray and Nairn, Feb. 1974–1979; contested (SNP) Orkney and Shetland, 1983. MEP (SNP), 1975–99, elected Mem. for Highlands and Is, 1979–99; Vice-Pres., Animal Welfare Intergp, EP, 1989–99. President: Scottish National Party, 1987–2005; European Free Alliance, 1991–; Mem., Lomé Assembly, 1981–. Pres., Glasgow Central Soroptimist Club, 1966–67. FRSA 1990. DUniv: Open, 1993; Stirling, 2012; Hon. LLD Glasgow, 1995; Hon. LLD Aberdeen, 2004. Freeman, City of Avignon, 1985; Comptroller of Scottish Privileges, Veere, Netherlands, 1997–2011. Médaille d'Or, Fondation du Mérite Européen, 2014.

See also A. J. Ewing.

EWINS, Prof. David John, FRS 2006; FREng, FIMechE; Professor of Vibration Engineering and Director, Bristol Laboratory for Advanced Dynamic Engineering, University of Bristol, since 2007; Professor of Vibration Engineering, 1983–2013, Distinguished Research Fellow, since 2014, Imperial College London (formerly Imperial College of Science, Technology and Medicine); *b* 25 March 1942; *s* of W. J. and P. Ewins; *m* 1964, Brenda Rene (*née* Chalk) (marr. diss. 1997); three *d*. *Educ:* Kingswood Grammar Sch., Bristol; Imperial Coll., London (BScEng, ACGI, DScEng); Trinity Coll., Cambridge (PhD). FIMechE 1990; FREng (FEng 1995). Res. Asst for Rolls-Royce Ltd, Cambridge Univ., 1966–67; Imperial College, London University: Lectr, then Reader, in Mech. Engrg, 1967–83; formed Modal Testing Unit, 1981; Dir, Rolls-Royce sponsored Centre of Vibration Engrg, 1990–2002; Pro-Rector, Internat. Relations, 2001–05. Temasek Prof., and Dir, Centre for Mechanics of Microsystems, Nanyang Technol Univ., Singapore, 1999–2002. Sen. Lectr, Chulalongkorn Univ., Bangkok, 1968–69; Maître de Conférences, INSA, Lyon, 1974–75; Visiting Professor: Virginia Poly and State Univ., USA, 1981; ETH, Zürich, 1986; Inst. Nat. Polytechnique de Grenoble, 1990; Nanyang Technol Univ., Singapore, 1994, 1997; Hon. Professor: Nanjing Aero Inst., 1988; Shandong Polytechnic Inst., 1991. Partner, ICATS, 1989–. Consultant to: Rolls-Royce, 1969–; MoD, 1977–, and other organisations in Europe, S America and USA. Chm., then Pres., Dynamic Testing Agency, 1990–99; Chm., EU CleanSky Sci. and Technol. Adv. Bd, 2010–. FCGI 2002. Foreign Fellow, Indian Nat. Acad. of Engrg, 2012; Fellow, Soc. of Experimental Mechanics (USA), 2014. *Publications:* Modal Testing: theory and practice, 1984, 9th edn 1996; Modal Testing: theory, practice and application, 2000; (ed with D. J. Inman) Structural Dynamics, 2000; papers on vibration engrg in technical jls in UK, USA, France. *Recreations:* music (piano, choral singing), moorland walking, travel, good food, French, Italian. *Address:* Imperial College, Exhibition Road, SW7 2AZ. *T:* (020) 7594 7068.

EWINS, Peter David, CB 2001; FREng; FRAeS; Chief Executive, Meteorological Office, 1997–2004; *b* 20 March 1943; *s* of John Samuel Ewins and Kathleen Ewins; *m* 1968, Barbara Irene Howland; two *s* one *d*. *Educ:* Imperial College London (BSc Eng); Cranfield Inst. of Technology (MSc). FREng (FEng 1996); FRAeS 1996. Joined RAE Farnborough, 1966, research on structl applications of composite materials; section head, 1974; staff of Chief Scientist, RAF, MoD, 1978; Head of Helicopters Res. Div., RAE, 1981; seconded to Cabinet Office (Civil Service personnel policy), 1984; Dir, Nuclear Projects, MoD, 1987; Dir, ARE, MoD (PE), 1988; Man. Dir (Maritime and Electronics), 1991, Man. Dir, Command and Maritime Systems Gp, 1992, Man. Dir (Ops), 1993–94, DRA; Chief Scientist, MoD, 1994–97. Mem. Council, Royal Acad. of Engrg, 1999–. Hon. DSc Exeter, 2006. *Publications:* technical papers on structural composite materials in learned jls. *Recreations:* horticulture, bee-keeping, walking.

EXETER, 8th Marquess of, *cr* 1801; **William Michael Anthony Cecil;** Baron Burghley 1571; Earl of Exeter 1605; *b* 1 Sept. 1935; *s* of 7th Marquess of Exeter and Edith Lilian Csanady de Telegd (*d* 1954); *S* father, 1988; *m* 1st, 1967, Nancy Rose (marr. diss. 1992), *d* of Lloyd Arthur Meeker; one *s* one *d*; 2nd, 1999, Barbara Anne, *d* of Eugene Magat. *Educ:* Eton. Rancher and businessman in 100 Mile House, BC, Canada, 1954–96. Pres., Ashland Inst., 1999–. *Publications:* (jtly) Spirit of Sunrise, 1979; The Long View, 1985; The Rising Tide of Change, 1986; Living at the Heart of Creation, 1990. *Heir:* *s* Lord Burghley, *qv*. *Address:* 2290 Morada Lane, Ashland, OR 97520–3639, USA. *T:* (541) 488 3646. *E:* mcecil@mind.net.

EXETER, Bishop of, since 2014; **Rt Rev. Robert Ronald Atwell;** *b* Ilford, Essex, 3 Aug. 1954; s of Ronald Victor Atwell and Marcia Blanche Atwell (*née* Newton). *Educ:* Wanstead High Sch.; St John's Coll., Durham Univ. (BA 1975; MLitt 1979); Westcott House, Cambridge; Venerable English Coll., Rome. Ordained deacon, 1978, priest, 1979; Asst Curate, John Keble, Mill Hill, 1978–81; Chaplain, Trinity Coll., Cambridge, 1981–87; Benedictine Monk, Burford Priory, 1987–98; Vicar, St Mary-the-Virgin, Primrose Hill, 1998–2008; Bishop Suffragan of Stockport, 2008–14. *Publications:* Spiritual Classics from the Early Church, 1995; Celebrating the Saints, 1998, enlarged edn, 2004; Celebrating the Seasons, 1998; Gift: 100 readings - celebration of birth and parenthood, 2005; Love: 100 readings - celebration of marriage and love, 2005; Remember: 100 readings for those in grief and bereavement, 2005; The Contented Life: spirituality and the gift of years, 2011; The Good Worship Guide, 2013; Peace at the Last: leading funerals well, 2014. *Recreations:* theatre, gardening, hill-walking. *Address:* The Palace, Exeter EX1 1HY. *T:* (01392) 272362. *E:* bishop.of.exeter@exeter.anglican.org.

EXETER, Dean of; *see* Draper, Very Rev. J. L.

EXETER, Archdeacon of; *see* Futcher, Ven. C. D.

EXLEY, Margaret, CBE 2001; Chief Executive, SCT Consultants Ltd, since 2011; *b* 9 Feb. 1949; *d* of Ernest and Elsie Exley; *m* 1984, Malcolm Grant (*d* 2007); one *s* one *d*. *Educ:* Univ. of Manchester (BA Hons Econ); Univ. of Warwick (MBA). Res. Fellow, Manchester Business Sch., 1971–73; Principal, Cabinet Office, 1973–80; Dir, Hay Mgt Consultants, 1980–84; Chief Exec., Kinsley Lord Ltd, 1984–95; European Managing Partner, Towers Perrin, 1995–2001; Chm., Mercer Delta UK Ltd, 2001–07; Founder and Chm., Stonecourt Consulting Ltd, 2007–11. Non-executive Director: St Mary's NHS Trust, 1997–2000; Field Gp, 1997–99; HM Treasury, 1999–2005. Mem., Employment Appeal Tribunal, 1992–95. Mem., Charter Renewal Steering Gp, BBC, 2006–07. Chm., Corporate Adv. Bd, NPG, 2000–; Trustee, NPG Portrait Fund, 2012–. FRSA 1996. *Publications:* various, on strategy and leadership, in learned and popular jls. *Recreations:* social history, politics, music. *Address:* 11 Launceston Place, Kensington, W8 5RL. *T:* (020) 7376 1973, *Fax:* (020) 7376 1985. *E:* margaret.exley@sctconsultants.com. *Club:* Reform.

EXMOUTH, 10th Viscount *cr* 1816; **Paul Edward Pellew;** Bt 1796 (Pellew of Treverry); Baron 1814; Marqués de Olias (Spain *cr* 1652); *b* 8 Oct. 1940; *s* of 9th Viscount Exmouth and Maria Luisa (*d* 1994), *d* of late Luis de Urquijo, Marqués de Amurrio, Madrid; *S* father, 1970; *m* 1st, 1964, Krystina Garay-Marques (marr. diss. 1974); one *d*; 2nd, 1975, Rosemary Countess of Burford (marr. diss. 2000); twin *s*. *Educ:* Downside. Formerly cross bencher, House of Lords. *Heir:* *er twin s* Hon. Edward Francis Pellew, *b* 30 Oct. 1978. *E:* PaulExmouth@aol.com.

EXNER, Most Rev. Adam; Archbishop of Vancouver, (RC), 1991–2004, now Archbishop Emeritus; *b* 24 Dec. 1928. *Educ:* St Joseph's Coll., Yorkton, Sask; Gregorian Univ., Rome (LPH 1954; STB 1956 STL 1958). Ottawa Univ. (STD 1960). Entered novitiate, Oblates of Mary Immaculate, St Norbert, Manitoba, 1950; ordained Roviano, Rome, 1957; St Charles Scholasticate, Battleford, Saskatchewan: Prof., 1960–64 and 1971–72; Rector and Superior, 1965–71; Prof. of Moral Theology, Newman Theol Coll., Edmonton, Alberta, 1972–74; Bishop of Kamloops, BC, 1974–82; Archbishop of Winnipeg, 1982–91. Secretary: BC and Yukon Conf. of Bishops, 1974–79 (Chm., 1991–); Conf. of Catholic Bishops, 1974–80. Canadian Conference of Catholic Bishops: Mem., Admin. Bd, 1976–83; Rep. of Western Conf. of Bishops, 1981–83; Mem., Episcopal Commn for Christian Educn, 1983–88; Mem., Social Communications Commn, 1989–91; Rep. of W Reg. of Bishops on Permanent Council, 1989–93; Mem., Cttee on Sexual Abuse, 1990–92; Mem., Theol. Commn, 1991–93, 1995– (Pres., 1993–95); Mem., Working Gp Residential Schs, 1992–95; Mem., Progs and Priorities Cttee, 1993–95; Chm., Catholic Orgn for Life and Family, 1995. Chm., Conf. of Bishops of Manitoba, 1983–91; Member: Sacred Congregation for Bishops, 1984–90; Nat. Catholic-Lutheran Dialogue, 1987–89. Chaplain, Knight of Columbus, 1974–82; Liaison Bp and Chaplain, Catholic Sch. Trustees Assoc. of BC, 1974–82; Mem., St Paul's Coll. Bd, Univ. of Manitoba, 1982. *Publications:* contrib. to Catholic Press, 1960–82. *Recreations:* playing piano and accordion, golf, working out, cross country ski-ing, jogging. *Address:* c/o 150 Robson Street, Vancouver, BC V6B 2A7, Canada.

EXON, Richard Douglas; Co-founder, Joint, since 2012; *b* Birmingham, 12 Aug. 1971; *s* of Dr and Mrs Peter Exon; *m* 2001, Melanie Copeland; two *d*. *Educ:* Yarlet Hall; Shrewsbury Sch.; Univ. of Durham (BA Hons 1993). Account Exec., Ogilvy & Mather, 1993; Account Manager to Global Business Develt Dir, Bartle Bogle Hegarty, 1994–2007; Man. Dir, 2007, CEO, 2007–12, Rainey Kelly Campbell Roalfe/Y&R. IPA Effectiveness Award, 1998. *Recreations:* winter sports, field sports, ball sports, cooking. *Address:* Joint, 8–10 Lower James Street, W1F 9EL. *T:* (020) 3651 1149. *Clubs:* Ivy, Every House.

EXTON-SMITH, Jasmine; *see* Whitbread, J.

EYERS, Patrick Howard Caines, CMG 1985; LVO 1966; HM Diplomatic Service, retired; *b* 4 Sept. 1933; *s* of late Arthur Leopold Caines Eyers and Nora Lilian Eyers; *m* 1960, Heidi, *d* of Werner Rüsch, Dipl. Ing, and Helene (*née* Feil); two *s* one *d*. *Educ:* Clifton Coll.; Gonville and Caius Coll., Cambridge (BA Hons 1957); Institut Universitaire de Hautes Etudes Internationales, Geneva. RA, 1952–54. Asst Editor, Grolier Soc. Inc., New York, 1957; HM Foreign (now Diplomatic) Service, 1959; ME Centre for Arabic Studies, 1960; Dubai, 1961; Brussels, 1964; FO, 1966; Aden, 1969; Abidjan, 1970; British Mil. Govt, Berlin, 1971; FCO, 1974; Counsellor, Bonn, 1977; Head, Republic of Ireland Dept, FCO, 1981; RCDS, 1984; Ambassador: to Zaire, the Congo, Rwanda and Burundi, 1985–87; to Algeria, 1987–89; to GDR, 1990; to Jordan, 1991–93. Officer, Order of Leopold, Belgium, 1966. *Recreations:* music, sailing. *Address:* c/o Barclays Bank, 86 Queens Road, Bristol BS8 1RB. *Club:* Hurlingham.

EYKYN, George William; Director of Communications, British Gas, since 2014; *b* Oxford, 4 May 1966; *s* of Jamie and Angela Eykyn; *m* 1993, Anne Lennon; one *s* one *d*. *Educ:* Radley Coll., Oxon; Magdalen Coll., Oxford (MA Hons Modern Langs). Joined BBC, 1987: trainee, News, 1987–89; regl journalist, then TV reporter, NI, 1989–92; reporter, Breakfast News, 1992–94; news corresp., BBC News, 1994–2004; presenter, BBC World, 1997–2004; Sen. Consultant, PricewaterhouseCoopers LLP, 2004–08; Dir of Communication, DCLG, 2008–14. *Recreations:* cricket, ski-ing, motorcycling. *E:* geykyn@btopenworld.com. *Club:* MCC (playing Mem.).

EYRE, Prof. Deborah Mary; Chief Executive Officer, DEL International Consultancy; *b* 22 Jan. 1954; *d* of Philip and Mary Davis; *m* 1976, John Eyre; one *s* one *d*. *Educ:* Hunmanby Hall Sch., Filey; Westminster Coll., Oxford (Cert Ed); Univ. of Reading (MEd). Teacher, primary schs, 1976–83; educn consultant on gifted and talented, 1983–89; advr on gifted and talented, Oxon LEA, 1989–97; Oxford Brookes University: Dir, Res. Centre for Able Pupils, and Dep. Dean of Educn, 1997–2002; Prof. of Educn, 2002; University of Warwick: Dir, Nat. Acad. for Gifted and Talented Youth, 2002–07; Prof. of Educn, 2007–08, now Hon. Prof. Chief Executive, Deborah Eyre Ltd, 2008–10; Educn Dir, Nord Anglia Educn Ltd, 2010–14. Member, Executive Board: Center for Talented Youth, Johns Hopkins Univ., 2005–; Trng and Develt Agency for Schs, 2006–09; Governing Council Observer, Nat. Coll. for Sch. Leadership, 2006–09; Vice-Pres., World Council for Gifted and Talented Children, 2006–09; Educn Dir, Mawhiba Schs Partnership Initiative, King Abdulaziz and his Companions Foundn for the Gifted, Saudi Arabia, 2009–. Non-executive Director: Inspiring Futures Foundn, 2007–; Kingshurst CTC Acad., Birmingham, 2009–; Mem. Bd, 21st Century Learning Alliance, 2007–. Vis. Senior Res. Fellow, St Hugh's Coll., Univ. of Oxford, 2007–; Adv. Prof., Hong Kong Inst. of Educn, 2008–09. Adviser: Educn Select Cttee, H of C, 1998–99; Ministerial Task Force for Gifted and Talented, DfES, 1998–2001. FRSA. *Publications:* School Governors and More Able Children, 1995; Able Children in Ordinary Schools, 1997; (ed jtly) Curriculum Provision for the Gifted and Talented in the Primary School, 2001; (ed jtly) Curriculum Provision for the Gifted and Talented in the Secondary School, 2002; Gifted and Talented International: international handbook for gifted education, 2007; (ed) Major Themes in Gifted Education (4 vols), 2009; Room at the Top: inclusive education for high performance, 2010. *Recreations:* modern fiction, food and wine, family and friends. *Address:* 59 Linkside Avenue, Oxford OX2 8JE. *T:* (01865) 510045. *E:* DeborahEyre@nordanglia.com.

EYRE, James Henry Robert, OBE 2003; Director, Wilkinson Eyre Architects Ltd, since 1989; *b* 24 Jan. 1959; *s* of late Michael Robert Giles Eyre and of Susan Bennett; *m* 1983, Karen Fiona Turner; one *s* one *d*. *Educ:* Oundle Sch.; Liverpool Univ. (BA Hons 1980); Architectural Assoc. (AA Dip. 1983). RIBA 1985. Architect, Michael Hopkins & Partners, 1980–85; joined Chris Wilkinson Architects, subseq. Wilkinson Eyre Architects, 1985, Partner, 1986–; *projects include:* Stratford Market Depot for Jubilee Line Extension, 1996; South Dock Footbridge for LDDC, 1997; Hulme Arch, Manchester, 1997; Stratford Station for Jubilee Line Extension, 2000; Gateshead Millennium Bridge, 2001; Making the Modern World gall., Science Mus.; Bridge of Aspiration, Floral Street, for Royal Ballet Sch., 2003; Mus. of London entrance and gall., 2003; Ceramics Gall. Bridge, V&A Mus., 2010; 435m Guangzhou Internat. Finance Centre Tower, 2011; Gardens by the Bay Conservatories, Singapore, 2011. Comr, Royal Commn for the Exhibition 1851, 2014–. Trustee, Design Council CABE, 2011–. Pres., AA, 2007–09. Hon. DLaws Liverpool, 2009. *Publications:* (contrib.) The Architecture of Bridge Design, 1997; (jtly) Bridging Art and Science, 2001; Exploring Boundaries, 2007; contribs World Architecture, Architects Jl, The Architecture of Bridge Design. *Recreations:* designing, making, reading, game fishing. *Address:* (office) 33 Bowling Green Lane, EC1R 0BJ. *T:* (020) 7608 7900.

EYRE, Major John Vickers; JP; DL; Vice Lord-Lieutenant of Gloucestershire, 2007–11; *b* 30 April 1936; *s* of Nevill Cathcart Eyre and Maud Evelyn Eyre (*née* Truscott); *m* 1974, Sarah Margaret Aline Heywood; one *s* one *d*. *Educ:* Winchester; Staff Coll., Camberley. Commnd, 1955, RHA, 1957, 14th/20th Kings Hussars, 1962; retd, 1973. Asst to Chm., Savoy Hotel, 1973–75; Administrator, Brian Colquhoun and Partners, consulting engrs, 1975–79; Proprietor, Haresfield Garden Centre, 1981–86; Man. Dir, George Truscott Ltd, 1986–2003. Royal Glos Hussars, TA, 1980–83 (Patron, 1997–). Dist Comr, Berkeley Hunt Pony Club, 1986–95; Chm., Berkeley Hunt, 2005–11. Gloucestershire: JP 1987; DL 2000; High Sheriff, 2000–01. Pres., Glos, RBL, 2008–11. *Recreation:* country pursuits. *Address:* Barn Cottage, Tytherington, Wotton-under-Edge, Glos GL12 8UG. *T:* (01454) 412220. *E:* jve@boyts.co.uk. *Club:* Army and Navy.

EYRE, Patrick Giles Andrew; Master of the Senior (formerly Supreme) Court, Queen's Bench Division, 1992–2012; *b* 11 March 1940; *s* of late Edward Joseph Eyre and Hon. Dorothy Elizabeth Anne Pelline Lyon-Dalberg-Acton; *m* 1977, Victoria Mary Bathurst Barthorp; one *s*, and one step *d*. *Educ:* Downside; Trinity Coll., Oxford (MA). Farmer, 1965–72. Called to the Bar, Inner Temple, 1974. *Publications:* articles on law, computers, horses and country pursuits. *Recreations:* books, horses, hunting, music.

EYRE, Sir Reginald (Edwin), Kt 1984; President, Birmingham Heartlands Business Forum, 2000–05; Consultant, Eyre & Co., solicitors, 1992–2002; *b* 28 May 1924; *s* of late Edwin Eyre and Mary Eyre (*née* Moseley); *m* 1978, Anne Clements; one *d*. *Educ:* King Edward's Camp Hill Sch., Birmingham; Emmanuel Coll., Cambridge (MA). RNVR, 1942–45 (Sub-Lt). Admitted a Solicitor, 1950; Senior Partner, Eyre & Co., solicitors, Birmingham, 1951–91. Chairman: Birmingham Heartlands Develt Corp. (formerly Birmingham Heartlands Ltd (East Birmingham Urban Develt Agency)), 1987–98; Birmingham Cable Corp. Ltd, 1988–99; Dep. Chm., Commn for New Towns, 1988–92. Hon. Consultant, Poor Man's Lawyer, 1948–58. Conservative Political Centre: Chm., W Midlands Area, 1960–63; Chm., National Advisory Cttee, 1964–66. Contested (C) Birmingham (Northfield) 1959; MP (C) Birmingham Hall Green, May 1965–87. Opposition Whip, 1966–70; a Lord Comr of the Treasury, June–Sept. 1970; Comptroller of HM Household, 1970–72; Parliamentary Under-Secretary of State: DoE, 1972–74; Dept of Trade, 1978–82; Dept of Transport, 1982–83. A Vice Chm., Cons. Party Organisation, 1975–79; Founder Chm., Cons. Parly Urban Affairs Cttee, 1974–79. Freeman, City of Birmingham, 1991. DUniv UCE, 1997. *Publications:* Hope for our Towns and Cities, 1977. *Address:* c/o Eyre & Co., 1041 Stratford Road, Hall Green, Birmingham B28 8AS.

EYRE, Richard Anthony, CBE 2014; Chairman, Internet Advertising Bureau Ltd, since 2003; Founder, RadioCrimson.com, since 2014; *b* 3 May 1954; *s* of Edgar Gabriel Eyre and Marjorie (*née* Corp); *m* 1977, Sheelagh Colquhoun; one *s* one *d*. *Educ:* King's Coll. Sch., Wimbledon; Lincoln Coll., Oxford (MA); Harvard Business Sch. (AMP). Media buyer, Benton & Bowles, 1975–79; TV airtime salesman, Scottish TV, 1979–80; media planner, Benton & Bowles, 1980–84; Media Director: Aspect, 1984–86; Bartle Bogle Hegarty, 1986–91; Chief Executive: Capital Radio plc, 1991–97; ITV, 1997–2000; Pearson Television, 2000–01; Dir, Strategy and Content, RTL Gp, 2000–01. Chairman: RDF Media plc, 2001–09; GCap Media plc, 2007–08; Rapid Mobile, 2008–11; Eden Project Ltd, 2009–13 (non-exec. Dir, 2003–09); Next 15 plc, 2011–; non-executive Director: Guardian Media Gp, 2004–07; MGt, 2007–; Results Internat. Gp, 2007–; Grant Thornton LLP, 2010–. FRSA 1997. Chm., Media Trust, 2014–; Trustee, Walking with the Wounded, 2013–. Mackintosh Medal, Advertising Assoc., 2013. *Publications:* The Club (novel), 2005. *Recreations:* music, travel. *Address:* Internet Advertising Bureau, 14 Macklin Street, WC2B 5NF. *Club:* Thirty.

EYRE, Sir Richard (Charles Hastings), Kt 1997; CBE 1992; theatre, film and TV director; Artistic Director, Royal National Theatre, 1988–97 (Associate Director, 1981–88); *b* 28 March 1943; *m* 1973, Susan Elizabeth Birtwistle, *qv*; one *d*. *Educ:* Sherborne Sch.; Peterhouse, Cambridge (BA; Hon. Fellow, 2001). Asst Dir, Phoenix Theatre, Leicester, 1966; Lyceum Theatre, Edinburgh: Associate Dir, 1967–70; Dir of Productions, 1970–72; freelance director: Liverpool, 7:84 Co., West End; tours for British Council: W Africa, 1971; SE Asia, 1972; Artistic Dir, Nottingham Playhouse, 1973–78; Prod./Dir, Play for Today, BBC TV, 1978–80. A Gov., BBC, 1995–2003. Director: The Churchill Play, Nottingham, 1974; Comedians, Old Vic and Wyndhams, 1976; Touched, Nottingham, 1977; Hamlet, Royal Court, 1980; Edmond, Royal Court, 1985; Kafka's Dick, Royal Court, 1986; National Theatre: Guys and Dolls, 1982, revived 1996 (SWET Director of the Year, 1982, Standard Best Director, 1982, Critics' Circle Best Dir Award, 1997); The Beggar's Opera, and Schweyk in the Second World War, 1982; The Government Inspector, 1985; Futurists, 1986 (Best Production Award, Time Out, 1986); The Changeling, Bartholomew Fair, 1988; Hamlet, The Voysey Inheritance, 1989; Racing Demon, Richard III, 1990; White Chameleon, Napoli Milionaria, Murmuring Judges, 1991; Night of the Iguana, 1992; Macbeth, The Absence of War, 1993; Johnny on a Spot, Sweet Bird of Youth, 1994; La Grande Magia, 1995; Skylight, 1995, transf. Wyndham's, then NY, 1996, UK tour, then Vaudeville, 1997; The Prince's Play, John Gabriel Borkman (Critics' Circle Best Dir Award, 1997), 1996; Amy's View, 1997, NY, 1999; King Lear (Olivier Award, 1998), The Invention of Love (Evening Standard Award, 1997), 1997; Vincent in Brixton, transf. Wyndham's, 2002, NY, 2003 (Drama League Award); The Reporter, 2007; The Observer, 2009; Welcome to Thebes, 2010; Liolà, 2013; The Judas Kiss, Playhouse, transf. NY, 1998; (also trans.) The Novice, Almeida, 2000; The Crucible, NY, 2002; Mary Poppins, Prince Edward, 2004; (also trans.) Hedda Gabler, Almeida, transf. Duke of York's, 2005 (Olivier Award, 2006); The Last Cigarette, Minerva, Chichester, 2009; Private Lives, Vaudeville, 2010; A Flea in Her Ear, Old Vic, 2010; Betty Blue Eyes, Novello, 2011; The Last of the Duchess, Hampstead Th., 2011; The Dark Earth and the Light Sky, Almeida, 2012; Quartermaine's Terms, Wyndham's, 2013; The Pajama Game, Minerva, Chichester, 2013, transf. Shaftesbury Th., 2014; Ghosts, Almeida, 2013, transf. Trafalgar Studios, 2014 (Evening Standard Award for Best Dir, 2013; Olivier Award for Best Revival, 2014); Stephen Ward, Aldwych, 2013; Mr Foote's Other Leg, Hampstead Th., 2015. *Opera:* La Traviata, Covent Gdn, 1994; Le Nozze di Figaro, Aix-en-Provence, 2001; Carmen, 2009, Werther, Le Nozze di Figaro, 2014, Metropolitan Opera, NY; Manon Lescaut, Baden-Baden Festspielhaus, 2014. *Films:* The Ploughman's Lunch (Evening Standard Award for Best Film, 1983), Loose Connections, 1983; Laughterhouse, 1984, released as Singleton's Pluck, USA, 1985 (TV Prize, Venice Film Fest.); Iris, 2002 (Humanitas Prize; Efebo d'Oro Award); Stage Beauty, 2004; Notes on a Scandal, 2007; The Other Man, 2009; *for television:* The Imitation Game, Pasmore, 1980; Country, 1981; The Insurance Man, 1986 (Special Prize, Tokyo TV Fest., 1986); Past Caring, 1986; Tumbledown, 1988 (BAFTA Award for best single drama, Italia RAI Prize, RTS Award, Press Guild Award, Tokyo Prize); v., 1988 (RTS Award); Suddenly Last Summer, 1992; The Absence of War, 1995; King Lear, 1998 (Peabody Award, 1999); writer and presenter, Changing Stages (series), 2000; Henry IV, 2012. Cameron Mackintosh Vis. Prof. of Contemporary Theatre, Oxford Univ., 1997. Hon. Fellow: Goldsmiths' Coll., 1993; KCL, 1994. Hon. DLitt: Nottingham Trent, 1992; South Bank, 1994; Liverpool, 2003; Nottingham, 2008; DUniv Surrey, 1998; Hon. DDra RSAMD, 2000; Hon. Dr Oxford Brookes, 2003. STV Awards for Best Production, 1969, 1970 and 1971; De Sica Award, Sorrento Film Fest., 1986; Laurence Olivier and South Bank Show Awards for Outstanding Achievement, 1997; Lifetime Achievement Awards, Critics' Circle, and Directors' Guild, 1997. Officier de l'ordre des Arts et des Lettres (France), 1998. *Publications:* Utopia and Other Places, 1993; The Eyre Review (report of inquiry into running of Royal Opera House), 1998; (with Nicholas Wright) Changing Stages: a view of British theatre in the twentieth century, 2000; Iris (screenplay), 2002; National Service, 2003 (Theatre Bk Award, 2004); Hedda Gabler (adaptation), 2005; Talking Theatre: interviews with theatre people, 2009; Ghosts (adaptation), 2013; What Do I Know? (essays), 2014. *Address:* c/o Judy Daish Associates, 2 St Charles Place, W10 6EG. *T:* (020) 8964 8811.

EYRE, Stephen John Arthur; QC 2015; **His Honour Judge Eyre;** a Circuit Judge, since 2015; *b* Stourbridge, 17 Oct. 1957; *s* of Leslie Eyre and Joyce Eyre (*née* Whitehouse); *m* 1989, Margaret Goodman. *Educ:* Solihull Sch.; New Coll., Oxford (BA 1979; BCL 1980; MA); Cardiff Univ. (LLM 2010). Called to the Bar, Inner Temple, 1981; barrister, 1 Fountain Court, 1982–2002, St Philips Chambers, 2002–15; a Recorder, 2005–15; a Judge, First-tier Tribunal (Mental Health) (formerly Legal Mem., Mental Health Review Tribunal), 2007–15. Dep. Chancellor, dio. of Southwell, 2007–12; Chancellor: dio. of Coventry, 2009–; dio. of Lichfield, 2012–. Mem. (C), Solihull MBC, 1983–91, 1992–96. Contested (C) Birmingham Hodge Hill, 1987, July 2004, Strangford, 1992, Stourbridge, 2001. *Recreations:* reading, opera, theatre, walking, gardening. *Address:* Birmingham Crown Court, Queen Elizabeth II Law Courts, 1 Newton Street, Birmingham B4 7NA.

EYRE, Susan Elizabeth, (Lady Eyre); *see* Birtwistle, S. E.

EYSENCK, Prof. Michael William; Professor of Psychology, Royal Holloway (formerly Royal Holloway and Bedford New College), University of London, 1987–2009, now Emeritus (Head of Department of Psychology, 1987–2005), Honorary Fellow, 2013; Professorial Fellow, Roehampton University, since 2010; *b* 8 Feb. 1944; *s* of late Prof. Hans Jürgen Eysenck and Margaret Malcolm Eysenck (*née* Davies); *m* 1975, Mary Christine Kabyn; one *s* two *d*. *Educ:* Dulwich Coll.; University College London (BA Psych, 1st cl. Hons; Rosa Morrison Medal for outstanding arts graduate, 1965); Birkbeck Coll., London (PhD Psych). Asst Lectr, Lectr and Reader in Psychology, Birkbeck Coll., Univ. of London, 1965–87. Vis. Prof., Univ. of S Florida, Tampa, 1980. Chm., Cognitive Psych. Section, BPsS, 1982–87; Pres., Internat. Soc. for Stress and Anxiety, 2006–08 (Pres.-elect, 2004–06; Past Pres., 2008–10). Editor, European Jl of Cognitive Psych., 1989–91. *Publications:* Human Memory, 1977; (with H. J. Eysenck) Mindwatching, 1981; Attention and Arousal: cognition and performance, 1982; A Handbook of Cognitive Psychology, 1984; (with H. J. Eysenck) Personality and Individual Differences, 1985; (with J. T. Richardson and D. W. Piper) Student Learning: research in education and cognitive psychology, 1987; (with H. J. Eysenck) Mindwatching: why we behave the way we do, 1989; Happiness: facts and myths, 1990; (ed) The Blackwell Dictionary of Cognitive Psychology, 1990; International Review of Cognitive Psychology, 1990; (with M. T. Keane) Cognitive Psychology: a student's handbook, 1990; Anxiety: the cognitive perspective, 1992; (with M. Weller) The Scientific Basis of Psychiatry, 1992; (with A. Gale) Handbook of Individual Differences: biological perspectives, 1992; Principles of Cognitive Psychology, 1993; Perspectives on Psychology, 1994; Individual Differences: normal and abnormal, 1994; Simply Psychology, 1996; Anxiety and Cognition:

a unified theory, 1997; Psychology: an integrated approach, 1998; Psychology: a student's handbook, 2000; (with C. Flanagan) Psychology for A2 Level, 2001; Key Topics in A2 Psychology, 2003; Psychology for AS Level, 2003; Perspectives in Psychology, 2004; Fundamentals of Cognition, 2006; (with P. Buchwald and T. Ringeisen) Stress and Anxiety owns the life span: recent developments and challenges, 2008; Fundamentals of Psychology, 2009; (with A. Baddeley and M. C. Anderson) Memory, 2009; (with T. Marusz and M. Fajkowska) Warsaw Lectures on Personality and Social Psychology, vol 1: personality from biological, cognitive and social perspectives, 2009; (jtly) Handbook of Managerial Behaviour and Occupational Health, 2009; (with M. Fajkowska and T. Marusgewski) Warsaw Lectures on Personality and Social Psychology, vol. 2: personality, cognition and emotion, 2012, vol. 4: anxiety, depression and attentional control, 2014; (with D. Groome) Cognitive Psychology: revisiting the classic studies, 2015; numerous book chapters and contribs to Qly Jl of Exptl Psychology, Jl of Exptl Psychology, Jl of Abnormal Psychology, British Jl of Clin. Psychology, Jl of Personality and Social Psychology, Psychol Bull., Emotion, and others. *Recreations:* travel, tennis, golf, walking, bridge, croquet. *Address:* Department of Psychology, Roehampton University, Whitelands College, Holybourne Avenue, SW15 4JD. *T:* (020) 8392 3510. *Clubs:* Campden Hill Lawn Tennis; Surbiton Croquet.

EYTON, Anthony John Plowden, RA 1986 (ARA 1976); RWS 1988 (ARWS 1985); RWA 1984; RCA 1993; NEAC 1985; *b* 17 May 1923; *s* of late Captain John Seymour Eyton, ICS, author, and Phyllis Annie Tyser, artist; *m* 1960, Frances Mary Capell, MA (marr. diss.); three *d*. *Educ:* Twyford Sch.; Canford Sch.; Dept of Fine Art, Reading Univ.; Camberwell Sch. of Art (NDD). Served War, 1939–45, Cameronians (Scottish Rifles), Hampshire Regt, and Army Educn Corps. Abbey Major Scholarship in Painting, 1950–51. Elected Mem., London Gp, 1958. One Man Exhibitions: St George's Gall., 1955; Galerie de Seine, 1957; New Art Centre, 1959, 1961, 1968; New Grafton Gall., 1973; William Darby Gall., 1975; Newcastle Polytechnic Art Gall., 1978; Browse & Darby, 1978, 1981, 1985, 1987, 1990, 1993, 1996, 2000, 2005, 2009, 2013; Austin Desmond Gall., 1990; A. T. Kearney Ltd, 1997; King's Road Gall., 2002; Woodlands Art Gall., 2003; Eleven Spitalfields Gall., 2011, 2015; Retrospective Exhibn, S London Art Gall., Towner Art Gall., Eastbourne, and Plymouth Art Gall., 1981; Hong Kong and the New Territories exhibn, Imperial War Museum, 1983 (subsequent to commission); Evolution of a Cornish China Clay Pit exhibn, Eden Project, 2009–10 (resident artist, 1999–2009); work included in British Painting 1945–77, RA; Drawing Inspiration, Abbot Hall Art Gall., Lakeland Arts Trust, 2006. Work in public collections: Tate Gall.; Arts Council; Plymouth Art Gall.; Towner Art Gall., Eastbourne; Carlisle Art Gall.; DoE; RA; Government Picture Coll.; BR; Contemp. Art Soc.; Guildhall Art Gall. Fellowship awarded by Grocers' Co. (for work and travel in Italy), 1974. Hon. Fellow, Univ. of Arts, London, 2011. Hon. Mem., Pastel Soc., 1986; Hon. ROI 1988. Prize, John Moore's Exhibn, Liverpool, 1972; First Prize, Second British Internat. Drawing Biennale, Middlesbrough, 1975; Charles Wollaston Award, RA, 1981. *Relevant publication:* Eyton's Eye, by Jenny Pery, 2005. *Recreation:* gardening. *Address:* c/o Browse & Darby Ltd, 19 Cork Street, W1S 3LP.

EZRA, family name of **Baron Ezra**.

EZRA, Baron *cr* 1983 (Life Peer), of Horsham in the County of West Sussex; **Derek Ezra,** Kt 1974; MBE 1945; President, National Home Improvement Council, 1986–2005 (Hon. Vice-President, since 2005); *b* 23 Feb. 1919; *s* of David and Lillie Ezra; *m* 1950, Julia Elizabeth Wilkins (*d* 2011). *Educ:* Monmouth Sch.; Magdalene Coll., Cambridge (MA, Hon. Fellow, 1977). Army, 1939–47. Joined NCB, 1947; representative of NCB at Cttees of OEEC and ECE, 1948–52; Mem. of UK Delegn to High Authority of European Coal and Steel Community, 1952–56; Dep. Regional Sales Manager, NCB, 1956–58; Regional Sales Manager, 1958–60; Dir-Gen. of Marketing, NCB, 1960–65; NCB Bd Mem., 1965–67; Dep. Chm., 1967–71; Chm., 1971–82. Chairman: Associated Heat Services plc, 1966–99; J. H. Sankey & Son Ltd, 1977–82; Petrolex PLC, 1982–85; Throgmorton Trust PLC, 1984–91; Sheffield Heat and Power Ltd, 1985–2000; Associated Gas Supplies Ltd, 1987–95; Energy and Technical Services Gp plc, 1990–99; Micropower Ltd, 2000–05 (Patron, Micropower Council, 2005–); Director: British Fuel Co., 1966–82; Solvay SA, 1979–90; Redland PLC, 1982–89; Supervisory Bd, Royal Boskalis Westminster NV, 1982–85. Industrial Advr, Morgan Grenfell & Co. Ltd, 1982–88. Chm., NICG, 1972 and 1980–81; President: Nat. Materials Handling Centre, 1979; Coal Industry Soc., 1981–86 (Chm., 1961); W European Coal Producers' Assoc., 1976–79; BSI, 1983–86; Economic Res. Council, 1985–2000; Inst. of Trading Standards Admin, 1987–92; Vice-Pres., BIM, 1978 (Chm., 1976–78); Chm., British Iron and Steel Consumers' Council, 1983–86; Member: BOTB, 1972–82 (Chm., European Trade Cttee); Cons. Cttee, ECSC, 1973–82 (Pres., 1978–79); Adv. Council for Energy Conservation, 1974–79; Adv. Bd, Petrofina SA, 1982–90; Internat. Adv. Bd, Creditanstalt Bankverein, 1982–90; Energy Commn, 1977–79; Ct of Governors, Administrative Staff Coll., 1971–82; Internat. Adv. Bd, Banca Nazionale del Lavoro, 1984–94; Governor, London Business Sch., 1973–82. Pres., Keep Britain Tidy Gp, 1985–89 (Chm., 1979–85). Hon. Liveryman, Haberdashers' Co., 1982; Liveryman, Fuellers' Co., 1987. Hon. DSc Cranfield, 1979; Hon. LLD Leeds, 1982. Bronze Star (USA), 1945; Grand Officer, Italian Order of Merit, 1979; Comdr, Luxembourg Order of Merit, 1981; Officer of Légion d'Honneur, 1981. *Publications:* Coal and Energy, 1978; The Energy Debate, 1983. *Address:* House of Lords, Westminster, SW1A 0PW. *T:* (020) 7219 3180.

F

FABER, David James Christian; writer; Headmaster, Summer Fields School, Oxford, since 2010; *b* 7 July 1961; *s* of late Julian Tufnell Faber and of Lady (Ann) Caroline Faber, *e d* of 1st Earl of Stockton, OM, PC, FRS; *m* 1st, 1988, Sally Elizabeth Gilbert (marr. diss. 1996); one *s*; 2nd, 1998, Sophie Amanda Hedley; two *d*. *Educ:* Summer Fields Sch., Oxford; Eton Coll.; Balliol Coll., Oxford (MA Mod. Langs). Conservative Central Office, 1985–87; Director: Sterling Marketing Ltd, 1987–2002; Freestream Aircraft Ltd, 1998–; Quintus Public Affairs Ltd, 2006–09. Contested (C) Stockton North, 1987; MP (C) Westbury, 1992–2001. PPS to Min. of State, Foreign Office, 1994–96, to Sec. of State for Health, 1996–97; Opposition frontbench spokesman on foreign and commonwealth affairs, 1997–98. Member: Social Security Select Cttee, 1992–97; Culture, Media and Sport Select Cttee, 1998–2001; Public Accounts Cttee, 2000–01; Sec., Cons. back bench Educn Cttee, 1992–94. Trustee: Rehabilitation for Addicted Prisoners Trust, 1993–2001; Clouds House, 1992–2007 (Chm., 2003–07). Member, Board of Governors: Summer Fields Sch., Oxford, 2001–09; Aysgarth Sch., 2012–. *Publications:* Speaking for England, 2005; Munich, 2008. *Recreations:* Chelsea FC, cricket, golf. *Address:* Summer Fields, Mayfield Road, Oxford OX2 7EN. *Clubs:* Garrick, MCC (Mem. Cttee, 1997–2000, 2001–04, 2005–08, 2011–; Chm., Arts and Library Cttee, 2013–), Lord's Taverners; Vincent's (Oxford); Sunningdale Golf; Royal and Ancient Golf (St Andrews).

FABER, Diana; Her Honour Judge Faber; a Circuit Judge, since 2000; *b* 23 Oct. 1955; *d* of T. G. Faber and Mrs D. Swan, and step *d* of A. C. Swan. *Educ:* Putney High Sch.; University Coll. London (LLB Hons). Called to the Bar, Gray's Inn, 1977; barrister, 1977–82; admitted solicitor, 1983; joined Richards Butler, 1982, Partner, 1987–93; a Law Comr, 1994–2000; a Recorder, 1998–2000. Bencher, Lincoln's Inn, 2009. *Publications:* (General Ed.) Multimodal Transport: avoiding legal problems, 1997; numerous articles in legal and commercial jls and newspapers. *Recreations:* painting, visiting art galleries.

FABER, His Honour Trevor Martyn; a Circuit Judge, 2001–12; *b* 9 Oct. 1946; *s* of Harry Faber and Millicent Faber (*née* Waxman); *m* 1985, Katrina Sally Clay. *Educ:* Clifton Coll.; Merton Coll., Oxford (MA; 3 boxing blues and Capt.). Called to the Bar, Gray's Inn, 1970; in practice, Midland and Oxford Circuit, 1970–2001; a Recorder, 1989–2001. *Recreations:* music, sport, theatre, literature, cooking. *Club:* Vincent's (Oxford).

FABIAN, Prof. Andrew Christopher, OBE 2006; FRS 1996; Director, Institute of Astronomy, University of Cambridge, since 2013; Fellow of Darwin College, Cambridge, since 1983 (Vice-Master, 1997–2012); *b* 20 Feb. 1948; *s* of John Archibald and Daphne Monica Fabian; *m* 1st, 1971 (marr. diss. 1991); one *s* one *d*; 2nd, 1991, Prof. Carolin Susan Crawford, *qv*; two *s*. *Educ:* Daventry Grammar Sch.; King's Coll., London (BSc Physics); University Coll. London (PhD). SRC post doctoral research asst, University Coll. London, 1972–73; Institute of Astronomy, Cambridge: SRC post doctoral Fellow, 1973–75; SRC PDRA, 1975–77; Radcliffe Fellow in Astronomy, 1977–81; Royal Soc. Res. Prof., 1982–2002, Prof., 2002–13. Pres., RAS, 2008–10. (Jtly) Rossi Prize, AAS, 2001; Dannie Heineman Prize for Astrophysics, Amer. Inst. Physics and AAS, 2008; Gold Medal, RAS, 2012; Mohler Prize, Univ. of Michigan, 2012. *Publications:* contribs to Monthly Notices RAS, Astrophys. Jl, Nature, etc. *Address:* Institute of Astronomy, Madingley Road, Cambridge CB3 0HA.

FABIAN, (Andrew) Paul; HM Diplomatic Service, retired; Chief Secretary, Turks and Caicos Islands, 1990–91; *b* 23 May 1930; *s* of late Andrew Taggart Fabian and Edith Mary Whorwell; *m* 1st, Elisabeth Vivien Chapman (*d* 2015); one *s* two *d*; 2nd, 1983, Eryll Francesca Dickinson. *Educ:* Mitcham County School; Reading Sch.; St Paul's Sch.; Wadham College, Oxford (scholar; MA). Singapore Engineer Regt, 1953–54; Tanganyika, 1955–64 (on secondment to Foreign Office, serving at Usumbura, 1961–64); HM Diplomatic Service, 1964; served Lusaka, Ankara, New Delhi, FCO (Hd of Guidance), Islamabad, Karachi; High Comr, Nuku'alofa, Tonga, 1987–90. *Publications:* Delhi Post Bedside Book (ed), 1977. *Recreations:* chess (Pres., Tunbridge Wells Chess Club, 2006–14), reading, bird-watching. *Address:* 5 Broadwater Court, Broadwater Down, Tunbridge Wells, Kent TN2 5PB.

FABIAN, Carolin Susan; *see* Crawford, C. S.

FABIANI, Linda; Member (SNP) East Kilbride, Scottish Parliament, since 2011 (Central Scotland, 1999–2011); *b* 14 Dec. 1956; *d* of late Giovanni Aldo Fabiani and Claire Fabiani (*née* Smith). *Educ:* Napier Coll., Edinburgh (SHND); Glasgow Univ. (Dip Housing 1988). FCIH 2007. Admin. Sec., Yoker Housing Assoc., Glasgow, 1982–85; Housing Officer, Clydebank Housing Assoc., 1985–88; Develt Manager, Bute Housing Assoc., Rothesay, 1988–94; Dir, E Kilbride Housing Assoc., 1994–99. Scottish Parliament: Dep. shadow spokesperson on social justice, housing and urban regeneration, 1999–2003; SNP Dep. Business Manager and Whip, 2003–05; Convenor, European and External Relations Cttee, 2005–07; Minister for Europe, Ext. Affairs and Culture, 2007–09; Mem., Scottish Parlt Corporate Body, 2011–; Convenor, Scotland Bill Cttee, 2011–13; Member: Referendum Bill Cttee, 2012–; Welfare Reform Cttee, 2012–13. Hon. FRIAS 2009. Cavaliere, Order of Star of Italian Solidarity (Italy), 2007. *Recreations:* reading, theatre, music, holidays. *Address:* Scottish Parliament, Edinburgh EH99 1SP. *T:* (0131) 348 5698.

FABIUS, Laurent; Minister of Foreign and European Affairs, France, since 2012; *b* 20 Aug. 1946; *s* of André Fabius and Louise Fabius (*née* Mortimer). *Educ:* Lycée Janson-de-Sailly; Lycée Louis-le-Grand; Ecole Normale Supérieure, Paris; Institut d'Etudes Politiques, Paris (Agrégé des lettres); Ecole Nationale d'Administration. Conseil d'Etat, 1973–81; Deputy for Seine Maritime, French Nat. Assembly, 1978–81, re-elected 1981, 1986, 1993, 1997, 2002, 2007 (Pres., 1988–92, 1997–2000); Nat. Sec., Parti Socialiste (responsible for the press), 1979–81; Junior Minister, Ministry of Economy and Finance (responsible for the budget), 1981–83; Minister of Industry and Research, 1983–84; Prime Minister of France, 1984–86; MEP, 1989–92; Finance Minister and Dep. Prime Minister, 2000–02; First Sec., Socialist Party, 1992–93; Pres., Socialist Gp, Nat. Assembly, 1995–97. Mem., Conseil d'Etat, 1981–93. First Dep. Mayor, 1977–95 and 2000–, Mayor, 1995–2000, Grand Quevilly. *Publications:* La France inégale, 1975; Le Coeur du Futur, 1985; C'est en allant vers la mer, 1990; Les Blessures de la Vérité, 1995; Cela commence par une balade, 2003; Une certaine idée de l'Europe, 2005; Le Cabinet des Douze: regards sur des tableaux qui font la France, 2010. *Address:* Ministère des Affaires étrangères et européennes, 37 quai d'Orsay, 75007 Paris, France.

FABRE, Prof. Cécile, DPhil; FBA 2011; Professor of Political Philosophy, University of Oxford, since 2010; Senior Research Fellow, All Souls College, Oxford, since 2014; *b* Paris, France, 2 Feb. 1971; *d* of Francois Fabre and Geneviève Fabre (*née* Thélot); one *s*. *Educ:* Univ. of La Sorbonne, Paris (BA Hist. 1992); Univ. of York (MA Pol Theory 1993); Univ. of Oxford (DPhil Pols 1997). Postdoctoral Fellow, Nuffield Coll., Oxford, 1998–2000; Lectr, then Sen. Lectr, LSE, 2000–07; Prof. of Pol Theory, Univ. of Edinburgh, 2007–10; Fellow, and Tutor in Philosophy, Lincoln Coll., Oxford, 2010–14. *Publications:* Social Rights under the Constitution, 2000; Whose Body is it Anyway?, 2006; Justice in a Changing World, 2007; Cosmopolitan War, 2012; articles in Ethics, Jl of Pol Philos., British Jl of Pol Sci., Utilitas. *Recreations:* reading and watching thrillers, doing nothing. *Address:* All Souls College, Oxford OX1 4AL. *T:* (01865) 279282. *E:* cecile.fabre@all-souls.ox.ac.uk.

FÁBREGA, Daniel Eduardo; Ambassador of Panama to the Court of St James's, since 2014; *b* Panama, 15 March 1975; *s* of Julio J. Fábrega III and Mary Faith Fábrega Venier; *m* 2001, Amparo Arrocha; one *s* one *d*. *Educ:* Valley Forge Mil. Acad., Wayne (Bachelor of Sci. and Letters 1993); ITESO, Univ. Jesuita de Guadalajara; Clarkson Univ., Potsdam; Loyola Univ. (Bachelor of Business Admin 1997); Univ. Latinoamericana de Ciencia y Tecnología (MBA 2004). Brand Manager, Ron Bacardi, 1998–2000; Commercial Vice Pres. of Exports, Varela Hermanos, SA, 2000–14. *Recreations:* ski-ing, boxing, swimming, general fitness. *Address:* Embassy of Panama, 40 Hertford Street, W1J 7SH. *T:* (020) 7493 4646, *Fax:* (020) 7493 4333. *E:* dfabrega@mire.gob.pa. *Clubs:* Naval and Military; Union (Panama).

FABREGAT, Fernando L.; *see* Lopez-Fabregat.

FABRICANT, Michael Louis David; MP (C) Lichfield, since 1997 (Mid-Staffordshire, 1992–97); *b* 12 June 1950; *s* of late Isaac Nathan Fabricant and of Helena (*née* Freed). *Educ:* Loughborough Univ. (BA Law and Econs); Univ. of Sussex (MSc Systems). CEng, FIET. Postgrad. doctoral res., mathematical econs, London Univ., Oxford Univ. and Univ. of S California, LA. Formerly: Broadcaster, current affairs, BBC Radio; Man. Dir, Commercial Radio Gp; Founder Dir, Internat. Broadcast Electronics and Investment Gp, 1979–91. PPS to Financial Sec., HM Treasury, 1996–97; Opposition front-bench spokesman on economic affairs, 2003–05; an Opposition Whip, 2005–10; a Lord Comr of HM Treasury (Govt Whip), 2010–12. Member, Select Committee: Nat. Heritage, 1993–96, 1997–2005; Culture, Media and Sport, 1997–99, 2001–05; Home Affairs, 1999–2001; Information, 2001–03 (Chm., 2001–03); Member: European Legislation Scrutiny Cttee B, 1993–97; Finance and Services Cttee, 2001–03; Liaison Cttee, 2001–03; Admin Cttee, 2015–; Dep. Chm., All Party Cable and Satellite Gp, 1997–99 (Treas., 1995–97); Vice Chairman: All Party Gp on Smoking and Health, 1997–2010; All Party Anglo-German Gp, 1997–2010; All Party Gp on Film Industry, 1997–2010; Jt Chm., All Party Internet Gp, 1998–2003; Chairman: Royal Marines All Party Parly Gp, 2005–10 (Jt Chm., 1999–2005); Cons. Friends of America, 2008–; Dep. Chm., Cons. Parly Media Cttee, 1992–96. Vice Chm., Cons. Party, 2012–14. FCMI; FRSA. *Publications:* various newspaper articles and pamphlets. *Recreations:* fell-walking, reading, music (Mozart to rock), ski-ing, listening to the Archers. *Address:* House of Commons, SW1A 0AA. *Club:* Rottingdean (Sussex).

FACER, Roger Lawrence Lowe, CB 1992; Deputy Under-Secretary of State, Ministry of Defence, 1988–93; *b* 28 June 1933; *s* of late John Ernest Facer and Phyllis Facer; *m* 1960, Ruth Margaret, *o d* of late Herbert Mostyn Lewis, PhD, Gresford, Clwyd; three *d*. *Educ:* Rugby; St John's Coll., Oxford (MA); Royal Holloway, Univ. of London (MA 2000). HM Forces, 2nd Lieut, East Surrey Regt, 1951–53. War Office, 1957; Asst Private Sec. to Secretary of State, 1958; Private Sec. to Permanent Under-Sec., 1958; Principal, 1961; Cabinet Office, 1966; Ministry of Defence, 1968–93: Private Sec. to Minister of State (Equipment), 1970; Asst Sec., 1970; Internat. Inst. for Strategic Studies, 1972–73; Counsellor, UK Delegn, MBFR Vienna, 1973–75; Private Sec. to Sec. of State for Defence, 1976–79; Asst Under-Sec. of State, 1979–81; Under Sec., Cabinet Office, 1981–83; Rand Corporation, Santa Monica, USA, 1984; Asst Under-Sec. of State, MoD, 1984–87. *Publications:* Weapons Procurement in Europe—Capabilities and Choices, 1975; Conventional Forces and the NATO Strategy of Flexible Response, 1985; articles in Alpine Garden Soc. Bulletin. *Recreations:* Alpine gardening, opera. *Address:* Kennett Lodge, Hambledon, Hants PO7 4SA.

FACEY, Dr Karen Maria, (Mrs Philip Gaskell); evidence based health policy consultant, since 2003; *b* Braunton, Devon, 13 Dec. 1963; *d* of Frederick Facey and Ivy Facey; *m* 2006, Dr Philip Gaskell. *Educ:* Braunton Sch. and Community Coll.; North Devon Coll.; City Univ., London (BSc 1st Cl. Stats); Univ. of Reading (PhD Stats 1991). CStat 1997. Statistician, Pfizer, 1986–87; Res. Fellow, Univ. of Reading, 1990–92; Statistics Manager, Roche UK, 1992–95; Sen. Statistical Assessor, MHRA, 1995–99; Chief Exec., Health Technol. Bd for Scotland, 2000–03. Chm., Acute Services, Tech. Adv. Gp on Resource Allocation, NHS Scotland, 2013–; Mem., Scottish Health Technologies Gp, 2011–. Coordinator, Methods and Impact Wkg Gp, Patient Involvement, Health Technol. Assessment Internat., 2014–. FRSocMed 2002. Hon. MFPH 2006. *Publications:* articles in Internat. Jl of Technol. Assessment in Health Care, Patient, New England Jl of Medicine. *Recreations:* Scottish Episcopal Church, classical concerts, enjoying Scottish countryside. *Address:* Woodlands Lodge, Buchanan Castle Estate, Drymen G63 0HX. *T:* and *Fax:* (01360) 660316. *E:* k.facey@btinternet.com.

FAGAN, Anne Marie, CBE 2000; Head Teacher, John Ogilvie High School, Hamilton, 1991–2007; *b* 17 Dec. 1947; *d* of Edward Irons and Helen (née Muir); *m* 1969, Bernard Fagan; two *c*. *Educ:* St Patrick's High Sch., Coatbridge; Strathclyde Univ. (BA); Jordanhill Coll. (PGCE Dist.). Teacher of Business Educn, Columba High Sch., Coatbridge, 1969–79; Principal Teacher of Business Educn, Cardinal Newman High Sch., 1979–84; Asst Hd Teacher, Curriculum/Middle Sch., John Ogilvie High Sch., 1984–91. Pres., Catholic Headteachers Assoc. of Scotland, 2000–02 (Vice-Pres., 1998–2000); Mem. Exec., Head Teachers Assoc. of Scotland. Chair, Conforti Inst. (formerly Global Educn Centre) (Bd Mem., 2005–10); Mem., Nat. Adv. Gp, Schs of Ambition Prog., 2005–. GTC Rep. on Bd of Govs, St Andrew's Coll. of Educn, Bearsden, Glasgow. Mem. Bd, Lanarkshire Orchestral Soc., 1996–98. FRSA. *Recreations:* singing (leading lady in light operatic society, 1986–96), playing piano, keep fit, running, painting, golf.

FAGAN, Dame (Florence) Mary, DCVO 2009; JP; Lord-Lieutenant of Hampshire, 1994–2014; *b* 11 Sept. 1939; *o d* of Col George Vere-Laurie, JP, DL, Carlton Hall, Newark, Notts and Judith Caroline Vere-Laurie (*née* Franklin); *m* 1960, Capt. Christopher Fagan, Grenadier Guards; one *s* (and one *s* decd). *Educ:* Southover Manor, Sussex. Chm., Countess of Brecknock Hospice Trust and Home Care Service Appeal, Andover, 1989–. Former Mem., Sch. Adv. Cttee, N Hants; Chm., Hants Magistrates Adv. Cttee, 1994–. President: Hants Council of Community Service, 1994–; Hants and IoW Youth Options, 1994–; Hants Br., Army Benevolent Fund, 1994–; Vice-President: Southern Regl Assoc. for the Blind, 1994–; Mary Rose Trust, 1994–; Fortune Centre of Riding Therapy, 1994–; SSAFA; Patron: Rowans Hospice, Portsmouth, 1994–; Hants Music Trust, 1994–; Hants Br., BRCS, 1994–; Oakhaven Hospice, 1995–; The Children's Hospice, 1996–; Home-Start Eastleigh, 2002–; Marwell Zoo. Chm., Portsmouth Cathedral Develt Trust, 2004–; Trustee: Andover Med. Fund, 1994–; Hants Gardens Trust, 1994–. Chancellor, Univ. of Winchester, 2006–. Hon. Colonel: ACF, 1995–; 457 Battery, RA, 1998–2010; REME (Vol.) 4th Div., 2010–; Hon. Cdre, RN, 2007– (Hon. Captain, 2001–07). Liveryman, Saddlers' Co., 1996–. JP Hants, 1994. Hon. DLitt Southampton, 1997; Hon. Dr jur Portsmouth, 2000. DStJ 1994 (Pres. Council, Hants, 1994–). *Recreation:* country activities. *Address:* Deane Hill House, Deane, near Basingstoke, Hants RG25 3AX. *T:* (01256) 780591.

FAGGE, Sir John Christopher, 12th Bt *cr* 1660, of Wiston, Sussex; *b* 30 April 1942; *o s* of Sir John William Frederick Fagge, 11th Bt and Ivy Gertrude (*née* Frier); *S* father, 2000; *m* 1974, Evelyn Joy Golding.

FAHEY, Hon. John Joseph, AC 2002; Chairman, World Anti-Doping Agency, 2007–13; *b* 10 Jan. 1945; *s* of Stephen Fahey and Annie (*née* Fahey); *m* 1968, Colleen Maree McGurren; one *s* two *d*. *Educ:* St Anthony's Convent, Picton, NSW; Chevalier Coll., Bowral, NSW; Univ. of Sydney Law Extension Cttee (Dip. Law). Practised law, Camden, NSW, 1971–86. New South Wales: MLA (L) Camden, 1984–88, Southern Highlands, 1988–96; Minister for Ind. Relns and Minister assisting the Premier, 1988–90; Minister for Ind. Relns, Further Educn, Trng and Employment, 1990–92; Premier, 1992–95; Treasurer, 1992–93; Minister for Econ. Develt, 1993–95. Australia: MHR (L) Macarthur, NSW, 1996–2001; Minister for Finance, 1996–2001, for Admin, 1997–2001. Chairman: Australian Rugby League Develt, 2002–12; Commonwealth Reconstruction Authy, 2011–; Assetinsure Hldgs Pty Ltd, 2003–. Sen. Advr, Business Adv. Council, J. P. Morgan Australia, 2002–. Director: Avant Insurance Gp, 2004–; Endeavour Energy Ltd, 2002–12. Chancellor, Australian Catholic Univ., 2014–. Hon. DLitt Western Sydney, 2013. Centenary Medal (Australia), 2001. *Recreations:* tennis, Rugby, cricket, gardening, reading.

FAHY, Sir Peter, Kt 2012; QPM 2004; Chief Constable of Greater Manchester Police, 2008–15; *b* London, 18 Jan. 1959; *m* 1981, Jenny; four *c*. *Educ:* Univ. of Hull (BA Hons 1981); Univ. of E Anglia (MA 1998). Joined Police Force, 1981; Asst Chief Constable, Surrey, 1997–2002; Chief Constable, Cheshire Constabulary, 2002–08. *Recreations:* running, charity work, theatre, singing.

FAINT, John Anthony Leonard, (Tony), CBE 2002; consultant on international development, since 2003; Director (International), Department for International Development, 1997–2002; *b* 24 Nov. 1942; *s* of Thomas Leonard Faint and Josephine Rosey Faint (*née* Dunkerley); *m* 1st, 1978, Elizabeth Theresa Winter (*d* 2002); 2nd, 2004, Dorothy Isobelle Rankin (*d* 2015). *Educ:* Chigwell Sch.; Magdalen Coll., Oxford (BA Lit.Hum. 1965); MA Development Economics, Fletcher Sch., Mass, 1969. Ministry of Overseas Development (later Overseas Development Administration), London, 1965–71 (study leave in Cambridge, Mass, 1968–69); First Secretary (Aid), Blantyre, Malawi, 1971–73; ODM/ODA, London, 1974–80; Head of SE Asia Develt Div., Bangkok, 1980–83; Head of Finance Dept, ODA, FCO, 1983–86; Alternate Exec. Dir, World Bank, Washington, 1986–89; Head, E Asia Dept, 1989–90, Under Sec., Internat. Div., 1990–91, ODA; on secondment as UK Dir, EBRD, 1991–92; Under Sec. (Eastern Europe), ODA, 1991–93; Under Sec. (Eastern Europe and Western Hemisphere), ODA, later DFID, 1993–97. *Recreations:* music, bridge, walking, skiing. *Address:* 7 The Leyes, Deddington, Oxon OX15 0TX.

FAIRBAIRN, Alasdair Chisholm; Chief Executive, Sea Fish Industry Authority, 1997–2002; *b* 23 Jan. 1940; *s* of late Douglas Chisholm Fairbairn, CIE, CBE and Agnes Fairbairn (*née* Arnott); *m* 1964, Charlotte Henriette Tichelman; two *s* one *d*. *Educ:* Trinity Coll., Glenalmond, Perthshire; Corpus Christi Coll., Cambridge (MA Hons). Man. Dir, Conimex BV, Netherlands, 1975–78; Reckitt & Colman plc: Chief Manager, Planning and Evaluation, 1978–80; Regl Dir, 1980–84; Dir, LR Overseas Ltd, 1984–91; Chief Exec., Potato Mktg Bd, 1991–97. *Recreations:* walking, computers, concerts.

FAIRBAIRN, Andrew Finlay, FRCPsych; Consultant in Old Age Psychiatry, Newcastle General Hospital, 1989–2008; Medical Director, Northumberland, Tyne and Wear NHS Trust, 2006–08 (Acting Chief Executive, 2007–08); *b* 16 April 1950; *s* of Thomas Andrew Fairbairn and Pauline Mary Fairbairn; *m* 1971, Andrea Mary Hudson; one *s* two *d*. *Educ:* George Watson's Coll., Edinburgh; Newcastle upon Tyne Univ. (MB BS 1974). FRCPsych 1989. Consultant Psychiatrist, St Nicholas' Hosp., Newcastle upon Tyne, 1981–88. Medical Director: Newcastle Mental Health Trust, 1992–94; Newcastle City Health, 2000–01; Newcastle, N Tyneside and Northumberland Mental Health Trust, 2002–06 (Jt Med. Dir, 2001–02). Sen. Policy Advr (pt-time), 1994–98, Mem., Nat. Taskforce for Older People, 2000–04, DoH; Chm., Jt NICE/SCIE Guidelines Develt Gp on Dementia, 2004–06. Non-exec. Dir, Gateshead Hosps NHS Foundn Trust, 2009–. Hon. Chm., Faculty for Psychiatry of Old Age, 1998–2002, Hon. Registrar, 2002–05, RCPsych. *Recreations:* house in France, 19th century history and biography. *Address:* 3 Killiebrigs, Heddon on the Wall, Northumberland NE15 0DD. *T:* (01661) 852686.

FAIRBAIRN, Sir Brooke; *see* Fairbairn, Sir J. B.

FAIRBAIRN, Carolyn Julie; Director-General, Confederation of British Industry, since 2015; *b* 13 Dec. 1960; *d* of David Ritchie Fairbairn, *qv*; *m* 1991, Peter Harrison Chittick; one *s* two *d*. *Educ:* Wycombe High Sch. for Girls; Bryanston (Schol.); Gonville and Caius Coll., Cambridge (Hon. Sen. Scholar, MA); Univ. of Pennsylvania (Thouron Schol., MA); INSEAD, Fontainebleau (MBA). Economist, World Bank, Washington, 1984–85; financial writer, The Economist, 1985–87; Mgt Consultant, McKinsey & Co., London and Paris, 1988–94; Mem., Prime Minister's Policy Unit, 1995–97; Dir of Strategy, BBC Worldwide, 1997–99; Dir of Strategy, then of Strategy and Distribution, BBC, 2000–04; Principal, McKinsey & Co., London, 2006–07; Dir of Gp Develt and Strategy, ITV, 2007–11. Non-executive Director: FSA, 2008–11; UK Statistics Authy, 2013–; Competition and Mkts Authy, 2013–. Non-executive Director: Vitec Gp plc, 2012–; Lloyds Banking Gp, 2012–; Capita plc, 2014–. Mem., Cttee on Standards in Public Life, 2014–. Chair, RTS, 2010–11 (Vice-Chair, 2008–10). Trustee, Marie Curie Cancer Care, 2012–. *Recreations:* tennis, travel. *Address:* 24 St Thomas Street, Winchester, Hants SO23 9HJ.

FAIRBAIRN, David Ritchie, OBE 1990; Chairman, Headstrong Inc., 2000–02; *b* 4 July 1934; *s* of G. F. Fairbairn; *m* 1958, Hon. Susan Hill, *d* of Baron Hill of Luton, PC; one *s* two *d*. *Educ:* Mill Hill Sch.; Gonville and Caius Coll., Cambridge (BAEcon). FBCS; FIDPM, FInstD. President, Cambridge Union Soc. Overseas Marketing Manager, Arthur Guinness Son & Co. Ltd, 1960; President, Guinness-Harp Corp., New York, 1964; Marketing Dir, Guinness Overseas Ltd, 1969; Man. Dir, Dataset Ltd (ICL), 1970; Manager, Retail and Distribution Sector, International Computers Ltd, 1975; Dir of Marketing, EMI Medical Ltd, 1976; Dir, Nat. Computing Centre, 1980–86; Man. Dir, James Martin Associates UK, 1985–89; Gp Man. Dir, James Martin Associates Ltd, 1989–92; Man. Dir, JMA Information Engineering Ltd, 1992–94; Vice-Chm., James Martin Holdings Ltd, 1994–99; Chm., James Martin Worldwide plc, 1999–2000; Vice Pres., Europe, Texas Instruments Inc., 1993–94. Pres., Inst. of Data Processing Management, 1982–96 (Vice-Pres., 1980–82). Vice-Chm., Parly IT Cttee, 1982. Member: Patent Office Steering Bd, 1989–2000; Telecommunications Panel, Monopoly and Mergers Commn, 1991–99. Freeman, City of London, 1990. FRSA. *Recreation:* sailing. *Address:* 11 Oak Way, West Common, Harpenden, Herts AL5 2NT. *T:* (01582) 715820, *Fax:* (01582) 468339.

See also C. J. Fairbairn.

FAIRBAIRN, Erik; Founder and Chief Executive Officer, POD Point Ltd, since 2009; *b* Redhill, 27 Feb. 1977. *Educ:* Univ. of Sheffield (BEng Hons 1999). Engr, MSX Internat., 2000–03; Innovation Manager, Britvic Soft Drinks, 2004–05; Founder and CEO, ecurie25 Ltd, 2005–09. Mem., Young Presidents' Orgn. *Recreation:* cycling. *Address:* POD Point Ltd, 145–157 St John Street, EC1V 4PW. *E:* erik.fairbairn@pod-point.com.

FAIRBAIRN, James Bennett, OBE 2007; FREng; Executive Director, Howden Group Ltd, since 2011; *b* Edinburgh, 18 Oct. 1968; *s* of James and Mary Fairbairn; *m* 2002, Teresa Turner; one *d*. *Educ:* Denny High Sch.; Univ. of Strathclyde (BEng Mech. Engrg 1992); Loughborough Univ. (MBA 2002). FREng 2013. Lead Engr, Wood Gp, 1995–96; Engrg Dir, 1996–2000, Man. Dir, 2000–07, Clyde Bergemann; Divl CEO, Clyde Process Solutions, 2008–09; Man. Dir, Howden Compressors, 2009–11. *Publications:* Nothing Changes Until You Do, 2004. *Recreations:* golf, football, ski-ing, running. *Address:* Howden Group Ltd, Old Govan Road, Renfrew PA4 8XJ. *T:* (0141) 885 7543. *E:* jim.fairbairn@howden.com. *Club:* Turnberry Golf.

FAIRBAIRN, Sir (James) Brooke, 6th Bt *cr* 1869, of Ardwick; Proprietor of J. Brooke Fairbairn & Co., textile converters and wholesalers dealing in furnishing fabrics, until 2009; *b* 10 Dec. 1930; *s* of Sir William Albert Fairbairn, 5th Bt, and Christine Renée Cotton, *d* of late Rev. Canon Robert William Croft; *S* father, 1972; *m* 1st, 1960, Mary Russell (*d* 1992), *d* of late William Russell Scott, MB, ChB, FFARCS; two *s* one *d*; 2nd, 1997, Rosemary Anne Victoria, *d* of late Edwin Henderson, FRCSE. *Educ:* Stowe. Upper Bailiff, Weavers' Co., 1992–93. *Heir: s* Robert William Fairbairn [*b* 10 April 1965; *m* 1990, Sarah, *e d* of Roger Griffin, BVSc, MRCVS; two *s* two *d*]. *Address:* Barkway House, Bury Road, Newmarket, Suffolk CB8 7BT. *T:* (01638) 662733.

FAIRBAIRN, John Sydney; Trustee, 1966–2008, and Chairman, 1988–2003, Esmée Fairbairn Foundation (formerly Esmée Fairbairn Charitable Trust); *b* 15 Jan. 1934; *s* of Sydney George Fairbairn, MC and Angela Maude Fairbairn (*née* Fane); *m* 1968, Mrs Camilla Fry (*d* 2000), *d* of late G. N. Grinling; one *s* two *d*, and two step *s* two step *d*; *m* 2001, Felicity, *widow* of 3rd Baron Milford; two step *s* three step *d*. *Educ:* Eton; Trinity College, Cambridge (MA). 2nd Lt, 17/21 Lancers, 1952–54. ACA 1960. With M & G Group, 1961–99: Dep. Chm., 1979–89; non-exec. Dir, 1989–99. Dep. Chm., Lautro, 1986–89. Chairman: Unit Trust Assoc., 1989–91; Central European Growth Fund plc, 1994–2000. Council Mem. and Treasurer, King's College London, 1972–84 (Fellow 1978); Council Member: Univ. of Buckingham, 1986–95; Policy Studies Inst., 1991–97. Trustee: Monteverdi Trust, 1991–96; Royal Pavilion, Art Gall. and Mus of Brighton, 1993–2001; Dulwich Picture Gall., 1994–97. DL West Sussex, 1996–2001. DUniv Buckingham, 1992. *Address:* The Old Vicarage, Powerstock, Dorset DT6 3TE. *Clubs:* Beefsteak, Brooks's.

FAIRBANK, Judith; *see* Pallot, J.

FAIRBURN, Prof. Christopher James Alfred Granville; Wellcome Principal Research Fellow, and Professor of Psychiatry, University of Oxford, since 1996; *b* 20 Sept. 1950; *s* of Ernest Alfred Fairburn and Margaret Isabel Fairburn; *m* 1st, 1979, Susan Margaret Russam (marr. diss. 2007); one *s* one *d*; 2nd, 2009, Kristin Sonja Bohn; one *s*. *Educ:* Malvern Coll.; Worcester Coll., Oxford (BM BCh). University of Oxford: Res. Psychiatrist, 1981–84; Wellcome Trust Sen. Lectr, 1984–96; Hon. Clinical Reader, 1991–96. Hon. Consultant Psychiatrist, Oxford Health NHS Foundn Trust (formerly Oxfordshire Mental Healthcare NHS Trust), 1984–. Gov., Wellcome Trust, 2008. *Publications:* Binge Eating: nature, assessment and treatment, 1993; Eating Disorders and Obesity: a comprehensive handbook, 1995, 2nd edn 2002; Science and Practice of Cognitive Behaviour Therapy, 1997; Cognitive Behavior Therapy and Eating Disorders, 2008; contrib. numerous articles to learned jls. *Recreations:* design, wine, travelling off the beaten track.

FAIRCLOUGH, Oliver Noel Francis, FSA; Keeper of Art, Amgueddfa Cymru—National Museum Wales (formerly National Museums and Galleries of Wales), Cardiff, since 1998; *b* 27 March 1950; *s* of late Arthur Basil Rowland Fairclough and Jean McKenzie Fairclough (*née* Fraser); *m* 1977, Caroline Mary Latta; one *s* two *d*. *Educ:* Bryanston Sch.; Trinity Coll., Oxford (BA); Univ. of Keele (MA). AMA 1978; FSA 2009. Asst, Liverpool Mus., 1971–74; Asst Keeper, Art, 1975–79, Dep. Keeper, Applied Art, 1979–86, Birmingham Museums and Art Gall.; Asst Keeper, Applied Art, Nat. Mus. of Wales, 1986–98. Lectr and author. Mem., various adv. bodies and learned socs. Ed., French Porcelain Soc., 2001–. *Publications:* (with E. Leary) Textiles by William Morris, 1981; The Grand Old Mansion, 1984; (with M. Evans) Companion Guide to the National Art Gallery, 1993, 2nd edn 1997; contribs to exhibn catalogues; contrib. to Burlington Mag. and other art Jls. *Recreations:* walking, travel, architectural history, naval and military history. *Address:* Tyn y Llwyn, Partrishow, Crickhowell, Breconshire NP7 7LT. *T:* (01873) 890540.

FAIREY, Michael Edward; Chairman: Vertex Data Science Ltd, since 2012 (Director, since 2007); One Savings Bank, since 2014; *b* 17 June 1948; *s* of late Douglas and Marjorie Fairey; 1973, Patricia Ann Dolby; two *s*. *Educ:* King Edward VI Grammar Sch., Louth. ACIB 1974. Barclays Bank, 1967–92: Asst Dir, Watford Gp, 1986; Ops Dir, Barclaycard, 1986–88; Exec. Dir, Barclays Card Services, 1988–92; Dir, Retail Credit, and Gp Credit Dir, 1992, Gp Dir, Credit and Ops, 1993–96, TSB Gp; Lloyds TSB Group plc: IT and Ops Dir, 1996–97; Gp Dir, Central Services, 1997–98; Dep. Gp Chief Exec., 1998–2008. Chm., APR Energy plc (formerly Horizon), 2010–14; non-executive Director: Energy Saving Trust; VTX Bidco. Chm., Race for Opportunity; Bd Mem., Business in the Community. Pres., British Quality Foundn. *Recreations:* tennis, opera, football.

FAIREY, Michael John, CB 1989; Chief Executive, The Royal London Hospital and Associated Community NHS Trust, 1991–94; *b* 20 Sept. 1933; *s* of late Ernest John Saunder Fairey and Lily Emily (*née* Pateman); *m* 1st, 1958 (marr. diss. 1989); two *s* one *d*; 2nd, 1990, Victoria Frances Hardman. *Educ:* Queen Elizabeth's Sch., Barnet; Jesus Coll., Cambridge (MA). Served RA, 1952–53. Jun. Administrator, St Thomas' Hosp., 1957–60; Gp Devel Sec., Westminster Hosp., 1960–62; Deputy House Governor, The London Hosp., 1962, House Governor 1972; Regional Administrator, NE Thames RHA, 1973; Dir, Planning and Inf., NHS Management Bd, DHSS, later Dept of Health, 1984–89; Dir of Information Systems, NHS Management Exec., Dept of Health, 1989–91. Sec., London Hospital Med. Coll., 1994–96. Gov., St Catherine's Sch., Ware, 1995– (Chm., 1997–2000). *Publications:* various articles in med. and computing jls. *Recreations:* church music, history of medieval exploration, Rugby football. *Club:* Athenæum.

FAIRFAX, family name of **Lord Fairfax of Cameron**.

FAIRFAX OF CAMERON, 14th Lord *cr* 1627; **Nicholas John Albert Fairfax;** Director: Sovcomflot (UK) Ltd, since 2005 (Member, Executive Board, since 2007); North of England P&I Association Ltd, 2012–; *b* 4 Jan. 1956; *e s* of 13th Lord Fairfax of Cameron and of Sonia, *yr d* of late Capt. Cecil Gunston, MC; *S* father, 1964; *m* 1982, Annabel, *er d* of late Nicholas and of Sarah Gilham Morriss; three *s*. *Educ:* Eton; Downing Coll., Cambridge (LLB in international law subjects, 1981). Called to the Bar, Gray's Inn, 1977. Director: Thomas Miller P and I, and Thomas Miller Defence, 1987–90; Sedgwick Marine & Cargo Ltd, 1995–96; British-Georgian Soc. Ltd, 2006–08. Patron, AMUR Tiger and Leopard Charity, 2006–. *Recreation:* sailing. *Heir: s* Hon. Edward Nicholas Thomas Fairfax, *b* 20 Sept. 1984. *Address:* 10 Orlando Road, SW4 0LF. *Club:* Royal Yacht Squadron (Cowes).

FAIRFAX, James Oswald, AC 2010 (AO 1993); Chairman, John Fairfax Ltd, Sydney, 1977–87; *b* 27 March 1933; *s* of Sir Warwick Oswald Fairfax and late Marcie Elizabeth Fairfax (*née* Wilson). *Educ:* Geelong Grammar School; Balliol College, Oxford (MA; Hon. Fellow, 1992). Director, John Fairfax, 1957–87; Chm., Amalgamated Television Services Pty Ltd, 1975–87 (Dir, 1958); Chm., David Syme & Co., 1984–87 (Dir, 1977). Member: Bd of Management, Royal Alexandra Hosp. for Children, 1967–85 (Bd, Children's Med. Res. Foundn, 1986–88); Council, International House, Sydney Univ., 1967–79; Internat. Council, Museum of Modern Art, NY, 1971–99; Council, Australian Nat. Gallery, 1976–84; Dir, Art Exhibns Australia Ltd, 1994–98. Governor: Qld Art Gall. Foundn, 1995–; Art Gall. of WA Foundn, 2008–; Life Governor: Art Gallery of NSW, 1991; Australian Nat. Gall. Foundn, 1992. Life Member: Nat. Trust of NSW, 1957; Nat. Gall. of Vic, 1992. *Publications:* My Regards to Broadway: a memoir, 1991. *Address:* Retford Park, Old South Road, Bowral, NSW 2576, Australia. *Clubs:* Garrick; Union, Australian (Sydney); Melbourne (Melbourne).

FAIRFAX-LUCY, Sir Edmund (John William Hugh Cameron-Ramsay-), 6th Bt *cr* 1836; painter, chiefly of still-life and interiors; *b* 4 May 1945; *s* of Sir Brian Fulke Cameron-Ramsay-Fairfax-Lucy, 5th Bt and Hon. Alice Caroline Helen Buchan (*d* 1993), *o d* of 1st Baron Tweedsmuir, PC, GCMG, GCVO, CH; *S* father, 1974; *m* 1994, Erica, *d* of Warren Loane, Crocknaerieve, Enniskillen; two *s*. *Educ:* City and Guilds of London Art Sch.; Royal Academy Schs of Art. Regular exhibitor, RA Summer Exhibn, 1967–; one-man shows, numerous mixed exhibitions. *Heir: s* Patrick Samuel Thomas Fulke Fairfax-Lucy, *b* 3 April 1995.

FAIRHAVEN, 3rd Baron *cr* 1929 and 1961 (new creation); **Ailwyn Henry George Broughton;** JP; Vice Lord-Lieutenant, Cambridgeshire, 1977–85; *b* 16 Nov. 1936; *s* of 2nd Baron Fairhaven and Hon. Diana Rosamond (*d* 1937), *o d* of late Captain Hon. Coulson Fellowes; *S* father, 1973; *m* 1960, Kathleen Patricia, *d* of late Col James Henry Magill, OBE; three *s* two *d* (and one *s* decd). *Educ:* Eton; RMA, Sandhurst. Royal Horse Guards, 1957–71. Mem., Jockey Club, 1977– (Steward, 1981–82, Sen. Steward, 1985–89). DL Cambridgeshire and Isle of Ely, 1973; JP South Cambridgeshire, 1975. KStJ 1992. *Recreations:* gardening, cooking. *Heir: s* Major Hon. James Henry Ailwyn Broughton [*b* 25 May 1963; *m* 1990, Sarah Olivia, *d* of late Harold Digby Fitzgerald Creighton; one *s* two *d*]. *Address:* Kirtling Tower, Cambs CB8 9PA. *Club:* White's.

FAIRLEY, Douglas; QC (Scot.) 2012; *b* Glasgow, 20 Feb. 1968; *s* of late John A. Fairley and of Marjorie Fairley; *m* 2000, Una Doherty; one *s* one *d*. *Educ:* Hutcheson's Grammar Sch., Glasgow; Glasgow Univ. (LLB Hons). Admitted as solicitor, 1992; Solicitor, Maclay Murray & Spens, 1992–98; called to Faculty of Advocates, 1999; Employment Judge, Scotland and England, 2009–13; Advocate Depute, 2011–15. Dir, Tennis Scotland, 2014–. *Publications:* Contempt of Court in Scotland, 2000. *Recreations:* tennis, ski-ing, music. *Address:* Advocates Library, Parliament House, Edinburgh EH1 1RF. *T:* (0131) 226 5071. *E:* douglas.fairley@advocates.org.uk. *Clubs:* Victory Services; New (Edinburgh).

FAIRLEY, John Alexander; Chairman: Highflyer Productions, since 1996; Trainers House Enterprises, since 2004; *s* of Alexander Miller Fairley and Madge Irene Fairley; *m*; three *d*. *Educ:* Merchant Taylors' Sch., Crosby; Queen's Coll., Oxford (MA). Midshipman, RNVR. Journalist: Bristol Evening Post, 1963; London Evening Standard, 1964; Producer: BBC Radio, 1965–68; Yorkshire TV, 1968–78; freelance writer and broadcaster, 1979–84; Dir of Programmes, Yorkshire TV, 1984–92; Managing Director: Yorkshire TV Programmes, 1992–93; Yorkshire TV, 1993–95; Chief Exec., UK TV, 1995–96; Chairman: ITV Broadcast Bd, 1995; K Max Radio, 1995–97; Channel 4 Racing, 1997–2012; Highfield Racing, 2006. TV presenter, Mysterious World, 2015. Mem., British Horseracing Bd Stud and Stable Staff Commn, 2004. Trustee, Injured Jockeys Fund, 1999–. FRTS 1994; FRSA. *Publications:* (jtly) The Monocled Mutineer, 1978; (jtly) Arthur C. Clarke's Mysterious World, 1980, and subseq. vols, 1984, 1987; Great Racehorses In Art, 1984; Racing In Art, 1990; (jtly) The Cabinet of Curiosities, 1991; The Art of the Horse, 1995; Horses of the Great War: the story in art, 2015. *Recreations:* writing, racing, hunting. *Address:* Trainers House, Eddlethorpe, Malton, Yorks YO17 9QS.

FAIRLEY, Josephine; *b* London, 10 July 1956; *d* of Peter Alan Fairley and Vivienne Fairley; *m* 1991, Craig Lynn Sams, *qv*. *Educ:* Bromley High Sch. for Girls. Editor: Look Now mag., 1979–82; Honey mag., 1982–85; columnist, Ecosphere, The Times, 1988–91; Co-Founder: Green & Black's Chocolate, 1991; The Perfume Society, 2014. Hon. DBA Kingston, 2006. *Publications:* The Ultimate Natural Beauty Book, 2004; (with Craig Sams) Sweet Dreams: the story of Green & Black's, 2008; (with Sarah Stacey) The Green Beauty Bible, 2008; (with Sarah Stacey) The Anti-Ageing Beauty Bible, 2011; Yoga for Life, 2012; (with Sarah Stacey) The Ultimate Natural Beauty Bible, 2014; The Perfume Bible, 2016. *Recreations:* sea bathing, yoga, kindle reading, travel. *Address:* 106 High Street, Hastings, E Sussex TN34 3ES. *T:* (01424) 203751. *E:* jo@josephinefairley.com. *Clubs:* Groucho, One Alfred Place.

FAIRLIE-CUNINGHAME, Sir Robert (Henry), 17th Bt *cr* 1630, of Robertland, Ayrshire; *b* 19 July 1974; *o s* of Sir William Henry Fairlie-Cuninghame, 16th Bt and of Janet Menzies, *d* of R. M. Saddington; *S* father, 1999; *m* 2005, Mary Louise, *d* of Captain Geoffrey Hugh Belasyse-Smith, Broadstairs; one *d*. *Heir: cousin* David Hastings Fairlie-Cuninghame [*b* June 1937; *m* 1963, Susan Gai White; one *s* one *d*]. *Address:* 29a Orinoco Street, Pymble, NSW 2073, Australia.

FAIRWEATHER, Prof. Denys Vivian Ivor, MD; FRCOG; Secretary-General of International Federation of Gynaecology and Obstetrics, 1985–94; Professor and Head of Department of Obstetrics and Gynaecology, 1966–90, and Vice-Provost, 1984–90, University College London; Pro-Vice-Chancellor for Medicine and Dentistry, University of London, 1989–92; *b* 25 Oct. 1927; *s* of late Albert James Ivor Fairweather and Gertrude Mary Forbes; *m* 1956, (Gwendolen) Yvonne Hubbard (*d* 2014); one *s* two *d*. *Educ:* Forfar Acad.; Websters Seminary, Kirriemuir; St Andrews Univ. (MB, ChB 1949; MD 1966). FRCOG 1967 (MRCOG 1958). Served RAF Med. Br., 1950–55, Sqn Leader. Sen. Lectr, Univ. of Newcastle upon Tyne, 1959–66; Fulbright Scholar, Western Reserve Univ., USA, 1963–64; Dean, Faculty of Clinical Science, UCL, 1982–84; Vice Provost (Medicine) and Head, University Coll. London Sch. of Medicine, later University Coll. and Middx Sch. of Medicine of UCL, 1984–89; Hon. Fellow, UCL, 1985. Member: GMC, 1988–92; Internat. Med. Adv. Panel, IPPF, 1988–94; Vice Pres., FPA, 1985–98 (Patron, 1998). Hon. FAARM 1969; Hon. FACOG 1993. Freeman, City of Krakow, 1989. Dist. Service Award, FIGO, 1997. *Publications:* Amniotic Fluid Research and Clinical Applications, 1973, 2nd edn 1978; Labour Ward Manual, 1985; over 160 pubns in scientific jls, on perinatal mortality, rhesus disease, genetics, antenatal diagnosis, very low birthweight, medical education. *Recreations:* gardening, fishing, do-it-yourself. *Address:* 4 Kingston Farm Road, Woodbridge, Suffolk IP12 4BD.

FAIRWEATHER, Eric John, FCIB; financial consultant; Senior Consultant, Corporate Finance and Business Recovery, Ultraforce Group, since 2011; *b* 9 Nov. 1942; *s* of late John Walter William Fairweather and Lilian Emma Fairweather; *m* 1st, 1966, Frances Mary Ewer (marr. diss.); two *d*; 2nd, 1991, Deborah Chubb; two *s*. *Educ:* Carlisle Grammar Sch. CeMAP 2005; CeRGI 2006. Entered Midland Bank at Carlisle, 1961; Manager, Corporate Finance Div., 1978–81; Sen. Asst Man., Poultry and Princes Street, 1981–84; on secondment as Dir, Industrial Develt Unit, DTI (Under Sec.), 1984–86; Manager, UK Business Sector, Midland Bank, 1986; Manager, Central Management and Planning, 1986–87; Corporate Banking Area Manager, Manchester, 1987–93; Area Manager: Manchester, 1993–94; Sheffield, 1994–95; Regl Gen. Manager, NW, Co-operative Bank, 1995–98; Hd of Asset Finance, Co-operative Bank PLC, 1999–2002. Non-executive Director: Cartel Mktg Ltd, 2004–07; Cartel Gp Hldgs plc, 2004–07; SD Healthcare Ltd, 2008–09. Director: Sheffield TEC, 1994–95; Wigan Borough Partnership, 1996–2002. Gov., Bolton Sch., 2006–. *Recreations:* classical music, Association football (Bolton Wanderers), golf. *Address:* 5 The Hamlet, Lostock, Bolton BL6 4QT.

FAIRWEATHER, Dr Frank Arthur; consultant in toxicology and pathology; *b* 2 May 1928; *s* of Frank and Maud Harriet Fairweather; *m* 1st, 1953, Christine Winifred Hobbs (*d* 2008); two *s*; 2nd, 2011, Mrs Dorothy Clifford. *Educ:* City of Norwich Sch.; Middlesex Hospital. MB, BS 1954; MRCPath 1963, FRCPath 1975; FRSB (FIBiol 1972). Clinical house appts, Ipswich Gp of Hosps, 1955–56; Pathologist, Bland Sutton Inst. of Pathology, and Courtauld Inst. of Biochem., Middlesex Hosp., Soho Hosp. for Women, 1956–60; Jt Sen. Registrar in Histopathology, Middlesex and West Middlesex Hosps, 1961–62; Chief Med. Adviser and Cons. Pathologist, Benger Labs, 1962–63; Chief Pathologist and Nuffield Scholar, British Industrial Biological Res. Assoc., Carshalton, and Hon. Sen. Lectr, RCS, 1963–65; Associate Res. Dir, Wyeth Labs, Taplow, 1965–69; Sen. Med. Officer, DHSS, and Principal Med. Officer, Cttee on Safety of Medicines, 1969–72; SPMO, DHSS, 1972–82; Head of Safety and Envmt Res. Div., Unilever, 1982–93. Mem., EEC Scientific Cttee for Food, 1976–84 (Chm., Sci. Cttee for Cosmetology); Consultant Adviser in Toxicology to DHSS, 1978–81; Dir, DHSS Toxicological Lab., St Bartholomew's Hosp., 1978–82, Hon. Dir, 1982–84; Hon. Prof. of Toxicology, Dept of Biochemistry, Univ. of Surrey, 1978–84; Hon. Prof. of Toxicology and Pathology, Sch. of Pharmacy, Univ. of London, 1982–88. Chief Examiner in Toxicology, Inst. of Biology, 1989–2006. Chm., BIBRA, 1987–93. Hon. FFOM 1991. QHP, 1977–80. *Publications:* various toxicological and medical papers. *Recreations:* angling, gardening, water colours. *Address:* 2 Bramblewood, off Heron Gardens, Stalham, Norfolk NR12 9SZ. *T:* (01692) 583373.

FAIRWEATHER, Sir Patrick (Stanislaus), KCMG 1992 (CMG 1986); HM Diplomatic Service, retired; Senior Adviser, Citigroup (formerly Schroders, then Schroder Salomon Smith Barney), 1996–2007; Director, Butrint Foundation, 1997–2004; *b* 17 June 1936; *s* of John George Fairweather and Dorothy Jane (*née* Boanas); *m* 1962, Maria (*née* Merica) (*d* 2010); two *d*. *Educ:* Ottershaw Sch., Surrey; Trinity Coll., Cambridge (Hons History). National Service in Royal Marines and Parachute Regt, 1955–57. Entered FCO, 1965; 2nd Secretary, Rome, 1966–69; FCO, 1969–70; 1st Secretary (Economic), Paris, 1970–73; FCO, 1973–75; 1st Sec. and Head of Chancery, Vientiane, 1975–76; 1st Sec., UK Representation to EEC, Brussels, 1976–78; Counsellor (Economic and Commercial), Athens, 1978–83; Head of European Community Dept (Internal), FCO, 1983–85; Ambassador to Angola, 1985–87; Asst Under-Sec. of State, FCO, 1987–90; Dep. Under-Sec. of State (ME/Africa), FCO, 1990–92; Ambassador to Italy and (non-resident) to Albania, 1992–96. *Recreations:* travel, gardening, photography. *Club:* Garrick.

FAIRWOOD, Ian Stuart; a District Judge, 1996–2014; a Recorder, since 2001; *b* 16 May 1951; *s* of George Centenus Fairwood and Kathleen Florence Fairwood; *m* 1976, Hilary Joan Middleton; two *s*. *Educ:* Carlton Cavendish Secondary Modern; UCL (LLB). Bar Sch., 1974–75; called to the Bar, Middle Temple, 1974; Dep. Dist Judge, 1993–96; NE Circuit. *Recreations:* golf, tennis, gardening. *Clubs:* Notts County Football; Easingwold Golf.

FAIZAL, Dr Farahanaz, PhD; High Commissioner for the Maldives in the United Kingdom, 2009–12; *m* Dr Mohamed Ahmed Didi; one *d*. *Educ:* Univ. of Keele (BA Internat. Relns 1989); Queens' Coll., Cambridge (MPhil Internat. Relns 1991); Univ. of Hull (PhD Politics 1996). Res. Officer, 1989–91, Sen. Res. Officer, 1991–92, For. Relns Section, President's Office, Malé; Nat. Programme Officer, UN Population Fund, 1996–98; independent analyst and consultant with res. speciality of security problems of small island states, gender and internat. relns, 1998–2008; Advr to Min. of For. Affairs, 2008–09. Mem., Maldivian Democratic Party, 2006–. *Address:* c/o High Commission of the Maldives, 22 Nottingham Place, W1U 5NJ.

FALCON, David; international public management consultant, 1992–2014; *b* 3 Jan. 1946; *s* of Arnold and Barbara Falcon; *m* 1st, 1967 (marr. diss. 1991); two *s*; 2nd, 1998, Simoné Mondesir. *Educ:* Helston County Grammar Sch.; University College London (BSc); Lancaster Univ. (MA); Univ. of Pennsylvania. Research Associate, Univ. of Lancaster, 1969–72; Lectr, Leeds Polytechnic, 1972–74; Sen. Lectr, Sheffield Polytechnic, 1974–76; Asst Dir, Sen. Asst Dir, Dep. Dir of Education, Humberside CC, 1976–85; Dir of Education, ILEA, 1985–88; Dir-Gen., RIPA, 1988–92. Mem., Manchester United Supporters' Trust, 2006–. *Publications:* articles in educn and management jls. *Recreations:* music, opera, photography, travel, bricolage. *Address:* 45 rue du Pérou, 66500 Prades, France. *T:* (4) 68057458.

FALCONER, family name of **Baron Falconer of Thoroton**.

FALCONER OF THOROTON, Baron *cr* 1997 (Life Peer), of Thoroton in the co. of Nottinghamshire; **Charles Leslie Falconer;** PC 2003; QC 1991; Secretary of State for Justice (formerly for Constitutional Affairs) and Lord Chancellor, 2003–07; a Senior Counsel, Gibson Dunn, since 2008; *b* 19 Nov. 1951; *s* of John Leslie Falconer and late Anne Mansel Falconer; *m* 1985, Marianna Catherine Thoroton Hildyard, *qv*; three *s* one *d*. *Educ:* Trinity Coll., Glenalmond; Queens' Coll., Cambridge (Hon. Fellow, 2003). Called to the Bar, Inner Temple, 1974, Bencher, 1997. Solicitor-General, 1997–98; Minister of State: Cabinet Office, 1998–2001; for Housing, Planning and Regeneration, DTLR, 2001–02; for Criminal Justice, Sentencing and Law Reform, Home Office, 2002–03; Shadow Lord Chancellor and Shadow Sec. of State for Justice, 2015–. Chairman: Amicus Horizon Gp Financing Ltd, 2008–12; 1NG Ltd, 2009–15. Chm., John Smith Meml Trust, 2007–. Visitor, Queens' Coll., Cambridge, 2007–. Hon. DCL Northumbria, 2015. *Address:* House of Lords, SW1A 0PW. *E:* falconerc@parliament.uk.

FALCONER OF THOROTON, Lady; *see* Hildyard, M. C. T.

FALCONER, Anthony Dale, OBE 2014; DM; FRCOG; Consultant Obstetrician and Gynaecologist, Derriford Hospital, Plymouth, 1986–2013; President, Royal College of Obstetricians and Gynaecologists, 2010–13; *b* Edinburgh, 11 March 1949; *s* of Dale Falconer and Hermione Falconer; *m* 1979, Elizabeth Mallaband, three *s* one *d*. *Educ:* Wellington Coll., Berks; Napier Coll., Edinburgh; Univ. of Bristol (MB ChB 1972); Univ. of Nottingham (DM 1984). FRCOG 1991. Trainee Obstetrician and Gynaecologist, Edinburgh, Nottingham and Cape Town, 1974–86; Lectr in Physiology and Pharmacology, Univ. of Nottingham, 1979–81. Sen. Vice Pres., RCOG, 2007–10. Trustee, Acad. of Med. Royal Colls, 2011–. Mem. Court, Queen Margaret Univ., Edinburgh, 2013–. FRCPE 2012. Hon. FICOG 2012;

Hon. FCOG(SA) 2012; Hon. FACOG 2012. Hon. DSc: Plymouth, 2011; Bristol, 2013. *Publications:* articles on sympatho-adrenal activity in fetuses, cancer and global health issues affecting maternity. *Recreations:* hockey, golf, walking, music. *Club:* Murrayfield Golf.

FALCONER, Prof. Roger Alexander, FREng; FLSW; CH2M HILL (formerly Hyder, then Halcrow) Professor of Water Management, Cardiff School of Engineering, Cardiff University, since 1997; *b* 12 Dec. 1951; *s* of late Cyril Thomas Falconer and Winifred Mary Matilda Falconer (*née* Rudge); *m* 1977, Nicola Jane Wonson; two *s* one *d. Educ:* King's Coll., London (BSc(Eng)); Univ. of Washington, USA (MScEng); Imperial Coll., London (PhD 1976; DIC 1976); Univ. of Birmingham (DEng 1992); Univ. of London (DSc(Eng) 1994). CEng 1982; Eur Ing 1990; FCIWEM 1990; FICE 1992; FREng (FEng 1997). Engr, Sir M. MacDonald and Partners, Cambridge, 1976–77; Lectr in Hydraulic Engrg, Dept of Civil Engrg, Univ. of Birmingham, 1977–86; University of Bradford: Prof. of Water Engrg, 1987–97; Dep. Hd, 1987–94, Hd, 1994–97, Dept of Civil and Envmtl Engrg. Guest Prof., Tianjin Univ., China, 1999–; Hon. Prof., China Inst. of Water Resources and Hydropower Research, 2013–. Co-Chm., Gp of Experts, Internat. Tribunal for Law of the Sea Malaysia *v* Singapore Land Reclamation Case, 2003–05. Member: Govt Expert Panel on Severn Tidal Power Studies, 2008–10; Expert Panel and Regl Cttee, Hafren Power, 2012–14. Pres., Internat. Assoc. for Hydro-Envmt Engrg and Res. (formerly Internat. Assoc. for Hydraulic Res.), 2011– (Mem. Council, 1999–2007); Member, Council: CIWEM, 1997–2002; ICE, 2000–03. FASCE 1993; FCGI 1997; FLSW 2011. Ippen Award, Internat. Assoc. Hydraulic Res., 1991; Telford Premium, 1994, Robert Carr Prize, 2003, 2007, ICE; Silver Medal, Royal Acad. of Engrg, 1999; Hai He Award, China, 2004. *Publications: edited:* (jtly) Hydraulic and Environmental Modelling of Coastal, Estuarine and River Waters, 1989, 1992; (jtly) Wetland Management, 1994; over 400 book chapters, jl and conf. papers, and tech. reports on hydro-envmtl modelling of coastal, estuarine and river waters. *Recreations:* music, walking, travel, Formula 1. *Address:* School of Engineering, Cardiff University, The Parade, Cardiff CF24 3AA. *T:* (029) 2087 4280. *E:* FalconerRA@cf.ac.uk; 3 Clos Cradog, Penarth, South Glamorgan CF64 3RJ. *T:* (029) 2035 0250. *E:* rogerfalconer@btinternet.com.

FALDO, Sir Nicholas Alexander, (Sir Nick), Kt 2009; MBE 1988; professional golfer; Chairman, Faldo Design, since 1991; lead golf analyst for CBS Sports and The Golf Channel, since 2007; *b* 18 July 1957; *s* of George and Joyce Faldo; *m* (marr. diss.); one *s* three *d. Educ:* Welwyn Garden City. Won English Amateur Golf Championship, 1975; Professional golfer, 1976; Mem., Ryder Cup team, 1977–97, Captain, 2008; many championship titles include: Open, Muirfield, 1987, 1992, St Andrews, 1990; US Masters, 1989, 1990, 1996; French Open, 1983, 1988, 1989; GA Eur. Open, 1992; World Match Play Championship, 1992; Irish Open, 1991, 1992, 1993. *Publications:* Golf: the winning formula, 1989; In Search of Perfection, 1994; A Swing for Life, 1995; Life Swings, 2004. *Recreations:* helicopter flying, fly fishing, motor sports, cycling, photography. *E:* info@nickfaldo.com.

FALKENDER, Baroness *cr* 1974 (Life Peer), of West Haddon, Northants; **Marcia Matilda Falkender,** CBE 1970; Private and Political Secretary to Lord Wilson of Rievaulx, 1956–83 (at 10 Downing Street, 1964–70 and 1974–76); *b* March 1932; *d* of Harry Field. *Educ:* Northampton High School; Queen Mary Coll., Univ. of London (BA Hons Hist). Secretary to Gen. Sec., Labour Party, 1955–56. Member: Prime Minister's Film Industry Working Party, 1975–76; Interim Cttee on Film Industry, 1977–82; British Screen Adv. Council, 1985–. Chm., Canvasback Productions, 1989–91. Director: Peckham Building Soc., 1986–91; South London Investment and Mortgage Corp., 1986–91; General Mediterranean Holding Group (UK). Political columnist, Mail on Sunday, 1982–88. Trustee, Silver Trust, 1988–. Mem., External Relations Cttee, QMW (formerly QMC), London Univ., 1987–97; Governor, QMW, 1987–93. FRSA. *Publications:* Inside Number 10, 1972; Downing Street in Perspective, 1983. *Address:* House of Lords, SW1A 0PW.

FALKINER, Sir Benjamin (Simon) Patrick, 10th Bt *cr* 1778, of Annemount, Cork; *b* 16 Jan. 1962; *s* of Sir Edmond Charles Falkiner, 9th Bt and of his 1st wife, Janet Iris, *d* of Arthur Edward Bruce Derby; *S* father, 1997, but his name does not appear on the Official Roll of the Baronetage; *m* 1998, Linda Louise Mason (*d* 2006); one *s* one *d. Educ:* Queen Elizabeth's Grammar Sch. for Boys, Barnet. *Heir: b* Matthew Terence Falkiner, *b* 9 Jan. 1964. *Address:* 29 Glebeland, Hatfield, Herts AL10 8AA.

FALKLAND, 15th Viscount *cr* 1620 (Scot.), of Falkland, Co. Fife; **Lucius Edward William Plantagenet Cary;** Lord Cary 1620; Premier Viscount of Scotland on the Roll; *b* 8 May 1935; *s* of 14th Viscount Falkland, and Constance Mary (*d* 1995), *d* of late Captain Edward Berry; *S* father, 1984; *m* 1st, 1962, Caroline Anne (marr. diss. 1990), *o d* of late Lt-Comdr Gerald Butler, DSC, RN, and late Mrs Patrick Parish; one *s* two *d* (and one *d* decd); 2nd, 1990, Nicole, *o d* of late Milburn Mackey; one *s. Educ:* Wellington Coll.; Alliance Française, Paris. Late 2nd Lieut 8th Hussars. Export marketing consultant, formerly Chief Executive, C. T. Bowring Trading (Holdings) Ltd. House of Lords: Mem., Select Cttee on Overseas Trade, 1984–85; Dep. Whip, Lib Dem, 1989–2002; spokesman on culture, media and sport (formerly nat. heritage), 1995–2005; elected Mem., 1999; Mem., Pre-legislative Jt Cttee on Gambling, 2006–07; Chm., Works of Art Cttee, 2008–10; crossbencher, 2012–. *Recreations:* reading, golf, motorcycling, racing, cinema. *Heir: s* Master of Falkland, *qv. Address:* c/o House of Lords, SW1A 0PW. *Clubs:* Brooks's; Sunningdale Golf; Cercle de Deauville.

FALKLAND, Master of; Hon. Lucius Alexander Plantagenet Cary; Co-Executive Producer, Homeland, US TV, 2011–14; *b* 1 Feb. 1963; *s* and *heir* of 15th Viscount Falkland, *qv*; *m* 1993, Linda (marr.diss. 1999), *d* of Raymond Purl, Colorado City, USA; one *s*; one *s* by another relationship. *Educ:* Loretto School; RMA Sandhurst. Late Captain, 2nd Battalion, Scots Guards. Exec. Prod., US TV series, Lie to Me, 2010–11. *Recreations:* ski-ing, golf. *Club:* Cavalry and Guards.

FALKNER, family name of **Baroness Falkner of Margravine**.

FALKNER OF MARGRAVINE, Baroness *cr* 2004 (Life Peer), of Barons Court in the London Borough of Hammersmith and Fulham; **Kishwer Falkner;** *b* 9 March 1955; *m* 1996, Robert Falkner; one *d. Educ:* St Joseph's Convent Sch., Karachi; LSE (BSc(Econ) 1992); Univ. of Kent (MA). Dir, Internat. Affairs, Lib Dems, 1993–99; Chief Prog. Officer, Political Affairs Div., Commonwealth Secretariat, 1999–2003; Chief Exec., Students Partnership Worldwide, 2003–04. Mem., H of L/H of C Jt Cttee on Human Rights, 2005. Contested (Lib Dem): Kensington and Chelsea, 2001; London, European Parlt, 2004. *Address:* House of Lords, SW1A 0PW.

FALL, Sir Brian (James Proetel), GCVO 1994; KCMG 1992 (CMG 1984); HM Diplomatic Service, retired; British Government Special Representative for the South Caucasus, 2002–12; *b* 13 Dec. 1937; *s* of John William Fall, Hull, Yorkshire, and Edith Juliette (*née* Proetel); *m* 1962, Delmar Alexandra Roos; three *d. Educ:* St Paul's Sch.; Magdalen Coll., Oxford; Univ. of Michigan Law Sch. Served HM Forces, 1955–57. Joined HM Foreign (now Diplomatic) Service, 1962; served in Foreign Office UN Dept, 1963; Moscow, 1965; Geneva, 1968; Civil Service Coll., 1970; FO Eastern European and Soviet Dept and Western Organisations Dept, 1971; New York, 1975; Harvard Univ. Center for Internat. Affairs, 1976; Counsellor, Moscow, 1977–79; Head of Energy, Science and Space Dept, FCO, 1979–80; Head of Eastern European and Soviet Dept, FCO, 1980–81; Prin. Private Sec. to Sec. of State for Foreign and Commonwealth Affairs, 1981–84; Dir, Cabinet, Sec. Gen. of NATO, 1984–86; Asst Under-Sec. of State (Defence), FCO, 1986–88; Minister, Washington, 1988–89; High Comr to Canada, 1989–92; Ambassador to Russian Fedn, and to Republics of Armenia, Georgia, Moldova and Turkmenistan, 1992–95, also to Azerbaijan, Belarus, Kazakhstan, Kyrgyzstan and Uzbekistan, 1992–93; Principal, LMH, Oxford, 1995–2002 (Hon. Fellow, 2002). Advr, Rio Tinto, 1996–2010; Chm., MC Russian Market Fund, 1996–2002; Mem., Internat. Adv. Bd, La Poste, 2006–14; Dir, Rio Tinto Alcan Fund, 2008–10. Chm., ICC (UK) Cttee on Anti-Corruption, 2005–11. Gov., ESU, 2002–08. Dir, UK Foundn, Univ. of BC, 2005–08. Gov., St Mary's Sch., Calne, 1996–2005. Hon. LLD York Univ., Toronto, 2002. *Recreation:* France. *Address:* 2 St Helena Terrace, Richmond, Surrey TW9 1NR. *Club:* Garrick.

See also C. Fall.

FALL, Catherine; Deputy Chief of Staff to the Prime Minister, since 2010; *d* of Sir Brian (James Proetel) Fall, *qv*; *m* 1996, Ralph Ward-Jackson (marr. diss.); one *s* one *d. Educ:* King's Sch., Canterbury (music schol.); St Hilda's Coll., Oxford (BA PPE 1986). Res. asst to Patricia Rawlings, MEP; Special Advr to Dep. Dir Gen., CBI; Conservative Research Department: desk officer for Europe and agric., 1995–97; work for Shadow Foreign Sec., then Hd, Home Affairs Section, 1997; Dep. COS to Leader of the Opposition, 2005–10. Dir, Atlantic Partnership, until 2006. *Address:* Prime Minister's Office, 10 Downing Street, SW1A 2AA.

[Created a Baroness (Life Peer) 2015 but title not yet gazetted at time of going to press.]

FALL, David William, CMG 2007; HM Diplomatic Service, retired; Ambassador to Thailand and Laos, 2003–07; *b* 10 March 1948; *s* of George William Fall and Susan Fall; *m* 1973, Margaret Gwendolyn Richards; three *s. Educ:* St Bartholomew's Grammar Sch., Newbury; New Coll., Oxford (MA Mod. Hist.). VSO, Papua-New Guinea, 1970–71; joined FCO, 1971; language student, later 2nd then 1st Sec., Bangkok, 1973–77; seconded to Cabinet Office, 1977–78; FCO, 1978–80; 1st Sec., Cape Town and Pretoria, 1981–85; FCO, 1985–90; Counsellor, 1989; Head of Narcotics Control and AIDS Dept, FCO, 1989–90; Dep. Hd of Mission, Bangkok, 1990–93; Dep. High Comr, Canberra, 1993–97; Ambassador to Socialist Republic of Vietnam, 1997–2000; Estate Sales Prog., subseq. Estate Modernisation, Manager, FCO, 2000–03. Board Member: POWER International, 2008–09; Anglo-Thai Society, 2008– (Chm., 2009–12). Internat. Trustee, British Red Cross, 2008–13 (Vice Chm., 2011–13). Mem. Council, Royal Over-Seas League, 2012–. *Recreations:* long distance walking, 19th century military and naval history, War of 1812, Monty Python.

FALLAS, Diana Elizabeth Jane; *see* Burrell, D. E. J.

FALLICK, Prof. Anthony Edward, PhD; FRSE; Professor of Isotope Geosciences, University of Glasgow, 1996–2012; *b* 21 April 1950; *s* of Edward Henry Fallick and Helen Fallick (*née* Murray); partner, Dr Charlotte Bryant; one *d. Educ:* Univ. of Glasgow (BSc Hons Natural Philosophy 1971; PhD Nuclear Geochem. 1975). Research Fellow, McMaster Univ., 1975–78; Vis. Schol., Cambridge Univ., 1978–80; Res. Fellow, 1980–85, Lectr, 1985–90, Reader, 1990–96, Univ. of Glasgow; Dir, Scottish Univs Envmtl Res. Centre, 1999–2007. FRSE 1993; FRSA 1997; FMinSoc 1998 (Schlumberger Medal, 1998; Dist. Lectr, 2009–10); Founding Fellow, Inst. of Contemp. Scotland, 2000. Richard A. Glenn Award, ACS, 2001; Coke Medal, Geol Soc., 2004; Clough Medal, Edinburgh Geol Soc., 2014. *Publications:* contrib. numerous articles and papers to peer-reviewed jls and symposia vols. *Recreations:* wine, song. *Address:* SUERC, Scottish Enterprise Technology Park, E Kilbride, Glasgow G75 0QF. *T:* (01355) 223332. *E:* t.fallick@suerc.gla.ac.uk. *Club:* Four Forty Five (Hamilton, Ont.).

FALLON, Her Honour Hazel Rosemary; a Circuit Judge, 1978–96; *b* 7 Jan. 1931; *d* of late Arthur Henry Counsell and Elsie Winifred Counsell; *m* 1980, Peter Fallon, *qv. Educ:* Clifton High Sch.; Switzerland; Univ. of Bristol (LLB). Called to the Bar, Gray's Inn, 1956; Western Circuit, 1956–96; a Recorder of the Crown Court, 1976–77. Legal Dept, Min. of Labour, 1959–62. Mem. of Council, Univ. of Bristol, 1992–97. Hon. LLD UWE, 1996. *Recreations:* reading, swimming, travel. *Address:* c/o The Law Courts, Small Street, Bristol BS1 1DA.

FALLON, Ivan Gregory; Deputy Chairman, N. Brown Group plc, since 2009 (Director, since 1994); *b* 26 June 1944; *s* of Padraic and Dorothea Fallon; *m* 1st, 1967, Susan Mary Lurring (marr. diss. 1997); one *s* two *d*; 2nd, 1997, Elizabeth Rees-Jones. *Educ:* St Peter's Coll., Wexford; Trinity Coll., Dublin (BBS). Irish Times, 1964–66; Thomson Provincial Newspapers, 1966–67; Daily Mirror, 1967–68; Sunday Telegraph, 1968–70; Deputy City Editor, Sunday Express, 1970–71; Sunday Telegraph, 1971–84: City Editor, 1979–84; Dep. Editor, Sunday Times, 1984–94; Chief Executive Officer: Ind. Newspapers of S Africa, then Ind. News & Media of SA, 1994–2002; Independent News & Media UK, 2002–10. Chm., iTouch plc, 1998–2005; Dir, Independent Newspapers plc, Ireland, 1995–2010. Mem., Council of Governors, United Med. and Dental Schs of Guy's and St Thomas' Hosps, 1985–94; Trustee, Project Trust, 1984–. *Publications:* (with James L. Srodes) DeLorean: the rise and fall of a dream-maker, 1983; (with James L. Srodes) Takeovers, 1987; The Brothers: the rise and rise of Saatchi and Saatchi, 1988; Billionaire: the life and times of Sir James Goldsmith, 1991; Paper Chase, 1993; The Player: the life of Tony O'Reilly, 1994; (with James B. Sherwood) Orient Express: a personal journey, 2012; Black Horse Ride: the inside story of Lloyds and the banking crisis, 2015. *Recreations:* walking, tennis. *Address:* 17 Kensington Mansions, Trebovir Road, SW5 9TF; Prospect House, Klein Constantia Road, Constantia, Cape Town 7806, South Africa. *Clubs:* Garrick, Beefsteak, Political Economy.

FALLON, John Joseph; Chief Executive Officer, Pearson plc, since 2013; *b* Blackpool, 25 Aug. 1962; *s* of Jack and Maureen Fallon; *m* 1988, Della Broome; two *d. Educ:* Cardinal Langley Sch., Middleton, Gtr Manchester; Hull Univ. (BA Hons Econs, Politics and Sociol.). Communications and public policy rôles with local govt and Parliament; Communications Director: Powergen plc, 1995–97; Pearson plc, 1997–2003; Chief Executive Officer: Pearson Educn, EMEA, 2003–08; Pearson Internat., 2008–13. *Recreations:* running, football, golf. *Address:* Pearson plc, 80 Strand, WC2R 0RL.

FALLON, Kieren; flat race jockey; *b* Crusheen, Co. Clare, 22 Feb. 1965; *s* of Frank and Maureen Fallon; *m* 1993, Julie Bowker; one *s* two *d.* With Lynda Ramsden stable, 1993–97; stable jockey for Henry Cecil, 1997–2000, for Michael Stoute, 2000–05, for Aidan O'Brien, 2005–07; rode first British winner, 1988; rode 200 winners in season, 1997. Winner: Lincoln Handicap, on High Premium, 1993; 1,000 Guineas, on Sleepytime, 1997, on Wince, 1999, on Russian Rhythm, 2003, on Virginia Waters, 2005; Oaks, on Reams of Verse, 1997, on Ramruna, 1999, on Ouija Board, 2004; Grosser Preis von Baden, Germany, on Borgia, 1997; Prix de la Forêt, France, on Tomba, 1998; Derby, on Oath, 1999, on Kris Kin, 2003, on North Light, 2004; Irish Oaks, on Ramruna, 1999, on Ouija Board, 2004, on Alexandrova, 2006; Tattersalls Gold Cup, Ireland, on Shiva, 1999; 2,000 Guineas, on King's Best, 2000, on Golan, 2001, on Footstepsinthesand, 2005, on George Washington, 2006, on Night of Thunder, 2014; King George VI and Queen Elizabeth Diamond Stakes, on Golan, 2002; Filly and Mare Turf, Breeders' Cup, on Islington, 2003, on Ouija Board, 2004; Irish Derby, on Hurricane Run, 2005, on Dylan Thomas, 2006; Prix de l'Arc de Triomphe, on Hurricane Run, 2005, on Dylan Thomas, 2007; French 2,000 Guineas, on Aussie Rules, 2006. Champion Jockey, 1997, 1998, 1999, 2001, 2002, 2003. *Address:* c/o Jockey Club, 151 Shaftesbury Avenue, WC2H 8AL.

FALLON, Martin; *see* Patterson, H.

FALLON, Rt Hon. Michael; PC 2012; MP (C) Sevenoaks, since 1997; Secretary of State for Defence, since 2014; *b* 14 May 1952; *s* of late Martin Fallon, OBE, FRCSI and of Hazel Fallon; *m* 1986, Wendy Elisabeth, *e d* of late Peter Payne, Holme-on-Spalding Moor, Yorks; two *s. Educ:* St Andrews Univ. (MA Hons 1974). European Educnl Res. Trust, 1974–75; Opposition Whips Office, House of Lords, 1975–77; EEC Officer, Cons. Res. Dept,

1977–79; Jt Man. Dir, European Consultants Ltd, 1979–81; Dir, Quality Care Homes plc, 1992–97; Chief Exec., Quality Care Develts Ltd, 1996–97; Man. Dir, Just Learning Ltd, 1996–2006; Director: Bannatyne Fitness Ltd, 1999–2000; Collins Stewart Tullett plc, 2004–06; Tullett Prebon plc, 2006–12; Attendo AB, 2008–12. Sec., Lord Home's Cttee on future of House of Lords, 1977–78; Assistant to Baroness Elles, 1979–83. MP (C) Darlington, 1983–92; contested (C) Darlington, 1992. PPS to Sec. of State for Energy, 1987–88; an Asst Govt Whip, 1988–90; a Lord Comr of HM Treasury, 1990; Parly Under-Sec. of State, DES, 1990–92; Opposition spokesman on trade and industry, 1997, on Treasury matters, 1997–98; Minister of State: BIS, 2012–14; DECC, 2013–14; Minister for Portsmouth, 2014. Mem., Treasury Select Cttee, 1999–2012; Chm., All Party Classics Gp, 2005–09. Mem., Exec., 1922 Cttee, 2005–07. Dep. Chm., Cons. and Unionist Party, 2010–12. Member: HEFCE, 1993–97; Adv. Council, Social Market Foundn, 1994–2001; Govt's Deregulation Task Force, 1994–97; Council, Centre for Policy Studies, 2009–. Dir, Internat. Care and Relief, 1997–2003; Pres., Royal London Soc. for the Blind, 2010–. Gov., Whitefield Schs, 1994–99. *Publications:* The Quango Explosion (jtly), 1978; Sovereign Members?, 1982; The Rise of the Euroquango, 1982; Brighter Schools, 1993; Social Mobility, 2007; contribs to journals. *Recreations:* books, ski-ing, visiting classical sites. *Address:* House of Commons, SW1A 0AA. *Club:* Academy.

FALLON, Paul Michael, OBE 2014; JP; independent health and social care consultant, since 2007; Head of Children's Services and Director of Social Services, London Borough of Barnet, 2001–07; *b* 11 July 1952; *s* of Michael and Doreen Fallon; *m* 2003, Joanne (*née* Katz); one *s*. *Educ:* Barking Abbey Grammar Sch.; Redbridge Tech. Coll.; Southampton Univ. (BSc, CQSW, DASS). Youth and Community Worker, 1975–78, Sen. Social Worker and Team Leader, 1978–82, Solihull MBC; Principal Officer (Child Care), 1982–89, Operational Services Manager, 1989–94, Coventry CC; Asst Dir (Child Care), Islington LBC, 1994–99; Quality Protects Develt Officer, DoH, 1999–2000. Co-Chm., ADSS Children and Families Policy Cttee, 2005–07; Ind. Chm., Croydon Safeguarding Children Bd, 2011–; Dir, Assoc. of Independent LSCB Chairs, 2013–. Non-exec. Dir, Pathway Care, 2008–11. Trustee and Board Member: Crime Reduction Initiatives, 2009–; Ambitious about Autism, 2011–14. JP Sussex Central, 2009. *Recreation:* playing the guitar. *E:* paulfallonuk@yahoo.co.uk.

FALLON, His Honour Peter; QC 1971; a Circuit Judge, 1979–96; a Senior Circuit Judge, 1980–96; *b* 1 March 1931; *s* of Frederick and Mary Fallon; *m* 1st, 1955, Zina Mary (*née* Judd); one *s* two *d*; 2nd, 1980, Hazel Rosemary Counsell (*see* Her Honour H. R. Fallon). *Educ:* Leigh Grammar Sch.; St Joseph's Coll., Blackpool; Bristol Univ. (LLB Hons). Called to Bar, Gray's Inn, 1953. Commissioned in RAF for three years. A Recorder of the Crown Court, 1972–79; Hon. Recorder of Bristol, 1995–96. Chm., Cttee of Inquiry into the Personality Disorder Unit, Ashworth Special Hosp., 1997–99. *Publications:* Crown Court Practice: Sentencing, 1974; Crown Court Practice: Trial, 1978; contrib. Proc. RSM. *Recreation:* reading. *Address:* c/o The Law Courts, Small Street, Bristol BS1 1DA.

FALLOWELL, Duncan Richard, FRSL; author; *b* London, 26 Sept. 1948; *s* of Thomas Edgar Fallowell and Celia Fallowell (*née* Waller). *Educ:* Palmer's Sch.; St Paul's Sch.; Magdalen Coll., Oxford (BA Hist. 1970; MA 2010). FRSL 2015. *Publications:* Drug Tales, 1979; April Ashley's Odyssey, 1982; Satyrday, 1986; The Underbelly, 1987; To Noto, 1989; One Hot Summer in Saint Petersburg, 1994; Twentieth Century Characters, 1994; A History of Facelifting, 2003; Going As Far As I Can, 2008; How To Disappear, 2011 (PEN Ackerley Prize, 2012); *e-publications:* Three Romes, 2014; The Rise and Fall of the Celebrity Interview, 2014; opera libretto: Gormenghast, composer, Irmin Schmidt, 1998. *Recreations:* swimming, rural motoring. *Address:* c/o Aitken Alexander Associates, 291 Gray's Inn Road, WC1X 8EB. *E:* reception@aitkenalexander.co.uk. *Club:* Groucho.

FALLOWS, Albert Bennett, CB 1987; Hon. RICS; Chief Valuer, Inland Revenue Valuation Office and Commissioner of Inland Revenue, 1984–88; *b* 7 Dec. 1928; *s* of Bennett and May Fallows; *m* 1955, Maureen James; two *d*. *Educ:* Leek High School. Private practice, surveying, 1945–56; local govt service, Staffs, 1956–63; joined CS, 1963; Dist Valuer, Basingstoke, 1973–75; Superintending Valuer, Liaison Officer, DoE/Dept of Transport, 1975–77; Board of Inland Revenue: Superintending Valuer, North West, Preston, 1977–80; Asst Chief Valuer, 1980–83; Dep. Chief Valuer, 1983. *Address:* 1 Meadow Drive, Bude, Cornwall EX23 8HZ. *T:* (01288) 354434.

FALLOWS, Prof. David Nicholas, PhD; FBA 1997; Professor of Musicology, University of Manchester, 1997–2010, now Emeritus; *b* 20 Dec. 1945; *yr s* of late William John Fallows and Winifred Joan Fallows (*née* Sanderson); *m* 1st, 1976, Paulène Oliver (marr. diss. 2008); one *s* one *d*; 2nd, 2013, Dagmar Hoffmann-Axthelm. *Educ:* Shrewsbury Sch.; Jesus Coll., Cambridge (BA 1967); King's Coll., London (MMus 1968); Univ. of Calif at Berkeley (PhD 1978). Assistant, Studio der Frühen Musik, Munich, 1968–70; Lectr, Univ. of Wisconsin-Madison, 1973–74; Lectr, 1976–82, Sen. Lectr, 1982–92, Reader in Music, 1992–97, Univ. of Manchester. Vis. Associate Prof., Univ. of N Carolina, Chapel Hill, 1982–83; Prof. invité de musicologie, Ecole Normale Supérieure, Paris, 1993; visiting posts: Univ. of Basel, 1996, 2004, 2009; Univ. of Vienna, 1999; Harvard Univ., 2002. Pres., Internat. Musicological Soc., 2002–07; Vice-Pres., Royal Musical Assoc., 2000–10. Corresp. Mem., Amer. Musicol Soc., 1999. Reviews Editor, Early Music, 1976–95, 1999–2000; Gen. Editor and Founder, Royal Musical Assoc. Monographs, 1982–98; Member, Editorial Board: Musica Britannica, 1985–; Jl of Royal Musical Assoc., 1986–88; Basler Jahrbuch für historische Musikpraxis, 1988–; Early Music History, 1991–; Muziek en Wetenschap, 1992–2001; Early English Church Music, 1994–. Dr *hc* Tours, 2010. Chevalier, Ordre des Arts et des Lettres (France), 1994. *Publications:* Dufay, 1982, 2nd edn 1987; (jtly) Chansonnier de Jean de Montchenu, 1991; (ed jtly) Companion to Medieval and Renaissance Music, 1992, 2nd edn 1997; The Songs of Guillaume Dufay, 1995; (ed and introd) Oxford Bodleian Library MS Canon Misc. 213 (Late Medieval and Early Renaissance music in facsimile, vol. 1), 1995; Songs and Musicians in the Fifteenth Century, 1996; The Songbook of Fridolin Sicher, 1996; A Catalogue of Polyphonic Songs 1415–1480, 1999; (ed) Josquin des Prez, Secular Works for Four Voices (New Josquin Edn vol. 28), 2005; Chansonnier de Jean de Montchenu (ca. 1475): commentary to the facsimile, 2008; Josquin, 2009; Composers and their Songs, 1400–1521, 2010; The Henry VIII Book: facsimile with introduction, 2014; (ed) Secular Polyphony 1380–1480, Musica Britannica, vol. 97, 2014. *Address:* Martin Harris Centre for Music and Drama, University of Manchester, Bridgeford Street, Manchester M13 9PL. *T:* 07714 184655. *E:* david.fallows@manchester.ac.uk.

FALLOWS, Geoffrey Michael; Headteacher, Camden School for Girls, 1989–2000; *b* 28 Sept. 1941; *er s* of late Rt Rev. William Gordon Fallows and of Edna (*née* Blakeman); *m* 1st, 1968, Carolyn (*d* 2000), *d* of late Dr William Brian Littler, CB and Pearl Littler; two *d*; 2nd, 2002, Johanna Koolhaas Revers, *d* of late Johann Koolhaas Revers and Maria Darley (*née* Buur). *Educ:* Shrewsbury Sch.; Wadham Coll., Oxford (MA); London Univ. Inst. of Education (PGCE). Vis. Classics Fellow, Marlboro Coll., Vermont, 1964–65; Asst Master, Latymer Upper Sch., 1966–69; Head of Classics, Crown Woods Sch., 1969–75; Dep. Head, Camden Sch. for Girls, 1975–89. Dir, Huron Univ., USA, in London, 1998–2005. Exec. Sec., 1978–81, Pres., 2003–05, JACT. Co-founder, Omnibus magazine, 1981. FRSA 1994. *Publications:* (ed jtly) Modern Stories of Ancient Greece, 1968; (contrib.) Intellegenda, 1970; articles in Omnibus mag. *Recreations:* theatre, gardening, Lake District. *Address:* 53 Byng Road, Barnet, Herts EN5 4NW. *T:* (020) 8449 2980, *Fax:* (020) 8440 7629.

FALMOUTH, 9th Viscount *cr* 1720; **George Hugh Boscawen;** 26th Baron Le Despencer, 1264; Baron Boscawen-Ros, 1720; Lord-Lieutenant of Cornwall, 1977–94; *b* 31 Oct. 1919; 2nd but *e* surv. *s* of 8th Viscount Falmouth; *S* father, 1962; *m* 1953, Elizabeth Price Browne (*d* 2007), OBE 2002, DL; four *s*. *Educ:* Eton Coll.; Trinity Coll., Cambridge. Served War, 1939–46, Italy. Capt., Coldstream Guards. DL Cornwall, 1968. *Heir:* *s* Hon. Evelyn Arthur Hugh Boscawen [*b* 13 May 1955; *m* 1st, 1977, Lucia Vivian-Neal (marr. diss. 1995), *e d* of R. W. Vivian-Neal; one *s* one *d*; 2nd, 1995, Katharine Maley; two *s* one *d*].

FALVEY, Dr David Alan, FGS; Managing Director: Research Connect Pty Ltd, since 2008; Palatine Energy, since 2011; *b* Sydney, 19 Dec. 1945; *s* of late Keith Falvey and Ella Falvey (*née* Hendley); *m* 1969, Margaret Kaye (*d* 1984); one *s* one *d*; *m* 1986, Gillian Tidey. *Educ:* Univ. of Sydney (BSc Hons 1967); Univ. of New South Wales (PhD 1972). FGS 1998. Explorationist, Shell Develt, Australia, 1972–74; Lectr, then Sen. Lectr, Univ. of Sydney, 1974–82; Chief, Marine Div., Bureau of Mineral Resources, 1982–89; Associate Dir, Petroleum and Marine Geoscis, Australian Geol Survey Orgn, 1989–94; Dir, Ocean Drilling Program, Jt Oceanographic Instns, Washington, 1994–98; Executive Director: British Geological Survey, NERC, 1998–2006; Physics, Chem. and Geosci., Australian Res. Council, 2006–08. Man. Dir, Tamboran, 2009–11. CCMI 2003. Hon. DSc Nottingham Trent, 2001. *Publications:* numerous scientific contribs to learned jls. *Recreation:* golf. *Club:* Royal Canberra Golf.

FAME, Georgie; musician, vocalist, songwriter; *b* 26 June 1943; *s* of James and Mary Anne Powell; *né* Clive Powell, name changed by impresario Larry Parnes, 1960; *m* 1971, Nicolette (*d* 1993); two *s*. *Educ:* Leigh Central Co. Secondary Sch., Lancs. Professional musician, 1959–; toured with Eddie Cochran, Gene Vincent and Billy Fury, 1960; leader of own band, The Blue Flames, 1962–; toured with Count Basie Orch., 1967 and 1968; rep. UK, Fest. Internat. da Cançao Popular, Brazil, 1967; in partnership with Alan Price, 1970–73; collaborated with Van Morrison, 1988–98; Founder Mem., Bill Wyman's Rhythm Kings, 1998; hosted own series, BBC Radio 2, 2000; featured guest soloist with all of Europe's major jazz orchs; has composed and performed music for various feature films, television and radio commercials. Over 30 albums released under own name inc. Poet in New York, 2000 (Prix Billie Holiday, Acad. du Jazz de France); 13 hit singles, incl. 3 Number Ones: Yeh Yeh, 1965; Getaway, 1966; Ballad of Bonnie and Clyde, 1968. Hon. Mem. Swedish Exec. Jazz Soc., 2002. *Recreations:* aviation, crosswords.

FANCOURT, Timothy Miles; QC 2003; a Recorder, since 2009; a Deputy High Court Judge, since 2013; *b* 30 Aug. 1964; *s* of Dr Philip Fancourt and Georgina Mary Fancourt (*née* Brown); *m* 2000, Emily Windsor; one *d*. *Educ:* Whitgift Sch.; Gonville and Caius Coll., Cambridge (MA). Called to the Bar, Lincoln's Inn, 1987. Chm., Chancery Bar Assoc., 2012–14 (Vice-Chm., 2010–12). *Publications:* Enforceability of Landlord and Tenant Covenants, 1997, 3rd edn 2014; Megarry's Assured Tenancies, 2nd edn 1999. *Recreations:* cricket, classical music. *Address:* Falcon Chambers, Falcon Court, EC4Y 1AA. *T:* (020) 7353 2484, *Fax:* (020) 7353 1261. *E:* fancourt@falcon-chambers.com.

FANE, family name of **Earl of Westmorland**.

FANE, Andrew William Mildmay, FCA; President, Emmanuel Society, since 2009; *b* 9 Aug. 1949; *s* of late Robert Fane and Valerie Fane (*née* Borthwick); *m* 1989, Clare Lucy Marx, *qv*. *Educ:* Radley Coll.; Emmanuel Coll., Cambridge (MA Law; Hon. Fellow 2012). FCA 1974. Chief Exec., Whitburgh Investments Ltd, 1982–92; Dep. Chm., Borthwicks plc, 1988–92. Non-exec. Dir, Great Ormond St Hosp. for Children NHS Trust, 2001–11 (Chm., Audit Cttee, 2006–08; Chm., Clinical Governance Cttee, 2008–11). Chairman: Friends of the Children of Gt Ormond St Hosp., 1992–2012; Special Trustees, Gt Ormond St Hosp. Children's Charity, 1999–2006 (Special Trustee, 1996–2007); Govs, The Children's Hosp. Sch. at Gt Ormond St Hosp. and UCH, 2000–12. Councillor, RBK&C, 1987–94 (Chm., Planning Cttee). Mem., Royal Commn on Histl Monuments of England, 1999–2003; English Heritage: Comr, 1995–2004; Dep. Chm., 2001–04; Chm., Audit Cttee, 2002–11. Chairman: Historic Bldgs and Areas Adv. Cttee, 1995–2001; London Adv. Cttee, 1999–2004 (Mem., 1994–2004). Mem., E Anglia Regl Cttee, NT, 1994–2002. Chm., Bd of Govs, Framlingham Coll., Suffolk, 2001– (Gov., 1995–); Mem. Council, Radley Coll., Oxon, 2003–11. Chm. Trustees, Inst. of Child Health, 2006– (Hon. Fellow, 2001); Trustee: Radley Foundn, 2002–14; Foundling Mus., 2007–12 (Chm., 2009–12); Britten-Pears Foundn, 2009– (Chm., Bldg Cttee, 2009–13); Gerald Coke Handel Foundn, 2010–; Chairman: Stowe House Preservation Trust, 2007–; Chiswick House and Gardens Trust, 2011–; Suffolk Preservation Soc., 2013–; Vice Chm., League of Remembrance, 2011– (Mem. Council, 2001–). *Recreations:* farming, conservation. *Address:* Hoo House, Woodbridge, Suffolk; 64 Ladbroke Road, W11 3NR. *T:* (020) 7221 2748.

FANE, Clare Lucy; *see* Marx, C. L.

FANE, Mark William; Co-Founder and Chief Executive, Crocus.co.uk Ltd, since 2003; *b* London, 21 June 1958; *s* of Michael Francis Fane and Carole Daisy Fane; *m* 1986, Emma Mary Bonnor-Maurice; one *s* one *d*. *Educ:* Eton Coll.; Univ. of Exeter (BA Politics and Econs); INSEAD Business Sch. (MBA 1986). Dir, Foreign & Colonial Ventures, 1987–91; Chm., Waterers Landscape plc, 1991–2003. Non-exec. Chm., Graphite Enterprise plc, 2010–. Non-exec. Chm., Garden Mus., 2011–; Mem., Council, RHS, 2009–. Freeman, Grocers' Co. *Address:* Fryern Court, Upper Burgate, Fordingbridge, Hants SP6 1NF. *E:* mark.fane@crocus.co.uk. *Clubs:* White's, Royal Thames Yacht; Sunningdale Golf.

FANE TREFUSIS, family name of **Baron Clinton**.

FANELLI, Sara; artist and illustrator; *b* 20 July 1969; *d* of Giovanni Fanelli and Rosalia (*née* Bonito); one *d* by Dario Marianelli. *Educ:* Liceo Classico Michelangelo, Florence (Maturità Classica); Camberwell Coll. of Art (BA Hons Graphic Design); Royal Coll. of Art (MA Illustration). Projects include: stamp design for Royal Millennium Collection, 1999 (D&AD Silver Award); timeline 40 metres long and design of 4 gallery entrances at Tate Modern, 2005–; (with Thomas Heatherwick) mural design for Nanyang Technology Univ., Singapore, 2014; book jackets for Penguin, Orion, Bloomsbury, Random House, Pan MacMillan and Faber and Faber; magazine illustrations for: New Yorker, NY Times, New Scientist, Guardian, TES, Radio Times, Daily Telegraph, Independent on Sunday; work for: BBC English; BBC Worldwide; British Council; Amnesty; Virgin Classics; Orange; Edinburgh Fest.; Royal Exchange Th., Manchester; Lyric Th., London; Nat. Westminster Bank; Nickelodeon (US); Alessi; Issey Miyake; Ron Arad. Mem., AGI, 2000–. Hon. RDI 2006. Numerous awards including: Parallel Prize, 1995; Nat. Art Liby Illustration Award, V&A, 1995, Commended Winner, 1997, 1998, 2000; D&AD Silver Award, for poster illustration, 2003; V&A Illustration Award, 2004; TITAN Internat. Illustration in Design Prize, 2009. *Publications: written and illustrated:* Button, 1994 (MacMillan Prize for a Children's Picture Book, 1992); My Map Book, 1995, 2nd edn 2006; Cinderella: Picture Box, 1996; Pinocchio: Picture Box, 1996; Wolf!, 1997; A Dog's Life, 1998; It's Dreamtime, 1999; Dear Diary, 2000; First Flight, 2002; Mythological Monsters, 2002; The Onion's Great Escape, 2012; *illustrated:* Dibby Dubby Dhu, 1997; The Folio Book of Short Novels, 1998; The New Faber Book of Children's Verse, 2001; Pinocchio, 2003; Sometimes I Think, Sometimes I Am, 2007 (D&AD Silver Award, for book design/illustration, 2008). *Recreations:* film, music, reading, travelling, flea markets, playing games, the moon. *Address:* c/o Walker Books, 87 Vauxhall Walk, SE11 5HJ. *W:* www.sarafanelli.com.

FANNING, Michael Leonard; a District Judge (Magistrates' Courts), since 2012; *b* Edinburgh, 18 Sept. 1967; *s* of Brian and Patricia Fanning; *m* 1993 (marr. diss.); two *d*. *Educ:* Keswick Sch., Cumbria; Leeds Poly. (LLB Hons). Admitted as solicitor, 1993; Solicitor,

1993–2012; a Dep. Dist Judge (pt-time) (Magistrates' Courts), 2008–12. Solicitor Mem. (pt-time), Solicitors' Disciplinary Tribunal, 2009–12. *Recreations:* fell-running (Member, Borrowdale Fell Runners and Holmfirth Harriers), Member, Keswick Mountain Rescue Team, 1989–2006. *Address:* Kirklees Magistrates' Court, The Court House, Civic Centre, Huddersfield, W Yorks HD1 2NH.

FANTONI, Prof. Barry Ernest; writer, performer, jazz musician; Member of editorial staff of Private Eye, 1963–2010; Professor of Communications and Media Studies, University of Salerno, since 1997; Director, All This Time Theatre Co., since 1998; *b* 28 Feb. 1940; *s* of late Peter Nello Secondo Fantoni and Sarah Catherine Fantoni; became Italian citizen, 1997; *m* 1972, Teresa Frances, (Tessa), Reidy (separated 1998). *Educ:* Archbishop Temple Sch.; Camberwell Sch. of Arts and Crafts (Wedgwood Scholar). Cartoonist of The Listener, 1968–88; contrib. art criticism to The Times, 1973–77; record reviewer, Punch, 1976–77; Diary cartoonist, The Times, 1983–90; Dir, Barry Fantoni Merchandising Co., 1985–93; designer of film and theatre posters and illustrator of book jackets; mural for Queen Elizabeth II Conf. Centre, London, 1985; film and television actor; From the Dragon's Mouth (one-man show for stage), 1991–; plays: Jeanne, performed Battersea Arts Centre, 1997; Modigliani, My Love, Paris, 1999; Rooms of the House, 2001; The Piano Tuner, 2005, Extra Time, 2006, (with Barry Booth) Café de Paris, 2006, (adapted and dir) Lady Windermere's Fan, 2006, (dir) Death of an Elephant, 2007, Loving Art, 2008, Put On a Happy Face - The Life and Songs of Charles Strouse, 2009, Landor Th.; Picasso is Coming, Pentameters and St James Th., 2013; (writer and dir) Seven Paintings of Joan de Llum, Heatherley School of Fine Art, 2010; creator, Ronnie's Horns (perf. with O. T. Fagbenly), RADA, 2002; travelling act (with Dominic Alldis) An Evening with E. J. Thribb; presenter and writer, Barry Fantoni's Chinese Horoscopes, BBC Radio 4 series, 1986; writer, My Turn for Lunch, Radio 4, 2015. One-man shows: Woodstock Gall., London, 1963; Comara Gall., LA, 1964; Brunel Univ., 1974; Times cartoon exhibition, Charlotte Lampard Gall., 1990; retrospective: Cadogan Contemporary Gall., 1991; Caricatures by Barry Fantoni, NPG, 2007; Thomas Williams Fine Art Gall., 2009; two-man shows (with Peter Fantoni): Langton Gall., London, 1977; Annexe Gall., London, 1978; Katherine House Gall., 1983; Fulford Cartoon Gall., 1983; New Grafton Gall., 1985; Green & Stone, Cirencester, 1986; work exhibited: AIA Gall., London, 1958, 1961 and 1964; D and AD Annual Exhibn, London, 1964; Royal Acad. Summer Exhibn, 1963 (as Stuart Harris, with William Rushton), 1964, 1975 and 1978 (with Richard Napper); Tate Gall., 1973; Bradford Print Biennale, 1974; National Theatre, 1977; Browse and Darby, 1977; Gillian Jason Gall., 1983; Three Decades of Art Schools, RA, 1983; Piers Feetham Gall., 2002; Chris Beetles Gall., 2014. Founder, Dépêchism art movement, 2012, exhibn (with Andrew Aarons), Thomas Williams Fine Art, 2014. Collections of work at London Museum, 1980; V&A, 1984; Cartoon Museum, 1993; Univ. of Kent, 2005; BL, 2006; NPG, 2007. Musical compositions include: popular songs (also popular songs with Marianne Faithfull and with Stanley Myers); The Cantors Crucifixion (musical improvisation for 13 instruments), 1977; (with John Wells) Lionel (musical), 1977; (with Barry Booth) We Are Your Future (official Unicef anthem), 1996; Mass of the Holy Spirit, 1999. Formed: (with John Butler) Barry Fantoni Duo, 1990–; Barry Fantoni's Jazz Circus, 1992 (a performance jazz trio). Patron: Landor Th., 2005–; British Musical Archive, 2011–. Editor, St Martin's Review, 1969–74; weekly columnist on Chinese Horoscopes: Today, 1986–87; Woman, 1987–88; Plus magazine, 1989; The Guardian, 1990. Male TV Personality of the Year, 1966. *Publications:* (with Richard Ingrams) Private Pop Eye, 1968; (as Old Jowett, with Richard Ingrams) The Bible for Motorists, 1970; Tomorrow's Nicodemus, 1974; (as Sylvie Krin, with Richard Ingrams) Love in the Saddle, 1974; Private Eye Cartoon Library 5, 1975; (as E. J. Thribb, with Richard Ingrams) So Farewell Then…and Other Poems, 1978; Mike Dime, 1980; (as Sylvie Krin, with Richard Ingrams) Born to be Queen, 1981; Stickman, 1982; (ed) Colemanballs, 1982; (ed) Colemanballs 2, 1984; The Times Diary Cartoons, 1984; Barry Fantoni's Chinese Horoscope, annually 1985–, retitled Barry Fantoni's Complete Chinese Horoscope, 1991; (ed) Colemanballs 3, 1986; Barry Fantoni Cartoons: a personal selection from The Times and The Listener, 1987; The Royal Family's Chinese Horoscopes, 1988; (ed) Colemanballs 4, 1988; Chinese Horoscope Guide to Love, Marriage and Friendship, 1989; (ed) Colemanballs 5, 1990; (ed) Colemanballs 6, 1992; (ed) Colemanballs 7, 1994; (ed) A Hundred Years of Neasden Football Club, 1995; (ed) Colemanballs 8, 1996; (ed) Colemanballs 9, 1998; (ed) Colemanballs 10, 2000; (ed) Colemanballs 11, 2002; (ed) Colemanballs 12, 2004; (ed) Colemanballs 13, 2006; (ed) Colemanballs 14, 2008; Scenes You Seldom See, 2005; (ed) Colemanballs 15, 2010; Harry Lipkin P.I., 2010; *illustrations for:* How To Be a Jewish Mother, 1966; The BP Festivals and Events in Britain, 1966; (with George Melly) The Media Mob, 1980; The Best of Barry Fantoni Cartoons, 1990. *Recreation:* animal welfare. *Address:* c/o MBA Literary Agents Ltd, 62 Grafton Way, W1T 5DW. *T:* (020) 7387 2076, *Fax:* (020) 7387 2042. *E:* info@mbalit.co.uk; 7 Boulevard Léon Gambetta, 62100 Calais, France. *Clubs:* Arts, Chelsea Arts (Chm., 1978–80).

FARAGE, Nigel Paul; Member (UK Ind) South East Region, England, European Parliament, since 1999; *b* 3 April 1964; *s* of Guy Farage and Barbara Stevens; *m* 1st, 1988 (marr. diss. 1997); two *s*; 2nd, 1999, Kirsten Mehr; two *d*. *Educ:* Dulwich Coll. Commodity Broker: Drexel Burnham Lambert, 1982–86; Credit Lyonnais Rouse Ltd, 1986–93; Refco Overseas Ltd, 1994–2002; Natexis Metals, 2003–04. UK Independence Party: Founder Mem., 1993; Chm., 1998–2000; Spokesman, 2000–; Leader, 2006–09 and 2010–. Co-Pres., Ind./Dem Gp, 2004–09, Europe of Freedom and Democracy Gp, 2009–, EP. Contested (UK Ind): Eastleigh, June 1994; Salisbury, 1997; Bexhill & Battle, 2001; Buckingham, 2010; S Thanet, 2015; Itchen, Test & Avon, EP elecns, 1994. Pres., Gadfly Club, 2006–. *Publications:* The Purple Revolution: the year that changed everything, 2015. *Recreations:* military history 1914–18, sea angling, proper English pubs. *Address:* 1 Darwin Villas, Single Street, Berrys Green, Westerham, Kent TN16 3AA. *T:* (office) (01903) 885573. *Club:* East India.

FARAH, Mohamed, (Mo), CBE 2013; athlete; *b* Mogadishu, Somalia, 23 March 1983; *m* 2010, Tania Nell; twin *d* and one step *d*. Gold Medal: for 5000m, Eur. Jun. Championships, 2001; Eur. Jun. Cross Country Championships, 2001; Silver Medal for 5000m, Eur. Under 23 Championships, 2003; debut for GB, 2005; Silver Medal for 5000m, Eur. T&F Championships, 2006; Gold Medal, 2006, Silver Medal, 2008, 2009, Eur. Cross Country Championships; Gold Medal for 3000m, Eur. Indoor Championships, 2009, 2011; Gold Medal for 5000m and for 10,000m, 2010, Gold Medal for 5000m, 2012, Gold Medal for 10,000m, 2014, Gold Medal for 5000m, 2014, Eur. Athletics Championships; Gold Medal for 5000m, Silver Medal for 10,000m, World Athletics Championships, 2011; Gold Medal for 5000m and for 10,000m, Olympic Games, London, 2012; Gold Medal for 5000m and for 10,000m, World Athletics Championships, 2013, 2015; winner: New York Half Marathon, 2011; New Orleans Half Marathon, 2013; Great North Run, 2014, 2015; Lisbon Half Marathon, 2015. Founder, Mo Farah Foundn, 2011. Male Athlete of Year, British Athletics Writers' Assoc., 2006, 2010, 2011, 2013; Sen. Athlete of Year, UK Athletics, 2010; Eur. Athlete of Year, Eur. Athletics Assoc., 2011, 2012. *Publications:* Twin Ambitions (autobiog.), 2013. *Address:* c/o PACE Sports Management, 6 The Causeway, Teddington, Middx TW11 0HE.

FARBEY, Judith Sarah; QC 2011; *b* London, 21 Oct. 1965; *d* of Alan David Farbey and Barbara Astrid Farbey; *m* 2011, Prabhat Vaze. *Educ:* Magdalen Coll., Oxford (BA Hons 1989); City Univ., London (DipLaw 1991). Called to the Bar, Middle Temple, 1992, Bencher, 2013. A Dep. Judge (part-time), Upper Tribunal (Administrative Appeals Chamber), 2014–. Member: Bar Law Reform Cttee, 2003–; Middle Temple Educn and Trng Cttee, 2014–. Asst Boundary Comr (Lead, London Reg.), 2011–12. Bar Pro Bono Award (first winner), 1997. *Publications:* (jtly) The Law of Habeas Corpus, 3rd edn 2011. *Recreations:* watching plays at Hampstead Theatre, using English Heritage membership, hanging out with Prabhat in Camden Town. *Address:* Doughty Street Chambers, 53–54 Doughty Street, WC1N 2LS. *T:* (020) 7404 1313, *Fax:* (020) 7404 2283.

FARDON, Prof. Richard Osborne, PhD; FBA 2004; Professor of West African Anthropology, since 1996, and Head, Doctoral School, since 2012, School of Oriental and African Studies, University of London; *b* 16 Jan. 1952; *s* of Arthur Dennis Fardon and Hilda Fardon (*née* Davidson); partner, Prof. Catherine Davies; one *s*, and two step *d*. *Educ:* Sir Roger Manwood's Grammar Sch., Sandwich; UCL (BSc (Econs) 1973; PhD 1980). Lectr in Social Anthropol., Univ. of St Andrews, 1980–88; Lectr in W African and Caribbean Anthropol., 1988–91, Reader, 1991–96, SOAS; Chm., Centre of African Studies, Univ. of London, 1993–97 and 2001–05. Chair, Assoc. of Social Anthropologists of UK and Commonwealth, 2001–05. Hon. Ed., Africa: Jl of Internat. African Inst., 2001–07. *Publications:* (ed) Power and Knowledge, 1985; Raiders and Refugees: trends in Chamba political development 1750–1950, 1988; (ed) Localizing Strategies, 1990; Between God, the Dead and the Wild, 1991; (ed with P. T. Baxter) Voice, Genre, Text, 1991; (ed with Graham Furniss) African Languages, Development and the State, 1994; (ed) Counterworks: managing the diversity of knowledge, 1995; Mary Douglas: an intellectual biography, 1999; (ed and introd with Jeremy Adler) Franz Baermann Steiner: selected writings, vol. 1, Taboo, Truth and Religion, vol. 2, Orientpolitik, Value and Civilisation, 1999; (ed jtly) Modernity on a Shoestring, 1999; (ed with Graham Furniss) African Broadcast Culture, 2000; (ed jtly) From Prague Poet to Oxford Anthropologist Franz Baermann Steiner Celebrated: essays and translations, 2003; (with Christine Stelzig) Column to Volume, 2005; Lela in Bali: history through ceremony in Cameroon, 2006; Fusions: masquerades and thought style east of the Niger-Benue confluence, West Africa, 2007; (with Marla Berns and Sidney Kasfir) Central Nigeria Unmasked: arts of the Benue River valley, 2011; (ed jtly) Sage Handbook of Social Anthropology, 2012; (ed with Maria Berns) Nigéria: arts de la vallée de la Bénoué, 2012; (ed) Mary Douglas—A Very Personal Method: anthropological writings drawn from life, 2013; (ed) Mary Douglas—Cultures and Crises: understanding risk and resolution, 2013; Tiger in an African Palace, and other thoughts about identification and transformation, 2014. *Recreations:* following opera and the fortunes of Tottenham Hotspur FC. *Address:* Department of Anthropology and Sociology, School of Oriental and African Studies, Thornhaugh Street, Russell Square, WC1H 0XG. *T:* (020) 7898 4406. *E:* rf@soas.ac.uk.

FARHI, Nicole, (Lady Hare), Hon. CBE 2007; sculptor, since 2012; *b* 25 July 1946; *d* of Ephraim Farhi and Marcelle (*née* Babani); one *d* by Stephen Marks; *m* 1992, Sir David Hare, *qv*. *Educ:* Lycée Calmette, Nice; Cours Berçot Art Sch., Paris. Fashion designer; first designed for Pierre d'Albi, 1968; founded French Connection with Stephen Marks, 1973; founder and designer, Nicole Farhi Co., 1983–2012; launched Nicole Farhi For Men, 1989; opened Nicole's Restaurant, 1994; opened Nicole Farhi US flagship store, NY, 1999. Solo exhibn, Bowman Sculpture, Duke St, 2014. British Classics award, 1989, Best Contemporary Designer, 1995, 1996 and 1997, British Fashion Awards; Menswear Designer of the Year, FHM Awards, 2000; British Designer of the Year, Maxim Awards, 2001; Lifetime Achievement Award, CBI, 2008; French Woman of the Year, Grandes Ecoles City Circle, 2008. Chevalier, Legion d'Honneur (France), 2010.

FARINGDON, 3rd Baron *cr* 1916; **Charles Michael Henderson,** KCVO 2008; Bt 1902; Partner, Cazenove & Co., 1968–96; Chairman, Witan Investment Trust (formerly Witan Investment Company) plc, 1980–2003; a Lord in Waiting to the Queen, 1998–2008; *b* 3 July 1937; *s* of Lt-Col Hon. Michael Thomas Henderson (*d* 1953) (2nd *s* of Col Hon. Harold Greenwood Henderson, CVO, and *g s* of 1st Baron) and Oonagh Evelyn Henderson, *er d* of late Lt-Col Harold Ernest Brassey; *S* uncle, 1977; *m* 1959, Sarah Caroline, *d* of late J. M. E. Askew, CBE; three *s* one *d*. *Educ:* Eton College; Trinity College, Cambridge (BA). Treasurer, Nat. Art Collections Fund, 1984–91; Chm., RCHME, 1994–99; Comr, English Heritage, 1998–2001. Chm. Bd of Governors, Royal Marsden Hosp., 1980–85 (Mem., 1975–85); Chm., Bd of Management, 2001–05 (Mem., 1980–2000), Fellow, 2000, Inst. of Cancer Res. Pro-Chancellor, Univ. of West London, 2014–. *Heir:* *s* Hon. James Harold Henderson [*b* 14 July 1961; *m* 1986, Lucinda, *y d* of late Desmond Hanson, Knipton, Lincs; two *s* one *d*]. *Address:* Plantation House, Buscot Park, Faringdon, Oxon SN7 8BU. *E:* farbuscot@aol.com.

FARISH, William Stamps, III; Ambassador of the United States of America to the Court of St James's, 2001–04; *b* Houston, Tex, 1938; *m* Sarah Sharp; one *s* three *d*. *Educ:* Univ. of Virginia. Formerly: Stockbroker, Underwood, Neuhaus & Co., Houston; Pres., Navarro Exploration Co.; Founding Director: Eurus Inc., NY; Capital Nat. Bank, Houston; Pres., W. S. Farish & Co., Houston. Owner, Lane's End Farm, Versailles, Ky, 1980–; formerly Chairman: Churchill Downs Inc., Ky; Exec. Cttee, Breeders Cup Ltd; Vice-Chm., US Jockey Club; Dir, Thoroughbred Breeders and Owners Assoc.

FARLEY, Prof. Francis James Macdonald, FRS 1972; Professor Emeritus, Royal Military College of Science (Dean, 1967–82); Visiting Professor, School of Engineering and the Environment, University of Southampton, since 2008; *b* 13 Oct. 1920; *er s* of late Brig. Edward Lionel Farley, CBE, MC; *m* 1st, 1945, Josephine Maisie Hayden (marr. diss.); three *s* one *d*; 2nd, 1977, Margaret Ann Pearce (marr. diss.); 3rd, 2000, Irina Melyushina. *Educ:* Clifton Coll.; Clare Coll., Cambridge. MA 1945; PhD 1950; ScD Cantab 1967. FInstP. Air Defence Research and Development Establishment, 1941–45 (first 3cm ground radar, Doppler radar); Chalk River Laboratories, 1945–46; Research Student, Cavendish Lab., Cambridge, 1946–49; Auckland Univ. Coll., NZ, 1950–57; attached AERE, 1955; CERN, Geneva, 1957–67 (muon g-2 experiment). Vis. Lectr, Univ. of Bristol, 1965–66; Vis. Scientist, CERN, 1967– (muon storage ring, tests of relativity); Vis. Sen. Res. Physicist, Yale Univ., 1984–92; Visiting Professor: Swiss Inst. of Nuclear Research, 1976–77; Univ. of Reading, 1982–86; Consultant, Centre Antoine Lacassagne, Nice, 1986–92. Rep. NZ at UN Conf. on Atomic Energy for Peaceful Purposes, 1955. Governor: Clifton Coll., to 1994; Welbeck Coll., 1970–82; Member Court: Univ. of Bath, 1974–82; Cranfield Inst. of Technology, 1989–93. Inventor: Anaconda, wave power converter, 2006; Ocean Energy Trawler, 2014. Hon. Mem., Instn of Royal Engineers. Hon. Fellow, TCD, 1986. Hughes Medal, Royal Soc., 1980. *Publications:* Elements of Pulse Circuits, 1955; Progress in Nuclear Techniques and Instrumentation, Vol. I, 1966, Vol. II, 1967, Vol. III, 1968; Catalysed Fusion (novel), 2012; scientific papers on nuclear physics, electronics, high energy particle physics, wave energy, cosmology. *Recreations:* gliding (FAI gold and diamond), ski-ing. *Address:* 8 chemin de Saint Pierre, 06620 Le Bar sur Loup, France. *T:* 0493424512. *E:* F.Farley@Soton.ac.uk.

FARLEY, Henry Edward, (Rob); Group Deputy Chief Executive, Royal Bank of Scotland Group, 1986–90; Director, Nationwide Building Society, 1990–97; *b* 28 Sept. 1930; *s* of late William and Frances Elizabeth Farley; *m* 1955, Audrey Joyce Shelvey (*d* 2012); one *s* one *d*. *Educ:* Harrow County Sch. for Boys. FCIB (FIB 1966). Entered National Bank, 1947; Head of UK Banking, 1978, Dir, 1981, Williams & Glyn's Bank; Chairman: Williams & Glyn's Bank (IOM) Ltd, 1973–76; Joint Credit Card Co. Ltd, 1982–84; Royal Bank of Scotland Gp Insce, 1988–90; Mem. Bd, Mastercard International Inc., 1982–84; Director: Royal Bank of Scotland Group plc, 1985–90; Royal Bank of Scotland, 1985–90 (Man. Dir, 1985–86); Charterhouse Japhet, 1985–86; Charterhouse Development, 1985–86; Charterhouse plc, 1986–90; Chm., Royscot Finance Gp, 1987–90; Dep. Chm., Supervisory Bd of CC Bank, Germany, 1989–90. Director: EFT-POS (UK) Ltd, 1986–88; A. T. Mays Gp, 1987–90; (Alternate) Citizens Financial Gp (USA), 1989–90; John Maunders Gp, 1989–99; Banque Rivaud, Paris, 1990–97; High Table Ltd, 1991–95; Davenham Gp, 1992–97. Mem. Develt Bd, Special Olympics, 1997–99. Member: Council, Inst. of Bankers, 1985–90; APACS

Council, 1983–90; Exec. Cttee, British Bankers Assoc., 1983–90. UMIST: Gov., 1990–2000; Vice-Chm. Council, 1994–2000; Chm., Students Assoc., 2000–02; Dir, UMIST Foundn, 1999–2000; Mem., Gen. Assembly, 2004–, and Mem., Nominations Cttee, Manchester Univ.; Mem. Bd, Manchester Federal Sch. of Business and Management, 1994–99. Sen. Vice-Pres., Knutsford RFC, 2004–. FRSA 1995. Liveryman: Marketors' Co., 1987– (Dir, Marketors' Hall Ltd, 1992–95); Guild of Internat. Bankers, 2005–. *Publications:* The Clearing Banks and Housing Finance, 1983; Competition and Deregulation: branch networks, 1984; The Role of Branches in a Changing Environment, 1985; Deregulation and the Clearing Banks, 1986; The Happy Cookers (poetry), 2003; Cheshire Sets and Matches (poetry), 2003; The Best of Ten (poetry), 2012. *Recreations:* all forms of rough sport, travel, modern literature. *Address:* Sylvan Lodge, Leycester Road, Knutsford, Cheshire WA16 8QR. *Clubs:* MCC; St James, Racquets (Manchester); Pitt (Chester).

FARLEY, Mary-Rose Christine, (Mrs R. D. Farley); *see* Bateman, M.-R. C.

FARLEY, Rob; *see* Farley, H. E.

FARMELO, Dr Graham Paul; author and consultant in science communication, since 2003; Adjunct Professor of Physics, Northeastern University, Boston, since 1990; Bye-Fellow, Churchill College, Cambridge, since 2010; *b* London, 18 May 1953; *s* of Cyril Albert John Farmelo and Joyce Alice Farmelo (*née* Puttock). *Educ:* Tubbenden Lane Primary Sch., Orpington; Cray Valley Tech. Sch., Sidcup; Univ. of Liverpool (BSc Mathematical Physics 1974; PhD Theoretical Physics 1977). Lectr in Physics, Open Univ., 1977–90; Hd, contemp. sci. exhibns and progs, Science Mus., London, 1990–2002. Has led internat. initiatives in sci. engagement in Europe and US; co-dir, internat. confs, incl. Sci. and Society: Closing the Gap (in collaboration with AAAS), 2007; has participated in strategic cttees, incl. Sci. and Technol. Facility Council Large Hadron Collider public engagement policy cttee, 2007–08; Chair, Internat. Rev. Panel on Communications and Engagement in Sci. Foundn Ireland, for Irish Govt, 2012. Senator James E. O'Neill Meml Lectr, Saginaw Valley State Univ., Michigan, 2014. Director's Visitor, Inst. for Advanced Study, Princeton Univ., 2014–15. Writer-in-residence, Kavli Inst., UCSB, 2015. Hon. Fellow, British Sci. Assoc., 2011. Kelvin Prize and Medal, Inst. of Physics, 2012. *Publications:* (ed with S. Bicknell) Visitor Studies in the 90s, 1993; (ed with J. Carding) Here and Now, 1996; (ed) It Must be Beautiful, 2003; (ed) Creating Connections: museums and the public understanding of research, 2004; The Strangest Man, 2007 (Costa Prize for Biography, Book of Year, Physics World, 2009); Churchill's Bomb, 2013; contrib. papers to specialist physics jls; articles and book reviews in mags and newspapers, incl. Nature and Scientific American. *Recreations:* books, theatre, art-house movies, music, exhibitions, walking, eating well, searching for the perfect espresso, not writing. *E:* graham@grahamfarmelo.com. *W:* www.grahamfarmelo.com, www.twitter.com/grahamfarmelo.

FARMER, family name of **Baron Farmer**.

FARMER, Baron *cr* 2014 (Life Peer), of Bishopsgate in the City of London; **Michael Stahel Farmer;** Founding Partner, RK Capital Management LLP, since 2004; *b* Dec. 1944; *m* Jennifer Dorothy Rochfort; one *s* two *d. Educ:* King Alfred's Grammar Sch., Wantage. Global Hd, Base Metals, Phibro Salomon, 1986–88; Man. Dir, The Metal and Commodity Co. Ltd, 1989–2002. Co-Treas., Cons. Party, 2012–. Trustee: Kingham Hill Trust, 2002–; The Cross Trust, 2008–. *Recreations:* military and political history, Biblical studies, running, cycling. *Club:* Royal Automobile.

FARMER, Bruce; *see* Farmer, E. B.

FARMER, Prof. David Malcolm, PhD; FRS 2006; FRSC; Dean and Professor of Oceanography, Graduate School of Oceanography, University of Rhode Island, 2001–11, now Dean and Professor Emeritus. *Educ:* McGill Univ. (MS 1969); Univ. of British Columbia (PhD 1972). FRSC 1993. Physical Oceanographer, Inst. of Ocean Scis, Sidney, BC, now Scientist Emeritus. Adjunct Prof., Sch. of Earth and Ocean Scis, Univ. of Victoria, BC. *Publications:* 113 articles in learned jls.

FARMER, Dr (Edwin) Bruce, CBE 1997; FREng; FIMMM; Chairman: Scottish & Southern Energy plc, 2000–05 (Deputy Chairman, 1999–2000); Southern Electric, 1998; *b* 18 Sept. 1936; *s* of Edwin Bruce Farmer and Doris Farmer; *m* 1962, Beryl Ann Griffiths; one *s* one *d. Educ:* King Edward's, Birmingham; Univ. of Birmingham (BSc, PhD). CEng 1994; FIMMM (FIM 1994); FREng (FEng 1997). Dir and Gen. Manager, Brico Metals, 1967–69; Man. Dir, Brico Engineering, 1970–76; Man. Dir, Wellworthy, 1976–81; The Morgan Crucible Co. plc: Dir, 1981–83; Chm., Thermal Ceramics Div., 1981–83; Man. Dir and Chief Exec., 1983–97; Chm., 1998–2003. Chairman: Allied Colloids Gp plc, 1996–98; Devro plc, 1998–2001; Bodycote Internat. plc, 1999–2002; Director: Scapa Gp plc, 1993–99; Foreign & Colonial Smaller Cos plc, 1999–2007 (Sen. Ind. Dir, 2005–07). Member: Council, CBI, 1990–2002; Adv. Bd, Imperial Coll. Management Sch., 1991–2003; Finance Cttee, Cancer Res. UK (formerly ICRF), 1997–2008; Court, Surrey Univ., 1998–2005. Pres., Inst. of Materials, 1999–2002 (Sen. Vice-Pres., 1997–99); Chm., Mgt Bd, 2002–04 (Platinum Medal, 2004), Chm., Communications Bd, 2006–, IMMM. CCMI (CIMgt 1984); FRSA 1995. Freeman, City of London, 1994; Liveryman, Scientific Instrument Makers' Co., 1995–. *Recreations:* music, cricket, hill walking. *Address:* Weston House, Bracken Close, Wonersh, Surrey GU5 0QS. *Club:* Athenæum.

FARMER, George Wallace; President, Immigration Appeal Tribunal, 1991–97 (Vice President, 1982–91); *b* 4 June 1929; *s* of George Lawrence Farmer and Blanche Amy (*née* Niccolls); *m* 1961, Patricia Mary Joyce (*d* 2012); three *d. Educ:* The Lodge, Barbados; Harrison Coll., Barbados. Called to the Bar, Middle Temple, 1950. Private practice, Barbados, 1950–52; Magistrate, Barbados, 1952–56; Resident Magistrate, Uganda, 1956–63, Sen. Resident Magistrate, 1963–64; Dir of Public Prosecutions, Uganda, 1964–65; attached to Cottle Catford & Co., Solicitors, Barbados, 1965–67; Legal Manager, Road Transport Industry Trng Bd, 1967–70; Adjudicator, Immigration Appeals, 1970–82. *Recreation:* enjoying the company of grandchildren. *Address:* 7 Coney Acre, West Dulwich, SE21 8LL.

FARMER, Ian Peter; Chief Executive Officer, Lonmin plc, 2008–12; *b* Petersfield, Hants, 25 March 1962; *s* of Brian John Farmer and Alice Kathleen Farmer; *m* 1994, Diane Chilangwa; three *s* one *d. Educ:* Springs Boys' High Sch.; Univ. of S Africa (BCompt Hons). CA S Africa. Audit Senior: Campbell, Bode, Brown & Stewart, 1980–84; Coopers & Lybrand, 1985–86; Gp Accountant and Treas., Lonmin plc, 1986–89; Financial Controller, Lonmin Zambia, 1990–95; Finance Dir, Lonmin Platinum, 1995–2000; Chief Strategic Officer, Lonmin plc, 2001–08. *Recreations:* family time, reading, travelling, Rugby spectator.

FARMER, Paul David Charles; Chief Executive, Mind, since 2006; *b* 8 Oct. 1966; *s* of David and Ann Farmer; *m* 1994, Claire Dwyer; two *s. Educ:* Oratory Sch., Reading; St Peter's Coll., Oxford (BA Modern Hist.). Communications Manager, Samaritans, 1994–97; Dir, Public Affairs, Rethink, 1997–2006. Chm., Mental Health Alliance, 2000–06. Mem., BBC Appeals Adv. Cttee, 2007–12. Chm., Disability Charities Consortium, 2009–14. Member: Catholic Bishops Mental Health Reference Gp, 2008–; Harrington Review on Disability Benefits, 2010–12; Ind. Commn on Mental Health and Policing, 2012–13; Bd, ACEVO, 2014– (Chm., 2015–). Trustee: Samaritans, 1998–2001; Directory of Social Change, 2000–10 (Chm., 2003–05); Mental Health Providers Forum, 2006–14; Lloyds Bank Foundn, 2014–. FRSA. Hon. DSc East London, 2012. Co-author, Realising Ambitions, DWP, 2009. *Publications:* contribs to jls on anti-discrimination and stigma. *Recreations:* cricket, Rugby, tennis, film, cookery, listening. *Address:* c/o Mind, 15–19 Broadway, Stratford, E15 4BQ. *T:* (020) 8215 2295. *E:* p.farmer@mind.org.uk.

FARMER, Peter John; Planning Director, Office of the Legal Services Complaints Commissioner, 2004–05; *b* 5 Nov. 1952; *s* of Alec and Norah Farmer; *m* 1986, Christine Ann Tetley. *Educ:* King Edward VI Sch., Southampton; Gonville and Caius College, Cambridge (Maths; MA); London Univ. (Cert. Psych.); Open Univ. (DipEcon 2007; BSc 2009). Joined HM Customs and Excise, 1975; HM Treasury, 1979; Lord Chancellor's Dept, 1981; Circuit Principal, Leeds, 1983; Asst Sec., 1987; Asst Public Trustee, 1988; Public Trustee and Accountant Gen. of Supreme Court, 1991; Circuit Administrator, NE Circuit, 1994–2002; Tribunal Appts Project Dir, LCD, 2002–03; Judicial Inf. and Planning Dir, Dept for Constitutional Affairs, 2003–04. Mem., Lord Chancellor's Adv. Cttee on Justices of the Peace for Leeds, 2005–11, for W Yorks, 2011–14 (Mem., sub-cttee for Leeds, 2011–14). Chm., Judicial Appts Panels, DCA, 2005–06; Panel Chm., Judicial Appts Commn, 2006–08. Consultant, Office of the Legal Services Complaints Comr, 2006–09. *Recreations:* English folk dancing, hill walking, choral music, photography (LRPS 2011).

FARMER, Sir Thomas, Kt 1997; CVO 2009; CBE 1990; FRSE; DL; Founder, Kwik-Fit, 1971; *b* 10 July 1940; *s* of John Farmer and Margaret (*née* Mackie); *m* 1966, Anne Drury Scott; one *s* one *d. Educ:* St Mary's Primary Sch., Edinburgh; Holy Cross Acad., Edinburgh. Chm. and Chief Exec., Kwik-Fit, 1984–2002. Chairman: Scottish BITC, 1990–2000; Investors in People Scotland, 1991–97; Mem. Bd, Scottish Enterprise, 1990–96. Chm., Bd of Trustees, Duke of Edinburgh Award, 2001–10. Chancellor, Queen Margaret Univ., Edinburgh, 2007–. FRSE 2009. DL Edinburgh, 1996. KCSG 1997. *Recreations:* tennis, swimming, ski-ing. *T:* (0131) 315 2830.

FARNELL, Graeme, FMA; Managing Director, Heritage Development Ltd, 1996–2008; Director: Heritage Business International, 2005–08; Heritage Development International, 2006–08; MuseumsEtc Ltd, since 2009; *b* 11 July 1947; *s* of Wilson Elliot Farnell and Mary Montgomerie Wishart Farnell (*née* Crichton); *m* 1969, Jennifer Gerda (*née* Huddlestone); one *s. Educ:* Loughborough Grammar Sch.; Edinburgh Univ. (MA); London Film Sch. (DipFilm Studies). FMA 1989; FSAScot 1976; MBIM. Asst Keeper, Mus. of East Anglian Life, 1973–76; Curator, Inverness Mus. and Art Gall., 1976–79; Dir, Scottish Museums Council, 1979–86; Dir Gen., Museums Assoc., 1986–89; Man. Dir, The Development (formerly Museum Development) Co. Ltd, 1989–94; Publishing Ed., IMS Publications, 1994–96; Publisher: New Heritage (formerly Heritage Development) magazine, 1996–2003; Heritage Business.net (formerly Heritage Insider, then Heritage Business) newsletter, 1998–2008; Heritage Retail mag., 1999–2003; Heritage Restoration mag., 2000–03; Heritage 365 mag., 2003–08. Director of films: Documentary, 1970; Jagger, 1971; Capital, 1972. *Publications:* (ed) The American Museum Experience, 1986; The Handbook of Grants, 1990, 2nd edn, 1993; (ed) The European Heritage Directory, 1998; (ed) New Museums in China, 2005; (ed) Museums of Ideas: commitment and conflict, 2011; (ed) The Photographer and the Collection, 2013; High Ground, 2013; contribs to Museums Jl, Internat. Jl of Mus. Management and Curatorship, Museum (Unesco), Industrial Soc. *Recreations:* baroque opera, contemporary music, photography.

FARNELL, John Bernard Patrick; writer and researcher on China-EU economic relations; Director, Coordination and International Affairs, Enterprise and Industry Directorate-General, European Commission, 2008–12 (Director, Competitiveness, 2006–07); *b* 24 Aug. 1948; *s* of James Farnell and Laura (*née* O'Connell); *m* 1976, Susan Mary Janus; two *s. Educ:* Downside Sch.; Christ's Coll., Cambridge (MA Hist.); London Sch. of Econs (MSc Econ). Economist, BEA, 1970–72; CBI, 1973–74; with European Commission, 1975–2012: Ext. Relns, 1975–77; Fisheries, 1977–82; Industry, 1982–93 (Internat. Questions Unit, 1982–87; Head: Standardisation and Certification Unit, 1987–93; Tech. Legislation Unit, 1993); Hd, Operation of Internal Mkt and Econ. Analysis Unit, Directorate-Gen. of Internal Mkt and Financial Services, 1993–97; Dir, Horizontal Measures and Markets, 1997–2001, Conservation Policy, 2001–06, Fisheries Directorate-General. Mem., Impact Assessment Bd, EC, 2008–12; Sen. Advr, EU-Asia Centre, Brussels, 2013–. EU Fellow, 2011–12, Academic Visitor, 2014–, St Antony's Coll., Oxford. *Publications:* Public and Private Britain, 1975; (with James Elles) In Search of a Common Fisheries Policy, 1984. *Recreations:* opera, fly-fishing, sailing. *Address:* 33 Rue du Châtelain, 1050 Brussels, Belgium.

FARNES, Richard Haworth; Music Director, Opera North, Leeds, 2004–July 2016; *b* Cuckfield, Sussex, 15 Jan. 1964; *s* of Alexander and Christine Farnes; *m* 2001, Juliet Welchman; two *s. Educ:* King's Coll. Sch., Cambridge; Eton Coll.; King's Coll., Cambridge (BA Music 1986). Freelance conductor, Glyndebourne, Scottish Opera, Royal Opera and ENO, 1988–. *Recreations:* earth sciences, astronomy, photography, walking, travel. *Address:* (until July 2016) c/o Opera North, Grand Theatre, 46 New Briggate, Leeds LS1 6NU. *T:* (0113) 243 9999, *Fax:* (0113) 244 0418; c/o Ingpen & Williams Ltd, 7 St George's Court, 131 Putney Bridge Road, SW15 2PA. *T:* (020) 8874 3222.

FARNHAM, 13th Baron *cr* 1756; **Simon Kenlis Maxwell;** Bt (NS) 1627; *b* 12 Dec. 1933; *s* of late Hon. Somerset Arthur Maxwell, MP and Angela Susan (*née* Roberts); *S* brother, 2001; *m* 1964, Karol Anne (*d* 2014), *d* of Maj.-Gen. George Erroll Prior-Palmer, CB, DSO; two *s* one *d* (of whom one *s* one *d* are twins). *Educ:* Eton. Late Lt, 10th Royal Hussars. *Heir: s* Hon. Robin Somerset Maxwell [*b* 15 Sept. 1965; *m* 1993, Tessa Shepherd; two *s* one *d*]. *Address:* The Dower House, Church Westcote, near Chipping Norton, Oxon OX7 6SF.

See also Viscountess Knollys.

FARNHAM, Diana, Lady; Diana Marion Maxwell, DCVO 2010 (CVO 1998); Lady of the Bedchamber to the Queen, since 1987; *b* London, 24 May 1931; *d* of Nigel Eric Murray Gunnis and Elizabeth Gunnis (*née* Morrison); *m* 1959, 12th Baron Farnham; two adopted *d. Educ:* Hatherop Castle Sch.; House of Citizenship. Vice-Pres., Dance Teachers' Benevolent Fund, 2012 (Trustee, 1989–2012); Trustee, British Kidney Patient Assoc., 2003–11; Patron, Friends of the Elderly, 1990–. *Address:* 3 Astell House, Astell Street, SW3 3RX.

FARNISH, Christine, (Mrs J. Hayes), CBE 2013; a Civil Service Commissioner, 2012–14; *b* 21 April 1950; *d* of Harry Farnish and Agnes Monica Farnish; *m* John Hayes; three *s* one *d. Educ:* Ipswich High Sch.; Manchester Univ. (BSc Botany and Geog. 1971); University Coll. London (MSc Conservation 1972). Asst Chief Exec., Cambridge CC, 1988–94; Consumer Dir, 1992–97, Actg Dep. Dir Gen., 1998, OFTEL; Consumer Dir, FSA, 1998–2002; Chief Exec., Nat. Assoc. of Pension Funds, 2002–06; Man. Dir, Public Policy, Barclays PLC, 2006–11. Mem. Council, ASA, 2002–08; non-exec. Dir, OFT, 2003–06; Director: Consumer Focus (formerly NCC), 2008–14 (Chm., 2010–14); ABTA, 2010–; Aggregate Industries, 2012–14; Brighton and Sussex Univ. Hosps NHS Trust, 2013–; Ofwat, 2014–; Payments Council, 2014–. Chm., Peer-to-Peer Finance Assoc., 2012–. Chm., Family and Parenting Inst., 2010–13. *Recreations:* singing, trekking, family. *Address:* Flat 3, 3 Palmeira Square, Hove, East Sussex BN3 2JA. *T:* (020) 7116 6094.

FARNSWORTH, Ian Ross; Director, Coutts & Co., 1992–97 (Deputy Chairman and Chief Executive, 1992–95); *b* 15 Feb. 1938; *s* of Frederick Sutcliffe and Winifred Ruby Bryan; *m* 1964, Rosalind Amanda Baker; one *s* one *d. Educ:* Nottingham High Sch. ACIB. Westminster Bank, later National Westminster Bank: joined 1954; seconded Nat. Bank of N America, 1979–80; Exec. Vice-Pres., NatWest N America, 1981–84; Asst Gen. Manager, NatWest, 1987–88; Dir, European Businesses, 1988–90; Gen. Manager, NatWest, 1990–91; Dep. Chm., Coutts & Co. AG, Zürich, 1991–94; Mem., Supervisory Bd, F. van Lanschot Bankiers, Holland, 1991–95. Chm., Willowbrite Ltd, 1997–2010; Dir, Finsbury Foods plc, 1997–2014.

Director: PEC Concerts Ltd, 1995–2000; New Sadler's Wells Ltd, 1996–2002; Gov., Sadler's Wells Foundn, 1995–2004. Mem., Develt Cttee, 1996–2008, Mem. Court, 2008–14, Univ. of Herts. Liveryman, Information Technologists' Co., 1994–2005. *Recreations:* music, golf. *Address:* 15 Dellcroft Way, Harpenden, Herts AL5 2NQ. *T:* (01582) 712518.

FARNWORTH, His Honour John David; a Circuit Judge, 1991–2008; *b* 20 June 1935; *s* of George Arthur Farnworth and Mary Lilian Farnworth; *m* 1964, Carol Gay Mallett; one *s* two *d*. *Educ:* Bedford Sch.; St Edmund Hall, Oxford (BA). Bigelow Teaching Fellow, Univ. of Chicago Law Sch., 1958–59. Admitted Solicitor, 1962; a Recorder, 1986–91. *Recreations:* golf, cricket, snooker, art galleries. *Clubs:* MCC; Bedfordshire Golf.

FARNWORTH, Judith Margaret; HM Diplomatic Service; Ambassador to Armenia, since 2015; *b* Sutton Coldfield, 25 April 1966; *d* of Roy Farnworth and Kathleen Mary Hulme. *Educ:* Univ. of Durham (BA Hons Russian 1988); Univ. of East Anglia (MA Internat. Relns 1990). Joined FCO, 1991; Sen. Res. Analyst, Res. and Analysis Dept, FCO, 1991–95; Second Sec., Political/Press Public Affairs, Kyiv, 1996–2000; Hd, Political Section, Prague, 2000–04; Deputy Head of Mission and Consul: Riga, 2005–08; Kyiv, 2008–12; Ambassador to the Kyrgyz Republic, 2012–15. *Address:* c/o Foreign and Commonwealth Office, King Charles Street, SW1A 2AH. *E:* judith.farnworth@fco.gov.uk.

FAROOKHI, Imtiaz; entrepreneur; Strategy Director, DragonGate, since 2012; *b* 17 Jan. 1951; *s* of Mumtaz and Anwar Farookhi; two *s* one *d*. *Educ:* King Alfred Sch.; Acton Tech. Coll.; Univ. of Kent at Canterbury; Birkbeck Coll., London Univ. FRICS 2011. Asst Chief Exec., Hackney LBC, 1983–88; Head of Co-ordination, Wakefield MDC, 1988–89; Dir of Policy and Admin, Southwark LBC, 1988–91; Chief Executive: Leicester CC, 1991–96; Nat. House-Building Council, 1997–2012. Member: Bd, Envmt Agency, 1995–97; BURA, 1998–2004; British Bd of Agrément, 1999–; LSC, 2001–04; CITB Construction Skills Council, 2004–; SEEDA, 2004–12; London Thames Gateway UDC, 2004–13; Chm., Vistage, 2013–14. Chm., Forum for Construction Skills, 2003–06. FRSA 1994. *Publications:* articles in jls. *Recreations:* cycling, family life. *Club:* QPR Supporters'.

FARQUHAR, Maj. Gen. Andrew Peter, CBE 2003 (MBE 1981); DL; Managing Director, UK, GardaWorld Consulting (UK) Ltd, since 2011; *b* Leeds, 1953; *s* of John and Elizabeth Farquhar; *m* 1981, Alison Jane Grey; three *s* one *d*. *Educ:* Pocklington Sch., Yorks; Sheffield Univ. (BEng Hons Mech. Engrg 1975); Army Staff Coll. (psc† 1985). Commnd Green Howards, 1975; MA to ACDS (I), 1986–88; Chief Instructor, RMA Sandhurst, 1990–92; CO, 1 Green Howards, 1994–96; MA to Adjt Gen., 1996–98; COS, HQ Infantry, 1998–2000; Commander: 15 (NE) Bde (York), 2000–02; Multinat. Div. (SW), Bosnia Herzegovina, 2002–03; COS to Comdr Regl Forces, 2003–04; Dep. Comdg Gen., Multi-Nat. Corps Iraq, 2004–05; GOC 5th Div., 2005–08. Man. Partner, Millbrook Partnership, 2008–10. Dep. Col, then Col, Green Howards, 2001–06; Dep. Col, Yorks Regt, 2006–11; Col, Royal Mercian and Lancastrian Yeomanry, 2008–14. Trustee, Green Howards Trust, 2001–; Chm., Adv. Bd, Nat. Meml Arboretum, 2011–. Vice Pres., Pocklington RFC, 2001–. FCMI 2008. Shrewsbury Drapers' Co., 2010–. DL Staffs, 2009. QCVS 1995. Officer, Legion of Merit (USA), 2005. *Recreations:* offshore sailing (Yachtmaster Offshore), slowly running marathons, shooting, carpentry, horology, classical music, watching cricket and Rugby. *Address:* GardaWorld Consulting (UK) Ltd, 2nd Floor, 23 Bruton Street, W1J 6QF. *Club:* MCC.

FARQUHAR, Charles Don Petrie, OBE 1999; JP; DL; engineer; *b* 4 Aug. 1937; *s* of late William Sandeman Farquhar and Annie Preston Young Farquhar; *m*; two *d*. *Educ:* Liff Road and St Michael's Primary Schs, Dundee; Stobswell Secondary Sch., Dundee. Served with Royal Engineers (Trng NCO); subseq. supervisory staff, plant engrg, NCR Ltd, Area Manager, Community Industry, Dundee/Fife, 1972–91. City Councillor, Dundee, 1965–74 (ex-Convener, Museums, Works and Housing Cttees); Mem., Dundee DC, 1974–96 (Chm., Leisure and Recreation Cttees, 1992–96); Lord Provost and Lord Lieutenant of City of Dundee, 1975–77; Mem., Dundee City Council, 1995–2008 (Chm., Leisure Services Cttee). Chairman: Dundee Dist Licensing Bd, Dundee Dist Licensing Cttee, 1984–93; Cttee for Employment of Disabled People (formerly Disabled Adv. Cttee), Tayside and Fife, 1979–94. JP Dundee, 1974; DL Dundee, 1978. *Recreations:* fresh-water angling, gardening, numismatics, do-it-yourself. *Address:* 2 Killin Avenue, Dundee DD3 6EB.

FARQUHAR, Prof. Graham Douglas, AO 2013; PhD; FRS 1995; FAA; Distinguished Professor, Australian National University, Canberra, since 2003; *b* 8 Dec. 1947. *Educ:* Australian Nat. Univ. (BSc 1968; PhD 1973); Queensland Univ. (BSc Hons Biophysics 1969). FAA 1988. Dept of Energy Plant Res. Lab., Michigan State Univ., 1973–76; Australian National University: Res. Fellow, 1976–80; Sen. Res. Fellow, 1980–; Fellow, 1980–83; Sen. Fellow, 1983–88; Prof. of Biology, 1988–2003; Research School of Biological Sciences, later Research School of Biology: Leader, Plant Envmtl Biology Gp, 1988–89; Envmtl Biology Gp, 1994–2009; Associate Dir, 2005–09; Lab. Leader, Plant Sci. Div., 2010–. *Publications:* (ed jtly) Stomatal Function, 1987; (ed jtly) Perspectives of Plant Carbon and Water Relations for Stable Isotopes, 1993; numerous research texts. *Address:* RN Robertson Building 46, Plant Science Division, Research School of Biology, Australian National University, GPO Box 475, Canberra, ACT 0200, Australia. *T:* (2) 61253743, *Fax:* (2) 61244919.

FARQUHAR, Margaret (Elizabeth), CBE 1999; JP; Lord Provost and Lord-Lieutenant of Aberdeen, 1996–99; *b* Aberdeen, 1930; *née* Burnett; *m* 1951, William Farquhar (*d* 1993); one *s* one *d*. *Educ:* Ruthrieston Secondary Sch., Aberdeen; Webster's Coll., Aberdeen. Clerical work: N of Scotland Coll. of Agric., 1947–48; Charles Michie, haulage contractor, 1948–51; Cordiners Sawmills, 1963–65; William Walker, haulage contractor, 1969–77. Member (Lab): Aberdeen DC, 1971–96 (Vice-Chm., 1994–96); Aberdeen CC, 1995–99. Mem., Planning Cttee, 1985–86, 1988–92, Aberdeen Council rep., 1992–99, COSLA. Dir, Grampian Enterprise, 1991–92. Member: Mgt Cttee, Aberdeen CAB, 1986–; Mgt Cttee, Northfield Community Centre, 1993–. Labour Party: Sec., Bridge of Don Br., 1980–81; Sec. and Chm., Cummings Pk Br., 1971–79; Chm., Aberdeen Women's Council, 1971–72. Hon. Pres., Grampian Girls' Bde, 1988–. Chm., Aberdeen Br., RNLI, 2003–. Chm., Friends of Gordon Highlanders Mus., 2001–. JP Aberdeen, 1972. Hon. LLD: Aberdeen, 1996; Robert Gordon, 1998. Paul Harris Fellowship, Rotary Internat., 1998. *Recreations:* working with the elderly and the young, bowling, driving, watching television.

FARQUHAR, Sir Michael (Fitzroy Henry), 7th Bt *cr* 1796, of Cadogan House, Middlesex; farmer; *b* 29 June 1938; *s* of Sir Peter Walter Farquhar, 6th Bt, DSO, OBE, and Elizabeth Evelyn (*d* 1983), *d* of Francis Cecil Albert Hurt; *S* father, 1986; *m* 1963, Veronica Geraldine Hornidge; two *s*. *Educ:* Eton; Royal Agricultural College. *Recreations:* fishing, shooting. *Heir:* *s* Charles Walter Fitzroy Farquhar [*b* 21 Feb. 1964; *m* 2004, Sarah Josephine Wynne-Williams; one *s* one *d*]. *Address:* Manor Farm, West Kington, Chippenham, Wilts SN14 7JG. *T:* (01249) 782671. *Club:* White's.

FARQUHAR, Stuart Alastair; His Honour Judge Farquhar; a Circuit Judge, since 2013; Judge of the Court of Protection, since 2013; *b* Weybridge, 4 June 1962; *s* of late Laurence Farquhar and of Grace Fairweather Farquhar; *m* 1991, Rebecca Jane Saunders; one *s* one *d*. *Educ:* Esher Grammar Sch.; Univ. of Manchester (LLB 1983); Inns of Court Sch. of Law. Called to the Bar, Inner Temple, 1985; in practice as barrister, 1985–2005; Dep. Dist Judge, 1999–2005; Dist Judge, 2005–13; Recorder, 2009–13. *Recreations:* supporting AFC Wimbledon, walking my dog in the rain, preferably past a real ale pub. *Address:* Brighton Family Court, 1 Edward Street, Brighton BN2 0JD. *T:* (01273) 811333.

FARQUHARSON of Invercauld, Captain Alwyne Arthur Compton, MC 1944; JP; Head of Clan Farquharson; *b* 1 May 1919; *er s* of late Major Edward Robert Francis Compton, JP, DL, Newby Hall, Ripon, and Torloisk, Isle of Mull, and Sylvia, *y d* of A. H. Farquharson; recognised by Lord Lyon King of Arms as Laird of Invercauld (16th Baron of Invercauld *S* aunt 1941), also as Chief of name of Farquharson and Head of Clan, since 1949; assumed (surname) Compton as a third forename and assumed surname of Farquharson of Invercauld, by warrant granted in Lyon Court, Edinburgh, 1949; *m* 1st, 1949, Frances Strickland Lovell (*d* 1991), *d* of Robert Pollard Oldham, Seattle, Washington, USA; 2nd, 1993, Patricia Gabrielle Estelle Parry de Winton, *d* of Henry Norman Simms-Adams, Brancaster Hall, Norfolk. *Educ:* Eton; Magdalen Coll., Oxford. Joined Royal Scots Greys, 1940. Served War, 1940–45, Palestine, N Africa, Italy, France (wounded); Captain 1943. County Councillor, Aberdeenshire, 1949–75, JP 1951. *Address:* Valley Farm, Brancaster Staithe, King's Lynn, Norfolk PE31 8DB.

FARQUHARSON, Sir Angus (Durie Miller), KCVO 2010; OBE 1995; Lord-Lieutenant of Aberdeenshire, 1998–2010 (Vice Lord-Lieutenant, 1987–98); *b* 27 March 1935; *s* of Dr Hugo Miller and Elsie (*née* Duthie); adopted surname of Farquharson, 1961; *m* 1961, Alison Mary Farquharson of Finzean, *o d* of W. M. Farquharson-Lang, CBE, 14th Laird of Finzean; two *s* one *d*. *Educ:* Glenalmond; Downing Coll., Cambridge (BA 1956; MA). Factor, farmer, forester, chartered surveyor. Member: Council, Scottish Landowners Fedn, 1980–88; Regl Adv. Cttee, Forestry Commn, 1980–94 (Chm., North Conservancy, 1993–94); Red Deer Commn, 1986–92; Nature Conservancy Cttee for Scotland, 1986–91; SNH NE Cttee, 1992–94. Vice Pres., Clan Farquharson Assoc., 2007–. Elder, 1969–, and Gen. Trustee, 1994–2006, Church of Scotland. Hon. Pres., Deeside (formerly Kincardine Deeside) Scouts, 1985. Director: Lathallan Sch., 1982–98; Scottish Traditional Skills Trng Centre, 2006–11. Chm., Finzean Sch. of Piping, 2011–. Aberdeenshire: DL 1984; JP 1998. CStJ 2009 (OStJ 2002). *Publications:* Finzean - The Fair Place, 2008. *Recreations:* gardening, walking, local history. *Address:* Glenferrick Lodge, Finzean, Banchory, Aberdeenshire AB31 6NG. *T:* (01330) 850229. *Club:* New (Edinburgh).

FARQUHARSON, Very Rev. Hunter Buchanan; Provost, St Ninian's Cathedral, Perth, since 1999; *b* 19 July 1958; *s* of Cameron Bruce Farquharson and Thelma Alice Buchanan Farquharson. *Educ:* Birmingham Sch. of Speech (ALAM, LLAM); Edinburgh Theol Coll. (General Ministerial Exams; Luscombe Scholar, 1989). Deacon 1988, priest 1989; Curate, West Fife Team, 1988–91; Rector, St Luke's, Glenrothes, 1991–97; Leader of Central Fife Team, 1995–97; Rector, Holy Trinity, Dunfermline and Leader of West Fife Team, 1997–99. Chm., Perth and Kinross Assoc. of Voluntary Services, 2000–08 (Advr to Bd, 2008–). Chm., Scottish Flat-Coated Retriever Club, 2005–11 (Vice-Chm., 2002–05). Dir, 2005–10, Vice-Chm., 2007–10, Chm., 2010–11, Ochil Tower Sch. (Camphill), Auchterarder. *Recreations:* showing and breeding flat-coated retrievers and Toulouse Geese, fishing, hill-walking. *Address:* Upper Greenside, by Abernethy, Perthshire KY14 6EL. *T:* (01738) 850987. *E:* huntfar@gmail.com. *Clubs:* Scottish Arts (Edinburgh); Flat-coated Retriever Society; Scottish Kennel (Edinburgh).

FARQUHARSON, Jonathan, CBE 1997; Charity Commissioner, 1985–96; *b* 27 Dec. 1937; *s* of Alan George Farquharson and Winifred Mary Farquharson (*née* Wilson); *m* 1963, Maureen Elsie Bright; two *d*. *Educ:* St Albans School; Manchester Univ. (LLB). Solicitor, 1962; with D. Herbert, Banbury, 1962–64; Charity Commission, 1964–96. FRSA. *Recreations:* geology, photography, reading, record collecting, gardening. *Address:* 30 Ennerdale Road, Formby, Merseyside L37 2EA. *T:* (01704) 871820.

FARQUHARSON, Paul Hiram, QPM; High Commissioner of the Bahamas to the United Kingdom, and Ambassador to the European Union, Belgium, France, Germany and Italy, 2008–12; *b* 10 Jan. 1949; *s* of late Ural Farquharson and Martha Deveaux; *m* 1969, Sharon Major; one *s* two *d*. *Educ:* Univ. of Louisiana (BAppSci); Univ. of Cambridge (Dip. Applied Criminol. and Police Studies); Atlanta Univ., Georgia (Cert. Criminal Justice, Admin and Principles of Mgt); Police Staff Coll., Bramshill (Strategic Comd Course; Overseas Comd Course). Enlisted Royal Bahamas Police Force, 1966: Corporal, 1971; Sergeant, 1974; Inspector, 1981; Chief Inspector, 1985; Asst Superintendent, 1988; Chief Superintendent, 1994; Asst Comr, 1998; Actg Comr of Police, 2000; Comr of Police, 2001–08. Aide-de-Camp: to Gov. Gen. of the Bahamas, 1984–88; to Rt Hon. Dr Robert Runcie, 1984–88; to Robert Mugabe, 1989; to HRH Duke of Edinburgh, 1993. Pres., Assoc. of Caribbean Comrs of Police, 2005; International Association of Chiefs of Police: Exec. Mem.; Mem., Firearms Cttee; Regl Chm. for Caribbean and Central America; Mem., Internat. Assoc. of Police Community Relns Officers. Mem., Bahamas Film and TV Commn. Salvation Army: Mem., Exec. Bd; Mem., Adv. Bd, Bahamas Div.

FARQUHARSON-ROBERTS, Surgeon Rear Adm. Michael Atholl, CBE 2001; FRCS; Medical Director General (Navy), 2003–07; Associate Research Fellow, National Museum of the Royal Navy, since 2014; *b* 23 Sept. 1947; *s* of Rev. Donald Arthur Farquharson-Roberts (Captain, RM) and Violet Farquharson-Roberts (*née* Crooks); *m* 1974, Jean Neilsen (*née* Harding); three *s* three *d*. *Educ:* Dorking County Grammar Sch.; Westminster Hosp. Sch. of Medicine (MB BS); RCDS/KCL (MA 2002); Exeter Univ. (PhD Maritime Hist. 2013). FRCS 1976. Orthopaedic trng, Nuffield Orthopaedic Centre, Oxford, Addenbrooke's Hosp., Cambridge and Royal Nat. Orthopaedic Hosp.; Consultant Orthopaedic Surgeon, Royal Hosp. Haslar, 1983–84 and 1986–2000; Principal Med. Officer, HMS Illustrious, 1985–86; rcds, 2001; Change Manager, Defence Med. Trng Orgn, 2001–02; Dir Med. Ops (Navy), 2002–03. Defence Consultant Advr in Orthopaedics, 1996–2000; Mem., Intercollegiate Specialist Adv. Cttee in Orthopaedics, 1996–2000. QHS 1997–2007. Gov., Royal Star and Garter Homes, 2003–; Trustee, Help for Heroes, 2007–08. Freeman: Apothecaries' Soc.; City of London, 2011. OStJ 2002. Gulf War Medal, 1991. *Publications:* A History of the Royal Navy: World War I, 2014; From War to War: the executive branch of the Royal Navy 1918–1939, 2015; articles in learned jls incl. Jl of Bone and Joint Surgery, BMJ and Jl of RUSI. *Recreations:* golf (badly), sailing, ship modelling. *Address:* 45 Bury Road, Gosport, Hants PO12 3UE. *E:* mfr@globalnet.co.uk. *Clubs:* Army and Navy; Hornet Sailing.

FARR, Clarissa Mary; High Mistress, St Paul's Girls' School, since 2006; *b* 30 June 1958; *d* of late Alan Farr and Wendy Farr; *m* 1993, John Goodbody; one *s* one *d*. *Educ:* Bruton Sch. for Girls; Exeter Univ. (BA Hons Eng. Lit., MA); Bristol Univ. (PGCE). Teacher: Farnborough Sixth Form Coll., 1981–83; Filton High Sch., 1983–86; Head of Sixth Form, Shatin Coll., Hong Kong, 1986–89; Sen. Mistress, Leicester GS, 1990–92; Dep. Head, 1992–96, Principal, 1996–2006, Queenswood Sch., Hatfield. Chm., Boarding Schs' Assoc., 2001–02; Pres., GSA, 2005. Trustee, African Gifted Foundn, 2014–. Gov., Royal Ballet Sch., 2010–. Fellow, Winchester Coll., 2013. *Recreations:* running, literature, theatre. *Address:* St Paul's Girls' School, Brook Green, W6 7BS. *T:* (020) 7603 2288.

FARR, David Charles; playwright; Associate Director, Royal Shakespeare Company, since 2009; *b* 29 Oct. 1969; *s* of Martin and Maureen Farr; *m* 2000, Anne Siddons; two *d*. *Educ:* Trinity Hall, Cambridge (BA double 1st cl. Hons (English) 1991). Associate Dir, Gate Th., London, and freelance Dir, Almeida Opera, 1991–95; Artistic Director: Gate Th., 1995–98; (Jt) Bristol Old Vic, 2003–05; Lyric Th., Hammersmith, 2005–08. Director: Coriolanus, 2002, Julius Caesar, 2004, The Winter's Tale, 2009 and 2010, King Lear, 2010, The Homecoming, 2011, Twelfth Night, The Tempest, 2012, Hamlet, 2013, RSC; A Midsummer Night's Dream, 2003 (TMA Award for Best Dir), (also adapted) The Odyssey, 2005, Bristol Old Vic; writer/director: The Nativity, Young Vic, 1999; Crime and Punishment in Dalston, Arcola Th. and radio, 2002; Night of the Soul, RSC, 2002; The UN

Inspector, NT, 2005; dir/adapter, Tamburlaine, Barbican/Young Vic, 2005; writer, The Heart of Robin Hood, RSC, 2011. *Publications: plays:* Elton John's Glasses, 1998 (Writers' Guild Best Play); The Nativity, 1999; The Danny Crowe Show, 2001; Night of the Soul, 2001; Plays 1, 2005. *Recreations:* guitar, cinema, football, walking, Shamanism. *Address:* c/o Curtis Brown, 5th Floor, Haymarket House, 28-29 Haymarket, SW1Y 4SP. *Club:* Anorak.

FARR, Jennifer Margaret, MBE 2003; Vice Lord-Lieutenant of Nottinghamshire, 1999–2008; *b* 20 July 1933; *d* of late Charles Percival Holliday and Vera Margaret Emily (*née* Burchell); *m* 1956, Sydney Hordern Farr (*d* 1981); two *s* one *d*. *Educ:* Nottingham Girls' High Sch.; Middlesex Hosp.; Royal Victoria Hosp., Newcastle upon Tyne. Physiotherapist, Nottingham City Hosp., 1954–56. National Society for Prevention of Cruelty to Children: Mem., Nottingham & Dist Cttee, 1959–; Nat. Council Mem., 1973–94; a Nat. Vice-Pres., 1994–; Member: Notts Centenary Appeal, 1983–85; Midlands Regions Bd, 2003–07; Chairman: Nottingham Br., 1983–98 (Pres., 1998–); Notts Full Stop Appeal, 1999–2004; Pres., Child's Voice Appeal, E Midlands, 2009–11. Pres., League of Friends, Queen's Med. Centre, 1999–2012. Member: Nottingham Convent Council, 1992–98; Southwell 2000 Appeal, 1992–96; Develt Bd, Nottingham Trent Univ., 2008–; Cttee, Motor Neurone Disease Appeal for Specialised Wheelchairs, 2010–12. Trustee, Mary Potter Convent Hosp. Trust, 1998–2014. Master Patron, Notts, Public Catalogue Foundn, 2007–09. Pres., Newark and Notts Agricl Soc., 2003 (Hon. Mem. Council, 2004). Gov., Nottingham High Sch. for Girls, 2001–10. Pres., Thurgarton Cricket Club, 1981–99. JP Notts, 1979–89; DL 1993, High Sheriff 1998–99, Notts. Hon. DLitt, Nottingham Trent, 2011. *Recreations:* bridge, gardening, music, sports, theatre, family life. *Address:* Lanesmeet, Epperstone, Notts NG14 6AU. *T:* (0115) 966 4584. *Club:* Sloane.

FARR, Susan Jane; Executive Director, Chime Communications plc, since 2003; *b* Yorks, 29 Feb. 1956; *d* of Derek Fairburn and Margaret, (Peggy), Fairburn; *m* 1st, 1979, Richard Peter Farr (marr. diss. 2002); 2nd, 2009, Anthony Christopher Mair. *Educ:* Sheffield High Sch. for Girls; Univ. of Reading (BA Hons Politics). Grad. trainee, Northern Foods plc, 1977–79; Mktg Consultant, KAE and Mintel, 1979–84; Account Director: Dorlands, 1984–86; CDP, 1986–87; WCRS, 1987–89; Dir, Corporate Communications, Thames TV plc, 1989–91; Mktg Dir, UK Gold, 1991–92; Director of Marketing: BBC Radio, 1993–95; BBC, 1995–2000; Chm., Golin Harris, 2000–02; Dir, Corporate Affairs, Vauxhall, 2002–03. Non-executive Director: New Look plc, 1994–96; Motivcom plc, 2008–; Dairy Crest plc, 2011–; Millennium and Copthorne Hotels plc, 2013–; Accsys, 2014–; British American Tobacco, 2015–. Trustee, Historic Royal Palaces, 2007–13. Chm., Mktg Soc., 1990–92; Mem., Mktg Gp of GB, 1993– (Chm., 1999–2001). Hon. DBA Bedfordshire, 2010. *Recreations:* horse riding, travelling, reading, enjoying life. *Address:* E1, Montevetro, 100 Battersea Church Road, SW11 3YL; Chime Communications plc, 6th Floor Southside, 105 Victoria Street, SW1E 6QT. *E:* sfarr@chimeplc.com.

FARRAN, Rt Rev. Brian George; Bishop of Newcastle, NSW, 2005–12; *b* 15 Dec. 1944; *s* of George Farran and Dorothy Barnes; *m* 1971, Robin Jeanne Marsden; one *s* two *d*. *Educ:* ANU (BA); St John's Theol Coll., Morpeth (ThL); Deakin Univ. (BLitt Hons); Melbourne Coll. of Divinity (DMin Studies 2005). Ordained deacon, 1967, priest, 1968; Curate: St Phillips, O'Connor, 1968; St Alban's, Griffith, 1969–71; Rector: Ch of the Epiphany, Lake Cargelligo, 1972–75; St Barnabas, N Rockhampton, 1975–79; St Saviour's, Gladstone, 1979–82; Dean of St Paul's Cathedral, Rockhampton, Queensland, 1983–89; Regl Dir, Australian Bd of Missions, Province of Victoria, 1989–92; an Asst Bp of Perth, WA, 1992–2005 (Bp of Goldfields Region, 1992–98, of Northern Region, 1998–2005). Vice-Chm., Gen. Bd of Religious Educn, Anglican Church of Australia, Vic, 1984–2000. Chm., Commn on Ministry, 2001–; Mem., Standing Cttee, Gen. Synod, 1998–. Chm. Council, Peter Moyes Anglican Community Sch., Mindarie, Perth, WA, 2000–; President: Bishop Tyrrell Anglican Coll., 2005–12; Lakes Grammar, 2005–12; Manning Valley Anglican Coll., 2005–12; Scone Grammar Sch., 2005–12. Fellow, Guildford Grammar Sch., Guildford, Perth, WA, 2001. *Recreations:* gardening, music, films, reading. *Address:* 4 Leicester Close, Raworth, NSW 2321, Australia.

FARRANCE, Roger Arthur, CBE 1988; Chief Executive, Electricity Association, 1990–93; Chairman: Electricity Association Services Ltd, 1991–93; Electricity Association Technology Ltd, 1991–93; *b* 10 Nov. 1933; *s* of Ernest Thomas Farrance and Alexandra Hilda May (*née* Finch); *m* 1956, Kathleen Sheila (*née* Owen); one *d*. *Educ:* Trinity School of John Whitgift, Croydon; London School of Economics (BScEcon). CCIPD; FIET (FIEE 2002). HM Inspector of Factories, Manchester, Doncaster and Walsall, 1956–64; Asst Sec., West of England Engineering Employers' Assoc., Bristol, 1964–67; Industrial Relations and Personnel Manager, Foster Wheeler John Brown Boilers Ltd, 1967–68; Dep. Director, Coventry and District Engineering Employers' Assoc., also Coventry Management Trng Centre, 1968–75; Electricity Council: Dep. Industrial Relations Adviser (Negotiating), 1975–76; Industrial Relations Adviser, 1976–79; Mem., 1979–88; Dep. Chm., 1989–90. Chm., Power Aid Logistics, 1993–94. Dir, Caswell Bay Court Mgt Co. Ltd, 2000–05 (Chm., 2002–05). Member Council: ACAS, 1983–89; CBI, 1983–93 (Chm., Health and Safety Policy Cttee, 1990–93); Mem., Directing Cttee, Union Internationale des Producteurs et Distributeurs d'Energie Electrique, 1991–94 (Chm., Human Factors Cttee, 1991–94). President: IPM, 1991–93; Electricity Supply Industry Ambulance Centre, St John's Amb. Assoc., 1979–93; St John's 210 (London Electricity) Combined Div., 1989–94. Chairman: Devonshire House Management Trustees, 1989–94; Management Bd, Electrical and Electronics Industry Benevolent Assoc., 1987–93. Councillor (C), London Borough of Merton, 1994–98. Chm. Govs, Pentyrch Primary Sch., 2002–06. Freeman, City of London, 1985; Liveryman, Basketmakers' Co., 1986–98. FRSA 1985. OStJ 1983. *Recreations:* painting, woodwork, music, walking. *Address:* The Rise, Heol-y-Parc, Pentyrch, Cardiff CF15 9NB.

FARRAND, Julian Thomas; legal editor and writer; *b* 13 Aug. 1935; *s* of J. and E. A. Farrand; *m* 1st, 1957, Winifred Joan Charles (marr. diss. 1992); one *s* two *d*; 2nd, 1992, Brenda Marjorie Hoggett (*see* Baroness Hale of Richmond). *Educ:* Haberdashers' Aske's Sch.; University Coll. London (LLB 1957, LLD 1966). Admitted Solicitor, 1960. Asst Lectr, then Lectr, KCL, 1960–63; Lectr, Sheffield Univ., 1963–65; Reader in Law, QMC, 1965–68; Prof. of Law, 1968–88, Dean of Faculty of Law, 1970–72, 1976–78, Manchester Univ. Visiting Professor: UCL, 1990–2001; London Guildhall, subseq. London Metropolitan Univ., 2001–06. A Law Comr, 1984–88; Insce Ombudsman, 1989–94; Pensions Ombudsman, 1994–2001. Chairman: Gtr Manchester and Lancs Area, Rent Assessment Panel, 1973–84 (Vice-Pres., 1977–84); Supplementary Benefit Appeals Tribunal, 1977–80; Nat. Insce Local Tribunal, 1980–83; Social Security Appeal Tribunal, 1983–88; Leasehold Valuation Tribunals and RACs for London Area, Rent Assessment Panel, 1984–2010; Govt Conveyancing Cttee, 1984–85; Disciplinary Sub-Cttee, Banking Code Standards Bd, 2001–05; Adjudicator, Ind. Cttee for Supervision of Standards of Telephone Inf. Services, subseq. PhonepayPlus, 2001–08. Chm., Pensions Compensation Bd, 1996–2001; Mem. Adv. Cttee, English Longitudinal Study of Ageing, 2001–05. Non-exec. Dir, First Title plc, 1996–2005 (Consultant, 2010–11). Mem., ADR Chambers (UK) Ltd, 2000–14. Mem., Consumer Policy Adv. Council, Brunel Univ., 2001–05. Hon. Prof. of Law, Essex Univ., 2000–12. FCIArb 1994. Hon. QC 1994. Hon. LLD Sheffield, 1990. Editor: Emmet & Farrand on Title, 1967–; Conveyancer and Property Lawyer, 1974–84. *Publications:* Contract and Conveyance, 1963–64, 4th edn 1983; (ed) Wolstenholme and Cherry, Conveyancing Statutes, 13th edn (vols 1–6) 1972, Consultant Ed., revd edn of vol. 6 as Wolstenholme and Cherry's Land Registration Act 2002, 2004; The Rent Acts and Regulations, 1978, 2nd edn (with A. Arden) 1981; (novel) Love at all Risks, 2001. *Recreations:* chess, bridge, wine, fiction. *Address:* Sandford House, Easby, Richmond, N Yorks DL10 7EW.

FARRANT, Graham Barry; Chief Executive and Chief Land Registrar, Land Registry, since 2015; *b* London, 7 June 1960; *s* of John Farrant and Barbara Farrant; *m* 1997, Linda Lillis; four *d*. *Educ:* Thames Poly. (BSc Hons); Brunel Univ., London (MSc). Student Envmtl Health Officer, 1978–82, Envmtl Health Officer, 1982–85, Westminster CC; Asst Principal Envmtl Health Officer, RBK&C, 1985–86; Asst Divl Dir of Housing, Westminster CC, 1986–90; Birmingham City Council: Asst Dir, 1990–94; Chief Exec., City Challenge, 1994–97; Dir of Housing, 1997–2000; Chief Executive: London Bor. of Barking and Dagenham, 2000–04; Leisure Connection Ltd, 2004–09; pmpgenesis, 2009–10; Thurrock Council, 2010–15; London Bor. of Barking and Dagenham, 2012–14. *Recreations:* hockey, tennis, angling. *Address:* Land Registry, Trafalgar House, Bedford Park, Croydon CR0 2AQ. *E:* graham.farrant@landregistry.gsi.gov.uk.

FARRAR, Catherine; *see* Finnegan, R. H.

FARRAR, Dr Jeremy James, OBE 2005; FMedSci; FRS 2015; Director, Wellcome Trust, since 2013; *b* Singapore, 1 Sept. 1961; *s* of Eric Farrar and Anne Farrar (*née* Melton); *m* 1998, Christiane Dolecek; two *s* one *d*. *Educ:* University Coll. London (BSc; MB BS); New Coll., Oxford (DPhil). Dir, Oxford Univ. Clin. Res. Unit, Hosp. for Tropical Diseases, Ho Chi Minh City, Viet Nam, 1996–2013; Prof. of Tropical Medicine and Global Health, Univ. of Oxford, 2000–13. Adv. roles on several WHO cttees. Co-Founder and Chm., Farrar Foundn, 2011–. FMedSci 2007. Ho Chi Minh City Medal, 2004; Frederick Murgatroyd Prize for Tropical Medicine, RCP, 2006; Bailey Ashford Award, Amer. Soc. for Tropical Medicine and Hygiene, 2006. Meml Medal (Viet Nam), 2013. *Publications:* 500 scientific papers on infectious diseases, global health and emerging infections. *Recreations:* all sports, walking in the Alps. *Address:* Wellcome Trust, 215 Euston Road, NW1 2BE. *T:* (020) 7611 8888.

FARRAR, Mark Jonathan, FCA; Chief Executive, Association of Accounting Technicians, since 2014; *b* 14 Aug. 1961; *s* of Ronald and late Doreen Farrar; *m* 2005, Francesca Ann Beckerleg; one *s* one *d*, and two step *s*. *Educ:* Univ. of Wales, Swansea (BSc Hons). FCA 1988. Finance Dir, Corporate and Instns Gp, Barclays Bank, 1992–94; Asst Dir of Finance, Allied Dunbar, 1994–95; Hd, Planning and Analysis, Norwich Union, 1995–2000; Finance and Resources Dir, 2000–04, Chief Exec., 2004–07, CEFAS; Corporate Services Dir, 2007–08, Chief Exec., 2008–13, ConstructionSkills. Mem., Adv. Bd, Skills Funding Agency, 2011–. Trustee, BRE, 2009–13. Mem., ACT. *Recreation:* sailing (RYA Yachtmaster: Ocean). *Address:* Association of Accounting Technicians, 40 Aldersgate Street, EC1A 4HY. *E:* mark.farrar@aat.org.uk.

FARRAR, Michael, CBE 2005; Chief Executive, NHS Confederation, 2011–13; *b* Rochdale, 31 July 1960; *s* of Jack and Betty Farrar; partner, Rosamond Roughton; one *s* three *d*. *Educ:* Bury Grammar Sch.; Nottingham Univ. (BA Hons Geog. 1981); Leeds Univ. (Postgrad. Dip. Health Educn 1985). Middle and sen. mgt appts, NHS, 1982–98; Hd of Primary Care, DoH, 1998–2000; Chief Executive Officer: Tees HA, 2000–02; S Yorks Strategic HA, 2002–05; W Yorks Strategic HA, 2005–06; NW Strategic HA, 2006–11. Director: York Health Econs Consortium, 2000–; Unique Health Solutions, 2012–13. Chm., Strategic HAs CEO Gp (NHS), 2002–09. Mem. Bd, Sport England, 2005–13 (Interim Chm., 2008–09). Hon. FRCGP 2009. Hon. Fellow, Univ. of Central Lancs, 2011. *Recreations:* all sports, films, family life.

FARRAR-HOCKLEY, Maj.-Gen. (Charles) Dair, MC 1982; Senior Fellow, Institute for Statecraft, since 2013; Director General (formerly Secretary General), Chartered Institute of Arbitrators, 1999–2006; *b* 2 Dec. 1946; *s* of Gen. Sir Anthony Farrar-Hockley, GBE, KCB, DSO, MC and Margaret Bernadette (*née* Wells); *m* 1969, Vicki King; two *s* one *d*. *Educ:* Exeter Sch. Commissioned Parachute Regt, 1967; Staff Coll., 1978–79; BM, Berlin, 1979–81; Co. Comdr, 2nd Para Bn, 1982, incl. Falkland Islands campaign; MA to Sec. to Chiefs of Staff Cttee, SHAPE, 1983; Directing Staff, Staff Coll., 1984; CO 3rd Para Bn, 1984–86; Special Briefer to COS, SHAPE, 1987; Higher Command and Staff Course, and Service Fellowship, KCL, 1988; Comdr 19 Inf. Bde, 1989–91; RCDS, 1992; Comdr Inf. Training, 1993–95; British Liaison Officer to Czech Chief of Defence, 1995–96; GOC 2nd Div., 1996–99. Consultant in commercial dispute resolution, 2006–15. Trustee: Airborne Forces Museum, 1993–98 (Chm., 1998–2008); Airborne Forces Security Fund, 1998–2014; Chm., Appeal Bd, Airborne Assault, 2004–09; Patron, Second World War Experience Centre, 1999–. Special Comr, Duke of York's Royal Mil. Sch., 2005–10. Trustee, Holy Trinity Monastery, 2012–. FCMI (FIMgt 1999); MCIArb 1999. Freeman, City of London, 1991. *Publications:* articles on causes and effects of human migration. *Recreations:* cricket, wine, photography, supporting Arsenal Football Club. *Address:* c/o Personal Banking Office, National Westminster Bank, Farnborough, Hants GU14 7YU. *Clubs:* Moulsford Cricket (Pres., 2007–); Travellers' Hockey.

FARRELL, David Anthony; QC 2000; **His Honour Judge Farrell;** a Circuit Judge, since 2011; *b* 27 May 1956; *s* of Joseph Anthony Farrell and Valerie Mabel Farrell; *m* 1981, Sandra Nicole Hibble; four *s* one *d*. *Educ:* Ashby-de-la-Zouch Grammar Sch.; Manchester Univ. (LLB Hons 1977). Called to the Bar, Inner Temple, 1978; Asst Recorder, 1996–2000; Recorder, 2000–11. *Recreations:* tennis, sailing, walking, music. *Address:* Luton Crown Court, 7 George Street, Luton, Beds LU1 2AA.

FARRELL, James Aloysius; QC (Scot.) 2013; Sheriff of Lothian and Borders at Edinburgh, 1986–2009; *b* 14 May 1943; *s* of James Stoddart Farrell and Harriet Louise McDonnell; *m* 1st, 1967, Jacqueline Allen (marr. diss.); two *d*; 2nd, 1996, Patricia McLaren. *Educ:* St Aloysius College; Glasgow University (MA); Dundee University (LLB). Admitted to Faculty of Advocates, 1974; Advocate-Depute, 1979–83; Sheriff: Glasgow and Strathkelvin, 1984; S Strathclyde, Dumfries and Galloway, 1985; Temporary Sheriff Principal: Glasgow and Strathkelvin, 2010; Tayside, Central and Fife, 2010, 2011; S Strathclyde, Dumfries and Galloway, 2012, 2013; Temp. High Court Judge, 2012, 2013. *Recreations:* sailing, hillwalking, cycling. *Address:* 8B Merchiston Park, Edinburgh EH10 4PN. *Club:* New (Edinburgh).

FARRELL, Michael Arthur; *b* 27 April 1933; *s* of Herbert and Marjorie Farrell; *m* 1st, 1957, Myra Shilton (*d* 1973); two *d*; 2nd, 1976, Beryl Browne (*d* 2011). *Educ:* Beverley Grammar Sch., Yorks; Holly Lodge Grammar Sch., Birmingham. Design Draughtsman, 1949–51; Nat. Service, RASC, 1951–53; Planning Engineer, 1953–61; Representative, 1961–74; Sales Manager, Lillywhites Cantabrian, 1974–80; Sales Executive, En-Tout-Cas, 1980–82; Gen. Sec., AAA, subseq. British Athletic Fedn, 1982–91; Export Sales Dir, Cantabrian Athletics Ltd, 1992–93; consultant, 1994–96; restaurateur, 1996–99. Mem., South Cams DC, 1994–96. Fifth position, 800m final (track and field), 1956 Olympics. *Recreations:* painting, walking, cycling.

FARRELL, Prof. Paul James, PhD; FMedSci; Professor of Tumour Virology, Imperial College, London, since 1994; *b* 10 July 1953; *s* of James Patrick Farrell and Audrey Winifred Farrell; *m* 1977, Diana Elizabeth Hamilton Kirby; one *s* one *d*. *Educ:* Churchill Coll., Cambridge (BA 1974); Clare Hall, Cambridge (PhD 1978). FRCPath 1995. Res. Fellow, Yale Univ., 1977–80; Res. Scientist, MRC Lab. of Molecular Biology and Ludwig Inst., Cambridge, 1980–86; Dir, St Mary's Br., Ludwig Inst. for Cancer Research, 1986–2005. Chm., Res. Cttee, Leukaemia and Lymphoma Res., 2009–. FMedSci 2003. *Publications:* res. pubns on molecular biology of viruses and cancer, particularly Epstein-Barr virus. *Recreations:* sailing (Sec., 2009–13, Chm., 2013–15, Gerrards Cross Sailing Assoc.), gardening. *Address:*

Section of Virology, Faculty of Medicine, Imperial College, St Mary's Campus, Norfolk Place, W2 1PG. *T:* (020) 7594 2005, *Fax:* (020) 7594 3973. *E:* p.farrell@imperial.ac.uk.

FARRELL, Simon Henry; QC 2003; a Recorder, since 2006; *b* 17 Jan. 1960; *s* of Thomas and Joyce Farrell; *m* 1988, Kathryn Wood; three *s* one *d. Educ:* King's Sch., Canterbury; Gonville and Caius Coll., Cambridge (MA 1981); City Univ. (Dip. Law). Called to the Bar, Lincoln's Inn, 1983; barrister specialising in law of commercial fraud, money laundering, tax evasion, civil and criminal confiscation of assets. *Publications:* (jtly) The Proceeds of Crime Act 2002, 2002; (jtly) Asset Recovery, Criminal Confiscation and Civil Recovery, 2003; (jtly) The Fraud Act 2006, 2007. *Recreations:* squash, running, watching Tottenham Hotspur FC, wine, family. *Address:* 3 Raymond Buildings, Gray's Inn, WC1R 5BH.

FARRELL, Sir Terence, (Sir Terry), Kt 2001; CBE 1996 (OBE 1978); Principal, Farrells (formerly Terry Farrell & Partners), since 1980; *b* 12 May 1938; *s* of Thomas and Molly Farrell (*née* Maguire); *m* 1st, 1960, Angela Rosemarie Mallam; two *d*; 2nd, 1973, Susan Hilary Aplin; two *s* one *d*; 3rd, 2007, Mei Xin Wang; one step *s. Educ:* St Cuthbert's Grammar Sch., Newcastle; Newcastle Univ. (BArch, 1st class hons); Univ. of Pennsylvania (MArch, MCP). ARIBA 1963; MRTPI 1970; FCSD (FSIAD 1981). Harkness Fellow, Commonwealth Fund, USA, 1962–64. Partner in Farrell Grimshaw Partnership, 1965–80. Major projects include: redevelt of Charing Cross Station; Edinburgh Internat. Conf. Centre; British Consulate-Gen., Hong Kong; Vauxhall Cross (MI6), London; Kowloon Station, Hong Kong; Internat. Centre for Life, Newcastle; Deep Aquarium, Hull; Greenwich Peninsular masterplan; Home Office HQ, London; regeneration of Marylebone-Euston Road, London; Transportation Centre, Inchon Internat. airport, Seoul; Univ. of Newcastle masterplan; Manchester Southern Gateway masterplan; Manchester Univ. masterplan; Regent's Place, London; Great North Museum, Newcastle upon Tyne; The Royal Institution, London; Beijing South Station. *Exhibitions:* RIBA Heinz Gall., London, 1987; RIBA, London, 1995; V&A Mus., 2011. Design Champion: City of Edinburgh, 2004–09; Thames Gateway, 2007–; Ashford's Future, 2009–; Vision Champion, Kent CC, 2009–. Comr, English Heritage, 1990–96; Member: Royal Parks Adv. Bd, 2003–; Mayor of London's Design Adv. Panel, 2009–. Chm., Walking Co-ordination Gp, Central London Partnership, 2003–. Vis. Prof., Univ. of Westminster, 1998–2001. Hon. FRIAS 1996; Hon. FAIA 1998. Hon. DCL Newcastle, 2000; Hon. DA Lincoln, 2003. *Publications:* Architectural Monograph, 1985; Urban Design Monograph, 1993; Place: a story of modelmaking, menageries and paper rounds (life and work: early years to 1981), 2004; Shaping London: the patterns and forms that make the metropolis, 2009; Terry Farrell Interiors and the Legacy of Postmodernism, 2011; articles in numerous British and foreign jls; *relevant publications:* Terry Farrell: selected and current works, 1994; Ten Years: Ten Cities: the work of Terry Farrell & Partners 1991–2001, 2002; Continuum, 2012; Collage & Context, 2013. *Recreations:* walking, swimming. *Address:* (office) 7 Hatton Street, NW8 8PL.

FARRELL, Timothy Robert Warwick; Organist, Liberal Jewish Synagogue, St John's Wood, since 1975; *b* 5 Oct. 1943; *m* 1st, 1975, Penelope Walmsley-Clark (marr. diss. 1995); one *s*; 2nd, 1996, Jane Emmanuel. *Educ:* Diocesan Coll., Cape Town; Royal Coll. of Music, London; Paris, etc. FRCO, ARCM (piano and organ). Asst Organist, St Paul's, Knightsbridge, 1962–66; Asst Organist, St Paul's Cath., 1966–67; Sub-organist, Westminster Abbey, 1967–74; Organ Tutor at Addington Palace, RSCM, 1966–73; Organist, Choirmaster and Composer, HM Chapels Royal, 1974–79. Broadcaster, recordings, electronic and orchestral music, etc. *Recreations:* golf, walking, sailing, flying. *Address:* Liberal Jewish Synagogue, 28 St John's Wood Road, NW8 7HA. *T:* (020) 7286 5181.

FARRELLY, (Christopher) Paul; MP (Lab) Newcastle-under-Lyme, since 2001; *b* Newcastle-under-Lyme, 2 March 1962; *s* of late Thomas Farrelly and of Anne Farrelly (*née* King); *m* 1998, Victoria Perry; one *s* two *d. Educ:* St Edmund Hall, Oxford (BA Hons PPE). Manager, Corporate Finance Div., Barclays de Zoete Wedd, 1984–90; Corresp., Reuters Ltd, 1990–95; Dep. City and Business Ed., Independent on Sunday, 1995–97; City Ed., The Observer, 1997–2001. Mem., Culture, Media and Sport Select Cttee, 2005–. *Recreations:* Rugby, football, writing. *Address:* House of Commons, SW1A 0AA. *T:* (020) 7219 8262. *Clubs:* Holy Trinity Catholic, Halmer End Working Men's (Newcastle-under-Lyme); Trentham Rugby Union Football, Finchley Rugby Football, Commons and Lords Rugby Union Football.

FARREN, Dr Sean; Member (SDLP) Antrim North, Northern Ireland Assembly, 1998–2007; *m* 1967, Patricia Clarke; one *s* three *d. Educ:* National Univ. of Ireland (BA 1960; HDE 1961); Essex Univ. (MA 1970); Univ. of Ulster (DPhil 1989). Teacher, Sierra Leone, Switzerland, Ireland, 1961–68; University Lectr in Educn, Univ. of Ulster, 1970–98. Fellow, Saltzburg Internat. Seminar, 1989. Minister of Higher and Further Educn, Trng and Employment, 1999–2001, of Finance and Personnel, 2001–02, NI. Contested (SDLP) Antrim N, 2001. *Publications:* The Politics of Irish Education 1920–1965, 1995; (with Robert Mulvihill) Paths to a Settlement in Northern Ireland, 1999; The SDLP: the struggle for agreement in Northern Ireland 1970–2000, 2010; (ed jtly) John Hume - Peacemaker, 2015; contributed to: Motivating the Majority—Modern Languages, Northern Ireland, 1991; Whose English, 1994; Irish Educational Documents, Vol. III, 1995; Language, Education and Society in a Changing World, 1996; A New History of Ireland, Vol. VII, 1998; Fiction, Multi-media and Intertextuality in Mother Tongue Education, 1998; contribs to Aspects of Educn, History of Educn, Etudes Irlandaises, Lang. Culture and Curriculum, Oxford Internat. Rev., Southeastern Pol Rev.; res. reports. *Recreations:* reading, swimming, cycling, theatre. *Address:* 3 Mill Square, Lissadell Avenue, Portstewart, Co. Derry BT55 7TB. *T:* (028) 7083 3042.

FARRER, His Honour Brian Ainsworth; QC 1978; a Circuit Judge, 1985–2001; *b* 7 April 1930; *s* of A. E. V. A. Farrer and Gertrude (*née* Hall); *m* 1960, Gwendoline Valerie (*née* Waddoup), JP; two *s* one *d. Educ:* King's Coll., Taunton; University Coll., London (LLB). Called to the Bar, Gray's Inn, 1957. A Recorder, 1974–85. Chm., Standards Cttee, Coventry CC, 2000–08. *Recreations:* golf, music, chess, bridge. *Address:* 2 Badminton House, Chepstow Place, Streetly, Sutton Coldfield B74 3TL. *Club:* Aberdovey Golf.

See also P. A. Farrer.

FARRER, Sir (Charles) Matthew, GCVO 1994 (KCVO 1983; CVO 1973); Private Solicitor to the Queen, 1965–94; Partner in Messrs Farrer & Co., Solicitors, 1959–94; *b* 3 Dec. 1929; *s* of late Sir (Walter) Leslie Farrer, KCVO, and Hon. Lady Farrer; *m* 1962, Johanna Creszentia Maria Dorothea Bennhold; one *s* one *d. Educ:* Bryanston Sch.; Balliol Coll., Oxford (MA). A Trustee, British Museum, 1989–99; Comr, Royal Commn on Historical Manuscripts, 1991–2002; Mem., British Library Bd, 1994–2000. Trustee, Lambeth Palace Library, 1991–2002. Pres., Selden Soc., 2001–03. Mem., Ct of Assts, Fishmongers' Co., 1995– (Prime Warden, 2007–08). *Address:* 6 Priory Avenue, Bedford Park, W4 1TX. *T:* (020) 8994 6052.

FARRER, Rt Rev. David; *see* Farrer, Rt Rev. R. D.

FARRER, David John; QC 1986; a Recorder, 1983; *b* 15 March 1943; *s* of John Hall Farrer and Mary Farrer; *m* 1969, Hilary Jean Bryson; two *s* one *d. Educ:* Queen Elizabeth's Grammar Sch., Barnet; Downing Coll., Cambridge (MA, LLB). Called to the Bar, Middle Temple, 1967, Bencher, 1998. Dep. Chm., Information Tribunal, 2005. Mem., Bar Council, 1986–94; Chm., Bar Services Cttee, 1989–94. Contested (L): Melton, 1979; Rutland and Melton, 1983. *Recreations:* tennis, cricket, Liberal Party politics. *Club:* National Liberal.

FARRER, Sir Matthew; *see* Farrer, Sir C. M.

FARRER, Paul Ainsworth; QC 2006; **His Honour Judge Farrer;** a Circuit Judge, since 2011; *b* 15 March 1965; *s* of Brian Ainsworth Farrer, *qv*; *m* 2004, Emma Louise Kelly; two *d. Educ:* Nottingham Univ. (LLB Hons 1986); Inns of Court Sch. of Law. Called to the Bar, Gray's Inn, 1988; in practice as barrister, 1988–2011, specialising in criminal law; Recorder, 2004–11. *Recreations:* golf (handicap 3), ski-ing, tennis, travel. *Address:* Warwickshire Justice Centre, Newbold Terrace, Leamington Spa, Warwickshire CV32 4EL. *Clubs:* Little Aston Golf, Aberdovey Golf.

FARRER, Rt Rev. (Ralph) David; Vicar, St Nicholas, Arundel, with Tortington and South Stoke, since 2008; an Honorary Assistant Bishop, Diocese of Chichester, since 2008; *b* 7 May 1944; *s* of Alexander John Farrer and Jacquelyn Mary Westacott Farrer (*née* Pattison); *m* 1969, Helen Belfield Walker; two *s. Educ:* Mentone Grammar Sch.; Ringwood High Sch.; St Barnabas Theol Coll. (ThL Hons; ThSchol Hons). Asst Curate, Good Shepherd, Plympton, SA, 1968–71; ordained priest, 1969; Priest i/c, St John the Baptist, Hillcrest, SA, 1971–73; Asst Priest, St Peter, Eastern Hill, Melbourne, 1973–75; Vicar: Christ Church, Brunswick, Vic, 1975–90; St Mary, Nottingham, 1988–89 (exchange); St Peter, Eastern Hill, 1990–98. Canon, St Paul's Cathedral, Melbourne, 1985–98; Archdeacon: La Trobe, Vic, 1994–96; Melbourne, 1996–98; Bishop of Wangaratta, Vic, 1998–2008. Dir, Inst. for Spiritual Studies, Melbourne, 1990–98. Chaplain to Parlt, Vic, 1992–98. CHLJ 1991; CMLJ 1996. *Publications:* Orthodoxy Down Under: tracts for our times, 1983; Wilderness Transformed, 1992. *Recreations:* reading, travel, golf. *Address:* The Vicarage, 26 Maltravers Street, Arundel BN18 9BU. *Club:* Melbourne (Melbourne).

FARRINGTON, family name of **Baroness Farrington of Ribbleton**.

FARRINGTON OF RIBBLETON, Baroness *cr* 1994 (Life Peer), of Fulwood in the County of Lancashire; **Josephine Farrington;** *b* 29 June 1940; *m* 1960, Michael James Farrington; three *s.* Lancashire County Council: Mem., 1977; Chm., 1992; Chm., Educn Cttee, 1981–91. Association of County Councils: Chm., Policy Cttee, 1993–94; Leader, Labour Gp, 1987–94; Vice-Chm., 1990–94; Chm., 1994–96. A Baroness in Waiting (Govt Whip), 1997–2010. Mem., Consultative Council for Local Govt Finance, 1987–. UK Rep., Cttee of the Regions, 1994– (Chm., Educn and Trng Cttee, 1994–). Pres., Council of Europe Cttee for culture, educn and the media, 1989–94. UK European Woman of the Year, 1994. *Address:* 114 Victoria Road, Fulwood, Preston, Lancs PR2 8NN. *T:* (01772) 718836.

FARRINGTON, Rev. Canon Christine Marion; Vicar of St Mark's, Cambridge, 1996–2002; Chaplain to the Queen, 1998–2012; *b* 11 June 1942; *d* of late Wilfred Bourne Farrington and Doris Violet Farrington. *Educ:* Cheshunt Grammar Sch.; Birkbeck Coll., London (BA Hons); Univ. of Nottingham (Dip. in Applied Social Studies); Univ. of Middlesex (MA in Deviancy and Social Policy); St Albans MTS. Ordained deaconess 1982, deacon, 1987, priest, 1994. Asst librarian, 1960–62; primary school teacher, 1962–65; probation officer, Hemel Hempstead, 1967–71; social work lectr, Middlesex Poly., 1971–79; sen. probation officer, Harrow, 1979–86; asst prison chaplain, 1986–87; Asst Dir of Pastoral Studies, Lincoln Theol Coll., 1986–87; Deacon, Salisbury Cathedral, 1987–93; Dir, Sarum Christian Centre, 1987–93; Co-Diocesan Dir of Ordinands and Dir of Women's Ministry, Dio. of Ely, 1993–2002; Hon. Canon, Ely Cathedral, 1993–2002, now Canon Emeritus; Chaplain, N Thames Ministerial Trng Course, 2003–07; RD, Wheathampstead, 2004–07; Associate Minister, Kirkwall Cathedral, Orkney, 2007–08. Hon. Chaplain: Wolfson Coll., Cambridge, 1993–2002; St John Ambulance Bde, Cambs, 2000–02. *Recreations:* gardening, walking, entertaining, reading, theatre and concerts. *Address:* 42 East Common, Redbourn, St Albans, Herts AL3 7NQ.

FARRINGTON, Prof. David Philip, OBE 2004; PhD; FBA 1997; FMedSci; Professor of Psychological Criminology, University of Cambridge, 1992–2012, now Emeritus; Leverhulme Trust Emeritus Fellow, 2012–15; *b* 7 March 1944; *s* of William Farrington and Gladys Holden (*née* Spurr); *m* 1966, Sally Chamberlain; three *d. Educ:* Clare Coll., Cambridge (BA, MA; PhD Psychology 1970). Joined staff of Cambridge Univ. Inst. of Criminology, 1969; Reader in Psychol Criminology, 1988–92; Fellow, Darwin Coll., Cambridge, 1980–83. Mem., Parole Bd for England and Wales, 1984–87. Chm., Div. of Criminological and Legal Psychology, British Psychological Soc., 1983–85; President: British Soc. of Criminology, 1990–93; Eur. Assoc. of Psychology and Law, 1997–99; Amer. Soc. of Criminology, 1998–99 (Chm., Div. of Develt and Life-Course Criminology, 2012–); Acad. of Experimental Criminology, 2001–03. Vice-Chm., US Nat. Acad. of Scis Panel on Violence, 1989–92; Co-Chairman: US Office of Juvenile Justice and Delinquency Prevention Study Gp on Serious and Violent Juvenile Offenders, 1995–97, on Very Young Offenders, 1998–2000; High Security Psychiatric Services Commng Bd, Network on Primary Prevention of Adult Antisocial Behaviour, DoH, 1997; US Center for Disease Control Expert Panel on Promotive and Protective Factors for Youth Violence, 2007–12; US Nat. Inst. of Justice Study Gp on Transitions from Juvenile Delinquency to Adult Crime, 2008–12; Chm., UK DoH Adv. Cttee, Nat. Prog. on Forensic Mental Health, 2000–03. FMedSci 2000. Hon. FBPsS, 2012. Hon. ScD Trinity Coll., Dublin, 2008. Sellin-Glueck Award, 1984, Sutherland Award, 2002, Vollner Award, 2014, Amer. Soc. of Criminology; Amer. Sociol Assoc. Prize for Dist. Scholarship, 1988; Award for Dist. Contribns, US Office of Juvenile Justice and Delinquency Prevention, 1998; Joan McCord Award, Acad. of Experimental Criminology, 2005; Beccaria Gold Medal of Criminology, Soc. of German-Speaking Countries, 2005; Sen. Prize, Div. of Forensic Psychology, BPsS, 2007; Award for Outstanding Career-long Contribs to the Scientific Study of Law and Human Behaviour, Eur. Assoc. of Psychol. and Law, 2009; Jerry Lee Award, Div. of Experimental Criminology, American Soc. of Criminology, 2010; Robert Boruch Award, Campbell Collaboration, 2012; Stockholm Prize in Criminology, Sweden, 2013; Freda Adler Dist. Scholar Award, Amer. Soc. of Criminology, 2013; Internat. Award, Juvenile Justice Without Borders, 2014. *Publications:* Who Becomes Delinquent?, 1973; The Delinquent Way of Life, 1977; Behaviour Modification with Offenders, 1979; Psychology, Law and Legal Processes, 1979; Abnormal Offenders, Delinquency and the Criminal Justice System, 1982; Aggression and Dangerousness, 1985; Reactions to Crime, 1985; Prediction in Criminology, 1985; Understanding and Controlling Crime, 1986; Human Development and Criminal Behaviour, 1991; Offenders and Victims, 1992; Integrating Individual and Ecological Aspects of Crime, 1993; Psychological Explanations of Crime, 1994; Building a Safer Society, 1995; Understanding and Preventing Youth Crime, 1996; Biosocial Bases of Violence, 1997; Serious and Violent Juvenile Offenders, 1998; Antisocial Behaviour and Mental Health Problems, 1998; Evaluating Criminology and Criminal Justice, 1998; Sex and Violence, 2001; Offender Rehabilitation in Practice, 2001; Child Delinquents, 2001; Costs and Benefits of Preventing Crime, 2001; Evidence-Based Crime Prevention, 2002; Early Prevention of Adult Antisocial Behaviour, 2003; Crime and Punishment in Western Countries, 2005; Integrated Developmental and Life-course Theories of Offending, 2005; Reducing Crime, 2006; Preventing Crime, 2006; Key Issues in Criminal Career Research, 2007; Saving Children from a Life of Crime, 2007; Violence and Serious Theft, 2008; (ed) Dictionary of Forensic Psychology, 2008; Making Public Places Safer, 2009; Young Homicide Offenders and Victims, 2011; Oxford Handbook of Crime Prevention, 2012; From Juvenile Delinquency to Adult Crime, 2012; Young Adult Offenders, 2012; Scholarly Influence in Criminology and Criminal Justice, 2012; Explaining Criminal Careers, 2012; Offending from Childhood to Middle Age, 2013; Labelling Theory: empirical tests, 2014; Most-Cited Scholars in Criminology and Criminal Justice, 2014; Effects of Parental Incarceration on Children, 2014. *Address:* Institute of Criminology, Sidgwick Avenue, Cambridge CB3 9DA. *T:* (01223) 335360.

FARRINGTON, Sir Henry (William), 8th Bt *cr* 1818, of Blackheath, Kent; *b* 27 March 1951; *s* of Sir Henry Francis Colden Farrington, 7th Bt and Anne, *e d* of Major W. A. Gillam, DSO; *S* father, 2004; *m* 1979, Diana Donne, *yr d* of late Geoffrey Broughton; two *s*. *Educ:* Haileybury; RAC Cirencester. MRICS. *Heir: s* Henry John Albert Farrington, *b* 4 Jan. 1985. *Address:* Castle, Wiveliscombe, Taunton, Somerset TA4 2TJ.

FARRINGTON, Paul; freelance vocal coach and consultant, and specialist remedial voice therapist; *b* 25 Feb. 1959; *s* of Brian and Mary Farrington. *Educ:* Birmingham Sch. of Music (GBSM, ABSM). Dir of Music, Birmingham Sch. of Speech and Drama, 1986–96; Opera Dir, Guildford Sch. of Acting, 1990–95; Vocal Tutor: Welsh Coll. of Music and Drama, 1990–97; RAM, 1994–99; Clinical Vocal Consultant, University Hosp., Birmingham, 1990–; Vocal Consultant: Samling Foundn, 1996–; Birmingham Sch. of Acting, 2001–; Internat. Vocal Tutor, NZ Opera Sch. for Emerging Artists, 2006–; Technical Vocal Coach, Young Artists Prog., Royal Opera, Covent Gdn, 2007–. Visiting Vocal Coach: Göteborgs Operan, 2004–; Tokyo New Nat. Th., 2009–; Frankfurt Neue Opera, 2010–; Lindemann Young Artists Prog., Met. Opera, NY, 2010–. Vis. Prof., Operahogskolan, Stockholm, 2010–; Prof. of Opera and Vocal Pedagogy, Kunsthogskolan, Oslo, 2014–. Vocal Coach and Musical Dir, film, Quartet, 2012; Music Consultant, Vocal Coach and Orchestral Cond., film, The Theory of Everything, 2015. *Recreations:* dining, gym, travel, theatre, fine wine, cooking, gardening, Pilates (keeping fit). *T:* 07970 268933. *E:* paulfarrington@me.com. *W:* www.paulfarrington.org.

FARRON, Timothy James; MP (Lib Dem) Westmorland and Lonsdale, since 2005; Leader, Liberal Democrats, since 2015; *b* 27 May 1970; *s* of Christopher Farron and Susan Farron (*née* Trenchard); *m* 2000, Rosemary Alison Cantley; two *s* two *d*. *Educ:* Univ. of Newcastle upon Tyne (BA Hons Politics 1991). Lancaster University: Adult Educn Officer, 1992–96; Special Needs Student Advr, 1996–98; Asst to Acad. Registrar, 1998–2002; Hd, Faculty Admin, St Martin's Coll., 2002–05. Member (Lib Dem): Lancs CC, 1993–2000; S Ribble BC, 1995–99; S Lakeland DC, 2004–08. Pres., Liberal Democrats, 2011–14. Mem., Amnesty Internat., 1993–. Mem., Cumbria Wildlife Trust, 2003–. Mem. PCC, Milnthorpe St Thomas, 2004–. Chm., Milnthorpe Youth Gp, 2004–. *Recreations:* walking, football (both playing and watching, respectively as an average goalkeeper and a Blackburn Rovers fan), music. *Address:* House of Commons, SW1A 0AA; Acland House, Yard 2, Strickland Gate, Kendal LA9 4ND. *T:* (01539) 723403, *Fax:* (01539) 740800. *E:* tim@timfarron.co.uk. *Club:* Kendal and South Westmorland Liberal (Pres.).

FARROW, Christopher John; Chairman, Aga Foodservice Group, 2001–04; *b* 29 July 1937; *s* of late Thomas and Evangeline Dorothea Farrow; *m* 1961, Alison Brown; one *s* one *d*. *Educ:* Cranleigh Sch.; King's Coll., Cambridge (BA). Board of Trade, 1961; Harkness Fellowship and visiting scholar, Stanford Univ., USA, 1968–69; Private Sec. to Pres. of BoT and Minister for Trade, 1970–72; Dept of Trade and Industry, 1972–74; Cabinet Office, 1975–77; Dept of Industry, 1977–83; Asst Dir, Bank of England, 1983–87; Dir, Kleinwort, Benson Ltd, 1987–92; Dir-Gen., British Merchant Banking and Securities Houses, then London Investment Banking, Assoc., 1993–99. Director: London Metal Exchange Ltd, 1987–99 (Vice Chm., 1997–99); Glynwed International, 1993–2001 (Chm., 2000–01). Member: Engrg Council, 1984–86; Financial Reporting Review Panel, 1992–2002. *Recreation:* gardening.

FARROW, Christopher John; Deputy Chairman, Ellesmere Port Development Board, since 2014 (Member, since 2010); *b* 19 Nov. 1947; *s* of Sydney A. Farrow; *m* 1980, Susan Thomas; three *d*. *Educ:* Clayesmore Sch., Dorset; Univ. of London (BA Hons); Polytechnic of Central London (DipTP Dist.). Planner, London Borough of Newham, 1974–81; Dir, LDDC, 1981–91; Chief Exec., Merseyside Develt Corp., 1991–98; Man. Dir, North, then Exec. Dir, N Wales, WDA, 1998–2006; Chief Exec., Central Salford Urban Regeneration Co., 2006–11. Director: Greenland Dock Develt Co., 1985–90; Mersey Partnership, 1992–98. MRTPI. FRSA 1993. *Publications:* planning papers on urban develt and economy.

FARROW, Gary, OBE 2011; Founder, Chairman and Chief Executive Officer, The Corporation, since 2005; *b* Orpington, 25 Aug. 1955; *s* of late Lesley Farrow and Evelyn Joyce Farrow; *m* 2002, Jane Moore; two *d*, and one step *d*. *Educ:* Midfield Sch. for Boys, later Walsingham Boys' Sch., Orpington; St Martin's Sch. of Art. Worked in shop, One Stop Records, London, 1973; runner, Rocket Records, 1974; joined EMI records, 1976; Man. Dir, Chinnichap, songwriting partnership, 1978; Founder, Gary Farrow Enterprises Media Mgt Co., 1980; Vice Pres., Communications, Sony Music Entertainment, 1995–2004. Deputy Chairman: Music Industry Trust, 1994–2010; Radio Acad., 1996–2004; PR Cttee, BPI, 2001–; Member: Cttee, HMV Charities, 1994; Cttee, BRITs, 1994–; Patron: Elton John Aids Foundn; Nordoff Robins; Fashion Rocks. Fellow, Radio Acad. Outstanding Achievement Award, Nordoff Robins, 2006; Scott Piering Award, Music Industry Trust, 2006. *Recreations:* photography, music, films, Chelsea Football Club, cooking. *Address:* (office) 18 Soho Square, W1D 3QL. *E:* garyfarrow@corporationltd.com. *Clubs:* Groucho, Soho House, Mark's.

FARROW, Mia (Villiers); actress; *b* 9 Feb. 1945; *d* of late John Villiers Farrow and Maureen O'Sullivan; *m* 1st, 1966, Frank Sinatra (marr. diss. 1968; he *d* 1998); 2nd, 1970, André Previn, *qv* (marr. diss. 1979); three *s*, two adopted *d* (and one adopted *d* decd); one *s* by Woody Allen, *qv*; three adopted *s* three adopted *d* (and one adopted *d* decd). *TV series:* Peyton Place, 1965; A Girl Thing, 2001; *films:* Secret Ceremony, 1968; Rosemary's Baby, 1969; John and Mary, 1970; The Public Eye, 1972; The Great Gatsby, 1974; Full Circle, Death on the Nile, A Wedding, 1978; Hurricane, 1980; A Midsummer Night's Sex Comedy, 1982; Zelig, 1983; Broadway Danny Rose, 1984; The Purple Rose of Cairo, 1985; Hannah and her Sisters, 1986; Radio Days, 1987; September, 1988; Another Woman, 1989; Crimes and Misdemeanours, 1990; Alice, 1990; Husbands and Wives, 1992; Shadows and Fog, 1992; Widows' Peak, 1994; Miami Rhapsody, 1995; Reckless, 1995; Angela Mooney, 1996; Coming Soon, 1999; Purpose, 2002; The Omen, 2006; Be Kind Rewind, 2008; Dark Horse, 2012; *stage:* The Importance of Being Earnest, NY, 1963; Mary Rose, Shaw, 1973; The Three Sisters, Greenwich, 1974; The House of Bernarda Alba, Greenwich, 1974; Peter Pan, 1975; The Marrying of Ann Leete, RSC, 1975; The Zykovs, Ivanov, RSC, 1976; A Midsummer Night's Dream, Leicester, 1976; Romantic Comedy, NY, 1979. David Donatello Award, Italy, 1969; Best Actress awards: French Academy, 1969; San Sebastian, 1969; Rio de Janeiro, 1970. *Publications:* What Falls Away (memoirs), 1997. *Address:* Bridgewater, CT, USA.

FARRY, Stephen Anthony, PhD; Member (Alliance) North Down, Northern Ireland Assembly, since 2007; Minister for Employment and Learning, since 2011; *b* 22 April 1971; *s* of Vincent Farry and Margaret Farry (*née* Greer); *m* 2005, Wendy Watt, PhD. *Educ:* Queen's Univ., Belfast (BSocSc 1st Cl. Pols 1992; PhD Internat. Relns 2000). Mem. (Alliance), N Down BC, 1993– (Dep. Mayor, 2002–03; Mayor, 2007–08). Gen. Sec., Alliance Party of NI, 2000–07. Contested (Alliance) N Down, 2010. Mem., Finance and Personnel Cttee, NI Assembly, 2007–11. Mem., Community Relns Council, 2007–11; Dep. Chm., Cttee for the Office of First Minister and Dep. First Minister, 2010–11. Sen. Fellow, US Inst. of Peace, 2005–06. *Publications:* various jl and newspaper articles. *Recreations:* travel, international affairs. *Address:* Parliament Buildings, Stormont, Belfast BT4 3XX. *E:* stephen.farry@allianceparty.org.

FARTHING, Alan John, MD; FRCOG; Consultant Gynaecological Surgeon, Imperial College Healthcare NHS Trust (formerly St Mary's NHS Trust), since 1997; Surgeon Gynaecologist to the Royal Household, since 2008; *b* Winchester, 8 June 1963; *s* of John Farthing and Barbara Farthing; *m* 2008, Janet Stowell; one *s*. *Educ:* Queen Elizabeth Sch., Wimborne; St George's Hosp. Med. Sch., London (MB BS 1986; MD 1996). MRCOG 1991, FRCOG 2003. Postgrad. trng posts, St Mary's NHS Trust, Guy's Hosp. and Perth, WA; Res. into human papillomavirus in cervical cancer, Ludwig Inst. of Cancer Res., 1992–94. Hon. Sen. Lectr, Imperial Coll. London, 1997–. *Publications:* articles on laparoscopic surgery in gynaecology and fertility sparing surgery in gynaecological cancer. *Recreations:* golf, cricket, Western Australian wine. *Address:* 148 Harley Street, W1G 7LG. *E:* alanfarthing@aol.com.

FARTHING, Prof. Michael John Godfrey, MD, DSc (Med); FRCP, FRCPE, FRCPGlas, FMedSci; Vice-Chancellor, University of Sussex, since 2007; *b* 2 March 1948; *s* of Dennis Jack Farthing and Joan Margaret Farthing (*née* Godfrey); *m* 1979, Alison Mary McLean; two *s*. *Educ:* Henry Thornton Sch., London; University Coll., London (BSc); UCH Med. Sch. (MB BS); MD London 1981; DSc (Med) London 2001. FRCP 1988; FRCPE 2001; FRCPGlas 2001. Res. Fellow, St Mark's Hosp., 1974; Med. Registrar, Addenbrooke's Hosp., 1975–77; Res. Fellow and Hon. Lectr, 1977–80, Wellcome Tropical Lectr, 1980–83, St Bart's Hosp.; Vis. Asst Prof., Tufts Univ. Sch. of Medicine, 1981–83; St Bartholomew's Hospital Medical College, subseq. St Bartholomew's and Royal London Hospital School of Medicine and Dentistry, QMW: Wellcome Sen. Lectr, 1983–91; Prof. and Head of Dept of Gastroenterology, 1990–2000; Dir, Digestive Diseases Res. Centre, 1990–2000; Dean, Faculty of Clin. Medicine, 1995–97; Prof. of Medicine and Exec. Dean, Faculty of Medicine, Univ. of Glasgow, 2000–03; Prof. of Medicine and Principal, St George's Hosp. Med. Sch., subseq. St George's, Univ. of London, 2003–07; Pro-Vice-Chancellor for Medicine, Univ. of London, 2005–07. Hon. Cons. Gastroenterologist, St George's Healthcare NHS Trust, 2003–07; Hon. Consultant: St Mark's Hosp., 1987–; St Luke's Hosp. for Clergy, 1990–; to the Army, 1991–. Non-executive Director: E London and City HA, 1998–2000; Greater Glasgow NHS Bd, 2001–03; SW London Strategic HA, 2004–06; Brighton and Sussex Univ. Hosp. Trust, 2010–15. Editor, Gut, 1996–2002. Mem., GMC, 2001–08, 2013– (Mem., Educn Cttee, 2001–08). Chairman: Cttee on Publication Ethics, 1997–2003; Scientific Cttee, United European Gastroenterology Fedn, 2004–09; Health and Soc. Care Policy Cttee, Universities UK, 2009–; 1994 Gp of Universities, 2011–13; Vice Chm., UK Res. Integrity Office, 2006–; Hon. Sec., 1990–94, Pres., 2007–08, British Soc. of Gastroenterology; Pres., Eur. Assoc. of Gastroenterology and Endoscopy, 1998–2001; Pres., United Eur. Gastroenterology Fedn, 2014–15; Vice-Pres., World Orgn of Gastroenterology, 2005–09. Trustee, Digestive Disorders Foundn, 2003–08. Founder FMedSci 1998. Mem. Ct of Assistants, Apothecaries' Soc., 2003–. *Publications:* Enteric Infection: mechanisms, manifestations and management, vol. 1 1989, vol. 2 1995; Clinical Challenges in Gastroenterology, 1996; Drug Therapy for Gastrointestinal and Liver Diseases, 2001; Fraud and Misconduct in Biomedical Research, 2008; many papers on intestinal disorders. *Recreations:* theatre, modern literature, jazz, running, watersports. *Address:* University of Sussex, Sussex House, Falmer, Brighton BN1 9RH. *Club:* Glasgow Art.

See also S. F. G. Farthing.

FARTHING, Stephen Frederick Godfrey, RA 1998; artist; Rootstein Hopkins Chair of Drawing, University of the Arts London, since 2004; *b* 16 Sept. 1950; *s* of Dennis Jack Farthing and Joan Margaret (*née* Godfrey); *m* 1st, 1975, Joni Elizabeth Jackson (marr. diss. 2004); one *d*; 2nd, 2010, Ami Jihan Abou-bakr. *Educ:* St Martin's Sch. of Art; Royal Coll. of Art; British Sch. at Rome. Lectr in Painting, Canterbury Coll. of Art, 1977–79; Tutor in Painting, RCA, 1980–85; Head of Painting, W Surrey Coll. of Art and Design, Farnham, 1985–90; Ruskin Master of Drawing, Oxford Univ., and Professorial Fellow, St Edmund Hall, Oxford, 1990–2000, now Emeritus Fellow; Exec. Dir, NY Acad. of Art, 2000–04. Artist in Residence, Hayward Gall., London, 1989. *One-man shows* include: Nat. Mus. of Modern Art, Kyoto; Museo Carrillo Gil, Mexico City; Arnolfini, Bristol; Edward Totah Gall., London; Royal Acad. of Arts; Royal W of England Acad., Bristol; represented in London by Purdy Hicks Gall. British School at Rome: Chm., Arts Faculty, 1996–2000; Mem., Council, 1998–2009. Mem., Bd of Dirs, MBNA Europe Bank Ltd, 2003–06. Chm., Exhibns Cttee, Royal Acad. of Arts, 2012–. *Publications:* The Intelligent Persons Guide to Modern Art, 2000; (ed) 1001 Paintings You Must See Before You Die, 2006; (ed) 501 Artists, 2008; Art: the whole story, 2010; Derek Jarman: the sketchbooks, 2013. *Recreations:* watercolours, tennis. *Address:* Chelsea College of Art and Design, University of the Arts London, 16 John Islip Street, SW1P 4JU.

See also M. J. G. Farthing.

FARWELL, Prof. Ruth Sarah, CBE 2015; PhD; DL; Professor and Vice Chancellor, Buckinghamshire New University (formerly Buckinghamshire Chilterns University College), 2006–15; *b* Leigh-on-Sea, Essex, 22 Feb. 1954; *d* of Frederick Farwell and Vera Farwell; *m* 2001, Dr Martin Daniels. *Educ:* Westcliff High Sch.; Univ. of Kent (BSc Hons Maths; PhD Applied Maths 1980). Sen. Lectr, Maths, 1982–86, Hd, Maths Dept, 1986–89, St Mary's University Coll.; Dir of Studies, 1990–93, Univ. Modular Co-ordinator, 1993–95, Hd, Strategic Planning, 1995–98, Univ. of Brighton; Pro Vice Chancellor, London South Bank Univ., 1998–2006. Mem. Bd, HEFCE, 2009–. Member, Board: Buckinghamshire Business First, 2011–14; Buckinghamshire Thames Valley LEP, 2012–15; Aylesbury Coll., 2012–; ifs University Coll. (formerly ifs Sch. of Finance), 2012–. Trustee: GuildHE, 2007–14 (Chair, 2009–13); Univs and Colls Employers Assoc., 2008–11; SE Reg., Open Coll. Network, 2008–12; Buckinghamshire Univ. Tech. Coll., 2012–; Buckinghamshire Educn Skills and Trng, 2013–15. Hon. Pres., AUA, 2014–. DL Bucks, 2015. *Publications:* over 20 papers in jls of physics and maths, 14 papers in conf. procs; chapters in books. *Recreations:* gardening, jazz music, bee keeping, cinema.

FASSENFELT, John Arthur, OBE 2014; JP; Chairman, Magistrates' Association, 2011–13 (Deputy Chairman, 2009–11); *b* Stepney, 17 May 1947; *s* of Arthur Edward and Joyce Fassenfelt; partner, Julie Evans; one *s* one *d*. *Educ:* Abbs Cross Tech. High Sch.; Medway and Maidstone Coll. (Dip. Mgt Studies 1985). CStat 1977. Section Engr, Kent CC, 1985–88; Sen. Manager, 1989, Asst Chief Personnel Officer, 1989–99, London Borough of Bexley. Mem., Kent Magistrates' Cttee, 1998–2001; Dep. Chm., Sittingbourne Bench, 2002–04; Magistrates' Association: Chm., Youth Courts Cttee, 2005–07; Trustee, 2008–13; Vice Pres., Kent Br., 2010–. Chairman: Govs, Sittingbourne Community Coll., 2013–; Swale Acads Trust, 2014– (Dir, 2010–). JP Maidstone, 1992. *Recreations:* golf, walking, going on holiday. *E:* john@fassenfelt.wanadoo.co.uk. *Club:* Durban (S Africa).

FASSETT, Kaffe; textile designer; *b* 7 Dec. 1937; *s* of William Elliot Fassett and Madeleine Fassett. Self-educated. Retrospective exhibitions: Tokyo, 1986; V&A Museum, 1989; Copenhagen, Stockholm, Oslo, Melbourne, Toronto and Helsinki, 1990; Vancouver, Holland, 1993; Osaka, Iceland, 1996; Minneapolis, 1997; Fashion and Textile Mus., London, 2013. *Publications:* Glorious Knitting, 1985; Glorious Needlepoint, 1987; Kaffe Fassett at the V & A, 1988, 4th edn, as Glorious Colour, 1991; Family Album, 1989; Glorious Inspiration, 1991; Kaffe's Classics, 1994; Glorious Interiors, 1995; Mosaics, 1997; Glorious Patchwork, 1999; Passionate Patchwork, 2001; Kaffe's Pattern Library, 2003; Kaffe Fassett's V & A Patchwork Quilts, 2005; Simple Shapes Spectacular Quilts, 2010; (with B. Mably) Knitting with The Color Guys, 2012; Dreaming in Colour (autobiog.), 2012. *Address:* c/o Random House, 20 Vauxhall Bridge Road, SW1V 2SA.

FATTORINI, Maj. Gen. Charles Sebastian; Senior British Loan Service Officer, Oman, since 2014; *b* Harrogate, N Yorks, 4 July 1962; *s* of late David William Fattorini and of Jennifer Susan Melville Fattorini (*née* Wills; she *m* 2nd, 17th Viscount Mountgarret); *m* 1993, Cecilia Antice Birkmyre; one *s* one *d* (and one *s* decd). *Educ:* Ampleforth Coll.; RMA, Sandhurst; Royal Mil. Coll. of Sci. (MA Mil. Studies 1993). Commnd Army, 1982; psc 1994; Comdr, Queen's Royal Lancers, 2002–04; Sen. British Liaison Officer, Pakistan, 2006; Dep.

Asst COS - Trng, HQ Land Forces, 2006–09; Col Officer, Liabilities, Army Personnel Centre, 2009–10; Defence Advisor, British High Commission: Islamabad, 2010–12; Nairobi and Dar-es-Salaam, 2012–14. *Recreations:* photography, wild life conservation, travel, fishing, kayaking. *Address:* c/o Army Personnel Centre, Kentigern House, 65 Brown Street, Glasgow G2 8EX. *Club:* Muthaiga Country (Nairobi).

FAUCONBERG, Barony *cr* 1295, **AND CONYERS**, Barony *cr* 1509; in abeyance. *Co-heiresses:* Hon. Anthea Theresa Lycett [*b* 21 June 1954; *née* Marcia Anne Miller; renamed on adoption by Major Michael Lycett, CBE but retains her right to the succession]; Hon. Beatrix Diana Armstrong [*b* 23 Aug. 1955; *m* 1991, Simon William Jones Armstrong (*d* 2012); two *s*].

FAULKNER, family name of **Baron Faulkner of Worcester**.

FAULKNER OF WORCESTER, Baron *cr* 1999 (Life Peer), of Wimbledon in the London Borough of Merton; **Richard Oliver Faulkner;** *b* 22 March 1946; *s* of late Harold Ewart and Mabel Faulkner; *m* 1968, Susan Heyes; two *d*. *Educ:* Merchant Taylors' Sch., Northwood; Worcester Coll., Oxford (MA PPE; Hon. Fellow, 2002). Research asst and journalist, Labour Party, 1967–69; PRO, Construction Ind. Trng Bd, 1969–70; Editor, Steel News, 1971; Account dir, F. J. Lyons (PR) Ltd, 1971–73; Dir, PPR International, 1973–76; communications advisor: to Leader of the Opposition and Labour Party (unpaid), gen. elections, 1987, 1992, 1997; to the Bishop at Lambeth, 1990; Govt relations adviser: rly trade unions, 1975–76; C. A. Parsons & Co., 1976–77; Pool Promoters Assoc., 1977–99; British Rlys Bd, 1977–97; Prudential Assurance Co., 1978–88; IPU, 1988–90; Southampton City Council, 1989–91; CAMRA, 1989; Barclays de Zoete Wedd, 1990–92; Standard Life Assurance, 1990–99; S Glam CC, 1991–96; Cardiff CC, 1996–99; Cardiff Bay Develt Corp., 1993–98; Littlewoods Orgn, 1994–99; FSA, 1998–99; Actg Hd of Communications, SIB, 1997; Jt Man. Dir, Westminster Communications Gp, 1989–97; Deputy Chairman: Citigate, Westminster, 1997–99; Cardiff Millennium Stadium, 2004–08 (Dir, 1997–2004); Strategy Adviser: Sportech Gp plc (formerly Littlewoods Pools), 1999–2009; Dept of Transport, NSW Govt, 2012; Chairman: Adv. Bd, First Great Western, 2014– (Mem., 2009, 2010–); Alderney Gambling Control Commn, 2014– (Strategy Advr, 2005–08; Mem., 2013–). A Dep. Chm., 2007–09 and Dep. Speaker, 2008–09, 2010–, H of L; a Lord in Waiting (Govt Whip), 2009–10; Dept Liaison Peer, DETR, 2000–01, Cabinet Office, 2001–05; House of Lords: Member: Sub-cttee B, 2000–03, Sub-cttee F, 2009 and 2013–15, EC Select Cttee; Delegated Powers and Regulatory Reform Cttee, 2007–09; Rookery South (Resource Recovery Facility) Order 2011 Cttee, 2012–13; Cttee of Selection, 2013–; EU Home Affairs Sub-cttee, 2015–; Information Cttee, 2015–; Equality Act 2010 and Disability Select Cttee, 2015–; Jt Scrutiny Cttee, Draft Gambling Bill, 2003–04; London Local Authy Private Bill Cttee, 2006; Chm., London Local Authorities and Transport for London Private Bill Cttee, 2009; Mem., Olympic Legacy Select Cttee, 2013; Chm., Inquiry into Betting on Sport, 2005. Treas., All Party Railways Gp, 2000–09, 2010–15; Graduate Mem., Armed Forces Parly Scheme, attached to RN, 2002–07; Sec., British-Namibian Parly Gp, 2004–09; Vice-Chairman: Football Gp, 2004–09, 2010–; British-Cyprus Gp, 2005–09; Betting and Gaming Gp, 2005–09; Abolition of Death Penalty Gp, 2007–09, 2010–; British Caribbean Gp, 2000–09; British-S African Gp, 2002–09; British-Danish Parly Gp, 2005–09; British-Channel Islands Gp, 2007–09, 2015–; Heritage Rail Gp, 2011–; East-West Rail Gp, 2015–; British-Norwegian Parly Gp, 2015– (Sec., 2000–09, 2010–15); British-Argentine Parly Gp, 2015 (Sec., 2001–09, 2010–15); Jt Treas., British-Swedish Parly Gp, 2001–09; Chairman: All Party War Graves and Battlefields Heritage Gp, 2002–09; All Party Sustainable Aviation Gp, 2003–09; Co-Chm., British-Taiwanese Parly Gp, 2005–09, 2010– (Sec., 2000–05); War Heritage Gp, 2015– (Chm., 2010–15). Mem., Govt Adv. Bd on WW1 Centenary Commemoration, 2013–. Football Trust: Foundn Trustee, 1979–82; Sec., 1983–86; First Dep. Chm., 1986–98; Chm., Sports Grounds Initiative, 1995–2000; Vice Chm., Govt's Football Task Force, 1997–99; Member: Sports Council, 1986–88; Football League enquiry into membership schemes, 1984, anti-hooliganism cttee, 1987–90; FIFA Wkg Gp on betting, 2006–09; Chm., Women's Football Assoc., 1988–91; non-exec. Dir, Football Assoc. of Wales, 2007–09. Vice-Chm., 1986–99, Vice-Pres., 2000–09, 2010–, Campaign for Better Transport (formerly Transport 2000 Ltd); Chm., Worcester Live, 2014– (Dir, 2011–); Mem., Railway Heritage Cttee, 2002–09 (Chm., 2004–09); President: Heritage Railway Assoc., 2011–; Cotswold Line Promotion Gp, 2007–09, 2010–. Pres., 2001–04, Vice Pres., 2004–, RoSPA; Vice-President: Football Conf., 2007–09, 2010–15; Level Playing Field (formerly Nat. Assoc. for Disabled Supporters), 2007–09, 2010–; Nat. League, 2015–. Trustee: Foundn for Sport and the Arts, 2000–12; Gamcare, 2005–09; Nat. Mus. for Sci. and Industry, 2007–09; Sci. Mus. Gp, 2011– (Vice-Chm., 2015–; Chairman: MOSI Adv. Bd, 2013; Railway Designation Adv. Bd, 2013–); Nat. Football Mus., 2007–09, 2011–; ASH, 2007–09; Patron: Roy Castle Lung Cancer Foundn, 1999– (Trustee, 2003–07); Myriad Centre Worcester, 2012–; Guild of Battlefield Guides, 2013–. Chairman: Worcester Coll. Appeal, 1996–2003; Adv. Cttee, Worcester Coll. Soc., 2003–13, Pres., 2013–; Mem. Ct, Bedfordshire Univ. (formerly Luton Univ.), 1999–2009; Pres., Old Merchant Taylors' Soc., 2011–12 (Vice-Pres., 2006–11). Mem., Merton Borough Council, 1971–78; contested (Lab) Devizes 1970, Feb. 1974, Monmouth, Oct. 1974, Huddersfield W, 1979. Co-founder, parly jl The House mag. (Mem., Editl Bd, 2003–). Fellow, Univ. of Worcester, 2008– (Mem., Develt Cttee, 2009–14; Pres., Coll. of Fellows, 2014–). Hon. LLD Beds (formerly Luton), 2003. Friendship Medal of Diplomacy (Taiwan), 2004; Order of the Brilliant Star with Grand Cordon (Taiwan), 2008. *Publications:* (with Chris Austin) Holding the Line: how Britain's railways were saved, 2012 (Railway and Canal Historical Soc. Award, 2014); Disconnected!: broken links in Britain's Rail Policy, 2015. *Recreations:* collecting Lloyd George memorabilia, tinplate trains, watching Association Football, travelling by railway. *Address:* House of Lords, SW1A 0PW. *E:* faulknerro@parliament.uk.
See also D. E. R. Faulkner.

FAULKNER, David Ewart Riley, CB 1985; Senior Research Associate, University of Oxford Centre for Criminology (formerly for Criminological Research), since 1992; *b* 23 Oct. 1934; *s* of Harold Ewart and Mabel Faulkner; *m* 1961, Sheila Jean Stevenson; one *s* one *d*. *Educ:* Manchester Grammar Sch.; Merchant Taylors' Sch., Northwood; St John's Coll., Oxford (MA Lit Hum). Home Office: Asst Principal, 1959; Private Sec. to Parly Under-Sec. of State, 1961–63; Principal, 1963; Jt Sec. to Inter-Party Conf. on House of Lords Reform, 1968; Private Sec. to Home Sec., 1969–70; Asst Sec., Prison Dept, 1970, Establishment Dept, 1974, Police Dept, 1976; Asst Under-Sec. of State, 1976; Under Sec., Cabinet Office, 1978–80; Home Office; Asst Under-Sec. of State, Dir of Operational Policy, Prison Dept, 1980–82; Dep. Under-Sec. of State, 1982; Head of Criminal and Res. and Statistical Depts, 1982–90; Principal Estab. Officer, 1990–92. Fellow, St John's Coll., Oxford, 1992–99. Chm., Howard League for Penal Reform, 1999–2002. Member: UN Cttee on Crime Prevention and Control, 1984–91; Adv. Bd, Helsinki Inst. for Crime Prevention and Control, 1988–93; Council, Magistrates' Assoc., 1992–98; Council, Justice, 1993–97; Commn on the Future of Multi-Ethnic Britain, 1998–2000. Trustee, Gilbert Murray Trust, 1992–, Thames Valley Partnership, 1992–, and other charities. *Publications:* Darkness and Light, 1996; Crime, State and Citizen, 2001, 2nd edn 2006; Civil Renewal, Diversity and Social Capital in a Multi-Ethnic Britain, 2004; Better Government: more justice, 2009; (with R. Burnett) Where Next for Criminal Justice?, 2011; Servant of the Crown: a civil servant's story of criminal justice and public service reform, 2014; contribs to jls. *Recreations:* railways, birds. *Address:* c/o Centre for Criminology, Manor Road, Oxford OX1 3UR.
See also Baron Faulkner of Worcester.

FAULKNER, Sir Dennis; *see* Faulkner, Sir J. D. C.

FAULKNER, Graham John; Chief Executive, National Society for Epilepsy, 2000–13; *b* 26 Sept. 1948; *s* of William and Edna Faulkner; *m* 1st, 1975, Jennifer Barkway (marr. diss. 1998); one *s* one *d*; 2nd, 1999, Dorothy, (Dee), Napier (marr. diss. 2002). *Educ:* UC of Swansea (BSc Hons Psychol. 1970); Univ. of Leicester (postgrad. res.); Univ. of Birmingham (CQSW 1984; MSocSc). Local Govt O R Unit, RIPA, 1973–75; Planning Dept, 1975–77, Social Services Dept, 1977–85, Warwickshire CC; Dir, Retirement Security Ltd, 1985–92; Dir and Gen. Sec., Leonard Cheshire Foundn, 1992–98; Chief Exec., Rehab UK, 1999–2000. Chm., Queen Square Enterprises, 2011–; Dir, Healthwatch Bucks. Gov., UCLH NHS Foundn Trust, 2004–11. Trustee: Roald Dahl Marvellous Children's Charity; Daisy Garland, epilepsy charity; Chm. Trustees, St Loye's Foundn, 2013–. *Publications:* contributor to: White Media and Black Britain, 1975; Solving Local Government Problems, 1981; This Caring Business, 1988; contrib. jls and res. reports. *Recreations:* theatre, music, Rugby, watching Coventry City.

FAULKNER, Gregory; *see* Faulkner, L. G.

FAULKNER, Sir (James) Dennis (Compton), Kt 1991; CBE 1980; VRD 1960; DL; Chairman, Marlowe Cleaners Ltd, 1973–2005; *b* 22 Oct. 1926; *s* of James and Nora Faulkner; *m* 1952, Janet Cunningham (*d* 1994); three *d*. *Educ:* College of St Columba, Co. Dublin. Served RNVR, 1946–71; UDR, 1971–92 (Col Comdt, 1986–92). Chairman: Belfast Collar Co. Ltd, 1957–63; Belfast Savings Bank, 1960–61; NI Develt Agency, 1978–82; Board Member: Gallaher NI, 1980–89 (Chm., 1982–89); Northern Bank Ltd, 1983–96; Chm., Ladybird (NI) Ltd, 1963–88; Dir, Giants Causeway and Bushmills Railway Co. Ltd, 1999–2005. Farming, 1946–. Mem., Strangford Lough Management Cttee, 1992–2004 (Chm., 1992–97); Chm., Ulster, North Down and Ards Hosp. Trust, 1993–94. Mem., RBL, 1971– (Chm., RBL NI, 1992–2000); President: Regtl Assoc. of UDR, 1986–2005 (Patron, 2005–); UDR Benevolent Fund, 2008– (Chm., 1986–2008); Trustee, Royal Irish Regtl Benevolent Fund, 1992–2005. DL County Down, 1988. *Recreations:* sailing, hunting, ocean racing, exploring in Arctic and Antarctic. *Address:* Northern Ireland. *Clubs:* Royal Ocean Racing, Royal Cruising; Royal Yacht Squadron; Irish Cruising; Strangford Lough Yacht; Cruising Club of America (New York).

FAULKNER, John Richard Hayward; theatre and management consultant; international impresario; *b* 29 May 1941; *s* of Capt. Richard Hayward Ollerton and Lilian Elizabeth (*née* Carrigan), and step *s* of late Herbert Andrew Faulkner; *m* 1st, 1970, Janet Gill (*née* Cummings) (*d* 1994); two *d*, and two step *d*; 2nd, 2001, Christie Dickason; two step *s*. *Educ:* Archbishop Holgate's Sch., York; Keble Coll., Oxford (BA). Worked with a number of theatre companies, Prospect Productions, Meadow Players, Century Theatre, Sixty-Nine Theatre Co., Cambridge Theatre Co., toured extensively, UK, Europe, Indian Sub-Continent, Australia, 1960–72; Drama Director: Scottish Arts Council, 1972–77; Arts Council of GB, 1977–83; Head, Artistic Planning, Nat. Theatre, 1983–88. Touring Consultant, The Entertainment Corp., 1988–92; Associate: Prince Res. Consultants, 2001–09; Theatre Futures Ltd, 2003–. Mem., Assessors' Panel, Nat. Lottery Dept, Arts Council, 1995–2001. Director: Minotaur Films, 1988–92; Visionhaven Ltd, 1991–2003; New Zoo Develts Ltd, 1992–. Proprietor, Ollerton Press, 2006–. Member: Pubns & Communication Commn, Orgn Internat. des Scénographes, Techniciens et Architectes de Théâtre, 1994– (Chm., 1999–2001); Internat. Soc. for the Performing Arts, 1997–; Council, Assoc. of British Theatre Technicians, 1998–2001 (sometime Chm.); Sec., Pleasance Theatre Trust, 1997–. Trustee: The Arts Educational Schools, 1986–92; The Arts for Nature, 1990–99; Performing Arts Labs, 1991–2001; Pension Scheme for Admin. and Tech. Staff in the Arts, 1996–2012; Orange Tree Th. Trust, 1998–2008 (Jt Chm., 1999–2004, Chm., 2004–08 and 2010–11). *Recreations:* intricacies and wildernesses. *Address:* 28 Ellesmere Road, Chiswick, W4 4QH. *T:* (020) 8995 3041.

FAULKNER, (Leo) Gregory; HM Diplomatic Service, retired; Ambassador to Chile, 2000–03; *b* 21 Sept. 1943; *s* of late James and Teresa Faulkner; *m* 1970, Fiona Hardie (*née* Birkett); three *d*. *Educ:* Manchester Univ. (BA Hons Spanish). FCO, 1968–72; Lima, 1972–76; Lagos, 1976–79; EC Internal Dept, FCO, 1979–82; Head of Chancery, Madrid, 1982–84; Head, Internat. Telecoms Br., DTI, 1984–86, on secondment; Commercial Counsellor, The Hague, 1986–90; Dep. Head of Mission, Buenos Aires, 1990–93; Head, Latin America Dept, FCO, 1993–96; High Commissioner, Trinidad and Tobago, 1996–99. Consultant (pt-time), UK Trade and Investment, 2009–. *Recreations:* tennis, golf, watching cricket, football and Rugby. *Club:* Canning.

FAULKNER, Most Rev. Leonard Anthony; Archbishop of Adelaide, (RC), 1985–2001; *b* Booleroo Centre, South Australia, 5 Dec. 1926. *Educ:* Sacred Heart Coll., Glenelg; Corpus Christi Coll., Werribee; Pontifical Urban University, Rome. Ordained Propaganda Fide Coll., Rome, 1 Jan. 1950; Asst Priest, Woodville, SA, 1950–57; Administrator, St Francis Xavier Cathedral, Adelaide, 1957–67; Diocesan Chaplain, Young Christian Workers, 1955–67; Mem., Nat. Fitness Council of SA, 1958–67; Bishop of Townsville, 1967–83; Coadjutor Archbishop of Adelaide, 1983–85. Chairman: Aust. Catholic Bishops' Conf. Cttee for the Family and for Life, 1993–2001; S Australian Ministerial Adv. Bd on Ageing, 2002–06. *Address:* 11 Debra Court, Netley, SA 5037, Australia.

FAULKNER, Sarah Donaldson; *see* Wootton, S. D.

FAULKS, family name of **Baron Faulks**.

FAULKS, Baron *cr* 2010 (Life Peer), of Donnington in the Royal County of Berkshire; **Edward Peter Lawless Faulks;** QC 1996; Minister of State, Ministry of Justice, since 2014; *b* 19 Aug. 1950; *s* of His Honour Peter Ronald Faulks, MC and Pamela Faulks (*née* Lawless); *m* 1990, Catherine Frances Turner, *d* of Lindsay Turner and Anthea Cadbury; two *s*. *Educ:* Wellington Coll.; Jesus Coll., Oxford (MA; Hon. Fellow 2014). FCIArb. Called to the Bar, Middle Temple, 1973, Bencher, 2002. Literary Agent, Curtis Brown, 1980–81; Asst Recorder, 1996–2000; Recorder, 2000–10. Chairman: Professional Negligence Bar Assoc., 2002–04; Res. Soc. of Conservative Lawyers, 2010–12. Special Advr to DCA on compensation culture, 2005–06. Mem., Commn on a Bill of Rights, 2012. *Publications:* (contributing ed.) Local Authority Liabilities, 1998, 5th edn 2012. *Recreations:* sports, the arts. *Address:* 33 Ladbroke Grove, W11 3AY; 1 Chancery Lane, WC2A 1LF. *T:* 0845 634 6666; House of Lords, SW1A 0PW. *Club:* Garrick.
See also S. C. Faulks.

FAULKS, His Honour Esmond James; a Circuit Judge, 1993–2011; *b* 11 June 1946; *s* of Hon. Sir Neville Faulks, MBE, TD and Bridget Marigold (*née* Bodley); *m* 1972, Pamela Margaret Ives; one *s* one *d*. *Educ:* Uppingham Sch.; Sidney Sussex Coll., Cambridge (Exhibitioner; MA). Called to the Bar, Inner Temple, 1968; a Recorder, 1987–93. Member: Parole Bd, 2002–08; Mental Health Rev. Tribunal, 2011–. Hon. Vis. Prof. of Law, Samford Univ., Ala, 2005. *Recreation:* country pursuits.

FAULKS, Sebastian Charles, CBE 2002; author; *b* 20 April 1953; *s* of His Honour Peter Ronald Faulks, MC and Pamela Faulks (*née* Lawless); *m* 1989, Veronica Youlten; two *s* one *d*. *Educ:* Wellington Coll. (Scholar); Emmanuel Coll., Cambridge (Exhibnr; BA 1974; Hon. Fellow 2007). Editor, New Fiction Society, 1978–81; Daily Telegraph, 1978–82; feature writer, Sunday Telegraph, 1983–86; Literary Editor, Independent, 1986–89; Dep. Editor, 1989–90, Associate Editor, 1990–91, Independent on Sunday; columnist: The Guardian, 1992–98; London Evening Standard, 1997–99; Mail on Sunday, 1999–2000. Writer and presenter: Churchill's Secret Army (television), 2000; Faulks on Fiction (television), 2011; panellist, The Write Stuff, Radio 4, 1998–. FRSL 1995. Hon. DLitt: Tavistock Clinic/UEL,

2007; Hertfordshire, 2012. Hon. Bencher, Middle Temple, 2015. *Publications:* A Trick of the Light, 1984; The Girl at the Lion d'Or, 1989; A Fool's Alphabet, 1992; Birdsong, 1993; The Fatal Englishman, 1996; Charlotte Gray, 1998 (filmed 2002); (ed with Jörg Hensgen) The Vintage Book of War Stories, 1999; On Green Dolphin Street, 2001; Human Traces, 2005; Pistache, 2006; Engleby, 2007; Devil May Care, 2008; A Week in December, 2009; Faulks on Fiction, 2011; A Possible Life, 2012; Jeeves and the Wedding Bells, 2013; (ed with Hope Wolf) A Broken World: letters, diaries and memories of the Great War, 2014; Where My Heart Used to Beat, 2015; contribs to newspapers and magazines. *Address:* c/o Aitken Alexander Associates, 291 Gray's Inn Road, WC1X 8EB.

See also Baron Faulks.

FAULL, Jonathan Michael Howard; Director General, Financial Stability, Financial Services and Capital Markets Union, European Commission, since 2015; *b* 20 Aug. 1954; *s* of Gerald Faull and June Faull (*née* Shepherd); *m* 1979, Sabine Garrel; two *s*. *Educ:* Univ. of Sussex (BA); Coll. of Europe, Bruges (MA). European Commission, 1978–: Administrator, then Principal Administrator, various depts, 1978–87; Asst to Dir Gen., Directorate Gen. for Competition, 1987–89; Mem., Cabinet of Sir Leon Brittan, Vice-Pres., EC, 1989–92; Directorate General for Competition: Hd, Transport and Tourism Unit, 1992–93; Hd, Co-ordination and Gen. Policy Unit, 1993–95; Dir, Competition Policy, Co-ordination, Internat. Affairs and Relns with other Instns, 1995–99; Dep. Dir Gen. of Competition, 1999; Hd of Press and Communication Service, later Dir Gen., Press and Communication, 1999–2003; Dir Gen., Justice and Home Affairs, later Justice, Freedom and Security, 2003–10; Dir Gen., Internal Market and Services, 2010–15. Advr to British Chamber of Commerce, Belgium, 2003–. Prof. of Law, Free Univ. of Brussels, 1989–2012, now Emeritus; Visiting Professor: Coll. of Europe, Bruges, 2008–; King's Policy Inst., KCL, 2014–; Vis. Lectr, Inst. d'Etudes Politiques, Paris, 1992–95; Vis. Fellow, Centre for Eur. Legal Studies, Cambridge Univ., 1997–2001. Member: Bd, Inst. of European Studies, Brussels, 2005–; Adv. Bd, Security and Defence Agenda, Brussels, 2006–. Mem., editl or adv. boards of various law jls, incl. Common Market Law Reports, Eur. Business Law Rev., UK Competition Law Reports, and World Competition Review; EC corresp., Eur. Law Review, 1980–89. *Publications:* The EC Law of Competition, 1999, 3rd edn 2014; contrib. articles on various topics of EC law and policy. *Address:* European Commission, 1049 Brussels, Belgium. *T:* (322) 2958658.

FAULL, Dr Margaret Lindsay, OBE 2009; Museum Director and Company Secretary, National Coal Mining Museum for England, since 1986; *b* Sydney, Australia, 4 April 1946; *d* of Norman Augustus Faull and Myra Beryl Faull (*née* Smith). *Educ:* Fort St Girls' High Sch., Sydney; Sydney Univ. (BA Archaeol. 1966; DipEd 1967); Macquarie Univ. (MA Hons English Lang. 1970); Leeds Univ. (PhD Archaeol. 1979); Sheffield Univ. (MA Leisure Mgt 1990). Teacher of English and History, NSW, 1970–71; Sub-Warden, Oxley Hall, Univ. of Leeds, 1972–75; field archaeologist, 1975–83, Dep. Co. Archaeologist, 1983–85, W Yorks MCC; Project Manager, Thwaite Mills Industrial Mus., 1985–86. Non-executive Director: Wakefield HA, 2000–02; Local Care Direct, 2005–; Mid Yorks Hosps NHS Trust, 2008–12. Ind. Mem., Wakefield Dist Housing, 2003–. Chair: Wakefield Dist Med. Res. Ethics Cttee, 2000–07; Leeds Central Med. Res. Ethics Cttee, 2007–13. Mem., Deptl Adv. Bd, Univ. of Bradford Archaeol Scis, 1998–2010; Trustee, 2000–04, Vice Pres., 2004–08, Council for British Archaeol.; Vice-Pres., Archaeol. Section, Assoc. for Advancement of Sci., 1997. Chair, Soc. for Church Archaeol., 2005–10. Vice-Chair and Trustee, Soc. for Landscape Studies, 1986–; Sec., Chair and Agent, Thwaite Mills Soc., 1986–2011. *Publications:* (ed with M. Stinson) Domesday Book, 30: Yorkshire, 2 vols, 1986. *Recreations:* watching cricket, attending opera and ballet, collecting African carvings. *Address:* National Coal Mining Museum for England, Caphouse Colliery, New Road, Overton, Wakefield, W Yorks WF4 4RH. *T:* (01924) 844554, *Fax:* (01924) 844567. *E:* managing.director@ncm.org.uk.

FAULL, Very Rev. Vivienne Frances; Dean of York, since 2012; *b* 20 May 1955; *d* of William Baines Faull and Pamela June Faull (*née* Dell); *m* 1993, Dr Michael Duddridge. *Educ:* Queen's Sch., Chester; St Hilda's Coll., Oxford; St John's Coll., Nottingham; Open Univ. Teacher, N India, 1977–79; youth worker, Everton, 1979. Ordained deaconess, 1982, deacon, 1987, priest, 1994; Deaconess, St Matthew and St James, Mossley Hill, 1982–85; Chaplain: Clare Coll., Cambridge, 1985–90; Gloucester Cathedral, 1990–94; Canon Pastor, 1994–2000, Vice Provost, 1995–2000, Coventry Cathedral; Dean of Leicester, 2000–12. Mem., Gen. Synod of C of E, 2003–12. Chairman: Assoc. of English Cathedrals, 2009–15; Deans' Conf., 2015–. Hon. Fellow, Clare Coll., Cambridge, 2012. Hon. DPhil Gloucester, 2014; Hon. Litt Chester, DUniv York, 2015. *Address:* Church House, 10–14 Ogleforth, York YO1 7JN.

FAURE WALKER, Rev. Edward William; Vice Lord-Lieutenant, Hertfordshire, 2001–10; farmer; Curate, All Saints, Pin Green, Stevenage, since 2004; *b* 14 Sept. 1946; *s* of Lt Col Henry W. Faure Walker and Elizabeth A. C. Faure Walker (*née* Fordham); *m* 1974, Louise Mary Robinson; two *s* one *d*. *Educ:* Eton; RMA, Sandhurst; St Albans and Oxford Ministry Course. Commnd Coldstream Guards, 1966–74 (C-in-C's Commendation for Courage and Leadership 1971). Farmer at Sandon Bury, 1974–. Chm., 1980–2000, Pres., 2000–08, Herts Assoc. for Young People; Trustee, UK Youth, 1998–2007. Chm., Boxworth Exptl Husbandry Farm, 1988–93. Conservator of Therfield Heath, 2015–. Ordained deacon, 2004, priest, 2005. Agricl Chaplain for Herts, 2006–08. Pres., Herts, SSAFA, 2008–. Hon. Col, Herts ACF, 2002–08. DL 1983, High Sheriff 2000–01, Herts. *Recreations:* country sports, mountaineering, reading, travelling, being at home with family. *Address:* Sandon Bury, Sandon, Buntingford, Herts SG9 0QY. *T:* (01763) 287224. *Clubs:* Alpine; Leander (Henley).

FAUSET, Ian David, CB 2002; *b* 8 Dec. 1943; *s* of late George William Fauset and Margaret Fauset (*née* Davies); *m* 1972, Susan, *d* of late Donald and Gwendolen Best; two *s* one *d*. *Educ:* Chester City Grammar Sch.; King Edward VI Sch., Lichfield; University of London (BSc); UCW Aberystwyth (Dip. Statistics). CEng, FRAeS. Dept of Chief Scientist (RAF), MoD, 1968–78; Head of Air Studies, Defence Optl Analysis Orgn, Germany, 1978–82; fast jet aircraft and helicopter projects, MoD (PE), 1982–87; Civilian Management (Specialists), MoD, 1987–89; Project Dir, Tornado Aircraft, 1989, EH 101 Helicopter, 1989–91, MoD (PE); Asst Under-Sec. of State, Civilian Mgt (Personnel), MoD, 1991–96; Dir Gen. Aircraft Systems, MoD (PE), 1996–99; Exec. Dir, Defence Procurement Agency, MoD, 1999–2003. Non-exec. Dir, GEC Avery, 1991–94. *Recreations:* bridge, tennis, squash. *Club:* Royal Air Force.

FAVELL, Anthony Rowland, MBE 2013; solicitor; *b* 29 May 1939; *s* of Arnold Rowland Favell and Hildegard Favell; *m* 1966, Susan Rosemary Taylor; one *s* one *d*. *Educ:* St Bees School, Cumbria; Sheffield University (LLB). Founder and Sen. Partner, Favell, Smith & Lawson solicitors, Sheffield, 1966–87. MP (C) Stockport, 1983–92; PPS to Rt Hon. John Major, MP, 1986–90. Contested (C) Stockport, 1992. Chm., Tameside and Glossop Acute Services NHS Trust, 1993–97. Part-time Chairman: Mental Health Review Tribunals, 1995–2008; FHSA Appeal Tribunals, 1996–2002; Mem., Criminal Injuries Appeal Panel, 2000–08; Tribunal Judge, 2008–09. Member: High Peak BC, 2007–; Peak Dist Nat. Park Authy, 2007– (Chm., 2011–14); E Midlands Regl Assembly, 2009–10; Chm., National Parks UK, 2013–14. *Recreations:* music, gardening, hill walking, dry stone walling. *Address:* Skinners Hall, Edale, Hope Valley S33 7ZE. *T:* (01433) 670281. *Club:* Lansdowne.

FAWCETT, Dame Amelia (Chilcott), DBE 2010 (CBE 2002); Chairman, Hedge Fund Standards Board, since 2011; non-executive Director, HM Treasury, since 2012; *b* 16 Sept. 1956; *d* of Frederick John Fawcett, II and Betsey Sargent Chilcott. *Educ:* Pingree Sch., Mass; Wellesley Coll. (BA 1978); Univ. of Virginia Sch. of Law (JD 1983). Admitted to New York Bar, 1984. Sullivan & Cromwell: NY, 1983–85; Paris, 1986–87; Morgan Stanley International, 1987–2007: Vice Pres., 1990; Exec. Dir, 1992; Man. Dir and Chief Admin. Officer, 1996–2002; Mem., Eur. Exec. Cttee, 1996–2007; Vice Chm. and Chief Operating Officer, 2002–06; Sen. Adviser, 2006–07. Chairman: Pensions First LLP, 2007–10; Guardian Media Gp plc, 2009–13 (non-exec. Dir, 2007–13). Non-executive Director: State St Corp., Boston, 2006– (Chm., Risk Cttee, 2010–); Investment A/B Kinnevik, 2011– (Dep. Chm., 2013–); Millicom Internat. Cellular SA, Luxembourg, 2014–. Mem. Court, Bank of England, 2004–09 (Chm., Audit Cttee, 2005–09). Chm., Financial Services Subcttee, Amer. Chamber of Commerce, Brussels, 1995–96. Member: Competitiveness Subcttee on Investment, DTI, 1997–98; London Employers Coalition, 1998–2002; Practitioner Forum, FSA, 1998–2001; Competitiveness Council, DTI, 1999–2000; New Deal Task Force, 1999–2001; Dep. Chm., Nat. Employment Panel, 2001–04. Member: Adv. Bd, Community Links, 1992–2001; Board of Directors: Bright Red Dot Foundn, 1998–2001; London First, 1997–2002; BITC, 2005–09. Trustee: Nat. Portrait Gall., 2003–11 (Chm., Develt Bd, 2002–11; Dep. Chm., 2005–11); Nat. Maritime Mus., Cornwall, 2004–06; Prince of Wales's Charitable Foundn, 2011– (Chm., 2012–). Chm., London Internat. Fest. of Theatre, 2002–10; Dir, Spitalfields Fest., 1998–2001. Mem. Council, Univ. of London, 2002–08 (Chm., Audit Cttee, 2003–08); Gov., London Business Sch., 2010–; Comr, UK-US Fulbright Commn, 2010–. Lady Usher of the Purple Rod, Order of the British Empire, 2013–. Hon. DIB American Univ., Richmond, 2006. Prince of Wales' Ambassador Award, 2004. *Recreations:* fly fishing, hill walking, sailing, photography. *Address:* Hedge Fund Standards Board Ltd, Somerset House, New Wing, Strand, WC2R 1LA. *E:* amelia@acfawcett.com. *Clubs:* Reform, 5 Hertford Street; Cradoc Golf; St Mawes Sailing; Manchester Yacht (USA).

FAWCETT, Prof. James William, PhD; FRCP; Chairman, Cambridge University Centre for Brain Repair, since 2001, and Merck Company Professor of Experimental Neurology, since 2002, University of Cambridge; Fellow, since 1986, and Director of Studies in Medicine, since 1999, King's College, Cambridge; *b* 13 March 1950; *s* of late Edward Fawcett, OBE and of Jane Fawcett; *m* 1980, Kay-Tee Khaw, *qv*; one *s* one *d*. *Educ:* Westminster Sch.; Balliol Coll., Oxford, (BA 1972); St Thomas's Hospital Med. Sch. (MB BS 1975); PhD London Univ. 1982. MRCP 1979, FRCP 2000. House Surgeon, St Thomas' Hosp., 1976; House Physician, Addenbrooke's Hosp., 1977; SHO Intensive Care, St Thomas' Hosp., 1977–78; SHO Immunology, Northwick Park Hosp., 1978–79; Scientist, NIMR, London, 1979–82; Asst Prof., Salk Inst., La Jolla, 1982–86; Lectr in Physiol., Cambridge Univ., 1986–2001. FMedSci 2003. *Publications:* (jtly) Formation and Regeneration of Nerve Connections, 1992; (jtly) Brain Damage, Brain Repair, 2002. *Recreations:* bagpiping, sailing, old machinery. *Address:* Cambridge University Centre for Brain Repair, Robinson Way, Cambridge CB2 2PY. *T:* (01223) 331160. *E:* JF108@cam.ac.uk. *Clubs:* Pinstripe Highlanders; Brancaster Staithe Sailing.

FAWCETT, Prof. Jeremy James, PhD; FBA 2010; Professor of International Commercial Law, University of Nottingham, 1995–2013, now Emeritus; *b* Isleworth, 18 May 1949; *s* of Sydney and Kathleen Fawcett; *m* 1971, Jane Rowe; two *d*. *Educ:* Altrincham Grammar Sch.; Univ. of Nottingham (LLB 1970); Univ. of Bristol (PhD 1980). Admitted as solicitor, 1973; Lectr in Law, 1973–87, Reader in Law, 1988, Univ. of Bristol; Prof. of Law, 1988–95, Dean, Faculty of Law, 1993–95, Univ. of Leicester. Vis. Sen. Fellow, NUS, 1987–88. Mem., Wine Soc. *Publications:* (with P. M. North) Cheshire and North's Private International Law, 11th edn 1987, 14th edn (with J. M. Carruthers) 2008; Declining Jurisdiction in Private International Law, 1995; (with P. Torremans) Intellectual Property and Private International Law, 1998, 2nd edn 2011; (jtly) International Sale of Goods in the Conflict of Laws, 2005. *Recreations:* gardening, art, walking coastal paths, theatre. *Address:* School of Law, University of Nottingham, University Park, Nottingham NG7 2RD. *T:* (0115) 951 5737. *E:* james.fawcett@nottingham.ac.uk.

FAWCETT, John Harold, CMG 1986; HM Diplomatic Service, retired; *b* 4 May 1929; *yr s* of late Comdr Harold William Fawcett, OBE, RN, and of late Una Isobel Dalrymple Fawcett (*née* Gairdner); *m* 1st, 1961, Elizabeth Shaw (*d* 2002); one *s*; 2nd, 2004, Linda Garnett. *Educ:* Radley (Scholar); University Coll., Oxford (Scholar). 1st cl. Hon. Mods 1951, 2nd cl. Lit. Hum. 1953. Nat. Service, RN (Radio Electrician's Mate), 1947–49. British Oxygen Co., 1954–63 (S Africa, 1955–57). Entered Foreign Service, 1963; FO, 1963–66; 1st Sec. (Commercial), Bombay, 1966–69; 1st Sec. and Head of Chancery, Port-of-Spain, 1969–70; Asst, Caribbean Dept, FCO, 1971–72; Head of Icelandic Fisheries Unit, Western European Dept, FCO, 1973; Amb. to Democratic Republic of Vietnam, 1974; Counsellor and Head of Chancery, Warsaw, 1975–78; Dep. High Comr, Wellington, 1978–86; Counsellor (Commercial and Economic, 1978–83, Political and Economic, 1983–86), and Head of Chancery, 1983–86, Wellington; Amb. to Bulgaria, 1986–89. Mem., 1998–2002, Chm., 2000–02, Dent Parish Council. Mem., 1989–94, Lay Chm., 1994–99, 2008–11, Ewecross Deanery Synod, dio. of Bradford; Member: Bradford Diocesan Synod, 2009–11; Kendal Deanery Synod, Dio. of Carlisle, 2012–. Trustee: Bradford Dio. Church Buildings Fund, 1996–99; Sedbergh and Dist Community Trust, 1998–2005. Chm., Morecambe Bay Gp, CS Pensioners' Alliance, 1994–2000. Clerk, 1989–94, Chm. of Govs, 1994–2001, Dent Grammar Sch. Educnl Foundn; Governor, Dent C of E Primary Sch., 1994–99. Pres., Dent CC, 2001–05. One of the Twenty-four Sidesmen of Dent. *Recreations:* gardening, collecting books, mathematical models, fractal development of the octagon, design of experimental multi-hull sailing craft. *Address:* Strait End, Dent, Cumbria LA10 5QW. *Clubs:* Savile, MCC; Wellington Racing (Wellington); Royal Bombay Yacht.

FAWCETT, Kay-Tee; *see* Khaw, Kay-Tee.

FAWCUS, Maj.-Gen. Graham Ben, CB 1991; Chief of Staff and Head of UK Delegation, Live Oak, SHAPE, 1989–91, retired; *b* 17 Dec. 1937; *s* of late Col Geoffrey Arthur Ross Fawcus, RE and Helen Sybil Graham (*née* Stronach); *m* 1966, Diana Valerie, *d* of Dr P. J. Spencer-Phillips of Bildeston, Suffolk; two *s* one *d*. *Educ:* Wycliffe College; RMA Sandhurst (Sword of Honour); King's College, Cambridge (BA 1963, MA 1968). Commissioned RE, 1958; served UK, Cyprus, BAOR, MoD; OC 39 Field Squadron RE, BAOR, 1973–74; MoD, 1975–76; GSO1 (DS), Staff College, 1977–78; CO 25 Engineer Regt, BAOR, 1978–81; Cabinet Office, 1981; Comdt, RSME, 1982–83; ACOS, HQ 1 (Br) Corps, 1984–85; Chief, Jt Services Liaison Orgn, Bonn, 1986–89. Col Comdt RE, 1991–2000. Chm., RE Widows Soc., 1992–2000. Chm., Ipswich & Suffolk Small Business Assoc., 1996–99. Gov., 1995–2006, Chm. of Govs, 2006–09, Wycliffe Coll. *Recreations:* ski-ing, tennis, Scottish country dancing, furniture restoration, bridge. *Address:* Church Cottage, The Green, Flowton, Ipswich, Suffolk IP8 4LG.

FAWKES, Wally; cartoonist, 1945–2005; *b* 21 June 1924; *m* 1st, 1949, Sandra Boyce-Carmichele (marr. diss. 1964; she *d* 2005); one *s* two *d* (and one *d* decd); 2nd, 1965, Susan Clifford; one *s* one *d*. *Educ:* Sidcup Central Sch.; Sidcup Sch. of Art; Camberwell Sch. of Art. Came from Vancouver, BC, to England, 1931. Joined Daily Mail, 1945; started Flook strip, 1949, transferred to The Mirror, 1984. Political cartoons for: Spectator, 1959; Private Eye, and New Statesman, 1965; Observer, 1965–95; Punch, 1971–92; Today, 1986–87; London Daily News, 1987; Times mag., 1995–96; Sunday Telegraph, 1996–2005; cartoons for Daily Express, 1994; caricatures for Oldie mag., 1996–2005; covers for The Week, 1997. Co-Founder, Humphrey Lyttelton Band, 1948. Hon. DLitt Kent, 2001. Cartoonist of the Year, British Press Awards, 2004. *Publications:* World of Trog, 1977; Trog Shots, 1984; Trog: 40 Graphic Years, 1987; collections of Flook strips. *Recreations:* playing jazz (clarinet and soprano saxophone), cooking, cricket. *Address:* 8 Glenhurst Avenue, NW5 1PS. *T:* (020) 7267 2979.

FAY, Dr Christopher Ernest, CBE 1999; FREng; Chairman: Brightside plc, 2008–14; Iofina plc, 2009–14 (non-executive Director, 2008–14); *b* 4 April 1945; *s* of Harry Thomas Fay and Edith Margaret Fay (*née* Messenger); *m* 1971, Jennifer Olive Knight; one *s* two *d*. *Educ:* Leeds Univ. (BSc Civil Eng. 1967; PhD 1970). CEng 1974; FICE 1994 (MICE 1973; Hon. FICE 1998); FEI (FInstPet 1994); FREng (FEng 1996). Joined Shell Internat. Petroleum Co., 1970, as offshore design engr; Shell-BP Develt Co., Nigeria, 1971–74; Head, Engrg Planning and Design and Offshore Construction, Sarawak Shell Berhad, Malaysia, 1974–78; Develt Manager, Dansk Undergrunds Consortium, Copenhagen, on secondment from Dansk Shell, 1978–81; Technical Manager, Norske Shell Exploration and Production, Stavanger, 1981–84; Dir, Exploration and Production, Norway, 1984–86; Gen. Manager and Chief Exec., Shell Cos, Turkey, 1986–89; Man. Dir, Shell UK Exploration and Production and a Man. Dir, Shell UK, 1989–93; Chm. and Chief Exec., Shell UK, 1993–98. Chairman: Expro Internat. Gp plc, 1999–2008; Tuscan Energy Gp Ltd, 2002–05; non-executive Director: BAA, 1998–2006; Stena Internat., 1999– (Chm.); Stena Drilling Ltd, 1999–; Anglo American plc, 1999–2010; Weir Gp plc, 2001–03; Conister Financial Gp plc, 2006–08. Chm., Adv. Cttee on Business and the Envmt, 1999–2003. Member: CBI President's Cttee, 1993–98; INSEAD UK Cttee, 1993–95; British Cttee, Det Norske Veritas, 1994–95 and 1996–2001; Bd, Oil, Gas and Petrochemicals Supplies (formerly Oil and Gas Projects and Supplies) Office, 1994–98; Exec. Cttee, British Energy Assoc., 1994–98; Chm., Oil Industries Emergency Cttee, 1993–98. Gov., Motability, 1999–2001 (Mem. Council, 1993–98). CCMI (CIMgt 1994); FRSE 1996; FRSA 1994. *Recreations:* gardening, ski-ing, golf, tennis. *Address:* Merrifield, Links Road, Bramley, Guildford GU5 0AL. *Clubs:* Sunningdale Golf, Bramley Golf.

FAY, Sir (Humphrey) Michael (Gerard), Kt 1990; Principal, Fay, Richwhite & Co. Ltd, Merchant Bankers, since 1974 (Joint Chief Executive, 1990–96); *b* 10 April 1949; *s* of James and Margaret Fay; *m* 1983, Sarah Williams; one *s* two *d*. *Educ:* St Patrick's Coll., Silverstream, Wellington; Victoria Univ., Wellington (LLB 1971). Jt Chief Exec., Capital Markets, 1986–90; Dir, Bank of New Zealand, 1989–92. Chairman: Australia/NZ Bicentennial Commn, 1988; Expo 1988 Commn, 1987–88; Expo 1992 Commn, 1989–92; NZ Ireland Fund, 1995–98. Hon. Consul General for Thailand, 1996–98. Chm., NZ Americas Cup Challenges, 1987, 1988, 1992. Chm., Manu Samoa Rugby Club, 1997–. *Recreations:* horse breeding and racing, fishing, swimming, running, golf. *Clubs:* Royal New Zealand Yacht Squadron, Auckland Racing, Mercury Bay Boating.

FAY, Margaret, CBE 2010 (OBE 2004); DL; Chairman, One NorthEast, 2003–10; *b* 21 May 1949; *d* of Oswald and Joan Allen; *m* 1st, 1968, Matthew Stoker (marr. diss. 1978); one *s*; 2nd, 1982, Peter Fay (marr. diss. 1993). *Educ:* South Shields Grammar Sch. for Girls. Joined Tyne Tees TV, 1981; Dir of Ops, 1995–97; Man. Dir, 1997–2003. Dir, Newcastle Gateshead Initiative, 1999–2003; Member Board: English Partnerships, 2004–08; Homes and Communities Agency, 2008–10. Non-executive Director: Darlington Building Soc., 2000–08; Northumbrian Water, 2010–; Fabrick Gp, 2011–14; Thirteen Group, 2014–. Vice Chm., The Sage Gateshead, 2010–. Governor: Teesside Univ., 1998–2007; Sunderland Univ., 2011–. DL Tyne and Wear, 2011. *Recreations:* travel, theatre, wine, grandchildren, food.

FAY, Sir Michael; *see* Fay, Sir H. M. G.

FAY, Stephen Francis John; journalist and author; *b* 14 Aug. 1938; *s* of Gerard Fay and Alice (*née* Bentley); *m* 1964, Prudence Butcher; one *s* one *d*. *Educ:* Highgate Sch.; Univ. of New Brunswick, Canada (BA, MA). On editl staff: Glasgow Herald, 1961–64; Sunday Times, 1964–84; freelance writer, 1984–86, 1991–96; Ed., Business Mag., 1986–89; Dep. Ed., Independent on Sunday, 1989–91 and 1996–99; Ed., Wisden Cricket Monthly, 2000–03. British Press Special Award, 1978, 1979. *Publications:* Measure for Measure: reform in the Trade Unions, 1970; (with L. Chester and M. Linklater) Hoax, 1972 (Edgar Award for Best Crime Fact Book, 1973); (with P. Knightley) The Death of Venice, 1976; The Great Silver Bubble, 1980; The Ring: anatomy of an opera, 1984; Portrait of an Old Lady: turmoil at the Bank of England, 1987; Power Play: the life and times of Peter Hall, 1995; The Collapse of Barings, 1996; (contrib.) The Secrets of the Press, 1999; Tom Graveney at Lord's, 2005. *Recreations:* theatre, watching sport, reading broadsheets. *Address:* 5A Furlong Road, N7 8LS. *T:* (020) 7607 8950. *E:* stephen@sandpfay.co.uk. *Clubs:* Garrick, Beefsteak, MCC.

FAYERS, Norman Owen; City Treasurer and Director of Financial Services, Bristol City Council, 1990–96; Managing Director, Norman Fayers Consultancy Ltd, 2002–09; *b* 8 Jan. 1945; *s* of Claude Lance Fayers and Winifred Joyce (*née* Reynolds); *m* 1966, Patricia Ann Rudd; two *s*. *Educ:* Northgate Grammar Sch. for Boys, Ipswich; BA Open Univ. CPFA 1967; IRRV 1990; FMAAT 1999. Ipswich CBC, 1961–66; Eastbourne CBC, 1966–70; Group Accountant (Educn), Royal Borough of Kingston upon Thames, 1970–73; Chief Accountant, RBK & C, 1973–77; Chief Officer, Finance, London Borough of Ealing, 1977–90. Chartered Institute of Public Finance and Accountancy: Mem. Council, 1991–92; Pres., S Wales and W England Reg., 1993–95 (Vice Pres., 1991–93); Association of Accounting Technicians: Mem. Council, 1992–2001, 2004–07; Chm., Bristol Br., 2000–03. Treas., Life Educn Centres Bristol Ltd, 2009–. Gov., Orchard Sch., Bristol, 2011–. *Recreations:* golf, music, bridge. *Clubs:* Rotary (Bristol; Pres., 2008–09; Treas., 2009–); Kendleshire Golf.

FAYRER, Sir John (Lang Macpherson), 4th Bt *cr* 1896; *b* 18 Oct. 1944; *s* of Sir Joseph Herbert Spens Fayrer, 3rd Bt, DSC, and Helen Diana Scott (*d* 1960), *d* of late John Lang; *S* father, 1976. *Educ:* Edinburgh Academy; Scottish Hotel School, Univ. of Strathclyde. Research Officer: Moray House Inst., 1991–95; Univ. of Edinburgh, 1995–2001. *Publications:* Child Development from Birth to Adolescence, 1992; ed reports of Scotplay confs, 1993, 1994. *Heir:* none. *Address:* 21/2 Lady Nairne Crescent, Edinburgh EH8 7PE.

FAZAKERLEY, Prof. John Kneale, PhD; FRCPath; FRSB; Director, Pirbright Institute (formerly Institute for Animal Health), since 2011; *b* Liverpool, 23 July 1957; *s* of John Ernest Fazakerley and Edna Fazakerley (*née* Kneale); *m* 1986, Ann Walker. *Educ:* Wilmslow Grammar Sch.; Univ. of Durham (BSc Hons); St Thomas' Hosp. Med. Sch. (PhD 1985); Univ. of Edinburgh (MBA). FRCPath 2005; FRSB (FSB 2011). Postdoctoral Fellow, Dept of Microbiol., Univ. of Pennsylvania, 1986–88; Sen. Res. Associate, Neuropharmacol., Scripps Res. Inst., La Jolla, Calif, 1988–91; Sen. Res. Fellow, Pathol., Univ. of Cambridge, 1991–94; University of Edinburgh: Veterinary Pathol., and Centre for Infectious Diseases, 1994–2011; Prof. of Virol., Coll. of Medicine and Veterinary Medicine, 2004–11, now Hon. Prof.; Gp Leader, Roslin Inst., 2009–11. Vis. Fellow, Nuffield Dept of Medicine, Univ. of Oxford. *Address:* Pirbright Institute, Pirbright, Woking, Surrey GU24 0NF. *T:* (01483) 231001. *E:* John.Fazakerley@pirbright.ac.uk.

FAZIO, Antonio; Governor, Bank of Italy, 1993–2005; *b* 11 Oct. 1936; *m* Maria Cristina Rosati; one *s* four *d*. *Educ:* Univ. of Rome (BSc *summa cum laude* Econs and Business 1960); MIT. Asst Prof. of Demography, Univ. of Rome, 1961–66; Consultant to Res. Dept, Bank of Italy, 1961–66; Bank of Italy: Dep. Head, subseq. Head, Unit of Econometric Res., 1966–72; Dep. Dir, Monetary Sector, 1972, Head, 1973–79, Res. Dept; Central Manager for Economic Res., 1980–82; Dep. Dir Gen., 1982–93. Chm., Italian Foreign Exchange Office, 1993–2005; Member: Bd of Dirs, BIS, 1993–2005; Governing Council, Eur. Central Bank (formerly Eur. Monetary Inst.), 1993–2005. Hon. Mem., Circolo San Tommaso d'Aquino, 2009. Hon. Dr Econs and Business Bari, 1994; Hon. DHL Johns Hopkins, 1995; Hon. Dr Pol Sci. Macerata, 1996; Hon. LLB Cassino, 1999; Hon. Dr Stats and Econs Milan, 1999; Hon. Dr Computer Engrg Lecce, 2000; Hon. Dr Banking Econs Verona, 2002; Hon. LLD St John's, 2002; Hon. DPhil Catania, 2002; Hon. Dr Moral Theol. Pontificia Salesiana, 2003. Ezio Tarantelli Prize for most original theory in Economic Policy, Club dell'Economia, 1995; Saint Vincent Prize for Economics, Centro Culturale Saint-Vincent, 1997; Pico della Mirandola Prize for Econs, Finance and Business, Fondazione Cassa di Risparmio di Mirandola, 1997–98; Internat. Award in the Humanities, Accad. di Studi Mediterranei, 1999; Keynes-Sraffa Prize, London, 2003; Fiaccola d'oro, Circolo San Tommaso d'Aquino, 2012. Kt Grand Cross, Order of Merit (Italy), 1993. *Publications:* Razionalità economica e solidarietà, 1996; Globalizzazione: politica economica e dottrina sociale, 2008; L'enciclica Caritas in Veritate: Prospettiva storica e attualità, 2011; Sviluppo e declino demografico in Europa e nel Mondo, 2012; scientific articles, mainly on monetary theory and monetary policy issues. *Address:* c/o Bank of Italy, Via Nazionale 91, 00184 Rome, Italy.

FEACHEM, Sir Richard (George Andrew), KBE 2007 (CBE 1995); PhD, DSc (Med); FREng; Professor of Global Health (formerly International Health), since 1999, and Director, Global Health Group, since 2007, University of California, San Francisco and Berkeley; *b* 10 April 1947; *s* of late Charles George Paulin Feachem and Margaret Flora Denise Greenhow; *m* 1st, 1970, Zuzana Sedlarova (marr. diss. 1999); one *s* one *d*; 2nd, 1999, Neelam Sekhri. *Educ:* Wellington Coll.; Univ. of Birmingham (BSc 1969); Univ. of NSW (PhD 1974); DSc (Med) London, 1991. MICE 1980; FIWEM 1987; FICE 1990; FREng (FEng 1994). Volunteer, Solomon Is, 1965–66; Research Fellow: Univ. of NSW, 1970–74; Univ. of Birmingham, 1974–76; London School of Hygiene and Tropical Medicine: Lectr and Sen. Lectr, 1976–82; Reader, 1983–87; Prof. of Tropical Envmtl Health, 1987–95; Dean, 1989–95; Dir, Health, Nutrition and Population, World Bank, 1995–99; Prof. of Internat. Health, Univ. of Calif, San Francisco and Berkeley, and founding Dir, Inst. for Global Health, 1999–2002; founding Exec. Dir, Global Fund to Fight AIDS, Tuberculosis and Malaria, and Under Sec.-Gen., UN, 2002–07 (on leave of absence). Vis. Prof., LSHTM, 1995–; Adjunct Professor: Johns Hopkins Univ., 1996–2001; George Washington Univ., 1997–2001; Hon. Prof., Univ. of Qld, 2005–. Consultant, WHO, 1982–83; Principal Public Health Specialist, World Bank, 1988–89; Chairman: Adv. Cttee, World Develt Report, 1992–93; Adv. Cttee, TB Programme, WHO, 1992–95; Bd, Initiative on Public Private Partnerships for Health, 2000–02; Bd, Global Forum for Health Res., 2001–04; Malaria Elimination Gp, 2008–; Co-Chair, Asia Pacific Malaria Elimination Network, 2008–; Member: Adv. Cttee, Caribbean Epidemiology Centre, 1990–95; Mgt Cttee, Inst. of Child Health, 1989–91; Bd on Internat. Health, US NAS, 1992–97, 2001–03; Bd, Internat. AIDS Vaccine Initiative, 1996–2003; Adv. Cttee, Aust. Nat. Centre for Epidemiology and Public Health, 1996–2001; Commn on Macroeconomics and Health, 2000–02; Commn on HIV/AIDS and Governance in Africa, 2003–06; Commn on Investing in Health, 2012–. Member Council: RSTM&H, 1978–81; VSO, 1991–2007; Water Aid, 1994–95; Patron, Assoc. for Promotion of Healthcare in former Soviet Union, 1992–96. Trustee, Internat. Centre for Diarrhoeal Diseases Research, Bangladesh, 1985–89. Chm., Health Policy Adv. Bd, Gilead Sciences Inc., 2010– (Mem., 2007–); Member: Adv. Bd, Sure Chill Ltd, 2011–; Bd, Vital Connect Inc., 2011–. Mem., Inst. of Medicine, 2002. Hon. FFPH (Hon. FFPHM 1990); Hon. Fellow, LSHTM, 2000. Hon. DEng Birmingham, 2007. Dean's Medal, Johns Hopkins Sch. of Public Health, 2003. Member, Editorial Board: Transactions of the RSTM&H, 1979–88; Jl of Tropical Medicine and Hygiene, 1979–96; Current Issues in Public Health, 1993–2002; Health and Human Rights, 1993–2002; Tropical Medicine and Internat. Health, 1996–2001; Global Public Health, 2005–; Editor-in-Chief, WHO Bulletin, 1999–2002. *Publications:* Water, Wastes and Health in Hot Climates, 1977; Subsistence and Survival: rural ecology in the Pacific, 1977; Water, Health and Development, 1978; Evaluation for Village Water Supply Planning, 1980; Sanitation and Disease, 1983; Environmental Health Engineering in the Tropics, 1983; Evaluating Health Impact, 1986; Disease and Mortality in Sub-Saharan Africa, 1991; The Health of Adults in the Developing World, 1992; Shrinking the Malaria Map, 2009; over 220 papers in scientific jls. *Recreations:* mountaineering, ski-ing. *Club:* Travellers.

FEALY, Michael; QC 2014; *b* Drogheda, Ireland, 6 May 1970; *s* of Peter and Rose Fealy; *m* 2003, Della Burnside. *Educ:* National Univ. of Ireland (BCL); Sidney Sussex Coll., Cambridge (LLM 1992). Called to the Bar: King's Inns, Dublin, 1995; Middle Temple, 1997. Lectr, QMW, subseq. QMUL, 1992–97; in practice as barrister, 1998–. Mem., Chatham House (RIIA). *Publications:* (with I. Grainger) An Introduction to the Civil Procedure Rules, 1999. *Recreations:* reading, running, travel. *Address:* 1 Essex Court, Temple, EC4Y 9AR. *T:* (020) 7583 2000. *E:* mfealy@oeclaw.co.uk. *Clubs:* Reform, Ivy.

FEAN, Sir (Thomas) Vincent, KCVO 2005; HM Diplomatic Service, retired; Consul General, Jerusalem, 2010–13; *b* 20 Nov. 1952; *s* of Joseph Peter Fean and Brigid Fean (*née* Walsh); *m* 1978, Anne Stewart; one *s* two *d*. *Educ:* St Theodore's RC Secondary Sch., Burnley; Sheffield Univ. (BA French and German 1975). Joined FCO, 1975; Second Sec., Baghdad, 1978; First Sec., Damascus, 1979–82; EU and Berlin issues, FCO, 1982–85; UK Repn to EU, Brussels, 1985–89; Personnel Mgt Dept, FCO, 1989–92; Counsellor, Press and Public Affairs, Paris, 1992–96; Head, Counter-Terrorism Policy Dept, FCO, 1996–99; Dir, Asia Pacific, Internat. Gp, Trade Partners UK, 1999–2002; High Comr, Malta, 2002–06; Ambassador to Libya, 2006–10. *Recreations:* supporting Burnley FC and Lancashire CCC, travel, walking, cycling, folk music. *Club:* Burnley Football.

FEAR, Kevin David; Headmaster, Nottingham High School, since 2007; *b* Watford, 12 June 1963; *s* of late Derek Fear and of Gwen Fear; *m* 1986, Denise Wilson; one *s* one *d*. *Educ:* Douai Sch.; Southampton Univ. (BA Hons Hist.); Nottingham Univ. (PGCE). Hd of Hist., King's Sch., Chester, 1986–2000; Sen. Teacher, 2000–04, Dep. Hd, 2004–07, Nottingham High Sch. *Recreations:* following fortunes of Arsenal FC, running local football team, children. *Address:* Nottingham High School, Waverley Mount, Nottingham NG7 4ED. *T:* (0115) 978 6056, *Fax:* (0115) 924 9716. *E:* fear.kd@nottinghamhigh.co.uk. *Clubs:* East India, Lansdowne.

FEARN, family name of **Baron Fearn**.

FEARN, Baron *cr* 2001 (Life Peer), of Southport in the County of Merseyside; **Ronald Cyril Fearn, (Ronnie),** OBE 1985; *b* 6 Feb. 1931; *s* of James Fearn and Martha Ellen Fearn; *m* 1955, Joyce Edna Dugan; one *s* one *d*. *Educ:* King George V Grammar School. FCIB. Banker with Williams Deacons Bank, later Williams & Glyn's Bank, later Royal Bank of Scotland. MP (L 1987–88, Lib Dem 1988–92 and 1997–2001) Southport; contested (Lib Dem) Southport, 1992. Lib Dem spokesman on health and tourism, 1988–89, on local govt, 1989–90, on transport, housing and tourism, 1990–92. Mem., Select Cttee on Culture, Media and Sport, 1997–2001. Councillor, Sefton MBC, 1974–. *Recreations:* badminton, amateur dramatics, athletics. *Address:* House of Lords, SW1A 0PW; Norcliffe, 56 Norwood Avenue, Southport, Merseyside PR9 7EQ. *T:* (01704) 228577.

FEARNLEY-WHITTINGSTALL, Hugh Christopher Edmund; writer, broadcaster, cook and food campaigner, since 1989; *b* 14 Jan. 1965; *s* of Robert and Jane Fearnley-Whittingstall; *m* 2001, Marie Derôme; two *s* two *d*. *Educ:* Eton Coll.; St Peter's Coll., Oxford (BA Hons Philos. and Psychol.). Sous chef, River Cafe, 1989; journalist: Punch, 1989–92; Sunday Times, 1990–92; Daily Telegraph, 1993–98; Independent on Sunday, 2000–02; Observer, 2002. Television includes series: A Cook on the Wild Side, 1995, 1997; Escape to River Cottage, 1998–99; Return to River Cottage, 2000; River Cottage Forever, 2002; Beyond River Cottage, 2004; River Cottage Road Trip, 2005; The View from River Cottage, 2005; The River Cottage Treatment, 2006; River Cottage Spring, 2008; River Cottage Autumn, 2008; River Cottage: Summer's Here, 2009, Winter's on the Way, 2009; River Cottage Every Day, 2010; Hugh's Fish Fight, 2011; River Cottage Veg, 2011; Three Good Things, 2012; Hugh's Fish Fight: Save Our Seas, 2013; River Cottage to the Core,

2013; Scandimania, 2014; Hugh's Fish Fight: Hugh's Last Stand, 2014; Waste, 2015. Member: Devon Cattle Breeders' Assoc., 2004–; Greenpeace, 2010–. Patron: FARMA; Switchback. Food columnist: Observer (monthly), 2003–06; Guardian Weekend Mag., 2006–13. *Publications:* A Cook on the Wild Side, 1995; The River Cottage Cookbook, 2001; The River Cottage Year, 2003; The River Cottage Meat Book, 2004; The River Cottage Family Cookbook, 2005; (with Nick Fisher) The River Cottage Fish Book, 2007; Hugh Fearlessly Eats It All, 2007; River Cottage Every Day, 2009; River Cottage Veg Every Day!, 2011; Hugh's Three Good Things on a Plate, 2012; River Cottage Fruit Every Day!, 2013; River Cottage Light & Easy, 2014; Love Your Leftovers, 2015. *Recreations:* fishing, diving, growing vegetables, charcuterie. *Address:* c/o Antony Topping, Greene & Heaton, 37 Goldhawk Road, W12 8QQ. *Clubs:* Century, Soho House.

FEARON, Prof. Douglas Thomas, MD; FRS 1999; FRCP, FMedSci; Sheila Joan Smith Professor of Immunology, 2003–10, now Professor Emeritus, and Senior Group Leader, CRUK Cambridge Research Institute, since 2011, University of Cambridge; Fellow, Trinity College, Cambridge, since 2001; *b* 16 Oct. 1942; *s* of late Dr Henry Dana Fearon and of Frances Hudson (*née* Eubanks); *m* 1st, 1972, Margaret Andrews (marr. diss. 1975); 2nd, 1977, Clare MacIntyre (*née* Wheless); one *s* one *d.* *Educ:* Williams Coll. (BA 1964); Johns Hopkins Med. Sch. (MD 1968). FRCP 1994. Major, US Army Med. Corps, 1970–72 (Bronze Star and Army Commendation Medal, 1972). Med. Res., Johns Hopkins Hosp., 1968–70; Helen Hay Whitney Foundn Post-Doctoral Res. Fellow, 1974–77; Harvard Medical School: Res. Fellow in Medicine, 1972–75; Instr in Medicine, 1975–76; Asst Prof., 1976–79, Associate Prof., 1979–84, Prof., 1984–87, of Medicine; Prof. of Medicine, and Director, Div. of Rheumatology and of Grad. Prog. in Immunology, Johns Hopkins Univ. Sch. of Medicine, 1987–93; University of Cambridge: Wellcome Trust Prof. of Medicine, 1993–2003; Dir, Wellcome Trust PhD Prog. in Infection and Immunity, 2005–10. Principal Res. Fellow, Wellcome Trust, 1993–2001; Hon. Consultant in Medicine, Addenbrooke's Hosp., 1993–. Member: Scientific Adv. Bd, Babraham Inst., 1998; Scientific Bd, Ludwig Inst. for Cancer Res., 1998–; Scientific Adv. Bd, Max Planck Institut für Immunobiologie, 2001; Scientific Adv. Cttee, Rita Allen Foundn, 2002–. Member: EMBO, 2001; NAS, USA, 2001; Hon. For. Mem., Amer. Acad. of Arts and Scis, 1999. Founder FMedSci 1998. Hon. MA Harvard, 1984. Merit Award, NIH, 1991. *Publications:* articles on immunology in learned jls. *Recreation:* golf. *Address:* Salix, Conduit Head Road, Cambridge CB3 0EY. *T:* (01223) 570067. *Clubs:* Gog Magog Golf; The Country (Brookline, USA).

FEAST, Prof. William James, (Jim), CBE 2007; FRS 1996; CChem, FRSC; Courtaulds Professor of Polymer Chemistry, Durham University, 1989–2003, now Emeritus Professor; *b* 25 June 1938; *s* of William Edward Feast and Lucy Mary Feast (*née* Willis); *m* 1967, Jenneke Elizabeth Catherina van der Kuijl, Middelburg, Netherlands; two *d.* *Educ:* Sheffield Univ. (BSc 1960); Birmingham Univ. (PhD 1963). CChem, FRSC 1981; FIM 1994. Durham University: Lectr, 1965–76; Sen. Lectr, 1976–86; Prof., 1986–2003; Dir, IRC in Polymer Sci. and Technol., 1994–2002. Gillette Internat. Res. Fellow, Leuven, Belgium, 1968–69; Vis. Prof., Max Planck Institut für Polymerforschungs, 1984–88. Pres., RSC, 2006–08. *Publications:* numerous res. papers, reviews in learned jls. *Recreations:* walking, gardening, theatre, fine arts. *Address:* Chemistry Department, Durham University, South Road, Durham DH1 3LE. *T:* (0191) 386 8646. *E:* w.j.feast@durham.ac.uk.

FEATES, Prof. Francis Stanley, CB 1991; PhD; CEng, FIChemE; FRSC; CChem; Professor of Environmental Engineering, University of Manchester Institute of Science and Technology, 1991–95; *b* 21 Feb. 1932; *s* of Stanley James Feates and Dorothy Marguerite Jenny Feates (*née* Orford); *m* 1953, Gwenda Grace Goodchild; one *s* three *d.* *Educ:* John Ruskin Sch., Croydon; Birkbeck Coll. London (BSc Special Chem.; PhD). FRSC 1972; FIChemE 1991; CEng 1991. Wellcome Res. Foundn, 1949–52; Chester-Beatty Cancer Res. Inst., Univ. of London, 1952–54. Chemistry Lectr, Goldsmiths' Coll., London, 1954–56; AERE, Harwell, UKAEA, 1956–78; Argonne Nat. Lab., Univ. of Chicago, Illinois, 1965–67; Department of the Environment: Dir, Nuclear Waste Management, 1978–83; Chief Radiochemical Inspector, 1983–86; Chief Inspector, Radioactive Substances, HM Inspectorate of Pollution, 1986–88; Dir and Chief Inspector, HM Inspectorate of Pollution, 1989–91. Consultant to EC (formerly EEC) on nuclear matters, 1991–. Director: Sir Alexander Gibb & Partners, 1991–94; Siemens Plessey Controls Ltd, 1991–92; Grundon Waste Management, 1991–92. Expert Mem., Scientific and Technical Cttee, EEC, Brussels, 1989–92; Member: Steering Cttee, Nuclear Energy Agency, OECD, Paris, 1988–91; Steering Bd, Lab. of Govt Chemist, 1991–94; Observer Mem., NRPB, 1988–91. Founder Editor, Jl of Hazardous Materials, 1975–85. *Publications:* Hazardous Materials Spills Handbook, 1982; Integrated Pollution Management, 1995; numerous scientific papers on pollution issues, nuclear power, electrochemistry, thermodynamics, waste management, electron microscopy. *Recreations:* walking, cycling, travel.

FEATHER, Prof. John Pliny; Professor of Book History, School of Arts, English and Drama, Loughborough University, 2013–14, now Emeritus Professor (Professor of Information and Library Studies, 1988–2013); *b* 20 Dec. 1947; *m* 1971, Sarah, *d* of late Rev. A. W. Rees and Mrs S. M. Rees. *Educ:* Heath Sch., Halifax; Queen's Coll., Oxford (BLitt, MA); MA Cambridge, PhD Loughborough. FCLIP (FLA 1986). Asst Librarian, Bodleian Liby, Oxford, 1972–79; Munby Fellow in Bibliography, Cambridge Univ., 1977–78; Loughborough University: Lectr, then Sen. Lectr, 1979–88; Hd, Dept of Information and Liby Studies, then Information Sci., 1990–94 and 2003–06; Dean of Educn and Humanities, 1994–96; Pro-Vice-Chancellor, 1996–2000; Dean, Graduate Sch., 2010–13. Vis. Prof., UCLA, 1982. Pres., Oxford Bibliographical Soc., 1988–92. Mem., many nat. and internat. professional cttees; consultancy and teaching in many countries and for UNESCO, EEC and British Council, 1977–. FRSA 1994. *Publications:* The Provincial Book Trade in Eighteenth-Century England, 1985; A Dictionary of Book History, 1987; A History of British Publishing, 1988, 2nd edn 2005; Preservation and the Management of Library Collections, 1991, 2nd edn 1996; Index to Selected Bibliographical Journals 1971–1985, 1991; Publishing, Piracy and Politics: a history of copyright in the British book trade, 1994; The Information Society, 1994, 6th edn 2013; (with James Dearnley) The Wired World, 2001; Managing Preservation in Libraries and Archives, 2002; Publishing: communicating knowledge in the 21st century, 2003; articles and reviews in academic and professional jls, conf. procs, etc. *Recreations:* photography, music, travel, cooking. *Address:* 36 Farnham Street, Quorn, Leicestershire LE12 8DR. *Club:* Athenæum.

FEATHERBY, William Alan; QC 2008; a Recorder, since 2002; *b* Clifton, Bristol, 16 May 1956; *s* of Joseph Alan Featherby and Patricia Annie Featherby (*née* Davies); *m* 1980, Clare Frances, JP, *d* of Ian Richard Posgate; five *s* five *d.* *Educ:* Ripley Court Sch., Ripley; Haileybury; Trinity Coll., Oxford (MA, Scholar). Called to the Bar, Middle Temple, 1978 (Astbury Law Scholar); practises in common law, esp. personal injury and clinical negligence. Member: Professional Conduct Cttee, Bar Council, 1995–2000; Civil Procedure Rules Cttee, 2008–14. Mem., Southwark Dio. Synod, 2006–10. *Publications:* A Yorkshire Furrow, 1992. *Recreations:* opera, Richard Strauss, reading, walking. *Address:* 12 King's Bench Walk, Temple, EC4Y 7EL. *Club:* Carlton.

FEATHERSTONE, Jane Elizabeth; *b* 24 March 1969; *d* of John Robert Featherstone and Elizabeth Ann Featherstone. *Educ:* Old Palace Sch., Croydon; Leeds Univ. (BA Jt Hons Hist. and German). PA, Paul Gascoigne Promotions, 1991–92; Producer: Hat Trick Prodns, 1992–95; United TV, 1995–97; Wall to Wall, 1998–99; Kudos Film and Television Ltd: Hd of Drama, 2000–02; Exec. Producer, 2002; Jt Man. Dir, 2002; Creative Dir, 2008; CEO, 2011–15; Jt Chm., UK Shine Gp, 2012–15; Producer or Executive Producer: Touching Evil; Glasgow Kiss; Sex 'n' Death; Spooks (series 1–6); Hustle (series 1–4); Life on Mars (series 1–2); Tsunami, the Aftermath; Secret Life; The Hour; Pleasureland; Wide Sargasso Sea; Ashes to Ashes; Broadchurch; The River. *Recreations:* family, friends, shops full of old things, ski-ing averagely, saying "quite frankly", good food and wine, the beach, wonderful writing.

FEATHERSTONE, Rt Hon. Lynne (Choona); PC 2014; *b* 20 Dec. 1951; *d* of Joseph and Gladys Ryness; *m* 1982, Stephen Featherstone (marr. diss. 2003); two *d.* *Educ:* South Hampstead High Sch.; Oxford Poly. (Dip. in Communications and Design). Various design posts, 1975–80; Man. Dir, own design co., Inhouse Outhouse Design, 1980–87; strategic design consultant, 1987–97. Dir, Ryness Electrical Supplies Ltd, 1991–2002. Member (Lib Dem): Haringey LBC, 1998–2006 (Leader of the Opposition, 1998–2002); London Assembly, GLA, 2000–05. MP (Lib Dem) Hornsey and Wood Green, 2005–15; contested (Lib Dem) same seat, 2015. Lib Dem Shadow Sec. of State for Internat. Devlt, 2006–10; Lib Dem Spokesperson for Youth and Equalities, 2007–10; Parliamentary Under-Secretary of State: (Minister for Equalities and Criminal Information), Home Office, 2010–12; DFID, 2012–14; Minister of State, Home Office, 2014–15. Lib Dem spokesperson for energy, 2015–. Contested (Lib Dem) Hornsey and Wood Green, 2001. *Publications:* (as Lynne Choona Ryness) Marketing and Communication Techniques for Architects, 1992. *Recreations:* tennis, food, architecture, writing.

[Created a Baroness (Life Peer) 2015 but title not yet gazetted at time of going to press.]

FEATHERSTONE-WITTY, Mark, OBE 2014; Founding Principal and Chief Executive Officer, Liverpool Institute for Performing Arts, since 1994; *b* 2 June 1946; *s* of late Philip and Evy Featherstone-Witty; *m* 1972, Alison Thomas; one *s.* *Educ:* Univ. of Durham (BA, PGCE); Rollins Coll., Florida (MEd). Asst Ed., Macmillan Educnl Publishing, 1974–76; English teaching jobs in both private and maintained sector, 1976–80; Founder and Principal, Capital Coll., 1980–89; Chief Exec., London Sch. of Publishing, 1982–89; Co-founder and Principal, London Sch. of Insce, 1983–89; Co-founder, Rainbow Educn Prodns, 1983–86; Consultative Educn Ed., Quartet Books, 1984–86; Founder, and Sen. Educnl Advr, Brit Sch., 1989–91. Chair, Assoc. of Tutors, 1985–88. Founder Trustee, Schs for Performing Arts Trust, 1985–2009; Trustee: Liverpool Royal Court Th. Foundn, 2000–; Nat. Acad. of Writing, 2003–11; Member, Board: The Music Lives Foundn, 2006–08; Drama UK, 2012–; Dir, Conference of Drama Schs, 2010–12. Chm., Sefton Park Palm House Preservation Trust, 2004–12. Member and Director: LIPA Primary Sch., 2012–; LIPA Sixth Form Coll., 2013–. Royal Norwegian Order of Merit, 2014. *Publications:* Optimistic, Even Then, 2000; LIPA in Pictures: the first ten years, 2006. *Recreations:* reading comic crime books, entertainment, walking, projects. *Address:* Liverpool Institute for Performing Arts, Mount Street, Liverpool L1 9HF. *T:* (0151) 330 3000. *E:* m.featherstone-witty@lipa.ac.uk. *Club:* Lansdowne.

FEAVER, (Mary Frances) Clare; *see* Harvey, M. F. C.

FEAVER, William Andrew; writer, art critic and painter; *b* 1 Dec. 1942; *s* of Rt Rev. Douglas Russell Feaver; *m* 1st, 1964, Victoria Turton (marr. diss.); one *s* three *d*; 2nd, 1985, Andrea Rose; two *d.* *Educ:* St Albans School; Nottingham High School; Keble College, Oxford. Teacher: South Stanley Boys' Modern Sch., Co. Durham, 1964–65; Newcastle Royal Grammar Sch., 1965–71; Sir James Knott Res. Fellow, Newcastle Univ., 1971–73; art critic: The Listener, 1971–75; Financial Times, 1974–75; art adviser, Sunday Times Magazine, 1974–75; art critic, The Observer, 1975–98. Vis. Prof., Nottingham Trent Univ., 1994–. Exhibitions curated include: George Cruikshank, V&A, 1974; Thirties, Hayward Gall., 1979; The Ashington Gp, Beijing, 1980; Lucian Freud, Kendal, 1996, Tate Gall., and La Caixa, Barcelona, 2002, Mus. of Contemp. Art, LA, 2002–03, Museo Correr, Venice, 2005; Michael Andrews: lights, Thyssen-Bornemisza Mus., Madrid, 2000; Michael Andrews, Tate Gall., 2001; John Constable, Grand Palais, Paris, 2002. Trustee, Ashington Gp, 1989–. Critic of the Year, 1983, Commended, 1986, UK Press Awards. *Publications:* The Art of John Martin, 1975; When We Were Young, 1976; Masters of Caricature, 1981; Pitmen Painters, 1988; James Boswell: unofficial war artist, 2006; Lucian Freud, 2007; Frank Auerbach, 2009. *Address:* 1 Rhodesia Road, SW9 9EJ. *T:* (020) 7737 3386.

See also W. Horbury.

FEDERER, Roger; professional tennis player, since 1998; *b* Basle, 8 Aug. 1981; *s* of Robert Federer and Lynette Federer (*née* Durand); *m* 2009, Mirka Vavrinec; twin *s* twin *d.* Ranked World No. 1 as Jun., 1998; winner: Wimbledon Jun. title, 1998; singles titles include: Milan, 2001; Hamburg TMS, 2002, 2005; Sydney, 2002; Vienna, 2002, 2003; Marseilles, 2003; Tennis Masters Cup, Houston, 2003, 2004; Wimbledon, 2003, 2004, 2005, 2006, 2007, 2009, 2012; Halle, Germany, 2003, 2004, 2005, 2006, 2008, 2013, 2014, 2015; Munich, 2003; Dubai, 2003, 2004, 2005, 2007, 2012, 2014; Australian Open, 2004, 2006, 2007, 2010; Bangkok, 2004, 2005; Canada AMS, 2004; Gstaad, 2004; Hamburg AMS, 2004, 2007; Toronto, 2004, 2006; US Open, 2004, 2005, 2006, 2007, 2008; Cincinnati, 2005, 2007, 2010, 2012, 2014; 2015; Doha, 2005, 2006, 2011; Miami, 2005, 2006; Rotterdam, 2005; Basle, 2006, 2007, 2008, 2010, 2014; Madrid, 2006, 2012; Masters Cup, Shanghai, 2006, 2007, 2014; Tokyo, 2006; Estoril, 2008; French Open, 2009; Stockholm Open, 2010; Istanbul Open, 2014; Barclays ATP World Tour Finals, London, 2010, 2011; Silver Medal, London Olympics, 2012; doubles titles: Rotterdam, 2001, 2002; Gstaad, 2001; Moscow, 2002; Vienna, 2003; Miami TMS, 2003; Halle, 2005; Beijing Olympics, 2008; 27 Davis Cup ties, 1999– (40 singles wins, 12 doubles wins; winning Swiss team, 2014). Founder, Roger Federer Foundn, 2003. Pres., ATP Player Council, 2008–. Swiss Personality of Year, 2003; ATP Eur. Player of Year, 2004; BBC Overseas Sports Personality of Year, 2004, 2006; Laureus World Sportsman of Year, 2005, 2006, 2007, 2008. *Recreations:* golf, soccer, ski-ing, friends, PlayStation, music, playing cards. *Address:* c/o Lynette Federer, POB 209, 4103 Bottmingen, Switzerland.

FEDOTOV, Yury Viktorovich; Executive Director, United Nations Office on Drugs and Crime, and Director-General, United Nations Office, Vienna, since 2010; *b* 14 Dec. 1947; *m* 1973, Elena Fedotova; one *s* one *d.* *Educ:* Moscow State Inst. of Internat. Relns. Joined USSR Diplomatic Service, 1971; served: Algeria, 1974–80; Ministry of For. Affairs, Moscow, 1980–83; India, 1983–88; Ministry of For. Affairs, Moscow, 1988–94; Dep. Perm. Rep., then Actg First Dep. Perm. Rep. of Russian Fedn to UN, NY, 1994–99; Ministry of For. Affairs, Moscow, 1999–2002; Dep. Minister of Foreign Affairs, 2002–05; Ambassador of the Russian Federation to the Court of St James's, 2005–10. Order of Friendship (Russia); Distinguished Mem. of Diplomatic Service (Russia). *Address:* United Nations Office on Drugs and Crime, Vienna International Centre, PO Box 500, 1400 Vienna, Austria. *Club:* Athenæum.

FEEHAN, Francis Thomas, (Frank); QC 2010; a Recorder, since 2005; *b* Liverpool, 26 Oct. 1964; *s* of Francis John Feehan and Angela Feehan (*née* Wilson); civil partnership 2006, Simon Owers. *Educ:* All Saints RC Comp. Sch., Sheffield; Emmanuel Coll., Cambridge (BA Hons 1987). Called to the Bar, Lincoln's Inn, 1988; in practice as a barrister, 1988–. *Recreations:* travel, friends. *Address:* 42 Bedford Row, WC1R 4LL. *T:* (020) 7831 0222, *Fax:* (020) 7831 2239. *E:* clerks@42br.com. *Club:* Travellers'.

FEENY, Patrick, (Paddy); Head of Communications, Europe, Middle East, Russia and India, Christie's, since 2014; *b* 27 June 1965; *s* of Victor Francis Foy Feeny and Joan Aïda (*née* Dunbar-Stuart); partner, Alan Davey, *qv.* *Educ:* St Brendan's Coll., Bristol; King's Coll., London (BD 1987). Asst Press Sec., Prime Minister's Office, 1993–96; Press. Sec., DFID, 1996–98; Policy and Commns Manager, Social Exclusion Unit, Cabinet Office, 1998–2000; Commns Advr, Teenage Pregnancy Unit, DoH, 2000–01; Hd of News, 2001–05, Communications Dir, later External Relations Dir, 2005–08, DCMS; Communications Dir,

DECC, 2008–11; Head of Communications, BBC News, 2012–14. *Recreations:* music, theatre, books and walking. *Address:* Christie's, 8 King Street, SW1Y 6QT. *E:* paddy.feeny@btinternet.com. *Club:* 2 Brydges.

FEESEY, Air Vice-Marshal John David Leonard, AFC 1977; retired, 1999; *b* 11 Oct. 1942; *s* of Leonard Ewart Feesey and Maisie Veronica Lillian Feesey; *m* 1968, Glenda Doris Barker; two *s*. *Educ:* Oldershaw Grammar Sch., Wallasey, Cheshire. RAF Officer Cadet, 1961; commnd General Duties Br., 1962; RAF pilot (Hunter, Harrier), 1962–83; OC No 1 (Fighter) Sqdn (Harrier), 1983–86; Stn Comdr, RAF Wittering, 1986–88; Comd Exec. Officer, HQ AAFCE, 1989–91; Dir Airspace Policy, 1991–93, Dir Gen., Policy and Plans, 1993–96, HQ NATS; Dep. Comdr, Combined Air Ops Centre 4, 1996–98. Vice-Pres., CCF Assoc., 1999–2009; President: No. 1 (Fighter) Sqdn Assoc., 2006–12; Pelynt and Lanreath Br., RBL, 2006–. Chm., Lanreath Community Assoc., 2014–. *Recreations:* hill walking, fishing, gardening. *Club:* Royal Air Force.

FEEST, Terry George, MD; FRCP; Consultant Nephrologist, Richard Bright Renal Unit, 1991–2009, and Clinical Director, Renal and Transplant Services, 1991–2006, Southmead Hospital, North Bristol NHS Trust; *b* 16 Feb. 1944; *s* of Sydney George Feest and Doris May Feest; *m* 1991, Kathleen Alexis Blosick; two *s* one *d*. *Educ:* Sidney Sussex Coll., Cambridge (BA 1965; MB BChir 1968; MD 1980); King's Coll. Hosp., London. FRCP 1986. Consultant Physician and Nephrologist, Royal Devon and Exeter Hosp., 1978–91. Hon. Prof. of Clinical Nephrology, Univ. of Bristol, 1995–. Renal Physician, Auckland City Hosp., 2009–10. Asst Dir, UK Renal Registry, Renal Assoc., 2011–13 (Chm., 1990–2006; Dir, 2010–11); Mem. Appraisal Cttees, NICE, 2000–06. *Publications:* UK Renal Registry Annual Report, 1998–2013; papers in internat. renal and gen. med. jls. *Recreations:* travel, walking, cooking, theatre, music, gardening, chess, swimming. *E:* terry@feest.co.uk.

FEILDEN, Sir Henry (Rudyard), 7th Bt *cr* 1846 of Feniscowles, Lancashire; Principal of Small Animal Practice, Poole Road Veterinary Surgery, since 1998; *b* Burwash, E Sussex, 26 Sept. 1951; *o s* of Sir Henry Wemyss Feilden, 6th Bt and Ethel May (*née* Atkinson); *S* father, 2010; *m* 1st, 1982, Anne, *d* of William Frank Bonner Shepperd (marr. diss. 1997); one *s*; 2nd, 1998, Geraldine, *d* of late Major Gerald Rayland Kendall; one *s* one *d*. *Educ:* Kent Coll., Canterbury; Bristol Univ. (BVSc 1975). MRCVS. Veterinary Surgeon: Tuckett Gray and Partners, Aylesbury, Bucks, 1976–78; Fraser and Smith, Binfield, Berks, 1978–83; L. A. Gould, Rossendale, Lancs, 1983–84; Riverside Veterinary Surgery, Bishopstoke, Eastleigh, Hants, 1996–98. Veterinary Advr, Solvay-Duphar Veterinary, Southampton, 1984–96. *Recreations:* DIY, natural history, military history, travel, fine wine, antiques, digital photography, genealogy, good company, visiting Bath. *Heir:* *s* William Henry Feilden, *b* 5 April 1983. *Address:* 340 Poole Road, Branksome, Poole, Dorset BH12 1AW. *T:* (01202) 765431. *Club:* Old Canterburians.

FEILDING, family name of **Earl of Denbigh**.

FEILDING, Viscount; Peregrine Rudolph Henry Feilding; *b* 19 Feb. 2005; *s* and *heir* of Earl of Denbigh, *qv*.

FEINSTEIN, Elaine Barbara, FRSL; writer, since 1966; *b* 24 Oct. 1930; *d* of Isidore Cooklin and Fay Cooklin (*née* Compton); *m* 1956, Arnold Feinstein; three *s*. *Educ:* Wyggeston Grammar Sch. for Girls, Leicester; Newnham Coll., Cambridge (Exhibnr; English Tripos; MA). Mem., editl staff, CUP, 1959–62; Asst Lectr, Comparative Lit. Dept, Univ. of Essex, 1968–71. Rockefeller Foundn Fellow, Bellagio, 1998. Writer of reviews for The Times, Daily Telegraph, TLS, The Guardian and other newspapers, 1975–2002; Writer in Residence: for British Council, Singapore, 1993; Tromsø, 1995. Mem. Council, RSL, 2004–11. Writer: *for television:* Breath, 1975; Lunch, 1981; The Edwardian Country Gentlewoman's Diary (12 part series), 1984; A Brave Face, 1985; *for radio:* Echoes, 1980; A Late Spring, 1981; A Day Off, 1983; Marina Tsvetaeva: a life, 1985; If I Ever Get On My Feet Again, 1987; The Man in Her Life, 1990; Foreign Girls (trilogy), 1993; A Winter Meeting, 1994; Lawrence's Women in Love (4 part adaptation), 1996; Cloudberries, 1999. Chm. Judges, T. S. Eliot Award, 1995. FRSL 1981. Hon. DLitt Leicester, 1990. Cholmondeley Award for Poetry, 1990; Soc. of Authors Travel Award, 1991. *Publications:* *novels:* The Circle, 1970; The Amberstone Exit, 1972; The Glass Alembic, 1973 (US edn as The Crystal Garden, 1974); Children of the Rose, 1975; The Ecstasy of Dr Miriam Garner, 1976; The Shadow Master, 1978; The Survivors, 1982; The Border, 1984; Mother's Girl, 1988; All You Need, 1989; Loving Brecht, 1992; Dreamers, 1994; Lady Chatterley's Confession, 1996; Dark Inheritance, 2001; The Russian Jerusalem, 2008; *poems:* In a Green Eye, 1966; The Magic Apple Tree, 1971; At the Edge, 1972; The Celebrants and Other Poems, 1973; Some Unease and Angels, 1977; Selected Poems, 1977; The Feast of Euridice, 1980; Badlands, 1987; City Music, 1990; Selected Poems, 1994; Daylight, 1997; (ed) After Pushkin, 1999; Gold, 2000; Collected Poems, 2002; Talking to the Dead, 2007; Cities, 2010; Portraits, 2015; *poems in translation:* The Selected Poems of Marina Tsvetaeva, 1971, 5th revd edn 1999 (Arts Council Translation Awards, 1970, 1972); Three Russian Poets: Margarite Aliger, Yunna Morits, Bella Akhmadulina, 1976; Bride of Ice: new selected poems by Marina Tsvetaeva, 2009; *biography:* Bessie Smith, 1986; A Captive Lion: the life of Marina Tsvetaeva, 1987; Lawrence's Women, 1993 (US edn as Lawrence and The Women, 1993); Pushkin, 1998; Ted Hughes: the life of a poet, 2001; Anna of All the Russias: a life of Anna Akhmatova, 2005; *short stories:* Matters of Chance, 1972; The Silent Areas, 1980; *autobiography:* It Goes with the Territory: memoirs of a poet, 2013; *editor:* Selected Poems of John Clare, 1968; (with Fay Weldon) New Stories, 1979; New Poetry, 1988. *Recreations:* books, music, travel, the conversation of friends. *Address:* c/o Rogers Coleridge & White, 20 Powis Mews, W11 1JN. *T:* (020) 7722 3688. *E:* ebfeinstein@btinternet.com. *Clubs:* Groucho, PEN.

FELDMAN, family name of **Barons Feldman** and **Feldman of Elstree**.

FELDMAN, Baron *cr* 1995 (Life Peer), of Frognal in the London Borough of Camden; **Basil Feldman,** Kt 1982; a Party Treasurer, Conservative and Unionist Party, since 1996; *b* 23 Sept. 1926; *s* of late Philip and Tilly Feldman; *m* 1952, Gita Julius; two *s* one *d*. *Educ:* Grocers' School. National Union of Conservative and Unionist Associations: Mem., 1975–98, Chm., 1991–96, Exec. Cttee; Vice-Chm., 1982–85, Chm., 1985–86; Vice-Pres., 1986–98; Jt Nat. Chm., Cons. Party's Impact 80s Campaign, 1982–87; Chairman: Team 1000, 1989–93; Renaissance Forum, 1996–2010; Member: Policy Gp for London, 1975–81, 1984–87; Nat. Campaign Cttee, 1976 and 1978; Adv. Cttee on Policy, 1981–86; Cttee for London, 1984–87; Greater London area: Dep. Chm., 1975–78; Chm., 1978–81; Pres., 1981–85; Vice Pres., 1985–; Vice-Pres., Greater London Young Conservatives, 1975–77; President: Richmond and Barnes Cons. Assoc., 1976–84; Hornsey Cons. Assoc., 1978–82; Patron, Hampstead Cons. Assoc., 1981–86. Contested GLC Elections, Richmond, 1973; Member: GLC Housing Management Cttee, 1973–77; GLC Arts Cttee, 1976–81. Mem., Free Enterprise Loan Soc., 1977–84. Chairman: Martlet Services Gp Ltd, 1973–81; Solport Ltd, 1980–85; The Quality Mark, 1987–92. Chairman: Better Made in Britain Campaign, 1983–98 (organising 22 exhibns in 14 different business sectors); Market Opportunities Adv. Gp, DTI, 1991–93; Shopping Hours Reform Council, 1988–93 (Pres., 1993–95); Better Business Opportunities, 1990–96; Watchpost Ltd, 1983–; Dir, Young Entrepreneurs Fund, 1985–95. Underwriting Mem. of Lloyd's, 1979–96. Membre Consultatif, Institut Internat. de Promotion et de Prestige, Geneva (affiliated to Unesco), 1978–96. Member: Post Office Users National Council, 1978–81 (Mem., Tariffs Sub-Cttee, 1980–81); English Tourist Board, 1986–96; Chairman: Clothing EDC (NEDO), 1978–85; Maker/User Working Party (NEDO), 1988–89. Gov., Sports Aid Foundn, 1990–2002. Chairman: London Arts Season 1993–97; Festival of Arts and Culture, 1995; Salzburg Festival Trust, London, 2000–03 (Vice Chm., 1997–2000); Mem., Internat. Council, Los Angeles Philharmonic, 1995–. Chm., Fresh Hope Trust, 2003–. Freeman, City of London, 1984. FRSA 1987. Silver Decoration of Honour, Salzburg, 2003. *Publications:* Some Thoughts on Job Creation (for NEDO), 1984; Constituency Campaigning: a guide for Conservative Party workers; several other Party booklets and pamphlets. *Recreations:* golf, tennis, theatre, opera, travel, watching football. *Club:* Carlton.

FELDMAN OF ELSTREE, Baron *cr* 2010 (Life Peer), of Elstree in the County of Hertfordshire; **Andrew Simon Feldman;** Chairman: Conservative Party, since 2010; Conservative Party Board, since 2010; *b* London, 25 Feb. 1966; *s* of Malcolm Roger Feldman and Marcia Feldman (*née* Summers); *m* 1999, Gabrielle Josephine Gourgey; two *s* one *d*. *Educ:* Haberdashers' Aske's Sch., Elstree; Brasenose Coll., Oxford (BA 1st Cl. Juris.); Inns of Court Sch. of Law. Mgt Consultant, Bain & Co., 1988–90; commercial barrister, 1 Essex Court, 1991–95. Dir, Jayroma (London) Ltd, 1995–. Dep. Treas., 2005–08, Chief Exec., 2008–10, Cons. Party; Mem. Bd, Cons. Party Foundn, 2010–. *Recreations:* tennis, golf, ski-ing, reading. *Address:* House of Lords, SW1A 0PW. *Clubs:* Carlton, George.

FELDMAN, Prof. David John, FBA 2006; Rouse Ball Professor of English Law, since 2004, and Fellow of Downing College, since 2003, University of Cambridge; *b* 12 July 1953; *s* of late Alec Feldman and Valerie Feldman (*née* Michaelson); *m* 1983, Naomi Jill Newman; one *s* one *d*. *Educ:* Brighton, Hove and Sussex Grammar Sch.; Exeter Coll., Oxford (MA, DCL). Lectr in Law, 1976–89, Reader, 1989–92, Bristol Univ.; University of Birmingham: Barber Prof. of Jurisprudence, 1992–2000; Dean of Law, 1997–2000; Prof. of Law, 2000–04; Chm., Faculty Bd of Law, Univ. of Cambridge, 2006–09. Vis. Fellow, ANU, 1989; Miegunyah Dist. Vis. Fellow, Univ. of Melbourne, 2006; Sir J. C. Smith Sen. Vis. Scholar, Univ. of Nottingham, 2010. Legal Advr to Jt Select Cttee on Human Rights, Houses of Parlt, 2000–04. A Judge of Constitutional Court of Bosnia and Herzegovina, 2002–10 (a Vice-Pres., 2006–09). Pres., Soc. of Legal Scholars, 2010–11. FRSA. Hon. Bencher, Lincoln's Inn, 2003. Hon. QC 2008. Hon. LLD Bristol, 2013. *Publications:* Law Relating to Entry, Search and Seizure, 1986; Criminal Confiscation Orders: the new law, 1988; (ed) Criminal Investigation: reform and control, 1991; Civil Liberties and Human Rights in England and Wales, 1993, 2nd edn 2002; (ed jtly) Corporate and Commercial Law: modern developments, 1996; (ed) English Public Law, 2004, 2nd edn 2009; (ed) Law in Politics, Politics in Law, 2013; contrib. articles on public law, human rights and criminal procedure. *Recreations:* music, dog-walking, cooking, history, theatre. *Address:* Downing College, Cambridge CB2 1DQ. *T:* (01223) 762122.

FELDMAN, Sally Joy; media trainer, journalist, humanist celebrant; Senior Fellow, Creative Industries, University of Westminster, since 2012 (Dean, School of Media, Arts and Design, 2003–12); *b* 10 March 1948; *d* of Reuben Feldman and Karola Landau; *m* 1st, 1981, Tony Russell (marr. diss. 2010); one *s* one *d*; 2nd, 2010, Prof. Laurence John, (Laurie), Taylor, *qv*. *Educ:* Univ. of Reading (BA Hons English 1970); Univ. of Manitoba (MA English 1972). Freelance and editorial posts, 1970s; Press Officer, CRC and CRE, 1976–78; Editor, range of magazines: Love Affair, New Love, Loving, Woman's World, 1978–83; Woman's Hour, BBC Radio 4: Producer, 1983–86; Dep. Editor, 1986–89; Presenter, Weekend Edition, 1986; Editor, 1990–97, and Editor, range of other progs; Launch Editor, Treasure Islands; Dean, Sch. of Media, London Coll. of Printing, 1998–2002. Freelance broadcaster, and journalist and reviewer. Mem. Council, Media Soc. Associate Ed., New Humanist Mag. *Publications:* The Complete Desk Book, 1978; *novels for teenagers* (as Amber Vane): Hopelessly Devoted, 1995; Blazing Kisses, 1996; Freezing Heart, 1996; Follow the Sun, 1996; I Taught Him a Lesson He'll Never Forget, 1998. *Recreations:* voracious reading, talking, film, clothes, travel, friends and family. *T:* 07930 314259. *E:* feldmas@wmin.ac.uk, sallyjoyfeldman@gmail.com.

FELDMAN, Prof. Stanley, FRCA; Professor of Anaesthetics, Charing Cross and Westminster Medical School, University of London, 1989–95, now Emeritus; *b* 10 Aug. 1930; *s* of Israel and Lilly Feldman; *m* 1957, Carole Bowman; one *s* one *d*. *Educ:* London Univ. (BSc 1950); Westminster Med. Sch. (MB BS 1955). FRCA (FFARCS 1962). Fellow (Fulbright Schol.), Univ. of Washington, Seattle, 1957–58; Westminster Hospital: Registrar, 1958–62; Consultant Anaesthetist, 1962–89; Sen. Lectr, RPMS, 1963–66. Postgrad. Advr in Anaesthetics, RCS, 1966–72; Res. Consultant, Royal Nat. Orthopaedic Hosp. NHS Trust, 1995–98. Vis. Prof., Stanford Univ., 1967–68. Hon. Member: Australasian Soc. Anaesthetists; Spanish Portuguese Soc. Anaesth.; Belgian Soc. Anaesth.; Netherlands Soc. Anaesthetists; Israeli Soc. Anaesth.; Assoc. Anaesthetists of GB and Ireland, 2013. Editor, Review of Anaesthetic Pharmacology, 1992–97. *Publications:* Anatomy for Anaesthetists, 1963, 8th edn 2008; Scientific Foundations of Anaesthesia, 1971, 4th edn 1990; Muscle Relaxants, 1973, 2nd edn 1981; Drug Mechanisms in Anaesthesia, 1981, 2nd edn 1993; Neuromuscular Block, 1997; Organophosphates and Health, 2001; Poison Arrows, 2005; Panic Nation, 2005, 2nd edn 2006; Life Begins At..., 2007; Poison Arrows to Prozac, 2009; Global Warming and Other Bollocks, 2009; A Doctor's Story, 2010. *Recreations:* sailing, travel. *Address:* 28 Moore Street, SW3 2QW. *Clubs:* Royal Society of Medicine, Lansdowne.

FELDMANN, Sir Marc, Kt 2010; AC 2014; PhD; FRCP, FRCPath; FMedSci; FRS 2006; FAA; Professor, Kennedy Institute of Rheumatology, University of Oxford, 2011–14, now Emeritus; Head, Kennedy Institute of Rheumatology, University of Oxford (formerly at Faculty of Medicine, Imperial College London), 2002–14 (Head, Cytokine Biology and Immunology, 1992); *b* 2 Dec. 1944; *s* of Elie and Cyla Feldmann; *m* 1966, Tania Gudinski; one *s* one *d*. *Educ:* Univ. of Melbourne (MB BS 1967, BSc Med Hons 1970; PhD 1972). FRCPath 1984; FRCP 1998. Sen. Scientist, 1974–77, Principal Scientist, 1977–85, ICRF; Prof. of Cellular Immunology, Univ. of London, 1985–2011; Dep. Dir, Charing Cross Sunley Res. Centre, 1985–92. Pres., Internat. Cytokine Soc., 2002–03. Mem., EMBO, 2006–. FMedSci 2001; FAA 2005. Crafoord Prize (with Sir R. Maini), Royal Swedish Acad. of Sci., 2000; Albert Lasker Award for Clin. Med. Res. (with Sir R. Maini), NY, 2003; Cameron Prize for Therapeutics (with Sir R. Maini), Edinburgh Univ., 2004; Internat. Rheumatoid Arthritis Award (with Sir R. Maini), Japan Rheumatism Foundn, 2007; Curtin Medal, ANU, 2007; Dr Paul Janssen Award for Biomed. Res. (with Sir R. Maini), Johnson & Johnson, New York, 2008; Ernst Schering Prize (with Sir R. Maini), Ernst Schering Foundn, 2010; Canada Gairdner Award, Gairdner Foundn, 2014. *Publications:* (ed with J. J. Oppenheim) Cytokine Reference, 2001; (with R. N. Maini) Pocket Reference to TNFα Antagonist and Rheumatoid Arthritis, 2001; numerous contribs to scientific literature. *Recreations:* tennis, hiking, keeping fit, art, theatre. *Address:* Kennedy Institute of Rheumatology, Nuffield Department of Orthopaedics, Rheumatology and Musculoskeletal Sciences, University of Oxford, Botnar Research Centre, Windmill Road, Headington, Oxford OX3 7LD. *E:* marc.feldmann@kennedy.ox.ac.uk. *Club:* Queen's.

FELDSTEIN, Prof. Martin Stuart; Professor, Harvard University, since 1969; *b* 25 Nov. 1939; *m* Kathleen Foley; two *d*. *Educ:* Harvard Coll. (AB *summa cum laude* 1961); Oxford Univ. (BLitt 1963, MA 1964, DPhil 1967). Nuffield College, Oxford University: Research Fellow, 1964–65; Official Fellow, 1965–67; Hon. Fellow, 1998; Lectr in Public Finance, Oxford Univ., 1965–67; Harvard University: Asst Professor, 1967–68; Associate Professor, 1968–69. President, National Bureau of Economic Research, 1977–82 and 1984–2008; Chm., Council of Economic Advrs, 1982–84. Mem., US President's Foreign Intelligence Adv. Bd, 2007–09, Economic Recovery Adv. Bd, 2009–11. Dir, Eli Lilly. Pres., American Econ. Assoc., 2004. Member: Amer. Philosophical Soc.; Amer. Acad. of Arts and Scis; Trilateral Commn; Council on Foreign Relations. Corresp. FBA, 1998. Hon. Fellow, Brasenose Coll., Oxford. *Publications:* (ed) The American Economy in Transition, 1980; Hospital Costs and Health Insurance, 1981; Inflation, Tax Rules, and Capital Formation,

1983; Capital Taxation, 1983; Effects of Taxation on Capital Formation, 1986; United States in the World Economy, 1988; International Economic Co-operation, 1988; American Economic Policy in the 1980s, 1994; International Capital Flows, 1999; articles on econs. *Address:* National Bureau of Economic Research, 1050 Massachusetts Avenue, Cambridge, MA 02138, USA.

FELL, Sir David, KCB 1995 (CB 1990); novelist; Pro-Chancellor, Queen's University Belfast, 2005–14; *b* 20 Jan. 1943; *s* of Ernest Fell and Jessie (*née* McCreedy); *m* 1967, Sandra Jesse (*née* Moore); one *s* one *d*. *Educ:* Royal Belfast Academical Instn; The Queen's University of Belfast (BSc: Pure and Applied Mathematics, also (1st Cl. Hons) Physics). Sales Manager, Rank Hovis McDougall Ltd, 1965–66; Teacher, 1966–67; Research Associate, 1967–69; Civil Servant, 1969–97: Dept of Agriculture (NI), 1969–72; Dept of Commerce (NI), 1972–82 (Under Secretary, 1981); Under Secretary, Dept of Economic Development (NI), 1982; Dep. Chief Exec., Industrial Develt Bd for NI, 1982–84; Permanent Sec., Dept of Economic Develt (NI), 1984–91; Hd of NICS, and Second Perm. Under Sec. of State, NI Office, 1991–97. Chairman: Northern Bank, 1998–2005; Boxmore Internat. plc, 1998–2000; Nat. Irish Bank, 1999–2005; Harland & Wolff Gp plc, 2001–02; Titanic Quarter Ltd, 2001–03; Titanic Properties Ltd, 2001–03; Canal Corp. (USA), 2009–11; Novenso (formerly Litelighting) Ltd, 2010–12; non-exec. Chm., Goldblatt McGuigan, 2005–12; non-executive Director: Dunloe Ewart plc, 1998–2002; Nat. Australia Gp (Europe) Ltd, 1998–2012; Fred Olsen Energy ASA, 1999–2003; Chesapeake Corp. (USA), 2000–09 (Chm., 2005–09); Clydesdale Bank plc, 2004–12. Chairman: Opera NI, 1998–99; Prince's Trust Volunteers (NI), 1998–99; Prince's Trust (NI), 1999–2005; Pres., Extern Orgn, 1998–. Mem. Council, Industrial Soc., 1998–2001. CCMI; FRSA; FCIB. DUniv Ulster, 2003; Hon. LLD QUB, 2014. *Recreations:* music (opera), reading, Rugby Union, writing. *Club:* Old Instonians (Belfast).

FELL, Richard Taylor, CVO 1996; HM Diplomatic Service, retired; *b* 11 Nov. 1948; *s* of late Eric Whineray Fell and Margaret Farrer Fell (*née* Taylor); *m* 1981, Claire Gates; three *s*. *Educ:* Bootham Sch., York; Bristol Univ. (BSc); Univ. of London (MA). Joined HM Diplomatic Service, 1971; Ottawa, 1972–74; Saigon, 1974–75; Vientiane, 1975; First Sec. and Chargé d'Affaires *ai*, Hanoi, 1979; First Sec., UK Delegn to NATO, 1979–83; First Sec. and Head of Chancery, Kuala Lumpur, 1983–86; FCO, 1986–88; on secondment to Thorn EMI, 1988–89; Counsellor, Ottawa, 1989–93; Dep. Hd of Mission, Bangkok, 1993–96; Counsellor, FCO, 1997–2000; Acting Consul-Gen., Toronto, 2000; RCDS, 2001; High Comr, New Zealand, Governor (non-res.) of Pitcairn, Henderson, Ducie and Oeno Is, and High Comr (non-res.), Samoa, 2001–06. Chm., NZ-UK Link Foundn, 2008–11. Book Reviews Editor and ex officio Mem. Council, RSAA, 2010–. *Publications:* Early Maps of South-East Asia, 1988. *Recreations:* antiques, reading, sport.

FELL, William Varley, CMG 2002; International Affairs Adviser, Cathay Pacific Airways, since 2009; Adviser, Aegis Defence Services Ltd, since 2009; *b* 4 March 1948; *s* of late John Richmond Fell and of Cicely Juliet Fell (*née* Varley); *m* 1970, Jill Pauline Warren; two *s* one *d*. *Educ:* Charterhouse; Bristol Univ. (BA Hons). With Hambros Bank, 1969–71; entered HM Diplomatic Service, 1971; 3rd Sec., Vienna, 1973–75; 2nd Sec., Havana, 1976–78; 1st Secretary: Warsaw, 1979–82; FCO, 1982–88; Counsellor, Athens, 1988–92; FCO, 1992–2002. Internat. Risk Advr, British Airways, 2002–08. Gov., Skinners' Sch., Tunbridge Wells, 2006–12 (Chm., Finance and Gen. Purposes Cttee, 2008–12). Liveryman, Skinners' Co., 2003– (Extra Mem. Ct, 2006–08; Master, 2012–13; Second Warden, 2015–16; Chm., Lawrence Atwell's Charity, 2011–). *Recreations:* walking, especially on Dartmoor and in Greece, history, travel. *Club:* Travellers.

FELLGETT, (Terence) Robin, CB 2007; PhD; Deputy Head, Economic and Domestic Affairs Secretariat, Cabinet Office, 2003–11; *b* 1 Oct. 1950; *s* of Prof. Peter Berners Fellgett, FRS, and Mary Briggs; *m* 1976, Patti Douglas (marr. diss.); one *s* one *d*; *m* 2009, Rebecca Collings; one step *s*. *Educ:* Univ. of Warwick (PhD Maths 1976); Birkbeck Coll., London Univ. (MSc Econs 1984); INSEAD (AMP 1995). BP Chemicals, 1969; Asst Prof., Univ. of Maryland, 1976–78; MSC, 1979; CSD 1979–83; joined HM Treasury, 1983: held posts in expenditure, privatisation and internat. finance; Dep. Dir, then Dir, Financial Sector, 1998–2003. *Recreations:* music, travel, relaxation. *Clubs:* Jazz Café, Vortex.

FELLNER, Eric, CBE 2005; film producer; Co-Chairman, Working Title Films, since 1992; *b* 10 Oct. 1959; *m* (marr. diss.); three *s*; partner, Laura Bailey; one *s* one *d*. *Educ:* Cranleigh Sch.; Guildhall Sch. of Music and Drama. *Films include:* Sid and Nancy, 1986; Pascali's Island, 1988; The Rachel Papers, 1989; Hidden Agenda, 1990; A Kiss Before Dying, Liebestraum, 1991; Wild West, 1992; Posse, Romeo is Bleeding, 1993; Four Weddings and a Funeral, The Hudsucker Proxy, 1994; Loch Ness, French Kiss, Dead Man Walking, 1995; Fargo, 1996; Bean, The Borrowers, 1997; Elizabeth, The Big Lebowski, 1998; Notting Hill, Plunkett & Macleane, 1999; O Brother, Where Art Thou?, Billy Elliot, The Man Who Cried, 2000; Bridget Jones's Diary, Captain Corelli's Mandolin, The Man Who Wasn't There, Long Time Dead, 2001; 40 Days and 40 Nights, About A Boy, Ali G Indahouse, The Guru, My Little Eye, 2002; Love Actually, Calcium Kid, Ned Kelly, Shape of Things, Johnny English, Thirteen, 2003; Thunderbirds, Bridget Jones: The Edge of Reason, Shaun of the Dead, Wimbledon, Inside I'm Dancing, 2004; Mickybo and Me, Pride and Prejudice, Nanny McPhee, The Interpreter, 2005; Sixty Six, United 93, Hot Stuff, 2006; The Golden Age, Atonement, Mr Bean's Holiday, Hot Fuzz, Gone, Smokin' Aces, 2007; Definitely Maybe, Wild Child, Burn After Reading, 2008; Frost/Nixon, State of Play, The Soloist, The Boat That Rocked, Hippie Hippie Shake, A Serious Man, 2009; Green Zone, Nanny McPhee and the Big Bang, 2010; Paul, Senna, Johnny English Reborn, Tinker, Tailor, Soldier, Spy, 2011; Anna Karenina, Les Misérables, 2012; I Give It a Year, Closed Circuit, About Time, Rush, 2013; Two Faces of January, 2014; The Theory of Everything, Trash, 2015. Four Academy Awards; 36 BAFTA awards. *Address:* Working Title Films, 26 Aybrook Street, W1U 4AN. *T:* (020) 7307 3000; Working Title Films, 4th Floor, 9720 Wilshire Boulevard, Beverly Hills, CA 90212, USA. *T:* (310) 777 3100.

FELLNER, Dr Peter John; Chairman, Vernalis (formerly British Biotech) plc, since 2002 (Director, 1988–90); *b* 31 Dec. 1943; *s* of late Hans Julius Fellner and Jessica (*née* Thompson); *m* 1st, 1969, Sandra Head (*née* Smith); one *d* and one step *s*; 2nd, 1982, Jennifer Mary Zabel (*née* Butler); two step *s*. *Educ:* Sheffield Univ. (BSc Biochem. 1965); Trinity Coll., Cambridge (PhD 1968). Post-doctoral Res. Fellow, 1968–70, Associate Prof., 1970–73, Strasbourg Univ.; Searle UK Research Laboratories: Sen. Res. Investigator, 1973–77; Dir of Chem., 1977–80; Dir of Res., 1980–84; Dir of Res., Roche UK Res. Centre, 1984–86; Man. Dir, Roche UK, 1986–90; Chief Exec., 1990–2003, Chm., 2003–04, Celltech, then Celltech Chiroscі., subseq. Celltech Gp. Chairman: Astex Pharmaceuticals (formerly Astex Technol., then Astex Therapeutics) Ltd, 2002–11 (Vice-Chm., 2011–13); Ionix Pharmaceuticals Ltd, 2002–05; Acambis plc, 2006–08; Premier Research Gp plc, 2007–08; Optos plc, 2010–15; Biotie Therapies Corp., 2010–14; Ablynx NV, 2013; non-executive Director: Colborn Dawes Ltd, 1986–90; Synaptica Ltd, 1999–2002; QinetiQ Gp plc, 2004–09; UCB SA, 2005–14; Evotec AG, 2005–11; Consort Medical (formerly Bespak) plc, 2005– (Chm., 2009–). Mem., MRC, 2000–07. *Address:* Vernalis plc, 100 Berkshire Place, Wharfedale Road, Winnersh, Berkshire RG41 5RD. *T:* (0118) 938 0019.

FELLOWES; *see* Kitchener-Fellowes, family name of Baron Fellowes of West Stafford.

FELLOWES, family name of **Barons De Ramsey** and **Fellowes**.

FELLOWES, Baron *cr* 1999 (Life Peer), of Shotesham in the county of Norfolk; **Robert Fellowes,** GCB 1998 (KCB 1991; CB 1987); GCVO 1996 (KCVO 1989; LVO 1983); QSO 1999; PC 1990; Chairman, Barclays Private Bank (formerly Barclays Private Banking), 2000–09 (Vice-Chairman, 1999–2000); Secretary and Registrar of the Order of Merit, since 2003; *b* 11 Dec. 1941; *s* of Sir William Fellowes, KCVO; *m* 1978, Lady Jane Spencer, *d* of 8th Earl Spencer, LVO; one *s* two *d*. *Educ:* Eton. Scots Guards (short service commission), 1960–63. Director, Allen Harvey & Ross Ltd, Discount Brokers and Bankers, 1968–77; Asst Private Sec. to the Queen, 1977–86, Dep. Private Sec., 1986–90; Private Sec. to the Queen and Keeper of the Queen's Archives, 1990–99. Non-exec. Dir, SABMiller (formerly South African Breweries), 1999–2010. Mem., UK Governing Body, Internat. Chamber of Commerce, 2004–. Vice-Chm., Commonwealth Educn Trust (formerly Commonwealth Inst.), 2000–; Chm., Prison Reform Trust, 2001–08; Mem., British Liby Bd, 2007–. Trustee: Rhodes Trust, 2000–10; Winston Churchill Meml Trust, 2001– (Chm., 2009–); Mandela-Rhodes Trust, 2003–10; Chm., Voices Foundn, 2004–12. Pres., Adv. Council, Goodenough Coll., 2008–13. Gov., King Edward VII Hosp., Sister Agnes, 2010–13. *Recreations:* reading, watching cricket, golf. *Address:* No 1 Millbank, House of Lords, SW1P 3JU. *Clubs:* White's, Pratt's, Royal Over-Seas League, MCC.

FELLOWES OF WEST STAFFORD, Baron *cr* 2011 (Life Peer), of West Stafford in the County of Dorset; **Julian Alexander Kitchener-Fellowes;** DL; screenwriter, actor, producer, director and lecturer (as **Julian Fellowes**); *b* 17 Aug. 1949; *s* of late Peregrine Edward Launcelot Fellowes and Olwen Mary (*née* Stuart-Jones); *m* 1990, Emma Kitchener, LVO (Lady-in-Waiting to HRH Princess Michael of Kent), *d* of Hon. Charles Kitchener; one *s*. *Educ:* Ampleforth Coll., Yorkshire; Magdalene Coll., Cambridge (BA, MA); Webber Douglas Acad. As actor: *theatre includes:* Joking Apart, Queen's, 1978; Present Laughter, Vaudeville, 1981; Futurists, RNT; *television includes:* For the Greater Good, 1991; Our Friends in the North, 1996; Aristocrats, 1999; Monarch of the Glen, 1999–2005; *films include:* Shadowlands, 1993; Damage, 1993; Tomorrow Never Dies, 1997; Place Vendôme, 1998; (co-prod.) A Married Man, 1982. As writer: *television:* Little Lord Fauntleroy, 1994 (Internat. Emmy, 1995); The Prince and the Pauper (also co-prod.), 1997; Downton Abbey (also exec. prod.), 2010, 2011, 2012 (Emmy Award for writing, 2011), 2013, 2014, 2015; Titanic, 2012; *films:* Gosford Park, 2001 (NY Film Critics' Circle Award, Best Screenplay, 2001; Nat. Soc. of Film Critics of America Award, Best Screenplay, 2001; Screenwriter of Year, ShoWest, 2002; Writer's Guild Award, Best Orig. Screenplay, 2002; Academy Award, Best Orig. Screenplay, 2002); Separate Lies (also dir), 2005 (Best Directorial Debut, Nat. Bd of Review, 2006); Vanity Fair, 2005; The Young Victoria, 2009; From Time to Time, 2010 (Best Picture, Chicago Children's Film Fest., Seattle Internat. Film Fest. Youth Jury Award, Fiuggi Family Fest., Rome, Cinemagic Belfast Young Jury Award, 2010); The Tourist, 2010; Romeo & Juliet, 2013; *theatre:* Mary Poppins, Prince Edward Th., 2004, New Amsterdam, NY, 2006. Chm., RNIB Talking Books Appeal, 2005–; Vice-Pres., Weldmar Hospicecare Trust, 2006–; Pres., Thomas Hardy Soc., 2007–; Patron, Help the Aged, Dorset, 2007–. Paul Harris Fellowship, Rotary Club, 2007. DL Dorset, 2008. Hon. DLitt Bournemouth, 2007; Hon. DArts Southampton Solent, 2010. *Publications:* Snobs (novel), 2004; The Curious Adventures of the Abandoned Toys (children's stories), 2007; Past Imperfect (novel), 2008; Downton Abbey: the complete scripts, Season One, 2012, Season Two, 2013, Season Three, 2014. *Recreation:* too little sport and too much eating. *Address:* c/o Independent Talent Group Ltd, 40 Whitfield Street, W1T 2RH. *Clubs:* Boodle's, Annabel's, Pratt's.

FELLOWES, Julian; *see* Baron Fellowes of West Stafford.

FELLOWS, Derek Edward, FIA; Executive Director, Securities and Investments Board, 1989–91; *b* 23 Oct. 1927; *s* of late Edward Frederick Fellows and of Gladys Fellows; *m* 1948, Mary Watkins (*d* 2013); two *d*. *Educ:* Mercers' Sch. FIA 1956. Entered Prudential Assurance Co. Ltd, 1943; Gp Pensions Manager, 1973–81; Chief Actuary, 1981–88; Man. Dir, Gp Pension Div., 1984–88; Dir, Prudential Corp. plc, 1985–88; non-exec. Dir, Countrywide Assured (formerly Hambro Guardian Assurance, then Hambro Assured), 1992–99. Mem., Occupational Pensions Bd, 1974–78; Chm., Bd of Trustees, South Bank Centre Retirement Plan, 1993–2001; Trustee, C of E Pensions Bd, 1998–2002. Church Comr, 1996–2002 (Mem., Audit Cttee, 1994–2001). FPMI 1976; Vice Pres., Inst. of Actuaries, 1980–83. *Publications:* contrib. Jl of Inst. of Actuaries. *Recreations:* music, theatre, gardening, bridge. *Club:* Actuaries'.

FELLOWS, Jeffrey Keith; Technical Consultant, BAE Systems, since 1999; *b* 17 Sept. 1940; *s* of Albert and Hilda May Fellows; *m* 1965, Mary Ewins; one *s*. *Educ:* Handsworth Grammar Sch.; Birmingham Univ. (BSc (Phys) Hons 1962). Royal Aircraft Establishment: joined Weapons Dept, 1962, Sect. Leader, 1973; Div. Leader, Systems Assessment Dept, 1976; Head of: Combat Mission Systems Div., 1981; Flight Systems Dept, 1983; seconded to BNSC as Dir (Projects and Technol.), 1986; Dep. Dir (Mission Systems), RAE, Farnborough, 1988–89; Asst Under Sec. of State, MoD, 1989–95; Technical Planning Dir, BAe plc, 1995–99; retired. *Publications:* various, for AGARD, IBA, US Nat. Space Foundn, etc. *Recreations:* tennis, aeromodelling.

FELLOWS, John Walter, CEng, FICE, FCIHT; independent transportation consultant, since 1996; *b* 27 July 1938; *s* of William Leslie Fellows and Lavinia Keziah (*née* Chilton); *m* 1964, Maureen Joyce Lewis; two *s*. *Educ:* Dudley Technical High Sch.; Wolverhampton Polytechnic; Birmingham Univ. (MSc). FICE 1990; FCIHT (FIHT 1989). Civil Engineer (pupil), Contractors Wilson Lovatt & Sons Ltd, 1954–59; Civil Engineer: CBs of Wolverhampton, Coventry and Dudley, 1959–69; joined Department of Transport, 1969: Asst Sec., Highway Maintenance Div., 1984–88; Dir, SE, 1988–90; Regl Dir (SE), DoE/DoT, 1990–94; Bd Dir, Highway Agency, 1994–96. *Publications:* papers to ICE and IHT. *Recreations:* boating, sailing, golf, music, theatre. *Address:* 17 Chinthurst Park, Shalford, Guildford, Surrey GU4 8JH. *E:* jwfellows@btopenworld.com.

FELLOWS, Marion; MP (SNP) Motherwell and Wishaw, since 2015; *b* 5 May 1949. *Educ:* Heriot-Watt Univ. (Accountancy and Finance). Lectr in Business Studies, W Lothian Coll. Mem. (SNP), N Lanarkshire Council, 2012–15. *Address:* House of Commons, SW1A 0AA.

FELLS, Prof. Ian, CBE 2000; FREng; FRSE; Professor of Energy Conversion, University of Newcastle upon Tyne, 1975–90, now Emeritus; *b* 5 Sept. 1932; *s* of late Dr Henry Alexander Fells, MBE and Clarice Fells, Sheffield; *m* 1957, Hazel Denton Scott; four *s*. *Educ:* King Edward VII School, Sheffield; Trinity College, Cambridge. MA, PhD. FInstE, FIChemE; FREng (FEng 1979); FRSE 1996. Chief Wireless Officer, British Troops in Austria, 1951–52; Lectr and Dir of Studies, Dept of Fuel Technology and Chem. Engineering, Univ. of Sheffield, 1958–62; Reader in Fuel Science, King's Coll., Univ. of Durham, 1962; Public Orator, Univ. of Newcastle upon Tyne, 1970–73. Lectures: Brough, Paisley Coll., 1977; Allerdale Wylde, Cumbria Science Socs, 1986; Fawley, Southampton Univ., 1987; Robert Spence, RSC, 1988 and 1990; Charles Parsons' Meml, Royal Soc., 1988; Clancey, City Univ., 1992; Erasmus Darwin, Lichfield Sci. and Engrg Soc., 1994; Hunter Meml, IEE, 1999; Higginson, Durham Univ., 2000; Idris Jones Meml, Cardiff, 2000; Hawksley Meml, IMechE, 2001. Pres., Inst. of Energy, 1978–79; Scientific Advr, World Energy Council, 1990–98; Special Advisor: to H of L Select Cttee for the European Communities, 1991–92; to H of C Select Cttee on Envmt, 1993–94, and on Trade and Industry, 1995–96; on Energy, Commonwealth Business Council, 2011–14. Member: Electricity Supply Res. Council, 1979–90; Sci. Consultative Gp, BBC, 1976–81; CNAA, 1987–93. Chm., New and Renewable Energy Centre, Blyth, Northumberland, 2002–05. Technical Dir, Penultimate Power UK Ltd, 2013–. Hon. Life Vice Pres., Internat. Centre for Life, 2010– (Trustee,

1995–2010). Hatfield Meml Prize, 1974; Beilby Meml Medal and Prize, 1976; Faraday Award and Lect., 1993, Collier Medal and Lect., 1999, Royal Soc.; Melchett Medal and Lect., Royal Instn, 1999; Kelvin Medal, Royal Philosophical Soc. of Glasgow, 2002. Participator in TV series: Young Scientist of the Year, 1970; The Great Egg Race, 1970–85; Earth Year 2050, 1983; Men of Science, 1984; Take Nobody's Word For It, 1987, 1989; QED, 1987, 1991; The Human Element, 1992; What If... the Lights Go Out?, 2004. *Publications:* Energy for the Future, 1973, 2nd edn 1986; UK Energy Policy Post-Privatisation, 1991; Energy for the Future, 1995; World Energy 1923–98 and Beyond, 1998; A Pragmatic Energy Policy for the UK, 2008; contribs to professional jls. *Recreations:* sailing, cross-country ski-ing, energy conversation. *Address:* 29 Rectory Terrace, Newcastle upon Tyne NE3 1YB. *T:* (0191) 285 5343. *Club:* Naval and Military.

FELTON, Ian; HM Diplomatic Service; Deputy High Commissioner, Bangalore, India, since 2011; *b* 16 May 1966; *m* Judith Fairbairn. Entered FCO, 1986; Southern Eur. Dept, FCO, 1986–87; Chancery, Brussels, 1987–89; worldwide floater, 1990–95, UN Dept, FCO, 1993–95; UK Mission to UN, NY, 1995–99; Dep. Hd of Mission, Cambodia, 2000–03; Prog. Manager, Engaging with the Islamic World, FCO, 2003–06; Team Leader, SE Asia and Pacific Gp, FCO, 2006–08; Ambassador to Guinea, 2008–11. *Address:* c/o Foreign and Commonwealth Office, King Charles Street, SW1A 2AH.

FELTON, Maj. Gen. Richard Friedrich Patrick, CBE 2011 (OBE 2006; MBE 1997); Commander, Joint Helicopter Command, since 2014; *b* Irvine, Scotland, 13 June 1964; *s* of Richard and Marga Felton; *m* 2007, Mia Shackleton; one *s*. *Educ:* West Buckland Sch.; Hull Univ. (BSc Hons); Cranfield Univ. (MA). Joined Army, 1985; Glos Regt, NI, Germany and Canada, 1986–92 (mentioned in despatches, 1990); Recce Flt Comdr, Hildesheim, 1992–95; COS 7 Armd Bde, 1996–99; Chief of Ops, HQ Multi-Nat. Div. (SE), Bosnia, 1997; OC 669 Sqdn AAC, 1999–2001; SO Directorate of Operational Capability, MoD, 2001–03; CO 9 Regt, AAC, 2004–06; Comdr, Jt Helicopter Force, Afghanistan, 2006; Chief of Staff: 1st (UK) Armd Div., 2007–09; Multi-Nat. Div. (SW), Iraq, 2007–08; Commander: 4th Mechanized Bde, 2009–11; Task Force Helmand, Afghanistan, 2010; Chief, Jt Force Ops, 2011–13. *Recreations:* fine art (Aidan Meller Galleries), scuba diving, running, poker and backgammon. *Address:* 3 The Terrace, Royal Military Academy Sandhurst, Camberley, Surrey GU15 4NS. *T:* (01276) 685920, 07880 730736. *E:* rfpf2@aol.com.

FELWICK, Wing Comdr David Leonard, CBE 2004; RAF retired; Deputy Chairman, John Lewis Partnership, 2002–04 (Director of Trading (Food), 1991–2002); *b* 9 Nov. 1944; *s* of Leonard Felwick and Mary J. Felwick (*née* Rolling); *m* 1970, Lynne Margaret Yeardley; two *s*. *Educ:* Devonport High Sch., Plymouth; RAF Coll., Cranwell. Served RAF, 1962–82. Joined John Lewis Partnership, 1982; Man. Dir, John Lewis, Welwyn, 1985–87; Dir of Selling, 1987–91, Man. Dir, 1991–2002, Waitrose Ltd. MInstD 1985. *Recreations:* ski-ing, shooting, tennis, golf. *Address:* Grange Barn, Moulsford, Wallingford OX10 9JD. *Club:* Royal Air Force.

FENBY, Jonathan Theodore Starmer, CBE 2000; author, analyst and journalist; *b* 11 Nov. 1942; *s* of late Charles Fenby and June (*née* Head); *m* 1967, Renée Wartski; one *s* one *d*. *Educ:* West House Sch., Birmingham; King Edward VI Sch., Birmingham; Westminster Sch.; New Coll., Oxford (BA). Reuters, 1963–77, Ed., Reuters World Service, 1973–77; correspondent in France and Germany, Economist, 1982–86; Asst Ed. and Home Ed., The Independent, 1986–88; Dep. Ed., The Guardian, 1988–93; Editor: The Observer, 1993–95; South China Morning Post and Sunday Morning Post, Hong Kong, 1995–99; Business Europe.com, 2000–01; Associate Ed., Sunday Business, 2000–01; Man. Partner, China, Trusted Sources, 2006–; contrib. to press and broadcasting in UK, Europe, US, Canada and Far East. Res. Associate, SOAS, 2002–. Member Board: Journalists in Europe, 2000–02; European Journalism Centre, 2002–; British-Belgian Conf., 2006–; China Dialogue, 2012–. Chevalier: Ordre Nat. du Mérite (France), 1992; Légion d'Honneur (France), 2013. *Publications:* Fall of the House of Beaverbrook, 1979; Piracy and the Public, 1983; International News Services, 1986; On the Brink: the trouble with France, 1998, 2nd edn 2002, updated edn as France on the Brink, 2014; Comment peut-on être français, 1999; Dealing with the Dragon: a year in the new Hong Kong, 2000; Generalissimo: Chiang Kai-shek and the China he lost, 2003; The Sinking of the Lancastria, 2005; Alliance, 2007; 70 Wonders of China, 2007; The Dragon Throne, 2008; China's Journey, 2008; The Penguin History of Modern China, 2008; The General: Charles de Gaulle and the France he saved, 2010; Tiger Head, Snake Tails: today's China, how it got there and where it is heading, 2012; Will China Dominate the 21st Century?, 2014; The Siege of Tsingtao, 2014; A History of Modern France, 2015. *Recreations:* walking, belote, jazz. *Address:* 101 Ridgmount Gardens, Torrington Place, WC1E 7AZ.

FENDER, Sir Brian (Edward Frederick), Kt 1999; CMG 1985; Chairman, BTG plc, 2003–08 (Board Member, British Technology Group, then BTG, 1992–2003); Chief Executive, Higher Education Funding Council for England, 1995–2001; *b* 15 Sept. 1934; *s* of late George Clements and of Emily Fender; *m* 1st, 1956; one *s* three *d*; 2nd, 1986, Ann Linscott (*d* 2011). *Educ:* Carlisle Grammar Sch.; Sale County Grammar Sch.; Imperial College London (ARCS, BSc 1956; DIC, PhD 1959; FIC 1997); MA Oxon 1963. FRSC; FInstP. Research Instructor, Univ. of Washington, Seattle, 1959–61; Senior Research Fellow, Nat. Chem. Lab. (now NPL), 1961–63; University of Oxford: Dept Demonstrator in Inorganic Chemistry, 1963–65; Lectr, 1965–84; Senior Proctor, 1975–76; Mem., Hebdomadal Council, 1977–80; St Catherine's College: Fellow, 1963–84 (Hon. Fellow 1986); Sen. Tutor, 1965–69; Chm., Management Cttee, Oxford Colls Admissions Office, 1973–80; Vice-Chancellor, Univ. of Keele, 1985–95. Institut Laue-Langevin, Grenoble: Asst Dir, 1980–82; Dir, 1982–85; Mem., Steering Cttee, 1974–77; Mem., Scientific Council, 1977–80. Member: SERC, 1985–90; CERN Review Cttee, 1986–87; Chairman: Science Board, SERC, 1985–90 (Mem., 1974–77); Neutron Beam Res. Cttee, 1974–77 (Mem., 1969–71); Science Planning Group for Rutherford Lab. Neutron Scattering Source, 1977–80; Member: Defence Meteorol Bd, subseq. UK Meteorol Bd, 1991–2004; Adv. Cttee, Tate Gall., Liverpool, 1988–93; West Midlands Arts Bd, 1995–2002; Bd of Conservatoire for Dance and Drama, 2002–04; Dir, Higher Aims Ltd, 2002–; Chairman: Univs and Colls Employers Assoc., 1994–95; New Victoria Th. Trust, Staffs, 2003–; Nat. Council for Drama Trng, 2004–11; Waterways Partnership (London), 2012–. Pres., NFER, 1999–2007; Pres., Inst. of Knowledge Transfer, 2006–14 (Chm., 2006–11). Chm. Trustees, Willoughbridge Garden Trust, Staffs, 2008–. Member: HK UGC, 2003–07; Canals and Rivers Trust Council, 2012–. CCMI (CBIM 1989). FInstKT 2011. Hon. Fellow, Univ. of Wales, Cardiff, 1996; Hon. FRVC 2001; Hon. FTCL 2001; Hon. FRCA 2003. DUniv: Keele, 1996; Staffordshire, 2001; Hon. DSc Ulster, 2001; Hon. DCL Northumbria, 2001; Hon. Dr jur Lincoln, 2002; Hon. DEd UWE, 2002. *Publications:* scientific articles on neutron scattering and solid state chemistry. *Recreations:* theatre, gardening, watching Manchester United. *Address:* Bishops Offley Manor, Bishops Offley, Stafford ST21 6ET. *Club:* Athenæum.

FENECH-ADAMI, Hon. Dr Edward, KUOM 1990; LLD; President of Malta, 2004–09; *b* Birkirkara, Malta, 7 Feb. 1934; *s* of late Luigi Fenech-Adami and Josephine (*née* Pace); *m* 1965, Mary (*née* Sciberras); four *s* one *d*. *Educ:* St Aloysius Coll., Malta; Royal Univ. of Malta (BA 1955, LLD 1958). Entered legal practice in Malta, 1959. Nationalist Party: Mem. Nat. Exec., 1961; Asst Gen. Sec., 1962–75; Pres., Gen. and Admin. Council, 1975–77; Leader, 1977–2004. MP Malta, 1969–2004; Shadow Minister for Labour and Social Services, 1971–77; Leader of the Opposition, 1977–82, 1983–87, 1996–98; Prime Minister, 1987–96, 1998–2004; Foreign Minister, 1989–90. Vice-Pres., European Union of Christian Democrat Parties, 1979–99. Editor, Il-Poplu (Party Newspaper), 1962–69. *Publications:* (with Steve Mallia) Eddie: my journey (autobiog.), 2014.

FENHALLS, Richard Dorian; Adviser, Hannam and Partners LLP (formerly Strand Partners Ltd), since 2014 (Chief Executive and Deputy Chairman, 2009–13); Chairman, After Strand Ltd, since 2012; *b* 14 July 1943; *s* of Roydon Myers and Maureen Rosa Fenhalls; *m* 1967, Angela Sarah Allen; one *s* one *d*. *Educ:* Hilton Coll., Univ. of Natal (BA); Christ's Coll., Cambridge (MA, LLM). Attorney, S Africa, 1969. Goodricke & Son, Attorney, S Africa, 1969–70; Citibank, 1970–72; Senior Vice President: Marine Midland Bank, 1972–77; American Express Bank, 1977–81; Dep. Chm. and Chief Exec., Guinness Mahon & Co. Ltd, 1981–85; Chief Exec., Henry Ansbacher Hldgs, 1985–93; Chm., Henry Ansbacher & Co. Ltd, 1985–93; Chief Exec., 1993–2007, Dep. Chm., 2006–07, Exec. Chm., 2007–09, Strand Partners, later Strand Hanson Ltd. *Recreations:* sailing, veteran cars, historic car rallying. *Address:* 8b St James's Gardens, W11 4RB. *Clubs:* Royal Ocean Racing, Royal Thames Yacht; Royal Southern Yacht (Hamble); Veteran Car of GB.

FENLON, Prof. Iain Alexander, FSA; Professor of Historical Musicology, University of Cambridge, since 2005; Fellow, King's College, Cambridge, since 1976; *b* 26 Oct. 1949; *s* of Albert Fenlon and Joan (*née* Rainey); *m* 1st, 1993, Nicoletta Guidobaldi (marr. diss. 2008); 2nd, 2014, Maria José de la Torre Molina. *Educ:* Reading Univ. (BA); Birmingham Univ. (MA); St Catharine's Coll., Cambridge; King's Coll., Cambridge (MA; PhD 1977). FSA 1989. Hayward Research Fellow, Birmingham Univ., 1974–75; Fellow, Villa I Tatti (Harvard Univ. Center for Italian Renaissance Studies), Florence, 1975–76; King's College, Cambridge: Jun. Res. Fellow, 1976–79; Sen. Res. Fellow, 1979–83; Vice-Provost, 1986–91; Sen. Tutor, 2005–08; University of Cambridge: Asst Lectr, 1979–84; Lectr, 1984–96; Reader in Historical Musicology, 1995–2005. Vis. Scholar, Harvard Univ., 1984–85; Visiting Fellow: All Souls Coll., Oxford, 1991–92; New Coll., Oxford, 1992; British Acad. Res. Reader, 1996–98; Visiting Professor: Ecole Normale Supérieure, Paris, 1998–99; Univ. of Bologna, 1999–2000. Leverhulme Res. Award, 2000–03. Founding Ed., Early Music History, 1981–. Dent Medal, Internat. Musicological Soc./Royal Musical Assoc., 1984. *Publications:* Music and Patronage in Sixteenth-Century Mantua, 2 vols, 1980, 1982; (ed) Music in Medieval and Early Modern Europe, 1981; (with J. Haar) The Early Sixteenth-Century Italian Madrigal, 1988; (with P. Miller) The Song of the Soul: understanding Poppea, 1992; Music, Print and Culture in Early Sixteenth-Century Italy, 1995; Giaches de Wert: letters and documents, 1999; Music and Culture in Late Renaissance Italy, 2002; The Ceremonial City: history, memory and myth in Renaissance Venice, 2007; Piazza San Marco, 2009; (ed with I. Groote) Heinrich Glarean's Books: the intellectual world of a sixteenth-century musical humanist, 2013; articles in various musicol jls, TLS, London Review of Books, etc. *Recreations:* travel, wine. *Address:* King's College, Cambridge CB2 1ST. *T:* (01223) 331100.

FENN, Sir Nicholas (Maxted), GCMG 1995 (KCMG 1989; CMG 1980); HM Diplomatic Service, retired; *b* 19 Feb. 1936; *s* of late Rev. Prof. J. Eric Fenn and of Kathleen (*née* Harrison); *m* 1959, Susan Clare (*née* Russell); two *s* one *d*. *Educ:* Kingswood Sch., Bath; Peterhouse, Cambridge (MA; Hon. Fellow, 2001). Pilot Officer, RAF, 1954–56. Third Sec., British Embassy, Rangoon, 1959–63; Asst Private Sec. to Sec. of State for Foreign Affairs, 1963–67; First Secretary: British Interests Sect., Swiss Embassy, Algiers, 1967–69; Public Relations, UK Mission to UN, NY, 1969–72; Dep. Head, Energy Dept, FCO, 1972–75; Counsellor, Peking, 1975–77; Head of News Dept and FCO Spokesman, 1979–82; Spokesman to last Governor of Rhodesia, 1979–80; Ambassador: Rangoon, 1982–86; Dublin, 1986–91; High Comr, India, 1991–96. Marie Curie Cancer Care: Chief Exec., 1997–2000; Chm., 2000–06; Vice-Pres., 2006–. Jt Chm., Anglo-Irish Encounter, 1998–2003. Vice-Pres., Leprosy Mission, 1996–2002; Trustee: Sightsavers Internat., 1996–2005 (Vice Pres., 2006–); Guide Dogs for the Blind Assoc., 2002–06; Patron: Arpana UK, 2000–; Village Service Trust, 2009–; Hon. Pres., Safe Anaesthesia Worldwide, 2011–; Governor: Jawaharlal Nehru Meml Trust, 1997–2006; Kingswood Sch., Bath, 1996–2006. Churchwarden, Marden Parish Ch, 2001–06. *Club:* Oxford and Cambridge.

See also R. D. R. Fenn.

FENN, Robert Dominic Russell; HM Diplomatic Service; Head, Human Rights and Democracy Department, since 2014; *b* 28 Jan. 1962; *s* of Sir Nicholas Maxted Fenn, *qv*; *m* 2002, Julia Lloyd Williams; two *s*. *Educ:* Kingswood Sch., Bath; Peterhouse, Cambridge (BA 1st Cl. Hons Classics 1983). Entered FCO, 1983; Third Sec., The Hague, 1985–88; Second Sec., Lagos, 1988–89; First Secretary: S Africa Desk, FCO, 1989–92; Human Rights, UKMIS, NY, 1992–97; (EU/Econ.), Rome, 1997–2001; Dep. Hd, Southern Eur. Dept, later Team Leader, E Mediterranean (Cyprus/Greece/Turkey), FCO, 2001–04; Dep. High Comr, Nicosia, 2004–08; High Comr, Brunei, 2009–13. *Recreations:* reading, poetry, armchair architecture. *Address:* c/o Foreign and Commonwealth Office, King Charles Street, SW1A 2AH. *E:* rob.fenn@fco.gov.uk.

FENNELL, Alister Theodore, (Theo); jewellery designer; Creative Director, Theo Fennell Ltd, since 1997; Founder, Original Design Partnership, 2008; *b* Egypt; *s* of Maj. Alister Fennell and Verity Fennell (*née* Frith); *m* 1977, Louise MacGregor; two *d*. *Educ:* Eton Coll.; Byam Shaw Sch. of Art. Office boy, Edward Barnard & Sons, 1973–75; formed Theo Fennell, 1975; Man. Dir, Theo Fennell Ltd, 1982–97; designer and Man. Dir, Theo Fennell plc, 1997. *Recreations:* most sports and games, music, art, drawing, reading, strumming guitar with tuneless vocals, musical theatre. *Address:* Theo Fennell Ltd, 2B Pond Place, SW3 6TF. *E:* theo.fennell@theofennell.com. *Clubs:* Chelsea Arts, Saints and Sinners, Tramp; MCC, I Zingari.

FENNEY, Roger Johnson, CBE 1973 (MBE (mil.) 1945); Chairman, Special Trustees, Charing Cross Hospital, 1980–88; *b* 11 Sept. 1916; *m* 1942, Dorothy Porteus (*d* 1989); two *d*. *Educ:* Cowley Sch., St Helens; Univ. of Manchester (BA Admin 1939). Served War, 1939–46: Gunner to Major, Field Artillery; served N Africa and Italy (mentioned in despatches). Secretary, Central Midwives Board, 1947–82; Governor, Charing Cross Hosp., 1958–74 (Mem. Council, Med. Sch., 1970–80); Governor, Hammersmith Hosp., 1956–74; Chm., W London Hosp., 1957–68; First Nuffield Fellow for Health Affairs, USA, 1968; Dep. Chm., Kennedy Inst. of Rheumatol., 1970–77. Member: Exec., Arthritis and Rheumatism Council, 1978–98; Field Dir, Jt Study Gp (FIGO/ICM), Accra, Yaoundé, Nairobi, Dakar, San José and Bogotá, 1972–76. *Address:* 11 Gilray House, Gloucester Terrace, W2 3DF. *T:* (020) 7262 8313.

FENTEM, Prof. Peter Harold, MBE 2011; FRCP; Emeritus Professor, University of Nottingham, 1997 (Stroke Association Professor of Stroke Medicine, 1992–97); Hon. Consultant, Nottingham City Hospital NHS Trust (formerly Nottingham Health Authority), 1976–97; *b* 12 Sept. 1933; *s* of Harold and Agnes Fentem; *m* 1958, Rosemary Hodson; two *s* two *d*. *Educ:* Bury Grammar Sch.; Univ. of Manchester (BSc 1st cl. hons 1955; MSc 1956; MB ChB Hons 1959). FRCP 1989. Hosp. appts, Manchester Royal Inf., 1959–60; Demonstrator in Path., Univ. of Manchester, 1960–61; Manchester and Cardiff Royal Infs, 1961–64; Lectr in Physiol., St Mary's Hosp. Med. Sch., 1964–68; University of Nottingham: Sen. Lectr in Physiol., 1968; Reader, 1975; Prof. of Physiol., 1975–92; Dean of Medicine, 1987–93. Chm., BSI Tech. Sub-Cttee on Compression Hosiery, 1978–89; Sci. Sec., Fitness and Health Adv. Gp, Sports Council, 1981; Civil Consultant to RAF, 1983–2000; Hon. Consultant to Army, 1989–97; Member: Army Personnel Res. Cttee, 1983–93 (Chm., Applied Physiol. Panel, 1986–93); GMC, 1988–93; Trent RHA, 1988–90; DoH Physical Activity Task Force, 1993–96; Nat. Alliance for Physical Activity, 1997–99; Nat. Heart Forum, 1997–. Trustee: Age Concern Essex, 1999–2008; Stroke Assoc., 2000–08. *Publications:* (jt author): Exercise: the facts, 1981; Work Physiology, in Principles and Practice of Human Physiology, 1981; The New Case for Exercise, 1988; Benefits of Exercise: the evidence, 1990; (Adv. Editor) Physiology Integrated Clinical Science, 1983. *Recreations:* gardening, walking.

FENTIMAN, Prof. Richard Griffith; Professor of Private International Law, University of Cambridge, since 2011; Fellow, Queens' College, Cambridge, since 1981; *b* Sevenoaks, Kent, 3 April 1956; *s* of Denis and Olwen Fentiman; *m* 1986, Alicia Jewett. *Educ:* St John's Sch., Leatherhead; Brasenose Coll., Oxford (Collins Schol.; BA 1977; BCL 1978; MA 1980). Admitted as solicitor, 1981; Articled Clerk and Solicitor, Clifford Chance, 1979–81; University of Cambridge: Asst Lectr in Law, 1985–89; Lectr in Law, 1989–2000; Reader in Private Internat. Law, 2000–12; Chm. Bd, Faculty of Law, 2015–. Vis. Fellow in Private Internat. Law, British Inst. of Internat. and Comparative Law, 1989–97; Visiting Professor: Inst. of Comparative Law in Japan, Tokyo, 1989; Cornell Law Sch., 1992; Walter Ganshof van der Meersch Prof., Univ. Libre de Bruxelles, 2001; delivered Special Course, Hague Acad. of Internat. Law, 2002. Member: Internat. Acad. of Comparative Law, 2004–; Amer. Law Inst., 2007–. Member, Editorial Board: Jl Private Internat. Law, 2005–; Law and Financial Mkts Rev., 2010–; Cambridge Yearbook of Eur. Legal Studies, 2012–. Pilkington Prize, Univ. of Cambridge, 2014. *Publications:* (ed) Conflict of Laws, 1996; Foreign Law in English Courts, 1998; (ed jtly) L'espace judicaire européen en matières civile et commercial, 1999; International Commercial Litigation, 2010, 2nd edn 2015; contrib. articles on private internat. law and internat. civil procedure. *Recreations:* wine, conversation, travel. *Address:* Queens' College, Cambridge CB3 9ET. *T:* (01223) 335511. *E:* rgf1000@cam.ac.uk.

FENTON, Ernest John; Director General, Association of Investment Trust Companies, 1993–97; *b* 14 Oct. 1938; *s* of Forbes Duncan Campbell Fenton and Janet Burnfield Fenton (*née* Easson); *m* 1965, Ann Ishbel Ramsay; one *s* two *d*. *Educ:* Harris Acad., Scotland. CA 1961; CFA (AIIMR 1972). Partner, W. Greenwell & Co., 1968–87; Chm. and Chief Exec., Greenwell Montagu Stockbrokers, 1987–92. Non-executive Director: Fleming Income & Capital Investment Trust PLC, 1991–2002; Cotesworth & Co. Ltd (Lloyd's Managing Agents), 1994–2001; Renaissance US Growth and Income Trust PLC, 1996– (Chm., 2004–14); US Special Opportunities (formerly BFS US Special Opportunities) Trust plc, 2001–08. Farmer, Kent and Sussex, 1973–. Proprietor, Fenton's Rink, Kent, 2004–. Mem. Investment Cttee, CRC, 1995–98. MCSI (MSI 1986); MInstD 1994. FRSA 1993. *Recreation:* curling. *Address:* Dundale Farm, Dundale Road, Tunbridge Wells, Kent TN3 9AQ.

FENTON, James Martin, FRSL; FSA; writer; Professor of Poetry, University of Oxford, 1994–99; *b* 25 April 1949; *s* of late Rev. Canon John Charles Fenton and Mary Hamilton (*née* Ingoldby). *Educ:* Durham Choristers Sch.; Repton Sch.; Magdalen Coll., Oxford (MA; Hon. Fellow, 1999). FRSL 1983; FSA 2006. Asst Literary Editor, 1971, Editorial Asst, 1972, New Statesman; freelance correspondent in Indo-China, 1973–75; Political Columnist, New Statesman, 1976–78; German Correspondent, The Guardian, 1978–79; Theatre Critic, Sunday Times, 1979–84; Chief Book Reviewer, The Times, 1984–86; Far East Corresp., 1986–88, columnist, 1993–95, The Independent. Trustee, Nat. Gall., 2002–09; Visitor, Ashmolean Mus., 2002. FRSA 2003. Queen's Gold Medal for Poetry, 2007. *Publications:* Our Western Furniture, 1968; Terminal Moraine, 1972; A Vacant Possession, 1978; A German Requiem, 1980; Dead Soldiers, 1981; The Memory of War, 1982; (trans.) Rigoletto, 1982; You Were Marvellous, 1983; (ed) The Original Michael Frayn, 1983; Children in Exile, 1984; Poems 1968–83, 1985; (trans.) Simon Boccanegra, 1985; The Fall of Saigon, in Granta 15, 1985; The Snap Revolution, in Granta 18, 1986; (ed) Cambodian Witness: the autobiography of Someth May, 1986; (with John Fuller) Partingtime Hall (poems), 1987; All the Wrong Places: adrift in the politics of Asia, 1988; Manila Envelope, 1989; (ed) Underground in Japan, by Rey Ventura, 1992; Out of Danger (poems), 1993; Leonardo's Nephew, 1998; The Strength of Poetry, 2001; A Garden from a Hundred Packets of Seed, 2001; An Introduction to English Poetry, 2002; The Love Bomb (3 dramatic works for music), 2003; Selected Poems, 2006; Samuel Taylor Coleridge: poems selected by James Fenton, 2006; School of Genius: a history of the Royal Academy, 2006; (ed) The New Faber Book of Love Poems, 2006; (ed) D. H. Lawrence: selected poems, 2008; Yellow Tulips: poems 1968–2011, 2012; (adapted) The Orphan of Zhao, 2012. *Address:* United Agents Ltd, 12–26 Lexington Street, W1F 0LE. *E:* wasserman@kwlit.com.

FENTON, Mark Alexander, PhD; Headmaster, Dr Challoner's Grammar School, Amersham, since 2001; Executive Headteacher, Ealing Fields Academy Trust, since 2014; *b* 20 Oct. 1965; *s* of Prof. George and Dr Sylvia Fenton. *Educ:* Peterhouse, Cambridge (BA 1987; MA); Anglia Poly. Univ. (MSc 1993; PhD 1997); Univ. of Buckingham (DipEd Law 1998). Teacher of Hist., Boswells Sch., Chelmsford, 1988–91; Head of Hist. and Politics, 1991–97, Sen. Teacher, 1994–97, King Edward VI Grammar Sch., Chelmsford; Dep. Headteacher, Sir Joseph Williamson's Mathematical Sch., Rochester, 1997–2001. Chm., Grammar Sch. Hds Assoc., 2012–13 (Nat. Vice Chm., 2011–12 and 2013–14). Addnl Mem., HMC, 2010. Bd Mem., Bucks Acad. of Sch. Leadership, 2004–10 (Chm., 2005–08); a Nat. Leader of Educn, 2009–. Gov., Berkhamsted Schs Gp, 2014–. Trustee: The Cricket Foundn, 2005–08; Internat. Boys' Schs Coalition, 2014–. Dir, Ramsey Singers, 1987–; Manager, Bucks County U13 Cricket, 2001–05, U15 Cricket, 2005–; Schools' Rep., 2002–10, Youth Cricket Dir, 2012–, Bucks Cricket Bd; Chm., Bucks Schs Cricket Assoc., 2004– (on secondment to British Council SLANT Project (Trinidad and Tobago), 2006–11). *Publications:* articles in educn mgt jls. *Recreations:* singing in and conducting choirs; watching, coaching, umpiring and talking about cricket; golf. *Address:* Dr Challoner's Grammar School, Chesham Road, Amersham, Bucks HP6 5HA. *T:* (01494) 787525, *Fax:* (01494) 721862. *E:* headmaster@challoners.com. *Clubs:* East India, Lansdowne, MCC.

FENTON, Shaun Alan, MA, MEd; Headmaster, Reigate Grammar School, since 2012; *b* Liverpool, 1969; *s* of late Shane Fenton (*né* Bernard William Jewry), (Alvin Stardust) and Iris Fenton; *m* 1997, Anna Heslop; two *s*. *Educ:* Haberdashers' Aske's Sch., Elstree; Keble Coll., Oxford (BA, MA PPE; MEd Educnl Leadership; PGCE); Nat. Coll. for Sch. Leadership (NPQH). Teacher: Bishopshalt Sch., 1994–96; The Ridings Sch., Yorks, 1996–98; Dep. Headteacher, Sandringham Sch., 1998–2000; Mem., Sch. Mgt and Improvement Service, Herts Educn Authy, 2000–01; Headteacher, Sir John Lawes Sch., Harpenden, 2001–06; Headmaster, Pate's Grammar Sch., Cheltenham, 2006–12; Principal, Pate's Acad., 2010–12. Partner, Cheltenham All Saints Acad. (Gov., 2011). Mem., Partnership Adv. Gp, Univ. of Herts, 2004–06. Chm., Nat. GS Heads' Assoc., 2008–10; Member: Nat. GS Assoc., 2006–; Nat. Headteacher Steering Gp for Sci. Colls, 2010–; Cttee, Freedom and Autonomy for Schs - Nat. Assoc. (formerly Foundn, Aided Schs and Academies Nat. Assoc.); Partnership Gp, UCAS. Addnl Mem., HMC, 2007–. Local Leader of Educn, 2010–11, Nat. Leader, 2011–. Mem., Royal Soc. of St George, 2010–. FRSA. *Recreations:* loving God, Anna and my two boys, Noah and Joseph. *Address:* Reigate Grammar School, Reigate Road, Reigate, Surrey RH2 0QS. *Club:* Lansdowne.

FENWICK, John James, CBE 2013; Vice Lord-Lieutenant, Tyne and Wear, 2002–07; Deputy Chairman, Fenwick Ltd, 1972–79 and 1997–2013 (Managing Director, 1972–82; Chairman, 1979–97); Director, Northern Rock plc (formerly Northern Rock Building Society), 1984–99; *b* 9 Aug. 1932; *e s* of James Frederick Trevor Fenwick; *m* 1957, Muriel Gillian Hodnett; three *s*. *Educ:* Rugby Sch.; Pembroke Coll., Cambridge (MA). Chairman: Northumberland Assoc. of Youth Clubs, 1966–71; Retail Distributors Assoc., 1977–79; Vice Chm., National Assoc. of Citizens Advice Bureaux, 1971–79; Regional Dir, Northern Bd, Lloyds Bank, 1982–85. Member: Newcastle Diocesan Bd of Finance, 1964–69; Retail Consortium Council, 1976–79; Post Office Users' Nat. Council, 1980–82; Civic Trust for NE, 1979–96. Governor: Royal Grammar Sch., Newcastle upon Tyne, 1975–2000 (Chm. Govs, 1987–2000); St Paul's Girls' Sch., 1988–2001 (Chm. Govs, 1995–2001); Moorfields Eye Hosp., 1981–86; Royal Shakespeare Theatre, 1985–2002. Master, Mercers' Co., 1991–92. DL Tyne and Wear, 1986. Hon. DCL Northumbria, 1993. *Recreations:* travel, reading, walking. *Address:* 63 New Bond Street, W1A 3BS. *Clubs:* Garrick, MCC.

FENWICK, Justin Francis Quintus; QC 1993; a Recorder, since 1999; a Deputy High Court Judge, since 2003; *b* 11 Sept. 1949; *s* of David and Maita Fenwick; *m* 1975, Marcia Mary Dunn; one *s* three *d*. *Educ:* Ampleforth Coll., York; Clare Coll., Cambridge (MA Mod. Langs and Architectural Hist.). Commnd Grenadier Guards, 1968; Adjt, 2nd Battalion, 1977–79; Temp. Equerry to HRH the Duke of Edinburgh, 1979–81. Called to the Bar, Inner Temple, 1980, Bencher, 1997. Hd of Chambers, 4 New Square, 2000–05. Dir, Bar Mutual Indemnity Fund Ltd, 1997–2013 (Chm., 1999–2013); Dir, 1982–, Man. Dir, 2006–, By Pass Nurseries Ltd; Dir, 1984–, Man. Dir, 2006–, Chelsea Gardener Ltd. Comr, Royal Hospital Chelsea, 2011–. *Recreations:* wine, shooting, reading. *Address:* 4 New Square, Lincoln's Inn, WC2A 3RJ. *T:* (020) 7822 2000. *Club:* Garrick.

FENWICK, Sir Leonard (Raymond), Kt 2008; CBE 2000; Chief Executive, Newcastle upon Tyne Hospitals NHS Foundation Trust (formerly NHS Trust), since 1998; *b* Newcastle upon Tyne, 10 Aug. 1947; *s* of late Leo Stanislaws Fenwick and Hilda May Fenwick (*née* Downey); *m* 1969, Jacqueline Simpson; one *d*. Joined NHS as mgt trainee; mgt roles at Newcastle Gen. Hosp., then at Freeman Hosp.; Chief Exec., Freeman Gp of Hosps NHS Trust, 1990–98. Hon. DSc Newcastle upon Tyne, 2006. *Address:* Newcastle upon Tyne Hospitals NHS Foundation Trust, Freeman Hospital, Freeman Road, High Heaton, Newcastle upon Tyne NE7 7DN.

FENWICK, Lex; Chief Executive Officer, Dow Jones & Company, 2012–14; *b* 21 March 1959; *s* of Benedict and Deirdre Fenwick; *m* 1990, Sophie Crichton-Stuart; two *d*. Bloomberg LP, 1996–2012: Man. Dir, Bloomberg Europe, ME and Africa, 1996–2000; Chief Operating Officer, 2001–02; CEO, 2002–08; Founder and CEO, Bloomberg Ventures, 2008–12. *Recreations:* art, music.

FENWICK, Mark Anthony; Director, since 1977, and Chairman, since 1997, Fenwick Ltd; Manager of Roger Waters, since 1991; *b* Newcastle upon Tyne, 11 May 1948; *s* of John Fenwick and Sheila Fenwick; *m* 1972, Margaret Kathleen Hue-Williams; one *s* one *d*. *Educ:* Millfield. Joined EG Management; on tour with T-Rex; Manager: Emerson Lake and Palmer; Roxy Music and Bryan Ferry, 1972–85; worked in the property business, 1985–91. *Recreations:* shooting, music. *Address:* Fenwick Ltd, 63 New Bond Street, W1S 1RQ. *T:* (020) 7629 9161. *E:* markfenwick@mfm.demon.co.uk. *Club:* George.

FENWICK, Mary; *see* Nightingale, M.

FENWICK, Peter Brooke Cadogan, FRCPsych; Consultant Neuropsychiatrist, Maudsley Hospital, 1977–96, now Emeritus; President, Scientific and Medical Network, since 2003 (Chairman, 1987–2000); *b* 25 May 1935; *s* of Anthony Fenwick and Betty (*née* Darling); *m* 1963, Elizabeth Roberts; one *s* two *d*. *Educ:* Stowe Sch.; Trinity Coll., Cambridge (BA 1957; MB BChir 1960); DPM London 1966. FRCPsych 1986. House Officer, St Thomas' Hosp., 1960–62; SHO in Psychiatry, Middlesex Hosp., 1962–64; MRC Fellow, Nat. Hosp., 1964–66; Registrar, then Sen. Registrar, Maudsley Hosp., 1967–74; Consultant Neurophysiologist: Westminster Hosp., 1974–77; St Thomas' Hosp., 1974–96, now Hon. Consulting Neurophysiologist; Cons. Neuropsychiatrist, Radcliffe Infirmary, Oxford, 1989–2002, now Emeritus; Hon. Cons. Neurophysiologist, Broadmoor Special Hosp., 1972–; Hon. Sen. Lectr, Inst. of Psychiatry, London Univ., 1974–; RIKEN Inst. of Neurosci., Japan, 2000–09. Forensic expert on automatism and sleep disorders; has given expert neuropsychiatric evidence in many civil and criminal legal cases; res. into experiences of dying in hospices and nursing homes in UK and Holland; internat. lectr. Consultant, Music and the Brain documentary series, 1986. Ver Hayden de Lancey Prize, Cambridge Univ., 1987. *Publications:* with Elizabeth Fenwick: The Truth in the Light, 1995; The Hidden Door, 1997; Past Lives, 1999; The Art of Dying, 2008; over 200 contribs to learned jls. *Recreations:* flying, hill walking, wind and water turbines, the study of consciousness. *Address:* 42 Herne Hill, SE24 9QP. *T:* (020) 7274 3154.

FENWICK, Rt Rev. Dr Richard David; *see* St Helena, Bishop of.

FERGUS, Prof. Sir Howard (Archibald), KBE 2001 (CBE 1995; OBE 1979); PhD; Deputy Governor, Montserrat, 1976–2009; Professor, University of West Indies, 2001–04; *b* 22 July 1937; *s* of Simon and Priscilla Fergus; *m* 1970, Eudora Edgecombe; one *s* two *d*. *Educ:* Univ. of W Indies (BA, PhD 1984); Univ. of Bristol (CertEd); Univ. of Manchester (MEd). Primary sch. teacher, 1955–64; secondary sch. teacher, 1964–70; Chief Educn Officer, Montserrat, 1970–74; Lectr, 1974–81, Sen. Lectr, 1981–2001, Sch. of Continuing Studies, Univ. of WI. Mem. and Speaker, Legislative Council, Montserrat, 1975–2001; Speaker, Legislative Assembly, 2014–15. Supervisor of Elections, 1978–2009. Hon. DD WI Sch. of Theology, Trinidad and Tobago, 2010. *Publications:* Calabash of Gold (poetry), 1993; Montserrat: history of a Caribbean colony, 1994, 2nd edn 2004; Gallery Montserrat: prominent people in our history, 1996; Montserrat Versus Volcano, 1996; Hope (poetry), 1998; Lara Rains and Colonial Rites (poetry), 1998; (jtly) Montserrat: report of the election commissioners, 1999; Volcano Song: poems of an island in agony, 2000; Montserrat in the Twentieth Century: trials and triumphs, 2001; Volcano Verses, 2003; A History of Education in the British Leeward Islands, 1838–1945, 2003; (jtly) Montserrat and Montserratians, 2005; Love, Labor, Liberation in Lasana Sekou, 2007; (jtly) Breaking down the Walls, 2007; I Believe (poetry), 2008; Death in the Family: E. A. Markham 1939–2008, 2008; The Arrow Poems and Saturday Soup, 2010; Poems From Behind God Back, 2011; Obama and Other Poems, 2012; Festival at Fifty, 1962–2012, 2012; Road from Long Ground: my personal path (autobiog.), 2005; A Cloud of Witnesses: some Pentecostal Pastors of Montserrat, 2014; September Remember (poems), 2014; contrib. several book chapters and articles to learned jls. *Recreations:* reading, writing, poetry. *Address:* (home) Olveston, Montserrat, W Indies. *T:* 4912414, 4962888.

FERGUSON, Sir Alexander Chapman, Kt 1999; CBE 1995 (OBE 1984); Director, Manchester United Football Club Ltd, since 2013; Manager, Manchester United Football Club, 1986–2013; *b* Govan, Glasgow, 31 Dec. 1941; *s* of Alexander and Elizabeth Ferguson; *m* 1966, Catherine Holding; three *s*. *Educ:* Govan High Sch., Glasgow. Footballer; played for: Queen's Park, 1957–60; St Johnstone, 1960–64; Dunfermline Athletic, 1964–67; Glasgow Rangers, 1967–69; Falkirk, 1969–73; Ayr United, 1973–74; Manager: East Stirlingshire, 1974; St Mirren, 1974–78 (Scottish First Div. 1977); Aberdeen, 1978–86 (Scottish Premier League, 1980, 1984, 1985; Scottish Cup, 1982, 1983, 1984, 1986; Scottish League Cup, 1986; European Cup Winners Cup, 1983; UEFA Super Cup, 1983); wins with Manchester United: FA Cup, 1990, 1994, 1996, 1999, 2004; Charity Shield, later Community Shield, 1990, 1993, 1994, 1996, 1997, 2003, 2007, 2008, 2010, 2011; Premier Div., 1992–93, 1993–94, 1995–96, 1996–97, 1998–99, 1999–2000, 2000–01, 2002–03, 2006–07, 2007–08, 2008–09, 2010–11, 2012–13; League Cup, 1992, 2006, 2009, 2010; European Cup Winners Cup, 1991; UEFA Super Cup, 1991; UEFA Champions League, 1999, 2008; European-S American Cup, 1999; FIFA Club World Cup, 2008. Lectr, Business of Entertainment, Media and Sports, Harvard Business Sch., 2014–. *Publications:* A Light in the North, 1985; Six Years at United, 1992; Just Champion, 1993; A Year in the Life: the Manager's diary, 1995; (with David Meek) A Will to Win: the Manager's diary, 1997; (with Hugh McIlvanney) Managing My Life: my autobiography, 1999; The Unique Treble: achieving our goals, 2000; Alex Ferguson: my autobiography, 2013; (with Sir Michael Moritz) Leading, 2015. *Recreations:* golf, snooker.

FERGUSON, Dr Archibald Thomas Graham, CPhys, FInstP; Nuclear Weapons Safety Advisor, Ministry of Defence, 1994–97; *b* 27 Dec. 1928; *s* of Francis Ferguson and Annie Orr Ferguson (*née* Graham); *m* 1956, Margaret Watson; two *d. Educ:* Irvine Royal Acad.; Glasgow Univ. (MA 1950; PhD 1954). CPhys 1974; FInstP 1974. United Kingdom Atomic Energy Authority, Harwell Laboratory, 1953–93: Nuclear Physics Div., 1953–65; Gp Leader, High Voltage Lab., 1961–81; on secondment to Neils Bohr Inst., Copenhagen, 1965–66; Head: Scientific Admin, 1982–85; Nuclear Physics Div., 1985–90; Safety, Culham and Harwell, 1990–93. *Publications:* contrib. numerous articles in learned jls; conf. proceedings. *Recreations:* sailing, gardening.

FERGUSON, Duncan George Robin, FIA; Senior Independent Director, Royal London Mutual Insurance Society, since 2010; *b* 12 May 1942; *s* of Dr R. L. Ferguson and K. I. Ferguson; *m* 1966, Alison Margaret Simpson; one *s* one *d* (and one *s* decd). *Educ:* Fettes Coll., Edinburgh; Trinity Coll., Cambridge (MA Maths and Econs 1964; DipAgSci (Agricl Econs) 1965). FIA 1970. Actuarial student, Bacon & Woodrow, 1965–69; Actuary and Asst Gen. Manager, Metropolitan Life, Cape Town, 1969–72; Actuary and Dir, Nation Life, 1972–75; Dir, Internat. Div., Eagle Star, 1975–88; Partner, 1988, Sen. Partner, 1994–2001, Bacon & Woodrow; Sen. Partner, B & W Deloitte, and Partner, Deloitte & Touche, 2001–03. Non-executive Director: HBOS Financial Services (formerly Halifax), 1994–2007; Illium Insce, 2003–05; Windsor Life, 2004–11; Henderson, 2004–13; non-exec. Chm., Phoenix Life Assurance Ltd (formerly Resolution Gp Life Assurance Co.), 2003–09. Pres., Inst. of Actuaries, 1996–98. *Publications:* Unit Linked Life Assurance in South Africa, 1972; Life Assurance Solvency and Insolvency, 1976; Business Projections: a critical appraisal, 1980; Review of Law Relating to Insolvent Life Assurance Companies and Proposals for Reform, 1984; Reasonable Expectations of Policy Holders, 1984. *E:* dferguson@europe.com.

FERGUSON, Edward Alexander de Poulton; HM Diplomatic Service; Ambassador to Bosnia and Herzegovina, since 2014; *b* Oslo, 15 March 1978; *s* of Brig. John Gordon Goddard de Poulton Ferguson, OBE, DL and Celia Mary Ferguson, MBE; *m* 2007, Caroline Evelyn Vera Harris; one *s* one *d. Educ:* Trinity Coll., Oxford (BA 1st Cl. Hons Lit.Hum. 2001); London Sch. of Econs and Pol Sci. (MSc Dist. Diplomacy and Internat. Strategy 2012). Ministry of Defence: fast-stream grad. posts, 2001–04; Proj. Manager, Defence Estates, 2004–06; Political Advr, Maysaan Battlegroup, Iraq, 2006; Asst Hd, N America and Western Europe, 2006–07; Private Sec. to Sec. of State for Defence, 2007–09; Head: Afghanistan and Pakistan Policy, 2009–11; Defence Strategy and Priorities, 2011–14. *Recreations:* family, singing, theatre, long walks and a good book. *Address:* British Embassy, 39a Hamdije Čemerlića, Sarajevo, Bosnia and Herzegovina. *T:* (33) 282214, *Fax:* (33) 282203. *E:* edward.ferguson@fco.gov.uk.

FERGUSON, George Robin Paget, CBE 2010; Mayor of Bristol, since 2012; Director, since 1988, and Chairman, 2002–12, Ferguson Mann (formerly Acanthus Ferguson Mann) Architects; *b* 22 March 1947; *s* of late Robert Spencer Ferguson and Eve Mary Ferguson; *m* 1969, Lavinia (*née* Clerk) (marr. diss. 2000); one *s* two *d. Educ:* Wellington Coll.; Univ. of Bristol (BA, BArch). RIBA. Mem. (L), Bristol CC, 1973–79. Contested (Lib/Alliance) Bristol West, 1983, 1987. Commenced own architectural practice as sole practitioner, 1971; Founder and Dir, Acanthus Associated Architectural Practices Ltd, 1986–; Dir, Concept Planning Gp, 1991–2003; Founder and Owner, Tobacco Factory Arts Centre, S Bristol, 1995–. Pres., RIBA, 2003–05. Dir, Acad. of Urbanism, 2006–11. Chm., Bristol Beer Factory (Bristol Brewing Co. Ltd), 2006–; Dir, Pierian Centre Community Interest Co., 2008–11. Presenter: The Architecture Show, TV, 1998; Demolition, C4, 2005–06; Building Britain, BBC, 2007; Columnist, Bristol Evening Post, 2008–10. Chm., Bristol Exploratory, 1993–2001; Pres., Avon Youth Assoc., 1999–2015; Dir, Canteen West Ltd, 2010–; Trustee: Greater Bristol Foundn, 1995–2001; Bristol Cathedral Trust, 1999–2002; Demos, 2008–10; Arnolfini Art Gall., 2009–12; Bristol Univ. Student Union, 2011–15. Gov., UWE, 1995–99. Architect to RWA, 1997–2007. High Sheriff, Bristol, 1996–97. Hon. FRIAS 2011; Hon. AIA. Hon. MA Bristol, 1999; Hon. DDes UWE, 2003. RIBA Awards; Civic Trust Awards; RICS Awards. *Publications:* Races Against Time, 1983. *Recreations:* the arts, travel, people, ideas, challenging the establishment, making things happen. *Address:* Tobacco Factory, Raleigh Road, Bristol BS3 1TF; City Hall, College Green, Bristol BS1 5TR. *E:* mayor@bristol.gov.uk.

FERGUSON, Air Vice-Marshal Gordon MacArthur, CB 1993; CBE 1990; FRAeS; Chairman, Suffolk Probation Board, 2001–04; *b* 15 April 1938; *s* of late James Miller Ferguson and Elizabeth Thomson Ferguson (*née* Barron); *m* 1966, Alison Mary Saxby; one *s* one *d. Educ:* King Edward VI Sch., Southampton. Commissioned, RAF, 1960; served Mobile Air Movements, RAF Pergamos and Nicosia, HQ 38 Group, RAF Stafford and Fylingdales, MoD Supply Policy, HQ 2nd ATAF; RAF Staff Coll., 1977; OC Tac Supply Wing, 1977–79; MoD Supply Policy, 1979–81; Air Warfare Course, 1981; MoD Supply Policy, 1981–85; Dep. Dir, Supply Management, 1985–87, Dir, 1987–89; Dir, AMSO Reorgn Implementation Team, 1989–91; AOA, HQ Strike Comd, 1991–94. Man. Dir, Taylor Curnow Ltd, 1994–99. Trustee, Royal Patriotic Fund Corp., 1995–2004. FRAeS 2004. *Recreations:* bridge, walking. *Address:* Paseo Maritimo 53, Apt 1A, Esc. 1, Edf. Catamaran, Aguadulce, 04720 Almeria, Spain. *Club:* Royal Air Force.

FERGUSON, Iain William Findlay; QC (Scot.) 2000; *b* 31 July 1961; *s* of James Thomas Ferguson and Catherine Doris (*née* Findlay); *m* 1992, Valérie Laplanche; two *s. Educ:* Univ. of Dundee (LLB Hons; DipLP). Admitted Faculty of Advocates, 1987; Standing Junior Counsel: MoD (Army), 1991–98; Scottish Exec., Planning, 1998–2000. *Recreations:* cycling, Rugby, cooking. *Address:* 16 McLaren Road, Edinburgh EH9 2BN. *T:* (0131) 667 1751.

FERGUSON, Sir Ian Edward J.; *see* Johnson-Ferguson.

FERGUSON, Ian Stewart, CBE 2005; Chairman of Trustees, Employee Benefit Trust, Metaswitch Networks (formerly Data Connection Ltd), since 1988 (Chief Executive, 1981–2008; Chairman, 1981–2010); *b* 22 Feb. 1943; *s* of John Smith Ferguson and Victoria Alexandra Ferguson (*née* Luscombe); *m* 1st, 1967, Wilma Murray (marr. diss. 1991); one *s* one *d*; 2nd, 1995, Catherine Tessa Marston (marr. diss. 2014). *Educ:* High Sch. of Glasgow; Univ. of Glasgow (BSc Hons Maths 1965). Unilever, 1965–70; IBM, 1970–81. Dir, Business Link London, 1995–97. Member: Modern Apprenticeship Adv. Cttee, DfES, 2001; LSC, 2001–10 (Chm., Young Peoples' Learning Cttee, 2004–07); 14–19 Govt Wkg Gp, 2003–04; Talent and Enterprise Taskforce, 2008–10; Skills Commn, 2011–; Adv. Bd, Educn Funding Agency, 2012–; Deputy Chairman: Apprenticeship Task Force, 2003–05; Apprenticeship Ambassadors Network, 2006–; Educnl Technology Taskforce, 2010–; Member, Board: QCA, 2003–08 (Chm., Qualifications and Skills Adv. Gp, 2003–08); UK Skills, 2004–; Trng and Develt Agency for Schs, 2006–09; Mem., Young People's Learning Agency, 2010–12. Confederation of British Industry: Mem., Nat. Council, 1998–99; Member: Educn and Skills (formerly Educn and Trng Affairs) Cttee, 2003–; Educn Funding Agency Adv. Gp, 2012–. Mem., Educn Adv. Gp, RSC, 2012–. FRSA 2006. *Recreations:* theatre, opera, music, ski-ing, food, wine, family, philosophy, human condition. *Address:* Metaswitch Networks, 100 Church Street, Enfield EN2 6BQ. *T:* (020) 8366 1177, *Fax:* (020) 8363 5062. *E:* ian.ferguson@metaswitch.com.

FERGUSON, Prof. Mark William James, CBE 1999; PhD; FMedSci; FDSRCSE, FFDRCSI; Professor, Faculty of Life Sciences (formerly School of Biological Sciences), University of Manchester, 1984–2012, now Honorary Professor of Life Sciences; Director General, Science Foundation Ireland, and Chief Scientific Adviser to the Government of Ireland, since 2012; *b* 11 Oct. 1955; *s* of late James Ferguson and of Elenor Gwendoline Ferguson; *m* (marr. diss.); three *d. Educ:* Queen's Univ., Belfast (BSc 1st Cl. Hons Anatomy 1976; BDS 1st Cl. Hons Dentistry 1978; PhD Anatomy and Embryology 1982). FFDRCSI 1990; FDSRCSE 1997. Winston Churchill Travelling Fellow, 1978; Lectr in Anatomy, QUB, 1979–84; Head, Dept of Cell and Structural Biology, 1986–92, Dean, Sch. of Biol Scis, 1994–96, Univ. of Manchester. Founder and Chm. of Bd, Manchester Biotechnology Ltd, 1997–99; Founder, 1998, CEO, 2000–11, non-exec. Chm., 2011–12, Renovo Ltd, later Renovo Gp plc. Chm., Health and Life Scis Panel, Tech. Foresight Prog., OST, 1994–99; Member: Lord Sainsbury's Biotech. Cluster Cttee, DTI, 1999; Biol Sub Cttee, Cttee of Safety of Medicines, 1999–2005; Genome Valley Steering Gp, DTI, 2000–01; Preclinical Medicine, Anatomy, Physiol. and Pharmacol. Panel, RAE 2001, HEFCE; Life Sci. Mktg Bd, UK Trade & Investment, 2008–11; Bd, Sci. Foundn Ireland, 2012–; Bd, Forfás, 2012–. President: Med. Scis Section, BAAS, 1997; Bd, BioIndustry Assoc., 2001–03; European Tissue Repair Soc., 2002–03 (Sec., 1996–2007); Manchester Med. Soc., 2009–10. Gov., Res. into Ageing, 1995–2000. Steeger Vis. Prof. and Lectr, NY Univ. Med. Center, 1992; Lectures: Teale, RCP, 1994; Kelvin, IEE, 1995; Broadhurst, Harvard Med. Sch., 1996; Distinguished, Amer. Soc. of Human Genetics, 1998; Northcroft, British Orthodontic Soc., 2001; Langdon-Brown, RCP, 2002; Cairns, British Soc. Neurol Surgery, 2008; British Council lecture tours: India, 1999, China, 2002. Founder FMedSci 1998. Mem., World Econ. Forum, Davos, 2007– (Tech. Pioneer, 2007–09). FIAE 2014. Hon. DMedSci QUB, 2002. John Tomes Prize and Medal, 1990, Charles Tomes Prize and Medal, 1998, RCS; Carter Medal, Clin. Genetics Soc., 1997; Internat. Assoc. for Dental Res. Award, 2000; Körber European Science Award, 2002; N. Rowe Lecture and Prize, BAOMS, 2003; Eur. Biotechnia Award, Eur. Biotechnol. Orgn, 2007; Fergal Nally Lect. and Medal, RCSI, 2013. *Publications:* The Structure, Development and Evolution of Reptiles, 1984; Egg Incubation: its effects on embryonic development in birds and reptiles, 1991; (ed) Gray's Anatomy, 38th edn, 1995; more than 350 scientific papers, patents and contribs to books on wound healing, prevention of scarring, cleft palate and sex determination. *Recreations:* travel, wildlife, reading, antiques, scientific research. *Address:* Science Foundation Ireland, Wilton Park House, Wilton Place, Dublin 2, Ireland. *T:* (1) 6073175.

FERGUSON, Martin John, AM 1996; MP (ALP) Batman, Australia, 1996–2013; Minister for Resources and Energy, and Minister for Tourism, 2007–13; Group Executive, Seven Group Holdings, since 2013; *b* 12 Dec. 1953; *s* of Laurie John Ferguson and Mary Ellen Clare Ferguson (*née* Bett); *m* 1981, Patricia Jane Waller; one *s* one *d. Educ:* St Patrick's Convent, Guildford; St Patrick's Coll., Strathfield; Sydney Univ. (BEc Hons). Federated Miscellaneous Workers Union of Australia: Federal Research Officer, 1975–81; Asst Gen. Sec., 1981–84; Gen. Sec., 1984–90; Pres., ACTU, 1990–96. Asst to Ldr of Opposition on multicultural affairs, 1997–98; Opposition Shadow Minister, Australian Parliament: for employment and trng, 1996–98; for population, 1997–2001; for immigration, 1997–98; for regl develt and infrastructure, 1999–2002; for regl services, 1999–2001; for transport, 1999–2002; for urban develt, 2001–03; for regl develt, transport infrastructure and tourism, 2002–03; for urban and regl develt, transport and infrastructure, 2003–04; for resources, forestry and tourism, 2004–06, and for primary industries, 2005–06; for transport, roads and tourism, 2006–07. Non-exec. Dir, BG Group, 2014–. Chairman: Adv. Bd, APPEA, 2013–; CO_2 Co-operative Res. Centre, 2013–. Mem., Governing Body, ILO, 1990–96. Member: Trade Develt Council, 1990–96; Econ. Planning Adv. Council, 1990–96; Australian Govt's Agric. Food Council, 1992–96; Exec. Bd, Construction Ind. Develt Agency, 1992–96. Member: Bd, Nat. Liby of Australia, 1999–2007; Bd of Trustees, Energy and Minerals Inst., Univ. of Western Australia, 2013–.

FERGUSON, Prof. Michael Anthony John, CBE 2008; PhD; FRS 2000; FRSE; Regius Professor of Life Sciences, since 2013, and Professor of Molecular Parasitology, since 1994, University of Dundee (Dean of Research, 2007–14); *b* 6 Feb. 1957; *s* of Dr Anthony John Alexander Ferguson and Pamela Mary (*née* Gray); *m* 1st, 1982, Sheila Duxbury (marr. diss. 1988); 2nd, 1992, Dr Maria Lucia Sampaio Güther; one *s. Educ:* St Peter's Sch., York; UMIST (BSc Hons Biochem. 1979); Charing Cross Hosp. Med. Sch., Univ. of London (PhD Biochem. 1982). Post-doctoral Research Fellow: Rockefeller Univ., NY, 1982–85; Oxford Univ., 1985–88; Res. Fellow, Pembroke Coll., Oxford, 1986–88; University of Dundee: Lectr, 1988–91; Reader, 1991–94. Member: Bd of Govs, Wellcome Trust, 2012–; Bd of Dirs, Medicines for Malaria Venture, 2012–. FRSE 1994; FMedSci 2007. Colworth Medal, Biochemical Soc., 1991; Royal Medal, Royal Soc. of Edinburgh, 2013. *Recreation:* travel. *Address:* Division of Biological Chemistry and Drug Discovery, College of Life Sciences, University of Dundee, Dundee DD1 5EH. *T:* (01382) 384219.

FERGUSON, Prof. Niall Campbell, DPhil; Laurence A. Tisch Professor of History, Harvard University, since 2004; Senior Fellow, Hoover Institution, Stanford University, since 2003; Senior Research Fellow, Jesus College, Oxford, since 2003; *b* 18 April 1964; *s* of late Dr James Campbell Ferguson and of Molly Archibald Ferguson (*née* Hamilton); *m* 1st, 1994, Susan Margaret Douglas, *qv* (marr. diss. 2011); two *s* one *d*; 2nd, 2011, Ayaan Hirsi Ali; one *s. Educ:* Glasgow Acad.; Magdalen Coll., Oxford (BA 1st Cl. Hons; DPhil 1989). Hanseatic Schol., Hamburg, 1986–88; Research Fellow, Christ's Coll., Cambridge, 1989–90; Official Fellow and Lectr, Peterhouse, Cambridge, 1990–92; University of Oxford: Lectr in Mod. Hist., 1992–2000; Prof. of Pol and Financial Hist., 2000–02; Vis. Prof. in Modern Eur. Hist., 2003–; John E. Herzog Prof. of Financial History, Leonard N. Stern Sch. of Business, NY Univ., 2002–04; William Ziegler Prof. of Business Admin, Harvard Business Sch., 2006–11; Philippe Roman Prof. of History and Internat. Affairs, LSE, 2010–11. Houblon-Norman Fellow, Bank of England, 1998–99. Reith Lectr, BBC, 2012. Dir, Chimerica Media Ltd, 2007–; CEO, Greenmantle LLC, 2011–. Presenter, TV series: Empire, 2003; American Colossus, 2004; War of the World, 2006; The Ascent of Money, 2008; Civilization: Is the West History?, 2011; China: Triumph and Turmoil, 2012; The Pity of War, 2014. Ed., Jl of Contemp. History, 2004–08; contributing ed., FT, 2008–11. *Publications:* Paper and Iron: Hamburg business and German politics in the era of inflation 1897–1927, 1995; (ed) Virtual History: alternatives and counterfactuals, 1997; The World's Banker: the history of the house of Rothschild, 1998; The Pity of War, 1998; The Cash Nexus, 2001; Empire: how Britain made the modern world, 2003; Colossus: the rise and fall of the American Empire, 2004; The War of the World: history's age of hatred, 2006; The Ascent of Money: a financial history of the world, 2008; High Financier: the lives and time of Siegmund Warburg, 2010; Civilization: the West and the rest, 2011; Kissinger, vol. 1, 2015; contrib. English Historical Rev., Past & Present, Econ. Hist. Rev., Jl of Econ. Hist. *Recreations:* double bass, surfing, ski-ing. *Address:* Minda de Gunzburg Center for European Studies, Harvard University, 27 Kirkland Street, Cambridge, MA 02138, USA. *Clubs:* Beefsteak, Savile, Royal Automobile; Gridiron (Oxford); Brook (New York).

FERGUSON, Nicholas Eustace Haddon, CBE 2013; Chairman, Sky (formerly BSkyB) plc, since 2012 (Director, since 2004); *b* 24 Oct. 1948; *s* of Captain Derrick Ferguson, RN and Betsy Ferguson; *m* 1976, Margaret Jane Dura Collin; two *s* one *d. Educ:* Univ. of Edinburgh (BSc Econs 1970); Harvard Business Sch. (MBA 1975, Baker Scholar). CEO, Singapore Internat. Merchant Bankers, 1980–83; Chm., Schroder Ventures, 1983–2001; CEO, 2001–06, Chm., 2006–12, SVG Capital plc (formerly Schroder Ventures Internat. Investment Trust). Non-executive Director: Schroders plc, 1998–2001; Tamar Energy Ltd, 2010–; Maris Ltd, 2014–; Chm., Alta Hldgs Ltd, 2008–. Chairman: Courtauld Inst. of Art, 2002–12; Inst. for Philanthropy, 2003–11. Chm., Kilfinan Trust, 2004–; Trustee, EDF, 2014–. *Recreations:* collecting and studying Medieval art, country pursuits, ski-ing, gardening. *Club:* Brooks's.

FERGUSON, Patricia Josephine; Member (Lab) Glasgow Maryhill and Springburn, Scottish Parliament, since 2011 (Glasgow Maryhill, 1999–2011); *b* 24 Sept. 1958; *d* of John

Ferguson and Andrewina Ferguson (*née* Power); *m* 1988, William Gerard Butler, *qv*. *Educ:* Garnethill Convent Secondary Sch., Glasgow; Glasgow Coll. of Technology (part-time) (SHNC Public Admin). Greater Glasgow Health Board: Admin. Trainee, 1976–78; Administrator, 1978–83; Sec., Greater Glasgow SE Local Health Council, 1983–85; Administrator: Capital Services, Lanarkshire Health Bd, 1985–90; Scottish TUC, 1990–94; Organiser, South West of Scotland Lab. Party, 1994–96; Scottish Officer, Scottish Lab. Party, 1996–99. Scottish Parliament: Dep. Presiding Officer, 1999–2001; Minister: for Parly Business, and Govt Chief Whip, 2001–04; for Tourism, Culture and Sport, 2004–07; Shadow Minister for Europe, External Affairs and Culture, 2007; Shadow Cabinet Sec. for Culture and External Affairs, 2011–14. *Recreations:* reading, driving, travel, theatre, music. *Address:* 43 Atlas Road, Glasgow G21 4TA. *T:* (0141) 558 9483.

FERGUSON, Rt Rev. Paul John; *see* Whitby, Bishop Suffragan of.

FERGUSON, Peter William; QC (Scot.) 2005; Advocate, since 1987; *b* 22 March 1961; *er s* of late John Lambie Ferguson and of Joyce Robertson Ferguson (*née* Carrol). *Educ:* Portobello High Sch., Edinburgh; Univ. of Edinburgh (LLB Hons 1983; MSc Dist. 1998); Univ. of Strathclyde (DipLP 1984). Admitted Advocate, 1987. Mem., Scottish Criminal Cases Review Commn, 2011–. *Publications:* Crimes Against the Person, 1989, 2nd edn 1998; contrib. legal pubns. *Address:* Advocates' Library, Parliament Square, Edinburgh EH1 1RF. *Club:* Scottish Arts (Edinburgh).

FERGUSON, Susan Margaret; *see* Douglas, S. M.

FERGUSON, Veronica Mary Geneste, LVO 2014; FRCS, FRCOphth; Consultant Ophthalmic Surgeon, Imperial College Healthcare NHS Trust (formerly Hammersmith Hospitals NHS Trust and St Mary's Hospital NHS Trust), since 1996; Surgeon Oculist to HM Household, since 2002; *b* 18 May 1960; *d* of late Geoffrey Crosby Ambrose and of Dympna Mary Ambrose (*née* Bourke); *m* 1988, James Malcolm Ferguson, TD. *Educ:* Convent of the Sacred Heart, Woldingham; Guy's Hosp. Med. Sch., London Univ. (MB BS 1983). FRCS 1987; FRCOphth 1989. Sen. House Officer, Guy's Hosp., Royal Free Hosp., Southampton Eye Hosp., and St Thomas' Hosp., 1984–89; Registrar, Southern Gen. Hosp., Glasgow, 1989–91; Sen. Registrar, St George's Hosp. and Moorfields Eye Hosp., 1991–96; Consultant Ophthalmic Surgeon: King Edward VII's Hosp. (Sr Agnes), 1997–; St Luke's Hosp. for the Clergy, 2002–; Ophthalmologist, Blind Veterans UK (formerly St Dunstan's Charity for Blind Ex-servicemen), 2004–. Hon. Sen. Lectr, Imperial Coll., London, 1996–. Mem. Council, Royal Coll. Ophthalmologists, 1999–2005. *Publications:* contribs on cataract surgery, ocular inflammation and strabismus to ophthalmic jls. *Recreations:* horses, gardening, bee-keeping, ski-ing. *Address:* 70 Harley Street, W1G 7HF. *T:* (020) 7580 0285, *Fax:* (020) 7580 0286. *E:* v.ferguson@doctors.org.uk.

FERGUSON, William James, OBE 1996; FEAgS; farmer; Vice Lord-Lieutenant of Aberdeenshire, 1998–2008; Chairman, Aberdeen Milk Company, since 1994; *b* 3 April 1933; *s* of William Adam Ferguson and Violet (*née* Wiseman); *m* 1961, Carroll Isabella Milne; one *s* three *d*. *Educ:* Turriff Acad.; North of Scotland Coll. of Agriculture (Cert. of Agric.). Nat. Service, 1st Bn Gordon Highlanders, serving in Malaya, 1952–54. Chm., North of Scotland Coll. of Agric., 1986–91; Vice Chm., Scottish Agricl Colls, 1991–97 (Hon. Fellow, 1999). Former Chm., Grampian Farm Wildlife Adv. Gp; Member: Rowett Res. Inst., 1980–82; Technical Cttee, Crichton Royal Dairy Farm, Dumfries, 1980–83; Macaulay Inst. of Soil Res., 1983–85; Scottish Farm Bldgs Investigation Unit, 1984–86; Scottish Country Life Mus., 1986–96; Trustee, Aberdeen Endowments Trust, 2003– (Convenor, Land and Finance Cttee, 2003–). FRAgS 1995. DL Aberdeenshire, 1988. *Recreations:* golf, ski-ing, field sports. *Address:* Nether Darley, Auchterless, Turriff, Aberdeenshire AB53 8LH. *Club:* Farmers.

FERGUSON DAVIE, Sir Michael, 8th Bt *cr* 1847, of Creedy, Devonshire; retired stockbroker; *b* 10 Jan. 1944; *er s* of Sir John Ferguson Davie, 7th Bt and (Joan) Zoë (Charlotte), *d* of Raymond Hoole, Vancouver, BC; *S* father, 2000; *m* 1st, 1968, (Margaret) Jean (marr. diss. 1992), *d* of Douglas Macbeth; one *s* decd; 2nd, 2001, Sarah, *d* of John Seyfried and Lady Cathleen Hudson (*née* Eliot), and former wife of Peter M. Smith; two step *s*. *Educ:* St Edward's Sch., Oxford. Grenfell & Co. (later Grenfell & Colegrave), 1961–79; Fielding Newson-Smith & Co., 1979–86; Dir, NatWest Markets, 1986–95; Consultant, Madoff Securities Ltd, 1995–98; Partner, Footloose, 1997–2003. Trustee: SCF Endowment, 2006–10; Somerset Community Foundn, 2007–13 (Treas., 2007–10); Somerset Sight, 2010–15. Mem., Treasury Cttee, Lord's Taverners, 2014–. *Recreations:* writing, bridge, Real tennis, cricket, Rugby football. *Heir:* *b* Julian Anthony Ferguson Davie [*b* 6 July 1950; *m* 1976, Louise, *d* of John Marsden; three *s*]. *Address:* Sherston Lodge, Evercreech, Somerset BA4 6LG. *T:* (01749) 830930. *Clubs:* Pratt's, City of London, MCC.

FERGUSON-SMITH, Prof. Anne Carla, PhD; FMedSci; Professor of Genetics, since 2012, and Head, Department of Genetics, since 2013, University of Cambridge; Fellow, Darwin College, Cambridge, since 1997; *b* Baltimore, USA, 23 July 1961; *d* of Prof. Malcolm Andrew Ferguson-Smith, *qv*; *m* 1988, Mark Gregory McHarg; one *s* one *d*. *Educ:* Univ. of Glasgow (BSc Hons); Yale Univ. (PhD 1989). FMedSci 2012. *Address:* Department of Genetics, University of Cambridge, Downing Street, Cambridge CB2 3EH.

FERGUSON-SMITH, Prof. Malcolm Andrew, FRS 1983; FRSE 1978; Professor of Pathology, University of Cambridge, 1987–98, now Emeritus; Professorial Fellow, Peterhouse, Cambridge, 1987–98, now Emeritus; Director, Cambridge University Centre for Medical Genetics, 1989–98; *b* 5 Sept. 1931; *s* of John Ferguson-Smith, MA, MD, FRCP and Ethel May (*née* Thorne); *m* 1960, Marie Eva Gzowska; one *s* three *d*. *Educ:* Stowe Sch.; Univ. of Glasgow (MB ChB 1955). MRCPath 1966, FRCPath 1978; MRCPGlas 1972, FRCPGlas 1974; FRCOG 1993. Registrar in Lab. Medicine, Dept of Pathology, Western Infirmary, Glasgow, 1958–59; Fellow in Medicine and Instructor, Johns Hopkins Univ. Sch. of Medicine, 1959–61; Lectr, Sen. Lectr and Reader in Med. Genetics, Univ. of Glasgow, 1961–73, Prof. of Med. Genetics, 1973–87; Hon. Consultant: in Med. Paediatrics, Royal Hosp. for Sick Children, Glasgow, 1966–73; in Clin. Genetics, Yorkhill and Associated Hosps, 1973–87; in Med. Genetics, Addenbrooke's NHS Trust, 1987–98; Director: W of Scotland Med. Genetics Service, 1973–87; E Anglian Regl Clin. Genetics Service, 1987–95. President: Clinical Genetics Soc., 1979–81; Eur. Soc. of Human Genetics, 1997–98; Internat. Soc. for Prenatal Diagnosis, 1998–2002; Assoc. of Clinical Cytogeneticists, 2002–05. Mem., Johns Hopkins Univ. Soc. of Scholars, 1983; For. Mem., Polish Acad. of Scis, 1988; For. Corresp. Mem., Nat. Acad. of Medicine of Buenos Aires, 2002. Founder FMedSci 1998; Hon. ARCVS 2002. Hon. DSc: Strathclyde, 1992; Glasgow, 2002. Bronze Medal, Univ. of Helsinki, 1968; Makdougall-Brisbane Prize, RSE, 1988; San Remo Internat. Prize for Genetic Res., 1990; Baschirotto Award, Eur. Soc. of Human Genetics, 1996. Founding Editor, Prenatal Diagnosis, 1980–2006. *Publications:* (ed) Early Prenatal Diagnosis, 1983; (jtly) Essential Medical Genetics, 1984, 6th edn 2011; (ed) Prenatal Diagnosis and Screening, 1992; papers on cytogenetics, gene mapping, human genetics and evolutionary biology in med. and biol. jls. *Recreations:* swimming, sailing, fishing. *Address:* Department of Veterinary Medicine, Cambridge University, Madingley Road, Cambridge CB3 0ES.

See also A. C. Ferguson-Smith.

FERGUSSON, Adam (Dugdale), FRSL; writer; *b* 10 July 1932; *yr s* of Sir James Fergusson of Kilkerran, 8th Bt, LLD, FRSE, and Frances Dugdale; *m* 1965, Penelope (*d* 2009), *e d* of Peter Hughes, Furneaux Pelham Hall; two *s* two *d*. *Educ:* Eton; Trinity Coll., Cambridge (BA History, 1955). Glasgow Herald, 1956–61: Leader-writer, 1957–58; Diplomatic Corresp., 1959–61; Statist, 1961–67: Foreign Editor, 1964–67; Feature-writer for The Times on political, economic and environmental matters, 1967–77. Special Advr on European Affairs, FCO, 1985–89; consultant on European affairs, 1989–. European Parliament: Member (C) West Strathclyde, 1979–84; Spokesman on Political Affairs for European Democratic Gp, 1979–82; Vice-Chm., Political Affairs Cttee, 1982–84; Mem., Jt Cttee of ACP/EEC Consultative Assembly, 1979–84; contested (C) London Central, European elecn, 1984. Vice-Pres., Pan-European Union, 1981–2004; Mem., Scotland Says No Referendum Campaign Cttee, 1978–79. Dir, Murray International Trust PLC, 1995–2001. Gov., Howick Trust, 1976–2002; Vice-Pres., Bath Preservation Trust, 1997–. FRSL 2009. *Publications:* Roman Go Home, 1969; The Lost Embassy, 1972; The Sack of Bath, 1973; When Money Dies, 1975; Scone: a likely tale, 2004; *musical comedies:* book and lyrics for: State of Emergency, 1962; Gibbon Slept Here, 1964; Just One of those Thanes, 2009; various pamphlets; articles in national and internat. jls and magazines. *Address:* 15 Warwick Gardens, W14 8PH. *T:* (020) 7603 7900.

FERGUSSON, Rt Hon. Alexander (Charles Onslow); PC 2010; Member (C) Galloway and Dumfries West, Scottish Parliament, since 2011 (Scotland South, 1999–2003, Galloway and Upper Nithsdale, 2003–11); Presiding Officer, Scottish Parliament, 2007–11; *b* 8 April 1949; *s* of Lt Col Rev. Simon Charles David Fergusson and Auriole Kathleen Fergusson (*née* Hughes Onslow); *m* 1974, Jane Merryn Barthold; three *s*. *Educ:* Eton Coll.; West of Scotland Agricl Coll. (ONDA). Farmer, 1971–99. JP S Ayrshire, 1997–99; DL Ayrshire and Arran, 1997–99. *Recreations:* curling, Rugby, folk music. *Address:* Grennan, Dalry, Kirkcudbrightshire DG7 3PL.

FERGUSSON of Kilkerran, Sir Charles, 9th Bt *cr* 1703; *b* 10 May 1931; *s* of Sir James Fergusson of Kilkerran, 8th Bt, and Frances (*d* 1988), *d* of Edgar Dugdale; *S* father, 1973; *m* 1961, Hon. Amanda Mary Noel-Paton, *d* of Lord Ferrier, ED; two *s*. *Educ:* Eton; Edinburgh and East of Scotland Coll. of Agriculture. *Heir:* *s* Maj. Adam Fergusson [*b* 29 Dec. 1962; *m* 1989, Jenifer, *yr d* of Adam Thomson; one *s* two *d*].

FERGUSSON, Rev. Prof. David Alexander Syme, DPhil; FBA 2013; FRSE; Professor of Divinity, since 2000, and Principal of New College, since 2008, University of Edinburgh (Vice-Principal, 2009–11); a Chaplain to the Queen in Scotland, since 2015; *b* Glasgow, 3 Aug. 1956; *s* of Thomas Fergusson and Charis Fergusson; *m* 1985, Margot Evelyn McIndoe; two *s*. *Educ:* Univ. of Glasgow (MA 1977); Univ. of Edinburgh (BD 1980); Univ. of Oxford (DPhil 1984). Licensed, 1980, ordained, 1984, C of S; Asst Minister, St Nicholas, Lanark, 1983–84; Associate Minister, St Mungo's, Cumbernauld, 1984–86; Lectr in Systematic Theol., Univ. of Edinburgh, 1986–90; Prof. of Systematic Theol., Univ. of Aberdeen, 1990–2000. Lectures: Cunningham, Univ. of Edinburgh, 1996; Bampton, Univ. of Oxford, 2001; Gifford, Univ. of Glasgow, 2008; Warfield, Princeton Theol Seminary, 2009; Birks, McGill Univ., 2013. FRSE 2004. Hon. DD Aberdeen, 2014. *Publications:* Bultmann, 1992; Christ, Church and Society, 1993; John and Donald Baillie, 1997; The Cosmos and the Creator, 1998; Community, Liberation and Christian Ethics, 1998; John Macmurray: critical perspectives, 2002; Church, State and Civil Society, 2004; Scottish Philosophical Theology, 2007; Faith and Its Critics, 2009; (ed) Blackwell Companion to 19th Century Theology, 2010; (ed) Cambridge Dictionary of Christian Theology, 2011; Creation, 2014. *Recreations:* golf, football. *Address:* 23 Riselaw Crescent, Edinburgh EH10 6HN. *T:* (0131) 447 4022. *E:* David.Fergusson@ed.ac.uk. *Clubs:* New, Mortonhall Golf (Edinburgh).

FERGUSSON, Sir Ewen (Alastair John), GCMG 1993 (KCMG 1987); GCVO 1992; HM Diplomatic Service, retired; King of Arms, Most Distinguished Order of St Michael and St George, 1996–2007; *b* 28 Oct. 1932; *er s* of late Sir Ewen MacGregor Field Fergusson; *m* 1959, Sara Carolyn, *d* of late Brig.-Gen. Lord Esmé Gordon Lennox, KCVO, CMG, DSO and *widow* of Sir William Andrew Montgomery-Cuninghame, 11th Bt; one *s* two *d*. *Educ:* Geelong Grammar Sch., Australia; Rugby; Oriel Coll., Oxford (MA; Hon. Fellow, 1988). Played Rugby Football for Oxford Univ., 1952 and 1953, and for Scotland, 1954. 2nd Lieut, 60th Rifles (KRRC), 1954–56. Joined Foreign (later Diplomatic) Service, 1956; Asst Private Sec. to Minister of Defence, 1957–59; British Embassy, Addis Ababa, 1960; FO, 1963; British Trade Development Office, New York, 1967; Counsellor and Head of Chancery, Office of UK Permanent Rep. to European Communities, 1972–75; Private Sec. to Foreign and Commonwealth Sec., 1975–78; Asst Under Sec. of State, FCO, 1978–82; Ambassador to S Africa, 1982–84; Dep. Under-Sec. of State (Middle East and Africa), FCO, 1984–87; Ambassador to France, 1987–92. Chairman: Coutts & Co. Gp, 1993–99; Savoy Hotel, 1995–98 (Dir, 1993–98; Co-Chm., Internat. Adv. Bd, Savoy Gp, 1999–2004). Director: British Telecom, 1993–99; Sun Alliance Gp, 1993–95. Chm., Govt Wine Adv. Cttee, 1993–2003. Governor, Rugby Sch., 1985–2002 (Chm. Govs, 1995–2002; Chm., Arnold Foundn, 2002–07); Trustee: Nat. Gall., 1995–2002; Henry Moore Foundn, 1998–2007 (Chm., 2001–07). Hon. LLD Aberdeen, 1995. Grand Officier, Légion d'Honneur (France), 1992. *Address:* 111 Iverna Court, W8 6TX. *T:* (020) 7937 2240; Les Baumériaux, 1131 Chemin des Essareaux, 84340 Entrechaux, France. *T:* 490460496. *Clubs:* Beefsteak, Pratt's; Jockey (Paris).

FERGUSSON, George Duncan Raukawa; HM Diplomatic Service; Governor and Commander-in-Chief of Bermuda, since 2012; *b* 30 Sept. 1955; *s* of Brig. Bernard Fergusson, later Baron Ballantrae, KT, GCMG, GCVO, DSO, OBE; *m* 1981, Margaret Sheila Wookey; three *d* (one *s* decd). *Educ:* Ballantrae Jun. Secondary Sch.; Hereworth Sch., NZ; Eton Coll.; Magdalen Coll., Oxford. Murray and Tait, Solicitors, 1977–78; joined Northern Ireland Office, 1978; seconded to NI Dept of Commerce, 1979–80; Private Sec. to Min. of State for NI, 1982–83; First Sec., Dublin, 1988–91; joined Diplomatic Service, 1990; FCO, 1991–93; First Sec., Seoul, 1994–96; FCO, 1996–99; Head: Republic of Ireland Dept, 1997–99; Devolved Admins Dept, 1999; Consul Gen., Boston, 1999–2003; Counsellor, Cabinet Office, 2003–06; High Comr, New Zealand, Governor (non-res.) of Pitcairn, Henderson, Ducie and Oeno Is, and High Comr (non-res.), Samoa, 2006–10; FCO, 2010–12. *Address:* Government House, 11 Langton Hill, Pembroke, HM13, Bermuda.

FERGUSSON, Kenneth James, CEng, FIMechE; Chief Executive, Coal Authority, 1997–2001; Trustee, UCG Association, 2010–12 (Senior Adviser, Underground Coal Gasification Partnership, 2008–10); *b* 1938; *s* of Robert Brown Millar Fergusson and Agnes Tattersall Fergusson; *m* 1961, Beryl Foster; two *s* one *d*. *Educ:* Robert Gordon's Coll., Aberdeen; Harrow County Grammar Sch.; Imperial Coll., London (BSc 1st cl. Hons Engrg); Harvard Business Sch. (AMP). CEng 1966; FIMechE 1976; FIMMM until 2015 (FIMM 1999). ICI Agricl Div., 1959–68; RTZ Gp, 1968–86: Geschäftsführer, Duisburger Kupferhütte, 1981–85; Man. Dir, Rio Tinto Zimbabwe, 1985–86; Project Dir, European Transonic Windtunnel, Cologne, 1986–88; Man. Dir, Docklands Light Railway, 1988–90; Chief Exec., Hub Power Co., Karachi, 1992–93; Regl Dir, BESO, 1995–97. Trustee, Industrial Trust, 1998–2010. Pres., Combustion Engrg Assoc., 2002–06. FIMgt 1984–2002; MInstD 1987–2010; FRSA 1998–2002. Freeman, City of London, 1990; Liveryman, Co. of Engineers, 1995–2014. *Recreations:* advanced motoring and motorcycling, swimming, archaeology, music, current affairs, travel. *Address:* 24F Thorney Crescent, Morgans Walk, SW11 3TT. *T:* (020) 7585 1294.

FERLEGER BRADES, Susan Deborah; Director, Hayward Gallery, London, 1996–2004; *b* 7 July 1954; *d* of Alvin Ferleger and Beatrice Ferleger (*née* Supnick); *m* 1st, 1979, Peter Eric Brades (*d* 2001); one *s*; 2nd, 2006, Rhett Davies. *Educ:* Courtauld Inst. of Art (MA); Univ. of Mass, Amherst (BA 1976; magna cum laude; Phi Beta Kappa); Barnard Coll., Columbia Univ., NY. Curatorial Co-ordinator, Solomon R. Guggenheim Mus., NY, 1975–79; Nat. Endowment for Arts Fellowship, 1975–76; Researcher, British Sculpture in the Twentieth

Century, Whitechapel Art Gall., London, 1979–80; Hayward Gallery: Exhibn Organiser, Arts Council of GB, S Bank Centre, 1980–88; Sen. Exhibn Organiser, Exhibns Dept, S Bank Centre, 1988–93 (Public Art Programme Co-ordinator, 1990); Dep. Dir, Hayward Gall., S Bank Centre, 1993–96. Purchaser, Arts Council Collection, 1983–2004; Visual Arts Advr, John Lyons Charity, 2004–; Consultant, Bldg Project and Artist Engagement, London Liby, 2005–10. Trustee, IVAM Centro Julio Gonzalez, Valencia, 2000–04; Review Panel Mem., Course Validation Panel, Academic Standards, RCA, 2009–11. *E:* susanbrades@gmail.com.

FERMOR-HESKETH, family name of **Baron Hesketh**.

FERMOY, 6th Baron *cr* 1856; **Maurice Burke Roche;** *b* 11 Oct. 1967; *s* of 5th Baron Fermoy and of Lavinia Frances Elizabeth, *o d* of late Captain John Pitman; name changed from Patrick Maurice Burke Roche by deed poll, 2010; *S* father, 1984; *m* 1998, Tessa Fiona Ledger, *d* of Major David Pelham Kayll; two *d*. *Educ:* Eton. A Page of Honour to the Queen Mother, 1982–85. Commnd, Blues and Royals, 1987–95; Capt. With Bass Taverns, 1996–99; Director: Arrow Pubs Ltd, 1999–; Oxford Street Connections Ltd, 2009–. Mem., Cherwell DC, 2000–04. *Recreation:* country sports. *Heir: b* Hon. (Edmund) Hugh Burke Roche [*b* 5 Feb. 1972; *m* 2004, Phillipa Long; one *s* two *d*]. *Address:* Handywater Farm, Sibford Gower, Banbury, Oxon OX15 5AE.

FERN, Georgina Jane; *see* Harrisson, G. J.

FERNANDES, Anthony Francis, Hon. CBE 2011; Group Chief Executive Officer, AirAsia Berhad, 2001–12 and since 2013 (non-executive Director, 2012–13; Executive Director, since 2013). *Educ:* ACCA 1991, FCCA 1996; ACA 2008. Financial Controller, Virgin Communications London, 1987–89; Sen. Financial Analyst, 1989–92, Man. Dir, 1992–96, Warner Music Internat. London; Dir, Warner Music, Malaysia, 1992–96; Regl Man. Dir, ASEAN, 1996–99; Vice Pres., Warner Music SE Asia, 1999–2001. Co-Founder, Tune Gp of Cos, 2001. Principal, Caterham F1 Team, 2010–12; Chm., Caterham Gp; Chm., Queens Park Rangers FC, 2011–. Commandeur, Légion d'Honneur (France), 2013 (Officier, 2010). *Recreations:* sports, football, hockey. *Address:* AirAsia Berhad, LCC Terminal, Jalan Klia S3, Southern Support Zone, Klia, 64000 Sepang, Selangor Darul Ehsan, Malaysia. *T:* 386604333, *Fax:* 386601100. *E:* tonyfernandes@airasia.com.

FERNANDES, Suella; MP (C) Fareham, since 2015; *b* London, 3 April 1980; *d* of Chris Fernandes and Uma Fernandes. *Educ:* Heathfield Sch., Pinner; Queens' Coll., Cambridge (BA Hons Law 2002); Panthéon-Sorbonne Univ., Paris (LLM 2003); BVC 2005. Called to the Bar, Middle Temple, 2005; admitted to State Bar, NY, 2006; in practice as barrister specialising in planning, judicial review, immigration, No5 Chambers; Mem., Attorney Gen.'s C Panel of Treasury Counsel, 2010–15. Mem., Educn Select Cttee, 2015–. Parly Patron, Westminster Strategic Studies Gp, 2015–. Founder and Trustee, Africa Justice Foundn, 2010–14. Co-Founder and Gov., Michaela Community Sch., 2010–. *Address:* House of Commons, SW1A 0AA. *T:* (020) 7219 3000. *E:* suella.fernandes.mp@parliament.uk.

FERNÁNDEZ, Mariano; Ambassador of Chile to Germany, since 2014; consultant on international affairs; *b* Santiago, 21 April 1945; *s* of Mariano Fernández and María Angélica Amunategui; *m* 1969, María Angélica Morales; two *s* one *d*. *Educ:* Universidad Católica de Santiago (law degree 1970); Bonn Univ. (major in pol sociol.). Mem., Foreign Service, Chile, 1967–74; Third Sec., Embassy of Chile, Germany, 1971–74; in exile, Bonn, 1974–82: Ed., Develt and Co-opn Mag.; Chief Editor: IPS-Dritte welt Nachrichtenagentur (news agency); Handbuch der Entwicklungshilfe; returned to Chile, 1982; Researcher and Mem. Exec. Cttee, Centre of Studies for Develt, 1982–90; Ambassador: to EC, 1990–92; to Italy and (non-resident) to Malta, 1992–94; Vice Minister for Foreign Affairs, 1994–2000; Ambassador: to Spain and (non-resident) to Andorra, 2000–02; to UK, 2002–06, and (non-resident) to Libya, 2005–06; to USA, 2006–09; Minister of Foreign Affairs, Chile, 2009–10; Under-Sec.-Gen. and Special Rep. to Haiti, and Hd of Peacekeeping Mission in Haiti, UN, 2011–13. Board Member: Fintesa Financial Agency, 1982–84; Radio Cooperativa, 1982–90; Editorial Board Member: Mensaje, 1984–86; Fortin Mapocho, 1986–88; Apsi, 1986–89. President: European-Latin American Relations Inst., Madrid, 1992–93 (Vice-Pres., 1992); Internat. Council, Latin-American Centre for Relations with Europe, 1996–98; Vice-Pres., Italo-Latin American Inst., Rome, 1994; Mem. Exec. Cttee, Jacques Maritain Inst., Rome, 1994–96. Hd, Chilean Commn, Internat. Whaling Commn, 2003–07; Chilean Rep., IMO, 2006. Member: Pol Sci. Assoc. of Chile; Acad. Internat. du Vin (Pres.); Cofradía del Mérito Vitivinícola de Chile; Jurade de St Emilion; Commanderie de Médoc et Graves; Europaische Weinritterschaft; Slow Food. Mem. Bd, Universidad Mayor, Santiago, until 2011. Hon. Pres., Chilean Assoc. of Sommeliers. Grand Cross of: Argentina; Brazil; Colombia; Ecuador; Finland; Germany; the Holy See; Italy; Mexico; Netherlands; Panama; Peru; Portugal; Spain; Grand Officer of: Croatia; Germany; Sweden. *Publications:* articles in mags and jls, mainly on internat. policy and on wine tasting. *Address:* Embassy of Chile, Mohrenstrasse 42, 10117 Berlin, Germany.

FERNANDO, Most Rev. Nicholas Marcus; Archbishop of Colombo, (RC), 1977–2002, now Emeritus; *b* 6 Dec. 1932. *Educ:* St Aloysius' Seminary, Colombo; Universitas Propaganda Fide, Rome. BA (London); PhL (Rome); STD (Rome). Ordained priest, 1959. Pres., Catholic Bishops' Conf. of Sri Lanka, 1989–95. Former Mem., Sacred Congregation for Evangelization of Peoples. *Address:* Emmaus, No 202, National Basilica Mawatha, Tewatta, Ragama, Sri Lanka.

FERNEYHOUGH, Prof. Brian John Peter, FRAM; composer; William H. Bonsall Professor in Music, Stanford University, since 2000; *b* 16 Jan. 1943; *s* of Frederick George Ferneyhough and Emily May (*née* Hopwood); *m* 1990, Stephany Jan Hurtik. *Educ:* Birmingham Sch. of Music; RAM (FRAM 1998); Sweelinck Conservatory, Amsterdam; Musikakademie, Basel. Mendelssohn Schol., 1968; Stipend: City of Basle, 1969; Heinrich-Strobel-Stiftung des Südwestfunks, 1972; Composition teacher, Musikhochschule, Freiburg, 1973–86 (Prof., 1978–86); Principal Composition Teacher, Royal Conservatory, The Hague, 1986–87; Prof. of Music, UCSD, 1987–99. Guest Artist, Artists' Exchange Scheme, Deutsche Akad. Austauschdienst, Berlin, 1976–77; Lectr, Darmstadt Summer Sch., 1976–96 and 2004 (Comp. course co-ordinator, 1984–94); Guest Prof., Royal Conservatory, Stockholm, 1981–83, 1985; Vis. Prof., Univ. of Chicago, 1986; Fellow, Birmingham Conservatoire, 1996. Master Class, Civica Scuola di Musica di Milano, 1985–87. Mem., ISCM Internat. Jury, 1977, 1988. Hon. DMus Goldsmiths, Univ. of London, 2012. Prizes, Gaudeamus Internat. Comp., 1968, 1969; First Prize, ISCM Internat. Comp., Rome, 1974; Koussevitsky Prize, 1978; Royal Philharmonic Soc. Award, 1996, 2011; Ernst von Siemens Music Prize, 2007. Chevalier, l'Ordre des Arts et des Lettres, 1984. *Compositions include:* Sonatas for String Quartet, 1967; Epicycle, for 20 solo strings, 1968; Firecycle Beta, for large orch. with 5 conductors, 1971; Time and Motion Studies I–III, 1974–76; Unity Capsule, for solo flute, 1975; Funérailles, for 7 strings and harp, 1978; La Terre est un Homme, for orch., 1979; 2nd String Quartet, 1980; Lemma-Icon-Epigram, for solo piano, 1981; Carceri d'Invenzione, for various ensembles, 1981–86; 3rd String Quartet, 1987; Kurze Schatten II, for guitar, 1988; La Chute d'Icare, for clarinet ensemble, 1988; Trittico per G. S., 1989; 4th String Quartet, 1990; Bone Alphabet, for percussionist, 1991; Terrain, for violin and eight instruments, 1992; On Stellar Magnitudes, for voice and ensemble, 1994; String Trio, 1995; Incipits, for viola, percussion and small ensemble, 1996; Kranichtänze II, for piano, 1996; Maisons Noires, for ensemble, 1997; Unsichtbare Farben, for solo violin, 1999; Doctrine of Similarity, for choir and instruments, 2000; Opus Contra Naturam, for speaking pianist, 2000; Stele for Failed Time, for choir and electronics, 2001; Shadowtime, 1999–2004; Dum transisset I–IV, for string quartet, 2005–06; 5th String Quartet, 2006; Plötzlichkeit, for orch., 2006; Chronos-Aion, for large ensemble, 2008; Exordium, 2008; 6th String Quartet, 2010, Renvoi/Shards, 2009; Sisyphus Redux, for alto flute, 2009; Liber Scintillarum, for six instruments, 2012; Finis Terrae, for six voices and ensemble, 2012; Quirl, for solo piano, 2013. *Publications:* Collected Writings, 1996; articles in Contrechamps, Musiktexte, and Contemp. Music Rev. *Recreations:* reading, wine, cats. *Address:* Department of Music, Braun Music Center, Stanford University, Stanford, CA 94305–3076, USA.

FERNIE, Prof. Eric Campbell, CBE 1995; FBA 2002; FSA; FSA (Scot.); FRSE; Director, Courtauld Institute of Art, University of London, 1995–2003, now Honorary Fellow; *b* Edinburgh, 9 June 1939; *s* of Sydney Robert and Catherine Reid Fernie; *m* 1964, Margaret Lorraine French; one *s* two *d*. *Educ:* Univ. of the Witwatersrand (BA Hons Fine Arts); Univ. of London (Academic Diploma). FSA 1973; FSA (Scot.) 1984; FRSE 1993. Lectr, Univ. of the Witwatersrand, 1963–67; University of East Anglia: Lectr and Sen. Lectr, 1967–84; Dean, Sch. of Fine Art and Music, 1977–81; Public Orator, 1982–84; Watson Gordon Prof. of Fine Art, Univ. of Edinburgh, 1984–95 (Dean, Faculty of Arts, 1989–92). Chm., Ancient Monuments Bd for Scotland, 1989–95; Trustee: Nat. Galleries of Scotland, 1991–97; Scotland Inheritance Fund, 1992–2005; Samuel Courtauld Trust, 1995–2003; Heather Trust for the Arts, 1997–2001; Comr, English Heritage, 1995–2001; Mem., RCHME, 1997–99. Pres., Soc. of Antiquaries of London, 2004–07 (Vice-Pres., 1992–95). Hon. DLitt UEA, 2011. *Publications:* An Introduction to the Communar and Pitcaner Rolls of Norwich Cathedral Priory (with A. B. Whittingham), 1973; The Architecture of the Anglo-Saxons, 1983; An Architectural History of Norwich Cathedral, 1993; Art History and its Methods, 1995; The Architecture of Norman England, 2000; Romanesque Architecture: the first style of the European Age, 2014; contribs to British and overseas architectural jls. *Address:* 82 Bradmore Way, Old Coulsdon, Surrey CR5 1PB. *T:* (01737) 559553.

FERRAN, Brian; Chief Executive, Arts Council of Northern Ireland, 1991–2000; *b* 19 Oct. 1940; *s* of late Bernard and Susan Ferran; *m* 1963, Denise Devine; one *s* one *d*. *Educ:* St Columb's Coll., Derry; St Mary's Coll., Belfast (ATD); Courtauld Inst., London Univ. (BA 1973); Queen's Univ., Belfast (DBA 1975). Art Teacher, Derry, 1963–66; Visual Arts Dir, Arts Council of NI, 1966–91. Commissioner: Paris Biennale, 1980; São Paolo Biennial, 1985; Orgnr, exhibn of NI artists, Houston Internat. Fest. and US tour, 1990. HRUA 1980; HRHA 1998. Leverhulme European Award, 1969; Douglas Hyde Gold Medal for historical painting, 1965, 1976; Conor Prize, Royal Ulster Acad., 1979. *Publications:* Basil Blackshaw: painter, 1995. *Recreation:* visiting museums. *Address:* Goorey Rocks, Malin, Inishowen, Co. Donegal, Ireland. *T:* 749370934.

FERRAN, Prof. Eilís Veronica, (Mrs Roderick Cantrill), PhD; FBA 2013; Professor of Company and Securities Law, University of Cambridge, since 2005; Fellow, St Catharine's College, Cambridge, since 1987; *b* Belfast, 14 March 1962; *d* of Edward Gerald and Kathleen Ferran; *m* 1992, Roderick Cantrill; one *s* one *d*. *Educ:* St Dominic's RC High Sch., Belfast; St Catharine's Coll., Cambridge (BA 1983; MA 1986; PhD 1992). Articled clerk, Coward Chance, 1984–86; admitted as solicitor, 1986; Lectr, St Catharine's Coll., Cambridge, 1986–88; Asst Lectr, 1988–91, Lectr, 1991–2000, Reader in Corporate Law and Financial Regulation, 2000–05, Univ. of Cambridge. *Publications:* Mortgage Securitisation, 1992; Building an EU Securities Market, 2004; Principles of Corporate Finance Law, 2008, 2nd edn 2014; (jtly) The Regulatory Aftermath of the Global Financial Crisis, 2012. *Recreation:* family activities. *Address:* St Catharine's College, Cambridge CB2 1RL. *T:* (01223) 338335, 330041, *Fax:* (01223) 338400. *E:* evf1000@cam.ac.uk.

FERRANTI, Sebastian Basil Joseph Ziani de; *see* de Ferranti.

FERRAROLI, Jennifer Fitzgerald; *see* Edwards, J. F.

FERRERO-WALDNER, Benita Maria; Member, European Commission, 2004–10; President, EU-LAC Foundation, since 2011; *b* 5 Sept. 1948; *d* of Bruno and Emilie Waldner; *m* 1993, Prof. Francisco Ferrero Campos. *Educ:* Univ. of Salzburg (DIur). Export Dept, Paul Kiefel, Freilassing, Germany, 1971–72; Dir for Export Promotion, Gerns and Gahler, Freilassing, 1972–78; Sales Dir for Europe, P. Kaufmann Inc., NY, 1978–81; Chief Mgt Asst, Gerns and Gahler, 1981–83; Special Consultancy, Austrian Embassy, Madrid, 1984; Federal Ministry for Foreign Affairs, Austria: Depts of Econ. Affairs, Political Affairs and Consular Affairs, 1984–86; First Sec., Dakar, 1986; Dept for Develt Co-operation, 1986–87; Counsellor for Econ. Affairs, 1987–90, Minister-Counsellor, Dep. Chief of Mission and Chargé d'Affaires, 1990–93, Paris; Dep. Chief of Protocol, 1993; Chief of Protocol, Exec. Office of Sec. Gen., UN Secretariat, NY, 1994–95; State Sec. for Foreign Affairs, 1995–2000; Minister for Foreign Affairs, Austria, 2000–04. Member, Advisory Board: Bertelsmann Foundn, 2011–; Munich Re, 2011–. Mem., Fundación Principe de Girona, 2011–. Grand Decoration of Honour in Gold with Sash (Austria), 1999; holds numerous foreign decorations, including: Grand Cross: Order of Isabel la Católica (Spain), 1995; Royal Order of Merit (Norway), 1996; 2nd Cl., Order of Merit (FRG), 1997; SMO (Malta), 1999. *Publications:* Globale Ethik, 1998; Zukunft der Entwicklungszusammenarbeit, 1999; Die Entwicklungzusammenarbeit – Herausforderungen und Visionen (Development Cooperation: challenges and visions), 1999; Kurs setzen in einer veränderten-Welt (Charting Course in a Changing World), 2002; Biregional Relations: European Union, Latin America and the Caribbean: speeches, 2012; contrib. articles and essays to internat. and European books and jls. *Recreations:* reading, travelling, theatre, concerts, swimming, yoga.

FERRERS, 14th Earl *cr* 1711; **Robert William Saswalo Shirley,** FCA; Viscount Tamworth 1711; Bt 1611; Managing Director: Ruffer Management (formerly Ruffer Investment Management) Ltd, 1999–2011 (Director, since 1994); Ruffer LLP, 2004–11, now Director; *b* 29 Dec. 1952; *s* of 13th Earl Ferrers, PC and Annabel Mary (*née* Carr); *S* father, 2012; *m* 1980, Susannah, *y d* of late C. E. W. Sheepshanks, Arthington Hall, Yorks; two *s* one *d*. *Educ:* Ampleforth. Teaching in Kenya, under CMS's Youth Service Abroad Scheme, 1971–72. Admitted to ICAEW, 1976. Articled to Whinney Murray & Co., CA, 1972–76; employed at Ernst & Whinney, 1976–82, Asst Manager, 1981–82; Gp Auditor, 1982–85, Sen. Treasury Analyst, 1986, BICC plc; Director: Viking Property Gp Ltd, 1987–88 (Financial Controller and Company Sec., 1986–87); Ashby Securities, subseq. Norseman Hldgs, 1987–92; Derbyshire Student Residences Ltd, 1996–2003. Dir, Assoc. of Private Client Investment Managers and Stockbrokers, 2007–13. Trustee: Auckland Castle Trust, 2012–; Orders of St John Care Trust, 2013–. Kt SMO Malta, 2005. *Recreations:* the British countryside and related activities, the garden. *Heir: s* Viscount Tamworth, *qv*. *Address:* Ditchingham Hall, Ditchingham, Norfolk NR35 2JX. *Clubs:* Boodle's, Pratt's.

FERRIE, Dr John, CBE 2004; CEng, FREng; FRAeS; FIMechE; Executive Director and Group Managing Director, Aerospace, Smiths Group plc, 2000–07; *b* 17 Jan. 1947; *s* of Hugh Ferrie and Barbara Ferrie (*née* Miller); *m* 1968, Helen Allan; two *s*. *Educ:* Univ. of Strathclyde (BSc 1st Cl. Hons Mech. Eng. 1970); Univ. of Warwick (DEng 1998). CEng, FREng 2000; FRAeS 1995; FIMechE 1996. With Rolls Royce, 1964–2000: Director: Manufacturing, 1992–96; Mil. Engines, 1996–98; Exec. Vice-Pres., Business Ops, 1998–2000; Company Officer, GE Aviation, 2007–08. Non-exec. Dir, Westbury plc, 2004–06. Mem. Council, Univ. of Warwick, 2014–. *Recreations:* golf, music, world travel. *E:* john.ferrie17@btinternet.com.

FERRIER, Margaret; MP (SNP) Rutherglen and Hamilton West, since 2015; *b* Glasgow; one *d*. Commercial Sales Supervisor, Terex Equipt Ltd, Motherwell, until 2015. *Address:* House of Commons, SW1A 0AA.

FERRIS, Hon. Sir Francis (Mursell), Kt 1990; TD 1965; Judge of the High Court of Justice, Chancery Division, 1990–2003; Judge of Restrictive Practices Court, 1990–98; *b* 19 Aug. 1932; *s* of Francis William Ferris and Elsie Lilian May Ferris (*née* Mursell); *m* 1957, Sheila Elizabeth Hester Falloon Bedford; three *s* one *d*. *Educ:* Bryanston Sch.; Oriel Coll., Oxford (BA (Modern History) 1955, MA 1979; Hon. Fellow, 2000). Served RA, 1951–52; 299 Field Regt (RBY QOOH and Berks) RA, TA 1952–67, Major 1964. Called to the Bar, Lincoln's Inn, 1956, Bencher, 1987; practice at Chancery Bar, 1958–90; Standing Counsel to Dir Gen. of Fair Trading, 1966–80; QC 1980; a Recorder, 1989–90. Member: Bar Council, 1966–70; Senate of Inns of Court and the Bar, 1979–82. *Recreation:* gardening without bending. *Address:* White Gables, New Road, Shiplake, Oxfordshire RG9 3LB. *Club:* Marlow Rowing.

FERRIS, Paul Frederick; author and journalist; *b* 15 Feb. 1929; *oc* of late Frederick Morgan Ferris and of Olga Ferris; *m* 1st, 1953, Gloria Moreton (marr. diss. 1995); one *s* one *d*; 2nd, 1996, Mary Turnbull. *Educ:* Swansea Gram. Sch. Staff of South Wales Evening Post, 1949–52; Woman's Own, 1953; Observer Foreign News Service, 1953–54. *Publications: novels:* A Changed Man, 1958; Then We Fall, 1960; A Family Affair, 1963; The Destroyer, 1965; The Dam, 1967; Very Personal Problems, 1973; The Cure, 1974; The Detective, 1976; Talk to Me About England, 1979; A Distant Country, 1983; Children of Dust, 1988; The Divining Heart, 1995; Infidelity, 1999; Cora Crane, 2003; *non-fiction:* The City, 1960; The Church of England, 1962; The Doctors, 1965; The Nameless: abortion in Britain today, 1966; Men and Money: financial Europe today, 1968; The House of Northcliffe, 1971; The New Militants, 1972; Dylan Thomas, 1977, rev. edn 2006; Richard Burton, 1981; Gentlemen of Fortune: the world's investment bankers, 1984; (ed) The Collected Letters of Dylan Thomas, 1986, rev. edn 2000; Sir Huge: the life of Huw Wheldon, 1990; Sex and the British: a 20th century history, 1993; Caitlin, 1993; Dr Freud, 1997; Gower in History: myth, people, landscape, 2009; *television plays:* The Revivalist, 1975; Dylan, 1978; Nye, 1982; The Extremist, 1984; The Fasting Girl, 1984. *Address:* c/o Sinclair-Stephenson, South Terrace, SW7 2TB. *T:* (home) (01874) 754446.

FERRIS, Rt Rev. Ronald Curry; Bishop of Algoma, 1996–2008; Assisting Bishop, Anglican Network in Canada, since 2009; *b* 2 July 1945; *s* of Herald Bland Ferris and Marjorie May Ferris; *m* 1965, Janet Agnes (*née* Waller); two *s* four *d*. *Educ:* Toronto Teachers' Coll. (diploma); Univ. of W Ontario (BA); Huron Coll., London, Ont. (MDiv); Pacific Sch. of Religion (DMin 1995). Teacher, Pape Avenue Elem. School, Toronto, 1965; Principal Teacher, Carcross Elem. School, Yukon, 1966–68. Incumbent, St Luke's Church, Old Crow, Yukon, 1970–72; Rector, St Stephen's Memorial Church, London, Ont., 1973–81; Bishop of Yukon, 1981–95; Rector, Anglican Church of the Ascension, Langley, BC, 2009–. Hon. DD Huron Coll., London, Ont, 1982; Hon. STD Thorneloe Univ., Ont, 1995. *Address:* 7137 194B Street, Surrey, BC V4N 5Z3, Canada.

FERRIS, William Stephen, OBE 2011; Chief Executive, Chatham Historic Dockyard Trust, since 2000; *b* 3 June 1958; *s* of Harold Sydney Ferris and Grace Eileen Ferris; *m* 1982, Honor Margaret Gregory; two *s*. *Educ:* Tavistock Comprehensive Sch.; Aston Univ. (BSc 1st Cl. Hons Managerial and Admin. Studies). Self-employed baker, 1982–88; Commercial Manager, Yorkshire Mining Mus., 1988–90; various posts, Heritage Projects (Mgt) Ltd, 1990–2000 (Ops Dir, 1996–2000). Chm., Assoc. of Ind. Mus, 2002–. Vice Chm., Tourism SE, 2003–11; Bd Mem., Visit Kent Ltd, 2008–. *Recreations:* trout fishing, mountain walking, ski-ing, Rugby football, gardening, family. *Address:* Chatham Historic Dockyard Trust, Historic Dockyard, Chatham ME4 4TZ. *T:* (01634) 823806, *Fax:* (01634) 823801. *E:* bferris@chdt.org.uk.

FERRY, Bryan, CBE 2011; musician; *b* 26 Sept. 1945; *s* of late Frederick Charles Ferry and Mary Ann Ferry (*née* Armstrong); *m* 1st, 1982, Lucy Helmore (marr. diss. 2003); four *s*; 2nd, 2012, Amanda Sheppard (marr. diss. 2014). *Educ:* Newcastle upon Tyne Univ. (BA Fine Art). Vocalist and founder mem., Roxy Music, 1971–83, subseq. solo recording artist; *albums* include: (with Roxy Music): Roxy Music, 1972; For Your Pleasure, 1973 (Grand Prix du Disque, Montreux, 1973); Stranded, 1973; Country Life, 1974; Siren, 1975; Viva Roxy Music, 1976; Manifesto, 1979; Flesh & Blood, 1980; Avalon, 1982; The High Road, 1983; Streetlife, 1986; (solo): These Foolish Things, 1973; Another Time Another Place, 1974; Let's Stick Together, 1976; In Your Mind, 1977; The Bride Stripped Bare, 1978; Boys and Girls, 1985; Bête Noire, 1987; Taxi, 1993; Mamouna, 1994; As Time Goes By, 2000; Frantic, 2002; Dylanesque, 2007; Olympia, 2010; The Jazz Age, 2012; Yellow Cocktail Music, 2013; Avonmore, 2014; numerous singles. Hon. DMus Newcastle, 2014. Officier, Ordre des Arts et des Lettres (France), 2012. *Recreations:* tennis, reading, shooting. *Address:* Studio 1, Avonmore Place, W14 8RW.

FERRY, Joe David; creative director and inventor; Development Director, Merlin Entertainments, since 2015; *b* Southampton, 20 April 1969; *s* of late Alan James Ferry and of Gillian Clare Ferry. *Educ:* Bitterne Park Comp. Sch., Southampton; Richard Taunton Coll., Southampton; Brunel Univ. (BSc Hons Industrial Design 1993; Hon. Fellow 2010); Royal Coll. of Art (MA Industrial Design Engrg 1996); Imperial Coll., London (DIC 1996). Jun. Designer, P I Global, 1994; Designer, Nokia Mobile Phones, 1995; Virgin Atlantic Airways: Sen. Designer, 1996–99; Industrial Design Manager, 1999–2001; Head of Design, 2001–10; Intercontinental Hotels Group: Sen. Vice Pres., Guest Experience and Design, 2010–12; Sen. Vice Pres., Global Design and Innovation, 2010–11; Hd of Brand Experience, Vertu, 2012–13; Global Hd of Design, Mars, 2013–15. Member: Design Council, 2009–11; Cabinet Office Innovators Council, 2009–10. Mem., Exec. Bd, D&AD, 2009–12. Vis. Tutor, RCA, 2013–. FRSA 2011–15. *Publications:* 9 patents on aircraft seating and vehicle accommodation. *Recreations:* ski-ing, cycling, triathlons, travelling, supporting Southampton FC and England Football Team. *Address:* Patty's Farm House, Brook Lane, Cropthorne, Worcs WR10 3JX. *T:* 07973 657476. *E:* joeferry@me.com. *Club:* Soho House.

FERSHT, Sir Alan (Roy), Kt 2003; MA, PhD; FRS 1983; Herchel Smith Professor of Organic Chemistry, University of Cambridge, 1988–2010; Fellow, since 1988, and Master, since 2012, Gonville and Caius College, Cambridge; Hon. Director, Cambridge Centre for Protein Engineering (formerly MRC Unit for Protein Function and Design), 1989–2010; Emeritus Group Leader, MRC Laboratory of Molecular Biology, Cambridge, since 2010; *b* 21 April 1943; *s* of Philip and Betty Fersht; *m* 1966, Marilyn Persell; one *s* one *d*. *Educ:* Sir George Monoux Grammar Sch.; Gonville and Caius Coll., Cambridge (MA, PhD). Res. Fellow, Brandeis Univ., 1968; Scientific Staff, MRC Lab. of Molecular Biology, Cambridge, 1969–77; Fellow, Jesus Coll., Cambridge, 1969–72; Eleanor Roosevelt Fellow, Stanford Univ., 1978; Wolfson Res. Prof. of Royal Society, Dept of Chemistry, Imperial Coll. of Science and Technology, 1978–89 (FIC 2004). Wellcome Vis. Prof. in Basic Med. Scis, Univ. of Calif, San Francisco, 1997–98; Manchot Prof., Munich, 2009–. Lectures: Smith Kline & French, Berkeley, 1984; Edsall, Harvard, 1984; B. R. Baker, Univ. of California at Santa Barbara, 1986; Frank Mathers, Univ. of Indiana, 1986; Cornell Biotechnol Program, 1987; Ferdinand Springer, FEBS, 1988–89; Calvin, Berkeley, 1990; Walker, Edinburgh, 1990; Max Tishler Prize, Harvard Univ., 1991–92; Jubilee, Biochemical Soc., E. Gordon Young Meml, Canada, and Brändström, Gothenberg, 1993; Sternbach, Yale, 1994; Sunner Meml, Lund, 1994; Heatley, Oxford, Chan, Berkeley, Rudin, Columbia, and Hofmann, German Chemical Soc., 1995; Herriott, Johns Hopkins, Fritz Lipmann, German Biol Chem. Soc., and Merck-Frosst, Montreal, 1996; Hong Kong Advanced Chems Ltd Dist., Dewey-Kelley Internat. Award, Univ. of Nebraska, Kolthoff, Univ. of Minn, Max Gruber, Groningen, 1998; Upper Rhine, NIH Dir's, 1999; Stauffer, Stanford, 2000; W. H. Stein, Rockefeller, 2003; Walker Ames, Seattle Univ., Albert Neuberger Meml, Jerusalem, 2005; Robert Robinson Meml, Oxford, Drummond, Queen Mary Coll., Kendrew, Weizmann Inst., 2006; Henry Kamin, Duke Univ., 2007; Marion Koshland, and G. N. Lewis, Berkeley, 2008; Summer, Cornell, 2009. Hon. Treas., Fedn of European Biochemical Socs, 2012–. Mem., EMBO, 1980; MAE 1989; FMedSci 2007. Hon. For. Mem., Amer. Acad. of Arts and Sci., 1988; For. Associate, Nat. Acad. of Scis, USA, 1993; Foreign Member: Amer. Philosophical Soc., 2008; Accademia Nazionale dei Lincei, 2013. Essex County Jun. Chess Champion, 1961; Pres., Cambridge Univ. Chess Club, 1964 (Half Blue, 1965). Hon. DPhil: Uppsala, 1999; Weizmann Inst., 2004; Dr *hc*: Free Univ. of Brussels, 1999; Hebrew Univ., 2006; Aarhus Univ., 2008. FEBS Anniversary Prize, 1980; Novo Biotechnology Prize, 1986; Charmian Medal, 1986, Natural Products Award, 1999, RSC; Gabor Medal, 1991, Davy Medal, 1998, Royal Medal, 2008, Royal Soc.; Harden Medal, Biochemical Soc., 1993; Feldberg Foundn Prize, 1996; Distinguished Service Award, Miami, 1997; Anfinsen Award, 1999, Stein and Moore Award, 2001, Protein Soc.; Bader Award, Amer. Chem. Soc., 2005; Linderstrøm-Lang Prize and Medal, 2005; Bijvoet Medal, Utrecht Univ., 2008; G. N. Lewis Medal, Berkeley, 2008; Wilhelm Exner Medal (Austria), Österreichischer Gewerbeverein, 2009. *Publications:* Enzyme Structure and Mechanism, 1977, 2nd edn 1984; Structure and Mechanism in Protein Science, 1999; Jaques Staunton Chess Sets 1849–1939, 2007; Jaques and British Chess Company Chess Sets, 2010; papers in scientific jls. *Recreations:* chess, horology. *Address:* Gonville and Caius College, Cambridge CB2 1TA. *T:* (01223) 332431; MRC Laboratory of Molecular Biology, Francis Crick Avenue, Cambridge CB2 0QH. *T:* (01223) 267088.

FERT, Prof. Albert, Grand Officier, Ordre National du Mérite, 2008; Commandeur de la Légion d'Honneur, 2012; DèsSc; Professor of Physics, University of Paris Sud 11, since 1976; Scientific Director, Unité Mixte de Physique CNRS/Thales, since 1995; *b* Carcassonne, France, 7 March 1938; *s* of Charles and Irmine Fert; *m* 1967, Marie-Josée; one *s* one *d*. *Educ:* Ecole Normale Supérieure, Paris (DèsSc). Lectr, Univ. of Grenoble, 1962–70; Asst Prof., Univ. of Paris Sud, 1970–76. (Jtly) Nobel Prize in Physics, 2007. *Publications:* 400 contribs to books and learned jls. *Recreations:* music (jazz), windsurfing, mountaineering. *Address:* Unité Mixte de Physique, CNRS/Thales, 1 Avenue Fresnel, 91767 Palaiseau, France. *T:* (1) 69415864. *E:* albert.fert@thalesgroup.com.

FESTING, Andrew Thomas, MBE 2008; RP 1992; painter, since 1981; President, Royal Society of Portrait Painters, 2002–08; *b* 30 Nov. 1941; *s* of Field Marshal Sir Francis Wogan Festing, GCB, KBE, DSO and Mary Festing (*née* Riddell); *m* 1968, Virginia Fyffe; one *d*. *Educ:* Ampleforth; RMA Sandhurst. Commnd Rifle Bde, 1961. Joined Sotheby & Co., 1969, Dir, English Picture Dept, 1977–81. Paintings in permanent collections incl. Nat. Gall. of Ireland, Palace of Westminster, Royal Collection, NPG. Notable commissions include HM the Queen, Queen Elizabeth the Queen Mother, group portrait of whole Royal family; group picture of MPs in Library at Palace of Westminster, H of L in Session, Speakers Boothroyd and Martin; set of five pictures of famous cricketers for Lord's. Hon. DLitt Northumbria, 2010. *Recreations:* country sports, gardening. *Address:* 3 Hillsleigh Road, W8 7LE. *T:* (020) 7727 9287.

FETHERSTON-DILKE, Mary Stella, CBE 1968; RRC 1966; Organiser, Citizens' Advice Bureau, 1971–83, retired; *b* 21 Sept. 1918; *d* of late B. A. Fetherston-Dilke, MBE. *Educ:* Kingsley Sch., Leamington Spa; St George's Hospital, London (SRN). Joined QARNNS, 1942; Matron-in-Chief, QARNNS, 1966–70, retired. OStJ 1966. *Recreation:* antiques.

FETHERSTONHAUGH, Guy Cuthbert Charles; QC 2003; *b* 29 Jan. 1955; *s* of late Theobald Henry Robert Fetherstonhaugh and Genevieve Fetherstonhaugh (*née* Moreau); *m* 1991, Alexia Jane Musson Lees; two *s* one *d*. *Educ:* Stonyhurst Coll.; Bristol Univ. (BSc). FCIArb 2014. Served 2nd Bn, RGJ, 1978–81. Called to the Bar, Inner Temple, 1983, Bencher, 2009. Hon. RICS 2011; Hon. Arbrix 2012. *Publications:* (jtly) Handbook of Rent Review, 1991 and Supplements; (contrib.) The Litigation Practice, 1999–2003; Commonhold, 2004. *Recreations:* my family, woodwork, gardening, cycling. *Address:* Falcon Chambers, Falcon Court, EC4Y 1AA. *T:* (020) 7353 2484. *Clubs:* Rifles Officers', Royal Automobile.

FETHERSTONHAUGH, Henry George, OBE 2001; FRAgS; farmer, forester and property manager; Lord-Lieutenant of Clwyd, since 2013; *b* 16 Oct. 1954; *s* of David Henry Fetherstonhaugh and Hon. Maria Victoria, *d* of 8th Viscount Galway, PC, GCMG, DSO, OBE; *m* 1st, 1978, Nicola Payne-Gallwey (marr. diss. 1994); two *s*; 2nd, 1996, Davina MacLeod; two *s*. *Educ:* Eton Coll.; Royal Agricl Coll., Cirencester. Game business, 1974–78; farming and forestry enterprises, 1978–; Finance Dir, Timber Growers UK, 1989–94. Forestry Comr for Wales, 1995–2001. Mem., Home Grown Timber Adv. Cttee, 1990–95. Royal Welsh Agricultural Society, 1978–: Hon. Show Dir, 1994–; Vice-Chm., Bd of Dirs, 1994–; Chair, Show Admin, 1994–; Chair, Livestock, 1998–2000; Chm., Finance; Chm., Bd of Dirs, 2002–04. Chm. Govs, Ysgol-Y-Plas Voluntary Aided Sch., 1979–2014. Pres., Denbigh and Flints Agricultural Assoc., 2014. *Recreations:* shooting, ornithology, tennis. *Address:* Coed Coch, Dolwen, Abergele, N Wales LL22 8AY. *T:* and *Fax:* (01492) 680357. *Club:* Boodle's.

FETTIPLACE, Prof. Robert, FRS 1990; Steenbock Professor of Neural and Behavioral Sciences, University of Wisconsin, since 1991; *b* 24 Feb. 1946; *s* of George Robert Fettiplace and Maisie Fettiplace (*née* Rolson); *m* 1977, Merriel Cleone Kruse. *Educ:* Nottingham High Sch.; Sidney Sussex Coll., Cambridge (BA 1968; MA 1972; PhD 1974). Research Fellow: Sidney Sussex Coll., Cambridge, 1971–74; Stanford Univ., 1974–76; Elmore Res. Fellow, Cambridge, 1976–79; Howe Sen. Res. Fellow, Royal Soc., 1979–90. Fellow, Amer. Acad. of Arts and Scis, 2012. *Publications:* contribs to Jl Physiology, Jl Neuroscience and other learned jls. *Recreations:* bird watching, listening to music. *Address:* Department of Neuroscience, University of Wisconsin, 1300 University Avenue, Madison, WI 53706–1510, USA.

FEVERSHAM, 7th Baron *cr* 1826; **Jasper Orlando Slingsby Duncombe;** *b* 14 March 1968; *e s* of 6th Baron Feversham and Shannon (*d* 1976), *d* of Sir Thomas Foy, CSI, CIE; *S* father, 2009; *m* 2009, Candida, *d* of Clive Boddington; one *s*. *Heir:* *s* Hon. Orlando Balthazar Duncombe, *b* 16 July 2009.

FEWSTER, Dr Kevin John, AM 2001; Director, Royal Museums Greenwich (formerly National Maritime Museum), since 2007; *b* Perth, WA, 1 Dec. 1953; *s* of Geoffrey and Audrey Fewster; *m* 1996, Carol Scott; one *d*. *Educ:* Glyn Grammar Sch., Ewell; Haileybury Coll., Melbourne; Australian National Univ. (BA Hons); Univ. of New South Wales (PhD 1980). Teaching Fellow, Royal Mil. Coll. Duntroon, Univ. of NSW, 1976–80; Tutor, 1981–82, Sen. Tutor, 1983–84, History Dept, Monash Univ.; Director: S Australian Maritime Mus., Port Adelaide, 1984–89; Australian Nat. Maritime Mus., Sydney, 1989–2000; Powerhouse Mus., Sydney, 2000–07. Dir, Royal Greenwich Destination Mgt Co., 2013–. Mem., Collections Council of Australia, 2004–07. Chm., Council of Australian Mus. Dirs, 2004–07. Vice Pres., 1993–96, Pres., 1996–99 and 2014–15, Internat. Congress of Maritime Mus. Pres., Darling Harbour Business Assoc., 2000–02. FRSA. *Publications:* Gallipoli Correspondent: the frontline diary of C. E. W. Bean, 1983, 3rd edn 2007; (jtly) A Turkish View of Gallipoli: Canakkale, 1985, 2nd edn 2005. *Recreations:* tennis, football. *Address:* Royal Museums Greenwich, Greenwich, SE10 9NF. *Club:* Sydney Cricket Ground.

FFOLKES, Sir Robert (Francis Alexander), 7th Bt *cr* 1774; OBE 1990; Save the Children UK, 1974–2003; *b* 2 Dec. 1943; *o s* of Captain Sir (Edward John) Patrick (Boschetti) ffolkes, 6th Bt, and Geraldine (*d* 1978), *d* of late William Roffey, Writtle, Essex; *S* father, 1960. *Educ:* Stowe Sch.; Christ Church, Oxford. *Recreations:* mountain ecology development and conservation, esp. in the Himalayas and Central Asia. *Address:* Coast Guard House, Morston, Holt, Norfolk NR25 7BH.

FFOWCS WILLIAMS, Prof. John Eirwyn, FREng; Rank Professor of Engineering, University of Cambridge, 1972–2002, now Emeritus; Master, Emmanuel College, Cambridge, 1996–2002 (Professorial Fellow, 1972–96; Life Fellow, 2002); *b* 25 May 1935; *m* 1959, Anne Beatrice Mason; two *s* one *d*. *Educ:* Friends Sch., Great Ayton; Derby Techn. Coll.; Univ. of Southampton (BSc, PhD 1960); MA, ScD Cantab 1986. CEng, FREng (FEng 1988); FRAeS, FInstP, FIMA, FIOA, Fellow Acoustical Soc. of America, FAIAA. Engrg Apprentice, Rolls-Royce Ltd, 1951–55; Spitfire Mitchell Meml Schol. to Southampton Univ., 1955–60 (Pres., Students' Union, 1957–58); Aerodynamics Div., NPL, 1960–62; Bolt, Beranek & Newman Inc., 1962–64; Reader in Applied Maths, Imperial Coll. of Science and Technology, 1964–69; Rolls Royce Prof. of Theoretical Acoustics, Imperial Coll., 1969–72. Chairman: Concorde Noise Panel, 1965–75; Topexpress Ltd, 1979–89; Dir, VSEL Consortium plc, 1987–95. Chm., Noise Research Cttee, ARC, 1969–76. FRSA; FLSW 2012. Honour Prof., Beijing Inst. of Aeronautics and Astronautics, 1992–; Emeritus Hon. Prof., Wales Inst. of Math. and Computational Scis, 2011. Foreign Hon. Mem., Amer. Acad. Arts and Scis, 1989; Foreign Associate, NAE, USA, 1995. Gov., Felsted Sch., 1980–94. Hon. ScD Southampton 2003. AIAA Aero-Acoustics Medal, 1977; Rayleigh Medal, Inst. of Acoustics, 1984; Silver Medal, Société Française d'Acoustique, 1989; Gold Medal, RAeS, 1990; Per Bruel Gold Medal, ASME, 1997; Sir Frank Whittle Medal, Royal Acad. Engrg, 2002; Aeroacoustics Award, Confedn of European Aerospace Socs, 2004. *Publications:* (with A. P. Dowling) Sound and Sources of Sound, 1983; articles in Philosophical Trans Royal Soc., Jl of Fluid Mechanics, Jl IMA, Jl of Sound Vibration, Annual Reviews of Fluid Mechanics, Random Vibration, Financial Times; (jtly) film on Aerodynamic Sound. *Recreations:* friends, vintage cars, thinking. *Address:* Emmanuel College, Cambridge CB2 3AP.

FFRENCH, family name of **Baron ffrench**.

FFRENCH, 8th Baron *cr* 1798; **Robuck John Peter Charles Mario ffrench;** Bt 1779; *b* 14 March 1956; *s* of 7th Baron ffrench and of Sonia Katherine, *d* of late Major Digby Cayley; *S* father, 1986; *m* 1987, Dörthe Marie-Louise, *d* of Captain Wilhelm Schauer; one *d*. *Educ:* Blackrock, Co. Dublin; Ampleforth College, Yorks. *Heir:* none.

ffRENCH BLAKE, Col Robert John William; Extra Equerry to the Prince of Wales, since 1995; international sporting consultant, since 1991; *b* Salisbury, Wilts, 21 June 1940; *s* of late Lt Col Desmond O'Brien Evelyn ffrench Blake and Elizabeth Iris (*née* Cardale, later Mrs Anthony Hogg); *m* 1976, Ilynne Sabina Mary Eyston; three *d*. *Educ:* Eton; RMA Sandhurst; Army Staff Coll. Commnd 13th/18th Royal Hussars, 1960; psc 1972; CO, 1981–83. Asst Mil. Attaché, Washington, 1985–88. Chief Exec., Guards Polo Club, 1989–91. Hon. Colonel: 13th/18th Royal Hussars, 1990–93; Light Dragoons, 1993–95. Mem., HM Body Guard, Hon. Corps of Gentlemen-at-Arms, 1990–2010 (Harbinger, 2007–10). *Recreations:* shooting, ski-ing, polo, Alpaca farmer. *Address:* Gillans, Minterne Parva, Dorchester, Dorset DT2 7AP. *T:* 07970 444447. *E:* rfb@gillans.net. *Clubs:* Cavalry and Guards, Pratt's.

FFRENCH-CONSTANT, Prof. Charles Kenvyn, PhD; FRCP; Professor of Medical Neurology and Director, Centre for Multiple Sclerosis Research, since 2008, Director, MRC Centre for Regenerative Medicine, since 2011, and Director, Anne Rowling Regenerative Neurology Clinic, since 2013, University of Edinburgh; *b* 5 Nov. 1954; *m* Jennifer Wimperis, DM, FRCP, FRCPath; one *s* one *d*. *Educ:* Pembroke Coll., Cambridge (BA 1976; BChir 1979; MA 1980; MB 1980); University College London (PhD 1986). MRCP 1982, FRCP 1999. Lucille Markey Postdoctoral Fellow, MIT, 1986–88; Wellcome Trust Sen. Res. Fellow, Wellcome/CRC Inst. of Develtl Biol., 1991–96, Prof. of Neurological Genetics, 1999–2008, Univ. of Cambridge; Fellow, Pembroke Coll., Cambridge, 1999–2008; Hon. Consultant in Med. Genetics, Addenbrooke's Hosp., Cambridge, 1996–2008; Dep. Dir, MRC Centre for Regenerative Medicine, Univ. of Edinburgh, 2008–11. *Publications:* papers on develtl and regenerative biol. *Recreation:* fishing. *Address:* Scottish Centre for Regenerative Medicine, Edinburgh bioQuarter, 5a Little France Drive, Edinburgh EH16 4UU; 420 Unthank Road, Norwich NR4 7QH.

FFYTCHE, Timothy John, LVO 1997; FRCS; Surgeon-Oculist to the Queen, 1999–2001; Consultant Ophthalmologist: Moorfields Eye Hospital, 1975–2001; Hospital for Tropical Diseases, 1988–2006; Consultant Ophthalmic Surgeon to King Edward VIIth Hospital for Officers, 1980–2006; *b* 11 Sept. 1936; *s* of late Louis ffytche and Margaret (*née* Law); *m* 1961, Bärbl, *d* of late Günther Fischer; two *s*. *Educ:* Lancing Coll.; St George's Hosp., London. MB, BS; DO 1961; FRCS 1968. Registrar, Moorfields Eye Hosp., 1966–69; Wellcome Lectr, Hammersmith Hosp., 1969–70; Sen. Registrar, Middlesex Hosp., 1970–73; Ophthalmic Surgeon, St Thomas' Hosp., 1973–99; Surgeon-Oculist to HM Household, 1980–99. Sec., OSUK, 1980–82. Mem., Medical Adv. Bd, LEPRA, 1982–2008; Vice-Pres., Ophthalmol Sect., RSocMed, 1985–88; UK rep. to Internat. Fedn of Ophthalmic Socs, 1985–89; Mem., Adv. Cttee to Internat. Council of Ophthalmology, 1985–2002. Founder, Ophthalmic Aid to Eastern Europe, 1990–; Chm., European Sect., Internat. Agency for Prevention of Blindness, 1999–2008 (Co-Chm., 1994–99); President: Med. Soc. of London, 2001–02; Moorfields Alumni Assoc., 2010–. Clayton Meml Lectr, LEPRA, 1984. Hon. FRCOphth 2011. Editorial Committee: Ophthalmic Literature, 1968–82; Transactions of OSUK, 1984–89, Eye, 1989–96; European Jl of Ophthalmology, 1990–2006. *Publications:* articles on retinal diagnosis and therapy, retinal photography and the ocular complications of leprosy, in The Lancet, British Jl of Ophthalmol., Trans OSUK, Proc. Royal Soc. Med., Leprosy Review and other specialist jls. *Recreation:* occasional fishing. *Address:* (home) 1 Wellington Square, SW3 4NJ.

FIDDES, Rev. Prof. Paul Stuart, DPhil, DD; Professor of Systematic Theology, University of Oxford, since 2002; Professorial Research Fellow and Director of Research, Regent's Park College, Oxford, since 2007; Ecumenical Canon, Christ Church, Oxford, since 2012; Ecumenical Prebendary, Collegiate Church of St Endelienta, North Cornwall, since 2012; *b* 30 April 1947; *s* of James Stuart Fiddes and Lois Sleeman Fiddes; *m* 1973, Marion Downing Anness; one *s* (and one *s* decd). *Educ:* Drayton Manor Grammar Sch.; St Peter's Coll., Oxford (BA Eng. Lang. and Lit. 1968; Theol 1970, MA 1972; Hon. Fellow 2004); Regent's Park Coll., Oxford (DPhil 1975; DD 2004). Ordained to Baptist Ministry, 1972; Regent's Park College, Oxford: Res. Fellow in OT, 1972–75; Tutorial Fellow in Christian Doctrine, 1975–89; Principal, 1989–2007, now Principal Emeritus; Lectr in Theol., St Peter's Coll., Oxford, 1979–85; Chm. Bd, Faculty of Theology, Oxford Univ., 1996–98. Gen. Ed., Regent's Study Guides; Jt Ed., Ecclesiology. Hon. Dr Bucharest, 2004. *Publications:* The Creative Suffering of God, 1988; Past Event and Present Salvation: the Christian idea of atonement, 1989; Freedom and Limit: a dialogue between literature and Christian doctrine, 1991; (ed) Reflections on the Water: understanding God and the world through the baptism of believers, 1996; (ed jtly) Pilgrim Pathways, 1999; The Promised End, 2000; Participating in God: a pastoral doctrine of the Trinity, 2000; (ed) The Novel, Spirituality and Modern Culture, 2000; (ed) Faith in the Centre: Christianity and culture, 2001; Tracks and Traces: baptist identity in church and theology, 2003; (ed jtly) Flickering Images: theology and film in dialogue, 2005; (ed) Under the Rule of Christ, 2008; (ed) The Spirit and the Letter, 2013; (ed jtly) The Rhetoric of Evil, 2013; Seeing the World and Knowing God: Hebrew wisdom and Christian doctrine in a late-modern context, 2013. *Recreations:* music, literature, travel, inland waterways. *Address:* Regent's Park College, Oxford OX1 2LB. *E:* paul.fiddes@regents.ox.ac.uk.

FIDDICK, Peter Ronald; journalist and broadcaster; *b* 21 Oct. 1938; *s* of late Wing-Comdr Ronald Fiddick and Phyllis Fiddick (*née* Wherry); *m* 1966, Jane Mary Hodlin; one *s* one *d*. *Educ:* Reading Sch.; Magdalen Coll., Oxford (BA English Lang. and Lit.). Journalist, Liverpool Daily Post, 1962–65; Leader writer, Westminster Press, 1965–66; Asst Editor, Nova, 1968; The Guardian: reporter, 1966–67 and 1969; Asst Features Editor, 1970–75; Television Columnist, 1971–84; Media Editor, 1984–88; Editor: The Listener, 1989–91; Television (RTS), 1991–2001; Research (Market Res. Soc.), 1992–99; RADA, The Magazine, 1993–2006; Media Columnist, Admap, 1997–2002. Newspaper Reviewer, BBC Breakfast News, 1989–99; Media Critic, BBC Radio Arts Programme, 1990–2001. Mem., Bd, George Foster Peabody Awards, USA, 2000–06 (Chm., 2005–06). FRTS 1992; Associate, RADA. Wrote and presented television series: Looking at Television, 1975–76; The Television Programme, 1979–80; Soviet Television - Fact and Fiction, 1985. *Publications:* (with B. Smithies) Enoch Powell on Immigration, 1969. *Recreations:* music, food, theatre, Saturdays.

FIDLER, John Allan, RIBA; FSA; Principal, John Fidler Preservation Technology Inc., Los Angeles, since 2012; *b* 1 Sept. 1952; *s* of late Eddie Fidler and Joan Margaret Fidler (*née* Edwards); *m* 1992, Jeanne Marie Teutonico. *Educ:* Sheffield Univ. (BA Hons; DipArch, MA Arch); Manchester Univ. (MA Conservation); Architectural Assoc., London (Grad. Dip. Conservation). RIBA 1979; IHBC 1998. Casework officer, Historic Bldgs Div., GLC, 1978–83; Historic Bldgs architect, City of London Corp., 1983–84; English Heritage: Conservation Officer for bldgs at risk, 1984–86; Superintending Architect, 1986–90; Head: Architectural and Survey Services, 1990–91; Bldg Conservation and Res., 1991–2002; Conservation Dir, 2002–06; Staff Consultant, 2006–12, Practice Leader, 2007–12, Preservation Technol., Simpson Gumpertz & Heger Inc., LA. Chm., Cttee B/209-7 drafting codes of practice, BSI, 2001–06. Member: Council, ICCROM, 2001–07 (Vice Pres., 2005–07); Conservation Cttee, Getty Foundn (formerly J. P. Getty Trust Grants Prog.), 2001–07. FAPT 2000; FSA 2002; FIIC 2006; FRICS 2007. FRSA 1980. *Publications:* (ed) English Heritage Directory of Building Sands and Aggregates, 2000; (ed) Stone, Vol. 2, English Heritage Research Trans, 2002; contrib. technical papers to ASCHB Trans, Bull. Assoc. for Preservation Technol. *Recreations:* hiking, visiting historic sites. *Address:* (office) 4640 Admiralty Way, Suite 500, Marina Del Rey, CA 90292, USA. *T:* (310) 4965730. *E:* johnfidler@jf-pt.com.

FIDLER, Prof. (John) Kelvin, PhD; FREng, Hon. FIET; consultant on engineering and higher education, since 2008; Vice-Chancellor and Chief Executive, University of Northumbria at Newcastle, 2001–08; *b* 11 May 1944; *s* of Samuel Fidler and Barbara Fidler; *m* 1st, 1966, Jadwiga Sorokowska (marr. diss. 1995); one *s* one *d*; 2nd, 2002, Nadine Cleaver. *Educ:* Harrow Co. Sch. for Boys; King's Coll., Univ. of Durham (BSc); Univ. of Newcastle upon Tyne (PhD 1968). CEng 1972, FREng 2005; FIET (FIEE 1982), Hon. FIET 2010. Sen. Res. Associate, Univ. of Newcastle upon Tyne, 1968–69; Lectr, 1969–74, Sen. Lectr, 1974–80, Reader, 1980–83, Univ. of Essex; Professor of Electronics: Open Univ., 1984–88; Univ. of York, 1989–2001. Chm., Engineering Council, 2005–11; Member: EngineeringUK (formerly Engrg and Technol. Bd), 2005–11; Standing Cttee on Educn and Trng, Royal Acad. of Engrg, 2011–. Mem., Prime Minister's Adv. Cttee, Queen's Award for Enterprise, 2005–11. Non-exec. Dir, Resource Develt Internat. Ltd, 2010–. Chm., Ind. Commn on Northumberland, 2008–09. Chm., Subject Benchmark Rev. Gp for Engrg, QAA, 2013–. Chm., Associates of Discovery Mus., 2008–11. Hon. Consultant, Graduate Excellence Curriculum Gp, Food and Drink Fedn, 2012–. Chm., Industrial Adv. Cttee, Univ. of Huddersfield, 2012–14. Mem., Fellows Standing Panel, 2013–, Scholarships and Awards Cttee, 2014–, IET. Hon. DSc Huddersfield, 2007; DUniv York, 2009; Hon. DCL Northumbria, 2010. *Publications:* Computer Aided Circuit Design, 1978; Introductory Circuit Theory, 1980, 2nd edn 1989; Continuous Time Active Filter Design, 1998; Skills for the Nation: engineering undergraduates in the UK, 2013; numerous contribs on electronics to learned jls. *Recreations:* varied. *Address:* c/o Resource Development International, 1A Brandon Lane, Coventry CV3 3RD.

FIDLER, Prof. Peter Michael, CBE 2012 (MBE 1993); DL; President, University of Sunderland, 2014–Jan. 2016 (Vice-Chancellor and Chief Executive, 1999–2014). *Educ:* Univ. of Salford (MSc). Town planner. Formerly: Dean, Dept of Built Envmt, UWE; Dep. Vice-Chancellor (Academic Affairs), Oxford Brookes Univ.; Past Pres., Royal Town Planning Inst. DL Tyne and Wear, 2005. *Address:* Office of the President, University of Sunderland, Edinburgh Building, City Campus, Chester Road, Sunderland SR1 3SD.

FIDLER-SIMPSON, John Cody; *see* Simpson.

FIELD, Barry John Anthony, TD 1984; *b* 4 July 1946; *s* of Ernest Field and late Marguerite Eugenie Field; *m* 1969, Jaqueline Anne Miller; one *s* one *d*. *Educ:* Collingwood Boys' Sch.; Mitcham Grammar Sch.; Bembridge Sch.; Victoria Street Coll. Chm., J. D. Field & Sons Ltd, 1993–94 (Dir, 1981–94); Dir, Great Southern Cemetery & Crematorium Co. Ltd, 1969–94. Councillor, Horsham Dist Council, 1983–86 (Vice-Chm., Housing, 1984–85, Chm., Housing, 1985–86); Mem., IoW CC, 1986–89. MP (C) Isle of Wight, 1987–97. Chm., H of C Deregulation Cttee, 1995–97. Major RCT TA; Liveryman, Turners' Co.; Mem., Watermen and Lightermen's Co. *Recreations:* sailing, theatre, ski-ing. *Address:* Medina Lodge, 25 Birmingham Road, Cowes, Isle of Wight PO31 7BH. *T:* (01983) 292871. *Club:* Island Sailing (Cowes).

FIELD, Dr Clive Douglas, OBE 2007; FRHistS; FEA; Director of Scholarship and Collections, British Library, 2001–06; *b* 27 June 1950; *o s* of Joseph Stanley Field and Lily Field (*née* Battams); *m* 1972, Verena Duss; one *s*. *Educ:* Dunstable Grammar Sch.; Wadham Coll., Oxford (BA Modern History 1971; MA 1975; DPhil Modern History 1975); Westminster Coll., Oxford (PGCE 1975). FRHistS 2001; FEA 2008. SSRC Post-Doctoral Fellow, Wadham Coll., Oxford, 1975–77; Asst Librarian, 1977–87, Sub-Librarian, 1987–90, John Rylands Univ. Liby of Manchester; University of Birmingham: Dep. Librarian, 1990–95; Librarian and Dir of Inf. Services, 1995–2001; Associate Mem., 1992–2001, Hon. Res. Fellow, 2006–, Dept of Modern History. Hon. Res. Fellow, Inst. for Social Change, Univ. of Manchester, 2010–. Project Director: Ensemble: towards a distributed nat. liby resource for music, 1999–2002; Revelation: unlocking research resources for 19th and 20th century church history and Christian theology, 2000–02. Co-Dir, British Religion in Numbers, 2008–. Chairman: Internat. English Short Title Catalogue Cttee, 2001–06; Full Disclosure Implementation Gp, 2001–05; Jt Cttee on Voluntary Deposit, 2001–03; Jt Cttee on Legal Deposit, 2004–06; Member: Bd of Dirs, Consortium of Univ. Res. Libraries, 1996–2001, 2003–06 (Chm., 2000–01); Cttee on Electronic Inf., 1999–2001, Cttee for Content Services, 2002–05, and Cttee for Support of Res., 2003–04, Jt Inf. Systems Cttee; Midlands Metropolitan Area Network Mgt Cttee, 1999–2001; HEFCE Strategic Adv. Cttee for Res., 2003–06; Legal Deposit Adv. Panel, 2005–06; Adv. Council on Nat. Records and Archives, 2007–14; Forum on Historical Manuscripts and Academic Res., 2010–14; Academic Adv. Cttee, Ushaw Coll. Liby, 2011–; Bd of Dirs, Birmingham Res. Park Ltd, 1999–2001. Dir and Trustee, Pastoral Res. Centre Trust, 2008–. Pres., Religious Archives Gp, 2007–. Bibliography Ed., Wesley Historical Soc., 1976–; Ed., The People Called Methodists microfiche project, 1988–98; Chm., Editl Bd, Bulletin of John Rylands Univ. Liby, Univ. of Manchester, 2008–12. Hon. DLitt Birmingham, 2006. *Publications:* Non-Recurrent Christian Data: reviews of UK Statistical Sources, 1987; Anti-Methodist Publications of the Eighteenth Century, 1991; Church and Chapel in Early Victorian Shropshire, 2004; Lutonian Odyssey, 2008; Britain's Last Religious Revival?, 2015; professional papers; articles, bibliographies and reviews on the social history of religion in Great Britain since 1689, with special reference to religious statistics, religious practice, and the history of Methodism. *Recreations:* historical research and writing, visiting (incl. virtually) secondhand bookshops. *Address:* 35 Elvetham Road, Edgbaston, Birmingham B15 2LZ. *E:* c.d.field@bham.ac.uk.

FIELD, David Anthony; Zoological Director, Zoological Society of London, since 2006; *b* 9 Jan. 1967; *s* of Derek and Jean Field; *m* 1997, Dr Lesley Dickie. *Educ:* Foxyards Primary Sch.; Dudley Sch.; University Coll., Cardiff (BSc Hons Zool.); Open Univ. (MBA). SO, UFAW, 1988–90; Senior Zookeeper: Penscynor Wildlife Park, 1990–93; Edinburgh Zoo, 1993–98; Asst Dir, Dublin Zoo, 1998–2002; Curator, Whipsnade Zoo, 2002–03; Curator of Mammals, 2003–04, Hd of Animal Care, 2004–06, Zool Soc. of London. Member: Council, British and Irish Assoc. of Zoos and Aquaria, 2005– (Chm., 2011–); Bd, Internat. Species Information Systems, 2008– (Chm., 2010–); DEFRA Zoos Forum, 2008–. Trustee: Wild Vets Internat., 2006–07; Gorilla Orgn, 2010–12. FLS 2010; FRSB (FSB 2010). *Recreations:* zoo history, golf. *Address:* Zoological Society of London, Regent's Park, NW1 4RY. *T:* (020) 7449 6500, *Fax:* (020) 7449 6283. *E:* david.field@zsl.org.

FIELD, Prof. David John, DM; FRCPE, FRCPCH; Professor of Neonatal Medicine, University of Leicester, since 1996; Hon. Consultant Neonatologist, University Hospitals of Leicester, since 1989; *b* Barnet, Herts, 12 March 1953; *s* of George and Joan Field; *m* 1974, Caroline Stainer; one *s* one *d*. *Educ:* Sandown Grammar Sch., IoW; King's Coll. Hosp., London (MB BS 1976). DCH 1978; FRCPE 1988; FRCPCH 1996. MRC Res. Fellow, Nottingham Univ., 1983–85; Lectr, 1985–89, Sen. Lectr, 1989–96, Univ. of Leicester. Neonatal Lead for MBBRACE-UK Collaboration, 2013–. Hon. Sec., 2001–04, Pres., 2008–11, British Assoc. of Perinatal Medicine. *Publications:* (with J. Stroobnant) Case Studies in Paediatrics, 1987; (jtly) Tutorials in Differential Diagnosis, 1989; (jtly) Paediatric Grey Courses, 1994; (ed jtly) Paediatrics: an illustrated colour text, 1997 (internat. edn 2002); (ed with J. Stroobnant) Handbook of Paediatric Investigations, 2001; (ed jtly) Paediatric Differential Diagnosis, 2nd edn 2005; (ed jtly) Multiple Pregnancy, 2006; contrib. chapters in books; contribs to Seminars in Neonatol., Paediatric Pulmonol., Archives of Diseases in Childhood, BMJ, Early Human Develt, Jl Perinatal Medicine, Lancet, Acta Paediatrica, etc. *Recreations:* gardening, travel, walking, opera and ballet. *Address:* Department of Health Sciences, University of Leicester, 22–28 Princess Road West, Leicester LE1 6TP. *T:* (0116) 252 5468. *E:* df63@le.ac.uk.

FIELD, His Honour Douglas John; a Circuit Judge, 2006–15; *b* 17 April 1947; twin *s* of Robert Henry Field and Ivy May Field (*née* Dicketts); *m* 1969, Karen Heather Strubbe; one *s* one *d*. *Educ:* Ottershaw Sch.; Coll. of Law, Guildford. Admitted solicitor, 1972; called to Bermuda Bar, 1974; in practice as barrister and attorney, Bermuda, 1972–76; a District Judge, 1995–2006; Resident Judge, Swindon Combined Court, 2007–14. *Recreations:* watching cricket and Rugby, playing golf, cinema.

See also Hon. Sir R. A. Field.

FIELD, (Edward) John, CMG 1991; HM Diplomatic Service, retired; High Commissioner, Sri Lanka, 1991–96; *b* 11 June 1936; *s* of late Arthur Field, OBE, MC, TD, and Dorothy Agnes Field; *m* 1960, Irene Sophie du Pont Darden; one *s* one *d*. *Educ:* Highgate Sch.; Corpus Christi Coll., Oxford; Univ. of Virginia. Courtaulds Ltd, 1960–62; FCO, 1963–96: 2nd, later 1st Sec., Tokyo, 1963–68; Amer. Dept, FCO, 1968–70; Cultural Attaché, Moscow, 1970–72; 1st Sec. (Commercial), Tokyo, 1973–76; Asst Head, S Asian Dept, FCO, 1976–77; Dept of Trade, 1977–79 (Head, Exports to Japan Unit); Counsellor: (Commercial), Seoul, 1980–83; at Harvard Univ., 1983–84; UK Mission to UN, 1984–87; Minister, Tokyo, 1988–91. Mem. Bd, WHRO, Virginia, 2011–. Pres., Virginia Opera Assoc., 2003–05. Trustee, Chrysler Mus. of Art, Norfolk, Virginia, 2002–10. *Recreations:* riding, listening to music. *Address:* 21 Dawson Place, W2 4TH; Jericho Farm, 19637 Governor Darden Road, Courtland, VA 23837, USA. *Club:* Travellers.

FIELD, Rt Hon. Frank; PC 1997; DL; MP (Lab) Birkenhead, since 1979; *b* 16 July 1942; *s* of late Walter and of Annie Field. *Educ:* St Clement Danes Grammar Sch.; Univ. of Hull (BSc (Econ)). Director: Child Poverty Action Gp, 1969–79; Low Pay Unit, 1974–80. Minister of State (Minister for Welfare Reform), DSS, 1997–98. Chairman: Select Cttee on Social Services, 1987–90; Select Cttee on Social Security, 1991–97; Jt Select Cttee on Draft Modern Slavery Bill, 2014; Select Cttee on Work and Pensions, 2015–; Co-Chm., All Party Parly Inquiry into hunger in UK, 2014. Chm., Pensions Reform Gp, 1999– (reports: Universal Protected Pension: modernising pensions for the millennium, 2001; Universal Protected Pension: the following report, 2002). Chairman: Ind. Review on Poverty and Life Chances, 2010 (report, Preventing Poor Children becoming Poor Adults, 2010); Modern Slavery Bill Evidence Rev., 2013 (report, Establishing Britain as a World Leader in the Fight against Modern Slavery, 2013). Vice Chm., Human Trafficking Foundn, 2011–. Co-Founder, Cool Earth, 2007. Chm., King James Bible Trust, 2007–. DL Merseyside, 2011. *Publications:* (ed jtly) Twentieth Century State Education, 1971; (ed jtly) Black Britons, 1971; (ed) Low Pay, 1973; Unequal Britain, 1974; (ed) Are Low Wages Inevitable?, 1976; (ed) Education and the Urban Crisis, 1976; (ed) The Conscript Army: a study of Britain's unemployed, 1976; (jtly) To Him Who Hath: a study of poverty and taxation, 1976; (with Ruth Lister) Wasted Labour, 1978 (Social Concern Book Award); (ed) The Wealth Report, 1979; Inequality in Britain: freedom, welfare and the state, 1981; Poverty and Politics, 1982; The Wealth Report—2, 1983; (ed) Policies against Low Pay, 1984; The Minimum Wage: its potential and dangers, 1984; Freedom and Wealth in a Socialist Future, 1987; The Politics of Paradise, 1987; Losing Out: the emergence of Britain's underclass, 1989; An Agenda for Britain, 1993; (jtly) Europe Isn't Working, 1994; (jtly) Beyond Punishment: pathways from workfare, 1994; Making Welfare Work, 1995; How to Pay for the Future: building a stakeholders welfare, 1996; Stakeholder Welfare, 1997; Reforming Welfare, 1997; Reflections on Welfare Reform, 1998; The State of Dependency: welfare under Labour, 2000; Making Welfare Work: reconstructing welfare for the millennium, 2001; Neighbours from Hell: the politics of behaviour, 2003; The Ethic of Respect: a left wing cause, 2006; Attlee's Great Contemporaries, 2009; Saints and Heroes, 2010. *Address:* House of Commons, SW1A 0AA. *T:* (020) 7219 5193.

FIELD, Maj.-Gen. Geoffrey William, CB 1993; CVO 2005; OBE 1983 (MBE 1976); Resident Governor and Keeper of the Jewel House, HM Tower of London, 1994–2006; Service Member, War Pensions and Armed Forces Compensation Tribunal (formerly Service Member, Pensions Appeal Tribunals), 2005–12; *b* 30 Nov. 1941; *s* of William Edwin Field and Ellen Campbell Field (*née* Forsyth); *m* 1966, Janice Anne Olsen; one *s* two *d*. *Educ:* Daniel Stewart's College, Edinburgh; RMA Sandhurst; RMCS Shrivenham; Australian Staff College; RCDS. Commissioned RE 1961; OC 59 Ind. Cdo Sqn, RE, 1976–78; CO 36 Engr Regt, 1980–83 (comd RE, Falkland Islands, 1982); Asst Dir Defence Policy, MoD, 1983–85; Comd 11 Engr Gp, 1986–87; Dir Defence Programmes, MoD, 1989–90; Dir Gen. Logistic Policy (Army), 1990–93; Engr-in-Chief (Army), 1993–94. Colonel Commandant: RPC, 1991–93; RLC, 1993–96; RE, 1996–2006; Hon. Col, RE Vols (Specialist Units), 1992–96. Comr, Royal Hosp., Chelsea, 1990–93. Dir, Historic Royal Palaces Enterprises, 1998–2006. Trustee: Ulysses Trust, 1994–2005; Tower Hill Trust, 2009–; Gov., St Katharine's and Shadwell Trust, 1999–2006. Freeman, City of London, 1995. *Recreation:* golf. *Address:* c/o Lloyds Bank, Cox's and King's Branch, 8–10 Waterloo Place, SW1Y 4BE. *Club:* Rye Golf.

FIELD, Brig. Jill Margaret, CBE 1992; RRC 1988; Matron-in-Chief (Army) and Director of Defence Nursing Services, 1989–92; *b* 20 June 1934; *d* of late Major Charles Euston Field, Royal Signals, and Mrs Eva Gladys Field (*née* Watson). *Educ:* High School for Girls, Southend-on-Sea; St Bartholomew's Hosp., London (SRN). Joined QARANC, 1957; appointments include: service in Mil. Hosps in UK, BAOR, N Africa, Cyprus, Singapore; Instructor, QARANC Trng Centre, 1971–74; Liaison Officer QARANC, MoD, 1980–83; Matron, BMH Hannover, 1984–85; Dep. Medical (Nursing), BAOR, 1985–87; Matron, Cambridge Mil. Hosp., Aldershot and Chief Medical (Nursing) SE and SW Dist, 1987–89. QHNS 1989–92. *Recreations:* gardening, reading, music.

FIELD, John; *see* Field, E. J.

FIELD, Prof. John Edwin, OBE 1987; PhD; FRS 1994; Professor of Applied Physics, Department of Physics, University of Cambridge, 1994–2003, now Emeritus; Head of Physics and Chemistry of Solids Section, Cavendish Laboratory, Cambridge, 1987–2003; Fellow of Magdalene College, Cambridge, 1964–2003, now Emeritus; *b* 20 Sept. 1936; *s* of William Edwin Field and Madge (*née* Normansell); *m* 1963, Ineke Tjan; two *s* one *d*. *Educ:* Univ. of London (BSc); Univ. of Cambridge (PhD 1962). Graduate Tutor, Magdalene Coll., Cambridge, 1974–87; Asst Lectr, 1966–71, Lectr, 1971–90, Reader, 1990–94, Dept of Physics, Univ. of Cambridge. Hon. FRSSAf 2002. Hon. DSc: Univ. of Luleå, Sweden, 1989; Cranfield, 2002. Duddell Medal, Inst. of Physics, 1990; John S. Rinehart Award, DYMAT Assoc., 2009. *Publications:* (ed) The Properties of Diamond, 1979, 2nd edn 1991; (ed) The Properties of Natural and Synthetic Diamond, 1992; (ed) 3 conf. proc.; over 440 scientific papers. *Recreations:* mountain walking, running, ski-ing. *Address:* 11A Church Street, Stapleford, Cambs CB22 5DS. *T:* (01223) 846515.

FIELD, Sir Malcolm (David), Kt 1991; Senior non-executive Director, Hochschild Mining plc, since 2006; non-executive Director: Odgers Berndston (formerly Odgers), since 2002; Petropavlovsk, since 2009; *b* 25 Aug. 1937; *s* of Stanley Herbert Raynor Field and Constance Frances (*née* Watson); *m* (marr. diss.); one *d*; *m* 2001, Anne Charlton. *Educ:* Highgate Sch.; London Business Sch. National Service, commnd Welsh Guards (2nd Lieut), 1955–57 (served in Cyprus and Germany). PA to Dir, ICI (Paints Div.), 1957; joined family business, 1960 (taken over by W. H. Smith, 1963); Wholesale Dir, 1970–82, Man. Dir, Retail Gp, 1978–82, Gp Man. Dir, 1982–93, Chief Exec., 1994–96, W. H. Smith. Chairman: Bd of Management, NAAFI, 1986–93 (Mem., Bd of Management, 1973–86; Dep. Chm., 1985–86); CAA, 1996–2001; Sofa Workshop, 1998–2002; Tube Lines Ltd, 2003–06; Aricom plc, 2004–06 (Sen. non-exec. Dir, 2006–09); non-executive Director: MEPC, 1989–99; Scottish & Newcastle Breweries, 1993–98; Phoenix Group Ltd, 1995–97; Stationery Office, 1996–2001; Walker Greenbank, 1997–2002; Evolution Beeson Gregory (formerly Beeson Gregory), 2000–04; Garden Centre Gp, 2011–12. Ext. Policy Advr, DfT, 2001–06. Mem. Council, RCA, 1991–2001; Mem. Bd, English Nat. Ballet Sch., 1997–2007; Gov., Highgate Sch., 1994–2004 (Dep. Chm., 1999–2004). CCMI (CBIM 1988); CRAeS 1997; FRSA 1989. *Recreations:* watching cricket, tennis, golf, restoring an orangery and garden in Devon, reading biographies, collecting modern art, grandchildren, playing golf and tennis. *Address:* 21 Embankment Gardens, SW3 4LH. *Clubs:* Garrick, MCC.

FIELD, Rt Hon. Mark (Christopher); PC 2015; MP (C) Cities of London and Westminster, since 2001; *b* 6 Oct. 1964; *s* of late Maj. Peter Field and Ulrike Field (*née* Peipe); *m* 1st, 1994, Michele Louise Acton (marr. diss. 2006); 2nd, 2007, Victoria Margaret Philadelphia Elphicke; one *s* one *d*. *Educ:* Reading Sch.; St Edmund Hall, Oxford (MA Hons Juris.); Coll. of Law, Chester. Trainee solicitor, Richards Butler, 1988–90; Solicitor, Freshfields, 1990–92; employment consultant, 1992–94; Man. Dir, Kellyfield Consulting (publishing/recruiting firm), 1994–2001. Adviser: Bd, Ellwood Atfield, 2011–; Cains, 2011–. Councillor (C), RBK&C, 1994–2002. An Opposition Whip, 2003–04; Shadow Minister for London, 2003–05; Shadow Financial Sec. to the Treasury, 2005; Shadow Minister for Culture, 2005–06. Member: Select Cttee on LCD, 2003, on Procedure, 2008–10; Intelligence and Security Cttee, 2010–15. Chm., All Party Parly Gp on Venture Capital and Private Equity, 2010–15 (Vice Chm., 2004–10); Vice-Chm., All Party Parly Gp on Bangladesh, 2009–, on Football, 2010–. Member Standing Committee for: Proceeds of Crime Act, 2002; Enterprise Act, 2002; Finance Act, 2002; Licensing Act, 2003; Housing Act, 2004; Railways Act, 2005; Finance Act (No. 2), 2005; Regn of Financial Services (Land Transactions) Act, 2006; Nat. Insurance Contributions Act, 2006; National Lottery Act, 2006; Crossrail Act, 2008; Finance Act, 2008; Nat. Insce Contribns Act, 2008; Dormant Bank and Building Socs Accounts Act, 2008; Business Rates Supplements Act, 2009; Finance Act, 2009. Mem., Adv. Cttee, London Sch. of Commerce, 2005–. Regular broadcaster on radio and TV and occasional newspaper columnist on H of C, economic and financial affairs, and London issues. *Publications:* Reforming the City (contrib.), 2009; Between the Crashes, 2013. *Recreations:* cricket, football, researching local history, reading political biographies and diaries, walking in London, listening to popular/rock music. *Address:* House of Commons, SW1A 0AA. *T:* (020) 7219 8155.

FIELD, Marshall Hayward, CBE 1985; Director, Phoenix Assurance, 1980–85 (Actuary, 1964–85, General Manager, 1972–85); *b* 19 April 1930; *s* of Harold Hayward Field and Hilda Maud Field; *m* 1960, Barbara Evelyn Harris (*d* 1998); two *d*. *Educ:* Dulwich College. FIA 1957. With Pearl Assce, 1948–58; joined Phoenix Assurance, 1958. Director: TSB Trust Co. Ltd, 1985–89; TSB Gp, 1990–95; Ark Life Assurance Co., Dublin, 1991–2003; Consultant, Bacon & Woodrow, 1986–2000. Institute of Actuaries: Hon. Sec., 1975–77; Vice-Pres., 1979–82; Pres., 1986–88; Vice Pres., International Actuarial Assoc., 1984–90; Chm., Life Offices' Assoc., 1983–85. Mem., Fowler Inquiry into Provision for Retirement, 1984; Consultant, Marketing of Investments Bd Organising Cttee, 1985–86. Mem., Dulwich Picture Gall. Cttee, 1985–94; Trustee, Dulwich Picture Gall., 1994–2002; Chm., Dulwich DFAS, 2002–05. Governor: Dulwich Coll. Estates, 1973–95 (Chm., 1988–90); Dulwich Coll., 1987–97; James Allen's Girls' School, 1981–95. Mem., Ct of Assistants, Actuaries' Co., 1989– (Master, 1996–97). *Recreations:* theatre, architecture. *Address:* 12 Gainsborough Court, College Road, SE21 7LT. *Club:* Bembridge Sailing.

FIELD, Hon. Michael Walter, AC 2003; Chancellor, University of Tasmania, since 2013; *b* 28 May 1948; *s* of William Field and Blanche (*née* Burrows); *m* 1975, Janette Elizabeth Mary Fone; one *s* two *d*. *Educ:* Railton Primary Sch., Tasmania; Devonport High Sch., Tasmania; Univ. of Tasmania (BA Pol Sci./History). Teacher, 1971–75; Community Develt Officer, 1975–76. Government of Tasmania: MHA (Lab) Braddon, 1976–97; Minister for Transport, Main Roads, Construction and Local Govt, 1979–82; Shadow Minister for: Transport, 1982–83; Education and Ind. Relns, 1982–86; State Development, 1992–97; Dep. Leader of Opposition and Shadow Minister for Forestry, Ind. Relns and Energy, 1986–88; Leader of the Opposition, 1988–89 and 1992–97; Premier, Treas. and Minister for State Develt and Finance, 1989–92; Shadow Minister for Educn, Trng, and Youth Affairs, 1996–97. Board Member: John Curtin House Ltd, 1997–2012; Tasmanian Electricity Code Change Panel, 1999–2005. Chairman: Tasmanian Innovations Adv. Bd, 1999–2009; Bd, Australian Innovation Res. Centre, 2006–12. Dir, Port Arthur Historic Site Mgt Authy, 2005–. Life Mem. ALP, 2001. Hon. LLD Tasmania, 2000. *Recreations:* fishing, reading, music, kayaking.

FIELD, Patrick John; QC 2000; **His Honour Judge Patrick Field;** a Circuit Judge, since 2012; *b* 19 March 1959; *s* of late Michael Edward and Patricia Field; *m* Helen McCubbin; one *s* two *d*. *Educ:* Wilmslow Co. Grammar Sch.; King's Coll. London (LLB Hons). Called to the Bar, Gray's Inn, 1981, Bencher, 2007; Northern Circuit, 1982– (Junior, 1985); a Recorder, 2001–12. *Recreations:* fishing, travel. *Address:* Courts of Justice, Crown Square, Manchester M3 3FL.

FIELD, Hon. Sir Richard (Alan), Kt 2002; a Judge of the High Court, Queen's Bench Division, 2002–14; Judge in charge of Commercial List, 2014; *b* 17 April 1947; twin *s* of Robert Henry Field and Ivy May Field; *m* 1st, 1968, Lynne Hauskind (*d* 2007); two *s* two *d*; 2nd, 2009, Marion Nitch-Smith. *Educ:* Ottershaw Sch.; Bristol Univ. (LLB); London School of Economics (LLM with Dist.). Asst Prof., Univ. of British Columbia, 1969–71; Lectr in Law, Hong Kong Univ., 1971–73; Associate Prof., McGill Univ., Montreal, 1973–77; called to the Bar, Inner Temple, 1977, Bencher, 1998. QC 1987; a Dep. High Court Judge, 1998–2001; a Recorder, 1999–2001; a Presiding Judge, Western Circuit, 2009–13. Cheng Yu Tung Vis. Prof., Faculty of Law, Hong Kong Univ., 2014–15. *Recreations:* cricket, opera, theatre, learning Italian. *Club:* Garrick.

See also D. J. Field.

FIELD, Stephen Brian; UK Executive Director, International Monetary Fund, since 2013; *b* London, 30 May 1972; *s* of Brian Albert Field and Jean Alice Field (*née* Ixer); *m* 2013, Helen Mary Lewis; one *s* one *d. Educ:* Dame Alice Owen's Sch.; British Sch. of Brussels; Queen's Coll., Cambridge (BA Hons Econs 1994). HM Customs and Excise, 1994–95; HM Treasury: Economic Asst, 1995–97; Private Sec. to Paymaster Gen., 1997–99; Economic Advr, 1999–2005, various posts incl. Dep. Press Sec., 2001–04; Dep. Dir, Europe, 2005–07; Press Sec. to Chancellor of the Exchequer, 2007–09; Dir, Strategy and Communication, 2009–10; Prime Minister's Spokesman, 2010–12. *Recreations:* cooking, piano, playing with my children, Arsenal FC. *Address:* International Monetary Fund, 700 19th Street NW, Washington, DC 20431, USA. *T:* (202) 6234560. *E:* sfield@imf.org.

FIELD, Stephen John, CBE 2010; FRCP, FRCGP, FFPH; Principal in General Practice (part-time), Bellevue Medical Centre, Edgbaston, Birmingham, since 1997; Chief Inspector of General Practice, Care Quality Commission, since 2013; Chairman, National Inclusion Health Board, since 2010; *b* Stourbridge, Worcs, 22 June 1959; *s* of Derek and Yvonne Field; *m* 1992, Lynn Kennedy; twin *d. Educ:* Univ. of Birmingham Med. Sch. (MB ChB with Dist. in Social Medicine 1982); Univ. of Dundee (Dip. Med. Educn 1994; MMEd 2001). Family Planning Cert. 1986; DRCOG 1987; JCPTGP Cert. 1987; MRCGP 1987, FRCGP 1997; FRCP 2009; FFPH 2011. Hse surgeon, Worcester Royal Infirmary, 1982–83; Hse physician, Kidderminster Gen. Hosp., 1983; Worcester Royal Infirmary: Senior House Officer: Anaesthetics, 1983–84; Paediatrics, 1984–85; Obstetrics and Gynaecol., 1985–86; Worcester Vocational Trng Scheme for Gen. Practice, 1986–87; GP, Qld, 1986; SHO, A&E, Worcester Royal Infirmary, 1987; Principal in Gen. Practice (Sen. Partner), Corbett Med. Practice, Droitwich Spa, Worcs, 1987–97. Regl Advr and Dir, Postgrad. Gen. Practice Educn, W Midlands, 1995–2001. Regl Postgrad. Med. and Dental Dean, 2001–10, Hd of Workforce Develt, 2006–07, NHS W Midlands; Dep. Nat. Med. Dir, NHS England, 2012–13; Chm., NHS Future Forum, 2011–13. Chm. Council, RCGP, 2007–10. Hon. Professor: of Med. Educn, Univ. of Warwick, 2002–; Sch. of Medicine, Univ. of Birmingham, 2003–. Mem. Faculty, Harvard Macy Inst. Prog. for Leaders in Health Care Innovation and Educn, Harvard Univ., 2003–. Broadcaster; contrib. radio and TV progs on ethical and health issues, UK and overseas, 2007–. FHEA 2007; Mem., Acad. Med. Educators, 2008. DUniv: Staffordshire, 2006; Birmingham City, 2012; Hon. MSc Worcester, 2010; Hon. DSc: Keele, 2011; Exeter, 2015. Gold Award, Adv. Cttee on Clin. Excellence Awards, DoH, 2005. *Publications:* (jtly) Watching You, Watching Me…: an introduction to communication skills in general practice, 1996, 2nd edn 1998; (jtly) Those Things You Say…: consultation skills and the MRCGP examination (interactive video and workbook), 1998; (jtly) Sexual Health History Taking, 1998; (jtly) Medical Careers: opportunities and options, 2000; (jtly) Quality in General Practice, 2000; (jtly) Continuing Professional Development in Primary Care: making it happen, 2000; (with P. Middleton) The GP Trainer's Handbook, 2000; (ed jtly) The General Practice Jigsaw, 2001; (jtly) Prescription for Learning: getting the message across, 2002; (jtly) Appraisal for the Apprehensive - or, being appraised and making it work for you, 2002; (jtly) Guiding Doctors in Managing Careers: a toolkit for tutors, trainers, mentors and appraisers, 2006; (jtly) The Future Direction of General Practice: a roadmap, 2007; (jtly) The Condensed Curriculum Guide for GP Training and the New MRCGP, 2007; (jtly) Primary Care Federations: putting patients first, 2008; contrib. educn and res. papers to learned jls on med. educn, continuing professional develt, revalidation, leadership, primary care and health policy. *Recreations:* tennis, hillwalking, supporting W Bromwich Albion, watching England win Test matches!

FIELD, Stuart, MBE 2013; FRCR; Consultant Radiologist, Kent and Canterbury Hospital, 1974–2004; Director, Kent Breast Screening Programme, 1988–2004; *b* 22 June 1944; *s* of Walter Frederick William Field and Maisie Field (*née* Marlow); *m* 1968, Margaret Shirley Dawes; two *d. Educ:* Watford Grammar Sch. (Head Boy); Gonville and Caius Coll., Cambridge (BA 1st Cl. Hons Natural Sci. Tripos, MA, MB BChir). DMRD 1972; FRCR 1974. Houseman to Professorial Med. and Surgical Units, 1969–70, Registrar in Radiol., 1970–74, KCH. Royal College of Radiologists: Dean, Faculty of Clinical Radiology, 1991–93, Vice-Pres., 1993; Pres. Kent Postgrad. Med. Centre, 1994–2000; Hon. Prof., Kent Inst. of Medicine and Health Scis, Univ. of Kent at Canterbury, 1998–2007. Mem., DoH Adv. Cttee for Breast Cancer Screening, 1994–2003. Chairman: Breast Gp, 1997–99; League of Friends, Kent and Canterbury Hosp., 2007–. Gov., E Kent Hosps Univ. NHS Foundn Trust, 2009–12. Hon. Mem., Romanian Radiol. Soc., 1993. President's Medal, RCR, 2002. *Publications:* numerous chapters in textbooks of radiol. on the plain abdominal radiograph in the acute abdomen; contrib. articles on breast cancer screening and other radiol topics to specialist radiol. jls. *Recreations:* gardening, walking, DIY, classical music, the family. *Address:* Bournes Corner, Bekesbourne Road, Bridge, Canterbury, Kent CT4 5AE.

FIELD-SMITH, Robin, MBE 1983; Lay Member, Equality and Diversity Committee, Bar Standards Board, since 2009; Independent Member, Chief Police Officer Appointments, since 2012; HM Inspector of Constabulary, 2000–09; Senior Police Assessor, since 2009; *b* Brighton, 24 Jan. 1948; *s* of John and Meriel Field-Smith; *m* 1970, Mary Paffett; two *s* one *d. Educ:* Manor House Sch.; Hurstpierpoint Coll.; Univ. of Liverpool (BA 1970); Churchill Coll., Cambridge (PGCE 1971); Open Univ. (MA 1993). FCIPD 1999. Commissioned: TA, 1970; RAEC, 1971; regtl duties, 1972–79; Staff Coll., 1980; SO2 HQ BAOR, 1981–82; BAOR and MoD, 1983–86; JSDC 1986; SO1 HQ AFCENT, 1987–89; Comd ETS, Berlin, 1990–92; SO1 HQ AGC, 1992–93; Comd ETS, BAOR, 1993–94; CO ASTS, 1995–97; Dep. Dir, ETS(A), 1997–99; Defence Trng Review, 1999–2000. Lay Chm., Army Synod, 1990–2000; Lay Member: GDC, 2009–13; Employment Tribunals (England and Wales), 2010–14. Vice-Pres., Nat. Assoc. of Chaplains to the Police, 2008–. Vis. Prof., Univ. of Portsmouth, 2010–. Dir, Wilts TEC, 1996–2000; Gov., Chippenham Coll., 1997–2001; Chair of Trustees, Royal Sch. Hampstead Trust, 2009– (Trustee, 2003–09); Trustee: Learning from Experience Trust, 2003– (Chair, 2008–10); Eric Frank Trust, 2010–. CCMI 2007; CMgr 2013. Freeman, City of London, 2008. Hon. MCGI 2004. *Publications:* over 60 inspection and independent member reports. *Recreations:* choral singing, family, steam railways, walking, DIY. *E:* robin@field-smith.com.

FIELDER, Prof. Alistair Richard, FRCS, FRCP, FRCOphth; Professor of Ophthalmology, City University, 2005–07, now Emeritus; Hon. Consultant Ophthalmologist: St Mary's Hospital NHS Trust, 1995–2007; Hillingdon Hospital NHS Trust, 1996–2007; *b* 3 Sept. 1942; *s* of late Alfred Emmanuel Hugh Fielder and Elizabeth Rachel Fielder (*née* Hutchinson); *m* 1965, Gillian Muriel Slough; one *s* three *d. Educ:* St George's Hosp. Med. Sch., London Univ. (MB BS 1966). FRCS 1974; FRCOphth (FCOphth 1988), Hon. FRCOphth 2012; MRCP 1991, FRCP 1994; FRCPCH 1999. RSO, Moorfields Eye Hosp., 1973–76; Consultant Ophthalmologist, Derby Hosps, 1977–82; Reader in Ophthalmology, Leicester Univ., 1982–88; Professor of Ophthalmology: Birmingham Univ., 1988–95; ICSTM, later ICL, 1995–2004. Vice Pres., 1995–99, Sen. Vice Pres., 1997–99, Royal Coll. of Ophthalmologists (Hon. Fellow, 2012); British Rep., Societas Ophthalmologica Europæa, 1998–2009. Trustee: RNIB, 1990–2002 (Mem., Nat. Assembly, 2002–09); Fight for Sight, 2003–; Nat. Fedn of Families with Visually Impaired Children (LOOK), 2003–09 (Chm. Trustees, 2003–07); Action for Blind People, 2006–; Vice Chm. Trustees, Vision 2020 UK, 2002–07. *Publications:* scientific articles and contribs to books on the developing visual system and paediatric ophthalmology. *Recreation:* escaping on narrow boats and Dutch barges. *Address:* 18 Melrose Gardens, W6 7RW. *T:* (020) 7602 4790, 07850 742900. *Club:* Royal Society of Medicine.

FIELDHOUSE, Brian; DL; Chief Executive, West Sussex County Council, 1990–95; *b* 1 May 1933; *s* of late Harry and Florence Fieldhouse; *m* 1959, Sonia J. Browne; one *s* one *d. Educ:* Barnsley Holgate Grammar Sch.; Keble Coll., Oxford (MA PPE). IPFA 1960. Formerly, Treasurer's Departments: Herts CC; Hants CC; Flints CC; County Treasurer: Lincs parts of Lindsey CC, 1970–73; W Sussex CC, 1973–90. Comr, Public Works Loans Bd, 1988–92. Principal Financial Advr, ACC, 1980–85. Pres., Soc. of Co. Treasurers, 1983. Dir, Chichester Fest. Theatre Trust, 1995–97. Sec., Rees Jeffreys Road Fund, 1995–2005. DL West Sussex, 1996. FRSA 1984. *Recreations:* hill farming, theatre going. *Address:* 13 The Avenue, Chichester PO19 5PX. *Club:* Farmers.

FIELDHOUSE, Prof. David Kenneth, FBA 1996; Vere Harmsworth Professor of Imperial and Naval History, Cambridge University, 1981–92; Fellow, Jesus College, Cambridge, 1981–92, subseq. Emeritus; *b* 7 June 1925; *s* of Rev. Ernest Fieldhouse and Clara Hilda Beatrice Fieldhouse; *m* 1952, Sheila Elizabeth Lyon; one *s* two *d. Educ:* Dean Close Sch., Cheltenham; Queen's Coll., Oxford (MA, DLitt). War Service: RN, Sub-Lt (A), 1943–47. History master, Haileybury Coll., 1950–52; Lectr in Modern History, Univ. of Canterbury, NZ, 1953–57; Beit Lectr in Commonwealth History, Oxford Univ., 1958–81; Fellow, Nuffield Coll., Oxford, 1966–81. *Publications:* The Colonial Empires, 1966, 2nd edn, 1982; The Theory of Capitalist Imperialism, 1967, 2nd edn 1969; Economics and Empire, 1973, 2nd edn 1984; Unilever Overseas, 1978; Colonialism 1870–1945, 1981; Black Africa 1945–80, 1986; Merchant Capital and Economic Decolonization, 1994; The West and the Third World, 1999; Kurds, Arabs and Britons, 2001; Western Imperialism in the Middle East, 1914–1958, 2006. *Recreations:* music, reading fiction. *Address:* Jesus College, Cambridge CB5 8BL. *T:* (01223) 339339.

FIELDING, Emma Georgina Annalies; actress; *b* 7 Oct. 1971; *d* of late Johnny Fielding, CBE and of Sheila Fielding (*née* Brown); *m* 2004, Michael Ashcroft; one *s. Educ:* Royal Scottish Acad. of Music and Drama (Dip. Dramatic Art). BBC Radio Drama Co., 1991; Sheffield Crucible, 1992; Almeida Th., 1993, 1995, 1997, 2005; NT, 1993, 1999, 2005; RSC, 1994, 1998, 2003; *plays* include: Private Lives, Albery Th., 2001, NY, 2002 (Theater World Award, outstanding Broadway debut, 2002); Rock 'n' Roll, Duke of York's, 2007; Decade, Headlong Th., 2011; The King's Speech, Yvonne Arnaud, Guildford and tour, 2012; Heartbreak House, Chichester, 2012; In the Republic of Happiness, Royal Court, 2012; Rapture, Blister, Burn, Hampstead Th., 2014; *films* include: Pandaemonium, 2000; The Discovery of Heaven, 2001; Shooters, 2002; The Great Ghost Rescue, 2011; Twenty8K, Fast Girls, 2012; *television* includes: Tell Tale Hearts, 1992; The Maitlands, 1993; A Dance to the Music of Time, 1997; A Respectable Trade, 1998; Big Bad World, 1999; Other People's Children, 2000; My Uncle Silas, 2003; The Government Inspector, The Ghost Squad, 2005; Cranford, 2007; Return to Cranford, 2009; The Suspicions of Mr Whicher, 2011; Kidnap and Ransom, 2011; many radio performances. Associate Artist, RSC. London Critics' Circle Award, most promising newcomer, 1993. *Publications:* Twelfth Night: actors on Shakespeare, 2002. *Recreation:* walking. *Address:* c/o Rebecca Blond Associates, 69a Kings Road, SW3 4NX. *T:* (020) 7351 4100.

FIELDING, Fenella Marion; actress; *b* London, 17 Nov. 1934. *Educ:* North London Collegiate School. Began acting career in 1954; *plays include:* Cockles and Champagne, Saville, 1954; Pay the Piper, Saville, 1954; Jubilee Girl, Victoria Palace, 1956; Valmouth, Lyric, Hammersmith, 1958, Saville, 1959, and Chichester Fest., 1982; Pieces of Eight, Apollo, 1959; Five Plus One, Edinburgh Fest., 1961; Twists, Arts, 1962 (Best Revue Performance of the Year in Variety); Doctors of Philosophy, New Arts, 1962; Luv, New Arts, 1963; So Much to Remember—The Life Story of a Great Lady, Establishment, transf. to Vaudeville, 1963; Let's Get a Divorce, Mermaid, transf. to Comedy, 1966; The Beaux Stratagem and The Italian Straw Hat, Chichester Fest., 1967; The High Bid, Mermaid, 1967; Façade, Queen Elizabeth Hall, 1970; Colette, Ellen Stewart, NY, 1970 (first appearance in NY); Fish Out of Water, Greenwich, 1971; The Old Man's Comforts, Open Space, 1972; The Provok'd Wife, Greenwich, 1973; Absurd Person Singular, Criterion, 1974, transf. to Vaudeville, 1975; Fielding Convertible, Edinburgh Fest., 1976; Jubilee Jeunesse, Royal Opera House, 1977; Look After Lulu, Chichester Fest., transf. to Haymarket, 1978; A Personal Choice, Edinburgh Fest., 1978; Fenella on Broadway, W6, Studio, Lyric, Hammersmith, 1979; Wizard of Oz, Bromley, 1983; The Jungle Book, Adelphi, 1984; The Country Wife, Mermaid, 1990; A Dangerous Woman, New End Th., 1998; Blithe Spirit, Salisbury, 1999; *films include:* Drop Dead, Darling; Lock Up Your Daughters; Carry On Screaming; Carry On Regardless; Doctor in Clover; Doctor in Distress; Doctor in Trouble; No Love for Johnnie; Robin Hood; Guest House Paradiso; *television series:* That Was The Week That Was; A Touch of Venus; Ooh La La; Stories from Saki; Dean Martin and the Gold-Diggers; Comedy Tonight; Rhyme and Reason; numerous appearances in UK and USA. *Recreations:* reading, diarising. *Address:* c/o Langford Associates Ltd, 17 Westfields Avenue, Barnes, SW13 0AT.

FIELDING, Helen Elizabeth; novelist and screenwriter; *b* Yorkshire, 19 Feb. 1958; *d* of late Michael Fielding and of Nellie Fielding; partner, Kevin Curran; one *s* one *d. Educ:* Wakefield Girls' High Sch.; St Anne's Coll., Oxford (MA English 1979). BBC TV researcher and producer, 1979–90; journalist, Independent, Sunday Times, Guardian, Telegraph, 1990–. Ambassador, Save the Children, 2013–. Writer of screenplays: Bridget Jones's Diary, 2001 (Evening Standard Award for Best Screenpaly, 2002); Bridget Jones: The Edge of Reason, 2004. *Publications: novels*: Cause Celeb, 1994; Bridget Jones's Diary, 1996 (British Book of Year, Nat. Book Awards, 1997); Bridget Jones: The Edge of Reason, 1999; Olivia Joules and the Overactive Imagination, 2003; Bridget Jones: Mad About the Boy, 2013; *short stories:* Ox-Tales, 2009. *Recreations:* hiking, salsa, scuba, ski-ing, Googling imaginary holidays. *Address:* c/o Aitken Alexander Associates Ltd, 291 Gray's Inn Road, WC1X 8EB. *Club:* Soho House.

FIELDING, Sir Leslie, KCMG 1988; Vice-Chancellor, University of Sussex, 1987–92; *b* 29 July 1932; *o s* of late Percy Archer Fielding and of Margaret (*née* Calder Horry); *m* 1978, Dr Sally P. J. Harvey, FSA, FRHistS, sometime Fellow of St Hilda's Coll., Oxford; one *s* one *d. Educ:* Queen Elizabeth's Sch., Barnet; Emmanuel Coll., Cambridge (First in History; MA; Hon. Fellow 1990); School of Oriental and African Studies, London; St Antony's Coll., Oxford (MA; Vis. Fellow, 1977–78). Served with Royal Regt of Artillery, 1951–53; TA, 1953–56. Entered HM Diplomatic Service, 1956; served in: Tehran, 1957–60; Foreign Office, 1960–64; Singapore, 1964; Phnom Penh (Chargé d'Affaires), 1964–66; Paris, 1967–70; Dep. Head of Planning Staff, FCO, 1970–73; seconded for service with European Commn in Brussels, 1973; Dir (External Relns Directorate Gen.), 1973–77; permanent transfer 1979; Head of Delegn of Commn in Tokyo, 1978–82; Dir-Gen. for External Relns, Brussels, 1982–87. UK Mem., High Council of European Univ. Inst. in Florence, 1988–92. Chm., Nat. Curriculum Geography Wkg Gp, 1989–90. Adviser: IBM Europe, 1989–95; Panasonic Europe, 1990–96. Hon. Pres., Univ. Assoc. for Contemporary European Studies, 1990–2000; Founder Mem., Japan-EC Assoc., then Europe-Japan Business Forum, 1988–98; Mem., UK-Japan 2000 Gp, 1993–2001. Mem. Ct, Univ. of Sussex, 2000–. Mem., Gen. Synod, C of E, 1990–92. Admitted to office of Reader by Bishop of Exeter, 1981; served dios of Exeter, Tokyo, Gibraltar, Chichester and Hereford; Reader Emeritus, 2007. Patron, Soc. of King Charles the Martyr, 1992–. Mem., Soc. of Authors, 2006–. FRSA 1989; FRGS 1991 (Mem. Council, 1992–95). Hon. Fellow, Sussex European Inst., 1993. Hon. LLD Sussex, 1992. Grand Officer, Order of St Agatha (San Marino), 1987; Knight Commander Order of the White Rose (Finland), 1988; Grand Silver Medal of Honour with Star (Austria), 1989. *Publications:* Europe as a global partner: the external relations of the European Community, 1991; (contrib.) Travellers' Tales, 1999; (contrib.) More Travellers' Tales, 2005; Before the Killing Fields: witness to Cambodia and the Vietnam War, 2008; Kindly Call Me God: the misadventures of Fielding of the FO, Eurocrat Extraordinaire and Vice-Chancellor Semipotentiary, 2009; Twilight Over The Temples: the close of Cambodia's Belle Epoque, 2011; The Mistress of the Bees, 2011; Mentioned in Dispatches - Phnom Penh, Paris, Tokyo, Brussels: Is Diplomacy Dead?, 2012; (contrib.) Changing Horizons: memories of Britain's European pioneers 1973, 2013; Is Diplomacy Dead?, 2014; Germansweek and its Parish Church, 2014; articles on internat. relations, higher educn and ecclesiastical matters. *Recreations:* life in the country, theology. *Address:* Wild Cherry Farm, Elton, Ludlow, Shropshire SY8 2HQ. *Club:* Travellers.

FIELDING, Dame Pauline, DBE 1999; PhD; Professional Adviser to the Healthcare Commission, 2002–09; Director of Nursing: Preston Acute Hospitals NHS Trust, 1993–2003; Chorley and South Ribble NHS Trust, 1998–2003; *m* Rev. Michael Fielding; one *s* one *d*. *Educ:* Univ. of Southampton (BSc Hons; PhD 1981). Ward Sister, 1982, Sen. Nurse, then Dir of Clinical Nursing Res., Middx Hosp.; formerly Nursing Dir, Forest Healthcare Trust. Hon. Professor of Nursing: Univ. of Central Lancashire, 2000; Southampton Univ., 2003. Chm., Lancaster and Morecambe Univ. of the Third Age, 2008–11. DUniv Southampton, 2003. *E:* paulinefielding@aol.com.

FIELDING, Richard Walter; Chairman, Richard Fielding Ltd, 1992–2000; *b* 9 July 1933; *s* of late Walter Harrison Fielding, MBE, and Marjorie Octavia Adair (*née* Roberts); *m* 1st, 1961, Felicity Ann Jones (*d* 1981); one *s* three *d*; 2nd, 1983, Jacqueline Winifred Digby (*née* Hussey). *Educ:* Clifton Coll., Bristol. National Service, Royal Engineers (Lieut), 1951–53. Broker to Dir, Bland Welch & Co. Ltd, 1954–68; Dir to Man. Dir, C. E. Heath & Co. Ltd, 1968–75; Founder and Chm., Fielding and Partners, 1975–86; Chairman: C. E. Heath PLC, 1987–92; Sharelink PLC, 1993–95. Chm., Syndicate Capital Trust, 1996–98 (Dir, 1993–96); Dir, Hambros Insurance Services, 1993–98. High Sheriff, Dorset, 1997. *Recreations:* hunting, country sports. *Address:* 104 Cambridge Street, SW1V 4QG.

FIELDS, Sir Allan (Clifford), KCMG 2005; Chairman, Banks Holdings Ltd, 1999–2012 (Managing Director, 1988–99); *b* 19 Sept. 1942; *s* of James Percival Fields and Gwendolyn Fields; *m* 1964, Irene Elizabeth Smith; one *s* one *d*. *Educ:* Harrison Coll., Barbados; Stow Coll. of Engrg, Glasgow. Engr, Barbados Light & Power, 1966–78; Managing Director: Neal & Massy, 1978–88; Barbados Shipping & Trading, 1999–2005 (Chm., 2005–07). Chairman: Cable & Wireless (Barbados), 2002–; Tower Hill Merchants plc. Chm., Private Sector Assoc., 1999–2004. Senator (Ind) Barbados Parlt, 2003–08. *Recreations:* reading, gardening, cooking. *Address:* Morning Mist, Stepney, St George, Barbados. *T:* 4265195, *Fax:* 4294664. *E:* afields@caribsurf.com.

FIELDSEND, Sir John (Charles Rowell), KBE 1998; Judge, Court of Appeal: St Helena, Falkland Islands and British Antarctic Territory, 1985–99; Gibraltar, 1985–97 (President, 1991–97); *b* 13 Sept. 1921; *s* of C. E. Fieldsend, MC, and Phyllis (*née* Brucesmith); *m* 1945, Muriel Gedling (*d* 2010); one *s* one *d*. *Educ:* Michaelhouse, Natal; Rhodes University Coll., Grahamstown, SA (BA 1942, LLB 1947). Served RA, 1943–45. Called to the Bar, S Rhodesia, 1947; advocate in private practice, 1947–63; QC S Rhodesia, 1959; Pres., Special Income Tax Court for Fedn of Rhodesia and Nyasaland, 1958–63; High Court Judge, S Rhodesia, 1963, resigned 1968; Asst Solicitor, Law Commn, 1968–78, Sec., 1978–80; Chief Justice: of Zimbabwe, 1980–83; of Turks and Caicos Islands, 1985–87; of British Indian Ocean Territory, 1987–99 (Principal Legal Advr, 1984–87). *Recreations:* home-making, travel. *Address:* Great Dewes, Ardingly, Sussex RH17 6UP.

FIENNES, family name of **Baron Saye and Sele**.

FIENNES, Joseph Alberic; actor; *b* 27 May 1970; *s* of late Mark Fiennes and Jennifer Fiennes (*née* Lash); *m* 2009, María Dolores Diéguez; two *d*. *Educ:* Guildhall Sch. of Music and Drama. *Theatre includes:* The Woman in Black, Fortune, 1993; A Month in the Country, Albery, 1994; A View from the Bridge, Strand, 1995; Real Classy Affair, Royal Court, 1998; Edward II, Crucible, Sheffield, 2001; Love's Labour's Lost, NT, 2003; Epitaph for George Dillon, Comedy, 2005; Unicorns, Almost (one-man play), Old Vic, 2006; 2,000 Feet Away, Bush Th., 2008; Cyrano de Bergerac, Chichester, 2009; Royal Shakespeare Company: Son of Man, Les Enfants du Paradis, Troilus and Cressida, The Herbal Bed, 1996; As You Like It, 1997. *Television includes:* The Vacillations of Poppy Carew, 1995; FlashForward (series), 2009; Camelot (series), 2011. *Films include:* Stealing Beauty, 1996; Elizabeth, Martha - Meet Frank, Daniel and Laurence, 1998; Shakespeare in Love, Forever Mine, 1999; Rancid Aluminium, 2000; Enemy at the Gates, Dust, 2001; Killing Me Softly, Leo, 2002; Luther, 2003; The Merchant of Venice, 2004; Man to Man, The Great Raid, 2005; The Darwin Awards, 2006; Running with Scissors, Goodbye Bafana, 2007; The Escapist, Spring 41, 2008; Red Baron, 2008; Against the Current, 2009; dir, The Spirit, 2008 (Best Short Film, Cinema for Peace); Hercules 3D, 2014. *Address:* c/o The Artists Partnership, 101 Finsbury Pavement, EC2A 1RS.

See also R. N. Fiennes.

FIENNES, Ralph Nathanial; actor; *b* 22 Dec. 1962; *s* of late Mark Fiennes and Jennifer Fiennes (*née* Lash). *Educ:* Bishop Wordsworth's Sch., Salisbury; RADA. *Theatre* includes: Open Air Theatre, Regent's Park: Twelfth Night, Ring Round the Moon, 1985; A Midsummer Night's Dream, 1985, 1986; Romeo and Juliet, 1986; Royal National Theatre: Six Characters in Search of an Author, Fathers and Sons, Ting Tang Mine, 1987; The Talking Cure, 2002; Oedipus, 2008; Man and Superman, 2015; Royal Shakespeare Company: The Plantagenets, Much Ado About Nothing, 1988; Playing With Trains, 1989; Troilus and Cressida, King Lear, 1990; The Man Who Came to Dinner, 1991; Brand, transf. Th. Royal Haymarket, 2003; Almeida Theatre: Hamlet, 1995 (also Hackney Empire and Belasco, NY); Ivanov, 1997; Richard II, Coriolanus (transf. NY), 2000; Julius Caesar, Barbican, 2005; Faith Healer, Gate Th., Dublin, transf. NY, 2006; God of Carnage, Gielgud, 2008; The Tempest, Th. Royal, Haymarket, 2011; *films:* Wuthering Heights, 1992; Baby of Macon, Schindler's List, 1993; Quiz Show, 1994; Strange Days, 1995; The English Patient, 1997; Oscar and Lucinda, The Avengers, 1998; Onegin, 1999 (also exec. producer); Sunshine, The End of the Affair, 2000; Red Dragon, Maid in Manhattan, 2002; Spider, 2003; Chromophobia, The Constant Gardener, Wallace and Gromit in the Curse of the Were-Rabbit, Harry Potter and the Goblet of Fire, 2005; The White Countess, Land of the Blind, 2006; Harry Potter and the Order of the Phoenix, Bernard and Doris, The Chumscrubber, 2007; In Bruges, The Duchess, 2008; The Reader, The Hurt Locker, 2009; Cemetery Junction, Nanny McPhee and the Big Bang, Clash of the Titans, 2010; Harry Potter and the Deathly Hallows, Pt 1, 2010, Pt 2, 2011; Coriolanus (also dir), Wrath of the Titans, Skyfall, Great Expectations, 2012; The Invisible Woman (also dir), The Grand Budapest Hotel, 2014; *television* includes: A Dangerous Man, 1991; The Cormorant, 1992; Page Eight, 2011; Turks & Caicos, Salting the Battlefield, 2014. *Recreation:* books. *Address:* c/o Dalzell & Beresford Ltd, Paddock Suite, The Courtyard, 55 Charterhouse Street, EC1M 6HA. *T:* (020) 336 0531.

See also J. A. Fiennes.

FIENNES, Sir Ranulph Twisleton-Wykeham-, 3rd Bt *cr* 1916; OBE 1993; *b* 7 March 1944; *s* of Lieut-Col Sir Ranulph Twisleton-Wykeham-Fiennes, DSO, 2nd Bt (died of wounds, 1943) and Audrey Joan (*d* 2004), *yr d* of Sir Percy Newson, 1st Bt; *S* father 1944; *m* 1st, 1970, Virginia Pepper (*d* 2004) (first female member of Antarctic Club, 1985; first woman to be awarded Polar Medal, 1987); 2nd, 2005, Louise Millington; one *d*. *Educ:* Eton. Liveryman, Vintners' Company, 1960. French Parachutist Wings, 1965. Lieut, Royal Scots Greys, 1966, Captain 1968 (retd 1970). Attached 22 SAS Regt, 1966, Sultan of Muscat's Armed Forces, 1968 (Dhofar Campaign Medal, 1969; Sultan's Bravery Medal, 1970). T&AVR 1971, Captain RAC. Leader of British expeditions: White Nile, 1969; Jostedalsbre Glacier, 1970; Headless Valley, BC, 1971; (Towards) North Pole, 1977; (with Charles Burton) Transglobe (first surface journey around the world's polar axis), 1979–82, reached South Pole, 15 Dec. 1980, reached North Pole, 11 April 1982 (first man in history to reach both Poles by surface travel); North Polar Unsupported Expeditions: reached 84°48′N on 16 April 1986; reached 88°58′N on 14 April 1990 (Furthest North Unsupported record); (with Dr Mike Stroud) South Polar Unsupported Expedition: first crossing of Antarctic Continent and longest unsupported polar journey in history (1,345 miles), 1992–93; (with Dr Mike Stroud) Land Rover 7x7x7 Challenge (7 marathons in 7 days on 7 continents), 2003; climbed North Face of Eiger, 2007; climbed Everest, 2009 (first OAP to scale highest summit). Life Mem., Highland Soc. of London, 2010. Hon. MRIN 1997. Hon. Fellow, Univ. of Glamorgan, 2012. Hon. DSc: Loughborough, 1986; Portsmouth, 2000; Sheffield, 2005; Abertay Dundee, 2007; Plymouth, 2011; DUniv Birmingham, 1995; Hon. DLitt Glasgow Caledonian, 2002. Inst. of Navigation Award, 1977; elected to Guinness Hall of Fame, 1987. Livingstone Gold Medal, RSGS, 1983; Explorers' Club of New York Medal (and Hon. Life Membership), 1983; Founder's Medal, RGS, 1984; Polar Medal, 1987, clasp 1995; ITN Award, for the Event of the Decade, 1990; Millennium Award for Polar Exploration, British Chapter, Explorers' Club; Oldies of the Year Award, 2004; Great British Sportsman of Year Award, ITV, 2007. *Films:* (cameraman) To the Ends of the Earth, 1983; (writer) Killer Elite, 2011. Just Giving Award, 2011. *Publications:* A Talent for Trouble, 1970; Ice Fall in Norway, 1972; The Headless Valley, 1973; Where Soldiers Fear To Tread, 1975; Hell on Ice, 1979; To the Ends of the Earth, 1983; (with Virginia Fiennes) Bothie, the Polar Dog, 1984; Living Dangerously (autobiog.), 1987, rev. and expanded 1994; The Feather Men, 1991; Atlantis of the Sands, 1992; Mind Over Matter, 1993; The Sett, 1996; Fit for Life, 1998; Beyond the Limits, 2000; The Secret Hunters, 2001; Captain Scott, 2003; Mad, Bad and Dangerous to Know: the autobiography, 2007; Mad Dogs and Englishmen, 2009; My Heroes, 2011; Cold, 2013; Agincourt: my family, the battle and the fight for France, 2014. *Recreations:* langlauf, photography. *Heir:* none. *Club:* Travellers (Hon. Mem.).

FIENNES-CLINTON, family name of **Earl of Lincoln**.

FIETH, Robin Paul, FCA; Chief Executive, Building Societies Association, since 2013; *b* Sheffield, Yorks, 8 Dec. 1963; *s* of Eric and Eileen Fieth; *m* 1991, Fiona MacGregor; one *s* two *d*. *Educ:* Downside Sch.; Durham Univ. (BA Hons Geog.). FCA 1990. Price Waterhouse, 1986–96; Finance Dir, Girovend Cashless Systems plc, 1996–2000; Gp Finance Dir, Transacsys plc, 2000–01; Finance Dir, 2002–07, Exec. Dir, 2007–13, ICAEW. Trustee, Chartered Accountants Benevolent Assoc., 2010–. *Recreations:* cycle touring, philately. *Address:* Building Societies Association, York House, 23 Kingsway, WC2B 6UJ. *T:* (020) 7520 5900. *E:* robin.fieth@bsa.org.uk.

FIFE, 4th Duke of, *cr* 1899; **David Charles Carnegie;** Lord Carnegie of Kinnaird (Scot.), 1616; Earl of Southesk and Lord Carnegie of Kinnaird and Leuchars (Scot.), 1633; Bt (NS), 1663; Baron Balinhard, 1869; Earl of Macduff, 1899; Chairman, Elsick Development Co., since 2008; *b* 3 March 1961; *s* of 3rd Duke of Fife and of Hon. Caroline Cicely Dewar (now Hon. Lady Worsley), *er d* of 3rd Baron Forteviot, MBE; *S* father, 2015; *m* 1987, Caroline, *d* of Martin Bunting, *qv*; three *s*. *Educ:* Eton; Pembroke Coll., Cambridge (BA Law 1982; MA 1986); Royal Agricultural College, Cirencester; Edinburgh Univ. (MBA 1990). Cazenove & Co., 1982–85; Bell Lawrie & Co., 1988–89; chartered accountant, Reeves & Neylan, to 1997. Partner, Southesk Farms. Mem. Council, HHA for Scotland; Vice Chm., Angus Cons. and Unionist Assoc. Hon. President: Montrose and Dist Angling Club; Angus Show; Hon. Patron, Edinburgh Angus Club. *Heir:* *s* Earl of Southesk, *qv*.

FIFE, Robert Donald Mathieson; Sheriff of North Strathclyde at Paisley, since 2014; *b* Edinburgh, 2 Sept. 1955; *s* of Robert and Kathleen Fife; *m* 1975, Jean McVitie; two *s*. *Educ:* Edinburgh Acad.; Univ. of Edinburgh (LLB). Admitted solicitor, 1978; Partner, Strathern & Blair WS, subseq. Anderson Strathern LLP, 1982–2014. Temp. Sheriff, 1998–2000, pt-time Sheriff, 2000–14. Chair, Appeals Cttee, Inst. of Chartered Accountants of Scotland, 1999–2013. *Recreations:* travel, walking, sports, cultural events. *Address:* Paisley Sheriff Court, St James Street, Paisley PA3 2HW. *T:* (0141) 887 5291, *Fax:* (0141) 887 6702. *E:* sheriffrdmfife@scotcourts.gov.uk.

FIGEL, Ján; Leader, Christian Democratic Movement, Slovakia, since 2009; *b* 20 Jan. 1960; *s* of Stefan Figel and Mária Figelova; *m* 1983, Maria; three *s* one *d*. *Educ:* Tech. Univ., Kosice (MSc Electronic Engrg); Georgetown Univ., Washington (Internat. Affairs); UFSIA, Antwerp (European Econ. Integration). MP, Slovak Republic, 1992–98; State Sec., Min. of Foreign Affairs, 1998–2002; Chm., Internat. Cttee, 2002–04. Mem., Parly Assembly to Council of Europe, Strasbourg, 1993–98 (Vice Chm., Agric. and Rural Develt; Chm., Internat. Econ. Relns). Chief Negotiator of Slovak Republic for accession to EU, 1998–2002. Mem., Eur. Commn, 2004–09. Dep. Prime Minister, and Minister of Transport, Posts and Telecommunications, 2010–12. *Publications:* European Foreign Affairs Review: Slovakia's difficult but promising task, 1999; (jtly) Slovakia on the Road to the EU, 2002; (ed and contrib.) Slovakia on the Road to the European Union, 2003.

FIGES, Prof. Orlando Guy, PhD; FRSL; Professor of History, Birkbeck College, London University, since 1999; *b* 20 Nov. 1959; *s* of late John Figes and Eva Figes (*née* Unger); *m* 1990, Stephanie Palmer; two *d*. *Educ:* Gonville and Caius Coll., Cambridge (BA History 1982); Trinity Coll., Cambridge (PhD 1987). Fellow, 1984–99, Dir of Studies in History, 1988–98, Trinity Coll., Cambridge; University Lectr in History, Cambridge, 1987–99. FRSL 2003. *Publications:* Peasant Russia Civil War: the Volga countryside in revolution 1917–21, 1989, 3rd edn 2000; A People's Tragedy: the Russian Revolution 1891–1924, 1996 (Wolfson History Prize, W. H. Smith Lit. Award, NCR Book Award, Los Angeles Times Book Prize, 1997); (with B. Kolonitskii) Interpreting the Russian Revolution: the language and symbols of 1917, 1999; Natasha's Dance: a cultural history of Russia, 2002; The Whisperers: private life in Stalin's Russia, 2007; Crimea: the last crusade, 2010; Just Send Me Word: a true story of love and survival in the Gulag, 2012; Revolutionary Russia, 1891–1991, 2014. *Recreations:* soccer, music, gardening, wine, anything Italian. *Address:* Birkbeck College, Malet Street, WC1E 7HX.

FIGGIS, Sir Anthony (St John Howard), KCVO 1996; CMG 1993; HM Diplomatic Service, retired; HM Marshal of the Diplomatic Corps, 2001–08; *b* 12 Oct. 1940; *s* of Roberts Richmond Figgis and Philippa Maria Young; *m* 1964, Miriam Ellen, (Mayella), Hardt; two *s* one *d*. *Educ:* Rugby Sch.; King's Coll., Cambridge (Mod Langs). Joined HM Foreign (later Diplomatic) Service, 1962; Third Sec., Belgrade, 1963–65; Commonwealth Office, 1965–68; Second Sec., Pol Residency, Bahrain, 1968–70; FCO, 1970–71; First Sec. (Commercial), Madrid, 1971–74; CSCE delegn, Geneva, 1974–75; FCO, 1975–79; Madrid: Head of Chancery, 1979–80; Commercial Counsellor, 1980–82; Counsellor, Belgrade, 1982–85; Head of E European Dept, FCO, 1986–88; Counsellor and Head of Chancery, Bonn, 1988–89; Dir of Res., subseq. of Res. and Analysis, FCO, 1989–91; Asst Under-Sec. of State, FCO, and HM Vice-Marshal of the Diplomatic Corps, 1991–96; Ambassador to Austria, 1996–2000. Pres., Internat. Social Service (UK), 2001–08 (Patron, 2008–); Patron, Curriculum for Cohesion, 2011–. Trustee: Guildhall Sch. Trust, 2001–09; Swinfen Charitable Trust, 2008–; Gov., Goodenough Coll. for Overseas Graduates, 2004–; Royal Over-Seas League: Mem., Central Council, 2004–, Exec. Cttee, 2006–; Vice-Chm., 2007–09; Chm.,

2009–. Gentleman Usher of the Blue Rod, Order of St Michael and St George, 2002–. Freeman, City of London, 1996. *Recreations:* family, fly-fishing, tennis, music (piano). *Address:* 5 Bellevue Road, SW13 0BJ. *Club:* Royal Over-Seas League.

FIGGURES, Lt-Gen. Andrew Collingwood, CB 2009; CBE 1998; FREng; Chief Executive, British Transport Police Authority, since 2010; *b* 13 Nov. 1950; *s* of Colin Norman Figgures and Ethel Barbara Figgures (*née* Wilks); *m* 1978, Poppy Felicity Ann Ogley; one *d*. *Educ:* Loughborough Grammar Sch.; Welbeck Coll.; RMA Sandhurst; St Catharine's Coll., Cambridge (MA); Open Univ. (MBA). CEng 1991; MIEE 1991, FIET (FIEE 2005); FIMechE 1992; FREng 2011. Commnd, REME, 1970; served UK, Cyprus, BAOR, Former Republic of Yugoslavia, Iraq; attended Army Staff Coll., HCSC and RCDS; Comdr, Equipment Support, Land Comd, 1995; DOR (Land), Defence Systems, MoD, 1999–2000; Capability Manager (Manoeuvre), MoD, 2000–03; Dep. Commanding Gen., Jt Task Force 7, Iraq, 2003–04; Master Gen. of the Ordnance, and Tech. Dir, Defence Procurement Agency and Defence Logistics Orgn, MoD, 2004–06; Dep. Chief of Defence Staff (Equipment Capability), 2006–09. Col Comdt, 2002–11, Master Gen., 2012–, REME. MAPM 2005; FRAeS 2006; FCGI 2014. QCVS 2004. Hon. DSc Cranfield, 2008. *Address:* British Transport Police Authority, The Forum, 5th Floor North, 74–80 Camden Street, NW1 0EG. *Clubs:* Royal Over-Seas League; Leander.

FIGUERES, Christiana; Executive Secretary, UN Framework Convention on Climate Change, since 2010; *b* San Jose, Costa Rica, 7 Aug. 1956; *d* of Jose Figueres Ferrer and Karen Olsen; two *d*. *Educ:* London Sch. of Econs and Pol Sci. (MA Anthropol.). Minister Counsellor, Embassy of Costa Rica in Bonn, 1982–85; Dir, Internat. Cooperation, Min. of Planning, Costa Rica, 1987–88; COS to Minister of Agric., 1988–90; Dir, Tech. Secretariat, Renewable Energy in the Americas, 1993–94; Founder and Exec. Dir, Center for Sustainable Develt of the Americas, 1995–2003; Mem., Costa Rican climate change negotiating team, 1995–2009; Mem. Exec. Bd, Clean Develt Mechanism, and Vice Pres., Bureau of Conf. of the Parties, 2008–09. Hero for the Planet, 2001; Energy Efficiency Visionary, Energy Efficiency Global Forum, 2011; Climate Leadership Award, American Carbon Registry, 2013; Leadership Award, Climate Gp, 2014; Global Citizen Award, Unilever, 2015. *Publications:* chapters in: The UN Framework Convention on Climate Change Activities Implemented Jointly Pilot, 1999; Global Environmental Governance: options and opportunities, 2002; Global Environmental Governance: perspectives on the current debate, 2007; contribs to jls incl. Climate Policy, Envmtl Finance, Our Planet, Jl Envmt and Develt, Jl Sustainable Develt, Law and Policy. *Recreations:* long distance running, biking, hiking. *Address:* UN Framework Convention on Climate Change, PO Box 260124, 53153 Bonn, Germany. *E:* christianafigueres@gmail.com.

FILBEY, Air Vice-Marshal Keith David, CBE 1993; FRAeS; Chairman, since 2008, and Managing Director, since 2015, AirTanker Services Ltd (Chief Executive, 2004–08); *b* 16 Dec. 1947; *s* of late Sqn Ldr Cecil Hayward Filbey and of Barbara Filbey; *m* 1982, Anne Feaver; one *s* one *d*. *Educ:* Brentwood Sch.; Royal Air Force Coll., Cranwell. Royal Air Force: Pilot, 214 Sqn, 1969–76; Flt Comdr 51 Sqn, 1976–78; Personnel Officer, 1978–79; RAF Staff Coll., 1980; Staff Officer, HQ 1 Gp, 1981–83; OC, 216 Sqn, 1983–86; staff appts, MoD and HQ 1 Gp, 1986–90; OC, RAF Brize Norton, 1990–92; RCDS, 1993; Dep. Chief of Assessments Staff, Cabinet Office, 1993–96; Dir, Air Ops, 1997; Sen. DS (Air), RCDS, 1998–99; AOC No 38 Gp, 2000; AOC No 2 Gp, 2000–02. Business Develt Advr, Cobham PLC, 2003–04. Mem., Air League, 1999–. Pres., RAF Cricket Assoc., 2000–02. Gov., Sherborne Sch. for Girls, 2005–09. FRAeS 2000. Upper Freeman, Hon. Co. of Air Pilots (formerly GAPAN), 2000–. *Recreations:* walking, tennis, golf, choral music, ski-ing. *Clubs:* Royal Air Force, Innominate; Adastrian Cricket; Aero Golfing Soc. (Capt., 2013–14), Lilley Brook Golf.

FILDES, (David) Christopher, OBE 1994; financial journalist; *b* 10 Nov. 1934; *s* of late David Garland Fildes and Shelagh Fildes (*née* Jones), Manley, Cheshire; *m* 1st, 1969, Susan Patricia Mottram (*d* 1978); one *d* decd; 2nd, 1986, Frederica Bement Lord (*d* 1992); one step *d*. *Educ:* Clifton; Balliol Coll., Oxford. Financial journalist, 1963–; columnist, editor and broadcaster (The Times, Spectator, Daily Mail, Euromoney, Evening News, Investors Chronicle, Business Prog.); financial columnist: Euromoney, 1969–98; Daily Telegraph, 1984–2005; Spectator, 1984–2006; Evening Standard, 2005–09. Director: The Spectator (1828) Ltd, 1990–2004; London Mozart Players, 2000–09. Member: Council, GDST, 1999–2008; Rly Heritage Cttee, 1999–2010. Hon. Freeman, Drapers' Co., 2010. Hon. LittD Sheffield, 1999. Wincott Award for financial journalism, 1978 and 1986. *Publications:* A City Spectator, 2004. *Recreations:* racing, railways. *Address:* 4 Scarsdale Villas, W8 6PR. *Club:* Garrick.

FILER, Denis Edwin, CBE 1992; TD 1965 and 1977; FREng, FIMechE, FIChemE; Director of Engineering, ICI, 1981–88; *b* 19 May 1932; *s* of Francis and Sarah Filer; *m* 1957, Pamela Armitage; one *s* two *d*. *Educ:* Manchester Central Grammar Sch.; Manchester Univ. (Hons BSc Mech. Eng.); BA Open 1987. Commissioned REME (Nat. Service); served in Germany; REME TA, 1955–: Col, 1975–77; Hon. Col, 1978–87. ICI: Works Maintenance Engineer, 1960–67; Project Manager, Manchester, 1967–71; Project Manager, Holland (ICI Europa), 1971–73; Div. Maintenance Advisor, Organics Div., 1973; Plastics Div., Wilton Works: Works Engineer, 1973–76; Engineering Manager, Welwyn Garden City, 1976–78; Engineering & Production Dir, 1978–81; Dir-Gen., Engrg Council, 1988–95 (Mem., 1986–88; Chm., Continuing Educn and Trng Cttee; Mem., Standing Cttee for Industry). Chairman: Rolinx, 1978–81; Adwest Gp, then Adwest Automotive plc, 1994–97 (Dir, 1991–97); Electra Innvotec Corporate Ventures Ltd, then Innvotec Corporate Ventures Ltd, 2000–01 (Dir, 1989–2001); Director: Bexford, 1978–80; Engineering Services Wilton, 1978–81; Eur. Adv. Dir, Callidus Technologies Inc., 1991–99. Member: Council, IMechE, 1983–89 (Vice-Pres., 1987–89, 1996–98; Dep. Pres., 1998–2000; Pres., 2000–01; Chm., Process Industries Div. Bd, 1985–87); Board, Lloyd's Register of Quality Assurance, 1986–88, Gen. Cttee, Lloyd's Register, 1988–95. Chm., F and GP Cttee, 2002–04. Gov., Univ. of Hertfordshire, 1996– (Vice-Chm., 2002–04; Chm., 2004–07). FREng (FEng 1985). Liveryman, Engineers' Co., 1990– (Mem. Court, 1995–). Hon. DSc Herts, 1993. *Recreations:* tennis, sport, reading. *Address:* Brambles, Perrywood Lane, Watton Green, Watton-at-Stone, Hertford SG14 3RB. *T:* (01920) 830207. *Club:* Army and Navy.

FILER, (Douglas) Roger, FCA; Chairman, D & S Travel Supplies Ltd, since 2012 (Managing Director, 1997–2012); *b* 25 Feb. 1942; *s* of Horace Filer and Raie (*née* Behrman); *m* 1979, Vivienne Sara Green; one *s* one *d*. *Educ:* Clifton Coll.; St John's Coll., Oxford (MA); FCA 1970. Called to the Bar, Gray's Inn, 1979. Joined Association Television Group, 1967; Chief Accountant, Ambassador Bowling, 1967–69; Financial Controller, Bentray Investments, 1969–70; Financial Dir, M. Berman then Bermans & Nathans, 1971–73; Financial Controller, Stoll Theatres Corp./Moss Empires, 1974; Dir, 1982–92, Man. Dir, 1990–92, Stoll Moss Theatres; Man. Dir, Maybox Gp, subseq. Mayfair Theatres and Cinemas Ltd, 1993–96. *Recreations:* golf, history, walking. *Address:* Four Brim Hill, Hampstead Garden Suburb, N2 0HF. *T:* (020) 8455 7392.

FILKIN, family name of **Baron Filkin**.

FILKIN, Baron *cr* 1999 (Life Peer), of Pimlico in the City of Westminster; **David Geoffrey Nigel Filkin,** CBE 1997; Chairman, Centre for Ageing Better, since 2013; *b* 1 July 1944; *s* of Donald Geoffrey and Winifred Filkin; *m* 1974, Elizabeth Tompkins (*see* Elizabeth Filkin) (marr. diss. 1994); three *d*; *m* 2005, Brigitte Paupy. *Educ:* King Edward VI Sch., Five Ways, Birmingham; Clare Coll., Cambridge (MA Hist.); Manchester Univ. (DipTP); Birmingham Univ. (postgrad. study). Formerly MRTPI. Teacher on VSO, Ghana, 1966–67; Planner, Redditch Develt Corp., 1969–72; Manager, Brent Housing Aid Centre, London Borough of Brent, 1972–75; Dep. Chief Exec., Merseyside Improved Houses, 1975–79; Borough Housing Officer, Ellesmere Port and Neston Council, 1979–82; Dir of Housing, London Borough of Greenwich, 1982–88; Chief Exec., Reading BC, 1988–91; Sec., ADC, 1991–97. Dir, New Local Govt Network, 1995–2001. A Lord in Waiting (Govt Whip), 2001–02; Parliamentary Under-Secretary of State: Home Office, 2002–03; DCA, 2003–04; DFES, 2004–05. Chairman: All Party Parly Business Services Gp, 2000; H of L Merits Cttee, 2005–09; H of L Select Cttee on Public Services and Demographic Change, 2012–13; Founder and Chairman: The Parlt Choir, All Party Parly Gp, 2000–; Public Sector Res. Gp, 2005–07; 2020 Public Services Trust, 2007–11. Non-exec. Dir, Accord, 2005–07. Chairman: Beacon Council Adv. Panel, 1999–2001; St Albans Cathedral Music Trust, 2006–10. Adviser: on local govt, Joseph Rowntree Foundn, 1997–2001; H of C Envmt Cttee, 1998; Capgemini, 2005–; NSL (Services) (formerly NCP), 2006–12; Serco (Civil Govt), 2006–13. Trustee, Southbank Sinfonia, 2008–. *Publications:* (jtly) Better Outcomes, 2009; pamphlets, papers and articles on housing and local govt policy. *Recreations:* music, walking, swimming. *Address:* c/o House of Lords, SW1A 0PW. *T:* (020) 7219 0640.

FILKIN, Elizabeth Jill, CBE 2014; Chairman: Annington (formerly Annington Homes) Ltd, since 2008; Appointments Committee, General Pharmaceutical Council, since 2010; Independent Adviser, Metropolitan Police Service, 2011–12; *b* 24 Nov. 1940; *d* of Frances Trollope and John Tompkins; *m* 1974, David Geoffrey Nigel Filkin (marr. diss. 1994); three *d*; *m* 1996, Michael John Honey, *qv*. *Educ:* Birmingham Univ. (BSocSci). Organiser, Sparkbrook Assoc., 1961–64; Whyndham Deedes Fellowship, Israel, 1964; Res. Asst, Associate Lectr, Birmingham Univ., 1964–68; Lectr and Community Worker, Nat. Inst. for Social Work, 1968–71; Community Work Services Officer, London Borough of Brent, 1971–75; Lectr in Social Studies, Liverpool Univ., 1975–83; Chief Exec., Nat. Assoc. of CABx, 1983–88; Dir of Community Services, 1988–90, Asst Chief Exec., 1990–92, LDDC; Revenue Adjudicator, 1993–95; The Adjudicator, Inland Revenue, Customs and Excise, and Contribs Agency, 1995–99; Parly Comr for Standards, 1999–2002; Comr, Audit Commn, 1999–2004; Mem., 2002–08, Dep. Chm., 2005–08, Regulatory Decisions Cttee, FSA. Non-executive Director: Britannia Bldg Soc., 1992–98; Hay Management Consultants, 1992–98; Logica, 1995–98; Weatherall, Green & Smith, 1997–99; Jarvis plc, 2003–10; Sen. Ind. non-exec. Dir, Stanelco plc, 2003–10 (Chm., 2002–03); Chm., HBS, 2005–08. Chm., Lord Chancellor's Adv. Cttee on Legal Aid, 1991–94. Chairman: Rainer Foundn, 2004–08; Television (formerly Video) on Demand Assoc., 2004–10; Appts Gp, RPSGB, 2005–10; Advertising Adv. Cttee, 2005–11. Trustee: Tiri, 2008–12; Vodafone Foundn, 2009–. Dep. Chm. Council, Univ. of E London, 1999–2004. City Fellow, Hughes Hall, Cambridge Univ., 2003–06. *Publications:* The New Villagers, 1968; What a Community Worker Needs to Know, 1974; Community Work and Caring for Children, 1979; Caring for Children, 1979; (ed) Women and Children First, 1984. *Recreations:* walking, swimming.

FILLINGHAM, David James, CBE 2005; Chief Executive, Advancing Quality Alliance, since 2010; Senior Visiting Fellow, King's Fund, since 2012; *b* 28 March 1960; *s* of Thomas Fillingham and Irene Fillingham (*née* Webster); *m* 1982, Janet Green; two *d*. *Educ:* Cowley High Sch.; Peterhouse, Cambridge (MA History 1982); Henley Coll. (MBA 1993). Personnel Officer, Pilkington plc, 1982–84; Personnel Manager, 1984–88, Product Develt Manager, 1988–89, Pilkington Glass; Regl Personnel Manager, Mersey RHA, 1989–91; Gen. Manager, Wirral FHSA, 1991–93; Chief Executive: St Helens and Knowsley HA, 1993–97; N Staffordshire Hosp. NHS Trust, 1997–2001; Dir, NHS Modernisation Agency, 2001–04; Chief Exec., Royal Bolton Hosp. NHS Foundn Trust (formerly Bolton Hosps NHS Trust), 2004–10. Non-exec. Dir, Aintree Hosp. NHS Foundn Trust, 2013–. MIPM 1986. FRSA 2005. *Publications:* Lean Healthcare, 2008; various articles in mgt jls and health service pubns. *Recreations:* hill-walking, watching Rugby League, keen but inexpert skier. *Address:* Advancing Quality Alliance, St James's House, Pendleton Way, Salford M6 5FW; Springfield, Millbrow, St Helens, Merseyside WA10 4QQ. *T:* (01744) 29600.

FILLON, François Charles Amand; Member (UMP) Paris, National Assembly, since 2012; Prime Minister of France, 2007–12; *b* Le Mans, 4 March 1954; *m* 1980, Penelope Clarke; four *s* one *d*. *Educ:* Univ. du Maine, Le Mans (Master's degree Public Law 1976); Univ. René Descartes, Paris (Dip. d'études appliquées Public Law 1977). Intern, Agence France-Presse, Paris, 1976; Parly Asst to Joël Le Theule, MP, 1976–77; Dep. Hd, private office of Joël Le Theule, 1978–80; Hd, legislation dept, private office of André Giraud, 1981. Mayor, Sablé-sur-Sarthe, 1983–2001; Chm., Sarthe Gen. Council, 1992–98; Pays de la Loire Regional Council: Chm., 1998–2002; First Vice-Chm., 2002–04; Mem., 2004–07; Chm., Community of Communes of Sablé sur Sarthe, 2001–. MP (RPR) Sarthe, 1981–93, 1997–2002, 2007; Mem. of Senate for Sarthe, 2004–07. Minister: of Higher Educn and Res., 1993–95; for Information Technol. and the Post Office, 1995; Minister Delegate with responsibility for the Post Office, Telecommns and Space, 1995–97; Minister: of Social Affairs, Labour and Solidarity, 2002–04; for Nat. Educn, Higher Educn and Res., 2004–05. Pol Advr to Nicolas Sarkozy, UMP, 2004–07. Chm., France.9 think-tank, 2002; Founder Mem., Union en Mouvement, 2002. Nat. Sec., 1997, Spokesman, 1998, RPR. *Publications:* La France peut supporter la vérité, 2006. *Recreations:* mountain climbing, ski-ing, hiking, motor racing, running, mountain biking, cinema, reading.

FILMER-SANKEY, Dr William Patrick, FSA; Partner, Alan Baxter & Associates, since 2008 (Senior Engineer, 2000; Associate, since 2002; Senior Associate, 2005–08); *b* 13 Oct. 1957; *s* of late Patrick Hugh Filmer-Sankey and Josephine Filmer-Sankey; *m* 1981, Caroline Frances Sparrow; one *s* one *d*. *Educ:* Downside Sch.; New Coll., Oxford (BA Hons Mod. Hist. 1979); Inst. of Archaeology, Oxford (Dip. European Archaeol. 1981; DPhil 1989). Associate Archaeol Consultant, Oxford Archaeological Associates Ltd, 1990–93; Dir, Victorian Soc., 1993–2000. Dir, Snape Historical Trust, 1987–95; Hon. Sec., 1994–2000, Vice Pres., 2000–, British Archaeol Assoc.; Mem. Council, Soc. of Antiquaries, 2002–05. Vis. Fellow, Dept of Archaeol., Univ. of York, 2005–08. FSA 1997; FRSA 1998. Editor, Anglo-Saxon Studies in Archaeology and History, 1991–94. *Publications:* From the Dust of the Earth Returning: excavations of the Anglo-Saxon cemetery at Snape, Suffolk, 1990; (contrib.) Maritime Celts, Frisians and Saxons, 1991; (contrib.) The Age of Sutton Hoo, 1992; Snape Anglo-Saxon Cemetery: excavations and surveys 1824–1992, 2001; articles and papers. *Recreations:* archaeology, ornithology, sailing, deer stalking, Germany. *Address:* 57 Lavington Road, Ealing, W13 9LS. *T:* (020) 8579 0425.

FILOCHOWSKI, Jan; writer and speaker; Chief Executive Officer, Great Ormond Street Hospital for Children NHS Foundation Trust, 2012–13; *b* England, 27 April 1950; *s* of Tadeusz Filochowski and Jean Filochowski (*née* Royce); *m* 2006, Prof. Naomi Fulop; one *s* one *d* from a former marriage. *Educ:* Churchill Coll., Cambridge (BA 1972); Newcastle Univ. (MA 1973); Linacre Coll., Oxford. Civil Servant, DoH, 1975–85; United General Manager: Southend HA, 1986–87; Barts and St Mark's Hosps, 1987–88; Chief Executive Officer: Poole Hosps NHS Trust, 1989–97; Southmead Hosp. NHS Trust, 1998–99; Medway Hosps NHS Trust, 1999–2002; Royal United Hosps, Bath NHS Trust, 2002–03; Sen. Mgt Advr, NHS Authorities, SE, 2003–07; Advr to Prime Minister's Delivery Unit (pt-time), 2004–06; CEO, W Herts Hosps NHS Trust, 2007–12. Vis. Prof., Brunel Univ., 2004–; Vis. Fellow, Harvard Univ., 1997–98; NHS Univ. Fellow and Associate, Judge Business Sch., Univ. of Cambridge, 2004–05; Sen. Mem., Wolfson Coll., Cambridge, 2004–. *Publications:* Too Good to Fail?,

2013 (trans. Korean, 2014, Chinese, 2015). *Recreations:* swimming, ski-ing, walking, Real tennis.

See also Julian Filochowski.

FILOCHOWSKI, Julian, CMG 2004; OBE 1998; international development consultant, 2005–14; former Strategic Development and Advocacy Adviser, Jesuit Missions (GB); *b* 9 Dec. 1947; *s* of Tadeusz Filochowski and Jean Filochowski (*née* Royce); civil partnership 2006, Martin Pendergast. *Educ:* St Michael's Coll., Leeds; Churchill Coll., Cambridge (MA Econs). Economic Planning Advr, Min. of Finance, Belize, 1969–70; Central America Regl Co-ordinator, British Volunteer Prog., 1970–73; Co-ordinator, Educn Dept, Catholic Inst. for Internat. Relations, 1973–82; Dir, CAFOD, 1982–2003. Dir, Tablet Publishing Co., 2003–. Vis. Fellow, Clare Coll., Cambridge, 2005. Chm., Archbp Romero Trust, 2005–; Trustee: Thomson Foundn, 2008–12; Denis Hurley Assoc., 2011–; The Friars Aylesford, 2011–. Patron, Nat. Justice and Peace Network, 2012–. Dr *hc*: Univ. Centroamericana, San Salvador, 2004; Roehampton, 2006. *Publications:* Reflections on Puebla, 1980; Archbishop Romero, Ten Years On, 1991; (ed jtly) Opening Up: speaking out in the Church, 2005. *Recreations:* swimming, reading. *Address:* 57 Lyme Grove, E9 6PX.

See also Jan Filochowski.

FINALDI, Dr Gabriele Maria; Director, National Gallery, since 2015; *b* Barnet, 28 Nov. 1965; *s* of Remo and Iwonka Finaldi; *m* 1987, Maria Inés Luisa Irene Guerrero Parra; one *s* five *d*. *Educ:* St Joseph's Acad., Blackheath; Istituto Cristoforo Colombo, Piacenza, Italy; Dulwich Coll.; Courtauld Inst. of Art, London Univ. (BA 1987; MA 1989; PhD Hist. of Art 1995). Curator, Later Italian and Spanish Painting, National Gall., 1992–2002; Dep. Dir for Collections and Res., Museo del Prado, Madrid, 2002–15. Cavaliere dell'Ordine al Merito (Italy), 2006; Medalla de Oro al Merito de las Bellas Artes (Spain), 2015. *Publications:* Discovering the Italian Baroque: the Denis Mahon collection, 1997; Orazio Gentileschi at the Court of Charles I, 1999; The Image of Christ, 2000; El trazo oculto: dibujos subyacentes en pinturas de los siglos XV y XVI, 2006; The Art of Friendship, Murillo and Justino de Neve, 2012; contrib. articles to Burlington Mag., Apollo, Boletín del Museo del Prado. *Recreation:* playing the piano. *Address:* National Gallery, Trafalgar Square, WC2N 5DN.

FINCH, Hilary Ann; freelance writer and broadcaster, since 1980; *b* 2 May 1951; *d* of Francis Richard Finch and Hilda Grace (*née* Davey). *Educ:* Univ. of Exeter (MA); Hughes Hall, Cambridge (PGCE). Asst to Arts Editor, TES, 1976–80; feature writer and Music Critic, The Times, 1980–2015. *Recreation:* walking in Iceland. *Address:* 51 Victoria Road, Mortlake, SW14 8EX. *T:* (020) 8878 0957.

FINCH, Dame Janet (Valerie), DBE 2008 (CBE 1999); DL; PhD; FAcSS; Vice-Chancellor, Keele University, 1995–2010; *b* 13 Feb. 1946; *d* of Robert Bleakley Finch and Evelyn Muriel (*née* Smith); *m* 1st, 1967, Geoffrey O. Spedding (marr. diss. 1982); 2nd, 1994, David H. J. Morgan. *Educ:* Merchant Taylors' Sch. for Girls, Crosby; Bedford Coll., London (BA Hons Sociol.; Hon. Fellow, RHC, 1999); Univ. of Bradford (PhD Sociol. 1975). Lectr, Endsleigh Coll., Hull, 1974–76; Lancaster University: Lectr, then Sen. Lectr, 1976–88; Prof. of Social Relations, 1988–95; Pro-Vice-Chancellor, 1992–95. Non-executive Director: NW Regl HA, 1992–96; ONS, 1999–2008; HM Passport Service (formerly Identity and Passport Service), 2008–13; Office of the Health Professions Adjudicator, 2010–12; Chm., Ombudsman Services Ltd, 2010–; Member: Bd, QAA, 1997–2004; Council for Science and Technology, 2004–11 (Ind. Co-Chm., 2007–11); Ind. Panel, BBC Charter Review, 2004–05; Sci. and Technol. Honours Cttee, 2009–; Chairman: Health Cttee, Universities UK, 2003–06; Social Scis, REF, 2010–14; Rev. on Expanding Access to Res. Pubns, 2012–13; Chm., Nursing and Midwifery Council, 2015–. Chm., Preston CRC, 1980–85; Mem. Bd, Staffs Environmental Fund Ltd, 2000–04; Chm., Staffs Connexions Ltd, 2002–04. Member: ESRC, 1993–97 (Chm., Res. Grants Bd, 1994–97); MRC, 2014–. Chm. Exec., Brit. Sociol. Assoc., 1983–84. Governor: City of Stoke-on-Trent Sixth Form Coll., 1999–2002; Manchester Metropolitan Univ., 2002–10; Chm., Governing Bd, Life Study, 2011–. Trustee, Nat. Centre for Soc. Res., 2002–12 (Chm., 2007–12). DL Staffs, 1999. FAcSS (AcSS 1999). Hon. Fellow, Liverpool John Moores Univ., 2001. Hon. DLitt UWE, 1997; Hon. DSc: Edinburgh, 2000; Southampton, 2001; Hon. DEd: Lincoln, 2002; Queen Margaret UC, Edinburgh, 2003. *Publications:* Married to the Job, 1983, reprint 2012; Education as Social Policy, 1984; Research and Policy, 1986; Family Obligations and Social Change, 1989; Negotiating Family Responsibilities, 1993; Wills, Inheritance and Families, 1996; Passing On, 2000. *Recreation:* theatre-going. *Address:* The Cottage, 39 Millfields, Nantwich, Cheshire CW5 5HR. *Club:* Athenæum.

FINCH, John; Executive Director, Information Services and Technology, and Chief Information Officer, Bank of England, since 2013; *b* UK, 8 Sept. 1965; *m* 1994, Hilary; one *d*. *Educ:* Aireborough Grammar Sch., Leeds; Univ. of Hull (BSc (Econ) Hons Business Econs 1987). Mercury Communications, Cable & Wireless, 1988–95; Sen. Business Analyst, Heinz, 1995–97; Hd of Intranet Develt, Unipart, 1997–98; Hd of Internet/Intranet Develt, Nat. Bank of Kuwait, 1998–2001; Hd of Develt, SHL plc, 2002–05; Global Hd of Product Develt, 2005–11, Chief Information Officer, 2011–13, Experian. Non-exec. Dir, OPP Ltd, 2011–. Mem. Council, Nottingham Univ., 2014– (Mem., Audit Cttee, 2012–). *Recreations:* Leeds United FC supporter, England cricket watcher. *Address:* Bank of England, Threadneedle Street, EC2R 8AH. *E:* john.finch@bankofengland.co.uk.

FINCH, (John) Russell, FCIArb; Judge, Royal Court of Guernsey, since 2005; *b* 15 Feb. 1950; *s* of Reginald John Peter Fergusson Finch and Winifred Joan Finch (*née* Woods); *m* 1990, Anne Elizabeth Sergeant (*née* Lowe), *widow* of Peter Sergeant; one step *s*. *Educ:* Southern Grammar Sch. for Boys, Portsmouth; Queen Mary Coll., London (LLB); Univ. de Caen; Open Univ. (BA Hons, DipEurHum); Sheffield Hallam Univ. (MA 2004). FCIArb 1999. Articled to Clerk to Fareham and Gosport Justices, 1972–74; admitted solicitor, 1974; Court Clerk, 1974–75; Principal Asst, Aylesbury Gp of Magistrates' Courts, 1975–79; joined Dept of DPP, 1979; served on S, Metropolitan and Police Complaints Divs, 1979–86; Asst Br. Crown Prosecutor, Inner London CPS (Sen. Principal), 1986–88; joined Chambers of HM's Procureur (Attorney-Gen.) for Guernsey, 1988; Advocate, Royal Court of Guernsey, 1993; Crown Advocate, 1994; Stipendiary Magistrate and Coroner, 1997–2005, Sen. Magistrate, 2004–05, Guernsey; Lt-Bailiff and Judge, Matrimonial Causes Div., 1999–2011. Examr in Family Law and Criminal Law, Guernsey Bar, 2000–. Chm., Guernsey Inf. Exchange, 1999–2005. Member: US Naval Inst., Annapolis; HMS Hood Assoc. *Publications:* Practical Police Prosecuting, 1977; contrib. articles to various jls on magisterial law and practice. *Recreations:* chess (mainly correspondence) (former Vice-Pres., English Chess Fedn), history, listening to opera recordings. *Address:* Royal Court House, St Peter Port, Guernsey GY1 2NZ. *T:* (01481) 726161. *E:* russell.finch@gov.gg. *Club:* Civil Service.

FINCH, Karen Solveig Sinding Møller, OBE 1976; FIIC; Founder, 1975, and Principal, 1975–86, Textile Conservation Centre, Hampton Court Palace, subseq. at Winchester College of Art, Southampton University; *b* 8 May 1921; *d* of Søren Møller and Ellen Sinding Møller, Viborg, Denmark; *m* 1946, Norman Frank Finch (*d* 1996); one *d*. *Educ:* Kunsthaandvarkerskolen, Copenhagen. FIIC 1962 (Hon. Fellow 2004). Royal Sch. of Needlework, 1946–48; artwork room, V&A Mus., 1954–59; Independent Textile Conservation Services (based on textiles as historic documents), 1960–75; teacher, hist. of textile techniques, Courtauld Inst. of Art, 1969–86 (jtly inaugurated postgrad. course in textile conservation, 1973), Hon. Sen. Lectr, 1975–86. Dedication of Karen Finch Liby and Ref. Collection, Winchester Coll., 1993. Mem. Council, Leather Conservation Centre, UC Northampton (formerly Nene Coll.), 1978–. Emeritus Mem., Embroiderers' Guild, 1980. Hon. DLitt Southampton, 1999. Award for Lifetime Service to the Arts, NACF, 1987; Festschrift from colleagues and friends, 1999. *Publications:* Caring for Textiles, 1977; The Care and Preservation of Textiles, 1985, 2nd edn 1991; contrib. papers and articles to textile related societies and to professional jls. *Recreations:* family and friends, reading, the arts, TV. *Address:* 37 Bisterne Avenue, Walthamstow, E17 3QR. *T:* (020) 8520 7680.

FINCH, Hon. Lance (Sidney George); Associate Counsel, Guild Yule LLP, since 2014; *b* 16 June 1938; *s* of Herbert George and Rita Muriel Finch; *m* 1963, Judith A. C. Jack; one *s* two *d*. *Educ:* Univ. of British Columbia (LLB 1962). Barrister and solicitor, 1963–83; Justice: Supreme Court of BC, 1983–93; BC and Yukon Courts of Appeal, 1993–2001; Chief Justice of BC and Yukon Courts of Appeal, Chief Justice of BC, and Adminr of Govt, Province of BC, 2001–13. Hon. QC 2014. *Club:* Vancouver.

FINCH, Paul, OBE 2002; Director, World Architecture Festival, since 2008; Editorial Director, Architectural Review and Architects' Journal, since 2009; *b* 2 March 1949; *s* of William and Nancy Finch; *m* 1973, Susanna Phillips; one *s*. *Educ:* Woolverstone Hall, Suffolk; Selwyn Coll., Cambridge (MA). Dep. Ed., Estates Times, 1976–83; Ed., Building Design, 1983–94; Jt Ed., Planning in London, qly jl, 1991–; Ed., Architects' Jl, 1994–99; Editl Dir, Emap Construct, 1999–2008; Ed., The Architectural Rev., 2005–08. Dep. Chm., 1999–2005, Chm., 2009–14, CABE, then Design Council Cabe. Hon. Mem., Architectural Assoc., 2014. Hon. FRIBA 1994; Hon. Fellow, UCL, 2006. Hon. DSc Westminster, 2007. *Recreations:* cinema, novels, weekend cooking. *Address:* (office) Telephone House, 69–77 Paul Street, EC2A 4NA. *E:* paul.finch@emap.com. *Club:* Reform.

FINCH, Raymond Terence; Member (UK Ind) South East England, European Parliament, since 2014; *b* Liverpool, 2 June 1963; *s* of Raymond Walter and Lily Finch; *m* 1989, Debra Anne; one *s*. *Educ:* Cantril Farm Primary Sch.; Liverpool Inst. High Sch. for Boys. Mem. (UK Ind) Hants CC, 2013–. Fisheries spokesman, 2014–, Dep. Whip, 2014–, UKIP Gp, EP. Contested (UK Ind): SE England, EP, 2009; Eastleigh, 2010; Lewes, 2015. Hon. Sec., Gadfly Club. *Recreation:* watching Everton FC. *Address:* European Parliament, Rue Wiertz, Brussels 1047, Belgium. *E:* Raymond.finch@europarl.europa.eu.

FINCH, Sir Robert Gerard, Kt 2005; DL; Chairman, Royal Brompton and Harefield NHS Trust, 2009; Lord Mayor of London, 2003–04; *b* 20 Aug. 1944; *s* of late Brig. J. R. G. Finch; *m* 1971, Patricia Ann Ross; two *d*. *Educ:* Felsted Sch. Articled Clerk, Monro Pennefather & Co., 1963; joined Linklaters & Paines (later Linklaters), 1969; Partner, 1974–2005; Head of Property Dept, 1996–99. Chm., Liberty International plc, 2005–08. Director: IFSL, 2001–03; FF&P (Russia) Ltd, 2002–. A Church Comr, 1999–2008. St Paul's Cathedral: Mem. Council, 2000–08; Chairman: Endowment Trust, 2006–11; Mall Fund, 2009–; Property Industry Alliance, 2010–. Mem. Council, Lloyd's of London, 2009–12. Member Court: HAC, 1992–; King Edward's Sch., Witley, 1992– (Vice-Pres., 2006–); Christ's Hosp., 1992–. Governor: Legal Educn Foundn (formerly Coll. of Law), 2000–; St Paul's Sch., 2005–08. Trustee: Morden Coll., 2002–; Chichester Harbour Trust, 2009–; Nat. Heart and Lung Inst., 2009–. Mem., Corporate Bd, RA, 2005–08. Hon. Mem., LSO, 2004– (Mem. Adv. Council, 2005–). Hon. Bencher, Lincoln's Inn, 2012. Hon. Colonel: 31 Signal City of London Regt, 2007–10; Inns of Court, City & Essex Yeomanry, 2010–. Alderman, 1992, Sheriff, 1999–2000, City of London; Liveryman: Solicitors' Co., 1986– (Master, 1999–2000); Innholders' Co., 1991– (Mem. Ct Assts, 2001–; Master, 2010–11); Hon. Liveryman: Envmtl Cleaners' Co., 1998; Chartered Surveyors' Co., 2001; Leathersellers' Co., 2005. JP 1993, DL 2003, City of London. Hon. Fellow, Coll. of Estate Mgt, 2007–; Hon. FRICS 1999. DCL *hc* City Univ., 2003. *Recreations:* sailing, ski-ing, climbing. *Clubs:* Garrick, Ski Club of GB, Alpine Ski, East India; Itchenor Sailing (W Sussex).

FINCH, Russell; *see* Finch, J. R.

FINCH, Stephen Clark, OBE 1989; independent consultant, since 1989; *b* 7 March 1929; *s* of Frank Finch and Doris Finch (*née* Lloyd), Haywards Heath; *m* 1975, Sarah Rosemary Ann, *d* of Adm. Sir Anthony T. F. G. Griffin, GCB; two *d*. *Educ:* Ardingly; Sch. of Signals; RMCS. FInstAM; FCMA. Commnd Royal Signals 1948; served Korea, UK and BAOR; retired 1968. Joined British Petroleum Co. Ltd, 1968: Gp Telecommunications Manager, 1968–81; Sen. Adviser, Regulatory Affairs, 1981–84; Asst Co-ordinator, Inf. Systems Admin, 1984–89. Member: Adv. Panel on Licensing Value Added Network Services, 1982–87; Competition (formerly Monopolies and Mergers) Commn, 1985–2000. Member: Inst. of Administrative Management, 1968– (Mem. Council, 1981–84; Medallist, 1985); Communications Mgt Assoc. (formerly Telecommunications Managers Assoc.), 1968– (Exec. Cttee, 1971–91; Chm., 1981–84; Regulatory Affairs Exec., 1984–87; Dir, External Affairs, 1988–91); Council, Internat. Telecommunications Users Gp, 1981–94 (Chm., 1987–89). Member: City of London Deanery Synod, 1981– (Lay Chm., 1994–2008); London Diocesan Synod, 1994– (Bishop's Council, 1994–); City Churches Grants Cttee, 1994–2008; London DAC for Care of Churches, 1995–2006; City Churches Develt Gp, 1997–2002; Two Cities Area Council, 1997–2008 (Vice-Chm., 2001–07); Archdeacon of London's Finance Adv. Gp, 1999–2008; City Deanery Bishop's Adv. Gp, 2003–08. Trustee: Oxford Churches Trust, 1996– (Sec., 1997–); Dick Lucas Trust, 1999– (Chm., 1999–). Churchwarden, St Martin Outwich, 1987–2010. Freeman, City of London, 1975. FCMI. *Publications:* occasional contribs to learned jls. *Recreations:* sailing, ski-ing, swimming, music. *Address:* 97 Englefield Road, Canonbury, N1 3LJ. *T:* (020) 7226 2803. *Club:* National.

FINCH, Stephen John; Consultant, Locke Lord LLP, since 2014 (Partner, and Member, Global Executive Committee, 2012–13); *b* Carshalton, 28 Nov. 1950; *s* of Harry John and Evelyn Louise Finch; three *s* one *d*. *Educ:* London Univ. (LLB). Admitted solicitor, 1975; Solicitor: practising in Sydney and London, 1975–78; Lloyds Bowmaker, 1978–82; Citibank Internat., 1982–85; Partner: Hill Bailey, 1985–89; Salans, 1989–2012 (Chm., 2005–10). *Publications:* (contrib.) Practical Commercial Precedents. *Recreations:* anything involving mainstream sports, spending time with family and friends, restaurant owner. *Address:* c/o Locke Lord LLP, 201 Bishopsgate, EC2M 3AB. *T:* (020) 7861 9011, *Fax:* (020) 7785 9016. *E:* sfinch@lockelord.com.

FINCH HATTON, family name of **Earl of Winchilsea and Nottingham**.

FINCH-KNIGHTLEY, family name of **Earl of Aylesford**.

FINCHAM, Peter Arthur; Director of Television, ITV, since 2008; *b* 26 July 1956; *s* of late Arthur and Joan Fincham; *m* 1995, Clare Lewthwaite; two *s* two *d*. *Educ:* Tonbridge Sch.; Churchill Coll., Cambridge (BA English 1977). Man. Dir, TalkBack Prodns, 1986–2002; Chief Exec., talkbackThames, 2003–05; Controller, BBC1, 2005–07. *Address:* ITV plc, 21st Floor, London Television Centre, 58–72 Upper Ground, SE1 9LT.

FINDLATER, (John) Donald; child protection worker and commentator; Director, Research and Development, Lucy Faithfull Foundation, since 2008 (Manager, Wolvercote Clinic, 1995–2002; Deputy Director, 1997–2007); Director, Stop it Now! UK and Ireland, since 2008 (Manager, UK and Ireland helpline, 2002–07); *b* 23 March 1955; *s* of Robert and Mary Findlater; *m* 1977, Jacqueline Durrant; four *s* one *d*. *Educ:* King George V Grammar Sch., Southport; Univ. of Kent, Canterbury (BA Hons Law 1976); Univ. of East Anglia (MA Soc. Work 1981; CQSW 1981). Probation Officer, Hereford and Worcester Probation Service, 1981–85; Probation Officer, then Sen. Probation Officer, Surrey Probation Service, 1985–97. Consultant: to Home Office, DfES, later DCSF, and DoH on sexual abuse prevention; to RC, Anglican and Methodist Churches on sexual abuse prevention and sex offender rehabilitation; Member: Sir Roger Singleton's panel of child protection experts,

2006–08; Ind. Safeguarding Authy, 2008–12; Disclosure and Barring Service, 2012–13. Trustee: Langley House Trust, 2003–08; Sanctuary, 2006–08. FRSA. *Publications:* contrib. to professional jls and ref. texts. *Recreations:* spending time with my family, DIY, gardening, walking, visiting historic buildings, finding and sharing hope. *Address:* Lucy Faithfull Foundation, Nightingale House, 46–48 East Street, Epsom, Surrey KT17 1HB. *T:* 07778 532851. *E:* dfindlater@lucyfaithfull.org.

FINDLAY, Alastair Donald Fraser, FCIWEM; Chief Executive, North of Scotland Water Authority, 1995–2000; *b* 3 Feb. 1944; *s* of late Rev. Donald Fraser Findlay and Isobel Ellis Findlay (*née* Louden); *m* 1969, Morag Cumming Peden; one *s* three *d*. *Educ:* Pitlochry High Sch.; Kelso High Sch.; Univ. of Edinburgh (MA (Hons) Mental Philosophy). FCIWEM 1996. Asst Principal, Dept of Agriculture and Fisheries for Scotland, 1966–70; Private Sec. to Jt Parly Under Sec. of State, Scottish Office, 1970–71; Principal, Scottish Office, 1971–74; on loan to FCO as First Sec. (Agric. and Food), The Hague, 1975–78; Asst Sec., Higher Educn Div., Scottish Educn Dept, 1979–82; Fisheries Div., 1982–85, Livestock Products Div., 1985–88, Dept of Agric. and Fisheries for Scotland; Under Sec., IDS, then Scottish Office Industry Dept, 1988–93; Fisheries Sec., Scottish Office Agric. and Fisheries Dept, 1993–95. Advr to Scottish Fishermen's Orgn, 2005–. Mem., Barnardo's Scottish Cttee, 2002–05. Trustee: Lloyds TSB Foundn for Scotland, 1998–2004 (Dep. Chm., 2003–04); Univ. of Highlands and Islands Develt Trust (formerly Univ. of Highlands and Islands Millennium Inst. Develt Trust), 2003–08; The Queen Mother's Memorial Fund for Scotland, 2003–09. Treas., Boroughmuir RFC, 2001–08 (Dir, 2004–09). *Recreations:* walking, motor cars, Rugby spectating.

FINDLAY, Donald Russell; QC (Scot.) 1988; after dinner and motivational speaker; *b* 17 March 1951; *s* of James Findlay and Mabel Findlay (*née* Muirhead); *m* 1982, Jennifer Edith (*née* Borrowman). *Educ:* Harris Academy, Dundee; Univ. of Dundee (LLB 1st cl. Hons); Univ. of Glasgow (MPhil). Mem., Faculty of Advocates, 1975– (Chm., Faculty Services Ltd, 2003–05; Chm., Criminal Bar Assoc., 2010–12); Lectr in Law, Heriot-Watt Univ., 1976–77. Mem., Lothian Health Bd, 1987–91. Vice Chm., Glasgow Rangers FC, 1992–99 (Dir, 1991–99); Chm., Cowdenbeath FC, 2010–. Vice Chairman: N Cunninghame Cons. and Unionist Assoc., 1989–92; Leith Cons. and Unionist Assoc., 1985–88. Rector, St Andrews Univ., 1993–99. Vice Pres., Assoc. for Internat. Cancer Res., 1996–. Columnist, Scottish Daily Express, 1995–97; radio and television broadcaster. FRSA 1997. *Publications:* Three Verdicts (novel), 1998; contribs to Scots Law Times and various medico-legal publications. *Recreations:* Glasgow Rangers FC, Egyptology, malt whisky, photography, cooking, drinking claret, politics, ethics; challenging authority. *Address:* Faculty of Advocates, Parliament House, Edinburgh EH1 1RF. *T:* (0131) 226 2881; Mackinnon Stable, Glasgow High Court, 1 Mart Street, Saltmarket, Glasgow G1 5NA.

FINDLAY, Irene, OBE 2004; executive coach, since 2011; Managing Director, Hurria, since 2011; *b* Greenock, Scotland; 24 Oct.; *d* of John Kerrigan Findlay and Olive Findlay (*née* Maddock). *Educ:* Greenock Acad.; Univ. of E Anglia (CQSW); John Moores Univ., Liverpool (MBA). Asst Dir of Social Services, Wirral MBC, 1991–2000; Dep. Dir, Social Services Inspectorate, 2001–03; Advr on Social Care Reconstruction, Iraq, 2003–04; Dir of Adult Social Services, 2004–10, Dir of Health Integration, 2010–11, London Bor. of Barnet. FRSA 2005–12. *Recreations:* sailing (crewed Tall Ships Race, 2011), ski-ing, internet/ technology, wine (currently studying for wine qualification). *T:* 07867 537535, (UAE) 501405236. *E:* irenefindlay@thewatergardenslondon.com.

FINDLAY, James de Cardonnel; QC 2008; *b* Girvan, 27 June 1961; *s* of John Findlay and Rosemary Findlay; *m* 1994, Caroline Pedersen; two *s* one *d*. *Educ:* Trinity Coll., Glenalmond; Magdalene Coll., Cambridge (BA 1983). Called to the Bar, Middle Temple, 1984; admitted Advocate, 2008; in practice as barrister specialising in administrative, planning and licensing law in England and Scotland. *Recreations:* walking, supporting Scottish Rugby. *Address:* Cornerstone Barristers, 2–3 Gray's Inn Square, WC1R 5JH. *T:* (020) 7242 4986. *E:* jamesf@cornerstonebarristers.com. *Club:* Lansdowne.

FINDLAY, Neil; Member (Lab) Lothian, Scottish Parliament, since 2011; *b* Broxburn, 6 March 1969; *s* of Ian Findlay and Margaret Findlay (*née* McAuley); *m* 1998, Fiona Miller; one *d*. *Educ:* St Kentigern's Acad., Blackburn; Univ. of Strathclyde (BA 1996); Univ. of Glasgow (PGCE 2003). Apprentice and tradesman bricklayer, 1986–93; Housing Official, various housing orgns, 1996–2002; teacher, several schs, Falkirk Council, 2003–11. Mem. (Lab), West Lothian Council, 2003–12. Member: UNITE; EIS; Campaign for Socialism; Cuba Solidarity Campaign. *Recreations:* golf, cooking, going for a pint, gardening. *Address:* Scottish Parliament, Edinburgh EH99 1SP. *T:* (0131) 348 6896. *E:* neil.findlay.msp@scottish.parliament.uk. *Club:* Greenburn Golf.

FINDLAY, Ralph Graham; Chief Executive, Marston's plc (formerly The Wolverhampton & Dudley Breweries plc), since 2001; *b* 9 Jan. 1961; *s* of James Findlay and Margaret Findlay (*née* Teesdale); *m* 1990, Louise MacKenzie; one *s* one *d*. *Educ:* James Gillespie's High Sch., Edinburgh; Univ. of Edinburgh (BSc Hons 1983). FCA 1988; MCT (Dip). Price Waterhouse, 1984–90; Treasury Manager, Bass plc, 1990–92; Chief Accountant, Geest plc, 1992–94; joined Wolverhampton & Dudley Breweries plc, 1994, Gp Finance Dir, 1996–2001. Non-exec. Dir, Bovis Homes Gp plc, 2015–. Chm., British Beer and Pub Assoc., 2009–11. *Recreations:* family, reading, music, running, sport. *Address:* Marston's plc, Marston's House, Brewery Road, Wolverhampton WV1 4JT. *T:* (01902) 329530, *Fax:* (01902) 778007. *E:* ralph.findlay@marstons.co.uk. *Clubs:* South Staffordshire Golf (Wolverhampton); Wolverhampton and Newbridge Lawn Tennis and Squash.

FINDLAY, Richard, CBE 2013; Chairman, Creative Scotland, since 2015; *b* Berlin, 5 Nov. 1943; *s* of Rudi and Inge Barth; *m* 1971, Elspeth Macbeth; two *s* one *d*. *Educ:* Royal Scottish Acad. of Music and Drama. Chief Exec., Scottish Radio Hldgs plc, 1996–2004. Chairman: Scottish Television plc, 2007–13; Innovate Financial Services, 2008–; Youth Media Gp Ltd, 2010–; New Wave Media Ltd, 2013–. Founding Chairman, Nat. Theatre of Scotland, 2003–13. *Recreation:* boating. *Address:* Creative Scotland, Waverley Gate, 2–4 Waterloo Place, Edinburgh EH1 3EG. *T:* (0131) 333 2000. *Club:* Scottish Arts (Edinburgh).

FINDLAY, Richard Martin; entertainment lawyer and business affairs consultant, since 2012; Entertainment Law Partner, 1990–2012, Head of Hospitality and Leisure and Charity Law Team, 2009–12, Tods Murray, LLP; *b* 18 Dec. 1951; *s* of late Ian Macdonald Semple Findlay and Kathleen Lightfoot or Findlay. *Educ:* Gordon Schs, Huntly; Univ. of Aberdeen (LLB). Trainee Solicitor, Wilsone & Duffus, Advocates, Aberdeen, 1973–75; Asst Solicitor, Maclay Murray & Spens, Glasgow, 1975–79; Partner, Ranken & Reid, SSC, Edinburgh, 1979–90. Mem., Business in the Arts Placement Scheme, 1994–2012; Associate Mem., 1996–2000, Mem., 2000–13, Theatrical Management Assoc. Chm., Red FM Ltd, 2004–05; Director: Krazy Kat Theatre Co., 1984–86; Edinburgh Music Theatre Co. Ltd, 1985–88; Gallus Theatre Co. Ltd, 1996–98; Dance Base Ltd, 1997–98; Royal Lyceum Theatre Co. Ltd, 1999–2013 (Vice-Chm., 2002–13); Audio Description Film Fund Ltd, 2000–09; Hill Adamson (formerly Scottish Nat. Photography Centre Ltd), 2002–12; Scottish Screen, 2003–07; Scottish Screen Enterprises, 2003–07; Luxury Edinburgh Ltd, 2006–12; David Hughes Dance Productions Ltd, 2010– (Chm., 2012–); Angel Scene Ltd, 2011–12; Scottish Documentary Inst., 2014–; Stills Gallery, 2015–. Company Secretary: Edinburgh Arts and Entertainment Ltd, 1987–2000; Duddingston Coachworks Ltd, 1988–91; Edinburgh Internat. Jazz and Blues Fest. Ltd, 1988–2012; Edinburgh Capital Gp Ltd, 1989–2001; French Film Fest. Ltd, 1992–2000; Centre for Moving Image, 1993–95; Filmhouse Trading Ltd, 1993–95; Italian Film Fest. Ltd, 1994–2002; Great Distribution Ltd, 1995–2000; Scottish Screen Locations 1996–2000; Moonstone Ltd, 1997–2008; Assoc. of Integrated Media, Highlands and Islands Ltd, 2002–09. Dir, Lothian Gay and Lesbian Switchboard Ltd, 1998–2002; Company Secretary: Gay Men's Health Ltd, 1995–2012; Positive Voice, 1999–2006. Member: Internat. Assoc. of Entertainment Lawyers, 1990–2012; Internat. Entertainment & Multimedia Law & Business Network, 1995–2012; Scottish Media Lawyers Soc., 1995–2012; IBA, 1993–99; BAFTA, 1990– (Mem. Mgt Cttee, BAFTA (Scotland), 1998–2004); Writers' Guild, 1993–2002; New Producers Alliance, 1993–98; Inst. of Art and Law, 1996–98; RTS, 2003–05. Mem., Fedn of Scottish Theatre, 1997–2012; Founder Mem., Screen Academy Scotland Adv. Bd, 2006–12. Hon. Patron, Pitlochry Fest. Th., 2013–. Trustee: Peter Darrell Trust, 1996–2004; Frank Mullen Trust, 2004–08. Part-time Lectr on Law of Film, Napier Univ., then Screen Acad., Scotland, 1997–. Man. Editor, i-2-i–the business journal for the international film industry (formerly Internat. Film Business, Finance and Law Rev.), 1995–97; Scotland Ed., Methuen Amateur Theatre Handbook; Mem., Editl Bd, The Firm Mag., 2009–12. *Recreations:* photography, theatre, cycling, film, music, Highland Games, genealogy. *Address:* 1 Darnaway Street, Edinburgh EH3 6DW. *T:* (0131) 226 3253, 07850 327725. *E:* richard@darnaway.co.uk.

FINE, Anne, OBE 2003; FRSL; writer; Children's Laureate, 2001–03; *b* 7 Dec. 1947; *d* of Brian Laker and Mary Baker; *m* 1968, Kit Fine (marr. diss. 1991); two *d*. *Educ:* Northampton High School for Girls; Univ. of Warwick (BA Hons History and Politics). Guardian Children's Fiction Award, 1990; Carnegie Medal, 1990, 1993; Children's Author of the Year, Publishing News, 1990, 1993. FRSL 2003. *Publications: for older children:* The Summer House Loon, 1978; The Other Darker Ned, 1978; The Stone Menagerie, 1980; Round Behind the Icehouse, 1981; The Granny Project, 1983; Madame Doubtfire, 1987; Goggle-Eyes, 1989; The Book of the Banshee, 1991; Flour Babies, 1992 (Whitbread Award, 1993); Step by Wicked Step, 1995; The Tulip Touch, 1996 (Whitbread Award, 1997); Very Different, 2001; Up on Cloud Nine, 2002; The Road of Bones, 2006; The Devil Walks, 2011; Blood Family, 2013; Blue Moon Day, 2014; *for younger children:* Scaredy-Cat, 1985; Anneli the Art Hater, 1986; Crummy Mummy and Me, 1988; A Pack of Liars, 1988; Stranger Danger, 1989; Bill's New Frock, 1989 (Smarties Award, 1990); The Country Pancake, 1989; A Sudden Puff of Glittering Smoke, 1989; A Sudden Swirl of Icy Wind, 1990; Only a Show, 1990; Design-a-Pram, 1991; A Sudden Glow of Gold, 1991; The Worst Child I Ever Had, 1991; The Angel of Nitshill Road, 1991; Same Old Story Every Year, 1992; The Chicken Gave it to Me, 1992; The Haunting of Pip Parker, 1992; How To Write Really Badly, 1996; Press Play, 1996; Jennifer's Diary, 1997; Loudmouth Louis, 1998; Roll Over, Roly, 1999; Charm School, 1999; Bad Dreams, 2000; The Jamie and Angus Stories, 2002 (Boston Globe Horn Book Award, 2003); The More the Merrier, 2003; Return of The Killer Cat, 2003; Frozen Billy, 2004; Nag Club, 2004; The Killer Cat Strikes Back, 2006; Ivan the Terrible, 2007; The Killer Cat's Birthday Bash, 2008; The Killer Cat's Christmas, 2009; Eating Things on Sticks, 2009; Under a Silver Moon, 2010; Trouble in Toadpool, 2012; The Killer Cat Runs Away, 2013; The Only Child Club, 2013; Party Club, 2015; Under the Bed, 2015; *picture books:* Poor Monty, 1991; Ruggles, 2002; *novels:* The Killjoy, 1986; Taking the Devil's Advice, 1990; In Cold Domain, 1994; Telling Liddy, 1997; All Bones and Lies, 2001; Raking the Ashes, 2005; Fly in the Ointment, 2008; Our Precious Lulu, 2009. *Recreations:* reading, walking. *Address:* c/o David Higham Associates, 7th Floor, Waverley House, 7–12 Noel Street, W1F 8GQ.

FINE, Prof. Leon Gerald, FRCP, FRCPGlas, FACP, FMedSci; Chairman, Department of Biomedical Sciences, since 2007, and Vice-Dean for Research and Graduate Research Education, Cedars-Sinai Medical Center and University of California, Los Angeles; *b* 16 June 1943; *s* of Matthew Fine and Jeanette (*née* Lipshitz); *m* 1966, Brenda Sakinovsky; two *d*. *Educ:* Univ. of Cape Town, SA (MB, ChB). FACP 1978; FRCP 1986; FRCPGlas 1993. Internship and Residency in Internal Medicine, Tel Aviv Univ. Med. Sch., Israel, 1967–70; Asst Prof. of Medicine, Albert Einstein Coll. of Medicine, NY, 1975–76; University of Miami School of Medicine: Asst Prof., 1976–78; Associate Prof., 1978–82; Prof. of Medicine and Chief, Div. of Nephrology, UCLA, 1982–91; University College London: Prof. and Hd, Dept of Medicine, 1991–2002; Dean, Faculty of Clinical Sci., Royal Free and UC Med. Sch., 2002–06. Founder FMedSci 1998. Editor-in-Chief, Nephron, 2003–14. *Publications:* contribs in professional jls on pathophysiology of chronic renal disease, renal growth control, renal growth responses to acute and chronic injury, genetic manipulation of the kidney, and history of medicine. *Recreations:* collecting rare books on the history of medicine, fine printing and photography, book-binding. *Address:* Department of Biomedical Sciences, Cedars-Sinai Medical Center, Davis Building, Room 5093, 8700 Beverly Boulevard, Los Angeles, CA 90048, USA. *T:* (310) 4236457. *E:* leon.fine@cshs.org. *Club:* Athenæum.

FINE, Nigel, CEng, FICE, FIET; Chief Executive, Institution of Engineering and Technology, since 2009; *b* Cardiff, 21 June 1957; *s* of Mossey and Esther Fine; *m* 1982, Ruth; two *s* one *d*. *Educ:* Cardiff High Sch.; Univ. of Manchester Inst. of Sci. and Technol. (BSc Civil Engrg); London Business Sch. (MBA 1984). MICE 1982, FICE 2011; CEng 1983; FIET 2009. Grad. and Project Engr, John Laing plc, 1978–82; EMEA Strategy and Business Develt Dir, Internat. Paint Ltd, 1984–94; Associate Partner, Andersen Consulting (Accenture), 1994–99; Man. Dir, EMEA and Asia Pacific, Experian plc, 1999–2009. *Recreations:* family, theatre, travel, sport. *Address:* Institution of Engineering and Technology, Savoy Place, WC2R 0BL. *T:* (020) 7344 5400. *E:* nfine@theiet.org.

FINER, Dr Elliot Geoffrey, FRSC; Director General, Chemical Industries Association, 1996–2002; *b* 30 March 1944; *s* of Reuben and Pauline Finer; *m* 1970, Viviane Kibrit; two *s*. *Educ:* Royal Grammar Sch., High Wycombe; Cheadle Hulme Sch.; East Barnet Grammar Sch.; St Catharine's Coll., Cambridge (BA 1965); Univ. of East Anglia (MSc 1966; PhD 1968). CChem, FRSC 1993. Unilever Research, Welwyn, 1968–75; Dept of Energy, 1975–90; Dir for Industry and Commerce, 1983–86, Dir Gen., 1988–90, Energy Efficiency Office; Under Secretary, 1988; Head of Management Develt Gp, Cabinet Office, 1990–92; Head of Chemicals and Biotechnology Div., DTI, 1992–95. Director: Spillers Foods Ltd, 1989–92; Vestry Court Ltd, 1997–. Dir, Enfield PCT, 2003–08. Mem., BBSRC, 1994–95. Pres., Assembly of European Chemical Industry Fedns, 1998–2000. Mem. Council, RSC, 2002–09 (Hon. Treas., 2005–09). Chm., Ramsay Meml Fellowship Trust, 2007–15. Hon. FEI (CIE 1985). *Publications:* scientific papers and articles in learned jls. *Recreations:* home and family, reading, DIY. *Club:* Athenæum.

FINESTEIN, Jonathon Eli; a District Judge (Magistrates' Courts), Manchester and Salford, 2012–15; *b* 9 April 1950; *s* of Gustav Finestein and Esther Finestein; *m* 1985, Elaine March; one *d*. *Educ:* Hull Grammar Sch.; Leeds Univ. (LLB). Called to the Bar, Gray's Inn, 1973; practice in Hull; Asst Stipendiary Magistrate, 1989–92; Stipendiary Magistrate for Lancs and Merseyside, 1992–2001; Stipendiary Magistrate, later a District Judge (Magistrates' Courts), Salford, 2001–12; Asst Recorder, 1992–96; Recorder, 1996–2008. *Recreations:* watching all sports, walking. *E:* jfinestein@gmail.com.

FINGLETON, John, DPhil; Senior Adviser: Cabinet Office, since 2012; HM Treasury, since 2012; company director, since 2013; *b* 21 Sept. 1965. *Educ:* Trinity Coll., Dublin (BA Mod 1987); Nuffield Coll., Oxford (MPhil Econs 1989, DPhil 1991). Researcher, LSE, 1991; Lectr in Econs, Trinity Coll., Dublin, 1991–2000; Chm., Competition Authy of Ireland, 2000–05; CEO, OFT, 2005–12. Visiting Scholar: Université Libre de Bruxelles, 1995; Univ. of Chicago, 1998–2000. *Publications:* (jtly) Competition Policy and the Transformation of Central Europe, 1996; (jtly) The Dublin Taxi Market: re-regulate or stay queuing?, 1998; contrib. Global Agenda.

FINGRET, His Honour Peter; a Circuit Judge, 1992–2005; *b* 13 Sept. 1934; *s* of late Iser and Irene Fingret; *m* 1st, 1960, June Moss (marr. diss. 1980); one *s* one *d*; 2nd, 1980, Dr Ann

Lilian Mary Hollingworth (*née* Field) (*d* 2011). *Educ:* Leeds Modern Sch.; Leeds Univ. (LLB Hons); Open Univ. (BA). President, Leeds Univ. Union, 1957–58. Admitted Solicitor, 1960. Partner: Willey Hargrave & Co., Leeds, 1964–75; Fingret, Paterson & Co., Leeds, 1975–82. Stipendiary Magistrate for Co. of Humberside sitting at Kingston-upon-Hull, 1982–85; Metropolitan Stipendiary Magistrate, 1985–92; a Recorder, 1987–92; a Pres., Mental Health Rev. Tribunal, 1993–2005. Mem., Parole Bd, 2003–. Chm., Lord Chancellor's Adv. Cttee on JPs for Cities of London and Westminster, 2005–07. Councillor, Leeds City Council, 1967–72; Member: Court, Univ. of Leeds, 1975–85; Cttee, Leeds Internat. Piano Competition, 1981–85. Freeman: Musicians' Co., 2002– (Liveryman, 2010–); City of London, 2004–. *Recreations:* golf, music, theatre. *E:* peterfingret@hotmail.com. *Clubs:* Garrick, MCC.

FINK, family name of **Baron Fink**.

FINK, Baron *cr* 2011 (Life Peer), of Northwood in the County of Middlesex; **Stanley Fink;** Chief Executive, International Standard Asset Management, since 2008; *b* 15 Sept. 1957; *s* of Louis and Janet Fink; *m* 1981, Barbara Paskin; two *s* one *d*. *Educ:* Manchester Grammar Sch.; Trinity Hall, Cambridge (MA Law). ACA. Qualified chartered accountant, Arthur Andersen, 1979–82; Financial Planning, Mars Confectionery, 1982–83; Vice Pres., Citibank NA, 1983–86; Man Group plc: Dir, 1987–2008; Gp Finance Dir, 1992–96; Man. Dir, Asset Mgt, 1996–2000; Chief Exec., 2000–07; Dep. Chm., 2007–08; Chm., Man Investments, 2002–07. Principal Treas., Cons. Party, 2010–13 (Co-Treas., 2010–11). *Recreations:* golf, tennis, ski-ing. *Address:* House of Lords, SW1A 0PW. *E:* stanley.fink@isam.com.

FINK, Prof. George, FRCPE; FRSE; FRSB; Professorial Research Fellow, University of Melbourne and Mental Health Research Institute of Victoria, Australia, 2007 (Director, 2004–06; Director of Laboratory Research, 2003–04); Honorary Professorial Research Fellow, Florey Institute of Neuroscience and Mental Health, University of Melbourne, since 2014; Hon. Professor, University of Melbourne Centre for Neuroscience, 2008–13; *b* 13 Nov. 1936; *s* of John H. Fink and Therese (*née* Weiss); *m* 1959, Ann Elizabeth Langsam; one *s* one *d*. *Educ:* Melbourne High Sch. (Dist. Old Boy); Univ. of Melbourne (MB BS Hons 1960; MD 1978); Hertford Coll., Univ. of Oxford (DPhil 1967). FRSE 1989; FRCPE 1998. Jun. and sen. house officer, Royal Melbourne and Alfred Hosps, Victoria, Australia, 1961–62; Demonstrator in Anatomy, Monash Univ., Victoria, 1963–64; Nuffield Dominions Demonstrator, Oxford Univ., 1965–67; Sen. Lectr in Anatomy, Monash Univ., 1968–71; Univ. Lectr 1971–80, Official Fellow in Physiology and Med., Brasenose Coll., 1974–80, Oxford Univ.; Dir, MRC Brain Metabolism Unit, 1980–99, Hon. Prof., 1984–, Univ. of Edinburgh; Vice-Pres. of Res., 1999–2003, consultant, 2003–04, Pharmos Corp. Royal Soc.-Israel Acad. Exchange Fellow, 1979, Vis. Scientist, Neurobiol., 2009–11, Weizmann Inst. of Sci., Israel; Walter Cottman Fellow and Vis. Prof., Monash Univ., 1985, 1989; Arthur Fishberg Prof., Mt Sinai Med. Sch., NY, 1988; Visiting Professor: Neurobiol., Mayo Clinic, Minnesota, 1993; Neurobiol. and Behavior, Rockefeller Univ., NY, 1996–2000. Prosector in Anatomy, Melbourne Univ., 1956; Wolfson Lectr, Univ. of Oxford, 1982; first G. W. Harris Lectr, Physiol Soc., Cambridge, 1987. Pres., European Neuroendocrine Assoc., 1991–95; Member: Council, European Neuroscience Assoc., 1980–82, 1994–98; Mental Health Panel, Wellcome Trust, 1984–89; Steering Cttee, British Neuroendocrine Group, 1984–88 (Trustee, BNG, 1990–); Co-ordinating Cttee, ESF Network on Neuroimmunomodulation, 1990–93. Chm., 5 Year Assessment Biomed. Prog., 1991–96; Monitor, EU Biomed. 2 Prog., 1995. Senior Member: Physiological Soc., 1967; Soc. for Endocrinology, 1967; British Pharmacological Soc., 1990; Mem., Internat. Coll. of Neuropsychopharmacology, 2010. FRSB (FSB 2015). Hon. Mem., British Neuroendocrine Soc., 2005. Emeritus Member: Soc. for Neurosci., 2008; Endocrine Soc., 2008; Genetics Soc. of America, 2009. Lifetime Achievement Award, Internat. Soc. of Psychoneuroendocrinology, 2000. Trustee, Jl of Neuroendocrinology, 1990–2003. *Publications:* (ed with L. J. Whalley) Neuropeptides: Basic and Clinical Aspects, 1982; (ed with A. J. Harmar and K. W. McKerns) Neuroendocrine Molecular Biology, 1986; (ed) Transmitter Molecules in the Brain, 1987; (ed with A. J. Harmar) Neuropeptides: A Methodology, 1989; (Ed. in Chief) Encyclopedia of Stress, 2000, 2nd edn 2007; (ed) Stress Science: neuroendocrinology, 2010; (ed) Stress Consequences: mental, neuropsychological and socioeconomic, 2010; (ed) Stress of War, Conflict and Disaster, 2010; (ed with D. W. Pfaff and J. Levine) Handbook of Neuroendocrinology, 2011; more than 360 scientific publications on neuroendocrinol., molecular neuroendocrinol., neuropharmacol. and psychopharmacol. *Recreations:* ski-ing, scuba diving. *Address:* Mental Health Research Institute, Florey Institute of Neuroscience and Mental Health, University of Melbourne, 30 Royal Parade (corner of Genetics Lane), Melbourne, Vic 3010, Australia. *T:* (3) 90356634, *Fax:* (3) 90358768. *E:* gfink@mhri.edu.au. *W:* www.georgefink.com.

FINK, Laurence Douglas, (Larry); Co-Founder, Chairman and Chief Executive, BlackRock, since 1988; *m* Lori; three *c*. *Educ:* Univ. of Calif, Los Angeles (BA Pol Sci. 1974; MBA 1976). First Boston Corporation, 1976–88: Mem., Mgt Cttee; a Man. Dir; Co-Head, Taxable Fixed Income Div.; started Financial Futures and Options Dept. Co-Chm., Partnership for New York City. Mem., Bd of Trustees, New York Univ.; Co-Chm., Bd of Trustees, New York Univ. Langone Med. Center. Member, Board: MOMA; Council on Foreign Relns; Robin Hood. *Address:* BlackRock, 55 East 52nd Street, New York, NY 10055, USA. *T:* (212) 8105300.

FINKELSTEIN, family name of **Baron Finkelstein**.

FINKELSTEIN, Baron *cr* 2013 (Life Peer), of Pinner in the County of Middlesex; **Daniel William Finkelstein,** OBE 1997; Associate Editor, 2001–10 and since 2013, and Columnist, since 2013, The Times (Executive Editor, 2010–13; Chief Leader Writer, 2008–13; Comment Editor, 2004–08); *b* 30 Aug. 1962; *s* of late Prof. Ludwik Finkelstein, OBE and of Mirjam Emma Finkelstein (*née* Wiener); *m* 1993, Dr Nicola Ruth, *d* of Henry and Frances Connor; three *s*. *Educ:* Hendon Prep. Sch.; University College Sch.; London School of Economics (BSc Econs 1984); City Univ. (MSc 1986). Journalist, Network magazine, 1987–89; Editor, Connexion, 1989–92; Columnist, Jewish Chronicle, 2004–; Editor, Comment Central (weblog), Times Online, 2006–. Director: Social Market Foundn, 1992–95; Conservative Res. Dept, 1995–98; Policy Unit, Conservative Central Office, 1999–2001; Associate Editor, New Moon magazine, 1990–97. Res. Asst, RCA, 1984–87; Political Advr to Dr David Owen, MP, 1986–91. Contested: (SDP) Brent E, 1987; (C) Harrow W, 2001. Mem., Nat. Cttee, SDP, 1986–90. Founder and Bd Mem., Enterprise Europe, 1990– (Chm., 1990–95). *Publications:* (with Craig Arnall) The Open Network and its Enemies, 1990; Conservatives in Opposition: Republicans in the US, 1994. *Recreations:* US political memorabilia, Chinese food. *Address:* c/o The Times, 1 London Bridge Street, SE1 9GF. *T:* (020) 7782 7188. *Club:* Reform.

See also A. C. W. Finkelstein, T. M. Finkelstein.

FINKELSTEIN, Prof. Anthony Charles Wiener, PhD; CEng, FIET, FREng; CITP; FBCS; FCGI; Professor of Software Systems Engineering, since 1997, and Dean, Faculty of Engineering Sciences, since 2010, University College London (Head of Computer Science, 2002–10); *b* London, 28 July 1959; *s* of late Prof. Ludwik Finkelstein, OBE and of Mirjam Emma Finkelstein (*née* Wiener); *m* 1985, Judith Fishman; two *s*. *Educ:* Univ. of Bradford (BEng); London Sch. of Econs and Pol Sci. (MSc); Royal Coll. of Art (PhD 1985). FREng 2012. Post-doctoral Res. Fellow, 1985–88, Lectr, 1988–94, Imperial Coll., London; Prof. of Computer Sci., 1994–97, Hd, Computer Sci., 1995–97, City Univ. Dist. Vis. Prof., Nat. Inst. of Informatics, Tokyo, 2007–; Vis. Prof., Imperial Coll., London, 2008–. Mem., EPSRC, 2013–. MAE 2013. FCGI 2013. *Publications:* contrib. IEEE Transactions on Software Engrg, ACM Transactions on Software Engrg Methods, Internat. Conf. on Software Engrg and other learned jls. *Recreations:* capoeira, reading, art, antiques, family life. *Address:* University College London, Faculty of Engineering Sciences, Gower Street, WC1E 6BT. *E:* a.finkelstein@ucl.ac.uk. *Club:* Athenæum.

See also Baron Finkelstein, T. M. Finkelstein.

FINKELSTEIN, Tamara Margaret, (Mrs M. Isaacs); Chief Operating Officer and Director General, Group Operations, Department of Health, since 2014; *b* 24 May 1967; *d* of late Prof. Ludwik Finkelstein, OBE and of Mirjam Emma Finkelstein (*née* Wiener); *m* 1997, Michael Isaacs; one *s* two *d*. *Educ:* Haberdashers' Aske's Sch. for Girls; Balliol Coll., Oxford (BA Engrg Sci. 1989); London Sch. of Econs (MSc Econs 1992). HM Treasury: Economic Advr, 1992–97; Private Sec. and Speechwriter to Chancellor of the Exchequer, 1997–99; Sen. Advr, Gen. Expenditure Policy, 2000–01; Dep. Dir, Sure Start, 2001–04; HM Treasury: Hd, Permt Sec.'s Strategy Team, 2004; Dir of Ops, 2005; Dir, Govt Treasury Mgt, 2006–08; Dir, UK Border Agency Integration Prog., 2008–10; Dir, Ind. Public Service Pension Commn, HM Treasury, 2010–11; Dir, Public Services, HM Treasury, 2011–14. *Recreations:* family, book club, women's group. *Address:* Department of Health, Richmond House, 79 Whitehall, SW1A 2NS.

See also Baron Finkelstein, A. C. W. Finkelstein.

FINLAY OF LLANDAFF, Baroness *cr* 2001 (Life Peer), of Llandaff in the County of South Glamorgan; **Ilora Gillian Finlay,** FRCP, FRCGP; Hon. Professor in Palliative Medicine, since 1996, and Vice-Dean, School of Medicine, 2000–05, Cardiff University (formerly University of Wales College of Medicine); President: Royal Society of Medicine, 2006–08; British Medical Association, 2014–15; *b* 23 Feb. 1949; *d* of Charles Beaumont Benoy Downman and Thaïs Helène Downman (*née* Barakan); *m* 1972, Andrew Yule Finlay; one *s* one *d*. *Educ:* Wimbledon High Sch.; St Mary's Hosp. Med. Sch., Univ. of London (MB, BS 1972). DObstRCOG 1974; DCH 1975. FRCGP 1992; FRCP 1999. GP, 1981–86; first Med. Dir, Holme Tower Marie Curie Centre, Cardiff, 1987–2000. Consultant in Palliative Medicine, Velindre NHS Trust, Cardiff, 1994–. Course Dir, Dip. and MSc in Palliative Medicine, Cardiff Univ. (formerly UWCM), 1989–2014. Non-exec. Dir, Gwent HA, 1995–2001. Founder Mem., Cancer Res. UK, 2002–04 (Mem., Sci. and Educn Cttee). Mem., Internat. Scientific Expert Panel, Cicely Saunders Foundn. House of Lords: Mem., Select Cttee on Sci. and Technol., 2002–06, and on Assisted Dying for Terminally Ill Bill, 2003–05; Chm., Allergy Inquiry, 2006–07. Chairman: Allergy Services: still not meeting the unmet need, RCP, 2008–10; Commn on Generalism, RCGP, 2010–11. Chm., Nat. Council for Palliative Care, 2015–; Co-Chm., Living and Dying Well, 2010–. President: Medical Women's Fedn, 2001–02; CSP, 2002–; Vice Pres., Marie Curie Cancer Care, 2009–. Gov., Howell's Sch., Llandaff, GDST, 2000–05; Ind. Gov., Cardiff Metropolitan Univ., 2012–14. Patron: Shalom Hospice, St David's, Pembrokeshire, 2001–; Coping and Living in Pain; MND Assoc. Member, Editorial Board: Lancet Oncology, 2002–; Quality in Healthcare, 2002–; Medical Humanities, 2002–. FMedSci 2014; Hon. Fellow, Cardiff Univ., 2002. Hon. Prof., Groningen Univ., 2006–07 (Vis. Prof., 2000–02). Hon. DSc: Glamorgan, 2002; UWIC, 2005. *Publications:* (ed jtly) Medical Humanities, 2001; (ed jtly) Oral Care in Advanced Disease, 2005; (ed jtly) Handbook of Communication in Oncology and Palliative Care, 2010. *Address:* House of Lords, SW1A 0PW; Velindre NHS Trust, Cardiff CF14 2TL.

FINLAY, Amanda Jane, CBE 2001; Director, Legal Aid Strategy, Ministry of Justice (formerly Department for Constitutional Affairs), 2005–09; *b* 3 Sept. 1949; *d* of John Alexander Robertson Finlay, QC (His Honour Judge Finlay) and Jane Little Hepburn, CBE; *m* 1975, Richard Bevan Butt, *qv*; two *s*. *Educ:* Newnham Coll., Cambridge (BA English 1971). Lord Chancellor's Department, then Department for Constitutional Affairs, subseq. Ministry of Justice: fast stream entrant, 1971; Principal, 1976; Sec. to Legal Aid Adv. Cttee, 1981; Asst Sec., 1993; Sec. to Lord Woolf's inquiry, Access to Justice, 1994–96; implementation of Human Rights Act, 1997–99; Grade 3, 1999; Director: Public and Private Rights, 1999–2004; Legal Services and Civil and Administrative Justice, 2004–05. Member: Council, Justice, 2009– (Mem., Exec. Bd, 2010–; Mem., Wkg Gp, Justice in an Age of Austerity, 2014–); Civil Justice Council, 2009–13 (Mem., Working Gp on Self Represented Litigants, 2011–); Public Legal Educn Strategy Gp, MoJ, 2009–10; Vice Chair, Low Commn on the Future of Advice and Legal Support, 2012–. Public Gov., Oxleas NHS Foundn Trust, 2008–; Trustee: Law Works, 2009–; Law for Life, 2011–. *Recreations:* gardening and entertaining in England and France, travel, opera. *E:* amandajfinlay@gmail.com.

FINLAY, Prof. Bland James, PhD; FRS 2004; Professor of Microbial Ecology, Queen Mary University of London, since 2007; *b* 16 March 1952; *s* of Bland and Mabel Finlay; *m* 1996, Genoveva Esteban; one *s* one *d*. *Educ:* Univ. of Stirling (BA; PhD). Lectr in Biol., Univ. of Jos, Nigeria, 1977; PSO, Freshwater Biol Assoc., UK, 1984–92; NERC, 1992–2007 (Dep. CSO, 2005–07). Guest Prof., Univ. of Aarhus, 1982. Field work and expeditions in field of protozoology: Nigeria, 1977–78; Kenya (soda lakes), 1985; Spain (solution lakes), 1987 and 1990; Australia (volcanic crater lakes), 1997. Chm., Grant Cttee, Royal Soc., 2005–07. Fellow, Royal Danish Acad. of Scis and Letters. Scientific Medal, Zool Soc. of London, 1991. *Publications:* Ecology and Evolution in Anoxic Worlds (with T. Fenchel), 1995; over 200 scientific articles. *Recreations:* being on holiday with my wife, listening to J. S. Bach, continuously searching for my spectacles. *Address:* c/o The River Laboratory, Wareham, Dorset BH20 6BB. *T:* (01929) 401885. *E:* b.j.finlay@qmul.ac.uk.

FINLAY, Sir David (Ronald James Bell), 2nd Bt *cr* 1964, of Epping, Co. Essex; *b* 16 Nov. 1963; *s* of Sir Graeme Bell Finlay, 1st Bt, ERD and of June Evangeline, *y d* of Col Francis Collingwood Drake, OBE, MC, DL; *S* father, 1987; *m* 1998, Camilla, *d* of Peter Newton Acheson; one *s* one *d*. *Educ:* Marlborough College; Bristol Univ. (BSc Hons Economics/ Philosophy). Peat Marwick McLintock, 1986–91; Hill Samuel Financial Services, 1992–94; Gerrard Vivian Gray, 1994–97; Greig Middleton, 1997; Cater Allen Asset Management, 1998–2001; RBC, 2002–11; Coutts & Co. Channel Islands, 2011–. Freeman, City of London, 1991. *Recreations:* ski-ing, shooting. *Heir: s* Tristan James Bell Finlay, *b* 5 April 2001.

FINLAY, Frank, CBE 1984; actor; *b* Farnworth, Lancs, 6 Aug. 1926; *s* of Josiah Finlay; *m* 1954, Doreen Shepherd; two *s* one *d*. *Educ:* St Gregory the Great, Farnworth; RADA (Sir James Knott Schol.). *Stage:* repertory, 1950–52 and 1954–57; Belgrade, Coventry, 1958; Epitaph for George Dillon, NY, 1958; Royal Court, 1958, 1959–62: Sugar in the Morning; Sergeant Musgrave's Dance; Chicken Soup with Barley, Roots, I'm Talking About Jerusalem; The Happy Haven; Platonov; Chips with Everything, Royal Court, transf. to Vaudeville Theatre, 1962 (Clarence Derwent Best Actor Award); Chichester Festival, 1963: St Joan; The Workhouse Donkey; *with National Theatre Co.:* St Joan, 1963; Willie Mossop in Hobson's Choice, and Iago in Othello (both also Chichester Fest., 1964, Berlin and Moscow, 1965), The Dutch Courtesan (also Chichester Fest.), 1964; Giles Corey in The Crucible, Dogberry in Much Ado About Nothing, Mother Courage, 1965; Joxer Daly in Juno and the Paycock, Dikoy in The Storm, 1966; Peppino in Saturday, Sunday, Monday, 1973; Sloman in The Party, 1973; Freddy Malone in Plunder, Ben Prosser in Watch It Come Down, Josef Frank in Weapons of Happiness, 1976; Amadeus, 1982; *other productions include:* Bernard in After Haggerty, Aldwych, Criterion, Jesus Christ in Son of Man, Leicester Theatre and Round House (first actor ever to play Jesus Christ on stage in English theatre), 1970; Kings and Clowns (musical), Phoenix, 1978; Filumena, Lyric, 1978, US tour, 1979–80, and NY, 1980; The Girl in Melanie Klein, Palace Th., Watford, 1980; The Cherry Orchard, tour and Haymarket, 1983; Mutiny (musical), Piccadilly, 1985–86; Beyond Reasonable Doubt, Queen's, 1987, Australian tour, 1988–89, UK tour, 1989–90; Black Angel, King's Head,

Islington, 1990; A Slight Hangover, 1991, The Heiress, 1992, Bromley and UK tour; The Woman in Black, UK tour, 1993–94; Peter Pan, Chichester and UK tour; Gaslight, Richmond, 1995; The Handyman, Chichester, 1996; The Cherry Orchard, Chichester, 2008; *films include*, 1962–: The Longest Day, Private Potter, The Informers, A Life for Ruth, Loneliness of the Long Distance Runner, Hot Enough for June, The Comedy Man, The Sandwich Man, A Study in Terror, Othello (nominated for Amer. Acad. award; best actor award, San Sebastian, 1966), The Jokers, I'll Never Forget What's 'Is Name, The Shoes of the Fisherman, Deadly Bees, Robbery, Inspector Clouseau, Twisted Nerve, Cromwell, The Molly Maguires (in Hollywood), Assault, Victory for Danny Jones, Gumshoe, Shaft in Africa, Van Der Valk and the Girl, Van Der Valk and the Rich; Van Der Valk and the Dead; The Three Musketeers; The Ring of Darkness, The Wild Geese, The Thief of Baghdad, Sherlock Holmes—Murder by Decree; Enigma; Return of the Soldier; The Ploughman's Lunch, 1982; La Chiave (The Key), Italy, 1983; Sakharov, 1983; Christmas Carol, Arch of Triumph, 1919, 1984; Lifeforce, 1985; Casanova, 1986; The Return of the Musketeers, 1988; Cthulhu Mansion, 1992; Charlemagne, 1993; The Sparrow, 1993; The Pianist, 2002; The Statement, 2003; *TV appearances include:* Julius Caesar, Les Misérables, This Happy Breed, The Lie (SFTA Award), Casanova (series), The Death of Adolf Hitler, Don Quixote (SFTA Award), Voltaire, Merchant of Venice, Bouquet of Barbed Wire (series) (Best Actor Award), 84 Charing Cross Road, Saturday Sunday Monday, Count Dracula, The Last Campaign, Napoleon in Betzi, Dear Brutus, Tales of the Unexpected, Tales from 1001 Nights, Aspects of Love—Mona, In the Secret State, Verdict on Erebus (NZ), King of the Wind, Mountain of Diamonds (series), Stalin (US), Sherlock Holmes, How Do You Want Me (series), The Sins (series), The Lost Prince, Station Jim, Prime Suspect, Eroica, Life Begins (series), Johnny and the Bomb (series), Merlin, Four Seasons (series). Hon. Fellow, Bolton Inst., 1992. Hon DA Bolton, 2010. *Address:* c/o The Artists Partnership, 101 Finsbury Pavement, EC2A 1RS. *Club:* Garrick.

FINLAY, Larry; Managing Director, Transworld Publishers, since 2001; *b* London, 20 Jan. 1960; *s* of Harry Finlay and Tess Matz; *m* 2002, Claire Calman; one *s*. *Educ:* University College Sch., London; Univ. of Manchester (BA Econ. and Soc. Studies). Transworld Publishers: copywriter, 1983–86; Advertising and Promotions Dir, 1986–90; Mktg Dir, 1990–96; Paperback Publisher, 1997–99; Dep. Publisher, 1999–2001. *Recreations:* reading, gardening, reading to my son, arguing about God, eating my wife's wonderful food, shouting at the TV, teaching my son to swim, unleashing nematodes on unsuspecting slugs. *Address:* Transworld Publishers, 61–63 Uxbridge Road, W5 5SA. *T:* (020) 8579 2652.

FINLAY, Most Rev. Terence Edward; Archbishop of Toronto and Metropolitan of the Ecclesiastical Province of Ontario, 2000–04; *b* 19 May 1937; *s* of Terence John Finlay and Sarah McBryan; *m* 1962, Alice-Jean Cracknell; two *d*. *Educ:* Univ. of Western Ontario (BA); Huron Coll., London, Ont (BTh); Cambridge Univ., Eng. (MA). Deacon 1961, priest 1962; Dean of Residence, Renison Coll., Waterloo, Canada; Incumbent: All Saints, Waterloo, 1964–66; St Aidan's, London, Canada, 1966–68; Rector: St John the Evangelist, London, 1968–78; Grace Church, Brantford, 1978–82; Archdeacon of Brant, 1978–82; Incumbent, St Clement's, Eglinton, Toronto, 1982–86; a Suffragan Bishop, Diocese of Toronto, 1986; Coadjutor Bishop, 1987; Bishop of Toronto, 1989–2004. Primate's Special Envoy for Residential Schs Settlement, Healing and Reconciliation, 2004–. DD: (*jure dignitatis*) Huron Coll., 1987; (*hc*) Wycliffe Coll., 1988; (*hc*) Trinity Coll., 1989. *Recreations:* music, travel. *Address:* 1602–62 Wellesley Street West, Toronto, ON M5S 2X3, Canada.

FINLAY, Thomas Aloysius; Chief Justice of Ireland, 1985–94; *b* 17 Sept. 1922; *s* of Thomas A. Finlay and Eva Finlay; *m* 1948, Alice Blayney; two *s* three *d*. *Educ:* Xavier Sch., Dublin; Clongowes Wood Coll.; University Coll. Dublin. BA Legal and Political Science, NUI. Called to the Bar, King's Inns, 1944 (Bencher, 1972); Hon. Bencher: Inn of Court of NI, 1985; Middle Temple, 1986. Mem., Dáil Éireann, 1954–57; Sen. Counsel, 1961; Judge of the High Court, 1972, Pres. of the High Court, 1974. *Recreations:* fishing, shooting, conversation. *Address:* 22 Ailesbury Drive, Dublin 4, Ireland. *T:* (1) 693395.

See also H. Geoghegan.

FINLAYSON, Sir Garet (Orlando), KCMG 2007; OBE 1999; Chairman and Chief Executive, Associated Bahamian Distillers & Brewers Ltd, since 1981; *b* Andros, Bahamas, 4 Aug. 1937; *s* of Hastings and Maud Finlayson; *m* 1963, Rowena Frances Rolle; two *s* two *d*. *Educ:* Evelyn Wood Inst.; La Salle Univ., Chicago (home study course in business); Bahamas Teachers' Coll., Nassau. Primary sch. teacher, 1949–52; tailor, 1950–61; waiter, 1961–68; car salesman, 1968–71; owner: car dealerships, 1972–92; Bahamas Catering Ltd, 1972–; Davinci Restaurant, 1973–94; Atlantis Hotel and Night Club, 1974–93; Bethell Robertson & Co. Ltd, 1981–; City Markets Food Stores, 2010–. Owner and Chairman: Burns House Ltd, 1980–; Bahamas Distillers Ltd, 1981–; Butler & Sands Ltd, 2004–; Solomon's Mines Ltd, 2004–; Chairman: Gen. Bahamian Cos Ltd, 1981–; Wholesale Wines & Spirits Ltd, 2004–; Todhunter-Mitchell Co. Ltd, 2004–; Deputy Chairman: Bahamas In-Flight Ltd, 1972–; Commonwealth Brewery Ltd, 1988–. Mem., World Presidents Orgn. Silver Jubilee Award in Business, Bahamas, 1998. *Recreations:* reading, yachting, fishing. *Address:* PO Box N1019, Nassau, Bahamas. *T:* 3282833, *Fax:* 3233211. *E:* gfinlayson@abdab.bs.

FINLAYSON, George; HM Diplomatic Service, retired; *b* 22 April 1943; *s* of late George Finlayson and Alison Boath (*née* Barclay); *m* 1966, Patricia Grace Ballantine; two *s*. *Educ:* Tynecastle High Sch., Edinburgh. Joined HM Diplomatic Service, 1965; Reykjavik, 1967–69; Prague, 1969–71; Lagos, 1971–75; FCO, 1975–78; 2nd Sec., New Delhi, 1978–81; 1st Sec., FCO, 1981–83; 1st Sec. and Head of Chancery, Montevideo, 1983–87; Consul (Commercial) and Dep. Dir for Trade Promotion, New York, 1987–90; Dep. High Comr, Dhaka, 1990–93; Consul-Gen., Melbourne, 1994–98; High Comr to Malaŵi, 1998–2001. Mem., Internat. Develt Adv. Gp, Scottish Govt, 2008–12. Advr, Challenges Worldwide, 2008–15; Dir, Challenges Africa, 2012–. Dep. Chm., Scots Australian Council, 2002–14. Trustee: Malaŵi Tomorrow, 2005–; Scotland Malaŵi Business Gp, 2007–. Mem., Scottish Charity Appeals Panel, 2006–10. *Recreations:* drawing, painting. *Address:* 12 Eglinton Crescent, Edinburgh EH12 5DD.

FINLAYSON, George Ferguson, CMG 1979; CVO 1983; HM Diplomatic Service, retired; *b* 28 Nov. 1924; *s* of late G. B. Finlayson; *m* 1st, 1951, Rosslyn Evelyn (*d* 1972), *d* of late E. N. James; one *d*; 2nd, 1982, Anthea Judith (*d* 2014), *d* of late F. D. Perry. *Educ:* North Berwick High Sch. Royal Air Force, 1943–47. Apptd HM Foreign (later Diplomatic) Service, 1949; 2nd Sec. (Inf.), HM Embassy, Rangoon, 1952–54; FO, 1955–59; First Sec., 1959; HM Consul, Algiers, 1959–61; First Sec., HM Embassy, Bamako, 1961–63; HM Consul (Commercial), New York, 1964–68; Counsellor, 1968; Counsellor (Commercial), British High Commn, Singapore, 1969–72; Head of Trade Relations and Exports Dept, FCO, 1972–73; Counsellor (Commercial) Paris, 1973–78; Consul-General: Toronto, 1978–81; Los Angeles, 1981–84. *Recreations:* travel, walking, swimming. *Address:* 141b Ashley Gardens, SW1P 1HN. *T:* (020) 7834 6227. *Club:* Oriental.

FINLAYSON, Niall Diarmid Campbell, OBE 1998; PhD; FRCSE, FRCP, FRCPE; Chief Medical Officer, Royal London Insurance, since 2004; Chairman, LifeCare, Edinburgh, since 2006; *b* 21 April 1939; *s* of Duncan Iain Campbell Finlayson and Helen Rita Blackney; *m* 1972, Dale Kristin Anderson; one *s* one *d*. *Educ:* Loretto Sch., Musselburgh; Edinburgh Univ. (BSc (Hons) 1962; MB, ChB 1964; PhD 1972). FRCPE 1977; FRCP 1982; FRCSE 1999. Asst Prof. of Medicine, New York Hospital-Cornell Medical Center, NY, 1969–73; Consultant Physician, Centre for Liver and Digestive Disorders, Royal Infirmary Edinburgh, 1973–2003. Hon. Sen. Lectr, Edinburgh Univ. Medical Sch., 1973–2003; Hon. Fellow (Clinical Teaching), Edinburgh Univ., 2004–. Pres., RCPE, 2001–04. *Publications:* (ed jtly) Diseases of the Gastrointestinal Tract and Liver, 1982, 3rd edn 1997; about 100 publications in learned jls and as contributions to books. *Recreations:* music, history. *Address:* 10 Queens Crescent, Edinburgh EH9 2AZ. *T:* (0131) 667 9369. *E:* ndc.finlayson@which.net.

FINLEY, Gerald Hunter, OC 2014; FRCM; baritone; *b* Montreal, 1960; *s* of Eric Gault Finley and Catherine Rae Finley; *m* 1st, 1990, Louise Winter, opera singer (marr. diss. 2009); two *s*; 2nd, 2010, Heulwen Keyte, artist agent. *Educ:* Glebe Collegiate Inst., Ottawa; Univ. of Ottawa; Royal Coll. of Music (ARCM 1980; Dip. 1986); King's Coll., Cambridge (BA 1983; MA 1986); Nat. Opera Studio. FRCM 2007. St Matthew's Church Choir, Ottawa, 1970–79; Ottawa Choral Soc., 1976–79; Ontario Youth Choir, 1977–78; King's Coll. Choir, 1981–83; Glyndebourne Chorus, 1986–88; *débuts:* Figaro in Le Nozze di Figaro, Downland Opera, 1984; Antonio in Le Nozze di Figaro, Nat. Arts Centre Opera, 1987; Graf Dominik in Arabella, Glyndebourne, 1989; Graf in Capriccio, Chicago Lyric Opera, 1994; Figaro in Le Nozze di Figaro, LA Music Centre, 1994, Royal Opera House, Covent Garden, 1995; Valentin in Faust, Opéra de Paris, 1997; Papageno in Die Zauberflöte, NY Met., 1998; Mr Fox in Fantastic Mr Fox, LA Opera, 1998; Harry Heegan in The Silver Tassie, ENO, 2000; Robert Oppenheimer in Doctor Atomic, San Francisco Opera, 2005; Iago in Otello, Barbican, 2009; Don Giovanni, Munich State Opera, 2010; Graf Almaviva, Vienna State Opera, 2012; *other rôles include:* Forester in Cunning Little Vixen, title rôle in Don Giovanni, Royal Opera, 2003; Guglielmo in Così fan tutte, Salzburg, Olivier in Capriccio, Paris Opera, and Jaufre Rudel in L'amour de Loin (Sariaaho), Helsinki, 2004; Giorgio Germont in La Traviata, Royal Opera, and title rôle in Eugene Onegin, ENO, 2005; Count in Le Nozze di Figaro, Royal Opera, 2006 and 2014; Guillaume Tell Accademia di Santa Cecilia, Rome, 2010, Royal Opera, 2015; Howard K. Stern in Anna Nicole, Royal Opera, and Hans Sachs in Die Meistersinger, Glyndebourne, 2011; Don Giovanni, Salzburg Fest., 2011, Royal Opera, Metropolitan Opera, 2012; Il Prigioniero, NY Philharmonic, Don Alfonso in Così fan tutte, Salzburg Fest., and Amfortas in Parsifal, Royal Opera, 2013; Falstaff, Canadian Opera, 2014; Wolfram in Tannhäuser, Lyric Opera, Chicago, 2015; Nick Shadow in Rake's Progress, NY Met, 2015. Vis. Prof., Royal Coll. of Music, 2000. Numerous opera and recital recordings, and recitals and masterclasses at festivals and music institutions worldwide. John Christie Award, Glyndebourne, 1989; Juno Award, Canadian Acad. of Recording Arts, 1998, 2011, 2015; Singer's Award, Royal Philharmonic Soc., 2000; Editor's Choice Award, Gramophone mag./Classic FM, 2006; Vocal Award, Gramophone mag., 2008, 2009, 2011; Oscar della Lirica—baritono 2012, Internat. Opera Award, Confederazione Italiana Associazioni e Fondazioni per al Musica Lirica e Sinfonica. *Recreations:* wine, cooking, astronomy. *Address:* c/o IMG Artists Europe, The Light Box, 111 Power Road, Chiswick, W4 5PY. *T:* (020) 7957 5800; c/o Alison Pybus, IMG Artists, 152 W 57th Street, New York, NY 10019, USA. *T:* (212) 9943500. *Club:* Two Brydges.

FINLEY, Michael John; Governor, International Press Foundation, 1988–97; *b* 22 Sept. 1932; *s* of late Walter Finley and Grace Marie Butler; *m* 1st, 1955, Sheila Elizabeth Cole (*d* 1992); four *s*; 2nd, 2001, Maureen Elizabeth Crocker. *Educ:* King Edward VII Sch., Sheffield. Editor, 1964–69, Sheffield Morning Telegraph (formerly Sheffield Telegraph); Editorial Dir, 1969–79, and Dir and Gen. Man., 1979–82, Kent Messenger Gp; Exec. Dir, Periodical Publishers Assoc., 1983–88; Dir, Internat. Fedn of Periodical Publishers, 1989–92. Hon. Mem. and Past Chm., Parly and Legal Cttee, Guild of British Newspaper Editors. Chm., Inst. of Dirs (Kent branch), 1980–83. Member: BBC Regional Adv. Council, 1967–69; BBC Gen. Adv. Council, 1971–77; Exec. Cttee, Internat. Fedn of Periodical Publishers, 1983–89; Bd, Fedn of Periodical Publishers in EEC, 1984–92; Bd, Internat. Press Centre, London, 1984–88; Gov., Cranbrook Sch., 1978–98. *Publications:* contrib. Advertising and the Community, 1968. *Recreations:* golf, Rugby (spectator), snooker, walking. *Address:* 22 Rochester Close, Eastbourne BN20 7TW.

FINN, Benjamin James, OBE 2007; Co-founder and Director, Sibelius Software Ltd, 1993–2006; *b* 29 Nov. 1968; *s* of Timothy Finn and Anthea, (Widget), Finn (*née* Fox-Male). *Educ:* King's Coll. Choir Sch., Cambridge; King's Sch., Canterbury; Royal Coll. of Music; King's Coll., Cambridge (BA 1991; MPhil). *Recreations:* thinking, dabbling.

See also J. H. Finn.

FINN, Jonathan Humbert, OBE 2007; Co-Founder and Director, Sibelius Software Ltd, 1993–2006; *b* 29 Nov. 1968; *s* of Timothy Finn and Anthea, (Widget), Finn (*née* Fox-Male). *Educ:* King's Coll. Choir Sch., Cambridge; King's Sch., Canterbury; Christ Church, Oxford (BA Music 1990). Vis. Prof. of Notation Technol., Royal Acad. Music, 1995. *Publications:* The Scorpion Control Computer, 1987. *Recreation:* paying the exact change.

See also B. J. Finn.

FINN, Leo Peter; Chief Executive, Northern Rock PLC, 1997–2001; *b* 13 July 1938; *s* of Thomas Leo Finn and Jenny Finn (*née* Davison); *m* 1963, Alice Patricia Harold; two *s* two *d*. *Educ:* Carlisle Grammar Sch.; Newcastle upon Tyne Polytechnic (BA Hons). FCIB. Sec., 1982–89, Exec. Dir, 1989–91, Dep. Man. Dir, 1991–97, Northern Rock Building Soc.; Dir, Bellway plc, 1995–09. Chairman: Newcastle/Gateshead Housing Market Restructure Pathfinder, 2002–05; Northern Recruitment Group PLC, 2005–09; Dir, Eden Housing Assoc., 2005–12 (Vice Chm., 2008–11; Chm., 2011–12). Lay Mem., Public Protection Panel Cumbria, 2002–10. Chm., Joseph Rowntree Enquiry into home ownership 2010 and beyond, 2004–05. Chm., Newcastle Coll., 2001–06. Chm., Northern Rock Foundn, 2004–06 (Trustee, 1997–2006). Hon. DCL Northumbria, 2005. *Recreations:* walking, opera, cooking.

FINN, Simone Jari; Special Advisor to Minister for Trade and Investment, since 2015; *b* 10 June 1968; *d* of Prof. Jan Kubes and Morwenna Talfan Davies (*née* Lewis); *m* 1996, Alexander William Galletly Finn; one *s* one *d*. *Educ:* Lady Margaret Hall, Oxford (BA Hist.). ACA 1995. Manager, Coopers & Lybrand, later PricewaterhouseCoopers, 1991–98; Sen. Acct, Financial Services Authy, 1998–2001; Advr on industrial relations to Cabinet Office, 2010–11; Special Advr to Minister for the Cabinet Office, 2012–15. *Address:* House of Lords, SW1A 0PW.

[Created a Baroness (Life Peer) 2015 but title not yet gazetted at time of going to press.]

FINNEGAN, Joseph; a Judge of the Supreme Court of Ireland, 2006–12; *b* 1 Oct. 1942; *s* of Isaac Finnegan and Charlotte Finnegan (*née* Sheridan); *m* 1968, Kathleen Gilligan; one *s* three *d*. *Educ:* Marist Coll., Dundalk; University Coll., Dublin (BCL, LLB). Admitted solicitor, Ireland; called to the Bar, King's Inns, Dublin (Bencher, 1999); in practice as solicitor, 1966–68 and 1973–78; Asst Sec., Incorporated Law Soc. of Ireland, 1968–73; Jun. Counsel, 1978–90; Sen. Counsel, 1990–99; Judge of the High Court of Ireland, 1992–2001; Pres. of the High Court, 2001–06. Bencher, Middle Temple, 2006. *Recreations:* National Hunt racing, golf. *Address:* Ardara, Killarney Road, Bray, Co. Wicklow, Ireland. *T:* (1) 2866710. *Clubs:* Blackrock College Rugby Football; Bray Golf, El Saler Golf (Valencia, Spain).

FINNEGAN, Kevin James; QC (NI) 1985; **His Honour Judge Finnegan;** a County Court Judge, Northern Ireland, since 2001; *b* 3 June 1947; *s* of James Finnegan and Sheila Finnegan; *m* 1976, Anne Frances Aubrey; six *s*. *Educ:* St Malachy's Coll., Belfast; Queen's Univ., Belfast (LLB Hons 1970). Called to the Bar, NI, 1973. *Recreations:* golf, reading, listening to the radio, sleeping, going to Van Morrison, John Prine and Ray Davies concerts. *Address:* Royal Courts of Justice, Belfast BT1 3JF. *Club:* Malone Golf.

FINNEGAN, Prof. Ruth Hilary, OBE 2000; DPhil; FBA 1996; Visiting Research Professor, Open University, since 1999 (Professor in Comparative Social Institutions, 1988–99, Emeritus Professor, 2002); *b* 31 Dec. 1933; *d* of Tom Finnegan and Agnes (*née* Campbell); *m* 1963, David John Murray; three *d*. *Educ:* Mount Sch., York; Somerville Coll., Oxford (BA 1956;

Dip in Anthropology 1959; BLitt 1960; Hon. Fellow, 1997); Nuffield Coll., Oxford (DPhil 1963). Teacher, Malvern Girls' Coll., 1956–58; Lectr in Social Anthropol., UC of Rhodesia and Nyasaland, 1963–64; Lectr in Sociol., 1965–67, Sen. Lectr, 1967–69, Ibadan Univ.; Open University: Lectr in Sociol., 1969–72; Sen. Lectr in Comparative Social Instns, 1972–75 and 1978–82; Reader, 1982–88; Reader in Sociol. and Head of Sociol. Discipline, Univ. of S Pacific, Suva, 1975–78. Vis. Prof., Univ. of Texas at Austin, 1989. Mem., Internat. Res. Council on Humanities and Social Scis Studies on Africa, 2013. Mem., Governing Body, SOAS, 1999–2007 (Vice-Chm., 2003–06). Trustee, Mass-Observation Archive, 1998–2011. Pres., Mount Old Scholars' Assoc., 2003–05. Associate Mem., Finnish Lit. Soc., 1989; Folklore Fellow, Finnish Acad. of Sci. and Letters, 1991; Hon. Mem., Assoc. of Social Anthropologists of UK and Commonwealth, 2002. *Publications:* Survey of the Limba people of Northern Sierra Leone, 1965; Limba Stories and Story-telling, 1967; Oral Literature in Africa, 1970, 1976, 2nd (illustrated) edn 2012; Oral Poetry, 1977, 2nd edn 1992; Literacy and Orality, 1988; The Hidden Musicians, 1989, 2nd edn 2007; Oral Traditions and the Verbal Arts, 1992; Tales of the City, 1998; Communicating: the multiple modes of human interconnection, 2002, 2nd edn 2014; The Oral and Beyond: doing things with words in Africa, 2007; Why Do We Quote?: the culture and history of the quotation, 2011; The Search for African Orality, 2012; Music and Creation, 2012; Thoughts and Reflections on Language, Literature and Performance, 2013; Love Enpictured, 2013; Studying Oral Texts, 2013; Where is Language?, 2015; Black Inked Pearl, 2015; Entrancement, 2016; *edited:* The Penguin Book of Oral Poetry, 1978, reissued as A World Treasury of Oral Poetry, 1982; Participating in the Knowledge Society: researchers beyond the university walls, 2005; Cato's Distichs: the oldest Latin primer, 2012; Peace Writing, 2013; Short Story Writing, 2013; He Came All So Stille: the home anthology of beautiful verse, 2014; *edited jointly:* Modes of Thought, 1973, 2nd edn 2013; Essays on Pacific Literature, 1978; Conceptions of Inquiry, 1981; New Approaches to Economic Life, 1985; Information Technology: social issues, 1987; From Family Tree to Family History, 1994; Sources and Methods for Family and Community Historians, 1994; South Pacific Oral Traditions, 1995; as Catherine Farrar (fiction): The Little Angel and the Three Wisdoms, 2012; Three Ways of Loving, 2012; L'il Ole Lil the Heavenly Rocker, 2012; The Dragon's Tale, 2012; The Wild Thorn Rose, 2012; contrib. to learned jls. *Recreations:* singing, walking with dogs (and husband), learning with and from grandchildren, visiting New Zealand, dreaming, running independent Callender Press (founder, director and senior editor), learning clarinet. *Address:* Faculty of Social Sciences, Open University, Milton Keynes MK7 6AA.

FINNERTY, Angela Catherine; Her Honour Judge Finnerty; a Circuit Judge, since 2000; Designated Family Judge for York, since 2011; *b* 22 March 1954; *d* of late Michael Peter Finnerty and of Mary Elizabeth Finnerty; *m* 1st (marr. diss.); one *s* one *d*; 2nd, 2012, Clive William Heaton, *qv*. *Educ:* Bury Convent Grammar Sch.; Leeds Univ. (LLB 1st Cl. Hons); Coll. of Law, London. Called to the Bar, Middle Temple, 1976 (Harmsworth Scholar); in practice as barrister, 1976–2000. *Address:* York County Court, Piccadilly House, 55 Piccadilly, York YO1 9WL.

FINNEY, Albert; actor, stage and film; film director; *b* 9 May 1936; *s* of Albert Finney, turf accountant, and Alice (*née* Hobson); *m* 1st, 1957, Jane Wenham, actress (marr. diss.); one *s*; 2nd, 1970, Anouk Aimée (marr. diss.); 3rd, 2006, Pene Delmage. Associate Artistic Dir, English Stage Co., 1972–75; a Dir, United British Artists, 1983–86. *Stage:* London appearance in The Party, New, 1958; Cassio in Othello, and Lysander, Stratford-on-Avon, 1959; subsequently in: The Lily White Boys, Royal Court, 1960; Billy Liar, Cambridge Theatre, 1960; Luther, in Luther: Royal Court Theatre and Phoenix Theatre, 1961–62; New York, 1963; Armstrong in Armstrong's Last Goodnight, Miss Julie and Black Comedy, Chichester, 1965, Old Vic, 1966; A Day in the Death of Joe Egg, NY, 1968; Alpha Beta, Royal Court and Apollo, 1972; Krapp's Last Tape, Royal Court, 1973; Cromwell, Royal Court, 1973; Chez Nous, Globe, 1974; Uncle Vanya, and Present Laughter, Royal Exchange, Manchester, 1977; Orphans, Hampstead, transf. to Apollo, 1986; J. J. Farr, Phoenix, 1987; Another Time, Wyndham's, 1989, Chicago, 1991; Reflected Glory, Vaudeville, 1992; Art, Wyndham's, 1996; *National Theatre:* Love for Love, 1965; Much Ado About Nothing, 1965; A Flea in Her Ear, 1966; Hamlet, 1975; Tamburlaine, 1976; The Country Wife, 1977; The Cherry Orchard, Macbeth, Has "Washington" Legs?, 1978; *Directed for stage:* The Freedom of the City, Royal Court, 1973; Loot, Royal Court, 1975; *Directed for stage and appeared in:* The Biko Inquest, Riverside, 1984; Serjeant Musgrave's Dance, Old Vic, 1984; *Films include:* Saturday Night and Sunday Morning, 1960; Tom Jones, 1963; Night Must Fall, 1964; Two for the Road, 1967; Scrooge, 1970; Murder on the Orient Express, 1974; Loophole, 1980; Wolfen, 1981; Looker, 1981; Shoot the Moon, 1982; Annie, 1982; The Dresser, 1983; Under the Volcano, 1984; Orphans, 1987; Miller's Crossing, 1990; The Playboys, 1992; Rich in Love, 1992; The Browning Version, 1994; A Man of No Importance, 1994; The Run of the Country, 1995; Washington Square, 1997; Simpatico, 1999; Delivering Milo, 2000; Erin Brockovich, 2000; Breakfast of Champions, 2000; Big Fish, 2004; Amazing Grace, 2006; A Good Year, 2006; The Bourne Ultimatum, 2007; Before the Devil Knows You're Dead, 2008; The Bourne Legacy, 2012; Skyfall, 2012; founded Memorial Films, 1965: co-produced with Michael Medwin: Charlie Bubbles (also actor/dir); If…; Bleak Moments; Spring and Port Wine; Gumshoe (also actor); In Loving Memory; O Lucky Man; The Day; Alpha Beta (also actor); The Engagement; Law and Disorder; Memoirs of a Survivor; *TV films:* John Paul II, 1984; The Endless Game, 1990; The Image, 1990; A Rather English Marriage, 1998; The Gathering Storm, 2002; *serials:* The Green Man, 1990; Karaoke, 1996; Nostromo, 1997; My Uncle Silas, 2001. Hon. LittD: Sussex, 1965; Salford, 1979. *Address:* c/o Nigel Bennett, Michael Simkins LLP, Lynton House, 7–12 Tavistock Square, WC1H 9LT.

FINNEY, Prof. David John, CBE 1978; MA, ScD Cantab; FRS 1955; FRSE; consultant biometrician; Professor of Statistics, University of Edinburgh, 1966–84; Director, Agricultural and Food Research Council (formerly Agricultural Research Council) Unit of Statistics, 1954–84; *b* Latchford, Warrington, 3 Jan. 1917; *e s* of late Robert G. S. Finney and late Bessie E. Whitlow; *m* 1950, Mary Elizabeth Connolly (*d* 2006); one *s* two *d*. *Educ:* Lymm and Manchester Grammar Schools; Clare Coll., Cambridge; Galton Laboratory, Univ. of London. Asst Statistician, Rothamsted Experimental Station, 1939–45; Lecturer in the Design and Analysis of Scientific Experiment, University of Oxford, 1945–54; Reader in Statistics, University of Aberdeen, 1954–63, Professor, 1963–66. Dir, ISI Res. Centre, Netherlands, 1987–88. Vis. Prof. of Biomathematics, Harvard Univ., 1962–63; Vis. Scientist, Internat. Rice Res. Inst., 1984–85. United Nations FAO expert attached to Indian Council of Agricultural Research, 1952–53; FAO Key Consultant, Indian Agricl Stats Res. Inst., 1984–90. Scientific Consultant, Cotton Research Corporation, 1959–75. Chm., Computer Bd for Univs and Research Councils, 1970–74 (Mem., 1966–74); Member: Adverse Reactions Sub-Cttee, Cttee on Safety of Medicines, 1963–81; BBC General Adv. Council, 1969–76. Trustee, Drug Safety Res. Trust, Bursledon Hall, Southampton, 1986–97. President of Biometric Society, 1964–65 (Vice-President, 1963, 1966); Fellow: Royal Statistical Soc. (Pres., 1973–74); American Statistical Assoc.; Mem., Internat. Statistical Inst.; Hon. Fellow Eugenics Society; Hon. Member: Société Adolphe Quetelet; Internat. Soc. of Pharmacovigilance, 2002. Weldon Memorial Prize, 1956; Paul Martini Prize, Deutsche Ges. für Medizinische Dokumentation und Statistik, 1971. Dr *hc* Faculté des Sciences Agronomiques de l'Etat à Gembloux, Belgium, 1967; Hon. DSc: City, 1976; Heriot-Watt, 1981; Hon. Dr Math Waterloo (Ont), 1989. *Publications:* Probit Analysis, 1947 (facsimile edn 2009), 3rd edn 1971; Biological Standardization (with J. H. Burn, L. G. Goodwin), 1950; Statistical Method in Biological Assay, 1952, 3rd edn 1978; An Introduction to Statistical Science in Agriculture, 1953, 4th edn 1972; Experimental Design and its Statistical Basis, 1955; Técnica y Teoría en el diseño de Experimentos, 1957; An Introduction to the Theory of Experimental Design, 1960; Statistics for Mathematicians: An Introduction, 1968; Statistics for Biologists, 1980; Writings on Pharmacovigilance, 2006; over 300 papers in statistical and biological journals. *Recreations:* travel (active), music (passive), and the 3 R's. *Address:* 13 Oswald Court, South Oswald Road, Edinburgh EH9 2HY. *T:* (0131) 667 0135. *E:* david.finney@freeuk.com.

FINNEY, Rt Rev. John Thornley; Bishop Suffragan of Pontefract, 1993–98; Hon. Assistant Bishop, diocese of Southwell and Nottingham (formerly diocese of Southwell), since 1998; *b* 1 May 1932; *s* of Arthur Frederick and Elaine Mary Finney; *m* 1959, Sheila Elizabeth Russell; three *d*. *Educ:* Charterhouse; Hertford College, Oxford (BA Jurisp.; Dip. Theol.). Ordained 1958; Curate, All Saints, Headington, 1958–61; Curate in Charge, Aylesbury, 1961–65; Rector, Tollerton, Notts, 1965–71; Vicar, St Margaret's, Aspley, Nottingham, 1971–80; Adviser in Evangelism to Bishop of Southwell, 1980–89; Officer for Decade of Evangelism, 1990–93. Manager, Research Project in Evangelism, BCC, 1989–92. Chm. Council, Lee Abbey, 1999–2003. *Publications:* Saints Alive!, 1983; Understanding Leadership, 1989; The Well Church Book, 1991; Church on the Move, 1992; Finding Faith Today, 1992; Stories of Faith, 1995; Recovering the Past: Celtic and Roman mission, 1996; Fading Splendour?, 2000; Emerging Evangelism, 2004; To Germany with Love: die evangelische Kirche in Deutschland aus der Sicht eines Anglikaners, 2011. *Recreations:* golf, growing old gracefully. *Address:* Greenacre, Crow Lane, South Muskham, Newark, Notts NG23 6DZ. *T:* and *Fax:* (01636) 679791. *E:* john.finney@virgin.net.

FINNIE, (James) Ross, CA; Chairman, Food Standards Scotland, since 2015; *b* 11 Feb. 1947; *s* of late James Ross Finnie and Elizabeth Main Finnie; *m* 1971, Phyllis Sinclair; one *s* one *d*. *Educ:* Greenock Acad. Director: James Finlay Bank Ltd, 1975–86; Singer & Friedlander Ltd, 1986–91; Partner, Ross Finnie & Co., Chartered Accountants, 1991–99. Mem., Exec. Cttee, Scottish Council (Develt and Industry), 1976–87. Member (L then Lib Dem): Inverclyde DC, 1977–96; Inverclyde Council, 1995–99. Mem. (Lib Dem) W of Scotland, Scottish Parlt, 1999–2011; contested (Lib Dem) Greenock and Inverclyde, 2011. Minister for Rural Affairs, then for Envmt and Rural Develt, Scottish Exec., 1999–2007; Lib Dem Shadow Cabinet Sec. for Health and Wellbeing, 2007–11. Vice Convenor, Health and Sport Cttee, 2007–11, Convenor, End of Life Assistance Bill Cttee, 2010, Scottish Parlt. Chm., Scottish Lib Party, 1982–86. Contested: (L) Renfrewshire W, 1979; (L/All) Stirling, 1983. Dir, Scotland's Futures Forum Ltd, 2009–11. Non-executive Member: Water Industry Commn for Scotland, 2012–; NHS Greater Glasgow and Clyde Health Bd, 2012–. *Address:* 91 Octavia Terrace, Greenock PA16 1PY. *T:* (01475) 631495. *E:* finnie80@btinternet.com.

FINNIE, John Bradford; Member for Highlands and Islands, Scottish Parliament, since 2011 (SNP, 2011–12, Ind, since 2012); *b* Clunes, Inverness-shire, 31 Dec. 1956; *m* Bernadette; one *s* one *d*. *Educ:* Achnacarry Primary Sch.; Lochaber High Sch.; Oban High Sch. Constable: Lothian and Borders Police, 1976–79; Northern Constabulary, 1979–2006. Sec., Northern Br., Scottish Police Fedn, 1992–2006. Mem. (SNP), Highland Council, 2007–12. *Recreations:* family, football, music. *Address:* Scottish Parliament, Edinburgh EH99 1SP. *T:* (0131) 348 6898. *E:* john.finnie.msp@scottish.parliament.uk.

FINNIE, Ross; *see* Finnie, J. R.

FINNIGAN, Judith, (Judy); television presenter; *b* 16 May 1948; *d* of late John Finnigan and of Anne Finnigan; *m* 1986, Richard Holt Madeley, *qv*; one *s* one *d*, and two *s* from previous marriage. Researcher, Granada TV, 1971–73; reporter, Anglia TV, 1974–77; presenter: Granada TV, 1980–2001; Channel 4, 2001–08; programmes include: This Morning, 1988–2001; Richard and Judy, 2001–08; British Book Awards, 2004–; Richard and Judy's New Position, Watch, 2008–09. *Publications:* (with R. Madeley) Richard & Judy: the autobiography, 2001; (novel) Eloise, 2012; (novel) I Do Not Sleep, 2015. *Address:* c/o James Grant Management, 94 Strand on the Green, Chiswick, W4 3NN. *T:* (020) 8742 4950.

FINNIGAN, Peter Anthony; QC 2009; *b* Leigh, Lancs, 14 Sept. 1955; *s* of Geoffrey Finnigan and Anne Finnigan; *m* 1982, Sarah Jane Farmbrough; one *s* two *d*. *Educ:* Sevenoaks Sch.; Univ. of Newcastle upon Tyne (LLB Hons). Called to the Bar, Lincoln's Inn, 1979; Standing Counsel to HMRC, 1996–2006. Mem., Glyndebourne Fest. Soc. *Recreations:* opera, travel, ski-ing, sailing, watching and supporting lacrosse and Rugby. *Address:* QEB Hollis Whiteman Chambers, 1–2 Laurence Pountney Hill, EC4R 0EU. *T:* (020) 7933 8855. *E:* peter.finnigan@qebholliswhiteman.co.uk. *Club:* Harlequin Football.

FINNIGAN, Stephen James, CBE 2010; QPM 2006; Chief Constable, Lancashire Constabulary, since 2005; *b* Liverpool, 29 June 1957; *s* of James Francis Finnigan and late Veronica Finnigan (*née* Ramsey); *m* 1992, Jaqueline Marie Brammer; one *s* one *d*. *Educ:* Maricourt Comprehensive Sch.; St John's Coll., Cambridge (BA 1992); Univ. of Cambridge (Dip. Applied Criminol. and Police Studies 2000). Merseyside Police, 1976–2001: Sergeant, 1980–87; Inspector, 1987–93; Chief Inspector, 1993–96; Superintendent, 1996–2001; Lancashire Constabulary: Asst Chief Constable, 2001–02, Dep. Chief Constable, 2002–05. *Recreations:* running, watching football (Everton FC), spending time with young family. *Address:* Lancashire Constabulary, PO Box 77, Saunders Lane, Hutton, Preston PR4 5SB. *T:* (01772) 412221, *Fax:* (01772) 614916. *E:* steve.finnigan@lancashire.pnn.police.uk.

FINNIS, Jane; Chief Executive, Culture24 (formerly 24 Hour Museum), since 2001; *b* Walton-on-Thames, Oct. 1965; *d* of Richard Finnis and Hazel Finnis (*née* Hoare); *m* 2006, Nick Brown; one *s* one *d*. *Educ:* Brighton Poly. (BA Hons 1st Cl. Expressive Arts 1987). Freelance video and TV prod. and dir, 1987–90; Dir, Lighthouse Arts & Training Ltd, 1989–2001. Mem., Adv. Bd, Place To Be, Brighton and Hove Council, 2000–03. Chm. and Founder Mem., Internat. Steering Cttee, Culturemondo, 2003–. Mem. Bd and Trustee, South East Dance Agency, 1998–2001; Member: South East Film Task Force, 2000–01; Prog. Cttee, Museums and the Web, 2010–. Trustee, Photoworks, 2007–. *Publications:* (contrib.) Learning to Live: museums, young people and education, 2009; (contrib.) Digital Culture: the changing dynamics, 2009; (contrib.) Let's Get Real - how to evaluate online success, 2011; (contrib.) Let's Get Real 2: a journey towards understanding and measuring online engagement, 2013. *Recreations:* family, singing, writing, travel. *Address:* c/o Culture24, 28 Kensington Street, Brighton BN1 4AJ. *E:* jane@culture24.org.uk. *W:* www.janefinnis.co.uk.

FINNIS, Prof. John Mitchell, DPhil; FBA 1990; Professor of Law and Legal Philosophy, Oxford University, 1989–2010, now Emeritus; Fellow and Praelector in Jurisprudence, 1966–2010, Stowell Civil Law Fellow, 1973–2010, Vice Master, 2001–10, University College, Oxford (Honorary Fellow, since 2011); *b* 28 July 1940; *s* of Maurice and Margaret Finnis; *m* 1964, Marie Carmel McNally; three *s* three *d* (and one *d* decd). *Educ:* St Peter's Coll., Adelaide, SA; St Mark's Coll., Univ. of Adelaide (LLB 1961); University Coll., Oxford (Rhodes Scholar for SA, 1962; DPhil 1965). Called to the Bar, Gray's Inn, 1970. Associate in Law, Univ. of Calif at Berkeley, 1965–66; Rhodes Reader in Laws of British Commonwealth and United States, Oxford Univ., 1972–89; Prof. and Head of Dept of Law, Univ. of Malaŵi, 1976–78; Biolchini Family Prof. of Law, Univ. of Notre Dame, USA, 1995–. Huber Distinguished Vis. Prof., Boston Coll. Law Sch., 1993–94. Special Adviser to Foreign Affairs Cttee, House of Commons, on role of UK Parlt in Canadian Constitution, 1980–82; Consultor, Pontifical Commn, Iustitia et Pax, 1977–89; Member: Pontifical Council de Iustitia et Pace, 1990–95; Catholic Bishops' Jt Cttee on Bio-Ethical Issues, 1981–88; Internat. Theol Commn, The Vatican, 1986–92; Pontifical Acad. for Life, 2001–. Governor, Anscombe Centre, Oxford (formerly Linacre Centre, London), 1981–96, 1998–2007, 2010– (Vice-Chm., 1987–96, 2002–07). Hon. LLD Notre Dame, Australia, 2011. *Publications:* Commonwealth and Dependencies, in Halsbury's Laws of England, 4th edn, Vol. 6, 1974, revised 1991, 2003, 5th edn, Vol. 13, 2009; Natural Law and Natural Rights, 1980, 2nd edn 2011; Fundamentals of Ethics, 1983; (with Joseph Boyle and Germain Grisez) Nuclear Deterrence, Morality and Realism, 1987; Moral Absolutes, 1991; Aquinas: moral, political, and legal theory, 1998; Collected Essays, Vols I–V, 2011. *Address:* University College, Oxford OX1 4BH.

FINNISSY, Prof. Michael Peter; composer; Professor of Composition, University of Southampton, since 1999; *b* 17 March 1946; *s* of George Norman Finnissy and Rita Isolene Finnissy (*née* Parsonson). *Educ:* Hawes Down Jun. Sch.; Bromley Tech. High Sch.; Beckenham and Penge Grammar Sch.; Royal Coll. of Music. Lectr, Music Dept, London Sch. of Contemporary Dance, 1969–74; Artist-in-Residence, Victorian Coll. of the Arts, Melbourne, Australia, 1982–83; Lectr, Dartington Summer Sch., 1981, 1990, 1992–; Consultant Tutor in Composition, Winchester Coll., 1988–; Res. Fellow in Music, Univ. of Sussex, 1989–99; Mem., Composition Faculty, Royal Acad. of Music, 1990–2001; KBC Prof. of New Music, Katholieke Univ., Leuven, 1999–2001. Pres., ISCM, 1990–96 (Hon. Mem., 1998–). Hon. FRCM 2008. *Compositions include:* Beat Generation Ballads (piano), 1961–2014; Four Organ Symphonies, 1962–2008; Eighteen Songs, 1963–76; World (vocal/orchestral), 1968–74; Tsuru-Kame (stage work), 1971–73; Mysteries (stage work), 1972–79; Verdi Transcriptions (piano), 1972–88; Cipriano (choral), 1974; Seven Piano Concertos, 1975–81; Pathways of Sun & Stars (orchestral), 1976; English Country-Tunes (piano), 1977; Alongside (orchestral), 1979; Sea and Sky (orchestral), 1979–80; Kelir (choral), 1981; The Undivine Comedy (stage work), 1985–88; Thérèse Raquin (stage work), 1992; Folklore (piano), 1993–94; Liturgy of S Paul (vocal), 1993–95; Shameful Vice (stage work), 1994; Speak its Name! (orchestral), 1996; The History of Photography in Sound (piano), 1993–2000; This Church (choral), 2000–03; Six Sexy Minuets Three Trios (string quartet), 2003; Molly-House (open ensemble), 2004; Second String Quartet, 2006–07; Grieg Quintettsatz, 2007; Mankind (stage work), 2007–08; Third String Quartet, 2007–09; The Transgressive Gospel, 2008–09; Three Piano Quartets, 2009–10; Completion of Grieg's Piano Quintet in B Flat, 2007–12; Awaz-e Niyaz (for lupophone doubling quarter-tone oboe and piano), 2012–13; Sesto Libro di Gesualdo (vocal), 2012–13; Remembrance Day, 2013–14; Janne (orchestra), 2014–15. *Address:* c/o Oxford University Press, Walton Street, Oxford OX2 6DP. *T:* (01865) 556767.

FINUCANE, Brendan Godfrey Eamonn; QC 2003; a Recorder, since 2000; *b* 16 March 1952; *s* of Raymond and Feardar Finucane; *m* 1998, Fiona Rosalie Horlick; two *s* two *d* from former marriage. *Educ:* Bedford Coll., Univ. of London (BSc Hons Sociol. and Social Admin). Called to the Bar, Middle Temple, 1976, Bencher, 2006; in practice, specialising in criminal law and regulatory and professional discipline work. Member Council: Tate Members, 2001–11; Friends of BM, 2002–12. Chm., Equipment for Independent Living (Charity), 1996–2011. Member: Bd of Dirs, City & Guilds of London Art Sch., 2006– (Chm., Develt Cttee, 2004–); Bd of Advrs, Delfina Foundn, 2007–; Finance and Gen. Purposes Cttee, Art Fund, 2011–; non-exec. Dir, Design and Artists Copyright Soc., 2010–. Mem. Council, RA, 2013–. Trustee: Paintings in Hosps, 2007–14; Pallant House Gall., 2009–; East Malling Trust, 2014–. *Recreations:* collecting art, architecture, theatre, cinema, visiting art galleries, music. *Address:* Outer Temple Chambers, Outer Temple, 222 Strand, WC2R 1BA. *T:* (020) 7353 6381, *Fax:* (020) 7583 1786. *E:* brendan.finucaneqc@outertemple.com. *Clubs:* Athenæum, Chelsea Arts.

FINUCANE, Joanne; *see* Lomas, J.

FINZI, Claudio V.; *see* Vita-Finzi.

FIORINA, Carleton S., (Carly); Chairman and Chief Executive Officer, Carly Fiorina Enterprises; *b* Austin, Texas, 6 Sept. 1954. *Educ:* Stanford Univ. (BA 1976); Univ. of Maryland (MBA 1980); Sloan Sch. of Mgt, MIT (MSc 1989); UCLA. Joined AT&T, 1980: posts included account exec., Sen. Vice-Pres. of Global Mktg, and Pres., Atlantic and Canadian Region; Lucent Technologies (formerly subsid. of AT&T), 1996–99: Vice-Pres. of Corp. Ops; Pres., Global Service Provider Business; Chm. and CEO, Hewlett-Packard Co., 1999–2005. Formerly Director: Kellogg Co.; Merck & Co. Inc.; Cybertrust, 2005–07; Revolution Health Gp, 2005–08; non-exec. Dir, Cisco Systems Inc., 2001. Chm., Good360, 2012–. Mem., US China Bd of Trade. *Publications:* Tough Choices: a memoir, 2006.

FIRE, Prof. Andrew Zachary, PhD; Professor of Pathology and of Genetics, Stanford University School of Medicine, since 2003; *b* Santa Clara Co., Calif, 27 April 1959. *Educ:* Fremont High Sch.; Univ. of Calif, Berkeley (AB 1978); Massachusetts Inst. of Technol. (PhD 1983). Helen Hay Whitney Foundn Fellow, MRC Lab. of Molecular Biol., Cambridge, 1983–86; Staff Associate, 1986–89, Staff Mem., 1989–2003, Dept of Embryology, Carnegie Instn of Washington, Baltimore. Adjunct Prof., Dept of Biol., Johns Hopkins Univ., 1989–. (Jtly) Nobel Prize in Physiol. or Medicine, 2006. *Publications:* articles in learned jls. *Address:* Departments of Pathology and Genetics, Stanford University School of Medicine, 300 Pasteur Drive - L235, Stanford, CA 94305–5324, USA.

FIRMIN, Carlene Emma, MBE 2011; Senior Research Fellow and Head of MsUnderstood Programme, University of Bedfordshire, since 2013; *b* London, Oct. 1983; *d* of John Firmin and Anita Pearson. *Educ:* St Michael's Catholic Grammar Sch.; Univ. of Cambridge (BA Hons Philosophy 2005); London Sch. of Econs and Pol Sci. (MSc Social Policy and Planning 2008). Race on the Agenda: Building Bridges Coordinator and Office Adminr, 2005–08; Senior Policy Officer, 2008–09; Female Voice in Violence Coordinator, 2009–11; Asst Dir, Policy and Res., Youth Justice and Child Sexual Exploitation, Barnardo's, 2011; Principal Policy Advr and Hd of Secretariat, Office of the Children's Comr's Inquiry into Child Sexual Exploitation in Gangs and Gps, Office of the Children's Comr, 2011–13. Columnist, Society Guardian, 2010–. Founder Bd of Dirs, GAG Project. Trustee: Prison Reform Trust; Hibiscus. *Recreations:* funky dance classes, looking after my Godchildren, baking, cooking for friends and family. *Address:* University of Bedfordshire, University Square, Luton, Beds LU1 3JU. *E:* carlenefirmin@hotmail.com.

FIRRELL, Hon. Dame Lucy Morgan; *see* Theis, Hon. Dame L. M.

FIRTH, Colin, CBE 2011; actor; *b* 10 Sept. 1960; *s* of David and Shirley Firth; one *s* by Meg Tilly; *m* 1997, Livia Giuggioli; two *s*. *Educ:* Montgomery of Alamein Sch., Winchester; London Drama Centre. *Stage* includes: Another Country, Queen's, 1983; The Lonely Road, Old Vic, 1985; The Elms, Greenwich, 1987; The Caretaker, Almeida, 1991; Chatsky, Almeida, 1993; Three Days of Rain, Donmar Warehouse, 1999; *films* include: Another Country, 1983; A Month in the Country, 1986; Valmont, 1988; Wings of Fame, 1989; The Hour of the Pig, 1992; Circle of Friends, 1995; The English Patient, 1996; Fever Pitch, 1997; Shakespeare in Love, The Secret Laughter of Women, 1999; My Life So Far, Relative Values, 2000; Bridget Jones's Diary, 2001; The Importance of Being Earnest, 2002; Hope Springs, What A Girl Wants, Love Actually, 2003; Girl with a Pearl Earring, Trauma, Bridget Jones: The Edge of Reason, 2004; Nanny McPhee, Where the Truth Lies, 2005; And When Did You Last See Your Father?, The Last Legion, St Trinian's, 2007; The Accidental Husband, Mamma Mia!, Easy Virtue, 2008; Genova, Dorian Gray, St Trinian's 2: the Legend of Fritton's Gold, 2009; A Single Man (BAFTA Award for Best Actor), 2010; The King's Speech (Academy, Golden Globe and BAFTA Awards for Best Actor), Tinker, Tailor, Soldier, Spy, 2011; Gambit, 2012; The Railway Man, 2013; Devil's Knot, 2014; Arthur & Mike, 2014; Before I Go to Sleep, 2014; Magic in the Moonlight, 2014; Kingsman, 2015; *television* includes: Dutch Girls, 1984; Tumbledown, 1987; Out of the Blue, 1990; The Deep Blue Sea, 1994; Pride and Prejudice, 1995; Nostromo, 1996; The Turn of the Screw, 1999; Donovan Quick, 2000. *Address:* c/o Independent Talent Group Ltd, 40 Whitfield Street, W1T 2RH. *T:* (020) 7636 6565.

FIRTH, Prof. David, PhD; FBA 2008; Professor of Statistics, University of Warwick, since 2003; *b* Wakefield, Yorks, 22 Dec. 1957; *s* of Allan Firth and Betty Firth (*née* Bailey); *m* 1987, Julie McCormack; one *s* two *d*. *Educ:* Trinity Hall, Cambridge (BA Maths 1980); Imperial Coll. London (MSc 1982; PhD Stats 1987). Asst Prof., Univ. of Texas at Austin, 1987–89; Lectr, Univ. of Southampton, 1989–93; Prof. of Social Stats, University of Oxford, 1993–2003. Professorial Fellow, ESRC, 2003–06. Guy Medal in Bronze, 1998, Guy Medal in Silver, 2012, Royal Statistical Soc. *Publications:* contrib. articles to learned jls incl. Biometrika, Jl Royal Statistical Soc., BMJ. *Recreations:* cycling, walking. *Address:* Department of Statistics, University of Warwick, Coventry CV4 7AL. *T:* (024) 7657 2581, *Fax:* (024) 7652 4532. *E:* d.firth@warwick.ac.uk.

FIRTH, Mrs Joan Margaret, CB 1995; PhD; Chair, Bradford Health Authority, 1998–2000 (Vice Chair, 1996–98); Deputy Director of NHS Finance, Department of Health, 1990–95; *b* 25 March 1935; *d* of Ernest Wilson and Ann (*née* Crowther); *m* 1955, Kenneth Firth. *Educ:* Lawnswood High Sch., Leeds; Univ. of Leeds (1st Cl. BSc Colour Chemistry; PhD Dyeing of Wool). Research Asst, Leeds Univ., 1958–60; Head of Science, Selby High Sch., 1960–62; Sen. Lecturer in General Science, Elizabeth Gaskell Coll., Manchester, 1962–66; Lectr in Organic Chemistry, Salford Univ., 1966–67; joined Civil Service as Direct Entry Principal, 1967; Asst Sec., 1974; Under-Sec., DHSS, 1981; Under-Sec., Social Security Div. C, DHSS, later DSS, 1987–90. Member: ESRC, 1988–92; Training Bd, 1990–92. Mem., Audit Cttee, Inst. Cancer Res., 1994–98. *Publications:* contrib. Jl Textile Inst., 1958. *Recreations:* wine, bridge.

FIRTH, Paul James; writer (part-time); a District Judge (Magistrates' Courts), Lancashire, 2001–05; *b* 2 June 1951; *s* of Albert and Violet Firth; *m* 1979, Ann Barbara Whitehead; one *s*. *Educ:* Bradford Grammar Sch.; Queen's Coll., Oxford (Hastings Exhibnr; MA 1973). Admitted solicitor, 1980; Trainee Court Clerk, Keighley Magistrates' Court, 1973–74; Trainee Court Clerk, Court Clerk, then Sen. Court Clerk, Leeds Magistrates' Court, 1975–81; Dep. Clerk to Justices (Legal), Manchester City Magistrates' Court, 1981–86; Clerk to Justices, Rotherham Magistrates' Court, 1986–95; Actg Stipendiary Magistrate, 1991–95; Stipendiary Magistrate, subseq. Dist Judge (Magistrates' Cts), Merseyside, 1995–2001. Pt-time Lectr, 2006–, Hon. Fellow in Criminal Justice Studies, Directorate of Social Scis, 2011–, Univ. of Salford. *Publications:* Four Minutes to Hell: the story of the Bradford City fire, 2005; Bobby Campbell: they don't make them like him any more, 2012; contrib. The City Gent, Boy from Brazil, Yorkshire Post. *Recreations:* running any distance up to 10 km, various sports (mainly watching, especially Bradford City), reading anything except law books. *E:* paulfirth@blueyonder.co.uk. *Club:* Yorkshire CC.

FIRTH, Rt Rev. Peter James; Bishop Suffragan of Malmesbury, 1983–94; Hon. Assistant Bishop, diocese of Gloucester, since 2003; *b* 12 July 1929; *s* of Atkinson Vernon Firth and Edith Pepper; *m* 1955, Felicity Mary Wilding; two *s* two *d* (and one long-term foster *d*). *Educ:* Stockport Grammar School; Emmanuel Coll., Cambridge (Open Exhibnr, MA, DipEd; Pres., Cambridge Footlights, 1953); St Stephen's House Theol Coll., Oxford. Ordained, 1955; Assistant Curate, St Stephen's, Barbourne in Worcester, 1955–58; Priest-in-charge, Church of the Ascension, Parish of St Matthias, Malvern Link, Worcs, 1958–62; Rector of St George's, Abbey Hey, Gorton in Manchester, 1962–66; Religious Broadcasting Assistant, North Region, BBC, 1966–67; Religious Broadcasting Organiser and Senior Producer, Religious Programmes, BBC South and West, Bristol, 1967–83. Religious Advr to HTV West, 1983–2003; Mem., W of England TV Council, 2003–. Pres., Religious Drama Soc. of GB, 1994–2009. Trustee, Bristol Cancer Help Centre, 1995–2007. Governor: Millfield Sch., 1994–2002. Clifton Coll., 1995–2007; Internat. Radio Festival winner, Seville, 1975. *Publications:* Lord of the Seasons, 1978; The Love that moves the Sun, 1996; As Far As I Can See (poetry), 2013. *Recreations:* theatre, photography, music, travel, Manchester United. *Address:* Mill House, Silk Mill Lane, Winchcombe GL54 5HZ. *T:* (01242) 603669. *E:* peter.united4@btinternet.com.

FIRTH, Tazeena Mary; designer; *b* 1 Nov. 1935; *d* of Denis Gordon Firth and Irene (*née* Morris). *Educ:* St Mary's, Wantage; Châtelard Sch. Theatre Royal, Windsor, 1954–57; English Stage Co., Royal Court, 1957–60; partnership in stage design with Timothy O'Brien estabd 1961; output incl.: The Bartered Bride, The Girl of the Golden West, 1962; West End prodns of new plays, 1963–64; London scene of Shakespeare Exhibn, 1964; Tango, Days in the Trees, Staircase, RSC, and Trafalgar at Madame Tussaud's, 1966; All's Well that Ends Well, As You Like It, Romeo and Juliet, RSC, 1967; The Merry Wives of Windsor, Troilus and Cressida (also Nat. Theatre, 1976), The Latent Heterosexual, RSC, 1968; Pericles (also Comédie Française, 1974), Women Beware Women, Bartholomew Fair, RSC, 1969; Measure for Measure, RSC, Madame Tussaud's in Amsterdam, and The Knot Garden, Royal Opera, 1970; Enemies, Man of Mode, RSC, 1971; La Cenerentola, Oslo, Lower Depths, and The Island of the Mighty, RSC, As You Like It, OCSC, 1972; Richard II, Love's Labour's Lost, RSC, 1973; Next of Kin, NT, Summerfolk, RSC, and The Bassarids, ENO, 1974; John Gabriel Borkman, NT, Peter Grimes, Royal Opera (later in Paris), The Marrying of Ann Leete, RSC, 1975; Wozzeck, Adelaide Fest., The Zykovs, RSC, and The Force of Habit, NT, 1976; Tales from the Vienna Woods, Bedroom Farce, NT, and Falstaff, Berlin Opera, 1977; The Cunning Little Vixen, Göteborg, Evita, London (later in USA, Australia, Vienna), A Midsummer Night's Dream, Sydney Opera House, 1978; Peter Grimes, Göteborg, The Rake's Progress, Royal Opera, 1979; Turandot, Vienna State Opera, 1983. Designed independently: The Two Gentlemen of Verona, RSC, 1969; Occupations, RSC, 1971; The Rape of Lucretia, Karlstad, 1982; Katherina Ismailova, Göteborg, 1984; La Traviata, Umeå, The Trojan Woman, Göteborg, and Bluebeard's Castle, Copenhagen, 1985; Il Seraglio, Göteborg, 1986; The Magic Flute, Rigoletto, Umeå, 1987; Romeo and Juliet, Malmö, 1988; The Rake's Progress, Göteborg, and, Dido and Aeneas, Copenhagen, 1989; From the House of the Dead, Göteborg, and, Barbarians, RSC, 1990; Macbeth, Göteborg, 1990; Lady Macbeth of Mtsensk, Copenhagen, La Bohème, Malmö, and Il Seraglio, Stockholm, 1991; Don Giovanni, Prague, 1991; Rigoletto, Oslo, and Carmen, Copenhagen, 1992; Carmen, Stockholm, Drot og Mask, Copenhagen, Magic Flute, Prague and Peter Grimes, Copenhagen, 1993; Vox Humana, Göteborg, 1994; Don Giovanni, Japan, Dido and Aeneas, and Oh Come Ye Sons of Art, Dröttningholm, Bluebeard's Castle, and Jenůfa, Göteborg, 1995; Peter Grimes, Göteborg and Finnish Nat. Opera, and Jenůfa, Copenhagen, 1998; Peter Grimes, New Israeli Opera, Tel Aviv, 2002. (Jtly) Gold Medal for Set Design, Prague Quadriennale, 1975. *Recreations:* sailing, walking. *Address:* Faraway, Keyhaven Marshes, Lymington SO41 0TR.

FISCHEL, David Andrew; Chief Executive, Intu Properties (formerly TransAtlantic Holdings, then Liberty International, then Capital Shopping Centres Group) plc, since 2001; *b* 1 April 1958. ACA 1983. Touche Ross & Co., 1980–85; with TransAtlantic Holdings, later Liberty International, then Capital Shopping Centres Group plc, subseq. Intu Properties plc, 1985–: Man. Dir, 1992–2001. *Address:* c/o Intu Properties plc, 40 Broadway, SW1H 0BT. *T:* (020) 7960 1200.

FISCHEL, Robert Gustav; QC 1998; Chambers of Robert Fischel, QC, Estepona, Spain; Consultant: Governor's Street Chambers, Gibraltar; Chambers of Stephen Bullock, Gibraltar; *b* 12 Jan. 1953; *s* of Bruno Rolf Fischel and Sophie Fischel (*née* Kruml); *m* 1st, 1989, Louise Kim Halsall (marr. diss. 1997); 2nd, 1999, Anna Louise (*d* 2012), *d* of Patrick Landucci; two *d. Educ:* City of London Sch.; Univ. of London (LLB). Called to the Bar, Middle Temple, 1975; in practice at the Bar, 1975–; called to the Gibraltar Bar, 2012. Former proprietor, El Molino de la Cala hotel, Estepona. Freeman, City of London, 1974. *Recreations:* cooking, horse riding, ski-ing, travel.

FISCHELIS, Suzy; *see* Klein, S.

FISCHER, Dr Edmond Henri; Professor Emeritus, University of Washington, since 1990; *b* Shanghai, China, 6 April 1920; *s* of Oscar Fischer and Renee Tapernoux; *m* 1st, Nelly Gagnaux (*d* 1961); two *s*; 2nd, 1963, Beverley Bullock (*d* 2006). *Educ:* Univ. of Geneva (Licencié ès Sciences 1943; Diplôme d'Ingénieur 1944; DSc 1947). Asst, Labs of Organic Chem., Univ. of Geneva, 1946–47; Fellow, Swiss Nat. Foundn, 1948–50; Res. Fellow, Rockefeller Foundn, 1950–53; Res. Associate, Div. of Biol., CIT, 1953; University of Washington: Asst Prof. of Biochem., 1953–56; Associate Prof., 1956–61; Prof., 1961–90. Associate, Neurosciences Res. Prog., Neuroscience Res. Inst., La Jolla, Calif, 1995–. Member: Biochem. Section, NIH, 1959–64; Editl Adv. Bd, Biochemistry, Jl of ACS, 1961–66 (Associate Editor, 1966–92); Adv. Bd, ACS, 1962; Sci. Adv. Bd, Friedrich Miescher Inst. CIBA-GEIGY, 1976–84 (Chm., 1981–84); Council, Amer. Soc. Biol Chemists, 1980–83; Scientific Council on Basic Sci., Amer. Heart Assoc., 1977–80; Bd of Scientific Govs, Scripps Res. Inst., 1987–; Scientific Adv. Cttee, Muscular Dystrophy Assoc., 1980–89; Scientific Adv. Bd, Basel Inst. for Immunology, 1996–; Bd Govs, Weizmann Inst. of Sci., Israel, 1997–; Chm., Task Force, Muscular Dystrophy Assoc. Res. Centres, 1985–89. Member: Amer. Soc. Biol Chemists; ACS; Amer. Acad. of Arts and Scis, 1972; AAAS 1972; NAS 1973; Amer. Assoc. of Univ. Profs. Foreign Mem., Royal Society, 2010. Pres., Pole Universitaire de Montpellier, 1993–96. Hon. PhD: Montpellier 1985; Basel 1988; Med. Coll. of Ohio, 1993; Indiana, 1993; Ruhr-Univ., 1994. Numerous awards, medals and prizes; Nobel Prize in Physiology or Medicine, 1992. *Publications:* numerous. *Recreations:* playing classical piano, private pilot. *Address:* Department of Biochemistry, Box 357350, University of Washington, Seattle, WA 98195–7350, USA. *T:* (206) 5431741.

FISCHER, Iván; conductor; Founder and Music Director, Budapest Festival Orchestra, since 1983; Music Director, Konzerthaus Berlin, and Principal Conductor, Konzerthaus Orchester, Berlin, since 2012; *b* Budapest, 20 Jan. 1951; *s* of Sándor Fischer and Éva Boschán; two *s* two *d. Educ:* Béla Bartók Music Conservatory, Budapest; Wiener Hochschule für Musik; Mozarteum, Salzburg. Début in London with RPO, 1976; Music Director: Northern Sinfonia, Newcastle, 1979–82; Kent Opera, 1984–89; Lyon Opera House, 1999–2003; Principal Guest Conductor, Cincinnati SO, 1989–96; Principal Guest Conductor, 2006–08, Principal Conductor, 2008–10, Nat. SO, Washington. Concert tours with LSO, to Spain, 1981, USA, 1982, world tour, 1983; concerts with orchestras, including: Berlin Philharmonic, Concertgebouw; Munich Philharmonic; Israel Philharmonic; Orch. de Paris; Orch. of Age of Enlightenment; LA and NY Philharmonics; Cleveland; Philadelphia; San Francisco Symphony; Chicago Symphony; opera prodns in London, Paris, Vienna. Has made over 70 recordings. Patron, British Kódaly Acad.; Founder, Hungarian Mahler Soc. Premio Firenze, 1974; Rupert Foundn Award, BBC, 1976; Gramophone Award for Best Orchestral Recording of Year, 1998; Crystal Award, World Econ. Forum, 1998. Golden Medal Award (Hungary), 1998; Kossuth Prize (Hungary), 2006; Royal Philharmonic Award, 2011; Dutch Ovatie Prize, 2011. Chevalier des Arts et des Lettres (France). *Address:* Budapest Festival Orchestra, Polgár u. 8–10, 1033 Budapest, Hungary.

FISCHER, Joseph Martin, (Joschka); Minister of Foreign Affairs and Deputy Chancellor, Germany, 1998–2005; Managing Partner, Joschka Fischer and Company, since 2009; *b* 12 April 1948; *m* 1st, 1967, Edeltraud (marr. diss. 1984); 2nd, 1984, Inge (marr. diss. 1987); one *s* one *d*; 3rd, 1987, Claudia Bohm (marr. diss. 1999); 4th, 1999, Nicola Leske (marr. diss. 2003); 5th, 2005, Minu Barati. Mem., Green Party, Germany, 1982– (former Leader). State of Hesse: Minister for the Envmt and Energy, 1985–87; Mem., Landtag, 1987–91 (Chm., Green Party); Minister for the Envmt, Energy and Fed. Affairs, and Dep. to Minister-Pres., 1991–94; Mem., Bundestag, 1983–85, 1994–2006; Dep. Mem., Bundesrat, 1985–87; Parly spokesman, Alliance '90/Green Party, Bundestag, 1994–98. Vis. Lectr, Woodrow Wilson Sch. of Public and Internat. Affairs, Princeton Univ., 2006–07. *Publications:* The Red-Green Years (autobiog.), 2007.

FISCHER, Hon. Timothy Andrew, AC 2005; Ambassador of Australia to the Holy See, 2009–12; Vice President, Global Crop Diversity Trust; *b* 3 May 1946; *s* of J. R. Fischer; *m* 1992, Judy, *d* of Harry Brewer; two *s. Educ:* Xavier Coll., Melbourne. Platoon Comdr and Transport Officer, RAR, 1967; Nat. Service, S Vietnam, 1968–69. Primary producer, Boree Creek, 1964–65, 1970. MLA Sturt, 1971–80, Murray, 1980–84, NSW; Nat. Party Whip, NSW, 1981–84; MP (Nat.) Farrer, NSW, 1984–2001; Shadow Minister: for Veterans' Affairs, 1985–90; for Energy and Resources, 1990–93; for Trade, 1993–96; Dep. Prime Minister and Minister for Trade, 1996–99; Leader, Nat. Party of Australia, 1990–99. Chm., Tourism Australia, 2004–07; Nat. Chm., Royal Flying Doctor Service, 2007–08. Dir, Australian Agricl Co., 2001–08. *Publications:* Seven Days in East Timor: ballot and bullets, 2000; (with Peter Rees) Outback Heroes and Communities that Count; Transcontinental Train Odyssey, 2004; (with Tshering Tashi) Bold Bhutan Beckons, 2009; Trains Unlimited in the 21st Century, 2011; Holy See, Unholy Me: 1,000 days in Rome, 2013; Maestro John Monash: Australia's greatest citizen general, 2014. *Recreations:* chess, tennis, trekking, bushwalking in Bhutan. *Address:* Grossotto, 189 Pini Lane, Mudgegonga, Vic 3737, Australia.

FISCHER BOEL, (Else) Mariann; Member, European Commission, 2004–10; *b* 15 April 1943; *d* of Hans Boel and Valborg Boel; *m* 1967, Hans Fischer Boel. Mgt Sec., 1965–67, Finance Manager, 1967–71, export co., Copenhagen. Mem., Munkebo Municipal Council, 1982–91, 1994–97. MP (L) Denmark, 1990–2004; Minister for Food, Agriculture and Fisheries, 2001–04.

FISCHLER, Dr Franz; Member, European Commission, 1995–2004; Consultant, Franz Fischler Consult GmbH, since 2004; President, European Forum Alpbach, since 2012; *b* 23 Sept. 1946; *s* of Josef Fischler and Theodora Fischler; *m* 1973, Adelheid Hausmann; two *s* two *d. Educ:* Univ. for Soil Sci., Vienna (Dr in Natural Scis 1978). Univ. Asst, Dept of Regl Agricl Planning, Inst. for Farm Mgt, Vienna, 1973–79; Tyrol Chamber of Agriculture: Mem., 1979–84; Dir, 1985–89; elected Mem., Nationalrat, 1990, 1994; Fed. Minister of Agric. and Forestry, 1989–94. Grosse Goldene Ehrenzeichen am Bande (Austria), 1993. *Address:* Dörferstrasse 30B, 6067 Absam, Austria.

FISH, David John, PhD; non-executive Chairman, United Biscuits, 2004–06 and 2011–14 (Executive Chairman, 2006–11); Director, Fishdance Ltd, since 2013; *b* 31 May 1948; *s* of George Henry and Edith Doreen Fish; *m* 1976, Linda Pamela Robinson; one *s* two *d. Educ:* Gateway Grammar Sch., Leicester; Univ. of Sheffield (BSc 1st cl. 1969, Mappin Medal; PhD Metal Physics 1972). Unilever, 1972–74; joined Mars, 1974; Operating Bd, Mars Inc., 1994–2001; Pres., European Snackfoods, 1998–2000; Jt Pres., Masterfoods Europe, 2000–01. Chm., Christian Salveson, 2003–07. Non-exec. Dir, Royal Mail, 2003–08. *Recreations:* cricket, football, ski-ing, golf. *Clubs:* Royal Automobile; Berkshire Golf.

FISH, Sir David Royden, Kt 2014; MD; FRCP; Professor of Clinical Neurophysiology and Epilepsy, University College London, 2000, now Hon. Professor; Managing Director, UCL Partners, since 2009; *b* 5 June 1956; *s* of George Henry Fish and Sadie Fish; *m* 1986, Glenda Joyce Parker; one *s* one *d* (twins). *Educ:* Selwyn Coll., Cambridge (BA 1978); King's Coll., London (MB BS 1981; MD 1989). FRCP 1994. Asst Prof., Neurology, McGill Univ., Montreal, 1988–89; Consultant Physician, Nat. Hosp. for Neurology and Neurosurgery, 1989–2010. Med. Dir (Specialist Hosps), UCL Hosps NHS Foundn Trust, 2001–09. *Publications:* contribs to learned jls and books on medical subjects incl. epilepsy, brain imaging, safety of video games and health care. *Recreations:* trekking, English music hall. *Address:* UCL Partners, 170 Tottenham Court Road, W1T 7HA.

FISH, David Stanley, CBE 2007; Head, Zimbabwe, Department for International Development, 2009–12; *b* 4 Oct. 1948; *s* of John and Phyllis Fish; *m* 1st, 1971, Sandra Templeton (marr. diss. 1990); two *d*; 2nd, 1992, Marion Fleming Semple; two *d. Educ:* Baines Grammar Sch., Poulton-le-Fylde. Department for International Development: Head: Develt Educn Unit, 1979–81; Manpower Policy Unit, 1981–84; Dependent Territories Section, British Develt Div. in the Caribbean, Barbados, 1985–86; Accounts Dept, 1986–88; Overseas Pensions Dept, 1988–92; Procurement, Appts and NGO Dept, 1993–97; Eastern Africa, Nairobi, 1997–99; Dir of Human Resources, 2000–04; Dir, Africa, then E and Central Africa, 2004–09. *Recreations:* sport, politics, dog walking, supporting Blackpool and Crystal Palace. *Address:* 34 Shawton Road, Chapelton, Strathaven, Lanarkshire ML10 6RY. *Club:* Chapelton Inn Racing.

FISH, David Thomas; QC 1997; a Recorder, 1994–2006; *b* 23 July 1949; *s* of Tom Fish and Gladys (*née* Durkin); *m* 1989, Angelina Brunhilde Dennett; one *s* one *d. Educ:* Ashton-under-Lyne Grammar Sch.; London Sch. of Econs (LLB). Called to the Bar, Inner Temple, 1973. *Recreations:* horse-racing, golf. *Address:* Deans Court Chambers, 24 St John Street, Manchester M3 4DF. *T:* (0161) 214 6000.

FISH, Dame Jocelyn (Barbara), DNZM 2009 (DCNZM 2001); CBE 1991; voluntary community worker, since 1959; farming partner, 1959–90; *b* 29 Sept. 1930; *d* of John Arthur Green and Edna Marion Green (*née* Garton); *m* 1959, Robert John Malthus Fish; one *s* two *d. Educ:* Hamilton High Sch., New Zealand; Auckland Univ. (BA); Auckland Teachers' College (cert.). Secondary school teacher, NZ and UK, 1953–59. Nat. Pres., Nat. Council of Women of NZ, 1986–90; (various offices) NZ Fedn of Univ. Women, and Anglican Women; Chm. Policy Cttee, survey, NZ Women—family, employment and education, Centre for Population Studies, Univ. of Waikato, 1995–98. NZ Deleg., UN Conf. on Women, Nairobi, 1985. Member: Film Censorship Bd of Review, 1981–84; Nat. Commn for Australian Bicentenary, 1987–88; Nat. Commn for UNESCO, 1989–94; Broadcasting Standards Authority, 1989–91; Transport Accident Investigation Commn, 1990–95; Hamilton Dist Legal Services Cttee, 1992–97; NZ Dental Council Complaints Assessment Cttee, 1995–2001. Member, Board: Waikato Br., Fedn of Univ. Women, 1991–99 (Chm.); Hamilton Community Law Centre Trust, 1994–2000 (Chm.); Hamilton Combined Christian Foodbank Trust, 1997–99; Waikato Anglican Social Services Trust, 2000–04 (Chm.). Councillor, Piako County Council, 1980–89. JP 1984–2010. Hon. Fellow, Waikato Inst. of Technol., 2003. NZ Sesquicentenary Commemoration Medal, 1990; NZ Suffrage Commemoration Medal, 1993; Univ. of Waikato Medal, 2012. *Recreations:* music, literature, family, travel, watching politics. *Address:* 63 Gilbass Avenue, Hamilton, New Zealand. *T:* (7) 839 1512.

FISH, His Honour Peter Stuart; a Circuit Judge, 1994–2005; *b* 18 Dec. 1938; *s* of Geoffrey Chadwick Fish and Emma (*née* Wood); *m* 1963, Nola Ann Worrall; two *s* one *d* (and one *d* decd). *Educ:* Rydal Sch.; Trinity Hall, Cambridge (MA). Admitted solicitor, 1963; practised in Southport, 1964–87; Dist Registrar, subseq. Dist Judge, Manchester, 1987–94; a Recorder, 1991–94. *Recreations:* music, gardening, golf, bridge, woodcarving.

FISH, Wendy; Director, British Architectural Library, Royal Institute of British Architects, since 2013; *b* Dulwich, London; *d* of John Alfred Fish and Elsie Joy Fish; *m* 2002, Andrew Geoffrey Greenhalgh. *Educ:* Kingsdale Comp. Sch., Dulwich; Leicester Poly. (BA Hons 1981); Poly. of North London (DipLib). Curator, 1984–89, Inf. Services Manager, 1989–96, Nat. Art Liby, V&A Mus.; Hd, User Services, Wellcome Liby, Wellcome Trust, 1996–2009; Dep. Dir, British Architl Liby, RIBA, 2010–13. *Recreations:* art, architecture, current affairs, walking, sport, Arsenal FC. *Address:* Royal Institute of British Architects, 66 Portland Place, W1B 1AD. *T:* (020) 7307 3695. *E:* wendy.fish@riba.org.

FISHBURN, (John) Dudley; Chairman: Bluecube Technology Ltd, since 2009; Mulvaney Capital Management, since 2011; Baring Vostok Investments Ltd, since 2013; *b* 8 June 1946; *s* of John Eskdale Fishburn and Bunting Fishburn; *m* 1981, Victoria, *y d* of Sir John Dennis, (Sir Jack), Boles, MBE; two *s* two *d. Educ:* Eton Coll.; Harvard Univ. (BA). Exec. Editor, The Economist, 1979–88. MP (C) Kensington, July 1988–1997. Parliamentary Private Secretary: FCO, 1989–90; DTI, 1990–93. Chairman: HFC Bank, 1998–2009; Henderson Smaller Cos Investment Trust plc, 2003–11. Non-executive Director: Saatchi & Saatchi, 1998–2003; Philip Morris Inc. (formerly Atria Inc.), 1998–2014; Beazley Gp plc, 2002–10; HSBC Bank plc, 2003–09; GFI Ltd, 2010–; Kyte Gp Ltd, 2010–15; Adviser: J. P. Morgan, 1988–96; T. T. Internat., 1997–2011; Baring Private Equity, 1997–2008. Chm., Standing Cttee on Social Scis, 1993–96, Library Cttee, 1996–2006, Harvard Univ.; Mem., Bd of Overseers, Harvard Univ., 1989–95; Pres., Harvard Club of London, 1970–90. Governor, English National Ballet, 1989–95; Chairman: Trustees, Open Univ., 1995–2001; Library Vis. Cttee, Cambridge Univ., 2005–14; Member of Council: Nat. Trust, 1993–2005 (Hon. Treas., 1996–2002); Prison Reform Trust, 1993–2000; Foundn for Liver Res. (formerly Liver Res. Trust), 1995–; Dulwich Picture Gall. Council, 1997–2001; Royal Oak Foundn (USA), 1997–2004; Reading Univ. Council, 2002–12. Chm., Theale Green Acad., 2013–. Gov., Peabody Trust, 2000–11; Trustee, Heritage of London Trust, 2010– (Chm., 2011–). Pres., W Berks Conservative Assoc., 2000–. Chm., Friends of Silchester Archaeological Site, 2003–. Fellow, Centre for the Advanced Study of India, Univ. of Penn, 2005–13. Editor, The Economist's World in 1993, and annually until 2003; Associate Editor, The Economist, 1989–2003. DUniv: Open, 2002; Reading, 2013. Parly Radical of the Year, 1992. *Recreations:* sailing, cooking. *Address:* The Old Rectory, Englefield, Berks RG7 5EP. *Club:* Brooks's.

See also N. E. C. Boles.

FISHER, family name of **Baron Fisher**.

FISHER, 4th Baron *cr* 1909, of Kilverstone, co. Norfolk; **Patrick Vavasseur Fisher;** *b* Cambridge, England, 14 June 1953; *er s* of 3rd Baron Fisher, DSC and of Elizabeth Ann Penelope Holt; *S* father, 2012; *m* 1977, Lady Karen Jean Carnegie, *er d* of 13th Earl of Northesk; three *s* four *d* (of whom one *s* one *d* are twins). *Educ:* Cheam Sch., Newbury; Stowe. *Recreations:* shooting, woodland management. *Heir: e s* Hon. John Carnegie Vavasseur Fisher, *b* 8 Dec. 1979. *Address:* Kilverstone Hall, Thetford, Norfolk IP24 2RL. *T:* (01842) 751122. *E:* patrick.fisher@kilverstonehall.com. *Clubs:* Naval and Military; Royal Thames Yacht.

FISHER, Adrian; maze designer, inventor and author; Founder and Chairman, Adrian Fisher Design (formerly Adrian Fisher Mazes) Ltd, since 1983; *b* 5 Aug. 1951; *s* of Dr James Frederick Fisher and Rosemary (*née* Sterling-Hill); *m* 1st, 1975, Dorothy Jane Pollard (marr. diss. 1996; she *d* 2009); two *d*; 2nd, 1997, Marie Ann Butterworth; one *s. Educ:* Oundle Sch.; Portsmouth Poly. Over 600 mazes created in 32 countries, 1979–; designer: world's first cornfield maize maze, Pennsylvania, 1993, and subseq. over 400 maize mazes; over 40 hedge mazes, including: Leeds Castle; Blenheim Palace; Scone Palace; Speke Hall; pioneer: of over 40 mirror mazes, including mazes at: Wookey Hole Caves; Hamburg Dungeon; Navy Pier, Chicago; Birmingham Sea Life Centre; Absolut Amaze, at Oxo Gall., London, 2002; Warwick Castle; Tokyo Dome; Hollywood Wax Mus., TN; PortAventura theme park, Spain; Tokyo Tower; of brick-path-in-grass mazes, and foaming fountain water mazes; walk-through parting waterfalls, foaming fountain gates and wrought-iron maze gates in mazes; inventor: 7-sided

Fisher Paver system for decorative brick paving; (jtly) Mitre Tile system for paving, tiling and decorative patterns, including 24ft high Mitre mosaic in SciTec Bldg, Oundle Sch.; designer of puzzles for 2000 and 2006 World Puzzle Championships; one-man show: An Amazing Art: Contemporary Labyrinths, Norton Mus. of Art, W Palm Beach, Florida, 1997. Set 6 Guinness world records for progressively larger cornfield mazes in USA and England, 1993–2003; Guinness world record (200 metres) for world's tallest maze on facades of Maze Tower, Dubai, 2015. Dir, 1991—The Year of the Maze, British tourism campaign. Mem., Eur. Bd, Themed Entertainment Assoc., 2005–08. Liveryman: Soc. of Apothecaries, 1979–; Gardeners' Co., 1991–. Gold Medal for Beatles' Maze, Liverpool Internat. Garden Fest., 1984; Resorgimento Award, Univ. of Tennessee at Knoxville, 2003. *Publications:* The Art of the Maze, 1990; Secrets of the Maze, 1997; Mazes and Follies, 2004; Mazes and Labyrinths, 2004; The Amazing Book of Mazes, 2006. *Recreations:* gardening, photography, water-colour painting, recreational mathematics, keeping sheep, flying quadcopter. *Address:* Adrian Fisher Design Ltd, Portman Lodge, Durweston, Dorset DT11 0QA. *T:* (01258) 458845. *E:* adrian@adrianfisherdesign.com. *W:* www.adrianfisherdesign.com.

FISHER, Andrew; *see* Fisher, J. A.

FISHER, Andrew Charles; Chief Executive, Towry Group (formerly JS & P Holdings, then Towry Law Group), 2006–14; *b* 22 June 1961; *s* of Harold Fisher and Jessie Fisher (now Stanley); *m*; two *s*; *m* 2009, Caroline Gina (*née* Moss); one *d*. *Educ:* Birmingham Univ. (BSc Hons Econs). Mktg Manager, Unilever PLC, 1982–87; Partner, Coopers & Lybrand Mgt Consultancy, 1987–91; Sales and Mktg Dir, Standard Chartered Bank, Equitor Div., 1991–94; Man. Dir, Rangeley Co. Ltd, 1994–97; Strategic Advr, NatWest Wealth Mgt, 1997–98; Gp Commercial Dir, Coutts NatWest Gp, 1998–2000; Chief Exec., Coutts Gp, 2000–02; Partner, Carlyle Gp, 2002–03; Chief Exec., CPP Gp, 2003–04; Gp CEO, Cox Insurance, 2004; Exec. Chm., JS & P Hldgs, 2005–06. Non-executive Director: Benfield Gp Ltd, 2003–08; C. Hoare & Co., 2015–; Adviser: Ondra Partners, 2014–; Davy Gp, 2015–. *Recreations:* ski-ing, golf, squash, scuba diving. *Clubs:* Mosimann's; Wentworth Golf.

FISHER, Carol Ann; Chief Executive, COI Communications (formerly Central Office of Information), 1999–2002; *b* 13 April 1954; *d* of Joseph and Gladys Fisher. *Educ:* Univ. of Birmingham (BA Hons Medieval and Modern Hist.). Brand Manager, Bisto, RHM Foods, 1979–81; Sen. Mktg Manager and various other posts, Grand Metropolitan Brewing, 1982–88; Mktg Dir, Holsten Distributors, 1989–94; Gen. Manager, Mktg and Commercial, Courage Internat., 1994–95; Man. Dir, CLT-UFA UK Radio Sales, 1996–98. Chief Advr to Govt on Mktg Commns, 2002. Member: Women in Advertising and Communications (Pres., 2000–01); Mktg Soc.; Mktg Gp GB. *Recreations:* walking, long haul travel.

FISHER, (Christopher) Mark, CBE 2010; Director, Office for Civil Society and Government Innovation Group, Cabinet Office, since 2014; *b* 8 Oct. 1960; *s* of late Christopher Forsyth Fisher and of (Nadia) Ruth Reeve Fisher (*née* Angel); *m* 1997, Helen, *d* of late Patrick Daniel Fitzgibbon and of Marie Fitzgibbon, Lymm, Cheshire. *Educ:* King Edward's Sch., Bath; Lady Margaret Hall, Oxford (BA Hons PPE). Jun. posts, DHSS, 1983–87; Principal: Social Security Policy Gp, DSS, 1988–90; Econ. Secretariat, Cabinet Office, 1990–92; speech writer for Sec. of State for Social Security, 1992; mgt posts, 1993–97, Personnel and Communications Dir, 1997–2000, Benefits Agency; Human Resources Dir, DSS, subseq. DWP, 2000–01; Dir, Performance and Product Mgt, then Business Strategy, Jobcentre Plus, DWP, 2001–05; Chief Exec., Sector Skills Develt Agency, 2005–08; Dir, Benefit Strategy and Skills, then Jobseekers and Skills, DWP, 2008–11; Social Justice Dir, DWP, 2011–14. *Recreations:* good company, railways, canals. *Address:* Cabinet Office, 1 Horse Guards Road, SW1A 2HQ. *Club:* Reform.

FISHER, David Paul; QC 1996; a Recorder, since 1991; *b* 30 April 1949; *s* of late Percy Laurence Fisher and Doris Mary Fisher; *m* 1st, 1971, Cary Maria Cicely Lamberton (*d* 1977); one *d*; 2nd, 1979, Diana Elizabeth Dolby. *Educ:* Felsted Sch. Called to the Bar, Gray's Inn, 1973, Bencher, 2003; Asst Recorder, 1987. Hd of Chambers, 2010–. Member: Gen. Council of the Bar, 1997–2000; Advocacy Studies Bd, 1997–2001; Criminal Procedure Rule Cttee, 2004–08. *Recreations:* travel, sport, gardening, cinema. *Address:* 21 College Hill, EC4R 2RP.

FISHER, Duncan Mark, OBE 2009; Project Director: Maternity Assist; Kids in the Middle, since 2012; MumsandDadsNet.com; Child&Family Blog, since 2014; *b* 3 Nov. 1961; *s* of Humphrey and Helga Fisher; *m* Clare; two *d*. *Educ:* Corpus Christi Coll., Cambridge (BA Natural Scis 1984; MPhil Theol 1986); School of Slavonic and East European Studies, London (MA Area Studies 1989). Founder and CEO, East West Environment, 1989–95; Founder and CEO, 1994–2003, Trustee, 2003–08, Action for Conservation through Tourism, subseq. Travel Foundn; Co-Founder and Chief Exec., Fathers Direct, subseq. Fatherhood Inst., 1999–2009; Co-Founder and Dir, Family Info Ltd, 2007–11. Mem., Equal Opportunities Commn, 2005–07. Hon. Fellow, Faculty of Health and Social Care, Univ. of Chester, 2009–14. *Recreations:* making lists, eating very good chocolate, driving my children to their activities, travelling with my children. *Address:* 37 Upper House Farm, Crickhowell, Powys NP8 1BZ. *T:* 07950 028704.

FISHER, Her Honour Elisabeth Neill; a Circuit Judge, 1989–2015; *b* 24 Nov. 1944; *d* of late Kenneth Neill Fisher and Lorna Charlotte Honor Fisher. *Educ:* Oxford High Sch. for Girls (GPDST); Cambridge Univ. (MA); Cardiff Univ. (LLM Canon Law, 2011). Called to the Bar, Inner Temple, 1968, Bencher, 2003. A Recorder, 1982–89. Mem. Senate, Inns of Court, 1983–86; Pres., Council of HM Circuit Judges, 2004. Member: Criminal Cttee, Judicial Studies Bd, 1995–98; Criminal Justice Consultative Council, 1992–99. Chm., Home Sec.'s Adv. Bd on Restricted Patients, 1998–2003. DUniv UCE, 1997. *Address:* c/o Queen Elizabeth II Law Courts, Newton Street, Birmingham B4 7NA.

FISHER, Dame Jacqueline, (Dame Jackie), DBE 2010 (CBE 2005); Chief Executive, NCG, until 2013; *b* 10 March 1956; *d* of Stanley and Anne Walton; *m* 1st, 1974, Thomas Fisher (marr. diss. 1978); two *s*; 2nd, 1996, David Collier. *Educ:* Leeds Univ. (BA Hons 1979; MA 1980; MSc 1989). Asst Principal, St Helen's Coll., 1989–94; Vice Principal, 1994–97, Chief Exec. and Principal, 1997–2000, Tameside Coll.; Chief Exec. and Principal, Newcastle Coll., 2000; interim Chief Exec., Barnfield Fedn, 2014. Member: Bd, One North East, RDA, 2000–07; Council, HEFCE, 2001–08. FCGI. *Recreations:* cinema, food, walking, travel in Central and Eastern Europe.

FISHER, (Jervis) Andrew; QC 2009; *b* 23 Oct. 1955; *s* of John George Fisher and Joyce Fisher (*née* Horton); *m* 1982, Catherine Maura Swatman; one *s* one *d*. *Educ:* Malvern; Queen Mary Coll., Univ. of London (LLB). Called to the Bar, Gray's Inn, 1980; in practice as a barrister, Midland Circuit, 1980–. *Address:* Citadel Chambers, 190 Corporation Street, Birmingham B4 6QD. *T:* (0121) 233 8500, *Fax:* (0121) 233 8501. *E:* andrew.fisher@citadelchambers.com.

FISHER, Joan; Headteacher, King Edward VI Camp Hill School for Girls, Birmingham, 1992–2003; *b* 24 Sept. 1939; *d* of R. and A. R. Bowler; *m* 1969, Ronald William Fisher; four *d* (incl. triplets). *Educ:* Univ. of Leeds (BA Modern Langs); Univ. of York (Schoolteacher Fellowship); Inst. of Educn, London (MA). Teacher in comprehensive schs, Yorkshire and Surrey, 1962–89: Holme Valley GS, 1962–66; Middlesbrough Girls' High, 1966–69; Acklam High, 1970–72; Framwellgate Moor, 1972–73; Glebelands, 1974–82; Tomlinscote, 1982–89; Dep. Headteacher, Westcliff High Sch. for Girls, 1989–92. Chm. Govs, Northway Infant Sch., Tewkesbury, 2007–. FRSA 1997. *Publications:* teaching materials for German, including: Achtung! Achtung!, 1985; Begegnungen, 1985; Lesekiste, A, 1987, B, 1988; Pack's An!, 1991.

FISHER, Prof. John, CBE 2011; PhD, DEng; CEng, FREng, FIMechE, FIPEM; FMedSci; Professor of Mechanical Engineering, since 1993, and Deputy Vice-Chancellor, since 2006, University of Leeds; *b* 10 Aug. 1955; *s* of James Fisher and Joan Fisher; *m* 1995, Eileen Ingham; two *d*. *Educ:* Univ. of Birmingham (BSc 1st Cl. Physics 1976); Univ. of Glasgow (PhD Bioengrg 1986); Univ. of Leeds (DEng 1996). CEng 1983; FIMechE 1995; FIPEM 1998; CSci 2005; FREng 2009. Bioengr, Dept of Clinical Phys and Bioengrg, Greater Glasgow Health Bd, 1978–87; University of Leeds: Lectr, 1987–93; Dir, Inst. of Med. and Biol Engrg, 2001–; Pro-Vice-Chancellor, 2001–06. Chm., Tissue Regenix Ltd, 2007–; Dir, Bitecic Ltd, 2006–. Mem., EPSRC, 2011–15. FMedSci 2012. *Publications:* 350 articles in jls. *Recreations:* walking, swimming, running. *Address:* School of Mechanical Engineering, University of Leeds, Leeds LS2 9JT. *T:* (0113) 343 2128. *E:* j.fisher@leeds.ac.uk.

FISHER, Jonathan Simon; QC 2003; *b* 24 Feb. 1958; *s* of Aubrey and Pauline Fisher; *m* 1980, Paula Goldberg; two *s* two *d*. *Educ:* Poly. of N London (BA 1st Cl. Hons); St Catharine's Coll., Cambridge (LLB). Called to the Bar, Gray's Inn, 1980; Lectr, Chelmer Inst., 1981–82; Mem. *ad eund*, Inner Temple, 1984; in practice as barrister, specialising in business crime and contentious tax cases, 1982–; Standing Counsel to IR, CCC and London Crown Courts, 1991–2003. Comr, Bill of Rights Commn, MoJ, 2011–12. Member: Steering Gp, Assets Recovery Agency, 2003–06; Legal Panel, Accountancy Investigation and Disciplinary, then Accountancy Actuarial and Discipline, Bd, 2005–09; Trustee Dir, Fraud Adv. Panel, 2006–10. Hon. Mem., Steering Gp, London Fraud Forum, 2007–. Exec. Mem., 2005–06 and 2011–, Chm. of Res., 2006–10, Soc. of Conservative Lawyers. Sen. Vis. Fellow, City Univ., 1986–2004; Visiting Professor: Cass Business Sch., City Univ., 2004–07; LSE, 2006– (Vis. Fellow, 2004–06); Hon. Vis. Prof., City Law Sch., City Univ., 2011–13. Fellow, Chartered Inst. of Taxation, 2009–; Accredited Trusts and Estates Practitioner, 2010–. Gen. Ed., Lloyds Law Reports: Financial Crime, 2008–; Mem., Editl Bd, Simon's Taxes, Butterworths Looseleaf, 2011–. *Publications:* (jtly) Pharmacy Law and Practice, 1995, 4th edn 2006; (jtly) Law of Investor Protection, 1997, 2nd edn 2003; (contrib.) Fighting Financial Crime in the Global Economic Crisis, 2014; contrib. articles to Conservative Liberty Forum, Policy Exchange, British Tax Review, Law and Financial Markets Review. *Recreations:* theatre, football, arts, history, travelling. *Address:* Devereux Chambers, Queen Elizabeth Building, Temple, EC4Y 9BS. *T:* (020) 7353 7534, *Fax:* (020) 7583 5150. *E:* fisher@devchambers.co.uk. *Club:* Carlton.

FISHER, Mark, FSA; *b* 29 Oct. 1944; *s* of Sir Nigel Fisher, MC and of Lady Gloria Flower; *m* 1971, Ingrid Geach (marr. diss. 1999); two *s* two *d*; *m* 2010, Gillian FitzHugh; two step *d*. *Educ:* Eton College; Trinity College, Cambridge (MA). Documentary film producer and script writer, 1966–75; Principal, Tattenhall Centre of Education, 1975–83. Mem., Staffs CC, 1981–85 (Chm., Libraries Cttee, 1981–83). Contested (Lab) Leek, 1979. MP (Lab) Stoke-on-Trent Central, 1983–2010. An Opposition Whip, 1985–87; Opposition spokesman on the arts, 1987–92, 1993–97, on Citizen's Charter, 1992–93; Parly Under-Sec. of State, Dept for Culture, Media and Sport, 1997–98. Mem., Treasury and CS Select Cttee, 1983–85. Chm., Parliament First, 2003–10. Dep. Pro-Chancellor, Keele Univ., 1989–97. Vis. Fellow, St Antony's Coll., Oxford, 2000–01. Member: BBC Gen. Adv. Council, 1988–95; Council, PSI, 1989–95; Acceptance in Lieu Panel, 1998–2012; Museums and Galls Commn, 1998–2002; Develt Cttee, RA, 2010–. Trustee: Britten-Pears Foundn, 1998–2007; Estorick Collection of Modern Italian Art, 2000–14; Hunterian Museum, 2005–14; Friends of the Nat. Libraries, 2005–09; British Sporting Art Trust, 2011–; Member: Bd, Qatar Mus Authy, 2007–10 (Mem., Internat. and Policy Cttees, 2010–); Fitzwilliam Mus. Develt Trust, 2011–. FSA 2006. Hon. FRIBA 1992; Hon. FRCA 1993. Author of stage plays: Brave New Town, 1974; The Cutting Room, 1990. Patron, Ledbury Poetry Fest., 2011–. *Publications:* City Centres, City Cultures, 1988; (ed jtly) Whose Cities?, 1991; (with Richard Rogers) A New London, 1992; Britain's Best Museums and Galleries, 2004. *Address:* 111 Sixth Avenue, W10 4HH. *T:* (020) 8969 4067. *Club:* Grillions.

FISHER, Mark; *see* Fisher, C. M.

FISHER, Prof. Michael Ellis, FRS 1971; Distinguished University Professor and Regents' Professor, Institute for Physical Science and Technology, University of Maryland, 1993–2012, now Emeritus (Wilson H. Elkins Distinguished Professor, 1987–93); *b* 3 Sept. 1931; *s* of Harold Wolf Fisher and Jeanne Marie Fisher (*née* Halter); *m* 1954, Sorrel Castillejo; three *s* one *d*. *Educ:* King's Coll., London. BSc 1951, PhD 1957, FKC 1981. Flying Officer (Educn), RAF, 1951–53; London Univ. Postgraduate Studentship, 1953–56; DSIR Sen. Research Fellow, 1956–58. King's Coll., London: Lectr in Theoretical Physics, 1958–62; Reader in Physics, 1962–64; Prof. of Physics, 1965–66; Cornell University: Prof. of Chemistry and Maths, 1966–73; Horace White Prof. of Chemistry, Physics and Maths, 1973–89; Chm., Dept of Chemistry, 1975–78. Guest Investigator, Rockefeller Inst., New York, 1963–64; Vis. Prof. in Applied Physics, Stanford Univ., 1970–71; Walker Ames Prof., Univ. of Washington, 1977; Vis. Prof. of Physics, MIT, 1979; Sherman Fairchild Disting. Scholar, CIT, 1984; Vis. Prof. in Theoretical Physics, Oxford, 1985; Lorentz Prof., Leiden, 1993; Vis. Prof., Nat. Inst. of Sci. and Technol., USA, 1994; Phi Beta Kappa Vis. Scholar, 1994. Lectures: Buhl, Carnegie-Mellon, 1971; 32nd Richtmyer Meml, 1973; 17th Fritz London Meml, 1975; Morris Loeb, Harvard, 1979; H. L. Welsh, Toronto, 1979; Bakerian, Royal Soc., 1979; Welch Foundn, Texas, 1979; Alpheas Smith, Ohio State Univ., 1982; Laird Meml, Univ. of Western Ontario, 1983; Fries, Rensselaer Polytechnic Inst., NY, 1984; Amos de-Shalit Meml, Weizmann Inst., Rehovoth, 1985; Cherwell-Simon, Oxford, 1985; Marker, Penn. State Univ., 1988; Nat. Sci. Council, Taiwan, 1989; Hamilton Meml, Princeton Univ., 1990; 65th J. W. Gibbs, Amer. Math. Soc., Condon, Univ. of Colorado, and M. S. Green Meml, Temple Univ., 1992; R. and B. Sackler, Tel Aviv, 1992; Lennard-Jones, RSC, 1995; G. N. Lewis, UC Berkeley, 1995; Hirschfelder, Wisconsin Univ., 1995; Baker, in Chemistry, Cornell Univ., 1997; F. G. Brickwedde, in Physics, Johns Hopkins Univ., 1998; Michelson, Case Western Reserve Univ., 1999; T. A. Edison Meml, Naval Res. Lab., Washington, 2000; J. R. Oppenheimer, Univ. of Calif, Berkeley, 2006; C. V. Raman Meml, Indian Inst. Sci., Bangalore, 2007; Homi Bhabha Meml, Tata Inst. Fundamental Res., Mumbai, 2007; E. L. Hudspeth Centennial, Univ. of Texas, Austin, 2007; Mark Kac Meml, Los Alamos Nat. Lab., 2008; Seymour Sherman Meml, Indiana Univ., 2009. Mem. Council and Vice-Pres., Royal Soc., 1993–95. Mem., Amer. Philos. Soc., 1993. John Simon Guggenheim Memorial Fellow, 1970–71, 1978–79; Fellow, Amer. Acad. of Arts and Scis, 1979; FAAAS 1986; For. Associate, National Acad. of Sciences, USA, 1983; Foreign Member: Brazilian Acad. of Scis, 1996; Royal Norwegian Soc. of Scis and Letters, 2003–. Hon. FRSE 1986; Hon. Fellow, Indian Acad. of Scis, Bangalore, 2000. Hon. DSc Yale, 1987; Hon. DPhil Tel Aviv, 1992; Hon. PhD Weizman Inst. of Sci., 2009; Dr *hc* École Normale Supérieure de Lyon, 2012. Irving Langmuir Prize in Chemical Physics, Amer. Phys. Soc., 1970; Award in Phys. and Math. Scis, NY Acad. of Scis, 1978; Guthrie Medal, Inst. of Physics, 1980; Wolf Prize in Physics, State of Israel, 1980; Michelson-Morley Award, Case-Western Reserve Univ., 1982; James Murray Luck Award, National Acad. of Sciences, USA, 1983; Boltzmann Medal, Internat. Union of Pure and Applied Physics, 1983; Lars Onsager Medal, Norwegian Inst. of Technol., 1993; Onsager Meml Prize, Amer. Phys. Soc., 1995; Hildebrand Award, Amer. Chem. Soc., 1995; Royal Medal, Royal Soc., 2005; Frontiers of Knowledge Award in Basic Scis, BBVA Foundn, Madrid, 2010. *Publications:* Analogue Computing at Ultra-High Speed (with D. M. MacKay), 1962; The Nature of Critical Points (Univ. of Colorado) 1964, (Moscow) 1968; contribs to Proc. Roy. Soc., Phys. Rev., Phys. Rev. Lett., Jl Sci. Insts, Jl Math. Phys., Arch. Rational Mech. Anal., Jl Chem. Phys., Commun. Math. Phys., Rept Prog. Phys., Rev. Mod. Phys.,

Physica, Proc. Nat. Acad. Sci., USA, Biophys. Jl, etc. *Recreations:* Flamenco guitar, travel. *Address:* Institute for Physical Science and Technology, University of Maryland, College Park, MD 20742–8510, USA. *T:* (301) 4054819.

FISHER, Dr Paul Gregory; Deputy Head, Prudential Regulation Authority, and Executive Director, Supervisory Risk Specialists and Regulatory Operations, Bank of England, since 2014; *b* Rochford, 7 Sept. 1958; *s* of late Jack Nichol Archibald Fisher and Maisie Joan Fisher; *m* 1983, Susan Mary Gill; one *s* one *d. Educ:* Univ. of Bristol (BSSocSci Econs with Stats 1980); Univ. of Warwick (MA Econs 1983; PhD Econs 1990). Res. Associate, ESRC Macroeconomic Modelling Bureau, Univ. of Warwick, 1983–90; Bank of England: Analyst, then Manager, 1990–94; Hd, Conjunctural Assessment and Projections Div., 1995–98; Private Sec. to Governor, 1999–2001; Hd, Foreign Exchange Div., 2002–08. Mem., Monetary Policy Cttee Secretariat, 1998 and 2006–08; Chm., Foreign Exchange Jt Standing Cttee, 2002–08; Exec. Dir, Mkts and Mem., Monetary Policy Cttee, 2009–14; Mem., Interim Financial Policy Cttee, 2011–13. Chm., ifs UC (formerly ifs Sch. of Finance), 2011–; Mem. Adv. Bd, Centre for Competition Policy, UEA, 2012–. Vis. Prof., Richmond, Amer. Internat. Univ. in London, 2012–. *Publications:* (contrib.) Models of the UK Economy: a review by the ESRC Macroeconomic Modelling Bureau, 1984, a second review, 1985, a third review, 1986, a fourth review, 1987; Rational Expectations in Macroeconomic Models, 1992; articles in Econ. Jl, Jl of Econ. Dynamics and Control, Econ. Modelling, Oxford Bulletin of Econ. Statistics, etc. *Address:* Bank of England, Threadneedle Street, EC2R 8AH. *T:* (020) 7601 4444. *E:* paul.fisher@bankofengland.co.uk.

FISHER, Paul Richard; Group Managing Director, Jockey Club Racecourses Ltd, since 2008; *b* Gillingham, Kent, 24 Jan. 1965; *s* of Victor and Sheila Fisher; *m* 1998, Jacqueline Schooling; one *s* one *d. Educ:* Poly. of Central London (BA Hons). CPFA 1991. Sen. Accountant, 1990–92, Asst Chief Exec., 1992–95, Rochester CC; Dep. Finance Dir, Medway Council, 1995–97; Finance Director: Gillingham FC, 1997–2000; United Racecourses, 2000–05; Man. Dir, Kempton Park Racecourse, 2005–08. *Recreations:* cricket, football, horseracing, all sports, family, wine! *Address:* Jockey Club, 75 High Holborn, WC1V 6LS. *E:* paul.fisher@thejockeyclub.co.uk. *Clubs:* Ivy; Bobbing Court Cricket; Reigatians Rugby Football.

FISHER, Peter Antony Goodwin, FRCP; Consultant Physician, since 1986, Director of Research, since 1996, and Clinical Director, since 1998, Royal London Hospital for Integrated Medicine (formerly at Royal London Homoeopathic Hospital); Physician to the Queen, since 2001; *b* 2 Sept. 1950; *s* of Antony Martin Fisher and Eve Fisher; *m* 1997, Nina Oxenham; two *d. Educ:* Tonbridge Sch.; Emmanuel Coll., Cambridge (BA 1972, MA 1975; MB BChir 1975); Westminster Hosp. Med. Sch. FFHom 1986 (Vice Pres., 1991 and 1999); FRCP 1997. Med. Dir, Royal London Homeopathic Hosp., 1998–99. FRSocMed 1984. Editor, Homeopathy (formerly British Homeopathic Jl), 1986–. Clinical Lead: NICE NHS Evidence - complementary and alternative medicine (formerly Specialist Liby, Nat. Liby for Health), 2005–11; Complementary and Alternative Medicine Specialist Liby and Information Service, 2007–; Expert Advr, NICE, 2011–. Mem., Expert Adv. Panel on Traditional Medicine, WHO, 2007–. President: European Congress for Integrative Medicine, 2010; Internat. Congress for Complementary Medical Res., 2013. Albert Schweitzer Gold Medal, Polish Acad. of Medicine, 2007. *Publications:* Alternative Answers to Arthritis and Rheumatism, 1999; numerous scientific and scholarly articles on homeopathy and other forms of complementary and integrative medicine. *Recreations:* gardening, swimming, sailing. *Address:* Royal London Hospital for Integrated Medicine, Great Ormond Street, WC1N 3HR. *T:* (020) 3448 8880. *E:* peter.fisher@uclh.nhs.uk.

FISHER, Rev. Canon Peter Timothy; Vicar, Maney, 2002–10; *b* 7 July 1944; *s* of late Rev. James Atherton Fisher; *m* 1968, Elizabeth Lacey; two *s. Educ:* City of London Sch.; Durham Univ. (BA, MA); Cuddesdon Coll., Oxford. Ordained deacon, 1970, priest 1971; Curate, St Andrew's, Bedford, 1970–74; Chaplain, Surrey Univ., 1974–78; Sub-Warden, Lincoln Theol Coll., 1978–83; Rector, Houghton-le-Spring, 1983–94; Principal, The Queen's Coll., subseq. The Queen's Foundn for Ecumenical Theol Educn, Birmingham, 1994–2002. Mem., Faith and Order Commn, WCC, 2008–. Hon. Canon, Birmingham Cathedral, 2000–. *Publications:* Outside Eden, 2009. *Recreations:* piano and water-colours, both strictly incognito. *Address:* Eden, Unicorn View, Bowes, Barnard Castle, County Durham DL12 9HW. *T:* (01833) 628001.

FISHER, Richard, (Rick); lighting designer (freelance), since 1980; Chairman, Association of Lighting Designers, 1995–2011 (Fellow, 2011); *b* Pennsylvania, 19 Oct. 1954; *s* of Samuel M. Fisher and Helene K. Fisher. *Educ:* Dickinson Coll., Carlisle, PA (BA 1976). Lighting designs for theatre and dance productions include: An Inspector Calls, NT, 1992, transf. NY (Tony Award, Drama Desk Award, 1994); Matthew Bourne's Swan Lake, London, 1995, transf. Los Angeles and NY, and Cinderella, London, 1997, transf. Los Angeles; Via Dolorosa, Royal Court, transf. NY, 1998; Disney's The Hunchback of Notre Dame, Berlin, 1999; Blue/Orange, NT, 2000, Duchess, 2001; A Number, Royal Court, 2002; Far Away, NY, 2002; Jerry Springer the Opera, NT, transf. Cambridge Th., 2003; Old Times, 2004, The Philanthropist, 2005, Donmar; Billy Elliot, Victoria Palace, 2005, transf. Australia, 2007, New York, 2008 (Tony Award, Drama Desk Award, 2009); Resurrection Blues, Old Vic, 2006; Landscape with Weapon, NT, 2007; The Family Reunion, Donmar Warehouse, 2008; Tribes, Royal Court, 2010; The Sound of Music, Buenos Aires, 2011; Hero, Royal Court, 2012; The Judas Kiss, Hampstead Th., transf. Duke of York's, 2012; Chariots of Fire, Hampstead Th., transf. Gielgud, 2012; The Audience, Gielgud, 2013, transf. Apollo Th. and NY, 2015; Inside Wagner's Head, Linbury Studio Th., 2013; The Herd, Bush Th., 2013; Sunny Afternoon, Hampstead Th., transf. Pinter, 2014; for Royal Shakespeare Company: Merchant of Venice, 2011, transf. Almeida, 2014; Richard III, 2012; Galileo, 2013; opera productions include: Opera North: La Bohème, 1996; Gloriana, 1999; Bolshoi: Turandot, 2002; The Fiery Angel, 2004; Royal Opera: Wozzeck, 2002; Tsarina's Slippers, 2009; A Midsummer Night's Dream, La Fenice, Venice, 2004; Santa Fe: Peter Grimes, 2005; Billy Budd, Radamisto, 2008; Madame Butterfly, Albert Herring, 2010; Wozzeck, La Bohème, The Last Savage, 2011; The Little Prince, Houston, 2003, NY, 2005; Betrothal in a Monastery, Glyndebourne, 2006; Sweeney Todd, Paris, 2011; King and I, 2014. Olivier Award for Best Lighting Design, 1994 and 1998; Bronze Medal for Lighting Design, World Stage Design Expo, Toronto, 2005; Helpmann Award, Australia, 2008; Stage Lighting Designer of Year, Live Design Internat., 2008. *Recreations:* theatre going, travel, eating!, camping. *Address:* c/o Dennis Lyne Agency, 503 Holloway Road, N19 4DD.

FISHER, Richard Alan; QC 2015; *b* Coventry, 14 Oct. 1971; *s* of Alan and Mai Fisher; *m* 2007; one *s* one *d. Educ:* King Henry VIII Sch., Coventry; Bristol Univ. (LLB 1993); Inns of Court Sch. of Law. Called to the Bar, Lincoln's Inn, 1994; in practice as barrister, specialising in fraud and in advice and litigation relating to proceeds of crime. *Publications:* (jtly) Blackstone's Guide to the Proceeds of Crime Act 2002, 2003, 5th edn 2015. *Recreation:* sports (former English schools sprint hurdles champion, representative Rugby, Warwickshire schools and Bristol University). *Address:* Doughty Street Chambers, 53–54 Doughty Street, WC1N 2LS. *T:* (020) 7404 1313, *Fax:* (020) 7404 2283. *E:* r.fisher@doughtystreet.co.uk.

FISHER, Robert Reginald James, AM 2003; JP; Agent General for Western Australia, 2001–05; *b* 13 Oct. 1942; *s* of Albert Reginald Fisher and Irene Fisher; *m* 1967, Lynette Fulford; one *s* one *d. Educ:* Univ. of Western Australia (BA, BEd). Member, Australian Trade Commissioner Service, 1970–80: Lima, 1971–73; Russian lang. trng, 1973–74; Moscow, 1974–76; New Delhi, 1976–77; San Francisco, 1977–80; Government of Western Australia, 1980–2005: Chief Executive: Dept of Industrial Develt, 1980–87; Countertrade Office, 1987–88; Dept of Trade Develt, 1988–91; Regl Develt, 1991–92; Family and Children's Services, 1993–2001. Chairman: Aquatic Adv. Cttee, WA, 2012–; Forest Products Commn, WA, 2013–. Comr, Nat. Commn of Audit, 2013–14. JP Western Australia, 2001. *Recreations:* swimming, golf. *Address:* 12 Sutcliffe Street, Dalkeith, WA 6009, Australia.

FISHER, Roger Anthony, FRCO(CHM); Organist and Master of Choristers, Chester Cathedral, 1967–96; *b* 18 Sept. 1936; *s* of Leslie Elgar Fisher and Vera Althea (*née* Salter); *m* 1st, 1967, Susan Mary Green (marr. diss. 1983); one *d*; 2nd, 1985, Gillian Rushforth (*née* Heywood). *Educ:* Bancroft's Sch., Woodford Green, Essex; Royal Coll. Music; Christ Church, Oxford (Organ schol.; MA). FRCO(CHM); ARCM; ATCL. Organist, St Mark's, Regent's Park, 1957–62; Asst Organist, Hereford Cathedral, 1962–67; Asst Lectr in Music, Hereford Coll. of Educn, 1963–67. Music Critic, Liverpool Echo, 1976–79; Associate Editor, Organists' Rev., 1996–2004. Recital tours incl. N America, Europe, Scandinavia, S Africa and Australia. Recordings in GB, Europe, USA and S Africa; BBC broadcasts as organist and with Chester Cathedral Choir. Conductor, choral socs and orchestras; Organ Consultant to churches and cathedrals. Geoffrey Tankard Prize for Solo Organ, RCM, 1959. *Publications:* Master Class with Roger Fisher, 2006; Towards Keyboard Fluency, 2010; articles about the organ and related subjects in several periodicals. *Recreations:* railway interests, walking, motoring. *Address:* The Old Chapel, Trelogan, Holywell, Flintshire CH8 9BD. *W:* www.rfisher.me.

FISHER, Steven Mark; HM Diplomatic Service; Ambassador to the Dominican Republic and (non-resident) to Haiti, 2009–15; *b* Stratford upon Avon, 7 Feb. 1965; *s* of Dennis John Fisher and Janet Mary Fisher; *m* 1990, Linda Westwood (marr. diss. 2010); three *s*; partner, Kriszta Fogarasi; one *d. Educ:* Cubbington C of E Jun. Sch.; Warwick Sch.; Wadham Coll., Oxford (BA French and Hist. 1987). IT Consultant, Andersen Consulting, 1987–92; bookseller, The Book Shop, Amersham, 1992–93; joined FCO, 1993; Second Sec. (Econ./Commercial), Singapore, 1995–98; Hd, Ukraine, Belarus, Moldova Sect., Eastern Dept, FCO, 1998–2001; Hd, Press Sect., EU Dept, FCO, 2001; Dep. Hd of Mission, Caracas, 2002–06; First Sec. EU, then Dep. Hd of Mission, Budapest, 2006–09. *Recreations:* keeping up with my children, sports (cricket, football, Rugby), cooking, eating, drinking, travelling, gardening, restoring a farmhouse in Spain, maintaining old friendships, teaching my dog Zoltan new tricks, reading and writing history, music. *Address:* c/o 20 Ladycroft, Cubbington, Leamington Spa CV32 7NH. *Fax:* 4727190. *E:* steven.fisher@fco.gov.uk, stevenfisher2009@gmail.com.

FISHLOCK, Trevor; journalist, foreign correspondent, author; *b* 21 Feb. 1941; *s* of Edward and Ada Fishlock; *m* 1st, 1965; two *s* one *d*; 2nd, 1978, Penelope Symon. *Educ:* Churcher's Coll., Petersfield; Southern Grammar Sch., Portsmouth. Portsmouth Evening News, 1957–62; freelance and news agency reporter, 1962–68; The Times: Wales and W England staff correspondent, 1968–77; London and foreign staff, 1978–80; S Asia correspondent, Delhi, 1980–83; New York correspondent, 1983–86; Daily Telegraph: roving foreign correspondent, 1986–89, 1993–96; Moscow correspondent, 1989–91; foreign correspondent, The Sunday Telegraph, 1991–93. Writer-presenter, Wild Tracks, 1995–2008 (BAFTA Award, 2000), Fishlock's Wales, 2009–13, ITV Wales. Fellow, World Press Inst., St Paul, Minnesota, 1977–78. Mem., Council for the Welsh Language, 1973–77. Hon. Fellow, Univ. of Wales, Lampeter, 2008. Hon. MA Wales, 2008. David Holden Award for foreign reporting (British Press Awards), 1983; Internat. Reporter of the Year (British Press Awards), 1986. *Publications:* Wales and the Welsh, 1972; Talking of Wales, 1975; Discovering Britain: Wales, 1979; Americans and Nothing Else, 1980; India File, 1983; The State of America, 1986; Indira Gandhi (for children), 1986; Out of Red Darkness: reports from the collapsing Soviet Empire, 1992; My Foreign Country: Trevor Fishlock's Britain, 1997; Cobra Road: an Indian journey, 1999; Conquerors of Time, 2004; In This Place, centenary vol. for Nat. Liby of Wales, 2007; Senedd: the National Assembly for Wales building, 2010; Pembrokeshire: journeys and stories, 2011; A Gift of Sunlight: the fortune and quest of the Davies sisters, 2014. *Recreation:* sailing. *Address:* 7 Teilo Street, Cardiff CF11 9JN. *Club:* Naval.

FISHWICK, Dr Nicholas Bernard Frank, CMG 2009; HM Diplomatic Service, retired; Counsellor, Foreign and Commonwealth Office, 2007–12; *b* Ashbourne, 23 Feb. 1958; *s* of Roland Frank Fishwick and Dorothy May Fishwick (*née* Ford); *m* 1987, Rouane Theresa Mendel; two *s* one *d. Educ:* Staveley Netherthorpe Grammar Sch.; Hertford Coll., Oxford (BA 1st Cl. Hons Mod. Hist. 1979; DPhil 1985). Entered FCO, 1983; First Sec. (Press and Inf.), Lagos, 1988–91; Consul (Pol), Istanbul, 1994–97; on secondment to HM Customs and Excise, 2001–04; Counsellor (Pol), Kabul, 2006–07. *Publications:* English Football and Society 1910–1950, 1989; (contrib.) New DNB. *Recreations:* family, walks, cycling, football, churches, music (Beethoven, Morrissey). *E:* nick.fishwick@hotmail.co.uk.

FISK, Prof. David John, CB 1999; ScD, PhD; FREng; Laing O'Rourke Professor, Systems Engineering and Innovation, Imperial College London, since 2010; *b* 9 Jan. 1947; *s* of late John Howard Fisk and of Rebecca Elizabeth Fisk (*née* Haynes); *m* 1972, A. Anne Thoday; one *s* one *d. Educ:* Stationers' Company's Sch., Hornsey; St John's Coll., Cambridge (BA, MA, ScD); Univ. of Manchester (PhD). FCIBSE 1983 (Hon. FCIBSE 1998); FREng (FEng 1998); FInstP 1999. Joined Building Res. Estabt (traffic noise res.), 1972; Higher Sci. Officer, 1972–73; Sen. Sci. Officer (energy conservation res.), 1973–75; PSO, 1975–78; SPSO, Hd Mechanical and Elec. Engrg Div., 1978–84; Department of the Environment: Asst Sec., Central Directorate of Environmental Protection, 1984–87; Under Sec., 1987; Dep. Chief Scientist, 1987–88; Chief Scientific Advr, OPDM (formerly Dept of the Envmt, then DETR, later DTLR), 1998–2006. Director: Air, Climate and Toxic Substances Directorate, 1990–95; Envmt & Internat. Directorate, 1995–98; Central Strategy Directorate, DETR, then DTLR, 1999–2002. RAEng Prof. of Engrg for Sustainable Develt, Imperial Coll. London, 2002–11. Mem., Gas and Electricity Mkts Authy, 2009–. Pres., CIBSE, 2011–12 (Vice Pres., 2010–11). Dir, Watford Palace Th., 2000–08. Hon. FRIBA 2009. *Publications:* Thermal Control of Buildings, 1981; numerous papers on technical innovation, bldg sci., systems theory and economics. *Recreations:* modern theatre, music. *Address:* Imperial College London, South Kensington Campus, SW7 2AZ. *Club:* Athenæum.

FISON, Sir Charles (William), 5th Bt *cr* 1905, of Greenholme, Burley-in-Wharfedale, West Riding of Yorkshire; *b* 6 Feb. 1954; *o s* of Sir (Richard) Guy Fison, 4th Bt, DSC, and Elyn Hartmann (*d* 1987); *S* father, 2008, but his name does not appear on the Official Roll of the Baronetage. *Educ:* Eton. *Heir:* none.

FISON, David Gareth, CEng, FICE; Chairman, Pontoonworks Ltd, since 2015; *b* Rochester, Kent, 14 March 1952; *s* of Joseph Edward Fison and Monica Irene Fison; *m* 1979, Honor Mary Borwick; one *s* one *d. Educ:* Marlborough Coll.; Trinity Hall, Cambridge (BA 1973). CEng 1978; FICE 1992. Managing Director: Balfour Beatty Civil Engrg, 1994–96; Balfour Beatty Rail, 1996–98; Chief Executive: Skanska UK plc, 2002–08; Geoffrey Osborne Ltd, 2009–15. Non-executive Director: Olympic Delivery Authy, 2009–14; Harwich Haven Authy, 2014–. *Recreations:* house in Suffolk, sailing, ski-ing. *E:* david.fison@ntlworld.com.

FITCHETT, Robert Duncan; HM Diplomatic Service; Foreign and Commonwealth Office, since 2011; *b* 10 June 1961; *s* of late John Charles Fitchett and of Sheila Mary Fitchett; *m* 1985, Adèle Thérèse Hajjar; one *s* two *d. Educ:* Northampton Sch. for Boys; Univ. of Bradford (BA Hons Mod. Langs (French and German) 1983). Joined FCO, 1983; Dakar, 1984–87; Bonn, 1987–90; FCO, 1990–93; Cabinet Office, 1993–94; First Sec., Paris, 1994–98; FCO, 1998–2003; Dep. Hd of Mission, Manila, 2003–06; FCO, 2007–08; Dep. Hd of Mission and Consul Gen., Mexico City, 2008–11. *Recreations:* horse racing, opera, classical music, reading, walking. *Address:* c/o Foreign and Commonwealth Office, King Charles Street, SW1A 2AH.

FITKIN, Graham; Composer in Residence, London Chamber Orchestra, since 2009; *b* Cornwall, 19 April 1963; *s* of Norman Wayland Fitkin and Joan Fitkin; partner, Ruth Wall. *Educ:* Humphry Davy Sch., Penzance; Univ. of Nottingham (BA Hons Music 1984); Koninklijk Conservatorium, The Hague (MMus Music Composition 1986). Founder, Nanquidno Gp, 1985; Composer in Association, Royal Liverpool Philharmonic Orch., 1994–96; compositions for Tokyo SO, BBC Philharmonic Orch., Royal Scottish Nat. Orch., NY City Ballet, Umeå Capital of Culture 2014, Decca Records; *compositions* include: Still Warm, 2007; Reel (for Royal Ballet), 2009; Cello Concerto (for Yo-Yo Ma and BBC Proms), 2011; Home (for Royal Opera Hse), 2012; Intimate Curve (for Royal Liverpool Philharmonic Orch.), 2015. Hon. Fellow, University Coll. Falmouth, 2010. UK Composer Award, 1990; British Composer Award, BASCA, 2009 and 2011. *Publications:* ballet, opera and orchestral works. *Recreations:* running, swimming, cycling. *Address:* c/o Jane Ward, 60 Shrewsbury Road, Oxton, Merseyside CH43 2HY. *T:* (0151) 513 2716. *E:* info@fitkin.com.

FITT, Prof. Alistair David, DPhil; Vice-Chancellor, Oxford Brookes University, since 2015; *b* London, 23 Nov. 1957; *s* of Kenneth Walter Fitt and late Enid Phyllis Fitt; *m* 2012, Prof. Anne Trefethen; one step *s* one step *d*. *Educ:* Dr Challoner's Grammar Sch., Amersham; Lincoln Coll., Oxford (MA, MSc; DPhil 1984). Sen. Res. Fellow, RMCS, Shrivenham, 1984–89; University of Southampton: Lectr, 1989–94; Sen. Lectr, 1994–96; Reader, 1996–99; Prof. of Maths, 1999–2011; Dean, Faculty of Maths, 2002–08; Pro Vice Chancellor (Internat.), 2008–11; Pro Vice-Chancellor (Res. and Knowledge Exchange), Oxford Brookes Univ., 2011–15. Mem. Bd, Oxon Local Enterprise Partnership, 2014–. Mem. Council, IMA, 2000–; Exec. Sec., Internat. Council for Industrial and Applied Maths, 2007–15. Trustee, Oxford Trust, 2014–. *Publications:* contrib. scientific papers to peer-reviewed jls. *Recreations:* golf, cricket. *Address:* Office of the Vice-Chancellor, Oxford Brookes University, Headington Campus, Oxford OX3 0BP.

FITTALL, William Robert; Secretary-General, Archbishop's Council and General Synod of the Church of England, 2002–15; *b* 26 July 1953; *s* of Arthur Fittall and Elsie Fittall; *m* 1978, Barbara Staples; two *s*. *Educ:* Dover Grammar Sch.; Christ Church, Oxford (MA). Entered Home Office, 1975; Private Sec. to Minister of State, 1979–80; Principal, 1980; Ecole Nationale d'Administration, Paris, 1980–81; Broadcasting Dept, 1981–85; Private Sec. to Home Sec., 1985–87; Asst Sec., 1987; Sec., Review of Parole System, 1987–88; Prison Service HQ, 1988–91; Principal Private Sec. to Sec. of State for NI, 1992–93; Police Dept, Home Office, 1993–95; Asst Under Sec. of State, 1995; Chief of Assessments Staff, Cabinet Office, 1995–97; Dir, Crime Reduction and Community Progs, Home Office, 1997–2000; Associate Political Dir, NI Office, 2000–02. Anglican Lay Reader, 1977–. *Recreations:* playing church organs, watching sport, reading.

FITTER, Prof. Alastair Hugh, CBE 2010; PhD; FRS 2005; Professor of Ecology, University of York, 1992–2013, now Emeritus; *b* 20 June 1948; *s* of late Richard Sidney Richmond Fitter and Alice Mary, (Maisie), Fitter; *m* 1969, Rosalind Morris (*d* 2014); two *s* one *d*. *Educ:* New Coll., Oxford (BA 1969); Univ. of Liverpool (PhD 1973). University of York: Lectr and Sen. Lectr in Ecology, 1972–92; Hd of Dept of Biol., 1997–2004; Pro-Vice-Chancellor for Res., 2004–10. Dir, UK Population Biology Network, 2004–07. Mem., NERC, 2005–11. Joint Editor: Advances in Ecological Research, vols 18–30, 1987–99; Jl of Ecology, 1992–96; Ed., New Phytologist, 1988–2013. Pres., British Ecol Soc., 2003–05; Vice-Pres., Internat. Assoc. for Ecology, 2009–13. Hon. Member: British Naturalists' Assoc., 2006; Botanical Soc. of British Isles, 2007; British Mycol Soc., 2007. Chair of Trustees, Castle Howard Arboretum Trust, 2011–. *Publications:* (with M. Blamey and R. Fitter) Wild Flowers of Britain and Northern Europe, 1974, 5th edn 1996; An Atlas of the Wild Flowers of Britain and Northern Europe, 1976; (with C. Smith) A Wood in Ascam: a study in wetland conservation, Askham Bog 1879–1979, 1979; Trees, 1980; (with R. K. M. Hay) Environmental Physiology of Plants, 1981, 3rd edn 2002; (with N. Arlott and R. Fitter) The Complete Guide to British Wildlife, 1981; (with R. Fitter and J. Wilkinson) Collins Guide to the Countryside, 1984; (with R. Fitter and A. Farrer) Grasses, Sedges, Rushes and Ferns of Britain and Northern Europe, 1984; (ed) Ecological Interactions in the Soil: plants, microbes and animals, 1985; (with R. Fitter) Collins Guide to the Countryside in Winter, 1988; (ed jtly) Mycorrhizas in Ecosystems, 1992; (with M. Blamey and R. Fitter) Wild Flowers of Britain and Ireland, 2003, 2nd edn 2013. *Address:* Department of Biology, University of York, York YO10 5DD.

FITTON, David John, CMG 2004; HM Diplomatic Service; High Commissioner to Jamaica and the Bahamas, since 2013; *b* 10 Jan. 1955; *s* of Jack and Joan Fitton; *m* 1989, Hisae Iijima; one *s* one *d*. *Educ:* Durham Univ. (BA Hons; MA). Entered FCO, 1980; appts in New Delhi, Tokyo and London, 1980–96; Political Counsellor, Tokyo, 1996–2000; Dep. Hd of Mission, Ankara, 2001–04; Actg Consul-Gen., Istanbul, 2003–04; Hd, Crisis Gp, Consular Directorate, FCO, 2004–07; Minister, Tokyo, 2008–12. *Recreations:* tennis, medieval French manuscripts, football, golf. *Address:* c/o Foreign and Commonwealth Office, SW1A 2AH. *E:* david.fitton@fco.gov.uk.

FITTON, Michael David Guy; QC 2006; **His Honour Judge Fitton;** a Circuit Judge, since 2015; *b* Nairobi, 28 April 1957; *s* of O. V. A. Fitton and E. N. Fitton; *m* 1981, Susan Booker; one *s* one *d*. *Educ:* King George V Grammar Sch., Southport, Lancs; Lincoln Coll., Oxford (MA Juris.). Admitted Solicitor, 1981; Partner, Bobbetts Mackan, Bristol, 1985–91; called to the Bar, Gray's Inn, 1991; a Recorder, 2000–15; Hd, Albion Chambers, Bristol, 2009–15. Legal Mem., Mental Health Rev. Tribunal, Wales, 2012–15. *Recreations:* walking, gardening, family, world music, early classical and Irish literature. *Address:* Cardiff Crown Court, The Law Courts, Cathays Park, Cardiff CF10 3PG.

FITTON-BROWN, Edmund Walter; HM Diplomatic Service; Ambassador to Yemen, since 2015; *b* 5 Oct. 1962; *s* of Anthony David and Daphne Mary Fitton-Brown; *m* 1995, Julie Ann Herring; two *s* one *d*. *Educ:* Wyggeston Boys' Sch., Leicester; Corpus Christi Coll., Cambridge (BA Hons Hist. 1984). Joined FCO, 1984; Third Sec., 1987–88, Second Sec., 1988–89, Helsinki; FCO, 1989–91; First Secretary: FCO, 1991–93; Cairo, 1993–96; FCO, 1996–98; Kuwait, 1998–2001; FCO, 2001–03; Counsellor: Cairo, 2003–05; Riyadh, 2005–06; FCO, 2006–09; Rome, 2009–11; Dubai, 2011–15. *Recreations:* squash, football, tennis, golf, bridge. *Address:* c/o Foreign and Commonwealth Office, King Charles Street, SW1A 2AH. *E:* edmund.fitton-brown@fco.gov.uk.

FITZALAN-HOWARD, family name of **Duke of Norfolk**.

FITZGERALD, family name of **Duke of Leinster**.

FitzGERALD, Sir Adrian (James Andrew Denis), 6th Bt *cr* 1880, of Valencia, Co. Kerry; 24th Knight of Kerry; *b* 24 June 1940; *o s* of Major Sir George FitzGerald, 5th Bt, MC and Angela Dora (*née* Mitchell); *S* father, 2001. *Educ:* Harrow. Editor, Monday World, political qly, 1967–74; hotelier, 1983–90. Mem. (C) Council, Royal Borough of Kensington and Chelsea, 1974–2002 (Mayor, 1984–85; Chief Whip, 1986–95; Chm., Educn and Libraries Cttee, 1995–98; Chm., Highways and Traffic Cttee, 1999–2001). Dep. Leader, London Fire and Civil Defence Authy, 1989–90. Pres., Anglo-Polish Soc., 2001– (Chm., 1989–92); Vice-Chm., London Chapter, Irish Georgian Soc., 1990–2009; Pres., Benevolent Soc. of St Patrick, 1997–2013; Patron, Latin Mass Soc., 2012–. Gov., Cardinal Vaughan Meml Sch., 1999–2009, 2010–13 (Vice-Chm., 2002–03, Chm., 2003–09). Kt of Honour and Devotion in Obedience, SMO, Malta (Pres., Irish Assoc., 2009–). *Publications:* (contrib.) Education, Church and State, ed M. R. O'Connell, 1992; (contrib.) The Knights of Glin: seven centuries of change, ed Tom Donovan, 2009. *Heir: cousin* Anthony Desmond FitzGerald [*b* 24 Dec. 1953; *m* 1986, Janine Miller (marr. diss. 2003); one *s*]. *Clubs:* Beefsteak, Pratt's; Kildare Street and University (Dublin).

FitzGERALD, Christopher Francis; Chairman, Regulatory Decisions Committee, Financial Services Authority, 2001–04; *b* 17 Nov. 1945; *s* of late Lt Comdr Michael Francis FitzGerald, RN and Anne Lise FitzGerald (*née* Winther); *m* 1st, 1968, Jennifer (*née* Willis) (marr. diss. 1984); one *s* two *d*; 2nd, 1986, Jill (*née* Freshwater); two step *d*. *Educ:* Downside Sch.; Lincoln Coll., Oxford (Classics Schol.; BA Juris.; MA 1967). Admitted solicitor, 1971; Partner, Slaughter and May, 1976–95; Gen. Counsel, and Mem., Exec. Dirs' Cttee, NatWest Gp, 1995–2000. Non-executive Director: Intercare Gp plc, 2001–03; City Merchants High Yield Trust plc, 2007–12; Mimecast Ltd, 2007–. Member: Finance Cttee, Lincoln Coll., Oxford, 2003–; Financial Reporting Review Panel, 2006–12. Chm., Macfarlane Trust, 2007–12. *Recreations:* travelling, opera, theatre and concert going, appreciating fine wines. *Address:* 26 Lower Addison Gardens, W14 8BQ.

FitzGERALD, Rev. (Sir) Daniel Patrick, SSC; (4th Bt *cr* 1903, of Geraldine Place, St Finn Barr, Co. Cork, but does not use the title); *b* 28 June 1916; *S* brother, Rev. (Sir) Edward Thomas FitzGerald (3rd Bt), 1988, but his name does not appear on the Official Roll of the Baronetage. Roman Catholic priest. *Heir: cousin* John Finnbarr FitzGerald [*b* 11 June 1918; *m* 1949, Margaret Hogg; one *s* one *d*].

FITZGERALD, Edward Hamilton, CBE 2008; QC 1995; a Recorder, since 2002; *b* 13 Aug. 1953; *s* of Carrol James Fitzgerald and Cornelia (*née* Claiborne); *m* 1988, Rebecca Fraser; three *d*. *Educ:* Downside; Corpus Christi Coll., Oxford (BA 1st cl. Hons Lit. Hum. 1975); MPhil Cantab 1979. Called to the Bar, Inner Temple, 1978, Bencher, 2002. Times Justice Award, 1998. *Recreations:* reading history and novels, visiting the seaside, travel. *Address:* (chambers) 54 Doughty Street, WC1N 2LS. *T:* (020) 7404 1313.

FITZGERALD, Frank, CBE 1989; PhD; FREng; consultant, since 1992; Director, Sheffield Forgemasters Ltd, 1993–98; *b* 11 Nov. 1929; *s* of George Arthur Fitzgerald and Sarah Ann (*née* Brook); *m* 1956, Dorothy Eileen Unwin (*d* 2010); two *s* one *d*. *Educ:* Barnsley Holgate Grammar Sch.; Univ. of Sheffield (BScTech; PhD). FEI (FInstE 1965); FREng (FEng 1977); FIMMM (FIM 2000; Dedicatee, Frank Fitzgerald Medal and Travel Award, IMMM). Ministry of Supply, RAE, Westcott, Bucks, 1955; United Steel Cos, Swinden Laboratories, Rotherham, 1960–68; British Steel plc (formerly British Steel Corporation), 1968–92: Process Res. Manager, Special Steels Div., 1970; Head Corporate Advanced Process Laboratory, 1972; Director, R&D, 1977; Man. Dir, Technical, 1981–92; Dir, 1986–92; Chairman: British Steel Corp. (Overseas Services), subseq. British Steel Consultants, 1981–89; British Steel Stainless, 1989–91. Hon. Fellow, Queen Mary, Univ. of London, 2004. Hon. DEng Sheffield, 1993. Hadfield Medal, Iron and Steel Inst., for work on application of combustion and heat transfer science to industrial furnaces, 1972; Melchett Medal, Inst. of Energy, 1988; Bessemer Gold Medal, Inst. of Metals, 1991; Esso Energy Award, Royal Soc., 1991. *Publications:* papers in learned jls on heat and mass transfer and metallurgical processes. *Recreation:* rock climbing and mountaineering. *Clubs:* Alpine; Climbers'.

FitzGERALD, Prof. Garret Adare, MD; FRS 2012; FRCPI, FACP; Professor of Medicine and Pharmacology, since 1994, McNeil Professor of Translational Medicine and Therapeutics, since 2007, Chair, Department of Pharmacology, since 1996, Director, Institute for Translational Medicine and Therapeutics, since 2004, and Associate Dean for Translational Research, since 2004, University of Pennsylvania; *b* Dublin. *Educ:* Belvedere Coll., Dublin; University Coll. Dublin (MB BCh 1974; MD (Pharmacol.) 1980); Sch. of Hygiene, Univ. of London (MSc Stats 1979). MRCPI 1976, FRCPI 1982; MRCP 1977; FACP 1984. Intern, 1974–75, SHO, 1975–76, St Vincent's Hosp., Dublin; SHO, 1976–77, Res. Registrar, 1977, Mater Hosp., Dublin; Res. Fellow, RPMS, 1977–79; Neurol. Res. Fellow, Univ. of Cologne, 1979–80; Vanderbilt University School of Medicine, Nashville: Res. Fellow, 1980; Asst Prof., 1981–84, Associate Prof., 1984–87, Medicine and Pharmacol.; Prof. of Medicine and Pharmacol., 1987–91; William Stokes Prof. of Experimental Therapeutics, 1989–91; Dir, Centre for Cardiovascular Sci., 1991–94, and Prof. and Chm., Dept of Experimental Therapeutics, 1991–94, UCD; Consultant Physician, Mater Hosp., Dublin, 1991–94; University of Pennsylvania: Dir, Center for Experimental Therapeutics, and Dir, Clin. Res. Centre, 1994–2004; Robinette Foundn Prof. of Cardiovascular Medicine, 1994–2004; Elmer Bobst Prof. of Pharmacol., 1999–2007. Adjunct Prof., RCSI, 1995–2004; Visiting Scientist: Wellcome Trust Centre for Human Genetics and Dept of Anatomy and Human Genetics, Oxford Univ., 2002–03; Scripps Res. Inst. and Genomics Inst. of Novartis Foundn, La Jolla, Calif, 2003. FAAAS 1998. Boyle Medal, Royal Dublin Soc., 2005. *Publications:* articles in learned jls. *Address:* 10th Floor, Room 122, 3400 Civic Center Boulevard Building 421, Institute for Translational Medicine and Therapeutics, University of Pennsylvania, Philadelphia, PA 19104–5158, USA.

FITZGERALD, Hon. Gerald Edward, (Hon. Tony), AC 1991; private dispute adjudicator; *b* Brisbane, 26 Nov. 1941; *m* 1968, Catherine Glynn-Connolly; one *s* two *d*. *Educ:* Univ. of Queensland (LLB). Admitted Queensland Bar, 1964; QC Queensland 1975 and subseq. QC NSW and Victoria; Judge of Federal Court of Australia, 1981–84; Judge of Supreme Court of ACT, 1981–84; Pres., Court of Appeal, Supreme Court of Qld, 1991–98; Judge of Ct of Appeal, Supreme Ct of NSW, 1998–2001. Presidential Mem., Administrative Appeals Tribunal, 1981–84; Mem., Australian Law Reform Commn, 1981–84; Chairman, Commission of Inquiry: into official corruption, Qld, 1987–89; into the Conservation, Management and Use of Fraser Is. and the Gt Sandy Reg., Qld, 1990–91; Chairman: Litigation Reform Commn, Qld, 1991–92; Cape York Justice Study, 2001; Nat. Pro Bono Resource Centre, 2004–06; former Chm., Law and Justice Foundn. Dir, Australian Res. Alliance for Children and Youth. Chm., Australian Heritage Commn, 1990–91. Chairman: Nat. Inst. for Law, Ethics and Public Affairs, 1992–95; Key Inst. for Ethics, Law, Justice and Governance, Griffith Univ., 1999– (Hon. Prof., 2003–); Vis. Scholar, New York Univ. Sch. of Law, 1997; Professorial Fellow, Univ. of Melbourne Law Sch., 1999–. Chancellor, Sunshine Coast UC, 1994–98. Dep. Chm., Gov. Bd, Mater Health Services, 1995–98. Mem., Adv. Bd, Legal Information Access Centre, State Liby of NSW, 2002–05. Jury Mem., Internat. Justice in the World Prize, Justice in the World Foundn, Internat. Assoc. of Judges, 2002–03. Fellow, Australian Centre for Internat. Commercial Arbitration Ltd. Mem., List of Neutrals, Arbitration and Mediation Center, WIPO. DUniv: Qld Univ. of Technol., 1995; Sunshine Coast, 1999; Griffith, 2003. *Recreations:* tennis, reading, music. *Address:* Level 7, Wentworth Chambers, 180 Phillip Street, Sydney, NSW 2000, Australia. *T:* (2) 82243030, *Fax:* (2) 92259541. *E:* tonyfitzgerald@disputeresolution.net.au.

FITZGERALD, Gerard, (Ged); Chief Executive, Liverpool City Council, since 2011; *b* Liverpool, 26 Aug. 1961; *s* of Timothy and Patricia Fitzgerald; *m* 1999, Karen Morris; one *d*. *Educ:* Goldsmiths' Coll., Univ. of London (BA Hons); Univ. of Salford (MBA). ACIS 1986; DMS 1992. Sefton MBC, 1983–87; Eur. Officer, Knowsley MBC, 1987–88; Policy Officer, Sefton MBC, 1988–91; Econ. Devel Manager, Knowsley MBC, 1991–94; Exec. Dir, Bootle City Challenge, 1994–96; Hd, Econ. Devel and Eur. Affairs, Liverpool CC, 1996–98; Dep. Chief Exec., Calderdale MBC, 1998–2001; Chief Executive: Rotherham MBC, 2001–04; Sunderland CC, 2004–08; Lancs CC, 2008–10. *Recreations:* family, football - Liverpool FC fan, travel. *Address:* Liverpool City Council, Municipal Buildings, Dale Street, Liverpool L69 2DH. *E:* ged.fitzgerald@liverpool.gov.uk.

FITZGERALD, Kevin Jeffrey, CMG 2013; FRGS; Chief Executive Officer, Copyright Licensing Agency, 2007–14; *b* Oxford, 16 Jan. 1960; *s* of Thomas John Fitzgerald and Pamela Rosemary Fitzgerald. *Educ:* Greyfriars Hall, Oxford (MA). With Thomas Cook plc, 1997–2002, incl. Man. Dir, Thomas Cook Publishing, and Hd of Content, ThomasCook.com; Man. Dir, Rough Guides, Pearson plc, 2002–06. Chm., Eur. Gp, 2008–, Dir, 2012–, Internat. Fedn of Reprodn Rights Orgns; Chm., Regulation Gp, British Copyright Council, 2010–. Non-exec. Dir, E of England Tourist Bd, 2006–11. Ind. Mem., Public Diplomacy Partners Gp, FCO, 2007–12. Trustee, Prisoners Abroad, 2009– (Chm., 2009–14). FRGS 2004. *Club:* Travellers.

FitzGERALD, Michael Frederick Clive, OBE 2002; QC 1980; *b* 9 June 1936; *s* of Sir William James FitzGerald, MC, QC, and Mrs E. J. Critchley; *m* 1st, 1966, Virginia Grace Cave (marr. diss. 1992); one *s* three *d;* 2nd, 1999, Nicola Mary Rountree (*née* Norman-Butler). *Educ:* Downside; Christ's Coll., Cambridge, 1956–59 (MA). 2nd Lieut 9th Queen's Royal Lancers, 1954–56. Called to the Bar, Middle Temple, 1961, Bencher, 1987. Leader, Parly Bar, 1997–2002. Chm., Adv. Panel on Standards for Planning Inspectorate Exec. Agency, 1992–2000. *Recreations:* opera, field sports. *Address:* Middledown House, Buttermere, Marlborough, Wilts SN8 3RQ. *Club:* Boodle's.

FitzGERALD, Niall William Arthur, Hon. KBE 2002; Deputy Chairman, Thomson Reuters, 2008–11 (Chairman, Reuters PLC, 2004–08; non-executive Director, Thomson Reuters (formerly Reuters PLC), 2003–11); Chairman, Michael Smurfit Graduate Business School, University College Dublin, since 2014; *b* 13 Sept. 1945; *s* of William FitzGerald and Doreen Chambers; *m* 1st, 1970, Monica Cusack (marr. diss. 2003); two *s* one *d;* 2nd, 2003, Ingrid Van Velzen; one *d. Educ:* St Munchin's Coll., Limerick; University College Dublin (MComm). FCT 1986. Unilever, 1968–2004: North America, 1978–80; Chief Exec. Officer, Foods, S Africa, 1981–85; Group Treasurer, 1985–86; Financial Dir, 1987–89; Exec. Dir, 1987–96; Vice-Chm., 1994–96; Chm., 1996–2004; Director: Unilever Foods, 1990–91; Unilever Detergents, 1992–96. Non-executive Director: Bank of Ireland, 1990–99; Prudential Corp., 1992–99; Ericsson, 2000–02; Merck, 2000–03; Chairman: Hakluyt & Co. Ltd, 2008–13; Adv. Bd, Hakluyt Internat., 2013–. A Sen. Advr, Allen & Co. LLP. Chairman: CBI Europe Cttee, 1995–2001; Conference Bd, 2003–05; Co-Chairman: Transatlantic Business Dialogue, 2004–05; Investment Climate Facility for Africa, 2005–10. Chm., Internat. Business Council, 2006–08; Member: EU-China Business Council, 1997; US Business Council, 1998–2006; Trilateral Commn, 1999; Council: Co-operation Ireland; World Econ. Forum, 1999–; Member: President of South Africa's Internat. Investment Adv. Council, 2000–07; Mitsubishi Internat. Adv. Cttee, 2014–; Adv. Bd, Chairman Mentors Internat.; Chm., Munster Rugby Commercial Bd, 2013–. Chairman: NiJaCo, 2006–; Brand Learning, 2013–. Pres., Advertising Assoc., 2000–05. CCMI. Chm., Bd of Trustees, BM, 2006–14. Chm., Nelson Mandela Legacy Trust (UK), 2005–08; Trustee, Leverhulme Trust, 1996– (Chm., 2013–). Chm., Bd of Govs, Cumnor House Sch., 2014–. FRSA. *Recreations:* observing humanity, music (opera and jazz), Irish Rugby, running, golf, creating an exotic garden in Sussex. *Club:* Royal Automobile.

FITZGERALD, Prof. Patrick John; Adjunct Professor of Law, Carleton University, Ottawa, since 1996 (Professor of Law, 1971–96); *b* 30 Sept. 1928; *s* of Dr Thomas Walter and Norah Josephine Fitzgerald; *m* 1959, Brigid Aileen Judge (*d* 2011); two *s* one *d. Educ:* Queen Mary's Grammar Sch., Walsall; University Coll., Oxford. Called to the Bar, Lincoln's Inn, 1951; Ontario Bar, 1984. Fellow, Trinity Coll., Oxford, 1956–60. Professor of Law: Leeds Univ., 1960–66; Univ. of Kent at Canterbury, 1966–71. Visiting Prof., University of Louisville, 1962–63. Consultant, Law Reform Commn of Canada, 1973–92. *Publications:* Criminal Law and Punishment, 1962; Salmond on Jurisprudence (12th edn), 1966; This Law of Ours, 1977; Looking at Law, 1979, 6th edn 2010; (ed) Crime, Justice and Codification, 1986. *Recreations:* music, bridge, creative writing. *Address:* 246–3310 Southgate Road, Ottawa, ON K1V 8X4, Canada.

FitzGERALD, Presiley Lamorna, (Mrs R. K. FitzGerald); *see* Baxendale, P. L.

FITZGERALD, Prof. Rebecca Clare, MD; FRCP; FMedSci; Professor of Cancer Prevention, since 2014, and Programme Leader, MRC Cancer Unit, Hutchison/MRC Research Centre, since 2002, University of Cambridge; Director of Studies in Medicine, and College Lecturer in Medical Sciences, Trinity College, Cambridge, since 2002; *b* Sheffield, 30 Sept. 1968; *d* of Robert Parker and Linda Parker (*née* McKinley); *m* 1992, Shaun David Fitzgerald, *qv;* four *s. Educ:* St Brandon's Sch., Clevedon, Avon; Girton Coll., Cambridge (BA Hons Med. Scis 1989; MB BChir 1991; MA 1993; MD 1997). MRCP 1995, FRCP 2006. Hse surgeon, Hinchinbrooke Hosp., Huntingdon, 1992; hse physician, 1992–93, SHO, 1993–95, Addenbrooke's Hosp., Cambridge; Res. Fellow, Dept of Gastroenterol., Stanford Univ. Center for Molecular Biol. in Medicine, 1995–97; Specialist Registrar Rotation, Gastroenterol. and Gen. Medicine, NE Thames, 1997–2001; Postdoctoral Res. Trng, Digestive Diseases Res. Centre, St Bart's and the Royal London NHS Trust, 1997–2001 (MRC Clinician Scientist, 1999); Sen. Clinician Scientist, Cancer Cell Unit, Hutchison/MRC Res. Centre, Cambridge, 2001–02; Speciality Registrar, 2001–03, Hon. Consultant in Gastroenterol., Addenbrooke's Hosp. and Dept. of Oncol., Univ. of Cambridge, 2003–. Vis. Postdoctoral Res. Fellow, Dept of Cellular and Molecular Medicine, Stanford Univ., 1999. FMedSci 2013. *Publications:* book chapters; contribs to jls, incl. Nat. Medicine, Nat. Genetics and Gastroenterology. *Recreations:* classical music (piano, clarinet, singing), organizing church and community musical fundraising events. *Address:* MRC Cancer Unit, Hutchison/MRC Research Centre, University of Cambridge, Box 197, Cambridge Biomedical Campus, Cambridge CB2 0XZ. *T:* (01223) 763287, *Fax:* (01223) 763241. *E:* rcf29@mrc-cu.cam.ac.uk.

FITZGERALD, Dr Shaun David, FREng; Chief Executive Officer, Breathing Buildings, since 2006; *b* Crawley, W Sussex, 12 Nov. 1966; *s* of Alan and Susan Fitzgerald; *m* 1992, Rebecca Clare Parker (*see* R. C. Fitzgerald); four *s. Educ:* Girton Coll., Cambridge (BA 1989; MA); Darwin Coll., Cambridge (PhD 1994). FREng 2014. Actg Asst Prof., Stanford Univ., 1995–97; Consultant, Bain & Co., 1997–2001; Researcher, Univ. of Cambridge, 2001–05; Tutor and Teaching Fellow, Girton Coll., Cambridge, 2004–. *Recreation:* trumpet with Prime Brass. *Address:* The Wix, 147 High Street, Harston, Cambs CB22 7QD. *T:* (01223) 870420; Girton College, Huntingdon Road, Cambridge CB3 0JG. *T:* (01223) 338999.

FitzGERALD, Susanna Patricia; QC 1999; *d* of late Frederick Patrick FitzGerald, FRCSI, PPICS and Zina Eveline FitzGerald (*née* Moncrieff), FRCP; *m* 1983, Wendell, (Nick), Clough; two *s. Educ:* Benenden Sch.; Bristol Univ. (LLB Hons). Called to the Bar, Inner Temple, 1973, Bencher, 2007; in practice at the Bar, 1973–; specialises in gambling and licensing law. Dir, Business in Sport and Leisure, 1994–2013. Dir, Inst. of Licensing, 2008–. Mem., Internat. Masters of Gaming Law, 2011–. Trustee, Gamcare. *Publications:* (contributing ed.) Law of Betting, Gaming and Lotteries, 2nd and 3rd edns; (contrib.) Gambling and Public Policy, 1991; contributing ed., Halsbury's Laws of England, vol. 4(1), Betting, Gaming and Lotteries, 4th edn reissue, 2002. *Recreations:* renovating old houses, ski-ing. *Address:* 1 Essex Court, Temple, EC4Y 9AR. *T:* (020) 7583 2000.

FitzGERALD, Sylvia Mary Denise, FLS; Head of Library and Archives (formerly Chief Librarian and Archivist), Royal Botanic Gardens, Kew, 1979–99; *b* 7 May 1939; *d* of Audoen Aengus FitzGerald and Doris Winifred (*née* Dickinson). *Educ:* Our Lady of Sion Sch., Worthing; Open Univ. (BA Hons 1977); Univ. of Surrey (MA Pastoral Theology 2005). MCLIP (ALA 1962). Assistant: Science Mus. Liby, 1956–57; Brit. Mus. (Natural Hist.) Zool. Liby, 1957–63; Assistant Librarian: Patent Office Liby, 1963–65; MAFF, 1965–67; Librarian-in-charge: MAFF Food & Nutrition Liby, 1967–72; MAFF Tolworth Liby for State Vet. Service and Vertebrate Pest Control, 1972–78. Member, Library Committee: Linnean Soc. of London, 1985–2003; RHS, 1993–. FLS 1992. *Publications:* contrib. State Librarian, Aslib Prog., Archives, etc. *Recreations:* friends, music. *Address:* 139 London Road, Ewell, Epsom, Surrey KT17 2BT.

FITZGERALD, Hon. Tony; *see* Fitzgerald, Hon. G. E.

FITZGERALD-LOMBARD, Rt Rev. Charles, OSB, **(James Michael Hubert Fitzgerald-Lombard);** Abbot of Downside, 1990–98; Parish Priest, St Edmund, Bungay, since 2006; Episcopal Vicar for Religious, Diocese of East Anglia, since 2014; *b* 29 Jan. 1941; *s* of late Col James C. R. Fitzgerald-Lombard and Winifred (*née* Woulfe Flanagan). *Educ:* Downside; Collegio Sant Anselmo, Rome; King's Coll., London (MPhil). Monk of Downside Abbey, 1962–; ordained priest, 1968; Teacher and Tutor, Downside Sch., 1968–75; Bursar and Sec. to the Trustees, 1975–90. Dep. Chm., Union of Monastic Superiors, 1998. Titular Abbot of Glastonbury, 1999–. Governor: Downside Sch., 1999–2003; St Edmund's Sch., Bungay, 2006–. Mem., Historic Churches Cttee, Dio. E Anglia, 2007–. Dir, Mid-Suffolk Light Rly, 2008–. Trustee, Waveney Foodbank, 2013–. Ecclesiastical CLJ, 1995–. Ed., The Downside Review, 2002–05. *Publications:* Prayers and Meditations, 1967, 3rd edn 1974; A Guide to the Church of St Gregory the Great, Downside Abbey, 1981, 4th edn 2000; English and Welsh Priests 1801–1914, 1993. *Address:* St Edmund's Presbytery, St Mary's Street, Bungay, Suffolk NR35 1AX.

FITZGIBBON, Dr Andrew William, FREng; Principal Researcher, Microsoft Research, Cambridge, since 2005; *b* Dublin, 1968; *s* of Frank and Barbara Fitzgibbon; *m* 2003, Elizabeth Barry; one *d. Educ:* University Coll., Cork (BSc 1986); Heriot Watt Univ. (MSc 1989); Univ. of Edinburgh (PhD 1997). FBCS 2012; FREng 2014. Res. Asst, Univ. of Edinburgh, 1990–96; Res. Associate, 1996–99, Royal Soc. Univ. Res. Fellow, 1999–2005, Univ. of Oxford. Chm., British Machine Vision Assoc., 2010–13. Roger Needham Award, BCS, 2006; (jtly) MacRobert Award, 2011, Silver Medal, 2013, RAEng. *Recreations:* Alpine ski-ing, ski touring. *Address:* Microsoft Research Ltd, 21 Station Road, Cambridge CB1 2FB. *E:* awf@microsoft.com.

FitzGIBBON, Francis George Herbert Dillon; QC 2010; *b* Dorchester, 18 July 1961; *s* of late Constantine FitzGibbon and Marion FitzGibbon (*née* Gutmann); *m* 1986, Camilla Beresford; one *s* one *d. Educ:* Westminster Sch.; Magdalen Coll., Oxford (BA Hons Lit.Hum.; MA). Called to the Bar, Middle Temple, 1986; Immigration Judge, 2002–. Trustee, Turner Contemp., Margate, 2008–. *Recreations:* family, music, running. *Address:* Doughty Street Chambers, 54 Doughty Street, WC1N 2LS. *T:* (020) 7404 1313, *Fax:* (020) 7404 2283. *E:* f.fitzgibbon@doughtystreet.co.uk.

FitzHARRIS, Viscount; James Hugh Carleton Harris; *b* 29 April 1970; *s* and *heir* of Earl of Malmesbury, *qv;* *m* 1997, Jemima, *e d* of Captain M. Fulford-Dobson, *qv;* two *s* one *d. Educ:* Eton; Christ Church, Oxford (MEng); RAC Cirencester (DipAgr). ACA 1997. *Heir: s* Hon. James Michael Oswald Harris, *b* 26 April 1999. *Address:* Sydling Court, Sydling St Nicholas, Dorchester, Dorset DT2 9PA.

FITZHARRIS, Ven. Robert Aidan; Archdeacon of Doncaster, 2001–11, Archdeacon Emeritus, since 2012; *b* 19 Aug. 1946; *s* of late John Joseph and Margaret Louisa Fitzharris; *m* 1971, Lesley Margaret Mary Rhind; three *d. Educ:* St Anselm's Coll., Birkenhead; Sheffield Univ. (BDS 1971); Lincoln Theol Coll. (Gen. Ministerial Exam. 1989). General dental practice, 1971–87; part-time Clinical Asst to Prof. of Child Dental Health, Charles Clifford Dental Hosp., Sheffield, 1978–85. Ordained deacon, 1989, priest, 1990; Asst Curate, Dinnington, 1989–92; Vicar of Bentley, 1992–2001; Substitute Chaplain, HMP Moorland, 1992–2001; Area Dean, Adwick-le-Street, 1995–2001. Hon. Associate Chaplain, Doncaster Royal Infirmary and Mexbrough Montague Hosp. Trust, 1995–2001; Hon. Canon, Sheffield Cathedral, 1998; Hon. Associate Priest, Doncaster Minster, 2014–; Hon. Chaplain to Civic Mayor of Doncaster, 2014–15; Hon. Chaplain to High Sheriff of S Yorks 2015–March 2016. Chairman: Sheffield Diocesan Strategy Gp, 1999–2001; Sheffield Diocesan Bd of Educn, 2001–11; Sheffield Diocesan Parsonages Cttee, 2001–11; Doncaster Minster Develt Cttee, 2005–07; Together for Regeneration Project, 2004–10; Refurnish Ltd (formerly Doncaster Refurnish Ltd), 2007–; Member: Doncaster Adv. Gp, Common Purpose S Yorks, 2004–; Res. Ethics Cttee, Sheffield Univ., 2007–. Founding Chm., Bentley Assoc. for Supportive Help, 1995–2001; Chm., Doncaster Cancer Detection Trust, 2003–; Vice Chm., Doncaster Freeman Gp, 2014–. Chm., Wildwood Project (Bentley) Ltd, 1998–2004. Chm., Friends of Doncaster Mansion House, 2015–; Vice-Patron, Doncaster and Dist Family Hist. Soc., 2006–. Life Mem., Royal and Ancient Polar Bear Soc. of Hammerfest, Norway, 2012. Hon. Freeman, Bor. of Doncaster, 2008. Occasional broadcaster, BBC Radio 2 Pause for Thought. *Recreations:* travel, reading, cooking. *Address:* Amberley, Old Bawtry Road, Finningley, Doncaster DN9 3BY. *T:* (01302) 773220. *E:* lesleyfitzharris@waitrose.com.

FITZHERBERT, family name of **Baron Stafford.**

FitzHERBERT, Giles Eden, CMG 1985; HM Diplomatic Service, retired; *b* Dublin, 8 March 1935; *e s* of late Captain H. C. FitzHerbert, Irish Guards, and Sheelah, *d* of J. X. Murphy; *m* 1st, 1962, Margaret Waugh (*d* 1986); two *s* three *d;* 2nd, 1988, Alexandra Eyre; three *s* one *d. Educ:* Ampleforth Coll.; Christ Church Oxford; Harvard Business Sch. 2nd Lieut, 8th King's Royal Irish Hussars, 1957–58. Vickers da Costa & Co., 1962–66. First Secretary: Foreign Office, 1966; Rome, 1968–71; FCO, 1972–75; Counsellor: Kuwait, 1975–77; Nicosia, 1977–78; Head of Eur. Community Dept (Ext.), FCO, 1978–82; on sabbatical leave, LSE, 1982; Inspector, FCO, 1983; Minister, Rome, 1983–87; Ambassador to Venezuela and concurrently (non-resident) to the Dominican Republic, 1988–93. Contested (L) Fermanagh and South Tyrone, Gen. Elect., 1964. *Address:* Woodbrook House, Killanne, Enniscorthy, Co. Wexford, Ireland. *Club:* Beefsteak.

FitzHERBERT, Sir Richard (Ranulph), 9th Bt *cr* 1784, of Tissington, Derbyshire; *b* 2 Nov. 1963; *s* of Rev. David Henry FitzHerbert, MC (*d* 1976) and Charmian Hyacinthe (*d* 2006), *yr d* of late Samuel Ranulph Allsopp, CBE; *S* uncle, 1989; *m* 1st, 1993, Caroline Louise (marr. diss. 2007), *d* of late Major and Mrs Patrick Shuter; one *s* one *d;* 2nd, 2011, Fiona Alison, *d* of late Dr and Mrs John Fitzgerald. *Educ:* Eton College. Mem. (C) Derbys Dales DC, 2011–. President: Derbys Community Foundn, 1995–; Derbys Rural Community Council, 1996–; Derbys Scouts, 2004–; Member, Board: E Midlands Tourism, 2004–07; Visit Peak District and Derbyshire Destination Mgt Partnership, 2005–; HHA, 2009– (Mem., 1995, Chm., 1999–2006, E Midlands HHA). Patron, Soc. of Derbys Golf Captains. *Recreations:* cricket, shooting, restoring family estate. *Heir: s* Frederick David FitzHerbert, *b* 23 March 1995. *Address:* Tissington Hall, Ashbourne, Derbys DE6 1RA. *E:* tisshall@dircon.co.uk. *Clubs:* White's, MCC; I Zingari, Stansted Hall Cricket, Parwich Royal British Legion Cricket, Strollers Cricket, Strawberry Cricket.

FitzHUGH, (Edmund Francis) Lloyd, OBE 1995; JP; landowner; Vice Lord-Lieutenant for the County of Clwyd, since 2008; *b* 2 Feb. 1951; *s* of late Godfrey Edmund FitzHugh and Burness Grace FitzHugh (*née* Clemson); *m* 1975, Pauline Davison; two *s. Educ:* Eton; Shuttleworth Agricl Coll. Chairman: Bd of Mgt, Royal Welsh Agricl Soc., 1991–98; NE Wales NHS Trust, 1999–2005. Dep. Chm., Local Govt Boundary Commn for Wales,

1995–2002. JP Wrexham 1990; DL 1996, High Sheriff, 2011–12, Clwyd. *Recreations:* church music, wining and dining. *Address:* Garden House, Plas Power, Bersham, Wrexham LL14 4LN. *T:* (01978) 263522.

FITZMAURICE; *see* Petty-Fitzmaurice, family name of Marquess of Lansdowne.

FITZPATRICK, Brian; advocate; *b* 9 June 1961; *s* of late Patrick Fitzpatrick and Kathleen (*née* Strong); *m* 1986, Marie Macdonald; one *s* two *d. Educ:* Univ. of Glasgow (LLB Juris 1984). Called to Scottish Bar, 1993; Solicitor, Glasgow, Edinburgh and London, 1984–92; Mem., Faculty of Advocates, 1993–. Hd of Policy, First Minister's Policy Unit, Scottish Parlt, 1999–2000. MSP (Lab) Strathkelvin and Bearsden, June 2001–2003. Contested (Lab) Strathkelvin and Bearsden, Scottish Parlt, 2003. *Recreations:* swimming, cinema, reading, poetry, travel, wine, politics. *Address:* c/o Advocates' Library, Parliament House, Edinburgh EH1 1RF.

FITZPATRICK, Francis Paul; QC 2015; *b* Birmingham, 16 April 1967; *s* of Thomas Fitzpatrick and Catherine Fitzpatrick (*née* Coote); *m* 1997, Jessica; one *s* one *d. Educ:* Handsworth Grammar Sch.; Worcester Coll., Oxford (BA 1st Cl. Hons Law; BCL). Called to the Bar, Inner Temple, 1990. *Recreations:* ski-ing, tennis, croquet, theatre. *Address:* 1st Floor, 11 New Square, Lincoln's Inn, WC2A 3QB.

FITZPATRICK, James, (Jim); MP (Lab) Poplar and Limehouse, since 2010 (Poplar and Canning Town, 1997–2010); *b* 4 April 1952; *s* of James Fitzpatrick and Jean Fitzpatrick (*née* Stones). *Educ:* Holyrood Sch., Glasgow. Trainee, Tytrak Ltd, Glasgow, 1970–73; driver, Mintex Ltd, 1973–74; Firefighter, London Fire Brigade, 1974–97. PPS to Sec. of State for Health, 1999–2001; an Asst Govt Whip, 2001–02; a Lord Comr of HM Treasury (Govt Whip), 2002–03; Vice-Chamberlain of HM Household, 2003–05; Parliamentary Under-Secretary of State: ODPM, 2005–06; DTI, 2006–07; DfT, 2007–09; Minister of State, DEFRA, 2009–10; Shadow Minister for Envmt, Food and Rural Affairs, 2010, for Transport, 2010–13. Mem., NEC, Fire Bdes Union, 1988–97. Mem. Exec., Gtr London Lab. Party, 1988–2000 (Chm., 1991–2000). Fire Bde Long Service and Good Conduct Medal, 1994. *Recreations:* cycling, reading, football (West Ham Utd), television and films. *Address:* House of Commons, SW1A 0AA. *T:* (020) 7219 5085.

FITZPATRICK, Air Marshal Sir John (Bernard), KBE 1984; CB 1982; Royal Air Force, retired; *b* 15 Dec. 1929; *s* of Joseph Fitzpatrick and Bridget Fitzpatrick; *m* 1954, Gwendoline Mary Abbott; two *s* one *d. Educ:* RAF Apprentice Sch., Halton; RAF Coll. Cranwell. Officer Commanding: No 81 Sqdn, 1966–68; No 35 Sqdn, 1971–72; Gp Captain Plans to AOC No 18 Gp, 1973; OC, RAF Scampton, 1974–75; RCDS, 1976; Dir of Ops (Strike), RAF, 1977–79; SASO, HQ Strike Command, 1980–82; Dir Gen. of Organisation, RAF, 1982–83; AOC No 18 Gp, RAF, and Comdr Maritime Air Eastern Atlantic and Channel, 1983–86. Ind. Panel Inspector, Depts of the Envmt and Transport, 1986–99. *Recreations:* good food with good company, DIY.

FitzPATRICK, Joseph Martin; Member (SNP) Dundee City West, Scottish Parliament, since 2011 (Dundee West, 2007–11); Minister for Parliamentary Business, since 2012; *b* 1 April 1967; *s* of Joseph K. FitzPatrick and Margaret M. FitzPatrick (*née* Crabb). *Educ:* Univ. of Abertay Dundee (BSc Hons). Mem., Dundee CC, 1999–2007. Contested (SNP) Dundee W, 2005. *Recreations:* hill-walking, trekking, scuba diving. *Address:* (office) 8 Old Glamis Road, Dundee DD3 8HP. *T:* (01382) 623200, *Fax:* (01382) 903205. *E:* dundee@joefitzpatrick.net.

FITZPATRICK, Prof. Raymond Michael, PhD; Professor of Public Health and Primary Care, University of Oxford, since 1996; Fellow, Nuffield College, Oxford, since 1986; *b* 8 Oct. 1950; *s* of James Fitzpatrick and Maureen Fitzpatrick; *m* 1979, Mary Boulton. *Educ:* UC, Oxford (BA); Bedford Coll., London Univ. (MSc; PhD 1986). Lecturer: Bedford Coll., London Univ., 1978–86; Oxford Univ., 1986–. Mem., MRC, 1998–2003 (Chm., Health Services and Public Health Res. Bd, 1998–2003). *Publications:* (jtly) The Experience of Illness, 1984; (ed with G. Albrecht) Quality of Life in Health Care, 1994; (jtly) Understanding Rheumatoid Arthritis, 1995; (ed jtly) Health Services Research Methods, 1998. *Recreations:* music, theatre. *Address:* Nuffield College, Oxford OX1 1NF. *T:* (01865) 278500.

FitzROY, family name of **Duke of Grafton** and of **Baron Southampton**.

FitzROY NEWDEGATE, family name of **Viscount Daventry**.

FITZSIMONS, Anthony; *see* Fitzsimons, P. A.

FITZSIMONS, Prof. James Thomas, FRS 1988; Professor of Medical Physiology, University of Cambridge, 1990–95, now Emeritus Professor; Fellow of Gonville and Caius College, Cambridge, since 1961 (President, 1997–2005); *b* 8 July 1928; *s* of Robert Allen Fitzsimons, FRCS and Dr Mary Patricia (*née* McKelvey); *m* 1961, Aude Irène Jeanne, *d* of Gén. Jean Etienne Valluy, DSO and Marie (*née* Bourdillon); two *s* one *d. Educ:* St Edmund's Coll., Ware; Gonville and Caius Coll., Cambridge (1st cl. Pts I and II, Nat. Sci. Tripos; BA 1949; BChir 1953; MB 1954; MA 1954; PhD 1960; MD 1967, Sir Lionel Whitby Medal; ScD 1979); Charing Cross Hosp. House appts, Leicester Gen. and Charing Cross Hosps, 1954–55; RAF, Inst. of Aviation Medicine, 1955–57 (Flight Lieut); Cambridge University: MRC Scholar, Physiol. Lab., 1957–59; Univ. Demonstrator in Physiol., 1959–64, Lectr, 1964–76, Reader, 1976–90; Gonville and Caius College: Tutor, 1964–72; Coll. Lectr in Physiol., 1964–93; Dir of Studies in Medicine, 1978–93. Visiting Scientist: CNRS Lab. des Régulations Alimentaires, Coll. de France, 1967; Inst. of Neurol Scis, Univ. of Pennsylvania, 1968, 1972; CNRS Lab. de Neurobiol., Coll. de France, 1975; Lectures: Stevenson Meml, Univ. of Western Ontario, 1979; Halliburton, KCL, 1982. Royal Soc. rep., British Nat. Cttee for Physiol. Scis, 1976–82; Mem., Physiol. Soc. Cttee, 1972–76 (Chm., 1975–76); Mem., IUPS Commn on Physiol. of Food and Fluid Intake, 1973–80 (Chm., 1979–80). Member, Editorial Boards: Jl of Physiol., 1977–84; Neuroendocrinology, 1979–84; Editor, Biological Reviews, 1984–95. Hon. MD Lausanne, 1978. Dist. Career Award, Soc. for Study of Ingestive Behavior, 1998. *Publications:* The Physiology of Thirst and Sodium Appetite, 1979; scientific papers in professional jls. *Recreations:* Irish language and literature, cats, music, photography, grandchildren. *Address:* Gonville and Caius College, Trinity Street, Cambridge CB2 1TA. *T:* (01223) 332429; 91 Thornton Road, Girton, Cambridge CB3 0NR. *T:* (01223) 276874.

FITZSIMONS, Lorna, (Mrs S. B. Cooney); Director, Lorna Fitzsimons Consulting Ltd, since 2013; *b* 6 Aug. 1967; *d* of late Derek Fitzsimons and of Barbara Jean Taylor; *m* 2000, Stephen Benedict Cooney; one *s,* and one step *s* one step *d. Educ:* Wardle High Sch.; Rochdale Coll. of Art and Design; Loughborough Coll. of Art and Design (BA Hons Textile Design 1988; a Vice Pres., Students' Union, 1988–89). National Union of Students: part-time Nat. Exec. Officer, 1989–90; Vice Pres., Educn, 1990–92; Pres., 1992–94; Rowland Public Affairs: Account Manager, 1994–95; Account Dir, 1995–96; Associate Dir, 1996–97. Mem. Bd, Endsleigh Insce, 1992–94. Chair, Student Forum, EU, 1990–94; Mem., Quality Cttee, FEFC, 1993–94. Member National Executive: Fabian Soc., 1996–97; Lab. Co-ordinating Cttee, 1995–97, Campaign of Electoral Reform, 1997, Labour Party. MP (Lab) Rochdale, 1997–2005; contested (Lab) same seat, 2005. PPS to Minister of State, FCO, 2000–01, to Leader of H of C, 2001–03. Treas., 1997–2003, Chm., 2003–05, All Party Parly Gp on Kashmir. Chair, 1997–2001, Vice Pres., 2001–05, Women's Cttee, PLP. Supporter, Labour Friends of Israel, 1997–2005. Lorna Fitzsimons Consulting, 2005–06: CEO, Britain Israel Communications & Res. Centre, 2006–12. Sen. Associate Fellow, UK Defence Acad. Advanced Res. and Assessment Gp, 2005. Co-Founder and Dir, MK-LF Partnership Ltd and Pipeline Prog., 2013–. Director: Alliance Project, 2013–; Regl Growth Fund, 2013–; Textile Growth Prog., 2013–. Governor: Wardle High Sch., 1982–83, 2003–; Loughborough Coll. of Art and Design, 1988–89; Sheffield Hallam Univ., 1995–96. *Recreations:* watching films, cooking, walking, travelling, dancing or listening to music. *E:* mail@lornafitzsimons.net.

FITZSIMONS, P. Anthony; Chairman: Ruton Management Ltd, since 1994; Prisoner Escort and Custody Services Lay Observers' National Council, since 2015; *b* 16 March 1946; two *s. Educ:* LSE (BSc Econ.). Rank Xerox: Australia, 1972–75; Southern Europe, 1975–76; Australasia, Middle East, 1976–79; Regional Control Dir, London, 1979–81; Grand Metropolitan: Finance Systems and Strategy Dir, Brewing and Retail Div., 1981–83; Man. Dir, Host Group, 1983–85; Man. Dir, Personal Banking, Citibank, 1985–89; Chief Exec. and Man. Dir, Bristol & West Bldg Soc., 1989–93. Chm., Avon TEC. Chairman: Great Western Ambulance Service NHS Trust, 2006–12; Gloucestershire Probation Trust, 2007–14. *Recreations:* squash, riding, music, sailing. *Address:* Hill House, Hannington, Wilts SN6 7RS.

FitzWALTER, 22nd Baron *cr* 1295; **Julian Brook Plumptre;** *b* 18 Oct. 1952; *s* of 21st Baron FitzWalter and Margaret Melesina (*née* Deedes); *S* father, 2004; *m* 1988, Sally, *o d* of late I. M. T. Quiney; three *s. Educ:* Radley; Wye Coll., London Univ. *Heir: s* Hon. Edward Brook Plumptre, *b* 26 April 1989.

FIVET, Edmond Charles Paul, CBE 2008; FRCM; Principal, Royal Welsh College of Music and Drama, 1989–2007; *b* 12 Feb. 1947; *s* of Paul Fivet and Lorna (*née* Edwards); *m* 1st, 1969, Christine Partington (marr. diss. 1976); one *s* one *d*; 2nd, 1978, Elizabeth Page. *Educ:* Royal Coll. of Music; Coll. of St Mark and St John; City Univ. (MA); Open Univ. (BA). FRCM 1988. Registrar, 1973–83, Dir, 1983–89, Jun. Dept, Royal Coll. of Music; Music Dir, Audi Jun. Musician, 1986–98. Member: Music Cttee, Welsh Arts Council, 1991–94; Steering Cttee, NYO of Wales, 1991–2002; Music Cttee, Cardiff Internat. Fest., 1992–95; Council, Arts Council of Wales, 2000–03; Vice-Pres., Richmond upon Thames Arts Council, 1986–98. Member: Assoc. of European Conservatoires, 1989–2007; Heads of Higher Educn, Wales, 1996–2007. Music Director: Aldeburgh Music Club, 2008–; Phoenix Singers, 2008–12; Conductor, Prometheus Orch., 2008–. Chairman: Bury St Edmunds Concert Club, 2008–; Making Music Concert Promoters Gp (formerly Cttee), 2010–; Adjudicators, Young Musicians Competition, 2012–. Gov., Dartington Coll. of Arts, 1997–2004. Trustee, Millennium Stadium Charitable Trust, 2001–06. Hon. FBC 2006; Fellow, RWCMD, 2007. DUniv Glamorgan, 2007. *Recreations:* golf, music, theatre, reading, current affairs. *Address:* Fair Winds, 11 North Warren, Aldeburgh, Suffolk IP15 5QF. *Clubs:* Savile; Aldeburgh Golf, Thorpeness Golf.

FLACH, Timothy Irvine; photographer, specialising in conceptual images of animals, since 1983; *b* London, 16 April 1958; *s* of late Robert Thomas Francis Flach and Mary Irvine Flach, TD (*née* Friend; she *m* 2nd 5th Baron Crofton); *m* 2008, Yu Sun; one *s. Educ:* Launceston Coll., Cornwall; North East London Poly. (BA Hons Communication Design 1980); St Martin's Sch. of Art (Postgrad. Photography and Painted Structures 1983). Works in public collections incl. Nat. Media Mus., UK. FBIPP 2013. Hon. FRPS 2013. Hon. Dr Norwich Univ. of Arts, 2013. Fine Art Photographer of Year, USA, Internat. Photography Awards, 2006; Best in Book, Creative Rev. Photography Annual UK, 2010, 2012, 2013. *Publications:* Equus, 2008 (German and French edns 2008, Chinese edn 2011); Dogs Gods, 2010 (German, French, Australian edns 2010, Chinese edn 2011); More Than Human, 2012 (German and Australian edns 2012); Stern Portfolio NI.74 Evolution, 2013; contribs to Nat. Geographic mag., NY Times, Sunday Times. *Recreations:* dancing, running, table tennis. *Address:* 58 Eastern Street, EC2A 3QR. *E:* tim@timflach.com.

FLACK, Rt Rev. John Robert; an Honorary Assistant Bishop: Diocese of Peterborough, since 2003; Diocese in Europe, since 2004; Diocese of Ely, since 2013; *b* 30 May 1942; *s* of Edwin John Flack and Joan Annie Flack; *m* 1968, Julia Clare Slaughter; one *s* one *d. Educ:* Hertford Grammar Sch.; Univ. of Leeds (BA 1964); Coll. of the Resurrection, Mirfield. Ordained, deacon, 1966, priest, 1967; Assistant Curate: St Bartholomew, Armley, Leeds, 1966–69; St Mary the Virgin, Northampton, 1969–72; Vicar: Chapelthorpe (Wakefield dio.), 1972–81; Ripponden with Rishworth and Barkisland with West Scammonden, 1981–85; Brighouse, 1985–92 (Team Rector, 1988–92); Rural Dean of Brighouse and Elland, 1986–92; Archdeacon of Pontefract, 1992–97; Bishop Suffragan of Huntingdon, 1997–2003; Dir, Anglican Centre in Rome, and Archbp of Canterbury's Rep. to the Holy See, 2003–08; Priest-in-charge, Nassington with Yarwell and Woodnewton, and of Apethorpe, 2008–12. Hon. Canon of Peterborough Cathedral, 2004–12, now Canon Emeritus. *Recreations:* cricket, Mozart. *Address:* 7 Cemetery Road, Whittlesey, Peterborough PE7 1SF. *E:* johnflack67@yahoo.com.

FLAHERTY, Patrick John; Chief Executive, Somerset County Council, since 2014; *b* Stoke-on-Trent, 23 Sept. 1968; *s* of Vincent and Rosemary Flaherty; *m* 1993, Alison Ball; one *s* one *d. Educ:* St Thomas More High Sch. and Sixth Form Coll., Stoke-on-Trent; Bolton Inst. of Higher Educn (BEng Hons Civil Engrg 1997); Univ. of Salford (MSc Transport Engrg 2000). Hd of Regeneration, Stafford BC, 2002–06; Somerset County Council: Hd of Regeneration, 2006–11; Dir, Envmt Services, 2011–12; Gp Dir Ops, 2012–14. Gov., Richard Huish Sixth Form Coll., Taunton, 2013–. *Recreations:* cycling, literature, family. *Address:* Somerset County Council, County Hall, The Crescent, Taunton, Som TA1 4DY.

FLAHIVE, Daniel Michael; His Honour Judge Flahive; a Circuit Judge, since 2009; *b* London, 1 Oct. 1958; *s* of Jeremiah and Eileen Flahive; *m* 1989, Cheryl Ulmer; two *s. Educ:* London Sch. of Econs (LLB Hons); Inns of Court Sch. of Law. Called to the Bar, Gray's Inn, 1982; in practice specialising in criminal law, London, 1982–2009; Recorder, 2003–09. Judicial Mem., Parole Bd, 2010–13. *Recreation:* travel. *Address:* Croydon Combined Court Centre, The Law Courts, Altyre Road, Croydon CR9 5AB. *T:* (020) 8410 4700.

FLANAGAN, Andrew Henry; a Civil Service Commissioner, since 2013; Director, NHS North and East London Commissioning Support Unit, since 2013; *b* 15 March 1956; *s* of Francis Desmond Flanagan and Martha Donaldson Flanagan; *m* 1992, Virginia Walker; two *s* one *d. Educ:* Glasgow Univ. (BAcc). CA. Touche Ross, 1976–79; Price Waterhouse, 1979–81; Financial Control Manager, ITT, 1981–86; Finance Dir, PA Consulting Gp, 1986–91; Gp Finance Dir and Chief Financial Officer, BIS Ltd, 1991–94; Finance Dir, Scottish Television plc, 1994–96; Man. Dir, Scottish Television plc, 1996–97; Chief Exec., SMG (formerly Scottish Media Gp) plc, 1997–2006; Chm., Fleming Media, 2007–08; Chief Exec., NSPCC, 2009–13. Chm., Heritage House Gp, 2008–12 (Dir, 2008–12); Dir, Phonepayplus, 2008–09. Non-executive Director: Criminal Injuries Compensation Authy; NHS Business Services Authy; CIPFA Business Services Ltd. Non-exec. Dir, Scottish RU, 2000–05. Trustee, NESTA, 2006–09. *Recreations:* golf, ski-ing, television. *Address:* 7 Collylinn Road, Bearsden, Glasgow G61 4PN.

FLANAGAN, Caroline Jane; Partner, Ross & Connel, Solicitors, Dunfermline, since 1990; President, Law Society of Scotland, 2005–06; *b* 12 Jan. 1961; *d* of Leslie and Sheila Ebbutt; *m* 1986, Roy Flanagan; one *s* one *d. Educ:* Dollar Acad.; Edinburgh Univ. (LLB, DipLP). Trainee, then asst solicitor, 1982–90. Dean, Dunfermline and Dist Soc. of Solicitors, 2000–02; Vice-Pres., Law Soc. of Scotland, 2004–05. *Recreations:* ski-ing, walking, reading, music. *Address:* Ross & Connel, 18 Viewfield Terrace, Dunfermline KY12 7JH. *T:* (01383) 721156. *E:* cflanagan@ross.connel.co.uk.

FLANAGAN, Charles; Member (FG) of the Dáil (TD) for Laois-Offaly, 1987–2002 and since 2007; Minister for Foreign Affairs and Trade, Ireland, since 2014; *b* Dublin, 1 Nov. 1956; *s* of Oliver J. Flanagan and Mai Flanagan (*née* McWey); *m* 1984, Mary McCormack; two *d. Educ:* University Coll., Dublin (BA Hist. and Politics 1977). Admitted as solicitor, Ireland, 1982; legal practice in Portlaoise specialising in family and criminal law, 1982–87. FG spokesperson on NI, 1997–2000; Chief Whip (FG), 2000–02; Opposition spokesperson: on Justice, Equality and Defence, 2007–10; on Children and Youth Affairs, 2010–11; Minister for Children and Youth Affairs, 2014. Chairperson, FG Parly Party, 2011–14. Vice-Chm., British-Irish Parly Gp, 1997–2000. Member (FG): Mountmellik Town Council, 1987–91; Laois CC, 1987–2004. Mem., FG Party Exec. Council, 1995–2002 and 2010–14. *Recreations:* hill walking, following football and Gaelic games. *Address:* Department of Foreign Affairs and Trade, Iveagh House, 80 St Stephen's Green, Dublin 2, Ireland. *T:* 014082000. *E:* charlie.flanagan@oir.ie. *Club:* Rotary (Portlaoise).

FLANAGAN, Michael Joseph; Director, Finance and Planning, Cheshire Constabulary, 1995–2000; Company Secretary, FFBA Ltd, since 2004; *b* 21 Nov. 1946; *s* of Daniel and Margaret Constance Flanagan; *m* 1968, Patricia Holland; two *s* one *d. Educ:* St Joseph's Coll., Blackpool; Southampton Coll. of Higher Educn. IPFA 1972; DMS 1983. Trainee Accountant, Lancs CC, 1965–69; Preston County Borough, 1969–70; Southampton City Council, 1970–72; Accountant, 1972, Asst Dir of Finance, 1981–87, Telford Develt Corp.; Dir of Finance and Tech. Services, 1987–90, Chief Exec., 1990–95, Develt Bd for Rural Wales. *Recreations:* sport, esp. football, golf, tennis; family activities. *Club:* Lancs CC.

FLANAGAN, Sir Ronald, GBE 2002 (OBE 1996); Kt 1999; QPM 2007; HM Chief Inspector of Constabulary, 2005–08; Strategic Adviser to the Minister of Interior, United Arab Emirates, since 2009; Chairman, Anti-Corruption and Security Unit, International Cricket Council, since 2010; *b* 25 March 1949; *s* of John Patrick Flanagan and Henrietta Flanagan; *m* 1968, Lorraine Nixon; three *s. Educ:* Belfast High Sch.; Univ. of Ulster (BA, MA); Graduate: FBI Nat. Acad., 1987; FBI Nat. Exec. Inst., 1996. Joined Royal Ulster Constabulary, as Constable, 1970: Sergeant, Belfast, 1973; Inspector, Londonderry, 1976, Belfast, 1977–81; Detective Inspector, 1981; Detective Chief Inspector, 1983; Detective Superintendent, Armagh, 1987; Chief Superintendent, Police Staff Coll., Bramshill, 1990; Asst Chief Constable, Belfast, 1992; Actg Dep. Chief Constable, 1995, affirmed Feb. 1996; Chief Constable, RUC, 1996–2002; HM Inspector of Constabulary, 2002–05. Advr on illegal tobacco trade, British American Tobacco, 2013–. *Recreations:* walking, Rugby, reading (particularly Yeats' poetry), music (particularly Van Morrison), but very varied taste. *Club:* Royal Ulster Yacht (Bangor, Co. Down).

FLANDERS, Stephanie Hope; Chief Market Strategist, Europe, JP Morgan Asset Management, since 2013; *b* 5 Aug. 1968; *d* of late Michael Flanders, OBE and Claudia Flanders, OBE; partner, John Arlidge; one *s* one *d. Educ:* St Paul's Girls' Sch., Hammersmith; Balliol Coll., Oxford (Schol.; BA 1st Cl. Hons PPE); John F. Kennedy Sch. of Govt, Harvard Univ. (Kennedy Schol.; MPA). Research Officer: London Business Sch., 1990–91; Inst. for Fiscal Studies, 1991–92; Teaching Fellow, Dept of Govt, Harvard Univ., and Kennedy Sch. of Govt, 1993–94; econs leader-writer and columnist, Financial Times, 1994–97; Sen. Advr and speechwriter to Lawrence H. Summers, US Treasury Dept, 1997–2001; reporter, NY Times, 2001; Econs Ed., Newsnight, BBC TV, 2002–08; Econs Ed., BBC, 2008–13; Stephanomics (series), BBC Radio 4, 2011–13. Mem., Council on Foreign Relns, 2001–. Mem., Gen. Council, REconS, 2007–. FRSA 2006. *Publications:* Principal Editor: World Bank World Development Reports, 1996, 1997; UN Human Development Report, 2002. *Recreations:* cycling, collecting jokes. *Address:* JP Morgan Asset Management, 60 Victoria Embankment, EC4Y 0JP. *Club:* Soho House.

FLAPAN, Andrew Daniel, MD; FRCP; Consultant Cardiologist, New Royal Infirmary of Edinburgh, since 1994; Physician to the Queen in Scotland, since 2009; *b* London, 20 Sept. 1956; *m* 1994, Christiane Thöennes; two *s. Educ:* Epsom Coll.; London Hosp. Med. Coll. (MB BS 1981); Univ. of London (MD 1993). FRCP 2008. *Recreations:* Fly Fishing, Association football (Chelsea FC). *Address:* New Royal Infirmary of Edinburgh, Little France, Edinburgh EH16 4SA. *T:* (0131) 242 1847. *E:* andrew.flapan@luht.scot.nhs.uk.

FLATHER, family name of **Baroness Flather**.

FLATHER, Baroness *cr* 1990 (Life Peer), of Windsor and Maidenhead in the Royal County of Berkshire; **Shreela Flather;** JP; DL; Councillor, Royal Borough of Windsor and Maidenhead, 1976–91 (first ethnic minority woman Councillor in UK), Mayor, 1986–87 (first Asian woman to hold this office); *b* Lahore, India; *née* Shreela Rai; *m* Gary Flather, *qv*; two *s. Educ:* University Coll. London (LLB; Fellow 1992). Called to the Bar, Inner Temple, 1962. Infant Teacher, ILEA, 1965–67; Teacher of English as a second lang., Altwood Comp. Sch., Maidenhead, 1968–74, Broadmoor Hosp., 1974–78. Chairman: Consortium for Street Children Charities, 1992–94; Disasters Emergency Cttee, 1993–96; Vice Chm., Refugee Council, 1991–94; Member: W Metropolitan Conciliation Cttee, Race Relations Bd, 1973–78; Cttee of Inquiry (Rampton, later Swann Cttee) into Educn of Children from Ethnic Minority Gps, 1979–85; Comr, CRE, 1980–86 (Chm., Educn, Housing and Services Cttee, and Welsh Consultative Cttee, 1980–86); UK Rep., EC Commn into Racism and Xenophobia, 1994–95. Member: Police Complaints Board, 1982–85; HRH Duke of Edinburgh's Inquiry into British Housing, 1984–85; Lord Chancellor's Legal Aid Adv. Cttee, 1985–88; Social Security Adv. Cttee, 1987–90; Econ. and Social Cttee, EC, 1987–90; Carnegie Inquiry into the Third Age, 1990–93; H of L Select Cttee on Med. Ethics, 1993–94; Equal Opportunities Cttee, Bar Council, 2002–03; Chm., Alcohol Educn and Res. Council, 1996–2002; Dir, Marie Stopes Internat., 1996–. President: Cambs, Chilterns and Thames Rent Assessment Panel, 1983–97; Community Council for Berks, 1991–98; Member: Thames and Chilterns Tourist Bd, 1987–88; Berks FPC, 1987–88; Jt Pres., FPA, 1995–98; Vice-Pres., BSA, 1988–91. Member: Cons. Women's Nat. Cttee (formerly Cons. Women's Nat. Adv. Cttee), 1978–89; Exec. Cttee, Anglo-Asian Cons. Soc., 1979–83; NEC, Cons. Party, 1989–90; Sec., Windsor and Maidenhead Cons. Gp, 1979–83. Chm., Star FM, 1992–97; Director: Daytime Television, 1978–79; Thames Valley Enterprise, 1990–93; Meridian Broadcasting, 1991–2001; Cable Corp., 1997–2000; Kiss FM, 2000–02; Pres., Global Money Transfer, 1997–2001. Member: BBC S and E Regl Adv. Cttee, 1987–89; Cttee of Management, Servite Houses Ltd, 1987–94; LWT Prog. Adv. Bd, 1990–94. Member: Bd of Visitors, Holloway Prison, 1981–83; Broadmoor Hosp. Bd, 1987–88 (Chm., Ethics Cttee, 1993–97; Equal Opportunities Cttee, 1994–97; Pres., League of Friends, 1991–98); Dir, Hillingdon Hosp. Trust, 1990–98. Vice President: Townswomen's Guilds; Servite Houses Housing Assoc.; Carers Nat. Assoc.; British Assoc. for Counselling and Psychotherapy, 1999–2009. Chm., Memorial Gates Trust, 1998–2009; Member Council: Winston Churchill Meml Trust, 1993–2008; St George's Hse, Windsor Castle, 1996–2002; Mem., UK Adv. Council, Asia House, 1996–; Chm., ClubAsia, 2002–07; Trustee: Berks Community Trust, 1978–90; Borlase Sch., Marlow, 1991–97; Rajiv Gandhi UK Foundn, 1993–2001; BookPower (formerly Educational Low Priced Sponsored Texts), 2001–07; Pan African Health Foundn, 2004–11; Patron: Population Matters, 2011–; JAN Trust, Asian Women's Resource Centre, 2012–. Governor: Commonwealth Inst., 1993–98; Altwood Comp. Sch., Maidenhead, 1978–86; Slough Coll. of Higher Educn, 1984–89; Mem. Council, Atlantic Coll., 1994–98. Pres., Alumni Assoc., 1998–2000, Lay Mem., Council, 2000–06, UCL. Sec./Organiser Maidenhead Ladies' Asian Club, 1968–78; Founder, LINK (club for Asian conservatives in H of L), 1994–98; Chm., New Star Boys' Club, 1969–79; Vice Chairman: Maidenhead CAB, 1982–88; Maidenhead CRC, 1969–72; formerly Vice Chairman: Maidenhead Police Consultative Cttee; Maidenhead Volunteer Centre. FRSA 1999. JP Maidenhead, 1971; DL Berks, 1994. DUniv Open, 1994; Hon. LLD Leeds, 2008; Hon. Dr Northampton, 2010. Asian of the Year, 1996; Asian Jewel Award, Lloyds TSB, 2003; Lifetime Achievement Award, Global NRI Inst., 2011. Pravasi Diwas Samman (India), 2009. *Publications:* Stepping Stones (Adult English Training Scheme), 1973; Woman—Acceptable Exploitation for Profit, 2010. *Recreations:* travel, cinema, swimming. *Address:* House of Lords, SW1A 0PW. *T:* (020) 7219 5353.

FLATHER, Gary Denis, OBE 1999; QC 1984; a Commissioner, Royal Hospital, Chelsea, 2005–11; a Recorder, 1986–2010; a Deputy High Court Judge, 1997–2007; *b* 4 Oct. 1937; *s* of Denis Flather and Joan Flather; *m* 1965, Shreela Rai (*see* Baroness Flather); two *s. Educ:* Oundle Sch.; Pembroke Coll., Oxford (MA 1958). Called to the Bar, Inner Temple, 1962, Bencher, 1995 (Mem., Scholarships Cttee); first Hon. Mem. Bar, 2002. National Service, Second Lieut 1st Bn York and Lancaster Regt, 1956–58; Lieut Hallamshire Bn, TA, 1958–61. Asst Parly Boundary Comr, 1982–90; Asst Recorder, 1983–86. Mem., Panel of Chairmen: for ILEA Teachers' Disciplinary Tribunal, 1974–90 (Chm., Disciplinary ILEA Tribunal, William Tyndale Jun. Sch. teachers, 1976); for Disciplinary Tribunal for London Polytechnics, 1982–90; a Chairman: Police Disciplinary Appeals, 1987–2015; MoD (Police) Disciplinary Appeals, 1992–2015; Special Educnl Needs and Disability Tribunal, 2004–07; Private Patients Forum, 2011–12. Legal Mem., Mental Health Review Tribunal (restricted patients), 1987–2010; a Financial Services Act Inspector, employees of Coutts Bank, 1987–88; a legal assessor: GMC and GDC, 1987–95; RCVS, 2000–08; Ind. Person under Localism Act 2011 for Royal Bor. of Windsor and Maidenhead, 2012–. Chairman: Statutory Cttee, RPharmS, 1990–2000 (Hon. MRPharmS 2001); Disciplinary Cttee, Chartered Inst. of Marketing, 1993–2014. Bar Council: Chm., Disability Panel, 1992–2002; Member: Chambers Arbitration Panel, 1995; Equal Opportunities Cttee, 1998–2002. Dir, W. Fearnehough (Bakewell) Ltd, 1991–2002. Pres., Maidenhead Rotary Club, 1990–91. Vice-Pres., Community Council for Berks, 1987–2001; Littlewick Green Show, 1997–. Trustee: ADAPT, 1995–2007; Disabled Living Foundn, 1997–2003. Escort to the Mayor of the Royal Borough of Windsor and Maidenhead, 1986–87. *Recreations:* travel, music, dogs, coping with multiple sclerosis, laughing with friends. *E:* garyflather@hotmail.co.uk.

FLATT, Julie; *see* James, J.

FLAUX, Hon. Sir Julian Martin, Kt 2007; **Hon. Mr Justice Flaux;** a Judge of the High Court, Queen's Bench Division, since 2007; *b* 11 May 1955; *s* of late Louis Michael Flaux and of Maureen Elizabeth Brenda Flaux; *m* 1983, Matilda Christian (*née* Gabb); three *s. Educ:* King's Sch., Worcester; Worcester Coll., Oxford (BCL, MA). Called to the Bar, Inner Temple, 1978, Bencher, 2002; in practice, 1979–2007; QC 1994; a Recorder, 2000–07; a Dep. High Ct Judge, 2002–07; a Presiding Judge, Midland Circuit, 2010–13. *Recreations:* opera, reading, walking. *Address:* Royal Courts of Justice, Strand, WC2A 2LL.

FLAVELL, Prof. Richard Anthony, PhD; FRS 1984; Chairman, since 1988, and Sterling Professor of Immunobiology, since 2002 (Professor of Immunobiology, since 1988), Yale University School of Medicine; Professor of Biology, Yale University, and Investigator of the Howard Hughes Medical Institute, since 1988; *b* 23 Aug. 1945; *s* of John T. and Iris Flavell; *m* Madlyn (*née* Nathanson); one *d*; two *s* of former *m. Educ:* Dept of Biochemistry, Univ. of Hull (BSc Hons Biochem. 1967; PhD 1970). Royal Soc. Eur. Fellow, Univ. of Amsterdam, 1970–72; EMBO Post-doctoral Fellow, Univ. of Zürich, 1972–73; Wetenschappelijk Medewerker, Univ. of Amsterdam, 1973–79; Head, Lab. of Gene Structure and Expression, NIMR, Mill Hill, 1979–82; Pres., Biogen Res. Corp., 1982–88; Principal Res. Officer and CSO, Biogen Gp, 1984–88. Darwin Trust Vis. Prof., Univ. of Edinburgh, 1995; Adjunct Prof., Scripps Res. Inst., Fla, 2009. Mem., EMBO, 1978–. MRI 1984–; Mem., Amer. Assoc. of Immunologists, 1990–; FAAAS 2000; MNAS 2002; Member: Inst. of Medicine, NAS, 2006; Henry Kunkel Soc., 2007; Eur. Res. Inst. for Integrated Cellular Pathology, 2009; Yale Comprehensive Cancer Center, Yale Univ., 2010; Eur. Acad. for Tumour Immunology, 2011; Bd of Hon. Advisors, IUBMB, 2012. Hon. Professor: Nan Kai Univ., China, 2007; Suzhou Univ., China, 2010; Div. of Infection and Immunity, UCL, 2011. Anniversary Prize, FEBS, 1980; Colworth Medal, Biochem. Soc., 1980; Rabbi Shai Shacknai Meml Prize in Immunology and Cancer Res., Lautenberg Center, Hebrew Univ. Med. Sch., 2008; AAI-Invitrogen Meritorious Career Award, 2008; Andrew Lazarovitz Award, Canadian Soc. of Transplantation, Quebec, 2011; Gold Medal and Cert. of Honor, Cell Signaling Networks, Merida, Yacatan, 2011; William B. Coley Award for Dist. Res. in Basic and Tumour Immunology, 2012; Vilcek Prize in Biomedical Sci., 2013. *Publications: chapters in:* Handbook of Biochemistry and Molecular Biology, ed Fasman, 3rd edn 1976; McGraw-Hill Yearbook of Science and Technology, 1980; Eukaryotic Genes: their structure, activity and regulation, ed jtly with Maclean and Gregory, 1983; Globin Gene Expression: hematopoietic differentiation, ed Stamatoyannopoulos and Nienhuis, 1983; Regulation of the Immune System, 1984; Lyme Disease: molecular and immunologic approaches, ed Schutzer, 1992; Tumor Necrosis Factor: molecular and cellular biology and clinical relevance, ed Fiers and Buurman, 1993; Analysis of the Immune System Utilizing Transgenesis and Targeted Mutagenesis, ed Blüthmann and Ohashi, 1994; Current Directions in Autoimmunity, ed von Herrath, 2001; Apoptosis and Autoimmunity: from mechanisms to treatments, ed Kalden and Herrmann, 2003; Therapeutic Targets of Airway Inflammation, ed Eissa and Huston, 2003; Cancer Immunotherapy: immune suppression and tumor growth, ed Prendergast and Jaffee, 2007; New Generation Vaccines, ed Levine, 4th edn, 2007; articles in numerous scientific jls, incl. Nature, Cell, Proc. Nat. Acad. Sci., EMBO Jl, Jl Exp. Med. Sci., Science, and Immunity; contrib. Proceedings of symposia. *Recreations:* music, tennis, horticulture. *Address:* Department of Immunobiology, Yale University School of Medicine, 300 Cedar Street, TAC S–569, New Haven, CT 06520–8011, USA. *E:* richard.flavell@yale.edu.

FLAVELL, Dr Richard Bailey, CBE 1999; FRS 1998; Chief Scientific Advisor, Ceres Inc., since 2013 (Chief Scientific Officer, 1998–2013); *b* 11 Oct. 1943; *s* of Sidney Flavell and Emily Gertrude Flavell (*née* Bailey); *m* 1966, Hazel New; two *d. Educ:* Univ. of Birmingham (BSc 1964); Univ. of East Anglia (PhD 1967). Research Associate, Univ. of Stanford, California, 1967; Plant Breeding Institute, 1969–88 (Head, Molecular Genetics Dept, 1985–88); Dir, John Innes Inst., subseq. Centre, and John Innes Prof. of Biology, UEA, 1988–98; Chm. Mgt Cttee, AFRC Inst. of Plant Sci. Res., 1990–94. Hon. Prof., King's College London, 1986–90. Fellow, EMBO, 1990; Pres., Internat. Soc. for Plant Molecular Biology, 1993–95. *Publications:* scientific papers and books. *Recreations:* music, gardening. *Address:* Ceres Inc., 1535 Rancho Conejo Boulevard, Thousand Oaks, CA 91320, USA. *T:* (805) 3766500. *E:* rflavell@ceres-inc.com.

FLAVELL, Prof. Wendy Ruth, DPhil; CChem, CPhys, FInstP; Professor of Surface Physics, University of Manchester (formerly University of Manchester Institute of Science and Technology), since 1998; *b* Bilston, W Midlands, 1 Sept. 1961; *d* of Maurice and June Flavell; partner, Stephen Allen. *Educ:* Wolverhampton Girls' High Sch.; St John's Coll., Oxford (BA Natural Scis (Chem.) 1983; MA 1983; DPhil 1986). CChem 1995; CPhys 1998; FInstP 1999. MRSC. SERC Postdoctoral Fellow, 1986–88, Royal Soc. Univ. Res. Fellow, 1988–90, Dept of Chem., Imperial Coll. London; University of Manchester Institute of Science and Technology: Lectr, 1990–94, Reader, 1994–96, Dept of Chem.; Reader, Dept of Physics, 1996–98. Chair, UK Synchrotron Radiation Source Sci. Adv. Council, 2002–04; Dep. Chair, Physics sub-panel REF, 2014; Mem., beamtime allocation panels for internat. synchrotron sources, including: SOLEIL, France, 2006–; SLS, Switzerland, 2009–11; MAX-lab, Sweden, 2012–; Member: Physical Sci. Strategic Adv. Team, EPSRC, 2007–09; Physics sub-panel, RAE, 2008. *Publications:* contribs to scientific jls on electronic structure of functional materials, incl. semiconductor nanocrystals, oxide catalysts and photocatalysts. *Recreations:* singing (St

George's Singers, Poynton), generally futile gardening, beachcombing, testing deck chairs. *Address:* Photon Science Institute, University of Manchester, Alan Turing Building, Oxford Road, Manchester M13 9PL. *T:* (0161) 306 4466, *Fax:* (0161) 275 1001. *E:* wendy.flavell@manchester.ac.uk.

FLAXEN, David William; Director of Statistics, Department of Transport, 1989–96; statistics consultant to overseas governments, especially in Central and Eastern Europe and Africa, 1996–2009; *b* 20 April 1941; *s* of late William Henry Flaxen and Beatrice Flaxen (*née* Laidlow); *m* 1969, Eleanor Marie Easton; two *d.* *Educ:* Manchester Grammar Sch.; Brasenose Coll., Oxford (MA Physics); University Coll. London (DipStat). Teacher, Leyton County High School for Boys, 1963; UK Government Statistical Service, 1963–96: Central Statistical Office and Min. of Labour, 1964–71; UNDP Advr, Swaziland, 1971–72; Statistician, Dept of Employment, 1973–75; Chief Statistician: Dept of Employment, 1975–76; Central Statistical Office, 1976–77 and 1981–83; Inland Revenue, 1977–81; Asst Dir (Under-Sec.), Central Statistical Office, 1983–89. Creator of Tax and Price Index, 1979. *Publications:* contribs to articles in Physics Letters, Economic Trends, Dept of Employment Gazette, etc. *Recreations:* bridge, wine, cooking, music. *Address:* 65 Corringham Road, NW11 7BS. *T:* (020) 8458 5451. *E:* dflaxen@easynet.co.uk.

FLECK, Andrew Arthur Peter, MA; Headmaster, Sedbergh School, since 2010; *b* Chichester, 18 Aug. 1962; *s* of Peter Hugo Fleck and Fiona Charis Elizabeth Fleck (*née* Miller); *m* 1987, Anne Judith Jennison; twin *d.* *Educ:* Marlborough Coll.; Nottingham Univ. (BSc Hons Geol. 1983); University Coll., N Wales (PGCE 1985); Sussex Univ. (MA Educn 1993). Kayak expedns around Newfoundland, Japan and Norway, 1986–88; Hd of Geog., Hurstpierpoint Coll., 1988–96; Dep. Headmaster, St Bedes Sch., 1996–2003; Headmaster, Ashville Coll., 2003–10. Dir, Eggbase Ltd, 2011–; Chm., Fibre GarDen Broadband Delivery CIC, 2012–. Governor: Westville Hse Sch., 2008–; Terra Nova Sch., 2012–; St Mary's, Melrose, 2014–. *Recreations:* sailing, writing. *Address:* Sedbergh School, Sedbergh, Cumbria LA10 5HG. *T:* (01539) 620535. *E:* hm@sedberghschool.org.

See also R. J. H. Fleck.

FLECK, Prof. Norman Andrew, PhD; FRS 2004; FREng, CEng, FIMMM; Professor of Mechanics of Materials, Cambridge University, since 1997; Fellow of Pembroke College, Cambridge, since 1982; *b* 11 May 1958; *s* of William and Roberta Fleck; *m* 1983, Vivien Christine Taylor (*d* 2007); one *s* one *d.* *Educ:* Jesus Coll., Cambridge (BA 1979; MA 1981); PhD Cantab 1982. FIMMM (FIM 1997); FREng 2008. Maudslay Res. Fellow, Pembroke Coll., Cambridge, 1983–84; Lindemann Fellow, Harvard Univ., 1984–85; Cambridge University: Lectr in Engineering, 1985–94; Reader in Mechanics of Materials, 1994–97; Dir, Cambridge Centre for Micromechanics, 1996–. For. Mem., US NAE, 2014. Hon. Dr Eindhoven, 2014. *Publications:* (jtly) Metal Foams: a design guide, 2000; numerous papers in mechanics and materials jls. *Recreations:* running, ski-ing, wine, church. *Address:* Cambridge University Engineering Department, Trumpington Street, Cambridge CB2 1PZ. *T:* (01223) 332650.

FLECK, Richard John Hugo, CBE 2009; Consultant, Herbert Smith Freehills (formerly Herbert Smith), since 2009 (Partner, 1980–2009); *b* Leamington, 30 March 1949; *s* of Peter Hugo Fleck and Fiona Charis Elizabeth Fleck (*née* Miller); *m* 1983, Mary Gardiner; one *s* one *d.* *Educ:* Marlborough Coll.; Southampton Univ. (LLB Hons). Solicitor, Herbert Smith, 1971–2009. Mem., Auditing Practices Bd, 1986–2012 (Chm., 2003–12); Dir, Financial Reporting Council Ltd, 2004–13 (Chm., Financial Reporting Review Panel, 2012–14; Chm., Conduct Div., 2012–14); Chm., Consulting and Adv. Gp, Internat. Ethic Standards Bd for Accountants, 2006–13. Non-exec. Dir, Nat. Audit Office, 2009–12. Mem., Council, Marlborough Coll., 1997–2010. *Recreations:* sailing, Real tennis, golf, shooting, rackets. *Address:* Hill Farm, Ebbesbourne Wake, Salisbury, Wilts SP5 5LW. *T:* (01722) 780644. *E:* richardfleck@btinternet.com. *Clubs:* Athenæum, MCC, Royal Yacht Squadron, Royal Ocean Racing, Jesters; City Law; Itchenor Sailing; Petworth Real Tennis.

See also A. A. P. Fleck.

FLECKER, James William, MA; Founder/Director, European Language Year, 2003–10; Headmaster, Ardingly College, 1980–98; *b* 15 Aug. 1939; *s* of Henry Lael Oswald Flecker, CBE, and Mary Patricia Flecker; *m* 1967, Mary Rose Firth; three *d.* *Educ:* Marlborough Coll.; Brasenose Coll., Oxford (BA, now MA Lit. Hum., 1962). Asst Master: Sydney Grammar Sch., 1962–63; Latymer Upper Sch., 1964–67; (and later Housemaster), Marlborough Coll., 1967–80. Recruitment Manager, Students Partnership Worldwide, 1998–2001 (Trustee, 2001–08); Recruiter, BESO, 2001–05; Short Term Placement Advr, VSO, 2005–06. Trustee: Alive and Kicking, 2003– (Chm., 2005–09); Good Earth Trust, 2006–13 (Chm., 2006–11). Governor: Reed's Sch., Cobham, 1998–2010; Royal Masonic Sch. for Girls, Rickmansworth, 2007–. Chm., Friends of Gt Bedwyn Ch, 2012–. *Recreations:* hockey, cricket, flute playing, writing children's operas, golf, vegetable gardening. *Address:* Easter Cottage, 42 Church Street, Great Bedwyn, Wilts SN3 3PQ. *T:* (01672) 870079. *E:* james@flecker.com.

FLEET, Dr Andrew James, FGS; Keeper of Mineralogy, 1996–2015, and Assistant Director of Science, 2013–15, Natural History Museum; *b* 14 June 1950; *s* of late Rupert Stanley Fleet and Margaret Rose Fleet (*née* Aitken); *m* 1976, Susan Mary Adamson; one *s* one *d.* *Educ:* Bryanston Sch.; Chelsea Coll., Univ. of London (BSc; PhD 1977). FGS 1976. UNESCO Fellow in Oceanography, Open Univ., 1975–79; Lectr in Geochem., Goldsmiths' Coll., Univ. of London, 1979–80; Research and Exploration, BP, 1980–95, Head, Petroleum Geochem. Res., 1987–95; Hd, Dept of Earth Scis, Natural Hist. Mus., 2012–13. Vis. Prof. in Geol., ICSTM, 1997–. Geological Society: Special Pubns Ed., 1993–2002; Mem. Council, 1997–2000, 2002–05 and 2006–11; Sec. (Publications), 2002–05; Treas., 2006–11; Mem., Finance and Planning Cttee, 2011–; Custodian Trustee, Mineralogical Soc. of GB and Ireland, 2012–. *Publications:* edited jointly: Marine petroleum source rocks, 1987; Lacustrine petroleum source rocks, 1988; Petroleum migration, 1991; Coal and coal-bearing strata as oil-prone source rocks?, 1994; Muds and mudstones: physical and fluid flow properties, 1999; Petroleum Geology of Northwest Europe: proceedings of the 5th conference, 1999; contrib. papers in scientific jls on petroleum and sedimentary geochemistry and marine geology. *Recreations:* archaeology, cricket, family, cooking, wine. *Address:* Stour Brook House, Cookswell, Shillingstone, Blandford Forum, Dorset DT11 0QZ.

FLEETWOOD, Gordon; Sheriff of Grampian, Highland and Islands at Inverness, since 2014; *b* Elgin, Moray, 3 Oct. 1951; *s* of John Fleetwood and Isabel Fleetwood; *m* 1975, Jean; two *d.* *Educ:* Elgin Acad.; Univ. of Edinburgh (LLB Hons 1973). Admitted Solicitor, 1975, Solicitor Advocate, 1994; Solicitor: More and Co., 1977–82; Sutherland and Co., 1982–86; Fleetwood and Robb, 1986–2004; principal in own practice, 2004–08; part-time Sheriff, 2003–14; Legal Mem., Parole Bd for Scotland, 2010–14. *Recreations:* salmon fishing, curling. *Address:* Sheriff Court House, The Castle, Inverness IV2 3EG. *T:* (01463) 230782.

FLEGG, Dr James John Maitland, OBE 1997; FCIHort; consultant on horticulture and environment; Chairman, Meiosis Ltd, since 2000; *b* Hong Kong, 23 April 1937; *s* of Jack Sydney Flegg and Lily Elizabeth (*née* Spooner); *m* 1976, Caroline Louise Coles; two *s.* *Educ:* Melbourne, Australia; Gillingham Grammar Sch.; Imperial Coll. of Science and Technol. (BSc, PhD). ARCS 1962; FCIHort (FIHort 1993). Nematologist, E Malling Res. Stn, 1956–66; MAFF, 1966–68; Dir, Brit. Trust for Ornithology, Tring, 1968–75; Hd, Zool. Dept, E Malling Res. Stn, 1976–87; Dir of Inf. Services, 1987–95, Hd of Stn, 1990–95, Dir, Ext. Affairs, 1995–97, Horticulture Res. Internat., East Malling. Presenter, Country Ways, Meridian TV. Sec., European Soc. of Nematologists, 1965–68; Mem. Council, RSPB, 1978–83; Pres., Kent Ornithol Soc., 1986–2004. MBOU 1966. Chm., Romney Marsh Res. Trust, 1990–2000; Mem., Conservation Panel, Nat. Trust, 2003–11. Freeman, City of London; Liveryman, Co. of Fruiterers. *Publications:* books include: In Search of Birds, 1983; Oakwatch, 1985; Birdlife, 1986; Field Guide to the Birds of Britain and Europe, 1990; Poles Apart, 1991; Deserts, 1993; Classic Birds (60 Years of Bird Photography): a biography of Eric Hosking, 1993; Photographic Field Guide to the Birds of Australia, 1996; Time to Fly: exploring bird migration, 2004; numerous papers and articles on nematological, ornithological and envmtl topics. *Recreations:* grandsons, wildlife, rural history, environmental affairs, gardening, music. *Address:* Divers Farm, E Sutton, Maidstone, Kent ME17 3DT.

FLELLO, Robert Charles Douglas; MP (Lab) Stoke-on-Trent South, since 2005; *b* 14 Jan. 1966; *s* of Douglas Flello and Valerie Swain; *m* 1990, Teresa (*née* Gifoli) (marr. diss.); one *d*, and one step *s.* *Educ:* University Coll. of N Wales, Bangor (BSc Hons). Consultant, Price Waterhouse, 1989–94; Manager, Arthur Andersen, 1994–99; Dir, Platts Flello Ltd, 1999–2003; CEO, Malachi Community Trust, 2003–04. Associate: Royal Inst. Taxation, 1990–; Soc. Financial Advrs, 1998–. *Recreations:* reading, running, ancient history, cooking, riding my motorbike. *Address:* House of Commons, SW1A 0AA; Ground Floor, Travers Court, City Road, Fenton, Stoke-on-Trent ST4 2PY. *T:* (01782) 844810, *Fax:* (01782) 593430.

FLEMING, Anne Elizabeth; film archive consultant, since 2005; *b* 12 Aug. 1944; *d* of Harry Gibb Fleming and Agnes Wilkie Fleming (*née* Clark); *m* 2003, Taylor Downing. *Educ:* Univ. of Edinburgh (MA Hons English Lit. and Lang.). Films Administrator, Edinburgh Film Fest., 1966, 1967, 1968, 1969; teacher of English as a foreign lang., Acad. of Langs, Catania, Sicily, 1967–68; Imperial War Museum; Res. Asst, Dept of Film Programming, 1970–72; Res. Asst, Dept of Film, 1972–73; Dep. Keeper, 1973–83, Keeper, 1983–90, Dept of Film; Dep. Curator, 1990–97, Curator, 1997–2000, BFI Nat. Film and TV Archive; Hd of Content, MAAS Media Online, British Univs Film and Video Council, 2001–05. Mem., Wellcome Trust Liby Adv. Cttee, 2006–09. Co-ordinating Juror, FOCAL Internat. Film Restoration and Preservation Award, 2003–15. *Publications:* contribs to catalogues and data-bases. *Recreations:* cinema, reading, walking, cooking, growing herbs. *E:* anneefleming@btinternet.com.

FLEMING, Ven. David; Chaplain-General to HM Prisons and Archdeacon of Prisons, 1993–2001; Chaplain to the Queen, 1995–2007; *b* 8 June 1937; *s* of John Frederick Fleming and Emma (*née* Casey); *m* 1966, Elizabeth Anne Marguerite Hughes; three *s* one *d.* *Educ:* Hunstanton County Primary School; King Edward VII Grammar School, King's Lynn; Kelham Theological Coll. National Service with Royal Norfolk Regt, 1956–58. Deacon 1963; Asst Curate, St Margaret, Walton on the Hill, Liverpool, 1963–67; priest 1964; attached to Sandringham group of churches, 1967–68; Vicar of Great Staughton, 1968–76; Chaplain of HM Borstal, Gaynes Hall, 1968–76; RD of St Neots, 1972–76; RD of March, 1977–82; Vicar of Whittlesey, 1976–85; Priest-in-Charge of Pondersbridge, 1983–85; Archdeacon of Wisbech, 1984–93; Vicar of Wisbech St Mary, 1985–88. Hon. Canon of Ely Cathedral, 1982–2001. Chm. of House of Clergy, Ely Diocesan Synod, 1982–85. *Recreations:* tennis, chess, extolling Hunstanton. *Address:* Fair Haven, 123 Wisbech Road, Littleport, Ely, Cambs CB6 1JJ. *Club:* Whittlesey Rotary.

FLEMING, Dr David, OBE 1997; Director, National Museums Liverpool (formerly National Museums and Galleries on Merseyside), since 2001; *b* 25 Dec. 1952; *s* of Jack and Doreen Fleming; *m* 2007, Alison Jane Hastings, *qv*; one *d*, and two *s* one *d* from a previous marriage. *Educ:* London Sch. of Econs; Leeds Univ. (BA Hons); Leicester Univ. (MA; PhD 1981). Curator: Yorkshire Mus. of Farming, 1981–83; Collection Services, Leeds Mus, 1983–85; Principal Keeper of Mus, Hull Mus, 1985–90; Asst Dir, 1990–91, Dir, 1991–2001, Tyne & Wear Museums. Vis. Prof., Liverpool Hope Univ., 2013–. Mem. Exec. Bd, ICOM (UK), 1997–2000 (Chm., Finance and Resources Cttee, 2011–). Chairman: Social History Curators Gp, 1986–87; Museum Professionals Gp, 1986–90; Liverpool Culture Partnership, 2003–05; Liverpool Heritage and Regeneration Adv. Gp, 2005–06; Liverpool Find Your Talent Mgt Cttee, 2008–11; Liverpool Mayor's Task Gp on Cultural Heritage, 2012–; Mem., Liverpool Mayor's Creative Commn, 2014–; Convenor: Gp for Large Local Authority Museums, 1998–2001; Social Justice Alliance of Mus, 2013–; Vice Chairman: Liverpool First Culture Task Gp, 2009–; European Mus. Forum, 2009– (Treas., 2012–13); Member: NW Cultural Consortium, 2003–04; Culture Cttee, UK Nat. Commn for UNESCO, 2005–09; Creative Apprenticeship Task Force, 2005–07. Mem. Adv. Cttee on the Export of Works of Art, 1991–93; Special Advisor: Min. of Educn, Culture and Sci., Netherlands, 2005–06; Mus. of Democracy, Rosario, Argentina, 2013–; Mem., Expert Panel, Stuttgart City Mus., 2007; Expert Advr, Grand Egyptian Mus. Project, 2008. Lecturer: Baltic Museology Sch., 2009; Lithuanian Cultural Administrators Trng Centre, 2011. External Examiner: Dept of Mus. Studies, Leicester Univ., 2003–; Dept of Heritage and Mus. Studies, Bournemouth Univ., 2010–. Trustee: Yorks and Humberside Museums Council, 1986–90; Nat. Mus. of Labour History, 1990–92; North of England Mus. Service, 1990–2001; Nat. Football Mus., 1996–2003; NE Cultural Consortium, 1999–2001; Cultural Heritage Nat. Trng Orgn, 2000–01; NE Museums, Libraries and Archives Council, 2001; NW Museums Service, 2001–02; Liverpool Capital of Culture Co., 2001–03; St George's Hall, 2001–08; Bluecoat Arts Centre, 2004–09; SS Daniel Adamson, 2015–. President: Museums Assoc., 2000–02 and 2015– (Trustee, 2011–; Chm., Ethics Cttee, 2014–); Internat. Cttee on Mus. Mgt, 2004–10; Fedn of Internat. Human Rights Museums, 2010–; Luciano Becchio Appreciation Soc., 2010–13. Patron, St James in the City, 2013–. *Recreations:* my family, history, travel, film, literature, Leeds United, collecting CDs. *Address:* World Museum, William Brown Street, Liverpool L3 8EN. *T:* (0151) 478 4201. *E:* david.fleming@liverpoolmuseums.org.uk.

FLEMING, Prof. David, DBA; Vice-Chancellor, 2010–15, and Professor of Land Economics, 2010–15, now Emeritus, York St John University; *b* Southport, 24 Sept. 1959; *s* of Norman Fleming and Shirley Fleming; *m* Lesley; one *s* one *d.* *Educ:* King William's Coll., IOM; Sheffield City Poly. (BSc Hons, PGDip, MBA, DBA 2001). FRICS 1986. Man. Dir, Pannon Pacific, 1988–91; Sen. Lectr, 1991–99, Principal Lectr, 1999–2002, Nottingham Trent Univ.; Dean, Sch. of Built Envmt, Northumbria Univ., 2002–07; Dep. Vice-Chancellor, Univ. of Sunderland, 2007–10. *Publications:* articles in jls on behavioural analysis of building occupants. *Recreations:* golf, sailing. *Address:* York St John University, Lord Mayor's Walk, York YO31 7EX.

FLEMING, Fergus Hermon Robert; writer, since 1991; *b* 13 Oct. 1959; *s* of Richard and Charm Fleming; partner, Elizabeth Hodgson; one *s* one *d.* *Educ:* Magdalen Coll., Oxford (MA); City Univ., London. Trainee accountant, Ernst & Whinney, 1981–82; acad. trng as barrister, 1982–83; furniture maker, Christopher Clark Workshops, 1984–85; writer and ed., Time-Life Books, 1985–91. Dir, Ian Fleming Pubns Ltd, 2003–; Publisher, Queen Anne Press, 2007–. *Publications:* Amaryllis Fleming, 1993; The Medieval Messenger, 1996; The Greek Gazette, 1997; The Viking Invader, 1997; Stone Age Sentinel, 1998; Barrow's Boys, 1998; Killing Dragons, 2000; Ninety Degrees North, 2001; The Sword and the Cross, 2003; Tales of Endurance, 2004; (ed) The Explorer's Eye, 2005; (ed) The Travellers Daybook, 2011. *Address:* c/o Aitken Alexander Associates, 291 Gray's Inn Road, WC1X 8EB. *T:* (020) 7373 8672. *Club:* Leander (Henley-on-Thames).

FLEMING, Prof. George, PhD; FREng, FICE; FCIWM; FRSE; Professor of Civil Engineering, University of Strathclyde, 1985–2003, now Emeritus; Chairman, EnviroCentre, since 2007 (Managing Director, 1993–2011); *b* Glasgow, 16 Aug. 1944; *s* of Felix and Catherine Fleming; *m* 1966, Irene MacDonald Cowan; two *s* one *d.* *Educ:* Univ. of Strathclyde (BSc 1st cl. Hons; PhD 1969). FICE 1982; FREng (FEng 1987); FRSE 1992;

FASCE 2000; FCIWM 2002 (MIWM 1987). Res. Fellow, Stanford Univ., 1967; University of Strathclyde: Res. Asst, 1966–69; Lectr, 1971–76; Sen. Lectr, 1976–82; Reader, 1982–85; Dir and Vice Pres., Hydrocomp Internat., 1969–77. Consultant, Watson Hawkesley, 1980–92; non-exec. Dir, WRAP, 2001–07. Member: Overseas Projects Bd, DTI, 1991–95; British Waterways Bd, 2001–07; Port of Tyne Bd, 2005–. Pres., ICE, 1999–2000; Mem., Smeatonian Soc. of Civil Engrs, 1998. Hon. Mem., British Hydrol Soc. *Publications:* Computer Simulation in Hydrology, 1971; The Sediment Problem, 1977; (ed) Recycling Derelict Land, 1991; (contrib.) Geochemical Approaches to Environmental Engineering of Metals, 1996; (contrib.) Energy and the Environment: geochemistry of fossil, nuclear and renewable resources, 1998. *Recreations:* DIY, travelling. *Address:* EnviroCentre, Unit 2B, Craighall Business Park, Eagle Street, Glasgow G4 9XA.

FLEMING, Prof. Graham Richard, PhD; FRS 1994; Melvin Calvin Distinguished Professor of Chemistry, University of California, Berkeley, since 1997; Berkeley Director, Institute for Quantitative Biomedical Research (QB3), University of California, since 2001; *b* 3 Dec. 1949; *s* of Maurice Norman Henry Fleming and Lovima Ena Winter; *m* 1977, Jean McKenzie; one *s*. *Educ:* Bristol Univ. (BSc Hons); Royal Instn (PhD London). Res. Fellow, CIT, 1974–75; Univ. Res. Fellow, Univ. of Melbourne, 1975–76; Leverhulme Fellow, Royal Instn, 1977–79; University of Chicago: Asst Prof., 1979–83; Associate Prof., 1983–85; Prof., 1985–87; Arthur Holly Compton Dist. Service Prof., Dept of Chem., 1987–97; Dep. Dir, Lawrence Berkeley Nat. Lab., Univ. of Calif, Berkeley, 2005–07. Member: NAS, 2007–; Amer. Philosophical Soc., 2011. Fellow, Amer. Acad. of Arts and Scis, 1991. Hon. DSc: Bristol, 2012; Vilnius, 2013. *Publications:* Chemical Applications of Ultrafast Spectroscopy, 1986; numerous articles in learned jls. *Recreation:* mountaineering. *Address:* Department of Chemistry, B84 Hildebrand #1460, University of California, Berkeley, CA 94720–1460, USA. *T:* (510) 6432735, *Fax:* (510) 6426340. *E:* fleming@cchem.berkeley.edu.

FLEMING, Grahame Ritchie; QC (Scot.) 1990; Sheriff of Lothian and Borders, 1993–2014; *b* 13 Feb. 1949; *s* of Ian Erskine Fleming and Helen Ritchie Wallace or Fleming; *m* 1st, 1984, Mopsa Dorcas Robbins (*d* 2008); one *d*; 2nd, 2013, Evelyn Mary Donaldson. *Educ:* Forfar Acad.; Univ. of Edinburgh (MA, LLB). Admitted Faculty of Advocates, 1976. Standing Jun. Counsel to Home Office in Scotland, 1986–89. *Recreations:* food, travel, supporting the Scottish Rugby team. *Address:* Advocates Library, Parliament House, Edinburgh EH1 1RF.

FLEMING, Iain Macdonald; Sheriff of North Strathclyde at Greenock, since 2014; *b* London, 24 Aug. 1962; *s* of Archibald Macdonald Fleming and Joan Moore; *m* 1990, Louise Alexandra Cumming; one *d*. *Educ:* High Sch. of Glasgow; Kelvinside Acad., Glasgow; Univ. of Strathclyde (LLB Hons 1983; DipLP 1984). Admitted Solicitor, 1986, Solicitor Advocate, 2001; part-time Sheriff, 2005–14; Convenor, Mental Health Tribunals, 2011. Mem., Judicial Panel, Scottish FA, 2011. President: Glasgow Bar Assoc., 1998–99; Part-Time Sheriffs' Assoc., 2011–13. *Recreations:* Association football, martial arts, golf, works of Robert Burns. *Address:* Greenock Sheriff Court, Nelson Street, Greenock PA15 1TR. *T:* 07957 818969. *E:* sheriffifleming@scotcourts.gov.uk. *Club:* Glasgow Golf.

FLEMING, Prof. Ian, FRS 1993; Professor of Organic Chemistry, University of Cambridge, 1998–2002, now Emeritus (Reader in Organic Chemistry, 1986–98); Fellow of Pembroke College, Cambridge, 1964–2002; *b* 4 Aug. 1935; *s* of David Alexander Fleming and Olwen Lloyd Fleming (*née* Jones); *m* 1st, 1959, Joan Morrison Irving (marr. diss. 1962); 2nd, 1965, Mary Lord Bernard. *Educ:* Pembroke Coll., Cambridge (MA, PhD 1963; ScD 1982). Cambridge University: Res. Fellow, Pembroke Coll., 1962; Univ. Demonstrator, 1964–65; Asst Dir of Research, 1965–80; Univ. Lectr, 1980–86. *Publications:* (with D. H. Williams) Spectroscopic Methods in Organic Chemistry, 1966, 6th edn 2007; (with D. H. Williams) Spectroscopic Problems in Organic Chemistry, 1967; Selected Organic Syntheses, 1973; Frontier Orbitals and Organic Chemical Reactions, 1976; Pericyclic Reactions, 1998; Molecular Orbitals and Organic Chemical Reactions: student edition, 2009, reference edition, 2010; 273 papers in chem. jls. *Recreations:* watching movies, reading, music. *Address:* Pembroke College, Cambridge CB2 1RF. *T:* (01223) 362862.

FLEMING, James Randolf G.; *see* Gibson Fleming.

FLEMING, Kenneth Anthony, DPhil; FRCPath; FRCP; Clinical Reader in Pathology, University of Oxford, 1981–2000 and 2008–10, now Emeritus; Fellow of Green Templeton College (formerly Green College), Oxford, 1981–2010, now Emeritus (Virginia Swanson Fellow in Pathology, 2004–10); Senior Consultant for Pathology, Center for Global Health, National Cancer Institute, Washington, DC, since 2015; *b* 7 Jan. 1945; *s* of Thomas and Margaret Fleming; *m* 1969, Jennifer; two *s* one *d*. *Educ:* Univ. of Glasgow (MB ChB); Merton Coll., Oxford (DPhil; MA). FRCPath 1988; FRCP 2007. University of Glasgow: Sen. House Officer, 1969–70; Registrar in Pathology, 1970–72; Lectr in Pathology, 1972–76; Wellcome Res. Fellow in Pathology, Univ. of Oxford, 1976–80; MRC Travelling Fellow, Roche Inst. for Molecular Biology, USA, 1980–81; University of Oxford: Dir of Planning and Develt, 1995–97; Dean, Faculty of Clinical Medicine, 1997–2000; Hd, Med. Scis Div., 2000–08. Hon. Consultant in Pathology, Oxford Radcliffe Hosps Trust, 1981–2008. Associate Hd, Academic Affairs, Oxford Deanery, 2009–12. Chair, Ind. Appt Panel, Bar Standards Bd, 2010–Jan. 2016. Member: Council, RVC, 2009–12; Adv. Bd, Li Ka Shing Res. Inst., Chinese Univ. of Hong Kong, 2010–15; UK Lead, Project to develop MMEd in Pathology, Univ. of Zambia, Tropical Health Educn Trust, 2010–15; Dir of Internat. Activities, RCPath, 2011–14. Sen. Res. Fellow, Inst. for Preventative Res., Lyon, 2010–; Co-founder, Global Health Policy and Mgt in Medicine Progs, 2012–, Health Advr, Emerging Markets Symposium, Green Templeton Coll., Oxford, 2010–. *Publications:* over 150 articles in learned jls on aspects of molecular biology and pathology. *Recreations:* walking, golf, reading. *Address:* 2 The Winnyards, Cumnor, Oxford OX2 9RJ. *T:* (01865) 864793. *E:* kennethfleming@myfastmail.com.

FLEMING, Prof. Peter John, CBE 2001; PhD; FRCP, FRCPC, FRCPCH; Professor of Infant Health and Developmental Physiology, University of Bristol, since 1995 (Head, Division of Child Health, 1996–2002); Consultant Paediatrician, Royal Hospital for Children, Bristol, since 1982; *b* 19 Aug. 1949; *s* of Nora Eileen Page and step *s* of Peter John Page; *m* 1973, Dr Josephine Olwen Allen; four *s*. *Educ:* Gillingham Grammar Sch., Kent; Univ. of Bristol (MB ChB 1972; PhD 1993). MRCP 1975, FRCP 1988; FRCPC 1981; FRCPCH 1997. Senior House Officer: Southmead Hosp., Bristol, 1974–75; Gt Ormond St Hosp., 1975–76; Sen. Resident, 1976–77, Fellow in Neonatal Medicine, 1977–78, Hosp. for Sick Children, Toronto; Sen. Registrar, Paediatrics, Royal Hosp. for Children, Bristol, 1978–81. Chm. of Overview Panel, and co-author of report, Confidential Inquiry into Premature Deaths of People with Learning Disabilities, 2013. Pres., Assoc. of Clinical Profs of Paediatrics, 2002–05; Member: Neonatal Soc., 1979–; British Assoc. Perinatal Medicine, 1980–; Paediatric Intensive Care Soc., 1987–. FRSA 1996. *Publications:* A Neonatal Vade Mecum, 1986, 3rd edn 1998; The Care of Critically Ill Children, 1993; Sudden Unexpected Death in Infancy, 2000; Unexpected Death in Childhood, 2007; contrib. numerous original and rev. articles on neonatal medicine, developmental physiology, the epidemiology and prevention of cot death and paediatric intensive care to learned jls. *Recreations:* being with my family, working on and caring for our land, running, listening to and playing music, reading. *Address:* Centre for Child and Adolescent Health, Level D, St Michael's Hospital, Southwell Street, Bristol BS2 8EG. *T:* (0117) 342 5144, *Fax:* (0117) 342 5154. *E:* peter.fleming@bris.ac.uk.

FLEMING, Raylton Arthur; freelance journalist specialising in international affairs, music and Mallorca; editorial adviser, Majorca Daily Bulletin; *b* 1 Sept. 1925; *s* of Arthur and Evelyn Fleming; *m* 1967, Leila el Doweini; one *s*. *Educ:* Worksop Coll. Associate Producer, World Wide Pictures Ltd, 1952; Head of Overseas Television Production, Central Office of Information, 1957; Dep. Dir, Films/Television Div., COI, 1961; Asst Controller (Overseas) COI, 1968; Actg Controller (Overseas), 1969; Dir, Exhibns Div. COI, 1971; Controller (Home), COI, 1972–76; Controller (Overseas), COI, 1976–78; Dir of Inf., UN Univ., Japan, 1978–83; Dir, UN Univ. Liaison Office, NY, 1983–84; Liaison Officer, UN Univ., World Inst. for Develt Econs Res., Helsinki, 1984–86. *Recreations:* music, opera. *Address:* Camino del Castillo, 07340 Alaro, Mallorca, Spain.

FLEMING, Renée L.; soprano; *b* 14 Feb. 1959; *d* of Edwin Davis Fleming and Patricia (Seymour) Alexander; *m* 1989, Richard Lee Ross (marr. diss. 2000); two *d*; *m* 2011, Timothy Jessell. *Educ:* Potsdam State Univ. (BM Music Educn 1981); Eastman Sch. of Music (MM 1983). Studied at Juilliard American Opera Center, 1983–84, 1985–87; Fulbright Schol., Frankfurt, 1984–85. *Débuts* include: Houston Grand Opera, 1988; NYC Opera, 1989; Covent Garden, 1989; San Francisco Opera, 1991; Met. Opera, Paris Opera, Bastille, 1991; Teatro Colon, Buenos Aires, 1991; La Scala, Milan, 1993; Lyric Opera, Chicago, 1993; performed at Nobel Peace Prize ceremony, 2006, and US Presidential inauguration, 2009; Creative Consultant, Lyric Opera, Chicago, 2010. Winner, Met. Opera Nat. Auditions, 1988; George London Prize, 1988; Richard Tucker Award, 1990; Solti Prize, 1998; Grammy Award, 1999, 2003, 2010; Classical Brit Award, 2004; Polar Music Prize, 2008. Hon. Mem., RAM, 2003; Hon. DMus: Juilliard, 2003; Eastman Sch. of Music, 2011. Commandeur des Arts et des Lettres (France), 2002; Chevalier de la Légion d'Honneur (France), 2005; Victoire d'Honneur, Victoires de la Musique, 2012. *Publications:* The Inner Voice, 2004.

FLEMING, Robert, (Robin), CBE 2013; DL; Chairman, Robert Fleming Holdings, 1990–97; *b* 18 Sept. 1932; *s* of late Major Philip Fleming and Joan Cecil Fleming (*née* Hunloke); *m* 1962, Victoria Margaret Aykroyd; two *s* one *d*. *Educ:* Eton College; Royal Military Academy, Sandhurst. Served The Royal Scots Greys, 1952–58. Joined Robert Fleming, 1958; Director: Robert Fleming Trustee Co., 1961– (Chm., 1985–91); Robert Fleming Holdings, 1974–97 (Dep. Chm., 1986–90). High Sheriff, 1980, DL 1990, Oxfordshire. *Recreation:* most country pursuits. *Address:* Church Farm, Steeple Barton, Bicester, Oxon OX25 4QR. *T:* (01869) 347177.

FLEMING, Roderick John; Director: Fleming Family & Partners, 2000–08; Highland Star Group, since 2000; Chairman, Robert Fleming Holdings Ltd, 2000 (Director, 1994–2000; Deputy Chairman, 1999–2000); *b* 12 Nov. 1953; *s* of Richard Evelyn Fleming and Hon. Dorothy Charmian Fleming; *m* 1979, Diana Julia Wake; twin *d*. *Educ:* Eton Coll.; Magdalen Coll., Oxford (MA History). Trainee: Cazenove, 1974–75; Morgan Guaranty, NY, 1975–76; Corporate Finance Dept, Robert Fleming, 1976–80; joined Jardine Fleming, Singapore, 1980, Man. Dir, 1982–84; Dir, Jardine Fleming Internat. Ltd, with responsibility for internat. corporate finance, Jardine Fleming, Tokyo, 1984–86; International Portfolios Gp, Robert Fleming: joined, 1986; est. Product Develt Gp, 1989; Product Develt Gp Dir, 1990–2000; Director: Capital Mkts, 1991–2000, Corporate Finance UK, 1993–2000, Robert Fleming; Robert Fleming Trustee Co. Ltd, 1991–; Dover Corp., 1995–2002; Ian Fleming (Glidrose) Pubns Ltd, 1996– (Chm., 2000–). *Recreation:* country pursuits. *Address:* Fleming Family & Partners (Liechtenstein) AG, AM Schrägen Weg 2, Postfach 740, 9490 Vaduz, Liechtenstein. *Clubs:* White's, Mark's.

FLENLEY, William David Wingate; QC 2010; *b* 28 April 1964; *s* of late Prof. David Caton Flenley and of Hilary Elizabeth Flenley (*née* Wingate); *m* 2001, Hannah Keturah Coombe; one *s* one *d*. *Educ:* Exeter Coll., Oxford (Open Exhibnr; MA; BCL; Editor, Isis mag.); Cornell Law Sch., NY (St Andrew's Soc. of State of NY Schol.; LLM). Called to the Bar, Middle Temple, 1988, Bencher, 2014; in practice, Hailsham Chambers, specialising in professional liability and insce law, 1990–. Lectr in Law (pt-time), LSE, 1988–89. Member: Mgt Cttee, Bondway Housing Assoc., 1990–2001; Bd of Mgt, Thames Reach Housing Assoc., 2001–. Vice Chm., 2011–13, Chm., 2014–, Professional Negligence Bar Assoc. Asst Gen. Ed., Lloyd's Reports: Professional Negligence, 2000–03. *Publications:* (jtly) The Mareva Injunction and Anton Piller Order, 2nd edn 1993; (ed and contrib.) Cordery on Legal Services (formerly Cordery on Solicitors), 9th edn, 1995–2011; (with T. Leech) Solicitors' Negligence and Liability, 1999, 3rd edn 2012; (contrib.) Professional Negligence and Liability, 2001. *Address:* Hailsham Chambers, 4 Paper Buildings, Temple, EC4Y 7EX.

FLESCH, Michael Charles; QC 1983; *b* 11 March 1940; *s* of late Carl and Ruth Flesch; *m* 1972, Gail Schrire; one *s* one *d*. *Educ:* Gordonstoun Sch.; University College London (LLB 1st Cl. Hons; Hon. Fellow, 2011). Called to the Bar, Gray's Inn, 1963 (Lord Justice Holker Sen. Schol.), Bencher, 1993. Bigelow Teaching Fellow, Univ. of Chicago, 1963–64; Lectr (part-time) in Revenue Law, University Coll. London, 1965–82. Practice at Revenue Bar, 1966–. Chairman: Taxation and Retirement Benefits Cttee, Bar Council, 1985–93; Revenue Bar Assoc., 1993–95. Governor of Gordonstoun Sch., 1976–96. *Publications:* various articles, notes and reviews concerning taxation, in legal periodicals. *Recreations:* all forms of sport, backgammon. *Address:* (home) 38 Farm Avenue, NW2 2BH. *T:* (020) 8452 4547; (chambers) Gray's Inn Chambers, 36 Queen Street, EC4R 1BN. *T:* (020) 7242 2642, *Fax:* (020) 7831 9017. *E:* mf@taxbar.com. *Clubs:* MCC, Arsenal Football, Brondesbury Lawn Tennis and Cricket.

See also S. B. Lucas.

FLESHER, Timothy James, CB 2002; adviser and consultant, since 2010; Director, CTC Consultants (UK) Ltd; *b* 25 July 1949; *s* of James Amos Flesher and Evelyn May Flesher (*née* Hale); *m* 1986, Margaret McCormack; two *d*. *Educ:* Hertford Coll., Oxford (BA). Lectr, Cambridge Coll. of Arts and Technol., 1972–74; Admin. Trainee/HEO, Home Office, 1974–79; Sec. to Prisons Bd, 1979–82; Private Sec. to Prime Minister, 1982–86; Home Office: Head of: After Entry and Refugee Div., 1986–89; Personnel Div., 1989–91; Probation Service Div., 1991–92; Dir of Admin, OFSTED, 1992–94; Dep. DG (Ops), Immigration and Nationality Directorate (formerly Dept), Home Office, and Chief Inspector, Immigration Service, 1994–98; a Comr, 1998–2003, a Dep. Chm., 1999–2003, Inland Revenue; Dep. Chief of Defence Logistics, MoD, 2003–07; Chief of Corporate Services, Defence Equipment and Support Orgn, MoD, 2007–10. Mem., Armed Forces Pay Rev. Body, 2014–. Trustee, Charity for Civil Servants, 2010– (Vice-Chm., 2012–).

FLETCHER; *see* Aubrey-Fletcher.

FLETCHER, Andrew Fitzroy Stephen; QC 2006; *b* 20 Dec. 1957; *s* of Fitzroy Fletcher and Brygid Fletcher (*née* Mahon); *m* 1st, 1984, Felicia Taylor (marr. diss. 1999); 2nd, 2010, Eri Aso, three *s* one *d*. *Educ:* Eton Coll.; Magdalene Coll., Cambridge (BA 1980; MA 1983). 2nd Lieut, Welsh Guards, 1976. Called to the Bar, Inner Temple, 1980; in practice specialising in commercial litigation. Liveryman, Grocers' Co., 1994–. *Recreations:* Real Tennis, travel, cricket, wine, reading. *Address:* 3 Verulam Buildings, Gray's Inn, WC1R 5NT. *T:* (020) 7831 8441. *E:* afletcher@3vb.com. *Clubs:* Boodle's, Pratt's, MCC.

FLETCHER, Dame Ann Elizabeth Mary; *see* Leslie, Dame A. E. M.

FLETCHER, Prof. Anthony John; Professor of English Social History, University of London, at the Institute of Historical Research, 2001–03, now Emeritus; *b* 24 April 1941; *s* of John Molyneux Fletcher and Delle Clare Chenevix-Trench; *m* 1st, 1967, Tresna Dawn Russell (marr. diss. 1999); two *s*; 2nd, 2006, Brenda Joan Lockhart-Smith (*née* Knibbs). *Educ:* Wellington Coll.; Merton Coll., Oxford (BA 1962). History Master, King's Coll. Sch., Wimbledon, 1964–67; Lectr, Sen. Lectr, then Reader in History, Sheffield Univ., 1967–87; Prof. of Modern History, Durham Univ., 1987–95; Prof. of History, Essex Univ., 1995–2000;

Dir and Gen. Ed., Victoria County History, Inst. of Histl Res., Univ. of London, 2001–03. Auditor, QAA (formerly HEQC), 1994–2001. Pres., Ecclesiast. Hist. Soc., 1996–97; Vice-Pres., RHistS, 1997–2001 (Mem. Council, 1992–96). Convenor, History at the Univs Defence Gp, 1997–2000; Chair, QAA History Subject Benchmarking Gp, 1998–99. *Publications:* Tudor Rebellions, 1967; A County Community in Peace and War, 1975; The Outbreak of the English Civil War, 1981; (ed jtly) Order and Disorder in Early Modern England, 1985; Reform in the Provinces, 1986; (ed jtly) Religion, Culture and Society in Early Modern Britain, 1994; Gender, Sex and Subordination in England 1500–1800, 1995; (ed jtly) Childhood in Question: children, parents and the state, 1999; Growing Up in England: the experience of childhood 1600–1914, 2008; Life, Death and Growing Up on the Western Front, 2013; articles and reviews in learned jls. *Recreations:* theatre, opera, travel, walking, gardening. *Address:* School House, South Newington, Banbury, Oxon OX15 4JJ. *E:* afletcher1@btinternet.com.

FLETCHER, Augustus James Voisey, OBE 1977; GM 1957; HM Diplomatic Service, retired; Foreign and Commonwealth Office, 1982–89; *b* 23 Dec. 1928; *s* of James Fletcher and Naomi Fletcher (*née* Dudden); *m* 1956, Enyd Gwynne Harries; one *s* one *d. Educ:* Weston-super-Mare Grammar Sch.; Oriental Language Institute, Malaya. Colonial Service, Palestine, 1946–48, Malaya, 1948–58; Min. of Defence, 1958–64; FCO, 1964–89: Hong Kong (seconded HQ Land Forces), 1966–70; FCO, 1970–73; Hong Kong, 1973–76; FCO, 1976–79; Counsellor, New Delhi, 1979–82. *Recreations:* trout fishing, walking, food/wine, theatre. *Club:* Travellers.

FLETCHER, Rt Rev. Colin William; *see* Dorchester, Area Bishop of.

FLETCHER, Colleen Margaret; MP (Lab) Coventry North East, since 2015; *b* Coventry, 23 Nov. 1954; *d* of William Charles Dalton and Dot Dalton; *m* Ian Richard Fletcher; two *s. Educ:* Lyng Hall Comprehensive Sch.; Henley Coll. GEC, Coventry; Customer Services Officer, Orbit Housing Gp. Mem. (Lab), Coventry CC, 1992–2000, 2002–04 and 2011–15. *Address:* House of Commons, SW1A 0AA.

FLETCHER, David Edwin, MBE 1986; Owner and Director, Hebden Bridge Mill, since 1972; President, Pennine Heritage Environmental Trust, since 2015 (Founder Chairman, 1979–2015); restoration and regeneration specialist; *b* 15 July 1933; *s* of Edwin and Winifred Fletcher; marr. diss. 1990; two *d*; *m* 2005, Hilary Darby. *Educ:* Hebden Bridge Grammar Sch.; Calder High Sch.; Sheffield Univ. (BSc Jt Hons); Leeds Univ. (PGCE); Bradford Univ. (MSc). Schoolmaster and Head of Biology, Bingley GS, 1957–60, Calder High Sch., 1960–69; Manchester Polytechnic: Sen. Lectr, 1970–74; Principal Lectr, 1974–80; Head, Envmt and Geographical Dept, 1980–88; Exec. Dir, Transpennine Campaign, 1988–2005. Mem., Hebden Royd UDC, 1967–74 (Chm., Planning Cttee, 1969–74). Founder Chm., Calder Civic Trust, 1965–75; Dir, Adv. Services, Civic Trust NW, 1970–76. Commissioner: Countryside Commn, 1988–96; Rural Develt Commn, 1993–2000. Chairman: Action for Market Towns, 1998–2005; Hebden Bridge (formerly Hebden Royd Town) Partnership, 2002–11; Upper Calder Valley Renaissance, 2003–07; Chm. of Trustees, X-PERT Health Charity, 2010–. Member: NW Council for Sport and Recreation, 1972–78; Yorks and Humber Cttee, Heritage Lottery Fund, 2001–06. *Publications:* ASK - Amenity, Society Knowhow, 1976; Industry Tourism, 1988; England's North West: a strategic vision for a European region, 1992; research and consultancy reports; contribs to acad. jls; environmental pamphlets. *Recreations:* walking, ski-ing, travel, meeting interesting people in interesting situations, restoring and finding new uses for wonderful old mills in the Pennines; engaged in returning 700 year old Bridge Mill, Hebden Bridge, to its sustainable energy origins, independent of the grid, through solar and hydropower solutions. *Address:* c/o Birchcliffe, Hebden Bridge, W Yorks HX7 8DG. *T:* (01422) 844450.

FLETCHER, Dr David John, CBE 2002; CEng, FREng, FIET; Chief Executive, British Waterways, 1996–2002; *b* 12 Dec. 1942; *s* of late John Fletcher and Edna Fletcher; *m* 1967, Irene Mary Luther; one *s* one *d. Educ:* The Crypt Grammar Sch., Gloucester; Univ. of Leeds (BSc (Elect. Eng, High Frequency Electronics), DEng). FCIWEM; FREng 2004. General Electric Company, 1965–95: GEC Applied Electronics Labs, Stanmore, 1965–80; Gen. Manager, Stanmore Unit, Marconi Space and Defence Systems, 1980–84; Man. Dir, Marconi Defence Systems, 1984–87; GEC Marconi, 1987–95 (Dep. Chm., 1993–95). Dir, Easynet Group PLC, 2001–06; Chm., Infrared Systems Ltd, 2004–06. Mem., Partnerships UK Adv. Council, 1999–2002. Chm., Assoc. of Inland Navigation Authorities, 1997–2003; Director: Co. of Proprietors Stroudwater Navigation, 2003–; Stroud Valley Canal Co., 2012–. President: Sleaford Navigation, 2003–; Wendover Arm Trust, 2003–; Vice-President: Inland Waterways Assoc., 2002–; Cotswold Canal Trust, 2003–; Bedford/Milton Keynes Canal Trust, 2003–06; Trustee, Waterways Trust, 1999–2012. Director Trustee, Nat. Coal Mining Mus., 1997–. Member: Rare Breed Survival Trust; Nat. Trust. *Recreations:* boating, classic cars. *Address:* Beverley House, Nettleden Road, Little Gaddesden, Herts HP4 1PP.

FLETCHER, David Robert, CBE 2010; **His Honour Judge David Fletcher;** a Circuit Judge, since 2004; *b* 6 May 1957; *s* of late Donald Fletcher and of Alice Fletcher (*née* Worrall); *m* 1982, Janet Powney; one *s* one *d. Educ:* Biddulph Grammar Sch.; Biddulph High Sch.; Univ. of Liverpool (LLB Hons 1978). Admitted solicitor, 1981; Higher Courts Advocate, 1999; Charltons, Solicitors: articled clerk, 1979–81; Asst Solicitor, 1981–84; Partner, 1984–96; Partner: Beswicks, Stoke-on-Trent, 1996–2001; Stevens, Stoke-on-Trent, Stafford and Wolverhampton, 2001–03. Actg Stipendiary Magistrate, 1998–2000; Dep. Dist Judge (Magistrates' Courts), 2000–03; a Dist Judge (Magistrates' Courts), Sheffield, 2003–04; Presiding Judge, N Liverpool Community Justice Centre, 2004–12. Mem. Bd, Internat. Assoc. of Drug Treatment Courts, 2008–. Mem. Council, Tate Liverpool, 2008–12. Chm. Govs, Biddulph High Sch., 1996–2004. *Recreations:* swimming, hill walking, travel, cooking, music, speaking and learning Spanish, watching Port Vale FC. *Address:* Trent Combined Court Centre, Bethesda Street, Hanley, Stoke on Trent ST1 3BP.

FLETCHER, Hugh Alasdair; Chairman, Fletcher Brothers Ltd, since 1997; Deputy Chairman, Reserve Bank of New Zealand, 2009–12 (Director, 2002–12); *b* 28 Nov. 1947; *s* of Sir James Muir Cameron Fletcher, ONZ and of Margery Vaughan Fletcher; *m* 1970, Sian Seerpoohi Elias (*see* Rt Hon. Dame Sian Elias); two *s. Educ:* Auckland Univ. (MCom Hons, BSc); Stanford Univ., USA (MBA 1972). Fletcher Holdings: Asst to Ops Res., 1969–70; PA to Man. Dir, 1972–76; Dep. Man. Dir, 1976–79; CEO, 1979–81; Fletcher Challenge Ltd: non-exec. Dir, 1981–2001; Man. Dir, 1981–87; CEO, 1987–97; Chairman: CGNU Australia Holdings Ltd (formerly CGU Insurance Australia), 1998–2003; New Zealand Insurance, 1998–2003. Non-exec. Chm., Air New Zealand Ltd, 1985–89; Director: Australasian Adv. Bd, Merrill Lynch, 1998–2000; Rubicon, 2001–; Fletcher Bldg, 2001–12; Ports of Auckland, 2002–06; IAG NZ, 2004–; IAG, 2007–; Vector, 2007–. Chairman: NZ Thoroughbred Marketing, 1998–2000; Ministerial Inquiry into Telecommunications, 2000; Member: Prime Minister's Enterprise Council, 1992–97; Asia Pacific Adv. Cttee, New York Stock Exchange, 1995–2005; World Business Council for Sustainable Develt, Geneva, 1993–96; Adv. Cttee, UN Office for Project Services, 2000–07. Chancellor, Univ. of Auckland, 2005–08 (Mem. Council, 2000–11). Hon. LLD Auckland, 2012. *Recreations:* horse riding, horse breeding and racing, chess, Go. *Address:* PO Box 11468, Ellerslie, Auckland 1542, New Zealand.

FLETCHER, Ian Raymond; Director, Government Communications Security Bureau, New Zealand, 2012–15; *b* New Zealand, 25 Aug. 1959; *s* of Raymond William Fletcher and Elizabeth Ruth (*née* Millin); *m* 1st, 1990, Lorna Windmill (marr. diss. 2007); 2nd, 2008 Elizabeth Claire McNabb. *Educ:* Burnside High Sch., Christchurch, NZ; Canterbury Univ. (MA Hons 1982). NZ Diplomatic Service, 1982–89; Monopolies and Mergers Commn, UK, 1989–91; Department of Trade and Industry: general trade policy, 1992–94; telecommunications policy, 1994–95; EC, on secondment, 1996–98; DTI and British Trade Internat., 1998–99; Dir-Gen., UN Customs Service and Hd, Dept of Trade and Industry, UN Admin, Kosovo, 2000; Dir, Gas and Electricity, DTI, 2000–02; Principal Private Sec. to Sec. of the Cabinet, 2002–04; Dir, Internat. Trade Develt, UK Trade and Investment, 2004–07; Chief Exec., Intellectual Property Office (Patent Office), 2007–09; Dir-Gen., Dept. of Employment, Econ. Develt and Innovation, Qld, 2009–12. *Address:* PO Box 12068, Wellington 6144, New Zealand.

FLETCHER, His Honour John Edwin; a Circuit Judge, 1986–2006; *b* 23 Feb. 1941; *s* of late Sydney Gerald Fletcher and Cecilia Lane Fletcher; *m* 1st, 1971, Felicity Jane Innes Dick (marr. diss.); 2nd, 1996, Mrs Susan Kennedy-Hawkes. *Educ:* Munro Coll., Jamaica; St Bees Sch., Cumbria; Clare Coll., Cambridge (MA). Called to the Bar, Inner Temple, 1964; Midland and Oxford Circuit, 1965–86; a Recorder, 1983–86. Mem. Panel of Chairmen, Medical Appeal Tribunals, 1981–86. *Recreations:* walking, photography, classical guitar.

FLETCHER, Kim Thomas; Partner, Brunswick, since 2011; *b* 17 Sept. 1956; *s* of Jack Fletcher and Agnes Fletcher (*née* Coulthwaite); *m* 1991, Sarah Sands; one *s* one *d*, and one step *s. Educ:* Heversham Grammar Sch., Westmorland; Hertford Coll., Oxford (BA Law); UC Cardiff (Dip. Journalism Studies). Journalist: The Star, Sheffield, 1978–81; Sunday Times, 1981–86; Daily Telegraph, 1986–87; Sunday Telegraph, 1988–98; Editor, Independent on Sunday, 1998–99; Editl Dir, Hollinger Telegraph New Media, 2000–03; Editl Dir, Telegraph Gp Ltd, 2003–05; Man. Dir, Trinity Mgt Communications, 2007–11. Chm., NCTJ, 2004–. Ed., British Journalism Rev., 2012–. *Publications:* The Journalist's Handbook, 2005. *Recreation:* family life. *Address:* (home) 16 Pembroke Place, W8 6ET. *E:* kim.fletcher@me.com. *Club:* Groucho.

FLETCHER, Malcolm Stanley, MBE 1982; FREng; FICE; Consultant, Halcrow Group (formerly Sir William Halcrow & Partners) Ltd, Consulting Civil Engineers, 1996–2012; *b* 25 Feb. 1936; *s* of Harold and Clarice Fletcher; *m* 1965, Rhona Christina Wood; one *s* two *d. Educ:* Manchester Grammar Sch.; Manchester Univ. (MSc); Imperial Coll., London (DIC). FGS 1968; FICE 1976; FREng (FEng 1993). Pupil, Binnie & Partners, 1957–60; Sir William Halcrow & Partners, 1968–96: Partner, 1985–96; Chm., 1990–96. Resident Engineer: Jhelum Bridge, Pakistan, 1965–67; Giuliana Bridge, Libya, 1968–74; Design Team Leader, Orwell Bridge, Ipswich, 1976–82; Dir of Design, Second Severn Crossing, 1988–96; Adviser: Dartford River Crossing, 1985–90; Lantau Fixed Crossing, Hong Kong, 1990–96. *Recreation:* cycling. *Address:* 8 The Green, Aldbourne, Marlborough, Wilts SN8 2BW.

FLETCHER, Margaret Ann; *see* Cable, M. A.

FLETCHER, Martin Guy; Chief Executive Officer, Australian Health Practitioner Regulation Agency, since 2010; *b* Sydney, Australia, 3 April 1961; *s* of Brian and Beverley Fletcher; *m* 1988, Therese Hanna; two *s* one *d. Educ:* Univ. of Sydney (BSocStud); Macquarie Univ. (BA Hons); Univ. of Technol., Sydney (MMan). Manager, Care Plus (ACT) Pty Ltd, 1996–98; Dir, Australian Dept of Health and Ageing, 1998–2000; Dir, Australian Council for Safety and Quality in Health Care, 2000–03; Asst Dir, Nat. Patient Safety Agency, 2003–04; Hd, Patient Safety, WHO World Alliance for Patient Safety, 2004–07; Chief Exec., Nat. Patient Safety Agency, 2007–10. *Publications:* contrib. articles on patient safety to jls incl. Med. Jl of Australia, Quality and Safety in Healthcare and Internat. Jl for Quality in Health Care. *Recreations:* swimming, reading, travel. *Address:* Australian Health Practitioner Regulation Agency, 111 Bourke Street, Melbourne, Vic 3001, Australia. *E:* Martin.Fletcher@ahpra.gov.au. *Club:* Royal Society of Medicine.

FLETCHER, Michael John; Sheriff of Tayside Central and Fife, 2000–14; *b* 5 Dec. 1945; *s* of Walter Fletcher and Elizabeth Fletcher (*née* Pringle); *m* 1968, Kathryn Mary Bain; two *s. Educ:* High Sch. of Dundee; Univ. of St Andrews (LLB). Admitted solicitor, 1968; apprenticeship, Kirk Mackie & Elliot, SSC, Edinburgh, 1966–68; Asst, then Partner, Ross Strachan & Co., Dundee, 1968–88; Partner, Hendry & Fenton, later Miller Hendry, Dundee, 1988–94; Sheriff of South Strathclyde, Dumfries and Galloway, 1994–99; Sheriff of Lothian and Borders, 1999–2000. Mem., Sheriff Court Rules Council, 2002–11; Pres., Sheriffs' Assoc., 2009–11. Lectr (part-time) in Civil and Criminal Procedure, Univ. of Dundee, 1974–94. Editor, Scottish Civil Law Reports, 1999–. *Publications:* (jtly) Delictual Damages, 2000. *Recreations:* golf, badminton, gardening.

FLETCHER, Neil; education consultant, since 2003; Head of Education, Local Government Association, 1998–2003; *b* 5 May 1944; *s* of Alan and Ruth Fletcher; *m* 1967, Margaret Monaghan; two *s. Educ:* Wyggeston Sch., Leicester; City of Leeds Coll. of Educn (Teachers' Cert.); London Univ. (BA Hons); London Business Sch. (MBA 1994). Charter FCP 1990. Schoolteacher, 1966–68; Lectr, 1969–76; Admin. Officer, 1976–91, Hd of Educn, 1991–94, NALGO; Hd of Strategic Projects, UNISON, 1994–95; mgt consultant, 1995–98. Member: Camden Bor. Council, 1978–86 (Dep. Leader, 1982–84); ILEA, 1979–90 (Chair, Further and Higher Educn Sub-Cttee, 1981–87; Leader, 1987–90); Chair: Council of Local Educn Authorities, 1987–88, 1989–90; Educn Cttee, AMA, 1987–90 (Vice-Chair, 1986–87). Advr, London Skills and Employment Bd, 2006–08; Chm., CLC Building Futures Bd, 2013–. Governor: Penn Sch., 1985–2006; London Inst., 1986–99; LSE, 1990–2001; City Literary Inst., 1996–2006 (Chair of Govs, 2003–06). FRSA 1989. *Recreations:* cricket, soccer, theatre, cookery, walking. *Address:* 42 Narcissus Road, NW6 1TH. *T:* (020) 7435 5306. *E:* neil@neilfletcher.org.uk.

FLETCHER, Nicholas Hugo Martin; QC 2014; barrister and arbitrator, 4 New Square, since 2014; *b* London, 8 Nov. 1958; *s* of Barbara Fletcher; *m* 1985, Geraldine Caruana; two *s. Educ:* Reed's Sch., Cobham; Balliol Coll., Oxford (BA Hons Juris 1980); London Sch. of Econs and Pol Sci. (LLM 1981). Called to the Bar, Lincoln's Inn, England and Wales, 1982; admitted to Bar of New York, 1985; admitted as solicitor, 1991; Associate, Haight Gardner Poor & Havens, NY, 1983–86; Associate, 1986–98, Partner, 1998–2009, Clifford Chance, subseq. Clifford Chance LLP; Partner, and Hd of Internat. Arbitration, Berwin Leighton Paisner LLP, 2009–14. Member: London Court of Internat. Arbitration, 2000–; Exec. Cttee, Foundn for Internat. Arbitration Advocacy, 2008–; ICC Task Force on New York Convention, 2008–; IBA, 2009–; ICCA, 2012–. *Recreations:* sailing, golf, opera, theatre, reading, travelling, supporting Chelsea Football Club. *Address:* 4 New Square, Lincoln's Inn, WC2A 3RJ. *T:* (020) 7822 212. *E:* n.fletcher@4newsquare.com. *Club:* Royal Southampton Yacht.

FLETCHER, Philip John, CBE 2006; Chairman, Water Services Regulation Authority (Ofwat), 2006–12 (Director General, Water Services, 2000–06); *b* 2 May 1946; *s* of late Alan Philip Fletcher, QC and Annette Grace Fletcher (*née* Wright); *m* 1977, Margaret Anne Boys; one *d* (and one *d* decd). *Educ:* Marlborough Coll.; Trinity Coll., Oxford (MA). Asst Principal, MPBW, 1968; Department of the Environment: Private Sec. to Permanent Sec., 1978; Asst Sec., Private Sector Housebuilding, 1980, local govt expenditure, 1982–85; Under Secretary: Housing, Water and Central Finance, 1986–90; Planning and Develt Control, 1990–93; Chief Exec., PSA Services, 1993–94, and Dep. Sec., Property Holdings, 1994; Dep. Sec., Cities and Countryside Gp, 1994–95; Receiver for the Metropolitan Police District, 1996–2000. Mem. Bd, Ofqual, 2010– (Mem. Cttee, 2008–10). Reader, Church of England; Mem., Archbishops' Council, 2007– (Chair, Mission and Public Affairs Council, 2012–). *Recreation:* walking.
See also Area Bishop of Dorchester.

FLETCHER, Richard George Hopper, CMG 1996; HM Diplomatic Service, retired; Senior Adviser, Anthem Corporate Finance, since 2010; *b* 8 Nov. 1944; *s* of late George Hopper Fletcher, CBE, FCA and Kathleen Mary Parsons; *m* 1967, Celia Rosemary Soord; two *d*. *Educ:* Leys Sch., Cambridge; Balliol Coll., Oxford. Joined Foreign Office, 1966–67; Athens, 1968; Nicosia, 1969–72; First Sec., Bucharest, 1973–76; FCO, 1977–83; Counsellor: Athens, 1984–88; FCO, 1989–98; Vice-Pres., Govt Relns and External Affairs, Europe, Nortel Networks, 1998–2001; Public Policy Advr, Cogent Defence and Security Networks Ltd, 2001–02; re-employed, FCO, 2003–05. Sen. Policy Advr, EADS Defence and Security Systems, 2005–09; Senior Adviser: Ernst & Young, 2010–11; Hakluyt, 2010–11. Dir, West Mercian Property Ltd, 2014–. *Recreations:* forestry, gardening, bridge, golf. *Clubs:* Wimbledon Park Golf (Dir, 2002–07; Capt., 2007); Sapey Golf.

FLETCHER, Robin Anthony, OBE 1984; DSC 1944; DPhil; Warden of Rhodes House, Oxford, 1980–89; Professorial Fellow, Trinity College, Oxford, 1980–89, now Emeritus; *b* 30 May 1922; *s* of Philip Cawthorne Fletcher, MC, and Edith Maud Fletcher (*née* Okell); *m* 1950, Jinny May (*née* Cornish) (*d* 2010); two *s*. *Educ:* Marlborough Coll.; Trinity Coll., Oxford (MA, DPhil). Served Royal Navy (Lieut RNVR), 1941–46. University Lecturer in Modern Greek, 1949–79; Domestic Bursar, Trinity Coll., Oxford, 1950–74; Senior Proctor, 1966–67; Member, Hebdomadal Council, 1967–74. Represented England at hockey, 1949–55 and GB, 1952 Olympic Games (Bronze Medal). *Publications:* Kostes Palamas, Athens, 1984; A Favouring Wind, 2007; various articles. *Recreations:* sport, music. *Address:* Lismore, St Mary's, Holm, Orkney KW17 2RT. *Clubs:* Naval; Vincent's (Oxford).

FLETCHER, Prof. Roger, PhD; FRS 2003; FRSE; Baxter Professor of Mathematics, 1993–2005, and Professor of Optimization, 1984–2005, University of Dundee, now Emeritus; *b* 29 Jan. 1939; *s* of Harry and Alice Fletcher; *m* 1963, Mary Marjorie Taylor; two *d*. *Educ:* Huddersfield Coll.; Selwyn Coll., Cambridge (MA); Univ. of Leeds (PhD 1963). FIMA 1971. Lectr, Leeds Univ., 1963–69; PSO, AERE Harwell, 1969–73; Sen. Lectr, then Reader, Univ. of Dundee, 1973–84. Hon. Prof., Univ. of Edinburgh, 2005–. FRSE 1988. *Publications:* Practical Methods of Optimization, Vol. 1, 1980, Vol. 2, 1981, 2nd edn as one vol. 1987; numerous contribs to jls. *Recreations:* hill-walking, bridge. *Address:* Department of Mathematics, University of Dundee, Dundee DD1 4HN. *T:* (01382) 384490, *Fax:* (01382) 385516. *E:* fletcher@maths.dundee.ac.uk.

FLETCHER, Prof. Ronald Stanley, FRAeS; Professor of Thermal Power, 1972–2003, now Emeritus, and Deputy Vice-Chancellor, 1994–2003, Cranfield University (formerly Cranfield Institute of Technology); *b* 12 Dec. 1937; *s* of Reginald and Dorothy Fletcher; *m* 1965, Pamela Alys, *d* of Gwilym and Alys Treharne; one *s* twin *d*. *Educ:* Imperial College, London Univ. (PhD, DIC); UMIST (BSc Tech). FRAeS 1994. Senior Engineer, Northern Research & Engineering Corp., Cambridge, USA, 1965–70; Consultant, Northern Research & Engineering Corp., Herts, 1970–72; Cranfield Institute of Technology: Head of Mechanical Engineering, 1977–87; Dean of Engineering, 1982–85; Pro-Vice-Chancellor, 1985–93; Head of Cranfield Campus, 1989–94; Chairman: Cranfield Mgt Develt Ltd, 1993–2004; Cranfield Aerospace Ltd, 1996–98. Visiting Professor: Cairo, 1975; Brazil, 1977; China (Beijing Inst. of Aero. and Astro.), 1979. Member: ARC, 1974–77; Governing Body, AFRC Inst. of Engrg Res. (formerly Nat. Inst. of Agricl Engrg), 1978–93 (Chm., Finance Cttee, 1982–86); Council, British Hydro. Res. Assoc., 1979–89; AGARD (NATO) Propulsion and Energetics Panel, 1980–99 (Chm., 1997–98); Scientific Bd, Univ. de Technologie de Compiègne, 1989–94; Conseil Scientifique, Inst. Méditerranéen de Technologie, 1989–94. Governor, Bedford Modern Sch., 1986–89. Médaille Gustave Trasenster, Liège, 1990; Prix Formation Etranger, Acad. Nat. de l'Air et de l'Espace, France, 1991. Chevalier, 1990, Officier, 1994, Ordre des Palmes Académiques (France). *Publications:* papers on combustion. *Recreations:* sailing, music. *Address:* 34 Brecon Way, Bedford MK41 8DD. *T:* (01234) 358483. *Club:* Parkstone Yacht.

FLETCHER, Sarah Kate; Head Teacher, City of London School, since 2014; *b* Wantage, 6 Feb. 1963; *d* of Dr Cedric Turberfield and Sheila Turberfield; *m* 1988, Andrew Fletcher; two *s*. *Educ:* King Alfred's Sch., Wantage; New Coll., Oxford (MA 1st Cl.); Univ. of Exeter (PGCE). NPQH 2006. Teacher of Hist., Wycombe Abbey, 1985–90; Hd, Hist. and Careers, St George's Sch., Montreux, 1990–92; Head of History: Haberdashers' Aske's Sch. for Girls, Elstree, 1992–94; Lawrence Sheriff Sch., Rugby, 1994–96; House Mistress, 1996–99, Dir of Studies and Dep. Head, 1999–2009, Rugby School; Head, Kingston Grammar Sch., 2009–14. *Publications:* (contrib.) Liberating Learning: widening participation, 2009; contrib. articles in SecEd mag. and New DNB. *Recreations:* clarinet (semi professional orchestral and chamber musician), music, theatre, opera, art, walking. *Address:* City of London School, Queen Victoria Street, EC4V 3AL. *T:* (020) 7489 0291. *E:* head@clsb.org.uk.

FLETCHER, Stuart Barron, OBE 2003; Chairman, Welsh Ambulance Services NHS Trust, 2006–13; *b* 28 July 1945; *s* of Arthur Barron Fletcher and Bertha Fletcher; *m* 1970, Dilys Roberts; two *s* one *d*. *Educ:* King George V Grammar Sch., Southport; Oriel Coll., Oxford (MA). MHSM, DipHSM. Entered Health Service as Nat. Trainee Administrator, 1968; NHS posts include: Hosp. Sec., Broadgreen Hosp., Liverpool, 1972–74; Area Gen. Administrator, St Helens and Knowsley HA, 1974–78; Dist Administrator, E Birmingham HA, 1978–82; Chief Exec., N Staffs HA, 1982–91; Regl Man. Dir, subseq. Chief Exec., W Midlands RHA, 1992–93; Chief Exec., Pembs, subseq. Pembs and Derwen, NHS Trust, 1994–2003; Chief Exec., Health Commn Wales, NHS Dept, Welsh Assembly Govt, 2003–05. Member: NHS Trng Authy, 1985–91; NHS Trng Adv. Bd, 1991–93. Pres., IHSM, 1991–92 (Mem., Nat. Council, 1981–95). Mem. Council and Trustee, Stroke Assoc., 2011–. Sec. to Trustees, Welsh Livery Guild Charitable Trust. Liveryman, Livery Co. of Wales (formerly Welsh Livery Guild), 2002 (Master, 2011–12; Dep. Master, 2012–13). Chm., St John Pembrokeshire Council. OStJ 2012. *Recreations:* Rugby, fell walking, photography, theatre. *Address:* 5 Douglas James Close, Haverfordwest, Pembrokeshire SA61 2UF. *T:* (01437) 760103. *Club:* Cardiff and County.

FLETCHER, Thomas Stuart Francis, CMG 2011; Visiting Professor of International Relations, New York University, since 2015; Chief Executive, Interpol Foundation, since 2015; Strategy Director, Global Business Coalition for Education, since 2015; *b* Kent, 27 March 1975; *s* of Mark and Deborah Fletcher; *m* 2006, Louise Fitzgerald; two *s*. *Educ:* Harvey Grammar Sch., Folkestone; Hertford Coll., Oxford (BA 1st Cl. Hons Hist.; MA Hist.; Hon. Fellow). Entered FCO, 1997; Second Sec., Nairobi, 1998–2001; Private Sec. to Parly Under Sec. of State, FCO, 2002–04; Hd, Internat. Policy, Paris, 2004–07; Private Sec., 2007, Private Sec. for Foreign Affairs and NI, 2007–10, Foreign Policy Advr, 2010–11, to the Prime Minister (on secondment); Ambassador to the Lebanon, 2011–15. Sen. Associate, St Antony's Coll., Oxford, 2011–. *Recreations:* mountains, cricket, history. *Address:* New York University Abu Dhabi, PO Box 129188, Saadiyat Island, Abu Dhabi, United Arab Emirates. *Clubs:* 2020 (Co-Pres., 2002–); Strollers Cricket (Cowden).

FLETCHER-VANE, family name of **Baron Inglewood**.

FLEWITT, Neil; QC 2003; **His Honour Judge Flewitt;** a Circuit Judge, since 2015; *b* 3 July 1959; *s* of Robert Arthur Flewitt and Caroline Mary Flewitt; *m* 1987, Melanie Ann Carter; two *s* one *d*. *Educ:* St Edward's Coll., Liverpool; Liverpool Univ. (LLB 1980). Called to the Bar, Middle Temple, 1981; joined chambers, Liverpool, 1981; in practice as a barrister in criminal law (prosecution and defence); a Recorder, 1998–2015. Mem., Criminal Bar Assoc. *Recreations:* films, food, football. *Address:* Liverpool Crown Court, Queen Elizabeth II Law Courts, Derby Square, Liverpool L2 1XA.

FLIGHT, family name of **Baron Flight**.

FLIGHT, Baron *cr* 2011 (Life Peer), of Worcester in the County of Worcestershire; **Howard Emerson Flight;** Chairman: Flight and Partners, since 2007; Aurora Investment Trust plc, since 2011; Director: Investec Asset Management Ltd (formerly Guinness Flight), since 1987 (Joint Chairman, 1999–2003); non-executive Director, Metro Bank plc, since 2010; *b* 16 June 1948; *s* of late Bernard Thomas Flight and Doris Mildred Emerson Flight; *m* 1973, Christabel Diana Beatrice Norbury; one *s* three *d*. *Educ:* Brentwood Sch.; Magdalene Coll., Cambridge (MA Hist. Pt 1, Econs Pt 2); Univ. of Michigan (MBA 1971). Investment Adviser: N. M. Rothschild & Sons, 1970–73; Cayzer Ltd, 1973–77; Wardley Ltd (Hong Kong Bank), Hong Kong and India, 1977–79; Investment Dir, Guinness Mahon Co. Ltd, 1979–86; Jt Man. Dir, Guinness Flight Global Asset Mgt, 1986–99; Dep. Chm., Guinness Flight Hambro, 1997–98. Contested (C) Bermondsey, Feb. and Oct. 1974. MP (C) Arundel and South Downs, 1997–2005. Shadow Econ. Sec. to Treasury, 1999–2001; Shadow Paymaster Gen., 2001–02; Shadow Chief Sec. to HM Treasury, 2002–04; Dep. Chm., Cons. Party, 2004–05. Mem., Envmt Select Cttee, 1997–98, Social Security Select Cttee, 1998–99. Jt Chm., All Party H of C Hong Kong Cttee, 1998–2005. Mem., EU Cttee, Econs and Financial Affairs, H of L, 2011–. Chairman: CIM Investment Mgt, 2006–; Loudwater Trust Ltd, 2007–12; CorporActive Fund (HK), 2008–13; Downing Structured (formerly Protected) Opportunities VCT 1 plc, 2009– (Dir, 2009–); Director: Marechale Capital Ltd (formerly St Helen's Capital), 2005–; R5 FX Trading, 2015–; Consultant: Tax Incentives Savings Assoc. (formerly PEP and ISA Mgt Assoc.), 1998–; Kinetic Partners, 2005–; Arden Partners, 2014–. Member: Adv. Council, Financial Services Forum, 2005–; Adv. Bd, Guinness Renewable Energy EIS Fund, 2011–. Mem., Guernsey Financial Services Commn, 2005–; Chm., Enterprise Investment Scheme Assoc., 2005–. Vice Pres., Elgar Foundn, 2005– (Trustee, 1979–); Trustee, Africa Res. Inst., 2006–. Governor, Brentwood Sch., 1989–. Liveryman, Carpenters' Co., 1999–. FRSA. *Publications:* All You Need to Know About Exchange Rates, 1988. *Recreations:* classical music, antiques, gardening, ski-ing. *Address:* 6 Barton Street, Westminster, SW1P 3NG. *E:* hflight@btinternet.com. *Clubs:* Carlton, Pratt's, Boodle's.

FLINDALL, Jacqueline; Regional Nursing Officer, Wessex Regional Health Authority, 1983–85; *b* 12 Oct. 1932; *d* of Harry and Lilian Flindall. *Educ:* St David's Sch., Ashford, Middx; University Coll. Hosp., London (DipN). SRN, SCM, UCH, 1950–54; Midwifery, St Luke's Mat. Hosp., Guildford and Watford, 1955; exchange student, Mount Sinai Hosp., NY, 1956; Ward Sister and Clinical Teacher, UCH, 1957–63; Asst Matron, Wexham Park Hosp., 1964–66; Dep. Supt of Nursing, Prince of Wales and St Anne's, 1967–69; Chief Nursing Officer: Northwick Park Hosp., 1969–73; Oxfordshire HA, 1973–83. Associate Consultant, PA Management Consultants, 1986–94. Non-exec. Dir, Royal Nat. Orth. Hosp. NHS Trust, Stanmore, 1991–95. Vice Chm., Hosp. Chaplaincies Council, 1997–2003. Professional Organization Mem., RCN; Hon. FRCN 1983. JP Oxford, 1982, Salisbury, 1987–2002; Mem., Wilts Magistrates' Courts Cttee, 1995–2002. *Recreations:* painting, voluntary work.

FLINDERS, Prof. Matthew Vincent, PhD; Professor of Parliamentary Government and Governance, since 2009, and Founding Director, Sir Bernard Crick Centre for Public Understanding of Politics, since 2013, University of Sheffield; *b* London, 19 Aug. 1972; *s* of Terence George Flinders and Margaret Anne Flinders (*née* Sadler); *m* 2001, Tamsin Jane Burton Ryder; one *s* three *d*. *Educ:* St Catherine's Sch., Swindon; St Joseph's Sch., Swindon; Swindon Coll.; Loughborough Univ. (BA Hons); Univ. of Sheffield (PhD 1999). Department of Politics, University of Sheffield: Lectr, 2000–03; Sen. Lectr, 2003–05; Reader, 2005–08; Dep. Dean, Faculty of Social Scis, 2004–05. Leverhulme Res. Fellow, 2005; Whitehall Fellow, Cabinet Office, 2006. Adjunct Dist. Prof. of Governance and Public Policy, Sir Walter Murdoch Sch. of Public Policy and Internat. Affairs, Murdoch Univ., Perth, 2013–. Gov., Sheffield Health and Social Care NHS Trust, 2008–11. Mem., Exec. Cttee, Political Studies Assoc., 2011– (Chm., 2014–). FAcSS (AcSS 2011). FRSA 2012. Harrison Prize, 2002, Richard Rose Prize, 2004, W. J. M. Mackenzie Prize, 2009, Pol Studies Assoc.; Communicator of Year Award, Pol Studies Assoc., 2012; Sam Aaronovitch Meml Prize, Local Econ. Jl, 2012; Impact Champion Prize, ESRC, 2013. *Publications:* Quangos, Accountability and Reform, 1999; The Politics of Accountability in the Modern State, 2001; Multi-Level Governance, 2004; New Politics, New Parliament?, 2005; Democratic Drift, 2008; Oxford Handbook of British Politics, 2009; Walking Without Order, 2009; Defending Politics, 2012; contrib. res. articles and book chapters. *Recreations:* fell running, Rugby. *Address:* Department of Politics, University of Sheffield, Elmfield, Northumberland Road, Sheffield S10 2TU. *T:* (0114) 222 1680, *Fax:* (0114) 222 1717. *E:* m.flinders@sheffield.ac.uk. *Club:* Penn.

FLINT; *see* Heyhoe Flint.

FLINT, Prof. Anthony Patrick Fielding, PhD, DSc; FRSB; Professor of Animal Physiology, School of Biosciences (formerly Department of Physiology and Environmental Science), University of Nottingham, 1993; *b* 31 Aug. 1943; *s* of Maurice Fielding Flint and Patricia Joan (*née* Ince); *m* 1967, Chan Mun Kwun; two *s*. *Educ:* Hill Crest Sch., Swanage; King's Sch., Bruton; Univ. of St Andrews (Queen's Coll., Dundee) (BSc 1966); Univ. of Bristol (PhD 1969; DSc 1984). FRSB (FIBiol 1982). Res. Fellow, Univ. of Western Ontario, 1969–72; Sen. Res. Biochemist in Obs and Gyn., Welsh Nat. Sch. of Medicine, Cardiff, 1972–73; Lectr, Nuffield Dept of Obs and Gyn., Oxford Univ., 1973–77; Staff Mem., AFRC Inst. of Animal Physiology and Genetics Res., Cambridge, 1977–87; Dir of Science and Dir of Inst. of Zool., Zool. Soc. of London, 1987–93. Special Lectr, 1985–87, Special Prof. in Molecular Biol., 1987–93, Univ. of Nottingham Sch. of Agric.; Visiting Professor: Dept of Biology, UCL, 1989–; Biosphere Scis Div., KCL, 1989–. Member: Cttee, Soc. for Study of Fertility, 1981–89 (Sec., 1985–89); Steering Cttee, WHO Task Force on Plants for Fertility Regulation, 1982–87 (Chm., 1985). Member: Council of Management, Journals of Reproduction and Fertility Ltd, 1981–87 (Mem. Exec. Cttee, 1983–87); Bd of Scientific Editors, Jl of Endocrinology, 1983–87. Medal, Soc. for Endocrinology, 1985. *Publications:* (ed jtly) Embryonic Diapause in Mammals, 1981; Reproduction in Domestic Ruminants, 1991; papers in physiol, endocrinol and biochemical jls. *Recreations:* playing Bach on the organ or cello, coasting in small ships. *Address:* School of Biosciences, University of Nottingham, Sutton Bonington, Loughborough, Leics LE12 5RD.

FLINT, Rt Hon. Caroline Louise; PC 2008; MP (Lab) Don Valley, since 1997; *b* 20 Sept. 1961; *d* of late Wendy Flint (*née* Beasley); *m* 1st, 1987 (marr. diss. 1990); one *s* one *d*; 2nd, 2001, Phil Cole; one step *s*. *Educ:* Univ. of East Anglia (BA Hons American History and Lit.). Mgt Trainee, 1983–84, Policy Officer, 1984–86, GLC/ILEA; Head of Women's Unit, NUS, 1988–89; Principal Officer, Lambeth, 1989–93; Sen. Researcher and Political Officer, GMB, 1994–97. Parliamentary Private Secretary: to Minister of State, FCO, 1999–2000 and 2001–02, Minister for Energy, DTI, 2001; to Minister without Portfolio and Labour Party Chair, 2003; Parly Under-Sec. of State, Home Office, 2003–05, DoH, 2005–06; Minister of State, DoH, 2006–07, DWP, 2007–08; Minister for Yorks and the Humber, 2007–08; Minister for Housing, DCLG, 2008; Minister of State (Minister for Europe), FCO, 2008–09; Shadow Sec. of State for Communities and Local Govt, 2010–11, for Energy and Climate Change, 2011–15. *Recreations:* cinema, family and friends. *Address:* House of Commons, SW1A 0AA. *T:* (020) 7219 4407.

FLINT, Charles John Raffles; QC 1995. *Educ:* Trinity College, Cambridge (BA 1973; MA 1980). Called to the Bar, Middle Temple, 1975, Bencher, 2001; Junior Counsel to the Crown (Common Law), 1991–95. *Address:* Blackstone Chambers, Blackstone House, Temple, EC4Y 9BW.

FLINT, Prof. David, TD; MA, BL, CA; Professor of Accountancy, 1964–85, (Johnstone Smith Chair, 1964–75), and Vice-Principal, 1981–85, University of Glasgow; *b* 24 Feb. 1919; *s* of David Flint, JP, and Agnes Strang Lambie; *m* 1953, Dorothy Mary Maclachlan Jardine; two *s* one *d*. *Educ:* Glasgow High Sch.; University of Glasgow. Served with Royal Signals, 1939–46, Major (despatches). Awarded distinction final examination of Institute of Chartered Accountants of Scotland, 1948. Lecturer, University of Glasgow, 1950–60; Dean of Faculty of Law, 1971–73. Partner, Mann Judd Gordon & Co. Chartered Accountants, Glasgow, 1951–71. Hon. Prof. of Accountancy, Stirling Univ., 1988–91. Hon. Pres. Glasgow Chartered Accountants Students Soc., 1959–60; Chm., Assoc. of Univ. Teachers of Accounting (now British Accounting Assoc.), 1969. Scottish Economic Society: Treas., 1954–62; Vice-Pres., 1977–88. Institute of Chartered Accountants of Scotland: Convener: Taxation Review and Res. Sub-Cttee, 1960–64; Res. Adv. Cttee, 1974–75 and 1977–84; Working Party on Future Policy, 1976–79; Public Sector Cttee, 1987–89; Vice-Pres., 1973–75; Pres., 1975–76. Member: Mgt Trng and Develt Cttee, Central Trng Council, 1966–70; Social Scis Panel, Scottish Univs Council on Entrance, 1968–72; Mgt and Industrial Relns Cttee, SRC, 1970–72 and 1978–80; Council, Scottish Business Sch., 1971–77; Company Law Cttee, Law Soc. of Scotland, 1976–85; Pres., European Accounting Assoc., 1983–84; Member: Management and Ind. Rel. Cttee, SSRC, 1970–72 and 1978–80; Commn for Local Authy Accounts in Scotland, 1978–80. Trustee, Scottish Chartered Accountants Trust for Educn, 1981–87. DUniv Glasgow, 2001. BAA Lifetime Achievement Award, 2004; Lifetime Achievement Award, ICAS, 2013. *Publications:* A True and Fair View in Company Accounts, 1982; Philosophy and Principles of Auditing: an introduction, 1988. *Recreation:* golf. *Address:* Wardside House, Muthill, Perthshire PH5 2AS.

FLINT, (David) Jonathan, CBE 2012; FREng, FInstP; Chief Executive Officer, Oxford Instruments plc, since 2005; *b* London, 8 Feb. 1961; *s* of Alan Flint and Gillian Flint; *m* 2012, Claire Goulding; one *s* two *d*. *Educ:* Imperial Coll. London (BSc Phys 1982); Univ. of Southampton (MBA 1998). FInstP 2007; FREng 2011. Marconi: Systems Engr, 1982–87; Business Develt Manager, 1987–91; Matra Marconi Space Systems: Divl Manager, 1991–94; Dir, Business Unit, 1994–96; Divisional Managing Director: GEC Marconi, 1996–98; BAE Systems, 1998–2002; Man. Dir, Vislink plc, 2002–04. Non-exec. Dir, Cobham plc, 2013–. Mem. Council, Inst. of Physics, 2009–12. *Recreations:* reading, hill walking and knowing about the bothy on Knoydart. *Address:* Oxford Instruments plc, Tubney Woods, Abingdon OX13 5QX. *T:* (01865) 393200. *Club:* Reform.

FLINT, Prof. Jonathan, FRCPsych; Michael Davys Professor of Neuroscience, University of Oxford, since 2007; Fellow of Merton College, Oxford, since 2007; *b* Sutton, 22 Jan. 1958; *s* of Michael Frederick Flint, *qv*; *m* 1980, Alison Shaw; one *s* two *d*. *Educ:* Westminster Sch.; Merton Coll., Oxford (BM BCh 1988). FRCPsych 2006. Registrar in Psychiatry, 1989–92, Sen. Registrar, 1992, Maudsley Hosp., London; University of Oxford: Wellcome Trust Career Develt Fellow, 1992–97; Wellcome Trust Sen. Fellow, 1997–2007; Wellcome Trust Principal Fellow, 2007–; Prof. of Molecular Psychiatry, 2005–07; Hon. Consultant Psychiatrist, Warneford Hosp., Oxford, 1996–. *Publications:* 200 articles in jls and contrib. to text books on the genetics of behaviour. *Recreation:* work. *Address:* Wellcome Trust Centre for Human Genetics, Roosevelt Drive, Oxford OX3 7BN. *T:* (01865) 287500, *Fax:* (01865) 287501. *E:* jf@well.ox.ac.uk.

FLINT, Jonathan; *see* Flint, D. J.

FLINT, Michael Frederick, FSA; artist printmaker; President, Orford Museum, since 2014 (Chairman, 1997–2014); *b* 7 May 1932; *s* of Frederick Nelson La Fargue Flint and Nell Dixon Smith; *m* 1st, 1954, Susan Kate Rhodes (marr. diss.) two *s* one *d*; 2nd, 1984, Phyllida Margaret Medwyn Hughes. *Educ:* St Peter's Sch., York; Kingswood Sch., Bath. Admitted Solicitor 1956; Denton Hall & Burgin, subseq. Denton Hall Burgin & Warrens, then Denton Wilde Sapte: Articled Clerk, 1951–56; Asst Solicitor, 1956–60; Partner, 1960–66 and 1972–93; Man. Partner, 1979–82; Chm., 1990–93; Consultant, 1993–2000. Paramount Pictures Corporation: Asst Vice-Pres., 1967; Vice-Pres., 1968–70; Consultant, Henry Ansbacher & Co., 1970; Chairman: London Screen Enterprises, 1970–72 (Exec. Producer, feature film, Glastonbury Fayre, 1972); Sudbourne Park Printmakers, 2003–13. Dir, Portman Entertainment Group Ltd, 1995–2001; Chm., Renaissance Films Ltd, 2002–04. Dir, and Chm. Council, 1995–99, Intellectual Property Inst. (formerly Council of Common Law Inst. of Intellectual Property; founder Mem.); Chm., Intellectual Property, Entertainment and Telecommunications Cttee, Internat. Bar Assoc., 1985–90. Vice-Pres., Brit. Archaeol Assoc., 1988–. Member: BAFTA, 1984–; British Screen Adv. Council, 1991– (Dep. Chm., 1995–); Council, Aldeburgh Music (formerly Aldeburgh Prodns), 1998–2009. Chm., Esmond House Day Care Centre, 2000–10. One-man exhibitions of etchings: Aldeburgh Cinema Gall.; Snape Maltings Concert Hall Gall.; other exhibitions: Peter Pears Gall.; Strand Gall.; Thackeray Gall.; Caroline Wiseman Prints; P-Dram Gall., Paris; Re+Art, Woodbridge. FSA 1965. *Publications:* A User's Guide to Copyright, 1979, (jtly) 6th edn 2006; (jtly) Television by Satellite: legal aspects, 1987; (jtly) Intellectual Property: the new law, 1989. *Recreations:* painting, etching, golf, opera. *Address:* Green Lane House, Castle Green, Orford, Suffolk IP12 2NF. *Clubs:* Garrick; Aldeburgh Golf; Orford Sailing.

See also J. Flint.

FLINT, Simon Coleridge R.; *see* Russell Flint.

FLÖCKINGER, Gerda, CBE 1991; designer/lecturer/photographer; *b* Innsbruck, 8 Dec. 1927; *d* of Karl Flöckinger and Anna (*née* Frankl); naturalised British citizen, 1946; *m* 1954, R. S. Houghton (marr. diss. 1962). *Educ:* Primary Sch., Innsbruck; Maidstone Girls' GS; Dorchester Co. High Sch. for Girls; S Hampstead High Sch.; St Martin's Sch. of Art; Central Sch. of Arts and Crafts. Came to England, 1938. Lectr, Hornsey Coll. of Art, 1962–68 (created New Modern Jewellery course). *Solo shows:* British Crafts Centre, London, 1968; V&A Mus., 1971 and 1986; Bristol City Art Gall. and Mus., 1971; Dartington Cider Press Gall., 1977; Crafts Council Shop at V&A, 1991; V&A, 2006; Electrum Gall., London, 2007; Boston Mus. of Fine Arts, MA, 2007–08; *numerous group shows* in UK and internationally, including: ICA, 1954–64; V&A Mus.; Arnolfini Gall., Bristol; Goldsmiths' Hall; Design Centre; Electrum Gall., London; Crafts Council, London; work in *collections:* Bristol City Mus. and Art Gall.; Crafts Council; Nottingham Castle Mus.; Royal Scottish Mus., Edinburgh; Pompidou Centre, Paris; Schmuckmuseum, Pforzheim, Germany; V&A Mus.; Goldsmiths' Co., London. Hon. Fellow, Univ. of the Arts London, 2006. Freeman, Goldsmiths' Co., 1998. *Recreations:* growing camellias, breeding Iris Germanica, pistol-shooting.

FLOOD, David Andrew; Organist and Master of the Choristers, Canterbury Cathedral, since 1988; *b* 10 Nov. 1955; *s* of Frederick Flood and June Flood (*née* Alexander); *m* 1976, Alayne Nicholas; two *s* two *d*. *Educ:* Royal Grammar School, Guildford; St John's Coll., Oxford (MA); Clare Coll., Cambridge (PGCE). FRCO(CHM). Assistant Organist, Canterbury Cathedral, 1978–86; Organist and Master of Choristers, Lincoln Cathedral, 1986–88. Vis. Prof., Canterbury Christ Ch Univ., 2012–; Vis. Fellow, St John's Coll., Durham, 2009–. Mem., Royal Soc. of Musicians, 1996–; Hon. Sen. Mem., Darwin Coll., Univ. of Kent, 1989–; Hon. Fellow, Canterbury Christ Church Univ., 2008. Hon. FGCM 2000. Hon. DMus Kent, 2002. *Recreations:* motoring, cooking, travel. *Address:* 6 The Precincts, Canterbury, Kent CT1 2EE. *T:* (01227) 865242. *E:* davidf@canterbury-cathedral.org.

FLOOD, Prof. John Lewis, PhD; FRHistS; Senior Research Fellow, University of London Institute of Modern Languages Research (formerly of Germanic Studies), since 2002 (Deputy Director, 1979–2002; Leverhulme Emeritus Research Fellow, 2002–04); Professor of German, University of London, 1993–2002, now Emeritus; *b* 22 Sept. 1938; *s* of late William Henry Flood and Ethel Mary Flood (*née* Daffern); *m* 1973, Ann Matthews, BA, MCLIP, *d* of late Edward Matthews; three *s*. *Educ:* Alderman Newton's Grammar Sch., Leicester; Univ. of Nottingham (BA 1961; MA 1963); Univ. of Munich; Univ. of Kiel; PhD London 1980. Lektor for English, Univ. of Erlangen-Nuremberg, 1963–64; Asst Lectr in German, Univ. of Nottingham, 1964–65; King's College London: Asst Lectr in German, 1965–67; Lectr, 1967–72; Sen. Lectr, 1972–79; Reader in German, Univ. of London, 1980–93. Chm., Panel for German, Dutch and Scandinavian Langs, RAEs 1996 and 2001, HEFCE; Mem., Coll. of Peer Review Assessors, AHRC (formerly AHRB), 2004–09; Peer Reviewer, European Res. Council, 2008–. Hon. Sec., Conf. of Univ. Teachers of German in GB and Ireland, 1971–92. Hon. Treas., 1984–2001, Vice-Pres., 2001–, Henry Sweet Soc. for Hist. of Linguistic Ideas; Vice-Pres., 1993–2004, Sen. Vice-Pres., 2002–04, Pres., 2004–06, Bibliographical Soc.; Member, Council: Philological Soc., 1998–2003; Viking Soc. for Northern Res., 2002–04. Adv. Ed., Oxford DNB, 2008–. Fellow, Centre for the Book, British Library, 1993–94. Corresp. Mem., Historical Commn, Börsenverein des Deutschen Buchhandels, Frankfurt am Main, 1995–. FRHistS 2002. Jacob und Wilhelm Grimm Prize, GDR, 1988. Officer's Cross, Order of Merit (FRG), 2002. *Publications:* (ed) Modern Swiss Literature, 1985; (ed) Ein Moment des erfahrenen Lebens, 1987; (ed) Mit regulu bithuungan, 1989; (ed) Kurz bevor der Vorhang fiel, 1990; (ed) Common Currency?, 1991; Die Historie von Herzog Ernst, 1992; (ed) The German Book 1450–1750, 1995; Johannes Sinapius 1505–1560, 1997; (with M. Davies) Proper Words in Proper Places: studies in lexicology and lexicography, 2001; Incunabula: German vernacular literature, 2003; Poets Laureate in the Holy Roman Empire: a bio-bibliographical handbook (4 vols), 2006; contrib. numerous essays in British, American, French, German, Italian, Hungarian and Estonian books and jls. *Recreation:* writing. *Address:* University of London School of Advanced Study, Institute of Modern Languages Research, Senate House, Malet Street, WC1E 7HU. *T:* (020) 7862 8966.

FLOOD, John Martin; Director, Weapons Systems Sector, 1991–93, Technical Director, 1993–94, Defence Research Agency; *b* 3 Oct. 1939; *s* of late Harry Flood and Rita Flood (*née* Martin); *m* 1962, Irene Edwards; one *s*. *Educ:* Merchant Taylors' School, Crosby; Leeds Univ. (BSc Physics, 1st cl.). CEng 1991; FRAeS 1991. Graduate Apprentice, English Electric, Stevenage, 1962; joined RAE, 1963; Asst Dir, Dir Air Guided Weapons and on Army Chief Scientist staff, 1978–83; joined RAE, 1983; Head, Attack Weapons and Defensive Systems Depts, RAE, 1985–89; Dep. Dir (Mission Systems), RAE, 1989–91; Technical Dir, RAE, 1991–92. Non-exec. Dir, Hunting Engrg Ltd, 1994–99. *Recreations:* bird watching, walking, theatre, reading (political biography). *Address:* Brandon, 38 Kings Road, Ilkley LS29 9AN.

FLOOD, Michael Donovan, (Mik); arts consultant, since 1997; *b* 7 May 1949; *s* of late Gp Capt. Donovan John Flood, DFC, AFC and of Vivien Ruth (*née* Alison); *m* 1st, 1975, Julie Ward (marr. diss. 1989); one *d*; 2nd, 2000, Ionela Nicolae (separated 2013). *Educ:* St George's Coll., Weybridge; Llangefni County Sch., Anglesey. Founder and Artistic Dir, Chapter Arts Centre, Cardiff, 1970–81; Develt Dir, Baltimore Theater Project, USA, 1981–82; Administrator, Pip Simmons Theatre Gp, 1982–83; Arts consultancy, 1983–85; Dir, Watermans Arts Centre, Brentford, 1985–90; Dir, ICA, 1990–97. Producer of large-scale events: Woyzeck, Cardiff, 1976; Deadwood, Kew Gdns, 1986; Offshore Rig, River Thames, 1987. Member: Film Cttee, Welsh Arts Council, 1976–80; Exec. Cttee, SE Wales Arts Assoc., 1980–81; Co-Founder, Nat. Assoc. of Arts Centres, 1976. Exec. Bd, European Forum for Arts and Heritage, 2004–08; Board of Directors: Pip Simmons Theatre Gp, 1977–83; Thames Fest., 2004–08. Pres., Informal European Theatre Meeting, 1998–2002. Mem., Ct of Govs, RCA, 1990–97. Silver Jubilee Medal, 1977. *Publications:* book reviews in nat. newspapers; contribs on arts and cultural politics to British and European periodicals. *Recreations:* sailing, ichthyology, travel. *Address:* 1 Marshall House, Dorncliffe Road, SW6 5LF. *T:* (020) 7736 8668. *E:* mik@mikflood.com.

FLOOD, Philip James, AO 1992; High Commissioner for Australia in the United Kingdom, 1998–2000; *b* 2 July 1935; *s* of Thomas and Maxine Flood; *m* 1990, Carole, *d* of Cuthbert and Nicole Henderson; two *s* one *d*. *Educ:* North Sydney Boys' High Sch.; Univ. of Sydney (BEc Hons). Australian Embassy and Mission to EC, Brussels, 1959–62; Australian Embassy and Mission to OECD, Paris, 1966–69; Asst Sec., Dept of Foreign Affairs, 1971–73; High Comr, Bangladesh, 1974–76; Minister, Washington, 1976–77; Special Trade Rep., 1977–80; First Asst Sec., Dept of Trade, 1981–84; Dep. Sec., Dept of Foreign Affairs and Trade, 1985–88; Ambassador to Indonesia, 1989–93; Director General: Australian Internat. Develt Assistance Bureau, 1993–95; Office of Nat. Assessments, 1995–96; Sec., Dept of Foreign Affairs and Trade, 1996–98. Mem., Minister's Foreign Affairs Council, 2004–07. Head: Inquiry into Immigration Detention, 2000–01; Inquiry into Australian Intelligence Agencies, 2004; Chm., Plasma Fractionation Review, 2006; Consulting Mem., Human Rights Inquiry, 2009. Vis. Fellow, ANU, 2001–06. Mem., Commonwealth War Graves Commn, 1998–2000; Trustee, Imperial War Mus., 1998–2000. Mem., 1996–2004, Chm., 2001–04, Australia Indonesia Inst.; Dir, 2004–05, Dep. Chm., 2006–09, Asialink. Dir and Dep. Chm., CARE Australia, 2003–11, FIPAA; FAIIA. Order of Merit (Indonesia), 1993. *Publications:* Odyssey by the Sea, 2005; Dancing with Warriors: a diplomatic memoir, 2011. *Recreations:* reading, theatre, walking, swimming. *Address:* 96 Jervois Street, Deakin, ACT 2600, Australia. *Club:* Commonwealth (Canberra).

FLOOD, Thomas Oliver, CBE 2004; Chief Executive, Conservation Volunteers (formerly British Trust for Conservation Volunteers), 2001–12 (Marketing Director, 1986–2001); *b* 21 May 1947; *s* of Thomas Joseph Flood and Elizabeth Gerard Flood (*née* Byrne); adopted British citizenship, 1999; civil partnership 2006, Paul Cornes. *Educ:* University Coll., Dublin (BA Eng, Metaphysics and Politics). Mkt res., W. S. Atkins Ltd, 1970–72; sales and mktg, 3M UK plc, 1972–86. Chm., Red Admiral Aids Charity, 1994–99. Member: Treasury Adv. Gp on Third Sector, 2008; Ministerial Taskforce on Climate Change, Envmt and Sustainable Develt, 2009–10; Partnership Bd, DCLG, 2011–12; Department for Environment, Food and Rural Affairs: Mem., Third Sector Adv. Bd, 2009–; Co-Chair, Civil Soc. Adv. Bd, 2009–14; Chairman: Water Sector Innovation Leadership Gp, 2013–15; DEFRA Civil Society Partnership Network, 2014–; Dir, UK Water Partnership, 2015–. Mem. Bd, Acevo, 2008–11 and 2011–12 (Chm., Special Interest Gp on Sustainable Develt, 2009–11); Chm., Acevo Solutions Ltd, 2011–; Ind. non-exec. Dir, EST Hldgs Ltd, 2015–. Mem. Cttee, Queen's Awards for Voluntary Service, 2013–. Patron, Charity Leaders' Exchange—Knowledge Peers, 2011–. Trustee, Energy Saving Trust, 2012– (Mem., Audit Cttee, 2013–); Trustee and Chm., Energy Saving Trust Foundn, 2015–; Mem. Council, NT, 2012–; Ambassador, FoodCycle, 2012–13. Vice Pres., CPRE, 2012–. FRSA 1995; CCMI 2010 (FCMI 1995). *Recreations:* walking, cooking, opera, cinema, reading my Kindle, growing fruit and vegetables. *Address:* Flat 18, 6 Pear Tree Court, EC1R 0DW. *T:* 07711 262198. *E:* tomnflood@hotmail.co.uk.

FLOOK, Adrian John; Consultant, CTF Corporate & Financial Communications, since 2013; *b* 9 July 1963; *s* of late John Harold Julian Flook and late Rosemary Ann Flook (*née* Richardson); *m* 2003, Frangelica O'Shea; one *d*. *Educ:* King Edward's Sch., Bath; Mansfield Coll., Oxford (MA Hons Mod. Hist.). Stockbroker, Warburg Securities, and others, 1985–98; Financial Dynamics (business communications consultancy), 1998–2003. MP (C) Taunton, 2001–05; contested (C) same seat, 2005. Consultant, M:Communications, 2005–13. *Address:* 37 Simpson Street, SW11 3HW.

FLORENCE, Prof. Alexander Taylor, CBE 1994; PhD, DSc; FRSE; FRPharmS, FRSC; Dean, School of Pharmacy, University of London, 1989–2006; *b* 9 Sept. 1940; *s* of late Alexander Charles Gerrard Florence and Margaret Florence; *m* 1st, 1964, Elizabeth Catherine McRae (marr. diss. 1995); two *s* one *d*; 2nd, 2000, Dr Florence Madsen, *d* of Bernard Madsen, Paris. *Educ:* Royal Coll. of Science and Technology, Glasgow and Univ. of Glasgow (BSc

Hons 1962; PhD 1965); DSc Strathclyde, 1984. FRSC 1977; FRPharmS 1987. University of Strathclyde: MRC Jun. Res. Fellow, 1965–66; Lectr in Pharmaceutical Chemistry, 1966–72; Sen. Lectr in Pharm. Chem., 1972–76; J. P. Todd Prof. of Pharmacy, 1976–88. Member: Cttee on Safety of Medicines, 1983–98 (Mem., Sub-cttee on Chemistry, Pharmacy and Standards of Cttee on Safety of Medicines, 1972–98); Nuffield Inquiry into Pharmacy, 1984–86. Pres., Eur. Assoc. of Faculties of Pharmacy, 1997–2001; Vice Pres., Internat. Pharmaceutical Fedn, 1998–2000 (Høst-Madsen Medal, 1996); Pres., Controlled Release Soc., 2002–03 (Vice Pres., 2001–02). Co-Editor in Chief, Jl of Drug Targeting, 1993–97; Ed.-in-Chief, Internat. Jl of Pharmaceutics, 2008– (Ed.-in-Chief (Europe), 1997–2008). FRSE 1987; FRSA 1989. DUniv: Hoshi, Tokyo, 2003; Strathclyde, 2004; Danish Univ. of Pharmaceutical Scis, 2006; Hon. ScD UEA, 2007; Hon. DSc London, 2009. British Pharmaceutical Conf. Science Award, 1972; Harrison Meml Medal, Royal Pharmaceutical Soc., 1986; Scheele Prize, Swedish Acad. of Pharmaceutical Scis, 1993; GlaxoSmithKline Internat. Achievement Award, 2001; Maurice-Marie Janot Award, Assoc. de Pharmacie Galénique Industrielle, France, 2006; Higuchi Prize, Acad. of Pharmaceutical Sci. and Technol., Japan, 2006; Founder's Award, Controlled Release Soc., 2009. *Publications:* Solubilization by Surface Active Agents, 1968; Physicochemical Principles of Pharmacy, 1981, 6th edn 2015; Surfactant Systems, 1983; (ed) Materials Used in Pharmaceutical Formulation, 1985; (ed) Formulation Factors in Adverse Reactions, 1990; (ed jtly) Liposomes in Drug Delivery, 1992; (ed jtly) Modern Pharmaceutics, 2009; Introduction to Clinical Pharmaceutics, 2010; pubns on drug delivery and targeting, surfactants, dendrimers and nanotechnology. *Recreations:* music, writing, painting. *Address:* 18 Marine Parade, City Quay, Dundee DD1 3BN. *T:* (01382) 200135; La Providence, 7G rue Sincaire, 06300, Nice, France. *T:* 493130397.

FLORENCE, Peter Kenrick, MBE 2005; Founder and Director, Hay Festival, since 1988; *b* 4 Oct. 1964; *s* of late Norman Samuel Florence and of Rhoda Lewis; *m* 1996, Becky Shaw; four *s*. *Educ:* Ipswich Sch.; Jesus Coll., Cambridge (BA Hons Mod. and Medieval Langs 1987, MA); Université Paris-Sorbonne (Paris IV). Designer: Festivaletteratura, Mantova, 1996; The Word, London, 1999; Festa Literária Internacional de Paraty (FLIP), Brazil, 2002; Beirut 39, Lebanon, 2010; Hay Festivals: Cartagena, Colombia, 2005; Segovia, Spain, 2006; Alhambra, Spain, 2008; Storymoja, Kenya, 2009; Belfast, 2009; Zacatecas, Mexico, 2010; Kerala, India, 2010; Xalapa, Mexico, 2011; Merthyr Rock, Wales, 2011; Beirut, Lebanon, 2011; Dhaka, Bangladesh, 2011; Budapest, Hungary, 2012; Kells, Ireland, 2013. Fellow: Hereford Art Coll., 2008; RWCMD, 2010; Hon. Fellow: Cardiff Univ., 2013; Bangor Univ., 2013. Gov., Fairfield High Sch., Herefords. Hon. DLitt: Glamorgan, 2004; Open, 2010. Colombiano de Corazón, 2010. *Publications:* OxTales, 2009; (ed jtly) OxTravels, 2011; OxCrimes, 2014. *Recreations:* walking, food, family. *Address:* Hay Festival, 25 Lion Street, Hay HR3 5AD. *E:* peter@hayfestival.org. *Clubs:* Groucho; Hawks (Cambridge).

FLOREY, Prof. Charles du Vé; Professor of Public Health Medicine (formerly Community Medicine), University of Dundee, 1983–99; *b* 11 Sept. 1934; *s* of Howard Walter Florey and Mary Ethel Florey; *m* 1966, Susan Jill Hopkins; one *s* one *d*. *Educ:* Univ. of Cambridge (MD); Yale Univ. (MPH). FFCM 1977; FRCPE 1986. Instructor, 1965, Asst Prof., 1966–69, Yale Univ. School of Medicine; Mem. Scientific Staff, MRC, Jamaica, 1969–71; St Thomas's Hospital Medical School, London: Sen. Lectr, 1971–78; Reader, 1978–81; Prof., 1981–83. Pres., Internat. Epidemiol Assoc., 1999–2002. *Publications:* (with S. R. Leeder) Methods for Cohort Studies of Chronic Airflow Limitation, 1982; (jtly) Introduction to Community Medicine, 1983; A European Concerted Action: maternal alcohol consumption and its relation to the outcome of pregnancy and child development at eighteen months, 1992; (ed) Epilex: a multilingual lexicon of epidemiological terms, 1993; (jtly) The Audit Handbook: improving health through clinical audit, 1993; (jtly) The Pocket Guide to Grant Applications, 1998. *Recreations:* photography, sailing, walking, computing. *Address:* 76 Alton Road, Poole, Dorset BH14 8SS.

FLÓREZ, Juan Diego; tenor; *b* Lima, Peru, 13 Jan. 1973; *s* of Ruben Flórez and Maria Teresa Flórez (*née* Salom, later French); *m* 2007, Julia Trappe; one *s* one *d*. *Educ:* Conservatory of Lima; Curtis Inst., Philadelphia. Début in Matilde di Shabran, Rossini Opera Fest., 1996; has performed at: La Scala, Milan; Comunale of Florence; Rossini Opera Fest., Pesaro; Opera of Rome; Metropolitan Opera, NY; Staatsoper, Vienna; San Francisco Opera; Royal Opera Hse, Covent Gdn; Bayerische Staatsoper, Munich; Gran Teatre del Liceu, Barcelona; Paris Opera; Lyric Opera, Chicago; Deutsche Oper, Berlin. UNESCO Goodwill Ambassador, 2012. Kammersänger, Austria, 2012. Abbiati Prize, Rossini d'Oro, Pesaro. Gran Cruz, Orden del Sol (Peru). *Address:* c/o Ernesto Palacio, Inart Management, Via San Gregorio 53, 20124 Milan, Italy. *E:* palacio@inartmanagement.com.

FLORMAN, (Carl Alan) Mark; Chairman and Chief Executive, Time Partners Ltd, since 2013; Chairman, Centre for Social Justice, since 2010; *b* London, 2 Nov. 1958; *s* of late Charles Florman and Madeleine Florman; *m* 1987, Alexia Anninos; three *d*. *Educ:* Harrow Sch.; London Sch. of Econs and Pol Sci. (BSc Econs of Industry and Trade 1981). Vice Pres., Northern Trust Co., 1981–85; Dir, Capital Mkts, County NatWest, 1985–87; Partner, Enskilda Securities, 1988–91; Founder and CEO, Maizels Westerberg, 1991–2000; Man. Dir, Doughty Hanson & Co., 2001–08. Chairman: LM Glasfiber, 2003–06; Spayne Lindsay, 2009–; Vice Chm., 8 Miles LLP, 2010–. CEO, BVCA, 2011–13. Dir, Swedish Chamber of Commerce, 2006–. Sen. Advr, MCF Corporate Finance, 2013–; Hon. Pres., B Lab UK, 2015–. Trustee: BBC Trust, 2015–; Foundn for Future London, 2015–; Commonwealth Educn Trust, 2015–; Dir, Africa Enterprise Challenge Fund; Mem. Adv. Cttee, Palaeontological Scientific Trust; Ambassador, Royal Albert Hall, 2004–. *Publications:* The Florman Guide to Europe's Best Restaurants, 2001. *Recreations:* inspecting my schools in Africa, politics, fast ski-ing, lunch in Courchevel, painting. *Address:* Time Partners Ltd, 24 Thurloe Square, SW7 2SD. *T:* 07767 420491. *E:* mark@florman.co.uk.

FLOUD, Sir Roderick (Castle), Kt 2005; FBA 2002; Provost, Gresham College, London, 2008–14 (Member of Council, 1998–2014); Vice-Chancellor, 2002–04, President, 2004–06, now President Emeritus, London Metropolitan University; *b* 1 April 1942; *s* of late Bernard Francis Castle Floud, MP and Ailsa (*née* Craig); *m* 1964, Cynthia Anne (*née* Smith); two *d*. *Educ:* Brentwood Sch.; Wadham Coll., Oxford (MA; Hon. Fellow, 1999); Nuffield Coll., Oxford (DPhil 1970). Asst Lectr in Economic History, UCL, 1966–69; Lectr in Economic History, Univ. of Cambridge and Fellow of Emmanuel Coll., Cambridge, 1969–75 (Hon. Fellow, 2003); Prof. of Modern History, Birkbeck Coll., Univ. of London, 1975–88; Provost, City of London Poly., subseq. London Guildhall Univ., 1998–2002; Acting Dean, Sch. of Advanced Study, Univ. of London, 2007–09. Vis. Prof. of European History and of Economics, Stanford Univ., Calif, 1980–81. Associate Mem., Nuffield Coll., Oxford, 2007–. Research Associate, Nat. Bureau of Economic Research, USA, 1978–; Research Programme Dir, Centre for Economic Policy Research, 1983–88. Member: Council: ESRC, 1993–97; UUK (formerly CVCP), 1997–2005 (Pres., 2001–03); Convenor, London Higher Educn Consortium, 1999–2001; Mem. Bd, European Univ. Assoc., 2001–07 (Vice-Pres., 2005–07). Chair, Sci. Rev. Gp (formerly Standing Cttee) for Social Scis, Eur. Sci. Foundn, 2007–. Mem., Lord Chancellor's Adv. Council on Public Records, 1978–84. Mem. Bd, London Develt Partnership, 1998–2001; Observer, London Develt Agency, 2001–06. Mem., Tower Hamlets Coll. Corp., 1997–2001. Trustee, Samaritans, 2006–08. Treas., Oxford Union Soc., 1966. Freeman: City of London, 1995; Information Technologists' Co., 1996 (Liveryman, 2005); Co. (formerly Guild) of Educators, 2000 (Master, 2005–06). MAE 2012. FCGI 2001. FAcSS (AcSS 2001). Hon. Fellow, Birkbeck Coll., 1994; Centenary Fellow, Historical Assoc., 2006. Hon. DLitt: City, 1999; Westminster, 2006. *Publications:* An Introduction to Quantitative Methods for Historians, 1973, 2nd edn 1980; (ed) Essays in Quantitative Economic History, 1974; The British Machine Tool Industry 1850–1914, 1976; (ed) The Economic History of Britain since 1700, 1981, 2nd edn 1994; (ed) The Power of the Past, 1984; (jtly) Height, Health and History, 1990; The People and the British Economy 1830–1914, 1997; (ed) Health and Welfare during Industrialisation, 1997; (ed) London Higher, 1998; (ed) The Cambridge Economic History of Modern Britain, 2004, 2nd edn 2014; (jtly) The Changing Body, 2011; articles in Economic History Review, Social Science History, etc. *Recreations:* family, walking, music. *Address:* 15 Flint Street, Haddenham, Bucks HP17 8AL. *T:* (01844) 291086. *Club:* Athenæum.

FLOWER, family name of **Viscount Ashbrook**.

FLOWER, Antony John Frank, (Tony), MA, PhD; Senior Fellow, The Young Foundation, since 2007 (Founding Chairman, 2005–07); *b* 2 Feb. 1951; *s* of late Frank Robert Edward Flower and Dorothy Elizabeth (*née* Williams). *Educ:* Chipping Sodbury Grammar Sch.; Univ. of Exeter (BA Hons Philosophy and Sociology; MA Sociology); Univ. of Leicester (PhD Mass Communications). Graphic Designer, 1973–76; Co-founder with Lord Young of Dartington, and first Gen. Sec., Tawney Soc., 1982–88; Dir, Res. Inst. for Econ. and Social Affairs, 1982–92. Co-ordinator, Argo Venture (Nat. Space Mus.), 1984–2002, Dir, Argo Trust, 1986–95; Director: Healthline Health Inf. Service, 1986–88; Health Information Trust, 1987–88 (Trustee, 1988–90); Environmental Concern Centre in Europe, 1990–92; Institute of Community Studies: Trustee, 1993–2005; Dep. Dir, 1994–96; Sen. Fellow, 1996–2001; Acting Dir, 2001; Chm., 2001–05; Dep. Dir, 1994–96, Chm., 2001–04, Mutual Aid Centre (Trustee, 1990–2004). Chm., ContinYou, 2003–05. Mem. Adv. Bd, The Earth Centre, 1990–2000; Sec., Ecological Studies Inst., 1990–92. Associate: Redesign Ltd, 1989–92; Nicholas Lacey & Partners (Architects), 1989–2005; Consultant: CIRIA, 1992–96; Rocklabs Geochemical Analysis CC, 1993–2005; Cambridge Female Educn Trust, 1999–2005. Co-ordinator, Campaign for Educnl Choice, 1988–89. Trustee: Gaia, 1988–2001; Educn Extra, 1995–2004 (Chm. of Trustees, 2001–03); Consultant, Joseph Rowntree Reform Trust Ltd, 1993–2003; Co-founder and Patron, Tower Hamlets Summer Univ. Trust, 1995–2005; Patron, Nat. Space Centre, 1996–. Mem., Council for Social Democracy, 1982–84; Dir of Develt, Green Alliance, 1991–92. Associate: Open Coll. of the Arts, 1988–2002; Inst. for Public Policy Res., 1989–95; Family Covenant Assoc., 1994–2000. Editor, Tawney Journal, 1982–88; Co-founder and Man. Editor, Samizdat Magazine, 1988–90. FRSA 1991. *Publications:* (with Graham Mort) Starting to Write: a course in creative writing, 1990; (ed with Ben Pimlott and Anthony Wright) The Alternative, 1990; (ed jtly) Young at Eighty: the prolific public life of Michael Young, 1995; Trusting in Change: a history of the Joseph Rowntree Reform Trust, 2004. *Recreations:* collecting junk, sailing, making and restoring musical instruments, attempting to write poetry. *Address:* c/o 18 Victoria Park Square, E2 9PF.

FLOWER, Gwynneth Gabrielle, CEng, FIET; Chairman, Werneth Enterprises, since 2001; *b* Chester, 29 June 1938; *d* of William Denis Flower and Gertrude Molly Flower (*née* Jacob). *Educ:* Royal Masonic Sch.; King's Coll. London (BSc Eng. Hons); Cranfield Univ. (MBA). CEng 1967; FIET (FIEE 1968). Served Army, 1965–80. Mktg Manager, Scicon Consultancy (BP), 1980–82; Commercial Dir, Plessey Electronics, 1982–85; Dir, Sales and Mktg, GEC Marconi, 1986–90; Chief Exec., Central London Training and Enterprise Council, 1990–97; Man. Dir, Action 2000, 1998–2000; Chairman: CMB Technologies, 2000–03; UK Transplant SHA, 2003–05. Dir, 2 Change, 2003–10; Nat. Meteorological Prog., Met Office, 2004–07. Non-executive Director: Ordnance Survey, 1997–2002; European Tech. Mktg Services, 2000–03; Army Base Repair Orgn, 2001–03. Hon. Treas., Royal Instn of GB, 2006–09 (Mem., 1998–). Mem., Forum UK, Internat. Women's Forum, 1995–. Liveryman: Engrs' Co., 2000–; Clockmakers' Co., 2010–. Chm., Govs, Our Lady of Victories Primary Sch., Kensington, 1996–; Vice Chm., Kensington and Chelsea FE Coll., 1997–2003. *Recreations:* arts, antique clocks, Victorian London, gardening, sailing, ski-ing. *Address:* Royal Institution of Great Britain, 21 Albemarle Street, W1S 4BS. *T:* (020) 7409 2992. *E:* gwynneth.flower@btinternet.com. *Club:* Defence Technology.

FLOWER, Robert Philip; HM Diplomatic Service, retired; Counsellor, Foreign and Commonwealth Office, 1994–96; *b* 12 May 1939; *s* of Philip Edward Flower and Dorothy Agnes Elizabeth (*née* Beukers); *m* 1964, Anne Daveen Tweddle (marr. diss. 2011); two *s*. *Educ:* Christ's Hosp.; Magdalene Coll., Cambridge (BA). Called to the Bar, Middle Temple, 1964. FCO, 1967–96; served in Malawi, Malaysia, UK Delegn to NATO, Bonn and London; Dep. Head of Mission, The Hague, 1990–93. *Recreations:* fell-walking, reading, music.

FLOWER, Prof. Roderick John, PhD, DSc; FMedSci; FRS 2003; FBPhS; Professor of Biochemical Pharmacology, and Joint Head, Department of Biochemical Pharmacology, William Harvey Research Institute, Barts and the London, Queen Mary's School of Medicine and Dentistry (formerly St Bartholomew's and the Royal London School of Medicine and Dentistry, Queen Mary and Westfield College), London, since 1994; *b* 29 Nov. 1945; *s* of Lesley Ralph Flower and Audrey Ellen Eckett; *m* 1994, Lindsay Joyce Riddell. *Educ:* Univ. of Sheffield (BSc 1st class Hons Physiol. 1971); PhD 1974, DSc 1985, London. Wellcome Res. Labs, Beckenham, 1973–84, Sen. Scientist, 1975–84; University of Bath: Prof. of Pharmacol., 1984–89; Hd, Sch. of Pharmacy and Pharmacol., 1987–89; Medical College of St Bartholomew's Hospital, London, then St Bartholomew's and Royal London Sch. of Medicine and Dentistry, QMW: Lilly Prof. of Biochem. Pharmacol., 1989–94; pt-time Actg Hd of Clinical Pharmacol., 1993–96; William Harvey Research Institute: a Dir and founding Mem., 1989–; Head of Inst., 1998–2002; Wellcome Trust Principal Res. Fellow, 1994–2007; a Dir and founding Mem., William Harvey Res. Ltd, 1989–. Pres., British Pharmacological Soc., 2000–01 (Fellow, 2005). Hon. Fellow, Sch. of Pharmacy, 2008. Hon. LLD Bath, 2011. *Publications:* (ed with N. J. Goulding) Glucocorticoids, 2001; (ed jtly) Rang & Dale's Pharmacology, 8th edn 2014; 320 peer reviewed articles and over 200 other publications incl. reviews, book chapters, abstracts, conf. procs, editorials and pubd correspondence. *Recreations:* the camera, history of science, travel. *Address:* Department of Biochemical Pharmacology, William Harvey Research Institute, Barts and the London School of Medicine, Charterhouse Square, EC1M 6BQ. *T:* (020) 7882 8781, *Fax:* (020) 7882 6076. *E:* r.j.flower@qmul.ac.uk.

FLOWERDEW, Robert John; horticultural consultant, since 1986; *b* Yaxley, Suffolk, 30 April 1953; *s* of Richard Flowerdew and late Pamela Flowerdew; *m* 2002, Vonnetta Angeleta Crossman; one *s* one *d* (twins). *Educ:* Hatfield Poly. (BA Hons Business Studies). Panellist, Gardeners' Question Time, BBC Radio 4, 1993–; presenter, Gardeners' World, BBC TV, 1995–97. Mem., 1983–, Ambassador, 2006–, Henry Doubleday Res. Assoc. (Garden Organic); Life Mem., Soil Assoc., 1989–; Pres., Norfolk Organic Gp (formerly Norfolk Organic Gardeners), 1996– (Mem., 1982–); Patron: NWA1 Rethink Rubbish campaign, 2002–; Send a Cow to Africa, 2007–; Dig It, 2007–; Cuddalore Health and Agriculture Trust India, 2008–; Paxton Horticl Soc., 2009–; Champion for: Millennium Greens, 1998–; Woodland Trust, 1999–. *Publications:* (jtly) The Complete Manual of Organic Gardening, 1992; The Organic Gardener, 1993; Bob Flowerdew's Organic Garden, 1993; The Complete Book of Companion Gardening, 1993; Complete Fruit Book, 1995; Organic Bible, 1998; (jtly) Gardeners' Question Time All Your Gardening Problems Solved, 2000; Go Organic, 2002; The No-Work Garden, 2002; (jtly) The Complete Book of Vegetables, Herbs and Fruit, 2002; (jtly) Gardeners' Question Time Plant Chooser, 2003; (jtly) Gardeners' Question Time Tips and Techniques, 2005; The Gourmet Gardener, 2005; Organic Garden Basics, 2007; Going Organic, 2007; Grow Your Own, Eat Your Own, 2008; Simple Green Pest and Disease Control, 2010; Composting, 2010; Pruning, Training and Tidying, 2010; Companion Planting, 2010; Weeding Without Chemicals, 2010; Re-cycle and Re-use Stuff in Your

Garden, 2014; contrib. Amateur Gardening, Kitchen Garden Mag., BBC Gardeners' World mag. *Recreations:* gardening!, scented plants, good food, cats, beautiful women, conversation, reading, etymology, inventing, outrageous ideas, public speaking, scuba diving, whingeing on about the state of things. *E:* bob@bobflowerdew.com. *W:* bobflowerdew.com.

FLOWERS, Angela Mary; Chairman, Angela Flowers Gallery Ltd, since 1989; *b* 19 Dec. 1932; *d* of Charles Geoffrey Holland and Olive Alexandra Holland (*née* Stiby); *m* 1st, 1952, Adrian Flowers (marr. diss. 1973); three *s* one *d*; 2nd, 2003, Robert Heller (partner, 1973–2003; *d* 2012); one *d*. *Educ:* Westonbirt Sch., Glos; Wychwood Sch., Oxford; Webber Douglas Sch. of Singing and Dramatic Art. Posts in stage, film and advertising, until 1967; founded Angela Flowers Gallery, 1970: Lisle St, 1970–71; Portland Mews, 1971–78; Tottenham Mews, 1978–88; Richmond Rd, 1988–2001; Kingsland Rd, 2001–. Mem. Bd, Nat. Youth Jazz Orch., 1988–93. Trustee, John Kobal Foundn, 1992–97. Sen. Fellow, RCA, 1994. Hon. DArt, E London, 1999. *Recreations:* piano, singing, trombone, cooking, jazz, collecting contemporary art. *Address:* Flowers East, 82 Kingsland Road, E2 8DP. *T:* (020) 7920 7777, *Fax:* (020) 7920 7770. *E:* angelaflowers1932@gmail.com.

FLOWERS, Michael James; Chief Executive Officer, Chemring Group plc, since 2014; *b* Melbourne, 2 Aug. 1961; *s* of Allan James Flowers and Margaret Mary Flowers; *m* 1990, Linda McCauley; two *d*. *Educ:* Christian Brothers' Coll., St Kilda, Melbourne; Univ. of New South Wales (Bachelor Mech. Engrg); Australian Army Comd and Staff Coll.; Royal Mil. Coll. of Sci.; Univ. of Queensland (MBA). Australian Army, 1979–2001; Prog. Manager, BAE Systems Australia, 2001–06; Man. Dir, Chemring Australia, 2006–13; Gp Dir Munitions, Chemring Gp plc, 2013–14. *Recreations:* travel, cricket, Australia football, art and its history, wine. *Address:* Chemring Group plc, Roke Manor, Old Salisbury Lane, Romsey, Hants SO51 0ZN. *T:* (01794) 833901.

FLOYD, Rt Hon. Sir Christopher (David), Kt 2007; PC 2013; **Rt Hon. Lord Justice Floyd;** a Lord Justice of Appeal, since 2013; *b* 20 Dec. 1951; *s* of David and Hana Floyd; *m* 1974, Rosalind Jane Arscott; one *s* two *d*. *Educ:* Westminster Sch.; Trinity Coll., Cambridge (MA Nat. Scis and Law). Called to the Bar, Inner Temple, 1975, Bencher, 2001; called to the Bar of Republic of Ireland, 1988. QC 1992; Asst Recorder, 1994–2000; a Dep. High Court Judge (Patents Court), 1998–2007; Recorder, 2000–07; a Judge of the High Ct of Justice, Chancery Div., 2007–13; Judge i/c, Patents Court, 2011–13. Dep. Chm., Copyright Tribunal, 1995–2007; Chm., Competition Appeal Tribunal, 2007–. Chm., QC's Complaints Cttee, 2013–; Member: Bar Council Chm.'s Arbitration/Conciliation Panel, 1996–2007; Bar Council Professional Conduct and Complaints Cttee, 1998–2002; Bar Council, 2000–04; Bar Council European Cttee, 2003–04; Litigation Accreditation Bd Appeal Panel, Chartered Inst. Patent Attorneys, 2005–07; Enlarged Bd of Appeal, European Patent Office, 2011–; Chm., Intellectual Property Bar Assoc., 1999–2004. Chm., Perm. Exhibn of Legal Costume, 2009–. Trustee, Rolls Bldg Art and Educnl Trust, 2011–. *Recreations:* Austin Sevens, cricket, ski-ing, walking. *Address:* Royal Courts of Justice, Strand, WC2A 2LL. *Club:* Garrick.

FLOYD, Sir Giles (Henry Charles), 7th Bt *cr* 1816; Director, Burghley Estate Farms, since 1958; *b* 27 Feb. 1932; *s* of Sir John Duckett Floyd, 6th Bt, TD, and Jocelin Evadne (*d* 1976), *d* of late Sir Edmund Wyldbore Smith; *S* father, 1975; *m* 1st, 1954, Lady Gillian Moyra Katherine Cecil (marr. diss. 1978), 2nd *d* of 6th Marquess of Exeter, KCMG; one *s* (and one *s* decd); 2nd, 1985, Judy Sophia Lane, *er d* of late W. L. Tregoning, CBE, and D. M. E. Tregoning. *Educ:* Eton College. High Sheriff of Rutland, 1968. *Heir: er s* David Henry Cecil Floyd [*b* 2 April 1956; *m* 1981, Caroline, *d* of John Beckly, Manor Farm, Bowerchalke, Salisbury, Wilts; two *d*]. *Address:* Tinwell Manor, Stamford, Lincs PE9 3UF. *T:* (01780) 762676. *Club:* Turf.

FLUCK, Nicholas Peter; Partner, Stapleton & Son, Solicitors, Stamford, since 1984; President, Law Society of England and Wales, 2013–14; *b* 11 Dec. 1956; *s* of Canon Peter Ernest Fluck and Jane Maureen Fluck (*née* Snaddon); *m* 1993, Dr Susan Ruth Wheatley; one *d* (and one *d* decd). *Educ:* Huddersfield Poly. (BA Hons Humanities 1979); Leeds Poly. (CPE 1981; Law Soc. Finals 1982). Admitted as solicitor, 1984. Dep. Vice-Pres., 2011–12, Vice-Pres., 2012–13, Law Soc. of England and Wales. DUniv Huddersfield, 2014. *Publications:* articles in legal press and online on gen. legal issues and land law matters. *Recreations:* reading, playing piano and church organ, listening to music, spending time with my family. *Address:* 16 Mayfair Gardens, Boston PE21 9NZ. *T:* 07836 792187. *E:* nick@fluck.org.

FLUCK, Peter Nigel; freelance artist; sculptor of abstract kinetics, since 1994; founded (with Roger Law) Spitting Image, 1982; *b* 7 April 1941; *s* of Herbert William Fluck and Ada Margaret (*née* Hughes); *m* 1963, Anne-Cécile de Bruyne; one *d* one *s*. *Educ:* Cambs High Sch. for Boys; Cambridge Sch. of Art. Artist-reporter, illustrator, 1961–70; cartoonist and caricaturist, 1970–82; Luck & Flaw (with Roger Law), 1974–82; Spitting Image (18 TV series), 1982–94. Exhibitions: Chaotic Constructions (with Tony Myatt) Tate Gall., St Ives and Edin. Fest., 1997, (expanded) RIBA, 1999, Study Gall., Poole, 2004; Yew Tree Gall., Cornwall, 2004; exhibn of mobiles, Kestle Barton Gall., Cornwall, 2011. *Recreations:* fly fishing, ceramics, print-making. *Address:* White Feather, Cadgwith, Cornwall TR12 7LB. *T:* (01326) 290546.

FLUGGE, Klaus; Founder, Publisher and Managing Director, Andersen Press Ltd, since 1976; *b* 29 Nov. 1934; *s* of Werner and Emmi Flügge; *m* 1964, Joëlle Dansac; one *s*. *Educ:* German Book Trade Sch., Leipzig (Dip.). Asst to Pres., Abelard-Schuman, NY, 1959–61; Man. Dir, Abelard-Schuman Ltd, 1963–76. Eleanor Farjeon Award for distinguished services to children's books, 1999. *Recreations:* book collecting, jazz, swimming. *Address:* c/o Andersen Press Ltd, 20 Vauxhall Bridge Road, SW1V 2SA. *T:* (020) 7840 8701. *Club:* Groucho.

FLYNN, Douglas Ronald; Chairman, Konekt Ltd, since 2012; *b* 8 June 1949; *s* of Ronald Norman Flynn and Rhona Ellen Flynn; *m* 1975, Lynne Cecily Harcombe; two *s*. *Educ:* Newcastle Boys' High Sch., Australia; Univ. of Newcastle, Australia (BEng Hons 1972); MBA Melbourne Univ. 1979. Australian Sales Manager, ICI Australia, Melbourne, 1975–80; Gen. Manager, ICI Explosives, Hong Kong, 1980–82; Regl Manager, Perth, 1982–85, Manager Strategic Planning, Melbourne, 1985–86, ICI Australia Ltd; Deloitte Haskins & Sells, 1986–87; Chief Exec., Hobart, Davies Bros Ltd, 1987–90; Man. Dir, News Ltd Suburban Newspapers, Sydney, 1990–94; Dep. Man. Dir, News Internat. Newspapers, London, 1994–95; Man. Dir, News Internat. plc, 1995–99; Chief Executive Officer: Aegis Gp, 1999–2005; Rentokil Initial plc, 2005–08. Non-exec. Dir, Seven West Media (formerly West Australian Newspapers) Ltd, 2008–. *Recreation:* sailing. *Clubs:* Tasmanian (Hobart); Royal Corinthian Yacht, Royal Hong Kong Yacht, Royal Sydney Yacht Squadron.

FLYNN, Sister Ellen Teresa, DSL; Sister of Charity of St Vincent de Paul; Chairman, The Passage, since 2009 (Chief Executive Officer, 2000–09); *b* Nairobi, 15 Feb. 1953; *d* of Daniel Flynn and Doris Flynn. *Educ:* St Mary's Sch., Hereford; Christ's Coll., Liverpool (BEd 1989; Dip Mgt Studies 2001). DSL 1989. Teaching, 1981–88; liturgy and music consultant, 1989–99. Provincial Councillor, British Province, Sisters of Charity of St Vincent de Paul, 2009–. Hon. Fellow, St Margaret's Univ. Coll., Twickenham, 2009. *Recreation:* music (grade 6 piano, grade 8 singing, Associated Bd RSM).

FLYNN, James Edward; QC 2003; barrister; *b* 21 June 1956; *s* of late Ronald Joseph Flynn and of Margaret Rose Flynn (*née* Crossland, now Harris); *m* 1st, 1983, Catherine Clare Gibson (marr. diss. 2008); one *s* one *d*; 2nd, 2013, Anna Margaret Morfey. *Educ:* Loughborough Grammar Sch.; Brasenose Coll., Oxford (BA Jurisprudence 1977; MA 2012). Called to the Bar, Middle Temple, 1978; admitted solicitor, 1984; with Linklaters & Paines, London and Brussels, 1982–86 and 1989–96; Legal Sec., European Court of Justice, 1986–89; Partner, Linklaters & Paines, Brussels, 1993–96; in practice as a barrister, London and Brussels, 1996–. Chm., Competition Law Assoc., 2009–; UK Mem., CCBE Perm. Delegn to European Cts. *Publications:* (jtly) Competition: understanding the 1998 Act, 1999; (jtly) The Law of State Aid in the EU, 2003; articles in jls and poems in literary reviews. *Recreations:* poetry, singing, music. *Address:* Brick Court Chambers, 7–8 Essex Street, WC2R 3LD. *T:* (020) 7379 3550. *E:* james.flynn@brickcourt.co.uk.

FLYNN, John Gerrard, CMG 1992; HM Diplomatic Service, retired; Ambassador to Venezuela, and concurrently (non-resident) to the Dominican Republic, 1993–97; *b* 23 April 1937; *s* of late Thomas Flynn and Mary Chisholm; *m* 1973, Drina Anne Coates (*d* 2015); one *s* one *d*. *Educ:* Glasgow Univ. (MA). Foreign Office, 1965; Second Sec., Lusaka, 1966; First Sec., FCO, 1968; seconded to Canning House as Asst Dir-Gen., 1970; First Sec. (Commercial) and Consul, Montevideo, 1971; Rhodesia Dept, FCO, 1976; Chargé d'Affaires, Luanda, 1978; Political Counsellor and Consul-Gen., Brasilia, 1979; Econ. Counsellor and Dir of Trade, Madrid, 1982; High Comr, Swaziland, 1987; Ambassador to Angola and (non-resident) to São Tomé and Príncipe, 1990–93. British Special Rep. for Sierra Leone, 1998. Pol Advr, Chevron, 1997–; Consultant, De La Rue, 2002–08. Chairman: Anglo Latin American Foundn, 1998–2003; Anglo-Venezuelan Soc., 1999–2005; British Venezuelan Chamber of Commerce, 1999–2003. Order of the Liberator Simon Bolivar (Venezuela), 1997. *Recreations:* hill-walking, golf. *Address:* 27 Parthenia Road, SW6 4BE. *Clubs:* Travellers, Caledonian.

FLYNN, Padraig; Member, European Commission (formerly Commission of the European Communities), 1993–99; *b* 9 May 1939; *m* 1963, Dorothy Tynan; one *s* three *d*. *Educ:* St Gerald's Secondary Sch., Castlebar, Co. Mayo; St Patrick's Trng Coll., Dublin (DipEd). Mayo County Council: Mem., 1967–87; Vice-Chm., 1975–77. TD (FF), 1977–93; Minister of State, Dept of Transport and Power, 1980–81; Minister for: Gaeltacht, March–Oct. 1982; Trade, Commerce and Tourism, Oct.–Dec. 1982; spokesman on trade, commerce and tourism, 1982–87; Minister for: the Envmt, 1987–91; Justice, Feb.–Dec. 1992; Industry and Commerce, Nov.–Dec. 1992. Mem., Irish Nat. Teachers' Orgn, 1957. Mem., Gaelic Athletic Assoc., 1959–. *Recreations:* golf, reading, world affairs. *Address:* Carrowbrinogue Lodge, Castlebar, Co. Mayo, Ireland.

FLYNN, Paul Phillip; MP (Lab) Newport West, since 1987; *b* 9 Feb. 1935; *s* of late James Flynn and Kathleen Williams; *m* 1st, 1962, Anne Harvey (marr. diss. 1984); one *s* (one *d* decd); 2nd, 1985, Samantha Morgan, *d* of Douglas and Elsie Cumpstone; one step *s* one step *d*. *Educ:* St Illtyd's Coll., Cardiff. Steelworker, 1955–84; Researcher, 1984–87. Mem., Gwent CC, 1974–82. Contested (Lab) Denbigh, Oct. 1974. Frontbench spokesman on Wales, 1987, on social security, 1988–90. Mem., Gorsedd of Bards, 1991. Campaign for Freedom of Information Parly Award, 1991. *Publications:* Commons Knowledge: how to be a backbencher, 1997; Baglu 'Mlaen (autobiog.), 1998; Dragons led by Poodles, 1999; The Unusual Suspect, 2010; How to be an MP, 2012; Clockwinder Who Wouldn't Say No: the life of David Taylor MP, 2012. *Address:* House of Commons, SW1A 0AA. *Club:* Ringland Labour (Newport, Gwent).

FLYNN, Roger; Chief Executive Officer, Springboard Group Ltd, since 2004; Chairman: Want2bethere Ltd, since 2011; Olive Communications Solutions, since 2013; *b* 4 Nov. 1962; *s* of Peter Flynn and late Shirley Flynn; *m* 1986, Lisa Eyre; two *d*. *Educ:* Imperial Coll., London (BSc 1st Cl. Hons Physics). ACA 1987. With Arthur Andersen, 1984–88; Corporate Finance Exec., Virgin Gp plc, 1988–91; Commercial Dir, Virgin Communications Ltd, 1991–95; Gen. Manager, World Sales and Distribution, BA plc, 1995–98; Man. Dir, Prudential Retail, 1998–2000; CEO, BBC Ventures Gp Ltd, 2001–04. Pres., Internat., SDI Media Gp Inc., 2006–09. MInstP 1985; MRI 1985. Trustee, Youth Culture Television, 1994–2007. Mem., Magic Circle. *Recreations:* Rugby, tennis ski-ing, film. *Address:* 29 Farm Street, Mayfair, W1J 5RL. *E:* roger@springboard.uk.com.

FLYNN, Most Rev. Thomas, DD; Bishop of Achonry, (RC), 1977–2007, now Bishop Emeritus; *b* 8 July 1931; *s* of Robert and Margaret Flynn. *Educ:* St Nathy's, Ballaghaderreen; Maynooth College. BD, LPh, MA. Diocesan Religious Inspector of Schools, 1957–64; teaching in St Nathy's College, Ballaghaderreen, 1964–73; President and Headmaster of St Nathy's Coll., 1973–77. DD 1977. *Recreations:* gardening, fishing, golf. *Address:* St Michael's, Cathedral Grounds, Ballaghaderreen, Co. Roscommon, Eire.

FLYNN, Vernon James Hennessy; QC 2008; *b* London, 1 Sept. 1966; *s* of James and Alice Flynn; *m* 1996, Angela Porta; one *s* two *d*. *Educ:* Trinity Coll., Cambridge (BA 1989). Called to the Bar, Lincoln's Inn, 1991. Vis. Fellow, LSE, 2003–09. *Address:* Essex Court Chambers, 24 Lincoln's Inn Fields, WC2A 3EG.

FLYVBJERG, Prof. Bent, PhD; BT Professor and Chair of Major Programme Management, Saïd Business School, University of Oxford, since 2009; *s* of Thorkild and Regina Flyvbjerg. *Educ:* Univ. of Aarhus (BSc Geog. and Econs 1975; MSc Geog. and Econs 1979); Univ. of Aarhus (PhD Econ. Geog. 1985); Aalborg Univ. (Dr Techn. 1991; Dr Scient. 2007). Department of Development and Planning, Aalborg University: Asst Prof., 1979–82; Associate Prof., 1983–92; Prof. of Planning, 1993–2009; non-exec. Dir, 1980–84; Prof. and Chair in Infrastructure Policy and Planning, Faculty of Technol., Policy and Mgt, Delft Univ. of Technol., 2006–09. Vis. Fulbright Scholar, UCLA, 1981–82 and 1985–86; Dist. Res. Scholar, Nat. Sci. Council, Copenhagen, 1985–88; Vis. Fellow, Eur. University Inst., Florence, 1994. Mem., Danish Govt Commn on Infrastructure, Copenhagen, 2006–08. Non-executive Director: Nordic Section, Regl Sci. Assoc., Aalborg, 1983–85; Nordic Inst. of Planning, Stockholm, 1990–98; Danish Court Admin, Copenhagen, 1999–2005. Knight, Order of the Dannebrog (Denmark), 2002. *Publications:* Rationality and Power: democracy in practice, 1998, 5th edn 2005; Making Social Science Matter: why social inquiry fails and how it can succeed again, 2001, 10th edn 2007; (with Nils Bruzelius and Werner Rothengatter) Megaprojects and Risk: an anatomy of ambition, 2003, 7th edn 2006; (ed jtly) Decision-Making on Mega-Projects: cost-benefit analysis, planning, and innovation, 2008; numerous book chapters and articles in learned jls. *Recreations:* jogging, bike-racing, ski-ing, music.

FO, Dario; Italian playwright and actor; *b* 24 March 1926; *s* of Felice Fo and Pina (*née* Rota); *m* 1954, Franca Rame (*d* 2013); one *s*. *Educ:* Acad. of Fine Arts, Milan. Joined a small theatre gp, 1950; wrote satirical radio series, Poer nano (Poor Dwarf), 1951, and performed selections from it, Teatro Odeon, Milan; appeared in Cocorico, Teatro Odeon, Milan, 1952; jt founder and performer, Il Dito Nell'Occhio (revue co.), 1953–55 (toured nationally); screenwriter, Rome, 1955–58; performer and writer, theatre gp, Compagnia Fo-Rame, 1958–68; artistic dir, Chi l'ha visto? (TV musical revue), 1959; performer and writer, Canzonissima (TV variety show); returned to theatre work, 1962; jt founder, theatre co-operative, Nuova Scena, 1968 (toured, 1968–69); jt founder, theatre gp, la Comune, 1970; Tricks of the Trade (TV series), 1985. *Plays include:* Gli Arcangeli non Giocano a Flipper, 1959 (Archangels Don't Play Pinball); Isabella, Tre Caravelle e un Cacciabelle, 1963 (Isabella, Three Sailing Ships and a Con Man); Mistero Buffo, 1969; Morte Accidentale di un Anarchico, 1970 (Accidental Death of an Anarchist); Non Si Paga, Non Si Paga!, 1974 (Can't Pay! Won't Pay!); (with Franca Rame) Tutta Casa Letto e Chiesa, 1977; Storia Della Tigre ed Altre Storie, 1979 (Tale of a Tiger and Other Stories); Clacson, Trombette e Pernacchi, 1980 (Trumpets and Raspberries); (with Franca Rame) Coppia Aperta, 1983 (Open Couple); Il Papa e La Strega, 1989 (The Pope and the Witch); (with Franca Rame) L'Eroina—Grassa è Bello, 1991; Johan Padan a la Descoverta de le Americhe, 1991; Discorsi sul Ruzzante, 1993; Il Diavolo con le Zinne, 1997; Da Tangentopoli all'Irrisistibile Ascesa di Ubu Bas, 2002; Ubu Bas Va alla Guerra, 2003; his plays have been translated into many languages and performed in many countries. Nobel Prize for Literature, 1997. *Publications:* The Tricks of the Trade, 1991; My First Seven Years (Plus a Few More) (memoir), 2005; many plays. *Address:* CTFR Srl, Corso di Porta Romana 132, 20122 Milan, Italy.

FOALE, (Colin) Michael, CBE 2005; PhD; Astronaut, US National Aeronautics and Space Administration, 1987–2013; *b* 6 Jan. 1957; dual UK/US nationality; *s* of late Air Cdre Colin Henry Foale and Mary Katherine Foale (*née* Harding); *m* 1987, Rhonda Butler; one *s* one *d*. *Educ:* King's Sch., Canterbury; Queens' Coll., Cambridge (BA 1st Cl. Hons Nat. Sci. Tripos 1978; PhD Lab. Astrophysics 1982; Hon. Fellow, 1998). National Aeronautics and Space Administration (US): Payload Officer, 1983–87; Space Shuttle Missions: Atlas 1, 1992; Atlas 2, 1993; Space Suit Test, 1995; Russian Space Station Mir, May–Oct. 1997; Hubble Telescope Repair, 1999; Asst Dir (Technical), 1998; Chief of Expedn Corps, Astronaut Office, Johnson Space Center, 1999; Comdr, Internat. Space Stn Expedn 8, 2003–04; Dep. Assoc. Adminr, Exploration Ops, NASA HQ, 2005–06; Chief, Soyuz Branch, Astronaut Office, 2010–13. Hon. FRAeS 1997. DUniv: Kent, 2000; Lincs and Humberside, 2000. Founder's Medal, Air League, 1993; Barnes Wallis Award, GAPAN, 1994. *Recreations:* flying, wind surfing, diving, ski-ing, theoretical physics, electric flight.

FOALE, Rodney Alan, FRCP, FACC, FESC, FCSANZ; Consultant Cardiologist, since 1985, and Clinical Director of Surgery, Cardiovascular Science and Clinical Care, 1999–2010, St Mary's Hospital, London; *b* 11 Sept. 1946; *s* of Maurice Foale; *m* 1st, 1981, Emma Gordon (marr. diss. 2007); two *s*; 2nd, 2010, Dr Samina Showghi; one *d*. *Educ:* Univ. of Melbourne (MB BS 1971). FACC 1985; FESC 1990; FRCP 1994; FCSANZ 2003. Sen. Clin. Fellow, Harvard Univ. and Massachusetts Gen. Hosp., 1980–82; Sen. Registrar (Cardiol.), Hammersmith Hosp., 1982–85. *Recreations:* sea, sand, rivers, field. *Address:* 66 Harley Street, W1G 7HD. *T:* (020) 7323 4687, *Fax:* (020) 7631 5341. *E:* raf@smht-foale.co.uk. *Clubs:* Flyfishers', Chelsea Arts.

FOCKE, His Honour Paul Everard Justus; QC 1982; a Circuit Judge, 1997–2007; a Senior Circuit Judge, 2000–07; *b* 14 May 1937; *s* of late Frederick Justus Focke and Muriel Focke; *m* 1973, Lady Tana Marie Alexander, *er d* of 6th Earl of Caledon; two *d*. *Educ:* Downside; Exeter Coll., Oxford; Trinity Coll., Dublin. National Service, 1955–57; Territorial Army, 1957–66, Cheshire Yeomanry (Captain). Called to the Bar, Gray's Inn, 1964 (Bencher, 1992), to the Bar of NSW and to the NZ Bar, 1982; QC NSW 1984; a Recorder, 1986–97. Dir, Bar Mutual Indemnity Fund, 1988–97. Judicial Mem., Parole Bd, 2007–. *Recreations:* travelling, aeroplanes. *Clubs:* Pratt's, Turf, Beefsteak, Cavalry and Guards.

FODEN, (Arthur) John; Chairman, PA Consulting Group, 1986–95; *b* 4 Oct. 1939; *s* of Air Vice-Marshal Arthur Foden, CB, CBE and Constance Muriel Foden (*née* Corkill); *m* 1963, Virginia Caroline Field; two *d*. *Educ:* Abingdon Sch., Oxon. Joined Whitbread and Co. Ltd, 1959, Industrial Relns Manager, 1967; PA Consulting Group, 1967–95: Gp Human Resources Dir, 1975–79; Chief Exec. of PA Germany, 1979–80, of PA Personnel Services, 1980–85; Chief Exec., 1985–92; Chm., 1986–95. Chm., Scottish Provident Instn, 1998–2001 (non-exec. Dir, 1995–2001); non-executive Director: Media Audits Ltd, 1992–2001; Scottish Mutual Assce plc, 2001–03. *Publications:* Paid to Decide, 1991. *Recreations:* travel, cooking.

FOËX, Prof. Pierre, DPhil; FRCA, FANZCA, FMedSci; Nuffield Professor of Anaesthetics, 1991–2002, and Fellow, 1991–2002, Supernumerary Fellow, since 2002, Pembroke College, University of Oxford; *b* 4 July 1935; *s* of Georges and Berthe Foëx; *m* 1958, Anne-Lise Schürch; two *s*. *Educ:* Univ. of Geneva (DM); professional qualifying Swiss State Exam. in Medicine and Surgery, 1960; DPhil Oxon 1973. FRCA (FFARCS 1985); FANZCA 1993. University Hospital, Geneva: Asst, 1961–62 and Chef de Clinique, 1962–63, Dept of Neurology; Asst, 1963–65, Chef de Clinique-adjoint, 1966–68 and Chef de Clinique, 1969–70, Dept of Medicine; Nuffield Department of Anaesthetics, University of Oxford: Res. Fellow, 1970–71; Lectr, 1971–73; Univ. Lectr, 1973–76; Clinical Reader and Hon. Consultant (Clinical Physiology), 1976–91; Emer. Fellow, Worcester Coll., Oxford, 1993 (Fellow, 1976–91). Mem., Exec. Cttee, Anaesthetic Res. Soc., 1982–86; Senator, European Acad. of Anaesthesiology, 1988–99 (Vice-Pres., 1991–93); Mem. Council, RCAnaes, 1996–2002. Non-exec. Dir, Oxford Radcliffe Hosps NHS Trust, 1992–99. Vis. Prof., univs in Australia, Canada, Europe, NZ, USA. Founder FMedSci 1998. Hon. FCA(SA) 2008. *Publications:* Anaesthesia for the Compromised Heart, 1989; Principles and Practice of Critical Care, 1997; Cardiovascular Drugs in the Perioperative Period, 1999; chapters and papers on cardiac physiology, cardiovascular physiology applied to anaesthesia, myocardial ischaemia, cardiovascular pharmacology, anaesthesia, hypertension, implications of coronary revascularisation and perioperative beta-blockade. *Recreations:* walking, foreign travel. *Address:* 26 Jack Straw's Lane, Oxford OX3 0DW. *T:* (01865) 761771.

FOGLE, Bruce, MBE 2004; DVM; veterinary surgeon, writer, broadcaster; *b* 17 Feb. 1944; *s* of Morris Fogle and Aileen (*née* Breslin); *m* 1973, Julia Foster; one *s* two *d*. *Educ:* Ontario Vet. Coll., Univ. of Guelph (DVM 1970). MRCVS 1970. Clinical Veterinary Surgeon, London Vet. Clinic (formerly Portman Vet. Clinic), London, 1973–; Founder and Partner, Emergency Vet. Clinic, London, 1980–; Partner, Elizabeth Street Vet. Clinic, London, 1980–. Co-Founder and Vice Chm., Hearing Dogs for Deaf People, 1982–. Television: Presenter: Petwatch, 1986; Good Companions, 1987; London Walkies, 1988; People and Pets, 1989–90; radio: Resident Vet, The Jimmy Young Prog., 1992–2003, The Jeremy Vine Show, 2003–, Radio 2; columnist: Today, 1986–89; Prima mag., 1986–92; Dogs Today mag., 1990–; Daily Telegraph, 1992–97; feature writer, The Times. Consultant to internat. pet food ind. cos, Pet Plan, Encyclopedia Britannica, Microsoft Encarta. Member: BVA, 1970; British Small Animal Vet. Assoc., 1970. Consumer Writer of Year, PPA, 1991. *Publications:* Interrelations Between People and Pets (ed and contrib.), 1981; Pets and their People, 1983; Games Pets Play, 1986; Paws Across London, 1989; The Dog's Mind, 1990; The Cat's Mind, 1991; People and Pets, 1991; Know Your Cat, 1991; Know Your Dog, 1992; The Complete Dog Care Manual, 1993; 101 Questions Your Cat Would Ask its Vet if Your Cat Could Talk, 1993; 101 Questions Your Dog Would Ask its Vet if Your Dog Could Talk, 1993; The Complete Dog Training Manual, 1994; 101 Essential Tips: caring for your dog, 1995; First Aid for Cat Owners, 1995; First Aid for Dog Owners, 1995; The Encyclopedia of the Dog, 1995; The Cocker Spaniel Handbook, 1996; The Golden Retriever Handbook, 1996; The Labrador Retriever Handbook, 1996; The German Shepherd Handbook, 1996; The Dachshund Handbook, 1997; The Poodle Handbook, 1997; The Secret Life of Cat Owners, 1997; The Secret Life of Dog Owners, 1997; 101 Essential Tips: training your dog, 1997; 101 Essential Tips: caring for your puppy, 1997; The Encyclopedia of the Cat, 1997; Cat's Christmas, 1998; Natural Dog Care, 1999; Natural Cat Care, 1999; The New Encyclopedia of the Dog, 2000; The New Encyclopedia of the Cat, 2001; The New Complete Dog Training Manual, 2001; What's up with my Dog?, 2001; What's up with my Cat?, 2001; The Dog Owner's Manual, 2002; The Cat Owner's Manual, 2002; Caring for your Dog, 2003; Dialogues with Dogs, 2004; Travels with Macy, 2005; If Only They Could Talk, 2006; A Dog Abroad, 2007; Eyewitness Companions: Dogs, 2006; Cats, 2006; Barefoot at the Lake: a memoir of summer people and water creatures, 2015; *contributions to:* New Perspectives on our Lives with Companion Animals, 1983; The Veterinary Annual, 1986; Eye to Eye: the psychology of relationships, 1988; Animals and People Sharing the World, 1988; contribs to learned jls in Eur. and N America, and to many newspapers and magazines. *Recreations:* stalking painted Gustavian furniture in rural Sweden, acting as putty in my dog's paws. *Address:* 86 York Street, W1H 1QS. *T:* (020) 7723 2068, *Fax:* (020) 7723 9009. *E:* bruce.fogle@clara.co.uk. *Club:* Garrick.

FOISTER, Dr Susan Rosemary, FSA; Curator of Early Netherlandish, German and British Paintings, since 1990, Deputy Director, since 2010, and Director of Public Engagement, since 2013, National Gallery (Director of Collections, 2004–13); *b* 12 May 1954; *d* of late Philip and Pamela Foister; *m* 1985, Richard Bulkeley Ritchie; two *s* one *d*. *Educ:* Hastings High Sch.; St Anne's Coll., Oxford (BA English 1975); Courtauld Inst. of Art (MA 1977; PhD 1982). FSA 2010. Jun. Res. Fellow, Warburg Inst., 1979–81; Curator, Victorian Portraits, NPG, 1983–89; Hd, Curatorial Dept, Nat. Gall., 2000–04. Dir, Nat. Gall. Co. Ltd, 2005–. Member: Adv. Bd, Renaissance Studies, 1997–2013; Adv. Panel, Public Catalogue Foundn, 2003–; Adv. Bd, Making Art in Tudor Britain Project, NPG, 2007–12; Peer Rev. Coll., AHRC, 2011–14. Chm., Soc. of Renaissance Studies, 1992–95. *Publications:* Drawings by Holbein from the Royal Library, Windsor Castle, 1983; Cardinal Newman, 1990; (jtly) Giotto to Dürer, 1991; (ed jtly) Robert Campin: new directions in scholarship, 1996; (jtly) Making and Meaning: Holbein's Ambassadors, 1997; (jtly) Dürer to Veronese, 1999; (ed jtly) Investigating Jan van Eyck, 2000; (jtly) Art in the Making: Renaissance underdrawing, 2002; Dürer and the Virgin in the Garden, 2004; Holbein and England, 2004; Holbein in England, 2006; Art of Light: German Renaissance stained glass, 2007; (jtly) Renaissance Faces: Van Eyck to Titian, 2008; contrib. articles to Burlington Mag., Apollo. *Address:* National Gallery, Trafalgar Square, WC2N 5DN. *T:* (020) 7839 3321, *Fax:* (020) 7742 2472.

FOKAS, Prof. Athanasios Spyridon, MD; PhD; Professor of Nonlinear Mathematical Science, University of Cambridge, since 2002; Fellow, Clare Hall, Cambridge, since 2005; *b* 30 June 1952; *s* of Spyridon and Anastasia Fokas; *m* 1996, Regina Karousou; one *s* two *d*. *Educ:* Imperial Coll., London (BS 1975); CIT (PhD 1979); Sch. of Medicine, Univ. of Miami (MD 1986). Saul Kaplun Res. Fellow in Applied Maths, CIT, 1979–80; Asst Prof., 1980–82, Prof. and Chm., 1986–93, Dept of Maths and Computer Sci., Clarkson Univ.; Prof., Dept of Maths, Univ. of Loughborough, 1993–95; Prof. of Applied Maths, Dept of Maths, Imperial Coll., London, 1996–2001. Vis. Prof., Dept of Maths, Stanford Univ., 1987–88. Ambassador of Hellenism, Greece, 2010. Member, Editorial Board: Jl Nonlinear Science, 1991–; Selecta Mathematica, 1998–; Proc. Royal Soc., 2002–; Jl Math. Physics, 2002–. Mem., Acad. of Athens, 2004. Guggenheim Fellow, 2009; Fellow, Eur. Acad. of Scis, 2010. Hon. DSc: Tech. Univ. of Crete, 2004; Athens, 2006; Western Macedonia, 2008; Hon. Dr: Applied Maths and Phys. Scis, Tech. Univ. of Athens, 2004; Maths Patras, 2005; Materials Sci. and Engrg Univ. Ioannina, 2013. Naylor Prize, LMS, 2000; Aristeion Prize: Acad. of Athens, 2004; Bodossaki Foundn (Greece), 2006. Comdr, Order of the Phoenix (Greece), 2005. *Publications:* (with M. J. Ablowitz) Introduction and Applications of Complex Variables, 1997; (jtly) Painlevé Transcendents, the Riemann-Hilbert Approach, 2006; A Unified Approach to Boundary Value Problems, 2008; edited jointly: Important Developments in Soliton Theory, 1993; Nonlinear Processes in Physics, 1993; Algebraic Aspects of Integrable Equations, 1996; conference procs; about 200 papers. *Address:* Department of Applied Mathematics and Theoretical Physics, University of Cambridge, Wilberforce Road, Cambridge CB3 0WA. *T:* (01223) 339733, *Fax:* (01223) 765900. *E:* t.fokas@damtp.cam.ac.uk.

FOKINE, Yuri Evgenievich; Adviser to Rector, Diplomatic Academy, Ministry of Foreign Affairs, Russian Federation, since 2006 (Rector, 2000–06); *b* 2 Sept. 1936; *s* of Evgeni G. Fokine and Ekaterina I. Fokine; *m* 1958, Maya E. Klimova; one *s* (one *d* decd). *Educ:* Moscow State Inst. for Internat. Relations (grad 1960). Entered Diplomatic Service, 1960; posts in USSR Perm. Mission to UN, Dept of Internat. Orgns, USSR Foreign Min., and Secretariat, USSR Foreign Min.; Dep. Perm. Rep. to UN, 1976–79; Ministry of Foreign Affairs: Dep. Sec.-Gen., 1979–80; Sec.-Gen. and Mem. of Collegium, 1980–86; Ambassador to Cyprus, 1986–90; Dir, 2nd Eur. Dept, Min. of Foreign Affairs, 1990–95; Ambassador to Norway, 1995–97, to UK, 1997–2000. Head, Assoc. for Contacts with UK. Member, Editorial Council: Internat. Affairs Mag., Moscow, 2000–; Diplomatic Service Mag., Moscow, 2009–; Ed., Diplomatic Yearbook, 2000–14. Grand Gold Cross, Order of Merit (Austria), 1995; Royal Order of Merit (Norway), 1997; also national decorations. *Publications:* A. Akaev: president, 2004; articles in jls. *Recreations:* art, ballet, reading, tennis. *Address:* Diplomatic Academy, 53/2 Ostozhenka, Moscow 119992, Russia.

FOLDES, Prof. Lucien Paul; Professor of Economics, University of London, at London School of Economics and Political Science, 1979–96, then Emeritus; *b* 19 Nov. 1930; *s* of Egon and Marta Foldes; *m* Carol Rosalind Hewlett. *Educ:* Bunce Court Sch.; Monkton Wyld Sch.; London School of Economics (BCom, MScEcon, DBA). National Service, 1952–54. London School of Economics and Political Science: Asst Lecturer in Economics, 1954–55; Lectr, 1955–61; Reader, 1961–79. Rockefeller Travelling Fellow, 1961–62. *Publications:* articles in Rev. of Economic Studies, Economica, Jl of Mathematical Economics, Stochastics, Mathematical Finance, Jl of Economic Dynamics and Control, and others. *Recreation:* mathematical analysis. *Address:* London School of Economics, Houghton Street, WC2A 2AE. *T:* (020) 7405 7686.

FOLEY, family name of **Baron Foley**.

FOLEY, 9th Baron *cr* 1776, of Kidderminster; **Thomas Henry Foley;** *b* 1 April 1961; *s* of 8th Baron Foley and of Patricia De Meek, *d* of Joseph Zoellner III; *S* father, 2012. *Heir: cousin* Rupert Thomas Foley, *b* 16 March 1970.

FOLEY, Rt Rev. Graham; *see* Foley, Rt Rev. R. G. G.

FOLEY, Hugh Smith; Principal Clerk of Session and Justiciary, Scotland, 1989–97. *Educ:* Dalkeith High Sch. (Joint Dux). Student Actuary, Standard Life Assce Co., 1956–59; nat. service, RAF, 1959–61; entered Scottish Court Service, Court of Session Br., 1962; Asst Clerk of Session, 1962–71; Depute Clerk of Session, 1972–80; seconded to Sheriff Court, Edinburgh, 1980–81; Prin. Sheriff Clerk Depute, Glasgow, 1981–82; Sheriff Clerk, Linlithgow, 1982; Dep. Prin. Clerk of Session, 1982–86; Sen. Dep. Principal Clerk, 1986–89. Member: Lord President's Cttee on Procedure in Personal Injuries Litigation in Court of Session, 1978–79; Lothian Valuation Appeal Panel, 1997–2007. *Recreations:* walking, painting, golf.

FOLEY, Johanna Mary, (Jo); journalist, editor and media consultant specialising in spa, health and wellness retreats, luxury travel and lifestyle; *b* 8 Dec. 1945; *d* of John and Monica Foley. *Educ:* St Joseph's Convent, Kenilworth; Manchester Univ. (BA Jt Hons English and Drama, 1968). Sen. Asst Editor, Woman's Own, 1978; Woman's Editor, The Sun, 1980; Editor, Woman, 1982; Exec. Editor (Features), The Times, 1984–85; Man. Editor, The Mirror, 1985–86; Editor: Observer Magazine, 1986–87; Options, 1988–91. Editor of the Year, British Soc. of Magazine Editors, 1983. *Recreations:* eating, reading, walking, cinema, opera, travel.

FOLEY, His Honour John Dominic; a Circuit Judge, 1994–2009; *b* 17 Jan. 1944; *s* of Cyril Patrick Foley and Winifred Hannah (*née* McAweeny); *m* 1978, Helena Frances McGowan (marr. diss. 1986); two *d*. *Educ:* St Brendan's Coll., Bristol; Exeter Univ. (LLB Hons). Called to the Bar, Inner Temple, 1968; Western Circuit, 1969–2009; Attorney-Gen. Special Prosecutor, NI, 1971–73; Asst Recorder, 1986–89; Recorder, 1990–93; an Investigating Judge (Judicial Discipline), 2006–09. Vice-Pres., Immigration Appeal Tribunal, 1998–2005; Mem., Special Immigration Appeal Commn, 2002–05. Ind. Arbitrator (Discipline), RFU and Internat. Rugby Bd, 2005–09. Pres., Bracton Law Soc., Exeter Univ., 1966–67. *Recreations:* Rugby (formerly 1st XV, Exeter Univ.), cricket, travel, rock. *Clubs:* Clifton Rugby Football, Bristol Rugby Football; Somerset County Cricket; Carlton Cricket (Barbados), Barbados Cricket Assoc.

FOLEY, Lt-Gen. Sir John (Paul), KCB 1994 (CB 1991); OBE 1979; MC 1976; Vice Lord-Lieutenant, Herefordshire, 2010–14; *b* 22 April 1939; *s* of Henry Thomas Hamilton Foley, MBE and Helen Constance Margaret Foley (*née* Pearson); *m* 1972, Ann Humphries; two *d*. *Educ:* Bradfield College; Mons OCS; Army Staff College (psc). Lieut, Royal Green Jackets, 1959; RMCS and Army Staff Coll., 1970–71; Regimental Duty, 1972–74; Chief of Staff, 51 Inf. Bde, Hong Kong, 1974–76; Instructor, Army Staff Coll., 1976–78; CO 3rd Bn RGJ, 1978–80; Comdt Jun. Div., Staff Coll., 1981–82. Dir, SAS, 1983–85; RCDS 1986; Chief, British Mission to Soviet Forces in Germany, 1987–89; Dir Gen. Intelligence (Rest of World), 1989–92; Comdr, British Forces Hong Kong, and Maj.-Gen. Brigade of Gurkhas, 1992–94; Chief of Defence Intelligence, MoD, 1994–97. Col Comdt, 1st Bn, Royal Green Jackets, 1991–94, The Light Div., 1994–97. Lieut Gov. and Comdr-in-Chief, Guernsey, Channel Is, 2000–05. Non-exec. Dir, AD Systems (UK) Ltd, 2010–11. Chm., British Greyhound Racing Bd, 1999–2000. Mem., Royal Patriotic Fund Corp., 2000–01. Pres., BRIXMIS Assoc., 2002–. Liveryman, Skinners' Co., 1972– (Mem. Court, 1995–2000). DL Herefords, 2006; High Sheriff, Herefords and Worcs, 2006–07. KSJ 2000. Officer, Legion of Merit (USA), 1997. *Recreations:* tennis, walking, shooting, reading. *Club:* Boodle's.

FOLEY, Prof. Robert Andrew, PhD, ScD; FBA 2007; Leverhulme Professor of Human Evolution, since 2003, and Co-Founder and Co-Director, Leverhulme Centre for Human Evolutionary Studies, since 2001, University of Cambridge; Fellow, King's College, Cambridge, since 1987; *b* 18 March 1953; *s* of late Nelson Foley and Jean Foley; *m* 2003, Marta Mirazon Lahr; two *s*, and two step *s*. *Educ:* Peterhouse, Cambridge (BA 1974; PhD 1980); King's Coll., Cambridge (ScD 1996). Lectr in Anthropology, Univ. of Durham, 1977–85; Lectr in Biol Anthropology, 1986–98, Reader in Evolutionary Anthropology, 1998–2003, Univ. of Cambridge. Vis. Prof., Centre for GeoGenetics, Univ. of Copenhagen, 2013–. *Publications:* Off-Site Archaeology, 1981; Hominid Evolution and Community Ecology, 1984; Another Unique Species, 1987; Comparative Socioecology of Humans and Other Mammals, 1989; The Origins of Human Behaviour, 1991; Humans Before Humanity, 1995; (with P. Donnelly) Genes, Fossils and Behaviour, 2001; (with R. Lewin) Principles of Human Evolution, 2003; many scientific papers. *Recreations:* travel, cricket, gadgets. *Address:* King's College, Cambridge CB2 1ST. *T:* (01223) 331459, *Fax:* (01223) 335460.

FOLEY, Rt Rev. (Ronald) Graham (Gregory); appointed Bishop Suffragan of Reading, 1982, Area Bishop, 1985, retired 1989; Assistant Bishop, Diocese of York, 1989–2007; *b* 13 June 1923; *s* of Theodore Gregory Foley and Cessan Florence Page; *m* 1944, Florence Redman; two *s* two *d*. *Educ:* King Edward's Grammar Sch., Aston, Birmingham; Wakefield Grammar Sch.; King's Coll., London; St John's Coll., Durham (BA Hons Theol., LTh). Curate, South Shore, Blackpool, 1950; Vicar, S Luke, Blackburn, 1954; Dir of Educn, Dio. of Durham, and Rector of Brancepeth, 1960; Chaplain, Aycliffe Approved Sch., 1962; Vicar of Leeds, 1971–82; Chaplain to the Queen, 1977–82. Hon. Canon: Durham Cathedral, 1965–71; Ripon Cath., 1971–82. Dir, Yorks Electricity Bd, 1976–82. Chm. of Trustees, Dorothy Kerin Trust, Burrswood, 1983–89. *Publications:* (jtly) Religion in Approved Schools, 1969. *Recreations:* journalism, reading detective stories, watching other people mow lawns. *Address:* Ramsey Cottage, 3 Poplar Avenue, Kirkbymoorside, York YO62 6ES. *T:* (01751) 432439.

FOLJAMBE, family name of **Earl of Liverpool**.

FOLKESTONE, Viscount; Jacob Pleydell-Bouverie; *b* 7 April 1999; *s* and *heir* of Earl of Radnor, *qv*.

FOLKSON, Richard, CEng, FIMechE; President, Institution of Mechanical Engineers, 2015–May 2016; *b* Westminster, London, 31 Jan. 1955; *s* of Dr Aleck Folkson and Sheila Sybil Folkson; *m* 1993, Patricia Carole Thomas; two *d*. *Educ:* Haywards Heath Grammar Sch.; Imperial Coll. London (BSc Engrg 1977). ACGI 1977; CEng 1986; FIMechE 1995. Ford Motor Co. Ltd: Supervisor, Product Strategy, 1990–92; Project Manager, Transit, 1992–98; Chief Program Engr, 1997–98; Manager, Product Verification and Testing, 1998–2004; Chief Engr, 2004–06. Engrg consultant, low carbon vehicle technol., 2006–. Non-exec. Dir, Evalu8 Transport Innovations, 2008–. Vis. Prof., 2004–, RAEng Vis. Prof., 2007–, Univ. of Hertfordshire. Member: Chelmsford Model Engrg Soc.; Romford Model Engrg Club; Aston Martin Owners Club. *Publications:* Alternative Fuels and Advanced Vehicle Technologies for Improved Environmental Performance, 2014. *Recreations:* model engineering, classic sports cars, motorcycling, Thundersley Brass Band (cornet), Big Band (trumpet). *Address:* President's Office, Institution of Mechanical Engineers, 1 Birdcage Walk, SW1H 9JJ. *T:* (020) 7973 6846. *E:* president@imeche.org; The Black Mill, Wheelers Lane, Navestock Side, Brentwood, Essex CM14 5RN. *T:* (01277) 374389. *E:* rfolkson@aol.com.

FOLLETT, Barbara; *see* Follett, D. B.

FOLLETT, Sir Brian (Keith), Kt 1992; DL; FRS 1984; Visiting Professor, Department of Zoology, University of Oxford, since 2001; *b* 22 Feb. 1939; *m* 1961, Deb (*née* Booth); one *s* one *d*. *Educ:* Bournemouth Sch.; Univ. of Bristol (BSc 1960, PhD 1964); Univ. of Wales (DSc 1975). Res. Fellow, Washington State Univ., 1964–65; Lectr in Zool., Univ. of Leeds, 1965–69; Lectr, subseq. Reader and Prof. of Zool., University Coll. of N Wales, Bangor, 1969–78; Bristol University: Prof. of Zool., 1978–93, AFRC Res. Prof., 1989–93; Hd of Dept of Zool., 1978–89; Chm., Sch. of Biol Scis, 1989–93; Vice-Chancellor, Warwick Univ., 1993–2001; Chairman: AHRB, then AHRC, 2001–07; TTA, then TDA, 2003–09. Chm., Infectious Diseases Inquiry, Royal Soc., 2001–02. Chairman: ESRC-British Acad. Working Party on the Future of Funding Res. in the Humanities, 1992; Adv. Bd, British Library, 2000–07; Res. Support Librarians Review Gp, 2001–03; Adv. Forum, STEM Strategy Gp, DfES, later DIUS, then BIS, 2007–11; Member: Biol Sci. Cttee, SERC, 1981–84; AFRC, 1984–88 (Mem., Animals Cttee, 1984–88); Biol Sci. Cttee, UGC, 1985–88; UFC, 1989–93; HEFCE, 1992–96 (Chairman: Libraries Review Gp, 1992–97; Strategic Subjects Adv. Gp, 2007–); Council, BBSRC, 1994–2001 (Chm., Sci. and Engrg Bd, 1994–97); Royal Commn on Envmtl Pollution, 2000–05. Trustee, BM (Natural Hist.), 1989–98. Biol Sec. and Vice-Pres., Royal Soc., 1987–93; Member of Council: Soc. for Study of Fertility, 1972–87 (Prog. Sec., 1976–78; Treas., 1982–87); Soc. for Endocrinology, 1974–77; Bristol Zoo, 1978–93; Wildfowl Trust, Slimbridge, 1983–86; Zool Soc. of London, 1983–86. Pres. ASE, 1997. Lectures: Amoroso, Soc. for Study of Fertility, 1985; Annual Zool., Liverpool Univ., 1991; Barrington Meml, Nottingham Univ., 1992. Gov., RSC, 2007–; Pres., Stratford-upon-Avon Soc., 2003–. Chm., Liby and Archive Gp, The Globe, 2013–14. Mem., Academia Europaea, 1988. DL West Midlands, 2000. Hon. FCLIP (Hon. FLA 1997); Hon. FZS 2004. Hon. Fellow: UCNW, Bangor, 1990; Worcester, 2008. Hon. LLD: Wales, 1992; Calgary, 2001; St Andrews, 2002; Bristol, 2005; Lancaster, 2012; Hon. DSc: Univ. Teknologi, Malaysia, 1999; Leicester, 2001; Warwick, 2002; East Anglia, 2003; London, 2004; Bedfordshire, 2008; Bournemouth, 2008; Hon DLitt Oxford, 2002. Scientific Medal, 1976, Frink Medal, 1993, Zool Soc. of London; Dale Medal, Soc. of Endocrinology, 1988. Editorial Bds: Jl of Endocrinology, 1971–78; Gen. & Comparative Endocrinology, 1974–82; Jl of Biol Rhythms, 1986–2000; Proc. of Royal Soc., 1987–90. *Publications:* over 260 scientific papers on biol clocks and reproductive physiology. *Address:* Department of Zoology, University of Oxford, Oxford OX1 3PS. *E:* brian.follett@zoo.ox.ac.uk; 120 Tiddington Road, Stratford-upon-Avon, Warwicks CV37 7BB.

FOLLETT, (Daphne) Barbara; *b* 25 Dec. 1942; *d* of late William Vernon Hubbard and Charlotte Hubbard (*née* Goulding); *m* 1st, 1963, Richard Turner (marr. diss. 1971); two *d*; 2nd, 1971, Gerald Stonestreet (marr. diss. 1974); 3rd, 1974, Leslie Broer (marr. diss. 1985); one *s*; 4th, 1985, Ken Follett, *qv*; one step *s* one step *d*. *Educ:* London Sch. of Economics (BSc Econ); Open Univ. Teacher, Berlitz Sch. of Language, Paris, 1963–64; Jt Manager, fruit farm, Stellenbosch, S Africa, 1966–77; acting Regl Sec., S African Inst. of Race Relations, Cape Town, 1970; Regl Manager (Cape and Namibia), 1971–74, Nat. Health Educn Dir, 1975–78, Kupugani; Asst Course Orgnr and Lectr, Centre for Internat. Briefing, Farnham, 1980–84; freelance lectr and consultant, 1984–92. Vis. Fellow, Inst. of Public Policy Research, 1993–95. Contested (Lab): Woking, 1983; Epsom and Ewell, 1987. MP (Lab) Stevenage, 1997–2010. Parliamentary Under-Secretary of State: DWP, 2007; Govt Equalities Office, 2008; DCMS, 2008–09; DCLG, 2009–10; Minister for E of England, 2007–10. CEO, The Follett Office, 2010–; Dir, Jumby Bay Island Co. Ltd, 2011–. Founder Member: EMILY's List UK, 1992– (also Dir); Women's Movt for Peace, S Africa, 1976; Labour Women's Network (Mem., Steering Cttee, 1988–); Member: Fawcett Soc., 1993; Nat. Alliance of Women's Orgns, 1993; Nat. Women's Network, 1993. Hon. LLD Hertfordshire, 2010. *Recreations:* photography, Scrabble, Star Trek.

FOLLETT, Ken; author, since 1977; *b* 5 June 1949; *s* of late Martin Dunsford Follett and Lavinia Cynthia (Veenie) Follett (*née* Evans); *m* 1st, 1968, Mary Elson (marr. diss. 1985); one *s* one *d*; 2nd, 1985, Barbara Broer (*see* D. B. Follett). *Educ:* Harrow Weald Grammar Sch.; Poole Tech. Coll.; University Coll. London (BA; Fellow 1994). Trainee journalist, S Wales Echo, 1970–73; Reporter, London Evening News, 1973–74; Everest Books: Editl Dir, 1974–76; Dep. Man. Dir, 1976–77. Dir, Stevenage Leisure Ltd, 1997–2005. Mem. Council, Nat. Literary Trust, 1996–2010 (Trustee, 2005–10); Chm., Nat. Year of Reading, 1998–99; Bd Dir, Nat. Acad. of Writing, 2003–10. Pres., Dyslexia Inst., 1998–2008. Vice-Pres., Stevenage Bor. FC, 2000–02; Trustee, Stevenage Community Trust, 2002– (Chm., 2005–13; Pres., 2013–); Patron, Stevenage Home-Start, 2000–. Chm. Govs, Roebuck Primary Sch. and Nursery, 2001–05. Mem., Yr Academi Gymreig, 2000 (Fellow, 2011). Hon. DLitt: Glamorgan, 2007; Saginaw Valley State, 2007; Exeter, 2008. Olaguibel Prize, Colegio Oficial de Arquitectos Vasco-Navarro, 2008; Thriller Master Award, Internat. Thriller Writers, 2010; Grand Master, Mystery Writers of America, 2013. *Publications:* Eye of the Needle (Edgar Award, Mystery Writers of Amer.), 1978; Triple, 1979; The Key to Rebecca, 1980; The Man from St Petersburg, 1982; On Wings of Eagles, 1983; Lie down with Lions, 1986; The Pillars of the Earth, 1989; Night over Water, 1991; Mrs Shiblak's Nightmare (pamphlet), 1992; A Dangerous Fortune, 1993; A Place Called Freedom, 1995; The Third Twin, 1997; The Hammer of Eden, 1998; Code to Zero, 2000; Jackdaws, 2001 (Corine Buchpreis, 2003); Hornet Flight, 2002; Whiteout, 2004; World Without End, 2007; Fall of Giants, 2010 (Libri Golden Book Award, Hungary, 2010; Que Leer Prize, 2011); Winter of the World, 2012; Edge of Eternity, 2014; various articles, screenplays and short stories. *Recreations:* bass guitarist in a blues band; Labour Party supporter and campaigner. *Address:* The Follett Office, Follett House, Primett Road, Stevenage, Herts SG1 3EE. *Clubs:* Athenæum, Groucho.

FONAGY, Prof. Peter, OBE 2013; PhD; FMedSci; FBA 1997; Freud Memorial Professor of Psychoanalysis, University of London, at University College, since 1992, and Head, Research Department of Clinical, Educational and Health Psychology, University College London, since 2008; Chief Executive, Anna Freud Centre, since 2003 (Director of Research, 1989–2003); National Clinical Lead, Children and Young People's Improving Access to Psychological Therapies Programme, Department of Health, then NHS England, since 2011; *b* 14 Aug. 1952; *s* of Ivan Fonagy and Judith (*née* Barath); *m* 1990, Dr Anna Higgitt; one *s* one *d*. *Educ:* UCL (BSc Hons 1974; PhD 1980). Dip. Clin. Psych. 1980. Lectr, 1977–88, Sen. Lectr, 1988–92, in Psychology, Univ. of London; Dir, Sub-Dept of Clin. Health Psychology, UCL, 1995–2007. Menninger Clinic: Co-ordinating Dir, Child and Family Center, 1995–2003, Clin. Protocols and Outcome Center, 1996; Voorhees Distinguished Prof., 1995; Consultant, Child and Family Prog., Menninger Dept of Psychiatry, Baylor Coll. of Medicine, Houston, 2003–. Prog. Dir, Integrated Mental Health Prog., UCLPartners, 2011– (Interim Prog. Dir, 2010–11). Interim Clinical Lead, IAPT for Children and Young People, DoH, 2011; NIHR Sen. Investigator, 2011–. Visiting Professor: Hebrew Univ. of Jerusalem, 1993; Univ. of Haifa, 1993, 1995; Cornell Med. Coll., NY, 1994; Adjunct Prof. of Clin. Psychol., Kansas Univ., 1995–2002; Marie and Scott S. Smith Chair in Child Develt, Karl Menninger Sch. of Psychiatry and Mental Health Scis, Kansas, 1999–2003; Adjunct Prof. of Psychiatry, Baylor Coll. of Medicine, 2003–; Clin. Prof. of Psychiatry, Sch. of Medicine, Yale Univ., 2005–; Vis. Clin. Prof., Harvard Univ., 2011–15. Hon. Principal Investigator, Tavistock and Portman NHS Foundn Trust, 2011–. Mem., 1988–, and Trng and Supervising Analyst, 1995–, British Psycho-Analytical Soc. FMedSci 2014. *Publications:* (with A. Higgitt) Personality Theory and Clinical Practice, 1985; (with A. D. Roth) What Works for Whom?: a critical review of psychotherapy research, 1996 (trans. Italian, 1996), 2nd edn 2005; (jtly) Psychodynamic Developmental Therapy for Children: a manual, 2000; Attachment Theory and Psychoanalysis, 2001 (trans. German 2003, French 2004, Danish 2006; Korean); (jtly) What Works for Whom?: a critical review of treatments for children and adolescents, 2002, 2nd edn 2014 (trans. Italian 2003); (jtly) Affect Regulation, Mentalization and the Development of the Self, 2002 (trans. German 2004, Italian 2005, Danish 2007); (jtly) Drawing on the Evidence: advice for mental health professionals working with children and adolescents, 2002; (with M. Target) Psychoanalytic Theories: perspectives from developmental psychopathology, 2003 (trans. Italian 2005, Hungarian 2005, Czech 2005); (with A. Bateman) Psychotherapy for Borderline Personality Disorder: mentalization based treatment, 2004 (trans. Spanish 2005, Italian 2006, German 2008); (with A. Bateman) Mentalization-Based Treatment for Borderline Personality Disorder: a practical guide, 2006 (trans. Dutch 2007, Norwegian 2007, Danish, Italian 2010, Korean 2010, Finnish 2014); (with J. G. Allen) Handbook of Mentalization-Based Treatment, 2006; (jtly) Development Science and Psychoanalysis: integration and innovation, 2007; (jtly) Mentalizing in Clinical Practice, 2008 (trans. Dutch 2009, Danish 2010, Italian 2010, Hungarian 2011, Japanese 2014, Polish 2014); (jtly) Social Cognition and Developmental Psychopathology, 2008; (with J. F. Clarkin and G. O. Gabbard) Psychodynamic Psychotherapy for Personality Disorders: a clinical handbook, 2010; (jtly) Brief Dynamic Interpersonal Therapy: a clinician's guide, 2011; (jtly) Mentalizing in Mental Health Practice, 2011; papers, contribs books. *Recreations:* ski-ing, theatre, gardening. *Address:* c/o Research Department of Clinical, Educational and Health Psychology, University College London, Gower Street, WC1E 6BT. *T:* (020) 7679 1943. *E:* p.fonagy@ucl.ac.uk.

FONE, Angela Mary, (Jill); *see* Tookey, A. M.

FONTAINE, Barbara Janet; Senior Master of the Senior Courts, Queen's Bench Division, and Queen's Remembrancer, since 2014; *b* 29 Dec. 1953; *d* of late John Fontaine and Brenda Fontaine (*née* Taylor); *m* 1990, Trevor John Watkins; twin *s*. *Educ:* Stockport High Sch. for Girls; KCL (LLB). Admitted solicitor, 1978; articled Bird & Bird, 1976–78; Solicitor: Hill, Dickinson, London, 1978–83; Coward Chance, later Clifford Chance, 1983–87; Baker & McKenzie, Hong Kong, 1987–93 (Partner, 1989); Dep. Queen's Bench Master, 1997–2003; Master of the Senior (formerly Supreme) Court, QBD, 2003–14. *Recreations:* theatre, art, cooking, travel. *Address:* Royal Courts of Justice, Strand, WC2A 2LL.

FONTAINE, Nicole Claude Marie; Member (EPP), European Parliament, 2004–09; *b* 16 Jan. 1942; *d* of Jean Garnier and Geneviève Garnier (*née* Lambert); *m* 1964, Jean-René Fontaine; one *d*; *m* 1995, Paul Aubret. *Educ:* Faculté de Droit, Paris (law degree, 1962); Inst. d'Etudes Politiques, Paris (Dip. 1964); DenD 1969. Teacher, 1963–64; Catholic Education Secretariat, France: Legal Advr, 1965; Dep. Sec.-Gen., 1972–81; Chief Rep., 1981–84. Member: Nat. Educn Council, France, 1975–81; Economic and Social Council, France, 1980–84. European Parliament: Mem. (UDF), 1984–2002; Vice Pres., 1989–94; First Vice Pres., 1994–99; Pres., 1999–2002; Member: Legal Affairs and Citizens' Rights Cttee,

1984–89; Women's Rights Cttee, 1984–89; Culture, Youth, Educn, Media and Sport Cttee, 1989–2002; Israel Delegn, 1989–97; Perm. Mem., Conciliation Cttee, 1994–99; Chm., Delegn to COSAC. Minister for Industry, France, 2002–04. Jean Monnet Professor *ad personam*, Univ. of Nice Sophia-Antipolis, 2010–13. Mem., Union des Démocrates et Indépendants (Mem., Founding Council and Exec. Cttee), 2012–. *Publications:* Les établissements d'enseignement privé associés à l'Etat par contrat, 1980; Les députés européens: qui sont-ils? que font-ils?, 1994; L'Europe de vos initiatives, 1997; Le traité d'Amsterdam, 1998; Mes combats à la présidence du Parlement européen, 2002. *Address:* 45 rue du Bois de Boulogne, 92200 Neuilly/Seine, France.

FOOKES, Baroness *cr* 1997 (Life Peer), of Plymouth in the co. of Devon; **Janet Evelyn Fookes,** DBE 1989; DL; *b* 21 Feb. 1936; *d* of late Lewis Aylmer Fookes and Evelyn Margery Fookes (*née* Holmes). *Educ:* Hastings and St Leonards Ladies' Coll.; High Sch. for Girls, Hastings; Royal Holloway Coll., Univ. of London (BA Hons; Hon. Fellow, 1998). Teacher, 1958–70. Councillor for County Borough of Hastings, 1960–61 and 1963–70 (Chm. Educn Cttee, 1967–70). MP (C): Merton and Morden, 1970–74; Plymouth, Drake, 1974–97. Mem., Speaker's Panel of Chairmen, 1976–97; Second Dep. Chm. of Ways and Means and Dep. Speaker, H of C, 1992–97. Sec., Cons. Parly Educn Cttee, 1971–75; Chairman: Educn, Arts and Home Affairs Sub-Cttee of the Expenditure Cttee, 1975–79; Parly Gp for Animal Welfare, 1985–92 (Sec., 1974–82); Member: Unopposed Bills Cttee, 1973–75; Services Cttee, 1974–76; Select Cttee on Home Affairs, 1984–92; Armed Forces Parly Scheme, 2001–. A Dep. Speaker, H of L, 2002–; a Dep. Chm. of Cttees, H of L, 2002–; Chm., Refreshment Cttee, H of L, 2003–07; Member: Jt Select Cttee on Draft Mental Capacity Bill (formerly Mental Incapacity Bill), 2003; Select Cttee on Crossrail Bill, 2008; Select Cttee on Communications, 2010–15; Delegated Powers and Regulatory Reform Select Cttee, 2013–; Chm., All Party Parly Gardening and Horticulture Gp, 2010–. Chm., Cons. West Country Mems Cttee, 1976–77, Vice-Chm., 1977. Fellow, Industry and Parlt Trust, 1978. Pres., Hastings and Rye Cons. Assoc., 1998–. Member: Council, RSPCA, 1975–92 (Chm., 1979–81; Vice-Pres., 1992–); Council, SSAFA, 1980–98 (Vice-Pres., 1998–); Council, Stonham Housing Assoc., 1980–92; Commonwealth War Graves Commn, 1987–97; Council, Coll. of St Mark and St John, 1989–2004. President: Hastings, St Leonards on Sea, Bexhill and Dist Br., NSPCC, 2000–; War Widows Assoc., 2005–. Chm., Plymouth Ambassadors' Gp of Tomorrow's People (formerly Patron, Plymouth Workroute, later Regl Patron, Tomorrow's People), 1998–. Gov., Kelly Coll., 2002–14. Hon. Freeman, Plymouth, 2000. Member: RHS; Nat. Trust; Art Fund. DL E Sussex, 2001. Hon. DLitt Plymouth, 1993. *Recreations:* theatre, gardening, swimming, yoga. *Address:* House of Lords, SW1A 0PW.

FOOT, David Lovell, CB 1998; FICFor; Head of Forestry Authority, 1995–99; *b* 20 May 1939; *s* of late John Bartram Lovell Foot, MBE and of Bertha Lilian Foot; *m* 1964, Verena Janine Walton; one *s* one *d*. *Educ:* John Lyon Sch., Harrow; Edinburgh Univ. (BSc Hons 1961). FICFor 1980. Dist Officer, Forestry Commn, 1961–64; Silviculturist, Dept of Forestry and Game, Govt of Malawi, 1964–70; Forestry Commission: various appts in S Scotland, N Wales and E Scotland, 1970–86; Comr, 1986–99. Trustee, Woodland Trust, 1999–2008. *Recreations:* walking, writing, photography.

FOOT, Michael David Kenneth Willoughby, CBE 2003; Global Vice-Chairman, Promontory Financial Group, since 2012; *b* 16 Dec. 1946; *s* of Kenneth Willoughby Foot and Ruth Joan (*née* Cornah); *m* 1972, Michele Annette Cynthia Macdonald; one *s* two *d*. *Educ:* Pembroke Coll., Cambridge (MA); Yale Univ., USA (MA). Joined Bank of England, 1969; manager, 1978; sen. man., 1985; seconded to IMF, Washington, as UK Alternate Exec. Dir, 1985–87; Head: Foreign Exchange Div., 1988–90; European Div., 1990–93; Banking Supervision Div., 1993–94; Dep. Dir, Supervision and Surveillance, 1994–96; Exec. Dir, Bank of England, 1996–98; Man. Dir, Deposit Takers and Mkts, FSA, 1998–2004; Inspector of Banks, Central Bank of the Bahamas, 2004–07. Chm., Promontory Financial Gp (UK) Ltd, 2007–12. *Publications:* contrib. essays on monetary econs to books and jls. *Recreations:* choral singing, tennis, voluntary youth work.

FOOT, Prof. Mirjam Michaela, DLitt; FSA; Professor of Library and Archive Studies, University College London, 2000–06, now Emeritus; *b* 11 Oct. 1941; *d* of Carl Paul Maria Romme and Anthonia Maria Wiegman; *m* 1972, Michael Richard Daniell Foot, CBE, TD (*d* 2012). *Educ:* Amsterdam Univ. (BA, MA, DLitt 1979). FSA 1986. Asst Lectr, Bedford Coll., Univ. of London, 1965–66; British Library: Asst Keeper, Rare Book Collection, 1966–84; Curator, Preservation Service, 1984–87; Dep. Dir, Hd of W European Collections and Hd of Acquisitions, 1987–90; Dir of Collections and Preservation, 1990–99. Associate, Clare Hall, Cambridge, 1970–72; Sandars Reader in Bibliography, Univ. of Cambridge, 2002–03; Hon. Sen. Res. Fellow, Sch. of Advanced Study, Univ. of London, 2006–. Ed., British Liby Jl, 1977–85. Bibliographical Society: Hon. Sec., 1975–94; Vice-Pres., 1990–2000; Pres., 2000–02; Gold Medal, 2014. Vice-Pres., Soc. of Antiquaries, 2001–05. Hon. Fellow, Designer Bookbinders, 1986. *Publications:* The Henry Davis Gift: Vol I: Studies in the History of Bookbinding, 1978; Vol II: North European Bindings, 1983; Vol III: South European Bindings, 2010; Pictorial Bookbindings, 1986; (with H. M. Nixon) The History of Decorated Bookbinding in England, 1992; Studies in the History of Bookbinding, 1993; The History of Bookbinding as a Mirror of Society, 1998; The Decorated Bindings in Marsh's Library, Dublin, 2004; (ed) Eloquent Witnesses: bookbindings and their history, 2004; Bookbinders at Work: their roles and methods, 2005; contrib. articles in Book Collector, The Liby, British Liby Jl, Revue française d'histoire du livre, Proc. and Bulletins of Assoc. Internat. de Bibliophilie, Paper Conservator. *Recreations:* music, reading, walking. *Address:* Martins Cottage, Bell Lane, Nuthampstead, Herts SG8 8ND.

FOOT, Prof. Rosemary June, PhD; FBA 1996; John Swire Senior Research Fellow in International Relations, St Antony's College, Oxford, 1990–2014, now Emeritus; Professor of International Relations, 1997–2014, now Emeritus, and Senior Research Fellow, Department of Politics and International Relations and Research Associate, China Centre, since 2014, University of Oxford; *b* 4 June 1948; *d* of Leslie William Foot, MBE and Margaret Lily Frances Foot; *m* 1996, Timothy C. S. Kennedy. *Educ:* Univ. of Essex (BA Hons Govt 1972); SOAS, London Univ. (MA Area Studies (Far East) 1973); LSE (PhD Internat. Relns 1977). Lectr in Internat. Relns, Univ. of Sussex, 1978–90. Fulbright Scholar and American Council of Learned Socs Fellow, E Asian Inst., Columbia Univ., NY, 1981–82; Vis. Scholar, Renmin Univ., Beijing, 1986; Sen. Fellow, Belfer Center, Kennedy Sch. of Govt, Harvard Univ., 2006; S. Rajaratnam Prof. of Strategic Studies, Nat. Tech. Univ., Singapore, 2006; Visiting Fellow: Dr Seaker Chan Center, Fudan Univ., 2013; Nobel Inst., 2014; Sir Howard Kippenberger Vis. Prof., Victoria Univ. of Wellington, 2014. *Publications:* The Wrong War: American policy and the dimensions of the Korean conflict 1950–1953, 1985; A Substitute for Victory: the politics of peacemaking at the Korean Armistice talks, 1990; (ed jtly) Migration: the Asian experience, 1994; The Practice of Power: US relations with China since 1949, 1995; (ed jtly) Hong Kong's Transitions 1842–1997, 1997; Rights Beyond Borders: the global community and the struggle over human rights in China, 2000; (ed jtly) Order and Justice in International Relations, 2003; (ed jtly) US Hegemony and International Organisations, 2003; Human Rights and Counter-terrorism in America's Asia Policy, 2004; (ed jtly) Does China Matter?: a reassessment, 2004; Framing Security Agendas: US counter-terrorist policies and Southeast Asian responses, 2008; (jtly) China, the United States, and Global Order, 2011; (ed) China Across the Divide: the domestic and global in politics and society, 2013; (ed jtly) The Oxford Handbook of the International Relations of Asia, 2014. *Recreations:* walking, music, swimming. *Address:* St Antony's College, Oxford OX2 6JF. *T:* (01865) 612868.

FOOT, Prof. Sarah Rosamund Irvine, PhD; FRHistS, FSA; Regius Professor of Ecclesiastical History, University of Oxford, since 2007; *b* 23 Feb. 1961; *d* of late Michael Richard Daniell Foot, CBE, TD, and Elizabeth Mary Irvine Foot (*née* King); *m* 1st, 1986, Geoffrey Martin Kenneth Schrecker (marr. diss. 1999); one *s*; 2nd, 2002, Prof. Michael John Bentley. *Educ:* Withington Girls' Sch., Manchester; Newnham Coll., Cambridge (BA 1984, MA 1986; PhD 1990). FSA 2001; FRHistS 2001. Res. Fellow, Gonville and Caius Coll., Cambridge, 1989–93; University of Sheffield: Lectr, 1993–2001; Sen. Lectr, 2001–04; Prof. of Early Medieval Hist., 2004–07. Lay Canon, Christ Ch, Oxford, 2007–. *Publications:* Veiled Women: the disappearance of nuns from Anglo-Saxon England, 2 vols, 2000; Monastic Life in Anglo-Saxon England *c* 600–900, 2006; Athelstan: the first King of England, 2011. *Recreations:* music, fiction, travel. *Address:* Christ Church, Oxford OX1 1DP. *T:* (01865) 286078. *E:* sarah.foot@chch.ox.ac.uk.

FOOTMAN, John Richard Evelegh; an Executive Director, Bank of England, since 2003; *b* 6 Sept. 1952; *s* of Jack and Joyce Footman; *m* 1983, Elaine Watkiss; two *s* three *d*. *Educ:* Clifton Coll., Bristol. Joined Bank of England, 1969; Private Sec. to Gov., 1986–89; Head of Information, 1989–94; Sec., 1994–97; Dep. Dir, 1997–99; Dir of Personnel, 1999–2003. *Address:* Bank of England, EC2R 8AH. *T:* (020) 7601 5765.

FOOTTIT, Rt Rev. Anthony Charles; Bishop Suffragan of Lynn, 1999–2003; an Honorary Assistant Bishop, Diocese of Norwich, since 2004; *b* 28 June 1935; *s* of Percival Frederick and Mildred Foottit; *m* 1977, Rosamond Mary Alyson Buxton; one *s* two *d*. *Educ:* Lancing Coll.; King's Coll., Cambridge (MA). Asst Curate, Wymondham, 1961–64; Vicar, Blakeney Group, 1964–71; Rector, Camelot Group, 1971–81; RD of Cary, 1979–81; St Hugh's Missioner for Lincolnshire, 1981–87; Hon. Canon of Lincoln Cathedral, 1986–87; Archdeacon of Lynn, 1987–98. *Publications:* Mission and Ministry in Rural France, 1967; A Gospel of Wild Flowers, 2006. *Recreations:* gardening, botany, rambling. *Address:* Ivy House, Whitwell Street, Reepham, Norfolk NR10 4RA. *T:* (01603) 870340.

FOPP, Dr Michael Anton; Director General (formerly Director), Royal Air Force Museum, 1988–2010; *b* 28 Oct. 1947; *s* of late Sqdn Ldr Desmond Fopp, AFC, AE and of Edna Meryl Fopp; *m* 1968, Rosemary Ann Hodgetts; one *s*. *Educ:* Reading Blue Coat Sch.; City Univ., London (MA 1984; PhD 1989). FMA; FRAeS. Dep. Keeper 1979–82, Keeper 1982–85, Battle of Britain Mus.; Co. Sec., Hendon Mus. Trading Co. Ltd, 1983–85; Dir, London Transport Mus., 1985–88. Hon. Sec. 1976–86, Chm. 1986–88, Soc. of Friends of RAF Mus. President: London Underground Rly Soc., 1987–88; Internat. Assoc. of Transport Museums, 1992–98. Chairman: Museums' Documentation Assoc., 1995–98; London Transport Flying Club Ltd, 1986–97. Dir, RAF Mus. Amer. Foundn, 2000–10. Trustee: Air Safety Trust, 2011– (Chm., 2012–); Air Pilots (formerly Guild of Air Pilots) Trust, 2011– (Chm., 2012–). Freeman, City of London, 1984; Liveryman, 2002–, Master, 2010–11, Hon. Co. of Air Pilots (formerly GAPAN). Hon. DSc City, 2011. Cruise ship lecturer, 2011–. *Publications:* The Boeing Washington, 1980; The Battle of Britain Museum Guide, 1980; The Bomber Command Museum Guide, 1982; The RAF Museum Guide, 1985; (ed) A Junior Guide to the RAF Museum, 1985; (ed) Battle of Britain Project Book, 1989; Royal Air Force Museum, 1992, 2nd edn 2003; (ed) High Flyers, 1993; Managing Museums and Galleries, 1997; The Implications of Emerging Technologies for Museums and Galleries, 1997; The Tradition is Safe, 2003; various articles on aviation, museums and management, in magazines and jls. *Recreations:* computers, flying, gliding, Chinese cookery, Radio Yacht Racing, bell ringing, model railways. *Address:* Honourable Company of Air Pilots, Cobham House, 9 Warwick Court, Gray's Inn, WC1R 5DJ. *T:* (020) 7404 4032. *Clubs:* Royal Air Force; Air Squadron.

FORAN, (Mary) Shirley; Sheriff of North Strathclyde at Kilmarnock, since 2014; *b* Glasgow, 6 July 1957; *d* of Alexander and Mary Stewart; *m* 1979, John Foran; one *s* two *d*. *Educ:* St Michael's Acad., Kilwinning; Glasgow Univ. (LLB). NP 1981. Admitted Solicitor, 1980; Asst, 1980–90, Litigation Partner, 1990–2014, Black Hay, Solicitors, Ayr and Prestwick; Sheriff (pt-time), 2006–14. Chm., Bd of Govs, Wellington Sch. (Ayr) Ltd, 2013–. *Recreations:* reading, gardening, watching and pretending to play tennis. *Address:* Kilmarnock Sheriff Court, St Marnock Street, Kilmarnock KA1 1ED. *T:* (01563) 550024.

FORBES, family name of **Lord Forbes** and of **Earl of Granard**.

FORBES, 23rd Lord *cr* 1445 or before; **Malcolm Nigel Forbes;** DL; Premier Lord of Scotland; landowner; *b* 6 May 1946; *s* of 22nd Lord Forbes and Hon. Rosemary Katharine Hamilton-Russell, *o d* of 9th Viscount Boyne; *S* father, 2013; *m* 1st, 1969, Carole Jennifer Andrée (marr. diss. 1982), *d* of N. S. Whitehead, Aberdeen; one *s* one *d*; 2nd, 1988, Jennifer Mary Gribbon, *d* of I. P. Whittington, Tunbridge Wells. *Educ:* Eton; Aberdeen Univ. Director, Instock Disposables Ltd, 1974–2009; Chm., Castle Forbes Collection Ltd, 1996–. DL Aberdeenshire, 1996. *Heir: s* Master of Forbes, *qv*. *Address:* Castle Forbes, Alford, Aberdeenshire AB33 8BL. *T:* (01975) 562574; 3 Steeple Close, SW6 3LE. *T:* (020) 7736 0730.

FORBES, Viscount; Jonathan Peter Hastings Forbes; *b* 24 Dec. 1981; *e s* and *heir* of Earl of Granard, *qv*.

FORBES, Master of; Hon. Neil Malcolm Ross Forbes; *b* 10 March 1970; *s* and *heir* of Lord Forbes, *qv*; *m* 2009, Maria Elfgyva Martell; one *s* one *d*. *Educ:* Eton Coll.; Bristol Univ. (BA Hons); Edinburgh Univ. (MSc). Partner, Harthill Farms. *Address:* Forbes Estate Office, Castle Forbes, Alford AB33 8BL.

FORBES, Major Sir Andrew (Iain Ochoncar), 13th Bt *cr* 1630 (NS), of Craigievar, Aberdeenshire and of Corse; *b* 28 Nov. 1945; *s* of Lt-Col Patrick Walter Forbes of Corse, OBE, DL and Margaret Hawthorne Forbes (*née* Lydall); *S* kinsman, 2000, but his name does not appear on the Official Roll of the Baronetage; *m* 1984, Jane Elizabeth Dunbar-Nasmith (*d* 2005); two *s* two *d*. *Educ:* Trinity Coll., Glenalmond; RMA Sandhurst; St Catherine's Coll., Oxford (BA 1969); Cranfield Sch. of Mgt (MBA 1979). Major, Gordon Highlanders, retired. *Heir: s* James Patrick Ochoncar Forbes, *b* 1 Nov. 1986.

FORBES, Andrew Malcolm; Founding Partner, Forbes Anderson Free (formerly Forbes Anderson), since 2001; *b* London, 15 April 1963; *s* of Gordon and Adriana Forbes; *m* 1997, Charlotte Matthews; one *s* two *d*. *Educ:* Belle Vue Boys' Sch., Bradford; Univ. of E Anglia (LLB 1986); Coll. of Law, Chancery Lane. Lead guitarist, punk band, The Wall, 1980–81. Admitted solicitor, 1989; Solicitor: Richards Butler, 1989–92; Simkins Partnership, 1992–96 (Partner, 1996–98); Partner, Statham Gill Davies, 1998–2001. *Recreations:* musician and songwriter, mountaineer and hill walker, polar adventurer, potholer, creator of The Spider. *Address:* Forbes Anderson Free, 60 Charlotte Street, W1T 2NU. *T:* (020) 7291 3500. *E:* aforbes@forbesanderson.com.

FORBES, Anthony David Arnold William; Joint Senior Partner, Cazenove & Co., 1980–94; *b* 15 Jan. 1938; *s* of late Lt-Col D. W. A. W. Forbes, MC, and Diana Mary (*née* Henderson), later Marchioness of Exeter; *m* 1st, 1962, Virginia June Ropner; one *s* one *d*; 2nd, 1973, Belinda Mary Drury-Lowe. *Educ:* Eton. Served Coldstream Guards, 1956–59. Joined Cazenove & Co., 1960; Member of Stock Exchange, subseq. MSI, 1965–2003. Director: Carlton Communications Plc, 1994–2002; The Merchants Trust PLC, 1994–2002; Royal & Sun Alliance Insurance Gp (formerly Royal Insurance Hldgs plc), 1994–2002 (Dep. Chm., 1998–2002); RTZ Pension Investment Ltd, 1994–2000; Watmoughs (Hldgs) PLC, 1994–98; Phoenix Group Ltd, 1995–97; Rio Tinto Pension Fund Trustees Ltd, 2000–06. Chairman: Hospital and Homes of St Giles, 1975–; Wellesley House Educnl Trust, 1983–94; Trustee, Botanic Gardens Conservation Internat., 1992–2005. Governor: Cobham Hall, 1975–94;

Royal Choral Soc., 1979–. FRSA 1993. Hon. DBA De Montfort Univ., 1994. *Recreations:* music, gardening. *Address:* Wakerley Manor, Wakerley, Oakham, Rutland LE15 8PA. *T:* (01572) 747549.

FORBES, Prof. Charles Douglas, MD, DSc; Professor of Medicine, University of Dundee, 1987–2004, now Emeritus; *b* 9 Oct. 1938; *s* of late John Forbes and Dr Annie Forbes (*née* Stuart); *m* 1965, Jannette MacDonald Robertson; two *s*. *Educ:* Univ. of Glasgow (MB ChB 1961; MD 1972; DSc 1986). Trng grades, Dept of Materia Medica, Univ. of Glasgow, 1961–65; Lectr in Medicine, Makerere Univ., Uganda, 1965–66; Registrar in Haemophilia, Royal Infirmary, Glasgow, 1966–68; American Heart Fellow/Fulbright Fellow, Cleveland, Ohio, 1968–70; Sen. Lectr, then Reader, Univ. of Glasgow, 1970–87. *Publications:* (with W. F. Jackson) Colour Atlas and Text of Clinical Medicine, 1993; (jtly) Haemophilia, 1997; articles and research papers on blood coagulation and thrombosis. *Recreations:* gardening, walking, DIY. *Address:* East Chattan, 108 Hepburn Gardens, St Andrews, Fife KY16 9LT. *T:* (01334) 472428.

See also J. S. Forbes.

FORBES, Colin, RDI 1974; Consulting Partner, Pentagram Design AG, since 1993; *b* 6 March 1928; *s* of Kathleen and John Forbes; *m* 1961, Wendy Schneider; one *s* one *d*, and one *d* by a previous marriage. *Educ:* Sir Antony Browne's, Brentwood; LCC Central Sch. of Arts and Crafts. Design Asst, Herbert Spencer, 1952; freelance practice and Lectr, LCC Central Sch. of Arts and Crafts, 1953–57; Art Dir, Stuart Advertising, London, 1957–58; Head of Graphic Design Dept, LCC Central Sch. of Arts and Crafts, 1958–61; freelance practice, London, 1961–62; Partner: Fletcher/Forbes/Gill, 1962–65; Crosby/Fletcher/Forbes, 1965–72; Pentagram Design Ltd, 1972–78; Pentagram Design Inc., NY, 1978–93. Mem., Alliance Graphique Internationale, 1965– (Internat. Pres. 1976–79); Pres., Amer. Inst. Graphic Arts, 1984–86. *Publications:* Graphic Design: visual comparisons, 1963; A Sign Systems Manual, 1970; Creativity and Communication, 1971; New Alphabets A to Z, 1973; Living by Design, 1978; Pentagram: the compendium, 1993. *Address:* Forbes Farm, 2879 Horseshoe Road, Westfield, NC 27053, USA. *T:* (336) 3513941.

FORBES, Very Rev. Graham John Thomson, CBE 2004; Provost, St Mary's Cathedral, Edinburgh, since 1990; *b* 10 June 1951; *s* of J. T. and D. D. Forbes; *m* 1973, Jane T. Miller; three *s*. *Educ:* George Heriot's School, Edinburgh; Univ. of Aberdeen (MA); Univ. of Edinburgh (BD). Curate, Old St Paul's Church, Edinburgh, 1976–82; Provost, St Ninian's Cathedral, Perth, 1982–90. Dir, Theol Inst. of Scottish Episcopal Ch, 2002–04. HM (Lay) Inspector of Constabulary, 1995–98. Member: Armed Forces Pay Rev. Body, 2009–14; Security Vetting Appeals Panel, 2009–15. Member: Parole Bd for Scotland, 1990–95; Scottish Consumer Council, 1995–98; GMC, 1996–2008; Scottish Criminal Cases Rev. Commn, 1998–2008 (Chm., 2001–08); Clinical Standards Bd for Scotland, 1999–2002; NHS Quality Improvement Scotland, 2002–05; Chairman: MMR Expert Gp, Scottish Exec., 2001–02; UK Cttee on Ethical Aspects of Pandemic Influenza, 2006–; Mental Welfare Commn for Scotland, 2011–; Office of Scottish Charity Regulator, 2011–. Mem., Historic Bldgs Council (Scotland), 2000–02. Chm., Court, Edinburgh Napier Univ., 2012–. DUniv Napier, 2006. *Recreations:* running, fly-fishing. *Address:* 8 Lansdowne Crescent, Edinburgh EH12 5EQ. *T:* (home) (0131) 225 2978, (office) (0131) 225 6293.

FORBES, Adm. Sir Ian (Andrew), KCB 2003; CBE 1994; Supreme Allied Commander Atlantic, 2002–03; Deputy Supreme Allied Commander Transformation, 2003–04; *b* 24 Oct. 1946; *s* of late James and Winifred Forbes; *m* 1975, Sally, *d* of late Ronald Statham and Cynthia Statham; two *d*. *Educ:* Eastbourne Coll.; BRNC. Sea-going appointments, 1969–83: HM Ships Hermes, Upton, HM Yacht Britannia, USS W. H. Stanley; RAF Staff Coll., 1982–83; HM Ships Whitby, Kingfisher (CO), Apollo, Juno, Glamorgan, Diomede (CO), 1984–86; Chatham (CO), 1989–91; MoD, 1991–94; RCDS 1994; HMS Invincible (CO), 1995–96; MA to UN High Rep., Sarajevo, 1996–97; Comdr, UK Task Gp and Comdr, Anti-Submarine Warfare Striking Force, 1997–2000; Flag Officer Surface Flotilla, 2000–01; Dep. SACLANT, 2002. Chm., Naval Review, 2007–13. Sen. Advr, Strategy& (formerly Booz Allen Hamilton, later Booz & Co.), 2006–. Chm. Council, Eastbourne Coll., later Eastbourne Coll. and St Andrews Sch., 2005–13; Gov., Portsmouth High Sch., 2001–09; Mem. Adv. Bd, Occidental Coll., Calif., 2001–. President: Portsmouth Sea Cadets, 2006–13; Forces Pension Soc., 2013–; Chm., Royal Navy Club of 1765 and 1785, 2010–13. Associate FRUSI, 2005–. Hon. Citizen, City of Norfolk, Va, 2004. QCVS 1996; Legion of Merit (US); NATO Meritorious Service Medal. *Recreations:* tennis, history, gardening. *Clubs:* Army and Navy, Pilgrims.

FORBES, James Alexander, CBE 2003; CEng; non-executive Director, Atlantis Resources Corporation and Chairman, Atlantis Operations (UK) Ltd, 2010–12; *b* 6 Aug. 1946; *s* of James A. Forbes and Verna Kelman; *m* 1969, Jean Clark; four *s*. *Educ:* Paisley Coll. of Technol. (BSc (1st cl. hons) Elect. Engrg); Loughborough Univ. of Technol. (MSc Electro-heat). MIEE. Scottish Power: Student Apprentice, 1964; Commercial Engr, 1973–84; Area Commercial Officer, 1984–86; Mktg Manager, 1986–89; Northern Electric: Commercial Dir, 1989–90; Distribn Dir, 1990–91; Southern Electric: Ops Dir, 1991–94; Man. Dir, Electricity, 1994–96; Chief Operating Officer, 1996; Chief Exec., 1996–98; Chief Exec., Scottish and Southern Energy plc, 1998–2002. Non-exec. Chm., Thames Water, 2006; non-exec. Dir, FirstGroup plc, 2000–09. *Recreation:* golf.

FORBES, Sir James Thomas Stewart, 8th Bt *cr* 1823, of Newe, Aberdeenshire; *b* 28 May 1957; *o s* of Major Sir Hamish Stewart Forbes, 7th Bt, MBE, MC and Jacynthe Elizabeth Mary (*née* Underwood); *S* father, 2007; *m* 1986, Kerry Lynne, *o d* of Rev. Lee Toms, Sacramento; two *d*. *Educ:* Eton; Bristol Univ. (BA). Patron, Lonach Highland and Friendly Soc., 2007–. Owner, Bear's Head Prodns, Napa Valley, 1997–; creator: This is Your Fridge, TV show, 1991–92 (Sweden, Germany, Norway), 2012 (Sweden); Dramophone, app for smartphone.

FORBES, Vice-Adm. Sir John Morrison, KCB 1978; *b* 16 Aug. 1925; *s* of late Lt-Col R. H. Forbes, OBE and Gladys M. Forbes (*née* Pollock); *m* 1950, Joyce Newenham Hadden (*d* 2004); two *s* two *d*. *Educ:* RNC, Dartmouth. Served War: HMS Mauritius, Verulam and Nelson, 1943–46. HMS Aisne, 1946–49; Gunnery course and staff of HMS Excellent, 1950–51; served in RAN, 1952–54; Staff of HMS Excellent, 1954–56; HMS Ceylon, 1956–58; Staff of Dir of Naval Ordnance, 1958–60; Comdr (G) HMS Excellent, 1960–61; Staff of Dir of Seaman Officers' Appts, 1962–64; Exec. Officer, Britannia RN Coll., 1964–66; Operational Comdr and 2nd in Comd, Royal Malaysian Navy, 1966–68; Asst Dir, Naval Plans, 1969–70; comd HMS Triumph, 1971–72; comd Britannia RN Coll., Dartmouth, 1972–74; Naval Secretary, 1974–76; Flag Officer, Plymouth, Port Adm., Devonport, Comdr, Central Sub Area, Eastern Atlantic, and Comdr, Plymouth Sub Area, Channel, 1977–79. Naval ADC to the Queen, 1974. Kesatria Manku Negara (Malaysia), 1968. *Recreation:* country pursuits. *Address:* Rosapenna, Tanfield Park, Wickham, Fareham, Hants PO17 5NP. *Club:* RN Sailing Association.

FORBES, John Stuart; Sheriff of Tayside, Central and Fife at Dunfermline, 1980–2002; part-time Sheriff, whole of Scotland, 2003–05; *b* 31 Jan. 1936; *s* of late John Forbes and Dr A. R. S. Forbes; *m* 1963, Marion Alcock; one *s* two *d*. *Educ:* Glasgow High Sch.; Glasgow Univ. (MA, LLB). RA, TA, 1958–63 (Lieut). Solicitor, 1959–61; Advocate, Scottish Bar, 1962–76; Standing Jun. Counsel, Forestry Commn, 1972–76; Sheriff of Lothian and Borders, 1976–80. Pres., Glasgow Juridical Soc., 1963–64. Life Trustee, Carnegie, Dunfermline and Hero Fund Trusts, 1985–2002; Trustee, Carnegie UK Trust, 1990–2002. *Recreations:* tennis, golf, curling, shooting, fishing. *Address:* 8 Croftwynd, Milnathort, Kinross KY13 9GH. *Clubs:* Royal Scots (Edinburgh), Edinburgh Sports.

See also C. D. Forbes.

FORBES, Matthew Keith, OBE 2007; HM Diplomatic Service; Deputy Consul General, Shanghai, since 2012; *b* Yateley, 19 April 1966; *s* of Keith Forbes and Angela Norris (*née* Parsons); *m* 1988, Lydia Mary Bagg; three *s* one *d*. *Educ:* Clark's Coll., Guildford. Practitioner, Inst. Internal Auditors. Joined FCO, 1987; Attaché, Peking, 1989–90; Vice Consul, Colombo, 1990–94; Dep. High Comr, Maseru, 1999–2002; First Sec., Wellington, NZ, and Dep. Gov., Pitcairn, 2002–06; Hd, Mexico, Central America, Cuba and Hispaniola Section, FCO, 2007–09; High Comr to the Seychelles, 2009–12. *Recreations:* scuba diving, flying (PPL S Africa 2002), football. *Address:* c/o Foreign and Commonwealth Office, King Charles Street, SW1A 2AH. *E:* matthew.forbes@fco.gov.uk.

FORBES, Nanette; *see* Newman, N.

FORBES, Hon. Sir Thayne (John), Kt 1993; a Judge of the High Court of Justice, Queen's Bench Division, 1993–2009; *b* 28 June 1938; *s* of late John Thomson Forbes and Jessie Kay Robertson Stewart; *m* 1960, Celia Joan; two *s* one *d*. *Educ:* Winchester College (Quirister); Wolverton Grammar Sch.; University College London (LLB, LLM). Served Royal Navy (Instructor Lieutenant), 1963–66. Called to Bar, Inner Temple, 1966, Governing Bencher, 1991; QC 1984; a Recorder, 1986–90; a Circuit Judge (Official Referee), 1990–93; Presiding Judge, Northern Circuit, 1995–99; Judge i/c Technology and Construction Ct, 2001–04. Chm., Al Sweady Public Inquiry, 2009–. *Recreations:* music, reading, sailing, bird watching, astronomy, beekeeping. *Club:* Garrick.

FORBES, Sir William (Daniel) Stuart-, 13th Bt *cr* 1626 (NS), of Pitsligo and of Monymusk, Aberdeenshire; *b* 21 Aug. 1935; *s* of William Kenneth Stuart-Forbes (*d* 1946), 3rd *s* of 10th Bt, and Marjory Gilchrist; *S* uncle, 1985; *m* 1st, 1956, Jannette (*d* 1997), *d* of late Hori Toki George MacDonald; three *s* two *d*; 2nd, 2001, Betty Dawn Ward, *d* of William Henry Gibson and Ellen Dorothy Neilson. *Heir: s* Kenneth Charles Stuart-Forbes [*b* 26 Dec. 1956; *m* 1981, Susan, *d* of Len Murray; one *s* two *d*]. *Address:* 169 Budge Street, Blenheim, Marlborough 7201, New Zealand.

FORBES, Captain William Frederick Eustace; Vice Lord-Lieutenant of Stirling and Falkirk, 1984–96; Forestry Commissioner, 1982–88; *b* 6 July 1932; *er s* of late Lt-Col W. H. D. C. Forbes of Callendar, CBE and Elisabeth Forbes; *m* 1st, 1956, Pamela Susan (*d* 1993), *er d* of Lord McCorquodale of Newton, KCVO, PC; two *d*; 2nd, 1995, Venetia, Hon. Lady Troubridge, *widow* of Sir Peter Troubridge, 6th Bt. *Educ:* Eton. Regular soldier, Coldstream Guards, 1950–59; farmer and company director, 1959–. Chairman: Scottish Woodland Owners' Assoc., 1974–77; Nat. Playing Fields Assoc., Scottish Branch, 1980–90. *Recreations:* country pastimes, golf, cricket, travel. *Address:* Earlstoun Lodge, Dalry, Castle Douglas, Kirkcudbrightshire DG7 3TY. *T:* (01644) 430213. *Clubs:* MCC; New (Edinburgh); Royal and Ancient Golf.

FORBES ADAM, Rev. Sir (Stephen) Timothy (Beilby), 4th Bt *cr* 1917, of Hankelow Court, co. Chester; Non-Stipendiary Minister, Escrick, Stillingfleet, Naburn, since 1991; *b* Bombay, 19 Nov. 1923; *s* of Colin Gurdon Forbes Adam, CSI (*d* 1982), 3rd *s* of 1st Bt and Hon. Irene Constance Lawley (*d* 1976), *d* of 3rd Baron Wenlock; *S* cousin, 2009; *m* 1954, Penelope, *d* of George Campbell Munday, MC; four *d*. *Educ:* Eton; Balliol Coll., Oxford; Chichester Theol Coll. Ordained deacon, 1961, priest, 1962; Curate, St Nicholas, Guisborough, 1960–64; Rector, Barton-in-Fabis with Thrumpton, 1964–70; Priest-in-Charge, Southstoke with Midford, 1970–83; NSM, Tadmarton, Epwell, Sibfords, 1985–91. *Recreations:* cricket, tennis, hunting, shooting, dancing. *Heir: brother* Nigel Colin Forbes Adam [*b* 7 Dec. 1930; *m* 1st, 1954, Teresa Hermione Idena Robertson (*d* 2005); four *s*; 2nd, 1987, Mrs Mildred Malise Hare Ropner (*née* Armitage)]. *Address:* Woodhouse Farm, Escrick, York YO19 6HT. *T:* (01904) 728827.

FORBES-LEITH of Fyvie, Sir George Ian David, 4th Bt *cr* 1923, of Jessfield, co. Midlothian; *b* 26 May 1967; *e s* of Sir Andrew George Forbes-Leith, 3rd Bt and Jane Kate (*née* McCall-McCowan); *S* father, 2000; *m* 1995, Camilla Frances Ely; two *s* one *d*. *Educ:* RAC, Cirencester. *Recreations:* shooting, ski-ing, fishing. *Heir: s* Alexander Philip George Forbes-Leith, *b* 4 Feb. 1999. *Address:* Tifty, Fyvie, Turriff AB53 8JT.

FORBES-MEYLER, John William, OBE 1990; HM Diplomatic Service, retired; Ambassador to Ecuador, 1997–2000; *b* 3 July 1942; *s* of late J. J. C. Forbes and Moira Patricia (*née* Garvey, who later *m* James Robert Meyler); changed name by Deed Poll, 1963 to Forbes-Meyler; *m* 1st, 1964, Margaret Goddard (marr. diss. 1979); (one *d* decd); 2nd, 1980, Mary Read (*née* Vlachou); one step *s*. *Educ:* grammar sch., etc. Joined HM Diplomatic Service, 1962: CRO, 1962–64; Lagos, 1964–68; Chicago, 1968–69; Boston, 1969–70; FCO, 1970–71; NY, 1971–72; FCO, 1972–75; Athens, 1975–80; FCO, 1980–83; 1st Sec. (Econ.), Bonn, 1983–86; on loan to MoD, 1986–88; Deputy Head of Mission: Bogota, 1988–92; Vienna, 1992–96. *Recreations:* walking, music, reading. *E:* johnforbesmeyler@gmail.com. *Club:* Special Forces.

FORBES SMITH, Michael; *see* Smith, M. F.

FORBES WATSON, Anthony David; Managing Director, Pan Macmillan Publishers Ltd, since 2008; *b* 25 Sept. 1954; *s* of late Ian and Evelyn Forbes Watson; *m* 1983, Jennifer Ann Curnow; one *s* one *d*. *Educ:* Charterhouse Sch.; York Univ. (BA English and Related Lit.). Internat. Sales, OUP, 1977–80; Harper Collins: Internat. Sales Mgt, 1980–86; Sales and Mktg Dir, 1986–90; Managing Director: Pitman Publishing, 1990–91; Ladybird Books Ltd, 1991–96; Chief Exec., Penguin Gp (UK), 1996–2005. Pres., Publishers' Assoc. of UK, 2002–03. Governor, Loughborough Coll. of Art and Design, 1993–95. *Recreations:* drawing, ski-ing, golf. *Address:* The Granary, 27–31 High Street, Watlington, Oxon OX49 5PZ. *Clubs:* Garrick; Huntercombe Golf.

FORD, family name of **Baroness Ford.**

FORD, Baroness *cr* 2006 (Life Peer), of Cunninghame in North Ayrshire; **Margaret Anne Ford;** Chairman, STV Group plc, since 2013; *b* 16 Dec. 1957; *d* of Edward and Susan Garland; *m* 1990, David Arthur Bolger; one *s* one *d* by a previous marriage. *Educ:* Glasgow Univ. (MA Hons, MPhil). Scottish Organiser, BIFU, 1982–87; Managing Consultant, Price Waterhouse & Co., 1987–90; Dir, Scottish Homes, 1990–93; Man. Dir, 1993–2000, Chm., 2000–02, Eglinton Mgt Centre; Chief Exec., Good Practice Ltd, 2000–04 (Dep. Chm., 2004–05); Chm., English Partnerships, 2002–07; Man. Dir, Royal Bank of Canada Capital Mkts, 2007–09. Chairman: Lothian Health Bd, 1997–2000; Irvine Bay URC, 2006–11; Olympic Park Legacy Co., 2009–12. Non-executive Director: Scottish Prison Service, 1994–98; Ofgem, 2000–03; Thus plc, 2002–05; Serco plc, 2003–10; Grainger plc, 2008–; Segro plc, 2013–; Taylor Wimpey plc, 2013–; Chairman: May Gurney plc, 2011–13; Barchester Healthcare Ltd, 2012–15. Nat. Pres., British Epilepsy Assoc., 2008–. Hon. Prof., Urban Studies Dept, Univ. of Glasgow, 2008–. Hon. DBA Napier, 2008; DUniv Stirling, 2008. Hon. MRICS 2008. *Recreations:* family, sport, fine art, travel. *Address:* House of Lords, SW1A 0PW.

FORD, Rev. Adam; Chaplain, St Paul's Girls' School, London, 1976–2001 (Head of Lower School, 1986–92); *b* 15 Sept. 1940; *s* of John Ford and Jean Beattie Ford (*née* Winstanley); *m* 1st, 1969, Veronica Rosemary Lucia Verey (marr. diss. 1993); two *s* two *d*; 2nd, 2011, Rosemary Roscoe. *Educ:* Minehead Grammar Sch.; King's Coll., Univ. of London (BD

Hons, AKC 1964); Lancaster Univ. (MA Indian Religion 1972). Asst, Ecumenical Inst. of World Council of Churches, Geneva, 1964; ordained deacon and priest, 1965; Curate, Cirencester Parish Church, Glos, 1965–69; Vicar of Hebden Bridge, W Yorkshire, 1969–76; Priest-in-Ordinary to the Queen, 1984–90. Regular contributor to Prayer for the Day, Radio 4, 1978–; writer and narrator, Whose World?, series of TV progs on sci. and religion, 1987. Hon. FRAS 1960. *Publications:* Spaceship Earth, 1981; Weather Watch, 1982; Star Gazers Guide to the Night Sky (audio guide to astronomy), 1982; Universe: God, Man and Science, 1986; The Cuckoo Plant, 1991; Mr Hi-Tech, 1993; Faith and Science, 1999; The Art of Mindful Walking, 2010; Seeking Silence in a Noisy World, 2011; Mindfulness and the Art of Urban Living, 2011; Galileo and the Art of Ageing Mindfully, 2015; articles in The Times and science jls on relationship between science and religion, also on dialogue between religions; regular contrib. Church Times. *Recreations:* painting birds, feathers and flints, travelling, writing. *Address:* Bramble Cottage, Weaver's Lane, Alfriston, E Sussex BN26 5TH.

See also Anna Ford.

FORD, Lt Col Sir Andrew (Charles), KCVO 2012; Comptroller, Lord Chamberlain's Office, since 2006; *b* 5 Feb. 1957; *s* of Charles and Irmgard Ford; *m* 1985, Rosalind Birkett; two *s*. *Educ:* King's Coll., Taunton; RMA Sandhurst; JSDC Greenwich. Commnd Grenadier Guards, 1977; Comd, 1st Bn Welsh Guards, 1999–2002; Extra Equerry to the Queen, 2005. *Address:* c/o Buckingham Palace, SW1A 1AA. *Clubs:* Pratt's, Cavalry and Guards.

FORD, Sir Andrew (Russell), 3rd Bt *cr* 1929, of Westerdunes, Co. of East Lothian; Head of Sport and Leisure, 1974–96, Senior Lecturer in English, 1996–2003, Wiltshire College (formerly Chippenham College); *b* 29 June 1943; *s* of Sir Henry Russell Ford, 2nd Bt, TD and Mary Elizabeth (*d* 1997), *d* of late Godfrey F. Wright; *S* father, 1989; *m* 1968, Penelope Anne, *d* of Harry Relph; two *s* one *d*. *Educ:* Winchester; New Coll., Oxford (half-blue, athletics, 1962); Loughborough Coll. (DLC); London Univ. (BA external); Birmingham Univ. (MA external). Schoolmaster: Blairmore Sch., Aberdeens, 1967–71; St Peter's Sch., Cambridge, NZ, 1971–74. Hon. BSc Loughborough, 2009. *Heir: s* Toby Russell Ford, *b* 11 Jan. 1973. *Address:* 20 Coniston Road, Chippenham, Wilts SN14 0PX. *T:* (01249) 655442.

FORD, Anna; broadcaster, BBC, 1989–2006; *b* 2 Oct. 1943; *d* of John Ford and Jean Beattie Winstanley; *m* 1st, 1970, Dr Alan Holland Bittles (marr. diss. 1976); 2nd, 1981, Charles Mark Edward Boxer (*d* 1988); two *d*. *Educ:* Manchester Univ. (BA Hons Econ 1966; DipAE 1970). Work with Internat. Students, Manchester Univ., 1966–69; Lecturer: Rupert Stanley Coll. of Further Educn, Belfast, 1970–72; NI Reg., Open Univ., 1972–74; presenter and reporter in news and current affairs for Granada TV, ITN and BBC, 1974–2006. Non-executive Director: Sainsbury's, 2006–12; N. Brown Gp plc, 2009–. Chair, Index on Censorship, 2005–08. Trustee: Royal Botanic Gardens, Kew, 1995–2002; Forum for the Future, 2006–09. Chancellor, 2001–04, Co-Chancellor, 2004–08, Univ. of Manchester. FRGS 1990; Hon. Fellow, Lucy Cavendish Coll., Cambridge, 2006. Hon. Bencher, Middle Temple, 2002. Hon. LLD Manchester, 1998; DUniv Open, 1998; Hon. DLit St Andrews, 2006. *Publications:* Men: a documentary, 1985. *Recreations:* gardening, walking, drawing.

See also Rev. Adam Ford.

FORD, Anthony; *see* Ford, J. A.

FORD, Antony, CMG 1997; HM Diplomatic Service, retired; Ambassador to Austria, 2000–03; *b* Bexley, 1 Oct. 1944; *s* of late William Ford and Grace Ford (*née* Smith); *m* 1970, Linda Gordon Joy; one *s* one *d*. *Educ:* St Dunstan's Coll., Catford; UCW, Aberystwyth (BA). Joined HM Diplomatic Service, 1967; Third, later Second, Sec., Bonn, 1968–71; Second Sec., Kuala Lumpur, 1971–73; First Secretary: FCO, 1973–77; Washington, 1977–81; FCO, 1981–84; Counsellor: East Berlin, 1984–87; FCO, 1987–90; Consul-Gen., San Francisco, 1990–94; Chm., CSSB, on secondment to RAS Agency, 1994–96; Minister, Berlin, 1996–99; on secondment to Andersen Consulting, 1999–2000. *Publications:* Learning to Suffer, 2010. *Recreations:* reading, golf, cricket. *Club:* Morgan Sports Car.

FORD, Benjamin Thomas; DL; *b* 1 April 1925; *s* of Benjamin Charles Ford and May Ethel (*née* Moorton); *m* 1950, Vera Ada (*née* Fawcett-Fancet); two *s* one *d*. *Educ:* Rowan Road Central Sch., Surrey. Apprenticed as compositor, 1941. War Service, 1943–47, Fleet Air Arm (Petty Officer). Electronic Fitter/Wireman, 1951–64; Convener of Shop Stewards, 1955–64. Pres., Harwich Constituency Labour Party, 1955–63; Mem., Clacton UDC, 1959–62; Alderman Essex CC, 1959–65; JP Essex, 1962–67. MP (Lab) Bradford N, 1964–83; contested (Lab Ind.) Bradford N, 1983. Mem., H of C Select Cttee (Services), 1970–83 (Chm., Accommodation and Admin Sub-Cttee, 1979–83); Chm., Jt Select Cttee on Sound Broadcasting, 1976–77; Chairman: British-Portuguese Parly Gp, 1965–83; British-Argentinian Parly Gp, 1974–81; British-Brazilian Parly Gp, 1974–79; British-Malaysian Parly Gp, 1975–83; British-Venezuelan Parly Gp, 1977–83; All-Party Wool Textile Parly Gp, 1974–83; Vice-Chairman: British-Latin American Parly Gp, 1974–79; PLP Defence Cttee, 1979–82; Mem. Exec. Cttee, IPU British Gp, 1971–83 (Chm., 1977–79); Sec., British-Namibian Parly Gp, 1980–83. Chm., Leeds NW Lib Dems, 1988–91; Pres., Leeds Fedn of Lib Dems, 1991–97. Bd Mem., Bradford & Northern Housing Assoc., 1975–95 (Chm., Yorks and Humberside Regl Cttee). President: English Shooting Council, 1996–2001 (Chm., 1982–96); English Target Shooting Fedn, 2001–04; Yorks Rifle Assoc., 2004–12 (Chm., 1999–2004); Vice-Pres., British Assoc. for Shooting and Conservation, 1983–; Mem. Council, Nat. Rifle Assoc., 1968–94 (Vice-Pres., 1984–). President: Yorks and Humberside Region, Mencap, 1986–91; Bradford Civic Soc., 1988–96; RBL, Bramhope, 2009–. Freeman, City of London, 1979; Liveryman, Gunmakers' Co., 1978–99. DL W Yorks, 1982. Hon. FAIA 1983. Grand Officer, Order of the Southern Cross (Brazil), 1976. *Publications:* Piecework, 1960. *Recreations:* music, shooting, family, reading. *Address:* 9 Wynmore Crescent, Bramhope, Leeds LS16 9DH. *Club:* East Ward Labour (Bradford).

FORD, Colin John, CBE 1993; lecturer, writer and broadcaster on films, theatre and photography; exhibition organiser; Chairman, PEEL Entertainment Group (formerly Partnership Events & Entertainment), 1999–2011; *b* 13 May 1934; *s* of John William and Hélène Martha Ford; *m* 1st, 1961, Margaret Elizabeth Cordwell (marr. diss.); one *s* one *d*; 2nd, 1984, Susan Joan Frances Grayson; one *s*. *Educ:* Enfield Grammar Sch.; University Coll., Oxford (MA). Manager and Producer, Kidderminster Playhouse, 1958–60; Gen. Man., Western Theatre Ballet, 1960–62; Vis. Lectr in English and Drama, California State Univ. at Long Beach and UCLA (Univ. Extension), 1962–64; Dep. Curator, Nat. Film Archive, 1965–72. Organiser, 30th Anniv. Congress of Internat. Fedn of Film Archives, London, 1968; Dir, Cinema City Exhibn, 1970; Programme Dir, London Shakespeare Film Festival, 1972; Keeper of Film and Photography, Nat. Portrait Gall., 1972–81; founding Hd, Nat. Mus. of Photography, Film and Television, 1982–93; Dir, Nat. Mus. of Wales, then Nat. Museums & Galls of Wales, 1993–98. Chm., Kraszna-Krausz Foundn, 2003–10; Vice-Pres., Julia Margaret Cameron Trust, 2005–. Hon. FRPS 1999. Hon. MA Bradford, 1989. *Film:* Masks and Faces, 1966 (BBC TV version, Omnibus, 1968). *Publications:* (with Roy Strong) An Early Victorian Album, 1974, 2nd edn 1977; The Cameron Collection, 1975; (principal contrib.) Oxford Companion to Film, 1975; (ed) Happy and Glorious: Six Reigns of Royal Photography, 1977; Rediscovering Mrs Cameron, 1979; People in Camera, 1979; (with Brian Harrison) A Hundred Years Ago (Britain in the 1880s), 1983; Portraits (Gallery of World Photography), 1983; (ed) The Story of Popular Photography, 1988; Lewis Carroll, 1998; André Kertész and the Avant Garde, 1999; (ed) Performance!, 2000; (with Julian Cox) Julia Margaret Cameron: the complete photographs, 2003; Julia Margaret Cameron: 19th century photographer of genius, 2003; (with Péter Baki and George Szirtes) Eyewitness: Hungarian photography in the twentieth century, 2011; (with Karl Steinorth): You Press the Button, We Do the Rest: the birth of snapshot photography, 1988; Lewis Carroll: photographs, 1991; Ferenc Berko: 60 Years of Photography, 1991; articles in many jls. *Recreations:* travel, music. *Address:* 7 Gentleman's Row, Enfield EN2 6PT.

FORD, Prof. David Frank, Hon. OBE 2013; PhD; Regius Professor of Divinity and Fellow of Selwyn College, Cambridge University, 1991–2015; *b* 23 Jan. 1948; *s* of George Ford and Phyllis (*née* Woodman); *m* 1982, Deborah Perrin Hardy, *d* of late Rev. Prof. Daniel Wayne Hardy; one *s* two *d* (and one *d* decd). *Educ:* Trinity Coll. Dublin (BA (Mod) 1970); St John's Coll., Cambridge (MA 1976; PhD 1977); Yale Univ. (STM 1973); Tübingen Univ. Lectr in Theology, Birmingham Univ., 1976–91; Cambridge University: Chairman: Faculty Bd of Divinity, 1993–95; Mgt Cttee, Centre for Advanced Religious and Theol Studies, 1995–2013; Dir, Cambridge Inter-faith Prog., 2002–15; Member: Arts and Humanities Personal Promotions Cttee, 2003–08; Gen. Bd Adv. Cttee on Sen. Appts, 2005–08. Mem., CUP Syndicate, 1993–2004. Pres., Soc. for Study of Theology, 1997–98. Member: World Econ. Forum Council of 100 Leaders, 2003–08; AHRC Peer Review Coll., 2005–12; Bd of Reference, Westminster Abbey Inst., 2014–. Trustee: Center of Theological Inquiry, Princeton, 2007–; Rose Castle Foundn, 2014–; Mem., Bd of Advrs, John Templeton Foundn, 2008–11. Hon. DD Birmingham, 2000. Gold Medallion for Inter-Faith Relns, Sternberg Foundn, 2008; Coventry Internat. Prize for Peace and Reconciliation, 2012. *Publications:* Barth and God's Story: biblical narrative and the theological method of Karl Barth in the Church Dogmatics, 1981; (with Daniel W. Hardy) Jubilate: Theology in praise, 1984; (with Frances M. Young) Meaning and Truth in 2 Corinthians, 1987; (ed) The Modern Theologians, vols I and II, 1989, 3rd edn 2005; (ed jtly) Essentials of Christian Community, 1996; The Shape of Living, 1997; Self and Salvation: being transformed, 1999; Theology: a very short introduction, 1999, 2nd edn 2013; (ed jtly) Jesus, 2002; (ed jtly and contrib.) Reading Texts, Seeking Wisdom: scripture and theology, 2003; (ed jtly) Fields of Faith: theology and religious studies for the twenty-first century, 2005; (ed jtly) The Promise of Scriptural Reasoning, 2006; Christian Wisdom: desiring God and learning in love, 2007; (ed jtly) Musics of Belonging: the poetry of Micheal O'Siadhail, 2007; Shaping Theology: engagements in a religious and secular world, 2007; (jtly) Wording a Radiance: parting conversations on God and the Church, 2010; The Future of Christian Theology, 2011; (ed jtly) The Modern Theologians Reader, 2012; (ed jtly) Interreligious Reading After Vatican II: scriptural reasoning, comparative theology and receptive ecumenism, 2013; The Drama of Living: becoming wise in the spirit, 2014; (ed jtly) Say But the Word: poetry as vision and voice, 2015. *Recreations:* gardening, poetry, drama, sports (especially ball games). *Address:* Selwyn College, Grange Road, Cambridge CB3 9DQ. *T:* (07879) 116894.

FORD, David R. J.; Member (Alliance) Antrim South, Northern Ireland Assembly, since 1998; Minister of Justice, since 2010; Leader, Alliance Party, since 2001; *b* 24 Feb. 1951; *s* of late Eric Ford and Jean Ford; *m* 1975, Anne Murdock; one *s* three *d*. *Educ:* Dulwich Coll.; Queen's Univ., Belfast (BSc Econ 1972); Northern Ireland Poly. (Cert. Social Work 1976). Social worker, then sen. social worker, Northern Health and Social Services Bd, Antrim, Newtownabbey and Carrickfergus, 1972–90; Gen. Sec., Alliance Party, 1990–98. Mem. (Alliance), Antrim BC, 1993–2010. Contested S Antrim, NI Forum, 1996. Contested (Alliance) S Antrim, 1997, Sept. 2000, 2001, 2005. Alliance Chief Whip, 1998–2001. *Address:* Northern Ireland Assembly, Parliament Buildings, Stormont, Belfast BT4 3XX.

FORD, Sir David (Robert), KBE 1988 (OBE 1976); LVO 1975; Chief Secretary, Hong Kong Government, 1986–93; Chairman: PCCW (Europe), since 2003; UK Broadband, since 2004; *b* 22 Feb. 1935; *s* of William Ewart and Edna Ford; *m* 1st, 1958, Elspeth Anne (*née* Muckart) (marr. diss. 1987); two *s* two *d*; 2nd, 1987, Gillian Petersen (*née* Monsarrat). *Educ:* Taunton's School. National Service, 1953–55; regular commn, RA, 1955; regimental duty, Malta, 1953–58; Lieut, UK, 1958–62; Captain, Commando Regt, 1962–66; active service: Borneo, 1964; Aden, 1966; Staff Coll., Quetta, 1967; seconded to Hong Kong Govt, 1967; retired from Army (Major), 1972. Dep. Dir, Hong Kong Govt Information Service, 1972–74, Dir, 1974–76; Dep. Sec., Govt Secretariat, Hong Kong, 1976; Under Sec., NI Office, 1977–79; Sec. for Information, Hong Kong Govt, 1979–80; Hong Kong Comr in London, 1980–81 and 1994–97; RCDS, 1982; Hong Kong Government: Dir of Housing, 1983–84; Sec. for Housing, 1985; Sec. for the Civil Service, 1985–86. Chm., Council for Protection of, subseq. Campaign to Protect, Rural England, 1998–2003. Vice-Pres., Rare Breeds Survival Trust, 2004–07. Chm., Hong Kong Soc., 2003–06. *Address:* Rosemary Cottage, Rampisham, Dorset DT2 0PX.

FORD, Prof. Gary Ashley, CBE 2013; FMedSci; Chief Executive Officer, Oxford Academic Health Science Network, since 2013; *b* Coventry, 18 Nov. 1958; *s* of Ashley Greg Ford and Eileen Mary Ford (*née* Painter); *m* 1987, Angela Mary Lewis; two *s* one *d*. *Educ:* King Henry VIII Sch., Coventry; Clare Coll., Cambridge (BA 1979); King's Coll. Hosp. Med. Sch., London (BA Hons; MB BChir 1983). MRCP 1985; FRCP 1996. Sen. House Officer, Addenbrooke's Hosp., Cambridge, 1983–85; Registrar, Glos Royal Hosp., 1985–87; Post-doctoral Res. Fellow in Clin. Pharmacol., Stanford Univ., Calif, 1987–89; Sen. Registrar in Geriatric and Gen. Medicine (Clin. Pharmacol.), Freeman Hosp., Newcastle upon Tyne, 1989–92; University of Newcastle upon Tyne and Newcastle upon Tyne Hospitals NHS Trust: Sen. Lectr and Cons. Physician in Clin. Pharmacol. and Geriatric Medicine, 1992–2000; Prof. of Pharmacology of Old Age, 2000–06; Hon. Consultant Physician in Stroke Medicine, 2000–; Director: Newcastle Clin. Res. Centre, 2005–08; NIHR (formerly UK) Stroke Res. Network, 2005–14; Jacobson Prof. of Clin. Pharmacol., 2006–13; Clin. Dir, R&D, Newcastle upon Tyne Hosps NHS Foundn Trust, 2006–13. Vis. Prof. of Clin. Pharmacol., Univ. of Oxford, 2013–. FBPhS (FBPharmacolS 2014); FMedSci 2014. *Recreations:* music, cooking, travel. *Address:* Oxford Academic Health Science Network, Magdalen Centre North, Oxford Science Park, Oxford OX4 4GA. *T:* (01865) 338439.

FORD, Dr Gillian Rachel, (Mrs N. I. MacKenzie), CB 1981; FRCP, FFPH; Medical Director, Marie Curie Cancer Care (formerly Marie Curie Memorial Foundation), 1991–97; *b* 18 March 1934; *d* of Cecil Ford and Grace Ford; *m* 1988, Prof. Norman I. MacKenzie (*d* 2013). *Educ:* Clarendon Sch., Abergele; St Hugh's Coll., Oxford; St Thomas' Hosp., London. MA, BM, BCh; FFCM 1976; FRCP 1985. Junior hospital posts, St Thomas', Oxford, Reading, 1959–64; Medical Officer, Min. of Health, 1965, Sen. Med. Officer, 1968; SPMO, 1974–77, Dep. Chief MO (Dep. Sec.), 1977–89, DHSS, later Dept of Health; on secondment as Dir of Studies, St Christopher's Hospice, Sydenham, 1985–88; Med. Sec., Standing Cttee on Postgrad. Med. Educn, 1989–90. Vice Pres., St Christopher's Hospice, 1999–; Vice Chm., Hospice in the Weald, 1999–2003. *Publications:* papers on health services research, terminal care, audit, palliative medicine and care in sundry med. publications. *Recreations:* music, ski-ing, children's literature, gardening. *Address:* 20 Winterbourne Mews, Lewes, E Sussex BN7 1HG. *T:* (01273) 479206.

FORD, Glyn; *see* Ford, J. G.

FORD, Harrison; actor; *b* Chicago, 13 July 1942; *m* 1st, Mary Ford (marr. diss. 1978); two *s*; 2nd, 1983, Melissa Mathison (marr. diss. 2004), screenwriter; one *s* one *d*; 3rd, 2010, Calista Flockhart. *Educ:* Ripon Coll., Wis. *Films* include: Dead Heat on a Merry-Go-Round, 1966; Journey to Shiloh, 1968; Getting Straight, 1970; The Conversation, 1974; American Graffiti, 1974; Star Wars, 1977; Force 10 from Navarone, 1978; Apocalypse Now, 1979; The Frisco Kid, 1979; The Empire Strikes Back, 1980; Raiders of the Lost Ark, 1981; Blade Runner, 1982; Return of the Jedi, 1983; Indiana Jones and the Temple of Doom, 1984; Witness, 1985; Mosquito Coast, 1986; Frantic, 1988; Indiana Jones and the Last Crusade, 1989; Presumed Innocent, 1990; Regarding Henry, 1991; The Fugitive, 1992; Patriot Games, 1992; Clear and

Present Danger, 1994; Sabrina, 1995; Devil's Own, 1996; Air Force One, 1997; Six Days, Seven Nights, 1998; Random Hearts, 1999; What Lies Beneath, 2000; K-19: The Widowmaker, 2002; Hollywood Homicide, 2003; Firewall, 2006; Indiana Jones and the Kingdom of the Crystal Skull, Crossing Over, 2008; Extraordinary Measures (also prod.), 2010; Morning Glory, Cowboys and Aliens, 2011; Ender's Game, 2013; Star Wars: the Force Awakens, The Age of Adeline, 2015; numerous TV appearances, including The Virginian, Gunsmoke, Ironside. *Address:* United Talent Agency, 9336 Civic Center Drive, Beverly Hills, CA 90212, USA.

FORD, (James) Glyn; *b* 28 Jan. 1950; *s* of late Ernest Benjamin Ford and Matilda Alberta Ford (*née* James); *m* 1st, 1973, Hazel Nancy Mahy (marr. diss. 1992); one *d*; 2nd, 1992, Daniela Zannelli (marr. diss. 2005); one *s*. *Educ:* Marling; Reading Univ. (BSc Geol. with Soil Sci.); UCL (MSc Marine Earth Sci.); Manchester Univ. Undergraduate Apprentice, BAC, 1967–68; Course Tutor in Oceanography, Open Univ., 1976–78; Teaching Asst, UMIST, 1977–78; Res. Fellow, Sussex Univ., 1978–79; Manchester University: Res. Asst, 1976–77; Res. Fellow, 1979; Lectr, 1979–80; Sen. Res. Fellow, Prog. of Policy Res. in Engrg Sci. and Technol., 1980–84; Hon. Vis. Res. Fellow, 1984–. Vis. Prof., Tokyo Univ., 1983. Mem., Lab Party NEC, 1989–93 (Member: Sci. and Technol. Policy Sub-Cttee, 1981–83; Review Gp on Trade Union/Labour Party Links, 1992–93). MEP (Lab): Gtr Manchester E, 1984–99; SW Region, England, 1999–2009. European Parliament: Chm., Cttee of Inquiry into Growth of Racism and Fascism in Europe, 1984–86; Vice-Chm., Sub-Cttee on Security and Disarmament, 1987–89; first Vice-Pres., Group of Party of European Socialists, 1989–93; Vice Chm., Delegn, Japanese Diet, 1992–94, 1996–99; Leader, 1989–93, Dep. Leader, 1993–94, Eur. PLP. Mem., Consultative Cttee on Racism and Xenophobia, Council of Ministers of EU, 1994–98. EU Chief Observer: Indonesian elections, 2004; Aceh, 2006–07. Mem., Exec. Cttee, Labour Movement for Europe, 2010– (Chm., SW, 2003–); SW Rep., Labour Party Nat. Policy Forum, 2010–. Treas., Anti Nazi League. Mem., Steering Cttee, UNITE Against Fascism. Contested (Lab), Hazel Grove, 1987. Founder, Polint, 2009. *Publications:* (with C. Niblett and L. Walker) The Future for Ocean Technology, 1987; Fascist Europe, 1992; The Evolution of a European, 1994; Changing States, 1996; Making European Progress, 2002; Left in Europe, 2008; (with S. Kwon) North Korea on the Brink, 2008; (ed with J. Priestley) Our Europe, Not Theirs, 2013. *Recreation:* Asia. *Clubs:* Groucho, Soho House.

FORD, John; *see* Ford, S. J.

FORD, (John) Anthony, OBE 1998; Director, Crafts Council, 1988–99 (Deputy Director, 1985–88); *b* 28 April 1938; *s* of Frank Everatt Ford and Dorothy Mary Ford; *m* 1st, 1963, Caroline Rosemary Wharrad (marr. diss.); one *d*; 2nd, 1984, Sandra Edith Williams. *Educ:* Epsom Coll.; St Edmund Hall, Oxford (MA). Admitted Solicitor, 1963. Dir, Art Services Grants, 1974–79; Crafts Council, 1979–99. Mem., Visual Arts Adv. Cttee, British Council, 1988–99. Vice-Pres. for Europe, World Crafts Council, 1987–93 (Advr, 1993–). Mem., Fabric Adv. Cttee, Rochester Cathedral, 1990–2004. Member: Court, RCA, 1989–99; Court of Govs, London Inst., 1993–2000; Board of Governors: Kent Inst. of Art and Design, 2001–05 (Dep. Chm., 2002–05); Univ. (formerly UC) for the Creative Arts at Canterbury, Epsom, Farnham, Maidstone and Rochester, 2005–10. Trustee: Craft Pottery Charitable Trust, 1991–2010 (Chm., 2004–10); Idlewild Trust, 2000– (Chm., 2009–). *Recreations:* theatre, cinema. *Address:* 64 Wood Vale, SE23 3ED. *T:* (020) 8693 4837.

FORD, Sir John (Archibald), KCMG 1977 (CMG 1967); MC 1945; HM Diplomatic Service, retired; *b* 19 Feb. 1922; *s* of Ronald Mylne Ford and Margaret Jesse Coghill, Newcastle-under-Lyme, Staffs; *m* 1956, Emaline Burnette (*d* 1989), Leesville, Virginia; two *d*. *Educ:* St Michael's Coll., Tenbury; Sedbergh Sch., Yorks; Oriel Coll., Oxford. Served in Royal Artillery, 1942–46 (temp. Major); demobilised, 1947. Joined Foreign (subseq. Diplomatic) Service, 1947. Third Sec., British Legation, Budapest, 1947–49; Third Sec. and a Resident Clerk, FO, 1949–52; Private Sec. to Permanent Under-Sec. of State, FO, 1952–54; HM Consul, San Francisco, 1954–56; seconded to HM Treasury, 1956–59; attended Course at Administrative Staff Coll., 1959; First Sec. and Head of Chancery, British Residency, Bahrain, 1959–61; Asst, FO Personnel Dept, 1961–63; Asst, FO Establishment and Organisation Dept, 1963; Head of Diplomatic Service Establishment and Organisation Dept, 1964–66; Counsellor (Commercial), Rome, 1966–70; Asst Under-Sec., FCO, 1970–71; Consul-Gen., New York, and Dir-Gen., British Trade Develt in USA, 1971–75; Ambassador to Indonesia, 1975–78; British High Comr in Canada, 1978–81. Lay Administrator, Guildford Cathedral, 1982–84. Mem., Exec. Cttee, VSO, 1982–87; Chm. of Trustees, Voluntary and Christian Service, 1985–88; Chm., AIDS Care Educn and Trng, 1989–93; Trustee: World in Need, 1987–95; Opportunity Trust, 1991–96; Opportunity Internat. (USA), 1994–95. *Publications:* Honest to Christ, 1988; The Answer is the Christ of AD 2000, 1996; Introducing the Young to the Christ of AD 2000, 1999; Searching for the Christ of AD 2000 in Saint John's Gospel, 1999; Seeking the Christ of AD 2000 through Francis of Assisi and Brother Lawrence, 1999; Praying in the Mystical Body of the Christ of AD 2000, 1999; Spiritual Exercises for AD 2000, 1999; Looking for the Christ of AD 2000 in the Recorded Sayings of Jesus, 2000; God's Project People, 2002; Love's Lure: God's project people, 2011. *Recreations:* walking, gardening, sailing. *Address:* Admiral 633, 8750 South Ocean Drive, Jensen Beach, FL 34957–2128, USA.

FORD, Rt Rev. John Frank; *see* Murray, Bishop of The.

FORD, Leigh-Ann Maria; *see* Mulcahy, L.-A. M.

FORD, Prof. Mark Nicholas, DPhil; Professor of English and American Literature, University College London, since 2005; *b* Nairobi, Kenya, 24 June 1962; *s* of Don and Mary Ford; *m* 2003, Kate Bomford; two *d*. *Educ:* St Paul's Sch., London; Lincoln Coll., Oxford (BA English Lit.; DPhil 1991). Lectr, UCL, 1988–90; Lectr, Kyoto Univ., 1991–93; Lectr, 1995–2002, Sen. Lectr, 2002–05, UCL. *Publications:* Landlocked, 1992; Raymond Roussel and the Republic of Dreams, 2000; Soft Sift, 2001; A Driftwood Altar, 2005; Mr and Mrs Stevens, 2011; Six Children, 2011; Selected Poems, 2014; This Dialogue of One, 2014. *Recreations:* tennis, football, music. *Address:* English Department, University College London, Gower Street, WC1E 6BT. *T:* (020) 7679 3129. *E:* m.ford@ucl.ac.uk.

FORD, Prof. Michael David; QC 2013; Professor of Law, University of Bristol, since 2015; *b* Cyprus, 1961; *s* of Michael and Maureen Ford; partner, Sarah Leverton; two *s*. *Educ:* Gravesend Grammar Sch.; Univ. of Bristol (LLB 1st Cl. Hons 1986; BSc 1st Cl. Hons 2010); Univ. of Sheffield (MA Socio-Legal Studies 1989). Mem., GB cycling squad, 1983–84. Solicitor, Slaughter and May, 1987–89; admitted as solicitor, 1989; Lectr, Univ. of Manchester, 1990–92; called to the Bar, Middle Temple, 1992; in practice as barrister, specialising in labour law, 1992–; Lectr, Univ. of London, 1996–98; an Employment Judge (pt-time), 2003–. Vis. Fellow, LSE, 1996–2006. Trustee, Bat Conservation Trust, 2003–13. *Publications:* (jtly) Redgrave's Health and Safety, 2nd edn 1996 to 7th edn 2010; Munkman on Employer's Liability, 12th edn 1995 to 13th edn 2001; Privacy and Surveillance at Work, 1998; contrib. articles to jls incl. Industrial Law Jl, Modern Law Rev. *Recreations:* cycling, wildlife, film, French, Spanish, my boys. *Address:* Old Square Chambers, 10–11 Bedford Row, WC1R 4BU. *T:* (020) 7269 0300; Old Square Chambers, 3 Orchard Court, St Augustine's Yard, Bristol BS1 5DP. *T:* (0117) 930 5100.

FORD, Peter George Tipping; Secretary, Medical Protection Society, 1983–90; *b* 18 Sept. 1931; *s* of late Raymond Eustace Ford, CBE; *m* 1958, Nancy Elizabeth Procter; four *d*. *Educ:* Epsom Coll.; St Bartholomew's Hosp. Med. Coll., Univ. of London (MB, BS); MRCGP, DObstRCOG. Nat. Service, RAMC, 1957–59. Gen. practice, Hythe, 1960–68; Asst Sec., Med. Protection Soc., 1968–72, Dep. Sec., 1972–83. Sec., Jt Co-ordinating Cttee, UK Defence Organizations, 1985–89. Mem., Soc. of Apothecaries. FRSocMed. Medal of Honour, Med. Defence Soc. of Queensland, 1984. *Publications:* contribs to medico-legal periodicals. *Recreations:* baroque choral music, gardening, bridge. *Address:* Braeside Cottage, Cannongate Road, Hythe, Kent CT21 5PT. *T:* (01303) 267896.

FORD, Peter John, CBE 1998; Chairman, London Transport, 1994–98; *b* 21 Nov. 1938; *s* of John Frederick Arthur Ford and Hazel Mary Ford; *m* 1966, Olivia Mary Temple; two *s* two *d*. *Educ:* King's Sch., Canterbury; Christ Church, Oxford (MA Chem.); Harvard Business Sch. (MBA). With Shell Chemical Co., 1961–65; McKinsey & Co., NY, 1967–70; Exec. Dir, Sterling Guarantee Trust, 1970–85; Exec. Dir, P&OSNCo., 1985–93. Director: Countrywide Assured Gp, 1994–2002; Palliser Furniture, Winnipeg, Canada, 2001–; Cambridge Biostability Ltd, 2004–09. Pres., Sheffield Chamber of Commerce, 1985–86; Dep. Pres., London Chamber of Commerce and Industry, 1998–2000. Chm., NW Surrey Short Stay Schools, 2009–; Governor: Kingston Univ., 1993–98; Collingwood Coll., 2001–10. *Recreations:* walking, music. *Address:* 2B The Downs, SW20 8HN. *T:* (020) 8944 7207. *Club:* Royal Automobile.

FORD, Peter William; HM Diplomatic Service, retired; Senior Regional Representative, United Nations Relief and Works Agency for Palestinian Refugees, since 2006; *b* 27 June 1947; *s* of Alec and Gertrude Ford; *m* 1st, 1974, Aurora Garcia Mingo (marr. diss. 1992); 2nd, 1992, Alganesh Haile Beyene. *Educ:* Helsby Grammar Sch.; Queen's Coll., Oxford (BA Hons). FCO, 1971–72; Beirut, 1972–73; Second, then First, Sec., Cairo, 1974–78; Eur. Integration Dept, FCO, 1978–80; First Sec., Paris, 1980–85; Asst Hd, EC Dept, FCO, 1985–87; Counsellor (Commercial), Riyadh, 1987–90; Vis. Fellow, Harvard Univ., 1990–91; Dep. High Comr and Counsellor (Econ. and Commercial), Singapore, 1991–94; Hd, Near East and N Africa Dept, FCO, 1994–99; Ambassador to Bahrain, 1999–2003; Ambassador to Syria, 2003–06. Internat. Fellow, Brandeis Univ., 2001–03. *Recreations:* sport, reading, travel.

FORD, Gen. Sir Robert (Cyril), GCB 1981 (KCB 1977; CB 1973); CBE 1971 (MBE 1958); Vice-Chairman, Commonwealth War Graves Commission, 1989–93 (Commissioner, 1981–93); *b* 29 Dec. 1923; *s* of late John Stranger Ford and Gladys Ford, Yealmpton, Devon; *m* 1st, 1949, Jean Claudia Pendlebury (*d* 2002), *d* of late Gp Capt. Claude Pendlebury, MC, TD; one *s*; 2nd, 2003, Caroline Margaret Peerless (*née* Leather) (*d* 2013). *Educ:* Musgrave's Coll. War of 1939–45: commissioned into 4th/7th Royal Dragoon Guards, from Sandhurst, 1943; served with Regt throughout NW European campaign, 1944–45 (despatches) and in Egypt and Palestine, 1947–48 (despatches). Instructor, Mons OCS, 1949–50; Training Officer, Scottish Horse (TA), 1952–54; Staff Coll., Camberley, 1955; GSO 2 Mil. Ops, War Office, 1956–57; Sqdn Ldr 4/7 RDG, 1958–59; Bde Major, 20th Armoured Bde, 1960–61; Brevet Lt-Col, 1962; Sqdn Ldr, 4/7 RDG, 1962–63; GSO1 to Chief of Defence Staff, 1964–65; commanded 4/7 RDG in S Arabia and N Ireland, 1966–67; Comdr, 7th Armd Bde, 1968–69; Principal Staff Officer to Chief of Defence Staff, 1970–71; Comdr Land Forces, N Ireland, 1971–73; Comdt, RMA Sandhurst, 1973–76; Military Secretary, 1976–78; Adjutant-General, 1978–81; ADC General to the Queen, 1980–81; Governor, Royal Hosp., Chelsea, 1981–87. Colonel Commandant: RAC, 1980–82; SAS Regt, 1980–85; Col 4th/7th Royal Dragoon Gds, 1984–88. President: Services Kinema Corp., 1978–81; Army Boxing Assoc., 1978–81. Chm., 1981–87, and Pres., 1986–97, Army Benevolent Fund; Chm., Royal Cambridge Home for Soldiers' Widows, 1981–87; Nat. Pres., Forces Help Soc. and Lord Roberts Workshops, 1981–91. Governor, Corps of Commissionaires, 1981–94. Freeman, City of London, 1981. CCMI. *Recreations:* watching cricket, tennis, war studies, theatre. *Clubs:* Cavalry and Guards, MCC.

FORD, Robert Stanley; HM Diplomatic Service, retired; *b* 30 Nov. 1929; *s* of late Robert Hempstead Ford and Janet Mabel Elliot; *m* 1957, Cynthia Valerie Arscott, *d* of late Ronald Prowse Arscott, Bexhill-on-Sea, Sussex; one *s* two *d*. *Educ:* Daniel Stewart's Coll., Edinburgh; Univ. of Edinburgh (MA). Joined HM Diplomatic Service, 1949; HM Forces, 1949; FCO, 1951; Third Sec., Moscow, 1955; Consul, Dakar, 1958; FCO, 1959; Information Officer, NY, 1963; First Sec., Managua, 1965; Consul, Naples, 1968; FCO, 1972; Consul-Gen., Madrid, 1978; FCO, 1982; Counsellor (Admin), Paris, 1984–86. *Recreations:* music, photography, travel. *Address:* 31 Seabright, West Parade, Worthing, W Sussex BN11 3QS. *T:* (01903) 537033.

FORD, Sir Robin Sam St C.; *see* St Clair-Ford.

FORD, Steven Charles; QC 2010; barrister; *b* London, 11 June 1965; *s* of Charles Ford and Pamela Ford; *m* 2000, Jane Elizabeth Ettridge; two *d*. *Educ:* Tiffin Boys' Sch.; Royal Acad. of Music (LRAM 1986); Kingston Univ. (LLB 1991). Called to the Bar, Middle Temple, 1992. *Recreations:* cooking, wine. *Address:* 7 Bedford Row, WC1R 4BS. *T:* (020) 7242 3555. *E:* clerks@7br.co.uk.

FORD, (Sydney) John, CBE 1999; PhD; Chief Executive, Driver and Vehicle Licensing Agency 1995–2000; *b* 23 Aug. 1936; *s* of Sidney James Ford and Barbara Ford (*née* Essenhigh); *m* 1st, 1960, Beryl Owen (marr. diss. 1990); two *s*; 2nd, 1990, Morag Munro. *Educ:* Bromsgrove High Sch.; Swansea Grammar Sch.; UC Swansea, Univ. of Wales (BSc Maths; PhD Maths; Hon. Fellow, 1999). British Aluminium Co. plc, 1966–82 (Dir, 1977–82; Man. Dir, 1982); Dep. Man. Dir, British Alcan Aluminium plc, 1982–85; UK Ops Dir, Williams Hldgs plc, 1985–88; Dir, European Distribn, Christian Salvesen plc, 1988–93; Chief Exec., Driving Standards Agency, 1993–94. Chm., Ofwat CSC Wales, subseq. WaterVoice Wales, 2001–05; Mem., Consumer Council for Water, Midlands, 2005–07. *Recreations:* artist and art tutor, qualified Rugby referee and coach. *Address:* Shenval, 1 Evertons Close, Droitwich Spa WR9 8AE.

FORD, Victoria Grace; Member (C) Eastern, European Parliament, since 2009; *b* Omagh, NI, 21 Sept. 1967; *d* of Dr Anthony Pollock and Deborah Marion (*née* Bliss, now Lady Cassidi); *m* 1996, Dr Hugo Ford; two *s* one *d*. *Educ:* Omagh Acad. Prep. Dept; St Paul's Girls' Sch.; Marlborough Coll.; Trinity Coll., Cambridge (BA 1989). JP Morgan, 1989–2001; Bear Stearns, 2001–03. Mem. (C) S Cambs DC, 2006–09. *Recreations:* fly fishing, music, gardening. *Address:* European Parliament, Rue Wiertz, 1047 Brussels, Belgium. *E:* vicky.ford@europarl.europa.eu.

FORD, William Clay, Jr; Executive Chairman, Ford Motor Company, since 2006 (Director, since 1988; Chairman, 1999; Chief Executive, 2001–06); *b* Detroit, 3 May 1957; *m*. *Educ:* Princeton Univ. (BA 1979); MIT (Alfred P. Sloan Fellow, 1983–84, MBA 1984). Ford Motor Company: Product Planning Analyst, Advanced Vehicle Develt, Design Center, then Manufg Engr, Automobile Assembly Div., subseq. NY Zone Manager, Ford Div., 1979–82; Mktg Strategy Analyst, N Amer. Automobile Ops, and Advertising Specialist, Ford Div., 1982–83; Internat. Finance Specialist, 1984–85; Planning Manager, Car Product Develt, 1985–86; Dir, Commercial Vehicle Mktg, Ford of Europe, 1986–87; Chm. and Man. Dir, Ford of Switzerland, 1987–89; Manager, Heavy Truck Engrg and Manufg, Ford Truck Ops, 1989–90; Dir, 1990–91, Exec. Dir, 1991–92, Business Strategy, Ford Auto Gp; Gen. Manager, Climate Control Div., 1992–94; Vice Pres., Commercial Truck Vehicle Center, Ford Automotive Ops, 1994–95; Chm., Finance Cttee, 1995–99. Mem., Bd of Trustees, The Henry Ford (formerly Henry Ford Mus. and Greenfield Village); Trustee, Henry Ford Health System; Chm., Detroit Economic Club, 2005–; Mem., Business Leaders for Michigan. Vice Chm., Detroit Lions (prof. football team); Mem., NFL Broadcasting Cttee. *Address:* Ford Motor Company, One American Road, Dearborn, MI 48126–2798, USA. *T:* (313) 3223000.

FORDE, Helen, PhD; FSA; archivist; lecturer; *b* Oxford, 26 May 1941; *d* of Antony Andrewes and Alison Andrewes (*née* Hope); *m* 1962, Thomas Middleton Forde; one *s* one *d*. *Educ:* Oxford High Sch. for Girls; University Coll. London (BA Hist. 1962); Univ. of Liverpool (DAA 1968); Univ. of Leicester (PhD 1977). FSA 2001. Archivist, Nottingham City, 1970–73; Urban Res. Asst, Council for British Archaeol., 1973–75; Archivist, Liby of the Soc. of Friends, 1978–79; Public Record Office: Asst Keeper, 1979–2001; Head: Liby and Mus., 1979–82; Conservation Dept, 1982–92; Preservation Services, 1992–2001. Extra mural tutor: Nottingham Univ., 1970–73; London Univ., 1975–89; Lectr, Sch. of Liby, Archive and Inf. Studies, 1989–2007, Hon. Res. Fellow, UCL, 2008–. Society of Archivists: Chm., 1993–95; Pres., 2002–05; Vice Pres., 2005–. Chm., Preservation Cttee, 1992–2000, Mem., Cttee of Prog. Mgt, 2000–04, Internat. Council on Archives; Museums, Libraries and Archives Council: Chm., Designation Panel, 2004–12; Chm., E Midlands, 2005–09; Mem. Bd, 2007–11; Member: Northants Archives Panel, 1994–2014; (and Vice Chm.) Lincoln Cath. Liby Council, 2001–06; (and Chm.) Expert Panel for Mus, Libraries and Archives, Heritage Lottery Fund, 2001–05; British Postal Mus. and Archive, 2001– (Chm., 2011–); Documentary Heritage Review of C of E, 2004–05; Member, Council: Soc. of Antiquaries of London, 2012– (Vice-Pres., 2014–); Friends of Nat. Archives, 2012–13. Trustee, Marc Fitch Fund, 2001–. Chm., Banbury Histl Soc., 2008–11; Mem., Banbury Mus. Trust, 2012– (Mem., Shadow Bd, 2012–13). *Publications:* Domesday Preserved, 1986; Preserving Archives, 2007, 2nd edn (with J. Rhys Lewis) 2013; contrib. archive, liby and historical jls; ed professional works and online information sources. *Recreations:* music, gardening, travelling. *Address:* Lovells, The Square, Kings Sutton, Banbury OX17 3RE. *T:* (01295) 811247. *E:* helenforde1@gmail.com.

FORDE, Martin Andrew; QC 2006; *b* 1961; *s* of Ralph and Cynthia Forde; *m* 2004, Nadège Vidal; one *s* three *d*. *Educ:* Langley Grammar Sch.; Brasenose Coll., Oxford (BA Hons Juris). Called to the Bar, Middle Temple, 1984 (Harmsworth Exhibnr, 1983), Bencher, 2010; in practice, specialising in professional negligence, employment, professional regulatory and public law. Mem., Judicial Appointments Commn, 2012–. *Recreations:* sport, music, travel. *Address:* 1 Crown Office Row, Temple, EC4Y 7HH. *E:* martin.forde@1cor.com.

FORDE, Hon. (Mary Marguerite) Leneen, AC 1993; Chancellor, Griffith University, Queensland, 2000–15; Governor of Queensland, 1992–97; *b* 12 May 1935; *d* of John Alfred Kavanagh and Evlyn Philomena Kavanagh (*née* Bujold); *m* 1st, 1955, Francis Gerard Forde (*d* 1966), *s* of Rt Hon. Francis Michael Forde, PC; three *s* two *d*; 2nd, 1983, (Albert) Angus McDonald (*d* 1999). *Educ:* Lisgar Collegiate, Ottawa (Dip.); Univ. of Queensland (LLB). Student Med. Lab. Technician, Ottawa Gen. Hosp., 1952–53; Med. Lab. Technician, Drs Rousell and Gagne, Ottawa, 1953–54; Haematol. Dept, Royal Brisbane Hosp., 1954–56; medical lab. work, 1956–58; articled Law Clerk, Alexander McGillivray, 1969–70; Solicitor, Cannan & Peterson, 1971–74; Partner, Sly, Weigall, Cannan & Peterson, subseq. Deakins, 1974–92. Comr, Royal Commn of Inquiry into Abuse of Children in Queensland Instns, 1998–99; Nat. Chm., Australian Defence Reserves Support Council, 2002–05. Board Member: St Leo's Coll., 1998–2000; Brisbane Coll. of Theol., 1999–2000; Brisbane City Council Arts and Envmt Trust, 1999–2000; Qld Ballet, 2000–11; Qld Govt Forde Foundn, 2000–07; Qld Community Foundn, 2008–; All Hallow's Sch., 2008–09; Searchlight Educn, 2008–11. Founder, Qld Women Lawyers' Assoc., 1976; Member: Qld Law Soc., 1971–; Women Chiefs of Enterprises Internat., 1989–; Zonta Club of Brisbane Inc., 1971–; President: Zonta Internat., 1990–92; Scout Assoc. of Aust., 1997–2003 (Vice-Pres., 2003–10). Patron, Nat. Pioneer Women's Hall of Fame, 1999–. Paul Harris Fellow, Rotary Club of Brisbane, 1990; Woman of Substance Award, Qld Girl Guides' Assoc., 1990; Queenslander of the Year, 1991; Queensland Great, 2007. DUniv: Griffith, 1992; Qld Univ. of Technology, 1993; Australian Catholic, 2000; Southern Qld, 2000; Hon. DLitt Queensland, 1996. DStJ 1992. *Publications:* Queensland Annual Law Review, 1991, 1992. *Recreations:* theatre, art, music, ballet, surfing.

FORDHAM, His Honour (John) Jeremy; a Circuit Judge, 1986–99; *b* 18 April 1933; *s* of John Hampden Fordham, CBE and Rowena Fordham (*née* Day, later Langran); *m* 1962, Rose Anita (*née* Brandon), *d* of Philip Brandon, Wellington, New Zealand; one *s* one *d*. *Educ:* Gresham's Sch.; Univ. of New Zealand. LLB (NZ). Merchant Navy, 1950–55 (2nd Mate (Foreign Going) Cert.); labourer, fireman etc, 1955–60; Barrister and Solicitor, New Zealand, 1960–64; called to Bar, Inner Temple, 1965; practised 1965–71, 1976–78; Sen. Magistrate, Gilbert and Ellice Islands, 1971–75; a Metropolitan Stipendiary Magistrate, 1978–86; a Recorder, 1986; a Dep. Circuit Judge, 1999–2001. Legal Chm., Immigration Appeal Tribunal, 1999–; Asst Surveillance Comr, 2001–07. *Recreations:* boats, games. *Club:* Garrick.

FORDHAM, Max; *see* Fordham, S. M.

FORDHAM, Michael John; QC 2006; a Recorder, since 2010; *b* 21 Dec. 1964; *s* of John and Margaret Fordham; *m* 1993, Alison Oxley; one *s* two *d*. *Educ:* Spalding Grammar Sch.; Hertford Coll., Oxford (BA Hons, BCL); Univ. of Virginia (LLM). Called to the Bar, Gray's Inn, 1990 (Prince of Wales Schol., Karmel Schol., Mould Schol., 1989), Bencher, 2009; Lectr, Hertford Coll., Oxford, 1989–; in practice as barrister, 1990–. Mem., Adv. Bd, British Inst. Internat. and Comparative Law, 2003–. Vis. Fellow, Bingham Centre for the Rule of Law, 2011–12. Human Rights Lawyer of the Year, 2005; Bar Pro Bono Award, 2006; Human Rights and Public Law Silk of the Year, 2008. Co-Ed., Judicial Rev., 1996–. *Publications:* Judicial Review Handbook, 1994, 6th edn 2012. *Recreations:* St Albans Hockey Club (Captain, Veterans' Team), Marlborough Road Methodist Church, St Albans (Youth Music Co-ordinator). *Address:* Blackstone Chambers, Temple, EC4Y 9BW. *T:* (020) 7583 1770. *E:* michaelfordham@blackstonechambers.com.

FORDHAM, (Sigurd) Max, OBE 1994; RDI 2008; FREng; Member, Max Fordham LLP, since 2001; Director, Max Fordham Consulting Ltd, since 2004; *b* Highgate, 17 June 1933; *s* of Dr Michael Scott Montague Fordham and Molly Fordham (*née* Swabey); *m* 1960, Thalia Aubrey Dyson; three *s*. *Educ:* DeCarteret Sch., Mandeville, Jamaica; Dartington Hall Sch., Totnes; Trinity Coll., Cambridge (BA 1957; MA 1960). CEng, FREng 1992. National Service, 1952–54: served RN, FAA (Temp. actg Sub-Lt (A) RNVR). Develt engr, Weatherfoil Ltd, 1958–61; engr, Arup Bldg Gp, later Arup Associates, 1961–66; Max Fordham Consulting Engr Building Services, 1966–73; Max Fordham & Partners, 1973–2001; Max Fordham Associates, 1985–2001. *Building projects* include: Alexandra Rd housing scheme, London, 1969; Royal Exchange Th., Manchester, 1977; Southern Water, Sparrow Grove, Hants, 1985; RMC Internat. HQ, Egham, 1992; Grove Rd Primary Sch., London, 1993 (HVCA/Independent on Sunday Green Bldg of Year); Queens Bldg, De Montfort Univ., 1995 (HVCA/Independent on Sunday Green Bldg of Year); Tate Gall., St Ives, 1995 (Civic Trust Award); MCC Cricket Sch., Lord's Ground, London, 1995 (Balthasar-Neumann Prize, Assoc. of German Master Builders, Architects and Engrs); Judge Inst. of Mgt Studies, Cambridge Univ., 1997; Bedales Sch. Th., Hants, 1998 (Royal Fine Arts Commn Bldg of Year); Royal Exchange, Manchester, 1999 (Lighting Project of Year, Bldg Services Awards); Nat. Botanic Gdn of Wales, 2000 (RICS Bldg Efficiency Award); Beaufort Court Zero Emissions Bldg, Kings Langley, 2005 (RICS Regl Sustainability Award). Vis. Prof., Building Design, Sch. of Civil Engrg and Architecture, Univ. of Bath, 1990–. Dir, Nestar Ltd, 1987–99. External Examiner: Univ. of Edinburgh, 1992–94; AA, 1995–97, 2007–12; Cambridge Univ., 1996–98. Mem., Judging Panel, RIBA Stirling Prize, 2005. Pres., CIBSE, 2001–02. MCIBS (MIHVE); FCIBSE. Hon. FRIBA 1996. Gold Medal, CIBSE, 1997; Prince Philip Designers Prize, 2008. *Publications:* (contrib.) European Directory of Sustainable and Energy Efficient Buildings, 1998; papers to conferences and contrib. papers and articles to jls incl. RSA Jl, Architectural Rev., Dubai. *Recreations:* mucking about in boats mostly on the East coast of England, walking in the Lake District, gardening, reading and writing about my work of improving the design of buildings. *Address:* 3 Camden Square, NW1 9UY. *T:* (020) 7485 5113. *E:* max@maxf.co.uk.

FOREMAN, Dr Amanda Lucy, (Mrs J. L. E. Barton); historian; *b* London, 30 June 1968; *d* of Carl Foreman, Hon. CBE and of Evelyn Foreman; *m* 2000, Jonathan Luke Elliott Barton; one *s* four *d*. *Educ:* Lady Margaret Hall, Oxford (MPhil; DPhil 1998). Writer, consultant and presenter, BBC TV documentaries, 1998–; journalist and contributor to US and UK newspapers and periodicals, 1998–; Adjunct Prof., Faculty of Writing, Gallatin Sch., New York Univ., 2002; Vis. Sen. Res. Fellow in Hist., Faculty of Arts, QMUL, 2004–. Member: Bd, Sarah Lawrence Coll., 2000–04; Adv. Council, Lady Margaret Hall, Oxford, 2005–; Adv. Council, NY Public Liby, 2009–. Judge: PEN/Hessell-Tiltman Prize for Hist., 2012; Man Booker Prize for Fiction, 2012. Member: Virginia Histl Soc.; Columbia Histl Soc. FRSA 2001. *Publications:* Georgiana, Duchess of Devonshire, 1998 (Whitbread Prize for Biog.); (contrib.) New Dictionary of National Biography, 2002; (Series Ed.) Making History, 2004; (contrib.) What Might Have Been, 2004; A World on Fire: an epic history of two nations divided, 2010 (Fletcher Pratt Award for Civil War Hist., Civil War Round Table of NY, 2011). *Recreations:* gardening, cooking, film, television, screenwriting, journalism. *Address:* The Wylie Agency, 17 Bedford Square, WC1B 3JA. *T:* (020) 7908 5901. *E:* mail@wylieagency.co.uk. *Clubs:* Colony, Century Association (NY).

FOREMAN, Michael, RDI 1985; AGI; writer and illustrator; *b* 21 March 1938; *s* of Walter and Gladys Mary Foreman; *m* 1st, 1959, Janet Charters (marr. diss. 1966); one *s*; 2nd, 1980, Louise Phillips; two *s*. *Educ:* Notley Road Secondary Modern Sch., Lowestoft; Royal College of Art, London (ARCA 1st Cl. Hons and Silver Medal). Freelance, 1963–; six animated films produced, 1967–68. Hon. FRCA 1989. Hon. DArts Plymouth, 1998. Awarded Aigle d'Argent, Festival International du Livre, Nice, 1972; (jtly) Kurt Maschler Award, 1982; Graphics Prize, Bologna, 1982; Kate Greenaway Medal, Library Assoc., 1983 and 1989. *Publications:* author and illustrator: The Perfect Present, 1967; The Two Giants, 1967; The Great Sleigh Robbery, 1968; Horatio, 1970; Moose, 1971; Dinosaurs and all that Rubbish, 1972 (Francis Williams Prize, 1972); War and Peas, 1974; All The King's Horses, 1976; Panda's Puzzle and his Voyage of Discovery, 1977 (Francis Williams Prize, 1977); Panda and the Odd Lion, 1980; Trick a Tracker, 1982; Land of Dreams, 1982; Panda and the Bunyips, 1984; Cat and Canary, 1984; Panda and the Bushfire, 1985; Ben's Box, 1986; Ben's Baby, 1987; The Angel and the Wild Animal, 1988; War Boy (autobiog.), 1989; One World, 1990; Michael Foreman's World of Fairytales, 1990; Michael Foreman's Mother Goose, 1991, reissued as Michael Foreman's Nursery Rhymes, 1998; The Boy Who Sailed with Columbus, 1991; Jack's Fantastic Voyage, 1992; War Game, 1993; Grandfather's Pencil and the Room of Stories, 1993; Dad! I Can't Sleep, 1994; Surprise! Surprise!, 1995; After the War Was Over, 1995; Panda (Panda's Puzzle, Panda and the Odd Lion), 1996; Seal Surfer, 1996; The Little Reindeer, 1996; Look! Look!, 1997; Angel and the Box of Time, 1997; Jack's Big Race, 1998; Chicken Licken, 1998; Little Red Hen, 1999; Michael Foreman's Christmas Treasury, 1999; Rock-a-Doodle Do!, 2000; Cat in the Manger, 2000; Memories of Childhood (War Boy, After the War was Over), 2000; Saving Sinbad!, 2001; Wonder Goal, 2002; Dinosaur Time, 2002; Michael Foreman's Playtime Rhymes, 2002; Evie and the Man who Helped God, 2003; Cat on the Hill, 2003; Hello World, 2003; Can't Catch Me, 2005; Classic Fairy Tales, 2005; Norman's Ark, 2006; Fox Tale, 2006; Mia's Story, 2006; The Littlest Dinosaur, 2008; A Child's Garden, 2009; The Littlest Dinosaur's Big Adventure, 2009; Why the Animals Came to Town, 2010; Fortunately, Unfortunately, 2010; Superfrog!, 2011; Oh! If Only…, 2011; Friends, 2012; Newspaper Boy and the Origami Girl!, 2012; Superfrog and the Big Stink!, 2013; I Love You Too!, 2013; The Amazing Tale of Ali Pasha, 2013; Cat and Dog, 2014; The Seeds of Friendship, 2015; The Little Bookshop and the Origami Army, 2015; illustrator of many books by other authors. *Recreations:* football, travelling. *Address:* 11 Howards Lane, SW15 6NX. *Club:* Chelsea Arts.

FORESTER; *see* Weld Forester, family name of Baron Forester.

FORESTER, 9th Baron *cr* 1821; **Charles Richard George Weld Forester;** land agent, since 2004; *b* 8 July 1975; *o s* of 8th Baron Forester and of Catherine Elizabeth Weld Forester; *S* father, 2004; *m* 2009, Lydia, *d* of George Baugh; one *s*. *Educ:* Harrow; RAC Cirencester. *Recreations:* sport (cricket, tennis ski-ing), bridge, reading, countryside pursuits. *Heir: s* Hon. Brook George Percival Weld Forester, *b* 29 March 2014.

FORESTIER-WALKER, Sir Michael (Leolin), 6th Bt *cr* 1835; General Manager, Leatherhead Theatre, 2003–10 (Development Manager, 2002–03); *b* 24 April 1949; *s* of Lt-Col Alan Ivor Forestier-Walker, MBE (*d* 1954) (*g s* of 2nd Bt), and Margaret Joan Forestier-Walker (*née* Marcoolyn) (*d* 1988); *S* cousin, 1983; *m* 1988, Elizabeth Hedley, *d* of Joseph Hedley, Bellingham, Northumberland; one *s* one *d*. *Educ:* Wellington College, Crowthorne; Royal Holloway College, London Univ. (BA Hons). Teacher, Feltonfleet Sch., 1975–2002. *Heir: s* Joseph Alan Forestier-Walker, *b* 2 May 1992. *Address:* Bibury, 116 Hogshill Lane, Cobham, Surrey KT11 2AW.

FORGAN, Dame Elizabeth (Anne Lucy), DBE 2006 (OBE 1999); writer and broadcaster; Chair, National Youth Orchestra of Great Britain, since 2013; *b* 31 Aug. 1944; *d* of late Thomas Moinet Forgan and Jean Margaret Muriel. *Educ:* Benenden Sch.; St Hugh's Coll., Oxford (BA; Hon. Fellow 2014). Journalist: Teheran Journal, 1967–68; Hampstead and Highgate Express, 1969–74; Evening Standard, 1974–78; The Guardian, 1978–81; Channel Four TV: Sen. Commissioning Editor, 1981–86; Dir of Progs, 1988–93; Man. Dir, Network Radio BBC, 1993–96. Dir, Guardian Media Gp, 1998–2004. Non-exec. Dir, DCMS, 2008–09. Member: HFEA, 1990–98; Churches Conservation Trust, 1998–2001 (Chm., 1999–2001); Chair: NHMF and HLF, 2001–08; Arts Council England, 2009–13; Scott Trust, 2004–16. Trustee: Conservatoire for Dance and Drama, 2002–09; British Mus., 2009– (Dep. Chm., 2012–); The Art Fund, 2012–. Patron: St Giles Trust, 2007–; Schola Cantorum of Oxford, 2011–; Pier Arts Centre, Stromness, 2013–. FRTS 1988; FRSA 1989; Hon. Fellow, Girton Coll., Cambridge, 2009; Hon. FBA 2014. Hon. DLitt: Keele, 1994; Kent, 2009; Hon. MA Salford, 1995; Hon. Dr Univ. of the Arts, 2013. Chevalier de l'ordre des arts et des lettres (France), 1990. *Recreations:* church music, cheap novels, Scottish islands. *Address:* Most Media Ltd, 112 Regent's Park Road, NW1 8UG. *Club:* Reform.

FORLIN, Gerard; QC 2010; *b* Ayrshire; *s* of late Prof. Joseph Forlin and Moira Forlin (*née* Conway). *Educ:* London Sch. of Econs and Pol Sci. (LLB Hons, LLM); Trinity Hall, Cambridge (MPhil); Inst. of World Affairs (Dip. Air and Space Law). Called to the Bar, Lincoln's Inn; in practice as barrister, specialising in corporate manslaughter, health and safety, envmtl, disaster litigation, aviation, public inquiries and inquests. Pt-time lectr and speaker, incl. internat. confs, in over 50 countries, lectures for FCO, UN and ASEAN corporate social responsibility on UK Bribery Act. *Publications:* (Gen. Ed.) Corporate Liability: work related deaths and criminal prosecutions, 2004, 3rd edn 2014; contrib. books and articles. *Recreations:* swimming, travel, amateur dramatics, script writing, music, after dinner speaking. *Address:* c/o Cornerstone Chambers, 2–3 Gray's Inn Square, Gray's Inn, WC1R 5JH; c/o Denman Chambers, Level 7/185 Elizabeth Street, Sydney, NSW 2000, Australia; c/o Maxwell Chambers, 3 Temasek Avenue, #16–01, Singapore 039190.

FORMAN, (Francis) Nigel; Hon. Senior Research Fellow, Constitution Unit, University College London, since 2002; Tutor, Wroxton College, since 1997; *b* 25 March 1943; *s* of late Brig. J. F. R. Forman and Mrs P. J. M. Forman; *m*. *Educ:* Dragon Sch., Oxford; Shrewsbury Sch.; New Coll., Oxford; College of Europe, Bruges; Kennedy Sch. of Govt, Harvard; Sussex Univ. Information Officer, CBI, 1970–71; Conservative Research Dept, 1971–76. Contested

(C) Coventry NE, Feb. 1974. MP (C) Carshalton, March 1976–1983, Carshalton and Wallington, 1983–97; contested (C) Carshalton and Wallington, 1997. PPS to Lord Privy Seal, 1979–81 and to Minister of State, FCO, 1979–83, to Chancellor of the Exchequer, 1987–89; Parly Under Sec. of State, Dept for Educn, 1992. Member: Select Cttee on Science and Technology, 1976–79; Select Cttee on Foreign Affairs, 1990–92; Vice-Chairman: Cons. Finance Cttee, 1983–87; All Party Social Sci. and Policy Cttee, 1984–97; Secretary: Cons. Education Cttee, 1976–79; Cons. Energy Cttee, 1977–79. Mem. Exec., 1922 Cttee, 1990–92. Director: HFC Bank plc, 1995–2008; Prospects Services Ltd, 2001–03. Mem., ESRC, 1991–92. Chm., GB-E Europe Centre, 1990–92; Hon. Dir, Job Ownership Ltd, 1993–2001; Mem. Council, Federal Trust, 1995–. Mem. Council, Tavistock Inst., 1993–2005. *Publications:* Towards a More Conservative Energy Policy, 1977; Another Britain, 1979; Mastering British Politics, 1985, 5th edn 2007; (with John Maples) Work to be Done, 1985; Constitutional Change in the United Kingdom, 2002.

FORMAN, Air Vice-Marshal Graham Neil, CB 1989; Director of Legal Services, Royal Air Force, 1982–89; *b* 29 Nov. 1930; *s* of Stanley M. Forman and Eva Forman (*née* Barrett); *m* 1957, Valerie Fay (*née* Shaw) (*d* 2011); one *s* two *d*. *Educ:* Boston Grammar School; Nottingham Univ. Law School; Law Society's School of Law; admitted solicitor 1953. Commissioned RAF Legal Branch, 1957; served HQ Far East Air Force, Singapore, 1960–63 and 1965–68; Dep. Dir, RAF Legal Services, HQ Near East Air Force, Cyprus, 1971–72 and 1973–76; Dep. Dir, RAF Legal Services, HQ RAF Germany, 1978; Dep. Dir, Legal Services (RAF), 1978–82. *Clubs:* Royal Air Force (Life Mem.), Middlesex CC (Life Mem.).

FORMAN, Miloš; film director; *b* Čáslav, 18 Feb. 1932; *m* Martina; four *s*. *Educ:* Acad. of Music and Dramatic Art, Prague. Director: Film Presentations, Czechoslovak Television, 1954–56; Laterna Magika, Prague, 1958–62. Co-Chm. and Prof., Film Div., Columbia Univ. Sch. of Arts, 1978–. Films directed include: Talent Competition; Peter and Pavla, 1963 (Czech. Film Critics' Award; Grand Prix, Locarno, 1964; Prize, Venice Festival, 1965); A Blonde in Love (Grand Prix, French Film Acad., 1966); The Fireman's Ball, 1967; Taking Off, 1971; (co-dir) Visions of Eight, 1973; One Flew Over the Cuckoo's Nest, 1975 (Academy Award, 1976; BAFTA Award, 1977); Hair, 1979; Ragtime, 1982; Amadeus, 1985 (Oscar Award, 1985); Valmont, 1988; The People vs Larry Flynt, 1996 (Golden Globe Award, 1997); Man on the Moon, 2000; Goya's Ghosts, 2006. *Publications:* Turnaround: a memoir, 1993. *Address:* Aspland Management, 245 West 55th Street, Suite 1102, New York, NY 10019, USA.

FORMAN, Nigel; *see* Forman, F. N.

FORMANTINE, Viscount; Ivo Alexander Ninian Gordon; *b* 18 July 2012; *s* and *heir* of Earl of Haddo, *qv*.

FORNA, Aminatta, FRSL; writer, since 1999; *b* Glasgow, 7 May 1964; *d* of late Mohamed Sorie Forna and of Maureen Margaret Forna (*née* Christison); *m* 1994, Simon John Westcott; one *s*. *Educ:* Malvern Girl's Coll.; University Coll. London (LLB Hons Laws); Univ. of California at Berkeley (Harkness Fellow 1996). FRSL 2012. Reporter, Arts, News and Current Affairs, BBC Television, 1989–99. Prof. of Creative Writing (part-time), Bath Spa Univ., 2013–. Member: Council, Caine Prize for African Writing, 2005–; Bd, Index on Censorship, 2007–09; Adv. Cttee, Royal Literary Fund, 2008–; Bd, National Th., 2012–15; Council, RSL, 2014–. *Publications:* The Devil that Danced on the Water (memoir), 2002; Ancestor Stones, 2006; The Memory of Love, 2010 (Commonwealth Writer's Prize for Best Book, 2011); The Hired Man, 2013. *Recreation:* running. *Address:* c/o David Godwin Associates Ltd, 55 Monmouth Street, WC2H 9DG. *T:* (020) 7240 9992. *E:* assistant@davidgodwinassociates.co.uk. *Clubs:* Groucho, Quo Vadis.

FORRES, 4th Baron *cr* 1922; **Alastair Stephen Grant Williamson,** MARAC; Bt 1909; Chairman, Agriscot Pty Ltd; Director, Jaga Trading Pty Ltd; *b* 16 May 1946; *s* of 3rd Baron Forres and of Gillian Ann Maclean, *d* of Major John Maclean Grant, RA; *S* father, 1978; *m* 1969, Margaret, *d* of late G. J. Mallam, Mullumbimby, NSW; two *s*. *Educ:* Eton. Alderman, Orange City Council, 1987. Pres., Big Brother Movt, 1986–. Patron, Sydney Scottish Week, 1981–. *Heir:* *s* Hon. George Archibald Mallam Williamson [*b* 16 Aug. 1972; *m* 2002, Charlotte, *e d* of Timothy and Sara Barrett; *m* 2009, Frances Louise, *d* of John Lindsay Merity; one *s* one *d*]. *Clubs:* Union, Australian Jockey, Sydney Turf (Sydney).

FORREST, Prof. (Alexander) Robert (Walker), FRCP, FRCPE, FRCPath; CSci, CChem, FRSC; HM Senior Coroner (formerly HM Coroner), South Lincolnshire, since 2012; Assistant Coroner (formerly Assistant Deputy Coroner), Central Lincolnshire, since 2012; *b* 5 July 1947; *s* of Alexander Muir Forrest and Rose Ellen Forrest (*née* Ringham); *m* 1999, Dr Wendy Susan Phillips; two *s*. *Educ:* Stamford Sch.; Univ. of Edinburgh (BSc Hons 1970; MB ChB 1973); Cardiff Law Sch. (LLM). DObstRCOG 1975; MCB 1981; CChem, FRSC 1983; FRCPE 1989; FRCP 1992; FRCPath 1992; Eurotox Registered Toxicologist 1997; CSci 2004. Sen. Registrar, Royal Infirmary, Glasgow, 1979–81; Consultant in Clin. Chem. and Toxicol., Sheffield Univ. Hosps NHS Trust at Royal Hallamshire Hosp., Sheffield, 1981–98 (Hon. Consultant, 1998–2005); Prof. of Forensic Toxicol., 1998–2005, Hon. Prof. of Forensic Chem., 2005–, Sheffield Univ. Assistant Deputy Coroner: S Yorks (W), 1989–2012; E Riding of Yorks and Kingston-upon-Hull, 2008–12. Mem., Sec. of State for Transport's Hon. Medical Adv. Panel for Alcohol, Drugs and Substance Misuse and Driving. Ed., Science and Justice, 1999–2006. Pres., Forensic Sci. Soc., 2005–07. Fellow, American Acad. of Forensic Scis, 2010–. *Publications:* numerous contribs to med. and scientific literature on forensic toxicology and related subjects. *Recreations:* family, cats, computers, books. *Address:* Office of HM Coroner, 1 Gilbert Drive, Boston PE21 9PT. *T:* (01522) 552064, *Fax:* (01522) 516717. *E:* toxicologist@mac.com. *Club:* Athenæum.

FORREST, Prof. Sir (Andrew) Patrick (McEwen), Kt 1986; Regius Professor of Clinical Surgery, University of Edinburgh, 1970–88, now Professor Emeritus; *b* 25 March 1923; *s* of Rev. Andrew James Forrest, BD, and Isabella Pearson; *m* 1955, Margaret Beryl Hall (*d* 1961); one *s* one *d*; *m* 1964, Margaret Anne Steward; one *d*. *Educ:* Dundee High Sch.; Univ. of St Andrews. BSc 1942; MB, ChB 1945; ChM hons, University Gold Medal, 1954; MD hons, Rutherford Gold Medal, 1958; FRCSE 1950; FRCS 1952; FRCSGlas 1962; FRSE 1976; FRSB (FIBiol 1986); FRCPE 1999. Surg.-Lt RNVR, 1946–48. Mayo Foundation Fellow, 1952–53; Lectr and Sen. Lectr, Univ. of Glasgow, 1955–62; Prof. of Surgery, Welsh Nat. Sch. of Medicine, 1962–70. Hon. Consultant Surgeon: Royal Inf. of Edinburgh, until 1988; Royal Prince Alfred Hosp., Sydney; Civilian Consultant to RN, 1977–88. Chief Scientist (pt-time), SHHD, 1981–87. McIlrath Vis. Prof., Royal Prince Alfred Hosp., Sydney, 1969; Nimmo Vis. Prof., Royal Adelaide Hosp., 1973; McLauchlin-Gallie Prof., RCP of Canada, 1974; numerous other visiting professorships; Vis. Scientist, Nat. Cancer Inst., 1989–90; Associate Dean, Internat. Med. Coll., Kuala Lumpur, 1993–96. Eponymous lectures include: Lister Meml, Canadian Med. Assoc., 1970; Inaugural Bruce Wellesley Hosp., Toronto, 1970; Inaugural Peter Lowe, RCP Glas., 1980. Member: Medical sub-cttee, UGC, 1967–76; MRC, 1974–79; Scientific Adv. Cttee, Cancer Res. Campaign, 1974–83; ABRC, 1982–85. Asst Editor and Editor, Scottish Med. Jl, 1957–61; Hon. Secretary: Scottish Soc. for Experimental Medicine, 1959–62; Surgical Research Soc., 1963–66, Pres., 1974–76; Chairman: British Breast Gp, 1974–77; Working Gp on Breast Cancer Screening (reported, 1986); Scottish Cancer Foundn, 1998–2003. Member Council: Assoc. of Surgeons of GB and Ireland, 1971–74 (Pres., 1988–89); RCSE, 1976–84, 1986–89; Member: Internat. Surgical Gp, 1963–; James IV Assoc. of Surgeons Inc., 1981–; Scottish Hosp. Endowments Res. Trust, 1990–94. Mem., Kirk Session, St Giles' Cathedral, 1979–. Hon. Fellow, Amer. Surgical Assoc., 1981; Hon. FACS 1978; Hon. FRACS 1987; Hon. FRCR 1988; Hon. FRCSCan 1989; Hon. FFPH (Hon. FFPHM 2001). Hon. DSc: Wales, 1981; Chinese Univ. of Hong Kong, 1986; Hon. LLD Dundee, 1986; Hon. MD Internat. Medical Univ., 2007. Lister Medal, RCS, 1987; Gold Medal, Netherlands Surgical Assoc., 1988; Gimbernat Prize, Catalan Soc. of Surg., 1996; Breast Cancer Award, European Inst. of Oncology, 2000. *Publications:* (ed jtly) Prognostic Factors in Breast Cancer, 1968; (jtly) Principles and Practice of Surgery, 1985; Breast Cancer: the decision to screen, 1991; various papers in surgical jls, mainly on gastro-intestinal disease and breast cancer. *Address:* 19 St Thomas Road, Edinburgh EH9 2LR. *T:* (0131) 667 3203.

FORREST, John Richard, CBE 2002; DPhil; FREng; FIET; Director, Cranfield Ventures Ltd, since 2014; *b* 21 April 1943; *s* of late John Samuel Forrest, FRS and Ivy May Olding; *m* 1st, 1973, Jane Patricia Robey Leech (marr. diss. 2000); two *s* one *d*; 2nd, 2006, Diane Martine James. *Educ:* Sidney Sussex Coll., Cambridge (MA); Keble Coll., Oxford (DPhil). Research Associate and Lectr, Stanford Univ., Calif, 1967–70; Lectr, later Prof., Electronic and Elect. Engrg Dept, UCL, 1970–84; Technical Dir, Marconi Defence Systems Ltd, 1984–86; Dir of Engrg, IBA, 1986–90; Chief Exec., 1990–94, Dep. Chm., 1994–96, National Transcommunications Ltd; Chairman: Brewton Group, 1994–99; Human IT Ltd, 2000–03; CDS Ltd, 2003–05; Adv. Bd, Interregnum plc, 2003–06; Zinwave Ltd, 2008–13; Mirics Ltd, 2010–12; Dep. Chm., Surrey Satellite Technology Ltd, 2006–14. Director: Egan Internat., 1994–98; Drake Automation, 1996–99; Loughborough Sound Images, 1996–98; Screen, 1997–2000; Tricorder Technology, 1997–2001; 3i Gp, 1997–2004; Blue Wave Systems Inc., 1998–2001 (Chm., 2000–01); Globecast (Northern Europe) Ltd, 1998–2000; Printable Field Emitters Ltd, 1999–2000; Morgan Howard Internat. Gp Ltd, 1999–2000; Cellular Design Services Ltd, 2001–02; System C Healthcare, 2005–11; Restore plc, 2010–15. Chm., UK Govt Spectrum Mgt Adv. Gp, 1998–2003; Member: UK Adv. Bd, Stanford Res. Inst. Internat., 1996–98; EC IT Rev. Bd, 1995–99; Steering Bd, Eur. Digital Video Broadcast Initiative, 1995–97. Sen. Vice-Pres., Royal Acad. of Engrg, 1999–2002 (FEng 1985; Hon. Sec. for Electrical Engrg, and Mem. Council, 1995–97; Vice-Pres., 1997–99); Vice-President: IEE, 1992–95; RTS, 1994–97. Pro-Chancellor, Surrey Univ., 2005–15. Mem. Council, Brunel Univ., 1996–99. FRSA 1986; FRTS 1990; FInstD 1991. Hon. Fellow, BKSTS. Hon. DSc City, 1992; Hon. DTech Brunel, 1995. Chevalier de l'ordre des arts et des lettres (France), 1990. *Publications:* papers and contribs to books on phased array radar, satellite communications, broadcasting and optoelectronics. *Recreations:* travel, sailing, mountain walking, literature, study of mankind. *T:* 07785 251734. *E:* johnrforrest1@btinternet.com.

FORREST, Prof. Sir Patrick; *see* Forrest, Prof. Sir A. P. M.

FORREST, Robert; *see* Forrest, A. R. W.

FORREST, Rev. Canon Robin Whyte; Dean of Moray, Ross and Caithness, 1992–98; Canon of St Andrew's Cathedral, Inverness, 1986–98, now Hon. Canon; Rector of St John's, Forres, 1979–98; *b* 1933. *Educ:* Edinburgh Theol Coll., 1958. Ordained deacon, 1961, priest, 1962; Asst Curate, St Mary, Glasgow, 1961–66; Rector: Renfrew, 1966–70; Motherwell, 1970–79, with Wishaw, 1975–79; St Columba's, Nairn, 1979–92. Synod Clerk, Moray, 1991–92. *Address:* Landeck, Cummingston, Elgin, Moray IV30 5XY. *T:* (01343) 835539.

FORRESTER, David Michael; education consultant; Director, Further Education and Youth Training, Department for Education and Employment, 1995–2001; *b* 22 June 1944; *s* of late Reginald Grant Forrester and Minnie Forrester (*née* Chaytow); *m* 1st, 1978, Diana Douglas (marr. diss. 1983); 2nd, 1993, Helen Mary Williams, *qv*; one *s* one *d*. *Educ:* St Paul's Sch.; King's Coll., Cambridge (BA Hons 1st Cl. 1966, MA); Kennedy Sch. of Govt, Harvard Univ. (an inaugural Kennedy Scholar, 1966–67). DES, 1967; Private Sec. to Parly Under Sec., 1971–72; Principal, DES, 1972–76; HM Treasury, 1976–78; Asst Sec., DES, 1979–85; DTI, 1985–87; Under Sec., DES, subseq. DFE, then DFEE, 1988; Hd of Further Educn Br., 1994–95. FRSA 1999. *Recreations:* cricket, squash, music, esp. opera, mountain walking. *Address:* 340 Liverpool Road, N7 8PZ. *T:* (020) 7607 1492. *E:* davidforrester@btinternet.com. *Club:* Pretenders'.

FORRESTER, Rev. Prof. Duncan Baillie, FRSE; Professor of Theology and Public Issues, 2000–01, Professor of Christian Ethics and Practical Theology, 1978–2000, and Dean, Faculty of Divinity, 1996–99, University of Edinburgh (Principal, New College, 1986–96); Director, Edinburgh University Centre for Theology and Public Issues, 1984–2000; *b* 10 Nov. 1933; *s* of Rev. Prof. William Forrester and Isobel McColl or Forrester; *m* 1964, Rev. Margaret R. McDonald or Forrester (former Minister of St Michael's Parish Church, Edinburgh); one *s* one *d*. *Educ:* Madras Coll., St Andrews; Univ. of St Andrews (MA Hons Mod. Hist. and Pol Sci.); Univ. of Chicago (Grad., Dept of Politics); Univ. of Edinburgh (BD); DPhil Sussex. Part-time Asst in Politics, Univ. of Edinburgh, 1957–58; Asst Minister, Hillside Church and Leader of St James Mission, 1960–61; Church of Scotland Missionary to S India, 1962, Lectr, then Prof. of Politics, Madras Christian Coll., Tambaram, 1962–70; ordained as Presbyter of Church of S India; part-time Lectr in Politics, Univ. of Edinburgh, 1966–67; Chaplain and Lectr in Politics and Religious Studies, Sch. of African and Asian Studies, Univ. of Sussex, 1970–78. Lectures: Lee, Edinburgh, 1980; Hensley Henson, Oxford, 1988; Bernard Gilpin, Durham, 1992; F. D. Maurice, KCL, 1995; Bishop Butler, Bristol, 1996; Richard Hooker, Exeter, 1999; Von Hügel, Cambridge, 2000; Ferguson, Manchester, 2002; Eric Abbott, Westminster, 2003; Boutwood, Cambridge, 2004. Chm., Edinburgh Council of Social Service, 1983–87. President: Soc. for the Study of Theol., 1991–93; Soc. for the Study of Christian Ethics, 1991–94; Church Service Soc., 1999–2001; Vice-Pres., Council on Christian Approaches to Defence and Disarmament, 1998–. Member: Faith and Order Commn, WCC, 1983–96; Center of Theol Inquiry, Princeton, 1992–; Nuffield Council on Bioethics, 1996–2002. FRSA 2000; FRSE 2007. Hon. Fellow, Harris Manchester Coll., Oxford, 2000. Hon. DTheol Univ. of Iceland, 1997; Hon. DD: Glasgow, 1999; St Andrews, 2000. Templeton UK Award, 1999. *Publications:* chapters on Luther, Calvin and Hooker, in History of Political Philosophy, ed Strauss and Cropsey, 1963, 3rd edn 1986; Caste and Christianity, 1980; (with J. I. H. McDonald and G. Tellini) Encounter with God, 1983; (ed with D. Murray) Studies in the History of Worship in Scotland, 1984; Christianity and the Future of Welfare, 1985; (ed with D. Skene and co-author) Just Sharing, 1988; Theology and Politics, 1988; Beliefs, Values and Policies: conviction politics in a secular age, 1989; (ed jtly) Worship Now, Book 2, 1989; (ed) Theology and Practice, 1990; The True Church and Morality, 1997; Christian Justice and Public Policy, 1997; Truthful Action: explorations in practical theology, 2000; On Human Worth: a Christian vindication of equality, 2001; Apocalypse Now? reflections on faith in a time of terror, 2005; Theological Fragments: explorations in unsystematic theology, 2005; Living and Loving the Mystery: exploring Christian worship, 2010; Forrester on Christian Ethics and Practical Theology, 2010; articles on Indian politics and religion, ethics and political theology. *Recreations:* hill-walking, ornithology. *Address:* 25 Kingsburgh Road, Edinburgh EH12 6DZ. *T:* (0131) 337 5646.

FORRESTER, His Honour Giles Charles Fielding; a Circuit Judge, 1986–2011; a Senior Circuit Judge and Permanent Judge at the Central Criminal Court, 1995–2011; *b* 18 Dec. 1939; *s* of late Basil Thomas Charles Forrester and Diana Florence Forrester (*née* Sandeman); *m* 1966, Georgina Elizabeth Garnett; one *s* one *d*. *Educ:* Rugby School; Grenoble Univ.; Trinity College, Oxford (MA Jurisp.). Account Exec., Pritchard Wood and Partners, 1962–66. Called to the Bar, Inner Temple, 1966, Bencher, 2008; practised, SE Circuit, 1966–86; Asst Recorder, 1981–86; Recorder of the Crown Court, 1986. Judicial Mem., Parole Bd, 2002–07. Mem., HAC Infantry Bn, 1963–67, Veteran Mem., 1994–; Pres., HAC RFC, 1994–98. Mem. Council, Magistrates' Assoc., 1998–2008 (Pres., SW London Br., 1991–2007). FRGS 2004. Freeman, City of London, 1997; Freedom, Weavers' Co., 1998

(Mem., Ct of Assts, 2008–; Upper Bailiff, 2011–12). *Recreations:* a wide variety, mainly sporting. *Address:* 21 Tideswell Road, Putney, SW15 6LJ. *T:* (020) 8789 7386. *E:* gcf.forrester@gmail.com. *Clubs:* Boodle's, Roehampton; Royal Western Yacht; St Enodoc Golf; New Zealand Golf (Weybridge).

FORRESTER, Helen Mary; *see* Williams, Helen M.

FORRESTER, Ian Stewart; QC (Scot.) 1988; *b* 13 Jan. 1945; *s* of late Alexander Roxburgh Forrester and Elizabeth Richardson Forrester (*née* Stewart); *m* 1981, Sandra Anne Therese Keegan, Louisiana lawyer; two *s*. *Educ:* Kelvinside Acad., Glasgow; Univ. of Glasgow (MA 1965; LLB 1967); Tulane Univ. of Louisiana (MCL 1969). Mem., British Univs debating team, 1966; Commonwealth expedn to India, 1967. Admitted Faculty of Advocates, Scots Bar, 1972; admitted Bar of State of NY, following order of NY Court of Appeals, 1977; admitted English Bar, Middle Temple, 1996, Bencher, 2012. With Maclay, Murray & Spens, 1968–69; Davis Polk & Wardwell, 1969–72; Cleary Gottlieb Steen & Hamilton, 1972–81; estab. ind. chambers, Brussels, 1981; co-founder, Forrester & Norall, 1981 (Forrester Norall & Sutton, 1989; White & Case, 1998), practising before European Commn and Courts. Chm., British Conservative Assoc., Belgium, 1982–86. Vis. Prof., European Law, Univ. of Glasgow, 1991–2010, now Hon. Prof. Mem., Eur. Adv. Bd, 1992–2006, Dean's Adv. Bd, Law Sch., 2006–, Tulane Univ. Trustee, EU Baroque Orch., 2005–. Elder, St Andrew's Church of Scotland, Brussels, 1992–. Hon. LLD Glasgow, 2009. *Publications:* numerous articles on EEC customs, dumping and trade law, competition law, German civil and commercial codes. *Recreations:* politics, wine, cooking, tree planting, sailing. *Address:* White & Case, 62 Rue de la Loi, 1040 Brussels, Belgium; Advocates' Library, Parliament House, Edinburgh EH1 1RF. *Clubs:* Athenæum; International Château Ste-Anne (Brussels); Royal Yacht Club of Belgium.

FORRESTER, James William; Executive Director, Manchester International Festival, since 2012; *b* 25 Feb. 1952; *s* of Dr Sam Forrester and Dr Marion Forrester; *m* 1988, Caroline Slinger (*d* 2008); one *s* one *d*. *Educ:* Univ. of Durham (BA Hons English Lit. and Lang. 1973); Univ. of Leicester (Mus Dip.). Apprentice boatbuilder, 1974–76; journeyman boatbuilder, 1976–84; Ship and Boat Conservator, 1984–88, Public Progs Officer, 1988–96, Merseyside Maritime Mus.; Gen. Manager, NMGM Trading Co., 1996–2001; Dir, Imperial War Mus. North, 2002–12. Chairman: N Wales and Borders Partnership Bd, Canal and River Trust, 2012–14; Bd of Trustees, Greater Manchester Arts Centre, 2012–. *Recreations:* travel, boats and fun with family, life's unfolding tapestry. *Address:* Rose Cottage, Utkinton Lane, Tarporley, Cheshire CW6 0JH. *E:* jim.forrester@btinternet.com.

FORRESTER, Prof. John Vincent, MD; FRCSE, FRCOphth, FRCSGlas, FRCPE, FMedSci, FRSE, FRSB; Cockburn Professor of Ophthalmology, University of Aberdeen, 1984–2011, now Emeritus; Professor of Ocular Immunology, University of Western Australia, since 2012; *b* 11 Sept. 1946; *m* Anne Gray; two *s* two *d*. *Educ:* St Aloysius Coll., Glasgow; Glasgow Univ. (MD Hons 1980). FRCSE 1975; FRCSGlas 1985; FRCOphth 1990; FRCPE 1996. FRSB (FIBiol 2009). Various hosp. appts, Glasgow, 1971–78; MRC Travelling Fellow, Columbia Univ., NY, 1976–77; Consultant Ophthalmologist, Southern Gen. Hosp., Glasgow, 1979–83. Spinoza Prof., Univ. of Amsterdam, 1997; Adjunct Prof., Univ. of Western Australia, 2010; Visiting Professor: Univ. of Pittsburgh, 2010; Univ. of Kentucky, 2012. Master, Oxford Ophthalmol Congress, 2000–02. Pres., European Assoc. of Eye and Vision Res., 2001–02. Ian Constable Lect., 2013. Ed., British Jl Ophthalmol., 1992–2000. FMedSci 1998; FRSE 2003; Fellow, Assoc. for Res. in Vision and Ophthalmol., 2009. McKenzie Medal, 2006; Doyne Medal, 2007; Mooney Medal, 2010; Bowman Medal, 2012; Donders Medal, 2012; Mildred Wiesenfeld Award, 2012. *Recreation:* family. *Address:* Division of Applied Medicine, Institute of Medical Sciences, Foresterhill, Aberdeen AB25 2ZD. *T:* (01224) 437505.

FORRESTER, Lisa; *see* Appignanesi, L.

FORRESTER-PATON, His Honour Douglas Shaw; QC 1965; a Circuit Judge (formerly a Judge of County Courts), 1970–86; *b* 22 June 1921; 3rd *s* of late Alexander Forrester-Paton, JP; *m* 1948, Agnete, *d* of Holger Tuxen; one *s* two *d*. *Educ:* Gresham's Sch., Holt; Queen's Coll., Oxford (BA). Called to Bar, Middle Temple, 1947; North East Circuit. Served RAF, 1941–45. Recorder: Middlesbrough, 1963–68; Teesside, 1968–70. *Address:* 11 The Dorkings, Great Broughton, Middlesbrough TS9 7NA. *T:* (01642) 712301; 5 King's Bench Walk, Temple, EC4Y 7DB.

FORSDICK, Prof. Charles Richard Allerton, PhD; James Barrow Professor of French, University of Liverpool, since 2001; *b* West Runton, 26 June 1969; *s* of late Michael Edward Forsdick and of Brenda Forsdick (*née* Whitehead, now Townsend); *m* 1994, Rev. Christine Margaret Dutton; two *s* one *d*. *Educ:* Norwich Sch.; New Coll., Oxford (BA 1992); Lancaster Univ. (PhD 1995). Lectr in French, Univ. of Glasgow, 1995–2001. British Acad. Sen. Res. Fellow, 2004–05; AHRC Theme Leadership Fellow, 2012–. Pres., Soc. for French Studies, 2012–14. MAE 2011. Philip Leverhulme Prize, Leverhulme Trust, 2005. *Publications:* Victor Segalen and the Aesthetics of Diversity, 2000; Travel in 20th-Century French and Francophone Cultures, 2005; Oasis Interdites, 2008. *Recreations:* travel, languages, ceramics, history of Norfolk. *Address:* Department of Modern Languages and Cultures: French, University of Liverpool, Liverpool L69 7ZR. *T:* (0151) 794 2740. *E:* craf@liv.ac.uk.

FORSDICK, David John; QC 2014; *b* Woking, Surrey, 11 Jan. 1969; *s* of Brian and Joan Forsdick; *m* 1999, Natalie O'Shea; one *s* one *d*. *Educ:* Heathside Co. Sch.; Strodes VIth Form Coll.; Warwick Univ. (BA Hons Modern Eur. Hist.). Called to the Bar: Gray's Inn, 1993; NI, 2012; in practice as barrister, specialising in envmtl, planning and public law, 1994–; Mem., A Panel of Jun. Counsel to the Crown, 2005–. Chm. Govs, St Luke's Primary Sch., Islington, 2001–. *Recreations:* ski-ing, walking. *Address:* Landmark Chambers, 180 Fleet Street, EC4A 2HG. *T:* (020) 7430 1221.

FORSHAW, Christian; saxophonist and composer; Professor of Saxophone, Guildhall School of Music and Drama, since 2002; *b* Harrogate, 22 May 1972; *s* of Brian Forshaw and Margaret Forshaw; *m* 2006, Sarah Allen; two *s*. *Educ:* Guildhall Sch. of Music and Drama (BMus Hons 1995). Founder, Sanctuary Ensemble (saxophone, voice, organ, percussion), 1996. Recordings incl. Sanctuary, 2004, Songs of Solace, 2012. *Recreations:* cooking, walking, cycling, family. *E:* mail@christianforshaw.com.

FORSHAW, Sarah Anne; QC 2008; *b* Gloucester, 2 July 1964; *d* of late Brig. Peter Forshaw, CBE and of Helen Forshaw (*née* Cliff); *m* 1991 (marr. diss. 2002); two *s*. *Educ:* King's Coll., Taunton; King's Coll. London (LLB). Called to the Bar, Middle Temple, 1987, Bencher, 2013; in practice as barrister specialising in crime. *Address:* 5 King's Bench Walk, Temple, EC4Y 7DN. *T:* (020) 7353 5638.

FORSTER, Prof. Anthony William, DPhil; Vice-Chancellor, University of Essex, since 2012; *b* Chiseldon, Wilts, 19 May 1964; *s* of William A. Forster and Patricia Forster; *m* 1994, Victoria. *Educ:* Denstone Coll., Uttoxeter; Univ. of Hull (BA 1st Cl. Hons Politics 1985); St Antony's Coll., Oxford (MPhil Eur. Politics and Society 1993); St Hugh's Coll., Oxford (DPhil 1996); Univ. of Nottingham (Postgrad. Cert. Acad. Practice 1999). Army Officer, RCT, 1985–91. Stipendiary Lectr, St Hilda's Coll., Oxford, 1995–96; Lectr, Sch. of Politics, Univ. of Nottingham, 1996–2000; Dir of Res. and Sen. Lectr, 2000–02, Reader, 2002, in Eur. Foreign and Security Policy, Defence Studies Dept, KCL; University of Bristol: Dir, Governance Res. Centre, 2002–06; Prof. of Politics, 2002–04; Hd, Dept of Politics, 2004–06; Durham University: Exec. Dean (Social Scis and Health), 2006–08; Prof. of Politics, 2006–08; Pro-Vice-Chancellor (Educn), 2008–11; Hon. Prof. of Politics, 2008–12; Dep. Vice-Chancellor, 2011–12. FHEA 2007; FAcSS (AcSS 2009); Fellow, Leadership Foundn for HE, 2014. FRSA 2010. *Publications:* Britain and the Maastricht Negotiations, 1999; (with A. Blair) The Making of Britain's European Foreign Policy, 2001; Euroscepticism in Contemporary British politics: opposition to Europe in the British Conservative and Labour Parties since 1945, 2002; (with A. Cottey) Reshaping Defence Diplomacy: new roles for military cooperation and assistance, 2004; Armed Forces and Society in Europe, 2006; (with T. Edmunds) Out of Step: the case for change in British armed forces, 2007; edited with T. Edmunds and A. Cottey: Democratic Control of the Military in Postcommunist Europe, 2001; The Challenge of Military Reform in Postcommunist Europe: building professional armed forces, 2002; Soldiers and Societies in Postcommunist Europe, Legitimacy and Change, 2003; Civil-Military Relations in Postcommunist Europe, 2006. *Recreations:* dog walking, twentieth century architecture. *Address:* University of Essex, Wivenhoe Park, Colchester, Essex CO4 3SQ. *T:* (01206) 872000, *Fax:* (01206) 869493. *E:* vc@essex.ac.uk. *Club:* Athenæum.

FORSTER, Donald, CBE 1988; Managing Director, 1945–81, and Chairman, 1981–86, B. Forster & Co. Ltd, Leigh (textile manufacturing company); *b* 18 Dec. 1920; *s* of Bernard and Rose Forster; *m* 1942, Muriel Steinman; one *s* two *d*. *Educ:* N Manchester Grammar School. Served War, RAF pilot (Flt Lieut), 1940–45. Mem., Skelmersdale Develt Corp., 1980–82; Chairman: Warrington/Runcorn Develt Corp., 1982–86; Merseyside Develt Corp., 1984–87. *Recreations:* golf, music, paintings. *Address:* 72A Elizabeth Street, SW1W 9PD. *Club:* Whitefield Golf.

See also L. C. Goldstone.

FORSTER, Jilly, (Mrs R. A. Lamond); Founder and Chair, The Forster Co., since 1996; *b* 8 Dec. 1955; *d* of Dr Matthew Forster and Dr Margaret Forster; *m* 1979, Robert Andrew Lamond; two *s*. *Educ:* N London Collegiate Sch.; The Priory, Lewes. Founding Dir, Munro & Forster, 1984–89; Dir, Body Shop Internat. plc, 1989–96; Dir, Big Issue, 1991–93. Trustee: Children on the Edge, 2004–09; Forgiveness Project, 2004–09; Royal Parks Foundn, 2004–08; Jamie Oliver Foundn, 2010–. *Recreations:* semiology, social enterprise, land art. *Address:* The Forster Co., 49 Southwark Street, SE1 1RU. *T:* (020) 7403 2230. *E:* jilly@forster.co.uk.

FORSTER, Margaret; author; *b* 25 May 1938; *d* of Arthur Gordon Forster and Lilian (*née* Hind); *m* 1960, Edward Hunter Davies, *qv*; one *s* two *d*. *Educ:* Carlisle and County High Sch. for Girls; Somerville Coll., Oxford (BA). FRSL. Teacher, Barnsbury Girls' Sch., Islington, 1961–63. Member: BBC Adv. Cttee on Social Effects of Television, 1975–77; Arts Council Literary Panel, 1978–81. Chief non-fiction reviewer, Evening Standard, 1977–80. *Publications: non-fiction:* The Rash Adventurer: the rise and fall of Charles Edward Stuart, 1973; William Makepeace Thackeray: memoirs of a Victorian gentleman, 1978; Significant Sisters: grassroots of active feminism 1839–1939, 1984; Elizabeth Barrett Browning: a biography, 1988; (ed, introd. and prefaces) Elizabeth Barrett Browning: selected poems, 1988; Daphne du Maurier, 1993; Hidden Lives (memoir), 1995; Rich Desserts and Captains Thin: a family and their times 1831–1931, 1997; Precious Lives, 1998; Good Wives? Mary, Fanny, Jennie and Me, 1845–2001, 2001; My Life in Houses (memoir), 2014; *novels:* Dames' Delight, 1964; Georgy Girl, 1965 (filmscript with Peter Nichols, 1966); The Bogeyman, 1965; The Travels of Maudie Tipstaff, 1967; The Park, 1968; Miss Owen-Owen is At Home, 1969; Fenella Phizackerley, 1970; Mr Bone's Retreat, 1971; The Seduction of Mrs Pendlebury, 1974; Mother, can you hear me?, 1979; The Bride of Lowther Fell, 1980; Marital Rites, 1981; Private Papers, 1986; Have the Men Had Enough?, 1989; Lady's Maid, 1990; The Battle for Christabel, 1991; Mothers' Boys, 1994; Shadow Baby, 1996; The Memory Box, 1999; Diary of an Ordinary Woman 1914–1995, 2003; Is There Anything You Want?, 2005; Keeping the World Away, 2006; Over, 2007; Isa and May, 2010; The Unknown Bridesmaid, 2013. *Recreations:* walking on Hampstead Heath, reading contemporary fiction. *Address:* 11 Boscastle Road, NW5 1EE. *T:* (020) 7485 3785; Grasmoor House, Loweswater, near Cockermouth, Cumbria CA13 0RU. *T:* (01900) 85303.

FORSTER, Rt Rev. Peter Robert; *see* Chester, Bishop of.

FORSTER, Prof. Piers Maxwell de Ferranti, PhD; Professor of Physical Climate Change, University of Leeds, since 2008; *b* Oxford, 1968; *s* of Roger and Trödissita Forster; *m* 2000, Stella; one *d*. *Educ:* Monkton Combe Sch., Bath; Imperial Coll. London (BSc Hons 1990; ARCS); Univ. of Reading (PhD Meteorol. 1994). NERC Advanced Res. Fellow, 2000–05; Res. Fellow, Univ. of Colorado, 2002; Reader, Univ. of Leeds, 2005–08. Royal Soc. Wolfson Merit Award Holder, 2011–. Mem., Expert Panel, Airport Commn, 2013–. Trustee and Dir, United Bank of Carbon Charity, 2009–. *Publications:* contrib. Intergovtl Panel for Climate Change Assessment Reports and peer-reviewed papers on aspects of climate change. *Recreations:* ski touring, hill walking, tennis, sleeping in the sun, marmalade, sheep farming. *Address:* School of Earth and Environment, University of Leeds, Leeds LS2 9JT. *T:* (0113) 343 6476. *E:* p.m.forster@leeds.ac.uk.

FORSYTH, family name of **Baron Forsyth of Drumlean**.

FORSYTH OF DRUMLEAN, Baron *cr* 1999 (Life Peer), of Drumlean in Stirling; **Michael Bruce Forsyth,** Kt 1997; PC 1995; *b* 16 Oct. 1954; *s* of John T. Forsyth and Mary Watson; *m* 1977, Susan Jane Clough; one *s* two *d*. *Educ:* Arbroath High School; St Andrews University (MA). Pres., St Andrews Univ. Cons. Assoc., 1972–75; Nat. Chm., Fedn of Cons. Students, 1976–77. Dir, Flemings, 1997–99; Vice-Chm., Investment Banking Europe, JP Morgan, 1999–2001; Dep. Chm., JP Morgan UK, 2002–05; Sen. Advr, 2006–07, Sen. Man. Dir, 2007–, Evercore Partners Ltd; non-executive Director: J & J Denholm Ltd, 2005–; Denholm Logistics Ltd, 2011–; Hyperion Insce Gp, 2012– (Chm., 2014–); Secure Trust Bank, 2014–. MP (C) Stirling, 1983–97; contested (C) same seat, 1997. PPS to Sec. of State for Foreign and Commonwealth Affairs, 1986–87; Parly Under-Sec. of State, 1987–90, Minister of State, 1990–92, Scottish Office; Minister of State: Dept of Employment, 1992–94; Home Office, 1994–95; Sec. of State for Scotland and Lord Keeper of the Great Seal of Scotland, 1995–97. Member: Select Cttee on Economic Affairs, H of L, 2009–13; Select Cttee on Soft Power, H of L, 2013–14; Jt Cttee on Nat. Security Strategy, 2014–. Chm., Scottish Cons. Party, 1989–90. Mem., Westminster City Council, 1978–83. Mem. Develt Bd, Nat. Portrait Gall., 1999–2003. Dir, Centre for Policy Studies, 2006–13. Pres., Royal Highland and Agricl Soc. of Scotland, 2015–16. Patron: Craighalbert Centre, 1999–; Children in Need Inst. UK, 2008–13. *Recreations:* photography, gardening, fly-fishing, mountaineering, ski-ing, amateur astronomy. *Address:* House of Lords, SW1A 0PW.

FORSYTH OF THAT ILK, Alistair Charles William; JP; FSCA, FSAScot; FInstPet; Baron of Ethie; Chief of the Name and Clan of Forsyth; *b* 7 Dec. 1929; *s* of Charles Forsyth of Strathendry, FCA, and Ella Millicent Hopkins; *m* 1958, Ann, OStJ, *d* of Col P. A. Hughes, IA; four *s*. *Educ:* St Paul's Sch.; Queen Mary Coll., London. FInstPet 1973; FSCA 1976; FSAScot 1979. National Service, 2nd Lieut The Queen's Bays, 1948–50; Lieut The Parachute Regt, TA, 1950–54. Chm., Hargreaves Reiss & Quinn Ltd, 1981–99. Mem., Angus DC, 1988–92. Mem., Standing Council of Scottish Chiefs, 1978–. Freeman, City of London, 1993; Liveryman, Scriveners' Co., 1993–. CStJ 1982 (OStJ 1974). JP NSW, 1965; JP Angus, 1987. KHS 1992. *Heir:* *s* Alistair James Menteith Forsyth, yr of that Ilk, barrister and advocate, *b* 21 Dec. 1960. *Address:* Dysart House, Kempton, Tas 7030, Australia; Monteleone, Condom-en-Armanac 32100, France.

FORSYTH, Bill; film director and script writer; *b* Glasgow, 1947; one *s* one *d*. *Educ:* National Film Sch. *Films directed:* That Sinking Feeling, 1980; Gregory's Girl, 1981; Local Hero, 1983; Comfort and Joy, 1984; Housekeeping, 1988; Breaking In, 1990; Being Human, 1993; Gregory's Two Girls, 1999. TV film, Andrina, 1981. BAFTA Award: best screenplay, 1982; best dir, 1983. Hon. DLitt Glasgow, 1984; DUniv Stirling, 1989. *Address:* c/o United Agents, 12–26 Lexington Street, W1F 0LE.

FORSYTH, Sir Bruce; *see* Forsyth-Johnson, Sir B. J.

FORSYTH, Frederick, CBE 1997; author; *b* 25 Aug. 1938; *m* 1st, 1973, Carole Cunningham; two *s*; 2nd, 1994, Sandy Molloy. *Educ:* Tonbridge Sch. RAF, 1956–58. Reporter, Eastern Daily Press, Norfolk, 1958–61; joined Reuters, 1961: Reporter, Paris, 1962–63; Chief of Bureau, E Berlin, 1963–64; joined BBC, 1965; radio and TV reporter, 1965–66; Asst Diplomatic Correspondent, BBC TV, 1967–68; freelance journalist, Nigeria and Biafra, 1968–69. *Publications: non fiction:* The Biafra Story, 1969, 2nd edn 1977; The Outsider: my life in intrigue (autobiog.), 2015; *fiction:* The Day of the Jackal, 1971 (filmed, 1973); The Odessa File, 1972 (filmed, 1975); The Dogs of War, 1974 (filmed, 1981); The Shepherd, 1975; The Devil's Alternative, 1979; No Comebacks (short stories), 1982; Emeka, 1982; The Fourth Protocol, 1984 (filmed, 1987); The Negotiator, 1988; The Deceiver, 1991; (ed) Great Flying Stories, 1991; The Fist of God, 1993; Icon, 1996; The Phantom of Manhattan, 1999; The Veteran and Other Stories, 2001; Avenger, 2003; The Afghan, 2006; The Cobra, 2010; The Kill List, 2013. *Address:* c/o Bantam Books, 62/63 Uxbridge Road, W5 5SA.

FORSYTH, Justin; *see* Forsyth, R. J. A.

FORSYTH, Prof. Murray Greensmith, FRHistS; Professor of Politics, University of Leicester, 1990–94, now Emeritus; *b* 30 Oct. 1936; *s* of Maj. Henry Russell Forsyth and Marie Elaine Forsyth; *m* 1964, Marie Denise Edelin de la Praudière; one *s* two *d*. *Educ:* Wellington Coll.; Balliol Coll., Oxford (BA Mod. Hist. 1959; MA 1964); College of Europe, Bruges. FRHistS 1991. Research Officer, Political and Econ. Planning, London, 1960–64; University of Leicester: Lectr in Politics, 1964–70; Reader in Internat. Politics, 1971–90; Dir, Centre for Federal Studies, 1988–94; Prof. of Govt and Pol Sci., Hong Kong Baptist Univ., 1995–97. British Acad. Wolfson Fellow, Paris, 1977; Bradlow Fellow, S African Inst. of Internat. Affairs, 1983; Vis. Prof., Coll. of Europe, Bruges, 1993–94; Robert Schuman Vis. Prof., Fudan Univ., Shanghai, 1998. Pres., European Consortium for Regl and Federal Studies, 1993–94. *Publications:* The Parliament of the European Communities, 1964; (jtly) Economic Planning and Policies in Britain, France and Germany, 1968; (ed jtly) The Theory of International Relations, 1970; Unions of States: the theory and practice of confederation, 1981; Reason and Revolution: the political theory of the Abbé Sieyes, 1987; (ed jtly) The Political Classics: Plato to Rousseau, 1988; (ed) Federalism and Nationalism, 1989; (trans.) The Spirit of the Revolution of 1789, 1989; (ed jtly) The Political Classics: Hamilton to Mill, 1993, Green to Dworkin, 1996. *Recreations:* collecting prints and watercolours, browsing in second-hand bookshops. *Address:* Blackmore House, Blackmore Park Road, Malvern, Worcs WR14 3LF. *T:* (01684) 560901.

FORSYTH, Rt Rev. Robert Charles; Bishop of South Sydney and an Assistant Bishop, Diocese of Sydney, since 2000; *b* 8 June 1949; *m* 1970, Margaret Diane Shelley; two *s* two *d*. *Educ:* Meadowbank Boys' High Sch.; Sydney Univ.; Moore Coll. Assistant Minister: Glenbrook, 1976–77; Holy Trinity, Adelaide, 1978–83; Rector, St Barnabas', Broadway and Chaplain, Sydney Univ., 1983–2000. Sydney Gen. Synod Rep., 1990– (Mem., Strategic Issues Adv. Panel, 1999–2001); Member: Sydney Standing Cttee, 1990–; Archbishop's Liturgical Panel, 1993–; St Andrew's Cathedral Chapter, 1993–2010; Sydney Doctrine Commn, 1994–; Archbishop's Selection Panel, 1996– (Examining Chaplain, 1991–94). Sydney Anglican Cursillo Spiritual Dir, 1995–97. Chairman: EU Graduates Fund, 1995–; Langham Partnership Australia, 2000–07. Columnist, Southern Cross newspaper, 1989–2000; co-author and developer, LifeWorks evangelism prog. *Address:* PO Box Q190, QVB Post Office, NSW 1230, Australia. *Club:* Australian (Sydney).

FORSYTH, (Robert) Justin (Alexander); Chief Executive, Save the Children UK, since 2010; *b* Paisley, 17 June 1965; *s* of Robert Forsyth and Maureen Forsyth (*née* Irvine); *m* 2012, Lisa Stevens; one *s*. *Educ:* Oxford Poly. (BA Hons Hist. and Pols 1988). Oxfam: Advr on Africa, 1989–95; Internat. Advocacy Dir, Washington, DC, 1995–99; Policy Dir, 1999–2002; Dep. Dir (Campaigns and Policy), 2003–05; Special Advr to the Prime Minister, 2005–08; Dir of Campaigns and Strategic Communications for the Prime Minister, 2008–10. *Recreations:* tennis, reading, African history and politics. *Address:* Save the Children UK, 1 St John's Lane, EC1M 4AR. *T:* (020) 7012 6400.

FORSYTH-JOHNSON, Sir Bruce Joseph, (Sir Bruce Forsyth), Kt 2011; CBE 2006 (OBE 1998); entertainer and comedian; *b* 22 Feb. 1928; *m* 1st, 1953, Penny Calvert (marr. diss. 1973; she *d* 2014); three *d*; 2nd, 1973, Anthea Redfern (marr. diss. 1982); two *d*; 3rd, 1983, Wilnelia Merced; one *s*. *Educ:* Higher Latimer Sch., Edmonton. Started stage career as Boy Bruce—The Mighty Atom, 1942; after the war, appeared in various double acts and did a 2 yr spell at Windmill Theatre; first television appearance, Music Hall, 1954; resident compère, Sunday Night at the London Palladium, 1958–60; own revue, London Palladium, 1962; leading role, Little Me, Cambridge Theatre, 1964; début at Talk of the Town (played there 7 times); compèred Royal Variety Show, 1971, and on subseq. occasions; London Palladium Show, 1973 (also Ottawa and Toronto) and 1980; commenced Generation Game, BBC TV series, 1971 (completed 7 series), and 1990–95; compèred Royal Windsor to mark BBC Jubilee Celebrations, 1977; One Man Show, Theatre Royal, Windsor, and Lakeside, 1977; Bruce Forsyth's Big Night, ITV, 1978; Play Your Cards Right, ITV, 1980–87, 1994–2000; Slinger's Day, ITV, 1986, 1987; You Bet!, 1988; Takeover Bid, BBC, 1990–91; Bruce's Guest Night, BBC, 1992–93; Bruce's Price is Right, 1996–2000; Strictly Come Dancing, BBC, 2004–14. Films include: Star; Can Hieronymus Merkin Ever Forget Mercy Humppe and Find True Happiness?; Bedknobs and Broomsticks; The Magnificent 7 Deadly Sins; Pavlova. Numerous records. Fellow, BAFTA, 2008. Show Business Personality of the Year, Variety Club of GB, 1975; TV Personality of the Year, Sun Newspaper, 1976 and 1977; Male TV Personality of the Year, TV Times, 1975, 1976, 1977 and 1978; Favourite Game Show Host, TV Times, 1984; BBC TV Personality of the Year, 1991; Lifetime Achievement Award, Comic Heritage, 2002. *Publications:* Bruce: the autobiography, 2001. *Recreation:* golf (handicap 10, Wentworth Golf Club).

FORSYTHE, John Leslie Robert, FRCS, FRCSEd, FRCPEd; Consultant Transplant Surgeon, Royal Infirmary of Edinburgh, since 1995; Honorary Professor in Surgery, School of Clinical Sciences and Community Health, University of Edinburgh, since 2011 (Reader in Surgery, 2006–11); Lead Clinician for Organ Donation and Transplantation Scotland, since 2008; *b* 27 Feb. 1958; *s* of Rev. Canon John Leslie Forsythe and Margaret Forsythe; *m* 1st, 1982, Jo-ann E. G. Harvey (marr. diss. 2007); one *s* two *d*; 2nd, 2008, Lorna P. Marson. *Educ:* Univ. of Newcastle upon Tyne (MB BS 1981; MD 1991). FRCSEd 1986; FRCS 2001; FRCPEd 2014. Surgical trng, Newcastle upon Tyne; Consultant Transplant Surgeon and Hon. Sen. Lectr, Royal Victoria Infirmary, Newcastle upon Tyne, 1991–95. Specialist Advr to CMO, Scotland, 2000–07. Chairman: Scottish Transplant Gp, 2001–; Kidney Pancreas Adv. Gp, UK Transplant SHA, 2002–06 (Mem., 1996–2001); Adv. Cttee on Safety of Blood, Tissues and Organs, DoH, 2007–15. Member: Bd, NHS Quality Improvements Scotland, 2003–08; Bd, NHS Blood and Transplant, 2006–14. Pres., British Transplantation Soc., 2005–07 (Vice-Pres., 2003–05); Gen. Sec., 2009–13, Pres., 2013–15, Eur. Soc. of Transplantation. FEBS 2009. *Publications:* A Companion to Specialist Surgical Practice, Vol. VII, 1997, 5th edn 2013; Principles and Practice in Surgery, 2002, 6th edn 2012; Abdominal Organ Retrieval and Transplantation Bench Surgery, 2013; numerous reviewed contribs to learned jls. *Address:* Transplant Unit, Royal Infirmary of Edinburgh, 51 Little France Crescent, Old Dalkeith Road, Edinburgh EH16 4SA. *T:* (0131) 242 1715, *Fax:* (0131) 242 1739. *E:* john.forsythe@luht.scot.nhs.uk.

FORSYTHE, Dr (John) Malcolm; Chairman, South West Kent Primary Care Trust (formerly Tunbridge Wells Primary Care Group), 1998–2004; *b* 11 July 1936; *s* of late Dr John Walter Joseph Forsythe and Dr Charlotte Constance Forsythe (*née* Beatty); *m* 1961, Delia Kathleen Moore (marr. diss. 1984); one *s* three *d*; *m* 1985, Patricia Mary Barnes. *Educ:* Repton Sch., Derby; Guy's Hosp. Med. Sch., London Univ. BSc(Hons), MB, BS, MSc; DObstRCOG, FRCP; FFPH. Area Medical Officer, Kent AHA, 1974–78; SE Thames Regional Health Authority: Dir of Planning, 1985–89; Regl MO, 1978–92; Regl Dir of Public Health and Service Develt, 1989–92; Professorial Fellow in Public Health, Kent Univ., 1992–2001; Sen. Lectr, King's Coll. Sch. of Medicine and Dentistry, 1992–2001. Hon. Consultant, Univ. of Kent Health Services Res. Unit, 1977–92. Vis. Prof., Univ. of N Carolina, Chapel Hill, 1973, 1976, 1993; Adjunct Prof., Univ. of St Georges, Grenada, 1995–; Jack Masur Fellow, Amer. Hosp. Assoc., 1976. Head, UK Deleg., Hospital Cttee, EEC, 1980–85, 1989–90; Consultant, Urwick Orr Ltd; Chm., GMC Wkg Pty on Performance Assessment in Public Health Medicine, 1995–97; Member: Resource Allocation Wkg Pty and Adv. Gp on Resource Allocation, 1975–78; Technical Sub Gp, Review of Resource Allocation Working Party Formula, 1986–87; DHSS Med. Manpower Planning Review, 1986–88; NHS Computer Policy Cttee, 1981–85; Standing Med. Adv. Cttee to Sec. of State, 1982–86; PHLS Bd, 1986–95; Central Council for Postgrad. Med. Educn, 1986–88; Health Services Res. Cttee, MRC, 1988–91; Bd of Governors, UMDS of Guy's and St Thomas', 1982–92; Delegacy, King's Coll. Hosp. Med. and Dental Schs, 1978–95. External Examiner to Univ. of London, 1987–89. Member: Bd of Mgt, Horder Health Care (formerly Horder Centre for Arthritis), Crowborough, 1992– (Chm., 1996–2000; Chm., Remuneration Cttee, 2011–); Tech. Bd, BUPA Ltd, 1992–2007; John Fry Cttee, KCL, 2011– (Treas., 2012–). Trustee, Sick Doctors Trust, 1996–. Vice-Pres., Epidemiology Sect., RSM, 2001–04 (Pres., 1998–2000); Mem. Editl Bd, RCP, 1999–2003. Member: Hyde Housing Assoc., 1999–2008; Bd, Chichester Diocesan Housing Assoc., 2001–07; Bd, In Touch, 2006–10. Chm., Ind. Remuneration Panel, Tonbridge & Malling BC, Sevenoaks DC and Tunbridge Wells BC, 2001–07. Council of Europe Fellowship, 1975; Silver Core Award, IFIP, 1977; KCL Alumni Award, 2012. *Publications:* (ed jtly) Information Processing of Medical Records, 1969; Proceedings of First World Conference on Medical Informatics, 1975. *Recreations:* golf, music, ornithology. *Address:* Buckingham House, 1 Royal Chase, Tunbridge Wells, Kent TN4 8AX. *T:* (01892) 522359. *Club:* Royal Society of Medicine (Hon. Sec., 2006–10, Vice-Chm., 2010–11, Retired Fellows Section).

FORSYTHE, William; choreographer; Professor of Dance and Artistic Advisor, Choreographic Institute, Glorya Kaufman School of Dance, University of Southern California, since 2015; Associate Choreographer, Paris Opera Ballet, since 2015; *b* NYC, 1949; *m*; two *s* one *d*. *Educ:* Jacksonville Univ., Florida; Joffrey Ballet Sch., NY. Joined Stuttgart Ballet as dancer, 1973, subseq. house choreographer and freelance choreographer; Dir, Frankfurt Ballet, 1984–2004; Artistic Dir, The Forsythe Co., 2005–15. A.D. White Prof.-at-Large, Cornell Univ. 2009–15. *Works choreographed* include: Urlicht, 1976; Gänge, 1983; France/Dance, 1983; Artifact, 1984; Steptext, 1985; Die Befragung des Robert Scott, 1986; In the Middle, Somewhat Elevated, 1988; Impressing the Czar, 1988; Limb's Theorem, 1991; The Loss of Small Detail, 1991; Herman Schmerman, 1992; Eidos: Telos, 1995; The Vertiginous Thrill of Exactitude, 1996; workwithinwork, 1998; Endless House, 1999; One Flat Thing, reproduced 2000; Kammer/Kammer, 2000; Decreation, 2003; Three Atmospheric Studies, 2005; You made me a monster, 2005; Human Writes, 2005; Heterotopia, 2006; The Defenders, 2007; Yes we can't, 2008; I don't believe in outer space, 2008; The Returns, Theatrical Arsenal II, 2009; Rearray, Sider, 2011; Stellenstellen, Study # 1, Neue Suite, Study # 3, 2012; works performed by NYC Ballet, Kirov Ballet, San Francisco Ballet, Nat. Ballet of Canada, Royal Ballet, Royal Ballet of Flanders, Royal Swedish Ballet, etc. Installation art works exhibited at the Louvre, Tate Modern Gall., Whitney Biennale, Venice Biennale, Munich Pinakothek der Moderne, NY MOMA, Hayward Gall., Hamburg Deichtorhallen, Zurich migrosmuseum für Gegenwartskunst, Centre Pompidou, Museo d'Arte Contemporanea Roma, etc. *Address:* Forsythe Productions GmbH, Basaltstrasse 58, 60487 Frankfurt am Main, Germany.

FORTE, Hon. Sir Rocco (John Vincent), Kt 1995; FCA; Chairman, Rocco Forte Hotels (formerly RF Hotels Ltd), since 1996; *b* 18 Jan. 1945; *s* of Baron Forte; *m* 1986, Aliai, *d* of Prof. Giovanni Ricci, Rome; one *s* two *d*. *Educ:* Downside Coll.; Pembroke Coll., Oxford (MA). Trusthouse Forte, subseq. Forte: Dir of Personnel, 1973–78; Dep. Chief Exec., 1978–82; Jt Chief Exec., 1982–83; Chief Exec., 1983–92; Chm., 1992–96. Pres., BHA. Dir, BTA, 1986–97. *Recreations:* triathlon, golf, country pursuits. *Address:* (office) 70 Jermyn Street, SW1Y 6NY.

See also Hon. O. Polizzi.

FORTESCUE, family name of **Earl Fortescue**.

FORTESCUE, 8th Earl *cr* 1789; **Charles Hugh Richard Fortescue;** Baron Fortescue, 1746; Viscount Ebrington, 1789; *b* 10 May 1951; *s* of 7th Earl and his 1st wife, Penelope Jane (*d* 1959), *d* of Robert Evelyn Henderson; *S* father, 1993; *m* 1974, Julia, *er d* of Air Commodore J. A. Sowrey; three *d*. *Heir: cousin* John Andrew Francis Fortescue [*b* 27 March 1955; *m* 1990, Phoebe Anne Cecilia, *d* of late Rev. John Eustace Burridge; two *s* one *d*].

FORTESCUE, Hon. Seymour Henry; Chairman, Short-term Lending Compliance Board, 2013–14; *b* 28 May 1942; *s* of 6th Earl Fortescue, MC, TD and late Sybil, *d* of 3rd Viscount Hardinge, CB; *m* 1st, 1966, Julia Mary Blair Pilcher (marr. diss. 1990); one *s* one *d*; 2nd, 1990, Jennifer Ann Simon; one *d*. *Educ:* Eton Coll.; Trinity Coll., Cambridge (MA); London Business Sch. (MSc). With Barclays Bank plc, 1964–91: Local Dir, Luton, 1972–77; Hd, Mktg, 1977–80; Chief Exec., Barclaycard, 1980–85; Dir, UK Personal Sector, 1986–91; Dir, Voluntary Income, ICRF, 1991–96; Chief Executive: HEA, 1996–99; Banking Code Standards Bd, 1999–2006. Chairman: UK Remittances Task Force, 2006–09; Portman Gp, 2009–13. Hon. Treas., LEPRA, 1985–96; Chm., BookPower (formerly Educnl Low-Priced Sponsored Texts), 2001–07. Mem. Council, London Univ., 2006–08; Governor, Oundle Sch., 1999–2004. Mem., Court of Assistants, Grocers' Co., 1987– (Master, 1997–98). *Recreations:* gardening, travel, opera, country activities. *Address:* Canon Bridge House, Madley, Hereford HR2 9JF. *T:* 07785 992453.

FORTEVIOT, 4th Baron *cr* 1917, of Dupplin, Perthshire; **John James Evelyn Dewar;** Bt 1907; farmer, landowner; *b* 5 April 1938; *s* of 3rd Baron Forteviot, MBE, and Cynthia Monica Starkie (*d* 1986); *S* father, 1993; *m* 1963, Lady Elisabeth Waldegrave (*d* 2003), 3rd *d* of 12th Earl Waldegrave, KG, GCVO; one *s* three *d*. *Educ:* Eton. Nat. Service, Black Watch (RHR), 1956–58. John Dewar & Sons Ltd, 1959–62; ADC to Governor General of NZ, 1962–63; John Dewar & Sons, 1963–98. *Recreations:* fishing, shooting, birdwatching, travel. *Heir: s* Hon. Alexander John Edward Dewar [*b* 4 March 1971; *m* 1997, Donryn (*née* Clement); two *s* one *d*]. *Club:* Royal Perth Golfing and Country and City.

FORTEY, Dr Richard Alan, FRS 1997; FRSL; Merit Researcher, since 1986, Research Associate, since 2006, Natural History Museum; *b* 15 Feb. 1946; *s* of Frank Allen Fortey and Margaret Fortey (*née* Wilshin); *m* 1st, 1968, Bridget Elizabeth Thomas (marr. diss.); one *s*; 2nd, 1977, Jacqueline Francis; one *s* two *d*. *Educ:* Ealing Grammar Sch.; King's Coll., Cambridge

(BA, MA; PhD 1971; ScD 1986). Res. Fellow, 1970–73, SSO, 1973–77, BM (Natural Hist.); PSO, Natural Hist. Mus., 1978–86. Howley Vis. Prof., Meml Univ. of Newfoundland, 1977–78; Vis. Prof. of Palaeobiology, Univ. of Oxford, 2000–09; Collier Prof. of Public Understanding of Sci. and Technol., Univ. of Bristol, 2002–03. Presenter, BBC TV series: Survivors, 2012; Fossil Wonderlands, 2014. Pres., Geol Soc. of London, 2006–08 (Mem., 1972–); Mem., Brit. Mycological Soc., 1980– (Vice-Pres., 2014–). FRSL 2010. Hon. Fellow, BAAS, 2008. Hon. DSc: St Andrews, 2006; Birmingham, 2010; Leicester, 2014; DUniv Open, 2006. Lyell Medal, Geol Soc., 1996; Frink Medal, Zool Soc. of London, 2001; Lewis Thomas Prize, Rockefeller Univ., 2003; Linnean Medal for Zoology, 2006; Michael Faraday Prize, Royal Soc., 2006; Linnean Legacy Award, State Univ. Arizona, 2009. *Publications:* Fossils: the key to the past, 1982, 4th edn 2009; The Hidden Landscape, 1993, 2nd edn 2010; Life: an unauthorized biography, 1997; Trilobite!, 2000; The Earth: an intimate history, 2004; Dry Store Room No 1: the secret life of the Natural History Museum, 2008; Survivors: the animals and plants that time has left behind, 2011; (as Roderick Masters) The Roderick Masters Book of Money Making Schemes, 1981. *Recreations:* mushrooms and toadstools, East Anglia, conviviality. *Address:* Natural History Museum, South Kensington, Cromwell Road, SW7 5BD. *T:* (020) 7942 5493.

FORTUNE, Robert Andrew; QC 2003; *b* 4 July 1953; *s* of Hamish Campbell Fortune and Hazel Phoebe Fortune. *Educ:* Millfield Sch.; London Sch. of Econs (LLB Hons). Called to the Bar, Middle Temple, 1976; barrister, specialising in criminal law. *Publications:* Alaric's Gold, 2014. *Recreations:* travel, reading, archaeology. *T:* 07973 117860. *E:* robert.fortune@btinternet.com.

FORTY, Prof. Arthur John, CBE 1991; PhD, DSc; FRSE; FRSA; Principal and Vice-Chancellor, Stirling University, 1986–94; *b* 4 Nov. 1928; *s* of Alfred Louis Forty and Elisabeth Forty; *m* 1950, Alicia Blanche Hart Gough; one *s*. *Educ:* Headlands Grammar Sch.; Bristol Univ. (BSc; PhD 1953; DSc 1967). FRSE 1988, FRSA 1989. Served RAF, 1953–56. Sen. Res. Scientist, Tube Investments Ltd, 1956–58; Lectr, Univ. of Bristol, 1958–64; University of Warwick: Foundn Prof. of Physics, 1964–86; Pro-Vice-Chancellor, 1970–86. Visiting scientist: Gen. Electric Co., USA; Boeing Co.; Nat. Bureau of Standards, Washington, USA. Member: SRC Physics Cttee, 1969–73; SRC Materials Cttee, 1970–73; Computer Bd, 1982–85; University Grants Committee: Mem., 1982–86, Vice-Chm., 1985–86; Chairman: Physical Sciences Sub-cttee, 1985–86; Equipment Sub-cttee, 1985–86; Chairman: Jt ABRC, Computer Bd and UGC Working Party on Future Facilities for Advanced Res. Computing (author, Forty Report), 1985; Management Cttee for Res. Councils' Supercomputer Facility, 1986–88; UFC Cttee for Information Systems (formerly Computer Bd for Univs and Res. Councils), 1988–91; Jt Policy Cttee for Advanced Res. Computing, 1988–94; Cttee of Scottish Univ. Principals, 1990–92; Edinburgh Parallel Computing Centre, 1994–97; Adv. Cttee, Scottish Science Liby, 1995–2001; Member: British Library Bd, 1987–94; Bd of Trustees, Nat. Liby of Scotland, 1995–2001; Academic Adv. Bd, Univ. of the Highlands and Islands, 1999–. Chm., ICIAM 99 Ltd, 1995–96. Hon. Fellow, Edinburgh Univ., 1994. Hon. LLD St Andrew's, 1989; DUniv Stirling, 1995; Hon. DSc Warwick, 2005. *Publications:* papers in Proc. Royal Soc., Phil Magazine and other learned jls. *Recreations:* sailing, gardening, the ancient metallurgy of gold. *Address:* Port Mor, St Fillans, by Crieff, Perthshire PH6 2NF.

FORWELL, Prof. George Dick, OBE 1993; PhD; FRCP; Chief Administrative Medical Officer, 1973–93, and Director of Public Health, 1989–93, Greater Glasgow Health Board; *b* 6 July 1928; *s* of Harold C. Forwell and Isabella L. Christie; *m* 1957, Catherine F. C. Cousland; two *d*. *Educ:* George Watson's Coll., Edinburgh; Edinburgh Univ. (MB, ChB 1950; PhD 1955). MRCPE 1957, DIH 1957, DPH 1959, FRCPE 1967, FFCM 1972, FRCPGlas 1974, FRCP 1985. House Officer and Univ. Clin. Asst, Edinburgh Royal Infirm., 1950–52; RAF Inst. of Aviation Med., 1952–54; MRC and RCPE grants, 1954–56; pneumoconiosis field res., 1956–57; Grad. Res. Fellow and Lectr, Edinburgh Univ. Dept of Public Health and Social Med., 1957–60; Asst Dean, Faculty of Med., Edinburgh Univ., 1960–63; Dep. Sen. and Sen. Admin. MO, Eastern Reg. Hosp. Bd, Dundee, 1963–67; PMO, Scottish Home and Health Dept, 1967–73. Vis. Prof., Dept of Public Health, Glasgow Univ., 1990–93; Hon. Prof., Sch. of Biol and Med. Scis, St Andrews Univ., 1993–98. QHP, 1980–83. Mem., GMC, 1984–89. *Publications:* papers on clin. res. and on health planning and services, in med. and other jls. *Recreation:* running. *Address:* 20 Irvine Crescent, St Andrews, Fife KY16 8LG. *Club:* Royal Air Force.

FORWOOD, family name of **Baroness Arlington**.

FORWOOD, Nicholas James; QC 1987. Judge, General Court of the European Union (formerly Court of First Instance, European Community), 1999–2015; *b* 22 June 1948; *s* of late Lt-Col Harry Forwood and Wendy Forwood. *Educ:* Stowe Sch.; St John's Coll., Cambridge (Open Schol., MA, Pt I Mechanical Scis, Pt II Law). Called to the Bar, Middle Temple, 1970, Bencher, 1998. Chm., Permanent Delegn of CCBE to European Courts, 1997–99. *Recreations:* ski-ing, golf, walking across Europe, opera. *Club:* Oxford and Cambridge.

FORWOOD, Sir Peter Noel, 4th Bt *cr* 1895; *b* 15 Oct. 1925; *s* of Arthur Noel Forwood, 3rd *s* of 1st Bt, and Hyacinth Forwood (*née* Pollard); *S* cousin, 2001; *m* 1950, Roy Murphy; six *d*. *Educ:* Radley. Served 1939–45 War, Welsh Guards. *Heir:* none. *Address:* Marsh Farm, Graffham, Petworth, W Sussex GU28 0NY.

FOSKETT, Hon. Sir David (Robert), Kt 2007; **Hon. Mr Justice Foskett;** a Judge of the High Court of Justice, Queen's Bench Division, since 2007; *b* 19 March 1949; *s* of late Robert Frederick Foskett and Ruth (*née* Waddington); *m* 1975, Angela Bridget Jacobs; two *d*. *Educ:* Warwick Sch.; King's Coll., London (LLB Hons; Pres., Faculty of Laws, 1969–70; Pres., Union Soc., 1970–71; Mem., Delegacy, 1970–72; FKC 2009). FCIArb 1992. Called to the Bar, Gray's Inn, 1972, Bencher, 1999; Mem., Midland Circuit; QC 1991; Asst Recorder, 1992–95; Recorder, 1995–2007; a Dep. High Ct Judge, 1998–2007. Member: Civil Procedure Rule Cttee, 1997–2001; Civil Justice Council, 2012–; Chm., Law Reform Cttee, Bar Council, 2005–07. President: KCL Assoc., 1997–2000; Old Warwickian Assoc., 2000, 2014; Mem. Council, KCL, 2010–. *Publications:* The Law and Practice of Compromise, 1980, 8th edn 2015; Settlement Under the Civil Procedure Rules, 1999; various articles. *Recreations:* theatre, music, poetry, cricket, golf. *Address:* Royal Courts of Justice, Strand, WC2A 2LL. *Clubs:* Athenæum, MCC; Woking Golf.

FOSKETT, Prof. Nicholas Hedley, PhD; Vice-Chancellor, Keele University, 2010–15; *b* Burslem, Stoke-on-Trent, 12 March 1955; *s* of Eric and Beryl Foskett; *m* 1979, Rosalind Arnold; one *s* one *d*. *Educ:* Wolstanton Co. Grammar Sch., Newcastle-under-Lyme; Keble Coll., Oxford (BA Hons 1977; PGCE 1978; MA 1981); Univ. of Southampton (PhD 1995). Geog. teacher, 1978–86, Hd of Geog., 1984–86, Haywards Heath Coll., W Sussex; Co-ordinator, Schools Prog., Aston Univ., 1987–89; University of Southampton: Lectr in Educn, 1989–95; Sen. Lectr, 1995–2000; Hd of Sch., 2000–05; Dean, Faculty of Law, Arts and Social Scis, 2005–10. *Publications:* (ed) Managing External Relations in Schools, 1992; (ed with A. R. Cook) Fieldwork, Development and Practice, 1996; (ed with B. Marsden) A Bibliography of Geographical Education 1970–1997, 1998 and Supplement 1998–1999, 2002; (ed with J. Lumby) Managing External Relations in Schools and Colleges, 1999; (with J. Hemsley-Brown) Choosing Futures: young people's decision-making in careers, education and training markets, 2001; (with J. Lumby) Leading and Managing Education: the international dimension, 2003; (with J. Lumby) 14–19 Education: policy, leadership and learning, 2005; (ed with F. Maringe) Globalisation and Internationalisation in Higher Education: theoretical, strategic and management perspectives, 2010; *with Rosalind Foskett*: Land, Man and Weather, 1981; The Wealden Landscape, 1983; Wealden Perspectives, 1984; People and the Rural Landscape, 1987; Conservation, 1999; (*et al.*) Geography AS/A2 Study Guide, 2001, 2nd edn 2005, rev. edn 2009; (and C. Burnett) Geography AS Fast Track, 2001; Postgraduate Study in the UK: the international student's guide, 2006; contrib. chapters in books; contrib. papers to acad. jls and res. reports. *Recreations:* sport, walking, family, theatre, music, travel.

FOSTER, family name of **Barons Foster of Bishop Auckland** and **Foster of Thames Bank**.

FOSTER OF BISHOP AUCKLAND, Baron *cr* 2005 (Life Peer), of Bishop Auckland in the County of Durham; **Derek Foster;** PC 1993; DL; *b* 25 June 1937; *s* of Joseph and Ethel Maud Foster; *m* 1972, Florence Anne Bulmer; three *s* one *d*. *Educ:* Bede Grammar Sch., Sunderland; Oxford Univ. (BA Hons PPE). In industry and commerce, 1960–70; Youth and Community Worker, 1970–73; Further Educn Organiser, Durham, 1973–74; Asst Dir of Educn, Sunderland Borough Council, 1974–79. Councillor: Sunderland Co. Borough, 1972–74; Tyne and Wear County Council, 1973–77 (Chm. Econ. Develt Cttee, 1973–76). Chm., North of England Develt Council, 1974–76. MP (Lab) Bishop Auckland, 1979–2005. North Regional Whip, 1981–82; opposition front bench spokesman on social security, 1982–83; PPS to Leader of Opposition, 1983–85; Opposition Chief Whip, 1985–95; opposition front bench spokesman on the Duchy of Lancaster, 1995–97. Member: Select Cttee on Trade and Industry, 1980–82, on Employment, 1997–2005 (Chm., 1997–2001), on Educn and Employment, 1997–2005 (Jt Chm., 1997–2001); Standards and Privileges Select Cttee, 2003–05. Member: H of C Liaison Cttee, 1997–2005; Parly Ecclesiastical Cttee, 1997–2005; Registration of Political Parties Adv. Gp, 1998–2005; Exec. Mem., British American Parly Gp, 1997–2005. Chairman: PLP Employment Cttee, 1980–81; PLP Econ. and Finance Cttee, 1981–82. Mem. (ex officio) Lab. Party NEC, 1985–95. Fellow, Industry and Parlt Trust. Chm., Bishop Auckland Develt Co., 2001–05; Mem., Co. Durham Develt Co., 2006–07. Chairman: Manufg Industry Gp, 1998–2001; N Regl Electronic Economy Prog.; non-executive Director: Northern Informatics, 1998–2001; Walker Hall Associates, 2006–07; HB Innovations, 2006–; Pres., SW Durham Engrg Training Ltd, 2003–. Vice Chm., Youthaid, 1979–86; Chairman: Northern Region Information Soc. Initiative, 1996; Pioneering Care Partnership, 1997–2005; Nat. Prayer Breakfast, 1997–99; non-exec. Dir, Health Express, 2014–; former Vice-Pres., Christian Socialist Movt; Mem., Nat. Adv. Bd, Salvation Army. Chm., Heritage Lottery Fund NE, 2006–. Chm., Bowes Mus., 2007–14. Trustee: Auckland Castle, 1996–; Nat. e^2 Learning Foundn, 2001–09 (Chm., e^2 Learning Foundn NE, 2004–08). Mem., Fabian Soc. CompILE 2001. Patron, Stockton and Darlington Railway Assoc., 2014–. DL Durham, 2001. Hon. DCL Durham, 2005. *Recreations:* brass bands, choirs, uniformed member Salvation Army. *Address:* 3 Linburn, Rickleton, Washington, Tyne and Wear NE38 9EB. *T:* (0191) 4171580.

FOSTER OF THAMES BANK, Baron *cr* 1999 (Life Peer), of Reddish in the county of Greater Manchester; **Norman Robert Foster,** OM 1997; Kt 1990; RA 1991 (ARA 1983); RWA 1994; RDI 1988; RIBA, FCSD, FAIA; architect; Founder and Chairman, Foster + Partners, London; *b* Reddish, 1 June 1935; *s* of late Robert Foster and Lilian Smith; *m* 3rd, 1996, Dr Elena Ochoa; one *s* one *d*. *Educ:* Univ. of Manchester Sch. of Architecture (DipArch 1961, CertTP); Yale Univ. Sch. of Architecture (Henry Fellow, Jonathan Edwards Coll., March 1962). Founded: Foster Associates, 1967; Foster and Partners, 1992; in collab. with Dr Buckminster Fuller, 1968–83; Cons. Architect, UEA, 1978–87. Mem. Council: AA, 1969–70, 1970–71 (Vice Pres., 1974); RCA, 1981. Taught at: Univ. of Pennsylvania; AA, London; Bath Acad. of Arts; London Polytechnic; Visiting Professor: Bartlett Sch. of Architecture, 1998; Harvard Univ. Grad. Scholar of Design, 2000; Sch. of Geog. and Envmt, Univ. of Oxford, 2010–. External Examr, 1971–73 and Mem. Visiting Bd of Educn, RIBA. Founder Trustee, Architecture Foundn, London, 1991–. Mem., H of L, 1999–2010. Major projects include: Head Office for Willis Faber & Dumas, Ipswich, 1975 (First Trustees', Medal, RIBA, 1990); Sainsbury Centre for Visual Arts, UEA, Norwich, 1977; UK headquarters for Renault, 1983; Nomos Furniture System, 1985; new HQ, Hongkong and Shanghai Banking Corp., Hong Kong, 1986; Millennium Tower, Tokyo, 1990; RA Sackler Galls, 1991; Terminal Zone, Stansted Airport, 1991; ITN HQ, 1991; Century Tower, Tokyo, 1991; inner harbour, Duisburg, 1991–2003; Barcelona Telecoms Tower, 1992; Arts Centre, Nîmes, 1993; school, Fréjus, 1993; German Parlt bldg (Reichstag), Berlin, 1993 and 1999; Bilbao Metro System, 1995; Univ. of Cambridge Faculty of Law, 1996; American Air Mus., Duxford, 1997; HQ for Commerzbank, Frankfurt, 1997; Hong Kong Internat. Airport, 1998; Congress Centre, Valencia, 1998; Great Court, BM redevelt, 2000; City Hall, London, 2002; Swiss Re Tower, London (RIBA Stirling Prize), 2004; McLaren Technol. Centre, Woking, 2004; Sage Centre, Gateshead, 2004; Millau Viaduct, France, 2004; Hearst Tower, NY, 2006; Wembley Stadium, 2007; Beijing Capital Internat. Airport, 2008; Elephant Hse, Copenhagen Zoo, 2008; Masdar masterplan, Abu Dhabi, 2008; Caja Madrid Tower, 2009; YachtPlus Boat Fleet, 2009; Winspear Opera Hse, Dallas, 2009; Circle Hosp. Bath, 2009; Bodegas Portia, Faustino Winery, Spain, 2010; Masdar Inst., Abu Dhabi, 2010; Boston Museum of Fine Art, 2010; Sperone Westwater, NY, 2010; Queen Alia Internat. Airport, 2012. Work exhibited: Antwerp, Barcelona, Berlin, Bordeaux, Hanover, London, Lyon, Manchester, Madrid, Milan, Munich, NY, Nîmes, Paris, Seville, Tokyo, Valencia, Zurich, Dallas, Copenhagen, Hong Kong, Beijing, Shanghai, Mexico City, Frankfurt, Venice; permanent collections: MOMA, NY, Centre Georges Pompidou, Paris. IBM Fellow, Aspen Conference, 1980; Hon. Prof., Buenos Aires, 1997; Hon. FAIA 1980; Hon. FREng; Hon. FIStructE; Hon. FRIAS 2000; Hon. Fellow, Inst. of Art and Design, Kent; Hon. Mem., Bund Deutscher Architekten, 1983; Member: Internat. Acad. of Architecture, Sofia; French Order of Architects; Eur. Acad. of Scis and Arts; Foreign Member: Royal Acad. of Fine Arts, Sweden; Amer. Acad. of Arts and Scis; Associate, Académie Royale de Belgique, 1990. Hon. Dr: E Anglia, Bath, Valencia, Humberside, Manchester, RCA, Eindhoven, Oxford, London, Negev, London Inst., Durham, Aberdeen, Dundee, Hong Kong, Yale, Madrid. Practice awards: over 600 for design excellence, including: R. S. Reynolds Internat. Awards, USA, 1976, 1979, 1986; 30 RIBA Awards and Commendations; 8 Financial Times Awards for outstanding Industrial Architecture; 9 Structural Steel Awards; Internat. Design Award; RSA Award, 1976; Ambrose Congreve Award, 1980; 15 Civic Trust Awards; 2 IStructE Special Awards; Premio Compasso d'Oro Award, 1987; 5 Interiors Awards (USA); 14 British Construction Industry Awards; 4 Aluminium Imagination Awards; Best Building of the Year Award, Royal Fine Art Commn/Sunday Times, 1992, 1993, Royal Fine Art Commn/BSkyB, (jtly) 1998; 15 BCO Awards; Queen's Award for Export, 1995; Regl Arch. Award, AIA, 1995. Personal awards include: RIBA Gold Medal, 1983; Kunstpreis, Berlin, 1989; Japan Design Foundn Award, 1987; Mies van der Rohe Award, Barcelona, 1991; Gold Medal, French Acad. of Arch., 1991; Brunner Meml Award, AAIL, 1992; Gold Medal, AIA, 1994; Gold Medal, Univ. Internacional Menéndez Pelayo, Santander, 1995; Best Internat. Promotion of Barcelona Award, 1997; Silver Medal, CSD, 1997; Berliner Zeitung Kulturpreis, 1998; special prize for positive contribution to British-German relations, German-British Forum, 1998; Pritzker Architecture Prize, 1999; special prize, 4th Internat. Biennial of Architecture, São Paulo, 1999; Walpole Medal of Excellence, 1999; Visual Arts Award, South Bank Show, 2001; Auguste Perret Prize, IUA, 2002; City of Rome Lifetime Achievement Award and Medaglia di Roma, 2003; Transatlantic Bridge Award, Friends of Free Univ. of Berlin, 2004; Prince Philip Designers Prize, Design Council, 2004; China Friendship Award, State Admin of Foreign Experts Affairs, 2008; Laureate, Prince of Asturias Award for the Arts, 2009; Humanitarian Award, UN Assoc. of New York, 2009; Save the Children Award, 2011. Officer, Order of Arts and Letters (France), 1994; Order of North Rhine Westphalia; Kt Comdr's Cross, OM (Germany), 2009 (Comdr's Cross 1999). *Relevant publications:* The Work of Foster Associates, 1979; Norman Foster, 1988; Stansted: Norman Foster and the architecture of flight, 1992; Norman Foster Sketches, 1992; Foster Associates, 1992; Foster and Partners, 1996; Sir Norman Foster, 1997; The Master Architect Series II: Norman Foster, 1997; Norman Foster 30 Colours, 1998; The Norman Foster Studio, 2000; On Foster…Foster On, 2000; Norman Foster Works: vol. 1, 2003, vol. 2, 2005, vol. 3, 2006, vol. 4, 2004, vol. 5, 2009, vol. 6, 2012; Foster Catalogue, 2001, 2005, 2008, 2012; Norman Foster: the architect's studio, 2001; Architecture is About People: Norman Foster, 2001; Norman Foster and the British Museum, 2001; Reichstag Berlin, 2002; Blade of Light: the story of the Millennium Bridge, 2002; Reichstag Graffiti, 2003; Reflections, 2005; 30 St Mary Axe: a tower for London, 2006; Foster 40, 2007; Wembley Stadium: venue of legends, 2008; Norman Foster: a life in architecture, 2010; Norman Foster: drawings 1958–2008, 2010. *Recreations:* running, flying, ski-ing. *Address:* (office) Riverside, 22 Hester Road, SW11 4AN. *T:* (020) 7738 0455, *Fax:* (020) 7738 1107. *E:* enquiries@fosterandpartners.com.

FOSTER, Alicia Christian, (Jodie); American film actress and director; *b* 19 Nov. 1962; *d* of Lucius Foster and Evelyn Foster (*née* Almond); two *s*; *m* 2014, Alexandra Hedison. *Educ:* Yale Univ. (BA Eng. Lit. 1985). *Films* include: Napoleon and Samantha, 1972; Kansas City Bomber, 1972; Tom Sawyer, 1973; Alice Doesn't Live Here Anymore, 1975; Taxi Driver, 1976; Bugsy Malone, 1976; The Little Girl Who Lives Down the Lane, 1977; Candleshoe, 1977; Foxes, 1980; Carny, 1980; Hotel New Hampshire, 1984; Siesta, 1987; Five Corners, 1988; The Accused, 1988 (Academy Award for Best Actress, 1989); Little Man Tate, 1991 (also dir); The Silence of the Lambs, 1991 (Academy Award for Best Actress, 1992); Shadows and Fog, 1991; Sommersby, 1993; Maverick, 1994; Nell, 1994 (also prod.); dir and prod., Home for the Holidays, 1995; Contact, 1997; Anna and the King, 1999; Panic Room, 2002; Flight Plan, 2005; Inside Man, 2006; The Brave One, 2007; Nim's Island, 2008; The Beaver, 2011 (also dir); Carnage, 2012; Elysium, 2013; *television* includes: Mayberry, 1969; Bonanza; Paper Moon, 1974–75. Cecil B. De Mille Award, Golden Globe Awards, 2013.

FOSTER, Alison Lee Caroline, (Lady Havelock-Allan); QC 2002; *b* 22 Jan. 1957; *o d* of Leslie Francis Foster and Marie Anne Foster (*née* McIntosh-Hudson); *m* 1986, (Anthony) Mark (David) Havelock-Allan (*see* Sir A. M. D. Havelock-Allan, Bt); one *s* two *d*. *Educ:* Bexhill Grammar Sch. for Girls; Jesus Coll., Oxford (BA Hons English 1979; MA); Courtauld Inst. of Art, London Univ. (MPhil 1981); City Univ. (Dip. Law 1983). Called to the Bar, Inner Temple, 1984, Bencher, 2002; in practice, specialising in administrative law regulation and tax; a Deputy High Court Judge, Chancery Div., 2007–. *Recreations:* painting, gardening. *Address:* c/o 39 Essex Street, WC2R 3AT. *T:* (020) 7832 1111, *Fax:* (020) 7353 3978. *Clubs:* Groucho, Royal Automobile.

FOSTER, Prof. Allan (Bentham); Professor of Chemistry, University of London, 1966–86, now Emeritus; *b* 21 July 1926; *s* of late Herbert and Martha Alice Foster; *m* 1949, Monica Binns (*d* 2012); two *s*. *Educ:* Nelson Grammar Sch., Lancs; University of Birmingham. Frankland Medal and Prize, 1947; PhD, 1950; DSc, 1957. University Res. Fellow, University of Birmingham, 1950–53; Fellow of Rockefeller Foundn, Ohio State Univ., 1953–54; University of Birmingham: ICI Res. Fellow, 1954–55; Lectr, 1955–62; Sen. Lectr, 1962–64; Reader in Organic Chemistry, 1964–66; Institute of Cancer Research: Head of Chemistry Div., Chester Beatty Res. Inst., 1966–82; Head, Drug Metabolism Team, Drug Develt Sect., 1982–86. Sec., British Technol. Gp, New Cancer Product Develt Adv. Bd, 1986–91. FChemSoc (Mem. Council, 1962–65, 1967–70); Corresp. Mem., Argentinian Chem. Soc. Editor, Carbohydrate Research, 1965–92. *Publications:* numerous scientific papers mainly in Jl Chem. Soc., Carbohydrate Research and cancer jls. *Recreations:* golf, theatre. *Club:* Banstead Downs.

FOSTER, Andrew Kevin, CBE 2005; Chief Executive, Wrightington, Wigan and Leigh NHS Foundation Trust, since 2007; *b* 3 March 1955; *s* of Kevin William Foster and late Doreen Foster; *m* 1981, Sara Gillian Daniels; one *s* two *d*. *Educ:* Millfield Sch.; Keble Coll., Oxford (BA Hons PPE, MA). Mktg Manager, Rowntree Mackintosh plc, 1976–81; Dir, Worldcrest Ltd, 1981–. Chairman: W Lancs NHS Trust, 1993–96; Wigan & Leigh NHS Trust, 1996–2001; Policy Dir, NHS Confedn, 1998–2001; Dir of Human Resources, then of Workforce, DoH, 2001–06; Dir of HR and Organisational Develt, Blackpool, Fylde and Wyre Hosps NHS Trust, 2006–07; Interim Chief Exec., Heart of England Foundn Trust, 2015. *Recreation:* golf.

FOSTER, Sir Andrew (William), Kt 2001; Deputy Chairman, Royal Bank of Canada, 2003–12; *b* 29 Dec. 1944; *s* of George William and Gladys Maria Foster; *m* 1st, 1967, Christine Marquiss (marr. diss. 2000); one *s* one *d*; 2nd, 2001, Jadranka Porter. *Educ:* Abingdon School; Newcastle Polytechnic (BSc Sociol.); LSE (Postgrad. Dip. Applied Social Studies). Social Worker, London, 1966–71; Area Social Services Officer, 1971–75; Asst Dir of Social Services, Haringey, 1975–79; Dir of Social Services, Greenwich, 1979–82, N Yorks, 1982–87; Regional Gen. Manager, Yorks RHA, 1987–91; Dep. Chief Exec., NHS Management Exec., 1991–92; Controller, Audit Commn, 1992–2003. Non-executive Director: Nestor Healthcare, 2004–11; Nat. Express Gp, 2004–; Prudential Health Ltd, 2004–. Chair: Foster Review Group Athletics, 2004; Further Education Review Gp, 2005; Commonwealth Games England, 2007–; 2020 Public Services Commn, 2008–10; Review of Capital Prog. in Further Educn, 2009; Review of Intercity Express Prog., DfT, 2010. Non-exec. Dir, Sport England, 2003–09. Hon. DCL Northumbria at Newcastle, 1996. *Recreations:* golf, walking, travel, theatre, food, wine. *Address:* 269 Lauderdale Mansions, Lauderdale Road, Maida Vale, W9 1LZ.

FOSTER, Angiolina, CBE 2011; Chief Executive, Healthcare Improvement Scotland, since 2014; *b* 1 Feb. 1956; *d* of Andrew Seath and Vera Seath; *m* 1983, Michael Foster; one *s* one *d*. *Educ:* Univ. of Glasgow (MA Hons); Glasgow Caledonian Univ. (Dip. Mgt Studies). Glasgow DC, 1979–85; Chief Housing Benefits Officer, Edinburgh DC, 1985–87; Depute Dir, Housing, City of Edinburgh Council, 1987–2001; Dir, Regulation and Inspection, Communities Scotland, 2001–02; Actg Chief Exec., Glasgow Housing Assoc., 2002–03; Chief Exec., Communities Scotland, 2004–07; Scottish Government: Dir, Strategy and Ministerial Support, 2007–12; Dir, Health and Social Care Integration, 2012–14. *Recreations:* long distance walks, charity runs, food and wine with good friends, cinema, theatre. *Address:* Healthcare Improvement Scotland, Delta House, 50 West Nile Street, Glasgow G1 2NP.

FOSTER, Ann; *see* Knowles, P. A.

FOSTER, Arlene Isobel; Member (DemU) Fermanagh and South Tyrone, Northern Ireland Assembly, since 2003; Acting First Minister, and Minister of Finance and Personnel, Northern Ireland, since 2015; *b* 17 July 1970; *d* of John William Kelly and Julia Georgina Kelly (*née* Sills); *m* 1995, William Brian Johnston Foster; two *s* one *d*. *Educ:* Collegiate Grammar Sch. for Girls, Enniskillen; Queen's Univ., Belfast (LLB Hons 1993; CPLS 1996). Solicitor, private practice, 1996–2005, pt-time, 2005–07. Mem. (DemU), Fermanagh DC, 2005–07. Minister of the Envmt, 2007–08, Minister of Enterprise, Trade and Investment, 2008–15, NI. Mem., NI Policing Bd, 2006–07. *Recreations:* reading (especially political and historical biographies), listening (and singing along to) music of all types. *Address:* (constituency office) 32a New Street, Enniskillen BT74 6AH. *T:* (028) 6632 0722. *E:* arlene@arlenefoster.org.uk.

FOSTER, Brendan, CBE 2008 (MBE 1976); television athletics commentator, since 1981; Chairman, Nova International Ltd, since 2000; *b* 12 Jan. 1948; *s* of Francis and Margaret Foster; *m* 1972; one *s* one *d*. *Educ:* St Joseph's Grammar Sch., Hebburn, Co. Durham; Sussex Univ. (BSc); Carnegie Coll., Leeds (DipEd). School Teacher, St Joseph's Grammar Sch., Hebburn, 1970–74; Sports and Recreation Manager, Gateshead Metropolitan Bor. Council, 1974–81; UK Man. Dir, Nike Internat., 1981–87; Chm., Nike (UK), 1981–86; Man. Dir, Nike Europe, 1985–87; Vice Pres. Marketing, Nike Inc. Oregon, USA, 1986–87. Commonwealth Games: Bronze medal: 1500m, 1970; 5000m, 1978; Silver medal, 5000m, 1974; Gold medal, 10,000m, 1978; European Games: Bronze medal, 1500m, 1971; Gold medal, 5000m, 1974; Olympic Games: Bronze medal, 10,000m, 1976; World Records: 2 miles, 1973; 3000m, 1974. BBC Sports Personality of the Year, 1974. Chm. and Founder, Great North Run, 1981–. Chancellor, Leeds Metropolitan Univ., 2005–09. Freeman, Metropolitan Bor. of Gateshead, 2009. Hon. Fellow, Sunderland Polytechnic, 1977; Hon. MEd Newcastle, 1978; Hon. DLitt Sussex, 1982; Hon. DArts Leeds Metropolitan, 2004; Hon. DCL Northumbria, 2003. *Publications:* Brendan Foster, 1978; Olympic Heroes 1896–1984, 1984. *Recreations:* running (now only a recreation), sport (as spectator).

FOSTER, Prof. Brian, OBE 2003; DPhil; FRS 2008; CPhys, FInstP; Professor of Experimental Physics, University of Oxford, since 2003; Fellow of Balliol College, Oxford, since 2003; Alexander von Humboldt Professor, University of Hamburg and Deutsches Elektronen-Synchrotron, since 2010; *b* 4 Jan. 1954; *s* of John and Annie Foster; *m* 1983, Sabine Margot Koch; two *s*. *Educ:* Wolsingham Secondary Sch.; Queen Elizabeth Coll., Univ. of London (BSc 1975); St John's Coll., Oxford (DPhil 1978); MA Oxon 2003. CPhys, FInstP 1992. Research Associate: Rutherford Appleton Lab., 1978–82; Imperial Coll. of Science and Technology, 1982–84; Bristol University: Lectr, 1984–92; SERC, subseq. PPARC, Advanced Fellow, 1991–97; Reader, 1992–96; Prof. of Experimental Physics, 1996–2003, Emeritus, 2004. Institute of Physics: Chm., Nuclear and Particle Physics Div., 1989–93; Mem. Council, 2009–13; Mem., Resources (formerly Investment) Cttee, 2009–13; Recorder, Physics Section, BAAS, 1994–97; Mem., PPARC, 2001–06 (Mem., 1995, and Chm., 1996–99, Particle Physics Cttee; Jt Chm., 1996–99, Mem., 2001–07, Science Cttee); Mem., Physics Sub-Panel, 2008 RAE; Chm., Physics Sub-Panel, 2014 REF. Chm., Mgt Cttee, Oxford e-Science Res. Centre, 2010–. Member: various adv. cttees, CERN, 1993–2000; Extended Scientific Council, Deutsches Elektronen-Synchrotron, 1998–2009; Evaluation Commn, Sci. Council of Germany, 2001–07; Scientific Policy Cttee, CERN Council, 2002–05; Chm., European Cttee for Future Accelerators, 2002–05. Spokesman, ZEUS Collaboration, 1999–2003; European Director: Global Design Effort for the Internat. Linear Collider, 2005–13; Linear Collider Collaboration, 2013–. Chm. Trustees and Admin Dir, Oxford May Music Fest., 2008–. Hon. Vice-Pres., Ernest Bloch Soc., 2008–. Alexander von Humboldt-Stiftung Res. Prize, 1999–2000; Max Born Medal, Inst. of Physics and German Physical Soc., 2003. *Publications:* (ed) Topics in High Energy Particle Physics, 1988; (ed jtly) Forty Years of Particle Physics, 1988; (ed and contrib.) Electron-Positron Annihilation Physics, 1990; numerous papers in learned jls, articles on science in popular press. *Recreations:* collecting first editions, violin playing, history and politics, hill walking. *Address:* Denys Wilkinson Building, Keble Road, Oxford OX1 3RH; 2 Hillview Cottage, Blackford, near Wedmore, Somerset BS28 4NL. *T:* (01934) 712699.

FOSTER, Sir Christopher (David), Kt 1986; MA; Member, Board of Governors, Better Government Initiative, since 2013 (Chairman, 2006–13); Vice-President: RAC, since 2003 (Vice-Chairman, 1998–99; non-executive Director, 1994–98); RAC Foundation, since 2003 (Chairman, 1999–2003); *b* 30 Oct. 1930; *s* of George Cecil Foster and Phyllis Joan Foster (*née* Mappin); *m* 1958, Kay Sheridan Bullock; two *s* three *d*. *Educ:* Merchant Taylors' Sch.; King's Coll., Cambridge (Scholar) (History Tripos Pt I, Economics Tripos Pt II, 1954; MA 1959). Commnd into 1st Bn Seaforth Highlanders, Malaya, 1949. Hallsworth Research Fellow, Manchester Univ., 1957–59; Senior Research Fellow, 1959–64, Official Fellow and Tutor, 1964–66, Hon. Fellow, 1992, Jesus Coll., Oxford; Dir-Gen. of Economic Planning, MoT, 1966–70; Head of Unit for Res. in Urban Economics, LSE, 1970–76; Prof. of Urban Studies and Economics, LSE, 1976–78; a Dir and Head of Econ. and Public Policy Div., Coopers & Lybrand Associates, 1978–84; a Dir, Public Sector Practice Leader and Economic Advr, Coopers & Lybrand, 1984–86; Commercial Adviser to British Telecom, 1986–88; Mem. Bd, Coopers & Lybrand, 1988–90; Sen. Public Sector and Econs Partner, Coopers & Lybrand Deloitte, later Coopers & Lybrand, 1990–98; Advr to Chm., Coopers & Lybrand, 1994–99. Governor, 1967–70, Dir, 1976–78, Centre for Environmental Studies; Visiting Professor: of Economics, MIT, 1970; LSE, 1978–86. Special Economic Adviser (part time), DoE, 1974–77; Special Advr on BR Privatisation to Sec. of State for Transport, 1992–94; Mem. Bd, Railtrack, 1994–2000. Member: (part time), PO Bd, 1975–77; Audit Commn, 1983–88; ESRC, 1985–89; Chm., NEDO Construction Industry Sector Gp, 1988–92. Chm., Cttee of Inquiry into Road Haulage Licensing, 1977–78; Mem., Cttee of Inquiry into Civil Service Pay, 1981–82; Economic Assessor, Sizewell B Inquiry, 1982–86. Member: Econ. and Financial Cttee, CBI, 1987–94; LDDC, 1988–96. Chairman: Circle 33 Housing Assoc., 1986–90; Construction Round Table, 1993–97. Governor: RSC, 1991–; Inst. for Govt, 2009–12. *Publications:* The Transport Problem, 1963; Politics, Finance and the Role of Economics: an essay on the control of public enterprise, 1972; (with R. Jackman and M. Perlman) Local Government Finance, 1980; Privatisation, Public Ownership and the Regulation of Natural Monopoly, 1993; (with F. J. Plowden) The State Under Stress, 1996; British Government in Crisis, 2005; papers in various economic, political and other journals. *Address:* 6 Holland Park Avenue, W11 3QU. *T:* (020) 7229 6581. *Clubs:* Reform, Royal Automobile.

FOSTER, Christopher Norman; consultant on horseracing matters, since 2006; Keeper of the Match Book, The Jockey Club, since 1983; *b* 30 Dec. 1946; *s* of Maj.-Gen. Norman Leslie Foster, CB, DSO; *m* 1981, Anthea Jane Sammons; two *s*. *Educ:* Westminster Sch. ACA 1969, FCA 1979. Cooper Brothers & Co., Chartered Accountants, 1965–73; Weatherbys, 1973–90; The Jockey Club: Sec., 1983–90; Exec. Dir, 1993–2006. Vice Chm., Internat. Fedn of Horseracing Authorities, 2000–08. Director: Wincanton Racecourse, 2006–13; The National Stud, 2008–. Trustee: Retraining of Racehorses, 2006–13; Home of Horseracing Trust, 2009–; Racing Welfare, 2013–. Governor, Westminster Sch., 1990–. *Recreations:* racing, shooting, fishing, gardening. *Address:* Jockey Club, 75 High Holborn, WC1V 6LS. *Club:* MCC.

FOSTER, Rt Rev. Christopher Richard James; *see* Portsmouth, Bishop of.

FOSTER, Prof. Christopher Stuart, MD; PhD, DSc; FRCPath; George Holt Professor of Pathology, and Director of Cellular Pathology and Molecular Genetics, University of Liverpool, 1994–2012, now Emeritus Professor; Consultant Histopathologist, Royal Liverpool and Broadgreen University Hospitals NHS Trust, 1993–2012; *b* Pilling, Lancs, 22 Oct. 1947; *s* of Geoffrey Stuart Foster and Dilys Joan Foster (*née* Hughes); *m* 1992, Joan Elizabeth Hardie; one *s* one *d*. *Educ:* Midsomer Norton Grammar Sch.; Dover Boys' Grammar Sch.; University Coll. London (BSc Physiol. and Biochem. 1966); Westminster Med. Sch. (MB BS 1974); Ludwig Inst. for Cancer Res., London (PhD 1983); Children's Hosp. of Philadelphia (MD 1987); Inst. of Cancer Res. (DSc 2002). LRCP, MRCS 1973; MRCPath 1984, FRCPath 1995. Exptl Officer, RN Physiol Lab., Alverstoke, 1966–68; SHO, Royal Marsden Hosp., Sutton, 1975–76; Registrar: in Gen. Medicine, Redhill Gen. Hosp., 1976–77; in Histopathol., Greenbank Hosp., 1977–79; Clin. Scientist, Ludwig Inst. for Cancer Res., London, 1979–83; Res. Fellow, ICRF and Sen. Registrar in Pathol., St Bartholomew's Hosp., London, 1983–85; Sen. Res. Fellow, Children's Hosp. of Philadelphia, 1985–87; Sen. Lectr in Pathol., RPMS and Hammersmith Hosp., London, 1987–94; Hd, Sch. of Clin. Lab. Scis, Univ. of Liverpool, 2004–06. Visiting Professor: Medunsa Univ., S Africa, 1990; Al Quds Med. Univ., Palestine, 1998; Univ. of Beijing, 2003–04. European Editor: Human Pathol., 1995–2005; Amer. Jl Clin. Pathol., 1999–2005. Chm., NHS-NW Reg. Pathol. Modernisation Cttee, 2000–01; Mem., Nat. Steering Cttee, Pathol. Modernisation,

DoH, 2001–06. Reference Pathologist, WHO Prostate Cancer, 1999–; Co-Chm., Pathol. Section, WHO Internat. Consultation on Prostate Cancer, 1999; Chm., Pathol. Section, WHO Cttee on Benign Prostatic Hyperplasia, 2000; Sen. Pathologist, Transatlantic Prostate Gp, 2004–. Dir, Workforce Planning, RCPath, 2004–07. Mem. Council, ACP, 1995–98. *Publications:* Diagnostic Liver Pathology, 1993; Pathology of the Prostate, 1997; Pathology of the Urinary Bladder, 2004; Molecular Oncology of Prostate Cancer, 2007; contrib. papers on tumour pathology, particularly develt of novel biomarkers applied to diagnosis and prognosis of cancer. *Recreations:* ski-ing, sailing, fly-fishing, cooking. *Club:* Athenæum.

FOSTER, Rt Hon. Donald (Michael Ellison); PC 2011; *b* 31 March 1947; *s* of late Rev. J. A. Foster and Iris Edith (*née* Ellison); *m* 1968, Victoria, 2nd *d* of late Major Kenneth Pettegree, OBE, TD and Jean Pettegree; one *s* one *d*. *Educ:* Lancaster Royal Grammar Sch.; Univ. of Keele (BA Hons; Cert Ed 1969); Univ. of Bath (MEd 1982). CPhys, MInstP. Science teacher, Sevenoaks Sch., Kent, 1969–75; Science Curriculum Proj. Dir, Avon LEA, 1975–81; Science Educn Lectr, Bristol Univ., 1981–89: Head, Science Educn Centre; teacher trainer; organiser of link with Univ. of Zambia; Managing Consultant, Pannell Kerr Forster, 1989–92. Mem., Avon CC, 1981–89 (Leader, Liberal Gp; Chm., Educn Cttee, 1987–89). Mem. Exec. Cttee, ACC, 1985–89. Contested (L/All) Bristol East, 1987. MP (Lib Dem) Bath, 1992–2015. Lib Dem spokesman: on educn, 1992–99; on envmt, transport and the regions, 1999–2001; on transport, local govt and the regions, 2001–02; on transport, 2002–03; Parly Under-Sec. of State, DCLG, 2012–13; Comptroller of HM Household (Dep. Chief Whip), 2013–15. Co-Chair, Lib Dem Parly Policy Cttee for culture, Olympics, media and sport, 2010–12; Member: Select Cttee on Educn and Employment, 1996–99; Bd, Westminster Foundn for Democracy, 2010–. Mem. Bd, Olympic and Paralympic Games 2012, 2010–12. Treas., All-Party Yugoslav Gp, 1994–97. Vice-Chm., British Assoc. for Central and Eastern Europe, 1994–97. Pres., Nat. Campaign for Nursery Educn, 1999–2001 (Vice-Chm., 1993–99); Hon. Pres., British Youth Council, 1992–99; Trustee: Open Sch., 1992–99; Educn Extra, 1992–99. Hon. Fellow, Bath Coll. of Further Educn, 1994. *Publications:* Resource-based Learning in Science, 1979; Science with Gas, 1981; (jtly) Aspects of Science, 1984; (jtly) Reading about Science, 1984; (jtly) Nuffield Science, 1986; (ed) Teaching Science 11–13, 1987; From the Three Rs to the Three Cs, 2003; science curriculum resources and educn papers. *Recreations:* watching all forms of sport (former rower and Rugby player), reading, films, music. *Address:* Myrtle Cottage, Northend, Bath BA1 8ES. *T:* (01225) 858093.

[Created a Baron (Life Peer) 2015 but title not yet gazetted at time of going to press.]

FOSTER, Ian Hampden; a Master of the Senior (formerly Supreme) Court, Queen's Bench Division, 1991–2011; a Recorder, 1998–2011; *b* 27 Feb. 1946; *s* of Eric Hampden Foster and Irene Foster (*née* Warman); *m* 1975, Fiona Jane (*d* 2011), *d* of Rev. J. N. and Mrs Robertson-Glasgow; one *s* one *d*. *Educ:* Battersea Grammar Sch.; Univ. of Exeter (LLB Hons 1968). Called to the Bar, Inner Temple, 1969; practice at common law bar, 1969–91. Adv. Editor, Atkin's Court Forms, 1991–2003; Jt Editor, Supreme Court Practice, 1993–98. *Recreation:* watching cricket. *Address:* c/o Royal Courts of Justice, Strand, WC2A 2LL. *Club:* Travellers.

FOSTER, Jacqueline; Member (C) North West Region, European Parliament, 1999–2004 and since 2009; *d* of late Samuel and Isabella Renshaw; *m* 1975, Peter Laurance Foster (marr. diss. 1981). *Educ:* Prescot Girls' Grammar Sch., Lancashire. Cabin Services, BEA, then British Airways, 1969–81; Area Manager, Austria, Horizon, 1981–85; Cabin Services, British Airways, 1985–99; Founder Mem. and Exec. Officer, Cabin Crew '89 (Airline Trade Union), 1989–99; aerospace consultant, Brussels, 2004–09. European Parliament: Chm., Cons. backbench cttee, 1999–2004; Mem. Industry and Transport (Aviation) Cttees, 1999–2004; Cons. spokesman on transport and tourism, 2001–04, 2009–; Vice-President, Parliamentary Intergroup: Sky and Space, 2009–; Animal Welfare, 2009–. Mem., Eur. Aviation Club, Brussels. *Recreations:* ski-ing, travel, golf. *Club:* Carlton.

FOSTER, Joan Mary; Under Secretary, Department of Transport, Highways Planning and Management, 1978–80, retired; *b* 20 Jan. 1923; *d* of John Whitfield Foster and Edith Foster (*née* Levett). *Educ:* Northampton School for Girls. Entered Civil Service (HM Office of Works), Oct. 1939; Ministry of Transport, 1955; Asst Secretary, 1970. *Recreations:* gardening, cooking, good wine. *Address:* 3 Hallfields, Shouldham, King's Lynn, Norfolk PE33 0DN. *T:* (01366) 347809.

FOSTER, Joanna Katharine, CBE 2002; Chair, Crafts Council, 2006–13; *b* 5 May 1939; *d* of late Michael and of Lesley Mead; *m* 1961, Jerome Foster (marr. diss. 2002); one *s* one *d*; partner, Nicholas Tresilian. *Educ:* Benenden School; Univ. of Grenoble. Sec. and Editl Asst, Vogue Magazine, London and NY, 1958–59; journalist, San Francisco Chronicle, 1959; Management Adviser, Industrial Soc., 1966–72; Dir, Centre Actif Bilingue, Fontainebleau, 1972–79; Press Attachée and Editor, INSEAD, Fontainebleau, 1972–79; Educn and Trng Dir, Corporate Services, Western Psychiatric Inst. and Clinic, Univ. of Pittsburgh, 1980–82; Management Adviser, 1982–85, Head of Pepperell Unit, 1985–88, Mem. Council, 1990–2000, Industrial Soc.; Chair: Equal Opportunities Commn, 1988–93; UK Council, UN Internat. Year of the Family 1994, 1993–95; Dir, 1995–97, Chm., 1997–2001, BT Communication Forum; Chm., Nat. Work-Life Forum, 1998–2002. Pres., European Commn Adv. Cttee on Equal Opportunities, 1991–92 (Vice Pres., 1990, 1991, 1993); Member: Nat. Adv. Council for Careers and Educnl Guidance, 1993–94; Sec. of State for Employment's Women's Issues Adv. Gp, 1991–93; Target Team for Business in the Community's Opportunity 2000 Initiative, 1992–99; Govt Adv. Gp on Work-Life Balance, 2000–02. Chair, Adv. Cttee, European Public Policy Inst., Warwick Univ., 1993–95. Chm., Lloyds TSB (formerly TSB) Foundn, 1997–2003 (Dep. Chm., 1991–97). Dir, WNO, 1990–94; Mem., Central TV Adv. Bd, 1991–95; Member, Advisory Board: Econ. Regl Analysis, 1997–; Common Purpose Oxfordshire, 2004–; What Next? prog., 2007–; Dir, Pennell Initiative for Women's Health, 1997– (Chm., 2003–); Chm., Nuffield Orthopaedic Centre NHS Trust, 2001–10. President: Relate, 1993–96; Oxfordshire Craft Guild, 2008–. Trustee: Employment Policy Inst., 1995–98; Open Univ. Foundn, 2004–. Mem., Adv. Council, Oxford Philomusica, 2006–. Associate Fellow, 2010, Dir, NHS Chairs' Forum, 2010, Saïd Business Sch., Oxford. Governor: Oxford Brookes Univ., 1993– (Dep. Chm., 1998–2003); Birkbeck Coll., Univ. of London, 1996–98. Hon. Fellow, St Hilda's Coll., Oxford, 1988. Hon. DLitt Kingston, 1993; DU Essex, 1993; Hon. LLD: Oxford Brookes, 1993; West of England, 1993; Strathclyde, 1994; Salford, 1994; Bristol, 1996. *Recreations:* family, friends, food. *Clubs:* Reform, International Women's Forum UK.

FOSTER, Jodie; *see* Foster, A. C.

FOSTER, John Edward, CBE 2008; Chief Executive, London Borough of Islington, 2008–11; *b* 30 Dec. 1948; *s* of John and Ethel Foster; *m* 2003, Pauline de Silva; one *s* three *d* from a former marriage. *Educ:* Univ. of London (BSc Hons ext. 1970); Univ. of Durham. Community worker, Northumberland CC, 1971; Community Develt Officer, Durham CC, 1972; Community Develt Project, Home Office, 1973–92; various rôles with N Tyneside MBC and NALGO, 1979–92; Exec. Dir, North Tyneside MBC, 1992–97; Chief Executive: Middlesbrough Council, 1998–2002; City of Wakefield MDC, 2003–08. Dir, New Local Govt Network, 2002. Trustee, Yorkshire Sculpture Park, 2011–. FRSA 2007. *Recreations:* weekends away from it all, Friends of the Royal Academy and the Tate. *Address:* West Royd Mill House, Wesley Street, Ossett, Wakefield WF5 8EZ.

FOSTER, John Graham; District Judge (Magistrates' Court), South Yorkshire, since 2001; *b* 28 April 1947; *s* of James Beaumont Foster and Margaret Foster; *m* 1971, Susan Boothroyd; three *s*. *Educ:* Woodhouse Grove Sch.; Sheffield Univ. (LLB Hons). Admitted Solicitor, 1973; in private practice with Morrish & Co., Solicitors, Leeds, 1970–2001 (Partner 1975–2001); Dep. Dist Judge, 1997–2001. *Recreations:* after dinner speaking, theatre, films, music, sport, especially badminton and cricket. *Address:* c/o Rotherham Magistrates' Court, The Statutes, PO Box 15, Rotherham S60 1YW. *T:* (01709) 839339.

FOSTER, His Honour Jonathan Rowe; QC 1989; a Circuit Judge, 2004–15; *b* 20 July 1947; *s* of Donald Foster and Hilda Eaton; *m* 1978, Sarah Ann Mary da Cunha; four *s*. *Educ:* Oundle Sch.; Keble Coll., Oxford (Exhibr). Called to the Bar, Gray's Inn, 1970, Bencher, 1998; a Recorder, 1988–2004; a Dep. High Ct Judge, 1994–; Hd of Chambers, 1997–2004. Treas., Northern Circuit, 1992–97. Mem., Criminal Injuries Compensation Bd and Appeal Panel, 1995–2004. Gov., Ryleys Sch., 1990–2006. Trustee, Acorn Recovery Service, 2012–. *Recreations:* outdoor pursuits, bridge. *Club:* St James's (Manchester).

FOSTER, Kevin John; MP (C) Torbay, since 2015; *b* Plymouth, 31 Dec. 1978; *s* of Michael Foster and late Linda Foster; partner, Hazel Noonan. *Educ:* Hele's Sch., Plympton; Univ. of Warwick (LLB Law 2000; LLM Internat. Econ. Law 2001); Inns of Court Sch. of Law (BVC 2002). Barman, Coventry Cons. Club, 2000–03; Asst to Philip Bradbourne, MEP, 2002–03; Paralegal, Howell and Co. Solicitors, 2003–04. Mem. (C), Coventry CC, 2002–14. Contested (C) Coventry S, 2010. *Recreations:* military history, cinema, music, church. *Address:* House of Commons, SW1A 0AA. *T:* 07985 446803. *E:* kevin.foster.mp@parliament.uk. *Clubs:* Preston Conservative (Paignton); Plympton Conservative (Plymouth).

FOSTER, Lawrence; conductor; Music Director, Gulbenkian Orchestra, Lisbon, since 2002; *b* Los Angeles, 23 Oct. 1941; *s* of Thomas Foster and Martha Wurmbrandt; *m* 1972, Angela Foster; one *d*. *Educ:* Univ. of California, LA; studied under Fritz Zweig, Bruno Walter and Karl Böhm. Asst Conductor, Los Angeles Philharmonic, 1965–68; British début, Royal Festival Hall, 1968; Covent Garden début, Troilus and Cressida, 1976; Chief Guest Conductor, Royal Philharmonic Orchestra, 1969–74; Music Dir and Chief Conductor, Houston Symphony Orchestra, 1971–78; Chief Conductor, Orchestre National (later Orchestre Philharmonique) of Monte Carlo, 1978–95; Gen. Music Dir, Duisburg concert series, 1982–86; Prin. Guest Conductor, Düsseldorf Opera, 1982–86; Music Director: Lausanne Chamber Orch., 1985–90; Aspen Fest., 1991–96; Barcelona SO and Nat. Orch. of Catalonia, 1996–2002; Orch. and Nat. Opera of Montpellier, 2009–12; Philharmonic Orch. of Marseille, 2012–; Artistic Dir, Georg Enescu Fest., 1998–2001; Guest Conductor: Deutsche Oper Berlin; LA Music Centre Opera; LA Philharmonic Orch.; Hallé Orch.; Pittsburgh, Chicago, Montreal, and Jerusalem Symphony Orchs; Orchestre de Paris. *Recreations:* reading European history, films. *Address:* c/o HarrisonParrott, 5–6 Albion Court, Albion Place, W6 0QT.

FOSTER, Michael George; active in range of non-executive roles and early stage companies; Chairman: Impression Technologies Ltd, since 2013; Microtech Ceramics Ltd, since 2014; *b* 17 Feb. 1953; *s* of Brian and Betty Foster; *m* 1977, Marion Frances Chambers; one *s* one *d*. *Educ:* Nottingham High Sch.; Peterhouse, Cambridge (BA 1975, MA 1979); Council of Legal Educn. Called to the Bar, Inner Temple, 1977; barrister in private practice, 1977–85; admitted solicitor, 1989; GKN plc: Sen. Commercial Lawyer, 1985–88; Asst Gp Treas., 1988–93; Dep. Hd, Corporate Finance, 1993–94; Gp Treas., Trafalgar House plc, 1994–95; Chief Executive: Kvaerner Metals (Davy), 1995–98; Kvaerner Engrg & Construction Div., 1998–2000; Exec. Dir, RMC plc, 2000–04; Commercial Dir, 2005–06, Chief Exec., 2006–11, Charter International (formerly Charter) plc. Non-executive Director: Charter plc, 2001–04; Chas A. Blatchford and Sons Ltd, 2011–13. Trustee, St Mungo's Broadway, 2013–. Fellow, ACT, 2007. *Recreations:* family, theatre and film, opera, blues, rock and roll, literature, travel, clay pigeon shooting.

FOSTER, Michael Jabez; DL; solicitor specialising in employment law; Principal, Michael Foster Law, since 2010; *b* Hastings, 26 Feb. 1946; *s* of Dorothy Foster; *m* 1969, Rosemary, *d* of Eric and Hilda Kemp; two *s*. *Educ:* Hastings Secondary Sch.; Hastings Grammar Sch.; Leicester Univ. (LLM). Admitted Solicitor, 1980; ACIArb 1997. Partner, 1980–99, Consultant, 1999–2009, Fynmores, solicitors, Bexhill-on-Sea. Member: Hastings CBC, 1971–74 (Ldr, Lab. Gp, 1973); Hastings BC, 1973–79, 1983–87 (Ldr, Lab. Gp and Dep. Ldr of Council, 1973–79); E Sussex CC, 1973–77, 1981–97 (Dep. Leader, Lab Gp, 1984–93); Mem., Sussex Police Authy, 1991–96; Mem., E Sussex AHA, later Hastings HA, 1974–91. Contested (Lab) Hastings, Feb. and Oct. 1974, 1979. MP (Lab) Hastings and Rye, 1997–2010; contested (Lab) same seat, 2010. PPS to Attorney General, 1999–2003; Parly Under-Sec. of State, Govt Equalities Office, 2009–10. Pres., Hastings Law Soc., 2014–15. DL 1993, High Sheriff 2016, E Sussex. Freeman, Bor. of Hastings, 2010. *Address:* Lacuna Place, Havelock Road, Hastings TN34 1BG. *T:* (01424) 203040. *E:* mail@michaelfosterlaw.co.uk.

FOSTER, Michael John; *b* 14 March 1963; *s* of Brian and Edna Foster; *m* 1985, Shauna Ogle; one *s* two *d*. *Educ:* Great Wyrley High Sch., Staffs; Wolverhampton Poly. (BA Hons Econs 1984); Univ. of Wolverhampton (PGCE 1995). ACMA. Management Accountant, Jaguar Cars, 1984–91; Lectr, Worcester Coll. of Technology, 1991–97. MP (Lab) Worcester, 1997–2010; contested (Lab) same seat, 2010. Department of Education and Skills: PPS to Minister of State for Lifelong Learning and Higher Educn, 2001–03, for Children, 2003–04; Departmental PPS, 2004–05; PPS to Sec. of State for NI, 2005–06; an Asst Govt Whip, 2006–08; Parly Under-Sec. of State, DFID, 2008–10. Mem., Educn Select Cttee, 1999–2001. *Recreations:* most sports, gardening. *Club:* Worcestershire County Cricket.

FOSTER, Richard John Samuel; His Honour Judge Foster; a Circuit Judge, since 2004; a Deputy High Court Judge, since 2003; *b* 28 May 1954; *s* of late Samuel Geoffrey Foster and Beryl Foster; *m* 1st, 1980, Ann Scott (*d* 2002); one *d*; 2nd, 2004, Susan Claire Sansome (*née* Brodie); one step *s* one step *d*. *Educ:* Bromsgrove Sch.; Coll. of Law, Guildford. Qualified solicitor, 1979; Partner, 1987–97, Jt Sen. Partner, 1997–98, Vizards, London; Sen. Partner, Vizard Oldham, London, 1998–2002; Partner and Hd, Health Care Law, Weightman Vizards, subseq. Weightmans Solicitors, 2002–04. Asst Recorder, 1997–2000; Recorder, 2000–04; Resident Judge, Luton Crown Court, 2012–. Hon. Recorder of Luton, 2013–. Mem., Beds Probation Bd, 2006–10. Chm. Trustees, Royal British Legion Pension Fund, 2004; Trustee, Bromsgrove Sch. Foundn, 2011–. Mem., Appeals Court, United Grand Lodge of England, 2011–. Lay Mem., Consistory Ct, Dio. of St Albans, 2000–04. *Publications:* (ed) Morrell and Foster on Local Authority Liability, 1998, 5th edn 2012. *Recreations:* golf, gardening, running smallholding, bridge. *Address:* c/o Luton Crown Court, 7 George Street, Luton LU1 2AA. *Clubs:* Reform; Andratx Golf (Mallorca).

FOSTER, Richard Scot, CBE 2007; Chairman, Criminal Cases Review Commission, since 2008; *b* 26 March 1950; *s* of Frank Walter Foster and Betty Lilian Foster; *m* 1997, Susan Warner Johnson; one *s* one *d*. *Educ:* Devonport High Sch.; Pembroke Coll., Cambridge (MA Hons Moral Scis). Joined Dept of Employment, 1973; Sec., MSC, 1975–77; Private Sec. to Minister, 1977–78; on secondment to FCO, Stockholm, 1981–84; Industrial Relations legislation, 1984–86; Head of Deptl Strategy Unit, 1986–88; Director: Finance and Planning, Employment Service, 1988–90; Trng Commn, 1990–92; Employment Service, 1992–98; Dir, Welfare to Work, DFEE, subseq. at DWP, 1998–2001; Chief Exec., CPS, 2002–07. Trustee, Refugee Council of GB, 2007– (Chm., 2013–). *Recreations:* ski-ing, climbing, opera, theatre, tennis. *Address:* c/o Criminal Cases Review Commission, 5 St Philip's Place, Birmingham B3 2PW.

FOSTER, Robert; Commissioner, Gambling Commission, since 2013 (Commissioner, National Lottery Commission, 2005–13); *b* 12 May 1943; *s* of David and Amelia Foster; *m* 1967, Judy Welsh; one *s* one *d*. *Educ:* Oundle Sch.; Corpus Christi Coll., Cambridge (BA 1964; MA 1967). CEng, FIET (FIEE 1993); FRAeS 1996. Parkinson Cowan, 1964–66;

Automation Ltd, 1966–71; Exec. Engineer, Post Office Telecommunications, 1971–76; DTI, 1977–92; Under Sec., OST, Cabinet Office, 1992–93, DTI, 1993–2000; Chief Exec. and Sec., Competition Commn, 2001–04. Non-exec. Dir, Jersey Competition Regulatory Authy, 2004–12; Vice Chair, KCH NHS Foundn Trust, 2004–12; Chm., Equinox Care, 2012–14. *Recreations:* theatre, golf, music. *Address:* 9 Holmdene Avenue, Herne Hill, SE24 9LB.

FOSTER, Prof. Robert Fitzroy, (Roy), PhD; FRSL; FRHistS; FBA 1989; Carroll Professor of Irish History, University of Oxford, since 1991; *b* 16 Jan. 1949; *s* of Frederick Ernest Foster and Elizabeth (*née* Fitzroy); *m* 1972, Aisling O'Conor Donelan; one *s* one *d*. *Educ:* Newtown Sch., Waterford; St Andrew's Sch., Middletown, Delaware, USA; Trinity Coll., Dublin (MA; PhD 1975). FRHistS 1979; FRSL 1992. Lectr, 1974, Reader, 1983, Professor of Modern British Hist., 1988–91, Hon. Fellow, 2005, Birkbeck Coll., London Univ. Alistair Horne Fellow, St Antony's Coll., Oxford, 1979–80; British Acad. Res. Reader in the Humanities, 1987–89; Fellow, IAS, Princeton, and Vis. Fellow, Dept of English, 1988–89, Whitney J. Oates Fellow, 2002, Princeton Univ. Wiles Lectr, QUB, 2004; Clark Lectr, Trinity Coll., Cambridge, 2009; Wolfson Foundn Res. Prof., 2009–12; Vis. Prof., UCD, 2010; James Ford Lectr, Univ. of Oxford, 2012. Parnell Fellow, Magdalen Coll., Cambridge, 2015–16. Hon. MRIA 2010. Hon. DLitt: Aberdeen, 1997; QUB, 1998; TCD, 2003; NUI, 2004; Hon. DLaws Queen's Univ., Ontario, 2007; Hon. LittD Edinburgh, 2013. Irish Post Community Award, 1982; Sunday Independent/Irish Life Arts Award, 1988; M. L. Rosenthal Award, Yeats Soc. of NY, 2003; James Joyce Award, Lit. and Histl Soc., UCD, 2012. *Publications:* Charles Stewart Parnell: the man and his family, 1976, 2nd edn 1979; Lord Randolph Churchill: a political life, 1981, 3rd edn 1987; Political Novels and Nineteenth Century History, 1983; Modern Ireland 1600–1972, 1988; (ed) The Oxford Illustrated History of Ireland, 1989; (ed) The Sub-Prefect Should Have Held His Tongue and other essays, by Hubert Butler, 1990; Paddy and Mr Punch: connections in English and Irish history, 1993; The Story of Ireland, 1995; W. B. Yeats: a life, Vol. 1 The Apprentice Mage 1865–1914, 1997 (James Tait Black Prize for biog., 1998), Vol. 2 The Arch-Poet 1915–1939, 2003; The Irish Story: telling tales and making it up in Ireland, 2001 (Christian Gauss Award for literary criticism, 2004); (with Fintan Cullen) Conquering England: Ireland in Victorian London, 2005; Luck and the Irish, 2007; Words Alone: Yeats and his inheritances, 2011; Vivid Faces: the revolutionary generation in Ireland, 2014; numerous essays and reviews. *Recreation:* recreation. *Address:* Hertford College, Oxford OX1 3BW.

FOSTER, Prof. Russell Grant, CBE 2015; PhD, DSc; FRS 2008; FMedSci; Professor of Circadian Neuroscience, since 2006, Chair, Nuffield Laboratory of Ophthalmology, since 2007, and Founder and Director, Sleep and Circadian Neuroscience Institute, since 2012, University of Oxford; Nicholas Kurti Senior Fellow, Brasenose College, Oxford, since 2006; *b* Aldershot, 19 Aug. 1959; *s* of Donald and Doreen Foster; *m* 1984, Elizabeth Ann Downes; one *s* two *d*. *Educ:* Heron Wood Sch., Aldershot; Farnborough 6th Form Coll.; Univ. of Bristol (BSc 1980; PhD 1984; DSc 2015). Asst Prof., Dept of Biol., Univ. of Va, 1988–95; Imperial College London: Governor's Lectr, Dept of Biol., 1995–97, Reader in Zool., 1997–99; Prof., Dept of Integrative and Molecular Neurosci., 2000–03; Dep. Chair, Dept of Visual Neurosci., 2003–06. Visiting Professor: Dept of Biomed. and Molecular Scis, Univ. of Surrey, 1999–; Dept of Biol Scis, Imperial Coll. London, 2006–; Dept of Biol Scis, Univ. of WA, 2007–. Biotechnology and Biological Sciences Research Council: Chm., Animal Scis Cttee, 2002–06; Mem., Strategy Bd, 2007–11; Mem., Council, 2011–15. Mem., UK Panel for Res. Integrity in Health and Biomed. Scis, 2006–15. Mem. Faculty, Lundbeck Internat. Neurosci. Foundn, Denmark, 2007–. Trustee, Sci. Mus. Gp, 2015–. Chair, Sci. Festival, 2011–; Mem. Bd, Cheltenham Festivals, 2011–. Royal Society: Chair, Public Engagement Cttee, 2013–; Chair, Sectional Cttee 8, 2014–. Pres., British Neurosci. Assoc., 2013–15. FMedSci 2013. *Publications:* (with L. Kreitzman) Rhythms of Life: the biological clocks that control the daily lives of every living thing, 2005 (multiple trans); (with L. Kreitzman) Seasons of Life: the biological rhythms that living things need to thrive and survive, 2009; (with S. Lockley) Sleep: a very short introduction, 2012; contrib. to research-related jls. *Recreations:* listening to opera, Wagner when possible, to compensate doing anything that involves laughter, hunting for fossils, swimming, being in or near the sea, food, cocktails and wine with family and friends. *Address:* Nuffield Laboratory of Ophthalmology, Levels 5 and 6 West Wing, John Radcliffe Hospital, Headley Way, Headington, Oxford OX3 9DU. *T:* (01865) 234777. *E:* russell.foster@eye.ox.ac.uk. *Club:* Athenæum.

FOSTER, Sir Saxby Gregory, 4th Bt *cr* 1930, of Bloomsbury, co. London; *b* 3 Sept. 1957; *s* of Sir John Gregory Foster, 3rd Bt, and of Jean Millicent, *d* of late Elwin Watts; *S* father, 2006; *m* 1989, Rowan Audrey, *d* of late Reginald Archibald Ford; two *s*. *Heir: s* Thomas James Gregory Foster, *b* 1 May 1991. *Address:* PO Box 37, Golden Beach, Qld 4551, Australia. *T:* (7) 54922942, *Fax:* (7) 54957655; 125 Landsborough Parade, Golden Beach, Qld 4551, Australia. *E:* fosters4mail@gmail.com, rfoster@smccab.qld.edu.au.

FOSTER, Simon Ridgeby; farmer; *b* 1 Sept. 1939; *s* of Sir Ridgeby Foster and of Lady Nancy Foster (*née* Godden); *m* 1st, 1966, Mairi Angela Chisholm (marr. diss.); one *s* two *d*; 2nd, 1990, Philippa Lucy Back (*see* P. L. Foster Back). *Educ:* Shrewsbury Sch.; Jesus Coll., Cambridge (MA Hist.); London Business Sch. (Sloane Fellow); Wye Coll., London Univ. (MSc Sustainable Agric. 1995). Pres. and Dir Gen., Dunlop France, 1983–88; Dir, SMMT, 1988–91; Man. Dir, Toyota GB, 1991–93. Médaille d'Allier, 1987. *Publications:* Politique Industrielle, 1990. *Recreations:* farming, Dutch sailing barges.

FOSTER BACK, Philippa Lucy, CBE 2014 (OBE 2006); Director, Institute of Business Ethics, since 2001; *b* Swardeston, Norwich, 13 Nov. 1954; *d* of Philip John Quarles Back and June Debenham Back; *m* 1990, Simon Ridgeby Foster, *qv*. *Educ:* Berkhamsted Sch. for Girls; University Coll. London (BA Hons Geog. 1976). CDipAF 1986; CDir 2006. Citibank NA, 1977–79; Bowater Industries plc, 1979–88; DC Gardner Gp plc, 1988–90; self-employed consultant, 1990–93; Thorn EMI plc, subseq. EMI Gp plc, 1993–2000. Member: Woolf Cttee, ethical business conduct in BAE Systems plc, 2007–08; Clause 7 MoJ UK Bribery Act Steering Cttee, 2009–10; ICSA review of Higgs Guidance Steering Gp, 2009–11; Whitehall Corporate Governance Steering Gp, 2009–11. Tax Comr, 1992–98; non-executive Director: MoD, 1994–2007 (Mem., Defence Bd, 2002–07; Chm., Defence Audit Cttee); Investors Compensation Scheme, 1995–2001; Highways Agency, 2001–05; Ind. Mem., Milk Develt Council, 1995–2001; Comr, UK Debt Mgt Office, 2004–09; Chm., UK Antarctic Place-names Cttee, 2009–. Non-exec. Dir, Barrier Biotech Ltd, 1996–; Mem., Adv. Bd, RAND Europe, 2008–. Non-exec. Dir, Norfolk and Norwich Univ. Foundn NHS Trust, 2007–11 (Chm., Audit Cttee, 2007–11). Assoc. of Corporate Treasurers, 1982– (Pres., 1999–2000; Hon. Fellow, 2015); IoD, 1999–2013 (Vice Chm. and Sen. Ind. Dir, 2010–13); Trustee and non-exec. Dir, Assoc. for Project Mgt, 2007–09. Trustee: UK Antarctic Heritage Trust, 2001–13 (Chm., 2006–13); South Georgia Heritage Trust, 2015– (Chm. designate, 2015–). Mem. Adv. Bd, Centre for Corporate Reputation, Saïd Business Sch., Univ. of Oxford, 2008–. FRGS. Hon. FInstD 2013. *Publications:* Corporate Cash Management: strategy and practice, 1987; Setting the Tone: ethical business leadership, 2005. *Recreations:* polar issues (former Chm., Friends of Scott Polar Research Inst., Cambridge), travelling (three trips to Antarctica and two to Barren Lands, N Canada), current affairs, corporate governance. *Address:* c/o Institute of Business Ethics, 24 Greencoat Place, SW1P 1BE. *T:* (020) 7798 6040. *E:* pfb@ibe.org.uk. *Clubs:* Royal Over-Seas League; Norfolk.

FOTHERBY, Gordon; *b* 15 Nov. 1950; *m* 1974, Victoria Eloise (marr. diss. 2014). *Educ:* Hull GS; Sheffield Univ. (LLB Hons 1972). Called to the Bar, Inner Temple, 1973; Capt., Army Legal Corps, 1973–77; Solicitor's Office, HM Customs and Excise, later HM Revenue and Customs, 1977–2005: Asst Sec., Legal, 1986–93; on secondment to EC, 1989–91; Dep. Solicitor and Hd of Advisory and European, 1993–99, Hd of Prosecutions, 1999–2005; Sen. Legal Counsellor, Internat. Policy, 2005; with The Khan Partnership, LLP, 2006–08; Sen. Manager for Tax, KPMG, 2008–09; legal consultant, 2009.

FOTHERGILL, Alastair David William; Director, Silverback Films, since 2012; *b* 10 April 1960; *s* of David and Jaqueline Fothergill; *m* 1994, Melinda Jane Barker; two *s*. *Educ:* Harrow Sch.; St Andrews Univ.; Durham Univ. (BSc). Joined BBC Natural History Unit, 1983, Head, 1992–98; series producer: Life in the Freezer, 1993; The Blue Planet, 2001; Planet Earth, 2006; exec. prod., Frozen Planet, 2011. Director of films: Deep Blue, 2004; Earth, 2007; DisneyNature African Cats, 2011; DisneyNature Chimpanzee, 2012; DisneyNature Bears, 2014. *Publications:* Life in the Freezer, 1993; The Blue Planet, 2001; Planet Earth, 2006; Frozen Planet, 2011. *Recreations:* painting, walking. *Address:* Lodge Farm, St Catherine, Bath BA1 8HA. *E:* Alastair.fothergill@silverbackfilms.tv.

FOU TS'ONG; concert pianist; *b* 10 March 1934; *m* 1st, 1960, Zamira Menuhin (marr. diss. 1970); one *s*; 2nd, 1973, Hijong Hyun (marr. diss. 1976); 3rd, 1987, Patsy Toh; one *s*. *Educ:* Shanghai and Warsaw. Debut, Shanghai, 1953. Concerts all over Eastern Europe including USSR up to 1958. Arrived in Great Britain, Dec. 1958; London debut, Feb. 1959, followed by concerts in England, Scotland and Ireland; subsequently has toured all five Continents. Recordings include: Chopin, Mozart, Schumann, Debussy, Scarlatti, Handel, Haydn and Bach. Hon. DLitt Hong Kong, 1983. *Recreations:* bridge, Scrabble, watching sport, Chinese painting. *Address:* 62 Aberdeen Park, N5 2BL. *T:* and *Fax:* (020) 7226 9589.

FOUBISTER, Stuart Russell; Head of Economy and Transport Division, Scottish Government Legal Directorate, since 2011; *b* 12 Oct. 1958; *s* of late John and Yvonne Foubister; *m* 2006, Kirsten Rosemary Davidson; one *s* one *d*. *Educ:* Stewart's Melville Coll., Edinburgh; Edinburgh Univ. (LLB Hons 1980). Admitted solicitor, 1983. Joined Office of Solicitor to Sec. of State for Scotland, 1985; Divl Solicitor, 1997–2001; Scottish Executive, later Scottish Government: Dep. Solicitor, 2001–03; Legal Sec. to Lord Advocate, 2003–05; Scottish Legislative Counsel, 2005–07; Hd, Food and Envmt Div., Legal Directorate, 2008–11. *Recreations:* hill-walking, golf, cricket, reading. *Address:* (office) Victoria Quay, Edinburgh EH6 6QQ. *T:* (0131) 244 1408, *Fax:* (0131) 244 0591. *E:* stuart.foubister@scotland.gsi.gov.uk.

FOULDS, Adam Samuel James, FRSL; novelist and poet; *b* London, 8 Oct. 1974; *s* of Rabbi Michael Foulds, OBE and Ruth Foulds; *m* 2012, Charla Jones. *Educ:* Bancroft's Sch., Woodford Green, Essex; St Catherine's Coll., Oxford (BA English Lang. and Lit.); Univ. of E Anglia (MA Creative Writing). FRSL 2009. Hon. Fellow, Univ. of Roehampton, 2015. Best of Young British Novelists list, Granta mag., 2013; Next Generation Poet, Poetry Book Soc., 2014. *Publications:* The Truth About These Strange Times, 2007; The Broken Word, 2008; The Quickening Maze, 2009; In the Wolf's Mouth, 2013. *Recreations:* internal martial arts, playing the violin, music, visual art, film. *Address:* c/o The Wylie Agency, 17 Bedford Square, WC1B 3JA. *T:* (020) 7908 5900. *E:* mail@wylieagency.co.uk.

FOULDS, (Hugh) Jon; Chairman: L Huntsworth plc, 2000–08; Fauchier Partners Ltd, 1995–2009; Halifax plc (formerly Halifax Building Society), 1990–99 (Director, 1986–99); *b* 2 May 1932; *s* of late Dr E. J. Foulds and Helen Shirley (*née* Smith); *m*; two *s*. *Educ:* Bootham Sch., York. Dir and Chief Exec., 1976–88, Dep. Chm., 1988–92, Investors in Industry, subseq. 3i Gp plc; Director: Brammer plc, 1980–91 (Chm., 1988–91); London Smaller Companies (formerly London Atlantic) Investment Trust, 1983–95; Pan-Holdings SA, 1986–2008; Eurotunnel plc, 1988–96; Mercury Asset Management Gp plc, 1989–98. Mem. Bd of Banking Supervision, Bank of England, 1993–96. Hon. MA Salford, 1987. *Recreations:* tennis, ski-ing, shooting, pictures. *Address:* 28 Grosvenor Crescent Mews, SW1X 7EX. *Clubs:* Chelsea Arts, Garrick, Hurlingham.

FOULGER, Keith, BSc(Eng); CEng, MIMechE; FRINA, RCNC; Chief Naval Architect, Ministry of Defence, 1983–85, retired; *b* 14 May 1925; *s* of Percy and Kate Foulger; *m* 1951, Joyce Mary Hart; one *s* one *d*. *Educ:* Univ. of London (Mech. Eng.); Royal Naval Coll., Greenwich. Asst Constructor, 1950; Constructor, 1955; Constructor Comdr, Dreadnought Project, 1959; Staff Constructor Officer to C-in-C Western Fleet, 1965–66; Chief Constructor, 1967; Asst Director, Submarines, 1973; Deputy Director: Naval Construction, 1979; Naval Ship Production, 1979–81; Submarines, Ship Dept, 1981–83; Asst Under-Sec. of State, 1983. *Recreations:* travel, gardening, photography. *Address:* Lindley, North Road, Bathwick, Bath BA2 6HW.

FOULIS, Lindsay David Robertson; Sheriff of Tayside, Central and Fife at Perth, since 2001; *b* 20 April 1956; *s* of Henry Edwards Foulis and Mary Robertson Foulis; *m* 1981, Ellenore Brown; two *s* one *d*. *Educ:* High Sch. of Dundee; Univ. of Edinburgh (LLB Hons 1978). Legal apprentice, 1978–80, legal asst, 1980–81, Balfour and Manson, Edinburgh; asst, 1981–84, Partner, 1984–2000, Reid Johnston Bell and Henderson, subseq. Blackadder Reid Johnston, Dundee; Temp. Sheriff, 1998–99; All Scotland Floating Sheriff, Perth, 2000–01. Dundee University: Lectr (pt-time), 1994–2000; Hon. Prof. in Scots Law, 2001–. Mem. Council, Sheriff Court Rules, 1996–2000. *Publications:* (jtly) Civil Court Practice materials for Diploma in Legal Practice, 2001; contrib. articles on civil procedure to Jl Law Soc. of Scotland. *Recreations:* sport, now mainly golf (played badly), music. *Address:* Sheriff's Chambers, Sheriff Court House, Tay Street, Perth PH2 8NL.

FOULIS, Michael Bruce, FRGS; Director, Children and Families, Scottish Government, since 2011; *b* 23 Aug. 1956; *s* of Kenneth Munro Foulis and Edith Lillian Sommerville (*née* Clark); *m* 1981, Gillian Margaret Tyson; one *s* one *d*. *Educ:* Kilmarnock Acad.; Edinburgh Univ. (BSc Geog.). Joined Scottish Office, 1978: Private Sec. to Parly Under Sec. of State, 1987–89; on secondment to Scottish Financial Enterprise as Asst Dir, 1989–91; Scottish Educn Dept, 1991–93; Principal Private Sec. to Sec. of State for Scotland, 1993–95; Hd of Div., Agric., Envmt and Fisheries Dept, 1995–97; on secondment to Cabinet Office as Dep. Hd, Devolution Team, Constitution Secretariat, 1997–98; Hd of Gp, Educn and Industry Dept, 1998–99; Scottish Executive, later Scottish Government: Hd of Gp, Enterprise and Lifelong Learning Dept, 1999–2001; Hd, Envmt Gp, Envmt and Rural Affairs Dept, 2001–05; on secondment to Mining (Scotland) Ltd, subseq. Scottish Resources Gp, to work on corp. strategy, 2006–07; Dir, Housing and Regeneration, 2007–10; Dir, Strategy and Performance, 2011. Board Member: Children 1st, 2002–08; Wasps Artists' Studios, 2008–11. FRGS 2010. *Recreations:* playing cello, appreciating lithographs, moderate exercise. *Address:* Scottish Government, Victoria Quay, Edinburgh EH6 6QQ.

FOULKES, family name of **Baron Foulkes of Cumnock**.

FOULKES OF CUMNOCK, Baron *cr* 2005 (Life Peer), of Cumnock in East Ayrshire; **George Foulkes;** PC 2002; JP; *b* 21 Jan. 1942; *s* of late George and Jessie M. A. W. Foulkes; *m* 1970, Elizabeth Anna Hope; two *s* one *d*. *Educ:* Keith Grammar Sch., Keith, Banffshire; Haberdashers' Aske's Sch.; Edinburgh Univ. (BSc 1964). President: Edinburgh Univ. SRC, 1963–64; Scottish Union of Students, 1965–67; Manager, Fund for Internat. Student Cooperation, 1967–68. Scottish Organiser, European Movement, 1968–69; Director: European League for Econ. Co-operation, 1969–70; Enterprise Youth, 1970–73; Age Concern, Scotland, 1973–79. Councillor: Edinburgh Corp., 1970–75; Lothian Regional Council, 1974–79; Chairman: Lothian Region Educn Cttee, 1974–79; Educn Cttee, Convention of Scottish Local Authorities, 1975–78. MP (Lab and Co-op) S Ayrshire, 1979–83, Carrick, Cumnock and Doon Valley, 1983–2005. Opposition spokesman on

European and Community Affairs, 1984–85, on Foreign Affairs, 1985–92, on Defence, 1992–93, on Overseas Develt, 1994–97; Parly Under-Sec. of State, DFID, 1997–2001; Minister of State, Scotland Office, 2001–02. Mem., Select Cttee on Foreign Affairs, 1981–83. Jt Chm., All Party Pensioners Cttee, 1983–97 (Sec./Treasurer 1979–83); Mem., Jt Select Cttee on Nat. Security Strategy, 2010–. UK Delegate to Parly Assembly of Council of Europe, 1979–81, 2002–05; Mem., Parly Assembly, WEU, 2002–05. MSP (Lab) Lothians, 2007–11. Member: Sub Cttee F, European Scrutiny Cttee, H of L, 2006–08; Intelligence & Security Cttee, H of L, 2007–10; EU Select Cttee, H of L, 2011–; EU Sub Cttee on Social Policy and Consumer Protection, 2011–12; Sub Cttee C, Foreign Affairs, Defence and Internat. Develt, 2012–. Treas., Parliamentarians for Global Action, 1993–97 (Mem. Council, 1987–97); Member: UK Exec., CPA, 1987–97, 2002–05, 2011–; IPU, 1989–97 (Mem., British Cttee, 2002–08). Member: Scottish Exec. Cttee, Labour Party, 1981–89; Exec., Socialist Internat., 2003–08; Chm., Labour Movt for Europe in Scotland, 2002–. President: Caribbean-Britain Business Council, 2002–11; Caribbean Council, 2011–; Vice-Chm., Cuba Initiative, 2005–. Rector's Assessor, Edinburgh Univ. Court, 1968–70, Local Authority Assessor, 1971–79. Chairman: Scottish Adult Literacy Agency, 1976–79; John Wheatley Centre, 1990–97. Mem. Exec., British/China Centre, 1987–93. Director: St Cuthbert's Co-op. Assoc., 1975–79; Co-op. Press Ltd, 1990–97. Trustee, Age Scotland, 2014– (Vice Chair, 2015–); Trustee and Treas., Climate Parliament, 2014–. JP Edinburgh, 1975. Wilberforce Medal, City of Hull, 1998. Order of Merit (Dominican Republic), 2006. *Publications:* Eighty Years On: history of Edinburgh University SRC, 1964; (contrib.) A Claim of Right, ed Owen Dudley Edwards, 1989. *Recreations:* boating, watching Heart of Midlothian FC (Chm., 2004–05). *Address:* House of Lords, SW1A 0PW. *T:* (020) 7219 3474.

FOULKES, Sir Arthur (Alexander), GCMG 2010 (KCMG 2001); Governor-General of the Bahamas, 2010–14 (Deputy Governor-General, 2008–10); *b* 11 May 1928; *s* of late Dr William Alexander Foulkes and Julie Blanche Foulkes (*née* Maisonneuve); *m* 1st, Naomi Louise Higgs; 2nd, Joan Eleanor Bullard. *Educ:* Public Sch., Inagua, Bahamas; Western Central Sch., Nassau, Bahamas; privately tutored in journalism. News Editor, The Tribune, 1950–62; Editor, Bahamian Times, 1962; Founder/Chm., Diversified Services (PR), 1967. MP Bahamas, 1967; Chm., Bahamas Telecommunications Corp., 1967; Cabinet Minister, 1968; Co-Founder, Free Nat. Movement, 1970; Mem., Senate, 1972. Delegate: Bahamas Petition to UN Cttee on Decolonization, 1965; Bahamas Constitutional Conf., London, 1972. High Comr to UK and Ambassador to France, Italy, Germany, Belgium and the EC, 1992–99; Ambassador (non-resident) to China and to Cuba, 1999–2002. Chairman: Bahamas Broadcasting Corp., 2001–02; Bahamas Parly Salaries Commn, 2001; Bahamas Order of Merit Cttee, 2001; Dir, Bahamas Information Services, 2007–10. Hon. LLD Saint John's Univ., Minnesota, 2010. *Recreations:* theatre, music, art, literature. *Address:* Gambier, West Bay Street, PO Box CB–12366, Nassau, Bahamas.

FOULKES, Brig. Thomas Howard Exton, OBE 2012; CEng; FICE; Chairman, Victoria Business Improvement District, since 2011; Director General, Institution of Civil Engineers, 2002–11; *b* 31 Aug. 1950; *s* of late Maj.-Gen. Thomas Herbert Fischer Foulkes, CB, OBE and of Delphine Foulkes (*née* Exton Smith); *m* 1976, Sally Winter; two *d. Educ:* Clifton Coll.; RMA Sandhurst; RMCS Shrivenham (BSc); Open Univ. (MBA 2001). FIMechE 1997; FICE 1998; MInstRE 2005; FIET 2008. Commnd RE, 1971; Troop Comdr, Ind. Field Troop, AMFL, 1976–79; OC, 1st Field Sqn RE, 1985–87; CO, 28 Amphibious Engr Regt, 1989–92; Project Manager, Gen. Engr Equipment, MoD PE, 1992–95; Col ES42, HQ QMG, 1995–98; rcds, 1998; Dir, Army Estates Orgn, 1999–2002. Dep. Chm., Thomas Telford Ltd, 2002–11; Chm., Cyntra Ltd, 2009–12. Sec.-Gen., 2002–09, Pres., 2009–11, Commonwealth Engrs Council. Vis. Prof. of Civil Engrg, Univ. of Surrey, 2010–. Mem., Smeatonian Soc., 2004–; Trustee, RE Museum Foundn, 2010–. Gov., Clifton Coll., 2010–. FAPM 2009. Liveryman, Engineers' Co., 2005. *Publications:* contribs to RE Jl, chiefly on military bridging and walks in Whitehall. *Recreations:* monuments in Whitehall, history of ideas, obituaries, football, photography, gardening, cycling. *Clubs:* Athenæum; Royal Engineers Assoc. Football (Pres., 1992–2002).

FOULSER, Jeff; Chairman and Chief Executive Officer, Sunset + Vine Productions, since 2005; *b* London, 21 Aug. 1952; *s* of George and Rose Foulser; *m* 1981, Clementine Robinson; one *s* one *d. Educ:* Claremont High Sch., Harrow. Asst Prod., LWT, 1970–73; Prod., The Big Match, 1973–76; Exec. Producer, ITV Sport, 1976–89; Exec. Producer, 1989–95, Man. Dir, 1995–2000, Sunset + Vine Prodns; Chief Exec., Television Corp. plc, 2000–05. *Recreations:* golf, walking, ski-ing, theatre, cinema. *Address:* 13 Spencer Road, Twickenham, Middx TW2 5TH. *T:* (020) 7478 7310. *E:* jeff.foulser@sunsetvine.com. *Clubs:* MCC, Annabel's; Royal Wimbledon Golf.

FOULSHAM, Richard Andrew, CMG 2006; HM Diplomatic Service, retired; *b* 24 Sept. 1950; *s* of William Foulsham and Lilian Elizabeth Foulsham (*née* Monro); *m* 1982, Deirdre Elizabeth Strathairn; one *s* one *d. Educ:* Univ. of St Andrews (MA Hons 1973). Argyll and Sutherland Highlanders, 1973–79; joined FCO, 1982; Second Sec., FCO, 1982–84; First Secretary: Brunei, 1984–86; Lagos, 1986–90; FCO, 1990–95; Counsellor (Political), Rome, 1995–99; Counsellor: FCO, 1999–2001; Ottawa, 2001–03; FCO, 2003–05. Chief Exec., Hope and Homes for Children, 2005–11. Trustee, Child Health Internat., 2005–. *Recreation:* walking in mountains. *Address:* Hope and Homes for Children, East Clyffe, Salisbury, Wilts SP3 4LZ.

FOUNTAIN, Alan; President, European Audiovisual Entrepreneurs, since 2012 (Head of Studies, 2000–11; Chief Executive, 2006–09); *b* 24 March 1946; *s* of Harold Fountain and Winifred Cecily Brown. *Educ:* Nottingham Univ. (BA Hons Philosophy). Film Officer, E Midlands Arts, 1976–79; producer, 1979–81; Channel Four TV, 1981–94 (Sen. Commissioning Editor, 1982–94); Head, Northern Media Sch., Sheffield Hallam Univ., 1995–98; Prog. Dir, Alfa TV, 1997–98; Founder and Man. Dir, Mondial TV and Mondialonline.com, 1998–2001; Prof. of TV Studies and Hd, Centre for Cultural Industries, Middlesex Univ., 2001–05. *Publications:* (ed) Ruff's Guide to the Turf, 1972; (ed jtly) The Alternative Media Handbook, 2008; contrib. film and TV pubns. *Recreations:* family, golf, watching sports. *Address:* 72 Sydney Road, Muswell Hill, N10 2RL.

FOUNTAIN, Anthony; Chief Executive Officer, Refining and Marketing, Reliance Industries Ltd, India, since 2011; *b* Newquay, Cornwall, 23 Sept. 1960; *s* of Air Cdre C. Fountain and Winifred Fountain; one *d. Educ:* Loughborough Grammar Sch.; Warwick Univ. (BSc Econs and Internat. Studies); St Antony's Coll., Oxford (MPhil Econs). Economist, latterly Gp Vice Pres., Refining and Mktg, BP, 1984–2009; CEO, Nuclear Decommissioning Authy, 2009–11. *Recreations:* horse riding, running, golf. *Address:* Little Pell Farm, Wadhurst, E Sussex TN5 6DN; Reliance Industries Ltd, Makers Chambers IV, Nariman Point, Mumbai 400 021, India. *Club:* Royal Automobile.

FOUNTAIN, Hon. Sir Cyril (Stanley Smith), Kt 1996; Chief Justice, Supreme Court of Bahamas, 1996, retired; *b* 26 Oct. 1929; *s* of Harold Jackson Fountain and Winifred Olive Helen Fountain (*née* Smith); *m* 1954, Dorothy Alicia Hanna; two *s* one *d. Educ:* St Benedict's Coll., Atchison, Kansas (BA *cum laude* Econs); King's Coll. London (LLB Hons 1962). Head Teacher, Bd of Educn, Bahamas, 1955–58; articled law student to Sir Leonard J. Knowles, 1958–59; called to the Bar: Gray's Inn, 1963; Bahamas, 1963; Partner, Cash, Fountain & Co., 1963–93; Supreme Court of Bahamas: Actg Judge, April 1985 and April–Aug. 1990; Justice, 1993–94; Sen. Justice, 1994–96. MP (FNM) Long Island, Rum Cay and San Salvador, 1972–77. *Recreations:* swimming, historical reading. *Address:* PO Box N 476, Nassau, Bahamas. *T:* (home) 3936493, (office) 3222956/7.

FOUNTAIN, Ian Matthew; concert pianist; Professor of Piano, Royal Academy of Music, since 2001; *b* Welwyn Garden City, 15 Oct. 1969; *s* of Nigel and Joan Fountain; partner, Erika Geldsetzer. *Educ:* New Coll. Sch., Oxford; Winchester Coll.; Royal Northern Coll. of Music (GRNCM 1991). ARCO 1985. Winner: Viotti-Valsesia Internat. piano competition, 1986; Arthur Rubinstein Internat. Piano Masters Competition, 1989. Has performed worldwide: London début, Queen Elizabeth Hall, 1991; NY, Berlin, Paris, Israel, Far East. Has made recordings. Hon. ARAM 2007; Hon. RAM 2014. Echo-Preis, Germany, 2014. *Recreations:* horse racing, literature. *Address:* Royal Academy of Music, Marylebone Road, NW1 5HT. *T:* (020) 7873 7405. *E:* fountain_ian@yahoo.co.uk.

FOURACRE, Joanna Dorothy; *see* Haigh, J. D.

FOURCADE, Jean-Pierre; Commandeur de l'ordre national du Mérite, 2011; Senator, French Republic, for Hauts-de-Seine, 1977–2011, now Honorary Senator; *b* 18 Oct. 1929; *s* of Raymond Fourcade (Médecin) and Mme Fourcade (*née* Germaine Raynal); *m* 1958, Odile Mion; one *s* two *d. Educ:* Collège de Sorèze; Bordeaux Univ. Faculté de Droit, Institut des Etudes politiques (Dip.); Ecole Nationale d'Administration; higher studies in Law (Dip.). Inspecteur des Finances, 1954–73. Cabinet of M. Valéry Giscard d'Estaing: Chargé de Mission, 1959–61; Conseiller technique, 1962, then Dir Adjoint to chef de service, Inspection gén. des Finances, 1962; Chef de service du commerce, 1966–68; Dir-gén. du Commerce intérieur et des Prix, 1968–70; Dir-gén. adjoint du Crédit industriel et commercial, 1970, Dir-gén., 1972, and Administrateur Dir-gén., 1973; Ministre de l'Economie et des Finances, 1974–76; Ministre de l'Equipement et de l'Aménagement du Territoire, 1976–77. Senate: Pres., Commn des Affaires Sociales, 1983–98; Mem., Commn des Affaires Etrangères, de la Défense et des Forces Armées, 2004–. Mayor of Saint-Cloud, 1971–92; Conseiller général of canton of Saint-Cloud, 1973–89; Conseiller régional d'Ile de France, 1976– (Vice-Président, 1982–95); Mayor of Boulogne-Billancourt, 1995–2007. Président: Clubs Perspectives et Réalités, 1975–82; Comité des Finances Locales, 1980–2004; Commn Consultative d'Evaluation des Changes, 2005–11. Vice-Pres., Union pour la Démocratie Française, 1978–86 (Mem. Bureau, 1986); Mem., UMP, 2002–. *Publications:* Et si nous parlions de demain, 1979; La tentation social-démocrate, 1985; Remèdes pour l'Assurance-Maladie, 1989; Mon expérience peut-elle éclairer l'avenir?, 2015. *Address:* 8 Parc de Béarn, 92210 Saint-Cloud, France.

FOURMAN, Prof. Michael Paul, DPhil; Professor of Computer Systems, University of Edinburgh, since 1988; *b* Oxford, 12 Sept. 1950; *s* of Lucien Paul Rollings Fourman and Julia Mary Fourman (*née* Hunton); *m* 1982, Jennifer Robin Head (marr. diss. 2001); two *s* one *d. Educ:* Univ. of Bristol (BSc Maths 1971); Univ. of Oxford (MSc Mathematical Logic 1972; DPhil 1974). Joseph Fels Ritt Asst Prof., Dept of Maths, Columbia Univ., NY, 1977–82; Reader, 1982–86, Prof. of Formal Systems, Dept of Electronic and Electrical Engrg, 1986–88, Brunel Univ. SRC Fellow, Univ. of Cambridge, 1979; Visiting Scientist: Sydney Univ., 1982; McGill Univ., Montreal, 1983. Founder and Technical Dir, Abstract Hardware Ltd, 1986–96; consultancies for Siemens, Soft Image Systems, Higher Order Logic, Showbusiness, etc. FBCS; CITP; FRSE. *Publications:* articles in jls incl. Pure and Applied Algebra and Automated Reasoning. *Recreations:* cooking, sailing. *Address:* School of Informatics, University of Edinburgh, Informatics Forum, 10 Crichton Street, Edinburgh EH8 9AB. *T:* (0131) 651 3266, *Fax:* (0131) 651 1426. *E:* Michael.Fourman@ed.ac.uk.

FOURNIER, Bernard; non-executive Chairman, Xerox Ltd, 1998–2001 (Chief Executive Officer, 1995–98); *b* 2 Dec. 1938; *s* of Jean Fournier and Solange Hervieu; *m* 1st; two *s*; 2nd, 1980, Françoise Chavailler; one *s. Educ:* Philo Lycée (Baccalauréat); Louis Le Grand, Paris; Ecole des Hautes Etudes Commerciales, Lille. Joined: Publiart SA, 1964; Sanglier SA, 1965; Rank Xerox, 1966: Regional Manager Africa, Eastern Europe, 1980; Gen. Manager, RX France, 1981; Pres., Amer. Ops, Xerox, 1988; Man. Dir, Rank Xerox Ltd, 1989–95. Non-exec. Dir, AEGIS, 2001–09. Chm. Govs and Mem., Internat. Adv. Bd, Ecole des Hautes Etudes Commercial du Nord, 2008–12. *Recreations:* cooking, oenology, stamps, antiques, golf.

FOVARGUE, Yvonne Helen; MP (Lab) Makerfield, since 2010; *b* Sale, 29 Nov. 1956; *d* of Kenneth Gibbon and Irene, (Renee), Gibbon (*née* Reed); one *d*; *m* 2009, Paul Kenny. *Educ:* Sale Girls Grammar Sch.; Leeds Univ. (BA Hons Eng.). Housing Officer, Manchester CC, 1979–86; Chief Exec., St Helens CAB, 1986–2010. Mem. (Lab) Warrington BC, 2004–10. Opposition Whip, 2011–13; Shadow Parly Under Sec. of State for Transport, 2013; Shadow Minister: for Defence, 2013–14, 2015; for Young People, 2014–15. Chm., All Party Parly Gp on Debt and Personal Finance, 2010–, on Legal Aid, 2010–. Mem., MENSA. *Recreations:* crime fiction, music of David Bowie. *Address:* (office) Wigan Investment Centre, Waterside Drive, Wigan WN3 5BA. *T:* (01942) 824029. *E:* yvonne.fovargue.mp@parliament.uk. *W:* www.twitter.com/Y_FovargueMP.

FOWKE, Sir David (Frederick Gustavus), 5th Bt *cr* 1814, of Lowesby, Leics; *b* 28 Aug. 1950; *s* of Lt-Col Gerrard George Fowke (*d* 1969) (2nd *s* of 3rd Bt) and Daphne (*née* Monasteriotis) (*d* 2010); *S* uncle, 1987. *Educ:* Cranbrook School, Sydney; Univ. of Sydney (BA 1971). *Heir:* none.

FOWLER, family name of **Baron Fowler**.

FOWLER, Baron *cr* 2001 (Life Peer), of Sutton Coldfield in the County of West Midlands; **Peter Norman Fowler,** Kt 1990; PC 1979; Chairman, Aggregate Industries, 2000–06 (non-executive Director, 2010–13); *b* 2 Feb. 1938; *s* of late N. F. Fowler and Katherine Fowler; *m* 1979, Fiona Poole, *d* of John Donald; two *d. Educ:* King Edward VI Sch., Chelmsford; Trinity Hall, Cambridge (MA). Nat. Service commn, Essex Regt, 1956–58; Cambridge, 1958–61; Chm., Cambridge Univ. Conservative Assoc., 1960. Joined staff of The Times, 1961; Special Corresp., 1962–66; Home Affairs Corresp., 1966–70; reported Middle East War, 1967. Mem. Council, Bow Group, 1967–69; Editorial Board, Crossbow, 1962–69; Vice-Chm., North Kensington Cons. Assoc., 1967–68; Chm., E Midlands Area, Cons. Political Centre, 1970–73. MP (C): Nottingham S, 1970–74; Sutton Coldfield, Feb. 1974–2001. Chief Opposition spokesman: Social Services, 1975–76; Transport, 1976–79; Opposition spokesman, Home Affairs, 1974–75; PPS, NI Office, 1972–74; Sec. of State for Transport, 1981 (Minister of Transport, 1979–81), for Social Services, 1981–87, for Employment, 1987–90; Chief Opposition front bench spokesman on the envmt, transport and the regions, 1997–98; Shadow Home Sec., 1998–99. Mem., Parly Select Cttee on Race Relations and Immigration, 1970–74; Jt Sec., Cons. Parly Home Affairs Cttee, 1971–72, 1974 (Vice-Chm., 1974); Chairman: Cons Parly Cttee on European Affairs, 1991–92; H of L Select Cttee on BBC, 2005; H of L Select Cttee on Communication, 2007–10. Special Advr to Prime Minister, 1992 Gen. Elecn; Chm., Cons. Party, 1992–94; Mem. Exec., Assoc. of Cons. Peers, 2001–04 (Vice Chm., 2004–10). Chairman: Midland Independent Newspapers, 1991–98; Regl Independent Media (Yorks Post gp of newspapers), 1998–2002; Numark Ltd, 1998–2005; Thomson Foundn, 2007–13; Director: NFC plc, 1990–97; Holcim Ltd, 2006–09; non-exec. Dir, ABTA, 2010–. Chm., NHBC, 1992–98. *Publications:* After the Riots: the police in Europe, 1979; Ministers Decide: a memoir of the Thatcher years, 1991; A Political Suicide, 2008; AIDS: don't die of prejudice, 2014; political pamphlets including: The Cost of Crime, 1973; The Right Track, 1977. *Address:* House of Lords, SW1A 0PW.

FOWLER, Prof. Alastair David Shaw, CBE 2014; FBA 1974; Professor of English, University of Virginia, 1990–98; Regius Professor of Rhetoric and English Literature, University of Edinburgh, 1972–84, now Emeritus (University Fellow, 1985–87 and since 2007); *b* 17 Aug. 1930; *s* of David Fowler and Maggie Shaw; *m* 1950, Jenny Catherine Simpson; one *s* one *d. Educ:* Queen's Park Sch., Glasgow; Univ. of Glasgow; Univ. of

Edinburgh; Pembroke Coll., Oxford. MA Edin. 1952 and Oxon 1955; DPhil Oxon 1957; DLitt Oxon 1972. Junior Res. Fellow, Queen's Coll., Oxford, 1955–59; Instructor, Indiana Univ., 1957–58; Lectr, UC Swansea, 1959–61; Fellow and Tutor in English Lit., Brasenose Coll., Oxford, 1962–71. Visiting Professor: Columbia Univ., 1964; Univ. of Virginia, 1969, 1979, 1985–90; Mem. Inst. for Advanced Study, Princeton, 1966, 1980; Visiting Fellow: Council of the Humanities, Princeton Univ., 1974; Humanities Research Centre, Canberra, 1980; All Souls Coll., Oxford, 1984. Lectures: Witter Bynner, Harvard, 1974; Churchill, Bristol Univ., 1979; Warton, British Acad., 1980; Ballard Matthews, Univ. of Wales, 1981; Coffin, UCL, 1984; Read-Tuckwell, Bristol Univ., 1991; Shakespeare, British Acad., 1995; Croston, Oxford, 2003; Bateson, Oxford, 2008; MacDiarmid, 2012. Mem., Agder Akademi, 2003. Mem., Scottish Arts Council, 1976–77. Milton Soc. of America Honoured Scholar, 2013. Adv. Editor, New Literary History, 1972–2003; Gen. Editor, Longman Annotated Anthologies of English Verse, 1977–80; Member, Editorial Board: English Literary Renaissance, 1978–2003; Word and Image, 1984–91, 1992–97; The Seventeenth Century, 1986–2003; Connotations, 1990–98; Translation and Literature, 1990–2014; English Review, 1990–98. *Publications:* (trans. and ed) Richard Wills, De re poetica, 1958; Spenser and the Numbers of Time, 1964; (ed) C. S. Lewis, Spenser's Images of Life, 1967; (ed with John Carey) The Poems of John Milton, 1968; Triumphal Forms, 1970; (ed) Silent Poetry, 1970; (ed with Christopher Butler) Topics in Criticism, 1971; Seventeen, 1971; Conceitful Thought, 1975; Catacomb Suburb, 1976; Edmund Spenser, 1977; From the Domain of Arnheim, 1982; Kinds of Literature, 1982; A History of English Literature, 1987; The New Oxford Book of Seventeenth Century Verse, 1991; The Country House Poem, 1994; Time's Purpled Masquers, 1996; (ed) Paradise Lost, 1998; Renaissance Realism, 2003; How to Write, 2006; Literary Names, 2012; contribs to jls and books. *Address:* 11 East Claremont Street, Edinburgh EH7 4HT.

FOWLER, Prof. (Christine) Mary Rutherford, PhD; Master, Darwin College, Cambridge, since 2012; *b* 1950; *d* of Peter and Rosemary Fowler; *m* 1975; one *s* two *d*. *Educ:* Girton Coll., Cambridge (BA 1st Cl. Maths 1972); Darwin Coll., Cambridge (PhD 1976). Royal Soc. Eur. Fellow, ETH Zürich, 1977–78; University of Saskatchewan: Professional Res. Associate, 1981–82, 1983–91; Asst Prof., 1982–83; Adjunct Prof., 1991–2001; Royal Holloway, University of London: Lectr, then Sen. Lectr (pt-time), 1992–2003; Prof. of Geophysics, 2003–12; Hd, Dept of Earth Scis, 2002–08; Deputy Dean Res. (Sci.), 2009–11; Dean of Science, 2011–12. Chm., Cttee Heads of Univ. Geosci Depts, 2010–11. Associate Editor: Reviews of Geophysics, 1991–94; Jl Geophysical Res., 1998–2004. Dir, Sask Energy, 1992. Mem. Council, 1998–2002, Vice-Pres., 2000–02, RAS; Mem. Council, Geol Soc., 2007–10; Mem., Adv. Cttee, British Geol Survey, 2012–15. Member: Bureau, Internat. Lithosphere Prog., 1997–2002; Governing Bd, Sch. of Cosmic Physics, Dublin Inst. for Advanced Studies, 2006–15. Hon. Fellow, RHUL, 2015. Prestwich Medal, Geol Soc., 1996. *Publications:* (ed with E. G. Nisbet) Heat Metamorphism and Tectonics, 1988; The Solid Earth: an introduction to global geophysics, 1990, 2nd edn 2005; (ed jtly) The Early Earth: physical, chemical and biological development, 2002; contrib. learned jls. *Address:* Darwin College, Silver Street, Cambridge CB3 9EU. *T:* (01223) 335660.

FOWLER, Christopher B.; *see* Brocklebank-Fowler.

FOWLER, Prof. David, CBE 2005; PhD; FRS 2002; FRSE; Senior Scientist, Biogeochemistry, Centre for Ecology and Hydrology, Natural Environment Research Council, Edinburgh, since 2008 (Science Director, 2003–08); *b* 1 June 1950; *s* of late Roy Fowler and of Phyllis Joan Fowler (*née* Lee); *m* 1976, Annette Francesca Odile Rossetti; one *s* two *d*. *Educ:* City Sch., Lincoln; Univ. of Nottingham (BSc 1972; PhD 1976). Institute of Terrestrial Ecology, subseq. Centre for Ecology and Hydrology, Edinburgh: HSO, 1975–78; SSO, 1978–85; PSO, 1985; Section Hd, Air Pollution, 1986; Grade 6, 1991; Grade 5, 1998; Hd, Atmospheric Scis Div., 2002–03. Hon. Lectr, Univ. of Edinburgh, 1988; Special Prof. of Envmtl Sci., Univ. of Nottingham, 1991. Chairman: UK Photochemical Oxidants Rev. Gp, 1990–98; UK Nat. Expert Gp on Transboundary Air Pollution, 1999. FRSE 1999. Member Editorial Board: Tellus, 1995; Environmental Pollution, 2000. *Publications:* (with M. H. Unsworth) Acid Deposition at High Elevation, 1988; Ozone in the United Kingdom, 1997; Acidification, Eutrophication and Ozone in the UK, 2001; (with C. E. R. Pitcairn and J. W. Erisman) Air-Surface Exchange of Gases and Particles; many scientific papers in Qly Jl RMetS, Atmospheric Envmt, Envmtl Pollution, Tellus, New Phytologist and Nature. *Recreations:* hill walking, gardening, music, photography, natural history, cycling. *Address:* Centre for Ecology and Hydrology, Bush Estate, Penicuik, Midlothian EH26 0QB. *T:* (0131) 445 4343, *Fax:* (0131) 445 3943. *E:* dfo@ceh.ac.uk.

FOWLER, Sir (Edward) Michael (Coulson), Kt 1981; Mayor of Wellington, New Zealand, 1974–83; architectural consultant, since 1989; former company chairman and director; *b* 19 Dec. 1929; *s* of William Coulson Fowler and Faith Agnes Netherclift; *m* 1953, Barbara Hamilton Hall (*d* 2009); two *s* one *d*. *Educ:* Christ's Coll., Christchurch, NZ; Auckland Univ. (MArch). Architect, London office, Ove Arup & Partners, 1954–55; own practice, Wellington, 1957–59; Partner, Calder Fowler Styles and Turner, 1959–89. Wellington buildings designed and supervised: Overseas Passenger Terminal, 1963; The Reserve Bank, 1970; Dalmuir House, 1971; Church of the Immaculate Conception, Taumarunui, 1975; St Andrew's Presbyterian Church, Blenheim, 1976; Greenock House, 1978; alterations and additions, Old St Mary's Convent, Blenheim, 1986; Highfield Winery, Marlborough, 1995–2000; many country and urban houses. Director: New Zealand Sugar Co., 1983–95; Cigna Insurance New Zealand Ltd, 1985–89. Chm., Queen Elizabeth II Arts Council, 1983–87. Wellington City Councillor, 1968–74. Nat. Pres., YHA of NZ, 1984–87. Medal of Honour, NZIA, 1983; Alfred O. Glasse Award, NZ Inst. of Planning, 1984. *Publications:* Wellington Sketches: Folio I, 1971, Folio II, 1974; Country Houses of New Zealand, 1972, 2nd edn 1977; The Architecture and Planning of Moscow, 1980; Eating Houses in Wellington, 1980; Wellington Wellington, 1981; Eating Houses of Canterbury, 1982; Wellington—A Celebration, 1983; The New Zealand House, 1983; Buildings of New Zealanders, 1984; Michael Fowler's University of Auckland, 1993. *Recreations:* sketching, reading, writing, history, politics. *Address:* 263 Tinakori Road, Thorndon, Wellington 6011, New Zealand; (office) Michael Fowler Gallery, 277 Tinakori Road, Thorndon, Wellington 6011, New Zealand. *E:* michael.fowler@xtra.co.nz. *Club:* Wellington (Wellington, NZ).

FOWLER, John Francis, DSc, PhD; FInstP; Professor, Departments of Human Oncology and Medical Physics, University of Wisconsin, USA, 1988–94 and 1999–2004, now Emeritus; Director of Cancer Research Campaign's Gray Laboratory, at Mount Vernon Hospital, Northwood, 1970–88; *b* 3 Feb. 1925; *er s* of Norman V. Fowler, Bridport, Dorset and Marjorie Vivian Fowler (*née* White); *m* 1st, 1953, Kathleen Hardcastle Sutton, MB, BS (marr. diss. 1984); two *s* five *d*; 2nd, 1992, Anna Edwards, BSc, MCSP, SRP. *Educ:* Bridport Grammar Sch.; University Coll. of the South-West, Exeter. BSc 1st class Hons (London) 1944; MSc (London) 1946; PhD (London) 1955; DSc (London) 1974; FInstP 1957. Research Physicist: Newalls Insulation Co., 1944; Metropolitan Vickers Electrical Co., 1947; Stage Dir, Th. Workshop, Manchester, 1947–49; Newcastle upon Tyne Regional Hosp. Board (Radiotherapy service), 1950; Principal Physicist at King's Coll. Hosp., SE5, 1956; Head of Physics Section in Medical Research Council Radiotherapeutic Res. Unit, Hammersmith Hosp., 1959 (later the Cyclotron Unit); Reader in Physics, London Univ. at Med. Coll. of St Bartholomew's Hosp., 1962; Prof. of Med. Physics, Royal Postgraduate Med. Sch., London Univ., Hammersmith Hosp., 1963–70, Vice-Dean, 1967–70. Visiting Professor: in Oncology, Middx Hosp. Med. Sch., 1977–88; Dept of Oncol., University Hosp. of Leuven, Belgium, 1994–99; Bush Vis. Prof., Ontario Cancer Inst., Toronto, 1991. President: Hosp. Physicists Assoc., 1966–67; Eur. Soc. Radiat. Biol., 1974–76; British Inst. Radiol., 1977–78. Hon. FBIR 1989; Hon. FIPEM 2005; Hon. FRCR 1999. Fellow, Amer. Soc. for Therapeutic Radiol. and Oncol., 2006; Hon. Fellow: Amer. Coll. of Radiology, 1981; Amer. Coll. of Radiation Oncology, 1994. Hon. Member: Amer. Assoc. of Med. Physicists, 1983; Assoc. of Radiation Res., 2008. Hon. MD Helsinki, 1981; Hon. DSc Med. Coll. Wisconsin, 1989. Roentgen Award, BIR, 1965; Röntgen Plakette, Deutsches Röntgen Museum, 1978; Heath Meml Award, Univ. of Texas, Houston, 1981; Breur Medal, European Soc. Therapeutic Radiology and Oncology, 1983; Barclay Medal, BIR, 1985; Marie Sklodowska-Curie Medal, Polish Radiation Res. Soc., 1986; Gold Medal, Amer. Soc. Therapeutic Radiol. and Oncol., 1995; Failla Award, US Radiation Res. Soc., 2003. *Publications:* Nuclear Particles in Cancer Treatment, 1981; (contrib.) Technical Basis of Radiation Therapy, 4th edn, and 5th edn 2012; papers on radiobiology applied to radiotherapy, in Brit. Jl Radiology, Clinical Oncology, Radiotherapy and Oncology, Internat. Jl Radiation Oncology Biol. Physics, etc. *Recreations:* theatre, getting into the countryside, reading. *Address:* Flat 1, 150 Lambeth Road, SE1 7DF. *E:* jackfowlersbox@gmail.com.

FOWLER, Mary Rutherford; *see* Fowler, C. M. R.

FOWLER, Sir Michael; *see* Fowler, Sir E. M. C.

FOWLER, Michael Glyn; His Honour Judge Fowler; a Circuit Judge, since 2009; *b* Wantage, Oxon, 20 Nov. 1951; *s* of Gordon Fowler and Elizabeth Aled Fowler; *m* 1977, Ruth Mary Adgey-Edgar; two *d*. *Educ:* King's Coll. London (LLB 1973); Chancery Lane Sch. of Law. Called to the Bar, Middle Temple, 1974; Asst Recorder, 1996–2000; Recorder, 2000–09. Member: Civil Service Sports Council; Civil Service Sailing Assoc. *Recreations:* motorbikes, sailing, family and friends. *Address:* Northampton Crown Court, 85–87 Lady's Lane, Northampton NN1 3HQ. *T:* (01604) 470400, *Fax:* (01604) 470445.

FOWLER, Neil Douglas; Associate Member, 2009–10 and since 2011, and Interim Bursar, since 2014, Nuffield College, Oxford (Guardian Research Fellow, 2010–11); media and communications adviser and researcher, since 2008; *b* 18 April 1956; *s* of late Arthur Vincent Fowler and Helen Pauline Fowler; *m* 1989, Carol Susan (*née* Cherry); one *d*, and one step *s*. *Educ:* Southend High Sch. for Boys; Univ. of Leicester (BA Social Scis). Reporter, Leicester Mercury, 1978–81; Dep. News Editor, then Asst Chief Sub-editor, Derby Evening Telegraph, 1981–84; Asst to Editor, Asst Editor, then Editor, Lincolnshire Echo, 1984–87; Editor: Derby Evening Telegraph, 1987–91; The Journal, Newcastle upon Tyne, 1991–94; The Western Mail, 1994–2002; Proprietor, Neil Fowler Communications, 2002–03; CEO and Publisher, Toronto Sun, 2003–05; Editor, Which? mag., 2006–08; media consultant, 2008–12; Dir, Creative and Content, then Publishing Dir, 2012–14, Man. Dir, 2014, Headlines Corporate News Ltd. Dir, Publishing NTO, 2000–03. Columnist, Publishing mag., 2011–. FRSA 1999. Pres., Society (formerly Guild) of Editors, 1999–2000 (Vice-Pres., 1998–99). Trustee, Northamptonshire Theatres Trust, 2009–. Mem., Audit Cttee, Nuffield Coll., Oxford, 2010–. Regional Editor of Year, Newspaper Focus magazines, 1994; BT Welsh Journalist, 1999. *Publications:* (contrib.) Face the Future: tools for the modern media age, 2011; (contrib.) Charitable and Trust Ownership of News Organisations, 2011; (contrib.) Investigative Journalism, 2011; (ed jtly) What We Mean by Local, 2012. *Recreations:* Essex cricket, cinema, bridge, music of Frank Zappa. *E:* neildfowler1@aol.com, neil.fowler@nuffield.ox.ac.uk.

FOWLER, Prof. Patrick William, PhD; FRS 2012; Professor of Theoretical Chemistry, University of Sheffield, since 2005. *Educ:* Univ. of Sheffield (BSc Chem. 1977; PhD 1980). SERC Postdoctoral Fellow, Univ. of Cambridge, 1980–83; Sen. Demonstrator, Durham Univ., 1984–85; Postdoctoral Res. Fellow, Univ. of Cambridge, 1985; University of Exeter: Lectr in Physical Chem., 1985–90; Reader, 1990–95; Prof., 1995–2005. Visiting Professor: Ecole Nationale Supérieure, Paris, 1996–2005; Univ. Paul Sabatier, Toulouse, 2007. Corday-Morgan Medal, 1992, Tilden Medal, 2004, RSC. *Address:* Department of Chemistry, University of Sheffield, Sheffield S3 7HF.

FOWLER, Peter James, CMG 1990; HM Diplomatic Service, retired; International Adviser, Cairn Energy PLC, since 2002 (Director, 1996–2001); *b* 26 Aug. 1936; *s* of James and Gladys Fowler; *m* 1962, Audrey June Smith; one *s* three *d*. *Educ:* Nunthorpe Grammar Sch., York; Trinity Coll., Oxford (BA). Army Service, 1954–56. FCO, 1962–64; Budapest, 1964–65; Lisbon, 1965–67; Calcutta, 1968–71; FCO, 1971–75; East Berlin, 1975–77; Counsellor, Cabinet Office, 1977–80; Comprehensive Test Ban Delegn, Geneva, 1980; Counsellor, Bonn, 1981–85; Head of N America Dept, FCO, 1985–88; Minister and Dep. High Comr, New Delhi, 1988–93; High Comr to Bangladesh, 1993–96. Vice-Chm., Diplomatic Service Appeal Bd, 1997–2003. Chm., Britain-Nepal Chamber of Commerce and Industry, 2010–14. Chm., Charles Wallace Trust (Bangladesh), 1996–; Hon. Pres., Bangladesh-British Chamber of Commerce, 1998–2007. *Recreations:* reading, South Asia, opera, grandchildren. *Address:* 33 Northdown Street, N1 9BL.

FOWLER, Peter Jon, PhD; FSA; Professor of Archaeology, University of Newcastle upon Tyne, 1985–96, now Emeritus; painter, since 2003; *b* 14 June 1936; *s* of W. J. Fowler and P. A. Fowler; *m* 1959, Elizabeth (*née* Burley) (marr. diss. 1993); three *d*. *Educ:* King Edward VI Grammar Sch., Morpeth, Northumberland; Lincoln Coll., Oxford (MA 1961); Univ. of Bristol (PhD 1977). FSA 1963. Investigator on staff of RCHM (England), Salisbury office, 1959–65; Staff Tutor in Archaeology, Dept of Extra-Mural Studies, 1965–79, and Reader in Arch., 1972–79, Univ. of Bristol; Sec., Royal Commn on Historical Monuments (England), 1979–85; Leverhulme Fellow, Univ. of Newcastle upon Tyne, 1996–99; world heritage consultant, 2000–11. Member: Historic Bldgs and Ancient Monuments Adv. Cttees, Historic Buildings and Monuments Commn, 1983–86 (Ancient Monuments Bd, 1979–83); Council, National Trust, 1983–2000; World Heritage Panel, DCMS, 2010–11; Pres., Council for British Archaeol., 1981–83 (Vice-Pres., 1979–81). Archaeological consultant, Forestry Commn, 1988–2000; Mem., Landscape Adv. Cttee, DoT, 1990–95. Chm., Jarrow 700AD Ltd, 1991–2000. *Publications:* Regional Archaeologies: Wessex, 1967; (ed) Archaeology and the Landscape, 1972; (ed) Recent Work in Rural Archaeology, 1975; (ed with K. Branigan) The Roman West Country, 1976; Approaches to Archaeology, 1977; (ed with H. C. Bowen) Early Land Allotment in the British Isles, 1978; (with S. Piggott and M. L. Ryder) Agrarian History of England and Wales, I, pt 1, 1981; The Farming of Prehistoric Britain, 1983, re-issued 2009; Farms in England, 1983; (with P. Boniface) Northumberland and Newcastle upon Tyne, 1989; (jtly) Who Owns Stonehenge?, 1990; (with M. Sharp) Images of Prehistory, 1990; The Past in Contemporary Society: then, now, 1992; (jtly) Cadbury Congresbury 1968–73: a late/post-Roman hilltop settlement in Somerset, 1992; (with P. Boniface) Heritage and Tourism in 'the global village', 1993; (jtly) The Experimental Earthwork Project 1960–1992, 1996; (with I. Blackwell) The Land of Lettice Sweetapple, 1998; Landscape Plotted and Pieced: landscape history and local archaeology in Fyfield and Overton, Wiltshire, 2000; (with I. Blackwell) An English Countryside Explored, 2000, re-issued 2009; Farming in the First Millennium AD, 2002; World Heritage Cultural Landscapes, 1992–2002, 2003; Landscapes for the World, 2004; (jtly) Inventory of Cultural and National Heritage Sites of Potential Outstanding Universal Value in Palestine, 2005, re-issued 2006 (Arabic), 2009 (English, Arabic); contribs to learned jls and numerous pubns. *Recreations:* writing, music, gardening, sport. *T:* (020) 7638 6762.

FOWLER, Robert Asa; Owner and Chairman, Fowler International, since 1986; Consul General for Sweden, 1989–99; *b* 5 Aug. 1928; *s* of Mr and Mrs William Henry Fowler; *m* 1987, Monica Elizabeth Heden; three *s* one *d* by a previous marriage. *Educ:* Princeton Univ. (BA Econs); Harvard Business Sch. (MBA). Lieut USNR, 1950–53. Various appts with

Continental Oil, 1955–75; Area Manager, Northwest Europe, Continental Oil Co., 1975–78; Chm. and Man. Dir, Conoco Ltd, 1979–81; Vice-Pres., Internat. Marketing, Conoco Inc., 1981–85. An Hon. Consul Gen. for Sweden. *Recreations:* tennis, ski-ing. *Address:* 2 Azalea Court, Princeton, NJ 08540, USA. *T:* (609) 5141511. *Clubs:* Hurlingham; River, Knickerbocker (New York); Allegheny Country (Pa); Chagrin Valley Hunt (Ohio).

FOWLER, Prof. Robert Louis Herbert, DPhil; FBA 2015; Henry Overton Wills Professor of Greek, University of Bristol, since 1996; *b* 19 May 1954; *s* of Rev. Dr Louis Heath Fowler and Helen Minto Fowler (*née* Wilson); *m* 1976, Judith Lee Evers; two *s*. *Educ:* Univ. of Toronto Schs; Univ. of Toronto (BA 1976, MA 1977); Wadham Coll., Oxford (DPhil 1980). Fellow, Calgary Inst. for the Humanities, 1980; Department of Classical Studies, University of Waterloo, Canada: Asst Prof., 1981–86; Associate Prof., 1986–94; Chm. of Dept, 1988–96; Prof., 1994–96; Dean of Arts, Univ. of Bristol, 2004–09. Chm. Council, Classical Assoc., 2002–07. Pres., Soc. for Promotion of Hellenic Studies, 2014–. Ed., Jl Hellenic Studies, 2001–05. *Publications:* The Nature of Early Greek Lyric, 1987; Early Greek Mythography, vol. I, 2000, vol. II, 2013; (ed) The Cambridge Companion to Homer, 2004; contrib. articles to learned jls. *Recreations:* piano, golf. *Address:* Department of Classics and Ancient History, University of Bristol, 11 Woodland Road, Bristol BS8 1TB. *T:* (0117) 928 8258.

FOWLER, Prof. Robert Stewart, OBE 2001; Principal and Chief Executive, Central School of Speech and Drama, 1986–2001; *b* 1 Feb. 1932; *s* of William Fowler and Breta Bell Fowler (*née* Stewart); *m* 1965, Penelope Jessie Hobbs; two *s* one *d*. *Educ:* Queen's Coll., Oxford (MA); Queen's Univ., Belfast (DipEd); Guildhall Sch. of Music and Drama (LGSM). Served RAEC, 1950–52. Asst in English, Drama and Latin, Royal Belfast Acad. Instn, 1955–58; Hd of Dept, Forest Gate Sch., 1958–60; Warden, Bretton Hall Coll., Wakefield, 1960–66; Dep. Principal and Principal Elect, Sittingbourne Coll. of Educn, 1966–76; HMI with resp. for theatre, the arts in teacher trng and staff inspector, teacher trng, 1976–86. Chief Ext. Examr (Theatre Design), Nottingham Trent Univ., 1996–98; Ext. Examr (Theatre Studies), TCD, 1997–99. Vis. Prof., Birmingham City Univ. (formerly Univ. of Central England), 1995–. Vice-Pres., European League Inst. of Arts, 1998–2002; Member: Bd, Univs and Colls Employers' Assoc., 1996–2000; Nat. Council for Drama Trng, 1996–2000. Panel Chm., Hong Kong Council for Academic Accreditation, 1996–. Chm. Govs, Keswick Sch., 2007–10 (Foundn Gov., 2004–; Trustee repr. Queen's Coll., Oxford, 2007–). Sec., Oxford Univ. Soc. Cumbria, 2005–14. FRSA 1990. NW Vision Film Writing Award, 2003. *Publications:* Themes in Life and Literature, 1967; (jtly) English 11/16, 5 books, 1971–73; The Hobbit Introduced for Schools, 1973; (jtly) English: a literary foundation course, 1975; Art Rush in Seattle in Blunter Edge, 2008; Private Verses, 2009; (jtly) Dreams of Longing: a song cycle, 2010; Tricky Trumtrot The Last Dragon Slayer, 2012. *Recreations:* living, loving, life-saving, laughing, Lake District, Provence, family, friends, writing. *Address:* Gutherscale, Newlands, Keswick, Cumbria CA12 5UE.

FOWLER, Sarah Hauldys; *see* Evans, S. H.

FOWLIE, John Kay; JP; Vice Lord-Lieutenant of Banffshire, 2003–11; *b* 28 Jan. 1936; *s* of late Spencer Stephen Fowlie, MC and Agnes Howatson (*née* Kay); *m* 1960, Catherine Ann Coull Flett; one *s* one *d* (and one *s* decd). *Educ:* Buckie High Sch.; Jordanhill Coll. of Educn, Glasgow (Teaching Dip. in PE 1960). Nat. Service, 3rd Bn Parachute Regt, Cyprus and Suez, 1955–57; served TA 3rd Bn Gordon Highlanders, 1964–68. Teacher, then Principal Teacher of PE, Keith Grammar Sch., 1960–77; Principal Teacher (Guidance), Buckie High Sch., 1977–96. Mem., then Chm., Moray Children's Panel Adv. Cttee, 1985–96. RNLI: fundraising, 1970–; Station Hon. Sec., Launch Authy, Buckie Lifeboat, 1985–2003; Member: Steering Gp Cttee for RNLI Family Assoc., 2002–03; Scottish Lifeboat Council, 1999–2003; Cttee Mem., Buckie & District Fishing Heritage Mus., 2002–; Bd Mem., Buckie and District Fishing Heritage Gp, 2002–. Elder, Buckie S & W Church, 1975–; Hon. Sec., Buckie & District Seamen's Meml Chapel, 2004– (Sec., 1998–2004). JP Moray, 1995; DL Banffshire, 1998. *Publications:* The Times, the People, and the Buckie Fishermen's Choir, 2005. *Recreations:* walking, gardening, local history, reading. *Address:* Dunedin, 16 Titness Street, Buckie, Banffshire AB56 1HR. *T:* (01542) 832429.

FOX, family name of **Baron Fox**.

FOX, Baron *cr* 2014 (Life Peer), of Leominster in the County of Herefordshire; **Christopher Francis Fox;** Director, Group Communications, GKN plc, since 2012; *b* Haslemere, 27 Sept. 1957; *s* of Andrew Fox and Elizabeth Fox; *m* Sarah, (Essie), Bengry; one *d*. *Educ:* Imperial Coll. London (BSc). ARCS 1980. Front of house, King's Head Th., 1980; Field Engr, 1981–85, Communications Manager, 1990–98, Schlumberger Oilfield Services; Editor, Offshore Engineer, 1985–90; Dir, Corporate Relns, Tate & Lyle, 1998–2005; Dir, Communications, Smiths Gp, 2005–09; Chief Exec., Lib Dems, 2009–11. *Recreations:* mountains, tai chi, cigars. *Address:* 9 Claremont Road, Windsor SL4 3AX. *E:* chrisffox9@gmail.com. *Clubs:* MCC, Arsenal Football.

FOX, Dr Alan Martin; Clerk to Trustees, St Marylebone Almshouses, since 1998; *b* 5 July 1938; *s* of Sidney Nathan Fox and Clarice Solov; *m* 1965, Sheila Naomi Pollard; one *s* two *d*. *Educ:* Bancroft's Sch., Essex; Queen Mary Coll., London (BSc Hons II1, Physics 1959; PhD Math. Phys. 1963). ACIArb 1997, MCIArb 1999. Home Civil Service by Open Competition, 1963; Ministry of Aviation: Private Sec. to Parly Sec., 1965–67; 1st Sec. (Aviation and Defence) on loan to FCO, Paris, 1973–75; MoD, 1975–78; RCDS, 1979; MoD, 1980–98; Asst Under Sec. of State (Ordnance), 1988–92; Vis. Fellow, Center for Internat. Affairs, Harvard, 1992–93; Asst Under-Sec. of State (Quartermaster), 1994–95, (Export Policy and Finance), 1995–98. Lectr (part-time), UCL, 1998–2000. Member: London Rent Assessment Panel, 1999–2008; Compliance and Supervision Cttee, 2000–01, Adjudication Panel, 2002–08, SRA (formerly Office for the Supervision of Solicitors); Review Cttee on Non-Competitive Contracts, 2000–07. Clerk to Governors: Henrietta Barnett Sch., 1998–2003; Jews Free Sch., 2000–02, 2009–; King Solomon High Sch., 2008–13. *Recreations:* grandchildren, computer games, watching Rugby, cricket, TV, travel. *Address:* 4 Woodside Avenue, N6 4SS.

FOX, Dr (Anthony) John, FFPH; Visiting Professor, University College London, since 2006; *b* 25 April 1946; *s* of Fred Frank Fox, OBE, and Gertrude Price; *m* 1971, Annemarie Revesz; one *s* two *d*. *Educ:* Dauntsey's School; University College London (BSc); Imperial College London (PhD, DIC). FFPH (FFPHM 2000). Statistician: Employment Medical Adv. Service, 1970–75; OPCS, 1975–79; Prof. of Social Statistics, City Univ., 1980–88; Chief Medical Statistician, OPCS, 1988–96; Dir, Census, Population and Health Gp, ONS, 1996–99; Dir of Statistics, DoH, 1999–2005; Strategic Advr, Research, Information Centre for Health and Social Care (formerly Dir, Customer and Stakeholder Engagement, NHS Health and Social Care Information Centre), 2005–06. Vis. Prof., LSHTM, 1990–. Trustee, N London Hospice, 2007–. Hon. DSc City, 1997. *Publications:* Occupational Mortality 1970–72, 1978; Socio-Demographic Mortality Differentials, 1982; Health Inequalities in European Countries, 1989; (jtly) Health and Class: The early years, 1991. *Recreations:* family, tennis, bridge, theatre. *Address:* Department of Epidemiology and Public Health, University College London, 1–19 Torrington Place, WC1E 6BT.

FOX, Ashley Peter; Member (C) South West England and Gibraltar, European Parliament, since 2009; *b* Sutton Coldfield, 15 Nov. 1969; *s* of Clive and Diana Fox; *m* 1997, Julia Glynis David; one *s* one *d*. *Educ:* The King's School, Worcester; Bristol Poly. (LLB (Hons)); Coll. of Law, Chester. Admitted solicitor, 1994; former Solicitor, Morgan Cole. Mem. (C) Bristol CC, 2002–10. *Recreations:* bridge, poker, swimming. *Address:* (office) 5 Westfield Park, Bristol BS6 6LT. *T:* (0117) 973 7050. *E:* ashley@ashleyfoxmep.co.uk.

FOX, Brian Michael, CB 1998; Head of Civil Service Corporate Management (Grade 2), Cabinet Office, 1998–2000; *b* 21 Sept. 1944; *s* of Walter Frederick and Audrey May Fox; *m* 1966, Maureen Ann Shrimpton; one *d*. *Educ:* East Ham Grammar School for Boys. Joined CS, HM Treasury, 1963–98: Private Sec. to Financial Sec., 1967–69; secondment to 3i Gp, 1981–82; Dep. Estabt Officer, 1983–87; Head of Defence Policy and Materiel Div., 1987–89; Principal Estabt and Finance Officer, 1989–93; Dir (Grade 3), Sen. and Public Appts Gp, later Sen. CS Gp, Cabinet Office (on loan), 1994–98. Trustee, Help The Aged, 1998–2009; Property Trustee, Civil Service Benevolent Fund, 2001–12. Chm., Anim-Mates, 2006–11. *Recreations:* bowls, soccer. *Club:* Elm Park Bowls.

FOX, Sir Christopher, Kt 2006; QPM 1996; Managing Director, Chris Fox Consulting Ltd, 2006–13; *b* 21 July 1949; *s* of late Douglas Charles Fox and Olive Eileen Fox (*née* Vigar); *m* 1972, Carol Ann Wortley; one *s* two *d*. *Educ:* Broomhill Primary Sch.; Robert Gordon's Coll., Aberdeen; W Bridgford GS, Nottingham; Loughborough Univ. (BSc Physics and Electronic Engrg; DIS); Cabinet Office (Top Mgt Prog. 1995). Joined Notts Constabulary, 1972; detective and uniform duties, 1972–83; Superintendent, Mansfield, 1984–87; Chief Supt, Nottingham N Div., 1987–90; Actg Asst Chief Constable, Nottingham, 1990–91; Asst Chief Constable, 1991–94, Dep. Chief Constable, 1994–96, Warwickshire; Chief Constable, Northants, 1996–2003; Pres., ACPO, 2003–06. Chm., Civil Nuclear Police Authy, 2009–11. Vice Pres., Endeavour Trng, 2009–. Trustee, Police Foundn, 2005–. *Recreations:* played Rugby at first class level (Nottingham), golf, laid back cruiser sailing. *T:* 07714 689219.

FOX, Claire; Founder and Director, Institute of Ideas, since 2000; *b* 5 June 1960; *d* of late John Fox and of Maura Fox. *Educ:* Warwick Univ. (BA Hons English and American Lit.); Thames Poly. (PGCE 1992). Mental health social worker for variety of orgns in voluntary sector, incl. Cyrenians and MIND, 1981–87; Lectr and Tutor in English Lang. and Lit., Thurrock Tech. Coll., 1987–90 and W Herts Coll., 1992–99; Publisher, Living Marxism, subseq. LM mag., 1997–2000. Panellist, Moral Maze, BBC Radio 4, 2000–; columnist, MJ mag., 2000–. Convenor, Battle of Ideas Fest., 2006–. *Publications:* contributed chapters to: Debating Education: issues for the new millennium, 1996; Dumbing Down, 2000; (also ed) Maybe I Do: marriage and commitment in the singleton society, 2002; The McDonaldisation of Higher Education, 2002; The Routledge Falmer Guide to Key Debates in Education, 2004; A Lecturer's Guide to Further Education, 2006; The Lottery Debate, 2006; Panic Attack, 2006; No Strings Attached!: why arts funding should say no to instrumentalism, 2008. *Recreations:* putting my head above the parapet, saying the unsayable and stirring up intellectual debate. *Address:* Institute of Ideas, Signet House, 49–51 Farringdon Road, EC1M 3JP. *T:* (020) 7269 9223, *Fax:* (020) 7269 9235. *E:* clairefox@instituteofideas.com.

FOX, Colin; Member (Scot Socialist) Lothians, Scottish Parliament, 2003–07; National Convenor, Scottish Socialist Party, since 2005; *b* 17 June 1959; *s* of John Fox and Agnes Fox (*née* Mackin); partner, Zillah Jones; one *s* one *d*. *Educ:* Our Lady's High Sch., Motherwell; Bell Coll., Hamilton (SHND Accounting); Open Univ. (BSc Hons Soc. Sci. 2012). Political organiser (militant), 1983–95; Scottish Socialist Alliance organiser, 1995–98; Scottish Socialist Party: Founder Mem., 1998; Organiser, 1998–2003. Contested (Scot Socialist): Edinburgh SW, 2010; Edinburgh S, 2015. Mem., 'Yes Scotland' Adv. Bd for Independence, 2012–. Co-organiser, Edinburgh Mayday Fest., 1998–; Founder/Organiser, Edinburgh People's Fest., 2002–. *Publications:* Motherwell is Won for Moscow, 1991; (jtly) Whose Justice, 2006; End Fuel Poverty and Power Company Profiteering, 2012. *Recreations:* golf, reading.

FOX, Edward, OBE 2003; actor; *b* 13 April 1937; *s* of late Robin and Angela Muriel Darita Fox; *m* 1st, 1958, Tracy (*née* Pelissier) (marr. diss. 1961); one *d*; 2nd, 2004, Joanna David; one *s* one *d*. *Educ:* Ashfold Sch.; Harrow Sch. RADA training, following National Service, 1956–58; entry into provincial repertory theatre, 1958, since when, films, TV films and plays, and plays in the theatre, have made up the sum of his working life. *Theatre includes:* Knuckle, Comedy, 1973; The Family Reunion, Vaudeville, 1979; Anyone for Denis, Whitehall, 1981; Quartermaine's Terms, Queen's, 1981; Hamlet, Young Vic, 1982; Interpreters, Queen's, 1985; Let Us Go Then, You and I, Lyric, 1987; The Admirable Crichton, Haymarket, 1988; (also dir) Another Love Story, Leicester Haymarket, 1990; The Philanthropist, Wyndham's, 1991; The Father, tour, 1995; A Letter of Resignation, Comedy, 1997; The Chiltern Hundreds, Vaudeville, 1999; The Browning Version, and The Twelve-Pound Look, Th. Royal, Bath, 2002; The Winslow Boy, tour, 2002; The Old Masters, Comedy, 2004; You Never Can Tell, Th. Royal, Bath, 2005, Garrick, 2005–06; Legal Fictions, tour, 2007; Lloyd George Knew My Father, tour, 2009–10; Trollope in Barsetshire, tour, 2010, Riverside Studios, 2011; The Audience, Gielgud, 2013; An Ideal Husband, Chichester Fest. Th., 2014. T. S. Eliot's Four Quartets, tours in provinces, 2000–, Riverside Studios, 2011. *Films include:* The Go-Between, 1971 (Soc. of Film and Television Arts Award for Best Supporting Actor, 1971); The Day of the Jackal, A Doll's House, 1973; Galileo, 1976; The Squeeze, A Bridge Too Far (BAFTA Award for Best Supporting Actor, 1977), The Duellists, The Cat and the Canary, 1977; Force Ten from Navarone, 1978; The Mirror Crack'd, 1980; Gandhi, 1982; Never Say Never Again, The Dresser, 1983; The Bounty, 1984; The Shooting Party, 1985; A Month by the Lake, 1996; Stage Beauty, 2004. *Television series include:* Hard Times, 1977; Edward and Mrs Simpson, 1978 (BAFTA Award for Best Actor, 1978; TV Times Top Ten Award for Best Actor, 1978–79; British Broadcasting Press Guild TV Award for Best Actor, 1978; Royal TV Soc. Performance Award, 1978–79); They Never Slept, 1991; A Dance to the Music of Time, 1997; Daniel Deronda, 2002; Oliver Twist, 2007. *Recreations:* music, reading, walking. *Club:* Savile.

See also J. Fox, R. M. J. Fox, Viscount Gormanston.

FOX, Fiona Bernadette, (Mrs Kevin Rooney), OBE 2013; Founding Director and Chief Executive, Science Media Centre, since 2001; *b* Mancot, Wales, 12 Nov. 1964; *d* of late John Fox and of Maura Fox; *m* 1996, Kevin Rooney; one *s*. *Educ:* St Richard Gwyn High Sch., Flint; Poly. of Central London (BA Hons Journalism). Press Manager, NCOPF, 1984–86; Press Officer, EOC, 1986–92; Asst Press Officer, Thames Poly., 1992–93; Sen. Press Manager, Brook Adv. Centres, 1993–95; Hd of Media, CAFOD, 1995–2001. Chair, Science and the Media: securing the future, BIS report, 2010. *Publications:* (contrib.) Communicating Biological Sciences, 2009. *Recreations:* news junkie, Celtic FC supporter. *Address:* Science Media Centre, 215 Euston Road, NW1 2BE. *T:* (020) 7611 8300. *E:* fiona@sciencemediacentre.org.

See also Claire Fox.

FOX, Hazel Mary, (Lady Fox), CMG 2006; Director, British Institute of International and Comparative Law, 1982–89; General Editor, International and Comparative Law Quarterly, 1987–98; *b* 22 Oct. 1928; *d* of J. M. B. Stuart, CIE; *m* 1954, Rt Hon. Sir Michael Fox, PC (*d* 2007); three *s* one *d*. *Educ:* Roedean Sch.; Somerville Coll., Oxford (1st Cl. Jurisprudence, 1949; MA). Called to the Bar, Lincoln's Inn, 1950 (Buchanan Prize; Bencher, 1989); practised at the Bar, 1950–54 and 1994–2011; Fellow of Somerville Coll., Oxford, 1976–81, Hon. Fellow 1988. Chairman: London Rent Assessment Panel, 1977–98; London Leasehold Valuation Tribunal, 1981–98; Mem., Home Office Deptl Cttee on Jury Service, 1963–65. Mem., Institut de droit international, 2001. Hon. QC 1993. JP London, 1959–77; Chm., Tower Hamlets Juvenile Court, 1968–76. *Publications:* (with J. L. Simpson) International Arbitration, 1959; (ed) International Economic Law and Developing States, vol. I 1988, vol. II 1992; (ed) Joint Development of Offshore Oil and Gas, vol. I 1989, vol. II 1990; (ed jtly)

Armed Conflict and the New Law, vol. II: Effecting Compliance, 1993; The Law of State Immunity, 2002, 3rd edn (with P. Webb) 2013. *Address:* 4/5 Gray's Inn Square, WC1R 5AH. *T:* (020) 7404 5252, *Fax:* (020) 7242 7803.

FOX, James; actor; *b* 19 May 1939; *s* of late Robin and Angela Fox; changed forename from William to James, 1962; *m* 1973, Mary Elizabeth Piper; four *s* one *d. Educ:* Harrow Sch.; Central Sch. of Speech and Drama. National Service, 1959–61. Entered acting as child, 1950; left acting to pursue Christian vocation, 1970–79; returned to acting, 1980. Main *films* include: The Servant, 1963; King Rat, 1964; Thoroughly Modern Millie, 1965; The Chase, 1966; Isadora, 1968; Performance, 1969; A Passage to India, 1984; Runners, 1984; Farewell to the King, 1987; Finding Mawbee (video film as The Mighty Quinn), 1988; She's Been Away, 1989; The Russia House, 1990; Afraid of the Dark, 1991; The Remains of the Day, 1993; Anna Karenina, 1997; Mickey Blue Eyes, 1999; Up the Villa, 1999; Sexy Beast, 1999; The Golden Bowl, 1999; The Prince and Me, 2004; Charlie and the Chocolate Factory, 2005; Mr Lonely, 2006; Sherlock Holmes, 2009; A Long Way From Home, 2012; The Double, 2012; Effie, 2013; *screenplay:* Under Western Eyes, 2009; *theatre* includes: Uncle Vanya, NY, 1995; Resurrection Blues, Old Vic, 2006; Dear Lupin, Apollo Th., 2015; *television* includes: The Choir (serial), 1995; Gulliver's Travels, 1996; The Lost World, 2001; The Falklands (play), 2002; Suez, 2006; Margaret, 2008. Writer and Dir, Lara and Zhivago, 2010; Utopia, 2012; London Spy, 2014. *Publications:* Comeback: an actor's direction, 1983. *Recreations:* Russian language and culture, wind surfing. *Address:* c/o Dalzell & Beresford Ltd, Paddock Suite, The Courtyard, 55 Charterhouse Street, EC1M 6HA.

See also E. Fox, R. M. J. Fox.

FOX, (James) Robert (Rutherford), MBE 1982; Defence Editor, Evening Standard, since 2013 (Defence Correspondent, since 1999); *b* Ratley, Warks, 21 Sept. 1945; *s* of George and Patricia Fox; *m* 1971, Fyne Marianne Ockinga; one *s* one *d. Educ:* Blundell's Sch.; Magdalen Coll., Oxford (BA Hons Modern Hist. 1967; MA 1970). News Producer, 1968–71, Producer, Talks and Documentaries, 1971–73, BBC Radio; Nat. Reporter, then Internat. Corresp., BBC, 1973–87; Defence Chief Foreign Corresp., Daily Telegraph, 1987–97; Special Corresp., Evening Standard, 1998–99. Churchill Fellow, 1982; Associate Fellow, Centre for Defence Studies, KCL, 2000–; Hon. Fellow, Strategic Studies Inst., Exeter Univ., 2013. Comr, Commonwealth War Graves Commn, 2012–. *Publications:* Eye Witness Falklands, 1982; Inner Sea: Mediterranean and its people, 1990; Camera in Conflict, 1995; Eyewitness to History, 2008. *Recreations:* small boats, Italy, standing and staring, music. *T:* (office) (020) 7607 6148. *E:* robfox45@gmail.com. *Clubs:* Garrick, Academy, Beefsteak, Frontline.

FOX, John; *see* Fox, A. J.

FOX, John Rupert Anselm; a Vice President, Immigration Appeal Tribunal, 2000–04 (Legal Member, 1996–2005); an Adjudicator, Immigration and Asylum Appeals, 1990–2005; *b* 10 Dec. 1935; *s* of John Arnold Fox, MBE (mil.) and Eleanor Margaret Fox (*née* Green); *m* 1965, Isabel June Mary Jermy Gwyn; three *s* one *d* (and two *s* one *d* decd). *Educ:* Stonyhurst Coll. 2nd Lieut, RASC, 1954; transf. to Cheshire Yeo., 1958; Capt. 1959; RAC Reserve of Officers, 1966. Admitted solicitor, 1960; articled to Simpson North Harley & Co., London and Liverpool, 1953, Solicitor, Liverpool, 1960–62; Partner, Whatley Weston & Fox, Worcester, Malvern and Hereford, 1963–76; Asst Dir/Legal Advr, Foreign Investment Agency of Canada, 1976–78; Partner, John Fox Solicitors, Broadway, Worcs, 1978–91. Mem., Special Immigration Adv. Commn, 1999–2005. Under Sheriff, City of Worcester, 1965–76. Jt Sec., Liverpool River Pilots' Assoc., 1960–62. KM 1975 (Officer of Merit, Civil Div., 1980). *Recreations:* gardening, painting. *Address:* Calumet Cottage, 23 Old Road, Bromyard, Herefordshire HR7 4BQ. *T:* (01885) 489469. *Club:* Cavalry and Guards.

FOX, Prof. Keith Alexander Arthur, FRCPE, FMedSci; Duke of Edinburgh Professor of Cardiology, since 1989, and Head, Cardiology Section, Centre for Cardiovascular Sciences, University of Edinburgh; *b* 27 Aug. 1949; *m* Aileen Fox; one *s* one *d. Educ:* Falcon Coll.; Univ. of Edinburgh (BSc 1972; MB ChB 1974). FRCPE 1987. Asst Prof. of Medicine, Univ. of Washington, 1980–85; Sen. Lectr in Cardiol. and Hon. Cons. Cardiologist, UWCM, 1985–89. Pres., British Cardiovascular Soc., 2009–12. FESC 1988 (Chm., Clinical Prog. Cttee, 2012–14); FMedSci 2001. *Address:* Centre for Cardiovascular Science, Chancellor's Building, 49 Little France Crescent, Edinburgh EH16 4SB; Flat 20, 21 Simpson Loan, Edinburgh EH3 9GD.

FOX, Kenneth Lambert, FCIPS; public sector consultant, since 1986; *b* 8 Nov. 1927; *s* of J. H. Fox, Grimsby, Lincolnshire; *m* 1959, P. E. Byrne; one *d. Educ:* City of London Coll.; Univ. of London. BSc (Hons); MIIM. Plant Manager, Rowntree Gp, 1950–63; Supply Manager, Ford Motor Co. (UK), 1963–67; Sen. Management Conslt, Cooper & Lybrand Ltd, 1967–70; Manager of Conslts (Europe), US Science Management Corp., 1971–72; Supply Management, British Gas Corp., 1972–75; Dir of Supplies, GLC, 1975–86. *Recreations:* tennis, painting, bird watching, DIY. *Address:* 9 Dolphin Lane, Melbourn, Royston, Herts SG8 6AF. *T:* (01763) 206573.

FOX, Prof. Kevin Dyson, PhD; FMedSci; Professor of Neuroscience, Cardiff University, since 1996; *b* London, 1957; *s* of Kenneth Fox and Peggy Fox; *m* 1st, 1990, Helena Williams (marr. diss. 2003); two *s*; 2nd, 2009, Anwen John; two *s. Educ:* Buckhurst Hill Co. High Sch.; Univ. of Bath (BSc Hons Electrical and Electronic Engrg); London Hosp. Medical Coll., Univ. of London (PhD Neurophysiol. 1986). McDonnell Fellow, Sch. of Medicine, Washington Univ., St Louis, 1987–90; Res. Asst Prof., Brown Univ., Providence, 1990–93; Asst Prof., Sch. of Medicine, Univ. of Minnesota, 1993–96. Dep. Chm., Neurosci. and Mental Health Bd, MRC, 2008–12. Mem., REF 2014 Assessment Panel, 2014. MAE 2010; FMedSci 2013. *Publications:* Barrel Cortex, 2008; articles in Nature, Sci., Nature Neurosci., Neuron, Procs NAS. *Recreations:* music, film, poetry, hiking, ski-ing. *Address:* Cardiff School of Biosciences, Sir Martin Evans Building, Museum Avenue, Cardiff CF10 3AX. *E:* foxkd@cardiff.ac.uk.

FOX, Dr the Rt Hon. Liam; PC 2010; MP (C) North Somerset, since 2010 (Woodspring, 1992–2010); *b* 22 Sept. 1961; *s* of William Fox and Catherine Young; *m* 2005, Dr Jesmé Baird. *Educ:* St Bride's High Sch., E Kilbride; Univ. of Glasgow (MB ChB 1983). MRCGP 1989. General Practitioner, Beaconsfield, 1987–91; Army MO (civilian), RAEC, 1981–91; Divl Surgeon, St John's Ambulance, 1987–91. Contested (C) Roxburgh and Berwickshire, 1987. PPS to Home Sec., 1993–94; an Asst Govt Whip, 1994–95; a Lord Comr of HM Treasury (Govt Whip), 1995–96; Parly Under-Sec. of State, FCO, 1996–97; Opposition spokesman on constitutional affairs, 1997–99, on health, 1999–2001; Shadow Health Sec., 2001–03; Co-Chm., Cons. Party, 2003–05; Shadow Foreign Sec., 2005; Shadow Defence Sec., 2005–10; Sec. of State for Defence, 2010–11. Mem., Select Cttee on Scottish Affairs, 1992; Secretary: Cons. back bench Health Cttee, 1992–93; Cons. West Country Members Group, 1992–93. *Publications:* Making Unionism Positive, 1988; (contrib.) Bearing the Standard, 1991; Rising Tides: facing the challenges of a new era, 2013; contrib. to House of Commons Magazine. *Recreations:* tennis, swimming, cinema, theatre. *Address:* House of Commons, SW1A 0AA. *T:* (020) 7219 4086.

FOX, Ven. Michael John; Archdeacon of West Ham, 1996–2007; *b* 28 April 1942; *s* of John and Dorothy Fox; *m* 1966, Susan Cooper; one *s* one *d. Educ:* Barking Abbey GS; Hull Univ. (BSc); Coll. of the Resurrection, Mirfield. Ordained deacon, 1966, priest, 1967; Curate: St Elizabeth, Becontree, 1966–70; Holy Trinity, S Woodford, 1970–72; Vicar: Ch. of the Ascension, Victoria Docks, and Missioner, Felsted Sch., 1972–76; All Saints, Chelmsford, 1976–88; Asst RD and RD, Chelmsford, 1982–88; Rector, St James, Colchester, 1988–93; Archdeacon of Harlow, 1993–96. Hon. Canon, Chelmsford Cathedral, 1991–. *Recreations:* walking, photography, West Ham. *Address:* 17A Northgate Street, Colchester, Essex CO1 1EZ. *T:* (01206) 710701.

FOX, Sir Paul (Leonard), Kt 1991; CBE 1985; Managing Director, BBC Television Network, 1988–91; *b* 27 Oct. 1925; *m* 1948, Betty Ruth (*née* Nathan) (*d* 2009); two *s. Educ:* Bournemouth Grammar Sch. Served War, Parachute Regt, 6th Airborne Division, 1943–46. Reporter, Kentish Times, 1946; Scriptwriter, Pathé News, 1947; joined BBC Television, 1950: Scriptwriter, Television Newsreel; first Editor, Sportsview, 1953, Panorama, 1961; Head, Public Affairs, 1963, Current Affairs, 1965; Controller, BBC1, 1967–73; Dir of Progs, 1973–84, Man. Dir, 1977–88, Yorkshire Television. Chairman: ITN, 1986–88 (Dir, 1980–86); BBC Enterprises Ltd, 1988–91; Stepgrades Consultants, 1991–2002; Director: Trident Television, 1973–80; Channel Four, 1985–88; World Television News, 1986–88; Thames Television, 1991–95. Sports columnist, The Daily Telegraph, 1991–2003. Chm., Racecourse Assoc. Ltd, 1993–97; Director: British Horseracing Bd, 1993–97; Horseracing Betting Levy Bd, 1993–97. Chm., Disasters Emergency Cttee, 1996–99; Member: Royal Commn on Criminal Procedure, 1978–80; Inquiry into Police Responsibilities and Rewards, 1992–93. Pres., RTS, 1985–92; Mem. Cttee, Nat. Mus. of Film, Photography and TV, 1985–95; Trustee, Cinema and Television Benevolent Fund, 1987–90 and 1995–2002 (Pres., 1992–95). BAFTA Fellow, 1990. CCMI (CBIM 1987). Hon. LLD Leeds, 1984; Hon. DLitt Bradford, 1991. Cyril Bennett Award, for outstanding television programming, 1984; Founders Award, Internat. Council, US Nat. Acad. of TV Arts and Scis, 1989; RTS Gold Medal, for outstanding services to television, 1992. *Recreations:* travel, theatre, films. *Address:* 20 The Rose Walk, Radlett, Herts WD7 7JS. *E:* fox.sirpaul@gmail.com. *Club:* Garrick.

FOX, Peter Kendrew; University Librarian, University of Cambridge, 1994–2009, now Emeritus Librarian; Fellow of Selwyn College, Cambridge, since 1994; *b* 23 March 1949; *s* of Thomas Kendrew Fox and Dorothy Fox; *m* 1983, Isobel McConnell; two *d. Educ:* Baines GS, Poulton-le-Fylde; King's Coll., London (BA, AKC 1971); Sheffield Univ. (MA 1973); MA Cantab 1976; MA Dublin, 1984. ALA 1974; ALAI 1989. Cambridge University Library: grad. trainee, 1971–72; Asst Liby Officer, 1973–77; Asst Under-Librarian, 1977–78; Under-Librarian, 1978–79; Trinity College Dublin: Dep. Librarian, 1979–84; Librarian and Coll. Archivist, 1984–94; Vis. Fellow, 2011. Curator, Oxford Univ. Library Services, 2007–09. Chairman: SCONUL Adv. Cttee on Inf. Services, 1987–90; Bd of Dirs, Consortium of Univ. Res. Libraries, 1997–2000; Brotherton Collection Adv. Cttee, 1999–2002 (Mem., 1995–2002, 2009–11); Wellcome Trust Liby Adv. Cttee, 2000–05 (Mem., 1996–2005); Bd, Nat. Preservation Office, 2002–05 (Member: Mgt Cttee, 1996–2002; Bd, 2002–09); Gen. Sec., 2003–06, Vice-Pres., 2007–08, LIBER; Member: An Chomhairle Leabharlanna, Dublin, 1982–94; Cttee on Liby Co-operation in Ireland, 1983–94; Nat. Preservation Adv. Cttee, 1984–95; Adv. Cttee for Document Supply, 1991–95, Arts, Humanities and Social Scis Adv. Cttee, 2000–02, British Liby; Lord Chancellor's Adv. Council on Nat. Records and Archives (formerly Public Records), 2001–06; Legal Deposit Adv. Panel, DCMS, 2005–08; Long Room Hub Ext. Adv. Bd, TCD, 2008–12. *Publications:* Reader Instruction Methods in British Academic Libraries, 1974; Trinity College Library, Dublin, 1982; Trinity College Library Dublin: a history, 2014; *edited:* Treasures of the Library: Trinity College Dublin, 1986; Book of Kells: commentary vol. to facsimile edn, 1990; Cambridge University Library: the great collections, 1998; Proc. Internat. Confs on Library User Education, 1980, 1982, 1984; contrib. learned jls. *Address:* Selwyn College, Cambridge CB3 9DQ.

FOX, Prof. Renée Claire, PhD; FAAAS; Annenberg Professor of the Social Sciences, University of Pennsylvania, 1969–98, now Emerita (also Professor of: Sociology in Psychiatry, 1969–98; Sociology in Medicine, 1972–98; Sociology, School of Nursing, 1978–98); Senior Fellow, Center for Bioethics, University of Pennsylvania, 1999–2005, now Emerita; *b* 15 Feb. 1928; *d* of Paul Fred Fox and Henrietta Gold Fox. *Educ:* Smith Coll., Northampton, Mass (BA *summa cum laude* 1949); Harvard Univ. (PhD Sociol. 1954). Teaching Fellow, Harvard Univ., 1950–51; Columbia University: Res. Asst, Bureau of Applied Social Res., 1953–55; Res. Associate, 1955–58; Barnard College, New York: Lectr in Sociol., 1955–58; Asst Prof., 1958–64; Associate Prof., 1964–66; Harvard University: Lectr in Sociol., 1967–69; Res. Fellow, Center for Internat. Affairs, 1967–68; Res. Associate, Program on Technol and Soc., 1968–71; Consultant, Social Sci. Curriculum, Lincoln Center Coll., Fordham Univ., NY, 1968–70; University of Pennsylvania: Faculty Asst to Pres., 1971–72; Chm., Dept of Sociol., 1972–78. Res. Associate, Queen Elizabeth House, Internat. Develt Centre, Univ. of Oxford, 1999–2006. Numerous distinguished visiting appointments and lectureships; George Eastman Vis. Prof., Oxford Univ., 1996–97. Fellow, Amer. Acad. of Arts and Scis, 1971; FAAAS 1978; Member: Inst. of Med., US NAS, 1975; Amer. Philosophical Soc., 2012. Fellow, Explorers Club, 2014. Hon. Mem., Alpha Omega Alpha Honor Med. Soc., 2004. Hon. Dr: Medical Coll. of Pennsylvania, 1974; Smith Coll., Northampton, Mass, 1975; Katholieke Univ., Leuven, 1978; St Joseph's Univ., Philadelphia, 1978; La Salle, 1988; Hahnemann, 1991; Nottingham, 2002; Harvard, 2010; KCL, 2010; Hon. DSc Pennsylvania, 2011. Chevalier, Order of Leopold II (Belgium), 1995. *Publications:* (with W. de Craemer) The Emerging Physician: a sociological approach to the development of a Congolese medical profession, 1968; Experiment Perilous: physicians and patients facing the unknown, 1974, repr. with new epilogue, 1997; (with J. P. Swazey) The Courage to Fail: a social view of organ transplants and dialysis, 1974, rev. edn 1978; Essays in Medical Sociology: journeys into the field, 1979, 2nd edn 1988; (ed) The Social Meaning of Death, 1980; L'Incertitude Médicale, 1988; (jtly) Spare Parts: organ replacement in American society, 1992 (trans. Japanese 1999); The Sociology of Medicine: a participant observer's view, 1989 (trans. Korean 1993); In the Belgian Château: the spirit and culture of European society in the age of change, 1994 (French edn, with new epilogue, 1997); (ed jtly) Meanings and Realities of Organ Transplantation, 1996; (ed jtly) After Parsons: a theory of social action for the twenty-first century, 2005; (with J. P. Swazey) Observing Bioethics, 2008; In the Field: a sociologist's journey, 2010; Doctors Without Borders: humanitarian quests, impossible dreams of Médecins Sans Frontières, 2014; contrib. numerous articles on medical sociology, incl. articles on organ donation and transplantation, bioethics, med. res. and educn, and med. humanitarian action, to scientific and learned jls worldwide. *Address:* Sociology Department, University of Pennsylvania, 3718 Locust Walk, Philadelphia, PA 19104–6299, USA; The Wellington # 1104, 135 South 19th Street, Philadelphia, PA 19103, USA. *T:* (215) 5634912.

FOX, Prof. Robert, FSA; Professor of the History of Science, University of Oxford, and Fellow of Linacre College, 1988–2006; *b* 7 Oct. 1938; *s* of Donald Fox and Audrey Hilda Fox (*née* Ramsell); *m* 1964, Catherine Mary Lilian Roper Power; three *d. Educ:* Doncaster Grammar Sch.; Oriel Coll., Oxford (BA 1961; MA 1965; DPhil 1967; Hon. Fellow 2006). Asst Master, Tonbridge Sch., 1961–63; Clifford Norton Junior Res. Fellow, Queen's Coll., Oxford, 1965–66; University of Lancaster: Lectr, 1966; Sen. Lectr, 1972; Reader, 1975; Prof. of History of Science, 1987. Mem., Inst. for Advanced Study, Princeton, 1974–75 and 1985; Vis. Prof. and Mem., Davis Center for Historical Studies, Princeton Univ., 1978–79; Visiting Professor: Ecole des Hautes Etudes en Scis Sociales, Paris, 1984 and 2000; Johns Hopkins Univ., Baltimore, 2007; East Carolina Univ., Greenville, 2009; Dir, Centre de Recherche en Histoire des Sciences et des Techniques, Cité des Sciences et de l'Industrie, Paris, and Dir de recherche associé, Centre Nat. de la Recherche Scientifique, 1986–88; Asst Dir, Science Museum, 1988. President: IUHPS, 1995–97 (Pres., Div. of History of Science, 1993–97); European Soc. for History of Science, 2004–06. Mem., Eur. Acad. of Scis, 2015. Chevalier de l'Ordre des Palmes Académiques (France), 1998; Chevalier de l'Ordre des Arts et des Lettres (France), 2005. *Publications:* The Caloric Theory of Gases from Lavoisier to Regnault, 1971; Sadi Carnot: Réflexions sur la puissance motrice du feu, 1978 (trans. English 1986,

German 1987, Italian 1992); (ed jtly) The Organization of Science and Technology in France 1808–1914, 1980; The Culture of Science in France 1700–1900, 1992; (ed jtly) Education, Technology and Industrial Performance in Europe 1850–1939, 1993; Science, Technology, and the Social Order in Post-revolutionary France, 1995; (ed) Technological Change: methods and themes in the history of technology, 1996; (ed jtly) Luxury Trades and Consumerism in Ancien Régime Paris, 1998; (ed jtly) Natural Dyestuffs and Industrial Culture in Europe 1750–1880, 1999; (jtly) Laboratories, Workshops and Sites, 1999; (ed) Thomas Harriot: an Elizabethan man of science, 2000; (ed jtly) Physics in Oxford 1839–1939, 2005; (ed) Thomas Harriot: mathematics, exploration and natural philosophy in Early Modern England, 2012; The Savant and the State, 2012; (ed jtly) Oxford Handbook of the History of Physics, 2013. *Address:* Museum of the History of Science, Broad Street, Oxford OX1 3AZ. *T:* (01865) 512787. *Club:* Athenæum.

FOX, Robert; *see* Fox, J. R. R.

FOX, Dr Robert McDougall, FRCP, FRCPE; Editor: The Lancet, 1990–95; Journal of the Royal Society of Medicine, 1996–2005; *b* 28 Dec. 1939; *s* of Sir Theodore Fortescue Fox and Margaret Evelyn McDougall; *m* 1969, Susan Clark; two *s* one *d*. *Educ:* Univ. of Edinburgh (MB ChB); Open Univ. (Dip. Music 2009). MRCP 1993, FRCP 1996; FRCPE 1990. House physician, Western Gen. Hosp., Edinburgh; house surgeon, Royal Infirmary, Edinburgh; joined staff of The Lancet, 1968, Dep. Editor, 1976–90. Associate Editor, Circulation, 1995–2005. *Recreation:* bassoon and hoe. *Address:* Green House, Rotherfield, Crowborough, East Sussex TN6 3QU. *T:* (01892) 852850.

FOX, Robert Michael John; theatre, film and television producer; Managing Director, Robert Fox Ltd, since 1980; *b* 25 March 1952; *s* of late Robin Fox and Angela Fox; *m* 1st, 1975, Celestia Sporborg (marr. diss. 1990); one *s* two *d*; 2nd, 1990, Natasha Jane Richardson (marr. diss. 1994; she *d* 2009); 3rd, 1996, Fiona Golfar; one *s* one *d*. *Educ:* Harrow. Actor; runner for John Heyman at World Film Services; Asst Dir, Royal Court Th., 1971–73; PA, Michael White Ltd, 1973–80. *Productions* include: *theatre:* Goose Pimples, Garrick, 1981; Anyone For Denis?, Whitehall, 1981; Another Country, Queen's, 1982; The Seagull, Queen's, 1985; Chess, Prince Edward, 1986; Lettice and Lovage, Globe, 1987, NY, 1990; A Madhouse In Goa, Apollo, 1989; Anything Goes, Prince Edward, 1989; Burn This, Lyric, 1990; The Big Love, NY, 1991; When She Danced, Globe, 1991; The Ride Down Mount Morgan, Wyndham's, 1991; The Importance of Being Earnest, Aldwych, 1993; Vita & Virginia, Ambassadors, 1992, NY, 1994; Three Tall Women, Wyndham's, 1994; Burning Blue, Haymarket, 1995; Skylight, Wyndham's, 1995, 2014, NY, 1996, 2015, Vaudeville, 1997; Who's Afraid of Virginia Woolf?, Almeida, transf. Aldwych, 1996; Master Class, Queen's, 1997; A Delicate Balance, Haymarket, 1997; Amy's View, RNT, transf. Aldwych, 1997, NY 1999; Closer, RNT, transf. Lyric, 1998, NY 1999; The Judas Kiss (co-producer), Almeida, transf. Playhouse, NY, 1998, Duke of York's, 2013; The Boy from Oz (co-producer), Australia, 1998; The Lady in the Van, Queen's, 1999; The Blue Room, NY, 1999; The Caretaker, Comedy, 2000; The Breath of Life, Haymarket, 2002; Salome: the reading, NY, 2003, LA, 2006; Gypsy, NY, 2003; The Boy From Oz, NY, 2003, arena tour, 2006; The Pillowman, NY, 2005; Hedda Gabler, Almeida, transf. Duke of York's, 2005; Frost/Nixon, Gielgud, 2006, NY, 2007; The Vertical Hour, NY, 2006; The Lady from Dubuque, Haymarket, 2007; The Harder They Come, Playhouse, 2008; God of Carnage, NY, 2009, LA, 2011; Exit The King, NY, 2009; A Behanding in Spokane, NY, 2010; Hugh Jackman Back on Broadway, 2011; South Downs and The Browning Version, Harold Pinter Th., 2012; The Audience, Gielgud, 2013, Apollo, 2015, NY, 2015; Stephen Ward, Aldwych, 2014; Fatal Attraction, Haymarket, 2014; *films:* A Month by the Lake, 1996; Iris, 2001; The Hours, 2002; Closer, 2004; Notes on a Scandal, 2006; Atonement, 2007; Wilde Salome, 2011; *television:* Oscar's Orchestra, 1996; Working with Pinter, 2007. *Address:* (office) 6 Beauchamp Place, SW3 1NG. *T:* (020) 7584 6855, *Fax:* (020) 7225 1638.

See also E. Fox, J. Fox.

FOX, Robert Trench, (Robin), CBE 1993; Chairman, Lombard Risk Consultants, since 2000; *b* 1 Jan. 1937; *s* of Waldo Trench Fox and Janet Mary Kennedy Fox (*née* Bassett); *m* 1962, Lindsay Garrett Anderson; two *s* two *d*. *Educ:* Winchester Coll.; University Coll., Oxford (MA). FCIB. Kleinwort Benson Group, 1961–99; Vice-Chm., Kleinwort Benson Gp, 1989–97; Pres., Kleinwort Benson Asia Ltd, 1997–99. Chairman: Whiteaway Laidlaw Bank, 1997–2008 (Dir, 1992–2008); Boyer Allan Pacific Fund, 1998–12; Stone Drum Pacific Opportunities Fund, 2012–; Gaman Greater Europe Opportunities Fund, 2012–; Dir, InvestUK Ltd, 2012–. Chm., Export Guarantees Adv. Council, 1992–98; Mem., Overseas Projects Bd, 1988–98. Chm. Council, City Univ. Business Sch., 1991–99. *Recreations:* sailing, theatre, reading. *Address:* Lombard Risk Consultants, 7th Floor 60 Gracechurch Street, EC3V 0HR. *T:* (020) 7593 6770. *Clubs:* Brooks's; Royal Cornwall Yacht.

FOX, Robin James L.; *see* Lane Fox.

FOX-PITT, William; international three day event rider, since 1993; *b* 2 Jan. 1969; *s* of late Oliver Fox-Pitt and of Marietta Fox-Pitt; *m* 2003, Alice Plunkett; two *s* two *d*. *Educ:* Eton Coll.; Goldsmiths' Coll., London Univ. (BA Hons French 1993). Three day event rider, first competed at jun. level, 1984, also trainer, 1993–; winner: Burghley Horse Trials, 1994, 2002, 2005, 2007, 2008, 2011; British Open Championships, 1995, 2000, 2005; Badminton Horse Trials, 2004, 2015; Open European Championships: team Gold Medal, 1995; team Gold and individual Bronze Medal, 1997; team Gold Medal, 2001, 2003; team Gold and individual Silver Medal, 2005; team Gold, 2009; World Championships: team Bronze Medal, 2002; team Silver Medal, 2006; team Gold and individual Silver Medal, 2010; team Silver Medal, Olympic Games, Athens, 2004; team Bronze Medal, Olympic Games, Beijing, 2008; team Silver Medal, Olympic Games, London, 2012; represented GB in team at Atlanta Olympics, 1996; ranked British No 1, 2001, 2002, 2003, 2004, 2005, 2006, 2008, 2010 and 2011, World No 1, 2002, 2008 and 2010, World No 2, 2003, 2004, 2005, 2006 and 2011. Board Director: Professional Event Riders' Assoc., 1998–; British Eventing (formerly British Horse Trials Assoc.), 2000–. *Publications:* Schooling for Success, 2004; What Will Be: the autobiography, 2007. *Recreations:* ski-ing, jogging, travel.

FOX-STRANGWAYS, family name of **Earl of Ilchester**.

FOXALL, Colin, CBE 1995; rail industry adviser; reinsurance consultant, since 1997; Chairman, Passenger Focus, 2005–15; *b* 6 Feb. 1947; *s* of Alfred George Foxall and Ethel Margaret Foxall; *m* 2013, Helen Patricia Kaye. *Educ:* Gillingham Grammar Sch., Kent. MIEx; FICM. Joined ECGD, 1966; Dept of Trade, 1974; ECGD, 1975–91: Underwriter, Eastern Bloc, 1975; Dep. Hd, For. Currency Branch, 1977; Hd, Financial Planning, 1979; Asst Sec., ME Project Gp, 1982; Under Sec., and Dir of Comprehensive Guarantee, subseq. Insce Services, Gp, 1986–91; Man. Dir and Chief Exec., NCM Credit Insurance Ltd, 1991–97; Vice-Chm., NCM (Hldg) NV, 1996–97. Dir, Radian Asset Assurance Ltd, 2003–08; Bd Advr, Classic Construction, 2003–04; Advr, Aon Benfield, 2007–10. Member: Rail Passengers Council, 2004–05; British Transport Police Authy, 2005–. *Recreations:* clay target shooting, farming. *Address:* Brynglas Cottage, Devauden, Chepstow, Mon NP16 6NT.

FOXCROFT, Victoria Jane; MP (Lab) Lewisham, Deptford, since 2015. *Educ:* De Montfort Univ. (BA 2000). Research Officer, AEEU, 2002–05; Political Officer, Amicus the Union, 2005–09; Finance Sector Officer, Unite the Union, 2009–. Mem. (Lab) Lewisham LBC, 2010–14. *Address:* House of Commons, SW1A 0AA.

FOXELL, Clive Arthur Peirson, CBE 1987; FREng; consultant; Managing Director, Engineering and Procurement, and Board Member, British Telecom, 1986–89; *b* 27 Feb. 1930; *s* of Arthur Turner Foxell and Lillian (*née* Ellerman); *m* 1956, Shirley Ann Patey Morris; one *d*. *Educ:* Harrow High Sch.; Univ. of London. (BSc). FREng (FEng 1985); FIET, FInstP (Hon. FInstP 2002), FCIPS. GEC Res. Labs, 1947–68; Man., GEC Semiconductor Labs, 1968–71; Man. Dir, GEC Semiconductors Ltd, 1971–75; Dep. Dir of Research, PO, 1975–78; Dep. Dir, Procurement Exec., 1978–79; Dir of Purchasing, PO, 1980; British Telecom: Dir of Procurement, 1981–84; Senior Dir, 1984; Chief Exec., Procurement, 1984–86; Dir, British Telecommunications Systems Ltd, 1982–89. Chairman: Fulcrum Communications Ltd, 1985–86; TSCR Ltd, 1986–88; Phonepoint Ltd, 1989–93; Dir, BT&D Technologies Ltd, 1986–88. Institution of Electrical Engineers: Mem. Council, 1975–78, 1982–85, 1987–90; Vice-Pres., 1996–99; Chm., Electronics Div., 1983–84. Member: SERC (formerly SRC) Engrg Bd, 1977–80 (Chm., Silicon Working Party, 1980–81; Chm., Microelectronics, 1982–86); SERC, 1986–90; NEDC (electronics), 1987–90; ACARD Working Party on IT, 1981; Council, Foundn for Sci. and Technol., 1996–2002. Senator, Engrg Council, 1999–2002. Pres., Mobile Radio Trng Trust, 1991–95. President: IBTE, 1987–90; Inst. of Physics, 1992–94. Hon. Treas., Nat. Electronics Council, 1994–99. Bulgin Premium, IERE, 1964. Liveryman, Engineers' Co. Hon. DSc Southampton, 1994. *Publications:* Low Noise Microwave Amplifiers, 1968; Chesham Shuttle, 1996; Chesham Branch Album, 1998; The Met & GC Joint Line, 2000; Memories of the Met & GC Joint Line, 2002; Rails to Metro-Land, 2005; The Metropolitan Line: London's first underground railway, 2010; The Ten Cinemas of Chesham, 2010; The Lowndes Chesham Estate: the early photographs, 2011; 150 Years of the Metropolitan Railway, 2012; Echoes of the 'MET' Line, 2014; articles and papers on electronics. *Recreations:* photography, railway history and engineering. *Address:* 4 Meades Lane, Chesham, Bucks HP5 1ND. *T:* (01494) 785737.

FOXON, Prof. (Charles) Thomas (Bayley), PhD; FRS 2006; Professor of Physics, University of Nottingham, 1991, now Emeritus Research Professor. *Educ:* BSc, PhD. Sen. Principal Scientist, Philips Res. Labs, until 1991. *Publications:* articles in learned jls. *Address:* School of Physics and Astronomy, University of Nottingham, University Park, Nottingham NG7 2RD.

FOXTON, David Andrew; QC 2006; PhD; a Recorder, since 2009; *b* 14 Oct. 1965; *s* of Adrian and Catherine Foxton; *m* 1992, Heather Crook; two *s* two *d*. *Educ:* Glasgow Acad.; Magdalen Coll., Oxford (MA, BCL); King's Coll. London (PhD). Called to the Bar, Gray's Inn, 1989, Bencher, 2009; in practice, specialising in commercial law. Vis. Prof. of Law, Univ. of Nottingham, 2007–. Mem. Cttee, Church Urban Fund, 2006–. Trustee: St Albans Cathedral Music Trust, 2009–; Magdalen Coll. Develt Trust, 2009–. Freeman, City of London, 2007. *Publications:* Scrutton on Charterparties, 20th edn 2008, 21st edn 2011; Revolutionary Lawyers: Sinn Fein and Crown Courts in Britain and Ireland 1916–1923, 2008; The Life of T. E. Scrutton, 2013; articles in legal jls. *Recreations:* Irish history, sport (especially cricket and football), dog walking, child-ferrying and other forms of travel. *Address:* Essex Court Chambers, 24 Lincoln's Inn Fields, WC2A 3EG. *T:* (020) 7813 8000, *Fax:* (020) 7813 8080. *Club:* Athenæum.

FOY, John Leonard; QC 1998; a Recorder, since 2000; *b* 1 June 1946; *s* of late Leonard James Foy and Edith Mary Foy; *m* 1972, Colleen Patricia Austin (*d* 2006); one *s*. *Educ:* Dartford GS; Birmingham Univ. (LLB Hons 1967). Called to the Bar, Gray's Inn, 1969, Bencher, 2004; in practice at the Bar, 1969–. Judge (formerly Mem.), Mental Health Review Tribunal, 2003–. *Publications:* contribs to various legal books and jls. *Recreations:* watching West Bromwich Albion, football, Rugby, reading modern literature. *Address:* 9 Gough Square, EC4A 3DG. *T:* (020) 7832 0500.

FRACKOWIAK, Prof. Richard Stanislaus Joseph, MD, DSc; FRCP, FMedSci; Professor of Neurology, Chairman of Department of Clinical Neurosciences, and Head of Neurology Service, Centre Hospitalier Universitaire Vaudois, University of Lausanne, 2009–15, now Professeur ordinaire ad hominem and médecin associé; Titular Professor, Faculty of Life Sciences, Ecole Polytechnique Fédérale de Lausanne, since 2013; Director (Medicine), Human Brain Project, European Union, since 2013; *b* 26 March 1950; *s* of Joseph Frackowiak and Wanda (*née* Majewska); *m* 1st, 1972, Christine Jeanne Françoise Thepot (marr. diss. 2004); one *s* two *d*; 2nd, 2004, Laura Frances Spinney. *Educ:* Latymer Upper Sch.; Peterhouse, Cambridge (Wilhelm Brauer Open Schol.; MA); Middlesex Hosp. Med. Sch. (MB BChir; MD 1983); DSc London 1996. FRCP 1987. Sen. Lectr, 1984–90, Prof. of Neurology, 1990–94, RPMS and Hammersmith Hosp.; Consultant Neurologist: Hammersmith Hosp., 1984–95; Nat. Hosp. for Neurology and Neurosurgery, 1984–; MRC Trng Fellow, 1980–81; MRC Clinical Scientist, 1984–94; Wellcome Principal Res. Fellow, 1994–2003; Institute of Neurology, London University: Prof. and Chm., Wellcome Dept of Cognitive Neurol., 1994–2002; Dir, Leopold Muller Functional Imaging Lab., 1994–2002; Dean, 1998–2002; Vice-Provost, UCL, 2002–09; Hd, Dépt d'Etudes Cognitives, Ecole Normale Supérieure, Paris, 2004–09. Adjunct Prof. of Neurology, Cornell Univ. Med. Sch., NY, 1990; Visiting Professor: Wellcome Lab. of Neurobiol., UCL, 1991–95; Cath. Univ., Louvain, Belgium, 1996–97; Harvard Med. Sch., 1999; Yale Med. Sch., 2001; Hon. Prof. and Advr to Provost-Pres., UCL, 2009–. Scientific Advr to Dir-Gen. and Pres., Inserm, Paris, 2007–; Consultant, Lab. di neuroimagine, IRCCS Santa Lucia, Rome, 2003–. Non-exec. Dir, UCLH NHS Foundn Trust Bd, 2003–08. Chair, Med. Scis Cttee, Science Europe, 2012–; Mem., Steering Cttee, Scientific Panel for Health, Eur. Commn, 2015–. Member: Assoc. of British Neurologists, 1984; American Neurological Assoc., 1988 (Hon. Mem., 2000); Soc. Française de Neurologie, 1993; Academia Europaea, 1995; L'Academie Royale de Médecine de Belgique, 1995. Foreign Associate, Acad. Nat. de Médecine de France, 2000; Foreign Mem., Inst. of Medicine, Amer. Nat. Acads, 2009; Corresp. Mem., Polish Acad. of Scis, 2013. Founder FMedSci 1998 (Mem. Council, 2000–). Hon. Dr Liège 1999. Wilhelm Feldberg Foundn Prize, 1996; (jtly) Ipsen Prize for Neuronal Plasticity, Ipsen Foundn, Paris, 1997; Klaus Joachim Zulch Prize, Gertrud Reemtsma Foundn and Max Planck Soc., 2004. *Publications:* (jtly) Human Brain Function, 1997, 2nd edn 2004; Brain Mapping: the disorders, 2000; numerous on functional anatomy and organisation of the human brain using non-invasive monitoring techniques. *Recreations:* motorcycling, reading. *Address:* Service de neurologie BH 10–137, Centre Hospitalier Universitaire Vaudois, 46 rue du Bugnon, 1011 Lausanne, Switzerland. *T:* (79) 5565404. *Club:* Athenæum.

FRADD, Dame Elizabeth (Harriet), DBE 2009; independent health service adviser, since 2004; *b* Worcester Park, Surrey; *d* of Rev. Dr Norman Alan Birtwhistle and Edith Harriet Birtwhistle (*née* Abey); *m* 1976, Simon Oakley Fradd (marr. diss. 1998). *Educ:* Westminster Hosp. (SRN 1970; RSCN 1971); King's College Hosp. (SCM 1973); Croydon Coll. (HVCert 1981); Nottingham Univ. (MSc 1994). Sen. Nurse Manager, Children's Services, Nottingham Hosps, 1983–94; Nursing Officer, Children, DoH, 1994–95; Dir of Nursing and Educn, NHS West Mid. Reg., 1995–99; Asst Chief Nurse, DoH, 1999–2000; Dir of Nursing and Dir for Review and Inspection, Commn for Health Improvement, 2000–04. Hon. Sen. Lectr, Univ. of Birmingham, 1995–2003; Vis. Prof. of Nursing, UCE, 1996; Special Prof. of Nursing, 2000, Vice Pres., 2012, Univ. of Nottingham. Chm., Health Visitor Taskforce, 2011–15; Mem., Children and Young People's Health Outcomes Forum, 2012–15. Trustee, Sue Ryder Care, 2004–10 (Vice-Chm., 2008–10); Vice-Pres., Rainbows Children's Hospice, 2005–; Patron, Together for Short Lives (formerly Ambassador, Children's Hospice UK), 2010–. Chm., Magdala Trust, 2000–15. Fellow, Queen's Nursing Inst., 2000. FRCN 2004. Hon. FRCPCH 2000. Hon. MFPH 2000. Mem., RSA, 2003–08. Mem. Court, Needlemakers' Co., 2008. Hon. DSc Wolverhampton, 2001; DUniv UCE, 2002; Hon. LLD

Nottingham, 2003. *Publications:* over 30 articles in professional jls incl. Nursing Times, Nursing Standard, Paediatric Nursing, Jl of Clin. Nursing, Community Outlook, Health Visitor, Senior Nurse, Nursing Mgt. *Recreations:* gardening, ski-ing, travel. *Address:* Greenways, 147 Tollerton Lane, Tollerton, Nottingham NG12 4FT. *T:* (0115) 937 5038. *E:* liz.fradd@btinternet.com.

FRAENKEL, Prof. Ludwig Edward, FRS 1993; Professor of Mathematics, School of Mathematical Sciences, University of Bath, since 1988; *b* 28 May 1927; *s* of Eduard David Mortier Fraenkel and Ruth (*née* von Velsen); *m* 1954, Beryl Jacqueline Margaret Currie; two *d. Educ:* Dragon Sch., Oxford; Univ. of Toronto Schs; Univ. of Toronto (BASc 1947; MASc 1948); MA Cantab 1964. SO, RAE, Farnborough, 1948–52; Res. Fellow, Univ. of Glasgow, 1952–53; Imperial College, London: Lectr, Aeronautics Dept, 1953–58, Reader 1958–61; Reader, Mathematics Dept, 1961–64; Lectr in Applied Maths, Univ. of Cambridge, 1964–75; Fellow, Queens' Coll., Cambridge, 1964–68; Prof., Maths Div., Univ. of Sussex, 1975–88. Sen. Whitehead Prize, London Math. Soc., 1989. *Publications:* An Introduction to Maximum Principles and Symmetry in Elliptic Problems, 2000; some 60 papers in jls ranging from Aeronautical Qly to Acta Mathematica. *Recreations:* ski-ing, cycling. *Address:* School of Mathematical Sciences, University of Bath, Bath BA2 7AY. *T:* (01225) 826249. *Club:* Ski of Great Britain.

FRAME, David William; Member, Baltic Exchange, since 1961 (Chairman, 1987–89); *b* 26 July 1934; *s* of William and Ursula Frame; *m* 1963, Margaret Anne Morrison; two *d. Educ:* Wellington College. Commissioned Royal Artillery, National Service. Qualified Chartered Accountant, 1960; joined Usborne & Son (London), 1961, Dir 1962; Dir, Usborne and Feedex subsid. cos and other cos. *Recreation:* golf (played for GB and Ireland in Walker Cup, 1961, for England, 1958–63). *Address:* Green Glades, 46 Frensham Vale, Lower Bourne, Farnham, Surrey GU10 3HT. *T:* (01252) 793272. *Clubs:* Royal and Ancient, Worplesdon Golf, Trevose Golf, Old Thorns Golf, Plettenberg Bay Golf.

FRAME, Frank Riddell; Deputy Chairman, Hongkong and Shanghai Banking Corporation, 1986–90; *b* 15 Feb. 1930; *s* of late William Graham Frame; *m* 1958, Maureen Willis Milligan; one *s* one *d. Educ:* Hamilton Academy; Univ. of Glasgow (MA, LLB); admitted solicitor, 1955. North of Scotland Hydro-Electric Board, 1955–60; UK Atomic Energy Authority, 1960–68; Weir Group plc, 1968–76 (Dir, 1971–76); joined Hongkong and Shanghai Banking Corp., as Gp Legal Advr, 1977, Exec. Dir, 1985–90; Advr to Bd, HSBC Hldgs plc, 1990–98. Chairman: South China Morning Post Ltd, 1981–87; Far Eastern Economic Review Ltd, 1981–87; Wallem Group Ltd, 1992–2004; Director: Marine Midland Banks Inc., 1986–90; The British Bank of the Middle East, 1986–91; Swire Pacific Ltd, 1986–90; Consolidated Press Internat. Ltd, 1988–91; Securities and Futures Commn, Hong Kong, 1989–90; Baxter Internat. Inc., 1992–2001; Edinburgh Dragon Trust plc, 1994–2011; Northern Gas Networks Ltd, 2004–11; Northumbrian Water Ltd, 2012–. DUniv Glasgow, 2001. *Publications:* (with Prof. Harry Street) The Law relating to Nuclear Energy, 1966. *Address:* The Old Rectory, Bepton, Midhurst, W Sussex GU29 0HX. *Club:* Brooks's.

FRAME, Rt Rev. John Timothy, DD; Dean of Columbia and Rector of Christ Church Cathedral, Victoria, BC, 1980–95; *b* 8 Dec. 1930; *m;* three *d. Educ:* Univ. of Toronto. Burns Lake Mission, Dio. Caledonia, 1957; Hon. Canon of Caledonia, 1965; Bishop of Yukon, 1968–80. *Address:* 2173 Tull Avenue, Courtenay, BC V9N 7S1, Canada.

FRAME, Ronald William Sutherland; author; *b* 23 May 1953; *s* of late Alexander D. Frame and Isobel D. Frame (*née* Sutherland). *Educ:* High Sch. of Glasgow; Univ. of Glasgow (MA Hons); Jesus Coll., Oxford (MLitt). Full-time author, 1981–; first Betty Trask Prize (jtly), 1984; Samuel Beckett Prize, 1986; Television Industries' Panel's Most Promising Writer New to TV Award, 1986. *Television* films: Paris, 1985; Out of Time, 1987; Ghost City, 1994; A Modern Man, 1996; M. R. James (Ghost Stories for Christmas), 2000; Darien: Disaster in Paradise, 2003; Cromwell, 2003; (contrib.) The Two Loves of Anthony Trollope, 2004; *radio* drama includes: Winter Journey, 1984; Cara, 1989; The Lantern Bearers, 1997; The Hydro (serial), 1997, 2nd series 1998, 3rd series 1999; Havisham, 1998; Maestro, 1999; Pharos, 2000; Sunday at Sant' Agata, 2001, 2013; Greyfriars, 2002; The Shell House, 2008; Blue Wonder, 2008; Pinkerton, 2010; The Dreamer, 2012; (adaptations): Don't Look Now, 2001; The Servant, 2005; The Razor's Edge, 2005; A Tiger for Malgudi, 2006; The Other Simenon: The Blue Room, 2007, Monsieur Monde Vanishes, 2009, Sunday, Striptease, 2010, In Case of Emergency, The Cat, The Little Man from Archangel, 2011; The Other Simenon 2: Teddy Bear, The Neighbours, The Venice Train, 2012; Before the Fact, 2013; The Other Simenon 3: Three Beds in Manhattan, The Confessional, A New Lease of Life, 2014. *Publications:* Winter Journey, 1984; Watching Mrs Gordon, 1985; A Long Weekend with Marcel Proust, 1986; Sandmouth People, 1987; A Woman of Judah, 1987; Paris, 1987; Penelope's Hat, 1989; Bluette, 1990; Underwood and After, 1991; Walking My Mistress in Deauville, 1992; The Sun on the Wall, 1994; The Lantern Bearers, 1999 (Scottish Book of the Year, Saltire Soc., 2000; Stonewall-Barbara Gittings Honor Award in Fiction, Amer. Liby Assoc., 2003); Permanent Violet, 2002; Time in Carnbeg, 2004; Unwritten Secrets, 2010; Havisham, 2012; contrib. weekly Carnbeg story, The Herald, 2008, The Scotsman, 2008–09; regular contrib. to Sunday Herald's Scottish Review of Bks. *Recreations:* swimming, walking in the wind, jazz. *Address:* c/o Faber & Faber Ltd (Authors), Bloomsbury House, 74–79 Great Russell Street, WC1B 3DA. *T:* (020) 7927 3800, *Fax:* (020) 7927 3801; c/o Laura Macdougall, Tibor Jones & Associates, 2nd Floor 2–6 Atlantic Road, SW9 8HY. *T:* (020) 7733 0555. *E:* laura@tiborjones.com. *W:* www.carnbeg.com.

FRAME, Rt Rev. Prof. Thomas Robert, PhD; Professor, School of Humanities and Social Sciences, since 2014, Director, Australian Centre for the Study of Armed Conflict and Society, since 2014, UNSW Australia (formerly University of New South Wales); *b* 7 Oct. 1962; *s* of Robert and Doreen Catherine Frame; *m* 1983, Helen Mary (*née* Bardsley); two *d. Educ:* Royal Australian Naval Coll. HMAS Creswell; Univ. of NSW (BA Hons 1985, PhD 1992); Univ. of Melbourne (DipEd 1986); MTh Sydney Coll. of Divinity 1993; Univ. of Kent at Canterbury (Lucas Tooth Schol., 1996–97; MA Hons 1997). Officer, RAN, 1979–92; ordained deacon, 1993, priest, 1994; Asst Priest, Wagga Wagga, 1993–95; Rector: Binda, 1995–99; Bungendore, 1999–2001; Anglican Bishop to Australian Defence Force, 2001–07; Dir, St Mark's Nat. Theol Centre, 2007–14. Res. Fellow, Mt Stromlo Observatory, ANU, 1999–2003; Lectr in Public Theol., St Mark's Nat. Theol Centre, 2000–02; Charles Sturt University: Vis. Fellow, Sch. of Humanities, 2000–06; Prof., 2007–14; Hd, Sch. of Theol., 2007–08. Vis. Prof., Sch. of Humanities and Social Scis, Univ. of NSW, 2013–14. W. J. Liu Prize for Excellence in Chinese Studies, Univ. of NSW, 1985. *Publications:* First In Last Out!: the Navy at Gallipoli, 1990; (with G. Swinden) The Garden Island, 1990; (ed jtly) Reflections on the RAN, 1991; Where Fate Calls: the HMAS Voyager tragedy, 1992; Pacific Partners: a history of Australian-American naval relations, 1992; HMAS Sydney: loss and controversy, 1993; Where the Rivers Run: a history of the Anglican parish of Wagga Wagga, 1995; (with G. Webster) Labouring in Vain: a history of Bishopthorpe, 1996; (with G. Webster) The Seven Churches of Binda, 1998; Binding Ties: an experience of adoption and reunion in Australia (autobiog.), 1999; The Shores of Gallipoli: naval aspects of the Anzac campaign, 2000; A Church for a Nation, 2000; (with K. Baker) Mutiny!: naval insurrections in Australia and New Zealand, 2001; (with D. Faulkner) Stromlo: an Australian observatory, 2003; Living by the Sword?: the ethics of armed intervention, 2004; 'No Pleasure Cruise': the story of the Royal Australian Navy, 2004; The Cruel Legacy: the tragedy of HMAS Voyager, 2005; The Life and Death of Harold Holt, 2005; (ed) Agendas for Australian Anglicanism, 2006; Church and State: Australia's imaginary wall, 2006; Anglicans in Australia, 2007; Children on Demand: the ethics of defying nature, 2008; Evolution in the Antipodes: Charles Darwin and Australia, 2009; Losing My Religion: unbelief in Australia, 2009; A House Divided: the Anglican quest for unity, 2010. *Recreations:* Rugby, reading biographies. *Address:* Australian Centre for the Study of Armed Conflict and Society, UNSW Australia, PO Box 7916, Canberra, ACT 2610, Australia. *E:* t.frame@adfa.edu.au.

FRAMLINGHAM, Baron *cr* 2011 (Life Peer), of Eye in the County of Suffolk; **Michael Nicholson Lord,** Kt 2001; *b* 17 Oct. 1938; *s* of John Lord and Jessie Lord (*née* Nicholson); *m* 1965, Jennifer Margaret (*née* Childs); one *s* one *d. Educ:* Christ's College, Cambridge. MA. FArborA. Arboricultural consultant. MP (C) Suffolk Central, 1983–97, Central Suffolk and N Ipswich, 1997–2010. PPS: to Minister of State, MAFF, 1984–85; to Chief Secretary to the Treasury, 1985–87; Second Dep. Chm. of Ways and Means and a Dep. Speaker, 1997–2010. Member: Select Cttee on Parly Comr for Admin, 1990–97; Council of Europe, 1987–91; WEU, 1987–91. *Recreations:* golf, sailing, gardening, trees.

See also Hon. T. M. Lord.

FRANCE, Annette Stephanie; Headteacher, Beaconsfield High School, since 2012; *b* Hitchin, Herts, 20 April 1952; *d* of Colin and Iris France; *m* (marr. diss.); two *d. Educ:* Thetford Grammar Sch. for Girls; Helsby Co. Grammar Sch. for Girls; Keele Univ. (BA Hons English and Psychol.); Nottingham Univ. (MEd; MSc). NPQH. Teaching posts in 14–19 Community Colls, Leics, 1975–2000; on secondment to Nat. Grid, 1995; Headteacher: Heart of England Sch., 2001–07; Chipping Campden Sch., 2007–12. Churchill Fellow, 1982. Nat. Leader of Educn, 2010–. *Publications:* Remembering and Forgetting, 1991; Perception, 1991. *Recreations:* travel, reading, writing, grandchildren. *Address:* 31 Whitebeam Close, Weston Turville, Bucks HP22 5YE. *T:* 07958 718325; Candle Cottage, Anchor Lane, Harvington, Worcs WR11 8NR. *E:* penlan52@gmail.com.

FRANCE, Elizabeth Irene, CBE 2002; Chairman: Security Industry Authority, since 2014; Police Advisory Board for England and Wales, since 2014; *b* 1 Feb. 1950; *d* of Ralph Salem and Elizabeth Joan Salem (*née* Bryan); *m* 1971, Dr Michael William France; two *s* one *d. Educ:* Beauchamp Sch., Leics; UCW, Aberystwyth (BScEcon Pol Sci.). Home Office: Admin. Trainee, 1971; Principal, 1977; Asst Sec., 1986; Police Dept, Criminal Justice and Constitutional Dept, IT and Pay Services, 1986–94; Data Protection Registrar, subseq. Comr, then Inf. Comr, 1994–2002; Telecommunications Ombudsman, 2002–09; Energy Supply Ombudsman, 2006–09; Surveyors Ombudsman, 2007–09; Chm., Office for Legal Complaints, 2009–14. Non-exec. Dir, Serious and Organised Crime Agency, 2005–10. Member: Commn for control of Interpol's files, 2001–05; Compliance Cttee, Aarhus Convention, 2003–05; British Transport Police Authy, 2010–; Ofgem Enforcement Decision Panel, 2014–; Chm., UK Public Affairs Council, 2010–13. Mem., Gen. Assembly (formerly Court), Univ. of Manchester, 2002–15; Vice-Pres., Aberystwyth Univ., 2008–. Fellow, Univ. of Wales, Aberystwyth, 2003. FRSA 1995. Hon. FICM 1999; Hon. Fellow, Inst. for Mgt of Inf. Systems, 2003. Hon. DSc De Montfort, 1996; Hon. DLitt Loughborough, 2000; Hon. LLD Bradford, 2002. *Address:* Security Industry Authority, PO Box 49768, London, WC1V 6WY.

FRANCE, Prof. Peter, DPhil; FBA 1989; FRSE; Professor of French, University of Edinburgh, 1980–90, now Emeritus (University Endowment Fellow, 1990–2000); *b* Londonderry, 19 Oct. 1935; *s* of Edgar France and Doris Woosnam Morgan; *m* 1961, Siân Reynolds; three *d. Educ:* Bridlington Sch.; Bradford Grammar Sch.; Magdalen Coll., Oxford (MA; DPhil). FRSE 2003. Lectr, then Reader, in French, Univ. of Sussex, 1963–80. French Editor, MLR, 1979–85. Jt Gen. Editor, Oxford History of Literary Translation in English (5 vol. series), 2005–. Mem., Chuvash Nat. Acad., 1991. Dr *hc* Chuvash State Univ., 1996. Officer de l'Ordre des Palmes Académiques (France), 1990; Chevalier, Légion d'Honneur (France), 2001. *Publications:* Racine's Rhetoric, 1965; Rhetoric and Truth in France, 1972; Poets of Modern Russia, 1982; Racine: Andromaque, 1977; Diderot, 1983; Rousseau: Confessions, 1987; trans., An Anthology of Chuvash Poetry, 1991; Politeness and its Discontents, 1992; (ed) New Oxford Companion to Literature in French, 1995; trans., Gennady Aygi, Selected Poems, 1997; (ed) Oxford Guide to Literature in English Translation, 2000; (ed) Mapping Lives: the uses of biography, 2002; (ed jtly) Oxford History of Literary Translation in English, vol. 4: 1790–1900, 2006; trans., Gennady Aygi, Field-Russia, 2007; (ed jtly) After Lermontov: translations for the bicentenary, 2014. *Address:* 10 Dryden Place, Edinburgh EH9 1RP. *T:* (0131) 667 1177.

FRANCE, Valerie Edith, (Lady France), OBE 1994; MA; Headmistress, City of London School for Girls, 1986–95; *b* 29 Oct. 1935; *d* of Neville Larman, DFC and Edith Larman; *m* 1961, Sir Christopher Walter France, GCB (*d* 2014); one *s* one *d. Educ:* St Hugh's Coll., Oxford (MA); CertEd Cantab. Deputy Headmistress, Bromley High Sch., GPDST, 1984–86; Acting Hd, Atherley Sch., Oct.–Dec. 1996. Mem., Eco-Schs Adv. Panel, 1996–2000. Member Council: Cheltenham Ladies' Coll., 1995–98; Francis Holland Schs Trust, 1997–2005 (Chm. Council, 1999–2005); Mem. Court, Whitgift Foundn, 1994–97; Gov., Trinity Sch., 1997–2003. FRGS 1959; FRSA 1991. Freeman, City of London, 1988; Liveryman, Needlemakers' Co., 1992–. *Recreations:* family, friends, places.

FRANCES DOMINICA, Sister; *see* Ritchie, Sister F. D. L.

FRANCIES, Michael Shaul; Managing Partner, London Office, Weil, Gotshal & Manges, since 1998; *b* Tiberius, Israel, 14 Oct. 1956; *s* of Anthony and Iris Francies; *m* 1979, Claire Heather Frome; three *s. Educ:* Kingsbury High Sch.; Manchester Univ. (LLB Hons); Coll. of Law, Lancaster Gate. Clifford Turner, subseq. Clifford Chance: articled clerk, 1979–81; Asst Solicitor, 1981–83 and 1984–86; Partner, 1986–98; Asst Dir and Co. Sec., Carlton Communications, 1983–84. *Recreations:* family, football, Rugby, reading, music. *Address:* Weil, Gotshal & Manges, 110 Fetter Lane, EC4A 1AT. *T:* (020) 7903 1000, *Fax:* (020) 7903 0990. *E:* michael.francies@weil.com.

FRANCIS, Arthur; *see* Francis, F. A. S.

FRANCIS, Barney; Managing Director, Sky Sports, since 2009; *b* Leicester, 23 June 1971; *s* of Tony and Jane Francis; *m* 2000, Amy; two *s. Educ:* Univ. of Liverpool (BA Hons Econ. Hist.). Granada TV, 1993–96; Sky TV, 1996–98; BBC, 1998–99; Sky TV, 1999–. *Address:* Sky Sports, British Sky Broadcasting Ltd, Grant Way, Isleworth, Middx TW7 5QD. *E:* barney.francis@bskyb.com.

FRANCIS, Clare Mary, MBE 1978; writer; *b* 17 April 1946; *d* of late Owen Francis, CB and Joan St Leger (*née* Norman); *m* 1977, Jacques Robert Redon (marr. diss. 1985); one *s. Educ:* Royal Ballet Sch.; University Coll. London (BScEcon; Fellow, 1978). Crossed Atlantic singlehanded, Falmouth to Newport, in 37 days, 1973; Observer Transatlantic Singlehanded Race: women's record (29 days), 1976; Whitbread Round the World Race (fully-crewed), first woman skipper, 1977–78. Chm., Soc. of Authors, 1997–99. Chm., Govt Adv. Cttee on PLR, 2000–03. Pres., Action for ME, 1990–. Hon. Fellow, UMIST, 1981. *Publications: non-fiction:* Come Hell or High Water, 1977; Come Wind or Weather, 1978; The Commanding Sea, 1981; *novels:* Night Sky, 1983; Red Crystal, 1985; Wolf Winter, 1987; Requiem, 1991; Deceit, 1993 (televised, 2000); Betrayal, 1995; A Dark Devotion, 1997; Keep Me Close, 1999; A Death Divided, 2001; Homeland, 2004; Unforgotten, 2008. *Recreations:* opera, walking. *Address:* c/o Johnson & Alcock Ltd, 45–47 Clerkenwell Green, EC1R 0HT.

FRANCIS, (David) Hywel, PhD; FRHistS; *b* 6 June 1946; *s* of late David Francis and of Catherine Francis (*née* Powell); *m* 1968, Mair Georgina Price; one *s* one *d* (and one *s* decd). *Educ:* UC, Swansea (BA 1968; PhD 1978). Admin. Asst, TUC, 1971–72; University College, Swansea, subseq. University of Wales Swansea: Sen. Res. Officer, 1972–74; Tutor/Lectr,

Contg Educn, 1974–87; Dir, Contg Educn, 1987–99; Prof., Contg Educn, 1992–99; Prof. Emeritus, 2006. Chm., Wales Congress in Support of Mining Communities, 1984–86; Nat. Convenor, Yes for Wales Campaign, 1997; Special Policy Advr, Sec. of State for Wales, 1999–2000. MP (Lab) Aberavon, 2001–15. Chair: Select Cttee on Welsh Affairs, 2005–10 (Mem., 2001–10); Jt Cttee on Human Rights, 2010–15; Member, All-Party Parliamentary Group: on Steel, 2001–15 (Sec., 2002–05; Chm., 2005–10); on Carers, 2005–15 (Chm., 2005–10); on Archives and History, 2010–15 (Chm., 2010–15); on Down's Syndrome, 2010–15 (Vice Chm., 2010–15). Introd Private Mem.'s Bill, Carers (Equal Opportunities), which received Royal Assent in 2004. Trustee: Paul Robeson Wales Trust, 2001– (Chm., 2001–08); Bevan Foundn, 2001–. Chm., Richard Burton Adv. Bd, 2005–, Hon. Prof., 2013–, Swansea Univ. Pres., S Wales Miners' Mus., 2001–. Mem., Gorsedd of Bards, 1986. FRSA 1987; FRHistS 2011. Hon. DLitt Swansea, 2012. *Publications:* (with David Smith) The Fed: a history of the South Wales miners in the twentieth century, 1980, 2nd edn 1998; Miners against Fascism: Wales and the Spanish Civil War, 1984, 3rd edn 2012; Wales: a learning country, 1999; History on Our Side: Wales and the 1984–85 miners' strike, 2009, 2nd edn 2015; (with Sian Williams) Do Miners Read Dickens?: origins and progress of the South Wales Miners' Library 1973–2013, 2013. *Recreations:* photography, walking, reading. *Address:* Swansea University, Singleton Park, Swansea SA2 8PP. *Clubs:* Port Talbot Cricket (Pres.); Aberavon Rugby Football (Vice-Pres.); Seven Sisters Rugby Football (Pres.); Onllwyn Miners' Welfare (Trustee).

FRANCIS, Elizabeth Ann, (Lisa); Member (C) Wales Mid and West, National Assembly for Wales, 2003–07; *b* 29 Nov. 1960; *d* of Thomas Foelwyn and Dilys Olwen Francis. *Educ:* Ardwyn Grammar Sch.; W London Inst. of Higher Educn. PA to Gp Chief Exec., Lead Industries Gp Ltd; Managerial Sec., African Dept, Glaxo Gp; Manager, Queensbridge Hotel, Aberystwyth, 1985–2002; Dir, Mid Wales Tourism Co., 2002–. *Recreations:* reading, travel, theatre, opera, swimming in the sea, cooking for friends.

FRANCIS, Canon Prof. (Frederick) Arthur (Stratton); Professor of Management and Dean, Bradford University School of Management, 1998–2010, now Emeritus Professor; *b* 16 Dec. 1944; *s* of late Arthur James Stratton Francis and Jessie Margery Francis; *m* 1969, Janice Mary Taylor; one *s* two *d*. *Educ:* Warwick Sch.; Imperial Coll., London (BSc Eng). Res. student and Res. Officer, Imperial Coll., London, 1967–73; Res. Officer, Nuffield Coll., Oxford, 1973–76; Lectr, then Sen. Lectr, Imperial Coll. Sch. of Mgt, 1976–92; University of Glasgow: Prof. of Corporate Strategy, Business Sch., 1992–98; Associate Dean (Res.), Faculty of Soc. Scis, 1992–98. Sen. Res. Fellow, ESRC, 1986–91; Member: ESRC Cttee on Mgt Res., 1991–93; ESRC Res. Progs Bd, 1991–94. Vis. Prof., Kobe Univ., 1989. Nat. Rep., European Gp for Organizational Studies, 1973–90; Chm., EC COST A3 Action on Mgt and New Technol., 1993–96. Vice Chm., then Chm., Assoc. of Business Schs, 2002–06 (Companion, 2008); Dean, Coll. of Fellows, British Acad. of Mgt, 2014. Chair, Abbeyfield The Dales Ltd, 2014–; Dir, Clarke-Foley Trust, 2014–. Chm. Council, Bradford Cathedral, 2000–14; Member: Bradford Diocesan Synod, 2012–, Diocesan Bd of Educn, 2013–14. Hon. Lay Canon, Bradford Cathedral, 2008–. Gov., Bradford Grammar Sch., 2008–. Fellow British Acad. of Mgt, 1997; CCMI 2000; FAcSS (AcSS 2009). *Publications:* (ed jtly) Power, Efficiency and Institutions, 1982; (jtly) Office Automation, Organisation and the Nature of Work, 1984; (jtly) Innovation and Management Control: labour relations at BL Cars, 1985; New Technology at Work, 1986; (ed jtly) New Technologies and Work: capitalist and socialist perspectives, 1989; (ed jtly) The Competitiveness of European Industry, 1989; (jtly) The Structure of Organizations, 1992; (ed jtly) Design, Networks and Strategies, 1995; articles in Sociology, Cambridge Jl of Econs, Organization Studies, Strategic Mgt Jl and Internat. Jl of Ops and Prodn Mgt. *Address:* High House, Main Street, Addingham, Ilkley, W Yorks LS29 0LY. *T:* (01943) 830264. *E:* a.francis@bradford.ac.uk.

FRANCIS, Gwyn Jones, CB 1990; Director-General and Deputy Chairman, Forestry Commission, 1986–90, retired; *b* 17 Sept. 1930; *s* of Daniel Brynmor Francis and Margaret Jane Francis (*née* Jones); *m* 1st, 1954, Margaretta Meryl Jeremy (*d* 1985); one *s* one *d* (and one *s* decd); 2nd, 1986, Audrey Gertrude (*née* Gill). *Educ:* Llanelli Grammar Sch.; University Coll. of N Wales, Bangor (BSc Hons 1952); Univ. of Toronto (MSc 1965). Served RE, 1952–54. Forestry Commission: Dist Officer, 1954; Principal, Forester Training Sch., 1962; Asst Conservator, 1969; Dir, Harvesting and Marketing Div., 1976; Comr, 1983–86. Mem. Council, 1992–98, and Chm., Scottish Cttee, 1992–98, RSPB. FICFor 1982; FIWSc 1984. Hon. Fellow, Univ. of Wales, 1991. *Recreations:* bird-watching, painting. *Address:* 2/16 Succoth Court, Succoth Park, Edinburgh EH12 6BZ. *T:* (0131) 337 5037. *Club:* New (Edinburgh).

FRANCIS, His Holiness Pope, (Jorge Mario Bergoglio), SJ; *b* Buenos Aires, 17 Dec. 1936; *s* of Mario Jose Bergoglio and Regina Maria Sivori. *Educ:* Escuela Nacional de Educación Técnica; Inmaculada Concepción Seminary, Villa Devoto, Buenos Aires; Colegio de San José, San Miguel (LPh 1960); Sankt Georgen Graduate Sch. of Philosophy and Theology, Frankfurt. Chemical Technician, Hickethier-Bachmann Laboratory; entered Soc. of Jesus, 1958; Teacher of Literature and Philosophy: Immaculate Conception Coll., Santa Fé, 1964–65; Colegio del Salvatore, Buenos Aires, 1966; ordained priest, 1969; Master of Novices and Prof. of Theology, Facultades de Filosofía y Teología de San Miguel; final profession, Soc. of Jesus, 1973; Provincial Superior, Soc. of Jesus, Argentina, 1973–79; Rector, Colegio de San José, San Miguel, 1980–86; Spiritual Dir and Confessor, Jesuit Church in Córdoba; Titular Bishop of Auca and Aux. Bishop of Buenos Aires, 1992–97; Episcopal Vicar, Flores District; Vicar-Gen., Archdiocese, 1993; Coadjutor Bishop of Buenos Aires, 1997; Archbishop and Primate of Argentina, 1998–2013; apptd Cardinal, 2001; elected Pope 13 March 2013. *Publications:* Meditaciones para religiosos, 1982; Reflexiones sobre la vida apostólica, 1992; Reflexiones de esperanza, 1992. *Address:* Apostolic Palace, 00120 Vatican City State.

FRANCIS, Sir (Horace) William (Alexander), Kt 1989; CBE 1976; FREng; FICE; Director, British Railways Board, 1994–97; *b* 31 Aug. 1926; *s* of Horace Fairie Francis and Jane McMinn Murray; *m* 1949, Gwendoline Maud Dorricott; two *s* two *d*. *Educ:* Royal Technical Coll., Glasgow. Dir, Tarmac Civil Engineering Ltd, 1960; Man. Dir, Tarmac Construction Ltd, 1963; Dir, Tarmac Ltd, 1964, Vice-Chm., 1974–77; Director: Trafalgar House Ltd, 1978–85; Trafalgar House Construction Hldgs, 1979–85; Trafalgar House Oil and Gas, 1986–88; Mining (Scotland) Ltd, 1995–98; Barr Holdings Ltd, 1994–2000; Chairman: Fitzpatrick Internat. Ltd, 1993–99; Enhanced Recovery Systems, 1999–2009. Member: Export Credit Guarantees Adv. Council, 1974–80; British Overseas Trade Bd, 1977–80; Chairman: Overseas Projects Bd, 1977–80; Black Country UDC, 1987–94; Midlands Enterprise Fund, 1996–99. Mem., Engrg Council, 1995–96. Pres., ICE, 1987–88 (Vice-Pres., 1984–87). Lt-Col, Engr and Transport Staff Corps, TA, 1982. FREng (FEng 1977). FRSA 1989. Hon. LLD Strathclyde, 1988; Hon. DSc Aston, 1990. *Recreations:* fishing, construction. *Address:* The Firs, Cruckton, near Shrewsbury, Shropshire SY5 8PW. *T:* (01743) 860796, *Fax:* (01743) 860969, *T:* (020) 7930 5008, *Fax:* (020) 7930 8473. *Clubs:* Army and Navy, Livery.

FRANCIS, Hywel; *see* Francis, D. H.

FRANCIS, Jennifer Faure; Executive Director of Marketing, Philadelphia Museum of Art, since 2012; *b* 13 July 1959; *d* of Luke Redmond Faure and Clytie Jeanne Francis; two *s*. *Educ:* St Augustine's C of E Sch., London; City Univ. (DipCAM; MA Cultural Leadership Policy and Mgt 2011). MCIPR (MIPR 1989). Br. Manager, Brook Street Bureau, 1980–83; PR, Cannons Sports Club, 1983–85; freelance PR, 1985–86; Man. Dir, Networking Public Relations, then Head of African, Caribbean, Asian and Pacific Gp, Pielle Public Relations, 1986–92; PR, LAPADA, 1999; Mktg Dir and Fest. Organiser, Carriacou Maroon Music. Fest., 2000–07; Diversity Project Manager, London Tourist Bd, 2003; Dir of Communications, The Drum, 2003–04; Hd of Press and Marketing, RA, 2004–12. Actg Hd of Media Relations, V&A Mus., 1998; Actg Dir of Public Relations—The Show, RCA, 1999. Member: Media Adv. Gp, CRE, 1990–91; Nat. Consumer Council, 1991–94; ITC Advertising Adv. Cttee, 1992–99; Prince's Youth Business Trust Ethnic Minority Adv. Gp, 1993–99; Radio Authority, 1994–99; London Regl Bd, Arts Council England, 2009–12; Chm., Women's Enterprise Develt Agency, 1990–93. Black Business Woman of the Year, 1989. *Publications:* contrib. to periodicals. *Recreations:* watercolours, travel, current affairs, music.

FRANCIS, Dr John Michael, FRSE; Consultant and Adviser, UNESCO, since 2000 (Chair: UK National Commission, 1999–2003; Sustainable Development, Peace and Human Rights, UK UNESCO, 1999–2003; Deputy Chair, Scotland Committee, since 2007); *b* 1 May 1939; *s* of late William Winston Francis and Beryl Margaret Francis (*née* Savage); *m* 1963, Eileen Sykes, Cyncoed, Cardiff; two *d*. *Educ:* Gowerton County Grammar Sch.; Royal Coll. of Sci., Imperial Coll. of Sci. and Technol., Univ. of London (BSc, ARCS, PhD, DIC). FRIC 1969; FRSGS 1990; FRSE 1991; FRZSScot 1992. Res. Officer, CEGB, R&D Dept, Berkeley Nuclear Labs, 1963–70; First Dir, Society, Religion and Tech. Project, Church of Scotland, 1970–74; Sen. Res. Fellow in Energy Studies, Heriot-Watt Univ., 1974–76; Scottish Office, Edinburgh, 1976–84; Dir Scotland, Nature Conservancy Council, 1984–91 (Mem., Adv. Cttee for Scotland, 1974–76); Chief Exec., NCC for Scotland, 1991–92; Asst Sec., Envmt Dept, 1992–95, Sen. Policy Advr, Home Dept, 1995–99, Scottish Office. Member: Oil Develt Council for Scotland, 1973–76; Ind. Commn on Transport, 1974; Adv. Cttee on Marine Fishfarming Crown Estate Commn, 1989–92. Chm., Francis Group (Consultants), 1992–99. Consultant on Sci., Tech. and Social Ethics, WCC, Geneva, 1971–83; Church of Scotland: Chm., Cttee on Society, Religion and Technol., 1980–94; Trustee, Society, Religion and Technol. Project Trust, 1998–2007; Member: Church and Nation Cttee, 2000–05; Church and Society Council, 2005–12. Chm., Edinburgh Forum, 1984–93. Mem. Council, Nat. Trust for Scotland, 1985–92. Mem., St Giles' Cathedral, Edinburgh. Associate, Scottish Inst. of Human Relations, 1974–94; Member: Scottish Univs Policy, Res. and Advice Network, 1999–2012; Internat. Develt Gp, Scottish Parlt, 2001–; Steering Gp, Scottish Sustainable Develt Forum, 2004–11; Exec. Bd, Centre for Theology and Public Issues, Univ. of Edinburgh, 2005–10; Governing Bd, UNESCO Centre for Water Law, Policy and Sci., Univ. of Dundee, 2008–; Internat. Cttee, RSE, 2009–12. Trustee, RSE Scotland Foundn, 2004–07. Fellow, Inst. for Advanced Studies in the Humanities, Edinburgh Univ., 1988; Hon. Fellow, Edinburgh Univ., 2000–10; Vis. Fellow, Centre for Values and Social Policy, Univ. of Colorado at Boulder, 1991; UK Rep., Millennium Proj., UN Univ., 1992–2004. Professional Mem., World Futures Soc., Washington DC, 1991–; Mem., UNA, 2004– (Convener, UNA Edinburgh, 2006–07). Mem., John Muir Trust, 1994–2010. *Publications:* Scotland in Turmoil, 1973; (jtly) Changing Directions, 1974; (jtly) The Future as an Academic Discipline, 1975; Facing up to Nuclear Power, 1976; (jtly) The Future of Scotland, 1977; (jtly) North Sea Oil and the Environment, 1992; (jtly) Democratic Contracts for Sustainable and Caring Societies, 2000; (jtly) Conserving Nature, 2005; contribs to scientific and professional jls and periodicals, and to RSE programmes on public understanding of science. *Recreations:* writing on environmental values and the ethics of science and technology, travels in France, walking, theatre.

FRANCIS, Rev. Canon Prof. Leslie John, PhD, ScD, DD, DLitt; CPsychol, FBPsS; Professor of Religions and Education, Centre for Education Studies (formerly Institute of Education), University of Warwick, since 2007; *b* 10 Sept. 1947; *s* of Ronald Arthur Francis and Joan Irene Francis. *Educ:* Colchester Royal Grammar Sch.; Pembroke Coll., Oxford (BA (Theol.) 1970, MA 1974); Westcott House, Cambridge; Queens' Coll., Cambridge (PhD (Educn) 1976); Univ. of Nottingham (MTh 1976); Inst. of Educn, Univ. of London (MSc (Psychol.) 1977); Oxford Univ. (BD (Theol.) 1990; DD 2001); Univ. of Cambridge (ScD 1997); Univ. of Wales, Bangor (DLitt 2007). FBPsS 1988; CPsychol 1989. Ordained deacon, 1973, priest, 1974; Curate, St Mary's, Haverhill, 1973–77; Leverhulme Res. Fellow, London Central YMCA/Westminster Med. Sch., 1977–82; non-stipendiary Priest-in-charge, St Mary's, Gt Bradley and Holy Trinity, Little Wratting, Suffolk, 1978–82; Res. Officer, 1982–86, Sen. Res. Officer, 1986–88, Culham Coll. Inst.; non-stipendiary Priest-in-charge, All Saints, N Cerney and St Margaret's, Bagendon, Glos, 1982–85; non-stipendiary Priest, Dio. of Oxford, 1985–88; Trinity College, Carmarthen: Mansel Jones Fellow, 1989–99; Principal Lectr in Religious Studies, 1989–91; Dir, Centre for Theol. and Educn and Dir of Res., 1992–99; Asst Chaplain, 1989–94; Dean of Chapel, 1994–99; D. J. James Prof. of Pastoral Theol., Univ. of Wales, Lampeter, 1992–99; Prof. of Practical Theol. and Dir, Welsh Nat. Centre for Religious Educn, Univ. of Wales, Bangor, 1999–2007; non-stipendiary Priest, Dio. of Bangor, 1999–2006; Hon. Asst Curate, Llanfairpwll and Llanddaniel-fab with Penmynydd, 2006–12; non-stipendiary Assoc. Priest, Seintiau Braint a Chefni, 2012–. Hon. Canon, St Davids Cathedral, 1998–99; Hon. Canon, 2006–11, Cursal Canon (Secundus), 2011–12, Canon Theologian, 2006–, Canon Treas., 2012–, Bangor Cathedral. Chairman: Census 2001 Wkg Party, CCBI, 1995–2001; Religious Affiliation Subgp, Census Content Wkg Gp, ONS, 1996–98; Religious Affiliation Gp, 2001 Census, 1998–. Church in Wales: Chairman: Continuing Ministerial Educn Cttee, 1992–2001; Children's Sector, 1995–; Mem., Governing Body, 1997–2001. National Council of YMCAs: Mem., Wkg Party on use and abuse of alcohol, 1983–84; Chm., Educn and Prog. Develt, 1985–90; Mem., Exec. Cttee and Nat. Bd, 1985–90. Consultant, Archbps' Commn on Rural Areas, 1989–90. British Psychological Society: Mem., Standing Cttee on teaching psychol. to other professional gps, 1990–2000; Trustee, Welfare Fund, 1992–. Trustee: Alister Hardy Trust, 1999– (Chm., 2002–; Chm., Res. Cttee, 1999–2002); St Deiniol's Liby, Hawarden, 2002–10; Network for the Study of Implicit Religion, 2002–; Internat. Seminar for Religious Educn and Values, 2003–; Intereuropean Commn on Church and School, 2005–. FCP 1994. *Publications:* Youth in Transit, 1982; Experience of Adulthood, 1982; Young and Unemployed, 1984; Teenagers and the Church, 1984; Rural Anglicanism: a future for young Christians?, 1985; Partnership in Rural Education: church schools and teacher attitudes, 1986; Religion in the Primary School, 1987; (with K. Williams) Churches in Fellowship: local councils of churches in England, 1991; (with W. K. Kay) Teenage Religion and Values, 1995; (with W. K. Kay) Drift from the Churches: attitudes towards Christianity during childhood and adolescence, 1996; Church Watch: Christianity in the countryside, 1996; (with J. Martineau) Rural Praise, 1996; Personality Type and Scripture: exploring Mark's Gospel, 1997; (with P. Richter) Gone but not Forgotten: church leaving and returning, 1998; (with M. Robbins) The Long Diaconate 1987–1994: women deacons and the delayed journey to priesthood, 1999; (jtly) Rural Ministry, 2000; (with P. Atkins) Exploring Luke's Gospel: a guide to the gospel readings in the Revised Common Lectionary, 2000; The Values Debate: a voice from the pupils, 2001; (with J. Martineau) Rural Visitors, 2001; (with J. Martineau) Rural Youth, 2001; (with P. Atkins) Exploring Matthew's Gospel: a guide to the gospel readings in the Revised Common Lectionary, 2001; (with J. Martineau) Rural Mission, 2002; (with J. Astley) Children, Churches and Christian Learning, 2002; (with P. Atkins) Exploring Mark's Gospel: an aid for readers and preachers using year B of the Revised Common Lectionary, 2002; (with S. H. Louden) The Naked Parish Priest: what priests really think they're doing, 2003; Faith and Psychology: personality, religion and the individual, 2005; (with M. Robbins and J. Astley) Fragmented Faith: exposing the fault-lines in the Church of England, 2005; (with M. Robbins) Urban Hope and Spiritual Health: the adolescent voice, 2005; (with J. M. Haley) British Methodism: what circuit ministers really think, 2006; (with P. Richter) Gone for Good?: church-leaving and returning in the 21st century, 2007; (with A. Village) Preaching with all our Souls: a study in hermeneutics and psychological type, 2008; The Gospel in the Willows, 2009; (with A. Village) The Mind of the Anglican Clergy: assessing attitudes and beliefs in the Church of England, 2009; (jtly) Ordained Local Ministry in the Church of England, 2012; *edited books:* (with A. Thatcher) Christian Perspectives for Education: a reader in the theology of education, 1990; (with J. Astley) Christian Perspectives on Faith Development: a reader, 1992; (with D. W. Lankshear) Christian Perspectives on Church Schools: a reader, 1993; (with J. Astley) Critical Perspectives on Christian Education, 1994; (jtly) Fast-moving Currents in Youth Culture, 1995; (with J. Astley) Christian Theology and Religious Education, 1996; (with S. H. Jones) Psychological Perspectives on Christian Ministry: a reader, 1996; (jtly) Research in Religious Education, 1996; (jtly) Theological Perspectives on Christian Formation: a reader on theology and Christian education, 1996; (with W. K. Kay) Religion in Education: vol. 1, 1997, vol. 2, 1998, vol. 3, 2000, vol. 4 (also with K. Watson), 2003; (with J. Francis) Tentmaking: perspectives on self-supporting ministry, 1998; Sociology, Theology and the Curriculum, 1999; (with Y. J. Katz) Joining and Leaving Religion: research perspectives, 2000; (jtly) The Fourth R for the Third Millennium: education in religion and values for the global future, 2001; (with J. Astley) Psychological Perspectives on Prayer: a reader, 2001; (jtly) Changing Rural Life: a Christian response to key rural issues, 2004; (jtly) Making Connections: a reader on preaching, 2005; (jtly) The Idea of a Christian University: essays on theology and higher education, 2005; (jtly) Religion, Education and Adolescence: international empirical perspectives, 2005; (jtly) Peace or Violence: the ends of religion and education, 2007; (jtly) Empirical Theology in Texts and Tables: qualitative, quantitative and comparative perspectives, 2009; (jtly) International Handbook of Education for Spirituality, Care and Wellbeing, 2009; (jtly) The Public Significance of Religion, 2011; (jtly) Teaching Religion, Teaching Truth: theoretical and empirical perspectives, 2012; (jtly) Rural Life and Rural Church: theological and empirical perspectives, 2012; (jtly) Religious Education and Freedom of Religion and Belief, 2012; (with J. Astley) Exploring Ordinary Theology: everyday Christian believing and the Church, 2013; has also written 14 bks for teachers and clergy, and over 30 bks for children, incl. (with N. M. Slee) Teddy Horsley Bible Books series. *Recreations:* music, the countryside and architecture, holder of licence to drive coaches and buses. *Address:* Warwick Religions and Education Research Unit, Centre for Education Studies, University of Warwick, Coventry CV4 7AL. *T:* (024) 7652 2539, *Fax:* (024) 7657 2638. *E:* leslie.francis@warwick.ac.uk.

FRANCIS, Lisa; *see* Francis, E. A.

FRANCIS, Mary Elizabeth, CBE 2005; LVO 1999; non-executive Director, Swiss Re Group, since 2013; *b* 24 July 1948; *d* of Frederick Henry George and Barbara Henrietta George (*née* Jeffs); *m* 1st, Dr Roger John Brown, *qv* (marr. diss.); 2nd, 1991, Prof. Peter William Francis (*d* 1999); 3rd, 2001, Ian Campbell Ferguson Rodger. *Educ:* James Allen's Girls' Sch., Dulwich; Newnham Coll., Cambridge (MA Hist.). Res. Asst to Prof. Max Beloff, All Souls Coll., Oxford, 1970–72; CS Dept and HM Treasury, 1972–90 incl. secondment to Hill Samuel & Co. Ltd, 1984–86, then Asst Sec., 1986–90; Economic Counsellor, British Embassy, Washington, 1990–92; Private Sec. to Prime Minister, 1992–95; Asst Private Sec. to the Queen, 1996–99, Dep. Private Sec., Feb.–June 1999; Dir-Gen., ABI, 1999–2005. Non-executive Director: Bank of England, 2001–07; Centrica plc, 2004–14 (Sen. Ind. Dir, 2006–14); St Modwen Properties Plc, 2005–09; Aviva plc, 2005–12; Alliance & Leicester plc, 2007–08; Cable and Wireless Communications plc, 2009–12; Swiss Re Zurich Ltd, 2012–; Ensco plc, 2013–. Member: Press Complaints Commn, 2001–05; Adv. Bd, NCC, 2002–08; Adv. Bd, Cambridge Univ. Centre for Business Res., 2006–10; Sen. Advr, Chatham House (RIIA), 2008–. Gov., Pensions Policy Inst., 2002–09. Trustee, Almeida Th., 2002–10 (Treas., 2008–10). Associate Fellow, Newnham Coll., Cambridge, 1995–98. Chm. of Govs, James Allen's Girls' Sch., Dulwich, 2009–13 (Gov., 1992–2001). *Recreations:* reading, swimming, ballet, walking. *Address:* 115 Ashley Gardens, SW1P 1HJ.

FRANCIS, Nicholas; *see* Francis, P. N.

FRANCIS, Paul Richard, FRICS, PPISVA; Surveyor Member, Upper Tribunal (Lands Chamber) (formerly Lands Tribunal), since 1998; *b* 14 Feb. 1948; *o s* of Richard Francis and Pamela Francis (*née* Rouse); *m* 2006, Mollie Labercombe. *Educ:* King's Sch., Harrow. FSVA 1974; FRICS 2000. Midland Marts (Banbury), 1967–70; E. J. Brooks & Son, Chartered Surveyors, 1970–75; Partner, A. C. Frost & Co., 1975–86; Nat. Survey and Valuation Dir, Prudential Property Services Ltd, 1986–98. Pres., ISVA, 1994–95. Chm. Adv. Bd, Cert. in Residential Estate Agency, Coll. of Estate Mgt, 1997–2000; Vice-Chm., RICS Dispute Resolution Faculty Bd, 2001–07. *Recreations:* motor sailing, golf, shooting. *Address:* Upper Tribunal (Lands Chamber), Royal Courts of Justice, Strand, WC2A 2LL. *Club:* Royal Southampton Yacht.

FRANCIS, Rev. Peter Brereton; Warden and Chief Librarian, Gladstone's (formerly St Deiniol's) Library, Hawarden, since 1997; *b* 18 June 1953; *s* of Richard and Pauline Francis; *m* 1st, 1976, Denise Steele (marr. diss. 1997); 2nd, Helen Grocott; one step *d. Educ:* Malvern Coll.; St Andrews Univ. (MTh 1977); Queen's Coll., Birmingham. Ordained deacon, 1978, priest, 1979; Curate, Hagley, Worcs, 1978–81; Chaplain, QMC, 1981–87; Rector, Holy Trinity, Ayr, 1987–92; Provost and Rector, St Mary's Cathedral, Glasgow, 1992–96. Vis. Prof., Glyndwr Univ., Wrexham, 2009–. Dir, Gladstone Project, 1997–. Trustee, Nat. Liberal Club, 2011–. Hon. DD Chester, 2012. *Publications:* The Grand Old Man, 2000; The Gladstone Umbrella, 2001; (ed jtly) Changing Rural Life, 2004; (ed Jtly) Cinema Divinité, 2005; (ed) Rebuilding Communion, 2007; (contrib.) Pieces of Ease and Grace, 2013; Bible and Cinema, 2013; (contrib.) Oxford Dictionary of Christian Art and Architecture, 2013. *Recreations:* cinema, theatre, contemporary literature. *Address:* The Warden's Lodge, Gladstone's Library, St Deiniol's, Church Lane, Hawarden, Flintshire CH5 3DF. *T:* (01244) 532350, 531659, *Fax:* (01244) 520643.

FRANCIS, (Peter) Nicholas; QC 2002; a Deputy High Court Judge, since 2011; *b* 22 April 1958; *s* of Peter and Jean Francis; *m* 2000, Penny Seguss; two *s*, and one *d* from previous marriage. *Educ:* Radley Coll.; Downing Coll., Cambridge (MA). Called to the Bar, Middle Temple, 1981; in practice, specialising in family law; Asst Recorder, 1997–99; a Recorder, 1999–; Head of Chambers, 29 Bedford Row, 2002–. *Recreations:* sailing, theatre, wine. *Address:* 29 Bedford Row, WC1R 4HE. *T:* (020) 7404 1044, *Fax:* (020) 7831 0626. *E:* nfrancis@29br.co.uk.

FRANCIS, Richard Mark; barn restorer and art historian; *b* 20 Nov. 1947; *s* of Ralph Lawrence and Eileen Francis; *m* 1976, Tamar Janine Helen Burchill; one *d. Educ:* Oakham Sch.; Cambridge Univ.; Courtauld Inst. Walker Art Gall., Liverpool, 1971–72; Arts Council of GB, 1973–80; Asst Keeper, Tate Gall., London, 1980–86; Curator, Tate Gall., Liverpool, 1986–90; Chief Curator, Mus. of Contemp. Art, Chicago, 1993–97; Christie's, NY, 1997–2002. *Publications:* Jasper Johns, 1984.

FRANCIS, Sir Robert (Anthony), Kt 2014; QC 1992; a Recorder, since 2000; a Deputy High Court Judge, since 2014; *b* 4 April 1950; *s* of late John Grimwade Francis and of Jean Isobel Francis; *m* 1st, 1976, Catherine Georgievsky (marr. diss. 2005); one *s* two *d*; 2nd, 2007, Alison Meek. *Educ:* Uppingham Sch.; Exeter Univ. (LLB Hons). Pres., Exeter Univ. Guild of Students, 1971–72. Called to the Bar, Inner Temple, 1973, Bencher, 2002. Asst Recorder, 1996–2000. Legal Assessor, Chartered Soc. of Physiotherapists, 1991. Mem. Exec. Cttee, Professional Negligence Bar Assoc., 2000–06 (Vice Chm., 2002; Chm., 2004); Chm., Educn and Trng Cttee, Inner Temple, 2010–13. Chairman: Mid Staffs NHS Foundn Trust Public Inquiry, 2010–13 (report, 2013); Freedom to Speak Up Rev., 2014–15 (report, 2015). Non-exec. Dir, Care Quality Commn, 2014–. Pres., Patients' Assoc., 2013–. Trustee: Peper Harow Orgn, 1992–2002; Prostate Cancer Res. Centre, 2014–; Point of Care Foundn, 2014–. Churchwarden, St John's Parish Church, Milford, Surrey, 1984–92. Hon. FRCAnaes 2014. Consultant Ed., Medical Law Reports (formerly Lloyd's Law Reports: Medical, later LS Law Medical), 1999–. *Publications:* (jtly) Medical Treatment Decisions and the Law, 2001, 2nd edn 2010. *Recreation:* cricket. *Address:* Serjeants' Inn Chambers, 85 Fleet Street, EC4Y 1AE. *T:* (020) 7427 5000.

FRANCIS, Sheena Vanessa; *see* Wagstaff, S. V.

FRANCIS, Stewart Alexander Clement, MA; Headmaster, Colchester Royal Grammar School, 1985–2000; *b* 25 Feb. 1938; *s* of Clement Francis and Patricia Francis (*née* Stewart); *m* 1965, Valerie Stead; one *s* one *d. Educ:* St Andrew's Sch., Eastbourne; St Edward's Sch., Oxford; St John's Coll., Cambridge (MA Classics, Cert Ed). Assistant Master: Mill Hill Sch., London, 1963; Maidenhead GS, 1963–66; temp. teaching posts in S Africa and England, 1966–67; Hd, Lower Sch., Maidenhead GS, 1967–69; Hd of English and Hd of Sixth Form, William Penn Sch., Rickmansworth, 1969–74; Dep. Head, Southgate Sch., London, 1974–79; Headmaster, Chenderit Sch., Middleton Cheney, Northants, 1979–84. OFSTED sch. inspector, 2005–08; sch. improvement partner, 2006–10. Pres., NE Essex Headteachers' Assoc., 1987–88. Trustee, Colchester Blue Coat Sch. Foundn, 1985–. Mem. Court, Univ. of Essex, 1996–2000. Gov., Philip Morant Sch. and Coll., Colchester, 2011–. FRSA 1995. Mem., Cricket Soc., 2005–; Men's squash champion, Bucks, 1970. Member: Johnian Soc., 1958–; Brightwine, 2000–; Colchester Breakfast Club, 2001–; Tate, 2010–12; Friend: Bankside Gall., 2006–; Rotary Club of Colchester, 2008– (Mem., 2001–08); Royal Acad., 2010–12; Chm., Colchester Twinning Soc., 2012–13. Paintings in group exhibitions: Bankside Gp, London, 2010–12; Mersea Is. Art Gp, Mersea Is. Mus., Essex, 2011–12. Chevalier du Sacavin d'Anjou, 2008. *Publications:* contrib. Cricket Qly; letters in nat. newspapers; poems in Cricket Soc. News Bulletin, The Eagle, Poetry Wivenhoe. *Recreations:* cricket and other sports, reading, writing, theatre, drawing and painting, visiting art galleries. *Address:* 32 The Lane, West Mersea, Essex CO5 8NT. *T:* (01206) 386084. *E:* stewartfrancis7@gmail.com. *Clubs:* Eagles, MCC, Jesters Cricket.

FRANCIS, Sir William; *see* Francis, Sir H. W. A.

FRANCKE, Ann P.; Chief Executive, Chartered Management Institute, since 2012; *m* Barry King; one *d. Educ:* Stanford Univ. (BA Distinction Russian and Politics 1980); Berlin Univ. (Deutscher Akademischer Austausch Dienst Schol.); Columbia Univ., NY (MBA, MS). Procter & Gamble, Inc., 1986–99; Eur. Vice Pres. (Petcare Portfolio), Mars, Inc., 1999–2002; Dir, Strategic Mktg, Boots Gp plc, 2003; Chief Mktg Officer, Yell Gp plc, 2004–06; Co-Founder and Pres., Beutorium LLC, 2007–09; Global Man. Dir, BSI Gp, 2009–12. *Publications:* FT Guide to Management: how to make a difference and get results, 2014. *Address:* 52 Antrobus Road, W4 5HZ. *E:* annpfrancke@gmail.com.

FRANCOIS, Rt Hon. Mark (Gino); PC 2010; MP (C) Rayleigh and Wickford, since 2010 (Rayleigh, 2001–10); Minister of State, Department for Communities and Local Government, since 2015; *b* London, 14 Aug. 1965; *m* 2000, Karen Thomas (marr. diss. 2006). *Educ:* Nicholas Comprehensive Sch., Basildon; Univ. of Bristol (BA 1986); King's Coll. London (MA 1987). Mgt trainee, Lloyds Bank, 1987; Consultant and Dir, Market Access Internat. Public Affairs Consultancy, 1988–95; Public Affairs Consultant, Francois Associates, 1996–2001. Mem. (C) Basildon DC, 1991–95. Opposition Jun. Whip, 2002; Shadow Econ. Sec., HM Treasury, 2004; Shadow Paymaster Gen., 2005–07; Opposition spokesman on Europe, 2007–09; Shadow Minister for Europe, 2009–10; Vice-Chamberlain of HM Household (Govt Whip), 2010–12; Minister of State, MoD, 2012–15. Mem., Envmtl Audit Cttee, H of C, 2001–05. Contested (C) Brent East, 1997. Served TA, 1983–89 (Lieut). Mem., RUSI. Fellow, Huguenot Soc. of GB and Ire., 2001–. Freeman, City of London, 2004; Liveryman, Co. of Wheelwrights, 2005–. Pres., Palace of Westminster Lions Club, 2006–12. *Recreations:* reading, travel, walking, history (including military history). *Address:* (office) 25 Bellingham Lane, Rayleigh, Essex SS6 7ED; c/o House of Commons, SW1A 0AA. *T:* (020) 7219 3000. *Clubs:* Carlton; Rayleigh Conservative (Pres., 2010–).

FRANCOME, John, MBE 1986; writer; racing presenter, Channel 4 Television, until 2012; first jockey to F. T. Winter, 1975–85; *b* 13 Dec. 1952; *s* of Norman and Lillian Francome; *m* 1976, Miriam Strigner. *Educ:* Park Senior High School, Swindon. First ride, Dec. 1970; Champion Jockey (National Hunt), 1975–76, 1978–79, 1980–81, 1981–82, 1982–83, 1983–84, 1984–85; record number of jumping winners (1,036), May 1984; retired March 1985 (1,138 winners). *Publications:* Born Lucky (autobiog.), 1985; How to Make Money Betting—or at least how not to lose too much, 1986; Twice Lucky: the lighter side of steeplechasing, 1988; *novels*: Blood Stock, 1989; Stud Poker, 1990; Stone Cold, 1991; Rough Ride, 1992; Outsider, 1993; Break Neck, 1994; Dead Ringer, 1995; False Start, 1996; High Flyer, 1997; Safe Bet, 1998; Tip Off, 1999; Lifeline, 2000; Dead Weight, 2001; Inside Track, 2002; Stalking Horse, 2003; Back Hander, 2004; Cover Up, 2005; Free Fall, 2006; Winner Takes All, 2006; Dark Horse, 2007; Final Break, 2008; Deadly Finish, 2009; Storm Rider, 2010; (with James MacGregor): Eavesdropper, 1986; Riding High, 1987; Declared Dead, 1988. *Recreations:* tennis, music. *Address:* Beechdown Farm, Sheepdrove, Lambourn, Berks RG17 7UN.

FRANK, Sir Andrew; *see* Frank, Sir R. A.

FRANK, David; Chief Executive, Dial Square 86, since 2013; Chairman, The RightsXchange, since 2014; *b* 24 Sept. 1958; *s* of late Peter James Frank and of Joyce Miriam Frank (*née* Sollis); *m* 1983, Isabelle Turquet de Beauregard; two *s* one *d. Educ:* Trinity Coll., Oxford (BA Juris.). Manager: Hill Samuel & Co. Ltd, 1982–85; Swiss Bank Corp. Internat., 1985–87; freelance journalist, 1987–89; reporter, BBC TV, 1989–92; Chief Exec., RDF Media, later Zodiak Media Gp, 1993–2013. *Recreations:* football, scuba-diving, golf, tennis, fly-fishing. *Address:* Dial Square 86, Somerset House, Strand, WC2R 1LA. *E:* david.frank@dialsquare86.com. *Clubs:* Roehampton, Soho House.

FRANK, Prof. John William, MD; FRSE; Director, Scottish Collaboration for Public Health Research and Policy, since 2008; Professor of Public Health Research and Policy, University of Edinburgh, since 2008; *b* Guelph, Ont, 23 June 1949; *s* of William Frank and Marion Frank; *m* 1976, Eden Anderson; three *s. Educ:* Univ. of Toronto (BSc 1971; MD 1974); Coll. of Family Physicians of Canada (Cert. Coll. of Family Practice 1976); London Sch. of Hygiene and Tropical Medicine (MSc 1981). FRCPC 1982. Med. Officer and MA Instructor, Mbeya, Tanzania, 1976–79; Staff Physician, York Community Services, Toronto, 1979–80; Prof., Faculty of Medicine, Univ. of Toronto, 1983–2008, now Emeritus; Dir, Res., Inst. for Work and Health, Toronto, 1991–97; Adjunct Prof., Sch. of Public Health, Univ. of Calif, Berkeley, 1997–2000; Inaugural Scientific Dir, CIHR Inst. of Popn and Public Health, 2000–08. FCAHS 2006; FFPH 2009; FRSE 2013. *Publications:* over 25 book chapters and monographs; 210 articles in jls. *Recreations:* natural history, singing, Scottish country dancing, travel. *Address:* Scottish Collaboration for Public Health Research and Policy, 1st Floor, 20 West Richmond Street, Edinburgh EH8 9DX. *T:* (0131) 651 1593. *E:* john.frank@ed.ac.uk.

FRANK, Sir (Robert) Andrew, 4th Bt *cr* 1920, of Withyham, Co. Sussex; freelance event management and training consultant, since 2000; owner, Baronet Communications, since 2009; *b* 16 May 1964; *s* of Sir Robert John Frank, 3rd Bt, FRICS, and Margaret Joyce (*d* 1995), *d* of Herbert Victor Truesdale; *S* father, 1987; *m* 1st, 1990, Zoë, *er d* of S. A. Hasan (marr. diss. 2010); 2nd, 2014, Dr Rehanwant Singh Gomez. *Educ:* Ludgrove Prep. School; Eton College. *Recreations:* travel, theatre, cinema. *Heir:* none.

FRANKEL, Dr Hans Ludwig, OBE 1993; FRCP; Consultant in Spinal Injuries, National Spinal Injuries Centre, Stoke Mandeville Hospital, 1966–2002, now Honorary Consultant; *b* 7 April 1932; *s* of late Dr Paul Frankel, CBE and Helen Frankel; *m* 1956, Mavis Anne Richardson; two *s*. *Educ:* Dauntsey's Sch.; University Coll. London; University Coll. Hosp. Med. Sch. (MB BS 1956). MRCS 1956; LRCP 1956, MRCP 1964, FRCP 1977. Casualty officer, Hampstead Gen. Hosp., 1957; Stoke Mandeville Hospital, 1957–: Hse Physician, 1957–58; National Spinal Injuries Centre: Registrar, 1958–62; Sen. Registrar, 1962–66; Dep. Dir, 1969–77; Mem., Exec. Bd, 1991–98; Clin. Dir, 1993–98. Hon. Consultant, Star & Garter Home, Richmond, 1979–. Vis. Prof., ICSTM, 2000–. Member: Editorial Board: Paraplegia; Annales de Readaptation et de Médecine Physique; Clinical Autonomic Res.; Editl Adv. Bd, Annals of Sports Medicine. Buckinghamshire Area Health Authority: Vice-Chm., 1976–77, Chm., 1978–80, Med. Adv. Cttee. International Medical Society of Paraplegia: Hon. Treas., 1966–78; Hon. Sec., 1976–87; Vice Pres., 1987–91; Pres., 1996–2000; Chm., Scientific Cttee, 1992–96. President: Brit. Cervical Spine Soc., 1990–92; Chiltern Gp, Spinal Injuries Assoc., 1989–98. Mem., Exec. Cttee, Brit. Paraplegic Sports Soc., 1977–91. Chm. Trustees, Internat. Spinal Res. Trust, 1983–97; Mem., Mgt Council, Brit. Neurol Res. Trust, 1989–. Numerous lectures in UK, Europe, USA and throughout the world, incl. Arnott Demonstrator, RCS 1987, Sandoz Lectr, Inst. of Neurol., London, 1988 and 1992. *Publications:* (ed) volume on Spinal Cord Injuries in Handbook of Clinical Neurology, 1992; contrib. chapters on spinal cord injuries to text books. *Recreations:* ski-ing, opera. *Address:* Seytons Manor, Terrick, Aylesbury, Bucks HP17 0UA.

FRANKEL, Prof. Stephen John, DM, PhD; FRCP, FFPH; Professor of Epidemiology and Public Health, University of Bristol, 1993–2007, now Emeritus; Chair, Board of Directors, Wadebridge Renewable Energy Network, since 2011; Visiting Professor, Energy Policy Group, University of Exeter, since 2011; *b* 4 Nov. 1946; *s* of Eric and Constance Frankel; *m* 1st, 1972, Hermione Jane Dennis (marr. diss. 2003); one *s* one *d*; 2nd, 2004, Elizabeth-Jane Grose. *Educ:* Corpus Christi Coll., Oxford (BM BCh 1970; MA 1970; DM 1983); Corpus Christi Coll., Cambridge (PhD 1981). MFPHM 1985, FFPH (FFPHM 1991); FRCP 2000. District Medical Officer, Papua New Guinea, 1972–74; Res. Officer, Dept of Social Anthropology, Cambridge Univ., 1977–81; Res. Fellow, Clare Hall, Cambridge, 1981–84; Senior Lecturer in Epidemiology: Univ. of Wales Coll. of Medicine, 1985–89; Univ. of Bristol, 1989–92. Consultant, WHO, 1985–2001; Director: Health Care Evaluation Unit, Univ. of Bristol, 1989–93; R&D, South Western Reg., NHS, 1992–96; NHS Cancer Res. Prog., 1993–96; MRC Health Services Res. Collaboration, 1996–97. Mem. Bd, Cornwall and Isles of Scilly Local Nature Partnership, 2013–. SW Sustainable Energy Champion, SW Green Energy Awards, 2013. *Publications:* The Huli Response to Illness, 1986; (ed jtly) A Continuing Trial of Treatment, 1988; (ed) The Community Health Worker, 1992; (ed jtly) Rationing and Rationality in the National Health Service: the persistence of waiting lists, 1993; (ed jtly) Priority Setting: the health care debate, 1996; numerous articles in med. and sci. jls concerning the aetiology of disease, disease prevention and health service research. *Recreations:* the usual things, plus windsurfing, gigging with Spot the Dog and the O'Frankel Family Band. *Address:* Carhart Mill, Wadebridge, Cornwall PL27 7HZ. *T:* (01208) 816818.

FRANKL, Peter; pianist; *b* Hungary, 2 Oct. 1935; *s* of Laura and Tibor Frankl; adopted British nationality, 1967; *m* 1958, Annie Feiner; one *s* one *d*. *Educ:* Liszt Ferenc Acad. of Music, Budapest. First Prize, several internat. competitions; London début, 1962; New York début, with Cleveland Orch. under George Szell, 1967; performances with Berlin Philharmonic, Amsterdam Concertgebouw, Israel Phil., Leipzig Gewandhaus, Orchestre de Paris, and with all London and major Amer. orchs (Chicago, Philadelphia, Boston, Washington, Los Angeles, San Francisco, Pittsburg, etc); many tours in Japan, Australia, NZ and SA, playing with orchs, in recitals and chamber music concerts; over 20 appearances, BBC Promenade Concerts, London; regular participant at Edinburgh, Cheltenham, Aldeburgh, Verbier and Kuhmo Fests; regular guest artist at summer fests in Aspen, Chautauqua, Hollywood Bowl, Marlboro, Norfolk, Ravinia, Santa Fé and Prades. Vis. Prof. of Piano, Yale Univ. Sch. of Music, 1987–. Hon. Prof., Liszt Acad., Budapest, 2006. Recordings include: complete solo works for piano by Schumann and Debussy; complete works for piano and orch. by Schumann; (with ECO) Mozart concerti; (with Tamás Vásáry) complete 4-hand works by Mozart; (with Lindsay Quartet) Brahms, Schumann, Dvorak and Martinu quintets; (with Kyung Wha Chung) Brahms Violin Sonatas; Brahms Piano Concerti; (with G. Pauk and R. Kirshbaum) Brahms Piano Trios; (with Fine Arts Quartet) Dohnanyi Quintets. Officer's Cross, Order of Merit (Hungary), 1995; Middle Cross Award (Hungary), 2005. *Recreations:* football, opera, theatre. *Address:* 5 Gresham Gardens, NW11 8NX. *T:* (020) 8455 5228. *E:* pafrankl@aol.com.

FRANKLAND, family name of **Baron Zouche**.

FRANKLAND, (Anthony) Noble, CB 1983; CBE 1976; DFC 1944; MA, DPhil; historian and biographer; *b* 4 July 1922; *s* of late Edward Frankland, Ravenstonedale, Westmorland; *m* 1st, 1944, Diana Madeline Fovargue (*d* 1981), *d* of late G. V. Tavernor, of Madras and Southern Mahratta Rly, India; one *s* one *d*; 2nd, 1982, Sarah Katharine, *d* of His Honour the late Sir David Davies, QC and late Lady Davies (Margaret Kennedy). *Educ:* Sedbergh; Trinity Coll., Oxford. Served Royal Air Force, 1941–45 (Bomber Command, 1943–45). Air Historical Branch Air Ministry, 1948–51; Official Military Historian, Cabinet Office, 1951–58. Rockefeller Fellow, 1953. Deputy Dir of Studies, Royal Institute of International Affairs, 1956–60; Dir, Imperial War Museum (at Southwark, 1960–82, Duxford Airfield, 1976–82, and HMS Belfast, 1978–82). Lees Knowles Lecturer, Trinity Coll., Cambridge, 1963. Historical advisor, Thames Television series, The World At War, 1971–74. Vice-Chm., British Nat. Cttee, Internat. Cttee for Study of Second World War, 1976–82. Mem., Council, Morley Coll., 1962–66; Trustee: Military Archives Centre, KCL, 1963–82; HMS Belfast Trust, 1971–78 (Vice-Chm., 1972–78); HMS Belfast Bd, 1978–82. *Publications:* Documents on International Affairs: for 1955, 1958; for 1956, 1959; for 1957, 1960; Crown of Tragedy, Nicholas II, 1960; The Strategic Air Offensive Against Germany, 1939–1945 (4 vols) jointly with Sir Charles Webster, 1961; The Bombing Offensive against Germany, Outlines and Perspectives, 1965; Bomber Offensive: the Devastation of Europe, 1970; (ed jtly) The Politics and Strategy of the Second World War (8 vols), 1974–78; (ed jtly) Decisive Battles of the Twentieth Century: Land, Sea, Air, 1976; Prince Henry, Duke of Gloucester, 1980; general editor and contributor, Encyclopaedia of 20th Century Warfare, 1989; Witness of a Century: the life and times of Prince Arthur Duke of Connaught, 1993; History at War: the campaigns of an historian, 1998; The Unseen War (novel), 2007; Belling's War (novel), 2008; historical chapter in Manual of Air Force Law, 1956; contrib. to Encyclopaedia Britannica; other articles and reviews; broadcasts on radio and TV. *Address:* 26/27 River View Terrace, Abingdon, Oxfordshire OX14 5AE. *T:* (01235) 521624.

See also M. D. P. O'Hanlon.

FRANKLIN, Andrew Cecil; Founder and Managing Director, Profile Books Ltd, since 1996; *b* 6 March 1957; *s* of Norman Albert Jessel Franklin and Jill (*née* Leslie); *m* 1981, Caroline Elton; two *s* one *d*. *Educ:* Leighton Park Sch.; Balliol Coll., Oxford (MA PPE). HM Factory Inspector, 1979–81; bookseller, Hatchards Bookshop, 1981–82; editl asst, Faber and Faber, 1982–83; editor: Methuen, 1983–84; Penguin Books, 1984–89; Publishing Dir, Hamish Hamilton, and Dir, Penguin Books, 1989–95. Vis. Prof., City Univ. London, 2011–. Chm., Jewish Community Centre for London, 2004–10. Fellow, Jerusalem Book Fair, 1985; Aspen Fellow, 1987. Trustee and Director: Jewish Literary Trust, 1987–2010 (Chm., 1994–96); Edinburgh Internat. Book Fest., 2006–14. Stanley Unwin Fellowship Award, Publishers Assoc., 1986; Friend of Jerusalem Award, City of Jerusalem, 2005. *Publications:* contrib. various newspapers. *Recreation:* my family and making trouble (separately and together). *Address:* Profile Books, 3 Holford Yard, Bevin Way, WC1X 9HD. *T:* (020) 7841 6300, *Fax:* (020) 7833 3969. *E:* andrew.franklin@profilebooks.com.

FRANKLIN, Caryn Dawn, MBE 2013; fashion commentator and campaigner for body diversity and emotionally considerate fashion practice; *b* Isleworth, 11 Jan. 1959; *d* of Brian Henry Charles Franklin and Pamela Ann Franklin (*née* Pollard); one *d* by Mandu Saldaan; *m* 2000, Ian Phillip Denyer; one *d*. *Educ:* Feltham Comprehensive Sch.; Richmond upon Thames Coll.; Kingston Poly. (BA Hons Graphic Design 1981); St Martin's School of Art. Fashion Ed. and Co-Ed., 1982–88, Contributing Ed., 1988–, i-D Mag.; presenter and researcher, SWANK, Channel 4, 1984; Fashion Ed., C4 Network 7, 1986; Presenter and Dir, World-wide-audience, The Clothes Show, BBC TV, 1986–98; Presenter and Educnl Ambassador, Clothes Show Live, 1989–; freelance producer and presenter, fashion documentary features, BBC, Channel 4, ITV, Discovery, Granada and UKTV Style, 1998–2006; Co-founder, Moet & Chandon Fashion Tributes, ITV, 1999–2003; contrib., nat. newspapers and magazines, 1984–; lectr, ext. assessor and course validator, 1984–. Co-Chair, Fashion Targets Breast Cancer, 1996–. Ambassador, Centre for Sustainable Fashion, London Coll. of Fashion, 2008–; Co-Founder, All Walks Beyond the Catwalk, 2009–; established: Diversity Network, Edinburgh Coll. of Art, 2011; Body Confidence Awards, All-Party Parly Gp on body image, 2012. Vis. Fellow, London Coll. of Fashion, 2011; Hon. Fellow, Arts Univ. Bournemouth, 2011. Hon. Dr Kingston, 2013. Ultimate Women Award, Cosmopolitan Mag., 2009; Red Hot Women Award, Red Mag., 2012. *Publications:* (with G. Goodman) Breast Health Handbook, 1996; Franklin on Fashion, 1997; Woman in the Mirror, 1998; Fashion UK, 2003. *Recreation:* feminist. *Address:* c/o Jo Wander, 110 Gloucester Avenue, Primrose Hill, NW1 8HX. *E:* caryn@carynfranklin.co.uk.

FRANKLIN, Daniel, PhD; Executive Editor, since 2006, and Editor, The World In series, since 2003, The Economist; *b* London, 27 Nov. 1955; *s* of Colin and Charlotte Franklin; *m* 1987, Gaby; one *s* one *d*. *Educ:* University College Sch., London; St John's Coll., Oxford (MA French and Russian); Aston Univ., Birmingham (PhD). Joined The Economist, 1983; Europe Ed., 1986–92; Britain Ed., 1992–93; Washington Bureau Chief, 1993–97; Editl Dir, Economist Intelligence Unit, 1997–2006; Ed. in Chief, economist.com, 2006–09; Business Affairs Ed., 2010–14. *Publications:* (ed jtly) Megachange: the World in 2050, 2012. *Recreations:* travel, learning languages. *Address:* The Economist, 25 St James's Street, SW1A 1HG. *T:* (020) 7576 1185, *Fax:* (020) 7925 0651. *E:* danielfranklin@economist.com. *Club:* Lansdowne.

FRANKLIN, John; *see* Franklin, W. J.

FRANKLIN, John Richard; Head Master, Christ's Hospital, since 2007; *b* 17 May 1953; *s* of late Richard Franklin and of Jean Franklin; *m* 1980, Kim Gillespie. *Educ:* Lockyer High Sch.; Ipswich Grammar Sch.; Univ. of Southern Qld (Dip. Teaching; BA); Univ. of New England, Australia (MEd Admin). Teacher: of English and Drama, Qld Educn Dept, 1976–79; and Housemaster and Hd of Sen. Sch., Toowoomba GS, 1980–88; Sedbergh Sch., 1989; Marlborough Coll., 1989–92; Dep. Headmaster, St Peter's Coll., Adelaide, 1993–98; Headmaster, Ardingly Coll., 1998–2007. *Recreations:* theatre, travel, golf. *Address:* Christ's Hospital, Horsham, W Sussex RH13 0LS. *T:* (01403) 211293. *Clubs:* East India, Lansdowne.

FRANKLIN, Lucy; *see* Hughes-Hallett, L.

FRANKLIN, Sir Michael (David Milroy), KCB 1983 (CB 1979); CMG 1972; Permanent Secretary, Ministry of Agriculture, Fisheries and Food, 1983–87; *b* 24 Aug. 1927; *o s* of late Milroy Franklin; *m* 1951, Dorothy Joan Fraser; two *s* one *d*. *Educ:* Taunton Sch.; Peterhouse, Cambridge (1st cl. hons Economics). Served with 4th RHA, BAOR. Asst Principal, Min. of Agric. and Fisheries, 1950; Economic Section, Cabinet Office (subseq. Treasury), 1952–55; Principal, Min. of Agric., Fisheries and Food, 1956; UK Delegn to OEEC (subseq. OECD), 1959–61; Private Sec. to Minister of Agric., Fisheries and Food, 1961–64; Asst Sec., Head of Sugar and Tropical Foodstuffs Div., 1965–68; Under-Sec. (EEC Gp), MAFF, 1968–73; a Dep. Dir Gen., Directorate Gen. for Agric., EC, Brussels, 1973–77; Dep. Sec., Head of the European Secretariat, Cabinet Office, 1977–81; Permanent Sec., Dept of Trade, 1982–83. Director: Agricultural Mortgage Corp., 1987–93; Barclays Bank, 1988–93; Barclays PLC, 1988–93; Whessoe plc, 1988–97; Whitbread plc, 1991–98; Co-Chm., UK Adv. Bd, Rabobank, 1996–2006. Pres., West India Cttee, 1987–95; Chm., Europe Cttee, British Invisibles (formerly BIEC), 1993–98 (Dep. Chm., 1988–93); Member: Council, Royal Inst. for Internat. Relations, 1988–95; Internat. Policy Council on Agric., Food and Trade, 1988–98; Chm., Jt Consultative Cttee, Potato Marketing Bd, 1990–97. Governor, Henley Management Coll. (formerly Henley Administrative Staff Coll.), 1983–93; Chm., Charlemagne Inst., 1996–99; Co-Chm., Wyndham Place Charlemagne Trust, 1999–2001. *Publications:* Rich Man's Farming: the crisis in agriculture, 1988; Britain's Future in Europe, 1990; The EC Budget, 1992; (with Jonathan Ockenden) European Agriculture: making the CAP fit the future, 1995; (ed) Joining the CAP: the agricultural negotiations for British accession to the European Economic Community, 1961–73, 2010. *Address:* 15 Galley Lane, Barnet, Herts EN5 4AR. *Club:* Oxford and Cambridge.

See also R. J. M. Franklin.

FRANKLIN, Prof. Raoul Norman, CBE 1995; FREng; FInstP, FIMA; Visiting Professor, Open University, 1998; Vice Chancellor, 1978–98, and Professor of Plasma Physics and Technology, 1986–98, The City University, London; *b* 3 June 1935; *s* of Norman George Franklin and Thelma Brinley Franklin (*née* Davis); *m* 1st, 1961, Faith (*d* 2004), *d* of Lt-Col H. T. C. Ivens and Eva (*née* Gray); two *s*; 2nd, 2005, Christine Penfold, *d* of Henry Harold and Irene Josephine (*née* Matthews). *Educ:* Howick District High Sch.; Auckland Grammar Sch., NZ (Augusta Award 2014); Univ. of Auckland (ME, DSc; Dist. Alumnus Award 2004); Christ Church, Oxford (MA, DPhil, DSc). FInstP 1968; FIMA 1970; FIET (FIEE 1986); FREng (FEng 1990). Officer, NZ Defence Scientific Corps, 1957–75. Sen. Res. Fellow, RMCS, Shrivenham, 1961–63; University of Oxford: Tutorial Fellow, 1963–78, Dean, 1966–71, Hon. Fellow, 1980, Keble Coll.; Univ. Lectr in Engrg Science, 1966–78; Mem., Gen. Bd, 1967–74 (Vice Chm., 1971–74); Mem., Hebdomadal Council, 1971–74, 1976–78. Chairman: Associated Examining Bd, 1994–98; Assessment and Qualifications Alliance, 1998–2003. Consultant, UKAEA Culham, 1968–2001. Dep. Editor, Jl of Physics D, 1986–90. Member: UGC Equipment Sub Cttee, 1975–78; Plasma Physics Commn, IUPAP, 1971–79; Science Bd, SERC, 1982–85; Exec. Council, Business in the Community, 1982–90; Management Cttee, Spallation Neutron Source, 1983–86; Technology Educn Project, 1986–88; UK-NZ 1990 Cttee, 1988–90; Internat. Scientific Cttee, Eur. Sectional Conf. on Atomic and Molecular Processes in Ionized Gases, 1993–97. Chairman: Internat. Science Cttee, Phenomena in Ionized Gases, 1976–77; City Technology Ltd, 1978–93 (Queen's Award for Technol., 1982, 1985, for Export, 1988, 1991). Mem., London Pensions Fund Authority, 1989–95. Trustee: Ruskin School of Drawing, 1975–78; Lloyds Tercentenary Foundn, 1990–2007. Member Council: Gresham Coll., 1981–98; C&G, 1994–2000. Governor: Ashridge Management Coll., 1986–99; Univ. of Buckingham, 2000–06. Freeman, City of London, 1981. Liveryman, Curriers' Co., 1984 (Master, 2002–03); Foundn Master, Educators' Co. (formerly Guild of Preceptors, then Guild of Educators), 1999–2002. Hon. Mem. RICS, 1992; Hon. GSMD 1993. CCMI (CBIM 1986); FRSA. Hon. DCL City, 1999. *Publications:* Plasma Phenomena in Gas Discharges, 1976; papers on plasmas, gas discharges and granular materials. *Recreations:* walking, gardening, sudoku.

FRANKLIN, Prof. Robin James Milroy, PhD; FRCPath; Professor of Stem Cell Medicine, since 2014, and Head of Translational Science, Wellcome Trust-MRC Cambridge Stem Cell Institute, University of Cambridge; Fellow, Pembroke College, Cambridge; *b* Barnet, Herts, 15 Aug. 1962; *s* of Sir Michael (David Milroy) Franklin, *qv*; two *s*. *Educ:* Haberdashers' Aske's Sch., Elstree; University Coll. London (BSc 1985); Royal Veterinary Coll. (BVetMed 1988); Univ. of Cambridge (PhD 1991). MRCVS 1988; FRCPath 2006. University of Cambridge: Wellcome Trust Res. Fellow, 1991–94; Wellcome Trust Res. Career Develt Fellow, 1994–99; Wellcome Trust Lectr, 1999–2000; Sen. Lectr in Exptl Neurol., 2000–02; Reader in Exptl Neurol., 2002–05; Prof. of Neurosci., 2005–13. *Publications:* contrib. articles to neurosci. and stem cell jls. *Recreations:* bird watching, running, music, reading, Liverpool Football Club. *Address:* Wellcome Trust-MRC Cambridge Stem Cell Institute, Clifford Allbutt Building, Cambridge Biomedical Campus, University of Cambridge, Cambridge CB2 0AH. *T:* (01223) 762034. *E:* rjf1000@cam.ac.uk.

FRANKLIN, Prof. Sarah Brooks, PhD; FRSB; Professor of Sociology, University of Cambridge, since 2011; Fellow, Christ's College, Cambridge, since 2012; *b* Cambridge, Mass, 9 Nov. 1960; *d* of John Thomas Franklin and Susan Brooks Franklin; partner, 2001, Sara Ahmed. *Educ:* Smith Coll., Mass (BA 1982); Univ. of Kent (MA 1984); New York Univ. (MA 1986); Univ. of Birmingham (PhD 1992). FRSB (FSB 2011). Res. Associate, Dept of Anthropol., Univ. of Manchester, 1990–93; Lancaster University: Lectr, 1993–97 (pt-time, 1990–93); Sen. Lectr, 1997–99; Reader in Cultural Anthropol., 1999–2001; Prof. of Anthropol. of Sci., 2001–04; Prof. of Social Study of Biomedicine, LSE, 2004–11. Mem., Presidential Adv. Bd, Smith Coll., 2007–13. Trustee, Anne McLaren Fund, 2011–. Smith Coll. Medal, 2011. *Publications:* (jtly) Off-Centre: feminism and cultural studies, 1991; (jtly) Technologies of Procreation: kinship in the age of assisted conception, 1993, 2nd edn 1999; The Sociology of Gender, 1996; Embodied Progress: a cultural account of assisted conception, 1997; (with H. Ragone) Reproducing Reproduction: kinship, power and technological innovation, 1998; (jtly) Global Nature, Global Culture, 2000; (with S. McKinnon) Relative Values: reconfiguring kinship study, 2001; (with M. Lock) Remaking Life and Death: toward an anthropology of the biosciences, 2003; (with C. Roberts) Born and Made: an ethnography of preimplantation genetic diagnosis, 2006; Dolly Mixtures: the remaking of genealogy, 2007; Biological Relatives: IVF, stem cells and the future of kinship, 2013. *Address:* Department of Sociology, Free School Lane, University of Cambridge, Cambridge CB2 3RQ.

FRANKLIN, Prof. Simon Colin, DPhil; FBA 2012; Professor of Slavonic Studies, since 2004, and Head, School of Arts and Humanities, 2009–14, University of Cambridge; Fellow, Clare College, Cambridge, since 1980; *b* 11 Aug. 1953; *s* of Colin and Charlotte Franklin; *m* 1975, Natasha Gokova; one *s* one *d*. *Educ:* University Coll. Sch.; King's Coll., Cambridge (BA 1976); St Antony's Coll., Oxford (DPhil 1981). Jun. Fellow, Dumbarton Oaks Center for Byzantine Studies, Washington, 1979–80; University of Cambridge: Res. Fellow, Clare Coll., 1980–83; Univ. Lectr in Russian, 1983–99; Reader, 1999–2003; Prof. of Russian Studies, 2003–04. Chm., Pushkin House Trust, 2004–09. Lomonosov Gold Medal, Russian Acad. of Scis, 2008. *Publications:* (trans with A. Boyars) The Face Behind the Face: new poems by Yevgeny Yevtushenko, 1979; (with A. Kazhdan) Studies in Byzantine Literature of the Eleventh and Twelfth Centuries, 1984; Sermons and Rhetoric of Kievan Rus, 1991; (with J. Shepard) The Emergence of Rus 750–1200, 1996; Writing, Society and Culture in Early Rus c.950–1300, 2002; (ed with E. Widdis) National Identity in Russian Culture: an introduction, 2004. *Recreations:* old books, watching football. *Address:* Clare College, Cambridge CB2 1TL. *T:* (01223) 333263. *E:* scf1000@cam.ac.uk.

See also D. Franklin.

FRANKLIN, Thomas Gerald; Chief Executive, Think Global, since 2012; *b* 24 June 1969; *s* of Gerald Joseph Franklin and Jillian Ruth Franklin. *Educ:* King Edward VI Upper Sch., Bury St Edmunds; Univ. of Hull (BA Politics). Account Dir, Rowland Public Affairs, 1996–2000; Chief Executive: Living Streets (The Pedestrians Assoc.), 2002–07; Rambler's Assoc., 2007–12. Mem. (Lab) Lambeth BC, 1994–06 (Leader, 2000–02). Trustee, Canal and River Trust, 2011–. *Recreations:* marathon running, cycling, walking, cinema, travelling. *Address:* Think Global, CAN Mezzanine, 32–36 Loman Street, SE1 0EH. *Club:* Constituency Labour (Streatham).

FRANKLIN, (William) John; DL; Deputy Chairman, Chartered Trust plc, 1986–97 (Director, 1982–97); Chairman: Howells Motors Ltd, 1986–89; Powell Duffryn Wagon, 1986–89; *b* 8 March 1927; *s* of late William Thomas Franklin and Edith Hannah Franklin; *m* 1951, Sally (*née* Davies) (*d* 2003); one *d*. *Educ:* Monkton House Sch., Cardiff. W. R. Gresty, Chartered Accountants, 1947–50; Peat Marwick Mitchell, Chartered Accountants, 1950–55; Powell Duffryn, 1956–86: Director, Cory Brothers, 1964; Man. Dir, Powell Duffryn Timber, 1967–70; Dir, 1970–86; Man. Dir and Chief Exec., 1976–85; Dep. Chm., Jan.–July 1986. Treas., UC of Swansea, 1989–92. DL Mid Glamorgan, 1989. *Recreation:* golf.

FRANKLYN, Prof. Jayne Agneta, (Mrs Michael Gammage), MD, PhD; FRCP; FMedSci; William Withering Professor of Medicine, 2011–14, now Emeritus (Professor of Medicine, 1995–2014), and Head, School of Clinical and Experimental Medicine, College of Medical and Dental Sciences, 2008–14, University of Birmingham; Consultant Physician, Queen Elizabeth Hospital, Birmingham, 1988–2014; *b* Birmingham, 7 July 1956; *d* of late Ivor George Franklyn and Joyce Helen Franklyn; *m* 1980, Prof. Michael Gammage; one *s* one *d*. *Educ:* Univ. of Birmingham (MB ChB Hons 1979; MD 1985; PhD 1988). MRCP 1982, FRCP 1991. University of Birmingham: MRC Trng Fellow, 1994–95; Wellcome Trust Sen. Res. Fellow in Clin. Sci., 1988–89; Sen. Lectr, then Reader in Medicine, 1989–95; Associate Dean, Grad. Sch., 2002–08. Chairman: Specialist Adv. Cttee in Endocrinol. and Diabetes, JRCPTB, 2006–09; Clinical Cttee, Soc. for Endocrinol., 2011; Mem. Council, Acad. of Med. Scis, 2012–14. Pres., British Thyroid Assoc., 2008–11. FMedSci 2000. *Publications:* contrib. papers on thyroid disease pathogenesis, treatment and long term effects. *Recreations:* gardening, enjoying the Devon coast and sea. *Address:* The Old Rectory, Plymouth, Devon EX15 2JP. *E:* j.a.franklyn@bham.ac.uk.

FRANKLYN, Rear-Adm. Peter Michael, CB 1999; MVO 1978; Chief Executive, Royal Hospital for Neuro-disability, 2000–09; Chairman, Royal National Hospital for Rheumatic Diseases NHS Foundation Trust, Bath, 2010–13; *b* 10 Sept. 1946; *s* of late Roy Vernon Bolton Franklyn and Yvonne Beryl Franklyn (*née* Hooper); *m* 1977, Caroline Barbara Anne Jenks; one *s* one *d*. *Educ:* King's Coll., Taunton. Joined RN, 1963; Comdr, 1980; CO, HMS Active, 1980–82; Trng Comdr, BRNC, Dartmouth, 1982–84; SO Ops FO 3rd Flotilla, 1984–86; Captain, 1986; Naval Asst to 1st Sea Lord, 1986–88; CO, HMS Bristol, 1988–90; RCDS, 1991; Capt., Sch. of Maritime Ops, 1992–93; Dir Naval Officers' Appts (Seaman), 1993–94; Rear-Adm., 1994; Comdr, UK Task Gp, 1994–96; Flag Officer, Sea Training, 1996–97; Flag Officer, Surface Flotilla, 1997–2000. Mem., RNSA, 1993–. Trustee, St John's Hospital Charitable Trust, Bath, 2010–. Younger Brother, Trinity House, 1996. *Recreation:* outdoor activities.

FRANKOPAN, Dr Peter Doimi de, FRHistS; Director, Oxford Centre for Byzantine Research, University of Oxford, since 2011; Senior Research Fellow, Worcester College, Oxford, since 2000; *b* London, 22 March 1971; *s* of Prince and Princess Louis Doimi de Frankopan Šubić; *m* 1997, Jessica, *d* of Rt Hon. Sir Timothy Alan Davan Sainsbury, *qv*; two *s* two *d*. *Educ:* Eton Coll.; Jesus Coll., Cambridge (BA Hist.); Corpus Christi Coll., Oxford (MPhil); Worcester Coll., Oxford (DPhil 1998). FRHistS 2012. Jun. Res. Fellow, Worcester Coll., Oxford, 1997–2000. Stanley J. Seeger Vis. Fellow in Hellenic Studies, Princeton Univ., 2002–03. Chair: A Curious Gp of Hotels, 1999–; Frankopan Nekretnine, 2001–; Peckwater PR, 2014–. Mem., Guild of Benefactors, Cambridge Univ., 2012–. Gov., Wellington Coll., 2006–. Trustee: Staples Trust, 1996–; Jerusalem Trust, 2008–; World Monument Fund, 2010–15; Oxford Philomusica, 2013–. FRSA 2001; FRAS 2014; FRAI 2014; Fellow, Sutton Trust, 2015. *Publications:* (trans.) Anna Komnene, The Alexiad, 2009; The First Crusade: the call from the East, 2012; The Silk Roads: a new history of the world, 2015. *Recreations:* off-piste ski-ing, sigillography, Vietnamese cooking. *Address:* Worcester College, Oxford OX1 2HB. *T:* (01865) 278300. *E:* peter.frankopan@history.ox.ac.uk. *Clubs:* Hurlingham, Authors' Cricket, Century.

FRANKS, Alan Lewis Duder; author and journalist; *b* London, 3 March 1948; *s* of Arthur Henry Franks and Vera Wilson Franks (*née* Duder); *m* 1st, 1976, Susan Law (marr. diss. 1987); two *s* one *d*; 2nd, 2006, Ruth Gledhill, *qv*; one *s*. *Educ:* Kings House, Richmond; Westminster Sch.; University Coll., Oxford (BA English). Reporter, sports and arts corresp., London local newspapers, 1971–75; Ed., Richmond Herald, 1976–78; sub-ed. and writer, THES, 1979; The Times: feature writer and columnist, 1980–2010; Alan Franks's Diary, 1983–84; Ed., PHS, Times Diary, 1986–87; contrib., Guardian, Observer, Radio Times, 2010–. Mem., Bd of Dirs, Shared Experience Th. Co., 2002–08. Writer of plays: The Changing, Irish Th. Co., 1984; Our Boys, Falcon Th. Co., Camden, 1984; A Wing and a Prayer, 1991, Augusta, 2008, New End, Hampstead; The Mother Tongue, Greenwich Th., 1992; The Edge of the Land, Eastern Angles, 2004; Previous Convictions, Orange Tree, Richmond, 2005; A World Elsewhere, Theatre503, Battersea, 2014; composer and performer of songs; albums with Patty Vetta: Will, 1995; Ladders of Daylight, 1997; The Arms of the Enemy, 2002; Bird in Flames, 2006; Only Natural, 2011. First Prize, Wigtown Internat. Poetry Competition, 2007; First Prize, Wilfred Owen Assoc. Poetry Competition, 2014. *Publications:* Real Life with Small Children Underfoot: collected episodes of Alan Franks's Diary, 1984; *novels:* Boychester's Bugle, 1982; Going Back, 2009; The Sins of the Sons, 2010; The Notes of Dr Newgate, 2013; *plays:* The Mother Tongue, 1992; A World Elsewhere, 2014; *poetry:* Unmade Roads, 2010. *Recreations:* singing, books, country walking. *Address:* c/o Curtis Brown, Haymarket House, 28–29 Haymarket, SW1Y 4SP. *T:* (020) 7393 4400. *E:* alan@alanfranks.com.

FRANKS, Jeremy Christopher Reynell; Deputy Chairman, DAKS Simpson Group plc, 2002–04; *b* 26 April 1937; *s* of late Geoffrey Charles Reynell Franks and Molly (*née* McCulloch); *m* 1959, Elizabeth Brown; one *d*. *Educ:* Lancing Coll. 2nd Lt, 1st Kings Dragoon Guards, 1956–57, Aide de Camp to British High Comr for Fedn of Malaya. Man. Dir, Simpson (Piccadilly) Ltd, 1985–86; Dir, DAKS Simpson Gp plc, 1986–87; Man. Dir, DAKS Simpson Ltd, 1987–91; Gp Man. Dir, 1991–92, Chief Exec. and Man. Dir, 1992–2002, DAKS Simpson Gp plc; Dir, Sankyo Seiko Co. Ltd, Japan, 1992–2002. Chm., British Menswear Guild, 1989–91 and 1993–95. Chm., Walpole Cttee, 1994–2000. Dir, Pony Club (GB), 2008–12. *Recreations:* Rugby, cricket, antiques, theatre. *Clubs:* Mark's; Petworth House Real Tennis.

FRANKS, Prof. Nicholas Peter, PhD; FRS 2011; FRSB, FRCA, FMedSci; Professor of Biophysics and Anaesthetics, Imperial College London, since 1993; *b* London, 14 Oct. 1949; *s* of Leonard Maurice Franks and Mary Franks; *m* 1975, Marie Ange de Vena; two *s*. *Educ:* Mill Hill Sch.; King's Coll., London (BSc 1972; PhD 1975). FRCA 2007. Lectr in Biophysics, 1977–89, Reader in Biophysics, 1989–93, Imperial Coll. London. Hon. Dr Montreal, 2011. FMedSci 2004. Gold Medal, RCAnaes, 2003. *Publications:* contribs to sci. and med. jls. *Recreations:* food and wine, watching almost any sport, collecting modern art. *Address:* Department of Life Sciences, Sir Ernst Chain Building, Wolfson Laboratories, Imperial College London, SW7 2AZ. *T:* (020) 7594 7629. *E:* n.franks@imperial.ac.uk.

FRANKS, Simon; Founder and Chairman, Redbus (media group), since 1998; Chairman, Lionsgate UK, since 2005; *b* 23 Aug. 1971; *s* of David and Brenda Franks. *Educ:* UMIST (BSc Hons). Executive: J. P. Morgan, 1992–95; BNP Paribas, 1995–97; Co-Founder and Chief Exec., Redbus Film Distribution, 1998–2005. *Recreations:* politics, film. *Address:* Redbus Group, 5th Floor, Orwell House, 16–18 Berners Street, W1T 3LN. *E:* sfassist@redbus.com.

FRANSMAN, Laurens François, (Laurie); QC 2000; *b* 4 July 1956; *s* of Henri Albert, (Harry), Fransman and Hannah Lena, (Helen), Fransman (*née* Bernstein); *m* 1st, 1977, Claire Frances Goodman (marr. diss. 1985); one *s*; 2nd, 1994, Helena Mary Cook; two *s*. *Educ:* King David High Sch., Johannesburg; Jerusalem Univ.; Leeds Univ. (LLB 1978). Called to the Bar, Middle Temple, 1979; in practice at the Bar, 1979–. Co-Founder, 1983 and Mem. Exec. Cttee, Immigration Law Practitioners' Assoc.; Member: Bar European Gp; Justice; Liberty. Participated in UNHCR and Open Soc. policy develt initiatives on nationality and statelessness, 2009–. Member, Editorial Board: Immigration and Nationality Law and Practice, 1987–; Immigration and Internat. Employment Law, 1999–2001. *Publications:* British Nationality Law and the 1981 Act, 1982; (jtly) Tribunals Practice and Procedure, 1985; (UK contrib. Ed.) Immigration Law and Practice Reporter, 1985; (jtly) Immigration Emergency Procedures, 1986; Fransman's British Nationality Law, 1989, 3rd edn 2011; Halsbury's Laws of England, 4th edn, cons., Nationality sect., 1991, Ed., and principal contrib., British Nationality, Immigration and Asylum, 2002, 5th edn (consultant ed) vol. 57, British Nationality, 2011; (jtly) Blackstone's Guide to The Borders, Citizenship and Immigration Act 2009, 2010; (contrib.) The Constitution of the United Kingdom, 1991; (contrib.) Strangers and Citizens, 1994; (contrib.) Citizenship and Nationality Status in the New Europe, 1998; (ed jtly and contrib.) Immigration, Nationality and Asylum under the Human Rights Act 1998, 1999; (contrib.) Immigration Law and Practice, 2001; (contrib.) Immigration Law and Practice in the United Kingdom, 7th edn 2008; (contrib.) Max Planck Encyclopedia of Public International Law, 2009; (jtly) Blackstone's Guide to the Borders, Citizenship and Immigration Act 2009, 2010; numerous articles on law practice, procedure and policy. *Recreations:* family, guitar, ski-ing, theatre, travel. *Address:* Garden Court Chambers, 57–60 Lincoln's Inn Fields, WC2A 3LJ. *T:* (020) 7993 7600.

FRANZ, Kevin Gerhard; Head, Department of Pastoral and Spiritual Care, Mental Health Partnerships, Greater Glasgow and Clyde Health Board, since 2009; *b* 16 June 1953; *m* 1976, Veda Fairley; one *s* one *d*. *Educ:* Univ. of Edinburgh (MA 1974; BD 1979; PhD 1992); Edinburgh Theol Coll. Ordained deacon, 1979, priest 1980; Curate, St Martin, Edinburgh, 1979–83; Rector, St John's, Selkirk, 1983–90; Provost, St Ninian's Cathedral, Perth, 1990–99, Canon, 2000–05; General Secretary: Action of Churches Together in Scotland, 1999–2007; Quaker Peace and Social Witness, 2007–09. Chm., Scottish Religious Adv. Cttee, BBC, 2002–05. Chm., Perth and Kinross Assoc. of Voluntary Services, 1995–2001. Trustee, Mindfulness Scotland, 2012–. *Publications:* (contrib.) Mental Health Ethics: the human context, 2010. *Address:* The Chaplaincy, Gartnavel Royal Hospital, 1055 Great Western Road, Glasgow G12 0XH. *T:* (0141) 211 3686. *E:* kevin.franz@ggc.scot.nhs.uk.

FRASER, family name of **Barons Lovat** and **Strathalmond**, and of **Lady Saltoun**.

FRASER, Alex; *see* Fraser, J. A.

FRASER, (Alexander) Malcolm; Founder, 1993, and Director, since 2006, Malcolm Fraser Architects; *b* 21 July 1959; *s* of William Fraser and Margaret (*née* Watters); *m* 1998, Helen Lucas; one *s* two *d*. *Educ:* George Watson's Coll., Edinburgh; Edinburgh Univ. (MA Hons; DipArch 1985). ARB. Vis. Prof., UWE, 2003–09; Geddes Hon. Professorial Fellow, Univ. of Edinburgh, 2009–. Dep. Chm., Architecture+Design Scotland, 2005–07. Chm., Scottish Govt's Town Centre Rev., 2013–. Principal buildings completed: Scottish Poetry Liby, Edinburgh, 1999; Dance Base, Edinburgh, 2001; Dance City, Newcastle, 2005; Scottish Storytelling Centre, Edinburgh, 2006; HBOS HQ, Edinburgh, 2006; Scottish Ballet, Glasgow, 2009; Dovecot Studios, Edinburgh, 2009; Royal Conservatoire of Scotland Speirs

Locks Studio, 2010; Burgh Halls, Linlithgow, 2011; Edinburgh Centre for Carbon Innovation, Edinburgh Univ., 2013. *Address:* Malcolm Fraser Architects, North Bridge Studios, 28 North Bridge, Edinburgh EH1 1QG. *T:* (0131) 225 2585, *Fax:* (0131) 226 1895. *E:* malcolm.fraser@malcolmfraser.co.uk.

FRASER, Andrew John, CMG 2001; Senior Adviser, Mitsubishi Corporation, since 2000; Director, Mitsubishi Corporation International (Europe) plc, since 2013; *b* 23 Oct. 1950; *s* of John and Mary Fraser; *m* 1st, 1976, Julia Savell (marr. diss. 1987); two *d*; 2nd, 1996, Jane Howard. *Educ:* Univ. of Sussex (BA); ESU Schol., Harvard Sch.; exchange schol., UCLA. Account Dir, Young and Rubicam, London, 1972–76; Man. Dir, McCann Erickson, Thailand, 1976–80; Exec. Vice Pres., Dir of Business Develt, Saatchi and Saatchi Worldwide, 1981–92; Man. Dir, cdp Europe (Dentsu Worldwide), 1992–94; Chief Exec., Invest in Britain Bureau, later INVEST.UK, 1994–2000. Dir, UK-Japan 21st Century Gp, 1998–2004; non-exec. Dir, English Partnerships, 1999–2000; Mem., Internat. Adv. Bd, FTI Consulting (Strategic Communications) (formerly Financial Dynamics), 2003–. Dir, Think London (formerly London First Centre), 2002–12. Advr, Arup Gp, 2001–05. Pres., Worldaware, 2002–05; Member: Develt Council, 2001–06, Trust Bd, 2006–14, Council, 2014–, Shakespeare's Globe; Council, Chatham House (RIIA), 2006–12; Council, Japan Soc., 2006–11 (Chm., Business Gp, 2006–). *Recreations:* sports, theatre, food and drink, conversation. *Clubs:* Royal Automobile, MCC, ESU, Pilgrims; V&A Cricket; Woking Golf; Royal Wimbledon Golf.

FRASER, Dr Andrew Kerr, FRCPE, FRCPGlas, FFPH; Director of Public Health Science, NHS Health Scotland, since 2012; *b* 10 Dec. 1958; *s* of Sir William (Kerr) Fraser, *qv* and of Lady Marion Fraser, *qv*; *m* 1st, 1985 (marr. diss. 2010); three *s* one *d*; 2nd, 2012, Barbara Pettigrew Allison. *Educ:* George Watson's Coll.; Univ. of Aberdeen (MB ChB 1981); Univ. of Glasgow (MPH 1990). FRCPE 1998; FFPH (FFPHM 1999); FRCPGlas 2001. Med. Dir, Nat. Services Div., CSA, 1993–94; Dir of Public Health, Highland Health Bd, 1994–97; Dep. CMO, Scottish Office, subseq. Scottish Exec., 1997–2003; Head of Health, 2003–06, Dir of Health and Care, 2006–12, Scottish Prison Service. *Recreations:* music, mountain walking. *Address:* NHS Health Scotland, Meridian Court, Cadogan Street, Glasgow G2 6QE. *T:* (0141) 414 2735.

FRASER, Angus Robert Charles, MBE 1999; Managing Director, Cricket, Middlesex County Cricket Club, since 2009; Selector, England Cricket Team, since 2014; *b* 8 Aug. 1965; *s* of Donald and Irene Fraser; *m* 1996, Denise Simmonds; one *s* one *d*. *Educ:* Gayton High Sch.; Orange Hill Sen. High Sch. Played for Middlesex CCC, 1984–2002 (Captain, 2000–02); England Test Cricketer, 1989–99: 46 Test matches (took 177 Test wickets); 42 One-day Internationals. Sponsorship consultant, Whittingdale, 1991–93 (whilst injured). Cricket Corresp., Independent, 2002–08. *Publications:* Fraser's Tour Diaries, 1998. *Recreations:* golf, wine, Liverpool FC, watching children play sport. *Address:* Middlesex County Cricket Club, Lord's Cricket Ground, NW8 8QN. *Clubs:* MCC, Stanmore Cricket, Middlesex County Cricket.

FRASER, Angus Simon James; Co-founder and Director, QuickVox Ltd, since 2009; *b* 28 Feb. 1945; *s* of Baron Fraser of Kilmorack, CBE and Elizabeth Chloë Fraser (*neé* Drummond); *m* 1970, Jennifer Ann, *d* of Colin McKean Craig, FRCS and Irene Joan Craig (*née* Yeldham); two *s* one *d*. *Educ:* Fettes Coll., Edinburgh; Selwyn Coll., Cambridge (MA); European Inst. of Business Admin (INSEAD), France (MBA). Dunlop Co. Ltd, 1968–70; Mercantile Credit Co. Ltd, 1971–76; Chloride Group PLC, 1976–2006: Chm., Chloride Europe, 1983–85; Exec. Dir, Industrial Operations, 1985–87, Corporate Operations, 1987–88; non-exec. Dir, 1988–2006; Man. Dir, Imperial Coll. of Sci., Technol. and Medicine, 1989–94 (Gov., 1990–94); Chief Exec., Scruttons plc, 1995–97; Chm., Benitec Ltd, 1998–2002. Non-executive Director: Davies, Laing and Dick Ltd, 1998–2002 (Chm., 2000–02); Technology Enterprise Kent, 1998–2005; Singapore Para Rubber Estates plc, 1999–2001; Bertam Hldgs plc, 2001–05 (Dep. Chm., 2001–05); Shepherd Bldg Gp Ltd, 2002–07; IdaTech plc, 2007–11; Chm., Alpha Plus (formerly DLD) Hldgs Ltd, 2002–07. Trustee, Caldecott Foundn, 2004–14 (Vice Chm., 2006–09; Chm., 2009–14). *Recreations:* opera, golf, fly-fishing, painting, walking, family and friends.

FRASER, Air Cdre Anthony Walkinshaw; company director; *b* 15 March 1934; *s* of late Robert Walkinshaw Fraser and Evelyn Elisabeth Fraser; *m* 1st, 1955, Angela Mary Graham Shaw (marr. diss. 1990); one *s* three *d*; 2nd, 1990, Grania Ruth Eleanor Stewart-Smith. *Educ:* Stowe Sch. MIL. RAF Pilot and Flying Instructor, 1952–66; sc Camberley, 1967; MA/VCDS, MoD, 1968–70; Chief Instructor Buccaneer OCU, 1971–72; Air Warfare Course, 1973; Directing Staff, National Defence Coll., 1973; Dep. Dir, Operational Requirements, MoD, 1974–76; Comdt, Central Flying Sch., 1977–79. ADC to the Queen, 1977–79. Dir, SMMT, 1980–88. Chairman: Personal Guard, 1992–94; Chlorella Products Ltd (formerly Nature's Balance Marketing), 1994–2007; Enhanced Office Environments Ltd, 2001–07; Dir, Nissan UK Ltd, 1989–91. President: Comité de Liaison de la Construction Automobile, 1980–83; Organisation (formerly Bureau Perm.) Internat. des Constructeurs d'Automobiles, 1983–87 (Vice-Pres., 1981–83). FCMI. *Recreations:* shooting, golf, fishing, languages. *Address:* 31 Grove End Road, NW8 9LY. *T:* (020) 7286 0521. *Clubs:* Royal Air Force, Sunningdale.

FRASER, Lady Antonia, (Lady Antonia Pinter), DBE 2011 (CBE 1999); writer; *b* 27 Aug. 1932; *d* of 7th Earl of Longford, KG, PC, and late Elizabeth, Countess of Longford, CBE; *m* 1st, 1956, Rt Hon. Sir Hugh Fraser, MBE, MP (marr. diss. 1977, he *d* 1984); three *s* three *d*; 2nd, 1980, Harold Pinter, CH, CBE (*d* 2008). *Educ:* Dragon School, Oxford; St Mary's Convent, Ascot; Lady Margaret Hall, Oxford (MA; Hon. Fellow, 2007). General Editor, Kings and Queens of England series. Chairman: Soc. of Authors, 1974–75; Crimewriters' Assoc., 1985–86; Vice Pres., English PEN, 1990– (Mem. Cttee, 1979–88; Pres., 1988–89; Chm., Writers in Prison Cttee, 1985–88, 1990). Goodman Lecture, 1997. Pres., Gaieties CC, 2011–. FRSL 2003; Centenary Fellow, Histl Assoc., 2006. Norton Medlicott Medal, Histl Assoc., 2000. Hon. DLitt: Hull, 1986; Sussex, 1990; Nottingham, 1993; St Andrews, 1994. Officier, Ordre des Palmes Académiques, 2012. *Publications:* (as Antonia Pakenham): King Arthur and the Knights of the Round Table, 1954 (reissued, 1970); Robin Hood, 1955 (reissued, 1971); (as Antonia Fraser): Dolls, 1963; A History of Toys, 1966; Mary Queen of Scots (James Tait Black Memorial Prize, 1969), 1969 (reissued illus. edn, 1978); Cromwell Our Chief of Men, (in USA, Cromwell the Lord Protector), 1973; King James: VI of Scotland, I of England, 1974; (ed) Kings and Queens of England, 1975 (reissued, 1988); (ed) Scottish Love Poems, a personal anthology, 1975 (reissued, 1988), new edn 2002; (ed) Love Letters: an anthology, 1976, rev. edn 2002; Quiet as a Nun (mystery), 1977, adapted for TV series, 1978; The Wild Island (mystery), 1978 (reissued as Tartan Tragedy, 2005); King Charles II, (in USA, Royal Charles), 1979; (ed) Heroes and Heroines, 1980; A Splash of Red (mystery), 1981 (basis for TV series Jemima Shore Investigates, 1983); (ed) Mary Queen of Scots: poetry anthology, 1981; (ed) Oxford and Oxfordshire in Verse: anthology, 1982; Cool Repentance (mystery), 1982; The Weaker Vessel: woman's lot in seventeenth century England, 1984 (Wolfson History Award, 1984; Prix Caumont-La Force, 1985); Oxford Blood (mystery), 1985; Jemima Shore's First Case (mystery short stories), 1986; Your Royal Hostage (mystery), 1987; Boadicea's Chariot: the Warrior Queens, 1988 (paperback, The Warrior Queens, 1989, in USA, The Warrior Queens, 1989); The Cavalier Case (mystery), 1990; Jemima Shore at the Sunny Grave (mystery short stories), 1991; The Six Wives of Henry VIII, 1992, reissued illus. edn, 1996 (Schloss Bauverein Preis, 1997; in USA, The Wives of Henry VIII); (ed) The Pleasure of Reading, 1992 (reissued 2015); Political Death (mystery), 1994; The Gunpowder Plot: terror and faith in 1605, 1996 (CWA Non Fiction Gold Dagger, 1996) (in USA, Treason and Faith: the story of the gunpowder plot; St Louis Literary Award, 1996); Marie Antoinette: the Journey, 2001 (Enid McLeod Lit. Award, Franco-British Soc., 2002); First Jemima Shore Anthology (Quiet as a Nun, Tartan Tragedy, A Splash of Red), 2005; Second Jemima Shore Anthology (Oxford Blood, Cool Repentance, Your Royal Hostage), 2006; Love and Louis XIV: the women in the life of the Sun King, 2006; Must You Go? My life with Harold Pinter, 2010 (Prix du meilleur livre étranger essai, 2010); Perilous Question: the drama of the Great Reform Bill 1832, 2013 (in USA, Perilous Question: reform or revolution? Britain on the brink); My History: a memoir of growing up, 2015; various mystery stories in anthols, incl. Have a Nice Death, 1983 (adapted for TV, 1984); TV plays: Charades, 1977; Mister Clay, Mister Clay (Time for Murder series), 1985. *Recreations:* swimming, grandchildren. *Address:* 52 Campden Hill Square, W8 7JR. *Clubs:* Athenæum, PEN; Literary Society.

See also F. Fraser, O. G. Fraser.

FRASER, Sir Charles (Annand), KCVO 1989 (CVO 1985; LVO 1968); WS; non-executive Vice Chairman, United Biscuits (Holdings), 1986–95 (Director, 1978–95); Partner, W & J Burness, WS, Edinburgh, 1956–92; *b* 16 Oct. 1928; *o s* of late Very Rev. John Annand Fraser, MBE, TD; *m* 1957, Ann Scott-Kerr; four *s*. *Educ:* Hamilton Academy; Edinburgh Univ. (MA, LLB). Purse Bearer to Lord High Commissioner to General Assembly of Church of Scotland, 1969–88. Chairman: Morgan Grenfell (Scotland), 1985–86; Adam & Co., 1989–98; Lothian & Edinburgh Enterprise Ltd, 1991–94; NSM, 1992–94; Director: Scottish Widows' Fund, 1978–94; British Assets Trust, 1969–; Scottish Media Group plc (formerly Scottish Television Ltd), 1979–98, and other companies. Chm., Sec. of State for Scotland's Adv. Cttee on Sustainable Develt, 1995–98. Trustee, WWF (UK), 1998–2000. Mem. Council, Law Society of Scotland, 1966–72; Governor of Fettes, 1976–86; Mem. Court, Heriot-Watt Univ., 1972–78. Hon. Res. Fellow, Royal Botanic Gardens, Edinburgh, 2008. WS 1959; DL East Lothian, 1984–2003. Dr *hc* Edinburgh, 1991; Hon. LLD Napier, 1992. *Recreations:* gardening, ski-ing, piping. *Address:* Shepherd House, Inveresk, Midlothian EH21 7TH. *T:* (0131) 665 2570. *Clubs:* New, Hon. Co. of Edinburgh Golfers (Edinburgh); Royal and Ancient (St Andrews).

FRASER, Christopher James, OBE 2013; Chairman, International Communications Group. Mem., Three Rivers DC, 1992–96. MP (C) Mid Dorset and N Poole, 1997–2001, SW Norfolk, 2005–10. PPS to Leader of the Opposition, H of L, 1999–2001. Member: Culture, Media and Sports Select Cttee, 1997–2001; NI Select Cttee, 2005–10; NI Grand Cttee; Speaker's Panel of Chairmen; Vice Chm., All-Party Forestry Gp, 1997–2001; Mem., Parly Inf. and Technol. Cttee, 1997–2001; Chm., Parly Mgt Consultancy Gp, 2000–01; Vice Chm., Cons. Trade and Industry Cttee, 2000–01; Chm., All Party Parly Gp on NI. Member: IPU, 1997–2010; CPA, 1997–2010; Council of Europe, 2005–07; WEU, 2005–07. Director: Small Business Bureau, 1997–2005; Genesis Foundn. Patron, Firmlink, 1995–2001. Appeals Chm., Pramacare, 1996–2007; Mem., County Cttee, Holton Lee Charity Appeal, 1997–2001. Mem., Soc. of Dorset Men, 1997–2001. Freeman, City of London, 1992.

FRASER, Prof. Derek, FRHistS; Vice-Chancellor, University of Teesside, 1992–2003; Independent Football Ombudsman, since 2008 (Chairman, Independent Football Commission, 2001–08); *b* 24 July 1940; *s* of Jacob and Dorothy Fraser; *m* 1962, Ruth Spector; two *s* one *d*. *Educ:* Univ. of Leeds (BA, MA, PhD). Schoolteacher, 1962–65; Lectr, Sen. Lectr, Reader and Prof. of Modern History, Univ. of Bradford, 1965–82; Prof. of English History, UCLA, 1982–84; HMI (History and Higher Educn), 1984–88; Staff Inspector (Higher Educn), DES, 1988–90; Asst/Dep. Principal, Sheffield City Polytechnic, 1990–92. Chairman: Graduate Apprenticeship Nat. Steering Cttee, 1998–2000; Univ. Vocational Awards Council, 1999–2001; Standards Verification UK, 2005–11; Member: NACETT, 1999–2001; One NorthEast RDA, 1999–2001; Educn Cttee, RICS, 2006–09; Lifelong Learning UK, 2011–12. Levinson Scholar in Residence, St Andrew's Sch., Delaware, 2014. Hon. LLD Teesside, 2003. *Publications:* The Evolution of the British Welfare State, 1973, 4th edn 2009; Urban Politics in Victorian England, 1976; Power and Authority in the Victorian City, 1979; (ed) A History of Modern Leeds, 1980; (ed jtly) The Pursuit of Urban History, 1980; (ed) Municipal Reform and the Industrial City, 1982; (ed) Cities, Class and Communication: essays in honour of Asa Briggs, 1990; The Welfare State, 2000. *Recreations:* cruising, bridge, music, football and other spectator sports. *Address:* Office of the Independent Football Ombudsman, Suite 49, 33 Great George Street, Leeds LS1 3AJ.

FRASER, Dame Dorothy (Rita), DBE 1987; QSO 1978; JP; Australasian Chairman, Community Systems Foundation Australasia, 1991–94 (New Zealand Director, 1975–91); *b* 3 May 1926; *d* of Ernest and Kate Tucker; *m* 1947, Hon. William Alex Fraser; one *s* one *d*. *Educ:* Gisborne High Sch. Chm., Otago Hosp. Bd, 1974–86 (Mem., 1953–56, 1962–86); Member: Nursing Council of NZ, 1981–87; Grading Review Cttee (Health Service Personnel Commn), 1984–87; Hosps Adv. Council, 1984–86; NZ Health Service Personnel Commn, 1987–88; Otago Plunket-Karitane Hosp. Bd, 1979–87; NZ Lottery Bd, 1985–90; Vice-Pres., NZ Hosp. Bds Assoc., 1981–86; Chairman: Southern Region Health Services Assoc., 1984–86; Hosp. and Specialist Services Cttee, NZ Bd of Health, 1985–88. Consultant, ADT Ltd Australasia, later Command Pacific Group, 1988–91. Chm., Otago Jt Tertiary Educn Liaison Cttee, 1988–99; Panel Chm., NZ Colls of Educn Accreditation Cttee, 1996–2004; Member: Council, Univ. of Otago, 1974–86; Otago High Schs Bd of Governors, 1964–85. Chm., Dunedin Airport Cttee, 1971–74; Member: Dunedin CC, 1970–74; NZ Exec. Marr. Guidance, 1969–75. Chairman: Montecillo Trust, 2001–08; Montecillo Veterans' Home and Hospital Ltd, 2001–08. Life Mem., NZ Labour Party; Gold Badge for Service to Labour Party. JP 1959. Hon. LLD Otago, 1994. Silver Jubilee Medal, 1977. *Recreations:* gardening, golf, reading. *Address:* 21 Ings Avenue, St Clair, Dunedin, New Zealand. *T:* (3) 4558663.

FRASER, Edward; *see* Fraser, J. E.

FRASER, Flora, (Mrs Flora Soros); writer; *b* 30 Oct. 1958; *d* of Rt Hon. Sir Hugh Charles Patrick Joseph Fraser, MBE, MP, and of Lady Antonia Fraser, *qv*; *m* 1st, 1980, Robert James Powell-Jones (marr. diss. 1989); one *d*; 2nd, 1997, Peter Ross Soros (marr. diss. 2010); two *s*. *Educ:* St Paul's Girls' Sch.; British Inst., Florence; Wadham Coll., Oxford (BA Lit. Hum.). Member: Exec. Cttee, Friends of Nat. Libraries, 1999–2003; Develt Council Exec., Wadham Coll., Oxford, 2011–. Trustee, NPG, 1999–2008. Co-Founder: Elizabeth Longford Prize for Historical Biog., 2003; Elizabeth Longford Grants for Historical Biographers, 2003. *Publications:* Tamgar, 1981; Double Portrait, 1983; Maud: the diaries of Maud Berkeley, 1985; Beloved Emma: the life of Emma, Lady Hamilton, 1986; The English Gentlewoman, 1987; The Unruly Queen: the life of Queen Caroline, 1996; Princesses: the six daughters of George III, 2004; Venus of Empire: the life of Pauline Bonaparte, 2009; George and Martha Washington: a revolutionary marriage, 2015. *Recreation:* swimming in Greece. *Address:* 15 Kensington Park Gardens, W11 3HD.

See also O. G. Fraser.

FRASER, Rev. Canon Dr Giles Anthony; Priest-in-charge, St Mary's, Newington, since 2012; columnist, Church Times, 2003–13; *b* 27 Nov. 1964; *s* of Wing Comdr Anthony Fraser and Gillian Fraser; *m* 1993, Sally Aagaard; one *s* two *d*. *Educ:* Uppingham Sch.; Univ. of Newcastle-upon-Tyne (BA Hons Philosophy 1984); Ripon Coll., Cuddesdon (BA Hons Theol. (Oxon) 1992; MA (Oxon) 1997); Univ. of Lancaster (PhD 1999). Ordained deacon, 1993, priest, 1994; Curate, All Saints, Streetly, 1993–97; Chaplain, Univ. Church of St Mary the Virgin, Oxford, 1997–2000; Wadham College, Oxford: Chaplain, 1997–2000; Lectr in Philosophy, 2000–07; Team Rector, Parish of Putney, 2000–09; Canon Chancellor, St Paul's Cathedral, 2009–11. Mem., Gen. Synod, C of E, 2003–09. Founder, 2003–, Pres., 2005–,

Inclusive Church. Regular contrib. to Radio 4's Thought for the Day, Guardian. *Publications:* Christianity and Violence, 2001; Redeeming Nietzsche, 2002; Christianity with Attitude, 2007. *Recreations:* golf, food, politics.

FRASER, Helen Jean Sutherland, CBE 2010; Chief Executive, Girls' Day School Trust, since 2010; *b* 8 June 1949; *d* of George Sutherland Fraser and Paddy Fraser; *m* 1982, Grant James McIntyre; two *d*, and two step *d*. *Educ:* St Anne's Coll., Oxford (BA Eng. Lang. and Lit. 1970, MA). Editor: Methuen Academic, 1972–74; Open Books, 1974–77; Editor, then Editl Dir, William Collins, 1977–87; Publisher, then Man. Dir, Reed Trade Books, 1987–97; Man. Dir, Penguin General, 1997–2001; Man. Dir, Penguin UK, 2001–09. Chm. of Judges, Bailey's Women's Prize for Fiction, 2014. Trustee, Spitalfields Music, 2008–14. Churchwarden, St Bride's Fleet St, 2013–. Hon. DLitt Bristol, 2010. *Recreations:* opera, ballet, theatre, concerts. *Address:* (office) 100 Rochester Row, SW1P 1JP.

See also B. P. K. McIntyre.

FRASER, Sir Iain (Michael Duncan), 3rd Bt *cr* 1943, of Tain, co. Ross; owner of The Elephant House chain of café/bistros, Edinburgh, since 1994; *b* 27 June 1951; *er s* of Prof. Sir James David Fraser, 2nd Bt and Edith Maureen, *d* of Rev. John Reay, MC; *S* father, 1997; *m* 1st, 1981, Sherylle Ann Gillespie (marr. diss. 1991), Wellington, NZ; one *s* one *d*; 2nd, 2004, Mrs Anne Ferguson (*née* Sim). *Educ:* Glenalmond; Edinburgh Univ. (BSc Business Studies 1974). Sales Manager, Edinburgh and Hong Kong, Ben Line Containers Ltd, 1974–80; Internat. Traffic Manager, Asia, Amerex International, 1980–84; Sales/Marketing management, Hong Kong, Singapore, New York and San Francisco, American President Lines, 1984–94. *Recreations:* photography, historical tourism, coffee. *Heir: s* Benjamin James Fraser, *b* 6 April 1986. *Address:* 36 Comely Bank, Edinburgh EH4 1AJ.

FRASER, (James) Edward, CB 1990; Secretary of Commissions for Scotland, 1992–94; an Assistant Local Government Boundary Commissioner for Scotland, 1997–2011; *b* 16 Dec. 1931; *s* of late Dr James F. Fraser, TD, Aberdeen, and late Dr Kathleen Blomfield; *m* 1959, Patricia Louise Stewart; two *s*. *Educ:* Aberdeen Grammar Sch.; Univ. of Aberdeen (MA); Christ's Coll., Cambridge (BA). FSAScot. RA, 1953; Staff Captain 'Q', Tel-el-Kebir, 1954–55. Asst Principal, Scottish Home Dept, 1957–60; Private Sec. to Permanent Under Sec. of State, 1960–62, and to Parly Under-Sec. of State, 1962; Principal: SHHD, 1962–64; Cabinet Office, 1964–66; HM Treasury, 1966–68; SHHD, 1968–69; Asst Sec., SHHD, 1970–76; Asst Sec., 1976, Under Sec., 1976–81, Local Govt Finance Gp, Scottish Office; Under Sec., SHHD, 1981–91. Pres., Scottish Hellenic Soc. of Edinburgh and Eastern Scotland, 1987–93. Pres., Former Pupils' Club, Aberdeen GS, 1997–98 (Hon. Vice-Pres., 1998–). *Recreations:* reading, music, walking, Greece ancient and modern, DIY. *Address:* 59 Murrayfield Gardens, Edinburgh EH12 6DH. *T:* (0131) 337 2274. *Club:* Scottish Arts (Edinburgh).

FRASER, James Mackenzie, CBE 2014; Principal, 2009–13, and Vice-Chancellor, 2011–13, University of the Highlands and Islands (formerly University of the Highlands and Islands Millennium Institute); *b* Poolewe, Ross-shire, 29 July 1948; *s* of Duncan Fraser and Anne Fraser; *m* 1st, 1975, Janet Sinclair (*d* 1986); one *d*; 2nd, 1987, Sheila Macfarlane; one *s* one *d*. *Educ:* Plockton High Sch., Ross-shire; Univ. of Edinburgh (MA Hons Mental Philos.); Univ. of Stirling (MEd). Lectr, Inverness Technical Coll., 1971–77; Tutor, Open Univ. in Scotland, 1971–77; Sen. Asst Registrar, Univ. of Stirling, 1977–87; Coll. Sec., Queen Margaret Coll., Edinburgh, 1987–89; Sec., Paisley Coll., subseq. Univ. of Paisley, 1989–2002; Sec., 2002–07, Depute Principal-Sec., 2007–09, UHI Millennium Inst. Dir, Free Church Nominees Co., 1989–; Chm., Bd of Trustees, Free Church of Scotland, 2007. *Recreations:* music, genealogy, cinema, travel. *Address:* The Old Manse, Camault Muir, Kiltarlity, Beauly IV4 7JH. *E:* jmfraserbusiness@gmail.com. *Club:* New (Edinburgh).

FRASER, James Owen Arthur; a Sheriff of Grampian, Highland and Islands, 1984–2002; *b* 9 May 1937; *s* of James and Effie Fraser; *m* 1961, Flora Shaw MacKenzie (*d* 2010); two *s*. *Educ:* Glasgow High Sch. (Classical Dux 1954); Glasgow Univ. (MA 1958; LlB 1961). Qualified as Solicitor, 1961; employed as solicitor, Edinburgh, 1961–65, Glasgow, 1965–66; Partner, Bird Son & Semple, later Bird Semple & Crawford Herron, Solicitors, Glasgow, 1967–84. Part-time Lectr in Evidence and Procedure, Glasgow Univ., 1976–83. Temp. Sheriff, 1983–84. *Recreation:* golf. *Address:* Ardmara, 18 Marine Terrace, Rosemarkie, Ross-shire IV10 8UL. *T:* (01381) 621011.

FRASER, Hon. John Allen; PC (Can.) 1979; OC 1995; OBC 1995; CD 1962; QC (Can.) 1983; Chairman, BC Pacific Salmon Forum, Canada, 2005–09; *b* Japan, 15 Dec. 1931; *m* 1960, Catherine Findlay; three *d*. *Educ:* Univ. of British Columbia (LLB 1954). Law practice, Victoria, Powell River, Vancouver, 1955–72. MP (PC) Vancouver S, 1972–94; Opposition Critic, Environment, 1972–74, Labour, 1974–79; Minister of Environment and Postmaster General, 1979–80; Opposition Critic, Environment, Fisheries, Post Office, and Solicitor-General, 1980–84; Minister of Fisheries and Oceans, 1984–85; Speaker of H of C, Canada, 1986–94; Ambassador for the Envmt, Dept of Foreign Affairs and Internat. Trade, Canada, 1994–98. Chm., Pacific Fisheries Resource Conservation Council, 1998–2005. Chairman: Nat. Defence Minister's Monitoring Cttee on Change, 1998–2005; Parly Precinct Oversight Adv. Cttee, 2000–. Hon. LLD: St Lawrence Univ., 1999; Simon Fraser Univ., 1999; British Columbia, 2004. Hon. Lt-Col, Seaforth Highlanders of Canada, 1994– (Hon. Col).

FRASER, John Denis; *b* 30 June 1934; *s* of Archibald and Frances Fraser; *m* 1960, Ann Hathaway; two *s* one *d*. *Educ:* Sloane Grammar Sch., Chelsea; Co-operative Coll., Loughborough; Law Soc. Sch. of Law (John Mackrell Prize). Entered Australia & New Zealand Bank Ltd, 1950; Army service, 1952–54, as Sgt, RAEC (educnl and resettlement work). Solicitor, 1960; practised with Lewis Silkin. Mem. Lambeth Borough Council, 1962–68 (Chm. Town Planning Cttee; Chm. Labour Gp). MP (Lab) Norwood, 1966–97. PPS to Rt Hon. Barbara Castle, 1968–70; Opposition front bench spokesman on Home Affairs, 1972–74; Parly Under-Sec. of State, Dept of Employment, 1974–76; Minister of State, Dept of Prices and Consumer Protection, 1976–79; opposition spokesman on trade, 1979–83, on housing and construction, 1983–87, on legal affairs, 1987–94. *Recreations:* athletics, football, music. *Address:* 24 Turney Road, SE21 8LU.

FRASER, John Stewart; Chairman and Chief Executive, Ciba-Geigy plc, 1990–96; *b* 18 July 1931; *s* of Donald Stewart Fraser and Ruth (*née* Dobinson); *m* 1st, 1955, Diane Louise Witt (marr. diss. 1996); two *s* one *d*; 2nd, 1996, Lynette Ann Murray. *Educ:* Royal Melbourne Inst. of Technology. ARACI. Technical Rep., Australian Sales Manager and Australian Marketing Manager, Monsanto Australia Ltd, 1953–68; Marketing Manager, Ilford (Australia) Pty Ltd, 1968–73; Ilford Ltd, UK: Marketing Dir, 1973–78; Man. Dir and Chief Exec., 1978–84; Corporate Man. Dir, Ciba-Geigy Plastics and Additives Co., UK, 1982–84; Ciba-Geigy plc, UK: Gp Man. Dir, 1984–87; Gp Man. Dir and Chief Exec., 1987–90. Non-exec. Dir, Westminster Health Care, 1993–99. Chm., Assoc. for Schools' Sci., Engrg and Technol. (formerly Standing Conf. on Schools' Sci. and Technol.), 1996–2000. Pres., Chemical Industries Assoc., 1994–95. *Recreations:* swimming, walking. *Address:* 124/1 The Inlet Drive, Carrara, Qld 4211, Australia.

FRASER, Julian Alexander, (Alex); Principal, ifs University College, since 2015; *b* 23 July 1959; *s* of Peter Marshall Fraser, MC, FBA and Ruth Fraser. *Educ:* Abingdon Sch., Oxon; Manchester Univ. (BA Hons Classics 1987). Teacher, Latin and Computer Studies, Lawrence House Sch., St Annes on Sea, Lancs, 1978–84; Database Researcher, CEDIM srl, Ancona, 1987–89; Information Consultant, Atefos SpA, Turin, 1989–90; Manager, Inf. Resource Centre, Merrill Lynch Europe Ltd, 1990–93; Asst Dir and Head of Inf. Systems, West Merchant Bank Ltd, 1993–95; J. Henry Schroder & Co. Ltd: Manager, Inf. Centre, 1995–96; Head of Ops, European Corporate Finance Div., 1996–97; Dir and Global Head, Corporate Finance Support Services, 1997–2000; Director: Logistics, HM Customs and Excise, 2000–03; Get Well UK Ltd, 2003–05; CEO, Land Data Ltd, 2005–09; Chief Operating Officer, Cass Business Sch., City Univ. London, 2009–15. *Recreation:* equine. *Address:* ifs University College, Peninsular House, 36 Monument Street, EC3R 8LJ.

FRASER, Kenneth John Alexander; international marketing consultant; *b* 22 Sept. 1929; *s* of Jack Sears Fraser and Marjorie Winifred (*née* Savery); *m* 1953, Kathleen Grace Booth (*d* 2013); two *s* one *d*. *Educ:* Thames Valley Grammar Sch., Twickenham; London School of Economics (BScEcon Hons). Joined Erwin Wasey & Co. Ltd, 1953, then Lintas Ltd, 1958; Managing Director, Research Bureau Ltd, 1962; Unilever: Head of Marketing Analysis and Evaluation Group, 1965; Head of Marketing Division, 1976–79, 1981–89; Hd of Internat. Affairs, 1985–89; Hd of External Affairs, 1989–90; seconded to NEDO as Industrial Dir, 1979–81. Advr, European Assoc. of Branded Goods Manufacturers, 1991–93. Member: Consumer Protection Adv. Cttee, Dept of Prices and Consumer Protection, 1975; Management Bd, ADAS, MAFF, 1986–92; Chairman: CBI Marketing and Consumer Affairs Cttee, 1977; Internat. Chamber of Commerce Marketing Commn, 1978; Vice Chm., Advertising Assoc., 1981–90; Dir, Direct Mail Services Standards Bd, 1991–94. Mem., Advocacy Cttee, Nat. Children's Home, 1987–95. FRSA 1980. *Recreations:* walking, music, reading. *T:* (office) (020) 8949 3760.

FRASER, Malcolm; *see* Fraser, A. M.

FRASER, Lady Marion Anne, LT 1996; Chair of the Board, Christian Aid, 1990–97; Lord High Commissioner, then HM High Commissioner, General Assembly, Church of Scotland, 1994–95; *b* 17 Oct. 1932; *d* of Robert Forbes and Elizabeth Taylor Watt; *m* 1956, Sir William (Kerr) Fraser, *qv*; three *s* one *d*. *Educ:* Hutchesons' Girls' Grammar Sch.; Univ. of Glasgow (MA); Royal Scottish Academy of Music. LRAM, ARCM. Chm., Scottish Internat. Piano Comp., 1995–99. Director: Friends of Royal Scottish Academy (Founder Chm., 1986–89); Scottish Opera, 1990–94; St Mary's Music School, 1989–95. Chm., Scottish Assoc. for Mental Health, 1995–99. President: Scotland's Churches Scheme, 1997–2009; Scotland's Churches Trust, 2013–. Trustee: Scottish Churches Architectural Heritage Trust, 1989–2013; Lamp of Lothian Collegiate Trust, 1996–2005; Gov., Laurel Bank Sch. for Girls, 1988–95. Hon. Mem., Co. of Merchants of City of Edinburgh, 1998. FRCPSGlas 2002. Hon. LLD Glasgow, 1995; DUniv Stirling, 1998. *Recreations:* family, friends, people and places. *Address:* Broadwood, Edinburgh Road, Gifford, East Lothian EH41 4JE. *Club:* New (Edinburgh).

See also A. K. Fraser.

FRASER, Mark Thomas, LVO 2014; OAM 2003; Official Secretary to Governor-General of Australia, since 2014; Secretary: Council for Order of Australia, since 2014; Australian Bravery Decorations Council, since 2014; National Emergency Medal Committee, since 2014; *b* Hobart, 6 March 1975; *s* of John and Sharyn Fraser; partner, 1998, Cüneyt Mermercan. *Educ:* Bond Univ. (BA Internal Relns, PR and Journalism 1994); Monash Univ. (MA Foreign Affairs and Trade 2001); Univ. of Sydney (Exec. MBA 2013). Grad. prog., Australian Taxation Office, 1995; entered Dept of Foreign Affairs and Trade, 1996; Cultural Relns Branch, then Internat. Media Centre, 1996–98; Consul, Ankara, 1998–2001; Southern Europe Sect., Ministerial and Exec. Liaison Sect., then Audit and Evaluation Sect., 2001–04; Consul-Gen., The Hague, 2004–07; Dir, Remuneration, Entitlements and Conditions Sect., 2007–09; Dep. Official Sec. to Gov.-Gen. of Australia, 2009–14. Co-Founder and CEO, Make A Mark Australia, 2009–. Chm., Rhodes Scholarship-At-Large Selection Cttee, 2014–. *Recreations:* charity works, travel. *Address:* Government House, Canberra, ACT 2600, Australia. *T:* (02) 62833508, *Fax:* (09) 62813760. *E:* Mark.Fraser@gg.gov.au.

FRASER, Prof. Maurice; Professor of Practice in European Politics, since 2012, and Head, European Institute, since 2013, London School of Economics and Political Science; *b* London, 2 March 1960; *s* of Maurice Fraser and Fanny Helena Fraser; *m* 1989, Nicolette Le Pelley; two *s* one *d*. *Educ:* French Lycée, London; London Sch. of Econs and Pol Sci. (BSc (Econ)). Conservative Research Department: Home Affairs Desk Officer, 1984–85; Hd, Pol Section, 1985–86; Asst Dir, 1986–88; Special Advr to Foreign Sec., 1989–95; Consultant: Internat. Relns, Unilever plc, 1996–98; Eur. Affairs, Merrill Lynch, 1996–98; Econ. and Monetary Union, EC, 1996–98; London School of Economics and Political Science: Vis. Fellow in Eur. Politics, 1996–2003; Fellow in Eur. Politics, 2003–08; Sen. Fellow, 2009–13. Sen. Counsellor, APCO worldwide, 1995–2013 (Mem., Internat. Adv. Council, 2008–13). Dir and Ed., Agenda Publishing, 1998–2003; Dir, Agora Projects, 2004–08. Associate Fellow, RIIA, 2007–. Dep. Chm., Franco-British Council, 2006–11 (Trustee, 2006–). Trustee, Forum for Eur. Philosophy, 1996–. Chevalier, Légion d'honneur (France), 2008. *Publications:* (ed) G8 Summit 2007, 2007; (ed) European Union: the next fifty years, 2007; (ed) European Union: policies and priorities, 2008; (ed jtly) Franco-British Academic Partnerships: the next chapter, 2011. *Recreations:* French chanson, Italian baroque opera, Greek rebetika, social and cultural history, my labradoodle. *Address:* European Institute, London School of Economics and Political Science, Houghton Street, WC2A 2AE. *T:* 07770 431725, *Fax:* (020) 7221 6600. *E:* m.fraser@lse.ac.uk. *Club:* Travellers.

FRASER, Murdo Mackenzie; Member (C) Scotland Mid and Fife, Scottish Parliament, since Aug. 2001; *b* 5 Sept. 1965; *s* of Sandy Fraser and Barbara Fraser (*née* MacPherson); *m* 1994, Emma Jarvis; one *s* one *d*. *Educ:* Inverness Royal Acad.; Univ. of Aberdeen (LLB 1986; Dip. Legal Studies). Admitted solicitor, 1988; practised in Aberdeen and Edinburgh; Associate Partner, Ketchen and Stevens WS, Edinburgh, 1994–2001. Chairman: Scottish Young Conservatives, 1989–92; Nat. Young Conservatives, 1991–92; former Dep. Chm., Edinburgh Central Cons. Assoc. Dep. Leader, Scottish Cons. and Unionist Party, 2005–11. Contested (C): East Lothian, 1997; N Tayside, 2001; N Tayside, 1999, 2003, 2007, Perthshire N, 2011, Scottish Parlt. *Recreations:* hillwalking, football, Scottish history, classic cars. *Address:* Scottish Parliament, Edinburgh EH99 1SP. *T:* (0131) 348 5293; (office) Control Tower, Perth Airport, Scone, Perth PH2 6PL. *T:* (01738) 553990. *E:* murdo.fraser.msp@scottish.parliament.uk.

FRASER, Prof. Murray, PhD; RIBA; Professor of Architecture and Global Culture, Bartlett School of Architecture, University College London, since 2011; *b* Glasgow, 7 July 1958; *s* of James Leslie Fraser and Amelia Ann Fraser; *m* (marr. diss.); two *s*. *Educ:* Hemel Hempstead Grammar Sch.; University Coll. London (BSc Architecture 1979; DipArch 1981; MSc Architectl Hist. 1983; Professional Practice 1983; PhD 1993). ARB 1984; RIBA 1984. Architectl Asst, Ansell Bailey Architects, 1981–84; Architect, London Borough of Haringey, 1985–86; Vis. Lectr, Bartlett Sch. of Architecture, UCL, 1987–85; Architect, Architype Ltd, 1989–90; Sen. Lectr, then Prof. of Architecture, Oxford Brookes Univ., 1990–2003; Prof. of Architecture, Univ. of Westminster, 2003–11. Chm., Res. and Innovation Gp, RIBA, 2011–. Mem., Council, Eur. Assoc. of Architectl Educn, 2012–; Founding Mem., Architectural Res. in Europe Network Assoc., 2013–. Co-Ed., Jl of Architecture, 2007–12. *Publications:* John Bull's Other Homes, 1996; Critical Architecture, 2007; Architecture and the Special Relationship, 2007; Design Research in Architecture, 2013; Architecture and Globalisation in the Persian Gulf, 2013; contrib. essays to internat. jls on architecture, architectl hist. and theory, and urbanism. *Recreations:* sport, watching football with my sons, cinema, dining out, socialising. *Address:* Bartlett School of Architecture, University College London, Wates House, 22 Gordon Street, WC1H 0QH. *T:* (020) 3108 5080. *E:* murray.fraser@ucl.ac.uk.

FRASER, Dr Nicholas Campbell; Keeper of Natural Sciences, National Museums Scotland, since 2007; *b* Nottingham, 14 Jan. 1956; *s* of Hugh Mckenzie Fraser and Patricia Margaret

Fraser; *m* 1982, Christine Mary; two *d. Educ:* Univ. of Aberdeen (BSc Zool. 1978; PhD Geol. 1984). Res. Fellow, Girton Coll., Cambridge, 1985–90; Curator of Vertebrate Paleontol., 1990–2007, Dir of Res. and Collections, 2004–07, Virginia Mus. of Natural Hist. Adjunct Professor of Geology: Virginia Tech, 1993–; N Carolina State Univ., 2007–. Ed., Memoirs Series, Soc. Vertebrate Paleontol. Hon. MA Cantab 1985. *Publications:* (ed with Hans-Dieter Sues) In the Shadow of the Dinosaurs, 1994; Dawn of the Dinosaurs, 2006; (with Hans-Dieter Sues) Triassic Life on Land: the great transition, 2010; contrib. peer-reviewed jls. *Recreations:* soccer, hill-walking, travel. *Address:* National Museums Scotland, Chambers Street, Edinburgh EH1 1JF. *T:* (0131) 247 4007, *Fax:* (0131) 220 4819. *E:* nick.fraser@nms.ac.uk.

FRASER, Orlando Gregory; QC 2014; *b* London, 9 May 1967; *s* of Rt Hon. Sir Hugh Charles Patrick Joseph Fraser, MBE, MP and of Lady Antonia Fraser, *qv*; *m* 2006, Clementine Hambro; three *d. Educ:* St Paul's Ind. Sch., Barnes; British Inst., Florence; Fitzwilliam Coll., Cambridge (BA Hons Hist. 1989). Asst to Patricia Rawlings, MEP, 1989; stagiaire, DG1, EC, 1990; GEC Plessey Telecommunications, Paris, Coventry, 1990–92; called to the Bar, Inner Temple, 1994; in practice as barrister, 1995–. Member: Adv. Council, NCVO, 2009–; Bd, Charity Commn of England and Wales, 2013–. Mem., Mgt Cttee, Westside Housing, 2001–03. Centre of Social Justice: Mem., Social Justice Commn, 2006–07; Founding Fellow, 2008. Contested (C) N Devon, 2005. Mem., Bd of Govs, Ilfracombe Community Coll., 2003–05. Chm., Bosnian Winter Appeal, 1992. *Recreations:* reading, tennis, Scrabble. *Address:* 4 Stone Buildings, Lincoln's Inn, WC2A 3XT. *T:* (020) 7242 5524. *E:* clerks@4stonebuildings.com. *Club:* MCC.

FRASER, Hon. Sir Peter Donald, Kt 2015; **Hon. Mr Justice Fraser;** a Judge of the High Court, Queen's Bench Division, since 2015; *b* Co. Down, Ireland, 6 Sept. 1963; *s* of Donald and Jean Fraser; *m* 2002, Samantha Hurrell; three *d. Educ:* Harrogate Grammar Sch.; St John's Coll., Cambridge (Open Exhibnr; BA 1986; LLM 1988). Called to the Bar, Middle Temple, 1989 (Harmsworth Exhibnr; Astbury Schol.); in practice as barrister, specialising in construction, engineering and international arbitration; a Recorder, 2002–15; QC 2009. *Publications:* How to Pass Law Exams, 1991; (Ed.) Building Law Reports, 1990–. *Recreations:* Rugby Union (London Scottish), triathlon, wine, shooting. *Address:* Royal Courts of Justice, Strand, WC2A 2LL. *Clubs:* Reform; Hawks (Cambridge); Leander (Henley-on-Thames).

FRASER, Peter John; photographer, since 1982; *b* Cardiff, 1 April 1953; *s* of Jack Fraser and Doreen Fraser (*née* Evans); *m* 1st, Claire McNamee; 2nd, 1992, Christy Johnson; 3rd, 2008, Urve Opik. *Educ:* Cardiff High Sch. for Boys; Manchester Poly. (Dip. Photography 1976). Solo exhibitions include: The Flower Bridge Impressions Gall., York, 1982; Photographers' Gall., London, 1986, 2002; St Louis Mus. of Art, 1995; Ffotogallery, Cardiff, 2010; Brancolini Grimaldi Gall., London, 2012; 30 year retrospective, Tate St Ives, 2013. Hon. FRPS 2013. *Publications:* Two Blue Buckets, 1988; Ice and Water, 1993; Deep Blue, 1997; Material, 2002; Lost for Words, 2010; A City in the Mind, 2012; photographs included in internat. pubns. *Recreation:* still searching for a hobby which my wife thinks would be good for me. *Address:* c/o Grimaldi Gavin Gallery, 27 Albemarle Street, W1S 4DW. *Club:* 2 Brydges.

FRASER, Robert William, MVO 1994; **His Honour Judge Fraser;** a Circuit Judge, since 2007; *b* Birkenhead, 23 Sept. 1955; *s* of Gordon Smith Fraser and Kathleen Mary Fraser; *m* 1990, Isobel Patricia Mary Clapham; two *d. Educ:* Birkenhead Sch.; Univ. of Liverpool (LLB Hons). Called to the Bar, Gray's Inn, 1984; Recorder, 2000–07. Royal Navy, 1974–2007: HMS Yarmouth, 1985–86; HMS Battleaxe, 1986–87; Equerry to the Prince of Wales, 1991–94; Briefing Officer to First Sea Lord, 1997–98; Dir of Staff, NATO HQ, Naples, 2000–02; rcds, 2002; Sec. to Chiefs of Staff Cttee, 2004–05; Cdre, 2005; Dir Naval Legal Services, 2005–07. *Publications:* (contrib.) Seaford House Papers, 2002. *Recreations:* sailing, ski-ing, motor cars. *Address:* c/o Inner London Crown Court, Sessions House, Newington Causeway, SE1 6AZ.

FRASER, Sir Simon James, KCMG 2013 (CMG 2009); Permanent Under-Secretary of State, Foreign and Commonwealth Office, and Head of the Diplomatic Service, 2010–15; *b* 3 June 1958; *s* of late James Stuart Fraser and of Joan Fraser; *m* Shireen; two *d. Educ:* St Paul's Sch.; Corpus Christi Coll., Cambridge (MA). Joined FCO, 1979; Second Secretary: Baghdad, 1982–84; Damascus, 1984–86; First Sec., FCO, 1986–88; Private Sec. to Minister of State, FCO, 1989–90; Policy Planning Staff, FCO, 1991–92; Asst Head, Non-Proliferation and Defence Dept, FCO, 1992–93; First Sec., Financial and Eur. Affairs, Paris, 1994–96; Dep. Chef de Cabinet of Vice-Pres. of EC, 1996–99; Pol Counsellor, Paris, 1999–2002; Dir for Strategy and Innovation, FCO, 2002–04; Chief of Staff to Peter Mandelson, EC, 2004–08; Dir Gen. for Europe and Globalisation, FCO, 2008–09; Permanent Sec., BERR, later BIS, 2009–10. *Recreations:* ski-ing, football, opera, art.

FRASER, Simon Joseph, CBE 2003; Chairman, 1984–2003, Director, 1990–2005, Fibrowatt Ltd; *b* 13 March 1929; *s* of late Maj. Hon. Alastair Thomas Joseph Fraser and Lady Sibyl Fraser (*née* Grimston); *m* 1956, E. Jane Mackintosh (*d* 2007); one *s* five *d. Educ:* Ampleforth Coll.; Magdalen Coll., Oxford (BA, MA Hist.). Man. Dir, Internat. Janitor, 1964–70; Dir, S. G. Warburg & Co. Ltd, 1970–75; Chm., Kirkhill Investment & Mgt Co. Ltd, 1975–84; Founder, Fibrowatt Ltd (gp of cos which developed UK's first 3 biomass fired power stations), 1984. *Recreations:* music, early church history, tackling environmental challenges. *Address:* 2 Hereford Mansions, Hereford Road, W2 5BA.

FRASER, Simon William Hetherington; Sheriff of North Strathclyde at Dumbarton, 1989–2014; *b* 2 April 1951; *s* of late George MacDonald Fraser, OBE, author and Kathleen Margarette (*née* Hetherington); *m* 1st, 1979, Sheena Janet Fraser (marr. diss. 2009); one *d*; 2nd, 2010, Fiona Petrie. *Educ:* Glasgow Acad.; Glasgow Univ. (LLB). Solicitor, 1973–89 (Partner, Flowers & Co., Glasgow, 1976–89). Temp. Sheriff, 1987–89. Pres., Glasgow Bar Assoc., 1981–82; Mem. Council, Sheriffs' Assoc., 2007–10. *Recreations:* watching Partick Thistle, cricket. *Club:* Avizandum (Glasgow).

FRASER, Stuart John, CBE 2012; Deputy Chairman, Policy and Resources Committee, City of London Corporation, 2012–13 (Chairman, 2008–12); *b* Bexley, Kent, 13 April 1946; *s* of Kenneth and Anne Fraser; *m* 1967, Laura Mary Byford. *Educ:* University Sch., Bexley; Cannock House Sch. Trainee stockbroker, 1963; James Capel, 1963–66; Charterhouse Gp, 1966–68; Sheppards & Co., 1968–73; Capel-Cure Myers, 1973–78; Williams de Broë, 1978–99; Divl Dir, Brewin Dolphin Securities Ltd, 1999– (Chm., Asset Allocation Cttee). Corporation of London, later City of London Corporation: Mem., Court of Common Council, 1993–; Chm., Planning and Transportation Cttee, 1997–2000. Mem., London Stock Exchange, 1982–86. Mem. Bd and Regl Chm., London & Quadrant Housing Assoc., 1997–2007. CFA (Associate, Soc. of Investment Analysts 1976); FCSI (FSI 1978). Chm., Greenwich Br., MS Soc., 1973–92; Director: Blackheath Concert Halls, 1987–90; Blackheath Rugby Club, 1988–91. Gov., Legacy Trust, 2007–10; Chm., Bd of Govs, City of London Freemans Sch., 2013–. Liveryman, Fletchers' Co., 1999 (Sen. Warden, 2014). *Recreations:* walking, golf, theatre, reading. *Address:* 19 Lock Chase, SE3 9HB. *T:* (020) 8852 6248. *E:* stuartfraser2@me.com. *Clubs:* Reform; Royal Blackheath Golf.

FRASER, Prof. Thomas Grant, MBE 2006; PhD; FRHistS; Professor of History, 1991–2006, now Professor Emeritus and Hon. Professor of Conflict Research, University of Ulster (Provost of Magee Campus, 2002–06); *b* 1 July 1944; *s* of Thomas Fraser and Annie Grant Alexander; *m* 1970, Grace Frances Armstrong; one *s* one *d. Educ:* Univ. of Glasgow (MA Medieval and Modern Hist. 1966; Ewing Prize); London Sch. of Economics (PhD 1974). New University of Ulster, subseq. University of Ulster: Lectr, 1969–85; Sen. Lectr, 1985–91; Hd, Dept of Hist., 1988–94; Hd, Sch. of Hist., Philosophy and Politics, 1994–98. Fulbright Scholar-in-Residence, Indiana Univ. South Bend, 1983–84. Advr, Cordia Educn Complex, Sanghol, India, 2012–. Chm., NI Museums Council, 1998–2006; Trustee, Nat. Museums and Galls of NI, 1998–2002. Dir, Playhouse Community Arts Centre, Derry, 2003–. FRHistS 1992; FRSA 2000; FRAS 2013. *Publications:* (ed) The Middle East 1914–1979, 1980; Partition in Ireland, India and Palestine, 1984; The USA and the Middle East since World War 2, 1989; (ed with P. Lowe) Conflict and Amity in East Asia: essays in honour of Ian Nish, 1992; (ed with K. Jeffery) Men, Women and War: historical studies XVIII, 1993; The Arab Israeli Conflict, 1995, new edn 2015 (Spanish edn 2008; Italian edn 2009); (ed with S. Dunn) Europe and Ethnicity: the First World War and contemporary ethnic conflict, 1996; (ed) The Irish Parading Tradition: following the drum, 2000; Ireland in Conflict 1922–1998, 2000; (with D. Murray) America and the World since 1945, 2002; Chaim Weizmann: the Zionist dream, 2009; (with A. Mango and R. McNamara) The Makers of the Modern Middle East, 2011, 2nd edn 2015 (Turkish edn 2011); (ed) India's Rural Transformation and Development: issues, processes and direction, 2012; (ed with J. Hume and L. Murray) Peacemaking in the 21st Century, 2013; (ed) The First World War and its Aftermath: the shaping of the Middle East, 2015. *Recreations:* travel, cooking. *Address:* 45 Blackthorn Manor, Londonderry BT47 5ST. *T:* (028) 7131 2290.

FRASER, Veronica Mary; Diocesan Director of Education, Diocese of Worcester, 1985–93; *b* 19 April 1933; *o d* of late Archibald Fraser. *Educ:* Richmond County Sch. for Girls; St Hugh's Coll., Oxford. Head of English Department: The Alice Ottley Sch., Worcester, 1962–65; Guildford County Sch. for Girls, 1965–67 (also Librarian); Headmistress, Godolphin Sch., Salisbury, 1968–80; Adviser on Schools to Bishop of Winchester, 1981–85. Pres., Assoc. of Sen. Members, St Hugh's Coll., Oxford, 1994–98. Gov., SPCK, 1994–98.

FRASER, Vincent; QC 2001; a Recorder, since 2002; a Deputy High Court Judge, since 2010; *b* 18 Oct. 1958; *s* of Martin and Monica Fraser; *m* 1994, Mary Elizabeth Sweeney; one *s* three *d. Educ:* St Mary's Coll., Crosby; University Coll., Oxford (Open Schol.; MA Juris.; Sweet & Maxwell Prize). Called to the Bar, Gray's Inn, 1981. *Publications:* Planning Decisions Digest, 1987, 2nd edn 1992. *Recreations:* literature, music, football. *Address:* Kings Chambers, 36 Young Street, Manchester M3 3FT. *T:* (0161) 832 9082, *Fax:* (0161) 835 2139. *E:* vfraser@kingschambers.com.

FRASER, Prof. William Irvine, CBE 1998; MD; FRCPE, FRCPsych, FMedSci; Professor of Developmental Disability, University of Wales College of Medicine, 1989–2002, now Emeritus; *b* 3 Feb. 1940; *s* of late Duncan Fraser and Muriel (*née* Macrae); *m* 1964, Joyce Carrol; two *s. Educ:* Greenock Acad.; Glasgow Univ. (MBChB 1963; DPM 1967; MD (with commendation) 1969). FRCPsych 1979; FRCPE 2000. Physician Superintendent, Mental Handicap Service, Fife, 1974–78; Hon. Sen. Lectr in Psychology, Univ. of St Andrews, 1973–89; pt-time Sen. Lectr, Psychiatry, Univ. of Edinburgh, 1973–89; Consultant Psychiatrist, Royal Edinburgh Hosp., 1978–89. Ed., Jl of Intellectual Disability Research, 1982–2003. Trustee, Bailey Thomas Charitable Fund, 1999–; Autism Cymru, 2001– (Chair, 2008–); Pres., Welsh Psychiatry Soc., 2006–. Res. Medallist, Burden Inst., 1989; Fellow, Internat. Assoc. for Scientific Study of Intellectual Disability, 1997 (Dist. Achievement Award, 1996); FMedSci 2001. *Publications:* (with R. McGillivray) Care of People with Intellectual Disabilities, 1974, 9th edn, 1998; (with R. Grieve) Communicating with Normal and Retarded Children, 1981; (with M. Kerr) Seminars in Learning Disabilities, 2003. *Recreation:* sailing. *Address:* 146 Wenallt Road, Cardiff CF14 6TQ. *T:* (029) 2052 1343.

FRASER, Sir William (Kerr), GCB 1984 (KCB 1979; CB 1978); Chancellor, University of Glasgow, 1996–2006 (Principal and Vice-Chancellor, 1988–95); *b* 18 March 1929; *s* of A. M. Fraser and Rachel Kerr; *m* 1956, Marion Anne Forbes (*see* Lady Marion Fraser); three *s* one *d. Educ:* Eastwood Sch., Clarkston; Glasgow Univ. (MA, LLB). Served RAF, 1952–55. Joined Scottish Home Dept, 1955; Private Sec. to Parliamentary Under-Sec., 1959, and to Secretary of State for Scotland, 1966–67; Civil Service Fellow, Univ. of Glasgow, 1963–64; Asst Sec., Regional Development Div., 1967–71; Under Sec., Scottish Home and Health Dept, 1971–75; Dep. Sec., 1975–78, Permanent Under-Sec. of State, 1978–88, Scottish Office. Chm., Scottish Mutual Assce, 1999 (Dir, 1990–99). Chm., Royal Commn on the Ancient and Historical Monuments of Scotland, 1995–2000. Gov., Caledonian Res. Foundn, 1990–99. FRSE 1985. FRCPS (Hon.) 1992; FRSAMD 1995. Hon. LLD: Glasgow, 1982; Strathclyde, 1991; Aberdeen, 1993; Dr *hc* Edinburgh, 1995. *Address:* Broadwood, Edinburgh Road, Gifford, East Lothian EH41 4JE. *T:* (01620) 810319. *Club:* New (Edinburgh).

See also A. K. Fraser.

FRASER-HOPEWELL, Peter David, CMG 2009; MBE 1986; Head, Group Security, Enrichment Technology, since 2008; *b* Sheldon, Warks, 26 Nov. 1953; *s* of David Hopewell and Isobel Hopewell (*née* Smart); *m* 1990, Clare Mary Steven; one *d. Educ:* Marshill Boys Grammar Sch., Birmingham; London Coll. of Printing (HND Business Studies 1975). Jun. mgt in printing industry, 1976–80. Commnd TA, 1974; Commnd Royal Scots, 1981, as regular officer; Co. Comdr, 1989–91 and 1993–96 (despatches 1983, 1991); CO, 1996–99; Chief Special Forces, HQ Allied Rapid Reaction Corps, 1999–2001; Deputy Commander: 3 Inf. Bde, 2001–03; 16 Air Assault Bde, 2003–05; COS UN Force in Cyprus and Comdr British Contingent, 2005–08. QCVS 1996. *Recreations:* ski-ing, running, triathlon, history. *E:* fraserhopewells@talktalk.net. *Club:* Royal Scots.

FRATTINI, Franco; President, Società Italiana per l'Organizzazione Internazionale, since 2012; *b* 14 March 1957. *Educ:* La Sapienza Univ., Rome (LLB). State Attorney, 1981; Attorney, State Attorney-Gen.'s Office, 1984; Magistrate, Regl Admin. Tribunal, Piedmont, 1984–86; Council of State Judge, 1986; Legal Adviser: to Minister of Treasury, 1986–90; to Dep. Prime Minister, 1990–91; to Prime Minister, 1992; Dep. Sec.-Gen., 1993, Sec.-Gen., 1994–95, Prime Minister's Office; Minister for the Civil Service and Regl Affairs, 1995–96; MP (Forza Italia), 1996–2004; Minister for Civil Service and for Co-ordination of Intelligence and Security Services, 2001–02; Minister for Foreign Affairs, 2002–04; MP (Popolo della Libertà) Italy, 2008–13; Minister for Foreign Affairs, 2008–11. Mem., EC, 2004–08. Mem., Rome CC, 1997–2000. *Address:* Società Italiana per l'Organizzazione Internazionale, Palazzetto Venezia, Piazza di San Marco 51, 00186 Rome, Italy.

FRAWLEY, Carolyn; *see* McCall, C.

FRAWLEY, Thomas Jude, CBE 2008; Assembly Ombudsman for Northern Ireland and Northern Ireland Commissioner for Complaints, since 2000; *b* Limerick, 4 Feb. 1949; *s* of Joseph and Bride Frawley; *m* 1983, Marie Mallon; two *s* one *d. Educ:* St Mary's Grammar Sch., Belfast; Trinity Coll., Dublin (BA). Grad. Trainee, NHS, 1971–73; Unit Administrator, Ulster Hosp., Dundonald, 1973–77; Asst Dist Administrator, Lisburn, 1977–80; Dist Administrator for Londonderry, Limavady and Strabane Dist, 1980; Chief Admin. Officer, 1980–85, Gen. Manager, 1985–2000, Western Health and Social Services Bd. Dir-Gen., Co-operation and Working Together Initiative, 1990–2000; led project to support health system in Zimbabwe, 1994. King's Fund Travel Bursary, 1983; King's Fund Internat. Fellowships, 1988 and 1992; Eisenhower Fellowship, 1989. Mem., Ministerial Adv. Bd on Health Estates, NI, 1998–2000; Chairman: Expert Panel on Review of Public Admin, 2002–; Gp on Review of Ambulance Service, NI, 1998–2000. Trustee, NHS Confedn, 1998–2000. Vice Pres., World Bd, Internat. Ombudsman Inst., 2006–. Mem., BITC, 1998–2000. Gov., Lumen Christi Coll., 1998–2000. Rep. of Ire., Alumni Adv. Council, Eisenhower Fellowship, 2004. DUniv Ulster, 2003. *Recreations:* current affairs, sport (played Rugby and Gaelic football). *Address:* Office of the Ombudsman for Northern Ireland, 33 Wellington Place, Belfast BT1 6HN.

FRAY, Prof. Derek John, FRS 2008; FREng; Professor of Materials Chemistry, Cambridge University, 1996–2007, now Emeritus (Head, Department of Materials Science and Metallurgy, 2001–05); Professorial Fellow, Fitzwilliam College, Cambridge, 1996–2007, now Life Fellow; *b* 26 Dec. 1939; *s* of Arthur Joseph Fray and Doris Lilian Fray; *m* 1965, Mirella Christine Kathleen Honey (marr. diss. 2004); one *s* one *d*. *Educ:* Emanuel Sch.; Imperial Coll., Univ. of London (BSc Eng, ARSM 1961; PhD, DIC 1965). FIMMM; FREng (FEng 1989); FRSC 2003. Asst Prof. of Metallurgy, MIT, 1965–68; Gp Leader, Imperial Smelting Corp., Bristol, 1968–71; Cambridge University: Lectr, Dept of Materials Sci. and Metallurgy, 1971–91; Fitzwilliam College: Fellow, 1972–90; Tutorial and Estates Bursar, 1974–86; Bursar, 1986–88; Investment and Estates Bursar, 1988–90; Prof. of Mineral Engrg, Univ. of Leeds, 1991–96 (Head of Dept). Hon. Professor: Beijing Univ. of Sci. and Technol., 1995–; Hubei Poly. Univ., 2006–; Liaoning Univ. of Sci. and Technol., 2009–; Vis. Prof., Univ. of Leeds, 1996–. Director: Cambridge Advanced Materials, 1989–2006; Ion Science Ltd, 1989–2010; British Titanium plc, 1998–2007; EMC Ltd, 2000–; Metalysis Ltd, 2002–04; Inotec AMD Ltd, 2005–; Camfridge Ltd, 2005–; Chinuka Ltd, 2007–; La Serena Technologies Ltd, 2012–; Welding Alloys Gp Ltd, 2012–. Numerous medals and awards, UK and overseas. *Publications:* (jtly) Worked Examples in Mass Heat Transfer in Materials Technology, 1983; numerous papers and granted patents on material chemistry and allied topics. *Recreations:* reading, cinema, walking. *Address:* 7 Woodlands Road, Great Shelford, Cambridge CB22 5LW. *T:* (01223) 842296.

FRAYLING, Sir Christopher (John), Kt 2001; MA, PhD; Professor of Cultural History, 1979–2009, now Emeritus, Rector and Vice-Provost, 1996–2009, Royal College of Art, London; Chairman, Arts Council England, 2004–09; *b* 25 Dec. 1946; *s* of late Arthur Frederick Frayling and Barbara Kathleen (*née* Imhof); *m* 1981, Helen Snowdon. *Educ:* Repton Sch.; Churchill Coll., Cambridge (BA, MA, PhD; Fellow, 2009). FCSD 1994. Churchill Research Studentship, 1968–71; Lectr in Modern History, Univ. of Exeter, 1971–72; Tutor, Dept of General Studies, Royal College of Art, 1972–73, Vis. Lectr, 1973–79; Research Asst, Dept of Information Retrieval, Imperial War Mus., 1973–74; Lectr in the History of Ideas and European Social History, Univ. of Bath, 1974–79; Royal College of Art: founder, 1979, and Head of Dept, 1979–96, Dept of Cultural History (ex General Studies); founded courses: History of Design, 1982; Conservation, 1987; Visual Arts Admin, subseq. Curating Contemporary Art, 1991; Pro-Rector, 1993–96. Visiting Professor: Shanghai Univ. of Technol., 1991; Univ. of Lancaster, 2010–; Hon. Prof., Richmond Univ., 2012–. Chancellor, Arts Univ., Bournemouth, 2014–. Historian, lectr, critic; regular contributor, as writer and presenter, to radio (incl. Kaleidoscope, Stop the Week, Meridian, Critics' Forum, Third Opinion, Third Ear, Nightwaves, Front Row, Back Row, The Film Programme; series: The American Cowboy; America: the movie (Silver Medal, NY Internat. Radio Fest., 1989); Britannia: the film; Print the Legend; Cinema Cities) and TV (incl. series Scene, Art of Persuasion (Gold Medal, NY Internat. Film and TV Fest., 1985), Busting the Block—or the Art of Pleasing People, Design Classics, Design Awards, Timewatch, Movie Profiles, The Face of Tutankhamun, Strange Landscape, and Nightmare: the birth of horror). Curator of exhibitions: (co-curator) Designs of the Times, RCA, 1996; Once Upon a Time in Italy, Autry Nat. Center, LA, 2005 (Humanities Prize for scholarship); (co-curator) Gothic Nightmares—Fuseli, Blake and the Romantic Imagination, Tate Britain, 2006; (co-curator) Hollywood Costume, V&A, 2012; Sergio Leone—c'era una volta in Italia, Nat. Mus. of Cinema, Turin, 2014. Chm., Design Council, 2000–04; Mem., Crafts Council, 1982–85. Arts Council of England (formerly of GB): Mem., 1987–2000; Mem., Art Panel, 1983–94 (Dep. Chm., 1984–87; Chm., 1987–94); Chm., Film, Video and Broadcasting Panel, 1994–97; Chm., Educn and Trng Panel, 1996–98; Chm., Combined Arts Cttee, 1989–95; Chm., New Collaborations Cttee, 1990–94. Chairman: Curriculum Develt Bd, Arts Technol. Centre, 1989–94; Design Sub-Gp, Liturgical Publishing Commn, 1999–2000; Royal Mint Design Adv. Cttee, 2000–11. Chm. of Trustees, Crafts Study Centre, Bath, 1982–2004; Foundn Trustee, Holburne of Menstrie Mus., Bath, 1985–2000; Chm., Free Form Arts Trust, 1984–88; Trustee: V&A Museum, 1984–2009 (Hon. Res. Fellow, 2011–; Member: Adv. Council, 1981–83; Sen. Staff Appts Cttee, 1987–91; S Kensington Jt Planning Cttee, 1989–95; Educn and Res. Cttees, 1990–97; Chm., Bethnal Green Mus. Cttee, 1995–99; Chm., Contemporary Projects Cttee, 1999–2002; Chm., S Kensington Cultural Gp, 1999–2004); Koestler Trustees for Art in Prisons, 1992–99; Royal Mint Mus., 2011–. Member: Litmus Gp for Millennium Dome, 1998–2000; Bd, Design Mus., 1999–2004 and 2009–; AHRB, 1999–2004; Council, Catalyst, 2004–09; Blue Plaques Cttee, English Heritage, 2009–; Royal Commn for 1851 Exhibn, 2009–; Royal Fine Art Commn Trust, 2014–; UK Supreme Court Arts Trust, 2014–. Governor, BFI, 1982–87 and 2009–12 (Mem., 1982–86, Chm. 1984–86, Educn Cttee); Member: Art and Design Sect., Leverhulme Team on Arts in Higher Educn, 1982; Working Party on art and design advising NAB, 1985–87. Chm., Soc. of Designer-Craftsmen, 1997–2004. Patron: Guild of Handicraft Trust, 1989–; Parnham Trust for Makers in Wood, 1989–2003. FRSA 1984 (Bicentennial Medal, 2001; Hon. Life Fellowship, 2006); Sen. Fellow, Hereford Coll. of Arts, 2010; Hon. Fellow, Cardiff Univ., 2013. Hon. FRIBA 2005; Hon. RCM 2007; Hon. FGSM 2010; Hon. FBKSTS. Hon. DLitt: NSW, 1999; Lancaster, 2008; Brighton, 2009; DUniv: Staffordshire, 2002; Sheffield Hallam, 2011; Hon. DArts: UWE, 2003; Bath, 2003; UAL, 2009; Hon. DHL Richmond, 2005; Hon. Dr Birmingham City, 2014; Hon. DArt Nottingham Trent, 2014. Sir Misha Black Medal, CSD, 2003; Maitland Medal, IStructE, 2006; Leonardo da Vinci Medal, Arts Club, 2009. Radio play, The Rime of the Bounty (Sony Radio Award, 1990). *Publications:* Napoleon Wrote Fiction, 1972; (ed) The Vampyre—Lord Ruthven to Count Dracula, 1978; Spaghetti Westerns: Cowboys and Europeans, from Karl May to Sergio Leone, 1981; The Schoolmaster and the Wheelwrights, 1983; The Royal College of Art: one hundred and fifty years of art and design, 1987; Vampyres, 1991; (ed) Beyond the Dovetail: essays on craft, skill and imagination, 1991; Clint Eastwood, 1992; The Face of Tutankhamun, 1992; (with Helen Frayling) The Art Pack, 1992; Research in Art and Design, 1994; Strange Landscape: a journey through the Middle Ages, 1995; Things to Come: a classic film, 1995; (ed jtly) Design of the Times: one hundred years of the Royal College of Art, 1996; Nightmare: the birth of horror, 1996 (Hamilton Deane Award, 1997); Tim Mara: the complete prints, 1998; Art and Design: 100 years at the Royal College of Art, 1999; Sergio Leone: something to do with death, 2000; (ed) The Hound of the Baskervilles, 2001; Ken Adam: the art of production design, 2005; Once Upon a Time in Italy, 2005; Mad, Bad and Dangerous?: images of the scientist in film, 2005; (with Sir Kenneth Adam) Ken Adam Designs the Movies, 2008; Horace Walpole's Cat, 2009; Bill Gold: posterworks, 2010; On Craftsmanship, 2011; The Innocents: a classic film, 2013; The Yellow Peril: Dr Fu Manchu and the rise of Chinaphobia, 2014; The 2001 File, 2015; Inside the Bloody Chamber, 2015; The Ken Adam Archive, 2015; contribs to: Reappraisals of Rousseau—studies in honour of R. A. Leigh, 1980; Cinema, Politics and Society in America, 1981; Rousseau et Voltaire en 1978, 1981; Rousseau After Two Hundred Years: Proc. of Cambridge Bicentennial Colloquium, 1982; Eduardo Paolozzi: perspectives and themes, 1984; Rape: an interdisciplinary study, 1987; The Cambridge Guide to the Arts in Britain, Vol. IX (post 1945), 1988; BFI Companion to the Western, 1988; Craft Classics since the 1940s, 1988; Eduardo Paolozzi: Noah's Ark, 1990; Ariel at Bay: reflections on broadcasting and the arts, 1990; Objects and Images: essay on design and advertising, 1992; BFI Companion to Horror, 1996; Fear: essays on the meaning and experience of fear, 2007; Age of Experience, 2009; It Came From the 1950s: popular culture, popular anxieties, 2012; Tanner Lectures: modern art and religion in the twentieth century, 2012; Hollywood Costume, 2012; Bram Stoker Centenary Essays, 2013; articles on film, popular culture and the visual arts/crafts in Cambridge Rev., Cinema, Film, Sight & Sound, London Magazine, New Statesman & Society, Crafts, Burlington Magazine, Art and Design, Designer, Design Week, Design, THES, TLS, Time Out, Punch, Designer, Craft History, Creative Review, Blueprint, Independent Magazine, Independent on Sunday, Culture Magazine, Listener, Times, Sunday Times, Guardian, Daily Telegraph, Christie's Magazine, RA Magazine, and various learned jls and catalogues. *Recreation:* finding time. *Address:* Garden House, Mill Lane, Bathampton, Bath, Avon BA2 6TS.

See also Very Rev. N. A. Frayling.

FRAYLING, Very Rev. Nicholas Arthur; Dean of Chichester, 2002–14, now Dean Emeritus; Dean, Priory of England and the Islands of the Most Venerable Order of the Hospital of St John of Jerusalem, since 2014; *b* 29 Feb. 1944; *s* of late Arthur Frederick Frayling, OBE and Barbara Kathleen (*née* Imhof). *Educ:* Repton Sch.; Exeter Univ. (BA Theology 1969); Cuddesdon Theol Coll., Oxford. Management training, retail trade, 1962–64; Temp. Probation Officer (prison welfare), Inner London Probation and After-Care Service, 1965–66, pt-time, 1966–71. Deacon, 1971; priest, 1972; Asst Curate, St John, Peckham, 1971–74; Vicar, All Saints, Tooting Graveney, 1974–83; Canon Residentiary and Precentor, Liverpool Cathedral, 1983–87, Hon. Canon, 1989–2002; Rector of Liverpool, 1987–2002. Chaplain: St Paul's Eye Hosp., Liverpool, 1987–90; Huyton Coll., 1987–91; to High Sheriff of Merseyside, 1992–93, 1997–98 and 1999–2000; Hon. Chaplain, British Nuclear Tests Veterans' Assoc., 1988–. Chairman: Southwark Diocesan Adv. Cttee for Care of Churches, 1980–83; Religious Adv. Panel, BBC Radio Merseyside, 1988–2002; Welfare Orgns Cttee, Liverpool CVS, 1992–2002; Mersey Mission to Seafarers, 2000–02; Church in Society Adv. Gp, Dio. of Chichester, 2003–09; Diocesan European Ecumenical Cttee, 2009–14. Trustee, Inst. of Food, Brain and Behaviour (formerly Natural Justice), 1995– (Chm., 2005–07). Chm. of Govs, Prebendal Sch., Chichester, 2002–14. Liveryman, Skinners' Co., 1980– (Chaplain, 2011–). Hon. Fellow, Liverpool John Moores Univ., 2003. Hon. LLD Liverpool, 2001. Hon. Freeman, City of Chichester, 2014. *Publications:* Pardon and Peace: a reflection on the making of peace in Ireland, 1996. *Recreations:* music, friends. *Address:* Flat 5, 27 South Parade, Southsea, Hants PO5 2JF. *T:* (023) 9281 7041. *E:* nicholasfrayling@gmail.com. *Clubs:* Oriental; Liverpool Artists (Life Mem.).

See also Sir C. J. Frayling.

FRAYN, Claire, (Mrs Michael Frayn); *see* Tomalin, C.

FRAYN, Michael, CLit 2007; writer; *b* 8 Sept. 1933; *s* of late Thomas Allen Frayn and Violet Alice Lawson; *m* 1st, 1960, Gillian Palmer (marr. diss. 1989); three *d*; 2nd, 1993, Claire Tomalin, *qv*. *Educ:* Kingston Gram. Sch.; Emmanuel Coll., Cambridge (Hon. Fellow, 1985). Reporter, Guardian, 1957–59; Columnist, Guardian, 1959–62; Columnist, Observer, 1962–68. Cameron Mackintosh Prof. of Contemporary Drama, Univ. of Oxford, 2009–10; Fellow, St Catherine's Coll., Oxford, 2009–10, now Emeritus. Foreign Hon. Mem., Amer. Acad. of Arts and Scis, 2000. Hon. DLitt Cambridge, 2001. *Television:* plays: Jamie, 1968 (filmed as Remember Me?, 1997); Birthday, 1969; First and Last, 1989 (Internat. Emmy Award, 1990); A Landing on the Sun, 1994; *documentaries:* Imagine a City Called Berlin, 1975; Vienna—the Mask of Gold, 1977; Three Streets in the Country, 1979; The Long Straight, 1980; Jerusalem, 1984; Prague—the Magic Lantern, 1993; Budapest: Written in Water, 1996; *stage plays:* The Two of Us, 1970; The Sandboy, 1971; Alphabetical Order, 1975 (Evening Standard Drama Award for Best Comedy); Donkeys' Years, 1976 (SWET Best Comedy Award); Clouds, 1976; Liberty Hall, 1980; Make and Break, 1980 (New Standard Best Comedy Award); Noises Off, 1982 (Standard Best Comedy Award; SWET Best Comedy Award); Benefactors, 1984 (Standard Best Play Award; Laurence Olivier (formerly SWET) Award for Play of the Year; Plays and Players London Theatre Critics' Best New Play); Look Look, 1990; Here, 1993; Now You Know, 1995; Copenhagen, 1998 (Evening Standard Best Play, South Bank Show Award for Theatre, Critics' Circle Best New Play, 1998; Prix Molière, 1999; Tony Award, Best Play, 2000); Alarms and Excursions, 1998; Democracy, 2003 (Best Play, Evening Standard, 2003; South Bank Show Award, 2003; Best New Play, Critics' Circle Awards, 2004); The Crimson Hotel, 2007; Afterlife, 2008; Matchbox Theatre, Hampstead Th., 2015; *opera:* La Belle Vivette, 1995; *filmscripts:* Clockwise, 1986; Remember Me?, 1997. Nat. Press Award, 1970; Heywood Hill Literary Prize, 2002; Golden PEN Award, 2003; Saint Louis Literary Award, 2006; McGovern Award, Cosmos Club Foundn, 2006; Writers' Guild Lifetime Achievement Award, 2011; Olivier Special Award, 2013. Bundesverdienstkreuz (Germany), 2004. *Publications:* collections of columns: The Day of the Dog, 1962; The Book of Fub, 1963; On the Outskirts, 1964; At Bay in Gear Street, 1967; The Original Michael Frayn, 1983; Speak After the Beep, 1995; The Additional Michael Frayn, 2000; Michael Frayn: collected columns, 2007; Stage Directions, 2008; Travels with a Typewriter, 2009; *non-fiction:* Constructions, 1974; (with David Burke) Celia's Secret, 2000; The Human Touch, 2006; My Father's Fortune: a life (memoir), 2010 (PEN/Ackerley Award); *novels:* The Tin Men, 1965 (Somerset Maugham Award); The Russian Interpreter, 1966 (Hawthornden Prize); Towards the End of the Morning, 1967; A Very Private Life, 1968; Sweet Dreams, 1973; The Trick of It, 1989; A Landing On the Sun, 1991 (Sunday Express Book of the Year Award, 1991); Now You Know, 1992; Headlong, 1999; Spies, 2002 (Bollinger Everyman Wodehouse Prize, 2002; Whitbread Novel of the Year, 2003); Skios, 2012; Matchbox Theatre (collection of sketches), 2014; *translations:* Tolstoy, The Fruits of Enlightenment, 1979 (prod. 1979); Anouilh, Number One, 1984; Chekhov: The Cherry Orchard, 1978 (prod. 1978, 1989); Three Sisters, 1983 (prod. 1985); Wild Honey, 1984 (prod. 1984); The Seagull, 1986 (prod. 1986); Uncle Vanya, 1988 (prod. 1988); The Sneeze (adapted from one-act plays and short stories), 1989 (prod. 1988); Trifonov, Exchange, 1986 (prod. 1986, 1990). *Address:* c/o Greene & Heaton Ltd, 37a Goldhawk Road, W12 8QQ.

FRAYNE, Very Rev. David; Dean (formerly Provost) of Blackburn, 1992–2001, now Emeritus; *b* 19 Oct. 1934; *s* of late Philip John Frayne and Daisy Morris Frayne (*née* Eade); *m* 1961, Elizabeth Ann Frayne (*née* Grant); one *s* two *d*. *Educ:* Reigate Grammar Sch.; St Edmund Hall, Oxford (BA 1958 (2nd cl. Hons PPE); MA 1962); The Queen's Coll., Birmingham (DTh 1960). Pilot Officer, RAF, 1954–55. Ordained deacon, 1960, priest, 1961; Asst Curate, St Michael, East Wickham, 1960–63; Priest-in-charge, St Barnabas, Downham, Lewisham, 1963–67; Vicar of N Sheen, Richmond, 1967–73; Rector of Caterham, 1973–83; Vicar of St Mary Redcliffe with Temple, Bristol and St John the Baptist, Bedminster, 1983–92. Rural Dean of Caterham, 1980–83; Hon. Canon, Southwark Cathedral, 1982, Emeritus, 1983; Rural Dean of Bedminster, 1986–92; Proctor in Convocation, 1987–90; Hon. Canon of Bristol Cathedral, 1991. A Church Comr, 1994–98; Mem., Redundant Churches Cttee, 1995–2001. *Recreations:* walking, camping, music. *Address:* 30 Coleridge Vale Road South, Clevedon BS21 6PB. *T:* (01275) 873799. *E:* davidfrayne666@btinternet.com. *Club:* Oxford Society.

FRAZER, Prof. Ian Hector, AC 2012; MD; FRCPE, FRCPA; FRS 2011; FAA; Chairman, TRI Foundation, Translational Research Institute Pty Ltd, Brisbane, since 2015 (Chief Executive Officer and Director of Research, 2011–15); *b* Glasgow, 6 Jan. 1953; *s* of Sam Frazer and Marion Frazer; *m* 1976, Caroline Nicoll; three *s*. *Educ:* George Watson's Coll., Edinburgh; Robert Gordon's Coll., Aberdeen; Univ. of Edinburgh (BSc Hons Pathol. 1974; MB ChB 1977); Univ. of Melbourne (MD 1988). FRCPE 1988; FRCPA 1988. Sen. Res. Officer and Asst Physician, Clin. Res. Unit, Walter and Eliza Hall Inst. of Medical Res., 1981–85; Sen. Lectr, Dept of Medicine, Univ. of Queensland, 1985–91; Dir, 1991–2011, Prof., 1993–2011, Univ. of Queensland Diamantina Inst. (formerly Centre for Immunol. and Cancer Res.). Pres., Cancer Council Australia, 2006–10; Chm., Scientific Adv. Council, Internat. Agency for Res. on Cancer, 2011. FAICD 2002; FTSE 2004; FAA 2005; FRACGP 2009; FASM 2011. *Publications:* over 200 res. articles. *Recreations:* snow ski-ing, classical music, bush walking, cycling. *Address:* Translational Research Institute Pty Ltd, 37 Kent Street,

Woolloongabba, Brisbane, Qld 4102, Australia. *T:* (7) 34436962, *Fax:* (7) 34437779. *E:* ianhfrazer@gmail.com. *Clubs:* Queensland, Brisbane (Brisbane).

FRAZER, Lucy Claire; QC 2013; MP (C) South East Cambridgeshire, since 2015; *d* of Colin and Jocelyn Frazer; *m* 2002, David Leigh; one *s* one *d. Educ:* Leeds Girls' High Sch.; Newnham Coll., Cambridge (BA 1994). Called to the Bar, Middle Temple, 1996; in practice as barrister, 1998–2015. *Publications:* (contrib.) Rowlatt on Principal and Surety. *Address:* House of Commons, SW1A 0AA.

FREAN, Jennifer Margaret, (Jenny), RDI 1998; Founder, and Head, First Eleven Studio, since 1986; *b* 17 April 1947; *d* of Theodore Farbridge and Isobel Farbridge (*née* Reid-Douglas); *m* 1970 (Christopher) Patrick Frean; one *d. Educ:* City of London Sch. for Girls; Hornsey Coll. of Art (BA Hons); Royal Coll. of Art (MA 1972). Design Consultant, Centro Design Montefibre, Milan, 1974; set up Jenny Frean Associates, textile design studio, 1975; portraitist, 1984–86; founded First Eleven Studio; working with textile manufacturers worldwide on every aspect of colour and surface decoration, 1986. *Recreations:* music (especially opera), all art forms, gardening. *Address:* Christmas Cottage, Ingrams Green, Midhurst, W Sussex GU29 0LJ. *T:* (01730) 812337.

FREARS, Stephen Arthur; film director; *b* 20 June 1941; *s* of late Dr Russell E. Frears and Ruth M. Frears; *m* 1st, 1968, Mary-Kay Wilmers, *qv* (marr. diss. 1974); two *s*; 2nd, 2002, Anne Rothenstein; one *s* one *d. Educ:* Gresham's Sch., Holt; Trinity Coll., Cambridge (BA Law). Director of films: Gumshoe, 1971; Bloody Kids, 1980; Going Gently, 1981; Walter, 1982; Saigon, 1983; The Hit, 1984; My Beautiful Laundrette, 1985; Prick Up Your Ears, 1986; Sammy and Rosie Get Laid, 1987; Dangerous Liaisons, 1989; The Grifters, 1990; Accidental Hero, 1992; The Snapper, 1993; Mary Reilly, 1996; The Van, 1996; The Hi-Lo Country, 1999; High Fidelity, 2000; Liam, 2001; Dirty Pretty Things, 2002; Mrs Henderson Presents, 2005; The Queen, 2006; Chéri, 2009; Tamara Drewe, 2010; Lay the Favorite, 2011; Mohammed Ali's Greatest Fight, 2012; Philomena, 2013; The Program, 2015; television: Fail Safe, 2000; The Deal, 2003. *Recreation:* reading. *Address:* c/o Casarotto Co. Ltd, 7–12 Noel Street, W1F 8GQ. *T:* (020) 7287 4450.

FRÉCHETTE, Louise, OC 1999; Deputy Secretary-General, United Nations, 1998–2006; *b* 16 July 1946. *Educ:* Collège Basile Moreau (BA 1966); Univ. of Montreal (LèsL Hist. 1970); Coll. of Europe, Bruges (Post-grad. Dip. Econ. Studies 1978). Joined Dept of External Affairs, Govt of Canada, 1971; Ambassador to Argentina and Uruguay, 1985–88; Assistant Deputy Minister: for Latin America and Caribbean, Min. of Foreign Affairs, 1988–91; for Internat. Econ. and Trade Policy, 1991–92; Ambassador to UN, 1992–94; Associate Dep. Minister, Dept of Finance, 1994–95; Dep. Minister of Defence, Canada, 1995–98. Member, Board: CARE Canada, 2007– (Chair, 2011–); Essilor Internat., France, 2012–. Distinguished Fellow, Centre for Internat. Governance Innovation, Canada, 2006–12. Hon. LLD St Mary's Univ., Halifax, 1993; hon. drs from Univs of Ottawa, Laval, Montreal, Carleton, Waterloo, Toronto, McGill, St Francis-Xavier, Guelph, Quebec, Kyung Hee, Turin. *Recreations:* golf, reading.

FREDERICK, Sir Christopher (St John), 11th Bt *cr* 1723, of Burwood House, Surrey; *b* 28 June 1950; *s* of Sir Charles Frederick, 10th Bt and of Rosemary, *er d* of Lt-Col R. J. H. Baddeley, MC; *S* father, 2001; *m* 1990, Camilla Elizabeth, *o d* of Sir Derek Gilbey, 3rd Bt; one *s* one *d. Heir: s* Benjamin St John Frederick, *b* 29 Dec. 1991.

FREDMAN, Prof. Sandra Debbe, FBA 2005; Rhodes Professor of the Laws of the British Commonwealth and the USA, University of Oxford, since 2011 (Professor of Law, 1999–2011); Fellow, Pembroke College, Oxford, since 2011; barrister; *b* 28 July 1957; *d* of Michael Geoffrey Fredman and Naomi Pauline Fredman (*née* Greenstein); *m* 1985, Alan Leslie Stein; two *s* one *d. Educ:* Univ. of Witwatersrand (BA 1st Cl. Maths and Philosophy 1977); Wadham Coll., Oxford (Rhodes Schol., 1979–82; BA 1st Cl. Hons Jurisp. 1981; BCL 1st Cl. Hons 1982). Political and econs journalist, Financial Mail, S Africa, 1978–79; articled clerk, Lawford & Co., Gray's Inn, 1983–84; Lectr in Law, KCL, 1984–88; Fellow and Lectr in Law, Exeter Coll., Oxford, 1988–2011. Leverhulme Major Res. Fellow, 2004–07. Scientific Dir, European Network of Legal Experts in the Non-Discrimination Field, 2005–07; Dir, Oxford Human Rights Hub, 2012. Fellow, Gray's Inn, 2007–. Hon. QC 2012. *Publications:* (with M. Nell and P. Randall) The Narrow Margin: how black and white South Africans view change in South Africa, 1983; (with B. Hepple) Labour Law and Industrial Relations in Great Britain, 1986, 2nd edn 1992; (with G. Morris) The State as Employer: labour law in the public services, 1989; Women and the Law, 1997; (ed) Discrimination and Human Rights, 2001; Discrimination Law, 2002, 2nd edn 2011; (ed with S. Spencer) Age as an Equality Issue, 2003; Human Rights Transformed: positive rights and positive duties, 2008; articles in legal jls. *Recreations:* outdoor activities, literature, theatre, travel. *Address:* Pembroke College, Oxford OX1 1DW. *T:* (01865) 276444; Old Square Chambers, 10–11 Bedford Row, WC1R 4BU. *T:* (020) 7269 0300.

FREE, Maj. Gen. Julian Richard, CBE 2009 (OBE 2006; MBE 2001); Commandant, Joint Services Command and Staff College, since 2014; *b* Plymouth, 30 Jan. 1963; *s* of Paul and Christine Free; *m* 1990, Barbara, (Babs), Woodward; one *s* one *d. Educ:* Queen's Coll., Taunton; St Luke's Coll., Exeter Univ. (BEd Hons 1986); RMA Sandhurst; Army Comd and Staff Coll., Camberley (psc, MA 1995). RA Young Officers' Course, Larkhill, 1987; Comd Post Officer, 1987–88, Gun Position Officer, 1989, Forward Observation Officer (Saudi Arabia, Kuwait), 1990–91, 1 RHA; Forward Observation Officer, 1991–92, Adjt, 1992–94, 7 Para. RHA; SO 2 (Weapons) c, Equipment Support 22a, 1995–98; Batt. Comdr, G Parachute Batt. (Mercer's Troop) RHA (Kosovo, Sierra Leone), 1998–2000; Batt. Comdr, Aviation Batt. 7 Para. RHA, 2000; MA to COS, HQ Kosovo Force 4, 2000–01; MA to QMG, 2001–03; CO, 26 Regt RA (Iraq, Cyprus), 2003–05; DACOS Future Structures, HQ Land, 2005–07; hcsc 2007; Comdr, 4 Mechanised Bde (Iraq), 2007–09; rcds 2009; Director: Collective Trng Gp, 2009–10; Campaign and Transition Assessment Gp, HQ ISAF Jt Comd, Afghanistan, 2011; COS, HQ ARRC, 2012–14. Legion of Merit (USA), 2011. *Recreation:* keen sportsman who enjoys chasing balls of all sorts and casting flies whilst furthering his arboreal knowledge. *Address:* Joint Services Command and Staff College, Defence Academy, Shrivenham, Swindon SN6 8LA.

FREEDBERG, Prof. David Adrian; Professor of Art History, since 1984, Pierre Matisse Professor of History of Art, since 2007, and Director, Italian Academy for Advanced Studies in America, since 2000, Columbia University; *b* 1 June 1948; *s* of William Freedberg and Eleonore Kupfer; one *s* one *d. Educ:* S African Coll. High Sch., Cape Town; Yale Univ. (BA); Balliol Coll., Oxford (DPhil). Rhodes Scholar, Oxford, 1969–72; Lectr in History of Art: Westfield Coll., Univ. of London, 1973–76; Courtauld Inst. of Art, Univ. of London, 1976–84; Slade Prof. of Fine Art, Univ. of Oxford, 1983–84. Baldwin Prof., Oberlin Coll., Ohio, 1979; Andrew W. Mellon Prof. of Fine Art, Nat. Gall. of Art, Washington, 1996–98; Nat Robertson Prof. of Sci. and Society, Emory Univ., 2006; Vis. Mem., Inst. for Advanced Study, Princeton, NJ, 1980–81; Gerson Lectr, Univ. of Groningen, 1983; VUB-Leerstoel, Brussels Univ., 1988–89; Wittkower Prof., Bibliotheca Hertziana, Rome, 2008–09; Vis. Fellow, Wissenschaftskolleg, Berlin, 2009. Fellow: Amer. Acad. of Arts and Scis, 1997; Amer. Philosophical Soc., 1997; Accademia Nazionale di Agricolture, 2003; Istituto Veneto di Scienze, Lettere e Arti, 2011; Stellenbosch Inst. for Advanced Study, 2012. *Publications:* Dutch Landscape Prints of the Seventeenth Century, 1980; The Life of Christ after the Passion (Corpus Rubenianum Ludwig Burchard, VII), 1983; Iconoclasts and their Motives, 1985; Iconoclasm and Painting in the Revolt of the Netherlands 1566–1609, 1988; The Power of Images, 1989 (many translations); (ed) The Prints of Pieter Bruegel the Elder, 1989; (ed with Jan De Vries) Art in History/History in Art: studies in seventeenth century Dutch culture, 1991; Joseph Kosuth: The Play of the Unmentionable, 1992; Peter Paul Rubens: paintings and oil sketches, 1995; (with Enrico Baldini) Citrus Fruit: the Paper Museum of Cassiano dal Pozzo B I, 1997; (with Andrew Scott) Fossil Woods and other Geological Specimens: the Paper Museum of Cassiano dal Pozzo B III, 2000; The Eye of the Lynx: Galileo, his friends, and the beginnings of modern natural history, 2003; (with David Pegler) Fungi vols I-III: the Paper Museum of Cassiano dal Pozzo B II, 2005; Las Mascaras de Aby Warburg, 2013; articles in Burlington Magazine, Revue de l'Art, Gentse Bijdragen, Art Bulletin, Münchner Jahrbuch der Bildenden Kunst, Jl of Warburg and Courtauld Insts, Print Quarterly, Quaderni Puteani, Trends in Cognitive Science, Frontiers in Human Neurosci. *Address:* Italian Academy for Advanced Studies in America, Columbia University, 1161 Amsterdam Avenue, New York, NY 10027, USA.

FREEDLAND, Jonathan Saul; Executive Editor, Opinion, since 2014, and Columnist, since 1997, The Guardian; *b* 25 Feb. 1967; *s* of Michael Freedland and late Sara Freedland; *m* 2000, Sarah Peters; two *s. Educ:* University Coll. Sch., London; Wadham Coll., Oxford (BA Hons PPE). Reporter, Sunday Correspondent, 1989–90; news trainee, BBC, 1990; reporter, BBC News and Current Affairs, 1991–93; Laurence Stern Fellow, as staff writer, Washington Post, 1992; Washington Corresp., 1993–97, Policy Editor, 1997–2014, The Guardian. Monthly Columnist: Jewish Chronicle, 1998–; Daily Mirror, 2002–04; Presenter, The Long View, Radio 4, 1999–. Dir and Trustee, Index on Censorship, 2002–09. Columnist of the Year, What the Papers Say Awards, 2002; David Watt Prize for Journalism, Rio Tinto, 2008. *Publications:* Bring Home the Revolution, 1998 (Somerset Maugham Award for Non-fiction); Jacob's Gift: a journey into the heart of belonging, 2005; The 3rd Woman, 2015; *as Sam Bourne*: The Righteous Men, 2006 (Gold Book Award, Neilsen, 2007); The Last Testament, 2007; The Final Reckoning, 2008; The Chosen One, 2010; Pantheon, 2012; contribs to NY Times. *Recreations:* family, music, movies. *Address:* The Guardian, Kings Place, 90 York Way, N1 9AG. *T:* (020) 3353 2000. *E:* Jonathan.freedland@guardian.co.uk.

FREEDLAND, Prof. Mark Robert, DPhil; FBA 2002; Professor of Employment Law, 1996–2012, now Emeritus and Research Fellow, Institute of European and Comparative Law, since 2014, University of Oxford (Senior Research Fellow, Law Faculty, 2012–14); Fellow and Tutor in Law, St John's College, Oxford, 1970–2012, now Emeritus Research Fellow; *b* 19 April 1945; *s* of Nathaniel Freedland and Esther (*née* Bendas); *m* 1st, 1973, Lalage Lewis (*d* 1976); one *s* one *d*; 2nd, 1997, Geraldine Field. *Educ:* Hendon Co. Grammar Sch.; University Coll. London (LLB); Brasenose Coll., Oxford (MA; DPhil 1970). Called to the Bar, Gray's Inn, 1971, Bencher, 1998; University of Oxford: Lectr, 1971–94; Reader, 1994–96; Dir, Inst. of European and Comparative Law, 2001–04; Leverhulme Major Res. Fellow, 2005–08. Visiting Professor: European Univ. Inst., Florence, 1995; Univ. of Paris I, 1996–98; Univ. of Paris II, 1999–2002; Hon. Prof., Faculty of Laws, UCL, 2012–. Hon. QC 2013. Dr *hc* Paris II, 2000. *Publications:* The Contract of Employment, 1976; (with P. L. Davies) Labour Law Text and Materials, 1979, 2nd edn 1983; (ed with P. L. Davies) Kahn-Freud's Labour and the Law, 1983; (with P. L. Davies) Labour Legislation and Public Policy, 1993; (jtly) Public Services and Citizenship in European Law, 1998; The Personal Employment Contract, 2003; (with P. L. Davies) Towards a Flexible Labour Market, 2005; (with N. Kountouris) The Legal Construction of Personal Work Relations, 2012; (with N. Kountouris) Resocialising Europe, 2013; (with C. Costello) Migrants at Work, 2014; (with J. Prassl) Viking, Laval and Beyond, 2015; contrib. articles to Public Law, Industrial Law Jl. *Recreation:* living village life in France. *Address:* St John's College, Oxford OX1 3JP. *T:* (01865) 277387. *E:* mark.freedland@sjc.ox.ac.uk.

FREEDMAN, Amelia, (Mrs Michael Miller), CBE 2006 (MBE 1989); FRAM; Artistic Director and Founder, Nash Ensemble, since 1964; Head of Classical Music, South Bank Centre, 1995–2006; *b* 21 Nov. 1940; *d* of Miriam Freedman (*née* Claret) and Henry Freedman; *m* 1970, Michael Miller; two *s* one *d. Educ:* St George's Sch., Harpenden; Henrietta Barnett, London; RAM (LRAM (piano), ARCM (clarinet); ARAM 1977, FRAM 1986). Music teacher, 1961–72: King's Sch., Cambridge; Perse Sch. for Girls, Cambridge; Chorleywood College for the Blind; Sir Philip Magnus Sch., London. Presented annual themed series, Wigmore Hall, 1979–; Artistic Director: Bath Internat. Fest., 1984–93; Bath Mozartfest, 1995–; Bath Bachfest, 2012–; Musical Adviser, Israel Fest., 1989–90; Programme Adviser, Philharmonia Orch., 1993–95; chamber music consultant for various projects at South Bank Centre and Barbican, and for LSO; has commnd 171 new works for Nash Ensemble and presented 270 world premières; sang in film, A Hard Day's Night, 1964. Trustee, Nash Concert Soc., 1968–. Freeman, City of London, 2003. FRSA 2004. Hon. DMus Bath, 1993. Walter Wilson Cobbett Gold Medal, Musicians' Co., 1996; Leslie Boosey Award, PRS/Royal Philharmonic Soc., 2000; Internat. Artist Managers' Assoc. Award, 2011. Chevalier, l'Ordre des Arts et des Lettres (France), 1983; Czech Govt Medal for services to Czech music in UK, 1984; Chevalier, l'Ordre National du Mérite (France), 1996; Officier, l'Ordre des Arts et des Lettres (France), 2009. *Recreations:* theatre, cinema, ballet, opera; spectator sport—cricket, rugger, football (supporting Arsenal); children. *Address:* 14 Cedars Close, Hendon, NW4 1TR. *T:* (020) 8203 3025, *Fax:* (020) 8203 9540. *E:* info@nashensemble.org.uk.

FREEDMAN, (Benjamin) Clive; QC 1997; a Recorder, since 2000; a Deputy High Court Judge, since 2003; *b* 16 Nov. 1955; *s* of Lionel and Freda Freedman; *m* 1980, Hadassa Helen Woolfson; one *s* three *d. Educ:* Manchester Grammar Sch.; Pembroke Coll., Cambridge (MA). Called to the Bar, Middle Temple, 1978, Bencher, 2005; Jt Hd, Littleton Chambers, 2006–13; Mem., Northern Circuit, 1980–; an Asst Recorder, 1997–2000. *Recreations:* Manchester City FC, Test Match Special. *Address:* 7 King's Bench Walk, Temple, EC4Y 7DS.

FREEDMAN, Charles, CB 1983; Commissioner, Customs and Excise, 1972–84; *b* 15 Oct. 1925; *s* of late Solomon Freedman, OBE, and Lilian Freedman; *m* 1949, Sarah Sadie King; one *s* two *d. Educ:* Westcliff High Sch.; Cheltenham Grammar Sch.; Trinity Coll., Cambridge (Sen. Schol., BA). Entered HM Customs and Excise, 1947; Asst Sec., 1963. *Address:* 10 Cliff Avenue, Leigh-on-Sea, Essex SS9 1HF. *T:* (01702) 473148.

FREEDMAN, Clive; *see* Freedman, B. C.

FREEDMAN, Her Honour Dawn Angela, (Mrs N. J. Shestopal); a Circuit Judge, 1991–2007; *b* 9 Dec. 1942; *d* of Julius and Celia Freedman; *m* 1970, Neil John Shestopal. *Educ:* Westcliff High Sch. for Girls; University Coll., London (LLB Hons). Called to the Bar, Gray's Inn, 1966; Metropolitan Stipendiary Magistrate, 1980–91; a Recorder, 1989–91. Mem. Parole Bd, 1992–96. Chm., Jewish Marriage Council, 1998–2002. Mem. Council, London Sch. of Jewish Studies, 1998–2002. Trustee, Jewish Women's Aid, 2008–. *Recreations:* theatre, television, cooking. *Address:* c/o Harrow Crown Court, Hailsham Drive, Harrow HA1 4TU.

FREEDMAN, Jeremy Stuart; His Honour Judge Jeremy Freedman; a Circuit Judge, since 2013; *b* Newcastle upon Tyne, 20 April 1959; *s* of Roland and Valerie Freedman; *m* 1989, Julia Anne Chapman; one *s* one *d. Educ:* Oundle Sch.; Manchester Univ. (BA Hons); City Univ. (DipLaw); Gray's Inn (Bar Vocational Course). Called to the Bar, Middle Temple, 1982; in practice as a barrister, specialising in personal injury and clinical negligence; Asst Recorder, 1998–2000; Recorder, 2000–13; Dep. Asst Coroner, Durham, 2010–13. *Recreations:* Real tennis, golf, ski-ing, reading, food and wine. *Address:* 10 North Avenue, Gosforth, Newcastle upon Tyne NE3 4DT. *E:* jeremy.freedman@btinternet.com, HHJudgejeremy.freedman@judiciary.gsi.gov.uk. *Clubs:* Northern Counties (Newcastle upon Tyne); Northumberland Golf.

FREEDMAN, Prof. Judith Anne, (Lady Freedman), CBE 2013; Professor of Tax Law, since 2001, and Director of Legal Research, Oxford University Centre for Taxation, since 2008, University of Oxford; Fellow of Worcester College, Oxford, since 2001; *b* 10 Aug. 1953; *d* of Harry Hill and Estella Hill; *m* 1974, Lawrence David Freedman (*see* Rt Hon. Prof. Sir Lawrence Freedman); one *s* one *d*. *Educ:* North London Collegiate Sch.; Lady Margaret Hall, Oxford (BA 1st Class Hons Jurisprudence, MA). Articled Clerk, Stanleys & Simpson North, 1976–78; Solicitor of Supreme Court, 1978; Solicitor, Corporate Tax Dept, Freshfields, 1978–80; Lectr in Law, Univ. of Surrey, 1980–82; London School of Economics: Lectr, Law Dept, 1982–91; Sen. Lectr, 1991–96; Reader in Law, 1996–2000; Prof. of Law, 2000–01; Sen. Res. Fellow in Company and Commercial Law, Inst. of Advanced Legal Studies, 1989–92. Anton Philips Vis. Prof., Tilburg Univ., 2007–08; Adjunct Prof., Australian Sch. of Business, Univ. of NSW, 2011–. Member: Tax Law Review Cttee, 1994–; DTI Company Law Review Working Party on Small Businesses, 1998–2000; Office of Tax Simplification Consultative Cttee on Small Business Taxation, 2010–12; Tax Avoidance Study Gp to advise Exchequer on Gen. Anti-avoidance Rule, 2010–12. Mem Council, Inst. for Fiscal Studies, 2003–. Gov., Wimbledon High Sch. (GDST), 2009–. European Editor, Palmer's Company Law, 1991–2003; Jt Editor, British Tax Review, 1997– (Asst Ed., 1988–97); Member, Editorial Board: Fiscal Studies, 2000–11; The Tax Jl, 2002–; eJournal of Tax Res., Univ. of NSW, 2003–; Modern Law Rev., 2004– (Mem., Editl Cttee, 1987–2004); Canadian Tax Jl, 2005–; Australian Tax Rev., 2011–. *Publications:* (jtly) Property and Marriage: an integrated approach, 1988; (ed jtly) Law and Accounting: competition and co-operation in the 1990s, 1992; Employed or Self-employed? tax classification of workers and the changing labour market, 2001; (ed jtly) Taxation: an interdisciplinary approach to research, 2005; (ed) Beyond Boundaries: developing approaches to tax avoidance and tax risk management, 2008; (ed jtly) The Delicate Balance: tax, discretion and the Rule of Law, 2011; contrib. articles to jls. *Recreations:* family, friends, doodling. *Address:* Worcester College, Oxford OX1 2HB. *W:* www.law.ox.ac.uk/profile/freedmanj.

FREEDMAN, Rt Hon. Prof. Sir Lawrence (David), KCMG 2003; CBE 1996; PC 2009; DPhil; FBA 1995; Professor of War Studies, King's College, London, 1982–2014, now Emeritus; *b* 7 Dec. 1948; *s* of late Lt-Comdr Julius Freedman and Myra Freedman; *m* 1974, Judith Anne Hill (*see* J. A. Freedman); one *s* one *d*. *Educ:* Whitley Bay Grammar Sch.; BAEcon Manchester; BPhil York; DPhil Oxford. Teaching Asst, York Univ., 1971–72; Research Fellow, Nuffield Coll., Oxford, 1974–75; Research Associate, IISS, 1975–76 (Mem. Council, 1984–92 and 1993–2002); Research Fellow, 1976–78, Head of Policy Studies, 1978–82, RIIA; King's College London: Hd, Dept of War Studies, 1982–97; Hd, Sch. of Social Sci. and Public Policy, 2000–03; Vice-Principal, 2003–13. Vis. Prof., Blavatnik Sch. of Govt, Univ. of Oxford, 2015–. Mem., Iraq Inquiry, 2009–. Hon. Dir, Centre for Defence Studies, 1990–. Chm., Cttee on Internat. Peace and Security, Social Science Res. Council (US), 1993–98. Trustee, Imperial War Mus., 2001–09. FKC 1992. FRSA 1991; FRHistS 2000. FAcSS (AcSS 2001). Chesney Gold Medal, RUSI, 2006; Dist. Scholar Award, Internat. Studies Assoc., 2007; George Webb Prize for Strategic Studies Leadership, Canadian Internat. Council, 2008. *Publications:* US Intelligence and the Soviet Strategic Threat, 1977, 2nd edn 1986; Britain and Nuclear Weapons, 1980; The Evolution of Nuclear Strategy, 1981, 2nd edn 2003; (jtly) Nuclear War & Nuclear Peace, 1983; (ed) The Troubled Alliance, 1983; The Atlas of Global Strategy, 1985; The Price of Peace, 1986; Britain and the Falklands War, 1988; (jtly) Signals of War, 1990; (ed) Population Change and European Security, 1991; (ed) Britain in the World, 1991; (jtly) The Gulf Conflict 1990–1991, 1993; War: a Reader, 1994; (ed) Military Intervention in Europe, 1994; (ed) Strategic Coercion, 1998; The Politics of British Defence, 1999; Kennedy's Wars, 2000; The Cold War, 2001; (ed) Superterrorism, 2002; Deterrence, 2004; The Official History of the Falklands Campaign, vols I and II, 2005; A Choice of Enemies, 2008 (Lionel Gelber Prize, 2009; Duke of Westminster Prize for Military Lit., RUSI, 2009); (ed) Scripting Middle East Leaders, 2013; Strategy: a history, 2013 (W. J. M. Mackenzie Book Prize, Pol Studies Assoc., 2014). *Recreation:* political caricature. *Address:* c/o Department of War Studies, King's College London, Strand, WC2R 2LS. *T:* 07920 221312.

FREEDMAN, Susan Rachel; *see* Prevezer, S. R.

FREELAND, Anne Elizabeth; *see* Studd, A. E.

FREELAND, Henry John, FSA; RIBA; Partner, Freeland Rees Roberts Architects, 1981–2005; Director, Freeland Rees Roberts Architects Ltd, since 2005; *b* 16 Jan. 1948; *s* of Lt-Gen. Sir Ian Henry Freeland, GBE, KCB, DSO and Mary Freeland; *m* 1971, Elizabeth Margaret Sarel Ling; one *s* three *d*. *Educ:* Eton Coll.; Bristol Univ. (BA 1st Cl. Hons Architecture 1970; BArch 1st Cl. Hons 1973). ARCUK, RIBA 1975; AABC. Twist and Whitley, Architects, Cambridge, 1972–74; Cecil Bourne, Architects, Cambs, 1974–77; Whitworth & Hall, Architects, Bury St Edmunds, 1977–81. Surveyor to the Fabric, King's Coll. Chapel, Cambridge, 1987–; Architect and Surveyor: Ickworth House, 1988–; Guildford Cath., 1995–2010; Norwich Cath., 1996–; Burghley House, 2003–; Millennium Project Architect, St Edmundsbury Cath., 2008–. Member: Ely DAC, 2001–; Fabric Adv. Cttee, Cath. and Abbey Ch of St Alban, 2006–; Fabric Adv. Cttee, St George's Chapel, Windsor, 2010–. Member: Ecclesiastical Architects' and Surveyors' Assoc., 1978–; Cathedral Architects' Assoc., 1995–; Life Mem., SPAB, 1970. FSA 2006. Freeman, City of London, 1985; Liveryman, Co. of Chartered Architects, 1986–. Trustee, D'Oyly Carte Trust, 2001–. *Recreations:* cooking, family, painting, cricket, archaeology, fossils, gardening. *Address:* Freeland Rees Roberts Architects, 25 City Road, Cambridge CB1 1DP. *T:* (01223) 366555, *Fax:* (01223) 312882. *E:* hf@frrarchitects.co.uk. *Club:* Surveyors' (Trustee, 2009–).

FREELAND, Simon Dennis Marsden; QC 2002; **His Honour Judge Freeland;** a Circuit Judge, since 2007; *b* 11 Feb. 1956; 2nd *s* of late Dennis Marsden Freeland and of Rosemary Turnbull Tarn; *m* 2000, Anne Elizabeth Studd, *qv*; one *s* one *d*. *Educ:* Malvern Coll.; Manchester Univ. (LLB Hons). Called to the Bar, Gray's Inn, 1978, Bencher, 2007; in practice at the Bar, 1978–2007, specialising in police law and civil liberties; Head of Chambers, 5 Essex Court, 2002–07; Recorder, 2000–07. *Recreations:* horse-racing, walking, good food and fine wine, family. *Address:* Central London County Court, Thomas More Building, Royal Courts of Justice, Strand, WC2A 2LL.

FREELING, Dr Anthony Nigel Stanley; President, Hughes Hall, Cambridge, since 2014 (Fellow, 2008–14); *b* London, 6 Aug. 1956; *s* of Dr Paul Freeling and Shirley Valerie Freeling; *m* 1989, Laurel Claire Powers (*see* L. C. Powers-Freeling); two *d*. *Educ:* Haberdashers' Aske's Sch., Elstree; St John's Coll., Cambridge (BA (1st Cl.) Maths 1978; MPhil Control Engrg and Operational Res. 1980; PhD Mgt Studies 1985). Decision Analyst, Decision Science Consortium, 1978–83; Sen. Mgt Scientist, Mars Inc., 1984–86; McKinsey & Company, 1986–2004: Principal, 1992–99; Dir, 1999–2004. Dir, Strategic Mgt Centre, Ashridge Business Sch., 2005–; Mem. Council, Open Univ., 2006–14. Res. Dir, Retailing Res. Councils, Asia and Europe, Coca-Cola Co. Inc., 2010–. Trustee: UnLtd, 2004–14; PHG Foundn, 2012–; Dir, Capacitybuilders, 2008–11. *Publications:* Agile Marketing, 2011. *Recreations:* food and wine, tennis, motor racing, music. *Address:* Hughes Hall, Cambridge CB1 2EW. *T:* (01223) 761087. *E:* president@hughes.cam.ac.uk. *Club:* Oxford and Cambridge.

FREELING, Laurel Claire P.; *see* Powers-Freeling.

FREEMAN, family name of **Baron Freeman**.

FREEMAN, Baron *cr* 1997 (Life Peer); **Roger Norman Freeman;** PC 1993; MA; FCA; Chairman: UK Advisory Board (formerly Corporate Finance Advisory Board), PricewaterhouseCoopers, since 1999; Skill Force Development Ltd, since 2004; Director, Parity Group plc, since 2007; *b* 27 May 1942; *s* of Norman and Marjorie Freeman; *m* 1969, Jennifer Margaret Watson (*see* Lady Freeman); one *s* one *d*. *Educ:* Whitgift Sch., Croydon; Balliol Coll., Oxford (MA PPE). Chartered Accountant, 1969; FCA 1979. Articled with Binder Hamlyn & Co., 1964–69 (Hons Prize, 1968); General Partner, Lehman Brothers, 1969–86. MP (C) Kettering, 1983–97; contested (C) same seat, 1997. Parliamentary Under-Secretary of State: for the Armed Forces, 1986–88; DoH, 1988–90; Minister of State: Dept of Transport, 1990–94; MoD, 1994–95; Chancellor of the Duchy of Lancaster, 1995–97. Partner, PricewaterhouseCoopers, 1997–99. Dir, Thales SA, 1997–2013; Chm., Thales UK Pension Fund, 2000–. A Vice-Chm., Cons. Party, 1997–2001. Chm., Cambridge Enterprise Ltd (formerly Cambridge Univ. Venture Bd), 2005–10. President: British Internat. Freight Assoc., 1999–2002; RFCA (formerly TAVRA) Council, 1999–2010. *Publications:* Professional Practice, 1968; Fair Deal for Water, 1985; (ed) UK Rail Privatisation 1992–1997, 2000; (ed) University Spin-out Technology Companies, 2004. *Address:* House of Lords, SW1A 0PW. *Club:* Carlton.

FREEMAN, Lady; Jennifer Margaret Freeman, OBE 2012; FSA; architectural historian, writer, specialist in building conservation and developer of listed buildings; Director, Historic Chapels Trust, 1993–2012; Chairman, Freeman Historic Properties Ltd, since 1992; *b* 28 Oct. 1944; *d* of Malcolm Woodward Watson and Margaret Hannah Watson; *m* 1969, Roger Norman Freeman (*see* Baron Freeman); one *s* one *d*. *Educ:* Withington Girls' Sch., Manchester; Univ. of Manchester (BA Hons); Architectural Assoc. (Dip. Building Conservation); Inst. of Historic Bldg Conservation. Project Co-ordinator, Save the City: a conservation study of the City of London, report published 1976, 2nd edn 1979. Member: Cttee, Save Britain's Heritage, 1977–; London Adv. Cttee, English Heritage, 1986–2003; Council for the Care of Churches, 1991–2003. Dir and Trustee, Waltham Abbey Royal Gunpowder Mills Operating Co., 2013–. Pres. and Trustee, Friends of Kensal Green Cemetery, 2004–; Vice-President: Friends of the City Churches, 1996–; Nat. Churches Trust (formerly Historic Churches Preservation Trust), 2003–. Sec., Victorian Soc., 1982–85. Trustee: Heritage Link, 2002–08; Constable Trust, 2003–10. Pres., Kettering Civic Soc., 2004–. Hon. Life Mem., Rothwell Preservation Trust, 1997. Assessor, City Heritage Award, 1978–. FRSA 2003; FSA 2005. Freeman, City of London, 1998. Hon. DArts De Montfort, 1997. *Publications:* (jtly) Kensal Green Cemetery, 2001; W. D. Caröe (1857–1938): his architectural achievement, 1990; contrib. various articles to learned jls. *Recreations:* embroidery, art gallery and museum-going, country walking, theatre, reading, travel. *E:* jmfhproperties@gmail.com.

FREEMAN, Catherine; Director, Dove Productions, since 1989; *b* 10 Aug. 1931; *d* of Harold Dove and Eileen Carroll; *m* 1st, 1958, Sir Charles Wheeler, CMG; 2nd, 1962, Rt Hon. John Freeman, MBE, PC (marr. diss. 1976; he *d* 2014); two *s* one *d*. *Educ:* Convent of the Assumption; St Anne's Coll., Oxford (MA Hons). Joined BBC as trainee producer, 1954; Producer/director: Panorama, Brains Trust, Monitor, Press Conference, 1954–58; joined Thames Television as Sen. Producer in Features Dept, 1976; Editor, Daytime progs, 1976–82; originator and series producer of Citizen 2000 for Channel 4; Controller, Documentaries, Features and Religion, 1982–86; Controller, Features and Religion, 1986–89. Member: Devlin Cttee on Identification Procedures, 1974–76; Literature Panel, Arts Council, 1981–84; Broadcasting, Film and Video panel, Arts Council, 1986–88; Council, ICA, 1983–93. Dir, One World Broadcasting Trust, 1990–95. *Address:* Davis Cottage, Torriano Cottages, NW5 2TA.

See also M. J. A. Freeman.

FREEMAN, David Charles; Founder/Director of Opera Factory; freelance opera and theatre director; *b* 1 May 1952; *s* of Howard Wilfred Freeman and Ruth Adair Nott; *m* 1985, Marie Angel (marr. diss. 2012); one *s* one *d*. *Educ:* Sydney Univ., NSW (BA Hons). Opera Factory Sydney, 1973–76; Opera Factory Zürich, 1976–95: directed 20 prodns, appearing in 5, writing the text of 4; Opera Factory London, 1981–98: directed 21 prodns (8 televised by Channel Four), writing text of two; founded Opera Factory Films, 1991; Associate Artist, ENO, 1981–95: prodns include world première of The Mask of Orpheus, 1986; directed: Goethe's Faust, Pts I and II, Lyric, Hammersmith, 1988; (also adapted) Malory's Morte d'Arthur, Lyric, Hammersmith, 1990; The Winter's Tale, Shakespeare's Globe (opening prodn), 1997; Madam Butterfly, 1998 (and six revivals), Tosca, 1999, Carmen, Royal Albert Hall, 2002 (and four revivals); Carmen, O2 Centre, 2010 (first opera prodn); Magic Flute, Sydney Opera House, 2006; Gadaffi (world première), ENO, 2006; Sweeney Todd, RFH, 2007; Wozzeck, Brussels, 2008; Messiah, Royal Danish Opera, 2012; The Wonderful Adventures of Nils (musical), China, 2013 (Golden Lion award, 2014); opera prodns in New York, Houston, Paris, Germany and St Petersburg; has also worked in Senegal and India (Zangoora). Founder, Factory Edge, 2011. Chevalier de l'Ordre des Arts et des Lettres, France, 1985.

FREEMAN, Prof. Ernest Michael, PhD; FREng; Professor of Applied Electromagnetics, Imperial College of Science, Technology and Medicine, London University, 1980–2003, now Emeritus Professor of Electromagnetics; *b* 10 Nov. 1937; *s* of Ernest Robert Freeman and Agnes Maud Freeman; *m* 1987, Helen Anne Rigby. *Educ:* Colfe's Grammar Sch., Lewisham; King's Coll., London (BScEng; PhD 1964). Lectr, King's Coll., London, 1960–63 and 1966–70; Engrg Designer, AEI, Rugby, 1964–65; Reader: Brighton Polytechnic, 1970–73; Imperial Coll. of Science and Technology, 1973–80. Chm., Infolytica Ltd, 1978–; Vice Pres., Infolytica Corp., 1978–. FREng (FEng 1987). *Publications:* papers in learned society jls on magnetics. *Recreations:* Anglo-Saxon period, pre-conquest churches, architecture, military and electrical engineering history, industrial archaeology. *Address:* Electrical and Electronic Engineering Department, Imperial College London, South Kensington Campus, SW7 2AZ. *E:* e.freeman@imperial.ac.uk.

FREEMAN, George William; MP (C) Mid Norfolk, since 2010; Parliamentary Under-Secretary of State, Department for Business, Innovation and Skills and Department of Health, since 2014; *b* Cambridge, 12 July 1967; *s* of Arthur Freeman and Joanna Stockbridge (*née* Philipson); *m* 1996, Eleanor Holmes; one *s* one *d*. *Educ:* Radley Coll., Oxon; Girton Coll., Cambridge (BA Geog. 1989; MA). Parly Officer, NFU, 1990–92; Founder, Local Identity Agency, 1992–96; Dir, Early Stage Ventures, Merlin Biosciences, 1997–2001; CEO, Amedis Pharmaceuticals, 2001–03; Man. Dir, 4D Biomedical, 2003–10. PPS to Minister of State, DECC, 2010–12. Chm., All Party Parly Gp on Agricl Sci. and Technol., 2010; Govt Advr on Life Scis, 2011–13; Prime Ministerial Trade Envoy, 2013. Mem. Bd, Gtr Cambridge Partnership, 2005–09. Trustee, Cambridge Union Soc., 2005–08. Chm., The Norfolk Way, 2007–11. Contested (C) Stevenage, 2005. *Recreations:* sailing, wildfowling. *Address:* House of Commons, SW1A 0AA. *T:* (020) 7219 1940. *E:* george.freeman.mp@parliament.uk. *Club:* Norfolk (Norwich).

FREEMAN, Sir James (Robin), 3rd Bt *cr* 1945; *b* 21 July 1955; *s* of Sir (John) Keith (Noel) Freeman, 2nd Bt and Patricia Denison (*née* Thomas); *S* father, 1981, but his name does not appear on the Official Roll of the Baronetage. *Heir:* none.

FREEMAN, Jennifer Margaret; *see* Freeman, Lady.

FREEMAN, Joan; *see* Freeman, S. J.

FREEMAN, John; a Judge of the Upper Tribunal (Immigration and Asylum Chamber) (formerly a Vice-President, Immigration Appeal Tribunal, later a Senior Immigration Judge, Asylum and Immigration Tribunal), since 2000; a Recorder, since 2003; *b* 13 July 1951; *s* of late E. A. Freeman, FRCS and Joan (*née* Horrell); *m* 1st, 1983, Alison Gwenllian Wornsnop (marr. diss. 1988); 2nd, 2015, Amanda Elaine Paul. *Educ:* Winchester Coll.; Corpus Christi Coll., Cambridge (MA); Univ. of Warwick (LLM). Practised at Bar, Midland and Oxford Circuit, 1976–83, 1986–89; Resident Magistrate, Registrar and Commissioner of High Court and Court of Appeal, actg Dir of Public, Prosecutions, Solomon Islands, 1983–86; consultant, ODA and UNHCR, 1987–92; Immigration Appeal Adjudicator, 1989–90, 1991–2000. Part-time Legal Mem., Special Immigration Appeals Commn, 2001–. *Recreation:* breeding Staffordshire bull terriers. *Address:* (office) Field House, 15–25 Bream's Buildings, EC4A 1DZ. *Club:* Royal Geographical Society.

FREEMAN, Prof. Kenneth Charles, PhD; FRS 1998; FAA; Duffield Professor, Research School of Astronomy and Astrophysics, since 2000 (Professor, Mount Stromlo and Siding Spring Observatories, 1987–2000), Institute of Advanced Studies, Australian National University; *b* 27 Aug. 1940; *s* of Herbert and Herta Freeman; *m* 1963, Margaret Leigh Cook; one *s* three *d*. *Educ:* Scotch Coll.; Univ. of Western Australia (BSc Hons Mathematics 1962); Trinity Coll., Cambridge (PhD 1965). FAA 1981. Res. Fellow, Trinity Coll., Cambridge, 1965–69; McDonald Postdoctoral Fellow in Astronomy, Univ. of Texas, 1966; Mount Stromlo and Siding Spring Observatories, Australian National University: Queen Elizabeth Fellow, 1967–70; Fellow, 1970–74; Sen. Fellow, 1974–81; Professorial Fellow, 1981–87. Sen. Scientist, Kapteyn Lab., Univ. of Groningen, 1976; Vis. Mem., IAS, Princeton, 1984, 1988; Distinguished Vis. Scientist, Space Telescope Science Inst., Baltimore, 1988–; Oort Prof., Univ. of Leiden, 1994; Vis. Fellow, Merton Coll., Oxford, 1997; Tinsley Prof., Univ. of Texas, 2001; Blaauw Prof., Univ. of Groningen, 2003; de Vaucouleurs Lectr, Univ. of Texas, 2003; Henry Norris Russell Lectr, AAS, 2013. Chm., Nat. Cttee on Astronomy, Australian Acad. of Science, 1984–86 (Pawsey Medal, 1972). ARAS 2002. Hon. DSc WA, 1999. Heineman Prize, Amer. Inst. of Physics and Amer. Astronomical Soc., 1999; Citation Laureate Award, Thomson ISI, 2001; Johann Wempe Award, Astrophysical Inst. Potsdam, 2008; Prime Minister's Sci. Prize, Australia, 2012; Matthew Flinders Medal, Australian Acad. of Sci., 2013; Gruber Cosmology Prize, 2014. *Publications:* (with G. McNamara) In Search of Dark Matter, 2006; (with D. Block) Shrouds of the Night, 2008; more than 750 articles in learned astronomical jls. *Recreations:* bushwalking, birdwatching, classical music. *Address:* Mount Stromlo Observatory, Cotter Road, Weston Creek, ACT 2611, Australia. *T:* (2) 61250264. *E:* kcf@mso.anu.edu.au.

FREEMAN, Dr Marie Joyce, FFCM; Health Service Management Consultant, 1988–95; *b* 14 April 1934; *d* of Wilfrid George Croxson and Ada Mildred (*née* Chiles); *m* 1958, Samuel Anthony Freeman (decd); one *s*. *Educ:* Royal Free Hospital Sch. of Medicine (MB BS, DPH). Specialist in Community Medicine, Avon AHA, 1974; District MO, Southmead HA, 1982; Actg Regl MD, SW RHA, 1986–88. *Address:* Wingfield House, Darlington Place, Bath BA2 6BY. *T:* (01225) 466670; Hameau de la Lauze, 84570 Blauvac, Vaucluse, France.

FREEMAN, Dr Matthew John Aylmer, FRS 2006; Professor of Pathology and Head of Department, Sir William Dunn School of Pathology, University of Oxford, since 2013; *b* 16 June 1961; *s* of Rt Hon. John Freeman, MBE, PC and of Catherine Freeman, *qv*; *m* 1990, Rose Taylor; one *s* one *d*. *Educ:* King Alfred's Sch.; Pembroke Coll., Oxford (BA Hons); Imperial Coll., London (PhD 1987). Postdoctoral Fellow, Univ. of Calif, Berkeley, 1987–92; MRC Laboratory of Molecular Biology, Cambridge: Mem., Perm. Scientific Staff, 1992–2012; Jt Hd, 2007–08, Hd, 2008–12, Div. of Cell Biol. Chairman: British Scientists Abroad, 1990–92; British Soc. for Develtl Biology, 2004–09; Member: Exec., Campaign for Sci. and Engrg (formerly Save British Sci.), 1992–2012; Agric. and Envmt Biotechnol. Commn, 2000–05; Council, Royal Soc., 2009–11; Dir, Co. of Biologists, 2003–. Ed., Develtl Biol., 2003–12. Mem., EMBO, 1999– (Gold Medal, 2001). Hooke Medal, British Soc. for Cell Biology, 2003; Novartis Medal and Prize, Biochemical Soc., 2015. *Publications:* contrib. primary res. articles and reviews in specialist and gen. sci. jls. *Recreation:* sailing. *Address:* Sir William Dunn School of Pathology, University of Oxford, South Parks Road, Oxford OX1 3RE. *T:* (01865) 275500.

FREEMAN, Michael Alexander Reykers, MD; FRCS; Consultant Orthopaedic Surgeon, The London Hospital, 1968–96; Hon. Consultant, Royal Hospitals NHS Trust, since 1996; *b* 17 Nov. 1931; *s* of Donald George and Florence Julia Freeman; *m* 1st, 1951, Elisabeth Jean; one *s* one *d*; 2nd, 1959, Janet Edith; one *s* one *d*; 3rd, 1968, Patricia; one *d* (and one *s* decd). *Educ:* Stowe Sch.; Corpus Christi Coll., Cambridge (open scholarship and closed exhibn); London Hospital Med. Coll. BA (1st cl. hons), MB BCh, MD (Cantab). FRCS 1959. Trained in medicine and surgery, London Hosp., and in orthopaedic and traumatic surgery, London, Westminster and Middlesex Hosps; co-founder, Biomechanics Unit, Imperial Coll., London, 1964; Cons. Surg. in Orth. and Traum. Surgery, London Hosp., also Res. Fellow, Imperial Coll., 1968; resigned from Imperial Coll., to devote more time to clinical activities, 1979. Special surgical interest in field of reconstructive surgery in lower limb, concentrating on joint replacement; originator of new surgical procedures for reconstruction and replacement of arthritic hip, knee, ankle and joints of foot; has lectured and demonstrated surgery, Canada, USA, Brazil, Japan, China, Australia, S Africa, continental Europe; guest speaker at nat. and internat. profess. congresses. Robert Jones Lectr, RCS, 1989. Visiting Professor: Sch. of Engrg Sci., Univ. of Southampton, 2001; Inst. of Orthopaedics, UCL, 2001. Mem., Editl Adv. Bd, 1986–97, Eur. Ed.-in-Chief, 1997–2001, Jl of Arthroplasty. Past Member: Scientific Co-ordinating Cttee, ARC; MRC; Clin. Res. Bd, London Hosp. Bd of Governors; Brent and Harrow AHA; DHSS working parties. President: Internat. Hip Soc., 1982–85; British Hip Soc., 1989–91; British Orthopaedic Assoc., 1992–93; Eur. Fedn of Nat. Assocs of Orthopaedics and Traumatol., 1994–95. Member: BMA; Amer. Acad. Orth. Surgs; Orth. Res. Soc.; SICOT; RSM; Health Unit, IEA; SIROT; European Orth. Res. Soc. Hon. Member: Danish Orth. Assoc.; Soc. Française de Chirurg. Orth. et Traum.; Canadian Orth. Assoc. Hon. Fellow, Soc. Belge de Chirurg. Orth. et de Traum. Bacon and Cunning Prizes and Copeman Medal, CCC; Andrew Clark and T. A. M. Ross Prize in Clin. Med., London Hosp. Med. Coll.; Robert Jones Medal, Brit. Orth. Assoc. *Publications:* editor and part-author: Adult Articular Cartilage, 1973, 2nd edn 1979; Scientific Basis of Joint Replacement, 1977; Arthritis of the Knee, 1980; chapters in: Bailey and Love's Short Practice of Surgery; Mason and Currey's Textbook of Rheumatology; papers in Proc. Royal Soc., Jl Bone and Joint Surgery, and med. jls. *Recreations:* gardening, reading, surgery. *Address:* 79 Albert Street, NW1 7LX. *T:* (020) 7387 0817.

FREEMAN, Prof. Michael David Alan, FBA 2009; Professor of English Law, University College London, 1984–2011, now Emeritus; *b* London, 25 Nov. 1943; *s* of Raphael and Florence Freeman; *m* 1967, Vivien Ruth Brook; one *s* one *d*. *Educ:* Hasmonean Grammar Sch., Hendon; University Coll. London (LLB, LLM; Fellow 2000). Called to the Bar, Gray's Inn, 1968. Lectr, E London Coll. of Commerce, 1965–66; Asst Lectr, 1966–67, Lectr, 1967–69, Univ. of Leeds; Lectr, 1969–79, Reader, 1979–84, UCL. Editor: Current Legal Problems, 1992–2004; Internat. Jl Children's Rights, 1993–; Current Legal Issues, 1997–2012; Internat. Jl of Law in Context, 2005–13. *Publications:* The Legal Structure, 1974; The Rights and Wrongs of Children, 1983; The Moral Status of Children, 1997; Understanding Family Law, 2007; Introduction to Jurisprudence, 3rd edn 1972 to 9th edn 2014; Law and Childhood Studies, 2012; Law and Language, 2013; Law and Global Health, 2014; The Human Rights of Children, 2015; A Magna Carta for Children?, 2015. *Recreations:* listening to the symphonies of Bruckner and the operas of Mozart, reading the plays of Ibsen and Brecht, watching first division county cricket, Jewish history. *Address:* Bentham House, Endsleigh Gardens, WC1H 0EG. *T:* (020) 7679 1443. *E:* mdaf@bamps.com. *Club:* Middlesex CC.

FREEMAN, Morgan Porterfield; actor; *b* Memphis, 1 June 1937; *m* 1st, 1967, Jeanette Adair Bradshaw (marr. diss. 1979); two *c*; 2nd, 1984, Myrna Colley-Lee (marr. diss. 2010); two *c*. *Educ:* LA City Coll. USAF, 1955–59. *Stage* productions include: The Nigger Lovers (debut), 1967; Hello Dolly, NY, 1969; Coriolanus, Julius Caesar, NY Shakespeare Fest., 1979; Mother Courage and Her Children, 1980; Othello, All's Well That Ends Well, Dallas Shakespeare Fest., 1982; The Country Girl, NY, 2008; *films* include: Who Says I Can't Ride a Rainbow, 1971; Brubaker, 1980; Eyewitness, 1981; Harry & Son, 1984; Street Smart, 1987; Clean and Sober, 1988; Lean on Me, Johnny Handsome, Driving Miss Daisy (Golden Globe Award), Glory, 1989; Bonfire of the Vanities, Robin Hood: Prince of Thieves, 1991; Unforgiven, 1992; The Shawshank Redemption, Outbreak, Se7en, 1995; Chain Reaction, 1996, Moll Flanders, Amistad, 1997; Deep Impact, 1998; Nurse Betty, 2000; Under Suspicion, Along Came a Spider, 2001; High Crimes, The Sum of All Fears, 2002; Dreamcatcher, Bruce Almighty, 2003; Levity, The Big Bounce, 2004, Million Dollar Baby (Screen Actors' Guild Award, Academy Award for Best Supporting Actor), Batman Begins, War of the Worlds (narrator), Edison, March of the Penguins (narrator), 2005; An Unfinished Life, Lucky Number Slevin, 2006; Gone Baby Gone, The Bucket List, Wanted, The Dark Knight, 2008; Thick as Thieves, 2009; Invictus, Red, 2010; The Dark Knight Rises, 2012; Oblivion, Olympus Has Fallen, Now You See Me, 2013; Transcendence, Lucy, 2014; Ted 2, Ruth & Alex, 2015; *television* includes: The Electric Company, 1971–77; Death of a Prophet, 1981; Ryan's Hope, 1981; Another World, 1982–84; The Atlanta Child Murders, 1985; The Civil War, 1990; Freedom: a history of Us, 2003; Slavery and the Making of America (narrator), 2005. *Address:* Creative Artists Agency, 2000 Avenue of the Stars, Los Angeles, CA 90067, USA.

FREEMAN, Paul Illife, CB 1992; PhD; Controller and Chief Executive of HM Stationery Office, and the Queen's Printer of Acts of Parliament, 1989–95; *b* 11 July 1935; *s* of late John Percy Freeman and Hilda Freeman; *m* 1959, Enid Ivy May Freeman; one *s* one *d*. *Educ:* Victoria University of Manchester (BSc (Hons) Chemistry, PhD). Post Doctoral Fellow, Nat. Research Council of Canada, 1959–61; Research Scientist, Dupont De Nemours Co. Ltd, Wilmington, Del, USA, 1961–64; Nat. Physical Laboratory: Sen. Scientific Officer, 1964–70; Principal Scientific Officer, 1970–74; Exec. Officer, Research Requirements Bds, DoI, 1973–77; Director: Computer Aided Design Centre, 1977–83; National Engrg Lab., 1980–83; Central Computer and Telecommunications Agency, HM Treasury, 1983–88. Member: CS Coll. Adv. Council, 1983–88; Bd, NCC, 1983–88; Bd, DVLA, 1990–92; Council, UEA, 1994–2003. Vis. Prof. Univ. of Strathclyde, 1981–86. CCMI (CIMgt 1995). *Publications:* scientific papers. *Recreations:* fishing, reading, walking, gardening.

FREEMAN, Peter David Mark, CBE 2001; Principal Finance Officer, Department for International Development, 2000–01; *b* 8 Dec. 1947; *s* of Dr Victor Freeman and Ethel (*née* Halpern); *m* 1980, Anne Tyndale; two *d*. *Educ:* Merton Coll., Oxford (BA Hons); Univ. of Toronto (MA). Asst Private Sec. to Minister for Overseas Develt, 1973–75; Office of UK Exec. Dir, World Bank, 1975–78; British High Commn, Zimbabwe, 1980–83; Overseas Development Administration, then Department for International Development: Head: EC Dept, 1984–88; Central and Southern Africa Dept, 1988–90; Aid Policy Dept, 1990–91; Internat. Div., 1991–93; Personnel, Orgn and Services Div., 1993–96; Dir, Africa Div., 1996–99. Non-executive Director: Shared Interest Soc. Ltd, 2003–13; Brighton Housing Trust, 2012–. Mem., Audit Cttee, Sightsavers Internat., 2001–09. Trustee: Internat. HIV/AIDS Alliance, 2002–11; Shared Interest Foundn, 2005–13; IDS, 2006–13; Brighton Peace and Envmt Centre, 2010–12. Governor: Stanford Jun. Sch., Brighton, 1988–2014 (Chm., 1992–96); Dorothy Stringer High Sch., Brighton, 1996–99; Brighton, Hove and Sussex Sixth Form Coll., 2001– (Chm., 2005–); Coombe Road Primary Sch., Brighton, 2014–; Chm., Brighton and Hove Schs Forum, 2003–. *Address:* 7 Windlesham Road, Brighton BN1 3AG.

FREEMAN, Peter John, CBE 2010; Chairman, Competition Appeal Tribunal, since 2013 (Member, 2011–13); *b* 2 Oct. 1948; *s* of Comdr John Kenneth Herbert Freeman, LVO, RN retd and Jean Forbes Freeman (*née* Irving); *m* 1972, Elizabeth Mary Rogers; two *s* two *d*. *Educ:* King Edward's Sch., Bath; Kingswood Sch., Bath; Goethe Inst., Berlin; Trinity Coll., Cambridge (Exhibnr; MA); Univ. Libre de Bruxelles (Licence Spéciale en Droit Européen). Called to the Bar, Middle Temple, 1972; admitted solicitor, 1977; Simmons & Simmons: asst, 1973; Partner, 1978–2003; Hd, EC and Competition Gp, 1987–2003; Managing Partner, Commercial and Trade Law Dept, 1994–99. Sen. Consultant, Cleary Gottlieb Steen & Hamilton LLP, 2011–13. Mem., 2003–11, Dep. Chm., 2003–05, Chm., 2006–11, Competition Commn. Chm., Regulatory Policy Inst., Oxford, 1998–2007. Jt Gen. Ed., 1991–2005, Cons. Ed., 2005–, Butterworth's Competition Law. Member of Advisory Board: ESRC Res. Centre for Competition Policy, 2007–; Internat. Competition Law Forum (St Gallen), 2007–; Mem. Sci. Bd, Concorrência e Regulação, Lisbon, 2010–. Hon. QC 2010. *Publications:* (with R. Whish) A Guide to the Competition Act 1998, 1999; articles on competition law. *Recreations:* studying naval history, painting in oils, playing the piano. *Address:* Competition Appeal Tribunal, Victoria House, Bloomsbury Place, WC1A 2EB. *E:* Peter.Freeman@catribunal.org.uk. *Clubs:* Oxford and Cambridge, Reform.

FREEMAN, Prof. Raymond, MA, DPhil, DSc (Oxon); FRS 1979; John Humphrey Plummer Professor of Magnetic Resonance, University of Cambridge, 1987–99, now Emeritus; Fellow of Jesus College, Cambridge, since 1987; *b* 6 Jan. 1932; *s* of late Albert and Hilda Frances Freeman; *m* 1958, Anne-Marie Périnet-Marquet; two *s* three *d*. *Educ:* Nottingham High Sch. (scholar); Lincoln Coll., Oxford (open scholar). Ingénieur, Centre d'Etudes Nucléaires de Saclay, Commissariat à l'Energie Atomique, France, 1957–59; Sen. Scientific Officer, Nat. Phys. Lab., Teddington, Middx, 1959–63; Man., Nuclear Magnetic Resonance Research, Varian Associates, Palo Alto, Calif, 1963–73; Lectr in Physical Chemistry, 1973–82, Aldrichian Praelector in Chemistry, 1982–87, and Fellow, Magdalen Coll., 1973–87, Oxford Univ. Fellow, Internat. Soc. of Magnetic Resonance, 2008. Hon. DSc Durham, 1988. Chem. Soc. Award in Theoretical Chem. and Spectroscopy, 1978; Leverhulme Medal, Royal Soc., 1990; Longstaff Medal, RSC, 1999; Queen's Medal, Royal Soc., 2002; Günther Laukien Prize, Experimental NMR Conf., 2006; Russell Varian Prize, Varian Inc., 2012. *Publications:* A Handbook of Nuclear Magnetic Resonance, 1987; Spin Choreography: basic steps in high resolution NMR, 1997; Magnetic Resonance in Chemistry and Medicine, 2003; articles on nuclear magnetic resonance spectroscopy in various scientific journals. *Recreations:* swimming, traditional jazz. *Address:* Jesus College, Cambridge CB5 8BL.

FREEMAN, Rt Rev. Robert John; *see* Penrith, Bishop Suffragan of.

FREEMAN, Dr (Sally) Joan, PhD; CPsychol, FBPsS; private psychology practice, London, since 1989; Visiting Professor, School of Lifelong Learning and Education, Middlesex University, since 1992; author; *b* 17 June 1935; *d* of late Phillip Casket and Rebecca (*née* Goldman); *m* 1957, Hugh Lionel Freeman (*d* 2011); three *s* one *d*. *Educ:* Broughton High Sch.; Univ. of Manchester (BSc, PhD 1980, MEd, DipEdGuidance). FBPsS 1985; CPsychol 1988; FCP 1990. Sen. Lectr in Applied Psychol., Preston Poly., 1975–81; Hon. Tutor, Dept of Educn, Univ. of Manchester, 1975–89; Hon. Lectr, Inst. of Educn, Univ. of London, 1988–94. Ed., High Ability Studies, 1995–98. Dir, Gulbenkian Res. Project on Gifted Children, 1973–88. Founder Pres., European Council for High Ability, 1987–92. Mem., various cttees and projects on the educn of children of high ability, incl. Adv. Bd on Exceptionally Able Pupils, SCAA, 1994–, and Govt Adv. Gp, Gifted and Talented Children,

1998–. Chair and Founder, Tower Educn Gp (UK), experts on gifts and talents, 2007–; consultant and contributor, Channel 4 TV series, Child Genius, 2006. Vis appts, scholarships and consultancies, Italy, Bulgaria, Canada, SA, Hong Kong and Australia; Executive: Eur. Talent Support Centres, Budapest, 2013–; Templeton Res. Project, Hungary, 2014–. College of Preceptors, now College of Teachers: Member: Bd of Examnrs, 1987–; Council, 1995–; Exec. Cttee, 1999–; Sen. Vice-Pres., 2002–; Chm., Publications Bd, 1998–; British Psychological Society: Mem., Nat. Council, 1975–86; Chm., Northern Br., 1978–86; Mem., Standing Press Cttee, 1980–85; Lifetime Achievement Award, 2007. Mem., Strategic Thinking Forum, Centre for British Teachers. Mem., Fawcett Soc., 1984–. Patron, Nat. Assoc. for Able Children in Educn, 2006–. Hon. FCollT 2006. Lifetime Achievement Award, Internat. Mensa, 2015. *Publications:* Human Biology and Hygiene, 1968, 2nd edn 1981; In and Out of School: an introduction to applied psychology in education, 1975 (trans. Portuguese, Hebrew and Spanish); Gifted Children: their identification and development in a social context, 1979; Clever Children: a parents' guide, 1983 (trans. German, Finnish and Thai); (ed) The Psychology of Gifted Children: perspectives on development and education, 1985 (trans. Spanish); Gifted Children Growing Up, 1991; Bright as a Button: how to encourage your children's talents 0–5 years, 1991 (trans. Indonesian); Quality Basic Education: the development of competence, 1992 (trans. French); (with S. Ojanen) The Attitudes and Experiences of Headteachers, Class-teachers and Highly Able Pupils Towards the Education of the Highly Able in Finland and Britain, 1994; (ed jtly) Actualising Talent: a lifelong challenge, 1995; Highly Able Girls and Boys, 1996; How to Raise a Bright Child, 1996 (trans. Russian and Chinese); Educating the Very Able: current international research, 1998 (trans. Thai); International Out-of-school Education for the Gifted and Talented, 1998; (with Z. C. Guenther) Educando os Mais Capazes: idéias e ações comprovadas, 2000; Gifted Children Grown Up, 2001; (with J. Fořtiková) Volnočasové aktivity: pro nadané a talentované u nás a ve světě, 2009; Gifted Lives: what happens when gifted children grow up, 2010; numerous academic papers and chapters in books; contrib. numerous articles and book reviews on child develt, psychol. and educn for both professional and lay jls. *Recreations:* photography, theatre, travel. *Address:* 21 Montagu Square, W1H 2LF. *T:* (020) 7486 2604. *E:* joan@joanfreeman.com. *W:* www.joanfreeman.com.

FREEMAN-ATTWOOD, Prof. Jonathan; Principal, Royal Academy of Music, since 2008 (Vice-Principal, 1995–2008); Professor, University of London, since 2001; *b* Woking, 4 Nov. 1961; *s* of late Harold Warren Freeman-Attwood and Marigold Diana Sneyd Freeman-Attwood (*née* Philips); *m* 1990, Henrietta Paula Christian Parham; one *s* one *d*. *Educ:* Univ. of Toronto (BMus Hons); Christ Church, Oxford (MPhil). Royal Academy of Music: GRSM Tutor, 1990–91; Associate Dean, 1991–92, Dean, 1992–95, of Undergraduate Studies; Dir of Studies, 1995–96. Vis. Prof., KCL, 2007–. Pres., RAM Club, 2006–07. Critic, Gramophone, 1992–; freelance writer mainly on 18th century music, esp. Bach, performance traditions and recordings; regular contrib. to CD Review, BBC Radio 3, 1992–. Trumpet player for many ensembles; solo recordings: Albinoni for Trumpet, 1993; Bach Connections, 1999; The Trumpets that Time Forgot, 2003; La Trompette Retrouvée, 2007; Trumpet Masque, 2008; Romantic Trumpet Sonatas, 2011; A Bach Notebook for Trumpet, 2013; (world premiere) Lydia's Vocalises, by Fauré, 2014; The Neoclassical Trumpet, 2015. Producer of over 200 commercial CDs (7 Gramophone Awards incl. Record of the Year, 2010 and several Diapason d'Ors). Cheltenham Fest. Adv. Cttee, 2011–. Trustee: Young Classical Artists (formerly Young Concert Artists) Trust, 2008–; Countess of Munster Trust, 2008–; Winifred Christie Trust, 2008–; Associated Bd of Royal Schs of Music, 2008–; Harriet Cohen Trust, 2008–; Lucille Graham Trust, 2008–; Mendelssohn and Boise Foundn, 2008–; British Library Saga Trust, 2008–; Christ Church Oxford Music Trust, 2011–; Univ. of London, 2011–15; Chair, Artistic Adv. Cttee, Garsington Opera, 2012–; Vice Pres., Nat. Youth Wind Orch. of GB, 2013–. Patron: London Youth Choirs, Cavatina Chamber Music Trust; Hon. Patron, Lionel Tertis Fest. and Competition. FRNCM 2013. Hon. RAM 1997 (Hon. ARAM 1993); Hon. FKC 2009. *Publications:* (contrib.) The New Grove Dictionary of Music and Musicians, 2nd edn 2000; (contrib.) The Cambridge Companion to Recorded Music, 2009. *Recreations:* lots of Bach, watching cricket, French wine châteaux from a distance, Liverpool FC, reading. *Address:* c/o Royal Academy of Music, Marylebone Road, NW1 5HT. *T:* (020) 7873 7377. *E:* j.freeman-attwood@ram.ac.uk.

FREEMAN-GRENVILLE, family name of **Lady Kinloss**.

FREEMANTLE, Andrew, CBE (civ.) 2007 (MBE (mil.) 1982); Chief Executive, Royal National Lifeboat Institution, 1999–2009; *b* 26 Sept. 1944; *s* of Lt-Col Arthur Freemantle and Peggy Frances Freemantle (*née* Wood); *m* 1972, Patricia Mary Thompson; four *d*. *Educ:* Framlingham Coll.; RMCS; RCDS; Sheffield Univ. Commnd Royal Hampshire Regt, 1965; Australian Army, 1969–72; Royal Hampshire Regt, 1972–76; sc, Camberley, 1978; Directing Staff, Staff Coll. Camberley, 1983–84; CO 1st Bn Royal Hampshire Regt, 1985–87 (despatches 1987); Brigadier 1987; Comd 19 Infantry Bde, 1987–89; Mem., RCDS, 1990. Chief Exec., Scottish Ambulance Service NHS Trust, 1991–99. Non-exec. Dir, Salisbury Foundn NHS Trust, 2013–. Freeman, City of London, 2001. CCMI 2003. Hon. DBA Bournemouth, 2007. Officier, Ordre du Mérite Maritime (France), 2010. *Recreations:* cycling, cooking.

FREEMONT, Prof. Anthony John, MD; FRCP, FRCPath; Professor of Osteoarticular Pathology, since 1993, and Head, Manchester Medical School, since 2011, University of Manchester; Honorary Consultant, Central Manchester Foundation Trust, since 1988; *b* Plymouth, 27 March 1953; *s* of Walter Freemont and Sarah Freemont; *m* 1976, Susan Murray; one *d*; *m* 2008, Cordelia Warr. *Educ:* Latymer Upper Sch., Hammersmith; St Thomas' Hosp. Med. Sch., London (BSc 1973; MB BS 1976; MD 1984). FRCP 1995; FRCPath 1996. ARC Lectr, 1983–88, Sen. Lectr, 1988–93, in Osteoarticular Pathology, Univ. of Manchester. *Publications:* Atlas of Synovial Fluid Cytopathology (with J. Denton), 1991 (Glaxo Med. Atlas Book Award, 1992); 46 book chapters; over 300 articles in jls on aspects of bone, joint and soft tissue pathology. *Recreations:* church bell ringing, collecting brass threepenny pieces. *Address:* Firwood, Turners Lane, Llynclys, Shropshire SY10 8LL. *T:* (01691) 831233. *E:* tonyfreemont@hotmail.com.

FREER, Maj. Gen. Adrian Robert, OBE 1994; Director, Civil Nuclear Security, Office for Nuclear Regulation (formerly Health and Safety Executive), since 2011 (Assistant Director, 2008–11); *b* 17 April 1952; *s* of Air Chief Marshal Sir Robert William George Freer, GBE, KCB and of Margaret Freer; *m* 1983, Caroline Mary Henderson; two *d*. *Educ:* Trent Coll., Long Eaton, Notts. Commnd Parachute Regt, 1972; served 1 Para, 1972–80; Instructor, NCO Tactical Wing, Brecon, 1980–81; served 3 Para, 1982–83; Army Staff Coll., 1984; COS, 48 Gurkha Bde, 1985–86; Co. Comd 3 Para, 1987–88; Chief Instructor, RMA Sandhurst, 1989–90; Directing Staff, Army Staff Coll., 1990–91; CO 2 Para, 1992–94; Comdt, Inf. Trng Centre, 1994–97; Comd 5 Airborne Bde, 1997–99; rcds 2000; ACOS, J7 PJHQ, 2001–02; Comd Internat. Military Adv. Team, Sierra Leone, 2003–04; Co-ordinator, Kosovo Protection Corps, 2004–05. Chm., Airborne Assault Mus., 2008–. *Recreations:* all sports, particularly golf! *E:* adrianfreer@btinternet.com. *Clubs:* MCC, Army and Navy; Crieff Golf.

FREER, Maj. Gen. Ian Lennox, CB 1994; CBE 1988 (OBE 1985); Principal, Lennox Freer and Associates Pty Ltd, since 1997; Director, since 2004, and Executive Chairman, since 2007, Ocean Software Pty Ltd (Managing Director, 2004–07); *b* 18 May 1941; *s* of late Lt-Col George Freer, OBE and Elizabeth (*née* Tallo), Edinburgh; *m* 1970, Karla Thwaites; one *s* two *d*. *Educ:* George Watson's Coll., Edinburgh; RMA Sandhurst; Royal College of Defence Studies. Commnd Staffordshire Regt (Prince of Wales's), 1961; served UK, Kenya, Germany, Gulf States, Belize, Gibraltar; Staff Capt. to QMG, 1972–73; MA to COS, BAOR, 1975–77; SO1, Instr Staff Coll., 1980–81; CO 1st Bn, Staffords Regt, 1982–84; Div. Col, Staff Coll., 1985; Comdr, 39 Inf. Bde (NI), 1986–87; Chief, BRIXMIS (Berlin), 1989–91; Comdr, Land Forces, NI, 1991–94; GOC Wales and Western Dist, later 5th Div., 1994–96. Col, Staffordshire Regt, 1990–96; Col Comdt, POW Div., 1993–96. Dir, Woodleigh Sch., Vic, 1999–; Mem. Council, RUSI, Vic, 1999–. Mem., Pacific Inst. of Aust. *Recreations:* sailing, gardening. *Clubs:* Melbourne; Royal Brighton Yacht.

FREER, Michael Whitney; MP (C) Finchley and Golders Green, since 2010; *b* Manchester, 29 May 1960; *s* of Herbert and Marian Freer; civil partnership 2007, Angelo Crolla. *Educ:* Chadderton Grammar Sch., Manchester; St Aidan's Sch., Carlisle. Mem. (C) Barnet LBC, 1990–94 and 2001–10 (Leader, 2006–09). Exec. Mem., London Councils, 2008–09. Non-exec. Dir, London Develt Agency, 2008–10. Contested (C) Harrow West, 2005. *Recreations:* cycling, keep fit, learning French. *Address:* House of Commons, SW1A 0AA. *T:* (020) 7219 7071, *Fax:* (020) 7219 2211. *E:* mike.freer.mp@parliament.uk.

FREER, Dame Yve Helen Elaine; *see* Buckland, Dame Y. H. E.

FREETH, Peter Stewart, RA 1991 (ARA 1990); RE 1991 (ARE 1987); Tutor, Etching, Royal Academy Schools, since 1966; *b* 15 April 1938; *s* of Alfred William Freeth and Olive Walker; *m* 1967, Mariolina Meliadò; two *s*. *Educ:* King Edward's Grammar School, Aston, Birmingham; Slade School, London (Dip Fine Art). Rome Scholar, Engraving, British Sch., Rome, 1960–62; teacher of Printmaking, Camden Inst., 1979–2007. One man shows: Christopher Mendez Gall., London, 1987–89; Friends' Room, RA, 1991; S Maria a Gradillo, Ravello, Italy, 1997; Word Play, RA, 2001; Christ Church Coll. Gall., Oxford, 2006; North House Gall., Manningtree, 2006; My Affair with Resin, Tennant Room, RA, 2008–09; Previous Conviction, Highgate Literary and Scientific Soc., 2013; represented in collections: British Museum; V&A; Fitzwilliam Mus., Cambridge; Arts Council; Metropolitan Mus., NY; Nat. Gall., Washington; Hunterian Mus., Glasgow; Ruth Borchard, Portrait Collection; Ashmolean Mus., Oxford; Pallant House, Chichester. Mem., Royal Soc. of Painter Printmakers. *Recreations:* music, books, yet more work. *Address:* 83 Muswell Hill Road, N10 3HT.

FREI, Matt; Europe Editor and Presenter, Channel 4 News (Chief Washington Correspondent, 2011–13); *b* 26 Nov. 1963; *s* of Peter and Anita Frei; *m* 1996, Penny Quested; one *s* three *d*. *Educ:* Westminster Sch.; St Peter's Coll., Oxford (MA Hist. and Spanish). Joined BBC, 1988; BBC Television: Southern Europe Corresp., 1991–96; Asia Corresp., 1996–2002; Chief Washington Corresp., 2002–11. Writer and presenter, TV series, Berlin, 2009. RTS Award, 2000. *Publications:* Italy: the unfinished revolution, 1996, 2nd edn 1998; Only in America, 2008. *Recreation:* painting.

FREIER, Most Rev. Philip Leslie; *see* Melbourne, Archbishop of.

FREMANTLE, family name of **Baron Cottesloe**.

FRÉMAUX, Louis Joseph Felix; conductor; *b* 13 Aug. 1921; *m* 1st, 1948, Nicole Petibon (*d* 1999); four *s* one *d*; 2nd, 1999, Cecily Hake. *Educ:* Conservatoire National Supérieur de Musique de Paris. Chef d'Orchestre Permanent et Directeur, l'Orchestre National de l'Opéra de Monte Carlo, 1956–66; Principal Conductor, Orchestre de Lyon, 1968–71; Musical Dir and Principal Conductor, City of Birmingham Symphony Orch., 1969–78; Music Dir and Principal Conductor, 1979–81, Principal Guest Conductor, 1982–85, Sydney Symph. Orch. First concert in England, with Bournemouth Symph. Orch., 1964. Guest appearances with all symph. orchs in GB; many recordings. Hon. RAM 1978. Hon. DMus Birmingham, 1978. Croix de Guerre, 1945, 1947; Chevalier de la Légion d'Honneur, 1969. *Recreations:* walking, photography.

FRENCH, family name of **Baron De Freyne**.

FRENCH, Prof. Anthony Philip, PhD; Professor of Physics, Massachusetts Institute of Technology, 1964–91, now Emeritus; *b* 19 Nov. 1920; *s* of Sydney James French and Elizabeth Margaret (*née* Hart); *m* 1st, 1946, Naomi Mary Livesay (*d* 2001); one *s* one *d*; 2nd, 2002, Dorothy Ada Jensen. *Educ:* Varndean Sch., Brighton; Sidney Sussex Coll., Cambridge (major schol.; BA Hons 1942, MA 1946, PhD 1948). British atomic bomb project, Tube Alloys, 1942–44; Manhattan Project, Los Alamos, USA, 1944–46; Scientific Officer, AERE, Harwell, 1946–48; Univ. Demonstrator in Physics, Cavendish Laboratory, Cambridge, 1948–51, Lectr 1951–55; Dir of Studies in Natural Sciences, Pembroke Coll., Cambridge, 1949–55, Fellow of Pembroke, 1950–55; Visiting research scholar: California Inst. of Technology, 1951; Univ. of Michigan, 1954; Prof. of Physics, Univ. of S Carolina, 1955–62 (Head of Dept, 1956–62); Guignard Lectr, 1958; Vis. Prof., MIT, 1962–64; Vis. Fellow of Pembroke Coll., Cambridge, 1975. Member, Internat. Commn on Physics Educn, 1972–84 (Chm., 1975–81); Pres., Amer. Assoc. of Physics Teachers, 1985–86. FInstP 1986; Fellow, Amer. Physical Soc., 1987. Hon. ScD Allegheny Coll., 1989. Bragg Medal, Institute of Physics, 1988; Oersted Medal, 1989, Melba Newell Phillips Award, 1993, Amer. Assoc. of Physics Teachers. *Publications:* Principles of Modern Physics, 1958; Special Relativity, 1968; Newtonian Mechanics, 1971; Vibrations and Waves, 1971; Introduction to Quantum Physics, 1978; Einstein: a centenary volume, 1979; Niels Bohr: a centenary volume, 1985; Introduction to Classical Mechanics, 1986; Physics in a Technological World, 1988; Physics History from AAPT Journals II, 1995. *Recreations:* music, reading, writing. *Address:* c/o Physics Department, Room 6C–435, Massachusetts Institute of Technology, Cambridge, MA 02139, USA.

FRENCH, Cecil Charles John, FREng; Group Technology Director, Ricardo International, 1990–92, retired; *b* 16 April 1926; *s* of Ernest French and Edith Hannah French (*née* Norris); *m* 1st, 1956, Olive Joyce Edwards (*d* 1969); two *d*; 2nd, 1971, Shirley Frances Outten; one *s* one *d*. *Educ:* King's Coll., Univ. of London (MScEng; DSc Eng 1987); Columbia Univ., New York. FIMechE, FIMarEST; FREng (FEng 1982). Graduate apprentice, CAV Ltd, 1948–50; Marshall Aid scholar, MIT, USA (research into combustion in engines), 1950–52; Ricardo Consulting Engineers, subseq. Ricardo Internat., 1952–92, Director, 1969, Vice-Chm., 1982, Man. Dir, 1989; Man. Dir, 1979–83, Chm., 1984–87, G. Cussons Ltd. President, Instn of Mechanical Engineers, 1988–89 (Vice-Pres., 1981–86, Dep. Pres., 1986–88). Hon. DSc Brighton, 2006. *Publications:* numerous articles on diesel engines in learned soc. jls world wide. *Recreations:* folk dancing, photography. *Address:* 303 Upper Shoreham Road, Shoreham-by-Sea, Sussex BN93 5QA. *T:* (01273) 452050.

FRENCH, David; Partner, Hilliard French Associates, executive coaching, since 2014; Associate Director, Transform, since 2011; Principal, Convener Associates, since 2009; Senior Advisor, European Partnership for Democracy, 2010–11; *b* 20 June 1947; *s* of late Captain Godfrey Alexander French, CBE, RN, and Margaret Annis French; *m* 1974, Sarah Anne, *d* of late Rt Rev. (Henry) David Halsey; four *s*. *Educ:* Sherborne Sch.; Durham Univ. (BA). MCIPD. Nat. Council of Social Service, 1971–74; Hd of Social Services Dept, RNID, 1974–78; Dir of Services, C of E Children's Soc., 1978–87; Dir, Nat. Marriage Guidance Council, then Relate, 1987–95; consultant on family policy, 1995–97; Dir Gen., subseq. Chief Exec., Commonwealth Inst., 1997–2002; Chief Exec., Westminster Foundn for Democracy, 2003–09. Exec. Dir, Alexandria Trust, 2011–14. Chairman: London Corrymeela Venture, 1973–76; St Albans Internat. Organ Fest., 1985–87; Twenty First Century Foundn, 1996–2001. Trustee: Charity Appts, 1984–91; British Empire and Commonwealth Mus., 1999–2003; The Round Table: Commonwealth Jl of Internat. Affairs, 2001–08. Mem. Governing Council, Family Policy Studies Centre, 1989–2001. Mem., St Albans Cathedral

Council, 1996–99. Liveryman, Glaziers' Co., 1990–. MRSocMed 1988, FRSocMed 2008 (Life Fellow, 2009). FRSA 1993. *Recreation:* challenging projects. *Address:* Molly Bawn, Stoke Abbott, Beaminster, Dorset DT8 3JT. *T:* (01308) 868241. *E:* david@conveners.eu.

FRENCH, Air Vice-Marshal David Rowthorne, CB 1993; MBE 1976; engineering consultant, 1994–2008; *b* 11 Dec. 1937; *s* of Norman Arthur French and late Edna Mary French (*née* Rowthorne); *m* 1st, 1963, Veronica Margaret Mead (marr. diss. 1982); two *s* one *d*; 2nd, 1984, Philippa Anne Pym, *d* of Sir Alexander Ross; one *s* one *d*. *Educ:* Gosport County Grammar Sch.; RAF Technical Coll., Henlow. CEng, MRAeS 1969. Commnd Engr Br., RAF, 1960; various engrg appts, 1960–69; Sen. Engrg Officer, No 14 Sqn, RAF Bruggen, 1970–71; OC Airframe Systems Sqn, CSDE, RAF Swanton Morley, 1971–72; RAF Staff Coll., Bracknell, 1973; Sen. Engrg Officer, No 54 Sqn, RAF Coltishall, 1974–76; OC Engrg Wg, RAF Lossiemouth, 1976–79; Air Warfare Coll., RAF Cranwell, 1979; SO for Offensive Support Aircraft, HQ Strike Comd, 1980; Dep. Dir of Engrg Policy, MoD, 1981–82; Comd Mech. Engr, HQ RAF Germany, 1983–86; Dir of Policy, Directorate Gen., Defence Quality Assurance, MoD (PE), 1986–87; AO Wales and Stn Comdr, RAF St Athan, 1988–90; Comd Mech. Engr, HQ Strike Comd, 1990–91; AO Maintenance and Chief Exec. Maintenance Gp Defence Support Agency, RAF Support Comd, 1991–94, retd. Mem. (C), Broadland DC, 2007–11. Chairman: RAF Germany Golf, 1983–86; RAF Support Comd Golf, 1988–90; Capt., RAF Germany Golf Club, 1985–86. *Recreations:* golf, ski-ing, gardening, wine. *Address:* Milestone Piece, 109 Yarmouth Road, Blofield, Norwich, Norfolk NR13 4LQ. *Clubs:* Royal Air Force; Royal Norwich Golf.

FRENCH, Douglas Charles; Chairman, Westminster and City Programmes, since 1997; *b* London, 20 March 1944; *s* of late Frederick Emil French and Charlotte Vera French; *m* 1978, Sue, *y d* of late Philip Arthur Phillips; two *s* one *d*. *Educ:* Glyn Grammar Sch., Epsom; St Catharine's Coll., Cambridge (MA). Called to the Bar, Inner Temple. Exec., then Dir, P. W. Merkle Ltd, 1966–87. Asst to Rt Hon. Sir Geoffrey Howe, Shadow Chancellor, 1976–79; Special Advr to Chancellor of the Exchequer, 1981–83. Contested (C) Sheffield, Attercliffe, 1979; MP (C) Gloucester, 1987–97; contested (C) same seat, 1997. PPS to Minister of State, FCO, 1988–89, ODA, 1989–90, MAFF, 1992–93, DoE, 1993–94, to Sec. of State for the Envmt, 1994–97. Chm., All Party Cttee on Building Socs, 1996–97. Initiated Building Socs (Jt Account Holders) Act 1995, and Building Socs (Distributions) Act 1997. Chm., Bow Gp, 1978–79. Pres., Gloucester Conservative Club, 1989–97. Pres., Glyn Old Boys' Assoc., 2005–11. Gov., Glyn Sch., Epsom, 2000–15 (Vice-Chm., 2003–05; Chm., 2006–09). *Publications:* articles and reviews. *Recreations:* gardening, renovating period houses, ski-ing, squash. *Address:* 231 Kennington Lane, SE11 5QU. *Club:* Royal Automobile.

FRENCH, Air Chief Marshal Sir Joseph Charles, (Sir Joe), KCB 2003; CBE 1991 (OBE); FRAeS; defence and security consultant, since 2007; Commander-in-Chief Strike Command, 2006–07; Air Aide-de-Camp to the Queen, 2006–07; *b* 15 July 1949. Joined RAF, 1967; rcds; psa; postings in ME, Germany, Hong Kong and UK; ADC to CDS; Central Trials and Tactics Orgn; OC, 7 Sqdn, RAF Odiham, 1984–86; PSO to AOC-in-C Strike Comd, 1986–88; Hd, RAF Presentation Team, RAF Staff Coll., Bracknell, 1988; Station Comdr, RAF Odiham, 1989–91; Dir, Air Force Staff Duties, MoD, 1992–95; ACDS (Policy), 1995–97; Dir Gen. Intelligence and Geographic Resources, MoD, 1997–2001; Chief of Defence Intelligence, 2001–03; Air Mem. for Personnel and C-in-C PTC, 2003–06. Comr, CWGC, 2008–. Trustee, Nuffield Trust for the Forces of the Crown, 2009–; Vice-Patron, Blind Veterans UK (formerly St Dunstan's), 2009–.

FRENCH, Ven. Judith Karen; Archdeacon of Dorchester, since 2014; *b* Portsmouth, 18 Nov. 1960. *Educ:* St David's Coll., Lampeter (BA 1989); St Stephen's House, Oxford; Sarum Coll., Salisbury (MA Univ. of Wales, Lampeter 2008). Ordained deacon, 1991, priest, 1994; Parish Deacon, All Saints, Botley, 1991–94; Asst Curate, St Mark, Bilton, 1994–97; Vicar, St Mary the Virgin, Charlbury, 1997–2014; Area Dean, Chipping Norton, 2007–12; Hon. Canon, Christ Church, 2012–14. *Address:* 11 Broad Field Road, Yarnton, Kidlington OX5 1UL.

FRENCH, Philip Neville, OBE 2013; writer and broadcaster; Film Critic, The Observer, 1978–2013; *b* Liverpool, 28 Aug. 1933; *s* of late John and Bessie French; *m* 1957, Kersti Elisabet Molin; three *s*. *Educ:* Bristol Grammar Sch.; Exeter Coll., Oxford (BA Law) (editor, The Isis, 1956); Indiana Univ. Nat. Service, 2nd Lieut Parachute Regt, 1952–54. Reporter, Bristol Evening Post, 1958–59; Producer, BBC N Amer. Service, 1959–61; Talks Producer, BBC Radio, 1961–67; New Statesman: Theatre Critic, 1967–68; Arts Columnist, 1967–72; Sen. Producer, BBC Radio, 1968–90: editor of The Arts This Week, Critics' Forum and other series, writer-presenter of arts documentaries, Radio 3. Vis. Prof., Univ. of Texas, 1972. Mem., BFI Prodn Bd, 1968–74; Jury Mem., Cannes Film Fest., 1986. Fellow, BFI, 2013. Hon. Life Mem., BAFTA, 2008; Hon. Associate, London Film Sch., 2011. Hon. DLitt Lancaster, 2006. Critic of the Year, Nat. Press Awards, 2009. *Publications:* Age of Austerity 1945–51 (ed with Michael Sissons), 1963; The Movie Moguls, 1969; Westerns: aspects of a movie genre, 1974, 3rd expanded edn as Westerns and Westerns Revisited, 2005; Three Honest Men: Edmund Wilson, F. R. Leavis, Lionel Trilling, 1980; (ed) The Third Dimension: voices from Radio Three, 1983; (ed with Deac Rossell) The Press: observed and projected, 1991; (ed) Malle on Malle, 1992; (ed with Ken Wlaschin) The Faber Book of Movie Verse, 1993; (with Kersti French) Wild Strawberries, 1995; (with Karl French) Cult Movies, 1999; (with Julian Petley) Censoring the Moving Image, 2007; I Found It At the Movies: reflections of a cinephile, 2011; numerous articles and essays in magazines, newspapers and anthologies. *Recreations:* woolgathering in England, picking wild strawberries in Sweden. *Address:* 62 Dartmouth Park Road, NW5 1SN. *T:* (020) 7485 1711.

FRENCH, Hon. Robert Shenton, AC 2010; **Hon. Chief Justice French;** Chief Justice of Australia, since 2008; *b* Perth, WA, 19 March 1947; *s* of Robert William Shenton French and Kathleen Carina French; *m* 1976, Valerie Jean Lumsden; three *s*. *Educ:* St Louis Sch.; Univ. of Western Australia (BSc, LLB). Admitted barrister and solicitor, WA, 1972; Chm., Aboriginal Legal Service of WA, 1973–75; commenced practice at Ind. Bar, 1983; Judge, Federal Court, 1986–2008; pt-time non-resident Mem., Supreme Court of Fiji, 2003–08; Addnl Judge, Supreme Court, ACT, 2004–08. Associate Mem., Trade Practices Commn, 1983–86; Dep. Chm., 1983–86, Chm., 1986, Town Planning Appeals Tribunal, WA; Member: Law Reform Commn, WA, 1986; (pt-time), Australian Law Reform Commn, 2006–08; Pres., Nat. Native Tribunal, 1994–98; Dep. Pres., Australian Competition Tribunal, 2005–08. Chm., 1988–90, Chancellor, 1991–97, WA Coll. of Advanced Educn, later Edith Cowan Univ.; Mem. Council, Australian Inst. of Judicial Admin, 1992–98. Mem. Council, John XXIII Coll., Perth, 1978–83. Foundn Mem., Australian Acad. of Law, 2007–; Pres., Australian Assoc. for Constitnl Law, 2001–05. Hon. FASSA, 2010. Hon. Bencher: Gray's Inn, 2008; Lincoln's Inn, 2008. Hon. DLaws: Edith Cowan Univ., WA, 1998; Univ. of WA, 2011. Centenary Medal, 2003. *Publications:* (jtly) Reflections on the Australian Constitution, 2003. *Recreation:* tennis. *Address:* Chief Justice's Chambers, High Court of Australia, PO Box 6309, Kingston, ACT 2604, Australia. *T:* (2) 62706948, *Fax:* (2) 62706947.

FRENCH, Roger; HM Diplomatic Service, retired; Counsellor (Management) and Consul-General, Tokyo, 2003–07; *b* 3 June 1947; *s* of Alfred Stephen George French and Margaret (*née* Brown); *m* 1969, Angela Cooper (*d* 2011); one *s* one *d*. *Educ:* County Grammar Sch., Dagenham. Joined Foreign and Commonwealth Office, 1965; Havana, 1970; Vice-Consul: Madrid, 1971–73; Puerto Rico, 1973–76; UN Dept, FCO, 1977–80; Second, later First, Sec., (Chancery), Washington, 1980–84; First Sec. (Commercial), Muscat, 1985–88; Dep. Hd of N America Dept, FCO, 1988–92; Dep. Consul-Gen., Milan, 1992–96; Counsellor (Mgt) and Consul-Gen., Washington, 1997–2001; Actg Dep. High Comr, Nigeria, 2001; Hd of Inf. Mgt Gp, FCO, 2001–03. Chm., SPUC, Milton Keynes, 2011–. Commnd Kentucky Col, 1998. *Recreation:* music. *E:* angrog1969@hotmail.co.uk.

FRENK, Prof. Carlos Silvestre, PhD; FRS 2004; Ogden Professor of Fundamental Physics and Director, Institute for Computational Cosmology, University of Durham, since 2002; *b* 27 Oct. 1951; *s* of Silvestre Frenk and Alicia Mora de Frenk; *m* 1978, Susan Frances Clarke; two *s*. *Educ:* Nat. Autonomous Univ. of Mexico (BSc Theoretical Physics 1976); King's Coll., Cambridge (Math. Tripos Part III 1977); Inst. of Astronomy, Univ. of Cambridge (PhD 1981). Postdoctoral Research Fellow: Dept of Astronomy, Univ. of Calif at Berkeley, 1981–83; Astronomy Centre, Univ. of Sussex, 1983–85; Asst Res. Physicist, Inst. for Theoretical Physics, Univ. of Calif at Santa Barbara, 1984; University of Durham: Lectr in Astronomy, Dept of Physics, 1985–91; Reader in Physics, 1991–93; Prof. of Astrophysics, 1993–2002. Withrow Lect., 2006, George Darwin Lect., 2010, RAS. Alexander von Humboldt Fellow, 2012; Oort Prof., Leiden Observatory, 2015. Occasional broadcasts, radio and television, 1988–. Mem. Council, Royal Soc., 2012–. Member: IAU, 1985; AAS, 1993. FRAS 1981. Wolfson Res. Merit Award, Royal Soc., 2006; Daniel Chalonge Medal, Internat. Sch. of Astrophysics, 2007; Hoyle Medal, Inst. of Physics, 2010; Advanced Investigator Award Grant, ERC, 2011; Gruber Cosmology Prize, Gruber Foundn, 2011; Humboldt Res. Award, Alexander von Humboldt Foundn, 2013; Gold Medal, RAS. *Publications:* (ed) The Epoch of Galaxy Formation, 1989; (ed) Observational Tests of Cosmological Inflation, 1991; more than 600 scientific papers in prof. jls, incl. Nature, Astrophys. Jl, Astronomical Jl. *Recreations:* literature, ski training. *Address:* Department of Physics, Ogden Centre for Fundamental Physics, University of Durham, Science Laboratories, South Road, Durham DH1 3LE. *T:* (0191) 334 3641.

FRENKEL, Prof. Daniel, PhD; FRSC; Professor of Theoretical Chemistry, since 2007, and Head, Department of Chemistry, since 2011, University of Cambridge; Fellow, Trinity College, Cambridge, since 2008; *b* Amsterdam, 27 July 1948; *s* of Maurits Frenkel and Herta G. Tietz; *m* 1st, 1986, Alida H. Bolliger (*d* 1995); two *d*; 2nd, 2004, Dr Erika Eiser. *Educ:* Barlaeus Gymnasium, Amsterdam; Univ. of Amsterdam (Masters degree in Phys. Chem. 1972; PhD 1977). FRSC 2010. Post-doctoral Res. Fellow, UCLA, 1977–80; Res. Scientist, Shell Res., Amsterdam, 1980–81; University of Utrecht: Lectr, then Reader, Dept of Physics, 1981–86; Prof. of Computational Chem. (pt-time), 1987–; Prof. of Macromolecular Simulations (pt-time), Univ. of Amsterdam, 1998–2007; Gp Leader, 1987–2007, Scientific Advr, 2007–, Inst. for Atomic and Molecular Physics, Foundn for Fundamental Res. on Matter, Amsterdam. Hon. Prof., Beijing Univ. of Chem. Technol., 2005–; Concurrent Prof. (Hon.), Nanjing Univ., 2011–. Chm., Amsterdam Centre for Multiscale Modelling, 2007–. Member: Royal Dutch Acad. of Scis, 1998; Hollandsche Maatschappij der Wetenschappen, Netherlands, 2002. Foreign Mem., Royal Soc. (London), 2006; Foreign Hon. Mem., Amer. Acad. Arts and Scis, 2008; Associate Fellow, World Acad. of Scis (formerly Acad. of Scis for Developing World), 2012. MAE 2013. Hon. DSc Edinburgh, 2007. *Publications:* (jtly) Simulation of Liquids and Solids, Molecular Dynamics and Monte Carlo Methods in Statistical Mechanics, 1987; (jtly) Understanding Molecular Simulation: from algorithms to applications, 1996, 2nd edn 2002; contrib. internat. jls. *Address:* Department of Chemistry, University of Cambridge, Lensfield Road, Cambridge CB2 1EW. *T:* (01223) 336376. *E:* df246@cam.ac.uk.

FRENNEAUX, Prof. Michael Paul, MD; FRCP, FRCPE, FMedSci; Dean, Norwich Medical School, University of East Anglia, since 2015; *b* Hull, 11 Feb. 1957; *s* of Jack Frenneaux and Margaret Frenneaux; *m* 1978, Cheryl Christina Lord; one *s* one *d*. *Educ:* Beverley Grammar Sch.; Westminster Hosp. Med. Sch., London (MB BS Hons, Gold Medal, 1980; MD 1991). FRCP 1998; FRCPE 2009. Hse Officer, Westminster Hosp., 1980–81; SHO, Hammersmith and Brompton Hosps, and Nat. Hosp. for Nervous Diseases, Queen Square, 1981–83; Registrar, Aberdeen, 1983–84; Registrar (Cardiology): Edinburgh, 1984–85; Hammersmith Hosp., 1985–88; Consultant Cardiologist, Canterbury Hosp. Bd, NZ, 1988–91; Prof. of Medicine and Dir of Cardiol., Univ. of Queensland and Royal Brisbane Hosp., 1991–96; BHF Sir Thomas Lewis Prof. of Cardiol., Univ. of Wales Coll. of Medicine, 1996–2004; BHF Prof. of Cardiovascular Medicine, Univ. of Birmingham, 2004–09; Regius Prof. of Medicine, Univ. of Aberdeen, 2009–15. FRACP 1988; FACC 1995; FESC; FMedSci 2008. *Publications:* papers on cardiovascular physiol. and pathophysiol., particularly in heart failure and the cardiomyopathies. *Address:* Norwich Medical School, University of East Anglia, Norwich Research Park, Norwich NR4 7TJ. *Club:* Athenæum.

FRERE, Vice-Adm. Sir Richard Tobias, (Sir Toby), KCB 1994; Chairman, Prison Service Pay Review Body, 2001–05; Member, Armed Forces Pay Review Body, 1997–2002; *b* 4 June 1938; *s* of late Alexander Stewart Frere and Patricia Frere; *m* 1968, Jane Barraclough; two *d*. *Educ:* Eton College; Britannia Royal Naval College. Joined RNVR as National Serviceman; transf. RN 1956; commissioned 1958; submarines 1960; served Canada, 1961–62, Australia, 1966–67, 1973; commanded HM Submarines Andrew, Odin and Revenge and Frigate HMS Brazen. JSSC Canberra, 1973; RCDS London, 1982; Dir Gen. Fleet Support, Policy and Services, 1988–91; Flag Officer Submarines, and Comdr Submarines Eastern Atlantic, 1991–93; Chief of Fleet Support and Mem., Admiralty Bd, 1994–97. Chm. Govs, Oundle Sch., 2007–10. Master, Grocers' Co., 2004–05. *Recreation:* sailing. *Address:* c/o Naval Secretary, Fleet Headquarters, Whale Island, Portsmouth PO2 8BY. *Clubs:* Garrick, Naval, MCC.

FRESKO, Adrienne Sheila, CBE 2003; Partner, GE Healthcare Finnamore, since 2014; *b* 22 Feb. 1957; *d* of Mendal and Esther Marcus; *m* 1979, Marc Marcos Fresko; two *d*. *Educ:* Manchester High Sch. for Girls; St Anne's Coll., Oxford (MA Exptl Psychol.); Birkbeck Coll., London (MSc Occupational Psychol.). Mem., BPsS, 1998. Vice-Pres., Human Resources, Citibank, 1985–86; Principal, Adrienne Fresko Consulting, 1989–97; Audit Commission: Mem., 1996–2000; Dep. Chair, 2000–03; Actg Chair, 2001–02; Hd, Centre for Public Governance, Office of Public Mgt, 2000–04; Co-founder and Dir, Foresight Partnership, 2004–14. Chairman: Croydon Dist HA, 1992–96; Croydon HA, 1996–2000; Lead Chm., Croydon Health Commng Agency, 1994–96. Dir, Accountancy Foundn, 1999–2003; Mem., 2004–13, Vice Chm., 2009–13, Health Foundn. Ind. Mem. Council, Univ. of Sussex, 2013–. MCIPD (MIPD 1991); FRSA 2000. *Publications:* Making a Difference: women in public appointments, 2001; The Good Governance Standard for Public Services, 2005; The Healthy NHS Board: principles for good governance, 2010, 2nd edn 2013; Governing GP Commissioning, 2011. *Recreations:* family, travel, community, choral singing.

FRETWELL, Sir (Major) John (Emsley), GCMG 1987 (KCMG 1982; CMG 1975); HM Diplomatic Service, retired; Political Director and Deputy to the Permanent Under-Secretary of State, Foreign and Commonwealth Office, 1987–90; *b* 15 June 1930; *s* of late Francis Thomas and Dorothy Fretwell; *m* 1959, Mary Ellen Eugenie Dubois (OBE 2001); one *s* one *d*. *Educ:* Chesterfield Grammar Sch.; Lausanne Univ.; King's Coll., Cambridge (MA). HM Forces, 1948–50. Diplomatic Service, 1953; 3rd Sec., Hong Kong, 1954–55; 2nd Sec., Peking, 1955–57; FO, 1957–59; 1st Sec., Moscow, 1959–62; FO, 1962–67; 1st Sec. (Commercial), Washington, 1967–70; Commercial Counsellor, Warsaw, 1971–73; Head of European Integration Dept (Internal), FCO, 1973–76; Asst Under-Sec. of State, FCO, 1976–79; Minister, Washington, 1980–81; Ambassador to France, 1982–87. Specialist Advr, H of L, 1992–93; Specialist Assessor, HEFC, 1995–96. Mem., Council of Lloyd's, 1991–92. Chm., Franco-British Soc., 1995–2005. *Recreations:* history, walking, wine. *Club:* Brooks's.

FREUD, family name of **Baron Freud**.

FREUD, Baron *cr* 2009 (Life Peer), of Eastry, in the County of Kent; **David Anthony Freud;** PC 2015; Minister of State (Minister for Welfare Reform), Department for Work and Pensions, since 2015; *b* London, 24 June 1950; *s* of Anton Walter Freud and Annette Vibeke Freud (*née* Krarup); *m* 1978, Priscilla Jane Dickinson; one *s* two *d*. *Educ:* Whitgift Sch.; Merton Coll., Oxford (BA PPE 1972; MA 1989). Journalist, Western Mail, 1972–75; Econs/Tax Reporter, and Lex Corresp., Financial Times, 1976–83; S. G. Warburg, later UBS Investment Bank, 1984–2003 (Vice Chm., Investment Banking, 2000–03); CEO, The Portland Trust, 2006–08. Author, ind. report for DWP, Reducing Dependency, Increasing Opportunity: options for the future of welfare to work, 2007; Advr, DWP, 2008. Shadow Minister for Welfare Reform, 2009–10; Parly Under-Sec. of State (Minister for Welfare Reform), DWP, 2010–15. *Publications:* Freud in the City, 2006. *Recreations:* swimming, cycling, ski-ing. *Address:* House of Lords, SW1A 0PW. *T:* (020) 7219 4907. *E:* freudd@parliament.uk. *Club:* Ski Club of GB.

FREUD, Anthony Peter, OBE 2006; General Director, Lyric Opera of Chicago, since 2011; *b* 30 Oct. 1957; *s* of Joseph Freud and Katalin Lowi. *Educ:* King's Coll. London (LLB 1978); Inns of Court Sch. of Law. Called to the Bar, Gray's Inn, 1979; Th. Manager, Sadler's Wells Th., 1980–84; Company Sec. and Dir, Opera Planning, WNO, 1984–92; Exec. Producer, Philips Classics, 1992–94; Gen. Dir, WNO, 1994–2005; Gen. Dir and CEO, Houston Grand Opera, 2006–11. Chairman: Opera Europa, 2003–05; Opera America, 2008–12. Honorary Fellow: Cardiff University, 2005; RWCMD, 2006. *Address:* Lyric Opera of Chicago, 20 N Wacker Drive, Chicago, IL 60606, USA. *T:* (312) 3322244, *Fax:* (312) 4190820. *E:* afreud@lyricopera.org.

FREUD, Elisabeth; *see* Murdoch, E.

FREUD, Emma Vallency, OBE 2011; associate film producer; script editor, broadcaster; Director, Red Nose Day, since 2000; *b* 25 Jan. 1962; *d* of Sir Clement (Raphael) Freud and June Beatrice, (Jill), Freud; partner, Richard Whalley Anthony Curtis, *qv*; three *s* one *d*. *Educ:* St Mary's Convent; Queen's College London; Bristol Univ.; Royal Holloway Coll., Univ. of London (BA Hons Drama and Film Studies). Played Vincent Price's daughter in Ardele, West End, 1975; backing singer for Mike Oldfield on Tubular Bells tour, 1978; Mem. of The Girls (cabaret band), 1984–2004; Co-Dir and Musical Dir, Open Air Th., Regents Park, 1985–86; presenter: *television:* 6 O'Clock Show, 1986–88, Pillowtalk, 1987–89, Theatreland, 1996–98, ITV; The Media Show, 1989–91, Turner Prize, 1991, Channel 4; Everyman, 1992–94, Edinburgh Nights, 1994–96, BAFTA Awards, 1994, BBC2; *radio:* Loose Ends, BBC Radio 4, 1987–; morning show, BBC GLR, 1988–90; lunchtime show, BBC Radio 1, 1995–96; *theatre*: National Theatre Live, NT, 2009–. Script editor to Richard Curtis on: *films:* Four Weddings and a Funeral, 1994; Bean, 1997; Notting Hill, 1999; Bridget Jones's Diary, 2001; Love Actually, 2004; About Time, 2013; *television:* The Vicar of Dibley, 1995–2007; Doctor Who, 2010; Associate Producer, film, The Boat That Rocked, 2009. Chm., Christmas Quiz, NT, 2000–. Key Mem., Make Poverty History campaign and co-prod., Live 8 concerts, 2005. Trustee, Comic Relief, 1998–; Patron, White Ribbon Alliance, 2008–. Columnist, Tatler, 2011–. *Publications:* contribs to The Times Mag., Guardian, Telegraph, Sunday Times, Mirror, Radio Times. *Recreations:* Lego, colouring in. *T:* (office) (020) 7221 9434.

See also M. R. Freud.

FREUD, Matthew Rupert; Chairman, Freuds (formerly Freud Associates, then Freud Communications), since 1985; *b* 2 Nov. 1963; *s* of Sir Clement Raphael Freud; *m* Caroline Victoria Hutton (marr. diss.); two *s*; *m* Elisabeth Murdoch, *qv*; one *s* one *d*. *Educ:* St Anthony's, Westminster. Trustee, Comic Relief, 2000–. *Address:* (office) 55 Newman Street, W1T 3EB. *T:* (020) 3003 6300.

See also E. V. Freud.

FREYBERG, family name of **Baron Freyberg**.

FREYBERG, 3rd Baron *cr* 1951, of Wellington, New Zealand and of Munstead, Co. Surrey; **Valerian Bernard Freyberg;** *b* 15 Dec. 1970; *o s* of 2nd Baron Freyberg, OBE, MC, and of Ivry Perronelle Katharine, *d* of Cyril Harrower Guild, Aspall Hall, Debenham, Suffolk; *S* father, 1993; *m* 2002, Dr Harriet Atkinson, *d* of late John Atkinson and of Jane (who *m* 2nd, John Watherston, *qv*); one *s* two *d*. *Educ:* Eton Coll.; Camberwell Coll. of Art; Slade Sch. of Fine Art (MA Fine Art 2006). Elected Mem., H of L, 1999. Mem., Design Council, 2001–04. *Heir: s* Hon. Joseph John Freyberg, *b* 21 March 2007. *Address:* House of Lords, SW1A 0PW.

FRICKER, His Honour (Anthony) Nigel; QC 1977; a Deputy Circuit Judge, 2001–05 (a Circuit Judge, 1984–2001); *b* 7 July 1937; *s* of late Dr William Shapland Fricker and Margaret Fricker; *m* 1960, Marilyn Ann, *d* of late A. L. Martin, Pa, USA; one *s* two *d*. *Educ:* King's School, Chester; Liverpool Univ. (LLB 1958). President of Guild of Undergraduates, Liverpool Univ., 1958–59. Called to Bar, Gray's Inn, 1960. Conf. Leader, Ford Motor Co. of Australia, Melbourne, 1960–61. Recorder, Crown Court, 1975–84; Prosecuting Counsel to DHSS, Wales and Chester Circuit, 1975–77; an asst comr, Boundary Commn for Wales, 1981–84; Mem. Bd, Children and Family Court Adv. and Support Service, 2001. Member: Bar Council, 1966–70; Senate and Bar Council, 1975–78; County Court Rule Cttee, 1988–92; Family Proceedings Rule Cttee, 1997–2001; Mental Health Review Tribunal, 2001–08. Pres., Council of HM Circuit Judges, 1997. Fellow, Internat. Acad. of Trial Lawyers, 1979–. Mem. Court: Liverpool Univ., 1977–2011; York Univ., 1984–2012. Confrérie des Chevaliers du Tastevin. *Publications:* (jtly) Family Courts: Emergency Remedies and Procedures, 1990, 3rd edn (loose-leaf) as Emergency Remedies in the Family Courts (Gen. Ed., 1990–99, Consulting Ed., 1999–2002); (with David Bean) Enforcement of Injunctions and Undertakings, 1991; (consulting ed.) The Family Court Practice, (annually) 1993–2002; contrib. legal periodicals in UK and USA (Family and Conciliation Courts Rev.). *Address:* 6 Park Square, Leeds LS1 2LW; Farrar's Building, Temple, EC4Y 7BD.

See also C. R. Burn.

FRICKER, Rt Rev. Joachim Carl; a Suffragan Bishop of Toronto (Bishop of Credit Valley), 1985–95; *b* Zweibrucken, Germany, 1 Dec. 1927; *s* of Carl and Caroline Fricker; *m* 1952, Shirley Joan (*née* Gill); three *s* two *d*. *Educ:* Niagara Falls Public Schools; Univ. of Western Ontario (BA); Huron College (LTh). Ordained deacon and priest, 1952; Rector: St Augustine's, Hamilton, 1952–59; St David's, Welland, 1959–65; St James, Dundas, 1965–73; Canon of Christ's Church Cathedral, Hamilton, 1964–73; Dean of Diocese of Niagara and Rector, Christ's Church Cathedral, 1973–85. Chm., Nat. Doctrine and Worship Cttee (Anglican Church of Canada), 1989–92. Hon. DD: Huron Coll., 1974; Trinity Coll., 1987; Hon. DSL, Wycliffe Coll., 1987. *Recreations:* theatre, gardening, reading, walking. *Address:* 5280 Lakeshore Road, Unit 1102, Burlington, ON L7L 5R1, Canada.

FRIED, Bradley; Managing Partner, Grovepoint Capital LLP, since 2010; Chief Executive Officer-in-Residence, Judge Business School, University of Cambridge, since 2010; Fellow Magdalene College, Cambridge, since 2010; *b* Cape Town, SA, 12 Aug. 1965; *s* of Louis and Joan Fried; *m* 1996, Lauren Roth; two *s*. *Educ:* Univ. of Cape Town (BCom with Dist.); Wharton Sch., Univ. of Pennsylvania (Palmer Scholar; MBA with Dist. 1993). Trainee Accountant, Arthur Andersen, 1988–91; CA, S Africa, 1991; Partner, McKinsey & Co., NY, 1993–99; Chief Operating Officer, 1999–2003, CEO, 2003–10, Investec Bank plc. Non-executive Director: London and Johannesburg Listed Investec Gp, 2010–; Court, Bank of England, 2012– (Dep. Chm., 2014–; Chm., Audit and Risk Cttee, 2014–). *Recreations:* family, visual arts. *Address:* 8–12 York Gate, NW1 4QG. *T:* (020) 7486 5954. *E:* bradley@grovepoint.co.uk.

FRIEDBERGER, Maj.-Gen. John Peter William, CB 1991; CBE 1986 (MBE 1975); Administrator, Sovereign Base Areas and Commander, British Forces, Cyprus, 1988–90; *b* 27 May 1937; *s* of late Brig. John Cameron Friedberger, DSO, DL and Phyllis Grace Friedberger, JP; *m* 1966, Joanna Mary, *d* of Andrew Thorne, ERD; one *s* two *d*. *Educ:* Red House School, York; Wellington College; RMA Sandhurst. Commissioned, 10th Royal Hussars (PWO), 1956; seconded to Northern Frontier Regt, Sultan's Armed Forces, Oman, 1961–63; Australian Army Staff Coll., 1969; CO The Royal Hussars (PWO), 1975–78; RCDS, 1978–79; Comdr, Royal Brunei Armed Forces, 1982–86; ACOS, HQ Northern Army Group, 1986–88. Chief Exec., British Helicopter Adv. Bd, 1992–2002. Hon. Colonel: The Royal Hussars (PWO), 1991–92; The King's Royal Hussars, 1992–97. Chm., Railfuture (Wessex), 2006–12. FRGS 1990. Dato, DPKT (Negara Brunei Darussalam) 1984. *Recreation:* travel. *Address:* c/o Home HQ, The King's Royal Hussars, Peninsula Barracks, Winchester, Hants SO23 8TS. *Club:* Cavalry and Guards.

FRIEDLAND, Prof. Jonathan Samuel, PhD; FRCP, FRCPE, FRCPI, FMedSci; Professor of Infectious Diseases and Head, Infectious Diseases and Immunity, since 2004, and Director (formerly Dean), Hammersmith campus, since 2010, Imperial College London; Honorary Consultant in Infectious Diseases and Medicine, Imperial College Healthcare (formerly Hammersmith Hospitals) NHS Trust, since 1994; *b* London, 6 Sept. 1960; *s* of Albert and Rosalind Friedland; *m* 1995, Joanna Catherine Porter; one *s* one *d*. *Educ:* St Paul's Sch., London; Corpus Christi Coll., Cambridge (BA 1981; MA 1985); King's Coll. Hosp. Med. Sch., Univ. of London (MB BS 1984); London Univ. (PhD 1993). FRCP 1999; FRCPE 1999; FRCPI 2010. Registrar, Nuffield Dept of Medicine, John Radcliffe Hosp., Oxford, 1987–89; MRC Trng Fellow, 1989–92; Univ. Lectr and Hon. Sen. Registrar in Communicable Diseases, St George's Hosp. and Med. Sch., 1992–94; Sen. Lectr in Infectious Diseases, 1994–2000, Reader in Infectious and Tropical Diseases, 2000–03, RPMS/Imperial Coll. London; Lead Clinician, Clinical Infection, Imperial Coll. Healthcare (formerly Hammersmith Hosps) NHS Trust, 2004–13. Member: Tropical Medicine Interest Gp, Wellcome Trust, 2002–04; UK Jt Cttee on Vaccination and Immunisation, 2005–13; Nat. Expert Panel of New and Emerging Infections, 2007–12; Clin. Trng and Career Develt Panel, MRC, 2009–13; Commn on Human Medicines, MHRA, 2014–. Pres., British Infection Soc., 2007–09. FMedSci 2008. Weber-Parkes Prize Medal, RCP, 2005. *Publications:* papers on infectious diseases and innate immunity focusing on tuberculosis. *Recreations:* family, chess, theatre. *Address:* Department of Infectious Diseases and Immunity, Imperial College London, Hammersmith Campus, Du Cane Road, W12 0NN. *T:* (020) 8383 8521, *Fax:* (020) 8383 3394. *E:* j.friedland@imperial.ac.uk.

FRIEDMAN, David Peter; QC 1990; *b* 1 June 1944; *s* of Wilfred Emanuel Friedman and Rosa Lees; *m* 1972, Sara Geraldine Linton. *Educ:* Tiffin Boys' School; Lincoln College, Oxford (BCL, MA). Called to the Bar, Inner Temple, 1968, Bencher, 1999; a Recorder, 1998–2005. *Recreations:* good food (cooked by others), reading. *Address:* 4 Pump Court, Temple, EC4Y 7AN. *T:* (020) 7842 5555. *Club:* Lansdowne.

FRIEDMAN, Prof. Jerome Isaac, PhD; Professor of Physics, 1967, William A. Coolidge Professor, 1988–90, Institute Professor, 1990, now Emeritus, Massachusetts Institute of Technology; *b* 28 March 1930; *m* Tania Baranovsky Friedman; two *s* two *d*. *Educ:* Univ. of Chicago (AB 1950; MS 1953; PhD Physics 1956). Research associate; Univ. of Chicago, 1956–57; Stanford Univ., 1957–60; MIT: Asst Prof. and Associate Prof., 1960–67; Dir, Nuclear Science Lab., 1980–83; Head of Dept of Physics, 1983–88. Fellow: Amer. Phys. Soc.; Nat. Acad. of Scis; Amer. Acad. of Arts and Scis. (Jtly) W. H. K. Panofsky Prize for Physics, 1989; (jtly) Nobel Prize for Physics, 1990. *Publications:* numerous papers in learned jls on particle physics, esp. the division of protons and neutrons into smaller particles, leading to different types of quarks. *Address:* Department of Physics, Massachusetts Institute of Technology, 77 Massachusetts Avenue, Cambridge, MA 02139–4307, USA.

FRIEDMAN, Sonia Anne Primrose; Producer, Sonia Friedman Productions, since 2002; *b* 19 April 1965; *d* of Leonard and Clair Friedman. *Educ:* St Christopher Sch., Letchworth; Central Sch. of Speech and Drama (HND Stage Mgt; Hon. Fellow, 2014). Hd of Mobile Prodns, RNT, 1990–93; Producer and Co-Founder, Out of Joint Theatre Co., 1993–98; Producer, Ambassador Theatre Gp, 1998–2002. *Address:* Duke of York's Theatre, 104 St Martins Lane, WC2N 4BG. *T:* (020) 7845 8750, *Fax:* (020) 7845 8759. *E:* office@soniafriedman.com.

FRIEDMANN, Prof. Peter Simon, MD; FRCP, FMedSci; Professor of Dermatology, University of Southampton, 1998–2008, now Emeritus; *b* 18 Nov. 1943; *s* of Charles Aubrey Friedmann and Atersia Friedmann (*née* Le Roux); *m* 1967, Bridget Ann Harding; one *s* one *d*. *Educ:* Trinity Coll., Cambridge (BA 1966); University Coll. Hosp., London (MB BChir 1969; MD 1977). FRCP 1984. Wellcome Trng Fellow, RCS, 1973–77; University of Newcastle upon Tyne: Lectr in Dermatology, 1977–81; Sen. Lectr, 1981–90; University of Liverpool: Prof. of Dermatology, 1990–97; Actg Hd, Dept of Medicine, 1996–97. Hon. Res. Fellow, Tufts Univ., Boston, 1985–86. Med. Advr to All-Party Parly Gp on Skin, 1996–2008. Chm., Scientific Cttee, Nat. Eczema Soc., 1995–2001. Founder FMedSci 1998. *Publications:* contrib. book chapters; numerous scientific papers. *Recreations:* music (playing flute), bird-watching, tennis. *Address:* Dermatology Unit, Southampton General Hospital, Tremona Road, Southampton SO16 6YD. *T:* (023) 8079 6142.

FRIEL, Anna; actress; *b* Rochdale, Lancs; one *d* by David Thewlis. *Stage* appearances: Look Europe, Almeida, 1997; Closer, NY, 1998 (Drama Desk Award for Outstanding Featured Actress in a Play, 1999); Lulu, Almeida, 2001, transf. NY (Helen Hayes Award for Outstanding Lead Actress, 2002); Breakfast at Tiffany's, Th. Royal, Haymarket, 2009; Uncle Vanya, Vaudeville Th., 2012; *films* include: The Tribe, The Stringer, Land Girls, 1998; All For Love, Rogue Trader, A Midsummer Night's Dream, Mad Cows, 1999; Sunset Strip, 2000; Everlasting Piece, Me Without You, 2001; War Bride, 2002; Timeline, 2003; Goal!, 2005; Niagara Motel, Irish Jam, 2006; Goal! II, 2007; Land of the Lost, 2009; London Boulevard, You Will Meet a Tall Dark Stranger, 2011; The Look of Love, 2013; *television* includes: GBH, 1991; Brookside, 1993–95 (Nat. Television Award for Most Popular Actress, 1995); Our Mutual Friend, 1998; The Jury, 2004; Pushing Daisies, 2007–09; The Street, 2009; Without You, 2011; Odyssey, 2015. *Address:* c/o The Artists Partnership, 101 Finsbury Pavement, EC2A 1RS.

FRIEL, Brian; writer; *b* 9 Jan. 1929; *s* of Patrick Friel and Christina Friel (*née* MacLoone); *m* 1954, Anne Morrison; one *s* four *d*. *Educ:* St Columb's Coll., Derry; St Patrick's Coll., Maynooth; St Joseph's Trng Coll., Belfast. Taught in various schools, 1950–60; writing full-time from 1960. Lived in Minnesota during first season of Tyrone Guthrie Theater, Minneapolis. Member: Irish Acad. of Letters, 1972; Aosdána, 1983–; Amer. Acad. of Arts and Letters. FRSL 1998. Hon. DLitt: Chicago, 1979; NUI, 1983; NUU, 1986. Hon. DLit: QUB, 2004; TCS, 2006; UCD, 2008. Ulysses Medal, UCD, 2010. *Publications: collected stories:* The Saucer of Larks, 1962; The Gold in the Sea, 1966; *plays:* Philadelphia, Here I Come!, 1965; The Loves of Cass McGuire, 1967; Lovers, 1968; The Mundy Scheme, 1969; Crystal and Fox, 1970; The Gentle Island, 1971; The Freedom of the City, 1973; Volunteers, 1975; Living Quarters, 1976; Aristocrats, 1979; Faith Healer, 1979; Translations, 1981 (Ewart-Biggs Meml Prize, British Theatre Assoc. Award); (trans.) Three Sisters, 1981; The Communication Cord, 1983; (trans.) Fathers and Sons, 1987; Making History, 1988; London Vertigo, 1989; Dancing at Lughnasa, 1990; A Month in the Country, 1990; Wonderful Tennessee, 1993; Molly Sweeney, 1995; Give Me Your Answer, Do!, 1997; (trans.) Uncle Vanya, 1998; (trans.) The Bear, 2002; The Yalta Game, 2002; Afterplay, 2002; Performances, 2003; The Home Place,

2005 (Best Play, Evening Standard Th. Awards, 2005); (trans.) Hedda Gabler, 2008. *Address:* Drumaweir House, Greencastle, Co. Donegal, Ireland.

FRIEL, (Michael) John; District Judge (Magistrates' Courts) (formerly Stipendiary Magistrate), Derbyshire, 1997–2011; *b* 3 Sept. 1942; *s* of Hugh and Madeline Friel; *m* 1980, Elizabeth Mary Jenkins; two *s* one *d*. *Educ:* Leeds Univ. (LLB). Admitted solicitor, 1969; Nottingham Magistrates' Court: Court Clerk, 1965–71; Dep. Clerk to the Justices, 1972–73; Clerk to the Justices: Isle of Ely, Cambs, 1973–76; Mansfield, Notts, 1976–97; also Clerk to: Worksop and E Retford Justices, 1977–97; Newark and Southwell Justices, 1986–97; Nottingham Justices, 1996–97. *Recreation:* sports (tennis, cricket, football, squash, ski-ing).

FRIEND, Andrew Erskine; Chairman, Balfour Beatty Infrastructure Partners, since 2010; *b* 25 June 1952; *s* of Philip Friend and Eileen (*née* Erskine); *m* 1985, Jennifer Elizabeth Keating; one *s* two *d*. *Educ:* Christ's Hosp.; Peterhouse, Cambridge (BA 1973). MAICD 1994; CCMI 2006. Policy Advr, GLC, 1982–84; City of Melbourne: Dir, Econ. Develt, 1985–89; Corporate Manager, 1990–95; Chief Exec., 1995–97; Associate Dir, Macquarie Bank, 1997–99; Man. Dir, Laing Investments, 1999–2003; Chief Exec., John Laing plc, 2003–06; Commercial Advr, DfT, 2006–08. Non-executive Director: ING European Infrastructure Fund, 2006–09; Partnerships UK, 2007–10; Financial Security Assurance (UK) Ltd, 2007–09; DfT, 2009–10; HS2 Ltd, 2009–12; Strategic Advr, India Infrastructure plc, 2008–10. Chm., Investment Cttee, InfraMed Infrastructure SAS, 2010–. Trustee, Oxfam, 2007–12. Mem. Council, City Univ., 2013–. *Publications:* Slump City: the politics of mass unemployment, 1981; res. pubns on housing, econ. and urban develt. *Recreations:* golf, walking, reading history, lino-cuts, growing vegetables.

FRIEND, John Richard, DM; FRCOG; Consultant Obstetrician and Gynaecologist, Plymouth General Hospital, 1973–2000 (Medical Director, 1999–2000); Senior Vice President, Royal College of Obstetricians and Gynaecologists, 1995–98; *b* 31 Jan. 1937; *s* of George Chamings Friend and Gwendoline Mary Lewis Friend; *m* 1971, Diana Margaret Fryer; one *s* two *d* (incl. twin *s* and *d*). *Educ:* St Edward's Sch. (schol.); St Edmund Hall, Oxford (MA; BM, BCh, DM); St Thomas' Hosp. MRCOG 1968, FRCOG 1987; MRCP 1999. Queen Charlotte's Hosp. and Chelsea Hosp., 1965–66; MRC Fellow, 1969–70; Hammersmith Hosp., 1966–67; KCH, 1967–73. Hon. Consultant Gynaecologist, RN, 1987–. *Publications:* articles in jls. *Recreations:* golf, tennis. *Address:* Holme House, Stoke Hill Lane, Crapstone, Yelverton, Devon PL20 7PP. *T:* (01822) 852527. *Clubs:* Royal Western Yacht; Yelverton Golf.

FRIEND, Lionel; conductor; Music Director, British Youth Opera, since 2015; *b* 13 March 1945; *s* of Moya and Norman A. C. Friend; *m* 1969, Jane Hyland; one *s* two *d*. *Educ:* Royal Grammar School, High Wycombe; Royal College of Music; London Opera Centre. LRAM; ARCM. Glyndebourne Opera, 1969–72; Welsh National Opera, 1969–72; Kapellmeister, Staatstheater, Kassel, Germany, 1972–75; Staff Conductor, ENO, 1978–89; Musical Dir, New Sussex Opera, 1989–96; Conductor-in-residence, Birmingham Conservatoire, 2003–10. Guest Conductor: BBC orchestras; Philharmonia; Royal Ballet; Oper Frankfurt; Opera Australia; Opéra National, Brussels; State Symphony, Hungary; Nash Ensemble, Royal Danish Opera, Polish Nat. Opera, etc. *Recreations:* reading, theatre. *Address:* 136 Rosendale Road, SE21 8LG. *T:* (020) 8761 7845.

FRIEND, Prof. Peter John, MD; FRCS; Professor of Transplantation, University of Oxford, since 1999; Fellow, Green Templeton College (formerly Green College), Oxford, since 1999; Hon. Consultant Surgeon, Oxford University Hospitals NHS Trust (formerly Oxford Radcliffe NHS Trust), since 1999; Co-Founder, and Medical Director, since 2008, OrganOx; *b* 5 Jan. 1954; *s* of late John Friend and (Dorothy) Jean Friend (*née* Brown); *m* 2001, Prof. Laurie Elizabeth Maguire. *Educ:* Rugby Sch.; Magdalene Coll., Cambridge (MA, MB, BChir, MD); St Thomas's Hosp. Med. Sch. FRCS 1983. St Thomas' Hosp., London, W Norwich Hosp., Bedford Gen. Hosp., Addenbrooke's Hosp., Cambridge, 1978–88; Vis. Asst Prof., Indiana Univ., USA, 1988–89; Lectr in Surgery, Univ. of Cambridge and Hon. Consultant Surgeon, Addenbrooke's Hosp., 1989–99; Fellow, Magdalene Coll., Cambridge, 1993–99. Pres., British Transplantation Soc., 2007–09. *Publications:* papers on transplantation and surgery in scientific jls. *Address:* Nuffield Department of Surgical Sciences, Oxford Transplant Centre, Churchill Hospital, Oxford OX3 7LE. *Club:* Oxford and Cambridge.

FRIEND, Sir Richard (Henry), Kt 2003; FRS 1993; FREng, FIET; Cavendish Professor of Physics, University of Cambridge, since 1995; Fellow, St John's College, Cambridge, since 1977; *b* 18 Jan. 1953; *s* of John Henry Friend and Dorothy Jean (*née* Brown); *m* 1979, Carol Anne Maxwell (*née* Beales); two *d*. *Educ:* Rugby Sch.; Trinity Coll., Cambridge (MA, PhD; Hon. Fellow, 2004). FInstP 1999 (Hon. FInstP 2008); FREng 2002; FIET (FIEE 2002). Res. Fellow, St John's Coll., Cambridge, 1977–80; University of Cambridge: Demonstrator in Physics, 1980–85; Lectr, 1985–93; Reader in Experimental Physics, 1993–95. R&D Dir, 1996–98, Chief Scientist, 1998–2007, Cambridge Display Technology; Chief Scientist, Plastic Logic Ltd, 2000–06. Vis. Prof., Univ. of Calif, Santa Barbara, 1986–87; Nuffield Science Res. Fellowship, 1992–93; Mary Shepard B. Upson Vis. Prof., Cornell Univ., 2003. Mem., EPSRC, 2012–. Lectures: Mott, Inst. of Physics, 1994; Kelvin, IEE, 2004; Holst Meml, Tech. Univ. of Eindhoven and Philips Res., 2004; (inaugural) Nakamura, Univ. of Calif, Santa Barbara, 2005; Clifford Paterson, Royal Soc., 2006; Menelaus, S Wales Inst. of Engineers, Cardiff, 2008; Kolthoff, Univ. of Minnesota, 2008; Leibniz, Kolleg Potsdam, 2008; Konarka-Tripathy, Univ. of Mass, Lowell, 2010; Georg Kanig, Berlin-Brandenburgischer Verband, Berlin, 2010; International, Internat. Centre for Materials Science, JNCASR, Bangalore, 2010; Golden Jubilee, Indian Inst. of Technol., Delhi, 2010. Hon. FRSC 2004; Hon. Fellow: Univ. of Wales, Bangor, 2006; Indian Acad. of Scis, 2011. Hon. DSc: Linköping, 2000; Mons, 2002; Heriot-Watt, 2006; Nijmegen, 2008; Montreal, 2009. C. V. Boys Prize, Inst. of Physics, 1988; Interdisciplinary Award, RSC, 1991; Hewlett-Packard Prize, European Physical Soc., 1996; Rumford Medal and Prize, Royal Soc., 1998; Italgas Prize for res. and technol innovation, 2001; Silver Medal, 2002, MacRobert Prize, 2002, Royal Acad. of Engrg; Faraday Medal, IEE, 2003; Gold Medal, Eur. Materials Res. Soc., 2003; Descartes Prize, Eur. Commn, 2003; Jan Rachmann Prize, Soc. for Information Displays, 2005; (jtly) Daniel E. Noble Award, IEEE, 2007; Inaugural Award, Rhodia de Gennes Prize for Sci. and Technol., Paris, 2008; (jtly) King Faisal Internat. Prize for Sci., 2009; (jtly) Business and Innovation Gold Medal, Inst. of Physics, 2009; Millennium Prize Laureate, Finnish Acad. of Technol., 2010; Harvey Prize, Israel Inst. of Technol., 2011. *Publications:* papers on chem. physics and solid-state physics in scientific jls. *Address:* Cavendish Laboratory, J. J. Thomson Avenue, Cambridge CB3 0HE. *T:* (01223) 337218. *E:* rhf10@cam.ac.uk.

FRIEND, Victoria; *see* Richardson, V.

FRIER, Prof. Brian Murray, MD; FRCPE, FRCPGlas; Consultant Physician, Royal Infirmary of Edinburgh, 1987–2012; Hon. Professor of Diabetes, University of Edinburgh, since 2001; *b* Edinburgh; *s* of Murray and Christina Frier; *m* 1985, Isobel Wilson; one *d*. *Educ:* George Heriot's Sch., Edinburgh; Univ. of Edinburgh (BSc 1st Cl. Hons Physiol. 1969; MB ChB 1972; MD 1981). MRCP(UK) 1974; FRCPE 1984; FRCPGlas 1986. Jun. med. posts, Edinburgh, 1972–74; Med. Registrar, Ninewells Hosp., Dundee, 1974–76; Clin. Res. Fellow, Cornell Univ. Med. Center, New York Hosp., NY, 1976–77; Sen. Med. Registrar, Royal Infirmary, Edinburgh, 1978–82; Consultant Physician, Western Infirmary and Gartnavel Gen. Hosp., Glasgow, 1982–87. Chair: Hon. Adv. Panel on Driving and Diabetes to Sec. of State for Transport, 2001–12 (Mem., 1993–2012); Diabetes Res. Gp, Chief Scientist Office, 2003–06. Mem. Council, 2002–08, Vice-Pres., 2008–12, RCPE. Member: Diabetes Panel, CAA, 2010–; Internat. Hypoglycemia Study Gp, 2013–. R. D. Lawrence Lectr, British Diabetic Assoc., 1986; Banting Meml Lectr, Diabetes UK, 2009. Somogyi Award, Hungarian Diabetes Assoc., 2004. Co-Ed., Diabetes/Metabolism Res. and Reviews, 1998–2008; Ed., Diabetic Hypoglycemia, 2008–14; Mem., Internat. Editl Bd, Clinical Diabetes and Endocrinology, 2014–. *Publications:* (ed with B. M. Fisher) Hypoglycaemia and Diabetes: clinical and physiological aspects, 1993; (ed with B. M. Fisher) Hypoglycaemia and Clinical Diabetes, 1999, 3rd edn (ed with S. R. Heller and R. J. McCrimmon) 2014; (with M. W. J. Strachan) Insulin Pocketbook, 2013. *Recreations:* appreciation of the arts, ancient and modern history, sport. *Address:* University of Edinburgh/BHF Centre for Cardiovascular Science, Queen's Medical Research Institute, 47 Little France Crescent, Edinburgh EH16 4TJ; 100 Morningside Drive, Edinburgh EH10 5NT. *Clubs:* Heriot's Former Pupils, Heriot's Rugby.

FRIES, Richard James; Chief Charity Commissioner, 1992–99; Visiting Fellow, Centre for Civil Society, London School of Economics, 2000–06; *b* 7 July 1940; *s* of late Felix Theodore Fries and Joan Mary Fries (subseq. Mrs John Harris); *m* 1970, Carole Anne Buick; one *s* two *d*. *Educ:* King's Coll., Cambridge. Home Office, 1965–92. Chm. Bd, Internat. Center for Not-for-Profit Law, Washington, 1999–2005. *Recreations:* chess, music.

FRISBY, Audrey Mary; *see* Jennings, A. M.

FRISBY, Terence; playwright, actor, producer, director, author; *b* 28 Nov. 1932; *s* of William and Kathleen Frisby; *m* 1963, Christine Vecchione (marr. diss.); one *s*. *Educ:* Dobwalls Village Sch.; Dartford Grammar Sch.; Central Sch. of Speech Training and Dramatic Art. Substantial repertory acting and directing experience, also TV, films and musicals, 1957–63; appeared in A Sense of Detachment, Royal Court, 1972–73 and X, Royal Court, 1974; Clive Popkiss, in Rookery Nook, Her Majesty's, 1979, and many since. Productions: Once a Catholic (tour), 1980–81; There's a Girl in My Soup (tour), 1982; Woza Albert!, Criterion, 1983; The Real Inspector Hound/Seaside Postcard (tour), 1983–84; Comic Cuts, 1984. Has written: many TV scripts, incl. series Lucky Feller, 1976; That's Love, 1988–92 (Gold Award, Houston Film Festival); film, There's A Girl in My Soup, 1970 (Writers Guild Award, Best British Comedy Screenplay); stage musical, Just Remember Two Things..., 2004, retitled as Kisses on a Postcard, Queen's Th., Barnstable, 2011. *Publications:* Outrageous Fortune (an autobiog. story), 1998; Kisses on a Postcard (childhood memoir), 2009; *plays:* The Subtopians, 1964; There's a Girl in My Soup, 1966; The Bandwagon, 1970; It's All Right if I Do It, 1977; Seaside Postcard, 1978; Just Remember Two Things: It's Not Fair And Don't Be Late, 1989 (radio play; Giles Cooper Award, 1988); Rough Justice, 1995; Funny About Love, 2002. *Address:* c/o The Agency, 24 Pottery Lane, Holland Park, W11 4LZ. *T:* (020) 7727 1346. *Club:* Richmond Golf.

FRISCHMANN, Wilem William, CBE 1990; PhD; FREng; FICE; FIStructE; FCGI; Chairman: Pell Frischmann Group: Pell Frischmann Consulting Engineers Ltd, since 1985; Pell Frischmann Consultants Ltd, since 1986; Conseco International, since 1985; *s* of Lajos Frischmann and Nelly Frischmann; *m* 1957, Sylvia Elvey; one *s* one *d*. *Educ:* Hungary; Hammersmith College of Art and Building; Imperial Coll. of Science and Technology (DIC); City University (PhD). MASCE. FIStructE 1964; FREng (FEng 1985); FCGI 1988; FConsE 1993; FICE 2004. Engineering training with F. J. Samuely and Partners and W. S. Atkins and Partners; joined C. J. Pell and Partners, 1958, Partner, 1961. Dep. Chm., Building & Property Management Services Ltd, 1993–96. Structural Engineer for Nat. Westminster Tower (ICE Telford Premium Award), Centre Point, Drapers Gardens tower (IStructE Oscar Faber Prize) and similar high buildings, leisure buildings, hotels and hospitals; Engineer for works at Bank of England, Mansion House and Alexandra Palace; particular interest and involvement in tall economic buildings, shear walls and diaphragm floors, large bored piles in London clay, deep basements, lightweight materials for large span bridges, monitoring and quality assurance procedures for offshore structures; advisory appts include: Hong Kong and Shanghai Bank HQ, Malayan Banking Berhad, Kuala Lumpur. Hon. DSc. Lifetime Achievement Award, Eur. CEO Awards, 2013; Outstanding Personal Contrib. Award, British Expertise Internat. Awards, 2013; Golden Global Excellence Award, Inst. of Economic Studies, India, 2013; Rashtriya Udyog Ratan Award, 2013. *Publications:* The use and behaviour of large diameter piles in London clay (IStructE paper), 1962; papers to learned socs and instns, originator of concepts: English Channel free-trade port; industrial complex based on Varne and Colbart sandbanks; two-mile high vertical city. *Recreations:* ski-ing, jogging, chess, architecture, design. *Address:* (office) 5 Manchester Square, W1A 1AU. *T:* (020) 7486 3661, *Fax:* (020) 7487 4153; Haversham Grange, Haversham Close, Twickenham, Middx TW1 2JP. *Club:* Arts.

FRISK, Monica Gunnel Constance C.; *see* Carss-Frisk.

FRISTON, Prof. Karl John, FRS 2006; Professor of Neuroscience, since 1998, and Wellcome Principal Research Fellow, Wellcome Trust Centre for Neuroimaging (formerly Wellcome Department of Imaging Neuroscience), since 1999, Institute of Neurology, University College London; *b* 12 July 1959; *s* of Anthony Harpham Friston and Audrey Agnes Friston (*née* Brocklesby); *m* 1987, Ann Elisabeth Leonard; three *s*. *Educ:* Gonville and Caius Coll., Cambridge (Exhibnr; BA Med. Scis Tripos 1980); King's Coll. Med. Sch., Univ. of London (MB BS 1983); MA Cantab 1985. MRCPsych 1988. Pre-registration, Surgery, Bromley Hosp. and Medicine, Farnborough Hosps, 1984–85; Post-registration, Rotational Trng Scheme in Psychiatry, Dept of Psychiatry, Univ. of Oxford, 1985–88; Hon. Senior Registrar: Dept of Psychiatry, Charing Cross and Westminster Med. Sch., 1988–91; RPMS, 1991–94 (Hon. Lectr, 1991–92); Sen. Lectr, 1994–97, Reader, 1997–98, Inst. Neurol., UCL. Research: Wellcome Trust Fellow, MRC Clin. Neuropharmacol. Unit, Oxford Univ., 1987–88; Wellcome Trust Res. Fellow, 1988–91, MRC Clin. Scientist (Sen. Grade), 1991–92, MRC Cyclotron Unit, Hammersmith Hosp.; W. M. Keck Foundn Fellow in Theoretical Neurobiol., Neuroscis Inst., La Jolla, Calif, 1992–94; Wellcome Sen. Res. Fellow in Clin. Sci., Inst. of Neurol., 1994–99. Hon. Consultant, Nat. Hosp. for Neurol. and Neurosurgery, Queen Sq., 1999–. FMedSci 1999. *Publications:* (ed jtly) Human Brain Function, 1997, 2nd edn 2004; (ed jtly) Statistical Parametric Mapping and Causal Models for Brain Imaging, 2006; contrib. numerous peer-reviewed articles to acad. lit. *Recreation:* painting. *Address:* Wellcome Trust Centre for Neuroimaging, 12 Queen Square, WC1N 3BG. *T:* (020) 3448 4347. *E:* k.friston@ucl.ac.uk.

FRITCHIE, family name of **Baroness Fritchie**.

FRITCHIE, Baroness *cr* 2005 (Life Peer), of Gloucester in the county of Gloucestershire; **Irene Tordoff Fritchie,** DBE 1996; Chair: 2gether Gloucestershire NHS Foundation Trust, 2008–12; Nominet, since 2010; Consultant on Leadership and Change, Mainstream Development, since 1991; *b* 29 April 1942; *d* of Charles Fredrick Fennell and Eva (*née* Tordoff); *m* 1960, Don Jamie Fritchie; one *s* (and one *s* decd). *Educ:* Ribston Hall Grammar Sch. for Girls. Admin. Officer, Endsleigh Insce Brokers, 1970–73; Sales Trng Officer, Trident Insce Ltd, 1973–76; Head of Trng Confs and Specialist Trng Advr on Women's Develt, Food and Drink ITB, 1976–80; Consultant, Social Ecology Associates, 1980–81; Dir, Transform Ltd, 1981–85; Rennie Fritchie Consultancy, 1985–89; Man. Dir, Working Choices Ltd, 1989–91; Vice Chair, Stroud and Swindon Bldg Soc., 2002–08 (Bd Mem., 1995–2008). Chair: Gloucester HA, 1988–92; South-Western RHA, 1992–94; S and W Region, NHS Executive (formerly S and W RHA), 1994–97. Member: NHS Policy Bd, 1994–97; GMC, 1996–99; Board, British Quality Foundn, 1994–99; Selection Panel, Glos Police Authy, 1994–99; Comr for Public Appts, 1999–2005; Civil Service Comr, 1999–2005; Chair: Ind. Appts Selection Bd, RICS, 2006–12; Adv. Bd, Web Sci. Res. Initiative, Southampton/MIT, 2006–09; Vice-Chm., Audit Cttee, Scottish Public Service Ombudsman, 2007–10; non-exec. Dir, UK Shared Business Service, 2013–. Mem., Forum UK, IHSM, 1993. Pres., Pennell Initiative for Women's Health in Later Life, 1999–2006 (Chair, 1997–99); Chm., Chronic

Pain Policy Coalition, 2006–08; Vice-Chm., British Lung Foundn, 2006–. Patron: Healing Arts, 1995–2002; SHARE young persons counselling service, 1997–2002; Meningitis Trust, 1998–2002; Westbank League of Friends, 1998–2002; Bart's Cancer Centre, 1998–2000; Effective Intelligence, 2000–02; SPACE, 2000–02; Swindon Arts Foundn, 2000–02; Lord Mayor's Appeal, 2000–01; Pied Piper Appeal, 2002–; Winston's Wish (grief support charity for children), 2002–06 (Pres., 1996–2000; Ambassador, 2006–); Women in Banking and Finance, 2008–11; Pres., Hosp. Caterers Assoc., 2009–10. Vis. Associate Prof., York Univ., 1996–; Pro-Chancellor, Southampton Univ., 1998–2008 (Chm. Council, 1998–2000). Mem., British and Irish Ombudsman Assoc., 2002–. Mem., Editl Adv. Bd, Revans Inst., 2002–. CCMI (CIMgt 2000). Fellow: Glos Univ. (formerly Cheltenham & Gloucester Coll. of Higher Educn), 1996– (Chancellor, 2012–); Sunningdale Inst., Nat. Sch. of Govt, 2006–; FCGI, 2002. Hon. PhD Southampton, 1996; DUniv: York, 1998; Oxford Brookes, 2001; Open, 2003; QUB, 2005; Hon. LLD St Andrews, 2002; Hon. DLitt Hull, 2006. *Publications:* Working Choices, 1988; The Business of Assertiveness, 1991; Resolving Conflicts in Organisations, 1998. *Recreations:* family, reading, gardening, swimming, theatre, cooking, the 'Archers'. *Address:* Mainstream Development, 51 St Paul's Road, Gloucester GL1 5AP. *T:* (01452) 414542.

FRITH, Prof. Christopher Donald, PhD; FRS 2000; FBA 2008; Professor in Neuropsychology, University College London, 1994–2008, now Emeritus; Visiting Professor, University of Aarhus, Denmark, since 2007; Quondam Fellow, All Souls College, Oxford, since 2013 (Fellow, 2011–13); *b* 16 March 1942; *s* of Donald Alfred Frith, OBE; *m* 1966, Uta Aurnhammer (*see* U. Frith); two *s*. *Educ:* Leys Sch., Cambridge; Christ's Coll., Cambridge (MA 1963); Inst. of Psychiatry, London Univ. (Dip. Psych. 1965; PhD 1969). Res. Asst, Inst. of Psychiatry, 1965–75; MRC Scientific Staff: Clin. Res. Centre, Div. of Psychiatry, Northwick Park Hosp., 1975–92; MRC Cyclotron Unit, Hammersmith Hosp., 1992–94; Wellcome Principal Res. Fellow, Wellcome Trust Centre for Neuroimaging (formerly Wellcome Dept of Cognitive Neurology), Inst. of Neurology, UCL, 1994–2008. FRSA 1996; FMedSci 1999; FAAAS 2000. Kenneth Craik Award, St John's Coll., Cambridge, 1999; (jtly) European Latsis Prize, Eur. Sci. Foundn, 2009; Internat. Fyssen Prize, Fyssen Foundn, 2009. *Publications:* Cognitive Neuropsychology of Schizophrenia, 1992; Schizophrenia: a very short introduction, 2003; Making up the Mind, 2007; papers on cognitive neuropsychology in various scientific jls. *Recreations:* music, study of consciousness, interacting minds. *Address:* Wellcome Trust Centre for Neuroimaging, 12 Queen Square, WC1N 3BG. *T:* (020) 7833 7457.

FRITH, David Edward John; cricket author and journalist; Founder, 1979, Editor and Editorial Director, 1979–96, Wisden Cricket Monthly; *b* 16 March 1937; *s* of Edward Frith and Patricia Lillian Ethel Frith (*née* Thomas); *m* 1957, Debbie Oriel Christina Pennell; two *s* one *d*. *Educ:* Canterbury High Sch., Sydney. First grade cricket, Sydney, 1960–64. Editor, The Cricketer, 1972–78. Vice-Pres., Cricket Memorabilia Soc., 1987–. Hon. Life Mem., Assoc. of Cricket Statisticians and Historians, 2013. Cricket Soc. Literary Award, 1970, 1987 and 2003; Cricket Writer of the Year, Wombwell Cricket Lovers Soc., 1984; Magazine Sports Writer of the Year, Sports Council, 1988; Ian Jackson Award for Dist. Service to Cricket, Cricket Soc., 2011. *Publications:* Runs in the Family (with John Edrich), 1969; (ed) Cricket Gallery, 1976; My Dear Victorious Stod, 1977; (with Greg Chappell) The Ashes '77, 1977; The Golden Age of Cricket 1890–1914, 1978; The Ashes '79, 1979; Thommo, 1980; The Fast Men, 1981; The Slow Men, 1984; (with Gerry Wright) Cricket's Golden Summer, 1985; (ed) England *v* Australia Test Match Records 1877–1985, 1986; Archie Jackson, 1987; Pageant of Cricket, 1987; Guildford Jubilee 1938–1988, 1988; England *v* Australia: A Pictorial History of the Test Matches since 1877, 1990; By His Own Hand, 1991; Stoddy's Mission, 1995; (ed) Test Match Year, 1997; Caught England, Bowled Australia (autobiog.), 1997; The Trailblazers, 1999; Silence of the Heart, 2001; Bodyline Autopsy, 2002; The Ross Gregory Story, 2003; The Battle for the Ashes, 2005; The Battle Renewed 2006–07, 2007; Inside Story: unlocking Australian cricket's archives, 2007 (Aust. Cricket Soc. Book Award, 2008); The David Frith Archive, 2009; Frith on Cricket, 2010; Cricket's Collectors, 2012; Guildford's Cricket Story, 2013; Frith's Encounters, 2014; 'Stoddy': England's finest sportsman, 2015. *Recreations:* collecting cricketana, watching documentaries. *Address:* 6 Beech Lane, Guildford, Surrey GU2 4ES. *T:* (01483) 532573. *Club:* MCC.

FRITH, Mark; Lifestyle Editorial Director, Bauer Media, 2011–12; *b* 22 May 1970; *s* of John and Monica Frith; partner, Gaby; one *s* one *d*. *Educ:* Norton Free Primary Sch., Sheffield; Gleadless Valley Secondary Sch., Sheffield; Univ. of E London. Editor: Overdraft mag. (UEL mag.), 1989–90; Smash Hits mag., 1994–95; Sky mag., 1995–97; Editor-in-Chief, heat mag., 1999–2008; Editor, Time Out, 2009–11; presenter, Liquid News, BBC TV, 2002–03. Contributing Ed., LOVE mag., 2008–09. *Publications:* (ed) The Best of Smash Hits: the eighties, 2006; The Celeb Diaries, 2008. *Recreations:* music, cinema, Sheffield UFC, talking too fast, clumsiness, finding things to read in other people's recycling bins, Dostoyevsky (not really!).

FRITH, Rt Rev. Richard Michael Cokayne; *see* Hereford, Bishop of.

FRITH, Prof. Simon Webster, PhD; FBA 2011; Tovey Professor of Music, Reid School of Music, Edinburgh College of Art, University of Edinburgh, since 2006; *b* 25 June 1946; *s* of Donald Frith and Mary Frith (*née* Tyler); *m* 1999, Jenny McKay; one *d*. *Educ:* Balliol Coll., Oxford (BA PPE); Univ. of Calif, Berkeley (MA; PhD Sociol. 1976). Lectr, then Sen. Lectr in Sociol., Warwick Univ., 1972–87; Professor: of English Studies, Univ. of Strathclyde, 1987–99; of Film and Media, Univ. of Stirling, 1999–2005. Dir, Media Econs and Media Culture Res. Prog., ESRC, 1995–2000. Chair of Judges, Mercury Music Prize, 1992–. *Publications:* Sound Effects, 1983; Music for Pleasure, 1988; Performing Rites, 1996; Music and Copyright, 2004; Taking Popular Music Seriously, 2007; The Art of Record Production, 2012; History of Live Music in Britain 1950–1967, 2013. *Recreation:* music. *Address:* Reid School of Music, Edinburgh College of Art, University of Edinburgh, Alison House, 12 Nicolson Square, Edinburgh EH8 9DF. *T:* (0131) 650 2426. *E:* simon.frith@ed.ac.uk.

FRITH, Prof. Uta, Hon. DBE 2012; PhD; FMedSci; FRS 2005; FBA 2001; Professor of Cognitive Development, Institute of Cognitive Neuroscience, University College London, 1996–2006, now Emeritus (Deputy Director, 1998–2006); Visiting Professor, Interacting Minds Centre (formerly Guest Professor, Niels Bohr Project on Interacting Minds), Aarhus University, since 2007; *b* 25 May 1941; *d* of Wilhelm Aurnhammer and Anne (*née* Goedel); *m* 1966, Prof. Christopher Donald Frith, *qv*; two *s*. *Educ:* Univ. des Saarlandes (Vordiplom. Psychol. 1964); Inst. of Psychiatry, Univ. of London (Dip. Abnormal Psychol. 1966; PhD Psychol. 1968). CPsychol. MRC Scientific Staff: Scientist, 1968–80; Sen. Scientist, 1980–98; Special Appt, 1998–. FMedSci 2001. Hon. FBPsS 2006. Hon. Fellow: UCL, 2007; Newnham Coll., Cambridge, 2008. Hon. DPhil: Göteborg, 1998; St Andrews, 2000; Palermo, 2005; York, 2005; Nottingham, 2007; Cambridge, 2012. *Publications:* Autism: explaining the enigma, 1989, 2nd edn 2003; (ed) Autism and Asperger's Syndrome, 1991; (with Rab Houston) Autism in History, 2000; (ed jtly) Autism: mind and brain, 2004; (with Sarah-Jayne Blakemore) The Learning Brain: Lessons for Education, 2005; Autism: a very short introduction, 2008. *Recreations:* collecting art and antiques, tidying and polishing, enjoying my husband's cooking. *Address:* Institute of Cognitive Neuroscience, University College London, Alexandra House, 17 Queen Square, WC1N 3AR. *T:* (020) 7679 1177.

FRITSCH, Elizabeth, CBE 1995; potter; *b* Shropshire, 1940; *d* of Welsh parents; one *s* one *d*. *Educ:* Royal Acad. of Music; Royal Coll. of Art (Silver Medallist, 1970). Established own workshop, E London, 1985. *One-woman exhibitions* include: Bing and Grondahl, Copenhagen, 1972; Waterloo Place Gall., London, 1974; British Craft Centre, 1976; Leeds Galls, Temple Newsham, 1978, touring to Glasgow, Bristol, Bolton and V & A; Cross Rhythms and Counterpoint, Edinburgh, 1990; Hetjens Mus., Dusseldorf, 1991; Retrospective, Pischeur Fine Art, London, 1992–93; Vessels from Another World, Northern Centre for Contemp. Art, Sunderland, touring to Aberdeen, Birmingham, Cardiff, London and Norwich, 1993–95, Osiris Gall., Brussels, 1994; Order and Chaos, Bellas Artes, Santa Fe, 1994–95; Metaphysical Pots, Bellrive Mus., 1995; Retrospective, touring to Munich, Karlsruhe, Halle and Bellerive, Zurich, 1995–96; Sea Pieces, Contemp. Applied Arts, London, 1998; Memory of Architecture, Pt II, Besson Gall., London, 2000; Metaphysical Vessels, Mobilia Gall., Cambridge, Mass, 2000; Anthony Hepworth Gall., Bath, 2007; Retrospective, Bonhams, London, 2007; Fine Art Soc., London, 2008; Dynamic Structures: Painted Vessels, Nat. Mus. of Wales, Cardiff, 2010; *group exhibitions* include: Oxford Gall., 1974; ICA, 1985; Künstlerhaus, Vienna, 1986; Fischer Fine Art, London, 1987; Kyoto and Tokyo Nat. Museums of Modern Art, 1988; Crafts Council, touring to Amsterdam, 1988; Sotheby's, 1988; 35 Connaught Square, London (Lord Queensberry), 1991; Stuttgart, 1991; Oriel Gall., Cardiff, 1991; Marianne Heller Gall., Heidelberg, 1999; Mus. of Modern Ceramic Art, Gifu, 2003; Hayward Gall., London, 2003–04; *works in public collections:* V & A; Crafts Council; Lotherton Hall, Leeds City Art Galls; Royal Mus. of Scotland; Glasgow, Bolton, Bristol and Birmingham City Art Galls. Judge, Fletcher Challenge Internat. Ceramics Competition, NZ, 1990. Major influences on work: music, fresco painting, topology. Sen. Fellow, RCA, 1995. Herbert Read Meml Prize, 1970; Winner, Royal Copenhagen Jubilee Competition, 1972; Gold Medal, Internat. Ceramics Competition, Sopot, Poland, 1976; Gold Medal, Internat. Handwerksmesse, Munich, 1993. *Recreations:* music, mountains, theatre.

FRIZZELL, Edward William, CB 2000; Head, Scottish Executive Enterprise, Transport and Lifelong Learning (formerly Enterprise and Lifelong Learning) Department, 1999–2006; *b* 4 May 1946; *s* of late Edward Frizzell, CBE, QPM and Mary McA. Russell; *m* 1969, Moira Calderwood; two *s* one *d*. *Educ:* Paisley Grammar School, Glasgow Univ. (MA Hons). Scottish Milk Marketing Board, 1968–73; Scottish Council (Develt and Industry), 1973–76; Scottish Office, 1976–78; First Sec., Fisheries, FCO UK Rep. Brussels, 1978–82; Scottish Office, then Scottish Executive, 1982–2006: SED, 1982–86; Finance Div., 1986–89; Industry Dept/SDA (Dir, Locate in Scotland), 1989–91; Under Sec., 1991; Chief Exec., Scottish Prison Service, 1991–99. Non-exec. Dir, Scottish Ambulance Service, 2011–. Vis. Prof. in Public Service Mgt, Queen Margaret Univ., Edinburgh, 2006–. Chm. Court, Abertay Univ. (formerly Univ. of Abertay, Dundee), 2013– (Mem. Court, 2006–12). Chm., Trefoil House, 2012–. *Recreations:* running, mountain biking, painting. *Club:* Mortonhall Golf.

FROGGATT, Anthony Grant; Chief Executive Officer, Scottish & Newcastle PLC, 2003–07; *b* 9 June 1948; *s* of Sir Leslie Trevor Froggatt and of Jessie Elizabeth Froggatt (*née* Grant); *m* 1999, Chris Bulmer; three *s*. *Educ:* Queen Mary Coll., Univ. of London (LLB Hons); Columbia Business Sch., NY (MBA). Man. Dir, Swift & Moore, Sydney, Australia, 1983–88; CEO, Cinzano Internat., Geneva, 1988–92; President: Asia Pacific, 1992–95, Europe, 1995–98, Internat. Distillers & Vintners; Europe and Africa, Seagram, 1999–2002. Consultant Dir, Rothschild Australia, 2003. Non-executive Director: Brambles Ltd, 2006–; Billabong Ltd, 2008–13; AXA Asia Pacific Hldgs Ltd, 2008–11; Coca-Cola Amatil Pty Ltd, 2010–. *Recreations:* tennis, travel, historical letters/signature collection. *Address:* 7 Eastbourne Road, Darling Point, Sydney, NSW 2027, Australia.

FROGGATT, Sir Peter, Kt 1985; MD; FRCP, FRCPI; Trustee, National Museums and Galleries of Northern Ireland, 1998–2003; Pro-Chancellor, University of Dublin, 1985–2003 (Senior Pro-Chancellor, since 1999); President and Vice-Chancellor, Queen's University of Belfast, 1976–86; *b* 12 June 1928; *s* of Albert Victor and Edith (*née* Curran); *m* 1958, Norma Cochrane; four *s* (and one *s* decd). *Educ:* Royal Belfast Academical Institution; Royal Sch., Armagh (Schol.); Trinity Coll., Dublin (BA; MB; BCh; BAO 1952; MA 1956; MD 1957; Welland Prize; Cunningham Medal; Begley Schol.); Queen's Univ., Belfast (DPH 1956; PhD 1967; Carnwath Prize). MRCPI 1972; FRCPI 1973; FFPH (FFCM 1973); MRCP 1974; FFOMI 1975; FFCMI 1976; MRIA 1978; FRCP 1980. House Surgeon and Physician, Sir Patrick Dun's Hosp., Dublin, 1952–53; Nuffield Res. Student, 1956–57; Med. Officer, Short Bros and Harland Ltd, 1957–59; Queen's University, Belfast: Lectr, 1959–65; Reader, 1965–68; Prof. of Epidemiology, 1968–76; Dean, Faculty of Medicine, 1971–76; Consultant, Eastern Health and Social Services Board, 1960–76. Hon. Prof., St Bartholomew's Hosp. Med. Sch., 1986–94. Chairman: Independent Scientific Cttee on Smoking and Health, 1980–91 (Mem., 1977–80); Tobacco Products Res. Trust, 1981–97; ASME, 1987–92; Central Ethical Compliance Gp, Unilever, 1991–97. Director: AIB Gp plc, 1984–95; TSB Bank (Northern Ireland), later First Trust Bank, 1991–98. President: Biol Scis Section, British Assoc., 1987–88; BMA, 1999–2000; Member: Bd, 1983–85, Adv. Cttee, NI, 1988–94, British Council; Gen. Adv. Cttee, BBC, 1986–88; Supervisory Bd, NHS NI, 1986–92; British Occupational Health Res. Foundn, 1991–2000. Hon. Member: Soc. for Social Medicine; Soc. of Occupational Medicine. Lectures: Robert Adams, 1977, Kirkpatrick, 1984, Abrahamson, 1986, RCSI; Apothecaries, SOM, 1978; Freyer, NUI, 1984; Bayliss, RCP, 1989; Smiley, FOMI, 1989; Bartholomew Mosse, Rotunda Hosp., 1992; John Snow, Assoc. of Anaesthetists, 2001; Doctors Award Redistribution Enterprise, FPHM, 2001. Trustee, Mater Infirmorum Hosp., Belfast, 1994–2002; Chm., Scotch-Irish Trust of Ulster, 1990–. Freeman, City of London, 1990. FSS 1963; Hon. FRCSI 1988; Hon. Fellow, Royal Acad. of Medicine in Ireland; CCMI (CBIM 1986). Hon. LLD: Dublin, 1981; QUB, 1991; Hon. DSc NUI, 1982. Dominic Corrigan Gold Medal, RCPI, 1981. *Publications:* (jtly) Causation of Bus-driver Accidents: Epidemiological Study, 1963; (ed jtly) Nicotine, Smoking and the Low Tar Programme, 1988; articles in jls on human genetics, occupational medicine, med. history, med. educn, epidemiology and smoking policies. *Recreations:* golf, music, travel. *Address:* Rathganley, 3 Strangford Avenue, Belfast BT9 6PG.

FROST, Alan John; DL; FIA; Chairman, Dorset Opera, since 2004; *b* 6 Oct. 1944; *s* of Edward George Frost and Ellen Lucy Jamieson; *m* 1973, Valerie Jean Bennett; two *s*. *Educ:* Stratford County Grammar Sch., London; Manchester Univ. (BSc Hons). FIA 1970. Pearl Assurance Co., 1966–67; Australian Mutual Provident Soc., 1967–72; Laurie, Milbank & Co., 1972–74; London & Manchester Assurance Gp, 1974–84; Sun Life Assurance Soc., 1984–86; Man. Dir, Abbey Life Assurance Co., 1986–98; Gp Chief Exec., United Assce Gp plc, 1998–2000; Dep. Chief Exec., Royal London Gp, 2000–01; Chm., Queen Mab Consultancy Ltd, 2001–04. Chm., Teachers' Bldg Soc., 2004–10 (non-exec. Dir, 2001–10); non-executive Director: INVESCO Pensions Ltd, 2001–; Bournemouth Univ., 2001–10 (Chm., 2004–10); NFU Mutual Insce Co., 2002–09; Car Crash Line Gp, 2002–06; Hamworthy plc, 2004–12. Chm., Bournemouth Chamber Music Soc., 2012–. Liveryman, Co. of Actuaries, 1986– (Master, 2004–05). DL 2010, High Sheriff, 2011–12, Dorset. Hon. DBA Bournemouth, 2011. *Publications:* (with D. P. Hager) A General Introduction to Institutional Investment, 1986; (with D. P. Hager) Debt Securities, 1990; A Light Frost, 2005; actuarial papers. *Recreation:* opera. *E:* mail@alanfrost.co.uk. *Club:* Reform.

FROST, (Angela) Jane, CBE 2011; Chief Executive, Market Research Society, since 2011; *b* 14 July 1957; *d* of Dr William Derek Walsh and Julia Margaret Walsh; *m* 1981, Martin John Frost; one *s* one *d*. *Educ:* New Hall, Cambridge (BA 1978). Trainee manager to Product Gp Manager, Lever Brothers Ltd, 1978–85; Hd of Mktg, Shell Middle East Ltd (Dubai), 1985–88; Shell International Trading Company plc: Brand Coordinator Lubricants, 1988–91; Internat. Brand Coordinator, 1991–94; Planning and Mktg Dir (Far East and Australasia), 1995; Controller, Brand Mktg, BBC, 1995–2000; Dir, Mktg and Strategy, BBC Technol. Ltd, 2000–01; Dir, Greystones Consulting, 2001–02; Dir, Consumer Strategy, subseq. Strategy,

DCA, 2003–06; Dir, Individual Customers, HMRC, 2006–11. Mem. Supervisory Bd, Wolters Kluwer NV, 2000–09. Chair, Legal Services Reform Consumer Panel, 2006–09; Dir, Audit Cttee, DirectGov, 2007–11; Mem., Governance Cttee, JobCentre Plus, 2008–11; Chm., Audit Cttee (Personal Tax Gp), HMRC, 2010–11. Dir, BBC Children in Need Ltd, 1997–. Non-exec. Dir, 2003–, Trustee, 2005–, Lowry Arts Centre; Mem. Council of Trustees, Heads, Teachers and Industry, 2003–11 (Vice Chair, 2008–11; Patron, 2011–); Chm., Heads, Teachers and Industry Trust, 2005–08; Vice Chm., Fairtrade Foundn, 2013–. FCIM; FRSA. *Recreations:* my children, my dogs, Georgian glass. *Address:* Market Research Society, 15 Northburgh Street, EC1V 0JR. *T:* (020) 7490 4911. *E:* janefrost@mrs.org.uk. *Club:* Women in Advertising and Communications London.

FROST, Christopher Ian; Co-Director, East West Offender Management Consultancy Services (supporting development of justice services and promoting human rights in developing countries), since 2008; *b* 17 April 1949; *s* of late Joffre and Emily Frost; *m* Sandra Lomax; one *s* two *d*. *Educ:* Lewes County Grammar Sch. for Boys; Nottingham Univ. (MEd). Teacher, subseq. Hd of Dept, Sir William Nottidge Sch., 1970–77; Hd, Community Educn, Wigan, 1977–81; Dep. Educn Officer, Notts LEA, 1981–84; Educn Officer, Leics LEA, 1984–91; NVQ Development Officer, Home Office, 1991–93; Dir, City Coll., Manchester, 1994–2001; Chief Exec., Rathbone (educn and trng for disadvantaged young people), 2001–04. Sen. expert on justice matters in European projects supporting develts in Russia, Georgia and Serbia, 2004–; expert in criminal justice for Council of Europe in Ukraine, Moldova and Kazakhstan, 2011–13, in Armenia and Bosnia, 2011–15. Conseiller municipale, Charlas, France, 2014–. *Publications:* Using Group Work in Anger Management Work (in Russian), 2008; reports and newspaper articles on supporting develt of democracy for offenders and of new trng initiatives for prison governors in Russia. *Recreations:* musical theatre, travel, ski-ing, performing folk music.

FROST, David George Hamilton, CMG 2006; Chief Executive, Scotch Whisky Association, since 2014; *b* 21 Feb. 1965; *s* of George Leonard Frost and Margaret Elsie Frost; *m* 1993, Jacqueline Elizabeth Dias; one *s* one *d*. *Educ:* St John's Coll., Oxford (BA Hons; MA). Entered FCO, 1987: London, 1987–89; Third Sec. (Political), Nicosia, 1989–90; KPMG Peat Marwick (on secondment), 1990–92; FCO, 1992–93: First Secretary (Economic): UK Repn to EU, 1993–96; UKMIS to UN, NY, 1996–98; Private Sec. to Perm. Under Sec., FCO, 1998–99; Dep. Hd, EU Dept, FCO, 1999–2001; Counsellor (Econ. and EU), Paris, 2001–03; Dir, EU (Internal) (formerly Dep. Dir, Europe), FCO, 2003–06; Ambassador to Denmark, 2006–08; Dir of Policy Planning Staff (formerly for Strategy, Policy Planning and Analysis), FCO, 2008–10; Dir, Europe, Trade and Internat. Affairs, BIS, 2010–13 (on secondment). Mem., Adv. Council of Open Europe, 2014–. *Recreations:* history, art and architecture, modern languages and historical linguistics, detective fiction, free-market economic theory, EU policy and politics. *Address:* Scotch Whisky Association, 20 Atholl Crescent, Edinburgh EH3 8HF. *T:* (0131) 222 9200. *E:* dfrost@swa.org.uk.

FROST, David Stuart, CBE 2011; DL; Chairman, Stoke on Trent and Staffordshire Local Enterprise Partnership, since 2014; *b* 22 Feb. 1953; *s* of George William Stuart Frost and Winifred Leslie Frost; *m* 1981, Mari Doyle; two *d*. *Educ:* Thames Poly. (BA Hons Pol Economy); Poly. of the South Bank (Dip Internat. Financial Studies). Economist, London Chamber of Commerce, 1976–79; Dir of Services, Walsall Chamber of Commerce, 1979–86; Chief Executive: Walsall Chamber of Commerce and Industry, 1986–96; East Mercia Chamber of Commerce, 1996–2000; Coventry and Warwickshire Chamber of Commerce, 2000–02; Dir-Gen., British Chambers of Commerce, 2002–11. Chairman: Nat. Centre for Entrepreneurship in Educn, 2006–; Studio Schs Trust, 2010–12, now Ambassador; Local Enterprise Partnership Network, 2011–14; vInspired, 2012–; National Numeracy, 2014–. Liveryman, Co. of Loriners, 1986 (Master, 2013). DL W Midlands, 2012. DUniv Birmingham City, 2008. *Recreations:* cycling, motorcycling, sailing. *Address:* 5 Norfolk Gardens, Sutton Coldfield, West Midlands B75 6SS. *T:* (0121) 355 7788. *E:* dsfrost@yahoo.com.

FROST, Ven. George; Archdeacon of Lichfield and Canon Treasurer of Lichfield Cathedral, 1998–2000; *b* 4 April 1935; *s* of William John Emson Frost and Emily Daisy Frost; *m* 1959, Joyce Pratt; four *s*. *Educ:* Hatfield Coll., Durham Univ. (BA 1956, MA 1961); Lincoln Theological Coll. Schoolmaster, Westcliff High School, 1956–57; labourer, Richard Thomas and Baldwin Steelworks, Scunthorpe, 1958–59; Asst Curate, St Margaret, Barking Parish Church, 1960–64; Minister, Ecclesiastical District of St Mark, Marks Gate, 1964–70; Vicar: St Matthew, Tipton, 1970–77; St Bartholomew, Penn, Wolverhampton, 1977–87; RD of Trysull, 1984–87; Archdeacon of Salop, 1987–98; Vicar of Tong, 1987–98. Prebendary of Lichfield Cathedral, 1985–87, Hon. Canon, 1987–98. *Recreations:* walking, wild flowers, photography. *Address:* 23 Darnford Lane, Lichfield, Staffs WS14 9RW. *T:* (01543) 415109.

FROST, Gerald Philip Anthony; author and journalist; *b* 8 Nov. 1943; *s* of Sidney and Flora Frost; *m* 1970, Margaret Miriam Freedman; two *s*. *Educ:* Univ. of Sussex (BA Hons; mature student). Junior reporter, Ilford and East London newspapers, 1960–64; reporter: Recorder Newspapers, Ilford, 1964–65; Yorkshire Post, 1965–67; Chief reporter, Morning Telegraph, 1967–68; Sub-editor: Daily Express, Manchester, 1968–69; Press Assoc., 1969–71; research staff, Centre for Policy Studies, 1974–80 (Sec. and Mem Bd, 1977–80); Chief Leader Writer, Evening Standard, 1979–80; Director: Inst. for European Defence and Strategic Studies, 1980–92; Centre for Policy Studies, 1992–95; Trade and Welfare Unit, IEA, 1997–2001. Ed., eurofacts, 2001–09. Consultant Dir, New Atlantic Initiative, 1996–98. *Publications:* Protest and Perish: a critique of unilateralism (with P. Towle and I. Eliott), 1983; Antony Fisher: champion of liberty, 2002; (with John Blundell) Friend or Foe?: what Americans should know about the European Union, 2004; (with Anthony Scholefield) Too 'Nice' to be Tories: how the modernisers have damaged the Conservative Party, 2011; *editor and contributor:* Europe in Turmoil, 1991; In search of Stability, 1992; Hubris: the tempting of modern conservatives, 1992; Loyalty Misplaced, 1997; Unfit to Fight: the cultural subversion of the armed forces in Britain and America, 1999; contribs to British and US newspapers and jls. *Recreations:* family pursuits, reading, wine. *Address:* Pear Tree Cottage, Downs Road, Epsom, Surrey KT18 5HN. *Club:* Reform.

FROST, Jane; *see* Frost, A. J.

FROST, Jeffrey Michael Torbet; Executive Director, London & Continental Bankers, 1983–89 (Associate Director, 1982–83); *b* 11 June 1938; *s* of late Basil Frost and Dorothy Frost. *Educ:* Diocesan Coll., Cape, South Africa; Radley Coll.; Oriel Coll., Oxford; Harvard Univ. Admin. Asst, Brazilian Traction, Light and Power Co., Toronto and Brazil, 1965–70; Economics Dept, Bank of London and S America, 1971–73; Asst Dir, 1974–75, Exec. Dir, 1976–81, Cttee on Invisible Exports. Hon. Sec., Anglo-Brazilian Soc., 1977–84. Liveryman, Worshipful Co. of Clockmakers. Freeman, City of London, 1980. FRSA. *Recreations:* bridge, ballet, walking. *Address:* 34 Paradise Walk, SW3 4JL. *T:* (020) 7352 8642; The Reading Room, Kintbury, near Hungerford, Berks RG17 9UP. *Clubs:* White's; Leander (Henley-on-Thames).

FROST, Rt Rev. Jonathan Hugh; *see* Southampton, Bishop Suffragan of.

FROST, Michael Edward, LVO 1983; HM Diplomatic Service, retired; Consul-General, San Francisco, 1998–2001; *b* 5 July 1941; *s* of Edward Lee Frost and Ivy Beatrice (*née* Langmead); *m* 1964, Carole Ann Beigel; three *s*. *Educ:* Torquay Grammar Sch. FCO, 1959–62; Algiers, 1962–67; Commercial Officer, Kuala Lumpur, 1967–71; 3rd Sec., later 2nd Sec. Commercial, Bucharest, 1972–75; FCO, 1975–78; Consul (Commercial), Seattle, 1978–83; FCO, 1983–84; on secondment to ICI, 1984–87; Dep. Head of Mission, Sofia, 1987–90; Dep. Consul Gen. and Dir (Investment), British Trade and Investment Office, NY, 1991–95; Head of Migration and Visa Dept, FCO, 1995–97. *Recreations:* watercolours, golf, travel. *Address:* 25 Waldens Park Road, Woking, Surrey GU21 4RN.

FROST, Ronald Edwin; Chairman, Hays plc, 1989–2001; *b* 19 March 1936; *s* of Charles Henry Frost and Doris (*née* Foggin); *m* 1959, Beryl Ward; one *s* two *d*. Founded Farmhouse Securities, 1965, Chm., 1979–81; Farmhouse Securities purchased by Hays Gp, 1981: Chief Exec., Distribn Div., 1981–83; Chief Exec. and Man. Dir, 1983–89. MInstD 1975; CIMgt (CBIM 1989). Freeman, City of London, 1983; Liveryman, Co. of Watermen & Lightermen, 1983–. *Recreations:* farming, game shooting, sailing. *Address:* The Grove, Le Mont Cambrai, St Lawrence, Jersey JE3 1JN. *Clubs:* Carlton, Royal Thames Yacht; Royal Channel Islands Yacht.

FROST, Thomas Pearson, FCIB; Group Chief Executive, National Westminster Bank, 1987–92; *b* 1 July 1933; *s* of James Watterson Frost and Enid Ella Crawte (*née* Pearson); *m* 1958, Elizabeth (*née* Morton); one *s* two *d*. *Educ:* Ormskirk Grammar Sch. FCIB (FIB 1976). Joined Westminster Bank, 1950; Chief Exec. Officer and Vice Chm., NBNA (later National Westminster Bank USA), 1980; National Westminster Bank: Gen. Man., Business Develt Div., 1982; Dir, 1984–93; Dep. Gp Chief Exec., 1985–87; Dep. Chm., 1992–93; Chm., London Clearing House Ltd, 1993–96. Chairman: Five Oaks Investments PLC, 1995–98 (non-exec. Dir, 1993–95); WSPA (UK), 2003–07 (Mem. Adv. Council, 2007–08); non-executive Director: Freedom Food Ltd, 1994–2003; Fenchurch PLC, 1993–97. Member: BOTB, 1986–93; UK Adv. Bd, British-American Chamber of Commerce, 1987–93; Business in the Cities, 1988–91; Policy Adv. Cttee, Tidy Britain Gp, 1988–92; Adv. Bd, World Economic Forum, 1990–93; Chairman: CBI Business & Urban Regeneration Task Force, 1987–88; Exec. Cttee, British Bankers' Assoc., 1991–92. Trustee, British Sports Trust, 1988–92; Gov., Royal Ballet Sch., 1988–98. Fellow, World Scout Foundn, 1984. Freeman, City of London, 1978. FCIM 1987; CompOR 1987; CCMI (CIMgt 1987); Companion, BITC, 1993; FRSA 1993. OStJ 1991. *Recreations:* orchids, theatre. *Clubs:* Carlton, MCC.

FROST, Vince; Graphic Designer, Creative Director and Chief Executive Officer, Frost Collective (formerly Frost Design), since 1994; *b* 23 Nov. 1964; *s* of Alan Frost and Irene Frost; *m* 1997, Sonia Della Grazia-Frost; two *s* one *d*. *Educ:* W Sussex Coll. of Art and Design. Joined Pentagram, 1989, Associate Dir, 1992; founded own practice, Frost Design, 1994. Exhibns incl. Frost*bite: Graphic Ideas by Vince Frost, Sydney Opera House Exhibn Hall, 2006. Member: D&AD; Chartered Soc. of Designers; Internat. Soc. of Typographic Designers; Aust. Graphic Design Assoc.; AGI. Over 300 design awards. *Publications:* Frost*(sorry trees), 2006; Design Your Life®, 2014. *Recreations:* surfing, walking, playing with my kids. *Address:* Frost Design, Level 1, 15 Foster Street, Surry Hills, Sydney, NSW 2010, Australia. *T:* (2) 92804233, *Fax:* (2) 92804266. *E:* vince@frostdesign.com.au.

FROSTICK, Prof. Lynne Elizabeth, PhD; Research Professor in Physical Geography, University of Hull, 2010–14, now Professor Emerita; *b* Gillingham, Kent, 2 Feb. 1949; *d* of Victor Alec John Frostick and Kathleen Frances Frostick; *m* Prof. Ian Reid; three *s*. *Educ:* Dartford Grammar Sch. for Girls; Univ. of Leicester (BSc (Hons) Geol. 1970); Univ. of East Anglia (PhD Envmtl Scis 1973). FGS 1976; CGeol 1989; FRGS 1996; CGeog 2002. Lectr in Geol., Birkbeck Coll., Univ. of London, 1973–85; Lectr, 1985–88, Sen. Lectr, 1989, in Geol., RHBNC; Sen. Lectr in Sedimentology, Univ. of Reading, 1989–96; Prof. of Physical Geog., 1996–2010, Pro Vice Chancellor, 2000–03, Univ. of Hull. Chm., Govt's Expert Gp for Women in Sci., Engrg and Technol., 2004–10; Member: Sub-panel 17, REF 2010–14; Equality and Diversity Adv. Panel, REF, 2011–14; Equalities Adv. Gp, BIS, 2011–; Bd, Envmt Agency, 2015–. Pres., Geol Soc., 2008–10; Chm., British Soc. for Geomomorph., 2008–09. Hon. DSc RHUL, 2014. Cuthbert Peek Award for Res., RGS, 2005. *Publications:* Sedimentation in the African Rifts, 1986; Desert Sediments: ancient and modern, 1987; Tectonic Controls and Signatures in Sedimentary Successions, 1993; (ed jtly) Sediment Flux to Basins: causes, control and consequences, 2002; (ed jtly) A Users Guide to Physical Modelling and Experimentation, 2011; (ed) A Users Guide to Ecohydraulic Modelling and Experimentation, 2014; over 100 papers in jls incl. Sedimentology, Sedimentary Res., Jl of Geol Soc., Jl of Hydraulic Res. *Recreations:* cycling, reading, walking, travelling on Caledonian MacBrayne ferries amongst islands off Oban in Scotland. *Address:* Department of Geography, Environment and Earth Sciences, University of Hull, Cottingham Road, Hull HU6 7RX. *T:* (01482) 466069. *E:* l.e.frostick@hull.ac.uk.

FROSTRUP, Mariella; journalist; television and radio presenter; Presenter: Open Book, BBC Radio 4; columnist, The Observer; *b* Oslo, 12 Nov. 1962; *d* of late Peter Trulls Frostrup and of Joan Drysdale McMurray Blair; *m* 2003, Jason Daniel McCue, *qv*; one *s* one *d*. *Educ:* schs in Ireland. Presenter, The Book Show, Sky Arts, until 2013. Founder and Trustee, The Great Initiative. Mem. Council, RA. Mem., BAFTA. Hon. DLit Nottingham Trent, 2008. *Publications:* Dear Mariella, 2005. *Recreations:* travelling, walking, reading, film, scuba diving. *T:* (020) 7221 5363. *E:* mariella.frostrup@observer.co.uk. *Clubs:* Groucho, Ivy, Soho House.

FROUDE, Ven. Christine Ann; Archdeacon of Malmesbury, since 2011; Acting Archdeacon of Bristol, since 2013; *b* 6 June 1947; *d* of Winifred Woolcock and Frederick Woolcock; *m* 1972, David Froude; one *s* one *d*. *Educ:* Southern Diocesan Ministerial Trng Scheme. Various roles with Midland Bank incl. Hd of Trng Res., City of London Internat. Div.; ordained deacon, 1995, priest, 1996; non-stipendiary Minister, St Mary Magdalene, Stoke Bishop, 1995–99; Chaplain, Univ. Hosps Bristol NHS Foundn Trust, 1999–2001; Dean, Women's Ministry, Dio. of Bristol, 2000–11; Priest-in-charge, St Mary, Shirehampton, 2001–11. Hon. Canon, Bristol Cathedral, 2001–11. *Address:* 1 Orchard Close, Winterbourne, Bristol BS36 1BF. *T:* (01454) 778366.

FROW, Prof. John Anthony, PhD; Professor of English, University of Sydney, since 2013; *b* 13 Nov. 1948; *s* of Anthony Gaunt Frow and Nola Marjorie Frow; *m* 1970, Mayerlene Engineer (marr. diss. 1985); one *s*; partner, 1978, Christine Alavi; one *d*; partner, 2001, Sandra Hawker. *Educ:* Australian National Univ. (BA); Cornell Univ. (MA 1974; PhD 1977). Lectr in American Lit., Universidad del Salvador, Buenos Aires, 1970; Lectr in English Lit., then Sen. Lectr, Murdoch Univ., WA, 1975–88; Visiting Professor: Univ. of Minnesota, 1988–89; Univ. of Qld, 1989–2000; Regius Prof. of Rhetoric and English Lit., Univ. of Edinburgh, 2000–04; Prof. of English, Univ. of Melbourne, 2004–12. FAHA 1998. *Publications:* Marxism and Literary History, 1986; Cultural Studies and Cultural Value, 1995; Time and Commodity Culture, 1997; (jtly) Accounting for Tastes, 1999; Genre, 2006; The Practice of Value, 2013; Character and Person, 2014. *Address:* Department of English, University of Sydney, NSW 2006, Australia.

FROY, Prof. Martin; Professor of Fine Art, University of Reading, 1972–91, now Emeritus; *b* 9 Feb. 1926; *s* of late William Alan Froy and Helen Elizabeth Spencer. *Educ:* St Paul's Sch.; Magdalene Coll., Cambridge (one year); Slade Sch. of Fine Art. Dipl. in Fine Art (London). Visiting Teacher of Engraving, Slade Sch. of Fine Art, 1952–55; taught at Bath Acad. of Art, latterly as Head of Fine Art, 1954–65; Head of Painting Sch., Chelsea Sch. of Art, 1965–72. Gregory Fellow in Painting, Univ. of Leeds, 1951–54; Leverhulme Research Award, six months study in Italy, 1963; Sabbatical Award, Arts Council, 1965. Mem., Fine Art Panel, 1962–71, Mem. Council, 1969–71, Nat. Council for Diplomas in Art and Design; Trustee: National Gall., 1972–79; Tate Gall., 1975–79. Fellow, UCL, 1978. *One-Artist Exhibitions:* Hanover Gall., London, 1952; Wakefield City Art Gall., 1953; Belgrade Theatre, Coventry, 1958; Leicester Galls, London, 1961; Royal West of England Acad., Bristol, 1964; Univ. of Sussex, 1968; Hanover Gall., London, 1969; Park Square Gall., Leeds, 1970; Arnolfini Gall.,

Bristol, 1970; City Art Gall., Bristol (seven paintings), 1972; Univ. of Reading, 1979; New Ashgate Gall., Surrey, 1979; Serpentine Gall., 1983; Stanley and Audrey Burton Gall., Univ. of Leeds, 2014. *Other Exhibitions:* Internat. Abstract Artists, Riverside Mus., NY, 1950; ICA, London, 1950; Ten English Painters, Brit. Council touring exhibn in Scandinavia, 1952; Drawings from Twelve Countries, Art Inst. of Chicago, 1952; Figures in their Setting, Contemp. Art Soc. Exhibn, Tate Gall., 1953; Beaux Arts Gall., London, 1953; British Painting and Sculpture, Whitechapel Art Gall., London, 1954; Le Congrès pour la Liberté de la Culture Exhibn, Rome, Paris, Brussels, 1955; Pittsburgh Internat., 1955; Six Young Painters, Arts Council touring Exhibn, 1956; ICA Gregory Meml Exhibn, Bradford City Art Gall., Leeds, 1958; City Art Gall., Bristol, 1960; Malerei der Gegenwart ans Südwestengland, Kunstverein, Hanover, 1962; Corsham Painters and Sculptors, Arts Council Touring Exhibn, 1965; Three Painters, Bath Fest. Exhibn, 1970; Park Square Gall., Leeds, 1978; Ruskin Sch., Univ. of Oxford, 1978; Newcastle Connection, Newcastle, 1980; Homage to Herbert Read, Canterbury, 1984. *Commissions, etc:* Artist Consultant for Arts Council to City Architect, Coventry, 1953–58; mosaic decoration, Belgrade Th., Coventry, 1957–58; two mural panels, Concert Hall, Morley Coll., London, 1958–59. *Works in Public Collections:* Tate Gall.; Mus. of Mod. Art, NY; Chicago Art Inst.; Arts Council; Contemp. Art Soc.; Royal W of England Acad.; Leeds Univ.; City Art Galls of Bristol, Carlisle, Leeds, Southampton and Wakefield; Reading Mus. and Art Gall. *Address:* Rich Fine Art, 111 Mount Street, Mayfair, W1K 2TT.

FRY, Anthony Michael; Chairman: Dairy Crest plc, 2010–14 (Deputy Chairman, 2009); CALA Group Ltd, since 2010; *b* Worthing; *s* of Denis Fry and Doris, (Trixie), Fry (*née* Barter); *m* 1985, Anne Elizabeth Birrell; two *s* one *d*. *Educ:* Stonyhurst Coll.; Magdalen Coll., Oxford (BA 1st Cl. Hons Mod. Hist. 1977); Harvard Business Sch. (AMP 2007). Mem., Exec. Bd, N M Rothschild & Sons, 1977–96; Man. Dir, Credit Suisse, 1996–2004; Hd, UK Investment Banking, Lehman Brothers, 2004–07; Sen. Advr, Evercore Partners, 2008–11. Non-executive Director: Southern Water, 1990–96; Mowlem, 2000–06; Control Risks, 2007–. Chairman: LCC Ventures, 2010–12; Banco Espirito Santo UK, 2011–12 (Sen. Advr to Bd, 2012–14); Premier League, 2013–14. Non-exec. Dir, BSI, 2000–04; Trustee, BBC, 2008–13. Vice Chm., British Lung Foundn, 1996–2002; Member Board: Natural Hist. Mus., 1992–2004; LAMDA, 1998–2004; Nat. Film and TV Sch., 2001–04; SOAS, 2004– (Chm., Develt Bd, 2009–); The Sixteen, 2006–; ENO, 2009–; Paintings in Hosps, 2009–; Twig World, 2010–; Member, Advisory Board: Project Associates, 2012–; Board Intelligence, 2012–. *Recreations:* discovering London monuments, cricket, opera, American Civil War, 18th century prints, political toby jugs. *T:* 07767 374567. *E:* amf@fryassociates.co.uk. *Clubs:* Soho House, Carlton, Century, Bonnetmakers; Armadillos Cricket, Incogniti Cricket, Sussex CC, Primrose Hill Cricket.

FRY, Sir Graham (Holbrook), KCMG 2006; HM Diplomatic Service, retired; Ambassador to Japan, 2004–08; *b* 20 Dec. 1949; *s* of Wing Comdr Richard Holbrook Fry and Marjorie Fry; *m* 1st, 1977, Mayko Iida (marr. diss. 1991); two *s*; 2nd, 1994, Toyoko Ando. *Educ:* Brasenose Coll., Oxford (BA 1972). Entered HM Diplomatic Service, 1972; Third, later Second, Sec., Tokyo, 1974–78; seconded to Invest in Britain Bureau, DoI, 1979–80; FCO, 1981–83; First Sec., Paris, 1983–87; FCO, 1987–88; Political Counsellor, Tokyo, 1989–93; Head, Far Eastern Dept, later Far Eastern and Pacific Dept, FCO, 1993–95; Dir, Northern Asia and Pacific, FCO, 1995–98; High Comr, Malaysia, 1998–2001; Dep. Under-Sec. of State, FCO, 2001–03; Dir Gen., Econ., FCO, 2003–04. Mem. Council, Wildfowl and Wetlands Trust, 2009–. Mem., Gov. Body, SOAS, Univ. of London, 2008–.

FRY, Gregory John; Executive Director, since 1986 and Chairman, since 2011, St George plc; Divisional Executive Director, The Berkeley Group plc, since 2011 (Director, 1996–2010); *b* 29 April 1957; *s* of Wilfred John Fry, Freeman of the City of London. *Educ:* Lord Wandsworth Coll., Hants. ACA 1983; FCA. Joined Berkeley Homes, 1982. Gov., Richmond upon Thames Coll., 2000–04. FInstD 1990. *Recreation:* Rugby. *Address:* St George plc, St George House, 76 Crown Road, Twickenham TW1 3EU. *T:* (020) 8917 4000. *E:* Greg.Fry@stgeorgeplc.com. *Club:* Harlequins Rugby.

FRY, Dr Ian Kelsey, DM, FRCP, FRCR; Dean, Medical College of St Bartholomew's Hospital, 1981–89; Consultant Radiologist, St Bartholomew's Hospital, 1966–87; *b* 25 Oct. 1923; *s* of Sir William and Lady Kelsey Fry; *m* 1951, Mary Josephine Casey; three *s* (one *d* decd). *Educ:* Radley Coll.; New Coll., Oxford; Guy's Hosp. Medical Sch. BM BCh 1948, DM Oxon 1961; MRCP 1956, FRCP 1972; DMRD 1961; FFR 1963; FRCR 1975. RAF Medical Services, 1949–50 (Sqdn Ldr). Director, Dept of Radiology, BUPA Medical Centre, 1973–86; Dir of Radiology, London Independent Hosp., 1986–94; Mem. Council, Royal College of Radiologists, 1979–82; Pres. and Chm. Bd, Med. Defence Union, 1993–97 (Mem. Bd, 1991–93); President, British Institute of Radiology, 1982–83. Gov., Charterhouse Sch., 1984–94. *Publications:* chapters and articles in books and jls. *Recreations:* golf, hill walking, racing. *Address:* 8 Kingsmere, 43 Chislehurst Road, Chislehurst, Kent BR7 5LE. *T:* (020) 8467 4150.

FRY, Jonathan Michael; Chairman, Control Risks Holdings Ltd, 2000–07; *b* 9 Aug. 1937; *s* of late Stephen Fry and Gladys Yvonne (*née* Blunt); *m* 1st, 1970, Caroline Mary Dunkerly (marr. diss. 1997); four *d*; 2nd, 1999, Marilyn Diana Russell. *Educ:* Repton Sch.; Trinity Coll., Oxford (Lit. Hum., MA). Engagement Manager and Consultant, McKinsey & Co., 1966–73; Unigate Foods Division: Man. Dir, 1973–76; Chm., 1976–78; Gp Planning Dir, Burmah Oil Trading Ltd, 1978–81; Chief Executive: Burmah Speciality Chemicals Ltd, 1981–87; Castrol Internat., 1987–93; Burmah Castrol: Man. Dir, 1990–93; Chief Exec., 1993–98; Chm., 1998–2000. Chm., Christian Salvesen plc, 1997–2003; non-executive Director: Northern Foods plc, 1991–2002 (Dep. Chm., 1996–2002); Elementis (formerly Harrisons & Crosfield), 1997–2004 (Chm., 1997–2004). Mem. Council, RIIA, 1998–2002. Chm. Govs, Repton Sch., 2003–12. *Recreations:* cricket, ski-ing, archaeology, wine, gardening. *Address:* Beechingstoke Manor, Pewsey, Wilts SN9 6HQ. *Clubs:* Beefsteak, MCC, Lord's Taverners; Vincent's (Oxford).

FRY, Dame Margaret (Louise), DBE 1989 (OBE 1982); Chairman, National Union of Conservative and Unionist Associations, 1990–91 (a Vice-Chairman, 1987–90); *b* 10 March 1931; *d* of Richard Reed Dawe and Ruth Dora Dawe; *m* 1955, Walter William John Fry; three *s*. *Educ:* Tavistock Grammar School. Conservative Women's Advisory Committee (Western Area): Vice-Chm., 1975–78; Chm., 1978–81; Conservative Women's National Committee: Vice-Chm., 1981–82; Chm., 1984–87; Chm., W Devon Cons. Assoc., 1982–85; Patron, Torridge and W Devon Cons. Assoc., 1999– (Pres., 1992–99; Pres., Women's Cttee, 1988–93); Pres., Western Area Cons, 1995–99. Chairman of Trustees: Peninsula Med. Sch. of Univs of Exeter and Plymouth, 2001–; Primrose Foundn for Breast Care, Derriford Hosp., Plymouth, 2001–. Hon. Dr Health Plymouth, 2011. *Recreations:* farming, conservation, church, sport (former member, Devon County Hockey XI). *Address:* Thorne Farm, Launceston, Cornwall PL15 9SN. *T:* (01566) 784308.

FRY, Lt-Gen. Sir Robert (Alan), KCB 2005; CBE 2001 (MBE 1981); Vice President, Hewlett Packard, since 2009; *b* 6 April 1951; *s* of Raymond and Elizabeth Fry; *m* 1977, Elizabeth Woolmore; two *d*. *Educ:* Bath Univ. (BScEcon); King's Coll., London (MA). Worked in commerce, NY, 1972–73; joined Royal Marines, 1973: COS, 3 Commando Bde, 1989–91; CO 45 Commando, 1995–97; Dir Naval Staff, MoD, 1997–99; Comdr 3 Commando Bde, 1999–2001; Comdt-Gen., Royal Marines, 2001–02; COS, Perm. Jt HQ, 2002–03; DCDS (Commitments), MoD, 2003–06; Dep. Comdg Gen., Multinational Force, Iraq, 2006. CEO, EDS Defence and Security, 2007–09. Director: Injazat Data Services, Abu Dhabi, 2008–; Meeza Corp., Doha, 2008–; McKinney Rogers Internat., 2008–13 (Exec. Chm., 2010–13); non-exec. Chm., Albany Associates, 2012–. Mem., RBS Middle East Adv. Gp, 2011–. Visiting Professor: Dept of Politics and Internat. Relns, Univ. of Reading, 2009–; Dept of War Studies, KCL, 2014; Fellow, Changing Character of War, Oxford Univ., 2009–. Trustee: Help for Heroes, 2009–; RUSI, 2010–. Freeman, City of London, 2003. Hon. LLD Bath, 2014. Officer, Legion of Merit (USA), 2006. Occasional columnist, Wall St Jl; Feature writer, Prospect Mag., 2012–. *Publications:* (contrib.) War in a Time of Peace, 2014; contrib. to RUSI Jl, US Naval Inst. Proc., Bull. d'Etudes de la Marine, Huffington Post, City AM, Forbes Mag., Wall Street Jl, Prospect Mag. *Recreations:* Welsh Rugby, cinema, photography, history, cooking. *Address:* Albany Associates, 18–24 Turnham Green Terrace, W4 1QP. *Club:* Special Forces.

FRY, Sir Roger (Gordon), Kt 2012; CBE 2002 (OBE 1993); Chairman, King's Group, since 1981; *b* Portsmouth, 10 Jan. 1943; *s* of Gordon Fry and Doris Fry (*née* Chopping); *m* 1st, 1966; one *s* one *d* (and one *s* decd); 2nd, 1983, Begoña Jauregui Campuzano; one *s* two *d*. *Educ:* primary and grammar schs, Portsmouth; King's Coll. London (BD; AKC); Inst. of Educn, Univ. of London (PGCE); Inst. of Dirs, London (Dip. Co. Direction). Lectr, Univ. of Comillas, Madrid, 1968–71; Founder, 1969, Headteacher, 1969–81, King's Coll., Madrid. Mem., Gen. Synod of C of E, 1990–95, 2005–10. Chm., Council of British Internat. Schs (formerly Council of British Ind. Schs in EC), 1996–2011 (Pres., 2011–); Dir, Ind. Schs Council, 2008–11. Nat. Pres., British Chamber of Commerce in Spain, 2006–08. Founder, 1981, Chm., 1981–93, British Hispanic Foundn. Member: Multi Academy Trust, Worcester Dio., 2015–; Educn Adv. Bd, British Council, 2015–. Gov., Royal Grammar Sch., Worcester, 1993–. Sir Thomas Pope Hon. Fellow, Trinity Coll., Oxford, 2009. Reader, C of E, 1969–. Freeman, City of London, 2002: Liveryman: Co. of Carmen, 2002–; Educators' Co., 2014–. Hon. DLitt Portsmouth, 2006. Internat. Medal, Complutense Univ., Madrid, 2009. Comdr, Order of Civil Merit (Spain), 1994. *Recreations:* study of world religions and cultures, current affairs, travel, family, classic cars, walking, gastronomy. *Address:* King's Group, Oldwood Road, St Michael's, Tenbury Wells, Worcs WR15 8PH. *E:* roger.fry@kingsgroup.org. *Clubs:* East India; Royal Naval, Royal Albert Yacht (Portsmouth); Rolls Royce Enthusiasts'; Financiero Genova, Gran Peña, Nuevo (Madrid).

FRY, Sarah McC.; *see* McCarthy-Fry.

FRY, Stephen John; writer, actor, comedian; *b* 24 Aug. 1957; *s* of Alan John Fry and Marianne Eve (*née* Newman); *m* 2015, Elliott Spencer. *Educ:* Uppingham Sch.; Queens' Coll., Cambridge (MA; Hon. Fellow, 2005). *TV series:* Blackadder, 1987–89; A Bit of Fry and Laurie, 1989–95; Jeeves in Jeeves and Wooster, 1990–92; Gormenghast, 2000; Absolute Power, 2003, 2005; Kingdom, 2007–09; Bones, 2007–09; 24: Live Another Day, 2014; presenter: QI, 2003–; Stephen Fry: Gadget Man, 2012; Stephen Fry's Key to the City, 2013; writer and presenter: Stephen Fry in America, 2008; Last Chance To See, 2009; Fry's Planet Word, 2011; *TV documentary:* Stephen Fry: the secret life of a manic depressive, 2006 (Emmy Award, 2007); Stephen Fry: Out There, 2013; Fry's Central America, 2015; *theatre:* Forty Years On, Queen's, 1984; The Common Pursuit, Phoenix, 1988; Twelfth Night, Shakespeare's Globe, transf. Apollo Th., 2012; *films:* Peter's Friends, 1992; I.Q., 1995; Wilde, 1997; Cold Comfort Farm, 1997; The Tichborne Claimant, 1998; Whatever Happened to Harold Smith?, 2000; Relative Values, 2000; Gosford Park, 2002; (dir) Bright Young Things, 2003; Tooth, 2004; The Life and Death of Peter Sellers, 2004; (for TV) Tom Brown's Schooldays, 2005; V for Vendetta, 2006; St Trinian's, 2007; Sherlock Holmes: A Game of Shadows, 2011; (for TV) The Borrowers, 2011; (for TV) Doors Open, 2012; The Look of Love, The Hobbit: The Desolation of Smaug, 2013; The Hobbit: The Battle of the Five Armies, 2014; The Man Who Knew Infinity, 2015; *radio series:* Fry's English Delight, 2008–. Numerous audiobook recordings incl. Harry Potter series. Columnist: The Listener, 1988–89; Daily Telegraph, 1990–91; The Guardian, 2007–. *Publications:* Me and My Girl, 1984 (musical performed in West End and on Broadway); A Bit of Fry and Laurie: collected scripts, 1990; Moab is My Washpot (autobiog.), 1997; The Ode Less Travelled, 2005; Stephen Fry in America, 2008; The Fry Chronicles: an autobiography, 2010; The Library Book, 2012; More Fool Me: a memoir, 2014; *novels:* The Liar, 1991; The Hippopotamus, 1994; Making History, 1996; The Stars' Tennis Balls, 2000. *Recreations:* smoking, drinking, swearing, pressing wild flowers. *Address:* c/o Hamilton Hodell Ltd, 20 Golden Square, W1F 9JL. *Clubs:* Savile, Oxford and Cambridge, Groucho, Chelsea Arts, Garrick.

FRYAR, Rt Rev. Godfrey Charles; *see* Rockhampton, Bishop of.

FRYER, Dr Geoffrey, FRS 1972; Deputy Chief Scientific Officer, Windermere Laboratory, Freshwater Biological Association, 1981–88; *b* 6 Aug. 1927; *s* of W. and M. Fryer; *m* 1953, Vivien Griffiths Hodgson; one *s* one *d*. *Educ:* Huddersfield College. DSc, PhD London. Royal Navy, 1946–48. Colonial Research Student, 1952–53; HM Overseas Research Service, 1953–60: Malawi, 1953–55; Zambia, 1955–57; Uganda, 1957–60; Sen., then Principal, then Sen. Principal Scientific Officer, Freshwater Biological Assoc., 1960–81. H. R. Macmillan Lectr, Univ. of British Columbia, 1963; Distinguished Vis. Schol., Univ. of Adelaide, 1985; Distinguished Lectr, Biol Scis Br., Dept Fisheries and Oceans, Canada, 1987; Hon. Prof., Inst. of Environmental and Natural (formerly Biol) Scis, Lancaster Univ., 1988–2008. Mem. Council, Royal Soc., 1978–80. Mem., Adv. Cttee on Science, Nature Conservancy Council, 1986–91. Pres., Yorks Naturalists' Union, 1993. Frink Medal, Zool Soc. of London, 1983; Linnean Medal for Zoology, Linnean Soc., 1987; Elsdon-Dew Medal, Parasitological Soc. of Southern Africa, 1998. *Publications:* (with T. D. Iles) The Cichlid Fishes of the Great Lakes of Africa: their biology and evolution, 1972; A natural history of the lakes, tarns and streams of the English Lake District, 1991; The Freshwater Crustacea of Yorkshire: a faunistic and ecological survey, 1993; (ed with V. R. Alexeev) Diapause in the Crustacea, 1996; numerous articles in scientific jls. *Recreations:* natural history, history of science, walking, church architecture, photography. *Address:* Greystones, Church Lane, Stonehouse, Glos GL10 2BG.

FRYER-SPEDDING, John Henry Fryer, CBE 2003 (OBE 1982); Vice Lord-Lieutenant of Cumbria, 2006–12; *b* 23 Jan. 1937; *s* of Lieut Col James Eustace Spedding, OBE and Mary Catherine Spedding (*née* Fryer); *m* 1968, Clare Caroline Ewbank, JP, *d* of Ven. Walter Frederick Ewbank; two *s*. *Educ:* Trinity Coll., Cambridge (BA 1958, MA 1961). Royal Green Jackets, 1958–68: served Germany, Cyprus and Borneo; retd Maj. 1968. Called to the Bar, Gray's Inn, 1970; a Recorder, 1990–97. Mem., Lake Dist Nat. Park Authy, 1997–2001. Pres., Royal Forestry Soc., 2003–05. Vice-Pres., Cumbria Community Foundn, 2007– (Trustee, 1997–2007; Chm., 1997–2002); Pres., Calvert Trusts (for disabled people), 2008– (Trustee, 1976–2006; Chm. Council, 2002–06; Vice-Pres., 2005–08). Fellow, Wordsworth Trust, 2000– (Trustee, 1978–2000); Vice-Pres., Tennyson Soc., 1984–. DL 1985, High Sheriff, 1997–98, Cumbria. DLI (TA), 1969–78: CO 7th Bn, 1976–78; retd Lt Col, 1978. *Recreations:* forestry, bee-keeping. *Club:* Lansdowne.

FUAD, Kerim Selchuk; QC 2010; *b* Kampala, Uganda, 19 Jan. 1968; *s* of late Kutlu Tekin Fuad, CBE; *m* 1998, Tania Danielle Stevenson. *Educ:* Charterhouse Sch.; London Univ. (LLB Hons 1990). Called to the Bar, Inner Temple, 1992; in practice as barrister, specialising in criminal defence, 1992–; Jt Hd of Chambers, 1 Inner Temple Lane, 2010–13; Hd of Chambers, Church Court Chambers, 2014–. Member, Executive: Criminal Bar Assoc., 2012–; S Eastern Circuit, 2013–. Co-founder and Co-Chm., Cypriot Lawyers Soc., 2013–. Chm., Herts and Beds Bar Mess, 2013–. *Recreations:* fire lighting, the works of Hergé, Liverpool FC, talk of exercise, friends, red wine, gardening, getting lost, making lists, enjoying my wife's great cooking, gnome collecting. *Address:* Church Court Chambers, Second Floor, Goldsmith Building, Temple, EC4Y 7BL. *T:* (020) 7936 3637. *E:* k.fuadqc@churchcourtchambers.co.uk.

FUGARD, Athol; playwright, director, actor; *b* 11 June 1932; *s* of Harold David Fugard and Elizabeth Magdalene Potgieter; *m* 1956, Sheila Meiring; one *d. Educ:* Univ. of Cape Town. Directed earliest plays, Nongogo, No Good Friday, Johannesburg, 1960; acted in The Blood Knot, touring S Africa, 1961; Hello and Goodbye, 1965; directed and acted in The Blood Knot, London, 1966; Boesman and Lena, S Africa, 1969; directed Boesman and Lena, London, 1971; directed Serpent Players in various prodns, Port Elizabeth, from 1963, directed co-authors John Kani and Winston Ntshona in Sizwe Bansi is Dead, SA, 1972, The Island, 1973, and London, 1973–74; acted in film, Boesman and Lena, 1972; directed and acted in Statements after an Arrest under the Immorality Act, in SA, 1972, directed in London, 1973; wrote Dimetos for Edinburgh Fest., 1975; directed and acted in, A Lesson from Aloes, SA, 1978, London, 1980 (directed, NY 1981, winning NY Critics Circle Award for Best Play); directed: Master Harold and the Boys, NY, 1982 (Drama Desk Award), Johannesburg, 1983, Nat. Theatre, 1983 (Standard award for Best Play); The Road to Mecca, Yale Repertory Theatre, 1984; (also wrote) My Children! My Africa!, NY, 1990; (also wrote) Playland, SA, 1992, NY and London, 1993; (also wrote and acted in) Valley Song, Royal Court, 1996; (also wrote and acted in) The Captain's Tiger, NY, 1999, London, 2000; (also wrote) Sorrows and Rejoicings, London, 2002; Exits and Entrances, LA, 2004; Victory, SA, 2006; Coming Home, 2009; The Train Driver, SA, 2010; (also wrote) The Painted Rocks at Revolver Creek, 2015. Hon. DLitt: Natal, 1981; Rhodes, 1983; Cape Town, 1984; Emory, 1992; Port Elizabeth, 1993; Hon. DFA Yale, 1983; Hon. DHL Georgetown, 1984. *Films:* Boesman and Lena, 1973; The Guest, 1977; (acted in) Meetings with Remarkable Men (dir, Peter Brook), 1979; (wrote and acted in) Marigolds in August (Silver Bear Award, Berlin), 1980; (acted in) Gandhi, 1982; (co-dir and acted in) Road to Mecca, 1991. Adjunct Prof. of Playwriting, Acting and Directing, Univ. of Calif, San Diego. *Publications:* The Blood Knot, 1962; People Are Living There, Hello and Goodbye, 1973; Boesman and Lena, 1973; (jtly) Three Port Elizabeth Plays: Sizwe Bansi is Dead, The Island, Statements after an Arrest under the Immorality Act, 1974; Tsotsi (novel), 1980 (also USA) (filmed 2005); A Lesson from Aloes, 1981 (also USA); Master Harold and the Boys, US 1982, UK 1983; Notebooks 1960–1977, 1983 (also USA); Road to Mecca, 1985; A Place with the Pigs, 1988; Cousins: a memoir, 1994. *Recreations:* angling, skin-diving, bird-watching. *Address:* c/o ICM Partners, 730 5th Avenue, New York, NY 10019, USA.

FUGGER, Prof. Lars, MD, PhD, DMSc; Professor of Neuroimmunology, University of Oxford, since 2007; Fellow of Oriel College, Oxford, since 2007; Honorary Consultant, Department of Clinical Immunology, John Radcliffe Hospital, Oxford, since 2003; *b* Copenhagen, 15 Aug. 1960; *s* of Henrik Fugger and Inger Fugger; *m* 1991, Astrid Kristine Nagel Iversen, MD, PhD; two *s* two *d. Educ:* Rungsted Gymnasium (BA Maths 1979); Univ. of Copenhagen (MD 1987; PhD 1990, DMSc 1993). Internships and residencies, various hosps, Denmark, 1987–90; Postdoctoral Fellow, Dept of Microbiol. and Immunol., Stanford Univ., 1990–94; Clin. Fellow, Dept of Clin. Immunol., Rigshospitalet, Copenhagen Univ. Hosp., 1994–96; Prof. of Clin. Immunology, Aarhus Univ. Hosp., 1996–; Sen. Clin. Fellow, MRC Human Immunol. Unit, Weatherall Inst. of Molecular Medicine, John Radcliffe Hosp., Oxford, 2002–07; Prof. of Clin. Immunol., Univ. of Oxford, 2004–. Chm., Danish MRC, 2007–. Mem. Bd of Dirs, Novo Nordisk Foundn, Denmark, 2013–. FMedSci 2010. Gold Medal, Univ. of Aarhus, 1985; Anders Jahre Nordic Med. Res. Prize for young scientists, 1998; Descartes Prize, EC, 2002; August Krogh Prize, Danish Med. Soc., 2003; Award for Excellence in Clin. Sci., Eur. Soc. of Clin. Investigation, 2005; Sobek Internat. Res. Prize, Sobek Foundn, Germany, 2009; MS Res. of Year Award, MS Soc. (UK), 2012. Knight, Order of Dannebrog (Denmark), 2011. *Address:* Department of Clinical Neurology and MRC Human Immunology Unit, Weatherall Institute of Molecular Medicine, John Radcliffe Hospital, University of Oxford, Oxford OX3 9DS. *T:* (01865) 222351, *Fax:* (01865) 222502. *E:* lars.fugger@imm.ox.ac.uk.

FUHR, Michael John, CBE 2012 (OBE 1999); Commercial Advisor (formerly Director), Department for Transport, since 2003; Chairman, ITSO Ltd, since 2011; *b* 5 June 1949; *s* of late Max Fuhr and of Betty Fuhr (*née* Neuman); *m* 1975, Susan Harrington; two *d. Educ:* Bradford Grammar Sch.; Univ. of Surrey (BSc Hons 1973). Admin. trainee, 1974, Principal, 1978, DoE; Department of Transport, then DETR, subseq. DTLR, 1979–2001; Asst Sec., 1989; Project Dir, Channel Tunnel Rail Link, 1996–99; Dir, London Underground Task Gp, 1999–2001; Dir of Corporate Strategy, Treasury Solicitor's Dept, 2001–03. Dir, Cross London Rail Links Ltd, 2004–09. Mem. Council, Univ. of Sussex, 2009–. *Recreations:* most sports, photography, technology, following the variable fortunes of Bradford City AFC. *Address:* Department for Transport, 33 Horseferry Road, SW1P 4DR.

FUJII, Hiroaki; Chairman, Mori Arts Center, Tokyo, since 2004; Senior Executive Adviser, Mori Building, since 2004; Adviser, Japan Foundation, Tokyo, since 2003 (President, 1997–2003); *b* 21 Aug. 1933; *m* 1963, Kiyoko Shimoda; three *d. Educ:* Tokyo Univ.; Amherst Coll., USA (BA 1958). Entered Min. of Foreign Affairs, Japan, 1956; Dir, Econ. Affairs Div., UN Bureau, 1971–72; Private Sec. to Minister for Foreign Affairs, 1972–74; Dir, 2nd Econ. Co-operation Div., Econ. Co-operation Bureau, 1974–75; Dir, 1st N American Div., American Affairs Bureau, 1975–76; Fellow, Center for Internat. Affairs, Harvard Univ., 1976; Counsellor, Embassy of Japan, Washington, 1977–79; Ministry of Foreign Affairs: Dir, Personnel Div., Minister's Secretariat, 1979–81; Dep. Dir Gen., Asian Affairs Bureau, 1981–83; Consul-Gen., Hong Kong, 1983–85; Ministry of Foreign Affairs: Dir Gen., N American Bureau, 1985–88; Dep. Vice-Minister, 1988–89; Ambassador to: OECD, Paris, 1989–92; Thailand, 1992–94; Court of St James's, 1994–97. Hon. DCL: Durham, 1997; UEA, 1999; Hon. LLD Birmingham, 1997. Kt Grand Cross (1st Cl.), Most Exalted Order of White Elephant (Thailand), 1994. *Address:* Mori Arts Center, Roppongi Hills Mori Tower, 6–10–1 Roppongi, Minato-ku, Tokyo 106–6150, Japan. *T:* (3) 64066133, *Fax:* (3) 64066518.

FULBROOK, Prof. Mary Jean Alexandra, PhD; FRHistS; FBA 2007; Professor of German History, since 1995, and Dean, Faculty of Social and Historical Sciences and Director, European Institute, since 2013, University College London; *b* 28 Nov. 1951; *d* of Prof. Arthur J. C. Wilson and Dr Harriett C. Wilson (*née* Friedeberg); *m* 1973, Dr Julian Fulbrook; two *s* one *d. Educ:* Sidcot Sch., Somerset; King Edward VI High Sch., Birmingham; Newnham Coll., Cambridge (BA 1973 Double 1st Cl. Hons; Schol., Sen. Schol., Helen Gladstone Meml Schol.; MA 1977); Harvard Univ. (AM 1975; PhD 1979). FRHistS 1987. Harvard Center for European Studies Krupp Fellow, LSE, 1976–77; Temporary Lecturer: LSE, 1977–78; Brunel Univ., 1978–79; Lady Margaret Res. Fellow, New Hall, Cambridge, 1979–82; Res. Associate, KCL, 1982–83; University College London: Lectr, 1983–91, Reader, 1991–95, in German Hist.; Dir, Centre for European Studies, 1991–2010; Hd, German Dept, 1995–2006; Mem., Council, 2003–07; Vice-Dean (Inter-Disciplinarity), Faculty of Arts and Humanities, 2010–13. Vis. Fellow, Forschungsschwerpunkt Zeithistorische Studien, Potsdam, 1994; Vis. Bye-Fellow, Newnham Coll., Cambridge, 1994; Vis. Prof., Univ. of Jena, 2013. Jt Founding Ed., German History, 1984–94. Member: Jt Cttee on W Europe of ACLS/SSRC, 1990–94; Adv. Bd, German Historical Inst., London, 2003–; AHRC (formerly AHRB) Res. Panel for Hist., 2004–07; Adv. Bd, Stiftung Gedenkstätten Buchenwald und Mittelbau-Dora, 2007–; Adv. Bd, Bundeskanzler-Willy-Brandt-Stiftung, 2008–. Chm., German Hist. Soc., 1996–99. Vice-Chairman of Governors: Great Ormond Street Hosp. Sch. for Sick Children, 1980–85; Haverstock Sch., 1999–2001; Chm. Govs, S Camden Community Sch., 1992–94. Mayoress, London Bor. of Camden, 1985–86. *Publications:* Piety and Politics: religion and the rise of absolutism in England, Württemberg and Prussia, 1983; A Concise History of Germany, 1990, 2nd edn 2004 (trans. Hungarian, Spanish, Swedish, Korean, Romanian, Chinese, Japanese); The Divided Nation: Germany 1918–1990, 1991 (trans. Italian), 3rd edn as A History of Germany 1918–2008: the divided nation, 2008; The Two Germanies 1945–1990: problems of interpretation, 1992, 2nd edn as Interpretations of the Two Germanies 1945–1990, 2000; (ed) National Histories and European History, 1993; Anatomy of a Dictatorship: inside the GDR 1949–89, 1995; (ed with D. Cesarani) Citizenship, Nationality and Migration in Europe, 1996; (ed with J. Breuilly) German History since 1800, 1997; German National Identity after the Holocaust, 1999 (trans. Hungarian); (ed) The Short Oxford History of Europe 1945–2000, 2000 (trans. Spanish and Polish); (ed with M. Swales) Representing the German Nation, 2000; (ed) Twentieth-century Germany: politics, culture and society 1918–1990, 2001; Historical Theory, 2002; Hitler, Book 1, 2004, Book 2, 2005; The People's State: East German Society from Hitler to Honecker, 2005 (trans. German 2008); (ed) Uncivilising Processes? Excess and Transgression in German Society and Culture, 2006; (ed) Power and Society in the GDR, 1961–1979, 2009; Dissonant Lives: generations and violence through the German dictatorships, 2011; A Small Town near Auschwitz: ordinary Nazis and the Holocaust, 2012 (Fraenkel Prize, Weiner Liby for Study of Holocaust and Genocide); (ed with A. Port) Becoming East German: socialist structures and sensibilities after Hitler, 2013; numerous articles in jls and chapters in books. *Recreations:* swimming, jogging (London marathon 2002), reading novels, spending time with my family. *Address:* Department of German, University College London, Gower Street, WC1E 6BT. *T:* (020) 7679 7120. *E:* m.fulbrook@ucl.ac.uk.

FÜLE, Štefan; Member, European Commission, 2010–14; *b* Sokolov, 24 May 1962; *m* Hana; one *s* two *d. Educ:* Charles Univ., Prague; Moscow State Inst. of Internat. Relns. Desk Officer, UN Dept, Czechoslovakian Min. of Foreign Affairs, 1987–90; First Sec., Czechoslovakian, subseq. Czech Perm. Delegn to the UN, 1990–95; Mem., Czech Delegn, and Alternate Rep. to UN Security Council, 1994–95; Czech Ministry of Foreign Affairs: Dir, UN Dept, 1995–96; Dir, Security Policy Dept, 1996–98; Ambassador to Lithuania, 2000–01; First Dep. Defence Minister, 2001–02; Ambassador to the UK, 2003–05; Perm. Rep. to NATO, 2005–09; Eur. Affairs Minister, 2009.

FULFORD, Rt Hon. Sir Adrian Bruce, Kt 2002; PC 2013; **Rt Hon. Lord Justice Fulford;** a Lord Justice of Appeal, since 2013; Senior Presiding Judge of England and Wales, from Jan. 2016 (Deputy Senior Presiding Judge, 2015); Judge in charge of Technology, since 2014; *b* 8 Jan. 1953; *s* of Gerald John Fulford and Marie Bettine (*née* Stevens). *Educ:* Elizabeth Coll., Guernsey; Southampton Univ. (BA Hons). Housing Advr, Shelter's Housing Aid Centre, 1974–75; called to the Bar, Middle Temple, 1978, Bencher, 2002; QC 1994; a Recorder, 2001–02; a Judge of the High Ct, QBD, 2002–13; a Judge of the Internat. Criminal Ct, The Hague, 2003–12 (Pres., Trial Div., 2008–12; Presiding Judge, Trial Chamber I, 2007–12); a Presiding Judge, S Eastern Circuit, 2010–13. Ed., UK Human Rights Reports, 2000–. Hon. DLaws Southampton, 2011. *Publications:* (contrib.) Atkin's Court Forms, 1987; (ed) Archbold Criminal Pleading and Practice, 1992; (jtly) A Criminal Practitioner's Guide to Judicial Review and Case Stated, 1999; (jtly) Judicial Review: a practical guide, 2004; (ed jtly) Archbold International Criminal Courts, 2005, 4th edn 2014. *Recreations:* riding, golf. *Address:* Royal Courts of Justice, Strand, WC2A 2LL. *Club:* Garrick.

FULFORD, Prof. Michael Gordon, CBE 2011; PhD; FSA; FBA 1994; Professor of Archaeology, University of Reading, since 1993; *b* 20 Oct. 1948; *s* of Comdr E. G. J. D. Fulford, RN (retd) and E. Z. Fulford (*née* Simpson); *m* 1972, Charlotte Jane Hobbs; one *s* one *d. Educ:* St Edwards Sch., Oxford; Univ. of Southampton (BA Hons 1970; PhD 1975). DES Res. Student, 1970; Research Assistant: Univ. of Southampton, 1971–72; Univ. of Oxford, 1972–74; University of Reading: Lectr in Archaeol., 1974–85; Reader, 1985–88; Leverhulme Res. Fellow, 1987; Personal Prof., 1988–93; Dean, Faculty of Letters and Social Scis, 1994–97; Pro-Vice-Chancellor, 1998–2004; Leverhulme Major Res. Fellow, 2004–07. Chm., Archaeol. Panel, RAE 2001, Main Panel H, RAE 2008, HEFCE. Dalrymple Lectr, Glasgow Univ., 1996. Pres., Soc. for Promotion of Roman Studies, 2005–08 (Vice-Pres., 2008–; Editor, Britannia, 1994–99); Chm., Roman Res. Trust, 2008–. Historic England (formerly English Heritage): Chm., Hadrian's Wall Adv. Panel, 1989–97 (Mem., 1985–97); Mem., Ancient Monuments Adv. Cttee, 1991–97; Comr, 2014–; Chm., Adv. Cttee, 2014–; Comr, RCHM, 1993–99; Member: Archaeology Adv. Cttee, Nat. Mus. of Wales, 1991–99; SE Mus., Library and Archive Council, 2002–06. Vice-President: Royal Archaeol Inst., 1996–2001; British Acad., 2006– (Mem. Council, 2003–; Mem., Humanities Res. Bd, 1995–98; Chm., Acad.-Sponsored Insts and Socs Cttee, 2005–10; Treas., 2010–15); Member: Council, British Sch. at Rome, 2003–05; Sen. Academic Promotions Cttee, Univ. of Cambridge, 2008–14. Chm., Aimhigher, Berks, 2004. FSA 1977. *Publications:* New Forest Roman Pottery, 1975; (with B. Cunliffe) CSIR Great Britain I: Bath and the Rest of Wessex, 1982; Silchester Defences, 1984; (with D. Peacock) Excavations at Carthage: The British Mission, The Pottery and other Ceramics, Vol. 1, 1984, Vol. 2, 1994; The Silchester Amphitheatre, 1989; Excavations at Sabratha 1948–1951, Vol. 2, pt i (ed with M. Hall), 1989, pt ii (ed with R. Tomber), 1994; (ed jtly) Developing Landscape of Lowland Britain: the archaeology of the British gravels, 1992; (ed jtly) England's Coastal Heritage, 1997; (with J. R. Timby) Late Iron Age and Roman Silchester: excavations on the site of the Forum-Basilica 1977 and 1980–86, 2000; (jtly) Life and Labour in Late Roman Silchester: excavations in Insula IX since 1997, 2006; (jtly) Iron Age and Romano-British Settlements and Landscapes of Salisbury Plain, 2006; (jtly) Silchester: city in transition, 2011; (jtly) Pevensey Castle, Sussex, 2011; (ed) Silchester and the Study of Romano-British Urbanism, 2012; (jtly) A Late Roman Town House and its Environs, 2014. *Recreations:* music, walking, sailing. *Address:* Department of Archaeology, University of Reading, PO Box 227, Reading, Berks RG6 6AB. *T:* (0118) 378 8048.

FULFORD-DOBSON, Captain Michael, CVO 1999; OBE 2008; JP; RN; Lord-Lieutenant of Dorset, 1999–2006; *b* 6 April 1931; *e s* of late Lt-Col Cyril Fulford-Dobson, OBE and Betty Bertha Fulford-Dobson (*née* Bendelack-Hudson-Barmby); *m* 1966, Elizabeth Barbara Mary Rose Tate; three *d. Educ:* Pangbourne Coll.; RN Coll., Dartmouth; RN Coll., Greenwich. Royal Navy, 1949–84 (served Korean War, Suez Operation, first Cod War; 3 Sea Comds); Gentleman Usher to the Queen, 1985–99, Extra Gentleman Usher, 1999–. Chm., W Dorset Hosps NHS Trust, 1991–98. Chm., Dorset Trust, 1991–2000; President: Dorset Br., CPRE, 1995–2008; Dorset Natural History and Archaeol Soc., 2010–14; Dorset Health Trust, 2011–; Poole Maritime Trust, 2013–; Trustee, Cancer Care Dorset, 1998–2007; Patron: Bournemouth Natural Sci. Soc., 1999–2006; Community Foundn for Dorset (formerly for Bournemouth, Dorset and Poole), 2000–; Bournemouth Soc. for Visually Impaired, 2001–; Pres., Dorset Scout Council, 2002–. Dir, In and Out Ltd, 1993–96. Member of Court: Exeter Univ., 1999–2007; Southampton Univ., 1999–2007; Governor, Sherborne Sch., 1999–2007. Patron, Dorset Yeomanry, 2002–. Church Warden, St Mary's Cerne Abbas, 1992–2012. High Sheriff of Dorset, 1994–95; DL 1995, JP 1999, Dorset. KStJ 1999 (Pres., St John Council for Dorset, 1999–2006). Hon. Dr Arts Bournemouth, 2007. *Recreations:* restoration of historic buildings, field sports. *Address:* Cerne Abbey, Dorset DT2 7JQ. *T:* (01300) 341284, *T:* and *Fax:* (01300) 341948. *E:* cerneabbey@talktalk.net. *Club:* White's.

See also Viscount FitzHarris.

FULHAM, Bishop Suffragan of, since 2013; **Rt Rev. Jonathan Mark Richard Baker;** Guild Vicar, St Andrew Holborn, since 2015; *b* 6 Oct. 1966; *s* of Sir John William Baker, *qv*; *m* 1992, Jacqueline Norton (marr. diss. 2013); two *s* one *d*; *m* 2015, Susie Page. *Educ:* Merchant Taylors' Sch., Northwood; St John's Coll., Oxford (BA 1988, MPhil 1990, MA (Eng. Lit.)); St Stephen's House, Oxford (BA Theol. 1992). Ordained deacon, 1993, priest, 1994; Asst Curate, All Saints, Ascot Heath, 1993–96; Priest i/c, 1996–99, Vicar, 1999–2003, Holy Trinity, Reading and St Mark, Reading; Principal, Pusey House, Oxford, 2003–13; Asst

Curate, St Thomas with St Frideswide, Oxford, 2008–11; Asst Bishop, Dioceses of Bath and Wells, Lichfield, Worcester, Oxford, and Salisbury, 2011–13; Bishop Suffragan of Ebbsfleet, 2011–13; Guild Vicar, St Dunstan-in-the-West, Fleet Street, 2013–15. Hon. DD Nashotah House, Wisconsin, 2009. *Publications:* (ed) Consecrated Women?, 2004; (ed jtly) Who Is This Man?, 2006. *Recreations:* music, theatre, poetry, crime fiction, continental holidays. *Address:* The Vicarage, 5 St Andrew Street, EC4A 3AF.

FULLBROOK, Lorraine; *b* Glasgow, 28 July 1959; *d* of late Ian and Margo; *m* 1987, Mark Fullbrook. *Educ:* Glasgow Caledonian Univ. Mem. (C) Hart DC, 2000–04 (Leader, 2001–04). Contested (C) S Ribble, 2005. MP (C) S Ribble, 2010–15. Mem., Home Affairs Select Cttee, 2010–15. FRSA.

FULLER, Anne Rosemary, OBE 2000; JP; Vice President, Magistrates' Association, since 1999 (Deputy Chairman of Council, 1993–96, Chairman, 1996–99); *b* 27 Sept. 1936; *d* of Ronald Clifford Dent and Clara Vera Dent (*née* Murray); *m* 1960, John Acland Fuller (*d* 2006); two *s* one *d*. *Educ:* St Anne's Sch., Windermere; Royal Holloway Coll., Univ. of London (BA Hons 1957); KCL and LSE (Dip. in Law 1992). Market Research Executive: McCann Erickson, then Marplan, 1958–60; Bureau of Commercial Research, 1960–65; freelance market res. consultant, 1965–. Member: Nat. Forum, SCAA, 1996–97; Home Secretary's Task Force on Youth Justice, 1997–98; Compliance and Supervision Cttee, Office for Supervision of Solicitors, 1998–2001; Sentencing Adv. Panel, 2000–10; Adjudication Panel: Law Soc., 2001–07; SRA, 2007–08; Tribunal Mem., Disciplinary Cttee, 2000–09, Review Panel, 2009–, ICAEW. Dir and Trustee, Soc. of Voluntary Associates, 2000–04. Asst Hosp. Manager, Priory Hosp., Roehampton, 2010–14. JP Kingston-upon-Thames, 1975 (Dep. Chm., 1991–95); Chm., Betting Licensing Cttee, 1986–89; Mem., Magistrates' Courts Cttee, 1987–96; Chm., Youth Panel, 1990–93; Vice Pres., Magistrates' Assoc., 1999– (Mem. Council, 1984–; Vice Chm., Sentencing Cttee, 1991–93); Mem., Magistrates' Courts Consultative Council, 1993–99 (Mem., Trial Issues Gp, 1996–99); Nat. Co-ordinator, Magistrates in Community Project, 1993–97. Mem., Chatham House, RIIA, 2009–. FRSA 1997. *Publications:* (ed jtly) International Directory of Market Research Organisations, 1974, 11th edn 1994; numerous articles on magisterial matters. *Recreations:* music, theatre, cookery, international affairs, travel. *Address:* 41 Savery Drive, Long Ditton, Surrey KT6 5RJ. *T:* (020) 8224 5308.

FULLER, Brian Leslie, CBE 1989; QFSM 1981; Commandant Chief Executive, Fire Service College, 1990–94; *b* 18 April 1936; *s* of Walter Leslie Victor Fuller and Eliza May Fuller; *m* 1957, Linda Peters; three *s*. *Educ:* St Albans County Grammar Sch. for Boys. FIFireE 1975. Station Officer: Herts Fire Brigade, 1960–66; Warwicks Fire Brigade, 1966–68; Asst Divl Officer, Notts Fire Brigade, 1968–69; Divl Commander, Essex Fire Brigade, 1969–72; Dep. Chief Fire Officer, Glamorgan Fire Brigade, 1972–74; Chief Fire Officer: Mid Glamorgan Fire Brigade, 1974–80; Notts Fire Brigade, 1980–81; W Midlands Fire Service, 1981–90. Gen. Manager and Principal, Fire Safety Engrg Coll., Oman, 1997–2001; Chm., BFA Devels Internat., 2001–04. Mem. (C), Bromsgrove DC, 2003–07. Hon. DSc South Bank, 1993. *Recreations:* cricket, music, reading. *Address:* Newlands, Aqueduct Lane, Alvechurch, Birmingham B48 7BP.

FULLER, Prof. Christopher John, PhD; FBA 2007; formerly Professor of Anthropology, London School of Economics and Political Science. *Educ:* Peterhouse, Cambridge (BA 1970; PhD 1974). Specialist on anthropology of India; fieldwork: Nayars and Syrian Christians, Kerala, 1971–72; Temple of Madurai, Tamilnadu, 1976–2001; ESRC research projects: on regionalism, nationalism and globalisation in India, 2003–05; on Tamil Brahman community, 2005–08. *Publications:* Servants of the Goddess: the priests of a South Indian temple, 1991; (with V. Bénéï) The Everyday State and Society in Modern India, 2001; The Renewal of the Priesthood: modernity and traditionalism in a South Indian temple, 2003; The Camphor Flame: popular Hinduism and Indian society, 2004; (ed with J. Assayag) Globalizing India: perspectives from below, 2005; contribs to jls incl. Contribs to Indian Sociol., Anthropol. Today, Social Anthropol., Modern Asian Studies, Econ. and Political Weekly, Comparative Studies in Society and Hist. *Address:* c/o Department of Anthropology, London School of Economics and Political Science, Houghton Street, WC2A 2AE.

FULLER, Eleanor Mary, OBE 2013; JP; HM Diplomatic Service, retired; Director of Advocacy and Commonwealth Engagement, Queen Elizabeth Diamond Jubilee Trust, since 2013; *b* Aldershot, 31 Dec. 1953; *d* of Peter and Ruth Breedon; *m* 1984, Simon William John Fuller, *qv*; three *s*. *Educ:* Somerville Coll., Oxford (MA Modern Langs). Joined FCO, 1975; FCO, 1975–77; Paris, 1978–81; FCO, 1981–83; on loan to ODA, 1983–86; Second, later First Sec., FCO, 1990–93; UNRWA for Palestine refugees in Near East, Vienna, 1993–96; First Sec., UK Delegn to OSCE, Vienna, 1998–99; First Sec., UK Mission to UN and WTO, Geneva, 2000–04; on loan to DFID, 2004–06; FCO, 2006–07; Perm. Rep. of UK to Council of Europe, Strasbourg, 2007–12; FCO, 2012. JP SE London 2014. *Recreations:* gardens, music. *Address:* Queen Elizabeth Diamond Jubilee Trust, 128 Buckingham Palace Road, SW1W 9SA. *E:* eleanor.fuller@qejubileetrust.org.

See also T. J. Breedon.

FULLER, Geoffrey Herbert, CEng, FRINA, FIMarEST; RCNC; defence and maritime consultant; Director, British Maritime Technology Ltd, Teddington, 1985–2000 (Deputy Chairman, 1985–95); *b* 16 Jan. 1927; *s* of late Major Herbert Thomas Fuller and Clarice Christine Fuller; *m* 1952, Pamela-Maria Quarrell (*d* 2008); one *d*. *Educ:* Merchant Taylors', Northwood, Middx; Royal Naval Engrg Coll., Keyham; Royal Naval Coll., Greenwich. FRINA 1965; FIMarEST (FIMarE 1974). Constructor Commander: Staff of Flag Officer (Submarines), 1958; British Navy Staff, Washington, 1960; RCDS, 1973; Support Manager Submarines, 1976; Dep. Dir, Submarines/Polaris, Ship Dept, MoD, 1979; Dir of Naval Ship Production, 1981–82; Dir, Manpower and Productivity, HM Dockyards, 1982–83; Mem. Bd, and Man. Dir, Warship Div., British Shipbuilders, 1983–85; Exec. Chm., 1984–86, Technical Adviser, 1986–87, Vickers Shipbuilding and Engrg Ltd, Barrow. Vice-Pres., RINA, 2004–07 (Chm. Council, 1994–96; Treas., 1999–2004). FRSA 1995. *Address:* Room 15, Oakfield, Weston Park, Bath BA1 4AS. *T:* (01225) 466054. *E:* casafuller@btinternet.com.

FULLER, Sir James (Henry Fleetwood), 4th Bt *cr* 1910, of Neston Park, Corsham, Wiltshire; manager, Neston Park; *b* 1 Nov. 1970; *e s* of Major Sir John William Fleetwood Fuller, 3rd Bt and of Lorna Marian (*née* Kemp-Potter); *S* father, 1998; *m* 2000, Venetia, *d* of Col Robin Mactaggart; two *s*. *Educ:* Milton Abbey Sch. Commnd The Life Guards, 1991; Belize, 1993; Bosnia, 1994; Knightsbridge, 1995–98; with Fuller Smith & Turner plc, 1998–2003 (non-exec. Dir, 2010–). *Heir: s* Archie Mungo Fleetwood Fuller, *b* 7 Aug. 2001. *Address:* Neston Park, Corsham, Wiltshire SN13 9TG. *T:* (01225) 810211.

FULLER, John Leopold, FRSL 1980; writer; Fellow of Magdalen College, Oxford, and Tutor in English, 1966–2002, now Fellow Emeritus; *b* 1 Jan. 1937; *s* of late Roy Broadbent Fuller, CBE, FRSL; *m* 1960, Cicely Prudence Martin; three *d*. *Educ:* St Paul's School; New Coll., Oxford (BLitt, MA). Vis. Lectr, State Univ. of NY at Buffalo, 1962–63; Asst Lectr, Univ. of Manchester, 1963–66. *Publications:* Fairground Music, 1961; The Tree that Walked, 1967; A Reader's Guide to W. H. Auden, 1970; The Sonnet, 1972; Cannibals and Missionaries, 1972, and Epistles to Several Persons, 1973 (Geoffrey Faber Meml Prize, 1974); Squeaking Crust, 1973; The Last Bid, 1975; The Mountain in the Sea, 1975; Lies and Secrets, 1979; The Illusionists (Southern Arts Lit. Prize), 1980; The Extraordinary Wool Mill and other stories, 1980; Waiting for the Music, 1982; Flying to Nowhere (Whitbread Prize for a First Novel), 1983; The Beautiful Inventions, 1983; (ed) The Dramatic Works of John Gay, 1983; Come Aboard and Sail Away, 1983; The Adventures of Speedfall, 1985; Selected Poems 1954–1982, 1985; (with James Fenton) Partingtime Hall, 1986; Tell It Me Again, 1988; The Grey Among the Green, 1988; The Burning Boys, 1989; (ed) The Chatto Book of Love Poetry, 1990; The Mechanical Body, 1991; Look Twice, 1991; The Worm and the Star, 1993; Stones and Fires, 1996 (Forward Prize, Forward Poetry Trust, 1997); Collected Poems, 1996; A Skin Diary, 1997; W. H. Auden: a commentary, 1998; (ed) The Oxford Book of Sonnets, 2000; The Memoirs of Laetitia Horsepole, 2001; Now and for a Time, 2002; Ghosts, 2004; Flawed Angel, 2005; The Space of Joy, 2006; Song & Dance, 2008; Pebble & I, 2010; (with David Hurn) Writing the Picture, 2010; Who is Ozymandias? and other Puzzles in Poetry, 2011; Dream Hunter (chamber opera libretto), 2011; New Selected Poems 1983–2008, 2012; Sketches from the Sierra de Tejeda, 2013; The Dice Cup, 2014; You're Having Me On, 2014. *Recreations:* correspondence chess, music. *Address:* Magdalen College, Oxford OX1 4AU.

FULLER, Jonathan Paul; QC 2002; **His Honour Judge Fuller;** a Circuit Judge, since 2014; *b* 27 Feb. 1954; *s* of Edward and Joan Fuller; *m* 1988, Karon J. Quinn; two *s* one *d*. *Educ:* Ampleforth; Liverpool Poly. (LLB Lond. (ext.)); Inns of Court Sch. of Law. Called to the Bar, Lincoln's Inn, 1977; a Recorder, 1999–2014. *Address:* Courts of Justice, Deansleigh Road, Bournemouth, Dorset BH7 7DS.

FULLER, Rev. Canon Dr Michael Jeremy; Teaching Fellow, New College, Edinburgh, since 2014; *b* 7 Jan. 1963; *s* of Peter Roy Fuller and Mary Eileen Fuller; *m* 1993, Sue Rigby; two *s*. *Educ:* King Edward VI Grammar Sch., Chelmsford; Worcester Coll., Oxford (BA 1985, MA 1989; DPhil 1989); Westcott House and Queens' Coll., Cambridge (BA 1991). Ordained deacon 1992, priest 1993; Curate, All Saints', High Wycombe, 1992–95; Associate Rector, St John's, Princes Street, Edinburgh, 1995–99; Theological Institute of Scottish Episcopal Church: Pantonian Prof., 2000–14; Principal, 2000–02; Initial Ministerial Educn Officer, 2002–04; Provincial Ministerial Develt Officer, 2004–14. Canon, 2000–14, Hon. Canon, 2015–, St Mary's Cathedral, Edinburgh. Chair, Science and Religion Forum, 2013–. Hon. Vis. Fellow, New Coll., Edinburgh, 1998–2014; Hon. Vis. Fellow, Univ. of Glasgow, 2008–. Vice Pres. for Publications, Eur. Soc. for Study of Sci. and Theol., 2014–. *Publications:* Atoms and Icons, 1995; Matter and Meaning, 2010; Is Religion Natural?, 2012; Inspiration in Science and Religion, 2012; The Concept of the Soul, 2014; What is Life?, 2015; articles and reviews in Theology, Modern Believing, New Blackfriars, Musical Times, Wagner Jl, etc. *Recreations:* opera, reading, walking. *Address:* New College, Mound Place, Edinburgh EH1 2LX. *Club:* New (Edinburgh).

FULLER, Michael John; Director and Chief Executive Officer, Bank of Kuwait and Middle East, 2003–06; *b* 20 July 1932; *s* of Thomas Frederick and Irene Emily Fuller; *m* 1st, 1955, Maureen Rita Slade (marr. diss. 1989); two *s* two *d*; 2nd, 1990, Elizabeth Frost. *Educ:* Wallington County Grammar Sch. FCIB 1980. National Service, commnd RAF, 1950–52. Midland Bank, 1948–90: various branch, regl and head office posts; Gp Public Affairs Advr, 1977–79; Regl Dir, Southampton, 1979–81; Gen. Manager, Midland and Wales, 1981–82; Gen. Manager, Business Develt Div., 1982–85; UK Operations Dir, 1985–87; Dep. Chief Exec., 1987–89, Chief Exec., 1989–90, UK Banking Sector; Gen. Man., Nat. Bank of Abu Dhabi, 1991–92; Dir and CEO, Al Ahli Commercial Bank BSC, subseq. Ahli United Bank (Bahrain) BSC(c), 1992–2002. Chm., ais>BrandLab, 2007–08. *Recreations:* reading, travelling. *Club:* Royal Air Force.

FULLER, Richard; MP (C) Bedford, since 2010; *b* Bedford. *Educ:* University Coll., Oxford (BA); Harvard Business Sch. (MBA). Former Partner: technol. venture capital firm; mgt consultancy. Contested (C) Bedford, 2005. Nat. Chm., Young Conservatives, 1985–87. *Address:* House of Commons, SW1A 0AA.

FULLER, Simon; Founder, XIX Entertainment Ltd, 2010; Co-founder, XIX Globosport, 2013; Founder and Chief Executive Officer, 19 Entertainment Ltd, 1985–2010; *b* 17 May 1960; *m* 2008, Natalie Swanston. Chrysalis Music, 1981–85; founder of 19 Entertainment, comprising management, merchandising, music recording and TV production operations; manager of artists incl. Annie Lennox, Cathy Dennis, Spice Girls, Emma Bunton, S Club 7, Will Young, Gareth Gates, David and Victoria Beckham, Carrie Underwood, Adam Lambert, Andy Murray, Daughtry, Lisa Marie Presley, Roland Mouret, Lewis Hamilton. Dir, CKX, 2005–09. Creator and producer, TV series, Pop Idol, 2001, American Idol, 2002–10, So You Think You Can Dance, 2005–10, If I Can Dream, 2010; exec. producer, Bel Ami (film), 2011.

FULLER, Simon William John, CMG 1994; HM Diplomatic Service, retired; UK Permanent Representative to the Office of the United Nations and other international organisations, Geneva, 2000–03; *b* 27 Nov. 1943; *s* of late Rowland William Bevis Fuller and Madeline Fuller (*née* Bailey); *m* 1984, Eleanor Mary Breedon (*see* E. M. Fuller); three *s*. *Educ:* Wellington College; Emmanuel College, Cambridge (BA Hist.). Served Singapore and Kinshasa, 1969–73; First Sec., Cabinet Office, 1973–75; FCO, 1975–77; UK Mission to UN, New York, 1977–80; FCO, 1980–86 (Counsellor, 1984); Dep. Hd of Mission, Tel Aviv, 1986–90; Hd of NE and N African Dept, FCO, 1990–93; Hd of UK Delegn to CSCE, then OSCE, Vienna, 1993–99. *Recreation:* cooking. *Address:* 27 Carlisle Mansions, Carlisle Place, SW1P 1EZ. *T:* (020) 7828 5484. *Clubs:* Brooks's, MCC.

FULLERTON, Hance, OBE 1995; Chairman: Grampian University Hospitals NHS Trust, 1996–2002; Angle plc (formerly AngleTechnology Ltd), 1996–2007; *b* 6 Dec. 1934; *s* of late Robert Fullerton and Jessie Fullerton (*née* Smith); *m* 1958, Jeannie Reid Cowie; three *d*. *Educ:* Anderson Educnl Inst., Lerwick; Aberdeen Univ. (BSc). Technical, prodn and operational mgt in paper industry, 1958–78; Gen. Manager, Aberdeen, 1978–81, Divl Dir, 1981–86, Wiggins Teape Ltd; Gen. Manager, Grampian Health Bd, 1986–91; Chief Exec., Grampian Enterprise Ltd, 1991–96. Chairman: Aberdeen Univ. Res. and Industrial Services Ltd, 1996–2000; Cordah Ltd, 1996–99. Hon. LLD Aberdeen, 1996. *Recreations:* golf, walking, reading, theatre.

FULLERTON, William Hugh, CMG 1989; HM Diplomatic Service, retired; Ambassador to Morocco and Mauritania, 1996–99; *b* 11 Feb. 1939; *s* of late Major Arthur Hugh Theodore Francis Fullerton, RAMC, and of Mary (*née* Parker); *m* 1968, Arlene Jacobowitz; one *d*. *Educ:* Cheltenham Coll.; Queens' Coll., Cambridge (MA Oriental Langs). Shell Internat. Petroleum Co., Uganda, 1963–65; FO, 1965; MECAS, Shemlan, Lebanon, 1965–66; Information Officer, Jedda, 1966–67; UK Mission to UN, New York, 1967; FCO, 1968–70; Head of Chancery, Kingston, Jamaica (also accredited to Haiti), 1970–73, and Ankara, 1973–77; FCO, 1977–80; Counsellor (Economic and Commercial), 1980–83 and Consul-Gen., 1981–83, Islamabad; Ambassador to Somalia, 1983–87; on loan to MoD, 1987–88; Gov., Falkland Is, and Comr for S Georgia and S Sandwich Is, 1988–92; High Comr, British Antarctic Territory, 1988–89; Ambassador to Kuwait, 1992–96. Mem. Adv. Bd, Intrinsic Value Investors LLP, 2011–. Trustee, Arab-British Centre, London, 2002–12 (Dir, 2000–02; Chm., 2002–07). Member: Falkland Is Assoc., 1992–; Friends of Kuwait, 2000–; Life Member: Nat. Trust, 1968; CPRE. Trustee: Soc. for Protection of Animals Abroad, 2000–15; Lord Caradon Lectures Trust, 2004–. Kuwait Medallion, First Class, 1995; Comdr, Ouissam Alaouite (Morocco), 1999. *Recreations:* travelling in remote areas, sailing, reading, walking. *Club:* Travellers.

FULTON, Andrew; *see* Fulton, R. A.

FULTON, Prof. Helen Elizabeth, PhD; FSA, FLSW; Professor of Medieval Literature, University of Bristol, since 2015; *b* Frankston, Vic, 3 June 1952; *d* of Sir Brian (John Maynard)

Tovey, *qv* and Elizabeth Mary Christopher; *m* 1st, 1971, Glenn Richard Fulton (marr. diss. 1985); two *s*; 2nd, 1988, Geraint Gwilym Evans. *Educ:* St Paul's Girls' Sch., Hammersmith, London; Narrabeen Girls' High Sch., Sydney; Univ. of Sydney (BA Hons 1st; PhD 1983); Linacre Coll., Oxford (Dip. Celtic). Postdoctoral Fellow, Univ. of Wales, Aberystwyth, 1985–87; Leverhulme Postdoctoral Fellow, 1987–88; Lectr, 1988–91, Associate Prof., 1991–2005, Univ. of Sydney; Prof. of English, Swansea Univ., 2005–10; Prof. of Medieval Literature, Univ. of York, 2010–15. Vis. Res. Fellow, Corpus Christi Coll., Cambridge, 2003–04; Sen. Vis. Res. Fellow, St John's Coll., Oxford, 2013–14. Mem., Peer Rev. Coll., AHRC, 2007–. Trustee, Swansea Univ. Pension Scheme, 2006–10. FSA 2014; FRSA 2014; FLSW 2015. Ed., Trans of Honourable Soc. of Cymmrodorion, 2007–; Series Ed., New Century Chaucer, 2012–. *Publications:* (ed) Medieval Celtic Literature and Society, 2005; Narrative and Media, 2005; (ed jtly) Medieval Cultural Studies, 2006; Welsh Prophecy and English Politics, 2008; (ed) Companion to Arthurian Literature, 2009, 2nd edn 2012; (ed) Urban Culture in Medieval Wales, 2012. *Recreations:* family, film, theatre, opera, reading, writing, afternoon tea. *Address:* Department of English, University of Bristol, 11 Woodland Road, Bristol BS8 1TB. *T:* (0117) 331 7932. *E:* helenefulton@me.com.

FULTON, Prof. John Francis; Secretary, Northern Ireland Fund for Reconciliation, 1999–2008; *b* 21 Sept. 1933; *s* of Robert Patrick Fulton and Anne Fulton (*née* McCambridge); *m* 1958, Elizabeth Mary Brennan; one *s* one *d*. *Educ:* St Malachy's College, Belfast; QUB (BA 1954, DipEd 1958, MA 1964); Univ. of Keele (PhD 1975). Lectr and Principal Lectr, St Joseph's Coll. of Educn, Belfast, 1961–73; Queen's University of Belfast: Lectr, Inst. of Educn, 1973–76; Prof. and Head of Dept of Educnl Studies, 1977–85; Dir, Sch. of Educn, 1985–93; Pro-Vice-Chancellor, 1987–92; Provost, Legal, Social and Educnl Scis, 1993–97; Dir of Develt, 1997–98; Prof. Emeritus, 1997. Mem., IBA, subseq. ITC, 1987–94. Mem., Trng and Employment Agency, 1993–98; Chairman: Strategy Gp for Health Services R&D, 1999–2003; Central Services Agency, Dept of Health and Social Services and Public Safety, NI, 2004–09 (non-exec. Dir, 1999–2003). FRSA. Hon. LLD QUB, 2000. *Publications:* contribs to: Education in Great Britain and Ireland, 1973; Educational Research and Development in Great Britain, 1982; Willingly to School, 1987; articles in learned jls. *Recreations:* golf, music. *Address:* c/o Queen's University of Belfast BT7 1NN.

FULTON, (Paul) Robert (Anthony); *b* 20 March 1951; *s* of George Alan Fulton and Margaret Fulton (*née* Foxton); *m* 1981, Lee Hong Tay. *Educ:* Nunthorpe Grammar Sch., York; Churchill Coll., Cambridge (BA Hons French and Russian). Home Office, 1973–2003: Private Sec. to Perm. Sec., 1977–78; Radio Regulatory Dept, 1978–83; Police Dept, 1984–88; Prison and Criminal Policy Depts, 1988–91; Dir of Prison Service Industries and Farms, 1991–96; Principal Finance Officer, 1996–2000; Dir, Strategy and Performance, 2000–02; Implementation Dir, Assets Recovery Agency, 2002–03. Chairman: CHAS (Central London) 2006–10 (Treas., 2004–06); Ducane Housing Assoc., 2004–11; Vice-Chm., SOVA (formerly Soc. of Voluntary Associates), 2004–12. Mem., Finance and Audit Cttee, Skills for Justice, 2008–10; Treasurer: Clinks, 2009–; Concern and Help for E Elmbridge Retired, 2009–. Trustee, Voluntary Action Elmbridge, 2010–12. *Recreations:* learning new things, re-learning old things. *Address:* 1 Meadow Close, Hinchley Wood, Esher, Surrey KT10 0AY.

FULTON, (Robert) Andrew; HM Diplomatic Service, retired; Chairman, GPW Ltd, since 2006; *b* 6 Feb. 1944; *s* of late Rev. Robert M. Fulton and Janet W. Fulton (*née* Mackenzie); *m* 1970, Patricia Mary Crowley; two *s* one *d*. *Educ:* Rothesay Academy; Glasgow University (MA, LLB). Foreign and Commonwealth Office, 1968; Third later Second Secretary, Saigon, 1969; FCO, 1972; First Sec., Rome, 1973; FCO, 1977; First Sec., E Berlin, 1978; FCO, 1981; Counsellor, Oslo, 1984; FCO, 1987; UK Mission to UN, NY, 1989; FCO, 1992; Counsellor: Washington, 1995–99; FCO, 1999. Dir, Scotland, Control Risks Gp, 2002–06; Internat. Business Advr, Memex Technology, 2003–12; Global Business Adviser: Dynamic Knowledge Corp., 2005–08; Armor Gp, 2006–08; Advr, G4S, 2008–10. Chairman: Scottish N American Business Council, 2000–10 (Pres., 2010–); Adv. Bd, Proudfoot Consulting, 2003–09; Edo Midas, 2004–09; nation 1, 2005–08; Huntswood, 2006–09; Scottish Conservative and Unionist Party, 2008–11. Senior Adviser: Source8, 2009–11; Indigo Vision, 2010–11 (non-exec. Dir, 2011–). Mem., Nat. Adv. Gp, Internat. Street Papers, 2013–. Vis. Prof., Univ. of Glasgow Sch. of Law, 1999–2003. *Recreations:* golf, racing, reading, cinema. *Address:* 7 Crown Road South, Glasgow G12 9DJ.

FULTON, Lt-Gen. Sir Robert (Henry Gervase), KBE 2005; Chief Executive, Global Leadership Foundation, since 2010; *b* 21 Dec. 1948; *s* of late James Fulton and Cynthia Fulton (*née* Shaw); *m* 1975, Midge Free; two *s*. *Educ:* Eton Coll.; Univ. of East Anglia (BA Hons). Entered RM, 1972: 42 Commando, 1973–75; 40 Commando, 1976–78; Instructor, Sch. of Signals, Blandford, 1978–80; student, Army Staff Coll., Camberley, 1980–81; Instructor, Jun. Div. Staff Coll., 1981–83; 42 Commando, 1983–85; SO2 Ops, HQ Training, Reserve and Special Forces, 1985–87; SO2 Commitments, Dept of Comdt Gen., 1987–90; SO1 DS, Army Staff Coll., Camberley, 1990–92; CO, 42 Commando, 1992–94; Asst Dir, CIS Operational Requirements, MoD, 1994–95; RCDS, 1996; Comdr, 3 Commando Bde, 1997–98, Comdt Gen., 1998–2001, RM; Capability Manager (Inf. Superiority), 2001–03; DCDS (Equipment Capability), 2003–06; Governor and C-in-C, Gibraltar, 2006–09. Chm. Govs, Haberdashers' Aske's Schs Elstree, 2012–. Mem. Council, White Ensign Assoc., 2006–; Vice Pres., RN and RM Charity, 2009–. Trustee, Nat. Mus. of RN, 2012–15. Liveryman, Haberdashers' Co. (Mem., Ct of Assts, 2012–). KStJ 2009. *Recreations:* playing and watching sport, military history. *Clubs:* Army and Navy, MCC.

FUNNELL, Christina Mary; Director, Christina Funnell (formerly Funnell Associates) Consultancy, 1997–2011; *b* 24 Aug. 1947; *d* of Joanna Christina Beaumont (*née* Lenes) and Norman Beaumont; *m* 1970 (marr. diss. 1994); one *s* one *d*. *Educ:* Hull Univ. (BA Spec. Hons Soc. Admin. 1968). W Riding CC Social Services, 1964; Methodist Assoc. of Youth Clubs, 1965–68; London Council of Social Service, 1971; Herts CC Youth Service, 1973; Nat. Eczema Soc., 1982–96 (Dir, 1987–96; Chief Exec., Skin Care Campaign, 1995–96). Mem., Standing Adv. Gp on consumer involvement in NHS R&D prog., 1996–98; Chm., Consumer Health Inf. Centre, 1997–99; Organising Sec., Health Coalition Initiative, 1997–2008; Sec. and Co-ordinator, Patient Information Forum, 2001–03; Patient and Public Involvement Consultant, Perf. Develt Team, NHS Modernisation Agency, 2003–05; Patient Consultant, N and E Yorks and N Lincs Strategic Health Authy, 2005–07; Patient Engagement Officer, Patient Opinion, 2007–10. Lay Member: Nat. Clin. Assessment Authy, 2001–05; NMC, 2002–08; Health Technol. Devices Prog., DoH, 2002–12; non-exec. Mem., BeIndependent, 2014–. Mem. Council, Gen. Pharmaceutical Council, 2010–; Mem., N Yorks Fire and Rescue Authy, 2009–11. Panel Mem., Richard Neale Inquiry, 2005. Feasibility Consultant to North Bank Estate, Muswell Hill, London, 1998–99. Vice-Chm., Socialist Health Assoc., 2005–13; Trustee: Pharmacy Practice Res. Trust, 2005–12; York Council of Voluntary Service, 2009–; St Nicholas Envmt Centre, 2009–14; Mem. Exec., York Older People's Assembly, 2008–10. Mem. (Labour), City of York Council, 2007– (Chm., Health Overview and Scrutiny Cttee, 2007–08, 2011–). Member: Wesley's Chapel, 1996–97; Christian Socialist Movt, 2009– (Mem. Exec., 1998–2003); Council, Socialist Health Assoc., 2015–; Associate Mem., Iona Community, 1997–2000. Gov., Burnholme Community Coll., 2008–14. Former Mem. and Chm. Cttee, Scarcroft Allotments; Chm., Tang Hall Community Centre, 2012–. *Publications:* (contrib.) Clinical and Experimental Dermatology, 1993; (contrib.) Developing New Clinical Roles: a guide for health professionals, 2000. *Recreations:* gardening, travel, social and political history, current affairs. *Address:* 6 Upper Price Street, off Scarcroft Road, York YO23 1BJ. *T:* and *Fax:* (01904) 613041. *E:* tinafunnell@btinternet.com.

FUNNELL, Philippa Rachel, MBE 2005; event rider; *b* 7 Oct. 1968; *d* of George and Jennifer Nolan; *m* 1993, William Funnell. *Educ:* Wadhurst Coll. Young Rider Gold Medallist, 1987; British Open Champion, 1992 and 2002; European Championships: Team and Individual Champion, 1991 and 2001; Team Champion and Individual Bronze Medallist, 2003; Olympic Games: Team Silver Medallist, Sydney, 2000; Team Silver and Individual Bronze Medallist, Athens, 2004; winner: Badminton Horse Trials, 2002, 2003, 2005; Rolex Grand Slam (Badminton, Burghley and Kentucky), 2003; Bramham Internat. Horse Trials, 2010. *Publications:* Training the Young Horse, 2002; My Story (autobiog.), 2004; Tilly's Ponytails (series for children), 2009–. *Recreations:* tennis, cooking. *Address:* c/o British Eventing, Stoneleigh Park, Kenilworth, Warwicks CV8 2RN.

FURBER, (Frank) Robert; retired solicitor; *b* 28 March 1921; *s* of late Percy John Furber and Edith Furber; *m* 1948, Anne Wilson McArthur (*d* 2015); three *s* one *d*. *Educ:* Willaston Sch.; Berkhamsted Sch.; University College London. LLB. Articled with Slaughter and May; solicitor 1945; Partner, Clifford-Turner, 1952–86. Mem., Planning Law Cttee, Law Society, 1964–69. Chairman: Blackheath Soc., 1968–89; Blackheath Preservation Trust, 1972–2000; Film Industry Defence Organization, 1968–89; Governor: Yehudi Menuhin Sch., 1964–91; Live Music Now!, 1977–87; Berkhamsted Sch., and Berkhamsted Sch. for Girls, 1976–91 (Chm., 1986–91); Board Member: Trinity Coll. of Music, 1974–91; Nat. Jazz Centre, 1982–87; Common Law Inst. of Intellectual Property, 1982–87; Chm., Rules of Golf Cttee, Royal and Ancient Golf Club, 1976–80; Trustee, Robert T. Jones Meml Trust, 1982–86; Mem. and Hon. Sec., R & A Golf Amateurism Commn of Inquiry, 1984–85; Mem., CCPR Cttee of Enquiry into Amateurism in Sport, 1986–88. Hon. Fellow, Trinity College, London. *Publications:* A Course for Heroes, 1996; History of The Moles GS, 2011. *Address:* 8 Pond Road, Blackheath, SE3 9JL. *T:* (020) 8852 8065. *Clubs:* Buck's; Royal Blackheath Golf, Royal St George's Golf.

See also S. A. Coakley, R. J. Furber, W. J. Furber.

FURBER, James; *see* Furber, W. J.

FURBER, (Robert) John; QC 1995; *b* 13 Oct. 1949; *s* of (Frank) Robert Furber, *qv*, and late Anne Wilson Furber (*née* McArthur); *m* 1st, 1977, Amanda Cherry Burgoyne Varney (marr. diss. 2010); one *s* two *d*; 2nd, 2011, Dr Virginia Taylor. *Educ:* Westminster Sch.; Gonville and Caius Coll., Cambridge (MA). Called to the Bar, Inner Temple, 1973. Chm., Field Lane Foundn, 2004–06, 2009–12. Chm., Property Bar Assoc., 2011–14. *Publications:* (ed jtly) Halsbury's Laws of England: Landlord and Tenant, 4th edn 1981, Compulsory Acquisition of Land, 4th edn reissue 1996; (ed jtly) Hill and Redman's Landlord and Tenant, 17th edn 1982, 18th edn (looseleaf) 1988–2015; (jtly) Guide to the Commonhold and Leasehold Reform Act, 2002. *Address:* Wilberforce Chambers, 8 New Square, Lincoln's Inn, WC2A 3QP. *T:* (020) 7306 0102; 1 Hallgate, Blackheath Park, SE3 9SG. *T:* (020) 8852 7633. *Clubs:* Buck's, Beefsteak, Pratt's.

See also S. A. Coakley, W. J. Furber.

FURBER, Prof. Stephen Byram, CBE 2008; FRS 2002; FREng; ICL Professor of Computer Engineering, University of Manchester, since 1990 (Head, Department of Computer Science, 2001–04); *b* 21 March 1953; *s* of Benjamin Neil Furber and Margaret Furber (*née* Schofield); *m* 1977, Valerie Margaret Elliott; two *d*. *Educ:* St John's Coll., Cambridge (BA Maths 1st Cl. 1974; PhD Aerodynamics 1980). FREng 1999. Rolls Royce Res. Fellow, Emmanuel Coll., Cambridge, 1978–81; Hardware Design Engr, then Design Manager, Acorn Computers Ltd, Cambridge, 1981–90. Non-executive Director: Manchester Informatics Ltd, 1994–2010; Cogency Technology Inc., 1997–99; Cogniscience Ltd, 2000–; Transitive Technologies Ltd, 2001–04; Silistix Ltd, 2004–06. *Publications:* VLSI RISC Architecture and Organization, 1989; (ed jtly) Asynchronous Design Methodologies, 1993; ARM System Architecture, 1996; ARM System-on-Chip Architecture, 2000; (ed jtly) Principles of Asynchronous Circuit Design: a systems perspective, 2001; over 100 conf. and jl papers. *Recreations:* 6-string and bass guitar (Church music group), badminton. *Address:* School of Computer Science, University of Manchester, Oxford Road, Manchester M13 9PL. *T:* (0161) 275 6129, *Fax:* (0161) 275 6236. *E:* steve.furber@manchester.ac.uk.

FURBER, (William) James; Partner, Farrer & Co., since 1985 (Senior Partner, 2008–11); *b* 1 Sept. 1954; *s* of (Frank) Robert Furber, *qv*; *m* 1982, Rosemary Elizabeth Johnston (marr. diss. 2010); two *s* one *d*. *Educ:* Westminster Sch.; Gonville and Caius Coll., Cambridge (BA 1975, MA 1979). Admitted solicitor, 1979; joined Farrer & Co. (Solicitors), 1976, Associate Partner, 1981. Solicitor to Duchy of Cornwall, 1994–. Trustee: Leonard Cheshire Foundn, 2000–06; Arvon Foundn, 2000–07; Trinity Coll. of Music, 2003–06; Trinity Coll. of Music Trust, 2006–; Cambridge Univ. Musical Soc., 2014–; Secretary: St Bartholomew's Med. Coll. Charitable Trust, 1996–2012; Art Workers Guild Trust, 2007–10. Reader, C of E, 1991–2010. Treas., Lowtonian Soc., 2003–. *Publications:* (contrib.) Encyclopedia of Forms and Precedents, vol. 36, 1990. *Recreations:* golf, literature, wine, cooking, avoiding boring people. *Address:* c/o Farrer & Co., 66 Lincoln's Inn Fields, WC2A 3LH. *T:* (020) 3375 7000, *Fax:* (020) 3375 7001. *E:* james.furber@farrer.co.uk. *Clubs:* Garrick; Bucks; Hawks (Cambridge); Royal & Ancient Golf (St Andrews), Royal St George's Golf (Sandwich), Royal West Norfolk Golf (Brancaster), Royal Blackheath Golf; Honourable Company of Edinburgh Golfers.

See also S. A. Coakley, R. J. Furber.

FUREDI, Ann Marie; Chief Executive Officer, British Pregnancy Advisory Service, since 2003; *b* Wolverhampton, 31 Oct. 1960; *d* of Joseph and Joan Bradley; *m* 1982, Ferenc, (Frank), Furedi; one *s*. *Educ:* Univ. of Kent (BA Hons 1982). Med. journalist and political activist, 1982–91 (Mem., Political Cttee, Revolutionary Communist Party); Press Officer, FPA, 1991–92; Dep. Dir, 1992–95, Dir, 1995–98, Birth Control Trust; Dir of Communications, British Pregnancy Adv. Service, 1998–2002; Dir, Policy and Communications, HFEA, 2002–03. Mem., Bd of Trustees, IBIS Reproductive Health, 2011–. Vice Chair, Bd of Govs, Mid Kent Coll., 2012–. *Publications:* Unplanned Pregnancy: your choices, 1995; The Moral Case for Abortion, 2016; contribs to BMJ, British Jl Med. Ethics, British Jl Family Planning. *Recreations:* wandering, wondering, cuddling cats, and avoiding alliteration. *Address:* 9 Newton Road, Faversham, Kent ME13 8DZ. *E:* ann.furedi@bpas.org.

FURLONG, Prof. (Vivian) John, PhD; FAcSS; Professor of Educational Studies, University of Oxford, 2003–12, now Emeritus (Director, Department of Educational Studies, later of Education, 2003–10); Fellow of Green Templeton College (formerly Green College), Oxford, 2003–12, now Emeritus; *b* 7 May 1947; *s* of late William James Furlong and Ann Furlong; *m* 1972, Ruth Roberts; two *s*. *Educ:* Hertford Grammar Sch.; Middx Poly. (BA 1968); City Univ. (PhD 1978); Corpus Christi Coll., Cambridge (MA 1984). Teacher, Paddington Sch., London, 1971–74; post-doctoral Res. Fellow, Univs of Manchester and Brunel, 1975–81; Lectr in Educn, Univ. of Cambridge, 1981–92; Professor and Head: Dept of Educn, Univ. of Swansea, 1992–95; Grad. Sch. of Educn, Univ. of Bristol, 1995–2000; Prof., Sch. of Social Scis, Cardiff Univ., 2000–03. Pres., British Educnl Res. Assoc., 2003–05. Member: Social Scis Panel, Internat. Evaluation of Sci. and Innovation Policy in Latvia, 2013; International Expert Panel for review of teacher educn in Rep. of Ireland, 2013, of teacher training infrastructure in NI, 2014; UK REF Educn Panel, 2014; Chair, BERA-RSA Inquiry into res. and teacher educn, 2014; Convenor, Hong Kong RAE Educn Panel, 2014; Expert Advr to Welsh Govt on Initial Teacher Training, 2014–. FRSA 1995; FAcSS (AcSS 2003).

Mem., Editl Bd, Cambridge Jl of Educn; Jt Ed., Oxford Rev. of Educn. *Publications:* The Language of Teaching (with A. D. Edwards), 1978; The Deviant Pupil: sociological perspectives, 1985; (jtly) Initial Teacher Training and the Role of the School, 1988; (with T. Maynard) Mentoring Student Teachers: the growth of professional knowledge, 1995; (ed jtly) The Role of Higher Education in Initial Teacher Education, 1996; (jtly) Teacher Education in Transition: re-forming professionalism?, 2000; (ed jtly) Education, Reform and the State: policy, politics and practice, 2001; (jtly) Screenplay: children and computing in the home, 2003; (jtly) Adult Learning in the Digital Age, 2005; (ed jtly) Understanding Quality in Applied and Practice-Based Research, 2007; (ed jtly) Politics and Policy in Teacher Education: international perspectives, 2008; (ed jtly) Disciplines of Education: their role in the future of education research, 2010; Education: an anatomy of the discipline, Rescuing the University project?, 2013; over 100 articles in educnl jls and books. *Recreations:* gardening, keeping chickens, cooking, travel, entertaining. *Address:* Department of Education, University of Oxford, 15 Norham Gardens, Oxford OX2 6PY. *T:* (01865) 274024, *Fax:* (01865) 274027. *E:* john.furlong@education.ox.ac.uk.

FURLONGER, Robert William, CB 1981; retired public servant, Australia; *b* 29 April 1921; *s* of George William Furlonger and Germaine Rose Furlonger; *m* 1944, Verna Hope Lewis; three *s* one *d*. *Educ:* Sydney High Sch.; Sydney Univ. (BA). Served War, AMF, 1941–45. Australian Dept of External (later Foreign) Affairs, 1945–69 and 1972–77 (IDC, 1960; Dir, Jt Intell. Org., Dept of Def., 1969–72); appointments included: High Comr, Nigeria, 1961; Aust. Perm. Rep. to the European Office of the UN, 1961–64; Minister, Aust. Embassy, Washington, 1965–69; Ambassador to Indonesia, 1972–74, and to Austria, Hungary and Czechoslovakia, 1975–77; Dir-Gen., Office of National Assessments, Canberra, 1977–81. *Address:* PO Box 548, Belconnen, ACT 2616, Australia. *T:* (2) 62531384. *Club:* Royal Canberra Golf.

FURMSTON, Prof. Michael Philip, TD 1966; Professor of Law, University of Bristol, 1978–98, now Emeritus; Professor of Law, Singapore Management University, since 2007 (Dean, School of Law, 2007–12); *b* 1 May 1933; *s* of late Joseph Philip Furmston and Phyllis (*née* Clowes); *m* 1964, Ashley Sandra Maria Cope; three *s* seven *d*. *Educ:* Wellington Sch., Somerset; Exeter Coll., Oxford (BA 1st Cl. Hons Jurisprudence, 1956; BCL 1st Cl. Hons 1957; MA 1960). LLM Birmingham, 1962. Called to the Bar, Gray's Inn, 1960 (1st Cl. Hons), Bencher, 1989. National Service, RA, 1951–53 (2nd Lieut); Major, TA, 1966–78, TAVR. Lecturer: Univ. of Birmingham, 1957–62; QUB, 1962–63; Fellow, Lincoln Coll., Oxford, 1964–78 (Sen. Dean, 1967–68; Sen. Tutor and Tutor for Admissions, 1969–74); Univ. Lectr in Law, 1964–78, Curator, University Chest, 1976–78, Oxford; Lectr in Common Law, Council of Legal Educn, 1965–78; Dean, Faculty of Law, 1980–84 and 1995–98, Pro-Vice-Chancellor, 1986–89, Univ. of Bristol. Chm., COMEC, 1996–2000. Visiting Professor: City Univ., 1978–82; Katholieke Universiteit, Leuven, 1980, 1986, 1992 and 1999; Nat. Univ. of Singapore, 1987, 1999; Singapore Mgt Univ., 2006; McWilliam Vis. Prof. of Commercial Law, Univ. of Sydney, 2005. Sen. Fellow, Univ. of Melbourne, 2003–05. Liveryman, Arbitrators' Co. Jt Editor, 1985–97, Editor, 1997–, Construction Law Reports. DUniv Open, 2010. *Publications:* (ed) Cheshire, Fifoot and Furmston's Law of Contract, 8th edn 1972, to 16th edn 2012; Contractors Guide to ICE Conditions of Contract, 1980; Misrepresentation and Fraud, in Halsbury's Law of England, 1980, 1998; Croner's Buying and Selling Law, 1982; (ed jtly) The Effect on English Domestic Law of Membership of the European Communities and Ratification of the European Convention on Human Rights, 1983; (jtly) A Building Contract Casebook, 1984, 5th edn 2012; (jtly) Cases and Materials on Contract, 1985, 5th edn 2007; (ed) The Law of Tort: policies and trends in liability for damage to property, 1986; (ed) You and the Law, 1987; Croner's Model Business Contracts, 1988; (jtly) 'A' Level Law, 1988, 4th edn 2002; Sale of Goods, 1990; Sale and Supply of Goods, 1994, 3rd edn 2000; (jtly) Commercial Law, 1995, 2nd edn 2001; Contract Formation and Letters of Intent, 1998; (ed) The Law of Contract, 1999, 5th edn 2015; (jtly) Contract Formation, Law and Practice, 2010; (jtly) Commercial and Consumer Law, 2010, 2nd edn 2013; (jtly) Privity of Contract, 2015. *Recreations:* chess (Member, English team, Postal Olympiads), watching cricket, dogs. *Address:* 51 Grenville Court, Bridgwater, Somerset TA6 3TY. *T:* (01278) 421676; Faculty of Law, University of Bristol, Wills Memorial Building, Queen's Road, Bristol BS8 1RJ; School of Law, Singapore Management University, 60 Stamford Road, Singapore 178900. *T:* 68280893. *Clubs:* Reform, Naval and Military, MCC.

FURNESS, Alan Edwin, CMG 1991; HM Diplomatic Service, retired; Secretary-General, British Association of the Order of Malta, since 2013; *b* 6 June 1937; *s* of late Edwin Furness and Marion Furness (*née* Senton); *m* 1971, Aline Elizabeth Janine Barrett; two *s*. *Educ:* Eltham Coll.; Jesus Coll., Cambridge (BA, MA). Researcher, University Coll. of W Indies, Jamaica, 1959–60; Commonwealth Relations Office, 1961; Private Sec. to Parliamentary Under-Secretary of State, 1961–62; Third, later Second Secretary, British High Commn, New Delhi, 1962–66; First Secretary, DSAO (later FCO), 1966–69; First Sec., UK Delegn to European Communities, Brussels, 1969–72; First Sec. and Head of Chancery, Dakar, 1972–75; First Sec., FCO, 1975–78; Counsellor and Head of Chancery, Jakarta, 1978–81; Counsellor and Head of Chancery, Warsaw, 1982–85; Head of S Pacific Dept, FCO, 1985–88; Dep. High Comr, Bombay, 1989–93; Ambassador to Senegal and, concurrently, to Cape Verde, Guinea, Guinea Bissau and Mali, 1993–97. Resident Rep. in Senegal, 1998–2008, Advr, 2008–, Business Council for Africa (W and Southern) (formerly W Africa Cttee). Ambassador of Order of Malta to Senegal, 2000–11. Knight of Magistral Grace, 1999, Grand Cross pro Merito Melitensi, 2011, Order of Malta. *Publications:* (trans.) Le Cavalier et son ombre by Boubacar Boris Diop, as The Knight and his Shadow, 2015. *Recreations:* music, literature. *Address:* 40 Brunswick Court, 89 Regency Street, SW1P 4AE. *Club:* Oxford and Cambridge.

FURNESS, (Hugh) Jonathan; QC 2003; a Recorder, since 1998; a Deputy High Court Judge, since 2008; *b* 8 Nov. 1956; *s* of late Thomas Hogg Batey Furness and Hilda Anita Furness; *m* 1984, Anne Margaret Jones; three *s* one *d*. *Educ:* St John's Coll., Cambridge (MA). Called to the Bar, Gray's Inn, 1979; in practice, specialising in divorce and child care work. *Recreations:* golf, cricket, music. *Address:* 30 Park Place, Cardiff CF10 3BS. *T:* (029) 2039 8421. *Clubs:* Cardiff and County; Mitres Cricket (Llandaff); Royal Porthcawl Golf.

FURNESS, Mark Richard; His Honour Judge Furness; a Circuit Judge, since 1998; *b* 28 Nov. 1948; *m* 1974, Margaretta Trevor Evans; one *s* one *d*. *Educ:* Hereford Cathedral Sch.; St John's Coll., Cambridge (BA 1970; MA 1972). Called to the Bar, Lincoln's Inn, 1970; an Asst Recorder, 1992–96; a Recorder, 1996–98. Chairman: Social Security Appeal Tribunal, 1987–94; Disability Appeal Tribunal, 1991–98. Chairman: Marie Curie Cttee for Wales, 2001–07; Trustees and Managing Cttee, Swansea Children Contact Centre, 2002–09; Mem., Marie Curie Welsh Devolt Bd, 2007–. *Recreations:* gardening, motoring, literature, music, DIY, travel. *Address:* Pontypridd County Court, The Courthouse, Courthouse Street, Pontypridd, S Wales CF37 1JR. *Clubs:* Cardiff and County (Cardiff); Saba Rock Yacht.

FURNESS, Michael James; QC 2000; a Deputy High Court Judge, since 2004; *b* 2 Sept. 1958; *s* of late Harry Furness and of Rosemary Nancy Furness; *m* 2008, Frances Marguerite Shore. *Educ:* Emmanuel Coll., Cambridge (MA); St Edmund Hall, Oxford (BCL). Called to the Bar, Lincoln's Inn, 1982, Bencher, 2009; First Standing Jun. Counsel to Inland Revenue, 1998–2000. *Recreations:* acting, walking. *Address:* Wilberforce Chambers, 8 New Square, Lincoln's Inn, WC2A 3QP. *T:* (020) 7306 0102.

FURNESS, Prof. Peter Norman, PhD; FRCPath; Consultant Histopathologist, since 1990, and Assistant Medical Director, since 2011, University Hospitals of Leicester; Hon. Professor of Renal Pathology, University of Leicester, since 2001; National Medical Examiner, since 2013; *b* Barnsley, S Yorks, 2 Sept. 1955; *s* of Harold and Kathleen Furness; *m* 1979, Sarah Haddon; one *d*. *Educ:* Fitzwilliam Coll., Cambridge (BA 1st Cl. Natural Scis 1977); Wolfson Coll., Oxford (BM BCh Clin. Medicine 1981); Univ. of Nottingham (PhD 1989). FRCPath 1989. Lectr in Pathol., Univ. of Nottingham, 1984–89; Sen. Lectr in Pathol., Univ. of Leicester, 1990–2001. Mem., Nuffield Council for Bioethics, 2013–. Pres., RCPath, 2008–11; Vice Chair, Acad. of Medical Royal Colls, 2009–11. *Recreations:* woodwork, house and car renovation, dogwalking, horology, beekeeping, making broken things work again. *Address:* Department of Histopathology, Sandringham Building, Leicester Royal Infirmary, Leicester LE1 5WW. *Club:* Athenæum.

FURNESS, Robin; *see* Furness, Sir S. R.

FURNESS, Col Simon John, MBE 2012; Vice Lord-Lieutenant of Berwickshire, 1990–2009; *b* 18 Aug. 1936; 2nd *s* of Sir Christopher Furness, 2nd Bt and Violet Flower Chipchase Furness, OBE (*d* 1988), *d* of Lieut-Col G. C. Roberts, Hollingside, Durham. *Educ:* Charterhouse; RMA Sandhurst; Royal Naval Staff College. Commissioned 2nd Lieut Durham Light Infantry, 1956; served Far East, UK, Germany; active service, Borneo and NI; Comd 5th Bn LI, 1976–78, retired 1978. Dep. Col (Durham), LI, 1989–93. Trustee, Gunsgreen Hse Trust, 2002–15 (Chm., 2012–15). DL Berwickshire, 1984. OStJ 2009. *Recreations:* gardening, country sports, fine arts. *Address:* The Garden House, Netherbyres, Eyemouth, Berwickshire TD14 5SE. *T:* (01890) 750337. *Club:* Army and Navy.

FURNESS, Sir Stephen (Roberts), 3rd Bt *cr* 1913, of Tunstall Grange, West Hartlepool; farmer and sporting/landscape artist (as Robin Furness); *b* 10 Oct. 1933; *e s* of Sir Christopher Furness, 2nd Bt, and Flower, Lady Furness, OBE (*d* 1988), *d* of late Col G. C. Roberts; *S* father, 1974; *m* 1961, Mary, *e d* of J. F. Cann, Cullompton, Devon; one *s* one *d*. *Educ:* Charterhouse. Entered RN, 1952; Observer, Fleet Air Arm, 1957; retired list, 1962. NCA, Newton Rigg Farm Inst., 1964. Member: Armed Forces Art Soc.; Darlington Art Soc.; Associate Mem., Soc. of Equestrian Artists. *Recreations:* looking at paintings, foxhunting, racing. *Heir: s* Michael Fitzroy Roberts Furness [*b* 12 Oct. 1962; *m* 1998, Katrine Oxtoby]. *Address:* Stanhow Farm, Great Langton, Northallerton, Yorks DL7 0TJ.

See also S. J. Furness.

FURNHAM, Prof. Adrian Frank, DSc, DPhil, DLitt; Professor of Psychology, University College London, since 1992; *b* 3 Feb. 1953; *s* of late Leslie Frank Furnham and of Lorna Audrey (*née* Cartwright); *m* 1990, Dr Alison Clare Green; one *s*. *Educ:* Natal Univ. (BA Hons, MA; DLitt 1997); LSE (MSc Econ 1976; DSc 1991); Strathclyde Univ. (MSc 1977); Wolfson Coll. and Pembroke Coll., Oxford (DPhil 1982). Oxford University: Res. Officer, Dept Exptl Psychol., 1979–81; Lectr in Psychol., Pembroke Coll., 1980–82; University College London: Lectr, 1981–87; Reader, 1988–92. Visiting Lecturer: Univ. of NSW, 1984; Univ. of WI, 1986; Univ. of Hong Kong, 1994–96; Vis. Prof., Henley Mgt Coll., 1999–2001; Adjunct Prof., Norwegian Sch. of Mgt, Oslo, 2009–; Hon. Prof., Univ. of KwaZulu-Natal, S Africa, 2015–. Founder Dir, ABRA, business consultancy, 1986–2002. Ext. Examr at various univs. Mem., Internat. Adv. Council, Social Affairs Unit, 1995–. Dir, Internat. Soc. for Study of Individual Differences, 1996–2001 (Pres., 2003–05). Mem., editl bd of 11 internat. scientific jls. *Publications:* books include: Culture Shock, 1986; Lay Theories, 1988; The Protestant Work Ethic, 1990; Personality at Work, 1992; Corporate Assessment, 1994; All in the Mind, 1996, 2nd edn 2001; The Myths of Management, 1996; The Psychology of Behaviour at Work, 1997; Complementary Medicine, 1997; The Psychology of Money, 1998; The Psychology of Managerial Incompetence, 1998; Children as Consumers, 1998; Personality and Social Behaviour, 1999; Body Language at Work, 1999; The Hopeless, Hapless and Helpless Manager, 2000; Designing and Analysing Questionnaires and Surveys, 2000; Children and Advertising, 2000; The Psychology of Culture Shock, 2001; Assessing Potential, 2001; The 3D Manager: dangerous, derailed and deranged, 2001; Mad, Sad and Bad Management, 2003; The Incompetent Manager, 2003; Management and Myths, 2004; The Dark Side of Behaviour at Work, 2004; Personality and Intellectual Competence, 2005; The People Business, 2005; Learning at Work, 2005; Just for the Money, 2005; Management Mumbo-Jumbo, 2006; The Body Beautiful, 2007; Dim Sum Management, 2008; The Psychology of Physical Attractiveness, 2008; Head and Heart Management, 2008; Personality and Intelligence at Work, 2008; Management Intelligence, 2008; The Economic Socialisation of Young People, 2008; 50 Psychology Ideas You Really Need to Know, 2009; The Psychology of Personnel Selection, 2010; The Elephant in the Board Room, 2010; Body Language in Business, 2010; Bad Apples, 2011; Managing People in a Downturn, 2011; Leadership: all you want to know, 2012; The Talented Manager, 2012; The Resilient Manager, 2013; The New Psychology of Money, 2014; Mental Illness at Work, 2014; High Potential, 2014; Backstabbers and Bullies, 2015; 1000 scientific papers; contrib. articles and columns to newspapers, incl. Daily Telegraph, Sunday Times. *Recreations:* travel, theatre, arguing at dinner parties and at work (because as Noël Coward wisely observed 'work is more fun than fun'). *Address:* 45 Thornhill Square, Islington, N1 1BE. *T:* (020) 7607 6265. *E:* ucjtsaf@ucl.ac.uk.

FURNISS, Prof. Graham Lytton, OBE 2013; PhD; FBA 2009; Professor of African-Language Literature, School of Oriental and African Studies, University of London, 1999–2014, now Emeritus; *b* 21 June 1949; *s* of Alfred Lytton and Margaret Elizabeth Furniss; *m* 1977, Wendy Jane de Beer; one *s* two *d*. *Educ:* Sch. of Oriental and African Studies, Univ. of London (BA; PhD 1977). Lectr, Dept of Langs and Linguistics, Univ. of Maiduguri, Nigeria, 1977–79; School of Oriental and African Studies, University of London: Lectr, then Sen. Lectr in Hausa, 1979–96; Reader in Hausa Cultural Studies, 1996–99; Hd, Lang. Centre, 1995–98; Dean: of Langs, 1995–97; Faculty of Langs and Cultures, 2002–04; Pro-Dir (Res. and Enterprise), 2008–13. Chm., Africa sub-panel, 2001 RAE Panel 46: African and ME Studies. Comr, Commonwealth Scholarship Commn, 2010–. Vice-Chm., Royal African Soc., 2000–08; President: Internat. Soc. for Oral Lit. in Africa, 1998–2002; African Studies Assoc. of UK, 2004–06. Gov. and Trustee, Harrow Sch. Foundn, 2007–; Trustee, Britain-Nigeria Educnl Trust, 2008–. *Publications:* (ed with R. Fardon) African Languages, Development and the State, 1994; (ed with E. Gunner) Power, Marginality and African Oral Literature, 1995; Ideology in Practice: Hausa poetry as exposition of values and viewpoints, 1995; Poetry, Prose and Popular Culture in Hausa, 1996; (ed with R. Fardon) African Broadcast Cultures: radio in transition, 2000; Orality: the power of the spoken word, 2004. *Recreations:* hill-walking, beach-combing, pottery, painting, tropical plants, gardening, cooking. *Address:* Faculty of Languages and Cultures, School of Oriental and African Studies, University of London, Thornhaugh Street, Russell Square, WC1H 0XG. *E:* gf1@soas.ac.uk.

FURNISS, (Mary) Jane, CBE 2012; Chief Executive, Independent Police Complaints Commission, 2006–13; *b* 28 March 1954; *d* of Eric Richard Sanders and late Catherine Lilly Sanders; *m* 1977, David Kenneth Furniss. *Educ:* Burton-on-Trent Girls' High Sch.; Bradford Univ. (BSc Hons 1975); York Univ. (MSW 1978). West Yorkshire: Probation Officer, 1975–76, 1978–85; Sen. Probation Officer, 1985–90; Asst Chief Probation Officer, 1990–95; Home Office: HM Inspector of Probation, 1995–97; HM Dep. Chief Inspector, 1997–2001; Hd, Justice and Victims Unit, 2001–02; Dir, Criminal Policy, then Criminal Justice, Gp, 2002–05; Dir, Criminal Justice, Office for Criminal Justice Reform, 2005–06. Mem., Audit and Risk Cttee, Children's Comr, 2010–11; Associate and Bd Mentor, Criticaleye, 2013– (Mem., Adv. Bd, 2010–12); Sen. Ind. Dir, Solicitors Regulation Authy, 2014–; non-exec. Dir, Nat. Crime Agency, 2013–. Judge, Contrarian Prize Panel, 2013–. Trustee, Crisis, 2006– (Dep. Chm., 2013–). *Recreations:* music (listening), art (viewing), the world (exploring), learnt to swim in 2013!

FURNIVALL, Barony *cr* 1295; in abeyance. *Co-heiresses:* Hon. Rosamond Mary Dent (Sister Ancilla, OSB); *b* 3 June 1933; Hon. Patricia Mary Dent [*b* 4 April 1935; *m* 1st, 1956, Captain Thomas Hornsby (marr. diss., 1963; he *d* 1967); one *s* one *d*; 2nd, 1970, Roger Thomas John Bence; one *s* one *d*].

FURR, Barrington John Albert, (Barry), OBE 2000; PhD; FMedSci; CBiol, FRSB; Consultant and Chairman, Llangarth Ltd, since 2006; *b* London, 1943; *s* of William Howard James Furr and Winifred Rosemary Furr; *m* 1970, Eileen Pamela Mahoney; one *s* two *d*. *Educ:* Reading Univ. (BSc Chem., Microbiol. and Physiol Chem. 1965; BSc Special Hons Physiol Chem.; PhD Reproductive Endocrinol. 1969); MA Cantab. CBiol 1998; FRSB (FIBiol 1998). British Egg Mktg Bd Fellow, Nat. Inst. for Res. into Dairying, 1969–71; Wellcome Vet. Fellow, Univ. of Reading, 1971–72; ICI Pharmaceuticals: Biologist, 1972–79; Sen. Scientist, 1979–87; Section Manager, Cancer and Immunol., 1984–86; Manager: Biosci. 1 Dept, 1987–93; Vascular Inflammatory and Musculoskeletal Res. Dept, 1993–95; Zeneca Ltd, later AstraZeneca Ltd: Manager, Cardiovascular and Musculoskeletal Res., 1996–97; Sen. Vice-Pres., Therapeutic Res., 1997–98; Chief Scientist and Hd, Project Evaluation, 1999–2006. Non-executive Director: Manchester Technology Fund, 2003–09; Genus Ltd, 2006–; Avesthagen, India, 2006–07; GTx, 2011–. Member, Scientific Advisory Board: Merlin Bioventures, 2002–05; Astex, 2006–12; Almirall, 2007–; Cambridge Univ. Life Scis, 2008–; Avila, 2008–12; Wales Cancer Bank, 2009–; Evgen Ltd, 2012–. Consultant to: Abingworth, 2005–; Sequella, 2007–; Shroders, Life Scis, 2007–; MVM, 2007–. Non-exec. Dir, Medicines and Healthcare Products Regulatory Agency, 2008–15. Hon. Prof., Sch. of Biol. Scis, 2002–06, Sch. of Life Scis, 2006–, Univ. of Manchester; William Pitt Fellow, Pembroke Coll., Cambridge, 2003–. Gen. Sec., 1990–93, Chm., 1993–96, Soc. for Endocrinol.; Chm., Med. Scis Forum, Acad. of Med. Scis, 2005–08 (Vice-Chm., 2003–05). Trustee: Breast Cancer Campaign, 2004–11; Cancer Res. UK, 2005–08. FMedSci 2002. Award for Drug Discovery, Soc. for Drug Res., 1991; Jubilee Medal, Soc. for Endocrinology, 1997. *Publications:* (ed) Clinics in Oncology on Hormone Therapy, 1982; (ed) Clinics in Oncology on Prostate Cancer, 1988; (ed with A. E. Wakeling) Pharmacology and Clinical Uses of Inhibitors of Hormone Secretion and Action, 1987; (ed) Aromatase Inhibitors, 2007, 2nd edn 2009; over 180 papers on reproductive endocrinology, anti-hormones and cancer. *Recreations:* listening to music, trying to solve crossword puzzles, organising local election campaigns for the Liberal Democrats. *E:* barry.furr@llangarth.com, barry.furr@yahoo.co.uk. *Club:* Royal Society of Medicine.

FURSDON, (Edward) David; a Crown Estate Commissioner, 2008–Jan. 2016; rural consultant, since 2008; Lord-Lieutenant of Devon, since 2015; *b* Sevenoaks, 20 Dec. 1952; *s* of Maj. Gen. (Francis William) Edward Fursdon, CB, MBE and Joan Fursdon; *m* 1978, Catriona Margaret McCreath; three *s*. *Educ:* Sherborne Sch.; St John's Coll., Oxford (Scholar; BA 1975; Cricket Blue); RAC, Cirencester. FRICS 1998. Owner/manager, Fursdon Estate, 1981–; Officer, 6th QEO Gurkha Rifles, 1971–72; civil servant, MoD and UN, Geneva, 1975–79; Teacher, Blundell's Sch., 1979–84; RAC, Cirencester, 1984–86; Land agent, 1986–94; Partner, Stags, 1994–2007. Chm., 2003–05, Pres., 2005–07, CLA. Comr, English Heritage, 2010–14; Mem. Bd, SW RDA, 2009–12. Chm., Future of Farming Rev., 2013–14. Chairman: SW Bd for 2012 Games, 2010–12; SW Rural and Farming Network, 2011–15; Beeswax Farming Ltd, 2014–. Gov., Blundell's Sch., 1984–2011 (Chm., 2000–11). FAAV 1988; FRAgS 2011 (ARAgS 2007). DL, 2004, High Sheriff, 2009–10, Devon. *Recreations:* planting trees, appreciating landscape, buildings and gardens, moving from playing to watching sport. *Address:* c/o The Crown Estate, 16 New Burlington Place, W1S 2HX. *T:* (020) 7851 5000. *E:* david.fursdon@fursdon.co.uk. *Clubs:* Farmers, MCC; Vincent's (Oxford).

FURSE, Dame Clara (Hedwig Frances), DBE 2008; Chief Executive, London Stock Exchange plc, 2001–09; *b* 16 Sept. 1957; 2nd *d* of Herman Werner Siemens and Cornélie Siemens-Gravin Schimmelpenninck; *m* 1981, Richard Furse; two *s* one *d*. *Educ:* St James's Sch., W Malvern; London Sch. of Econs (BScEcon). Joined UBS, 1983, Man. Dir, 1995–98; Gp Chief Exec., Credit Lyonnais Rouse, 1998–2000. Dep. Chm., LIFFE, 1997–99. Non-executive Director: Legal & General, 2009–13; Nomura International, 2009–13; Nomura Europe Hldgs, 2009–13; Nomura Hldgs, 2010–; Amadeus IT Hldgs SA, 2010–; DWP, 2011–; Vodafone, 2014–. Mem., Financial Policy Cttee, Bank of England, 2013–.

FURSSEDONN-WOOD, Scott; HM Diplomatic Service; Deputy High Commissioner, Kolkata, since 2013; *b* Harrow, 13 Feb. 1978; *s* of Leonard and Joan Furssedonn; *m* 2005, Elizabeth Wood; one *s* two *d*. *Educ:* Hatch End High Sch.; Northwood Sch.; Merton Coll., Oxford (BA Hons PPE); Open Univ. (MBA). Second, later First Sec., UK Perm. Representation to EU, 2001–06; Private Sec. to Minister of State for Middle East and S Asia, 2006–08; First Sec., Washington, 2008–13. *Recreations:* travel, being a dad, long walks with the dog. *Address:* c/o Foreign and Commonwealth Office, King Charles Street, SW1A 2AH. *E:* scott-furssedonn@fco.gov.uk. *Clubs:* Bengal; Calcutta, Tollygunge (Kolkata).

FURST, David Anthony; Director, Robert Hitchins Group Ltd, since 2012; Finance Director, Powell Gilbert LLP, since 2012; *b* London, 4 Sept. 1950; *s* of Arthur Gerald Furst and Aline Verity Furst; *m* 1987, Anne Elizabeth Fleming; two *s* two *d*. *Educ:* Leighton Park Sch., Reading. FCA 1973. Horwath Clark Whitehill, later Crowe Clark Whitehill: Partner, 1984–2012; Chief Exec., 1998–2004; Chm., 2004–12. Founder Mem. Cttee, Assoc. of Partnership Practitioners, 1998–2004. Mem. Bd, Crowe Horwarth (formerly Horwarth) Internat., 2002–08. Pres., ICAEW, 2008–09; Chm., CCAB, 2008–09. Mem., Takeover Panel, 2008–09. *Publications:* Essential Guide to Self Assessment, 1994; regular contrib. to legal and accountancy jls. *Recreations:* bridge, ski-ing, watching motor racing, Rugby, cricket and football. *Address:* Dial House, Shepperton Road, Laleham, Middx TW18 1SE. *Clubs:* MCC; Goodwood Road Racing, Silverstone Racing.

FURST, Stephen Andrew; QC 1991; a Recorder, since 1999; a Deputy High Court Judge, since 2010; *b* 8 Feb. 1951; *s* of Herbert and Viviane Furst; *m* 1979, Bridget Collins (marr. diss. 2013); one *s* one *d*. *Educ:* Edinburgh Academy; St Edmund Hall, Oxford (BA Hons); Leeds Univ. (LLB Hons). Called to the Bar, Middle Temple, 1975, Bencher, 2000. An Asst Recorder, 1993–99. Joint Editor, Construction Law Yearbook, 1994–. *Publications:* (ed jtly) Keating on Construction Contracts, 9th edn 2012, 2nd Supplement to 9th edn, 2015. *Recreations:* bee-keeping, watercolour painting. *Address:* Keating Chambers, 15 Essex Street, WC2R 3AA. *T:* (020) 7544 2600.

FURTADO, Peter Randall, FRHistS; Director, Shilbrook Associates, since 2012; *b* 20 May 1952; *s* of Robert Audley Furtado and Marcelle Elizabeth Furtado (*née* Whitteridge); *m* 1st, 1977, Roberta Jane Day (marr. diss.); 2nd, 1983, (Margaret Elizabeth) Ann Swoffer; three *d*. *Educ:* Whitgift Sch., Croydon; Oriel Coll., Oxford (BA 1st Cl. Hons 1973; Dip. Hist. Art 1974). Sen. ed., Hamlyn Books, 1977–83; freelance ed., 1983–87; sen. ed., Equinox Books, 1987–91; Exec. Ed., Andromeda Books, 1991–97; Ed., History Today, 1997–2008. Managing Editor: The Ordnance Survey Atlas of Great Britain, 1981; The Illustrated History of the 20th Century, 10 vols, 1989–92; The Cassell Atlas of World History, 1996. Chm., Bd of Dirs, Shintaido Foundn, 1994–97, 2002–09; Dir, Internat. Shintaido Foundn, 2003–12; Lead Consultant, SiftGroups Ltd, 2010–12. FRHistS 2002. Hon. DLitt Oxford Brookes, 2009. *Publications:* 1001 Days That Shaped the World, 2008; Living Histories: Restoration England, 2010; History's Daybook, 2011; The Histories of Nations, 2012. *Recreations:* life, liberty, pursuit of happiness. *Address:* 1 Marlborough Court, Duke Street, Oxford OX2 0QT. *T:* (01865) 251234. *E:* pfurtado1543@gmail.com.

FURY, Alexander Louis; Fashion Editor, The Independent and i, since 2013; *b* Bolton, 15 Dec. 1982; *s* of Paul and Janet Fury. *Educ:* Central St Martins Coll. of Art and Design (BA Hons Fashion Hist. and Theory). Fashion Dir, SHOWstudio.com, 2008–12; Ed., Love Mag., 2012–13. *Publications:* Pattern, 2013; (jtly) Isabella Blow: Fashion Galore!, 2014. *Recreations:* fashion, 18th century French history, rabbits. *Address:* The Independent, 2 Derry Street, W8 5HF. *T:* (020) 3615 2514.

FUTCHER, Ven. Christopher David; Archdeacon of Exeter, since 2012; *b* Luton, 6 Jan. 1958; *s* of David and Brenda Futcher; *m* 1986, Anne Myers; one *s* one *d*. *Educ:* Strode's Grammar Sch., Egham; Univ. of Edinburgh (BD 1980); Heythrop Coll., Univ. of London (MTh 2004); King's Coll. London (MA 2011). Ordained deacon, 1982, priest, 1983; Asst Curate, Borehamwood Team Ministry, 1982–85; Asst Curate, 1985–88, Vicar, 1988–96, All Saints, Pin Green, Stevenage; Vicar, St Stephen's, St Albans, 1996–2000; Rector, Harpenden, 2000–12. *Recreations:* reading, walking, sailing, music, theatre. *Address:* Emmanuel House, Station Road, Ide, Exeter EX2 9RS. *T:* (01392) 425577. *E:* archdeacon.of.exeter@exeter.anglican.org.

FYFE, Maria; Member, Scottish Policy Forum, since 2008, and Better Politics Commission, since 2010, Labour Party; *b* 25 Nov. 1938; *d* of James O'Neill and Margaret Lacey; *m* 1964, James Joseph Fyfe (decd); two *s*. *Educ:* Strathclyde Univ. (BA Hons Economic History 1975). Senior Lecturer, Trade Union Studies Unit, Glasgow Central College of Commerce, 1978–87. Mem., Labour Party, 1960–, Scottish Exec., 1981–88; Mem., Glasgow District Council, 1980–87 (Vice-Convener, Finance Cttee, 1980–84; Convener, Personnel Cttee, 1984–87). MP (Lab) Glasgow, Maryhill, 1987–2001. Dep. Shadow Minister for Women, 1988–91; Convener, Scottish Gp of Labour MPs, 1991–92; Scottish front bench spokesperson, 1992–95. Chair: Labour Deptl Cttee on Internat. Develt, 1997–2001; Labour Gp, UK Delegn to Council of Europe, 1997–2001; Mem., Nat. Policy Forum, Labour Party, 2010–. Vice-Chair, Glasgow Housing Assoc., 2001–06. DUniv Glasgow, 2002. Columnist on Scottish affairs, Tribune mag., 2014–. *Publications:* A Problem Like Maria: a woman's eye view of life as an MP, 2014; Women Saying No: making a positive case against independence, 2014. *Address:* 10 Ascot Avenue, Glasgow G12 0AX. *T:* (0141) 334 6737.

FYFE, William Stevenson, CBE 1992 (OBE 1987); FIIM; Chairman, Greater Glasgow Health Board, 1993; *b* Glasgow, 10 June 1935; *s* of Dr Andrew Fyfe and Janet Isabella Fyfe (*née* Soutar), New Cumnock; *m* 1986, Margaret H. H. Auld; one *s* one *d*. *Educ:* Dollar Acad.; Scottish Coll. of Commerce. FIIM 1985. Town Councillor (C), Prestwick, 1967–73; Co. Councillor (C), Ayrshire, 1970–73; Ayrshire and Arran Health Board: Financial Convener, 1973–81; Chm., 1981–93. Exec. Officer, Minerva Housing Assoc., Prestwick, 1997–2004. Chm., Scottish Health Services Adv. Council, 1989–93; Mem., General Whitley Council, 1989–93. *Recreation:* gardening. *Address:* 30 Kilbrandon Crescent, Doonfoot, Ayr KA7 4JX.

FYFIELD, Frances; novelist; solicitor; *b* 8 Nov. 1948; *d* of Dr Andrew George Hegarty and Winifred Doris Hegarty (*née* Fyfield). *Educ:* convent and grammar schools, Newcastle upon Tyne; Newcastle upon Tyne Univ. (BA English Lit. 1970); Coll. of Law. Admitted solicitor, 1973; a solicitor: for Metropolitan Police, 1973–80; for DPP, 1980–86; CPS, 1986–97, pt-time, 1997–2005; lawyer and novelist, 1987–2000. Registrar, Royal Literary Fund. Presenter, Tales from the Stave, Radio 4, 2007–09, 2011–15. *Publications:* A Question of Guilt, 1988 (televised 1994); Shadows on the Mirror, 1989; Trial by Fire, 1990 (televised 1999); Deep Sleep (Silver Dagger Award, CWA), 1990; Shadow Play, 1991; Perfectly Pure and Good, 1992; A Clear Conscience, 1994 (Grand Prix de Literature Policière, 1998); Without Consent, 1996; Blind Date, 1998 (televised 2000); Staring at the Light, 1999; Undercurrents, 2000; Helen West Omnibus, 2002 (televised, as Helen West, 2002); The Nature of the Beast, 2001; Seeking Sanctuary, 2003; Looking Down, 2004; Safer Than Houses, 2005; The Art of Drowning, 2006; Blood from Stone (Gold Dagger Award, CWA), 2008; Cold to the Touch, 2009; Gold Digger, 2013; Casting the First Stone, 2014; *as Frances Hegarty:* The Playroom, 1990; Half Light, 1992; Let's Dance, 1995. *Recreations:* tobacco and fine wine, paintings, company, watching the sea. *Address:* c/o Rogers Coleridge and White, 20 Powis Mews, W11 1JN.

FYSH, Marcus John Hudson; MP (C) Yeovil, since 2015; *b* Australia, 8 Nov. 1970; *m*; one *d*. Mercury Asset Mgt, 1993–2003; set up own business, 2003. Member (C): S Somerset DC; Somerset CC. *Address:* House of Commons, SW1A 0AA.

FYSH, His Honour (Robert) Michael; QC 1989; QC (NI) 1990; a Circuit Judge, Patents County Court, 2001–10; *b* 2 Aug. 1940; *s* of Dr Leslie Fysh and Margaret Fysh, Ashford, Kent; *m* 1971, Mary Bevan; three *s*. *Educ:* Downside Sch.; Exeter Coll., Oxford (MA). Called to the Bar, Inner Temple, 1965, Bencher, 1999; NI, 1974; NSW, 1975; Ireland, 1975; India, 1982; Pakistan, 1987; SC Trinidad and Tobago Bar, 1990; SC Dublin, 1994. A Dep. High Court Judge, Chancery Div., 1997–2010; an Additional Judge, Technol. and Construction Court, 2002–10. Chm., Copyright Tribunal, 2006–10. CEDR Mediator, 2011. Vis. Prof., Intellectual Property Inst., New Delhi, 2002. Hon. LLD Wolverhampton, 2005. *Publications:* Russell-Clarke on Registered Designs, 4th edn 1974; The Industrial Property Citator, 1982, 2nd edn 1996; (ed) The Spycatcher Cases, 1989; (consulting ed.) The Modern Law of Patents, 2005, 2nd edn 2010. *Recreations:* forestry, swimming, travel. *Address:* c/o 8 New Square, Lincoln's Inn, WC2A 3QP. *Club:* Kildare Street and University (Dublin).

FYSON, Anne Elizabeth; *see* Howells, A. E.

G

GABATHULER, Prof. Erwin, OBE 2001; FRS 1990; FInstP; Sir James Chadwick Professor of Physics, Liverpool University, 1991–2001, now Emeritus Professor (Professor of Experimental Physics, 1983–91); *b* 16 Nov. 1933; *s* of Hans and Lena Gabathuler; *m* 1962, Susan Dorothy Jones; two *s* one *d*. *Educ:* Queen's University Belfast (BSc 1956; MSc 1957); Univ. of Glasgow (PhD 1961). Research Fellow, Cornell Univ., 1961–64; Group Leader, Research, SERC, Daresbury Lab., 1964–73; CERN (European Organisation for Nuclear Research): Vis. Scientist, EMC Experiment, 1974–77; Leader, Exp. Physics Div., 1978–80; Dir of Research, 1981–83; Hd of Physics Dept, Liverpool Univ., 1986–91 and 1996–99. Chm., Particle Physics Cttee, SERC, 1985–88; Member: Nuclear Physics Bd, 1985–88; NATO Collaborative Research Grants Panels, 1990–93; Educn and Trng Cttee, PPARC, 1994–96. Dr *hc* Univ. of Uppsala, 1982; Hon. DSc QUB, 1997. Rutherford Medal, Inst. of Physics, 1992. *Publications:* articles in research jls. *Recreations:* music, walking. *Address:* 3 Danebank Road, Lymm, Cheshire WA13 9DQ. *T:* (01925) 752753.

GABBANA, Stefano; President, Dolce & Gabbana; *b* 14 Nov. 1962. Asst in design studio, Milan; with Domenico Dolce opened fashion consulting studio, 1982; Co-founder, Dolce & Gabbana, 1985; first major women's collection, 1986; knitwear, 1987; beachwear, lingerie, 1989; men's collection, 1990; women's fragrance, 1992; D&G line, men's fragrance, 1994; eyewear, 1995; opened boutiques in major cities in Europe, America and Asia. *Publications:* (with Domenico Dolce): 10 Years Dolce & Gabbana, 1996; Wildness, 1997; Mémoires de la Mode, 1998; Animal, 1998; Calcio, 2004; Music, 2005; 20 Years Dolce & Gabbana, 2005; (with Eve Claxton and Domenico Dolce) Hollywood, 2003. *Address:* Dolce & Gabbana, Via Goldoni 10, 20129 Milan, Italy.

GABBITAS, Peter; Director of Health and Social Care, Edinburgh City Council, since 2005; *b* 15 Aug. 1961; *s* of Robert and Mary Gabbitas; *m* 1986, Karen Brown; one *d*. *Educ:* St Thomas Aquinas RC Grammar Sch.; Durham Univ. (BA Gen. Arts 1984); Warwick Univ. (MBA Dist. 1994). DipHSM 1987. NHS gen. mgt trainee, 1984–86; Director: of Service Develt, Solihull Acute Trust, 1989–91; of Ops, Dudley Gp of Hosps, 1991–97; Chief Executive: E and Midlothian NHS Trust, 1997–99; W Lothian Healthcare NHS Trust, 1999–2005. *Recreations:* golf, gardening, swimming, stained and fused glass. *Address:* City of Edinburgh Council/NHS Lothian, Waverley Court, 4 East Market Street, Edinburgh EH8 8BG. *E:* peter.gabbitas@edinburgh.gov.uk. *Club:* Glen Golf.

GABER, Prof. Ivor Harold; Professor of Journalism, University of Sussex, since 2015; freelance journalist, consultant and trainer; *b* High Wycombe, 23 Nov. 1946; *s* of Jack Gaber and Alice Gaber; *m* 1974, Jane; three *d*. *Educ:* Woodberry Down Comp. Sch., London; Univ. of Warwick (BA Hist. and Pols 1970); Univ. of Sussex (MA Industrial Relns 1972); City Univ. London (PhD Journalism Studies 2013). Asst Ed., Drugs and Society mag., 1971–73; TV journalist, Reuters TV, London, Sydney and Rome, 1973–76; Industrial Corresp., Evening Post-Echo, Hemel Hempstead, 1976–78; scriptwriter and investigative reporter, ITN, 1978–82; producer and reporter, BBC TV Current Affairs, 1982–86; Prof. and Hd, Dept of Media and Communications, Goldsmiths' Coll., Univ. of London, 1986–2000, now Emeritus Prof. of Broadcast Journalism; Res. Prof. in Media and Politics, Univ. of Bedfordshire, 2006–14; Prof. of Political Journalism and Dir, Political Journalism MA Course, City Univ. London, 2008–14; freelance TV and radio presenter and editor, BBC, ITN, Channel 4 and Sky News, 1986–. Ind. Editl Advr, BBC Trust, 2010–. Member: UK Delegn to UNESCO Gen. Conf., Paris, 2001, 2003, 2007; Freedom of Expression Panel, FCO, 2004–; Internat. Adv. Bd, Centre for Study of Global Media and Democracy, 2006–; Munro Inquiry into Child Protection, 2011; Vice Chm., Communications Sector, UK UNESCO Nat. Commn, 2006–; UK Rep., Inter-Govtl Council, Internat. Prog. for Develt Communication, UNESCO, 2010–. Mem., Adv. Council, Hansard Soc., 2006–. Member: Jury, RTS Television News Awards, 2008, 2009; Judging Panel, One World Media Awards, 2011. FAcSS (AcSS 2009); FHEA 2013. *Publications:* (with J. Aldridge) In the Best Interests of the Child: culture, identity and transracial adoption, 1994; (jtly) Environmentalism and the Mass Media: the north-south divide, 1997; (with S. Barnett) The Westminster Tales: the 21st century crisis in political journalism, 2001; (jtly) Culture Wars: the media and the British Left, 2006; Live from Africa: a handbook for African radio journalists, 2007; articles on media, politics and public affairs in learned jls, nat. newspapers and magazines incl. Guardian, Sunday Times, New Statesman, Tribune and THES. *Recreations:* playing tennis, supporting Queens Park Rangers, ski-ing, visiting the cinema, theatre, opera, travel. *E:* ivorgaber@gmail.com.

GABITASS, Jonathan Roger, MA; Head Master, Merchant Taylors' School, 1991–2004; *b* 25 July 1944; *s* of William Gabitass and Nell Gabitass (*née* Chaffe); *m* 1967, Fiona Patricia Hoy; two *d*. *Educ:* Plymouth Coll.; St John's Coll., Oxford (MA English Lang. and Lit., PGCE). Asst English teacher, Clifton Coll., Bristol, 1967–73; Head of English, 1973–78, Second Master, 1978–91, Abingdon Sch., Oxon. Governor: Godolphin and Latymer Sch., 2004–; Abingdon Sch., 2005–; Abingdon Prep. Sch., 2005–; St Helen and St Katharine's Sch., 2007–. Liveryman, Merchant Taylors' Co., 2005–. *Recreations:* Rugby football, Cornish coastal path walking, 18th and 19th Century caricature, art galleries and theatre. *Clubs:* East India; Vincent's (Oxford).

GABRA, Prof. Hani, PhD; FRCP, FRCPE; Professor of Medical Oncology, since 2003, Director, Ovarian Cancer Action Research Centre, since 2006, and Deputy Head, Division of Cancer, since 2013, Imperial College London; Hon. Consultant Medical Oncologist, since 2003, and Head of Medical Oncology, since 2013, Imperial College Healthcare NHS Trust; *b* Cairo, 15 Jan. 1963; *s* of Gamal and Samira Gabra; *m* 1992, Laura Lee (separated 2013); two *s* one *d*. *Educ:* Carluke High Sch., Carluke, Lanarkshire; Univ. of Glasgow (BSc Hons 1984; MB ChB 1987); Univ. of Edinburgh (MSc 1993; PhD 1996). MRCP 1990, FRCP 2005; FRCPE 2003. ICRF Clin. Scientist and Hon. Consultant Med. Oncologist, CRUK Med. Oncol. Unit, Western Gen. Hosp., Edinburgh, 1998–2003; Lead for Cancer Clin. Trials, Imperial Coll. London, 2012–; Lead for Div. 1 and Associate Dir, NIHR Clinical Res. Network for NW London, 2014–. Pres., Eur. Translational Ovarian Cancer Network, 2010. *Recreations:* cycling, stargazing. *Address:* Department of Surgery and Cancer, 4th Floor, Institute of Reproductive and Developmental Biology, Imperial College London, Hammersmith Campus, Du Cane Road, W12 0NN. *T:* (020) 7594 2792, *Fax:* (020) 7594 2154. *E:* h.gabra@imperial.ac.uk. *Club:* Caledonian.

GABRIEL, Peter; singer, musician and songwriter; *b* 13 Feb. 1950; *m* 1st, 1971, Jill Moore (marr. diss.); two *d*; 2nd, 2002, Meabh Flynn; two *s*. *Educ:* Charterhouse. Mem., Genesis, 1966–75; solo artist, 1975–. Founder: World of Music, Arts and Dance (annual festivals), 1982; Real World Gp, 1985; Real World Studios, 1986; Real World Records, 1989; Real World Multimedia, 1994; Jt Founder, Witness (human rights programme), 1992; Co-founder, theElders.org, 2000. *Albums* include: *with Genesis:* From Genesis to Revelation, 1969; Nursery Crime, 1971; Foxtrot, 1972; Selling England by the Pound, 1973; The Lamb Lies Down on Broadway, 1974; *solo:* Peter Gabriel I, 1977, II, 1978, III, 1980, IV, 1982; So, 1986; Us, 1992; Ovo, 2000; Up, 2002; Scratch My Back, 2010; *film soundtracks:* Birdy, 1984; Last Temptation of Christ, 1988; Rabbit-Proof Fence, 2002; WALL·E, 2008. *Address:* Real World, Box Mill, Box, Wilts SN13 8PL.

GADD, (John) Staffan; Hon. Chairman, Gadd & Co. AB, Stockholm, 2005–09; Hon. Vice President, Swedish Chamber of Commerce for UK, since 1996 (Chairman, 1993–96); Chairman, Saga Securities Ltd, 1985–98; *b* 30 Sept. 1934; *s* of John Gadd and Ulla Olivecrona; *m* 1st, 1958, Margaretha Löfborg (marr. diss.); one *s* one *d*; 2nd, 1990, Kay McGreeghan. *Educ:* Stockholm Sch. of Econs. MBA. Sec., Confedn of Swedish Industries, 1958–61; Skandinaviska Banken, Stockholm, 1961–69 (London Rep., 1964–67); Dep. Man. Dir, Scandinavian Bank Ltd, London, 1969–71, Chief Exec. and Man. Dir, 1971–80; Chief Exec., 1980–84, Chm., 1982–84, Samuel Montagu & Co. Ltd; Chm., Montagu and Co. AB, Sweden, 1982–86; Dir, Guyerzeller Zurmont Bank AG, Switzerland, 1983–84; Chm., J. S. Gadd Cie SA, Geneva, 1989–98; Mem. Bd, Carta Corporate Advisors AB, 1990–98. *Recreations:* the arts, walking, travel. *Address:* Locks Manor, Hurstpierpoint, West Sussex BN6 9JZ.

GADD, Ruth Maria; *see* Kelly, Rt Hon. R. M.

GADDES, (John) Gordon; Chairman and Trustee, Langa Township Pre-Schools Trust UK, since 2011; *b* 22 May 1936; *s* of late James Graham Moscrop Gaddes and of Irene Gaddes (*née* Murray; who later married E. O. Kine); *m* 1958, Pamela Jean (*née* Marchbank); one *s* one *d*. *Educ:* Carre's Grammar Sch., Sleaford; Selwyn Coll., Cambridge (MA Hons Geography); London Univ. (BScEcon Hons 1966; MA Philosophy and Religion 2005). Asst Lectr in Business Studies, Peterborough Technical Coll., 1960–64; Lectr in Business Studies, later Head of Business Studies, then Vice-Principal, Dacorum Coll. of Further Educn, Hemel Hempstead, 1964–69; Head of Export Services: British Standards Instn, 1969–72; Quality Assurance Dept, 1972–73; Dir, BSI Hemel Hempstead Centre, 1973–77; Commercial Dir, BSI, 1977–81; Dir, Information, Marketing and Resources, BSI, 1981–82; Dir Gen., BEAMA, 1982–97; UK Deleg., 1997, Sec. Gen., 1998–2001, Pres., 2001–03, European Orgn for Testing and Certification, subseq. for Conformity Assessment; Dir, DENS Ltd (formerly Dacorum Emergency Night Shelter), 2003–10 (Chm., 2003–07). Dir, Gaddes Associates Ltd, 1998–2007. Secretary, BSI Quality Assurance Council, 1976–80; Member: Council, 1982–97, President's Cttee, 1984–86, Production Cttee, 1984–88, CBI; NACCB, 1984–90 (Chm., Assessment Panel, 1985–90); Project Leader for ISO/UNESCO inf. network study, 1974–75; variously, consultant to UNIDO, EC and HMG; UK Rep., ORGALIME, 1982–97 (Chairman: Electrical and Electronic Inds Liaison Cttee, 1982–86; Finance and Admin Cttee, 1986–88; Exec. Cttee, 1988–90); Pres., CENELEC, 1989–91 (Dep. Pres., 1987–89, 1994–95); Chairman: Eur. Electrotechnical Sectoral Cttee for Testing and Certification, 1992–95; ASTA Certification Services, 1994–98; UK Ex Forum, 1995–97; Kennedy Mgt Develt, 1998–99. Gov., Adeyfield Sch., 2001–12 (Vice-Chm., 2005–12). Mem., Fabian Soc., 2011–. Vice-Chm., 2005–08, Treas., 2015–, Parish of St Mary and St Paul, Hemel Hempstead. *Recreations:* golf, swimming, family, church and community affairs. *Clubs:* Athenæum; Whipsnade Park Golf.

GADHIA, Jayne-Anne, CBE 2014; Chief Executive Officer, Virgin Money, since 2007; *b* Stourbridge, 19 Oct. 1961; *d* of Geoffrey and Gwendoline Finch; *m* 1984, Ashou Gadhia; one *d*. *Educ:* Univ. of London (BA Hons Hist.). CA 1989. Trainee chartered accountant, Ernst & Young, 1982–87; Hd, Unit Trust Mktg/Business and Finance Manager, Norwich Union, 1987–94; Ops and Compliance Dir, Virgin Direct, 1994–98; Man. Dir, Virgin One Account, 1998–2001; Hd, Gp Mortgages, RBS, 2001–07. FCIB. *Recreations:* horses, music, film, France. *Address:* Virgin Money, 28 St Andrew Square, Edinburgh EH2 1AF.

GADHIA, Jitesh; Senior Managing Director, Blackstone Advisory Partners LP, since 2010; *b* Kampala, Uganda, 27 May 1970; *s* of Kishore and Hansa Gadhia; *m* 2001, Angeli Saujani. *Educ:* Fitzwilliam Coll., Cambridge (BA Hons Econs 1991); London Business Sch. (Sloan Fellow; MSc Mgt). Baring Bros, 1991–98; Manek Investment Mgt, 1998–99; ABN AMRO, 2001–08; Man. Dir, Global Head of Advisory, Barclays Capital, 2008–10. Mem. Bd, UK Financial Investments, 2014–. Trustee: Guy's and St Thomas' Charity, 1999–2009; NESTA, 2007–14. *Recreations:* charitable activities, reading, walking, cinema, travel. *Address:* The Blackstone Group, 40 Berkeley Square, W1J 5AL.

GADNEY, Jane Caroline Rebecca; *see* Parker-Smith, J. C. R.

GADSBY, Prof. David Christopher, PhD; FRS 2005; Patrick A. Gerschel Family Professor, Laboratory of Cardiac/Membrane Physiology, Rockefeller University, since 2007. *Educ:* Trinity Coll., Cambridge (BA 1969, MA 1973); University Coll. London (PhD 1978). Rockefeller University: Asst Prof., 1978–84, Associate Prof., 1984–91, Lab. of Cardiac Physiol.; Prof. and Hd, Lab. of Cardiac/Membrane Physiol., 1991–2007. *Publications:* contrib. learned jls. *Address:* Laboratory of Cardiac/Membrane Physiology, Rockefeller University, 1230 York Avenue, New York, NY 10065, USA.

GAFFNEY, James Anthony, CBE 1984; FREng; FICE; *b* Bargoed, Glam, 9 Aug. 1928; *s* of James Francis and Violet Mary Gaffney; *m* 1953, Margaret Mary, 2nd *d* of E. and G. J. Evans, Pontypridd; one *s* two *d*. *Educ:* De La Salle Coll.; St Illtyd's Coll., Cardiff; UWIST; UC, Cardiff (Fellow, 1984). BSc (Eng) London. FREng (FEng 1979); FICE 1968; FInstHE 1970. Highway Engr, Glam CC, 1948–60; Asst County Surveyor, Somerset CC, 1960–64; Deputy County Surveyor, Notts CC, 1964–69; County Engr and Surveyor, WR Yorks, 1969–74; Dir Engrg Services, W Yorks MCC, 1974–86. President: County Surveyors' Soc., 1977–78; Instn of Highway Engrs, 1978–79; ICE, 1983–84; Vice-Pres., Fellowship of

Engrg, 1989–92. Hon. DSc: Wales, 1982; Bradford, 1984. *Recreations:* golf, travel, supporting Rugby. *Address:* Drovers Cottage, 3 Boston Road, Wetherby, W Yorks LS22 5HA. *Club:* Alwoodley Golf (Leeds).

GAFFNEY, John Campion B.; *see* Burke-Gaffney.

GAGE, family name of **Viscount Gage**.

GAGE, 8th Viscount *cr* 1720 (Ire.); **Henry Nicholas Gage;** DL; Bt 1622; Baron Gage (Ire.) 1720; Baron Gage (GB) 1790; *b* 9 April 1934; *yr s* of 6th Viscount Gage, KCVO and his 1st wife, Hon. Alexandra Imogen Clare Grenfell (*d* 1969), *yr d* of 1st Baron Desborough, KG, GCVO; *S* brother, 1993; *m* 1st, 1974, Lady Diana Adrienne Beatty (marr. diss. 2002); two *s*; 2nd, 2009, Alexandra Murray Templeton; one *s*. *Educ:* Eton; Christ Church, Oxford. 2nd Lt Coldstream Guards, 1953. DL East Sussex, 1998. *Recreation:* country and other pursuits. *Heir: s* Hon. Henry William Gage, *b* 25 June 1975. *Address:* Firle Place, Lewes, East Sussex BN8 6LP. *T:* (01273) 858535.

GAGE, Rt Hon. Sir William (Marcus), Kt 1993; PC 2004; a Lord Justice of Appeal, 2004–08; a Surveillance Commissioner, 2009–15; *b* 22 April 1938; *s* of late His Honour Conolly Gage; *m* 1962, Penelope Mary Groves; three *s*. *Educ:* Repton; Sidney Sussex Coll., Cambridge. MA. National Service, Irish Guards, 1956–58. Called to the Bar, Inner Temple, 1963, Bencher, 1991; QC 1982; a Recorder, 1985–93; a Judge of the High Court of Justice, QBD, 1993–2004. Presiding Judge, S Eastern Circuit, 1997–2000. Chancellor, diocese of Coventry, 1980–2009, of Ely, 1989–2012. Chm., Baha Mousa Public Inquiry, 2008–11 (report published 2011); Member: Criminal Injuries Compensation Bd, 1987–93; Parole Bd, 2001–04. *Recreations:* shooting, fishing, travel. *Address:* Office of Surveillance Commissioners, PO Box 29105, SW1V 1ZU.

GAGEBY DENHAM, Susan; *see* Denham.

GAGEN, Heather Jacqueline; *see* Yasamee, H. J.

GAHAGAN, Michael Barclay, CB 2000; Director, Housing (formerly Housing, Private Policy and Analysis) Directorate, Office of the Deputy Prime Minister (formerly Department for the Environment, Transport and the Regions, then Department for Transport, Local Government and the Regions), 1997–2003; *b* 24 March 1943; *s* of Geoffrey and Doris Gahagan; *m* 1967, Anne Brown; two *s*. *Educ:* St Mary's Coll., Southampton; Univ. of Manchester (MA Econs, BA). MRICS. W. H. Robinson & Co., Chartered Surveyors, Manchester, 1964–66; DEA (NW), 1966–69; Min. of Housing and Local Govt (NW), 1969–71; DoE, Central Res. and Inner Cities Directorates, NW, SE and London Regl Offices, 1971–88; seconded to DTI Inner Cities Unit, 1988–91; Dir, Inner Cities, subseq. Cities and Countryside Policy, then Regeneration, Directorate, DoE, 1991–96. Pres., Internat. Urban Develt Assoc., 1995–99. Chairman: S Yorks Housing Market Renewal Pathfinder, 2003–11; Doncaster Housing Improvement Bd, 2011–12; Member, Board: Paradigm Housing Gp, 2003–13 (Chm., Homes (formerly Ops) Bd, 2008–13); Centre for Refurbishment Excellence, 2011– (Chm., 2012–); Chm., Paradigm Foundn, 2013–. *Recreations:* soccer, bridge.

GAIMSTER, Prof. David Richard Michael, PhD; FSA; Director, The Hunterian (formerly Hunterian Museum and Art Gallery), University of Glasgow, since 2010; *b* 3 Jan. 1962; *s* of late Rev. Leslie Rayner Gaimster and of Mareike Gaimster (*née* Döhler); *m* 1st 1990, Märit Thurborg (marr. diss. 2004); one *s* one *d*; 2nd, 2005, Amy Clarke; one *s* two *d*. *Educ:* Longsands Sch., St Neots, Cambs; Durham Univ. (BA Hons Archaeol. 1984); University Coll. London (PhD Medieval Archaeol. 1991). Asst Keeper, Dept of Medieval and Later Antiquities, BM, 1986–2001; Sen. Policy Advr, Cultural Property Unit, DCMS, 2002–04; Gen. Sec. and Chief Exec., Soc. of Antiquaries, 2004–10. Associate Prof. in Historical Archaeol., Dept of Cultural Scis, Univ. of Turku, Finland, 2000–; Vis. Prof., Sch. of Archaeol. and Ancient History, Leicester Univ., 2009–; Hon. Res. Fellow, Inst. of Archaeol., UCL, 2000–. Mem., Culture Cttee, 2005–11, Dir, 2009–11, UK Nat. Commn for UNESCO. Member, Board: Museums Galleries Scotland, 2012–; Historic Envmt Scotland, 2015–. FSA 1996; FMA 2008 (AMA 2001); MCIfA (MIFA 1987). OM, Soc. of Historical Archaeol of N America, 2005. *Publications:* German Stoneware 1200–1900: archaeology and cultural history, 1997; (ed jtly) The Age of Transition: the archaeology of English culture 1400–1600, 1997; (ed jtly) Pottery in the Making: world ceramic traditions, 1997; Maiolica in the North: the archaeology of tin-glazed earthenware in NW Europe *c* 1500–1600, 1999; (ed jtly) Novgorod: the archaeology of a Russian medieval city and its hinterland, 2001; (ed jtly) The Archaeology of Reformation 1480–1580, 2003; The Historical Archaeology of Pottery Supply and Demand in the Lower Rhineland, AD 1400–1800, 2006; (ed jtly) Making History: antiquaries in Britain 1707–2007, 2007; (ed jtly) International Handbook of Historical Archaeology, 2009; Director's Choice: the Hunterian, University of Glasgow, 2012; contribs to archaeol and historical monographs and learned jls. *Recreations:* antiques, historic buildings and interiors, travel in N Europe. *Address:* The Hunterian, University of Glasgow, University Avenue, Glasgow G12 8QQ. *T:* (0141) 330 3711, *Fax:* (0141) 330 3617. *E:* david.gaimster@glasgow.ac.uk.

GAINFORD, Barony of *cr* 1917; title not used by 4th Baron (*see* Pease, G.);

GAINS, Sir John (Christopher), Kt 2003; CEng, FICE; Chairman, CCS Group plc, since 2008; Chief Executive, Mowlem (formerly John Mowlem & Co.) PLC, 1995–2004 (Director, 1992–2005); *b* 22 April 1945; *s* of Albert Edward Gains and Grace (*née* Breckenridge); *m* 1st, 1969, Ann Murray (*d* 1999); one *s* one *d*; 2nd, 2012, Prof. Shirley Anne Pearce (DBE 2014). *Educ:* King Henry VIII Sch., Coventry; Loughborough Univ. (BSc). CEng 1970; FICE 1992. Joined John Mowlem & Co. PLC, 1966; Dir, Mowlem Civil Engineering, 1983–95. Chm., Aktrion Hldgs Ltd, 2005–09; non-executive Director: SGB plc, 1997–2000; Heiton Gp plc, 2002–05; Thames Water Utilities Ltd, 2005–06. Mem. Council, Loughborough Univ., 2006–. Hon. DTech Loughborough, 2004. *Recreations:* golf, sailing, walking. *Address:* Longridge, Farm Lane, East Markham, Newark, Notts NG22 0QH. *T:* (01777) 870616. *Clubs:* Reform; Lincoln Golf.

GAINSBOROUGH, 6th Earl of, (2nd) *cr* 1841; **Anthony Baptist Noel;** Bt 1781; Baron Barham, 1805; Viscount Campden, Baron Noel, 1841; *b* 16 Jan. 1950; *e s* of 5th Earl of Gainsborough and of Mary (*née* Stourton); *S* father, 2009; *m* 1972, Sarah Rose (LVO 1996, DL), *er d* of Col T. F. C. Winnington; one *s*. *Educ:* Ampleforth; Royal Agricultural Coll., Cirencester. *Heir: s* Viscount Campden, *qv*. *Address:* Hall Farmhouse, Cottesmore Road, Exton, Oakham, Rutland LE15 8AN. *T:* (01572) 812458.

GAINSBOROUGH, Michael; Commissioner, Royal Hospital, Chelsea, 2001–07 (Secretary, 1994–2001); *b* 13 March 1938; *s* of late George Fotheringham Gainsborough, CBE and Gwendoline Gainsborough (*née* Berry); *m* 1962, Sally, *yr d* of Rt Rev. John Hunter and Philippa Hunter; one *s* two *d*. *Educ:* St Paul's Sch.; Trinity Coll., Oxford. Air Ministry, 1959–64; Ministry of Defence, 1964–78; Defence Counsellor, UK Delegn to NATO, Brussels, FCO, 1978–81; Dir, Resources and Programmes (Strategic Systems), MoD, 1981–83; Asst Under-Sec. of State (Naval Staff), 1984, (Programmes), 1985–86, MoD; Center for Internat. Affairs, Harvard Univ., 1986–87; Asst Under-Sec. of State (Adjutant Gen.), 1987–91, (Service Personnel), 1992, MoD. Mem., Royal Patriotic Fund Corp., 1987–2000. Trustee and Gov., Royal Sch., Hampstead, 1997–2004. *Recreations:* walking, military history, rough gardening. *Address:* 3 Methley Street, SE11 4AL.

GAINSFORD, Sir Ian (Derek), Kt 1995; FDSRCS, FDSRCSE; Dean of King's College School of Medicine and Dentistry, King's College London, 1988–97; Vice-Principal, King's College London, 1994–97, Vice-Principal Emeritus, 2008; *b* 24 June 1930; *s* of late Rabbi Morris Ginsberg, MA, PhD, AKC, and Anne Freda; *m* 1957, Carmel Liebster; one *s* two *d*. *Educ:* Thames Valley Grammar Sch., Twickenham; King's Coll. and King's College Hosp. Med. Sch., London (BDS; FKC 1984); Toronto Univ., Canada (DDS Hons). FDSRCS 1967; FDSRCSE 1998. Junior Staff, King's College Hosp., 1955–57; Member staff, Dept of Conservative Dentistry, London Hosp. Med. Sch., 1957–70; Sen. Lectr/Consultant, Dept of Conservative Dentistry, King's College Hosp., 1970–97; Dep. Dean of Dental Studies, 1973–77; Dir of Clinical Dental Services, KCH, 1977–87 (Dean of Dental Studies, KCHMS, 1977–83); Dean, Faculty of Clinical Dentistry, KCL, 1983–87. President, British Soc. for Restorative Dentistry, 1973–74; Member: BDA, 1956– (Pres., Metropolitan Br., 1981–82); Internat. Dental Fedn, 1966–; American Dental Soc. of London, 1960– (Pres., 1982); Amer. Dental Soc. of Europe, 1965– (Hon. Treas. 1971–77; Pres., 1982); GDC, 1986–94 (Chm., Educn Cttee, 1990–94; Chm., Specialist Trng Adv. Cttee, 1996–2000). Examiner for Membership in General Dental Surgery, RCS, 1979–84 (Chm., 1982–84); External Examiner: Leeds Univ. Dental Sch., 1985–87; Hong Kong Dental Sch., 1988–90; Fellow, and Mem., 1967–, Hon. Mem., 1996, Pres., 1993–94, Odontological Sect., RSM; a Regent, RCSE, 2002–10, now Regent Emeritus. Non-exec. Dir, SE Thames RHA, 1988–93. President: Western Marble Arch Synagogue, 1998–2000; The Maccabaeans, 2000–07; St Marylebone Soc., 2001–04. Hon. Pres., British Friends of Magen David Adom, 1995–2009. Hon. Mem., Amer. Dental Assoc., 1983. Hon. Scientific Advr, British Dental Jl, 1982. FICD 1975; MGDS RCS 1979; FACD 1988; FRSA 1996. Hon. FRCSE 2006. *Publications:* Silver Amalgam in Clinical Practice, 1965, 3rd edn 1992. *Recreations:* theatre, canal cruising. *Address:* Flat 1, 12A Dor Vedorshav, Jerusalem 93117, Israel. *T:* (2) 563 3050. *Clubs:* Athenæum, Royal Society of Medicine.

GAIR, Hon. George Frederick, CMG 1994; QSO 1988; former New Zealand politician; *b* 13 Oct. 1926; *s* of Frederick James Gair and Roemer Elizabeth Elphege (*née* Boecking); *m* 1951, (Esther Mary) Fay Levy; one *s* two *d*. *Educ:* Wellington Coll.; Wairarapa Coll.; Victoria and Auckland Univ. Colls (BA 1949); Auckland Univ. of Technol. (MPhil 2010). Journalist: NZ Herald, 1945–47; BCON, Japan, 1947–48; Sun News Pictorial, Melbourne, 1949–50; Auckland Star, 1950–52; Auckland PRO, 1952–57; Staff Leader of Opposition, NZ, 1958; Press Officer and Personal Asst to Chief Exec., TEAL (later Air NZ), 1960–66. MP (Nat.) North Shore, 1966–90; Parly Under-Sec. to Minister of Educn, 1969–71; Minister of: Customs, and Associate Minister of Finance, 1972; Housing, and Dep. Minister of Finance, 1975–77; Energy, 1977–78; Health, and of Social Welfare, 1978–81; Transport, Railways, and Civil Aviation, 1981–84; Dep. Leader of Opposition, 1986–87; retd 1990. High Comr for NZ in UK, 1991–94, concurrently High Comr in Nigeria and Ambassador to Republic of Ireland. Mayor, North Shore City, NZ, 1995–98. Chm., NZ Ambulance Bd, 1995–2001. President: Alumni Assoc., Univ. of Auckland, 1994–96; Assoc. of Former MPs of NZ, 2002–03. *Recreation:* walking. *Address:* Villa 59 Mayfair Village, 14 Oteha Valley Road, Northcross, Auckland 0632, New Zealand.

GAISFORD, Rt Rev. John Scott; Bishop Suffragan of Beverley, 1994–2000; Episcopal Visitor for the Province of York, 1994–2000; Hon. Assistant Bishop of Ripon, 1996–2000; *b* 7 Oct. 1934; *s* of Joseph and Margaret Thompson Gaisford; *m* 1962, Gillian Maclean; one *s* one *d*. *Educ:* Univ. of Durham (Exhibnr, St Chad's Coll., Durham; BA Hons Theol. 1959, DipTh with Distinction 1960, MA 1976). Deacon 1960, priest 1961, Manchester; Assistant Curate: S Hilda, Audenshaw, 1960–62; S Michael, Bramhall, 1962–65; Vicar, S Andrew, Crewe, 1965–86; RD of Nantwich, 1974–85; Hon. Canon of Chester Cathedral, 1980–86; Archdeacon of Macclesfield, 1986–94. Proctor in Convocation, Mem. Gen. Synod, 1975–95; Church Commissioner, 1986–94; Member: Church of England Pensions Bd, 1982–97; Churches Conservation Trust (formerly Redundant Churches Fund), 1989–98. *Recreation:* fell walking. *Address:* 5 Trevone Close, Knutsford, Cheshire WA16 9EJ. *T:* (01565) 633531. *E:* jandg.gaisford@tiscali.co.uk. *Club:* Athenæum.

GAISMAN, Jonathan Nicholas Crispin; QC 1995; *b* 10 Aug. 1956; *o s* of Peter and Bea Gaisman; *m* 1982, Tessa Jardine Paterson (MBE 1990); one *s* two *d*. *Educ:* Summer Fields; Eton College (King's Scholar); Worcester Coll., Oxford (BCL; MA 1st cl Hons Jurisp.). Called to the Bar, Inner Temple, 1979, Bencher, 2004; Asst Recorder, 1998–2000; Recorder, 2000–08. Director: English Chamber Orchestra and Music Soc. Ltd, 1992–96; Internat. Musicians' Seminar, Prussia Cove, 1994–; Streetwise Opera, 2002–. FRSA 1997. *Recreations:* the arts, travel, country pursuits. *Address:* 7 King's Bench Walk, Temple, EC4Y 7DS. *T:* (020) 7910 8300. *Clubs:* Beefsteak; I Zingari.

GAITSKELL, Robert; QC 1994; PhD; CEng, FIET, FIMechE; FCIArb; a Recorder, 2000–10; Vice President, Institution of Electrical Engineers, 1998–2001; *b* 19 April 1948; *s* of late Stanley Gaitskell and late Thelma Phyllis Gaitskell (*née* Holmes); *m* 1974, Dr Deborah Lyndall Bates; one *d*. *Educ:* Hamilton High Sch., Bulawayo, Zimbabwe; Univ. of Cape Town (BSc Eng); KCL (PhD 1998; AKC 1998). CEng 1993; FIET (FIEE 1993); FCIArb 1995; FIMechE 1998. CEDR Accredited and Registered Mediator, 1999. Grad. trainee, Reyrolle Parsons, 1971–73; Engr, Electricity Dept, Bulawayo CC, Zimbabwe, 1973–75; Electrical Engr, GEC (South Africa), 1975–76; called to the Bar, Gray's Inn, 1978, Bencher, 2003; in practice at Bar in construction cases; arbitrator; Asst Recorder, 1997–2000. Lectr, Centre of Construction Law and Mgt, KCL, 1993–2003, for LLM, on Internat. Infrastructure Arbitration, 2006–08, and other professional bodies. Institution of Electrical Engineers: Mem. Council, 1994–2001; Chairman: Bd of Mgt and Design Div., 1995; Professional Gp on Engrg and the Law, 1994; Internat. Bd, 1998–99; Public Affairs Bd, 1999–2000; Professional Bd, 2000; Dispute Bd, ITER (F4E) nuclear fusion project, France, 2014–. Mem. Council, Inns of Ct Tribunal Appts Body, 2012–. Mem., Heilbron Cttee on Civil Procedure, 1993; Chm., IET/IMechE Jt Cttee on Model Forms, 2001–. Senator, Engrg Council, 1998–2002 (Chairman: Election Cttee, 1999–2001; Code of Conduct Cttee, 1999–2001). Member: Arbitration Panel, Dubai Internat. Arbitration Centre, 2006–; Dispute Resolution and Compensation Panel, Nat. Electricity Market of Singapore, 2008–. Member Committee: London Common Law and Commercial Bar Assoc., 1987–2000; Official Referees Bar Assoc., 1987–93; Gray's Inn Barristers, 2002–03. Legal columnist, Engrg Mgt Jl, 1994–2003; Mem. Editl Bd, Construction and Engrg Law Jl, 1998–2005. Methodist local preacher. Liveryman: Engineers' Co., 1997–; Arbitrators' Co., 2002– (Mem., Ct Assts, 2010–). *Publications:* (ed) Engineers' Dispute Resolution Handbook, 2006; (ed) Construction Dispute Resolution Handbook, 2nd edn 2011; papers and articles on law and engrg. *Recreations:* walking, theatre, travel. *Address:* Keating Chambers, 15 Essex Street, WC2R 3AA.

GALASKO, Prof. Charles Samuel Bernard; Professor of Orthopaedic Surgery, University of Manchester, 1976–2004, now Professor Emeritus; Consultant Orthopaedic Surgeon, Hope Hospital, 1976–2004 (Medical Director, 1993–96); Director of Education and Training, Salford Royal Hospitals NHS Trust, 2003–05; *b* 29 June 1939; *s* of David Isaac Galasko and Rose Galasko; *m* 1967, Carol Freyda Lapinsky; one *s* one *d*. *Educ:* King Edward VII Sch., Johannesburg; Univ. of Witwatersrand (MB BCh 1st Cl. Hons 1962; ChM 1969); MSc Manchester 1980. FRCS 1966; FRCSEd 1966. Med., surg. and orth. trng, Johannesburg Gen. Hosp. and Univ. of Witwatersrand, 1963–66; House Surgeon and Surg. Registrar, Hammersmith Hosp. and RPMS, 1966–69; Lord Nuffield Schol. in Orthopaedic Surgery, Univ. of Oxford, 1969; Orth. and Trauma Registrar and Sen. Registrar, Radcliffe Infirmary and Nuffield Orth. Centre, Oxford, 1970–73; Cons. Orth. Surgeon, Dir of Orth. Surgery, and Asst Dir, Div. of Surgery, RPMS and Hammersmith Hosp., 1973–76; Cons. Orth.

Surgeon, Royal Manchester Children's Hosp., 1976–2002. Member, Management Board: Royal Manchester Children's Hosp., 1989–92; Salford Royal Hosps NHS Trust, 1989–96; Gov., Stockport NHS Foundn Trust, 2013–. Hunterian Prof., RCS, 1971; Sir Arthur Sims Commonwealth Prof., 1998. Lectures: Hunterian, 1972; Annandale, 1979; Batson, 1979; Stanford Cade, 1993; Malkin, 1996; David Fuller, 1996; Chatterjee, 1997; Francois P. Fouche, 1999; Robert Jones, 1999; Hunterian Orator, 2003; Lord Henry Cohen, 2010; Naughton Dunn, 2010. Chm., Jt Cttee on Higher Surgical Trng, UK and Ire., 1997–2000. Member: Med. Sub-Cttee, British Olympic Assoc., 1988–2002; Internat. Cttee, 1990–93, Internat. Adv. Bd, 1994–96, SICOT (A. O. Internat. Award, 1981); President: SIROT, 1990–93; British Orthopaedic Assoc., 2000–01 (Vice Pres., 1999–2000; Mem. Council, 1988–91, 1998–2003); Faculty of Sport and Exercise Medicine, 2006–09 (Chm., Intercollegiate Academic Bd of Sport and Exercise Medicine, 2002–05); Vice President: Sect. of Oncology, RSM, 1987 (Mem. Council, 1980–87); RCS, 1999–2001 (Mem. Council, 1991–2003; Chm., Hosp. Recognition Cttee, 1992–95; Chm., Trauma Cttee, 1992–95; Chm., Trng Bd, 1995–99). Vice Pres., British Amateur Wrestling Assoc., 1996–2002 (Chm., 1992–96; Med. Advr, 1987–2002); Vice-Chm., English Olympic Wrestling Assoc., 1998–2000 (Med. Advr, 1987–2000). SICOT Fellow, 1972; ABC Fellow, 1978; Aust. Commonwealth Fellow, 1982. Hon. Fellow: British Orth. Assoc.; S African Orth. Assoc.; Amer. Fracture Assoc.; British Orthopaedics Res. Soc.; Emeritus Mem., Amer. Orth. Assoc.; Corresp. Mem., Columbian Soc. of Orth. Surgery and Traumatology. FMedSci 2002; FFSEM (Ireland) 2003; FFSEM (UK) 2006. Hon. FCMSA 2002. Moynihan Prize, Assoc. of Surgeons, 1969. *Publications:* (ed jtly) Radionuclide Scintigraphy Orthopaedics, 1984; (ed) Principles of Fracture Management, 1984; Skeletal Metastases, 1986; (ed) Neuromuscular Problems in Orthopaedics, 1987; (ed jtly) Recent Developments in Orthopaedic Surgery, 1987; (ed jtly) Current Trends in Orthopaedic Surgery, 1988; (ed jtly) Imaging Techniques in Orthopaedics, 1989; (jtly) Competing for the Disabled, 1989; articles and contribs to books on aspects of orthopaedics and trauma, surgical educn, skeletal metastasis, neuromuscular conditions, sport and exercise medicine. *Recreations:* sport, opera, music. *Address:* 72 Gatley Road, Gatley, Cheadle, Cheshire SK8 4AA.

GALBRAITH, family name of **Baron Strathclyde**.

GALBRAITH, Anne, CBE 2010 (OBE 2005); Chairman, Valuation Tribunal Service, since 2004; *b* 7 July 1940; *d* of Edward and Hannah Wilks; *m* 1965, John Gordon Galbraith; one *s* one *d*. *Educ:* Blyth Grammar Sch.; Durham Univ. (LLB). Sen. Lectr in Law, Newcastle Coll. of Commerce, then Newcastle Poly., subseq. Univ. of Northumbria, 1965–97 (latterly pt-time); Chair, Newcastle CAB, 1983–88; Mem., Northern RHA, 1988–91; Chair, Royal Victoria Infirmary Hosp. Trust, Newcastle, 1991–97. Member: Prime Minister's Adv. Panel for Citizen's Charter, 1994–2001; Lord Chancellor's Council on Tribunals, 1997–2003; Chm., NHS Prescription Pricing Authy, 2000–06. Non-exec. Dir, NHS Business Authy, 2006–14. Chair, Council, Univ. of Durham, 2006–12. *Recreations:* gardening, reading. *Address:* The Vicarage, Beltingham, Northumberland NE47 7BZ.

GALBRAITH, Colin Archibald, PhD; Director, Colin Galbraith Environment Ltd, since 2010; *b* 4 Feb. 1959; *s* of Lorne Galbraith; *m* 1987, Maria; one *s* one *d*. *Educ:* Minard Primary Sch.; Lochgilphead Sec. Sch.; Oban High Sch.; Paisley Univ. (BSc Hons Biol. 1981); Univ. of Aberdeen (PhD Zool. 1987). Ecologist, Nature Conservancy Council, 1987–91; Joint Nature Conservation Committee: Hd, Vertebrate Ecology, 1991–96; Hd, Biodiversity Service, 1996–97; Scottish Natural Heritage: Hd, Adv. Services, 1997–2001; Dir, Scientific and Adv. Services, 2001–07; Dir of Policy and Advice, 2007–10. Hon. Prof., Univ. of Stirling, 2002–. Chm., 1999–2005, Vice Chm., 2005–, Scientific Council, Convention on Migratory Species; Chairman: intergovtl negotiations on develt of global agreement on Conservation of Birds of Prey, 2007–08; Bd of Dirs, Langholm Grouse Moor Recovery Project, 2007–; Cttee for Scotland, RSPB, 2013–. Member: Bd, Millennium Ecosystem Assessment, 2002–05; Exec. Bd, RZSScot, 2008–. *Publications:* (ed jtly) Mountains of Northern Europe, 2005; (ed jtly) Farming, Forestry and the Natural Heritage, 2006; (ed jtly) Waterbirds around the World, 2006; (ed jtly) Energy and the Natural Heritage, 2008; (ed jtly) Species Management: challenges and solutions for the 21st century, 2010. *Recreations:* bird watching, hill walking, photography, travel, antiques. *Address:* 45 Mounthooly Loan, Edinburgh EH10 7JD. *E:* colin@cgalbraith.freeserve.co.uk.

GALBRAITH, Prof. Graham Harold, PhD; CEng; Vice-Chancellor, University of Portsmouth, since 2013; *b* Scotland, 16 Oct. 1960; *s* of William Galbraith and late Jean Galbraith; *m* 1987, Caroline Wilson; two *s* one *d*. *Educ:* High Sch. of Glasgow; Shawlands Acad., Glasgow; Strathclyde Univ. (BSc 1st Cl. Hons Envmt Engrg 1981; MSc Mech. Engrg 1986; PhD Mech. Engrg 1992). CEng 1983; MCIBSE 1983. Scientific Officer, BRE, Scotland, 1981–83; Lectr, Strathclyde Univ., 1983–93; Tech. Dir, 3E Consultants and Dir, 3E Consultants Ltd: a Strathclyde Univ. co., 1991–93; Glasgow Caledonian University: Sen. Lectr, 1993–96, Reader, 1996–98, Prof. of Building Physics, 1998–2000, Dept of Building and Surveying; Actg Hd, Dept of Energy and Envmtl Technol., 2000–01; Exec. Dean, 2001–05, Asst Principal, 2004–05, Sch. of Engrg, Sci. and Design; Pro Vice-Chancellor, Univ. Exec., 2005–08; Dep. Vice-Chancellor, 2008–13. Vis. Prof., Tech. Univ. of Denmark, 2001–02; Vis. Schol., Faculty of Architecture, Inst. for Building Physics, Tech. Univ. of Dresden, 2002–05. Non-exec. Dir, Watford Enterprise Agency, 2010–14. Mem. Council, CBI E of England, 2011–. FHEA 2001. MInstD 2012. *Publications:* res. reports; contribs to scientific jls. *Recreations:* walking, reading, theatre going. *Address:* University of Portsmouth, University House, Winston Churchill Avenue, Portsmouth PO1 2UP. *T:* (023) 9284 3191, *Fax:* (023) 9284 3400. *E:* graham.galbraith@port.ac.uk.

GALBRAITH-MARTEN, Jason Nicholas; QC 2014; Director, Assurety Training, since 2011; *b* London, 7 Jan. 1967; *s* of Gavin and Lesley Galbraith-Marten; *m* 2010, Joanne White; one *s* two *d*. *Educ:* Campion Sch., Hornchurch; Magdalene Coll., Cambridge (BA 1989). Called to the Bar, Middle Temple, 1991; in practice as barrister, 1991–. Pegasus Schol., NZ, 1994. Chair, Industrial Law Soc., 2010–13. *Recreations:* fine wine and dining, motor racing, Manchester United. *Address:* Cloisters, 1 Pump Court, Temple, EC4Y 7AA. *T:* (020) 7827 4000. *E:* jgm@cloisters.com, jason@assuretytraining.com.

GALE, Baroness *cr* 1999 (Life Peer), of Blaenrhondda in the county of Mid Glamorgan; **Anita Gale;** General Secretary, Wales Labour Party, 1984–99; *b* 28 Nov. 1940; *d* of late Arthur and Lillian Gale; *m* 1959 (marr. diss. 1983); two *d*. *Educ:* Pontypridd Tech. Coll.; University Coll., Cardiff (BSc Econ). Machinist, clothing factory, 1955–56 and 1965–70; grocery shop asst, 1956–59; returned to full-time educn, 1970–76; Women's Officer and Asst Organiser, Wales Labour Party, 1976–84. Member: Inf. Select Cttee, H of L, 2001–04; Jt Cttee on Statutory Instruments, 2004–07; Sub Cttee G, EU Select Cttee, 2006–09; Parly Delegn, Council of Europe, 2008–10; Works of Art Cttee, H of L, 2010–. All Party Parliamentary Groups: Member: British/Taiwan, 2002–; Jt Sec., Children in Wales, 2008–12; Chm., Parkinson's, 2006–; Mem., Associate Parly Gp on animal welfare, 2000– (Vice-Chm., 2000–01; Jt Sec., 2001–05). Vice-Chm., Labour Animal Welfare Soc., 1990–; Co-Chair, PLP Women's Cttee, 2013–; Mem., CPA, 2004–. Mem., IPU, 1999–. Comr for Wales, Women's Nat. Commn, 2004–09. President: Treherbert and Dist Br., RBL, 2000–; Nat. Assoc. of Old Age Pensioners Wales, 2010–; Cardiff and Dist Rhondda Soc., 2014–; Patron: Kidney Wales Foundn, 2008–; Bees for Develt, 2013–. *Recreations:* walking, swimming, reading. *Address:* House of Lords, SW1A 0PW. *T:* (020) 7219 3000. *E:* galea@parliament.uk.

GALE, Audrey Olga Helen; *see* Sander, Her Honour A. O. H.

GALE, Benjamin Anthony; Co-founder and Managing Director, Little Gem, since 2014; *b* London, 23 March 1967; *m* 2001, Leeanne Vinson; one *s* two *d*. *Educ:* Pimlico Sch., London; Manchester Univ. (BA Politics and Modern Hist.). BBC Television: prodn trainee, 1990–92; series producer, documentaries, 1992–98; Exec. Producer, Lion Television, 1998–2003; Series Ed., Who Do You Think You Are?, Wall to Wall Television, 2003–04; Commng Exec., 2004–06, Commng Ed., 2007–08, BBC TV; Dir of Progs, Channel Five, 2008; Head, Bristol Factual, BBC Vision Productions, 2009–12; Dir of Progs, Maverick Television, 2012–14. *Recreations:* cooking, running, ski-ing, reading, primary school governor. *Address:* Little Gem, G12, Shepherds Building, Charecroft Way, W14 0EE.

GALE, Prof. Edwin Albert Merwood, FRCP; Professor of Diabetic Medicine, Bristol University, 1997, now Emeritus; *b* 21 March 1945; *s* of George Edwin Gale and Carole Fisher Gale; *m* 1982, Lone Brogaard; one *s* two *d*. *Educ:* Sevenoaks Sch.; Sidney Sussex Coll., Cambridge (MA, MB BChir). Sen. Lectr, 1984–92, Prof. of Diabetes, 1992–97, St Bartholomew's Hosp. *Publications:* (with R. B. Tattersall) Diabetes: clinical management, 1990; papers on causes, prediction and possible prevention of type 1 diabetes. *Recreations:* ancient coins, fossils.

GALE, John, OBE 1987; theatre producer; *b* 2 Aug. 1929; *s* of Frank Haith Gale and Martha Edith Gale (*née* Evans); *m* 1950, Liselotte Ann (*née* Wratten); two *s*. *Educ:* Christ's Hospital; Webber Douglas Academy of Dramatic Art. Formerly an actor; presented his first production, Inherit the Wind, London, 1960; has since produced or co-produced, in London, British provinces, USA, Australia, New Zealand and S Africa, over 150 plays, including: Candida, 1960; On the Brighter Side, 1961; Boeing-Boeing, 1962; Devil May Care, 1963; Windfall, 1963; Where Angels Fear to Tread, 1963; The Wings of the Dove, 1963; Amber for Anna, 1964; Present Laughter, 1964, 1981; Maigret and the Lady, 1965; The Platinum Cat, 1965; The Sacred Flame, 1966; An Evening with G. B. S., 1966; A Woman of No Importance, 1967; The Secretary Bird, 1968; Dear Charles, 1968; Highly Confidential, 1969; The Young Churchill, 1969; The Lionel Touch, 1969; Abelard and Héloïse, 1970; No Sex, Please—We're British, 1971; Lloyd George Knew My Father, 1972; The Mating Game, 1972; Parents' Day, 1972; At the End of the Day, 1973; Birds of Paradise, 1974; A Touch of Spring, 1975; Separate Tables, 1977; The Kingfisher, 1977; Sextet, 1977; Cause Célèbre, 1977; Shut Your Eyes and Think of England, 1977; Can You Hear Me at the Back?, 1979; Middle Age Spread, 1979; Private Lives, 1980; A Personal Affair, 1982. The Secretary Bird and No Sex, Please—We're British set records for the longest run at the Savoy and Strand Theatres respectively; No Sex, Please—We're British is the longest running comedy in the history of World Theatre and passed 6,000 performances at the Garrick Theatre in Nov. 1985. Chichester Festival Theatre: Exec. Producer, 1983–84; Director, 1984–89. Director: John Gale Productions Ltd, 1960–90; Gale Enterprises Ltd, 1960–90; West End Managers Ltd, 1972–89; Lisden Productions Ltd, 1975–90. President, Soc. of West End Theatre Managers, 1972–75; Chm., Theatres National Cttee, 1979–85. Governor, 1976–, and Almoner, 1978–95, Christ's Hospital; Chm. of Govs, Guildford Sch. of Acting, 1989–2000. Member, Amicable Soc. of Blues, 1981–. *Recreations:* travel, Rugby. *Address:* East Dean Cottage, East Dean, near Chichester, W Sussex PO18 0JA. *T:* (01243) 811407. *Club:* London Welsh Rugby Football (Richmond) (Chairman, 1979–81).

GALE, Michael; QC 1979; a Recorder of the Crown Court, 1977–97; *b* 12 Aug. 1932; *s* of Joseph Gale and Blossom Gale; *m* 1963, Joanna Stephanie Bloom; one *s* two *d*. *Educ:* Cheltenham Grammar Sch.; Grocers' Sch.; King's Coll., Cambridge (Exhibnr; BA History and Law, 1954, MA 1958). National Service, Royal Fusiliers and Jt Services Sch. for Linguists, 1956–58. Called to the Bar, Middle Temple, 1957, Bencher, 1988; Harmsworth Law Scholar, 1958. Mem., Gen. Council of the Bar, 1987–94; Legal Assessor: GMC, 1995–2002; GDC, 1995–2002; Gen. Osteopathic Council, 1998–2002; CIPFA, 2000–02; Chm., Review and Complaints Cttee, Nat. Heritage Meml Fund and Heritage Lottery Fund, 1996–2001. *Publications:* jointly: A Guide to the Crime (Sentences) Act, 1997; Fraud and the PLC, the Criminal Justice and Police Act 2001: a guide for practitioners, 1999. *Recreations:* the arts, country living. *Clubs:* Garrick, MCC.

GALE, Sir Roger (James), Kt 2012; MP (C) North Thanet, since 1983; *b* Poole, Dorset, 20 Aug. 1943; *s* of Richard Byrne Gale and Phyllis Mary (*née* Rowell); *m* 1st, 1964, Wendy Dawn Bowman (marr. diss. 1967); 2nd, 1971, Susan Sampson (marr. diss.); one *d*; 3rd, 1980, Susan Gabrielle Marks; two *s*. *Educ:* Southbourne Prep. Sch.; Hardye's Sch., Dorchester; Guildhall Sch. of Music and Drama (LGSM). Freelance broadcaster, 1963–72; freelance reporter, BBC Radio, London, 1972–73; Producer, Current Affairs Gp, BBC Radio (progs included Newsbeat and Today), 1973–76; Producer/Dir, BBC Children's Television, 1976–79; Producer/Dir, Thames TV, and Editor, teenage unit, 1979–83. Joined Conservative Party, 1964; Mem., Cttee, Greater London Young Conservatives, 1964–65. PPS to Minister of State for Armed Forces, 1992–94. Member: Select Cttee on Televising of Proceedings of the House, 1988–91; Home Affairs Select Cttee, 1990–92; Broadcasting Select Cttee, 1997–2005; Procedure Select Cttee, 2010–15; All Party Parly Gp, Fund for Replacement of Animals in Med. Experiments, 1983–86; Chm., All Party Animal Welfare Gp, 1992–98; Mem., Chairman's Panel, 1997–. Vice Chm., Cons. Party, 2001–03. Founding Mem., Police and Parlt Scheme, 1996. Delegate, Council of Europe, 1987–89 and 2011–15. Contested Birmingham, Northfield, Oct. 1982 (Lab. majority, 289). Mem., Gen. Council, BBC, 1992–94. Founder, East Kent Development Assoc., 1984–86. Fellow: Industry and Parlt Trust, 1985; Parlt and Armed Forces Fellowship, 1992; Postgrad. Fellowship, Parlt Armed Forces Scheme, 2001–02. Pres., Cons. Animal Welfare Gp, 2003–. Special Constable, British Transport Police, 2003–06. *Recreations:* swimming, sailing. *Address:* House of Commons, Westminster, SW1A 0AA. *E:* galerj@parliament.uk. *Clubs:* Farmers, Lord's Taverners.

GALE, William Stuart; QC (Scot) 1993; *b* 10 June 1955; *s* of William Grimshaw Gale and Patricia Sheila (*née* Nicol); *m* 1981, Michele Marie Keklak (marr. diss.); one *d*. *Educ:* Univ. of Dundee (LLB Hons 1977); Tulane Univ., New Orleans (LLM 1978). Advocate of Scottish Bar, 1980–93; Standing Jun. Counsel to FCO in Scotland, 1987–93. Chm., Police Appeals Tribunal Scotland, 2001–. *Recreation:* modern jazz. *Address:* Terra Firma Chambers, Parliament House, Edinburgh EH1 1RF.

GALIONE, Prof. Antony Giuseppe, PhD; FMedSci; Professor of Pharmacology and Head, Department of Pharmacology, University of Oxford, since 2006; Fellow, Lady Margaret Hall, Oxford and Extraordinary Lecturer in Biochemical Pharmacology, New College, Oxford, since 2006; *b* Chelmsford, 13 Sept. 1963; *s* of Angelo and Margaret Galione; *m* 1992, Angela Clayton. *Educ:* Felsted (Lord Butler of Saffron Walden Schol.); Trinity Coll., Cambridge (Sen. Schol.; BA 1985; PhD 1989). Harkness Fellow, 1989–91, Dmitri d'Arbeloff Fellow in Biol., 1990–91, John Hopkins Univ.; University of Oxford: Beit Meml Fellow for Med. Res., Dept of Pharmacol., 1991–94; Hayward Jun. Res. Fellow, Oriel Coll., 1992–95; Lectr in Med. Scis, St Hilda's Coll., 1993–95; Wellcome Trust Career Develt Fellow, Dept of Pharmacol., 1994–97; Staines Med. Res. Fellow, Exeter Coll., 1995–98; Lectr in Molecular and Cellular Biochem., St Catherine's Coll., 1997–98; Wellcome Trust Sen. Fellow in Basic Biomed. Sci., Dept of Pharmacol., 1997–2005; Fellow and Tutor in Biochem. Pharmacol., New Coll., 1998–2005; Titular Prof. of Pharmacol., 2002–05. Herbert Rand Vis. Fellow, Marine Biol Lab., Woods Hole, Mass, 1993; Vis. Sen. Fellow, Inst. of Advanced Studies, Hong Kong Univ. of Sci. and Technol., 2011–; Vis. Prof. of Pharmacol., Univ. of Kuwait, 2011–. Mem., Physiol. and Pharmacol. Panel, 2002–05, Basic Sci. Interest Cttee, 2006–09, Sen. Investigator, 2014–, Wellcome Trust. Co-Chair, Cttee of Heads of Pharmacol. and Therapeutics Depts UK, 2014–. Member: Amer. Biophysical Soc., 1995–; British Marine Biol Assoc., 1995–; British Pharmacol Soc., 1997– (Trustee and Council Mem., 2014–); British Neurosci. Assoc., 1997–. FMedSci 2010. Ed., Biochem. Jl, 1997–2006; Mem., Editl Bd, Zygote, 1998–. Dr *hc*

Univ. of Medicine and Pharmacy, Craiova, 2011. Novartis Prize, British Pharmacol Soc., 2001. *Publications:* contrib. scientific papers on cell signalling to jls incl. Nature, Science and Cell. *Recreations:* Egyptology, cats, Jack Russell terriers, gardening, Cotswold village life. *Address:* Department of Pharmacology, Oxford University, Mansfield Road, Oxford OX1 3QT. *T:* (01865) 271862, *Fax:* (01865) 271853. *E:* antony.galione@pharm.ox.ac.uk.

GALL, Anthony Robert S.; *see* Scott-Gall.

GALL, Henderson Alexander, (Sandy), CMG 2011; CBE 1988; freelance writer and broadcaster; Foreign Correspondent, Independent Television News, 1963–92 (Newscaster, 1968–90); *b* 1 Oct. 1927; *s* of Henderson Gall and Jean Begg; *m* 1958, Eleanor Mary Patricia Ann Smyth; one *s* three *d. Educ:* Glenalmond; Aberdeen Univ. (MA). Foreign Correspondent, Reuters, 1953–63, Germany, E Africa, Suez Invasion (1956), Hungary, S Africa, Congo; joined ITN, 1963, working in Middle East, Africa, USA, Vietnam, Far East, China, Afghanistan; Newscaster on News at Ten, 1970–90; Producer/Presenter/Writer, documentaries on: King Hussein, 1972; Afghanistan, 1982, 1984, 1986; Cresta Run, 1984; George Adamson: lord of the lions, 1989; Richard Leakey, the man who saved the animals, 1995; Empty Quarter, 1996; Veil of Fear (Taliban rule in Afghanistan), 1996; Imran's Final Test, 1997; Sandy's War: face of the Taliban, 2001; Afghanistan: war without end, 2004. Chm., Sandy Gall's Afghanistan Appeal, 1983–. Rector, Aberdeen Univ., 1978–81 (Hon. LLD, 1981). Sitara-i-Pakistan, 1986; Lawrence of Arabia Medal, RSAA, 1987. *Publications:* Gold Scoop, 1977; Chasing the Dragon, 1981; Don't Worry About the Money Now, 1983; Behind Russian Lines, 1983; Afghanistan: Agony of a Nation, 1988; Salang, 1989; Lord of the Lions, 1991; News from the Front, 1994; The Bushmen of Southern Africa: slaughter of the innocent, 2001; War Against the Taliban: why it all went wrong in Afghanistan, 2012. *Recreations:* gardening, swimming. *Address:* Doubleton Oast House, Penshurst, Tonbridge, Kent TN11 8JA. *Clubs:* Turf; St Moritz Tobogganing (Hon. Mem.).

GALLACHER, Bernard, OBE 1996; professional golfer; golf professional, Wentworth Golf Club, 1975–96; *b* 9 Feb. 1949; *s* of Bernard and Matilda Gallacher; *m* 1974, Lesley Elizabeth Wearmouth; one *s* two *d. Educ:* St Mary's Academy, Bathgate. Golf tournaments won: Scottish Open Amateur Championship, 1967; PGA Schweppes, W. D. & H. O. Wills Open, 1969; Martini Internat., 1971, 1982; Carrolls Internat., 1974; Dunlop Masters, 1974, 1975; Spanish Open, 1977; French Open, 1979; Tournament Players Championship, 1980; Gtr Manchester Open, 1981; Jersey Open, 1982, 1984. Harry Vardon Trophy, 1969. Scottish Professional Champion, 1971, 1973, 1974, 1977, 1984. Ryder Cup Team, 1969, 1971, 1973, 1975, 1977, 1979, 1981, 1983, European Captain, 1991, 1993, 1995. Pres., Golf Foundn, 1996–2001. *Publications:* (with Mark Wilson) Teach Yourself Golf, 1988; (with Renton Laidlaw) Captain at Kiawah, 1991. *Recreations:* walking dogs, reading. *Address:* c/o Wentworth Club, Virginia Water, Surrey GU25 4LS.

GALLAGHER, Ann; Head of Collections (British Art), Tate, since 2006; *b* Nottingham, 14 May 1957; *d* of Eugene Gallagher and Diana Gallagher (*née* Greaves); *m* 2001, David Batchelor. *Educ:* Mackie Acad., Stonehaven; Bedford Coll., Univ. of London (BA Hons). Nigel Greenwood Gall., London, 1984–89; Dir, Anthony Reynolds Gall., London, 1989–94; Sen. Curator, Visual Arts Dept, British Council, London, 1994–2005; Hd, British Art Post 1900, Tate Collection, London, 2005–06. Mem. of Faculty, British Sch. at Rome, 2005–10. Trustee, Whitechapel Art Gall., London, 2008–. *Publications:* (ed) Rachel Whiteread, 1997; Landscape, 2000; (ed) Mark Wallinger, 2001; Still Life, 2002; Sodio y Asfalto, 2004; Chris Ofili: the Upper Room, 2006; Rachel Whiteread Drawings, 2010; (ed) Susan Hiller, 2011; Damien Hirst, 2012. *Recreations:* architecture and design, film, literature. *Address:* c/o Tate, Millbank, SW1P 4RG.

GALLAGHER, Edward Patrick, CBE 2001; FREng, FIET, FCIWEM; Chair, Centre for Low Carbon Futures, 2009–14; *b* 4 Aug. 1944; *m* 1969, Helen Wilkinson; two *s. Educ:* Univ. of Sheffield (BEng Hons; Diploma in Business Studies; Mappin Medal, 1966; John Brown Award, 1966). MRI 1992. Systems Analyst, Vauxhall Motors, 1963–68; Corporate Planning Manager, Sandoz Products, 1968–70; Computer Services Manager, Robinson Willey, 1970–71; with Black and Decker, 1971–86: Director: Marketing Services, 1978–79; Service and Distribn, 1979–81; Business Analysis, 1981–83; Market and Product Develt, 1983–86; Amersham International: Dir of Corporate Develt, 1986–88; Divl Chief Exec., 1988–90; Mfg Dir, 1990–92; Chief Executive and Board Member: NRA, 1992–95; EA, 1995–2001. Dir, ECUS Ltd, 2001–11; Chm., Enviro-fresh Ltd, 2003–06. Chair: Energywatch, 2004–08; Renewable Fuels Agency, 2008–11; Mem., NCC, 2008; Mem. Bd, Consumer Focus, 2008–11. Vice-Pres., Council for Envmtl Educn, 1997–2006; Mem. Bd and Chm. Audit Cttee, English Nature, 2001–06. Chm., Pesticides Forum, DEFRA, 2003–06. A CS Comr, 2001–06. Middlesex University: Vis. Prof., Business Sch. and Faculty of Technol., 1994–97, Sch. of Health, Biol and Envmtl Sci., 1997–; Mem., Faculty of Technol. Adv. Gp, 1994–97; Gov., 1994–2004 (Chm., Bd of Govs, 2001–04); Chairman: Audit Cttee, 1995–2000; Planning and Resources Cttee, 2000–01; Governance Cttee, 2000–01; Bristol University: Mem. Council, 1994–98; Mem. Finance Adv. Gp, 1994–2001; Chm. Adv. Bd, Centre for Social and Econ. Res. on Global Envmt, UEA, 2004–08 (Mem., 2001–04). Mem. Council, 1998–2001, Mem., Envmt and Energy Policy Cttee, 1999–2002 (Chm., 2002–04), IEE; Royal Academy of Engineering: Mem., Sustainable Develt Educn Panel, 1999–2003; Mem., Awards Cttee, 2001–04; Chm., Health, Safety and Envmt Cttee, EEF, 2001–04. Advr, Maidenhead Waterways Restoration Gp, 2008–. Patron, Envmtl Industries Commn, 2001–13. Trustee: Living Again Trust, Royal Hosp. for Neurodisability (formerly Royal Hosp. and Home, Putney), 1993–2003; Envmtl Vision, 2001–11 (Chm., 2004–11). FRSA 1995–2007; CCMI (CIMgt 1996). Freeman, City of London; Liveryman, Co. of Water Conservators (Mem., Ct of Assistants, 1999–2001). Hon. DEng Sheffield, 1996; Hon. DSc: Tomsk, 1998; Plymouth, 1998; Brunel, 1999; DUniv Middx, 2005. *Recreations:* tennis, theatre, walking, guitar, clocks. *Address:* 154 Whyteladyes Lane, Cookham, Maidenhead, Berks SL6 9LA.

GALLAGHER, Eileen Rose, OBE 2010; Chief Executive, Shed Productions, since 2008 (Co-owner and co-founder, 1998; Managing Director, then Chief Executive, Shed Media, 1998–2008); *b* 26 Nov. 1959; *d* of Mathew Gallagher and Christine McAvoy. *Educ:* Glasgow Univ. (MA Hons Politics); UC Cardiff (Dip. Journalism). Freelance journalist, 1980–84; Scottish Television: Press Officer, 1984–87; Head of Programme Planning, 1987–91; Head of Broadcasting Div., 1991–92; Dir of Broadcasting, 1992–94; Man. Dir, Granada/LWT Broadcasting, then Man. Dir, LWT and Dep. Man. Dir, Granada UK Broadcasting, 1994–98; Man. Dir, Ginger TV, 1999. Director: Granada, 1995–98; LWT, 1995–98. Mem. Bd, Glasgow 2014, 2010–14. *Address:* Shed Productions, 85 Gray's Inn Road, WC1X 8TX.

GALLAGHER, Francis Xavier, OBE 1986; HM Diplomatic Service, retired; Head of Panel 2000 Unit, Foreign and Commonwealth Office, 1998; *b* 28 March 1946; *s* of F. P. H. Gallagher and Carmen Gallagher (*née* Wilson); *m* 1981, Marie-France Martine Guiller; one *d. Educ:* Oxford Univ. (Chancellor's Essay and Matthew Arnold Meml Prizes; BA, BPhil). Tutor, Villiers Park Educnl Trust, Oxon, 1970; joined FCO, 1971: MECAS, Lebanon, 1972–74; served FCO, NY, then Dep. Hd of Mission, Beirut, Khartoum, Kuwait, Copenhagen, 1974–98. Officier, Ordre National du Lion (Senegal), 1988. *Recreations:* music, walking. *Address:* 102 rue de la Tour, 75016 Paris, France.

GALLAGHER, James Daniel, CB 2005; FRSE; Associate Member, Nuffield College, Oxford, since 2014 (Gwilym Gibbon Fellow, 2010–14); Visiting Professor of Government, University of Glasgow, since 2005; *s* of William Gallagher and Bridget Gallagher (*née* Hart); *m* 1978, Una Mary Green; one *s* two *d. Educ:* Glasgow Univ. (BSc Hons Chemistry and Nat. Phil. 1976); Edinburgh Univ. (MSc Public Policy 1986). Joined Scottish Office, 1976: Private Sec. to Minister for Home Affairs, 1979; Head of Criminal Policy and Procedure Brs, 1981–85; Sec., Mgt Gp, 1985–88; Head of Urban Policy Div., 1988–89; Private Sec. to successive Secs of State for Scotland, 1989–91; Dir (Human Resources), Scottish Prison Service, 1991–96; Hd, Local Govt Finance Gp, later Local Govt and Europe Gp, Scottish Office, 1996–99; Dep. Head of Economic and Domestic Secretariat, Cabinet Office, 1999; Policy Advr, Prime Minister's Policy Unit, 1999–2000; Hd, Scottish Exec. Justice Dept, 2000–04; Prof. of Govt, Univ. of Glasgow, 2005–07 (on secondment); Dir Gen., Devolution, MoJ and Prime Minister's Office, 2007–10. Vis. Prof., 2005–08, Hon. Prof., 2007, Centre for Ethics in Public Policy and Corporate Life, Glasgow Caledonian Univ. Director: Scottish Mutual Assurance, 1999–2003; Abbey National Life, 1999–2003; Scottish Provident Life Assurance, 2001–03; Admin Re UK Services Ltd (formerly Admin Re UK Ltd), 2010–; ReAssureUK (formerly Windsor Life) Ltd, 2010–; Barclays Life Ltd, 2010–13. Chairman: Supervisory Cttee, Scottish Provident, 2003–09; With Profits Cttee, Police Mutual Assce Soc., 2015–; Member: Abbey Nat. Policy Holder Review Cttee, 2003–06; Fairness Cttee, Royal London Insce Gp, 2012–. Non-exec. Dir, Lothian and Borders Police, 2006–13. Mem. Council, Law Soc. of Scotland, 2011–. Dir, Scottish Catholic Internat. Aid Fund, 2013–. FRSE 2007. *Publications:* England and the Union, 2012; Scotland's Choices, 2013; Where Next for the UK and Scotland, 2014. *Address:* Nuffield College, University of Oxford OX1 1NF.

GALLAGHER, John David Edmund; barrister, since 1974; Chancellor and Vicar General, Diocese of Rochester, since 2005; *b* Wimbledon, 13 Sept. 1950; *s* of William Norman Gallagher, MA, ICS and Zoe Gallagher; *m* 1974, Gillian Amanda Battersby; three *s* two *d* (and one *d* decd). *Educ:* Mill Hill Sch.; King's Coll. London (Masom Scholar in Classics 1970; BA Classics, AKC Theol. 1972); Coll. of Law. Called to the Bar, Gray's Inn, 1974, Bencher, 2014; Asst Recorder, 1995; Recorder, 2000. Chm., Drugs Tribunal, ICC Champions Trophy, 2004; Professional Mem., Sports Dispute Resolution Panel, 1999–2007. Pres., ICS Assoc., 2006–. Life Mem., Pakistan Soc., 1998–. Trustee, Samaritans Purse, 2005–. Ct Asst, Co. of Pewterers, 2012–. *Recreations:* cricket, Rugby, theatre, horse-riding. *Address:* Hardwicke Building, New Square, Lincoln's Inn, WC2A 3SB. *T:* (020) 7242 2523. *E:* allgallaghers@hotmail.com. *Clubs:* MCC, HAC Cricket (Pres., 2008–13), Old Millhillians Rugby Football (Chm., 2014–).

GALLAGHER, Sister Maire Teresa, CBE 1992 (OBE 1987); SND; Sister Superior, Convent of Notre Dame, Dumbarton, 1987–94, retired; *b* 27 May 1933; *d* of Owen Gallagher and Annie McVeigh. *Educ:* Notre Dame High Sch., Glasgow; Glasgow Univ. (MA Hons 1965); Notre Dame Coll. of Educn (Dip. 1953). Principal Teacher of History, Notre Dame High Sch., Glasgow, 1965–72; Lectr in Secondary Educn, Notre Dame Coll., 1972–74; Head Teacher, Notre Dame High Sch., Dumbarton, 1974–87. Chair, Scottish Consultative Council (formerly Scottish Consultative Cttee) on the Curriculum, 1987–91 (Mem., 1976–91; Chair, Secondary Cttee, 1983–87); Mem., Sec. of State's Cttee of Enquiry into Teachers' Pay and Conditions of Service, (Main Cttee), 1986; Pres., Scottish Br., Secondary Heads Assoc., 1980–82. Member: Central Council, Action of Churches Together in Scotland, 1990–2003 (Convener, 1999–2003); Assembly, CCBI, 1990–2002; Steering Cttee, CTBI, 2004–06. Fellow: SCOTVEC, 1989; Scottish Qualifications Authority, 1997. Hon. MEd CNAA, 1992. *Publications:* papers and articles in jls on teaching and management of schools. *Recreations:* homemaking skills, reading. *Address:* Sisters of Notre Dame, 2/2 90 Beith Street, Glasgow G11 6DQ. *T:* (0141) 357 4576.

GALLAGHER, Michael; consultant, Bellway Homes Ltd; *b* 1 July 1934; *s* of Michael and Annie Gallagher; *m* 1959, Kathleen Mary Gallagher; two *s* three *d. Educ:* Univ. of Nottingham; Univ. of Wales. Dip. General Studies. Branch Official, NUM, 1967–70; day release, Univ. of Nottingham, 1967–69; TUC scholarship, Univ. of Wales, 1970–72; Univ. of Nottingham, 1972–74. Councillor: Mansfield Borough Council, 1970–74; Nottinghamshire CC, 1973–81. Contested (Lab) Rushcliffe, general election, Feb. 1974; Member (Lab) Nottingham, European Parlt, 1979–83, (SDP) 1983–84; contested (SDP) Lancs Central, European elecn, 1984. *Recreations:* leisure, sports. *Address:* 4 Mansfield Road, Mansfield Woodhouse, Mansfield, Notts NG19 9JN.

GALLAGHER, Paul, CBE 1996; General Secretary, Amalgamated Engineering and Electrical Union, 1995–96; *b* 16 Oct. 1944; *s* of Joe and Annie Gallagher; *m* 1974, Madeleine. *Educ:* St Anne's, Droylesden, Manchester. Electrical, Electronic, Telecommunication and Plumbing Union: full-time officer, 1966–78; Exec. Councillor for Manchester and N Wales, 1978–91; Pres., 1986–91; Gen. Sec., 1992–95. Mem., HSC, 1990–96. *Recreations:* gardening, music, reading.

GALLAGHER, Thomas Joseph; Member (SDLP) Fermanagh and South Tyrone, Northern Ireland Assembly, 1998–2011; *b* 17 Aug. 1942; *s* of Thomas and Nellie Gallagher; *m* 1968, Eileen Carty; two *s* one *d. Educ:* St Joseph's Coll.; Queen's Univ., Belfast. Mem., NI Forum, 1996. Mem. (SDLP), Fermanagh DC, 1989–2001. Contested (SDLP) Fermanagh and S Tyrone, 2001, 2005; contested (SDLP) Fermanagh and S Tyrone, NI Assembly, 2011. Mem., Western Educn and Library Bd, 1989–2001. *Recreations:* Gaelic games, horse racing. *Address:* Keenaghan, Belleek, Co. Fermanagh BT93 3ES. *T:* (028) 6865 8355. *Club:* Erne Gaels Gaelic Football.

GALLAGHER, Tony; Editor-in-Chief, The Sun, since 2015; *b* London, 2 Nov. 1963; *s* of Tony Gallagher and Winifred Gallagher; *m* 1991, Catherine Elliott; one *s* two *d. Educ:* Finchley Catholic High Sch., London; Univ. of Bristol (BA Hons); City Univ., London (Postgrad. Dip. Newspaper Journalism). Reporter: Southern Evening Echo, Southampton, 1985–86; South West News Service, Bristol, 1987–88; Today, 1988–89; Daily Mail: Reporter, 1990–96; NY Corresp., 1996–97; Dep. News Ed., 1997–99; News Ed., 1999–2006; Dep. Ed., 2007–09, Ed., 2009–14, Daily Telegraph; Dep. Ed., Daily Mail, 2014–15. *Recreations:* family, West Ham United.

GALLARD, Jill; HM Diplomatic Service; Human Resources Director, Foreign and Commonwealth Office, since 2014; *b* Omagh, 11 June 1968; *d* of Leslie Parkinson and Margaret Parkinson (*née* Thompson); *m* 2007, Dominic John Gallard; two *s. Educ:* Univ. of Edinburgh (MA Hons French and Spanish). Joined HM Diplomatic Service, 1991; FCO, 1991–94; on secondment to EC, 1994; Third Sec. (Pol), 1994–97, Second Sec. (EU/Econ.), 1997–99, Madrid; Hd, Turkey Section, FCO, 1999–2001; Dep. Hd, Common For. and Security Policy Team, FCO, 2001–03; Hd, Pol/EU/Econ. Sections, Prague, 2004–07; Private Sec. to Perm. Under-Sec. of State, FCO, 2007–08; Asst Dir, HR Ops, FCO, 2008–10; Ambassador to Portugal, 2011–14. *Address:* c/o Foreign and Commonwealth Office, King Charles Street, SW1A 2AH. *E:* jill.gallard@fco.gov.uk.

GALLEY, Roy; Director, Planning, Post Office Property Holdings, 1998–2006; *b* 8 Dec. 1947; *s* of late Kenneth Haslam Galley and Letitia Mary Chapman; *m* 1976, Helen Margaret Butcher; one *s* one *d. Educ:* King Edward VII Grammar Sch., Sheffield; Worcester Coll., Oxford (MA). North-East Postal Bd, 1969–83: started as management trainee; Asst Controller, Projects (regional manager), 1980–83; Head of Project Control, London Building and Estates Centre, Royal Mail Letters, 1987–91; Royal Mail, London: Dir, Facilities, 1992–95; Dir, Restructuring, 1995–96; Dir, Operations, 1996–98. Chm., Kingston and Richmond (formerly Kingston and Esher) DHA, 1989–98. Member: Calderdale MBC, 1980–83; Maresfield Parish Council, 2006–; Wealden DC, 2007– (Portfolio Holder, Economic Develt and Regeneration, 2013–); E Sussex CC, 2013–; E Sussex Fire Authy, 2013–. Mem., Bd of Conservators, Ashdown Forest, 2008– (Chm., 2013–). Chm., Yorks

Young Conservatives, 1974–76; contested (C): Dewsbury, 1979; Halifax, 1987. MP (C) Halifax, 1983–87. Sec., Cons. Backbench Health Cttee, 1983–87; Mem., Social Services Select Cttee, 1984–87. Chm., Kingston and St George's Coll. of Nursing, 1993–96. *Recreations:* history, European literature, theatre, music, gardening, riding. *Address:* Fairplace Farm, Nutley, Uckfield, East Sussex TN22 3HE.

GALLI, Paolo; Italian Ambassador to the Court of St James's, 1995–99; *b* 10 Aug. 1934; *s* of Carlo Galli and Bianca Metral-Lambert; *m* 1959, Maria Giuliana Calioni; two *d*. *Educ:* Univ. of Padua (law degree). Entered Italian Diplomatic Service, 1958; Minister of State's Private Office, 1958–61; Vice Consul, Cardiff, 1961–63; Second Sec., Washington, 1963–65; First Sec., Co-ordination Dept, Sec.-Gen's Office, Min. for Foreign Affairs, 1965–68; First Sec., later Counsellor and First Counsellor, London, 1968–72; First Counsellor, Warsaw, 1972–75; Min. for Foreign Affairs, Econ. Affairs Dept, 1975–79; Foreign Minister's Private Office, 1979–80; Minister-Counsellor, Dep. Perm. Rep. to EEC, Brussels, 1980–85; promoted to rank of Minister, 1985; Ambassador to Warsaw, 1986–88; Dir-Gen., Aid and Co-operation Dept, Min. for Foreign Affairs, 1988–91; promoted to rank of Ambassador, 1989; Ambassador to Tokyo, 1992–95. Cavaliere di Gran Croce, Ordine al Merito della Repubblica Italiana, 1997. *Recreations:* classical music, the arts, fencing. *Address:* Zattere 1404, 30123 Venice, Italy.

GALLIANO, John Charles, CBE 2001; RDI 2002; Company Director and Couturier for Maison John Galliano, since 1984; Artistic Director: L'Etoile, since 2014; Maison Martin Margiela, since 2014; *b* 28 Nov. 1960. *Educ:* Wilson's Grammar Sch. for Boys; St Martin's Sch. of Art and Design (BA; Hon. Fellow, London Inst., 1997). Regular seasonal collections, 1985–. Designer of Haute Couture and Prêt-à-Porter: for Givenchy, 1995–96; for Dior, 1996–2011. British Designer of the Year, British Fashion Council, 1987, 1994, 1995, 1997 (jtly); Telva Award for Best Internat. Designer, Mejor Creador International, 1995; VH1 Best Women's Wear Designer Award, 1998; Internat. Designer Award, Council of Fashion Designers of America, 1998. *Address:* 60 rue d'Avron, 75020 Paris, France. *T:* (1) 55251111, *Fax:* (1) 55251112.

GALLIE, Prof. Duncan Ian Dunbar, CBE 2009; DPhil; FBA 1995; Professor of Sociology, University of Oxford, since 1996; Official Fellow, Nuffield College, Oxford, 1985–2014, now Emeritus Fellow; *b* 16 Feb. 1946; *s* of Ian Gallie and Elsie (*née* Peers); *m* 1971, Martine Josephine Jurdant. *Educ:* St Paul's Sch., London (Scholar); Magdalen Coll., Oxford (Demyship; BA 1st Cl. Hons History); LSE (MSc); St Antony's Coll., Oxford (DPhil). Research Fellow, Nuffield Coll., Oxford, 1971–73; Lectr in Sociology, Univ. of Essex, 1973–79; Reader in Sociology, Univ. of Warwick, 1979–85; Dir, ESRC Social Change and Economic Life Initiative, 1985–90. Advr, Comité Nat. d'Evaluation de la Recherche, 1991; Member, Scientific Committee: IRESCO, 1989–93; IFRESI, 1993–98; Member: EU Adv. Gp on Social Scis and Humanities in European Res. Area, 2002–; Scientific Council, Paris Sch. of Econs, 2009–. Vice-Pres., 2004–, and Foreign Sec., 2006–11, British Acad. Dist. Contrib. to Scholarship Award, Amer. Sociol. Assoc., 1985. *Publications:* In Search of the New Working Class, 1978; Social Inequality and Class Radicalism in France and Britain, 1983; (ed jtly) New Approaches to Economic Life, 1985; (ed) Employment in Britain, 1988; (ed jtly) Social Change and the Experience of Unemployment, 1994; (ed jtly) Trade Unionism in Recession, 1996; (jtly) Restructuring the Employment Relationship, 1998; (ed jtly) Welfare Regimes and the Experience of Unemployment in Europe, 2000; (ed) Resisting Marginalization, 2004; (ed) Employment Regimes and the Quality of Work, 2007; (ed) Economic Crisis, Quality of Work and Social Integration: the European experience, 2013; articles in learned jls. *Recreations:* travelling, music, museum gazing. *Address:* Nuffield College, Oxford OX1 1NF. *T:* (01865) 278586; 149 Leam Terrace, Leamington Spa, Warwickshire CV31 1DF. *T:* (01926) 314941.

GALLIE, Gail Elizabeth; Co-founder and Creative Lead, Project Everyone, since 2015; *b* Newcastle, 12 March 1971; *d* of Gerard and Irene Nuttney; *m* 2003, James Duncan Gallie; one *s* one *d*. *Educ:* Dame Allan's Sch.; Balliol Coll., Oxford (BA Hons Modern Langs (Italian/French)). Advertising Exec., DMB&B, 1992–94; Advertising Dir, BMP DDB Needham, 1994–97; Hd of Mktg, BBC, 1997–2007; Founder, Gallie Godfrey, 2008–10; CEO, Fallon London, 2010–14. Founder, Outdoor Swimming Soc. *Recreations:* nature, travel, music, family. *E:* gailgallie@me.com.

GALLIERS, Margaret Mary, CBE 2009; Chair: Company Board, National Institute of Adult Continuing Education, since 2012 (Board Member, since 2007); City College Coventry, since 2013; *b* Coventry, 17 April 1952; *d* of Alexander Michael Donald and Ella Mary Donald; *m* 1st, 1973, Simon Godfrey (marr. diss. 1987); two *s* one *d*; 2nd, 1987, David John Galliers; one *s*. *Educ:* Barr's Hill Sch., Coventry; Univ. of Exeter (BA Social Policy and Social Admin); Univ. of Warwick (PGCE). Teacher/lectr, 1974–90; Dep. Associate Principal, 1990–92, Dep. Principal, 1992–97, Tile Hill Coll.; Principal, Henley Coll., Coventry, 1997–2002; Principal and Chief Exec., Leicester Coll., 2002–13. Pres., Assoc. of Colleges, 2012–13. Member: Quality Assessment Cttee, FEFC, 1998–2001; Young People's Cttee, LSC, 2001–07; Apprenticeship Task Force, 2003–05; Bd, Quality Improvement Agency, 2006–09; Teaching Quality and Student Experience Cttee, HEFCE, 2007–13; Nat. Learning and Skills Council, 2008–10; Bd, QCA, 2008–10; Bd, Office of Qualifications and Exams Regulation, 2010– (Chm., Audit and Risk Cttee, 2015–). Nat. Leader in Governance, 2014–. *Recreations:* walking, gardening, kayaking. *Address:* National Institute of Adult Continuing Education, 21 De Montfort Street, Leicester LE1 7GE. *E:* helen.prew@niace.org.uk.

GALLIFORD, Rt Rev. David George; Bishop Suffragan of Bolton, 1984–91; *b* 20 June 1925; *s* of Alfred Edward Bruce and Amy Doris Galliford; *m* 1st, 1954, Enid May Drax (*d* 1983); one *d*; 2nd, 1987, Claire Margaret Phoenix. *Educ:* Bede Coll., Sunderland; Clare Coll., Cambridge (Organ Scholar, 1942, BA 1949, MA 1951); Westcott House, Cambridge. Served 5th Royal Inniskilling Dragoon Guards, 1943–47. Curate of St John Newland, Hull, 1951–54; Minor Canon of Windsor, 1954–56; Vicar of St Oswald, Middlesbrough, 1956–61; Rector of Bolton Percy and Diocesan Training Officer, 1961–70; Canon of York Minster, 1969; Canon Residentiary and Treasurer of York Minster, 1970–75; Bishop Suffragan of Hulme, 1975–84. Asst Bishop, dio. York, 1991–2011. SBStJ 1992. *Publications:* God and Christian Caring, 1973; Pastor's Post, 1975; (ed) Diocese in Mission, 1968. *Recreations:* music, composition, water colours. *Address:* Connaught Court, Royal Masonic Benevolent Institution, St Oswalds Road, Fulford, York YO10 4FA. *T:* (01904) 626208.

GALLIGAN, Prof. Denis James, DCL; Professor of Socio-Legal Studies, and Director, Centre for Socio-Legal Studies, University of Oxford, since 1993; Fellow, Wolfson College, Oxford, since 1993; *b* 4 June 1947; *s* of John Felix Galligan and Muriel Maud Galligan; *m* 1972, Martha Louise Martinuzzi; one *s* one *d*. *Educ:* Univ. of Queensland (LLB 1970); Univ. of Oxford (BCL 1974; MA 1976; DCL 2000). Barrister, Supreme Court of Qld, 1970; called to the Bar, Gray's Inn, 1996. Rhodes Scholar, Magdalen Coll., Oxford, 1971–74; Lectr, Faculty of Law, UCL, 1974–76; Fellow, Jesus Coll., and CUF Lectr, Oxford Univ., 1976–81; Sen. Lectr, Univ. of Melbourne, 1982–84; Prof. of Law, Univ. of Southampton, 1985–92 (Dean, Law Faculty, 1987–90); Prof. of Law, Univ. of Sydney, 1990–92. Visiting Professor: Central European Univ., 1993–2004; Princeton Univ., 2002–; Jean Monnet Prof., Univ. of Siena, 2003–. AcSS 2000. *Publications:* Essays in Legal Theory, 1984; Law, Rights and the Welfare State, 1986; Discretionary Powers, 1986; Australian Administrative Law, 1993; Socio-Legal Readings in Administrative Law, 1995; Socio-Legal Studies in Context, 1995; Due Process and Fair Procedures, 1996; Administrative Justice in the New Democracies, 1998; Western Concepts of Administrative Law, 2002; Law and Informal Practices, 2003; Law and Modern Society, 2006. *Recreations:* reading, gardening. *Address:* Wolfson College, Linton Road, Oxford OX2 6UD; The Rosary, Beckley, Oxford OX3 9UU. *T:* (01865) 284220 and 351281.

GALLIVER, Philippa Ann; *see* Helme, P. A.

GALLOP, Prof. Hon. Geoffrey (Ian), AC 2008; DPhil; Professor and Director, Graduate School of Government, University of Sydney, since 2006; *b* 27 Sept. 1951; *s* of Douglas and Eunice Gallop; *m* 1st, 1975, Beverley Jones (*d* 2009); two *s*; 2nd, 2010, Ingrid van Beek. *Educ:* Univ. of Western Australia (BEc); Murdoch Univ. (MPhil); St John's and Nuffield Colls, Oxford (MA, DPhil). Res. Fellow, Nuffield Coll., Oxford, 1979–81; Lectr in Social and Political Theory, Murdoch Univ., 1981–86. MLA (ALP) Victoria Park, WA, 1986–2006; Minister: for Educn, and Parly and Electoral Reform, 1990–91; for Fuel and Energy, Microecon. Reform, Parly and Electoral Reform, and Assisting the Treas., 1991–93; Leader of the Opposition, WA, 1996–2001; Premier of WA, 2001–06. Dep. Chm., Council of Australian Govts Reform Council, 2007–11. Chm., Australian Awards Bd, 2011–. FIPAA. Hon. DLitt Murdoch, 2006. *Publications:* (ed) Pigs' Meat: selected writings of Thomas Spence, 1982; A State of Reform: essays for a better future, 1998; Politics, Society, Self, 2012. *Recreations:* swimming, cricket, football. *Address:* Graduate School of Government, University of Sydney, Sydney, NSW 2006, Australia. *Clubs:* Swan Districts Football, West Coast Eagles.

GALLOWAY, 13th Earl of, *cr* 1623; **Randolph Keith Reginald Stewart;** Lord Garlies, 1607; Bt 1627, 1687; Baron Stewart of Garlies (GB), 1796; *b* 14 Oct. 1928; *s* of 12th Earl of Galloway, and Philippa Fendall (*d* 1974), *d* of late Jacob Wendell, New York; *S* father, 1978; *m* 1975, Mrs Lily May Budge, DLJ (*d* 1999), *y d* of late Andrew Miller, Duns, Berwickshire. *Educ:* Harrow. KLJ. *Heir: cousin* Andrew Clyde Stewart [*b* 13 March 1949; *m* 1st, 1977, Sara (marr. diss. 2001), *o d* of Brig. Patrick Pollock; one *s* two *d*; 2nd, 2008, Christine Merrick Andersson]. *Address:* Castle Douglas, Kirkcudbrightshire.

GALLOWAY, Bishop of, (RC), since 2015; **Rt Rev. William Nolan;** *b* Motherwell, 26 Jan. 1954; *s* of late William and Catherine Nolan. *Educ:* St Vincent's Coll., Langbank; St Mary's Coll., Blairs; Pontifical Scots Coll., Rome; Gregorian Univ. (STL 1978). Ordained priest, 1977; Assistant Priest: Our Lady of Lourdes, E Kilbride, 1978–80; St David's Plains, 1980–83; Vice-Rector, Scots Coll., Rome, 1983–90; Asst Priest, St Bridget's, Baillieston, 1990–94; Parish Priest, Our Lady of Lourdes, E Kilbride, 1994–2015; Administrator, St John Ogilvie Parish, Blantyre, 2013–15; Vicar Gen., Dio. of Motherwell, 2014–15. *Address:* Diocesan and Pastoral Office, Candida Casa, 8 Corsehill Road, Ayr KA7 2ST.

GALLOWAY, Alexander Kippen, CVO 2006; Clerk of the Privy Council, 1998–2006; *b* 29 April 1952; *s* of late Alexander Kippen Galloway and Vera Eleanor Galloway; *m* 1st, 1973, Elaine Margaret Watkinson (marr. diss. 2005); three *s*; 2nd, 2006, Suzanne Lesley Phillips. *Educ:* Birkenhead Sch.; Jesus Coll., Oxford (MA Lit.Hum.); LLB Hons Open Univ. 2006. Department of the Environment: Exec. Officer, 1974; Principal, 1982; Private Sec. to Chancellor of Duchy of Lancaster, 1982–84, to Paymaster Gen., 1982–83 and 1984–85; Secretariat, Cabinet Office, 1992–93; Asst Sec., DoE, 1994–98. CEO, Soc. for the Envmt, 2012–14. Mem., Edtl Bd, Sustain mag., 2013–. Member: Architects' Registration Bd, 2007–13 (Chm., Investigations Cttee, 2008–13); Professional Regulation Exec. Cttee (formerly Affairs Bd), Inst. and Faculty of Actuaries (formerly Actuarial Profession), 2007–12; Council, IoD, 2007–13. Formerly Trustee, Projects in Partnership (Chm., 1999–2004); Trustee, Southwark Charities, 2008–12. Advr, Assoc. of Lord Lieutenants, 2007–. Pres., London Br., Oxford Univ. Soc., 2007–. Clerk, Co. of Glaziers and Painters of Glass, 2007–12 (Master, 2014–15). Juror, Court Leet of the King's Manor, Southwark, 2008– (Foreman, 2011–12). FRSA 2002. Hon. FSE 2004. *Recreations:* playing the cello, choral singing, ski-ing. *Address:* 19 Frythe Close, Kenilworth, Warwickshire CV8 2SY. *T:* (01926) 777569. *Clubs:* City Livery, Scribes, Royal Over-Seas League.

GALLOWAY, Prof. David Malcolm, PhD; FBPsS; Professor of Education, University of Durham, 1992–2001, now Emeritus (Head of School of Education, 1993–2000); *b* 5 July 1942; *s* of late Malcolm Ashby Galloway and Joan Dorah Frances Galloway (*née* Slater); *m* 1971, Christina Mary King; two *s* one *d*. *Educ:* St Edmund Hall, Oxford (BA Psychol., Phil. and Physiol. 1970; MA 1974); UCL (MSc Educnl Psychol. 1972); Sheffield City Poly. (PhD 1980). FBPsS 1983. Educnl Psychologist and Sen. Educnl Psychologist, Sheffield LEA, 1972–79; Sen. Lectr, Victoria Univ. of Wellington, NZ, 1980–83; Lectr, UC Cardiff, 1983–87; Lectr and Reader in Educnl Res., Lancaster Univ., 1987–91. Chm., Assoc. for Child Psychology and Psychiatry, 1999–2001. *Publications:* books include: Schools and Persistent Absentees, 1985; (with C. Goodwin) The Education of Disturbing Children: pupils with learning and adjustment difficulties, 1987; (with A. Edwards) Primary School Teaching and Educational Psychology, 1991; (jtly) The Assessment of Special Educational Needs: whose problem?, 1994; (jtly) Motivating the Difficult to Teach, 1998; (jtly) Academies and Educational Reform, 2010; numerous articles in acad. and professional jls. *Recreations:* bee-keeping, fell search and mountain rescue (Chm., Kirkby Stephen Mountain Rescue Team, 2002–07). *Address:* Crosby Mill Cottage, Smardale, Kirkby Stephen, Cumbria CA17 4HQ.

GALLOWAY, George; *b* 16 Aug. 1954; *s* of George and Sheila Galloway; *m* 1st, 1979, Elaine Fyffe (marr. diss. 1999); one *d*; 2nd, Dr Amineh Abu-Zayyad (marr. diss. 2009); one *s* by Rima Husseini; *m* 2012, Putri Gayatri Pertiwi. *Educ:* Charleston Primary Sch.; Harris Acad., Dundee. Engrg worker, 1973; organiser, Labour Party, 1977; Gen. Sec., War on Want, 1983–87. MP Glasgow, Hillhead, 1987–97, Glasgow Kelvin, 1997–2005, Bethnal Green and Bow, 2005–10 (Lab, 1987–2003, Ind Lab, 2003–04, Respect, 2004–10); contested (Respect) Poplar and Limehouse, 2010; MP (Respect) Bradford W, March 2012–2015; contested (Respect) same seat, 2015. Contested (Respect) London reg., EP elections, 2004. HQA (Pakistan), 1990; HPK (Pakistan), 1995. *Publications:* (jtly) Downfall: the Ceausescus and the Romanian revolution, 1991; I'm Not the Only One, 2004; Fidel Castro Handbook, 2007. *Recreations:* boxing, football, films, music.

GALLOWAY, Peter George, CBE 2006; Rector, Trinity Academy, Edinburgh, 1983–2008; *b* 21 March 1944; *s* of John and Mary Galloway; *m* 1971, Elizabeth Taylor; one *d*. *Educ:* Buckhaven High Sch.; Heriot-Watt Univ. (Dip Commerce 1966; BA 1970); Moray House Coll. Asst Rector, Royal High Sch., Edinburgh, 1976–80; Depute Head, James Gillespie's High, Edinburgh, 1980–83. Chm., Partnership Planning Gp, Enterprise in Educn, 2004–; Member: UK Council for European Educn, 1995–2000; Determined to Succeed Gp, 2001; Smith Gp, 2005–. Dir, Schools Enterprise Scotland Ltd, 2003–05. FRSA. *Recreations:* all sports, particularly Rugby, cricket and football as a spectator, golf as a player, travel, cooking. *Address:* 32 Bramdean Rise, Braids, Edinburgh EH10 6JR. *T:* (0131) 447 3070. *E:* peterggallowaycbe@hotmail.co.uk. *Clubs:* Mortonhall Golf, Trinity Academicals Rugby (Edinburgh).

GALLOWAY, Rev. Dr Peter John, OBE 1996; JP; Chaplain of the Queen's Chapel of the Savoy and of the Royal Victorian Order, since 2008; Secretary for Church Livings, Duchy of Lancaster, since 2008; Visiting Professor in Politics and History, Brunel University, since 2008; *b* 19 July 1954; *s* of late Henry John Galloway and Mary Selina (*née* Beshaw); civil partnership 2008, Michael Russell Stewart Turner. *Educ:* Westminster City Sch.; Goldsmiths' Coll., Univ. of London (BA 1976); King's Coll., London (PhD 1987); St Stephen's House, Oxford. Ordained deacon, 1983; priest, 1984; Curate: St John's Wood, 1983–86; St Giles-in-the-Fields, 1986–90; Priest-in-charge, 1990–95, Vicar, 1995–2008, Emmanuel Church, W Hampstead; Warden of Readers, London Episcopal Area, 1987–92; Area Dean, N Camden, 2002–07; Surrogate, 2006–. Member: London Dio. Synod, 1997–2000; London Dio. Adv.

Cttee, 2007–13. St John Ambulance: Asst Dir-Gen., 1985–91; Dep. Dir-Gen., 1991–99; Chm., Nat. Publications Cttee, 1988–95; Order of St John: Mem., Chapter Gen., 1996–99; Mem., Priory of England Chapter, 1999–2013; Sub Dean, Priory of England, 1999–2007; Registrar, 2007–. Mem., Lord Chancellor's Adv. Cttee, City of London, 1994–2000 and 2005–11 (Vice Chm., 2008–11), Central and S London, 2012–13. London University: Mem. Council, 1999–2008; Vice Chm. Convocation, 1999–2003 (Acting Chm., 2001–03); Chm., Convocation Trust, 2005–12 (Trustee, 2003–); Mem. Council, Goldsmiths' Coll., 1993–99 (Hon. Fellow, 1999); Chm., Goldsmiths' Soc., 1997–2007 (Vice-Chm., 1991–97); Mem. Council, Heythrop Coll., 2006–14. Mem., Adv. Bd, Magna Carta Inst., Brunel Univ., 2009–. Gov., Soho Parish Sch., 1989–91; Chm. of Governors, Emmanuel Sch., W Hampstead, 1990–2008; Gov., St Olave's and St Saviour's GS, 2009– (Vice Chm., 2012–13; Chm., 2013–); Mem., Ct of Govs, St Olave's and St Saviour's Schs Foundn, 2014–. Patron, English Schs Orch., 1998–. Trustee: League of Mercy Foundn, 1999–; St Gabriel's Trust, 2001–04. Provost (formerly Chaplain), Imperial Soc. of Knights Bachelor, 2006–; Chaplain to HRH the Princess Royal as Master, Butchers' Co., 2010–11. Freeman, City of London, 1995. JP: City of London, 1989–2011 (Dep. Chm., 2000, Chm., 2001–04, Bench); Central London, 2012. Dep. Chm., 2003, Chm., 2004, Gtr London Bench Chairmen's Forum. FSA 2000. Hon. DLitt Brunel, 2009. KStJ 1997. Award of Merit, Orders and Medals Res. Soc., 2013. Officer, Order of the Crown (Romania), 2013. *Publications:* The Order of St Patrick 1783–1983, 1983; Henry Falconar Barclay Mackay, 1983; (with Christopher Rawll) Good and Faithful Servants, 1988; The Cathedrals of Ireland, 1992; The Order of the British Empire, 1996; (jtly) Royal Service, 1996; The Most Illustrious Order, 1999; A Passionate Humility: Frederick Oakeley and the Oxford movement, 1999; The Cathedrals of Scotland, 2000; The Order of St Michael and St George, 2000; Companions of Honour, 2002; The Order of the Bath, 2006; The Order of the Thistle, 2009; The Queen's Chapel of the Savoy, 2009; Exalted, Eminent and Imperial, Honours of the British Raj, 2014. *Recreations:* reading, writing, book collecting, solitude. *Address:* The Queen's Chapel of the Savoy, Savoy Hill, Strand, WC2R 0DA. *Clubs:* Athenæum, Beefsteak.

GALLOWAY, Prof. Tamara Susan, PhD; Professor of Ecotoxicology, University of Exeter, since 2007; Honorary Chair, University of Exeter Medical School, since 2007; *b* Bognor Regis, 6 Feb. 1963; *d* of Anatole Scobie and Wendy Scobie; *m* (marr. diss.); three *s*. *Educ:* Bishopbriggs High Sch., Glasgow; Univ. of Glasgow (BSc Hons Biochem. 1979); Univ. of Edinburgh (PhD Biochem. 1983). Proj. Leader, Clin. Reagents Res. and Develt, Amersham Internat. plc, 1986–90; pt-time Res. Asst to Prof. Peter Mitchell, FRS, Glynn Res. Inst., 1991–92; Sen. Lectr, 1997–2005, Reader, 2005–07, in Biochem., Univ. of Plymouth. *Publications:* approx. 200 scientific articles and book chapters on envmtl pollution. *Recreations:* swimming, shopping for clothes, hanging about with friends, cooking, worrying about things. *Address:* College of Life and Environmental Sciences, University of Exeter, Exeter EX4 4QD. *T:* (01392) 263436. *E:* t.s.galloway@exeter.ac.uk.

GALSWORTHY, Sir Anthony (Charles), KCMG 1999 (CMG 1985); HM Diplomatic Service, retired; Ambassador to the People's Republic of China, 1997–2002; *b* 20 Dec. 1944; *s* of Sir Arthur Norman Galsworthy, KCMG, and Margaret Agnes Galsworthy (*née* Hiscocks); *m* 1970, Jan Dawson-Grove; one *s* one *d*. *Educ:* St Paul's Sch.; Corpus Christi Coll., Cambridge (MA). FCO, 1966–67; Hong Kong (language training), 1967–69; Peking, 1970–72; FCO, 1972–77; Rome, 1977–81; Counsellor, Peking, 1981–84; Head of Hong Kong Dept, FCO, 1984–86; Principal Private Sec. to Sec. of State for Foreign and Commonwealth Affairs, 1986–88; seconded to RIIA, 1988–89; Sen. British Rep., Sino-British Jt Liaison Gp, Hong Kong, 1989–93; Chief of Assessments Staff, Cabinet Office, 1993–95; Dep. Under Sec. of State, FCO, 1995–97. Scientific Associate, Natural Hist. Mus., 2001–. Member Council: British Trust for Ornithology, 2002–06; Wildfowl and Wetlands Trust, 2002–09. Advr, Standard Chartered Bank, 2002–14; Director: Bekaert SA, 2004–14; WTT Consulting, 2009–. Dir, Earthwatch (Europe), 2002–06. Hon. Prof., Kunming Inst. of Botany, Chinese Acad. of Scis. Hon. Fellow, Royal Botanic Gdns, Edinburgh, 2001. *Publications:* (jtly) The Genus Eupithecia in China, 2013. *Recreations:* bird-watching, wildlife. *Club:* Oxford and Cambridge.

GALSWORTHY, (Arthur) Michael (Johnstone), CVO 2002; CBE 1999; Chairman, Trewithen Estates Management Co., since 1979; Vice Lord-Lieutenant, Cornwall, 2002–14; *b* 10 April 1944; *s* of Sir John Galsworthy, KCVO, CMG and late Jennifer Ruth Johnstone; *m* 1st, 1972, Charlotte Helena Prudence Roberts (*d* 1989); one *s* two *d*; 2nd, 1991, Sarah Christian Durnford; one *s* one *d*. *Educ:* Radley; St Andrews Univ. (MA Hons). International Harvester Corp., 1967–69; English China Clays PLC, 1970–82; Man. Dir, Hawkins Wright Associates, 1982–86. Local Adv. Dir, Barclays Bank, 1987–98. Mem., Prince of Wales Council, 1985–2002; Dir, CoSIRA, 1985–88; a Develt Comr, 1987–92; Trustee, Rural Housing Trust, 1986–92; Chairman: Cornwall Rural Housing Assoc., 1985–95; Royal Cornwall Hosps NHS Trust, 1991–93; Chm., In Pursuit of Excellence Partnership for Cornwall, 1994–2000. Chm., Cornwall Co. Playing Fields, 1978–96; Dir, Woodard Corp. (W Region), 1983–87. Vice Pres., Royal Cornwall Agricl Assoc., 1987–. FRAgS 2007; FZS 2008. Mem., Court of Assts, Goldsmiths' Co., 1998– (Prime Warden, 2010–11). Chm. Council, Order of St John for Cornwall, 1995–99. DL Cornwall, 1993; High Sheriff, Cornwall, 1994. *Publications:* In Pursuit of Excellence: testimonial of business in Cornwall, 1994; The IPE Business Journal, 1996; The IPE Green Book Testimonial, 1997; A Wealth of Talent: the best of crafts in Cornwall, 1998. *Recreations:* gardening, fishing, shooting, walking. *Address:* Trewithen, Grampound Road, near Truro, Cornwall TR2 4DD. *T:* (01726) 882418. *Clubs:* Brooks's, Farmers.

GALTON, Bernard John; Director General, Workforce and Organisational Development, NHS Wales, 2013–14; *b* 5 July 1956; *s* of Roy and Kathleen Galton; *m* 1978, Susan Fox; two *s*. *Educ:* City of Bath Boys' Sch. Ministry of Defence, 1973–2004: Dir, HR Policy, 1996–98; HR Dir, Defence Aviation Repair Agency, 1998–2004; Dir, HR Gp, Welsh Assembly Govt, 2004–09; Dir Gen., People, Places and Corporate Services, Welsh Assembly Govt, later Welsh Govt, 2009–13. Strategic Advr, Sapienti, 2014–. Non-exec. Dir, Royal Nat. Hosp. for Rheumatic Diseases, 2014–. Chartered FCIPD (FCIPD 2001); Mem., BPsS. *Recreations:* reading, travelling, gym, good food and wine, family. *T:* (.

GALTON, Raymond Percy, OBE 2000; author and scriptwriter, since 1951; *b* 17 July 1930; *s* of Herbert and Christina Galton; *m* 1956, Tonia Phillips (*d* 1995); one *s* two *d*. *Educ:* Garth Sch., Morden. *Television:* with Alan Simpson: Hancock's Half Hour, 1954–61 (adaptation and translation, Fleksnes, Scandinavian TV, film and stage); Comedy Playhouse, 1962–63; Steptoe and Son, 1962–74 (adaptations and translations: Sanford and Son, US TV; Stiefbeen and Zoon, Dutch TV; Albert och Herbert, Scandinavian TV, film and stage; Camilo y Filho, Portugal TV (Golden Globe Award, 1996)); Galton-Simpson Comedy, 1969; Clochemerle, 1971; Casanova '74, 1974; Dawson's Weekly, 1975; The Galton and Simpson Playhouse, 1976–77; Paul Merton in Galton and Simpson's…, 1996, 1997; Fleksnes Fataliteter, Scandinavian TV, 2002; with Johnny Speight: Tea Ladies, 1979; Spooner's Patch, 1979–80; with John Antrobus: Room at the Bottom, 1986–87 (Banff TV Fest. Award for Best Comedy, 1987); Get Well Soon, 1997; *films:* with Alan Simpson: The Rebel, 1960; The Bargee, 1963; The Spy with a Cold Nose, 1966; Loot, 1969; Steptoe and Son, 1971; Steptoe and Son Ride Again, 1973; Den Siste Fleksnes (Scandinavia), 1974; Die Skraphandlerne (Scandinavia), 1975; with Alan Simpson and John Antrobus: The Wrong Arm of the Law, 1963; with Andrew Galton: Camping (Denmark), 1990; *theatre:* with Alan Simpson: Way Out in Piccadilly, 1966; The Wind in the Sassafras Trees, 1968; Albert och Herbert (Sweden), 1981; Fleksnes (Norway), 1983; Mordet på Skolgatan 15 (Sweden), 1984; Steptoe and Son (Kneehigh version), 2012–13; with John Antrobus: When Did You Last See Your Trousers?, 1986, UK tour, 1994; Steptoe and Son in Murder at Oil Drum Lane, Comedy Th., 2006; Des Pieds et Des Mains, Paris, 2013–14; *radio:* Galton and Simpson's Half Hour, Radio 2, 2009. Awards, with Alan Simpson: Scriptwriters of the Year, 1959 (Guild of TV Producers and Directors); Best TV Comedy Series, Steptoe and Son, 1962/3/4/5 (Screenwriters Guild); John Logie Baird Award (for outstanding contribution to Television), 1964; Best Comedy Series (Steptoe and Son, Dutch TV), 1966; Best comedy screenplay, Steptoe and Son, 1972 (Screenwriters Guild); Lifetime Achievement Award, Writers' Guild of GB, 1997. *Publications:* (with Alan Simpson): Hancock, 1961; Steptoe and Son, 1963; The Reunion and Other Plays, 1966; Hancock Scripts, 1974; The Best of Hancock, 1986; The Best of Steptoe and Son, 1988; The Lost Hancock Scripts, 2010; The Masters of Sitcom: from Hancock to Steptoe, 2011. *Recreations:* reading, worrying. *Address:* The Ivy House, Hampton Court, Middx KT8 9DD. *T:* (020) 8977 1236; Tessa Le Bars Management, 54 Birchwood Road, Petts Wood, Kent BR5 1NZ. *T:* (01689) 837084. *W:* www.galtonandsimpson.com.

GALVIN, John Rogers; General, United States Army, retired; Supreme Allied Commander, Europe, and Commander-in-Chief, US European Command, Stuttgart, 1987–92; Dean, Fletcher School of Law and Diplomacy, Tufts University, 1995–2000, now Emeritus; *b* 13 May 1929; *s* of John J. Galvin and Mary Josephine Logan; *m* 1961, Virginia Lee Brennan; four *d*. *Educ:* US Mil. Acad. (BS); Columbia Univ. (MA); US Army Command and General Staff Coll.; Univ. of Pennsylvania; US Army War Coll.; Fletcher Sch. of Law and Diplomacy (US Army War Coll. Fellowship). Platoon Leader, I Co., 65 Inf. Regt, Puerto Rico, 1955–56; Instructor, Ranger Sch., Colombia, 1956–58; Co. Comdr, 501 Airborne Battle Group, 101 Airborne Div., 1958–60; Instructor, US Mil. Acad., 1962–65; DACOS, Plans, 1st Cavalry Div., Vietnam, 1966–67; MA and Aide to Sec. of US Army, 1967–69; Comdr, 1st Bn, 8th Cavalry, 1st Cavalry Div., Vietnam, 1969–70; Dep. Sec., Jt Staff, US European Comd, Stuttgart, 1973–74; MA to SACEUR, 1974–75; Comdr, Div. Support Comd, 1975–77; COS, 3rd Inf. Div. (Mechanized), Würzburg, 1977–78; Asst Div. Comdr, 8th Inf. Div. (Mechanized), Mainz, 1978–80; Asst DCOS for Training, US Army Training and Doctrine Comd, 1980–81; Comdg Gen., 24 Inf. Div. (Mechanized), and Fort Stewart, 1981–83; Comdg Gen., VII Corps, Stuttgart, 1983–85; C-in-C, US Southern Comd, Panama, 1985–87. Olin Dist. Prof. of Nat. Security, W Point, 1992–94; Dist. Policy Analyst, Mershon Center, Ohio State Univ., 1994–95. Defense DSM, Army DSM, Navy DSM, Air Force DSM, Silver Star, Legion of Merit (with 2 Oak Leaf Clusters), DFC, Soldier's Medal, Bronze Star (with 2 Oak Leaf Clusters), Combat Infantryman Badge, Ranger Tab, foreign decorations. *Publications:* The Minute Men, 1967; Air Assault: the development of airmobility, 1969; Three Men of Boston, 1975. *Recreations:* walking, jogging. *Address:* 2714 Lake Jodeco Circle, Jonesboro, GA 30236–5326, USA.

GALVIN, William; Group Chief Executive, Universities Superannuation Scheme, since 2013; *b* Waterford, Ireland, 1968; *m* 2010, Clemence Bourdariat; two *d*. *Educ:* Univ. of Limerick (BA 1989); University Coll. Cork (Postgrad. Dip. 1995); Univ. of Manchester (MBA 2001). IBM (UK), 2001–06: Strategy consultant, IBM Consulting; strategy and mktg, IBM Global Services; pensions protection policy, DWP, 2006–08; Exec. Dir for Strategic Develt, 2008–10, CEO, 2011–13, Pensions Regulator. Non-executive Director: Pensions Adv. Service, 2010–13; Solicitors Regulation Authy, 2011–; Mem. Bd, Eur. Insce and Occupational Pensions Authy, 2010–13. Gov., Pensions Policy Inst., 2010–. *Address:* Universities Superannuation Scheme, Royal Liver Building, Liverpool L3 1PY.

GALWAY, 12th Viscount *cr* 1727; **George Rupert Monckton-Arundell;** Baron Killard, 1727; Lieut Comdr RCN, retired; *b* 13 Oct. 1922; *s* of Philip Marmaduke Monckton (*d* 1965) (*g g s* of 5th Viscount) and Lavender, *d* of W. J. O'Hara; *S* cousin, 1980; *m* 1944, Fiona Margaret (*d* 2010), *d* of late Captain P. W. de P. Taylor; one *s* three *d*. *Heir: s* Hon. John Philip Monckton [*b* 8 April 1952; *m* 1st, 1980, Deborah Holmes (marr. diss. 1992); 2nd, 2002, Tracey Jean Black; one *s* two *d*]. *Address:* 787 Berkshire Drive, London, ON N6J 3S5, Canada.

GALWAY, Sir James, Kt 2001; OBE 1977; FRCM 1983; fluteplayer; *b* 8 Dec. 1939; *s* of James Galway and Ethel Stewart Clarke; *m* 1st, 1965; one *s*; 2nd, 1972; one *s* twin *d*; 3rd, 1984, Jeanne Cinnante. *Educ:* St Paul's Sch., and Mountcollyer Secondary Modern Sch., Belfast; RCM, and Guildhall Sch. of Music, London; Conservatoire National Supérieur de Musique, Paris. First post in wind band of Royal Shakespeare Theatre, Stratford-upon-Avon; later worked with Sadler's Wells Orch., Royal Opera House Orch. and BBC Symphony Orch.; Principal Flute, London Symphony Orch., 1966, Royal Philharmonic Orch., 1967–69; Principal Solo Flute, Berlin Philharmonic Orch., 1969–75; international soloist, 1975–. Principal Guest Conductor, London Mozart Players, 1999–. Recordings of works by C. P. E. Bach, J. S. Bach, Beethoven, Corigliano, Debussy, Franck, Handel, Khachaturian, Mancini, Mozart, Nielsen, Prokoviev, Reicha, Reincke, Rodrigo, Schubert, Stamitz, Telemann and Vivaldi; also albums of flute showpieces, Australian, Irish and Japanese collections. Grand Prix du Disque, 1976, 1989. Hon. FGSM 2003. Hon. MA Open, 1979; Hon. DMus: QUB, 1979; New England Conservatory of Music, 1980; St Andrews, 2003. Officier des Arts et des Lettres (France), 1987. *Publications:* James Galway: an autobiography, 1978; Flute (Menuhin Music Guide), 1982; James Galway's Music in Time, 1983 (TV series, 1983); Masterclass: performance editions of great flute literature, 1987; Flute Studies, 2003; (with Linda Bridges) The Man with the Golden Flute: Sir James, a Celtic minstrel, 2009. *Recreations:* music, walking, swimming, films, theatre, TV, chess, backgammon, computing, talking to people.

GAMBACCINI, Paul Matthew; broadcaster, since 1973; *b* New York, 2 April 1949; *s* of Mario and Dorothy Gambaccini. *Educ:* Dartmouth Coll., USA; University Coll., Oxford (MA PPE). British corresp., Rolling Stone mag., 1970–78; presenter: BBC Radio One, 1973–86 and 1990–93; BBC Radio Four, 1974–; Classic FM, 1992–2008; BBC Radio Three, 1995–96; BBC Radio Two, 1998–; television: The Old Grey Whistle Test, 1978–85; Top of the Pops; The Other Side of the Tracks, 1983–85; TV-AM, 1983–92; Television's Greatest Hits, 1992–93; GMTV, 1992–94. Presenter: Ivor Novello Awards, 1988–; Sony Radio Awards, 1999–2008; Parly Jazz Awards, 2005–12. News Internat. Vis. Prof. of Broadcasting Media, Oxford Univ., 2009. Prince's Trust Ambassador, 2009–. Philanthropist of Year, Nat. Charity Fundraisers, 1995; Sony Awards for Music Broadcaster, 2003, Music Documentary, 2004, Career Achievement, 2007. Winner, Celebrity Mastermind, BBC TV, 2010. *Publications:* (jtly) Guinness Book of British Hit Singles, 1977, 10th edn 1996; (jtly) Guinness Book of British Hit Albums, 1982, 6th edn 1994; Radio Boy, 1986; (jtly) Television's Greatest Hits, 1993; Love Letters, 1996. *Recreations:* film and theatre, softball (Inaugural Inductee, British Softball Federation Hall of Fame, 2007). *Address:* 1225 The Whitehouse Apartments, 9 Belvedere Road, SE1 8YW. *T:* (020) 7401 6753. *E:* paulgambaccini@hotmail.com.

GAMBETTA, Prof. Diego, PhD; FBA 2000; Professor of Sociology, University of Oxford, since 2002, on leave as Professor of Social Theory, European University Institute, Florence, since 2012; Official Fellow, Nuffield College, Oxford, since 2003; *b* 30 Jan. 1952; *s* of Carlo Gambetta and Giovanna (*née* Giavelli); *m* 1992, Dr Valeria Pizzini; one *s* one *d*. *Educ:* Chieri, Turin; Univ. of Turin (BA Philosophy); King's Coll., Cambridge (PhD 1983). Civil servant, Regl Admin, Piedmont, Italy, 1978–84; Jun. Res. Fellow, 1984–88, Sen. Res. Fellow, 1988–91, King's Coll., Cambridge; University of Oxford: Fellow, St Anne's Coll. and Lectr in Sociology, 1991–95 (*ad hominem* Reader, 1993); Reader in Sociology, 1995–2002; Fellow, All Souls Coll., 1995–2003. Vis. Prof. in Social Orgn, Grad. Sch. of Business and Dept of Sociol., Univ. of Chicago, 1994; Inaugural Fellow, Italian Acad. for Advanced Studies, Columbia Univ., 1996–97; Vis. Prof., Sciences Po, Paris, 2005, 2008; Guest Lectr, Collège de France, Paris, 2007; Internat. Scholar, Humanities Center and Freeman Spogli Inst., Stanford Univ., 2010. *Publications:* Were they pushed or did they jump?: individual decision mechanisms in education, 1987 (trans. Italian 1990), 2nd edn 1996; (ed) Trust: making and breaking co-operative relations, 1988 (trans. Italian 1989); The Sicilian mafia: the business of private protection (Premio Iglesias), 1993 (trans. Italian, 1992, German, 1994, Spanish, 2007, Polish, 2009), 2nd edn 1996 (Premio Borsellino, 2003); (with S. Warner) La retorica della riforma: fine del sistema proporzionale in Italia, 1994; (ed) Making Sense of Suicide Missions, 2005; (with H. Hamill) Streetwise: how taxi drivers establish the trustworthiness of their customers, 2005; Codes of the Underworld: how criminals communicate, 2009; contribs to anthologies and social scientific jls. *Recreations:* mountaineering, ski-ing, yoga, cinema. *Address:* Nuffield College, Oxford OX1 1NF; European University Institute, Badia Fiesolana, Via dei Roccettini 9, I-50014 San Domenico di Fiesole (FI), Italy.

GAMBLE, Alan James; an Upper Tribunal Judge (Administrative Appeals Chamber) (formerly Social Security and Child Support Commissioner), since 2008; *b* Glasgow, 29 April 1951; *s* of Frank Gamble and Nancy Gamble (*née* Johnston); *m* 1977, Elizabeth Rodger Waugh; two *s* one *d*. *Educ:* High Sch. of Glasgow; Univ. of Glasgow (LLB); Harvard Law Sch. (LLM). Advocate, 1978; Lectr, 1976–86, Sen. Lectr, 1986–93, in Private Law, Univ. of Glasgow; District Chm., Appeal Tribunals, 1993–2008; Dep. Social Security and Child Support Comr, 1994–2008; Convener, Mental Health Tribunal for Scotland, 2005–; Dep. Social Security and Child Support Comr for NI, 2011–. *Publications:* (contrib.) Legal Issues in Medicine, 1981; (contrib.) The Law of Property in Scotland, 1996; (ed) Obligations in Context, 2000; articles on legal topics. *Recreations:* reading, hill walking. *Address:* (office) George House, 126 George Street, Edinburgh EH3 7PW. *T:* (0131) 271 4310, *Fax:* (0131) 271 4398.

GAMBLE, Prof. Andrew Michael, PhD; FBA 2000; FAcSS; Professor of Politics, University of Cambridge, 2007–14, now Emeritus; Fellow of Queens' College, Cambridge, 2007–14, now Emeritus; Professor of Politics, University of Sheffield, since 2014; *b* 15 Aug. 1947; *s* of Marcus Elkington Gamble and Joan (*née* Westall); *m* 1974, Christine Jennifer Rodway; one *s* two *d*. *Educ:* Brighton Coll.; Queens' Coll., Cambridge (BA Econs 1968); Univ. of Durham (MA Pol Theory 1969); Gonville and Caius Coll., Cambridge (PhD Social and Pol Scis 1975). University of Sheffield: Lectr in Politics, 1973–82; Reader, 1982–86; Prof. of Politics, 1986–2006; Pro-Vice-Chancellor, 1994–98; Dir, Pol Economy Res. Centre, 1999–2004; Leverhulme Res. Fellow, 2004–07. Visiting Professor: Univ. of Kobe, 1990; Univ. of Hitotsubashi, 1992; Univ. of Chuo, 1994; ANU, 2005. Mem. Exec., 1988–91, Vice-Chair, 1989–91, Political Studies Assoc. Joint Editor: New Political Economy, 1996–2008; Political Qly, 1997–2012. FRSA 1999; FAcSS (AcSS 2002). Mitchell Prize, 1977; Sir Isaiah Berlin Prize for Lifetime Contrib. to Pol Studies, Pol Studies Assoc., 2005. *Publications:* (jtly) From Alienation to Surplus Value (Isaac Deutscher Meml Prize), 1972; The Conservative Nation, 1974; (jtly) Capitalism in Crisis, 1976; Britain in Decline, 1981, 4th edn 1994; An Introduction to Modern Social and Political Thought, 1981; (ed jtly) Developments in British Politics, vol. 1, 1983, vol. 2, 1986, vol. 3, 1990, vol. 4, 1993, vol. 5, 1997, vol. 6, 2000, vol. 7, 2003; (jtly) The British Party System and Economic Policy, 1984; (ed jtly) The Social Economy and the Democratic State, 1987; The Free Economy and the Strong State, 1988, 2nd edn 1994; (ed jtly) Thatcher's Law, 1989; Hayek: the iron cage of liberty, 1996; (ed jtly) Regionalism and World Order, 1996; (ed jtly) Stakeholder Capitalism, 1997; (ed jtly) Fundamentals in British Politics, 1999; (ed jtly) Marxism and Social Science, 1999; (ed jtly) The New Social Democracy, 1999; Politics and Fate, 2000; (ed jtly) The Political Economy of the Company, 2000; Between Europe and America: the future of British politics, 2003 (W. J. M. Mackenzie Prize, Pol Studies Assoc., 2005); (ed jtly) Restating the State, 2004; The Spectre at the Feast, 2009; Crisis without end?: the unravelling of western prosperity, 2014; articles in learned jls. *Recreations:* music, growing tomatoes. *Address:* Department of Politics, University of Sheffield, Sheffield S10 2TN.

See also C. S. Gamble.

GAMBLE, Dr Christine Elizabeth; Director, Royal Institute of International Affairs, 1998–2001; *b* 1950; *d* of late Albert Edward Gamble and Kathleen Laura (*née* Wallis); *m* 1989, Edward Barry Antony Craxton. *Educ:* Royal Holloway Coll., London Univ. (BA 1st Cl. Hons; PhD 1977). English-French Cultural Orgn, 1974–75; British Embassy, Moscow, 1975–76; with British Council, 1977–98: New Delhi, 1977–79; Stratford-on-Avon, 1979–80; Harare, 1980–82; Regl Officer for Soviet Union in London, 1982–85; Dep. Dir, Athens, 1985–87; Dir General's Dept, 1988–90; Head, Project Pursuit Dept and Dir, Chancellor's Financial Sector Scheme for Former Soviet Union, 1991–92; Dir, Visitors' Dept, 1992–93; Gen. Manager, Country Services Gp, 1993–95 and Hd, European Series, 1994–96; Cultural Counsellor, Paris and Dir, France, 1996–98. Co. Sec., Ind. Football Commn, 2002–05; Consultant on equality and diversity issues, 2005–10. Dir, Japan 21st Century Gp, 1999–2005; Mem., Franco-British Council, 2000–06. Order of Rio Branco (Brazil), 2000. *Recreations:* collecting wine, sports, music, theatre. *Address:* 25 Abbey Street, Faversham ME13 7BE.

GAMBLE, Prof. Clive Stephen, PhD; FBA 2000; FSA; Professor of Archaeology, University of Southampton, since 2011; *b* 10 March 1951; *s* of Marcus Elkington Gamble and Joan Gamble (*née* Westall); *m* 1981, Dr Elaine Lisk Morris. *Educ:* Brighton Coll.; Jesus Coll., Cambridge (BA 1972, MA 1975; PhD 1978). FSA 1981; MCIfA (MIFA 1987). Department of Archaeology, University of Southampton: exptl officer, 1975; Lectr, 1976–86; Sen. Lectr, 1986–90; Reader, 1990–95; Prof. of Archaeol., 1995–2004; British Acad. Res. Reader, 2000–02; Dir, Centre for Archaeol. of Human Origins, 1999–2004; Prof. of Geog., Royal Holloway, Univ. of London, 2004–11. Pres., RAI, 2011–14. Trustee, BM, 2010–. *Publications:* The Palaeolithic Settlement of Europe, 1986; Timewalkers: the prehistory of global colonisation, 1993; (with C. Stringer) In Search of the Neanderthals, 1993; The Palaeolithic Societies of Europe, 1999; Archaeology: the basics, 2001; Origins and Revolutions, 2007; Settling the Earth, 2013; Thinking Big, 2014. *Recreations:* cats, cricket, gardening. *Address:* Department of Archaeology, University of Southampton, Highfield, Southampton SO17 1BF.

See also A. M. Gamble.

GAMBLE, Sir David (Hugh Norman), 6th Bt *cr* 1897, of Windlehurst, St Helens, Co. Palatine of Lancashire; *b* 1 July 1966; *s* of Sir David Gamble, 5th Bt and of Dawn Adrienne, *d* of late David Hugh Gittins; *S* father, 1984. *Educ:* Shiplake College, Henley-on-Thames. *Heir: cousin* Hugh Robert George Gamble [*b* 3 March 1946; *m* 1989, Rebecca Jane, *d* of Lt Comdr David Odell, RN; one *s* one *d*]. *Address:* Keinton House, Keinton Mandeville, Somerton, Somerset TA11 6DX. *T:* (01458) 223964.

GAMBLE, Richard Arthur; non-executive Director: Highway Insurance Group (formerly Highway Insurance Holdings) plc, 2003–08 (Executive Chairman, 2006–07; non-executive Chairman, 2007–08); Equity Syndicate Management, 2011–13; *b* 19 Sept. 1939; *s* of late Arthur Gamble and of Grace Emily Gamble (*née* Little); *m* 1966, Elizabeth Ann, *d* of Edward Godwin-Atkyns; two *s*. *Educ:* Raynes Park Co. Grammar Sch. FCA 1962. Articled clerk, W. J. Gilbert & Co., London, 1957–62; Asst Manager, Turquand Youngs & Co., 1962–66; Dir and Co. Sec., Lee Davy Gp Ltd, 1966–68; Dir and Sec., Hamilton Smith, Lloyd's Brokers, 1968–70; Finance Dir, Lowndes Lambert Internat., Lloyd's Brokers, 1970–76; European Finance Dir, Data100/Northern Telecom Systems, 1976–80; Finance Dir, McDonnell Douglas Inf. Systems and Dir, McDonnell Douglas UK, 1980–84; Dep. Chief Financial Officer, British Airways, 1984–89; Royal Insurance Holdings PLC: Gp Finance Dir, 1989–91; Gp Chief Operating Officer, 1991; Gp Chief Exec., 1992–96; Gp Chief Exec., Royal & Sun Alliance Insurance Gp plc, 1996–97. Non-executive Chm., Denne Gp Ltd, 2001–03 (Advr, 1999–2001); non-executive Dir, Excel Airways Gp plc, 2003–05. Mem. Bd, ABI, 1994–96; Chm., Policy Holders Protection Bd, 1994–98. Mem., Adv. Cttee on Business in the Envmt and Chm., Financial Services Working Gp, 1993–96. Mem., Educnl Nat. Leadership Team, BITC, 1995–97. Trustee, Crimestoppers, 1995–; Pres., GB Wheelchair Basketball Assoc., 1997–; Gov., RSC, 1997–2002. CCMI (CIMgt 1992). *Recreations:* all sport, particularly golf, walking with dogs, theatre, family. *Address:* 77 St John's Road, Penn, High Wycombe, Bucks HP10 8HU. *T:* (01494) 815103. *Clubs:* Beaconsfield Golf; Falmouth Rugby Football (Life Vice Pres.); Falmouth Cricket (Vice Pres.).

GAMBLES, Dr Ian Christopher; Director, England, Forestry Commission, since 2013; *b* Crosby, 17 Oct. 1962; *s* of Robert Henry Gambles and Hanna Hermana Gambles; *m* 2011, Helen Adlard; two *s* one *d* and two step *d*. *Educ:* Merchant Taylors' Sch., Crosby; Balliol Coll., Oxford (BA Hons Ancient and Modern Hist. 1983); Georgetown Univ. (MSc Foreign Service 1988); Princeton Univ. (PhD Politics 1991). FCMA 2000. Grad. trainee, Shell UK Ltd, 1984–86; Res. Associate, Internat. Inst. for Strategic Studies, 1988–89; HM Treasury: Principal (sovereign debt mgt and co-ordination of Budget), 1991–94; Principal (defence expenditure control), 1995–97; Vis. Fellow, Budapest Univ. of Econs, 1994–95; Principal Consultant, KPMG Consulting, 1997–2001; Sen. Manager, Deloitte Consulting, 2001–02; Dir, Frontline Consultants, 2002–03; Man. Dir, Enodian Ltd, 2003–09; Director: Infrastructure Planning Commn, 2009–12; Nat. Infrastructure, Planning Inspectorate, 2012–13. *Publications:* Making the Business Case, 2009. *Recreations:* fell-walking, Real Tennis, gardening, chess. *Address:* Forestry Commission, 620 Bristol Business Park, Coldharbour Lane, Bristol BS16 1EJ. *T:* 0300 067 4061. *E:* ian.gambles@forestry.gsi.gov.uk.

GAMBLIN, Dr Steven John, FRS 2011; FMedSci; Director of Science Operations, Crick Institute, since 2013; *b* 7 Jan. 1962; *s* of Anthony Edward Gamblin and late Pamela Joy Gamblin; *m* 1996, Priscilla J. C. Meigh; two *s* one *d*. *Educ:* Univ. of Bristol (BSc Biochem. 1983; PhD 1986). Post-doctoral researcher: Bristol Univ., 1988–90; Harvard Univ., 1990–94; National Institute for Medical Research: Prog. Leader, Div. of Protein Structure, 1994–2005; Jt Hd, Div. of Molecular Structure, 2005–15; Dir of Res., 2011–15. Mem., EMBO, FMedSci 2008. Feldberg Prize, Feldberg Foundn, 2012. *Publications:* contribs to scientific jls incl. Nature. *Recreations:* gardening, history, music. *Address:* Francis Crick Institute, The Ridgeway, Mill Hill, NW7 1AA.

GAMBLING, Prof. (William) Alex(ander), PhD, DSc; FRS 1983; FREng; Founder and Director, Optoelectronics Research Centre, University of Southampton, 1989–95; *b* 11 Oct. 1926; *s* of George Alexander Gambling and Muriel Clara Gambling; *m* 1st, 1952, Margaret Pooley (marr. diss. 1994); one *s* two *d*; 2nd, 1994, Barbara Colleen O'Neil. *Educ:* Univ. of Bristol (BSc, Alfred Fry Prize, DSc); Univ. of Liverpool (PhD). FIERE 1964; CEng, Hon. FIET (FIEE 1967); FREng (FEng 1979); FHKAES 2000. Lectr in Electric Power Engrg, Univ. of Liverpool, 1950–55; National Res. Council Fellow, Univ. of BC, 1955–57; Univ. of Southampton: Lectr, Sen. Lectr, and Reader, 1957–64; Prof. of Electronics, 1964–80; Dean of Engrg and Applied Science, 1972–75; Hd of Dept, 1974–79; BT Prof. of Optical Communication, 1980–95; Royal Soc. Kan Tong Po Prof. and Dir, Optoelectronics Res. Centre, City Univ., Hong Kong, 1996–2001. Dir, York Ltd, 1980–97. Vis. Professor: Univ. of Colo, USA, 1966–67; Bhabha Atomic Res. Centre, India, 1970; Osaka Univ., Japan, 1977; City Univ. of Hong Kong, 1995; Hon. Professor: Huazhong Univ. of Sci. and Technol., Wuhan, China, 1986–; Beijing Univ. of Posts and Telecommunications, 1987–; Shanghai Univ., 1991–; Shandong Univ., 1999–; Hon. Dir, Beijing Optical Fibre Inst., 1987–. Member: Electronics Res. Council, 1977–80 (Mem., Optics and Infra-Red Cttee, 1965–69 and 1974–80); Board, Council of Engrg Instns, 1974–79; National Electronics Council, 1977–78, 1984–95; Technol. Sub-Cttee of UGC, 1973–83; British Nat. Cttee for Radio Science, 1978–87; Nat. Adv. Bd for Local Authority Higher Educn, Engrg Working Gp, 1982–84; Engineering Council, 1983–88; British Nat. Cttee for Internat. Engineering Affairs, 1984–88; Council, Royal Acad. of Engrg, 1989–92; Chairman: Commn D, Internat. Union of Radio Science, 1984–87 (Vice-Chm., 1981–84); Nat. DTI/SERC Optoelectronics Cttee, 1988–91. Pres., IERE, 1977–78 (Hon. Fellow 1983); Vice Pres., Hong Kong Acad. of Engrg Scis, 2004–08. Selby Fellow, Australian Acad. of Science, 1982; For. Mem., Polish Acad. of Scis, 1985. Freeman, City of London, 1987; Liveryman, Worshipful Co. of Engrs, 1988. Dr *hc* Univ. Politécnica de Madrid, 1994; Hon. DSc: Aston, 1995; Southampton, 2005. Hon. DEng Bristol, 1999. Bulgin Premium, IERE, 1961, Lord Rutherford Premium, IERE, 1964, Electronics Div. Premium, IEE, 1976 and 1978, Oliver Lodge Premium, IEE, 1981, Heinrich Hertz Premium, IERE, 1981, for research papers; J. J. Thomson Medal, IEE, 1982, Faraday Medal, IEE, 1983, Churchill Medal, Soc. of Engineers, 1984 and Simms Medal, Soc. of Engineers, 1989, for research innovation and leadership; Academic Enterprise Award, 1982; Micro-optics Award, Japan, 1989; Dennis Gabor Award, Internat. Soc. for Optical Engrg, USA, 1990; Rank Prize for Optoelectronics, 1991; Medal and Prize, Foundn for Computer and Communications Promotion, Japan, 1993; Mountbatten Medal, Nat. Electronics Council, 1993; James Alfred Ewing Medal, ICE/Royal Soc., 2002. *Publications:* 300 papers on electronics and optical fibre communications. *Recreations:* music, reading.

GAMBON, Sir Michael (John), Kt 1998; CBE 1990; actor; *b* 19 Oct. 1940; *s* of Edward and Mary Gambon; *m* 1962, Anne Miller; one *s*; two *s* by Philippa Hart. *Educ:* St Aloysius School for Boys, Somers Town, London. Served 7 year apprenticeship in engineering; first appeared on stage with Edwards/MácLiammoir Co., Dublin, 1962; Nat. Theatre, Old Vic, 1963–67; Birmingham Rep. and other provincial theatres, 1967–69 (title rôles incl. Othello, Macbeth, Coriolanus); RSC Aldwych, 1970–71; Norman Conquests, Globe, 1974; Otherwise Engaged, Queen's, 1976; Just Between Ourselves, Queen's 1977; Alice's Boys, Savoy, 1978; King Lear and Antony and Cleopatra (title rôles), RSC Stratford and Barbican, 1982–83; Old Times, Haymarket, 1985; Uncle Vanya, Vaudeville, 1988; Veterans Day, Haymarket, 1989; Man of the Moment, Globe, 1990; Othello and Taking Steps, Scarborough, 1990; Tom and Clem, Aldwych, 1997; The Unexpected Man, Barbican Pit, transf. Duchess, 1998; Juno and the Paycock, Gaiety, Dublin, 1999; Cressida, Albery, 2000; The Caretaker, Comedy (Variety Club Best Actor, Critics' Circle Best Actor), 2000; A Number, Royal Court, 2002; Endgame, Albery, 2004; Eh Joe, Duke of York's, 2006, Royal Lyceum, 2013; No Man's Land, Duke of York's, 2008; Krapp's Last Tape, Duchess, 2010; All That Fall, Jermyn Street Th., 2012; National Theatre: Galileo, 1980 (London Theatre Critics' Award, Best Actor); Betrayal, 1980; Tales From Hollywood, 1980; Chorus of Disapproval, 1985 (Olivier Award, Best Comedy Performance); Tons of Money, 1986; A View from the Bridge, 1987, transf. Aldwych (Best Actor, Evening Standard Awards, Olivier Awards, and Plays and Players London Theatre Critics' Awards; Best Stage Actor, Variety Club Awards); A Small Family Business, 1987; Mountain Language, 1988; Skylight, transf. Wyndhams, then NY, and Volpone (Best Actor, Evening Standard Awards), 1995; Henry IV, Parts 1 and 2, 2005. *Television* includes: The Singing Detective, 1986 (BAFTA Award, Best Actor, 1987); Maigret, 1992, 1993; Faith, 1994; Wives and Daughters, 1999 (BAFTA Award, Best Actor, 2000); Longitude, 2000 (BAFTA Award, Best Actor, 2001); Perfect Strangers, 2001 (BAFTA Award, Best Actor, 2002); The Lost Prince, 2003; Angels in America, 2004; Cranford, 2007; Emma, 2009; Page Eight, 2011; Restless, 2012; Quirke, 2014; Fortitude, The Casual Vacancy, 2015. *Films* include: The Cook, The Thief, His Wife and Her Lover, The Heat of the Day, Paris by Night, 1989; A Dry White Season, 1990; Mobsters, Toys, 1992; The Browning Version, 1993; A Man of No Importance, Midnight in Moscow, 1994; The Innocent Sleep, All Our Fault, 1995; Mary Reilly, Two Deaths, Nothing Personal, The Gambler, 1996; The Wings of the Dove, Dancing at Lughnasa, 1997; Plunkett and Macleane, 1999; The Last September, Sleepy Hollow, The Insider, 2000; End Game, High Heels and Low Lifes, 2001; Gosford Park, Charlotte Gray, Ali G Indahouse, Path to War, 2002; The Actors, 2003; Sylvia, Being Julia, Layer Cake, Open Range, Harry Potter and the Prisoner of Azkaban, Sky Captain and the World of Tomorrow, 2004; The Life Aquatic with Steve Zissou, Harry Potter and the Goblet of Fire, 2005; Amazing Grace, 2006; The Good Shepherd, Harry Potter and the Order of the Phoenix, 2007; Harry Potter and the Half-Blood Prince, 2009; The Book of Eli, Harry Potter and the Deathly Hallows, Pt 1, 2010, Pt 2, 2011; The King's Speech, 2011; Quartet, 2013. Trustee, Royal Armouries, 1995. Liveryman, Gunmakers' Co. Hon. DLitt Southampton, 2002. *Recreations:* flying, gun collecting, clock making. *Address:* Independent Talent Group Ltd, 40 Whitfield Street, W1T 2RH. *Club:* Garrick.

GAME, Amanda, (Mrs A. O. E. Raven); independent curator and producer, since 2008; Co-Founder, 2005, Consulting Lead Director, 2008–10, IC: Innovative Craft; *b* 22 Aug. 1958; *d* of John Game and Margaret Newman Game (*née* Smith); *m* 1987, Andrew Owen Earle Raven, OBE (*d* 2005). *Educ:* Open Univ. (BA 1st Cl. Hons Humanities Art Hist. and Lit.). Asst, Oxford Gall., 1984–86; Scottish Gallery, Edinburgh: Manager for Contemporary Craft, 1986–95; Dir of Applied Art, 1995–2007. Curator, Jewellery Moves, 1997–99, Res. Associate, 1998–, Nat. Mus of Scotland. Crafts Advr, Scottish Arts Council, 1995–2001; Advisor: Inches Carr Trust, Edinburgh, 1999–; Goldsmiths' Trust, Edinburgh, 2002–. Associate, PALlabs, 2013–15. Mem., Modern Plate Cttee, Goldsmiths' Hall, 2009–. Founder Trustee, 2008–, Chm., 2010–, Andrew Raven Trust. Freeman, 1995, Liveryman, 2007, Goldsmiths' Co. Chair, Judging Panel, Jerwood Applied Arts Prize, Textiles, 1997; Judge: Young Designer Silversmith Award, Goldsmiths' Hall, 1994–2004; Leonardo Prize, 2004. MPhil researcher, Sch. of Humanities, RCA, 2011–. *Publications:* Jewellery Moves, 1998, 3rd edn 2001; (contrib.) Silver from Scotland, 2008. *Recreations:* hill-walking, classical music, opera, literature, film, gardens, architecture. *E:* amandaraven2005@yahoo.co.uk.

GAMMAGE, Jayne Agneta; *see* Franklyn, J. A.

GAMMELL, Sir William Benjamin Bowring, (Sir Bill), Kt 2006; Chairman, Cairn Energy PLC, 2011–14 (Chief Executive, 1989–2011); *b* 29 Dec. 1952; *s* of late James Gilbert Sidney Gammell and Patricia Bowring Gammell (*née* Toms). *Educ:* Stirling Univ. (BA Econ). Founded Cairn Energy Mgt, 1980, Man. Dir, 1980–89. Director: Scottish Inst. of Sport, 1998–2008; Artemis Aim VCT Trust, 2001–08; Chairman: Winning Scotland Foundn (formerly Scottish Inst. of Sport Foundn), 2006–; Genius Foods, 2012–. Dir, Glasgow 2014, 2009–14. *Recreations:* Rugby (Scotland Rugby Internat., 1977–78), squash, football, golf, skiing. *Club:* Golf House (Elie, Fife).

GAMMIE, Malcolm James, CBE 2005; QC 2002; *b* 18 Feb. 1951; *s* of Maj. James Ian Gammie, MC, and Florence Mary Gammie (*née* Wiggs); *m* 1974, Rosalind Anne Rowe; one *s* three *d*. *Educ:* Edge Grove Sch., Aldenham; Merchant Taylors' Sch.; Sidney Sussex Coll., Cambridge (MA). Linklaters & Paines: articled clerk, 1973–75; solicitor, Tax Dept, 1975–78 and 1985–87; Partner, 1987–97; Dep. Hd, Tax Dept, CBI, 1978–79; Director: Nat. Tax Office, Thomson McLintock & Co., 1979–84; Nat. Tax Services, KMG Thomson McLintock, 1984–85; called to the Bar, Middle Temple, 1997, Bencher, 2010; in practice as barrister, 1997–. Dep. Special Comr and pt-time VAT and Duties Tribunal Chm., 2002–. Vis. Professorial Fellow, Centre for Commercial Law Studies, QMW, 1997–; Res. Fellow, Inst. for Fiscal Studies, 1997–; Unilever Prof. of Internat. Business Law, Leiden Univ., 1998; Visiting Professor: of Tax Law, LSE, 2000–; of Internat. Tax Law, Sydney Univ., 2000 and 2002. Editor: Law and Tax Rev., 1982–88; Land Taxation, 1985–; Consulting Ed., Butterworth's Tax Handbook, 1994–2004. Cabinet Office: Member: Taxation Deregulation Gp, 1993–97; Fiscal Studies Wkg Party Adv. Council on Sci. and Technol., 1993; Mem., 1994–97, Res. Dir, 1997–2014, Tax Law Rev. Cttee; Mem., Special Cttee of Tax Law Consultative Bodies, Taxation Cttee, IOD, 1987–97. Chartered Institute of Taxation: Mem. Council, 1985–2001; Chm., Capital Taxes Wkg Party, 1986–92; Chm., Exec. Cttee, 1991–97. London Chamber of Commerce and Industry: Mem., 1976–; Mem. Council, 1989–92; Chm., Taxation Cttee, 1989–92. Chm., Revenue Law Cttee, Law Soc., 1996–97; Mem., Soc. for Advanced Legal Studies, 1997–. Mem., Perm. Scientific Cttee, Internat. Fiscal Assoc., 1998–2008 (Vice-Chm., British Br. Cttee). FRSA 1993. *Publications:* (with S. Ball) Taxation Publishing, Tax on Company Reorganisations, 1980, 2nd edn 1982; Tax Strategy for Companies, 1981, 3rd edn 1986; (with D. Williams) Stock Relief, 1981; (with D. Williams) Tax Focus on Interest and Discounts, 1983; Tax Strategy for Directors, Executives and Employees, 1983, 2nd edn 1985; (jtly) Whiteman on Capital Gains Tax, 1988; The Process of Tax Reform in the United Kingdom, 1990. *Recreations:* music, church architecture. *Address:* (chambers) 1 Essex Court, Temple, EC4Y 9AR. *T:* (020) 7583 2000, *Fax:* (020) 7583 0118. *E:* mgammie@oeclaw.co.uk.

GAMON, Hugh Wynell, CBE 1979; MC 1944; formerly Partner, Winckworth & Pemberton (incorporating Sherwood & Co., 1991); HM Government Agent, 1970–89; *b* 31 March 1921; *s* of Judge Hugh R. P. Gamon and E. Margaret Gamon; *m* 1949, June Elizabeth (*d* 2003), *d* of William and Florence Temple; one *s* three *d*. *Educ:* St Edward's Sch., Oxford; Exeter Coll., Oxford, 1946–48. MA 1st Cl. Hons Jurisprudence; Law Society Hons; Edmund Thomas Childe Prize. Served War, 1940–46: Royal Corps of Signals, N Africa, Italy and Palestine, with 1st Division. Articled to Clerk of Cumberland CC, 1949–51; joined Sherwood & Co., 1951; Parly Agent, 1954; Sen. Partner, Sherwood & Co., 1972; retd from Winckworth & Pemberton, 1995. *Recreation:* gardening. *Address:* Claygate, Shipbourne, Kent TN11 9RL. *T:* (01732) 810308.

GAMON, Maj.-Gen. John Anthony, CBE 2003; Special Project Officer Deputy Chief of Defence Staff (Health), 2005–06; *b* 13 March 1946; *s* of James Davidson Gamon and Dorothy Gamon (*née* Radford); *m* 1968, Mary Patricia Medicke; one *s* one *d*. *Educ:* Penlan Multilateral Sch., Swansea; Royal Dental Hosp., London (BDS 1969); Eastman Dental Inst., London (MSc 1978). MGDSRCS 1982; DRD RCSEd 1983. Gen. clinical appts, Army Dental Service, 1970–92; Deputy Director: Defence Dental Services, 1993–96; Army Dental Service, 1996–97; Director: Army Dental Service, 1997–2001; Clinical Services, 1997–99; Corporate Develt, 1999–2001, Defence Dental Agency; Dir Gen., Defence Dental Services and Chief Exec., Defence Dental Agency, 2001–05. QHDS, 1997–2006. Pres., British Soc. for Gen. Dental Surgery, 2001–02. Chm., Thames Valley Crimestoppers, 2008–12. Sec., English Fly Fishing Assoc., 2012–. FInstD 2002. *Recreations:* fly fishing, hill walking, gardening, reading. *Address:* 1 Bushmead Close, Whitchurch, Aylesbury, Bucks HP22 4SH. *Club:* Naval and Military.

GANDEE, Jane Sara; Headmistress, St Swithun's School, Winchester, since 2010; *b* Welwyn Garden City, 12 May 1968; *d* of John Gandee and Sara, (Sally), Gandee; *m* 1998, Richard Morgan; one *s* two *d*. *Educ:* Presdales Sch.; Girton Coll., Cambridge (BA French and Spanish 1990); Open Univ. (PGCE). Accountant, 1991–93; Teacher (French and Spanish): Lord Wandsworth, Hants, 1993–95; Oakham Sch., 1995–97; Hd of Langs, Queenswood, 1997–2005; Dir of Studies, City of London Sch. for Girls, 2005–10. Gov., Twyford Sch., 2011–. *Recreations:* running, reading, Latin America, being irritated by female stereotyping. *Address:* St Swithun's School, Alresford Road, Winchester, Hants SO21 1HA. *E:* headmistress@stswithuns.com.

GANDHI, Gopalkrishna; Governor of West Bengal, India, 2004–09; *b* 22 April 1945; *s* of Devadas Mohandas Gandhi and Lakshmi Rajagopalachari; *m* Tara Ananth; two *d*. *Educ:* St Stephen's Coll., Delhi Univ. (BA Hons 1964; MA English Lit 1964). Member, Indian Administrative Service, 1968–92: various positions, Tamil Nadu, 1969–77; First Sec., Asst High Commn of India, Kandy, Sri Lanka, 1978–82; Dir of Handlooms and Textiles, Govt of Tamil Nadu, 1982–83; Sec. to Governor of Tamil Nadu, 1983–85; Sec. to Vice-Pres. of India, 1985–87; Jt Sec. to Pres. of India, 1987–92; voluntary retirement, 1992; Minister (Culture) and Dir, Nehru Centre, London, 1992–96; High Comr in S Africa, 1996–97; Sec. to Pres. of India, 1997–2000; High Comr in Sri Lanka, 2000–02; Ambassador to Norway, 2002–04. Sen. Fellow, Centre for Public Affairs and Critical Theory, New Delhi, 2014–. Hon. Distinguished Prof., Indian Inst. of Technol. Madras, 2011–; Distinguished Prof., Ashoka Univ., 2015–. Hon. LLD Natal, 1999; Hon. DLitt Peradeniya, Kandy, 2001. *Publications:* Saranam (novel), 1985, reprinted as Refuge, 1987; Dara Shukoh (play), 1993; trans. Hindustani, Seth, A Suitable Boy, 1998; (ed) The Oxford Gandhi, 2008; (ed) A Frank Friendship, 2008; Of a Certain Age: twenty life sketches, 2012; (ed) My Dear Bapu: letters from Rajagopalachari to Gandhi, 2012. *Club:* India International Centre (New Delhi).

GANDHI, Sonia; President: Congress Party, India, since 1998; Indian National Congress, since 2005; MP (Congress) Raebareli, UP, Lok Sabha, 2004–March 2006 and since May 2006 (MP for Amethi, 1999–2004); *b* Italy, 9 Dec. 1947; adopted Indian nationality, 1983; *d* of Stefano and Paola Maino; *m* 1968, Rajiv Gandhi (*d* 1991); one *s* one *d*. *Educ:* language sch., Cambridge; Art restoration course, Nat. Gall. of Modern Art, New Delhi. Pres., Rajiv Gandhi Foundn. Mem., Congress Party, 1997–. Leader of the Opposition, Lok Sabha, 1999–2004. *Publications:* (ed) Freedom's Daughter, 1989; (ed) Two Alone, Two Together, 1992; Rajiv, 1992; Rajiv's World, 1994. *Address:* 10 Janpath, New Delhi 110011, India; All India Congress Committee, 24 Akbar Road, New Delhi 110011, India.

GANDY, David James; model; *b* London; *s* of Christopher and Brenda Gandy. *Educ:* Billericay Sch.; Gloucestershire Univ. Modelling contracts with: Dolce & Gabbana, 2006–, incl. Light Blue fragrance campaign, 2007, Light Blue 2, 2009; Martini, 2011; M&S, 2012; magazine covers include: V Man, by Mario Testino, 2008; L'Optimum, GQ, 2011. Creator, David Gandy Men's Style Guide app, 2010. Designer, underwear and nightwear collection with Marks and Spencer, 2014. Fashion Ambassador, Comic Relief, 2012. Face of Today Award, Shortlist, 2011. *Relevant publication:* David by Dolce & Gabbana, 2011. *Recreations:* car racing, ski-ing. *T:* (Monsta PR) 07958 458733. *E:* charl@monsta.biz.

GANDY, David Stewart, CB 1989; OBE 1981; Consultant, Pannone and Partners, solicitors, since 1993; Deputy Director of Public Prosecutions and Chief Executive, Crown Prosecution Service, 1987–93; *b* 19 Sept. 1932; *s* of Percy Gandy and Elizabeth Mary (*née* Fox); *m* 1956, Mabel Sheldon; one *s* one *d*. *Educ:* Manchester Grammar Sch.; Manchester Univ. Nat. Service, Intell. Corps (Germany and Austria), 1954–56. Admitted Solicitor, 1954; Asst Solicitor, Town Clerk, Manchester, 1956–59; Chief Prosecuting Solicitor: Manchester, 1959–68; Manchester and Salford, 1968–74; Gtr Manchester, 1974–85; Head of Field Management, Crown Prosecution Service, 1985–87; Acting DPP, Oct. 1991–May 1992. Mem., Home Office Assessment Consultancy Unit, 1993–2005. Mem. Council, Criminal Law Solicitors Assoc., 1992–2001. Lect. tour on English Criminal Justice System, for Amer. Bar Assoc., USA and Canada, 1976; Lecturer: UN Asia and FE Inst. for Prevention of Crime and Treatment of Offenders, Tokyo, 1990, 1995; Internat. Congress of Criminal Lawyers on Penal Reform, La Plata, 1995. Law Society: Mem., Criminal Law Standing Cttee, 1969–97 (Vice Chm., 1995–96); Mem., Council, 1984–96; Prosecuting Solicitors' Society of England and Wales: Mem., Exec. Council, 1966–85; Pres., 1976–78; Chm., Heads of Office, 1982–83; President: Manchester Law Soc., 1980–81; Manchester and Dist Medico-Legal Soc., 1982–84; Manchester Trainee Lawyers Gp, 1982–84. Non-exec. Dir, Mancunian Community Health NHS Trust, 1993–98. Mem. Council, Order of St John, 1978–85. *Recreations:* cricket, theatre, bridge, walking. *Address:* The Ridgeway, Broad Lane, Hale, Altrincham, Cheshire WA15 0DD.

GANE, Barrie Charles, CMG 1988; OBE 1978; HM Diplomatic Service, retired; Director Group Research, Group 4 Securitas, 1993–2000; *b* 19 Sept. 1935; *s* of Charles Ernest Gane and Margaret Gane; *m* 1974, Jennifer Anne Pitt; two *d* of former marriage. *Educ:* King Edward's School, Birmingham; Corpus Christi College, Cambridge. MA. Foreign Office, 1960; served Vientiane, Kuching and Warsaw; First Sec., Kampala, 1967; FCO, 1970; First Sec., later Counsellor, seconded to HQ British Forces, Hong Kong, 1977; Counsellor, FCO, 1982–92. *Recreations:* walking, reading. *Club:* Brooks's.

GANE, Michael, DPhil, MA; economic and environmental consultant; *b* 29 July 1927; *s* of late Rudolf E. Gane and Helen Gane; *m* 1954, Madge Stewart Taylor; one *d*. *Educ:* Colyton Grammar Sch., Devon; Edinburgh Univ. (BSc Forestry 1948); London Univ. (BSc Econ 1963); Oxford Univ. (DPhil, MA 1967). Asst Conservator of Forests, Tanganyika, 1948–62; Sen. Research Officer, Commonwealth Forestry Inst., Oxford, 1963–69; Dir, Project Planning Centre for Developing Countries, Bradford Univ., 1969–74; Dir, England, Nature Conservancy Council, 1974–81. *Publications:* Forest Strategy, 2007; various contribs to scientific and technical jls. *Recreations:* natural history, gardening. *Address:* Coast Watchers Cottage, 6 Avalanche Road, Southwell, Portland, Dorset DT5 2DJ.

GANELLIN, (Charon) Robin, PhD, DSc; FRS 1986; CSci; CChem, FRSC; Smith Kline and French Professor of Medicinal Chemistry, University College London, 1986–2002, now Emeritus; *b* 25 Jan. 1934; *s* of Leon Ganellin and Beila Cluer; *m* 1st, 1956, Tamara Greene (*d* 1997); one *s* one *d*; 2nd, 2003, Dr Monique Garbarg (*née* Lehmann). *Educ:* Harrow County Grammar School for Boys; Queen Mary Coll., London Univ. (BSc, PhD, DSc; Fellow, QMW, 1992). FRSC 1968; CChem 1976; CSci 2003. Res. Associate, MIT, 1960; Res. Chemist, then Dept Hd in Medicinal Chem., Smith Kline & French Labs Ltd, 1958–59, 1961–75; Smith Kline & French Research Ltd: Dir, Histamine Res., 1975–80; Vice-President: Research, 1980–84; Chem. Res., 1984–86. Hon. Lectr, Dept of Pharmacol., UCL, 1975–86; Hon. Prof. of Medicinal Chem., Univ. of Kent at Canterbury, 1979–89. Tilden Lectr and Medal, 1982, Adrien Albert Lectr and Medal, 1999, RSC. Pres., Section on Medicinal Chemistry, 2000–01, Chm., Subcttee on Medicinal Chem. and Drug Develt, IUPAC, 2002– (Emeritus Fellow, Chem. and Human Health Div. VII, IUPAC, 2014); Chm., Soc. for Drug Res., 1985–87; Hon. Member: Soc. Española de Quimica Terapeutica, 1982; European Histamine Res. Soc., 2007; Corresp. Academician, Real Academia Nacional de Farmacia, Spain, 2006. Hon. DSc Aston, 1995. Medicinal Chem. Award, RSC, 1977; Prix Charles Mentzer, Soc. de Chimie Therap., 1978; Div. of Medicinal Chem. Award, ACS, 1980; Messel Medal, SCI, 1988; Award for Drug Discovery, Soc. for Drug Res., 1989; USA Nat. Inventors' Hall of Fame, 1990; Nauta Prize for Pharmacochem., European Fedn for Medicinal Chem., 2004; Pratesi Gold Medal, Medicinal Chem. Div., Italian Chem. Soc., 2006; ACS Div. of Medicinal Chem. Hall of Fame, 2007. *Publications:* Pharmacology of Histamine Receptors, 1982; Frontiers in Histamine Research, 1985; Dictionary of Drugs, 1990; (jtly) Medicinal Chemistry, 1993; Dictionary of Pharmacological Agents, 1997; (with J. Fischer) Analogue-based Drug Discovery, 2006, vol. II, 2010, vol. III, 2013; Practical Studies in Medicinal Chemistry, 2007; (ed jtly) Introduction to Biological and Small Molecule Drug Research and Development, 2013; res. papers and reviews in various jls, incl. Jl Med. Chem., Jl Chem. Soc., Brit. Jl Pharmacol. *Recreations:* music, sailing, walking. *Address:* Department of Chemistry, University College London, 20 Gordon Street, WC1H 0AJ.

GANI, Prof. David, DPhil; CChem, FRSC; FRSE; Trustee and Governor, CRAC Ltd, since 2011; Deputy Principal, University of Strathclyde, 2009–12; Chief Executive, Glasgow City of Science, 2011–13 (on secondment, 2011–12); *b* 29 Sept. 1957; one *s* two *d*. *Educ:* Sussex Univ. (BSc; DPhil 1983). Technician, Wellcome Res. Labs, 1974–76; Southampton University: Royal Soc. Res. Fellow and Lectr in Organic Chem., 1983–89; Sen. Lectr, 1989–90; St Andrews University: Prof. of Chemistry, 1990–98, Purdie Prof., and Res. Dir, Sch. of Chemistry, 1997–98; Dir, Centre for Biomolecular Scis, 1995–98; Prof. of Organic Chem., Birmingham Univ., 1998–2001 (Hon. Prof. of Organic Chem., 2001–09); Dir of Res. Policy, Scottish Funding Councils for Further and Higher Educn, later Dir of Res. Policy and Strategy, SFC, 2002–09. Mem., Strategy Bd, BBSRC, 1997–2002. *Publications:* (jtly) Enzymic Catalysis, 1991; contrib. to learned jls. *Address:* CRAC Ltd, Castle Park, Cambridge CB3 0AX.

GANT, Andrew John, PhD; composer; Organist, Choirmaster and Composer, Chapels Royal, 2000–13; *b* 6 Aug. 1963; *s* of John Gant and Vivien Gant (*née* Christian); *m* 1992, Dr Katherine Willis; two *s* one *d*. *Educ:* Radley Coll.; St John's Coll., Cambridge (Choral Schol.; BA 1984; MA 1994); Royal Acad. of Music (MMus 1993; ARAM 2003); PhD Goldsmiths Coll., London 2000. Lay Vicar, Westminster Abbey, 1988–90; Dir of Music in Chapel, Selwyn Coll., Cambridge, 1993–98; Organist and Master of Choir, Royal Military Chapel, Wellington Barracks, 1997–2000. Tutor in Music, Univ. of Oxford, 1998–. *Compositions include:* May We Borrow Your Husband (opera), 1999; (with Andrew Motion) A Hymn for the Golden Jubilee, 2002; The Vision of Piers Ploughman (oratorio), 2002; A Good-Night (anthem), 2002. Mem. (Lib Dem) Oxford CC, 2014–. *Publications:* Christmas Carols, 2014. *Recreations:* golf, walking, cycling. *Address:* 55 Middle Way, Summertown, Oxford OX2 7LE. *T:* (01865) 558841. *E:* andrew.gant@btopenworld.com.

GANT, Diana Jillian; Headmistress, Mount School, York, 2001–09; *b* 25 April 1948; *d* of John Edward Wakeham Scutt and Lucy Helen Scutt; *m* 1969, Rev. Canon Brian Leonard Gant; two *d*. *Educ:* Harrow Co. Grammar Sch. for Girls; King's Coll. London (BD Hons 1970); Christ Ch Coll., Canterbury (PGCE 1973). Various teaching posts, 1973–84; Hd of Religious Studies, King's Sch., Worcester, 1984–89; Hd of Careers and Dep. Hd of 6th Form, Tonbridge GS for Girls, 1989–95; Dep. Headmistress, Norwich High Sch. for Girls (GDST), 1995–2000. Gov., York St John Univ. (formerly Coll., then UC), 2005–14. *Recreations:* walking, cooking, reading. *Address:* 122 Henwick Road, Worcester WR2 5PB. *E:* dianajgant@aol.com.

GANT, John, CB 2003; Chairman, NHS Leicestershire County and Rutland (formerly Leicestershire County and Rutland Primary Care Trust), 2006–10; *b* 25 Feb. 1944; *s* of William and Barbara Gant; *m* 1967, Annette Sonia Cobb; two *s*. *Educ:* Univ. of Newcastle upon Tyne (BA Hons French and German). Inland Revenue: Inspector of Taxes, 1966; Dist Inspector, 1972–74; Head Office Adviser, 1974–77; Dist Inspector, 1977–81; Group Controller, 1981–83; Asst Dir, Ops, 1983–88; Regl Controller, 1988–90; Dep. Dir, Ops, 1990–92; Dir of Human Resources, 1992–2000; Dir of Finance, 2000–03. Mem., Audit Cttee, Statistics Commn, 2004–08. Chm., Melton, Rutland and Harborough PCT, 2003–06. *Recreations:* opera, ballet, theatre, travel, horse racing, importing and enjoying wine. *Address:* PO Box 9378, Melton Mowbray LE13 9DT.

GAO XINGJIAN; writer, artist and film maker; *b* Ganzhou, Jiangxi Province, China, 4 Jan. 1940. Formerly translator: China Reconstructs mag.; Chinese Writers' Assoc. Left China, 1987; now a French citizen. Solo and group exhibns and works in public collections in Europe, Asia and USA. Films include: Silhouette/Shadow, 2003; After the Flood, 2009; Requiem for Beauty. Nobel Prize for Literature, 2000. Chevalier de l'Ordre des Arts et des Lettres (France), 1992. *Publications:* A Preliminary Discussion of the Art of Modern Fiction, 1981; A Pigeon Called Red Beak, 1985; In Search of a Modern Form of Dramatic Representation, 1987; Gao Xingjian: aesthetics and creation, 2012; *novels:* Soul Mountain, 1999; One Man's Bible, 2002; *stories:* Buying a Fishing Rod for My Father, 2004; *plays:* Signal Alarm, 1982; Bus Stop, 1983; Wild Man, 1985; Collected Plays, 1985; The Other Shore, 1986; Fugitives; Summer Rain in Peking; articles in jls. *Address:* c/o HarperCollins Publishers Ltd, 77–85 Fulham Palace Road, W6 8JB.

GAPES, Michael John; MP (Lab and Co-op) Ilford South, since 1992; *b* 4 Sept. 1952; *s* of late Frank William Gapes and of Emily Florence Gapes (*née* Jackson). *Educ:* Staples Road Infants' Sch., Loughton; Manford County Primary Sch., Chigwell; Buckhurst Hill County High Sch., Essex; Fitzwilliam Coll., Cambridge (MA Hons Econs 1975); Middlesex Polytechnic (Dip. Indust. Relations and Trade Union Studies 1976). VSO teacher, Swaziland, 1971–72; Sec., Cambridge Students' Union, 1973–74; Chm., Nat. Orgn of Labour Students, 1976–77. Admin. Officer, Middlesex Hosp., 1977; Nat. Student Organiser, Lab. Party, 1977–80; Res. Officer, Internat. Dept, Lab. Party, 1980–88; Sen. Internat. Officer, Lab. Party, 1988–92. Contested (Lab) Ilford North, 1983. PPS to Minister of State: NI Office, 1997–99; Home Office, 2001–02. Member: Foreign Affairs Select Cttee, 1992–97, 2010– (Chm., 2005–10); Defence Select Cttee, 1999–2001, 2003–05; Treas., 2010–13, Vice Chm., 2013–, British Gp, IPU; Chairman: UN All Party Parly Gp, 1997–2001; All Party Crossrail Gp, 2005–; Vice-Chm., All Party Parly Gp against Anti-Semitism, 1992–2005; Member: All Party Pakistan Gp, 1998; All Party Gp for the Tamils, 2009; Co-Chm., All Party EU Gp, 2010–12; Chm., PLP Children and Families' Cttee, 1994–95; Vice-Chm., PLP Defence Cttee, 1992–95 and 1996–97. Dep. Chm., Labour Friends of Israel, 1997–2005; Member: Labour Nat. Policy Forum, 1998–2005; Labour Friends of India, 1999–, of Palestine and the ME, 2009–, of the Czech Republic, 2012–; Labour ME Council, 2002–05. Mem., NATO Parly Assembly, 2002–05, 2010–. Chm., Westminster Foundn for Democracy, 2002–05. Member: Unite the Union; Co-operative Party. Member, Council: RIIA, 1996–99; VSO, 1997–2011. Vice Pres., Valentines Park Conservationists, 1998–2010; Member: Friends of Valentines Mansion, 2009–; Friends of Ilford Hosp. Chapel, 2000–. *Publications:* co-author of books on defence policy; Labour Party and Fabian Society pamphlets. *Recreations:* blues and jazz music, supporting West Ham United FC. *Address:* House of Commons, SW1A 0AA.

GARBETT, Mark Edward; Headteacher, Latymer School, since 2005; *b* 14 May 1957; *s* of Edward and Mary Garbett; two *d*. *Educ:* Tividale Sch.; Selwyn Coll., Cambridge (BA Maths 1978; PGCE); Open Univ. (MEd). NPQH. Hd of Maths and Housemaster, Framlingham Coll., 1986–91; Hd of Maths and ICT, Royal Belfast Academical Instn, 1991–97; Dep. Head, Skegness GS, 1997–2000; Head, Stretford GS, 2000–05. *Recreations:* creek crawling on the East coast, running, playing piano. *Address:* Latymer School, Haselbury Road, Edmonton, N9 9TN. *T:* (020) 8807 4037, *Fax:* (020) 8887 8111. *E:* gar@latymer.co.uk.

GARBUTT, Graham Bernard; Chief Executive, Commission for Rural Communities, 2006–09; Visiting Professor of Governance and Development, University of the West of England, since 2010; *b* 16 June 1947; *s* of Alfred Garbutt and Rhoda Garbutt (*née* Jones); *m* 1986, Lyda Patricia Jadresić, MD; one *s* two *d*. *Educ:* Grove Sch., Market Drayton; Univ. of Bath (BSc 1970; BArch (1st cl.) 1972); Univ. of Sheffield (MA Town and Regl Planning 1974). Urban Renewal Co-ordinator, Haringey BC, 1974–80; Policy and Prog. Planning Officer, Hackney BC, 1980–87; Dir, S Canning Town and Custom House Project, Newham BC, 1987–90; Chief Exec., Gloucester CC, 1990–2001; Regl Dir, Govt Office for W Midlands, ODPM, 2001–05 (Chairman: Eur. Prog. Monitoring Cttee, 2001–05; Regl Housing Bd, 2004–05; Regl Resilience Forum, 2004–05); Chief Exec., Countryside Agency, 2005–06. Planning and housing consultant, Nigeria, 1976–77. Vis. Lectr, AA Grad. Sch., London, 1976–82. England rep., 2002–, Pres., 2004–05, European Assoc. of State Territorial Reps; Advr to OECD territorial review of Chile, 2008–09; Vice-Pres. and UK Rep., Entretiens Universitaires Réguliers pour l'Administration en Europe univs network, 2011–. Ind. Chm., Cheltenham Develt Task Force, 2010–; Chm., Ind. Inquiry into Cotswold Water Park, 2011–12; Chair, Neighbourhood Develt Plan steering gp, Tewkesbury Parishes, 2014–. Patron, Friends of CAB, Cheltenham, 2010–12. *Recreations:* family, stone and wood sculpture, visual arts, architecture, travel, garden. *Address:* University of the West of England, Faculty of Environment and Technology, Frenchay Campus, Coldharbour Lane, Bristol BS16 1QY. *E:* graham.garbutt@uwe.ac.uk.

GARDAM, Jane Mary, OBE 2009; novelist; *d* of William Pearson, Coatham Sch., Redcar and Kathleen Mary Pearson (*née* Helm); *m* 1954, David Hill Gardam, QC (*d* 2010); two *s* (one *d* decd). *Educ:* Saltburn High Sch. for Girls; Bedford Coll., London Univ. Red Cross Travelling Librarian, Hospital Libraries, 1951; Sub-Editor, Weldon's Ladies Jl, 1952; Asst Literary Editor, Time and Tide, 1952–54. FRSL 1976. Hon. DLitt: Teesside, 2003; Royal Holloway, 2010. Heywood Hill Award for lifetime's contrib. to enjoyment of books, 2000. *Publications:* A Long Way From Verona, 1971 (Phoenix Award, Children's Literature Assoc., 1991); The Summer After The Funeral, 1973; Bilgewater, 1977; God on the Rocks, 1978 (Prix Baudelaire, 1989; televised, 1992); The Hollow Land (Whitbread Literary Award), 1981; Bridget and William, 1981; Horse, 1982; Kit, 1983; Crusoe's Daughter, 1985; Kit in Boots, 1986; Swan, 1987; Through the Doll's House Door, 1987; The Queen of the Tambourine (Whitbread Novel Award), 1991; Faith Fox, 1996; Tufty Bear, 1996; The Green Man, 1998; The Flight of the Maidens, 2000; Old Filth, 2004; The Man in the Wooden Hat, 2009; Last Friends, 2013; *non-fiction:* The Iron Coast, 1994; *short stories:* A Few Fair Days, 1971; Black Faces, White Faces (David Higham Award, Winifred Holtby Award), 1975; The Sidmouth Letters, 1980; The Pangs of Love, 1983 (Katherine Mansfield Award, 1984); Showing the Flag, 1989; Going into a Dark House, 1994; Missing the Midnight, 1997; The People on Privilege Hill, 2007; The Stories, 2014. *Address:* Haven House, 29 Harnet Street, Sandwich, Kent CT13 9ES. *Club:* PEN.

See also T. D. Gardam.

GARDAM, Timothy David; Principal, St Anne's College, Oxford, since 2004; *b* 14 Jan. 1956; *s* of David Hill Gardam, QC and of Jane Mary Gardam, *qv*; *m* 1982, Kim Scott Walwyn (*d* 2002); one *d*; one *d* with Prof. Helen Small. *Educ:* Westminster Sch.; Gonville and Caius Coll., Cambridge (MA). Joined BBC as trainee researcher, 1977; Asst Producer, Nationwide, 1977–79; Producer, Newsnight, 1979–82; Executive Producer: Timewatch, 1982–85; Bookmark, 1984–85; Dep. Editor, Election Programmes, 1985–87; Editor: Panorama, 1987–90; Newsnight, 1990–93; Hd, Weekly Programmes, BBC News and Current Affairs, 1993–96; Controller, News, Current Affairs and Documentaries, Channel Five, 1996–98; Dir of Programmes, 1998–2002, Dir of Television, 2002–03, Channel 4. Non-exec. Dir, OFCOM, 2008– (Chm., Content Bd, 2012–). University of Oxford: Chm., Reuters Inst. for Study of Journalism, 2006–; Chm., Admissions Exec., 2009–. Dir, Oxford Playhouse, 2005–. Chm., Voltaire Foundn, 2005–09. *Recreations:* history, gardens. *Address:* The Principal's Lodgings, St Anne's College, Oxford OX2 6HS.

GARDEN, family name of **Baroness Garden of Frognal**.

GARDEN OF FROGNAL, Baroness *cr* 2007 (Life Peer), of Hampstead, in the London Borough of Camden; **Susan Elizabeth Garden;** PC 2015; *b* 22 Feb. 1944; *d* of late Henry George Button, author, and Edith Margaret Heslop; *m* 1965, Timothy Garden (later Baron Garden (Life Peer), KCB) (*d* 2007); two *d*. *Educ:* Westonbirt Sch., Glos; St Hilda's Coll., Oxford (BA 1965; MA 1982). Secondary sch. teacher in UK and Germany; City and Guilds of London Institute, 1988–2008: Manager, 1990–2000; consultant, 2000–08. Chm., ASM, St Hilda's Coll., Oxford, 1996–2000; Trustee, Oxford Univ. Soc., 2001–08 (Vice-Chm., 2005–08). Contested (Lib Dem) Finchley and Golders Green, 2005. Lib Dem Spokesman on univs and skills, H of L, 2009–10; government spokesman: DCMS (sport, Olympics, media), DfE, BIS (higher educn), 2010–12; BIS (HE and Skills), DfE, MoD, 2012–13; women and equalities, educn, DEFRA, 2014–15; a Baroness in Waiting (Govt Whip), 2010–13 and 2014–15. Pres., Camden Lib Dems, 2008–. Mem., Co. of World Traders, 2000– (Master, 2008–09). Mem. Council, Air League, 2012–. Dir, UK-Japan 21st Century Gp, 2013–. CAB Advr, 1982–87; Pres., Relate, Central Middx, 1997–2002; SSAFA Caseworker, 2001–05; Vice-Pres., War Widows Assoc., 2014–. Patron, Hampstead Counselling Service, 2009–. FRSA 1993; FCGI 2010. Hon. FCIL 2012. *Address:* House of Lords, SW1A 0PW. *E:* gardens@parliament.uk, sue.garden@blueyonder.co.uk. *Clubs:* National Liberal, Royal Air Force.

GARDEN, Ian Harrison; barrister; *b* 18 June 1961; *s* of late Norman Harrison Garden and Jean Elizabeth Garden; *m* 1986, Alexandra Helen Grounds; two *s*. *Educ:* Sedbergh Sch.; UC Wales, Aberystwyth (LLB Hons 1982). Barrister in private practice, 1989–2012. Dep. Chancellor, Dio. of Sheffield, 1999–2013. Mem., Gen. Synod, C of E, 1995–2005 (Member: Legislative Cttee, 1996–2000; Legal Adv. Commn, 2001–); Member: Bishop's Council and Standing Cttee, Dio. of Blackburn, 1996–2004; Crown Appts, then Crown Nominations, Commn, 1997–2005; Archbishops' Council, 2000–05; C of E Appts Cttee, 2001–05; Chm., Dio. of Blackburn Vacancy-in-See Cttee, 2001–. Lay Canon, Blackburn Cathedral, 2003–. Member, Appeals Tribunal Panels, 1996–2001: Pastoral Measure (1983); Incumbents (Vacation of Benefices) Measure (1977); Ordination of Women (Financial Provisions) Measure (1993). Director: Walsingham Coll. Trust Assoc., 1999–2013; Walsingham Coll. (Yorks Properties) Ltd, 2001–14; Mem. Bd Dirs, Manchester Camerata Ltd, 2003–09. Guardian, Shrine of Our Lady of Walsingham, 1996–2013. Gov., Quainton Hall Sch., Harrow, 1999–2001. *Recreations:* orchestral and choral conducting, organ playing, driving classic cars on the continent, golf. *Address:* Old Church Cottage, 29 Church Road, Rufford, near Ormskirk, Lancs L40 1TA. *T:* (01704) 821303.

GARDEN, James; *see* Garden, O. J.

GARDEN, Malcolm; Sheriff of Grampian Highland and Islands at Aberdeen, since 2008; *b* 7 Aug. 1952; *s* of George Garden and Phillippa Mary Hills or Garden; *m* 1984, Sandra Moles; two *s* one *d*. *Educ:* Robert Gordon's Coll., Aberdeen; Univ. of Aberdeen (LLB). NP 1976. Apprentice, then Asst Solicitor, Watt and Cumine, Aberdeen, 1973–76; Asst Solicitor, 1976–79, Partner, 1979–2001, Clark-Wallace, Aberdeen; Temp. Sheriff, 1994–99; Sheriff (pt-time), 2000–01; Sheriff, Grampian Highland and Islands at Peterhead, 2001–08. Tutor (pt-time), Univ. of Aberdeen, 1980–85. Mem., Aberdeen and NE Legal Aid Cttee, 1984–86; Reporter to Scottish Legal Aid Bd, 1986–96. Member: Law Soc. of Scotland, 1976–; Soc. of Advocates, Aberdeen, 1978–. *Recreations:* family, golf, football, tennis. *Address:* Sheriff Court House, Aberdeen AB10 1WP. *T:* (01224) 657200. *E:* Sheriff.MGarden@scotcourts.gov.uk.

GARDEN, Prof. (Olivier) James, CBE 2014; MD; FRCSEd, FRCPEd, FRSE; Regius Professor of Clinical Surgery, since 2000, and Director of Masters Surgical Programmes (formerly Masters in Surgical Sciences), since 2007, University of Edinburgh; Surgeon to the Queen in Scotland, since 2004; *b* 13 Nov. 1953; *s* of late James Garden and Marguerite Marie Jeanne Garden (*née* Vourch); *m* 1977, Amanda Gillian Merrills; one *s* one *d*. *Educ:* Lanark Grammar Sch.; Univ. of Edinburgh (BSc 1974; MB ChB 1977; MD 1988). FRCSGlas 1981; FRCSEd 1994; FRCPEd 2003; FRSE 2013. Lectr in Surgery, Univ. of Glasgow, 1985; Chef de Clinique, Univ. de Paris-Sud, 1986–88; University of Edinburgh: Sen. Lectr in Surgery, 1988–98; Prof. of Hepatobiliary Surgery, 1998–2000; Head: Dept of Clin. and Surgical Scis, 1999–2003; Sch. of Clin. Scis and Community Health, 2003–06. Hon. Consultant Surgeon: Royal Infirmary of Edinburgh, 1988–; and Head, Scottish Liver Transplant Unit, 1992–2006. Ext. Examr, univs incl. Glasgow, Newcastle, Bristol, Hong Kong, Dublin, Oxford, Singapore, Malaysia. Member: James IV Assoc. of Surgeons, 1996– (Hon. Sec., 1999–); Assoc. Upper Gastrointestinal Surgeons, 1996– (Pres., 2002–04); Internat. Hepato-Pancreato-Biliary Assoc., 1998–2006 (Pres., 2012–14). Chm., British Jl of Surgery Soc. Ltd, 2012– (Co. Sec., 2003–12). Ed. in Chief, HPB, 2009–. Hon. Mem., Amer. Surgical Assoc., 2010. Hon. FRACS 2007; Hon. FRCSCan 2008; Hon. FACS 2014; Hon. FRCS 2014; Hon. FCSHK 2015. *Publications:* Principles and Practice of Surgical Laparoscopy, 1994; Intraoperative and Laparoscopic Ultrasonography, 1995; Color Atlas of Surgical Diagnosis, 1995; A Companion to Specialist Surgical Practice (7 vols), 1997, 5th edn 2014; Liver Metastasis: biology, diagnosis and treatment, 1998; Principles and Practice of Surgery, 2000, 6th edn 2012; General Surgery: principles and international practice (2 vols), 2009; numerous contribs to surgical and gastroenterological jls. *Recreations:* ski-ing, golf, food, wine. *Address:* 22 Moston Terrace, Edinburgh EH9 2DE. *T:* (0131) 667 3715. *Club:* New (Edinburgh).

GARDINER OF KIMBLE, Baron *cr* 2010 (Life Peer), of Kimble in the County of Buckinghamshire; **John Eric Gardiner;** Captain of the Yeoman of the Guard (Deputy Chief Whip, House of Lords), since 2015; *b* London, 17 March 1956; *s* of Anthony Ernest Fiddes Gardiner and Heather Joan Gardiner (*née* Robarts); *m* 2004, Olivia Mirabel, sculptor, *e d* of Sir Richard Musgrave, 7th Bt. *Educ:* Uppingham Sch.; Royal Holloway Coll., Univ. of London (BA Mod. History and Politics). Farmer; Partner, C. M. Robarts and Son, 1992–. Countryside Alliance: Dir, Political Affairs, 1995–2004; Dep. Chief Exec., 2004–10; Bd Mem. and Exec. Dir, 2010–12. Chm., FACE (Fedn of Assocs for Hunting and Conservation) (UK), 1998–2012; Treas. Gen., FACE (Europe), 2000–12. Private Sec. to Chm., Cons. Party, 1989–95. A Lord in Waiting (Govt Whip), 2012–15; H of L Spokesperson for DCMS, 2012–; H of L Whip for Cabinet Office and DECC, 2012–. Mem., Select Cttee on HIV and Aids in UK, 2011. Cons. Party Whip, 2011–12; Cons. Dep. Chief Whip, 2013–. Chm., Vale of Aylesbury with Garth and S Berks Hunt, 1992–2006. Pres., Bucks Agricl Assoc., 2007. *Recreations:* hunting, gardening. *Address:* House of Lords, SW1A 0PW. *E:* gardinerj@parliament.uk. *Club:* Pratt's.

GARDINER, Barry Strachan; MP (Lab) Brent North, since 1997; *b* 10 March 1957; *s* of late John Flannegan Gardiner and Sylvia Jean Strachan; *m* 1979, Caroline Anne Smith; three *s* one *d*. *Educ:* Haileybury; St Andrews Univ. (MA Hons). Corpus Christi Coll., Cambridge. ACII. Scottish Sec., SCM, 1979–81. John F. Kennedy Schol., Harvard Univ., 1983; General Average Adjuster, 1987–97. Parliamentary Under-Secretary of State: NI Office, 2004–05; DTI, 2005–06; DEFRA, 2006–07. Prime Minister's Special Envoy for Forests, 2007–08; Leader of Opposition's Special Envoy for Climate Change and the Envmt, 2010–15. *Publications:* articles in Philosophical Qly, Science, Lloyd's List, Insurance Internat. *Recreations:* music, bird watching, hill walking. *Address:* House of Commons, SW1A 0AA.

GARDINER, Elizabeth Anne Finlay, CB 2013; Parliamentary Counsel, since 2003; *b* 19 March 1966; *m* 1990, Alan Gardiner; one *s* one *d*. *Educ:* Edinburgh Univ. (LLB 1987; DLP). Admitted as solicitor, Scotland, 1990, England and Wales, 1991; Asst Parly Counsel, 1991–95; Sen. Asst Parly Counsel, 1995–2000; Dep. Parly Counsel, 2000–03. *Address:* Office of the Parliamentary Counsel, Cabinet Office, 1 Horse Guards Road, SW1A 2HQ. *T:* (020) 7276 6541.

GARDINER, George; Director General, 2007, Head of Delivery for Land and Maritime, 2008–11, Intelligence Surveillance Target Acquisition and Reconnaissance Capability, Ministry of Defence; *b* 25 Oct. 1955; *s* of George Gardiner and Isabella Colquhoun Gardiner; *m* 1981, Colleen May Holbrow; three *d*. *Educ:* Paisley Grammar Sch. MoD, 1974–2011: Asst Dir, Above Water Secretariat, 1991–92; Principal (Finance and Secretariat), Military Communications Systems, 1992–94; jsdc (No. 17), 1994; Asst Dir, Commercial Policy, 1996–98; Hd, Secretariat Smart Procurement Implementation Team, 1999; Dir, Commercial Policy, 2000; Support Dir IJ, 2002–04; Dir, Information Systems, 2004–06. *Recreations:* creating electronic music, shooting, fly fishing. *Address:* Langley Burrell, Wilts SN15 4LQ. *E:* geo-gardiner@lineone.net.

GARDINER, Sir John Eliot, Kt 1998; CBE 1990; conductor; Founder and Artistic Director, English Baroque Soloists, Monteverdi Choir, and Orchestre Révolutionnaire et Romantique; *b* 20 April 1943; *s* of Rolf Gardiner and late Marabel Gardiner (*née* Hodgkin); *m* 1st, 1972, Cherryl ffoulkes (marr. diss. 1980); 2nd, 1981, Elizabeth Suzanne Wilcock (marr. diss. 1997); three *d*; 3rd, 2001, Isabella de Sabata. *Educ:* Pinewood Sch.; Bryanston Sch.; King's Coll., Cambridge (MA History; Hon. Fellow 2015); King's Coll., London (Certif. of Advanced Studies in Music, 1966; Hon. FKC 1992). French Govt Scholarship to study in Paris and Fontainebleau with Nadia Boulanger, 1966–68. Founded: Monteverdi Choir, following performance of Monteverdi's Vespers of 1610, King's Coll. Chapel, Cambridge, 1964; Monteverdi Orchestra, 1968; English Baroque Soloists (period instruments), 1978; Orchestre Révolutionnaire et Romantique, 1989. Guest Conductor (opera): Sadler's Wells; Royal Opera House, Covent Garden; Glyndebourne; La Scala, Milan; La Fenice, Venice; Zurich; Guest Conductor (symphonic): LSO; LPO; Philharmonia; Vienna Phil.; Berlin Phil.; Czech Phil.; Orch. Nat. de France; Concertgebouw; Dresden Staatskapelle; Bavarian Radio SO; Gewandhaus; Boston SO; Cleveland Orch., Pittsburgh. Principal Conductor: CBC Vancouver Orchestra, 1980–83; NDR SO, Hamburg, 1991–94; Music Dir, Opéra de Lyon Orch., 1983–88 (Chef fondateur, 1988). Artistic Director: Göttingen Handel Fest., 1981–90; Veneto Music Fest., 1986. Vis. Fellow, Peterhouse, Cambridge, 2008–09; (first) C. Wolff Dist. Vis. Scholar, Music Dept, Harvard Univ., 2015. Pres., Bach-Archive, Leipzig, 2014–. Hon. FRAM 1992; Hon. FBA 2015. DUniv Univ. Lumière Lyon, 1987; Hon. Dr New England Conservatory of Music, Boston, 2005; Hon. Dr Musicol. Pavia, 2006; Hon. DMus: St Andrews, 2014; Cambridge, 2015. Numerous awards include: Grand Prix du Disque; Deutscher Schallplattenpreis; Edison Awards; Gramophone Record of the Year, 1991, 2005; Gramophone Artist of the Year, 1994; La Medalla internacional, Complutense Univ. of Madrid, 2001; Léonie Sonnings Prize, Denmark, 2005; Bach-Medaille, City of Leipzig, 2005; RAM and Kohn Foundn Bach Prize, 2008; Gramophone Special Achievement Award, 2010; Harvard Glee Club Medal, 2015; Premier Prix, Prix des Muses, Fondation Singer-Polignac, 2015. Commandeur, Ordre des Arts et des Lettres (France), 1997 (Officier, 1988); Verdienstkreuz, 1st Class (Germany), 2005; Chevalier, Légion d'Honneur (France), 2010. *Publications:* Music in the Castle of Heaven: a portrait of Johann Sebastian Bach, 2013. *Recreations:* organic farming, forestry. *Address:* c/o Intermusica Artists' Management Ltd, 36 Graham Street, Crystal Wharf, N1 8GJ.

GARDINER, Prof. John Graham, PhD; FIET; FREng; Professor of Electronic Engineering, 1986–94, and Dean of Engineering and Physical Sciences, 1996–2002, University of Bradford; Director, Wireless Technologies CIC, since 2006; *b* 24 May 1939; *s* of William Clement Gardiner and Ellen (*née* Adey); *m* 1962, Sheila Joyce Andrews; one *s* two *d*. *Educ:* Univ. of Birmingham (BSc 1st Cl. Hons; PhD 1964). FIET (FIEE 1988); FREng (FEng 1994). Software designer, Racal Res. Ltd, 1966–68; University of Bradford: Lectr, 1968–72; Sen Lectr, 1972–78; Reader, 1978–86; Hd, Dept of Electronic and Electrical Engrg, 1994–96. Hon. Pres., British Royal Univ., Kurdistan, 2009–. SMIEE 1995; FRSA 1997. *Publications:* (with J. D. Parsons) Mobile Communication Systems, 1989; (with B. West) Personal Communication Systems and Technologies, 1995. *Recreation:* music. *Address:* 1 Queen's Drive Lane, Ilkley, W Yorks LS29 9QS. *T:* (01943) 609581.

GARDINER, John Ralph; QC 1982; *b* 28 Feb. 1946; *s* of late Cyril Ralph Gardiner and Mary Gardiner (*née* Garibaldi); *m* 1976, Pascal Mary Issard-Davies; one *d*. *Educ:* Bancroft's Sch., Woodford; Fitzwilliam Coll., Cambridge (BA (Law Tripos), MA, LLM). Called to the Bar, Middle Temple, 1968 (Harmsworth Entrance Scholar and Harmsworth Law Scholar; Bencher, 1992); practice at the Bar, 1970–; Mem., Senate of Inns of Court and Bar, 1982–86 (Treasurer, 1985–86); Chm., Taxation and Retirement Benefits Cttee, Bar Council, 1982–85. FRSA 2001. *Publications:* contributor to Pinson on Revenue Law, 6th to 15th (1982) edns. *Recreations:* tennis, horse racing. *Address:* 11 New Square, Lincoln's Inn, WC2A 3QB. *T:* (020) 7242 3981; Admiral's House, Admiral's Walk, Hampstead, NW3 6RS. *T:* (020) 7435 0597.

GARDINER, Juliet; writer and historian; *b* 24 June 1943; *d* of Charles and Dorothy Wells; *m* 1st, 1961, George Arthur Gardiner (later Sir George Gardiner) (marr. diss. 1980; he *d* 2002); two *s* one *d*; 2nd, 1990, Henry Horwitz. *Educ:* Berkhamsted Sch. for Girls; University Coll. London (BA 1st Cl. Hons Hist.). Ed., History Today, 1981–85; Acad. Dir, then Publisher, Weidenfield & Nicolson, 1985–89; Middlesex University: Principal Lectr, 1992–97; Acad. Chair, Communication, Cultural and Media Studies, 1997–2000; Hd, Publishing Studies, Oxford Brookes Univ., 2000–01. Res. Fellow, Inst. Histl Res., Univ. of London, 1979–81; Hon. Res. Fellow, IAS, Univ. of Edinburgh, 2006; Hon. Vis. Prof., Sch. of Arts, Middlesex Univ., 2004–07. Member: Mgt Cttee, Soc. of Authors, 2011–14; Academic Adv. Panel, Nat. Army Mus., 2014–. Trustee, History Today, 1998–. Historical adviser: Atonement (film), 2006; Upstairs Downstairs (BBC TV), 2010; Turn Back Time - The High Street (BBC TV), 2010; Turn Back Time - The Family (BBC TV), 2012; Mr Selfridge (ITV). Occasional presenter, Night Waves, BBC Radio 3; writer and presenter: A History of the Future, 2012, Presenting the Past, 2013, BBC Radio 4. *Publications:* Over Here: GIs in wartime Britain 1942–45, 1992; The World Within: the Brontës at Haworth, 1992; (ed) Women's Voices: the new woman 1880–1914, 1993; Picture Post Women, 1994; (ed) The History Today Companion to British History, 1995; Oscar Wilde: a life in letters, writings and wit, 1995; Queen Victoria, 1997; From the Bomb to the Beatles: the changing face of post-war Britain 1945–65, 1999; The Penguin Dictionary of British History, 2000; The History Today Who's Who in British History, 2000; The 1940s House, 2000; The Edwardian Country House, 2002; Wartime: Britain 1939–1945, 2004; The Children's War, 2005; The Animals' War, 2006; War on the Home Front, 2007; The Thirties: an intimate history, 2010; The Blitz: the British under attack, 2010; Memories of Britain Past, 2011; (contrib.) Hackney: an uncommon history, 2012. *Recreation:* London. *E:* juliet@julietgardiner.com.

GARDINER, Air Vice-Marshal Martyn John, OBE 1987; FRAeS; *b* 13 June 1946; *s* of late John Glen Gardiner and Edith Eleanor Gardiner (*née* Howley); *m* 1971, Anne Dunlop Thom; two *s* one *d*. *Educ:* Frimley and Camberley Grammar Sch.; Southampton Univ. (BScEng (Hons) Aeronautics and Astronautics 1967). FRAeS 2000. Flying and staff appointments include: Coll. of Air Warfare, 1969–71; No 99 Sqdn, Brize Norton, 1971–75; Dept of Air Warfare, Gen. Duties Aero-Systems Course, 1976; No 72 Sqdn, Odiham, 1977–80; HQ 2 Armd Div., Germany, 1980–82; RAF Staff Coll., Bracknell, 1983; OC 32 Sqdn, RAF Northolt, 1984–87; HQ STC, 1987–88; Defence Policy and Commitments Staffs, MoD, 1988–91; OC RAF Northolt, 1991–93; SASO, HQ 38 Gp, 1994–96; COS Reaction Force Air Staff Kalkar, 1996–98; Dep. Comdr, Combined Air Ops Centre 4, Messstetten, 1998–2001; Mil. Advr to High Rep. for Bosnia and Herzegovina, 2001–02. Non-executive Director: Singleton Birch Ltd, 2013–; Estuary TV, 2014–. Chairman: NE Lincs Aircrew Assoc., 2004–; Louth RAFA, 2004–. Dir, Grimsby Inst. Corp., 2004–13; Dir and Trustee, Katherine Martin Charitable Trust, 2006–; Chm. of Govs, Duke of Kent Sch., Ewhurst, 2002–08; Chm., Alexander Duckham Meml Schs Trust, 2004–. *Recreations:* golf, ski-ing, walking, Rugby-watching. *Address:* Heronsbrook, Stewton Lane, Louth, Lincolnshire LN11 8SB. *Club:* Royal Air Force.

GARDINER, Peter Dod Robin; First Deputy Head, Stanborough School, Hertfordshire, 1979–92, retired; *b* 23 Dec. 1927; *s* of late Brig. R. Gardiner, CB, CBE; *m* 1959, Juliet Wright; one *s* one *d*. *Educ:* Radley College; Trinity Coll., Cambridge. Asst Master, Charterhouse, 1952–67, and Housemaster, Charterhouse, 1965–67; Headmaster, St Peter's School, York, 1967–79. *Publications:* (ed) Twentieth-Century Travel, 1963; (with B. W. M. Young) Intelligent Reading, 1964; (with W. A. Gibson) The Design of Prose, 1971. *Recreations:* reading, music, walking, acting. *Address:* 1 Court Gardens, Cleeve Road, Goring on Thames, Reading RG8 9BZ.

GARDINER, Victor Alec, OBE 1977; Director and General Manager, London Weekend Television, 1971–87; *b* 9 Aug. 1929; *m*; one *s* two *d*. *Educ:* Whitgift Middle Sch., Croydon; City and Guilds (radio and telecommunications). Techn. Asst, GPO Engrg, 1947–49; RAF Nat. Service, 1949–51; BBC Sound Radio Engr, 1951–53; BBC TV Cameraman, 1953–55; Rediffusion TV Sen. Cameraman, 1955–61; Malta TV Trng Man., 1961–62; Head of Studio Prodn, Rediffusion TV, 1962–67; Man. Dir, GPA Productions, 1967–69; Production Controller, London Weekend Television, 1969–71; Director: LWT (Hldgs) Ltd, 1976–87; London Weekend Services Ltd, 1976–87; Richard Price Television Associates, 1981–87; Chairman: Dynamic Technology Ltd, 1972–87; Standard Music Ltd, 1972–87; LWT Internat., 1981–87. Mem., Royal Television Soc., 1970– (Vice-Chm. Council, 1974–75; Chm. Papers Cttee, 1975; Chm. Council, 1976–77; Fellow, 1977). *Recreations:* Big Band music, travelling, sound and video constructions.

GARDNER, family name of **Baroness Gardner of Parkes**.

GARDNER OF PARKES, Baroness *cr* 1981 (Life Peer), of Southgate, Greater London, and of Parkes, NSW; **(Rachel) Trixie (Anne) Gardner,** AM 2003; JP; dental surgeon; Chairman, Plan International (UK) Ltd, 1990–2003; *b* Parkes, NSW, Australia, 17 July 1927; eighth *c* of late Hon. J. J. Gregory McGirr and Rachel McGirr, OBE, LC; *m* 1956, Kevin Anthony Gardner (*d* 2007), *o s* of late George and Rita Gardner, Sydney, Australia; three *d*. *Educ:* Monte Sant Angelo Coll., N Sydney; East Sydney Technical Coll.; Univ. of Sydney (BDS 1954; Hon. Fellow 2005). Cordon Bleu de Paris, Diplôme 1956. Came to UK, 1954. Member: Westminster City Council, 1968–78 (Lady Mayoress, 1987–88); GLC, for Havering, 1970–73, for Enfield-Southgate, 1977–86. Contested (C) Blackburn, 1970; N Cornwall, Feb. 1974. House of Lords: a Dep. Speaker, 1999–2002; Dep. Chm. of Cttees, 1999–2002. Chm., Royal Free Hampstead NHS Trust, 1994–97; Vice-Chm., NE Thames RHA, 1990–94; Member: Inner London Exec. Council, NHS, 1966–71; Standing Dental Adv. Cttee for England and Wales, 1968–76; Westminster, Kensington and Chelsea Area Health Authority, 1974–82; Industrial Tribunal Panel for London, 1974–97; N Thames Gas Consumer Council, 1980–82; Dept of Employment's Adv. Cttee on Women's Employment, 1980–88; Britain–Australia Bicentennial Cttee, 1984–88; London Electricity Bd, 1984–90. British Chm., European Union of Women, 1978–82; UK Rep., UN Status of Women Commn, 1982–88. Director: Gateway Building Soc., 1987–88; Woolwich Building Soc., 1988–93. Chm., Suzy Lamplugh Trust, 1993–97. Governor: Eastman Dental Hosp., 1971–80; Nat. Heart Hosp., 1974–90. Fellow, Sancta Sophia Coll., Univ. of Sydney, 2011. Hon. Pres., War Widows Assoc. of GB, 1984–87; Hon. Vice-Pres., Women's Sect., RBL, 2000–06. JP North Westminster, 1971. DUniv Middlesex, 1997. Univ. of Sydney Award for Internat. Achievement, 2010. *Recreations:* gardening, reading, travel, needlework. *Address:* House of Lords, SW1A 0PW.

See also Hon. S. L. Joiner.

GARDNER, Brigid Catherine Brennan, OBE 2002; Principal, St George's British International (formerly English) School, Rome, 1994–2004; *b* 5 May 1941; *d* of John Henthorn Cantrell Brennan and Rosamond Harriet Brennan (*née* Gardner); *m* 1963, Michael Henry Davies (marr. diss. 1980); three *d*. *Educ:* The Alice Ottley Sch., Worcester; Girton Coll., Cambridge (MA). English and History teacher, Harrogate High Sch., 1963–66; English teacher, Hong Kong, 1967–69; James Allen's Girls' School: Head of History, 1976–83; Dep. Head, 1981–83; Headmistress, 1984–94. Governor: Oundle Sch., 1992–94; Whitgift Foundn, 1992–94; Charter Sch., Dulwich, 2009–13. *Recreations:* gardening, politics (Liberal Democrat). *Address:* Ash Cottage, Court Lane, Dulwich Village, SE21 7DH.

GARDNER, Caroline Jane; Auditor General for Scotland, since 2012; *b* London, 1 May 1963; *d* of Dennis and Pauline Bradley; *m* 1989, Edward Paul Gardner. *Educ:* Univ. of Aston (BSc Combined Hons 1985); Warwick Business Sch. (MBA 1995); Open Univ. (BA 1st Cl.

Hons English Lit. 2006). CIPFA 1988; FT Non-exec. Dir Dip. 2012. Trainee accountant, Wolverhampton MBC, 1985–88; Special Projects Officer, District Audit, 1988–92; Sen. Manager, Audit Commn, 1992–95; Dir, Health and Social Work Studies, Accounts Commn, 1995–2000; Audit Scotland: Dep. Auditor Gen., 2000–10; Controller of Audit, 2004–10; Chief Financial Officer, Turks and Caicos Is Govt, 2010–11; Ind. Consultant in Public Financial Mgt, 2011–12. Mem. Bd, Public Service Audit Appointments, 2014–. Pres., CIPFA, 2006–07. Mem., Internat. Ethics Standards Bd for Accountants, 2010–. *Address:* Audit Scotland, 110 George Street, Edinburgh EH2 4LH. *T:* (0131) 625 1605. *E:* cgardner@audit-scotland.gov.uk.

GARDNER, Charlotte Ann; *see* Roberts, C. A.

GARDNER, Christopher James Ellis; QC 1994; Chief Justice of the Falkland Islands, South Sandwich, South Georgia, British Antarctic Territory and British Indian Ocean Territory, 2007–15; *b* 6 April 1945; *s* of James Charles Gardner and Phillis May Gardner (*née* Wilkinson); *m* 1972, Arlene Sellers; one *s* one *d*. *Educ:* Rossall Sch., Lancs; Fitzwilliam Coll., Cambridge (MA). Called to the Bar, Gray's Inn, 1968; a Recorder, 1993–; Chief Justice, Turks and Caicos Islands, 2004–07. FCIArb 1999; Chartered Arbitrator, 2003; Accredited Mediator, 2000. Liveryman, Arbitrators' Co., 2003. Fellow, Soc. for Advanced Legal Studies, 1999; FRSocMed 2000; FCJEI 2013. *Recreations:* theatre, ballet, bell ringing, golf, cooking curries. *Address:* Old Rose Cottage, Cheriton, Hants SO24 0QA. *Clubs:* Dartmouth Yacht; Royal Dart Yacht.

GARDNER, Prof. David Pierpont, PhD; President, The William and Flora Hewlett Foundation, 1993–99; President, University of California, 1983–92; Professor of Education, University of California at Berkeley, 1983–92; *b* 24 March 1933; *s* of Reed S. Gardner and Margaret (*née* Pierpont); *m* 1st, 1958, Elizabeth Fuhriman (*d* 1991); four *d*; 2nd, 1995, Sheila S. Rodgers. *Educ:* Brigham Young Univ. (BS 1955); Univ. of Calif, Berkeley (MA 1959, PhD 1966). Dir, Calif Alumni Foundn, Calif Alumni Assoc., Univ. of Calif, Berkeley, 1962–64. University of California, Santa Barbara: Asst Prof. of Higher Educn, 1964–69; Associate Prof. of Higher Educn, 1969–70; Prof. of Higher Educn (on leave), 1971–73; Asst to the Chancellor, 1964–67; Asst Chancellor, 1967–69; Vice Chancellor and Exec. Asst, 1969–70; Vice Pres., Univ. of Calif, 1971–73; Pres., and Prof. of Higher Educn, Univ. of Utah, 1973–83, Pres. Emeritus, 1985. Chm., Nat. Commn on Excellence in Educn, 1981–83. Vis. Fellow, Clare Hall, Univ. of Cambridge, 1979 (Hon. Fellow, 2002). Fellow, Nat. Acad. of Public Administration; Member: Amer. Philosophical Soc.; Nat. Acad. of Educn. Chm., J. Paul Getty Trust, 2000–04. Trustee, Tanner Lectures on Human Values, 1975–2004. Fulbright 40th Anniversary Distinguished Fellow, Japan, 1986; Fellow, Amer. Acad. of Arts and Scis, 1986. Hon. LLD: Univ. of The Pacific, 1983; Nevada, Las Vegas, 1984; Westminster Coll., 1987; Brown, 1989; Notre Dame, 1989; Hon. DH Brigham Young, 1981; Hon. DLitt Utah, 1983; Hon. HHD Utah State, 1987; Hon. Dr Bordeaux II, 1988; Hon. DHL Internat. Christian Univ. Benjamin P. Cheney Medal, Eastern Washington Univ., 1984; James Bryant Conant Award, Educn Commn of the States, 1985; Hall of Fame Award, Calif. Sch. Bd Res Foundn, 1988. Chevalier, Légion d'Honneur (France), 1985; Knight Commander, Order of Merit (Germany), 1992. *Publications:* The California Oath Controversy, 1967; Earning My Degree: memoirs of an American university president, 2005; contrib. articles to professional jls. *Address:* (office) Center for Studies in Higher Education, 771 Evans Hall, University of California, Berkeley, CA 94720–4650, USA.

GARDNER, Douglas Frank; Chairman, Industrial Realisation plc, since 2000; *b* 20 Dec. 1943; *s* of late Ernest Frank Gardner and Mary Gardner; *m* 1978, Adèle (*née* Alexander); one *s* two *d*. *Educ:* Woolverstone Hall; College of Estate Management, London Univ. (BSc). FRICS. Chief Exec., Properties Div., Tarmac plc, 1976–83; Man. Dir, 1983–93, Chm., 1993–2000, Brixton Estate plc. Chairman: Industrial Develt Partnership, 2000–07; GPT Halverton Ltd (formerly Halverton REIM LLP), 2004–08; Director: Invesco UK Property Income Trust, 2004–; Hirco plc, 2006–11; Invista Real Estate Investment Mgt plc, 2010–12; Prime plc, 2010–11; Mem., Investment Cttee, Eur. Industrial Property Fund, 2001–04. Chm., Bd of Govs, Nuffield Hospitals, subseq. Nuffield Health, 2001–09 (Gov., 1995–2009). Mem. Council, RCM. *Recreations:* tennis, theatre. *Address:* Flat 10 Stavordale Lodge, 10–12 Melbury Road, W14 8WL.

GARDNER, Edward James, OBE 2012; conductor; Music Director, English National Opera, 2007–15; Principal Guest Conductor, City of Birmingham Symphony Orchestra, since 2010; Chief Conductor, Bergen Philharmonic Orchestra, since 2015 (Principal Guest Conductor, 2013–15); *b* Gloucester, 22 Nov. 1974; *s* of Kingsley and Helen Gardner; one *s*. *Educ:* Eton; King's Coll., Cambridge (BA 1996); Royal Acad. of Music. Asst to Music Dir, Hallé Orch., 2000–03; Founder, Hallé Youth Orch., 2002; Musical Dir, Glyndebourne Touring Opera, 2004–07. Débuts: Paris Opera, 2004; BBC SO, 2005; Metropolitan Opera, NY, 2010; La Scala, Milan, 2011; has worked with orchestras incl. NHK SO, Melbourne SO, St Louis SO, Nat. Arts Centre Orch., Ottawa, Mahler Chamber Orch., Bamberg SO, Netherlands Radio Philharmonic, Philharmonia, LPO, Orch. of the Age of Enlightenment, Royal Concertgebouw, Deutsches SO Berlin, Orchestre Philharmonique de Radio France, Accademia Nazionale di Santa Cecilia, Orchestra Filarmonica della Scala, Czech Philharmonic, Swedish Radio Orch., Danish Nat. Symphony, Gothenberg Symphony, Rotterdam Philharmonic, Royal Scottish Nat. Orch. Conductor, Last Night of the Proms, 2011. *Address:* c/o Askonas Holt, Lincoln House, 300 High Holborn, WC1V 7JH.

GARDNER, Francis Rolleston, OBE 2005; BBC Security Correspondent, since 2002; *b* 31 July 1961; *s* of Robert Neil Gardner and Grace Rolleston Gardner; *m* 1997, Amanda Jane Pearson; two *d*. *Educ:* Marlborough Coll.; Exeter Univ. (BA Hons Arabic and Islamic Studies 1984). Marketing Manager, Gulf Exports, 1984–86; Trading and Sales, Saudi Internat. Bank, 1986–90; Dir, Robert Fleming, 1990–95; joined BBC News, 1995: World TV, 1995–97; Gulf Corresp., 1997–99; ME Corresp., 1999–2002. Dist. Vis. Prof. of 2015, USC. Platoon Comdr 4th (V) Bn, RGJ, 1984–90. FRGS 2006. Hon. LLD: Staffordshire, 2006; Nottingham, 2006; Exeter, 2007; East Anglia, 2009; Open, 2009; London, 2013. Person of the Year, Press Gazette, 2005; El Mundo Internat. Journalism Prize, 2006; McWhirter Award for Bravery, 2006; Zayed Medal for Journalism, UAE, 2007; AIM Ability Media Internat. Award, 2009; Master Wheelrights' Award, 2011; Journalist of the Year, Eur. Diversity Awards, 2011. *Publications:* Blood and Sand, 2006; Far Horizons, 2009. *Recreations:* ski-ing (Pres., Ski Club of GB, 2011–), scuba diving, birdwatching, rifle shooting. *Address:* BBC News Centre, Portland Place, W1A 1AA. *Clubs:* Rifles Officers London, Ivy.

GARDNER, James Jesse, CVO 1995; CBE 1986; DL; consultant, since 1986; Chairman, OFWAT National Consumer Council, 1993–98; *b* 7 April 1932; *s* of James and Elizabeth Rubina Gardner; *m* 1st, 1955, Diana Sotheran (*d* 1999); three *s* one *d*; 2nd, 2002, Joan Adamson. *Educ:* Kirkham Grammar Sch.; Victoria Univ., Manchester (LLB). Nat. Service, 1955–57. Articled to Town Clerk, Preston, 1952–55; Legal Asst, Preston Co. Borough Council, 1955; Crosby Borough Council: Asst Solicitor, 1957–59; Chief Asst Solicitor, 1959–61; Chief Asst Solicitor, Warrington Co. Borough Council, 1961–65; Stockton-on-Tees Borough Council: Dep. Town Clerk, 1966; Town Clerk, 1966–68; Asst Town Clerk, Teesside Co. Borough Council, 1968; Associate Town Clerk and Solicitor, London Borough of Greenwich, 1968–69; Town Clerk and Chief Exec. Officer, Co. Borough of Sunderland, 1970–73; Chief Exec., Tyne and Wear CC, 1973–86; Chm., Tyne and Wear PTE, 1983–86. Chief Exec., Northern Develt Co. Ltd, 1986–87; Chairman: Sunderland DHA, 1988–90; Northumbrian Water Customer Services Cttee, 1990–2001; North East Television, 1991–92; Dir, Birtley Enterprise Action Management (BEAM) Ltd, 1989–93; Sec., Northern Region Councils Assoc., 1986. Clerk to Lieutenancy, Tyne and Wear, 1974–91. Dir, Garrod Pitkin (1986) Ltd, 1991–93. Chairman: Prince's Trust Trustees, 1986–94; Prince's Trust and Royal Jubilee Trust Management Bd, 1989–93 (former Chm., Northumbria Cttee, Royal Jubilee and Prince's Trusts); Prince's Trust Events Ltd, 1987–94; Director: Threshold (formerly Prince's Trust Training & Employment Ltd), 1991–95 (Chm., 1992); NE Civic Trust, 1986–92. Chairman: Century Radio, 1993–2000; St Benedict's Hospice, Sunderland, 1993–2008; Royalty Theatre, 2001–05; Trustee: Tyne Tees Telethon Trust, 1988–91; Great North Air Ambulance Service Appeal, 1991–95. DL Tyne and Wear, 1976. FRSA 1976; CCMI (CIMgt 1987). Hon. Fellow, Sunderland Polytechnic, 1986. *Recreations:* golf, music, theatre, food and drink. *Address:* Wayside, 121 Queen Alexandra Road, Sunderland, Tyne and Wear SR2 9HR.

GARDNER, (James) Piers; barrister; *b* 26 March 1954; *s* of Michael Clement Gardner and Brigitte Elsa Gardner (*née* Ekrut); *m* 1978, Penelope Helen Chloros; three *s* one *d*. *Educ:* Bryanston Sch.; Brasenose Coll., Oxford (MA Jurisp. 1st Class). Solicitor of the Supreme Court, 1979–2000; called to the Bar, Gray's Inn, 2000. Articled and in private practice as solicitor, with Stephenson Harwood, London, 1977–80; Secretariat, European Commn of Human Rights, Council of Europe, Strasbourg, 1980–87; Exec. Dir, 1987–89, Dir, 1989–2000, British Inst. of Internat. and Comparative Law. *Recreations:* foreign property, arguing. *Address:* Monckton Chambers, 1–2 Raymond Buildings, Gray's Inn, WC1R 5NR. *T:* (020) 7405 7211. *Club:* Athenæum.

GARDNER, Prof. John, DPhil; FBA 2013; Professor of Jurisprudence, University of Oxford, since 2000; Fellow, University College, Oxford, since 2000; *b* 23 March 1965. *Educ:* New Coll., Oxford (BA 1986; Vinerian Schol.; BCL 1987); Inns of Court Sch. of Law; All Souls Coll., Oxford (DPhil 1993). Called to the Bar, Inner Temple, 1988, Bencher, 2003; Fellow, All Souls Coll., Oxford, 1986–91; Fellow and Tutor, Brasenose Coll., Oxford, 1991–96; Reader in Legal Philosophy, KCL, 1996–2000; Fellow, All Souls Coll., Oxford, 1998–2000. Visiting Professor: Columbia Univ. Sch. of Law, NY, 2000; Yale Law Sch., 2002–03, 2005; Univ. of Texas, 2006; Princeton Univ., 2008; ANU, 2008; Univ. of Auckland, 2010. *Publications:* Action and Value in Criminal Law, 1993; Relating to Responsibility, 2001; Offences and Defences, 2007; Punishment and Responsibility, 2008; Law as a Leap of Faith, 2012; contrib. jls incl. Oxford Jl Legal Studies, Cambridge Law Jl, Univ. of Toronto Law Jl. *Recreations:* cooking, web design. *Address:* University College, Oxford OX1 4BH. *T:* (01865) 276638.

GARDNER, Julie Anne; *see* Etchingham, J. A.

GARDNER, Ven. Paul Douglas, PhD; Senior Minister, Christ Church Presbyterian Church, Atlanta, Georgia, since 2005; *b* 28 May 1950; *s* of late Rev. David Gardner and Dr Joy M. Gardner; *m* 1971, Sharon Anne Bickford; two *s* one *d*. *Educ:* Leeds Grammar Sch.; KCL (BA 1972, AKC 1972); Reformed Theol Seminary, USA (MDiv 1979); Ridley Hall, Cambridge; Sidney Sussex Coll., Cambridge (PhD 1989). Company dir, 1972–77. Ordained deacon, 1980, priest, 1981; Curate, St Martin's, Cambridge, 1980–83; Lectr in NT and Acad. Registrar, Oak Hill Theol Coll., 1983–90; Vicar, St John the Baptist, Hartford, Cheshire, 1990–2003; Archdeacon of Exeter, 2003–05. RD, Middlewich, 1994–99. *Publications:* The Gifts of God and the Authentication of a Christian, 1994; The Complete Who's Who in the Bible, 1995; (ed and contrib.) New International Encyclopedia of Bible Characters, 1995, 4th edn 2002; Focus on the Bible series: 2 Peter and Jude, 1998, new edn as 1 Peter, 2 Peter and Jude, 2012; Revelation, 2001; Ephesians, 2006. *Recreations:* alpine walking, ski-ing, writing, photography. *Address:* 143 Ridgeland Way, Atlanta, GA 30305, USA.

GARDNER, Piers; *see* Gardner, J. P.

GARDNER, Sir Richard (Lavenham), Kt 2005; PhD; FRS 1979; Royal Society Edward Penley Abraham Research Professor, Department of Zoology, University of Oxford, 2003–08, now Academic Visitor, Sir William Dunn School of Pathology; Student of Christ Church, Oxford, 1974–2008, now Emeritus; *b* 10 June 1943; *s* of late Allan Constant and Eileen May Gardner; *m* 1968, Wendy Joy Cresswell; one *s*. *Educ:* St John's Sch., Leatherhead; North East Surrey Coll. of Technology; St Catharine's Coll., Cambridge (BA 1st Cl. Hons Physiol., 1966; MA; PhD 1971; Hon. Fellow, 2008). Res. Asst, Physiological Lab., Cambridge, 1970–73; Oxford University: Lectr in Developmental and Reproductive Biology, Dept of Zoology, 1973–77; Res. Student, Christ Church, 1974–77; Royal Soc. Henry Dale Res. Prof., Dept of Zool., 1978–2003; Hon. Dir, ICRF Develtl Biol. Unit, 1986–96. Associate, and Hon. Vis. Prof., Dept of Biol., Univ. of York, 2007–. Ind. Mem., ABRC, 1990–93. Pres., Inst. Biol., 2006–08. Chm., Animals in Science Educn Trust, 2009–; Trustee, Edwards and Steptoe Res. Trust, 2010–. Patrick Steptoe Meml Lect., British Fertility Soc., 2015. Hon. ScD Cambridge, 2012. Scientific Medal, Zoological Soc. of London, 1977; March of Dimes Prize in Develtl Biology, 1999; Royal Medal, Royal Soc., 2001; Albert Brachet Prize, Royal Acad. of Belgium, 2004. *Publications:* contribs to Jl of Embryology and Experimental Morphology, Nature, Jl of Cell Science, and various other jls and symposia. *Recreations:* ornithology, music, sailing, painting, gardening. *Address:* Christ Church, Oxford OX1 1DP.

GARDNER, Dr Rita Ann Moden, CBE 2003; Director and Secretary, Royal Geographical Society (with the Institute of British Geographers), since 1996; *b* 10 Nov. 1955; *d* of John William Gardner and Evelyn Gardner (*née* Moden); partner, 1982, Dr Martin Eugene Frost. *Educ:* Huntingdon Grammar Sch.; Hinchingbrooke Sch.; University Coll. London (BSc 1st cl. Hons Geog.); Wolfson Coll., Oxford (DPhil 1981). Lectr in Physical Geog., St Catherine's Coll., Oxford, 1978–79; Lectr in Geog., KCL, 1979–94; Dir, Envmtl Sci. Unit and Reader in Envmtl Sci., QMW, 1994–96. Advr to Schools Minister, DFES, then DCSF, 2006–09; Member: Archives Task Force, DCMS, 2002–03; Geography Advisors Gp, DfE, 2011–13; Working Gp on Open Access to Scholarly Publishing, BIS, 2011–13. Non-exec. Dir, British Antarctic Survey, 2011–14. Member, Council: ALPSP, 2008–11; Acad. of Social Scis, 2013–. Co-Chair, Exhibition Road Cultural Gp, 2004–09; Trustee: WWF-UK, 2000–04; World Conservation Monitoring Centre, 2008–11. Ed., Geographical Jl, 1989–93. Hon. Sec., RGS, 1991–96. Hon. Fellow, QMUL, 2004. Hon. DSc Southampton, 2004; Hon. Dr Gloucester, 2004. Busk Medal, RGS, 1995; Ronald F. Abler Distinguished Service Honor, Assoc. of Amer. Geographers, 2015. *Publications:* Landscape in England and Wales, 1981, 2nd edn 1994; Mega-geomorphology, 1981; Land Shapes, 1986; numerous academic papers in learned jls specialising in geomorphology, physical geog., sedimentology and Quaternary envmtl change. *Recreations:* restoration of historic vernacular buildings, contemporary architecture and furniture, gardening, travel, good food and wine, dance. *Address:* Royal Geographical Society (with IBG), 1 Kensington Gore, SW7 2AR. *T:* (020) 7591 3010. *E:* director@rgs.org.

GARDNER, Sir Robert Henry B.; *see* Bruce-Gardner.

GARDNER, Sir Roy Alan, Kt 2002; FCCA; Chairman: Mainstream Renewable Power Ltd, since 2011 (non-executive Director, since 2008); Chairman, Serco Group plc, since 2015; Senior Advisor, Credit Suisse, since 2006; *b* 20 Aug. 1945; *s* of Roy Thomas Gardner and Iris Joan Gardner; *m* 1969, Carol Ann Barker; one *s* two *d*. *Educ:* Strode's Sch., Egham. FCCA 1980. Works Acct, later Concorde Project Acct, BAC Ltd, 1963–75; Chief Acct, Asst Finance Dir, then Finance Dir, Marconi Space & Defence Systems, 1975–84; Finance Dir, Marconi Co. Ltd, 1984–85; STC plc: Finance Dir, 1986–89; Dir, 1986–91; Man. Dir, STC Communications Ltd, 1989–91; Chief Operating Officer, Northern Telecom Europe Ltd, 1991–92; Man. Dir, GEC-Marconi Ltd, 1992–94; Dir, GEC plc, 1994; Exec. Dir, British Gas plc, 1994–97; Chief Exec., Centrica plc, 1997–2006. Chairman: Manchester United plc,

2002–05 (non-exec. Dir, 1999–2005); Compass Gp PLC, 2006–14 (non-exec. Dir, 2005–14); Plymouth Argyle FC, 2009–10; Connaught plc, 2010; EnServe Gp Ltd (formerly Spice Ltd), 2010–14; non-executive Director: Laporte plc, 1997–2001; Willis Gp Hldgs Ltd, 2006–. Chairman: Employers' Forum on Disability, 2000–03; Modern Apprenticeship Task Force, 2002–05; Apprentices Ambassadors Network UK, 2006–14; British Olympic Appeal for Beijing Games 2008, 2007–08. Mem., Council for Ind. and Higher Educn, 1996–99. Chm., Adv. Bd, Energy Futures Lab, Imperial Coll., 2007–. Member Council: RUSI, 1992–96; Brunel Univ., 1998–2001. Pres., Carers UK (formerly Carers Nat. Assoc.), 1998–2014. Trustee, Develt Trust, 1997–. Mem. Bd, Enemy Within appeal, Combat Stress, 2010–. CCMI; FCGI; FRSA 1995. *Recreations:* golf, running. *Address:* Serco Group plc, Serco House, 16 Bartley Wood Business Park, Bartley Way, Hook, Hants RG27 9UY. *Clubs:* Brooks's, Annabel's, Mark's, Harry's Bar, 5 Hertford Street, George.

GARDNER, Sally Ann Collins; author of books for children and young people, since 2005; *b* Birmingham, 2 Oct. 1953; *d* of Sir Edward Lucas Gardner, QC and of Her Honour Noreen Margaret, (Nina), Lowry, *qv*; *m* 1981, Adrian Corry (marr. diss. 1999); one *s* two *d*. *Educ:* Central St Martins (BA Hons Theatre 1975). Theatre designer, 1975–88; illustrator, 1989–2005. *Publications: illustrator:* Robert and the Giant, 1990; Suzi, Sam, George & Alice, 1993; Gynormous!: the ultimate book of giants, 1996; Hello? Is Anybody There?, 1997 (Norwegian edn as Hallo? Er det noen her?, 1996); The Real Fairy Storybook, 1998; Polly's Running Away Book, 2000; Polly's Absolutely Worst Birthday Ever, 2001; Polly's Really Secret Diary, 2002; *writer and illustrator:* The Little Nut Tree, 1993; My Little Princess, 1994; Playtime Rhymes, 1995; A Book of Princesses, 1997; The Strongest Girl in the World, 1999; The Fairy Catalogue: everything you need to know to make a fairy tale, 2000; The Smallest Girl Ever, 2000; The Boy Who Could Fly, 2001; The Glass Heart: a tale of three princesses, 2001; Mama, Don't Go Out Tonight, 2002; The Invisible Boy, 2002; Boolar's Big Day Out, 2003; Fairy Shopping, 2003; The Boy with the Magic Numbers, 2003; The Countess's Calamity, 2003; The Boy with the Lightning Feet, 2006; *writer:* I, Coriander, 2005 (Nestlé Smarties Book Prize, Booktrust); Lucy Willow, 2006; The Red Necklace: a story of the French Revolution, 2007; The Silver Blade, 2008; The Double Shadow, 2011; Maggot Moon, 2012 (Carnegie Maedal, CLIP); Wings & Co: Operation Bunny: the fairy detective agency's first case, 2012, Three Pickled Herrings, 2012, The Vanishing of Billy Buckle, 2013; Tinder, 2013; The Matchbox Mysteries, 2014; The Door That Led to Where, 2015. *Recreations:* walking the dog, searching for peace and quiet. *Address:* c/o Orion Children's Books/Indigo, Carmelite House, 50 Victoria Embankment, EC4Y 0DZ; c/o Hot Key Books Ltd, 10 Northburgh Street, EC1V 0AT. *Club:* Union.

GAREL-JONES, family name of **Baron Garel-Jones**.

GAREL-JONES, Baron *cr* 1997 (Life Peer), of Watford in the co. of Hertfordshire; **William Armand Thomas Tristan Garel-Jones;** PC 1992; Managing Director, 1999–2008, Senior Advisor, since 2009, UBS Investment Bank (formerly Warburg Dillon Read); *b* 28 Feb. 1941; *s* of Bernard Garel-Jones and Meriel Garel-Jones (*née* Williams); *m* 1966, Catalina (*née* Garrigues); four *s* one *d*. *Educ:* The King's Sch., Canterbury. Principal, Language Sch., Madrid, Spain, 1960–70; Merchant Banker, 1970–74; worked for Cons. Party, 1974–79 (Personal Asst to Party Chm., 1978–79). Contested (C): Caernarvon, Feb. 1974; Watford, Oct. 1974. MP (C) Watford, 1979–97. PPS to Minister of State, CSD, 1981; Asst Govt Whip, 1982–83; a Lord Comr of HM Treasury, 1983–86; Vice-Chamberlain of HM Household, 1986–88; Comptroller of HM Household, 1988–89; Treasurer of HM Household and Dep. Chief Whip, 1989–90; Minister of State, FCO, 1990–93. *Recreation:* collecting books. *Address:* House of Lords, SW1A 0PW.

GARFORTH, Prof. Christopher James, PhD; Professor of Agricultural Extension and Rural Development, University of Reading, 1995–2013, now Emeritus; *b* Hull, 15 Nov. 1950; *s* of Francis William Garforth and Francesca Mary Garforth; *m* 1971, Sally Boyes; three *d*. *Educ:* Hymers Coll., Hull; Queens' Coll., Cambridge (BA Classics and Land Econ. 1972; PhD 1977). Sen. Res. Officer, Newcastle upon Tyne CC, 1975–77; Action Res. Officer, Min. of Agric., Botswana, 1977–80; Lectr, 1980–87, Sen. Lectr, 1987–95, Univ. of Reading. Chm., Tropical Agric. Assoc., 2008–12; Mem., Develt Studies Assoc., 1990–. *Publications:* contrib. papers to internat. jls. *Recreations:* walking, music, allotment gardening. *Address:* Pear Tree Cottage, Wrench Green, Hackness, Scarborough YO13 9AB. *T:* (01723) 882159, 07730 532746. *E:* c.j.garforth@reading.ac.uk.

GARGAN, Nicholas James, QPM 2012; Chief Constable, Avon and Somerset Constabulary, since 2013; *b* York, 7 Dec. 1966; *s* of Anthony Patrick and Jean Anne Gargan. *Educ:* Bar Grammar Sch., York; Univ. of Leicester (BA Hons French and Politics 1988). Leicestershire Constabulary: Police Constable, 1988–91; Sergeant, 1991–93; Inspector, 1993–95; on secondment to the Nat. Criminal Intelligence Service (Interpol), 1995–98; Chief Inspector, 1998–2001; Detective Superintendent, 2001–03; Chief Superintendent, E Area Comdr, 2003–06; Asst Chief Constable, Thames Valley Police, 2006–09; Dep. CEO, 2010, Chief Constable and Chief Exec., 2010–13, Nat. Policing Improvement Agency. *Recreations:* running, cycling, watching Leicester City FC, opera. *Address:* Avon and Somerset Constabulary, PO Box 37, Valley Road, Portishead, Bristol BS20 8QJ. *T:* (01275) 816007. *E:* nick.gargan@avonandsomerset.police.uk.

GARLAND, Basil; Registrar, Family Division of High Court of Justice (formerly Probate, Divorce and Admiralty Division), 1969–85; *b* 30 May 1920; *oc* of late Herbert George Garland and Grace Alice Mary Martha Garland; *m* 1942, Dora Mary Sudell Hope (*d* 2008); one *s*. *Educ:* Dulwich Coll.; Pembroke Coll., Oxford (MA). Served in Royal Artillery, 1940–46: commnd 1941; Staff Officer, HQ RA, Gibraltar, 1943–45; Hon. Major 1946. Called to Bar, Middle Temple, 1948; Treasury Junior Counsel (Probate), 1965; Registrar, Principal Probate Registry, 1969. *Publications:* articles in Law Jl. *Recreations:* sailing, drama, painting. *Address:* Christmas Cottage, Blyth's Lane, Wivenhoe, Colchester, Essex CO7 9BG. *T:* (01206) 827566. *Club:* Bar Yacht.

GARLAND, Nicholas Withycombe, OBE 1998; Political Cartoonist, The Daily Telegraph, 1966–86 and 1991–2011; *b* 1 Sept. 1935; *s* of Tom and Peggy Garland; *m* 1st, 1964, Harriet Crittall (marr. diss. 1968); 2nd, 1969, Caroline Beatrice (marr. diss. 1994), *d* of Sir Peter Medawar, OM, CH, CBE, FRS; three *s* one *d*; 3rd, 1995, Priscilla Roth (*née* Brandchaft). *Educ:* Slade School of Fine Art. Worked in theatre as stage man. and dir, 1958–64; Political Cartoonist: New Statesman, 1971–78; The Independent, 1986–91; drew regularly for The Spectator, 1979–95; with Barry Humphries created and drew comic strip, Barry McKenzie, in Private Eye. *Publications:* (illustrated) Horatius, by T. B. Macaulay, 1977; An Indian Journal, 1983; Twenty Years of Cartoons by Garland, 1984; Travels with my Sketchbook, 1987; Not Many Dead, 1990; (illustrated) The Coma, by Alex Garland, 2004; I Wish..., 2007. *E:* nicholasgarland@blueyonder.co.uk.

GARLAND, Sir Patrick (Neville), Kt 1985; a Judge of the High Court, Queen's Bench Division, 1985–2002; Senior Trial Judge, England and Wales, 2000–02; *b* 22 July 1929; *s* of Frank Neville Garland and Marjorie Garland; *m* 1955, Jane Elizabeth Bird; two *s* one *d*. *Educ:* Uppingham Sch. (Scholar); Sidney Sussex Coll., Cambridge (Exhibnr and Prizeman; MA, LLM; Hon. Fellow, 1991). Called to the Bar, Middle Temple, 1953, Bencher, 1979. Asst Recorder, Norwich, 1971; a Recorder, 1972–85; QC 1972; Dep. High Court Judge, 1981–85; a Judge of the Employment Appeal Tribunal, 1986–95; Presiding Judge, SE Circuit, 1989–93. Mem., Judges' Council, 1993–94. President: Central Probation Council (formerly Central Council of Probation Cttees), 1986–2001; Technol. and Construction Bar Assoc., 1985–2002; Mem., Parole Bd, 1988–91 (Vice-Chm., 1989–91). *Publications:* articles in legal and technical jls. *Recreations:* shooting, gardening, industrial archaeology. *Address:* 9 Ranulf Road, NW2 2BT. *Clubs:* Savage, Royal Over-Seas League; Norfolk (Norwich); Cumberland Lawn Tennis.

GARLAND, Prof. Peter Bryan, CBE 1999; PhD; FRSE; Professor of Biochemistry, Institute of Cancer Research, University of London, 1992–99, now Emeritus Professor (Chief Executive, 1989–99); *b* 31 Jan. 1934; *s* of Frederick George Garland and Molly Kate Jones; *m* 1959, Ann Bathurst; one *s* two *d*. *Educ:* Hardye's Sch., Dorchester; Downing Coll., Cambridge (BA 1st Class Hons in Physical Anthropol., 1955; BChir 1958, MB 1959; PhD 1964); King's Coll. Hosp. Med. Sch. (Burney Yeo Schol.). MRC Res. Schol., Chem. Pathol. Dept, KCH Med. Sch., and Biochem. Dept, UCL, 1959–61; British Insulin Manufacturers' Fellow, Biochem. Dept, Cambridge Univ., 1961–64; Lectr, 1964–68, Reader, 1969–70 in Biochem., Bristol Univ.; Prof. of Biochem., Dundee Univ., 1970–84; Principal Scientist and Hd, Biosciences Div., Unilever Research, 1984–87; Dir of Research, Amersham Internat., 1987–89. Vis. Prof., Johnson Res. Foundn, Philadelphia, 1967–69; Vis. Fellow, ANU, 1983. Member: MRC, 1980–84 (Chm., Cell Biol.-Disorders Bd, 1980–82); EMBO, 1981; CRC Scientific Policy Cttee, 1985–92. Director: CRC Technology Ltd, 1988–96 (Chm., 1988–91); CAT plc, 1990–2004 (Chm., 1995–2004). FRSE 1977. Hon. Fellow, UCL, 1999. Hon. LLD Dundee, 1990; Hon. DSc London, 2012. Colworth Medal, Biochem. Soc., 1970. *Publications:* numerous articles in biochemistry and biophysics. *Recreations:* sport (athletics blue, Cambridge, 1954–55), ski-ing, sailing, windsurfing, reading. *Address:* Hope Cottage, Sunny Way, Bosham, W Sussex PO18 8HQ. *Club:* Bosham Sailing.

GARLAND, Peter Leslie, CB 2002; Director, Health and Social Care (Northern), Department of Health, 2002–03; *b* 21 Sept. 1946; *s* of Leslie and Stella Garland; *m* 1979, Janet Rosemary Prescott; three *d*. *Educ:* Bristol Cathedral Sch.; Manchester Univ. Joined DHSS, 1974; Asst Sec. 1989; Under Sec. and Dep. Dir of Finance, 1993–99, Regl Dir, Northern and Yorks Reg., 1999–2002, NHS Exec., DoH. *Recreations:* family, gardening. *Address:* 140 Curly Hill, Ilkley, W Yorks LS29 0DS.

GARLAND, Hon. Sir (Ransley) Victor, KBE 1982; High Commissioner for Australia in the United Kingdom, 1981–83; *b* 5 May 1934; *m* 1960, Lynette Jamieson, BMus (Melb.); two *s* one *d*. *Educ:* Univ. of Western Australia. BA(Econ); FCA. Practised as Chartered Accountant, 1958–70. Director: Prudential Corp., 1984–93; Mitchell Cotts PLC, 1984–86; Govett Funds Inc., 1991–2000 (Pres., 1997–2000). MP for Curtin, Australian Federal Parliament, 1969–81; Minister for Supply, 1971–72; Executive Councillor, 1971–; Minister Asstg Treasurer, 1972; Chief Opposition Whip, 1974–75; Minister for Special Trade Representations, also Minister Asstg Minister for Trade and Resources, 1977–79; Minister for Business and Consumer Affairs, 1979–80. Govt Representative Minister: at Commonwealth Ministerial Meeting for Common Fund, London, 1978; at Ministerial Meetings of ESCAP, New Delhi, 1978; Minister representing Treas., at Ministerial Meeting of OECD, Paris, 1978; Leader, Aust. Delegn to UNCTAD V and Chm. Commonwealth Delegns to UNCTAD V, Manila, 1979; attended, with Premier, Commonwealth Heads of Govt meeting, Lusaka, 1979. Parly Adviser, Aust. Mission to UN Gen. Assembly, New York, 1973; Chairman: House of Reps Expenditure Cttee, 1976–77; Govt Members' Treasury Cttee, 1977. Director: Henderson Far East Income Trust PLC, 1984–2006 (Chm., 1990–2006); Throgmorton Trust PLC, 1985–2006; Signet Gp, 1991–92; Nelson Hurst PLC, 1993–94; Fidelity Asian Values PLC, 1996–2010 (Chm., 2000–10). Vice-Chm., South Bank Bd (RFH Complex), 1985–2000; Dir, South Bank Foundn, 1996–2001. Councillor, UK, Royal Commonwealth Society for the Blind, 1988. Freeman, City of London, 1982. *Recreations:* music (chorister, St George's Cathedral, 1942–46), reading, writing, travel.

GARLAND, William George; Editor, Official Report (Hansard), House of Commons, 2002–05; *b* 9 March 1946; *s* of George and Evelyn Garland; *m* 1st, 1969, Sally Doyle (marr. diss. 1985); one *s* one *d*; 2nd, 1993, Mary Frances Finch. *Educ:* Sir Joseph Williamson's Mathematical Sch., Rochester. Jun. Cttee Clerk, Northfleet Council, 1963–65; News Reporter, Kent Messenger Gp, 1965–70; Parly Reporter, Press Assoc., 1970–75; Hansard, 1975–2005. Sec., Commonwealth Hansard Editors Assoc., 2002–05. *Recreations:* theatre, watching cricket and football.

GARLAND-THOMAS, Jane Elizabeth; Her Honour Judge Garland-Thomas; a Circuit Judge, since 2014; *b* Swansea, 15 July 1956; *d* of Griffith Thomas Mepham David and Barbara Doris David; *m* 1st, 1979, William Paul Garland-Thomas (marr. diss. 1996); one *s* one *d*; 2nd, 1999, Jason Paul Thomas. *Educ:* Glanmor Girls' Grammar Sch., Swansea; Bishop Gore Comp. Sch., Swansea; Univ. of Bristol (LLB Hons 1977); Swansea Univ. (BA Hons Ancient Hist. 2009). Admitted solicitor, 1980; solicitor, 1980–2001; a Dep. Dist Judge, 1999–2001; Dist Judge, 2001–14. *Recreations:* walking, ancient history, cooking, reading. *Address:* Swansea Civil Justice Centre, Caravella House, Quay West, Quay Parade, Swansea SA1 1SP. *T:* (01792) 485800, *Fax:* (01792) 485810.

GARLICK, Rev. Preb. Kathleen Beatrice, (Kay); DL; Chaplain to the Queen, since 2011; *b* 26 Feb. 1949; *d* of Arthur and Beatrice Harris; *m* 1973, Dr Peter Garlick; one *s* three *d*. *Educ:* Prendergast Grammar Sch.; Leeds Univ. (BA Hons Music); Birmingham Univ. (PGCE); Gloucester Sch. for Ministry. Music teacher, Kidbrooke Comprehensive Sch., 1973–75; mother and housewife, 1975–87; ordained priest, 1990; NSM, Birch Gp of parishes, Hereford dio., 1990–96; Chaplain, Hereford Sixth Form Coll., 1996–2002; Rector, Wormelow Hundred Benefice, 2002–09; Cathedral Chaplain, Hereford Cathedral, 2009–13. Member: Gen. Synod of C of E, 1995–2010 (Chair, Business Cttee, 2006–10); Archbishop's Council, 2006–10. DL Herefordshire, 2013. *Recreations:* playing and singing Early Music (Medieval and Renaissance), directing choirs and persuading and encouraging even the least confident to sing. *Address:* Birch Lodge, Much Birch, Herefordshire HR2 8HT. *T:* (01981) 540666. *E:* kaygarlick@hotmail.com.

GARLICK, Paul Richard; QC 1996; a Recorder, since 1997; *b* 14 Aug. 1952; *s* of late Arthur Garlick and of Dorothy Garlick (*née* Allan). *Educ:* Liverpool Univ. (LLB 1973). Called to the Bar, Middle Temple, 1974, Bencher, 2005; Standing Counsel to HM Customs and Excise, 1990–96; Asst Recorder, 1993–97. Internat. Judge, War Crimes Chamber of State Court of Bosnia and Herzegovina, 2005–06. Trustee, Redress, 2004–09. Mem., Justice, 2003–. *Recreations:* music, cooking, walking, travel. *Address:* Furnival Chambers, 30–32 Furnival Street, EC4A 1JQ. *T:* (020) 7405 3322.

GARLING, David John Haldane, (Ben), ScD; Reader in Mathematical Analysis, Cambridge University, 1978–99, now Emeritus; Fellow of St John's College, Cambridge, since 1963; *b* 26 July 1937; *s* of Leslie Ernest Garling and Frances Margaret Garling; *m* 1963, Anthea Mary Eileen Dixon; two *s* one *d*. *Educ:* Highgate Sch.; St John's Coll., Cambridge (BA, MA, PhD; ScD 1978). Cambridge University: Asst Lectr, 1963–64; Lectr, 1964–78; Head of Dept of Pure Maths and Math. Stats, 1984–91; Pro-Proctor, 1995–96, Sen. Proctor, 1996–97, Dep. Proctor, 1997–98; Tutor, 1971–78, Pres., 1987–91, St John's Coll. Mem., SERC Mathematics Cttee, 1983–86. Exec. Sec., London Mathematical Soc., 1998–2002 (Mem. Council, 1986–88 and 1995–98; Meetings and Membership Sec., 1995–98). *Publications:* A Course in Galois Theory, 1987; Inequalities, 2007; Clifford Algebras, 2011; papers in sci. jls. *Address:* St John's College, Cambridge CB2 1TP. *T:* (01223) 338600.

GARMOYLE, Viscount; Hugh Sebastian Frederick Cairns; Partner, Venrex Investment Management, since 2009; Director: Hampden Agencies Ltd, since 2010; Hampden Capital Ltd, since 2010; Devonshire Homes (Bracken) Ltd, since 2010; RateSetter, since 2011; Red Savannah, since 2011; *b* 26 March 1965; *s* and *heir* of Earl Cairns, *qv*; *m* 1991, Juliet, *d* of

Andrew Eustace Palmer, *qv*; one *s* two *d*. *Educ:* Eton; Edinburgh Univ. (MA Hons); London Coll. of Law. With Freshfields, solicitors, 1990–94; Partner, 1999–2001, Man. Dir, 2002–08, Cazenove, stockbrokers, subseq. JPMorgan Cazenove. *Heir: s* Hon. Oliver David Andrew Cairns, *b* 7 March 1993.

GARNER, Alan, OBE 2001; FSA, FRSL; author; *b* 17 Oct. 1934; *s* of Colin and Marjorie Garner; *m* 1st, 1956, Ann Cook; one *s* two *d*; 2nd, 1972, Griselda Greaves; one *s* one *d*. *Educ:* Alderley Edge Council Sch.; Manchester Grammar Sch.; Magdalen Coll., Oxford. Writer and presenter, documentary films: Places and Things, 1978; Images, 1981 (First Prize, Chicago Internat. Film Fest.). Vis. Prof., Sch. of Applied Scis, Univ. of Huddersfield, 2012. Mem. Internat. Editl Bd, Detskaya Literatura Publishers, Moscow, 1991–. Co-Founder, Blackden Trust, 2004. Garner Lect., Jodrell Bank Discovery Centre, 2015. FSA 2007; FRSL 2012. Hon. DLitt: Warwick, 2010; Salford, 2011; Manchester Metropolitan, 2013; DUniv Huddersfield, 2012. Karl Edward Wagner Special Award, British Fantasy Soc., 2003; World Fantasy Lifetime Award, World Fantasy Convention, Toronto, 2012. *Publications:* The Weirdstone of Brisingamen, 1960 (Lewis Carroll Shelf Award, USA, 1970); The Moon of Gomrath, 1963; Elidor, 1965; Holly from the Bongs, 1966; The Old Man of Mow, 1967; The Owl Service, 1967 (Library Assoc. Carnegie Medal 1967, Guardian Award 1968); The Hamish Hamilton Book of Goblins, 1969; Red Shift, 1973 (with John Mackenzie, filmed 1978); (with Albin Trowski) The Breadhorse, 1975; The Guizer, 1975; The Stone Book, 1976 (Phoenix Award, Children's Lit. Assoc. of Amer., 1996); Tom Fobble's Day, 1977; Granny Reardun, 1977; The Aimer Gate, 1978; Fairy Tales of Gold, 1979; The Lad of the Gad, 1980; Alan Garner's Book of British Fairy Tales, 1984; A Bag of Moonshine, 1986; Jack and the Beanstalk, 1992; Once Upon a Time, 1993; Strandloper, 1996; The Voice That Thunders, 1997; The Little Red Hen, 1997; The Well of the Wind, 1998; Grey Wolf, Prince Jack and the Firebird, 1998; Approach to the Edge, 1998; Thursbitch, 2003; By Seven Firs and Goldenstone, 2010; Collected Folk Tales, 2011; Boneland, 2012; *plays:* Lamaload, 1978; Lurga Lom, 1980; To Kill a King, 1980; Sally Water, 1982; The Keeper, 1983; Out of the Dark, 2015; *dance drama:* The Green Mist, 1970; *libretti:* The Bellybag, 1971 (music by Richard Morris); Potter Thompson, 1972 (music by Gordon Crosse); Lord Flame, 1995; *screenplay:* Strandloper, 1992. *Recreation:* work. *Address:* Blackden, Cheshire CW4 8BY. *Club:* Portico Library (Manchester).

GARNER, Prof. (Christopher) David, PhD; FRS 1997; CChem, FRSC; Professor of Biological Inorganic Chemistry, University of Nottingham, 1999–2010, now Emeritus; *b* 9 Nov. 1941; *s* of Richard Norman Garner and Chrystabel (*née* Potts); *m* 1968, Pamela Eva Kershaw; one *s* one *d*. *Educ:* Cheadle Hulme Warehousemen & Clerk's Orphans' Sch.; Nottingham Univ. (BSc 1st Cl. Hons Chem. 1963; PhD 1966). CChem 1982; FRSC 1982. Post-doctoral Res. Fellow, CIT, 1966–67; ICI Res. Fellow, Univ. of Nottingham, 1967–68; University of Manchester: Lectr in Chemistry, 1968–78; Sen. Lectr, 1978–84; Prof. of Inorganic Chemistry, 1984–99; Hd of Chemistry, 1988–96; Mem. Court, 1995–99; Mem. Council, 1996–99. Vis. Prof., Univ. of Lausanne, 1977; Frontiers in Chem. Res. Vis. Prof., Texas A&M Univ., 1987; Visiting Professor: Strasbourg Univ., 1990–92; Univ. of Florence, 1995; Univ. of Arizona, 1998; Sydney Univ., 2000; Wilsmore Fellow, Univ. of Melbourne, 1994; Bye Fellow and Fellow, Robinson Coll., Cambridge, 1997. Chm., Metbio Prog., ESF, 1994–98. Royal Society of Chemistry: Pres., Dalton Div., 2001–04; Mem. Council, 2005–; Pres., 2008–10; Tilden Medal, 1985; Chatt Lectr, 1999; Inorganic Biochem. Award, 2002; Ludwig Mond Lectr, 2007–08. Founding Pres., Soc. Biol Inorganic Chem., 1996–98. Hon. Fellow, Chinese Chemical Soc., 2009. Elder, URC, Bramhall, and Chm., Devlt Gp, 1990–98. Ed., Phil. Trans A, Royal Soc., 2011–; Ed.-in-Chief, RSC Metallobiol. textbook series. *Publications:* over 400 original res. papers and reviews, primarily concerned with roles of transition metals in biological systems and devlt of chemical analogues for centres which occur in nature. *Recreations:* spending time with family and friends, attending theatre, dining out, listening to classical music and popular music of 1960s and 1970s. *Address:* School of Chemistry, Nottingham University, Nottingham NG7 2RD. *T:* (0115) 921 2711.

GARNER, John Donald, CMG 1988; CVO 1991 (LVO 1979); HM Diplomatic Service, retired; *b* 15 April 1931; *s* of late Ronald Garner and Doris Ethel Garner (*née* Norton); *m* Karen Maria Conway; two *d*. *Educ:* Trinity Grammar Sch., N22. Royal Navy, National Service, 1949–51. Foreign Office, 1952–55; Third Secretary: Seoul, 1955; Bangkok, 1957; Foreign Office, 1959–63; Second Secretary: Benghazi and Tripoli, 1963–67; Sydney, 1967–69; First Sec., Tel Aviv, 1969–73; FCO, 1973–76; NDC 1976; Dep. High Commissioner, Lilongwe, 1977–80; Chargé d'affaires, Kabul, 1981–84; High Comr, The Gambia, 1984–87; Consul-Gen., Houston, 1988–91. Rep. of Sec. of State for Foreign and Commonwealth Affairs, 1996–2011. *Recreation:* golf. *Address:* 30 The Green, N14 6EN. *T:* (020) 8882 6808. *Club:* South Herts Golf.

GARNER, His Honour Michael Scott; a Circuit Judge, 1988–2004; *b* 10 April 1939; *s* of William Garner and Doris Mary (*née* Scott); *m* 1st, 1964, Sheila Margaret (*d* 1981) (*née* Garland); one *s* one *d*; 2nd, 1982, Margaret Anne (*née* Senior). *Educ:* Huddersfield Coll.; Manchester Univ. (LLB). Admitted Solicitor, 1965. Asst Recorder, 1978–85; a Recorder, 1985–88. *Recreations:* reading, walking, gardening, motoring, cooking.

GARNER, Rosamund; Headteacher, Newport Girls' High School, since 2011; *b* Wolverhampton, 17 March 1958; *d* of Kenneth and Jean Hodgkiss; *m* 1981, Kevin Garner; two *c*. *Educ:* Highfields Sch.; Wolverhampton Univ. (BA Hons Humanities); W Midlands Coll. (PGCE); Nottingham Univ. (MBA Public Services (Educn)). NPQH. Queen Mary's High Sch., 1980–2011. *Recreations:* walking, gardening, ski-ing, family. *Address:* Newport Girls' High School, Wellington Road, Newport, Shropshire TF10 7HL. *T:* (01952) 797552. *E:* r.garner@nghs.org.uk. *Club:* Lansdowne.

GARNETT, Ven. David Christopher; Archdeacon of Chesterfield, 1996–2009, now Archdeacon Emeritus; Priest-in-charge, Beeley and Edensor, 2007–12; *b* 26 Sept. 1945; *s* of Douglas and Audrey Garnett; *m* 1974, Susanne Crawford; two *s*. *Educ:* Giggleswick Sch.; Nottingham Univ. (BA Hons); Fitzwilliam Coll., Cambridge (BA Hons); Westcott House, Cambridge; MA Cantab. Curate of Cottingham, E Yorks, 1969–72; Chaplain, Fellow, Tutor, Selwyn Coll. and Pastoral Advr, Newnham Coll., Cambridge, 1972–77; Rector of Patterdale and Diocesan Dir of Ordinands, Carlisle, 1977–80; Vicar of Heald Green, Dio. Chester and Chaplain, St Ann's Hospice, 1980–87; Rector of Christleton and Chm., Bishop's Theol Adv. Gp, 1987–92; Team Rector, Ellesmere Port, 1992–96; Canon of Derby Cathedral, 1996–2009, now Canon Emeritus. Mem. Gen. Synod, 1990–96, 2000–05. Chm., Univ. Chaplaincy Council, 1996–2013; Mem. Council, Derby Univ., 2004–12. *Recreations:* clarinet playing, dog training, gardening. *Club:* Poultry of Great Britain.

GARNETT, Adm. Sir Ian (David Graham), KCB 1998; Commandant, Royal College of Defence Studies, 2005–08; *b* 27 Sept. 1944; *s* of late Capt. Ian Graham Hartt Garnett, DSC, RN and Barbara Anne Langrishe (*née* Hackett); *m* 1973, Charlotte Mary Anderson; one *s* two *d*. *Educ:* Canford Sch.; BRNC, Dartmouth. Entered RN, 1962; Lt 1967; flying trng, 1968–69; HMS Hermes, 814 Sqdn, 1969–70; Loan Service, RAN, 1971–72; HMS Tiger, 826 Sqdn, 1973–74; Warfare Officer, 1974–76; HMS Blake, Sen. Pilot, 820 Sqdn, 1977–78; Dep. Dir, JMOTS, 1978–80; in comd, HMS Amazon, 1981–82; RN staff course, 1983; Asst Dir, Operational Requirements, 1983–86; Captain Fourth Frigate Sqdn (HMS Active), 1986–88; RN Presentation Team, 1988–89; Dir Operational Requirements, 1989–92; FO Naval Aviation, 1993–95; Dep. SACLANT, 1995–98; Chief of Jt Ops, MoD, 1999–2001; COS SHAPE, 2001–04. Chm., Chatham Historic Dockyard Trust, 2005–; Mem., Commonwealth War Graves Commn, 2006–11 (Vice-Chm., 2008–11). Mem., Fleet Air Arm Officers Assoc., 1992–. *Recreation:* my family and other matters. *Address:* Haslemere, Surrey. *Clubs:* Royal Navy of 1765 and 1785, Army and Navy.

GARNETT, Dame Julia Charity; *see* Cleverdon, Dame J. C.

GARNETT, Kevin Mitchell; QC 1991; Legal Member, Boards of Appeal, 2005–15, and Enlarged Board of Appeal, 2010–15, European Patent Office; *b* 22 June 1950; *s* of Frank Raymond Garnett and Cynthia Ruby Eberstein; *m* 1980, Susan Jane Louise (*née* Diboll); one *s*. *Educ:* Bradfield Coll., Berks; University Coll., Oxford (MA). Called to the Bar, Middle Temple, 1975; Bencher, Lincoln's Inn, 2000. Asst Recorder, 1996–2000; Recorder, 2000–05; a Dep. High Court Judge, 2000–05. Vice-Chm., Cartoon Art Trust, 1994–2005. *Publications:* (ed jtly) Williams, Mortimer and Sunnucks on Executors, Administrators and Probate, 16th edn 1982, 17th edn 1993; (ed jtly) Copinger and Skone James on Copyright, 13th edn 1991 to 16th edn 2010; (contrib.) Copyright and Free Speech, 2005; (jtly) Moral Rights, 2010. *Recreations:* singing, mountain walking, tennis, ski-ing.

GARNHAM, Diana Anjoli; Chief Executive, Science Council, since 2006; *b* 17 Nov. 1954; *d* of George Leslie John Garnham and Monisha Vida (*née* Mander); *m* 2003, Rodney Stewart Buse. *Educ:* Christ's Hosp., Hertford; Lady Margaret Sch., London; Univ. of Leicester (BSocSc (Politics)); King's Coll. London (MA War Studies); University Coll. of Wales, Aberystwyth. Admin. Sec., Council on Christian Approaches to Defence and Disarmament, 1983–87; Association of Medical Research Charities: Exec. Officer, 1987–89; Asst Sec.-Gen., 1989–91; Gen. Sec., then Chief Exec., AMRC, 1991–2005. Member: BBC Appeals Cttee, 1992–98; Bd, Groundwork Southwark, 1995–2002; NHS Standing Cttee (formerly Adv. Gp) on Consumer Involvement in NHS R&D, 1997–2002; Chief Scientist Cttee, Scottish Exec., 1999–2005; COPUS, Royal Soc., 2001–03; HEFCE Res. Strategy Cttee, 2003–06; Panel, UK Stem Cell Initiative, 2005; Nat. Adv. Gp, UK Resource Centre for Women in SET, 2006–10; Forensic Sci. Occupational Cttee, 2006–08; Nat. Scis Cttee, UK Nat. Commn for UNESCO, 2006–11; Chairman: Mgt Bd, Coalition for Med. Progress, 2003–05; Sci. for Careers Expert Gp, DIUS, then BIS, 2009–11; Mem., Technician Council, 2010–14; Ind. Mem., CITB, 2015–. Member: Adv. Cttee, Inst. of Psychiatry, 2003–08; Council, Nottingham Univ., 2003–11; Corp. of South Coast Coll., 2012–; Vice-Chm., Alumni Giving Cttee, KCL, 2011–. Trustee: Sense about Science, 2003–; Internat. Spinal Res. Trust, 2008–11; Mem., Bd, Benevolent Soc. of Blues, 2000–13 (Dep. Chm., 2009–13); Patron, Cae Dai Trust, 2008–; also involved in other charity sector gps. Hon. DLaws Leicester, 2013. *Recreations:* family, friends, music, needlecraft, travel, gardening. *Address:* Science Council, Hodgkin Huxley House, 30 Farringdon Lane, EC1R 3AW. *T:* (020) 3434 2020. *E:* d.garnham@sciencecouncil.org.

GARNHAM, Neil Stephen; QC 2001; barrister; a Recorder, since 2001; a Deputy High Court Judge, since 2008; *b* 11 Feb. 1959; *s* of Geoffrey Arthur Garnham and Cynthia Avril Rose Garnham; *m* 1991, Gillian Mary Shaw; two *s*. *Educ:* Ipswich Sch.; Peterhouse, Cambridge (MA). Called to the Bar, Middle Temple, 1982, Bencher, 2008; a Jun. Counsel to the Crown, 1995–2001. *Address:* 1 Crown Office Row, Temple, EC4Y 7HH. *T:* (020) 7797 7500.

GARNIER, Rt Hon. Sir Edward (Henry), Kt 2012; PC 2015; QC 1995; MP (C) Harborough, since 1992; *b* 26 Oct. 1952; *s* of late Col William d'Arcy Garnier and Hon. Lavender Hyacinth (*née* de Grey); *m* 1982, Anna Caroline Mellows; two *s* one *d*. *Educ:* Wellington Coll.; Jesus Coll., Oxford (BA, MA). Called to the Bar, Middle Temple, 1976, Bencher, 2001; Asst Recorder, 1998–2000; a Recorder, 2000–. Vice-Pres., Hemsworth Assoc., 1987–. Contested: Wandsworth BC by-election, 1984; Tooting ILEA election, 1986; (C) Hemsworth, Gen. Election, 1987. PPS to Ministers of State, FCO, 1994–95; PPS to Attorney General and to Solicitor General, 1995–97, and to Chancellor of the Duchy of Lancaster, 1996–97; Opposition spokesman, Lord Chancellor's Dept, 1997–99; Shadow Attorney-Gen., 1999–2001; Shadow Minister: for Home Affairs, 2005–07; for Justice, 2007–09; Shadow Attorney-Gen., 2009–10; Solicitor Gen., 2010–12. Member: Home Affairs Select Cttee, 1992–95; Jt Cttee on Human Rights, 2014–; Sec., Cons. Foreign Affairs Cttee, 1992–94. Mem., Exec. Cttee, 1922 Cttee, 2001–05. Member: Howard League Commn on Sex in Prison, 2012–; Adv. Bd, Samaritans, 2013–. Patron, Ridley Eye Foundn, 2011–. UK Election Observer: Kenya, 1992; Bosnia, 1996. Vis. Parly Fellow, St Antony's Coll., Oxford, 1996–97. Mem. Bd, Great Britain-China Centre, 1998–2010; Trustee, China-Oxford Scholarship Fund, 2006–10, 2012–. Mem., Leics and Rutland Cttee, 1992–, Legal and Parly Cttee, 1994–2000, CLA. *Publications:* (contrib.) Halsbury's Laws of England, 4th edn, 1985; (contrib.) Bearing the Standard, 1991; (contrib.) Facing the Future, 1993; (contrib.) Lissack and Horlick on Bribery, 2nd edn 2014. *Recreations:* cricket, shooting, opera. *Address:* House of Commons, SW1A 0AA. *T:* (020) 7219 3000. *Clubs:* White's, Pratt's, Beefsteak; Vincent's (Oxford).

GARNIER, Jean-Pierre, Hon. KBE 2008; PhD; Chief Executive, GlaxoSmithKline, 2000–08; *b* 31 Oct. 1947; *m* Danyele; three *d*. *Educ:* Univ. of Louis Pasteur, France (MS, PhD); Stanford Univ., Calif (Fulbright Scholar; MBA 1974). Schering Plough: Gen. Manager of overseas subsidiaries, 1975–83; Sen. Dir of Mktg, 1983–84, Vice-Pres. of Mktg, 1984–85, Sen. Vice-Pres. and Gen. Manager for Sales and Mktg, 1987–88, Pres., 1989–90, US Pharmaceutical Products Div.; SmithKline Beecham: Pres., pharmaceutical business in N America, 1990–93; Exec. Dir, 1992–2000; Exec. Vice-Pres., 1993–94, Chm., 1994–95, Pharmaceuticals; Chief Operating Officer, 1995–2000; Chief Exec., 2000; Chief Exec., Pierre Fabre Group, 2008–10. Dir, United Technologies Corp., 1997–. Mem., Adv. Bd, Dubai Internat. Capital, 2008. Officier de la Légion d'Honneur (France), 2007 (Chevalier, 1997).

GARNIER, Rear-Adm. Sir John, KCVO 1990 (LVO 1965); CBE 1982; Extra Equerry to the Queen, since 1988; *b* 10 March 1934; *s* of Rev. Thomas Vernon Garnier and Helen Stenhouse; *m* 1966, Joanna Jane Cadbury; two *s* one *d*. *Educ:* Berkhamsted School; Britannia Royal Naval College. Joined RN 1950; served HM Yacht Britannia, 1956–57; HMS Tyne (Suez Operation) 1956; qualified navigation specialist, 1959; Naval Equerry to HM Queen, 1962–65; Comd HMS Dundas, 1968–69; Directorate of Naval Ops and Trade, 1969–71; Comd HMS Minerva, 1972–73; Defence Policy Staff, 1973–75; HMS Intrepid, 1976; Asst Dir, Naval Manpower Planning, 1976–78; RCDS 1979; Comd HMS London, 1980–81; Dir, Naval Ops and Trade, 1982–84; Commodore Amphibious Warfare, 1985; Flag Officer Royal Yachts, 1985–90. Private Sec. and Comptroller to HRH Princess Alexandra, 1991–95. Younger Brother of Trinity House, 1974. Mem., Council, Shipwrecked Fishermen and Mariners' Royal Benevolent Soc., 1996–2004. Gov., Sherborne Sch. for Girls, 1985–2004. Freeman of City of London, 1982. *Recreations:* sailing, golf, gardening, opera. *Address:* Bembury Farm, Thornford, Sherborne, Dorset DT9 6QF.

GARNIER, Mark Robert Timothy; MP (C) Wyre Forest, since 2010; *b* London, 26 Feb. 1963; *s* of Peter Garnier and Patricia Garnier (*née* Dowden); *m* 2001, Caroline Louise Joyce; two *s* one *d*. *Educ:* Charterhouse. Associate Director: W. I. Carr (Overseas Ltd), 1982–86; Swiss Bank Corp. Internat., 1986–88; Man. Dir, S China Securities (UK) Ltd, 1988–95; Exec. Dir, Daiwa (Europe Ltd), 1995–96; Associate Director: L. C. F. Edmond de Rothschild Securities, 1996–97; Bear Stearns, 1998; Dir, Meilen Asset Mgt, 1999–2005; Partner: CGR Capital LLP, 2006–08; Severn-Capital LLP, 2008–. Member: Treasury Select Cttee, 2010–; Finance Select Cttee, 2015–; Parly Commn on Banking Standards, 2012–13. FCSI (FSI 2007). Mem. Ct, Coachmakers' Co., 2003. *Recreations:* historic motor sport and aviation, target rifle shooting, photography, ski-ing. *Address:* House of Commons, SW1A 0AA. *T:* (020) 7219 7198. *E:* mark.garnier.mp@parliament.uk. *Clubs:* Carlton, Royal Automobile; North London Rifle.

GARNOCK, Viscount; William James Lindesay-Bethune; *b* 30 Dec. 1990; *s* and *heir* of Earl of Lindsay, *qv*.

GARNON, Tudor Mansel; Employment Judge (formerly Chairman of Employment Tribunals), Newcastle Region, since 2002; *b* 19 Oct. 1953; *s* of David Carey Garnon and Marian Garnon; *m* 1976, Jean Davina Hewet; one *d*. *Educ:* Trinity Hall, Cambridge (MA). Admitted as solicitor, 1978; Partner, Richard Reed and Co., Solicitors, 1980–92; sole practitioner, Garnon and Co., 1993–99; Partner, McArdles, Solicitors, 2000–01; Chm., Employment Tribunals, London NW, 2001–02. *Recreation:* various sports. *Address:* 139 Priors Grange, High Pittington, Durham DH6 1DF. *T:* (0191) 372 0367.

GARNSEY, Prof. Peter David Arthur, FBA 1993; Fellow of Jesus College, Cambridge, 1974–2006, now Emeritus; *b* 22 Oct. 1938; *m* 1967, Elizabeth Franklin; one *s* two *d*. *Educ:* Sydney Univ. (BA); Rhodes Scholar, 1961; MA 1967, DPhil 1967, Oxon; PhD Cantab 1974. Jun. Fellow, University Coll., Oxford, 1964–67; Asst, then Associate, Prof., Univ. of Calif, Berkeley, 1967–73; Cambridge University: Lectr, 1974–90; Reader in Ancient History, 1990–97; Prof. of the Hist. of Classical Antiquity, 1997–2006; Dir of Res., 2006–07. Hon. FAHA 2001. *Publications:* Social Status and Legal Privilege in the Roman Empire, 1970; (ed jtly) Imperialism in the Ancient World, 1978; (ed jtly) Trade and Famine in Classical Antiquity, 1983; (ed) Nonslave Labour in the Graeco-Roman World, 1980; (jtly) Early Principate: Augustus to Trajan, 1982; (ed jtly) Trade in the Ancient Economy, 1983; (jtly) Roman Empire: economy, society and culture, 1987; Famine and Food Supply in the Graeco-Roman World, 1988; (ed) Food, Health and Culture in Classical Antiquity, 1989; Ideas of Slavery from Aristotle to Augustine, 1996; (ed jtly) Hellenistic Constructs: essays in culture, history and historiography, 1997; (ed jtly) Cambridge Ancient History XIII: the Late Empire AD325–425, 1998; Cities, Peasants and Food in Classical Antiquity, 1998; Food and Society in Classical Antiquity, 1999; (ed jtly) Cambridge Ancient History XI: the High Empire AD70–192, 2000; (jtly) The Evolution of the Late Antique World, 2001; (jtly) Lactantius, Divine Institutes (trans. with introduction and notes), 2003; (ed jtly) Cambridge Ancient History XII: the crisis of empire AD193–337, 2005; Thinking about Property: from antiquity to the age of revolution, 2007. *Address:* Jesus College, Cambridge CB5 8BL.

GARRAD, Dr Andrew Douglas, CEng, FREng; FIMechE, FRAeS; Member, Supervisory Board, DNV GL Energy, since 2013; Chairman, GL Garrad Hassan, 2012–13 (President, 2009–12); *b* Braunston, Northants, 8 Nov. 1953; *s* of John Douglas Garrad and Mary Ann Garrad; *m* 1982, Emma Balfour; one *s* three *d*. *Educ:* Marlborough Coll., Wilts; New Coll., Oxford (BA Engrg Sci. 1974; Hon. Fellow 2014); Univ. of Exeter (PhD 1979). CEng 1982; FIMechE 2006. Man. Dir, Garrad Hassan Gp Ltd, 1984–2009; merged with Germanischer Lloyd AS, to become GL Garrad Hassan, 2009. Chm., British Wind Energy Assoc., 1994; Board Member: Eur. Wind Energy Assoc., 1999– (Pres., 2013–); Global Wind Energy Council, 2005–. Chm., Bristol European Green Capital 2015, 2014–March 2016. Mem. Council, Univ. of Bristol, 2012–. Trustee, Centre for Sustainable Energy, 2005–. FEI 2005; FRAeS 2007; FREng 2011. Hon. DEng Bristol, 2009. Mem., Soc. of Merchant Venturers, 2007–. Poul la Cour Prize, Eur. Wind Energy Assoc., 2006; AIOLOS Prize, Helenic Wind Energy Assoc., 2015. *Publications:* Wind Energy Conversion Systems, 1990; Wind Energy: the facts, 2004. *Recreations:* farming, mowing, croquet, mathematics. *Address:* DNV GL, St Vincent's Works, Silverthorne Lane, Bristol BS2 0QD. *T:* (0117) 972 9948. *E:* andrew.garrad@dnvgl.com.

GARRARD, Rt Rev. Richard; an Hon. Assistant Bishop: Diocese of Europe, since 2001; Diocese of Norwich, since 2003; Hon. Assisting Bishop, American Episcopal Convocation of Churches, since 2001; *b* 24 May 1937; *s* of Charles John Garrard and Marjorie Louise (*née* Pow); *m* 1961, Elizabeth Ann Sewell; one *s* one *d*. *Educ:* Northampton Grammar Sch.; King's Coll., Univ. of London (BD, AKC). Ordained deacon, 1961, priest, 1962; Assistant Curate: St Mary's, Woolwich, 1961–66; Great St Mary's, Cambridge, 1966–68; Chaplain/Lectr, Keswick Hall Coll. of Educn, Norwich, 1968–74; Principal, Church Army Training Coll., 1974–79; Canon Chancellor, Southwark Cathedral and Dir of Training, dio. of Southwark, 1979–87; Canon Residentiary, St James's Cathedral, Bury St Edmunds and Advr for Clergy Training, dio. of St Edmundsbury and Ipswich, 1987–91; Archdeacon of Sudbury, 1991–94; Suffragan Bp of Penrith, 1994–2001; Dir, Anglican Centre in Rome, and Archbp of Canterbury's Rep. to the Holy See, 2001–03. *Publications:* Lent with St Mark, 1992; A Time to Pray, 1993; Love on the Cross, 1995. *Recreations:* cats, crosswords, Italy, the fells. *Address:* 26 Carol Close, Stoke Holy Cross, Norwich, Norfolk NR14 8NN.

GARRARD, Susan Björg; Senior Vice President of Global Communications, since 2011, and of Sustainable Business Development, since 2014, Unilever; *b* Birmingham, 30 Aug. 1960; *d* of George Robert Anderson and Evelyn Björg Anderson; *m* 1988, Dr Martin Peyton Garrard. *Educ:* Malvern Girls' Coll. Dept of Energy, 1979–86; Young & Rubicam, 1986–91; Director: Abbott Mead Vickers, 1991–2001; Fishburn Hedges, 2001–07; Communications Dir, 2007–09, Dir Gen., Communications and Customer Strategy, 2009–10, DWP. Member: British Dressage; British Horse Soc. *Recreations:* dressage, dog walking, cooking, reading. *Address:* Unilever plc, 100 Victoria Embankment, Blackfriars, EC4Y 0DY. *Club:* Women in Advertising and Communications London.

GARRÉ, Philomene Korinna Kornelia S.; *see* Magers, P. K. K.

GARRETA, Caroline; *see* Dinenage, C.

GARRETT, Sir Anthony (Peter), Kt 1997; CBE 1992; General Secretary, Association of British Dispensing Opticians, since 1999; *b* Jersey, 28 Nov. 1952; *m* 1st, 1974 (marr. diss. 1985); twin *d*; 2nd, 1989, Jane Wight Scott; two *d*. *Educ:* Canterbury Tech. High Sch. for Boys. Conservative Party Organisation, 1971–98: Constituency Agent, Rochester and Chatham, 1973–79; Cons. Central Office, 1979–98: SE Area Office, 1979–86; Asst Dir, Campaigning, 1986–92; Dir of Campaigning, 1992–98; Mem., Cons. Bd of Mgt, 1993–98. Pres., Cons. Agents' Benevolent Fund, 1992–98 and 2014– (Trustee, 2001–); Trustee, Cons. Agents' Superannuation Fund, 1992–98. *Recreations:* cricket, travel. *Address:* c/o Association of British Dispensing Opticians, 199 Gloucester Terrace, W2 6HX. *Clubs:* Carlton; Kent CC (Life Mem.).

GARRETT, Charles Edmund; HM Diplomatic Service; Ambassador to Macedonia, since 2014; *b* Helsinki, 16 April 1963; *s* of Terence Garrett, *qv*; *m* 1991, Véronique Barnes; three *s* two *d*. *Educ:* Winchester Coll.; Sch. of Slavonic and E European Studies, Univ. of London (BA Hons Russian Studies). With Barclays Bank Internat., 1985–87; entered FCO, 1987; Econ. Relns Dept, FCO, 1987–88; Sino-British Jt Liaison Gp, Hong Kong, 1988–89 and 1990–93; Third Sec., Nicosia, 1989; Hong Kong Dept, FCO, 1993–95; Head: Balkans Team, UK Know How Fund, FCO, 1995–97; Political and Public Affairs, Berne, 1997–2001; Dep. Hd, Central Eur. Dept, FCO, 2001–03; Hd, EU Enlargement Team, FCO, 2003–05; Dep. Dir, British Trade and Cultural Office, Taipei, 2005–09; Strategic Finance Team, FCO, 2009–10; on secondment as: Hd, Internat. Relns, LOCOG, 2010–12; Foreign Affairs Liaison, Queen Elizabeth Diamond Jubilee Trust, 2012–14. *Recreations:* mountaineering, cycling. *Address:* c/o Foreign and Commonwealth Office, King Charles Street, SW1A 2AH. *E:* cegarrett33@gmail.com.

GARRETT, Godfrey John, OBE 1982; HM Diplomatic Service, retired; consultant on Central and Eastern Europe, since 1996, and on Global Conflict Prevention Policy to HM Government, 2004–06; *b* 24 July 1937; *s* of Thomas and May Garrett; *m* 1963, Elisabeth Margaret Hall; four *s* one *d*. *Educ:* Dulwich Coll.; Cambridge Univ. (MA). Joined FO, 1961; Third Sec., Leopoldville (later Kinshasa), 1963; Second Sec. (Commercial), Prague, 1965; FCO, 1968; First Sec., Buenos Aires, 1971; FCO, 1973; First Sec., later Counsellor, Stockholm, 1981; Counsellor: Bonn, 1983; FCO, 1988; E Berlin, 1990; Prague, 1990–92; FCO, 1992–93; Head of UK Delegn to EC Monitoring Mission, Zagreb, 1993–94; Hd, OSCE Mission to Ukraine, 1995. Consultant, Control Risks Group Ltd, 1996–98. Order of the Northern Star, Sweden, 1983. *Recreations:* all outdoor activities, especially ski-ing; travel, gardening, languages. *Address:* White Cottage, Henley, Haslemere, Surrey GU27 3HQ. *T:* (01428) 652172; Mains of Glenlochy, Bridge of Brown, Tomintoul, Ballindalloch, Banff AB37 9HR. *T:* (01807) 580257.

GARRETT, Maj.-Gen. Henry Edmund Melvill Lennox, CBE 1975; *b* 31 Jan. 1924; *s* of John Edmund Garrett and Mary Garrett; *m* 1973, Rachel Ann Beadon; one step *s* one step *d*. *Educ:* Wellington Coll.; Clare Coll., Cambridge (MA). Commnd 1944; psc 1956; DAAG, HQ BAOR, 1957–60; US Armed Forces Staff Coll., 1960; OC 7 Field Sqdn RE, 1961–63; GSO2 WO, 1963–65; CO 35 Engr Regt, 1965–68; Col GS MoD, 1968–69; Comdr 12 Engr Bde, 1969–71; RCDS, 1972; Chief of Staff HQ N Ireland, 1972–75; Maj.-Gen. i/c Administration, HQ UKLF, 1975–76; Vice Adjutant General, MoD, 1976–78; Dir of Security (Army), MoD, 1978–89. Chm., Forces Help Soc. and Lord Roberts Workshops, 1991–96; Vice-President: SSAFA, 1991–96; SSAFA/Forces Help, 1997–2013; Lady Grover's Hosp. Fund for Officers' Families, 2002–. Col Comdt RE, 1982–90. Chm., RE Assoc., 1989–93. Chm. Governors, Royal Soldiers' Daughters Sch., 1983–86. *Recreations:* reading, walking. *Address:* c/o National Westminster Bank, 7 Hustlegate, Bradford, W Yorkshire BD1 1PP. *Club:* Army and Navy.

GARRETT, Lesley, CBE 2002; FRAM; Principal Soprano, English National Opera, 1984–98; *b* 10 April 1955; *d* of Derek Arthur Garrett and Margaret Garrett (*née* Wall); *m* 1991; one *s* one *d*. *Educ:* Thorne Grammar Sch.; Royal Acad. of Music (FRAM 1995); Nat. Opera Studio (Post-grad.). Winner, Kathleen Ferrier Meml Competition, 1979. Performed with WNO, Opera North and at Wexford and Buxton Fests and Glyndebourne; joined ENO, 1984; début with Royal Opera, 1997; has appeared in opera houses in Geneva, São Paulo, Boboli Gdns, Florence, Bolshoi Theatre, Moscow and Kirov Theatre, St Petersburg; major roles include: Susanna in Marriage of Figaro; Despina in Così Fan Tutte; Musetta in La Bohème; Jenny in The Rise and Fall of The City of Mahaggony; Atalanta in Xerxes; Zerlinda in Don Giovanni; Yum-Yum in The Mikado; Adèle in Die Fledermaus; Oscar in A Masked Ball; Dalinda in Ariodante; Rose in Street Scene; Bella in A Midsummer Marriage; Eurydice in Orpheus and Eurydice; Rosina in The Barber of Seville; Elle in La Voix Humaine; title rôles in The Cunning Little Vixen, La Belle Vivette, and The Merry Widow; Mother Superior in The Sound of Music; Nettie in Carousel; concert hall appearances in UK and abroad include: Royal Variety Performance, 1993, Last Night of the Proms, Royal Albert Hall, Royal Fest. Hall, Centre Pompidou, Paris; numerous recordings and TV and radio appearances. Hon. DArts Plymouth, 1995. Best selling classical artist, Gramophone award, 1996. *Recreation:* watching cricket. *Address:* The Music Partnership Ltd, Eaton House, 126A Chester Road, Helsby, Cheshire WA6 0QS.

GARRETT, Richard Anthony, (Tony), CBE 1987; company director; Chairman, National Association of Boys' Clubs, 1980–87, retired; *b* 4 July 1918; 3rd *s* of Charles Victor Garrett and Blanche Michell; *m* 1st, 1946, Marie Louise Dalglish (*d* 1999); one *s* two *d* (and one *d* decd); 2nd, 2000, Nancy Rae Wise. *Educ:* King's Sch., Worcester. Served War, 1939–45 (despatches, 1945). Joined W.D. & H.O. Wills, 1936; Chm., ITL, retd 1979; Chm. and Man. Dir, John Player & Sons, 1968–71; Chm., Dataday Ltd, 1978–83; Director: HTV Gp plc, 1976–89 (Vice-Chm., 1978–83); Standard Commercial (formerly Standard Commercial Tobacco) Corp., 1980–95. Vice Pres., (Founder), Arts & Business (formerly Assoc. of Business Sponsorship of the Arts). Chm., Bath Festival, 1986–87; Trustee, Glyndebourne Arts Trust, 1976–88. Liveryman, Worshipful Co. of Tobacco Pipe Makers and Tobacco Blenders. MInstD; CCMI (CBIM 1979). *Recreations:* golf, gardening, music, opera, reading. *Address:* Ground Floor Flat, Rivers House, Russell Street, Bath BA1 2QF. *T:* (01225) 445613. *Clubs:* MCC, XL; Bath and County; Bristol and Clifton Golf.

GARRETT, Terence, CMG 1990; CBE 1967; Assistant Secretary (International Affairs), Royal Society, 1991–94; *b* 27 Sept. 1929; *e s* of late Percy Herbert Garrett and Gladys Annie Garrett (*née* Budd); *m* 1960, Grace Elizabeth Bridgman Braund, *yr d* of Rev. Basil Kelly Braund; two *s* three *d*. *Educ:* Alleyn's Sch.; Gonville and Caius Coll., Cambridge (Scholar; 1st Cl. Hons, Mathematics; DipMathStat.). Instructor Lieut RN, 1952–55. Lecturer, Ewell County Technical Coll., 1955–56; Sen. Lectr, RMCS, Shrivenham, 1957–62; Counsellor (Sci. and Technol.), Moscow, 1962–66 and 1970–74; Programmes Analysis Unit, Min. of Technology, 1967–70; Internat. Technological Collaboration Unit, Dept of Trade, 1974–76; Sec. to Bd of Governors and to Gen. Conf. of Internat. Atomic Energy Agency, Vienna, 1976–78; Counsellor (Science and Technology), Bonn, 1978–82; DCSO, Research and Technology Policy Div., DTI, 1982–87; Counsellor (Sci. and Technol.), Moscow, 1987–91. *Recreation:* travel. *Address:* Lime Tree Farmhouse, Chilton, Didcot, Oxon OX11 0SW. *Club:* Hawks (Cambridge).

See also C. E. Garrett.

GARRETT, Tony; *see* Garrett, R. A.

GARRICK, Sir Ronald, Kt 1994; CBE 1986; DL; FREng; FRSE; Deputy Chairman, HBOS plc, 2003–09 (Director, 2001–09); *b* 21 Aug. 1940; *s* of Thomas Garrick and Anne (*née* McKay); *m* 1965, Janet Elizabeth Taylor Lind; two *s* one *d*. *Educ:* Royal College of Science and Technology, Glasgow; Glasgow University (BSc MechEng, 1st cl. hons). FIMechE; FREng (FEng 1984); FRSE 1992. Joined G. & J. Weir Ltd, 1962; Weir Pumps: Dir, Industrial Div., 1973; Dir Production Div., 1976; Managing Dir, 1981; Dir, 1981, Man. Dir and Chief Exec., 1982–99, Chm., 1999–2002, Weir Group. Vis. Prof., Dept of Mech. Engrg, Univ. of Strathclyde, 1991–96. Member: Scottish Council, CBI, 1982–90; Gen. Convocation, 1985–96, Court, 1990–96, Univ. of Strathclyde; Restrictive Practices Court, 1986–96; Offshore Industry Adv. Bd, 1989–97; Scottish Economic Council, 1989–98; Scottish Business Forum, 1998–99; Dep. Chm., Scottish Enterprise Bd, 1991–96; Dearing Cttee of Inquiry into Higher Educn, 1996–97 (Chm., Scottish Cttee). Non-executive Director: Supervisory Bd, NEL, 1989–92; Strathclyde Graduate Business Sch., 1990–96; Scottish Power PLC, 1992–99; Shell UK Ltd, 1993–98; Bank of Scotland, 2000–01. DL Renfrewshire, 1996. DUniv: Paisley, 1993; Strathclyde, 1994; Hon. DEng Glasgow, 1998. *Recreations:* golf, reading. *Address:* 14 Roddinghead Road, Giffnock, Glasgow G46 6TN.

GARRIDO, Damian Robin Leon; QC 2015; a Recorder, since 2012; *b* Manchester, 7 June 1969; *s* of Robin John Garrido and Karen Margaret Garrido; *m* 2015, Lucy Watts. *Educ:* Manchester Grammar Sch.; Univ. of Kent at Canterbury (BA Hons); City Univ., London (DipLaw); Inns of Court Sch. of Law. Called to the Bar, Middle Temple, 1993; in practice as barrister, specialising in family law, 1993–. *Publications:* Relocation: a practical guide, 2013. *Recreations:* motor racing, ski-ing, politics. *Address:* 2 Harcourt Buildings, Temple, EC4Y 9DB. *T:* (020) 7353 6961. *E:* clerks@harcourtchambers.co.uk.

GARSIDE, Bernhard Herbert; HM Diplomatic Service; Ambassador to El Salvador, since 2015; *b* Germany, 21 Jan. 1962; *s* of Capt. Roy B. Garside and Gertrud Hedwig Garside (Blome); *m* 1989, Jennifer Susan Yard; one *s* two *d*. *Educ:* Chase Bridge Jun. Sch., Whitton;

St Joseph's Coll., Dumfries; Univ. of Glasgow (MA Politics, German, Philos.). Joined FCO, 1983; Consul, Havana, 1999–2002; Consul-Gen., Amsterdam, 2003–07; First Sec., Migration, Khartoum, 2007–08; FCO, 2008–11; Dep. Hd of Mission, Algiers, 2011–14. *Recreations:* diving, golf, shooting, cinema, gardening. *Address:* British Embassy, Edificio 14, Torre Futura, San Salvador, El Salvador.

GARSIDE, Charles Alexander; Assistant Editor, Daily Mail, since 2006 (Managing Editor, 2004–06); Proprietor, Miller Howe Hotel and Restaurant, Windermere, 1998–2006; *b* 9 April 1951; *s* of John Robert Garside and Florence Garside (*née* Wilson); *m* 1st, 1972, Shirley May Reynolds (marr. diss.); 2nd, 1984, Carole Anne Short (marr. diss.); one *s* one *d*; 3rd, 2010, Gail Graham. *Educ:* Queen Elizabeth's Grammar Sch., Blackburn; Harris Coll., Preston. News Editor, London Evening News, 1979–80; News Editor, 1981–85, Asst Editor, 1986, Evening Standard; Dep. News Editor, The Times, 1987; Dep. Editor, Sunday Express, 1988–89; Asst Editor, The Times, 1989–90; Dep. Editor, 1991–92, Editor and Gen. Manager, 1992–94, Editor in Chief, 1994–97, The European. Man. Dir, 649 Service Ltd, 1997–2006. *Recreations:* fly fishing, theatres, classic cars. *Address:* The Daily Mail, 2 Derry Street, W8 5TT. *T:* (020) 7938 6125. *E:* managingeditor@dailymail.co.uk.

GARSIDE, Charles Roger; QC 1993; a Recorder, since 1994; *b* 13 Aug. 1948; *s* of Richard Murray Garside and Jane Garside (*née* Boby); *m* 1973, Sophie Shem-Tov; two *s* one *d*. *Educ:* Tonbridge Sch. Called to the Bar, Gray's Inn, 1971. Mem., Manchester Pedestrian Club, 1993–. *Recreations:* gardening, cricket, Rugby. *Address:* 9 St John Street, Manchester M3 4DN. *T:* (0161) 955 9000. *Clubs:* Lancashire County Cricket; Manchester Pedestrian.

GARSIDE, Prof. John, CBE 2005; PhD, DSc(Eng); FREng, FIChemE; Professor of Chemical Engineering, 1982–2004, now Emeritus, and Principal and Vice-Chancellor, 2000–04, University of Manchester Institute of Science and Technology; *b* 9 Oct. 1941; *s* of Eric and Ada Garside; *m* 1965, Patricia Louise Holtom; one *s* one *d*. *Educ:* Christ's Coll., Finchley; University Coll. London (BSc(Eng), PhD, DSc(Eng); Fellow, 1994). FIChemE 1986; FREng (FEng 1988). ICI Agricl Div., 1966–69; Lectr, later Reader, UCL, 1969–81; Vice-Principal, UMIST, 1985–87. Vis. Prof., Iowa State Univ., 1976–77. Mem., various cttees and Engrg Bd, SERC, 1989–93. Institution of Chemical Engineers: Mem. Council, 1992–; Pres., 1994–95. Exec. Vice-Pres., EFCE, 2006–09. Dep. Pro-Chancellor, Lancaster Univ., 2014–. *Publications:* (ed) Advances in Industrial Crystallization, 1991; Precipitation: basic principles and industrial application, 1992; From Molecules to Crystallizers, 2000; papers in Chem. Engrg Sci., Trans IChemE, Amer. Instn Chem. Engrs, Jl Crystal Growth, etc. *Recreations:* music, sailing, gardening. *Address:* Bryham House, Low Knipe, Askham, Penrith CA10 2PU.

GARSIDE, (Pamela) Jane, CBE 1995; JP; Chief Commissioner, The Guide (formerly Girl Guides) Association of the United Kingdom and the Commonwealth, 1990–95; *b* 20 Aug. 1936; *d* of Ronald and Nellie Whitwam; *m* 1958, Adrian Fielding Garside; two *s* (two *d* decd). *Educ:* Royds Hall Grammar Sch., Huddersfield; Yorkshire Trng Coll. of Housecraft, Leeds Inst. of Educn (Teaching Dip. 1957). Teacher, Deighton Secondary Sch., 1957–58; Co. Sec. 1959–, Dir 1964–, Highfield Funeral Service Ltd. Girl Guides: Dist Comr, Huddersfield N, 1973–77; County Comr, W Yorks S, 1977–83 (County Pres., 1996–2001); Chief Comr, NE England, 1984–89 (Vice-Pres., 1990–2000; Pres., 2000–05). Nat. Pres., Trefoil Guild, 2004–08. *Recreations:* reading, gardening, music.

GARSIDE, Roger Ramsay; Executive Chairman, GMA Capital Markets Ltd (formerly Garside, Miller Associates), advisers to emerging financial markets, 1990–2000; *b* 29 March 1938; *s* of late Captain F. R. Garside, CBE, RN and Mrs Peggie Garside; *m* 1st, 1969, Evelyne Guérin (marr. diss. 2001); three *d*; 2nd, 2004, Mariota Rosanna Theresa, *d* of Keith and Oonagh Kinross. *Educ:* Eton; Clare Coll., Cambridge (BA EngLit, MA); Sloan Fellow in Management, Massachusetts Inst. of Technology. 2nd Lieut, 6th Gurkha Rifles, 1958–59; entered HM Foreign Service, 1962; served, Rangoon, 1964–65; Mandarin Chinese Lang. Student, Hong Kong, 1965–67; Second Secretary, Peking, 1968–70; FCO, 1970–71, resigned 1971; World Bank, 1972–74; rejoined Foreign Service, 1975; served FCO, 1975; First Sec., Peking, 1976–79; on leave of absence, as Vis. Professor of East Asian Studies, US Naval Postgrad. Sch., Monterey, Calif, 1979–80; Dep. Head, Planning Staff, FCO, 1980–81; seconded, HM Treasury, 1981–82; Financial and Commercial Counsellor, Paris, 1982–87, resigned 1987; Dir, Public Affairs, Internat. Stock Exchange of UK and Rep. of Ireland (now London Stock Exchange), 1987–90. *Publications:* Coming Alive: China after Mao, 1981. *Recreations:* reading, writing, walking. *Club:* Reform.

GARTH, Andrew John; HM Diplomatic Service; Ambassador to Slovakia, since 2014; *b* Bradford, 28 Sept. 1969; one *d*. *Educ:* Tong Sch. Entered FCO, 1988; Attaché, Warsaw, 1990–92; SE Asia/Far East Floater, 1992–95; Desk Officer (Asia Policy), FCO, 1995–97; Turkey Desk, UKTI, 1997–99; Sci. and Technol. Officer, Taipei, 1999–2002; on secondment to S Yorks Internat. Trade Centre, 2003–04; First Sec. (Trade Develt), Bucharest, 2004–07; Head: Political and Econ. Section, Bangkok, 2008; EU Enlargement and Pre-Accession Team, FCO, 2008–10; Commercial Develt Unit, UKTI, 2010–14. *Recreations:* football, hiking, golf. *Address:* c/o Foreign and Commonwealth Office, King Charles Street, SW1A 2AH. *E:* Andy.Garth@fco.gov.uk.

GARTHWAITE, Sir (William) Mark (Charles), 3rd Bt *cr* 1919, of Durham; Director, Willis Ltd (formerly Willis Faber), Lloyds Brokers, 1997–2009; *b* 4 Nov. 1946; *s* of Sir William Francis Cuthbert Garthwaite, 2nd Bt, DSC and Bar and his 2nd wife, Patricia Beatrice Eden (*née* Neate); *S* father, 1993; *m* 1979, Victoria Lisette Hohler, *e d* of Gen. Sir Harry Tuzo, GCB, OBE, MC; one *s* two *d*. *Educ:* Dragon Sch.; Gordonstoun; Univ. of Pennsylvania (Wharton Sch.; BSc Econ.). Seascope Insurance Services, Lloyds Brokers, 1970–87 (Man. Dir, 1980–87); Brandram and Garthwaite Ltd, 1987–88; Director: Regis Low Ltd, Lloyds Brokers, 1988–92; Steel Burrill Jones Ltd, Lloyds Brokers, 1992–97. Chm., London Market Insurance Brokers Cttee Marine, 2000–02. *Recreations:* sailing, ski-ing, trekking. *Heir: s* William Tuzo Garthwaite, *b* 14 May 1982. *Club:* Royal Yacht Squadron.

GARTON, Rt Rev. John Henry; Bishop Suffragan of Plymouth, 1996–2005; Hon. Assistant Bishop, Diocese of Oxford, 2006; *b* 3 Oct. 1941; *s* of Henry and Dorothy Garton; *m* 1969, Pauline (*née* George) (*d* 2006); two *s*. *Educ:* RMA Sandhurst; Worcester Coll., Oxford (MA); Cuddesdon Coll., Oxford. Commissioned in Royal Tank Regt, 1962. Ordained, 1969; CF, 1969–73; Lectr, Lincoln Theol Coll., 1973–78; Rector of Coventry East Team Ministry, 1978–86; Principal, Ripon Coll., Cuddesdon, 1986–96; Vicar, All Saints, Cuddesdon, 1986–96. Hon. Canon of Worcester Cathedral, 1988–96. *Address:* St John's Home, St Mary's Road, Oxford OX4 1QE. *T:* (01865) 247725.

GARTON ASH, Prof. Timothy John, CMG 2000; writer; Professor of European Studies, University of Oxford, since 2004; Fellow, since 1989, Isaiah Berlin Professorial Fellow, since 2006, St Antony's College, Oxford; *b* 12 July 1955; *s* of late John Garton Ash and of Lorna (*née* Freke); *m* 1982, Danuta Maria Brudnik; two *s*. *Educ:* Sherborne; Exeter Coll., Oxford (BA 1st Cl. Hons Mod. Hist., MA); St Antony's Coll., Oxford; Free Univ., W Berlin; Humboldt Univ., E Berlin. Foreign Editor, Spectator, 1984–90; editl writer on Central Europe, The Times, 1984–86; Fellow, Woodrow Wilson Center, Washington, 1986–87; columnist: Independent, 1988–90; Guardian, 2002–; Dir, European Studies Centre, St Antony's Coll., Oxford, 2001–06; Sen. Fellow, Hoover Instn, Stanford Univ., 2001–. Gov., Westminster Foundn for Democracy, 1992–2000. FRSA; FRHistS; FRSL; Fellow: Berlin-Brandenburg Acad. of Scis, European Acad. of Scis; Institut für die Wissenschaften vom Menschen, Vienna. Hon. DLitt: St Andrews, 2004; Sheffield Hallam, 2005; Leuven, 2011. Commentator of Year, What the Papers Say awards, 1989; David Watt Meml Prize, RTZ, 1990; Premio Napoli, 1995; OSCE Prize for Journalism and Democracy, 1998; George Orwell Prize, 2006; Médaille Charlemagne pour les Médias Européens, 2013. Order of Merit (Poland), 1992; Bundesverdienstkreuz (FRG), 1995; Order of Merit (Czech Republic), 2003. *Publications:* 'Und willst Du nicht mein Bruder sein ...' Die DDR heute, 1981; The Polish Revolution: Solidarity, 1983, 3rd edn 1999 (Somerset Maugham Award, 1984); The Uses of Adversity, 1989, 2nd edn 1991 (Prix Européen de l'Essai, 1989); We the People, 1990, 2nd edn 1999; In Europe's Name: Germany and the divided continent, 1993; The File: a personal history, 1997; History of the Present, 1999, 2nd edn 2000; Free World, 2004; Facts are Subversive: political writing from a decade without a name, 2009. *Address:* St Antony's College, Oxford OX2 6JF. *T:* (01865) 274474, *Fax:* (01865) 274478.

GARTRY, David Stanley, MD; FCOptom, FRCS, FRCOphth; Consultant Ophthalmic Surgeon, since 1995, and Director, Refractive Surgical Service, since 2007, Moorfields Eye Hospital, London; *b* 23 June 1956; *s* of Stanley and Phyllis Gartry; *m* 1980, Lily Giacoman; three *s*. *Educ:* Glasgow Coll. of Technol. (BSc 1st Cl. Hons Optometry 1978); University Coll. London (Suckling Prize in Neuroanatomy, 1981; Duke-Elder undergrad. prize in Ophthalmol., 1983; MB BS 1984); DO 1988; MD London 1995. FCOptom 1979; FRCS 1988; FRCOphth 1988. Sen. Lectr, UCL, 1995–. Discourse Lectr, Royal Instn, 1995; Vis. Lectr, 1997–2006, Vis. Prof., 2006–, City Univ.; Vis. Prof., Glasgow Caledonian Univ., 2010–. External Examiner: City Univ., 2006; Anglia Ruskin Univ., 2008–; Examr, RCOphth. Mem., Ophthalmic Technol. Assessment Panel, Amer. Acad. of Ophthalmol., 2010–. First surgeon in UK to perform laser refractive surgery, 1989. Pres., British Soc. for Refractive Surgery, 1999–2002. Hon. DSc Glasgow Caledonian, 2010. Master's (SMC), Colebrook and Porter Prizes, BOA, 1979; Iris Fund Triennial Award, 1995; Honor Award, Amer. Acad. Ophthalmol., 1999. *Publications:* Excimer Lasers in Ophthalmology, 1997; Cataract Surgery, 2003; numerous scientific contribs and book chapters. *Recreations:* formerly enthusiastic squash player (quite good, Middlesex ranked, Cumberland Cup), guitar (not bad), piano (poor!), golf, Ferrari enthusiast! *Address:* Moorfields Eye Hospital, 162 City Road, EC1V 2PD. *T:* (020) 7490 7222; The London Clinic Eye Centre, 119 Harley Street, W1G 6AU. *T:* (020) 7486 3112. *E:* david@gartry.com. *Club:* Cumberland Lawn Tennis and Squash.

GARTSIDE, Timothy James; Head Master, Altrincham Grammar School for Boys, since 2003; *b* Rochdale, Lancs, 21 Jan. 1961; *s* of John Gartside and Mary Gartside; *m* 1984, Hilary Robb; two *s* one *d*. *Educ:* Hulme Grammar Sch. for Boys, Oldham; Univ. of Edinburgh (MA Hons); Univ. of Sheffield (PGCE); Inst. of Educn, Univ. of London (NPQH). Teacher of History and Politics, Hulme Grammar Sch. for Boys, 1984–89; Hd of History, Wisbech Grammar Sch., 1989–95; Hd of History and Politics, Newcastle under Lyme Sch., 1995–98; Dep. Hd, Westcliff High Sch., 1998–2003. *Recreations:* family and friends, history, reading, cycling, supporting Rochdale AFC, camping. *Address:* Altrincham Grammar School for Boys, Marlborough Road, Bowdon, Altrincham WA14 2RS. *T:* (0161) 928 0858, *Fax:* (0161) 924 3888. *E:* tgartside@agsb.co.uk.

GARVAGH, 6th Baron *cr* 1818; **Spencer George Stratford de Redcliffe Canning;** *b* 12 Feb. 1953; *s* of 5th Baron Garvagh and Christine Edith Canning (*née* Cooper); *S* father 2013; *m* 1979 Julia Margery Morison Bye (*d* 2009), *er d* of Col F. C. E. Bye; one *s* two *d*. *Educ:* Cranleigh; Univ. of London (Dip. Surveying). MRICS. Founded Asset Plus One Ltd, 1999. *Heir: s* Hon. Stratford George Edward de Redcliffe Canning, *b* 7 Feb. 1990.

GARVEY, Angela Josepha, (Mrs D. G. Daly), FRCP, FRCPE; Lord-Lieutenant of Londonderry, since 2013; *b* Armagh, NI, 1 June 1953; *d* of James Edward Garvey and Mary Elizabeth Garvey (*née* Savage); *m* 1984, John Gerard Daly; two *s* two *d*. *Educ:* Our Lady's Grammar Sch., Newry, Co. Down; Queen's Univ. Belfast (BCh BAO 1977). MRCPE 1982, FRCPE 1995; FRCP 2000. Various posts, jun. doctor trng, 1977–86; Med. Dir, NI Hospice, Belfast, 1986–87; career break, 1987–98; Consultant, NI Hospice, 1998–2000; Consultant in Palliative Medicine, Western Health and Social Care Trust, Londonderry, 2000–13. Specialist Advr on end of life care, Care Quality Commn, 2014–. *Publications:* contrib. articles to peer-reviewed jls on aspects of palliative medicine and evidence-based guidelines for lymphoedema. *Recreations:* walking, Irish art and literature, Gaelic games. *Address:* 9 Coolafinny Road, Eglinton, Co. Londonderry, Northern Ireland BT47 3PG. *T:* 07739 072627. *E:* a.daly489@btinternet.com.

GARVEY, Arnold James; Editor, Horse and Hound, 1995–2001; *b* 7 Aug. 1946; *s* of late James Adamson Garvey and Esme Muriel (*née* Noble); *m* 1st, 1969, Kathleen Gordon (marr. diss. 1996); two *d*; 2nd, 1997, Marta-Lisà Conversi; two *s* one *d*. *Educ:* Bramston, Witham, Essex; Braintree Coll., Essex. Joined Horse and Hound, as sub-editor, 1971: Dep. Ed., 1987–94; Actg Ed., 1994–95. *Recreations:* horse riding, theatre, walking. *Address:* 27 Cornel Close, Witham, Essex CM8 2XH. *Club:* Farmers.

GARVIE, Wayne Fernley, PhD; Chief Creative Officer, International Production, Sony Pictures Television, since 2012; *b* Plymouth, 9 Sept. 1963; *s* of George Garvie and Frances Garvie; two *d*. *Educ:* Woodbridge Sch.; Univ. of Kent at Canterbury (BA Hons 1st Cl.); Univ. of Sheffield (PhD Econ. and Social Hist. 1989). Granada Television: producer, 1988–96; Dir of Broadcasting, 1996–98; BBC: Hd, Entertainment and Features, 1998–2002; Hd, Entertainment Gp, 2002–06; Man. Dir, Content and Prodn, BBC Worldwide, 2006–10; Man. Dir, Internat. Prodn, All3Media, 2011–12. Chm., RTS, 2008–. Trustee, People's History Mus., 2007–. Vis. Prof. of Media, Univ. of Chester, 2008–. *Recreations:* football, Roman history, being relentlessly optimistic and enjoying life, in all its messy glory. *Address:* Sony Pictures Television, 25 Golden Square, W1F 9LU. *E:* wayne_garvie@spe.sony.com. *Club:* Soho House.

GARWOOD, Air Marshal Richard Frank, CB 2010; CBE 2002; DFC 1991; Director General, Military Aviation Authority, since 2013; *b* 10 Jan. 1959; *s* of Sidney Richard Garwood and Queenie Blanche May Garwood (*née* Bradfield); *m* 1981, Susan Ann Trendell; one *s*. *Educ:* Smithdon High Sch., Hunstanton; Norfolk Coll. of Arts and Technol.; King's Coll. London (MA Defence Studies). Pilot, RAF, grad. RAF Coll., Cranwell, 1979; Fighter Reconnaissance pilot, 41 (Fighter) Sqdn, 1982–85; Instructor pilot, 234 Sqdn, RAF Brawdy, 1985–87; exchange pilot, USAF, 1987–90; Flight Comdr, No II (AC) Sqdn, 1990–93; Staff Officer, Operational Requirements, MoD, 1993–96; Army Comd and Staff Coll., 1995; OC II (AC) Sqdn, 1996–98; SO, PJHQ, Northwood, 1998–2000; CO, RAF Marham, 2000–02; rcds 2003; HQ 1Gp, 2003–04; HQ 1 Gp SO, Dir of Air Staff, 2004–07; CDS Liaison Officer to US Chm. of Jt Chiefs of Staff, 2007; AOC 22 (Trng) Gp, 2007–09; COS (Ops), 2009–10, Dep. C-in-C (Ops), 2010–12, Dep. Comdr (Ops), 2012–13, HQ Air Comd; Mem. for Ops, Air Force Bd, Defence Council, 2012–13. *Recreations:* game fishing, shooting. *Address:* c/o Military Aviation Authority, Ministry of Defence, Main Building, Whitehall, SW1A 2HB. *Club:* Royal Air Force.

GASCOIGNE, Bamber; author and broadcaster; Editor-in-Chief, www.historyworld.net, since 2000; *b* 24 Jan. 1935; *s* of late Derick Gascoigne and Midi (*née* O'Neill); *m* 1965, Christina Ditchburn. *Educ:* Eton; Magdalene Coll., Cambridge (Hon. Fellow, 1996). Commonwealth Fund Fellow, Yale, 1958–59. Theatre Critic, Spectator, 1961–63, and Observer, 1963–64; Co-editor, Theatre Notebook, 1968–74. Founded Saint Helena Press, 1977; Chm., Ackermann Publishing, 1981–85; Co-founder and Chm., HistoryWorld, 2000. Trustee: Nat. Gall., 1988–95; Tate Gall., 1993–95; Chm., Friends of Covent Garden, 1991–95; Member: Bd of Dirs, Royal Opera House, Covent Garden, 1988–95; Council, Nat. Trust, 1989–94. Sandars Lectr in Bibliography, Cambridge, 1993–94. FRSL 1976. *Theatre:*

Share My Lettuce, London, 1957–58; Leda Had a Little Swan, New York, 1968; The Feydeau Farce Festival of Nineteen Nine, Greenwich, 1972; Big in Brazil, Old Vic, 1984. *Television:* presenter of: University Challenge, (weekly) 1962–87; Cinema, 1964; (also author) The Christians, 1977; Victorian Values, 1987; Man and Music, 1987–89; The Great Moghuls, 1990; Brother Felix and the Virgin Saint, 1992; deviser and presenter of Connoisseur, 1988–89; author of: The Four Freedoms, 1962; Dig This Rhubarb, 1963; The Auction Game, 1968. *Publications:* (many with photographs or watercolour illustrations by Christina Gascoigne): Twentieth Century Drama, 1962; World Theatre, 1968; The Great Moghuls, 1971; Murgatreud's Empire, 1972; The Heyday, 1973; The Treasures and Dynasties of China, 1973; Ticker Khan, 1974; The Christians, 1977; Images of Richmond, 1978; Images of Twickenham, 1981; Why the Rope went Tight, 1981; Fearless Freddy's Magic Wish, 1982; Fearless Freddy's Sunken Treasure, 1982; Quest for the Golden Hare, 1983; Cod Streuth, 1986; How to Identify Prints, 1986; Amazing Facts, 1988; Encyclopedia of Britain, 1993; Milestones in Colour Printing, 1997; HistoryWorld's Pocket History series: The First World War, 2010; The Second World War, 2010; Science, Ancient World to 1800, 2011; Maya, Aztecs, Incas and Conquistadors, 2011; Napoleon Bonaparte, 2011. *Address:* Saint Helena Terrace, Richmond, Surrey TW9 1NR.

GASCOYNE-CECIL, family name of **Marquess of Salisbury**.

GASH, Haydon Boyd W.; *see* Warren-Gash.

GASKELL, Dr Colin Simister, CBE 1988; FREng; Chairman, Ferranti Technologies Ltd, 2000–05; *b* 19 May 1937; *s* of James and Carrie Gaskell; *m* 1961, Jill (*née* Haward); one *s* one *d*. *Educ:* Manchester Grammar Sch.; Manchester Univ. (BSc); St Edmund Hall, Oxford (DPhil). CEng, FREng (FEng 1989); FIET (Hon. Treas., IEE, 1996–99). Research Fellow, Oxford Univ., 1960–61; Central Electricity Res. Labs, 1961–62; Microwave Associates, 1962–67; Chief Engineer, Microwave Div., Marconi Instruments, 1967–71; Technical Dir, Herbert Controls, 1971–74; Marconi Instruments: Technical Management, 1974–77; Technical Dir, 1977–79; Man. Dir, 1979–90; Gp Man. Dir, 1990–96, Chief Exec., 1996–97, 600 Group plc; Chm., Telemetrix plc, 1997–2003. *Recreations:* reading, walking, theatre, family pursuits.

GASKELL, His Honour Joseph William; a Circuit Judge, 1996–2015; *b* 5 June 1947; *s* of Joseph Gerald Gaskell and Maureen Elizabeth Jane Gaskell (*née* Thomas); *m* 1970, Rowena Gillian Case; one *s* one *d*. *Educ:* Harrow Sch.; Clare Coll., Cambridge. Called to the Bar, Inner Temple, 1970; in private practice, Cardiff, 1971–96; Asst Recorder, 1990; Recorder, 1993–96; Asst Parly Boundary Comr, 1994. Mem., Parole Bd, 2010–13. *Recreations:* the arts, sailing, dog walking. *Clubs:* Cardiff and County; Penarth Yacht; Cardiff Bay Yacht.

GASKELL, Karen Maria; *see* Facey, K. M.

GASKELL, Prof. Simon James, PhD; FRSC; President and Principal, Queen Mary University of London, since 2009; *b* Lancs, 2 May 1950; *s* of Leo Gaskell and Olive Gaskell (*née* Bennett); *m* 1974, Deirdre Jane Ellison; one *s* one *d*. *Educ:* Haberdashers' Aske's Elstree Sch.; Univ. of Bristol (BSc Chem.; PhD 1974). FRSC 1991. Res. Scientist, Tenovus Inst. for Cancer Res., Univ. of Wales Coll. of Medicine, 1977–86; Prof. of Exptl Medicine, Baylor Coll. of Medicine, Houston, Texas, 1987–93; Prof. of Mass Spectrometry, UMIST, then Univ. of Manchester, 1993–2009; Vice-Pres. for Res., Univ. of Manchester, 2006–09. Chair, HE Statistics Agency, 2012–. *Publications:* Mass Spectrometry in Biomedical Research, 1986; contrib. articles to biochem. and analytical sci. res. jls. *Recreations:* theatre, physical exercise. *Address:* Office of the Principal, Queen Mary University of London, Mile End Road, E1 4NS. *T:* (020) 7882 5061, *Fax:* (020) 8981 2848. *E:* principal@qmul.ac.uk.

GASKELL, Vincent; Executive Director for New Service Implementation and Communications and Marketing, Identity and Passport Service, 2009–10; *b* 17 June 1952; *s* of late John Rigby Gaskell and Eilleen Winnifred Gaskell; *m* 1972, Anne Frances Neil; one *s* two *d*. *Educ:* W Park Grammar Sch., St Helens; Salford Univ.; Open Univ. (BA). Area Dir, Benefits Agency, 1994–96; Prog. Dir, DSS, 1996–99; Mem. Bd, CSA, 1999–2003; Chief Exec., Criminal Records Bureau, 2003–09. Mem., Agency Chief Executives Assoc., 2005–. *Recreations:* mountaineering, mountain biking. *T:* 07919 115140. *E:* vincegaskell@msn.com. *Club:* Pannal Wheelers.

GASKILL, William; freelance stage director; *b* 24 June 1930; *s* of Joseph Linnaeus Gaskill and Maggie Simpson. *Educ:* Salt High Sch., Shipley; Hertford Coll., Oxford. Asst Artistic Dir, English Stage Co., 1957–59; freelance Dir with Royal Shakespeare Co., 1961–62; Assoc. Dir, National Theatre, 1963–65, and 1979; Artistic Director, English Stage Company, 1965–72, Mem. Council, 1978–87; Dir, Joint Stock Theatre Gp, 1973–83. *Publications:* A Sense of Direction: life at the Royal Court (autobiog.), 1988; Words into Action: finding the life of the play, 2010. *Address:* 124A Leighton Road, NW5 2RG.

GASKIN, John Martin; Director, Escrick Education Associates, since 2010; *b* 27 Jan. 1951; *s* of Les and Gwen Gaskin; *m* 1980, Rosemary (marr. diss. 2005); two *d*; *m* 2005, Jean Samuel. *Educ:* City Coll. of Educn, Sheffield (CertEd); Sheffield City Poly. (BEd Hons); Univ. of Sheffield (AdvDipEd). Headteacher: Swavesey Primary Sch., Cambs, 1984–86; Concord Middle Sch., Sheffield, 1986–89; Advr, 1989–92, Chief Advr, 1992–95, Hd, Educn Services, 1995–97, Barnsley LEA; HM Inspector of Schs, 1997–98; City Educn Officer, Portsmouth LEA, 1998–2002; Dir of Educn and Lifelong Learning, Bristol CC, 2002–04; Dir, Learning Services, Prospects Services, 2004–05; Man. Dir, Education Bradford, 2005–09. *Recreations:* late comer to running, fishing, but not often enough, wondering why and concentrating on why not! *Address:* Nor Riddings, Escrick Park Gardens, York YO19 6LZ.

GASPARINI, Robert Lincoln; Partner, President and Managing Director, Monticello Partners LLC, since 2003; Operating Partner, Compass Partners International, since 2011; *b* 22 Oct. 1950; *s* of late Baron Carlo Gasparini, sometime Italian Ambassador to Nato, and Gloria Gasparini, *d* of Marquis A. Ferrante di Ruffano and Virginia MacVeagh; *m* 1979, Marilyn Varnell Murphy; one *s*. *Educ:* French Baccalaureat, Brussels; Univ. of Rome (BA Pol Scis); Columbia Univ. (MBA 1977). Product Mgt, Colgate Palmolive, NY, 1977–79; Management Consultant: Booz Allen & Hamilton, London, 1979–83; Strategy Res. Associates, London, 1983–85; Man. Dir, European Ops, Fort Howard Corp., London, 1985–88; Williams plc: Man. Dir, Europe, Paris, 1988–91; Man. Dir, Consumer & Building Products, NY, 1992–94; Man. Dir, Global Systems & Services, NY, 1994–2000; Main Bd Dir, 1999–2000; CEO, Chubb plc, 2000–03; Chm., CEO and Pres., Drake Beam Morin Inc., 2007–11. Dir, Compass Partners Internat. *Recreations:* tennis, sailing, cinema. *Address:* 164 Kirby Lane, Rye, New York, NY 10580, USA. *T:* (914) 9672865. *Club:* La Caccia (Rome).

GASS, Dame Elizabeth (Periam Acland Hood), DCVO 2014; JP; Lord-Lieutenant of Somerset, 1998–2015 (Vice Lord-Lieutenant, 1996–98); *b* 2 March 1940; *d* of late Hon. John Acland-Hood, barrister, *yr s* of 1st Baron St Audries, PC and of Dr Phyllis Acland-Hood (*née* Hallett); *m* 1975, Sir Michael Gass, KCMG (*d* 1983). *Educ:* Cheltenham Ladies' Coll.; Girton Coll., Cambridge (MA). Somerset County Council: Member, 1985–97; Chm., Exmoor Nat. Park Cttee, 1989–93; Vice-Chm., Social Services Cttee, 1989–93. Dir, Avalon NHS Trust, 1993–96. Comr, English Heritage, 1995–2001. Member: Rail Users' Consultative Cttee for Western England, 1992–99; Nat. Trust Wessex Cttee, 1994–2002; Nat. Exec. Cttee, CLA, 1998–2003; Wessex Cttee, HHA, 1998–; Wells Cathedral Council, 2004–. Member, Council: Cheltenham Ladies' Coll., 1992–2001; Bath Univ., 1999–2002. Trustee, West of England Sch. for Children with Little or no Sight, 1996–2008. Pres., Royal Bath and W of England Soc., 2002–03; Patron, Pres. and Mem. of many Somerset charitable orgns. High Sheriff 1994, DL 1995, JP 1996, Somerset. *Recreations:* gardening, music, archaeology. *Address:* Fairfield, Stogursey, Bridgwater, Somerset TA5 1PU. *T:* (01278) 732251, *Fax:* (01278) 732277.

GASS, James Ronald, CMG 1989; Consultant, European Economic Commission, since 1989; *b* 25 March 1924; *s* of Harold Amos Gass and Cherry (*née* Taylor); *m* 1950, Colette Alice Jeanne Lejeune; two *s* one *d*. *Educ:* Birkenhead Park High Sch.; Liverpool Univ. (BA Hons); Nuffield and Balliol Colls, Oxford. Flight Lieut Pilot, RAF, service in US, India and Burma, 1942–46. PSO, DSIR Intelligence Div., 1951–57; Special Asst to Chm., Task Force on Western Scientific Co-operation, NATO, Paris, 1957; OEEC, subsequently OECD, Paris: Head of Div., Scientific and Tech. Personnel, 1958–61; Dep. Dir for Scientific Affairs, 1961–68; Director: Centre for Educnl Res. and Innovation, 1968–89; Social Affairs, Manpower and Educn, 1974–89; retired 1989. *Recreations:* restoration of antiques, gymnastics, philosophy. *Address:* 2 avenue du Vert Bois, Ville d'Avray, 92410 Paris, France. *T:* 47095481.

GASS, Sir Simon (Lawrance), KCMG 2011 (CMG 1998); CVO 1999; HM Diplomatic Service; Political Director, Foreign and Commonwealth Office, since 2013; *b* 2 Nov. 1956; *s* of late Geoffrey Gass and of Brenda Gass (*née* Lawrance); *m* 1980, Marianne Enid Stott; two *s* one *d*. *Educ:* Eltham Coll.; Reading Univ. (LLB 1977). Joined FCO, 1977; Lagos, 1979–83; Athens, 1984–87; FCO, 1987–90; Asst Private Sec. to Foreign Sec., 1990–92; Rome, 1992–95; Counsellor, FCO, 1995–98; Dep. High Comr, S Africa, 1998–2001; Dir, Resources, then Finance, FCO, 2001–04; Ambassador to Greece, 2004–09; Ambassador to Iran, 2009–11; NATO Sen. Civilian Rep. in Afghanistan, 2011–12; UK Special Rep. for Afghanistan and Pakistan, 2013–15. *Address:* c/o Foreign and Commonwealth Office, King Charles Street, SW1A 2AH.

GASSON, (Gordon) Barry, OBE 1985; RSA; Principal, Barry Gasson, Architects; biodynamic farmer, France; *b* 27 Aug. 1935; *s* of late Gladys Godfrey (previously Gasson; *née* Byrne) and Stanley Gasson; *m* Rosemary Mulligan; one *s* two *d*. *Educ:* Solihull Sch.; Birmingham Sch. of Architecture (Dip. Arch. 1958); RIBA (Owen Jones Student); Columbia Univ., NY (MS 1961); Q. W. Boese English Speaking Fellowship; MA Cantab 1963. ARIAS, RIBA. Lectr, Univ. of Cambridge, 1963–73; visiting critic: University Coll., Dublin, 1969–72; California State Poly., 1969; Mackintosh Sch. of Arch., 1978–85; Edinburgh Coll. of Art, 1986–92; Vis. Prof., Univ. of Manchester, 1987–95. Former Mem., Royal Fine Art Commn for Scotland. Assessor, Civic Trust Awards, RIBA student medals, nat. competitions; Chm., RIBA regional awards. Designed galleries for Burrell Collection, Glasgow (won in open comp., 1972); awards: Stone Fedn, 1983; Arch. Design; RA Premier Arch., 1984; Museum of the Year; British Tourist Trophy; Sotheby Fine Art; Services in Building; Civic Trust; Eternit Internat., 1985; RIBA 1986; RSA Gold Medal, 1983; World Biennale of Arch. Gold Medal, 1987. *Publications:* contrib. to The Burrell Collection, 1983.

GASTON, Prof. John Stanley Hill, PhD; FRCP, FMedSci; Professor of Rheumatology, University of Cambridge, since 1995; Fellow, St Edmund's College, Cambridge, since 2000; *b* 24 June 1952; *s* of John Gaston, CBE and Elizabeth Gaston (*née* Gordon); *m* 1975, Christine Mary Arthur; one *s* one *d*. *Educ:* Royal Belfast Academical Instn; Lincoln Coll., Oxford (MA); Oxford Univ. Med. Sch. (BM BCh); Univ. of Bristol (PhD 1983). FRCP 1995. SHO, then Registrar posts at Hammersmith Hosp., Bristol Hosps and Torbay, 1977–80; Sir Michael Sobell Cancer Res. Fellow, Univ. of Bristol, 1980–83; MRC Travelling Fellowship, Stanford Univ. Med. Centre, 1983–85; University of Birmingham: MRC Res. Trng Fellow, 1985–87; Wellcome Sen. Res. Fellow in Clinical Sci., 1987–92; Sen. Lectr, then Reader in Rheumatology, 1992–95. Hon. Consultant in Rheumatology, S Birmingham HA, 1987–95. FMedSci 2001. *Publications:* papers on immunology and immunological aspects of rheumatic diseases. *Recreations:* music, reading biographies. *Address:* University of Cambridge School of Clinical Medicine, Box 157, Level 5, Addenbrooke's Hospital, Hills Road, Cambridge CB2 0QQ. *T:* (01223) 330161. *E:* jshg2@medschl.cam.ac.uk; 6 Parsonage Court, Whittlesford, Cambs CB22 4PH.

GASTON, Prof. Kevin John, DPhil; Professor of Biodiversity and Conservation, and Director of the Environment and Sustainability Institute, University of Exeter, since 2011; *b* 5 Nov. 1964; *s* of Mervyn John and Ann Grace Gaston; *m* 1987, Sian Roberts; one *d*. *Educ:* Tunbridge Wells Tech. High Sch.; Univ. of Sheffield (BSc 1986); Univ. of York (DPhil 1989). Department of Entomology, Natural History Museum, London: Jun. Res. Fellow, 1989–91; Sen. Res. Fellow, 1991–93; Principal Res. Fellow, 1993–94; Hon. Res. Fellow, 1999–2005; Royal Soc. Univ. Res. Fellow, Dept of Biol., Imperial Coll., London, 1994–95; Royal Soc. Univ. Res. Fellow, Dept of Animal and Plant Scis, 1995–2002, Prof. of Biodiversity and Conservation, 2000–11, Univ. of Sheffield; Royal Soc. Wolfson Res. Merit Award, 2006–11. Prof. Extraordinary in Zool., Univ. of Stellenbosch, 2002–14. MAE 2011. Internat. Recognition of Professional Excellence Prize, Ecology Inst., 1999; Marsh Award in Ecology, British Ecological Soc., 2013. *Publications:* Perspectives on Insect Conservation (ed jtly), 1993; Rarity, 1994; (ed) Biodiversity: a biology of numbers and difference, 1996; (ed jtly) The Biology of Rarity: causes and consequences of rare-common differences, 1987; (jtly) Biodiversity: an introduction, 1998, 2nd edn 2004; (jtly) Physiological Diversity and its Ecological Implications, 1999; (jtly) Pattern and Process in Macroecology, 2000; The Structure and Dynamics of Geographic Ranges, 2003; (ed jtly) Macroecology: concepts and consequences, 2003; (jtly) Gough Island: a natural history, 2005; (jtly) Endemic plants of the Altai mountain country, 2008; (ed) Urban Ecology, 2010; over 450 sci. papers in peer-reviewed jls. *Recreations:* kayaking, natural history, travel. *Address:* Environment and Sustainability Institute, University of Exeter, Cornwall Campus, Penryn, Cornwall TR10 9FE.

GASZTOWICZ, Steven; QC 2009; a Recorder, since 2009; *b* Blackpool, 22 July 1959; *s* of Lucjan and Edna Gasztowicz; *m* 1994, Sally Louise Barnett; one *s* one *d*. *Educ:* Univ. of Nottingham (LLB Hons 1980). Called to the Bar, Gray's Inn, 1981; barrister specialising in admin. and planning matters, land law, and contract and commercial litigation. Trustee, Leicester GS, 2009–. *Recreations:* art, swimming, books (collecting and reading), equestrian events (watching), wine (learning about, collecting and enjoying). *Address:* Cornerstone Barristers, 2–3 Gray's Inn Square, WC1R 5JH. *T:* (020) 7242 4986, *Fax:* (020) 7405 1166. *E:* sg@cornerstonebarristers.com. *Club:* Guards Polo.

GATEHOUSE, Graham Gould; Director, Orchard Lane Initiatives Ltd, 1995–2010; *b* 17 July 1935; *s* of G. and G. M. Gatehouse; *m* 1st, 1960, Gillian M. Newell (marr. diss. 2012); two *s* one *d*; 2nd, 2013, Wanda M. Kwilecka; one *d*. *Educ:* Crewkerne Sch., Somerset; Exeter Univ., Devon (DSA); London School of Economics (Dip. Mental Health). Served Royal Artillery, 1954–56. Somerset County Council, 1957–67; Worcestershire CC, 1967–70; Norfolk CC, 1970–73; West Sussex CC, 1973–81; Dir of Social Services, Surrey CC, 1981–95. FRSA 1987. *Recreations:* Rugby football, cricket, theatre. *Address:* 6 Millbrook Court, Prigg Lane, South Petherton, Som TA13 5ED.

GATENBY, Michael Richard Brock, FCA; Vice Chairman, Charterhouse Bank Ltd, 1989–95; *b* 5 Oct. 1944; *s* of Arthur Duncan Gatenby and Dora Ethel (*née* Brock); *m* 1990, Lesley Ann Harding; two step *s*. *Educ:* Haileybury; Trinity Hall, Cambridge (BA 1966). ACA 1970. With Peat Marwick Mitchell, 1966–71; Hill Samuel & Co. Ltd, 1971–85 (Dir, 1975–85); Charterhouse Bank Ltd, 1985–95: Man. Dir, 1986–89; Director: Staveley Industries plc, 1980–96; Bridport plc, 1980–99; Scholl plc, 1996–98; Philip Harris plc, 1996–97; SGB Gp plc, 1997–2000; Protherics (formerly Proteus International) plc, 1997–2004; Powell Duffryn plc, 1997–2000; Tarmac plc, 1999–2000; SRS Technology Gp plc, 2002–06; Porvair plc, 2002–13; Johnson Service Gp plc, 2002–10; Cobra Biomanufacturing plc, 2003–10; Chm., Alliance Pharma plc, 2004–. *Recreations:* golf, ski-ing. *Address:* Norfolk House, Chiswick Mall, W4 2PS. *T:* (020) 8994 4600.

GATES, Hon. Robert M.; Secretary of Defense, USA, 2006–11; *b* Kansas, 25 Sept. 1943; *m* Becky; two *c*. *Educ:* Coll. of William and Mary (BA 1965); Indiana Univ. (MA History, 1966); Georgetown Univ. (PhD Russian and Soviet History, 1974). Joined CIA, 1966; intelligence analyst; Asst Nat. Intell. Officer for Strategic Programs; staff, Nat. Security Council, 1974–79; rejoined CIA, 1979: admin. posts; Nat. Intell. Officer for Soviet Union; Dep. Dir for Intell., 1982–86; Chm., Nat. Intell. Council, 1983–86; Dep. Dir, 1986–89, Actg Dir, 1986–87, Dir, 1991–93, Central Intelligence; Asst to the President, and Dep. for Nat. Security Affairs, Nat. Security Council, 1986–91. Pres., Texas A&M Univ., 2002–06; Chancellor, Coll. of William & Mary, 2011–. Presidential Citizens Medal; Nat. Intell. Distinguished Service Medal; Distinguished Intell. Medal, CIA; Intell. Medal of Merit; Arthur S. Flemming Award. *Publications:* From the Shadows, 1996; Duty: memoirs of a Secretary at war, 2014. *Address:* c/o 1000 Pentagon, Washington, DC 20301, USA.

GATES, Emeritus Prof. Ronald Cecil, AO 1978; FASSA; Vice-Chancellor, University of New England, 1977–85; *b* 8 Jan. 1923; *s* of Earle Nelson Gates and Elsie Edith (*née* Tucker); *m* 1953, Barbara Mann; one *s* two *d* (and one *s* decd). *Educ:* East Launceston State Sch., Tas; Launceston C of E Grammar Sch., Tas; Univ. of Tas (BCom Econs and Commercial Law); Oxford Univ. (MA PPE). FASSA 1968. Served War, 1942–45: Private, AIF. Clerk, Aust. Taxation Office, Hobart, 1941–42; Rhodes Scholar (Tas), Oxford, 1946–48; Historian, Aust. Taxation Office, Canberra, 1949–52; Univ. of Sydney: Sen. Lectr in Econs, 1952–64; Associate Prof., 1964–65; Rockefeller Fellow in Social Sciences, 1955; Carnegie Travel Grant, 1960; Prof. of Econs, Univ. of Qld, 1966–77 (Pres., Professorial Bd, 1975–77). Pres., Econ. Soc. of Australia and NZ, 1969–72. Chairman: statutory Consumer Affairs Council of Qld, 1971–73; Aust. Inst. of Urban Studies, 1975–77. Comr, Commonwealth Commn of Inquiry into Poverty, 1973–77. Chairman: Aust. Nat. Commn for Unesco, 1981–83 (Vice-Chm., 1979); Adv. Council for Inter-govt Relations, 1979–85; Internat. Relations Cttee, Cttee of Australian Vice-Chancellors, 1981–84; Local Govt Trng Council (formerly Nat. Local Govt Industry Trng Cttee), 1983–92; Armidale-Dumaresq Jt Planning Cttee, 1992–97. Pres., Australian Esperanto Assoc., 1998–2001 (Vice-Pres., 1995–98). Hon. FRAPI 1976; Hon. Fellow, Aust. Inst. of Urban Studies, 1979. Hon. DEcon Qld, 1978; Hon. DLitt New England, 1987. *Publications:* (with H. R. Edwards and N. T. Drane) Survey of Consumer Finances, Sydney 1963–65: Vol. 2, 1965; Vols 1, 3 and 4, 1966; Vols 5, 6 and 7, 1967; (jtly) The Price of Land, 1971; (jtly) New Cities for Australia, 1972; (jtly) Land for the Cities, 1973; (with P. A. Cassidy) Simulation, Uncertainty and Public Investment Analysis, 1977; *in Esperanto:* detective novels: La Septaga Murdenigmo, 1991; Kolera Afero, 1993; Morto de Sciencisto, 1994; Mortiga Ekskurso, 2006; Bri?o kun Veneno, 2014; La Vidvino kaj la Profesoro (romantic novel), 1997; short stories: Sep Krimnoveloj, 1993; Refoje Krimnoveloj Sep, 1994; Tria Kolekto da Krimnoveloj, 1996; chapters in books and articles in learned jls. *Recreations:* music, Esperanto, bridge. *Address:* Wangarang, 182 Kelly's Plains Road, Armidale, NSW 2350, Australia.

GATES, Ven. Simon Philip; Archdeacon of Lambeth, since 2013; *b* Bromley, 12 July 1960; *s* of Michael and Ann Gates; *m* 1996, Helen Rosalind Shepherd; one *s* two *d*. *Educ:* Univ. of St Andrews (MA Classical Studies 1982); Durham Univ. (BA Theol. 1986). Ordained deacon, 1987, priest, 1988; Asst Curate, St John, Southall Green, 1987–91; Associate Minister, St Andrews, Kowloon, Hong Kong, 1991–95; Vicar: St Stephen, Clapham Park, 1996–2006; St Thomas with St Stephen, Telford Park, 2006–13; Area Dean, Lambeth South, 2006–13. *Recreations:* gardening, hill-walking, cooking. *Address:* 7 Hoadly Road, Streatham, SW16 1AE. *T:* (020) 8545 2440, *Fax:* (020) 8545 2441. *E:* simon.gates@southwark.anglican.org.

GATES, William Henry, III, Hon. KBE 2004; Technology Adviser, Microsoft Corp., since 2014 (Chairman, 1976–2014); Co-Founder and Co-Chair, Bill & Melinda Gates Foundation (formerly William H. Gates Foundation), since 1994; *b* 28 Oct. 1955; *s* of William Henry and Mary Maxwell Gates; *m* 1994, Melinda French (Hon. DBE 2013); one *s* two *d*. *Educ:* Lakeside High Sch., Seattle; Harvard Univ. Co-founder, Micro Soft, later Microsoft Corp., 1975; Chief Software Architect, 2000–08. *Publications:* The Road Ahead, 1995; (with C. Hemingway) Business @ the Speed of Thought: using a digital nervous system, 1999. *Address:* Microsoft Corp., 1 Microsoft Way, Redmond, WA 98052–8300, USA.

GATFORD, Ven. Ian; Archdeacon of Derby, 1993–2005; *b* 15 June 1940; *s* of Frederick Ernest and Chrissie Lilian Gatford; *m* 1965, Anne Maire (*née* Whitehead); one *s* three *d*. *Educ:* King's Coll. London (AKC 1965); St Boniface Coll., Warminster. Management Trainee, Taylor Woodrow Gp, 1959–62; Accounts and Admin, Farr's (Construction) Ltd, 1965–66; ordained deacon 1967, priest 1968; Curate, St Mary, Clifton, Nottingham, 1967–71; Team Vicar, Holy Trinity, Clifton, 1971–75; Vicar, St Martin, Sherwood, 1975–84; Canon Residentiary, Derby Cathedral, 1984–2000; Sub-Provost, Derby Cathedral, 1990–93. Presenter of weekly help-line programmes, BBC Radio Nottingham, 1972–84; presenter of religious affairs programmes, BBC Radio Derby, 1984–93; Chairman: BBC Local Adv. Council, 1998–2001; Derbys Area Cttee, RSCM, 2007–13. *Recreations:* playing the piano, classical music, German and French literature and conversation, walking, cycling and cycle training with Cycle Derby 2006–08. *Address:* 9 Poplar Nook, Derby DE22 2DW.

GATHERCOLE, Prof. Susan E., PhD; FBA 2014; Director, MRC Cognition and Brain Sciences Unit, Cambridge, since 2011; MRC Research Professor, University of Cambridge. *Educ:* York Univ. (BSc Psychol.); City Univ., London (PhD). Postdoctoral res., Oxford Univ., 1982–84; jun. scientist, MRC Applied Psychol. Unit, 1984–88; Lectr, Lancaster Univ., 1988–93; Reader, 1993–95, Prof. of Psychol., 1995–2001, Bristol Univ.; Professor of Psychology: Durham Univ., 2001–06; Univ. of York, 2006–11. Spearman Medal, 1989, President's Award, 2007, BPsS. *Publications:* (ed jtly) Theories of Memory, 1993; (with A. D. Baddeley) Working Memory and Language: essays in cognitive psychology, 1993; (ed with R. McCarthy) Memory Tests and Techniques, 1994; (ed) Models of Short-Term Memory, 1996; (ed jtly) Theories of Memory II, 1998; (ed) Short-term and Working Memory, 2001; (with T. P. Alloway) Working Memory in Neurodevelopmental Conditions, 2006; Working Memory and Learning: a practical guide for teachers, 2008; contribs to jls incl. Jl Child Psychol. Psychiatry, Child Neuropsychol., Jl Exptl Child Psychol., Develtl Sci., Jl Speech, Lang. and Hearing Res., Memory, Qly Jl Exptl Psychol. *Address:* MRC Cognition and Brain Sciences Unit, University of Cambridge, 15 Chaucer Road, Cambridge CB2 7EF.

GATHORNE-HARDY, family name of **Earl of Cranbrook**.

GATT, Colin, CMG 1993; Director, Managed Projects, Commonwealth Development Corporation, 1989–94; *b* 16 Aug. 1934; *s* of late William John Sim Gatt and Margaret Whyte-Hepburn; *m* 1st, 1957, Sheena Carstairs (*d* 1996); one *s* one *d* (and one *s* decd); 2nd, 1998, Susan Tessa Jennifer (*née* Lewis-Antill). *Educ:* state schs in Scotland. Engineer, 1955–71: manager, gen. manager and consultant, agricl businesses in Africa and Asia; Commonwealth Development Corporation, 1971–94: managed businesses in third world countries in Asia, Africa and Pacific regions, 1971–88. Independence Medal (Solomon Is), 1978. *Recreations:* reading, golf, wine, basic survival cookery. *Address:* Cobblestones, 16A East Street, Thame, Oxon OX9 3JS. *Club:* Oxfordshire Golf (Thame).

GATT, Ian Andrew; QC 2002; a Recorder of the Crown Court, since 2000; Partner, Herbert Smith Freehills LLP (formerly Herbert Smith LLP), since 2005; *b* 21 April 1963; *s* of John Alexander Gatt and Marie Gatt; *m* 1987, Nicola Jane Gatt (*née* Cherry); one *s* two *d*. *Educ:* Hertford Coll., Oxford (BA (Hons) Jurisprudence 1st cl.). Called to the Bar, Lincoln's Inn, 1985. *Publications:* (jtly) Arlidge and Parry on Fraud, 2nd edn, 1996; (with John Bowers) Procedure in Courts and Tribunals, 2nd edn 2000. *Recreations:* family, friends, Rugby, cars, Apostrophe Chambers. *Address:* Herbert Smith Freehills LLP, Exchange House, Primrose Street, EC2A 2EG. *T:* (020) 7466 3576, *Fax:* (020) 7374 0888. *E:* ian.gatt@hsf.com. *Club:* Goodwood Road Racing.

GATTI, Daniele; conductor; Music Director, Orchestre National de France, since 2008; *b* Milan, 6 Nov. 1961. *Educ:* Milan Conservatory. Founder and Music Dir, Stradivari Chamber Orch., 1986–92; débuts: La Scala, Milan, 1987–88; in USA with American Symphony Orch., Carnegie Hall, NY, 1990; Covent Gdn, 1992; Metropolitan Opera, NY, 1994–95; with RPO, 1994; with NY Philharmonic, 1995; Bayreuth Fest., 2008; Music Dir, Accad. di Santa Cecilia, Rome, 1992–97; Principal Guest Conductor, Covent Gdn, 1994–96; Music Director: RPO, 1996–2009; Teatro Communale, Bologna, 1997–2007; Principal Conductor, Zurich Opera, 2009–12; has worked with leading opera cos incl. Vienna State Opera, La Scala, Munich State Opera; has conducted leading internat. orchestras incl. New York Philharmonic, Boston Symphony, Wiener Philharmoniker, Royal Concertgebouw, Bayerischer Rundfunk, Chicago Symphony, LPO. Has toured extensively and made numerous recordings. *Recreations:* reading, walking, football, chess. *Address:* c/o Orchestre National de France, 116 Avenue du President Kennedy, 75016 Paris, France; CAMI Music LLC, 1790 Broadway, New York, NY 10019–1412, USA.

GATTING, Michael William, OBE 1987; Managing Director, Cricket Partnerships, England and Wales Cricket Board, since 2007; *b* 6 June 1957; *s* of William Alfred Gatting and Vera Mavis Gatting; *m* 1980, Elaine Mabbott; two *s*. *Educ:* John Kelly Boys' High Sch. Middlesex County Cricket team, 1975–98: début, 1975; county cap, 1977; Captain, 1988–97; retired from 1st XI, 1998; scored 77 hundreds, 8 double hundreds, 1000 runs in a season 17 times; highest score 258, 1984; also took 129 wickets and 393 catches. Test début, 1977; England Captain, 1986–88; overseas tours with England: NZ and Pakistan, 1977–78, 1983–84; W Indies, 1980–81, 1985–86; India and Sri Lanka, 1981–82, 1992–93; India, 1984–85; Australia, 1986–87; Australia and NZ, 1987–88; Australia, 1994–95; also, World Cup, 1987–88, *v* India, Pakistan, Australia and NZ; scored ten Test centuries; highest score 207, 1984–85. England A team coach, Australia tour, 1996–97, Kenya and Sri Lanka tour, 1997–98; Dir of Coaching, Middx CCC, 1998–2000; Manager: England Under 19 team, NZ tour, 1999; England A team, NZ tour, 1999. Mem., Selection Panel, ECB, 1997–99. Dir, Ashwell Leisure Group, 2001–03. President: Lord's Taverners, 2003–06; MCC, 2013–14. Hon. Dr Middlesex. Freedom, London Borough of Enfield, 2003. *Publications:* Limited Overs, 1986; Triumph in Australia, 1987; Leading from the Front, 1988. *Recreations:* golf, swimming, reading, music. *Address:* c/o Middlesex County Cricket Club, Lord's Cricket Ground, St John's Wood Road, NW8 8QN.

GATTY, Trevor Thomas, OBE 1974; HM Diplomatic Service, retired; international business consultant, arbitrator and mediator; President, TGC Group (formerly MGT International), since 1989; *b* 8 June 1930; *s* of Thomas Alfred Gatty and Lillian Gatty (*née* Wood); *m* 1st, 1956, Jemima Bowman (marr. diss. 1983); two *s* one *d*; 2nd, 1989, Myrna Saturn; one step *s* one step *d*. *Educ:* King Edward's Sch., Birmingham. Served Army, 1948–50, 2/Lieut Royal Warwickshire Regt, later Lieut Royal Fusiliers (TA), 1950–53. Foreign Office, 1950; Vice-Consul, Leopoldville, 1954; FO, 1958–61; Second (later First) Sec., Bangkok, 1961–64; Consul, San Francisco, 1965–66; Commercial Consul, San Francisco, 1967–68; FCO, 1968–73; Commercial Consul, Zürich, 1973–75; FCO, 1975–76; Counsellor (Diplomatic Service Inspector), 1977–80; Head, Migration and Visa Dept, FCO, 1980–81; Consul-General, Atlanta, 1981–85. Protocol Advr, Atlanta Organising Cttee for Olympic Games, 1996; Co-founder and Bd Mem., Internat. Soc. of Protocol and Etiquette Professionals, 2002–. Hon. British Consul for N Carolina, 1994–2001. *Address:* 229 North Poplar Street (#15), Charlotte, NC 28202, USA. *T:* (704) 3381372, (UK) (020) 7993 6587. *E:* ttgatty@gmail.com.

GATWARD, (Anthony) James; Chairman, Shape Up Studios Ltd, since 2011; *b* 4 March 1938; *s* of George James Gatward and Lillian Georgina (*née* Strutton); *m* 1969, Isobel Anne Stuart Black, actress; three *d*. *Educ:* George Gascoigne Sch., Walthamstow; South West Essex Technical Coll. and Sch. of Art (drama course). Entered TV industry, 1957; freelance drama producer/director: Canada and USA, 1959–65; BBC and most ITV cos, 1966–70; partner in prodn co., acting as Exec. Prod. and often Dir of many internat. co-prodns in UK, Ceylon, Australia and Germany, 1970–78; instigated and led preparation of application for S and SE England television franchise, 1979–80 (awarded Dec. 1980); Man. Dir, 1979–84, Chief Exec., 1984–91, Television South, subseq. TVS Entertainment PLC; Dep. Chm. and Chief Exec., 1984–90, Chm., 1990–91, TVS Television; Chief Exec., 1993–96, Chm., 1996–2000, Complete Media Mgt Ltd; Chm., Digital Television Network Ltd, 1996–99; Dep. Chm., Premium TV Ltd, 2000–03. Director: Southstar, Scottish and Global TV, 1971–78; Ind. TV Publications Ltd, 1982–88; Oracle Teletext Ltd, 1982–88; Solent Cablevision Ltd, 1983–89; Channel 4 TV Co., 1984–89; Ind. TV News Ltd, 1986–91; Super Channel Ltd, 1986–88; ITV Super Channel Ltd, 1986–89; Chm., TVS Production, 1984–89; Chm. and Chief Exec., TVS N American Hldgs, 1988–91; Pres., Telso Communications Inc., 1987–90; Chairman: Telso Communications Ltd, 1987–91; Telso Overseas Ltd, 1987–91; Midem Orgn SA, 1987–89; MTM Entertainment Inc., 1988–91 (Chief Exec. Officer, 1989–91); Redgrave Theatre, 1995–98. Member: Council, Operation Raleigh; Court of the Mary Rose. Pres., SE Agricl Soc., 1992; Governor, S of England Agricl Soc. *Recreations:* sailing, music. *Clubs:* Royal Thames Yacht; Porquerolles Yacht (Hyères).

GAU, John Glen Mackay, CBE 1989; former independent television producer; Managing Director, 1981–88, Chief Executive, 1990–2002, John Gau Productions; *b* 25 March 1940; *s* of late Cullis William Gau and Nan Munro; *m* 1966, Susan Tebbs; two *s*. *Educ:* Haileybury and ISC; Trinity Hall, Cambridge; Univ. of Wisconsin. BBC TV: Asst Film Ed., 1963; Current Affairs Producer, 24 Hours, Panorama, 1965–72; Dep. Ed., Midweek, 1973–74; Ed., Nationwide, 1975–78; Head of Current Affairs Progs, 1978–81; Dep. Chief Exec. and Dir of Progs, British Satellite Broadcasting, 1988–90. Dir, Channel 4, 1984–88. Chm., Ind. Programme Producers' Assoc., 1983–86. FRTS 1986 (Chm. Council, 1986–88; Hon. Sec., 1993–2002; Gold Medal, 2003). *Publications:* (jtly) Soldiers, 1985; Lights, Camera, Action!, 1995. *Address:* 15 St Albans Mansion, Kensington Court Place, W8 5QH. *T:* (020) 7937 4033. *E:* johngau@hotmail.com.

GAUCK, Joachim; President, Federal Republic of Germany, since 2012; *b* Rostock, 24 Jan. 1940. Mem. (Alliance 90), GDR Parlt, 1990. Federal Comr, Files of State Security Service of former GDR, 1991–2000. *Address:* Bundespräsidialamt, Referat Z1, 11010 Berlin, Germany.

GAUKE, David Michael; MP (C) South West Hertfordshire, since 2005; Financial Secretary, HM Treasury, since 2014; *b* 8 Oct. 1971; *s* of Jim Gauke and Susan Gauke (now Hall); *m* 2000, Rachel Katherine Rank; three *s*. *Educ:* Northgate High Sch., Ipswich; St Edmund Hall, Oxford; Chester Coll. of Law. Trainee solicitor and solicitor, Richards Butler, 1995–98; admitted, 1997; solicitor, Macfarlanes, 1999–2005. Exchequer Sec., HM Treasury, 2010–14. *Recreations:* cricket, football, walking, reading, family. *Address:* House of Commons, SW1A 0AA. *T:* (020) 7219 3000. *E:* david@davidgauke.com. *Clubs:* Rickmansworth Conservative; Tring Conservative.

GAULT, David Hamilton; Executive Chairman, Gallic Management Co. Ltd, 1974–93; *b* 9 April 1928; *s* of Leslie Hamilton Gault and Iris Hilda Gordon Young; *m* 1950, Felicity Jane Gribble; three *s* two *d*. *Educ:* Fettes Coll., Edinburgh. Nat. Service, commnd in RA, 1946–48;

Clerk, C. H. Rugg & Co. Ltd, Shipbrokers, 1948–52; H. Clarkson & Co. Ltd, Shipbrokers: Man. 1952–56; Dir 1956–62; Jt Man. Dir 1962–72; Gp Man. Dir, Shipping Industrial Holdings Ltd, 1972–74; Chm., Jebsen (UK) Ltd, 1962–81; Chm., Seabridge Shipping Ltd, 1965–73. *Recreations:* gardening, walking. *Address:* Kent House, East Harting, near Petersfield, Hants GU31 5LS. *T:* (01730) 825206. *Club:* Boodle's.

GAULT, David Thomas, FRCS; Consultant Plastic Surgeon, The Portland Hospital, since 2006; Founder, London Centre for Ear Reconstruction, Portland Hospital, 2006; *b* 21 March 1954; *s* of William and Irene Mabel Bebe Gault; *m* 1989, Debra Hastings-Nield; two *s* two *d.* *Educ:* Edinburgh Univ. (MB ChB 1977). FRCS 1982. MRC French Exchange Fellow, 1987; Craniofacial Fellow, Hôpital des Enfants Malades, Paris, 1987; Sen. Registrar, Plastic Surgery, St Thomas' Hosp., Gt Ormond St Hosp. for Sick Children and Royal Marsden Hosp., 1988–91; Consultant Plastic Surgeon: Mt Vernon Hosp., 1991–2006; Gt Ormond St Hosp. for Sick Children, 2000–06; Consultant: Bishops Wood Hosp., 1991–; Wellington Hosp., 1992–. Hon. Sen. Lectr, UCL, 1999–; Vis. Prof., Chinese Univ. of Hong Kong, 2004–05. Ethicon Foundn Travelling Schol., 1987; Wellington Foundn Schol., 1989; BAPS Travelling Bursary, 1990. Developer, Ear Buddies, 1990. *Publications:* contribs to books and articles on laser and plastic surgery, particularly on ear reconstruction and depilation laser treatment. *Recreations:* rowing, painting, sculpting, planting. *Address:* The Portland Hospital, Great Portland Street, W1W 5AH. *T:* (020) 7935 7665. *Club:* Cliveden (Taplow).

GAULT, Michael, OBE 2008; pistol shooter; Test and Measuring Equipment Controller, Ministry of Defence, since 1997; *b* 2 May 1954; *s* of Elizabeth Gault; *m* 1974, Janet Mary Manning; one *s* two *d.* *Educ:* St Bede's Jun. Sch.; St Newman's Sch., Carlisle. RAF, 1969–96: trained as electronics technician, RAF Cosford; served with 29 Sqn (Lightnings), 57 Sqn (Victors), 14 and 20 Sqns (Jaguars). Pistol shooter: British Champion, annually, 1992–96, 1998–99, and 2001–12; Commonwealth Games medals: Victoria, 1994: Gold, Free Pistol; Silver, Men's 25m Centre Fire Pistol; Bronze, Free Pistol pairs (with P. Leatherdale); Kuala Lumpur, 1998: Gold: Free Pistol; Free Pistol pairs (with N. Baxter); Men's 10m Air Pistol; 10m Air Pistol pairs (with N. Baxter); Manchester, 2002: Gold: Men's 10m Air Pistol; Men's 50m Pistol; Men's 10m Air Pistol pairs (with N. Baxter); Bronze, Men's 25m Standard Pistol; Melbourne, 2006: Gold, Men's 25m Standard Pistol; Silver: Men's 10m Air Pistol pairs (with N. Baxter); Men's 50m Pistol; Bronze, 50m Pistol pairs (with N. Baxter); New Delhi, 2010: Silver, Men's Air Pistol pairs (with N. Baxter); Bronze, Men's 25m Standard Pistol pairs (with I. Ubhi). Hon. Life Member: London and Middlesex Rifle Assoc.; Norwich City Pistol and Rifle Club; British Pistol Club; Holt and District Rifle and Pistol Club (Hon. Life Pres.); Nat. Small-bore Rifle Assoc. (Gold Medal, 2006); Blackburn Rifle and Pistol Club; Civil Service Sports Council Target Shooting Assoc.; Life Vice-Pres., Co. of Lancaster Small-Bore Target Shooting Assoc., 2012. Dereham Citizen of the Year, 2006–07. Civil Service Sportsman of the Year, 2006; Sportsperson of the Year, Eastern Daily Press, 2007; Lifetime Achievement Award, BBC Eastern, 2007. RAF Long Service and Good Conduct Medal, 1987; Lifetime Achievement Award, Pride in Breckland Awards, 2011. *Recreations:* qualified as a Regional Pistol Coach, looking for spare time, now a grandad with four grandchildren to play with. *E:* mickey.g@talktalk.net.

GAULT, Rt Hon. Sir Thomas (Munro), KNZM 2009 (DCNZM 2001); PC 1992; Judge of the Supreme Court of New Zealand, 2004–06, temporary, 2006–14; *b* 31 Oct. 1938; *s* of Thomas Gordon Gault and Evelyn Jane Gault (*née* Paulmeir); *m* 1963, Barbara Pauline Stewart; one *s.* *Educ:* Wellington Coll.; Victoria University Coll. (LLB); Victoria Univ. of Wellington (LLM). Solicitor of Supreme Court of NZ, 1961; A. J. Park & Son, 1961–81; practised at NZ Bar, 1981–87; QC 1984; Judge of High Court of NZ, 1987–91; Judge, 1991–2004, Pres., 2002–04, Court of Appeal, NZ. Judge (non-permanent), Court of Final Appeal, Hong Kong, 2006. Mem. of Honour, Internat. Assoc. for Protection of Industrial Property, 1990. *Recreation:* golf (Capt., Royal and Ancient Golf Club of St Andrews, 2005–06). *Address:* 2 Mamie Street, Remuera, Auckland, New Zealand. *T:* (9) 5246906.

GAULTER, Derek Vivian, CBE 1978; Chairman, Construction Industry Training Board, 1985–90; *b* 10 Dec. 1924; *s* of late Jack Rudolf Gaulter, MC and Muriel Gaulter (*née* Westworth); *m* 1st, 1949, Edith Irene Shackleton (*d* 1996); one *s* three *d*; 2nd, 2000, Marion Bowker (marr. diss. 2009). *Educ:* Denstone College; Peterhouse, Cambridge (MA). RNVR, Sub Lieut MTBs/Minesweepers, 1943–46. Lord Justice Holker Sen. Scholarship, Gray's Inn; called to the Bar, Gray's Inn, 1949; Common Law Bar, Manchester, 1950–55. Federation of Civil Engineering Contractors: Legal Sec., General Sec., Dep. Dir Gen., 1955–67; Dir Gen., 1967–86. Trustee, Woodland Trust, 1995–2000. *Recreations:* gardening, travel, opera. *Address:* 4 Abbotts Lea Cottages, Worthy Road, Winchester SO23 7HB.

GAULTIER, Jean-Paul; fashion designer; *b* 24 April 1952; *s* of Paul Gaultier and Solange Gaultier (*née* Garrabe). *Educ:* Lycée, Arcueil, Paris. Assistant: to Pierre Cardin, 1970; to Jacques Esterel, 1971–73; designer of US collections for Pierre Cardin, 1974–75; ind. designer, 1976–82; founder, Jean-Paul Gaultier SA, 1978; Artistic Dir, Hermès, 2004–10. Début collection, 1976; first collection for men, 1984, Junior Gaultier, 1988; also perfumes, 1993, 1995, 1999 and 2006. Designed costumes: for ballet, Le Défilé de Régine Chopinot, 1985; for films: The Cook, the Thief, His Wife and her Lover, 1989; Kika, 1994; La Cité des Enfants Perdus, 1995; The Fifth Element, 1996; Bad Education, 2004; The Skin I Live In, 2011; for Madonna's Blond Ambition tour, 1990. Chevalier des Arts et des Lettres (France); Chevalier de la Légion d'Honneur (France). *Address:* Jean-Paul Gaultier SA, 325 rue Saint-Martin, 75003 Paris, France.

GAUMOND, Most Rev. Mgr André; Archbishop of Sherbrooke, (RC), 1996–2011; *b* 3 June 1936. *Educ:* Ste Anne de la Pocatière, PQ (BA); St Paul's Seminary, Ottawa (LTh); Institut Catholique, Paris (LPh). Teacher of Philosophy: Ste Anne de la Pocatière, 1966–69; Coll. d'Enseignement Général et Professionnel de la Pocatière, 1969–80; Parish Priest, St Pamphile and St Omer, PQ, 1980–85; Bishop of Ste Anne de la Pocatière, 1985–95; Coadjutor Archbishop of Sherbrooke, 1995–96. *Recreation:* golf.

GAUNT, Jonathan Robert; QC 1991; a Deputy High Court Judge, since 2002; *b* 3 Nov. 1947; *s* of late Dr Brian Gaunt and Dr Mary Gaunt (*née* Hudson); *m* 1975, Lynn Dennis; one *d.* *Educ:* St Peter's Coll.; Radley; University Coll., Oxford (BA). Called to the Bar, Lincoln's Inn, 1972, Bencher, 1998. Jt Head, Falcon Chambers, 1993–. *Publications:* (ed) Halsbury's Laws of England, Vol. 27, 4th edn 1981, rev. 1994; (ed) Gale on Easements, 16th edn 1996 to 19th edn 2012. *Recreations:* golf, sailing. *Address:* Falcon Chambers, Falcon Court, EC4Y 1AA. *T:* (020) 7353 2484.

GAUNT, Maj. Gen. Mark Jarvis; Director Support, Army Headquarters, since 2015; *b* Beverley, E Yorks, 24 Dec. 1965; *s* of late Edwin Gaunt and Ida Gaunt; *m* 1991, Catherine Alice Humphrey; two *d.* *Educ:* Beverley Grammar Sch.; Welbeck Coll.; Royal Mil. Acad. Sandhurst; Royal Mil. Coll. of Sci. (MSc 1997); King's Coll. London (MA); Saïd Business Sch., Univ. of Oxford. Commnd REME, 1985; Platoon Comd 14 Berlin Field Workshop, 1984–86; NI Regt AAC, 1990–93; BEME 24 Airmobile Bde, 1993–95; Army Tech. Support Agency, 1995–96; Defence Technol. Course, 1997; acsc 1998; SO2 Prog. Directorate Equipment Capability Direct Battlefield Engagement, 1998–2000; Co. Comd 3 Bn REME, 2000–02; Dep. COS BRITFOR, Bosnia, 2002; MA to Dep. Supreme Allied Comdr Transformation, 2003–05; CO 1 Bn REME, 2005–07; Div. Dir Intermediate Comd and Staff Course (Land), 2007–08; Future Rapid Effects System Integrated Project Team, 2008; Prog. Support Function Hd of Capability Ground Manoeuvre, 2008–10; Comdr Equipment Capability, Afghanistan, 2010–11; Hd, Soldier System Prog., Defence Equipment and Support, 2011–13; Dir Equipment, Army HQ, 2013–15. *Recreations:* motorsport, running, hiking, squash.

GAUTEL, Prof. Mathias Sebastian, MD PhD; FMedSci; Professor of Molecular Cardiology, since 2002, and British Heart Foundation Professor of Molecular Cardiology, since 2008, King's College London; *b* Karlsruhe, Germany, 31 March 1963; *s* of Peter and Uta Gautel; *m* 1992, Dr Gudrun Kunst; two *s* one *d.* *Educ:* Fichte-Gymnasium, Karlsruhe; Heidelberg Univ. (MD *summa cum laude* 1991; accreditation as med. doctor 1993; MD PhD 1998). Habilitation Fellow, German Res. Foundn, and Vis. Gp Leader, Structl Biol. Div., EMBL Heidelberg, 1996–98; Heisenberg Fellow and Gp Leader, Max-Planck-Inst. for Molecular Physiol., Dept of Physical Biochem., Dortmund, 1999–2002; Hd, Muscle Signalling Section, Randall Div. for Cell and Molecular Biophysics, KCL, 2003–. Ed.-in-Chief, Jl Muscle Res. and Cell Motility, 2010–. FMedSci 2010. Outstanding Investigator Award, Internat. Soc. for Heart Res., 2009. *Publications:* contribs to learned jls, incl. Nature, Science, Cell, Proc. NAS (USA), EMBO Jl. *Recreations:* family, sport diving (BSAC dive leader and assistant club instructor), art, theatre and opera, antiquity. *Address:* Randall Division for Cell and Molecular Biophysics, and Cardiovascular Division, King's College London, New Hunt's House, Guy's Campus, 18–20 Newcomen Street, SE1 1UL. *T:* (020) 7848 6434. *E:* mathias.gautel@kcl.ac.uk.

GAUTIER-SMITH, Peter Claudius, FRCP; Consultant Neurologist, National Hospitals for Nervous Diseases, Queen Square and Maida Vale, 1962–89; *b* 1 March 1929; *s* of late Claudius Gautier-Smith and Madeleine (*née* Ferguson); *m* 1960, Nesta Mary Wroth; two *d.* *Educ:* Cheltenham Coll. (Exhibnr); King's Coll., Cambridge; St Thomas's Hosp. Med. Sch. MA, MD. Casualty Officer, House Physician, St Thomas' Hosp., 1955–56; Medical Registrar, University Coll. Hosp., 1958; Registrar, National Hosp., Queen Square, 1960–62; Consultant Neurologist, St George's Hosp., 1962–75; Dean, Inst. of Neurology, 1975–82. Mem., Bd of Governors, Nat. Hosps for Nervous Diseases, 1975–89. Hon. Neurologist, Dispensaire Français, London, 1983–89. *Publications:* Parasagittal and Falx Meningiomas, 1970; papers in learned jls on neurology; (as Peter Conway) over 30 novels incl.: Locked In, 2006; Evil Streak, 2006; Unwillingly to School, 2007; Deserving Death, 2007; Deadly Obsession, 2008; Family Fallout, 2011. *Recreations:* literary; French language; squash (played for Cambridge v Oxford, 1951; Captain, London Univ., 1954); tennis (played for King's Coll., Cambridge, 1952, St Thomas' Hosp., 1953–55). *Clubs:* Hawks (Cambridge); Jesters.

GAVASKAR, Sunil Manohar; Padma Bhushan; cricketer; business executive; Chairman, Cricket Committee, International Cricket Council, 2000–08; *b* 10 July 1949; *s* of Manohar Keshav Gavaskar and Meenal Manohar Gavaskar; *m* 1974, Marshniel Mehrotra; one *s.* *Educ:* St Xavier's High Sch.; St Xavier's Coll.; Bombay Univ. (BA). Represented India in cricket, 1971–88; Captain, Indian Team, 1978, 1979–80, 1980–82 and 1984–85; made 10,122 runs, incl. 34 centuries, in 125 Test matches; passed world records for no of runs in Test matches, 1983, and no of Test centuries, 1984; first batsman to score over 10,000 Test runs, 1987. Sheriff of Mumbai, 1994–95. *Publications:* Sunny Days, 1976; Idols, 1983; Runs 'n Ruins, 1984; One-day Wonders, 1985. *Clubs:* Cricket Club of India, Bombay Gymkhana.

GAVIN, (Alexander) Rupert; Executive Chairman, Incidental Colman, since 1996; Chief Executive, Odeon and UCI Cinema Group, 2005–14; *b* 1 Oct. 1954; *s* of late David Maitland Gavin and Helen Gavin (who *m* 1991, Sir Hugh Hambling, 3rd Bt); *m* 1991, Ellen Janet Miller; two *d.* *Educ:* Magdalene Coll., Cambridge (BA Hons 1975; MA). Dir and Partner, Sharps Advertising, 1981–85; Dir, Saatchi & Saatchi Gp, 1985–87; Dep. Man. Dir, Dixons Stores Gp, 1987–94; Man. Dir, Consumer Div., British Telecom, 1994–98; Chm. and Chief Exec., BBC Worldwide, 1998–2004; Chm., Contender Entertainment Gp, 2004–06; Chief Exec., Kingdom Media, 2005–06 (Dir, 2004–06). Dir, Ambassador Theatre Gp, 1999–2009 (Dir, Adv. Gp, 2009–); non-executive Director: Virgin Mobile, 2004–06; Garden Centre Gp, 2014–; Countrywide plc, 2014–; L'Escargot Ltd, 2014–. Chm., Historic Royal Palaces, 2015–. Liveryman, Grocers' Co., 1986–; Mem., Ct of Assts, Grocers' Co., 2010–. FRTS 2005 (Vice-Pres., 1997–2006). Olivier Awards: for Best Entertainment, 1999, 2000 and 2002; for Best New Play, 2003 and 2011; for Best New Musical, 2011. *Recreations:* theatre producing, songwriting, gardening. *Clubs:* Royal Automobile, Thirty.

GAVRON, Lady; Katharine Susan Gavron, (Kate), PhD; Chair: Carcanet Press Ltd, since 1989; Folio Society, since 2015; Folio Holdings Ltd, since 2015; *b* 19 Jan. 1955; *d* of His Honour (Maurice John) Peter Macnair and of Vickie Macnair; *m* 1st, 1975, Gerrard Gardiner (marr. diss. 1982); 2nd, 1989, Robert Gavron (Baron Gavron, CBE) (*d* 2015). *Educ:* Francis Holland Sch.; London Sch. of Econs (BSc; PhD 1997). William Heinemann Ltd, 1974–88 (Dir, 1984–88); Director: Secker & Warburg Ltd, 1984–88; Virago Press Ltd, 1994–96; Folio Hldgs Ltd, 2009–. Dir, Mutual Aid Centre, 1996–2005; Trustee and Research Fellow: Inst. Community Studies, 1992–2005; Young Foundn, 2005–09. Trustee: Runnymede Trust, 1997–2009; The Poetry Archive, 2001–08; Ballet Boyz (formerly George Piper Dances), 2001–; Helen Hamlyn Trust, 2001–; Reprieve, 2010–. *Publications:* (with G. Dench and T. Flower) Young at Eighty: the prolific public life of Michael Young, 1995; (with G. Dench and M. Young) The New East End: kinship, race and conflict, 2006. *Address:* c/o The Folio Society, 44 Eagle Street, WC1R 4FS.

GAVRON, Felicia Nicolette, (Nicky); Member (Lab), London Assembly, Greater London Authority, since 2000 (Member for Enfield and Haringey, 2000–04); Deputy Mayor of London, 2000–03 and 2004–08; *d* of Clayton English Coates and Elisabet Charlotta Horstmeyer; *m* 1967, Robert Gavron (Baron Gavron, CBE) (marr. diss. 1987; he *d* 2015); two *d.* *Educ:* Worcester Girls' Grammar Sch.; Courtauld Inst. Lectr, Camberwell Sch. of Art and St Martin's Sch. of Art. Mem. (Lab) Haringey BC, 1986–2002 (Chm., Develt Control, Planning Tech. and Envmtl Services Cttees). Mem., London Planning Adv. Cttee, 1989–97 and 1998–2000 (Dep. Chm., 1989–94; Chm., 1994–97 and 1998–2000; Leader, Lab Gp, 1989–2000); Local Government Association: Chm., 1997–99, Vice Chm., 1999–2000, Planning Cttee; Mem., Policy and Strategy Cttee, and Envmt and Regeneration Bd, 1997–2000; Chm., Reforming Local Planning, 1997–2002; Member: Exec., GLAA, 1986–92 (Vice Chm., London Arts Bd, 1992–2000); ALA, 1988–94 (Vice Chm., Envmtl Services Cttee); AMA, 1988–96 (Mem., Urban Policy Cttee; Vice Chm., Develt and Transport Cttee, 1995–96); SE Regl Planning Conf., 1989–2001 (Leader, Lab Gp, 1993–97; Vice Chm., 1997–2000); London Res. Centre Cttee, 1992–2000; Assoc. of London Govt, 1994–2000 (Mem., Envmt Cttee); London Pride Partnership, 1994–97 (Convener, Arts and Culture Gp; Co-Vice Chm., London Pride Housing Initiative; Co-Chm., London Pride Waste Action Prog., 1995–97); Bd, London First, 1995–2000. Chm., Children and Young People's Strategy Gp, GLA, 2000–02; Chm. and Dep. Chm. (alternate years), Planning and Housing Cttee, London Assembly, 2008–; Mayor of London's lead on London Plan and Strategic Planning, 2000–08, on Climate Change, 2004–08. Convener and Chairman: Land Use and Transport Interaction Working Gp, 1996–99; Brownfield Policy and Implementation Gp, 1997–98; Chairman: Nat. Planning Forum, 1999–2002; Commn for Integrated Transport, 1999–2002; Mayor's London Hydrogen Partnership, 2004–08; Dep. Chm., Mayor's London Climate Change Agency, 2006–; Vice Chm., Global Urban Develt, 2010–; Member: Thames Adv. Gp, 1994–97; Sounding Bd on Design, DoE, subseq. DETR, 1997–99; Metropolitan Police Authy, 2000–08; Sustainable Develt Commn, 2001–03; Internat. Adv. Bd, Rotterdam, 2009–; Advr, Urban Task Force, 1998–2000; Hon. Advr, Jt US-China Collaboration on Clean Energy, 2010–; Chief Project Advr, Economics of Green Cities, 2011–. Co-Founder,

C40 (formerly C20) Large Cities Climate Change Leadership Gp, 2005. Founding Trustee, Jackson's Lane Community Centre, 1975–. Hon. FRIBA 2001. Hon. Dr London Guildhall, 2001. *Address:* Greater London Authority, City Hall, More London, Queen's Walk, SE1 2AA.

GAWN, Ryan Marshall; Deployable Civilian Expert, Stabilisation Unit, UK Government, since 2009; Director, Stratagem International, since 2011; Head of International Communications, ActionAid International, since 2013; *b* Belfast, 6 April 1979; *s* of Richard Gawn and Iris Gawn (*née* Marshall); *m* 2014, Anna Wansbrough-Jones. *Educ:* Stirling Univ. (BA 1st Cl. Hons Politics 2001); Univ. of Salvador, Buenos Aires (MA Internat. Relns 2007). Ed., Santiago News Rev., Santiago, Chile, 2003; Business Develt Manager, Procter & Gamble UK, 2003–04; Pol Admin. Officer, Strategic Planning Unit, Exec. Office of Sec.-Gen., UN, NY, 2005; Internat. Ext. Relns Coordinator, Save the Children UK, 2006–09; Regl Manager, Eastern Afghanistan, Peace Dividend Trust, 2009–10; Dir, Penn Schoen Berland, 2010–11; Strategic Communications Advr, FCO, 2011–12, Strategic Campaigns Advr, DFID, 2012–13, British High Commn, Pakistan. Member: Council, RIIA, 2008–; Adv. Panel, NI Foundn, 2008–; Transatlantic Network, British Council, 2008–14. Hon. Sec., 2007, Hon. Treas., 2008–09, UN Assoc. Trustee, Concordis Internat., 2010–14. Arthur D. Tripp Meml Schol., Pennsylvania, 2001–02, World Peace Fellow, Buenos Aires, 2004–06, Rotary Internat.; Salzburg Global Seminar Fellow, Salzburg, 2007. *Publications:* Economics in Peacemaking: lessons from Northern Ireland, 2007; Where Peace Begins: education's role in conflict prevention and peacemaking, 2008; contribs to jls incl. Foreign Policy Mag., Public Affairs News, Strategic Analysis, Irish Pol Studies, Peace and Conflict Rev., Internat. Affairs Forum. *Recreations:* Rugby, squash, tennis, polo, sailing, theatre, travel. *Address:* Stratagem International, Carnegie Building, 121 Donegall Road, Belfast BT12 5JL. *T:* (028) 9087 2800, *Fax:* (028) 9087 2801. *E:* ryan@stratagemint.com.

GAY, Mark Edward; Partner, Burges Salmon LLP, since 2011; *b* London, 25 June 1962; *s* of Eamon and Hannah Gay; *m* 1997, Susan Elizabeth Holmes; two *d*. *Educ:* Clapham Coll., London; Lady Margaret Hall, Oxford (BA Juris. 1984). Trainee solicitor, 1985–88, Associate, 1988–91, Linklaters & Paines; Associate, 1991–95, Partner, 1995–99, Herbert Smith; Partner, Denton Hall, 1999; Solicitor Advocate, 2007; Partner and Head, Sports Gp, DLA Piper LLP, 2005–11. *Recreations:* chauffeuring my children, fine wine, Buffy the Vampire Slayer. *Address:* Burges Salmon LLP, 6 New Street Square, EC4A 3BF. *Club:* Richmond Football.

GAYMER, Dame Janet (Marion), DBE 2010 (CBE 2004); Commissioner for Public Appointments, 2006–10; a Civil Service Commissioner, 2006–10; *b* 11 July 1947; *d* of late Ronald Frank Craddock and Marion Clara Craddock (*née* Stringer); *m* 1971, John Michael Gaymer; two *d*. *Educ:* Nuneaton High Sch. for Girls; St Hilda's Coll., Oxford (MA Jurisprudence; Hon. Fellow 2002); LSE (LLM). Simmons & Simmons: admitted solicitor, 1973; Head, Employment Law Dept, 1973–2001; Partner, 1977–2001; Sen. Partner, 2001–06. Chm., Employment Tribunal System Taskforce, 2001–02 and 2003–06; Member: Justice Cttee, Industrial Tribunals, 1987; Council, ACAS, 1995–2001; Steering Bd, Employment Tribunals Service, 2001–06; Bd, Financial Ombudsman Service, 2011–13; Ind. Mem., Speaker's Cttee, Ind. Parly Standards Authy, 2011–; non-exec. Mem., Mgt Bd, H of C, 2013– (Actg Chm., 2014–; Chm., Admin Estimate and Members Estimate Audit Cttees, 2013–). Chairman: Employment Law Sub Cttee, City of London Law Soc., 1987; Employment Law Cttee, Law Soc., 1993–96; Founder Chm. and Life Vice-Pres., Employment Lawyers Assoc., 1993; Founder Chm. and Hon. Chm., European Employment Lawyers Assoc., 1998; Mem., Exec. Bd, 1995–2003, Council, 1995–, Justice. Member: Bd, RSC, 1999–2006; Bd, Internat. Women of Excellence, 2005–; Co-Chm., Consultation Steering Panel, Legal Educn and Training Rev., 2010–13; Chair, CEO Network, Winmark Europe, 2014–. Mem., Adv. Bd, Excello Law LLP, 2014–. Member Editorial Advisory Board: Sweet & Maxwell's Encyclopedia of Employment Law, 1987; Tolley's Health and Safety at Work, 1995–2006. Patron: Assoc. of Women Solicitors, 2000–13; City Women's Network, 2006–13. Hon. Vis. Prof., Faculty of Mgt, Cass Business Sch., 2008. Hon. QC 2008; Hon. Bencher, Gray's Inn, 2012. Hon. LLD: Nottingham, 2004; College of Law, 2009; Westminster, 2013; BPP Univ., 2013; DUniv Surrey, 2006. The Times Woman of Achievement in the Law Award, 1997; Lifetime Achievement Award, City of London Law Soc., 2006; Lifetime Achievement Award, Europe Women in Business Law Awards, 2012. *Publications:* The Employment Relationship, 2001. *Recreations:* watercolour painting, music, theatre, opera, swimming. *Address:* The Nutcracker House, Effingham Common Road, Effingham, Surrey KT24 5JG. *T:* and *Fax:* (01372) 452639. *E:* janet@janetgaymer.com. *Club:* Athenæum.

GAYOOM, Maumoon Abdul, Hon. GCMG 1997; President and Commander-in-Chief of the Armed Forces and of the Police, Republic of Maldives, 1978–2008; Co-Founder and Chairman, The Maumoon Foundation, since 2010; *b* 29 Dec. 1937; *s* of late Abdul Gayoom Ibrahim and Khadeeja Moosa; *m* 1969, Nasreena Ibrahim; two *s* twin *d*. *Educ:* Al-Azhar Univ., Cairo. Res. Asst, Amer. Univ. of Cairo, 1967–69; Lectr in Islamic Studies and Philosophy, Abdullahi Bayero Coll., Ahmadu Bello Univ., 1969–71; teacher, Aminiya Sch., 1971–72; Manager, Govt Shipping Dept, 1972–73; writer and translator, President's Office, 1972–74; Under-Sec., Telecommunications Dept, 1974; Special Under-Sec., Office of the Prime Minister, 1974–75; Dep. Ambassador to Sri Lanka, 1975–76; Under-Sec., Dept of External Affairs, 1976; Dep. Minister of Transport, 1976; Perm. Rep. to UN, 1976–77; Minister of Transport, 1977–78; Governor, Maldives Monetary Authy, 1981–2004; Minister: of Defence and Nat. Security, 1982–2004; of Finance, 1989–93; of Finance and Treasury, 1993–2004. Numerous hon. degrees. *Publications:* The Maldives: a nation in peril, 1998. *Recreations:* reading, poetry, astronomy, calligraphy, photography, badminton, cricket. *Address:* Ma. Ki'nbigasdhoshuge, Malé 20229, Republic of Maldives.

GAZDAR, Prof. Gerald James Michael; Professor of Computational Linguistics, University of Sussex, 1985–2002, now Emeritus; *b* 24 Feb. 1950; *s* of John and Kathleen Gazdar. *Educ:* Heath Mount; Bradfield Coll.; Univ. of East Anglia (BA Phil with Econ); Reading Univ. (MA Linguistics, PhD). Sussex University: Lectr 1975–80; Reader 1980–85; Dean, Sch. of Cognitive and Computing Scis, 1988–93. Fellow, Center for Advanced Study in the Behavioral Sciences, Stanford Univ., California, 1984–85. Vis. Prof., Univ. of Brighton, 2007–. FBA 1988–2002. *Publications:* (with Klein, Pullum) A Bibliography of Contemporary Linguistic Research, 1978; Pragmatics, 1979; (with Klein, Pullum) Order, Concord, and Constituency, 1983; (with Klein, Pullum, Sag) Generalized Phrase Structure Grammar, 1985; (with Coates, Deuchar, Lyons) New Horizons in Linguistics II, 1987; (with Franz, Osborne, Evans) Natural Language Processing in the 1980s, 1987; (with Mellish): Natural Language Processing in Prolog, An Introduction to Computational Linguistics, 1989; Natural Language Processing in LISP, An Introduction to Computational Linguistics, 1989; Natural Language Processing in POP-11, An Introduction to Computational Linguistics, 1989. *Address:* Department of Informatics, University of Sussex, Brighton BN1 9QH. *T:* (01273) 678030.

GAZZARD, Prof. Brian George, CBE 2011; FRCP; Clinical Research Director, HIV Unit, Chelsea and Westminster Hospital, since 1978; Professor of HIV Medicine, Imperial College, University of London, since 1998; *b* 4 April 1946; *s* of Edward George Gazzard and Elizabeth (*née* Hill); *m*; four *s*. *Educ:* Queens' Coll., Cambridge (MA); King's Coll. Hosp., London (MD 1976). FRCP 1983. Senior Registrar: Liver Unit, KCH, 1974–76; Gastroenterology Unit, St Bartholomew's Hosp., 1976–78; Consultant Physician, Westminster and St Stephen's Hosps, 1978–. Prin. UK Investigator, various collaborative AIDS studies incl. MRC Delta Trial, 1978–. *Publications:* Treatment of Peptic Ulcer, 1989; Common Symptoms in Gastroenterology, 1990; Gastroenterological Manifestations in AIDS Patients, 1992. *Recreation:* gardening. *Address:* The Old Rectory, Down Street, Dummer, Hants RG25 2AD.

GAZZARD, Michael John; Managing Director, Tee to Green Marketing, since 1997; Director, British Homes Awards, since 2007; *b* Bournemouth, 20 June 1949; *s* of Kenneth Howard and Nancy Campbell Gazzard; *m* 1993, Brenda Porth; one *s* one *d*. *Educ:* Oakham Sch., Rutland; Enfield Coll. of Technol. (BA Hons Business Studies); City Univ. London (MSc Mgt Scis). VW Mktg Manager, Volkswagen (GB) Ltd, 1974–78; Area Sales Manager, 1978–81, Audi Mktg Manager, 1981–83, V. A. G. UK Ltd; Dir, Mktg Ops, 1983–94, Corporate Affairs, 1994–95, Toyota (GB) Ltd; Sen. Exec., Sales and Mktg, Europe, Rolls-Royce Internat. SA, 1995–97. Hon. FRIBA 2011. *Publications:* Design: the key to a better place, 2007, 5th edn 2012. *Recreations:* golf, tennis, squash. *Address:* Oakham House, Farm Lane, E Horsley, Surrey KT24 5AB. *T:* (01483) 286895. *E:* mike@teetogreen.com. *Clubs:* Old Oakhamian; Clandon Regis Golf, Effingham Golf.

GAZZARD, Roy James Albert, FRIBA; FRTPI; Pro-Director, 1982–84, Director, 1984–86, Hon. Fellow, 1987, Centre for Middle Eastern and Islamic Studies, Durham University; *b* 19 July 1923; *s* of James Henry Gazzard, MBE, and Ada Gwendoline Gazzard (*née* Willis); *m* 1947, Muriel Joy Morgan (*d* 2010); one *s* two *d* (and one *s* decd). *Educ:* Stationers' Company's Sch.; Architectural Assoc. Sch. of Architecture (Dip.); School of Planning and Research for Regl Develt (Dip.). Commissioned, Middx Regt, 1943; service Palestine and ME (Hon. Major). Acting Govt Town Planner, Uganda, 1950; Staff Architect, Barclays Bank Ltd, 1954; Chief Architect, Peterlee Develt Corp., 1960; Dir of Develt, Northumberland CC, 1962; Chief Professional Adviser to Sec. of State's Environmental Bd, 1976; Under Sec., DoE, 1976–79. Prepared: Jinja (Uganda) Outline Scheme, 1954; Municipality of Sur (Oman) Develt Plan, 1975. Renter Warden, Worshipful Co. of Stationers and Newspaper Makers, 1985–86. Captain, Durham City Mayoral Bodyguard, 2007–08. Govt medals for Good Design in Housing; Civic Trust awards for Townscape and Conservation. *Publications:* Durham: portrait of a cathedral city, 1983; contribs to HMSO pubns on built environment. *Recreations:* Islamic art and architecture, fortifications, dry-stone walling.

GBOWEE, Leymah Roberta; Liberian peace activist, social worker and women's rights advocate; Founder and President, Gbowee Peace Foundation Africa, since 2012; *b* Liberia; two *s* three *d* and one adopted *d*. *Educ:* Eastern Mennonite Univ., Va, USA (MA Conflict Transformation 2007). Case worker and counsellor for refugees, Ministry of Health Displaced Shelter, Liberia, 1995–96; volunteer, Trauma Healing and Reconciliation Prog., 1998–2003; Founding Mem. and Liberian Prog. Co-ordinator, Women in Peacebuilding Network, W Africa Network for Peacebuilding, 2001–05 (spokesperson, Women of Liberia Mass Action for Peace); Co-founder, 2006, Regl Consultant, 2006–07, and Executive Dir, 2007–13, Women Peace and Security Network Africa. Comr Designate, Liberia Truth and Reconciliation Commn, 2004–05. Oxfam Global Ambassador, 2013–. Dist. Fellow in Social Justice, Barnard Coll., Columbia Univ., 2013–14. Mem., African Women Leaders' Network for Reproductive Health and Family Planning. Member, Board of Directors: Nobel Women's Initiative; Peacejam Foundn. Hon. LLD: Rhodes, SA; Alberta, Canada; Dr *hc* Speciality Mgt and Conflict Resolution, Poly. Univ., Mozambique. Blue Ribbon for Peace Award, Kennedy Sch. of Govt, Harvard Univ., 2007; Gruber Prize for Women's Rights, Gruber Foundn, 2009; John F. Kennedy Profile in Courage Award, 2009; (jtly) Nobel Prize for Peace, 2011. *Publications:* (with C. Mithers) Mighty Be Our Powers (memoir), 2011. *Address:* Gbowee Peace Foundation Africa, 123 ABC Street, Monrovia, Liberia.

GEAKE, His Honour Jonathan Richard Barr; a Circuit Judge, Northern Circuit, 1994–2012; *b* 27 May 1946; *s* of late Michael and of Margaret Geake; *m* 1978, Sally Louise Dines; three *s*. *Educ:* Sherborne Sch.; Fitzwilliam Coll., Cambridge (BA). Called to the Bar, Inner Temple, 1969; practised on Northern Circuit; a Recorder, 1989; Standing Counsel for Customs & Excise, 1989. *Recreations:* golf and various other sporting activities, gardening. *Clubs:* Knutsford Golf, St Enodoc Golf; Alderley Edge Cricket.

GEAR, Alan, MBE 2003; author; *b* 12 June 1949; *s* of Harold Archibald Gear and Nora Esme Gear; *m* 1971, Jacqueline Anne Parker (*see* J. A. Gear). *Educ:* University Coll. of Wales, Swansea (BSc Hons 1970, MSc Civil Engrg 1971). Graduate Engr, West Glamorgan Water Bd, 1971–74; Deputy Dir, 1974–85, Chief Exec., 1985–2003, Henry Doubleday Res. Assoc. Mem., Adv. Cttee on Organic Standards, DEFRA, 2003–05. Hon. MRHS 2006. *Publications:* The Organic Food Guide, 1983, repr. as The New Organic Food Guide, 1986; (ed jtly) Thorsons Organic Consumer Guide, 1990; *contributions to:* Thorsons Organic Wine Guide, 1991; A Future for the Land: organic practice from a global perspective, 1992; Environmental Issues and the Food Industry, 1994, 2nd edn 1999; (with Jackie Gear) Organic Gardening: the whole story, 2009; (with Jackie Gear) Organic Vegetable and Fruit Growing and Preserving Month by Month, 2011. *Recreations:* listening to classical music, reading, gardening, model-making. *Address:* 12 Queens Gardens, Hunstanton, Norfolk PE36 6HD. *T:* (01485) 532219.

GEAR, Jacqueline Anne, MBE 2003; author; *b* 18 Dec. 1949; *d* of Stephen Edward Parker and Phyllis Mary Parker; *m* 1971, Alan Gear, *qv*. *Educ:* University Coll. of Wales, Swansea (BSc Hons Zoology 1971). Biologist, Gower RDC, 1971–74; Dir, Analytical Res., Henry Doubleday Res. Assoc., 1974–80; R&D Manager, F. H. Nash Ltd, 1981–84; Exec. Dir, Henry Doubleday Res. Assoc., 1985–2003. Hon. MRHS 2006. *Publications:* (jtly) Ryton Gardens Recipe Book, 1988; (jtly) Thorsons Organic Consumer Guide, 1990; (jtly) Thorsons Organic Wine Guide, 1991; (jtly) Organic Gardening: your questions answered, 1993; (jtly) The Chilli and Pepper Cookbook, 1995; (contrib.) Encyclopaedia of Organic Gardening, 2001; (with Alan Gear) Organic Gardening: the whole story, 2009; (with Alan Gear) Organic Vegetable and Fruit Growing and Preserving Month by Month, 2011. *Recreations:* classical music, reading, cooking, walking, the countryside. *Address:* 12 Queens Gardens, Hunstanton, Norfolk PE36 6HD. *T:* (01485) 532219.

GEAR, Rt Rev. Michael Frederick; Bishop Suffragan of Doncaster, 1993–99; an Hon. Assistant Bishop: Diocese of Rochester, since 1999; Diocese of Canterbury, since 2000; *b* 27 Nov. 1934; *s* of Frederick Augustus and Lillian Hannah Gear; *m* 1961, Daphne, *d* of Norman and Millicent Earl; two *d*. *Educ:* St John's College and Cranmer Hall, Durham. BA Social Studies, 1st cl., 1959; DipTh 1961. Assistant Curate: Christ Church, Bexleyheath, 1961–64; St Aldates, Oxford, 1964–67; Vicar of St Andrew, Clubmoor, Liverpool, 1967–71; Rector, Avondale, Salisbury, Rhodesia, 1971–76; Tutor, Wycliffe Hall, Oxford, 1976–80; Team Rector, Macclesfield, 1980–88; Archdeacon of Chester, 1988–93. Hon. Chaplain, Mothers' Union, 1996–99. Chairman: Cranmer Hall Cttee, St John's Coll., Durham, 1994–98; Northern Ordination Course, 1995–99; Member: Scargill Council, 1993–99; Bd, Church Army, 1993–99. *Recreations:* photography, golf, history and contemporary politics of Southern Africa. *Address:* 10 Acott Fields, Yalding, Maidstone ME18 6DQ.

GEARING, Matthew Peter; QC 2014; Partner, Hong Kong Office, since 2005, and Global Co-Head, International Arbitration Group, since 2013, Allen & Overy; *b* Croydon, 6 July 1972; *s* of Peter and Susan Gearing; *m* 1999, Katherine Brigg; two *s*. *Educ:* New Coll., Oxford (BA Hons Juris 1993); Coll. of Law, Chester. Admitted as solicitor: England and Wales, 1997; Hong Kong, 2001. Solicitor, Slaughter & May, 1995–97, Allen & Overy, 1997–. Member, Panel of Arbitrators: Singapore Internat. Arbitration Centre, 2009–; Hong Kong Internat. Arbitration Centre, 2010–; Kuala Lumpur Regl Centre for Arbitration, 2013–. Hong Kong International Arbitration Centre: Mem. Council, 2008–; Mem., Exec. Cttee, 2014–; London Court of International Arbitration: Co-Chm., Young Internat. Arbitration Gp, 2005–09;

Vice-Pres., Asia Pacific Users' Council, 2013–. *Publications:* (jtly) Russell on Arbitration, 23rd edn 2007. *Recreations:* sailing, running, walking. *Address:* 9th Floor, Three Exchange Square, Central, Hong Kong. *T:* 29747000, *Fax:* 30880088; One Bishops Square, E1 6AD. *T:* (020) 3088 0000, *Fax:* (020) 3088 0088. *Club:* Royal Hong Kong Yacht.

GEARTY, Prof. Conor Anthony, PhD; FBA 2010; Professor of Human Rights Law, since 2002, and Director, Institute of Public Affairs, since 2013, London School of Economics; barrister; *b* Dublin, 4 Nov. 1957; *s* of Enda and Margot Gearty; *m* 1986, Diane Wales (*d* 2011); one *s* one *d*. *Educ:* Castleknock Coll.; University Coll. Dublin (BCL 1978); Wolfson Coll., Cambridge (LLB 1980); Emmanuel Coll., Cambridge (PhD 1986). Fellow, Emmanuel Coll., Cambridge, 1983–90; King's College London: Sen. Lectr, 1990–93; Reader, 1993–95; Prof. of Human Rights Law, 1995–2002; Dir, Centre for Study of Human Rights, LSE, 2002–09. Called to the Bar, Middle Temple, 1995; in practice as barrister, Matrix Chambers, 2000–. Gov., William Ellis Sch. *Publications:* (with K. D. Ewing) Freedom Under Thatcher, 1990; Terror, 1991; (ed with A. Tomkins) Understanding Human Rights, 1995; (ed) Terrorism, 1996; The Future of Terrorism, 1997; (with K. D. Ewing) The Struggle for Civil Liberties, 2000; Principles of Human Rights Adjudication, 2004; Can Human Rights Survive?, 2006; Civil Liberties, 2007; Selected Essays, 2008; (with V. Mantouvalou) Debating Social Rights, 2011; The Rights' Future, 2010; (with C. Douzinas) Cambridge Companion to Human Rights Law, 2012; Liberty and Security, 2013; (with C. Douzinas) The Meanings of Rights, 2014. *Recreations:* tennis, reading, learning Italian. *Address:* London School of Economics, Houghton Street, WC2A 2AE. *T:* (020) 7849 4643. *E:* c.a.gearty@lse.ac.uk. *W:* www.conorgearty.com, www.twitter.com/conorgearty.

GEATER, Sara; Chairman, Emerald Films, since 2014; *b* Coventry, 18 March 1955; *d* of Jack and Patricia Geater; civil partnership 2007, Felicity Milton; one *s* one *d*. *Educ:* Farnham Common CP Sch.; Beaconsfield High Sch.; Leamington Coll. for Girls; City of London Poly.; Holborn Law Sch. (LLB). Called to the Bar, Middle Temple, 1998. CEDR Accredited Mediator, 2006. Prodn Accountant, LWT, 1977–84; producer, Business as Usual (film), 1985; line producer, Mr Pye (film), 1986; Head: of Production, Drama and Film, Channel 4, 1987–97; of Production, HAL/Miramax, 1997–98; of Film and TV, Avalon, 1998–2000; Dir, Rights and Business Affairs, BBC, 2000–04; Hd, Commercial Affairs, Channel 4, 2004–07; Chief Operating Officer, 2007–10, Chief Exec., 2010–14, talkbackThames, later FremantleMedia UK. Chm., Women in Film and TV, 1994–97. Chairman: BAFTA Prodns, 2007–; Pact, 2014–. Gov., London Film Sch., 2007. Mem., RTS. FRSA 2006. *Recreations:* being with family, golf, being with friends, theatre, talking to my mother daily, being in Portugal. *Clubs:* Groucho, Soho House, Ivy.

GEDDES, family name of **Baron Geddes**.

GEDDES, 3rd Baron *cr* 1942; **Euan Michael Ross Geddes;** Company Director, since 1964; *b* 3 Sept. 1937; *s* of 2nd Baron Geddes, KBE, and Enid Mary, Lady Geddes (*d* 1999), *d* of late Clarance H. Butler; *S* father, 1975; *m* 1st, 1966, Gillian (*d* 1995), *d* of late William Arthur Butler; one *s* one *d*; 2nd, 1996, Susan Margaret Hunter, *d* of late George Harold Carter. *Educ:* Rugby; Gonville and Caius Coll., Cambridge (MA 1964); Harvard Business School. Elected Mem., H of L, 1999; a Dep. Speaker, 2000–; Mem., Procedure Cttee, 2002–07. Treas., Assoc. of Cons. Peers, 2000–. *Recreations:* golf, bridge, music, gardening, shooting. *Heir:* *s* Hon. James George Neil Geddes [*b* 10 Sept. 1969; *m* 2004, Alice Arabella Alexander; three *s*]. *Address:* House of Lords, SW1A 0PW. *T:* (020) 7219 6400. *Clubs:* Brooks's; Hong Kong (Hong Kong); Noblemen and Gentlemen's Catch; Hong Kong Golf.

GEDDES, Prof. Alexander MacIntosh, (Alasdair), CBE 1996; FRCP, FRCPE, FRCPath, FFPH, FMedSci; Professor of Infection, 1991–99, and Deputy Dean, Faculty of Medicine and Dentistry, 1994–99, University of Birmingham (Professor of Infectious Diseases, 1982–91; Associate Dean, 1999–2002); *b* 14 May 1934; *s* of Angus and Isabella Geddes; *m* 1984, Angela Lewis; two *s*. *Educ:* Fortrose Acad.; Univ. of Edinburgh (MB ChB). FRCPE 1971; FRCP 1981; FRCPath 1995; FFPH (FFPHM 1998). Served RAMC, Captain, 1958–60. Med. Registrar, Aberdeen Hosps, 1961–63; Sen. Registrar, City Hosp. and Royal Infirmary, Edinburgh, 1963–67; Cons. Phys., E Birmingham Hosp., 1967–91; Hon. Cons. Phys., S Birmingham Health Dist, 1991–99. Examiner: MRCP (UK), 1972–99; Final MB, Univs of Birmingham, Glasgow, London, Sheffield, 1975–99. Forbes Vis. Fellow, Fairfield Hosp., Melbourne, Aust., 1988; Sir Edward Finch Vis. Prof., Univ. of Sheffield, 1989. Chairman: Sub-Cttee on Communicable and Trop. Diseases, Jt Cttee on Higher Med. Trng, 1984–94; Isolation Beds Working Party, DoH, 1989–95; Member: Birmingham AHA, 1977–81; Health Educn Authority, 1987–98; Sub-Cttee on Efficacy and Adverse Reactions, Cttee on Safety of Medicines, 1978–85; DHSS Expert Adv. Gp on AIDS, 1985–92; DoH (formerly DHSS) Jt Cttee on Vaccination and Immunization, 1986–95; Trop. Med. Res. Bd, MRC, 1984–88; Ministerial Inquiry into the Public Health Function, 1985–87; DoH Cttee on Safety of Medicines, 1993–96; Consultant Advr in Infectious Diseases, DoH, 1990–94; Civilian Consultant, Infectious Diseases and Tropical Medicine, RN, 1991–. Non-exec. Dir, City Hosp. NHS Trust, 1999–. Chm., Brit. Soc. for Antimicrobial Therapy, 1982–85; Chm., Communicable and Tropical Diseases Cttee, 1983–93, Censor, 1987–89, RCP; Mem., Assoc. of Physicians of GB and Ire., 1976–; President: Internat. Soc. for Infectious Diseases, 1994–96; 21st Internat. Chemotherapy Congress, 1999. Lectures: Honyman-Gillespie, Univ. of Edinburgh, 1975; Public, Univ. of Warwick, 1980; Davidson, RCPE, 1981; Watson-Smith, 1988; Lister, RCPE, 1990. FMedSci 2000. Chm., Editorial Bd, Jl of Antimicrobial Therapy, 1975–85; Ed.-in-Chief, Internat. Jl of Antimicrobial Agents, 2005–. *Publications:* (ed) Control of Hospital Infection, 1975, 5th edn 2000; (ed) Recent Advances in Infection, 1975, 3rd edn 1988; (contrib.) Davidson, Principles and Practice of Medicine, 16th edn 1991, 17th edn 1995; (contrib.) Kumar and Clark, Clinical Medicine, 6th edn 2005; (contrib.) Grayson et al, The Use of Antibiotics, 6th edn 2010; papers on infectious diseases, immunology, antibiotic therapy and epidemiology in learned jls. *Recreations:* gardening, literature, history of science. *Address:* 34 The Crescent, Solihull, West Midlands B91 1JR. *T:* (0121) 705 8844, *Fax:* (0121) 705 2314. *E:* a.m.geddes@bham.ac.uk. *Club:* Athenæum.

GEDDES, Prof. Duncan Mackay, CBE 2012; MD, FRCP; Professor of Respiratory Medicine, Imperial College School of Medicine, since 1996; Consultant Physician, Royal Brompton Hospital, 1978–2007, now Honorary Consultant; *b* 6 Jan. 1942; *s* of Sir Reay Geddes, KBE and Lady Geddes (Imogen, *d* of late Captain Hay Matthey); *m* 1968, Donatella Flaccomio Nardi Dei; two *s* one *d*. *Educ:* Eton Coll.; Magdalene Coll., Cambridge (MA); Westminster Hosp. Med. Sch. (MB, BS 1971; MD 1978). FRCP 1982. Hon. Consultant: Royal London Hosp., 1982–2007; Royal Marsden Hosp., 1990–2007; Civilian Consultant in chest disease to the Army and Navy, 1986–2007. Director: Finsbury Worldwide Pharmaceutical Trust, 1995–2012; SR Pharma plc, 2000–02; India Pharma Fund, 2005–09. Chm. Council, Nat. Asthma Campaign, 1996–2003. Mem., Med. Adv. Bd, Transgene, France, 1997–2002. Pres., British Thoracic Soc., 2000–01 (Vice-Pres., 1999–2000). Trustee: Garfield Weston Trust for Res. into Heart Surgery, 2005–; Paintings in Hospitals, 2008–13; Royal Brompton and Harefield Hosps Charity, 2013–; All Saints Farnborough Supporters, 2014–. Vice Chm., Linari Classic Internat. Music Fest., 2014–. *Publications:* Practical Medicine, 1976; Airways Obstruction, 1981; Respiratory Medicine, 1990; Cystic Fibrosis, 1995; numerous papers in med. and scientific jls. *Recreations:* tennis, golf, painting, cabinet making. *Address:* 57 Addison Avenue, W11 4QU. *Clubs:* Boodle's, Queen's; Denham Golf.

GEDDES, Prof. John Richard, MD; FRCPsych; Professor of Epidemiological Psychiatry, since 2002, and Head, Department of Psychiatry, since 2011, University of Oxford; *b* 28 Oct. 1961; *s* of William Watt Geddes and Carol Geddes (*née* Blomerley). *Educ:* Manchester Grammar Sch.; Leeds Univ. (MB ChB 1985; MD 1994). FRCPsych 2000. Registrar, Sheffield Hosps, 1986–90; Sen. Registrar, Royal Edinburgh Hosp., 1990–95; Clinical Lectr, Dept of Psychiatry, Univ. of Oxford, 1995. Hon. Consultant Psychiatrist, 1995–, Dir of Res. and Develt and Associate Medical Dir, 2012–, Oxford NHS Foundn Trust. Hon. Fellow, Amer. Coll. of Psychiatrists, 2008. *Publications:* (jtly) Psychiatry, 2nd edn 1999, 4th edn 2012; (jtly) Lecture Notes on Psychiatry, 8th edn 1998, 10th edn 2010; (jtly) New Oxford Textbook of Psychiatry, 2nd edn 2009; papers in gen. and specialist med. jls on clinical epidemiol. and psychiatry. *Address:* Department of Psychiatry, University of Oxford, Warneford Hospital, Oxford OX3 7JX. *T:* (01865) 226451, *Fax:* (01865) 204198. *E:* john.geddes@psych.ox.ac.uk.

GEDDES, Keith Taylor, CBE 1998; Policy Director, Pagoda PR (formerly P. S. Communication Consultants) Ltd, since 1999; *b* 8 Aug. 1952. *Educ:* Galashiels Acad.; Edinburgh Univ. (BEd 1975); Moray House Coll. of Educn (Cert. in Youth and Community work 1977); Heriot-Watt Univ. (Dip. in Housing 1986). Worker, Shelter Housing Aid (Scotland), 1977–84. Lothian Regional Council: Mem. (Lab), 1982–96; Chair, Educn Cttee, 1987–90; Leader, Labour Gp, 1990–96; Leader, City of Edinburgh Council, 1995–99. Bd Mem., Accounts Commn, 2002–08. Sen. Vice Pres., 1994–96, Pres., 1996–99, COSLA. Chairman: Greenspace Scotland, 2003–09; Central Scotland Green Network Trust (formerly Central Scotland Green Network), 2010–. Contested (Lab) Tweeddale, Ettrick and Lauderdale, 2001. Dep. Chm. Bd, Scottish Natural Heritage, 2005–10 (Mem., 2001–10). *Recreations:* hill walking, golf, cricket, film. *Address:* 12 Woodmill Terrace, Dunfermline, Fife KY11 4SR. *T:* (01383) 623947.

GEDDES, Michael Dawson; Executive Director, Milton Keynes Economic Partnership, 1995–2003; *b* 9 March 1944; *s* of late David Geddes and Audrey Geddes; *m* 1966, Leslie Rose Webb; two *s*. *Educ:* Sherborne Sch., Dorset; Univ. of BC (Goldsmith's Exhibitioner) (BA). Cranfield Institute of Technology: Admin. Asst, 1968–71; Planning Officer, 1971–77; Develt and Estates Officer, 1977–83; Financial Controller, RMCS, 1983–84; Sec., Ashridge (Bonar Law Meml) Trust; Dir, Admin, Ashridge Management Coll. and Dir, Ashridge subsids, 1984–90; Chief Exec., Recruitment and Assessment Services Agency, 1990–95; Civil Service Comr, 1990–97. Gov., Tring Park Sch. for the Performing Arts (formerly Arts Educnl Sch., Tring), 2006– (Chm., 2009–). *Publications:* (with W. Briner and C. Hastings) Project Leadership, 1990; Making Public Private Partnerships Work, 2005; papers on resource allocation in univs and on project management. *Recreations:* golf, bridge. *Address:* 2 Tidbury Close, Woburn Sands, Milton Keynes MK17 8QW. *T:* (01908) 282830.

GEDDES, Paul Robert; Chief Executive, Direct Line Group, since 2009; *b* Redhill, 4 June 1969; *s* of Keith Geddes, OBE and Anne Geddes; *m* 1994, Fiona Slater; two *d*. *Educ:* Wilson's Sch., Wallington; St Peter's Coll., Oxford (MA Hons PPE). Brand Manager to Mktg Manager, UK Cosmetics, Procter & Gamble, 1990–97; Hd of Mktg, Superdrug Stores plc, 1997–99; Mktg and Develt Dir, Comet Gp plc, 1999–2001; Mktg Dir, Argos, 2001–04; joined RBS Group, 2004: Man. Dir, Mktg and Strategy, Retail Banking, 2004–06; CEO, UK Retail Banking (NatWest and RBS), 2006–09. Member: Bd, ABI, 2011–; Practitioner Panel, FSA, 2011–. FCIBS. *Recreations:* playing the violin, travel, family. *Address:* Direct Line Group plc, Churchill Court, Westmoreland Road, Bromley, Kent BR1 1DP. *T:* (01651) 832303. *E:* paul.geddes@directlinegroup.co.uk.

GEE, David Charles Laycock; Senior Advisor, Science, Policy Emerging Issues (formerly Co-ordinator, Emerging Issues and Scientific Liaison), European Environment Agency, Copenhagen, 1995–2013; consultant, environmental and occupational risk, since 1992; *b* 18 April 1947; *s* of Charles Laycock Gee and Theresa Gee (*née* Garrick); *m* 1974, Vivienne Taylor Gee; four *d*. *Educ:* Thomas Linacre and Wigan Grammar Schs; York Univ. (BA Politics). MIOSH 1985. Res. Dept, AUEW, 1970–73; Educn Service, TUC, 1973–78; Nat. Health/Safety Officer, GMB, 1978–88; Occupational/Environmental Cons., 1988–89; Campaign Co-ordinator, 1989–90, Dir, 1990–91, Friends of the Earth; Partner, WBMG Envmtl Communications, 1992–94. Vis. Fellow, Inst. of Envmt, Health and Societies, Brunel Univ. Fellow, Collegium Ramazzini, Italy, 1984; FRSA 1990. *Publications:* (with John Cox and Dave Leon) Cancer and Work, 1982; (with Lesley Doyal et al) Cancer in Britain, 1983; Economic Tax Reform: a primer, 1994; (with Penny Allen and Christophe Bonazzi) Metaphors for Change: partnerships, tools and civic action for sustainability, 2001; *contributions to:* Radiation and Health—Biological Effects of Low Level Exposure to Ionising Radiation, 1987; Transport and Health, ed Fletcher and McMichael, 1995; Ecotaxation, ed O'Riordan, 1997; The Market and the Environment, ed Sterner, 1999; The Daily Globe: environmental change, the public and the media, ed Smith, 2000; Late Lessons from Early Warnings, vol 1: the precautionary principle 1896–2000, 2001, vol. 2: science, precaution, innovation, 2013; The Politics of Scientific Advice, ed Lentsch and Weingart, 2011; pubns for EEA, MSF and GMB on scientific uncertainty, ecological tax reform, anticipatory res. *Recreations:* family, swimming, tennis, running, entertaining, theatre, music. *Address:* 24 Broomwood Road, SW11 6HT.

GEE, His Honour David Stephenson; a Circuit Judge, 1992–2007; a Deputy Circuit Judge, 2007–14; *b* 16 Dec. 1944; *s* of William and Marianne Gee; *m* 1972, Susan Margaret Hiley; two *s* two *d*. *Educ:* William Hulme's Grammar Sch., Manchester; Leeds Univ. (LLB Hons). Admitted Solicitor, 1970; Registrar, Manchester County Court and Dist Registry, 1982–90; Dist Judge, 1991–92; a Recorder of the Crown Court, 1991; Designated Family Judge: Blackburn Care Centre, 1994–2005; Lancs, 2005–07. Chairman: Selcare (Greater Manchester) Trust, 1989–95; Rhodes Foundn Scholarship Trust, 1989–2005. Adv. Editor, Atkins' Court Forms, 1989–2003; Editor, Butterworth's Family Law Service, 1990–98. *Recreations:* music, walking, reading, travelling. *Address:* c/o Regional Director, 1 Bridge Street, Manchester M60 1TE.

GEE, James; Director of Counter Fraud Services, BDO LLP (formerly PKF (UK) LLP), since 2010; Visiting Professor and Chair, Centre for Counter Fraud Studies, University of Portsmouth, since 2010; *b* 1 Oct. 1957; *m* 1992, Lesley Ann White. *Educ:* London Sch. of Econs (BSc Econs 1978); CPE Law 1995. Civil servant, 1978–90; Counter Fraud Manager, London Boroughs of: Islington, 1990–94; Haringey, 1994–96; Lambeth, 1996–98. Advr to Social Security Select Cttee, H of C, 1995–97; Counter Fraud Advr to Minister of State for Welfare Reform, 1997–98; Dir, Counter Fraud Services, DoH, 1998–2002; Chief Exec., NHS Counter Fraud and Security Mgt Service, 2003–06; Dir of Fraud Services, KPMG, 2007–08; Dir of Counter Fraud Services, MacIntyre Hudson LLP, 2009–10. Hon. Mem., CIPFA. *Recreations:* military history, gardening, tennis. *Address:* BDO LLP, 55 Baker Street, W1V 7EU. *Club:* Manchester United Football.

GEE, Dr Maggie Mary, OBE 2012; FRSL; writer; Professor of Creative Writing, Bath Spa University, since 2012; Vice President, Royal Society of Literature, since 2008 (Chair, 2004–08); *b* 2 Nov. 1948; *d* of Victor Gee and Aileen Gee (*née* Church); *m* 1983, Nicholas Rankin; one *d*. *Educ:* Somerville Coll., Oxford (BA, MA, MLitt); Wolverhampton Polytech. (PhD 1980). FRSL 1994. Writing Fellow, UEA, 1982; Northern Arts Writer-in-Residence, 1996. Vis. Fellow, Sussex Univ., 1986–; Hawthornden Fellow, 1989, 2002, 2009, 2014; Vis. Prof., Sheffield Hallam Univ., 2006–09. Mem., Govt PLR Cttee, 1999–2006. Member: Council, RSL, 1999–2008; Mgt Cttee, Soc. of Authors, 1991–94. Judge, Booker Prize, 1989. Best of Young British Novelists, Granta, 1982. *Publications:* Dying in Other Words, 1981, 3rd edn 1993; The Burning Book, 1983, 2nd edn 1993; Light Years, 1985, 3rd edn 2004; Grace, 1988; Where Are the Snows, 1991, 2nd edn 2006; Lost Children, 1994; The Ice People, 1998, 3rd edn 2008; The White Family, 2002; The Flood, 2004; My Cleaner, 2005; The Blue: short stories, 2006; (ed with Bernardine Evaristo) NW15: anthology of new writing, 2007; My Driver, 2009; My Animal Life (memoir), 2010; Virginia Woolf in Manhattan, 2014. *Recreations:* music, walking, film, theatre, looking at pictures, dancing. *Address:* c/o Karolina Sutton, Curtis Brown, 5th Floor, Haymarket House, 28-29 Haymarket, SW1Y 4SP.

GEE, Mark Norman K.; *see* Kemp-Gee.

GEE, Nigel Ian, RDI 2007; FREng; Managing Director, BMT Nigel Gee and Associates, 2003–06 (Founder and Managing Director, Nigel Gee and Associates, 1986–2003); *b* 30 July 1947; *s* of Saville and Betty Gee; *m* 1969, Susan Margaret Campbell Stewart; one *s* one *d*. *Educ:* Univ. of Newcastle upon Tyne (BSc Hons (Naval Architecture) 1969). CEng 1974, FREng 2006; FRINA 1993. Engrg Manager, Hovermarine, 1976–79; Sen. Lectr in Naval Architecture, Southampton Inst., 1979–83; Technical Gen. Manager, Vosper Hovermarine, 1983–86. Innovator-in-residence, Curtin Univ. of Technol., Perth, WA, 2008–09. Pres., RINA, 2004–07. Trustee, Charity Care of Destitute Children in India, 2009–. FRSA 2008. Hon. DEng Southampton Solent, 2005. *Publications:* 21 papers on fast ships and boats for a variety of worldwide confs. *Recreations:* cruising under sail, painting, solving Araucaria, tennis. *Address:* Ashlake Farmhouse, Ashlake Farm Lane, Wootton Bridge, Ryde, Isle of Wight PO33 4LF. *E:* nigelgee@btopenworld.com. *Clubs:* Royal Victoria Yacht; Island Sailing (Cowes).

GEE, Richard; a Circuit Judge, 1991–99; *b* 25 July 1942; *s* of John and Marie Gee; *m* 1st, 1965; three *s*; 2nd, 1995, Mrs Marilyn Gross. *Educ:* Kilburn Grammar School; University College London (LLB Hons). Admitted Solicitor, 1966; Assistant Recorder, 1983; Recorder, 1988. Mem., Main Board, Judicial Studies Board, 1988–93 (Mem., Ethnic Minorities Adv. Cttee, 1991–93). *Recreations:* golf, the arts.

GEE, Ruth; Director of Strategic Human Resources, INTO University Partnerships, 2012–14; *b* 21 May 1948; *d* of late George Gaskin and Florence Ann Gaskin; *m* 1972 (marr. diss. 2003); one *s* one *d*. *Educ:* Stoneraise Primary Sch., Cumbria; Whitehouse Sch., Brampton, Cumbria; Manchester Polytech. (London Univ. ext. BA Gen. Arts); Newcastle upon Tyne Univ. (Postgrad. DipEd). Teacher of English in comprehensive schs, 1970–80; Asst Dir, Polytech. of N London, 1986–89; Dir/Chief Exec., Edgehill Coll. of Higher Educn, 1989–93; Chief Executive: Assoc. for Colls, 1993–96; British Trng Internat., 1997–2000; British Council: Educn Manager, London, 2000–03; Director: Hong Kong, 2003–09; India and Sri Lanka, 2009–10. Dir, Geelinks Ltd, 2011–12. Mem. (Lab) Hackney LBC, 1978–86. Co-opted Mem., 1980, Mem., 1981–86, ILEA (Dep. Leader, 1983–86). Non-executive posts: Basic Skills Agency, 1993–2003; Consumers' Assoc., 1996–2003. Mem., Hong Kong Women's Commn, 2006–08. *Recreations:* health farm addict, art gallery and exhibition enthusiast. *Address:* Flat 1, 39 Canonbury Park North, N1 2JU.

GEE, Steven Mark; QC 1993; a Recorder, since 2000; *b* 24 Aug. 1953; *yr s* of Dr Sidney Gee and Dr Hilda Elman; *m* 1999, Meryll Emilie Bacri; two *s*. *Educ:* Tonbridge Sch.; Brasenose Coll., Oxford (Open Scholar; MA 1st Cl. Hons Jurisprudence; Gibbs Prize for Law). Called to the Bar, Middle Temple, 1975 (Inns of Court Prize, Harmsworth Scholar); admitted NY Bar, 1999. Standing Jun. Counsel, ECGD, DTI, 1986–93. Hd of Chambers. *Publications:* Mareva Injunctions and Anton Piller Relief, 1995, 4th edn 1998; Commercial Injunctions, 5th edn, 2004. *Recreations:* marathon running, bridge. *Address:* 4 Field Court, Gray's Inn, WC1R 5EF. *T:* (020) 7440 6900. *Club:* MCC.

GEEKIE, Charles Nairn; QC 2006; a Recorder, since 2006; *b* 7 Feb. 1962; *s* of David Nairn Geekie and Gillian Mary Geekie (*née* Dind); *m* 1993, Geeta Manglani; one *s* one *d*. *Educ:* Hawford Lodge; Malvern Coll.; Bristol Univ. (LLB). Called to the Bar, Inner Temple, 1985; in practice as barrister, 1985–, specialising in family law; Jt Hd of Chambers, 2013–. *Recreations:* cycling, hill walking, theatre. *Address:* 1 Garden Court, Temple, EC4Y 9BJ. *T:* (020) 7797 7900. *E:* geekie@1gc.com.

GEER, Katherine Emma; *see* Smith, K. E.

GEERING, Ian Walter; QC 1991. *Educ:* Bedford Sch.; Univ. of Edinburgh (BVMS). Called to the Bar, Inner Temple, 1974. *Recreations:* walking, reading, sailing, photography.

GEERING, Rev. Prof. Sir Lloyd (George), ONZ 2007; GNZM 2009 (PCNZM 2001); CBE 1989; Foundation Professor of Religious Studies, Victoria University of Wellington, 1971–84, now Professor Emeritus; *b* 26 Feb. 1918; *s* of George Frederick Thomas Geering and Alice Geering; *m* 1st, 1943, Nancy McKenzie (*d* 1949); one *s* one *d*; 2nd, 1951, Elaine Parker (*d* 2001); one *d*; 3rd, 2004, Shirley White. *Educ:* Univ. of Otago (MA 1st Cl. Hons Maths; BD Hons OT); Melbourne Coll. of Divinity. Presbyterian Parish Minister, 1943–55; Professor of Old Testament: Emmanuel Coll., Brisbane, 1956–59; Theol Hall, Knox Coll., Dunedin, 1960–71 (Principal, 1963–71). Hon. DD Otago, 1976. *Publications:* God in the New World, 1968; Resurrection: a symbol of hope, 1971; Faith's New Age, 1981; In the World Today, 1988; Tomorrow's God, 1994; The World to Come, 1999; Christianity without God, 2002; Every Moment Must Be Lived, 2003; Wrestling with God, 2006; Coming Back to Earth, 2009; Such is Life!, 2010; From the Big Bang to God, 2013; Reimagining God: the faith journey of a modern heretic, 2014. *Address:* 5B Herbert Gardens, 186 The Terrace, Wellington 6011, New Zealand. *T:* (4) 4730188.

GEFFEN, Charles Slade Henry; Chair, London Corporate, Gibson Dunn & Crutcher, since 2014; *b* London, 19 Sept. 1959; *s* of Ernest, (Bill), Geffen and Bridget Geffen; *m* 1986, Rosemary Anne Valder; three *s* one *d*. *Educ:* Leicester Univ. (LLB). Admitted solicitor, 1984. Ashurst LLP: joined, 1982; corporate lawyer; Partner, 1991–2014; Hd, Private Equity, 1999–2008; Sen. Partner, 2009–14. Trustee: Inst. of Cancer Res., 2014–; City Year UK, 2014–. *Address:* Gibson Dunn & Crutcher, Telephone House, 2–4 Temple Avenue, EC4Y 0HB. *T:* (020) 7071 4225. *E:* cgeffen@gibsondunn.com.

GEFFEN, Dr Terence John; Medical Adviser, Capsticks Solicitors, 1990–99; *b* 17 Sept. 1921; *s* of late Maximilian W. Geffen and Maia Geffen (later Reid); *m* 1965, Judith Anne Steward; two *s*. *Educ:* St Paul's Sch.; University Coll., London; UCH. MD, FRCP. House Phys., UCH, 1943; RAMC, 1944–47; hosp. posts, Edgware Gen. Hosp., Hampstead Gen. Hosp., UCH, 1947–55; Min. of Health (later DHSS), 1956–82, SPMO, 1972–82; Consultant in Public Health Medicine, NW Thames RHA, 1982–90. FRSocMed 1991. *Publications:* various in BMJ, Lancet, Clinical Science, etc. *Recreations:* music, reading, bridge. *Address:* 2 Stonehill Close, SW14 8RP. *T:* (020) 8878 0516.

GEHRELS, Jürgen Carlos, Hon. KBE 1997; non-executive Chairman, Siemens Holdings plc, 1998–2007 (Chief Executive, 1986–98); *b* 24 July 1935; *s* of Dr Hans Gehrels and Ursula (*née* da Rocha); *m* 1963, Sigrid Kausch; one *s* one *d*. *Educ:* Technical Univs, Berlin and Munich (Dipl. Ing.). Siemens AG, Germany, 1965–79; Pres., General Numeric Corp., Chicago, USA, 1979–82; Dir, Factory Automation, Siemens AG, Germany, 1982–86. Chairman: Siemens Communication Systems Ltd, 1986–92; Siemens Financial Services Ltd, 1988–92; Siemens Controls Ltd, 1990–98; Siemens-Nixdorf Inf. Systems Ltd, 1990–98; Director: Siemens Domestic Appliances Ltd, 1987–98; Comparex Ltd, 1988–92; Alfred Engelmann Ltd, 1989–98; Plessey UK, 1989–98; Plessey Overseas, 1989–98; Siemens Business Communication Systems Ltd, 1996–98; non-executive Director: Nammo AS, Norway, 1989–2003; Management Engineers, Germany, 1997–2006; Plus Plan (UK) Ltd, 2001–03. Pres., German-British Chamber of Industry and Commerce in UK, 1997–2002 (Chm., 1992–97). Gov., Henley Mgt Coll., 1998–2003. FIET (FIEE 1991). FRSA 1993. *Recreations:* golf, gardening, architecture. *Address:* Al Ruscello, Via Panoramica 32, 22010 Piano Di, Porlezza, Italy. *Club:* Reform.

GEHRY, Frank Owen, CC 2002; architect; Principal, Gehry Partners LLP (formerly Frank O. Gehry & Associates), since 1962; *b* Toronto, 28 Feb. 1929; *s* of late Irving and Thelma Gehry; *m* 1975, Berta Aguilera; two *s*, and one *d* (and one *d* decd) by a previous marriage. *Educ:* Univ. of Southern Calif (BArch 1954); Grad. Sch. of Design, Harvard Univ. Designer, 1953–54, Planning, Design and Project Dir, 1958–61, Victor Gruen Associates, LA; Project Designer and Planner, Pereira & Luckman, LA, 1957–58. Projects include: Loyola Law Sch., 1981–84; Calif Aerospace Mus., 1984; Inf. and Computer Sci./Engrg Res. Lab., Univ. of Calif, Irvine, 1986–88; Centre for Visual Arts, Univ. of Toledo, 1992; Frederick R. Weisman Art Mus., Minneapolis, 1993; American Centre, Paris, 1994; Vitra Internat. HQ, Basel, 1994; EMR Communication and Tech. Centre, Bad Oeynhausen, Germany, 1995; Nationale Nederlanden bldg, Prague, 1996; Guggenheim Mus., Bilbao, 1997; Experience Music Project, Seattle, 2000; Weatherhead Sch. of Mgt, Case Western Reserve Univ., 2001; Walt Disney Concert Hall, LA, 2003; Maggie's Cancer Care Centre, Ninewells Hosp., Dundee, 2003 (Royal Fine Art Commn Trust Bldg of Year, 2004); Jay Pritzker Pavilion, Chicago, 2004; IAC Building, NY, 2007; Serpentine Gall. Pavilion, Kensington, 2008; New York by Gehry, NY, 2011; Louis Vuitton Foundn, Paris, 2013. Charlotte Davenport Prof. of Architecture, Yale Univ., 1982, 1985, 1987–89; Eliot Noyes Prof. of Design, Harvard Univ., 1984. FAIA 1974. Hon. RA 1998. Prizes include: Arnold W. Brunner Meml Prize in Architecture, 1983; Gold Medal, RIBA, 2000. *Publications:* (with Thomas Hines) Franklin D. Israel: buildings and projects, 1992; (with L. William Zahner) Architectural Metals: a guide to selection, specification and performance, 1995; Individual Imagination and Cultural Conservatism, 1995.

GEIDT, Rt Hon. Sir Christopher, KCB 2014; KCVO 2011 (CVO 2007); OBE 1997; PC 2007; Private Secretary to The Queen and Keeper of The Queen's Archives, since 2007; *b* 1961; *s* of late Mervyn Bernard Geidt and Diana Cecil, *d* of Alexander John MacKenzie, OBE, DSC (and 2 bars); *m* Emma, *d* of Baron Neill of Bladen, *qv*; two *d*. *Educ:* Dragon Sch., Oxford; Trinity Coll., Glenalmond; King's Coll. London (FKC 2011); Trinity Hall, Cambridge. RMA Sandhurst (invalided), 1982–83; small business, 1983–86; RUSI, 1987–90; Army (commnd Intelligence Corps), 1990–94; Foreign and Commonwealth Office: Political Liaison Officer, EC Monitor Mission, Sarajevo, 1994–95; Political Advr, Internat. Conf. on former Yugoslavia, Geneva, 1995–96; Political Advr, later Sen. Advr, Office of High Rep., Sarajevo and Brussels, 1996–99; Private Sec. to UN Sec.-Gen.'s Special Envoy for the Balkans, Geneva, 1999–2001; Magdalen Coll., Oxford, 2001–02; Asst Private Sec. to The Queen, 2002–05, Dep. Private Sec., 2005–07. *Address:* Buckingham Palace, SW1A 1AA.

GEIM, Sir Andre (Konstantin), Kt 2012; FRS 2007; Royal Society 2010 Anniversary Research Professor, since 2010, Regius Professor of Physics, since 2013, and Director, Manchester Centre for Mesoscience and Nanotechnology, since 2003, University of Manchester; *b* 21 Oct. 1958. *Educ:* Moscow Phys-Tech. Univ. (MSc 1982); Inst. of Solid State Physics, Moscow (PhD Physics 1987). Research Scientist: Russian Acad., 1987–90; Univs of Copenhagen, Bath, and Nottingham, 1990–94; Associate Prof., Nijmegen Univ., Netherlands, 1994–2000; Prof. of Physics, 2001–13, Langworthy Prof. of Physics, 2007–13, Manchester Univ.; EPSRC Sen. Res. Fellow, 2007–10. Ig Nobel Prize for levitation, 2000; Mott Medal and Prize, Inst. Physics, 2007; Europhysics Prize, European Phys. Soc., 2008; Körber Prize, Körber Foundn, 2009; J. J. Carty Award, US NAS, 2010; (jtly) Nobel Prize in Physics, 2010; Hughes Medal, Royal Soc., 2010; Niels Bohr Medal, Denmark, 2011; Copley Medal, Royal Soc., 2013. Kt Comdr, Order of the Lion (Netherlands), 2010. *Recreation:* hiking in high mountains.

GEKOSKI, Dr Richard Abraham; dealer in rare books and manuscripts; writer, broadcaster and publisher; *b* St Louis, Mo, 25 Aug. 1944; *s* of Bernard Gekoski and Edith Gekoski (*née* Kornblueh); *m* 1st, 1969, Barbara Pettifer (marr. diss. 2000); one *s* one *d*; 2nd, 2004, Belinda Jane Kitchin. *Educ:* Huntington High Sch., NY; Univ. of Pennsylvania (BA *summa cum laude* 1966); Merton Coll., Oxford (BPhil English 1968; DPhil English 1972). English Department, University of Warwick: Lectr, 1971–83; Sen. Lectr in English, 1983–84; Chm., Faculty of Arts, 1978–82; Founder: R. A. Gekoski Rare Books and Manuscripts, 1982; Sixth Chamber Press, 1983; (with T. G. Rosenthal) Bridgewater Press, 1998. Writer and presenter, series, Rare Books, Rare People, 1999–2009, Lost, Stolen or Shredded, 2006–09, BBC Radio 4. Tutor, Arvon Foundn Creative Non-fiction course, 2009–; Mem., Arvon Foundn Develt Bd, 2008–; Trustee, English PEN, 2010–13 (Curator, charity auction, First Editions, Second Thoughts, 2013; Hon. Vice-Pres., 2014). Judge, Man Booker Prize, 2005; Chm. Judges, Man Booker Internat. Prize, 2009–11; Mem., Man Booker Internat. Prize e-Council, 2013–. Columnist, Finger on the Page, online Guardian, 2010–. Participant in internat. literary festivals. Creative writing teacher, Spread the Word. *Publications:* Joseph Conrad: the moral world of the novelist, 1978; (with P. A. Grogan) William Golding: a bibliography, 1994; Staying Up: a fan behind the scenes in the Premiership, 1998; Tolkien's Gown and Other Stories of Great Authors and Rare Books, 2004; Outside of a Dog: a bibliomemoir, 2009; Lost, Stolen or Shredded: stories of missing works of art and literature, 2013; contrib. articles and reviews to books, jls and newspapers on topics related to books. *Recreations:* watching sport unless it involves a horse or water, golf, travelling, buying pictures and antiques, doing up houses, reading thrillers. *Address:* 13 Bathurst Mews, W2 2SB. *T:* (020) 7706 2735, *Fax:* (020) 7706 4640; The River Houses, 565 Kahuranaki Road, Havelock North, New Zealand. *E:* rick@gekoski.com. *W:* www.gekoski.com.

GELDER, Prof. Michael Graham; W. A. Handley Professor of Psychiatry, University of Oxford, 1969–96, now Emeritus Professor; Fellow of Merton College, Oxford, 1969–96, now Emeritus Fellow (Subwarden, 1992–94); *b* 2 July 1929; *s* of Philip Graham Gelder and Margaret Gelder (*née* Graham); *m* 1954, Margaret (*née* Anderson); one *s* two *d*. *Educ:* Bradford Grammar Sch.; Queen's Coll., Oxford. Scholar, Theodore Williams Prize 1949 and first class Hons, Physiology finals, 1950; MA, DM Oxon, FRCP, FRCPsych (Hon. FRCPsych 2011); DPM London (with distinction) 1961. Goldsmit Schol., UCH London, 1951. House Physician, Sen. House Physician, UCH, 1955–57; Registrar, Maudsley Hosp., 1958–61; MRC Fellow in Clinical Research, 1962–63; Sen. Lectr, Inst. of Psychiatry, 1965–67 (Vice-Dean, 1967–68); Physician, Bethlem Royal and Maudsley Hosps, 1967–68. Hon. Consultant Psychiatrist, Oxford RHA, later DHA, 1969–96; Mem., Oxford DHA, 1985–92; Dir, Oxford Mental Health Care NHS Trust, 1993–97. Dir, WHO Collaborating Centre, 1994–96. Mem., MRC, 1978–79 (Chm., 1978–79, Mem., 1975–78 and 1987–90, Neurosciences Bd). Chm., Wellcome Trust Neuroscience Panel, 1990–95 (Mem., 1984–88). Chairman: Assoc. of Univ. Teachers of Psychiatry, 1979–82; Jt Cttee on Higher Psychiatric Trng, 1981–85. Eur. Vice-Pres., Soc. for Psychotherapy Research, 1977–82. Advisor, WHO, 1992–2001. Mem., Assoc. of Physicians, 1983–2007. Mem. Council, RCPsych, 1981–90 (Vice Pres. 1982–83; Sen. Vice-Pres., 1983–84; Chm. Res. Cttee, 1986–91). Founder FMedSci 1998. Mayne Guest Prof., Univ. of Queensland, 1990. Lectures: Malcolm Millar, Univ. of Aberdeen, 1984; Yap Meml, Hong Kong, 1987; Guze, Univ. of Washington, 1993; Curran, St George's Hosp. Med. Sch., 1996; Sargant, RCPsych, 1996. Gold Medal, Royal Medico-Psychol Assoc., 1962. *Publications:* (jtly) Agoraphobia: nature and treatment, 1981; (jtly) The Oxford Textbook of Psychiatry, 1983 (Russian edn 1997), 5th edn as Shorter Oxford Textbook of Psychiatry, 2006 (Chinese and French edns 2005); (jtly) Concise Oxford Textbook of Psychiatry, 1994; Psychiatry: an Oxford core text, 1999 (Portuguese edn 2002, Japanese edn 2007), 3rd edn 2005; (ed jtly) New Oxford Textbook of Psychiatry, 2 vols, 2000 (Spanish edn 2003, Greek edn 2009), 2nd edn 2009 (BMA Prize, 2011); chapters in books and articles in medical jls. *Recreations:* photography, travel. *Address:* Merton College, Oxford OX1 4JD.

GELDOF, Bob, Hon. KBE 1986; singer; songwriter; initiator and organiser, Band Aid, Live Aid, Live 8 and Sport Aid fund-raising events; *b* Dublin, 5 Oct. 1951; *m* 1986, Paula Yates (marr. diss. 1996; she *d* 2000); two *d* (and one *d* decd); *m* 2015, Jeanne Marine. *Educ:* Blackrock Coll. Sometime journalist: Georgia Straight, Vancouver; New Musical Express; Melody Maker. Jt Founder, Boomtown Rats, rock band, 1975; *albums:* Boomtown Rats: Boomtown Rats, 1977; A Tonic for the Troups, 1978; The Fine Art of Surfacing, 1979; Mondo Bongo, 1980; V Deep, 1982; In the Long Grass, 1984; Loudmouth, 1994; solo: Deep in the Heart of Nowhere, 1986; The Vegetarians of Love, 1990; The Happy Club, 1992; Sex, Age and Death, 2001; How to Compose Popular Songs That Will Sell, 2011. Acted in films: Pink Floyd—The Wall, 1982; Number One, 1985. Organised Band Aid, 1984, to record Do They Know It's Christmas, sales from which raised £8 million for famine relief in Ethiopia; organised simultaneous Live Aid concerts in London and Philadelphia to raise £50 million, 1985; organised Sport Aid to raise further £18 million, 1986. Chm., Band Aid Trust, 1985–; Founder, Live Aid Foundn, USA, 1985–; Co-founder and non-exec. Dir, Ten Alps plc, 1999–. Freeman: Borough of Swale, 1985; Newcastle. Hon. MA Kent, 1985; Hon. DSc(Econ) London, 1987; Hon. DPh Ghent. TV film: The Price of Progress, 1987. Awards include: UN World Hunger Award, FAO Medal; EEC Gold Medal; Irish Peace Prize; music awards include: Ivor Novello (four times); Brit Award for Outstanding Contribution to Music, 2005; several gold and platinum discs. Order of Two Niles (Sudan); Cavalier, Order of Leopold II (Belgium). *Publications:* Is That It? (autobiog.), 1986; Geldof in Africa, 2005.

GELL-MANN, Murray; Professor and Distinguished Fellow, Santa Fe Institute, since 1993; Robert Andrews Millikan Professor of Theoretical Physics at the California Institute of Technology, 1967–93, now Emeritus; *b* 15 Sept. 1929; *s* of Arthur and Pauline Gell-Mann; *m* 1st, 1955, J. Margaret Dow (*d* 1981); one *s* one *d*; 2nd, 1992, Marcia Southwick (marr. diss. 2005); one step *s*. *Educ:* Yale Univ.; Massachusetts Inst. of Technology. Mem., Inst. for Advanced Study, Princeton, 1951; Instructor, Asst Prof., and Assoc. Prof., Univ. of Chicago, 1952–55; Assoc. Prof. 1955–56, Prof. 1956–66, California Inst. of Technology. Vis. Prof., Collège de France and Univ. of Paris, 1959–60. Overseas Fellow, Churchill Coll., Cambridge, 1966. Member: President's Science Adv. Cttee, 1969–72; President's Council of Advrs on Sci. and Technol., 1994–2001. Regent, Smithsonian Instn, 1974–88; Chm. of Bd, Aspen Center for Physics, 1973–79; Dir, J. D. and C. T. MacArthur Foundn, 1979–2002; Vice-Pres. and Chm. of Western Center, Amer. Acad. of Arts and Sciences, 1970–76; Member: Nat. Acad. of Sciences, 1960–; Sci. and Grants Cttee, Leakey Foundn, 1977–90; Sci. Adv. Cttee, Conservation Internat., 1993–2003. Santa Fe Institute: Founding Trustee, 1982–; Chm., Bd of Trustees, 1982–85; Co-Chm., Sci. Bd, 1985–2000. Member Board: California Nature Conservancy, 1984–93; Wildlife Conservation Soc., 1993–2004. Foreign Mem., Royal Society, 1978. Hon. ScD: Yale, 1959; Chicago, 1967; Illinois, 1968; Wesleyan, 1968; Utah, 1970; Columbia, 1977; Southern Illinois, 1993; (Nat. Resources), Florida, 1994; Southern Methodist, 1999; Hon. DSc: Cantab, 1980; Oxon, 1992; Hon. Dr, Turin, 1969. Listed on UN Envmtl Program Roll of Honor for Envmtl Achievement (Global 500), 1988. Dannie Heineman Prize (Amer. Phys. Soc.), 1959; Ernest O. Lawrence Award, 1966; Franklin Medal (Franklin Inst., Philadelphia), 1967; John J. Carty Medal (Nat. Acad. Scis), 1968; Research Corp. Award, 1969; Nobel Prize in Physics, 1969; Erice Science for Peace Prize, 1990; Procter Prize for Scientific Achievement, Sigma Xi, 2004; Albert Einstein Medal, Einstein Soc., 2005. *Publications:* (with Yuval Ne'eman) The Eightfold Way, 1964; The Quark and the Jaguar, 1994; various articles in learned jls on topics referring to classification and description of elementary particles of physics and their interactions; also articles on complexity, information and entropy. *Recreations:* walking in wild country, study of natural history, languages. *Address:* Santa Fe Institute, 1399 Hyde Park Road, Santa Fe, NM 87501, USA. *T:* (505) 9848800. *E:* mgm@santafe.edu. *Clubs:* Cosmos (Washington), Explorers, Century (New York); Athenæum (Pasadena).

GELLER, Laurence Stephen, CBE 2012; President and Chief Executive Officer, Strategic Hotels & Resorts, Chicago, Illinois, 1997–2012; *b* Middx, 22 Nov. 1947; *s* of Harold and Ruth Geller; *m* (marr. diss.); one *s* two *d*. *Educ:* Orange Hill Grammar Sch.; Ealing Tech. Coll. (Nat. Dip. in Hotel Keep-up and Mgt). Dir, Grand Metropolitan Hotels, 1971–76; Sen. Vice Pres., Holiday Inns, Inc., 1976–81; Exec. Vice Pres. and Chief Operating Officer, Hyatt Develt Corp., 1985–89; Chm. and CEO, Geller & Co., 1989–97. Non-exec. Dir, Michels & Taylor, 2013–. Chancellor, Univ. of W London, 2011–. Chm., Bd of Trustees, Churchill Centre, 2007–. *Publications:* Do Not Disturb, 2006; The Last Resort, 2012. *Recreations:* marathon running, multi-national philanthropic and civic activities.

GELLETLY, Prof. William, OBE 1993; PhD; CPhys, FInstP; Professor of Physics, University of Surrey, 1993–2009, now Emeritus; *b* Edinburgh, 11 Dec. 1939; *s* of William Gelletly and Agnes Gelletly; *m* 1965, Alexandra Bain. *Educ:* Broughton Sen. Secondary Sch.; Univ. of Edinburgh (BSc 1st Cl. 1961; PhD 1965). Asst Lectr, Univ. of Edinburgh, 1964–65; Fellow, Chalk River Nuclear Labs, 1965–67; Associate Scientist, Brookhaven Nat. Lab., 1967–70; Lectr, 1970–78, Sen. Lectr, 1978–93, Univ. of Manchester. Hd, Nuclear Structure Facility, SERC, 1988–93; Mem. Bd, NRPB, 1997–2005; non-exec. Dir, HPA, 2005–13. *Publications:* approx. 250 articles in learned jls. *Recreations:* history, golf, theatre, music, reading. *Address:* Physics Department, University of Surrey, Stag Hill, Guildford, Surrey GU2 7XH. *T:* (01483) 682733. *E:* w.gelletly@surrey.ac.uk.

GELLING, Donald James, CBE 2002; Member of the Legislative Council, Isle of Man, 2002–06; Chief Minister, Isle of Man, 1996–2001 and 2004–06; *b* 5 July 1938; *s* of John Cyril Gelling and Gladys Gelling (*née* Maddrell); *m* 1960, Joan Frances Kelly; three *s* one *d*. *Educ:* Santon Primary Sch.; Murrays Road Junior; Douglas High Sch. for Boys. Comr, Santon Parish, 1961–86. MHK, 1986–2002; Minister: of Agriculture and Fisheries, 1987–89; of the Treasury, 1989–96. Chairman, Insce and Pensions Authy, 2002–. Mem., British-Irish Council, 2004–. Captain of the Parish, Santan, 2002–. Mem., Isle of Man Past Rotarians Club. *Recreations:* golf, DIY. *Address:* Grenaugh Beg, Santon, Isle of Man IM4 1HF. *T:* (01624) 823482, *Fax:* (01624) 827178. *Club:* Castletown Golf.

GELLING, William John, OBE 2013; HM Diplomatic Service; High Commissioner to Rwanda and Ambassador (non-resident) to Burundi, since 2014; *b* Pembury, Kent, 30 Dec. 1977; *s* of John Gelling and Bridget Gelling; *m* 2013, Lucy Elizabeth Barker. *Educ:* Tonbridge Sch.; Univ. of Edinburgh (MA Hons Econs and Politics 2000); Univ. of Pennsylvania. Joined FCO, 2001; G8 Desk Officer, FCO, 2001–02; Urdu lang. trng, 2002–03; Second Sec. (Pol), Islamabad, 2003–06; First Sec. (Pol and Mil.), Baghdad, 2006–07; Hd, Iran Nuclear Section, FCO, 2008–10; Private Sec. to Sec. of State for Foreign Affairs, FCO, 2010–13. *Recreations:* walking, singing. *Address:* c/o Foreign and Commonwealth Office, King Charles Street, SW1A 2AH. *T:* (020) 7008 1000. *E:* william.gelling@fco.gov.uk.

GEM, Dr Richard David Harvey, OBE 2002; FSA; Secretary, Cathedrals Fabric Commission for England, 1991–2002; *b* 10 Jan. 1945. *Educ:* Eastbourne Coll.; Peterhouse, Cambridge (MA, PhD). Inspector of Ancient Monuments, DoE, 1970–80; Res. Officer, Council for Care of Churches, 1981–88; Dep. Sec., then Sec., Cathedrals Adv. Commn for England, subseq. Cathedrals Fabric Commn for England, 1988–91. Mem., RCHM, 1987–99. President: British Archaeol Assoc., 1983–89; Soc. for Church Archaeol., 2006–12; Bucks Archaeol Soc., 2008–. *Publications:* Studies in English Pre-Romanesque and Romanesque Architecture, 2004; numerous papers on early medieval architecture in British and foreign learned jls. *Recreations:* gardening, theatre, music, foreign travel, philosophy and theology. *Address:* The Bothy, Mentmore, Leighton Buzzard, Beds LU7 0QG.

GEMMELL, Campbell; *see* Gemmell, J. C.

GEMMELL, Gavin John Norman, CBE 1998; CA; Director, Archangel Informal Investments, since 2001 (Chairman, 2008–14); *b* 7 Sept. 1941; *s* of late Gilbert A. S. Gemmell and of Dorothy M. Gemmell; *m* 1967, Kathleen Fiona Drysdale; one *s* two *d*. *Educ:* George Watson's Coll., Edinburgh. CA 1964. Baillie Gifford & Co., 1964–2002: investment trainee, 1964–67; Partner, 1967; Partner, Pension Funds, 1973–89; Sen. Partner, 1998–2001. Chairman: Scottish Widows, 2002–07 (Dep. Chm., 1995–2002); Gyne Ideas, 2006–10; Mpathy Medical Devices, 2007–10; Net Things, 2014–; non-executive Director: Scottish Enterprise Edinburgh and Lothian, 1995–2003; Scottish Financial Enterprise, 1998–2002; Lloyds TSB Gp, 2002–07; Flexitricity, 2009–14; Ateeda, 2014–. Trustee, Nat. Galls of Scotland, 1999–2007. Chm., Standing Cttee, Scottish Episcopal Ch, 1997–2002. Chm. Ct, Heriot-Watt Univ., 2002–08. Non-exec. Dir, St Mary's Music Sch., Edinburgh, 2010–. DUniv Heriot-Watt, 2009. *Recreations:* golf, foreign travel. *Address:* 14 Midmar Gardens, Edinburgh EH10 6DZ. *T:* (0131) 466 6367. *E:* gavingemmell@blueyonder.co.uk. *Clubs:* Hon. Co. of Edinburgh Golfers (Muirfield); Gullane Golf.

GEMMELL, Dr (James) Campbell; consultant; Chief Executive, Environment Protection Authority South Australia, 2012–14; *b* 24 Jan. 1959; *s* of late James Stewart Gemmell and Agnes Campbell Little; *m* 1992, Avril Gold. *Educ:* High Sch. of Stirling; Univ. of Aberdeen (BSc 1st cl. Hons; PhD 1985); MA Oxon 1985. Res. Lectr in Glaciol., Christ Church, Oxford, 1985–89; Exec., Scottish Develt Agency, Glasgow, 1988–90; Sen. Consultant, Ecotec Res. and Consulting Ltd, 1990–91; Policy Manager, then Strategist, Scottish Enterprise, 1991–94; Chief Exec., Central Scotland Countryside Trust, 1994–2001; Dir, Strategic Planning, 2001–03, Chief Exec., 2003–11, SEPA. Chm., Dounreay Particles Adv. Gp, 2001–03. Mem., Minister's Rural Focus Gp, Scottish Office, 1992–96. Chm., Landwise, and Mem. Gp Bd, Wise, 1999–2001. Hon. Prof., Faculties of Phys. and Mathematical Scis, 2007–10, Hon. Prof. of Envmtl Regulation and Governance, 2010–, Univ. of Glasgow; Adjunct Prof., Centre for Environmental Risk and Remediation, Univ. of S Australia, 2013–. Mem. Court, Stirling Univ., 2010–12; non-exec. Dir, Scottish Agricultural Coll., 2011–12. Mediator. FRSA 2008. *Publications:* (contrib.) Environmental Enforcement Networks, 2015; earth science papers in environmental risk and regulation, water policy, and glaciol. and glacial geomorphology (winner, Wiley Earth Sci. Paper, 1991) in jls incl. Sustainability Jl, Risk Mgt Jl, Statistica, etc. *Recreations:* eating fine seafood and drinking fine beverages, combined, if possible, with leisure time in Australia, Scotland, California and New Zealand; passionate about Norway, Belgian beers and writing. *E:* campbell.gemmell@btinternet.com.

GEMMELL, Roderick, OBE 2002; HM Diplomatic Service, retired; *b* 19 Aug. 1950; *s* of Matthew and Ethel Gemmell; *m* 1975, Janet Bruce Mitchell; one *d*. *Educ:* Craigbank Secondary Sch., Glasgow. PO Savings Bank, 1966; joined FCO, 1967; Bahrain, 1971–72; Washington, 1972–74; The Hague, 1975–79; FCO, 1979–82; Mbabane, 1982–84; Stockholm, 1984–87; Second Sec. (Commercial/Econ), Ankara, 1987–91; Second Sec., FCO, 1991–94; First Sec. (Mgt), Kampala, 1994–97; First Sec. (Consular/Immigration), then Dir of Entry Clearance, Lagos, 1998–2002; High Comr, Bahamas, 2003–05. *Recreations:* travel, reading, bowling. *E:* gemmellrj@ntlworld.com. *Club:* Rutherglen Bowling.

GENDERS, Rev. Nigel Mark; Chief Education Officer, Church of England, since 2014; *b* St Albans, 1965; *s* of Derek and Audrey Genders; *m* 1989, Sarah Hewitt; one *s* two *d*. *Educ:* Oak Hill Theol Coll. (BA Hons Theol. 1992). Quality Assurance Manager, Royal Mail, 1986–89; ordained deacon, 1992, priest, 1993; Curate: New Malden and Coombe, 1992–96; Enfield, 1996–98; Priest-in-charge: Eastry Benefice, 1998–2003; Woodnesborough and Staple, 2003–08; Minister to Sandwich Secondary Schs, 2006–08; Area Dean of Sandwich, 2006–08; Dir of Educn, Dio. of Canterbury, 2008–12; Hd of Sch. Policy, C of E, 2012–14. *Address:* Church House, Great Smith Street, SW1P 3AZ. *T:* (020) 7898 1500. *E:* nigel.genders@churchofengland.org.

GENGE, Rt Rev. Mark; Bishop of Central Newfoundland, 1976–90; Pastoral Associate, St John's, Yorkmills, Ontario, 1990–92; *b* 18 March 1927; *s* of Lambert and Lily Genge; *m* 1959, Maxine Clara (*née* Major); five *d*. *Educ:* Queen's Coll. and Memorial Univ., Newfoundland; Univ. of Durham (MA); BD Gen. Synod of Canada. Deacon, Corner Brook, Newfoundland, 1951; priest, Stephenville, 1952; Durham, 1953–55; Vice-Principal, Queen's Coll., St John's, Newfoundland, 1955–57; Curate, St Mary's Church, St John's, 1957–59; Rector: Foxtrap, 1959–64; Mary's Harbour, 1964–65; Burgeo, 1965–69; Curate, Marbleton, PQ, 1969–71; Rector, South River, Port-de-Grave, 1971–73; District Sec., Canadian Bible Soc., 1973–76. Chaplain, Queen's Coll., Newfoundland, 1993–98. *Recreations:* badminton, swimming, rollerblading. *Address:* 6 Maypark Place, St John's, NL A1B 2E3, Canada.

GENN, Dame Hazel (Gillian), DBE 2006 (CBE 2000); LLD; FBA 2000; Professor of Socio-Legal Studies, since 1994, Dean, Faculty of Laws, since 2008, and Co-Director, Judicial Institute, since 2010, University College London; *b* 17 March 1949; *d* of Lionel Isaac Genn and Dorothy Rebecca Genn; *m* 1973, Daniel David Appleby; one *s* one *d*. *Educ:* Univ. of Hull (BA Hons 1971); CNAA (LLB 1985); Univ. of London (LLD 1992). Res. Asst, Cambridge Inst. of Criminology, 1972–74; Sen. Res. Officer, Oxford Univ. Centre for Socio-Legal Studies, 1974–85; Lectr, 1985–88, Reader, 1988–91, Prof. and Head of Law Dept, 1991–94, Queen Mary and Westfield Coll., London Univ. Member: Cttee on Standards in Public Life, 2003–07; Judicial Appts Commn, 2006–12; Chair, Judicial Sub-Cttee, Sen. Salaries Rev. Bd, 2013–. Hon. QC 2006; Hon. Bencher, Gray's Inn, 2008. *Publications:* Surveying Victims, 1978; Hard Bargaining, 1987; Personal Injury Compensation: how much is enough?, 1994; Mediation in Action, 1999; Paths to Justice, 1999; Paths to Justice Scotland, 2001; Tribunals for Diverse Users, 2006; Twisting Arms, 2007; Judging Civil Justice: Hamlyn lectures, 2008. *Recreations:* music, walking, spending time with my family. *Address:* Faculty of Laws, University College London, Bentham House, Endsleigh Gardens, WC1H 0EG. *T:* (020) 7679 1436.

GENSCHER, Hans-Dietrich; lawyer, with Büsing, Müffelmann & Theye, Berlin, 1999–2010; Managing Partner, Hans-Dietrich Genscher Consult GmbH, since 2000; Federal Minister for Foreign Affairs and Deputy Chancellor, Federal Republic of Germany, 1974–92 (in government of Helmut Schmidt, to Oct. 1982, then in government of Helmut Kohl);; *b* Reideburg/Saalkreis, 21 March 1927; *m* Barbara; one *d*. *Educ:* Higher Sch. Certif. (Abitur); studied law and economics in Halle/Saale and Leipzig Univs, 1946–49. Served War, 1943–45. Mem., state-level org. of LDP, 1946. Re-settled in W Germany, 1952: practical legal training in Bremen and Mem. Free Democratic Party (FDP); FDP Asst in Parly Group, 1956; Gen. Sec.: FDP Parly Group, 1959–65; FDP at nat. level, 1962–64. Mem., Bundestag, 1965–98. A Parly Sec., FDP Parly Group, 1965–69; Hon. Chm., FDP, 1992 (Dep. Chm., 1968–74; Chm., 1974–85); Federal Minister of the Interior, Oct. 1969 (Brandt-Scheel Cabinet); re-apptd Federal Minister of the Interior, Dec. 1972. He was instrumental in maintaining pure air and water; gave a modern structure to the Federal Police Authority; Federal Border Guard Act passed; revised weapons laws, etc; in promoting relations between West and East, prominent role in CSCE, Helsinki, 1975, Madrid, 1980–83, Stockholm, 1984–86 and in setting up conferences on Conventional Armed Forces, Confidence and Security Building Measures, Vienna, 1989; an initiator of reform process that led to the inclusion of the Single European Act 1986. Co-initiator: 'Eureka' initiative; independence process in Namibia. Promotes co-operation between EC and other regional gps, ASEAN, Central Amer. States, (San José Conferences), Golf Co-operation Council. Chm., Bd of Trustees, Franckesche Stiftungen, Halle, 1992–94. Chm., Assoc. of Friends and Patrons, State Opera, Berlin. Hon. Prof., Free Univ., Berlin, 1994. Hon. Dr: Madras, 1977; Salamanca, Athens, Seoul, Budapest, 1988; Georgetown, Washington, Heidelberg, Maryland, 1990; Columbia, S Carolina, Ottawa, 1991; Kattowitz, 1992; Essex, Moscow, Warsaw, Medford, Massachusetts, Durham,

1993; Tiflis, 1998; Szczecin, 2002; Hon. Master, German Handicrafts 1975. Hon. citizen Costa Rica, 1987. Grand Fed. Cross of Merit 1973, 1975 with star and sash; Wolfgang-Döring Medal 1976; numerous foreign decorations. *Publications:* Umweltschutz: Das Umweltschutzprogramm der Bundesregierung, 1972; Bundestagsreden, 1972; Aussenpolitik im Dienste von Sicherheit und Freiheit, 1975; Deutsche Aussenpolitik, 1977, 3rd edn 1985; Bundestagsreden und Zeitdokumente, 1979; Zukunftsverantwortung, 1990; Erinnerungen, 1995; Die Chance der Deutschen, 2008. *Recreations:* reading, walking, swimming. *Address:* PO Box 200655, 53136 Bonn, Germany.

GENT, Sir Christopher (Charles), Kt 2001; Chairman, GlaxoSmithKline, 2005–15; Senior Adviser, Bain & Co. Inc.; *b* 10 May 1948; *s* of late Charles Arthur Gent and of Kathleen Dorothy Gent; *m* 1st, Lynda Marion Tobin (marr. diss. 1999); two *d*; 2nd, 1999, Kate Elisabeth Lock; two *s*. *Educ:* Archbishop Tenison's Grammar Sch. With Nat West Bank, 1967–71; Schroder Computer Services, 1971–79; Man. Dir, Baric Computing Services, 1979–84; Dir, Network Services Div., ICL, 1983–84; Man. Dir, Vodafone, 1985–97; Dir, Racal Telecom plc, 1988–91; Dir, 1991–97, Chief Exec., 1997–2003, Vodafone Gp plc; Chm., Supervisory Bd, Vodafone AG. Mem. Bd Reps, Verizon Wireless Partnership; non-executive Director: China Mobile (Hong Kong) Ltd; Lehman Brothers Holdings Inc., 2003–08; Ferrari SpA. Vice-Pres., Computer Services Assoc., 1984. Nat. Chm., Young Conservatives, 1977–79. *Recreations:* family, cricket, politics, horseracing. *Clubs:* Carlton, MCC; Goodwood (Sussex); Royal Ascot Racing; Lord's Taverners.

GENT, (John) David (Wright), FIMI; Director General, Retail Motor Industry Federation, 1985–95; *b* 25 April 1935; *s* of late Reginald Philip Gent and Stella Eva Parker; *m* 1970, Anne Elaine Hanson. *Educ:* Lancing Coll. Admitted a Solicitor, 1959. Joined Soc. of Motor Manufacturers as Legal Advr, 1961; Asst Sec., 1964; Sec., 1965; Dep. Dir, 1971–80; joined Lucas Industries as Gen. Man., Lucas Service UK, 1981; Gp PR Man., 1982–83; Dir, British Road Fedn, 1983–84. Director: DC Cook Hldgs, 1995–2001; Autofil Properties Ltd, 2002–05. Member: Road Transport ITB, 1985–91; Vehicle Security Installation Bd, 1994–95. FRSA 1995. Freeman, City of London, 1985; Liveryman, Coach Makers and Coach Harness Makers' Co., 1985. *Recreation:* gardening. *Address:* 44 Ursula Street, SW11 3DW. *T:* (020) 7228 8126.

GENTLEMAN, David (William), RDI 1970; artist and designer; *b* 11 March 1930; *s* of late Tom and Winifred Gentleman; *m* 1st, 1953, Rosalind Dease (marr. diss. 1966; she *d* 1997); one *d*; 2nd, 1968, Susan, *d* of late George Ewart Evans; two *d* one *s*. *Educ:* Hertford Grammar Sch.; St Albans Sch. of Art; Royal College of Art. Work includes: painting in watercolour, lithography, wood engraving, illustration and graphic design; commissions include Eleanor Cross mural designs for Charing Cross underground station, 1979; illustrations for many publishers; postage stamps for Royal Mail, including, 1962–: Shakespeare, Churchill, Darwin, Ely Cathedral, Abbotsbury Swans, Millennium, etc; coins for Royal Mint: Entente Cordiale, 2004; Slave Trade Abolition, 2007; posters for London Transport, National Trust, and Stop the War Coalition; symbols for British Steel, Bodleian Library, etc. Solo exhibitions: at Mercury Gallery: watercolours of: India, 1970; S Carolina, 1973; Kenya and Zanzibar, 1976; Pacific, 1981; Britain, 1982; London, 1985; British coastline, 1988; Paris, 1991; India, 1994; Italy, 1997; City of London, 2000; watercolours and designs, RCA, 2002; watercolours, Fine Art Soc., 2004 (retrospective), 2007, 2010, 2012, 2014. Editions of lithographs of architecture and landscape, 1967–2008. Work in public collections incl. Tate Gall., V&A, BM, Fitzwilliam Mus., and Nat. Maritime Mus., and also in private collections. Member: Nat. Trust Properties Cttee, 1985–2005; Alliance Graphique Internat.; Council, Artists' Gen. Benevolent Instn. Master of Faculty, RDI, 1989–91. Hon. Fellow, RCA, 1981; Hon. FRIBA 1996. Prince Philip Designers Prize, Design Council, 2007. *Publications:* author and illustrator: Design in Miniature, 1972; David Gentleman's Britain, 1982; David Gentleman's London, 1985; A Special Relationship, 1987; David Gentleman's Coastline, 1988; David Gentleman's Paris, 1991; David Gentleman's India, 1994; David Gentleman's Italy, 1997; The Wood Engravings of David Gentleman, 2000; Artwork, 2002; London, You're Beautiful—An Artist's Year, 2012; In the Country, 2014; *for children:* Fenella in Greece, 1967; Fenella in Spain, 1967; Fenella in Ireland, 1967; Fenella in the South of France, 1967; *illustrator:* Plats du Jour, 1957; Bridges on the Backs, 1961; Swiss Family Robinson, 1963 (USA); The Shepherd's Calendar, 1964; Poems of John Keats, 1966 (USA); The Pattern Under the Plough, 1966; covers for New Penguin Shakespeare, 1968–78; The Jungle Book, 1968 (USA); Robin Hood, 1977 (USA); The Dancing Tigers, 1979; Westminster Abbey, 1987; The Illustrated Poems of John Betjeman, 1995; Inwards where all the battle is, 1997; The Key Keeper, 2001; Ask the Fellows Who Cut the Hay, 2010; *illustrator and editor:* The Crooked Scythe, 1993; *relevant publication:* David Gentleman: Design, by Brian Webb and Peyton Skipwith, 2009. *Address:* 25 Gloucester Crescent, NW1 7DL. *T:* (020) 7485 8824. *E:* d@gentleman.demon.co.uk. *W:* www.davidgentleman.com.

GEOGHEGAN, Hugh; a Judge of the Supreme Court of Ireland, 2000–10; *b* 16 May 1938; *s* of late Hon. James Geoghegan (a Judge of the Supreme Court of Ireland, 1936–50) and Eileen Geoghegan (*née* Murphy); *m* 1981, Mary Finlay Geoghegan, Judge of High Court of Ireland, *d* of Thomas Aloysius Finlay, *qv*; one *s* two *d*. *Educ:* Clongowes Wood Coll.; University Coll., Dublin (BCL, LLB). Called to the Bar: King's Inns, 1962 (Bencher, 1992); Middle Temple, 1975 (Bencher, 2006); Inn of Court of NI, 1989; Sen. Counsel 1977; Judge of High Court of Ireland, 1992–2000. Arbitrator of Public Service staff claims, 1984–92. Chm., Barristers Professional Conduct Appeals Bd; former Ind. Appeals Comr, Royal Coll. of Surgeons Ireland. Former Mem., Bar Council. Former Mem. Council, Royal Victoria Eye and Ear Hosp., Dublin. Mem. Council, Irish Legal Hist. Soc. Gov., Clongowes Wood Coll., 1995–2002. *Recreations:* history, genealogy, music. *Address:* Carne Lodge, Cowper Gardens, Dublin 6, Ireland. *Clubs:* Kildare Street and University, Royal Dublin Society, Fitzwilliam Lawn Tennis (Dublin).

GEOGHEGAN, Michael Francis, CBE 2003; Group Chief Executive, HSBC Holdings plc, 2006–10 (an Executive Director, 2004–10); Chairman, The Hongkong and Shanghai Banking Corporation Ltd, 2010; *b* 4 Oct. 1953; *m*; two *s*. Joined HSBC Gp, 1973; Pres. and CEO, HSBC Bank Brazil S.A. - Banco Múltiplo, HSBC Investment Bank Brazil S.A. and HSBC Seguros S.A., 1997–2003; Chief Exec., HSBC Bank plc, 2004–06 (Dep. Chm., 2006–10). Dir, HSBC N America Hldgs Inc., 2006–10; Chm. and Dir, HSBC Bank Canada, 2007–10; Dir, HSBC Latin America Hldgs (UK) Ltd, 2008–10. Chm., Young Enterprise UK, 2004–09.

GEORGE; *see* Lloyd George and Lloyd-George.

GEORGE; *see* Passmore, G.

GEORGE, Andrew Henry; researcher and writer; Director, Cornwall Community Land Trust, since 2015; *b* Mullion, Cornwall, 2 Dec. 1958; *s* of late Reginald Hugh George and of Diana May (*née* Petherick); *m* 1987, Jill Elizabeth, *d* of late William and Margery Marshall; one *s* one *d*. *Educ:* Helston Grammar (subseq. Comprehensive) Sch.; Sussex Univ. (BA); University Coll., Oxford (MSc). Rural Officer, Notts Rural Community Council, 1981–84; housing, farming and charity work, Notts, Devon and Cornwall, 1984–89; Dep. Dir, Cornwall Rural Community Council, 1989–97. Contested (Lib Dem) St Ives, 1992. MP (Lib Dem) St Ives, 1997–2015; contested (Lib Dem) same seat, 2015. Lib Dem spokesman: on fisheries, 1997–2005; on disabilities, 2000–01; on rural affairs, 2002–05; on internat. develt, 2005–06; PPS to Leader of Lib Dem Party, 2001–02. Chm., Lib Dem Parly DEFRA/DECC Team, 2010–12. *Publications:* The Natives are Revolting Down in the Cornwall Theme Park, 1986; (jtly) Cornwall at the Crossroads, 1989; A Vision of Cornwall (Cornwall Blind Assoc.), 1995; A view from the bottom left hand corner, 2002; housing and planning pubns and res. reports. *Recreations:* football, Rugby, cricket, gardening, cycling, walking, singing, poetry, running, rowing. *Address:* 1 Riviere Cottages, Hayle, Cornwall TR27 5AA. *T:* (01736) 757070. *Clubs:* Penzance and Newlyn Rugby, Leedstown Cricket, Hayle Rugby (Vice-Pres.).

GEORGE, Andrew James; QC 2015; *b* London, 11 Dec. 1973; *s* of James George and Mary George; *m* 2003, Sara Phillp; one *d*. *Educ:* Windsor Boys' Sch.; St Catherine's Coll., Oxford (BA Eng. Lang. and Lit.); City Univ. (DipLaw). Called to the Bar, Gray's Inn, 1997; in practice as a barrister, specialising in commercial law, esp. financial services, Blackstone Chambers, 1997–. Chm., Trustees, Spitalfields City Farm, 2009–. *Publications:* Milk Round, 2015. *Recreations:* poetry, theatre, city farming. *Address:* Blackstone Chambers, Blackstone House, Temple, EC4Y 9BW. *E:* andrewgeorge@blackstonechambers.com.

GEORGE, Prof. Andrew John Timothy, PhD, DSc; FRCPath; Professor of Immunology and Deputy Vice Chancellor (Education and International), Brunel University London, since 2013; *b* Hong Kong, 12 May 1963; *s* of Timothy John Burr George, *qv*; *m* 1992, Dr Catherine E. Urch; one *s* one *d*. *Educ:* Clifton Coll., Bristol; Trinity Coll., Cambridge (BA 1984; MA 1995); Univ. of Southampton (PhD 1987); Imperial Coll. London (DSc 2012). MRCPath 1999, FRCPath 2005; FRSB (FSB 2011). Beit Meml Fellow, Univ. of Southampton, 1987–90; Res. Fellow, NIH, Md, 1990–92; Royal Postgraduate Medical School, subseq. part of Imperial College London: Lectr, 1992–96; Sen. Lectr, 1996–99; Reader in Molecular Immunol., 1999–2002; Prof. of Molecular Immunol., 2002–13; Director: Grad. Sch. of Life Scis and Medicine, 2010–11; Sch. of Professional Develt, 2010–13; Grad. Sch., 2011–13. Hon. Reader, 2002–05, Hon. Prof., 2005–13, Inst. of Ophthalmol., UCL; Vis. Prof., Flinders Univ., Adelaide, 2005; Hon. Prof., Hubei Univ. of Medicine, 2013. Mem., Clin. Trials Biologicals and Vaccines Expert Adv. Gp (formerly Clin. Trials Expert Adv. Gp), MHRA, 2007–; Chair: Nat. Res. Ethics Advrs' Panel, 2009–; Gene Therapy Adv. Cttee, 2012. Mem., 1998–2000, Chm., 2000–10, Res. Ethics Cttee, Hammersmith, Queen Charlotte's and Chelsea and Acton Hosps; Mem. Council, British Soc. for Immunol., 2007–10; Trustee, Action Med. Res., 2008–15 (Mem., 2005–08, Chm., 2008–12, Scientific Adv. Panel). Governor: Richmond Adult Community Coll., 2011–; John Hampden Grammar Sch., 2014–. FRSA 2006; FHEA 2007. Editor and mem. of editl bds of various learned jls. *Publications:* Diagnostic and Therapeutic Antibodies (with C. E. Urch), 2000; articles on immunol., transplantation and cancer res. in jls and books. *Recreations:* gardening, theatre, family. *Address:* Brunel University London, Kingston Lane, Uxbridge, Middx UB8 3PH. *T:* (01895) 266249. *E:* andrew.george@brunel.ac.uk.

GEORGE, Andrew Neil; HM Diplomatic Service, retired; Governor of Anguilla, 2006–09; *b* 9 Oct. 1952; *s* of Walter George and late Madeleine George (*née* Lacey); *m* 1977, Watanalak Chaovieng; one *s* one *d*. *Educ:* Royal High Sch., Edinburgh; Univ. of Edinburgh (MA Politics and Modern History 1974). Entered HM Diplomatic Service, 1974; W Africa Dept, FCO, and Third Sec., Chad, 1974–75; SOAS, London Univ., 1975–76; Third, subseq. Second, Sec., Bangkok, 1976–80; S America Dept, 1980–81, W Africa Dept, 1981–82, Perm. Under-Sec.'s Dept, 1982–84, FCO; First Sec., Canberra, 1984–88; First Sec. and Head of Chancery, Bangkok, 1988–92; Republic of Ireland Dept, 1993–94, Eastern Dept, 1994–95, Non-Proliferation Dept, 1995–98, FCO; Ambassador to Paraguay, 1998–2001; Counsellor (Commercial), Jakarta, 2002; Asst Dir, Health and Welfare, HR Directorate, FCO, 2003–06. *Recreations:* reading, watching football. *Address:* c/o Foreign and Commonwealth Office, King Charles Street, SW1A 2AH.

GEORGE, Prof. Andrew Robert, PhD; FBA 2006; Professor of Babylonian, School of Oriental and African Studies, University of London, since 2000; *b* 3 July 1955; *s* of Eric and Frances George; *m* 1996, Junko Taniguchi; three *s*. *Educ:* Christ's Hosp., Horsham; Univ. of Birmingham (BA; PhD 1985). School of Oriental and African Studies, University of London: Lectr in Ancient Near Eastern Studies, 1985–94; Reader in Assyriology, 1994–2000. Hon. Res. Fellow, 1995–98, Hon. Lectr, 1998–2002, Hon. Prof., 2002, Inst. of Archaeol., UCL. Vis. Prof., Univ. of Heidelberg, 2000. Mem., Inst. for Advanced Study, Princeton, 2004–05. Res. Associate, Rikkyo Univ., Tokyo, 2009. Jt Ed., Iraq jl, 1994–2011. *Publications:* Babylonian Topographical Texts, 1992; House Most High: the temples of Ancient Mesopotamia, 1993, 2nd edn 2004; The Epic of Gilgamesh: a new translation, 1999, 3rd edn 2003; The Babylonian Gilgamesh Epic: introduction, critical edition and cuneiform texts, 2003, 2nd edn 2004; Babylonian Literary Texts in the Schøyen Collection, 2009; Cuneiform Royal Inscriptions and Related Texts in the Schøyen Collection, 2011; Babylonian Divinatory Texts Chiefly in the Schøyen Collection, 2013. *Recreation:* Assyriology. *Address:* School of Oriental and African Studies, University of London, Russell Square, WC1H 0XG. *T:* (020) 7898 4335. *E:* ag5@soas.ac.uk.

GEORGE, Rt Hon. Bruce Thomas; PC 2001; *b* 1 June 1942; *m* 1992, Lisa Toelle. *Educ:* Mountain Ash Grammar Sch.; UCW Swansea (Hon. Fellow, 2001); Univ. of Warwick. BA Politics Wales 1964, MA Warwick 1968. Asst Lectr in Social Studies, Glamorgan Polytechnic, 1964–66; Lectr in Politics, Manchester Polytechnic, 1968–70; Senior Lectr, Birmingham Polytechnic, 1970–74. Vis. Lectr, Univ. of Essex, 1985–86; Vis. Prof., Univ. of Portsmouth, 2009–. MP (Lab) Walsall S, Feb. 1974–2010. Member: Select Cttee on Violence in the Family; Select Cttee on Defence, 1979–2005 (Chm., 1997–2005); Chm., All Party Parly Maritime Gp. Mem., NATO Parly Assembly (formerly North Atlantic Assembly), 1981–2010 (Chm., Mediterranean Special Gp). OSCE Parliamentary Assembly: Mem., 1992–2010; Gen. Rapporteur, 1992–95; Chm., 1996–99; Vice Pres., 1999–2002; Pres., 2002–04; Pres. Emeritus, 2004–06; Hd, Election Observation Missions, Office of Democratic Instns and Human Rights, OSCE. Member: RIIA; IISS; RUSI (Mem. Council); Vice Pres., Security Inst., 2010–. Hon. Pres., Internat. Professional Security Assoc., 2013–. Hon. Advr, Royal British Legion, 1997. Co-founder, Sec., House of Commons FC. Fellow, Parliament and Industry Trust, 1977–78. Ed., Jane's NATO Handbook, 1988–91. Freedom of Walsall BC, 2011. Order of Honour (Georgia), 2011; Civilian Medal for contribn to OSCE mission, OSCE, Vienna, 2012. *Publications:* numerous books and articles on defence and foreign affairs. *Recreations:* Association football, private security and democratization, student of American Indians, eating Indian food. *E:* brucetgeorge@gmail.com.

GEORGE, Sir Charles (Frederick), Kt 1998; MD; FRCP, FFPM; Chairman, Stroke Association, 2009–13; Emeritus Professor of Clinical Pharmacology, University of Southampton, since 1999; *b* 3 April 1941; *s* of William and Evelyn George; *m* 1969, Rosemary Moore (marr. diss. 1973). *Educ:* Univ. of Birmingham Med. Sch. (BSc 1962; MB ChB 1965; MD 1974). MRCP 1968; FRCP 1978; FFPM 1989. Med. Registrar, United Birmingham Hosps, 1967–69; Hammersmith Hospital, London: Med. Registrar, 1969–71; Sen. Registrar, 1971–73; University of Southampton: Sen. Lectr, 1973–75; Prof. of Clinical Pharmacology, 1975–99; Dean, Faculty of Medicine, Health and Biol Scis, 1993–98; Med. Dir, BHF, 1999–2004; Chm., Bd of Sci. and Educn, BMA, 2005–09. Non-exec. Chm., Fulcrum Pharma plc, 2000–08; non-exec. Dir, BMJ Publishing Gp, 2006–08. Pres., BMA, 2004–05. Founder FMedSci 1998. FRSA 1993; FESC 2000, Emeritus FESC 2005; Hon. FFPH 2004; Hon. FBPhS (Hon. FBPharmacolS 2006). Hon. DSc: Birmingham, 2003; Leicester, 2007; Hon. DM Southampton, 2004. Gold Medal, BMA, 2010. *Publications:* Topics in Clinical Pharmacology, 1980; (ed) Presystemic Drug Metabolism, 1982; (ed) Clinical Pharmacology and Therapeutics, vol. 1, 1982; (ed) Drug Therapy in the Elderly, 1998. *Recreations:* music, walking, wind surfing. *Address:* 15 Westgate Street, Southampton SO14 2AY.

GEORGE, Charles Richard; QC 1992; a Recorder, since 1997; Dean, Arches Court of Canterbury and Auditor, Chancery Court of York, since 2009; a Deputy High Court Judge, since 2010; *b* 8 June 1945; *s* of Hugh Shaw George, CIE and Joan George (*née* Stokes); *m* 1976, Joyce Tehmina Barnard; two *d*. *Educ:* Bradfield Coll.; Magdalen Coll., Oxford (MA 1st Cl. Hons Modern History); Corpus Christi Coll., Cambridge. Asst Master, Eton Coll., 1967–72; called to the Bar, Inner Temple, 1974, Bencher, 2001; an Asst Recorder, 1994–97. Chancellor, Dio. of Southwark, 1996–2009; Mem., Legal Adv. Commn, Gen. Synod of C of E, 2003–. Mem., Council, St Stephen's House, Oxford, 1999–2012. Hon. Fellow, Centre of Eur. Law, KCL, and Vis. Lectr in EU Envmtl Law, KCL, 2007–. *Publications:* The Stuarts: an age of experiment, 1973. *Recreations:* architecture, travel. *Address:* Church Field, 2 Oak Lane, Sevenoaks, Kent TN13 1NF. *T:* (01732) 451875; Francis Taylor Building, Inner Temple, EC4Y 7BY. *T:* (020) 7353 8415. *Club:* Garrick.

GEORGE, Hywel, CMG 1968; OBE 1963; Fellow, Churchill College, Cambridge, since 1971 (Bursar, 1972–90); *b* 10 May 1924; *s* of Rev. W. M. George and Catherine M. George; *m* 1955, Edith Pirchl; three *d*. *Educ:* Llanelli Grammar Sch.; UCW Aberystwyth; Pembroke Coll., Cambridge; SOAS, London. MA Cantab 1971. RAF, 1943–46. Cadet, Colonial Admin. Service, N Borneo, 1949–52; District Officer, 1952–58; Secretariat, 1959–62; Resident, Sabah, Malaysia, 1963–66; Administrator, 1967–69, Governor, 1969–70, St Vincent; Administrator, British Virgin Is, 1971. Mem. Court and Council, Univ. of Wales, Bangor, 1999–2007. Panglima Darjah Kinabalu (with title of Datuk), Sabah, 1964; JMN, Malaysia, 1966. CStJ 1969. *Address:* 46 St Margaret's Road, Girton, Cambridge CB3 0LT. *T:* (01223) 563766; Tu Hwnt ir Afon, The Close, Llanfairfechan LL33 0AG. *T:* (01248) 681509.

GEORGE, Rt Rev. Ian Gordon Combe, AO 2001 (AM 1989); Archbishop of Adelaide and Metropolitan of South Australia, 1991–2004; George Mitchell Fellow and Assistant Chaplain, Trinity College, University of Melbourne, since 2014; *b* 12 Aug. 1934; *s* of late Gordon Frank George and Kathleen Mary George (*née* Combe); *m* 1964, Barbara Dorothy (*née* Peterson); one *d* (one *s* decd). *Educ:* St Peter's Coll., Adelaide; Univ. of Adelaide (LLB 1957); Gen. Theol Seminary, NY (MDiv 1964). Judges' Associate, Supreme Court of S Australia, 1955–57; barrister and solicitor, S Australia, 1957–61. Ordained deacon and priest, New York, 1964; Assistant Curate: St Thomas', Mamaroneck, NY, USA, 1964–65; St David's, Burnside, SA, 1966–67; Priest-in-charge, St Barbara's, Woomera, SA and Chaplain and Welfare Officer, Australian Regular Army, 1967–69; Sub-Warden and Chaplain, St George's Coll., 1969–73, Lectr in History, 1969–73, Univ. of W Australia; Dean of Brisbane, Qld, 1973–81; Senior Chaplain (Army), Qld, 1975–81; Lectr in Theol., Univ. of Queensland, 1975–81; Archdeacon of Canberra, 1981–89; Rector, St John's Church, Canberra, 1981–89; Lectr in Theol., St Mark's Coll., 1982–91; Asst Bp, Dio. of Canberra and Goulburn, 1989–91. Locum, Holy Trinity, E Melbourne, 2012–14. Member: Australian Liturgical Commn, 1973–89; Community Arts Bd, Australia Council, 1974–77, 1981–84; Anglican Consultative Council, 1982–89; SA Multicultural Forum, 1991–2000; Internat. Year of Family Council (SA), 1993–95; SA Heritage Authy, 1993–2005. Chairman: Christian World Service Commn, Nat. Council of Chs of Australia, 1994–2002; SA Govt Community Housing Council, 1994–97; Anglican Internat. Affairs Commn, 1988–98; Anglican Communion Internat. Migrant and Refugee Network, 1998–2008; Member: Minister for For. Affairs, Overseas Aid Adv. Council, 1996–2002; Adv. Council, Burmese Border Consortium, 2000–02. Art Critic, The News, Adelaide, 1965–67. Vice-Pres., Qld Fest. of the Arts, 1975–81. Occasional Lecturer: Art Gall. of Qld, 1975– (Trustee, 1974–81); Nat. Gall. of Australia, 1983–; Art Gall. of SA, 1994–; Nat. Gall. of Victoria, 2010–; Johnston Collection, 2012–. Founding Pres., Alcohol and Drug Problems Assoc. of Qld, 1975–81; Vice Pres., Australian Foundn for Alcohol and Drug Dependence, 1976–82. Patron: Royal SA Soc. for Arts, 1991–2012; Port Power FC, 1997–2005; SA Migrant Resource Centre, 1999–2006; Ambassador, Australian Refugee Assoc., 2009–12. Mem., SA Cricket Assoc., 1951–. Mem., Griffith Univ. Council, 1975–80. Hon. DD Gen. Theol Seminary, NY, 1990. SChStJ 1998 (ChStJ 1992); EGCLJ 2007 (ChLJ 1995; Dep. Nat. Chaplain, 2002–07; Nat. Chaplain, 2007–13). Queen's Jubilee Medal, 1976; Centenary Medal, 2003. *Publications:* Meditations on the Life of Jesus, 1991; Making Worship Work, 1992; articles in theol, church and aesthetics jls on art and religion. *Recreations:* gardening, reading, the Arts, wine, tennis. *Address:* 93/145 Canterbury Road, Toorak, Vic 3142, Australia. *T:* (3) 9827 7772, (4) 1305 5644. *Clubs:* Adelaide; University House (Melbourne).

GEORGE, Jane Elizabeth; Her Honour Judge George; a Circuit Judge, since 2014; *b* Redhill, Surrey, 1959; *d* of Maurice and Margaret Peterson; *m* 1984, Charles George; two *s*. *Educ:* Girton Coll., Cambridge (BA Law 1981). Admitted Solicitor, 1984; Partner, Rothera-Dowson Solicitors, Nottingham, 1990–2006; Pres. (pt-time), Mental Health Rev. Tribunal, 1996–2006; a Dep. Dist Judge, 1998–2006; a Dist Judge, 2007–14. Dep. Diocesan Registrar, Dio. of Southwell and Nottingham, 1996–2006. Founder Mem., Assoc. of Road Transport Lawyers, 1995. *Recreations:* gardening, walking, cricket, reading, theatre, cinema. *Address:* Leicester County Court, 90 Wellington Street, Leicester LE1 6HJ. *E:* HHJudge.JaneGeorge@judiciary.gsi.gov.uk.

GEORGE, Prof. Kenneth Desmond; Professor of Economics, 1988–98, now Emeritus, and Pro Vice-Chancellor (formerly Vice-Principal), 1993–98, University of Wales Swansea (formerly University College of Swansea); *b* 11 Jan. 1937; *s* of Horace Avory George and Dorothy Margaret (*née* Hughes); *m* 1959, Elizabeth Vida (*née* Harries); two *s* one *d*. *Educ:* Ystalyfera Grammar Sch.; University Coll. of Wales, Aberystwyth (MA). Res. Asst, then Lectr in Econs, Univ. of Western Australia, 1959–63; Lectr in Econs, University Coll. of N Wales, Bangor, 1963–64; Univ. Asst Lectr, Univ. of Cambridge, 1964–66, Univ. Lectr, 1966–73; Fellow and Dir of Studies in Econs, Sidney Sussex Coll., Cambridge, 1965–73; Prof. and Head of Dept of Econs, 1973–88, and Dep. Principal, 1980–83, UC, Cardiff; Head of Dept of Economics, 1988–95 and Dean, Faculty of Econ. and Soc. Studies, 1992–93, UC Swansea. Vis. Prof., McMaster Univ., 1970–71. Part-time Mem., Monopolies and Mergers Commn, 1978–86; Member: Ind. panel on public appointments, Welsh Office, 1996–2000; Parly Boundary Commn for Wales, 1998–2006. Editor, Jl of Industrial Economics, 1970–83; Mem. Adv. Bd, Antitrust Law and Econs Rev., 1988–92. *Publications:* Productivity in Distribution, 1966; Productivity and Capital Expenditure in Retailing, 1968; Industrial Organisation, 1971, 4th edn (with C. Joll and E. Lynk), 1992; (with T. S. Ward) The Structure of Industry in the EEC, 1975; (ed with C. Joll) Competition Policy in the UK and EEC, 1975; (with J. Shorey) The Allocation of Resources, 1978; (ed with L. Mainwaring) The Welsh Economy, 1988; articles in Econ. Jl, Oxford Econ. Papers, Aust. Econ. Papers, Jl Indust. Econs, Rev. of Econs and Stats, Oxford Bull., Scottish Jl Polit. Econ., and British Jl Indust. Relations. *Recreations:* walking, music.

GEORGE, Dame (Lesley) Anne; *see* Glover, Dame L. A.

GEORGE, Michael; freelance classical singer, bass-baritone; *b* 10 Aug. 1950; *s* of late John James George and Elizabeth (*née* Holmes, now Clayton); *m* 1972, Julie Elizabeth Kennard; one *s* two *d*. *Educ:* King's Coll. Choir Sch., Cambridge; Oakham Sch.; Royal Coll. of Music (ARCM Hons). Opera appearances with ENO, Buxton Opera and Scottish Opera incl. Fidelio, Semele and Orfeo, and St John Passion. Has performed in concerts worldwide and worked with leading conductors. Numerous recordings incl. Dream of Gerontius, The Creation, St Matthew Passion, Messiah, complete sacred works of Purcell. *Recreations:* golf, dog walking. *Address:* c/o Davies Music, 23 Church Street, Tewkesbury GL20 5PD. *Club:* Royal Mid-Surrey Golf.

GEORGE, Patrick Herbert; artist; Emeritus Professor of Fine Art, University of London, since 1988; *b* 28 July 1923; *s* of A. H. George and N. George (*née* Richards); *m* 1st, 1953, June Griffith (marr. diss. 1980); four *d*; 2nd, 1981, Susan Ward (marr. diss. 2009); partner, Susan Castillejo. *Educ:* Downs Sch.; Bryanston Sch.; Edinburgh Coll. of Art; Camberwell Sch. of Art (NDD). Served War, RNVR, 1942–46. Asst, Slade Sch. of Fine Art, London, 1949–. Head, Dept of Fine Art, Nigerian Coll. of Art, Zaria, 1958–59; Slade School of Fine Art: Lectr, 1962; Reader in Fine Art, 1976; Prof. of Fine Art, Univ. of London, 1983; Slade Prof. of Fine Art, 1985–88. Works in public collections in GB and USA; one-man exhibn, Gainsborough's House, Sudbury, 1975; retrospective exhibn, Serpentine Gall., London, 1980; exhibn, Browse & Darby, 1984, 1989, 1994, 1998 and 2003; dealer, Browse & Darby. *Recreation:* make do and mend. *Address:* Grandfathers', Great Saxham, Bury St Edmunds, Suffolk IP29 5JW. *T:* (01284) 810997.

GEORGE, Paul; Executive Director, Conduct Division, since 2011, and Board Member, since 2012, Financial Reporting Council; *b* Dartford, 19 Dec. 1960; *s* of late Derek John George and Jeannette George; *m* 1991, Phillipa Jane Brown; two *s* one *d*. *Educ:* Langtree Sch., Woodcote; Orpington Sixth Form Coll.; Warwick Univ. (BSc Hons Accountancy and Financial Analysis). ACA 1986. With KPMG, 1982–99 (Partner, 1995–99); Main Bd Dir, Mgt Consulting Gp plc, 2000–03; Dir, Professional Oversight Bd, Financial Reporting Council, 2004–11. Gov., Alleyn's Sch., 2006–13. Trustee, Dulwich Estates, 2003–08. *Recreations:* golf, squash, cricket, Rugby, football, theatre. *Address:* Financial Reporting Council, 5th Floor, Aldwych House, 71–91 Aldwych, WC2B 4HN. *T:* (020) 7492 2300. *E:* p.george@frc.org.uk. *Clubs:* Dulwich and Sydenham Hill Golf, Dulwich Squash.

GEORGE, Sir Richard (William), Kt 1995; CVO 1998; Director, 1972–2008, Chairman, 1982–2008, Weetabix Ltd (Managing Director, 1982–2004); *b* 24 April 1944; *m* Patricia Jane Ogden; two *s* one *d*. *Educ:* Repton Sch.; Kansas State Univ. (BSc). Joined Weetabix Ltd, 1968: Dep. Man. Dir, 1976–82; Chm., Whitworths Holdings Ltd, 1987–97. Dep. Chm., Envmt Agency, 1995–98. Member: Exec. Cttee, Assoc. of Cereal Food Mfrs, 1977–2005 (Chm., 1983–85); Council, Food and Drink Fedn (formerly Food Mfrs Fedn), 1982–2004 (Mem., Exec. Cttee, 1984–2001 and 2003–04); Dep. Pres., 1990–92; Pres., 1993–95; Vice-Pres., 2001–02); Exec. Cttee, Ceereal (European Breakfast Cereal Assoc.), 1992–96 (Pres., 1994–96). Chm., Governing Body, Inst. of Food Res. (formerly Adv. Bd, Inst. of Food Res.), 1993–98; Mem., Food from Britain Council, 1993–98. Mem., Council, Royal Warrant Holders' Assoc., 1983– (Pres., 1993; Hon. Treas., 1998–2003). Prince's Trust: Mem., Mgt Bd, 1993–99 (Vice Chm., 1996–99); Mem., Northants Cttee, 1985–94 (Chm., 1985–88, 1991–94); Pres., Northants Prince's Youth Business Trust, 1998 (Vice-Chm., 1986–98); Mem., Prince's Charities Council, 2009–10. Non-exec. Dir, Enjoy E Lothian Ltd, 2009–14 (Chm., 2012–14). Chm., RAF Benevolent Fund, 2001–05. Hon. Air Cdre, 504 (Co. of Nottingham) Sqn (formerly Offensive Support Role Support Sqn), RAF Cottesmore, 1998–2008. FIGD 1983; FInstD 1981; FRSA 1991. Freeman, City of London, 2001; Liveryman, Hon. Co. of Air Pilots (formerly GAPAN), 2001– (Freeman, 1982). Hon. LLD Leicester, 1997. *Recreations:* family, golf. *Clubs:* Saints and Sinners; Royal and Ancient (St Andrews); Hon. Co. of Edinburgh Golfers (Muirfield).

GEORGE, Russell Ian; Member (C) Montgomeryshire, National Assembly for Wales, since 2011; *b* Welshpool, Montgomeryshire, 27 April 1974; *s* of Richard Thomas George and Janet Elizabeth George (*née* Haynes). *Educ:* Clatter Co. Primary Sch.; Caersws Co. Primary Sch.; Newtown High Sch.; Coleg Powys; Univ. of Glamorgan (HNC Business and Finance 1994); Univ. of Central England (BA Hons Information and Media Studies 1999). Mem. (C) Powys CC, 2008– (Bd Mem., 2008–11). Shadow Minister for Envmt and Sustainable Develt, 2011–14, for Agriculture and Rural Affairs, 2014–, Nat. Assembly for Wales. *Recreations:* walking, cycling, member of Hope Church, Newtown, Powys. *Address:* National Assembly for Wales, Cardiff Bay, Cardiff CF99 1NA. *T:* 0300 200 7206. *E:* Russell.George@assembly.wales.

GEORGE, Prof. Stephen Alan; Professor, Department of Politics, University of Sheffield, 1994–2004, now Emeritus; *b* 14 Oct. 1949; *s* of Arthur George and Florence Lilian George (*née* Jefferson); *m* 1970, Linda Margaret Booth; one *s* one *d*. *Educ:* Univ. of Leicester (BA 1st cl. Hons Social Scis 1971; MPhil 1974). Res. Asst in European Affairs, Huddersfield Poly., 1971–72; Lectr, 1973–90, Sen. Lectr, 1991–92, Reader, 1992–94, in Politics, Univ. of Sheffield. Chair, Univ. Assoc. for Contemporary European Studies, 1996–2000. Dir, S Yorks Neighbourhood Watch Assoc., 2007–10. *Publications:* Politics and Policy in the European Community, 1985, 3rd edn, as Politics and Policy in the European Union, 1996; An Awkward Partner: Britain in the European Community, 1990, 3rd edn 1998; (jtly) Politics in the European Union, 2001, 4th edn 2015. *Recreations:* walking, reading history, poetry and novels. *Address:* 33 St Quentin Drive, Bradway, Sheffield S17 4PN. *T:* (0114) 236 4564.

GEORGE, Timothy John Burr, CMG 1991; HM Diplomatic Service, retired; *b* 14 July 1937; *s* of late Brig. J. B. George, late RAMC and M. Brenda George (*née* Harrison); *m* 1962, Richenda Mary, *d* of late Alan Reed, FRIBA and Ann Reed (*née* Rowntree); one *s* two *d*. *Educ:* Aldenham Sch.; Christ's Coll., Cambridge (MA). National Service, 2nd Lieut RA, 1956–58; Cambridge Univ., 1958. FCO, 1961; 3rd Secretary: Hong Kong, 1962; Peking, 1963; 2nd, later 1st Sec., FCO, 1966; 1st Sec. (Economic), New Delhi, 1969; Asst Political Adviser, Hong Kong, 1972; Asst European Integration Dept (Internal), FCO, 1974; Counsellor and Head of Chancery, Peking, 1978–80; Res. Associate, IISS, 1980–81; Counsellor and Hd of Chancery, UK Perm. Delegn to OECD, 1982–86; Hd, Republic of Ireland Dept, FCO, 1986–90; Ambassador to Nepal, 1990–95; FCO, 1996–99. Mem. Bd, CARE Internat. UK, 1998–2004. Gov., Ogbourne Sch., 2004–10, 2012–14 (Chm., 2006–08). Reader/Lay Minister, C of E, 2002–. *Publications:* (jtly) Security in Southern Asia, 1984. *Address:* Martlets, Ogbourne St George, Marlborough, Wilts SN8 1SL. *T:* (01672) 841278.

See also A. J. T. George.

GEORGE, His Honour William; a Circuit Judge, 1995–2012; *b* 28 Sept. 1944; *s* of William Henry George and Elizabeth George; *m* 1973, Susan Isabel Pennington; two *d*. *Educ:* Herbert Strutt Grammar Sch.; Victoria Univ. of Manchester (LLB, LLM). Called to the Bar, Lincoln's Inn (Mansfield Scholar), 1968, Bencher, 2003; Chancery Bar, Liverpool, 1968–95; Head, Chancery Chambers, Liverpool, 1985–95; Asst Recorder, 1990–93; Recorder, 1993–95. Chm., Northern Chancery Bar Assoc., 1992–94. *Recreations:* history (military history and the American Civil War), contemporary British art, gardening, watching Rugby. *Address:* Queen Elizabeth II Law Courts, Derby Square, Liverpool L2 1XA. *Club:* Athenæum (Liverpool).

GEORGE, Prof. William David, CBE 2008; FRCS; Regius Professor of Surgery, University of Glasgow, 1999–2006 (Professor of Surgery, 1981–99), now Honorary Professor, Faculty of Medicine; *b* 22 March 1943; *s* of William Abel George and Peggy Eileen George; *m* 1st, 1967, Helen Marie (*née* Moran) (*d* 1986); one *s* three *d*; 2nd, 1990, Pauline (*née* Mooney). *Educ:* Reading Blue Coat Sch.; Henley Grammar Sch.; Univ. of London (MB, BS 1966; MS 1977). FRCS 1970. Jun. surgical jobs, 1966–71; Registrar in Surgery, Royal Postgrad. Med. Sch., 1971–73; Lectr in Surg., Univ. of Manchester, 1973–77; Sen. Lectr in Surg., Univ. of Liverpool, 1977–81. *Publications:* articles in BMJ, Lancet, British Jl of Surg. *Recreations:* veteran rowing, fishing, squash. *Club:* Clyde Amateur Rowing (Glasgow).

GEORGIEVA, Kristalina; Member, since 2010, and a Vice-President, since 2014, European Commission; *b* Sofia, Bulgaria, 13 Aug. 1953; *m*; one *c*. *Educ:* Univ. of National and World Economy, Sofia (MA Pol Econ. and Sociol. 1976; PhD Economic Scis 1986); Harvard Business Sch. (Corp. Finance Cert. Prog. 1997; World Bank Exec. Develt Prog. 1998). Asst

Prof./Associate Prof., Dept of Econs, Univ. of Nat. and World Economy, Sofia, 1977–93; Res. Fellow, Dept of Econs, LSE, 1987–88; Consultant, Environomics and Merser Mgt Consulting, Inc., 1992; World Bank Group: Envmtl Economist, then Sen. Envmtl Economist, Envmt Div., Europe and Central Asia, 1993–97; Sector Manager, Envmt, 1997–98, Sector Dir, Envmt and Social Develt, 1998–99, E Asia and Pacific Reg.; Dir, Envmt Dept, 2000–04; Dir and Resident Rep., Russian Fedn, Moscow, 2004–07; Dir, Strategy and Ops, Sustainable Develt, 2007–08; Vice Pres. and Corporate Sec., 2008–10. Visiting Professor: Univ. of South Pacific, Fiji, 1991; ANU, 1991; Vis. Scholar, Special Prog. in Urban Studies, MIT, 1991–92. Member Board of Trustees: Inst. for Sustainable Communities, 2003–05; LEAD Internat., 2003–09; Univ. of Nat. and World Economy, Sofia, 2009–. European of the Year and European Comr of the Year, European Voice, 2010. *Publications:* textbook on microeconomics; over 100 papers. *Address:* European Commission, Rue de la Loi 200, 1049 Brussels, Belgium.

GEORGY, Orla; *see* Guerin, O.

GERADA, Clare, (Lady Wessely), MBE 2000; FRCP, FRCGP, FRCPsych; Chair of Council, Royal College of General Practitioners, 2010–13; *b* Nigeria, 8 Nov. 1959; *d* of Dr Anthony Gerada and Josephine Gerada; *m* 1988, Simon Charles Wessely (*see* Sir Simon Wessely); two *s*. *Educ:* Peterborough Co. Girls Comprehensive Sch.; University Coll. London (MB BS 1983); PGCE (Merit). MRCPsych 1988, FRCPsych 2012; MRCGP 1995, FRCGP 2000; FRCP 2008. GP Partner, Hurley Gp, 1992–; Med. Dir, Practitioner Health Prog., 2008–. Chair, N Lambeth Practice Based Commng Gp, 2006–09. Nat. Order of Merit Award (Malta), 2012. *Recreations:* running, secret love of knitting. *Address:* c/o Royal College of General Practitioners, 30 Euston Square, NW1 2FB. *T:* (020) 3188 7410.

GERALD, Nigel Mortimer; His Honour Judge Gerald; a Circuit Judge, since 2009; *b* Guildford, 2 Jan. 1959; *s* of Terry John Gerald and Stella Mortimer Gerald; partner, Katie Jane Young; two *d*. *Educ:* Highfield Sch.; Oundle Sch.; University Coll. London (LLB 1982). Called to the Bar, Gray's Inn, 1985; Recorder, 2004–09. Chairman: Residential Property Tribunal Service, 2006–; Charity Tribunal, 2008–. *Recreations:* opera, theatre, films, yoga.

GERARD, family name of **Baron Gerard**.

GERARD, 5th Baron *cr* 1876; **Anthony Robert Hugo Gerard;** Bt 1611; *b* 3 Dec. 1949; *er s* of Maj. Rupert Charles Frederick Gerard, MBE (*ggs* of 1st Baron), and of Huguette Reiss-Brian; *S* cousin, 1992; *m* 1976, Kathleen (marr. diss. 1997), *e d* of Dr Bernard Ryan, New York; two *s*. *Educ:* Harvard. Dir and Mem., Investment Cttee, Azimuth Investment Mgt LLC; Man. Mem., Gerard Partners LLC; Chm., SupplyPro Inc. Sen. Advr to Chm. and CEO, New York Private Bank and Trust. Director: Nicklaus Cos; Zola Brazilian Superfruits. Former Mem., Adv. Council, Conservation Trust of Puerto Rico. Former Trustee, Cardigan Mountain Sch. Dir and Sec., Wellness Foundn of E Hampton. *Heir: s* Hon. Rupert Bernard Charles Gerard, *b* 17 Dec. 1981. *Address:* PO Box 2308, East Hampton, NY 11937, USA.

GERARD-PEARSE, Rear-Adm. John Roger Southey, CB 1979; Group Personnel Manager, Jardine Matheson Co. Ltd, Hong Kong, 1980–84; *b* 10 May 1924; *s* of Dr Gerard-Pearse; *m* 1955, Barbara Jean Mercer; two *s* two *d*. *Educ:* Clifton College. Joined RN, 1943; comd HM Ships Tumult, Grafton, Defender, Fearless and Ark Royal; Flag Officer, Sea Training, 1975–76; Asst Chief, Naval Staff (Ops), 1977–79. *Recreations:* sailing, carpentry. *Address:* 1 Fromandez Drive, Horsmonden, Kent TN12 8LN. *T:* (01892) 724830.

GERE, Richard Tiffany; actor; Founder and Director, Healing the Divide Foundation, since 2001; *b* 31 Aug. 1949; *s* of Homer and Doris Gere; *m* 1st, 1991, Cindy Crawford (marr. diss. 1995); 2nd, 2002, Carey Lowell; one *s*. *Educ:* Univ. of Massachusetts. Played trumpet, piano, guitar and bass and composed music with various gps; stage performances: with Provincetown Playhouse, Seattle Rep. Theatre; Richard Farina, Long Time Coming and Long Time Gone, Back Bog Beat Bait, off-Broadway; Soon, Habeas Corpus and Grease on Broadway; A Midsummer Night's Dream, Lincoln Center; Taming of the Shrew, Young Vic, London; Bent, on Broadway (Theatre World Award); *films* include: Report to the Commissioner, 1975; Baby Blue Marine, 1976; Looking for Mr Goodbar, 1977; Days of Heaven, Blood Brothers, 1978; Yanks, American Gigolo, 1979; An Officer and a Gentleman, 1982; Breathless, Beyond the Limit, 1983; The Cotton Club, 1984; King David, 1985; Power, No Mercy, 1986; Miles From Home, 1989; Pretty Woman, Internal Affairs, 1990; Rhapsody in August, 1991; Final Analysis, 1992; Mr Jones, Sommersby, 1993; And the Band Played On, Intersection, 1994; First Knight, 1995; Primal Fear, 1996; The Jackal, Red Corner, 1998; The Runaway Bride, 1999; Autumn in New York, Dr T and the Women, 2000; The Mothman Prophecies, Unfaithful, Chicago, 2002; Shall We Dance?, 2005; Bee Season, 2006; The Hoax, I'm Not There, 2007; Nights in Rodanthe, 2008; Amelia, 2009; Brooklyn's Finest, 2010; Arbitrage, 2012; The Second Best Exotic Marigold Hotel, 2015. Founding Chm. and Pres., Tibet House, NY; Founder, Gere Foundn, 1991. Eleanor Roosevelt Humanitarian Award, 2000; Marian Anderson Award, 2007. *Publications:* Pilgrim, 1997. *Address:* c/o William Morris Endeavor Entertainment LLC, 9601 Wilshire Boulevard, Beverly Hills, CA 90210, USA.

GERGIEV, Valery Abesalovich; Artistic Director and Principal Conductor, Kirov Opera, since 1988; Director, Mariinsky Theatre, St Petersburg, since 1996; Music Director, Munich Philharmonic Orchestra, since 2015; *b* Moscow, 2 May 1953. *Educ:* studied conducting under Ilya Musin, Rimsky-Korsakov Conservatory, Leningrad. Asst Conductor, Kirov Opera, 1977–88 (début, War and Peace, 1978); Chief Conductor, Armenian State Orch., 1981–85; has appeared with numerous major internat. orchs, incl. Bayerische Rundfunk, Berlin Philharmonic, Boston SO, LPO, LSO, BBC Symphony, Philharmonia, NY Philharmonic, Vienna Philharmonic; tours with Kirov Opera. Principal Conductor: Rotterdam Philharmonic Orch., 1995–2008; LSO, 2007–15; Principal Guest Conductor, Metropolitan Opera, NY, 1997–2008; Artistic Director: Stars of the White Nights Fest., St Petersburg, 1993–; Rotterdam Philharmonic/Gergiev/Philips Fest., 1996–; Director and Founder: Mikkeli Internat. Fest., Finland, 1992–; Peace to the Caucasus Fest., 1996–; Red Sea Internat. Music Fest., Eilat, Israel, 1996–. Has made numerous recordings. Winner, Herbert von Karajan Conductors Competition, Berlin; Dmitri Shostakovich Award; Golden Mask Award; People's Artist of Russia. *Address:* c/o Columbia Artists Management Inc., 1790 Broadway, New York, NY 10019–1412, USA.

GERHOLD, Dorian James, FRHistS, FSA; historian; Secretary, House of Commons Commission, 2008–12; *b* 7 March 1957; *s* of late Peter Kenneth Gerhold and Nancy Melinda Gerhold (*née* Jones); *m* 2013, Elisabeth Partridge. *Educ:* King's Coll. Sch., Wimbledon; Merton Coll., Oxford (MA Hist.). Clerk, House of Commons, 1978–2012: Energy Cttee, 1989–92; Trade and Industry Cttee, 1992–96; Table Office, 1996–2000; Eur. Scrutiny Cttee, 2000–05; Hd, Scrutiny Unit, 2005–06; Principal Clerk, Select Cttees, 2006–08. Presidential Advr, Parly Assembly of Council of Europe, 2001–04. Hon. Res. Fellow, Roehampton Univ., 2005–08. Mem. Cttee, Southern History Soc., 2013–. Chm., Transport Hist. Res. Trust, 1997–2000; Trustee: Wandsworth Mus. Co., 2007–; County History Trust, 2013–. FRHistS 1996; FSA 2006. Fellow, Industry and Parlt Trust, 1992. Mem. Editl Bd, Jl Transport Hist., 1992–. *Publications:* Road Transport Before the Railways: Russell's London flying waggons, 1993; (with T. Barker) The Rise and Rise of Road Transport 1700–1990, 1993, 2nd edn 1995; (ed) Putney and Roehampton Past, 1994; (ed) Road Transport in the Horse-drawn Era, 1996; Wandsworth Past, 1998; Westminster Hall, 1999; Carriers and Coachmasters: trade and travel before the turnpikes, 2005 (Transport Book of the Year, 2007); The Putney Debates 1647, 2007; Bristol's Stage Coaches, 2012; articles in jls. *Recreations:* travel, walking. *Address:* 19 Montserrat Road, SW15 2LD.

GERKEN, Ian, LVO 1992; HM Diplomatic Service, retired; Ambassador to Ecuador, 2000–03; *b* 1 Dec. 1943; *s* of late Alfred Gerken and Esther Mary (*née* Chesworth); *m* 1976, Susana Drucker; two *s*, and one step *d*. *Educ:* Liverpool Collegiate. Entered Foreign Office, 1962: served in Budapest, 1965; Buenos Aires, 1966–68; FCO, 1968–71; Caracas, 1971–75; FCO, 1975–79; Lima, 1979–84; UN Gen. Assembly, 1984; FCO, 1985–88; Dep. High Comr, Valletta, 1988–92; Counsellor and Dep. Head, Perm. Under Sec's Dept, FCO, 1992–95; Ambassador to El Salvador, 1995–99.

GERKEN, Vice-Adm. Sir Robert (William Frank), KCB 1986; CBE 1975; Royal Navy, retired 1987; *b* 11 June 1932; *s* of Francis Sydney and Gladys Gerken; *m* 1st, 1966, Christine Stephenson (*d* 1981); two *d*; 2nd, 1983, Mrs Ann Fermor. *Educ:* Chigwell Sch.; Royal Naval Coll., Dartmouth. Cadet, HMS Devonshire, 1950–51; Midshipman: HMS Ocean, 1951–52; HMS Morecambe Bay, 1952; Sub-Lieut, Royal Naval Coll., Greenwich, 1953; Sea service as Lieut and Lt-Comdr, 1953–66; RN Staff Course, 1967; in command HMS Yarmouth, 1968–69; Commander Sea Training, 1970–71; Naval Staff, 1972–73; in command: Sixth Frigate Sqdn, 1974–75; HMS Raleigh, 1976–77; Captain of the Fleet, 1978–81; Flag Officer Second Flotilla, 1981–83; Dir Gen., Naval Manpower and Trng, 1983–85; Flag Officer Plymouth, Port Admiral Devonport, Comdr Central Sub Area Eastern Atlantic, Comdr Plymouth Sub Area Channel, 1985–87. Chm., Plymouth Develt Corp., 1993–96; Dir, 1988–2001, Chm., 1994–2001, Corps of Commissionaires. Chm., China Fleet Trust (formerly China Fleet Club (UK) Charitable Trust), 1987–2013. President: British Korean Veterans' Assoc. (Devon and Cornwall), 1986–2014; Plymouth Lifeboat, RNLI, 1988–2007; SSAFA (formerly SSAFA Forces Help) Plymouth, 1998–. Governor, Chigwell Sch., 1987–2000. DL Devon, 1995. Hon. DSc Plymouth, 1993. *Recreation:* travel and family. *Address:* 22 Custom House Lane, Plymouth, Devon PL1 3TG. *T:* (01752) 665104. *Club:* Royal Western Yacht (Cdre, 1993–97).

GERMAN, family name of **Baron German**.

GERMAN, Baron *cr* 2010 (Life Peer), of Llanfrechfa in the County Borough of Torfaen; **Michael James German,** OBE 1996; *b* 8 May 1945; *s* of Arthur Ronald German and Molly German; *m* 1970 (marr. diss. 1996); two *d*; *m* 2006, Veronica Watkins. *Educ:* St Mary's Coll., London (CertEd 1966); BA Open Univ. 1972; Bristol Poly. (Postgrad. Dip. in Educn Mgt 1973). Primary sch. teacher, 1966–67; Secondary sch. teacher, Mostyn High Sch., 1967–70; Head of Music: Lady Mary High Sch., Cardiff, 1970–86; Corpus Christi High Sch., Cardiff, 1986–91; Dir, European Div., Welsh Jt Educn Cttee, 1991–99. Mem., Cardiff CC, 1983–96 (Jt Leader, 1987–91; Leader, Liberal Democrats, 1983–96). National Assembly for Wales: Mem. (Lib Dem) S Wales East, 1999–2010; Sec., subseq. Minister, for Econ. Develt, 2000–01; Dep. First Minister, 2000–01 and 2002–03; Minister for Rural Develt and Wales Abroad, 2002–03; Chairman: Legislation Cttee, 1999–2000; Sustainability Cttee, 2009–10; Leader: Liberal Democrats, 1999–2008; Welsh Liberal Democrats, 2007–08. Co-Chair, Lib Dem Parly Cttee for Work and Pensions, H of L, 2010–15; Mem., Adv. Cttee on Business Appts, 2014–. Chm., Anglo-Azerbaijani Soc.; President: Dolen Cymru, Wales-Lesotho Link, 2008–; Monmouth, Brecon and Abergavenny Canals Trust, 2011–. Vice Chm., Parliament Choir, 2013–. *Publications:* articles in political and educnl jls. *Recreations:* music, travel. *Address:* Hycona, Crown Road, Llanfrechfa, Cwmbran NP44 8UF. *T:* (01633) 970075; House of Lords, SW1A 0PW. *T:* (020) 7219 6942.

GERMAN, Lt-Col David John Keeling, TD 1972; JP; Vice Lord-Lieutenant of Staffordshire, 1995–2007; *b* 25 May 1932; *s* of Col Guy German, DSO and Rosemary German (*née* Keeling), MBE; *m* 1961, Anita Blanche Jupp; one *s* one *d*. *Educ:* Winchester; RMA, Sandhurst. Served Grenadier Guards, 1952–59; Keeling & Walker Ltd, Stoke on Trent, Chem. Mfrs, 1959–90, Man. Dir, 1974–90. Served Staffs Yeomanry, 1960–70, commanded QO Mercian Yeomanry, 1972–75. Founder and Curator, Mus. of Staffs Yeomanry, 1993–2007. Freeman, City of London, 1983. JP 1972, DL 1979, High Sheriff 1982–83, Staffs. *Recreations:* yachting, military history, France. *Address:* Ridgecombe, Penton Grafton, Andover SP11 0RR. *Clubs:* Army and Navy; Royal Yacht Squadron, Household Division Yacht (Cdre, 1993–98).

GERMOND, Rt Rev. Brian Charles; Bishop of Johannesburg, 2000–13; *b* 21 Jan. 1947; *s* of Charles Alfred Germond and Dorothy Eileen Germond (*née* Impey); *m* 1971, Susan Patricia Strong; one *s* two *d*. *Educ:* King Edward VII Sch.; Univ. of SA (BA); St Paul's Theol Coll. (DipTh); Univ. of London (BD); McCormack Seminary (DMin). Ordained deacon, 1976, priest, 1977; Curate, St Martin-in-the-Veld, Johannesburg, 1976–80; Rector: St Barnabas Lichtenburg, St Andrews, Lichtenburg, and St John's, Zeerust, 1980–85; St Martin-in-the-Veld, 1987–2000; Archdeacon of Rosebank, 1989–2000. *Recreations:* birdwatching, woodworking. *Address:* c/o PO Box 1131, Johannesburg 2000, RSA. *T:* (011) 3368724.

GERMOND, (Catherine) Siân; *see* Maddrell, C. S.

GEROSA, Peter Norman; Trustee, Tree Council, 1991–2003 (Secretary, 1983–91); *b* 1 Nov. 1928; *s* of late Enrico Cecil and Olive Doris Gerosa; *m* 1955, Dorothy Eleanor Griffin; two *d*. *Educ:* Whitgift Sch.; London Univ. (Birkbeck). BA (Hons) 1st Cl., Classics. Civil Service, 1945–82; Foreign Office, 1945; Home Office, 1949; HM Customs and Excise, 1953; Min. of Transport, 1966; DoE, 1970; Under Secretary: DoE, 1972; Dept of Transport, 1977; Dir of Rural Affairs, DoE, 1981–82. *Recreations:* singing, gardening, walking. *Address:* Sunnyside, 2 Chart Lane, Reigate, Surrey RH2 7BW.

GERRARD, Ven. David Keith Robin; Archdeacon of Wandsworth, 1989–2004, now Emeritus; *b* 15 June 1939; *s* of Eric Henry and Doris Jane Gerrard; *m* 1963, Jennifer Mary Hartley; two *s* two *d*. *Educ:* Royal Grammar School, Guildford; St Edmund Hall, Oxford (BA); Lincoln Theol Coll. Curate: St Olave, Woodberry Down, N16, 1963–66; St Mary, Primrose Hill, NW3, 1966–69; Vicar: St Paul, Lorrimore Square, SE17, 1969–79; St Andrew and St Mark, Surbiton, Surrey, 1979–89; RD of Kingston upon Thames, 1983–88. *Publications:* (co-author) Urban Ghetto, 1976. *Recreations:* embroidery, Proust, Yorkshire, statistics. *Address:* 15 Woodbourne Drive, Claygate, Surrey KT10 0DR. *T:* (01372) 467295. *E:* david.gerrard@btinternet.com.

GERRARD, Neil Francis; *b* 3 July 1942; *m* 1968, Marian Fitzgerald (marr. diss. 1983); two *s*. *Educ:* Manchester Grammar Sch.; Wadham Coll., Oxford (BA Hons); Chelsea Coll., London (MEd). Teacher, Queen Elizabeth's Sch., Barnet, 1965–68; Lectr in Computing, Hackney Coll., 1968–92. Mem. (Lab) Waltham Forest BC, 1973–90 (Leader of Council, 1986–90). Contested (Lab) Chingford, 1979. MP (Lab) Walthamstow, 1992–2010.

GERRARD, Peter Noël, CBE 1991; General Counsel, London Stock Exchange, 1991–94; *b* 19 May 1930; *oc* of Sir Denis Gerrard and of Hilda Goodwin (*née* Jones, who *m* 2nd, Sir Joseph Cantley, OBE); *m* 1957, Prudence Lipson-Ward; one *s* two *d*. *Educ:* Rugby; Christ Church, Oxford (MA). 2nd Lieut, XII Royal Lancers, Malaya, 1953–54. Solicitor, 1959; Partner, Lovell, White & King, 1960, Sen. Partner, 1980–88; Sen. Partner, Lovell White Durrant, 1988–91. Member: Bd of Banking Supervision, 1990–2001; City Capital Markets Cttee, 1974–91. Member: Council, Law Society, 1972–82; Bd, Inst. of Advanced Legal Studies, 1985–96; Council, St George's Hosp. Med. Sch., 1982–94. *Recreations:* music, walking (restricted). *Address:* Pightle Cottage, Ashdon, Saffron Walden, Essex CB10 2HG. *T:* (01799) 584374.

GERRIE, Malcolm; Chief Executive, Whizz Kid Entertainment, since 2006; *b* Newcastle upon Tyne, 9 May 1950; *s* of Athelstan Ross Gerrie and Evelyn Gerrie (*née* Nesbitt); three *s*. *Educ:* Durham Univ. (BA); Sunderland Univ. (BEd). Schoolteacher, 1971–76; researcher and producer, Tyne Tees TV, 1976–87; Dir, 1988, Man. Dir, 1988–2006, Initial Film & TV. Hon. DArts Sunderland, 2006. *Recreation:* anything ending in '…ing'. *Address:* Whizz Kid Entertainment, 4 Kingly Street, W1B 5PE. *T:* (020) 7440 2550, *Fax:* (020) 7440 2599. *Clubs:* Royal Automobile, Groucho, Soho House, Bureau, Ivy.

GERRISH, Prof. Catherine Anne, PhD; CBE 2014; FRCN; Professor of Nursing Research, University of Sheffield and Sheffield Teaching Hospitals NHS Foundation Trust, since 2011; *b* Stourbridge, 10 April 1955; *d* of Arthur Walker and Gudrun Walker; *m* 1986, Paul Gerrish. *Educ:* Stourbridge Co. High Sch. for Girls; Welsh Nat. Sch. of Medicine, Univ. of Wales (Bachelor of Nursing 1977); Univ. of Manchester (MSc 1986); Univ. of Nottingham (PhD 1998). RN 1977; Specialist Practitioner Dist Nursing 1977; RM 1979; FRCN 2014. Nursing Sister, Kalene Hosp., Zambia, 1978; Student Midwife, Univ. Hosp. of Wales, 1978–79; Staff Nurse, Singleton Hosp., 1979–81; Sister, Northern Gen. Hosp., 1981–84; Nurse Tutor, Sheffield Sch. of Nursing, 1984–89; Sen. Lectr, 1989–90, Principal Lectr, 1990–92, Univ. of Huddersfield; Asst Dir, Bradford and Airedale Coll. of Health, 1992–95; Sen. Res. Fellow, Sheffield Hallam Univ., 1995–2000; Reader in Nursing Practice Develt, 2000–02, Prof. of Nursing Practice Develt, 2002–06, Univ. of Sheffield and Northern Gen. Hosp. NHS Trust; Res. Prof. in Nursing, Sheffield Hallam Univ. and Sheffield Teaching Hosps NHS Foundn Trust, 2006–11. Adjunct Prof., Karolinska Inst., 2006–14; Hon. Prof., Univ. of Sheffield, 2009–11; Vis. Sen. Acad. Scholar, Univ. of British Columbia, 2013. Chm., Res. Soc., RCN, 2002–10. Trustee, Gen. Nursing Council Trust for Eng. and Wales, 2011–. *Publications:* Nursing in a Multi-ethnic Society, 2006; The Research Process in Nursing, 5th edn 2006 to 7th edn 2015; approx. 150 articles in learned jls. *Recreations:* cycle touring, walking, gardening, needlework, theatre. *Address:* School of Nursing and Midwifery, University of Sheffield, Barber House Annexe, 3a Clarkehouse Road, Sheffield S10 2LA. *T:* (0114) 222 2036. *E:* kate.gerrish@sheffield.ac.uk.

GERRY, Felicity Ruth; QC 2014; *b* Dagenham, 11 March 1968; *d* of Robin Gerry and Edith Tyler; *m* 1999; one *s* one *d* and one step *s*. *Educ:* Manning Girls Sch., Nottingham; Kingston Univ. (LLB Hons 1993). Called to the Bar, Middle Temple, 1994; Accredited Mediator, Australia, 2014. Legal media commentator, 2008–. Lectr in Law, Charles Darwin Univ., 2013–. Mem., Public Affairs Cttee, Bar Council, 2012–13. Member: Bd, Halsbury's Law Exchange, 2012–; Mgt Cttee, Advocates' Gateway, 2014–. *Publications:* The Sexual Offences Handbook, 2010, 2nd edn 2014; contribs to legal press. *Recreations:* dragon boating, horse riding, Twitter @felicitygerry. *Address:* 36 Bedford Row, WC1R 4JH. *T:* (020) 7421 8000. *E:* fgerry@36bedfordrow.co.uk.

GERSHON, Sir Peter (Oliver), Kt 2004; CBE 2000; FREng; Chairman: Tate & Lyle plc, since 2009; National Grid plc, since 2012; Aircraft Alliance Management Board, since 2014; *b* 10 Jan. 1947; *s* of late Alfred Joseph Gershon and Gerta Gershon; *m* 1971, Eileen Elizabeth Walker; one *s* two *d*. *Educ:* Reigate Grammar Sch.; Churchill Coll., Cambridge (MA). FIEE 1998, Hon. FIET (Hon. FIEE 2005); FRAeS 2000; FCIPS 2000; FREng 2001. Joined ICL, 1969; Mem. Mgt Bd, and Dir of Network Systems, 1985; Managing Director: STC Telecommunications Ltd, 1987–90; GPT Ltd, 1990–94; Marconi Electronic Systems Ltd, 1994–99; Chief Operating Officer, BAE Systems, 1999–2000; Chief Exec., Office of Govt Commerce, 2000–04; Chairman: Symbian Ltd, 2004–08; General Healthcare Gp, 2006–12; Premier Farnell plc, 2005–11; Vertex Data Sciences, 2007–. Mem. Ct and Council, Imperial Coll., London, 2002–10. CCMI (CIMgt 1996); FBCS 2005. Hon. Fellow: Cardiff Univ., 2007; Imperial Coll. London, 2011. Hon. DTech Kingston, 2005. *Publications:* Review of Civil Procurement in Central Government, 1999; Independent Review of Public Sector Efficiency, 2004; Independent Review of Royal Family and Ministerial Air Travel, 2006; Review of the Australian Government's Use of Information and Communication Technology, 2008. *Recreations:* cycling, reading, ski-ing, swimming, theatre. *T:* (01494) 723792.

GERSHUNY, Prof. Jonathan Israel, DPhil; FBA 2002; FAcSS; Professor of Economic Sociology, and Director, ESRC Centre for Time Use Research, University of Oxford, since 2012; Senior Research Fellow of Nuffield College, Oxford, since 2012; *b* 16 Sept. 1949; *s* of Charles and Cynthia Gershuny; *m* 1974, Esther Gershuny; one *s* one *d*. *Educ:* Loughborough Univ. (BSc Econs and Politics 1971); Strathclyde Univ. (MSc 1972); Sussex Univ. (DPhil 1977). Res. Officer, Dept of Transport Technology, Loughborough Univ., 1973–74; Science Policy Research Unit, Sussex University: Fellow, 1974–81; Sen. Fellow, 1981–84; Vis. Professorial Fellow, 1986–91; on secondment as pt-time Res. Fellow, Res. Unit on Ethnic Relations, Univ. of Bristol, 1978–79; University of Bath: Prof. of Sociology, 1984–89; Head: Sociology and Social Policy Gp, 1984–88; Sch. of Social Scis, 1988–89; Univ. Lectr, Dept of Social and Admin. Studies, and Fellow of Nuffield Coll., Univ. of Oxford, 1990–93; Prof. of Econ. Sociology and Dir, ESRC Res. Centre on Micro-social Change, subseq. Inst. for Social and Econ. Res., Univ. of Essex, 1993–2006; Prof. of Sociology, 2006–11, Hd, Dept of Sociology, 2008–09, Univ. of Oxford; Fellow, St Hugh's Coll., Oxford, 2006–11. Chm., Sect. S4 (Sociol., Demography, Social Stats), British Acad., 2006–09. FAcSS (AcSS 2011). Silver Medal, Market Res. Soc., 1986. *Publications:* After Industrial Society?, 1978 (trans. German, 1981, Italian, 1985); Social Innovation and the Division of Labour, 1983 (trans. Swedish 1986); (with I. D. Miles) The New Service Economy, 1983 (trans. Japanese 1983, Spanish 1988); (ed jtly) Time Use Studies World Wide, 1991; L'innovazione Sociale: tempo, produzione e consumi, 1993; (jtly) Changing Households, 1994; (ed jtly) The Social and Political Economy of the Household, 1994; Changing Times: the social and political economy of post industrial society, 2000; (ed jtly) Seven Years in the Lives of British Households, 2000; (ed jtly) Information and Communication Technologies in Society, 2007. *Recreations:* classical music, travel. *Address:* Nuffield College, New Road, Oxford OX1 1NF. *T:* (01865) 286175. *E:* jonathan.gershuny@sociology.ox.ac.uk.

GERSON, John Henry Cary, CMG 1999; Head of Government and Political Affairs, BP plc, 2007–12 (Group Political Adviser, 2000–07); *b* 25 April 1945; *s* of late Henry and of Benedicta Joan Gerson; *m* 1968, Mary Alison, *d* of late George Ewart Evans; one *s* one *d*. *Educ:* Bradfield; King's Coll., Cambridge (MA). HM Diplomatic Service, 1968–99: Third Sec., FCO, 1968; language student, Hong Kong, 1969–71; Second Secretary: Singapore, 1971–73; FCO, 1973–74; First Sec. and HM Consul, Peking, 1974–77; First Sec., FCO, 1978; on loan to Home CS, 1978–79; First Sec., later Counsellor, FCO, 1979–87; Counsellor, Hong Kong, 1987–92; Vis. Fellow, Princeton Univ., 1992; Counsellor, FCO, 1992–99. Mem. Bd, Handeni Gold, 2012–. Mem. Simuri Tribe, Manokwari, Irian Jaya, 2001. *Recreations:* ornithology, sinology, literature. *Club:* Athenæum.

GERSTENBERG, Frank Eric, MA; Principal, George Watson's College, Edinburgh, 1985–2001; *b* 23 Feb. 1941; *s* of late Eric Gustav Gerstenberg and Janie Willis Gerstenberg; *m* 1966, Valerie Myra (*née* MacLellan); one *s* twin *d*. *Educ:* Trinity College, Glenalmond; Clare College, Cambridge (MA); Inst. of Education, Univ. of London (PGCE). Asst History Teacher, Kelly Coll., Tavistock, 1963–67; Housemaster and Head of History, Millfield School, 1967–74; Headmaster, Oswestry School, 1974–85. Chm. of Govs, Glenalmond Coll., 2005–11; Governor: Compass Sch., Haddington, 2007–; Loretto Sch., 2012–. Elder, Ch of Scotland. *Recreations:* ski-ing, golf, visiting scattered children throughout the world. *Address:* Craigmore, Whim Road, Gullane, East Lothian EH31 2BD. *Clubs:* Royal Scots (Edinburgh); Luffness New Golf.

GERSTLE, Prof. (C.) Andrew, PhD; FBA 2015; Professor of Japanese Studies, School of Oriental and African Studies, University of London, since 1993; *b* 18 June 1951. *Educ:* Columbia Univ. (BA 1973); Waseda Univ., Tokyo (MA 1979); Harvard Univ. (PhD 1980). Lectr, 1980–89, Prof. of Japanese, 1989–93, ANU; Dir, AHRC (formerly AHRB) Centre for Asian and African Studies, SOAS, 2000–05. Guest Curator: Kabuki Heroes on the Osaka Stage 1780–1830 (special exhibn), BM, 2005; Shunga: Sex and Pleasure in Japanese Art (special exhibn), BM, 2013. *Publications:* Circles of Fantasy: convention in the plays of Chikamatsu, 1986, 2nd edn 1996; (ed) Eighteenth Century Japan: culture and society, 1989; (with K. Inobe and W. Malm) Theatre as Music: the Bunraku play 'Mt Imo and Mt Se: An Exemplary Tale of Womanly Virtue', 1990; (ed with A. Milner) Recovering the Orient: artists, scholars, appropriations, 1994; Chikamatsu: five late plays, 2001; Kabuki Heroes on the Osaka Stage 1780–1830, 2005; Edo onna no shungabon (Erotic parodies of Japanese conduct books), 2011; (ed) Shunga: sex and pleasure in Japanese Art, 2013. *Address:* School of Oriental and African Studies, University of London, Russell Square, WC1H 0XG. *E:* ag4@soas.ac.uk.

GERSTNER, Louis Vincent, Jr; Hon. KBE 2001; Chairman, 2003–08, Senior Advisor, since 2008, Carlyle Group; *b* NY, 1 March 1942. *Educ:* Dartmouth Coll. (BA Engrg 1963); Harvard Business Sch. (MBA 1965). Dir, McKinsey & Co., Inc., 1965–78; Pres., American Express Co., 1978–89; Chairman and Chief Executive Officer: RJR Nabisco Inc., 1989–93; IBM, 1993–2002. Director: NY Times Co., 1986–97; Bristol-Myers Squibb Co. Dir, New American Schs Develt Corp. Dir, Japan Soc., 1992–. Founder and Chm., Teaching Commn, 2003–06. Chm., Bd of Dirs, Broad Inst., 2013–; Vice Chm., American Mus. of Natural Hist. Mem. Bd, Lincoln Center for Performing Arts, 1984–2002. *Publications:* Re-inventing Education: entrepreneurship in America's public schools (jtly), 1994; Who Says Elephants Can't Dance: inside IBM's historic turnaround, 2002.

GERVAIS, Most Rev. Marcel; Archbishop of Ottawa, (RC), 1989–2007, now Archbishop Emeritus; *b* 21 Sept. 1931; *s* of Frédéric Pierre Gervais and Marie-Louise Beaudry. *Educ:* St Peter's Seminary, London, Ont.; Angelicum Athenæum Pontifical Inst., Rome; Pontifical Biblical Inst., Rome; Ecole Biblique et Archéologique Française de Jérusalem. Ordained priest, 1958; Prof. of Sacred Scriptures, St Peter's Seminary, London, 1962–76; Dir of Divine Word Internat. Centre of Religious Educn, London, 1974–80; Auxiliary Bishop of London, Ontario, 1980–85; Bishop of Sault Sainte-Marie, 1985–89; Coadjutor Archbishop of Ottawa, June–Sept. 1989. Pres., Canadian Conf. of Catholic Bishops, 1991–93. *Address:* 1243 Kilborn Place, Ottawa, ON K1H 6K9, Canada.

GERVAIS, Ricky Dene; comedian, actor, director, producer and author; *b* Reading, 25 June 1961; *s* of late Jerry and Eva Gervais; partner, Jane Fallon. *Educ:* Ashmead Comprehensive Sch., Reading; University Coll. London (BA Hons Philosophy). With Xfm, until 1998; *television:* actor: The 11 O'clock Show, 1998; (also writer with Stephen Merchant) Meet Ricky Gervais, 2000; (also writer, dir and exec. prod. with S. Merchant): The Office, 2001–03 (British Comedy Awards, 2002, 2004; RTS Award, 2002; BAFTA Awards, 2001, 2002, 2003; Golden Globe Awards, 2004; Emmy Award, 2006); Extras, 2005–07 (BAFTA Awards, 2005, 2006, 2007; Emmy Award, 2007; British Comedy Award, 2008; Golden Globe Award, 2008); Life's Too Short, 2011; writer: Stromberg, 2004; Le bureau, 2006; writer and exec. prod., with S. Merchant, The Office (US version), 2005–09; one episode, The Simpsons, 2006; executive producer: The Ricky Gervais Show, 2010–11; An Idiot Abroad, 2010; An Idiot Abroad 2, 2011; An Idiot Abroad 3, 2012; actor, writer, dir and exec. prod., Derek, 2012, 2014; *films:* actor: Dog Eat Dog, 2001; For Your Consideration, Night at the Museum, 2006; Stardust, 2007; Ghost Town, 2008; Night at the Museum: Battle of the Smithsonian, 2009; (also co-writer and dir) The Invention of Lying, 2009; (also co-writer, dir and exec. prod.) Cemetery Junction, 2010; Muppets Most Wanted, 2014; Night at the Museum: Secret of the Tomb, 2014. Stand-up comedy shows: Ricky Gervais Live: Animals, 2003; Politics, 2004; Fame, 2007; Out of England, 2008; Science, 2009–10; Out of England 2, 2010; David Brent and the Foregone Conclusion, 2013. *Publications:* with Rob Steen: Flanimals, 2004; More Flanimals, 2005; Flanimals of the Deep, 2006 (Galaxy British Book Award, 2007); Day of the Bletching, 2007; Flanimals Pop Up, 2009; with Stephen Merchant: The Office, Series 1, 2002; The Office, Series 2, 2003; Extras, 2006; The World of Karl Pilkington, 2006. *Address:* c/o United Agents Ltd, 12–26 Lexington Street, W1F 0LE.

GERVIS MEYRICK; *see* Meyrick.

GERY, Laura W.; *see* Wade-Gery.

GESTETNER, Jonathan; Chairman, Marlborough Rare Books Ltd, since 1990; *b* 11 March 1940; *s* of late Sigmund Gestetner and Henny Gestetner, OBE; *m* 1965, Jacqueline Margaret Strasmore; two *s* one *d*. *Educ:* Bryanston Sch.; Massachusetts Institute of Technology (BScMechEngrg). Joined Gestetner Ltd, 1962; Jt Chm., Gestetner Hldgs PLC, 1972–87; Director: DRS, USA, 1987–89; Klein Associates, USA, 1987–90. Member: Executive Council, Engineering Employers' London Assoc., 1972–77 (Vice-Pres., 1975–77); Maplin Development Authority, 1973–74; SSRC, 1979–82; Dir, Centre for Policy Studies, 1982–96. Member: Educnl Council, MIT, 1973–; Vis. Cttee, Cambridge Univ. Liby, 2009–; Liby Cttee, Oxford Centre for Hebrew and Jewish Studies (formerly Yarnton Centre for Postgrad. Hebrew Studies), 2009–. Trustee, Jewish Mus., 2000–. *Recreations:* the visual arts, Real tennis. *Clubs:* Brooks's, MCC; Grolier (New York).

GETHIN, Sir Richard (Joseph St Lawrence), 10th Bt *cr* 1665, of Gethinsgrott, Cork; civil engineer; Community Liaison Manager, Crossrail, since 2011; *b* 29 Sept. 1949; *s* of Sir Richard Patrick St Lawrence Gethin, 9th Bt and of Fara, *y d* of late J. H. Bartlett; *S* father, 1988; *m* 1974, Jacqueline Torfrida, *d* of Comdr David Cox; three *d*. *Educ:* The Oratory School; RMA Sandhurst; RMCS Shrivenham; Cranfield Inst. of Technology (BSc(Eng), MSc). Joined first unit, 1971; served in Germany and UK; retd in rank of Major, 1990. *Recreations:* gardening, woodwork. *Heir:* *cousin* Antony Michael Gethin [*b* 10 Jan. 1939; *m* 1965, Vanse, *d* of late Col C. D. Barlow, OBE, KSLI; two *s* one *d*]. *T:* (01474) 814231.

GETHINS, Stephen Patrick; MP (SNP) Fife North East, since 2015; *b* Glasgow, 28 March 1976; *s* of James Gethins and Rhona Gethins; *m* 2013, Anya Hart Dyke; one *d*. *Educ:* Perth Acad.; Univ. of Dundee (LLB Hons); Univ. of Kent (MA Res.). EU Cttee of the Regions, 2005–07; Scotland Europa, 2007–09; Special Advr to First Minister, Scottish Govt, 2009–13; Chm., Adv. Bd, Scottish Global Forum, 2013–15. *Address:* House of Commons, SW1A 0AA. *T:* (020) 7219 5671. *E:* stephen.gethins.mp@parliament.uk. *Club:* Dundee United Football.

GETTY, Hon. Donald Ross; PC (Can.) 1985; OC 1998; President and Chief Executive Officer, Sunnybank Investments Ltd, since 1993; Premier of Alberta, 1985–93; MLA Edmonton Whitemud, 1967–79, 1985–93; *b* 30 Aug. 1933; *s* of Charles Ross Getty and Beatrice Lillian Getty; *m* 1955, Margaret Inez Mitchell; four *s*. *Educ:* Univ. of Western Ontario (BBA 1955). MLA Alberta 1967; Minister of Federal and Intergovernmental Affairs, 1971; Minister of Energy and Natural Resources, 1975; resigned 1979; re-elected MLA, 1985. Joined Imperial Oil, 1955; Midwestern Industrial Gas, 1961; formed Baldonnel Oil & Gas, 1964 (Pres. and Man. Dir); Partner, Doherty Roadhouse & McCuaig, 1967; Pres., D. Getty Investments, 1979; Chm., Ipsco, 1981–85; former Chm. and Chief Exec., Nortek Energy Corp.; director of other cos. Played quarterback for Edmonton Eskimos Canadian Football team for 10 years. *Recreations:* horse racing, golf, hunting. *Address:* 1273 Potter Greens Drive NW, Edmonton, AB T5T 5Y8, Canada.

GETTY, Mark Harris; Chairman, Getty Images Inc., 1995–2015; *b* 9 July 1960; *s* of Sir (John) Paul Getty, KBE and of Gail Harris Getty; *m* 1982, Domitilla Lante Harding; three *s*. *Educ:* Taunton Sch.; St Catherine's Coll., Oxford (BA). Kidder, Peabody, Inc., 1984–88; Hambros Bank, 1990–93; Getty Images Inc., 1994–2015. Chm., John Wisden & Co., 2006–08. Trustee, Nat. Gall., 2001–15 (Chm. Trustees, 2008–15).

GEUSS, Prof. Raymond, PhD; FBA 2011; Professor of Philosophy, University of Cambridge, 2007, now Emeritus; *b* Evansville, Indiana, 10 Dec. 1946; *s* of Raymond Geuss and Helen Geuss; *m* 1st, 1987, Heda Šegvić (marr. diss. 1994); 2nd, 2010, Hilary Gaskin. *Educ:* Devon Prep. Sch., Penn; Columbia Univ. (BA *summa cum laude* 1966; PhD 1971). Heidelberg, 1971–73; Assistant Professor of Philosophy: Columbia Univ., 1973–76; Princeton Univ., 1976–79; Associate Prof. of Philos., Univ. of Chicago, 1979–83; Associate Prof., 1983–86, Prof., 1986–87, of Philos., Princeton Univ.; Prof. of Philos., 1987–91, Prof. of Political Sci., 1991–93, Columbia Univ.; University of Cambridge: Lectr, Faculty of Social and Pol Scis, 1993–97, Faculty of Philos., 1997–2000; Reader in Philos., 2000–07. Visiting appointments: Bielefeld, 1981; Hamburg, 1986, 1989; Yale, 1990–91; Freiburg, 1992; Frankfurt, 1992, 1999. Fellow, Wissenschaftskolleg zu Berlin, 1982–83. *Publications:* The Idea of a Critical Theory, 1981; History and Illusion in Politics, 2001; Public Goods, Private Goods, 2001; Outside Ethics, 2005; Philosophy and Real Politics, 2008; Politics and the Imagination, 2010; A World Without Why, 2014. *Address:* Faculty of Philosophy, University of Cambridge, Sidgwick Avenue, Cambridge CB3 9DA. *T:* (01223) 335090, *Fax:* (01223) 335091.

GHAFFUR, Tarique, CBE 2004; QPM 2001; Chairman, CSD Global (UK) Ltd, since 2009; *b* 8 June 1955; *m* 1990, Shehla (*née* Aslam); one *s* one *d*. *Educ:* Uganda; Manchester Poly. (BA); Keele Univ. (MA). Greater Manchester Police: uniform and CID posts, 1974–78; Sergeant, 1978; Inspector, 1982; Chief Inspector, 1988; Superintendent, Leics Constabulary, 1989–96; Asst Chief Constable, Lancs Constabulary, 1996–99; Dep. Chief Constable, Police Inf. Technol. Orgn, 1999; a Dep. Asst Comr, 1999–2001, an Asst Comr, 2001–08, Hd of Central Ops and Olympics Security, 2006–08, Metropolitan Police; Director: Specialist Crime, 2003–08; Policing Inst. Abu Dhabi Police, 2012–13. *Publications:* articles on crime, diversity, security and IT. *Address:* CSD Global Ltd, 48–49 Russell Square, WC1B 4JP.

GHAHRAMANI, Prof. Zoubin, PhD; FRS 2015; Professor of Information Engineering, University of Cambridge, since 2006; Fellow, St John's College, Cambridge, since 2009; *b* 8 Feb. 1970; *s* of Ghahraman Ghahramani and Manijeh Dabiri. *Educ:* American Sch. of Madrid, Spain; Univ. of Pennsylvania (BA Cognitive Sci. 1990; BSE Computer Sci. 1990); Massachusetts Inst. of Technol. (PhD 1995). Postdoctoral Fellow, Univ. of Toronto, 1995–98; Lectr, Gatsby Unit, 1998–2003, Reader, 2003–06, Adjunct Faculty, Gatsby Unit, 2006–, UCL. Associate Res. Prof., Carnegie Mellon Univ., 2003–12. *Publications:* (ed) Advances in Neural Information Processing Systems, 2002, 2013, 2014; 10th International Workshop on Artificial Intelligence and Statistics, 2005; (ed) Proceedings of the International Conference on Machine Learning, 2007; contrib. to Science, Nature, Jl Machine Learning Res., Phil. Trans, Royal Soc. B, Neural Computation, Bioinformatics. *Address:* Department of Engineering, University of Cambridge, Trumpington Street, Cambridge CB2 1PZ. *E:* zoubin@eng.cam.ac.uk.

GHALI, Boutros B.; *see* Boutros-Ghali.

GHANI, Nusrat; MP (C) Wealden, since 2015; *d* of Abdul Ghani and Farzand Begum; *m* 2002, David Wheeldon; one *d*. *Educ:* Bordesley Green Girls' Sch.; Cadbury Sixth Form Coll.; Univ. of Central England; Univ. of Leeds (MA Internat. Relns). Health campaigner: Age UK; Breakthrough Breast Cancer; Strategic Communications and Public Affairs, BBC World Service and BBC World Service Trust. Mem., Home Affairs Select Cttee, 2015–; Chairman, All Party Parliamentary Group: on Ageing and Older People, 2015–; on Eye Health and Visual Impairment, 2015–; Member, All Party Parliamentary Group: on Domestic Violence, 2015–; on Women in Parlt, 2015–. Contested (C) Birmingham Ladywood, 2010. *Recreations:* cinema, music, reading, ski-ing, sailing, travel, walking on Ashdown Forest. *Address:* House of Commons, SW1A 0AA. *E:* nusrat.ghani.mp@parliament.uk.

GHEORGHIU, Angela; soprano; *b* 1965; *m* 1st, 1988, Andrei Gheorghiu (marr. diss.); 2nd, 1996, Roberto Alagna, *qv*; one step *d*. *Educ:* Bucharest Acad. Débuts: Nat. Opera, Cluj, 1990; Royal Opera, Covent Garden, 1992; Vienna State Opera, 1992; Metropolitan Opera, NY, 1993. Rôles include: Mimi in La Bohème; Violetta in La Traviata; Micaela in Carmen; title rôle in Turandot; Adina in L'elisir d'amore; Juliette in Roméo et Juliette; Amelia in Simon Boccanegra; Marguerite in Faust; title rôle in Adriana Lecouvreur. Film, Tosca, 2002. Performs worldwide and has made numerous recordings. *Address:* c/o Royal Opera House, Covent Garden, WC2E 9DD; c/o Alexander Gerdanovits, Seenstrasse 28a, 9081 Reifnitz, Austria. *E:* agerdanovits@gmx.net.

GHOSE, Katie Sushila Ratna; Chief Executive, Electoral Reform Society, since 2010; *b* Shoreham-by-Sea, Sussex, 13 July 1970; *d* of Toon Ghose and Daphne Ghose (now Wall); partner, Andrew Jonathan Gilbert Harrop, *qv*; one *d*. *Educ:* Boundstone Community Coll.; Brighton, Hove and Sussex Sixth Form Coll.; Somerville Coll., Oxford (BA Hons Law 1991); Univ. of Calif, Riverside (MA Pol Sci. 1992); Council of Legal Educn; Birkbeck, Univ. of London (Dip. Mgt (Merit) 2002). Parly researcher to Greville Janner, QC, MP, 1992–94; Parly Officer, NACAB, 1994–95; called to the bar, Middle Temple, 1996; barrister, 1 Pump Court Chambers, London, 1997–99; Campaigns Manager, Child Accident Prevention Trust, 2000–01; Parly Officer, 2001–03, Campaigns and Parly Manager, 2003–05, Age Concern England; Dir, British Inst. of Human Rights, 2005–10. Mem., Ind. Asylum Commn, 2006–08. Chair: Asylum Aid, 1997–99; Bail for Immigration Detainees, 2002–04; Yes to Fairer Votes, 2010–11. Trustee and Co. Sec., Stonewall, 2005–11; Trustee, Fair Vote, 2011–. *Publications:* Beyond the Courtroom: a lawyer's guide to campaigning, 2005. *Recreations:* hiking, dance. *Address:* Electoral Reform Society, 2–6 Boundary Row, SE1 8HP. *T:* (020) 3724 4070. *E:* katie.ghose@electoral-reform.org.uk.

GHOSH, Dame Helen Frances, DCB 2008; Director-General, National Trust, since 2012; *b* 21 Feb. 1956; *d* of William and Eileen Kirkby; *m* 1979, Peter Robin Ghosh; one *s* one *d*. *Educ:* St Hugh's Coll., Oxford (BA (Mod. Hist.) 1976); Hertford Coll., Oxford (MLitt (6th century Italian Hist.) 1980). Admin. trainee, DoE, 1979; variety of posts in local govt finance, housing, urban regeneration, 1979–95, inc. Prin. Private Sec. to Minister of State for Housing, 1986–88; Dep. Dir, Efficiency Unit, Cabinet Office, 1995–97; Dir of Regeneration for E London, Govt Office for London, 1997–99; Dir Children's Gp, DSS, subseq. DWP, 1999–2001; Dir Gen., Machinery of Govt Secretariat, Cabinet Office, 2001–03; Dir Gen. for Corporate Services, 2003–05, and a Comr, 2003–05, Bd of Inland Revenue, later HM Revenue and Customs; Permanent Secretary: DEFRA, 2005–10; Home Office, 2011–12. *Publications:* (contrib.) Boethius: his life, thought and influence, 1981. *Recreations:* family life, ballet, gardening. *Address:* National Trust, Heelis, Kemble Drive, Swindon SN2 2NA.

GHOSH, (Indranil) Julian, DPhil; QC 2006; QC (Scot.) 2010; *m* 1994, Catherine Elizabeth Waring. *Educ:* Univ. of Edinburgh (LLB); London Sch. of Econs (LLM); Birkbeck Coll., London (MA); St Edmund Hall, Oxford (DPhil). Called to the Bar, Lincoln's Inn, 1993; a Dep. Judge, Tax, First-tier and Upper Tribunal, 2009– (a Dep. Special Comr, 2002–09). Sen. Vis. Fellow, Queen Mary and Westfield Coll., London, 1994–2006; Vis. Prof., Univ. of Leiden, 2005–; Lector, Trinity Coll., Cambridge, 2008; Vis. Fellow, Fitzwilliam Coll., Cambridge, 2009. *Publications:* Taxation of Loan Relationships and Derivatives, 1996; Principles of the Internal Market and Direct Taxation, 2007. *Recreations:* music, chess, fencing, cricket. *Address:* Pump Court Tax Chambers, 16 Bedford Row, WC1R 4EF. *Clubs:* Athenæum, Arts, Lansdowne, Two Brydges; New (Edinburgh).

GHOSH, Shaks, CBE 2015; Chief Executive, Private Equity Foundation, 2007–13; *b* 17 Jan. 1957; *d* of Samir Ghosh and Maria Rheinhold. *Educ:* Frank Anthony Public Sch.; Calcutta Univ. (BA 1st cl. Hons Geog. 1978); Salford Univ. (MSc Urban Studies 1980). Urban Renewal Officer, Leicester CC, 1980–84; Improvement Officer, Islington LBC, 1984–86; Supported Housing Officer, Community Housing Assoc., Camden and Westminster, 1986–89; Asst Dir, Centrepoint, 1989–92; Supported Housing Manager, NFHA, 1992–94; Head of London Region, Nat. Housing Fedn, 1994–97; Chief Exec., Crisis, 1997–2006. *Recreations:* gardening, travel, current affairs.

GHOSN, Carlos, Hon. KBE 2007; President, since 2000, and Chief Executive Officer, since 2001, and Chairman, Board of Directors, since 2008 (Co-Chairman, 2003–08), Nissan Motor Co. Ltd; President and Chief Executive Officer, since 2005, and Chairman, Board of Directors, since 2009, Renault (Co-Chairman, 2005–09); *b* Brazil, 9 March 1954; *s* of late Jorges Ghosn and of Rose Ghosn; *m* 1985, Rita; one *s* three *d*. *Educ:* Ecole Polytechnique, Paris (engrg degree 1974); Ecole des Mines de Paris (engrg degree 1978). Michelin: joined, 1978; Plant Manager, Le Puy Plant, France, 1981–84; Hd, R&D for industrial tyres, 1984; Chief Op. Officer, S Amer. Ops, Brazil, 1985–90; Chm. and CEO, N America, 1990–96; Exec. Vice Pres., Renault, 1996–99; Chief Op. Officer, Nissan Motor Co. Ltd, 1999–2001. Mem. Bd of Dirs, Alcoa. Internat. FREng 2013. Légion d'Honneur (France), 2002; Ordem de Rio Branco (Brazil), 2002; Medal of Blue Ribbon, Emperor of Japan, 2004. *Publications:* Renaissance (autobiog.), 2001; Shift: inside Nissan's historic revival (autobiog.), 2005. *Recreations:* swimming, playing tennis, reading, playing contract bridge. *Address:* Nissan Motor Co. Ltd, Takashima 1-chome, Nishi-ku, Yokohama-shi, Kanagawa 220–8686, Japan. *T:* (3) 35435523.

GIACCONI, Prof. Riccardo; President, Associated Universities Inc., 1999–2004; University Professor, Johns Hopkins University, since 2004; *b* 6 Oct. 1931; *s* of Antonio Giacconi and Elsa Canni Giacconi; *m* 1957, Mirella Manaira; one *s* two *d*. *Educ:* Univ. of Milan (Doctorate in Physics 1954). Asst Prof. of Physics, Univ. of Milan, 1954–56; Res. Associate (Fulbright Fellow), Indiana Univ., 1956–58; Res. Associate, Cosmic Ray Lab., Princeton Univ., 1958–59; American Science & Engineering Inc., Cambridge, Mass., 1959–73: Sen. Scientist and Mem. Bd of Dirs, 1966–73; Exec. Vice Pres., 1969–73; Associate Dir, High Energy Astrophysics Div., Harvard-Smithsonian Center for Astrophysics, 1973–81; Prof. of Astronomy, Harvard Univ., 1973–82; Johns Hopkins University: Prof. of Astronomy, 1981–99; Res. Prof., 1999–2004; Dir, Space Telescope Sci. Inst., Baltimore, 1981–92. Chm. Bd, Instituto Donegani, Italy, 1987–88; Prof. of Physics and Astronomy, Univ. of Milan, 1991–99; Dir Gen., European Southern Observatory, Germany, 1993–99. Prin. Investigator on NASA progs including: SAS-A (UHURU), 1960–81; SO-54 (SKYLAB); HEAO-2 (Einstein); AXAF Interdisciplinary Scientist (Chandra), 1986–. Hon. DSc: Chicago, 1983; Warsaw, 1996; Laurea *hc:* in Astronomia, Padua, 1984; in Physics, Rome, 1998; Hon. DScTech Uppsala, 2000. Helen B. Warner Award, AAS; Como Prize, Italian Physical Soc., 1967; Röntgen Prize in Astrophysics, Physikalisch-Medizinische Ges., Wurzburg, 1971; NASA Medal for Exceptional Scientific Achievement, 1971, 1980; NASA Distinguished Public Service Award, 1972, 2003; Richtmyer Meml Lectr, American Assoc. of Physics Teachers, 1975; Space Sci. Award, AIAA, 1976; Elliott Cresson Medal, Franklin Inst., Philadelphia, 1980; Catherine Wolfe Bruce Gold Medal, Astronomical Soc. of the Pacific, 1981; Dannie Heineman Prize for Astrophysics, AAS/AIP, 1981; Henry Norris Russell Lectr, AAS, 1981; Gold Medal, RAS, 1982; A. Cressy Morrison Award in Natural Scis, NY Acad. of Scis, 1982; Wolf Prize in Physics, 1987; Targhe d'Oro della Regione Puglia, 1996; (jtly) Nobel Prize in Physics, 2002; Nat. Medal of Science, USA, 2003. Cavaliere di Gran Croce Ordine al Merito (Italy), 2003. *Publications:* (ed jtly) X-ray Astronomy, 1974; (ed jtly) Physics and Astrophysics of Neutron Stars and Black Holes, 1978; (ed jtly) A Face of Extremes: the X-ray universe, 1985; Secrets of the Hoary Deep: a personal history of modern astronomy, 2008; contrib. more than 300 articles in prof. jls. *Recreation:* painting. *Address:* Department of Physics and Astronomy, Johns Hopkins University, 3400 N Charles Street, Baltimore, MD 21218–2686, USA. *Clubs:* Cosmos (Washington); Johns Hopkins (Baltimore).

GIACHARDI, Dr David John, FRSC; Secretary General and Chief Executive, Royal Society of Chemistry, 2000–06; *b* 17 May 1948; *o s* of Thomas and Kathleen Giachardi; *m* 1971, Helen Margaret Fraser; one *d*. *Educ:* Watford Boys' Grammar Sch.; Merton Coll., Oxford (BA Chem. 1971); St John's Coll., Oxford (MA, DPhil 1974). FRSC 1990. Boston Consulting Group, 1975–79; Courtaulds, 1979–98: Dir of Research, 1982–94; Exec. Dir, 1987–98; Human Resources Dir, 1994–98; Dir of Policy and Assoc. Affairs, EEF, 1998–2000. Member: Nat. Commn on Educn, 1991–93; European Science and Technology Assembly, 1994–97; EPSRC, 1994–99; Quality Assurance Cttee, HEFCE, 1999–2003; Vice-Chm., Industrial R&D Adv. Cttee to Commn for EC, 1991–94. Chm. Adv. Council, ASE, 1996–2001 (Pres., 1994); Mem. Council, Royal Instn of GB, 1995–98 (Chm., 1997–98). Court Asst, Horners' Co., 2012–. *Address:* Laburnum, Cheverells Green, Markyate, St Albans, Herts AL3 8RN. *Club:* Oxford and Cambridge.

GIAEVER, Prof. Ivar; Institute Professor, Physics Department, Rensselaer Polytechnic Institute, Troy, New York, 1988–2005, now Emeritus; Professor-at-large, University of Oslo, Norway, since 1988; Chief Technical Officer, Applied BioPhysics, since 2008; *b* 5 April 1929; *s* of John A. Giaever and Gudrun (*née* Skaarud); *m* 1952, Inger Skramstad; one *s* three *d*. *Educ:* Norwegian Inst. of Tech.; Rensselear Polytechnical Inst. ME 1952; PhD 1964. Norwegian Army, 1952–53; Norwegian Patent Office, 1953–54; Canadian General Electric, 1954–56; General Electric, 1956–58; Staff Mem., Gen. Electric R&D Center, 1958–88. Member: Nat. Acad. of Sciences; Nat. Acad. of Engineering; Amer. Acad. of Arts and Scis; Norwegian Acad. of Scis; Norwegian Acad. of Technology; Norwegian Profl Engrs; Swedish Acad. of Engrg. Hon. DSc: Trondheim, 1973; RPI, 1974; Union Coll., 1974; Clarkson, Potsdam, NY, 1983; Hon. DEng, Michigan Tech. Univ., 1976; Hon. DPhys: Oslo, 1976; State Univ. of NY, 1984. Oliver E. Buckley Prize, 1964; Nobel Prize for Physics, 1973; Zworykin Award, 1974; Onsager Medal, Norwegian Univ. of Sci. and Technol., 2003; Gunnerus Medal, Royal Norwegian Soc. of Sci. and Letters, 2010. *Publications:* contrib. Physical Review, Jl Immunology. *Recreations:* ski-ing, tennis, camping, hiking. *Address:* Applied BioPhysics, 185 Jordan Road, Troy, NY 12180, USA. *T:* (518) 8806860, *Fax:* (518) 8806865. *E:* giaever@biophysics.com.

GIBB, Andrew Thomas Fotheringham; Consultant, Balfour and Manson, Solicitors, Edinburgh, since 2012 (Partner, 1975–2012; Chairman, 1996–2005); President, Law Society of Scotland, 1990–91; *b* 17 Aug. 1947; *s* of Thomas Fotheringham Gibb and Isabel Gow McKenzie or Gibb; *m* 1971, Mrs Patricia Anne Eggo or Gibb; two *s*. *Educ:* Perth Acad.; Edinburgh Univ. (LLB Hons). Temporary Sheriff, 1989–99. Member: Lothian and Borders Legal Aid Cttee, 1977–84; Legal Aid Central Cttee, 1984–86; Council, Law Soc. of Scotland, 1981–94. Chm. Management Cttee, Lothian Allellon Soc., 1984–97 (Mem., Bd of Govs, 1984–2001). Accredited family law specialist; accredited collaborative lawyer. Trustee, Family Mediation Lothian, 2012–. Mem. Bd, Birthlink, 2012–. Session Clerk, St Ninian's Church, Corstorphine, Edinburgh. *Recreations:* music, church organist, golf. *Address:* 58 Frederick Street, Edinburgh EH2 1LS. *Clubs:* New (Edinburgh); Royal Burgess Golfing Soc.

GIBB, Frances Rebecca; Legal Editor, The Times, since 1999; *b* 24 Feb. 1951; *d* of late Matthew Gibb and of Bettina Mary Gibb (*née* Dawson); *m* 1978, Joseph Cahill (*d* 2009); three *s*. *Educ:* St Margaret's Sch., Bushey; Univ. of E Anglia (BA 1st Cl. Hons English). News researcher, Visnews, 1973; reporter, THES, 1974–78; Art Sales corresp., Daily Telegraph, 1978–80; The Times: reporter, 1980–82; Legal Corresp., 1982–99. Vis. Prof., QMC, 2003–. Gov., King's College Sch., Wimbledon, 2002–. MUniv Open, 2000. *Recreations:* my family, gardening, theatre. *Address:* The Times, 1 London Bridge Street, SE1 9GF. *Club:* Reform.

GIBB, Ian Pashley; Director of Public Services, Planning and Administration, British Library (Humanities and Social Sciences), 1985–87; *b* 17 April 1926; *s* of late John Pashley Gibb and Mary (*née* Owen); *m* 1953, Patricia Mary Butler (*d* 1993); two *s*. *Educ:* Latymer Upper Sch.; UCL (BA). MCLIP. Sen. Library Asst, Univ. of London, 1951–52; Asst Librarian, UCL, 1952–58; Dep. Librarian, National Central Library, 1958–73; British Library: Dep. Dir, Science Reference Library, 1973–75; Head of Divl Office, Reference Div., 1975–77; Dir and Keeper, Reference Div., 1977–85. Part-time Lectr, UCL, 1967–77, Hon. Research Fellow, 1977–85, Examiner, 1985–87. Hon. Treasurer, Bibliographical Soc., 1961–67; Member Council: Library Assoc., 1980–82; Friends of British Library, 1989–2001 (Dep. Chm., 1989–93). Chm., Dacorum NT Assoc., 1993–97 (Vice-Pres., 2010–). *Publications:* (ed) Newspaper Preservation and Access, 2 vols, 1988; various articles. *Recreations:* music, watching cricket, wine-tasting, travel especially to Austria and Greece, cruising. *Address:* The Old Cottage, 16 Tile Kiln Lane, Leverstock Green, Hemel Hempstead, Herts HP3 8ND. *T:* (01442) 256352.

GIBB, Dame Moira, DBE 2012 (CBE 2001); a Civil Service Commissioner, since 2012; *d* of James Bogan and Catherine Bogan (*née* McTaggart); *m* 1990, Henry Blythe; one *s*. *Educ:* Glasgow Univ. (MA); Edinburgh Univ. (Dip. Soc. Admin; CQSW); Univ. of Newcastle upon Tyne (PQCCC). Social worker and teacher, 1970–80; Lectr, Preston Polytech., 1980–81; Child Care Inspector, Surrey CC, 1981–84; Asst Dir, London Bor. of Ealing, 1984–88; Royal Borough of Kensington and Chelsea: Dep. Dir, 1988–91, Dir, 1991–2000, Social Services; Exec. Dir, Housing and Social Services, 2000–03; Chief Exec., London Bor. of Camden, 2003–11. Non-exec. Mem., UK Statistics Authy, 2008–; non-exec. Dir, NHS Commng Bd, 2012–; Mem., Ind. Panel Inquiry into Child Sexual Abuse, 2014–. Chair: Social Work Task Force, 2009; Social Work Reform Bd, 2010–13. Pres., Assoc. of Dirs of Social Services, 2000–01. Governor: Our Lady of Victories Sch., SW15, 1996–2004; Coram Family, 2002–05. Mem. Council, Reading Univ., 2013–; Chair, City Lit, 2013–. Dir, London Marathon, 2005–11. FCGI 2011. Hon. DCL UEA, 2012; Hon. DSc Kingston, 2013. *Recreations:* walking, running, detective fiction.

GIBB, Nicolas John; MP (C) Bognor Regis and Littlehampton, since 1997; Minister of State, Department for Education, 2010–12 and since 2014; *b* 3 Sept. 1960; *s* of late John McLean Gibb and Eileen Mavern Gibb. *Educ:* Maidstone Grammar Sch.; Roundhay Sch., Leeds; Thornes House Sch., Wakefield; Univ. of Durham (BA Hons). ACA 1987. Chartered Accountant, KPMG, 1984–97. Opposition spokesman: on HM Treasury, 1998–99; on trade and industry, 1999–2001; on education, 2005–10. Member: Social Security Select Cttee, 1997–98; Public Accounts Cttee, 2001–03; Educn and Skills Select Cttee, 2003–05. Contested (C): Stoke-on-Trent Central, 1992; Rotherham, May 1994. *Address:* House of Commons, SW1A 0AA.

GIBBENS, Nigel Paul; Chief Veterinary Officer, Department for Environment, Food and Rural Affairs, since 2008; *b* Dover, 1 March 1958; *s* of Francis Bernard Gibbens and Pauline Carol Gibbens; *m* 1981, Jane Stirling. *Educ:* Royal Veterinary Coll. (BVetMed); Edinburgh Univ. (MSc Tropical Vet. Medicine 1984). Gen. vet. practice in Alfreton, Derbys, 1981–83; Govt vet. services in Belize, 1985–88, Yemen, 1988–90; Vet. Field Service, MAFF, Winchester, 1990–96; veterinary posts in Animal Health and Welfare Policy Gp, MAFF, 1996–2002; Department for Environment, Food and Rural Affairs: Head: Internat. Animal Health Div., 2002–04; BSE and Animal By-products Div., 2005–06; Animal Welfare Div., 2006–07; Internat. Relns Core Team, Food and Farming Gp, 2007–08. Hon. Prof., RVC, 2009–. *Recreations:* walking, cycling, gardening, travel. *Address:* Department for Environment, Food and Rural Affairs, Nobel House, 17 Smith Square, SW1P 3JR. *T:* (020) 7238 6495. *E:* nigel.gibbens@defra.gsi.gov.uk.

GIBBINGS, Sir Peter (Walter), Kt 1989; Chairman, Radio Authority, 1995–99; *b* 25 March 1929; *s* of late Walter White Gibbings and Margaret Russell Gibbings (*née* Torrance); *m* 1st, Elspeth Felicia Macintosh; two *d*; 2nd, Hon. Louise Barbara, *d* of 2nd Viscount Lambert, TD; one *s*. *Educ:* Rugby; Wadham Coll., Oxford. Called to the Bar, Middle Temple, 1953. Served in 9th Queen's Royal Lancers, 1951–52. The Observer, 1960–67 (Deputy Manager and Dir, 1965–67); Man. Dir, Guardian Newspapers Ltd, 1967–73; Dir, Manchester Guardian and Evening News Ltd, 1967–73; Chm., Guardian and Manchester Evening News plc, 1973–88; Anglia Television Gp: Dir, 1981–94; Dep. Chm., 1986–88; Chm., 1988–94. Director: Press Assoc. Ltd, 1982–88 (Chm., 1986–87); Reuters Holdings PLC, 1984–88; The Economist, 1987–99; Rothschild Trust Corp. Ltd, 1989–96; Council, UEA, 1989–96. Mem., Press Council, 1970–74; Pres., CPU, 1989–91. *Recreations:* fishing, music. *Address:* 9 Physic Place, SW3 4HQ.

GIBBINS, Rev. Dr Ronald Charles; Methodist Minister; Superintendent Minister, Wesley's Chapel, London, 1978–88; *s* of Charles and Anne Gibbins; *m* 1949, Olive Ruth (*née* Patchett); one *s* two *d*. *Educ:* London Univ. (BScSociol); Wesley Theological Coll., Bristol; Eden Theological Seminary, US (DMin). Methodist Minister: Bradford, 1948–49; Spennymoor, 1949–50; Middlesbrough, 1950–57; Basildon, 1957–64; East End Mission, London, 1964–78. *Publications:* Mission for the Secular City, 1976; The Lumpen Proletariat, 1979; The Stations of the Resurrection, 1987. *Recreations:* travel, journalism.

GIBBON, Anthony David; Partner, GM Real Estate, since 2010; *b* 11 Aug. 1965; *s* of Thomas David Gibbon and Iris Patricia Gibbon; *m*, Sarah Newell; two *s* one *d*. *Educ:* Gable Hall Co. Secondary Sch., Corringham; South Bank Poly. Junior positions: Prudential Portfolio Managers, 1981–86; Bates Richards & Co., 1986–88; Partner, Lambert Smith Hampton, 1988–94; Founding Partner, BH2, 1994–2010. *Publications:* numerous articles in jls. *Recreations:* boxing, football, ski-ing, golf. *Address:* GM Real Estate, 6–7–8 Tokenhouse Yard, EC2R 7AS. *T:* (020) 7600 5000, 07770 721002. *E:* lisad@gmreal.com.

GIBBON, Gary; Political Editor, Channel 4 News, since 2005; *b* 15 March 1965; *s* of Robert Philip Gibbon and Elizabeth Mary Gibbon (*née* Harries); *m* 1994, Laura Kate Pulay; two *s*. *Educ:* John Lyon Sch., Harrow; Balliol Coll., Oxford (BA). Researcher, Viewpoint Productions, 1987–89; Producer, BBC Business Breakfast, 1989–90; Political Prod., 1990–94, Political Corresp., 1994–2005, Channel 4 News. Home News Award, RTS, 2006; Political Broadcaster of the Year Award, Political Studies Assoc., 2008; Specialist Journalist of the Year, RTS, 2010. *Address:* c/o Channel 4 News, Parliamentary Press Gallery, House of Commons, SW1A 0AA. *T:* (020) 7430 4990. *E:* gary.gibbon@itn.co.uk.

GIBBON, Michael Neil; QC 2011; *b* Berkeley, Glos, 14 Nov. 1964; *s* of Bill and Lynne Gibbon; *m* 1991, Amanda, *d* of David Harold Owen Owen, *qv*; two *s* two *d*. *Educ:* Conyers Sch., Yarm; Uppingham Sch. (Sixth Form Schol.); Magdalen Coll., Oxford (Exhibnr and Academical Clerk; BA 1st Cl. Mod. Hist. 1986); King's Coll., Cambridge (Choral Volunteer; MPhil Internat. Relns 1987); City of London Poly. (CPE 1992). Called to the Bar, Gray's Inn, 1993. Investment banker, BZW, 1987–91; in practice as a barrister, specialising in chancery, commercial and revenue law, 1995–; Mem., Attorney Gen.'s Panel of Jun. Counsel to the Crown, 1999–2011. Gov., King's College Sch., Cambridge, 2010–. An Ed., Civil Procedure (The White Book), 2003–. *Publications:* articles in Montgomeryshire Collections and in various legal pubns. *Recreations:* family, choral singing, Cyfeiliog local history. *Address:* Maitland Chambers, 7 Stone Buildings, Lincoln's Inn, WC2A 3SZ. *T:* (020) 7406 1200, *Fax:* (020) 7406 1300. *E:* mgibbon@maitlandchambers.com. *Club:* Reform.

GIBBONS, Brian Joseph, FRCGP; Member (Lab) Aberavon, National Assembly for Wales, 1999–2011; *b* 25 Aug. 1950. *Educ:* National Univ. of Ireland (MB BCh, BAO 1974). DRCOG 1979; Cert. FPA 1979; MRCGP 1980, FRCGP 1995. Jun. hosp. doctor, Galway, Roscommon and Sheffield, 1974–76; Calderdale GP Vocation Trng Scheme, 1977–80; GP, Blaengwynfi, 1980–99. Sec., W Glamorgan/Morgannwg LMC, 1994–99. National Assembly for Wales: Dep. Minister for Health and Social Services, 2000–03, for Economic Develt and Transport, 2003–05; Minister for Health and Social Services, 2005–07, for the Econ. and Transport, 2007, for Social Justice and Local Govt, 2007–09. Dir, Gwynfi Community Co-operative Ltd, 2013–. Chm. and Dir, Gwynfi Miners Community Hall, 2013–; Vice-President: Port Talbot Little Th.; Roger Chilcott Music in the Community; South Wales Miners Mus. *Club:* Gwynfi Social and Athletic.

GIBBONS, Prof. Gary William, PhD; FRS 1999; Professor of Theoretical Physics, University of Cambridge, 1997, now Emeritus; Fellow of Trinity College, Cambridge, since 2002; *b* 1 July 1946; *s* of Archibald Gibbons and Bertha Gibbons (*née* Bunn); *m* 1972, Christine Howden; two *s*. *Educ:* Purley County Grammar Sch.; St Catharine's Coll., Cambridge (BA 1968; MA 1972); Clare Coll., Cambridge (PhD 1973). University of Cambridge: Lectr in Maths, 1980–90; Reader in Theoretical Physics, 1990–97. *Publications:* (with S. W. Hawking) Euclidean Quantum Gravity, 1993. *Recreations:* listening to music, looking at paintings. *Address:* 52 Hurst Park Avenue, Cambridge CB4 2AE. *T:* (01223) 363036.

GIBBONS, Giles Christopher; Founder and Chief Executive Officer, Good Business Ltd, since 1996; *b* Woking, Surrey, 18 Nov. 1969; *s* of Richard Gibbons and Susan Gibbons (now Gill); *m* 1996, Laura Jackson; two *s* one *d*. Marketing, Cadbury, 1989–90; Director: Saatchi & Saatchi Advertising, 1990–95; M & C Saatchi, 1995–97. Dir, Shift Design (formerly We Are What We Do), 2001–. Founder, Sustainable Restaurant Assoc., 2009–. Dir, Paraorchestra, 2012–. Fellow, Wellington Coll., 2009. *Publications:* Good Business: your world needs you, 2002; The Economist Book of Brands and Branding, 2007. *Recreations:* cooking and eating, running, opera. *Address:* Good Business Ltd, 25 Gerrard Street, W1D 6JL. *T:* (020) 7494 0565. *E:* giles@goodbusiness.co.uk.

GIBBONS, Prof. Ian Read, FRS 1983; Research Cell Biologist, University of California, Berkeley, 1997–2010; *b* 30 Oct. 1931; *s* of Arthur Alwyn Gibbons and Hilda Read Cake; *m* 1961, Barbara Ruth Hollingworth; one *s* one *d*. *Educ:* Faversham Grammar School; Cambridge Univ. (BA, PhD). Research Fellow, 1958–63, Asst Prof., 1963–67, Harvard Univ.; Associate Prof., 1967–69, Prof. of Biophysics, 1969–97, Univ. of Hawaii. *Publications:* contribs to learned jls. *Recreations:* gardening, computer programming, music. *Address:* 79 Estates Drive, Orinda, CA 94563, USA.

GIBBONS, Jeremy Stewart; QC 1995; a Recorder, since 1993; *b* 15 July 1949; *s* of Geoffrey Gibbons and Rosemary Gibbons (*née* Stewart); *m* 1st, 1974, Mary Mercia Bradley; two *s* one *d* (and one *d* decd); 2nd, 1998, Sarah Valerie Jenkins. *Educ:* Oakmount Sch., Southampton; St Edward's Sch., Oxford. Called to the Bar, Gray's Inn, 1973; Asst Recorder, 1989–93. *Recreations:* cooking, gardening, ski-ing, carpentry. *Address:* 12 College Place, Southampton SO15 2FE.

GIBBONS, Dr John Ernest, CBE 2000; Architectural Adviser, Scottish Parliament, since 2001; *b* Halesowen, Worcs, 20 April 1940; *s* of late John Howard Gibbons and Lilian Alice Gibbons (*née* Shale); *m* 1963, Patricia Mitchell; one *s* two *d*. *Educ:* Oldbury Grammar Sch.; Birmingham Sch. of Architecture; Edinburgh Univ. PhD; DipArch; DipTP; ARIBA; ARIAS; FSA(Scot). In private practice, 1962–65; Lectr, Birmingham Sch. of Architecture and Univ. of Aston, 1964–66; Res. Fellow, 1967–69, Lectr, 1969–72, Edinburgh Univ.; Scottish Development Department: Prin. Architect, 1972–78; Asst Dir, Building Directorate, 1978–82; Dep. Dir and Dep. Chief Architect, 1982–84; Dir of Building and Chief Architect, Scottish Office, 1984–99; Chief Architect, Scottish Exec., 1999–2005. Vis. Res. Scientist, CSIRO, Melbourne, 1974–75; Vis. Prof., Mackintosh Sch. of Architecture, 2000. Member, Council: EAA and RIAS, 1977–80; ARCUK, 1984. FRSA 1979. DUniv UCE, 1999. *Publications:* contribs on architectural and planning matters to professional and technical jls. *Recreations:* reading, photography, music, travel. *Club:* New (Edinburgh).

GIBBONS, Ven. Kenneth Harry; Archdeacon of Lancaster, 1981–97, now Emeritus; *b* 24 Dec. 1931; *s* of Harry and Phyllis Gibbons; *m* 1962, Margaret Ann Tomlinson; two *s*. *Educ:* Blackpool and Chesterfield Grammar Schools; Manchester Univ. (BSc); Cuddesdon Coll., Oxford. RAF, 1952–54. Ordained, 1956; Assistant Curate of Fleetwood, 1956–60; Secretary for Student Christian Movement in Schools, 1960–62; Senior Curate, St Martin-in-the-Fields, Westminster, 1962–65; Vicar of St Edward, New Addington, 1965–70; Vicar of Portsea, 1970–81; RD of Portsmouth, 1973–79; Priest-in-charge of Weeton, 1981–85; Vicar, St Michael's-on-Wyre, 1985–97; Diocesan Dir of Ordinands, Blackburn, 1982–90; Priest i/c, St Magnus the Martyr, Lower Thames St with St Margaret, Fish St, and St Michael, Crooked Lane, 1997–2003, St Clement, Eastcheap, 1999–2007, City of London. Acting Chaplain to HM Forces, 1981–85. *Address:* Flat 84, Whitgift House, 76 Brighton Road, South Croydon CR2 6AB. *T:* (020) 8686 7505. *Club:* Reform.

GIBBONS, Michael Gordon, MBE 2002; PhD; Director, Science and Technology Policy Research, University of Sussex, 2004–06; Secretary General, Association of Commonwealth Universities, 1996–2004; *b* 15 April 1939; *m* 1968, Gillian Monks; one *s* one *d*. *Educ:* Concordia Univ., Montreal (BSc Maths and Physics); McGill Univ., Montreal (BEng); Queen's Univ., Ont (MSc Radio Astronomy); Manchester Univ. (PhD 1967). Department of Science and Technology Policy, University of Manchester: Lectr, 1967–72; Sen. Lectr, 1972–75; Prof., 1975–92; Hd of Dept, 1975–92; Dir, Univ./UMIST Pollution Res. Unit, 1979–86; Chm. and Founding Dir, Policy Res. in Engrg, Sci. and Technol., 1979–92; Dir, Res., Exploitation and Develt, Vice-Chancellor's Office, 1984–92; University of Sussex: Dean, Grad. Sch. and Dir, Science Policy Res. Unit, 1992–96; Mem., Senate and Mgt Cttee, 1992–96; Mem., Court and Council, 1994–96; Hon. Prof., 1994. Visiting Professor: Univ. of Montreal, 1976 and 1977–81; Univ. of Calif, Berkeley, 1992. Chm., Marinetech NW, 1981–91. Special Advr, H of C Sci. and Technol. Cttee, 1993–. Mem. Council, ESRC, 1997–2001 (Mem., 1994–97, Chm., 1997–2001, Res. Priorities Bd). Consultant, Cttee of Sci. and Technol. Policy, OECD, Paris, 1979–. Founding Bd Mem., Quest Univ., Canada (Chm., Bd of Govs, 2006–09); Cttee Mem., Nat. Centres of Excellence in Res. (Canada), 2010–Dec. 2016. Fellow, Royal Swedish Acad. of Engrg Scis, 2000. Member, Editorial Board: Technovation, 1984–; Prometheus, 1992–. Hon. LLD: Ghana, 1999; Concordia, 2004; DUniv Surrey, 2005. Golden Jubilee Medal (Canada), 2002. *Publications:* (jtly) Wealth from Knowledge, 1972; (jtly) Future of University Research, 1981; (ed jtly) Science Studies Today, 1983; (jtly) New Forms of Communication and Collaboration between Universities and Industry, 1985; (jtly) Post-Innovation Performance: technological development and competition, 1986; (with L. Georghiou) The Evaluation of Research: a synthesis of current practice, 1987; (jtly) The New Production of Knowledge: the dynamics of science and research in contemporary societies, 1994; (jtly) Re-Thinking Science: knowledge and the public in an age of uncertainty, 2001; contrib. numerous papers and articles on science policy. *Address:* 24 Fletsand Road, Wilmslow, Cheshire SK9 2AB.

GIBBONS, Prof. Simon, PhD; FRSC, FLS; Professor of Medicinal Phytochemistry and Head, Research Department of Pharmaceutical and Biological Chemistry, University College London, since 2012; *b* Gosport, 6 June 1966; *s* of Brian and Gillian Gibbons. *Educ:* Britannia Royal Naval Coll., Dartmouth; Kingston Poly. (BSc Hons Applied Chemistry 1989; BP Prize); Strathclyde Univ. (PhD 1994). CChem 1995; CSci 2004; FRSC 2005. Asst Prof. of Pharmaceutical Chem., Kuwait Univ., 1997; School of Pharmacy, University of London: Lectr in Pharmacognosy, 1999; teacher, 2002; Sen. Lectr in Phytochem., 2004; Reader in Phytochem., 2005; Prof. of Medicinal Phytochem., 2007–12. Adjunct Prof., Universiti Kebangsaan Malaysia, 2013–15. Member: Adv. Council on Misuse of Drugs, Home Office,

2010– (Chm., Novel Psychoactive Substances Work Gp, 2011–); Herbal Medicines Adv. Cttee, Medicines and Healthcare Regulatory Products Agency, 2010–12; British Pharmacopoeia Expert Work Gp on Herbal Medicines, 2015–. Pres., Phytochem. Soc. of Europe, 2012–14 (Vice Pres. 2010–12, 2014–Dec. 2016). Fellow, Prince of Wales' Foundn for Integrated Health, 2009–10. Mem., Governing Council, Coll. of Medicine, 2010– (Vice-Chm., Scientific Adv. Council, 2010–). Founding Ed.-in-Chief, Phytochemistry Letters, 2008–; Co-Ed., Progress in the Chem. of Organic Natural Products, 2015– (Mem., Editl Bd, 2009–); Member, Editorial Board: Phytotherapy Res., 2005–; Planta Medica, 2009–; Phytochem. Reviews, 2009–; Fitoterapia, 2009–; Chinese Jl Natural Medicines, 2009–; Natural Product Reports, 2010–; Phytochem. Analysis, 2010–; Scientia Pharmaceutica, 2010–. FLS 1995. Richard J. Cannell Biodiversity Award Lect., 2013. Pierre Fabre Prize for Phytochem., Phytochem. Soc. of Europe, 2005; Vice-Chancellor's Seminar Award, Tshwane Univ. of Technol., 2010; Pharmanex Prize for Phytochem., Phytochem. Soc. of Europe, 2012. *Publications:* (jtly) Fundamentals of Pharmacognosy and Phytotherapy, 2004, 2nd edn 2012; contrib. papers on phytochemistry, structure elucidation and biol evaluation of Novel Psychoactive Substances (NPS; 'Legal Highs'), and antibacterials from natural sources and bacterial resistance modifying agents. *Recreations:* ski-ing, drinking red wine and real ale, holidays in Austria, fishing, walking in the Cotswolds. *Address:* Research Department of Pharmaceutical and Biological Chemistry, UCL School of Pharmacy, 29–39 Brunswick Square, WC1N 1AX. *T:* (020) 7753 5913, *Fax:* (020) 7753 5964. *E:* simon.gibbons@ucl.ac.uk.

GIBBONS, Sir William Edward Doran, 9th Bt *cr* 1752; JP; cruise and ferry consultant; Director: Passenger Shipping Association, 1994–2013; Discover Ferries, since 2013; Membership Director, European Cruise Council, 2011–13 (Marketing Director, 2004–11); *b* 13 Jan. 1948; *s* of Sir John Edward Gibbons, 8th Bt, and of Mersa Wentworth, *y d* of late Major Edward Baynton Grove Foster; *S* father, 1982; *m* 1st, 1972, Patricia Geraldine Archer (marr. diss. 2004), *d* of Roland Archer Howse; one *s* one *d*; 2nd, 2004, Maggie Moone. *Educ:* Pangbourne; RNC Dartmouth; Bristol Univ. (BSc); Southampton Univ. Management Sch. (MBA 1996). Asst Shipping and Port Manager, Sealink UK, Parkeston Quay, 1979–82; Service Manager (Anglo-Dutch), Sealink UK Ltd, 1982–85; Ferry Line Manager (Harwich-Hook), 1985–87, Gen. Manager, IoW Services, 1987–90, Sealink British Ferries. Transport and management consultant, 1990–94. Chm., Council of Travel and Tourism, 1996–2001 (Vice Chm., 1995–96); Mem. Bd, Duty Free Confedn, 1996–2000. Non-exec. Mem., IoW DHA, 1990–94. Mem., Manningtree Parish Council, 1981–87 (Chm., 1985–87). Mem., Poundbury Residents Cttee, 2014–. JP: Portsmouth, 1990–94; Westminster Div., Inner London, 1994–2011 (Probation Liaison Justice, 1998–2006); W Dorset, 2011. Freeman, 2008, Liveryman, 2011, Shipwrights' Co.; Younger Brother, Trinity House, 2011. *Recreations:* opera, Dorset cottage. *Heir: s* Charles William Edwin Gibbons, *b* 28 Jan. 1983. *Address:* 3 St John Way, Dorchester, Dorset DT1 2FG.

GIBBS, family name of **Barons Aldenham** and **Wraxall**.

GIBBS, Alexander; Manager, Policy and Operations, World Bank Group, since 2013; *b* Leicester, 22 April 1964; *s* of Michael John Gibbs and Pamela Jesse Gibbs; *m* 1986, Sonja Elizabeth Grueter; one *s* two *d*. *Educ:* Charterhouse Sch.; Wadham Coll., Oxford (BA PPE); London Sch. of Econs (MSc Econs 1988). HM Treasury, 1985–: Econ. Advr, Public Services, 1985–87, Internat., 1988–90, Macroecon. Forecast, 1990–91; First Sec. (Econ.), British Embassy, Washington, 1991–95; Private Sec. to Chancellor of the Exchequer, 1995–97; Head: Internat. Instns, 1997–2000; Tax Policy, 2000–02; Econ. Counsellor, Washington, 2002–07; Exec. Dir for UK, IMF, and Minister (Economic), Washington, 2007–13. *Recreations:* horse-racing, music. *Address:* World Bank, 1818 H Street NW, Washington, DC 20433, USA. *T:* (202) 7631700. *E:* alexgibbs@mac.com.

GIBBS, Barbara Lynn; education consultant, since 2006; Head Teacher, British School in The Netherlands, 2001–06; *b* 8 Nov. 1945; *d* of William Newill and Mabel Till; *m* 1967, John Colin Gibbs; two *d*. *Educ:* Bromley Grammar Sch. for Girls; Univ. of Hull (BSc Hons Chem.); Univ. of E Anglia (MA; PGCE). Teaching and lecturing, mainly on chem. and maths, in various educnl estabts in Yorks, Notts, Norfolk and Barnet, 1967–86; Sen. Teacher, Henrietta Barnett Sch., 1986–90; Vice Principal, Havering Sixth Form Coll., 1990–94; Head Teacher, Newstead Wood Sch. for Girls, 1994–2001. OFSTED Inspector, 1998–2002; Strategic Dir, Prospects Educn Services, 1999–2001; ISI Inspector, 2003–; NPQH tutor. Millennium Awards Fellow, for work on osteoporosis educn in schools, 2000–. Chm., Gerrards Cross Cons. Assoc. Gov., Beaconsfield High Sch. FRSA 1994 (Life Fellow). *Recreations:* music, literature, travel, swimming, Rugby Union, bridge. *Clubs:* Royal Air Force; Royal Scots (Edinburgh); Stoke Park; Rotary.

GIBBS, Air Vice-Marshal Charles Melvin, CB 1976; CBE 1966; DFC 1943; RAF retd; Recruiting Consultant with Selleck Associates, Colchester, 1977–86; *b* 11 June 1921; American father, New Zealand mother; *m* 1947, Emma Pamela Pollard (*d* 1991); one *d*; *m* 1999, Adrienne Ryan (marr. diss. 2003). *Educ:* Taumarunui, New Zealand. MECI 1980. Joined RNZAF, 1941; service in Western Desert and Mediterranean, 1942–44; Coastal Comd, 1945; India, 1946–47; commanded Tropical Experimental Unit, 1950–52; RAF Staff Coll., 1953; commanded No 118 Squadron, 1954–55; Directing Staff, RAF Staff Coll., 1956–58; Pakistan, 1958–61; Chief Instructor, RAF Chivenor, 1961–63; CO, Wattisham, 1963–66; idc 1967; Defence Policy Staff, 1968–69; Dir of Quartering, 1970–72; AOA, Germany, 1972–74; Dir-Gen. Personal Services, RAF, 1974–76. *Recreations:* fishing, golf. *Address:* 20 Brompton Close, Taupo 3330, New Zealand. *T:* (7) 3771957.

GIBBS, Dame Jennifer (Barbara), DNZM 2009 (CNZM 2002); Deputy Chair, Regional Facilities Auckland, since 2010; Member, Ministerial Task Force on Philanthropy, since 2009; *b* Lower Hutt, NZ, 14 Sept. 1940; *d* of Ross Digby Gore and Barbara Mary Gore (*née* Standish); *m* 1961, Alan Timothy Gibbs (marr. diss. 1997); one *s* three *d*. *Educ:* Victoria Univ. of Wellington (BA 1961); Canterbury Univ. (MA Hons Hist. 1962). Jun. Lectr, Dept of Hist., Victoria Univ., 1962 and 1966–67; has travelled extensively and been involved in wide range of community, health, educnl and arts activities. Comr for NZ at Venice Biennale, 2001 and 2003. Member: Council, Auckland Univ., 1975–95 and 2000–08 (Pro-Chancellor, 1984 and 2004); Univ. Med. Sch. Admission Cttee, 1983–95; Founding Mem., Auckland Med. Sch. Foundn, 1993–. Founder and Chair: Patrons of Auckland Art Gall., 1986–; Auckland Contemporary Art Trust, 1993–; Patron and Founding Trustee, Auckland Univ. Foundn Appeal Cttee, 1996–; Founding Trustee: NZ Arts Foundn, 1999–2005; Auckland Art Gall. Foundn, 2001–; Founding Bd Mem., NZ Opera Co., 1999–2005. Invited Member: Internat. Council, MOMA, NY, 1989–; Internat. Council, Asia Soc., NY, 2001–. Fellow, Univ. of Auckland, 1995. Hon. DLitt Auckland, 2008. *Recreations:* art - looking and collecting, reading, opera, travel, walking poodles, food and wine. *Address:* 31 Paritai Drive, Orakei, Auckland 1071, New Zealand. *E:* jennygibbs@xtra.co.nz.

GIBBS, Rt Rev. Dr Jonathan Robert; *see* Huddersfield, Area Bishop of.

GIBBS, Marion Olive, CBE 2012; Headmistress, James Allen's Girls' School, Dulwich, 1994–2015; Co-Founder and Co-Director, Southwark Schools Learning Partnership, 2003–15; *b* 16 Sept. 1951; *d* of Harry Norman Smith and Olive Mabel (*née* Lewis). *Educ:* Pate's Grammar Sch. for Girls, Cheltenham; Bristol Univ. (BA 1st cl. Hons Classics 1973; PGCE 1974; MLitt 1981). Assistant Mistress: City of Worcester Girls' Grammar Sch., 1974–76; Chailey Comprehensive Sch., 1977; Hd of Sixth Form, Dir of Studies and Hd of Classics, Burgess Hill Sch. for Girls, 1977–89; Hd of Sixth Form and Classics, Haberdashers' Aske's Girls' Sch., Elstree, 1989–91; HMI of Schools, 1992–94. Tutor, Open Univ., 1979–91. Member Council: Classical Assoc., 1984–87, 1995–98 (Hon. Jt Sec., 1989–92); Hellenic Soc., 1997–2000, 2008–11; Chm. Council, JACT, 2001–04. Columnist, SecEd, 2004–15. Trustee: Dulwich Picture Gall., 2008–11; Arvon Foundn, 2008–; Mem., Educn Cttee, Woodward Trust, 2015–. FRSA 1997. *Publications:* Greek Tragedy: an introduction, 1989; (contrib.) Two Sectors, One Purpose, 2002; (contrib.) The Teaching of Classics, 2003; (contrib.) Heads: leading schools in the 21st century, 2007. *Recreations:* music, gardening, drama, keeping informed about the developing world.

GIBBS, Patrick Michael Evan; QC 2006; *b* 24 April 1962; *s* of Michael Edmund Hubert Gibbs and Helen Antonia Gibbs; *m* 1989, Catherine Clare Barroll; one *s* one *d*. *Educ:* Eton; Christ Church, Oxford; City Univ. Called to the Bar, Middle Temple, 1986. *Address:* 3 Raymond Buildings, Gray's Inn, WC1R 5BH.

GIBBS, Dr Richard John; management consultant, since 2002; Chief Executive, Kingston and Richmond (formerly Kingston and Esher) Health Authority, 1990–2002; *b* 15 May 1943; *s* of Leslie and Mary Gibbs; *m* 1968, Laura Wanda Olasmi; one *d*. *Educ:* Merchant Taylors' Sch., Northwood; Pembroke Coll., Cambridge (BA 1965); Warwick Univ. (PhD 1974). Teacher, City of London Sch. for Boys, 1965; Scientific Officer, Home Office, 1968; Sen. Scientific Officer, 1970, PSO, 1972, DHSS; Res. Schol., Internat. Inst. for Applied Systems Analysis, Austria, 1977; SPSO, DHSS, 1978; Central Policy Review Staff, 1980; Dir of Operational Res. (DCSO), 1982, CSO, 1985, DHSS; Under Sec. and Dir of Stats and Management, DHSS, then DoH, 1986–90. Vis. Prof., UCL, 1985. Non-exec. Dir, Southwark PCT, 2007–13 (Vice Chair, 2010–13); Vice Chair, Southwark Clinical Commissioning Gp, 2013–. *Publications:* contribs to Jl of ORS. *Recreations:* windsurfing, cooking. *E:* rjgibbs@ntlworld.com.

GIBBS, Hon. Sir Richard (John Hedley), Kt 2000; a Judge of the High Court of Justice, Queen's Bench Division, 2000–08; Presiding Judge, Midland Circuit, 2004–07; *b* 2 Sept. 1941; *s* of late Brian Conaway Gibbs and Mabel Joan Gibbs; *m* 1965, Janet (*née* Whittall); one *s* two *d* (and one *d* decd). *Educ:* Oundle Sch.; Trinity Hall, Cambridge (MA). Called to the Bar, Inner Temple, 1965, Bencher, 2000; a Recorder, 1981–90; QC 1984; a Circuit Judge, 1990–2000. Chm. Council, Lincoln Cathedral, 2008–14. *Address:* 12 The Redlands, Manor Road, Sidmouth, Devon EX10 8RT.

GIBBS, Sir Roger (Geoffrey), Kt 1994; Director: Fleming Family & Partners, 2000–07 (Chairman, 2000–03); Gerrard & National Holdings PLC (formerly Gerrard & National Discount Co. Ltd), 1971–94 (Chairman, 1975–89); Chairman, The Wellcome Trust, 1989–99 (Governor, 1983–99); *b* 13 Oct. 1934; 4th *s* of Hon. Sir Geoffrey Gibbs, KCMG, and Hon. Lady Gibbs, CBE; *m* 2005, Mrs Jane Patricia Lee. *Educ:* Eton; Millfield. Jessel Toynbee & Co. Ltd, 1954–64, Dir 1960–64; de Zoete & Gorton, later de Zoete & Bevan, Stockbrokers, 1964–71, Partner 1966. Chm., London Discount Market Assoc., 1984–86. Director: Arsenal FC, 1980–2006; Colville Estate Ltd, 1989–2005; Howard de Walden Estates Ltd, 1989–2001 (Chm., 1993–98). Member of Council: Royal Nat. Pension Fund for Nurses, 1975–2002; ICRF, 1982–2002. Chm., St Paul's Cathedral Foundn, 2000–06; Trustee, Winston Churchill Meml Trust, 2001–09. Governor, London Clinic, 1983–93; Special Trustee, Guy's Hosp., 1983–92. Freeman, City of London; Liveryman, Merchant Taylors' Co. Trustee, Arundel Castle Cricket Foundn, 1987–2005 (Chm., 1987–95). *Publications:* The Cresta Run 1885–1985, 1984. *Recreations:* travel, sport. *Clubs:* Boodle's, Pratt's, MCC; Swinley Forest Golf (Chm., 1993–97).

GIBRALTAR, Dean of; *see* Paddock, Very Rev. Dr J. A. B.

GIBRALTAR, Archdeacon of; *no new appointment at time of going to press.*

GIBRALTAR IN EUROPE, Bishop of, since 2014; **Rt Rev. Dr Robert Neil Innes;** *b* Wolverhampton, 1959; *s* of Frank Innes and Christine Innes; *m* 1985, Helen Alexandra Bennett; one *s* three *d*. *Educ:* Royal Grammar Sch., Guildford; King's Coll., Cambridge (BA Engrg 1982); Cranmer Hall, St John's Coll., Durham (BA Theol. 1991); Durham Univ. (PhD Theol. 1995). Engrg Trainee, Central Electricity Generating Bd, 1979–83; Consultant, later Manager, Arthur Andersen Mgt Consultants, 1983–89; ordination trng and theol res., 1989–95; ordained deacon, 1995, priest, 1996; Lectr, Systematic Theology, St John's Coll., Durham, 1995–99; Curate, Sherburn, Pittington and Shadforth, 1997–99; Vicar, Belmont, 1999–2005; Chancellor and Sen. Chaplain, Pro-Cathedral of Holy Trinity, Brussels, 2005–14; a Chaplain to the Queen, 2012–14. Pres., Central Cttee, Anglican Church in Belgium, 2007–14. Chm., Grove Bks Ltd, 1999–2014. *Publications:* God at Work, 1994; Personality Indicators and the Spiritual Life, 1996; Medical Vocation and Generation X, 1997; Discourses of the Self, 1999; Augustine and the Journey to Wholeness, 2004. *Recreations:* walking, tennis, fine Belgian food and beer. *Address:* (office) 47 rue Capitaine Crespel - box 49, 1050 Brussels, Belgium. *T:* (2) 2137480. *E:* bishop.europe@churchofengland.org.

GIBRALTAR IN EUROPE, Suffragan Bishop of, since 2002; **Rt Rev. David Hamid;** *b* 18 June 1955; *s* of Ebrahim Hamid and Patricia (*née* Smith); *m* 1978, Colleen Gwen Moore; two *s*. *Educ:* Nelson High Sch., Burlington, Canada; McMaster Univ. (BSc Hons); Univ. of Trinity Coll., Toronto (MDiv 1981). Ordained deacon, 1981, priest, 1982; Asst Curate, St Christopher's, Burlington, 1981–83; Rector, St John's, Burlington, 1983–87; Mission Co-ordinator for Latin Amer. and Caribbean, Anglican Ch of Canada, 1987–96; Dir, Ecumenical Affairs and Studies, ACC, 1996–2002. Canon, Santo Domingo, 1992–. Hon. Asst Bishop, Dio. of Rochester, 2003–11. Archbishop of Canterbury's Rep. for Muslim-led Interfaith Initiatives, 2008–13. Member: Faith and Order Adv. Gp, C of E, 1996–2002; Anglican-Old Catholic Internat. Co-ordinating Council, 2005– (Co-Sec., 1999–2002); Porvoo Panel, C of E, 2005– (Chm., 2009–); Co-Sec., Internat. Anglican-Baptist Conversations, 2000–02; Consultant: Jt Working Gp, WCC and RC Ch, 1998–2004; Internat. Anglican-RC Commn for Unity and Mission, 2002– (Anglican Co-chair, 2012–); Porvoo Ch Leaders' Consultations, 2006, 2010, 2014. Secretary: Metropolitical Council, Cuba, 1987–96; Inter Anglican Theol Doctrinal Commn, 2000–02; Inter Anglican Standing Cttee on Ecumenical Relns, 2000–02; Co-Secretary: ARCIC, 1996–2002; Internat. Commn of Anglican Orthodox Theol Dialogue, 1996–2002; Anglican-Lutheran Internat. Working Gp, 1999–2002. Trustee, CTBI, 2013–. Gov., Anglican Centre in Rome, 2014–. Treasurer: Anglican Council of N America and Caribbean, 1983–87; Canadian Interch Cttee on Human Rights in Latin America, 1987–96. Mem. Council, Us (formerly USPG, later USPG: Anglicans in World Mission), 2002–. Mem., Adv. Gp, Older People Residing Abroad, 2007–13. Hon. DD Trinity Coll., Univ. of Toronto, 2005. *Publications:* (contrib.) Beyond Colonial Anglicanism: the Anglican Communion in the Twenty-First Century, ed I. Douglas, 2001; contrib. to Ecclesiastical Law Jl, Unité des Chrétiens, Internationale Kirchliche Zeitschrift. *Recreations:* music, languages, history, travel. *Address:* Diocese in Europe, 14 Tufton Street, SW1P 3QZ. *T:* (020) 7898 1160, *Fax:* (020) 7898 1166. *E:* david.hamid@churchofengland.org. *W:* www.eurobishop.blogspot.com. *Club:* Army and Navy.

GIBSON, family name of **Baron Ashbourne**.

GIBSON OF MARKET RASEN, Baroness *cr* 2000 (Life Peer), of Market Rasen in the Co. of Lincolnshire; **Anne Bartell,** OBE 1998; National Secretary, (Union for) Manufacturing, Science, Finance, 1987–2000; *b* 10 Dec. 1940; *d* of Harry Tasker and Jessie Tasker (*née* Roberts); *m* 1st, 1962, John Donald Gibson (marr. diss. 1985); one *d*; 2nd, 1988, John Bartell; one step *d*. *Educ:* Market Rasen C of E Sch.; Caistor Grammar Sch., Lincs; Chelmsford Coll. of Further Educn, 1970–71; Univ. of Essex, 1972–76 (BA Hons II1, Govt). Sec., Penney and Porter Engrg Co., Lincoln, 1956; Cashier, Midland Bank, Market Rasen, 1959–62.

Organiser, Saffron Walden Labour Party, 1966–70; Asst Sec., Organisation and Industrial Relns Dept, TUC, 1977–87. Member: TUC Gen. Council, 1989–2000; EOC, 1991–98; Dept of Employment Adv. Gp on Older Workers, 1993–96; HSC, 1996–2000; Chm., DTI Wkg Gp on Bullying at Work, 2005–08. Dep. Chm., 2008–, Dep. Speaker, 2009–, H of L; Chm., All-Party Parly Gp on Bullying and Violence at Work, 2011–. Mem., Lab. Party Nat. Constitutional Cttee, 1997–2000. Mem., RoSPA, 2008– (EC Mem., 2000–08; Pres., 2004–08). Member Council: Air League, 2005–; ATC, 2005–. Patron, Happy Child Internat., 2010–. Hon. Pres., Yeadon Sqdn Air Cadets, 2002–. Hon. Dr Portsmouth, 2008. *Recreations:* Francophile, embroidery, reading, theatre, interest in Latin America. *Address:* House of Lords, SW1A 0PW.

GIBSON, His Honour Charles Andrew Hamilton; a Circuit Judge, 1996–2010; *b* 9 July 1941; *s* of late Rev. Preb. Leslie Andrew Gibson and Kathleen Anne Frances Gibson; *m* 1969, Susan Judith Rowntree; two *d. Educ:* Sherborne Prep. Sch.; Sherborne Sch.; Hertford Coll., Oxford (MA). Called to the Bar, Lincoln's Inn, 1966; practised at the Bar, 1966–96; Asst Recorder, 1987–91; a Recorder, 1991–96. Mem., Mental Health Review Tribunal (Restricted Patients Panel), 2002–12. Chm., Southwark Diocesan Pastoral Cttee, 1993–2003. Vice Pres., Hertford Soc., 2012– (Chm., 2004–12). *Publications:* (with Prof. M. R. A. Hollis) Surveying Buildings, 1983, 5th edn 2005; The Winetasters, 2013. *Recreations:* music, theatre, wine. *Address:* c/o Lambeth County Court, Cleaver Street, SE11 4DZ. *T:* (020) 7091 4410. *Club:* Oxford and Cambridge.

GIBSON, Charles Anthony Warneford; QC 2001; a Recorder, since 2001; *b* 25 Sept. 1960; *s* of Philip Gaythorne Gibson and Margaret Elizabeth (*née* Mellotte, now Sim); *m* 1989, Mary Ann Frances, *e d* of Sir John Albert Leigh Morgan, KCMG; three *s* one *d. Educ:* Wellington Coll.; Durham Univ. (BA Hons Classics); Dip. Law, Central London. Called to the Bar, Inner Temple, 1984, Bencher, 2008. Hd of Chambers, 2007–. *Recreations:* family, sport, ballet, boxing, theatre, food, comedy. *Address:* 2 Harcourt Buildings, Temple, EC4Y 9DB. *T:* (020) 7583 9020.

GIBSON, Christopher Allen Wood; QC 1995; a Recorder, since 2002; *b* 5 July 1953; *s* of Rt Hon. Sir Ralph Brian Gibson and Ann Gibson; *m* 1984, Alarys Mary Calvert Eaton; two *d. Educ:* St Paul's Sch.; Brasenose Coll., Oxford. FCIArb 1992. Called to the Bar, Middle Temple, 1976, Bencher, 2003. *Recreations:* Whitstable, motorcycles, family. *Address:* Outer Temple Chambers, The Outer Temple, 222 Strand, WC2R 1BA. *T:* (020) 7353 6381.

GIBSON, Rev. Sir Christopher (Herbert), 4th Bt *cr* 1931, of Linconia, Argentina, and of Faccombe, Southampton; CP; *b* 17 July 1948; *o s* of Sir Christopher Herbert Gibson, 3rd Bt and Lilian Lake Young, *d* of Dr George Byron Young; *S* father, 1994, but his name does not appear on the Official Roll of the Baronetage. Ordained priest, 1975. *Heir: cousin* Robert Herbert Gibson [*b* 21 Dec. 1966; *m* 1992, Catherine Grace, *d* of E. W. Pugh; three *s* one *d*].

GIBSON, Christopher Jeremy Patrick; Director, CERT-UK (UK National Computer Emergency Response Team), since 2013; *b* Kent, 15 Oct. 1963; *s* of Brian Leslie Gibson and Jenefer Anne Gibson (*née* Gray); *m* 1990, Natasha Caroline Quinn; two *s* one *d. Educ:* Maidstone Grammar Sch.; North East London Poly. Lead Surveyor, Geophysical Services Inc., 1984–88; Technol. Manager, Saudi American Bank, 1988–95; Citigroup: Vice Pres., Citibank, 1995–2005; Sen. Vice Pres., 2005–11; Dir, eCrime, 2011–13. Mem. Bd, Internat. Forum of Incident Response and Security Teams, 2004–14 (Chief Financial Officer, 2005–10; Pres., 2011–13). *Recreations:* sailing, reading, theatre, music, loud shirts. *Address:* Cabinet Office, 70 Whitehall, SW1A 2AS.

GIBSON, Dr Christopher John; Head, National School of Healthcare Science, since 2014; *b* Malta, 16 Nov. 1956; *s* of Walter and Audrey Gibson; *m* 1981, Yvonne Johnson; one *s* one *d. Educ:* Emmanuel Coll., Cambridge (BA Natural Scis 1977); Univ. of Aberdeen (MSc Med. Physics 1978); Univ. of Durham (PhD Med. Imaging 1988). CSci 2002; FIPEM 2002. Med. Physicist, Northern Regl HA, Durham, 1981–95; Director: N Wales Med. Physics, 1995–2002; Med. Physics, Oxford Radcliffe Hosps NHS Trust, 2002–11; Scientific Dir, NHS S of England (Central), 2011–; Professional Lead for Physical Scis, and Dep. Hd, Nat. Sch. of Healthcare Sci., 2011–14. Pres., Inst. of Physics and Engrg in Medicine, 2010–11. *Recreations:* music, sailing, natural history. *E:* chris.gibson@nhs.net.

GIBSON, David, CB 1997; *b* 8 Sept. 1939; *s* of Frank Edward Gibson and Nora Jessie Gibson (*née* Gurnhill); *m* 1963, Roberta Alexandra (*née* McMaster); one *s* two *d. Educ:* King Edward VI Grammar Sch., Retford. FCCA. GPO, 1958–63; MAFF, 1963–68; Belfast City Council, 1968–72; Dept of Commerce, NI, 1972–82; Dir of Accountancy Services, 1982–85, Asst Sec., 1985–87, Under Sec., then Dep. Sec., 1987–99, Dept of Economic Develt, NI; Dep. Chm., NI Sci. Park Foundn, 1999–2002; Sec., NI in Europe, 2002–04. Pres., Irish Region, Assoc. of Chartered Certified Accountants, 1982–83. Trustee, The Bytes Project, 2000–05. *Recreations:* reading, music, walking. *Address:* 14 Bramble Grange, Newtownabbey, Co. Antrim BT37 0XH. *T:* (028) 9086 2237.

GIBSON, Dennis; *see* Gibson, R. D.

GIBSON, Lt-Col Edgar Matheson, (Gary), MBE 1986; TD 1975; DL; self-employed artist - painting and sculpture, since 1990; Vice Lord-Lieutenant of Orkney, 2007–11; *b* Kirkwall, Orkney, 1 Nov. 1934; *s* of James Edgar Gibson and Margaret Johnston Gibson (*née* Matheson); *m* 1960, Jean McCarrick; two *s* two *d. Educ:* Kirkwall Grammar Sch.; Gray's Coll. of Art, Aberdeen (DA 1957); Teachers' Training Coll., Aberdeen. National Service, Army, 1958–60. Principal Art Master, 1974–88, Asst Headmaster, 1988–90, Kirkwall Grammar Sch. Examiner in Higher Art and Design, Scottish Cert. of Educn Examn Bd, Dalkeith, 1978–93. Mem., Orkney Health Bd, 1991–99. TA and TAVR, Lovat Scouts (Lt-Col), 1961–85, JSLO, Orkney, 1980–85; Cadet Comdt, Orkney Lovat Scouts ACF, 1979–86; Hon. Col, Orkney Lovat Scouts, 1986–2004; Chm., N Area Highland TAVRA, 1987–93. Pres., Orkney Br., SSAFA, 1997–2013 (Chm., 1990–97). Mem., Selection Cttee, 1983–91, County Co-ordinator, 1991–93, Operation Raleigh. Chairman: St Magnus Cathedral Fair, 1982–2004; Preservation Cttee, Italian POW Chapel, 2006 (Mem., 1976–); Hon. President: Soc. of Friends of St Magnus Cathedral, 1994–; Orkney Craftsmen's Guild, 1997–2002 (Chm., 1962–82). DL Orkney, 1976. Hon. Sheriff, Grampian, Highland and Is, 1992–. *Recreations:* ba playing (old Norse game), whisky tasting. *Address:* Transcona, New Scapa Road, Kirkwall, Orkney KW15 1BN. *T:* (01856) 872849. *Club:* Highland and Lowland Brigades'.

GIBSON, Ven. (George) Granville; Archdeacon of Auckland, Diocese of Durham, 1993–2001, now Archdeacon Emeritus; *b* 28 May 1936; *s* of late George Henry and Jessie Gibson (*née* Farrand); *m* 1958, Edna (*née* Jackson); two *s* one *d* (and one *s* decd). *Educ:* Queen Elizabeth Grammar Sch., Wakefield; Barnsley Coll. of Technology; Cuddesdon Coll., Oxford. Mining Surveyor, NCB, 1952–62; Field Officer, The Boys' Brigade, 1962–69. Ordained deacon, 1971, priest, 1972; Curate, St Paul, Cullercoats, 1971–73; Team Vicar, Cramlington, 1973–77; Vicar, St Clare, Newton Aycliffe, 1977–85; Rector of Bishopwearmouth and RD of Wearmouth, 1985–93; Hon. Canon of Durham, 1988–2001, now Emeritus; Interim Priest, St James the Great, Darlington, 2012–14. Proctor in Convocation, 1980–2000; Church Comr, 1991–98 (Mem., Bd of Govs, 1993–98). Stavrofor, Romanian Orthodox Church, 1997–. Mem., Archbishop of Canterbury's Romania Liaison Gp, 1994–. Trustee, Church Urban Fund, 1991–2003. Chm. Govs, St Aidan's (formerly Eastbourne) C of E Acad., Darlington, 2007–11 (Gov., 2011–14). *Recreations:* gardening, cactus plants, cookery, grandchildren. *Address:* 12 West Crescent, Darlington DL3 7PR. *T:* (01325) 462526. *E:* gib65@aol.com.

GIBSON, Prof. (Gerald) John, MD; FRCP, FRCPE; Professor of Respiratory Medicine, University of Newcastle upon Tyne, 1993–2009, now Emeritus; Consultant Physician (Respiratory Medicine), Freeman Hospital, Newcastle upon Tyne, 1978–2009; *b* 3 April 1944; *s* of Maurice Gibson and Margaret Gibson (*née* Cronin); *m* 1977, Dr Mary Teresa Cunningham; three *s. Educ:* St Michael's Coll., Leeds; Guy's Hosp. Med. Sch., Univ. of London (BSc 1st Class Hons Physiol. 1965; MB BS Hons 1968; MD 1976). FRCP 1982; FRCPE 2000. Hse Physician, Guy's Hosp., 1968; Hse Surgeon, Leeds Gen. Infirmary, 1969; Resident Physician, McMaster Univ., Ont, 1970–71; Registrar and Sen. Registrar, Hammersmith Hosp. and RPMS, 1971–77. Mem. Council, RCP, 2000–03; President: Brit. Thoracic Soc., 2004–05 (Hon. Sec., 1986–88; Chm., 1997–99); Eur. Respiratory Soc., 2002–03. FERS 2014. British Thoracic Soc. Medal, 2012. *Publications:* Clinical Tests of Respiratory Function, 1984, 3rd edn 2009; Respiratory Medicine, 1990, 3rd edn 2003; contrib. papers on several aspects of respiratory medicine, sleep apnoea and clinical respiratory physiology. *Recreations:* photography, opera and singers. *E:* john.gibson@ncl.ac.uk.

GIBSON, Ven. Granville; *see* Gibson, Ven. G. G.

GIBSON, Ian, PhD; Journalist, Evening News, Norwich, 2009–13; *b* 26 Sept. 1938; *s* of late William and Winifred Gibson; *m* 1977, Elizabeth Frances (*née* Lubbock); two *d. Educ:* Dumfries Acad.; Edinburgh Univ. (BSc, PhD). MIBiol 2000; CBiol 2000. Indiana Univ., 1963–64; Univ. of Washington, 1964–65. Lectr, 1968–71, Sen. Lectr, and Dean, Sch. of Biol Scis, 1991–97, Hon. Prof., 2003, UEA. Vis. Prof., MIT, 2012; Lectr, Univs of Cambridge, Hull, Durham, UEA, Inst. of Physics and UCL, 2009–14. Contested (Lab) Norwich N, 1992; MP (Lab) Norwich N, 1997–June 2009. Chm., Select Cttee on Sci. and Technol., 2001–05. Chairman: Parly OST, 1998–2001; All Party Parly Gp on Cancer, 1998–2009; All Party Parly Gp on Cuba, 2004–09; All Party Parly Writers Gp, 2008–09. Non-exec. Dir, Stem Cell Foundn, 2005–09; Director, Eur. Cervical Cancer Assoc., 2010–; Community Telemedicine, 2010–. Chairman: Nanotechnology Task Force; UK Brain Tumour Consortium, 2011–12. Jt Manager, Parly football squad, 1999–2005. Governor: Hellesdon High Sch., 1992–97; Sprowston High Sch., 1995–97 (Chm.); Parkside Sch., Norwich, 2011–. President: Newton's Apple Charity, 2007–; Norfolk Carers Forum, 2007–11; UN Assoc. (Norwich), 2009–; Norwich City Power Chair Football, 2009–. Hon. Fellow: British Sci. Assoc., 2005; Wellcome Trust, 2006. Trustee, Children with Leukaemia, 2009–11. Hon. DCL UEA, 2011. Macmillan Cancer Relief Champion, 2003; E-Politix Health Champion, 2003–05; Parly Award, Royal Soc. Chemistry, 2004; Backbencher of Year, House mag., 2004. *Publications:* Anti-sense Technology, 1997; (with D. Turner) Best when we are Labour?, 2011. *Recreations:* football coaching, watching, listening and questioning.

GIBSON, Sir Ian, Kt 1999; CBE 1990; FInstP; Chairman: Trinity Mirror plc, 2006–12; William Morrison Supermarkets plc, 2008–15 (Deputy Chairman 2007–08); *b* 1 Feb. 1947; *s* of Charley Gibson and Kate Gibson (*née* Hare); *m* 1st, 1969, Joy Musker (marr. diss. 1985); two *d*; 2nd, 1988, Susan Wilson (marr. diss. 2009); one *s*; 3rd, 2010, Jane Blackburn. *Educ:* UMIST (BSc Physics 1969). FInstP 1999. Ford Motor Co. and Ford Werke AG: various posts in industrial relns and gen. mgt, 1969–79; General Manager: Halewood Ops, 1979–82; Saarlouis, 1982–83; Nissan Motor Manufacturing: Dir, 1984–2000; Dep. Man. Dir, 1987–89; Man. Dir, 1989–98; Chm., UK, 1999–2000; Vice-Pres., 1994–98, Pres., 1999–2000, Nissan Europe; Sen. Vice-Pres., Nissan Motor Co. Ltd and Supervisory Bd Mem., Nissan Europe NV, 2000–01. Dep. Chm., ASDA plc, 1994–99; non-exec. Dir, 2001–05, Dep. Chm., 2003–04, Chm., 2004–05, BPB plc. Mem. Court, Bank of England, 1999–2004. Non-executive Director: GKN plc, 2002–07; Northern Rock plc, 2002–08; Greggs plc, 2006–08. Mem., Public Interest Body, PricewaterhouseCoopers LLP, 2010–14. CCMI (CBIM 1990; Gold Medal, 2001). Hon. DBA: Sunderland Poly., 1990; York St John, 2014. Mensforth Gold Medal, IEE, 1998. *Recreations:* sailing and working on my boat, reading. *Club:* Royal Automobile.

GIBSON, John; *see* Gibson, G. J.

GIBSON, John Peter; Chief Executive, Seaforth Maritime, 1986–88 (Deputy Chairman, 1978–83; Chairman, 1983–86); *b* 21 Aug. 1929; *s* of John Leighton Gibson and Norah Gibson; *m* 1954, Patricia Anne Thomas; two *s* three *d. Educ:* Caterham Sch.; Imperial Coll., London (BSc (Hons Mech. Engrg), ACGI). Post-grad. apprenticeship Rolls Royce Derby, 1953–55; ICI (Billingham and Petrochemicals Div.), 1955–69; Man. Dir, Lummus Co., 1969–73; Dir Gen. Offshore Supplies Office, Dept of Energy, 1973–76. Dir, Taylor Woodrow Construction Ltd, 1989–90. *Recreations:* gardening, handyman. *Address:* No 5, The Clockhouse, 192 High Road, Byfleet, Surrey KT14 7BT.

GIBSON, Jonathan Hedley; His Honour Judge Jonathan Gibson; a Circuit Judge, since 2008; *b* Harrogate, 30 March 1960; *s* of Hedley and Margaret Gibson; *m* 1984, Helen Downs; one *s* one *d. Educ:* Harrogate Grammar Sch.; Univ. of Nottingham (LLB 1981); Inns of Court Sch. of Law. Called to the Bar, Gray's Inn, 1982; Barrister, Broadway House Chambers, Bradford, 1982–2008; Asst Recorder, 1999–2000; Recorder, 2000–08. Legal Mem., Mental Health Rev. Tribunal, 2002–. Legal Assessor, GMC, 2002–08. *Recreations:* Church activities, reading. *Address:* Preston Combined Court Centre, The Law Courts, Ring Way, Preston, Lancs PR1 2LL.

GIBSON, Kenneth James; Member (SNP) Cunninghame North, Scottish Parliament, since 2007; *b* Paisley, 8 Sept. 1961; *s* of Kenneth George Gibson and Iris Gibson; *m* 1st, 1989, Lynda Dorothy Payne (marr. diss. 2006); two *s* one *d*; 2nd, 2007, Patricia Duffy (*see* P. Gibson). *Educ:* Bellahouston Acad., Glasgow; Univ. of Stirling (BA Econs). Member (SNP): Glasgow DC, 1992–96; Glasgow CC, 1995–99 (Leader of Opposition, 1998–99). Scottish Parliament: MSP (SNP) Glasgow, 1999–2003; Shadow Minister for Local Govt, 1999–2001, for Social Justice, Housing, Urban Regeneration and Planning, 2001–03; Mem., Local Govt Cttee; Deputy Convenor: Social Justice Cttee, 2001–03; Local Govt and Communities Cttee, 2007–08; Educn, Lifelong Learning and Culture Cttee, 2008–11; Convenor, Finance Cttee, 2011–; contested (SNP) Glasgow, Pollok, 2003. Mem., SNP Nat. Exec. Cttee, 1997–99. *Recreations:* cinema, theatre, swimming, classical history. *Address:* Scottish Parliament, Edinburgh EH99 1SP; (constituency office) 15 Main Street, Dalry KA24 5DL.

GIBSON, Mark, CB 2005; Chief Executive, Whitehall and Industry Group, 2009–15; *b* 2 Jan. 1953; *m* 1981, Jane Norma Lindley (*d* 2007); *m* 2013, Rachel Jenkinson. *Educ:* University Coll., Oxford (BA 1974); London Business Sch. (MSc). Entered Department of Trade and Industry, 1974: Dep. Project Manager, Next Steps team, Cabinet Office, 1990–92; Asst Sec. Competitiveness Unit, 1992–94; Principal Private Sec. to Pres., BoT, and Dep. Prime Minister, 1994–97; Dir, British Trade Internat., 1997–2000; Director General: Enterprise and Innovation, DTI, 2000–02; Business Gp, later Enterprise and Business Gp, DTI, later BERR, 2002–09.

GIBSON, Mel Columcille Gerard, AO 1997; actor, director and producer; *b* Peekskill, NY, 3 Jan. 1956; *s* of Hutton Gibson and late Anne Gibson; *m* 1980, Robyn Moore; six *s* one *d* (incl. twin *s*); one *d* by Oksana Grigorieva. *Educ:* Nat. Inst. of Dramatic Art, Univ. of NSW. Joined State Theatre Co. of SA, 1977; theatre includes: Waiting for Godot, Sydney, 1979; Death of a Salesman, Nimrod Th., Sydney, 1982; No Names, No Pack Drill; Romeo and Juliet. Co-founder and Partner, Icon Entertainment Internat., 1989–. *Films include:* Summer City, 1977; Mad Max, Tim, 1979; The Z Men, 1980; Gallipoli, Mad Max 2: The Road Warrior, 1981; The Year of Living Dangerously, 1982; The Bounty, The River, Mrs Soffell, 1984; Mad Max: Beyond Thunderdome, 1985; Lethal Weapon, 1987; Tequila Sunrise, 1988; Lethal Weapon 2, 1989; Bird on a Wire, Air America, 1990; Hamlet, 1991; Lethal Weapon

3, Forever Young, 1992; The Man Without a Face (also dir), 1993; Maverick, 1994; Braveheart (also dir and co-prod.), 1995 (Academy, Golden Globe and BAFTA Awards for best dir, 1996); Ransom, 1997; Conspiracy Theory, 1997; Lethal Weapon 4, 1998; Payback, 1999; The Million Dollar Hotel, The Patriot, 2000; What Women Want, 2001; We Were Soldiers, Signs, 2002; The Singing Detective (also prod.), 2004; Edge of Darkness, 2010; The Beaver, 2011; Dark Shadows, 2012; Machete Kills, 2013; The Expendables 3, 2014; dir, prod. and writer, The Passion of the Christ, 2004; dir and prod., Apocalypto, 2007. *Address:* c/o Shanahan Management Pty Ltd, PO Box 1509, Darlinghurst, NSW 1300, Australia.

GIBSON, Air Vice-Marshal Michael John, CB 1994; OBE 1979; FRAeS; Head of Aviation Regulation Enforcement, Civil Aviation Authority, 1996–99; *b* 2 Jan. 1939; *m* 1961, Dorothy Russell; one *s* one *d*. *Educ:* Imperial Coll., London (BSc); Selwyn Coll., Cambridge; National Defense Univ., Washington, DC. ACGI; FRAeS. Commnd RAFVR, 1959; commnd RAF, 1961; various appointments as fighter pilot and instructor; Personal Air Sec. to Air Force Minister, 1972–73; Officer Commanding: 45 Sqdn (Hunter), 1974–76; 20 Sqdn (Jaguar), 1976–79; RAF Brawdy, 1982–84; RAF Stanley, 1984–85; Air Officer Plans, HQ Strike Comd, 1987–88; Dir, Airspace Policy, 1988–91, Dir Gen. of Policy and Plans, 1991–94, Head of Mgt Support Unit, 1994–96, NATS. *Recreation:* music (singing and church organ playing). *Address:* 12 Watling Street, Radlett, Herts WD7 7NH. *Club:* Royal Air Force.

GIBSON, Patricia; MP (SNP) North Ayrshire and Arran, since 2015; *b* 12 May 1968; *née* Duffy; *m* 2007, Kenneth James Gibson, *qv*. *Educ:* Univ. of Glasgow (MA 1991). Teacher of English, St Ninians High Sch., Giffnock, until 2015. Mem. (SNP), Glasgow CC, 2007–15. *Address:* House of Commons, SW1A 0AA.

GIBSON, Paul Alexander; Founder, 1973, Partner, 1973–2001, later Consultant, Sidell Gibson Partnership, Architects; *b* 11 Oct. 1941; *s* of Wing-Comdr Leslie Gibson and Betty Gibson (later Betty Stephens); *m* 1969, Julia Atkinson. *Educ:* Kingswood Sch., Bath; King's Coll., London; Canterbury Sch. of Architecture; Regent Street Polytechnic Sch. of Architecture (DipArch 1968). Worked for Farrell Grimshaw Partnership, 1968–69; Lectr, North Dakota State Univ., 1969; worked for Foster Associates, 1970–73. 3 RIBA awards, Good Housing, 1986; won open competition for redevelt of Grand Buildings, Trafalgar Square, 1986; won competition for redevelt of Winchester Barracks, 1988; expansion of Jewel House, HM Tower of London, 1992–94; Woolgate House, Northgate House and Governor's House, City of London, 1996–2001. Judge, Nat. Stone Awards, 2004–10. *Recreations:* printmaking, etching and photography.

GIBSON, Rt Hon. Sir Peter (Leslie), Kt 1981; PC 1993; a Lord Justice of Appeal, 1993–2005; Intelligence Services Commissioner, 2006–10; *b* 10 June 1934; *s* of late Harold Leslie Gibson and Martha Lucy Gibson (*née* Diercking); *m* 1968, Katharine Mary Beatrice Hadow, PhD (*d* 2002); two *s* one *d*. *Educ:* Malvern Coll.; Worcester Coll., Oxford (Scholar; Hon. Fellow, 1993). 2nd Lieut RA, 1953–55 (National Service). Called to the Bar, Inner Temple, 1960; Bencher, Lincoln's Inn, 1975; Treas., Lincoln's Inn, 1996. 2nd Jun. Counsel to Inland Revenue (Chancery), 1970–72; Jun. Counsel to the Treasury (Chancery), 1972–81; a Judge of the High Court of Justice, Chancery Div., 1981–93. A Judge of the Employment Appeal Tribunal, 1984–86. A Judge of Qatar Financial Centre Civil and Commercial Court, 2007–15. Chairman: Law Commn, 1990–92; Trust Law Cttee, 2004–12; Detainee Inquiry, 2010–12. Conducted Omagh Bombing Intelligence Review, 2008. *Address:* c/o Royal Courts of Justice, Strand, WC2A 2LL.

GIBSON, Prof. (Robert) Dennis, AO 2002; PhD, DSc; FTS, FAICD; Member, Board of Governors, Torrens University, Adelaide, since 2013; *b* 13 April 1942; *m*; one *s* two *d*; *m* 1994, Catherin Bull. *Educ:* Hull Univ. (BSc Hons); Newcastle upon Tyne Univ. (MSc, PhD); DSc CNAA 1987. FAIM 1982; FTS 1993. Asst Lectr, Maths Dept, Univ. of Newcastle upon Tyne, 1966–67; Scientific Officer, Culham Plasma Lab., UKAEA, 1967–68; Lectr in Maths, Univ. of Newcastle upon Tyne, 1968–69; Sen. Lectr, Maths and Statistics, Teesside Polytechnic, 1969–77; Head, Dept of Maths, Stats and Computing (later Sch. of Maths, Stats and Computing), Newcastle upon Tyne Polytechnic, 1977–82; Queensland Institute of Technology: Dep. Dir then Actg Dir, 1982–83; Dir, 1983–88; first Vice-Chancellor, Qld Univ. of Technol., 1989–2003, now Emeritus Prof.; Chancellor: RMIT, 2003–10; INTI Internat. Univ., Kuala Lumpur, 2011–12. Mem., 1988–92, Dep. Chm., 1991–92, Aust. Res. Council; Chm., Grad. Careers Council of Aust., 2000–06. Chairman: M & MD Pty Ltd, 2003–09; RDDT Pty Ltd, 2007–10. Academic Advr, Laureate Educn Inc., 2010–. Mem. Council, 2005–10, Professorial Fellow, 2010–, Bond Univ.; Mem. Bd of Govs, St Thomas Univ., Osaka, 2011–13. FAICD 1995. DUniv: Southern Qld, 1999; Qld Univ. of Technol., 2003. *Publications:* numerous research papers on various aspects of mathematical modelling. *Recreations:* jogging, cricket. *Address:* 10/82 Macquarie Street, St Lucia, Qld 4067, Australia. *Club:* Brisbane.

GIBSON, Prof. Robert Donald Davidson, AO 2002; PhD; Professor of French, University of Kent at Canterbury, 1965–94, now Emeritus (Master of Rutherford College, 1985–90); *b* Hackney, London, 21 Aug. 1927; *o s* of Nicol and Ann Gibson, Leyton, London; *m* 1953, Sheila Elaine, *o d* of Bertie and Ada Goldsworthy, Exeter, Devon; three *s*. *Educ:* Leyton County High Sch. for Boys; King's Coll., London; Magdalene Coll., Cambridge; Ecole Normale Supérieure, Paris. BA (First Class Hons. French) London, 1948; PhD Cantab. 1953. Asst Lecturer, St Salvator's Coll., University of St Andrews, 1954–55; Lecturer, Queen's Coll., Dundee, 1955–58; Lecturer, Aberdeen Univ., 1958–61; Prof., Queen's Univ. of Belfast, 1961–65. *Publications:* The Quest of Alain-Fournier, 1953; Modern French Poets on Poetry, 1961; (ed) Le Bestiaire Inattendu, 1961; Roger Martin du Gard, 1961; La Mésentente Cordiale, 1963; (ed) Brouart et le Désordre, 1964; (ed) Provinciales, 1965; (ed) Le Grand Meaulnes, 1968; The Land Without a Name, 1975; Alain-Fournier and Le Grand Meaulnes, 1986; (ed) Studies in French Fiction, 1988; Annals of Ashdon, 1988; The Best of Enemies, 1995, 2nd edn 2004; The End of Youth, 2005; reviews and articles in: French Studies, Modern Language Review, The London Magazine, Times Literary Supplement, Encyclopædia Britannica, Collier's Encyclopædia. *Recreations:* reading, writing, talking. *Address:* Thalassa!, Cliff Road, Sidmouth, Devon EX10 8JN.

GIBSON, Robert McKay; Member (SNP) Caithness, Sutherland and Ross, Scottish Parliament, since 2011 (Highlands and Islands, 2003–11); *b* 16 Oct. 1945; *s* of John and Elsie Gibson; partner, Dr Eleanor Roberta Scott, *qv*. *Educ:* Dundee Univ. (MA Hons Modern Hist.); Dundee Coll. of Educn (DipEd 1973; Secondary Teaching Dip. 1973). Teacher, Geog. and Modern Studies, 1973–74, Asst Principal Teacher of Guidance, 1974–77, Invergordon Acad.; Principal Teacher of Guidance, Alness Acad., 1977–95; writer and researcher, 1995–2003. Vice-Pres., Brittany Scotland Assoc., 2005–; Hon. Pres., Kilt Soc. of France, 2006–. *Publications:* The Promised Land, 1974; Highland Clearances Trail, 1983, new edn 2006; Toppling the Duke: outrage on Ben Bhraggie, 1996; Plaids and Bandanas, 2003; Highland Cowboys, 2010. *Recreations:* traditional music singer, organic gardener, hill walker, traveller. *Address:* Scottish Parliament, Edinburgh EH99 1SP. *E:* rob.gibson.msp@scottish,parliament.uk; Tir Nan Oran, 8 Culcairn Road, Evanton, Ross-shire IV16 9YT. *T:* (01349) 830388. *E:* robgibson273@btinternet.com.

GIBSON, Robert Winnington, CMG 2011; HM Diplomatic Service; High Commissioner, Bangladesh, since 2011; *b* Neath, W Glamorgan, 7 Feb. 1956; *s* of Peter Winnington Gibson and Olive May Gibson (*née* Taylor). *Educ:* Dyffryn Sch., Port Talbot; University Coll., London (BSc Hons Zool. 1978). Entered HM Diplomatic Service, 1978; Desk Officer, Eur. Integration Dept, FCO, 1978–79; ME Centre for Arabic Studies, 1979–80; Vice Consul, Jeddah, 1981–84; Second Secretary: UK Representation, Brussels, 1984–85; (Chancery), Port of Spain, 1986–89; Head: Peacekeeping and Finance Section, UN Dept, FCO, 1989–93; Saudi Arabian and Gulf Section, ME Dept, FCO, 1993–95; First Sec., UK Delegn to OECD, Paris, 1995–99; Dep. Hd, Whitehall Liaison Dept, FCO, 1999–2001; Dep. High Comr and Commercial Counsellor, Dhaka, 2002–05; Dep. Hd of Mission, Baghdad, 2006–07; Dep. High Comr, Karachi, and Dir, UK Trade and Investment, Pakistan, 2008–11. *Recreations:* music, reading, food and travel. *Address:* c/o Foreign and Commonwealth Office, King Charles Street, SW1A 2AH. *Clubs:* Sindh (Karachi); Dhaka (Dhaka).

GIBSON, Roy; aerospace consultant, since 1980; Director General, British National Space Centre, 1985–87; *b* 4 July 1924; *s* of Fred and Jessie Gibson; *m* 1st, 1946, Jean Fallowes (marr. diss. 1971); one *s* one *d*; 2nd, 1971, Inga Elgerus. *Educ:* Chorlton Grammar Sch.; Wadham College, Oxford; SOAS. Malayan Civil Service, 1948–58; Health and Safety Br., UKAEA, 1958–66; European Space Research Orgn, 1967–75 (Dir of Admin, 1970–75); Dir Gen., European Space Agency, 1975–80. DSC (Kedah, Malaysia), 1953; Das Grosse Silberne Ehrenzeichen mit Stern (Austria), 1977. *Publications:* Space, 1992; Recollections, 2011; numerous articles in aerospace technical jls. *Recreations:* music, chess, walking. *Address:* Résidence les Hespérides, 51 Allée J. de Beins, Montpellier 34000, France. *T:* 467648181.

GIBSON, Prof. Susan Elizabeth, OBE 2013; DPhil; Professor of Chemistry, Imperial College, London, since 2003; *b* 3 Nov. 1960; *d* of late Arnold Sutcliffe Thomas and of Kathleen Thomas; *m* 1994, Vernon Charles Gibson, *qv*; one *s* one *d*. *Educ:* Darwen Vale High Sch.; Sidney Sussex Coll., Cambridge (BA 1981); New Coll., Oxford (DPhil 1984). Lecturer: Univ. of Warwick, 1985–90; ICSTM, London, 1990–99; Daniell Prof. of Chemistry, KCL, 1999–2003. Mem. Council, EPSRC, 2003–06. Pres., Organic Chemistry Div., RSC, 2007–10. Rosalind Franklin Award, Royal Soc., 2003–04. *Publications:* Organic Synthesis: the roles of boron and silicon, 1991; more than 130 articles in learned jls. *Recreations:* hill-walking, sailing. *Address:* Department of Chemistry, Imperial College, London, South Kensington Campus, SW7 2AZ. *T:* (020) 7594 1140. *E:* s.gibson@imperial.ac.uk.

GIBSON, Ven. Terence Allen; Archdeacon of Ipswich, 1987–2005, now Archdeacon Emeritus; *b* 23 Oct. 1937; *s* of Fred William Allen and Joan Hazel Gibson. *Educ:* Jesus Coll., Cambridge (MA); Cuddesdon Coll., Oxford. Curate of St Chad, Kirkby, 1963–66; Warden of Centre 63, Kirkby C of E Youth Centre, 1966–75; Rector of Kirkby, Liverpool, 1975–84; RD of Walton, Liverpool, 1979–84; Archdeacon of Suffolk, 1984–87. *Address:* 5 Berry Close, Purdis Farm, Ipswich IP3 8SP. *T:* (01473) 714756.

GIBSON, Prof. Vernon Charles, DPhil; FRS 2004; Chief Scientific Adviser, Ministry of Defence, since 2012; *b* 15 Nov. 1958; *s* of Dennis Charles Gibson and Pamela Gibson (*née* Lambley); *m* 1994, Susan Elizabeth Thomas (*see* S. E. Gibson); one *s* one *d*. *Educ:* Huntingtower Rd County Primary Sch.; King's Sch., Grantham; Univ. of Sheffield (R. D. Haworth Medal, 1980; BSc); Balliol Coll., Oxford (DPhil 1984). Lectr in Inorganic Chem., 1986–93, Prof. of Chem., 1993–95, Univ. of Durham; Imperial College London: Prof. of Polymer Synthesis and Catalysis, 1995–98; Sir Geoffrey Wilkinson Chair of Chem., 1998–2001; Sir Edward Frankland BP Prof. of Inorganic Chem., 2001–08; Hon. Prof., 2008–; Chief Chemist, BP plc, 2008–12. Hon. DSc Sheffield, 2010. Royal Society of Chemistry: BP Chemicals Young Univ. Lectr Award, 1990–93; Sir Edward Frankland Prize Fellowship, 1992–93; Corday-Morgan Medal and Prize, 1993–94; Monsanto Organometallic Chemistry Award, 1999; Joseph Chatt Lectr, 2001–02; Tilden Lectr, 2004–05. *Publications:* numerous book chapters; approx. 300 papers in learned jls and 30 published patents. *Recreations:* jogging around Hyde Park and Kensington Gardens, ski-ing, reading, old vintage claret. *Club:* Athenæum.

GIBSON-CRAIG-CARMICHAEL, Sir David Peter William, 15th Bt *cr* 1702 (Gibson Carmichael) and 8th Bt *cr* 1831; *b* 21 July 1946; *s* of Sir Archibald Henry William Gibson-Craig-Carmichael, 14th Bt and Rosemary Anita (*d* 1979), *d* of George Duncan Crew, Santiago, Chile; *S* father, 1969; *m* 1973, Patricia, *d* of Marcos Skarnic, Santiago, Chile; two *s* two *d*. *Educ:* Queen's Univ., Canada (BSc Hons Geology, 1971). *Heir:* *s* Peter William Gibson-Craig-Carmichael, *b* 29 Dec. 1975.

GIBSON FLEMING, James Randolf; Vice Lord-Lieutenant of Dorset, since 2006; *b* 27 July 1958; *s* of late Maj. William H. Gibson Fleming and Selina Littlehales Gibson Fleming (*née* Baker); *m* 1986, Fiona Lucy Don; two *s* one *d*. *Educ:* Eton; RMA Sandhurst; RAC Cirencester. SSC, Royal Hussars, PWO, 1977–81; served NI and W Berlin. Partner/dir, farming, property and asset mgt firms/cos, 1981–; Chief Exec., Hanford plc, 1987–93. Chm., CLA Game Fair Bd, 1992–97. Trustee: Talbot Village Trust, 1991–; Cancercare Dorset, 1994–2004 (Chm., 2000–04); Joseph Weld and Trimar Hospice and Cancercare Dorset, 2004–06 (Vice-Chm., 2004–06); Devonshire and Dorset Military Museums Charity, 2012–. Pres., Queen's Own Dorset Yeomanry Assoc., 2010–. DL Dorset, 2005. *Recreations:* field sports, flying, ski-ing, holidaying on Isle of Mull. *Address:* Ranston, Blandford, Dorset DT11 8PU. *Clubs:* Cavalry and Guards, Air Squadron, MCC, Shikar, Pratt's.

GIBSON-SMITH, Christopher Shaw, CBE 2011; PhD; Chairman: London Stock Exchange Group (formerly London Stock Exchange), 2003–15; JRP (formerly Partnership Assurance), since 2013; *b* 8 Sept. 1945; *s* of late John Gibson-Smith and Winifred Agnes Gibson-Smith; *m* 1969, Marjorie Hadwin Reed; two *d*. *Educ:* Durham Univ. (BSc Geol); Newcastle Univ. (PhD Geochem. 1970); Stanford Univ. (MSc Business Sci). Joined BP, 1970; CEO Europe, BP Exploration, 1992–95; Chief Operating Officer, BP Chemicals, 1995–97; Gp Man. Dir, BP, 1997–2001. Chm., NATS, 2001–05. Non-executive Director: Lloyds TSB, 1999–2005; Powergen, 2000–01; Chm., British Land plc, 2006–12. Hon. Fellow, UCD, 2006. *Recreations:* art, music, opera, ski-ing, golf, tennis. *Address:* Lansdowne, White Lane, Guildford, Surrey GU4 8PR. *T:* (01483) 571442, *Fax:* (01483) 455548.

GIDDEN, Mark Robert; Master of the Administrative Court, Queen's Bench Division, since 2012; *b* Reading, 5 Oct. 1964; *s* of late Michael John Gidden and of Patricia Gidden; *m* 1986, Nicola Alice (marr. diss. 2013); three *s* one *d*. *Educ:* Univ. of Birmingham (LLB). Admitted solicitor, 1991; solicitor, Govt Legal Service, 1991–2012, a Dir, Legal Services, DWP, 2010–11. *Recreations:* walking, gardening, history, travelling, fresh air and being quiet—but not necessarily all at once. *Address:* Administrative Court, Royal Courts of Justice, Strand, WC2A 2LL. *T:* (020) 7947 6003. *E:* master.gidden@hmcts.x.gsi.gov.uk.

GIDDENS, Baron *cr* 2004 (Life Peer), of Southgate in the London Borough of Enfield; **Anthony Giddens,** PhD; Director, London School of Economics, 1997–2003, now Emeritus; *b* 18 Jan. 1938; *s* of T. G. Giddens; *m* 1963, Jane M. Ellwood. *Educ:* Hull Univ. (BA); LSE (MA); MA 1970, PhD 1974, Cantab. Cambridge University: Lectr in Sociology, subseq. Reader, 1969–85; Prof. of Sociology, Faculty of Econs and Politics, 1985–96; Fellow, King's Coll., 1969–96. Reith Lectr, BBC, 1999. *Publications:* Capitalism and Modern Social Theory, 1971; (ed) Sociology of Suicide, 1972; Politics and Sociology in the Thought of Max Weber, 1972; (ed and trans) Emile Durkheim: Selected Writings, 1972; (ed) Positivism and Sociology, 1974; New Rules of Sociological Method, 1976; Studies in Social and Political Theory, 1976; Central Problems in Social Theory, 1979; Class Structure of the Advanced Societies, 2nd edn 1981; Contemporary Critique of Historical Materialism: vol. 1, Power, Property and State, 1981, vol. 2, Nation, State and Violence, 1985; (jtly) Classes, Power and Conflict, 1982; Profiles and Critiques in Social Theory, 1983; (ed jtly) Social Class and the Division of Labour, 1983; Constitution of Society, 1984; Durkheim, 1985; Sociology: a brief but critical introduction, 1986; Social Theory and Modern Sociology, 1987; (ed jtly) Social Theory Today, 1987; Sociology, 1989; The Consequences of Modernity, 1990; Modernity and Self-Identity, 1991; The Transformation of Intimacy, 1992; Beyond Left and Right,

1994; In Defence of Sociology, 1996; The Third Way, 1998, 2nd edn 2010; Runaway World (Reith Lectures), 1999; (with Will Hutton) On the Edge: living with global capitalism, 2000; The Third Way and its Critics, 2000; Europe in the Global Age, 2007; Over to You Mr Brown: how Labour can win again, 2007; The Politics of Climate Change, 2009. *Recreations:* theatre, cinema, playing tennis, supporting Tottenham Hotspur. *Address:* House of Lords, SW1A 0PW.

GIDDINGS, Anthony Edward Buckland, MD; FRCS; Consultant Surgeon in General and Vascular Surgery, Guy's, King's and St Thomas' Hospitals, 1997–2004; *b* 8 Feb. 1939; *s* of Edward Walter Giddings and Doris Margaret Giddings; *m* 1966, Maureen Ann Williams; one *s* one *d*. *Educ:* Cathedral Sch., Bristol; Univ. of Bristol (MB ChB 1966; MD 1978). FRCS 1971. Consultant Surgeon, Royal Surrey Co. Hosp., 1979–97. Non-exec. Dir, Nat. Clinical Assessment Authy, 2001–05. MRCS Course Dir, St Thomas' Hosp., 2003–05. Founding Pres., Assoc. of Surgeons in Training, 1976; President: Sect. of Surgery, RSM, 1994; Assoc. of Surgeons of GB and Ireland, 1997–98; Dir, James IV Assoc. of Surgeons Inc., 1998–2001; Chairman: Specialist Adv. Cttee in Gen. Surgery, 1998–2001; Fedn of Surgical Specialist Assocs, 1998–2001; Mem. Council, RCS, 2001–07. Hunterian Prof., RCS, 1978; James IV Assoc. of Surgeons Inc. Travelling Fellow, 1979; Visiting Professor: Univ. of Texas, 1980; Oregon Health Scis Univ., 1996; Lectures: A. B. Mitchell, QUB, 1996; Moynihan, RCS, 2007. Work on med. perf. and assessment, Nat. Clinical Assessment Authy, GMC and RCS, 1997–2007; work on orgn of surgical services, NHS Modernization Agency and DoH, 2001–08; clinical res. and educn and trng develt in safety and leadership for surgeons, 1997–2008; Surgical Adviser: Performance Support Team, DoH, 2006–08; Nat. Clinical Adv. Team, DoH, 2007–15; Healthcare Commn, 2008–09; Specialist Advr, Parly Health Cttee, 2008–09; Mem., Surgical Adv. Gp, John Radcliffe Hosp., 2009–10; Chairman: Alliance for Safety of Patients, RCS, 2006–09; Clin. Reference Gp, NW sector surgical proj., Manchester, 2014–. Founding Co-Organiser, Risky Business Confs, 2006–. Distinguished Fellow, Soc. for Vascular Surgery, 1999. Mem., Editl Bd, British Jl of Surgery, 1994–2000. *Publications:* contrib. papers and book chapters on surgical science, the safety of patients and the orgn of surgical services. *Recreations:* theatre, music, flying light aircraft. *Address:* 6 Fairway, Guildford, Surrey GU1 2XG. *T:* (01483) 561826. *E:* tonygiddings@btinternet.com. *Club:* Royal Automobile.

GIDDINGS, Dr Philip James; Senior Lecturer in Politics, 1998–2011, and Head, School of Politics and International Relations (formerly School of Sociology, Politics and International Relations), 2006–11, University of Reading; *b* 5 April 1946; *s* of Albert Edward Robert Giddings and Irene Trustrail Giddings (*née* Dunstan); *m* 1st, 1970, Margaret Anne Mulrenan (*d* 1978); one *d*; 2nd, 1979, Myfanwy Hughes; one *s*. *Educ:* Sir Thomas Rich's Sch., Gloucester; Worcester Coll., Oxford (BA Hons PPE); Nuffield Coll., Oxford (DPhil 1970). Lectr in Public Admin, Univ. of Exeter, 1970–72; Lectr in Politics, Reading Univ., 1972–98. Member: Crown Appointments Commn, 1992–97; Archbishops' Council, 1999–2015 (Chairman: Church and World Div., 1999–2002; Mission and Public Affairs Div., 2003–11). Mem., Gen. Synod of C of E, 1985–2015 (Vice-Chm., 1995–2000, 2006–10, Chm., 2010–15, House of Laity; Dep. Chm., Legislative Cttee, 2005–10); Lay Vice-Pres., Oxford Diocesan Synod, 1988–2000. Convenor and Chair of Trustees, Anglican Mainstream UK, 2003–14. *Publications:* Marketing Boards and Ministers, 1974; Parliamentary Accountability, 1995; (with G. Drewry) Westminster and Europe, 1996; (with R. Gregory) Righting Wrongs: the ombudsman in six continents, 2000; (with R. Gregory) The Ombudsman, the Citizen and Parliament, 2002; Britain in the European Union, 2004; The Future of Parliament, 2005; (ed with M. Rush) The Palgrave Review of British Politics 2005, 2006; (ed with M. Rush) The Palgrave Review of British Politics 2006, 2007; (ed with M. Rush) When Gordon Took the Helm: the Palgrave review of British politics 2007–08, 2008; (with M. Rush) Parliamentary Socialisation: learning the ropes or determining behaviour?, 2011. *Recreations:* light gardening, short walks. *Address:* 5 Clifton Park Road, Caversham, Reading, Berks RG4 7PD. *T:* (0118) 954 3892.

GIDLEY, Sandra Julia; *b* 26 March 1957; *d* of Frank Henry and Maud Ellen Rawson; *m* 1979, William Arthur Gidley; one *s* one *d*. *Educ:* Eggars Grammar Sch., Alton; AFCENT Internat., Brunssum, Netherlands; Windsor Girls' Sch., Hamm, Germany; Bath Univ. (BPharm). MRPharmS 1979, FRPharmS 2008. Pharmacist, Cheltenham, 1979–80; Pharmacy Manager, Gloucester, then Cheltenham, 1980–82; locum pharmacist, 1982–92; Pharmacy Manager: Safeway, 1992–99; Tesco, 1999–2000. Mem. (Lib Dem) Test Valley BC, 1995–2003; Mayor of Romsey, 1997–98. MP (Lib Dem) Romsey, May 2000–2010; contested (Lib Dem) Romsey and Southampton N, 2010. Lib Dem spokesman for women, 2002–06, for older people, 2003–06, for health, 2006–10. Trustee, Beadworkers Guild. *Recreations:* food, photography. *Address:* 15 Sycamore Close, Romsey, Hants SO51 5SB. *T:* (01794) 517652.

GIDOOMAL, Balram, (Ram), CBE 1998; Chairman: Winning Communications Partnership Ltd, since 1992; Allia (formerly Citylife Ltd), since 2005; Traidcraft plc, Traidcraft Exchange, since 2011; Office of the Independent Adjudicator for Higher Education, since 2009; European Network of Ombudsmen in Higher Education, since 2013; *b* 23 Dec. 1950; *s* of late Gagandas Gidoomal and Vasanti Gidoomal; *m* 1976, Sunita Shivdasani; two *s* one *d*. *Educ:* Aga Khan Sch., Mombasa; Christopher Wren Sch., London; Imperial Coll., London (BSc Hons Physics; Fellow, 2010). ARCS 1972. Inlaks Group: Dep. Gp Chief Exec., Head Office, France, then Geneva, 1978–85; UK Gp Chief Exec. and Vice Chm., 1985–92. Non-executive Director: Amsphere Ltd, 2006– (Chairman: Audit Cttee; Remuneration Cttee); Nirmaan Bharati SAAVS, 2007–09; Dulas Ltd, 2014–; non-exec. Adv. Bd Mem., Six Senses BVI, 2007–09. Board Member: Covent Gdn Mkt Authy, 1998–2004; English Partnerships, 2000–03; Think London (formerly London First Centre), 2001–09; Postmaster.net, 2003–06; Dir, Far Pavilions Ltd, 1998–2008. Member: Better Regulation Task Force, Cabinet Office, 1997–2002; Complaints Audit Cttee, UK Border Agency (formerly Immigration Nationality Directorate, then Border and Immigration Agency), Home Office, 2006–08; Bd, Food Standards Agency, 2014–. Mem., Royal Mail Stamp Adv. Cttee, 2002–11. Mem., Nat. Leadership Team and Chm., London Exec., Race for Opportunity, 1993–99; Founder Chm., Business Links London South, 1995–98; Director: Business Links-Nat. Accreditation Adv. Bd, 1995–2000; Business Links London, 1995–98 (Chm., CEO's Gp, 1996–98); Mem., SRI Adv. Cttee, Hendersons Global Investments, 2004–10. Patron, Small Business Bureau, 1998–. Mem. Council, Britain in Europe, 1999–2005. Chm., S Asian Develt Partnership, 1991–. Vis. Prof., Middx Univ., 2001–14. Member: Council, RSA, 1993–2002, 2004–08 (Trustee, 1999–2002); Council, Inst. of Employment Studies, 2001–10 (Bd Mem., 2003–10). Chairman: Christmas Cracker Trust, 1989–2000; London Community Foundn, 2001–03; London Sustainability Exchange, 2001–07. Leader, Christian Peoples Alliance, 2001–04; Pres., Nat. Information Forum, 2003–08; Vice President: Leprosy Mission, 1999–; Livability (formerly Shaftesbury Soc.), 2003–; Employee Ownership Assoc., 2009–. Member: Adv. Bd for ethics in the workplace, 2002–06, Adv. Bd, 2009–, Inst. of Business Ethics (Hon. Vice Pres., 2015–); Adv. Council for Clinical Excellence Awards, 2004–06; Adv. Council, Friends of the Elderly, 2003–08; Internat. Health Partners, 2006–11; Internat. Justice Mission, 2008–14; External Relns Gp, Water UK, 2009–; External Mem., Audit and Risk Cttee, Equality and Human Rights Commn, 2010–14. Gov., Health Foundn (formerly PPP Medical Healthcare Trust, subseq. PPP Foundn), 2000–05. Trustee: Inst. of Citizenship, 2000–05; Employability Forum, 2000–09 (Chm., 2003–09); Timebank, 2001–04; Forum for the Future, 2001–11; Trng for Life, 2001–04; Care for Children Trust, 2011–13. Mem. Ct of Govs, Luton Univ., 2001–08; Gov. and Mem., Ct and Council, Imperial Coll. London, 2002–09 (Chairman: Res. Ethics Cttee, 2006–09; Student Trustee Bd, 2007–09); Lay Mem. Council, St George's, Univ. of London (formerly St George's Hosp. Med. Sch.), 2002–09 (Vice-Chm., 2007–09; Chairman: Estates Project Bd, 2006–08; Audit Cttee, 2006–09). Governor: James Allen's Girls' Sch., Dulwich, 1997–2002; King's Coll. Sch., Wimbledon, 1998–2011. Freeman, City of London, 1997; Liveryman, Co. of Inf. Technologists, 2003–14 (Mem., 1998–2014; Mem., Court of Assistants, 2003–05). CCMI (CIMgt 2001; Mem. Bd of Companions, 2002–11); FRSA 1993; FCGI 2008; FIC 2010. Hon. Mem., Faculty of Divinity, Cambridge Univ., 1998–. Dehejia Fellow, Sidwell Friends Sch., Washington, DC, 2008. Hon. LLD Bristol, 2002; Hon. DLitt Nottingham Trent, 2003; DUniv Middlesex, 2003. *Publications:* Sari 'n' Chips, 1993; Karma 'n' Chips, 1994; Chapatis for Tea, 1994; Lions, Princesses and Gurus, 1996; The UK Maharajahs, 1997; Hinduism: a way of life, 1997; Building on Success: the South Asian contribution to UK competitiveness, 1997; (jtly) How Would Jesus Vote?, 2001; The British and How to Deal With Them: doing business with Britain's ethnic communities, 2001; various reports and lectures. *Recreations:* music, current affairs, swimming. *Address:* 14 The Causeway, Sutton, Surrey SM2 5RS.

GIELGUD, Maina; free-lance ballerina; ballet producer; guest répétiteur; *b* 14 Jan. 1945; *d* of late Lewis Gielgud and Elisabeth Grussner, (stage name, Zita Sutton). *Educ:* BEPC (French). Ballet du Marquis de Cuevas, 1962–63; Ballet Classique de France, 1965–67; Ballet du XXème Siècle, Maurice Béjart, 1967–72; London Festival Ballet, 1972–77; Royal Ballet, 1977–78; free-lance, 1978–; rehearsal director, London City Ballet, 1981–82; Artistic Dir, Australian Ballet, 1983–96; Dir, Royal Danish Ballet, Copenhagen, 1997–99; Artistic Associate, Houston Ballet, 2003–05; Artistic Advr, Hungarian Nat. Ballet, 2015–. Guest Répétiteur and Artistic Advisor: English National Ballet; Tokyo Ballet; Béjart Ballet, Lausanne; Ballet du Rhin; Boston Ballet; Munich Ballet; Paris Opera Ballet; Australian Ballet; guest teacher and coach: WA Ballet, 2014; Qld Ballet, 2014, 2015; Australian Ballet, 2014, 2015; Ellison Ballet, NY, 2014, 2015; Tokyo Ballet, 2015; American Ballet Th., 2015. Hon. AO 1991. Staged: Don Quixote, Australian Ballet, 1984, Royal Danish Ballet, 1998, Boston Ballet, 2011; (also prod.) Giselle, Australian Ballet, 1984 and 2015, Boston Ballet, 2002, Ballet du Rhin, 2003, Houston Ballet, 2005; Song of a Wayfarer, Australian Ballet, 1985, Nat. Ballet of Canada, 2011; Suite en Blanc, Australian Ballet, 1984, Houston Ballet, 2005, Hong Kong Ballet, 2008, English Nat. Ballet, 2011–12, San Francisco Ballet, 2013; (also prod., with additional choreography) The Sleeping Beauty, Australian Ballet, 1985; Four Last Songs, Paris Opera, 2007; Les Sylphides, English Nat. Ballet, 2011; Spectre de la Rose, English Nat. Ballet, 2011; Coppelia, Australian Conservatoire of Ballet, 2015. *Address:* 1/9 Stirling Court, 3 Marshall Street, W1F 9BD. *T:* (020) 7734 6612.

GIEVE, Sir (Edward) John (Watson), KCB 2005 (CB 1999); Chairman, VocaLink, since 2009; *b* 20 Feb. 1950; *s* of late David Watson Gieve, OBE and Susan Gieve; *m* 1972, Katherine Vereker; two *s*. *Educ:* Charterhouse; New Coll., Oxford (BA PPE, BPhil). Dept of Employment, 1974–78; HM Treasury: Principal, Industrial Policy Div., 1979–81; Energy Div., 1981–82; Private Sec., 1982–84; Investment Controller, Investors in Industry, 1984–86 (on secondment); Public Expenditure Survey Div., 1986–88; Press Sec., 1988–89; Principal Private Sec. to Chancellor of the Exchequer, 1989–91; Under Sec., Banking Gp, 1991–94; Dep. Dir, then Dir, Budget and Public Finances, 1994–98; Dir, then Man. Dir, Public Services, 1998–2001; Man. Dir, Finance, Regulation and Industry, 2001; Permanent Under-Sec. of State, Home Office, 2001–05; Dep. Gov., Bank of England, 2006–09. Non-exec. Dir, Homerton Univ. Hosp. NHS Foundn Trust, 2011–; Independent Director: CLS Gp Hldgs, 2012–; Morgan Stanley Internat., 2012–. Chm., Clore Social Leadership Prog., 2010–14. Trustee, NESTA, 2012– (non-exec. Dir, 2011). Vis. Prof., UCL, 2012–. *Recreations:* golf (playing), football (watching).

GIFFARD, Sir (Charles) Sydney (Rycroft), KCMG 1984 (CMG 1976); HM Diplomatic Service, retired; *b* 30 Oct. 1926; *s* of Walter Giffard and Minna Giffard (*née* Cotton); *m* 1st, 1951, Wendy Vidal (marr. diss. 1976); one *s* one *d*; 2nd, 1976, Hazel Roberts, OBE. *Educ:* Repton Sch.; Wadham Coll., Oxford (Hon. Fellow, 1991). Served in Japan, 1952; Foreign Office, 1957; Berne, 1961; Tokyo, 1964; Counsellor, FCO, 1968; Royal Coll. of Defence Studies, 1971; Counsellor, Tel Aviv, 1972; Minister in Tokyo, 1975–80; Ambassador to Switzerland, 1980–82; Dep. Under-Sec. of State, FCO, 1982–84; Ambassador to Japan, 1984–86. Grand Cordon, Order of the Rising Sun (Japan), 2003. *Publications:* Japan Among the Powers 1890–1990, 1994; (ed) Guns, Kites and Horses, 2003. *Address:* Flat 2, Hays Park, Sedgehill, Shaftesbury, Dorset SP7 9JR. *Club:* Lansdowne.

GIFFARD, John William, CBE 2003; QPM 1997; DL; Chief Constable, Staffordshire Police, 1996–2006; *b* 25 March 1952; *s* of late Peter Richard de Longueville Giffard and of (Mary) Roana (Borwick) Giffard; *m* 1978, Crescent Vail; two *s*. *Educ:* Eton; Univ. of Southampton (BA Hons 1973). With Staffordshire Police, 1973–91: Grad. Entrant 1973; Chief Supt, 1991; Asst Chief Constable, N Yorks Police, 1991–96. Mem. Court, Drapers' Co., 2007–. DL Staffs, 1999. *Recreations:* cricket, shooting, bridge. *Address:* Chillington Hall, Codsall Wood, Wolverhampton WV8 1RE. *T:* (01902) 850236. *Clubs:* MCC, I Zingari; Staffs Gents Cricket, Yorks Gents Cricket.

GIFFARD, Sir Sydney; *see* Giffard, Sir C. S. R.

GIFFORD, family name of **Baron Gifford**.

GIFFORD, 6th Baron *cr* 1824; **Anthony Maurice Gifford;** QC 1982; Barrister at Law, practising since 1966; Attorney-at-Law, Jamaica, since 1990; *b* 1 May 1940; *s* of 5th Baron Gifford and Lady Gifford (*née* Margaret Allen) (*d* 1990), Sydney, NSW; *S* father, 1961; *m* 1st, 1965, Katherine Ann (marr. diss. 1988), *o d* of Dr Mundy; one *s* one *d*; 2nd, 1988, Elean Roslyn (marr. diss. 1998), *d* of Bishop David Thomas, Kingston, Jamaica; one *d*; 3rd, 1998, Tina Natalia Goulbourne, Kingston, Jamaica. *Educ:* Winchester Coll. (scholar); King's Coll., Cambridge (scholar; BA 1961). Student at Middle Temple, 1959–62, called to the Bar, 1962. Sen. Partner, Gifford Thompson & Bright, Jamaica, 1991–. Chairman: Cttee for Freedom in Mozambique, Angola and Guiné, 1968–75; Mozambique Angola Cttee, 1982–90; Mem., Nat. Cttee on Reparations, Jamaica, 2009–. Chairman: N Kensington Neighbourhood Law Centre, 1974–77 (Hon. Sec., 1970–74); Legal Action Gp, 1978–83; Vice-Chm., Defence and Aid Fund (UK), 1983–94. Pres., Cttee for Human Rights, Grenada, 1987–; Vice-Pres., Haldane Soc. of Socialist Lawyers, 1986–. Chairman: Broadwater Farm Inquiry, 1986; Liverpool 8 Inquiry, 1988–89. *Publications:* Where's the Justice?, 1986; The Passionate Advocate, 2007. *Heir:* *s* Hon. Thomas Adam Gifford, *b* 1 Dec. 1967. *Address:* 122–126 Tower Street, Kingston, Jamaica. *T:* 922 6056, *Fax:* 967 0225; 1 MCB, Third Floor, 15 New Bridge Street, EC4V 6AU. *T:* (020) 7452 8900, *Fax:* (020) 7452 8999. *E:* anthony.gifford@btinternet.com.

GIFFORD, Andrew Graham; Partner, Gifford & Partners, since 2002; adviser to British record industry, since 1982; *b* 3 Feb. 1953; *s* of Charles Henry Pearson Gifford, OBE and Laetitia Gifford (*née* Lyell), MBE; *m* 1990, Charlotte Montrésor; four *s*. *Educ:* Bedales; Edinburgh Univ. (BSc). Personal Assistant: to Rt Hon. David Steel, MP, 1975–76; office of Leader of Liberal Party, 1976–80; ran election tours for Leader of Liberal Party, 1979, and of Lib Dem Party, 1983 and 1987. Founder Partner and Chief Exec., GJW Govt Relns, 1980–2002; Founder Director: 4th Estate Publishing, 1983–2000; Heritage Oil & Gas, 1989–95; Director: Fleming Mid Cap Investment Trust, 1994–2005; Second London American Growth, 1997–; Moneyweek mag., 2000–02. Founder Chm., Assoc. of Professional Political Consultants, 1989–95. Hon. Treas., Green Alliance, 1990–2002. *Publications:* Handbook of World Development, 1985. *Recreations:* fishing, shooting. *Clubs:* Beefsteak; New (Edinburgh).

GIFFORD, Michael John; HM Diplomatic Service; Counsellor, Foreign and Commonwealth Office, from Jan. 2016; *b* 2 April 1961; *s* of Henry Gifford and Gladys Mary Gifford (*née* Culverhouse); *m* 1986, Patricia Anne Owen; one *s* one *d*. *Educ:* Hastings Grammar Sch. Entered FCO, 1981; Arabic lang. trng, SOAS, 1982–83; Third Sec. (Commercial), Abu Dhabi, 1983–87; Second Sec. (Chancery), Oslo, 1988–90; on loan to Secretariat-Gen., EC, Brussels, 1990; Second, later First, Sec., FCO, 1991–93; First Secretary: (Econ.), Riyadh, 1993–97; FCO, 1997–2000; Counsellor and Dep. Hd of Mission, Cairo, 2001–04; Ambassador, Yemen, 2004–07; Counsellor, FCO, 2007–12; Ambassador to Democratic People's Republic of Korea, 2012–15. *Recreations:* reading, family. *Address:* c/o Foreign and Commonwealth Office, King Charles Street, SW1A 2AH.

GIFFORD, Sir (Michael) Roger, Kt 2014; UK Country Head (formerly UK Country Manager), SEB, since 2000; Lord Mayor of London, 2012–13; *b* St Andrews, 3 Aug. 1955; *s* of late Douglas John and Hazel Mary Gifford; *m* 1st, 1983, Jane Lunzer (marr. diss. 2004); three *s* one *d* (and one *d* decd); 2nd, 2008, Clare Taylor. *Educ:* Sedbergh; Trinity Coll., Oxford (MA Hons). SG Warburg & Co. Ltd, 1978–82; SEB: Corp. Finance, then Primary Debt, later Equity Capital Markets, Enskilda Securities, 1982–90; Hd, Debt Capital Markets, 1990–93; Hd, London Br., 1992–94; Hd, Tokyo Br., 1994–99. Chairman: Swedish Chamber of Commerce UK, 2003–07; Assoc. of Foreign Banks UK, 2007–11. Alderman, Cordwainer Ward, 2004–; Sheriff, City of London, 2008–09. Liveryman: Co. of Musicians, 2005–; Co. of Internat. Bankers, 2005–; Sponsoring Alderman, Guild of PR Practitioners, 2007–. Mem., City of London Br., Royal Soc. of St George. Trustee: St Paul's Cath. Foundn, 2006–; St Paul's Cath. Choir Sch., 2006–12; Barbican Centre Trust, 2014–; Governor: Summer Fields Sch., Oxford, 2001–07; King Edward's Sch., Witley, 2005–; Bridewell Hosp., 2005–. Chairman: English Chamber Orch. and Music Soc., 2001–; From Sweden Fest., 2004–06; Sibelius and Beyond Fest., 2007; Tenebrae Choir, 2011–; City Music Foundn, 2012–. Hon. LLD St Andrews; Hon. DSc City. Comdr, Order of Polar Star (Sweden), 2007; Comdr, Order of the Lion (Finland), 2011. *Recreations:* chamber music, singing, walking. *Address:* Ayton House, Perth; 40 Inverness Street, NW1 7HB; Ware House, Lyme Regis. *E:* roger.gifford@seb.co.uk. *Clubs:* Garrick; Royal Perth.

GIL-ROBLES GIL-DELGADO, José María; Member, European Parliament, 1989–2004 (President, 1997–99); *b* 17 June 1935; *m* 1963, Magdalena Casanueva (*d* 1999); *m* 2001, Rosario. *Educ:* Univ. of Deusto; Univ. of Salamanca. Legal Advr, Spanish Parlt, 1958; barrister, Madrid, Barcelona, Bilbao and Salamanca, 1959; Lectr in Law, Univ. of Complutense, 1959; Comité Director, Fedn of Christian Democrats, Spain, 1972. European Parliament: Pres., Institutional Affairs Cttee, 1991; Vice-Pres., 1994. President: European Movt Internat., 1999–2005; European Parlt Former Mems Assoc., 2006–09; Jean Monnet European Foundn, 2009–14. Mem., Royal Acad. of Econ. and Financial Scis, Barcelona. Freeman, City of Salamanca, 1998. Hon. Fellow, Catholic Univ. of Chile, 1998. Dr *hc* State Inst. for Internat. Relations, Moscow, 1998. Robert Schuman Medal; Gold Medal, City of Athens; Order of Francisco Morazán (Central American Parlt), 1997; Silver Medal of Galicia, 2000. Medalla del Mérito Agrícola (Spain); Grand Cross, Order of Isabel la Católica (Spain), 2000; Order of European Merit (Spain), 2006; Medal of the Republic (Uruguay), 1998; Grand Cross: Order of Merit (Chile), 1998; Order of Liberator San Martin (Argentina), 1998; Order Antonio José de Irizarri (Guatemala), 1999; Officer, Legion of Honour (France), 2000. *Publications:* Derecho de huelga, 1961; Commentarios a la ley de arrendamientos rústicos, 1981; Legislación agraria básica, 1986; Control y autonomías, 1986; Los derechos del europeo, 1993; Los Parlamentos de Europa y el Parlamento Europeo, 1997; Pasión por Europa, 2002. *Recreations:* reading, golf.

GILBART, Hon. Sir Andrew James, Kt 2014; **Hon. Mr Justice Gilbart;** a Judge of the High Court of Justice, Queen's Bench Division, since 2014; *b* 13 Feb. 1950; *s* of late Albert Thomas Gilbart and Carol Christie Gilbart, Vinehall Sch., Robertsbridge, Sussex; *m* 1st, 1979, Morag Williamson (marr. diss. 2001); one *s* one *d*; 2nd, 2003, Paula Doone Whittell; two step *s* one step *d*. *Educ:* Westminster Sch.; Trinity Hall, Cambridge (MA). Called to the Bar, Middle Temple, 1972, Bencher, 2000; elected to Northern Circuit, 1973; QC 1991; Hd of Chambers, Kings Chambers, Manchester and Leeds, 2001–04. An Asst Recorder, 1992–96; a Recorder, 1996–2004; a Circuit Judge, 2004–13; a Dep. High Court Judge (Admin. Court), 2004–14; a Sen. Circuit Judge, Hon. Recorder of Manchester and Resident Judge, Manchester Crown Ct, 2008–13. Member: Restricted Patients Presidents Panel, Mental Health Review Tribunal, 2000–06; Lands Tribunal, 2006–08. Member: Planning and Envmt Bar Assoc. (formerly Local Govt, Planning and Envmtl Bar Assoc.), 1986–2004 (Mem. Cttee, 1988–92); UK Envmtl Law Assoc., 1996–2004; Admin. Law Bar Assoc., 1999–; Eur. Circuit of the Bar, 2002–04; Internat. Associate Mem., Amer. Bar Assoc., 1994–2004. *Publications:* articles in Jl of Planning and Environment Law and Local Govt Chronicle. *Recreations:* history, walking, theatre, computers, all music (and especially blues), enjoying the Ariège. *Address:* Royal Courts of Justice, Strand, WC2A 2LL.

GILBART-DENHAM, Lt-Col Sir Seymour (Vivian), KCVO 2002 (CVO 1994); Crown Equerry, 1987–2002, an Extra Equerry to the Queen, since 2002; *b* 10 Oct. 1939; *s* of Major Vivian Vandeleur Gilbart-Denham (killed in action, Narvik, 1940), Irish Guards and Diana Mary Beaumont; *m* 1976, Patricia Caroline, *e d* of Lt Col and Mrs Granville Brooking; two *d*. Commissioned, Life Guards, 1960; served UK, Germany, Cyprus and Far East; Adjutant, Life Guards, 1965–67; commanded Household Cavalry Regt, 1986–87. Vice-President: Royal Windsor Horse Show, 1988–; Royal Parks Equitation Trust, 1992–2002; Gtr London Region, Riding for the Disabled, 1994–2002; Pres., Coaching Club, 2001–02. Freeman, City of London, 1988. *Recreations:* golf, gardening. *Address:* Trinity House, 8 Trinity Street, Bungay, Suffolk NR35 1EH. *Club:* White's.

GILBERD, Rt Rev. Bruce Carlyle, CNZM 2002; Bishop of Auckland, 1985–94; Chaplain, King's School, Remuera, 1997–2000; retired; *b* 22 April 1938; *s* of Carlyle Bond Gilberd and Dorothy Annie Gilberd; *m* 1963, Patricia Molly Tanton; two *s* one *d*. *Educ:* King's College, Auckland; Auckland Univ. (BSc); St John's Coll., Auckland (LTh Hons, STh). Deacon 1962, priest 1963, Auckland; Assistant Curate: Devonport, 1962–64; Ponsonby and Grey Lynn, 1965; Panmure, 1965–68; Vicar of Avondale, 1968–71; trainee Industrial Chaplain, Tees-side Industrial Mission, and Asst Curate of Egglescliffe, 1971–73; visited industrial missions in UK and Europe; Director, Interchurch Trade and Industrial Mission, Wellington, 1973–79; founding Mem., Wellington Industrial Relations Soc.; Hon. Asst Curate, Lower Hutt 1973–77, Waiwhetu 1977–79; Lectr, St John's Coll., Auckland, 1980–85; Priest-in-charge, Albany Greenhithe Mission Dist, 1995, St Thomas, Tamaki, 1996, dio. of Auckland. Pres., Christian Res. Assoc., Aotearoa, NZ, 1996–2000; Vice-Pres., Home and Family Soc., 1986–. Mem. Gen. Synod, NZ. Has travelled widely in UK, Europe, China, USA, S Africa and Pacific. NZ Commemorative Medal, 1990. *Publications:* (ed) Christian Ministry: a definition, 1984; (with Richard Whitfield) Taproots for Transformation, 2006; Future Focus, 2007; Life - is there more?, 2011; Guarding Paaku Bay, 2012; Ka the Falcon. *Recreations:* fishing, surfing, travel, reading, writing, golf. *Address:* 81 Manaia Road, Tairua, 3508, New Zealand.

GILBERT; *see* Proesch, G.

GILBERT OF PANTEG, Baron *cr* 2015 (Life Peer), of Panteg in the County of Monmouthshire; **Stephen Gilbert;** Deputy Chairman, Conservative Party, since 2015. Political Sec. to the Prime Minister, 2010–15. *Address:* Conservative and Unionist Party, 4 Matthew Parker Street, SW1H 9HQ.

GILBERT, Prof. Fiona Jane, FRCR, FRCPE, FRCPGlas; Professor of Radiology, University of Cambridge, since 2011; *b* Edinburgh, 1 May 1956; *d* of Dr John Knight Davidson and Edith Elizabeth Davidson; *m* 1982, Martin James Gilbert, *qv*; one *s* two *d*. *Educ:* Hutchesons' Girls' Grammar Sch., Glasgow; Univ. of Glasgow (MB ChB 1978); Univ. of Aberdeen (DMRD 1984). MRCP 1981; FRCR 1986; FRCPGlas 1991; FRCPE 1994. Consultant Radiologist, Aberdeen Royal Infirmary, 1989–96; University of Aberdeen: Hon. Sen. Lectr, 1989–96; Prof. of Radiol. and Hd, Dept of Radiol., 1996–2006; Hd, Imaging Res. Prog., 2006–11; Clin. Dir, NE Scotland Breast Screening Prog., 1989–2001. Chairman: RCR Breast Gp, 2009–11; Academic Cttee, RCR, 2010–. Mem. Bd, Royal Scottish Nat. Orch., 2002–08. Gov., Robert Gordon's Coll., Aberdeen, 1998–2011. *Publications:* articles in New England Jl of Medicine, Lancet Oncol., Health Technol. Assessment. *Recreations:* ski-ing, sailing, classical music. *Address:* Department of Radiology, University of Cambridge, Box 218, Level 5, Addenbrooke's Hospital, Hills Road, Cambridge CB2 0QQ. *T:* (01223) 336890, *Fax:* (01223) 330915.

GILBERT, Francis Humphrey Shubrick; QC 1992; **His Honour Judge Gilbert;** a Circuit Judge, since 2001; *b* 25 Jan. 1946; *s* of late Comdr Walter Raleigh Gilbert, RN, DL, Compton Castle, Devon and Joan Mary Boileau Gilbert; *m* 1975, Sarah Marian Kaye, *d* of late Col Douglas Kaye, DSO, DL, Brinkley Hall, Newmarket; one *s* two *d*. *Educ:* Stowe; Trinity Coll., Dublin (MA). Called to the Bar, Lincoln's Inn, 1970, Bencher, 2000. A Recorder, 1994–2001; Hd of Chambers, 1995–2001; Res. Judge, Plymouth Crown Court, 2006–12; Recorder of Exeter, 2012–. Devon County Councillor, 1977–85. Pres., Pegasus Club, 2001. *Recreations:* sailing, shooting and gardening. *Address:* Exeter Combined Court, Southernhay Gardens, Exeter EX1 1UH. *Club:* Royal Yacht Squadron.

GILBERT, Rt Rev. Hugh; *see* Aberdeen, Bishop of, (RC).

GILBERT, Ian Grant; Under Secretary, International Relations Division, Department of Health and Social Security, 1979–85; retired; *b* Kikuyu, Kenya, 18 June 1925; *s* of Captain Alexander Grant Gilbert, DCM, indust. missionary, Lossiemouth and Kenya, and Marion Patrick Cruickshank; *m* 1st, 1960, Heather Margaret Donald, PhD (*d* 1999) (biographer of Lord Mount Stephen), *y d* of Rev. Francis Cantlie and Mary Donald, Lumphanan, Aberdeenshire; 2nd, 2001, Mrs Shirley Ann Parr. *Educ:* Fordyce Acad., Banffshire; Royal High Sch. of Edinburgh; Univ. of Edinburgh (MA 1950). Served HM Forces (Captain Indian Artillery), 1943–47. Entered Home Civil Service as Asst Principal and joined Min. of National Insurance, 1950; Private Sec. to Perm. Sec., 1953, and to Parly Sec., 1955; Principal, Min. of Pensions and Nat. Insce, 1956; seconded to HM Treasury, 1962–66; Asst Sec., Min. of Social Security (later DHSS), 1967; Head of War and Civilian Disabled Branches, DHSS, 1974–79. UK Member: Social Security, Health and Social Affairs Cttees, Council of Europe, Strasbourg, 1979–85; EEC Adv. Cttee on Social Security for Migrant Workers, Brussels, 1979–85; UK Delegate, Governing Body, Internat. Soc. Security Assoc., Geneva, 1979–85; Mem., UK Delegn to World Health Assembly, Geneva, 1983–84; Clerk/Advr to Select Cttee on European Legislation, House of Commons, 1987–90. Hon. Treasurer, Presbytery of England (Church of Scotland), 1965–77; Session Clerk, Crown Court Ch. of Scotland, Covent Garden, 1975–80. A Ch. of Scotland Mem., The Churches Main Cttee, 1986–2002. Chm., Caledonian Christian Club, 1984–86. Clerk to Govs, St Gregory's Sch., Marnhull, 1991–2002. *Recreations:* keeping half-an-acre in good heart, local and natural history, choral singing, France. *Address:* Wellpark, Moorside, Sturminster Newton, Dorset DT10 1HJ. *T:* (01258) 820306.

GILBERT, Air Chief Marshal Sir Joseph (Alfred), KCB 1985 (CB 1983); CBE 1974; Deputy Commander-in-Chief, Allied Forces Central Europe, 1986–89; retired; *b* 15 June 1931; *s* of late Ernest and Mildred Gilbert; *m* 1955, Betty, *yr d* of late William and Eva Lishman; two *d*. *Educ:* William Hulme's Sch., Manchester; Univ. of Leeds (BA Hons, Econ. and Pol Science; Hon. LLD 1989). Commnd into RAF, 1952; Fighter Sqdns, 1953–61; Air Secretary's Dept, 1961–63; RAF Staff Coll., 1964; CO 92 (Lightning) Sqdn, 1965–67; jssc 1968; Sec., Defence Policy Staff, and Asst Dir of Defence Policy, 1968–71; CO, RAF Coltishall, 1971–73; RCDS, 1974; Dir of Forward Policy (RAF), 1975; ACAS (Policy), MoD, 1975–77; AOC 38 Group, 1977–80; ACDS (Policy), 1980–82; Asst Chief of Staff (Policy), SHAPE, 1983–84; Dep. C-in-C, RAF Strike Command, 1984–86. Vice Chm., Commonwealth War Graves Commn, 1993–98 (Comr, 1991–98); Trustee, Imperial War Mus., 1997–2002. Life Vice-Pres., RAFA, 1995. *Publications:* articles in defence jls. *Recreations:* grandchildren, Rugby, strategic affairs. *Address:* Brook House, Salisbury Road, Shrewton, Salisbury, Wiltshire SP3 4EQ. *T:* (01980) 620627. *Club:* Royal Air Force.

GILBERT, Martin James, CA; Chief Executive, Aberdeen Asset Management PLC, since 1991; *b* 13 July 1955; *m* 1982, Prof. Fiona Jane Davidson (*see* F. J. Gilbert); one *s* two *d*. *Educ:* Robert Gordon's Coll.; Aberdeen Univ. (MA, LLB). CA 1983. Deloitte Haskins & Sells, 1978–82; Brander & Cruickshank, 1982–83; Director: Aberdeen Asian Smaller Co. Investment Trust, 1995–; FirstBus, then FirstGroup, 1995–2013 (non-exec. Chm., 2000–13); Aberdeen Global, 1998; Aberdeen Asia Pacific Income Fund, 2000. Non-exec. Dir, Sky (formerly BSkyB), 2011–. Chm., Prudential Regulation Authy Practitioner Panel, 2013–; Member: Internat. Adv. Panel, Monetary Authy of Singapore, 2013; Financial Services Trade and Investment Bd, 2013–15. Jun. Vice-Pres., ICAS, 2002–03. *Recreations:* golf, ski-ing, sailing. *Address:* Aberdeen Asset Management PLC, 10 Queens Terrace, Aberdeen AB10 1YG. *Clubs:* Royal Thames Yacht; Gordonians Hockey (Aberdeen); Leander; Royal & Ancient Golf (St Andrews); Royal Aberdeen Golf; Wimbledon Golf; Royal Selangor Golf; Deeside Golf; Loch Lomond Golf.

GILBERT, Rev. Canon Roger Geoffrey; Rector of Falmouth, 1986–2002; Chaplain to the Queen, 1995–2002; *b* 18 June 1937; *s* of Geoffrey and Ruth Gilbert; *m* 1965, Marie-Pascale (*née* Berthelot); three *d*. *Educ:* Truro Secondary Modern Sch. for Boys; St Peter's Coll., Birmingham; King's Coll. London (BD; AKC); St Augustine's Coll., Canterbury. RAF, 1957–59. Asst Master, Hinchley Wood Sch., 1963–67; ordained deacon, 1970, priest, 1971; Asst Curate, Walton-on-Thames, 1970–74; Licensed to Officiate, Dio. of Europe, 1973–; Rector, St Mabyn with Helland, 1974–81; Priest-in-charge, Madron with Morvah, 1981–86. Hon. Canon of Truro Cathedral, 1994–2002, now Emeritus; Rural Dean of Carnmarth South, 1994–2000. Fellow, Woodard Corp., 1988–2002. *Recreations:* travel, Cornish-Breton history and culture, post-Impressionist painters, antiques, books. *Address:* 2 rue de Plouzon, 22690 Pleudihen-sur-Rance, Brittany, France. *T:* (2) 96882869.

GILBERT, Stephen; *b* Truro, 6 Nov. 1976. *Educ:* Fowey Community Sch.; St Austell Coll.; Univ. of Wales, Aberystwyth (BSc Econ Internat. Politics); London Sch. of Econs and Pol Sci. (MSc Internat. Relns). Parly asst to Lembit Öpik, MP, 1998; res. and media asst to Robin Teverson, MEP, 1998–99; Account Exec., PPS, 2000–02; Public Affairs Manager: IMA, 2002–04; Fidelity Investments, 2004–05; Account Manager, Deborah Clark Associates, 2005–07. Member (Lib Dem): Restormel BC, 1998–2002; Haringey LBC, 2002–06. MP (Lib Dem) St Austell and Newquay, 2010–15; contested (Lib Dem) same seat, 2015. Mem., Communities and Local Govt Select Cttee, 2010–12; PPS to Sec. of State for Energy and Climate Change, 2012–13.

GILBERT, Prof. Walter; Carl M. Loeb University Professor, Department of Molecular and Cellular Biology (formerly of Cellular and Developmental Biology), Harvard University, 1985–2005, now Carl M. Loeb Professor Emeritus; Vice Chairman, Myriad Genetics Inc., since 1992; Managing Director, BioVentures Investors; *b* Boston, 21 March 1932; *s* of Richard V. Gilbert and Emma (*née* Cohen); *m* 1953, Celia Stone; one *s* one *d*. *Educ:* Harvard Coll. (AB *summa cum laude* Chem. and Phys., 1953); Harvard Univ. (AM Phys., 1954);

Cambridge Univ. (PhD Maths, 1957). National Science Foundn pre-doctoral Fellow, Harvard Univ. and Cambridge Univ., 1953–57, post-doctoral Fellow in Phys., Harvard, 1957–58; Harvard University: Asst Prof. in Phys., 1959–64; Associate Prof. of Biophys., 1964–68; Prof. of Biochem., 1968–72; Amer. Cancer Soc. Prof. of Molecular Biology, 1972–81; H. H. Timken Prof. of Science, 1986–87. Jt Founder, 1978, and Dir, 1978–84, Biogen NV (Chm. and Principal Exec. Officer, 1981–84). Guggenheim Fellow, Paris, 1968–69. Member: Amer. Acad. of Arts and Sciences, 1968; National Acad. of Sciences, 1976; Amer. Phys. Soc.; Amer. Soc. of Biol Chemists; Foreign Mem., Royal Soc., 1987–. Hon. DSc: Chicago, 1978; Columbia, 1978; Rochester, 1979; Yeshiva, 1981; Tulane, 2011. Many prizes and awards, incl. (jtly) Nobel Prize for Chemistry, 1980. *Publications:* chapters, articles and papers on theoretical physics and molecular biology, and catalogues and work on photographic art. *Address:* BioVentures Investors, 70 Walnut Street # 302, Wellesley, MA 02481, USA; 15 Gray Gardens West, Cambridge, MA 02138, USA. *T:* (617) 8648778.

GILBERTSON, Barry Gordon; Principal, Barry Gilbertson Consultancy, since 2011; President, Royal Institution of Chartered Surveyors, 2004–05; *b* 6 June 1951; *s* of Bertram David Gilbertson and Joan Marion Ivy Gilbertson (*née* Gordon); *m* 1974, Yvonne Gunning; one *s*. *Educ:* Westcliff High Sch. for Boys; Coll. of Estate Management. FRICS 1974; ACIArb 1976; Registered Property (formerly Fixed Charge) Receiver 1999–2011; Counselor of Real Estate 2000. Partner, Butler & Hatch Waterman, 1983–86; Dir, Cherrydeal Ltd, 1986–87; Man. Dir, Claridge Gp, 1988–91; Nat. Property Advr, Coopers & Lybrand, 1992–96; Partner, PricewaterhouseCoopers, 1996–2011. Vis. Prof. of Built Envmt, Univ. of Northumbria, 2003–. Mem., Bank of England Property Forum, 2003–11. Ind. non-exec. Dir and Trustee, Granite REIT (formerly MI Develts Inc., then Granite Real Estate Inc.), 2011– (Chm., Real Estate Investment Cttee, 2012–13; Chm., Compensation Cttee, 2014–); Independent non-executive Director: RONA Inc., 2013–; Custodian REIT plc, 2014– (Sen. Ind. Dir, 2014–; Chm., Mgt Engagement Cttee); non-exec. Dir, Deeley Freed Estates, 2014–. Non-exec. Consultant, Knight Frank LLP, 2011–12. Mem., UN Real Estate Adv. Gp, 2000–05 (Chm., Valuation Cttee, 2003–05). Fellow: Property Consultants Soc., 1987; Non-Administrative Receivers Assoc., 1995– (Founding Chm., 1995–96); Internat. Real Estate Fedn, 2003 (Mem., 2002–05); Founding Dep. Chm., World Assoc. of Valuation Orgns, 2002–04. Internat. Associate Ed., Counselors of Real Estate, 2006–08. Trustee, Coll. of Estate Mgt, 2006–14 (Chm., Internat. Adv. Gp, 2008–11; Chm., Business Adv. Gp, 2011–13). Vis. Prof. of Real Estate and Land Mgt, Royal Agricultural Univ., 2014–. Mem., Council and Court, Univ. of Bath, 2014–. Governor: Sidney Street Primary Sch., Folkestone, 1987–90; Westcliff High Sch. for Boys, 2007–08. Mem., Nat. Scout Adv. Bd, Scout Assoc., 1983–87. Dir, Cranmer Court Tenants (Chelsea) Ltd, 2006–12. Mem., Architecture and Planning Cttee, Bath Preservation Trust, 2015–. Trustee, Fulham FC Supporters Trust, 2012–14. FICPD 1998; MInstD 1983; FRSA 2009. Hon. Member: Assoc. of S African Quantity Surveyors, 2005; S African Council for Quantity Surveying Profession, 2005; Assoc. of Valuers in Romania, 2006; Assoc. of Property and Fixed Charge Receivers, 2010. Mem., MENSA, 1976–; Folkestone Junior Chamber of Commerce, 1975–85 (Pres., 1979; SE Regl Chm., 1985). Pres., Rotary Club of Folkestone, 2003 (Mem., 1990–2004); Mem., Committee Club, 2002– (Hon. Sec., 2009–); Chm., Property & Finance Gp, 2010–. Freeman, City of London, 1996; Liveryman, Co. of Chartered Surveyors, 1996–. *Publications:* Vision for Valuation, 2004; RICS Presidential Nuggets, 2007; (jtly) Design Economics and Sustainability, 2015; travelogues and book reviews; contrib. articles to learned jls in UK and abroad. *Recreations:* family and friends, jogging, black and white digital photography, Fulham Football Club, Bath Rugby Club, the arts and architecture (especially Georgian), fun, oh, and of course, The Archers! *Address:* 12 Gay Street, Bath, Somerset BA1 2PH. *T:* 07710 073456. *E:* barry@barrygilbertson.com.

GILBERTSON, Prof. David Dennis; Emeritus Professor, University of Wales, since 1998; *b* Stratford, London, 1 Sept. 1945; *s* of late Thomas Gilbertson and of Ivy Florence Joyce Gilbertson; *m* 1970, Barbara Mary Mitchell; one *s* two *d*. *Educ:* South West Ham Tech. Sch.; Univ. of Lancaster (BA Hons 1968); Univ. of Exeter (PGCE 1969); Univ. of Bristol (PhD 1974; DSc 1991). FGS 1983. Teacher, Pretoria Sch., London, 1964–65; Res. Asst in Geology, Univ. of Bristol, 1969–71; Lectr in Geography, Plymouth Poly., 1971–74, Univ. of Adelaide, 1974–77; Sheffield University: Lectr, 1977–85; Sen. Lectr, 1985–88; Reader, 1988–92; Prof., and Hd of Res. Sch. of Archaeology and Archaeol Scis, 1992–94; Prof. of Physical Geography, Inst. of Geography and Earth Scis, and Dir, Inst. of Earth Studies, 1994–97, Univ. of Wales, Aberystwyth, 1994–98; Prof. of Envmtl Science, Nene Centre for Res., UC Northampton, 1998–2000; Hd, Sch. of Conservation Scis, Bournemouth Univ., 2000–02. Vis. Prof. and Fulbright Schol., Univ. of Arizona, 1981–82; Munro Lectr, Edinburgh Univ., 1999; Dist. Vis. Schol., Adelaide Univ., 1999; Vis. Prof., Univ. of Plymouth, 2001–. Co-Director: UNESCO Libyan Valleys Archaeol Survey, 1988–96; Wadi Faynan Survey, Jordan, 1994–2007; Niah Caves Proj., Borneo, 1998–; Chm., Univ. of Wales Subject Panel for Envmtl Studies, 1996–98. Jt Founder and Associate Ed., Applied Geography, 1981–88; Sen. UK Ed., 1992–98, Ed. Emeritus, 2009, Jl of Archaeol Sci. J. R. Wiseman Prize, Archaeol Inst. of Amer., 2001. *Publications:* (jtly) The Pleistocene Succession at Kenn, Somerset, 1978; (jtly) In the Shadow of Extinction, 1984; Late Quaternary Environments and Man in Holderness, 1984; (jtly) Practical Ecology, 1985; (jtly) The Chronology and Environment of Early Man: a new framework, 1985; (jtly) Farming the Desert: the UNESCO Libyan Valley survey, 1996; (jtly) The Outer Hebrides: the last 14000 years, 1996; (ed jtly) The Archaeology of Drylands: living on the margins, 2000; The Human Use of Caves in Island and Peninsula South East Asia, 2005; Archaeology and Desertification, 2007; contribs to books, and papers in learned jls. *Recreations:* walking, railways—large and small, West Ham United, the Teign Estuary. *Address:* c/o School of Geography, Earth and Environmental Sciences, University of Plymouth, Drake Circus, Plymouth PL4 8AA. *E:* dave.gilbertson@plymouth.ac.uk.

GILBERTSON, David Stuart; Chairman: MLex Market Intelligence, since 2012; Gambling Compliance, since 2012; Briefing Media Ltd, since 2013; World Trade Group, since 2014; *b* 21 Sept. 1956; *s* of Donald Stuart Gilbertson and Jocelyn Mary Gilbertson (*née* Sim); *m* 1991, Danielle Donougher; one *s* one *d*. *Educ:* Trinity Hall, Cambridge (BA 1978). Editl and mgt posts with Metal Bulletin, Reuters and Reed Elsevier; joined LLP, 1987: Ed., Lloyd's List, 1987–94; Dir, 1992–96; Chief Exec., 1997–98; Chief Exec., 1998–2004, Man. Dir, 2004–07, Informa Gp plc; Chief Executive: Informa plc, 2007–08; EMAP plc, 2008–11. Non-exec. Dir, Sigaria, 2012–; Sen. Ind. Dir, Tarsus Gp, 2014–; Chairman: Green Power Conferences, 2012–; Old St Labs, 2014–. Business Gov., City and Islington Coll., 2011–. FRSA. *Recreations:* sport, especially football.

GILBERTSON, Ven. Dr Michael Robert; Archdeacon of Chester, since 2010; *b* Stockport, 18 Aug. 1961; *s* of late John and Beryl Gilbertson; *m* 1985, Jenny Gates; two *s*. *Educ:* Stockport Grammar Sch.; New Coll., Oxford (BA Hons 1982; MA 1992); St John's Coll., Durham (BA Hons 1993; PhD 1997). Department of Trade and Industry: Admin trainee, 1982–84; Higher Exec. Officer (Develt), Regl Policy Div. and Cabinet Office, 1984–85; Private Sec. to Sec. of State for Trade and Industry, 1985–87; Principal, Eur. Policy Div., 1987–89, Radiocommunications Agency, 1989–91; ordained deacon, 1997, priest, 1998; Curate, St Matthew's, Surbiton, 1997–2000; Vicar, All Saints, Stranton, Hartlepool, 2000–10; Area Dean of Hartlepool, 2002–10. Non-residentiary Canon, Durham Cathedral, 2008–10. Dir, Grove Bks Ltd, 1997–2000; Ed., Anvil, 1998–2003. *Publications:* God and History in the Book of Revelation: New Testament studies in dialogue with Pannenberg and Moltmann, 2003. *Recreations:* music, watching sport, hill-walking, cooking. *Address:* c/o Church House, 5500 Daresbury Park, Daresbury, Cheshire WA4 4GE. *T:* (01928) 718834.

GILBEY, family name of **Baron Vaux of Harrowden**.

GILBEY, Sir (Walter) Gavin, 4th Bt *cr* 1893, of Elsenham Hall, Essex; *b* 14 April 1949; *s* of Sir (Walter) Derek Gilbey, 3rd Bt and of Elizabeth Mary, *d* of Col K. G. Campbell; *S* father, 1991, but his name does not yet appear on the Official Roll of the Baronetage; *m* 1st, 1980, Mary (marr. diss. 1984), *d* of late William E. E. Pacetti; 2nd, 1984, Anna (marr. diss. 1995), *d* of Edmund Prosser. *Educ:* Eton. *Clubs:* Army and Navy; Royal Dornoch Golf.

GILCHRIST, Andrew Charles; National Education Officer, Rail, Maritime and Transport Union, since 2010; *b* 5 Dec. 1960; *s* of late Edward Gilchrist and of Shirley Gilchrist; *m* 1985, Loretta Borman; one *s* one *d*. *Educ:* Bedford Modern Sch. Bedfordshire Fire Service, 1979–96; Mem., Exec. Council, 1993–2000, Nat. Officer, 1996–2000, Gen. Sec., 2000–05, Fire Bde Union; UK Co-ordinator: Service Employees Internat. Union, 2006–08; Internat. Brotherhood Teamsters, 2006–08; Project Manager, 2008, Internat. Progs Co-ordinator, 2009–10, Unite. Mem., Gen. Council, TUC 2000–05 (Mem., Exec. Cttee, 2004–05). *Recreations:* global politics, classical history, aquariums. *E:* painewon@msn.com.

GILCHRIST, Archibald, OBE 1996; Managing Director, 1971–79, and Chairman, 1978–79, Govan Shipbuilders; *b* 17 Dec. 1929; *m* 1958, Elizabeth Jean Greenlees; two *s* one *d*. *Educ:* Loretto; Pembroke Coll., Cambridge (MA). Barclay Curle & Co. Ltd, Glasgow, 1954–64, various managerial posts; ultimately Dir, Swan Hunter Group; Brown Bros & Co. Ltd, Edinburgh, 1964–72: Dep. Man. Dir, 1964; Man. Dir, 1969; Man. Dir, Vosper Private, Singapore, 1980–86; Dir, Management Search Internat. Ltd, 1986–89; Pt-time Bd Mem., Scottish Legal Aid Bd, 1986–96; non-executive Director: F. J. C. Lilley plc, 1987–93; RMJM Ltd, 1988–98; Scottish Friendly Assurance Soc. Ltd (formerly Glasgow Friendly Soc.), 1988–2000; Caledonian MacBrayne Ltd, 1990–97. Mem., BBC Council for Scotland, 1990–95. Vice Chm., Royal Scottish National (formerly Royal Scottish) Orchestra, 1989–94 (Dir, 1987–94). Former Chm., Cargilfield Sch.; Chm. Council, St Leonard's Sch., 1989–95; Gov., Glasgow Polytechnic, 1987–93. *Recreations:* golf, shooting, fishing, music. *Address:* Inchmaholm, 35 Barnton Avenue, Edinburgh EH4 6JJ. *Club:* Hon. Company of Edinburgh Golfers.

GILCHRIST, Maj. Gen. Peter, CB 2004; non-executive Chairman: Push Technology Ltd, since 2009; Enterprise Control Systems Ltd, since 2012; Director, Synergie Business Ltd, since 2009; *b* 28 Feb. 1952; *s* of late Col David A. Gilchrist and of Rosemary Gilchrist (*née* Drewe); *m* 1981, Sarah-Jane Poyntz; one *s* one *d*. *Educ:* Marlborough Coll.; Sandhurst. Commnd Royal Tank Regiment, 1972; Troop Leader, 3RTR, Germany and NI, 1972–76; aic 1977; Schools Gunnery Instructor, Lulworth, 1978–80; Ops Officer and Adjutant, 3RTR, 1980–82; Div. II, Army Staff Course (psc†), 1983–84; COS, 20th Armd Bde, 1985–87; Comdr, Ind. Recce Sqn, Cyprus, 1986; Sqn Comdr (Challenger), 3RTR, 1988; Mil. Sec.'s Staff, 1989; Directing Staff, RMCS, 1990–93; CO, 1 RTR, 1993–95; HCSC, 1996; Dep. DOR (Armour and Combat Support Vehicles), 1996–98; Prog. Dir, Armd Systems, MoD PE, 1998–2000; Exec. Dir, 2000–04, Tech. Dir, 2004, Defence Procurement Agency, and Master Gen. of the Ordnance; Dep. Comdr Combined Forces Comd, Afghanistan, 2004–05; Defence Attaché, Washington, and Hd, British Defence Staff, USA, 2005–08; retd 2009. Col Comdt, RAC, 2000–04; Dep. Col Comdt, RTR, 2000–08. Non-executive Director: DERA Facilities Bd, 2000–01; DSTL, 2001–04; Ricardo plc, 2010– (Chm., Remuneration Cttee, 2013–); Anova Power BV, 2015–; Chm., Electranet Gp Ltd, 2010–12. Chm., Tank Mus., 2010–. Bronze Star Medal (USA), 2006. *Recreations:* sailing, ski-ing, field sports, gardening, DIY. *Address:* Chapel Cottage, Netherhope Lane, Tidenham, Chepstow, Mon NP16 7JD. *Club:* Army and Navy.

GILCHRIST, Prof. Roberta Lynn, DPhil; FSA; FBA 2008; Professor of Archaeology, University of Reading, since 1996; *b* 28 June 1965; *d* of John James Gilchrist and Gail Ann Foreman (*née* Campbell); *m* 2000, Dr John Miles Preston. *Educ:* Univ. of York (BA 1986; DPhil 1990). MCIfA (MIFA 1990). Lectr, UEA, 1990–95; Archaeologist, Norwich Cathedral, 1993–2005. Ed., World Archaeol., 1997–2006; Mem., Editl Bd, Social Archaeol., 1999–. Acad. Advr, Mus. of London Archaeol. Service, 1991–. TV presenter, Down to Earth, 1991–92. Member: Adv. Bd for Redundant Churches, 1998–2001; Ancient Monuments Adv. Cttee, English Heritage, 1998–2001. Member: Churches Cttee, Council for British Archaeol., 1989–95; Archaeol. Section Cttee, 2009–, Pubns Cttee, 2010–, British Acad.; Council: Soc. for Medieval Archaeol., 1990–93 (Pres., 2004–07); Inst. of Field Archaeol., 1992–98; British Archaeol Assoc., 1995–98; Soc. of Antiquaries of London, 2007–10 (Mem., Res. Cttee, 2008–11). Trustee, Glastonbury Abbey, 2009–. Keeley Fellow, Wadham Coll., Oxford, 2008–09. FSA 2002. Martyn Jope Prize, Soc. for Medieval Archaeol., 2008. *Publications:* Gender and Material Culture: the archaeology of religious women, 1994; Contemplation and Action: the other monasticism, 1995; Gender and Archaeology: contesting the past, 1999; Norwich Cathedral Close: the evolution of the English cathedral landscape, 2005 (Outstanding Acad. Title Award, Choice, 2007); (with B. Sloane) Requiem: the medieval monastic cemetery in Britain, 2005 (Scholarly Pubn Award, British Archaeol Awards, 2006); Medieval Life: archaeology and the life course, 2012; (with C. Green) Glastonbury Abbey: archaeological excavations, 1904–1979, 2015; contrib. articles to World Archaeol., Antiquity, Medieval Archaeol., Archaeol Jl, Jl British Archaeol Assoc. *Recreations:* singing, walking, gardening, cats, travel, food and wine. *Address:* Department of Archaeology, University of Reading, Whiteknights, Reading RG6 6AB. *T:* (0118) 931 6381, *Fax:* (0118) 931 6718. *E:* r.l.gilchrist@reading.ac.uk.

GILCHRIST, Susan; Group Chief Executive, Brunswick Group, since 2012; *b* London, 26 May 1966; *d* of Robert David Gilchrist and Constance May Gilchrist (*née* Hodgson); *m* 2007, Andrew Roberts, *qv*; one step *s* one step *d*. *Educ:* Millfield Sch.; King's Coll., London (BA 1st Cl. Hons Eng. Lang. and Lit. 1987; FKC 2014). Mgt Consultant, Bain & Co., 1987–91; journalist: Mail on Sunday, 1991–93; The Times, 1993–95; Brunswick Group: Associate Partner, 1995–96; Partner, 1996–2005; Sen. Partner, London, 2005–10; US Man. Partner, 2010–12. Gov. (pt-time), Southbank Centre, 2008–; Mem. Bd, Old Vic, 2015–. *Recreations:* music, art, theatre, literature, women in business. *Address:* Brunswick Group, 16 Lincoln's Inn Fields, WC2A 3ED. *T:* (020) 7404 5959. *E:* sgilchrist@brunswickgroup.com.

GILCHRIST, William Alexander; Sheriff of Tayside, Central and Fife at Stirling, since 2006; *b* 15 Nov. 1951; *s* of William Gilchrist and Helen Lang Gilchrist (*née* Thomson). *Educ:* Stirling High Sch.; Edinburgh Univ. (LLB). Admitted solicitor, 1976; Crown Office and Procurator Fiscal Service, 1976–2006: Regl Procurator Fiscal, N Strathclyde, 1998–2002; Dep. Crown Agent, 2002–05; Area Procurator Fiscal, Lothian and Borders, 2005–06. Mem., Sentencing Commn, 2003–07. *Recreations:* tennis, ski-ing. *Address:* Sheriff's Chambers, Sheriff Court House, Viewfield Place, Stirling FK8 1NH. *T:* (01786) 462191. *E:* sheriffwagilchrist@scotcourts.gov.uk.

GILDEA, Prof. Robert Nigel, DPhil; FRHistS; FBA 2010; Professor of Modern History, University of Oxford, and Fellow, Worcester College, Oxford, since 2006; *b* 12 Sept. 1952; *s* of Denis and Hazel Gildea; *m* 1987, Lucy Jean Lloyd; two *s* two *d*. *Educ:* Merton Coll., Oxford (BA, MA); St Antony's Coll., Oxford; St John's Coll., Oxford (DPhil 1978). FRHistS 1986. Jun. Res. Fellow, St John's Coll., Oxford, 1976–78; Lectr in Hist., KCL, 1978–79; University of Oxford: CUF Lectr in Modern Hist., 1979–96; Reader in Modern Hist., 1996–2002; Prof. of Modern French Hist., 2002–06; Fellow and Tutor in Modern Hist., Merton Coll., 1979–2006. Élie Halévy Vis. Prof., Inst. d'Etudes Politiques, Paris, 1999–2000. Chevalier, Ordre des Palmes Académiques (France), 1997. *Publications:* Education in Provincial France 1800–1914: a study of three departments, 1983; Barricades and Borders: Europe 1800–1914, 1987, 3rd edn 2002; The Third Republic from 1870 to 1914, 1988; The

Past in French History, 1994; France since 1945, 1996, 2nd edn 2002 (Enid McLeod Prize, Franco-British Soc.); Marianne in Chains: in search of the German Occupation (Wolfson Hist. Prize), 2002; (ed jtly) Surviving Hitler and Mussolini: daily life in Occupied Europe, 2006; Children of the Revolution, 2008; (ed jtly) Writing Contemporary History, 2008; (ed jtly) Europe's 1968: voices of revolt, 2013; Fighters in the Shadows: a new history of the French Resistance, 2015. *Recreations:* walking, swimming, music, theatre, cooking, Oxford United. *Address:* Worcester College, Oxford OX1 2HB. *T:* (01865) 278348, *Fax:* (01865) 278303.

GILDERNEW, Michelle; *m* Jimmy; two *s* one *d. Educ:* Univ. of Ulster. Press Officer, Sinn Féin, 1997. Northern Ireland Assembly: Mem. (SF) Fermanagh and S Tyrone, 1998–July 2012; Minister for Agriculture and Rural Develt, 2007–11; Dep. Chm., Social Develt Cttee, 1999–2002; Mem., Centre Cttee, 2000–02. MP (SF) Fermanagh and S Tyrone, 2001–15; contested (SF) same seat, 2015.

GILES, Alan James; Chairman, Fat Face, 2006–13; *b* 4 June 1954; *s* of Ronald Arthur Giles and Christine Joyce Giles; *m* 1978, Gillian Margaret Rosser; two *d. Educ:* Merton Coll., Oxford (MA Physics); Graduate Sch. of Business, Stanford Univ. (MSc Mgt). Various buying roles, Boots the Chemists, 1975–82; Retail Develt Manager, 1982–84, Gen. Manager (Books), 1985–87, W. H. Smith; Ops and Develt Manager, Do It All, 1988–92; Managing Dir, Waterstone's, 1993–98; CEO, HMV Gp plc, 1998–2006. Non-executive Director: Somerfield plc, 1993–2004; Wilson Bowden plc, 2004–07; Rentokil Initial plc, 2006–; OFT, 2007–14; Competition and Mkts Authy, 2013–. *Recreations:* cycling, watching soccer.

GILES, Bill; *see* Giles, W. G.

GILES, Christopher Thomas; Economics Editor, Financial Times, since 2004; *b* 9 Nov. 1969; *s* of Gerald David Norman Giles and Rotraud Ursula Giles; *m* 2000, Katie Anne Roden; two *d. Educ:* Jesus Coll., Cambridge (BA 1991); Birkbeck Coll., London (MSc). Sen. Res. Economist, Inst. for Fiscal Studies, 1991–98; econs reporter, BBC, 1998–2000; Leader Writer, Financial Times, 2000–04. Royal Statistical Soc. Prize for Excellence in Journalism, 2008; Business Journalist of the Year, Press Gazette British Journalism Awards, 2012. *Recreations:* family, cycling, marathon running, theatre. *Address:* Financial Times, One Southwark Bridge, SE1 9HL. *T:* (020) 7873 4315, *Fax:* (020) 7873 3083. *E:* chris.giles@ft.com. *Clubs:* Tuesday, Political Economy.

GILES, Frank Thomas Robertson; Editor, The Sunday Times, 1981–83 (Deputy Editor, 1967–81); *b* 31 July 1919; *s* of late Col F. L. N. Giles, DSO, OBE, and Mrs Giles; *m* 1946, Lady Katharine Pamela Sackville (*d* 2010), *o d* of 9th Earl De La Warr and Countess De La Warr; one *s* one *d* (and one *d* decd). *Educ:* Wellington Coll.; Brasenose Coll., Oxford (Open Scholarship in History; MA 1946). ADC to Governor of Bermuda, 1939–42; Directorate of Mil. Ops, WO, 1942–45; temp. mem. of HM Foreign Service, 1945–46 (Private Sec. to Ernest Bevin; Mem. of Sir Archibald Clark Kerr's mission to Java); joined editorial staff of The Times, 1946; Asst Correspondent, Paris, 1947; Chief Corresp., Rome, 1950–53, Paris, 1953–60; Foreign Editor, Sunday Times, 1961–77; Dir, Times Newspapers Ltd, 1981–85. Lectures: tours, USA, 1975, FRG, 1984; Gritti, Venice, 1985. Chm., Library Cttee, Britain-Russia Centre, 1993–99. Chm., Painshill Park Trust, 1985–96; Mem., Governing Body, British Inst. of Florence, 1986–2001; Governor: Wellington Coll., 1965–89; Sevenoaks Sch., 1967–92. *Publications:* A Prince of Journalists: the life and times of de Blowitz, 1962; Sundry Times (autobiog.), 1986; The Locust Years: the story of the Fourth French Republic 1946–1958, 1991 (Franco-British Soc. award); (ed) Corfu, the Garden Isle, 1994; Napoleon Bonaparte, England's Prisoner, 2001. *Recreations:* going to the opera; collecting, talking about, consuming the vintage wines of Bordeaux and Burgundy. *Address:* 42 Blomfield Road, W9 2PF; Bunns Cottage, Lye Green, Crowborough, East Sussex TN6 1UY. *Clubs:* Brooks's, Beefsteak.

GILES, Hugh Peter; Director of Legal Services, Metropolitan Police Service, since 2012; *b* 25 Jan. 1964; *s* of late Peter Giles and of Mary Giles (*née* Cope); *m* 1997, Karen Duke; one *s* one *d. Educ:* Brentwood Sch.; Univ. of Nottingham (BA 1986). Admitted solicitor, 1991; Legal Adviser's Br., Home Office, 1991–99; Legal Secretariat to the Law Officers, 1999–2001; team leader, Treasury Solicitor's Dept, 2001–03; a legal dir, DTI, 2003–06; Dir, Legal Services Gp, DTI, subseq. BERR, 2006–08; Hd, Litigation and Employment Gp, then Litigation Gp, Treasury Solicitor's Dept, 2008–12. *Recreations:* family, cricket, Tottenham Hotspur. *Address:* New Scotland Yard, Broadway, SW1H 0BG.

GILES, Roy Curtis, MA; Administrative Consultant, Busoga Trust, 1991–2011; Head Master, Highgate School, 1974–89; *b* 6 Dec. 1932; *s* of Herbert Henry Giles and Dorothy Alexandra Potter; *m* 1963, Christine von Alten; two *s* one *d. Educ:* Queen Elizabeth's Sch., Barnet; Jesus Coll., Cambridge (Open Scholar). Asst Master, Dean Close Sch., 1956–60; Lektor, Hamburg Univ., 1960–63; Asst Master, Eton Coll., 1963–74, Head of Modern Languages, 1970–74. Educnl Selector, ABM (formerly ACCM), 1979–92; Mem., House of Bishops' Panel on Marriage Educn, 1983–89. Mem., Council of Management, Vernon Educnl Trust (formerly Davies's Educn Services), 1975–2005; Governor: The Hall, Hampstead, 1976–89; Channing Sch., 1977–89. *Recreations:* music, theatre, Central Europe. *Address:* Chattan Court, Woodbury Lane, Axminster, Devon EX13 5TL. *T:* (01297) 33720.

GILES, William George, (Bill Giles), OBE 1995; Chairman, The Weather People Ltd, since 1998; *b* 18 Nov. 1939; *s* of Albert William George Giles and Florence Ellen Christina Giles; *m* 1st, 1961, Eileen Myrtle Lake (marr. diss. 1991); one *s* one *d*; 2nd, 1993, Patricia Maureen Stafford. *Educ:* Queen Elizabeth's Sch., Crediton; Bristol Coll. of Sci. and Technol.; Meteorological Office Coll. Meteorological Office, 1959; radio broadcaster, 1972; television broadcaster, 1975; Head, BBC Weather Centre, 1983–2000. Chm., Thame Bowls Club, 2011–. Patron, Iain Rennie Hospice at Home, 2007–. Prix des Scientifiques, Fest. Internat. de Météo, Paris, 1994. *Publications:* Weather Observations, 1978; The Story of Weather, 1990. *Recreations:* gardening, golf, One Man Weather Show, after dinner speaker. *Address:* 73 Lower Icknield Way, Chinnor, Oxon OX39 4EA.

GILHOOLY, John, OBE 2013; Artistic and Executive Director, Wigmore Hall, since 2005 (Executive Director, 2000–05); *b* 15 Aug. 1973; *s* of Owen Gilhooly and Helena (*née* Conway). *Educ:* University Coll., Dublin (BA Hons). Administrator, University Coll., Dublin, 1994–97; Manager, Harrogate Internat. Centre, 1997–2000. Chm., Kohn Foundn Internat. Song Competition, 2006–; Trustee, London Internat. String Quartet Competition, 2006–. Chm., Royal Philharmonic Soc., 2010– (Hon. Sec., 2007–10). Trustee: The Opera Group, 2007–; London Music Masters, 2009–; Internat. Musicians Seminar, Prussia Cove, 2015–; Chm., Mahogany Opera Gp, 2014–. Patron: Irish Heritage, 2010–; Cavatina Chamber Music Trust, 2010–; Restoration of Corpus Christi Maiden Lane, 2011–. Hon. FRAM 2006; Hon. RCM 2012. *Address:* Wigmore Hall, 36 Wigmore Street, W1U 2BP. *E:* jgilhooly@wigmore-hall.org.uk.

GILHOOLY, John Francis, CB 2005; Chief Executive, Office of the Parliamentary Counsel, 2000–08; Associate Research Fellow, Institute of Advanced Legal Studies, University of London, 2007–14; occasional lecturer; *b* 26 April 1945; *s* of Francis Gilhooly and Sarah Gilhooly (*née* Gavigan); *m* 1971, Gillian Marie (*née* Cunningham); two *s* two *d. Educ:* Clapham Coll. Grammar Sch. (RC); King's Coll., Cambridge (BA Econ 1970). Clerical Officer, then Exec. Officer, ODM, 1965–70; Econ. Asst, then Sen. Econ. Asst, ODA, 1970–74; Econ. Adviser, Royal Commn on the Distribution of Income and Wealth, 1974–78; HM Treasury: Econ. Adviser, then Principal, 1978–84; Asst Sec. Pay Policy, Tax Policy, Gen. Expenditure Policy, Training Review, 1984–92; Asst Dir (on loan), Capital Allowances Policy, Tax Law Rewrite, Inland Revenue, 1992–96; Mgt Advr, Office of Parly Counsel, 1996–99. FRSA 2004. *Recreations:* reading, walking, family, friends. *Address:* c/o Institute of Advanced Legal Studies, Charles Clore House, 17 Russell Square, WC1B 5DR. *Club:* Civil Service.

GILL, Rt Hon. Lord; Brian Gill; PC 2002; Lord Justice General of Scotland and Lord President of the Court of Session, 2012–15; *b* 25 Feb. 1942; *s* of Thomas and Mary Gill, Glasgow; *m* 1969, Catherine Fox; five *s* one *d. Educ:* St Aloysius' Coll., Glasgow; Glasgow Univ. (MA 1962, LLB 1964); Edinburgh Univ. (PhD 1975). Asst Lectr, 1964–65, Lectr, 1965–69 and 1972–77, Faculty of Law, Edinburgh Univ.; Advocate, 1967; Advocate Depute, 1977–79; Standing Junior Counsel: Foreign and Commonwealth Office (Scotland), 1974–77; Home Office (Scotland), 1979–81; Scottish Education Dept, 1979–81; QC (Scot.) 1981; a Senator of the Coll. of Justice in Scotland, 1994–2015; Lord Justice Clerk and Pres., Second Div., Court of Session, 2001–12. Chairman: Scottish Law Commn, 1996–2001; Scottish Civil Courts Review, 2007–09. Called to the Bar, Lincoln's Inn, 1991, Hon. Bencher, 2002. Keeper of the Advocates' Library, 1987–94. Dep. Chm., Copyright Tribunal, 1989–94. Vice-Pres., RSAMD, later Royal Conservatoire of Scotland, 2006– (Chm., 1999–2006); Chm., RSCM, 2010–. FRSAMD 2002; FRSE 2004. Hon. LLD: Glasgow, 1998; Strathclyde, 2003; St Andrews, 2006; Edinburgh, 2007; Abertay, 2008; Hon. DAcad RSAMD, 2006. KSG 2011. *Publications:* The Law of Agricultural Holdings in Scotland, 1982, 3rd edn 1997; (ed) Scottish Planning Encyclopedia, 1996; articles in legal jls. *Recreation:* church music. *E:* lord.bgill@gmail.com. *Clubs:* Athenæum, MCC.

GILL, Adrian Anthony; journalist, Restaurant Critic, Television Critic and features writer, Sunday Times; *b* 28 June 1954; *s* of George Michael Gill and Yvonne Gilan Gill; *m* 1st, 1983, Cressida Connoly; 2nd, 1991, Amber Rudd (marr. diss.); one *s* one *d. Educ:* St Christopher Sch., Letchworth; St Martin's Sch. of Art; Slade Sch. of Fine Art. Sometime illustrator, muralist, graphic designer, portrait painter, artist material salesman, warehouseman, gents' outfitter, pizza chef, waiter, painter and decorator, gardener, pornography salesman, maitre d', film lectr, moonshine runner, nanny, sugar cane cutter, theatrical scene shifter, drawing master, plongeur, barman, male model, cookery teacher, writer and journalist. *Publications:* Sap Rising (fiction), 1996; The Ivy: the restaurant and its recipes, 1997; The Caprice, 1998; Starcrossed (fiction), 1999; A. A. Gill is Away, 2002; Table Talk, 2007; Paper View, 2008. *Recreation:* journalism. *Address:* c/o Ed Victor, 6 Bayley Street, Bedford Square, WC1B 3HB. *Clubs:* Chelsea Arts, Gerry's.

GILL, Sir Anthony (Keith), Kt 1991; FREng; Chairman, Docklands Light Railway, 1994–99; *b* 1 April 1930; *s* of Frederick William and Ellen Gill; *m* 1953, Phyllis Cook; one *s* two *d. Educ:* High Sch., Colchester; Imperial Coll., London (BScEng Hons). National Service officer, REME, 1954–56. Joined Bryce Berger Ltd, 1956, subseq. Director and Gen. Manager until 1972; Lucas CAV Ltd, 1972, subseq. Director and Gen. Manager until 1978; Divisional Managing Director, Joseph Lucas Ltd, 1978; Lucas Industries: Jt Gp Man. Dir, 1980–83; Gp Man. Dir, 1984–87 and Dep. Chm., 1986–87; Chm. and Chief Exec., 1987–94. Non-executive Director: Post Office Bd, 1989–91; National Power, 1990–98; Tarmac, 1992–2000. Chm., Teaching Co. Scheme Bd, 1991–96; Member: Adv. Council on Science and Technology (formerly Adv. Council for Applied R&D), 1985–91; DTI Technology Requirements Bd, 1986–88; Engineering Council, 1988–96 (Dep. Chm., 1994–95); Nat. Trng Task Force, 1991–93. Pres., IProdE, 1986–87; Mem., Council, IMechE, 1986–92; Vice-Pres., Inst. of Management, 1993 (Chm. Council, 1996–99; Pres., 1998–99). Member Court: Univ. of Warwick, 1986–94; Cranfield Univ. (formerly Inst. of Technology), 1991– (Pro-Chancellor, 1991–2001). FREng (FEng 1983); FCGI 1979; Fellow, City of Birmingham Polytechnic, 1989. Hon. FIET. Hon. DEng Birmingham, 1990; Hon. DSc: Cranfield, 1991; Southampton, 1992; Warwick, 1992; Hon. DTech Coventry, 1992; DUniv Sheffield Hallam, 1993. *Recreations:* boating, music. *Address:* The Point House, Astra Court, Hythe Marina Village, Hythe, Southampton SO45 6DZ. *T:* (023) 8084 0165. *Club:* Royal Southampton Yacht.

GILL, Brian; *see* Gill, Rt Hon. Lord.

GILL, Charan Singh, MBE 1998; Chairman, Harlequin Leisure Investments Ltd, since 2005; *b* 8 Dec. 1954; *s* of Mehar Singh Gill and Bhajan Kaur Gill; *m* 1974, Parminder Kaur Brar; one *s* four *d.* Engr, Yarrows Shipbuilder, 1969–79; restaurant manager, 1979–83; Asst Manager of insce co., 1983–86; insurance salesman, 1986–89; Man. Dir, Harlequin Leisure Gp, 1989–2005. Vice-Chm., Entrepreneurial Exchange, 2005–. Chm., Glasgow Restaurateurs Assoc., 2005–. Hon. Dr Paisley, 2004; DUniv Glasgow, 2010. *Recreations:* bhangra music, charity work. *Address:* Harlequin Leisure Investments Ltd, 1313 Argyle Street, Glasgow G3 8TL. *T:* (0141) 334 4633. *E:* charangillmbe@yahoo.com.

GILL, Prof. Christopher John, PhD; Professor of Ancient Thought, University of Exeter, 1997–2013, now Emeritus; *b* 2 May 1946; *s* of Ross and Phyllis Gill; *m* 1981, Karen Ann Brown (*d* 2010); four *s. Educ:* Cowbridge Grammar Sch., Glamorgan; St John's Coll., Cambridge (BA 1967, MA 1971); Yale Univ. (PhD 1970). Teaching asst, 1967–70, Instructor, 1970–71, Yale Univ.; Lectr, Univ. of Bristol, 1971–72; Lectr, 1972–83, Sen. Lectr, 1983–89, UCW, Aberystwyth; Sen. Lectr, 1989–94, Reader, 1994–97, Univ. of Exeter. Res. Fellow, Nat. Humanities Center, USA, 1981–82; Leverhulme Maj. Res. Fellow, 2003–06; Leverhulme Emeritus Fellow, 2014–16. *Publications:* Plato: the Atlantis story, 1980; (ed) The Person and the Human Mind: issues in ancient and modern philosophy, 1990; Greek Thought, 1995; Personality in Greek Epic, Tragedy and Philosophy: the self in dialogue, 1996; Plato: the symposium, 1999; (ed) Virtue, Norms, and Objectivity: issues in ancient and modern ethics, 2005; The Structured Self in Hellenistic and Roman Thought, 2006; Naturalistic Psychology in Galen and Stoicism, 2010; Marcus Aurelius, Meditations Books 1–6 (trans. with introdn and commentary), 2013; co-ed vols of essays. *Recreations:* swimming, hill-walking, listening to 16th century choral music. *Address:* Department of Classics and Ancient History, University of Exeter, Exeter EX4 4RJ. *E:* C.J.Gill@exeter.ac.uk.

GILL, Christopher John Fred, RD 1971; retired butcher and farmer; Hon. President, Freedom Association Ltd, since 2007 (Hon. Chairman, 2001–07); *b* 28 Oct. 1936; *m* 1960, Patricia M. (*née* Greenway); one *s* two *d. Educ:* Shrewsbury School. Chm., F. A. Gill Ltd, 1968–2006. Councillor, Wolverhampton BC, 1965–72. MP (C) Ludlow, 1987–2001. Member: Agriculture Select Cttee, 1989–95; Welsh Affairs Select Cttee, 1996–97. Vice Chairman: Cons. European Affairs Cttee, 1989–91 (Sec., 1988–89); Cons. Agric. Cttee, 1991–94 (Sec., 1990–91); Pres., Midlands W European Cons. Council, 1984–85. Member: Exec., 1922 Cttee, 1997–99; Council of Europe, 1997–99. Contested (UK Ind) Ludlow, 2010. *Publications:* Whips' Nightmare, 2003; Cracking the Whip, 2012. *Address:* Talbot Court, Bridgnorth, Shropshire WV16 5BR.

GILL, Devinder Kaur; a Judge of the Upper Tribunal (Immigration and Asylum Chamber) (formerly a Vice President, Immigration Appeal Tribunal, later a Senior Immigration Judge, Asylum and Immigration Tribunal), since 2003; a Recorder, since 2004; a Deputy Judge of the High Court, since 2013; *d* of I. S. G. Mahinder Gill. *Educ:* Wolfson Coll., Cambridge (LLM); Univ. of London (LLB ext.). Called to the Bar, Middle Temple, 1984; with various banks, including Singer & Friedlander, Samuel Montagu and HSBC; In-house Counsel, Emerging Mkts, 1986–94; In-house Gp Legal Advr, Finance, 1996–97; Legal Consultant, Emerging Mkts, 1997–2000. Adjudicator, Immigration Appellate Authy, 1995–2003. *Recreations:* theatre, gardening, music, reading, walking.

GILL, (Evelyn) Margaret, OBE 2011; PhD; FRSE; Professor of Integrated Land Use, University of Aberdeen, since 2006, on secondment (part-time) as Senior Research Fellow, Department for International Development, since 2009, and to World Bank as Chair, Independent Science and Partnership Council, Consultative Group on International Agricultural Research, since 2014 (Member, 2011–14); *b* 10 Jan. 1951; *d* of late William Alexander Morrison Gill and Eveline Elizabeth Gill (*née* Duthie). *Educ:* Univ. of Edinburgh (BSc Hons Agricl Sci.); Massey Univ., New Zealand (PhD); Open Univ. (BA Maths). Researcher, Grassland Res. Inst., AFRC, 1976–89; Researcher, 1989–94, Dir of Res., 1994–96, Natural Resources Inst., ODA; Chief Exec., Natural Resources Internat. Ltd, 1996–2000; Chief Exec. and Dir of Res., Macaulay Land Use Res. Inst., 2000–05. Chief Scientific Advr, Scottish Govt (formerly Exec.) Envmt and Rural Affairs, 2006–11. Hon. Prof., Univ. of Aberdeen, 2001. FRSE 2003. *Recreations:* hill-walking, classical music. *E:* m.gill@abdn.ac.uk.

GILL, (George) Malcolm, FCIB; Head, Banking Department, Bank for International Settlements, 1995–99 (Deputy Head, 1991–95); *b* 23 May 1934; *s* of late Thomas Woodman Gill and Alice Muriel Gill (*née* Le Grice); *m* 1966, Monica Kennedy Brooks; one *s* one *d*. *Educ:* Cambridgeshire High Sch.; Sidney Sussex Coll., Cambridge (MA). Entered Bank of England, 1957: seconded to UK Treasury Delegation, Washington DC, 1966–68; Private Sec. to Governor, 1970–72; Asst Chief Cashier, 1975; seconded to HM Treasury, 1977–80; Chief Manager, Banking and Credit Markets, 1980–82; Head of Foreign Exchange Div., 1982–88; Asst Dir, 1987–88; Chief of the Banking Dept and Chief Cashier, 1988–91. *Recreations:* reading, gardening, music. *Address:* 3 Scotscraig, Radlett, Herts WD7 8LH.

GILL, Guy Serle G.; *see* Goodwin-Gill.

GILL, Jack, CB 1984; Chief Executive (formerly Secretary), Export Credits Guarantee Department, 1983–87; Executive Director (part-time), Government Relations, BICC plc, 1987–91; *b* 20 Feb. 1930; *s* of Jack and Elizabeth Gill; *m* 1954, Alma Dorothy; three *d*. *Educ:* Bolton Sch. Export Credits Guarantee Department: Clerical Officer, 1946; Principal, 1962; Asst Sec., 1970; Asst Sec., DTI, 1972–75; Export Credits Guarantee Department: Under Sec., 1975–79; Principal Finance Officer, 1978–79; Sec., Monopolies and Mergers Commn, 1979–81; Dep. Sec., and Dir of Industrial Develt Unit, DoI, 1981–83. Mem., BOTB, 1981–87. Consultant: NEI Power Projects Ltd, 1987–90; British Aerospace plc, 1987–89; CBI Council, 1988–91 (Chm., Public Procurement Contact Gp, 1990–91; Mem., Overseas Cttee, 1990–91). National Service, REME, 1948–50. *Recreations:* music (Bass, St Paul's Cath. Sunday Evening and Special Service Choirs, 1951–60), chess; occasional crossword setter for The Listener. *Address:* 9 Ridley Road, Warlingham, Surrey CR6 9LR. *T:* (01883) 622688.

GILL, John William; Editor, Times Higher Education, since 2012; *b* Cambridge, 15 Dec. 1980; *s* of Andrew Gill and Chloe Gill. *Educ:* Netherhall Sch., Cambridge; Hills Road Sixth Form Coll., Cambridge; Univ. of Nottingham (BA Hons Hist.). Reporter, then Crime Reporter, Cambridge Evening News, 2003–07; Times Higher Education: reporter, 2007–08; Dep. News Editor, 2008; News Editor, 2008–12. *Address:* Times Higher Education, 26 Red Lion Square, WC1R 4HQ. *T:* (020) 3194 3077. *E:* john.gill@tsleducation.com.

GILL, Judith Ann Elizabeth; QC 2009; FCIArb; Partner, Allen & Overy LLP, since 1992; *b* Shepperton, 30 Sept. 1959; *d* of Desmond and Valerie Leighton; *m* 1984, Clifford William Gill; one *s* one *d*. *Educ:* Henley Grammar Sch.; S Oxfordshire Tech. Coll.; Worcester Coll., Oxford (MA Juris.); Queen Mary and Westfield Coll., Univ. of London (Dip. Internat. Commercial Arbitration). Admitted solicitor, 1985; with Allen & Overy LLP, 1985–. Dir, 1998–, Mem. Court, 2003–08, London Court of Internat. Arbitration; Director: Singapore Internat. Arbitration Centre, 2009–; American Arbitration Assoc., 2009–. Chm., Internat. Arbitration Club, 2009–14. Fellow, Inst. Advanced Legal Studies, 1998. FCIArb 1999. *Publications:* (jtly) Russell on Arbitration, 21st edn 1997 to 24th edn 2015; (ed and contrib.) State Entities in International Arbitration, 2008; contribs to Jl Internat. Arbitration, Transnat. Dispute Mgt, Internat. Business Litigation and Arbitration, Global Arbitration Rev., Internat. Arbitration Law Rev. *Recreations:* yachting, ski-ing. *Address:* Allen & Overy LLP, One Bishops Square, E1 6AD. *T:* (020) 3088 0000, *Fax:* (020) 3088 0088. *E:* judith.gill@allenovery.com.

GILL, Malcolm; *see* Gill, G. M.

GILL, Margaret; *see* Gill, E. M.

GILL, Nathan Lee; Member (UK Ind) Wales, European Parliament, since 2014; *b* Kingston upon Hull, 6 July 1973; *s* of Michael R. and Elaine Gill; *m* 2002, Jana Lyn King; three *s* four *d*. *Educ:* Ysgol David Hughes, Menai Bridge; Coleg Menai, Bangor. England London Mission, 1991–93; Man. Dir, Community Careline Services, Hull and E Yorks, 1996–2000; Man. Dir, Gill Enterprises Yorkshire Ltd, 2000–05; Campaign Manager, UKIP Wales, 2009; PA to John Bufton, MEP, 2009–14. Leader, UKIP Wales, 2014–. *Recreations:* reading, history, gardening. *Address:* 29 Ponc y Fron, Llangefni, Anglesey LL77 7NY. *T:* (01248) 723580. *E:* nathan.gill@ukipwales.org. *Club:* Gadfly.

GILL, Neena; Member (Lab) West Midlands Region, European Parliament, 1999–2009 and since 2014; *b* 24 Dec. 1956; *d* of late Jasmer S. Gill and of Birjinder K. Gill; *m* 1982, Dr John Towner (marr. diss. 2009); one *s*. *Educ:* Liverpool Poly.; London Business Sch. (BA Hons); Chartered Inst. of Housing (postgrad. dip. Public Sector Mgt). Admin. Officer, Ealing LBC, 1981–83; Principal Housing Officer, UK Housing Trust, 1983–86; Chief Executive: ASRA Greater London Housing Assoc., 1986–90; Newlon Housing Gp, 1990–99. Chair, S Asia Delegn, 2004–07, India Delegn, 2007–09, EP. Man. Dir, Public Affairs, Wrigglesworth Consultancy, 2009–10; Vice Pres., Corporate Affairs, Europe and Asia Pacific, SAS Inc., 2010–14. Member: Transatlantic Policy Network; Eur. Energy Foundn; Pres., Friends of Nepal; Patron, Friends of India. FRSA. *Recreations:* hill walking, football, minor bird watching, cinema, opera. *Address:* European Parliament, Rue Wiertz, 1047 Brussels, Belgium.

GILL, Parmjit Singh; information management consultant; Member (Lib Dem), Leicester City Council, 2003–11; *b* 20 Dec. 1966; *s* of Mohinder Singh Gill and Gurdev Kaur Gill; *m* 2006, Juliet; one *s* one *d*. *Educ:* Univ. of East London (BSc Hons Biochem. 1992); Univ. of Leicester (MSc Security Mgt and IT 1995). Inf. Mgt and Security Consultant, Leicester CC, 1999–2003; Inf. Security Manager, Charnwood BC, 2003–04; information consultant, 2005–. Contested (Lib Dem) Leicester S, 2001. MP (Lib Dem) Leicester S, July 2004–2005; contested (Lib Dem) same seat, 2005, 2010. *Address:* 17 Scholars Walk, London Road, Stoneygate, Leicester LE2 1RR.

GILL, Peter, OBE 1980; FRWCMD; dramatic author; Associate Director, Royal National Theatre, 1989–97; *b* Cardiff, 7 Sept. 1939; *s* of George John Gill and Margaret Mary Browne. *Educ:* St Illtyd's Coll., Cardiff. FRWCMD (FWCMD 1992). Associate Dir, Royal Court Theatre, 1970–72; Dir, 1976–80, Associate Dir, 1980, Riverside Studios, Hammersmith; Dir, Royal Nat. Theatre Studio, 1984–90. Productions include: *Royal Court:* A Collier's Friday Night, 1965; The Local Stigmatic, A Provincial Life, 1966 (for Nat. Th. Wales, Sherman Cymru, Cardiff, 2012); A Soldier's Fortune, The Daughter-in-law, Crimes of Passion, 1967; The Widowing of Mrs Holroyd, 1968; Life Price, Over Gardens Out, The Sleepers' Den, 1969; The Duchess of Malfi, 1971; Crete & Sergeant Pepper, 1972; The Merry-go-round, 1973; Small Change, The Fool, 1976; The York Realist, 2002; *Riverside Studios:* As You Like It, 1976; Small Change, 1977; The Cherry Orchard (own version), The Changeling, 1978; Measure for Measure, 1979; Julius Caesar, 1980; Scrape off the Black, 1980; Hens, for Sky Arts TV, 2010; *Royal National Theatre:* A Month in the Country, Don Juan, Scrape off the Black, Much Ado about Nothing, 1981; Danton's Death, Major Barbara, 1982; Kick for Touch, Tales from Hollywood, Antigone (co-dir), 1983; Venice Preserv'd, Fool for Love (transf. Lyric), 1984; The Murderers, As I Lay Dying (also adapted), A Twist of Lemon, In the Blue, Bouncing, Up for None, The Garden of England (co-dir), 1985; Mean Tears, 1987; Mrs Klein, 1988 (transf. Apollo, 1989); Juno and the Paycock, 1989; Cardiff East (also wrote), 1997; Friendly Fire, 1999; Luther, 2001; Scenes from the Big Picture, 2003; The Voysey Inheritance, 2006; *other London theatres:* O'Flaherty VC, Mermaid, 1966; The Way of the World, Lyric, Hammersmith, 1992; Uncle Vanya, Tricycle, 1995; Tongue of a Bird, Almeida, 1997; Certain Young Men, Almeida, 1999; Speed the Plow, New Ambassadors, 2000; Days of Wine and Roses, Donmar, 2005; George Dillon, Comedy Th., 2006; Gaslight, Old Vic, 2007; The Importance of Being Earnest, Vaudeville, 2008; Aliens, Bush Th., 2010; Versailles (also wrote), Donmar Warehouse, 2014; As Good a Time As Any (also wrote), Print Room at Coronet, 2015; *other theatres:* Another Door Closed, Th. Royal, Bath, 2009; The Breath of Life, Sheffield Th., 2011; *Royal Shakespeare Co.:* Twelfth Night, 1974; New England, 1994; A Patriot for Me, 1995; Romeo and Juliet, transf. Albery, 2004; has also produced plays by Shakespeare and modern writers at Nottingham, Edinburgh and in Canada, Germany, Switzerland and USA; *music theatre and opera* includes: Down By the Green Wood Side (co-dir), Bow Down (co-dir), Queen Elizabeth Hall, 1987; Marriage of Figaro, Opera North, 1987; *television* productions include: Grace, 1972; Girl, 1973; A Matter of Taste, Fugitive, 1974; Hitting Town, 1976; *radio* productions include: The Look Across the Eyes, 2001; Lovely Evening, 2001. *Publications:* plays: The Sleepers' Den, 1965; Over Gardens Out, 1969; Small Change, 1976; Small Change, Kick for Touch, 1985; In the Blue, Mean Tears, 1987; Cherry Orchard, 1996; The Look Across the Eyes, 1997; Cardiff East, 1997; Certain Young Men, 1999; The Seagull, 2000; The York Realist, 2001; Original Sin, 2002; The Look Across the Eyes, 2002; Lovely Evening, 2002. *Address:* c/o Casarotto Ramsay & Associates, Waverley House, 7–12 Noel Street, W1F 8GQ.

GILL, Sir Robin (Denys), KCVO 2010 (CVO 1993); Founder and Chairman of Executive, 1990–2010 and Chairman, 2002–10, Royal Anniversary Trust; Founder and Chairman, The Queen's Anniversary Prizes for Higher and Further Education, 1993–2010; *b* 7 Oct. 1927; *s* of Thomas Henry Gill and Marjorie Mary (*née* Butler); *m* 1st, 1951, Mary Hope Alexander (*d* 1986); three *s*; 2nd, 1991, Denise Spencer Waterhouse. *Educ:* Dulwich Coll.; Brasenose Coll., Oxford (MA; Hon. Fellow, 2005). Unilever plc, 1949–54; British Internat. Paper Ltd, 1954–59; Founder and Man. Dir, Border TV Ltd, 1960–64; Man. Dir, ATV Corp. Ltd, 1964–69; Chairman: ITCA, 1966–67; ITN, 1968–69; 1970 Trust Ltd, 1970–93; Ansvar Insce Co. Ltd, 1975–98; Standard Ind. Trust Ltd, 1970–81; various internat. private equity funds; Director: Reed Paper Gp Ltd, 1970–75; Hewlett Packard Ltd, 1975–92; Yarrow Plc, 1979–88; Baring Hambrecht Alpine Ltd, 1986–98; SD-Scicon plc, 1988–90. Member: Nat. Adv. Bd for Higher Educn; Oxford Univ. Appts Cttee; Vis. Cttee, RCA; Cttee, Royal Family Film, 1968–70. Pres., Brasenose Soc., 1995–96. Hon. DLitt Loughborough, 2010. *Recreations:* golf, sport, travel, art collecting, new projects. *Address:* PO Box 1, East Horsley, Surrey KT24 6RE. *T:* (01483) 285290. *Clubs:* Vincent's (Oxford); St George's Hill Golf; Free Foresters Cricket.

GILL, Rev. Prof. Robin Morton, PhD; Professor of Applied Theology, University of Kent, 2011–13, now Emeritus (Michael Ramsey Professor of Modern Theology, University of Kent at Canterbury, later University of Kent, 1992–2011); Non-Stipendiary Minister, Hollingbourne and Hucking, with Leeds and Broomfield, Diocese of Canterbury, 2003–14; *b* 18 July 1944; *s* of Alan Morton Gill and Mary Grace (*née* Hammond); *m* 1967, Jennifer Margaret Sheppard; one *s* one *d*. *Educ:* Westminster Sch.; King's Coll., London (BD 1966; PhD 1969); Birmingham Univ. (MSocSc 1972). Deacon, 1968; priest, 1969; Curate, Rugby St Andrews, 1968–71; Lectr, Newton Theol Coll., PNG, 1971–72; Edinburgh University: Lectr in Christian Ethics, 1972–86; Associate Dean, Faculty of Theol., 1985–88; Sen. Lectr, 1986–88; William Leech Res. Prof. in Applied Theol., Newcastle Univ., 1988–92. Priest-in-charge: St Philip, Edinburgh, 1972–75; Ford with Etal, Northumberland, 1975–87; St Mary, Coldstream, 1987–92; Area Dean, N Downs, Dio. of Canterbury, 2002–09. Canon Theologian, Dio. in Europe, Gibraltar, 2012–. Hon. Provincial Canon, Canterbury Cathedral, 1992–. *Publications:* The Social Context of Theology, 1975; Theology and Social Structure, 1977; Faith in Christ, 1978; Prophecy and Praxis, 1981; The Cross Against the Bomb, 1984; A Textbook of Christian Ethics, 1985, 4th edn 2014; Theology and Sociology, 1987, 2nd edn 1995; Beyond Decline, 1988; Competing Convictions, 1989; Christian Ethics in Secular Worlds, 1991; Gifts of Love, 1991; Moral Communities, 1992; The Myth of the Empty Church, 1993; A Vision for Growth, 1994; Readings in Modern Theology, 1995; (with Lorna Kendall) Michael Ramsey as Theologian, 1995; (with Derek Burke) Strategic Church Leadership, 1996; Moral Leadership in a Postmodern Age, 1997; Euthanasia and the Churches, 1998; Churchgoing and Christian Ethics, 1999; (ed) The Cambridge Companion to Christian Ethics, 2000, 2nd edn 2011; (ed jtly) The New Dictionary of Pastoral Studies, 2002; A Sense of Grace, 2004; Health Care and Christian Ethics, 2006; (ed) Reflecting Theologically on AIDS, 2007; A Bit Like Jesus, 2009; New Challenges for Christians: from test-tube babies to euthanasia, 2010; Sociological Theology, vol. 1, Theology in a Social Context, 2012, vol. 2, Theology Shaped by Society, 2012, vol. 3, Society Shaped by Theology, 2013. *Recreations:* running churches, playing the trumpet. *E:* r.gill@kent.ac.uk.

GILL, Stuart William; HM Diplomatic Service; Ambassador to Iceland, since 2012; *b* 6 Aug. 1958; *s* of William and Isabella Gill; *m* 1982, Maggie Denby; two *d*. *Educ:* Univ. of Kent (BA Politics and Govt 1980). DTI, 1980–94, incl. Asst Private Sec. to Minister of State, and Private Sec. to Parly Under Sec. of State; joined FCO, 1994; First Sec., and Hd, Inward Investment, Chicago, 1994–98; First Sec., and Hd of Section, UK Repn to EU, Brussels, 1998–2002; Hd of Section, EU-Asia and EU-US, Europe Directorate, 2002–06, Dep. Hd, Far Eastern Gp, Asia Pacific Directorate, 2006–08, FCO; Consul-General, Melbourne, 2008–12. *Publications:* Blood in the Sea: HMS Dunedin and the Enigma Code, 2003. *Address:* c/o Foreign and Commonwealth Office, King Charles Street, SW1A 2AH.

GILLAM, Sir Patrick (John), Kt 1998; Chairman, Asia House, 2003–05; Board Mentor, Career Management International; *b* 15 April 1933; *s* of late Cyril B. Gillam and Mary J. Gillam; *m* 1963, Diana Echlin; one *s* one *d*. *Educ:* London School of Economics (BA Hons History; Hon. Fellow, 1999). Foreign Office, 1956–57; British Petroleum Co. Ltd, 1957–91; Vice-Pres., BP North America Inc., 1971–74; General Manager, Supply Dept, 1974–78; Dir, BP International Ltd (formerly BP Trading Ltd), 1978–82; Man. Dir, BP, 1981–91; Chairman: BP Shipping Ltd, 1987–88; BP Minerals Internat. Ltd/Selection Trust Ltd, 1982–89; BP Coal Ltd, 1986–88; BP Coal Inc., 1988–90; BP America Inc., 1989–91; BP Nutrition, 1989–91; BP Oil International, 1990–91. Chairman: Booker Tate Ltd, 1991–93; Standard Chartered PLC, 1993–2003 (Dir, 1988–2003; Dep. Chm., 1991–93); Asda Gp, 1991–96; Royal & Sun Alliance Insurance Gp, 1997–2003. Chm., ICC UK, 1989–98; Mem. Exec. Bd, ICC Worldwide, 1991–98; Dir, Commercial Union, 1991–96. Mem., Court of Governors, LSE, 1989–2010, now Emeritus Governor; Trustee, Queen Elizabeth's Foundn for Disabled Develt Trust, 1984–2003. *Recreation:* gardening. *Address:* 3 St Leonard's Terrace, SW3 4QA.

GILLAN, Rt Hon. Cheryl (Elise Kendall); PC 2010; MP (C) Chesham and Amersham, since 1992; *b* 21 April 1952; *d* of Major Adam Mitchell Gillan and Mona Elsie Gillan (*née* Freeman); *m* 1985, John Coates Leeming, *qv*. *Educ:* Cheltenham Ladies' Coll.; Coll. of Law. FCIM DipM. International Management Group, 1976–84; British Film Year, 1984–86; Ernst & Young, 1986–91; Dir, Kidsons Impey, 1991–93. PPS to Lord Privy Seal, 1994–95; Parly Under-Sec. of State, DFEE, 1995–97; Opposition frontbench spokesman: on trade and industry, 1997–98; on foreign and commonwealth affairs and overseas develt, 1998–2001; on home affairs, 2003–05; an Opposition Whip, 2001–03; Shadow Sec. of State for Wales, 2005–10; Sec. of State for Wales, 2010–12. Chm., Bow Group, 1987. Freeman, City of London, 1991; Liveryman, Marketors' Co., 1991. *Recreations:* golf, music, gardening, animals. *Address:* House of Commons, SW1A 0AA. *T:* (020) 7219 3000. *Club:* Royal Automobile.

GILLAN, Prof. Michael John, DPhil; Professor of Physics, University College London, 1998–2009, now Emeritus; *b* Birmingham, 3 Jan. 1944; *s* of Robert Urquhart Gillan and Margaret Jennings Gillan; *m* 1st, 1969, Mary Torrenza Paterson (*d* 1998); two *s* one *d*; 2nd, 2009, Hilary Jane Wigmore. *Educ:* Christ Church, Oxford (BA Physics 1965; DPhil Theoretical Physics 1968). SSO, Theoretical Physics Div., AERE Harwell, 1970–88; Prof. of Theoretical Physics, Univ. of Keele, 1988–98. Chm., Thomas Young Centre, London Centre for Theory and Simulation of Materials, 2009–11. Dirac Medal and Prize, Inst. of Physics, 2006. *Publications:* approx. 250 articles in learned jls. *Recreations:* languages, music, travel.

GILLARD, Hon. Julia Eileen; MP (ALP) Lalor, Victoria, 1998–2013; Prime Minister of Australia, 2010–13; Chair, Global Partnership for Education, since 2014; *b* Barry, Wales, 29 Sept. 1961; *d* of John Oliver and Moira Gillard; partner, Tim Mathieson. *Educ:* Unley High Sch., SA; Univ. of Adelaide; Univ. of Melbourne (BA, LLB). Pres., Australian Union of Students. Solicitor, 1987–95, Partner, 1990–95, Slater & Gordon; COS to Leader of the Opposition, Vic, 1995–98. Shadow Minister: for Popn and Immigration, 2001–03; for Reconciliation and Indigenous Affairs, 2003; for Health, 2003–06; for Employment and Industrial Relns, 2006–07; for Social Inclusion, 2006–07; Dep. Manager, 2003, Manager, 2003–06, of Opposition Business, House of Reps; Dep. Leader of the Opposition, 2006–07; Minister for Educn, for Employment and Workplace Relns and for Social Inclusion, 2007–10; Dep. Prime Minister, 2007–10. Dep. Leader, 2007–10, Leader, 2010–13, ALP. Hon. Vis. Prof., Univ. of Adelaide, 2013–; Sen. Fellow, Brookings Instn, 2013–. *Publications:* My Story, 2014.

GILLEN, Rt Hon. Sir John, Kt 1999; PC 2014; **Rt Hon. Lord Justice Gillen;** a Lord Justice of Appeal, Supreme Court of Judicature, Northern Ireland, since 2014; *b* 18 Nov. 1947; *s* of John Gillen and Susan Letitia Gillen; *m* 1976, Claire; two *d*. *Educ:* Methodist Coll., Belfast; The Queen's Coll., Oxford (BA 1969; BL). Called to the Bar, Gray's Inn, 1970; Barrister, 1970–83; QC (NI), 1983–99; a Judge of the High Court of Justice, NI, 1999–2014. *Recreations:* reading, music, sports. *Address:* Royal Courts of Justice, Chichester Street, Belfast BT1 3JF. *T:* (028) 9023 5111.

GILLES, Prof. Chevalier Herbert Michael Joseph, CMG 2005; MD; FRCP, FFPH; Alfred Jones and Warrington Yorke Professor of Tropical Medicine, University of Liverpool, 1972–86, now Emeritus; *b* 10 Sept. 1921; *s* of Joseph and Clementine Gilles; *m* 1955, Wilhelmina Caruana (*d* 1972); three *s* one *d*; *m* 1979, Dr Mejra Kačić-Dimitri. *Educ:* St Edward's Coll., Malta; Royal Univ. of Malta (MD). Rhodes Schol. 1943. MSc Oxon; FMCPH (Nig.), DTM&H. Served War of 1939–45 (1939–45 Star, Africa Star, VM). Mem., Scientific Staff, MRC Lab., Gambia, 1954–58; University of Ibadan: Lectr, Tropical Med., 1958–63; Prof. of Preventive and Social Med., 1963–65; Liverpool University: Sen. Lectr, Tropical Med., 1965–70; Prof. of Tropical Med. (Personal Chair), 1970; Dean, Liverpool Sch. of Tropical Medicine, 1978–83. Vis. Prof., Tropical Medicine, Univ. of Lagos, 1965–68; Royal Society Overseas Vis. Prof., Univ. of Khartoum, Sudan, 1979–80; Hon. Prof. of Tropical Medicine, Sun-Yat-Sen Med. Coll., Guangzhou, People's Republic of China, 1984; Visiting Professor: Public Health, Univ. of Malta, 1989–; Internat. Health, Royal Colls of Surgeons, Ireland, 1994–; Tropical Medicine, Mahidol Univ., Bangkok, 1994–. Consultant Physician in Tropical Medicine, Liverpool AHA(T) and Mersey RHA, 1965–86; Consultant in Malariology to the Army, 1974–86; Consultant in Tropical Medicine to the RAF, 1978–86, to the DHSS, 1980–86. Pres., RSTM&H, 1985–87; Vice President: Internat. Fedn of Tropical Medicine, 1988–92; Liverpool Sch. of Tropical Medicine, 1991; Hon. Pres., Malta Assoc. of Public Health Physicians, 2001. Hon. MD Karolinska Inst., 1979; Hon. DSc Malta, 1984. Darling Foundn Medal and Prize, WHO, 1990; Mary Kingsley Medal, Liverpool Sch. of Tropical Medicine, 1994; Manson Medal, RSTM&H, 2007. KJSJ 2006. Title of Chevalier awarded for medical work in the tropics. Officer, Nat. Order of Merit (Malta), 2003; Companion, Order of White Elephant (Thailand), 2008. *Publications:* Tropical Medicine for Nurses, 1955, 4th edn 1975; Pathology in the Tropics, 1969, 2nd edn 1976; Management and Treatment of Tropical Diseases, 1971; (jtly) A Short Textbook of Preventive Medicine for the Tropics, 1973, 4th edn, as A Short Textbook of Public Health Medicine for the Tropics, 2003; Atlas of Tropical Medicine and Parasitology, 1976, 4th edn 1995 (BMA Book Prize, 1996); Recent Advances in Tropical Medicine, 1984; Human Antiparasitic Drugs, Pharmacology and Usage, 1985; The Epidemiology and Control of Tropical Diseases, 1987; Management of Severe and Complicated Malaria, 1991; Hookworm Infections, 1991; *edited:* Protozoal Diseases, 1999; Tropical Medicine—a clinical text, 4th edn 2006; Essential Malariology, 4th edn 2002. *Recreations:* swimming, music.

GILLESPIE, Dr Alan Raymond, CBE 2003; Chairman, Economic and Social Research Council, since 2009; *b* 31 July 1950; *s* of Charles Gillespie and Doreen Gillespie (*née* Murtagh); *m* 1973, (Georgina) Ruth Milne (*d* 2011); one *s* one *d*; *m* 2014, Caroline Sainsot. *Educ:* Grosvenor High Sch., Belfast; Clare Coll., Cambridge (BA 1972; MA 1973; PhD 1977; Hon. Fellow 2007). Citicorp International Bank Ltd, London and Geneva, 1976–86; Goldman Sachs & Co., NY, 1986–87; Goldman Sachs International, London, 1987–99 (Partner and Man. Dir, 1990–99); Chief Exec., CDC Gp plc, 1999–2002; Chm., Ulster Bank Gp, 2001–08. Non-executive Director: Elan Corp. plc, 1996–2007; United Business Media plc, 2007–; Old Mutual plc, 2010–. Chm., Internat. Finance Facility for Immunization, 2005–12. Chm., NI IDB, 1998–2002; Member: NI Econ. Strategy Steering Gp, 1998–99; NI Econ. Council, 1999–2001. Pres., European Develt Finance Instns, 2001–02. Member: Adv. Bd, Judge Inst. of Mgt Studies, Univ. of Cambridge, 1996–2003; Adv. Council, Prince's Trust, 1999–2002. Chm., Univ. Challenge Fund, NI, 1999–2007. DUniv Ulster, 2001; Hon. LLD QUB, 2005. *Recreations:* golf, tennis, ski-ing. *Address:* Economic and Social Research Council, Polaris House, North Star Avenue, Swindon SN2 1UJ. *Clubs:* Wisley Golf, Maison Blanche Golf (Geneva), Kiawah Island.

GILLESPIE, Prof. Iain Erskine, MD, MSc, FRCS; Professor of Surgery, University of Manchester, 1970–92 (Dean of Medical School, 1983–86); *b* 4 Sept. 1931; *s* of John Gillespie and Flora McQuarie; *m* 1957, Mary Muriel McIntyre; one *s* one *d*. *Educ:* Hillhead High Sch., Glasgow; Univ. of Glasgow. MB ChB, 1953; MD (Hons) 1963; MSc Manchester 1974; FRCSE 1959; FRCS 1963; FRCSGlas 1970. Series of progressive surgical appts in Univs of Glasgow, Sheffield, Glasgow (again), 1953–70. Nat. service, RAMC, 1954–56; MRC grantee, 1956–58; US Postdoctoral Research Fellow, Los Angeles, 1961–62; Titular Prof. of Surgery, Univ. of Glasgow, 1969. Vis. Prof. in USA, Canada, S America, Kenya, S Africa, Australia and New Zealand. Member: Cttee of Surgical Res. Soc. of GB and Ireland, 1975–; Medical Sub-Cttee, UGC, 1975–86; Univs and Polytechnics Grants Cttee, Hong Kong, 1984–89. Non-exec. Mem., Central Manchester HA, 1991–94. President: Manchester Med. Soc., 1994–95; Manchester Lit. and Phil Soc., 1999–2001 (Mem. Council, 1995–98); Manchester Luncheon Club, 2005–07. *Publications:* jt editor and contributor to several surgical and gastroenterological books; numerous articles in various med. jls of GB, USA, Europe. *Recreation:* golf. *Address:* 27 Athol Road, Bramhall, Cheshire SK7 1BR. *T:* (0161) 439 2811.

GILLESPIE, Ian; District Judge (Magistrates' Courts) (formerly Stipendiary Magistrate), West Midlands Area, 1991–2015; West Midlands Member, Council of District Judges (Magistrates' Courts), 2005–15; Family Court Judge, 2014–15; *b* 8 Oct. 1945; *s* of James Alexander and Margaret Cicely Gillespie; *m* 1974, Diana Mary Stevens. *Educ:* King Henry VIII Sch., Coventry. Admitted Solicitor of Supreme Court, 1973; Partner, Brindley Twist Tafft & James, Solicitors, Coventry, 1974–91; Actg Stipendiary Magistrate, Wolverhampton, 1989–91. *Recreations:* walking, theatre, music, ballet, reading (especially British Naval history), kitchen gardening. *E:* ian.gillespie45@icloud.com.

GILLESPIE, Jonathan William James, MA; Headmaster, St Albans School, since 2014; *b* 6 Dec. 1966; *s* of J. M. Gillespie and P. D. Gillespie; *m* 1992, Caroline Hotchkiss; two *s*. *Educ:* Bedford Modern Sch.; Selwyn Coll., Cambridge (BA Hons 1989; PGCE 1990; MA 1992). Asst Master, Highgate Sch., London, 1990–97; Hd of Modern Langs, 1997–2001, Housemaster, Moredun House, 2001–06, Fettes Coll., Edinburgh; Head Master, Lancing Coll., 2006–14. FRSA. *Recreations:* Highland bagpipe, hockey, golf, cricket, hillwalking. *Address:* St Albans School, Abbey Gateway, St Albans, Herts AL3 4HB. *T:* (01727) 515085, *Fax:* (01727) 843447. *E:* hm@st-albans-school.org.uk.

GILLESPIE, Robert Andrew Joseph; Partner, Evercore Partners Inc., 2009, on secondment as Director-General, Takeover Panel, 2010–13; *b* Nottingham, 14 April 1955; *s* of late John Robert Gillespie and Honora Margaret Littlefair; *m* Carolyn Sarah Powell (separated); three *d*. *Educ:* Nottingham High Sch.; Univ. of Durham (BA Hons Econs 1977). ACA. Price Waterhouse, 1977–81; S. G. Warburg, subseq. SBC Warburg 1981–97: Dir, 1987–97; Hd, Eur. Investment Banking, 1995–97; UBS Investment Bank, 1997–2008: Jt Hd, Global Investment Banking, 1999–2005; Chief Exec., Europe, Middle East and Africa, 2004–06; Vice Chm., 2005–08. Ind. Dir, Ashurst LLP; non-exec. Dir, Royal Bank of Scotland, 2013–. Chm., Somerset House Trust, 2006–15. Chm., The Boat Race Company Ltd, 2009–. Mem., Stop Organised Abuse Bd, NSPCC; Vice Pres., Save the Children. Mem. Council, Durham Univ., 2007–. *Recreations:* sailing, shooting, golf, rowing, reading. *Address:* 51 Lansdowne Road, W11 2LG. *T:* 07785 255542. *E:* gillespieraj@msn.com. *Clubs:* Oriental; Leander.

GILLESPIE, Prof. Ronald James, CM 2007; PhD, DSc; FRS 1977; FRSC; FRSC (UK); FCIC; Professor of Chemistry, McMaster University, Hamilton, Ont, 1960–88, now Emeritus; *b* London, England, 21 Aug. 1924; Canadian citizen; *s* of James A. Gillespie and Miriam G. (*née* Kirk); *m* 1950, Madge Ena Garner; two *d*. *Educ:* London Univ. (BSc 1945, PhD 1949, DSc 1957). FRSC 1965; FCIC 1960; FRIC; Mem., Amer. Chem. Soc. Asst Lectr, Dept of Chemistry, 1948–50, Lectr, 1950–58, UCL; Commonwealth Fund Fellow, Brown Univ., RI, USA, 1953–54; McMaster University: Associate Prof., Dept of Chem., 1958–60; Prof., 1960–62; Chm., Dept of Chem., 1962–65. Professeur Associé, l'Univ. des Sciences et Techniques de Languedoc, Montpellier, 1972–73; Visiting Professor: Univ. of Geneva, 1976; Univ. of Göttingen, 1978. Nyholm Lectr, RSC, 1979. Faraday Soc. Hon. LLD: Dalhousie Univ., 1988; Concordia Univ., 1988; Dr *hc* Montpellier, 1991; Hon. DSc: McMaster, 1993; Lethbridge, 2007. Medals: Ramsay, UCL, 1949; Harrison Meml, Chem. Soc., 1954; Canadian Centennial, 1967; Chem. Inst. of Canada, 1977; Silver Jubilee, 1978; Henry Marshall Tory, Royal Soc. of Canada, 1983. Awards: Noranda, Chem. Inst. of Canada, 1966 (for inorganic chem.); Amer. Chem. Soc. N-Eastern Reg., 1971 (in phys. chem.); Manufg Chemists Assoc. Coll. Chem. Teacher, 1972; Amer. Chem. Soc., 1973 (for distinguished service in advancement of inorganic chem.), 1980 (for creative work in fluorine chem.); Chem. Inst. of Canada/Union Carbide, 1976 (for chemical educn); Izaak Walton Killam Meml, Canada Council (for outstanding contrib. to advancement of res. in chemistry), 1987. *Publications:* Molecular Geometry, 1972 (London; German and Russian trans, 1975); (jtly) Chemistry, 1986, 2nd edn, 1989; The VSEPR Model of Molecular Geometry, 1990 (trans. Russian, 1992; Italian, 1994); (jtly) Atoms, Molecules and Reactions: an introduction to chemistry, 1994; (jtly) The Chemical Bond and Molecular Geometry: from Lewis to electron densities, 2001; papers in Jl Amer. Chem. Soc., Canadian Jl of Chem., and Inorganic Chem. *Recreations:* swimming, walking, reading, chess. *Address:* Department of Chemistry, McMaster University, Hamilton, ON L8S 4M1, Canada. *T:* (905) 6336042; 327–18 Plains Road West, Burlington, ON L7T 0B3, Canada. *E:* ronald.gillespie@sympatico.ca.

GILLESPIE, Simon Maxwell; Chief Executive, British Heart Foundation, since 2013; *b* Bromley, 17 Nov. 1959; *s* of Gordon Maxwell Gillespie and Margaret Cecilia Gillespie; *m* 1989, Dr Rosemary James. *Educ:* Corpus Christi Coll., Cambridge (BA 1981; MA 1994; MPhil 1994); Henley Mgt Coll. (MBA 1994). Served RN, 1977–2000: CO, HMS Sheffield; Mil. Asst to Minister for the Armed Forces. Dir of Ops, Charity Commn, 2000–04; Hd of Ops, Healthcare Commn, 2004–06; Chief Exec., Multiple Sclerosis Soc., 2006–13. Pres., European Heart Network, 2014–. *Recreations:* hill-walking, jogging, recreational golf. *Address:* British Heart Foundation, Greater London House, 180 Hampstead Road, NW1 7AW. *E:* gillespies@bhf.org.uk.

GILLESPIE, Prof. Vincent Anthony, DPhil; FBA 2013; FSA, FRHistS, FEA; J. R. R. Tolkien Professor of English Literature and Language (formerly J. R. R. Tolkien Professor of Medieval English Literature and Language), University of Oxford, and Fellow of Lady Margaret Hall, Oxford, since 2004; *b* 11 Feb. 1954; *s* of George Anthony Gillespie and Florence Doreen Gillespie (*née* Preston); *m* 1979, Margaret, (Peggy), Powell; two *s*. *Educ:* St Edward's Coll., Liverpool; Keble Coll., Oxford (BA, MA; DPhil 1981). Lectr in English, Univ. of Reading, 1977–80; University of Oxford: Lectr in English, 1980–98; Reader, 1998–2004; Fellow and Tutor in English, St Anne's Coll., 1980–2004 (Hon. Fellow, 2004). Distinguished Vis. Prof. of Medieval Studies, Univ. of Calif, Berkeley, 2009–10; William Evans Fellow, Univ. of Otago, 2013. FRHistS 2003; FEA 2003; FSA 2004. *Publications:* (jtly) The English Medieval Book, 2001; Syon Abbey, 2002; (ed jtly) The Cambridge Companion to Medieval English Mysticism, 2011; (ed jtly) After Arundel: religious writing in fifteenth-century England, 2011; Looking in Holy Books, 2012; (ed jtly) Probable Truth: editing medieval texts from Britain in the twenty-first century, 2013; (ed jtly) A Companion to the Early Printed Book in Britain, 1476–1558, 2014; articles in learned jls and collaborative books. *Recreations:* theatre, wine, music, retired double-bass player. *Address:* Lady Margaret Hall, Oxford OX2 6QA. *E:* vincent.gillespie@ell.ox.ac.uk.

GILLETT, Rt Rev. David Keith; Bishop Suffragan of Bolton, 1999–2008; an Honorary Assistant Bishop, since 2008, and Interfaith Adviser, since 2010, Diocese of Norwich; *b* 25 Jan. 1945; *s* of Norman and Kathleen Gillett; *m* 1988, Valerie Shannon (*d* 2013). *Educ:* Leeds Univ. (BA Theol. 1st cl. 1965; MPhil 1968). Curate, St Luke's, Watford, 1968–71; Northern Sec., Pathfinders and Church Youth Fellowship's Assoc., 1971–74; Lectr, St John's Coll., Nottingham, 1974–79; Co-Leader, Christian Renewal Centre for Reconciliation, NI, 1979–82; Vicar of St Hugh's, Luton, 1982–88; Principal, Trinity Theol Coll., Bristol, 1988–99. Mem., Gen. Synod of C of E, 1985–88, 1990–99. Vice Pres., Christian Muslim Forum, 2012–. Trustee, Council of Christians and Jews, 2011–. Hon. Canon of Bristol Cathedral, 1991–99. *Publications:* Learning in the Local Congregation, 1979; The Darkness where God is, 1983; Trust and Obey, 1993; (ed jtly) Treasure in the Field: the Archbishops' Companion to the Decade of Evangelism, 1993; co-author and contributor to various books and reference works. *Recreations:* photography, gardening, travel, especially visiting friends and former students around the world. *Address:* 10 Burton Close, Diss, Norfolk IP22 4YJ. *T:* (01379) 640309. *E:* dkgillett@btinternet.com.

GILLETT, Sir Nicholas (Danvers Penrose), 3rd Bt *cr* 1959, of Bassishaw Ward, City of London; Product Director - High Energy Systems, Astrophysics Inc., USA, since 2013; *b* S Kensington, London, 24 Sept. 1955; *er s* of Sir Robin Danvers Penrose Gillett, 2nd Bt, GBE, RD and Elizabeth Marion Grace, *e d* of late John Findlay, JP; *S* father, 2009; *m* 1987, Haylie Brooks (marr. diss. 1997). *Educ:* Pangbourne Coll.; Imperial Coll., London (BSc Hons Physics 1977). ARCS. Trials Engr, then Product Assurance Manager, Project Manager, Business Develt Manager, British Aerospace, Filton, 1977–91; EU Exec. Trng Prog., Japan, 1991–92;

Project Manager and Business Develt Manager, British Aerospace, Stevenage, 1993–96; Dir, Technology Sales, EG&G Astrophysics, Bristol, 1997–98; Dir, Technical Mktg, Cargo Products, EG&G Astrophysics, USA, 1999–2002; Dir, Engrg Applications, 2003–04, Dir, Technical Mktg - Cargo Systems, 2005–09, Product Manager - Cargo Imaging Systems, 2009–12, L-3 Communications Security & Detection Systems, USA. *Recreations:* ski-ing, beach volleyball, photography, diving. *Heir: b* Christopher John Gillett [*b* 16 May 1958; *m* 1st, 1984, Julia Anne Holmes (marr. diss. 1996); one *s* one *d*; 2nd, 1996, Lucy Marie Schaufer]. *Address:* 1507 7th Street #47, Santa Monica, CA 90404, USA. *T:* (424) 2418117. *E:* mail@nick-g.com. *Club:* Beach Cities Ski (Hermosa Beach).

GILLETT, Sarah, CMG 2009; CVO 2009 (MVO 1986); HM Diplomatic Service; Ambassador to Norway, since 2014; *b* 21 July 1956; *d* of Sir Michael Cavenagh Gillett, KBE, CMG and Margaret Gillett. *Educ:* St Anthony's Leweston, Sherborne; Aberdeen Univ. (MA Hons). Joined HM Diplomatic Service, 1976: Third Sec., Washington, 1984–87; Third, later Second, Sec., Paris, 1987–90; on secondment to ODA, 1990–91; Central Eur. Dept, FCO, 1991–92; Vice-Consul (Inward Investment), Los Angeles, 1992–94; SE Asia Dept, FCO, 1994–97; First Sec., Brasilia, 1997–99; Counsellor and Dep. Head of Mission, Brasilia, 1999–2001; Consul-Gen., Montreal, 2002–05; Vice-Marshal of the Diplomatic Corps, and Dir of Protocol, FCO, 2006–09; Ambassador to Switzerland and (non-resident) to Liechtenstein, 2009–13. *Recreation:* outdoor exercise. *Address:* c/o Foreign and Commonwealth Office, King Charles Street, SW1A 2AH.

GILLFORD, Lord; John Maximillian Meade; *b* 28 Jan. 1998; *s* and heir of Earl of Clanwilliam, *qv*.

GILLHAM, Geoffrey Charles; HM Diplomatic Service, retired; consultant; *b* 1 June 1954; *s* of Peter George Gee Gillham and Alison Mary (*née* Jackman); *m* 1991, Nicola Mary Brewer (*see* Dame N. M. Brewer); one *s* one *d*. *Educ:* UWIST (BScEcon). Joined FCO, 1981: Second Sec., Caracas, 1983–85; on loan to Cabinet Office, 1986–88; FCO, 1988–89; First Secretary: Madrid, 1989–91; UK Delegn, OECD, Paris, 1991–95; First Sec., later Counsellor, FCO, 1995–98; Counsellor, New Delhi, 1998–2001; Hd, S European Dept, FCO, 2001–03; Asst Dir, EU (Mediterranean), FCO, 2003–04; Hd, Estate Strategy Unit, later Dir, Estates, FCO, 2004–08. Sec., UK-India Round Table, 2008–11; S Africa, 2009–13. Ind. Mem., Lord Chancellor's Adv. Cttee, Central and S London, 2014–. *Publications:* Burn Before Reading: undiplomatic tales (collected short stories), 2014. *Recreations:* music, travel, writing, sailing.

GILLHAM, Dame Nicola Mary; *see* Brewer, Dame N. M.

GILLIAM, Terry; animator, actor, writer; film director, since 1973; *b* Minneapolis, USA, 22 Nov. 1940; *s* of James H. and Beatrice Gilliam; *m* 1973, Maggie Weston; one *s* two *d*. *Educ:* Occidental Coll., LA, Calif. *Television:* resident cartoonist, We Have Ways of Making You Laugh, 1968; animator: Do Not Adjust Your Set, 1968–69; (also actor and co-writer), Monty Python's Flying Circus, 1969–74 and 1979; The Marty Feldman Comedy Machine, 1971–72; The Do-It-Yourself Film Animation, 1974; presenter, The Last Machine, 1995; *films:* co-writer, actor and animator: And Now For Something Completely Different, 1971; (also co-dir) Monty Python and the Holy Grail, 1974; Monty Python's Life of Brian, 1979; Monty Python Live at the Hollywood Bowl, 1982; Monty Python's The Meaning of Life, 1983; (animator, writer) The Miracle of Flight, 1974; (writer, dir) Jabberwocky, 1977; (co-writer, prod., dir) Time Bandits, 1981; (co-writer, dir) Brazil, 1985; (co-writer, dir) The Adventures of Baron Münchhausen, 1989; (dir) The Fisher King, 1991; (dir) Twelve Monkeys, 1996; (co-writer, dir) Fear and Loathing in Las Vegas, 1998; Lost in La Mancha, 2002; (co-writer, dir) The Brothers Grimm, 2005; (co-writer, dir) Tideland, 2005; (co-writer, prod., dir) The Imaginarium of Doctor Parnassus, 2009; (writer, dir) The Wholly Family, 2011; (dir) The Zero Theorem, 2013; *opera:* (dir) The Damnation of Faust, ENO, 2011; Benvenuto Cellini, ENO, 2014; *live show:* Monty Python Live (Mostly), 02 Arena, 2014. Public art installation, Past People of Potsdamer Platz, Potsdamer Platz, Berlin, 2006. Fellow, BAFTA, 2009. Hon. DFA Occidental Coll., 1987; Hon. Dr: RCA, 1989; Nat. Univ. of Drama and Cinematography, Bucharest, 2013; Hon. DA Wimbledon Sch. of Arts, 2004. Chevalier, Order of Arts and Letters (France), 2013. *Publications:* Animations of Mortality, 1978; Time Bandits, 1981; (jtly) The Adventures of Baron Münchhausen, 1989; Fear and Loathing in Las Vegas: not the screenplay, 1998; Gilliam on Gilliam, 1999; Dark Knights and Holy Fools, 1999; *contributed to:* Monty Python's Big Red Book, 1971; The Brand New Monty Python Book, 1973, Monty Python and the Holy Grail, 1977; Monty Python's Life of Brian, 1979; Monty Python's The Meaning of Life, 1983; The Pythons Autobiography by The Pythons, 2003; Gilliamesque, 2015. *Recreations:* too busy. *Address:* c/o The Casarotto Co., Waverley House, 7–12 Noel Street, W1F 8GQ.

GILLIBRAND, Philip Martin Mangnall; District Judge (Magistrates' Courts), Hampshire, since 2005 (Inner London, 2001–05); *b* 28 June 1951; *s* of late Frank Ivor Croft Gillibrand, Chorley, Lancs and Marjorie Joyce Gillibrand (*née* Golding); *m* 1979, Felicity Alexandra Augusta Priefert; one *s* one *d*. *Educ:* Reading Blue Coat Sch. (Aldsworth's Hosp.); Poly. of Central London (LLB Hons London (ext.) 1974). Called to the Bar, Gray's Inn, 1975; in practice at the Bar, London and on Western Circuit, 1975–2000: Bristol, 1982–93; Winchester, 1993–2000; Dep. Stipendiary Magistrate, Leicester, 1997–2000; Prison Adjudicator, 2004–11; Diversity and Community Relns Judge, 2011–15. Mem., Family Proceedings and Youth Court Panels, 2001–; Chm., Judicial Complaints Panel, 2009–15. Parish Councillor, Crawley, Hants, 1998–2013. Pres., Old Blues Assoc., 2015–. *Recreations:* classic and historic motoring (Mem., Brooklands Soc.; E-Type register correspondent, Jaguar Drivers' Club, 2012–), motor racing (Mem., Mini Seven Racing Club; Steward, RAC Motor Sports Assoc., 2015–), reading from 19th and early 20th century, music (Mem., Elgar Soc.), campanology, the countryside, family life. *Address:* c/o Westminster Magistrates' Court, 181 Marylebone Road, NW1 5BR.

GILLIBRAND, Sydney, CBE 1991; FREng; Chairman, TAG Aviation (UK) Ltd, since 1998; Director, TAG Aviation (Holdings) SA, since 2001; *b* 2 June 1934; *s* of Sydney and Maud Gillibrand; *m* 1960, Angela Ellen Williams; three *s* (and one *s* decd). *Educ:* Preston Grammar Sch.; Harris Coll., Preston; College of Aeronautics, Cranfield (MSc). FRAeS 1975 (Hon. FRAeS 1994); FREng (FEng 1987). English Electric: apprentice, Preston, 1950; Chief Stress Engr, 1966; Works Man., Preston, 1974; Special Dir, BAC (Preston) Ltd, 1974; Dir of Manufacturing, Mil. Aircraft Div., 1977; British Aerospace Aircraft Group: Div. Prodn Dir, Warton, 1978; Dep. Man. Dir, Warton Div., and Bd Mem., Aircraft Gp, 1981; Div. Man. Dir, Kingston/Brough Div., 1983, Weybridge Div., 1984; British Aerospace PLC: Man. Dir, Civil Aircraft Div., 1986; Dir, 1987–95; Vice-Chm., 1991–95; Sen. Corporate Advr, 1995–99; Chairman: British Aerospace (Commercial Aircraft) Ltd, 1988–89; Aerospace Companies, 1989–92. Chm., AMEC plc, 1997–2004 (Dir, 1995–2004); Director: ICL plc, 1996–2002; Messier-Dowty Internat. Ltd, 1998–2003; Powergen, 1999–2002. Pres., SBAC, 1990–91. Hon. FIIE 2000. CCMI. Silver Medal, RAeS, 1981; James Watt Gold Medal, IMechE, 1997. *Recreation:* golf.

GILLICK, Liam; artist; *b* Aylesbury, 1964; *s* of G. V. T. Gillick and G. L. Gillick; *m* 1998, Sarah Dunbar Morris (marr. diss. 2013); one *s*. *Educ:* Goldsmiths' Coll., Univ. of London (BA Hons). Lectr, Goldsmiths' Coll., Univ. of London, 1994–97; Adjunct Professor: Columbia Univ., NY, 1997–2012; Bard Coll., Annandale-on-Hudson, 2007–. Exhibitions include: Whitechapel Gall., 2002; Mus. of Contemporary Art, Chicago, 2009. Work in permanent collections incl. Tate, MOMA, NY, Guggenheim, Centre Pompidou. Actor, Exhibition (film), 2014. *Publications:* Erasmus is Late, 1995; Discussion Island/Big Conference Centre, 1997; Five or Six, 2000; Literally No Place, 2002; Proxemics: selected writings, 1988–2004, 2005; (ed jtly) Factories in the Snow, 2006; All Books, 2009. *Recreations:* motorsports, agricultural history, early socialist literature. *Address:* c/o Maureen Paley, 21 Herald Street, E2 6JT. *T:* (020) 7729 4112.

GILLIES, Crawford Scott; Chairman, Scottish Enterprise, since 2009; *b* Edinburgh, 1 May 1956; *s* of Robert and Netta Gillies; *m* 1978, Alison Farquhar; three *s*. *Educ:* Perth Acad.; Univ. of Edinburgh (LLB); Harvard Business Sch. (MBA). ACA 1980. Accountant, Peat, Marwick, Mitchell, 1977–80; Bain & Co.: Consultant, 1983–86; Manager, 1986–88; Partner, 1988–2005; Man. Partner UK, 1996–2000; Man. Dir, Europe, 2001–05. Non-executive Chairman: Control Risks Gp Hldgs Ltd, 2006–; Hammonds LLP, 2006–09; non-executive Director: Standard Life plc, 2007–; Mitie Gp plc, 2012–; Barclays, 2014–. *Recreations:* Rugby, golf, football, trees. *Address:* 101 George Street, Edinburgh EH2 3ES. *T:* (0131) 220 5420, *Fax:* (0131) 226 6997. *E:* cg@crawfordgillies.co.uk. *Club:* Caledonian.

GILLIES, Prof. Malcolm George William, AM 2013; PhD, DMus; Vice-Chancellor and Chief Executive, London Metropolitan University, 2010–14, now Emeritus Professor; *b* 23 Dec. 1954; *s* of Frank Douglas Gillies and Beatrice Mary Belle Gillies (*née* Copeman); partner, 1980, Dr David Pear. *Educ:* Royal Coll. of Music; Australian National Univ. (BA 1978); Univ. of Queensland (DipEd 1978); Clare Coll., Cambridge (BA 1980; MA 1984); King's Coll. London (MMus 1981); Univ. of London (PhD 1987); Univ. of Melbourne (DMus 2004). Tutor, Lectr, then Sen. Lectr in Music, Univ. of Melbourne, 1981–92; Prof. of Music, 1992–99, Dean of Music, 1992–97, Univ. of Queensland; Exec. Dean and Pro-Vice-Chancellor, Univ. of Adelaide, 1999–2001; Australian National University: Dep. Vice-Chancellor (Educn), 2002–06; Vice-Pres. (Develt), 2006–07; Vice-Chancellor and Pres., 2007–09, and Prof. of Music, 2007–10, City Univ. London. President: Australian Acad. of Humanities, 1998–2001; Nat. Acads Forum, 1998–2002; Australian Council for the Humanities, Arts and Soc. Scis, 2004–06; Chm., Nat. Scholarly Communications Forum, 2001–07; Vice-Chm., 2008–09, Chm., 2010–14, London Higher. Member Council: Gresham Coll., 2009–10; Specialist Schs and Academies Trust, 2010; Mem., Foundn Bd, Nyenrode Business Univ., Netherlands, 2010–. Ed., Studies in Musical Genesis, Structure and Interpretation, 1997–. FLCM 1973; FAHA 1993; FACE 2006. *Publications:* Bartók in Britain: a guided tour, 1989; Notation and Tonal Structure in Bartók's Later Works, 1989; Bartók Remembered, 1990 (German edn, 1991; Spanish edn, 2004); (ed) Halsey Stevens, The Life and Music of Béla Bartók, 3rd edn 1993; (ed) The Bartók Companion, 1993; (ed with David Pear) The All-Round Man: selected letters of Percy Grainger 1914–1961, 1994; (ed) Northern Exposures, 1997; (ed jtly) Grainger On Music, 1999; (with David Pear) Portrait of Percy Grainger, 2002; (ed jtly) Self-Portrait of Percy Grainger, 2006; Bartók Connections, 2007. *Recreations:* swimming, arts, the 1890s. *Address:* 42 Lauderdale Tower, EC2Y 8BY.

GILLIES, Prof. Norman Neil Nicolson, OBE 2003; independent consultant, since 2012; *b* Stenscholl, Isle of Skye, 1 March 1947; *s* of Angus and Peggy Gillies; *m* 1977, Jean Brown Nixon; one *s* two *d*. *Educ:* Portree High Sch.; Ross Hall Scottish Hotel Sch.; Glasgow Coll. of Technol. (Cert. Accounting); Open Univ. (BA). Asst to Owner, Flodigarry Hotel, Isle of Skye, 1969–75; Admin. Manager, Allscott (CES) Ltd, 1975–83; Coll. Sec., 1983–86, Dir, 1986–2008, Sabhal Mòr Ostaig (Nat. Centre for Gaelic Lang. and Culture); Develt Dir, Clan Donald Lands Trust, 2009–11. Hon. Prof., Contemporary Highland Studies, Univ. of Aberdeen, 2002; Emeritus Prof., Univ. of Highlands and Islands, 2010. Gov., Royal Conservatoire of Scotland, 2010–. *Recreations:* reading, television, walking, films. *Address:* Innis Ard, Ardvasar, Sleat, Isle of Skye IV45 8RU. *T:* (01471) 844281. *E:* tormod281@btinternet.com.

GILLIES, Prof. Pamela A., CBE 2013; PhD; FFPH; Principal and Vice-Chancellor, Glasgow Caledonian University, since 2006; *b* Dundee, 13 Feb. 1957. *Educ:* Univ. of Aberdeen (BSc Physiol.; PGCE; MEd); Univ. of Nottingham (MMedSci 1978; PhD Epidemiol. 1986). FFPH 2002. Posts in Sheffield evaluating health promotion initiatives, 1978–84; University of Nottingham, 1984–2006: Lectr in Public Health Medicine, then Prof. of Public Health Medicine; Pro Vice-Chancellor, 2001–06; Exec. Dir of Res., Health Educn Authy for England (on secondment), 1996–99. Abbott Fellow for AIDS Res., San Francisco, 1988; Harkness Fellow and Vis. Prof. in Health and Human Rights, Harvard Univ., 1992–93. Mem., Global Prog. on AIDS, WHO, Geneva, 1989–90. Chair: Glasgow Task Force, 2010–; Glasgow Health Commn. Member: Bd, Scottish Inst. for Excellence in Social Work Educn, 2006–08; W Regl Adv. Bd, Scottish Enterprise; Bioscis Wkg Gp on Public Health, Nuffield Inst. Mem. Council, CBI Scotland. Trustee: British Council; Saltire Foundn. FAcSS (AcSS 2005). FRSA. Hon. FRCPSGlas 2007. *Publications:* contribs to acad. jls and to Govt reports. *Address:* Office of the Vice-Chancellor, Glasgow Caledonian University, Britannia Building, City Campus, Cowcaddens Road, Glasgow G4 0BA.

GILLIES, Rt Rev. Robert Arthur; *see* Aberdeen and Orkney, Bishop of.

GILLIGAN, Andrew Paul; London Editor, Telegraph Media Group, since 2009; Cycling Commissioner for London, Greater London Authority, since 2013; *b* London, 22 Nov. 1968; *s* of Kevin and Ann Gilligan. *Educ:* Grey Court Sch., Richmond; Kingston Coll. of Further Educn; St John's Coll., Cambridge. Defence corresp., Sunday Telegraph, 1995–99; Defence and Diplomatic corresp., Today Prog., BBC News, 1999–2004; reporter and columnist, London Evening Standard, 2004–09. *Recreation:* cycling. *Address:* Telegraph Media Group, 111 Buckingham Palace Road, SW1W 0DT. *E:* andrew.gilligan@telegraph.co.uk; City Hall, SE1 2AA.

GILLIGAN, Prof. Christopher Aidan, CBE 2015; DPhil, ScD; Professor of Mathematical Biology, University of Cambridge, since 1999 (Deputy Head, 2008–09, Head, 2009–13, School of Biological Sciences); Fellow, King's College, Cambridge, since 1988; *b* 9 Jan. 1953; *s* of William Christopher Gilligan and Kathleen Mary Gilligan (*née* Doyle); *m* 1974, Joan Flood; one *s* three *d*. *Educ:* St Mary's Coll., Crosby; Keble Coll., Oxford (BA 1974; MA 1978); Wolfson Coll., Oxford (DPhil 1978); Univ. of Cambridge (ScD 1999). University of Cambridge: Univ. Demonstrator, 1977; Lectr, Dept of Applied Biol., 1982–89, Dept of Plant Scis, 1989–95; Reader in Mathematical Biol., 1995–99; Royal Soc. Leverhulme Trust Sen. Res. Fellow, 1998–99; BBSRC Professorial Fellow, Dept of Plant Scis, 2004–10. King's College, Cambridge: Tutor, 1988–94; Mem. Coll. Council, 1988–91; Dir of Studies in Natural Sci., 1990–2004; Mem. Electors, 1995–98. Vis. Prof., Dept of Botany and Plant Pathol., Colorado State Univ., 1982. Chair: Sci. Adv. Council, DEFRA, 2011–14; Bd, Cambridge Prog. for Sustainability Leadership, 2011–; JNCC, 2014–. Member: Council, Nat. Inst. Agricl Botany, 1985–91; Governing Body, Silsoe Res. Inst., 1998–2006; Council, BBSRC, 2003–09 (Mem., Strategy Bd, 2005–09); Adv. Cttee on Forest Res., Forestry Commn, 2006–09; Chairman: BBSRC Crop Sci. Review, 2003–04; Commn of Evaluation on Plant Health and Envmt, Institut Nat. de la Recherche Agronomique, France, 2003; Adviser on agricl systems research: Scottish Exec. Envmt and Rural Affairs Dept, 1998–2003; Institut Nat. de la Recherche Agronomique, 2003–05. Pres., British Soc. for Plant Pathol., 2001. Fisher Lectr, Rothamsted Res., 2009; R. W. Holley Lectr, Cornell Univ., 2011. Fellow, Royal Statistical Soc., 1995; Rothamsted Fellow, 1998–; Hon. Fellow, Amer. Phytopathol Soc., 2005. Trustee, Natural Hist. Mus., 2011–. *Publications:* (ed) Mathematical Modelling of Crop Disease, 1985; numerous articles on botanical epidemiol. and modelling in biol. and mathematical biol. jls. *Recreations:* family, running, reading, travel. *Address:* Department of Plant Sciences, University of Cambridge, Downing Street, Cambridge CB2 3EA. *T:* (01223) 333900. *E:* cag1@cam.ac.uk.

GILLILAND, David; *see* Gilliland, His Honour J. A. D.

GILLILAND, David Jervois Thetford; solicitor and farmer, 1957–2013; *b* 14 July 1932; *s* of late Major W. H. Gilliland and of Mrs N. H. Gilliland; *m* 1st, 1958, Patricia, *o d* of late J. S. Wilson and Mrs Wilson (marr. diss. 1976); two *s* three *d*; 2nd, 1976, Jennifer Johnston, *qv*. *Educ:* Rockport Prep. Sch.; Wrekin Coll.; Trinity Coll., Dublin (BA 1954, LLB 1955). Qualified as solicitor, NI, 1957, own practice, until 2013. Mem. ITA, 1965–70; Chm., N Ireland Adv. Cttee of ITA, 1965–70. Chm., NI Heritage Gardens Cttee, 1991–; Mem. Council, Internat. Dendrology Soc., 1966–75, 2008–13 (Vice Pres., Ireland, 2008–13); etc. *Recreations:* gardening, photography. *Address:* Brook Hall, 65 Culmore Road, Londonderry, Northern Ireland BT48 8JE. *T:* (028) 7135 1297.

GILLILAND, His Honour (James Andrew) David; QC 1984; a Circuit Judge, 1992–2007; a Judge, Technology and Construction Court, 2000–07; an Arbitrator, since 2007; *b* 29 Dec. 1937; *s* of James Albin Gilliland and Mary Gilliland (*née* Gray); *m* 1961, Elsie McCully; two *s*. *Educ:* Campbell College; Queen's University Belfast. LLB (1st Class Hons) 1960. Called to the Bar, Gray's Inn, 1964 (Holt Scholar, Atkin Scholar, Macaskie Scholar); Lectr in Law, Manchester University, 1960–72; a Recorder, 1989–92. *Recreations:* music, opera, stamp collecting. *Address:* Kings Chambers, 36 Young Street, Manchester M3 3FT. *T:* (0161) 832 9082. *Club:* Athenæum (Liverpool).

GILLILAND, Jennifer, (Mrs David Gilliland); *see* Johnston, J.

GILLINGHAM, Prof. John Bennett, FBA 2007; historian; Professor of History, London School of Economics and Political Science, 1995–98, now Emeritus; *b* 3 Aug. 1940; *s* of Arthur Gillingham and Irene Gillingham; *m* 1966, June Guy (marr. diss. 1978); two *d*. *Educ:* Rottingdean Primary Sch.; Brighton, Hove and Sussex Grammar Sch.; Queen's Coll., Oxford (BA Hons Modern Hist.; BPhil Medieval Hist.). Laming Travelling Fellow, Queen's Coll., Oxford, 1963–65; Lectr, then Sen. Lectr, LSE, 1965–95. Dir, Battle Conf. on Anglo-Norman Studies, 2000–04; Ed., Anglo-Norman Studies, 2000–04. *Publications:* Cromwell: portrait of a soldier, 1976; Richard the Lionheart, 1978, 2nd edn 1989 (trans. German, French; Prix Guillaume le Conquérant, 1997); The Wars of the Roses, 1981 (trans. Hungarian); (ed with Malcolm Falkus) Historical Atlas of Britain, 1981 (trans. Japanese); The Angevin Empire, 1984, 2nd edn 2001; (ed) Richard III: a medieval kingship, 1993; Richard Coeur de Lion: kingship, chivalry and war in the twelfth century, 1994; Richard I, 1999, 2nd edn 2001 (trans. Spanish); The English in the Twelfth Century, 2000; (with Ralph Griffiths) Medieval Britain: a very short introduction, 2000 (trans. Chinese); Medieval Kingdoms, 2001; (with Danny Danziger) 1215 The Year of Magna Carta, 2003; Conquests, Catastrophe and Recovery: Britain and Ireland 1066–1485, 2014. *Recreation:* walking.

GILLINGS, Ven. Richard John; Archdeacon of Macclesfield, 1994–2010, now Archdeacon Emeritus; Priest, St Columba's, Grantown-on-Spey, and St John's Rothiemurchus, Diocese of Moray, since 2011; *b* 17 Sept. 1945; *s* of John Albert Gillings and Constance Ford Gillings; *m* 1972, Kathryn Mary Hill; two *s* two *d*. *Educ:* Sale GS; St Chad's Coll., Durham (BA, Dip Biblical Studies); Lincoln Theol Coll. Ordained deacon 1970, priest 1971; Curate, St George's, Altrincham, 1970–75; Priest i/c, then Rector, St Thomas', Stockport, 1975–83, and Priest i/c, St Peter's, Stockport, 1978–83; Rector, Birkenhead Priory, 1983–93; Vicar, Bramhall, 1993–2005. RD, Birkenhead, 1985–93; Hon. Canon, Chester Cathedral, 1992–94. Mem., Gen. Synod, 1980–2005. *Recreations:* music, cinema, theatre, railways. *Address:* Culvardie, Desher Road, Boat of Garten, Inverness-shire PH24 3BN.

GILLINGWATER, Richard Dunnell, CBE 2008; Chairman, Henderson Group, since 2013; *b* 21 July 1956; *s* of Malcolm and Olive Gillingwater; *m* 1981, Helen Margaret Leighton Davies; one *s* three *d*. *Educ:* Chesterfield Grammar Sch.; St Edmund Hall, Oxford (MA Jurisprudence); Inst. for Mgt Develt, Lausanne (MBA). Articled Clerk, Lovell, White and King, Solicitors, 1978–80; admitted solicitor, 1980; with Kleinwort Benson Ltd, 1980–90 (Dir, 1990); Barclays De Zoete Wedd: Dir, Corporate Finance, 1990–92; Man. Dir, 1992; Jt Hd, Global Corporate Finance, 1995–98; Jt Dep. Hd, 1998–2001, Chm., 2001–03, European Investment Banking, Credit Suisse First Boston; Chief Exec., 2003–06, Chm., 2006–07, Shareholder Exec., Cabinet Office; Dean, Cass Business Sch., City Univ., 2007–12. Chairman: Faber Music, 2002–07; CDC, 2009–13; non-executive Director: Kidde, 2004–05; QinetiQ, 2004–06; Tomkins, 2005–10; P&O, 2005–06; Debenhams, 2006–09; SSE (formerly Scottish and Southern Energy), 2007– (Chm., 2015–); Hiscox, 2010–; Helical Bar, 2012–; Wm Morrison Supermarkets plc, 2013–; Mem., Adv. Council, City UK, 2010–. Trustee, British Council, 2012–14. Chm., Malcolm Arnold Fest., 2010–. Mem., Adv. Bd, St Edmund Hall, Oxford, 2004–10; Pro-Chancellor, Open Univ., 2014–. *Recreations:* music, reading, walking, travelling.

GILLINSON, Sir Clive (Daniel), Kt 2005; CBE 1998; Executive and Artistic Director, Carnegie Hall, New York, since 2005; *b* 7 March 1946; *s* of Stanley Gillinson and Regina Schein; *m* 1979, Penelope Morsley; one *s* two *d*. *Educ:* Frensham Heights Sch.; Queen Mary Coll., London; Royal Acad. of Music (Recital Dip., May Mukle Prize). Mem., Cello Section, LSO, 1970–84. Jt owner, Clive Daniel Antiques, 1978–86. Founding Partner, Masterprize, 1997. Chm., Assoc. of British Orchestras, 1992–95; Gov. and Mem. Exec. Cttee, NYO of GB, 1995–2004; Man. Dir, LSO, 1984–2005. *Recreations:* tennis, ski-ing, reading, theatre, cinema, carpentry. *Address:* Carnegie Hall, 881 7th Avenue, New York, NY 10019–3210, USA.

GILLION, Rt Rev. (Alan) Robert; *see* Riverina, Bishop of.

GILLMAN, Bernard Arthur, (Gerry); General Secretary, Society of Civil and Public Servants, 1973–85; *b* 14 April 1927; *s* of Elias Gillman and Gladys Gillman; *m* 1951, Catherine Mary Antonia Harvey (*d* 2012). *Educ:* Archbishop Tenison's Grammar Sch. Civil Service, 1946–53; Society of Civil Servants, 1953–85. Mem., Police Complaints Authy, 1986–91. *Address:* 2 Burnham Street, Kingston-upon-Thames, Surrey KT2 6QR. *T:* (020) 8546 6905. *Clubs:* Royal Over-Seas League, MCC.

GILLMAN, Derek Anthony; Chairman, Impressionist and Modern Art, and Senior Vice President, Christie's, since 2015; Distinguished Visiting Professor, Westphal College of Media Arts and Design, Drexel University, since 2014; *b* 7 Dec. 1952; *s* of Abraham Gillman and Esther Gillman; *m* 1987, Yael Joanna Hirsch; one *s* two *d*. *Educ:* Clifton Coll., Bristol; Magdalen Coll., Oxford (MA); Beijing Langs Inst.; Univ. of E Anglia (LLM). Chinese specialist, Christie's Auctioneers, London, 1977–81; Res. Asst, Dept of Oriental Antiquities, BM, 1981–85; Keeper, Sainsbury Centre for Visual Arts, UEA, 1985–95; Dep. Dir, Internat. Art and Collection Mgt, 1995–96, Curatorial and Educn Services, 1996–99, Nat. Gall. of Victoria; Exec. Dir and Provost, 1999–2000, Pres. and Edna S. Tuttleman Dir, 2001–06, Pennsylvania Acad. of Fine Arts; Exec. Dir and Pres., Barnes Foundn, 2006–13. Sen. Fellow, Melbourne Inst. of Asian Langs and Socs, 1998–2003; Consulting Scholar, Asian Sect., Penn Mus., 2009–; Marina Kellen French Dist. Visitor, Amer. Acad. in Berlin, 2013. *Publications:* The Idea of Cultural Heritage, 2006, 2nd edn 2010; contrib. to exhibn catalogues; articles and reviews for Art, Antiquity and Law, SOAS Bull., Buddhist Forum, Apollo, Orientations, Trans Oriental Ceramic Soc. *Recreations:* reading, drawing. *Address:* Christie's, 20 Rockefeller Plaza, New York, NY 10020, USA.

GILLMAN, Gerry; *see* Gillman, B. A.

GILLON, John Christopher M.; *see* Moore-Gillon.

GILLON, Karen Macdonald; Member (Lab) Clydesdale, Scottish Parliament, 1999–2011; *b* 18 Aug. 1967; *d* of Edith Turnbull (*née* Macdonald); *m* 1999, James Gillon; two *s* one *d*. *Educ:* Jedburgh Grammar Sch.; Birmingham Univ. (Cert. Youth and Community Work 1991). Project Worker, Terminal One youth project, Blantyre, 1991–94; Community Educn Worker, N Lanarkshire Council, 1994–97; PA to Rt Hon. Helen Liddell, MP, 1997–99. Contested (Lab) Clydesdale, Scottish Parlt, 2011. *Recreations:* sport, cooking, flower arranging, music.

GILLON, Prof. Raanan Evelyn Zvi, FRCP; Professor of Medical Ethics, School of Medicine, Imperial College, London, 1995–99, now Emeritus (Visiting Professor, 1989–94); part-time general practitioner, 1974–2002; NHS Senior Partner, Imperial College Medical Partnership, 1991–2002; *b* Jerusalem, 15 April 1941; *s* of Diana Gillon and late Meir Gillon; *m* 1966, Angela Spear; one *d*. *Educ:* Christ's Hospital; University College London (MB BS 1964); Christ Church, Oxford; Birkbeck College London (BA Phil 1st cl. Hons 1979; philosophy prize). MRCP 1974, FRCP 1988. Medical journalism, 1964–71 (Ed., Medical Tribune); part-time GP, part-time philosophy student then teacher, 1974–2006; Dir, Imperial Coll. Health Service, 1982–95; Dir of Teaching in Medical Ethics (for MA course), KCL, 1986–89. Vis. Prof. in Med. Ethics, KCL, 1988–91. Chm., Imperial Coll. Ethics Cttee, 1984–93. Member: BMA, 1964 (Mem., 1998–, Vice-Chm., 2002–06, Ethics Cttee); Archbp of Canterbury's Adv. Gp on Med. Ethics, 1999–2006. Mem. Governing Body, 1989–, Chm., 2000–11, a Vice Pres., 2011–13, Pres., 2013–, Inst. of Medical Ethics; Pres., Health Care Ethics Forum, 2005–13. Ed., Jl of Med. Ethics, 1980–2001. FRSocMed 1966; Fellow, Hastings Center, USA, 2005. Hon. RCM 1986. Hon. DSc Oxon, 2006. Henry Beecher Award, Hastings Center, USA, 1999; Millennium Award, Norwegian Univ. of Sci and Tech., 2001. *Publications:* Philosophical Medical Ethics, 1986 (13 reprints); (Sen. Ed. and contrib.) Principles of Health Care Ethics, 1994; numerous papers on medical ethics. *Recreations:* enjoying the company of wife and daughter, thinking and writing about medical ethics; reading moral philosophy and, intermittently, thrillers and novels, mostly recommended by Angela; playing (blowing?) own trumpet, or rather, Uncle Peter's trumpet, kindly lent in 1954 and bequested to me by his executor Cousin Stephen; singing in a small choir, ski-ing, swimming, occasional active walks on a golf course, cooking, winetasting, arguing and good company. *Address:* 42 Brynmaer Road, SW11 4EW. *T:* (020) 7622 1450.

GILMORE, Brian Terence, CB 1992; *b* 25 May 1937; *s* of late John Henry Gilmore and of Edith Alice Gilmore; *m* 1962, Rosalind Edith Jean Fraser (*see* R. E. J. Gilmore). *Educ:* Wolverhampton Grammar Sch.; Christ Church, Oxford (Passmore-Edwards Prize, 1956; BA Lit. Hum.; MA 1961). CRO and Diplomatic Service Admin Office, 1958–65: Private Sec. to Perm. Sec., 1960–61, to Parly Under Sec., 1961–62; Asst Private Sec. to Sec. of State, 1962–64; British Embassy, Washington, 1965–68; Min. of Technology and DTI, 1968–72: Private Sec. to Minister of State, Industry, 1969–70, and to Lord Privy Seal and Leader of the House of Lords, 1971–72; CSD, 1972–81; Under Sec., 1979; Principal, CS Coll., 1979–81; HM Treasury, 1981–88; Principal Estabt Officer and Principal Finance Officer, 1982–84; Dep. Sec., Office of Minister for CS, Cabinet Office, 1988–92; Dep. Sec., DSS, 1992–94. Chairman: PYBT (E London), 1996–2000; Bart's and the London NHS Trust, 1999–2000. Vice-Pres., Soc. for Promotion of Hellenic Studies, 2000–. *Recreations:* music, walking, Greece. *Address:* 3 Clarendon Mews, W2 2NR. *Club:* Athenæum (Chm., 2000–03; Trustee, 2006–).

GILMORE, Eamon; Member of the Dáil (TD) for Dún Laoghaire, since 1989 (Workers', 1989–92, Democratic Left, 1992–99, Lab, since 1999); Tánaiste (Deputy Prime Minister) and Minister for Foreign Affairs and Trade, Ireland, 2011–14; Leader, Irish Labour Party, 2007–14; *b* Caltra, Co. Galway, 24 April 1955; *s* of John and Celia Gilmore; *m* Carol Hanney; two *s* one *d*. *Educ:* Garbally Coll., Ballinasloe, Galway; University Coll., Galway (BA Psychol.). Pres., Union of Students in Ireland, 1976–78. Trade union organiser, Irish Transport and Gen. Workers' Union, 1978–89. Mem., Dublin CC, 1985–2003. *Publications:* Leading Lights: people who've inspired me, 2010. *Recreations:* sport, family, cooking. *Address:* Leinster House, Kildare Street, Dublin 2, Republic of Ireland. *T:* (01) 6183566.

GILMORE, Prof. Gerard Francis, PhD, ScD; FRS 2013; FRAS, FInstP; Professor of Experimental Philosophy, University of Cambridge, since 2000; *b* Timaru, NZ, 7 Nov. 1951; *s* of Joseph and Eva Gilmore; *m* 1975, Annette Mary Connolly; one *s* one *d*. *Educ:* St Bede's Coll., Christchurch, NZ; Canterbury Univ., NZ (BSc 1st Cl. Hons 1973; PhD 1979); Clare Hall, Cambridge (MA; ScD 2002). FInstP 2000; FRAS 2009. Sen. Res. Fellow, Royal Observatory, Edinburgh, 1979–84; University of Cambridge: Advanced Res. Fellow, 1984–89; Royal Soc. Smithson Fellow, 1987–91; Fellow, King's Coll., 1987–91; John Couch Adams Astronomer, 1989–95; Reader in Astrophysics, 1995–2000; Dep. Dir, Inst. of Astronomy, 1996–2006. UK Principal Investigator, ESA Gaia mission, 2000–; Co-ordinator, Opticon, 2002–. Mem. Council, Eur. Southern Observatory, 2002–07; Member, Advisory Board: Iran Nat. Observatory, 2007–; Aarhus Univ., 2013–. MAE 2004. *Publications:* (ed jtly) The Galaxy, 1987; (jtly) The Milky Way as a Galaxy, 1989; (ed jtly) Baryonic Dark Matter, 1990; (ed jtly) Galactic and Solar System Optical Astrometry, 1994; (ed jtly) Stellar Populations, 1994; (ed jtly) Stellar Initial Mass Function, 1998; contrib. scientific articles. *Recreations:* sport, visiting historical sites, being a good dad, cooking, thinking, weighing galaxies, watching Shaun the Sheep. *Address:* Institute of Astronomy, University of Cambridge, Madingley Road, Cambridge CB3 0HA. *T:* (01223) 337506. *E:* gil@ast.cam.ac.uk.

GILMORE, Sir Ian (Thomas), Kt 2010; MD; FRCP; Consultant Physician, Royal Liverpool Hospital, 1980–2011, now Honorary Consultant Physician; Professor of Medicine, University of Liverpool, since 1999; Chair, Liverpool Health Partners, since 2011; *b* 25 Sept. 1946; *s* of James M. and Jean M. Gilmore; *m* 1975, Hilary Elizabeth Douglas; two *s* one *d*. *Educ:* Royal Grammar Sch., Newcastle upon Tyne; King's Coll., Cambridge (BA 1968; MB BChir 1971; MD 1979); St Thomas' Hosp., London. FRCP 1985. MRC Trng Fellow, St Thomas' Hosp., 1976–77; MRC Travelling Fellow, Univ. of Calif, San Diego, 1979–80. President: RCP, 2006–10; British Gastroenterology Soc., 2012–14; Alcohol Concern, 2014–. Chm., Alcohol Health Alliance, 2009–. *Publications:* (ed) Gastrointestinal Emergencies, 1992; contrib. original articles, chapters and invited reviews on gastrointestinal and liver diseases. *Recreations:* golf, travel. *Address:* Liverpool Health Partners, University of Liverpool, 1st Floor, Liverpool Science Park, 131 Mount Pleasant, Liverpool L3 5TF. *Clubs:* Artists (Liverpool); Royal Liverpool Golf.

GILMORE, Margaret, (Mrs Eamonn Matthews); writer, broadcaster and analyst; *b* 9 Feb. 1956; *d* of late Rev. Canon Norman and of Barbara Gilmore; *m* 1993, Eamonn Matthews; one *s*. *Educ:* North London Collegiate Sch., Middlesex; Westfield Coll., London (BA Hons English). Reporter: Kensington Post, 1977–79; Independent Radio News, 1979–84; BBC N Ireland, 1984–85; Newsnight, BBC, 1986–89; This Week, ITV, 1989–92; Panorama, BBC, 1993–95; news corresp., 1995–97, envmt corresp., 1997–2000, home and legal affairs corresp., 2000–07, BBC. Member: Bd, Food Standards Agency, 2008–14; HFEA, 2015–. Sen. Associate Fellow, RUSI, 2014– (Associate Fellow, 2007–09; Sen. Res. Fellow, 2009–14). *Publications:* (with A. Hayman) The Terrorist Hunters, 2009. *Recreations:* friends and family, playing the piano, supporting Reading Football Club. *Address:* c/o Knight Ayton Management, 35 Great James Street, WC1N 3HB. *E:* MargaretGilmore@btinternet.com. *W:* www.MargaretGilmore.com.

GILMORE, Rosalind Edith Jean, (Mrs B. T. Gilmore), CB 1995; Independent Director, Prudential Regulation Authority, Bank of England, since 2013; *b* 23 March 1937; *oc* of Sir Robert Brown Fraser, OBE, and Betty Fraser; *m* 1962, Brian Terence Gilmore, *qv*. *Educ:* King Alfred Sch.; University Coll. London (BA; Hon. Fellow (Fellow, 1989)); Newnham Coll., Cambridge (BA, MA; Associate Fellow, 1986–95, Hon. Fellow, 1995). Asst Principal, HM Treasury, 1960–65; IBRD, 1966–67; Principal, HM Treasury, 1968–73; Prin. Pvte Sec. to Chancellor of Duchy of Lancaster, Cabinet Office, 1974; HM Treasury: Asst Sec., 1975–80; Press Sec. and Hd of Inf., 1980–82; Gen. Man., Corporate Planning, Dunlop Ltd, 1982–83; Dir of Marketing, Nat. Girobank, 1983–86; Directing Fellow, St George's House, Windsor Castle, 1986–89; re-instated, HM Treasury, and seconded to Bldg Socs Commn, 1989; Dep. Chm., 1989–91, Chm. (First Comr), 1991–94, Bldg Socs Commn; Chief Registrar of Friendly Socs, 1991–94; Industrial Assurance Comr, 1991–94; Dir of Regulation, Lloyd's of London, 1995; Dir, Zurich Financial Services AG, 1998–2007. Chairman: Arrow Broadcasting, 1994–97; Homeowners Friendly Soc., 1996–98; Director: Mercantile Gp plc, 1986–89; London and Manchester Gp plc, 1988–89; BAT Industries, 1996–98; TU Fund Managers, 2000–06; Cons. Man., FI Gp plc, 1987–89. Mem., SIB, 1993–96; Comr, Nat. Lottery Commn, 2000–02. Director: Leadership Foundn, Washington, 1997– (Chm., 2005–07); Internat. Women's Forum, 2005–07 (Vice Pres., 1997–2001). Member: Board: Opera North, 1993–97; Moorfields Eye Hosp. NHS Trust, 1994–2000; Council, RCM, 1997–2007; Court, Cranfield Univ., 1992– (Mem. Adv. Bd, Sch. of Mgt, 2010–; Vis. Fellow, 2013–); Adv. Bd, Winton Centre for Financial History, 2011–. FRSA 1985; CCMI (CIMgt 1992); Hon. RCM 2009. *Publications:* Mutuality for the Twenty-first Century, 1998. *Recreations:* swimming (Half Blue, Cambridge Univ.), music, languages. *Address:* 3 Clarendon Mews, W2 2NR. *Club:* Athenæum.

GILMORE, Sheila; *b* Aberdeen, 1 Oct. 1949; *d* of Harry Hawthorne and Elizabeth McDonald; *m* 1969, Brian Gilmore; three *s* one *d*. *Educ:* Univ. of Kent (Hist. and Pols 1970); Univ. of Edinburgh (LLB 1977). Teacher, 1971–73; family lawyer, 1977–2001. Mem., Edinburgh CC, 1991–2007 (Housing Convenor, 1999–2007). MP (Lab) Edinburgh E, 2010–15; contested (Lab) same seat, 2015. *Recreations:* cycling, reading.

GILMOUR, David Jon, CBE 2003; singer, guitarist and songwriter; *b* Cambridge, 6 March 1946; *s* of Douglas Gilmour and Sylvia Gilmour (*née* Wilson); *m* 1st, 1975, Virginia, (Ginger), Hasenbein (marr. diss.); one *s* three *d*; 2nd, 1994, Polly Samson, *qv*; two *s* one *d* and one step *s*. *Educ:* Perse Sch. for Boys; Cambridgeshire Coll. of Arts and Technol. Joined Pink Floyd, 1968; albums include: A Saucerful of Secrets, 1968; Atom Heart Mother, 1970; Meddle, 1971; Obscured by Clouds, 1972; The Dark Side of the Moon, 1973; Wish You Were Here, 1975; Animals, 1977; The Wall, 1979; The Final Cut, 1983; A Momentary Lapse of Reason, 1987; The Division Bell, 1994; The Endless River, 2014; solo albums: David Gilmour, 1978; About Face, 1984; On an Island, 2006; Live in Gdansk, 2008; Rattle that Lock, 2015. Ivor Novello Award for Lifetime Achievement, 2008. *Address:* c/o One Fifteen, 1 Globe House, Middle Lane Mews, N8 8PN.

GILMOUR, Sir David (Robert), 4th Bt *cr* 1926; writer; *b* 14 Nov. 1952; *er s* of Lord Gilmour of Craigmillar, PC (Life Peer) and of Lady Caroline Gilmour (*née* Montagu-Douglas-Scott); *S* to father's Btcy, 2007; *m* 1975, Sarah Anne, *d* of late M. H. G. Bradstock; one *s* three *d*. *Educ:* Eton; Balliol Coll., Oxford (BA Hons). FRSL 1990. Dep. Ed., 1979–81, Contributing Ed., 1981–85, Middle East International; Res. Fellow, St Antony's Coll., Oxford, 1996–97; Sen. Res. Associate, Balliol Coll., Oxford, 2011–13. *Publications:* Lebanon: the fractured country, 1983, 3rd edn 1987; The Transformation of Spain: from Franco to the constitutional monarchy, 1985; The Last Leopard: a life of Giuseppe di Lampedusa, 1988 (Marsh Biography Award, 1989), 5th edn 2007; The Hungry Generations, 1991; Cities of Spain, 1992; Curzon, 1994 (Duff Cooper Prize, 1995), 2nd edn 2003; (ed) The French and their Revolution, 1998; (ed) Paris and Elsewhere, 1998; The Long Recessional: the Imperial life of Rudyard Kipling, 2002 (Elizabeth Longford Prize for Historical Biography, 2003); The Ruling Caste: Imperial lives in the Victorian Raj, 2005; The Pursuit of Italy: a history of a land, its regions and their peoples, 2011; contrib. Spectator, Literary Review, Times Literary Supplement and The New York Review of Books. *Recreations:* gardening, baking, cricket, opera. *Heir:* *s* Alexander Ian Michael Gilmour, *b* 19 Feb. 1980. *Address:* The Barn House, Alkerton, Oxon OX15 6NL. *Clubs:* Brooks's, Grillions.

GILMOUR, Sir (John) Nicholas, 5th Bt *cr* 1897, of Lundin and Montrave, co. Fife; *b* 15 Dec. 1970; *s* of Sir John Gilmour, 4th Bt and of Valerie Jardine Gilmour (*née* Russell); *S* father, 2013; *m* 1996, Airin Thamrin; two *s*. *Heir:* *s* John Edward Arief Gilmour, *b* 23 July 2001. *Address:* Montrave House, Leven, Fife KY8 5QF.

GILMOUR, His Honour Nigel Benjamin Douglas; QC 1990; a Circuit Judge, 2000–13; *b* 21 Nov. 1947; *s* of late Benjamin Waterfall Gilmour and Barbara Mary Gilmour (subseq. Mrs E. Harborow); *m* 1972, Isobel Anne, *d* of E. Harborow; two *d*. *Educ:* Tettenhall Coll., Staffordshire; Liverpool Univ. (LLB Hons). Called to the Bar, Inner Temple, 1970; an Asst Recorder, 1984–90; a Recorder, 1990–2000. *Recreations:* wine, food.

GILMOUR, Polly; *see* Samson, P.

GILMOUR, Dr Roger Hugh, FIFST; consultant, 2008–10; *b* 24 March 1942; *s* of late William Gilmour and Elizabeth Gilmour; *m* 1968, Margaret Jean Chisholm; one *s* one *d*. *Educ:* Ross High Sch.; Edinburgh Univ. (BSc); Heriot-Watt Univ. (PhD 1969). FIFST 1989. Griffith Laboratories: Canada, 1969; UK/Internat., 1970–79; Pres., USA, 1979–83; CEO Agricl Genetics Co. Ltd, 1983–93; Business Develt Dir, Centre for Applied Microbiol. and Res., 1994–96; Chief Exec., Microbiol Res. Authy, and Centre for Applied Microbiol. and Res., 1996–2003; Dir, Business Div. and Porton Down site, HPA, 2003–04; Dir, 2004–07, Consultant, 2007–09, Centre for Emergency Preparedness and Response, HPA. Dir, MRC Collaborative Centre, 1992–99. Chm., NMT Gp plc, 1998–2004; Dir, Syntaxin Ltd, 2005–07. Trustee, SCI, 2012–. Mem. Council, Univ. of Third Age, Cambridge, 2012–. *Recreations:* walking, ski-ing, gardening, cycling, photography. *Address:* Prospect Villa, Kirtling, Newmarket, Suffolk CB8 9HH. *Club:* Farmers.

GILMOUR, Soutra; theatre designer, since 1995; *b* London; *d* of Angus and Ruth Gilmour. *Educ:* Wimbledon Sch. of Art (BA 1st Cl. Theatre Design). Theatre designs, 1999–, incl. for Gate Th., London, Glasgow Citizens, Royal Court, Almeida, Old Vic, Young Vic, Traverse, Donmar, Wiltons Music Hall, NT (Cottesloe, Lyttleton, Olivier), Royal Opera Hse, RSC, Palace, Comedy, Vaudeville and Apollo theatres; productions include: Hair, Gate Th., 2005; The Caretaker, Crucible, 2006; The Pride, Royal Court, 2008; Piaf, Donmar, transf. Vaudeville, 2008; The Lover and the Collection, Comedy, 2008; Three Days of Rain, Apollo, 2009; Inadmissible Evidence, Donmar, 2011; Antigone, Olivier, 2012 (Evening Standard Award for Best Design, 2012); The Commitments, Palace Th., 2013; Macbeth, 2013, Richard III, 2014, Transformed@Trafalgar Studios; Urinetown, St James Th., transf. Apollo, 2014; Assassins, Menier Chocolate Factory, 2014; The Ruling Class, Trafalgar Studios, 2015; Bull, Young Vic, 2015. *Recreations:* bookbinding, architectural walks, photographing the urban fabric, London, amateur gardening. *W:* www.soutragilmour.com.

GILPIN, Ven. Richard Thomas; Archdeacon of Totnes, 1996–2005, now Archdeacon Emeritus; *b* 25 July 1939; *s* of Thomas and Winifred Gilpin; *m* 1966, Marian Moeller; one *s* one *d*. *Educ:* Ashburton Coll.; Lichfield Theol Coll. Ordained deacon, 1963, priest, 1964; Assistant Curate: Whipton, 1963–66; Tavistock and Gulworthy, 1966–69; Vicar, Swimbridge, 1969–73; Priest-in-charge, W Buckland, 1970–73; Vicar, Tavistock and Gulworthy, 1973–91; Diocesan Dir of Ordinands, 1990–96, and Advr for Vocations, 1991–96, Exeter; Sub-Dean, Exeter Cathedral, 1992–96. Rural Dean, Tavistock, 1987–90. Prebendary, Exeter Cathedral, 1982–2001, now Prebendary Emeritus; Proctor in Convocation, 1995–2000, 2002–05. Ex-officio Mem., Coll. of Canons, Exeter Cathedral, 2001–05. *Recreations:* family, music, art, theatre, walking.

GILROY, Linda; *b* 19 July 1949; *d* of late William Jarvie and Gwendoline Jarvie (*née* Grey); *m* 1987, Bernard Gilroy. *Educ:* Edinburgh Univ. (MA Hons History 1971); Strathclyde Univ. (Postgrad. Secl Dip. 1972), MITSA (Dip. in Consumer Affairs 1990). Dep. Dir, Age Concern Scotland, 1972–79; Regl Sec., subseq. Regl Manager, SW Office, Gas Consumers' Council, 1979–97. MP (Lab and Co-op) Plymouth Sutton, 1997–2010; contested (Lab and Co-op) Plymouth, Sutton and Devonport, 2010. PPS to Minister of State for Local Govt, Dept of Transport, Local Govt and the Regions, 2000–05. Mem., Defence Select Cttee, 2005–10. Hon. DBus Plymouth, 2011. *Recreations:* swimming, walking, keep fit. *E:* gilroyl@hotmail.co.uk.

GILROY, Paul; QC 2006; barrister; *b* 1 May 1962; *s* of George Gilroy and Joan Gilroy (*née* McConnell); two *s* one *d*. *Educ:* Hutchesons' Grammar Sch., Glasgow; Univ. of Dundee (LLB Hons 1984). Called to the Bar, Gray's Inn, 1985; in practice as a barrister, 1985–, specialising in employment, sport, professional discipline and public inquiries. Attorney General's Provincial Panel, 2000–; an Employment Judge (pt-time) (formerly a Chm. (pt-time), Employment Tribunals), 2000–. Chairperson's list, Sport Resolutions (UK) Panel (formerly Sports Dispute Resolution Panel), 2007–; Specialist Mem., Judicial Panel, 2007–, Mem., Appeal Panel, 2008–, FA; Legal Mem., Nat. Anti-Doping Panel, 2009–. *Recreations:* ski-ing, Manchester United FC, travel. *Address:* 9 St John Street, Manchester M3 4DN. *T:* (0161) 955 9000, *Fax:* (0161) 955 9001. *E:* paul.gilroy@9sjs.com; Old Square Chambers, 10–11 Bedford Row, WC1R 4BU. *T:* (020) 7269 0300, *Fax:* (020) 7269 5281. *E:* gilroyqc@oldsquare.co.uk.

GILSENAN, Prof. Michael Dermot Cole; David B. Kriser Professor of Middle Eastern Studies and Anthropology, New York University, since 1995 (Director, Kevorkian Center for Near Eastern Studies, 2007–15); *b* 6 Feb. 1940; *s* of Michael Eugene Cole Gilsenan and Joyce Russell Horn. *Educ:* Eastbourne Grammar Sch.; Oxford Univ. BA (Oriental Studies), Dip. Anth., MA, DPhil (Soc. Anthropology). Research Fellow, Amer. Univ. in Cairo, 1964–66; Research studentship, St Antony's Coll., Oxford, 1966–67; Research Fellow, Harvard Middle East Center, 1967–68; Asst Prof., Dept of Anthropology, UCLA, 1968–70; Research Lectr, Univ. of Manchester, 1970–73; Associate Fellow, St Antony's Coll., Oxford, 1970–73; Lectr, 1973–78, Reader, 1978–83, Dept of Anthropology, University College London; Mem., Sch. of Social Sci., Inst. for Advanced Study, Princeton, 1979–80; Khalid bin Abdullah al Saud Prof. for study of contemp. Arab world, and Fellow of Magdalen Coll., Oxford Univ., 1984–95, Emeritus Fellow, 1995. Anthrop. field work, Egypt, 1964–66, Lebanon, 1971–72, Java and Singapore, 1999–2000, Singapore and Malaysia, 2001–02, 2003–05. Carnegie Corp. Scholar, 2003–05. Mem. Editl Bd, History and Anthropology and Ethnos, Arabian Humanities, Comparative Studies in S Asia, Africa and Middle East, and formerly of Past and Present, Man, and Internat. Jl of Middle Eastern Studies; Series Editor, Society and Culture in the Modern Middle East, 1987–96. *Publications:* Saint and Sufi in Modern Egypt, 1973; Recognizing Islam, 1982; Lords of the Lebanese Marches, 1996. *Recreations:* music, theatre, being elsewhere. *Address:* Department of Middle Eastern and Islamic Studies, New York University, 50 Washington Square South, New York, NY 10012–1073, USA.

GILSON, Michael; Group Editor, Newsquest Sussex, and Editor, The Argus, since 2015; *b* 1 March 1963; *s* of Kenneth and Janet Gilson; *m* 1988, Susan Hunt; two *s*. *Educ:* Temple Secondary Sch., Strood, Kent; Poly. of Wales (BA Hons Communication Studies). With local newspapers, Kent, 1985–88; travel in Peru, 1988–89; News Ed., Hull Daily Mail, 1989–94; Night Ed., Western Mail, 1994–96; Editor: Peterborough Evening Telegraph, 1996–2000; The News, Portsmouth, 2000–06; The Scotsman, 2006–09; Belfast Telegraph, 2009–15. Mem., Code Cttee, Press Complaints Commn, 2004–09. Dir, Regulatory Funding Co., 2014–. Mem., Johnston Press Editl Rev. Gp, 2003–09. *Recreations:* football (player and sons' team coach), tennis, S American travel, trying to interest anyone in obscure 80's indie group, Orange Juice.

GILVARY, Dr Brian; Group Chief Financial Officer and Director, BP plc, since 2012; *b* Liverpool, 12 Feb. 1962; *s* of John and Gladys Gilvary; *m* 1988, Jo Roycroft; two *s*. *Educ:* Univ. of Sheffield (BSc Maths 1983); Univ. of Manchester (MSc Maths; PhD Maths 1986). Upstream Technol., BP Res., Sunbury, 1986–90; Strategy and Planning, Europe, BP Europe, Brussels, 1990–95; Hd, North Sea Crude Oil Trading, 1995–96, Oil Products Trading, 1996–97, BP Internat. Ltd; Hd, Oil Products Trading, BP America, NY, 1997–98; Commercial Vice Pres., Amoco Natural Gas Liquids, BP America, Chicago, 1999–2000; BP plc: COS, 2000–01, Vice Pres. Strategy, 2001, Downstream; Exec. Asst to CEO, 2001–02; Mem. Exec. Cttee and Chief Financial Officer, Refining and Mktg, 2002–05; Mem. Exec. Cttee, Gas, Power and Renewables, 2005–09; CEO, Internat. Supply and Trading, BP Internat. Ltd, 2005–09; Dep. Chief Financial Officer, BP plc, 2010–11. Dir, TNK-BP, Moscow, 2003–05 and 2010–13. Vis. Prof., Manchester Univ., 2013–. Advr, Business in the Community Prince of Wales' Initiatives, Farmers' Mktg, Hill Farming and Supporting local economy, community and heritage, 2007–09; Ext. Advr to Dir Gen. (Spending and Finance), HM Treasury Financial Mgt Rev. Bd. Freeman, Tallow Chandlers' Co., 2013. Award for Best Young Researcher, Tallow Chandlers, 1990. *Recreations:* swimming, cycling, running, football, Rugby, Speakers for School charity. *Address:* BP plc, 1 St James's Square, SW1Y 4PD. *Club:* Royal Automobile.

GIMBLETT, (Catherine) Margaret (Alexandra Forbes); Sheriff of North Strathclyde at Dunoon, 1999–2005; part-time Sheriff, 2005–09; *b* 24 Sept. 1939; *d* of Alexander Forbes Hendry and Margaret Hendry (*née* Whitehead); *m* 1965, Iain McNicol Gimblett; one *s* one *d*. *Educ:* St Leonard's Sch., St Andrews; Edinburgh Univ. (MA); Glasgow Univ. Sec. and PA, Humphreys & Glasgow Ltd, London, 1960–63; Staff Manager, John Lewis Partnership, London, 1963–67; Partner, Alexander Hendry & Son, subseq. Russel & Aitken, Denny, Solicitors, 1972–95; admitted solicitor, 1974; Temp. Sheriff, 1992–95; Sheriff, Glasgow and Strathkelvin, 1995–99. Churchill Fellowship, 1986. *Recreations:* gardening, walking, people, travelling.

GIMINGHAM, Prof. Charles Henry, OBE 1990; FRSE 1961; Regius Professor of Botany, University of Aberdeen, 1981–88 (Professor of Botany, since 1969); *b* 28 April 1923; *s* of late Conrad Theodore Gimingham and Muriel Elizabeth (*née* Blake), Harpenden; *m* 1948, Elizabeth Caroline, *o d* of late Rev. J. Wilson Baird, DD, Minister of St Machar's Cathedral, Aberdeen; three *d*. *Educ:* Gresham's Sch., Holt, Norfolk; Emmanuel Coll., Cambridge (Open scholarship; BA 1944; ScD 1977); PhD Aberdeen 1948. FRSB (FIBiol 1967). Research Asst, Imperial Coll., Univ. of London, 1944–45; University of Aberdeen: Asst, 1946–48, Lectr, 1948–61, Sen. Lectr, 1961–64, Reader, 1964–69, Dept of Botany. Vice Chm., NE Regl Bd, NCC for Scot., 1991–92; Member: Countryside Commn for Scotland, 1980–92; Sci Adv. Cttee, Scottish Natural Heritage, 1996–99 (Mem., NE Regl Bd, 1992–96); Bd of Management, Hill Farming Res. Organisation, 1981–87; Council of Management, Macaulay Inst. for Soil Research, 1983–87; Governing Body, Macaulay Land Use Res. Inst., 1987–90. Mem. Governing Body, Aberdeen Coll. of Educn, 1979–87. President: Botanical Soc. of Edinburgh, 1982–84 (Hon. British Fellow, Botanical Soc. of Scotland, 2004); British Ecological Soc., 1986–87 (Hon. Mem., 2004); Heather Trust, 2004–07. Founding Fellow, Inst. of Contemporary Scotland, 2000. Patron, Inst. of Ecology and Envmtl Mgt, 2000–

(Medal, 2008). *Publications:* Ecology of Heathlands, 1972; An Introduction to Heathland Ecology, 1975; The Lowland Heathland Management Handbook, 1992; (ed) The Ecology, Land Use and Conservation of the Cairngorms, 2002; papers, mainly in botanical and ecological jls. *Recreations:* hill walking, photography, foreign travel, history and culture of Japan. *Address:* 9 Florence Court, 402 North Deeside Road, Cults, Aberdeen AB15 9TD.

GIMZEWSKI, Prof. James Kazimierz, PhD; FRS 2009; FREng, FInstP; Professor of Chemistry, since 2001, Director, Nano and Pico Characterization Core Facility, California NanoSystems Institute, since 2003, and Scientific Director, Art|Sci Center, since 2005, University of California, Los Angeles; Satellite Director and Principal Investigator, National Institute for Materials Science and International Centre for Materials Nanoarchitectronics, Japan, since 2008. *Educ:* Univ. of Strathclyde (BS 1974; PhD 1977). FInstP 1995; FREng 2001. Post-doctoral Research Fellow: Oregon State Univ., 1977–79; Inst. of Inorganic Chem., Univ. of Zurich, 1979–83; Gp Leader, IBM Zurich Res. Lab., 1983–2001. Prof. of Physics, Univ. of Bristol, 2013–15. PhD *hc* Univ. de la Mediterranée, Aix-Marseille II, 2008; Hon. DSc Strathclyde, 2010. *Publications:* articles in jls. *Address:* Department of Chemistry and Biochemistry, University of California, Los Angeles, Charles E. Young Drive East, Los Angeles, CA 90095–1569, USA.

GINGELL, Maj.-Gen. Laurie William Albert, CB 1980; OBE 1966 (MBE 1959); General Secretary, Officers' Pensions Society, 1979–90; *b* 29 Oct. 1925; *s* of late Major William George Gingell, MBE, MM, and of Elsie Grace Gingell; *m* 1949, Nancy Margaret Wadsworth; one *s* one *d. Educ:* Farnborough Grammar Sch.; Oriel Coll., Oxford. Commissioned into Royal Gloucestershire Hussars, 1945; transf. Royal Tank Regt, 1947; psc 1956; jssc 1961; Commanded: 1st Royal Tank Regt, 1966–67; 7th Armoured Bde, 1970–71; DQMG, HQ BAOR, 1973–76; Maj.-Gen. Admin, HQ UKLF, 1976–79. ADC to the Queen, 1974–76. Vice-Pres., Victory Services Club, 1997–2006 (Chm., 1989–97) FCMI (FBIM 1979). Freeman, City of London, 1979. *Recreation:* reading. *Address:* 49 Albion Crescent, Lincoln LN1 1EB. *T:* (01522) 875965.

GINGRICH, Newton Leroy, (Newt); Chief Executive Officer, Gingrich Group, 1999–2011; *b* 17 June 1943; *s* of late Robert Bruce Gingrich and of Kathleen (*née* Daugherty); *m* 1st, 1962, Jacqueline Battley (marr. diss. 1981); two *d*; 2nd, 1981, Marianne Ginther (marr. diss. 2000); 3rd, 2000, Callista Bisek. *Educ:* Emory Univ. (BA); Tulane Univ. (MA; PhD 1971). Taught history, W Georgia Coll., Carrollton, 1970–78; Mem. from 6th Dist of Georgia, US Congress, 1979–99 (Republican Whip, 1989–94); Speaker, US House of Representatives, 1995–99. Founder, Center for Health Transformation, 2003. Gen. Chm., American Solutions for Winning the Future, 2007–11. *Publications:* (jtly) Window of Opportunity: a blueprint for the future, 1984; (jtly) 1945, 1995; To Renew America, 1995; Lessons Learned the Hard Way, 1998; (jtly) Saving Lives and Saving Money, 2006; Winning the Future: a 21st contract with America, 2006; Rediscovering God in America, 2006; (with Nancy Desmond) The Art of Transformation, 2006; (with T. L. Maple) A Contract with the Earth, 2007; Real Change: from the world that fails to the world that works, 2008; *novels* (with William Forstchen): Grant Comes East, 2004; Gettysburg, 2004; Never Call Retreat, 2007; Pearl Harbor: a novel of December the 8th, 2007; Days of Infamy, 2008.

GINNEVER, John Anthony; Director of Education, Leisure and Libraries, East Riding of Yorkshire, 1995–2002; *b* 24 June 1948; *s* of George Edward Ginnever and Olive Ginnever; *m* 1971, Wendy Marian Brown; one *s* one *d. Educ:* Hatfield Coll., Durham Univ. (BSc Hons 1970; PGCE 1971); Newcastle Univ. (MEd 1977). Teacher, 1971–77; Education Officer: Leeds MBC, 1978–82; Bucks CC, 1982–87; N Yorks CC, 1987–89; Dep. Dir of Educn, Newcastle MBC, 1989–95. Chm., Yorks and Humber Regl Adv. Cttee, Duke of Edinburgh's Award, 1998–2009; Member: Cttee, RSPB Richmondshire and Hambleton Local Gp, 2009–; Mgt Gp, Foxglove Covert Local Nature Reserve, 2010–. *Recreations:* birdwatching, hill walking, globetrotting, volunteering.

GINSBURG, Ruth Bader; Associate Justice of the Supreme Court of the United States, since 1993; *b* 15 March 1933; *d* of Nathan Bader and Celia Amster Bader; *m* 1954, Martin D. Ginsburg (*d* 2010); one *s* one *d. Educ:* James Madison High Sch., Brooklyn; Cornell Univ. (BA Hons 1954); Harvard Law Sch.; Columbia Law Sch. (Kent Scholar; LLB, JD 1959). Clerk, Southern Dist, NY, 1959–61; Columbia Law Sch. Project on Internat. Procedure, 1961–63; Professor: Rutgers Univ. Sch. of Law, 1963–72; Columbia Law Sch., 1972–80; Circuit Judge, Court of Appeals for Dist of Columbia, 1980–93. American Civil Liberties Union: Gen. Counsel, 1973–80; Nat. Board, 1974–80; Counsel to Women's Rights Project, 1972–80. Fellow: Amer. Bar Foundn, 1978– (Exec. Cttee and Sec., 1979–89); Amer. Acad. of Arts and Scis, 1982– (Mem. Council, Foreign Relations, 1975–). *Publications:* (with A. Bruzelius) Civil Procedure in Sweden, 1965; (with A. Bruzelius) Swedish Code of Judicial Procedure, 1968; (jtly) Text, Cases and Materials on Sex-Based Discrimination, 1974, Supp. 1978; numerous contribs to learned jls. *Address:* Supreme Court, 1 First Street NE, Washington, DC 20543, USA.

GIORDANO, Sir Richard (Vincent), KBE 1989; Chairman, BG Group plc, 2000–03 (Chairman, BG (formerly British Gas) plc, 1994–2000); *b* March 1934; *s* of late Vincent Giordano and of Cynthia Giordano (*née* Cardetta); granted British citizenship, 2002; *m* 1st, 1956 (marr. diss. 1993); one *s* two *d*; 2nd, 2000, Susan Ware (*d* 2001); 3rd, 2002, Marguerite Rule Johnstone. *Educ:* Harvard Coll., Cambridge, Mass, USA (BA); Columbia Univ. Law Sch. (LLB). Shearman & Sterling, 1959; Airco, Inc., 1963–78: Gp Vice Pres., 1967; Gp Pres. and Chief Operating Officer, 1971; Chief Exec. Officer, Airco, Inc., 1978; Chief Exec. Officer, BOC Gp, 1979–91; Chm., BOC, 1985–92, 1994–96; Grand Metropolitan plc: Bd Mem., 1985–97; Dep. Chm., 1991–97. Mem., CEGB, 1982–92; part-time Board Member: Rio Tinto plc (formerly RTZ Corp.), 1992–2005 (Dep. Chm., 2000–05); Georgia Pacific Corp., Atlanta, Ga, 1984–; Reuters, 1991–94; non-executive Director: Lucas Industries, 1993–94; Nat. Power. Hon. Fellow, London Business Sch., 1994. Hon. Dr of Commercial Science, St John's Univ., 1975; Hon. LLD Bath, 1998. *Recreations:* ocean sailing, tennis. *Address:* PO Box 1598, Lakeville, CT 06039, USA. *T:* (860) 4356617. *Clubs:* The Links, New York Yacht (New York).

GIPPS, Prof. Caroline Victoria, PhD; Vice Chancellor, University of Wolverhampton, 2005–11; *b* 2 Feb. 1948; *d* of John Stephen Davis and Adriaantje de Baat; *m* 1970, Dr Jonathan Henry William Gipps, *qv*; two *s. Educ:* St Winifred's Sch. for Girls, Llanfairfechan; Univ. of Bristol (BSc Psychol 1968); Inst. of Education, London (MSc 1973, PhD Psychol of Educn 1980). Primary sch. teacher, 1968–70; Researcher: Nat. Foundn for Educnl Res., 1970–74; Nat. Children's Bureau, London, 1975–77; Teaching Asst, Psychol. Dept, Univ. of British Columbia, 1977–79; Institute of Education, London: Researcher, Lectr and Reader, 1980–94; Nuffield Res. Fellow, 1992; Hd, Curriculum Studies Dept, 1993–94; Prof. of Educn, 1994–2000; Dean of Res., 1994–99; Dep. Vice Chancellor, Kingston Univ., 2000–05. Pres., British Educnl Res. Assoc., 1992; Member: Panel for Educn, 1996 RAE; Steering Cttee, ESRC Teaching and Learning Res. Prog., 1999–2004; Adv. Cttee, Staff and Educn Develt Assoc., 2002–05; Gen. Teaching Council for England, 2003–05; Ext. Cttee on Examination Standards, QCA, 2003–05; Adv. Cttee, Thomas Coram Res. Unit, Inst. of Educn, London, 2004–11; ESRC Strategic Res. Bd, 2005–08; Advr, Wingate Foundn Scholarships, 1995–2012. Mem. Bd, Kingston Univ. Trustee, Buttle UK. AcSS 2001. Hon. LLD Bristol 2010. *Publications:* (jtly) Language Proficiency in the Multiracial Junior School: a comparative study, 1975; (jtly) Combined Nursery Centres, 1981; (jtly) Testing Children: standardised testing in Local Education Authorities and schools, 1983; (jtly) Warnock's 18%: children with special needs in the primary school, 1987; Beyond Testing: towards a theory of educational assessment, 1994 (Japanese edn 2001); (with P. Murphy) A Fair Test?: assessment, achievement and equity, 1994 (Standing Council for Studies in Educn prize for best educnl book); Intuition or Evidence?: teachers and national assessment of seven year olds, 1995; (ed with P. Murphy) Equity in the Classroom: towards effective pedagogy for girls and boys, 1996; (with G. Stobart) Assessment: a teachers' guide to the issues, 3rd edn 1997; (jtly) What Makes a Good Primary School Teacher?, 2000. *Recreations:* sailing, sea-bathing, Handel opera, Mozart. *Address:* 2 Beech Close, SW15 4HW. *T:* (020) 8789 4306. *Clubs:* Athenæum; Trearddur Bay Sailing.

See also Sir P. J. Davis.

GIPPS, Dr Jonathan Henry William, OBE 2000; Director, Bristol Zoo Gardens, and Bristol, Clifton and West of England Zoological Society Ltd, 2001–10; *b* 7 July 1947; *s* of late Capt. Louis H. F. P. Gipps, RN and Molly Joyce Gipps; *m* 1970, Caroline Victoria Davis (*see* C. V. Gipps); two *s. Educ:* Imperial Coll., Univ. of London (BSc Zool. 1973); Royal Holloway Coll., Univ. of London (PhD 1977). RN, 1966–70. Post-doctoral Research Fellow, Univ. of British Columbia, 1977–79; Lectr in Biology, Univ. of Bath, 1980–81; Res. Fellow, RHBNC, 1981–84; Educn Officer, Computer Centre, Kingston Poly., 1984–87; London Zoo: Curator of Mammals, 1987–91; General Curator, 1991–93; Dir, 1993–2001. Co-keeper, Giant Panda Internat. Studbook, 1988–2010. Member, Council: UK Fedn of Zoos, subseq. British and Irish Assoc. of Zoos and Aquariums, 1995–2010 (Hon. Treas., 1998–2001); European Assoc. of Zoos and Aquaria, 1999–2006 (Chm., Conservation Cttee, 1999–2002); World Assoc. of Zoos and Aquariums, 2005–10 (Chm., Conservation Cttee, 2002–10); Chm., Adv. Bd, 2009–, Chm., Global Conservation Network, 2010–, Conservation Breeding Specialist Gp, IUCN. Pres., Anchor Soc., Bristol, 2010–11. Chm. Trustees, Bristol Natural Hist. Consortium, 2006–11; Trustee: Internat. Species Inf. System, 2000–05; SS Great Britain Trust, 2007–12; St George's, Bristol, 2010–; Early Opera Co., 2011– (Chm., 2012–); La Nuova Musica, 2011–. FRSA 1998. Hon. DSc: Kingston, 1993; Bristol, 2011. *Publications:* (ed jtly) The Ecology of Woodland Rodents, 1981; (ed) Beyond Captive Breeding: re-introducing endangered mammals to the wild, 1989. *Recreations:* fly-fishing, making jewellery, sailing, baroque opera, ski-ing, cooking, travelling.

GIPPSLAND, Bishop of, since 2015; **Rt Rev. Kay Goldsworthy;** *b* Melbourne, 18 Aug. 1956; *d* of George Raymond Goldsworthy and Esther Gertrude Goldsworthy (*née* Holt); *m* 1988, Benjamin James; two *s. Educ:* CPE (Basic) Instep 1983; Alfred Hosp. (CPE 1984); Melbourne Coll. of Divinity, Trinity Coll., Melbourne (BTh 1985); CPE (Advanced) Instep 1987. Ordained deaconess, 1984, deacon, 1986, priest, 1992; Asst Deaconess, Thomastown/Epping, Melbourne, 1984–85; Asst Deaconess, 1985–86, Asst Curate, 1986–88, St Alban's Deer Park, Keilor; Chaplain, Perth Coll., 1988–95; Rector, Parish of Applecross, 1995–2007; Archdeacon: Fremantle, 1998–99; Southern Region, 1999–2003; Archdeacon of Perth and Registrar, 2007–08; Asst Bishop, Dio. of Perth, WA, 2008–15. Administrator, Dio. of Perth, 2006–13. Canon, St George's Cathedral, Perth, 1994–98. *Address:* Anglican Diocese of Gippsland, PO Box 928, Sale, Vic 3853, Australia. *E:* BishopKay@gippsanglican.org.au.

GIRDWOOD, David Greenshields; DL; Rector, St Columba's School, Kilmacolm, since 2002; *b* 14 Oct. 1957; *s* of Alexander and Margaret Girdwood; *m* 1985, Lisa Greig; two *d. Educ:* St Andrews Univ. (BSc 1978); Jordanhill Coll. of Educn, Glasgow (PGCE 1979); Stirling Univ. (MEd 1985); Scottish Qualification for Headship, 2001. Teacher of Chemistry, 1979–85, Asst Hd of Science, 1985–87, Lornshill Acad., Alloa; Principal Teacher of Chemistry and Hd of Scis, 1987–96, Hd of Upper Sch., 1996–2002, Stewart's Melville Coll., Edinburgh. Associate Assessor, HM Inspectorate of Educn, 1999–2002. Member: Erskine Stewart's Melville Governing Council, 2006–; Scottish Strategic Adv. Cttee, Duke of Edinburgh Award, 2010–13. DL Renfrewshire, 2009. *Recreations:* family activities, walking. *Address:* St Columba's School, Duchal Road, Kilmacolm PA13 4AU. *Club:* East India.

GIRET, Joseph John Bela Leslie; QC 2010; *b* Paddington, London, 30 Sept. 1954; *s* of Joseph and Elizabeth Giret; *m* 2006, Magdalena Szajtek; one *s* one *d. Educ:* St Marylebone Grammar Sch.; Warwick Univ. (LLB); Inns of Court Sch. of Law. Called to the Bar, Gray's Inn, 1985; in practice: at Common Law Bar, specialising in military and criminal law, regulatory and sport. Freeman, City of London, 2006; Mem., Co. of Watermen and Lightermen, 2006. Mem., British Jun. Decathlon Squad, 1972. *Recreations:* opera, especially at Glyndebourne and Royal Opera House, Rugby (3 England caps and Captain Middx and London Counties at schoolboy level), sailing (qualified Yacht Master Ocean, 1988; has sailed across Atlantic twice), fair-weather sculling on River Thames, dedicated cyclist and follower of Tour de France, historic Formula single seater and sports car events (held International Racing Drivers Licence). *Address:* PortoBello, 3 HollyCross, Crazies Hill, Reading, Berks RG10 8QB. *E:* joseph@giret.co.uk. *Clubs:* Royal London Yacht; Archer Road Cycling; Gruppo Sportivo Henley Cycling; Leander, Upper Thames Rowing.

GIRET, (Josephine) Jane; QC 2001; *b* 6 June 1944; *d* of late Bernard Leslie Barker and of Josephine Mamie Barker; *m* 1985, Joseph John Bela Leslie Giret, QC (marr. diss.). *Educ:* Queen Anne's Sch., Caversham, Berks. Called to the Bar, Inner Temple, 1981; Mem. *ad eund*, Lincoln's Inn, 1992 (Bencher, 2004). *Recreations:* following the English Cricket Team, Barbados, yoga. *Address:* 74 Alder Lodge, River Gardens, Stevenage Road, SW6 6NR. *T:* (020) 7831 6381.

GIRI, Anu; Co-Director, English National Ballet School, since 2010; *b* Hyderabad, India, 11 Feb. 1968; *d* of Dr Ganjeti Yada Giri and Dr Arcot Kishori; *m* 2004, Paul Martindale; two *d. Educ:* King's High Sch. for Girls, Warwick; Liverpool Poly. (BA Hons Drama and Sociol. 1990); Birkbeck Coll., Univ. of London (Dip. Mgt 2001). Presenter, Network East, BBC2, 1992–93; Projects Asst, Dance 4, 1992–93; Administrator, Claire Russ Ensemble and Chitralekha and Co., 1993–94; Educn Manager, Birmingham Royal Ballet, 1994–97; Gen. Manager, Shobana Jeyasingh Dance Co., 1997–2000; Sen. Dance Officer, 2000–03, Hd of Dance, 2003–10, Arts Council England. *Recreations:* dance, theatre, gym, reading, family. *Address:* 47 Bective Road, Putney, SW15 2QA. *T:* (020) 8870 6679, 07989 404428. *E:* anugiri11@hotmail.com.

GIRLING, (John) Anthony; President of the Law Society, 1996–97; *b* 21 Aug. 1943; *s* of James William Girling, OBE and Annie Doris (*née* Reeves); *m* 1965, Lynne Margaret Davis; one *s* one *d. Educ:* Tonbridge Sch.; Guildford Coll. of Law. Admitted Solicitor, 1966; Girlings, Solicitors: Partner, 1968; Man. Partner, 1982–96; Chm., 1997–2000; Consultant, 2000–09. Hon. Sec., 1974–80, Pres., 1980–81, Kent Law Soc.; Mem. for Kent, Council of Law Soc., 1980–99. Hon. Sen. Mem., Darwin Coll., Univ. of Kent, 1984. Fellow, Inst. of Advanced Legal Studies, Univ. of London, 1997–2009. Hon. LLD Kent, 1998. *Publications:* contrib. to Law Soc. Gazette and other legal jls. *Recreations:* golf, ski-ing, the countryside. *Address:* 14 Ripple Court, Barton Mill Road, Canterbury, Kent CT1 1GN. *Clubs:* Canterbury Golf; El Paraíso Golf.

GIRLING, Julie McCulloch; Member (C) South West England and Gibraltar, European Parliament, since 2009; *b* London, 21 Dec. 1956; *m* 1981, Warren Glyn Girling; one *s. Educ:* Twickenham Co. Grammar Sch.; Liverpool Univ. (BA Hist. and Politics 1979). Grad. trainee, Ford Motor Co., 1979–82; Buyer and Merchandise Controller, Argos Catalogue Gp, 1982–88; Mktg Manager, Dixons Stores Gp, 1988–90; Marketing and Buying Manager: Boots, 1991; Halfords, until 1993; freelance trainer, 1995–2009. Member (C): Cotswold DC, 1999–2009 (Leader, 2003–06); Glos CC, 2000–09. *Address:* European Parliament, Rue Wiertz, 1047 Brussels, Belgium.

GIROLAMI, Sir Paul, Kt 1988; Chief Executive, 1980–86, and Chairman, 1985–94, Glaxo Holdings; *b* 25 Jan. 1926; *m* 1952, Christabel Mary Gwynne Lewis (*d* 2009); two *s* one *d*. *Educ:* London School of Economics (Hon. Fellow, 1989); FREconS; FIMC 1990. Chantrey & Button, Chartered Accountants, 1950–54; Coopers & Lybrand, Chartered Accountants, 1954–65; Glaxo Holdings: Financial Controller, 1965; Finance Director, 1968. Director: Inner London Board of National Westminster Bank, 1974–89; Credito Italiano Internat. UK, 1990–93; Forte plc, 1992–96; UIS France, 1994–. Member: Bd of Dirs, Amer. Chamber of Commerce (UK), 1983–; CBI Council, 1986–93; Appeal Cttee, ICA, 1987–; Stock Exchange Listed Cos Adv. Cttee, 1987–92. Chm., Senate for Chartered Accountants in Business, 1990–2000. Chm. Council, Goldsmiths' Coll., Univ. of London, 1994–2003; Mem. Open Univ. Vis. Cttee, 1987–89. Gov., NIESR, 1992–. Freeman, City of London; Liveryman, Goldsmiths' Co., 1980– (Mem., Ct of Assistants, 1986–; Prime Warden, 1995–96); Mem., Soc. of Apothecaries, 1993–. Hon. FCGI 1994; FCMI (FBIM 1986); FRSA 1986. Hon. DSc: Aston, 1990; Trieste, 1991; Sunderland, 1991; Bradford, 1993; Hon. LLD: Singapore, 1993; Warwick, 1996; Hon. DBA Strathclyde, 1993. Centenary Medal, UK SCI, 1992; Centenary Award, UK Founding Socs, 1992. Grand Cross, Order of the Holy Sepulchre, 1994. Grande Ufficiale, Ordine al Merito della Repubblica Italiana, 1987; Cavaliere al Merito del Lavoro, Italy, 1991; Insignia of the Order of the Rising Sun, Japan, 1991; Public Service Star, Singapore, 2000. *Recreations:* reading, music.

See also P. J. Girolami.

GIROLAMI, Paul Julian; QC 2002; barrister; *b* 5 Dec. 1959; *s* of Sir Paul Girolami, *qv*; *m* 1991, Deborah Bookman; one *s* two *d*. *Educ:* St Paul's Sch., London; Corpus Christi Coll., Cambridge. Called to the Bar, Middle Temple, 1983; Jun. Counsel to the Crown, Chancery, 1991–2000; a Dep. High Court Judge, 2006–. Freeman, City of London; Liveryman, Goldsmiths' Co. *Address:* Maitland Chambers, 7 Stone Buildings, Lincoln's Inn, WC2A 3SZ. *T:* (020) 7406 1200, *Fax:* (020) 7406 1300. *E:* clerks@maitlandchambers.com.

GIROUARD, Mark, PhD; FRSL; writer and architectural historian; Slade Professor of Fine Art, University of Oxford, 1975–76; *b* 7 Oct. 1931; *s* of late Richard D. Girouard and Lady Blanche Girouard; *m* 1970, Dorothy N. Dorf; one *d*. *Educ:* Ampleforth; Christ Church, Oxford (MA); Courtauld Inst. of Art (PhD); Bartlett Sch., UCL (BSc, Dip. Arc). Staff of Country Life, 1958–66; studied architecture, Bartlett Sch., UCL, 1966–71; staff of Architectural Review, 1971–75. George Lurcy Vis. Prof., Columbia Univ., NY, 1987. Member: Council, Victorian Soc., 1979– (Founder Mem. 1958; Mem. Cttee, 1958–66); Royal Fine Art Commn, 1972–96; Royal Commn on Historical Monuments (England), 1976–81; Historic Buildings Council (England), 1978–84; Commn for Historic Buildings and Monuments, 1984–90 (Mem., Buildings Adv. Cttee, 1984–86; Mem., Historic Areas Adv. Cttee, 1985–89; Mem., Historic Bldgs Cttee, 1988–90); Council, Spitalfields Historic Buildings Trust, 1983– (Chm., 1977–83); Trustee, Architecture Foundn, 1992–99. Mem., Adv. Council, Paul Mellon Centre for Studies in British Art, 1990–96. Hon. Student, Christ Ch, Oxford, 2002. FSA 1986; FRSL 2012. Hon. FRIBA, 1980. Hon. DLitt: Leicester, 1982; Buckingham, 1991. *Publications:* Robert Smythson and the Architecture of the Elizabethan Era, 1966, 2nd edn, Robert Smythson and the Elizabethan Country House, 1983; The Victorian Country House, 1971, 2nd edn 1979; Victorian Pubs, 1975, 2nd edn 1984; (jtly) Spirit of the Age, 1975 (based on BBC TV series); Sweetness and Light: the 'Queen Anne' movement 1860–1900, 1977; Life in the English Country House, 1978 (Duff Cooper Meml Prize; W. H. Smith Award, 1979); Historic Houses of Britain, 1979; Alfred Waterhouse and the Natural History Museum, 1981; The Return to Camelot: chivalry and the English gentleman, 1981; Cities and People, 1985; A Country House Companion, 1987; The English Town, 1990; Town and Country, 1992; Windsor: the most romantic castle, 1993; Big Jim: the life and work of James Stirling, 1998; Life in the French Country House, 2000; Elizabethan Architecture: its rise and fall, 1540–1640, 2009; Enthusiasms, 2011; articles in Country Life, Architect. Rev., Listener. *Address:* 35 Colville Road, W11 2BT.

GIRVAN, Rt Hon. Sir (Frederick) Paul, Kt 1995; PC 2007; a Lord Justice of Appeal, Supreme Court of Judicature, Northern Ireland, 2007–15; *b* 20 Oct. 1948; *s* of Robert Frederick Girvan and Martha Elizabeth (*née* Barron); *m* 1974, Karen Elizabeth Joyce (MBE 2013); two *s* one *d*. *Educ:* Belfast Royal Acad.; Clare Coll., Cambridge (BA); Queen's Univ., Belfast; Gray's Inn. Called to the Bar: NI, 1971; Inner Bar (NI), 1982; Jun. Crown Counsel, NI, 1979–82; Justice of the High Court, NI, 1995–2007. Chancellor, Archdio. of Armagh, 1999–. Chairman: Council of Law Reporting for NI, 1994–2001; Law Reform Adv. Cttee for NI, 1997–2004 (Mem., 1994–2004). Hon. Bencher, Gray's Inn, 1999. *Recreations:* badminton, walking, swimming, reading, modern languages, gardening, cooking, golf, painting.

GISBOROUGH, 3rd Baron *cr* 1917; **Thomas Richard John Long Chaloner;** Lord-Lieutenant of Cleveland, 1981–96; Lieutenant of North Yorkshire, 1996–2001; *b* 1 July 1927; *s* of 2nd Baron and Esther Isabella Madeleine (*d* 1970), *yr d* of late Charles O. Hall, Eddlethorpe; *S* father, 1951; *m* 1960, Shane, *e d* of late Sidney Newton, London, and *gd* of Sir Louis Newton, 1st Bt; two *s*. *Educ:* Eton; Royal Agricultural Coll. 16th/5th Lancers, 1948–52; Captain Northumberland Hussars, 1955–61; Lt-Col Green Howards (Territorials), 1967–69. Mem., Rural Develt Commn, 1985–89. CC NR Yorks, 1964–74, Cleveland, 1974–77. Hon. Col, Cleveland County Army Cadet Force, 1981–92. President: British Ski Fedn, 1985–90; Assoc. of Professional Foresters, 1998–2001. DL N Riding of Yorks and Cleveland, 1973; JP Langbaurgh East, 1981–94. KStJ 1981. *Recreations:* shooting, fishing, tennis, bridge, piano. *Heir: s* Hon. Thomas Peregrine Long Chaloner [*b* 17 Jan. 1961; *m* 1992, Karen, *o d* of Alan Thomas]. *Address:* Gisborough House, Guisborough, Cleveland TS14 6PT. *T:* (01287) 632002, 07717 411110.

GISBY, Jonathan Hugh; Executive Vice President Business Development, Magine.com, since 2012; *b* Salisbury, 27 May 1968; *s* of John Gisby and Rosalie Gisby (*née* Uwins); *m* 1996, Kate Wilson; two *s* one *d*. *Educ:* Exeter Coll., Oxford (BA Hons Mod. Hist. 1990); Johns Hopkins SAIS, Bologna (Dip. Internat. Relns 1991); Harvard Univ. (MBA 1996). Sen. Advr, Corporate Strategy, BBC, 1997–99; Man. Dir, Portals, Freeserve plc, 1999–2004; Man. Dir, Yahoo UK, 2004–06; Vice Pres. Media, Yahoo Europe, 2005–07; Dir, Future Media and Technol., Channel 4, 2007–10. Mem. Bd, Artichoke Prodns, 2009–. *Recreation:* adventures.

GISCARD d'ESTAING, Valéry; Grand Croix de la Légion d'Honneur; Croix de Guerre (1939–45); Member, Académie Française, 2003; President of the French Republic, 1974–81; Member, Constitutional Council, since 1981; President, European Convention, 2001–03; *b* Coblence, 2 Feb. 1926; *s* of late Edmond Giscard d'Estaing and May Bardoux; *m* 1952, Anne-Aymone de Brantes; two *s* two *d*. *Educ:* Lycée Janson-de-Sailly, Paris; Ecole Polytechnique; Ecole Nationale d'Administration. Inspection of Finances: Deputy, 1952; Inspector, 1954; Dep. Dir, Cabinet of Président du Conseil, June–Dec. 1954. Elected Deputy for Puy-de-Dôme, 1956; re-elected for Clermont N and SW, Nov. 1958, Nov.–Dec. 1962, March 1967, June 1968, March 1973, 1984, 1986 and 1988–89; Deputy for Puy-de-Dôme, 1993–2002; Sec. of State for Finance, 1959; Minister of Finance, Jan.–April 1962; Minister of Finance and Economic Affairs, April–Nov. 1962 and Dec. 1962–Jan. 1966; Minister of Economy and Finance, 1969–74. Pres., Nat. Fedn of Ind. Republicans, 1966–73 (also a Founder); Pres., comm. des finances de l'économie générale et du plan de l'Assemblée nationale, 1967–68; Chm., Commn of Foreign Affairs, Nat. Assembly, 1987–89, 1993–97. Mem., Eur. Parlt, 1989–93. President: Conseil Régional d'Auvergne, 1986–2004; Eur. Movt Internat., 1989–97; Council of Eur. Municipalities and Regions, 1997–2004. Mayor of Chamalières, 1967–74. Deleg. to Assembly of UN, 1956, 1957, 1958. Mem., Real Acad. de Ciencias Económicas y Financieras, Spain, 1995–. Nansen Medal, UNHCR, 1979; Gold Medal, Jean Monnet Foundn, 2001; Karl Prize, Aachen, 2003. *Publications:* Démocratie Française, 1976 (Towards a New Democracy, 1977); 2 Français sur 3, 1984; Le Pouvoir et la Vie (memoirs), 1988; L'Affrontement, 1991; Le Passage (novel), 1994; Dans 5 ans l'an 2000, 1995; La princesse et le président (novel), 2009. *Clubs:* Polo (Paris); Union Interalliée.

GISSING, Jason; Co-Founder, and Director, 2000–14, Ocado.com (Chief Financial and Marketing Officer, 2000–09; Commercial Director, 2011–14); *b* UK, 25 Oct. 1970; *s* of Graham and Mikiko Gissing; *m* 2002, Katinka, *d* of late Arne Naess; two *s* two *d*. *Educ:* Oundle Sch., Northants; Worcester Coll., Oxford (BA Juris.). Goldman Sachs, 1992–2000. *Recreations:* tennis, ski-ing, football, yoga, history, the environment. *Clubs:* Queen's, Campden Hill Lawn Tennis, 5 Hertford Street.

GITTINGS, (Harold) John; financial consultant and writer; *b* 3 Sept. 1947; *s* of Harold William Gittings and Doris Marjorie Gittings (*née* Whiting); *m* 1st, 1988, Andrea (*née* Fisher) (*d* 1995); 2nd, 2002, Barbara (*née* Lowenstein). *Educ:* Duke of York's Royal Military School, Dover. ACIS. Beecham Group, 1971–73; Peat Marwick Mitchell, Hong Kong, 1973–74; N. M. Rothschild & Sons, 1974–81; Continental Bank, 1981–82; Target Group, 1982–85; Man. Dir, Touche Remnant & Co., 1986–90; Chm., Greenfield Marketing, subseq. Greenfield Gp, 1992–96; Dir, Meltemi Entertainment Ltd, 1996–2000. Trustee, CAB Brighton, 2014–. Gov., St Peter's Sch., Portslade, 2014–. *Recreations:* travel, collecting, film. *Address:* 27 Cambridge Road, Hove BN3 1DE.

GITTUS, John Henry, DSc, DTech; FREng; Senior Technical Consultant: Chaucer plc, since 2002; NECSA (South Africa), since 2006; Klydon (South Africa), since 2009; *b* 25 July 1930; *s* of Henry Gittus and Amy Gittus; *m* 1953, Rosemary Ann Geeves; one *s* two *d*. *Educ:* Alcester Grammar Sch.; DSc Phys London 1976; DTech Metall Stockholm 1975. CEng, FREng (FEng 1989); FIMechE, FIS, FIMMM. British Cast Iron Res. Assoc., 1947–55; Mond Nickel Co., R&D Labs, Birmingham, 1955–60 (develt Nimonic series high temp. super alloys for aircraft gas turbine engines); United Kingdom Atomic Energy Authority, 1960–89: Research Manager, Springfields (develt nuclear fuel); Head, Water Reactor fuel develt; Head, Atomic Energy Tech. Br., Harwell; Director: Water Reactor Safety Research; Safety and Reliability Directorate, Culcheth; Communication and Information; Dir Gen., British Nuclear Forum, 1990–93; Senior Partner: SPA Consultants, 1993–; NUSYS Consultants, Paris, 1994–; AEA Technol., 1996–; Amersham, 1999–; Sumitomo Corp., 1999–; Senior Technical Consultant: Cox Power Hldgs, 1996–2002; Eskom, 1998–2002; Amersham Health plc, later GE Healthcare, Amersham, 2000–08. Working Mem., Lloyd's Nuclear Syndicate, 1996–. Consultant: Argonne Nat. Lab., USA, 1968; Oak Ridge Nat. Lab., 1969. Visiting Professor: Ecole Polytechnique Fédérale, Lausanne, 1976; Univ. de Nancy, 1984; Regents' Prof., UCLA, 1990–91; Prof. of Risk Mgt, 1997–2006, Royal Acad. of Engrg Prof. of Integrated Business Develt, 2006–, Plymouth Univ. Editor-in-Chief, Res Mechanica, 1980–91. *Publications:* Uranium, 1962; Creep, Viscoelasticity and Creep-fracture in Solids, 1979; Irradiation Effects in Crystalline Solids, 1979; (with W. Crosbie) Medical Response to Effects of Ionizing Radiation, 1989; numerous articles in learned jls. *Recreations:* old houses, old motor cars, old friends. *Address:* (office) 9 Devonshire Square, Cutlers Gardens, EC2M 4WL. *T:* (020) 7397 9700; (home) The Rectory, 19 Butter Street, Alcester, Stratford-upon-Avon B49 5AL. *E:* john@gittus.com. *Club:* Royal Society of Medicine.

GIUDICE, Hon. Geoffrey Michael, AO 2010; Judge of the Federal Court, Australia, 1997–2012; Consultant, Ashurst Australia, since 2013; *b* 16 Dec. 1947; *s* of Rupert Emanuel Giudice and Emily Muriel Giudice; *m* 1970, Beth Hayden; three *s* one *d*. *Educ:* Xavier Coll., Melbourne; Univ. of Melbourne (BA 1970; LLB). Res. Officer, Hosp. Employees Union, 1971; IR Manager, Myer Emporium Ltd, 1972–78; Partner, Moule Hamilton and Derham, solicitors, 1979–84; Barrister, Victoria Bar, 1984–97. Pres., Fair Work Australia (formerly Australian Industrial Relns Commn), 1997–2012. Hon. Professorial Fellow, Univ. of Melbourne, 2012–. *Recreations:* tennis, bridge. *Address:* Ashurst Australia, 181 William Street, Melbourne, Vic 3000, Australia. *Clubs:* Athenæum (Melbourne); Melbourne Cricket, Victoria Racing.

GIULIANI, Rudolph William, Hon. KBE 2001; Mayor, City of New York, 1994–2001; founder, Chairman and Chief Executive, Giuliani Partners, since 2002; Partner, Bracewell & Giuliani, since 2005; *b* 28 May 1944; *m* 1984; one *s* one *d*. *Educ:* Manhattan Coll. (AB); New York Univ. (JD). Legal Clerk to US Dist Court Judge, NYC, 1968–70; Asst Attorney, S Dist, NY, 1970–73; Exec. Asst Attorney, Dept of Justice, 1973–75; Associate Dep. Attorney Gen., 1975–77; with Patterson, Belknap, Webb and Tyler, 1977–81; Associate Attorney Gen., 1981–83; US Attorney, US Dist Court, S Dist, NY, 1983–89; with White & Case, 1989–90; with Anderson Kill Olick & Oshinsky PC, 1990–93. Republican Candidate for Mayor, NY, 1989. *Publications:* Leadership, 2002. *Address:* Giuliani Partners LLC, 1251 Avenue of the Americas, 9th Floor, New York, NY 10020–1104, USA.

GIUSSANI, Bruno; European Director, TED and Curator, TEDGlobal, since 2005; *b* Faido, Switzerland, 26 April 1964. *Educ:* Univ. of Geneva (Econ. and Social Scis 1989). Political Editor, 1992–93, Technol. Editor, 1994–97, l'Hebdo mag.; Cybertimes columnist, New York Times, 1996–2000; Hd, Online Strategy, WEF, 1998–2000; Eur. Editor, Industry Standard mag., 2000–01; Dir, Innovation, 3G Mobile, 2002; Knight Fellow, Stanford Univ., 2003–04. Producer and Host, Forum des 100, 2005–13. Vice-Chm., Tinext, 2001–13. *Publications:* ROAM: making sense of the wireless internet, 2001. *W:* www.giussani.com.

GLADDEN, Prof. Lynn Faith, CBE 2009 (OBE 2001); PhD; FRS 2004; FREng; Shell Professor of Chemical Engineering, since 2004, and Pro-Vice-Chancellor for Research, since 2010, University of Cambridge; Fellow, Trinity College, Cambridge, since 1999; *b* 30 July 1961; *d* of John Montague Gladden and Sheila Faith (*née* Deverell); partner, Prof. Paul Alexander, *qv*. *Educ:* Heathfield Sch., Harrow; Univ. of Bristol (BSc 1st cl. Hons (Chemical Physics) 1982); Keble Coll., Oxford (PGCE 1983); Trinity Coll., Cambridge (PhD 1987). FIChemE 1996; FRSC 2000; FInstP 2003. Pickering Res. Fellow, Royal Soc., 1986; University of Cambridge: Asst Lectr, 1987–91, Lectr, 1991–95; Reader in Process Engrg Sci., 1995–99; Prof. of Chem. Engrg Sci., 1999–2004; Hd, Dept of Chem. Engrg, later Chem. Engrg and Biotechnol., 2006–10. Miller Vis. Prof., Univ. of Calif., Berkeley, 1996; Hon. Prof., Beijing Univ. of Chem. Technol., 2010–. Member: Royal Soc./Royal Acad. of Engrg Adv. Gp to NPL, 2003–; EPSRC, 2006–12; Council, Royal Soc., 2006–08. Comr, Royal Commn for Exhibn of 1851, 2010–. FREng 2003. Beilby Medal, Inst. of Materials, Minerals and Mining, RSC, and Soc. of Chem. Industry, 1995; Tilden Lect. and Silver Medal, RSC, 2001. *Recreations:* reading, wine, modern art. *Address:* Jasmine Cottage, 79 Green End, Landbeach, Cambridge CB25 9FD. *T:* (01223) 334762, *Fax:* (01223) 334796. *E:* Gladden@cheng.cam.ac.uk.

GLADSTONE, David Arthur Steuart, CMG 1988; HM Diplomatic Service, retired; *b* 1 April 1935; *s* of late Thomas Steuart Gladstone and Muriel Irene Heron Gladstone; *m* 1961, April (*née* Brunner); one *s* one *d*. *Educ:* Eton; Christ Church, Oxford (MA History). National Service, 1954–56; Oxford Univ., 1956–59. Annan, Dexter & Co. (Chartered Accountants), 1959–60; FO, 1960; MECAS, Lebanon, 1960–62; Bahrain, 1962–63; FO, 1963–65; Bonn, 1965–69; FCO, 1969–72; Cairo, 1972–75; British Mil. Govt, Berlin, 1976–79; Head of Western European Dept, FCO, 1979–82; Consul-Gen., Marseilles, 1983–87; High Comr, Colombo, 1987–91; Chargé d'Affaires *ai*, Kiev, 1992. Dir, SANE, 2002–. *Publications:* What shall we do with the Crown Prerogative?, 1998. *Recreations:* music, theatre, cinema, dreaming, landscape gardening. *Address:* 1 Mountfort Terrace, N1 1JJ.

GLADSTONE, Emma Ace; Artistic Director and Chief Executive, Dance Umbrella, since 2013; *b* London, 12 Nov. 1960; *d* of Tim Gladstone and Caroline Gladstone; *m* 2004, Barnaby Stone; one *d*, and one step *s* one step *d*. *Educ:* Camden Sch. for Girls; Manchester Univ. (BA Hist. 1984); Laban Dance Centre (Postgrad. Cert. 1985; Advanced Performance Course 1986). Freelance dancer with Arlene Philips, 1977–79, Lea Anderson, 1989–97; Co-Founder and Dir, Adventures in Motion Pictures, 1986–89; Associate Dir, The Place Th., 1997–2003; Artistic Programmer and Producer, Sadler's Wells, 2005–13. Artistic Dir, Rolex Mentor Protégé Arts Weekend, 2013. Mentor, Dance UK, 2011–; Advisor: Family Arts Campaign, 2012–; Akademi, 2013–; PAL Labs, 2014–. Series Ed., body:language, booklets, 2013. Hon. Fellow, Trinity Laban Conservatoire of Music and Dance, 2014. *Recreations:* running, modern design, art, reading, surfing badly. *Address:* Dance Umbrella, 1 Brewery Square, SE1 2LF. *T:* (020) 7407 1200. *E:* emmag@danceumbrella.co.uk. *Club:* Two Brydges Place.

GLADSTONE, Sir (Erskine) William, 7th Bt *cr* 1846; KG 1999; JP; Lord-Lieutenant of Clwyd, 1985–2000; *b* 29 Oct. 1925; *s* of Charles Andrew Gladstone, (6th Bt), and Isla Margaret (*d* 1987), *d* of late Sir Walter Erskine Crum; *S* father, 1968; *m* 1962, Rosamund Anne, *yr d* of late Major A. Hambro; two *s* one *d*. *Educ:* Eton; Christ Church, Oxford. Served RNVR, 1943–46. Asst Master at Shrewsbury, 1949–50, and at Eton, 1951–61; Head Master of Lancing Coll., 1961–69 (Hon. Fellow 2009). Chief Scout of UK and Overseas Branches, 1972–82; Mem., World Scout Cttee, 1977–83 (Chm., 1979–81). DL Flintshire, 1969, Clwyd, 1974, Vice Lord-Lieut, 1984; Alderman, Flintshire CC, 1970–74. Chm., Rep. Body of Church in Wales 1977–92; Chairman: Council of Glenalmond Coll. (formerly Trinity Coll., Glenalmond), 1982–86; Govs, Ruthin Sch., 1987–92 (Patron, 1998–). JP Clwyd 1982. Hon. LLD Liverpool, 1998. *Publications:* The Shropshire Yeomanry, 1953; Gladstone: a bicentenary portrait, 2009; The Hawarden Events Books, 2009; People in Places, 2013; Family, Friends and Fervours, 2015; The Origins and Purpose of the Order of the Garter, 2015; various school textbooks. *Recreations:* reading history, watercolours, shooting, gardening. *Heir: s* Charles Angus Gladstone [*b* 11 April 1964; *m* 1988, Caroline, *o d* of Sir Derek Thomas, *qv*; two *s* four *d*]. *Address:* The Gardener's Cottage, Hawarden Castle, Flintshire CH5 3NY. *T:* (01244) 520987.

GLADWIN, Rt Rev. John Warren; Bishop of Chelmsford, 2003–09; Chair, Citizens Advice, since 2009; Honorary Assistant Bishop, Diocese of St Albans, since 2010; *b* 30 May 1942; *s* of Thomas Valentine and Muriel Joan Gladwin; *m* 1981, Lydia Elizabeth Adam. *Educ:* Hertford Grammar School; Churchill Coll., Cambridge (BA History and Theology, MA 1969); St John's Coll., Durham (Dip. Theol). Asst Curate, St John the Baptist Parish Church, Kirkheaton, Huddersfield, 1967–71; Tutor, St John's Coll., Durham and Hon. Chaplain to Students, St Nicholas Church, Durham, 1971–77; Director, Shaftesbury Project on Christian Involvement in Society, 1977–82; Secretary, Gen. Synod Board for Social Responsibility, 1982–88; Prebendary, St Paul's Cathedral, 1984–88; Provost of Sheffield, 1988–94; Bishop of Guildford, 1994–2003. Mem., Gen. Synod of C of E, 1990–2009. Jt Pres., Church Nat. Housing Coalition, 1997–2006; Chm. Bd, Christian Aid, 1998–2008. Chair, St Albans and District Bereavement Network, 2014–. Hon. DTh Anglia Ruskin, 2009. *Publications:* God's People in God's World, 1979; The Good of the People, 1988; Love and Liberty, 1998. *Recreations:* gardening, travel, beekeeping. *Address:* 131a Marford Road, Wheathampstead, Herts AL4 8NH. *T:* (01582) 834223.

GLADWYN, 2nd Baron *cr* 1960, of Bramfield, co. Suffolk; **Miles Alvery Gladwyn Jebb;** *b* 3 March 1930; *s* of 1st Baron Gladwyn, GCMG, GCVO, CB and Cynthia (*d* 1990), *d* of Sir Saxton Noble, 3rd Bt; *S* father, 1996. *Educ:* Eton; Magdalen Coll., Oxford (MA). Served as 2nd Lieut, Welsh Guards and Pilot Officer, RAFVR. Sen. management, BOAC, later British Airways, 1961–83. *Publications:* (as Miles Jebb): The Thames Valley Heritage Walk, 1980; A Guide to the South Downs Way, 1984; Walkers, 1986; A Guide to the Thames Path, 1988; East Anglia, 1990; The Colleges of Oxford, 1992; Suffolk, 1995; (ed) The Diaries of Cynthia Gladwyn, 1995; The Lord-Lieutenants and their Deputies, 2007; Patrick Shaw Stewart, 2010. *Heir:* none. *Address:* E1 Albany, Piccadilly, W1J 0AR. *Clubs:* Brooks's, Beefsteak.

GLAISTER, Lesley Gillian, FRSL; writer; *b* 4 Oct. 1956; *d* of Leonard Oliver Richard Glaister and Maureen Jillian Glaister (*née* Crowley); three *s*; *m* 2001, Andrew Greig. *Educ:* Open Univ. (BA 1st Cl. Hons Humanities); Univ. of Sheffield (MA Socio-Legal Studies). Adult Educn Tutor (pt-time), Sheffield, 1982–90; Lectr (pt-time), for MA in Writing, Sheffield Hallam Univ., 1993–2011. Writer-in-Residence: Cheltenham Fest. of Literature, and Univ. of Gloucester, 2002–03; Univ. of Edinburgh, 2008–11; Lectr, Univ. of St Andrews, 2011–. FRSL 1994. Author of the Year, Yorkshire Post, 1994. *Play:* Bird Calls, Crucible Th., Sheffield, 2003. *Publications:* Honour Thy Father (Somerset Maugham Award, Betty Trask Award), 1990; Trick or Treat, 1991; Digging to Australia, 1992; Limestone and Clay, 1993; Partial Eclipse, 1994; The Private Parts of Women, 1996; Easy Peasy, 1997; Sheer Blue Bliss, 1999; Now You See Me, 2001; As Far As You Can Go, 2004; Nina Todd Has Gone, 2007; Chosen, 2010; Little Egypt, 2014 (Jerwood Fiction Uncovered Prize). *Recreations:* walking, yoga, theatre, cinema, knitting, crochet. *Address:* 8 Greenbank Loan, Edinburgh EH10 5SH; Pentland View, Stromness, Orkney KW16 3JW.

GLAISTER, Prof. Stephen, CBE 1998; PhD; Professor of Transport and Infrastructure, Department of Civil and Environmental Engineering, 1998–2009, now Emeritus, and Chairman, Railway Technology Strategy Centre, since 2009 (Director, 1998–2009), Imperial College, London; Director, RAC Foundation, 2008–15; *b* 21 June 1946; *s* of Kenneth Goodall Glaister and Mary Glaister (*née* Jones); *m* 1977, Alison Sarah Linning; one *s*. *Educ:* Univ. of Essex (BA 1967); LSE (MSc 1968; PhD 1976). Lectr in Econs, 1969–78, Cassel Reader, 1978–98, LSE. Member, Board: LRT, 1984–93; Transport for London, 2000–. Advisor: DfT (various dates); Rail Regulator, 1994–2001. Trustee, Rees Jeffreys Road Fund, 1979–. *Publications:* Mathematical Methods for Economists, 1972, 3rd edn 1984; Fundamentals of Transport Economics, 1981; Urban Public Transport Subsidies, 1982; (with C. M. Mulley) Public Control of the Bus and Coach Industry, 1983; (jtly) Application of Social Cost Benefit Analysis to London Transport Policies, 1983; (with Tony Travers) Meeting the Transport Needs of the City, 1993; (with Tony Travers) New Directions for British Railways?: the political economy of privatisation and regulation, 1993; (with R. Layard) Cost Benefit Analysis, 1994; (with Tony Travers) Tolls and Shadow Tolls, 1994; (with Tony Travers) An Infrastructure Fund for London, 1994; (jtly) London Bus Tendering, 1995; (jtly) London's Size and Diversity: the advantages in a competitive world, 1996; (with Dan Graham) Who Spends What on Motoring in the UK?, 1996; (jtly) Transport Policy in Britain, 1998; (jtly) Getting Partnerships Going: public private partnerships in transport, 2000; (with T. Grayling) A New Fares Contract for London, 2000; (jtly) Capital Asset: London's healthy contribution to jobs and services, 2000; (with Dan Graham) The Effect of Fuel Prices on Motorists, 2000; (jtly) A Reassessment of the Economic Case for CrossRail, 2001; (jtly) Streets Ahead: safe and liveable streets for children, 2002; (with T. Travers) Treasurehouse and Powerhouse, 2004; (with D. Graham) Pricing Our Roads: vision and reality, 2004; (with D. Graham) National Road Pricing: is it fair and practical?, 2006; (jtly) Roads and Reality, 2007; numerous articles in learned jls. *Recreation:* playing the oboe. *Address:* 39 Huntingdon Street, N1 1BP. *T:* (020) 7609 1401. *E:* s.glaister@imperial.ac.uk.

GLAISYER, Ven. Hugh; Archdeacon of Lewes and Hastings, 1991–97, Archdeacon Emeritus, since 2007; *b* 20 Jan. 1930; *s* of Rev. Canon Hugh Glaisyer and Edith Glaisyer; *m* 1962, Alison Marion Heap; one *s* two *d*. *Educ:* Tonbridge Sch.; Oriel Coll., Oxford (MA 2nd cl. Hon. Mods, 2nd Cl. Theol.); St Stephen's House, Oxford. FO, RAF, 1954. Ordained, Manchester, 1956; Curate: St Augustine's, Tonge Moor, Bolton, 1956–62; Sidcup, 1962–64; Vicar, Christ Church, Milton-next-Gravesend, 1964–81; RD, Gravesend, 1974–81; Vicar, Hove, 1981–91; RD, Hove, 1982–91; Canon of Chichester Cathedral, 1982–91. *Recreations:* British shorthair cats, gardening. *Address:* Florence Villa, Hangleton Lane, Ferring, W Sussex BN12 6PP. *T:* (01903) 244688.

GLAMIS, Lord; Simon Patrick Bowes Lyon; *b* 18 June 1986; *s* and *heir* of Earl of Strathmore and Kinghorne, *qv*. *Club:* Turf.

GLAMORGAN, Earl of; Robert Somerset; *b* 20 Jan. 1989; *s* and *heir* of Marquess of Worcester, *qv*.

GLANCY, Robert Peter; QC 1997; a Recorder, since 1999; a Judge of the First Tier Tribunal (Mental Health) (formerly a President, Mental Health Review Tribunal), since 1999; *b* 25 March 1950; *s* of Dr Cecil Jacob Glancy, JP and Anita Glancy; *m* 1976, Linda Simons; one *s* two *d*. *Educ:* Manchester Grammar Sch.; St John's Coll., Cambridge (MA). Called to the Bar, Middle Temple, 1972, Bencher, 2007; in practice at the Bar, 1973–; Asst Recorder, 1993–99. *Publications:* (jtly) The Personal Injury Handbook. *Recreations:* theatre, cinema, reading, watching Manchester United. *Address:* 26 Litchfield Way, Hampstead Garden Suburb, NW11 6NJ. *T:* (020) 8933 1938.

GLANUSK, 5th Baron *cr* 1899; **Christopher Russell Bailey,** TD 1977; Bt 1852; *b* 18 March 1942; *o s* of 4th Baron Glanusk and Lorna Dorothy (*d* 1997), *o d* of Capt. E. C. H. N. Andrews, MBE, RA; *S* father, 1997; *m* 1974, Frances Elizabeth, *o d* of Air Chief Marshal Sir Douglas Lowe, *qv*; one *s* one *d*. *Educ:* Summer Fields, Oxford; Eton Coll.; Clare Coll., Cambridge (BA 1964). Design Engr, English Electric Leo Ltd, 1964–66; Product Mkting Manager, Ferranti Ltd, 1966–78; Internat. Product Manager, Bestobell Mobrey Ltd, 1978–83; Sales Engr, STC Telecommunication Ltd, 1984–86; General Manager: Autocar Equipment Ltd, 1986–97; Woolfram Research Europe Ltd, 1997–98. Territorial Army: Captain, Berks Yeo. Signal Sqdn, 1967–76, Cheshire Yeo. Signal Sqdn, 1976–79; Maj., HQ2 Signal Bde, 1979–83. *Heir: s* Hon. Charles Henry Bailey, *b* 12 Aug. 1976. *Address:* 51 Chertsey Road, Chobham, Surrey GU24 8PD.

GLANVILLE, Brian Lester; author and journalist since 1949; *b* 24 Sept. 1931; *s* of James Arthur Glanville and Florence Glanville (*née* Manches); *m* 1959, Elizabeth Pamela de Boer (*née* Manasse), *d* of Fritz Manasse and Grace Manasse (*née* Howden); two *s* two *d*. *Educ:* Newlands Sch.; Charterhouse. Literary Advr, Bodley Head, 1958–62; Sunday Times (football correspondent), 1958–92; sports columnist, 1960–66; The People (sports columnist), 1992–96; The Times (football writer), 1996–98; Sunday Times, 1998–. *Publications:* The Reluctant Dictator, 1952; Henry Sows the Wind, 1954; Soccer Nemesis, 1955; Along the Arno, 1956; The Bankrupts, 1958; After Rome, Africa, 1959; A Bad Streak, 1961; Diamond, 1962; (ed) The Footballer's Companion, 1962; The Director's Wife, 1963; The King of Hackney Marshes, 1965; A Second Home, 1965; A Roman Marriage, 1966; The Artist Type, 1967; The Olympian, 1969; A Cry of Crickets, 1970; The Financiers, 1972; The History of the World Cup, 1973; The Thing He Loves, 1973; The Comic, 1974; The Dying of the Light, 1976; Never Look Back, 1980; (jtly) Underneath The Arches (musical), 1981; A Visit to the Villa (play), 1981; The Rise of Gerry Logan, 1983; Kissing America, 1985; Love is Not Love, 1985; (ed) The Joy of Football, 1986; The Catacomb, 1988; Champions of Europe, 1991; Story of the World Cup, 1993; Football Memories, 1999; Dictators, 2001; The Arsenal Stadium History, 2006; England's Managers, 2007; For Club and Country, 2008; The Real Arsenal, 2009; *juvenile:* Goalkeepers are Different (novel), 1971; Target Man (novel), 1978; The Puffin Book of Football, 1978; The Puffin Book of Tennis, 1981. *Address:* 160 Holland Park Avenue, W11 4UH. *T:* (020) 7603 6908.

See also J. Glanville.

GLANVILLE, Josephine; Director, English PEN, since 2012; *b* London, 1 Sept. 1963; *d* of Brian Lester Glanville, *qv*. *Educ:* Worcester Coll., Oxford (1st Cl. Hon. Mods Classics 1985); School of Oriental and African Studies, Univ. of London (BA 1st Cl. Hons Hebrew 1995). Freelance journalist and teacher, 1985–91; freelance journalist, 1995–98; Producer, BBC Current Affairs, 1998–2006; Ed., Index on Censorship, 2006–12. Amnesty Media Award, 2008. *Publications:* (ed) Qissat, 2006. *Recreations:* hill walking, reading, music. *E:* joglanville@gmail.com.

GLANVILLE, Philippa Jane, OBE 2015; FSA; Academic Director (formerly Director), Waddesdon Manor, Buckinghamshire, 1999–2003; *b* 16 Aug. 1943; *d* of late Wilfred Henry Fox-Robinson and of Jane Mary (*née* Home); *m* 1968, Dr Gordon Harris Glanville; two *s*. *Educ:* Talbot Heath, Bournemouth; Girton Coll., Cambridge (MA Hist.); University Coll. London (Archives Admin). FSA 1968. Tudor and Stuart Curator, London Mus., 1966–72; Hd, Tudor and Stuart Dept, Mus. of London, 1972–80; Victoria and Albert Museum: Asst Keeper, Metalwork Dept, 1980–89; Curator, 1989–96, Chief Curator, 1996–99, Metalwork, Silver and Jewellery Dept. Consultant Curator, Gilbert Collection, 2001–03; Sen. Res. Fellow, 2004–07; Guest Curator, Nat. Archives, Drink: a History, 2006; Curatorial Advr, Harley Foundn, 2005–14. Member: Council for Care of Churches, 1997–2001; Westminster Abbey Fabric Commn, 1998–; Arts Council, Nat. Museums of Wales, 2002–11. Trustee: Bishopsland Educnl Trust, 2003–12; Geffrye Mus., 2005–14; Art Fund, 2011–; Vice-Pres., NADFAS, 2009–; Mem., Reviewing Cttee on Export of Works of Art, 2010–. Mem. Cttee, Court Dining Res. Gp, 1989–; contributor, Henry VIII inventory project, 1992–. Associate Fellow, Univ. of Warwick, 2003–06. Liveryman, Co. of Goldsmiths, 1991–; Master, Co. of Art Scholars, 2011–12. Mem., Editl Bd, Apollo, 2004–11. *Publications:* London in Maps, 1972; Silver in England, 1987; Silver in Tudor and Early Stuart England, 1990; (with J. Goldsborough) Women Silversmiths 1685–1845, 1991; (ed and contrib.) Silver, 1996, 2nd edn 1999; (ed with Hilary Young and contrib.) Elegant Eating, 2002; (contrib.) City Merchants and the Arts 1670–1720, 2004; (contrib.) East Anglian Silver 1550–1750, 2004; (contrib.) Britannia and Muscovy, 2006; (contrib.) Feeding Desire, 2006; The Art of Drinking, 2007; (contrib.) Quand Versailles était meublé, 2007; (contrib.) Treasures of the Church, 2008; Dinner with a Duke: decoding food and drink at Welbeck Abbey 1695–1914, 2010; (contrib.) Gold Power and Allure, 2012; contrib. articles in Antiquaries Jl, Burlington Mag., Silver Society Jl, Country Life, World of Interiors, etc, and in exhibn catalogues. *Address:* 4 Topiary Square, Stanmore Road, Richmond TW9 2DB.

GLASBY, John Hamilton; Treasurer, Devon and Cornwall Police Authority, 1993–2009; *b* 29 March 1950; *s* of James Ronald Glasby and Lucie Lillian Glasby (*née* Baxter); *m* 1st, 1971 (marr. diss. 1989); two *s* one *d*; 2nd, 2003, Vivienne Amanda Lloyd. *Educ:* Univ. of Sheffield (BA); Univ. of Birmingham (MSocSc); Liverpool Poly. Mem., CIPFA, 1982. Lectr in Econs, Univ. of E Anglia, 1972–73; Economist: Central Lancs New Town, 1973–76; Shropshire CC, 1976–82; Asst Dir of Finance, Dudley Metropolitan Borough, 1982–84; Devon County Council: Dep. Co. Treas., 1984–93; Co. Treas., 1993–96; Dir of Resources, 1996–2000. Treasurer: Dartmoor Nat. Park Authy, 1997–2000; Devon Fire Authy, 1998–2000. Trustee, Devon Community Foundn, 2010–. *Recreation:* amateur author.

GLASCOCK, Prof. John Leslie, PhD; Professor of Real Estate Finance, and Director, Center for Real Estate and Urban Economic Studies, University of Connecticut, since 2011; *b* 2 Jan. 1950; *s* of Leslie Albert Glascock and Clara Jean Glascock; *m* 1961, Linda Diane Brown; one *s* three *d*. *Educ:* Tennessee Technol Univ. (BSc (Business Admin (Econs)) 1971); Stetson Univ. (MBA 1974); Virginia Poly. Inst. and State Univ. (MEc 1978); Univ. of N Texas (PhD (Finance) 1984). Louisiana Real Estate Commn Endowed Chair of Real Estate and Prof. of Finance, 1988–96, Interim Dean, 1994–95, Orso Coll. of Business Admin, Louisiana State Univ.; Prof. of Finance and Real Estate and Hd, Dept of Finance, Sch. of Business Admin, Univ. of Connecticut, 1996–98; Oliver T. Carr Dist. Prof. of Real Estate

Finance, Sch. of Business and Public Mgt, 1998–2003, Associate Dean for Res. and Doctoral Progs, 2001–03, George Washington Univ.; Grosvenor Prof. of Real Estate Finance, Univ. of Cambridge, and Fellow, Pembroke Coll., Cambridge, 2003–09; West Shell Prof. of Real Estate Finance, and Dir, Real Estate Center, Univ. of Cincinnati, 2009–11. Sec.-Treas., Amer. Real Estate and Urban Econs Assoc., 1993; Pres., Southwest Finance Assoc., 1996–97; Bd Mem., Asian Real Estate Soc., 1999–. Member Editorial Board: Jl of Real Estate Finance and Econs, 1992– (Special Issue Ed., March 2000); Jl of Real Estate Practice and Educn, 1998–. *Publications:* over 50 refereed articles in jls and numerous reports and monographs. *Recreations:* travel, reading. *Address:* School of Business, University of Connecticut, 2100 Hillside Road, U1041RE, Storrs, CT 06269, USA.

GLASER, Dr Daniel Eduard; Director of Science Gallery London, King's College London, since 2013; *b* 1 April 1968; *s* of Denis Victor Glaser and Danya Ruth Glaser (*née* Samson); *m* 1996, Nathalie Claire Bloomberg; three *d*. *Educ:* George Eliot Jun. Sch.; Jews' Free Sch.; Westminster Sch.; Trinity Coll., Cambridge (BA Pt 1 Pure Maths, Pt 2 English Lit 1990); Sussex Univ. (MSc Knowledge Based Systems 1991); Weizmann Inst., Rehovot, Israel (PhD Neurobiol. 1999). University College London: Res. Fellow, Inst. of Ophthalmol., 1999–2000; Sen. Res. Fellow, Inst. of Cognitive Neurosci., 2000–06; Hon. Sen. Res. Fellow, 2006–; Develt Manager, 2006–07, Hd of Special Projects, Public Engagement, 2007–13, Wellcome Trust. Scientist in Residence, ICA, 2001–02; Chair, London Café Scientifique, 2002–. Presenter, Under Laboratory Conditions, BBC TV, 2006. Mem., Camden Cycling Campaign, 2000–. A Judge, Man Booker Prize, 2014. NESTA Cultural Leadership Award, Nassau, Bahamas, 2005. *Publications:* Trust Me I'm a Scientist, 2004; contrib. scientific papers on visual cortex, brain imaging techniques and effect of experience on vision. *Recreations:* fatherhood, restaurants, berating motorists, egosurfing. *Address:* King's Cultural Institute, Somerset House East Wing, Strand, WC2R 2LS.

GLASER, Milton; graphic designer; *b* 26 June 1929; *s* of Eugene and Eleanor Glaser; *m* 1957, Shirley Girton. *Educ:* High Sch. of Music and Art, NY; Cooper Union Art Sch., NY; Acad. of Fine Arts, Bologna (Fulbright Schol.). Joint Founder: Pushpin Studios, 1954; New York mag., 1968 (Pres. and Design Dir, 1968–77); WBMG, pubn design co., 1983; Milton Glaser Inc., 1974; *projects* include: 600 foot mural, New Federal Office Building, Indianapolis, 1974; Observation Deck and Perm. Exhibn, Twin Towers, World Trade Center, NY, 1975; Sesame Place, Pennsylvania, 1981–83; Grand Union Co. architecture, interiors and packaging; Internat. AIDS symbol and poster, WHO, 1987; Trattoria dell'Arte, NY, 1988; New York Unearthed mus., 1990; *solo exhibitions* include: MOMA, NY, 1975; Centre Georges Pompidou, Paris, 1977; Lincoln Center Gall., NY, 1981; Posters, Vicenza Mus., 1989; Art Inst. of Boston, 1995; *work in public collections* including: MOMA, NY; Israel Mus., Jerusalem; Nat. Archive, Smithsonian Instn, Washington; Cooper Hewitt Nat. Design Mus., NY. Member: Bd, Sch. of Visual Arts, NY, 1961–; Bd of Dirs, Cooper Union, NY; Amer. Inst. of Graphic Arts. Gold Medal, Soc. of Illustrators; St Gauden's Medal, Cooper Union; Prix Savignac, Urban Art Internat. and UNESCO, 1996; Honors Award, AIA, 1992; Lifetime Achievement Award, Cooper Hewitt Nat. Design Mus., 2004; Nat. Medal of Arts, USA, 2010. *Address:* Milton Glaser Inc., 207 East 32nd Street, New York, NY 10016, USA. *T:* (212) 8893161, *Fax:* (212) 2134072. *E:* studio@miltonglaser.com.

GLASGOW, 10th Earl of, *cr* 1703; **Patrick Robin Archibald Boyle;** DL; Lord Boyle, 1699; Viscount of Kelburn, 1703; Baron Fairlie (UK), 1897; television director/producer; *b* 30 July 1939; *s* of 9th Earl of Glasgow, CB, DSC, and Dorothea, *o d* of Sir Archibald Lyle, 2nd Bt; *S* father, 1984; *m* 1975, Isabel Mary James; one *s* one *d*. *Educ:* Eton; Paris Univ. National Service in Navy; Sub-Lt, RNR, 1959–60. Worked in Associated Rediffusion Television, 1961; worked at various times for Woodfall Film Productions; Asst on Film Productions, 1962–64; Asst Dir in film industry, 1962–67; producer/director of documentary films, Yorkshire TV, 1968–70; freelance film producer, 1971–, making network television documentaries for BBC Yorkshire Television, ATV and Scottish Television. Formed Kelburn Country Centre, May 1977, opening Kelburn estate and gardens in Ayrshire to the public. Elected Mem. (Lib Dem), H of L, Jan. 2005. DL Ayrshire and Arran, 1995. *Recreations:* theatre and performing arts, railways. *Heir: s* David Michael Douglas Boyle, *b* 15 Oct. 1978. *Address:* Kelburn, Fairlie, Ayrshire KA29 0BE. *T:* (01475) 568204; (office) South Offices, Kelburn Estate, Fairlie, Ayrshire KA29 0BE. *T:* (01475) 568685.

GLASGOW, Archbishop of, (RC), since 2012; **Most Rev. Philip Tartaglia,** STD; *b* 11 Jan. 1951; *s* of Guido and Annita Tartaglia. *Educ:* St Mungo's Acad., Glasgow; St Vincent's Coll., Langbank; St Mary's Coll., Blairs; Pontifical Scots Coll., Rome; Pontifical Gregorian Univ., Rome (PhB; STD 1980). Ordained priest, 1975; Dean of Studies, Pontifical Scots Coll., Rome, 1978–79; Asst Priest, Our Lady of Lourdes, Cardonald, 1980–81; Lectr, 1981–83, Dir of Studies, 1983–85, St Peter's Coll., Newlands, Glasgow; Vice-Rector, 1985–87, Rector, 1987–93, Chesters Coll., Bearsden, Glasgow; Asst Priest, St Patrick's, Dumbarton, 1993–95; Parish Priest, St Mary's, Duntocher, 1995–2004; Rector, Pontifical Scots Coll., Rome, 2004–05; Bishop of Paisley, (RC), 2005–12. *Address:* c/o Curial Offices, 196 Clyde Street, Glasgow G1 4JY.

GLASGOW, (St Mary's Cathedral), Provost of; *see* Holdsworth, Very Rev. K.

GLASGOW, Edwin John, CBE 1998; QC 1987; *b* 3 Aug. 1945; *s* of late Richard Edwin, (Dick), Glasgow and Diana Geraldine Mary Glasgow (*née* Markby); *m* 1967, Janet Coleman; one *s* one *d*. *Educ:* St Joseph's Coll., Ipswich; University Coll. London (LLB; Fellow, 2004). Called to the Bar, Gray's Inn, 1969, Bencher, 1994. Pres., Internat. Tribunal, Fedn Internat. de l'Automobile, 2011– (Vice-Pres., Court of Appeal, 2009–14). Chm., Stafford Corporate Consulting, 2000–. Chairman: Financial Reporting Review Panel, 1992–97; Advocacy Trng (formerly Teaching) Council, 2005–08 (Fellow, 2009–); Singapore Internat. Mediation Centre, 2014–; Mem., Singapore Internat. Arbitration Centre, 2014–; Pres., Internat. Advocacy Trng Council, 2011–15. Member: Adv. Council, Public Concern at Work, 2001– (Trustee, 1994–); Le Demi-Siècle de Londres, 2002–. Chm., Bentham Club, UCL, 2000–14; Trustee: Mary Glasgow Language Trust, 1978–2014 (Chm., 1984–2014); London Opera Players, 1985–2008. FCIL 2010; FCIArb 2012. *Recreations:* family, friends, France, music. *Address:* 39 Essex Street, WC2R 3AT. *T:* (020) 7832 1111; Copper Hall, Watts Road, Thames Ditton, Surrey KT7 0BX; Entrechaux, Vaucluse, France. *Clubs:* Garrick, Royal Automobile (Chm. Stewards, 2005–); Harlequins FC (Chm. Trustees, 1995–2004); Thames Ditton Cricket (Vice-Pres., 2001–).

GLASGOW AND GALLOWAY, Bishop of, since 2010; **Rt Rev. Dr Gregor Duthie Duncan;** *b* 11 Oct. 1950; *s* of Edwin John Duncan and Janet Brown Duncan. *Educ:* Univ. of Glasgow (MA Hons 1972); Clare Coll., Cambridge (PhD 1977); Oriel Coll., Oxford (BA Hons 1983); Ripon Coll., Cuddesdon. Ordained deacon, 1983, priest, 1984; Asst Curate, Oakham with Hambleton and Egleton, and Braunston with Brooke, 1983–86; Chaplain, Edinburgh Theol Coll., 1987–89; Rector of St Columba's, Largs, 1989–99; Dean, Dio. of Glasgow and Galloway, 1996–2010; Rector, St Ninian's, Pollokshields, 1999–2010. *Recreations:* collecting gramophone records, cooking. *Address:* 25 Quadrant Road, Newlands, Glasgow G43 2QP. *T:* (0141) 633 5877. *E:* bishop@glasgow.anglican.org.

GLASGOW AND GALLOWAY, Dean of; *see* Barcroft, Very Rev. I. D.

GLASHOW, Prof. Sheldon Lee, PhD; Metcalf Professor of Mathematics and Science, Boston University, since 2000; Higgins Professor of Physics, Harvard University, 1979–2000, now Emeritus (Professor of Physics, 1966–84); *b* 5 Dec. 1932; *s* of Lewis and Bella Glashow; *m* 1972, Joan (*née* Alexander); three *s* one *d*. *Educ:* Cornell Univ. (AB); Harvard Univ. (AM, PhD). National Science Foundn Fellow, Copenhagen and Geneva, 1958–60; Res. Fellow, Calif Inst. of Technol., 1960–61; Asst Prof., Stanford Univ., 1961–62; Associate Prof., Univ. of Calif at Berkeley, 1962–66. Visiting Professor: CERN, 1968; Marseille, 1971; MIT, 1974 and 1980; Boston Univ., 1983; Univ. Schol., Texas A&M Univ., 1983–86. Consultant, Brookhaven Nat. Lab., 1966–80; Affiliated Senior Scientist, Univ. of Houston, 1983–96. Pres., Sakharov Internat. Cttee, Washington, 1980–85. Hon. DSc: Yeshiva, 1978; Aix-Marseille, 1982. Nobel Prize for Physics (jtly), 1979. *Publications:* (jtly) Interactions, 1988; The Charm of Physics, 1990; From Alchemy to Quarks, 1994; articles in learned jls. *Recreations:* scuba diving, tennis. *Address:* Physics Research Building, Boston University, 3 Cummington Mall, Boston, MA 02215, USA; 30 Prescott Street, Brookline, MA 02446, USA.

GLASMAN, family name of **Baron Glasman.**

GLASMAN, Baron *cr* 2011 (Life Peer), of Stoke Newington and of Stamford Hill in the London Borough of Hackney; **Maurice Mark Glasman,** PhD; Reader in Political Theory, London Metropolitan University, since 2011; *b* Walthamstow, London, 8 March 1961; *s* of Coleman Glasman and Rivie Glasman (*née* Pressberg); *m* Catherine Green; two *s* one *d*. *Educ:* Clapton Jewish Day Sch.; J. F. S. Comprehensive Sch.; St Catharine's Coll., Cambridge (BA Modern Hist. 1982; MA 1986); York Univ. (MA Political Philos. 1987); European Univ. Inst. (PhD 1995). Sen. Lectr in Political Theory, London Guildhall Univ., later London Metropolitan Univ., 1995–2011. *Publications:* Unnecessary Suffering, 1996. *Recreations:* Tottenham Hotspur FC, writing songs, playing jazz trumpet. *Address:* House of Lords, SW1A 0PW. *T:* 07795 283810. *E:* glasmanm@parliament.uk.

GLASS, Anthony Trevor; QC 1986; a Recorder of the Crown Court, 1985–2005; *b* 6 June 1940. *Educ:* Royal Masonic School; Lincoln College, Oxford (MA). Called to the Bar, Inner Temple, 1965, Bencher, 1995. *Club:* Garrick.

GLASS, Patricia; MP (Lab) North West Durham, since 2010; *b* Esh Winning, Co. Durham; *m* Bob Glass; two *s*. Assistant Director of Education: Sunderland, 2004–06; Greenwich, 2006–08; Govt Advr on SEN for Yorks and Humber Reg., 2009–10. Mem., Educn Select Cttee, 2010–15. Mem., Lanchester Parish Council, 2007. *Address:* House of Commons, SW1A 0AA.

GLASS, Philip; American composer and performer; *b* 31 Jan. 1937; *s* of Benjamin Glass and Ida Glass (*née* Gouline); *m* 1st, JoAnne Akalaitis; one *s* one *d*; 2nd, Luba Burtyk; 3rd, Candy Jernigan; 4th, Holly Critchlow; two *s*. *Educ:* Peabody Conservatory; Univ. of Chicago; Juilliard Sch. of Music. Has worked as a taxi-driver, plumber and furniture mover. Composer-in-Residence, Pittsburgh Public Schs, 1962–64; studied with Nadia Boulanger, Paris, 1964–66; Musical Dir, Mabou Mines Co., 1965–74; Founder: Philip Glass Ensemble, 1968; record companies: Chatham Square Productions, 1972; Point Music, 1991; music publishers: Dunvagen, Inc., 1982. *Compositions include: operas:* Einstein on the Beach, 1976; Satyagraha, 1980; The Photographer, 1982; The Civil Wars, 1984; Akhnaten, 1984; The Juniper Tree, 1986; The Making of the Representative for Planet 8, 1986; The Fall of the House of Usher, 1988; 1000 Airplanes on the Roof, 1988; The Hydrogen Jukebox, 1990; White Raven, 1991; The Voyage, 1992; Orphée, 1993; La Belle et la Bête, 1994; Les Enfants Terribles, 1996; Monsters of Grace, 1998; In the Penal Colony, 2000; Galileo Galilei, 2002; Appomattox, 2007; The Perfect American, 2013; The Trial, 2014; *film scores:* Koyaanisqatsi, 1982; Mishima (Cannes Special Jury Prize), 1985; Powaqqatsi, 1987; The Thin Blue Line, 1989; Hamburger Hill, 1989; Mindwalk, 1990; A Brief History of Time, 1991; Anima Mundi, 1991; Candyman, 1992; Compassion in Exile, 1992; Candyman II, 1995; Jenipapo, 1995; Secret Agent, 1995; Bent, 1998; Kundun, 1998; The Truman Show (Golden Globe award for best score), 1998; Dracula, 1998; Naqoyqatsi, 2001; The Man in the Bath, 2001; Notes, 2001; Passage, 2001; Diaspora, 2001; The Hours, 2003; Taking Lives, 2004; Secret Windows, 2004; Notes on a Scandal, 2007; Icarus at the Edge of Time, 2010; *theatre music:* Endgame, 1984; Cymbeline, 1989; (with Foday Musa Suso) The Screens, 1990; Henry IV, 1992; Woyzeck (Drama Desk Award), 1992; The Mysteries & What's So Funny?, 1992; The Elephant Man, 2002; *dance music:* In the Upper Room, 1986; Witches of Venice, 1995; *instrumental works:* String Quartet no 1, 1966; Piece in the Shape of a Square, 1967; Strung Out, 1969; Music in Similar Motion, 1969; Music in Fifths, 1969; Music with Changing Parts, 1970; Music in Twelve Parts, 1974; Another Look at Harmony, 1974; North Star, 1977; Modern Love Waltz, 1979; Dance nos 1–5, 1979; Company, 1983; String Quartet no 2, 1983; String Quartet no 3, 1985; Songs from Liquid Days, 1986; Violin Concerto, 1987; The Light, 1987; Itaipu, 1988; Canyon, 1988; String Quartet no 4, 1989; Solo Piano, 1989; (with Ravi Shankar) Passages, 1990; String Quartet no 5, 1991; Low Symphony, 1992; Mato Grosso, 1992; Symphony no 2, 1994, no 3, 1995; Heroes Symphony, 1996; Symphony no 5, 1999; Concerto Fantasy, 2000; Concerto for Cello and Orchestra, 2001; Symphony no 6 (Plutonian Ode), 2001; Voices for Organ, Didgeridoo and Narrator, 2001; Dancissimo, 2001; Second Violin Concerto, 2010. Numerous awards and prizes, including: Benjamin Award, 1961; Fulbright Award, 1966–67. Officer, Order of Arts and Letters (France), 1995. *Publications:* Music by Philip Glass, ed R. T. Jones, 1987; Words Without Music: a memoir, 2015. *Address:* c/o Dunvagen Music Publishers, 40 Exchange Place, Suite 1906, New York, NY 10005, USA.

GLASSBROOK, Karen Margaret; *see* Steyn, K. M.

GLASSCOCK, John Lewis, FCIS; Director, British Aerospace PLC, 1982–87; *b* 12 July 1928; *s* of Edgar Henry and Maude Allison Glasscock; *m* 1959, Anne Doreen Baker; two *s*. *Educ:* Tiffin Sch.; University Coll. London (BA Hons). Served Royal Air Force, 1950–53. Joined Hawker Aircraft Ltd, 1953, Asst Sec., 1956, Commercial Man., 1961; Hawker Siddeley Aviation Ltd: Divl Commercial Man., 1964; Dir and Gen. Man. (Kingston), 1965–77; British Aerospace Aircraft Group: Admin. Dir, 1978; Commercial Dir, 1979; Man. Dir (Military), 1981; BAe PLC: Dep. Chief Exec., Aircraft Gp, and Man. Dir, Civil Aircraft Div., 1982–85; Commercial Dir, 1986–87. Mem. Supervisory Bd, Airbus Industrie, 1983–85. Mem. Council, SBAC, 1979–87. *Recreation:* golf. *Address:* The Apple Shaw, St Nicholas Hill, Leatherhead, Surrey KT22 8NE. *Club:* Royal Automobile.

GLASSER, Prof. Stanley; Head of Music, 1969–91, (first) Professor of Music, 1990–91, Goldsmiths' College, University of London, now Emeritus Professor; composer, ethnomusicologist and music consultant; *b* 28 Feb. 1926; *s* of Joe Glasser and Assia (*née* Kagan); *m* 1st 1951, Mona Vida Schwartz (marr. diss. 1965); one *s* one *d*; 2nd, 1971, Elizabeth Marianne Aylwin; two *s*. *Educ:* King Edward VII High Sch., Johannesburg; Univ. of the Witwatersrand (BComm (Econ) 1949); studied composition with Benjamin Frankel, 1950–52, Matyas Seiber, 1952–55; ethnomusicology res. under Dr Hugh Tracey, Internat. Liby of African Music, 1954–55; King's Coll., Cambridge (Music Tripos 1958; MA 1960). Music Dir, King Kong (African musical), 1958–60; Lectr and Asst Dir, Music Dept, Univ. of Cape Town, 1959–63; Music Critic, Cape Times, 1959–62; Goldsmiths' College, University of London: Music Tutor, Dept of Adult Studies, 1963–65; Lectr, 1966–69; established 1st UK electronic music teaching studio, 1971; Chm., Bd of Studies in Music, Univ. of London, 1981–83. Ext. examr, univs and music colls, 1973–. Reader, CUP, 1981–83. Composer-in-residence, Standard Bank Nat. Arts Fest., 2001. Mem. and Treas., Internat. Cttee, ISCM, 1951–55; Chairman: Composers' Guild of GB, 1975; UK Br., Internat. Cttee for Traditional Music, 1979–84; and Trustee, Dagarti Arts, 1996–2005; Founder and Trustee, Rand Educn Fund, 1964–98; Trustee, Classic FM Charitable Trust, 1994–2002; Academic Governor, Richmond, American Internat. Univ. in London, 1980–; Music Consultant to Nat. Council for Culture, Arts & Letters, Kuwait, 1994–2004; Dir, Poetry and Music, Indaba, S Africa House, London, 2009. Consultant, RAE in Drama, Dance and Performing Arts, 1996–97. Visiting Consultant Professor: Univ. of KwaZulu Natal, 2007; Univ. of Cyprus, 2010. Hon.

Fellow, Goldsmiths Coll., 2001. Hon. DMus Richmond, American Internat. Univ., 1997. Royal Philharmonic Soc. Prizeman, 1952; George Richards Prize, King's Coll., Cambridge, 1958; Kathleen Gurner Award, Goldsmiths' Coll., 1998. *Compositions include:* The Square (full-length ballet), 1961; Mr. Paljas (musical comedy, lyrics by Beryl Bloom), 1962; The Chameleon and The Lizard (choral, Zulu text by Lewis Nkosi), 1973; The Gift (one-act comic chamber opera, libretto by Ronald Duncan), 1976; Lalela Zulu (a cappella male sextet, Zulu poems by Lewis Nkosi), 1977; The Ward (song cycle, poems by Ronald Duncan), 1983; Zonkizizwe (large choir, wind band and percussion, text by composer), 1991; Magnificat & Nunc Dimittis (chapel double choir a cappella), 1995; Ezra (sacred drama, text by Elisabeth Ingles), 1996; Noon (tone poem for orch.), 1997; A Greenwich Symphony (choir and orch., text by Elisabeth Ingles), 1999; Concerto for flugelhorn and chamber orch., 2001, revd 2004; The Planet of Love (text by Adolf Wood), 2002; Celebration Dances (sinfonia and choir), 2002; Lewisham Hero (theatrical entertainment), 2003; Crossroads (clarinet and piano), 2003; Insumansemane (a capella male sextet), 2005; Karoo (for large orch.), 2008. *Publications:* (with Adolf Wood) 100 Songs of Southern Africa, 1968; (contrib.) The New Grove Dictionary of Music and Musicians, 7th edn 1980; The A-Z of Classical Music, 1994; various articles and reviews on music. *Recreations:* dining with family and friends, Walt Kelly's Pogo Possum books, cowboy films. *Address:* c/o Woza Music, 46 Weigall Road, SE12 8HE. *T:* (020) 8852 1997.

GLASSON, Jonathan Joseph; QC 2013; *b* Newport, 15 Feb. 1965; *s* of Bernard and Glythyn Glasson; partner, Jamie Lake. *Educ:* Maidstone Grammar Sch.; New Coll., Oxford (MA). Admitted Solicitor (Hons), 1995; called to the Bar, Middle Temple, 1996; in practice as barrister, 1996–. *Publications:* (Contrib. Ed.) Butterworth's Personal Injury Litigation Service, 2005–; (with J. B. Knowles) Blackstone's Guide to the Coroners and Justice Act 2009, 2010. *Recreations:* reading, theatre, Brecon Beacons. *Address:* Matrix Chambers, Griffin Building, Gray's Inn, WC1R 5LN. *T:* (020) 7404 3447. *E:* jonathanglasson@matrixlaw.co.uk.

GLASTONBURY, Virginia; Partner, since 1988, and Practice Group Leader, Real Estate London Practice, since 2014, Dentons UKMEA LLP (formerly Denton Hall, later Denton Wilde Sapte, then SNR Denton UK), Solicitors; *b* 25 Feb. 1957; *d* of Rt Hon. Sir Frank Cooper, GCB, CMG, PC and Peggie Cooper; *m* 1980, Richard Glastonbury; one step *s*. *Educ:* Bromley High Sch.; LMH, Oxford (BA (Modern Hist.) 1978). Admitted solicitor, 1982; Managing Partner, Denton Hall, 1999–2000; Man. Partner UK, 2000–02, Chief Exec., 2002–05, Denton Wilde Sapte. FRSA 2003; MInstD. *Recreations:* grandchildren, motor racing, travel. *Address:* Dentons UKMEA LLP, One Fleet Place, EC4M 7WS. *E:* virginia.glastonbury@dentons.com.

See also M. Cooper.

GLAUBER, Prof. Roy Jay, PhD; Mallinckrodt Professor of Physics, Harvard University, since 1976; *b* 1 Sept. 1925; *s* of Emanuel B. Glauber and Felicia Glauber (*née* Fox); *m* 1960, Cynthia Marshall Rich (marr. diss. 1976); one *s* one *d*. *Educ:* Harvard University (BS Physics 1946, MA 1947; PhD 1949). Staff mem., Theoretical Physics Div., Los Alamos, New Mexico, 1944–46; Mem., Inst. for Advanced Study, Princeton, NJ, 1949–51; Res. Fellow, Swiss Fed. Polytech. Dist., Zürich, 1950; Lectr, CIT, 1951–52; Harvard University: Lectr, 1952–53; Asst Prof., 1953–56; Associate Prof., 1956–62; Prof. of Physics, 1962–76. Member: Amer. Acad. Arts and Scis; NAS; Royal Soc. NZ; Foreign Mem., Royal Soc., 1997. Member: Phi Beta Kappa; Sigma Xi. Hon. Dr: Essen; Arizona; Erlangen; Ohio State; Valencia; Strathclyde. Max Born Award, Amer. Optical Soc., 1985; (jtly) Nobel Prize in Physics, 2005. *Publications:* Quantum Theory of Optical Coherence, 2006; numerous chapters in books, and articles in scientific jls. *Recreation:* gardening. *Address:* Department of Physics, Lyman 331, Harvard University, 17 Oxford Street, Cambridge, MA 02138, USA. *T:* (617) 4952869. *E:* glauber@physics.harvard.edu. *Club:* Shop (Harvard Univ.).

GLAVES-SMITH, Frank William, CB 1975; Deputy Director-General of Fair Trading, 1973–79, retired; *b* 27 Sept. 1919; *m* 1st, 1941, Audrey Glaves (*d* 1989); one *s* one *d*; 2nd, 1990, Ursula Mary Murray. *Educ:* Malet Lambert High Sch., Hull. War Service, 1940–46 (Captain, Royal Signals). Called to the Bar, Middle Temple, 1947. Board of Trade, 1947; Princ. Private Sec. to Pres. of Bd of Trade, 1952–57; Asst Secretary: HM Treasury, 1957–60; Cabinet Office, 1960–62; Bd of Trade, 1962–65; Under-Sec., BoT, 1965–69, Dept of Employment and Productivity, 1969–70, DTI, 1970–73; Dep. Sec., 1975. Mem., Export Guarantees Adv. Council, 1971–73. *Recreation:* fell-walking. *Address:* 8 Grange Park, Keswick, Cumbria CA12 4AY.

GLAZEBROOK, Hon. Dame Susan (Gwynfa Mary), DNZM 2014; a Judge of the Supreme Court of New Zealand, since 2012; *b* 1956; *d* of Harry Glazebrook and Megan Glazebrook; *m* 1992, Greg Kane; two *s*. *Educ:* Univ. of Auckland (BA 1975; MA 1st Cl. Hons 1978; LLB Hons 1980; Dip. Business (Finance) 1994); St Antony's Coll., Oxford (DPhil 1985). Jun. Lectr in Hist., Univ. of Auckland, 1976–79; Interpreter, Rouen, France, 1981–83; Res. Asst and Tutor, Univ. of Auckland, 1984; Partner, Simpson Grierson, Auckland, 1985–2000; a Judge of the High Court of NZ, 2000–02; a Judge of the Court of Appeal of NZ, 2002–12. Member: Bd of Trustees, Nat. Provident Fund, 1989–2000; Bd, South Auckland Health, 1993–2000. Pres., Inter-Pacific Bar Assoc., 1998. Mem., Adv. Council of Jurists, Asia Pacific Forum of Nat. Human Rights Instns, 2002–10. Chm., Inst. of Judicial Studies, NZ, 2007–12. Mem. Bd, Internat. Assoc. of Women Judges, 2006–08, 2012–14. *Publications:* The New Zealand Accrual Regime, 1989, 2nd edn 1999; numerous articles in jls incl. Victoria Univ. of Wellington Law Rev. and Otago Law Rev. *Recreations:* photography, cinema, music, theatre, reading, yoga, tramping, travel, family. *Address:* Supreme Court of New Zealand, 85 Lambton Quay, Wellington, New Zealand. *T:* (4) 9188222, *Fax:* (4) 9188495. *E:* Justice.Glazebrook@courts.govt.nz. *Club:* Wellington (Wellington).

GLEAN, Sir Carlyle (Arnold), GCMG 2008; Governor-General of Grenada, 2008–13; *b* St George's, 11 Feb. 1932; *s* of George Glean and Olive McBurnie; *m* 1955, Norma DeCoteau; one *s* five *d* (and one *d* decd). *Educ:* Grenada Teachers' Coll.; Univ. of Calgary (BEd 1970; MA (Ed) 1973); Univ. of East Anglia (MA (Ed) 1982). Primary sch. teacher, 1947–56, 1960–63, 1965–66, primary sch. principal, 1963–64, 1967; Grenada Teachers' College: Lectr, 1970–74; Principal, 1974–76; Lectr, Faculty of Educn, Univ. of the West Indies, 1976–86; educnl consultant, 1986–89. Minister of Educn, 1990–95; Senator, 1995–98. Asst Chief Examiner, Social Studies, Caribbean Exam. Council, 1979–84; Member: Conservation Educn Cttee, 1978–81; CARICOM Wkg Party on Family Life Educn, 1988–89. Volunteer teacher, Skills Trng Centre for Youth, New Life Orgn, 1995–2003; Chm., Mgt Cttee, Hillsview Home for the Elderly, 1997–2007. Founder, Camerhogne Foundn (Grenada) Inc., 2009. *Publications:* articles in Caribbean Jl of Educn, Bulletin of Eastern Caribbean Affairs, Curriculum and Caribbean Secondary and Primary Social Studies series. *Recreation:* walking. *Address:* St Dominic Street, Gouyave, Grenada. *E:* patogg@spiceisle.com.

GLEDHILL, Andreas Nikolaus; QC 2015; *b* London, 21 April 1967. *Educ:* Christ's Coll., Cambridge (BA 1988; MA). Called to the Bar, Middle Temple, 1992; in practice as barrister, 1992–. *Address:* Blackstone Chambers, Temple, EC4Y 9BW.

GLEDHILL, Anthony John, GC 1967; Divisional Auditor, NWS plc, 1993–97; cruise lecturer, since 2009; *b* 10 March 1938; *s* of Harold Victor and Marjorie Edith Gledhill; *m* 1958, Marie Lilian Hughes; one *s* one *d*. *Educ:* Doncaster Technical High Sch., Yorks. Accounts Clerk, Officers' Mess, RAF Bruggen, Germany, 1953–56. Metropolitan Police: Cadet, 1956–57; Police Constable, 1957–75; Detective Sergeant, 1976–87; Investigator, PO Investigation Dept, 1987–88. Vice Chm., Victoria Cross and George Cross Assoc., 2014– (Treas., 2000–14). *Recreations:* golf, bowls, DIY.

GLEDHILL, Prof. John E., FBA 2010; FAcSS; Max Gluckman Professor of Social Anthropology, University of Manchester, now Emeritus. *Educ:* University of Oxford (BA PPE). Sen. Lectr, then Reader, Dept of Anthropology, UCL; University of Manchester: Prof. of Social Anthropology, 1996; Hd of Dept, 1997–2001; former Co-Dir, Centre for Latin American and Caribbean Studies. Chm., Assoc. of Social Anthropologists of UK and Commonwealth, 2005–09; Vice Pres., Internat. Union of Anthropological and Ethnological Scis, 2009–13. FAcSS (AcSS 2001). *Publications:* (ed jtly) State and Society: the emergence and development of social hierarchy and political centralization, 1988; Casi Nada: a study of agrarian reform in the homeland of Cardenismo, 1991; Neoliberalism, Transnationalization and Rural Poverty, 1995; Power and Its Disguises: anthropological perspectives on politics, 2000; (ed with Patience A. Schell) New Approaches to Resistance in Brazil and Mexico, 2012; The New War on the Poor: the production of insecurity in Latin America, 2015. *Address:* Social Anthropology, Arthur Lewis Building, University of Manchester, Manchester M13 9PL.

GLEDHILL, Rt Rev. Jonathan Michael; Bishop of Lichfield, 2003–15; *b* 15 Feb. 1949; *s* of A. Gavan Gledhill and Susan M. (*née* Roberts); *m* 1971, S. Jane Street, PhD; one *s* one *d*. *Educ:* Keele Univ. (BA Hons 1972); Bristol Univ. (MA 1975); Trinity Coll., Bristol (BCTS 1975). Ordained deacon, 1975, priest, 1976; Curate, All Saints, Marple, Gtr Manchester, 1975–78; Priest-in-charge, St George's, Folkestone, 1978–83; Vicar, St Mary Bredin, Canterbury, 1983–96; Bp Suffragan of Southampton, 1996–2003. RD, Canterbury, 1988–94; Hon. Canon, Canterbury Cathedral, 1992–96. Tutor, Canterbury Sch. of Ministry, then SE Inst. for Theol Studies, 1983–96. Member: Gen. Synod, 1995–96; Meissen Commn, 1993–97; C of E Sen. Appts Gp, 2009–13. Chm., Nat. Coll. of Evangelists, 1998–2010. Link Bishop, Old Catholic Churches of Union of Utrecht, 1998–2014. Entered H of L, 2009. DUniv Keele, 2007. *Publications:* Leading a Local Church in the Age of the Spirit, 2003. *Recreations:* sailing, ski-ing.

GLEDHILL, Keith Ainsworth, MBE 1994; DL; President: Gledhill Building Products, since 2008; Gledhill Water Storage Ltd, 1998–2008; *b* 28 Aug. 1932; *s* of Norman Gledhill and Louise (*née* Ainsworth); *m* 1956, Margaret Irene Burton; one *s*. *Educ:* Arnold Sch., Blackpool. Jun. Officer, MN, 1950–54; Nat. Service, RAF, 1954–56. Dir, Norman Gledhill & Co. Ltd, 1956–65; Sen. Exec., Delta Metal Gp, 1965–72; Founder, Gledhill Water Storage Ltd, 1972. Vice Chm., Blackpool Fylde & Wyre Soc. for the Blind, 1990–2009; Chm., Foxton Trust, 1992–2005. Mem. Council, Blackburn Cathedral, 2000–06. Gov., Skelton Bounty, 1988–2005. Past District Gov., Rotary Internat.; Past Chm., St John Ambulance Council, Lancs. Chm., Gov. Council, Arnold Sch., Blackpool, 1983–97. FInstD 1968; MInstP 1970. DL 1986, High Sheriff, 1992–93, Vice Lord-Lieut, 2002–05, Lancs. Freeman, City of London, 1992; Liveryman, Co. of Plumbers, 1992–. KStJ 2002. *Recreations:* golf, travel. *Address:* c/o Gledhill Building Products Ltd, Sycamore Estate, Squires Gate, Blackpool, Lancs FY4 3RL. *T:* (01253) 474431. *E:* keithg@gledhill.net; 35 South Park Drive, Blackpool, Lancs FY3 9PZ. *T:* (01253) 764462. *Clubs:* Royal Lytham & St Anne's Golf; Fylde Rugby Union Football.

GLEDHILL, Michael Geoffrey James; QC 2001; **His Honour Judge Gledhill;** a Circuit Judge, since 2008; *b* 28 Dec. 1954; *s* of Geoffrey Gledhill and L. Barbara Gledhill (*née* Haigh); *m* 1988, Elizabeth Ann Miller Gordon. *Educ:* Christ Church, Oxford (MA Juris.). Called to the Bar, Middle Temple, 1976, Bencher, 2007; Asst Recorder, 1995–98; Recorder, 1998–2008; Hd of Chambers, 2 Dyers Buildings, 2002–08. Dep. Chancellor, Dio. of Salisbury, 2007–. *Address:* Southwark Crown Court, 1 English Grounds, SE1 2HU.

GLEDHILL, Ruth; Contributing Editor, Christian Today, since 2014; *b* 15 Dec. 1959; *d* of late Rev. Peter Gledhill and Bridget Mary Gledhill (*née* Rathbone), Anglesey, N Wales; *m* 1st, 1989, John Edward Stammers (marr. diss. 1994); 2nd, 1996, Andrew Daniels (marr. diss. 2003); 3rd, 2006, Alan Lewis Duder Franks, *qv*; one *s*. *Educ:* Thomas Alleyne's GS, Uttoxeter; London Coll. of Printing (HND); Birkbeck Coll., London (Cert. Religious Studies). With Uttoxeter Advertiser news service, 1980–81; Australasian Printer, Sydney, 1981–82; indentured, Birmingham Post & Mail, 1982–84; Industrial corresp., Birmingham Post, 1984; gen. news reporter and feature writer, Daily Mail, 1984–87; The Times: Home News Reporter, 1987–90; Religion Correspondent, 1990–2014; columnist, At Your Service, 1993–2002; also writer on dance sport for sports pages, 1997–2002; occasional corresp. on religion and new technology for Interface, 1998–2001; News Reporter, The Tablet, 2014. Columnist, Church of England Newspaper. Guest presenter: Good Worship Guide, Yorks TV, 1996; ITV Sunday Worship, 1999. Vis. Lectr, Sch. of Journalism, City Univ., 2008–. Member: IJA Commn on Rise of Neo-Fascism, 1993; BBC Governors' Independent Advice Panel: Religious Programmes, 1998. Mem., London Rotary, 1997–. Andrew Cross Award for Religious Journalism, 2005. Blog: ArticlesofFaith. *Publications:* (jtly) Birmingham is Not a Boring City, 1984; (ed and introd.) The Times Book of Best Sermons, annually 1995–2001; At A Service Near You, 1996; (ed) The Times Book of Prayers, 1997. *Recreations:* music, digital media. *T:* (home) (020) 8948 5871. *W:* www.ruthgledhill.com, www.twitter.com/ruthiegledhill.

GLEES, Ann Margaret; *see* Jefferson, A. M.

GLEESON, Hon. (Anthony) Murray, AC 1992 (AO 1986); Chief Justice of Australia, 1998–2008; *b* 30 Aug. 1938; *s* of Leo John Gleeson and Rachel Alice Gleeson; *m* 1965, Robyn Paterson; one *s* three *d*. *Educ:* St Joseph's Coll., Hunters Hill; Univ. of Sydney (BA, LLB). Called to the NSW Bar, 1963; QC 1974. Tutor in Law, St Paul's Coll., Sydney Univ., 1963–65; Part-time Lectr in Company Law, Sydney Univ., 1965–74. Chief Justice of NSW, 1988–98; Lt-Gov., NSW, 1989–98. Non-perm. Judge, HK Court of Final Appeal, 2009–. President: Judicial Commn, NSW, 1988–98; Australian Assoc. of Constit. Law, 2009–15. Mem., Perm. Court of Arbitration, 1999–2009. Mem. Council, NSW Bar Assoc., 1979–85 (Pres., 1984 and 1985). Hon. Bencher, Middle Temple, 1989. Patron, Chartered Inst. of Arbitrators (Australia) Ltd, 2009–. Hon. LLD Sydney, 1999; DUniv: Griffith, 2001; Aust. Catholic Univ., 2005. *Recreations:* tennis, golf. *Address:* Level 17, 115 Pitt Street, Sydney, NSW 2000, Australia. *Club:* Australian (Sydney).

GLEESON, Dermot James; non-executive Chairman, M. J. Gleeson Group plc, since 2005 (Executive Chairman, 1998–2005); *b* 5 Sept. 1949; *s* of late Patrick Joseph Gleeson and Margaret Mary Gleeson (*née* Higgins); *m* 1980, Rosalind Mary Catherine Moorhead; one *s* one *d*. *Educ:* Downside; Fitzwilliam Coll., Cambridge (MA). Conservative Res. Dept, 1974–77 (Dir, 1979); Mem., Cabinet of C. Tugendhat, EC, 1977–79; EEC Rep., Brussels, Midland Bank, 1979–81; Dep. Man. Dir, 1982–88, Chief Exec., 1988–98, M. J. Gleeson Gp plc. Chm., Major Contractors Gp, 2003–05. Mem. Bd, Housing Corp., 1986–92; Dir, CITB, 1996–2002. A Gov., BBC, 2000–06; Trustee, BBC Trust, 2007–08. Trustee: Inst. of Cancer Res., 2006–11; Fitzwilliam Mus. Develt Trust, 2006–08. Chm. of Govs, Rydes Hill Prep. Sch. *Recreations:* reading, family life - especially in the Outer Hebrides. *Address:* Hook Farm, White Hart Lane, Wood Street Village, Guildford, Surrey GU3 3EA. *Clubs:* Beefsteak (Chm., 2004–07), Royal Automobile, Brooks's.

GLEESON, Judith Amanda Jane; a Judge of the Upper Tribunal (Immigration and Asylum Chamber) (formerly a Vice President, Immigration Appeal Tribunal, later Senior Immigration Judge, Asylum and Immigration Tribunal), since 2002; *b* 24 Aug. 1955; *d* of late Derek Young Coomber and Jennifer Isabel Coomber (*née* Strudwick); *m* 1980, Donald Frank Gleeson (marr. diss. 2010); one *s*. *Educ:* Univ. Libre de Bruxelles (Weiner Anspach Schol.; Cert. Civil Law and Eur. Community Law 1976); Lady Margaret Hall, Oxford (MA Jurisprudence 1977); Coll. of Law. Articled Linklaters & Paines, 1978–80; Solicitor, 1981; Hedleys Solicitors,

1981–95; an Employment Judge (formerly a Chm., Employment Tribunals), 1993–2009; Immigration Adjudicator, 1995–2002. Vis. Industrial Fellow, Faculty of Business and Law, Kingston Univ., 1993–. *Recreations:* modern art, jazz and blues. *Address:* Upper Tribunal (Immigration and Asylum Chamber), Field House, 15–25 Bream's Buildings, EC4A 1DZ. *Club:* Athenæum.

GLEESON, Hon. Murray; *see* Gleeson, Hon. A. M.

GLEITZMAN, Morris; author; *b* 9 Jan. 1953; *s* of Philip and Pamela Gleitzman; *m* 1974, Christine McCaul (marr. diss. 1994); one *s* one *d*. *Publications:* The Other Facts of Life, 1985; Two Weeks with the Queen, 1990; Second Childhood, 1990; Misery Guts, 1991; Worry Warts, 1991; Blabber Mouth, 1992; Sticky Beak, 1993; Puppy Fat, 1994; Belly Flop, 1996; Water Wings, 1996; (with P. Jennings) Wicked!, 1997; Bumface, 1998; Gift of the Gab, 1999; Toad Rage, 1999; (with P. Jennings) Deadly!, 2000; Adults Only, 2001; Toad Heaven, 2001; Boy Overboard, 2002; Teacher's Pet, 2003; Toad Away, 2003; Girl Underground, 2004; Worm Story, 2004; Once, 2005; Aristotle's Nostril, 2005; Doubting Thomas, 2006; Give Peas a Chance, 2007; Then, 2008; Toad Surprise, 2008; Grace, 2009; Now, 2010; Too Small To Fail, 2011; Pizza Cake, 2011; After, 2012; Extra Time, 2013; Loyal Creatures, 2014. *Address:* c/o Penguin Books (Australia), 707 Collins Street, Melbourne, Vic 3008, Australia. *T:* (3) 98112400. *E:* morris@morrisgleitzman.com.

GLEN, Ian Douglas; QC 1996; a Recorder, since 2000; *b* 2 April 1951; *s* of Douglas and Patricia Glen; *m* 1st, 1978, Helen O'Dowd (marr. diss. 2010); two *s*; 2nd, 2010, Joan Welsh. *Educ:* five Lancs primary schs; Hutton Grammar Sch.; Wyggeston Grammar Sch.; King's Coll., London (LLB Hons). Called to the Bar, Gray's Inn, 1973, Bencher, 2003; Mem. *ad eundem*, Lincoln's Inn, 2005. Asst Recorder, 1996–2000. Mem., Bar Council, 2000–04. Hon. Res. Fellow, Bristol Univ., 1999. Mem. Court, Univ. of Bristol. FRSA. *Recreations:* seaside fairways, tranquil waters, after dinner speaking, dance music. *Address:* 5 King's Bench Walk, Temple, EC4Y 7DN. *Clubs:* Soho House, Chinawhite; India House (New York); Royal Cinque Ports Golf.

GLEN, John Philip; MP (C) Salisbury, since 2010; *b* Bath, 1 April 1974; *s* of Philip Glen and Thalia Glen (*née* Mitchenere); *m* 2008, Emma Caroline O'Brien (*née* Stephens); one step *s* one step *d*. *Educ:* King Edward's Sch., Bath (Hd Boy); Mansfield Coll., Oxford (BA Mod. Hist. 1996; Pres. JCR 1995); Judge Inst., Univ. of Cambridge (MBA 2003). Accounts Asst, Fleet Support Gp, Chippenham, 1992–93; Parly Researcher to Gary Streeter, MP and Michael Bates, MP, 1996–97; Strategy Consultant, Accenture, 1997–2004, on secondment to Hd, Political Section, Conservative Res. Dept, 2000–01; Dep. Dir, 2004–05, Dir, 2005–06, Conservative Res. Dept; Sen. Advr to Global Hd of Strategy, Accenture, 2006–10. PPS to Sec. of State for Communities and Local Govt, 2012–15, to Sec. of State for Business, Innovation and Skills, 2015–. Member: Defence Select Cttee, 2010–12; Cttee on Arms Exports, 2010–12; Downing St Policy Bd, 2014–. JP Westminster, 2006–11. *Publications:* (contrib.) There is Such a Thing as Society, 2002. *Recreations:* family, church, eating out, travel, squash. *Address:* (office) Morrison Hall, 12 Brown Street, Salisbury, Wilts SP1 1HE; House of Commons, SW1A 0AA. *T:* (020) 7219 3000. *E:* john.glen.mp@parliament.uk.

GLEN, Marlyn Laing; Member (Lab) Scotland North East, Scottish Parliament, 2003–11; *b* 30 Sept. 1951; *d* of Stewart and Rita Mitchell; *m* 1974, Neil Glen (*d* 2004); one *s* one *d*. *Educ:* Kirkton High Sch., Dundee; St Andrews Univ. (MA Hons); Dundee Univ. (DipEd; Dip Special Ed); Open Univ. (BA Hons; BSc Hons). Teacher, English, Stanley Park Comp. Sch., 1974–76, Belmont Acad., 1976–77; Asst Prin. Teacher of English, Ravenspark Acad., Irvine, 1977–82; Teacher of English and Learning Support (pt-time), Ravenspark Acad. and Auchenharvie Acad., Stevenston, 1982–90; Sen. Teacher, Craigie High Sch., Dundee, 1991–97; Principal Teacher, Support for Learning, Baldragon Acad., Dundee, 1997–2003. *Recreations:* music, theatre, literature, hill-walking.

GLENAPP, Viscount; Fergus James Kenneth Mackay; *b* 9 July 1979; *s* and *heir* of 4th Earl of Inchcape, *qv*; *m* 2010, Rebecca Margaret, *d* of Charles Jackson; one *d*. *Educ:* Radley Coll.; Edinburgh Univ. (MA); BPP Sch. of Law (CPE; BVC); Imperial Coll. London (MBA). *Address:* 40 Richford Street, W6 7HP.

GLENARTHUR, 4th Baron *cr* 1918; **Simon Mark Arthur;** DL; Bt 1903; *b* 7 Oct. 1944; *s* of 3rd Baron Glenarthur, OBE, and Margaret (*d* 1993), *d* of late Captain H. J. J. Howie; *S* father, 1976; *m* 1969, Susan, *yr d* of Comdr Hubert Wyndham Barry, RN; one *s* one *d*. *Educ:* Eton. Commissioned 10th Royal Hussars (PWO), 1963; ADC to High Comr, Aden, 1964–65; Captain 1970; Major 1973; retired 1975; Royal Hussars (PWO), TA, 1976–80. British Airways Helicopters Captain, 1976–82. A Lord in Waiting (Govt Whip), 1982–83; Parly Under Sec. of State, DHSS, 1983–85, Home Office, 1985–86; Minister of State: Scottish Office, 1986–87; FCO, 1987–89; elected Mem., H of L, 1999. Sen. Exec., 1989–96, Consultant, 1996–99, Hanson PLC; Dep. Chm., Hanson Pacific Ltd, 1994–96; Director: Aberdeen and Texas Corporate Finance Ltd, 1977–82; The Lewis Gp, 1993–95; Whirlybird Services Ltd, 1995–2004; Millennium Chemicals Inc., 1996–2004; Medical Defence Union Ltd, 2002–06; Audax Trading Ltd, subseq. Audax Global SARL, 2003– (Consultant, 2001–03); Chm., British European Aviation Ltd, 2015–. Consultant: BAe PLC, 1989–99; Chevron UK Ltd, 1994–97; Imperial Tobacco Gp, 1996–98. Chm., St Mary's Hosp., Paddington, NHS Trust, 1991–98 (Special Trustee, St Mary's Hosp., 1991–2000). Chm., Eur. Helicopter Assoc., 1996–2003; Dep. Chm., Internat. Fedn of Helicopter Assocs, 1996–97 and 2000–04 (Chm., 1997–2000); Pres., British Helicopter Assoc. (formerly Adv. Bd), 2004– (Chm., 1992–2004). Pres., Nat. Council for Civil Protection, 1991–2003; Mem. Council, Air League, 1994–2009; Mem., Nat. Employers Liaison Cttee for Britain's Reserve Forces, 1996–2002; Chm., Nat. Employer Adv. Bd for Britain's Reserve Forces, 2002–09. Scottish Patron, Butler Trust, 1994–2014; Trustee, RCO, 2014–. Governor: Nuffield Nursing Homes Trust, then Nuffield Hosps, later Nuffield Health, 2000–09; King Edward VII Hosp. (Sister Agnes), 2010–13 (Mem. Council and Trustee, 2011–13; Chm. Council, 2012–13); Sutton's Hosp. in Charterhouse, 2011–; Comr, Royal Hosp., Chelsea, 2001–07. Capt., Queen's Body Guard for Scotland (Royal Co. of Archers). FCILT until 2011 (FCIT 1999; MCIT 1979); FRAeS 1992–2011. Liveryman, GAPAN, 1996–2011. DL Aberdeenshire, 1988. *Recreations:* field sports, gardening, choral singing, organ-playing, barometers. *Heir: s* Hon. Edward Alexander Arthur, *b* 9 April 1973. *Address:* Northbrae Farmhouse, Crathes, Banchory, Kincardineshire AB31 6JQ. *Club:* Cavalry and Guards.

GLENCONNER, 4th Baron *cr* 1911; **Cody Charles Edward Tennant;** Bt 1885; *b* 2 Feb. 1994; *o s* of Hon. Charles Edward Pevensey Tennant (*d* 1996), and of Sheilagh, *y d* of Matthew Raymond Walker Scott; *S* grandfather, 2010. *Heir: cousin* Euan Lovell Tennant, *b* 22 July 1983.

GLENDAY, Craig Douglas; Editor-in-Chief, Guinness World Records, since 2002; *b* Dundee, 31 May 1973; *s* of Douglas and Sylvia Glenday. *Educ:* Balerno Primary Sch.; Powrie Primary Sch.; Craigie High Sch., Dundee; Royal Scottish Acad. of Music and Drama Jun. Sch., Glasgow; Napier Univ., Edinburgh (BA Publishing). Ed., Marshall Cavendish Publishing Ltd, 1992–97; Sen. Ed., Midsummer Books, 1997–2000; Producer: Trinity Mirror Digital Media, 2000–01; iVillage, 2001–02; publisher, Sondheim The Magazine, 2012–. Reviewer, Musical Th. Rev. mag., 2014–. Trustee, Stephen Sondheim Soc., 2014–. *Publications:* UFO Investigator's Handbook, 1999; Vampire Hunter's Notebook, 2003; (ed) Guinness World Records, annually, 2006–. *Recreations:* member, The Infamous Grouse band (drummer), theatre, script writing. *Address:* Guinness World Records, 184–192 Drummond Street, NW1 3HP. *T:* (020) 7891 4500, *Fax:* (020) 7891 4501. *E:* craig.glenday@guinnessworldrecords.com.

GLENDEVON, 3rd Baron *cr* 1964, of Midhope, Co. Linlithgow; **Jonathan Charles Hope;** *b* 23 April 1952; *yr s* of 1st Baron Glendevon and Elizabeth Mary (*d* 1998), *d* of (William) Somerset Maugham, CH; *S* brother, 2009.

GLENDINNING, Hon. Victoria, (Hon. Mrs O'Sullivan), CBE 1998; FRSL; author and journalist, since 1969; *b* 23 April 1937; *d* of Baron Seebohm, TD and Evangeline, *d* of Sir Gerald Hurst, QC; *m* 1st, 1958, Prof. (Oliver) Nigel (Valentine) Glendinning (marr. diss. 1981; he *d* 2013); four *s*; 2nd, 1982, Terence de Vere White (*d* 1994); 3rd, 1996, Kevin (Patrick) O'Sullivan. *Educ:* St Mary's Sch., Wantage; Millfield Sch.; Somerville Coll., Oxford (MA Mod. Langs; Hon. Fellow, 2004); Southampton Univ. (Dip. in Social Admin). Part-time teaching, 1960–69; part-time psychiatric social work, 1970–73; Editorial Asst, TLS, 1974–78. Trustee, Booker Prize Foundn, 2010–. FRSL 1982 (Vice-Pres., RSL, 2000–); Vice-Pres., English Centre, PEN, 2003 (Pres., 2001–03). Hon. DLitt: Southampton, 1994; Ulster, 1995; Dublin, 1995; York, 2000. *Publications:* A Suppressed Cry, 1969, re-published 2013; Elizabeth Bowen: portrait of a writer, 1977; Edith Sitwell: a unicorn among lions, 1981, repr. 2013; Vita: a biography of V. Sackville-West, 1983; Rebecca West: a life, 1987; The Grown-Ups (novel), 1989; Hertfordshire, 1989; Trollope, 1992; Electricity (novel), 1995; (ed with M. Glendinning) Sons and Mothers, 1996; Jonathan Swift, 1998; Flight (novel), 2002; Leonard Woolf: a life, 2006; (ed) Love's Civil War, 2008; Raffles and the Golden Opportunity, 2012; reviews and articles in newspapers and magazines in Britain, Ireland and USA. *Address:* c/o David Higham Associates, 7th Floor, Waverley House, 7–12 Noel Street, W1F 8GQ. *Club:* Athenæum.

GLENDONBROOK, Baron *cr* 2011 (Life Peer), of Bowdon in the County of Cheshire; **Michael David Bishop,** Kt 1991; CBE 1986; Chairman of Trustees, The Michael Bishop Foundation, since 1989; Chairman: British Midland Plc (formerly Airlines of Britain Holdings Plc), 1978–2009; British Regional Air Lines Group Plc, and Manx Airlines, 1982–2001; *b* 10 Feb. 1942; *s* of Clive Leonard Bishop. *Educ:* Mill Hill School. Joined: Mercury Airlines, Manchester, 1963; British Midland Airways, 1964; Director: Airtours plc, 1987–2001 (Dep. Chm., 1996–2001); Williams Plc, 1993–2000. Member: E Midlands Electricity Bd, 1980–83; E Midlands Reg. Bd, Central Television, 1981–89; Dep. Chm., 1991–93, Chm., 1993–97, Channel 4 Television Corp. Non-exec. Dir, Kidde plc, 2000–02. Chm., D'Oyly Carte Opera Trust Ltd, 1989–2008. Trustee and Dir, Friends in the UK, Royal Flying Doctor Service of Australia, 2005–14. Hon. Mem., Royal Soc. of Musicians of GB, 1989. *Address:* House of Lords, SW1A 0PW. *Clubs:* Brooks's; Australian (Sydney).

GLENDYNE, 4th Baron *cr* 1922; **John Nivison;** Bt 1914; *b* 18 Aug. 1960; *o s* of 3rd Baron Glendyne and of Elizabeth, *y d* of Sir Cecil Armitage, CBE; *S* father, 2008.

GLENFIELD, Rt Rev. Ferran; *see* Kilmore, Elphin and Ardagh, Bishop of.

GLENN, John H(erschel), Jr; US Senator from Ohio (Democrat), 1975–98; *b* Cambridge, Ohio, 18 July 1921; *s* of John H. and Clara Glenn; *m* 1943, Anna Castor; one *s* one *d*. *Educ:* Muskingum Coll., New Concord, Ohio. Joined US Marine Corps, 1943; Served War (2 DFCs, 10 Air Medals); Pacific Theater, 1944; home-based, Capt., 1945–46; Far East, 1947–49; Major, 1952; served Korea (5 DFCs, Air Medal with 18 clusters), 1953. First non-stop supersonic flight, Los Angeles–New York (DFC), 1957; Lieut-Col, 1959. In Jan. 1964, declared candidacy for US Senate from Ohio, but withdrew owing to an injury; recovered and promoted Col USMC, Oct. 1964; retired from USMC, Dec. 1964. Became one of 7 volunteer Astronauts, man-in-space program, 1959; made 3-orbit flight in Mercury capsule, Friendship 7, 20 Feb. 1962 (boosted by rocket; time 4 hrs 56 mins; distance 81,000 miles; altitude 160 miles; recovered by destroyer off Puerto Rico in Atlantic). Vice-Pres. (corporate develt), Royal Crown Cola Co., 1966–68; Pres., Royal Crown Internat., 1967–69. Holds hon. doctorates, US and foreign. Awarded DSM (Nat. Aeronautics and Space Admin.), Astronaut Wings (Navy), Astronaut Medal (Marine Corps), etc, 1962; Galabert Internat. Astronautical Prize (jointly with Lieut-Col Yuri Gagarin), 1963; Presidential Medal of Freedom (USA), 2012; also many other awards and citations from various countries and organizations. *Address:* John Glenn School of Public Affairs, 110 Page Hall, 1810 College Road, Columbus, OH 43210, USA.

GLENN, Sir Owen (George), KNZM 2013 (ONZM 2008); Executive Chairman and Owner, OTS Logistics Group, 1978–2011; Founder, Glenn Family Foundation, since 1984; *b* Calcutta, 19 Feb. 1940; *s* of Owen Arthur Glenn and Decima Irene Glenn; one *s* five *d*. *Educ:* Mt Roskill Grammar Sch.; Harvard Business Sch. (OPM 1990). With Trans-Tasman Airways, 1963–64; estabd McGregor Squire Air Services, 1969–75; consulting, 1975; estabd Pacific Forwarding, 1975–78; Founder: Direct Container Lines, 1978; NACA Logistics, 1981. Hon. LLD Auckland, 2012. *Publications:* Make a Difference, 2011. *Recreations:* hockey, Rugby, Rugby League, golf, cricket, philanthropy. *Address:* 314/121 Customs Street West, Auckland 1010, New Zealand; 1/17 Gladeswood Gardens, Double Bay, NSW 2028, Australia. *T:* (2) 9362 9096; Vale Levu, Molololailai, Fiji Islands. *T:* (1) 3103847043. *E:* sirowen.glenn@aol.com.

GLENN, Paul Anthony; His Honour Judge Glenn; a Circuit Judge, since 2004; *b* 14 Sept. 1957; *m* 1985, Diane Burgess; two *s*. *Educ:* Liverpool Univ. (LLB Hons 1979). Called to the Bar, Gray's Inn, 1983; Magistrates' Court Service, 1980–85; County Prosecuting Solicitor's Office, Cheshire, 1985–86; CPS, 1986–90; in practice as a barrister, 1990–2004; a Recorder, 2000–04. Hon. Recorder, Stoke-on-Trent, 2008. *Recreations:* sport, avid supporter of Stoke City FC and enjoys watching Rugby and cricket. *Address:* Stoke-on-Trent Combined Court, Bethesda Street, Hanley, Stoke-on-Trent ST1 3BP. *T:* (01782) 854000.

GLENNERSTER, Prof. Howard, FBA 2002; FAcSS; Co-Director, 1997–2007, Associate, since 2008, Centre for Analysis of Social Exclusion, and Professor of Social Administration, 1984–2001, now Professor Emeritus, London School of Economics; *b* 4 Oct. 1936; *s* of John Howard Glennerster and Charlotte Nellie Glennerster; *m* 1962, Ann Dunbar Craine; one *s* one *d*. *Educ:* Pixmore Secondary Modern Sch., Letchworth; Letchworth Grammar Sch.; Wadham Coll., Oxford (BA PPE). Res. Asst, Labour Party Res. Dept, 1959–64; London School of Economics: Res. Officer, Higher Educn Res. Unit, 1964–68; Lectr in Social Admin, 1968–79; Reader, 1979–84; Chm., Suntory and Toyota Internat. Centres for Econs and Related Disciplines, 1994–2000; Hon. Fellow, 2005. Vis. Prof. or acad. visitor, Brookings Instn, 1972, 1996, 2000, Univs of Berkeley, Calif, 1982, Washington State, 1982 and Chicago, 1989. Mem., Sec. of State for Health's Adv. Cttee on Resource Allocation, 1997–2010; Specialist Advr to H of L Cttee on Public Services and Demographic Change, 2012–13. Director: Basic Skills Agency, 1997–2007; Mgt Cttee, King's Fund, 2002–07. FAcSS (AcSS 2000); FRSA 1995. *Publications:* Social Service Budgets and Social Policy, 1974; Planning for Priority Groups, 1983; Paying for Welfare, 1984, 3rd edn 1997; Implementing GP Fundholding, 1994; British Social Policy since 1945, 1995, 3rd edn 2007; The State of Welfare: the economics of social spending, 1998; Understanding the Finance of Welfare, 2003, 2nd edn 2009; Wealth in the UK: distribution, accumulation, and policy, 2013; contrib. numerous papers on econs of social policy to acad. jls. *Recreations:* walking, bird-watching, gardening, tending an allotment, watching cricket, enjoying grandchildren. *Address:* London School of Economics, Houghton Street, WC2A 2AE. *E:* h.glennerster@lse.ac.uk. *Club:* Middlesex CC.

GLENNIE, Hon. Lord; Angus James Scott Glennie; a Senator of the College of Justice in Scotland, since 2005; farmer; *b* 3 Dec. 1950; *yr s* of late Robert Nigel Forbes Glennie and Barbara Scott (*née* Nicoll); *m* 1981, Patricia Jean Phelan, *er d* of His Honour Andrew Phelan; three *s* one *d*. *Educ:* Sherborne Sch.; Trinity Hall, Cambridge (MA Hons). Called to the Bar, Lincoln's Inn, 1974, Bencher, 2007; QC 1991; admitted to Faculty of Advocates, 1992; QC (Scot.) 1998. *Recreations:* sailing, ski-ing, Real tennis. *Address:* Parliament House, Parliament Square, Edinburgh EH1 1RQ.

GLENNIE, Dame Evelyn (Elizabeth Ann), DBE 2007 (OBE 1993); FRAM, FRCM; musician, motivational speaker, jewellery designer; *b* 19 July 1965; *d* of Isobel and Arthur Glennie. *Educ:* Ellon Acad., Aberdeenshire; Royal Academy of Music (GRSM Hons, LRAM, ARAM; FRAM 1992; Queen's Commendation Prize); FRCM 1991. Shell Gold Medal, 1984; Leonardo da Vinci Prize, 1987; début, Wigmore Hall, 1986; soloist in Europe, Asia, N and S America, Russia and Middle East; percussion and timpani concertos specially written; TV and radio presenting; numerous recordings and awards. Headline artist, London 2012 Olympic Games. Hon. DMus: Aberdeen, 1991; Bristol, 1995; Portsmouth, 1995; Leicester, Surrey, 1997; Belfast, Essex, Durham, 1998; Cambridge, 2010; Hon. DLitt: Warwick, 1993; Loughborough, 1995. Grammy Award, 1989, 2002, 2014; Polar Music Prize, 2015. *Publications:* Good Vibrations (autobiog.), 1990. *Recreations:* reading, walking, cycling, antiques. *Address:* 6 Ramsay Court, Hinchingbrooke Business Park, Huntingdon, Cambs PE29 6FY. *T:* (01480) 459279. *W:* www.evelyn.co.uk.

GLENNIE, Robert McDougall; Chief Executive, NewGalexy Partners Ltd, since 2008; Executive Chairman, NewGalexy Services Ltd, since 2012; *b* 4 April 1951. *Educ:* Jordanhill Coll. Sch., Glasgow; Univ. of Strathclyde (LLB). FCIS 2000 (MCIS). Admitted Solicitor, 1978. Joined McGrigor Donald, subseq. McGrigors, 1976; Partner, 1980–2002; Managing Partner of London Office, 1989–96; Sen. Partner, 2000–02; Chief Exec., KLegal Internat., 2002–04; Principal, Robert Glennie Legal Consulting, 2004–; Sen. Advr, Restructuring and Recovery, Pinsent Masons LLP (formerly McGrigors), 2010–13. Mem., Law Soc. of Scotland, 1977–. *Recreations:* hillwalking, cinema, travel, ayurvedic medicine and therapies. *Address:* NewGalexy Partners Ltd, Corunna House, 39 Cadogan Street, Glasgow G2 7AB. *T:* (0141) 280 1600; NewGalexy Services Ltd, Corunna House, 39 Cadogan Street, Glasgow G2 7AB.

GLENNY, Misha; journalist and historian; *b* 25 April 1958; *s* of late Michael V. G. Glenny and of Juliet Sydenham (*née* Crum); *m* 1987, Snezana Curcic (marr. diss. 2001); one *s* one *d*; *m* 2006, Kirsty Lang; one *s*. *Educ:* Bristol Univ. (BA Drama); Charles Univ., Prague. Rights editor, Verso publishing house, London, 1983–86; Central Europe Correspondent (based in Vienna): The Guardian, 1986–89; BBC World Service, 1989–93. Vis. Prof., Columbia Univ., NYC, 2012. Hon. Dr Hist. American Univ. in Bulgaria. Sony Special Award for Broadcasting, 1993; American Overseas Pressclub Award for Best Book on Foreign Affairs, 1993; Information Security Journalist of the Year, BT Information Security Journalism Awards, 2011. *Publications:* The Rebirth of History: Eastern Europe in the age of democracy, 1990, 2nd edn 1993; The Fall of Yugoslavia, 1992, 2nd edn 1993; The Balkans 1804–1999: nationalism, war and the great powers, 1999; McMafia: crime without frontiers, 2008; DarkMarket: cyberthieves, cybercops and you, 2011; Nemesis: one man and the battle for Rio, 2015. *Address:* 138 Percy Road, W12 9QL.

GLENNY, Ven. Olivia Josephine; *see* Graham, Ven. O. J.

GLENNY, Dr Robert Joseph Ervine, CEng, FIMMM; Consultant to UK Government, industry, and European Economic Community, 1983–2006; *b* 14 May 1923; *s* of late Robert and Elizabeth Rachel Glenny; *m* 1947, Joan Phillips Reid; one *s* one *d*. *Educ:* Methodist Coll., Belfast; QUB (BSc Chemistry); London Univ. (BSc Metallurgy, PhD). CEng, 1979; FIMMM (FIM 1958). Res. Metallurgist, English Electric Co. Ltd, Stafford, 1943–47; National Gas Turbine Establishment, 1947–70; Materials Dept, 1947–66; Head of Materials Dept, 1966–70; Supt, Div. of Materials Applications, National Physical Lab., 1970–73; Head of Materials Dept, RAE, 1973–79; Group Head of Aerodynamics, Structures and Materials Depts, RAE, 1979–83. *Publications:* research and review papers on materials science and technology, mainly related to gas turbines, in ARC (R&M series) and in Internat. Metallurgical Rev. *Recreations:* reading, gardening, walking. *Address:* 77 Gally Hill Road, Fleet, Hants GU52 6RU. *T:* (01252) 615877.

GLENTON, Anthony Arthur Edward, CBE 2000 (MBE mil. 1982); TD 1972 (bars 1980, 1986, 1992); FCA; Senior Partner, Ryecroft Glenton, Chartered Accountants, Newcastle, since 1967; Director, 1988–2005, Chairman, 1994–2005, Port of Tyne Authority; Vice Lord-Lieutenant of Northumberland, since 2013; *b* 21 March 1943; *s* of late Lt-Col Eric Cecil Glenton, Gosforth, Newcastle, and of Joan Lydia Glenton (*née* Taylor); *m* 1972, Caroline Ann, *d* of Maurice George Meade-King; one *s* one *d*. *Educ:* Merchiston Castle Sch., Edinburgh. FCA 1965. Chm., Charles W. Taylor & Son Ltd, Iron Founders, S Shields, 1995–2003; Dir, Newcastle Bldg Soc., 1987–2008 (Chm., 1992–97). Joined Royal Artillery, Territorial Army, 1961: Lieut Col 1984; CO 101 (Northumbrian) Field Regt RA (V), 1984–86; Col 1986; Dep. Comdr, 15 Inf. Bde, 1986–89; ADC to the Queen, 1987–89; TA Advr to GOC Eastern Dist, 1989–94; Hon. Col, 101 (Northumbrian) Regt RA (V), 2005–10. Chairman: N of England RFCA, 1999–2003 (Vice Chm., 1995–99); Northumberland Br., SSAFA (formerly SSAFA Forces Help), 1989–; Newcastle Cathedral Council, 2012–. Freeman, City of London, 1981; Liveryman, Co. of Chartered Accountants of England and Wales, 1981. DL Northumberland, 1993. *Recreations:* shooting, sailing, contemporary art. *Address:* Whinbank, Rothbury, Northumberland NE65 7YJ. *T:* (01669) 620361; Palace Hill Cottage, St Cuthbert's Square, Holy Island of Lindisfarne, Northumberland TD15 2SP. *T:* (01289) 389312; Ryecroft Glenton, 32 Portland Terrace, Newcastle upon Tyne NE2 1QP. *T:* (0191) 281 1292. *Club:* Army and Navy.

GLENTORAN, 3rd Baron *cr* 1939, of Ballyalolly, Co. Down; **Thomas Robin Valerian Dixon,** CBE 1992 (MBE 1969); DL; Bt 1903; *b* 21 April 1935; *er s* of 2nd Baron Glentoran, KBE, PC; *S* father, 1995; *m* 1959, Rona, *d* of Captain G. C. Colville; three *s*; *m* 1990, Margaret Rainey. *Educ:* Eton. Man. Dir, Redland (NI) Ltd, 1971–92. Mem., Millennium Fund Commn, 1994–2005. Elected Mem., H of L, 1999; front bench opposition spokesman, H of L, on NI, 1999–, on sport, 2005–06, on Olympics, 2007–, on Wales, 2007–. Non-executive Director: NHBC, 2001; BetonSports plc, 2004. Comr, Irish Light House Service, 1996–. Olympic Gold Medal for two-man bobsleigh, 1964. President: British Bobsleigh Assoc., 2012–; British Shooting Sports Council (former Chm.); Chm., Skiing with Heroes. DL Antrim, 1995. *Recreations:* sailing, golf. *Heir: s* Hon. Daniel George Dixon [*b* 26 July 1959; *m* 1983, Leslie Hope Brooke; two *s*]. *Address:* Drumadarragh House, Ballyclare, Co. Antrim BT39 0TA. *Clubs:* Boodles; Royal Yacht Squadron.

GLENVILLE, Dr Marilyn, CPsychol; nutritionist, since 1982; *b* London, 13 Aug. 1952; *d* of John and Margaret Eaton; *m* 1981, Kriss Glenville; two *s* one *d*. *Educ:* Highbury Hill High Sch., London; Avery Hill Coll., London Univ. (BEd); Leeds Univ. (MA); Darwin Coll., Cambridge (PhD 1980). CPsychol 1990. Mem. Council, Food and Health Forum, RSocMed, 2001– (Pres., 2007–09). Mem., Nutrition Soc., 2001–. Patron, Daisy Network, 2004–. FRSocMed 1999. *Publications:* (contrib.) Response to Stress, 1979; Natural Alternatives to HRT, 1997; Natural Alternatives to Dieting, 1999; Natural Alternatives to HRT Cookbook, 2000, re-issued as Healthy Eating for the Menopause, 2004; Natural Solutions to Infertility, 2000; Nutritional Health Handbook for Women, 2001; Natural Solutions to PMS, 2002; Osteoporosis - the silent epidemic, 2005; Fat Around the Middle, 2006; (contrib.) An Atlas of Endometriosis, 3rd edn, 2007; Getting Pregnancy Faster, 2008; Natural Health Bible for Women, 2010; Natural Solutions to Menopause, 2011; Natural Solutions to PCOS, 2012; Natural Solutions to IBS, 2013; contribs to jls incl. Sleep, Chronobiologia, Ergonomics, Current Opinion in Obstetrics and Gynaecology. *Recreations:* walking, reading, tennis, dancing. *Address:* Dr Marilyn Glenville Clinic, 14 St Johns Road, Tunbridge Wells, Kent TN4 9NP. *T:* 0870 532 9244, *Fax:* 0870 532 9255. *E:* health@marilynglenville.com.

GLERAWLY, Viscount; Michael Stephen Annesley; IT engineer; *b* 26 July 1957; *er s* and *heir* of Earl Annesley, *qv*; *m* 1st, 1983, Angela, *d* of David Matthews (marr. diss. 2000); one *s* one *d* (twins); 2nd, 2004, Karen Lesley Coolman, *d* of Ronald Fuller. *Educ:* Burford Grammar Sch. Man. Dir, Mikrotek Solutions Ltd, 1996–. *Recreation:* classic motorcycle racing. *Heir: s* Hon. Michael David Annesley, *b* 28 Jan. 1984.

GLESTER, John William; Managing Director (formerly Principal), John Glester Consultancy Services, since 1996; Consultant Director, Colliers CRE, since 2010; *b* 8 Sept. 1946; *o s* of late George Ernest Glester and Maude Emily Glester; *m* 1970, Ann Gleave Taylor (*d* 1998); two *s*. *Educ:* Plaistow Grammar Sch.; Reading Univ. (BA Hons); Open Univ. (Dip. Eur. Studies). Joined Civil Service 1968; served DEA, DoE and Merseyside Task Force; Regl Controller, NW, DoE, 1985–88; Chief Exec., Central Manchester Develt Corp., 1988–96; Trust Fund Adminr, Lord Mayor of Manchester's Emergency Appeal Fund, 1996–98; Dir (Regl Strategy), NW Regl Develt Agency, 1999–2000. Principal Associate (formerly Associate Dir), Locum Consulting, 2006–12. Chairman: Castlefield Management Co., 1992–2002; Castlefield Heritage Trust, 1996–2003; Hallogen Ltd (Bridgewater Hall), 1998–2004 (Dir, 1995–98); Ancoats Bldgs Preservation Trust, 2001–07 (Trustee, 2001–07); Commissions in the Environment, 2002–04; Urban Experience Ltd, 2002–04; Merseyside Housing Market Renewal, 2003–11; Manchester Salford Trafford NHS LIFT, 2003–07; Bolton, Rochdale and Heywood Middleton NHS LIFT, 2007–12; Heritage Works, 2007–; non-exec. Dir, Langtree Gp plc, 1999–2001; Consultant: Lloyds Metal Group plc, 1997–98; Dunlop Heywood, 1998–99; Valley and Vale Properties plc, 1998–2000. Chm., Network Space Consultative Cttee, 1999–2001. Director: Salford Phoenix, 1987–95; Manchester Arts Fest., 1989–93; Manchester 2000, 1992–94; Manchester City of Drama, 1992–94; Manchester Concert Hall Ltd, 1994–2004; Patterson Inst. for Cancer Res., 2001–03. Dep. Chair, Manchester Olympic Bid Cttee, 1990–93; Consultant, Commonwealth Games 2002, 2000–02. *Recreations:* cricket, football (West Ham United in particular), golf, music, theatre, cooking. *E:* johnglester27@gmail.com.

GLICK, Ian Bernard; QC 1987; a Recorder, 2000–06; *b* 18 July 1948; *s* of late Dr Louis Glick and Phyllis Esty Glick; *m* 1986, Roxane Eban; three *s*. *Educ:* Bradford Grammar School; Balliol College, Oxford (MA, BCL). President, Oxford Union Society, 1968. Called to the Bar, Inner Temple, 1970, Bencher, 1997. Junior Counsel to the Crown, Common Law, 1985–87; Standing Junior Counsel to DTI in Export Credit Cases, 1985–87. Chm., Commercial Bar Assoc., 1997–99. *Address:* 1 Essex Court, Temple, EC4Y 9AR.

GLICKSMAN, Brian Leslie, CB 2005; Treasury Officer of Accounts, HM Treasury, 2000–05; *b* 14 Dec. 1945; *s* of Henry and Kitty Glicksman; *m* 1971, Jackie Strachan; two *d*. *Educ:* Ealing Grammar Sch.; New Coll., Oxford (BA Maths); Warwick Univ. (MSc Mgt Sci. and OR). OR Scientist, CSD, 1969; Principal, DoE, 1976; Asst Dir, PSA, 1984; Sec. Royal Commn on Envmtl Pollution, 1987; Divl Manager, DoE, 1992. Mem., Audit Cttee, Office of Govt Commerce, 2001–07. Trustee, 2Care, 2004–11 (Vice-Chm., 2006–07; Chm., 2007–11). Trustee, 2Care Staff Pension Scheme, 2004–. Hon. Treas., CS Sports Council, 2006–. Chm., Phoenix Concert Band, 2008–. *Publications:* contrib. to Canadian Parly Rev. *Address:* 18 Worcester Road, Sutton, Surrey SM2 6PG.

GLIDEWELL, Rt Hon. Sir Iain (Derek Laing), Kt 1980; PC 1985; a Lord Justice of Appeal, 1985–95; a Justice of Appeal, 1998–2003, and President, 2003–04, Court of Appeal for Gibraltar; *b* 8 June 1924; *s* of late Charles Norman and Nora Glidewell; *m* 1950, Hilary, *d* of late Clinton D. Winant; one *s* two *d*. *Educ:* Bromsgrove Sch.; Worcester Coll., Oxford (Hon. Fellow 1986). Served RAFVR (pilot), 1942–46. Called to the Bar, Gray's Inn, 1949 (Bencher 1977, Treas. 1995). QC 1969; a Recorder of the Crown Court, 1976–80; Judge of Appeal, Isle of Man, 1979–80; a Judge of the High Court of Justice, Queen's Bench Division, 1980–85; Presiding Judge, NE Circuit, 1982–85. Chm., Judicial Studies Bd, 1989–92; Member: Senate of Inns of Court and the Bar, 1976–79; Supreme Court Rule Cttee, 1980–84. Chm., Panels for Examination of Structure Plans: Worcestershire, 1974; W Midlands, 1975; conducted: Heathrow Fourth Terminal Inquiry, 1978; Review of CPS, 1997–98. Hon. RICS, 1982. *Recreations:* gardening, walking, theatre. *Address:* 24 Beech Court, Willicombe Park, Tunbridge Wells, Kent TN2 3UX. *Club:* Garrick.

GLINDON, Mary; MP (Lab) North Tyneside, since 2010; *b* 13 Jan. 1957; *d* of Margaret and Cecil Mulgrove; *m* 2000, Raymond Glindon; one *d* and one step *s* one step *d*. *Educ:* Sacred Heart Grammar Sch., Fenham; Newcastle upon Tyne Poly. (BSc Sociol. 1979). Clerical officer, CS, 1980–85; adminr, local govt, 1987–88; adminr/community develt manager, Centre for Unemployment, 1988–2004; Adminr, NHS call centre, 2005; trainee dispenser, NHS, 2005–06; travel sales advr, call centre, 2006; sales asst in department store, 2006–08; Admin Officer, DWP and Child Maintenance and Enforcement Commn, 2008–10. Mem. (Lab) N Tyneside Council, 1995–2010 (Mayor, 1999–2000). Member: Envmt, Food and Rural Affairs Select Cttee, 2010–15; Transport Select Cttee, 2015–. *Address:* House of Commons, SW1A 0AA.

GLOAG, Ann Heron, OBE 2004; Director, Stagecoach Group (formerly Holdings) plc, since 1986 (Managing Director, 1986–94; Executive Director, 1986–2000); *b* 10 Dec. 1942; *d* of late Iain and Catherine Souter; *m* 1st, 1965, Robin N. Gloag (*d* 2007); one *d* (one *s* decd); 2nd, 1990, David McCleary. *Educ:* Caledonian Road Primary School; Perth High School. Trainee Nurse, Bridge of Earn Hosp., Perth, 1960–65; Ward Sister, Devonshire Royal Hosp., Buxton, 1965–69; Theatre Sister, Bridge of Earn Hosp., 1969–80; Founding Partner, Gloagtrotter, re-named Stagecoach Express Services, 1980–83; Co-Director, Stagecoach Ltd, 1983–86 (acquired parts of National Bus Co., 1987 and 1989 and Scottish Bus Group, 1991). Hon. Dr: Paisley, 1994; Napier, 1995; Dundee, 2014. Scottish Marketing Woman of the Year, Scottish Univs, 1989; UK Businesswoman of the Year, Veuve Cliquot and Inst. of Dirs, 1989–90; Susan B. Anthony Humanitarian of the Year Award, 2009; Eleanor Roosevelt Award for Outstanding Achievement, 2011. Order of the Star of Africa, 2009. *Recreations:* family, travel, charity support. *Address:* Stagecoach Group, 10 Dunkeld Road, Perth PH1 5TW.

See also Sir B. Souter.

GLOBE, Hon. Sir Henry (Brian), Kt 2011; **Hon. Mr Justice Globe;** a Judge of the High Court of Justice, Queen's Bench Division, since 2011; a Presiding Judge, North Eastern Circuit, since 2013; *b* 18 June 1949; *o s* of late Theodore Montague Globe and of Irene Rita Globe; *m* 1972, Estelle Levin; two *d*. *Educ:* Liverpool Coll.; Birmingham Univ. (LLB Hons). Called to the Bar, Middle Temple, 1972, Bencher, 2005; in practice on Northern Circuit, 1972–2003 (Junior, 1974; Treas., 2001–03); Standing Counsel to: DSS, 1985–94; HM Customs and Excise, 1992–94; Asst Recorder, 1987–90; a Recorder, 1991–2003; QC 1994; a Circuit Judge, then a Sen. Circuit Judge, 2003–11. Hon. Recorder, Liverpool, 2003–11. Member: Bar Council, 2001–03; Criminal Cttee, Judicial Studies Bd, 2001–05; Criminal Justice Council, 2004–10; Sentencing Council, 2010–15. Governor: King David Primary Sch., Liverpool, 1979–2001; King David High Sch., Liverpool, 1985–2000 (Chm., 1990–2000); Foundn Mem., Liverpool Coll., 2003–. Trustee, King David Foundn, 2001–13.

Hon. Fellow, Liverpool John Moores Univ., 2013; Hon. LLD Liverpool, 2015. *Recreations:* tennis, bridge, cycling. *Address:* Royal Courts of Justice, Strand, WC2A 2LL. *E:* mrjustice.globe@judiciary.gsi.gov.uk.

GLOCER, Thomas Henry; Chief Executive Officer, Thomson Reuters (formerly Reuters Group plc), 2001–12; *b* NYC, 8 Oct. 1959; *s* of Walter Glocer and Ursula Glocer (*née* Goodman); *m* 1988, Maarit Leso; one *s* one *d*. *Educ:* Columbia Coll. (BA *summa cum laude* 1981); Yale Law Sch. (JD 1984). Mergers and acquisitions lawyer, Davis Polk and Wardwell, NY, Paris and Tokyo, 1985–93; joined Reuters, 1993: mem., Legal Dept, Gen. Counsel, Reuters America Inc., NYC, 1993–96; Exec. Vice-Pres., Reuters America Inc. and CEO, Reuters Latin America, 1996–98; Chief Executive Officer: Reuters business in the Americas, 1998–2001; Reuters Inf., 2000–01. Director: NYC Investment Fund, 1999–2003 (Mem., Exec. Cttee); Instinet Corp., 2000–05. Mem., Adv. Bd, Singapore Monetary Authy, 2001–05. Director: Merck & Co., 2007–; Council on Foreign Relns; K2 Intelligence, 2013–. Member: Corporate Council, Whitney Mus. of American Art, 2000–03; Corporate Adv. Gp, Tate Britain, 2005–08. Author of computer software, incl. (jtly) Coney Island: a game of discovery, 1983. NY Hall of Sci. Award, 2000; John Jay Alumni Award, 2001. *Recreations:* tennis, windsurfing, ski-ing.

GLOSTER, Rt Hon. Dame Elizabeth, DBE 2004; PC 2013; **Rt Hon. Lady Justice Gloster;** a Lady Justice of Appeal, since 2013; *b* 5 June 1949; *d* of late Peter Gloster and Betty Gloster (*née* Read); *m* 1st, 1973, Stanley Eric Brodie, *qv* (marr. diss. 2005); one *s* one *d*; 2nd, 2008, Sir Oliver Popplewell, *qv*. *Educ:* Roedean Sch., Brighton; Girton Coll., Cambridge (BA Hons; Hon. Fellow 2011). Called to the Bar, Inner Temple, 1971, Bencher 1992; QC 1989; a Judge of the Courts of Appeal of Jersey and Guernsey, 1993–2004; a Recorder, 1995–2004; a Judge of the High Ct of Justice, QBD (Commercial Ct), 2004–13; Judge in Charge of Commercial Court, 2010–12. Mem., panel of Counsel who appear for DTI in company matters, 1982–89. Mem. Bd (non-exec.), CAA, 1992–93. Patron, CIArb, London Br. Hon. Fellow, Harris Manchester Coll., Oxford, 2006. *Address:* Royal Courts of Justice, Strand, WC2A 2LL.

GLOUCESTER, Bishop of, since 2015; **Rt Rev. Rachel Treweek;** *b* 4 Feb. 1963; *d* of Robert Steven Montgomery and Marian Montgomery; *m* 2006, Guy Matthew Treweek. *Educ:* Univ. of Reading (BA Linguistics and Lang. Pathol. (Speech Therapy) 1985); Wycliffe Hall, Oxford (BTh 1994). Paediatric Speech and Language Therapist, Hampstead Health Authority, 1985–91: Hampstead Child Develt Team, 1987–89; Manager for Therapists in Health Centres, Bloomsbury, Hampstead and Islington, 1989–91. Ordained deacon, 1994, priest, 1995; Curate, 1994–97, Associate Vicar, 1997–99, St George's, Tufnell Park; Vicar, St James-the-Less, Bethnal Green, 1999–2006; Archdeacon of Northolt, 2006–11; Archdeacon of Hackney, 2011–15. Mem., Gen. Synod, 2011–. *Address:* 2 College Green, Gloucester GL1 2LR.

GLOUCESTER, Dean of; *see* Lake, Very Rev. S. D.

GLOUCESTER, Archdeacon of; *see* Searle, Ven. J. A.

GLOVER, Dame Anne; *see* Glover, Dame L. A.

GLOVER, Anne Margaret, CBE 2006; Co-Founder and Chief Executive Officer, Amadeus Capital Partners Ltd, since 1997; *b* 6 Feb. 1954; *d* of John and Mary Glover. *Educ:* Clare Coll., Cambridge (BA 1st Cl. Metallurgy and Materials Sci. 1976); Yale Sch. of Mgt (MPPM 1978). Sen. Tech. Associate, Bell Telephone Labs, Murray Hill, 1977; Cummins Engine Company: Asst to Vice Pres., Affiliated Enterprises, 1978–79; Rod Line Foreman, 1979–80; Engine Order Mgt Consultant, NY, 1980–81; Customer Services Team Advr, NY, 1981–83; Bain & Co., Boston: Consultant, 1983–85; Sen. Consultant, 1985–86; Manager, 1986–88; Asst Dir, Apax Partners & Co. Ventures, London, 1989–93; Chief Op. Officer, Virtuality Gp plc, Leicester, 1994–95; Founder and non-exec. Dir, Calderstone Capital, 1996–97. Member Board: Glysure Ltd; Covestor Inc.; Nomad Digital Hldgs; Royal Soc. Enterprise Fund. Chm., British Venture Capital Assoc., 2004–05; Vice-Chm., Eur. Private Equity and Venture Capital Assoc. (Chm., Venture Capital Council). Mem., Eur. Res. and Innovation Area Bd, EC. Non-exec. Dir, Technol. Strategy Bd, 2005–12; Mem., Council for Sci. and Technol., 2014–. Hon. FREng 2008. *Address:* Amadeus Capital Partners Ltd, 16 St James's Street, SW1A 1ER. *T:* (020) 7024 6900, *Fax:* (020) 7024 6999. *E:* aglover@amadeuscapital.com.

GLOVER, Dame Audrey (Frances), DBE 2004; CMG 1997; barrister; Leader, UK Delegation to UN Human Rights Commission, 1998–2003; *d* of Robert John Victor Lush and Frances Lucy de la Roche; *m* 1971, Edward Charles Glover, *qv*; two *s* two *d* (and one *s* decd). *Educ:* St Anne's Coll., Sanderstead, Surrey; King's Coll. London (LLB Hons). Called to the Bar, Gray's Inn, 1961; LCD, 1965–67; HM Diplomatic Service, 1967–97: joined Foreign Office, as Asst Legal Advr, 1967; Asst (Temp.), Attorney Gen's Dept, Australia, 1972–73; Advr on British Law, Liby of Congress, Washington, 1974–77; Legal Advr (Asst), FCO, 1978–85; Legal Advr, British Mil. Govt, Berlin, 1985–89; Legal Counsellor, FCO, and UK Agent to EC and Ct of Human Rights, 1990–94; Dir (with rank of Ambassador), OSCE Office of Democratic Instns and Human Rights, Warsaw, 1994–97. Sen. Advr to Coalition Provisional Authy, Iraq and to Iraqi Minister of Human Rights, 2004–06. Head, OSCE Election Observation Mission: Belarus, 2004; Kazakhstan, 2005; former Yugoslav Republic of Macedonia, 2006; Ukraine, 2007; Italy, 2008; USA, 2008; Albania, 2009; Georgia, 2010; Azerbaijan, 2010; Slovenia, 2011; Ukraine, 2012. Member, Advisory Board: British Inst. of Human Rights, 2004–; Gender Aspects to Peace and Security, 2011–; Chm., Internat. Adv. Council, LINKS, 1999–; Mem. Bd, Electoral Reform Internat. Services, 2005–. Trustee, Prison Reform Trust, 2006–. *Recreations:* collecting paintings, sailing, travelling, theatre. *Address:* The Oak House, Thornham, Norfolk PE36 6LY. *Club:* Brancaster Staithe Sailing (Norfolk).

GLOVER, Prof. Beverley Jane, PhD; FLS; Professor of Plant Systematics and Evolution, University of Cambridge, since 2013; Director, Cambridge University Botanic Garden, since 2013; Fellow, Queens' College, Cambridge, since 1996; *b* Ely, 7 March 1972; *d* of Michael Glover and Margaret Glover (*née* Smith); *m* 2003, Stuart Nigel Bridge, *qv*; one *s* one *d*. *Educ:* Perth High Sch.; Univ. of St Andrews (BSc Plant and Envmtl Biol. 1993); John Innes Centre and Univ. of E Anglia (PhD 1997). Res. Fellow, Queens' Coll., Cambridge, 1996–99; University of Cambridge: Lectr, 1999–2005; Sen. Lectr, 2005–10; Reader, 2010–13; Admissions Tutor (Sci.), 2001–07; Dir of Studies, 2007–13. Member: Council, Eur. Soc. for Evolutionary Develtl Biol., 2010–; Botanical Soc. of America, 2009–; British Soc. for Develtl Biol., 2011–; Council, Systematics Assoc., 2014–. Trustee: Royal Botanic Garden Edinburgh, 2015–. FLS 2010. Bicentenary Medal, Linnean Soc., 2010; William Bate Hardy Prize, Cambridge Philosophical Soc., 2010. *Publications:* Understanding Flowers and Flowering: an integrated approach, 2007, 2nd edn 2014 (Marsh Book of Year Award, British Ecol Soc., 2009); contrib. papers on plant develt, evolution and function to scientific jls. *Recreations:* family, local community, reading, swimming in the sea. *Address:* University of Cambridge Botanic Garden, Brookside, Cambridge CB2 1JE. *T:* (01223) 333938. *E:* bjg26@cam.ac.uk.

GLOVER, Prof. David Moore, PhD; FRS 2009; FRSE; Arthur Balfour Professor of Genetics, University of Cambridge, since 1999 (Head, Department of Genetics, 1999–2004); Fellow, Fitzwilliam College, Cambridge, since 2004; Director, Cancer Research UK (formerly Cancer Research Campaign) Cell Cycle Genetics Group, since 1989; *b* 28 March 1948; *s* of Charles David Glover and Olivia Glover; *m* 2000, Magdalena Zernicka (*see* M. Zernicka-Goetz). *Educ:* Broadway Tech. Grammar Sch., Barnsley; Fitzwilliam Coll., Cambridge (BA 2nd Cl. Biochem.); ICRF and UCL (PhD 1972). FRSE 1992. Damon Runyon Cancer Res. Foundn Fellow, Stanford Univ., Calif, 1972–75; Imperial College, London: Lectr in Biochem., 1975–81; Sen. Lectr in Biochem., 1981–83; Reader in Molecular Genetics, 1983–86; Prof. of Molecular Genetics, 1986–89; Hd, Dept of Biochem., 1988–89; Prof. of Molecular Genetics, Dept of Biochem., 1989–92, Dept of Anatomy and Physiol., 1992–99, Univ. of Dundee. Jt Dir, 1979–86, Dir, 1986–89, CRC Eukaryotic Molecular Genetics Gp. Chief Scientist, Cyclacel Ltd, 1999–. Mem., EMBO, 1978. *Publications:* Genetic Engineering: cloning DNA, 1980; Gene Cloning: the mechanics of DNA manipulation, 1984; DNA Cloning: a practical approach (3 vols), 1985, 2nd edn (jtly with B. D. Hames) 1995; (with C. J. Hutchison) The Cell Cycle, 1995; (with S. Endow) Dynamics of Cell Division, 1998; contrib. over 250 scientific papers. *Recreations:* music, reading, walking. *Address:* University of Cambridge, Department of Genetics, Downing Street, Cambridge CB2 3EH. *T:* (01223) 333988.

GLOVER, Edward Charles, CMG 2003; MVO 1976; HM Diplomatic Service, retired; Associate Consultant, Public Administration International, 2009–13; *b* 4 March 1943; *s* of Edward and Mary Glover; *m* 1971, Audrey Frances Lush (*see* Dame A. F. Glover); two *s* two *d* (and one *s* decd). *Educ:* Goudhurst Sch. for Boys; Birkbeck Coll., London (BA Hons Hist., MPhil Hist.). Joined FO from BoT, 1967: Private Sec. to High Comr, Australia, 1971–73; Washington, 1973–77; Sec. to UK Delegn to UN Law of Sea Conf., 1978–80; on secondment to Guinness Peat Gp, 1981–83; Sect. Hd, Arms Control and Disarmament Dept, FCO, 1983–85; Senate Liaison Officer, BMG, Berlin, 1985–89; Dep. Hd, Near East and N Africa Dept, FCO, 1989–91; Hd, Mgt Rev. Staff, FCO, 1991–94; Dep. Hd of Mission and Consul-Gen., Brussels, 1994–98; High Comr to Guyana and Amb. to Suriname, 1998–2002; Quality and Efficiency Unit, FCO, 2002–03. Short term expert on Macedonia, Public Admin Internat., 2003–05; Adviser: on Foreign Affairs to Coalition Provisional Authy, Iraq, 2004; on Corporate Mgt Issues to Minister of Foreign Affairs, Iraq, 2004–05; on consular and visa matters to Foreign Minister, Bahamas, 2006; Associate Consultant, DFID Support: to Office of Prime Minister, Kosovo, 2006–07; to Min. of Foreign Affairs, Sierra Leone, 2008. Chm., Bd of Trustees, Iwokrama Internat. Centre for Rainforest Conservation and Develt, 2005–12; Trustee, Size of Wales, 2013–. Associate Fellow, Centre for Caribbean Studies, Univ. of Warwick, 2003–. Mem., RIIA, 1969–. Dir, FCO Assoc., 2013– (Mem. Cttee, 2011–13). Chm., NW Norfolk DFAS, 2003–06; Mem. Bd of Mgt, King's Lynn Preservation Trust, 2002–. Mem., Hakluyt Soc., 2003–. *Publications:* The Music Book (novel), 2014; Fortune's Sonata (novel), 2015; contrib. articles in jls on climate change. *Recreations:* writing, tennis, reading, water-colour painting, ran 2014 London Marathon. *Address:* The Oak House, Thornham, Norfolk PE36 6LY. *E:* edward.glover@btopenworld.com. *Clubs:* Brooks's; Norfolk (Norwich).

GLOVER, Prof. (Edward William) Nigel, PhD; FRS 2013; Professor of Physics, Durham University, since 2002; *b* Sunderland, 20 June 1961; *s* of late John Edward Glover and Iris Rebecca Glover (*née* Anderson); *m* Prof. Anne Taormina; one *s* one *d*. *Educ:* Downing Coll., Cambridge (BA 1982); Durham Univ. (PhD 1985). Research at: Univ. of Cambridge, 1985–87; CERN, Geneva, 1987–89; Fermi Nat. Accelerator Lab., Batavia, Ill, 1989–91; Durham University: Lectr, 1991–96; Reader, 1996–2002; Dir, Inst. for Particle Physics Phenomenology, 2005–10. PPARC Sen. Fellow, 2003–06. *Publications:* contribs to jls incl. Physical Rev. Letters, Jl High Energy Physics. *Address:* Department of Physics, Durham University, Science Laboratories, South Road, Durham DH1 3LE.

GLOVER, Rt Rev. (Elistan) Patrick; Bishop of the Diocese of the Free State (formerly Bishop of Bloemfontein), 1997–2012; an Assistant Bishop, Diocese of George, South Africa, since 2013; *b* 1 Feb. 1944; *s* of Rev. Chirho Glover and Sylvia Glover; *m* 1971, Kirsteen Marjorie Bain; two *s* two *d*. *Educ:* King Edward VII High Sch., Johannesburg; Rhodes Univ. (BA); Keble Coll., Oxford (BA Theol 1968; MA 1978); St Paul's Theol Coll., Grahamstown. Deacon 1969, priest 1970; Curate: St Peter's Church, Krugersdorp, 1969–71; St Martin's-in-Veld, Johannesburg, 1971–74; Rector: St Catherine's, Johannesburg, 1975–83; St George's, Johannesburg, 1983–86; Dean of Bloemfontein, 1987–94; Suffragan Bishop of Bloemfontein, 1994–97; Dean, Province of the Anglican Church of S Africa, 2009–12. *Recreations:* squash, jogging, cycling, tennis.

GLOVER, Eric; Secretary-General, Chartered Institute of Bankers (formerly Institute of Bankers), 1982–94; *b* 28 June 1935; *s* of William and Margaret Glover; *m* 1960, Adele Diane Hilliard; three *s*. *Educ:* Liverpool Institute High Sch.; Oriel Coll., Oxford (MA). Shell International Petroleum (Borneo and Uganda), 1957–63; Institute of Bankers, later Chartered Institute of Bankers, 1963–; Asst Sec., 1964–69; Dir of Studies, 1969–82. Chairman: Open and Distance Learning Quality Council (formerly Council for Accreditation of Correspondence Colls), 1993–98 (Mem., 1983–); Intrabank Expert Witness, 1998–2009. Treas., British Accreditation Council for Ind. Further and Higher Educn, 1987– (Mem., 1985–); Pres., Teachers & Trainers of Financial Services, 1998–2007. Hon. Fellow, Sheffield Hallam Univ., 1992. Hon. FCIB 1994. Hon. MBA City of London Polytechnic, 1991. *Publications:* articles on banking education and expert witness work. *Recreations:* golf, swimming. *Address:* 12 Manor Park, Tunbridge Wells, Kent TN4 8XP. *T:* (01892) 531221.

GLOVER, Fiona Susannah Grace; Presenter, The Listening Project, and Generations Apart, since 2010, and Shared Experience, since 2013, BBC Radio 4; *b* 27 Feb. 1969; *d* of William and Priscilla Glover; partner, Rick Jones; one *s* one *d*. *Educ:* Prince's Mead Sch., Winchester; St Swithun's Sch., Winchester; Univ. of Kent (BA Hons Classical Hist. and Philosophy). Trainee reporter scheme, BBC, 1993; presenter: Gtr London Radio Breakfast Show, 1994–95; Travel Show, BBC 2, 1995–97; Five Live, BBC Radio, 1997–2003; Radio 4: Broadcasting House, 2004–06; Travellers' Tree, 2006–07; Saturday Live, 2006–10. Columnist, Waitrose Weekend, 2009–. Mem. Bd, Sound Women, 2010–. Chair of Judges, Orange Prize, 2009. *Publications:* Travels with My Radio, 2000; (contrib.) Journey to the Sea, 2005; (contrib.) Modern Manners Defined, 2012. *Recreations:* cooking, domesticity, world wide radio. *Address:* c/o BBC Radio 4, W1A 1AA. *Club:* Shoreditch House.

GLOVER, Prof. Jane Alison, CBE 2003; DPhil; FRCM; conductor; Director of Opera (formerly Artistic Director of Opera), Royal Academy of Music, since 2009; Professor, University of London, since 2010; Music Director, Music of the Baroque, Chicago, since 2002; *b* 13 May 1949; *d* of late Robert Glover and Jean Glover. *Educ:* Monmouth School for Girls; St Hugh's Coll., Oxford (BA, MA, DPhil; Hon. Fellow, 1991). FRCM 1993. Oxford University: Junior Research Fellow, 1973–75, Sen. Res. Fellow, 1982–91, St Hugh's Coll.; Lecturer in Music: St Hugh's Coll., 1976–84; St Anne's Coll., 1976–80; Pembroke Coll., 1979–84; elected to OU Faculty of Music, 1979. Professional conducting début at Wexford Festival, 1975; thereafter, operas and concerts for: BBC; Glyndebourne (Musical Dir, Touring Opera, 1982–85); Royal Op. House, Covent Garden (début, 1988); ENO (début, 1989); Teatro la Fenice, Venice; Royal Danish Opera; Glimmerglass Opera, NY; Australian Opera; Chicago Opera; Berlin Staatsoper; London SO; London Philharmonic Orch.; Philharmonia Orch.; Royal Philharmonic Orch.; English Chamber Orch.; BBC SO; BBC Welsh SO; Scottish Nat. Orch.; Bournemouth SO; Toronto SO; Houston SO; St Louis SO; San Francisco SO; Philadelphia Orch.; Metropolitan Opera; Cleveland Orch.; and many others in Italy, Holland, Denmark, China, Hong Kong, Austria, Germany, France, Belgium, Australia, NZ, etc; Artistic Dir, London Mozart Players, 1984–91; Principal Conductor: London Choral Soc., 1983–99; Huddersfield Choral Soc., 1989–96. A Gov., BBC, 1990–95. Radio and television documentaries and series, and presentation for BBC and LWT, esp. Orchestra, 1983, Mozart, 1985, Opera House, 1995, Musical Dynasties, 2000. Governor, RAM, 1985–90. Hon. DMus: Exeter, 1986; London, 1992; City, 1994; Glasgow, 1997; Hon. DLitt:

Loughborough, 1988; Bradford, 1992; Brunel, 1996; DUniv Open, 1988; Hon. DMus CNAA, 1991. ABSA/Daily Telegraph Arts Award, 1990. *Publications:* Cavalli, 1978; Mozart's Women, 2005; contribs to: The New Monteverdi Companion, 1986; Monteverdi 'Orfeo' handbook, 1986; articles in Music and Letters, Proc. of Royal Musical Assoc., Musical Times, The Listener, TLS, Early Music, Opera, and others; many recordings. *Recreations:* theatre, skiing, walking. *Address:* Royal Academy of Music, Marylebone Road, NW1 5HT. *T:* (020) 7873 7404.

GLOVER, Julian Wyatt, CBE 2013; actor; *b* 27 March 1935; *s* of late (Claude) Gordon Glover and Honor Ellen Morgan (*née* Wyatt); *m* 1st, 1957, Eileen Atkins (now Dame Eileen Atkins, *qv*) (marr. diss. 1966); 2nd, 1968, Isla Blair; one *s*. *Educ:* St Paul's Sch., Hammersmith; Alleyn's Sch., Dulwich. Full-time actor, 1957–; *theatre includes:* Royal Shakespeare Co.: Coriolanus, Henry VI, 1977; Henry IV, pts I and II, 1991–92 (best supporting actor, Olivier award, 1993); Julius Caesar, Romeo and Juliet, Stratford, transf. Barbican, 1995–96; All My Sons, Palace, Watford, 1992; Cyrano de Bergerac, Haymarket, 1992–93; An Inspector Calls, Aldwych, 1993–94; Chips With Everything, RNT, 1996–97; Prayers of Sherkin, Old Vic, 1997; Waiting for Godot, Piccadilly, 1998; Phèdre, Britannicus, Albery, 1998; A Penny for a Song, Whitehall, 1999; The Tempest, Nuffield, 2000; In Praise of Love, UK tour, 2001; King Lear, Shakespeare's Globe, 2001; Macbeth, Albery, 2003; Taking Sides, UK tour, 2003–04; Galileo's Daughter (Peter Hall Co.), 2004; The Dresser, UK tour, 2004, Duke of York's, 2005; Richard II, The Soldier's Tale, Old Vic, 2005; The Voysey Inheritance, NT, 2006; Shadowlands, Salisbury Playhouse, 2007; The President's Holiday, Hampstead, 2008; Oliver, Theatre Royal, 2008–10; Maurice's Jubilee, The Pleasance, Edinburgh, 2012, UK tour, 2013; The Scottsboro Boys, Young Vic, 2013, transf. Garrick Th., 2014; Dir, Hamlet, Norwich Playhouse, 1996; *films include:* Tom Jones, 1963; I Was Happy Here, 1965; The Empire Strikes Back, 1980; For Your Eyes Only, 1981; The Fourth Protocol, Cry Freedom, 1987; Indiana Jones and the Last Crusade, 1989; Treasure Island, 1990; King Ralph, 1991; Vatel, 2000; Two Men Went to War, Harry Potter and the Chamber of Secrets, 2002; Troy, 2004; The Young Victoria, 2009; Battle for Britain, 2010; The Timber, 2012; *television includes:* Cover Her Face, 1985; The Chief, 1990; Born and Bred, 2002; In Search of Shakespeare, 2003; Waking the Dead, 2004; Trial and Retribution, 2005; The Impressionists, 2006; Michael Wood on Beowulf, 2008; Silent Witness, 2010; Game of Thrones, 2011–15; Spies of Warsaw, 2013; Holby City, 2014. *Publications:* Beowulf, 1987. *Address:* c/o Conway Van Gelder Grant Ltd, 8–12 Broadwick Street, W1F 8HW.

GLOVER, Prof. Keith, FRS 1993; FREng, FIEEE, FInstMC; Professor of Engineering, University of Cambridge, 1989–2013, now Emeritus; Fellow, Sidney Sussex College, Cambridge, 1976–2013, now Emeritus; *b* 23 April 1946; *s* of William Frank Glover and Helen Ruby Glover (*née* Higgs); *m* 1970, Jean Elizabeth Priestley; one *s* one *d*. *Educ:* Dartford Grammar Sch., Kent; Imperial College London (BSc(Eng)); MIT (PhD). FIEEE 1993; FInstMC 1999. Development engineer, Marconi Co., 1967–69; Kennedy Meml Fellow, MIT, 1969–71; Asst Prof. of Electrical Engineering, Univ. of S California, 1973–76; Department of Engineering, University of Cambridge: Lectr, 1976–87; Reader in Control Engineering, 1987–89; Head of Inf. Engrg Div., 1993–2001; Head of Dept, 2002–09. Non-exec. Dir, Sagentia Gp plc, 2011–. FREng 2000. Control Systems Award, IEEE, 2001. *Publications:* (with D. C. McFarlane) Robust Controller Design using Normalized Coprime Factor Plant Descriptions, 1989; (with D. Mustafa) Minimum Entropy H-infinity Control, 1990; (jtly) Robust and Optimal Control, 1996; contribs to control and systems jls. *Address:* Department of Engineering, Trumpington Street, Cambridge CB2 1PZ.

GLOVER, Kenneth Frank; Assistant Under-Secretary of State (Statistics), Ministry of Defence, 1974–81, retired; *b* 16 Dec. 1920; *s* of Frank Glover and Mabel Glover; *m* 1951, Iris Clare Holmes. *Educ:* Bideford Grammar Sch.; UC of South West, Exeter; LSE (MScEcon). Joined Statistics Div., MoT, 1946; Statistician, 1950; Statistical adviser to Cttee of Inquiry on Major Ports (Rochdale Cttee), 1961–62; Dir of Econs and Statistics at Nat. Ports Council, 1964–68; Chief Statistician, MoT and DoE, 1968–74. *Publications:* various papers; articles in JRSS, Dock and Harbour Authority. *Recreations:* boating, idleness. *Address:* Little Hamletts, 26 Platway Lane, Shaldon, Teignmouth, South Devon TQ14 0AR. *T:* (01626) 872700.

GLOVER, Dame (Lesley) Anne, DBE 2015 (CBE 2009); Professor of Molecular and Cell Biology, University of Aberdeen, since 2001; *b* 19 April 1956; *d* of Wesley and Mary Johnstone Glover; *m* 1996, Ian George. *Educ:* Dundee High Sch.; Edinburgh Univ. (BSc 1st Cl. Hons Biochem. 1978); King's Coll., Cambridge (MPhil 1979, PhD 1981). University of Aberdeen: Lectr in Biochem., 1983–94; Sen. Lectr, 1994–98; Reader in Molecular and Cell Biol., 1998–2001. Hon. Res. Fellow, Rowett Res. Inst., Aberdeen, 1992–; Res. Associate, Macaulay Land Use Res. Inst., Aberdeen, 2002–. Chief Scientific Advr for Scotland, 2006–11; Chief Scientific Advr to Pres., EC, 2012–15. Mem., NERC, 2001–11. Chm., UK Collaborative on Develt Scis, 2009–11. Mem. Council, Soc. of Gen. Microbiol., 1995–98. Mem., Bd of Trustees, Cl:aire, 2004–09. Fellow, Amer. Acad. of Microbiol., 1995; FRSE 2005; FRSA 2009. *Publications:* book chapters; numerous reviewed contribs to learned jls; invited reviews and conf. abstracts. *Recreations:* sailing, reading. *Address:* University Office, Room 180, University of Aberdeen, Aberdeen AB24 3FX.

GLOVER, Magdalena; *see* Zernicka-Goetz.

GLOVER, Nigel; *see* Glover, E. W. N.

GLOVER, Rt Rev. Patrick; *see* Glover, Rt Rev. E. P.

GLOVER, Richard Michael; QC 2009; *b* Woking, 12 Dec. 1961; *s* of William James Glover, *qv*; *m* 1988, Caroline Elizabeth de Rougemont; two *d*. *Educ:* Harrow; Gonville and Caius Coll., Cambridge (BA Hons 1983). Called to the Bar, Inner Temple, 1984. *Publications:* (ed) Ryde on Rating and the Council Tax. *Recreations:* books, theatre, music, horse racing and other things of beauty. *Address:* Francis Taylor Building, Temple, EC4Y 7BY. *T:* (020) 7353 8415. *E:* richard.glover@ftb.eu.com.

GLOVER, Stephen Charles Morton; journalist; *b* 13 Jan. 1952; *s* of Rev. Prebendary John Morton Glover and Helen Ruth Glover (*née* Jones); *m* 1982, Celia Elizabeth (*née* Montague); two *s*. *Educ:* Shrewsbury Sch.; Mansfield Coll., Oxford (MA). Daily Telegraph, 1978–85: leader writer and feature writer, 1978–85; parly sketch writer, 1979–81; Independent: Co-Founder, 1986; Foreign Editor, 1986–89; Editor, The Independent on Sunday, 1990–91; Associate Editor, Evening Standard, 1992–95; Columnist: Daily Telegraph, 1996–98; Spectator, 1996–2005; Daily Mail, 1998–; Independent, 2005–12. Dir, Newspaper Publishing, 1986–92. Vis. Prof. of Journalism, St Andrews Univ., 1992. *Publications:* Paper Dreams, 1993; (ed) Secrets of the Press, 1999. *Address:* c/o Aitken Alexander Associates, 291 Gray's Inn Road, WC1X 8EB. *Club:* Beefsteak.

GLOVER, Hon. Sir Victor (Joseph Patrick), Kt 1989; GOSK 1992; legal consultant; Chief Justice, Mauritius, 1988–94; *b* 5 Nov. 1932; *s* of Joseph George Harold Glover and Mary Catherine (*née* Reddy); *m* 1960, Marie Cecile Ginette Gauthier; two *s*. *Educ:* Collège du St Esprit; Royal Coll., Mauritius; Jesus Coll., Oxford (BA (Hons) Jurisprudence). Called to the Bar, Middle Temple, 1957. District Magistrate, 1962; Crown Counsel, 1964; Sen. Crown Counsel, 1966; Prin. Crown Counsel, 1970; Parly Counsel, 1972; Puisne Judge, 1976; Sen. Puisne Judge, 1982. Actg Governor General, July 1988, May 1989, June 1990 and Feb. 1991; Actg Pres. of the Republic, 1992. Chm., Tertiary Educn Commn, 1988–97; Pres., ESU, 1993–2007, now Patron. Hon. Prof. of Civil Law, Univ. of Mauritius, 1986. Hon. Bencher, Middle Temple, 1991. *Publications:* Abstract of Decisions of Supreme Court of Mauritius 1966–1981, 1982, Supplement 1982–1986, 1987; The Law of Seychelles through the Cases, 1999; The New Mauritius Digest, 2000. *Recreations:* reading, swimming, bridge. *Address:* River Court, Saint Denis Street, Port Louis, Mauritius. *Clubs:* Oxford Union Society; Oxford University Boat.

GLOVER, Prof. Vivette Ann Susan, PhD, DSc; Professor of Perinatal Psychobiology, Imperial College London, since 2000; *b* 9 Oct. 1942; *d* of William Fownes Luttrell and Marguerite Luttrell; *m* 1966, Jonathan Glover; two *s* one *d* (and one *d* decd). *Educ:* St Paul's Girls' Sch. (Foundn Schol.); Somerville Coll., Oxford (MA); University Coll. London (PhD 1970; DSc 1990). Res. Assistant, Chemistry Dept, UCL, 1971–76; Res. Biochemist, 1976–81, Clinical Biochemist, 1981–98, Queen Charlotte's Hosp., London; Reader in Perinatal Psychobiol., ICSTM, 1998–2000. Adjunct Prof., Univ. of Rochester, USA, 2004–. Hon. Sen. Lectr, Inst. of Psychiatry, London, 1994. Marcé Soc. Medal, 2004. *Publications:* numerous contribs to jls incl. Nature, Lancet, BMJ. *Recreations:* cycling (to Soho and in English counties), reading novels, opera, football. *Address:* 3 Chalcot Square, NW1 8YB. *T:* (020) 7586 5312. *E:* v.glover@imperial.ac.uk.

GLOVER, William James; QC 1969; a Recorder of the Crown Court, 1975–91; *b* 8 May 1924; *s* of late H. P. Glover, KC and Martha Glover; *m* 1956, Rosemary D. Long; two *s*. *Educ:* Harrow; Pembroke Coll., Cambridge. Served with Royal West African Frontier Force in West Africa and Burma, 1944–47. Called to the Bar, Inner Temple, 1950, Bencher, 1977. Second Junior Counsel to Inland Revenue (Rating Valuation), 1963–69. *Recreation:* photography. *Address:* Hamilton, The Heathers, Salisbury Road, Alderbury, Salisbury SP5 3AF.

See also R. M. Glover.

GLUBE, Hon. Constance Rachelle, OC 2006; ONS 2005; Chief Justice, Court of Appeal, Nova Scotia, 1998–2004; *b* 23 Nov. 1931; *d* of Samuel Lepofsky, QC and Pearl Lepofsky (*née* Slonemsky); *m* 1952, Richard Glube (*d* 1997); three *s* one *d*. *Educ:* McGill Univ. (BA 1952); Dalhousie Univ. (LLB 1955). Called to the Bar, Nova Scotia, 1956. Barrister and Solicitor: Kitz Matheson, 1960–64; Fitzgerald & Glube, 1964–68; City of Halifax: Sen. Solicitor, 1969–74; City Manager, 1974–77; QC (Can.) 1974; Puisne Judge, 1977–82, Chief Justice, 1982–98, Supreme Court of NS. Board Member: QE2 Foundn, 2005–11 (Chair, 2007–09); Halifax Learning Network, 2004–. Hon. Mem., Canadian Bar Assoc., 2003. Trustee, Canadian Museum for Human Rights, 2008–12. Hon. LLD: Dalhousie Law Sch., 1983; St Mary's, 2000; Hon. LHD Mt St Vincent Univ., 1998. Award of Merit, City of Halifax, 1977; Frances Fish Award (Women Lawyers), 1997; Justice Award, Canadian Inst. for Admin of Justice, 2003. Order of Nova Scotia, 2005. Confederation Medal, 1992; Golden Jubilee, 2002; Diamond Jubilee Award, 2012. *Recreations:* gardening, bridge. *Address:* 5920 Inglewood Drive, Halifax, NS B3H 1B1, Canada. *T:* (902) 423 2539.

GLUCK, Malcolm Richard; author and broadcaster; *b* Hornchurch, Essex, 23 Jan. 1942; *s* of late Harry Gluck and Ivy Gluck (*née* Messer); *m* 1st, 1969, Marilyn Janet Day (marr. diss. 1976); one *s* by Patricia Wellington; 2nd, 1984, Susan Ashley (marr. diss. 2003); one *s* one *d*. *Educ:* Drury Falls Sch., Hornchurch; Watford Coll. of Art. Lathe operator, Rotary Hoes Ltd, 1957; apprentice, Ford Motor Co., 1957–60; trainee salesman, Kingsland Shoes Ltd, 1960; poet, 1960–61; office boy, Stratford East Waste Paper Mill, cost clerk, Hackney Springs & Screws, clerk, Spillers Petfoods, Asst to Domestic Superintendent, Mile End Hosp., 1961; jun. sec., Motor Agents Assoc., 1961–62; trainee copywriter, S. H. Benson, 1963; copywriter: Press & General Publicity, 1963–64; Arks Publicity, 1964–65; Streets Advertising, 1965; Mclaren Dunkley Friedlander, 1965–66; Doyle Dane Bernbach: copywriter, London, 1966–69; Sen. Copywriter, NY, 1969; Gp Hd/Associate Dir, London, 1970–71; Copy Chief, 1971–73; Co-proprietor, Sales Dir and games developer, Intellect Games Ltd, 1973–75; Creative Dir, Drakes Jarvis Walsh & Gluck Ltd, 1973–75; script writer and contrib., Punch mag., 1976; Consultant Creative Dir, Pincus Vidler Arthur Fitzgerald, 1976–77; Dir and Sen. Copywriter, Abbott Mead Davies Vickers, 1977–80; Sen. Copywriter, Collet Dickenson Pearce, 1980–84; Dir, Ogilvy & Mather, 1984–85; Exec. Creative Dir, Lintas, 1986–88; Creative Dir, Priestley Marin-Guzman & Gluck, 1989–92; Wine Writer, Superplonk column, 1989–2004, Wine Corresp., 1996, The Guardian; Publisher, Adze Mag., 1992; Consultant Wine Editor, Sainsbury's Mag., 1993–2001; Wine Editor, Cosmopolitan mag., 1995–96; Co-proprietor, Superplonk Online Ltd, 2000–07. Presenter: Gluck, Gluck, Gluck, BBC TV, 1996. Compiler and presenter, Vintage Classics, Deutsche Grammophon, 1996. Over 200 advertising awards from Designers and Art Dirs Assoc., British Advertising Film Awards, British Creative Circle and overseas, 1966–92. *Publications:* Superplonk, (annually) 1991–2005; (with Anthony Worrall Thompson) Supernosh, 1993; Gluck's Guide to High Street Wine, 1995; Gluck on High, 1996; Gluck, Gluck, Gluck, 1996; Summerplonk, 1997, 1998; Streetplonk (annually), 1997–2000; The Sensational Liquid: Gluck's guide to wine tasting, 1999; Wine Matters: why water just won't do, 2003; (contrib.) New Media Language, 2003; Superplonk: the top one thousand, 2004; Supergrub, 2005; (with Mark Hix) The Simple Art of Matching Food and Wine, 2005; Malcolm Gluck's Brave New World, 2006; The Great Wine Swindle, 2008; Chateau Lafite 1953 and Other Stories, 2010; Five Tons of Jam: the poetry of John Orland, 2010; contrib. articles for Amateur Photographer, Punch, Guardian, Independent, Sunday Express, City Limits, Jl of ESU, Cosmopolitan, Living Well, Travel Spirit, Condé Nast Traveller and Hello! *Recreations:* novels (European and American), poetry, music (classical and jazz piano), chess, cooking (European, oriental), cycling through London cemeteries, photography, crosswords. *Address:* c/o Ed Victor Literary Agency, 6 Bayley Street, Bedford Square, WC1B 3HE. *T:* (020) 7304 4100, *Fax:* (020) 7304 4111. *E:* malcolm.gluck@gmail.com. *Clubs:* Groucho, Frontline.

GLUCKMAN, Sir Peter (David), ONZ 2015; KNZM 2009 (DCNZM 2008; CNZM 1997); DSc; FRACP, FRCPCH; FRS 2001; FRSNZ; Director, Liggins Institute, University of Auckland, 2001–09, now Director Emeritus and University Distinguished Professor; New Zealand Prime Minister's Chief Scientific Advisor, since 2009; *b* 8 Feb. 1949; *s* of Laurie Kalman Gluckman and Ann Jocelyn Gluckman (*née* Klippel); *m* 1970, Judith Lucy Nathan; one *s* one *d*. *Educ:* Univ. of Otago (MB ChB); Univ. of Auckland (MMedSci, DSc); Univ. of Calif, San Francisco. FRSNZ 1988; FRCPCH 2004. Res. Fellow, Univ. of Auckland, 1973–76; Res. Fellow, 1976–78, Asst Prof., 1978–80, Dept of Paediatrics, Univ. of Calif, San Francisco; University of Auckland: Sen. Res. Fellow, 1980–88, Prof. and Chair, 1988–92, Dept of Paediatrics; Dean, Faculty of Med. and Health Scis, 1992–2001. FMedSci 2006. *Publications:* contrib. numerous papers to scientific jls relating to fetal physiology, neurosci., endocrinology of growth and evolutionary medicine. *Recreations:* travel, nature photography. *Address:* Liggins Institute, University of Auckland, Private Bag 92019, Auckland 1142, New Zealand. *T:* (office) (9) 9236318. *Club:* Northern (Auckland).

GLUCKSMANN, Dame Margaret Myfanwy Wood; *see* Booth, Dame Margaret.

GLUCKSMANN, Prof. Miriam Anne, PhD; FBA 2005; FAcSS; Professor of Sociology, University of Essex, since 1996; *b* 8 April 1946; *d* of late Alfred Glucksmann, MD and Ilse Lasnitzki-Glucksmann, MD, PhD, DSc; partner, Prof. Mark Harvey. *Educ:* Perse Sch. for Girls, Cambridge; London Sch. of Econs and Political Sci. (BA, PhD 1972). Lecturer in Sociology: Brunel Univ., 1970–71; Univ. of Leicester, 1971–73; Sen. Lectr in Sociol., South Bank Poly., 1973–91; Sen. Lectr in Sociol., 1991–92, Reader in Sociol., 1992–96, Dept of Sociol., Univ. of Essex. Eur. Res. Council Advanced Investigator Grant, 2010–13. FAcSS (AcSS 2012). Hon. DSocSci Stockholm, 2011. *Publications:* Structuralist Analysis in Contemporary Social Thought, 1974, 2nd edn 2014; (as Ruth Cavendish) Women on the Line, 1982, 2nd edn 2009; Women Assemble: women workers and the new industries in inter-war Britain, 1990; Cottons and Casuals: the gendered organisation of labour in time and space, 2000; The New Sociology of Work, 2005. *Address:* Department of Sociology, University of Essex, Wivenhoe Park, Colchester CO4 3SQ.

GLYN, family name of **Baron Wolverton**.

GLYN, Caspar Hilary Gordon; QC 2012; *b* London, 6 Aug. 1969; *s* of James and Lucinda Glyn; *m* 1997, Christine Agnew, *qv*; two *s* one *d*. *Educ:* Ludgrove Sch.; Eton; Manchester Univ. (LLB Hons 1991). Called to the Bar, Inner Temple, 1992; in practice as barrister, 1992–. Chair, Industrial Law Soc., 2013–15 (Vice Chair, 2011–13). *Publications:* (jtly) Sweet & Maxwell's Small Claims Practice, 1999; (jtly) The Personal Injury Handbook, 2nd edn 2001; (jtly) Bullen & Leake Precedents and Pleading, 17th edn 2011. *Recreations:* contrarian, winning, losing gracelessly, auditioning for an obituary in the Daily Mail. *Address:* Cloisters, 1 Pump Court, Temple, EC4Y 7AA. *T:* (020) 7827 4052. *E:* cg@cloisters.com.

GLYN, Christine; *see* Agnew, C.

GLYN, Sir Richard (Lindsay), 10th Bt *cr* 1759, and 6th Bt *cr* 1800; *b* 3 Aug. 1943; *s* of Sir Richard Hamilton Glyn, 9th and 5th Bt, OBE, TD, and Lyndsay Mary (*d* 1971), *d* of T. H. Baker; *S* father, 1980; *m* 1970, Carolyn Ann Williams (marr. diss. 1979); one *s* one *d*. *Educ:* Eton. Co-Founder: Ashton Farm, 1976; High Lea Sch., 1982; Founder: Gaunts House Centre, 1989; Richard Glyn Foundn, 1995; Honeybrook Victorian Farm & Country Park, 2002. *Recreation:* tennis. *Heir: s* Richard Rufus Francis Glyn, *b* 8 Jan. 1971. *Address:* Ashton Farmhouse, Wimborne, Dorset BH21 4JD. *T:* (01258) 840585.

GLYNN, Faith Helen; *see* Wainwright, F. H.

GLYNN, Prof. Ian Michael, MD, PhD, FRS 1970; FRCP; Professor of Physiology, University of Cambridge, 1986–95, now Emeritus; Fellow, Trinity College, since 1955 (Vice-Master, 1980–86); *b* 3 June 1928; 2nd *s* of late Hyman and Charlotte Glynn; *m* 1958, Jenifer Muriel, 2nd *d* of Ellis and Muriel Franklin; one *s* two *d*. *Educ:* City of London Sch.; Trinity Coll., Cambridge; University Coll. Hosp. 1st cl. in Pts I and II of Nat. Sci. Tripos; BA (Cantab) 1949; MB, BChir, 1952; MD 1970; FRCP 1987. House Phys., Central Middx Hosp., 1952–53; MRC Scholar at Physiol. Lab., Cambridge; PhD 1956. Nat. Service in RAF Med. Br., 1956–57. Cambridge University: Res. Fellow, 1955–59, Staff Fellow and Dir of Med. Studies, 1961–73, Trinity Coll.; Univ. Demonstrator in Physiology, 1958–63; Lecturer, 1963–70; Reader, 1970–75; Prof. Membrane Physiology, 1975–86. Vis. Prof., Yale Univ., 1969. Member: MRC, 1976–80 (Chm., Physiological Systems and Disorders Bd, 1976–78); Council, Royal Soc., 1979–81, 1991–92; AFRC (formerly ARC), 1981–86. Chm., Editorial Bd, Jl of Physiology, 1968–70. Hon. Foreign Mem., Amer. Acad. of Arts and Scis, 1984. Hon. MD Aarhus, 1988. *Publications:* (with J. C. Ellory) The Sodium Pump, 1985; An Anatomy of Thought: the origin and machinery of the mind, 1999; (with J. M. Glynn) The Life and Death of Smallpox, 2004; Elegance in Science: the beauty of simplicity, 2010; scientific papers dealing with transport of ions across living membranes, mostly in Jl of Physiology. *Address:* Trinity College, Cambridge CB2 1TQ. *T:* (01223) 338415; Daylesford, Conduit Head Road, Cambridge CB3 0EY. *T:* (01223) 353079.

GLYNN, Joanna Elizabeth; QC 2002; *d* of Geraint David Vernet Glynn and Virginia Browell; *m* 1995, Christopher Tehrani; one *s*. Called to the Bar, Middle Temple, 1983; Bencher, 2011; in practice, specialising in professional regulatory work and related criminal litigation. Asst Recorder, 1997–2000; Recorder, 2000–13. Contrib. Ed., Archbold Criminal Pleading Evidence and Practice, annual edns, 1995–2006. *Publications:* (jtly) Fitness to Practise: health care regulatory law, principle and process, 2005; (jtly) The Regulation of Healthcare Professionals: law, principle and process, 2012. *Address:* 1 Crown Office Row, Temple, EC4Y 7HH. *T:* (020) 7797 7500, *Fax:* (020) 7797 7550. *E:* joanna.glynn@1cor.com.

GLYNN, Lucy Alexandra; *see* Davies, L. A.

GOAD, Dame Sarah (Jane Frances), DCVO 2012; JP; Lord-Lieutenant of Surrey, 1997–2015; *b* 23 Aug. 1940; *er d* of Uvedale Lambert and late Diana (*née* Grey) and step *d* of Melanie Grant Lambert, Denver, Colo; *m* 1961, Timothy Francis Goad, DL; two *s* one *d*. *Educ:* St Mary's, Wantage. Worked for Faber & Faber, 1959–70; Dir, Tilburstow Farms Co. Ltd, 1963–70; Partner, Lambert Farmers, 1970–94. JP Surrey, 1974; Dep. Chm., Family Panel, 1992–97; Mem., Surrey Magistrates' Soc., 1987–93. Trustee: St Mark's Foundn, 1971–; Love Walk (home for disabled), 1984–98 (Chm. Trustees, 1989–93); Surrey Care Trust, 1987–97 (Chm. Trustees, 1995–97); Chevening Estate, 2001–12. Chm., Southwark Cathedral Council, 2000–08; Lay Canon, Southwark Cathedral, 2004–15, now Hon. Lay Canon Emeritus. Pres., SE Reserve Forces' and Cadets' Assoc., 2006–11. Governor: local C of E sch., 1970–90; Hazelwood Sch., 1979–84. Patron, Yvonne Arnaud Theatre, 2004–15. Hon. Fellow, RHUL, 2013. DStJ 1997. *Recreations:* books, buildings, arts. *Address:* South Park, Bletchingley, Surrey RH1 4NE.

GOAD, Tina Gail; *see* Cook, T. G.

GOATER, Very Rev. Catherine; *see* Ogle, Very Rev. C.

GOBBO, Hon. Sir James (Augustine), AC 1993; Kt 1982; CVO 2000; Chairman, National Library of Australia, 2001–10; Commissioner for Italy, Victoria, 2001–06; *b* 22 March 1931; *s* of Antonio Gobbo and Regina Gobbo (*née* Tosetto); *m* 1957, Shirley Lewis; two *s* three *d*. *Educ:* Xavier Coll., Kew, Victoria; Melbourne Univ. (BA Hons); Magdalen Coll., Oxford Univ. (MA; Pres., OUBC, 1955; Mem., Boat Race Crew, 1954, 1955). Called to the Bar, Gray's Inn, London, 1956; Barrister and Solicitor, Victoria, Aust., 1956; signed Roll of Counsel, Victorian Bar, 1957; QC 1971; Supreme Court Judge, Victoria, 1978–94; Lt Gov., 1995–97, Governor, 1997–2000, of Victoria. Ind. Lectr in Evidence, Univ. of Melbourne, 1963–68. Comr, Victorian Law Reform Commn, 1985–88. Chairman: Aust. Refugee Council, 1977; Multicultural Taskforce for Aust. Bicentenary, 1982–84; Reference Gp into Public Liby Funding, 1987; Aust. Multicultural Affairs Council, 1987–91; Aust. Bicentennial Multicultural Foundn, 1988–97, 2001–; Palladio Foundn, 1989–97; Aust. Banking Industry Ombudsman Council, 1994–97; Electricity Industry Ombudsman Council, 1995–97; Council, Order of Australia, 2001–09 (Mem., 1982–92); Nat. Cttee of the Ageing, 2002–; Mercy Private Hosp., Melbourne, 1977–87 (Mem. Bd, Mercy Maternity Hosp., 1972–91); Caritas Christi Hospice, 1986–97; Order of Malta Hospice Home Care, 1986–97; Italian Historical Soc. of Vic, 1980–97. Member: Immigration Reform Gp, 1959–64; Aust. Inst. of Multicultural Affairs, 1979–86; Nat. Population Council, 1983–87; Victorian Health Promotion Foundn, 1989–97; Victorian Community Foundn, 1992–97; Nat. Adv. Cttee, Centenary of Fedn, 1994; Newman Coll. Council, 1970–85; Italo-Australian Educn Foundn, 1974–97; Palladio Trust, Univ. of Melbourne, 1989–; Cttee, Italian Services Inst., 1993–97, 2001–; Bd of Govs, Ian Potter Foundn, 2001–; Bd of Govs, CEDA, 2004–; Bd, Monash Inst. for Study of Global Movts, 2005–; Bd, St Vincent's Foundn, 2006; Bd, Internat. Specialised Skills Inst., 2010– (Chm., 1994–97); Pres., CO-AS-IT, 1979–84, 1986–94. Trustee: Victorian Opera Foundn, 1983–97; WWF, Australia, 1991–97. Vice-Pres., Aust. Assoc. of SMO Malta, 1984–87 and 2001–, Pres., 1987–97; Pres., Scout Assoc. of Victoria, 1987–97. Fellow, Rockefeller Foundn, Bellagio, 1994. Hon. Fellow Aust. Inst. of Valuers, 1985; Hon. Life Member: Aust. Inst. of Architects, 1997; Nat. Gall., Vic, 1999. Hon. LLD Monash, 1995; Hon. Dr Aust. Catholic Univ., 1996; Hon. Dr Jurisp. Bologna, 1998; Hon. LLD Melbourne, 2000. GCSG 2003. Commendatore, 1973, Grand Cross, 1998, Order of Merit, Republic of Italy; Kt Grand Cross, SMO Malta, 1982. *Publications:* (ed) Cross on Evidence (Australian edn), 1970–1978; Something to Declare: a memoir, 2010; various papers. *Address:* 8/25 Douglas Street, Toorak, Vic 3142, Australia. *T:* (3) 98266115.

GOBBY, Clive John; Director, South Africa and Regional Director, Southern Africa, British Council, 2000–03; *b* 2 June 1947; *m* 1978, Margaret Ann Edwards. *Educ:* Bective Secondary Mod. Sch., Northampton; Northampton GS; Leicester Univ. (BA 1968). Joined British Council, 1982; Dep. Manager, Enterprises, 1992–96; Network Manager, Grant in Aid Services, 1996; Dir, Turkey, 1997–2000. *Recreations:* walking, net surfing, dog training.

GOBLE, Prof. Carole Anne, CBE 2014; FREng; FBCS; Professor of Computer Science, University of Manchester, since 2000; *b* Maidstone, 10 April 1961; *d* of George Goble and Barbara Goble; *m* 2003, Ian Cottam. *Educ:* Maidstone Sch. for Girls; Univ. of Manchester (BSc Hons 1st Cl. Computing and Inf. Systems 1982). FBCS 2002. University of Manchester: Lectr, 1985–95; Sen. Lectr, 1995–2000. Mem., BBSRC, 2013–. *Publications:* over 250 articles in learned jls and confs in computer sci. and bioinformatics. *Recreations:* shopping, dining, music festivals. *Address:* School of Computer Science, University of Manchester, Kilburn Building, Oxford Road, Manchester M13 9PL. *E:* carole.goble@manchester.ac.uk.

GODARD, Jean-Luc; French film director; *b* 3 Dec. 1930; *s* of Paul Godard and Odile Godard (*née* Monad); *m* 1st, 1961, Anna Karina (marr. diss.); 2nd, 1967, Anne Wiazemsky. *Educ:* Collège de Nyon; Lycée Buffon; Faculté de Lettres, Paris. Former journalist and film critic: La Gazette du cinéma; Les Cahiers du cinéma. Mem., Conseil supérieur de la langue française, 1989. *Films include:* A bout de souffle, 1959 (prix Jean Vigo, 1960; Best Dir Award, Berlin Fest., 1960); Le Petit Soldat, 1960; Une femme est une femme, 1961 (Special Prize, Berlin Fest.); Les sept péchés capitaux, 1961; Vivre sa vie, 1962 (Special Prize, Venice Fest.); Les Carabiniers, 1963; Les plus belles escroqueries du Monde, 1963; Le Mépris, 1963; Paris vu par …, 1964; Une femme mariée, 1964; Alphaville, 1965; Pierrot le fou, 1965; Masculin-Féminin, 1966; Made in USA, 1966; Deux ou trois choses que je sais d'elle, 1966; La Chinoise, 1967 (Special Prize, Venice Fest.); Week-end, 1967; Loin du Vietnam, 1967; La Contestation, 1970; Ici et ailleurs, 1976; (jtly) Tout va bien, 1972; Moi je, 1974; Comment ça va?, 1975; Sauve qui peut, 1980; Passion, 1982; Prénom Carmen, 1983 (Golden Lion, Venice Fest.); Je vous salue Marie, 1985; Détective, 1985; Soigne ta droite, 1987; Le Roi Lear, 1987; Nouvelle vague, 1990; Hélas pour moi, 1993; JLG/JLG, 1995; For Ever Mozart, 1996; Eloge de l'amour, 2001; Notre Musique, 2005; Film Socialisme, 2010; Goodbye to Language, 2014. Hon. Academy Award, 2011. Chevalier de l'ordre national du Mérite. *Publications:* Introduction à une véritable histoire du cinéma.

GODBER, John Harry; playwright, since 1981; *b* 18 May 1956; *s* of Harry Godber and Dorothy (*née* Deakin); *m* 1993, Jane Thornton; two *d*. *Educ:* Leeds Univ. (CertEd, BEd Hons, MA, MPhil). School teacher, 1979–83; writing for TV, 1981–; Artistic Dir, Hull Truck Theatre Co., 1984–2010; Creative Dir, John Godber Co., Theatre Royal Wakefield, 2013–. Prof. of Contemporary Theatre, Liverpool Hope Univ., 2004–. *Plays include:* Up 'N' Under, 1984 (filmed, 1997); Bouncers, 1986; Teechers, 1987; On the Piste, 1993; April in Paris, 1994; Passion Killers, 1994; Shakers: the musical, 1994; Lucky Sods, 1995; Weekend Breaks, 1997; Perfect Pitch, 1998; Unleashed, 1998; It started with a Kiss, 1998; Thick as a Brick, 1999 (filmed, 2004); On a Night Like This, 1999; Departures, 2001; Reunion, 2002; Screaming Blue Murder, 2003; Black Tie and Tails, 2003; Fly Me to the Moon, 2004; Beef and Yorkshire Pudding, 2004; Going Dutch, 2004; Wrestling Mad, 2005; Crown Prince, 2007; Horrid Henry - Live and Horrid!, 2008; The Debt Collectors, 2011; (with Jane Thornton) Lost & Found, 2012; Muddy Cows, 2013; television series, Thunder Road (also filmed), 2002; television film, Oddsquad, 2005. Sunday Times Play-writing Award, 1981; Olivier Award for Comedy of Year, 1984. Hon. DLitt: Hull, 1988; Humberside, 1997. *Publications:* Up 'N' Under, 1985; Bouncers, 1986; John Godber: 5 plays, 1989; On the Piste, 1991; April in Paris, 1992; Blood Sweat and Tears, 1995; Lucky Sods, 1995; Passion Killers, 1995; Gym and Tonic, 1996; John Godber Plays: vols 1 and 2, 2001, vol. 3, 2003. *Recreations:* keep fit, reading, theatre, cinema, opera.

GODDARD OF STOCKPORT, Baron *cr* 2014 (Life Peer), of Stockport in the County of Greater Manchester; **David Goddard.** Mem. (Lib Dem) Stockport MC, 1990–2012 and 2014– (Leader, 2007–12). Former Mem., Greater Manchester Police Authy; former non-exec. Dir, Manchester Internat. Airport. Vice Chair: Exec. Bd, Assoc. of Gtr Manchester Authorities, 2007–12; Gtr Manchester Combined Authy; Envmt Comr for Gtr Manchester, 2008–12; Bd Mem., Gtr Manchester Enterprise Partnership, 2011–12.

GODDARD, Dr Andrew Francis, FRCP; Consultant Gastroenterologist, Royal Derby Hospital, since 2002; Registrar, Royal College of Physicians, since 2014; *b* Plymouth, 8 Nov. 1967; *m* 1994, Nicola; one *s* one *d*. *Educ:* City of London Freemen's Sch.; St John's Coll., Cambridge (BA 1988; BChir 1990, MB 1991; MD 1997). MRCP 1993, FRCP 2005. Dir, Derbys Bowel Cancer Screening Prog., 2007–. *Recreations:* cycling, golf, teenager negotiations. *Address:* Royal College of Physicians, 11 St Andrews Place, Regent's Park, NW1 4LE. *T:* (020) 3075 1234. *E:* andrew.goddard@rcplondon.ac.uk. *Club:* Stanton-on-the-Wolds Golf.

GODDARD, Andrew Stephen; QC 2003; *b* 5 Oct. 1959; *s* of Lt Col C. E. Goddard and Kathleen Goddard; one *s* two *d*. *Educ:* St John's Sch., Billericay; Chelmsford Coll. of Further Educn; Univ. of Sussex (BA 1st Cl. Hons Law); Inns of Court Sch. of Law. Called to the Bar, Inner Temple, 1985 (QE II Major Schol. 1984; Poland Prize 1985); barrister, specialising in internat. construction disputes, 1987–. *Recreations:* child rearing, peace and quiet. *Address:* 1 Atkin Building, Gray's Inn, WC1R 5AT. *T:* (020) 7404 0102, *Fax:* (020) 7405 7456. *E:* agoddard@atkinchambers.law.co.uk.

GODDARD, Harold Keith; QC 1979; barrister-at-law; a Recorder of the Crown Court, 1978–2001; a Deputy High Court Judge, 1993–2001; *b* 9 July 1936; *s* of late Harold Goddard and Edith Goddard, Stockport, Cheshire; *m* 1st, 1963, Susan Elizabeth (marr. diss.), *yr d* of late Ronald Stansfield and of Evelyn Stansfield, Wilmslow, Cheshire; two *s*; 2nd, 1983, Alicja Maria, *d* of late Czeslaw Lazuchiewicz and of Eleonora Lazuchiewicz, Lodz, Poland. *Educ:* Manchester Grammar Sch.; Corpus Christi Coll., Cambridge (Scholar; 1st Cl. Law Tripos 1957; MA, LLM). Bacon Scholar, Gray's Inn; called to the Bar, Gray's Inn, 1959. Practised on Northern Circuit, 1959–2001; Head of Chambers, 1983–2000. Member: CICB, 1993–2001; Mental Health Review Tribunal, 1998–2008. Chm., Disciplinary Appeals Cttee, 1974–80, Mem. Council, 1980–83, Mem. Ct of Governors, 1981, UMIST. *Recreation:* golf. *Address:* Deans Court Chambers, 24 St John Street, Manchester M3 4DF. *T:* (0161) 214 6000. *Club:* Wilmslow Golf.

GODDARD, Prof. John Burgess, OBE 1986; Henry Daysh Professor of Regional Development Studies, University of Newcastle upon Tyne, 1975–2008, now Emeritus (Deputy Vice-Chancellor, 2001–08; Leverhulme Emeritus Fellow, 2008–10); *b* 5 Aug. 1943; *s* of Burgess Goddard and Molly Goddard (*née* Bridge); *m* 1966, Janet Patricia (*née* Peddle); one *s* two *d*. *Educ:* Latymer Upper Sch.; University Coll. London (BA; Hon. Fellow, 2010); LSE (PhD). Lectr, LSE, 1968–75; Leverhulme Fellow, Univ. of Lund, 1974; University of Newcastle: Hon. Dir, Centre for Urban and Regional Develt Studies, 1978–; Dean, Faculty of Law, Envmt and Social Scis, 1994–98; Pro Vice-Chancellor, 1998–2001. Dir, ESRC Prog. on Inf. and Communications Technol., 1992–93. Vis. Fellow, NESTA, 2008–09. Advr, Trade and Industry Select Cttee, H of C, 1994–95. Chairman: Assoc. of Dirs of Res. Centres in Social Sciences, 1991–98; Assoc. of Res. Centres in the Social Scis, 1998–99. Member: Northern Economic Planning Council, 1976–79; Human Geography Cttee, SSRC, 1976–80;

Bd, Port of Tyne Authority, 1990–93; Bd, Tyne and Wear Sub-Regl Partnership, 2005–08; Bd, Newcastle City Centre Partnership, 2008–09; Lead Expert Gp, Foresight Project on Land Use Futures, 2008–10; Dir, Newcastle NE1 Ltd, 2009–; Trustee: Newcastle Together, 2013–; Newcastle Cathedral, 2015–. Chairman: NE Reg. Cttee, Community Fund, 2003–04; Voluntary and Community Sector Cttee, Big Lottery Fund, 2005–06. Member: Newcastle Cathedral Council, 2012–; Council, Acad. of Social Scis, 2013–; Bd, Campaign for Social Scis, 2014–. Governor, University of Northumbria at Newcastle (formerly Newcastle upon Tyne Poly.), 1989–98. Editor, Regional Studies, 1980–85; Member, Editorial Board: Jl of Higher Educn Policy and Mgt, 2008–10; 21st Century Society, 2008–. FAcSS (AcSS 2003). FRSA 1992. Victoria Medal, RGS, 1992. Lord Dearing Lifetime Achievement Award for Higher Educn, 2012. *Publications:* Office Linkages and Location, 1973; Office Location in Urban and Regional Development, 1975; The Urban and Regional Transformation of Britain, 1983; Technological Change, Industrial Restructuring and Regional Development, 1986; Urban Regeneration in a Changing Economy, 1992; (with Paul Vallance) The University and the City, 2013; articles in professional jls. *Club:* Athenæum.

GODDARD, Rt Rev. John William; Bishop Suffragan of Burnley, 2000–14; *b* 8 Sept. 1947; *s* of Rev. Canon William and Anna Elizabeth Goddard; *m* 1970, Vivienne Selby; two *s*. *Educ:* Durham Univ. (BA Hons Theol 1969; DipTh 1970). Ordained deacon, 1970, priest, 1971; Curate: St John, Southbank, 1970–74; Cayton with Eastfield, 1974–75; Vicar: Ascension, Middlesbrough, 1975–82; All Saints, Middlesbrough, 1982–88; RD, Middlesbrough, 1981–87; Canon and Prebend, York Minster, 1987–88, now Canon Emeritus; Vice-Principal, Edin. Theol Coll., 1988–92; Team Rector, Ribbleton, 1992–2000. *Recreations:* restoring old houses and working with wood, narrow boating. *Address:* 39 Kearsley Avenue, Tarleton, Preston PR4 6BP. *T:* (01772) 812532, 07779 786114.

GODDARD, Hon. Dame Lowell (Patria), DNZM 2014; **Hon. Justice Goddard;** QC (NZ) 1988; a Judge of the High Court of New Zealand, since 1995; *b* Auckland, 25 Nov. 1948; *d* of Pat Vaughan Goddard and Janet Frances Goddard (*née* Collinson); *m* 1992, Christopher John Hodson, QC. *Educ:* Diocesan High Sch., Auckland; Auckland Univ. (LLB 1975). Called to the Bar, NZ, 1975; in practice as barrister, 1977–89; Dep. Solicitor-Gen. for NZ, 1990–95. Chair: Ind. Police Conduct Authy, 2007–12; Ind. Panel Inquiry into Child Sexual Abuse, UK, 2015–. Expert Mem., UN Subcttee on Prevention of Torture, 2010–. Commemoration Medal (NZ), 1990; Suffrage Medal (NZ), 1994. *Recreations:* equestrian sport, thoroughbred racing and breeding, ski-ing, landscape and garden design. *Address:* High Court of New Zealand, PO Box 1091, Wellington 6140, New Zealand. *E:* justice.goddard@courts.govt.nz. *Club:* Wellington (Wellington, NZ).

GODDARD, Prof. Peter, CBE 2002; ScD; FRS 1989; Professor, Institute for Advanced Study, Princeton, since 2012 (Director, 2004–12); Fellow, St John's College, Cambridge, 1975–94 and since 2004 (Master, 1994–2004); *b* 3 Sept. 1945; *s* of Herbert Charles Goddard and Rosina Sarah Goddard (*née* Waite); *m* 1968, Helen Barbara Ross; one *s* one *d*. *Educ:* Emanuel Sch., London; Trinity Coll., Cambridge (BA 1966; MA, PhD 1971; Hon. Fellow, 2009); ScD Cantab 1996. FInstP 1990. Res. Fellow, Trinity Coll., Cambridge, 1969–73; Vis. Scientist, CERN, Geneva, 1970–72, 1978; Lectr in Applied Maths, Univ. of Durham, 1972–74; Mem., Inst. for Advanced Study, Princeton, NJ, 1974, 1988; Cambridge University: Asst Lectr 1975–76; Lectr 1976–89; Reader in Mathematical Physics, 1989–92; Prof. of Theoretical Physics, 1992–2004; Dep. Dir, Isaac Newton Inst. for Mathematical Scis, 1991–94 (Sen. Fellow, 1994–2010; Hon. Fellow, 2011); Mem., Univ. Council, 2000–03; St John's College: Lectr in Maths 1975–91; Tutor 1980–87; Sen. Tutor 1983–87. Vis. Prof. of Maths and Physics, Univ. of Virginia, 1983; SERC Vis. Fellow, Imperial Coll., 1987. Mem., Inst. for Theoretical Physics, Univ. of California, Santa Barbara, 1986, 1990. Pres., LMS, 2002–03. Chm., Univ. of Cambridge Local Exams Syndicate, 1998–2003. Governor: Berkhamsted Schs, 1985–96; Emanuel Sch., 1992–2003; Shrewsbury Sch., 1994–2003; Hills Road Sixth Form Coll., Cambridge, 1999–2003 (Chm., 2001–03). Hon. Fellow, TCD, 1995. Dirac Medal and Prize, Internat. Centre for Theoretical Physics, Trieste, 1997. *Publications:* articles on elementary particle physics and mathematical physics in sci. jls. *Recreations:* informal flower arranging, mathematical physics, idle thought. *Address:* Institute for Advanced Study, Einstein Drive, Princeton, NJ 08540, USA. *T:* (609) 7348335.

GODDARD, Air Vice-Marshal Peter John, CB 1998; AFC 1981; FRAeS; Senior Directing Staff (Air), Royal College of Defence Studies, 1996–98; *b* 17 Oct. 1943; *s* of John Bernard Goddard and Lily Goddard; *m* 1966, Valerie White; two *s*. *Educ:* Nottingham High Sch. qwi, ndc, aws, rcds. FRAeS 1997. Joined RAF 1963; served 54 and 4 Hunter Sqns, 233 Harrier and 226 Jaguar OCUs; OC, 54 Jaguar Sqn, 1978–80; MoD, 1981–83; OC, Tri-nat. Tornado Trng Estabt, RAF Cottesmore, 1984–86; RCDS 1988; Dir, Air Armament, 1989–93; Dep. Comdr, Interim Combined Air Ops Centre 4, 1993–96. *Recreations:* golf, gardening, walking. *Clubs:* Royal Air Force; Felixstowe Ferry Golf.

GODDARD, Roy; independent business consultant, since 1988; Member, Independent Television Commission, 1991–97; *b* 21 Feb. 1939; *s* of Roy Benjamin Goddard and Emma Annie Coronation (*née* Beckett); *m* 1961, Sally Anne Pain; one *s* one *d*. *Educ:* Henry Thornton Grammar Sch.; Regent Street Polytechnic. Cummins Engine Co., 1964–68; Partner, Alexander Hughes & Associates, executive search consultants, 1968–70; Founder, Goddard Kay Rogers & Associates, 1970–88. Chm., Network Gp of Cos, 1992–98; Mem. Adv. Bd, Private Equity Div., Mercury Asset Mgt, 1997–2000; Director: Hg Capital LLP (formerly Mercury Private Equity), 2001–11; Hg Investment Mgt, 2002–07; Hg Pooled Mgt, 2002–11. Member: IBA, 1990–91; GMC, 1994–99. Home Office selection panel appointee, Sussex Police Authy, 1994–2000; Ind. Assessor, Legal Aid Bd, 1996–98. Hon. Vice Pres., Dyslexia Inst., 1997–2014 (Chm., 1990–96). Freeman, City of London, 1981; Liveryman, Co. of Glaziers and Painters of Glass, 1981–. *Recreations:* water gardening, reading, eating, cinema, theatre. *Address:* Newells, Brighton Road, Lower Beeding, West Sussex RH13 6NQ. *T:* (01403) 891110. *Club:* Royal Automobile.

GODDARD, Suzanne Hazel Read; QC 2008; **Her Honour Judge Goddard;** a Circuit Judge, since 2015; *b* Manchester, 26 Sept. 1963; *d* of Geoffrey St John Lister Goddard and Phyllis Mary Goddard; *m* 1994, Richard Harrison Bevan. *Educ:* Dinas Bran Comp. Sch., Llangollen; Wrekin Coll., Wellington; Univ. of Manchester (LLB Hons 1985). Called to the Bar, Gray's Inn, 1986; Lincoln House Chambers, 1986–2015; Jun., N Circuit, 1989; a Recorder, 2002–15. *Recreations:* walking, ski-ing, theatre, cricket (Pres., Gentlemen Gardener's Cricket Club).

GODDEN, Charles Henry, CBE 1982; HM Diplomatic Service, retired; Governor (formerly HM Commissioner), Anguilla, 1978–83; *b* 19 Nov. 1922; *s* of late Charles Edward Godden and Catherine Alice Godden (*née* Roe); *m* 1943, Florence Louise Williams; two *d*. *Educ:* Tweeddale Sch., Carshalton; Morley Coll., Westminster. Served Army, 1941–46. Colonial Office, 1950–66 (seconded British Honduras, 1961–64: Perm. Sec., External Affairs; Dep. Chief Sec.; Clerk of Executive Council); FCO, 1966–: First Sec., 1968; Asst Private Sec. to Sec. of State for Colonies; Private Secretary: to Minister of State, FCO, 1967–70; to Parly Under Sec. of State, 1970; First Sec. (Commercial), Helsinki, 1971–75; First Sec., Belize, 1975–76; Dep. High Comr and Head of Chancery, Kingston, 1976–78. *Publications:* Trespassers Forgiven: memoirs of imperial service in an age of independence, 2009. *Recreations:* cricket, walking, reading. *Address:* Stoneleigh, Blackboys, Sussex TN22 5JL. *T:* (01825) 890410. *Club:* MCC.

GODDEN, Prof. Malcolm Reginald, PhD; FBA 2009; Rawlinson and Bosworth Professor of Anglo-Saxon, University of Oxford, 1991–2012; Fellow of Pembroke College, Oxford, 1991–2012; *b* 9 Oct. 1945. *Educ:* Devizes Grammar Sch.; Barton Peveril Sch., Eastleigh; Pembroke Coll., Cambridge (BA 1966; MA, PhD 1970). Res. Fellow, Pembroke Coll., Cambridge, 1969–72; Asst Prof., Cornell Univ., 1970–71; Lectr in English, Liverpool Univ., 1972–75; Univ. Lectr in English, and Fellow, Exeter Coll., Oxford, 1976–91. Exec. Editor, Anglo-Saxon England, 1989–2012. *Publications:* Ælfric's Catholic Homilies, (ed) second series, 1979, (ed jtly) first series, 1997, introduction, commentary and glossary, 2000 (Gollancz Prize, British Acad., 2001); The Making of Piers Plowman, 1990; (ed jtly) The Cambridge Companion to Old English Literature, 1991; (ed jtly) Anglo-Saxon England, vol. 27, 1999; (ed jtly) The Old English Boethius, 2009; contribs to Anglia, English Studies, Anglo-Saxon England, Rev. of English Studies.

GODDEN, Tony Richard Hillier, CB 1975; Secretary, Scottish Development Department, 1980–87, retired; *b* 13 Nov. 1927; *o s* of late Richard Godden and Gladys Eleanor Godden; *m* 1953, Marjorie Florence Snell; one *s* one *d* (and one *d* decd). *Educ:* Barnstaple Grammar Sch.; London Sch. of Economics (BSc (Econ.) 1st cl.). Commissioned, RAF Education Branch, 1950. Entered Colonial Office as Asst Principal, 1951; Private Sec. to Parly Under-Sec. of State, 1954–55; Principal, 1956; Cabinet Office, 1957–59; transferred to Scottish Home Dept, 1961; Asst Sec., Scottish Development Dept, 1964; Under-Sec., 1969; Sec., Scottish Economic Planning Dept, 1973–80. Member: Council on Tribunals, 1988–94; Ancient Monuments Board for Scotland, 1990–95. Sec., Friends of Royal Scottish Acad., 1987–2000. *Address:* Byways, Kiln Lane, Stokenham, Kingsbridge TQ7 2SQ. *T:* (0131) 667 6556.

GODFRAY, Prof. (Hugh) Charles (Jonathan), CBE 2011; PhD; FRS 2001; Hope Professor of Zoology (Entomology), and Fellow of Jesus College, University of Oxford, since 2006; *b* 27 Oct. 1958; *s* of Hugh and Annette Godfray; *m* 1992, Caroline Essil Margaret Elmslie. *Educ:* Millfield Sch., Som; St Peter's Coll., Oxford (MA; Hon. Fellow, 2001); Imperial Coll., London (PhD 1983). NERC Postdoctoral Fellow, Dept of Biol., Imperial Coll., London Univ., 1982–85; Demonstrator in Ecol., Dept of Zool., Univ. of Oxford, 1985–87; Imperial College, London University: Lectr, 1987–92, Reader, 1992–95, Dept of Biol Scis; Prof. of Evolutionary Biol., 1995–2006; Dir, NERC Centre for Population Biol., 1999–2006; Head, Div. of Biol., 2005–06. Mem., NERC, 2008–. Chm., BIS (formerly DIUS) Lead Expert Gp, Foresight Future of Food and Farming Project, 2009–11; Dir, Oxford Martin Prog. on Future of Food, 2012–; Chair, Sci. Adv. Council, DEFRA, 2015–. Pres., British Ecol Soc., 2009–11. Hon. Fellow, Nat. Hist. Mus., 2002–. Trustee, Royal Botanic Gdns, Kew, 2004–10; Trustee Dir, Rothamsted Research, 2012–. MAE 2012. For. Mem., American Acad. of Arts and Scis, 2009. Scientific Medal, 1994, Frink Medal, 2010, Zool. Soc.; Linnean Medal, Linnean Soc., 2011. *Publications:* Parasitoids, 1994; scientific papers in ecology and evolution. *Recreations:* natural history, gardening, opera, walking. *Address:* Department of Zoology, South Parks Road, Oxford OX1 3PS.

GODFREY, Daniel Charles; Chief Executive, Investment Association (formerly Investment Management Association), since 2012; *b* 30 June 1961; *s* of late Gerald Michael Godfrey, CBE; *m* 1994, Frederiki Androulla Perewiznyk; three *s* one *d*. *Educ:* Westminster Sch.; Victoria Univ. of Manchester (BA Hons Econs). Life Insp., UK Provident, 1982–85; Mktg Manager, Schroders, 1985–88; Project Manager, Mercury Asset Mgt, 1988–90; Mktg Manager, Laurentian Life, 1990–91; Proprietor, The Sharper Image, 1991–94; Mktg Dir, Flemings, 1994–98; Dir Gen., Assoc. of Investment Trust Cos, later Assoc. of Investment Cos, 1998–2009; Communications Dir, Phoenix Gp Hldgs (formerly Pearl Gp), 2009–12. Chm., Personal Finance Education Gp, 2000–03. Member: ICA, 1987–; IoD, 2001–; Internat. Bankers' Co. (formerly Guild of Internat. Bankers), 2001–. *Recreations:* theatre, children (raising), juggling, football. *E:* daniel@coburglodge.com.

GODFREY, David Warren; Chief Executive Officer, UK Export Finance, 2013–15 (non-executive Director, 2005–13); *b* Halifax, W Yorks, 22 Sept. 1950; *s* of Kenneth and Beryl Godfrey; *m* 2009, Theresa Froehlich; one *s* two *d*. *Educ:* Heath Grammar Sch., Halifax; Nottingham Univ. (BA Hons 1972). J. P. Morgan, 1994–2002; Mem., Exec. Bd, Swiss Re, 2002–09; Hd, Wholesale Risk, Lloyds Banking Gp, 2009–11; Chief Risk Officer, Pension Insce Corp., 2012–13. Non-exec. Dir, Charity Bank Ltd, 2013–. *Recreations:* theatre, opera, hill-walking. *Address:* 63 Cloudesley Road, N1 0EL. *T:* (020) 7913 9997, 07310 756442. *E:* dwgodfrey51@aol.com.

GODFREY, Rt Rev. (Harold) William; *see* Peru, Bishop of.

GODFREY, Howard Anthony; QC 1991; a Recorder, 1992–2005; *b* 17 Aug. 1946; *s* of late Emanuel and Amy Godfrey; *m* 1972, Barbara Ellinger; two *s*. *Educ:* William Ellis Sch.; LSE (LLB). Asst Lectr in Law, Univ. of Canterbury, NZ, 1969. Called to the Bar, Middle Temple, 1970 (Bencher, 2004), *ad eundem* Inner Temple, 1984; part-time Tutor, Law Dept, LSE, 1970–72; practising on SE Circuit, 1972–; called to the Bar, Turks and Caicos Is, 1996. Fellow, Soc. for Advanced Legal Studies, 1998. *Recreations:* wine and food, travel, humour, film and theatre. *Address:* 2 Bedford Row, WC1R 4BU. *T:* (020) 7440 8888, *Fax:* (020) 7242 1738. *E:* hgodfrey@2bedfordrow.co.uk. *Clubs:* MCC; Royal Corinthian Yacht.

GODFREY, James Eric, OBE 2002; FRAgS; Director: R. J. & A. E. Godfrey, since 1974; Elsham Linc Ltd, since 2006; *b* Lincs, 25 April 1953; *s* of Arthur Eric Godfrey and Etheldreda Godfrey (*née* Cadas); *m* 1975, Janet Barclay; two *s* one *d*. *Educ:* Epsom Coll.; Univ. of Reading (BSc 1974). FRAgS 2000. Chm., Sentry Farming Gp plc, subseq. Willisham Gp plc, 1997–2002. Director: Fen Peas Ltd, 1991–2013; Dream Direct Gp plc, 2002–06. Chairman: Potato Mktg Bd, 1992–93 (Mem., 1988–97); Sustainable Agric. and Food Innovation Platform, Technol. Strategy Bd, 2010–; Commercial Farmers Gp, 2013– (Mem., 2003–); Mem., BBSRC, 2009–15; non-exec. Dir, Rural Payments Agency, 2010–13. Dir, Lincs Rural Support Network, 2009–. Mem. Council, Humberside TEC, 1995–2000. Mem. Council, RASE, 1993– (Hon. Vice Pres., 2014–). Chairman: Internat. Potato Centre, Peru, 2003–08 (Trustee, 2000–08); Alliance of 15 Consultative Gp on Internat. Agricl Res. Centres, USA, 2006–07. Member: Ct, Univ. of Reading, 2008–; Steering Gp, Centre for Excellence in UK Farming, 2012–. Trustee, Nat. Inst. of Agricultural Botany, 2012–. Governor: Scottish Crop Res. Inst., 1991–2003 (Chm., 1999–2003); Roslin Res. Inst., 2006–08; Trustee, Internat. Rice Res. Inst., 2013–. FInstD 2004. Hon. DSc Reading, 2007. World Potato Congress Award, 2006; British Potato Council Award, 2008. *Recreations:* tennis, bridge, reading, travel. *Address:* Lautus Place, Silver Street, Barrow upon Humber, N Lincs DN19 7DN. *T:* (01469) 531521. *E:* Jim.Godfrey@godfrey.uk.com. *Club:* Farmers.

See also J. A. C. Godfrey.

GODFREY, John Arthur Cadas, CBE 1998; DL; FCA; farmer, since 1972; Chairman, Agriculture and Horticulture Development Board, 2011–14; *b* Caistor, 1948; *s* of Arthur Eric Godfrey and Ethelreda Godfrey (*née* Cadas); *m* 1979, Phoebe Ingleson. *Educ:* Epsom Coll.; St Mary's, Melrose. FCA 1971; FRAgS 2004. Chm., Nat. Pig Assoc., 1999–2001. President: Lincs Agricl Soc., 2007 (Treas., 2015–); Scunthorpe United FC, 2005–. Chm., Bd of Govs, Univ. of Lincoln, 2005–09. High Sheriff, 2010–11, DL, 2014, Lincs. DUniv Lincoln, 2009. *Recreations:* bridge, football, walking, wine. *Address:* Wootton Road, Elsham Top, Brigg DN20 0NU. *E:* john.godfrey@godfrey.uk.com.

GODFREY, Dr Malcolm Paul Weston, CBE 1986; Chairman, Public Health Laboratory Service Board, 1989–96; *b* 11 Aug. 1926; *s* of late Harry Godfrey and Rose Godfrey; *m* 1955, Barbara Goldstein; one *s* one *d* (and one *d* decd). *Educ:* Hertford Grammar Sch.; King's Coll.,

London Univ. (FKC 2000); KCH Med. Sch. (MB, BS (Hons and Univ. Medal) 1950); MRCP 1955, FRCP 1972. Hosp. posts at KCH, Nat. Heart and Brompton Hosps; RAF Med. Br., 1952–54; Fellow in Med. and Asst Physician (Fulbright Scholar), Johns Hopkins Hosp., USA, 1957–58; MRC Headquarters Staff, 1960–74: MO, 1960; Sen. MO, 1964; Principal MO, 1970; Sen. Principal MO, 1974; Dean, Royal Postgrad. Med. Sch., 1974–83 (Mem. Council, 1974–83, 1988–96; Chm., Audit Cttee, 1995–96; Hon. Fellow, 1985); Second Sec., MRC, 1983–88. University of London: Member: Senate, 1980–83; Court, 1981–83; Chm., Jt Med. Adv. Cttee, 1979–82. Mem., Faculty Bd of Clinical Medicine, Univ. of Cambridge, 1988–89. Chm., Brit. Council Med. Adv. Cttee, 1985–90; Member: Sci. Adv. Panel CIBA Foundn, 1974–91; Ealing, Hammersmith and Hounslow AHA(T), 1975–80; NW Thames RHA, 1980–83, 1985–88; Hammersmith SHA, 1982–83; Sec. of State's Adv. Gp on London Health Services, 1980–81; GMC, 1979–81. Lay Mem., Professional Standards Dept, Gen. Council of the Bar, 1990–95. Consultant Advr, WHO Human Reproduction Programme, 1979–90; Scientific Advr, Foulkes Foundn, 1983–89. Member, Council: Charing Cross Hosp. Med. Sch., 1975–80; St Mary's Hosp. Med. Sch., 1983–88; Royal Free Hosp. Sch. of Medicine, 1991–96; KCL, 1997–2001; Mem., Governing Body, BPMF, 1974–89; Chm., Council of Governors, UMDS of Guy's and St Thomas' Hosps, 1996–98 (Mem., 1990–96; Trustee, UMDS, 1998–2009); Mem., Special Trustees, Hammersmith Hosp., 1975–83. Pres., KCL Assoc., 2002–04 (Vice-Pres., 2000–02). Trustee, Florence Nightingale Fund, 1996–. Mem., Soc. of Scholars, Johns Hopkins Univ., USA, 2000. Gov., Quintin Kynaston Sch., 2000–03. Liveryman, Goldsmiths' Co., 1984– (Mem., Charity Cttee, 1998–2006); Mem. Court of Assts, Soc. of Apothecaries, 1979–94 (Master, 1989–90; Assistant Emeritus, 1995–). JP Wimbledon, 1972–92 (Chm. of the Bench and of Merton Magistrates' Courts Cttee, 1988–90 (Dep. Chm., 1987); Chm., Juvenile Panel, 1983–87). QHP, 1987–90. FRSA, 1989–92. Hon. Fellow, ICSM, 1999. *Publications:* contrib. med. jls on cardiac and respiratory disorders. *Recreations:* theatre, planning holidays (sometimes taking them), walking. *Address:* 23 Bentinck Close, 76–82 Prince Albert Road, NW8 7RY. *T:* (020) 3638 0196.

GODFREY, Very Rev. Nigel Philip; Dean of Sodor and Man, since 2011; Vicar, West Coast, since 2012; Leader, West Mission Partnership, since 2012; *b* Douglas, Isle of Man, 25 April 1951. *Educ:* Ripon Coll., Cuddesdon (BA 1978; MA 1984); London Guildhall Univ. (MBA 2000); King's Coll. London (MSc 2009). MRTPI 1976. Ordained deacon, 1979, priest, 1980; Asst Curate, St John the Divine, Kennington, 1979–89; Vicar, Christ Church, Brixton Road, 1989–2001; Principal, Ordained Local Ministry Training Scheme, Dio. of Southwark, 2001–07; Chaplain, Southwark Cathedral, 2002–07; Vicar and Vice-Dean, St German's Cathedral, 2007–11; Dir of Vocation and Training and Dir of Ordinands, Dio. of Sodor and Man, 2010–. Leader, Community of Christ the Servant, Christ Ch, Brixton, 1984–93. *Publications:* (ed with H. Morgan) Approaches to Prayer: a resource book for groups and individuals, 1991; (contrib.) Here to Stay: ordained local ministry in the Church of England, 2006. *Recreation:* landscape architecture. *Address:* The Deanery, Albany Road, Peel, Isle of Man IM5 1JS. *T:* (01624) 844830.

GODFREY, Peter, FCA; Senior Partner, Ernst & Whinney, Chartered Accountants, 1980–86, retired; Chairman, Accounting Standards Committee, 1984–86 (Member, 1983–86); *b* 23 March 1924; *m* 1951, Heather Taplin; two *s* one *d.* *Educ:* West Kensington Central Sch. Served Army, 1942, until released, rank Captain, 1947. Qual. as an Incorporated Accountant, 1949; joined Whinney Smith & Whinney, 1949; admitted to partnership, 1959; Chm., Ernst & Whinney Internat., 1981–83, 1985–86. Appointed: BoT Inspector into Affairs of Pinnock Finance Co. (GB) Ltd, Aug. 1967; DTI Inspector into Affairs of Rolls-Royce Ltd, April 1971; Mem., ODM Cttee of Inquiry on Crown Agents, April 1975. Institute of Chartered Accountants: Mem., Inflation Accounting Sub-Cttee, 1982–84; Mem., Council, 1984–86. *Recreation:* family. *Address:* 2N Maple Lodge, Lythe Hill Park, Haslemere, Surrey GU27 3TE. *T:* (01428) 656729.

GODFREY, Sarah; *see* Radclyffe, S.

GODFREY, Rt Rev. William; *see* Peru, Bishop of.

GODFREY, William Thomas; Chief Executive, Newport City Council, since 2013; *b* Darlington, Co. Durham, 1 April 1965; *s* of late Howard Godfrey and of Pat Godfrey; *m* 2002, Karen Arnott; one *s.* *Educ:* Richmond Sch., N Yorks; Univ. of Hull (BA Hons Politics and Sociol.); Univ. of Durham (MA Business Admin). CIPFA. Dir of Resources, Welsh LGA, 2002–03; Chief Exec., E Hants DC, 2003–09; Strategic Dir (Resources), then Strategic Dir (Corporate Services), Bristol CC, 2009–12. *Recreations:* walking, supporting Swansea City FC, reading modern history and political biographies, trying to keep up with my son's knowledge of technology. *Address:* Newport City Council, Civic Centre, Newport, South Wales NP20 4UR. *T:* (01633) 217925. *E:* will.godfrey@newport.gov.uk.

GODLEY, family name of **Baron Kilbracken**.

GODMAN, Norman Anthony, PhD; *b* 19 April 1938; *m* 1981, Patricia (*née* Leonard) (*see* Patricia Godman). *Educ:* Westbourne Street Boys' Sch., Hessle Road, Hull; Hull Univ. (BA); Heriot-Watt Univ. (PhD 1982). Nat. Service, Royal Mil. Police, 1958–60. Shipwright to trade teacher in Scottish further and higher educn; Contested (Lab) Aberdeen South, 1979. MP (Lab) Greenock and Port Glasgow, 1983–97, Greenock and Inverclyde, 1997–2001.

GODMAN, Patricia, (Trish); Member (Lab) West Renfrewshire, Scottish Parliament, 1999–2011; Deputy Presiding Officer, Scottish Parliament, 2003–11; *d* of Martin Leonard and Cathie Craig; *m* 1981, Norman Anthony Godman, *qv*; three *s* from previous marriage. *Educ:* St Gerard's Secondary Sch.; Jordanhill Coll. (CQSW 1976). Social worker, Strathclyde Reg. Member (Lab): Strathclyde Regl Council, 1994–96; Glasgow City Council, 1996–99. *Recreations:* gardening, theatre, music, cinema, reading.

GODSAL, Lady Elizabeth Cameron, MBE 2002; Vice Lord-Lieutenant of Berkshire, 2005–10; *b* 10 April 1939; *d* of 8th Earl of Courtown, OBE, TD and late Christina Margaret (*née* Cameron); *m* 1962, Alan Anthony Colleton Godsal (*d* 2011); one *s* two *d.* Comr, St John Ambulance, Berks, 1983–90; Chief Pres., St John Ambulance, 1990–96; Pres., St John Fellowship, 1996–2008. Mem., Indep. Monitoring Bd, HM YOI, Reading, 1993–2006 (Chm., 2000–03). High Sheriff, 1990–91, DL 1994, Berks. High Steward, Wokingham, 1992–. Patron and Pres., numerous orgns. GCStJ 2000. *Address:* Queen's Arbour, Hungerford Lane, Twyford, Berks RG10 0LZ. *T:* (0118) 932 0956.

GODSIFF, Roger Duncan; MP (Lab) Birmingham Hall Green, since 2010 (Birmingham, Small Heath, 1992–97; Birmingham Sparkbrook and Small Heath, 1997–2010); *b* 28 June 1946; *s* of late George and of Gladys Godsiff; *m* 1977, Julia Brenda Morris; one *s* one *d.* *Educ:* Catford Comprehensive Sch. Bank clerk, 1965–70; political officer, APEX, 1970–90; senior research officer, GMB, 1990–92. Mem. (Lab) Lewisham BC, 1971–90 (Mayor, 1977). Contested (Lab) Birmingham, Yardley, 1983. Chm., British-Japanese Parly Gp, 1994–. Chm., Charlton Athletic Charitable Trust, 2004–. Gold and Silver Star, Order of Rising Sun (Japan), 2014. *Recreations:* sport - particularly football and cricket, listening to music, spending time with family. *Address:* House of Commons, SW1A 0AA. *Clubs:* Rowley Regis Labour; Charlton Athletic Supporters.

GODSMARK, Nigel Graham; QC 2001; **His Honour Judge Godsmark;** a Circuit Judge, since 2012; Designated Civil Judge for Nottinghamshire, Derbyshire and Lincolnshire, since 2013; *b* 8 Dec. 1954; *s* of Derek and Betty Godsmark; *m* 1982, Priscilla Howitt; one *s* two *d.* *Educ:* Queen Mary's Grammar Sch., Basingstoke; Univ. of Nottingham (LLB 1978). Called to the Bar, Gray's Inn, 1979; Asst Recorder, 1998–2000; Recorder, 2000–12. Hon. Prof. of Law, Univ. of Nottingham, 2009. *Recreations:* sport (Rugby, cricket, sailing, ski-ing), wine, family. *Address:* Nottingham County Court, 60 Canal Street, Nottingham NG1 7EJ.

GODSON, Anthony; HM Diplomatic Service, retired; Specialist Adviser, Foreign and Commonwealth Office, since 2012; *b* 1 Feb. 1948; *s* of late Percival Lawrence Godson and Kathleen Elizabeth Godson (*née* Jennings); *m* 1977, Maryan Jane Margaret (*née* Hurst). Joined FCO, 1968; Attaché, Bucharest, 1970–72; Third Sec., Jakarta, 1972–76; Private Sec. to High Comr, Canberra, 1976–79; FCO, 1980–81; Second, later First, Sec., UKMIS to UN, NY, 1982–86; First Secretary: Kinshasa, 1987; FCO, 1988–89; Dep. Hd of Mission, Bucharest, 1990–92; UKMIS to UN, Geneva, 1992–95; FCO, 1996–97; Counsellor, later Dep. Hd of Mission and Consul Gen., Jakarta, 1998–2002; Counsellor, FCO, 2002–04; High Comr to Mauritius and Ambassador (non-res.) to Comoros, 2004–07. Exec. Dir, Prospect Burma, 2007–10. *Recreations:* tennis, ski-ing, walking, classical music, reading, photography.

GODSON, Rory James; Managing Partner, Powerscourt, since 2004; *b* Dublin, 2 Nov. 1962; *s* of Noel Anthony Godson and Bini Godson; *m* 1990, Hilary Hynes; three *s* one *d.* *Educ:* Rockwell Coll.; Dublin Inst. of Technol. (Cert. Journalism). Business and Finance mag., Dublin, then sports and business journalist, Sunday Tribune, 1985–90; Ed., Dublin Tribune, 1990–92; News Ed., Sunday Tribune, then Business Ed. and Chief Correspondent, Sunday Independent, 1992–95; Dep. Ed., Sunday Tribune, 1995; Ireland Ed., 1996–2000, Business Ed., 2000–02, Sunday Times; Dir, Corporate Affairs, Goldman Sachs Internat., 2003. *Address:* Powerscourt, 1 Tudor Street, EC4Y 0AH. *T:* (020) 7250 1446. *E:* rory.godson@powerscourt-group.com. *Clubs:* Soho House; Lansdowne Football (Dublin).

GODWIN, Joseph; Director, BBC Academy and BBC Birmingham, since 2015; *b* Leamington Spa, 7 July 1964; *s* of Stanley Godwin and Zena Godwin. *Educ:* Trinity Sch., Leamington Spa; Univ. of Manchester (BA Hons Hist. 1985). BBC: regl news, BBC Southampton, 1986; trainee, Children's Progs Dept, 1989; prod., Blue Peter, 1995–97; Ed., BBC Children's Presentation, 1997–2000; Hd, Original Prodn, Nickelodeon UK, 2000–05; BBC Children's: Hd of Entertainment, 2005–08; Hd of News, Factual and Entertainment, 2008–09; Dir, 2009–14. Mem., Adv. Panel on Children's Viewing, BBFC, 2004–. Trustee, Nat. Museums Liverpool, 2012–. *Recreations:* photography, cinema, wine. *Address:* BBC Birmingham, The Mailbox, Birmingham B1 1RF.

GODWIN-AUSTEN, Dr Richard Bertram, FRCP; Consultant Neurologist, Nottingham, Derby and South Lincolnshire Hospitals, 1970–97, Consultant Emeritus, since 1997; Secretary Treasurer-General, World Federation of Neurology, 1999–2006; *b* 4 Oct. 1935; *s* of late Annesley Godwin-Austen, CBE and Beryl Godwin-Austen; *m* 1st, 1961, Jennifer Jane (*d* 1996), *d* of Louis Himely; one *s* one *d*; 2nd, 1997, Deirdre, (Sally), *d* of FO Gerald Stark Toller. *Educ:* Charterhouse; St Thomas' Hosp., London (MB BS; MD 1968). FRCP 1976. Nat. Hosp. for Neurol., Queen Sq., 1964–70; clinical teacher in neurol., Faculty of Medicine, Univ. of Nottingham, 1970–97; Clinical Dir for Neuroservices, University Hosp., Nottingham, 1990–93. Chm., Sheffield Regl Adv. Cttee on Neurol. and Neurosurgery, 1990–93. Mem., Med. Adv. Panel, Parkinson's Disease Soc., 1970–97. Pres., Assoc. of British Neurologists, 1997–99; Vice-Pres., Eur. Fedn of Neurol Socs, 1996–2001; Mem., Eur. Bd of Neurol., 1996–2001. High Sheriff, Notts, 1994–95. *Publications:* The Neurology of the Elderly, 1990; The Parkinson's Disease Handbook, 1987, 2nd edn 1997; Seizing Opportunities: the reminiscences of a physician, 2008; numerous contribs to peer-reviewed med. jls. *Recreations:* water-colour painting, sweet wines, 20th century British painting. *Address:* 15 Westgate, Southwell, Notts NG25 0JN. *T:* (01636) 814126. *Clubs:* Garrick, Royal Society of Medicine.

GOEDERT, Michel, MD, PhD; FRS 2000; Member of Scientific Staff, since 1984, and Head, Division of Neurobiology, since 2007 (Joint Head, 2003–07), Medical Research Council Laboratory of Molecular Biology, Cambridge; *b* 22 May 1954; *s* of Pierre Goedert and Dr Marie-Antoinette Goedert (*née* Bové); partner, Prof. Maria Grazia Spillantini, *qv*; one *s.* *Educ:* Athénée, Luxembourg; Univ. of Basel (MD 1980); Trinity Coll., Cambridge (PhD 1984). Hon. Prof., Univ. of Cambridge, 2014. Mem., EMBO, 1997. FMedSci 2006. 1st Prize, Eur. Contest for Young Scientists and Inventors, 1973; Metropolitan Life Foundn Award for Med. Res., 1996; Potamkin Prize, Amer. Acad. Neurol., 1998; Prix Lions, Luxembourg, 2002; Eur. Grand Prix for Res., Foundn for Res. on Alzheimer's Disease, Paris, 2014. *Publications:* contrib. res. papers and reviews to scientific jls. *Recreations:* reading and writing, football. *Address:* MRC Laboratory of Molecular Biology, Francis Crick Avenue, Cambridge CB2 0QH. *T:* (01223) 267056.

GOEHR, Prof. Alexander; composer; Professor of Music, and Fellow of Trinity Hall, University of Cambridge, 1976–99, now Emeritus Professor and Fellow; *b* 10 Aug. 1932; *s* of Walter and Laelia Goehr. *Educ:* Berkhamsted; Royal Manchester Coll. of Music; Paris Conservatoire. Lectr, Morley Coll., 1955–57; Music Asst, BBC, 1960–67; Winston Churchill Trust Fellowship, 1968; Composer-in-residence, New England Conservatory, Boston, Mass, 1968–69; Associate Professor of Music, Yale University, 1969–70; West Riding Prof. of Music, Leeds Univ., 1971–76. Artistic Dir, Leeds Festival, 1975; Vis. Prof., Peking Conservatoire of Music, 1980. Reith Lectr, BBC, 1987. Mem., Bd of Dirs, Royal Opera House, 1982–84. Hon. Vice-Pres., SPNM, 1983–. Hon. Prof., Beijing Central Conservatory. Hon. Mem., Amer. Acad. and Inst. of Arts and Letters. Hon. FRMCM; Hon. FRAM 1975; Hon. FRNCM 1980; Hon. FRCM 1981. Hon. DMus: Southampton, 1973; Manchester, 1990; Nottingham, 1994; Siena, 1998; Cambridge, 2000. *Compositions include:* Songs of Babel, 1951; Fantasia Op. 4, 1954; String Quartet No. 1, 1957; La Belle Dame Sans Merci (ballet), 1958; Suite Op. 11, 1961; Hecuba's Lament, 1961; A Little Cantata of Proverbs, 1962; Concerto Op. 13, 1962; Little Symphony, 1963; Pastorals, 1965; Piano Trio, 1966; String Quartet No. 2, 1967; Romanza, 1968; Paraphrase, 1969; Symphony in One Movement, 1970; Concerto for Eleven, 1970; Concerto Op. 33, 1972; Chaconne for Wind, 1974; Lyric Pieces, 1974; Metamorphosis/Dance, 1974; String Quartet No. 3, 1976; Fugue on the notes of the Fourth Psalm, 1976; Romanza on the notes of the Fourth Psalm, 1977; Chaconne for Organ, 1979; Sinfonia, 1979; Kafka Fragments, 1979; Deux Etudes, 1981; Sonata, 1984; …a musical offering (JSB 1985), 1985; Symphony with Chaconne, 1986; …in real time, 1989; Still Lands, 1990; Bach Variations, 1990; Piano Quintet, 2000; …second musical offering (GFH 2001), 2001; Symmetry Disorders Reach, 2003; Marching to Carcassonne, 2003; Since Brass, no Stone…, 2008; TurmMusik, 2010; When Adam Fell, 2011; Largo Siciliano, 2012; between the Lines, 2014; *vocal:* The Deluge, 1958; Sutter's Gold, 1960; Virtutes, 1963; Arden Must Die (opera), 1966; Triptych (Naboth's Vineyard, 1968; Shadowplay, 1970; Sonata about Jerusalem, 1970); Psalm IV, 1976; Babylon the Great is Fallen, 1979; The Law of the Quadrille, 1979; Behold the Sun, 1981; Behold the Sun (opera), 1984; Eve Dreams in Paradise, 1988; Sing Ariel, 1990; The Death of Moses, 1992; Colossos or Panic, 1993; Arianna (opera), 1995; Schlussgesang, 1997; Kantan and Damask Drum (opera), 1999; Promised End (opera), 2010. *Address:* c/o Schott Music, 48 Great Marlborough Street, W1F 7BB.

GOERNE, Matthias; baritone; *b* Weimar, Germany, 31 March 1967. *Educ:* Studied under Prof. Beyer at Leipzig, Elizabeth Schwarzkopf and Dietrich Fischer-Dieskau. Début with Leipzig Radio SO; performances with Berlin Phil. Orch., Concentus Musicus, Concertgebouw; recitals in London, Amsterdam, Paris, Leipzig, Cologne and New York. Opera appearances include: Dresden Opera, and Komische Oper, Berlin, 1993; débuts, as Papageno, Salzburg Fest., 1997, Metropolitan Opera, NY, 1998; title rôle in Wozzeck,

Zürich, 1999. Numerous recordings. Gramophone Award; Diapason d'Or; Echo Prize, Germany; Cecilia Award, Belgium. *Address:* c/o Michael Kocyan Artists Management, Alt-Moabit 104A, 10559 Berlin, Germany.

GOFF, family name of **Baron Goff of Chieveley**.

GOFF OF CHIEVELEY, Baron *cr* 1986 (Life Peer), of Chieveley in the Royal County of Berkshire; **Robert Lionel Archibald Goff,** Kt 1975; PC 1982; DCL; FBA 1987; a Lord of Appeal in Ordinary, 1986–98; Senior Law Lord, 1996–98; *b* 12 Nov. 1926; *s* of Lt-Col L. T. Goff and Mrs Goff (*née* Denroche-Smith); *m* 1953, Sarah, *er d* of Capt. G. R. Cousins, DSC, RN; one *s* two *d* (and one *s* decd). *Educ:* Eton Coll.; New Coll., Oxford (MA 1953, DCL 1972; Hon. Fellow, 1986). Served in Scots Guards, 1945–48 (commnd 1945). 1st cl hons Jurisprudence, Oxon, 1950. Called to the Bar, Inner Temple, 1951; Bencher, 1975; QC 1967. Fellow and Tutor, Lincoln Coll., Oxford, 1951–55; in practice at the Bar, 1956–75; a Recorder, 1974–75; Judge of the High Ct, QBD, 1975–82; Judge i/c Commercial List, and Chm. Commercial Court Cttee, 1979–81; a Lord Justice of Appeal, 1982–86. Chm., Sub-Cttee E (Law and Instns), H of L Select Cttee on EC, 1986–88. Chairman: Council of Legal Educn, 1976–82 (Vice-Chm., 1972–76; Chm., Bd of Studies, 1970–76); Common Professional Examination Bd, 1976–78; Court, London Univ., 1986–91; Pegasus Scholarship Trust, 1987–2001. High Steward, Oxford Univ., 1991–2001. Hon. Prof. of Legal Ethics, Univ. of Birmingham, 1980–81; Lectures: Maccabean, British Acad., 1983; Lionel Cohen Meml, Hebrew Univ. of Jerusalem, 1987; Cassel, Stockholm Univ., 1993. Member: Gen. Council of the Bar, 1971–74; Senate of Inns of Court and Bar, 1974–82 (Chm., Law Reform and Procedure Cttee, 1974–76). Chm., British Inst. of Internat. and Comparative Law, 1986–2001 (Pres., 2001–08). President: CIArb, 1986–91; Bentham Club, 1986; Holdsworth Club, 1986–87. Hon. Fellow: Lincoln Coll., Oxford, 1985; Wolfson Coll., Oxford, 2001; Amer. Coll. of Trial Lawyers, 1997. Hon. DLitt: City, 1977; Reading, 1990; Hon. LLD: Buckingham, 1990; London, 1990; Bristol, 1996. Grand Cross (First Class), Order of Merit (Germany), 1999. *Publications:* (with Prof. Gareth Jones) The Law of Restitution, 1966. *Address:* House of Lords, Westminster, SW1A 0PW.

GOFF, Hon. Philip Bruce; MP (Lab) New Zealand, 1981–90 and since 1993, for Mount Roskill, since 1999; *b* 22 June 1953; *s* of Bruce Charles Goff and Elaine Loyola Goff; *m* 1979, Mary Ellen Moriarty; two *s* one *d*. *Educ:* Univ. of Auckland (MA 1st Cl. Hons); Nuffield Coll., Oxford. MP (Lab): Roskill, 1981–90 and 1993–96; New Lynn, 1996–99. Cabinet Minister: for Housing, Employment and Envmt, 1984–87; for Employment, Tourism, Youth Affairs and Associate Educn, 1987–89; for Educn, 1989–90; of Justice, and of For. Affairs and Trade, 1999–2005; of Pacific Is. Affairs, 2002–07; for Disarmament and Arms Control, 2005–08; of Defence and of Trade, 2005–08; Leader of the Opposition, 2008–11. Lab. spokesperson for defence, veterans' affairs, disarmament, ethnic communities and Auckland issues, 2014–. *Recreations:* motorbike riding, sport, gardening. *Address:* Parliament Buildings, Molesworth Street, Wellington 6160, New Zealand. *T:* (4) 8176775.

GOFF, Sir Robert (William Davis-), 4th Bt *cr* 1905; Director, O'Connor & Co., Art Dealers and Property Investment Co.; *b* 12 Sept. 1955; *s* of Sir Ernest William Davis-Goff, 3rd Bt, and of Alice Cynthia Davis-Goff (*née* Woodhouse); *S* father, 1980; *m* 1978, Nathalie Sheelagh, *d* of Terence Chadwick; three *s* one *d*. *Educ:* Cheltenham College, Glos. *Recreation:* shooting. *Heir: s* William Nathaniel Davis-Goff, *b* 20 April 1980. *Address:* Eairy Moar Farm, Glen Helen, Isle of Man IM4 3NP.

GOFFE, Judith Ann, FCA; independent business consultant, since 1991; *b* 6 March 1953; *d* of Albert Edward Goffe and Jennie Lucia Goffe (*née* Da Costa); *m* 1992, Peter Alexander Rose; one *s*. *Educ:* Immaculate Conception High Sch., Kingston, Jamaica; Reading Univ. (BSc 1976). Chartered Accountant, 1981; FCA 1991. Investment Dir, 3i Group plc, 1984–91. Director: Moorfields Eye Hosp. Trust, 1994–2004; Monitor (Indep. Regulator of NHS Foundn Trusts), 1994–2012. Mem., ITC, 1994–2003. Trustee, King's Fund, 2008–12. FRSA 1994. *Recreations:* collecting contemporary ceramics and jewellery, design, travel, family, food.

GOFFEE, Prof. Robert Edward, PhD; Professor of Organisational Behaviour, London Business School, 1994, now Emeritus; *b* Ilford, 18 April 1952; *s* of Edward William Goffee and Rose Elizabeth Goffee; *m* 1978, Victoria Julie Marriott; one *s* one *d*. *Educ:* Univ. of Kent (BA 1973; PhD 1978). Res. Officer, Sch. of Mgt, Univ. of Bath, 1976–78; Res. Fellow, Faculty of Social Scis, Univ. of Kent, 1978–81; Lectr in Mgt Studies, Faculty of Human Studies, Univ. of Surrey, 1981–83; London Business School: Lectr, 1983–87, Sen. Lectr, 1988–90, in Organisational Behaviour; Associate Prof. of Organisational Behaviour, 1990–94; Subject Area Chm., Organisational Behaviour, 1995–98; Dir, Innovation Exchange, 1997–2003; Faculty Advr, Exec. Educn, 1999–2001; Dep. Dean (Exec. Educn), 2001–04; Faculty Dir for Exec. Educn, 2004–06. Vis. Prof. of Organisational Behaviour, Australian Graduate Sch. of Mgt, Univ. of NSW, 1995, 2007. FRSA 1997. Series Ed., Organisational Behaviour and Mgt, 1989–96; Man. Ed., 2001–04, Contrib. Ed., 2004–, Business Strategy Rev. (Mem., Editl Bd, 1992–94); Member, Editorial Board: M@n@gement, 2005–; Leadership, 2006–. *Publications:* with R. Scase: The Real World of the Small Business Owner, 1980, 2nd edn 1989; The Entrepreneurial Middle Class, 1982; Women in Charge, 1985; (ed) Entrepreneurship in Europe: the social processes, 1987; Reluctant Managers, 1989; Corporate Realities: the dynamics of organisations - large and small, 1995; with G. Jones: The Character of a Corporation, 1998, 2nd edn 2003; Why Should Anyone be Led by You?, 2006; Clever: leading your smartest, most creative people, 2009; (ed jtly) Career Frontiers: new conceptions of working lives, 2000; articles in learned jls. *Recreations:* family, walking, good food and wine, football (supporting West Ham). *Address:* London Business School, Regent's Park, NW1 4SA. *T:* (020) 7000 7000. *E:* rgoffee@london.edu.

GOH CHOK TONG; Senior Minister, Prime Minister's Office, Singapore, 2004–11, now Emeritus; Senior Adviser, Monetary Authority of Singapore, since 2011 (Chairman, 2004–11); *b* 20 May 1941; *m* Tan Choo Leng; one *s* one *d* (twins). *Educ:* Raffles Instn; Univ. of Singapore (1st cl. Hons Econs); Williams Coll., USA. Admin. Service, Singapore Govt, 1964–69; Neptune Orient Lines, 1969–77. MP for Marine Parade, 1976–; Sen. Minister of State for Finance, 1977–79; Minister: for Trade and Industry, 1979–81; for Health, 1981–85; for Defence, 1981–91; First Dep. Prime Minister, 1985–90; Prime Minister, 1990–2004. People's Action Party: Mem., Central Exec. Cttee, 1979; First Organising Sec., 1979; Second Asst Sec. Gen., 1979–84; Asst Sec. Gen., 1984–89; First Asst Sec. Gen., 1989–92; Sec. Gen., 1992–2004. Formerly Chairman: Singapore Labour Foundn; NTUC Income, NTUC Fairprice. Medal of Honour, NTUC, 1987. *Recreations:* golf, tennis. *Address:* c/o Prime Minister's Office, Orchard Road, Istana Annexe, Istana, Singapore 238823.

GOLANT, Farah R.; *see* Ramzan Golant.

GOLD, family name of **Baron Gold**.

GOLD, Baron *cr* 2011 (Life Peer), of Westcliff-on-Sea in the County of Essex; **David Laurence Gold;** Principal, David Gold & Associates LLP, since 2011; *b* 1 March 1951; *s* of Michael Gold and Betty Gold; *m* 1978, Sharon Levy; two *s* one *d*. *Educ:* Westcliff High Sch. for Boys; London Sch. of Econs (LLB). Admitted Solicitor, 1975; Herbert Smith: Partner, 1983–2011; Head of Litigation, 2003–05; Senior Partner, 2005–10; Sen. Litigation Partner, 2010–11. Pres., Southend and Westcliff Hebrew Congregation, 1997–2006. CEDR Accredited Mediator, 2010–. Monitor, BAE Systems plc, 2010–13; Leader of governance review, Rolls-Royce plc, 2013–. Chm., Disciplinary Cttee, Conservative Party, 2010–12. Chm., Proven Ltd, 2013–14. Sen. Advr, G3, 2014–. Gov., LSE, 2009– (Mem., Finance Cttee, 2010–). Freeman: Solicitors' Co., 1977; City of London, 2010. *Recreations:* theatre, cinema, bridge, travel, family. *Address:* (office) 3 Fitzhardinge Street, W1H 6EF. *T:* (020) 3535 8989. *E:* David.Gold@davidgoldassociates.com.

GOLD, Jacqueline; Chief Executive: Ann Summers, since 1993; Knickerbox, since 2000; *b* 16 July 1960; *d* of David Gold and late Beryl Gold; *m* 1st, 1980, Tony D'Silva (marr. diss. 1990); 2nd, Daniel Cunningham; one *d*. Royal Doulton, 1979; joined Gold Gp as wages clerk, 1979; launched Ann Summers Party Plan, 1981; acquired Knickerbox, 2000. Business Communicator of the Year, British Assoc. of Communications in Business, 2004; Inspirational Women's Award, 2012; Female Entrepreneur of the Year, TiE Awards, 2013. *Publications:* Good Vibrations (autobiog.), 1995; A Woman's Courage (autobiog.), 2007. *Recreations:* travelling, watching football, partying, shopping. *Address:* Gold Group House, Godstone Road, Whyteleafe, Surrey CR3 0GG. *T:* (01883) 629629. *E:* shelley@pha-media.com.

GOLD, Jeremy Spencer; QC 2003; **His Honour Judge Gold;** a Circuit Judge, since 2009; *b* 15 July 1955; *s* of late Alfred Gold and Ruby Caroline Gold; *m* 1976, Joanne Driver. *Educ:* Brighton, Hove and Sussex Grammar Sch.; Univ. of Kent at Canterbury (BA Hons). Called to the Bar, Middle Temple, 1977; in practice as barrister specialising in criminal work, 1977–2009; Recorder, 2000–09. *Recreations:* theatre, good food, good company. *Address:* Croydon Crown Court, Altyre Road, Croydon CR9 5AB.

GOLD, John (Joseph Manson); Public Relations Consultant, 1979–90, retired; Manager of Public Relations, Hong Kong Mass Transit Railway (construction phase), 1975–79; *b* 2 Aug. 1925; *m* 1953, Berta Cordeiro; one *d*. *Educ:* Clayesmore Sch., Dorset. Yorkshire Evening News, 1944–47; London Evening News, 1947–52; Australian Associated Press (New York), 1952–55; New York Corresp., London Evening News, 1955–66; Editor, London Evening News, 1967–72; Dir, Harmsworth Publications Ltd, 1967–73. Free-lance writer and lectr, Far East, 1973–75.

GOLD, Murray Jonathan; writer and freelance composer; *b* Portsmouth, 28 Feb. 1969; *s* of Lenny and Suzanne Gold. *Educ:* Corpus Christi Coll., Cambridge (BA Hons Hist. 1991). Composer: for *films:* Beautiful Creatures, Wild About Harry, 2000; Miranda, 2002; Kiss of Life, 2003; Alien Autopsy, Mischief Night, 2006; Death at a Funeral, I Want Candy, 2007; for *television:* Vanity Fair, 1998; Queer As Folk, 1999 (RTS Award for Best Original Score); Randall & Hopkirk (Deceased), 2000–01; Clocking Off, 2000–02; Shameless, 2004–11; Casanova, 2005; Dr Who, 2005–12; Torchwood, 2006–11; Sarah Jane Adventures, 2007–11; The Devil's Whore, 2008; Single Father, 2010; Scott & Bailey, 2011–13; Last Tango in Halifax, 2012; writer: *plays:* Resolution, Battersea Arts Centre, 1994; 50 Revolutions, Whitehall, 2000; Electricity, Radio 3, 2000, W Yorkshire Playhouse, 2004 (Imison Award for Best New Radio Play, Soc. of Authors, 2002); radio play, Kafka the Musical, 2011 (Tinniswood Award for Best Original Radio Drama, Soc. of Authors, 2013). *Address:* c/o Cathy King, Independent Talent Group Ltd, 40 Whitfield Street, W1T 2RH; c/o Becky Bentham, Hot House Music, Abbey Road Studios, 3 Abbey Road, NW8 9AY.

GOLD, Nicholas Roger; *b* 11 Dec. 1951; *s* of Rev. (Guy) Alastair Whitmore Gold, TD, MA and Elizabeth Gold, JP; *m* 1983, Laura Arnold-Brown (marr. diss. 2005); one *s* two *d*. *Educ:* Felsted Sch.; Univ. of Kent; Coll. of Law. ACA 1977, FCA 1982. Chartered accountant, Touche Ross & Co., 1973–76; admitted solicitor, 1979; solicitor, Freshfields, 1977–86; Man. Dir, ING Bank NV (formerly Baring Bros and Co.), 1986–2008. Beach café proprietor, Winking Prawn brasserie, Salcombe, 1994–. Dir, BlackRock Income and Growth Investment Trust plc (formerly British Portfolio Trust plc), 2008–; Adviser: Pottinger Co. Pty (Sydney), 2009–; Edmond de Rothschild Ltd (London), 2011–. Member: Council, RADA, 2003–; Bd, RADA Enterprises Ltd, 2012–; Bd, Prince's Foundn for Integrated Health, 2004–08. Gov., Downe House Sch., 2008–. *Recreations:* the arts, portraiture, painting, drawing, sailing, country pursuits, tennis, travel, especially in India. *Address:* 14 Northumberland Place, W2 5BS; Avocets, Quay Street, Orford IP12 2NU. *E:* nicholasgold@aol.com, nicholas.gold@btinternet.com. *Clubs:* Garrick, Hurlingham; Orford Sailing.

GOLD, Stephen Charles, MA, MD, FRCP; Consulting Physician to: the Skin Department, St George's Hospital; St John's Hospital for Diseases of the Skin; King Edward VII Hospital for Officers; Former Hon. Consultant in Dermatology: to the Army; to Royal Hospital, Chelsea; *b* Bishops Stortford, Herts, 10 Aug. 1915; *yr s* of late Philip Gold, Stansted, Essex, and Amy Frances, *er d* of James and Mary Perry; *m* 1941, Betty Margaret, *o d* of late Dr T. P. Sheedy, OBE; three *s* one *d*. *Educ:* Radley Coll.; Gonville and Caius Coll., Cambridge; St George's Hosp. (Entrance Exhibnr); Zürich and Philadelphia. BA 1937; MRCS, LRCP 1940; MA, MB, BChir 1941; MRCP 1947; MD 1952; FRCP 1958. Served RAMC, 1941–46 (Major). First Asst to Out-Patients, St George's Hosp., Senior Registrar, Skin Dept, St George's Hosp., Sen. Registrar, St John's Hosp. for Diseases of the Skin; Lectr in Dermatology, Royal Postgraduate Med. Sch., 1949–69. Sec., Brit. Assoc. of Dermatology, 1965–70 (Pres., 1979). FRSocMed (late Sec. Dermatological Section, Pres., 1972–73); Fellow St John's Hosp. Dermatological Soc. (Pres., 1965–66). *Publications:* St George's and Dermatology: evolution and progress, 1993; A Biographical History of British Dermatology, 1996.

GOLDACRE, Dr Ben Michael; author; Research Fellow, London School of Hygiene and Tropical Medicine, since 2010; columnist, The Guardian, since 2003; *b* London, 1974; *s* of Michael Goldacre and Susan Goldacre. *Educ:* Church Cowley St James, Oxford; Temple Cowley St James, Oxford; Magdalen College Sch., Oxford; Magdalen Coll., Oxford (BA 1st Cl. Hons Physiol Scis 1995); King's Coll. London (MA Philos. 1997); University Coll. London (MB BS 2000); London Sch. of Hygiene and Tropical Medicine (MSc Epidemiol. 2010). MRCPsych 2005. Res. Fellow, Univ. of Milan, 1996; NHS, 2000–07; Research Fellow: KCL, 2008; Nuffield Coll., Oxford, 2009. *Publications:* Bad Science, 2008; Bad Pharma: how drug companies mislead doctors and harm patients, 2012; I Think You'll Find It's a Bit More Complicated Than That, 2014. *Recreations:* analogue modular synthesisers, blogging, abandoned buildings. *Address:* c/o Sarah Ballard, United Agents, 12–26 Lexington Street, W1F 0LE. *T:* (020) 3214 0800. *E:* ben@badscience.net.

GOLDBERG, David Gerard; QC 1987; *b* 12 Aug. 1947; *s* of late Arthur Goldberg and of Sylvia Goldberg; *m* 1981, Alison Ninette Lunzer (marr. diss. 2003); one *s* one *d*. *Educ:* Plymouth Coll.; London School of Economics (LLB, LLM). Called to the Bar, Lincoln's Inn, 1971, Bencher, 1997; practice at Revenue Bar, 1972–. Chm. Trustees, Surgical Workshop for Anatomical Prosection, 1994–. *Publications:* (jtly) Introduction to Company Law, 1971, 4th edn 1987; (jtly) The Law of Partnership Taxation, 1976, 2nd edn 1979; various articles and notes in legal periodicals mainly concerning taxation and company law. *Recreations:* reading, writing letters, thinking. *Address:* Gray's Inn Tax Chambers, 36 Queen Street, EC4R 1BN. *T:* (020) 7242 2642.

GOLDBERG, Rabbi David Julian, OBE 2004; Senior Rabbi, Liberal Jewish Synagogue, London, 1986–2004, now Emeritus Rabbi; *b* 25 Feb. 1939; *s* of Rabbi Dr Percy Selvin Goldberg and Frimette Goldberg; *m* 1969, Carole-Ann Marks; one *s* one *d*. *Educ:* Lincoln Coll., Oxford (MA); Leo Baeck Coll., London. Rabbinic ordination, 1971; Rabbi, Wembley and Dist Liberal Synagogue, 1971–75; Associate Rabbi, Liberal Jewish Synagogue, London, 1975–86. Hon. DD Manchester, 1999. *Publications:* (with John D. Rayner) The Jewish People: their history and their religion, 1987; To the Promised Land: a history of Zionist thought, 1996; The Divided Self: Israel and the Jewish psyche today, 2006; This is not the Way: Jews, Judaism and Israel, 2012; The Story of the Jews, 2013. *Recreations:* music, opera,

travel, walking, cricket, theatre. *Address:* c/o Liberal Jewish Synagogue, 28 St John's Wood Road, NW8 7HA. *E:* djg@bartvillas.org.uk.
See also J. J. Goldberg.

GOLDBERG, Sir David (Paul Brandes), Kt 1996; DM; FRCP, FRCPsych; Professor of Psychiatry, 1993–99, and Director of Research and Development, 1993–99, Institute of Psychiatry, University of London, now Professor Emeritus; *b* 28 Jan. 1934; *s* of Paul Goldberg and Ruby Dora Goldberg; *m* 1966, Ilfra Joy Pink; one *s* three *d*. *Educ:* William Ellis Sch., London; Hertford Coll., Oxford (MA 1956; DM 1970; Hon. Fellow 2002); St Thomas' Hosp.; Manchester Univ. (MSc 1974). FRCPsych 1974; FRCP 1976. Trained at Maudsley Hosp., 1962–69; Sen. Lectr, 1969–72, Prof., 1972–92, Univ. of Manchester. Visiting Professor: Medical Univ. of S Carolina, 1978–79; Univ. of WA, 1986. Non-exec. Chm., Psychiatry Res. Trust. Founder FMedSci 1998; FKC. Hon. FRSocMed 2008. Lifetime Achievement Award, RCPsych, 2009. *Publications:* Mental Illness in the Community: the pathway to psychiatric care, 1981; Common Mental Disorders: a biosocial model, 1991; Psychiatric Illness in Medical Practice, 1992; (with I. Goodyer) The Origins and Course of Common Mental Disorders, 2005; 350 papers. *Recreations:* walking, talking, travelling. *Address:* Institute of Psychiatry, Psychology and Neuroscience, King's College London, De Crespigny Park, SE5 8AF.

GOLDBERG, Jonathan Jacob; QC 1989; a Recorder, 1993–2013; *b* 13 Nov. 1947; *s* of late Rabbi Dr and Mrs P. Selvin Goldberg; *m* 1st, 1980, Alexis Jane (marr. diss. 1991), *e d* of Sir George Martin, *qv*; one *s* one *d*; 2nd, 2009, Mrs Regina Skyer, of New York. *Educ:* Manchester Grammar Sch.; Trinity Hall, Cambridge (MA, LLM). Called to the Bar, Middle Temple, 1971; Member, NY State Bar, 1985. Mem. Presidency, Internat. Assoc. of Jewish Lawyers and Jurists, 1999–. *Recreations:* music, cinema, wine, travel. *Address:* North Square Chambers, PO Box 67655, NW11 1HZ. *E:* jg@goldbergqc.com.
See also D. J. Goldberg.

GOLDBERG, Pamela Jill, OBE 2013; Chief Executive, Breast Cancer Campaign, 1995–2011; *b* 1945; *d* of late Jack and Norma Wolfowitz; *m* 1964, John Martin Goldberg; one *s* one *d*. *Educ:* Kingsmead Coll. for Girls, Johannesburg. Dir, Nordene Galls, S Africa, 1974–79; Talentmark Ltd, 1979–81; Res. Co-ordinator, Stephen Rose and Partners Ltd, 1981–88; London Partner, Lared Gp, 1988–95. Non-exec. Dir, Barnet FHSA, 1994–96. Mem., Human Tissue Authy, 2008–. Mem. Council and Vice-Chm., AMRC, 1999–2004. Trustee, Moorfields Eye Charity, 2011–. Liveryman, Needlemakers' Co., 1987– (Master, 2011–12). FRSA. *Recreations:* food, family, friends. *T:* 07973 195870. *E:* pamelajgoldberg@gmail.com.

GOLDBLATT, Prof. David, PhD; FRCP, FRCPCH; Consultant Paediatric Immunologist, since 1995, Director, Clinical Research and Development, since 2004, and Director, NIHR Biomedical Research Centre, since 2007, Great Ormond Street Hospital for Children; Professor of Vaccinology, Institute of Child Health, University College London, since 2003; Senior Investigator, National Institute for Health Research, since 2012; *b* 16 March 1960; *s* of Samuel Goldblatt and Betty (*née* Kramer); *m* 1994, Isobel Beatrice Pemberton; one *s* two *d*. *Educ:* Univ. of Cape Town (MB ChB); Univ. of London (PhD 1991). FRCPCH 2001; FRCP 2006. Trng as paediatrician and immunologist, Red Cross Children's Hosp., Cape Town, Queen Elizabeth Children's Hosp., Hackney, and Gt Ormond St Hosp. for Sick Children, 1983–95. *Publications:* (contrib.) Oxford Textbook of Medicine, 4th edn 2003; (contrib.) Oxford Handbook of Tropical Medicine, 2nd edn 2005; (contrib.) Harrisons Principles and Practice of Internal Medicine, 18th edn 2011, 19th edn 2014; contrib. numerous papers to learned jls incl. Lancet and BMJ. *Address:* Institute of Child Health, University College London, 30 Guilford Street, WC1N 1EH. *T:* (020) 7905 2886, *Fax:* (020) 7905 2882. *E:* d.goldblatt@ucl.ac.uk. *Club:* Arsenal Football.

GOLDBLATT, Simon; QC 1972. Called to the Bar, Gray's Inn, 1953 (Bencher, 1982). *Address:* 39 Essex Street, WC2R 3AT.

GOLDFRAPP, Alison E. M.; singer, songwriter and producer; *b* Enfield, Middx, 13 May 1966; *d* of Nicholas John Goldfrapp and Isabella Patricia Goldfrapp (*née* Barge). *Educ:* Middlesex Univ. (BA Hons Fine Art). Formed Goldfrapp music duo (with Will Gregory), 1999; albums: Felt Mountain, 2000; Black Cherry, 2002; Supernature, 2005; Seventh Tree, 2008; Head First, 2010; Tales of Us, 2013. *Recreations:* photography, travelling, wild swimming, reading, cooking, film and cinema. *Address:* c/o Fascination Management, First Floor, 6 South Hill Park, NW3 2SB. *T:* (020) 7986 6457. *E:* peter@fascinationmanagement.com.

GOLDHILL, Flora Taylor, CBE 2007; Director for Children, Families and Communities (formerly Maternity, and Health Inequalities, then Children, Families and Social Inclusion), Department of Health, since 2012. *Educ:* Morgan Academy, Dundee; Edinburgh Univ. (MA Hons). Civil Servant, DHSS and DoH, 1977–90; Chief Exec., HFEA, 1991–96; Department of Health: Head, Policy Mgt Unit, 1996–98; Dir of Personnel, 1999–2001; Dir, Chief Nursing Officer's Directorate, 2001–07; Dir, Workforce Directorate, 2007–10; acting Dir-Gen., Corporate Develt, 2010–12. Governor: Canonbury Primary Sch., 1994–2005 (Vice-Chm., 1996–2003); Islington Arts and Media Sch., 2012– (Chair, 2013–). *Recreations:* family, friends, hill walking, horse riding. *Address:* Department of Health, Richmond House, 79 Whitehall, SW1A 2NS. *T:* (020) 7210 5054.

GOLDIE, Baroness *cr* 2013 (Life Peer), of Bishopton in the County of Renfrewshire; **Annabel MacNicoll Goldie;** DL; Member (C) Scotland West, Scottish Parliament, since 1999; Leader, Scottish Conservative and Unionist Party, 2005–11 (Deputy Leader, 1998–2005); *b* 27 Feb. 1950; *d* of Alexander MacIntosh Goldie and Margaret MacNicoll Goldie. *Educ:* Greenock Acad.; Strathclyde Univ. (LLB; Hon. Fellow 2004). Admitted Solicitor, 1974; Notary Public, 1978–2007. Apprentice Solicitor, McClure Naismith Brodie & Co., Glasgow, 1971–73; Asst Solicitor, Haddow & McLay, Glasgow, subseq. Dickson, Haddow & Co., 1973–77; Partner, Dickson, Haddow & Co., subseq. Donaldson, Alexander, Russell & Haddow, 1978–2006. Scottish Parliament: Dep. Convener, Enterprise and Lifelong Learning Cttee, 1999–2003; Convener, Justice 2 Cttee, 2003–06. Dir, Prince's Scottish Youth Business Trust, 1995–2010. Vice-Chm., 1992–95, Dep. Chm., 1995–97 and 1997–98, Chm., March–July 1997, Scottish Cons. and Unionist Party. Mem., Adv. Bd, W Scotland Salvation Army. Mem., Charing Cross Rotary Club, Glasgow. DL Renfrew, 1993. Hon. FRIAS 2014. *Recreations:* gardening badly, walking happily, watching birds usually uncomprehendingly, listening to classical music enthusiastically, if not knowledgeably. *Address:* Scottish Parliament, Edinburgh EH99 1SP.

GOLDIN, Prof. Ian Andrew, DPhil; Director, Oxford Martin School (formerly James Martin 21st Century School), since 2006, and Professor of Globalisation and Development, since 2011, University of Oxford; Professorial Fellow, Balliol College, Oxford, since 2006; *b* Pretoria, SA, 3 March 1955; *s* of Harry Goldin and Alice Goldin (*née* Widrich); *m* 1992, Theresa Webber; one *s* one *d*. *Educ:* Univ. of Cape Town (BSc, BA Hons 1977); London Sch. of Econs (MSc 1979); Univ. of Oxford (DPhil 1983; MA 2007); INSEAD France (AMP 1999). Vis. Prof. and Actg Hd, Econs Dept, Univ. of Cape Town, 1980–81; Tutor in Econs, St Peter's Coll., Oxford, 1982–83; Commodities Analyst, Landell Mills Commodities Ltd, London and NY, 1984–88; Res. Dir of Progs, Develt Centre, OECD, Paris, 1988–92; Principal Economist: Country Ops, World Bank (IBRD), Washington, 1992–95; EBRD, London, 1995–96; Chief Exec. and Man. Dir, Develt Bank of SA, Johannesburg, 1996–2001; Dir, Develt Policy, 2001–03, Vice Pres., 2003–06, World Bank, Washington. Chevalier de l'Ordre Nationale du Mérite (France), 2000. *Publications:* Making Race: the economics and politics of coloured identity in South Africa, 1987; (with Gervasio Castro de Rezende) Economic Crisis: lessons from Brazil, 1990 (trans. French and Portuguese); (ed with Odin Knudsen) Trade Liberalization: implications for developing countries, 1990 (trans. French); (with Dominique van der Mensbrugghe) Trade Liberalisation: what's at stake?, 1992 (trans. French, Chinese and Indonesian); (ed with L. Alan Winters) Open Economies, 1992; (with Gervasio Castro de Rezende) Crescimento numa Economia em Crise, 1993 (trans. English); (jtly) Trade Liberalization: global economic implications, 1993 (trans. French and Chinese); (ed jtly) Modelling Economy-wide Reforms, 1994 (trans. French); (ed) Economic Reform, Trade and Agricultural Development, 1994; (ed with L. Alan Winters) The Economies of Sustainable Development, 1995; (jtly) The Case for Aid, 2002; (with Kenneth Reinert) Globalisation for Development: trade, finance, aid, migration and policy, 2006, rev. edn 2007 (trans. Spanish, Chinese, French); Exceptional People: how migration shaped our world and will define our future, 2011 (trans. Greek); Globalisation for Development: meeting new challenges, 2012; Divided Nations: why global governance is failing and what we can do about it, 2013; The Butterfly Defect: how globalisation creates systematic risk, and what we can do about it, 2014; (ed) Is the Planet Full?, 2014. *Recreations:* music, cycling, skiing, scuba, hiking. *Address:* Oxford Martin School, University of Oxford, Old Indian Institute, 34 Broad Street, Oxford OX1 3BD. *T:* (01865) 287430, *Fax:* (01865) 287435. *E:* info@oxfordmartin.ox.ac.uk.

GOLDING, Baroness *cr* 2001 (Life Peer), of Newcastle-under-Lyme in the County of Staffordshire; **Llinos Golding;** *b* 21 March 1933; *d* of Rt Hon. Ness Edwards, MP and Elina Victoria Edwards; *m* 1st, 1957, Dr John Roland Lewis; one *s* two *d*; 2nd, 1980, John Golding (*d* 1999). *Educ:* Caerphilly Girls' Grammar Sch.; Cardiff Royal Infirmary Sch. of Radiography. Mem., Soc. of Radiographers. Worked as a radiographer at various times; Assistant to John Golding, MP, 1972–86. MP (Lab) Newcastle-under-Lyme, July 1986–2001. An Opposition Whip, 1987–92; opposition spokesman: on social security, 1992–95; on children and the family, 1993–95; on agric., fisheries and food, 1995–97. Mem., Select Cttee on Culture, Media and Sport, 1997–2001. Former Chm., All Party Parly Gp on Children; Joint Chairman: All Party Parly Gp on Homeless, 1989–99; All Party Parly Gp on Drugs Misuse, until 1998; All Party Parly Betting and Gaming Gp, 2006–; former Treas., All Party Parly Gp on Racing and Bloodstock. Admin. Steward, BBB of C, 2004–. Member: BBC Gen. Adv. Council, 1988–91; Commonwealth War Graves Commn, 1992–2003. Chm., Angling Cttee, Countryside Alliance, 2004–. Chairman: Second Chance, children's charity, 2000–; Citizen Card, 2001–. Former Mem., Dist Manpower Services Cttee; Mem., N Staffs DHA, 1983–87. Sec., Newcastle (Dist) Trades Council, 1976–87. *Address:* House of Lords, SW1A 0PW.

GOLDING, Michael Redvers, OBE 2007; professional yachtsman, since 1992; Managing Director, Mike Golding Yacht Racing Ltd, since 2001; *b* 27 Aug. 1960; *s* of Jack Golding and late Margaret Golding; *m* 2002, Andrea Bacon; one *s*. *Educ:* Reading Blue Coat Sch., Sonning; Windsor and Eton Coll. Fire Officer, Royal Berks Fire and Rescue Service, 1979–92; professional yachtsman: skipper, British Admiral's Cup Team, 1995; Internat. Monohull Open Cl. Assoc. World Champion, 2004–05, 2005–06; Forum Internat. de la Course Océanique World Champion, 2005–06; has raced round the world 5 times, incl. 3 times solo; winner, BT Global Challenge Round the World Race, 1996–97; competitor: 7 consecutive Transat Jacques Vabre races, 1999–2011; 4 Vendée Globe non-stop solo circumnavigations, incl. 7th place, 2000–01 (dismasted day 1, restarted 8 days after main fleet), 3rd place, 2004–05; first non-stop solo in both directions round the world, 2001; *world records:* non-stop solo round the world E to W (125 days), 1993–94; single handed, non-stop circumnavigation W to E against prevailing winds and currents, 1994–2001; fastest single-handed transatlantic crossing E to W (12 days 15 hours), 2004–; fastest single-handed monohull crossing of Indian Ocean (14 days 2hrs 1 min.), 2004–; fastest single-handed monohull crossing of S Pacific Ocean (16 days 5hrs 26 mins), 2005–. *Publications:* No Law No God, 1993; Racing Skipper, 1999. *Recreations:* travel, cooking, mountain biking, cinema. *Address:* Mike Golding Yacht Racing Ltd, 24 Shore Road, Warsash, Hants SO31 9FU. *T:* (01489) 557960. *E:* info@mikegolding.com. *Clubs:* Royal London Yacht (Hon. Mem.); Royal Southampton Yacht (Hon. Mem.); Corinthian Yacht (Boston, Mass) (Hon. Mem.).

GOLDING, Ven. Simon Jefferies, CBE 2002; Hon. Priest, Diocese of West Yorkshire and the Dales, since 2014; *b* 30 March 1946; *s* of late George William Golding and Gladys Joyce Golding (*née* Henstridge); *m* 1968, Anne Reynolds; one *s* one *d*. *Educ:* HMS Conway Merchant Navy Cadet Sch.; Brasted Place Coll.; Lincoln Theol Coll. Navigating Officer, MN, and Lieut (X) RNR, 1963–69; ordained deacon 1974, priest 1975; Curate, St Cuthbert, Wilton, 1974–77; Chaplain, Royal Navy, 1977–2002; Chaplain of the Fleet, 1997–98; Archdeacon for RN and Principal Anglican Chaplain (Naval), 1998–2002; Dir Gen., Naval Chaplaincy Service and Chaplain of the Fleet, 2000–02. QHC 1997–2002; Hon. Canon, Gibraltar Cathedral, 1998–2002. Diocese of Ripon and Leeds: Hon. Priest, 2003–14; Convenor, Ministerial Rev. Scheme, 2003–08; Advr, Non-Stipendiary Ministry, 2008–11; Associate Minister, E Richmond Team Ministry, 2011–14; Hon. Chaplain to High Sheriff of Co. Durham, 2014–15. Lay Advr, N Yorks Multi Agency Public Protection Arrangements, 2005–. Mem., Gen. Council, Royal Nat. Mission to Deep-Sea Fishermen, 2007–. *Address:* Arlanza, Hornby Road, Appleton Wiske, Northallerton DL6 2AF. *T:* (01609) 881185.

GOLDING, Terence Edward, OBE 1992; FCA; Chief Executive, National Exhibition Centre, Birmingham, 1978–95; Deputy Chairman, Earls Court and Olympia Ltd, 1995–99; *b* 7 April 1932; *s* of Sydney Richard Golding and Elsie Golding; *m* 1955, Sheila Jean (*née* Francis); one *s* one *d*. *Educ:* Harrow County Grammar Sch. FCA 1967. Earls Court Ltd (Exhibition Hall Proprietors): Chief Accountant, 1960; Co. Sec., 1965; Financial Dir, 1972; Financial Dir, Olympia Ltd, and Earls Court & Olympia Ltd, 1973; Commercial Dir, Earls Court & Olympia Group of Cos, 1975; Chief Exec., Internat. Convention Centre, Birmingham, 1990–95; Dir, Alexandra Palace Trading Ltd, 2000–10; Chm., Expocentric plc, 2000–02. Member: Exhibition Liaison Cttee, 1979–97; Nat. Assoc. of Exhibn Hallowners, 1988–97. Director: British Exhibitions Promotion Council, 1981–83; Birmingham Convention and Visitor Bureau, 1981–93; Heart of England Tourist Bd, 1984–91; Central England, TEC, 1990–92; Birmingham Marketing Partnership, 1993–95; Chm., Exhibn Industry Fedn, 1995–97; Exhibition Venues Assoc., 1997–99. Hon. Mem. Council, Birmingham Chamber of Industry and Commerce, 1990–95. Midlander of the Year, 1990. *Recreation:* following sport. *Address:* Pinn Cottage, Pinner Hill, Pinner, Middx HA5 3XX. *T:* (020) 8866 2610.

GOLDINGAY, Rev. Prof. John Edgar, PhD; David Allan Hubbard Professor of Old Testament Studies, Fuller Theological Seminary, Pasadena, since 1997; Priest-in-Charge, St Barnabas, Pasadena, since 2011; *b* 20 June 1942; *s* of Edgar Charles and Ada Irene Goldingay; *m* 1st, 1967, Ann Elizabeth Wilson (*d* 2009); two *s*; 2nd, 2010, Kathleen Susan Scott. *Educ:* King Edward's School, Birmingham; Keble Coll., Oxford (BA); Nottingham University (PhD). Ordained deacon 1966, priest 1967; Asst Curate, Christ Church, Finchley, 1966–69; St John's College, Nottingham: Lectr, 1970–75; Dir of Acad. Studies, 1976–79; Registrar, 1979–85; Vice-Principal, 1985–88; Principal, 1988–97. DD Lambeth, 1997. *Publications:* Songs from a Strange Land, 1978; Approaches to Old Testament Interpretation, 1981; Theological Diversity and the Authority of the Old Testament, 1987; Daniel, 1989; (ed) Signs, Wonders and Healing, 1989; Models for Scripture, 1994; Models for the Interpretation of Scripture, 1995; (ed) Atonement Today, 1995; After Eating the Apricot, 1996; To The Usual Suspects, 1998; Men Behaving Badly, 2000; Isaiah, 2001; Walk On, 2002; Old Testament Theology, vol. 1, 2003, vol. 2, 2006, vol. 3, 2009; The Message of Isaiah 40–55,

2005; Isaiah 40–55, 2 vols, 2006; Psalms vol. 1, 2006, vol. 2, 2007, vol. 3, 2008; (ed) Uprooting and Planting, 2007; (with P. J. Scalise) Minor Prophets II, 2009; Genesis, 2 vols, 2010; Exodus and Leviticus, 2010; Numbers and Deuteronomy, 2010; Key Questions about Christian Faith, 2010; Joshua, Judges and Ruth, 2011; 1 and 2 Samuel, 2011; Remembering Ann, 2011; 1 and 2 Kings, 2011; Key Questions about Interpretation, 2011; 1 and 2 Chronicles, 2012; Ezra, Nehemiah, and Esther, 2012; Job, 2013; Isaiah 56–66, 2013; Psalms Part 1, 2013; Psalms Part 2, 2014; The Theology of the Book of Isaiah, 2014; Isaiah, 2015; Proverbs, Ecclesiastes, and Song of Songs, 2014; Do We Need the New Testament?, 2015. *Recreations:* family, Old Testament, rock music, jazz. *Address:* 111 South Orange Grove Boulevard, Apartment 108, Pasadena, CA 91105, USA. *T:* (626) 4050626, *Fax:* (626) 5845251. *E:* johngold@fuller.edu.

GOLDINGHAM, Claire Louise Margaret W.; *see* Wills-Goldingham.

GOLDMAN, Antony John, CB 1995; Director General, Civil Aviation, Department of the Environment, Transport and the Regions, 1996–99; *b* 28 Feb. 1940; *s* of Sir Samuel Goldman, KCB and step *s* of late Patricia Goldman (*née* Hodges); *m* 1964, Anne Rosemary Lane; three *s. Educ:* Marlborough College; Peterhouse, Cambridge (BA). International Computers Ltd, 1961–73; entered Civil Service, DoE, 1973; Private Sec. to Sec. of State for Transport, 1976–78; Asst Sec., 1977; seconded to HM Treasury, 1981–83; Under Sec., 1984. Non-exec. Dir, Hugh Baird & Sons, 1985–86. Chm., Eur. Air Traffic Control Harmonisation and Integration Prog., 1994–99; Vice-Pres., Eur. Civil Aviation Conf., 1997–99; Pres., Eurocontrol Council, 1998–99. Special Advr to H of L Select Cttee on Europe, 2001. Trustee, Watts Gall., 2004–. Hon. CRAeS 1997. Eur. Regl Airlines Award, 1993. *Recreations:* music, writing doggerel.

GOLDMAN, Dr Lawrence Neil, FRHistS; Director, Institute of Historical Research, School of Advanced Study, and Professor of History, University of London, since 2014; *b* 17 June 1957; *s* of Basil Benjamin Goldman and Hilda Hannah Goldman (*née* Schmerkin); *m* 1985, Madeleine Jean McDonald; two *s* one *d. Educ:* Haberdashers' Aske's Sch., Elstree; Jesus Coll., Cambridge (BA 1979); Trinity Coll., Cambridge (PhD 2003); Yale Univ. FRHistS 2002. Harkness Fellow, Commonwealth Fund of NY, 1979–80; Res. Fellow, Trinity Coll., Cambridge, 1982–85; Lectr in Hist. and Politics, Dept for Continuing Educn, Univ. of Oxford, 1985–90; Fellow and Tutor in Modern History, St Peter's Coll., Oxford, 1990–2014. Vis. Prof., Univ. of S Carolina, 1994; Vis. Fellow, Humanities Res. Centre, 2006, Dept of Hist., 2012, ANU. Assessor, Univ. of Oxford, 2000–01; External Mem., Cambridge History Faculty review, 2011. Member: Adv. Council, Warburg Inst.; Council, N Amer. Conf. on British Studies. Pres., Thames and Solent Dist, WEA, 2002–04. Governor: NLCS, 2006–11; Haberdashers' Aske's Schs, Elstree, 2011–. Editor: Oxford Dictionary of National Biography, 2004–14; Oxford Historical Monographs, 2009–14; Historical Research, 2014–. *Publications:* (ed) The Blind Victorian: Henry Fawcett and British Liberalism, 1989; Dons and Workers: Oxford and adult education since 1850, 1995; Science, Reform and Politics in Victorian Britain: the Social Science Association 1857–1886, 2002; (ed with P. Ghosh) Politics and Culture in Victorian Britain: essays in memory of Colin Matthew, 2006; (ed) The Federalist, 2008; The Life of R. H. Tawney: socialism and history, 2013; contribs to learned jls incl. English Histl Rev., Past and Present, Histl Jl. *Recreations:* walking, swimming, gardening, cricket, Suffolk. *Address:* Institute of Historical Research, School of Advanced Study, Senate House, Malet Street, WC1E 7HU. *T:* (020) 7862 8740. *E:* lawrence.goldman@sas.ac.uk; Flat 316, The Latitude, 130 Clapham Common Southside, SW4 9DX. *T:* (020) 8772 8305. *Club:* Southwold Sailors' Reading Room.

GOLDMARK, Peter Carl, Jr; Director, Climate and Air Program, Environmental Defense, 2003–10; *b* 2 Dec. 1940; *m* 1964, Aliette Misson. *Educ:* Harvard Univ. (BA Govt *magna cum laude* with Highest Hons 1962; Phi Beta Kappa). History teacher, Putney Sch., Vermont, 1962–64; US Office of Econ. Opportunity, Washington, 1965–66; City of New York: Exec. Asst to Dir of Budget, 1966–68; Asst Budget Dir for Prog. Planning and Analysis, 1968–70; Exec. Asst to Mayor, 1970–71; Sec. of Human Services, Commonwealth of Massachusetts, 1971–74; Dir of Budget, State of NY, 1975–77; Exec. Dir, Port Authy of NY and NJ, 1977–85; Sen. Vice Pres., Times Mirror Co., 1985–88; Pres., Rockefeller Foundn, 1988–97; Chm. and CEO, Internat. Herald Tribune, 1998–2003.

GOLDREIN, Iain Saville; QC 1997; a Recorder, since 1999; a Deputy High Court Judge, since 2008; Panel Deemster, Isle of Man, since 2012; *b* 10 Aug. 1952; *s* of Neville Clive Goldrein, *qv*; *m* 1980, Margaret de Haas, *qv*; one *s* one *d. Educ:* Merchant Taylors' Sch., Crosby; Hebrew Univ., Jerusalem; Pembroke Coll., Cambridge (exhibnr, Ziegler Prize for Law; Cambridge Squire Schol. for Law). Called to the Bar, Inner Temple, 1975 (Duke of Edinburgh Scholarship); Dep. Head, No 7 Harrington Street Chambers, Liverpool, 2003–12 (Jt Hd, 1989–2003); Asst Recorder, 1995–99. Mem., Mental Health Review Tribunal, 1999–2002. Vis. Prof., Nottingham Law Sch., 1991. Mediator: Acad. of Experts, 1992 (Companion, 1992); Commercial, 2009, Family, 2010, ADR Gp. Member: Council, Internat. Inst. of Experts, Hong Kong, 2010–; Adv. Bd, Centre for Opposition Studies, 2012–; Adv. Bd, Belief in Mediation and Arbitration, 2012–; Internat. Adv. Bd, Centre for Islamic Finance, Bolton Univ., 2014–. Mayoral Comr for City of Liverpool (Envmtl Sustainability), 2013–. Hon. Advr, Faith in the Future. Fellow, Soc. of Advanced Legal Studies, 1998. FRSA 1992. Jt Ed.-in-Chief, Genetics Law Monitor, 2000–02; Ed., In Brief, 2006–11; Adv. Ed., Hong Kong White Book, 2012; Internat. Adv. Ed., Malaysian White Book, 2013; Consulting Ed., Commercial Litigation in Hong Kong: a practical guide, 2013. Hon. DLaws Bolton, 2014. *Publications:* Personal Injury Litigation: practice and precedents, 1985; (with Clyde & Co.) Ship Sale and Purchase: law and technique, 1985, 6th edn 2012; (with K. H. P. Wilkinson) Commercial Litigation: pre-emptive remedies, 1987, 4th edn (with Sir Robin Jacob and P. M. Kershaw) 2003, internat. edn (with sub-editors) 2005, 2nd internat. edn 2011; with Sir J. Jacob: Bullen and Leake and Jacob's Precedents of Pleadings, 13th edn 1990 (supervisory ed.); Pleadings, Principles and Practice, 1990; (ed jtly) Insurance Disputes (loose-leaf), 1999–2003, hardback edn 2004, 3rd edn (with sub-editors) 2012; (ed jtly) Civil Court Practice, 1999–2013; (jtly) Human Rights and Judicial Review: case studies in context, 2001; with M. de Haas: Property Distribution on Divorce, 1983, 2nd edn 1985; Butterworths Personal Injury Litigation Service, 1988–; Structured Settlements, 1993, 2nd edn 1997; Medical Negligence: cost effective case management, 1997; (also ed jtly) Personal Injury Major Claims Handling: cost effective case management, 2000; (with J. Ryder) Child Case Management Practice, 2009, 2nd edn (with sub-editors) 2012; Media Access to the Family Courts, 2009; (ed jtly) Hong Kong Mediation Handbook, 2010; Privacy Injunctions and the Media: a practice manual, 2012. *Recreations:* Classical Hebrew, history, English legal history, new ideas, anything aeronautical or nautical, classical motor vehicles. *Address:* 7 Harrington Street, Liverpool L2 9YH. *T:* (0151) 242 0707; KCH Garden Square Chambers, 1 Oxford Street, Nottingham NG1 5BH; Church Court Chambers, Goldsmith Buildings, Inner Temple, EC4 7BL; Coram Chambers, 9–11 Fulwood Place, WC1V 6HG.

GOLDREIN, Margaret Ruth; *see* de Haas, M. R.

GOLDREIN, Neville Clive, CBE 1991; Senior Partner, Goldrein & Co., 1953–85; Consultant, Deacon Goldrein Green, Solicitors, 1985–92; *b* 28 Aug. 1924; *s* of Saville and Nina Goldrein; *m* 1949, Dr Sonia Sumner, MB, BS Dunelm; one *s* one *d. Educ:* Hymers Coll., Hull; Pembroke Coll., Cambridge (MA). Served Army: commnd E Yorks Regt; served East Africa Comd (Captain). Admitted Solicitor of the Supreme Court, 1949; former Dep. Circuit Judge. Mem., Crosby Bor. Council, 1957–71; Mayor of Crosby, 1966–67, Dep. Mayor, 1967–68; Mem., Lancs CC, 1965–74; Merseyside County Council: Mem., 1973–86; Dep. Leader, Cons. Gp, 1974–77; Vice-Chm. of Council, 1977–80; Leader, 1980–81; Leader, Cons. Gp, 1981–86. Chm., Crosby Constituency Cons. Assoc., 1986–89. Area Vice-Pres., Sefton, St John Ambulance, 1980–87 (Chm., S Sefton Div., 1975–87); Member: NW Econ. Planning Council, 1966–72; Bd of Deputies of British Jews, 1966–85, 1992–2001; Council, Liverpool Univ., 1977–81; Council, Merseyside Chamber of Commerce, 1987– (Chairman: Envmt and Energy Cttee, 1993–2006; Rivers Cttee, 1990–93; Police Liaison Cttee, 1994–2003; Mem., Arts and Culture Cttee, 2006–; Hon. Life Mem., 2006–); Regl Affairs Cttee, British Assoc. of Chambers of Commerce, 1993–97. Director: Merseyside Economic Develt Co. Ltd, 1981–87; Merseyside Waste Derived Fuels Ltd, 1983–86. Vice-Pres., Crosby Mencap, 1967–2011; Chm., Crosby Hall Residential Trust Appeal, 1989–91. Chm., Liverpool Royal Court Theatre Foundn, 1994–2005; Trustee, Liverpool Inst. for Performing Arts, 2008– (Mem. Council, 2005–08). Governor, Merchant Taylors' Sch., Crosby, 1965–74. *Publications:* Life is Too Serious to be Taken Seriously (autobiog.), 2010. *Recreations:* videography, photography, music, freelance journalism, travel. *Address:* Torreno, St Andrew's Road, Blundellsands, Merseyside L23 7UR. *T:* and *Fax:* (0151) 924 2065. *E:* goldrein@aol.com.

See also I. S. Goldrein.

GOLDRING, Jeremy Edward; QC 2013; *b* London, 22 April 1971; *s* of Rt Hon. Sir John Bernard Goldring, *qv* and Wendy Margaret Lancaster Goldring, *qv*; *m* 1997, Elizabeth Geren; one *d. Educ:* Oakham Sch.; Pembroke Coll., Oxford (BA, MA); Yale Univ. (MA; Henry Fellow). Called to the Bar, Lincoln's Inn, 1996; in practice as barrister, 1996–. *Recreations:* ski-ing, books. *Address:* 3–4 South Square, Gray's Inn, WC1R 5HP. *T:* (020) 7696 9900, *Fax:* (020) 7696 9911.

GOLDRING, Rt Hon. Sir John (Bernard), Kt 1999; PC 2008; a Lord Justice of Appeal, 2008–14; Senior Presiding Judge of England and Wales, 2010–12 (Deputy Senior Presiding Judge, 2008–09); *b* 9 Nov. 1944; *s* of Joseph and Marianne Goldring; *m* 1970, Wendy Margaret Lancaster Bennett (*see* W. M. L. Goldring); two *s. Educ:* Wyggeston Grammar Sch.; Exeter Univ. (LLB). Called to the Bar, Lincoln's Inn, 1969, Bencher, 1996 (Treas., Jan. 2016–). QC 1987; a Recorder, 1987–99; a Dep. Sen. Judge, Sovereign Base Areas, Cyprus, 1991–99; a Dep. High Court Judge, 1996–99; a Judge of the Courts of Appeal of Jersey and Guernsey, 1998–99; a Judge of the High Court of Justice, QBD, 1999–2008; a Presiding Judge, Midland Circuit, 2002–05. Asst Dep. Coroner for Hillsborough Inquests, 2012–. Comr, Judicial Appts Commn, 2006–08. Hon. LLD: Leicester, 2012; Exeter, 2015. *Recreations:* gardening, ski-ing. *Address:* Honourable Society of Lincoln's Inn, The Treasury Office, Lincoln's Inn, WC2A 3TL. *Club:* Athenæum.

See also J. E. Goldring.

GOLDRING, Mark Ian, CBE 2008; Chief Executive, Oxfam GB, since 2013; *b* 8 March 1957; *s* of Stephen and Pamela Goldring; *m* 1989, Rachel Carnegie; one *s* one *d. Educ:* Keble Coll., Oxford (BA Law 1979); LSE (MSc Social Policy and Planning in Developing Countries 1989). VSO Volunteer Teacher, Sarawak, 1979–81; Legal Researcher, Linklaters & Paines, 1982; Field Officer, Caribbean, 1983–85, Field Dir, Bhutan, 1985–88, VSO; UNDP Asst Rep., 1990–91, Oxfam Country Rep., 1991–94, Bangladesh; DFID Social Develt Advr, Pacific, 1994–95; VSO Overseas Dir, 1995–99; Chief Executive: VSO, 1999–2008; Mencap, 2008–13. Chairman: Revolving Doors Agency, 2002–05; Learning Disability Coalition, 2010–12; Member: Nat. Programme Bd, DoH, 2009–13; NHS Futures Forum, 2011–12; Foreign Sec.'s Human Rights Adv. Gp, 2013–15; Marks and Spencer Sustainability Adv. Bd, 2013–; Advr, Winterbourne View Rev. Team, 2011–12. Trustee: Accenture Develt Partnership, 2002–08; African Med. and Res. Foundn UK, 2008–13 (Vice-Chm., 2009–13); Bangladesh Rural Advancement Cttee (BRAC), 2009–13; Humanitarian Leadership Acad., 2015–. Chm., Thames Ditton Island (Maintenance and Service) Ltd, 2012–14. *Recreations:* cycling, Rugby, river life. *Address:* Oxfam GB, Oxfam House, John Smith Drive, Oxford OX4 2JY.

GOLDRING, Mary Sheila, OBE 1987; economist; presenter, Goldring Audit, Channel 4, 1992, 1993, 1994, 1995. *Educ:* Our Lady's Priory, Sussex; Lady Margaret Hall, Oxford (PPE). Air and Science correspondent, 1949–74, Business editor, 1966–74, Economist Newspaper; economist and broadcaster, 1974–; *television:* presenter: Analysis, BBC, 1977–87; Answering Back, Channel 4 interviews, 1989–91. Trustee, Science Museum, 1987–97. Fawley Foundn Lect., 1992. CRAeS 1995. Hon. DLitt UWE, 1994. Blue Circle Award for industrial journalism, 1979; Sony Radio Award for best current affairs programme (Analysis: Post-Recession Britain), 1985; Industrial Journalist Award, Industrial Soc., 1985; Outstanding Personal Contribution to Radio, Broadcasting Press Guild, 1986; Harold Wincott Award for Broadcasting, 1991; Industrial Journalist of the Year, Industrial Soc. and BP, 1991, 1995. *Publications:* Economics of Atomic Energy, 1957. *Recreation:* shopping.

GOLDRING, Wendy Margaret Lancaster, (Lady Goldring); Vice Lord-Lieutenant of Rutland, since 2006; *b* 10 July 1946; *d* of Ralph and Margaret Bennett; *m* 1970, John Bernard Goldring (*see* Rt Hon. Sir J. B. Goldring); two *s. Educ:* Farrington's Sch., Chislehurst; Univ. of Exeter (BA). Mem., Bd of Visitors, HMP Ashwell, 1984–92. Member: E Midlands Cttee, Nat. Lottery Charities Bd, 1995–99; County Bd, Prince's Trust, 2002–09. Trustee, Uppingham Sch., 2000–09. Pres., League of Friends, Rutland Meml Hosp., 2000–; Vice-Chm., Voluntary Action Rutland, 2001–12. JP Rutland, 1984–2012 (Chm. Bench, 1996–99); High Sheriff, 1999–2000, DL 2005, Rutland. *Recreations:* travel, gardening, history of art and architecture, reading. *Address:* c/o Lieutenancy Office, Catmose, Oakham, Rutland LE15 6HP.

See also J. E. Goldring.

GOLDSACK, His Honour Alan Raymond; QC 1990; DL; a Circuit Judge, 1994–2013; a Senior Circuit Judge, 2002–13; acting Judge, Grand Court of the Cayman Islands, since 2013; *b* 13 June 1947; *s* of Raymond Frederick Goldsack, MBE and Mildred Agnes Goldsack (*née* Jones); *m* 1971, Christine Marion Clarke; three *s* one *d. Educ:* Hastings Grammar School; Leicester Univ. (LLB). Called to the Bar, Gray's Inn, 1970, Bencher, 2003; a Recorder, 1988–94. Hon. Recorder, Sheffield, 2002–13. Mem., Parole Bd, 2009–. DL S Yorks, 2009. *Recreations:* gardening, walking. *Address:* The Old Rectory, Holy Well Lane, Braithwell, Botherham S66 7AF.

GOLDSACK, John Redman, MBE 1971; consultant in tropical agriculture and development, since 1993; *b* 15 Aug. 1932; 2nd *s* of late Bernard Frank and Dorothy Goldsack; *m* 1962, Madeleine Amelia Rowena, *d* of late Stanley and Grace Kibbler; two *s* one *d. Educ:* Sutton Grammar Sch., Surrey; Wye Coll., London Univ. (BScAgric); Queens' Coll., Cambridge (DipAgric); Imperial Coll. of Tropical Agric., Trinidad (DTA). Agricl Officer, HMOCS, Kenya, 1956; Hd of Soil Conservation and Planning Officer, Min. of Lands and Settlement, Kenya, 1963–67; Hd of Land Develt Div., Min. of Agriculture, Kenya, 1967–70; Asst Agric. Advr, ODM, 1970–74; Agriculture Adviser: S African Develt Div., 1974–78; ME Develt Div., 1979–81; E African Develt Div., 1981–83; Sen. Agric. Advr, Asia Div., ODA, 1983–86; Dep. Chief Natural Resources Advr and Prin. Agriculture Advr, ODA, 1986–88; Minister and UK Perm. Rep. to UNFAO, Rome, 1988–93. Chm., Prog. Adv. Cttee, Natural Resources Systems Progs, ODA, 1995–99. *Publications:* (with C. P. R. Nottidge) Million-Acre Settlement Scheme, Kenya, 1962–66, 1966. *Recreations:* cricket, golf, natural history. *Address:* 47 Peverell Avenue East, Poundbury, Dorchester, Dorset DT1 3RH. *T:* and *Fax:* (01305) 266543. *Clubs:* Farmers, MCC.

GOLDSCHMIED, Marco Lorenzo Sinnott, PPRIBA; Chairman, Thames Wharf Studios Ltd, 1984–2010; Managing Director, Rogers Architects Ltd, 1984–2004; Director, Shanghai Office, SPARK; *b* 28 March 1944; *s* of Guido Rodolfo Goldschmied and Elinor Violet (*née* Sinnott); *m* 1969, Andrea Halvorsen; four *s* one *d*. *Educ:* Architectural Assoc. (AA Dip. 1969); Reading Univ. (MSc 1986). RIBA 1971. Associate Partner, Piano & Rogers, 1971–77; Founder Partner, Rogers Partnership, 1977–84; Vice-Pres., Richard Rogers Japan KK, 1988–2004. Teacher: AA, 1971; Glasgow Sch. of Art, 1999; Lectr, RIBA, 1981–99 (Pres., 1999–2001). Mem., Architects Registration Bd, 1997–2000 (Mem., European Adv. Gp, 1998–2000); Trustee, Architectural Assoc., 1991–93; Chm., European Awards, 1996–99, Educn Review, 1998–99, C4 Stirling Prize, 2001, Chm., S and SE regions Awards, 2012–, RIBA. Royal Academy Summer Exhibitor, 2000. *Projects* include: Lloyd's HQ, City of London, 1978 (Civic Trust Award, 1987; RIBA Award, 1988); Fleetguard Manufg and Distribn Centre, Quimper, France, 1979–81; Inmos Microprocessor Factory, Newport, 1982 (British Steel Design Award, 1982; RIBA Award, 1983); PA Technology Res. Centre, Princeton, 1983; Linn-Sondek HQ, Glasgow, 1985 (RIBA Award); Billingsgate Mkt Restoration and Conversion, 1988 (Civic Trust Award, 1989); Reuters Computer Centre, London, 1988 (RIBA Award, 1990); Pumping Station, Victoria Docks, 1989; Terminal 5, Heathrow, 1990 (RIBA Award 2007); Channel 4 HQ, 1994 (RIBA Award, and RFAC Award, 1995); European Court of Human Rights, Strasbourg, 1995; Learning Resource Centre, Thames Valley Univ., 1996 (RIBA Award, 1998); Europier Passenger Terminal, Heathrow, 1996 (RIBA Award, and British Steel Award, 1997); Bordeaux Law Courts, 1998; Lloyd's Register of Shipping HQ, 1999; Daiwa Europe Office, 1999; 88 Wood Street, London, 1999 (RIBA Award, 2000); Millennium Dome, Greenwich, 1999; Offices and Laboratories, Gifu, Japan, 1999; Lloyd's Register of Shipping HQ, 1999; Montevetro Apartments, London (RIBA Award, 2000); Nat. Assembly of Wales, Cardiff, 2001; 16 Ha Masterplan, News Internat., 2004; The Albany Th., Deptford. Chair: Appeal for Care of Victims of Torture, Med. Foundn, 1999–2001; Leadership Gp, Amnesty Internat., 2003–05; Trustee, Marco Goldschmied Foundn, 2004– (Sponsor: Stephen Lawrence RIBA Award, 1998–; RIBA Stirling Prize, 2009). Patron, Stephen Lawrence Trust, 2004–. TV and radio interviews. Hon. Mem., AIA. Hon. FRSA. *Publications:* (jtly) Architecture 98, 1998; articles in jls. *Recreations:* twentieth century European history, etymology, ski-ing.

GOLDSMITH, family name of **Baron Goldsmith**.

GOLDSMITH, Baron *cr* 1999 (Life Peer), of Allerton in the county of Merseyside; **Peter Henry Goldsmith;** PC 2002; QC 1987; Chair of European and Asian Litigation (formerly European Chair of Litigation), since 2007, and Co-Managing Partner, since 2014, Debevoise & Plimpton LLP; *b* 5 Jan. 1950; *s* of late Sydney Elland Goldsmith, solicitor, and of Myra Nurick; *m* 1974, Joy; three *s* one *d*. *Educ:* Quarry Bank High Sch., Liverpool; Gonville and Caius Coll., Cambridge (Sen. Schol., Tapp Postgrad. Schol., Schuldham Plate, 1968–71; MA); UCL (LLM 1972; Fellow 2002). Called to the Bar, Gray's Inn (Birkenhead Schol.), 1972, Bencher, 1994; Avocat, Barreau de Paris, 1997; a Jun. Counsel to the Crown, Common Law, 1985–87; a Recorder, 1989–; HM Attorney Gen., 2001–07. Chairman: Bar Council, 1995 (Chairman: Legal Services Cttee, 1992–94; Internat. Relations Cttee, 1996); Bar Pro Bono Unit, 1996–2001 (Pres., 2001–); Financial Reporting Review Panel, 1997–99 (Mem., 1995–97); Mem. Council, 1996–2001, Co-Chm., Human Rights Inst., 1998–2001, Internat. Bar Assoc. Personal Rep. of Prime Minister to Convention to draft EU Charter of Fundamental Rights, 1999–2000. Member: Jt Human Rights Select Cttee, 2001; Constitution Select Cttee, 2011–15. Member: Council, Public Concern at Work, 1995–2001; Exec. Cttee, GB-China Centre, 1997–2001; Adv. Bd, Cambridge Centre for Commercial and Corporate Law, 1998–; Council, Internat. Law Section, ABA, 2008–; Bd, Rule of Law Initiative, 2010–; Council, Hong Kong Internat. Arbitration Centre, 2012– (Vice-Chm.). Chm., Access to Justice Foundn, 2009–. Non-exec. Dir, Westfield Gp, 2008–. Fellow, American Law Inst., 1997. Hon. LLD Univ. of Law, 2014. *Publications:* (contrib.) Common Law, Common Bond; articles in nat., internat. and legal press and jls. *Address:* House of Lords, SW1A 0PW; Debevoise & Plimpton LLP, 65 Gresham Street, EC2V 7NQ.

GOLDSMITH, Alexander Benedict Hayum; Director: Cavamont Holdings (formerly Cavamont Investment Advisers) Ltd, since 1998; Yetro Ltd, since 2001; *b* 10 Dec. 1960; *s* of late Edward René David Goldsmith and of Gillian Marion (*née* Pretty); *m* 1990, Louisa Kate Slack; two *s* one *d*. *Educ:* Westminster Sch.; Jesus Coll., Cambridge (MA Social Anthropol. 1986). Researcher and fundraiser for Survival Internat., 1986; Publisher and Editor, Envmt Digest, 1987–90; Editor: Geographical Magazine, 1991–94; People and Places in Peril series, 1995; Green Futures mag., 1996–98; Dir, Book Runner Ltd, 1999–2003. Chm., Weeding Technologies Ltd, 2011–13. Trustee: Ecology Trust, 2004–06; Cancer Prevention and Educn Soc. (formerly Cancer Prevention Soc.), 2000–05. FRGS 2002. *Recreations:* sailing, walking, ski-ing. *Clubs:* Groucho; Travellers (Paris).

GOLDSMITH, Alexander Kinglake, (Alick); HM Diplomatic Service, retired; *b* 16 Jan. 1938; *s* of Maj.-Gen. Robert Frederick Kinglake Goldsmith, CB, CBE and Brenda (*née* Bartlett); *m* 1971, Deirdre Stafford; one *s* one *d*. *Educ:* Sherborne; Trinity Coll., Oxford (MA Modern History). National Service, 1956–58 (DCLI and Queen's Own Nigeria Regt). Asst Principal, CRO, 1961; Hindi student, SOAS, 1962; Third Sec., New Delhi, 1963; FCO, 1967; First Sec. (Inf.), Wellington, NZ, 1971; FCO, 1975; Head of Chancery, E Berlin, 1978; FCO, 1980; Hd of Commonwealth Co-ordination Dept, FCO, 1982; seconded to Hong Kong Govt, 1984; Consul-Gen., Hamburg, 1986–90. Dir, Export Gp for the Constructional Industries, 1991–2001. *Recreations:* walking, swimming. *Address:* c/o Lloyds Bank, Butler Place, SW1H 0PR. *Club:* Royal Automobile.

GOLDSMITH, Benjamin James; Founding Partner, WHEB LLP, since 2002; *b* London, 28 Oct. 1980; *s* of late Sir James Michael Goldsmith and of Lady Annabel Goldsmith (formerly Lady Annabel Vane Tempest Stewart); *m* 1st, 2003, Kate Emma Rothschild (marr. diss. 2013); two *s* one *d*; 2nd, 2014, Jemima, *d* of Edward David Brynmor Jones, *qv*. *Educ:* Eton. Chm., Conservative Envmt Network, 2013–; Member, Advisory Board: JMG Foundn; Envmtl Funders Network. *Recreations:* cricket, the natural world, backgammon. *Address:* 2 Fitzhardinge Street, W1H 6EE. *E:* ben.goldsmith@whebgroup.com. *Clubs:* Brooks's, 5 Hertford Street.

See also F. Z. R. Goldsmith.

GOLDSMITH, Rt Rev. Christopher David; *see* St Germans, Bishop Suffragan of.

GOLDSMITH, Frank Zacharias Robin, (Zac); MP (C) Richmond Park, since 2010; *b* Westminster, 20 Jan. 1975; *s* of late Sir James Michael Goldsmith and of Lady Annabel Goldsmith (formerly Lady Annabel Vane Tempest Stewart); *m* 1st, 1999, Sheherazade Ventura-Bentley (marr. diss. 2012); one *s* two *d*; 2nd, 2013, Alice Miranda Rothschild; one *d*. *Educ:* Hawtreys; Eton Coll.; Internat. Honours Programme, Boston. Worked with Redefining Progress, San Francisco, 1994–95; joined Internat. Soc. for Ecology and Culture, 1995–97, based in Calif, Bristol and Ladakh, India (ran tourist educn prog. in Ladakh for part of time), later Assoc. Dir; Ed., 1997–2007, Dir, 2007–, The Ecologist mag. Co-founder, FARM, 2002. Dir, Ecosystems Ltd. Mem. Adv. Bd, JMG Foundn; Trustee: Royal Parks Foundn; Rainforest Foundn UK; Aspinall Foundn; Countryside Restoration Trust; Pres., Nat. Gardens Scheme, 2006–10. Speeches at numerous venues incl. Schumacher Meml Lects, Oxford Union, colls, schs and Think Tanks in UK. (Jtly) Beacon Prize for Young Philanthropist of the Year, 2003; Internat. Envmtl Leadership Award, Global Green USA, 2004. *Publications:* The Constant Economy: how to create a stable society, 2009; contrib. newspapers incl. The Times, Sunday Times, Daily Mail, Mail on Sunday, Independent, Guardian, Observer, Standard, Express, Daily Telegraph, Tribune and many regl newspapers; over 50 articles for The Ecologist; articles for other magazines incl. Country Life (contrib. and ed special edn, Dec. 2002), Big Issue, New Statesman, Spectator, Week, Global Agenda 2003, Geographical, Tatler and Vanity Fair. *Address:* House of Commons, SW1A 0AA. *Club:* Travellers.

See also B. J. Goldsmith.

GOLDSMITH, Harvey Anthony, CBE 1996; Managing Director, Artist Promotion Management (formerly Artiste Management Productions) Ltd, since 1973; *b* 4 March 1946; *s* of Sydney and Minnie Goldsmith; *m* 1971, Diana Gorman; one *s*. *Educ:* Christ's Coll.; Brighton Coll. of Technol. Partner, Big O Posters, 1966–67; organised first free open-air concert in Parliament Hill Fields, 1968; (with Michael Alfandary) opened Round House, Camden Town, 1968; Crystal Palace Gdn Party series of concerts, 1969–72; merged with John Smith Entertainments, 1970; formed Harvey Goldsmith Entertainments (rock tours promotions co.), 1976; acquired Allied Entertainments Gp (rock concert promotions co.), 1984; (with Mark McCormack) formed Classical Productions (to produce operas), 1986; Man. Dir, TBA Entertainment Corp. (Europe) Ltd, 2000–04. Promoter and producer of pop, rock and classical musical events, including: *concerts:* Bruce Springsteen; The Rolling Stones; Elton John; The Who; Pink Floyd; Led Zeppelin reunion, 2007; *opera:* Aida, 1988 and 1998, Carmen, 1989, Tosca, 1991, Earls Court; Pavarotti at Wembley, 1986; Pavarotti in the Park, 1991; The Three Tenors, 1996; Pavarotti World Tour, 2005; Salute Petra: Pavarotti tribute concert, 2008. Producer: Live Aid, 1985; Net Aid, 2000; Live 8, 2005; Executive Producer: Nokia New Year's Eve, 2006; Live Earth - SOS, 2007. Manager, Jeff Beck, 2008–. Chm., Ignition Internat., 2006–09. Dir, British Red Cross Events Ltd, 2000–03; Member: London Tourist Bd, 1994–2002 (Dir, 1993–2003); Prague Heritage Fund, 1994–2002; Mayor's Adv. Gp on Tourism, 2003. Chairman: Nat. Music Fest., 1991; Concert Promoters' Bd, 1994–99; Foundn and Bd, British Music Experience, 2007–; Co-Chm., President's Club, 1994–; Vice-Chm., Action Mgt Bd, Prince's Trust, 1993–2000; Trustee: Band Aid, 1985–; Live Aid, 1985–; Royal Opera House, 1995–2001; Vice-President: REACT, 1989–; Music Users' Council, 1994–; Mem., Communications Panel, BRCS, 1992–. Patron, Teenage Cancer Trust, 2006–. Lifetime Achievement Award, Nat. Outdoor Events Assoc., 2009; Internat. Music Person of the Year, Musexpo, 2010. Chevalier des Arts et Lettres (France), 2006. *Recreation:* golf. *Address:* Artist Promotion Management, 3rd Floor, 113 Great Portland Street, W1W 6QQ. *T:* (020) 7224 1992, *Fax:* (020) 7580 1853. *Clubs:* Royal Automobile, Home House; Century (NY); Vale de Lobo Golf.

GOLDSMITH, Jonathan; Secretary-General, Council of Bars and Law Societies of Europe, 2002–15 (Consultant, since 2015); *b* 22 Aug. 1953; *s* of Hans and Gisela Goldsmith; *m* 1978, Hermione St John Smith; two *d*. *Educ:* Trinity Coll., Oxford. Solicitor; Citizens Advice Bureaux: Advr, 1978–80; Community Lawyer, 1980–86; Law Society: Dep. Hd, Communications, 1986–95; Dir, Internat., 1995–2001.

GOLDSMITH, Philip; Director (observation of the Earth and its environment), European Space Agency, Paris, 1985–93; *b* 16 April 1930; *s* of late Stanley Thomas Goldsmith and Ida Goldsmith (*née* Rawlinson); *m* 1st, 1952, Daphne (*d* 1983), *d* of William Webb; two *s* two *d*; 2nd, 1990, Gail Lorraine. *Educ:* Almondbury Grammar Sch.; Pembroke Coll., Oxford (MA). Meteorologist with the Meteorological Office, 1947–54, incl. National Service, RAF, 1948–50; Research Scientist, AERE Harwell, 1957–67; Meteorological Office: Asst Director (Cloud Physics Research), 1967–76; Dep. Director (Physical Research), 1976–82; Dir (Res.), 1982–85. President: Royal Meteorological Society, 1980–82; Internat. Commn on Atmospheric Chem. and Global Pollution, 1979–83. *Publications:* articles in scientific jls mainly on atmospheric physics and chemistry and space research related to associated environmental concerns. *Recreations:* golf, gardening, antiques, old cars. *Address:* 50 Hapil Close, Sandford, Winscombe, Somerset BS25 5AA.

GOLDSMITH, Walter Kenneth, FCA; Chairman, Estates & Management Ltd, since 2006; *b* 19 Jan. 1938; *s* of late Lionel and of Phoebe Goldsmith; *m* 1961, Rosemary Adele, *d* of Joseph and Hannah Salter; two *s* two *d*. *Educ:* Merchant Taylors' School. Admitted Inst. of Chartered Accountants, 1960; Manager, Mann Judd & Co., 1964; joined Black & Decker Ltd, 1966: Dir of Investment, Finance and Administration, Europe, 1967; Gen. Man., 1970; Man. Dir, 1974; Chief Executive and European Dir, 1975; Black & Decker USA, 1976–79: Corporate Vice-Pres. and Pres. Pacific Internat. Operations; Dir Gen., Inst. of Dirs, 1979–84; Chm., Korn/Ferry International Ltd, 1984–86; Gp Planning and Marketing Dir, Trusthouse Forte plc, 1985–87; Chm., Food from Britain, 1987–90; Chm., British Food & Farming Ltd (Dep. Chm., 1990). Chairman: Ansoll Estates Ltd, 1989–98; Trident, later Flying Flowers, Ltd, 1990–99; Royal Stafford Tableware Ltd, 1997–2002; Asite plc, 2009– (Dep. Chm., 2001–09); Energy Technique plc, 2011–; Dep. Chm., MICE Gp, 1994–95; Director: Bank Leumi (UK) plc, 1984–2013; Trusthouse Forte Inc., 1985–87; The Winning Streak Ltd, 1985–2000; Isys plc (Dep. Chm.), 1987–99; CLS Group, 1992–2000; Chambers & Newman, 1994–2000; Betterware, 1995–97 (Chm., 1990–97); Fitness First plc, 1997–2003; Guiton Gp plc, 1998–2003; SCS Upholstery plc, 1998–2005; Visonic, 2004–10; KBH Media Ltd, 2005– (Chm.); Mercury Gp plc, 2006–09; Mem. Adv. Bd, Kalchas, 1990–97; Advisor to: Rotch Property Gp, 1996–2011; Consensus Business Gp, 2006–. Member: English Tourist Board, 1982–84; BTA, 1984–86; Vice-Pres., British Overseas Trade Gp for Israel, 1992–2000 (Chm., 1987–91). Mem., Internat. Adv. Bd, 2007–, Develt Adv. Bd, 2009–13, SOAS. Treas., Leo Baeck Coll., 1987–89; Chm., Jewish Music Inst., 2003–08 (Vice Pres., 2008–). Council Mem., RASE, 1988–95. Trustee, Israel Diaspora Trust, 1982–92; Chm., Grange Hospice Project, 1994–99. FRSA; CCMI. Liveryman, Worshipful Co. of Chartered Accountants in England and Wales, 1985. Free Enterprise Award, Aims for Industry, 1984. *Publications:* (with D. Clutterbuck): The Winning Streak, 1984; The Winning Streak Workout Book, 1985; The Winning Streak: Mark 2, 1997; (with Berry Ritchie) The New Elite, 1987. *Recreations:* music, walking, travel. *Address:* 35 Park Lane, W1K 1RB.

GOLDSMITH, Zac; *see* Goldsmith, F. Z. R.

GOLDSPRING, Paul; a District Judge (Magistrates' Courts), since 2013; *b* Greenwich, London, 11 Oct. 1971; *s* of Anthony George Goldspring and Maureen Ann Goldspring; *m* 1999, Joanne Naomi Jayne; two *s*. *Educ:* Eaglesfield Sch.; Univ. of Hertfordshire (LLB Hons 1993); Univ. of Cambridge (Dip. Legal Skills 1995). Admitted solicitor, 1997; a Dep. District Judge (Magistrates' Courts), 2009–13. *Recreations:* cricket, golf, football, jazz, wine. *Address:* Thames Magistrates' Court, 58 Bow Road, E3 4DJ.

GOLDSTAUB, Anthony (James); QC 1992; **His Honour Judge Goldstaub;** a Circuit Judge, since 2004; *b* 26 May 1949; *er s* of late Henry Goldstaub, engineer, and of Hilda (*née* Bendix); *m* 1st, 1982 (marr. diss. 1989); two *s*; 2nd, 1993, Moira Pooley; one *d*. *Educ:* Highgate Sch.; Nottingham Univ. (LLB 1971). Called to the Bar, Middle Temple, 1972; an Asst Recorder, 1995–98; a Recorder, 1999–2004. A Pres., Mental Health Review Tribunals, 2002–. *Address:* Chelmsford Crown Court, New Street, Chelmsford CM1 1EL.

GOLDSTAUB, Jane Hilary, (Mrs T. C. Goldstaub); *see* Procter, J. H.

GOLDSTEIN, Alfred, CBE 1977; FREng; consulting engineer, 1951–93; Senior Partner, Travers Morgan & Partners, 1972–85; Chairman, Travers Morgan Group, 1985–87; *b* 9 Oct. 1926; *s* of late Sigmund and Regina Goldstein; *m* 1959, Anne Milford, *d* of late Col R. A. M. Tweedy and Maureen Evans, and step *d* of Hubert Evans; two *s*. *Educ:* Rotherham Grammar Sch.; Imperial Coll., Univ. of London. BSc (Eng); ACGI 1946; DIC. FICE 1959; FIStructE 1959; FCIHT (FIHE 1959); FREng (FEng 1979); FCGI 1984. Partner, R. Travers Morgan

& Partners, 1951; early projects include: Oxford Univ. Parks Footbridge, 1949 (Grade II listed 1998); Bournemouth Bus Garage, 1950 (Grade II listed 1999); Winthorpe Bridge, Newark, 1962 (Grade II* listed 1998); responsible for planning, design and supervision of construction of major road and bridge projects and for planning and transport studies, incl. M23, Belfast Transportation Plan, Clifton Bridge, Nottingham, Elizabeth Bridge, Cambridge, Itchen Bridge, Southampton. Transport Consultant to Govt SE Jt Planning Team for SE Regional Plan; in charge London Docklands Redevelopment Study; Cost Benefit Study for 2nd Sydney Airport for Govt of Australia; Mem. Cttee on Review of Railway Finances, 1982; UK full mem., EC Article 83 Cttee (Transport), 1982–85; TRRL Visitor on Transport Res. and Safety, 1983–87. Member: Building Research Bd, subseq. Adv. Cttee on Building Research, 1963–66; Civil Engrg EDC on Contracting in Civil Engrg since Banwell, 1965–67; Baroness Sharp's Adv. Cttee on Urban Transport Manpower Study, 1967–69; Commn of Inquiry on Third London Airport, 1968–70; Urban Motorways Cttee, 1969–72; Genesys Bd, 1969–74; Chairman: DoE and Dept of Transport Planning and Transport Res. Adv. Council, 1973–79; DoE Environmental Bd, 1975–78; Mem., TRRL Adv. Cttee on Transport, 1974–80; Mem. Bd, Coll. of Estate Management, Reading Univ., 1979–92. *Publications:* papers and lectures, including: Criteria for the Siting of Major Airports, 4th World Airports Conf., 1973; Highways and Community Response, 9th Rees Jeffreys Triennial Lecture, RTPI, 1975; Environment and the Economic Use of Energy, (Plenary Paper, Hong Kong Transport Conf., 1982); Decision-taking under Uncertainty in the Roads Sector, PIARC Sydney, 1983; Investment in Transport (Keynote address, CIT Conf., 1983); Buses: social enterprise and business (main paper, 9th annual conf., Bus and Coach Council, 1983); Public Road Transport: a time for change (Keynote address, 6th Aust. passenger trans. conf., 1985); Private Enterprise and Highways (Nat. Res. Council conf., Baltimore, 1986); The Expert and the Public: local values and national choice (Florida Univ.), 1987; Travel in London: is chaos inevitable? (LRT), 1989. *Recreations:* carpentry, music, bridge. *Club:* Athenæum.

GOLDSTEIN, Prof. Harvey, FBA 1996; Professor of Social Statistics, University of Bristol, since 2005; *b* 30 Oct. 1939; *s* of Jack and Millicent Goldstein; *m* 1970, Barbara Collinge; one *s*. *Educ:* Oakthorpe Primary Sch., London; Hendon Grammar Sch.; Manchester Univ. (BSc Hons); University College London (Dip. Stats). Lectr in Statistics, Inst. of Child Health, 1964–71; Head of Statistics Section, Nat. Children's Bureau, 1971–76; Prof. of Statistical Methods, Inst. of Educn, Univ. of London, 1977–2005. *Publications:* (jtly) From Birth to Seven, 1972; (jtly) Assessment of Skeletal Maturity and Prediction of Adult Height, 1976; The Design and Analysis of Longitudinal Studies, 1979; (with C. Gipps) Monitoring Children, 1983; Multilevel Statistical Models, 1987, 4th edn 2011; (with T. Lewis) Assessment, 1996; (with A. Leyland) Multilevel Modelling of Health Statistics, 2001; (jtly) Measuring Success: league tables in the public sector, 2012. *Recreations:* playing the flute, walking, cycling, tennis. *Address:* Graduate School of Education, University of Bristol, Bristol BS8 1JA.

GOLDSTEIN, Janet Mary; *see* Ainley, J. M.

GOLDSTEIN, Prof. Joseph Leonard; physician, genetics educator; Paul J. Thomas Professor of Medicine, and Chairman, Department of Molecular Genetics, since 1977, Regental Professor, since 1985, University of Texas Southwestern Medical (formerly Health Science) Center at Dallas (Member of Faculty, since 1972); *b* 18 April 1940; *s* of Isadore E. and Fannie A. Goldstein. *Educ:* Washington and Lee University (BS); Univ. of Texas Health Science Center at Dallas (MD). Intern, then Resident in Medicine, Mass Gen. Hosp., Boston, 1966–88; clinical associate, NIH, 1968–70; Postdoctoral Fellow, Univ. of Washington, Seattle, 1970–72. Harvey Soc. Lecture, Rockefeller Univ., 1977. Member: Sci. Rev. Bd, Howard Hughes Med. Inst., 1978–84, Med. Adv. Bd, 1985–90 (Chm., 1995–2002; Trustee, 2002–); Bd of Dirs, Passano Foundn, 1985–; Sci. Adv. Bd, Welch Foundn, 1986–; Bd of Consultants, Meml Sloan-Kettering Cancer Center, 1992–; Bd of Trustees, Rockefeller Univ., 1994–; Bd of Govs, Scripps Res. Inst., 1996–; Bd of Sci. Advrs, Van Andel Res. Inst., 1996–; Sci. Adv. Cttee, Mass Gen. Hosp., 2005–; Bd of Dirs, Albert and Mary Lasker Foundn, 2007– (Chm., Awards Jury, 1996–). Fellow, Salk Inst., 1983–94. Member, editorial board: Jl Clin. Investigation, 1977–82; Annual Review of Genetics, 1980–85; Arteriosclerosis, 1981–87; Jl Biol Chemistry, 1981–85; Cell, 1983–; Science, 1985–98; Genomics, 1988–; Mol. Biol. of the Cell, 1992–97; Proc. Nat. Acad. Scis, 1992–. Member: Nat. Acad. of Scis (Lounsbery Award, 1979); Amer. Acad. of Arts and Scis, and other bodies; Foreign Mem., Royal Soc., 1991. Hon. DSc: Chicago, 1982; Rensselaer Polytechnic Inst., 1982; Washington and Lee, 1986; Paris-Sud, 1988; Buenos Aires, 1990; Southern Methodist, 1993; Miami, 1996; Rockefeller, 2001; Albany Med. Coll., 2004. Numerous awards from scientific instns, incl. Pfizer Award in Enzyme Chemistry, Amer. Chem. Soc., 1976; award in biol and med. scis, NY Acad. Scis, 1981; Albert Lasker Award in Basic Science (with Michael Brown), 1985; Nobel Prize (with Michael Brown) for Physiology or Medicine, 1985; Amer. Coll. of Physicians Award, 1986; US Nat. Medal of Science, 1988; Distinguished Alumni Award, NIH, 1991; Warren Alpert Foundn Prize, Harvard Med. Sch., 2000; Albany Med. Center Prize in Med. and Biomed. Res., 2003; Distinguished Scientist Award, American Heart Assoc., 2003; Woodrow Wilson Award for Public Service, 2005; Builders of Sci. Award, Research!America, 2007. *Publications:* (jtly) The Metabolic Basis of Inherited Diseases, 5th edn 1983; papers on genetics educn and science subjects. *Address:* Department of Molecular Genetics, University of Texas Southwestern Medical Center at Dallas, 5323 Harry Hines Boulevard, Dallas, TX 75390–9046, USA; 3831 Turtle Creek Boulevard, Apt 22–B, TX 75219, USA.

GOLDSTEIN, Dr Michael, CBE 1997; FRSC; higher education consultant, since 2004; author; *b* 1 May 1939; *s* of Sarah and Jacob Goldstein; *m* 1962, Janet Sandra Skevington (marr. diss. 2009); one *s*. *Educ:* Hackney Downs Grammar School; Northern Polytechnic, London. BSc, PhD, DSc; CChem. Lectr, sen. lectr, principal lectr, Polytechnic of N London, 1963–73; Head of Dept of Chemistry, 1974–83 and Dean of Faculty of Science, 1979–83, Sheffield City Polytechnic; Dep. Dir, Coventry Lanchester Polytechnic, 1983–87; Dir, Coventry Polytechnic, 1987–92; Vice-Chancellor, Coventry Univ., 1992–2004. Mem., cttees and bds, CNAA, 1975–93, incl. Chm., CNAA Chem. Bd, 1978–84; Dep. Chm., Polys and Colls Admissions System, 1989–94; Member: UCAS, 1993–2001 (Dep. Chm., 1995–97; Chm., 1997–2001); Univs and Colls Employers Assoc., 1994–2001. Director: Coventry and Warwicks TEC, 1992–97; City Centre Co. (Coventry) Ltd, 1997–2002 (Vice-Chm., 1999–2002); Coventry and Warwicks Chamber of Commerce, Trng and Enterprise, 1997–2001; CV One Ltd, 2002–08 (Dep. Chm., 2004–08); ContinYou Ltd, 2003–10; Chairman: Creative Partnerships Coventry, 2004–08; Heist Enterprises Ltd, 2004–06; Cre8us, 2008–10. Member: Adv. Cttee, Coventry Common Purpose, 1989–2004; Coventry is making it, 1992–95; Coventry and Warwicks LSC, 2001–07; Mgt Bd, Foundn Degree Forward, 2006–10. Non-exec. Dir, Coventry and Warwicks Partnership NHS Trust, 2006–11 (Chm., 2010–11). Member: RSC Council, 1983–86, 1993–99; other RSC cttees, 1975–99 (Pres., Educn Div., 1993–95; Chm., Educn and Quals Bd, 1995–99); Chairman: Council for Registration of Forensic Practitioners, 2005–08; Higher Educn Develt Gp, States of Jersey, 2005–08; Mem., Skills Bd, States of Jersey, 2008–. Panel Mem., Judicial Appts Commn, 2012–; Mem., HMP Ind. Monitoring Bd, 2012–. Trustee, Community Educn Develt Centre, 1996–2003. Emeritus Gov., Solihull Coll., 2012–. Hon. FCGI 1994. Hon. Fellow, Univ. of Worcester, 1998. Hon. DSc Warwick, 2003. *Publications:* (jtly) Three Lives in Education: reflections of an Anglo-Jewish Family, 2011; (jtly) John Hibbs: his journey by bus, coach and train, 2015; contribs to sci. jls, chapters in review books. *Recreations:* Coventry City FC, exercise, collector of classic Rupert items. *Address:* 19 Ryknild Drive, Thornhill Road, Streetly B74 2AZ. *T:* (0121) 352 0131.

GOLDSTEIN, Nathan Harold; a Judge of the Upper Tribunal (Immigration and Asylum Chamber) (formerly a Vice President, Immigration Appeal Tribunal, later a Senior Immigration Judge, Asylum and Immigration Tribunal), since 2003; *b* 21 Sept. 1944; *s* of Joseph and Fay Goldstein; *m* 1988, Shelley Katrina Sofier; one *s* two *d*. *Educ:* Carmel Coll.; Hasmonean Grammar Sch.; Coll. of Law. Admitted solicitor, 1987; Equity Partner, Nelsons Solicitors, 1988–95. Immigration Adjudicator (pt-time), 1996–97; Special Adjudicator (pt-time), 1997–99; Immigration Adjudicator, 1999–2003; Legal Mem., Special Immigration Appeals Commn, 2005–; an Investigating Judge and Mem., Review Bodies, 2006–. Mem., Law Soc., 1987–. Mem., BFI, 1964–. Mem., Knightsbridge Speakers Club, 1983–2004. *Publications:* papers on immigration matters. *Recreations:* family, cinema, theatre, jazz, football (lifelong Arsenal supporter), my grandchildren, reading (incl. subscribing to endless magazines which I never throw away). *Address:* Upper Tribunal (Immigration and Asylum Chamber), Field House, 15 Breams Buildings, EC4A 1DZ. *E:* Nathan.Goldstein@judiciary.gsi.gov.uk.

GOLDSTEIN, Prof. Raymond Ethan, PhD; FRS 2013; FInstP; Schlumberger Professor of Complex Physical Systems, University of Cambridge, since 2006. *Educ:* Massachusetts Inst. of Technol. (SB Physics and Chem. 1983); Cornell Univ. (MSc Physics 1986; PhD Physics 1988). FInstP 2009; FIMA 2010. Fannie and John Hertz Foundn Grad. Fellow, Cornell Univ., 1983–88; Vis. Scientist, Service de Physique Théorique, Centre d'Etudes Nucléaires de Saclay, Gif-sur-Yvette, France, 1988; Postdoctoral Res., James Franck and Enrico Fermi Insts, Univ. of Chicago, 1988–91; Asst Prof. of Physics, Princeton Univ., 1991–96; University of Arizona: Associate Prof. of Physics and Applied Maths, 1996–2002; Prof. of Physics and Applied Maths, 2002–10. Alfred P. Sloan Res. Fellow, Princeton Univ., 1992–96; NSF Presidential Faculty Fellow, Princeton Univ. and Univ. of Arizona, 1993–98. Fellow, Amer. Physical Soc., 2003. William Hopkins Prize, Cambridge Philosophical Soc., 2011; (jtly) Ig Nobel Prize in Physics, 2012. *Publications:* contribs to jls incl. Procs NAS, Physical Rev. Letters, Jl Fluid Mechanics. *Address:* Department of Applied Mathematics and Theoretical Physics, Centre for Mathematical Sciences, Wilberforce Road, Cambridge CB3 0WA.

GOLDSTEIN-JACKSON, Kevin Grierson; JP; writer; poet; artist; company director; *b* 1946; *s* of H. G. and W. M. E. Jackson; *m* 1975, Jenny Mei Leng, *e d* of Ufong Ng, Malaysia; two *d*. *Educ:* Reading Univ. (BA Phil. and Sociol.); Southampton Univ. (MPhil Law). Staff Relations Dept, London Transport (Railways), 1966; Scottish Widows Pension & Life Assurance Soc., 1967; Prog. Organizer, Southern TV, 1970–73; Asst Prod., HK-TVB, Hong Kong, 1973; freelance writer/TV prod., 1973–75; Head of Film, Dhofar Region TV Service, Sultanate of Oman, 1975–76; Founder and Dir, Thames Valley Radio, 1974–77; Asst to Head of Drama, Anglia TV, 1977–81; Founder, TSW-Television South West: Programme Controller and Dir of Progs, 1981–85; Jt Man. Dir, 1981–82; Chief Exec., 1982–85. Dir of private cos. Gov., Lilliput First Sch., Poole, 1988–93. FRSA 1978; FCMI (FBIM 1982); FInstD 1982; FFA 1988; FRGS 1989. Freeman, City of London, 1996. JP Poole, 1990. *Publications:* 18 books, including: The Right Joke for the Right Occasion, 1973; Encyclopaedia of Ridiculous Facts, 1975; Experiments with Everyday Objects, 1976; Things to make with Everyday Objects, 1978; Magic with Everyday Objects, 1979; Dictionary of Essential Quotations, 1983; Jokes for Telling, 1986; Share Millions, 1989; The Public Speaker's Joke Book, 1991; The Astute Private Investor, 1994; Quick Quips, 2002; contrib. financial and gen. pubns. *Recreations:* writing, TV, films, music, walking, philosophical and sociological investigation.

GOLDSTONE, Prof. Anthony Howard, CBE 2008; FRCP, FRCPE; FRCPath; Professor, Department of Haematology, University College London, since 1999; Director of Services, North London Cancer Network, 2000–09; Chairman, Royal National Orthopaedic Hospital NHS Trust, since 2011; *b* 13 Sept. 1944; *s* of Norman Goldstone and Edith Goldstone; *m* 1970, Jennifer Anne Krantz; one *s* one *d*. *Educ:* Bolton Sch.; St John's Coll., Oxford (BM BCh 1968; MA); University Coll. Hosp. Med. Sch. (Fellow, UCL, 1993). FRCPE 1979; FRCP 1983; FRCPath 1987. Sen. House Officer, Gastrointestinal Unit, Western General Infirmary, Edinburgh, 1969–70; Sen. Registrar in Haematology, Addenbrooke's Hosp., Cambridge, 1973–76; University College Hospital, London: Consultant Haematologist, 1976–2011, now Hon. Consultant Haematologist; Dir, Bone Marrow Transplantation, 1979–2000; Postgrad. Dean, UCH Med. Sch., 1984–87; Chm., UCH Med. Cttee, 1986–88; Med. Dir, 1992–2000, and Dir, Clinical Haematology and Cancer Services, 1997–2000, UCL Hosps NHS Trust. Chm., NE Thames Regl Haematologists, 1988–90. Mem. Bd, European Gp for Bone Marrow Transplantation, 1990–98; Nat. Co-ordinator, UK Adult Leukaemia Trials, 1987–2006. President: British Soc. for Blood and Bone Marrow Transplantation, 1999–2000; British Soc. for Haematology, 2000–01. Lifetime Achievement Award, UCLH NHS Foundn Trust, 2013. *Publications:* (jtly) Leukaemias, Lymphomas and Allied Disorders, 1976; Examination Haematology, 1977; (jtly) Synopsis of Haematology, 1983; Low Grade Lymphoma, 2005; 350 papers on leukaemia, lymphoma, myeloma and stem cell transplantation. *Recreations:* cuddling grandchildren, shouting at the dog, driving fast cars, still waiting for Manchester City to win Champions League. *Address:* 5th Floor, University College Hospital Macmillan Cancer Centre, Huntley Street, WC1E 6AG; 67 Loom Lane, Radlett, Herts WD7 8NX.

GOLDSTONE, David Joseph, CBE 2010; Chairman and Chief Executive, Regalian Properties Plc, 1970–2001; *b* 21 Feb. 1929; *s* of Solomon Goldstone and Rebecca Goldstone (*née* Degotts); *m* 1957, Cynthia (*née* Easton); one *s* two *d*. *Educ:* Dynevor Secondary Sch., Swansea; London School of Economics and Political Science (LLB Hons; Hon. Fellow, 1995). Admitted Solicitor (Hons), 1955. Legal practice, 1955–66. Mem., Capital Adv. Gp (formerly Strategic Capital Investment Panel), Welsh Assembly Govt, 2008–12. Dir, Swansea Sound Commercial Radio Ltd, 1974–96; Special Adviser (Estates) and Hon. Vice-Pres., Wales Millennium Centre Ltd, 2006– (Dir, 1998–2006). Mem., London First (formerly London Forum), 1993–97. Member Council: WNO, 1984–89; Royal Albert Hall, 1999–2006 (Hon. Vice Pres., 2007–). Mem., Court of Govs, LSE, 1985–2009, now Emeritus Gov.; Dep. Chm., Council, London Univ., 2002–06 (Mem., 1994–2006). Mem. Court, 1999–2005, Chm., 2001–05, Hon. Vice-Pres., 2006–, Coram Family. Adviser (Estates): Welsh Rugby Union, 2008–; NHS Wales, 2008–; Ind. Advr to Minister for Business, Enterprise, Technol. and Sci., Welsh Govt, 2008–. Hon. Vice Pres., London Welsh Male Voice Choir, 2007–. Trustee, Civil Liberties Trust, 2009–. *Recreations:* family, reading, sport. *Address:* Flat 4 Grosvenor Hill Court, 15 Bourdon Street, W1K 3PX. *Clubs:* Lansdowne, Bath & Racquets.

GOLDSTONE, David Julian; QC 2006; *b* 30 July 1962; *s* of Leslie and Barbara Goldstone; *m* 1991, Ruby Azhar; three *d*. *Educ:* Haberdashers' Aske's, Elstree; Emmanuel Coll., Cambridge (MA Law); New Coll., Oxford (BCL). Called to the Bar, Middle Temple, 1986; in practice at the Bar, 1989–: Queen Elizabeth Bldg, 1989–2002; Quadrant Chambers, 2002–. First Standing Counsel to the Admiralty, 1999–2006. Lectr (pt-time), LSE and KCL, 1985–88. *Recreations:* classical liberalism (Founding Mem., Soc. of liberal Lawyers, 2006), gardening, especially Mediterranean and sub-tropical plants, chess, Chelsea FC, off piste skiing. *Address:* Quadrant Chambers, 10 Fleet Street, EC4Y 1AU. *T:* (020) 7583 4444, *Fax:* (020) 7583 4455. *E:* david.goldstone@quadrantchambers.com.

GOLDSTONE, David Lionel Alexander, CBE 2013; Chief Executive, London Legacy Development Corporation, since 2014; *b* Manchester, 9 July 1962; *s* of His Honour Peter Walter Goldstone and of Patricia Goldstone; *m* 1990, Jenny Parry; three *s*. *Educ:* Haberdashers' Aske's Sch.; Hertford Coll., Oxford (BA PPE 1984); Univ. of Leicester (PGCE 1985). CIPFA 1990. Teacher of Politics, Econs and History, Whitgift Sch., 1985–86; Public Sector Audit Trainee, Audit Commn, 1986–89; Public Sector Auditor, then Financial Manager, Price Waterhouse, 1989–97 (on secondment to Private Finance Panel, 1995–97); Private Finance

Taskforce, HM Treasury, 1997–2000; Partnerships UK, 2000–07: on secondment as Chief Exec., Partnerships for Health, 2000–01; Finance Dir, 2001–07; on secondment as Chief Exec., Partnerships for Schs, 2004–05; Finance and Prog. Dir, Govt Olympic Exec., DCMS, 2007–12; Chief Finance Officer, TfL, 2013–14. Mem. Bd, Sport England, 2013–. *Recreations:* running, supporting my children's sports, going out with friends. *E:* davidgoldstone@londonlegacy.co.uk.

GOLDSTONE, Prof. Jeffrey, PhD; FRS 1977; Professor of Physics, Massachusetts Institute of Technology, 1977–2004, now Emeritus (Cecil and Ida Green Professor in Physics, 1983–2004; Director, Center for Theoretical Physics, 1983–89); *b* 3 Sept. 1933; *s* of Hyman Goldstone and Sophia Goldstone; *m* 1980, Roberta Gordon; one *s*. *Educ:* Manchester Grammar Sch.; Trinity Coll., Cambridge (MA 1956, PhD 1958). Trinity Coll., Cambridge: Entrance Scholar, 1951; Res. Fellow, 1956; Staff Fellow, 1962; Hon. Fellow, 2000; Cambridge University: Lectr, 1961; Reader in Math. Physics, 1976. Vis. appointments: Institut for Teoretisk Fysik, Copenhagen; CERN, Geneva; Harvard Univ.; MIT; Inst. for Theoretical Physics, Santa Barbara; Stanford Linear Accelerator Center; Lab. de Physique Théorique, L'Ecole Normale Supérieure, Paris; Università di Roma I. Smith's Prize, Cambridge Univ., 1955; Dannie Heineman Prize, Amer. Phys. Soc., 1981; Guthrie Medal, Inst. of Physics, 1983; Dirac Medal, Internat. Centre for Theoretical Physics, 1991. *Publications:* articles in learned jls. *Address:* Department of Physics, (6–407) Massachusetts Institute of Technology, Cambridge, MA 02139, USA. *T:* (office) (617) 2536263. *E:* goldston@mit.edu.

GOLDSTONE, Leonard Clement; QC 1993; **His Honour Judge Goldstone;** a Circuit Judge, since 2002; a Senior Circuit Judge, and Resident Judge, Liverpool, since 2011; *b* 20 April 1949; *s* of Maurice and Maree Goldstone; *m* 1972, Vanessa, *yr d* of Donald Forster, *qv*; three *s*. *Educ:* Manchester Grammar Sch.; Churchill Coll., Cambridge (BA). Called to the Bar, Middle Temple, 1971, Bencher, 2004; a Recorder, 1992–2002. Pres., Mental Health Review Tribunal (Restricted Cases), 1999–2004. Treas., Northern Circuit, 1998–2001. Hon. Recorder, Liverpool, 2011–. *Recreations:* golf, bridge, music, theatre. *Address:* Queen Elizabeth II Law Courts, Derby Square, Liverpool L2 1XA. *Club:* Dunham Forest Golf and Country (Altrincham).

GOLDSWORTHY, Andrew Charles, (Andy), OBE 2000; artist and sculptor; *b* 25 July 1956; *s* of Frederick Goldsworthy and Muriel Goldsworthy (*née* Stangar); *m* 1982, Judith Gregson (marr. diss. 2006); three *s* two *d*. *Educ:* Harrogate Secondary Mod. Sch.; Harrogate High Sch.; Bradford Coll. of Art; Lancashire Poly. Based in SW Scotland, has worked in many different countries, 1978–. Hon. Fellow, Central Lancashire Univ., 1995. Hon. MA Bradford, 1993; Hon. DLit Glasgow, 2005. *Publications:* Touching North, 1989; Leaves, 1989; Hand to Earth, 1990; Andy Goldsworthy, 1990; Snow and Ice Drawings, 1992; Two Autumns, 1993; Stone, 1994; Black Stones—Red Pools, 1995; Wood, 1996; Cairns, 1997; Andy Goldsworthy (Arches), 1998; Arch, 1999; Wall, 2000; Time, 2000; Midsummer Snowballs, 2001; Refuges D'Art, 2002; Passage, 2004; Enclosure, 2007; Ephemeral Works, 2015. *Address:* c/o Galerie Lelong, 528 West 26th Street, New York, NY 10001, USA.

GOLDSWORTHY, Rt Rev. (Arthur) Stanley; general licence to officiate, since 1992, sacramental and pastoral ministry, since 2010, Diocese of The Murray, SA; *b* 18 Feb. 1926; *s* of Arthur and Doris Irene Goldsworthy; *m* 1952, Gwen Elizabeth Reeves; one *s* one *d*. *Educ:* Dandenong High School, Vic; St Columb's Theological Coll., Wangaratta. Deacon 1951, priest 1952; Curate of Wodonga, in charge of Bethanga, 1951–52; Priest of Chiltern, 1952; Kensington, Melbourne, 1955; Yarrawonga, Wangaratta, 1959; Shepparton (and Archdeacon), 1972; Parish Priest of Wodonga, and Archdeacon of Diocese of Wangaratta, 1977; Bishop of Bunbury, 1977–83; an Assisting Bishop to Primate of Australia, 1983–84; Parish Priest: St John, Hendra, Brisbane, 1983–84; Gilgandra, Bathurst, 1986–89; Tailem Bend, Meningie, SA, 1989–92, retired. Chaplain, 1956–77, Visitor, 1977–84, Community of the Sisters of the Church. *Recreations:* music, reading, pastoral care.

GOLDSWORTHY, Julia Anne; Special Adviser, PwC, since 2014; *b* 10 Sept. 1978; *d* of Edward Douglas Goldsworthy and Margaret Joan Goldsworthy; *m* 2012, Christopher Church. *Educ:* Fitzwilliam Coll., Cambridge (BA Hist. 2000); Daiichi Univ. of Econs, Japan (Japanese Exchange Schol.); Birkbeck Coll., London (Postgrad. Cert. Econs 2002). Res. asst to Matthew Taylor, MP, 2001; Sen. Educn/Econ. Advr to Lib Dems, 2003; Res. Advr, Truro Coll. Business Centre, 2004; Regeneration Officer, Carrick DC, 2004–05. MP (Lib Dem) Falmouth and Camborne, 2005–10; contested (Lib Dem) Camborne and Redruth, 2010, 2015. Special Advr to Chief Sec. to the Treasury, 2010–14; Sen. Policy Advr, Hanover Communications, 2014–15. *Recreations:* pilot gig rowing, music (piano and clarinet). *Clubs:* Helford River Pilot Gig; Portreath Surf Lifesaving.

GOLDSWORTHY, Rt Rev. Kay; *see* Gippsland, Bishop of.

GOLDSWORTHY, Rt Rev. Stanley; *see* Goldsworthy, Rt Rev. A. S.

GOLDTHORPE, John Harry, CBE 2002; FBA 1984; Official Fellow, Nuffield College, Oxford, 1969–2002, now Emeritus; Distinguished Senior Research Fellow, Department of Social Policy and Intervention, University of Oxford, since 2012; *b* 27 May 1935; *s* of Harry Goldthorpe and Lilian Eliza Goldthorpe; *m* 1963, Rhiannon Esyllt (*née* Harry); one *s* one *d*. *Educ:* Wath-upon-Dearne Grammar School; University College London (BA Hons 1st Class Mod. Hist.); LSE. MA Cantab; MA Oxon. Asst Lectr, Dept of Sociology, Univ. of Leicester, 1957–60; Fellow of King's College, Cambridge, 1960–69; Asst Lectr and Lectr, Faculty of Economics and Politics, Cambridge, 1962–69. Vis. Prof. of Sociol., Cornell Univ., 2003–06; Vis. Professorial Fellow, Centre for Longitudinal Studies, Inst. of Educn, Univ. of London, 2009–12. Lectures: Fuller, Univ. of Essex, 1979; Marshall, Univ. of Southampton, 1989; Aubert, Oslo Univ., 1993; Geary, Econ. and Social Res. Inst., Dublin, 1998; Cummings, McGill Univ., Montreal, 2001. MAE 1988. For. Mem., Royal Swedish Acad. of Scis, 2001. Hon. Fellow, Eur. Acad. of Sociol., 2012. Hon. FilDr Stockholm Univ., 1990. (Jtly) Polanyi Prize, Hungarian Sociol Assoc., 2010. *Publications:* (with David Lockwood and others): The Affluent Worker: industrial attitudes and behaviour, 1968; The Affluent Worker: political attitudes and behaviour, 1968; The Affluent Worker in the Class Structure, 1969; (with Keith Hope) The Social Grading of Occupations, 1974; (with Fred Hirsch) The Political Economy of Inflation, 1978; Social Mobility and Class Structure in Modern Britain, 1980, 2nd edn 1987; Order and Conflict in Contemporary Capitalism, 1984; (with Hermann Strasser) Die Analyse Sozialer Ungleichheit, 1985; (contrib.) John H. Goldthorpe: consensus and controversy (ed Clark, Modgil and Modgil), 1990; (with Robert Erikson) The Constant Flux: a study of class mobility in industrial societies, 1992; (with Christopher Whelan) The Development of Industrial Society in Ireland, 1992; Causation, Statistics and Sociology, 1999; On Sociology, 2000, 2nd edn, 2 vols, 2007; (with Catherine Bunting and others) From Indifference to Enthusiasm: patterns of arts attendance in England, 2008; Sociology as a Population Science, 2016; papers in Acta Sociologica, American Jl of Sociology, American Sociological Rev., British Jl of Sociology, Comparative Soc. Res., Cultural Trends, Sociological Review, Sociology, European Jl of Sociology, European Sociological Rev., European Economic Rev., Jl of Economic Perspectives, Proc. NAS, National Institute Economic Rev., Poetics, Rationality and Society, Res. in Social Stratification and Mobility, Sociological Methods and Res., Sociologie du Travail, Rev. Française de Sociologie, Jl of Royal Statistical Soc., Quantity and Quality, European Societies, Longitudinal and Life-Course Studies, Jl of Social Policy. *Recreations:* bird watching, computer chess, cryptic crosswords. *Address:* 32 Leckford Road, Oxford OX2 6HX. *T:* (01865) 556602.

GOLLANCZ, Livia Ruth; Chairman, Victor Gollancz Ltd, 1983–89 (Governing Director, Joint Managing Director, 1965–85, Consultant, 1990–92); *b* 25 May 1920; *d* of Victor Gollancz and Ruth Lowy. *Educ:* St Paul's Girls' Sch.; Royal Coll. of Music (ARCM, solo horn). Horn player: LSO, 1940–43; Hallé Orch., 1943–45; Scottish Orch., 1945–46; BBC Scottish Orch., 1946–47; Covent Garden, 1947; Sadler's Wells, 1950–53. Joined Victor Gollancz Ltd as editorial asst and typographer, 1953; Dir, 1954. *Publications:* (ed and introd) Victor Gollancz, Reminiscences of Affection, 1968 (posthumous). *Recreations:* making music, gardening. *Address:* 26 Cholmeley Crescent, N6 5HA. *Club:* Alpine.

GOLOMBOK, Prof. Susan Esther, PhD; Professor of Family Research, and Director of Centre for Family Research, University of Cambridge, since 2006; Fellow, Newnham College, Cambridge, since 2006; *b* 11 Aug. 1954; *d* of Bennie and Kitty Golombok; *m* 1979, Prof. John Neville Rust, *qv*; one *s*. *Educ:* Hutchesons' Girls' Sch.; Univ. of Glasgow (BSc Hons 1976); Inst. of Educn, Univ. of London (MSc Child Develt 1977; PhD 1982). London University Institute of Psychiatry: Res. Psychologist, 1977–83; Lectr in Psychology, 1983–86; City University: Lectr, 1987–89; Sen. Lectr, 1989–90; Dir, Family and Child Psychology Res. Centre, 1989–2005; Reader, 1990–92; Prof. of Psychology, 1992–2005. Trustee: Laura Ashley Foundn, 1998–; One Plus One, 2005–. Freeman, City of London, 1986. *Publications:* (with Valerie Curran) Bottling It Up, 1985; (with John Rust) Modern Psychometrics, 1989, 3rd edn 2009; (with Robyn Fivush) Gender Development, 1994; (with Fiona Tasker) Growing Up in a Lesbian Family, 1997; Parenting: what really counts?, 2000; Modern Families: parents and children in new family forms, 2015; contribs to sci. jls. *Recreations:* reading, cinema, cooking, moving house. *Address:* Howe House, Huntingdon Road, Cambridge CB3 0LX. *T:* (01223) 277797.

GOMBRICH, Prof. Richard Francis; Boden Professor of Sanskrit, Oxford University, 1976–2004; Fellow of Balliol College, Oxford, 1976–2004, now Emeritus Fellow; Academic Director, 2004–09 and since 2011, and President, since 2009, Oxford Centre for Buddhist Studies; *b* 17 July 1937; *s* of Sir Ernst Hans Josef Gombrich, OM, CBE, FBA; *m* 1st, 1964, Dorothea Amanda Friedrich (marr. diss. 1984); one *s* one *d*; 2nd, 1985, Sanjukta Gupta. *Educ:* Magdalen Coll., Oxford (MA, DPhil); Harvard Univ. (AM). Univ. Lectr in Sanskrit and Pali, Oxford Univ., 1965–76; Fellow of Wolfson Coll., 1966–76, Emeritus Fellow, 1977. Stewart Fellow, Princeton Univ., 1986–87. President: Pali Text Soc., 1994–2002 (Hon. Sec., 1982–94); UK Assoc. of Buddhist Studies, 2007–; Hon. Life Mem., Internat. Assoc. of Buddhist Studies, 2008. Editor: Clay Sanskrit Library, 2004–08; Jl of Oxford Centre for Buddhist Studies, 2011–. Hon. Fellow, Internat. Assoc. of Buddhist Studies, 2008–. Hon. DLitt Kalyani Univ., West Bengal, 1991; Hon. DEd De Montfort, 1996; Vacaspati, Tirupati Univ., 1997. S. C. Chakraborty Medal, Asiatic Soc., Calcutta, 1993; Univ. Medal, Warsaw Univ., 1997. Sri Lanka Ranjana (Sri Lanka), 1994. *Publications:* Precept and Practice: traditional Buddhism in the rural highlands of Ceylon, 1971, 2nd edn, as Buddhist Precept and Practice, 1991; (with Margaret Cone) The Perfect Generosity of Prince Vessantara, 1977, 2nd edn 2011; On being Sanskritic, 1978; (ed with Heinz Bechert) The World of Buddhism, 1984; Theravada Buddhism: a social history from ancient Benares to modern Colombo, 1988, 2nd edn 2006; (with G. Obeyesekere) Buddhism Transformed, 1988; How Buddhism Began, 1996, 2nd edn 2006; What the Buddha Thought, 2009; contribs to oriental and anthropological journals. *Recreations:* singing, photography. *Address:* Oxford Centre for Buddhist Studies, Wolfson College, Linton Road, Oxford OX2 6UD.

GOMERSALL, Sir Stephen (John), KCMG 2000 (CMG 1997); HM Diplomatic Service, retired; Group Chairman for Europe and Member of Board, Hitachi Ltd, since 2011 (Chief Executive for Europe, 2004–11); *b* 17 Jan. 1948; *s* of Harry Raymond Gomersall and Helen Gomersall; *m* 1975 (marr. diss. 2006); two *s* one *d*. *Educ:* Forest Sch., Snaresbrook; Queens' Coll., Cambridge (Mod. Langs, MA); Stanford Univ., Calif (MA 1970). Entered HM Diplomatic Service, 1970; Tokyo, 1972–77; Rhodesia Dept, FCO, 1977–79; Private Sec. to Lord Privy Seal, 1979–82; Washington, 1982–85; Econ. Counsellor, Tokyo, 1986–90; Head of Security Policy Dept, FCO, 1990–94; Dep. Perm. Rep., UK Mission to UN, 1994–98; Dir, Internat. Security, FCO, 1998–99; Ambassador to Japan, 1999–2004. Mem., Adv. Council, LSO, 2005–. Hon. DLitt Sheffield, 2009. *Recreations:* music, golf, composing silly songs. *Address:* Hitachi Europe Ltd, Whitebrook Park, Lower Cookham Road, Maidenhead SL6 8YA. *T:* (01628) 585000. *E:* stephen.gomersall@hitachi-eu.com; 24 Windsor Court, Moscow Road, W2 4SN.

GOMEZ, Most Rev. Drexel Wellington, CMG 1994; Assistant Bishop of the Bahamas and the Turks and Caicos Islands, since 2009; Associate Priest, St Agnes, New Providence, since 2009; *b* Jan. 1937; *s* of late Rueben and Wealthy Gomez; *m* Carrol Gomez; four *c*. *Educ:* Codrington Coll., Barbados (DipTh 1957); Durham Univ. (BA 1959). Ordained 1959; parochial work, Bahamas, 1962–64; Tutor, Codrington Coll., 1964–68; Sec. and Treas., dio. of Bahamas, 1970–72; Bishop of Barbados, 1972–93; Asst Bishop, dio. of Bahamas, 1993–95; Bishop of Bahamas and Turks and Caicos Is (formerly Nassau and Bahamas), 1995–2008; Archbishop of the WI, 1998–2008. *Address:* c/o PO Box N–7107, Nassau, Bahamas.

GOMEZ, Jill, (Countess of Northesk); opera and concert singer; *b* New Amsterdam, British Guiana; *d* of late Albert Clyde Gomez and Denise Price Denham; *m* 2010, Earl of Northesk, (Dr Patrick Carnegy), *qv*. *Educ:* Royal Academy of Music (FRAM 1986); Guildhall School of Music, London. Operatic début as Adina in L'Elisir d'Amore with Glyndebourne Touring Opera, 1968 (after winning John Christie Award), then Mélisande, Glyndebourne Fest. Opera, 1969, and has subseq. sung leading rôles, incl. Calisto, 1970, Anne Trulove in The Rake's Progress, 1975, and Helena in A Midsummer Night's Dream, 1984; Royal Opera House début, 1970, creating role of Flora in Tippett's The Knot Garden, subseq. rôles incl. Tytania in A Midsummer Night's Dream, and Lauretta in Gianni Schicchi; rôles include: The Governess in The Turn of the Screw, Ilia in Idomeneo, English Opera Gp; The Governess in The Turn of the Screw, ENO; Jenifer in The Midsummer Marriage, WNO; with Scottish Opera: Pamina, Fiordiligi, The Countess in Figaro; Elizabeth in Elegy for Young Lovers; Anne Trulove; Leïla in Les Pêcheurs de Perles; with Kent Opera: Tatiana in Eugene Onegin, 1977; Violetta in La Traviata, 1979; Amyntas in Il Re Pastore, 1987; Donna Anna in Don Giovanni, 1988; created rôle of the Countess in Thea Musgrave's Voice of Ariadne, Aldeburgh, 1974; created title rôle in William Alwyn's Miss Julie for radio, 1977; title rôle BBC world première, Prokofiev's Maddalena, 1979; created rôle of Duchess, Adès' Powder Her Face, Cheltenham Fest. and Almeida Th., 1995; other rôles incl. Donna Elvira (Ludwigsburg), Cinna in Mozart's Lucio Silla (Zurich), Cleopatra in Giulio Cesare, Donna Anna (Frankfurt), Teresa in Benvenuto Cellini (Lyon), title rôle in Massenet's Thaïs (Wexford), Blanche in Dialogues des Carmélites (Hildesheim), Desdemona in Otello (London); première of Eighth Book of Madrigals, Monteverdi Fest., Zürich Opera, 1979. Also recitalist, progs incl. A Spanish Songbook, Night and Day (cabaret), Fortunes of Love and War, and A Bouquet from the Pleasure Gardens, Cambridge Spring Concerts, 2007; concert repertoire includes Rameau, Bach, Handel (Messiah and cantatas), Haydn's Creation and Seasons, Mozart's Requiem and concert arias, Beethoven's Ninth, Berlioz's Nuits d'Eté, Brahms's Requiem, Fauré's Requiem, Ravel's Shéhérazade, Mahler's Second, Fourth and Eighth Symphonies, Strauss's Four Last Songs, Britten's Les Illuminations, Spring Symphony and War Requiem, Tippett's A Child of Our Time, Messiaen's Poèmes pour Mi, Webern op. 13 and 14 songs, and Schubert songs orch. Webern. Commissioned Cantiga: the song of Inés de Castro (dramatic scena for soprano and orch.) from David Matthews (world première, BBC Prom., 1988). Concerts and recitals in Austria, Belgium, France, Germany, Holland, Hong Kong, Italy, Scandinavia, Spain, Switzerland, Thailand, West Indies, UK and USA; masterclasses; festival appearances incl. Aix-en-Provence, Aldeburgh, Bath, Bergen,

Cheltenham, Edinburgh, Flanders, Florence, Prague, Spoleto, Versailles, and BBC Prom. concerts. Recordings incl. three solo recitals (French, Spanish, and Mozart songs, with John Constable), Monteverdi's Vespro della Beata Vergine 1610, Ravel's Poèmes de Mallarmé, Handel's Admeto, Acis and Galatea, Elvira in Don Giovanni, Fauré's Pelléas et Mélisande, Handel's Ode on St Cecilia's Day, Rameau's La Danse, Britten's Les Illuminations, Canteloube's Songs of the Auvergne, Villa Lobos' Bachianas Brasileiras no 5, Samuel Barber's Knoxville—Summer of 1915, Cabaret Classics (with John Constable), South of the Border (…Down Mexico Way), A Spanish Songbook (with John Constable), Tippett's A Child of Our Time; première recordings: David Matthew's Cantiga: the Song of Inés de Castro, Mahler's Seven Early Songs, Britten's Quatre Chansons Françaises, Tippett's The Knot Garden, Alwyn's Miss Julie, Britten's Blues (incl. songs by Cole Porter), Adès' Powder her Face. *E:* jillgomez@btopenworld.com.

GÓMEZ PICKERING, Diego; Ambassador of Mexico to the Court of St James's, since 2013; *b* Mexico City, 6 Nov. 1977; *s* of Diego Gómez Soler and Patricia Pickering Chouza. *Educ:* Instituto Tecnológico Autónomo de México, Mexico City (BA Internat. Affairs); Columbia Univ. (Master Internat. Affairs). Protocol Officer, Mexican Pavilion, World Expo Hanover, 2000; freelance producer and reporter, Mexico City Bureau, CNN, 2001; Res. Fellow, Centro de Estudios Juan Marinello, Havana, 2001; Res. Fellow, Indian Inst. of Mass Communication, New Delhi, 2002; Consultant, UNESCO Global Alliance for Cultural Diversity, Paris, 2004; Consultant, Solana Consultores, Mexico City, 2005; Political, Cultural and Press Attaché, Embassy of Mexico, Kenya, 2006–07; Communications Consultant, UNRWA, Damascus, 2008–11; Foreign Press Officer, Presidential Office, Mexico City, 2012–13. Internat. Writers Award, Internat. Commn of Writers, 2014. *Publications:* La foto del recuerdo, 2006; Thursdays in Nairobi, 2010; La Primavera de Damasco, 2013. *Recreations:* tennis, cinema, hiking, cycling, travel, languages. *Address:* Embassy of Mexico, 16 St George Street, W1S 1FD. *T:* (020) 7499 8586. *E:* dgomezp@sre.gob.mx. *Clubs:* Royal Automobile, Athenæum, Groucho, Caledonian, Naval and Military, Harry's Bar, Mosimann, St Marks.

GOMME, Robert Anthony, CB 1990; Under Secretary, Department of the Environment, 1981–90, retired; *b* 19 Nov. 1930; *s* of Harold Kenelm Gomme and Alice Grace (*née* Jacques); *m* 1960, Helen Perris (*née* Moore); one *s* one *d*. *Educ:* Colfe's Grammar Sch., Lewisham; London School of Economics, Univ. of London (BScEcon 1955). National Service, Korean War, Corporal with Royal Norfolk Regt, 1951–52; Pirelli Ltd, 1955–66; NEDO, 1966–68; direct entrant Principal, Min. of Public Building and Works, 1968; Asst Sec., DoE, 1972–74, 1979–81; RCDS 1975; Cabinet Office, 1976–79; Department of the Environment: Dir of Defence Services, PSA, 1981–86; Prin. Finance Officer, 1987–90; Chief Exec., Crown Suppliers, 1990. Mem., Commonwealth War Graves Commn, 1981–86. Trustee: Friends of the National Libraries, 1991–97, 1999–2003; London Library, 1992–95, 1996–2000, 2001–05. Hon. Treas., Friends of Greenwich Park, 1992–95. *Publications:* George Herbert Perris: 1866–1920, the life and times of a radical, 2003; contrib. Oxford DNB and to learned jls. *Recreations:* historical research, music, theatre, travel. *Address:* 14 Vanbrugh Fields, Blackheath, SE3 7TZ. *T:* (020) 8858 5148.

GOMPERTZ, (Arthur John) Jeremy; QC 1988; *b* 16 Oct. 1937; *s* of late Col Arthur William Bean Gompertz and Muriel Annie Gompertz (*née* Smith). *Educ:* Beaumont Coll.; Trinity Coll., Cambridge (MA). Called to the Bar, Gray's Inn, 1962, Bencher, 1997; in practice, South East Circuit, 1963–2009; a Recorder, 1987–2002. Counsel for: Metropolitan Police, Stephen Lawrence Inquiry, 1998; Kelly family, Hutton Inquiry, 2003; Humberside Police, Bichard (Soham) Inquiry, 2004. Chm., Mental Health Review Tribunal, 1993–2010. Member: Jockey Club Security and Investigations Cttee, 2002–05; Council, Racehorse Owners' Assoc., 2007–; Disciplinary Rev. Gp, British Horseracing Authy, 2013–. *Recreations:* racing and breeding, travel, ski-ing. *Address:* 5 Essex Court, Temple, EC4Y 9AH. *T:* (020) 7410 2000.

GOMPERTZ, William Edward; Arts Editor, BBC, since 2009; *b* Tenterden, Kent, 25 Aug. 1965; *s* of Dr Hugh Gompertz, OBE and Frances Gompertz; *m* 1995, Kate Anderson; three *s* one *d*. *Educ:* Bedford Sch. Stage hand, Sadler's Wells, 1987–88; runner, Moving Picture Co., 1988–89; Co-Founder, Shots mag., 1990–96; Founder, Purple House, 1996–2002; Dir, Communications, 2002–06, Media, 2006–09, Tate. Mem. Bd, Nat. Campaign for the Arts, 2006–09. Hon. Fellow, Harris Manchester Coll., Oxford. *Publications:* What Are You Looking At?, 2012; Think Like an Artist, 2015. *E:* will.gompertz@bbc.co.uk. *Club:* Army and Navy.

GÖNCZ, Árpád, Hon. GCB 1999; Hon. KCMG 1991; President, Republic of Hungary, 1990–2000; *b* 10 Feb. 1922; *s* of Lajos Göncz and Ilona Heimann; *m* 1947, Mária Zsuzsanna Göntér; two *s* two *d*. *Educ:* Pázmány Péter Univ. (DJ 1944); Univ. of Agric. Scis. Nat. Land Bank, 1942–45; Independent Smallholders' Party: Sec. to Gen. Sec.; Leader, Independent Youth; Editor in Chief, Generation (weekly), 1947–48; jobless from 1948, worked as welder and metalsmith; sentenced to life imprisonment for political activity, 1957; released under general amnesty, 1963; freelance writer and literary translator, esp. of English works, 1963–; Pres., Hungarian Writers' Union, 1989–90; founding mem., Free Initiatives Network, Free Democratic Fedn, Historic Justice Cttee; MP, regional list, 1990; Speaker of Parliament and President *ai*, Republic of Hungary, May–Aug. 1990. József Attila Literary Prize, 1983; Wheatland Prize, 1989; Premio Mediterraneo, 1991. *Publications:* Men of God (novel), 1974; Hungarian Medea (play), Iron Bars (play), 1979; Encounters (short stories), 1980; Balance (6 plays, incl. A Pessimistic Comedy, and Persephone), 1990; Homecoming (short stories), 1991; Shavings (essays), 1991. *Recreations:* reading, walking. *Address:* Kossuth tér 4, 1055 Budapest, Hungary. *T:* 4413550.

GONZÁLEZ MÁRQUEZ, Felipe; Member for Madrid, 1977–2000, for Seville, 2000–04, Congress of Deputies; Prime Minister of Spain and President, Council of Ministers, 1982–96; *b* 5 March 1942; *s* of Felipe González and Juana Márquez; *m* 1969, Carmen Romero Lopez; two *s* one *d*. *Educ:* Univ. of Seville (Law degree); Univ. of Louvaine. Opened first labour law office, Seville, 1966; Spanish Socialist Party (PSOE), 1964–: Mem., Seville Provincial Cttee, 1965–69; Mem., Nat. Cttee, 1969–70; Mem., Exec. Bd, 1970; First Sec., 1974–79, resigned; re-elected, 1979; Sec.-Gen., 1974–97. Former Chm., Socialist Party Group. Co-Chm., Global Progress Council (formerly Fundación Socialismo XXI, then Global Progress Foundn). Grand Cross: Order of Military Merit (Spain), 1984; Order of Isabel the Catholic (Spain), 1996. *Publications:* What is Socialism?, 1976; PSOE, 1977. *Address:* Gobelas 31, 28023 Madrid, Spain.

GONZÁLEZ-PÁRAMO, Dr José Manuel; Professor of Economics, Universidad Complutense, Madrid, since 1988; Member, Executive Board, European Central Bank, 2004–12; *b* Madrid, 9 Aug. 1958. *Educ:* Univ. Complutense, Madrid (Econs degree 1980; PhD Econs 1985); Columbia Univ., New York (MA Econs 1983; MPhil Econs 1984; PhD Econs 1986). Universidad Complutense, Madrid: Res. Asst and Teaching Fellow, 1980–82; Associate Prof. of Econs, 1985–88; Hd, Public Finance Dept, 1986–94. Econ. Advr, Min. of Econ. and Finance, 1985–87; Banco de España: Sen. Econ. Advr, 1989–94; Gov., 1994–2004; Mem., Exec. Bd, 1998–2004. Advisory posts include: World Bank, Washington, 1984, 1989, 2000–02; Internat. Develt Bank, Argentina, 1998; EC, 1989, 1993; Spanish govt agencies, 1985–2004. Prof., World Bank Inst., 2001–02; Vis. Prof., Econs, IESE Business Sch., Univ. of Navarra, 2012–. Mem., Eur. Acad. Scis and Arts, 2000–. *Publications:* (jtly) The Spanish Financial System, 1982; (ed jtly) Argentina: tax policy for stabilization and economic recovery, 1990; (jtly) Public Management, 1997; Costs and Benefits of Fiscal Discipline: the budget stability law in perspective, 2001; (jtly) Taxation of Savings Products in Europe, 2001; (with B. Moreno-Dodson) The Role of the State and Economic Consequences of Alternative Forms of Public Expenditures Financing, 2003; (jtly) Public Economics, 2004; numerous contribs to books and to jls on monetary and financial policy and fiscal and structural policies. *E:* officegonzalezparamo@gmail.com.

GONZI, Hon. Dr Lawrence, KUOM 2004; Prime Minister of Malta, 2004–13; *b* 1 July 1953; *s* of Louis and Inez Gonzi; *m* 1977, Catherine Callus; two *s* one *d*. *Educ:* Univ. of Malta (LLD 1975). Practised law, 1975–88. Mem., Prisons Bd, 1987–88; Chairman: Pharmacy Board, 1987–88; Nat. Commn for Mental Health Reform, 1987–94 and 1994–96; Nat. Commn for Persons with Disabilities, 1987–94 (Pres., 1994–96); Electoral System (Revision) Commn, 1994–95. Chm., Bd of Dirs, Mizzi Orgn, 1989–97. Speaker, House of Reps, 1988–92 and 1992–96; elected to House of Reps, from 2nd Dist, 1996; Opposition Party Whip, Sec. to Parly Gp and Shadow Minister for Social Policy, 1996–98; Minister for Social Policy and Leader, House of Reps, 1998–99, Dep. Prime Minister, 1999–2004, Minister of Finance, 2004–08. Sec.-Gen., 1997–98, Dep. Leader, 1999–2004, Nationalist Party. Gen. Pres., Malta Catholic Action Movement, 1976–86.

GOOBY, Peter Frederick T.; *see* Taylor-Gooby.

GOOCH, Anthony John; HM Diplomatic Service, retired; Deputy High Commissioner and Economic and Commercial Counsellor, Singapore, 1997–2000; *b* 28 Nov. 1941; *s* of John Edgar Gooch and Mary Elizabeth (*née* Bricknell); *m* 1966, Jennifer Jane Harrison (*d* 1984); one *d*; *m* 1988, Cynthia Lee Barlow. *Educ:* Latymer Upper Sch.; St Catharine's Coll., Cambridge (BA Hist.); Open Univ. (MA 2002). Pubns Editor, Europa Pubns, 1964–70; joined FCO, 1970: attachment to SEATO, Bangkok, 1972–74; Second, later First, Sec., FCO, 1974–80; First Secretary: (Economic), Stockholm, 1980–83; (Labour), Pretoria, 1984–88; FCO, 1988–92; (Commercial), Warsaw, 1992–96; Dir, Trade Promotion, and Consul-Gen., Warsaw, 1996–97. Inquiry Sec., later Manager (panellist), Competition Commn, 2002–14. *Recreations:* tennis, gardening, cinema history. *Address:* 22 Trinity Place, Windsor, Berks SL4 3AT. *Club:* Windsor Lawn Tennis.

GOOCH, Brig. Sir Arthur (Brian Sherlock Heywood), 14th Bt *cr* 1746, of Benacre Hall, Suffolk; *b* 1 June 1937; *s* of late Col Brian Sherlock Gooch, DSO, TD and Monica Mary (*née* Heywood); *S* cousin, 2008; *m* 1963, Sarah Diana Rowena Perceval, JP; two *d*. *Educ:* Eton; RMA Sandhurst. Comdg The Life Guards, 1978–81. Hon. Col, Kent and Co. of London Yeomanry (Sharpshooters), 1992–99. DL Wilts 1998. *Recreation:* fishing. *Heir:* *b* Thomas Sherlock Heywood Gooch [*b* 12 Nov. 1943; *m* 1971, Elizabeth Clarice Joan Peyton; one *s* one *d*]. *Address:* Manor Farmhouse, Chitterne, Wilts BA12 0LG. *Club:* Army and Navy.

GOOCH, Graham Alan, OBE 1991; DL; Batting Coach, England cricket team, 2009–14; *b* 23 July 1953; *s* of late Alfred and of Rose Gooch; *m* 1976, Brenda Daniels; three *d* (incl. twins). *Educ:* Leytonstone. Batsman and bowler; first played for Essex CCC, 1973, Captain, 1986–94, retired, 1997; Member, England Test team, 1975–82 and 1986–Jan. 1995 (retired); played in S Africa, 1982; Captain of England, July 1988 and Sept. 1989–1993; 333 against India, highest score by a Test captain, 1990; 20 Test centuries; record no of runs (8900) in English Test cricket, 1995. England A team manager, Kenya and Sri Lanka tour, 1997–98; Manager, England Test tour, Australia, 1998–99. Chief Coach, 2001–05, Batting Coach, 2005–11, Essex CCC. Mem., Selection Panel, ECB, 1997–99. DL Essex, 2009. Hon. DArts E London, 2011. *Publications:* Batting, 1980; (with Alan Lee) My Cricket Diary 1981, 1982; (with Alan Lee) Out of the Wilderness, 1985; Testing Times (autobiog.), 1991; (with Frank Keating) Gooch: My Autobiography, 1995. *Address:* c/o England and Wales Cricket Board, Lord's Cricket Ground, NW8 8QZ.

GOOCH, Prof. John, PhD; FRHistS; Professor of International History, Leeds University, 1992–2010; *b* 25 Aug. 1945; *s* of George Gooch and Doris Evelyn (*née* Mottram); *m* 1967, Catherine Ann Staley; one *s* one *d*. *Educ:* Brockenhurst County High Sch.; King's Coll., Univ. of London (BA Hons History, class 1, 1966; PhD War Studies 1969). FRHistS 1975. Asst Lectr in History, 1966–67, Asst Lectr in War Studies, 1969, KCL; University of Lancaster: Lectr in History, 1969–81; Sen. Lectr, 1981–84; Reader in History, 1984–88; Prof. of History, 1988–92. Sec. of the Navy Sen. Res. Fellow, US Naval War Coll., 1985–86; Vis. Prof. of Military and Naval History, Yale Univ., 1988; Associate Fellow, Davenport Coll., Yale, 1988. Chm. of Council, Army Records Soc., 1983–2000; Vice-Pres., RHistS, 1990–94. Editor, Jl of Strategic Studies, 1978–2006; Gen. Editor, Internat. Relations of the Great Powers; Member of Editorial Board: European History Qly; Diplomacy and Statecraft; Terrorism and Small Wars; Security Studies; War in History. Premio Internazionale di Cultura, Città di Anghiari, 1983. Kt, Order of Vila Viçosa (Portugal), 1991; Cavaliere dell'Ordine della Stella della Solidarietà Italiana (Italy), 2010. *Publications:* The Plans of War: the general staff and British military strategy *c.* 1900–1916, 1974; Armies in Europe, 1980; The Prospect of War: studies in British defence policy 1847–1942, 1981; Politicians and Defence: studies in the formulation of British defence policy 1847–1970, 1981; Strategy and the Social Sciences, 1981; Military Deception and Strategic Surprise, 1982; Soldati e Borghesi nell'Europa Moderna, 1982; Army, State and Society in Italy 1870–1915, 1989 (trans. Italian); Decisive Campaigns of the Second World War, 1989; (with Eliot A. Cohen) Military Misfortunes: the anatomy of failure in war, 1990; Airpower: theory and practice, 1995; The Boer War: direction, experience and image, 2000; Mussolini and his Generals: the armed forces and fascist foreign policy, 1922–1940, 2007; The Italian Army and the First World War, 2014. *Recreation:* Italian food and wine. *Address:* Wellfield House, 15 Rutland Avenue, Matlock, Derbyshire DE4 3GQ. *T:* (01629) 593527.

GOOCH, Sir Miles (Peter), 6th Bt *cr* 1866, of Clewer Park, Berkshire; *b* 3 Feb. 1963; *s* of Sir Trevor Sherlock Gooch, 5th Bt and Denys Anne (*née* Venables); *S* father, 2003; *m* 2000, Louise Alicia Spiret; three *d*. *Educ:* Victoria Coll., Jersey; Preston Poly. (BEng). *Heir:* *kinsman* John Daniel Gooch, VRD [*b* 9 Dec. 1935; *m* 1972, Ann Patricia Lubbock; two *d*].

GOOD, Anthony Bruton Meyrick, OBE 2014; FCIPR; Group Chairman: Cox & Kings (UK) Ltd (formerly Cox and Kings (India) Ltd, later Cox & Kings Ltd), since 1975 (Director, since 1971); Flagship Group Ltd (formerly Millbank), 1994–2011; *b* 18 April 1933; *s* of Meyrick George Bruton Good and Amy Millicent Trussell; *m* (marr. diss.); one *d* (and one *d* decd); *m* 2010, Iris Shafir, PhD. *Educ:* Felsted Sch. Mgt Trainee, Distillers Gp, 1950–52; Editorial Asst, Temple Press Ltd, 1952–55; PRO, Silver City Airways, 1955–60; Founder Chm., Good Relations Gp plc, 1961–88; Chairman: Good Relations (India) Ltd, 1988–; Good Consultancy Ltd, 1988–; Tulip Star Hotels Ltd, 1989–; Outright Marketing and Distribution Ltd, 1999–2014; Outright Communication Ltd, 2008–15; I-Connections Ltd, 2007–; Obento Ltd, 2004–13; Benney Watches plc, 2007–13; Director: Nutrahealth plc, 2005– (Chm., 2011–); DQ Entertainment plc, 2008–13. Dir, UK India Business Council, 2005–15 (Chm., India, 2009–13). FCIPR (FIPR 1975); FInstD 1994. *Recreations:* travel, reading, theatre. *Address:* Clench House, Wootton Rivers, Marlborough, Wilts SN8 4NT. *T:* (01672) 810126, *Fax:* (01672) 810869. *Club:* Royal Automobile.

GOOD, Diana Frances; Commissioner, Independent Commission for Aid Impact, 2011–15; Chair, Mary Ward Settlement and Mary Ward Legal Centre, since 2008; *b* 16 July 1956; *d* of Michael and Valerie Hope; *m* 1981, Alexander Good; four *d*. *Educ:* Croydon High Sch., GPDST; St Anne's Coll., Oxford (BA Juris.); Chester Coll. of Law; Univ. of Aix-en-Provence (Dip. Etudes Supérieures). Admitted solicitor, 1981; a Recorder, 2001–11; joined Linklaters, 1979: Litigation Partner, 1988–2008; Litigation Partner, Brussels, 1989–92; Member: Finance and Policy Cttee, 1993–96; Diversity Cttee, 2000–08; Internat. Bd, 2001–04. Mem., Adv. Bd, Advocates for Internat. Develt, 2007–11. Trustee: British Inst.

Internat. and Comparative Law, 2000–08; Access to Justice Foundn, 2008–12. Mem. Bd, Red Shift Theatre Co., 2002–. *Recreations:* holidays/travelling, theatre and cinema, cycling, including 450 miles in NW Vietnam for Medical Foundation for Victims of Torture, reading and discussion with Book Club members.

GOOD, Sir John James Griffen, (Sir Ian), Kt 2008; CBE 1992; CA; Chairman, Edrington Group, 1994–2013 (Director, 1979–2013); *b* Renfrewshire. CA 1967. Price Waterhouse, 1967–69; joined Edrington Holdings Ltd, 1969: Man. Dir, Robertson and Baxter Ltd; Chief Exec., 1989–2004. Former Chm., Scottish Industrial Develt Adv. Bd. Chairman: Hamilton Park Racecourse; Scottish Racing Mktg Ltd. Non-exec. Dir, Horserace Totalisator Bd, 2006–08. Former Chm., Robertson Trust. Former Chm., Scotch Whisky Assoc. Dep. Sen. Steward, Jockey Club (Mem., 2005–; Steward, 2007–). Trustee, Racing Foundation, 2012–.

GOOD, Rt Rev. Kenneth Raymond; *see* Derry and Raphoe, Bishop of.

GOOD, Ven. Kenneth Roy; Archdeacon of Richmond, 1993–2006, now Emeritus; *b* 28 Sept. 1941; *s* of Isaac Edward Good and Florence Helen Good (*née* White); *m* 1970, Joan Thérèse Bennett; one *s* one *d*. *Educ:* Stamford Sch.; King's Coll., London (BD 1966; AKC). Ordained deacon 1967, priest 1968; Asst Curate, St Peter, Stockton on Tees, 1967–70; Missions to Seamen: Port Chaplain, Antwerp, 1970–74, Kobe, 1974–79; Asst Gen. Sec., 1979–85; Vicar of Nunthorpe, 1985–93; RD of Stokesley, 1989–93. Hon. Canon, Kobe, 1985. *Recreations:* gardening, photography. *Address:* 18 Fox Howe, Coulby Newham, Middlesbrough TS8 0RU.

GOODACRE, Peter Eliot, RD 1979, with clasp 1991; DL; chartered surveyor; Principal, College of Estate Management, Reading, 1992–2007, Hon. Fellow, 2007; *b* 4 Nov. 1945; *s* of late Edward Leslie Goodacre and of Cicely May (*née* Elliott); *m* 1971, Brita Christina Forsling; one *d* (and one *d* decd). *Educ:* Kingston Grammar Sch.; Coll. of Estate Management; Loughborough Univ. of Technology (MSc). FRICS 1980. Commnd RNR, 1965; Lt Comdr, 1979. In private practice, 1966–69; Lecturer: Coll. of Estate Mgt, 1970–73; Univ. of Reading, 1973–78, Sen. Lectr 1978–83; Vice-Principal, Coll. of Estate Mgt, 1984–92. Mem., Gen. Council, RICS, 1986–2009 (Vice-Pres., 2005–08, Sen. Vice-Pres., 2007–08, Pres., 2008–09); Vice-Chm., 1997–98, Pres., 1998–99, Quantity Surveyors' Divl Council). Mem., Gtr London RFCA (Chm., Works and Bldgs Sub-Cttee, 1997–2003). Chm., James Butcher Housing Assoc., 2006–10; Member: Bd, Southern Housing Assoc., 2006–10; NHBC Council, 2009–14; Bd, Central and Cecil Housing Trust, 2013–. Non-exec. Dir, Thames Valley Strategic Health Authy, 2004–06. Trustee: Harold Samuel Educn Trusts, 1992–; Guy Bigwood Trust, 2007–09; Sonning Volunteer Fire Brigade Trust, 2010–; Vice Patron, Commonwealth Housing Trust, 2010–. Pres., Berks, St John Ambulance, 2010–14. Chairman: Friends of St Andrew's Ch, Sonning, 2010–14 (Trustee, 2014–); Sonning Volunteer Fire Bde Trust, 2014–. FCIOB 1999. Freeman, City of London, 1994; Liveryman, Chartered Surveyors' Co., 1995–. DL Berks, 2011. *Publications:* Formula Method of Price Adjustment for Building Contracts, 1978, 2nd edn 1987; Cost Factors of Dimensional Co-ordination, 1981; Worked Examples in Quantity Surveying Measurement, 1982. *Recreations:* family, home and garden, visiting Sweden. *Address:* Kingsmead, West Drive, Sonning, Berks RG4 6GE. *T:* (0118) 969 2422. *Clubs:* Athenæum (Mem., Gen. Cttee, 2009–12), MCC; Phyllis Court (Henley).

GOODALE, Prof. Melvyn Alan, PhD; FRS 2013; FRSC 2001; Canada Research Chair in Visual Neuroscience, since 2001, and Director, Brain and Mind Institute, since 2005, University of Western Ontario; *b* Leigh-on-Sea, Essex, 22 Jan. 1943; *s* of Lawrence and Alice Goodale; *m* 1982, Joan Finegan; one *s* two *d*. *Educ:* Univ. of Alberta (BA Psychol. 1963); Univ. of Calgary (MA 1966); Univ. of Western Ontario (PhD Psychol. 1969). Postdoctoral Fellow, Univ. of Oxford, 1969–71; Lectr, Univ. of St Andrews, 1971–77; Associate Prof., 1977–83, Prof., 1983–, Univ. of Western Ont. Hon. Fellow, Durham Univ., 2003. *Publications:* (with A. D. Milner) The Visual Brain in Action, 1995, 2nd edn 2006; (with A. D. Milner) Sight Unseen: an exploration of conscious and unconscious vision, 2004, 2nd edn 2013; contrib. papers to jls. *Recreations:* walking, cinema, bicycling, hiking, travel. *Address:* Brain and Mind Institute, Natural Science Centre, University of Western Ontario, London, ON N6A 5B7, Canada. *T:* 5196612070, *Fax:* 5196613613. *E:* mgoodale@uwo.ca.

GOODALL, Sir (Arthur) David (Saunders), GCMG 1991 (KCMG 1987; CMG 1979); HM Diplomatic Service, retired; Chairman, Leonard Cheshire (the Leonard Cheshire Foundation), 1995–2000 (Chairman, International Committee, 1992–95); *b* 9 Oct. 1931; *oc* of late Arthur William and Maisie Josephine Goodall; *m* 1962, Morwenna, *y d* of late Percival George Beck Peecock; two *s* one *d*. *Educ:* Ampleforth; Trinity Coll., Oxford (1st Cl. Hons Lit. Hum., 1954; MA; Hon. Fellow, 1992). Served 1st Bn KOYLI (2nd Lieut), 1955–56. Entered HM Foreign (subseq. Diplomatic) Service, 1956; served at: Nicosia, 1956; FO, 1957–58; Djakarta, 1958–60; Bonn, 1961–63; FO, 1963–68; Nairobi, 1968–70; FCO, 1970–73; UK Delegn, MBFR, Vienna, 1973–75; Head of Western European Dept, FCO, 1975–79; Minister, Bonn, 1979–82; Dep. Sec., Cabinet Office, 1982–84; Dep. Under-Sec. of State, FCO, 1984–87; High Comr to India, 1987–91. Co-Chm., Anglo-Irish Encounter, 1992–97; Chm., British-Irish Assoc., 1997–2002. Vis. Prof., Inst. of Irish Studies, Univ. of Liverpool, 1996–2012. Vice-Chm., Council, Durham Univ., 1997–2000; Chairman: Governing Body, Heythrop Coll., Univ. of London, 2000–06; Abbot's Adv. Cttee, Ampleforth Coll., 2004–10; Gov., Westminster Cathedral Choir Sch., 1994–2007. Pres., Irish Genealogical Res. Soc., 1992–2010 (Fellow, 1978). Fellow, Heythrop Coll., Univ. of London, 2006. Hon. LLD Hull, 1994. Distinguished Friend of Oxford University, 2001. KSG 2007. *Publications:* Remembering India, 1997; Ryedale Pilgrimage, 2000; (with Gail Hudson) Seeds of Hope, 2013; contribs to: Ampleforth Jl; Tablet; Irish Genealogist; The Past. *Recreation:* painting in watercolours. *Address:* Greystones, Ampleforth, North Yorks YO62 4DU. *Clubs:* Garrick, Oxford and Cambridge.

GOODALL, Caroline Mary Helen; Consultant and Senior Adviser, Herbert Smith Freehills (formerly Herbert Smith) LLP, since 2009; *b* Dewsbury, 22 May 1955; *d* of late Peter Goodall, CBE, TD and Sonja Jeanne Goodall; *m* 1983, Vesey John Munnings Hill. *Educ:* Queen Ethelburga's Sch., Harrogate; Newnham Coll., Cambridge (BA 1977); Harvard Business Sch. (MA). Admitted solicitor; Herbert Smith LLP: Partner, 1987–2009; Global Hd, Corporate Practice, 2000–05. Non-executive Director: SVG Capital plc, 2010–14; Grant Thornton LLP, 2010–; Next plc, 2013–. Associate Fellow, Newnham Coll., Cambridge, 2003–08. Trustee, Woodland Trust, 2009–12; Mem. Council, Nat. Trust, 2010– (Trustee, 2012–). MInstD. FRSA. *Recreations:* tennis, walking, sailing, theatre. *Address:* Herbert Smith Freehills LLP, Exchange House, Primrose Street, EC2A 2EG. *T:* (020) 7374 8000. *E:* caroline.goodall@hsf.com. *Clubs:* Roehampton, Athenæum; Brancaster Staithe Sailing.

GOODALL, Sir David; *see* Goodall, Sir A. D. S.

GOODALL, David William, PhD (London); DSc (Melbourne); ARCS, DIC, FLS; FRSB; Hon. Research Fellow (formerly Hon. Research Associate), Centre for Ecosystem Management, Edith Cowan University, since 1998; *b* 4 April 1914; *s* of Henry William Goodall; *m* 1st, 1940, Audrey Veronica Kirwin (marr. diss. 1949); one *s*; 2nd, 1949, Muriel Grace King (marr. diss. 1974); two *s* one *d*; 3rd, 1976, Ivy Nelms (*née* Palmer). *Educ:* St Paul's Sch.; Imperial Coll. of Science and Technology (BSc). Research under Research Inst. of Plant Physiology, on secondment to Cheshunt and East Malling Research Stns, 1935–46; Plant Physiologist, W African Cacao Research Inst., 1946–48; Sen. Lectr in Botany, University of Melbourne, 1948–52; Reader in Botany, University Coll. of the Gold Coast, 1952–54; Prof. of Agricultural Botany, University of Reading, 1954–56; Dir, CSIRO Tobacco Research Institute, Mareeba, Qld, 1956–61; Senior Principal Research Officer, CSIRO Div. of Mathematical Statistics, Perth, Australia, 1961–67; Hon. Reader in Botany, Univ. of Western Australia, 1965–67; Prof. of Biological Science, Univ. of California Irvine, 1966–68; Dir, US/IBP Desert Biome, 1968–73; Prof. of Systems Ecology, Utah State Univ., 1969–74; Sen. Prin. Res. Scientist, 1974–79, Sen. Res. Fellow, 1979–83, Land Resources Management Div., CSIRO; Hon. Fellow, CSIRO Div. of Wildlife and Ecology, 1983–98. Hon. Dr in Natural Scis, Trieste Univ., 1990. Gold Medal, Ecological Soc. of Australia, 2008. *Publications:* Chemical Composition of Plants as an Index of their Nutritional Status (with F. G. Gregory), 1947; ed, Evolution of Desert Biota, 1976; editor-in-chief, Ecosystems of the World (series), 1977–2005; co-editor: Productivity of World Ecosystems, 1975; Simulation Modelling of Environmental Problems, 1977; Arid-land Ecosystems: Structure, Functioning and Management, vol. 1 1979, vol. 2 1981; Mediterranean-type Shrublands, 1981; Hot Deserts, 1985; numerous papers in scientific jls and symposium vols. *Recreations:* acting, reading. *Address:* Centre for Ecosystem Management, Edith Cowan University, 100 Joondalup Drive, Joondalup, WA 6027, Australia.

GOODALL, Howard Lindsay, CBE 2011; composer and broadcaster; *b* 26 May 1958; *s* of Geoffrey and Marion Goodall. *Educ:* New College Sch.; Stowe Sch.; Lord Williams' Sch., Thame; Christ Church, Oxford (MA 1979). ARCO 1975. Freelance composer, 1976–. Nat. Ambassador for Singing, 2007–11. *TV and film themes/scores* include: Blackadder; Red Dwarf; The Vicar of Dibley; The Thin Blue Line; 2.4 Children; Mr Bean; Rowan Atkinson in Revue; Q.I.; The Catherine Tate Show; *compositions* include: The Hired Man, 1984 (Ivor Novello Award for best musical, 1985); Girlfriends, 1987; Days of Hope, 1990; Silas Marner, 1993; Missa Aedis Christi, 1993; Marlborough Canticles, 1995; In Memoriam Anne Frank, 1995; The Kissing-Dance, 1998; We are the Burning Fire, 1998; The Dreaming, 2001; O Lord God of Time and Eternity, 2003; The Gathering Storm, 2003; Jason and the Argonauts, 2004; A Winter's Tale, 2005; Mr Bean's Holiday, 2007; Two Cities, 2006; Winter Lullabies, 2007; Eternal Light: a requiem, 2008 (Composer of the Year, Classical Brit Awards, 2009); Enchanted Voices: the beatitudes, 2009; Into the Storm, 2009; The Seasons, 2009; Love Story, 2010; Rigaudon for Diamond Jubilee, 2012; Sure of the Sky - Des Himmels sicher, commnd to be performed at St Symphorien Mil. Cemetery, 2014; (musical) Bend it Like Beckham, 2015. Presenter: BBC: Choir of the Year, 1990–; The Story of Music, 2013; Channel Four: Howard Goodall's Organ Works (RTS Award for best original title music), 1997; Four Goes to Glyndebourne, 1997–98; Howard Goodall's Choir Works, 1998; Howard Goodall's Big Bangs, 2000 (BAFTA Award, Huw Weldon Award for Arts, Religion, Hist. and Sci., Peabody Award for Mass Journalism and Communication, IMZ TV Award for Best Documentary); Howard Goodall's Great Dates, 2002; Howard Goodall's Twentieth Century Greats, 2004; How Music Works, 2006. Hon. DMus Bishop Grosseteste UC, 2006; Hon. DArts Bolton, 2008. Gold Badge, BACS, 2006; Making Music Sir Charles Grove Prize for Outstanding Contribn to British Music, 2007. *Publications:* The Story of Music, 2013. *Address:* c/o Caroline Chignell, PBJ Management, 22 Rathbone Street, W1T 1LG. *T:* (020) 7287 1112, *Fax:* (020) 7287 1191. *E:* PA@howardgoodall.info. *W:* www.howardgoodall.co.uk.

GOODALL, Dame Jane; *see* Goodall, Dame V. J.

GOODALL, Rt Rev. Jonathan Michael; *see* Ebbsfleet, Bishop Suffragan of.

GOODALL, Rt Rev. Lindsay; *see* Urwin, Rt Rev. L. G.

GOODALL, Patrick John; QC 2014; *b* Bury St Edmunds, 1 Jan. 1971; *s* of Robert Christopher Goodall and Bridget Anne Goodall (*née* Sadlier); *m* 1999, Emily Kate Bainbridge; one *s* three *d*. *Educ:* St Joseph's Coll., Ipswich (Hd of Sch.); Univ. of Southampton (LLB); Brasenose Coll., Oxford (BCL). Admitted solicitor, 1997; Freshfields, 1995–97; called to the Bar, Inner Temple, 1998; in practice as barrister, specialising in commercial law, 1998–; Jun. Counsel to the Crown (A Panel), 2011–14. *Publications:* (ed jtly) Commercial Court Procedure, 2001; (contrib.) Bullen and Leake and Jacob's Precedents of Pleadings, 2001, 17th ed 2012; (contrib.) Law of Bank Payments, 2004, 4th edn 2010; (contrib.) The Law of Privilege, 2006, 2nd edn 2011. *Recreations:* family, cinema, Isles of Scilly. *Address:* Fountain Court Chambers, Fountain Court, Temple, EC4Y 9DH. *T:* (020) 7583 3335, *Fax:* (020) 7353 0329. *Club:* Royal Automobile.

GOODALL, Air Marshal Sir Roderick Harvey, KBE 2001 (CBE 1990); CB 1999; AFC 1981, Bar 1987; Chief of Staff, Component Command Air North, NATO, 1999–2003; *b* 19 Jan. 1947; *s* of late Leonard George Harvey Goodall and Muriel Goodall (*née* Cooper); *m* 1973, Elizabeth Susan Haines; two *d*. *Educ:* Elizabeth Coll., Guernsey; RAF Coll., Cranwell. FRAeS 1997–2015. Commissioned 1968; served Bahrain, UK and Germany, to 1981; RAF Staff Coll., 1981; PMC Barnwood, 1982; OC 16 Sqn, Laarbruch, 1983–85; MoD, 1986–87; Station Comdr, RAF Bruggen, 1987–89; RCDS 1990; Station Comdr, RAF Detachment, Bahrain, 1990; Dir, Air Offensive and Air Force Ops, MoD, 1991–93; AOC No 2 Gp, 1994–96; COS Perm. Jt HQ, 1996–98; Leader, RAF Officers Branch Structure Review Team, 1998–99. Pres., RAF Golf Assoc., 1995–2003. Trustee, Lloyds TSB Foundn for the Channel Isles, 2005–11. *Recreations:* golf, photography, family. *Address:* c/o Lloyds Bank, 2 North Gate, Sleaford, Lincs NG34 7BL. *Club:* Royal Air Force.

GOODALL, Prof. Roger Morgan, PhD; FIET, FIMechE, FREng; Professor of Control Systems Engineering, Loughborough University, since 1994; Professor of Control, Institute of Railway Research, University of Huddersfield, since 2013; *b* Finchley, 7 May 1946; *s* of Philip Morgan and Gwynedd Marie Goodall; *m* 1987, Lesley Allison Page; one *s* three *d*. *Educ:* Ashville Coll., Harrogate; Peterhouse, Cambridge (BA 1968); Loughborough Univ. (PhD 1989). FIET (FIEE 1992); FIMechE 1995; FREng 2007. Jun. Engr, GEC-AEI Electronics Ltd, 1968–70; PSO, British Rail Res., Derby, 1970–82; Lectr, 1982–87, Sen. Lectr, 1987–94, Electronic & Electrical Engrg Dept, Loughborough Univ. Chm., UK Automatic Control Council, 2005–08. Member: Rolls-Royce Electrical Controls Systems and Electronics (formerly Electrical and Controls) Adv. Bd, 2003–13; Eur. Rail Res. Adv. Council, 2003–; Railway Tech. Strategy Leadership Gp (formerly Railway Tech. Strategy Adv. Gp), 2007–12; Scientific and Tech. Adv. Bd, Austrian Centre of Competence in Mechatronics, 2008–12. Vice-Pres., IFAC, 2008–14. Chm., Railway Div., IMechE, 2009–10 (Vice-Chm., 2005–09). James Watt Internat. Gold Medal, IMechE, 2011. *Publications:* Digital Control, 1991; contrib. learned jls incl. Proc. IEE, Proc. IMechE, Vehicle System Dynamics, Trans IEEE. *Recreations:* ski-ing, snowboarding, long walks with dogs, GPS gadgets, dining out, grandchildren. *Address:* School of Electronic, Electrical and Systems Engineering, Loughborough University, Ashby Road, Loughborough, Leics LE11 3TU. *T:* (01509) 227009, *Fax:* (01509) 227108. *E:* R.M.Goodall@lboro.ac.uk.

GOODALL, Dame (Valerie) Jane, DBE 2003 (CBE 1995); PhD; Scientific Director, Gombe Wildlife Research Institute, Tanzania, since 1967; *b* 3 April 1934; *er d* of Mortimer Herbert Morris-Goodall and Vanne Morris-Goodall (*née* Joseph); *m* 1st, 1964, Baron Hugo van Lawick (marr. diss. 1974); one *s*; 2nd, 1975, Hon. Derek Bryceson, Tanzanian MP (*d* 1980). *Educ:* Uplands Sch., Bournemouth; Cambridge Univ. (PhD 1965). Sec., Oxford Univ., 1952; worked as asst to Louis and Mary Leakey, Olduvai Gorge, 1957; engaged in res. into behaviour of chimpanzees, Gombe Stream Game Reserve, now Gombe Nat. Park, 1960–; res. in social behaviour of Spotted Hyena, Ngorongoro, 1968–69; dir. res. on behaviour of Olive Baboon, Gombe, 1972–82. Vis. Prof., Dept of Psychiatry and Program of Human Biology, Stanford Univ., 1971–75; Hon. Vis. Prof. in Zoology, Dar es Salaam Univ., 1973–; A. D. White Prof.-at-Large, Cornell Univ., 1996–. Vice-Pres., Animal Welfare Inst., BVA, 1987–; Mem. Adv. Bd, Albert Schweitzer Inst. for the Humanities, 1991–; Patron, Voiceless (Australia); Trustee, Jane Goodall Insts in UK, USA and Canada, and member of many other conservation and wildlife socs and foundns. Documentary films for television on research with chimpanzees incl. Fifi's Boys, BBC, 1995. Hon. FRAI 1991. UN Messenger for Peace, 2002–. Many hon. degrees. Numerous awards and prizes including: Franklin Burr Award for contrib. to Science, 1963, 1964, Centennial Award, 1988, Hubbard Medal, 1995, Nat. Geographic Soc.; Conservation Award, NY Zool Soc., 1974; Gold Medal, Soc. of Women Geographers, 1990; Kyoto Prize, 1990; Edinburgh Medal, 1991; Silver Medal, Zool Soc. of London, 1996; 60th Anniversary Medal, UNESCO, 2006. *Publications:* My Friends the Wild Chimpanzees, 1967; (with H. van Lawick) Innocent Killers, 1970; In the Shadow of Man, 1971; The Chimpanzees of Gombe: patterns of behaviour, 1986; Through A Window: 30 years observing the Gombe chimpanzees, 1990; (with Dale Peterson) Visions of Caliban, 1993; Jane Goodall: with love, 1994; Reason for Hope (autobiog.), 1999; (jtly) Hope for Animals and their World: how endangered species are being rescued from the brink, 2010; contribs to learned jls; *for children:* (with H. van Lawick) Grub: the bush baby, 1972; My Life with the Chimpanzees, 1988; The Chimpanzee Family Book, 1989; Jane Goodall's Animal World: chimps, 1989; Animal Family Series, 1991; The Eagle and the Wren, 2000. *Address:* Jane Goodall Institute UK, Suite 2, M Shed, Bath Road, Lymington, Hants SO41 3YL. *E:* info@janegoodall.org.uk. *Club:* Explorers (New York).

GOODBODY, Clarissa Mary; *see* Farr, C. M.

GOODBY, Prof. John William, PhD; FRS 2011; CChem, FRSC; Professor of Materials Chemistry, University of York, since 2005. CChem 1979; FRSC 1989. AT&T Bell Labs, USA; University of Hull, 1988–2005: Hd, Liquid Crystal Gp; Reader, then Prof., Dept of Chemistry. Mem., Editl Bd, Jl Liquid Crystals. Chair, British Liquid Crystal Soc., 2003–05 (Vice-Chair, 2000–03, 2005–06); Pres., Internat. Liquid Crystal Soc., 2000–04 (Vice-Pres., 1996–2000). Fellow: World Technol. Network, 2004; World Innovation Foundn, 2005. Hon. ScD TCD, 2002. Tilden Medal and Lectr, 2002, Interdisciplinary Award, 2007, Derek Birchall Medal, 2013, RSC; AkzoNobel UK Sci. Prize, 2014. *Publications:* (jtly) Smectic Liquid Crystals, 1984; (ed) Handbook of Liquid Crystals, 4 vols, 1998; (Sen. Ed.) Handbook of Liquid Crystals, 8 vols, 2014; contribs to scientific jls incl. Jl Materials Chem., Jl Structural Chem., Liquid Crystal, Physics Rev. E, Jl Amer. Chem. Soc. *Address:* Department of Chemistry, University of York, Heslington, York YO10 5DD.

GOODCHILD, David Lionel Napier, CMG 1986; a Director, Directorate-General of External Relations, Commission of the European Communities, 1985–86; *b* 20 July 1935; *s* of Hugh N. Goodchild and Beryl C. M. Goodchild. *Educ:* Eton College; King's College, Cambridge (MA). Joined Foreign Office, 1958; served Tehran, NATO (Paris), and FO, 1959–70; Dep. Political Adviser, British Mil. Govt, Berlin, 1970–72; transferred to EEC, Brussels, 1973; Head of Division, 1973, Principal Counsellor then Director, 1979–86. *Address:* Linden, Hall Road, Lavenham, Sudbury, Suffolk CO10 9QU. *T:* (01787) 248339.

GOODCHILD, Marianne, (Mrs Trevor Goodchild); *see* Rigge, M.

GOODCHILD, Peter Robert Edward; writer and film producer; *b* 18 Aug. 1939; *s* of Douglas Richard Geoffrey Goodchild, MBE and Lottie May Goodchild; *m* 1968, Penelope Jane, *d* of Dr William and Gwendoline Pointon-Dick; two *d*. *Educ:* Aldenham Sch., Elstree; St John's College, Oxford (MA). CChem, FRSC 1979. General trainee, BBC, 1963; BBC TV: Producer, Horizon, 1965–69, Editor, 1969–76; Editor, Special Features, 1977–80; Head, Science Features Dept, 1980–84; Head, Plays Dept, 1984–89; Exec. Producer, BBC Films, 1989–92. Producer, Television: The March, 1990; Trust Me, 1991; Adam Bede, 1992, Black Easter, 1994 (Gold Award, Chicago Film Fest., 1996); King of Chaos, 1998. Director: Screen Partners, 1992–94; Stone City Films, 1995–98; Green Umbrella Films, 1998–2005. Vis. Lectr, Nat. Film and TV Sch., 1995–2001. Pres., Dunchideock Treacle Mines, 2000–. Vice Pres., Exeter Rowing Club. Radio plays: Chicago Conspiracy Trial, 1993 (Gold Award, NY Radio Fest., 1995); Nuremberg, 1995; In the Name of Security, 1998; Lockerbie on Trial, 2001; The Putney Debates, 2002; The Real Dr Strangelove, 2006; stage plays: The Great Tennessee Monkey Trial, US tours, 2005–09; The Real Dr Strangelove, US tours, 2010–11. SFTA Mullard Award, for Horizon, 1967, 1968, 1969; BAFTA Awards: best factual series, for Horizon, 1972, 1974; best drama series, Marie Curie, 1977, Oppenheimer, 1980; Italia Prize for best factual prog., for Horizon, 1973, 1975. *Publications:* J. Robert Oppenheimer: 'shatterer of worlds', 1980; Edward Teller: the real Dr Strangelove, 2004. *Recreations:* music, painting, rowing. *Address:* Dunchideock House, Dunchideock, Exeter, Devon EX2 9TS. *Club:* Oxford and Cambridge.

GOODE, Cary; *see* Goode, P. C. A.

GOODE, Charles Barrington, AC 2001; Chairman, Flagstaff Partners, since 2009; *b* 26 Aug. 1938; *s* of Charles Thomas Goode and Jean Florence (*née* Robertson); *m* 1987, Cornelia Masters (*née* Ladd; former wife of Baron Baillieu, *qv*); one step *s*. *Educ:* Univ. of Melbourne (BCom Hons); Columbia Univ., NY (MBA). Joined Potter Partners, 1961: Partner, 1969; Sen. Partner, 1980–86; Chm., Potter Partners Gp Ltd, 1987–89. Chairman: Australian United Investment Co. Ltd, 1990–; Diversified United Investment Ltd, 1991–; Australia and New Zealand Banking Gp, 1995–2009 (Dir, 1991–2009); Woodside Petroleum Ltd, 1999–2007 (Dir, 1988–2007); Director: Pacific Dunlop Ltd, 1987–99; Qld Investment Corp. Ltd, 1991–99; CSR Ltd, 1993–2000; Singapore Airlines Ltd, 1999–2006. Chm., Ian Potter Foundn Ltd, 1994–. Member: Melbourne Cttee, Ludwig Inst. for Cancer Res., 1981–92; Exec. Cttee, Anti-Cancer Council of Victoria, 1981–84; Cttee of Mgt, Royal Victorian Eye and Ear Hosp., 1982–86; Chm., Howard Florey Inst. Exptl Physiol. and Medicine, 1997–2004. Pres., Inst. Public Affairs, 1984–93. Member of Council: Monash Univ., 1980–85 (Trustee, Monash Univ. Foundn, 1983–85); Australian Ballet Sch., 1980–86. Hon. LLD: Melbourne, 2001; Monash, 2002. Centenary Medal, 2003. *Recreations:* golf, reading. *Address:* 801/6 Victoria Street, St Kilda, Vic 3182, Australia. *T:* (3) 95348585, *Fax:* (3) 95341019. *Clubs:* Melbourne, Australian, Royal Melbourne Golf (Melbourne); Frankston Golf.

GOODE, Dr David Anthony, FLS; ecologist; Head of Environment, Greater London Authority, 2000–04; *b* 16 Jan. 1941; *s* of Rev. William Aubrey Goode and Vera Goode (*née* Parkinson); *m* 1966, Diana Lamble (*d* 2008); one *s* one *d*. *Educ:* Queen's Sch., Mönchen Gladbach, Germany; Malet Lambert High Sch., Hull; Univ. of Hull (BSc Sp. Hons Geol. 1963; PhD Botany 1970); University Coll. London (Postgrad. Dip. Conservation). MIEEM 1991, FCIEEM (FIEEM 2002) (Pres., 1994–97; Patron, 2010–); CEnv 2005. Peatland Officer, 1967–69, Hd, Peatland Ecology, 1969–73, Nature Conservancy; PSO, 1973–76, Asst Chief Scientist, 1976–82, NCC; Sen. Ecologist, GLC, 1982–86; Dir, London Ecology Unit, 1986–2000. Vis. Prof., UCL, 1994–; Hon. Prof., E China Normal Univ., Shanghai, 1996–2000. Brian Walker Lect., Green Coll., Oxford, 2003. Member: Envmt Panel, C of E Bd for Social Responsibility, 1983–92; Terrestrial Life Scis Grants Panel, 1984–87, Expert Rev. Gp on Urban Envmtl Sci., 1993–94, NERC; UK-Man and the Biosphere Urban Forum, 1987– (Vice Chm., 1990–94; Fellow, 2010); Adv. Cttee, Envmtl Law Foundn, 1991–2000; RHS Sci. and Horticulture Cttee, 1994–2002; UK Biodiversity Action Plan Steering Gp, 1994–95 (Chm., Public Awareness Gp, 1994–95); UK Agenda 21 Steering Gp, 1995–2000; UK Biodiversity Gp, 1996–2001 (Chm., Local Issues Gp, 1996–98); New Renaissance Gp, 1996–2002; Adv. Cttee, Darwin Initiative for Survival of the Species, 2000–06; UK Local Sustainability Gp, 2001–02; RHS Conservation and Envmt Cttee, 2001–11; England Biodiversity Gp, 2003–11 (Chm., Urban Gp, 2003–11); IUCN Task Force on Cities and Protected Areas, 2004–; Panel, UK Sustainable Develt, 2006–11. Member Board: Field Studies Council Exec., 1979–85; London Ecology Centre Trust, 1985–91; Think Green Campaign, 1985–91; Dir, Nat. Forest Co., 1998–2004; Chairman: Trust for Urban Ecology, 1987–91 (Pres., 1991–94); London Biodiversity Partnership, 1997–2004; Vice-Chm., 1991–92, Chm., 1992–94, Vice-Pres., 2002–06, Tree Council. Vice-Pres., British Assoc. Nature Conservationists, 1981–85; President: Reigate Soc., 1995–2000; Ecology and Conservation Studies Soc., 1999–2001; Biol Scis Section, BAAS, 2000. Advr, Landscape and Arts Network, 2001–11. Mem., British Ecol Soc., 1964– (Mem. Council, 1977–80 and 1988–92). FLS 1981 (Mem. Council, 1983–86); FRSA 1999. Heidelberg Award for Envmtl Excellence, 1999; Chartered Inst. of Ecol. and Envmtl Mgt Medal, 2015. *Publications:* Wild in London, 1986; (ed jtly) Ecology and Design in Landscape, 1986; (ed jtly) Routledge Handbook of Urban Ecology, 2011; Nature in Towns and Cities, 2014; contrib. numerous scientific papers and articles on envmtl topics. *Recreations:* photography, music, theatre, walking, ornithology, exploring the natural world. *Address:* Eastergate, 37a Lyncombe Hill, Bath BA2 4PQ. *Club:* Athenæum.

GOODE, (Penelope) Cary (Anne); freelance garden designer, since 1992; *b* 5 Dec. 1947; *d* of Ernest Edgar Spink and Rachel Atcherly Spink; *m* 1987, Richard Nicholas Goode. *Educ:* Westwing Sch. Royal Ascot Enclosure Office, 1971; MoD, 1973; Manager, retail business, 1978; Domestic and Social Sec., RCOG, 1980; Educn Administrator, British Heart Foundn, 1982; Dir, Asthma Res. Council, later Nat. Asthma Campaign, 1988–92. *Recreations:* gardening, vintage cars, dogs. *Address:* Rhodds Farm, Lyonshall, Hereford HR5 3LW. *T:* (01544) 340120.

GOODE, Sir Royston Miles, (Sir Roy), Kt 2000; CBE 1994 (OBE 1972); QC 1990; FBA 1988; Norton Rose Professor of English Law, Oxford University, 1990–98, now Emeritus Professor; Fellow, St John's College, Oxford, 1990–98, now Emeritus Fellow; *b* 6 April 1933; *s* of Samuel and Bloom Goode; *m* 1964, Catherine Anne Rueff; one *d*. *Educ:* Highgate School. LLB London, 1954; LLD London, 1976; DCL Oxon 2005. Admitted Solicitor, 1955. Partner, Victor Mishcon & Co., solicitors, 1966–71, Consultant 1971–88. Called to the Bar, Inner Temple, 1988; Hon. Bencher, 1992. Queen Mary College, University of London: Prof. of Law, 1971–73; Head of Dept and Dean of Faculty of Laws, 1976–80; Crowther Prof. of Credit and Commercial Law, 1973–89; Dir and Founder, Centre for Commercial Law Studies, 1980–89. Vis. Prof., Melbourne, 1975; Aust. Commonwealth Vis. Fellow, 1975. Chairman: Advertising Adv. Cttee, IBA, 1976–80; Pension Law Rev. Cttee, 1992–93; Member: Cttee on Consumer Credit, 1968–71; Monopolies and Mergers Commn, 1981–86; Deptl Cttee on Arbitration Law, DTI, 1986–; Governing Council, Internat. Inst. for Unification of Private Law, 1988–2003; Council of the Banking Ombudsman, 1989–92. Justice: Mem. Council, 1975; Chm. Exec. Cttee, 1994–96 (Vice-Chm., 1988–94); Mem., Council of Mgt, British Inst. of Internat. and Comparative Law, 1982. Hon. President: Centre for Commercial Law Studies, 1990–; Oxford Inst. of Legal Practice, 1994–96. Editor, Consumer Credit Law and Practice (looseleaf), 1999–. Hon. Fellow, QMW (Fellow, 1991). FRSA 1990. Hon. DSc (Econ) London, 1996; Hon. LLD: UEA, 2003; Coll. of Law, 2011. *Publications:* Hire-Purchase Law and Practice, 1962, 2nd edn 1970, with Supplement 1975; The Hire-Purchase Act 1964, 1964; (with J. S. Ziegel) Hire-Purchase and Conditional Sale: a Comparative Survey of Commonwealth and American Law, 1965; Introduction to the Consumer Credit Act, 1974; (ed) Consumer Credit Legislation, 1977, reissued as Consumer Credit Law and Practice (looseleaf), 1999; Consumer Credit, 1978; Commercial Law, 1982, 3rd edn 2004; Legal Problems of Credit and Security, 1982, 3rd edn 2003; Payment Obligations in Commercial and Financial Transactions, 1983; Proprietary Rights and Insolvency in Sales Transactions, 1985, 2nd edn 1989; Principles of Corporate Insolvency Law, 1990, 4th edn 2011; Convention on International Interests in Mobile Equipment and Protocol Thereto on Matters Specific to Aircraft Equipment: official commentary, 2002, 3rd edn 2013; (jtly) Transnational Commercial Law, 2007; Convention on International Interests in Mobile Equipment and Luxembourg Protocol Thereto on Matters Specific to Railway Rolling Stock: official commentary, 2008, 2nd edn 2014; Guide to ICC Uniform Rules for Demand Guarantees, 2011; Convention on International Interests in Mobile Equipment and Protocol Thereto on Matters Specific to Space Assets: official commentary, 2013. *Recreations:* chess, reading, walking, browsing in bookshops. *Address:* c/o St John's College, Oxford OX1 3JP; 42 St John Street, Oxford OX1 2LH. *Club:* Reform.

GOODENOUGH, Sir Anthony (Michael), KCMG 1997 (CMG 1990); HM Diplomatic Service, retired; High Commissioner to Canada, 1996–2000; *b* 5 July 1941; *s* of Rear-Adm. Michael Grant Goodenough, CBE, DSO, and Nancy, *d* of Sir Ransford Slater, GCMG, CBE; *m* 1967, Veronica Mary, *d* of Col Peter Pender-Cudlip, LVO; two *s* one *d*. *Educ:* Wellington Coll.; New Coll., Oxford (MA 1980). Voluntary Service Overseas, Sarawak, 1963–64; Foreign Office, 1964; Athens, 1967; Private Secretary to Parliamentary Under Secretary, 1971, and Minister of State, FCO, 1972; Paris, 1974; FCO, 1977; Counsellor on secondment to Cabinet Office, 1980; Hd of Chancery, Islamabad, 1982; Hd, Personnel Policy Dept, FCO, 1986–89; High Comr, Ghana and Ambassador (non-resident), Togo, 1989–92; Asst Under-Sec. of State (Africa and Commonwealth), FCO, 1992–95. Sec.-Gen., Order of St John, 2000–03. Governor: Goodenough Coll. for Overseas Graduates, 2000–12; Wellington Coll., 2002–10 (Vice-Pres., 2004–10). *Recreations:* reading, walking, gardening, travel. *Address:* The Old House, North Cheriton, Templecombe, Somerset BA8 0AE.

GOODENOUGH, Frederick Roger; DL; FCIB; Director, Barclays PLC, 1985–89; *b* 21 Dec. 1927; *s* of Sir William Macnamara Goodenough, 1st Bt, and late Lady (Dorothea Louisa) Goodenough; *m* 1954, Marguerite June Mackintosh (*d* 2015); one *s* two *d*. *Educ:* Eton; Magdalene Coll., Cambridge (MA). MA Oxon; FCIB (FIB 1968). Joined Barclays Bank Ltd, 1950; Local Director: Birmingham, 1958; Reading, 1960; Oxford, 1969–87; Director: Barclays Bank UK Ltd, 1971–87; Barclays Internat. Ltd, 1977–87; Barclays Bank PLC, 1979–89; Adv. Dir, Barclays Bank Thames Valley Region, 1988–89; Mem., London Cttee, Barclays Bank DCO, 1966–71, Barclays Bank Internat. Ltd, 1971–80. Supernumerary Fellow, Wolfson Coll., Oxford, 1989–95 (Hon. Fellow, 1995). Sen. Partner, Broadwell Manor Farm, 1968–; Curator, Oxford Univ. Chest, 1974–93; Trustee: Nuffield Med. Benefaction, 1968–2002 (Chm., 1987–2002); Nuffield Dominions Trust, 1968–2002 (Chm., 1987–2002); Nuffield Orthopaedic Centre Trust, 1978–2003 (Chm., 1981–2003); Nuffield Oxford Hospitals Fund (formerly Oxford and Dist Hosps Improvement and Develt Fund), 1968–2003 (Chm., 1982–88); Radcliffe Med. Foundn, 1987–98; Oxford Preservation Trust, 1980–89; Pres., Oxfordshire Rural Community Council, 1993–98. Governor: Shiplake Coll., 1963–74 (Chm., 1966–70); Wellington Coll., 1968–74; Goodenough Coll. (formerly London Hse for Overseas Graduates), 1985–2006. Patron, Anglo-Ghanaian Soc. (UK), 1991–. Churchwarden, Broadwell St Peter and St Paul, 1968–. FLS (Mem., Council, 1968–75, Finance Cttee, 1968–2008; Treasurer, 1970–75); FRSA. High Sheriff, 1987–88, DL 1989, Oxfordshire. *Recreations:* shooting, fishing, photography, ornithology. *Address:* Broadwell Manor, Lechlade, Glos GL7 3QS. *T:* (01367) 860326. *Club:* Brooks's.

GOODENOUGH, Prof. John Bannister; Virginia H. Cockrell Centennial Professor of Engineering, University of Texas at Austin, since 1986; *b* 25 July 1922; *s* of Erwin Ramsdell Goodenough and Helen Lewis Goodenough; *m* 1951, Irene Johnston Wiseman. *Educ:* Yale Univ. (AB, Maths); Univ. of Chicago (MS, PhD, Physics). Meteorologist, US Army Air Force, 1942–48; Research Engr, Westinghouse Corp., 1951–52; Research Physicist (Leader, Electronic Materials Gp), Lincoln Laboratory, MIT, 1952–76; Prof. and Hd of Dept of Inorganic Chemistry, Oxford Univ., 1976–86. Raman Prof., Indian Acad. of Science, 1982–83 (Hon. Mem., 1980–). Member: Nat. Acad. of Engrg, 1976–; Presidential Commn on Superconductivity, 1989–90; Nat. Acad. of Sci., USA, 2012. Foreign Associate: Acad. of Scis, Institut de France, 1992; Acad. de Ciencias Exactas, Físicas y Naturales, Spain, 2003. Foreign Mem., Royal Soc., 2010. Dr *hc*: Bordeaux, 1967; Santiago de Compostela, 2002. Von Hippel Award, Materials Res. Soc., 1989; Sen. Res. Award, Amer. Soc. of Engrg Educn,

1990; Univ. of Pennsylvania Medal for Dist. Achievement, 1996; John Bardeen Award, Minerals, Metals & Materials Soc., 1997; Olim Palladium Award, Electrochem. Soc., 1999–; Japan Prize, Sci. and Technol. Foundn of Japan, 2001; Enrico Fermi Award, US Dept of Energy, 2009; Nat. Medal of Sci., USA, 2011; Charles Stark Draper Prize for Engrg, NAE, 2014. Associate Editor: Materials Research Bulletin, 1966–; Jl Solid State Chemistry, 1969–; Structure and Bonding, 1978–; Solid State Ionics, 1980–94; Superconductor Science and Technology, 1987–; Jl of Materials Chem., 1990–95; Chem. of Materials, 1990–; Co-editor, International Series of Monographs on Chemistry, 1979–86; Member Executive, Editorial Board: Jl of Applied Electrochem., 1983–88; European Jl of Solid State and Inorganic Chem., 1992–. *Publications:* Magnetism and the Chemical Bond, 1963; Les oxydes des métaux de transition, 1973; Witness to Grace, 2008; (with K. Huang) Solid Oxide Fuel Cell Technology: principles, performance and operations, 2009; numerous research papers in learned jls. *Recreations:* walking, travel. *Address:* Texas Materials Institute, University of Texas at Austin, ETC 9.102, Austin, TX 78712, USA. *T:* (512) 4711646.

GOODENOUGH, Sir William (McLernon), 3rd Bt *cr* 1943, of Broadwell and Filkins, co. Oxford; Group Executive Chairman, Design Bridge Ltd, since 2002; *b* 5 Aug. 1954; *o s* of Sir Richard Edmund Goodenough, 2nd Bt and Jane Isobel Goodenough (*d* 1998); *S* father, 1996; *m* 1st, 1982, Louise Elizabeth Ortmans (marr. diss. 1998); one *s* two *d*; 2nd, 2002, Delia Mary, *d* of David Curzon-Price. *Educ:* Stanbridge Earls Sch.; Southampton Univ. Designer, 1980–83, Dir, 1984–87, Allied International Designers Ltd; Man. Dir, Allied International Designers (Singapore), 1983–86; Founding Partner and Man. Dir, 1986, Jt Man. Dir and Sales Dir, 1987–2002, Design Bridge Ltd. Trustee, Goodenough Coll., London, 2011–. *Recreations:* fishing, shooting, painting. *Heir: s* Samuel William Hector Goodenough, *b* 11 June 1992. *Address:* Beck Hall, Billingford, East Dereham, Norfolk NR20 4QZ. *Clubs:* Allsorts, Boodle's, Pratt's.

GOODERHAM, Peter Olaf, CMG 2007; PhD; Director, International Chamber of Commerce UK, since 2014; *b* 29 July 1954; *s* of Leonard Eric Gooderham and Gerd Gooderham; *m* 1985, Carol Anne Ward. *Educ:* Univ. of Newcastle (BA Hons); Univ. of Bristol (PhD 1981). Res. Fellow, Centre for Russian and E European Studies, Univ. of Birmingham, 1981–83; joined FCO, 1983; Falkland Is Dept, FCO, 1983–85; Second, later First, Sec., UK Delegn to NATO, Brussels, 1985–87; First Secretary: W Africa Dept, FCO, 1987–90; Riyadh, 1990–93; Dep. Hd, Security Policy Dept, FCO, 1993–96; Counsellor (Econ. and Social), UK Mission to UN, NY, 1996–99; Counsellor (Pol and Mil.), Washington, 1999–2003; UK Rep. to Pol and Security Cttee, EU, and UK Perm. Rep. to WEU, Brussels (with rank of Ambassador), 2003–04; Dir, Middle E and N Africa, FCO, 2004–07; UK Perm. Rep. to Office of the UN and other internat. orgns, Geneva, 2008–12; Internat. Dir, MoJ, 2012; Sen. Dir, RCDS, 2013–14. *Recreations:* travel, cinema, running.

GOODEY, Felicity Margaret Sue, CBE 2001; DL; Chairman, Buxton Festival, since 2015; *b* 25 July 1949; *d* of Henry Ernest Arthur and Susan Elsie Goodey; *m* 1973, John R. Marsh; two *s*. *Educ:* St Austell Grammar Sch.; St Hugh's Coll., Oxford (BA Hons Hist. Oxon 1971). Graduate trainee and reporter, World at One, BBC Radio, 1971–85; Northern Corresp., 1974–75, Northern Industrial Corresp., 1975–85, BBC TV; Presenter, 1987–99: File on Four, Punters, Sunday Programme, R4; Northwest Tonight, Northwestminster, BBC TV; owner and manager, Felicity Goodey & Associates, 1989–98; Director, Precise Communications, 1998–2004; Interim Chief Exec., Mediacity:UK, 2006–07. Chairman: The Lowry, 1994–2004 (Pres., 2004–); Lowry Operational & Develt Cos, 1994–2002; founder and non-exec. Dir, Excellence Northwest, 1993–2003; Bd Mem., Going for Green, 1994–98; Chairman: Cultural Consortium NW, 1999–2004; NW Tourism Forum, later Tourism NW England, 2004–11; Central Salford Urban Regeneration Co., 2005–11; University Hosp. of S Manchester NHS Foundn Trust, 2008–15; non-executive Director: Sustainability Northwest, 1994–98; Manchester Commonwealth Games Ltd, 1997–2002; Northwest Develt Agency, 1998–2002; Manchester Chamber of Commerce and Industry, 1999–2005 (Pres., 2001–02); Nord Anglia plc, 1999–2007; Gtr Manchester Chamber of Commerce and Industry, 2005–. Dir, Unique Communications Gp, 2004–07. Member: Private Investment Commn Northern Way, 2007–10; Panel, Regl Growth Fund, 2011–. Mem., AHRB, subseq. AHRC, 2003–07. Member Council: Salford Univ., 2006–12; Manchester Univ., 2008–. Member: Adv. Bd, Manchester Business Sch., 2008–; Bd, Royal Northern Sch. of Music, 2014–. Hon. Vice Pres., Northwest Riding for Disabled, 1978–; Trustee, Friends of Rosie (children's cancer res.), 1992–; Pres., Cheshire Wildlife Trust, 2011–; Hon. Col 207 (Manchester) Field Hosp. (V), 2009–14. Gov., Manchester Grammar Sch., 1994–2008. DL Greater Manchester, 1998. Hon. Fellow, Bolton Inst., 2002; Hon. FRIBA 2005. Hon. DLitt: Salford, 1996; Manchester Metropolitan, 2000; Hon. LLD Manchester, 2003. *Recreations:* the family, theatre, opera. *Address:* Buxton Festival, 3 The Square, Buxton, Derbys SK17 6AZ. *E:* felicity.goodey@buxtonfestival.co.uk.

GOODFELLOW, Giles William Jeremy; QC 2003; *b* 14 Nov. 1960; *s* of late Keith Frank Goodfellow, QC and Rosalind Erica Goodfellow, sometime Moderator, Gen. Assembly of URC; *m* 1990, Dr Maha Rosa Saif; three *s*. *Educ:* Harrow Sch.; Trinity Coll., Cambridge (MA; Capt., Univ. Boxing Team); Univ. of Virginia Law Sch. (LLM). Called to the Bar, Middle Temple, 1983 (Harmsworth Schol.). Mem., Pump Court Tax Chambers, 1985–. *Publications:* (jtly) Inheritance Tax Planning, 1986; (jtly) Financial Provision and Taxation in Marriage Breakdown, 1989. *Recreations:* field sports, sailing, exercising and being exercised by children. *Address:* Pump Court Tax Chambers, 16 Bedford Row, WC1R 4EF. *T:* (020) 7414 8080, *Fax:* (020) 7414 8099. *E:* clerks@pumptax.com. *Club:* Hawks (Cambridge).

GOODFELLOW, Dame Julia (Mary), DBE 2010 (CBE 2001); PhD; FMedSci; FRSB, FInstP; Vice-Chancellor, University of Kent, since 2007; *b* 1 July 1951; *d* of late Gerald Lansdall and Brenda Lansdall; *m* 1972, Peter Neville Goodfellow, *qv*; one *s* one *d*. *Educ:* Woking Co. Sch. for Girls; Reigate Co. Sch. for Girls; Univ. of Bristol (BSc Physics); Open Univ. (PhD Biophysics 1975). FRSB (FIBiol 2000); FInstP 2002. NATO Res. Fellow, Stanford Univ., 1976–78; Birkbeck College, University of London: Res. Fellow, 1979–83; Lectr, then Sen. Lectr and Reader, 1983–95; Prof. of Biomolecular Scis, 1995–2001; Chm., Dept of Crystallography, 1996–2001; Vice-Master, 1998–2001; Hon. Fellow, 2005; Chief Exec. and Dep. Chm., BBSRC, 2002–07 (Mem., 1997–2007). Wellcome Trust Res. Leave Fellow, 1990–93. Chm., Wellcome Trust Molecular and Cell Panel, 1995–98. Member: CCLRC, 2000–04; RURAL Council, 2003–07; NESTA, 2005–09; SE Sci., Technol. and Engrg Adv. Cttee, 2005–; HEFCE Res. and Innovation Adv. Bd, 2008–; STFC, 2011–; Council for Sci. and Technol., 2011–. Member Governing Body: St Paul's Girls Sch., 2001–08; Acad. Med. Scis, 2002–05. Trustee: STEMNET, 2008–11; John Innes Foundn, 2008–12; East Malling Trust, 2008–; Daphne Jackson Trust, 2008–. Chm., British Sci. Assoc., 2009–, Hon. Fellow (Hon. Fellow, BAAS, 2008); Hon. Fellow, Biochem. Soc., 2014. FRSA; FMedSci 2001. Hon. DSc: Strathclyde, 2002; Bristol, 2002; Durham, 2005; Manchester, 2009; London, 2009; DU Essex, 2004; Hon. DVSc Edinburgh, 2005. *Publications:* (ed) Molecular Dynamics: applications in molecular biology, 1990; (ed) Computer Modelling in Molecular Biology, 1992; (ed) Computer Simulation in Molecular Biology, 1995; numerous contribs to learned jls. *Recreations:* reading, family. *Address:* The Registry, University of Kent, Canterbury, Kent CT2 7NZ. *E:* j.m.goodfellow@kent.ac.uk.

GOODFELLOW, Michael Robert, PhD; Director, Goodfellow Consulting Ltd, since 2007; Divisional Managing Director, QinetiQ plc (formerly Defence Evaluation and Research Agency, Ministry of Defence), 1998–2007; *b* 7 Aug. 1948; *s* of Henry Goodfellow, MBE and Eileen Goodfellow (*née* Muff); *m* 1972, Karon Elizabeth Taylor; one *s* one *d*. *Educ:* St Bartholomew's Grammar Sch., Newbury; Imperial Coll., London (BSc 1st Cl. Hons Theoretical Physics 1970; ARCS 1970; DIC 1974; PhD 1974); Univ. of Surrey (MSc Dist. Econs 2013). CEng, FIET (FIEE 1988); FInstP 1999. Student Asst, Rutherford High Energy Lab., 1967; Res. Student, UKAEA, 1970–73; Sen. Analyst, Scicon Ltd, BP Gp, 1973–76; PSO, Systems Analysis Res. Unit, Depts of the Envmt and Transport, 1976–79; project manager, then staff manager, subseq. business gp manager, Sema Gp plc, 1979–95 (on secondment as Commercial Dir, DRA, 1992); Commercial Dir, DRA, MoD, 1995–98. Director, 1987–91: Yard Ltd; Sema Scientific Ltd; Dowty-Sema Ltd; Stephen Howe Ltd; VSEL-CAP Ltd; CAP-DBE Ltd; non-executive Director: Army Base Repair Orgn, MoD, 1998–2005; Met Office, 2007–13. Mem. Council, RUSI, 2006–. Mem., Audit Cttee, Univ. of Surrey, 2014–. Chm., Mgt Cttee, Surrey and NE Hants Industrial Mission, 1998–2004. Gov., Holy Trinity Sch., Guildford, 1989–97 (Chm., Finance Cttee). Mem., IAM. FCMI (FIMgt 1998). *Recreations:* walking, gardening. *E:* mike@goodfellows.org.uk.

GOODFELLOW, Prof. Peter Neville, DPhil; FRS 1992; Scientific Advisor, Abingworth LLP, since 2008; *b* 4 Aug. 1951; *s* of Bernard Clifford Roy Goodfellow and Doreen Olga (*née* Berry); *m* 1972, Julia Mary Lansdall (*see* Dame J. M. Goodfellow); one *s* one *d*. *Educ:* Bristol Univ. (BSc 1st Cl. Hons 1972); Oxford Univ. (DPhil 1975). MRC Postdoctoral Fellow, Oxford Univ., 1975–76; Stanford University: Jane Coffin Childs Postdoctoral Fellow, 1976–78; Amer. Cancer Soc. Sen. Fellow, 1978–79; Imperial Cancer Research Fund: Staff Scientist, 1979–83; Sen. Scientist, 1983–86; Principal Scientist, 1986–92; Arthur Balfour Prof. of Genetics, Cambridge Univ., 1992–96; Sen. Vice Pres., Biopharmaceuticals and Neuroscis, then Discovery, SmithKline Beecham Pharmaceuticals, 1996–2001; Sen. Vice Pres., Discovery Res., GlaxoSmithKline, 2001–06. Visiting Professor: Birkbeck, Univ. of London, 1996–; UCL, 2000–; Bristol Univ., 2005–; Univ. of Kent, 2008–; Rockefeller Univ., NY, 2008; Dr Mok Hing-Liu Vis. Prof., Hong Kong Univ., 2009–14. Mem., Bd, Prosensa BV, 2009–14. Trustee and Mem. Council, Inst. of Cancer Res., 2007–14. Founder FMedSci 1998. Hon. DSc Bristol, 2002. *Publications:* (ed) Genetic analysis of the cell surface in Receptors and Recognition, Vol. 16, 1984; (ed jtly) The Mammalian Y Chromosome: molecular search for the sex determining gene, 1987; (ed) Cystic Fibrosis, 1989; (ed jtly) Molecular genetics of muscle disease, 1989; (ed jtly) Sex determination and the Y chromosome, 1991; (ed jtly) Mammalian Genetics, 1992; numerous reviews and contribs to learned jls. *Recreations:* soccer, science, sex. *Address:* c/o Vice-Chancellor's Office, The Registry, University of Kent, Canterbury CT2 7NZ.

GOODHART, family name of **Baron Goodhart**.

GOODHART, Baron *cr* 1997 (Life Peer), of Youlbury in the co. of Oxfordshire; **William Howard Goodhart,** Kt 1989; QC 1979; *b* 18 Jan. 1933; *s* of late Prof. A. L. Goodhart, Hon. KBE, QC, FBA and Cecily (*née* Carter); *m* 1966, Hon. Celia McClare Herbert (*see* Lady Goodhart); one *s* two *d*. *Educ:* Eton; Trinity Coll., Cambridge (Scholar, MA); Harvard Law Sch. (Commonwealth Fund Fellow, LLM). Nat. Service, 1951–53 (2nd Lt, Oxford and Bucks Light Infantry). Called to the Bar, Lincoln's Inn, 1957, Bencher, 1986. Dir, Bar Mutual Indemnity Fund Ltd, 1988–97. Mem., H of L, 1997–2015. Member: Council of Legal Educn, 1986–92; Conveyancing Standing Cttee, Law Commn, 1987–89; Tax Law Review Cttee, 1994–2003; Cttee on Standards in Public Life, 1997–2003; Select Cttee on EU, H of L, 1998–2001 and 2005–06; Select Cttee on Delegated Powers and Regulatory Reform, H of L, 1998–2002, 2006–10 (Chm., 2006–10); Jt Cttee on Reform of H of L, 2002–03; Select Cttee on Econ. Affairs, H of L, 2003–05. Chm., Cambridge Univ. Court of Discipline, 1993–2000. Member: Internat. Commn of Jurists, 1993–2008 (Exec. Cttee, 1995–2002; Vice-Pres., 2002–06); Council, Justice, 1972–2008 (Vice Chm., 1978–88, Chm., 1988–94, Exec. Cttee; Chm., Council, 2006–08); Council, RIIA, 1999–2002; leader of Human Rights Missions: to Hong Kong, 1991; Kashmir, 1993; to Israel, and The West Bank, 1994; Kenya, 1996; Sri Lanka, 1997, 2009. Contested: Kensington: (SDP) 1983; (SDP/Alliance) 1987; (Lib Dem) July 1988; (Lib Dem) Oxford West and Abingdon, 1992. Chairman: SDP Council Arrangements Cttee, 1982–88; Lib Dem Conf. Cttee, 1988–91; Lib Dem Lawyers Assoc., 1988–91; Mem., Lib Dem Policy Cttee, 1988–97 (Vice-Chm., 1995–97). Trustee: Campden Charities, 1975–90; Airey Neave Trust, 1999–2004; Fair Trials Abroad, 2002–06. *Publications:* (with Prof. Gareth Jones) Specific Performance, 1986, 2nd edn 1996; reports of Human Rights Missions; contribs to Halsbury's Laws of England; articles in legal periodicals. *Recreations:* walking, ski-ing. *Club:* Brooks's.

See also C. A. E. Goodhart.

GOODHART, Lady; Celia McClare Goodhart; Principal, Queen's College, Harley Street, London, 1991–99; *b* 25 July 1939; *er d* of 2nd Baron Hemingford and Elizabeth (*née* Clark) (*d* 1979); *m* 1966, William Howard Goodhart (*see* Baron Goodhart); one *s* two *d*. *Educ:* St Michael's, Limpsfield; St Hilda's Coll., Oxford (MA; Hon. Fellow 1989). HM Civil Service, MAFF, seconded to Treasury, 1960–66; Hist. Tutor, Queen's Coll., London and Westminster Tutors, 1966–81. Contested: (SDP) Kettering, 1983; (SDP Liberal Alliance) Kettering, 1987; (SDP) Northants (for European Parlt), 1984. Chairman: SDP Envmt Policy Gp, 1985–87; Women for Social Democracy, 1986–88; Member: SDP Nat. and Policy Cttees, 1984–88; Liberal Democrats Fed. Exec. Cttee, 1988–90; Pres., E Midlands Liberal Democrats, 1988–91. Chm., Family Planning Assoc., 1999–2005. Member: Elizabeth Nuffield Educnl Fund, 1972–82; St Bartholomew's Hosp. Ethical Cttee, 1974–86; Lindop Cttee on Data Protection, 1976–78; Nat. Gas Consumer Councils, 1979–82 (also Chm., N Thames Gas Consumer Council); Women's Nat. Commn, 1986–89; Code Monitoring Cttee for Mkting of Infant Formulae in UK, 1986–90; Med. Audit Cttee, RCP, 1989–92; Council, GSA, 1997–99 (Sec., 1994–96, Chm., 1996–99, London Reg.); Council, Goldsmiths, Univ. of London, 2003–10 (Hon. Fellow 2010). President: Schoolmistresses and Governesses Benevolent Instn, 1991–2008; London Marriage Guidance Council, 1990–95; Chm., Youth Clubs, UK, 1988–91 (Vice-Pres., 1991–); Mem., First Forum (formerly Forum UK) (Chm., 2001–03). Gov., Compton Verney, 2006–. Chm. Bd Trustees, Oxford Univ. Soc. (formerly Oxford Soc.), 1996–2004; Trustee: CPRE, 1987–91; Oxford Univ. Nuffield Medical Benefaction, 1988–96; Childline, 1999–2004; Mem. Bd, Dignity in Dying, 2007–13. FRSA 1989. Hon. FCGI 2003. Distinguished Friend, Oxford Univ., 2001. *Recreations:* sociability, bridge, tapestry. *Address:* Youlbury House, Boars Hill, Oxford OX1 5HH. *T:* (01865) 735477. *Club:* Reform.

See also H. T. Moggridge.

GOODHART, Prof. Charles Albert Eric, CBE 1997; PhD; FBA 1990; Norman Sosnow Professor of Banking and Finance, London School of Economics and Political Science, 1985–2002, now Emeritus; Joint Founder, 1987, Deputy Director, 1987–2005, and Member, since 2005, Financial Markets Group, London School of Economics; *b* 23 Oct. 1936; *s* of late Prof. Arthur Goodhart, Hon. KBE, QC, FBA, and Cecily (*née* Carter); *m* 1960, Margaret, (Miffy), Ann Smith; one *s* three *d*. *Educ:* Eton; Trinity Coll., Cambridge (scholar; 1st Cl. Hons Econs Tripos); Harvard Grad. Sch. of Arts and Sciences (PhD 1963). National Service, 1955–57 (2nd Lieut KRRC). Prize Fellowship in Econs, Trinity Coll., Cambridge, 1963; Asst Lectr in Econs, Cambridge Univ., 1963–64; Econ. Adviser, DEA, 1965–67; Lectr in Monetary Econs, LSE, 1967–69; Bank of England: Adviser with particular reference to monetary policy, 1969–80; a Chief Adviser, 1980–85; External Mem., Monetary Policy Cttee, 1997–2000. Mem., Adv. Cttee, Hong Kong Exchange Fund, 1990–97. Hon. Fellow, LSE, 2006. *Publications:* The New York Money Market and the Finance of Trade 1900–13, 1968; The Business of Banking 1891–1914, 1972; Money, Information and Uncertainty, 1975, 2nd edn 1989; Monetary Theory and Practice: the UK experience, 1984; The Evolution of Central Banks, 1985, rev. edn 1988; (ed jtly) The Operation and Regulation of Financial Markets, 1987; (ed) EMU and ESCB after Maastricht, 1992; (jtly) The Future of

Central Banking, 1994; The Central Bank and the Financial System, 1995; (ed) The Emerging Framework of Financial Regulation, 1998; (jtly) Financial Regulation: why, how and where now?, 1998; (ed) Which Lender of Last Resort for Europe, 2000; (jtly) The Foreign Exchange Market, 2000; (ed jtly) Regulating Financial Services and Markets in the 21st Century, 2001; (ed jtly) Financial Crises, Contagion, and the Lender of Last Resort, 2002; (jtly) House Prices and the Macroeconomy, 2007; The Regulatory Response to the Financial Crisis, 2009; (jtly) Geneva Report on The Fundamental Principles of Financial Regulation, 2009; The Basel Committee on Banking Supervision, 2011; articles in econ. jls and papers contrib. to econ. books. *Recreation:* keeping sheep. *Address:* Financial Markets Group, London School of Economics and Political Science, Houghton Street, WC2A 2AE. *T:* (020) 7955 7555.

See also Baron Goodhart.

GOODHART, David Forbes; Chairman, Advisory Group, Demos, since 2014 (Director, 2011–14); Editor-at-Large, Prospect Magazine, since 2011 (Founder Editor, 1995–2011); *b* 12 Sept. 1956; *s* of Sir Philip Carter Goodhart; *m* 1990, Lucy Rosamond Kellaway; two *s* two *d.* *Educ:* Eton Coll.; York Univ. (BA 1st Cl. Hist./Politics 1979). Reporter, Yorkshire Evening Press, 1979–82; journalist, Financial Times, 1982–94 (incl. labour reporter, City reporter, Lex columnist, corresp. in Germany and employment ed.). FRSA. *Publications:* (with Patrick Wintour) Eddie Shah and the Newspaper Revolution, 1986; The Reshaping of the German Social Market, 1994; Progressive Nationalism: citizenship and the Left, 2006; The British Dream, 2013. *Recreations:* football, cricket, singing. *Address:* 52 Highbury Hill, N5 1AP. *T:* (020) 7704 1396. *E:* david.goodhart@demos.co.uk. *Clubs:* Academy, Groucho.

GOODHART, Sir Robert (Anthony Gordon), 4th Bt *cr* 1911; Medical Practitioner, retired; *b* 15 Dec. 1948; *s* of Sir John Gordon Goodhart, 3rd Bt, FRCGP, and of Margaret Mary Eileen, *d* of late Morgan Morgan; *S* father, 1979; *m* 1972, Kathleen Ellen, (Caitlin), *d* of late Rev. A. D. MacRae; two *s* two *d.* *Educ:* Rugby; Guy's Hospital Medical School, London Univ. MB BS (Lond.), MRCS, LRCP, MRCGP, DObstRCOG. Qualification, 1972. *Recreation:* sailing. *Heir:* *s* Martin Andrew Goodhart, *b* 9 Sept. 1974.

GOODHEW, David William; Head, Latymer Upper School, since 2012; *b* London, 1971; *m* 2012, Dr C. Haines. *Educ:* Cardinal Vaughan Meml Sch.; Corpus Christi Coll., Oxford (BA 1st Cl. Lit.Hum. 1993; MA 1996); Univ. of Nottingham (PGCE Classics 1994). Teacher of Classics: Bancroft's Sch., 1994–98; Eton Coll., 1998–2000; Hd of Classics, Bristol GS, 2000–05; Dir of Studies, Arnold Sch., 2005–08; Dep. Headmaster, Durham Sch., 2008–12. Governor: Glendower Prep Sch., 2013–; Dauntsey's Sch., 2014–. *Recreations:* cycling, classical music (violin). *Address:* Latymer Upper School, King Street, Hammersmith, W6 9LR. *T:* 0845 6385991, *Fax:* (020) 8748 5212. *E:* head@latymer-upper.org. *Clubs:* East India, Lansdowne.

GOODHEW, Duncan Alexander, MBE 1983; Director: Limelight Sports Ltd (formerly LEA Events & Marketing Group), since 1997; Premier Sports Ltd, since 2006; *b* 27 May 1957; *s* of late Donald Frederick Goodhew and of Dolores Perle Goodhew (*née* Venn); *m* 1984, Anne Patterson; one *s* one *d.* *Educ:* Millfield Sch.; North Carolina State Univ. (BA Business Mgt 1979). International swimmer, 1976–80; Captain, England and GB squads, 1978–80; competitions: Montreal Olympic Games, 1976; Commonwealth Games, 1978 (Silver Medal: 100m breast stroke; 200m breast stroke; 4×100 medley); World Championships, 1978 (Bronze Medal, 4×100 medley relay); Moscow Olympic Games, 1980 (Gold Medal, 100m breast stroke; Bronze Medal, 4×100 medley relay); Mem., 2-man and 4-man Bobsleigh teams, European Championships, 1981. Ambassador, Team GB. Pres., Swimathon, 1987–; Vice President: Dyslexia Action, 1994–; Youth Sport Trust, 1995–. Chm., Millfield Foundn. Patron: Disability Sport, England; Sparks; Cranial Facial Support Unit; James Powell Trust. Hon. Citizen, N Carolina. Royal Humane Soc. Award, 2001. *Publications:* Sink or Swim (with Victoria Hislop), 2001; contrib. Financial Times. *Recreations:* sport (including squash, aerobics, cycling), photography, cooking. *Address:* Limelight Sports, 29–35 Rathbone Street, W1T 1NJ. *T:* (020) 7299 4160.

GOODHEW, Most Rev. Richard Henry, (Harry), AO 2001; Archbishop of Sydney and Metropolitan of New South Wales, 1993–2001; *b* 19 March 1931; *s* of Baden Powell Richard Goodhew and Christina Delgarno Goodhew (*née* Fraser); *m* 1958, Pamela (*née* Coughlan); two *s* two *d.* *Educ:* Univ. of Wollongong (MA Hons; DLitt *hc*, 1993); Moore Theol Coll. (ThL 2nd cl. Hons, Diploma 2nd cl. Hons). Ordained 1958; Curate, St Matthew's, Bondi, NSW, 1958; Curate-in-charge, St Bede's, Beverly Hills, NSW, 1959–63; with Bush Church Aid, Ceduna, SA, 1963–66; Rector: St Paul's, Carlingford, NSW, 1966–71; St Stephen's, Coorparoo, Qld, 1971–76; Rector and Senior Canon, St Michael's Cathedral, Wollongong, 1976–79; Archdeacon of Wollongong and Camden, 1979–82; Bishop of Wollongong, Asst Bishop in dio. of Sydney, 1982–93. *Recreations:* walking, reading, swimming. *Address:* 239 Gipps Road, Keiraville, NSW 2500, Australia. *T:* (2) 42253332.

GOODIER, Gareth John; Chief Executive Officer, Melbourne Health, since 2012; *b* 5 Aug. 1951; *s* of Eric and Lilian Goodier; *m* 1st, 1970, Zena Edwards (marr. diss. 1976); 2nd, 1988, Georgina Hickling (marr. diss. 2003); one *s* one *d*; 3rd, 2004, Lynette Katherine Isabella Morero (*d* 2004); 4th, 2013, Joanne Pickard. *Educ:* Sheffield University Med. Sch. (MB ChB 1974); Univ. of NSW (Masters Health Admin 1993). FAFPHM 1990; FRACMA 1995 (Bernard Nicholson Prize, 1995). Regional Director: Kimberley Health Reg., 1989–91; Peninsula and Torres Strait Regl HA, 1991–93; Chief Executive Officer: Women's and Children's Health Service, WA, 1993–98; Royal Perth Hosp., 1998–2001; Royal Brompton and Harefield NHS Trust, 2003–04; North West London Strategic HA, 2004–06; Cambridge Univ. Hosps NHS Foundn Trust, 2006–12. Consultant, World Bank projects in Lebanon and Kuwait, 2001–03. Hon. Adv. Prof., Shanghai Jiao Tong Univ. Sch. of Medicine, 2015. Hon. DSc (Health) Anglia Ruskin, 2009. *Recreations:* art, art history, history, design/architecture, football, current affairs, travel, movies. *Address:* Melbourne Health, Royal Melbourne Hospital, Grattan Street, Parkville, Vic 3050, Australia. *T:* (3) 93427762. *E:* gareth.goodier@mh.org.au.

GOODIN, David Nigel; His Honour Judge Goodin; a Circuit Judge, since 2003; *b* 31 March 1953; *s* of Nigel Robin Fyson Goodin and Diana Goodin (*née* Luard); *m* 1st, 1993 (marr. diss. 2003); two *s*; 2nd, 2010, Catherine Mary, *d* of James Maurice Robson; one step *s* one step *d.* *Educ:* King's Sch., Ely; Coll. of Law. Admitted solicitor, 1980; Higher Courts Advocate, 1995; articled to Norton, Rose, Botterell & Roche, London; in practice as solicitor, Newmarket, Bury St Edmunds and Ipswich, 1980–2003; Founder, Saunders Goodin Riddleston, 2000; Asst Recorder, 1996–2000; Recorder, 2000–03. Mem., Funding Rev. Cttee, Legal Services Commn, 1995–2003. Chm., Local Duty Solicitor Cttee, 1987–95. *Recreation:* family and friends. *Address:* The Crown Court, 1 Russell Road, Ipswich IP1 2AG.

GOODING, Anthony James Joseph S.; *see* Simonds-Gooding.

GOODING, Mark, OBE 2011; HM Diplomatic Service; Minister Counsellor (Political), Beijing, since 2014; *b* Guildford, 17 Dec. 1974; *s* of Air Vice Marshal Keith Horace Gooding, CB, OBE and of Jean Gooding; civil partnership 2005, Dr Christopher McCormick. *Educ:* Royal Grammar Sch., Guildford; Lady Margaret Hall, Oxford (MA Modern Langs). Teacher, British Sch. in Colombo, Sri Lanka, 1996–98; Equinox Gp Pharma Consultancy, 1998–99; entered FCO, 1999; Mandarin lang. trng, 2000–02; Consul, Shanghai, 2002–04; Hd, EU Budget Team, FCO, 2004–06; Private Sec. to Foreign Sec., 2006–08; Dep. High Comr, Sri Lanka and the Maldives, 2008–11; Ambassador to Cambodia, 2011–14. *Recreations:* music, travel, running, swimming. *Address:* c/o Foreign and Commonwealth Office, King Charles Street, SW1A 2AH.

GOODING, Nigel Alexander; Deputy Director, Sea Fisheries and Conservation, Marine Programme, Department for Environment, Food and Rural Affairs, since 2015; UK Commissioner to the International Whaling Commission, since 2012; *b* 18 March 1956; *s* of Alexander Albert Gooding and Pearl Evelyn Gooding; *m* 1978, Anne Teresa Redwood; two *s* one *d.* *Educ:* Spencer Park Secondary Sch. Ministry of Agriculture, Fisheries and Food, 1974–2001: Policy Advr on Vet. Medicines, 1985–89, on Animal Health, zoonoses, 1989–92; Co-ordination of UK Presidency of EU, 1992; Head of Policy Br., UK Fisheries Enforcement, 1993; Chief Inspector of Fisheries, Eng. and Wales, DEFRA, 2003–05; Chief Exec., Marine and Fisheries Agency, 2005–10; Hd of Marine Biodiversity, Marine Prog., DEFRA, 2010–15. *Recreations:* football, golf, reading, theatre, music, walking. *Address:* Department for Environment, Food and Rural Affairs, Area 8A, 17 Smith Square, SW1P 3JR.

GOODING, Richard Ernest, OBE 2006; Chief Executive Officer, London City Airport, 1996–2012 (non-executive Director, since 2012); *b* Halesworth, 9 Oct. 1947; *s* of Frank Gooding and Gladys Gooding; one *d.* *Educ:* Leiston Grammar Sch.; Slough Technical Coll. CMILT (MCIT 1994). British European Airways, later British Airways, 1966–81: joined as apprentice, 1966; Sales Econs Officer; Activity Analyst; Ramp Supt; Overseas Area Manager; Ops Dir, Manchester Airport, 1981–86; Man. Dir, Oglen Allied Aviation Services, 1986–91; CEO, London Luton Airport, 1991–96. Non-exec. Dir, High Speed One, 2012–. Chm., Newham Homes, 2007–11. Hon. MBA LMU, 2003; Hon. DBA UEL, 2000. *Recreations:* charity, music, theatre. *T:* 07768 420501. *E:* richard@goodingobe.com.

See also V. F. Gooding.

GOODING, Stephen Leonard; Director, RAC Foundation, since 2015; *b* 20 Nov. 1960; *s* of Leonard Armstrong Gooding and Margaret Jane Gooding (*née* Horan); *m* 1985, Bernadette Kearns; two *s.* *Educ:* Colfe's Sch., Lee; Univ. of Durham (BA Hons Politics 1982). Brebner, Allen & Trapp (chartered accountants), 1982; PSA, DoE, 1983; Dept of Transport, 1987; Private Secretary: to Minister for Roads and Traffic, 1988; to Minister for Public Transport, 1989–91; Principal, 1991–97, Asst Sec., 1997–2000, Dept of Transport, subseq. DETR; Sec., CS Mgt Bd, Cabinet Office, 2000–01; Dir, Office of the Rail Regulator, 2001–04; Dir, Road Perf. and Strategy, then Roads and Road Pricing, 2004–08, Dir Gen., Motoring and Freight Services, then Domestic, later Roads, Traffic and Local, 2009–15, DfT. *Recreations:* motorcycles, film, cookery, early, baroque and heavy rock music. *Address:* c/o RAC Foundation, 89–91 Pall Mall, SW1Y 5HS. *T:* (020) 7747 3489. *E:* steve.gooding@racfoundation.org.

GOODING, Valerie Frances, CBE 2002; Chairman, Premier Farnell, since 2011; *b* 14 May 1950; *d* of Frank and Gladys Gooding; *m* 1986, Crawford Macdonald; two *s.* *Educ:* Leiston GS, Suffolk; Univ. of Warwick (BA Hons 1971); Kingston Univ. (Dip. Mgt Studies 1981). British Airways, 1973–96; Man. Dir, UK, 1996–98, CEO, 1998–2008, BUPA. Non-executive Director: Standard Chartered plc, 2005–13; J. Sainsbury plc, 2007–11; BBC, 2008–11; Home Office, 2011–14; Vodafone plc, 2014–; TUI Gp (formerly TUI Travel plc), 2014–. Dir, Lawn Tennis Assoc., 2005–13. Trustee: British Mus., 2004–11; Rose Theatre, Kingston upon Thames, 2009–11; Historic Royal Palaces, 2013–; English Nat. Ballet, 2014–; Royal Botanic Gdns, Kew, 2014–. Hon. DBA: Bournemouth, 1999; Middlesex, 2007; Hon. DSc Cranfield, 2009; Hon. DLaws Warwick, 2009. *Recreations:* tennis, theatre, travel, keeping fit, family life. *Club:* Athenæum.

See also R. E. Gooding.

GOODISON, Sir Nicholas (Proctor), Kt 1982; Chairman: Stock Exchange, 1976–88; TSB Group, 1989–95; Courtauld Institute of Art, 1982–2002 (Governor, 2002–09); National Art Collections Fund, 1986–2002; *b* 16 May 1934; *s* of Edmund Harold Goodison and Eileen Mary Carrington (*née* Proctor); *m* 1960, Judith Abel Smith; one *s* two *d.* *Educ:* Marlborough Coll.; King's Coll., Cambridge (Scholar; BA Classics 1958, MA; PhD Architecture and History of Art, 1981; Hon. Fellow, 2002). H. E. Goodison & Co., later Quilter Goodison, 1958–88: Partner, 1962; Chm., 1975–88; Chm., TSB Bank plc, 1989–2000; Dep. Chm., Lloyds TSB Gp plc, 1995–2000. Director: Ottoman Bank, 1986–92; Banque Paribas (Luxembourg) SA, 1986–88; Banque Paribas Capital Markets Ltd, 1986–88; Gen. Accident, 1987–95; British Steel, later Corus Gp plc, 1989–2002 (Dep. Chm., 1993–99). Mem. Council, Stock Exchange, 1968–88; President: Internat. Fedn of Stock Exchanges, 1985–86; British Bankers' Assoc., 1991–96; Vice Pres., Chartered Inst. of Bankers, 1989–2000 (FCIB 1989); Member: Panel on Takeovers and Mergers, 1976–88; Council of Securities Industry, 1978–85; Securities Assoc., 1986–88. Mem. Council, Industrial Soc., 1976–2000; Chairman: Crafts Council, 1997–2005; Burlington Magazine Ltd, 2002–07 (Dir, 1975–2007); Burlington Magazine Foundn, 2002–07 (Trustee, 1975–); Dir, ENO, 1977–98 (Vice-Chm., 1980–98); Trustee: ENO Trust, 1979–; Kathleen Ferrier Meml Scholarship Fund, 1987–; Nat. Heritage Meml Fund, 1988–97. Leader, Goodison Review, 2003 (report, Securing the Best for our Museums: Private Giving and Government Support for HM Treasury, published 2004). Mem., Royal Commn on the Long Term Care of the Elderly, 1997–99; Trustee, 2002–, Chm., 2003–, Nat. Life Story Collection. Hon. Keeper of Furniture, Fitzwilliam Museum, Cambridge; President: Furniture History Soc., 1990– (Hon. Treas., 1970–90); Antiquarian Horological Soc., 1986–93; Walpole Soc., 2007–. Chm., Review Steering Gp, Nat. Record of Achievement, 1996–97; Pres., Heads, Teachers and Industry, 1999–2002; Member: Adv. Bd, Judge Inst. of Mgt Studies, 1999–2003; FEFCE, 2000–01. Governor, Marlborough Coll., 1981–97. CCMI; FSA, FRSA, Sen. FRCA; Hon. Fellow RA, 1987; Hon. FRIBA 1992; Hon. FBA 2004; Hon. FCGI, 2007. Hon. DLitt: City, 1985; London, 2003; Hon. LLD Exeter, 1989; Hon. DSc Aston, 1994; Hon. DArt De Montfort, 1998; Hon. DCL Northumbria, 1999. CINOA Prize for lifetime achievement in arts, 2004; Robinson Medal, V&A Mus., 2007. Chevalier, Légion d'Honneur, 1990. *Publications:* English Barometers 1680–1860, 1968, 2nd edn 1977; Ormolu: The Work of Matthew Boulton, 1974, rev. edn as Matthew Boulton: Ormolu, 2002; (ed jtly) Hotspur: eighty years of antiques dealing, 2004; These Fragments, 2005; many papers and articles. *Recreations:* history of art, music, opera, walking. *Address:* PO Box 2512, W1A 5ZP. *Clubs:* Athenæum, Beefsteak, Brooks's, Arts.

GOODLAD, family name of **Baron Goodlad**.

GOODLAD, Baron *cr* 2005 (Life Peer), of Lincoln in the County of Lincolnshire; **Alastair Robertson Goodlad,** KCMG 1997; PC 1992; High Commissioner to Australia, 2000–05; *b* 4 July 1943; *y s* of late Dr John Goodlad and Isabel (*née* Sinclair); *m* 1968, Cecilia Barbara, 2nd *d* of late Col Richard Hurst and Lady Barbara Hurst; two *s.* *Educ:* Marlborough Coll.; King's Coll., Cambridge (MA, LLB). Contested (C) Crewe Div., 1970; MP (C) Northwich, Feb. 1974–1983, Eddisbury, 1983–99. An Asst Govt Whip, 1981–82; a Lord Commissioner of HM Treasury, 1982–84; Parly Under-Sec. of State, Dept of Energy, 1984–87; Comptroller of HM Household, 1989–90; Dep. Govt Chief Whip and Treasurer, HM Household, 1990–92; Minister of State, FCO, 1992–95; Parly Sec. to HM Treasury and Govt Chief Whip, 1995–97; Opposition frontbench spokesman on internat. devel, 1997–98. Chairman, H of L Select Cttees: on the Constitution, 2007–10; on Merits of Statutory Instruments, 2010–. *Address:* House of Lords, SW1A 0PW. *Clubs:* Brooks's, Beefsteak, Pratt's.

GOODLAND, Judith Mary; Head Mistress, Wycombe Abbey School, 1989–98; *b* 26 May 1938; *d* of Rolf Thornton Ferro and Joan (*née* O'Hanlon); *m* 1961, A. T. Goodland (marr. diss.); one *s* two *d.* *Educ:* Howell's Sch., Denbigh; Bristol Univ. (BA Hons); Charlotte Mason Coll., Ambleside (Cert Ed). Head, Modern Languages Dept, Cartmel Priory C of E Comprehensive Sch., 1968–72; Casterton Sch., Kirkby Lonsdale, 1980–83; Headmistress, St George's Sch., Ascot, 1983–88. Trustee, Bendrigg Trust, 2007– (Chm., 2011–14). Chm.,

U3A South Lakes, 2014–May 2016 (Vice-Chm., 2012–14). FRSA 1994. *Recreations:* bridge, quilting, church recording, bird watching. *Address:* 10 Starnthwaite Ghyll, Crosthwaite, Kendal, Cumbria LA8 8JN.

GOODMAN, Catherine Anne, LVO 2014; artist; Co-Founder and Artistic Director, Royal Drawing School (formerly Prince's Drawing School), since 2000; *b* London, 22 April 1961; *d* of Philip Goodman and Sonia Goodman. *Educ:* Queen's Coll., London; Camberwell Sch. of Arts and Crafts, London (Art Foundn; BA Fine Art Painting 1984); Royal Acad. Schs, London (Postgrad. Dip. 1987). Professional artist working in London and India, 1987–; Hd, Fine Art, Prince of Wales's Inst. for Architecture, 1992–2000. Gold Medal, RA, 1987; First Prize, BP Portrait Award, 2002. *Recreations:* walking, yoga. *Address:* Royal Drawing School, 19–22 Charlotte Road, EC2A 3SG. *T:* (020) 7613 8568. *E:* goodman-studio@royaldrawingschool.org.

GOODMAN, Elinor Mary; freelance journalist; *b* 11 Oct. 1946; *d* of Edward Weston Goodman and Pamela Longbottom. *Educ:* private schools, secretarial college. Financial Times: Consumer Affairs Corresp., 1971–78; Political Corresp., 1978–82; Channel Four News: Political Corresp., 1982–88; Political Ed., 1988–2005. Chm., Affordable Rural Housing Commn, 2005–06. Mem. Bd, Commn for Rural Communities, 2006–12. Assessor, Leveson Inquiry into culture, practice and ethics of the press, 2011–. *Recreations:* riding, walking.

GOODMAN, Helen Catherine; MP (Lab) Bishop Auckland, since 2005; *b* 2 Jan. 1958; *d* of Alan Goodman and Hanne Goodman; *m* 1988, Charles; two *c. Educ:* Lady Manners Sch., Bakewell; Somerville Coll., Oxford (BA 1979). HM Treasury, 1980–97, latterly Hd of Strategy Unit; Advr to Prime Minister of Czechoslovakia, 1990; Dir, Commn on Future of Multi Ethnic Britain, 1998; Hd of Strategy, Children's Soc., 1998–2002; Chief Exec., Nat. Assoc. of Toy and Leisure Libraries, 2002–05. Parly Sec., Office of the Leader of the H of C, 2007–08; Parly Under-Sec. of State, DWP, 2009–10. Shadow Minister: for Justice, 2010–11; for Culture, 2011–14; for Work and Pensions, 2014–15. Mem., Public Accounts Cttee, 2005–07. *Address:* House of Commons, SW1A 0AA. *T:* (020) 7219 4346. *E:* goodmanh@parliament.uk.

GOODMAN, Prof. John Francis Bradshaw, CBE 1995; PhD; CCIPD; Frank Thomas Professor of Industrial Relations, University of Manchester Institute of Science and Technology, 1975–2002 (Vice-Principal, 1979–81); *b* 2 Aug. 1940; *s* of Edwin and Amy Goodman; *m* 1967, Elizabeth Mary Towns; one *s* one *d. Educ:* Chesterfield Grammar Sch.; London Sch. of Economics (BSc Econ); MSc Manchester; PhD Nottingham. Personnel Officer, Ford Motor Co. Ltd, 1962–64; Lectr in Industrial Econs, Univ. of Nottingham, 1964–69; Industrial Relations Adviser, NBPI, 1969–70; Sen. Lectr in Industrial Relations, Univ. of Manchester, 1970–74; Chm., Manchester Sch. of Management, UMIST, 1977–79, 1986–94. Vis. Professor: Univ. of WA, 1981, 1984; McMaster Univ., 1985; Univ. of Auckland, 1996. Pres., British Univs Industrial Relations Assoc., 1983–86. Member: Council, ACAS, 1987–98; Training Bd, 1991–97, Council, 1993–97, ESRC. Dep. Chm., Central Arbitration Cttee, 1998–2011; Chairman: Professional Football Negotiating and Consultative Cttee, 2000–; Police Arbitration Tribunal, 2003–14. *Publications:* Shop Stewards in British Industry, 1969; Shop Stewards, 1973; Rulemaking and Industrial Peace, 1977; Ideology and Shop-floor Industrial Relations, 1981; Employment Relations in Industrial Society, 1984; Unfair Dismissal Law and Employment Practice, 1985; New Developments in Employee Involvement, 1992; Industrial Tribunals and Workplace Disciplinary Procedures, 1998; contribs to British Jl of Industrial Relations, ILR, Industrial Relations Jl, Jl of Management Studies, Personnel Management, etc. *Recreations:* hill walking (compleat Munroist, 1997), football, ornithology, golf. *Address:* 2 Pott Hall, Pott Shrigley, Macclesfield, Cheshire SK10 5RT. *T:* (01625) 572480.

GOODMAN, Prof. Martin David, DPhil, DLitt; FBA 1996; Professor of Jewish Studies, Oxford University, since 1996; Fellow of Wolfson College, Oxford, since 1991 (Viceregent, 2012–14); Fellow, since 1986, and President, since 2014, Oxford Centre for Hebrew and Jewish Studies; *b* 1 Aug. 1953; *s* of late Cyril Joshua Goodman and Ruth (*née* Sabel); *m* 1976, Sarah Jane Lock; two *s* two *d. Educ:* Rugby; Trinity Coll., Oxford (MA; DPhil 1980; DLitt 2009; Hon. Fellow 2010). Kaye Jun. Res. Fellow, Oxford Centre for Postgrad. Hebrew Studies, 1976–77; Lectr in Ancient Hist., Birmingham Univ., 1977–86; Oxford University: Sen. Res. Fellow, St Cross Coll., 1986–91; Lectr in Roman Hist., Christ Church, Oxford, 1988–; Reader in Jewish Studies, 1991–96. Fellow, Inst. for Advanced Studies, Hebrew Univ. of Jerusalem, 1993. Pres., British Assoc. for Jewish Studies, 1995. Jt Ed., Jl of Jewish Studies, 1995–99; Ed., Jl of Roman Studies, 2000–03. Hon. DLitt Southampton. *Publications:* State and Society in Roman Galilee, 1983, 2nd edn 2000; (trans. with Sarah Goodman) Johann Reuchlin, On the Art of the Kabbalah, 1983; (ed jtly) E. Schürer, The History of the Jewish People in the Age of Jesus Christ, vol. 3, pt 1 1986, pt 2 1987; The Ruling Class of Judaea, 1987; (with G. Vermes) The Essenes according to the Classical Sources, 1989; Mission and Conversion, 1994; The Roman World 44BC–AD180, 1997, 2nd edn 2012; (ed) Jews in a Graeco-Roman World, 1998; (ed jtly) Apologetics in the Roman Empire, 1999; (ed jtly) Representations of Empire: Rome and the Mediterranean world, 2002; (ed) The Oxford Handbook of Jewish Studies, 2002; Judaism in the Roman World: collected essays, 2007; Rome and Jerusalem: the clash of ancient civilizations, 2007; (ed jtly) Abraham, the Nations, and the Hagarites: Jewish, Christian and Islamic perspectives on kinship with Abraham, 2010; (ed jtly) Rabbinic Texts and the History of Late-Roman Palestine, 2010; (jtly) Toleration within Judaism, 2013. *Address:* Clarendon Institute, Walton Street, Oxford OX1 2HG; 57 Park Town, Oxford OX2 6SL.

See also Prof. R. J. Goodman.

GOODMAN, His Honour Michael Bradley; a Circuit Judge, 1983–99; *b* 3 May 1930; *s* of Marcus Gordon Goodman and Eunice Irene May Goodman (*née* Bradley); *m* 1967, Patricia Mary Gorringe; two *d* (one *s* decd). *Educ:* Aldenham; Sidney Sussex Coll., Cambridge (MA). Called to the Bar, Middle Temple, 1953; Western Circuit; a Recorder of the Crown Court, 1972–83. Prosecuting Counsel to DHSS, 1975–83; Pres., Wireless Telegraphy Appeals Tribunal, 1977–88. Chancellor: Dio. Guildford, 1968–2002; Dio. Lincoln, 1970–98; Dio. Rochester, 1971–2005; Vicar-Gen., Province of Canterbury, 1977–83. Member: Commn on Deployment and Payment of the Clergy, 1965–67; C of E Legal Adv. Commn, 1973–2006 (Chm., 1986–96); Faculty Jurisdiction Commn, 1980–83; General Synod, Church of England, 1977–83; Lay Chm., Dulwich Deanery Synod, 1970–73. Chairman: William Temple Assoc., 1963–66; Ecclesiastical Judges Assoc., 1987–97. President: SE London Magistrates' Assoc., 1989–96; SE London Family Mediation Bureau, 1999–2010. Governor: Liddon Trust, London, 1964–2004; Pusey Hse, Oxford, 1965–88; Trustee, Bromley and Sheppard's Colls for the Clergy, 1971–2010. President: The Madrigal Soc., 2007–09; St Paul's (Knightsbridge) Festival Choir, 2008–; Vice-Pres., Dulwich Choral Soc., 2011–. *Address:* c/o Lloyds Bank, BX3, BX1 1LT.

GOODMAN, Michael Jack, MA, PhD; Social Security Commissioner (formerly National Insurance Commissioner), 1979–98, and Child Support Commissioner, 1993–98, Deputy Commissioner, 1999–2002; *b* 3 Oct. 1931; *s* of Vivian Roy Goodman and Muriel Olive Goodman; *m* 1958, Susan Kerkham Wherry; two *s* one *d. Educ:* Sudbury Grammar Sch., Suffolk; Corpus Christi Coll., Oxford (MA). PhD Manchester. Solicitor. Lectr, Gibson & Weldon, 1957; solicitor, Lincoln, 1958–60; Lectr, Law Society's Sch., 1961–63; Lectr, then Sen. Lectr in Law, Manchester Univ., 1964–70; Prof. of Law, Durham Univ., 1971–76; Perm. Chm. of Indust. Tribunals, Newcastle upon Tyne, 1976–79. Gen. Editor, Encyclopedia of Health and Safety at Work, 1974–. *Publications:* Industrial Tribunals' Procedure, 1976, 3rd edn 1985; Health and Safety at Work: law and practice, 1988; contrib. Mod. Law Rev., and Conveyancer. *Recreations:* amateur radio (licence holder), National Trust volunteering.

GOODMAN, Sir Patrick (Ledger), GNZM 2009 (PCNZM 2002); Kt 1995; CBE 1990; Special Trade Ambassador of New Zealand, 1990; company director; President Emeritus, Goodman Fielder Ltd; *b* 6 April 1929; *s* of Athol Ledger Goodman and Delia Marion Goodman; *m* 1960, Hilary Gay Duncan; three *s. Educ:* St Patrick's Coll., Silverstream, NZ; Victoria University Coll., Wellington. Chairman: Heinz-Wattie, 1992–98; Quality Bakers of NZ, 1967–76; Goodman Group and subsidiaries, 1979–92; former Chm., Tourism Nelson. Founder Chm., NZ Business and Parlt Trust, 1991–92, now Patron; Trustee, Founders of Nelson; formerly Trustee, Massey Univ. Agric. Foundn; formerly Trustee and Patron, Bishop Suter Art Gall.; Patron, Massey Univ. Food Foundn. Foundn Mem., NZ Rugby Foundn. Dist. Fellow, NZ Inst. of Dirs, 2003. Hon. DSc Massey. NZ Business Hall of Fame, 2005. *Recreations:* golf, cricket, Rugby, boating, fishing. *Address:* 52 Tudor Street, Motueka, Nelson, New Zealand. *T:* (3) 5288314.

GOODMAN, Paul Alexander Cyril; Editor, Conservative Home, since 2010; *b* 17 Nov. 1959; *s* of Abel Goodman and Irene Goodman (*née* Rubens); *m* 1999, Fiona Gill; one *s. Educ:* Cranleigh Sch., Surrey; York Univ. (BA Hons Eng. Lit). Exec., Extel Consultancy, 1985–86; Res. Asst to Rt Hon. Tom King, MP, 1985–87; Mem., Policy Unit, Westminster CC, 1987–88; Novice, Quarr Abbey, 1988–90; Home Affairs Ed., Catholic Herald, 1991–92; Leader Writer, Daily Telegraph, 1992; reporter, Sunday Telegraph, 1992–95; Comment Ed., Daily Telegraph, 1995–2001. MP (C) Wycombe, 2001–10. Shadow Minister: for Work and Pensions, 2003–05; for Childcare, HM Treasury, 2005–07; DCLG, 2007–09. Member, Select Committee: on Work and Pensions, 2001–05; on Deregulation and Regulatory Reform, 2001–03.

GOODMAN, Perry; Director (Industry and Regions), The Engineering Council, 1990–92; *b* 26 Nov. 1932; *s* of Cyril Goodman and Anne (*née* Rosen); *m* 1958, Marcia Ann (*née* Morris); one *s* one *d. Educ:* Haberdashers' Aske's Hampstead Sch.; University Coll., London (BSc); Open Univ. (MSc). MIMMM (MICeram 1964). 2nd Lieut, Royal Corps of Signals, 1955–57; Jt Head, Chemistry Res. Lab., then Project Leader, Morgan Crucible Co. Ltd, 1957–64; Sen. Scientific Officer, DSIR, 1964–65; Principal Scientific Officer, Process Plant Br., Min. of Technology, 1965–67; 1st Sec. (Scientific), 1968–70, Counsellor (Scientific), 1970–74, British Embassy, Paris; Research Gp, DoI, 1974–79; Hd, Policy and Perspectives Unit, DoI, 1980–81; Department of Trade and Industry: Hd, Design Policy/Technical Adv. Services for Industry, 1981–86; Hd, Electrical Engrg Br., 1986–90. Mem. Bd, Northern Engrg Centre, 1990–92. FRSA 1986. *Recreations:* travel, walking, conversation. *Address:* 118 Westbourne Terrace Mews, W2 6QG. *T:* (020) 7262 0925.

GOODMAN, Prof. Roger James, DPhil; Nissan Professor of Modern Japanese Studies, since 2003, and Head, Social Sciences Division, since 2008, University of Oxford; Fellow, St Antony's College, Oxford, since 1993 (Acting Warden, 2006–07); *b* 26 May 1960; *s* of late Cyril Joshua Goodman and Ruth (*née* Sabel); partner, Carolyn Joy Dodd; two *s* one *d. Educ:* Rugby; King Edward VI Grammar Sch., Chelmsford; Univ. of Durham (BA 1981); St Antony's Coll., Oxford (DPhil 1987). Nissan Jun. Res. Fellow in Social Anthropol. of Japan, St Antony's Coll., Oxford, 1985–88; Lectr, Japan-Europe Ind. Res. Centre, Imperial Coll., Univ. of London, 1988–89; Reader in Japanese Studies, Dept of Sociol., Univ. of Essex, 1989–93; Lectr in Social Anthropol. of Japan, Univ. of Oxford, 1993–2003. Oxford University: Assessor, 1997–98; Chair, Japan Foundn Endowment Cttee, 1999–2006. *Publications:* Japan's International Youth: the emergence of a new class of schoolchildren, 1990; (ed jtly) Ideology and Practice in Modern Japan, 1992; (ed jtly) Case Studies on Human Rights in Japan, 1996; (ed jtly) The East Asian Welfare Model: welfare orientalism and the state, 1998; Children of the Japanese State: the changing role of child protection institutions in contemporary Japan, 2000; (ed) Family and Social Policy in Japan: anthropological approaches, 2002; (ed jtly) Can the Japanese Reform Their Education System?, 2003; (ed jtly) Global Japan: the experience of Japan's new minorities and overseas communities, 2003; (ed jtly) The Big Bang in Japanese Higher Education: the 2004 reforms and the dynamics of change, 2005; (ed jtly) Ageing in Asia, 2007; (ed jtly) A Sociology of Japanese Youth: from returnees to NEETs, 2012; (ed jtly) Higher Education and the State: changing relationships in Europe and East Asia, 2013. *Recreation:* hockey coach. *Address:* Nissan Institute of Japanese Studies, 27 Winchester Road, Oxford OX2 6NA. *T:* (01865) 274576. *E:* roger.goodman@nissan.ox.ac.uk.

See also Prof. M. D. Goodman.

GOODMAN, Roy Peter, FRCO; conductor; violinist; Principal Guest Conductor, English Chamber Orchestra, 2004–15; *b* 26 Jan. 1951; *s* of Peter and Mary Sheena Goodman; *m* 1st, 1970, Gillian Dey (marr. diss. 1992); two *s* one *d*; 2nd, 1992, Sally Jackson (marr. diss. 1999). *Educ:* King's Coll., Cambridge (chorister); Royal Coll. of Music; Berkshire Coll. of Educn. ARCO 1968, FRCO 1970; ARCM 1976. Head of Music: Alfred Sutton Boys' Sch., Reading, 1971–74; Bulmershe Comprehensive Sch., Reading, 1974–76; Sen. String Tutor, Berks, 1976–78; Dir of Music, Univ. of Kent, Canterbury, 1986–87; Dir, Early Music, RAM, 1987–89. Founder and Dir, Brandenburg Consort, 1975–2001; Co-Founder and Co-Dir, Parley of Instruments, 1979–86; Musical Dir, European Union Baroque Orch., 1988–2003; Principal Conductor: Hanover Band, 1986–94; Umeå Symphony Orchestra and Swedish Northern Opera, 1994–99; Manitoba Chamber Orch., Winnipeg, 1999–2005; Holland Symfonia, Amsterdam, 2003–06; Principal Guest Conductor: Västerås Sinfonietta, Sweden, 1995–2011; Auckland Philharmonia, NZ, 2007–11. Hon. FRCM 2005. Hon. DMus Hull, 2002. *Recreations:* squash, sailing, ski-ing. *Address:* 38 Blackbrook Road, Newark, Notts NG24 2ST. *E:* roy@roygoodman.com.

GOODMAN, Rupert Andrew Woodward, FRGS; DL; Chairman and Founder, FIRST, since 1985; *b* Kidderminster, 17 April 1963; *s* of Nigel and late Rachel Goodman (*née* Woodward); *m* 1991, Pamela Jane Blount; one *s* two *d. Educ:* Eton Coll.; Trinity Coll., Cambridge (BA Hons 1985). Founder, Responsible Capitalism Initiative, 2000–. Chairman: World Petroleum, 2000–; World Energy Insight, 2010–; Elmbridge Partners, 2014–. Vice Pres., FFI, 2011–. Mem., Develt Bd, Artes Mundi, 2009–. Founder Director: Equilibrium Golf, 2014–; Equilibrium Global, 2014–. Mem., Internat. Dendrol. Soc., 2008–. Founder Trustee, 2002–, Chm., 2013–, British Kazakh Soc.; Trustee, Nat. Botanic Gdns of Wales, 2005–08. DL Gtr London, 2012. Freeman, City of London, 2013. FRGS 1992. Metropolitan Police Comr's Award, 2012. *Publications:* (ed) The Critical Decade, 2003; (ed) The 21st Century: a view from the South, 2005; (ed with Baron Cormack) Responsible Capitalism: essays on morality, ethics and business, 2009; contrib. articles to jls. *Recreations:* hill walking, country pursuits, dendrology, sport, international affairs, Led Zeppelin. *Address:* c/o FIRST, Victory House, 99–101 Regent Street, W1B 4EZ. *T:* (020) 7440 3550, *Fax:* (020) 7440 3544. *Clubs:* Hawks, Brooks's, Pitt; Pitt (Cambridge).

GOODNOW, Prof. Christopher Carl, PhD; FRS 2009; FAA; Bill and Patricia Ritchie Foundation Professor, NH&MRC Australia Fellow, Deputy Director and Head, Division of Immunogenomics, Girvan Institute of Medical Research, since 2015; Adjunct Professor, John Curtin School of Medical Research, Australian National University, since 2015; *b* Hong Kong, 19 Sept. 1959. *Educ:* Univ. of Sydney (BVSc Hons, BSc (Vet) Hons 1984; Univ. Medal 1984). Vis. Student and Res. Asst, Stanford Univ. Med. Sch., 1985; NH&MRC Biomed. Scholar, Walter and Eliza Hall Inst., 1985; NH&MRC Biomed. Scholar, 1986–89, Medical Foundn Postdoctoral Fellow, 1989–90, Clinical Immunology Res. Centre, Univ. of Sydney;

Asst Investigator, Howard Hughes Med. Inst. and Asst Prof. of Microbiol. and Immunol., Stanford Univ. Med. Sch., 1990–97; John Curtin School of Medical Research, Australian National University: Prof. of Immunol. and Genetics, 1997–2014; Dir, Med. Genome Centre, 1997–2007; Founder Dir, Australian Phenomics Facility and ACRF Med. Genome Centre, 1997–2006; Hd, Div. of Genetics and Immunol., 2007–14. Founder and Chief Scientific Officer, Phenomix Corp. Searle Scholar, 1992–95. Pres., Australasian Soc. for Immunology, 2015–16. *Publications:* articles in jls. *Address:* Girvan Institute of Medical Research, 384 Victoria Street, Darlinghurst, Sydney, NSW 2010, Australia.

GOODSELL, (John) Andrew; Executive Chairman, Saga Group Ltd, since 2007; *b* 4 Jan. 1959; *s* of John Leonard Goodsell and Pamela Doris Goodsell; *m* 1st, 1983, Claire Hornsby (marr. diss.); one *s* one *d*; 2nd, 1999, Virginia Hubert; one *s* two *d*. *Educ:* West Kent Coll. Norwich Winterthur Reinsurance Co. Ltd, 1978–87; Lloyds of London, 1987–92; Saga Group Ltd: Business Develt Manager, 1992–95; Business Develt Dir, 1995–99; Chief Exec., Saga Services and Saga Investment Direct, 1999–2001; Dep. Gp Chief Exec., 2001–04; Gp Chief Exec., 2004–07; Exec. Chm., AA Ltd, 2007–14. Chm., Fundraising Bd, Age UK, 2009–. Hon. Fellow, Harris Manchester Coll., Oxford, 2002. *Recreations:* cooking, ski-ing, sailing. *Address:* (office) Enbrook Park, Folkestone, Kent CT20 3SE. *T:* (01303) 771702, *Fax:* (01303) 771175.

GOODSHIP, Prof. Allen Edward, PhD; Professor of Orthopaedic Sciences, Royal Veterinary College, London, and the Institute of Orthopaedics, 1996–2011, now Emeritus, and Professorial Research Associate in Orthopaedic Science, Institute of Musculoskeletal Science, 2012–14, University College London; Director and Head, Centre for Comparative and Clinical Anatomy, Vesalius Clinical Training Centre, 2012–15, Professorial Research Associate, Department of Physics and Bio-Engineering, since 2015, and Hon. Professor, since 2015, University of Bristol; *b* 1 Feb. 1949; *m* 1975, Dawn Taylor; two *d*. *Educ:* Reigate Grammar Sch.; Sch. of Vet. Sci., Univ. of Bristol (BVSc 1972; PhD 1977). MRCVS 1972. Res. Asst, RCVS Trust Fund Scholar, 1972–74; University of Bristol: Temp. Lectr in Vet. Anatomy, 1974–76; Res. Asst, Horserace Betting Levy Bd, 1976–78, Lectr, 1978–88, Dept of Anatomy; Reader in Vet. Anatomy, 1988; Prof. of Comparative Biomed. Scis, 1988–96 (Vis. Prof., 1996–); Hd, Dept of Anatomy, 1992–96; Dir, Inst. of Orthopaedics and Musculoskeletal Sci., UCL, 2009–11; Chm., Bd of Dirs, Vesalius Clin. Trng Centre, Univ. of Bristol, 2015–. Acad. Associate, QMW, 1996–; Convenor, Cell and Molecular Path. Res. Centre, Royal Nat. Orthopaedic Hosp. Trust, 1999–2003. Vis. Prof., Univ. of Guelph, 1989–; D. L. T. Smith Vis. Scientist, Univ. of Saskatoon, 1989–; Vis. Prof. of Pathol., Univ. of Adelaide, 2006–11. Trustee, Silsoe Res. Inst., 2002–06; Director: Stanmore Implants Worldwide, 2000–08; Bristol Zoo Enterprises Ltd; Consultant: Orthopaedic Div., Johnson & Johnson (DePuy); Res. Centre, Smith & Nephew Gp; Co-inventor, VetCell. Vice Pres. and Univ. Rep. to Council, and Chm., Welfare and Res. Adv. Bd, Bristol & SW Zool Soc.; Member: Med. Adv. Bd, General Orthopaedics, Boston; Adv. Bd, MRC. Member: Orthopaedic Res. Soc., USA (Mem. Prog. Cttee, 1997–98); British Vet. Zool Soc.; Anatomical Soc. of GB and Ire.; President: Internat. Soc. for Fracture Repair, 1994–96 (Chm. Memship Cttee, 1994–); British Orthopaedic Res. Soc., 2009–. Scientific Ed., Res. in Vet. Sci.; former Mem., Editl Adv. Bd, Clinical Materials; Member Editorial Board: Jl of Orthopaedic Trauma (Dep. Ed.); Equine & Comparative Exercise Physiology; Asst Ed., Equine Vet. Jl. Companion Fellow, British Orthopaedic Assoc. Hon. Mem., Uruguay Orthopaedic Assoc., 1994–. Prof. W. M. Mitchell Meml Fund Award, RCVS, 1976; Gary Hampson Meml Prize for Orthopaedic Res., 1984; Edwin Walker Prize, IMechE, 1988; Clinical Biomechanics Award, European Soc. of Biomechanics, 1990; Prize for Spinal Res., AcroMed, 1992; Medal, Nat. Back Pain Assoc., 1994; Open Award, Equine Vet. Jl, 1995; Scheering Plough Animal Health Vet. Achievement Award, Animal Health Trust, 2001; Meggers Award, Soc. for Applied Spectroscopy, 2006. *Publications:* (ed jtly) European Biomechanics: proceedings of the 6th meeting of the European Society of Biomechanics, 1988; book chapters and many articles in learned jls. *Recreations:* sailing, walking, gardening. *Address:* Institute of Orthopaedics and Musculoskeletal Science, University College London, Royal National Orthopaedic Hospital Trust, Brockley Hill, Stanmore, Middx HA7 4LP. *T:* (020) 8909 5535, *Fax:* (020) 8954 8560; Vesalius Clinical Training Centre, Centre for Comparative and Clinical Anatomy, University of Bristol, Southwell Street, Bristol BS2 8EJ.

GOODSMAN, James Melville, CBE 1993; Managing Director, 1995–97, Chairman, 1997–2002, Michael Fraser Associates Ltd; Director, Michael Fraser & Co. Ltd, 1997–2002; *b* 6 Feb. 1947; *s* of late James K. Goodsman and Euphemia Goodsman, Elgin, Moray; *m* 1990, Victoria, *y d* of late Col Philip Smitherman and Rosemary Smitherman, CBE. *Educ:* Elgin Academy. Joined Cons. Party organisation, 1966; Agent: to Rt Hon. Betty Harvie Anderson, 1970–74; to Rt Hon. Maurice Macmillan, 1974–80; Conservative Central Office: Dep. Agent, NW Area, 1980–84; Asst Dir (Community Affairs), 1984–90; Head, Community and Legal Affairs, May–Sept. 1990; Dir, Cons. Party in Scotland, 1990–93. Director: ICP Ltd, 1997–2001; Capitalize Ltd, 2001–02. Hon. Sec., One Nation Forum, 1986–90. Mem., Edinburgh Morayshire Club (Chm., 1996). *Publications:* contribs to Cons. party and community relations papers. *Recreation:* church music. *Address:* Le Bourg, 61170 Coulognes-sur-Sarthe, France. *E:* james.goodsman@orange.fr.

GOODSON, Sir Alan (Reginald), 4th Bt *cr* 1922, of Waddeton Court, Co. Devon; farmer; *b* Kelso, Roxburghshire, 15 May 1960; *s* of Sir Mark Weston Lassam Goodson, 3rd Bt and Barbara Mary Constantine Goodson (*née* Andrews); *S* father, 2015; *m* 1990, Melanie Jayne Lodder; one *s* one *d*. *Educ:* Ampleforth Coll.; Edinburgh Univ. (MA Hons English Lit.). *Recreations:* field sports, literary research. *Heir:* *s* Hugh Mark Edwin Goodson, *b* 31 May 1993. *Address:* Marlefield House, Kelso, Roxburghshire TD5 8ED. *T:* (01573) 440 506. *E:* alan.goodson@virgin.net.

GOODSON, Rear-Adm. Frederick Brian, CB 1996; OBE 1982; Chairman: Explora Security Ltd, 2002–11; Explora Security A&E Inc. (USA), 2010–12; Voyager Holding Group, 2008–11; Explora Foundation and Scholarship Fund, since 2012; *b* 21 May 1938; *m* 1965, Susan, (Sue), Mary Firmin; two *s* two *d*. *Educ:* Campbell Coll. Coastal Forces, 1958–60; HMS Gambia and HMS Lion, 1960–64; Aden, 1964–65; Supply Officer, HMS Diana, 1966–69; Staff, BRNC, Dartmouth, 1970–72; Exchange Service, USN, 1972–74; Comdr 1974; Exchange Service, Royal Naval Supply and Transport Service, 1975–78; Naval Sec's Dept, 1978–79; Supply Officer, HMS Invincible, 1980–81; Fleet Supply Officer, C-in-C Fleet, 1981–82; Capt. 1982; Sec., C-in-C Naval Home Comd, 1983–85; Dir, Naval Logistic Planning, 1985–87; Cdre comdg HMS Centurion, 1988–91; rcds 1992; Rear-Adm. 1993; ACDS (Logistics), 1993–96. Chairman: Bath and West Community NHS Trust, 1997–2001; South Glos Primary Care Trust, 2001–06; Trading Force Gp, 1999–2002; Explora Gp plc, 2003–07. Chm., Village Link, Wilts, 2012–. Pres., Calne Royal Naval Assoc., 2000–. MInstD 1996. KStJ 2013 (CStJ 2002); Chairman: Wilts, St John Ambulance, 1997–2005; Trustees, Explora Scholarship Fund, 2014–; Trustee, Orders of St John Care Trust, 2006–15 (Vice Chm., 2013–15). *Recreations:* offshore sailing, golf, country pursuits. *Address:* New Homestead Farm, Mountain Bower, North Wraxall, Chippenham, Wilts SN14 7AJ. *Clubs:* Bowood Golf and Country; Royal Naval Sailing Association.

GOODSON, Prof. Ivor Frederick, DPhil; Professor of Learning Theory, Education Research Centre, University of Brighton, since 2004; *b* 30 Sept. 1943; *s* of Frederick G. J. Goodson and Lily W. Goodson; *m* 1975, Mary L. Nuttall; one *s*. *Educ:* Forest Grammar Sch.; University Coll. London (BSc Econ); Inst. of Educn, Univ. of London; London Sch. of Econs; DPhil Sussex 1979. University of Sussex: Res. Fellow, 1975–78; Dir, Eur. Schools Unit, 1978–85; University of Western Ontario: Prof., Faculty of Educn, Faculty of Grad. Studies and Centre for Theory and Criticism, 1986–96; Dir, Educnl Res. Unit, 1989–96; Hon. Prof. of Sociol., 1993–98; Prof. of Educn, Sch. of Educn and Professional Develt, UEA, 1996–2004. Founding Ed. and Man. Ed., Jl Educn Policy, 1986–. Frederica Warner Schol., 1991–96, Susan B. Anthony Scholar in Residence and Prof., 1996–2001, Margaret Warner Grad. Sch. of Educn and Professional Develt, Univ. of Rochester, NY; Vis. Internat. Guest Scientist, Max Planck Inst. of Human Develt and Educn, Berlin, 1994; J. Woodrow Wilson Vis. Prof., Oppenheimer Foundn, Univ. of Witwatersrand, SA, 1996; Visiting Professor: Sch. of Educn, Univ. of Exeter, 2001–04; Centre for Educnl Innovation, Univ. of Sussex, 2002–03; STINT Foundn Prof., Uppsala Univ., Sweden, 2003–10; Res. Associate, Von Hügel Inst., St Edmund's Coll., Cambridge, 2004–; Catalan Res. Prof., Univ. of Barcelona, 2005; Joss Owen Chair of Education, Univ. of Plymouth, 2007–11; Sen. Vis. Fellow, Guerrand-Hermès Foundn for Peace, 2008–; Internat. Res. Prof., Univ. of Tallinn, 2012–15. Mem., Selection Cttee, Wellbeing in Social Contexts, Nat. Centre of Competence in Res., 2004–; CORE Societal Challenges Panel Expert, Fonds Nat. de la Recherche, Luxembourg, 2013–. Life Fellow, RSA, 2009. Dist. Vis. Professorial Award, Japanese Soc. for Promotion of Sci., Univ. of Tokyo, 1993. *Publications:* School Subjects and Curriculum Change, 1983, 3rd edn 1993; The Making of Curriculum: collected essays, 1988, 2nd edn 1995; Biography, Identity and Schooling, 1991; Through the Schoolhouse Door, 1993; Studying Curriculum: cases and methods, 1994; Currículo: teoria e história (Brazil), 1995, 3rd edn 1999; Historia del Curriculum (Spain), 1995; Att Starka Lararnas Roster: sex essaer om lararforskning och lararforskarsamarbete (Sweden), 1996; The Changing Curriculum: studies in social construction, 1997; Studying School Subjects, 1997; Subject Knowledge: readings for the study of school subjects, 1998; Das Schulfach als Handlungsrahmen: vergleichende Untersuchung zur Geschichte und Funktion der Schulfächer (Germany), 1999; La Crisis del Cambio Curricular (Spain), 2000; (with P. Sikes) Life History Research in Educational Settings: learning from lives, 2001; The Birth of Environmental Education (China), 2001; (jtly) Cyber Spaces/Social Spaces: culture clash in computerised classrooms, 2002; Estudio del Curriculum: casos y métodos (Argentina), 2003; Professional Knowledge, Professional Lives: studies in education and change, 2003; Learning Curriculum and Life Politics: selected works, 2005; Professional Knowledge, Professional Lives (China), 2007; Professionel Viden. Professionelt Liv (Denmark), 2007; (ed jtly) Education, Globalisation and New Times, 2007; Políticas do Conhecimento: vida e trabalho docente entre saberes e instituições, 2007; Investigating the Teacher's Life and Work, 2008 (Chinese edn 2014); As Políticas de Currículo e de Escolarização, 2008; Developing Professional Knowledge about Teachers, 2009; (jtly) Narrative Learning, 2010; Through the Schoolhouse Door, 2010; (jtly) Professional Knowledge and Educational Restructuring in Europe, 2011; (jtly) Narrative Pedagogy, 2011; Improving Learning Through the Lifecourse, 2011; Life Politics: conversations about education and culture, 2011; (jtly) The Life History of a School, 2011; (ed jtly) Explorations in Narrative Research, 2012; Developing Narrative Theory: life histories and personal representation, 2013; The Politics of Curriculum and Schooling, Chinese edn 2014; Curriculum, Personal Narrative and the Social Future, 2014; (with S. Gill) Critical Narrative as Pedagogy, 2014. *Recreations:* tennis, walking and birdwatching, jazz and rhythm and blues, Brighton and Hove FC supporter. *Address:* Education Research Centre, Room B323, Checkland Building, University of Brighton, Falmer, Brighton BN1 9PH. *T:* (01273) 644560.

GOODSON, Michael John; Assistant Auditor General, National Audit Office, 1984–93; *b* 4 Aug. 1937; *s* of late Herbert Edward William Goodson and Doris Maud Goodson; *m* 1958, Susan Elizabeth (*née* Higley) (*d* 2015); one *s* one *d*. *Educ:* King Henry VIII Sch., Coventry. Joined Exchequer and Audit Dept, 1955; Asst Auditor, 1955; Auditor, 1965; Private Sec. to Comptroller and Auditor Gen., 1967–70; Sen. Auditor, 1970; Health Service Ombudsman (on secondment), 1973–76; Chief Auditor, Exchequer and Audit Dept, 1976; Dep. Dir of Audit, 1978; Dir of Audit, 1981. *Recreations:* ornithology, model engineering. *Address:* 2 Bayley Mead, St John's Road, Boxmoor, Herts HP1 1US. *T:* (01442) 242611.

GOODSON-WICKES, Dr Charles; DL; consulting physician, company director, business consultant; *b* 7 Nov. 1945; *s* of late Ian Goodson Wickes, FRCP, Consultant Paediatrician and farmer, of Stock Harvard, Essex and of Monica Goodson-Wickes; *m* 1974, Judith Amanda Hopkinson, *d* of late Comdr John Hopkinson, RN, of Sutton Grange, near Stamford, Lincs; two *s*. *Educ:* Charterhouse; St Bartholomew's Hosp. (MB BS 1970). Called to the Bar, Inner Temple, 1972. Ho. Physician, Addenbrooke's Hosp., Cambridge, 1972; Surgeon-Capt., The Life Guards, 1973–77 (served BAOR, N Ireland, Cyprus); Silver Stick MO, Hsehold Cavalry, 1977; RARO, 1977–2000; re-enlisted as Lt-Col, 1991, for Gulf Campaign (served S Arabia, Iraq, Kuwait, with HQ 7 Armoured Bde). Clin. Asst, St Bart's Hosp., 1977–80; Consulting Phys., BUPA, 1977–86; Occupational Phys., 1980–94; formerly Med. advr to Barclays Bank, RTZ, McKinsey, Christie's, British Alcan, Collins, Meat & Livestock Commn etc; UK Advr, Norwegian Directorate of Health, 1983–94; Chm., Appeals Bd, Asbestos Licensing Regulations, 1982–87; Member: Med. Adv. Cttee, Industrial Soc., 1981–87; Fitness Adv. Panel, Inst. of Dirs, 1982–84; Adv. Council, Inst. for the Study of the Americas, Univ. of London, 2010–. Director: Medarc Ltd, 1981–; Thomas Greg and Sons Ltd, 1992– (Chm., 2011–); Nestor Healthcare Gp plc, 1993–99; Gyrus Gp plc, 1997–2007; RICS Business Develt Bd, 2010–; Ecohydra Technologies Ltd, 2014–, and other internat. cos. Contested (C) Islington Central, 1979. MP (C) Wimbledon, 1987–97; contested (C) same seat, 1997. Vice-Pres., Islington South and Finsbury Cons. Assoc., 1982–97. PPS to Minister of State for Housing and Planning, DoE, 1992–94, to Financial Sec. to HM Treasury, 1994–95, to Sec. of State for Transport, 1995–96. Mem., Select Cttee on Members' Interests, 1992–94; Vice-Chm., Constitutional Affairs Cttee, 1990–91; Sec., Arts and Heritage Cttee, 1990–92; Vice Chm., Defence Cttee, 1991–92; Mem., Jt Cttee, Consolidation of Bills, 1987–92; Founder Chm., All Party, British-Colombian Gp, 1995–97; Vice Chm., All Party British-Russian Gp, 1993–97; Treas., All Party British Chinese Gp, 1992–97. Fellow, Industry and Parlt Trust, 1991; Patron, Hansard Soc., 2003–. Vice Chm., Cons. Foreign and Commonwealth Council, 1997–2011. Dir Gen., Canning Hse, 2010–12. Treas., Dr Ian Goodson Wickes Fund for Handicapped Children, 1979–88; Vice-Pres., Combat Stress (formerly Ex-Services Mental Welfare Soc.), 1990–; Founder Chm., Countryside Alliance, 1997–99 (Patron, 2003–; Chm., 1994–98, Mem., Public Affairs Cttee, 1980–87, British Field Sports Soc.); Chm., 1997–98, Chief Exec., 1998–2007, London Playing Fields Soc., later Foundn; Chm., Rural Trust, 1999–; Mem., London Sports Bd, 2000–03 (Chm., Envmt Cttee, 2001–03); Vice-Pres., Gt Bustard Gp, 2008–. Governor, Highbury Grove Sch., 1977–85. Pte, The Parachute Regt (TA), 1963–65; Mem. HAC, 2013. Founder Chm., Essex Kit Cat Club, 1965. Freeman, City of London, 2014. DL Gtr London, 1999; Rep. DL Islington, 2011. *Publications:* The New Corruption, 1984; (contrib.) Another Country, 1999. *Recreations:* hunting, shooting, Real tennis, gardening, travel, history. *Address:* Watergate House, Bulford, Wilts SP4 9DY. *T:* (01980) 632344; 37 St James's Place, SW1A 1NS. *T:* (020) 7629 0981. *Clubs:* Boodle's, Pratt's, MCC.

GOODWAY, Russell; Member (Lab), County Council of the City and County of Cardiff, since 1995; Chief Executive, Community Pharmacy Wales, since 2009; *b* 23 Dec. 1955; *s* of Russell Donald Goodway and Barbara Mary Goodway (*née* Vizard); *m* 1979, Susan Yvonne Witchard; one *s*. *Educ:* Barry Boys' Comprehensive Sch.; University Coll., Swansea (BA Econs and Politics 1977). Partner, Keane Goodway & Co., Accountants, 1988–2000. Dep. Chm., Millennium Stadium plc, 1996–2004; Chief Exec., Cardiff Chamber of Commerce and Industry, 2005–07; Business Develt Dir, Paramount Office Interiors Ltd, 2008–09. Bd Mem., Cardiff Bay Develt Corp., 1993–2000. Member: Porthkerry Community Council, 1977–82 (Chm., 1980–81); Rhoose Community Council, 1982–87 (Chm., 1985–86);

S Glamorgan County Council: Mem., 1985–96; Chm., Property Services Cttee, 1988–89; Chm., Finance Cttee, 1989–92; Leader, and Chm. Policy Cttee, 1992–96; Dep. Chm., 1992–93; County Council of City and County of Cardiff: first Leader of the Council, 1995–2004, Exec. Leader, 2002–04; Chairman: Policy Cttee, 1995–99; Council's Cabinet, 1999–2004; Lord Mayor of Cardiff, 1999–2003; Cabinet Member: for Finance, Business and Local Economy, 2012–13; for Finance and Econ. Develt, 2013–14. Dep. Chm., Assembly of Welsh Counties, 1994–96. Chm., Millennium Stadium Charitable Trust, 2009–. OStJ 2004. *Recreations:* sport, especially Rugby and tennis, reading political biographies, music. *Address:* Singleton, 82 Colcot Road, Barry CF62 8HP. *T:* (01446) 749976.

GOODWILL, Robert; MP (C) Scarborough and Whitby, since 2005; Parliamentary Under-Secretary of State, Department for Transport, since 2013; *b* 31 Dec. 1956; *s* of late Robert W. Goodwill and Joan Goodwill; *m* 1987, Maureen (*née* Short); two *s* one *d. Educ:* Bootham Sch., York; Univ. of Newcastle upon Tyne (BSc Hons Agriculture). Farmer, 1979–. Contested (C): Redcar, 1992; NW Leics, 1997; Cleveland and Richmond, 1994, Yorks S, May 1998, EP elecns. MEP (C) Yorks and the Humber Reg., 1999–2004; Dep. Cons. Leader, EP, 2003–04. Opposition Whip, 2006–07; Shadow Transport Minister, 2007–10; an Asst Govt Whip, 2010–11; Govt Pairing Whip, 2011–13; a Lord Comr of HM Treasury (Govt Whip), 2012–13. *Recreations:* steam ploughing, travel, languages. *Address:* Southwood Farm, Terrington, York YO60 6QB. *T:* (01653) 648459; (constituency office) 21 Huntriss Row, Scarborough, N Yorks YO11 2ED. *E:* robert.goodwill.mp@parliament.uk.

GOODWIN, Christine, (Mrs Richard Goodwin); *see* Edzard, C.

GOODWIN, Daisy Georgia, (Mrs Marcus Wilford); television producer and writer; *b* London, 19 Dec. 1961; *d* of Richard Goodwin and late Jocasta Innes; *m* 1988, Marcus Wilford; two *d. Educ:* Westminster Sch.; Trinity Coll., Cambridge (BA Hist. 1983); Columbia Univ. (Harkness Fellow). Producer, BBC, 1985–98; programmes include: Homefront, Bookworm; Editl Dir, Talkback Thames, 1998–2005; programmes include: Grand Designs, Property Ladder, The Apprentice; Founder, Silver River Prodns, 2005; programmes include: The Supersizers, Pulling, Off By Heart, Hidden Talent, Shakespeare Off By Heart, If Walls Could Talk - an intimate history of the home; The Big Allotment Challenge, 2014. Presenter, Essential Poems, BBC, 2003–. Chair: Poetry Book Soc., 2003–07; Women Taking Action. FRSA. *Publications:* Silver River: memoir, 2007; My Last Duchess (novel), 2010; The Fortune Hunter (novel), 2014; edited: The Nation's Favourite Love Poems, 1997; 101 Poems to Save Your Life, 1998; 101 Poems to Get You Through Day and Night, 1999; Essential Poems to Fall in Love With, 2003; Poems for Life, 2004. *Recreations:* collecting books with Daisy in the title, avoiding meetings, quilting, making marmalade, reading poetry and classic crime.

GOODWIN, Dr Elizabeth Jane, OBE 2015; Chief Executive Officer, Waste and Resources Action Programme (WRAP), since 2007; *b* London, 6 June 1961; *d* of David Goodwin and Anna Goodwin (*née* Stretch, now Fitter); *m* 2011, Bruce Eggeling. *Educ:* Chichester High Sch. for Girls; University Coll. London (BSc 1st Cl.); Univ. of Exeter (PhD 1986). Technical Manager, ICI, 1986–92; Zeneca: Envmtl Advr, 1992–99; Envmtl Manager, 1999–2000; Eur. Envmtl Advr, 2000–01; Dir of Materials, WRAP, 2001–07. Hon. FSE 2013. Hon. DSc Cranfield, 2010. *Recreations:* running, walking, crosswords, sudokus, bridge, opera. *Address:* WRAP, The Old Academy, 21 Horsefair, Banbury, Oxon OX15 0AH. *T:* (01295) 819900.

GOODWIN, Frederick Anderson; Chief Executive, Royal Bank of Scotland Group plc, 2000–08 (Deputy Group Chief Executive, 1998–2000); Senior Adviser, RMJM, 2009–11; *b* 17 Aug. 1958; *s* of Frederick Anderson Goodwin and Marylyn Marshall Goodwin (*née* Mackintosh). *Educ:* Paisley GS; Univ. of Glasgow (LLB). CA 1983; FCIBS 1996; FCIB 2002. Joined Touche Ross & Co., 1979, Partner, 1988–95; Dep. Chief Exec., 1995, Chief Exec., 1996–98, Clydesdale Bank PLC; Chief Exec., Yorkshire Bank, 1997–98. Director: Bank of China, 2006–08; ABN AMRO, 2007–08. Dir, Scottish Business Achievement Award Trust, 2001–03. Chairman: Prince's Trust, Scotland, 1999–2003; Prince's Trust, 2003–09. DUniv: Paisley, 2001; Glasgow, 2002; Hon. LLD St Andrews, 2004. *Recreations:* restoring cars, golf.

GOODWIN, Prof. Graham Clifford, PhD; FRS 2002; FIEEE, FAA, FTSE; Professor of Electrical Engineering, 1983, now Laureate Professor, and Director, ARC Centre for Complex Dynamic Systems and Control, 2007–11, now Academic Researcher, University of Newcastle, New South Wales; *b* NSW, 20 April 1945; *s* of C. H. R. F. Goodwin; *m* 1967, Rosslyn Mackintosh; one *s* one *d. Educ:* Broken Hill High Sch.; Univ. of NSW (BSc 1964; BE 1966; PhD 1970). Lectr, Imperial Coll., Univ. of London, 1971–74; University of Newcastle, New South Wales: Lectr, 1974–75, Sen. Lectr, 1976, Associate Prof., 1977–83, Dept of Electrical Engrg; Hd, Dept of Electrical and Computer Engrg, 1979–84; Dir, Centre for Industrial Control Sci., 1988–96; Dean, Faculty of Engrg, 1994–96; Dir, Centre for Integrated Dynamics and Control, 1997–2001; ARC Fedn Fellow, 2002–06; Res. Dir, ARC Centre for Complex Dynamic Systems and Control, 2002–07. *Publications:* (jtly) Control Theory, 1970; (jtly) Dynamic System Identification, 1977; (jtly) Adaptive Filtering, Prediction and Control, 1984; (jtly) Digital Estimation and Control, 1990; (ed jtly) Adaptive Control Filtering and Signal Processing, 1994; (jtly) Sampling in Digital Signal Processing and Control, 1996; (jtly) Fundamental Limitations in Filtering and Control, 1996; (jtly) Control System Design, 2000; (jtly) Constrained Control and Estimation, 2003; chapters in books and articles in learned jls. *Address:* School of Electrical Engineering and Computer Science, University of Newcastle, University Drive, Callaghan, NSW 2308, Australia.

GOODWIN, Prof. Guy Manning, DPhil; FRCPsych, FMedSci; W. A. Handley Professor of Psychiatry, and Head, Department of Psychiatry, University of Oxford, 1996–2014, now Senior Research Fellow; Fellow of Merton College, Oxford, 1996–2014, now Emeritus; *b* 8 Nov. 1947; *s* of Kenneth M. Goodwin and Constance (*née* Hudson); *m* 1971, Philippa Catherine Georgeson; two *d. Educ:* Manchester GS; Exeter Coll., Oxford (open schol.; MA); Wolfson Coll., Oxford (Grad. Schol.; DPhil 1972); Magdalen Coll., Oxford (MB BCh 1978). FRCPE 1995–2000; FRCPsych 1995. Scholar, MRC, 1968–71; Fellow, Magdalen Coll., Oxford, 1971–76; House Physician, Nuffield Dept of Clin. Medicine, Oxford and House Surgeon, Horton Gen. Hosp., Banbury, 1978–79; Sen. House Officer, Nat. Hosp., Queen Sq., and Professorial Unit, Brompton Hosp., 1979–80; Registrar, Rotational Trng Scheme in Psychiatry, Oxford, 1980–83; MRC Clin. Trng Fellow, and Lectr, MRC Clin. Pharmacol. Unit, Oxford, 1983–86; MRC Clin. Scientist, Hon. Consultant Psychiatrist and Hon. Sen. Lectr, Edinburgh Univ., 1986–95; Prof. of Psychiatry, Edinburgh Univ., 1995–96. Res. Associate, Univ. of Washington, Seattle, 1972–74; Hobson Meml Schol., Oxford, 1975. Sen. Investigator, NIHR, 2011–. Mem., Neuroscis and Mental Health Grants and Fellowships Cttee, Wellcome Trust, 1992–97. Pres., British Assoc. for Psychopharmacol., 2002–04 (Mem. Council, 1993–97); Pres., Eur. Coll. of Neuropsychopharmacol., 2013–16. FMedSci 2006. *Publications:* contrib. learned jls on neurophysiol., psychopharmacol. and psychiatry. *Recreations:* football and opera passively, hillwalking actively. *Address:* Department of Psychiatry, Warneford Hospital, Oxford OX3 7JX.

GOODWIN, Jonathan; Founder, Lepe Partners, since 2011; *b* London, 12 Nov. 1972; *s* of Philip Goodwin and Ann Goodwin-Rooze; *m* 2011, Hon. Flora, *d* of Baron Hesketh, *qv*; three *s* one *d. Educ:* Charterhouse Sch.; Univ. of Nottingham (BA Geog.). Associate, Apax Partners, 1995–97; Man. Dir, Talk Radio, 1997; Gp Man. Dir, Wireless Gp plc, 1998–2000; Co-Founder, LongAcre Partners, 2000–07. Co-Founder: Founders Forum, 2005–; PROfounders Capital, 2010–. *Recreations:* shooting, sailing (J/109 class Cowes Week winner, 2012, 2013), tennis. *Address:* Lepe Partners, 17 Old Court Place, W8 4PL. *E:* rebecca@lepepartners.com. *Clubs:* Queen's, Royal Yacht Squadron.

GOODWIN, Dr Neil, CBE 2007; Chair: London Cancer Alliance, since 2012; Healthcare Support (Newcastle) Ltd, since 2014; Aintree University Hospitals NHS Foundation Trust, since 2014; *b* 1 March 1951; *s* of James and Dorothy Goodwin; *m* 1980, Sian Elizabeth Mary Holliday (marr. diss. 1992); two *s*; *m* 2006, Chris Hannah; one step *s* one step *d. Educ:* North Salford County Secondary Sch.; London Business Sch. (MBA); Manchester Business Sch. (PhD). FHSM, later FIHM, 1990–2014; CIHM, 2006–13. NHS mgt posts, London, Manchester, Liverpool, Southport, Bromsgrove, Hertfordshire, 1969–85; General Manager, Central Middlesex Hosp., 1985–88; Chief Executive: St Mary's Hosp., subseq. St Mary's Hosp. NHS Trust, 1988–94; Manchester HA, 1994–2002; Chief Exec., Gtr Manchester Strategic HA, 2002–06; Interim Chief Exec., N Cumbria Univ. Hosps NHS Trust, 2011–12. Vis. Prof. of Leadership Studies, Univ. of Manchester, 2004–15, Durham Univ., 2006–14, UCL, 2009–14. Dir, GoodwinHannah Ltd, 2006–14. Project Dir, UCL Partners Academic Health Science Partnership, 2008–09. Interim Dir, Nuffield Trust, 2007–08. Advisor: E. C. Harris LLP, 2006–08; Pinsent Masons, 2007–08; CHKS, 2007–12; Bd, Channel 3 Gp, 2015–. Non-exec. Dir, UK Transplant Authy, 2000–05. Member: Orgnl Audit Council and Accreditation Cttee, King's Fund Coll., 1993–2000; Manchester TEC Investors in People accreditation panel, 1995–99; Cabinet Office review of public sector leadership, 2000; Scientific Cttee, 2000–05, Bd, 2005–09, Eur. Health Mgt Assoc. Mem. Court, Manchester Univ., 2003–05. Advr, Serco Health, 2009–10. Editorial Adviser: British Jl of Health Care Mgt, 1998–2014; Jl of Mgt in Medicine, 1999–2014; Leadership in Health Services, 2008–14. MCMI (MBIM 1982), FCMI 2008. *Publications:* Leadership in Healthcare: a European perspective, 2005; (contrib.) Perspectives in Public Health, 2006; (contrib.) Health Care Management, 2006; academic papers and articles on corporate failure, public sector leadership, the contextual challenges of leadership, customer care in hosps, leadership develt needs of chief execs and public health professionals, and internat. healthcare. *Recreations:* Coronation Street, Friend of Lloyd George Museum, photography. *Address:* The Old School, Windmill Lane, Preston on the Hill, Cheshire WA4 4AZ. *E:* neil@goodwinhannah.co.uk.

GOODWIN, Nicholas Alexander John; QC 2014; a Recorder, since 2009; *b* London, 10 Nov. 1970; *s* of Frank and Mary Rose Goodwin; *m* 2006, Alison Marshall; one *d. Educ:* King's Sch., Canterbury; Oriel Coll., Oxford (MA English Lit.). Called to the Bar, Inner Temple, 1995; in practice as barrister, specialising in family law. *Recreations:* music, mountaineering. *Address:* Harcourt Chambers, 2 Harcourt Buildings, Temple, EC4Y 9DB. *T:* (020) 7353 6961. *E:* ngoodwin@harcourtchambers.co.uk.

GOODWIN, Paul; Artistic Director and Principal Conductor, Carmel Bach Festival, since 2011; *b* 2 Sept. 1956; *s* of Norman and Audrey Goodwin; *m* 1995, Helen Gough; two *s* one *d. Educ:* City of London Sch.; Univ. of Nottingham (BMus); Hochschule für Musik, Wien (Postgrad. Dip.); Guildhall Sch. of Music and Drama (Postgrad. Dip.). Chorister, Temple Ch Choir, London. Principal and solo oboist, English Consort, King's Consort, and London Classical Players, 1985–97; Prof. of Baroque Oboe, RCM, 1986–96; Musical Director: London Oboe band, 1985–97; Royal Coll. of Music baroque orch., 1993–99; Dartington Early Opera, 1995–2001; Associate Conductor, Acad. of Ancient Music, 1996–2008; Principal Guest Conductor, English Chamber Orch., 1997–2003; regular guest conductor in Europe and US, incl. Kammerorch. Basel, MDR Rundfunk Orch. Leipzig, Bayerischer Rundfunk, Munich, Saint Paul Chamber Orch., San Francisco SO, Minn, Spanish Nat. Orch., Scottish Chamber Orch., Scottish Nat. Orch., Hallé, CBSO, Philadelphia Orch., Nat. SO Washington; opera productions incl. Le Nozze di Figaro and Die Zauberflöte, Opera de Oviedo and Opera North, Iphigénie en Tauride, Komische Oper Berlin; Idomeneo, Graz Opera; Orlando, Scottish Opera, Flanders Opera, Opera Australia, Jeptha, Welsh Nat. Opera. Handel Hon. Prize, City of Halle, 2007. *Recreations:* sailing, racquet sports. *Address:* c/o Melanie Moult, Askonas Holt, Lincoln House, 300 High Holborn, WC1V 7JH. *T:* (020) 7400 1751, *Fax:* (020) 7400 1799. *E:* melanie.moult@askonasholt.co.uk.

GOODWIN, Dr Philip Paul; Chief Executive Officer, Voluntary Service Overseas International, since 2015; *b* 15 Feb. 1965; *s* of Dennis Paul Goodwin and Wendy Goodwin; *m* 1999, Annette Schwalbe; one *s* one *d. Educ:* Univ. of Reading (BSc Agricl Econs); Wye Coll., Univ. of London (MSc Rural Resource and Envmtl Policy; PhD Cultural Geog.). Professional musician and songwriter, 1989–93; volunteer, UNA Internat. Service, Mali, 1998; Res. Officer, ODI, 1999; British Council: Director: Develt Services, Pakistan, 1999–2002; Uganda, 2002–04; Regional Director: East and West Africa, 2004–08; Sub-Saharan Africa, 2008–09; Global Prog. Leader, Creative and Knowledge Economy, 2009–10; CEO, TREE AID, 2010–15. *Publications:* (with Tony Page) From Hippos to Gazelles: how leaders create leaders, 2008; contrib. refereed articles to Trans IBG, Society and Space: Envmt and Planning D, Jl Rural Studies. *Recreations:* songwriting, making records, my garden. *Address:* c/o VSO International, 100 London Road, Kingston upon Thames KT2 6QJ.

GOODWIN, Prof. Phillip Bramley, PhD; Professor of Transport Policy, Centre for Transport and Society, University of the West of England, 2005–12, now Emeritus Professor; *b* 6 March 1944; *s* of Dennis and Joan Goodwin; *m* 1966, Margaret Livesey (separated); one *d. Educ:* Henry Thornton Grammar Sch.; UCL (BSc Econs 1965; PhD Civil Engrg 1973). FCILT, FCIHT. Res. Asst, LRD Ltd, 1965–66; Res., UCL, 1966–74; Transport Planner, GLC, 1974–79; Dep. Dir, 1979–81, Dir, and Reader, 1981–95, Transport Studies Unit, Univ. of Oxford; Prof. of Transport Policy and Dir, ESRC Transport Studies Unit, UCL, 1996–2004, now Emeritus Prof. Mem., Standing Adv. Cttee on Trunk Road Assessment, 1979–2000; Chm., Ind. Adv. Panel for Transport White Paper, 1997–98. Non-exec. Dir, Dover Harbour Bd, 1989–2005. Distinguished Contrib. Award, Instn of Highways and Transportation, 1998. Founding Ed., Transport Policy, 1993; Ed.-in-chief, Jl Transportation Res. (A) Policy & Practice, 2005–10. *Publications:* Subsidised Public Transport and the Demand for Travel, 1983; Long Distance Transportation, 1983; (jtly) Transport and the Environment, 1991; (jtly) Trunk Roads and the Generation of Traffic, 1994; Car Dependence, 1995; (jtly) Transport and the Economy, 1999; approx. 200 articles in learned jls, conf. papers, and contribs to books on transport policy and travel behaviour. *Recreation:* Isla de el Hierro. *E:* philinelh@yahoo.com.

GOODWIN-GILL, Prof. Guy Serle, DPhil; Professor of International Refugee Law, University of Oxford, 1998–2014, now Emeritus; Senior Research Fellow, All Souls College, Oxford, 2002–14, now Emeritus; *b* Ealing, 25 Dec. 1946; *s* of Walter Booth Goodwin and Josephine Esther Goodwin (*née* Brown) and step *s* of Ian Arthur Gill; *m* 1991, Sharon Anne Rusu. *Educ:* Mill Hill Sch.; Wadham Coll., Oxford (BA Juris. 1968; DPhil 1974). Called to the Bar, Inner Temple, 1971; Lectr, 1971–74, Sen. Lectr, 1974–76, Coll. of Law, London; Legal Advr, UNHCR, UK, Australia and Geneva, 1976–88; Vis. Prof., Osgoode Hall Law Sch., 1988; Vis. Prof., 1988–89, Prof. of Law, 1989–97, Carleton Univ., Ottawa; Prof. of Asylum Law (pt-time), Univ. of Amsterdam, 1994–99; Rubin Dir of Res., Inst. of Eur. Studies, Oxford Univ., 1997–2002; in practice at the Bar, Blackstone Chambers, 2000–; Vis. Prof., Académie de droit humanitaire, Geneva, 2008–11; Julius Stone Vis. Fellow, Faculty of Law, Univ. of NSW, 2010; Dir, Hague Acad. of Internat. Law, Centre for Res. and Studies, 2010; W. J. Ganshof van der Meersch Chair, Univ. Libre de Bruxelles, 2010–11. Founding Ed. and Ed.-in-Chief, Internat. Jl Refugee Law, 1988–2001. Pres., Refugee and Migrant Justice (formerly Refugee Legal Centre), 1997–2010. Mem. Council, Overseas Develt Inst., 2007–13. Pres., Media Appeals Bd of Kosovo, 2000–03. Order of Independence (Jordan), 2007. *Publications:* International Law and the Movement of Persons Between States, 1978; The Refugee in International Law, 1983, 3rd edn with J. McAdam, 2007; Free and Fair Elections, 1994, 2nd edn 2006; (with I. Cohn) Child Soldiers, 1994; (ed with S. Talmon and contrib.) The Reality of International Law: essays in honour of Ian Brownlie, 1997; Codes of Conduct for Elections, 1998; (ed with I. Brownlie) Basic Documents on Human Rights, 4th edn 2002, 6th edn 2010; (ed with H. Lambert and contrib.) The Limits of Transnational Law, 2010. *Recreations:* music, cooking, gardening, cats, cycling. *Address:* All Souls College, Oxford OX1 4AL. *T:* (01865) 279379. *E:* guy.goodwin-gill@all-souls.ox.ac.uk.

GOODY, Juliet Constance Wyatt, (Lady Goody); *see* Mitchell, J. C. W.

GOODYEAR, Charles Waterhouse, (Chip); non-executive Chairman, Metallum Holding SA, since 2014; *b* 18 Jan. 1958; *s* of Charles and Linda Goodyear; *m* 1992, Elizabeth Dabezies; one *s* one *d*. *Educ:* Yale Univ. (BSc Geol., Geophys 1980); Wharton Sch. of Finance, Univ. of Pennsylvania (MBA 1983). Kidder, Peabody & Co.: Associate, 1983–85; Asst Vice Pres., 1985–86; Vice Pres., 1986–89; Freeport-McMoRan, Inc.: Vice Pres., Corporate Finance, 1989–93; Sen. Vice Pres. and Chief Investment Officer, 1993–95; Exec. Vice Pres. and Chief Financial Officer, 1995–97; Pres., Goodyear Capital Corp., 1997–99; Chief Financial Officer, BHP Ltd, 1999–2001; Exec. Dir and Chief Develt Officer, 2001–03, CEO, 2003–07, BHP Billiton. Non-exec. Dir, Anadarko Petroleum Corp., 2012–15. *Recreations:* bicycling, ski-ing, fishing.

GOODYEAR, Roger Maxwell, MBE 2015; Vice Lord-Lieutenant of Banffshire, since 2011; *b* Glasgow, 19 Oct. 1944; *s* of Max and Gwendoline Goodyear; *m* 1980, June Marshall; two *s*. *Educ:* Longrood Prep. Sch.; Wellingborough Sch. Trainee and Asst Manager, John West, Unilever, 1963–68; Product Manager: Nabisco, 1968–72; Baxters of Speyside, 1972–76; Sales and Mktg Manager, Harrison Barber, 1976–80; CWA: Account Dir, 1980–85; Dir, 1985–88; Man. Dir, 1988–2002. Dir, Banffshire Partnership, 2003–; Chm., Banffshire Coast Tourism Partnership, 2009–. Chm., Scottish Traditional Boat Fest., 2005–. DL Banffshire, 2009. *Recreations:* cycling (any weather), reading, travel, railway modelling. *Address:* Craigower House, Barbank Street, Portsoy, Banff AB45 2PD. *T:* (01261) 842894. *E:* rogergdy@aol.com.

GOODYER, Prof. Ian Michael, MD; FRCPsych, FMedSci; Foundation Professor of Child and Adolescent Psychiatry, Cambridge University, since 1992; Fellow of Wolfson College, Cambridge, since 1993; *b* 2 Nov. 1949; *s* of Mark and Belle Goodyer; *m* 1979, Jane Elizabeth Akister; one *s* one *d*. *Educ:* University College London; St George's Hosp.; Oxford Univ.; Newcastle Univ.; Brown Univ. MB BS, MD London; MRCPsych 1976, FRCPsych 1990; DCH 1978. Sen. Lectr, Child/Adolescent Psych. and Consultant, Univ. of Manchester and Salford HA, 1983–87; Cambridge University: Foundn Lectr in Child Psych., 1987–92; Head, Developmental Psych. Section, 1992–. FMedSci 1999. *Publications:* Life Experiences, Development and Child Psychopathology, 1991; The Depressed Child and Adolescent: developmental and clinical perspectives, 1995, 2nd edn 2000; Unipolar Depression: a lifespan perspective, 2003; (with David Goldberg) The Origins and Course of Common Mental Disorders, 2005; (jtly) Social Cognition and Developmental Psychopathology, 2008; contribs to learned jls. *Recreations:* keeping fit, guitar. *Address:* Developmental Psychiatry Section, Douglas House, 18 Trumpington Road, Cambridge CB2 8AH. *T:* (01223) 746066.

GOOLD, Sir George William, 8th Bt *cr* 1801, of Old Court, Cork; *b* 25 March 1950; *o s* of Sir George Leonard Goold, 7th Bt and of Joy Cecelia Goold (now Joy, Lady Goold); *S* father, 1997; *m* 1973, Julie Ann Crack; two *s*. *Heir: s* George Leonard Powell Goold [*b* 1 Dec. 1975; *m* 1999, Kirsty Ann Ling (marr. diss. 2014); one *s* one *d*]. *Address:* PO Box 176, Woollahra, NSW 1350, Australia. *T:* (2) 408421159.

GOOLEY, Michael David William, CBE 2007; FRGS; Founder and Chairman, Trailfinders Ltd, since 1970; *b* 13 Oct. 1936; *s* of late Denis David Gooley and Lennie Frances May Gooley (*née* Woodward); *m* 1st, 1961, Veronica Georgina Broad (marr. diss. 1970); two *d*; 2nd, 1971, Hilary Eila (marr. diss. 1981; she *d* 1993), *d* of Sir Paul Mallinson, 3rd Bt; one *s* one *d*; 3rd, 1983, Bernadette Mary Woodward (marr. diss. 1997); 4th, 2000, Fiona Kathleen Leslie. *Educ:* St John's Beaumont Prep. Sch.; St George's, Weybridge; RMA Sandhurst. Enlisted Regular Army, 1955: commnd 2nd Lieut, S Staffs Regt, 1956; joined 22 SAS, 1958; served Malaya and Arabian Peninsula; Adjt, 21 SAS, 1961–63; 1st Bn Staffords, 1963; served Kenya; 2nd tour, 22 SAS, 1964; served Malay Peninsula, Borneo and S Arabia; retd 1965. Mil. Advr to Royalist Yemini Army, 1965–69. Leader, expedition Trans Africa, 1971. Founder Trustee, Mike Gooley Trailfinders Charity, 1995. FInstD 1978; FRGS 1996. Hon. Life FRSA 2005. Patron, Prostate Cancer Charity, 1998–. Trustee, Special Forces Club, 1996–2007. *Publications:* Trans Africa Route Report, 1972. *Recreations:* travel, aviation, pragmatic entrepreneurialism, wining and dining, supporting Ealing Trailfinders RFC. *Address:* (office) 9 Abingdon Road, W8 6AH. *Club:* Special Forces.

GOOSE, Duncan; Founder and Chief Executive Officer, Global Ethics Group, since 2004; *b* Edinburgh, 1968; *s* of Dr David Goose and Joy Goose; *m* 2009, Dr Marta Boffito; one *s* one *d*. *Educ:* Wisbech Grammar Sch.; Framlingham Coll.; Coventry Poly. (HND Business Studies 1987). Business Develt Dir, Black Cat, 1994–98; global motorcycle odyssey (sabbatical), 1998–2000; Business Develt Dir, JWT, 2000–04. Launched One Water, 2004. Trustee: One Foundn, 2005–12; Coventry Univ., 2009–11; John Lewis Foundn, 2010–12. Hon. Mem., Path North, 2007–. Hon. DBA Sunderland, 2009. *Recreations:* motorbiking, travel, charitable causes, paragliding, painting, cookery. *Address:* Global Ethics Ltd, 13–17 Princes Road, Richmond, Surrey TW10 6DQ. *E:* duncan@global-ethics.com.

GOOSE, Julian Nicholas; QC 2002; **His Honour Judge Goose;** a Senior Circuit Judge and Resident Judge, Sheffield Combined Court Centre, and Honorary Recorder of Sheffield, since 2013; *b* 26 July 1961; *s* of Alan Charles Goose and Pauline Jean Goose; *m* 1987, Susan Frances Rose Bulmer; two *s* one *d*. *Educ:* Birkdale Sch.; Silverdale Sch.; Leeds Univ. (LLB Hons). Called to the Bar, Lincoln's Inn, 1984, Bencher, 2009. Junior, NE Circuit, 1992; Recorder 1998–2013. Hd of Zenith Chambers, 2004–13. Member: Advocacy Trng Council, 2004– (Vice Chm., 2012–14); Sentencing Council, 2014–. *Recreations:* golf, friends, family. *Address:* Sheffield Combined Court Centre, The Law Courts, 50 West Bar, Sheffield S3 8PH. *Club:* Alwoodley Golf.

GOOSE, Margaret Elizabeth, OBE 2004; Vice President, Stroke Association, since 2006 (Chief Executive, 1997–2004); *b* 10 Oct. 1945; *d* of late Leonard Charles Goose and Gladys Muriel Goose (*née* Smith). *Educ:* Blyth Sch., Norwich; Newnham Coll., Cambridge (BA 1967; MA 1971). FHSM 1991. Gen. mgt in hosps and health authorities, 1967–82; Chief Exec., N Beds HA, 1982–92; Hd of Health and Mgt Develt Div., Nuffield Inst. for Health, Univ. of Leeds, 1993–97. Lay Mem., Council, RCP, 2004–08 (Chm., Patient and Carer Involvement Steering Gp, 2004–08; Trustee, 2008–12). Gov., Health Foundn, 2007–; Mem., DoH Nat. Quality Bd, 2009–14. Trustee, Beds, Cambs, Northants, and Peterborough Wildlife Trust, 2005–14 (Vice-Chm., 2009–14). Pres., IHSM, 1989–90. Hon. MFPHM 1998. Hon. FRCP 2008. *Recreations:* walking, travel, theatre, music, friends.

GOOSEY, Michael William, PhD; FRSC; sustainable bioenergy and industrial biotechnology research and development consultant, since 2010; *b* Northampton, 18 Nov. 1955; *s* of Donald Joseph Goosey and Doris Edith Mary Goosey (*née* Line); *m* 1981, Elizabeth Ann Curtis; two *s* one *d*. *Educ:* Raunds Secondary Sch.; Univ. of Birmingham (BSc Hons Biochem. 1978; PhD Biochem. 1981). CChem 1997; FRSC 2007. Parkinson's Disease Res. Fellow, 1981–82; Sen. Res. Scientist, Dow Chemical Co. Ltd, King's Lynn and Letcombe Regis, 1982–88; Shell: Gp Leader, Sittingbourne Res. Centre, 1988–94, Resource and Prog. Manager, Analysis and Measurement Dept, Thornton Res. Centre, 1994–99, Shell Research Ltd; Business Gp Manager, Analytical Shell Global Solutions and Stanlow Oil and Petrochemicals Refinery, 1999–2005; Global Analytical Technol. Manager, Shell Global Solutions, 2005–07; Global Innovation Biodomain Technol. Manager, 2007–10. Member: Neurosci. Initiative Bd, SERC, 1989–93; Steering Gp, Industrial Biotechnol. Innovation and Growth Team (report to govt on Maximising UK Opportunities from Industrial Biotechnol. in a Low Carbon Econ.), 2009; Council, BBSRC, 2011–. Mem., Industrial Bd, Diamond Synchrotron Radiation Source, Oxford, 2005–07. Non-exec. Dir, Biosyntha Technol. Ltd, 2012– (Chm., 2013–); Mem., Adv. Bd, Algenuity, 2012–. Hon. Prof. of Sustainable Bioenergy, Univ. of Nottingham, 2011–. Mem., Editl Bd, Pesticide Jl, 1991–93. *Publications:* (ed jtly) Biochemistry of Cell Walls and Membranes in Fungi, 1989; papers on insect and fungal biochemical subjects. *Recreations:* bee keeper, fly fishing, World War 2 history, food and wine, travel. *Address:* Cherry Tree Cottage, The Orchard, Worthenbury, near Wrexham LL13 0BF. *T:* (01948) 770516. *E:* mikegoosey@hotmail.com.

GOPALAN, Coluthur, MD, DSc; FRCP, FRCPE; FRS 1987; President, Nutrition Foundation of India, New Delhi, since 1979; *b* 29 Nov. 1918; *s* of C. Doraiswami Iyengar and Mrs Pattammal; *m* 1940, Seetha Gopalan; one *s* one *d* (and one *s* decd). *Educ:* Univ. of Madras (MD); Univ. of London (PhD, DSc). Fellow, Acad. of Med. Scis, India, 1961; FIASc 1964; FNA 1966. Dir, Nat. Inst. of Nutrition, Hyderabad, 1960–74; Dir-Gen., Indian Council of Med. Res., New Delhi, 1975–79. Hon. DSc. Banares Hindu, 1982. *Publications:* Nutritive Value of Indian Foods, 1966; Nutrition and Health Care, 1984; Use of Growth Charts for Promoting Child Nutrition: a review of global experience, 1985; Combating Undernutrition: basic issues and practical approaches, 1987; Nutrition Problems and Programmes in South East Asia, 1987; Nutrition in Developmental Transition in South East Asia, 1992; Recent Trends in Nutrition, 1993; Towards Better Nutrition: problems and policies, 1993; Nutrition Research in South East Asia: the emerging agenda for the future, 1994; over 200 contribs to sci. jls; chapters on specific topics to several books on nutrition in internat. pubns on nutrition. *Recreation:* music. *Address:* Nutrition Foundation of India, C-13, Qutab Institutional Area, New Delhi 110016, India. *T:* (11) 6857814, 6965410; 39 Landon Road, Kilpauk, Chennai 600010, India. *Club:* India International Centre (New Delhi).

GORAI, Rt Rev. Dinesh Chandra; Bishop of Calcutta, 1982–99; *b* 15 Jan. 1934; *m* Binapani; two *c*. *Educ:* Calcutta Univ. (BA 1956). Serampore Theological Coll. (BD 1959). Ordained, 1962; Methodist Minister in Calcutta/Barrackpore, 1968–70; first Bishop, Church of N India Diocese of Barrackpore, 1970–82; Dep. Moderator, 1980, Moderator, 1983–86, Church of N India. Hon. DD: Bethel Coll., 1985; Serampore Coll., 1991. *Publications:* Society at the Cross Road, 1968; (ed) Transfer of Vision: a leadership development programme for the Church of North India 1983–1986, 1984; New Horizons in Christian Ministry, 1993. *Address:* Binapani Villa, 28 Mahatma Ghandi Road, Keorapukur M., Calcutta 700 082, India.

GORARD, Anthony John; *b* 15 July 1927; *s* of William James and Rose Mary Gorard; *m* 1954, Barbara Kathleen Hampton; one *s* three *d*. *Educ:* Ealing Grammar School. Chartered Accountant, 1951; Manufacturing Industry, 1952–58; Anglia Television Ltd, 1959–67, Executive Director and Member of Management Cttee; Managing Director, HTV Ltd, 1967–78; Chief Exec., HTV Gp Ltd, 1976–78; Director: Independent Television Publications Ltd, 1967–78; Independent Television News Ltd, 1973–78; Chief Exec., Cardiff Broadcasting Co. Ltd, 1979–81; Consultant, Mitchell Beazley Television, 1982–83; hotel proprietor, 1983–87; restaurant owner, 1987–94. Chm., British Regional Television Association, 1970–71. *Recreations:* gardening, pottery, rambling. *Address:* 6 Shetland Close, Leigh Park, Westbury, Wilts BA13 2GN. *T:* (01373) 824261.

GORBACHEV, Mikhail Sergeyevich; President: International Foundation for Socio-Economic and Political Studies (Gorbachev Foundation), since 1992; Green Cross International, since 1993; Executive President of the Soviet Union, 1990–91; *b* 2 March 1931; *m* 1953, Raisa Gorbacheva (*d* 1999); one *d*. *Educ:* Moscow State Univ. (law graduate); Stavropol Agric. Inst. Machine operator, 1946; joined CPSU 1952; First Sec., Stavropol Komsomol City Cttee, 1956–58, later Dep. Head of Propaganda; 2nd, later 1st Sec., Komsomol Territorial Cttee, 1958–62; Party Organizer, Stavropol Territorial Production Bd of Collective and State Farms, 1962; Head, Dept of party bodies, CPSU Territorial Cttee, 1963–66; 1st Sec., Stavropol City Party Cttee, 1966–68; 2nd Sec., 1968–70, 1st Sec., 1970–78, Stavropol Territorial CPSU Cttee; Central Committee, Communist Party of Soviet Union: Mem., 1971–91; Sec., with responsibility for agric., 1978–85; Alternate Mem., 1979–80, then Mem., Political Bureau; Gen. Sec., 1985–91. Deputy, Supreme Soviet: USSR, 1970–89 (Chm., Foreign Affairs Commn of the Soviet of the Union, 1984–85; Mem., 1985–88, Chm., 1988–89, Presidium); RSFSR, 1980–90; Deputy, Congress of Peoples' Deps, USSR, 1989; Chm., Supreme Soviet, USSR, 1989–90. Freeman of Aberdeen, 1993. Hon. Citizen of Berlin, 1992. Nobel Peace Prize, 1990; Ronald Reagan Freedom Award, 1992. Orders of Lenin, of Red Banner of Labour, Badge of Honour. *Publications:* A Time for Peace, 1985; The Coming Century of Peace, 1986; Speeches and Writings (7 vols), 1986–90; Peace has no Alternative, 1986; Moratorium, 1986; Perestroika: new thinking for our country and the world, 1987; The August Coup, 1991; December, 1991; My Stand, 1992; The Years of Hard Decisions, 1993; Life and Reforms, 1995 (UK edn, Memoirs, 1996); Reflections on the Past and Future, 1998; Alone With Myself, 2012. *Address:* (office) 39 Leningradsky Prospekt bdg14, Moscow 125167, Russia. *T:* (095) 9439990, *Fax:* (095) 9439594.

GORDHAN, Pravin Jamnadas; Minister of Cooperative Governance and Traditional Affairs, South Africa, since 2014; *b* Durban, 12 April 1949; *s* of Jamnadas Gordhan and Rumba Gordhan; *m* 1990, Vanitha Raju; two *d*. *Educ:* Sastri Coll., Durban; Univ. of Durban Westville (Bachelor of Pharmacy 1973). Organised and led student movement and civic structures during 1970s and 1980s; pharmacist, King Edward VII Hosp., Durban, 1974–81. Chm., multi-party talks, Convention for a Democratic SA, 1990; Co-Chm., Transitional Exec. Council, 1991–94. MP (ANC), SA, 1994–98; Chm., Constitutional Cttee, 1996–98. Dep. Comr, 1998–99, Comr, 1999–2009, SA Revenue Service; Minister of Finance, 2009–14. Chairman: World Customs Orgn, 2000–06; Forum on Tax Admin, OECD, 2008–. Hon. Dr Commerce South Africa, 2007; Hon. Dr Law Cape Town, 2007; DTech (Business Admin) Free State Central Univ. of Technol., 2009. Comdr, Order of the Crown (Belgium), 2002. *Recreations:* reading, gym, walks. *Address:* Ministry of Cooperative Governance and Traditional Affairs, Private Bag X802, Pretoria 0001, South Africa.

GORDIEVSKY, Oleg Antonovich, CMG 2007; writer on political affairs; lecturer; *b* Moscow, 10 Oct. 1938; *s* of Anton Lavrentyevich Gordievsky and Olga Nikolayevna Gordievsky; *m* (marr. diss.); two *d*. *Educ:* Inst. of Internat. Relations, Moscow (Bachelor Internat. Relns). Dep. Hd of Station, Copenhagen, 1974–78, Actg Hd of Station, London, 1984–85, KGB; Secret Agent, SIS, 1974–85; arrested by KGB, evacuated to Moscow and subseq. escaped back to UK, 1985. Hon. DLitt Buckingham, 2005. *Publications:* (with C. Andrew) KGB: the inside story of its foreign operations from Lenin to Gorbachev, 1990; (with C. Andrew) Instructions from the Centre, 1991; (with C. Andrew) More Instructions from the Centre, 1992; Next Stop Execution, 1995; (with I. Rogatchi) Opaque Mirror, 1997; (with J. Andersen) De Rode Spioner, 2002; contrib. internat. and political magazines. *Recreations:* cycling, collection of dictionaries of Germanic languages. *Address:* c/o A. M. Heath & Co. Ltd, 6 Warwick Court, WC1R 5DJ. *T:* and *Fax:* (01483) 417481. *E:* navole1@aol.com.

GORDON, family name of **Marquess of Huntly** and of **Baron Gordon of Strathblane**.

GORDON OF STRATHBLANE, Baron *cr* 1997 (Life Peer), of Deil's Craig in Stirling; **James Stuart Gordon,** CBE 1984; Chairman, Scottish Radio Holdings, 1996–2005; *b* 17 May 1936; *s* of James Gordon and Elsie (*née* Riach); *m* 1971, Margaret Anne Stevenson; two *s* one *d*. *Educ:* St Aloysius' Coll., Glasgow; Glasgow Univ. (MA Hons). Political Editor, STV, 1965–73; Man. Dir, Radio Clyde, 1973–96; Chief Exec., Radio Clyde Hldgs, subseq.

Scottish Radio Hldgs, 1991–96. Chairman: Scottish Exhibn Centre, 1983–89; Scottish Tourist Bd, 1998–2001 (Mem., 1997–98); Rajar, 2003–06; Vice-Chm., Melody Radio, 1991–97; Member: Scottish Develt Agency, 1981–90; Scottish Adv. Bd, BP, 1990–2003; Director: Clydeport Hldgs, 1992–98; Johnston Press plc, 1996–2007; Active Capital (formerly AIM) Trust plc, 1996–2009. Chm., Adv. Gp on Listed Sporting Events, 1997–98; Member: Cttee of Inquiry into Teachers' Pay and Conditions, 1986; Cttee to Review Funding of BBC, 1999. Trustee: John Smith Meml Trust, 1994–2007; Nat. Galls of Scotland, 1998–2002. Chm., Glasgow Common Purpose, 1995–97. Mem. Court, Univ. of Glasgow, 1984–97. Hon. DLitt Glasgow Caledonian, 1994; DUniv Glasgow, 1998. *Recreations:* ski-ing, walking, genealogy. *Address:* Deil's Craig, Strathblane, Glasgow G63 9ET. *T:* 07711 223149. *Clubs:* New (Edinburgh); Glasgow Art (Glasgow); Prestwick Golf.

GORDON, Very Rev. Canon Alexander Ronald; Chaplain, Holy Trinity, Geneva, since 2014; *b* 16 Dec. 1949; *s* of Alexander Donald and Norah May Gordon; *m* 1979, Geraldine Worrall; one *s* two *d*. *Educ:* Nottingham Univ. (BPharm 1971); Leeds Univ. (DipTh 1976); Coll. of the Resurrection, Mirfield. MRPharmS 1972. Ordained deacon, 1977, priest, 1978; Asst Curate, St Michael and All Angels, Headingley, 1977–80; Asst Priest, St Peter and St Paul, Fareham, 1980–83; Vicar, St John Baptist, Cudworth, 1983–85; *locum tenens*, St Andrew, Tain, 1985–87; Priest-in-charge, Lairg, Dornoch and Brora, 1987–2001; Diocesan Dir of Ordinands, Dio. Moray, Ross and Caithness, 1990–2001; Canon, St Andrew's Cathedral, Inverness, 1995–2001 (Hon. Canon, 2001–); Chaplain, St Alban, Strasbourg, 2001–05; Asst Dir of Ordinands, Dio. Gibraltar in Europe, 2004–05; Provost, St Andrew's Cathedral, Inverness, 2005–14. Associate Staff Mem., Church and Soc. Commn, Conf. of European Chs, 2004–. *Recreations:* music, travel, hill walking, reading detective and spy fiction, trying to get my computer to do what I want it to do, photography. *Address:* 84 rue de Montbrillant, 1202 Geneva, Switzerland. *T:* 227343817. *E:* canonalexgordon@holytrinitygeneva.org.

GORDON, Sir Andrew Cosmo Lewis D.; *see* Duff Gordon.

GORDON, Boyd; Fisheries Secretary, Department of Agriculture and Fisheries for Scotland, 1982–86; *b* 18 Sept. 1926; *er s* of David Gordon and Isabella (*née* Leishman); *m* 1951, Elizabeth Mabel (*née* Smith); two *d*. *Educ:* Musselburgh Grammar School. Following military service with the Royal Scots, joined the Civil Service, initially with Min. of Labour, then Inland Revenue; Department of Agriculture and Fisheries for Scotland: joined, 1953; Principal, Salmon and Freshwater Fisheries Administration and Fisheries R&D, 1962–73; Asst Secretary, Agriculture Economic Policy, EEC Co-ordination and Agriculture Marketing, 1973–82. *Recreations:* family and church affairs, gardening, sport of all kinds, reading, playing and writing Scottish fiddle music. *Address:* 87 Duddingston Road, Edinburgh EH15 1SP. *Club:* Civil Service.

GORDON, Brian William, OBE 1974; HM Diplomatic Service, 1949–81, retired; Commercial Counsellor, Caracas, 1980–81; *b* 24 Oct. 1926; *s* of William and Doris Margaret Gordon; *m* 1951, Sheila Graham Young; two *s* one *d*. *Educ:* Tynemouth Grammar School. HM Forces (Lieut in IA), 1944–47; joined HM Foreign Service (now Diplomatic Service), 1949; served in: Saigon; Libya; Second Sec. in Ethiopia, 1954–58 and in Peru, 1959–61; HM Consul: Leopoldville, Congo, 1962–64; New York, 1965–67; Puerto Rico, 1967–69; Consul-General, Bilbao, 1969–73; Asst Head, Trade Relations and Export Dept, FCO, 1974–77; Dep. Consul-Gen., Los Angeles, 1977–80. *Recreations:* golf, walking. *Address:* 4 Cragside, Corbridge, Northumberland NE45 5EU.

See also I. W. Gordon.

GORDON, Charles; Managing Director, Charlie Gordon Associates Ltd, since 2012; *b* 28 Oct. 1951; *m* 1st; two *s*; 2nd, Emma; one *s*. *Educ:* St Mungo's Acad., Glasgow. Member (Lab): Strathclyde Regl Council, 1987–96; Glasgow CC, 1995–2005 (Dep. Leader, 1997–99; Leader, 1999–2005). Mem. (Lab) Glasgow Cathcart, Scottish Parlt, Sept. 2005–2011; contested (Lab) same seat, 2011. Non-exec. Dir, Hampden Park Ltd, 2001–11. Chm., Develt Bd, Paddle Steamer Waverley, 2011–12.

GORDON, (Cosmo) Gerald (Maitland); His Honour Judge Gordon; a Circuit Judge, since 1990; a Senior Circuit Judge, Central Criminal Court, since 1994; *b* 26 March 1945; *s* of John Kenneth Maitland Gordon, CBE and Erica Martia Clayton-East; *m* 1973, Vanessa Maria Juliet Maxine Reilly-Morrison, LLB, AKC, barrister; two *s*. *Educ:* Eton. Called to the Bar, Middle Temple, 1966, Bencher, 2003. Asst Recorder, 1982–86; Recorder, 1986–90. Royal Borough of Kensington and Chelsea: Mem. Council, 1971–90; Chm., Works Cttee, 1978–80; Chm., Town Planning Cttee, 1988; Dep. Leader, 1982–88; Mayor, 1989–90. Chairman: Edwardes Square Scarsdale and Abingdon Assoc., 1990–2002; Westway Develt Trust (formerly N Kensington Amenity Trust), 1992–2002. Liveryman, Merchant Taylors' Co., 1995–. *Recreations:* food, wine, armchair sport. *Address:* Central Criminal Court, City of London, EC4M 7EH. *T:* (020) 7248 3277.

GORDON, Prof. David, FRCP, FMedSci; President, World Federation for Medical Education, since 2015 (Visiting Professor, since 2007); Professor of Medicine, University of Manchester, 1999–2008, now Emeritus; *b* 23 Feb. 1947; *s* of late Lawrence Gordon and Pattie Gordon (*née* Wood); *m* Dr C. Louise Jones; three *s* one *d*. *Educ:* Whitgift Sch.; Magdalene Coll., Cambridge (BA 1967, MA 1971; MB BChir 1970); Westminster Med. Sch. MRCP 1972, FRCP 1989. Clin. appts, Leicester and Cambridge, 1970–72; St Mary's Hospital Medical School: Res. Fellow, 1972–74; Lectr in Medicine, 1974–80; Sen. Lectr in Medicine, 1980–83; Hon. Sen. Lectr in Medicine, 1983–94; Hon. Cons. Physician, St Mary's Hosp., London, 1980–94; Wellcome Trust: Asst Dir, 1983–89; Prog. Dir, 1989–98; Dir of Special Initiatives, 1998–99; University of Manchester: Dean, Faculty of Medicine, Dentistry, Nursing and Pharmacy, Victoria Univ. of Manchester, then Faculty of Med. and Human Scis, 1999–2006; Vice-Pres., 2004–08. Hon. Consultant Physician, Manchester Royal Infirmary, Salford Royal Hosps and S Manchester Univ. Hosps, 1999–2006. Visiting Professor: Univ. of Copenhagen, 2007–; QMUL, 2008–11; State Medical and Pharmaceutical Univ., Chişinău, Moldova, 2009–; Kazakh Nat. Medical Univ., Almaty, 2014–. Consultant, Health Sector Reform Project, Min. of Health, Azerbaijan, 2010. Dir of several technol. transfer and biotech. cos, 2002–06. Member: Res. Sub-Gp, Task Force on Support of R&D in NHS, 1994; Academic Wkg Gp, HEFCE-CVCP-SCOP Cttee on Post Grad. Educn, 1995; Indep. Task Force on Clin. Academic Careers, CVCP, 1996–97; Res. Cttee, HEFCE, 1998–99; Chief Scientist Cttee, Scottish Office DoH, 1997–99; Pres., Assoc. of Med. Schs in Europe, 2004–14; Chm., Council of Heads of Medical Schs, 2003–06; Dep. Chm., ORPHEUS, 2005–10. Hon. Life Mem., St John Ambulance Assoc., 1983. FMedSci 1999. *Publications:* papers, reviews, etc on biomed. res., sci. policy, med. educn and other subjects in learned jls. *Recreations:* music (cello), books, food, finding out what is going on. *Address:* World Federation for Medical Education, 13A chemin du Levant, 01210 Ferney-Voltaire, France. *E:* president@wfme.org.

GORDON, David Sorrell; Principal, Gordon Advisory, LLC, since 2008; *b* 11 Sept. 1941; *s* of late Sholom and Tania Gordon; *m* 1st, 1963, Enid Albagli (marr. diss. 1969); 2nd, 1974, Maggi McCormick; two *s*. *Educ:* Clifton College; Balliol College, Oxford (PPE, BA 1963); LSE; Advanced Management Program, Harvard Business Sch. FCA. Articles with Thomson McLintock, 1965–68; The Economist: editorial staff, 1968–78; Production and Develt Dir, 1978–81; Gp Chief Exec., Economist Newspaper Ltd, 1981–93; Chief Exec., ITN, 1993–95; Sec., Royal Acad. of Arts, 1996–2002; CEO and Dir, Milwaukee Art Mus., Wisconsin, 2002–08. Director: Financial Times, 1983–93; eFinancial News, 1999–2006 (Chm., 2001–06); Profile Books, 1996–; Dice Holdings, Inc., 2006–. Dir, South Bank Bd, 1986–96; a Governor, BFI, 1983–91. Chm., Contemporary Art Soc., 1991–98; Trustee: Tate Gall., 1993–98; Architecture Foundn, 1993–2002; Architecture Assoc. Foundn, 1995–98; Assoc. of Art Mus. Dirs, 2006–08; Amer. Folk Art Mus., 2013–; Wende Mus. of Cold War, 2014–. Friends Council, Avery Architectural and Fine Arts Library, 2011–. Gov., LSE, 1990–2000. *Publications:* (with Fred Hirsch) Newspaper Money, 1975. *Recreation:* collecting stereoscopic photographs. *Address:* 460 Fairview Avenue, Sierra Madre, CA 91024, USA. *E:* david@gordonadvisory.com. *Club:* Garrick.

GORDON, Sir Donald, Kt 2005; Founder, Liberty International PLC (formerly TransAtlantic Holdings) (Chairman, 1981–2005; Life President, 2005–10; Life President, Intu Properties plc (formerly Capital Shopping Centres PLC) and Capital and Counties PLC, since 2010); *b* 24 June 1930; *s* of Nathan and Sheila Gordon; *m* 1958, Peggy Cowan (*d* 2014); two *s* one *d*. *Educ:* King Edward VII Sch., Johannesburg. CA (SA). Partner, Kessel Feinstein, 1955–57; Founder, Chm. and CEO, 1957–99, now Hon. Life Pres., Liberty Life Assoc. of Africa Ltd, subseq. Liberty Gp Ltd; Chairman: Liberty Hldgs, SA, 1968–99; Liberty Investors Ltd, 1971–99; Guardian Nat. Insce Co. Ltd, 1980–99; Capital & Counties (UK), 1982–2005; Continental & Industrial Trust, 1986–93; Capital Shopping Centres plc, 1994–2005; Deputy Chairman: Standard Bank Investment Corp., 1979–99; Premier Gp Ltd, 1983–96; SAB Miller plc, 1989–99; Beverage & Consumer Industry Hldgs, 1989–99; Sun Life Corp., UK, 1992–95. Director: Guardbank Mgt Corp. Ltd, 1969–99; Guardian Royal Exchange Assurance (UK), 1971–94; Charter Life Insce Co. Ltd, 1985–99; GFSA Hldgs, 1990–94. Hon. DEconSc Witwatersrand, 1991; Hon. DCom Pretoria, 2005. Business Man of Year Award, Financial Mail (SA), 1965; Sunday Times (SA) Businessman of the Year, 1969; Special Award for Lifetime Achievement, Entrepreneur of the Year Awards, 2000; (UK) Top 100 Lifetime Achievement Award, Sunday Times (SA), 2004. *Recreations:* opera, ballet. *Address:* Intu Properties plc, 40 Broadway, SW1H 0BT. *T:* (020) 7960 1200, *Fax:* (020) 7960 1333. *Clubs:* Rand, Johannesburg Country, Plettenberg Bay Country, Houghton Golf (SA).

GORDON, Douglas; *see* Gordon, Robert D.

GORDON, Douglas Lamont; artist; *b* Glasgow, 20 Sept. 1966; *s* of James Gordon and Mary Clements Gordon (*née* MacDougall). *Educ:* Glasgow Sch. of Art (BA Hons 1st cl. 1988); Slade Sch. of Art (Postgrad. Res. Dip. 1990). Former Vis. Prof. and John Florent Stone Fellow, Edinburgh Coll. of Art; Vis. Prof. of Fine Art, Glasgow Sch. of Art, Glasgow Univ., 1999–. Works in video, film, photography and sculpture include: List of Names; Something between My Mouth and Your Ear; 24 Hour Psycho, 1993; Hysterical; The Confessions of a Justified Sinner; Between Darkness and Light, 1997; Feature Film, 1999; Play Dead, Real Time, 2003; The Vanity of Allegory, Berlin, 2005; Zidane: a 21st century portrait, 2006. *Exhibitions* include: Lisson Gall., 1993, 1995 (solo), 1998, 2000; Hayward Gall., 1996, 1997, 2002; MOMA, Oxford, 1996; 10th Sydney Biennale, 1996; Venice Biennale (Premio 2000), 1997; Tate Liverpool, 2000; Sheep and Goats, Musée d'Art Moderne de la Ville de Paris, 2000; Mus. of Contemp. Art, LA, 2001; Van Abbemuseum, Eindhoven, 2003; Hirshhorn Mus. and Sculpture Garden, Washington, DC, 2004; The Vanity of Allegory, Deutsche Guggenheim Mus., Berlin, 2005; Mus. Morsbrich, Leverkusen, 2006; Timeline, MOMA, New York, 2006; Superhumanatural, Nat. Galls of Scotland, 2006; Between Darkness and Light, Kunstmuseum, Wolfsburg, 2007; Mus. of Contemp. Art, Chicago, 2007; Kunsthaus Bregenz, 2007; San Francisco MOMA, 2007; Timeline, Museo de Arte Latinoamericano de Buenos Aires, 2007; Pergamon Mus., Berlin, 2008; Où se trouvent les clefs?, La Collection Lambert en Avignon, 2008; Galerie Eva Presenhuber, Zürich, 2009; DVIR Gall., Israel, 2009; blood, sweat, tears, DOX, Prague, 2009; Art and the Sublime, TATE Britain, 2010; Museum fuer Moderne Kunst, Frankfurt, 2011; K.364, Gagosian Gall., London, 2011; Phantom, Yvon Lambert Gall., Paris, 2011; Galerie Niels Borch Jensen, Berlin, 2012; Douglas Gordon: Left Is Right and Right Is Wrong…, Inst. of Modern Art, Brisbane, 2012; Maestros, Mead Gall., Warwick, 2012; Schafstall Bisdorf, Bisdorf, 2012; Akademie der Künste, Berlin, 2012; Douglas Gordon: The End of Civilisation, Gagosian Gall., NY, 2012; Sharpening Fantasy, 2012, Blain|Southern, Berlin, 2013; I am also… Douglas Gordon, Tel Aviv Mus., Tel Aviv, 2013; (solo) NY Armory on Park, NY, 2014. Contrib., British Art Show and Spellbound, 1996. Turner Prize, 1996; Hugo Boss Prize, 1998; Roswitha Haftmann Prize, 2008. *Address:* Lost But Found, Wasps Artist's Studio, Room 238, 141 Bridgegate, Glasgow G1 5HZ; Lost But Found, Kurfürstenstrasse 13, 10785 Berlin, Germany.

GORDON, Eileen; *b* 22 Oct. 1946; *d* of late Charles Leatt and Margaret Rose Leatt; *m* 1969, Tony Gordon (*d* 2005); one *s* one *d*. *Educ:* Harold Hill Grammar Sch.; Shoreditch Comp. Sch.; Westminster Coll., Oxford (CertEd). Teacher; Asst to Tony Banks, MP, 1990–97. MP (Lab) Romford, 1997–2001. Contested (Lab) Romford, 1992 and 2001. Member: Broadcasting Select Cttee, 1998–2001; Health Select Cttee, 1999–2001.

GORDON, François; *see* Gordon, J. F.

GORDON, Gerald; *see* Gordon, C. G. M.

GORDON, Sir Gerald (Henry), Kt 2000; CBE 1995; QC (Scot.) 1972; LLD; Sheriff of Glasgow and Strathkelvin, 1978–99; Temporary Judge of Court of Session and High Court of Justiciary, 1992–2004; Member, Scottish Criminal Cases Review Commission, 1999–2009; *b* 17 June 1929; *er s* of Simon Gordon and Rebecca Gordon (*née* Bulbin), Glasgow; *m* 1957, Marjorie Joseph (*d* 1996), *yr d* of Isaac and Aimée Joseph (*née* Strump), Glasgow; one *s* two *d*. *Educ:* Queen's Park Senior Secondary Sch., Glasgow; Univ. of Glasgow (MA (1st cl. Hons Philosophy with English Literature) 1950; LLB (Distinction) 1953; PhD 1960); LLD Edinburgh 1968. National Service, RASC, 1953–55 (Staff-Sgt, Army Legal Aid, BAOR, 1955). Admitted Scottish Bar 1953; practice at Scottish Bar, 1953, 1956–59; Faulds Fellow, Univ. of Glasgow, 1956–59. Procurator Fiscal Depute, Edinburgh, 1960–65. University of Edinburgh: Sen. Lectr, 1965; Personal Prof. of Criminal Law, 1969–72; Head of Dept of Criminal Law and Criminology, 1965–72; Prof. of Scots Law, 1972–76; Dean of Faculty of Law, 1970–73; Vis. Prof., 2000–03. Sheriff of S Strathclyde, Dumfries and Galloway at Hamilton, 1976–77. Commonwealth Vis. Fellow and Vis. Res. Fellow, Centre of Criminology, Univ. of Toronto, 1974–75. Temporary Sheriff, 1973–76. Member: Interdepartmental Cttee on Scottish Criminal Procedure, 1970–77; Cttee on Appeals Criteria and Alleged Miscarriages of Justice Procedures, 1995–96. Hon. FRSE 2002. Hon. LLD: Glasgow, 1993; Aberdeen, 2003; Edinburgh, 2011. *Publications:* The Criminal Law of Scotland, 1967, 2nd edn 1978; (ed) Renton and Brown's Criminal Procedure, 4th edn 1972, to 6th edn 1996; (ed) Scottish Criminal Case Reports, 1981–; various articles. *Recreations:* Jewish studies, coffee conversation, crosswords.

GORDON, Hannah Campbell Grant; actress; *b* 9 April 1941; *d* of William Munro Gordon and Hannah Grant Gordon; *m* 1st, 1970, Norman Warwick (*d* 1994); one *s*; 2nd, 2009, Robert Lampitt. *Educ:* St Denis School for Girls, Edinburgh; Glasgow Univ. (Cert. Dramatic Studies); College of Dramatic Art, Glasgow (Dip. in speech and drama). FRSAMD 1980. Hon. DLitt Glasgow, 1993. Winner, James Bridie Gold Medal, Royal Coll. of Music and Dramatic Art, Glasgow, 1962. *Stage:* Dundee Rep., Glasgow Citizens Theatre, Belgrade Theatre, Coventry, Ipswich, Windsor; Can You Hear me at the Back, Piccadilly, 1979; The Killing Game, Apollo, 1980; The Jeweller's Shop, Westminster, 1982; The Country Girl, Apollo, 1983; Light Up the Sky, Old Vic, 1985; Mary Stuart, Edinburgh Fest., 1987; Shirley Valentine, Duke of York's, 1989; Hidden Laughter, Vaudeville, 1991; An Ideal Husband, Globe, 1992; The Aspern Papers, Wyndham's, 1996; My Fair Lady, Th. Royal, 2003, nat. tour, 2003–04; *television:* 1st TV appearance, Johnson Over Jordan, 1965; Great Expectations, 1969; Middlemarch, 1969; My Wife Next Door, 1972; Upstairs, Downstairs, 1976; Telford's Change, 1979; Goodbye Mr Kent, 1983; Gardener's Calendar, 1986; My Family and Other Animals, 1987; The Day after the Fair, 1987; Joint Account, 1989; Midsomer Murders, 1999;

One Foot in the Grave (final episode), 2000; Moving On, 2010; Hustle, 2011; presenter, Watercolour Challenge, 1998–2001; *films:* Spring and Port Wine, 1970; The Elephant Man, 1979; Made of Honour, 2008; numerous radio plays, recorded books and poetry and music recitals. *Recreations:* gardening, cooking, walking, sailing. *Address:* c/o Conway Van Gelder Grant Ltd, 8–12 Broadwick Street, W1F 8HW.

GORDON, Iain James, PhD; CBiol; FRSB; FRSE; Chief Executive Officer and Director, James Hutton Institute, since 2010; *b* Chester, 18 Oct. 1959; *s* of James William and Gillian Ann Gordon; *m* (marr. diss.); two *s* one *d.* *Educ:* Robert Gordon's Coll., Aberdeen; Univ. of Aberdeen (BSc Zool.); King's Coll., Cambridge (PhD Zool. 1986). CBiol 1983; FRSB (FIBiol 2003); FRSE 2012. Research Assistant: Large Animal Res. Gp, Dept of Zool., Univ. of Cambridge (red deer distrib. in Highlands of Scotland), 1986; Conservation Monitoring Centre, Cambridge (Biosphere Reserves Project), 1986; Res. Consultant, Zool Soc. of London (Scimitar-horned Oryx reintrod. project), 1986–96; Res. Associate, Station Biologique de la Tour du Valat, Carmargue, France, 1987–88; Res. Scientist, Macaulay Land Use Res. Inst., Aberdeen (Hd, prog. on ecol. of grazed ecosystems), 1988–2003; Officer-in-Charge, CSIRO Davies Lab., Townsville, 2003–10; Theme Leader, Bldg Resilient Biodiversity Assets, Canberra, 2009–10. Adjunct Associate Prof., Univ. of Qld, 2004; Adjunct Professor: Sch. of Tropical Biol., James Cook Univ., Australia, 2005; Sch. of Maths and Geospatial Scis, Royal Melbourne Inst. of Technol. Univ., 2005; ANU, 2010. Hon. Prof., Univ. of Aberdeen, 2000. Fellow, N American Acad. of Arts and Scis, 1996. Hon. Fellow, Univ. of Edinburgh, 1994. Hon. DSc Abertay, 2013. *Publications:* (ed with R. Rubino) Grazing Behaviour of Goats and Sheep, 1994; (with A. M. Sibbald) Tracking Animals with GPS, 2001; (ed with H. H. T. Prins) The Ecology of Grazing and Browsing, 2007; (ed) The Vicuna: the theory and practice of community based wildlife management, 2008; (ed with H. H. T. Prins) Invasion Biology and Ecological Theory, 2014; contrib. book chapters; contribs to learned jls incl. Jl Applied Ecol., Jl Zool., Oecologia, Functional Ecol., Animal Behaviour, Small Ruminant Res. *Recreations:* golf, book clubs, motorbike riding, collecting antique inkwells, collecting signed first edition science books. *Address:* James Hutton Institute, Invergowrie, Dundee DD2 5DA. *E:* iain.gordon@hutton.ac.uk. *Club:* Royal Over-Seas League.

GORDON, Ian William; Director, Service Policy and Planning, Scottish Executive Health Department, 2003–06; *b* 27 Dec. 1952; *s* of Brian William Gordon, *qv*; *m* 1979, Alison Margaret Bunting; two *s.* *Educ:* Strathallan Sch., Perth; Downing Coll., Cambridge (BA). Joined Civil Service, 1975: Dept of Energy, 1975–81; Scottish Office, 1981–99; Industry, 1981–85; Finance, 1985–86; Educn, 1986–90; Agriculture, 1990–93; Fisheries, 1993–99 (Fisheries Sec., 1995–99); Head of Dept, Scotland Office, 1999–2002. Non-exec. Dir, Cumbria PCT, 2007–13 (Chair, 2011–13); Chm., N Cumbria Univ. Hosp. Trust, 2013–14.

GORDON, Isabel; *see* Allende, I.

GORDON, Maj.-Gen. James Charles Mellish, CBE 1992; Chairman, Victory Services Association, since 2008 (Trustee, since 2005); *b* 3 Aug. 1941; *s* of Brig. Leonard Henry Gordon and Joyce Evelyn Mary Gordon (*née* Gurdon); *m* 1964, Rosemary Stella Kincaid; two *s* one *d.* *Educ:* Tonbridge Sch.; RMA Sandhurst. Commissioned RA 1961; served in UK, Germany, Singapore; RMCS, Shrivenham, 1972; Staff Coll., Camberley, 1973; MoD, 1974–75; Comdr, D Batt., RHA, UK and BAOR, 1976–78; MA to MGO, MoD, 1978–80; CO 45 Field Regt RA, BAOR, 1980–83; Col, ASD1, MoD, 1983–86; CRA 4th Armoured Div., BAOR, 1986–89; Dir, Mil. Ops, MoD, 1989–91; COS, HQ UKLF, 1991–94. Dir Gen., Assoc. of Train Operating Cos, 1994–99 (Director: Rail Settlement Plan Ltd; Rail Staff Travel Ltd; Nat. Rail Enquiry Service); Gen. Sec., Officers' Pensions Soc., later Forces Pension Soc., 2000–07; Dir, FPS Investment Co. Ltd, 2000–07; Man. Trustee, FPS Widows' Fund, 2000–07. FCILT (FCIT 1994–99); Corporate Fellow, Industry and Parlt Trust, 1998. Mem. Council Officers' Assoc., 2000–. Trustee: Haig Homes, 2003–09; Tall Ships Youth Trust, 2012–. Chm., Woodard Schs Corp., 2010; Gov., Oakwood Sch., 2010–11. *Recreations:* sailing, music, theatre, travel. *Club:* Victory Services.

GORDON, Maj. Gen. James Henry, CB 2013; CBE 2006 (MBE 1991); Senior British Loan Service Officer Oman, 2011–14; *b* London, 4 Dec. 1957; *s* of Graeme and Kirsten Gordon; *m* 1996, Fiona Fairbairn; three *s.* *Educ:* Trinity Coll., Glenalmond; RMA Sandhurst; Staff Coll. CO 2nd Bn, RGJ, 1995–98; Dep. Asst COS Operational Support PJHQ, 1998–2001; Comdr, British Forces, Falkland Is, 2002–03; COS, HQ NI, 2003–05; Dep. Comdr, Multinational Security Transition Comd, Iraq, 2006; Dir Personal Services (Army), 2006–08; Comdr British Forces Cyprus and Administrator Sovereign Base Areas, 2008–10. Queen's Body Guard for Scotland (Royal Co. of Archers), 2001–. Officer, Legion of Merit (USA), 2015. *Recreations:* field sports, ski-ing, sailing. *Club:* Boodle's.

GORDON, Jane-Anne Mary E.; *see* Evans-Gordon.

GORDON, (Jean) François, CMG 1999; CVO 2007; consultant and policy adviser, since 2013; European Strategy Adviser, Kent Police, 2009–13; *b* 16 April 1953; *s* of late Michael Colin Gordon and of Jeanine Marie Gordon (*née* Parizet); *m* 1977, Elaine Daniel; two *d.* *Educ:* Queen's Coll., Oxford (BA Hons Jurisprudence 1974); Université d'Aix et Marseille (Diplôme d'Etudes Supérieures 1975). Articled clerk, Ingledew Brown, 1975–78; admitted solicitor, 1979; joined HM Diplomatic Service, 1979: EU Dept, FCO, 1979–81; Second, later First Sec., Luanda, 1981–83; First Secretary: UK Delegn to UN Conf. on Disarmament, Geneva, 1983–88; UN Dept, FCO, 1988–90; (Political), Nairobi, 1990–92; Africa Dept (Southern), FCO, 1992–95; Dep. Hd, Drugs, Internat. Crime and Terrorism Dept, FCO, 1995–96; Hd, Drugs and Internat. Crime Dept, FCO, 1996; Ambassador to Algeria, 1996–99; RCDS, 2000; Ambassador to Côte d'Ivoire, and (non-resident) to Niger, Liberia and Burkina Faso, 2001–04; High Commissioner, Uganda, 2005–08. *Recreations:* reading, gardening, watching African wildlife, vintage cars, flying. *Club:* Alvis Owner.

GORDON, John Alexander, CB 1995; CEng; FRAeS; Partner, Gordon Consulting, since 1999; *b* 7 Nov. 1940; *s* of John and Eleanor Gordon; *m* 1962, Dyanne Calder; two *d.* *Educ:* RAF Colls, Henlow and Cranwell. CEng, MIMechE; FRAeS 1990. Engr Br., RAF, 1958–70; Ministry of Defence, Procurement Executive, 1970–95: mil. aircraft procurement, Dir Gen. Aircraft 1; projects incl. Harrier, Jaguar, Tornado and Eurofighter; Gen. Manager, NATO Eurofighter and Tornado Mgt Agency, 1996–99; Compliance Officer for Merger Undertakings, BAE Systems, 1999–2007. RAeS British Gold Medal, 1997. *Recreation:* carriage driving.

GORDON, John Keith; environmentalist; *b* 6 July 1940; *s* of late Prof. James Edward Gordon and Theodora (*née* Sinker); *m* 1965, Elizabeth Shanks; two *s.* *Educ:* Marlborough Coll.; Cambridge Univ. (1st Cl. Hons History). Henry Fellow, Yale Univ., 1962–63; research in Russian history, LSE, 1963–66; entered FCO, 1966; Budapest, 1968–70; seconded to Civil Service Coll., 1970–72; FCO, 1972–73; UK Mission, Geneva, 1973–74; Head of Chancery and Consul, Yaoundé, 1975–77; FCO, 1977–80; Cultural Attaché, Moscow, 1980–81; Office of UK Rep. to European Community, Brussels, 1982–83; UK Perm. Deleg. to UNESCO, Paris, 1983–85; Head of Nuclear Energy Dept, FCO, 1986–88; Imperial College, London: Academic Visitor, Centre for Envmtl Technol., 1988–90; Dep. and Policy Dir, Global Envmt Res. Centre, 1990–94. Special Advr, UK-UN Envmt and Develt Forum, 2000–04; Mem., UK Nat. Commn for UNESCO, 2004–07. Pres., Council for Educn in World Citizenship, 2004–08. Chm., S Oxon Sustainability Gp, 2011–; Co-Chm., Waterbird Cttee, 2012–. Contested (Lib Dem) Daventry, 1997. *Publications:* (with Caroline Fraser) Institutions and Sustainable Development, 1991; (with Tom Bigg) 2020 Vision, 1994; Canadian Round Tables, 1994; reports and articles on envmtl issues. *Recreations:* tree planting, canoeing, reading. *Address:* Well House, Reading Road, Wallingford, Oxon OX10 9HG.

GORDON, Kate; *see* Gordon, V. K.

GORDON, Sir Lionel Eldred Peter S.; *see* Smith-Gordon.

GORDON, Dr Lyndall Felicity, FRSL; writer; Senior Research Fellow, St Hilda's College, Oxford, since 1995; *b* 4 Nov. 1941; *d* of Harry Louis Getz and Rhoda Stella Getz (*née* Press); *m* 1963, Prof. Siamon Gordon, *qv*; two *d.* *Educ:* Univ. of Cape Town (BA Hons); Columbia Univ., NY (PhD 1973). Rhodes Vis. Fellow, St Hilda's Coll., Oxford, 1973–75; Asst Prof., Columbia Univ., NY, 1975–76; Lectr, Jesus Coll., Oxford, 1977–84; Fellow and Tutor, St Hilda's Coll., and CUF Lectr, Oxford Univ., 1984–95. FRSL 2003. *Publications:* Virginia Woolf: a writer's life, 1984, 4th edn 2006; Shared Lives, 1992, 2nd edn 2005; Charlotte Brontë: a passionate life, 1994, 2nd edn 2008; A Private Life of Henry James, 1998, reissued as Henry James: his women and his art, 2012; T. S. Eliot: an imperfect life, 1998, reissued as The Imperfect Life of T. S. Eliot, 2012; Mary Wollstonecraft: a new genus, 2005 (US edn and UK pbk edn as Vindication: a life of Mary Wollstonecraft); Lives Like Loaded Guns: Emily Dickinson and her family's feuds, 2010; Divided Lives: dreams of a mother and daughter, 2014. *Recreation:* reading. *Address:* St Hilda's College, Oxford OX4 1DY.

GORDON, Prof. Michael John Caldwell, PhD; FRS 1994; Professor of Computer Assisted Reasoning, Computer Laboratory, University of Cambridge, since 1996; *b* 28 Feb. 1948; *m* 1979, Avra Jean Cohn; two *s.* *Educ:* Bedales Sch.; Gonville and Caius Coll., Cambridge (BA Maths); King's Coll., Cambridge (Dip. Linguistics); Edinburgh Univ. (PhD). Research Associate, Stanford Univ., 1974–75; University of Edinburgh: Res. Fellow, 1975–78; SRC Advanced Res. Fellow, 1978–81; University of Cambridge: Lectr, 1981–88; Reader in Formal Methods, 1988–96; Royal Soc./SERC Industrial Fellow, SRI International, 1987–89. *Publications:* The Denotational Description of Programming Languages, 1979; Programming Language Theory and its Implementation, 1988. *Recreation:* mushroom hunting. *Address:* Computer Laboratory, University of Cambridge, William Gates Building, J J Thompson Avenue, Cambridge CB3 0FD. *T:* (01223) 334627, *Fax:* (01223) 334678. *E:* mjcg@cl.cam.ac.uk.

GORDON, Mildred; *b* 24 Aug. 1923; *d* of Dora and Judah Fellerman; *m* 1st, 1948, Sam Gordon (*d* 1982); one *s*; 2nd, 1985, Nils Kaare Dahl. *Educ:* Raine's Foundation School; Pitman's College; Forest Teacher Training College. Teacher, 1945–85. Mem. Exec., London Labour Party, 1983–86; Jt Chm., Greater London Labour Policy Cttee, 1985–86. MP (Lab) Bow and Poplar, 1987–97. Mem., Select Cttee on Educn, Science and Arts, 1991–97; Chm., All-Party Parly Child Support Agency Monitoring Group, 1995–97; Vice Chm., PLP Educn Cttee and Social Services Cttee, 1990–92, 1997. Formerly, Advr, GLC Women's Cttee. Member: Bd, Tower Hamlets Business and Educn Partnership; Nat. Council, National Pensioner Convention (Advr to Exec. Cttee, London and SE Branch); EC Barnet 55+; Co-op Party; Gen. Cttee Finchley and Golders Green Labour Party. Patron: Gtr London Pensioners' Assoc. (also Delegate); Dockland Singers; Danesford Trust. Founder, Schs' Public Speaking Competition, Tower Hamlets. Freeman, London Bor. of Tower Hamlets, 1999. *Publications:* essays and articles on education. *Recreations:* pottery, designing and making costume jewellery, painting, writing poetry. *Address:* 28 Cumbrian Gardens, NW2 1EF.

GORDON, Pamela Joan; Chief Executive, City of Sheffield Metropolitan District, 1989–97; *b* 13 Feb. 1936; *d* of Frederick Edward Bantick and Violet Elizabeth Bantick; *m* 1st, 1959, Wallace Henry Gordon (*d* 1980); two *s*; 2nd, 1997, Peter Charles Hoad. *Educ:* Richmond (Surrey) Grammar School for Girls; St Hilda's Coll., Oxford (MA). Variety of posts with ILEA, GLC and LCC, 1957–81; Greater London Council: Asst Dir Gen., 1981–83; Dep. Dir of Industry and Employment, 1983–85; Chief Exec., London Bor. of Hackney, 1985–89. Member: Adv. Cttee, Constitution Unit, 1995–97; Local Govt Commn for England, 1998–2002; Indep. Panel of Assessors for Public Appts, 1999–2007; Electoral Commn, 2001–07 (Chm., Boundary Cttee for England, 2002–07). Chm., Borders Exec. Cttee, Relationships Scotland, 2011– (Chm., Nat. Bd, 2012–15). Pres., SOLACE, 1996–97. Gov., Sheffield Hallam Univ., 1995–2003. Hon. Fellow, Inst. of Local Govt Studies, Birmingham Univ., 1990. Columnist, Local Government Chronicle. *Publications:* short stories and articles in various jls. *Recreations:* opera, theatre, foreign travel.

GORDON, Richard, (Dr Gordon Ostlere), FRCA; author; *b* 15 Sept. 1921; *m* 1951, Mary Patten; two *s* two *d.* *Educ:* Selwyn Coll., Cambridge; St Bartholomew's Hosp. Med. Sch. Formerly: anaesthetist at St Bartholomew's Hospital, and Nuffield Dept of Anaesthetics, Oxford; assistant editor, British Medical Jl; ship's surgeon. Mem., Punch Table. *Publications:* Anaesthetics for Medical Students; Doctor in the House, and 16 sequels; 32 other novels and non-fiction (adapted for 8 films and 4 plays, radio and TV series, and translated into 21 langs); (ed) The Literary Companion to Medicine; TV screenplay, The Good Dr Bodkin Adams; TV series, A Gentlemen's Club; contribs to Punch. *Recreation:* watching cricket and other sports. *Clubs:* Beefsteak, Garrick, MCC.

GORDON, Richard John Francis; QC 1994; a Recorder, since 2000; *b* 26 Nov. 1948; *s* of John Bernard Basil Gordon and Winifred Josephine (*née* Keenan); *m* 1975, Jane Belinda Lucey; two *s.* *Educ:* St Benedict's Sch., Ealing; Christ Church, Oxford (Open Schol.; MA); University Coll. London (LLM). Called to the Bar, Middle Temple, 1972, Bencher, 2003. Sen. Lectr in Admin. Law, KCL, 1991–93. Visiting Professor of Law: UCL, 1994–; Chinese Univ. of Hong Kong, 2008–11; Hong Kong Univ., 2012–. Member: Exec. Cttee, Admin. Law Bar Assoc., 1991; Adv. Bd, Constitution Soc. UK, 2010–. Trustee, Internat. Sen. Lawyers Project, 2013–. Editor-in-Chief, Administrative Court (formerly Crown Office) Digest, 1989–. *Publications:* The Law Relating to Mobile Homes and Caravans, 1978, 2nd edn 1985; Judicial Review: law and procedure, 1985, 2nd edn 1995; Crown Office Proceedings, 1990; Community Care Assessments, 1993, 2nd edn 1996; Human Rights in the United Kingdom, 1996; Judicial Review and Crown Office Practice, 2000; Judicial Review and the Human Rights Act, 2000; The Strasbourg Cases: leading cases from the European Human Rights Reports, 2001; (ed) Judicial Review in the New Millennium, 2003; EC Law in Judicial Review, 2006; Repairing British Politics: a blueprint for constitutional change, 2010; contrib. to numerous legal jls on admin. law. *Recreations:* reading, writing. *Address:* Brick Court Chambers, 7–8 Essex Street, WC2R 3LD. *T:* (020) 7379 3550. *Club:* MCC.

GORDON, Robert Anthony Eagleson, CMG 1999; OBE 1983; HM Diplomatic Service, retired; Chairman, Prospect Burma, since 2011; *b* 9 Feb. 1952; *s* of late Major Cyril Vivian Eagleson, MC, RE and of Clara Renata Romana Gordon (*née* Duse); *m* 1978, Pamela Jane Taylor; two *s* two *d.* *Educ:* King's Sch., Canterbury; Magdalen Coll., Oxford (MA Modern Langs). FCO 1973; Second Sec., Warsaw, 1975–77; First Sec., Santiago, 1978–83; FCO, 1983–87; First Sec., UK Deleg. to OECD, Paris, 1987–92; Counsellor and Dep. Head of Mission, Warsaw, 1992–95; Ambassador to Burma (Union of Myanmar), 1995–99; Head, SE Asia Dept, FCO, 1999–2003; Ambassador to the Socialist Republic of Vietnam, 2003–07. Dir, VinaLand, 2009–11. Pres., Britain-Burma Soc., 2011–.

GORDON, (Robert) Douglas, FRGS; HM Diplomatic Service, retired; Ambassador to Republic of Yemen, 1993–95 and (non-resident) to Republic of Djibouti, 1993; *b* 31 July 1936; *s* of Robert Gordon and Helen (*née* MacTaggart); *m* 1st, 1960, Margaret Bruckshaw (marr. diss. 1990); one *s*; 2nd, 1990, Valerie Janet Brownlee, MVO. *Educ:* Greenock Acad.; Cardiff High Sch. for Boys. FO, 1954. National Service with RM, 1955–57; commnd 2 Lieut

Wilts Regt, 1957. FO, 1958; Amman, 1958; MECAS, 1959; Abu Dhabi, 1961; Vienna, 1963; Second Sec. (Commercial), Kuwait, 1966; FCO, 1969; Second, later First Sec., Hd of Chancery and Consul, Doha, 1973; Asst to Dep. Gov., Gibraltar, 1976; FCO, 1979; HM Asst Marshal of the Diplomatic Corps, 1982; First Sec. (Commercial), Washington, 1984; Consul (Commercial), Cleveland, 1986; Ambassador, 1989–90, Consul-General, 1990, Aden; High Comr, Guyana, 1990–93, and Ambassador, Republic of Suriname, 1990–93. Diplomatic Consultant, Royal Garden Hotel, Kensington, 1996–2006. Chm., British-Yemeni Soc., 1999–2005 (Hon. Vice Pres., 2005–). FRGS 2012. Freeman, City of London, 1984. Order of: Gorkha Dakshina Bahu, 5th Cl. (Nepal), 1980; King Abdul Aziz ibn Saud, 4th Cl. (Saudi Arabia), 1982; Officier, l'Ordre Nat. du Mérite (France), 1984. *Recreations:* photography, walking. *Address:* 15 Kenton Court, 356 Kensington High Street, W14 8NN.

GORDON, Maj. Gen. Robert Duncan Seaton, CMG 2005; CBE 1994; Founder and Managing Director, RG Consulting Ltd, peace and security operations and senior leadership training, since 2006; *b* 23 Nov. 1950; *s* of Col Jack Gordon and Joan Gordon (*née* Seaton); *m* 1979, Virginia Brown, Toronto; two *s*. *Educ:* Wellington Coll.; St Catharine's Coll., Cambridge (BA Hons Modern Hist. 1974; MA 1978). Commnd 17th/21st Lancers, 1970; Army Staff Coll., 1982; COS, 4th Armoured Bde, 1983–84; MA (Lt-Col) to C-in-C BAOR/COMNORTHAG, 1987–90; CO 17th/21st Lancers, 1990–92; Sec. to Chiefs of Staff Cttee, MoD, 1992–94 (Col); Brig. 1993; HCSC 1994; Comdr, 19th Mechanized Bde, 1994–96; rcds 1996; DPR (Army), 1997–99; Maj.-Gen. 1999; GOC 2nd Div. in York, 1999–2000; GOC 2nd Div. in Edinburgh, and Gov. of Edinburgh Castle, 2000–02; Force Comdr, UN Mission in Ethiopia and Eritrea, 2002–04; retd 2005; Consultant to UN Peacekeeping, 2005–; Senior Adviser to: Challenges for Peace Forum, 2008–; Pearson Peacekeeping Centre of Canada, 2009–13; UNDP Iraq for Security Sector Reform, 2013–. Col Comdt, RAVC, 2001–07. *Recreations:* history, offshore sailing, international travel. *Address:* The Old Manor, Milton Road, Pewsey, Wilts SN9 5JJ. *Club:* Cavalry and Guards.

GORDON, Robert Ian Neilson, CBE 2012; DL; Member (C) Hertfordshire County Council, 1989–97 and since 2001 (Leader, since 2007); *b* 29 March 1952; *s* of late Louis George Gordon (formerly Smith) and Patricia Dunella Mackay Gordon (*née* Neilson); *m* 1984, Susan Elizabeth Leigh; three *d*. *Educ:* Watford Grammar Sch.; Univ. of Sussex; Coll. of Law, Guildford and Lancaster Gate; City Univ. Joined Maffey & Brentnall, solicitors, Watford, 1974, as Articled Clerk; admitted Solicitor, 1978; Partner, Brentnall & Cox, subseq. Bryan & Gordon, then Bryan, Furby & Gordon, 1978–92, Consultant, 1992–93. Dir, Soc. of Genealogists, 1998–2001; Mem. Exec. Cttee, Fedn of Family Hist. Socs, 1998–2001; Sec., Soc. of Genealogists Enterprises Ltd, 1999–2001; non-exec. Dir, W Herts Community Health NHS Trust, 1998–2001. Mem. (C), Watford BC, 1982–90, 2002–06 (Leader of Opposition, 1984–86, 1988–90; Chm., Finance and Resources Scrutiny Cttee, 2002–03; Vice-Chm., 2003–04; Chm., 2004–05); Hertfordshire County Council: Dep. Leader, 1991–93 and 2006–07; Leader of Opposition, 1993–96; Chm., Educn Cttee, 1992–93; Exec. Mem. for Children, Schs and Families, 2001–04, for Educn, 2004–06, for Perf. and Resources, 2006–07. Chairman: Herts Sch. Orgn Cttee, 2001–07; Herts Connexions Consortium Bd, 2002–05; E of England Strategic Authy Leaders, 2008–10; E of England Local Govt Assoc., 2010–11; Mem., 1995–97, 2001–05, 2007–12, Chm., 1995–97, Herts Police Authy; Mem., Herts Learning and Skills Council, 2003–07; Member: Exec. Council, ACC, 1991–93; Gen. Assembly, LGA, 2006– (Dep. Chm., 2011–13); Local Govt Gp Exec., 2010–13; European Cttee of the Regions, 2015–. Chm., County Councils Network, 2010–13 (Vice-Chm., 2008–10); Vice-Chm., Local Govt Improvement and Develt (formerly Improvement and Develt Agency), 2009–10. Mem., Gen. Teaching Council for England, 2006–12. Contested (C): Torfaen, 1987; Watford, 1997; Eastern Reg., England, EP, 1999. Chairman: Watford Cons. Assoc., 1990–92, 1995–96; Herts County Cons. Fedn, 1997–; Local Govt Bd, Cons. Councillors' Assoc., 2011–13 (Mem., 2010–13); Member: Cons. Nat. Local Govt Adv. Cttee, 1991–97; Bd, Cons. Party, 2011–13. Chm., Nat. Employers Orgn for Sch. Teachers, 2003–07. Member: Court, City Univ., 2001–06; Bd of Govs and Court, Univ. of Herts, 2010–; Chm. Govs, Watford GS for Girls, 1998–2001; Clerk to Trustees, Watford Grammar Schs Foundn, 2001–14. DL Hertford, 2009. *Publications:* (ed) Posterity's Blessing: the journey of the Watford School of Music to the Clarendon Muse, 2008. *Recreations:* choral music, walking, photography. *Address:* 6 Temple House, Old Park Ride, Waltham Cross, Herts EN7 5HY. *T:* (01992) 623971.

GORDON, Sir Robert James, 10th Bt *cr* 1706, of Afton and Earlston, Kirkcudbrightshire; farmer, since 1958; *b* 17 Aug. 1932; *s* of Sir John Charles Gordon, 9th Bt and of Marion, *d* of late James B. Wright; *S* father, 1982; *m* 1976, Helen Julia Weston Perry. *Educ:* Barker College, Sydney; North Sydney Boys' High School; Wagga Agricultural Coll., Wagga Wagga, NSW (Wagga Dip. of Agric., Hons I and Dux). *Recreations:* tennis, ski-ing, swimming. *Heir:* none. *Address:* 126 Earlstoun Road, Guyra, NSW 2365, Australia. *T:* (2) 67791343.

GORDON, Prof. Robert Patterson, PhD, LittD; FBA 2011; Regius Professor of Hebrew, Cambridge University, 1995–2012, now Professor Emeritus; Fellow, St Catharine's College, Cambridge, 1995–2012, now Emeritus Fellow; Foundation Member, Trinity College, Cambridge, 1995–2012; *b* 9 Nov. 1945; *s* of Robert Gordon and Eveline (*née* Shilliday); *m* 1970, Helen Ruth Lyttle; two *s* one *d*. *Educ:* Methodist Coll., Belfast; St Catharine's Coll., Cambridge (Jarrett Schol. in Oriental Studies, 1966; John Stewart of Rannoch Hebrew Schol., 1966; BA 1st Cl. Hons Oriental Studies 1968; Bender Hebrew Prize, 1968; Sen. Schol., 1968; Tyrwhitt Scholarship and Mason Hebrew Prize, 1969; MA 1972; PhD 1973; LittD 2001). Asst Lectr in Hebrew and Semitic Langs, 1969–70, Lectr, 1970–79, Glasgow Univ.; Cambridge University: Lectr in Divinity, 1979–95; Fellow, St Edmund's Coll., 1985–89 (Tutor, 1986–89); Univ. Preacher, 1999. Lectures include: McManis, Wheaton, 1990; Macbride Sermon, Oxford Univ., 2000; Didsbury, Manchester, 2001; 11th Annual Biblical Studies, Samford Univ., Alabama, 2004. Sec., Internat. Orgn for Study of OT, 2001–04; Pres., SOTS, 2003. Mem., Carrickfergus Gasworks Preservation Soc. Trustee, Spalding Trust, 2013–. Review Ed., Vetus Testamentum, 1998–2010; Ed., Hebrew Bible and its Versions, monograph series, 2001–15. *Publications:* 1 and 2 Samuel, 1984 (Chinese edn 2002); 1 and 2 Samuel: a commentary, 1986; (ed jtly) The Targum of the Minor Prophets, 1989; Studies in the Targum to the Twelve Prophets, 1994; (ed jtly) Wisdom in Ancient Israel, 1995; (ed) The Place is too Small for Us: the Israelite prophets in recent scholarship, 1995; (Consulting Ed.) New International Dictionary of Old Testament Theology and Exegesis, 1997; (ed) The Old Testament in Syriac: Chronicles, 1998; Hebrews: a new biblical commentary, 2000, 2nd edn, 2008; Holy Land, Holy City, 2004; (ed jtly) The Old Testament in its World, 2005; Hebrew Bible and Ancient Versions, 2006; (ed) The God of Israel, 2007; (ed jtly) Thus Speaks Ishtar of Arbela: prophecy in Israel, Assyria, and Egypt in the Neo-Assyrian period, 2013; (ed jtly) Leshon Limmudim: essays on the language and literature of the Hebrew Bible in honour of A. A. Macintosh, 2013; Genesis 1–11 in its Ancient Context, 2015; contrib. to learned jls incl. Jl Jewish Studies, Jewish Qly Rev., Jl Semitic Studies, Jl for Study of OT, Jl Theol Studies, Revue de Qumran, Vetus Testamentum, and to various composite vols. *Recreations:* jogging, otopianistics, local history (N Ireland). *Address:* St Catharine's College, Cambridge CB2 1RL. *Club:* National.

GORDON, Prof. Robert Samuel Clive, PhD; FBA 2015; Serena Professor of Italian, University of Cambridge, since 2012; Fellow of Gonville and Caius College, Cambridge, since 1998; *b* London, 13 March 1966; *s* of Lionel Lawrence Gordon and Jillian May Gordon; *m* 2001, Barbara Placido; two *s*. *Educ:* King's College Sch., Wimbledon; Pembroke Coll., Oxford (BA Hons); St John's Coll., Cambridge (PhD 1993). Lectr and Fellow, Pembroke Coll., Oxford, 1990–97; Lectr, 1998–2001, Sen. Lectr, 2001–06, Reader, 2006–11, Prof., 2011–12, Univ. of Cambridge. *Publications:* (ed) Ignazio Silone, Fontamara, 1994; Pasolini: forms of subjectivity, 1996; (ed) Primo Levi, The Voice of Memory, 2000; Primo Levi's Ordinary Virtues: from testimony to ethics, 2001; A Difficult Modernity, 2005; (ed) Culture, Censorship and the State in Twentieth-Century Italy, 2005; (ed) Leonardo De Benedetti and Primo Levi, Auschwitz Report, 2006; (ed) The Cambridge Companion to Primo Levi, 2007; Bicycle Thieves, 2008; Stacciata Fortuna, 2010; The Holocaust in Italian Culture, 2012; (ed) Holocaust Intersections, 2013. *Address:* Gonville and Caius College, Cambridge CB2 1TA. *E:* rscg1@cam.ac.uk.

GORDON, Robert Smith Benzie, CB 2000; Chair, Bethany Christian Trust, since 2009; executive coach and change consultant, since 2011; Associate, Kynesis, since 2011; *b* 7 Nov. 1950; *s* of William Gladstone Gordon and Helen Watt Gordon (*née* Benzie); *m* 1976, Joyce Ruth Cordiner; two *s* two *d*. *Educ:* Univ. of Aberdeen (MA Hons Italian Studies). Admin. trainee, Scottish Office, 1973–78; Principal, Scottish Develt Dept, 1979–85; Asst Sec., 1984; Principal Private Sec. to Sec. of State for Scotland, 1985–87; Dept of Agriculture and Fisheries for Scotland, 1987–90; Scottish Office, later Scottish Executive, then Scottish Government: Mgt Orgn and Industrial Relns, 1990–91; Dir of Admin. Services, 1991–97; Under Sec., 1993; Head of Constitution Gp, 1997–98; Dep. Sec., 1998; Hd of Exec. Secretariat, 1999–2001; Hd of Finance and Central Services Dept, 2001–02; Chief Exec., Crown Office and Procurator Fiscal Service, 2002–04; Hd of Legal and Parly Services, 2002–10, and Hd of Justice Dept, later Dir-Gen. of Justice and Communities, 2004–10. Dir, Inspiring Scotland, 2008–. Chair, Resources Gp, St Paul's and St George's Church, Edinburgh, 2011–. Warden, Incorporation of Goldsmiths, City of Edinburgh, 2000–. *Address:* c/o Bethany Christian Trust, 65 Bonnington Road, Edinburgh EH6 5JQ.

GORDON, Ronald Dingwall; Chairman, John Gordon & Son Ltd, since 2000; Vice Lord-Lieutenant of Nairnshire, 1999–2011; *b* 13 Nov. 1936; *s* of Ronald James Robertson Gordon and Mary Isabella Cardno Gordon; *m* 1961, Elizabeth Ancell Gordon; two *s* one *d*. *Educ:* Nairn Acad. Nat. Service, RAF, 1955–57. Joined John Gordon & Son, 1957; jt partner with father, 1961; sole trader, 1965–85; Man. Dir, 1985–2000. Dir, Nairn Museum Ltd, 2014–. DL Nairnshire, 1991. *Recreations:* golf, fishing, gardening. *Address:* Achareidh House, Nairn IV12 4UD. *T:* (01667) 452130. *Clubs:* Royal and Ancient Golf, Royal Dornoch Golf, Nairn Golf (Capt., 1980–82; Vice Pres., 2000–05; Pres., 2006–).

GORDON, Prof. Siamon, PhD; FRS 2007; Glaxo-Wellcome Professor of Cellular Pathology, Oxford University, 1991–2008, now Emeritus (Professor of Cellular Pathology, 1989–91); Fellow, Exeter College, Oxford, 1976–2006, now Emeritus Fellow; *b* 29 April 1938; *s* of Jonah and Liebe Gordon; *m* 1963, Lyndall Felicity Getz (*see* L. F. Gordon); two *d*. *Educ:* South African Coll. Sch., Cape Town; Univ. of Cape Town (MB ChB 1961); Rockefeller Univ. (PhD 1971). Res. Asst, Wright-Fleming Inst., St Mary's, London, 1964–65; Rockefeller University, NY: Res. Associate, 1965–71; Asst Prof. of Cellular Immunology, 1971–76; Adjunct Associate Prof., 1976–; Reader in Exptl Pathology, Sir Wm Dunn Sch. of Pathology, Univ. of Oxford, 1976–89, Actg Hd of Dept, 1989–90, 2000–01. University of Oxford: Chairman: Physiol Scis Bd, 1984–86; Search Cttee, E. P. Abraham Bldg, 1999–2003; Member: General Bd, 1989–92; Med. Scis Div., 2000–03. Member: Lister Scientific Adv. Cttee, 1987–92; Scientific Adv. Cttee, Inst. of Infection, Immunity and Molecular Medicine, Univ. of Cape Town, 2003– (Chm., 2003–08, 2013–). Special Fellow and Scholar, Leukaemia Soc. of America, 1971–76; Vis. Scientist, Genetics, Oxford Univ., 1974–75; Vis. Scholar, NIH, Bethesda, USA, 2009–10. FMedSci 2003. Hon. Mem., Amer. Assoc. of Immunologists, 2004. Hon. DSc Cape Town, 2003. Marie T. Bonazinga Award, Soc. of Leukocyte Biol., 2003. *Publications:* contribs to jls of exptl medicine, immunology, cell biology, AIDS educn in Southern Africa. *Recreations:* reading biography, medical history. *Address:* c/o Sir William Dunn School of Pathology, South Parks Road, Oxford OX1 3RE.

GORDON, (Vera) Kate, (Mrs E. W. Gordon), CB 1999; Chair, Queen Elizabeth Hospital NHS Foundation Trust, King's Lynn, 2007–13; *b* 8 Oct. 1944; *d* of late Kenneth Timms and Elsie Timms (*née* Cussans); *m* 1977, Ernest William Gordon; one step *d*. *Educ:* Queen Anne Grammar School, York; St Hilda's College, Oxford (PPE Hons). Economic Asst, NEDO, 1966–70; Ministry of Agriculture, Fisheries and Food, 1970; Asst Private Sec. to Minister of Agric., 1974–75; seconded to European Secretariat of Cabinet Office, 1976–79; Principal Private Sec. to Minister of Agric., 1980–82; Asst Sec. responsible for marketing policy, MAFF, 1982–84; Counsellor, Paris, seconded to HM Diplomatic Service, 1984–88; Asst Sec. and Head of Sugar and Oilseeds Div., MAFF, 1988–89; Under Sec., Arable Crops Gp, MAFF, 1989–90; Minister (Agriculture), Office of the UK Perm. Rep., Brussels, 1990–95; Principal Finance Officer, MAFF, 1995–96; Dep. Sec., Agriculture, Crops and Commodities, later Agriculture and Food Industry, MAFF, 1996–2001; Policy Dir, Health and Safety Exec., 2001–04. Member: Basic Skills Agency, 2004–07; Flagship Housing Gp (formerly Peddars Way Housing Assoc.), 2004–13; Passenger Focus (formerly Rail Passengers' Council), 2005–09. Ordre du Mérite Agricole (France), 1988. *Address:* Holly House, 62A London Street, Swaffham, Norfolk PE37 7DJ. *T:* (01760) 723034; 42 The Foreshore, SE8 3AG. *T:* (020) 8691 0823.

GORDON, William John, FCIB; Chief Executive (formerly Managing Director), UK Banking Services, Barclays Bank plc, 1992–98; *b* 24 April 1939; *s* of Sidney Frank Gordon and Grace Louie Gordon; *m* 1963, Patricia Rollason; two *s*. *Educ:* King Edward VI Sch., Fiveways, Birmingham. FCIB 1979. Joined Barclays Bank, 1955: branch and regl appts, 1955–80; Asst Gen. Manager, Barclaycard, 1980–83; Regl Gen. Manager, Central UK, 1983–87; Dir, UK Corporate Services, 1987–90; Gp Personnel Dir, 1990–92; Dir, 1995–98. Chm., Barclays Pension Fund Trustees Ltd, 1996–2005; Ind. Dir, Britannia Bldg Soc., 1999–2009 (Dep. Chm., 2004–09). Dir, Burdett Trust for Nursing, 2009–. Mem., Herts Bridge Assoc. *Recreations:* bridge, golf, chess, music. *Address:* 9 High Elms, Harpenden AL5 2JU. *Club:* Mid Herts Golf (Wheathampstead).

GORDON BANKS, Matthew Richard William; Director, Middle East and South Asia, International Institute for Strategic Affairs, since 2014; *b* 21 June 1961; *s* of Harry and Audrey Banks; *m* 1992, Jane, *d* of Michael Miller; one *s* one *d*. *Educ:* private; Sheffield City Polytechnic (BA Hons History and Econs); RMA Sandhurst; Donald Harrison Sch. of Business, SE Missouri State Univ., USA (MBA 2001). 1st Bn, 51st Highland Vols, 1979–81; Commnd, The Gordon Highlanders, 1981–83; War Disablement Pension, 1983. Barclays Bank, 1984–88; Private Sec. to Cecil Franks, MP, 1988–89. Dir, and Sen. Advr on ME Affairs, LBJ Ltd, 1989–. Mem., Wirral BC, 1984–90 (Chairman: Schs Cttee, 1985–86; Works Cttee, 1986–87). Contested (C) Manchester Central, 1987; MP (C) Southport, 1992–97; contested (C) same seat, 1997. PPS, DoE, 1996–97. Mem., Select Cttee on Transport, 1992–97; Chm., Anglo-Venezuela Parly Gp, 1993–97; Sec., Anglo-UAE Parly Gp, 1993–97. Advr, Jt Security Industry Council, 2002–06; Sen. Advr, Middle East and SE Asia, Advanced Res. Assessment Gp, Defence Acad., MoD, 2006–10; Dir, Internat. Relns and Public Affairs, Inst. of Islamic Strategic and Socio-Political Affairs, 2010–14; Advr, Internat. Inst. for Security Services, 2007–09; Foreign and Policy Advr to Tim Farron, MP, 2015–. Hon. Public Affairs Advr, Assoc. of Ophthalmologists, 2008–09. Mem. (C) Cotswold DC, 2001–04 (Chm., Overview and Scrutiny Cttee). FRGS 1983. *Recreations:* walking, travel, reading, flying, fishing. *Address:* Gordon Castle, Fochabers, Morayshire IV32 7PQ; The Green, Charlbury, Oxon OX7 3QB. *Club:* Caledonian.

GORDON-BROWN, Alexander Douglas, CB 1984; Receiver for the Metropolitan Police District, 1980–87; *b* 5 Dec. 1927; *s* of late Captain and Mrs D. S. Gordon-Brown; *m* 1959, Mary Hilton; three *s*. *Educ:* Bryanston Sch.; New Coll., Oxford (MA; 1st cl. hons PPE).

Entered Home Office, 1951; Sec., Franks Cttee on section 2 of Official Secrets Act 1911, 1971; Asst Under-Sec. of State, Home Office, 1972–75, 1978–80; Under Sec., Cabinet Office, 1975–78. Chm., Home Office Wkg Gp on Costs of Crime, 1988. Mem., Nat. Council, 1991–97, Trustee, 1998–2000, Victim Support. *Recreations:* music, walking.

GORDON CLARK, (Elizabeth) Jane; Founder/Designer, Ornamenta Ltd, since 1987; *m* 1981, Sam Gordon Clark. *Educ:* Ruskin Sch. of Art, Oxford. Consultant, Fine Art Develt plc, 1968–77; Founder/Designer: Davan Wetton Design, 1977–2008. Solo exhibition, Hothouse Flowers: The Gallery at Oxo, 2003; The Orangery, Holland Park, 2006; The Exhibition Gallery, SW7, 2007. Trustee, V&A Mus., 2000–08 (Mem. Develt Adv. Bd, 2011–); Chm., Friends of the V&A, 1994–2001; Member: Bd, V&A Enterprises, 2005–08; Cttee, Theatre Mus., 2003–06; Heatherley Sch. of Fine Art, 2015–. Mem., British Interior Design Assoc., 2003. Freeman, Painter Stainers' Co., 1981. *Publications:* Paper Magic, 1991; Italian Style, 1999; Wallpaper in Decoration, 2001. *Club:* Chelsea Arts.

GORDON CLARK, Robert Michael; Executive Chairman, London Communications Agency, since 2010 (Managing Director and Chairman, 1999–2010); *b* Derby, 8 May 1961; *s* of Rev. John Gordon Clark and late Jennifer Gordon Clark; *m* 1985, Lisa, *d* of Sir Michael John Day, *qv*; two *d*. *Educ:* St John's Sch., Leatherhead; Southampton Univ. (LLB Hons). Marketing Manager: Matthew Clark & Sons Ltd, 1983–89; CCA Galleries, 1989–90; Hd of Public Affairs, London Arts Bd, 1990–93; Dir of Communications, 1993–97, Dep. CEO, 1997–99, London First. Dir, Shannon & Clark Prodns Ltd, 2008–11. Non-exec. Dir, Hayes Davidson, 1999–2010. Chm., Mayor's Thames Fest., London, 2013– (Trustee, 2006–13). Presenter, The Business, LBC Radio, 1999–2002. Gov., St John's Sch., Leatherhead, 1996–2011. *Recreations:* cricket (Vice Pres., HAC CC), theatre (Questors Th., Ealing), singing. *Address:* London Communications Agency, 8th Floor, Berkshire House, 168–173 High Holborn, WC1V 7AA. *T:* (020) 7612 8480. *E:* rgc@londoncommunications.co.uk.

GORDON CUMMING, Sir Alexander Penrose, (Sir Alastair), 7th Bt *cr* 1804, of Altyre, Forres; *b* 15 April 1954; *s* of Sir William Gordon Cumming, 6th Bt and of Elisabeth Gordon Cumming (*née* Hinde); *S* father, 2002; *m* 1991, Louisa Clifton-Brown; two *s* one *d*. *Educ:* Ludgrove; Harrow. Insurance broker, 1976–95; Penrose Forbes Ltd, 1995–2000; Consultant, R. K. Harrison, 2000–14. *Recreation:* all country pursuits. *Heir: s* William Gordon Cumming, *b* 4 April 1993. *Address:* Altyre House, Forres, Morayshire IV36 2SH. *T:* (01309) 673774, *Fax:* (01309) 672270. *Clubs:* Turf, Pratt's; Shikar.

GORDON LENNOX, family name of **Duke of Richmond**.

GORDON LENNOX, Anthony Charles; Founder and Chief Executive Officer, AGL, since 2009; *b* Madrid, 29 April 1969; *s* of Lord Nicholas Charles Gordon Lennox, KCMG, KCVO and of Mary Gordon Lennox, LVO. *Educ:* Eton Coll.; Exeter Univ. (BA Sociol.). Producer: A Week in Politics, Channel 4, 1993–95; Question Time and political live events, BBC, 1995–2000; Founder and Sen. Partner, Company Agency, 2000–09. Vis. Fellow, Saïd Business Sch., Oxford Univ., 2010–. Founding Mem., Leadership Council, 2008–. Mem. Bd, LAMDA, 2009–. Trustee, New Schs Network, 2012–. *Recreations:* riding, tennis, swimming in the sea. *T:* 07767 686992. *E:* anthony@agordonlennox.co.uk. *Club:* Boodles.

GORDON LENNOX, Maj.-Gen. Bernard Charles, CB 1986; MBE 1968; *b* 19 Sept. 1932; *s* of Lt-Gen. Sir George Gordon Lennox and Nancy Brenda Darell; *m* 1958, Sally-Rose Warner; three *s*. *Educ:* Eton; Sandhurst. 2nd Lt, Grenadier Guards, 1953; Hong Kong, 1965; HQ Household Div., 1971; Commanding 1st Bn Grenadier Guards, 1974; Army Directing Staff, RAF Staff College, 1976–77; Command, Task Force H, 1978–79; RCDS, 1980; Dep. Commander and Chief of Staff, SE District, 1981–82; GOC Berlin (British Sector), 1983–85; Sen. Army Mem., RCDS, 1986–88, retd. Regtl Lt-Col, Grenadier Guards, 1989–95. Dir of Regions, Motor Agents Assoc., 1988–89. Chm., Guards' Polo Club, 1992–99. *Recreations:* field sports, cricket, squash, music. *Address:* c/o The Estate Office, Gordon Castle, Fochabers, Morayshire IV32 7PQ. *Clubs:* Army and Navy, MCC.

GORDON-MacLEOD, David Scott; HM Diplomatic Service; Chargé d'Affaires, Monrovia, Liberia; *b* 4 May 1948; *s* of Adam Denys Gordon-MacLeod and Margaret Rae Gordon-MacLeod (*née* Miller); *m* 1988, Adrienne Felicia Maria Atkins; two *s* two *d*. *Educ:* St Peter's Coll., Oxford (exhibitioner; BA); Carleton Univ., Canada (MA); Sarajevo Univ. (Dip. Islamic Studies). ODA, 1973–78; Mbabane, 1978–83; Second, later First Sec., Arms Control and Disarmament Dept, FCO, 1983–87; Dep. Hd of Mission, Maputo, 1987–91; First Sec., Equatorial Africa Dept, FCO, 1991–92; Hd of Missile Technol., Defence Dept, FCO, 1992–94; Dep. Hd of Mission, Bogotá, 1995–97; Dir, EU and Econ. Affairs, Athens, 1998–2003; High Comr to Papua New Guinea, 2003–07; Manager, FCO Global Response Centre, 2007; Dep. Ambassador, Bosnia and Herzegovina. FRGS 1975. *Recreations:* family, travel, environmental issues, climbing, tennis, writing.

GORDON-SAKER, Andrew Stephen; Costs Officer of the Supreme Court, since 2010; Senior Costs Judge of England and Wales, since 2014; *b* 4 Oct. 1958; *s* of Vincent Gordon-Saker and Gwendoline (*née* Remmers); *m* 1985, Liza Helen Marle (*see* L. H. Gordon-Saker); one *s* one *d*. *Educ:* Stonyhurst Coll.; Univ. of E Anglia (LLB). Called to the Bar, Middle Temple, 1981; in practice, SE Circuit, 1982–2003. Dep. Taxing Master of Supreme Court, 1994–2003; Master of the Sen. (formerly Supreme) Courts Costs Office, 2003–14. Mem., Cambridge Legal Aid Area Cttee, 1995–2003. Mem. (C) Camden LBC, 1982–86. Trustee, Jimmy's Night Shelter, Cambridge, 2000–03. Mem., Sen. Editl Bd, Civil Procedure (The White Book), 2015–. *Publications:* (ed) Butterworths Costs Service, 2006–; (contrib.) Civil Procedure (The White Book), 2012–. *Recreations:* gardening, construction. *Address:* Royal Courts of Justice, Strand, WC2A 2LL. *Club:* Trumpington Bridge.

GORDON-SAKER, Liza Helen; Her Honour Judge Gordon-Saker; a Circuit Judge, since 2014; *b* London, 30 Nov. 1959; *d* of William James Marle and Doreen Maud Marle; *m* 1985, Andrew Stephen Gordon-Saker, *qv*; one *s* one *d*. *Educ:* Farringtons Sch., Chislehurst; Univ. of E Anglia (LLB). Called to the Bar, Gray's Inn, 1982; in practice, SE Circuit, 1983–2009; Dep. Dist Judge, 2006–09; Dist Judge, Principal Registry of Family Div., 2010–14. Mem., Family Justice Council, 2013–. Dir, Bar Mutual Indemnity Fund, 1988–2002. Parish Councillor, 1998–2007. Trustee, Jimmy's Night Shelter, Cambridge, 2004–10. Chm., Univ. of E Anglia Soc. (Alumni Assoc.), 1985–88. Freeman, City of London, 1984. *Publications:* (contrib.) Atkin's Court Forms, 2011–. *Recreations:* golf, bridge, The Archers. *Address:* The Law Courts, Bishopgate, Norwich, Norfolk NR3 1UR.

GORDON-SMITH, David Gerard, CMG 1971; Director-General in Legal Service, Council of Ministers, European Communities, 1976–87; *b* 6 Oct. 1925; *s* of late Frederic Gordon-Smith, QC, and Elsie Gordon-Smith (*née* Foster); *m* 1952, Angela Kirkpatrick Pile; one *d* (and one *s* decd). *Educ:* Rugby Sch.; Trinity Coll., Oxford. Served in RNVR, 1944–46. BA (Oxford) 1948; called to the Bar, Inner Temple, 1949; Legal Asst, Colonial Office, 1950; Sen. Legal Asst, 1954; CRO, 1963–65; Asst Legal Adviser, CO, 1965–66; Legal Counsellor, CO, later FCO, 1966–72; Dep. Legal Advr, FCO, 1973–76. *Address:* Kingscote, Westcott, Surrey RH4 3NX.

GORDON-SMITH, Prof. Edward Colin, FRCP, FRCPE, FRCPath, FMedSci; Professor of Haematology, St George's, University of London (formerly St George's Hospital Medical School, London), 1987–2003, now Emeritus; *b* 26 June 1938; *s* of late Gordon John Gordon-Smith and Valentine (*née* Waddington); *m* 1968, Moira Phelan; two *s*. *Educ:* Oakham Sch.; Epsom Coll.; Exeter Coll., Oxford (MA, BSc, BM BCh); Westminster Med. Sch., London (MSc). FRCP 1978; FRCPath 1987; FRCPE 1999. House Officer, Westminster Hosp., 1964; Sen. House Officer, Nuffield Dept of Medicine, Radcliffe Infirmary, Oxford, 1966; Lectr in Neurology, Churchill Hosp., Oxford, 1966–67; Registrar in Haematology, Hammersmith Hosp., 1968–69; MRC Clinical Trng Fellow, RPMS Metabolic Unit, Oxford, 1970–71; Sen. Lectr 1972–83, Reader 1983–86, RPMS. Editor, Brit. Jl of Haematology, 1983–86. President: European Bone Marrow Transplant Gp, 1980; Internat. Soc. Exptl Haematology, 1990–92; British Soc. for Haematology, 1995; Vice-Pres., RCPath, 1996–99. Founder FMedSci 1998. Order of Prasidda Prabala Gorkha-Dakshin Bahu (2nd class), Nepal, 1984. *Publications:* papers on aplastic anaemia, bone marrow transplantation, inherited bone marrow disorders, culture of human bone marrow and drug induced blood disorders. *Recreations:* golf, music, gardening, arguing with the wireless. *Address:* 35 Park Road, Chiswick, W4 3EY. *T:* (020) 8994 2112, *Fax:* (020) 8995 6631. *Club:* Royal Society of Medicine.

GORDON-WATSON, Katherine Genevieve; *see* Reardon, K. G.

GORE; *see* Ormsby Gore.

GORE, family name of **Earl of Arran**.

GORE, Albert Arnold, Jr; Chairman, Current TV (formerly INdTV), 2004–12; Founding Partner and Chairman, Generation Investment Management, since 2004; *b* 31 March 1948; *s* of late Albert and Pauline Gore; *m* 1970, Mary Elizabeth, (Tipper), Aitcheson; one *s* three *d*. *Educ:* Harvard and Vanderbilt Univs. Served US Army in Vietnam, 1969–71. Reporter and editorial writer, The Tennessean, 1971–76; livestock farmer, 1971–. Democrat; Mem., US House of Representatives, 1977–85; Mem. for Tennessee, US Senate, 1985–92; Chm., US Senate Delegn to Earth Summit, Rio de Janeiro, 1992; Vice-President of USA, 1993–2001; Presidential cand., US elections, 2000. Dir, Apple, 2003–; Sen. Advr, Google, 2001–09. Visiting Professor: Fisk Univ., 2001; Middle Tenn State Univ., 2001; UCLA, 2001. (Jtly) Nobel Peace Prize, 2007. *Publications:* Earth in the Balance: ecology and the human spirit, 1992; (with Tipper Gore) Joined at the Heart: the transformation of the American family, 2002; The Spirit of Family (photographs), 2002; An Inconvenient Truth: the crisis of global warming, 2007; The Assault on Reason, 2007; Our Choice: a plan to solve the climate crisis, 2009; The Future: six drivers of global change, 2013. *Address:* 2100 West End Avenue, Nashville, TN 37203, USA.

GORE, Allan Peter; QC 2003; **His Honour Judge Gore;** a Circuit Judge, since 2010; a Senior Circuit Judge, since 2011; Designated Civil Judge for Manchester, since 2013; *b* 25 Aug. 1951; *s* of Gerry and Hansi Gore; *m* 1981 (marr. diss.); three *d*; partner, Alison Taylor. *Educ:* Trinity Hall, Cambridge (MA 1973; LLB 1st class 1974). Called to the Bar, Middle Temple, 1977; in practice, specialising in personal injury (particularly asbestos and other industrial disease), clinical negligence and related legal negligence litigation; Recorder, 2000–10. Pres., Assoc. of Personal Injury Lawyers, 2005–06. Mem., Editl Bd, Jl of Personal Injury Law, 2006–08. *Publications:* (ed jtly) Occupational Illness Litigation; contributions to: Personal Injury Pleadings, ed by Patrick Curran, 2001, 5th edn, 2014; Personal Injury Handbook, 2001; Butterworths Personal Injury Litigation Service; Butterworths Civil Court Precedents; Cordery on Legal Services; Jordan's Civil Court Service. *Recreations:* travel, sport, music, cooking. *Address:* Manchester Civil Justice Centre, 1 Bridge Street West, Manchester M60 9DJ.

GORE, Sir Hugh (Frederick Corbet), 15th Bt *cr* 1622 (Ire.), of Magherabegg, Co. Donegal; *b* Goondiwindi, Qld, 31 Dec. 1934; *s* of late Frederick Dundas Corbet Gore and Ella Maud, *d* of Charles Sydney Jones; *S* cousin, 2008; *m* 1963, Jennifer Mary Copp; one *s* two *d*. *Educ:* Church of England Grammar Sch., Brisbane; Univ. of Sydney. Qantas Airways Ltd: Traffic Handling, 1957–61; Ops Planning, 1961–68; Computer Systems Develt, 1968–90 (latterly Strategic Planning Manager, Systems Develt). *Recreations:* bridge, bushwalking. *Heir: s* Timothy Milton Corbet Gore [*b* 26 Nov. 1969; *m* 2009, Aya Tokito]. *Address:* 7 Romney Road, St Ives, Sydney, NSW 2075, Australia. *Clubs:* Australian, Union University and Schools, Australasian Pioneers', Tripe (Sydney).

GORE, Prof. Martin Eric, PhD; FRCP; Consultant Cancer Physician, since 1989, and Medical Director, since 2006, Royal Marsden Hospital; Professor of Cancer Medicine, Institute of Cancer Research, London, since 2002; *b* 18 Feb. 1951; *s* of late Bernard and Alexandra Gore; *m* 1979, Pauline Wren; three *s* one *d*. *Educ:* Summer Fields, Oxford; Bradfield Coll., Berks; St Bartholomew's Med. Coll. (MB BS 1974; PhD 1985). FRCP 1994. Hon. Sen. Lectr, Inst. Cancer Res., London, 1998–2002. Chair, Gene Therapy Adv. Cttee, DoH, 2006–12; Vice-Chair, Scientific Adv. Cttee on Genetically Modified Organisms, HSE, 2004–. *Publications:* joint editor: Biology of Gynaecological Cancer, 1995; Immunotherapy in Cancer, 1996; The Effective Management of Ovarian Cancer, 1999, 3rd edn 2004; Melanoma: critical debates, 2002; Cancer in Primary Care, 2003; Gynecologic Cancer: controversies in management, 2004; Renal Cell Carcinoma: a handbook, 2010; Emerging Therapeutic Targets in Ovarian Cancer, 2011; contrib. numerous articles on cancer. *Recreation:* agonising over Fulham FC. *Address:* Royal Marsden Hospital, Fulham Road, SW3 6JJ. *T:* (020) 7811 8576, *Fax:* (020) 7811 8103. *E:* martin.gore@rmh.nhs.uk.

GORE, Michael Edward John, CVO 1994; CBE 1991; HM Diplomatic Service, retired; Governor, Cayman Islands, 1992–95; *b* 20 Sept. 1935; *s* of late John Gore and Elsa Gore (*née* Dillon); *m* 1957, Monica Shellish; two *d* (and one *d* decd). *Educ:* Xaverian College, Brighton. Reporter, Portsmouth Evening News, 1952–55; Captain, Army Gen. List, 1955–59; Air Ministry, Dep. Comd. Inf. Officer, Cyprus and Aden, 1959–63; CRO, later FCO, 1963; served Jesselton, 1963–66, FCO, 1966–67, Seoul, 1967–71, Montevideo, 1971–74; First Sec., Banjul, 1974–78; FCO, 1978–81; Nairobi, 1981–84; Dep. High Comr, Lilongwe, 1984–87; Ambassador to Liberia, 1988–90; High Comr to the Bahamas, 1991–92. Mem., UK Dependent, then UK Overseas, Territories Conservation Forum, 1996–; Chm., Wider Caribbean Working Gp, 1997–2006. Member: Nature Photographers Portfolio, 1979– (Pres., 2001–13); Zool Photographic Club, 1992– (Pres., 2013–). Hon. Vice Pres., Birdlife Cyprus, 2003–. Distinguished Supporter, British Humanist Assoc., 2011–. FRPS. *Publications:* The Birds of Korea (with Pyong-Oh Won), 1971; Las Aves del Uruguay (with A. R. M. Gepp), 1978; Birds of the Gambia, 1981, 2nd edn 1991; On Safari in Kenya: a pictorial guide to the national parks and reserves, 1984, 2nd edn, 2007; papers on birds and conservation; wild-life photographs in books and magazines. *Recreations:* ornithology, wildlife photography, fishing. *Address:* 5 St Mary's Close, Fetcham, Surrey KT22 9HE. *W:* www.wildlife-photography.net.

GORE, Prof. Van Jonathan, CBE 2014; Vice-Chancellor, Southampton Solent University, 2007–14; *b* Birmingham; *s* of John and Daisy Gore; *m* Jill Helen; two *d*. *Educ:* Univ. of Sheffield (BA Hons Hist. and Politics; MA Modern British Politics). Sheffield Polytechnic, subseq. Sheffield Hallam University, 1972–2001: Prof. of Quality Mgt; Sen. Academic, Cultural Studies; Special Policy Advr to Vice-Chancellor; Sen. Vice-Principal, Southampton Inst., 2001–05; Dep. Vice-Chancellor, Southampton Solent Univ., 2005–07. *Recreations:* music, books, gardening, table tennis.

GORE-BOOTH, Sir Josslyn (Henry Robert), 9th Bt *cr* 1760 (Ire.), of Artarman, Sligo; *b* 5 Oct. 1950; *o s* of Sir Angus Gore-Booth, 8th Bt and Hon. Rosemary Myra Vane, *o d* of 10th Baron Barnard, CMG, OBE, MC, TD; *S* father, 1996; *m* 1980, Jane Mary, *o d* of Rt Hon. Sir Roualeyn Hovell-Thurlow-Cumming-Bruce; two *d*. *Educ:* Eton Coll.; Balliol Coll., Oxford (BA); Insead (MBA). Dir, Kiln Cotesworth Corporate Capital Fund plc, 1993–97. Chm., Herriot Hospice Homecare, 2007–13. Patron, living of Sacred Trinity, Salford.

Recreations: cooking, shooting. *Heir: cousin* (Paul Wyatt) Julian Gore-Booth [*b* 29 July 1968; *m* 1999, Amanda Marie McConnell; one *s* one *d*]. *Address:* Home Farm, Hartforth, Gilling West, Richmond, N Yorkshire DL10 5JS.

GORE-LANGTON; *see* Temple-Gore-Langton, family name of Earl Temple of Stowe.

GORE-RANDALL, Philip Allan, FCA; Chairman, Alvarez and Marsal Corporate Solutions (Europe) LLP, since 2013; *b* 16 Dec. 1952; *s* of late Alec Albert Gore-Randall and Joyce Margaret Gore-Randall; *m* 1984, Prof. Alison Elizabeth While; two *s*. *Educ:* Merchant Taylors' Sch., Northwood; University Coll., Oxford (MA 1975). FCA 1978. Arthur Andersen, subseq. Andersen, 1975–2002: Partner, 1986–2002; UK Man. Partner, Assurance and Business Advisory, 1995–97, Man. Partner, Assurance and Business Advisory, Europe, Africa, Middle East and India, 1996–97; UK Managing Partner, 1997–2001; Man. Partner, Global Ops, 2001–02; Chm. and CEO, Aon Risk Services, 2004–05; Dir, Aon Ltd, 2004–07; Chief Operating Officer, Aon UK, 2006–07; Chief Operating Officer and Dir, HBOS plc and Bank of Scotland plc, 2007–09. Chairman: Envmtl Resources Mgt Ltd, 2010–11; Fircroft Engrg Services Hldgs Ltd, 2013; Equiom Hldgs Ltd, 2014–. Non-executive Director: Compass Mgt Consulting Gp Hldgs Ltd, 2007–11; esure Ltd, 2009–10; Topaz Energy and Marine PLC, 2011 (Chm., Audit Cttee, 2013–); Ind. Mem., Internat. Exec. Cttee, Lovells, 2007–08; Advisor: Renaissance Services SAOG, 2011–13; RAK Ceramics PSC, 2014–; Chm., Audit and Ops Cttee, Chm., Competition Cttee, and non-exec. Mem., Exec. Cttee, Samena Capital, 2013–. *Recreations:* classical music/opera, good food, travel. *Club:* Vincent's (Oxford).

See also Rt Hon. Sir A. J. Randall.

GORELL, 5th Baron *cr* 1909, of Brampton, co. Derby; **John Picton Gorell Barnes;** Principal, Gorell Barnes, chartered surveyors, since 2009; *b* 29 July 1959; *s* of Hon. Ronald Alexander Henry Barnes, *yr s* of 3rd Baron, and Gillian Picton Barnes; *S* uncle, 2007; *m* 1989, Rosanne Duncan; one *s* one *d*. *Educ:* Mount House Sch., Tavistock; N Staffordshire Poly. (BSc Est. Mgt 1983). Assoc. Dir, Lambert Smith Hampton, 1984–89; Man. Dir, Barnes Noble Edwards, chartered surveyors, 1993–2009. Freeman, City of London. Upper Warden, Weavers' Co., 2014–15. *Recreations:* sailing, gun dog training, Stoke City FC. *Heir: s* Hon. Oliver Gorell Barnes, *b* 4 April 1993. *Address:* Fieldways, Great Addington, Northants NN14 4BW.

GORHAM, Ian David; Chief Executive Officer, Hargreaves Lansdown plc, since 2010 (Chief Operating Officer, 2009–10). *Educ:* Castle Rushen High Sch., I of M; Warwick Univ. (BSc Econs 1993). ACA 1996. Dir, Deloitte UK LLP, 1993–2003; Partner and Hd of UK Financial Services, Grant Thornton UK LLP, 2003–09. *Recreations:* golf, fitness. *Address:* Hargreaves Lansdown plc, 1 College Square South, Anchor Road, Bristol BS1 5HL. *T:* (0117) 988 9901. *E:* ian_gorham@hargreaveslansdown.co.uk. *Club:* Clevedon Golf.

GORHAM, Ven. Karen Marisa; Archdeacon of Buckingham, since 2007; *b* 24 June 1964. *Educ:* Mayflower Sch., Billericay; Trinity Coll., Bristol (BA 1995). Administrator: BTEC, 1982–86; RSA, 1986–88; ordained deacon, 1995, priest, 1996; Asst Curate, All Saints, Northallerton with Kirby Sigston, 1995–99; Priest-in-charge, St Paul's, Maidstone, 1999–2007; Area Dean, Maidstone, 2003–07; Asst Dir of Ordinands, Dio. of Canterbury, 2002–07. Hon. Canon, Canterbury Cathedral, 2006–07. Mem., Gen. Synod of C of E, 2003–07 and 2010–. FRSA 2011. *Recreations:* walking, travel, reading, theatre. *Address:* The Rectory, Stone, Aylesbury HP17 8RZ. *T:* (01865) 208264, *Fax:* (01296) 747424.

GORHAM, Martin Edwin, OBE 2005; Director: Gorham Partnership Ltd, 2007–13; Douglas-Gorham Partnership Ltd, 2008–15; *b* 18 June 1947; *s* of Clifford Edwin Gorham and Florence Ada Gorham; *m* 1st, 1968, Jean McNaughton Kerr (marr. diss. 1998); 2nd, 1998, Sally Ann Stevens (*née* Fletcher); one step *d*. *Educ:* Buckhurst Hill County High Sch.; Queen Mary Coll., Univ. of London (BA Hons History 1968). MHSM, DipHSM 1973. NHS Mgt Trainee, 1968; Deputy Hospital Secretary: Scarborough Gen. Hosp., 1970–72; Doncaster Royal Infirmary, 1972–75; Hosp. Manager, Northern Gen. Hosp., Sheffield, 1975–83; Dep. Dist Gen. Manager, Newcastle HA, 1983–86; Gen. Manager, Norfolk and Norwich Hosp., 1986–90; Dep. Regl Gen. Manager, SW Thames RHA, 1990–92; Chief Exec., London Ambulance Service, 1992–96; Dir of Projects, S Thames Regl Office, NHS Exec., DoH, 1996–98; Chief Executive: Nat. Blood Authy, 1998–2005; NHS Blood and Transplant, 2005–07. Pres., European Blood Alliance, 2001–07. Trustee, Princess Royal Trust for Carers, 2001–06; Mem. Bd, Foundn of the Internat. Soc. of Blood Transfusion, 2012–. *Recreations:* travel, music, books, art, ski-ing, food and wine, gardening, cricket. *Address:* 20 Grange Road, Bishop's Stortford, Herts CM23 5NQ. *T:* (01279) 501876. *Club:* Royal Society of Medicine.

GORHAM, Robin Stuart; HM Diplomatic Service, retired; Lecturer, University of East Anglia, since 2011; *b* 15 Feb. 1939; *s* of Stuart Gorham and Dorothy Gorham (*née* Stevens); *m* 1st, 1966, Barbara Fechner (marr. diss. 1991); three *d*; 2nd, 1992, Joanna Bradbury (marr. diss. 2004). *Educ:* Sutton Manor High Sch.; Oriel Coll., Oxford (MA). CRO, 1961–62; Ottawa, 1962–64; Centre for Econ. Studies, 1964–65; Bonn, 1965–66; Central European Dept, FCO, 1967–69; First Secretary: (External Affairs and Defence) and Dep. Hd of Chancery, Tokyo, 1970–74; (Commercial and Develt), Accra, 1974–77; ME Dept, FCO, 1977–79; Hd of Chancery, Helsinki, 1980–83; Counsellor and Dep. High Comr, Lusaka, 1983–86; rcds, 1987; Hd, W Indian and Atlantic Dept, FCO, 1988–91; Dep. Hd of Mission, Lagos, 1991–94; Head of Protocol Dept and Asst Marshal of Diplomatic Corps, FCO, 1994–98. *Recreations:* fox-hunting, tall ship sailing, Himalayan trekking. *Address:* The Arch, Thornham Hall Stables, Thornham Magna, Eye, Suffolk IP23 8HA. *T:* (01379) 783938; L'Oreneta, Barri d'Amunt, 66150 Corsavy, France. *T:* (4) 68834094.

GORICK, Ven. Martin Charles William; Archdeacon of Oxford, since 2013; *b* Liverpool, 23 June 1962; *s* of David Gorick and Janet Gorick; *m* 1985, Katharine Bentley; one *s* two *d*. *Educ:* West Bridgford Comp. Sch.; Selwyn Coll., Cambridge (BA 1984; MA 1988). Ordained deacon, 1987, priest, 1988; Curate, Birtley, 1987–91; Domestic Chaplain to Bishop of Oxford, 1991–94; Vicar, Smethwick, 1994–2001; Area Dean, Warley, 1997–2001; Vicar, Stratford-upon-Avon, 2001–13. *Publications:* (ed) Shakespeare's Church: a parish for the world, 2010; Eight Hundred Years: ten lifetimes, 2013. *Recreations:* family, walking, bird-watching, theatre, gardening. *Address:* Archdeacon's Lodging, Christ Church, Oxford OX1 1DP.

GORING, Sir William (Burton Nigel), 13th Bt *cr* 1627; Member of London Stock Exchange, since 1963; *b* 21 June 1933; *s* of Major Frederick Yelverton Goring (*d* 1938) (6th *s* of 11th Bt) and Freda Margaret (*d* 1993), *o d* of N. V. Ainsworth; *S* uncle, Sir Forster Gurney Goring, 12th Bt, 1956; *m* 1st, 1960, Hon. Caroline Thellusson (marr. diss. 1993; she *d* 2010), *d* of 8th Baron Rendlesham and of Mrs Patrick Barthropp; 2nd, 1993, Mrs Judith Rachel Walton Morison (*d* 1995), *d* of Rev. R. J. W. Morris, OBE; 3rd, 1998, Mrs Stephanie Bullock, *d* of George Carter, DFC. *Educ:* Wellington; RMA Sandhurst. Lieut, The Royal Sussex Regt. Master, Co. of Woolmen, 2000–01. *Recreation:* bridge. *Heir: kinsman* Richard Harry Goring [*b* 10 Sept. 1949; *m* 1972, Penelope Ann, *d* of J. K. Broadbent; three *s* three *d*]. *Address:* c/o Quilter Cheviot, One Kingsway, WC2B 6AN. *Club:* Hurlingham.

GORMALLY, Michael Anthony Peter Thomas; Headmaster, The Cardinal Vaughan Memorial School, Kensington, 1997–2010; *b* 30 Jan. 1956; *s* of Charles Gormally and Frances Edna Gormally. *Educ:* Inst. of Education, Univ. of London (BA Hons French). ACP 1986. Cardinal Vaughan Memorial School, 1981–2010: Asst Master, 1981–84; Hd, Modern Langs, 1984–90; Sen. Master, 1990–95; Dep. Headmaster, 1995–97. FRSA 1998. *Recreations:* reading, playing the piano, cooking. *Address:* c/o Cardinal Vaughan Memorial School, 89 Addison Road, W14 8BZ.

GORMAN, Christopher Nicoll; Partner, Linklaters & Paines, Solicitors, 1972–97 (Managing Partner, 1991–95); *b* 29 Aug. 1939; *s* of late James Gorman and Louise Barbara (*née* Rackham); *m* 1967, Anne Beech (*d* 1996); one *s* one *d*. *Educ:* Royal Liberty Sch., Romford; St Catharine's Coll., Cambridge (MA, LLM). Admitted Solicitor, 1965. *Publications:* (ed) Nelson's Tables of Company Procedure, 6th edn 1975 to 8th edn 1983; (ed) Westby Nunn's Company Secretarial Handbook, 7th edn 1977 to 11th edn 1992. *Recreations:* books and bookshops, outdoor activity, unfinished business. *Address:* 4 Windhill, Bishop's Stortford, Herts CM23 2NG. *T:* (01279) 656028. *Clubs:* Athenæum, Royal Automobile.

GORMAN, Justin; Head of Entertainment, Channel 4, since 2010; *b* Bromley, Kent, 25 April 1972; *s* of John Gorman and Sue Gorman; *m* 1999, Emily Tudor; two *d*. *Educ:* Goldsmith's Coll., Univ. of London (BA Hons Drama and Theatre Arts 1993). Researcher: Action Time, 1995–97; Hat Trick Prodns, 1996–97; BBC TV, 1997–98; Granada TV, 1999–2001; Executive Producer: Princess Prodns, 2001–05; Objective Prodns, 2005–10, prodns incl. Derren Brown, The Cube. *Recreations:* theatre, film, marathon running, drumming. *T:* 07940 797579. *E:* justingorman@mac.com.

GORMAN, Prof. Neil Thomson, PhD; FRCVS; DL; Vice-Chancellor, Nottingham Trent University, 2003–14; *b* 10 Sept. 1950; *s* of George Stewart Gorman and Madge Isobella Gorman; *m* 1975, Susan Mary (*née* Smith); one *s* one *d*. *Educ:* Univ. of Liverpool (BVSc 1974); Wolfson Coll., Cambridge (PhD 1977; Hon. Fellow, 2006). MRCVS 1974, FRCVS 1980. Asst Prof., Univ. of Florida, 1980–84; Lectr in Clinical Vet. Medicine, Univ. of Cambridge, 1984–87; Prof. of Vet. Surgery, Univ. of Glasgow, 1987–93; Hd of Res., Waltham, 1993–97; European Dir of R&D, 1997, Vice-Pres. of R&D, 1997–99, Mars Europe; Vice-Pres. of R&D, Masterfoods Europe, 2000–01; Global Dir, Sci. and Technol. Platforms, Mars Inc., 2001–03. President: British Small Animal Vet. Assoc., 1992–93; RCVS, 1997–98. Diplomate: American Coll. of Vet. Internal Medicine, 1988; Eur. Coll. of Vet. Internal Medicine, 2005. DL Notts, 2007. Hon. DVMS Glasgow, 2004; Hon. DVSc Liverpool, 2006; Hon. DVetMed RVC, 2012. FRSA. *Publications:* Advances in Veterinary Immunology, vol. 1 1983, vol. 2 1985; Contemporary Issues in Small Animal Medicine, 1986; Clinical Veterinary Immunology, 1988, 2nd edn 1990; Basic and Applied Chemotherapy, 1992; Canine Medicine and Therapeutics, 1998; 150 scientific articles. *Recreations:* sport, golf, opera, ballet.

GORMANSTON, 17th Viscount *cr* 1478; **Jenico Nicholas Dudley Preston;** Baron Gormanston (Ire.), 1365; Baron Gormanston (UK), 1868; Premier Viscount of Ireland; *b* 19 Nov. 1939; *s* of 16th Viscount and Pamela (who *m* 2nd, 1943, M. B. O'Connor, Irish Guards; he *d* 1961, she *d* 1975), *o d* of late Capt. Dudley Hanly, and Lady Marjorie Heath (by her 1st marriage); *S* father, who was officially presumed killed in action, France, 9 June 1940; *m* 1st, 1974, Eva Antoine Landzianowska (*d* 1984); two *s*; 2nd, 1997, Lucy Arabella, former wife of David Grenfell and *d* of Edward Fox, *qv* and of Tracy Reed. *Educ:* Downside. *Heir: s* Hon. Jenico Francis Tara Preston, *b* 30 April 1974. *Address:* 27A Ifield Road, SW10 9AZ.

GORMLEY, Sir Antony (Mark David), Kt 2014; OBE 1998; RA 2003; sculptor; *b* London, 30 Aug. 1950; *s* of Arthur John Constantine Gormley and Elspeth Gormley (*née* Brauninger); *m* 1980, Vicken Parsons; two *s* one *d*. *Educ:* Trinity Coll., Cambridge (BA Hist. of Art; Hon. Fellow 2003); Central Sch. of Art, London; Goldsmiths' Sch. of Art, London (BA Fine Art; Hon. Fellow, Goldsmiths Coll., 1998); Slade Sch. of Fine Art (Boise travelling scholar, 1979). Mem., Arts Council England (formerly Arts Council of England), 1998–. Trustee: Baltic Centre for Contemp. Art, 2004–07; British Mus., 2007–15. Numerous *solo exhibitions* in Europe, America, Japan and Australia, 1980–, including: Whitechapel Art Gall., 1981; Louisiana Mus. of Modern Art, Denmark, 1989; American Field, US touring exhibn, 1991; Recent Iron Works, LA, 1992; Tate Gall., Liverpool, 1993; European Field, touring exhibn, 1993–95; Irish Mus. of Modern Art, Dublin, 1994; Lost Subject, White Cube, London, 1994; Escultura, Portugal, 1994; Field for the British Isles, GB tour, 1994–95, Hayward Gall., 1996, Gt Court Gall., BM, 2002 and Yorks Sculpture Park, 2005; Kohji Ogura Gall., Nagoya, 1995; Drawings, San Antonio, USA, 1995; Critical Mass, Vienna, 1995, RA, 1998; New Work, Sarajevo, 1996; Inside the Inside, Brussels, 1996; Arts 04, St Rémy de Provence, France, 1996; Still Moving, retrospective tour, Japan, 1996–97; Drawings 1990–94, Ind. Art Space, London, 1996; Cuxhaven, and Total Strangers, Cologne, 1997; Neue Skulpturen, Cologne, 1998; Critical Mass, RA, 1998; Insiders, Brussels, 1999; Intimate Relations, Ontario and Cologne, 1999; European Field, Malmö, 1999; Quantum Clouds, Paris, 2000; Asian Field, China tour, 2003, ICA Singapore, Sydney Biennial, 2006; Baltic Centre, Gateshead, 2003; Clearing, White Cube, London, 2004; Display, Tate Britain, 2004; New Works, Sean Kelly Gall., NY, 2005; Certain Made Places, Tokyo, 2005; Inside Australia, Melbourne, 2005; Altered States, Naples, 2006; Breathing Room, Paris, 2006; Blind Light, Hayward Gallery, Sean Kelly Gall., NY, 2007; Bodies in Space, Berlin, 2007; Feeling Material, Berlin, 2007; Ataxia, Melbourne, 2007; Firmament, White Cube, London, 2008; Acts, States, Times, Perspectives, Copenhagen, 2008; Another Singularity, Gall. Andersson Sandstrom, Sweden, 2008; Lot, Guernsey, 2008; Drawings 1981–2001, Galerie Ropac, Paris, 2008; Between You and Me, Kunsthal Rotterdam, Musée d'Art Moderne St Etienne, 2008; Antony Gormley, Museo de Arte Contemporáneo, Monterrey, Mexico, 2008; One and Other, Fourth Plinth, Trafalgar Square, 2009; Test Sites, White Cube, London, 2010; Event Horizon, Madison Sq. Art, NY, 2010; Memes, Melbourne, 2011; Flare II, Salisbury Cath., 2011; For the Time Being, Galerie Ropac, Paris, 2011; Two States, Harewood House, Yorks, 2011; Still Standing, State Hermitage Mus., St Petersburg, 2011; Space Station and other Instruments, Galleria Continua Le Moulin, France, 2011; Model, White Cube, London, 2012; Horizon Field Hamburg, Deichtorhallen, Hamburg, 2012; Vessel, Galleria Continua, San Gimignano, 2012; Still Being, Centro Cultural Banco do Brasil, Rio de Janeiro, 2012; Bodyspace, Sean Kelly Gall., NY, 2012; according to a given mean, Xavier Hufkens, Brussels, 2013; Meter, Galerie Thaddeus Ropac, Salzburg, 2013; State and Conditions, White Cube, Hong Kong, 2014; Human, Forte di Belvedere, Florence, 2015; *group exhibitions* include: British Sculpture in the 20th Century, Whitechapel Art Gall., 1981; Biennale de Venezia, Venice, 1982 and 1986; An Internat. Survey of Recent Painting and Sculpture, Mus. of Modern Art, NY, 1984; Documenta 8, Kassel, 1987; Avant-garde in the Eighties, LA Co. Mus. of Art, 1987; Starlit Waters, Tate Gall., Liverpool, 1988; GB-USSR, Kiev, Moscow, 1990; British Art Now, touring Japan, 1990; Arte Amazonas, Rio de Janeiro, 1992, Berlin, 1993, Dresden, 1993, Aachen, 1993; From Beyond the Pale, Irish Mus. of Modern Art, Dublin, 1994; Un Siècle de Sculpture anglaise, Jeu de Paume, Paris, 1996; Malmö, Sweden, 1996; Sydney, Lisbon and Knislinge, Sweden, 1998; Presence, Liverpool, 1999; Trialogo, Rome, 2000; Tate Liverpool, 2004; Millennium Galls, Sheffield, 2005; Figure/Sculpture, Vienna, 2005; Henry Moore - Epoch und Echo, Künzelsau, Germany, 2005; Zero Degrees, Sadler's Wells, 2005; Space: Now & Then, Fundament Foundn, Tilburg, 2005; To the Human Future, Mito Contemporary Art Center, Japan, 2006; Asian Field, Sydney Biennale, 2006; 60 Years of Sculpture, Arts Council Collection, Yorks Sculpture Park, 2006; Turner Prize: a retrospective, Tate Britain, 2007; Reflection, Pinchuk Art Centre, Kiev, 2007; Fourth Plinth Proposals, Nat. Gall., 2008; Gravity: Ernesto Esposito Collection, Spain, 2008; Genesis - The Art of Creation, Bern, Switzerland, 2008; Locked In, Luxembourg, 2008; History in the Making, Mori Art Mus., Tokyo, 2008; En Perspective, Giacometti, Musée des Beaux-Arts de Caen, 2008; Kivik Art 08, Kivik Art Centre, Sweden, 2008; Statuephilia, British Mus., 2008; Earth: Art of a Changing World, RA, 2009; Visceral Bodies, Vancouver Art Gall., 2010; XIV Internat. Sculpture Biennale of Carrara, Italy, 2010; A Serpentine Gesture and Other

Prophecies, 49 Nord 6 Est Frac Lorraine, Metz, France, 2011; TRA: Edge of Becoming, Palazzo Fortuny, Venice, 2011; Summer Exhibn, Royal Acad. of Arts, 2011; Arte Torna Arte, Galleria dell'Accademia, Florence, 2012; Last Days of Pompeii, Getty Villa, Calif, 2012; Unlimited Bodies, Paris, 2012; Uncommon Ground, UK tour, 2013; Body and Void: Echoes of Henry Moore, Perry Green, 2014; work in private and public collections worldwide, including: Tate Gall., London; Scottish Gall. of Modern Art, Edinburgh; Jesus Coll., Cambridge; Art Gall. of NSW, Sydney; Louisiana Mus., Denmark; Israel Mus., Jerusalem; Sapporo Sculpture Park, Hokkaido, Japan; Mus. of Contemporary Art, LA; sculpture in public places: Out of the Dark, Kassel, Germany, 1987; Open Space, Rennes, France, 1993; Iron Man, Birmingham, 1994; Havmann, Mo I Rana, Norway, 1995; Angel of the North, Gateshead, 1998 (Civic Trust Award, 2000); Quantum Cloud, Greenwich, 2000; Sound II, Winchester Cathedral, 2001; Planets, British Library, 2002; Inside Australia, Lake Ballard, Australia, 2003; Broken Column, Stavanger, Norway, 2003; Fai Spazio, Poggibonsi, Italy, 2004; Another Place, Crosby Beach, Liverpool, 2005; You, Roundhouse, London, 2006; Resolution, Shoe Lane, London, 2007; Event Horizon, S Bank, London, 2007, NY, 2010; Flare II, St Paul's Cathedral, 2010; Exposure, Edinburgh, 2010; 6 Times, Edinburgh, 2010; Horizon Field, Austria, 2010–12; Transport, Canterbury Cathedral, 2011; Sculpture in the City, London, 2013. FRSA 2000. Hon. FRIBA 2001. Hon. doctorates incl. Sunderland, 1998; UCE, 1998; Open, 2001; Cambridge, 2003; Newcastle upon Tyne, 2004; Teesside, 2004; Liverpool, 2006; UCL, 2006. Turner Prize, 1994; South Bank Award, 1999; Bernard Heiliger Award for Sculpture, 2007; Praemium Imperiale (Japan), 2013.

See also Sir P. B. Gormley.

GORMLEY, Sir (Paul) Brendan, KCMG 2014; MBE 2001; international relief and development consultant, since 2012; Chairman, Communicating with Disaster Affected Communities Network, since 2012; *b* 2 Sept. 1947; *s* of Arthur John Constantine Gormley and Elspeth Gormley; *m* 1974, Sally Henderson; two *s* one *d*. *Educ:* Strasbourg Univ. (Bacc. en Théologie); Trinity Coll., Cambridge (BA Social and Pol Scis 1973). OXFAM: Country Dir, Niger, 1976–78; Regl Dir, W Africa, 1978–83; Country Dir, Egypt, 1983–85; Asst to Overseas Dir, Evaluation Officer, Area Co-ordinator for Africa (N), HQ based, 1985–91; Africa Dir, 1991–2000; Chief Exec., Disasters Emergency Cttee, 2000–12. Lead Expert, Risk and Horizon Scanning Expert Gp, Govt Office for Sci., 2012–; Mem., Ind. Rev. Panel, Internat. Non-Govtl Orgns Accountability Charter, Berlin, 2013–14; Chm., Internat. Non-Govtl Orgns Accountability Charter Co., 2014–. Mem. Council, ODI, 2012–14. Trustee: Noel Buxton Trust, 2002–; One World Broadcasting Trust, 2004–; Age Internat., 2012–. FRSA 2012. *Publications:* (contrib.) Indigenous Knowledge System and Development, ed David Brokenshaw, 1980. *Recreations:* sailing, golf. *Address:* Foxburrow Barn, Hailey, Witney, Oxon OX29 9UH. *T:* (01993) 773592. *E:* gormley.dec@btinternet.com.

See also Sir A. M. D. Gormley.

GORMLY, Allan Graham, CMG 2005; CBE 1991; Chairman, BPB plc (formerly BPB Industries), 1997–2004 (Deputy Chairman, 1996–97; Director, 1995–2004); *b* 18 Dec. 1937; *s* of William Gormly and Christina Swinton Flockhart Arnot; *m* 1962, Vera Margaret Grant; one *s* one *d*. *Educ:* Paisley Grammar School. CA. Peat Marwick Mitchell & Co., 1955–61; Rootes Group, 1961–65; John Brown PLC, 1965–68; Brownlee & Co. Ltd, 1968–70; John Brown PLC, 1970: Finance Director, John Brown Engineering Ltd, 1970–77; Director, Planning and Control, John Brown PLC, 1977–80; Dep. Chairman, John Brown Engineers and Constructors Ltd, 1980–83; Gp Man. Dir, John Brown PLC, 1983–92; Chief Exec., Trafalgar House, 1992–94 (Dir, 1986–95); Dir, 1990–96, Dep. Chm., 1992–94, Chm., 1994–96, Royal Insce Hldgs; Dir and Dep. Chm., Royal & Sun Alliance, 1996–98. Chm., Q-One Biotech Ltd, 1999–2003; Director: Brixton Estates, subseq. Brixton plc, 1994–2003 (Chm., 2000–03); European Capital Co., 1996–2000; Bank of Scotland, 1997–2001. Chm., Overseas Projects Bd, 1988–91; Dep. Chm., Export Guarantees Adv. Council, 1990–92; Member: BOTB, 1988–92; Review Body on Top Salaries, 1990–92; FCO Bd of Mgt, 2000–04. *Recreations:* golf, music. *Address:* 56 North Park, Gerrards Cross, Bucks SL9 8JR.

GORRINGE, Christopher John, CBE 1999; Chief Executive, All England Lawn Tennis and Croquet Club, Wimbledon, 1983–2005; *b* 13 Dec. 1945; *s* of late Maurice Sydney William Gorringe and Hilda Joyce Gorringe; *m* 1976, Jennifer Mary Chamberlain; two *d*. *Educ:* Bradfield Coll., Berks; Royal Agricl Coll., Cirencester. MRICS. Asst Land Agent, Iveagh Trustees Ltd (Guinness family), 1968–73; Asst Sec., 1973–79, Sec., 1979–83, All England Lawn Tennis and Croquet Club. Hon. Fellow, Roehampton Univ. (formerly Univ. of Surrey, Roehampton), 1998. *Publications:* Holding Court, 2009. *Recreations:* lawn tennis, golf. *Clubs:* All England Lawn Tennis and Croquet, International Lawn Tennis of GB, Queen's, St George's Hill Lawn Tennis, Rye Lawn Tennis (Pres.), Jesters.

GORRINGE, Rev. Prof. Timothy Jervis; St Luke's Professor of Theological Studies, University of Exeter, 1998–2013; *b* 12 Aug. 1946; *s* of R. C. and M. V. Gorringe; *m* 1st, 1972, Carol (*née* James) (*d* 2004); one *s* two *d*; 2nd, 2008, Gill (*née* Westcott). *Educ:* St Edmund Hall, Oxford (BA 1969); Univ. of Leeds (MPhil 1975); DD (Oxon) 2008. Ordained deacon, 1972, priest, 1973; Curate, St Matthew's, Chapel Allerton, 1972–75; Chaplain, Wadham Coll., Oxford, 1975–78; Lectr, Tamil Nadu Theol Seminary, India, 1979–86; Chaplain, Fellow and Tutor in Theol., St John's Coll., Oxford, 1986–95; Reader in Contextual Theol., Univ. of St Andrews, 1995–98. *Publications:* Redeeming Time, 1986; Discerning Spirit, 1990; God's Theatre: a theology of Providence, 1991; Capital and the Kingdom: theological ethics and economic order, 1994; Alan Ecclestone: priest as revolutionary, 1994; God's Just Vengeance: crime, violence and the rhetoric of salvation, 1996; The Sign of Love: reflections on the Eucharist, 1997; Karl Barth: against hegemony, 1999; The Education of Desire, 2001; A Theology of the Built Environment, 2002; Furthering Humanity: a theology of culture, 2004; Crime, 2004; Harvest: food, farming and the churches, 2006; The Common Good and the Global Emergency, 2011; Earthly Visions: theology and the challenges of art, 2011; (jtly) Transition Movement for Churches: a prophetic imperative for today, 2013. *Recreations:* bee keeping, wine-making, vegetable gardening, folk music, smallholding. *Address:* Venbridge House, Cheriton Bishop, Devon EX6 6HD. *T:* (01647) 24789. *E:* T.J.Gorringe@exeter.ac.uk.

GORROD, Prof. John William, FRCPath; CChem, FRSC; FRSB; Professor of Biopharmacy, King's College London, 1984–97, now Emeritus; Research Professor, Chelsea Department of Pharmacy, 1990–97; Visiting Professor of Toxicology, University of Essex, since 1997; *b* 11 Oct. 1931; *s* of Ernest Lionel and Carrie Rebecca Gorrod; *m* 1954, Doreen Mary Collins; two *s* one *d*. *Educ:* Brunel Coll. of Advanced Technology; Chelsea Coll. (DCC, PhD, DSc). FRSC 1980; FRCPath 1984; FRSB (FIBiol 1998). Biochem. Asst, Inst. of Cancer Res., 1954–64; Res. Fellow, Univ. of Bari, Italy, 1964; Sen. Student, Royal Commn for Exhibn of 1851, 1965–68; University of London: Lectr 1968–80, then Reader 1980–84, in Biopharmacy, Chelsea Coll.; Hd, Chelsea Dept of Pharmacy, King's Coll., 1984–90; Chm., Univ. Bd of Studies in Pharmacy, 1986–88; Hd of Div. of Health Science, KCL, 1988–89; FKC 1996. Dir, Drug Control and Teaching Centre, Sports Council, 1985–91. Member: Council, Internat. Soc. for Study of Xenobiotics (Pres., 2000–01); Educn Cttee, Pharmaceutical Soc. of GB, 1986–91; Assoc. for Res. in Indoor Air, 1989–95; Council, Indoor Air Internat., 1990–97; Associates for Res. in Substances of Enjoyment, 1990–92; Air Transport Users Cttee, CAA, 1990–93; Scientific Bd, Inst. of Drug and Pharmacokinetics Res., Develt and Applications, Ege Univ., Turkey, 1994–98; Council, Tobacco Sci. and Health Policy, Inst. for Sci. and Health, St Louis, USA, 2004–; Scientific Adv. Bd, Philip Morris Internat., Neuchâtel, 2006–. Vis. Prof., Univs of Bologna, Bari, and Kebangsaan, Malaysia; Canadian MRC Vis. Prof., Univs of Manitoba and Saskatchewan, 1988; Vis. Prof., Chinese Acad. of Preventive Medicine, 1991. Gov., Ipswich Hosp. Trust, 2010–14. Mem., Polstead Parish Council, 1999–2003. Hon. MPS, 1982; Corresp. Mem., German Pharm. Soc., 1985. Hon. Fellow: Greek Pharmaceutical Soc., 1987; Turkish Assoc. of Pharmacists, 1988; Sch. of Pharmacy, Univ. of London, 2002. Gold Medal, 1991, Silver Galen Medal, 2012, Comenius Univ., Bratislava. Editorial Board: Xenobiotica; Europ. Jl of Metabolism and Pharmacokinetics; Toxicology Letters; Anti-Cancer Res. *Publications:* Drug Metabolism in Man (ed jtly), 1978; Biological Oxidation of Nitrogen, 1978; Drug Toxicity, 1979; Testing for Toxicity, 1981; (ed jtly) Biological Oxidation of Nitrogen in Organic Molecules, 1985; (ed jtly) Development of Drugs and Modern Medicines, 1986; (ed jtly) Metabolism of Xenobiotics, 1987; (ed jtly) Molecular Aspects of Human Disease, 1989; (ed jtly) Molecular Basis of Neurological Disorders and their Treatment, 1991; (ed jtly) Nicotine and Related Alkaloids, 1993; Analytical Determination of Nicotine and Related Compounds and their Metabolites, 1999; contribs to Xenobiotica, Europ. Jl Drug Metabolism, Jl Pharm. Pharmacol, Mutation Res., Anti-Cancer Res., Jl Nat. Cancer Inst., Drug Metabolism Revs, Med. Sci. Res., Drug Metabolism & Drug Interact., Jl of Chromatography. *Recreations:* trying to understand government policies on tertiary education, travel, books, running (slowly!). *Address:* (home) The Rest Orchard, Polstead Heath, Suffolk CO6 5BG. *E:* jgorr@essex.ac.uk. *Clubs:* Athenæum; Hillingdon Athletic (Middx).

GORT, 9th Viscount *cr* 1816 (Ire.); **Foley Robert Standish Prendergast Vereker;** Baron Kiltarton 1810; photographer; *b* 24 Oct. 1951; *er s* of 8th Viscount Gort and Bettine Mary Mackenzie, *d* of Godfrey Greene; *S* father, 1995; *m* 1st, 1979, Julie Denise Jones (marr. diss. 1984); 2nd, 1991, Sharon Quayle; one *s* one *d*. *Educ:* Harrow. *Recreation:* golf. *Heir: s* Robert Foley Prendergast Vereker, *b* 5 April 1993. *Address:* The Coach House, Arbory Street, Castletown, Isle of Man IM9 1LN. *T:* (01624) 822295.

GOSCHEN, family name of **Viscount Goschen**.

GOSCHEN, 4th Viscount *cr* 1900; **Giles John Harry Goschen;** with Korn/Ferry International, since 2005; *b* 16 Nov. 1965; *s* of 3rd Viscount Goschen, KBE, and of Alvin Moyana Lesley, *yr d* of late Harry England, Durban, Natal; *S* father, 1977; *m* 1991, Sarah Penelope, *d* of late Alan Horsnail; one *s* two *d*. *Educ:* Eton. A Lord in Waiting (Govt Whip), 1992–94; Parly Under-Sec. of State, Dept of Transport, 1994–97; elected Mem., H of L, 1999. With Deutsche Bank, 1997–2000; Dir, Barchester Advisory, 2000–02. *Heir: s* Hon. Alexander John Edward Goschen, *b* 5 Oct. 2001.

GOSCHEN, Sir Edward (Alexander), 4th Bt *cr* 1916 of Beacon Lodge, Highcliffe, co. Southampton; *b* 13 March 1949; *s* of Sir Edward Goschen, 3rd Bt, DSO and Cynthia, *d* of Rt Hon. Sir Alexander Cadogan, OM, GCMG, KCB, PC; *S* father, 2001; *m* 1976, Louise Annette (*d* 2006), *d* of Lt-Col R. F. L. Chance, MC and Lady Ava Chance; one *d*. *Educ:* Eton. *Heir: cousin* Sebastian Bernard Goschen, *b* 1 Jan. 1959.

GOSDEN, Prof. Christine Margaret, PhD; FRCPath; Professor of Medical Genetics, University of Liverpool, 1993; *b* 25 April 1945; *d* of George G. H. Ford and Helena P. S. Ford; *m* 1971, Dr John Gosden. *Educ:* Univ. of Edinburgh (BSc Hons; PhD 1971). MRCPath, FRCPath. Res. Fellow, Univ. of Edinburgh, 1971–73; Mem., MRC Sen. Scientific Staff, MRC Human Genetics Unit, Western Gen. Hosp., Edinburgh, 1973–93; Vis. Prof. in Human Genetics, Harris Birthright Centre for Fetal Medicine, and Dept of Obstetrics and Gynaecology, King's Coll. Hosp. Sch. of Medicine and Dentistry, 1987–93; Hon. Consultant, Liverpool Women's Hosp., 1993. Mem., HFEA, 1996. Researcher, scriptwriter, co-presenter, etc of films (incl. contrib. to TV series Dispatches (Saddam's Secret Time Bomb) and 60 Minutes, 1998) and author of articles on med. effects of chemical and biological weapons use. *Publications:* (jtly) Is My Baby All Right?, 1994; numerous scientific papers, articles and contribs to books on human genetics, fetal medicine, mental illness, childhood and adult cancers and med. effects of chemical and biological weapons. *Recreations:* campaigner for human rights, whalewatching, alpine gardening, organ and harpsichord music, modern poetry.

GOSDEN, Prof. Christopher Hugh, PhD; FBA 2005; Professor of European Archaeology, University of Oxford, since 2006; Fellow, Keble College, Oxford, since 2006; *b* 6 Sept. 1955; *s* of Hugh and Margaret Gosden; *m* 1992, Jane Kaye; one *s* one *d*. *Educ:* Univ. of Sheffield (BA 1977; PhD 1983). Vis. Fellow, ANU, 1984–85; Lectr, then Sen. Lectr, Dept of Archaeol., La Trobe Univ., Melbourne, 1986–93; Oxford University: Lectr, 1994–2004, Prof. of Archaeology, 2004–06, Hd, 2004–07, Sch. of Archaeol.; Curator, Pitt Rivers Museum, 1994–2006; Fellow, St Cross Coll., 1994–2006. *Publications:* Social Being and Time: an archaeological perspective, 1994; Archaeology and Anthropology: a changing relationship, 1999; (with J. Hather) The Prehistory of Food, 1999; (with C. Knowles) Collecting Colonialism: material culture and colonial change in Papua New Guinea, 2001; Prehistory: a very short introduction, 2003; Archaeology and Colonialism, 2004; (with F. Larson) Knowing Things: exploring the collections of the Pitt Rivers Museum, 2007; (with D. Garrow) Technology of Enchantment, 2012; papers and monographs. *Recreations:* reading, running, travel. *Address:* School of Archaeology, 34 Beaumont Street, Oxford OX1 2PG. *T:* (01865) 278240, *Fax:* (01865) 278254. *E:* chris.gosden@arch.ox.ac.uk.

GOSDEN, John Harry Martin; racehorse trainer; *b* 30 March 1951; *s* of late John Montague Gosden and Peggie Gosden; *m* 1982, Rachel Dene Serena Hood; two *s* two *d*. *Educ:* Eastbourne Coll.; Emmanuel Coll., Cambridge (MA; athletics blue, 1970–73). Member: Cambridge Univ. Athletics Team, 1970; British Under-23 Rowing Squad, 1973. Assistant trainer to: Noel Murless, 1974–76; Vincent O'Brien, 1976–77; trainer, USA, 1979–88: trained 8 State champions, Calif, 3 Eclipse Award winners; in top 10 US trainers throughout 1980s; England, 1989–: by 2013, over 2000 UK winners (fastest 1000 winners trained in UK); over 150 Group Stakes winners, incl. Derby (Benny the Dip, 1997, Golden Horn, 2015), St Leger, English and French 1000 Guineas; winners trained include: Raven's Pass, Breeders' Cup Classic, 2008; two-year-old Breeders' Cup winners, Donativum, 2008, Pounced, 2009; Dar Re Mi, Dubai Sheema Classic, 2010; Debussy, Arlington Million, 2010; Arctic Cosmos, St Leger, 2010; Masked Marvel, St Leger, 2011; Duncan, Irish St Leger, 2011; Nathaniel, King George & Queen Elizabeth Diamond Stakes, 2011, Eclipse Stakes, 2012; Great Heavens, Irish Oaks, 2012; Fallen for You, Coronation Stakes, 2012; The Fugue, Irish Champion Stakes, 2013, Yorkshire Oaks, 2013; Seek Again, Hollywood Derby, 2013; Elusive Kate, Falmouth Stakes and Prix Rothschild, 2013; Champion Miler, Kingman, 2014; Champion Classic Filly, Taghrooda, 2014; Star of Seville, Prix de Diane, 2015; Golden Horn, Eclipse Stakes, 2015; leading trainer at Royal Ascot, 6 winners, 2012; champion flat racing trainer, 2012. *Recreations:* opera, polo, ski-ing, environmental issues. *Address:* Clarehaven Stables, Bury Road, Newmarket, Suffolk CB8 7BY.

GOSDEN, Prof. Roger Gordon; Professor, and Director of Research in Reproductive Biology, Weill Medical College, Cornell University, 2004–10; *b* 23 Sept. 1948; *s* of Gordon Conrad Jason Gosden and Peggy (*née* Butcher); *m* 1st, 1971, Carole Ann Walsh (marr. diss. 2003); two *s*; 2nd, 2004, Lucinda Leigh Veeck. *Educ:* Bristol Univ. (BSc); Darwin Coll., Cambridge (PhD 1974); Edinburgh Univ. (DSc 1989). CBiol, FRSB (FIBiol 1987). MRC Fellow, Physiological Lab., Cambridge, 1973–74, 1975–76; Population Council Fellow, Duke Univ., N Carolina, 1974–75; Lectr and Sen. Lectr and Dep. Head, Dept of Physiol., Edinburgh Univ. Med. Sch., 1976–94; Prof. of Reproductive Biol., Leeds Univ., 1994–99; Hon. Consultant, Leeds Gen. Infirmary and St James's Univ. Hosp., Leeds, 1994–99; Res. Dir, Dept of Obstetrics and Gynecology, McGill Univ., Montreal, 1999–2001; The Howard and Georgeanna Jones Prof. of Reproductive Med., and Scientific Dir, Jones Inst. for Reproductive Med., Eastern Virginia Med. Sch., 2001–04. Guest Scientist: Univ. of Southern

California, 1979, 1980, 1981, 1987; Univ. of Naples, 1989; Visiting Professor: Univ. of Washington, Seattle, 1999; Univ. of Leeds, 1999–2003; Sun Yat-Sen Univ. (Guangzhou), China, 2005–08; Adjunct Prof., McGill Univ., 2001–08. Scientific conf. organiser. Mem., Bd of Prison Visitors, Wetherby, 1996–99. Elder, Church of Scotland, 1982–. FRSA 1996. Occasional broadcasts. *Publications:* Biology of Menopause, 1985; Cheating Time, 1996; Transplantation of Ovarian and Testicular Tissues, 1996; Designer Babies, 1999; (ed jtly) Biology and Pathology of the Oocyte, 2003, 2nd edn 2013; (ed jtly) Preservation of Fertility, 2004; (ed with P. Walker) A Surgeon's Story: the autobiography of Robert T. Morris, 2013; technical articles and contribs to popular press. *Recreations:* Virginia Master Naturalist, creative writing, science writing and publishing. *Address:* 107 Paddock Lane, Williamsburg, VA 23188, USA. *W:* http://rogergosden.com.

GOSFORD, 7th Earl of, *cr* 1806; **Charles David Nicholas Alexander John Sparrow Acheson;** Bt (NS) 1628; Baron Gosford 1776; Viscount Gosford 1785; Baron Worlingham (UK) 1835; Baron Acheson (UK) 1847; *b* 13 July 1942; *o s* of 6th Earl of Gosford, OBE, and Francesca Augusta (*d* 2009), *er d* of Francesco Cagiati, New York; *S* father, 1966; *m* 1983, Lynnette Redmond. *Educ:* Harrow; Byam Shaw Sch. of drawing and painting; Royal Academy Schs. Chm., Artists Union, 1976–80; Mem. Visual Arts Panel, Greater London Arts Assoc., 1976–77; Council Member, British Copyright Council, 1977–80. Represented by: Barry Stern Gall., Sydney; Phillip Bacon Galls, Brisbane; Solander Gall., Canberra; Von Bertouch Gall., Newcastle, NSW. *Heir: cousin* Hon. Nicholas Hope Carter [*b* 29 Oct. 1957; *m* 1983, Patricia, *d* of James Beckford, Jacksonville Beach, Florida; one *s* one *d*].

GOSKIRK, (William) Ian (Macdonald), CBE 1986; Partner, Coopers & Lybrand Deloitte, 1990–92; *b* 2 March 1932; *s* of William Goskirk and Flora Macdonald; *m* 1969, Hope Ann Knaizuk; one *d*. *Educ:* Carlisle Grammar Sch.; Queen's Coll., Oxford (MA). Served REME, 1950–52. Shell Internat. Petroleum, 1956–74; Anschutz Corp., 1974–76; BNOC, 1976–85; Man. Dir, BNOC Trading, 1980–82; Chief Exec., BNOC, 1982–85; Dir, Coopers & Lybrand Associates, 1986–90. *Recreation:* gardening.

GOSLING, Allan Gladstone; Sales Director, PSA Projects, Property Services Agency, Department of the Environment, 1991–92, retired (Operational Director, 1990–91); Consultant to TBV Consult, 1992–95; *b* 4 July 1933; *s* of late Gladstone Gosling and of Elizabeth Gosling (*née* Ward); *m* 1961, Janet Pamela (*née* Gosling); one *s* one *d*. *Educ:* Kirkham Grammar Sch.; Birmingham Sch. of Architecture. DipArch; RIBA 1961; FRIAS 1988 (RIAS 1984); FFB 1991. Asst Architect, Lancs County Council, 1950–54; Birmingham Sch. of Architecture, 1954–57; Surman Kelly Surman, Architects, 1957–59; Royal Artillery, 1959–61; Army Works Organisation, 1961–63; Min. of Housing R&D Group, 1963–68; Suptg Architect, Birmingham Regional Office, Min. of Housing, 1968–72; Regional Works Officer, NW Region, PSA, 1972–76; Midland Regional Dir, PSA, 1976–83; Dir, Scottish Services, PSA, 1983–90. *Recreations:* walking, gardening, watercolour painting, DIY. *Address:* 11 The Moorlands, Four Oaks Park, Sutton Coldfield, West Midlands B74 2RF.

GOSLING, Sir Donald, KCVO 2004; Kt 1976; Joint Chairman, National Car Parks Ltd (formerly Central Car Parks), 1950–98; Chairman, Palmer & Harvey Ltd, since 1967; *b* 2 March 1929; *s* of Maisie Jordan; *m* 1959, Elizabeth Shauna (marr. diss. 1988), *d* of Dr Peter Ingram and Lecky Ingram; three *s*. Joined RN, 1944; served Mediterranean, HMS Leander. Mem., Council of Management, White Ensign Assoc. Ltd, 1970– (Chm., 1978–83; Vice Pres., 1983–93; Pres., 1993–); Mem., Exec. Cttee, Imperial Soc. of Kts Bachelor, 1977– (Hon. Dep. Kt Principal, 2007–). Chm., Berkeley Square Ball Trust, 1982–; Trustee: Fleet Air Arm Museum, Yeovilton, 1974–2000 (Chm., Mountbatten Meml Hall Appeals Cttee, 1980); RYA Seamanship Foundn, 1981–; Vice Pres., Seafarers UK (formerly King George's Fund for Sailors), 1993–; Patron: Submarine Meml Appeal, 1978–; HMS Ark Royal Welfare Trust, 1986–. Hon. Capt., 1993, Hon. Cdre, 2005, Hon. Rear Adm., 2009, Vice Adm. of the UK, 2012, Hon. Vice Adm., 2015, RNR. Younger Brother, Trinity House, 1998. Pres., TS Saumarez Sea Cadets, 1989–. Freeman, City of London, 1979; Hon. Freeman, Shipwrights' Co., 2007–. Mem., Grand Order of Water Rats, 1999. Hon. Dr Maritime Studies Southampton Solent, 2014. KJStJ 2009. *Recreations:* swimming, sailing, shooting. *Address:* (office) 21 Bryanston Street, Marble Arch, W1H 7PR. *T:* (020) 7499 7050. *Clubs:* Royal Thames Yacht, Royal London Yacht, Royal Naval Sailing Association, Thames Sailing, Royal Yacht Squadron; Saints and Sinners.

GOSLING, Jonathan Vincent Ronald; His Honour Judge Gosling; a Circuit Judge, since 2009; *b* Codsall, 28 April 1957; *s* of Gerard and Eileen Gosling; *m* 1987, Suzanne Kidson; two *s*. *Educ:* Ampleforth; Univ. of Wolverhampton (BA Law). Called to the Bar, Middle Temple, 1980; Standing Counsel, UK Register of Canine Behaviourists, 1993–2009; Actg Stipendiary Magistrate, 1997–2004; Recorder, 2000–09. *Recreations:* calligraphy, classic cars, game shooting, smallholding. *Address:* c/o Derby Combined Court, The Morledge, Derby DE1 2XE. *T:* (01332) 622533, *Fax:* (01332) 622529.

GOSLING, Justin Cyril Bertrand; Principal, St Edmund Hall, Oxford, 1982–96; *b* 26 April 1930; *s* of Vincent and Dorothy Gosling; *m* 1958, Margaret Clayton; two *s* two *d*. *Educ:* Ampleforth Coll.; Wadham Coll., Oxford (BPhil, MA). Univ. of Oxford: Fereday Fellow, St John's Coll., 1955–58; Lectr in Philosophy, Pembroke Coll. and Wadham Coll., 1958–60; Fellow in Philosophy, St Edmund Hall, 1960–82; Sen. Proctor, 1977–78. Barclay Acheson Prof., Macalester Coll., Minnesota, 1964; Vis. Res. Fellow, ANU, Canberra, 1970 (Pro-Vice-Chancellor, 1989–95). *Publications:* Pleasure and Desire, 1969; Plato, 1973; (ed) Plato, Philebus, 1975; (with C. C. W. Taylor) The Greeks on Pleasure, 1982; Weakness of the Will, 1990; The Jackdaw in the Jacaranda, 2008; articles in Mind, Phil Rev. and Proc. Aristotelian Soc. *Recreations:* gardening, intaglio printing, recorder music. *Address:* 124 Caldecott Road, Abingdon, Oxon OX14 5EP.

GOSLING, Prof. (Leonard) Morris, PhD; CBiol, FRSB; Professor of Animal Behaviour, University of Newcastle, 1999–2008, now Emeritus; *b* 22 Jan. 1943; *s* of William Richard Gosling and Marian (*née* Morris); *m* 1977, Dr Marion Petrie; two *d*. *Educ:* Wymondham Coll., Norfolk; Queen Mary Coll., London (BSc Zool. 1965); University Coll., Nairobi (PhD 1975). CBiol, FRSB (FIBiol 1989). Ministry of Agriculture, Fisheries and Food: SSO, Coypu Res. Lab., 1970–73; PSO, Mammal Ecology Gp, 1974–85; SPSO, Central Science Lab., 1986–93; Dir of Sci., Zool Soc. of London and Dir, Inst. of Zool., 1993–99. Hon. Lectr, UEA, 1978–81; Vis. Prof., UCL, 1994–99. Leader, Mt Zebra Project, Namibia Nature Foundn, 2005–. Member, Council: Mammal Soc., 1982–85; Assoc. for Study of Animal Behaviour, 1988–90 (Sec., Ethical Cttee, 1991–94); Royal Vet. Coll., 1994–99; Mem., Mgt Cttee, UCL Centre for Ecology and Evolution, 1995–99. *Publications:* (ed with M. Dawkins) Ethics in Research on Animal Behaviour, 1992; (ed with W. J. Sutherland) Behaviour and Conservation, 2000; numerous articles in learned jls and books on population biol. and behavioural ecology. *Recreations:* drawing, ditching, formerly Rugby. *Address:* Newcastle Institute for Research on Sustainability, Devonshire Building, University of Newcastle, Newcastle upon Tyne NE1 7RU. *E:* l.m.gosling@ncl.ac.uk.

GOSNELL, Mark; His Honour Judge Gosnell; a Senior Circuit Judge, since 2010; Designated Civil Judge for Leeds and North Yorkshire, since 2010, and for Bradford Group of Courts, since 2012; *b* Hyde, Cheshire, 23 Sept. 1957; *s* of Peter and Shirley Gosnell; *m* 2009, Sarah Jane Pritchard; one *s* one *d*. *Educ:* St Mary's Coll., Blackburn; Christ's Coll., Cambridge (BA 1978). Admitted Solicitor, 1981; Solicitor, Woodcocks, 1981–98; Dist Judge, 1998–2010; Recorder, 2005–10. *Recreations:* watching Burnley Football Club, playing guitar. *Address:* Leeds Combined Court Centre, Oxford Row, Leeds LS1 3BG. *T:* (0113) 306 2740. *E:* HHJudge.gosnell@judiciary.gsi.gov.uk. *Club:* Kimberley (Bacup).

GOSS, Hon. Sir James Richard William; Kt 2014; **Hon. Mr Justice Goss;** a Judge of the High Court, Queen's Bench Division, since 2014; *b* 12 May 1953; *s* of His Honour Judge William Alan Belcher Goss and of Yvonne Goss; *m* 1982, Dawna Elizabeth Davies; two *s* three *d*. *Educ:* Charterhouse; University Coll., Durham (BA). Called to the Bar, Inner Temple, 1975, Bencher, 2002; Recorder, 1994–2009; QC 1997; Circuit Judge, 2009–14; Senior Circuit Judge and Hon. Recorder of Newcastle upon Tyne, 2011–14. *Address:* Royal Courts of Justice, Strand, WC2A 2LL.

GOSS, Prof. Richard Oliver, PhD; Professor Emeritus, Cardiff University; *b* 4 Oct. 1929; *s* of late Leonard Arthur Goss and Hilda Nellie Goss (*née* Casson); *m* 1st, Lesley Elizabeth Thurbon (marr. diss. 1983); two *s* one *d*; 2nd, 1994, Gillian Mary (*née* Page). *Educ:* Christ's Coll., Finchley; HMS Worcester; King's Coll., Cambridge. Master Mariner 1956; BA 1958; MA 1961; PhD 1979. FCIT 1970; MNI (Founder) 1972; FNI 1977; FRINA 1998; FRSA 1993. Merchant Navy (apprentice and executive officer), 1947–55; NZ Shipping Co. Ltd, 1958–63; Economic Consultant (Shipping, Shipbuilding and Ports), MoT, 1963–64; Econ. Adviser, BoT (Shipping), 1964–67; Sen. Econ. Adviser (Shipping, Civil Aviation, etc), 1967–74; Econ. Adviser to Cttee of Inquiry into Shipping (Rochdale Cttee), 1967–70; Under-Sec., Depts of Industry and Trade, 1974–80; Prof., Dept of Maritime Studies, 1980–95, Dist. Res. Prof., 1995–96, UWIST, subseq. Univ. of Wales Coll. of Cardiff, Prof. Emeritus, Univ. of Wales, Cardiff, 1996. Nuffield/Leverhulme Travelling Fellow, 1977–78. Governor, Plymouth Polytechnic, 1973–84; Mem. Council: RINA, 1969–2002; Nautical Inst. (from foundn until 1976); Member: CNAA Nautical Studies Bd, 1971–81; CNAA Transport Bd, 1976–78. Pres. (first), Internat. Assoc. of Maritime Economists, 1992–94. Editor and Editor-in-Chief, Maritime Policy and Management, 1985–93. Hon. PhD Piraeus, 1999. Premio Internazionale delle Comunicazioni Cristoforo Colombo, Genoa, 1991; (jtly) Alexander Onassis Shipping Prize, Cass Business Sch., London and Alexander S. Onassis Public Benefit Foundn, 2012. *Publications:* Studies in Maritime Economics, 1968; (with C. D. Jones) The Economies of Size in Dry Bulk Carriers, 1971; (with M. C. Mann, et al) The Cost of Ships' Time, 1974; Advances in Maritime Economics, 1977; A Comparative Study of Seaport Management and Administration, 1979; Policies for Canadian Seaports, 1984; Port Authorities in Australia, 1987; Collected Papers, 1990; numerous papers in various jls, transactions and to conferences. *Recreations:* local history, travel. *Address:* 1 Weir Gardens, Pershore, Worcs WR10 1DX. *T:* (01386) 561140.

GOSSCHALK, His Honour Joseph Bernard; a Circuit Judge, 1991–2007; *b* 27 Aug. 1936; *s* of late Lionel Samuel Gosschalk and of Johanna (*née* Lion); *m* 1973, Ruth Sandra Jarvis; two *d*. *Educ:* East Ham Grammar Sch.; Magdalen Coll., Oxford (MA Jurisprudence). Called to the Bar, Gray's Inn, 1961; Asst Recorder, 1983–87; Head of Chambers, Francis Taylor Bldg, Temple, EC4, 1983–91; a Recorder, SE Circuit, 1987–91. *Recreations:* theatre, reading, foreign travel.

GOSTIN, Prof. Larry, DJur; Associate Dean and Linda D. and Timothy J. O'Neill Professor of Global Health Law, Law Center, since 1994, Faculty Director, O'Neill Institute for National and Global Health Law, since 2005, and University Professor, since 2012, Georgetown University; Professor of Health Policy, Johns Hopkins School of Public Health (formerly Hygiene and Public Health), since 1994; Director, World Health Organization Collaborating Center on Public Health Law and Human Rights, since 2006; *b* 19 Oct. 1949; *s* of Joseph and Sylvia Gostin; *m* 1977, Jean Catherine Allison; two *s*. *Educ:* State Univ. of New York, Brockport (BA Psychology); Duke Univ. (DJur 1974). Dir of Forensics and Debate, Duke Univ., 1973–74; Fulbright Fellow, Social Res. Unit, Univ. of London, 1974–75; Legal Dir, MIND (Nat. Assoc. for Mental Health), 1975–83; Gen. Sec., NCCL, 1983–85; Harvard University: Sen. Fellow of Health Law, 1985–86; Lectr, 1986–87; Adjunct Prof. in Health Law, Sch. of Public Health, 1988–94; Exec. Dir, Amer. Soc. of Law and Medicine, 1986–94. Legal Counsel in series of cases before Eur. Commn and Eur. Court of Human Rights, 1974–. Vis. Prof., Sch. of Social Policy, McMaster Univ., 1978–79; Vis. Fellow in Law and Psychiatry, Centre for Criminological Res., Oxford Univ., 1982–83. Chm., Advocacy Alliance, 1981–83; Member: National Cttee, UN Internat. Year for Disabled People, 1981; Legal Affairs Cttee, Internat. League of Socs for Mentally Handicapped People, 1980–; Cttee of Experts, Internat. Commn of Jurists to draft UN Human Rights Declarations, 1982–; Adv. Council, Interights, 1984–; AE Trust, 1984–85; WHO Expert Cttee on Guidelines on the Treatment of Drug and Alcohol Dependent Persons, 1985; WHO Steering Cttee, Internat. Ethical Guidelines for Human Population Res., 1990–; Nat. Bd of Dirs, Amer. Civil Liberties Union, 1986– (Mem. Exec. Cttee, 1988–). Mem., Inst. of Medicine, NAS, 2000. Western European and UK Editor, Internat. Jl of Law and Psychiatry, 1978–81; Exec. Ed., Amer. Jl of Law and Medicine, 1986–; Ed.-in-chief, Jl of Law, Medicine and Health Care, 1986–. Hon. LLD: SUNY, 1994; Sydney, 2012. Rosemary Delbridge Meml Award for most outstanding contribution to social policy, 1983. *Publications:* A Human Condition: vol. 1, 1975; vol. 2, 1977; A Practical Guide to Mental Health Law, 1983; The Court of Protection, 1983; (ed) Secure Provision: a review of special services for mentally ill and handicapped people in England and Wales, 1985; Mental Health Services: law and practice, 1986; Human Rights in Mental Health: an international report for the World Federation for Mental Health, 1988; Civil Liberties in Conflict, 1988; Surrogate Motherhood: politics and privacy, 1990; AIDS and the Health Care System, 1990; Implementing the Americans with Disabilities Act: rights and responsibilities of all Americans, 1993; Rights of Persons who are HIV Positive, 1996; Human Rights and Public Health in the AIDS Pandemic, 1997; Public Health Law: power, duty, restraint, 2000, 2nd edn 2008; Public Health Law and Ethics: a reader, 2002, 2nd edn 2010; The Human Rights of Persons with Intellectual Disabilities: different but equal, 2003; The AIDS Pandemic: complacency, injustice and unfulfilled expectations, 2004; Public Health Ethics, 2007; Biosecurity in the Global Age, 2008; Principles of Mental Health Law and Policy, 2010; Global Health Law, 2014; articles in learned jls. *Recreations:* family outings, walking on the mountains and fells of the Lake District. *Address:* Georgetown University Law Center, 600 New Jersey Avenue NW, Washington, DC 20001–2075, USA. *T:* (202) 6629373.

GOSWAMI, Prof. Usha Claire, DPhil; FBA 2013; Professor of Cognitive Developmental Neuroscience, Department of Psychology (formerly Department of Experimental Psychology), University of Cambridge, since 2010 (Professor of Education, 2003–10); Fellow, St John's College, Cambridge, 1990–97 and since 2003; *b* 21 Feb. 1960; *d* of late Roshan Lal Goswami and of Elisabeth Irene Goswami (*née* Zenner); *m* 1995, Mark Thomson (marr. diss. 2004); one *d*. *Educ:* St John's Coll., Oxford (BA Hons Exptl Psychol.; DPhil Psychol.); Univ. of London Inst. of Educn (PGCE Primary Educn). Res. Fellow, Merton Coll., Oxford, 1986–87 and 1988–89; Harkness Fellow, Univ. of Illinois, 1987–88; Lectr in Exptl Psychol., Univ. of Cambridge, 1990–97; Prof. of Cognitive Develtl Psychol., UCL, 1997–2002. Leverhulme Major Res. Fellow, 2009–11. AcSS 2004; FRSA; Fellow, Assoc. for Psychol Sci., 2009. *Publications:* (with P. Bryant) Phonological Skills and Learning to Read, 1990; Analogical Reasoning in Children, 1992; Cognition in Children, 1997; (ed) Blackwell Handbook of Childhood Cognitive Development, 2002, 2nd edn, 2010; (ed) Cognitive Development, 2007; Cognitive Development: the learning brain, 2008; (ed jtly) Mental Capital and Wellbeing, 2009; Child Psychology: a very short introduction, 2014; contrib. papers to scientific jls. *Recreations:* enjoying my daughter, travel, reading. *Address:* St John's College, Cambridge CB2 1TP. *T:* (01223) 338600, *Fax:* (01223) 337720. *E:* ucg10@cam.ac.uk.

GOTO, Prof. John Philip; artist; Professor of Fine Art, University of Derby, 2003–13, now Emeritus; *b* Stockport, 11 Feb. 1949; *s* of late Bernard Glithero and Catherine Glithero (*née* Craig); changed name by Deed Poll to Goto; *m* 1st, 1972, Linda Gowan (marr. diss. 1985); two *d*; 2nd, 1992, Celia Agnes Farrelly. *Educ:* Windsor Grammar Sch.; Berkshire Coll. of Art; St Martin's Sch. of Art (BA Hons Fine Art (Painting)); Ecole de Louis Lumière, Paris and Acad. of Performing Arts, Prague (British Council Schol. in Photography). Lectr, Oxford Brookes Univ., 1981–99. Visiting Lecturer: Poly. of Central London, 1979–87; Ruskin Sch. of Drawing and Fine Art, Univ. of Oxford, 1987–2002, and numerous art schs in UK and abroad. Artist Fellow, Girton Coll. and Kettle's Yard, Univ. of Cambridge, 1988–89; Artist-in-Residence, NPG, 1999–2000. Panellist, 1986–89, Vice Chair, 1989–90, Visual Arts Panel, Southern Arts Assoc.; Adv. Panellist, John Hansard Gall., Univ. of Southampton, 1991–96. *Solo exhibitions* include: Goto, Photographs 1971–81, Photographers' Gall., London, 1981; Goto, Photographs 1975–83, PPS Galerie Gundlac, Hamburg, ULUV Gall., Prague, Moravian Gall., Bruno and tour of Spain, 1983–85; Sites of Passage, Ashmolean Mus., Oxford, 1988; Terezin, Raab Gall., Berlin, John Hansard Gall., Univ. of Southampton, Cornerhouse Gall., Manchester, 1989; The Atomic Yard, Kettle's Yard, Cambridge, Raab Gall., London, 1990–91; The Scar, Benjamin Rhodes Gall., London, Manchester City Art Mus. and Gall., 1993; John Goto 94, touring Russia, 1994; The Framer's Collection, Portfolio Gall., Edinburgh, 1997; The Commissar of Space, MOMA, Oxford, 1998; NPG 2000, Photoworks, NPG, 1999; Capital Arcade, Andrew Mummery Gall., London, 2000; Loss of Face, Tate Britain, London, 2002–03; High Summer, British Acad., 2005–09; John Goto's New World Circus, Gallery On, Seoul, 2006; Green and Pleasant Land, 2008, Sweet Augmentations, 2013, Galerie Dominique Fiat, Paris; Mosaic, Edinburgh Printmakers Gall., 2011; Jazz, 2011, Three Series, 2014, Gallery On, Seoul; Dreams of Jelly Roll, Freud Mus., 2012; *group exhibitions* include: Summer Show 4, 1977, Blasphemies, Ecstasies, Cries, 1989, Serpentine Gall.; The Third Meaning, MOMA, Oxford, Painting/Photography, Richard de Marco Gall., Edinburgh, 1986; Romantic Visions, Camden Arts Centre, 1988; Photographic Art in Britain 1945–1989, Barbican Gall., 1989; John Moores Exhibition 18, Walker Art Gall., Liverpool (prizewinner), 1993; After Auschwitz, RFH and tour, Pretext: Heteronyms, Rear Window, London, 1995; Modern Times 3, Hasselblad Center, Goteborg, 2000; Trade, Fotomus., Winterthur, Netherlands Fotoinst., Rotterdam, 2001–02; Sight Seeing, Graz, 2003; Collage, Bloomberg Space, London, 2004; Experimentieren, Inst. Cervantes, Berlin, 2005; Fotofestiwal, Lodz, 2009; Abstracts, f5.6 Galerie, Munich, 2011; Imagine Earth, Hangaram Art Mus., Seoul, 2011; (curator and exhibitor) An Uncommon Past, New Media Gall., Sichuan Fine Art Inst., Chongqing, China, 2012; Medusa Caravage, Palais de Tokyo, Paris, 2013; *work in collections* includes: Arts Council of GB, Australian Nat. Gall., V&A Mus., MOMA, Valencia, Univ. of Warwick, Univ. of Sussex, St Anne's Coll., Oxford, Deutsche Bank, British Govt Art Collection, British Art Centre, Yale, NPG, British Acad., Chongqing Art Mus., China. *Recreations:* jazz, architecture, history, film, good cuisine. *Address:* c/o f5.6 Galerie f5.6, Ludwigstrasse 7, 80539 Munich, Germany; Galerie Dominique Fiat, 16 Rue Coutures St Gervais, 75003 Paris, France; Gallery On, B1 Young chung Boulevard, 69 Sagan-Dong, Chongno-Gu, Seoul 110-190, South Korea. *E:* johngoto@who.net. *W:* www.johngoto.org.uk.

GOTO, Midori; violinist; *b* Osaka, Japan, 25 Oct. 1971; *d* of Setsu Goto. *Educ:* Professional Children's Sch., New York; Juilliard Sch. of Music, New York; New York Univ. (BA 2000; MA Psychol. 2005). Début with New York Philharmonic Orch., 1982; concert and recital appearances worldwide. Numerous recordings. Founder: Midori & Friends Foundn, 1992; Partners in Performance, 2003; Orchestra Residencies Program, 2004; Music Sharing, 2004. Jascha Heifetz Chair in Violin, Thornton Sch. of Music, Univ. of S Calif, 2006–. UN Messenger of Peace, 2007. Fellow, American Acad. of Arts and Scis, 2012. Hon. DMus Yale, 2012. Japanese Govt Artist of the Year, 1988; Avery Fisher Prize, 2001; Deutsche Schallplattenpreis, 2002, 2003; Kennedy Center Gold Medal, 2010; Award of Merit for Achievement in Performing Arts, Assoc. Performing Arts Presenters, 2015. *Publications:* Einfach Midori (memoir), 2004. *Address:* c/o Intermusica, 36 Graham Street, Crystal Wharf, N1 8GJ.

GOTT, Haydn; a District Judge (Magistrates' Courts) (formerly Metropolitan Stipendiary Magistrate), 1992–2011; *b* 29 April 1946; *s* of Alan Gott and Delia Mary Gott (*née* Pugh); *m* 1975, Brigid Mary Kane (marr. diss. 2002); one *s* one *d*; *m* 2004, Susan Valerie Green, *qv*. *Educ:* Manchester Grammar Sch.; Oxford Univ. (MA). Admitted solicitor, 1972; Partner, Alexander & Partners, solicitors, 1975–92. Legal Mem., Mental Health Review Tribunal, 1986–. *Recreations:* sport, music. *Club:* Ronnie Scott's.

GOTT, Paul Andrew; QC 2012; *b* Essex, 1967; *s* of Prof. Geoffrey Gott and Hilary Gott; *m* 1991, Judith Ann Lee; three *d*. *Educ:* Marple Hall Comprehensive Sch.; Downing Coll., Cambridge (BA Law 1989); Brasenose Coll., Oxford (BCL 1990). Called to the Bar, Lincoln's Inn, 1991; in practice as a barrister, specialising in employment law and commercial law, especially industrial disputes; Jun. Counsel to the Crown, 1999–2012. Mem., Standards Bd for England, 2006–12. *Recreations:* family, numismatics, collecting (especially tat), Shuna, presents from Margate. *Address:* Fountain Court Chambers, Temple, EC4Y 9DH. *T:* (020) 7583 3335.

GOTT, Richard Willoughby; journalist; Literary Editor, The Guardian, 1992–94; *b* 28 Oct. 1938; *s* of Arthur Gott and Mary Moon; *m* 1st, 1966, Ann Zammit (marr. diss. 1981); one adopted *s* one adopted *d*; 2nd, 1985, Vivien Ashley. *Educ:* Winchester Coll.; Corpus Christi Coll., Oxford (MA). Res. Asst, RIIA, 1962–65; Leader Writer, Guardian, 1964–66; Res. Fellow, Inst. de Estudios Internacionales, Univ. of Chile, 1966–69; Foreign Editor, Tanzanian Standard, Dar es Salaam, 1970–71; Third World corresp., New Statesman, 1971–72; The Guardian: Latin American corresp., 1972–76; Foreign News Editor, 1977–78; Features Editor, 1978–89; Asst Editor, 1988–94. Editor, Pelican Latin American Library, 1969–78; Dir, Latin American Newsletters, 1973–79. Contested (Ind.) North Hull, by-election 1966. Order of Francisco Miranda, 1st cl. (Venezuela), 2002. *Publications:* The Appeasers (with Martin Gilbert), 1963; Guerrilla Movements in Latin America, 1970; Land Without Evil: Utopian journeys across the South American watershed, 1993; In the Shadow of the Liberator: Hugo Chavez and the transformation of Venezuela, 2000; Cuba: a new history, 2004; Britain's Empire: resistance, repression and revolt, 2011. *Recreation:* travelling. *Address:* 88 Ledbury Road, W11 2AH. *T:* (020) 7229 5467.

GOTT, Susan Valerie; *see* Green, S. V.

GÖTTGENS, Prof. Berthold, DPhil; Professor of Molecular Haematology, University of Cambridge, since 2011; *b* Mechernich, Germany, 25 March 1966; *s* of Hans-Peter and Marlene Göttgens; *m* 1994, Euphemia Mutasa; two *d*. *Educ:* Hermann Josef Kolleg Steinfeld (Abitur 1985); Univ. of Tübingen (Dip. Biochem. 1992); Linacre Coll., Oxford (DPhil 1994). University of Cambridge: Res. Associate, 1994–2000; Sen. Res. Associate, 2000–02; Leukaemia Res. Fund Lectr, 2003–06; Sen. Lectr, 2006–07; Reader in Molecular Haematol., 2007–11. *Publications:* contrib. res. articles on gene regulatory control of normal and leukaemic blood stem cells. *Recreations:* accomplished violinist, enjoying spending time with family. *Address:* Department of Haematology, University of Cambridge, Cambridge CB2 0XY. *T:* (01223) 336829, *Fax:* (01223) 762670. *E:* bg200@cam.ac.uk.

GOTTLIEB, Anthony John; author and journalist; *b* 26 May 1956; *s* of Felix Gottlieb and Jutta Gottlieb; *m* 1989, Miranda Seymour (marr. diss. 2005). *Educ:* John Lyon Sch., Harrow-on-the-Hill; Gonville and Caius Coll., Cambridge (MA Philos. 1979); University Coll. London. The Economist, 1984–2006: Science Ed., 1988–91; Surveys Ed., 1991–94; Exec. Ed., 1997–2006. Vis. Fellow, All Souls Coll., Oxford, 2013–14. Ivan Boesky Fellow, Harvard Univ., 1986. *Publications:* Socrates, 1997; The Dream of Reason: a history of Western philosophy, 2000. *Recreations:* music, reading. *Address:* 60 West 57th Street, New York, NY 10019, USA.

GOTTLIEB, Robert Adams; dance and book critic; Editor-in-Chief, The New Yorker, 1987–92; *b* 29 April 1931; *s* of Charles and Martha Gottlieb; *m* 1st, 1952, Muriel Higgins (marr. diss. 1965); one *s*; 2nd, 1969, Maria Tucci; one *s* one *d*. *Educ:* Columbia Coll., NY; Cambridge Univ. Simon & Schuster, publishers, 1955–68 (final positions, Editor-in-Chief and Vice-Pres.); Pres. and Editor-in-Chief, Alfred A. Knopf, publishers, 1968–87. Pres., Louis B. Mayes Foundn. *Publications:* Reading Jazz, 1996; (jtly) Reading Lyrics, 2000; George Balanchine: the ballet maker, 2004; Sarah: the life of Sarah Bernhardt, 2010; Great Expectations: the sons and daughters of Charles Dickens, 2012. *Recreations:* ballet, classic film, shopping.

GOTTLOB, Prof. Georg, PhD; FRS 2010; Professor of Informatics, University of Oxford, since 2012; Fellow, St John's College, Oxford, since 2012; *b* Vienna, 30 June 1956; *m* Dr Laura Carlotta; one *s* one *d*. *Educ:* Univ. of Technol., Vienna (Dipl Ing 1979; Dr phil 1981); Univ. of Oxford (MA). Italian Nat. Res. Council, Genoa; University of Technology, Vienna: Professor of Computer Sci., 1988–2006; Dir, Christian Doppler Laboratory for Expert Systems, 1989–96; Adjunct Prof., 2006–; Prof. of Computing Sci., Univ. of Oxford, 2006–11; Fellow, St Anne's Coll., Oxford, 2006–11 (Hon. Fellow, 2012). McKay Prof., Univ. of Calif, Berkeley, 1999. Co-Founder, Lixto Corp.; Founding Mem., Oxford-Man Inst. of Quantitative Finance, 2007–. Member: Austrian Acad. of Scis; German Acad. of Scis Leopoldina; MAE. Wittgenstein Award, Austrian Nat. Sci. Fund. *Publications:* (jtly) Hypertree Width and Related Hypergraph Invariants, 2007; (jtly) A Backtracking-based Algorithm for Computing Hypertree-Decompositions, 2007; (jtly) A General Datalog-based Framework for Tractable Query Answering Over Ontologies, 2010. *Address:* Department of Computer Science, University of Oxford, Wolfson Building, Parks Road, Oxford OX1 3QD.

GOTTS, Andrew James, MBE 2012; photographer, since 1991; Director, Dr Gotts Ltd, since 2013; *b* Erpingham, Norfolk, 9 Feb. 1971; *s* of Ivor Gotts and Enid Gotts. *Educ:* Norfolk Coll. of Arts and Technol. (BTEC Nat. Dip. Design Photography 1991); Univ. of Wolverhampton (HND Photography 1994); De Montfort Univ. (MA Photography 2007). Creative Dir, Ark, 2000–02. Pres., British Inst. of Professional Photographers, 2011–12. Ambassador for UK Now, China, 2012. *Exhibitions* include: Degrees, Getty Gall., London, 2005, Film Mus., Potsdam, 2006; Selected Works, Savoy Hotel, 2006–; Behind the Mask, Somerset House, Lowry, 2014, Williamson Gall., 2015; Unseen, Flemings Mayfair, 2015. Hon. DArts De Montfort, 2011. *Publications:* Degrees, 2005; iCons, 2014; Monty Python Live, 2014; Save the Arctic: Vivienne Westwood, 2014; Behind the Mask, 2015. *Recreations:* film, theatre, art galleries, travelling, champagne. *Address:* Dr Gotts Ltd, 7–8 Park Place, SW1A 1LP. *T:* 0845 045 0078. *E:* info@andygotts.com.

GOUCHER, Mark Terence; independent theatrical producer, since 1987; *b* Redhill, Surrey, 29 Aug. 1965; *s* of Terence and Barbara Goucher; partner, 1994, Andrew Mackie. *Educ:* St John's Church Sch.; Warlingham Secondary Sch.; Univ. of Leeds (BA Drama and Media). Produced first show, Edinburgh Fringe, 1987, West End, 1991; West End productions include: Kit and the Widow, Vaudeville, 1991; Steven Berkoff, Garrick, 1993; The Complete Works of Shakespeare (abridged), 1996, The Complete History of America (abridged), 1996, The Bible - the Complete Word of God (abridged), 2003, Reduced Shakespeare Co., Criterion; Trainspotting, Whitehall, 1995; Fever Pitch, Arts, 1996; Shopping and F***ing, 1997; Issey Ogata, Lyric, 1998; Rent - the Musical, Prince of Wales, 1999; Holy Mothers, Last Dance at Dum Dum, 1999, Fame - the Musical, Victoria Palace, Cambridge, Aldwych, 1999–2005; Frantic Assembly, 2000, Ambassadors; Dolly West's Kitchen, Old Vic, 2000; The Snowman, Peacock, 2000–; Vagina Monologues, New Ambassadors, 2001, Arts, 2002, Wyndhams, 2005; Elaine Stritch at Liberty, Old Vic, 2002; The Anniversary, Garrick, 2005; Amajuba, Criterion, 2005; High Society, Shaftesbury, 2005; Footloose - The Musical, Novello, 2006; Whipping it Up, New Ambassadors, 2007; Shout! - the Musical, Arts, 2007; Dickens Unplugged, Comedy, 2008; Yes, Prime Minister, Gielgud, Apollo, Trafalgar Studios, 2010–12; Crazy for You, Novello, 2011; Slava's Snowshow, Royal Festival Hall, 2012; A Chorus Line, Palladium, 2013; Jeeves and Wooster, Duke of York's, 2013; Taken at Midnight, Minerva, Chichester, 2014, Theatre Royal Haymarket, 2015; The King's Speech, UK tour, 2015. Mem., Soc. of London Theatres, 2004– (Mem. Bd, 2012–). *Recreation:* I ride with the Cotswold. *Address:* c/o Mark Goucher Ltd, 19 Garrick Street, WC2E 9AX. *E:* mark@markgoucher.com. *Clubs:* Groucho, Century.

GOUDIE, family name of **Baroness Goudie**.

GOUDIE, Baroness *cr* 1998 (Life Peer), of Roundwood in the London Borough of Brent; **Mary Teresa Goudie;** strategic and management consultant, since 1998; *b* 2 Sept. 1946; *d* of Martin Brick and Hannah Brick (*née* Foley); *m* 1969, Thomas James Cooper Goudie, *qv*; two *s*. *Educ:* Our Lady of the Visitation; Our Lady of St Anselm. Asst Dir, Brent Peoples' Housing Assoc., 1977–80; Sec. and Organiser, Labour Solidarity Campaign, 1980–84; Director: The Hansard Soc., 1985–89; The House Magazine, 1989–90; Public Affairs Dir, WWF, 1990–95; public affairs consultant, 1995–98. Mem. (Lab) Brent LBC, 1971–78. Vice Chm., Labour Peers, 2001–03. Vice Chairman: All-Party Parly Equality Gp; All-Party Gp on Global Educn. UK Dir, Centre for Talent Innovation, 2012–. Chair, Women Leaders' Council to Fight Human Trafficking, UN, 2007–; Founding Mem., 30% Club, 2010–; Member: Global Adv. Bd, WEConnect Internat., 2012–; Exec. and Bd of Dirs, Vital Voices Global Partnership. Trustee: E-Hibri Charitable Foundn, 2012–; Share Gift. Patron, Community Foundn of NI, 2000–. Hon. LLD Napier, 1999. Global Power Award, Center for Women Policy Studies, 2010. *Publications:* various articles. *Recreations:* family, gardening, travelling, art, food and wine, reading. *Address:* (office) 11 Groom Place, SW1X 7BA. *T:* (020) 7245 9181, *Fax:* (020) 7235 9879. *W:* www.baronessgoudie.com, www.twitter.com/BaronessGoudie.

GOUDIE, Prof. Andrew Shaw; Director, China Centre, University of Oxford, 2011–13; *b* 21 Aug. 1945; *s* of late William and Mary Goudie; *m* 1987, Heather (*née* Viles); two *d*. *Educ:* Dean Close Sch., Cheltenham; Trinity Hall, Cambridge. BA, PhD Cantab; MA, DSc 2002, Oxon. Oxford University: Departmental Demonstrator, 1970–76; Univ. Lectr, 1976–84; Prof. of Geography, 1984–2003, now Emeritus; Head: Dept of Geography, 1984–94; Sch. of Geography and the Envmt, 2002–03; Fellow, Hertford Coll., 1976–2003 (Hon. Fellow, 2003); Pro-Vice-Chancellor, 1995–97; Head of Develt Prog., 1995–97; Master, St Cross Coll., 2003–11, now Hon. Fellow. Hon. Secretary: British Geomorphological Res. Gp, 1977–80 (Chm., 1988–89); RGS, 1981–88; Member: Council, Inst. of British Geographers, 1980–83; British Nat. Cttee for Geography, 1982–87. Dep. Leader: Internat. Karakoram Project, 1980; Kora Project, 1983. President: Geographical Assoc., 1993–94; Section E, BAAS, 1995–96; Internat. Assoc. of Geomorphologists, 2005– (Vice-Pres., 2002–05; Hon. Fellow, 2013); British Inst. in Eastern Africa, 2011–Nov. 2016. Fellow, British Soc. for Geomorphology, 2014. Cuthbert Peek award, RGS, 1975; Geographic Soc. of Chicago Publication award, 1982; Founder's Medal, RGS, 1991; Mungo Park Medal, RSGS, 1991; Medal, Royal Belgian Acad., 2002; Farouk El-Baz Prize for Desert Res., Geol Soc. of America, 2007; David Linton Award, British Soc. for Geomorphology, 2009. *Publications:* Duricrusts of Tropical and Sub-tropical Landscapes, 1973; Environmental Change, 1976, 3rd edn 1992; The Warm Desert Environment, 1977; The Prehistory and Palaeogeography of the Great Indian Desert, 1978; Desert Geomorphology, 1980; The Human Impact, 1981, 7th edn 2013; Geomorphological Techniques, 1981, 3rd edn 1990; The Atlas of Swaziland, 1983;

Chemical Sediments and Geomorphology, 1983; The Nature of the Environment, 1984, 4th edn 2001; (jtly) Discovering Landscape in England and Wales, 1985; The Encyclopædic Dictionary of Physical Geography, 1985, 3rd edn 2000; (jtly) Landshapes, 1989; The Geomorphology of England and Wales, 1990; Techniques for Desert Reclamation, 1990; Climate, 1997; Great Warm Deserts of the World, 2002; Encyclopedia of Geomorphology, 2004; Desert Dust in the Global System, 2006; Global Environments through the Quaternary, 2007, 2nd edn 2013; Wheels across the Desert, 2008; The Oxford Companion to Global Change, 2009; Geomorphological Hazards and Disaster Prevention, 2010; Handbook of Geomorphology, 2011; Arid and Semi-Arid Geomorphology, 2013; Landscapes and Landforms of Namibia, 2014; contribs to learned jls. *Recreations:* bush life, old records, old books. *Address:* St Cross College, St Giles, Oxford OX1 3LZ. *Clubs:* Geographical; Gilbert (Oxford).

See also T. J. C. Goudie.

GOUDIE, Andrew William, CB 2011; PhD; FRSE; Chief Economic Adviser, 1999–2011, and Director-General of Economy (formerly Head, Finance and Central Services Department), 2003–11, Scottish Government (formerly Scottish Office, then Scottish Executive); Special Adviser to the Principal, and Visiting Professor, University of Strathclyde, Glasgow, since 2011; *b* 3 March 1955; *s* of Britton Goudie and Joan Goudie; *m* 1978, Christine Lynne Hurley; two *s* two *d. Educ:* Queens' Coll., Cambridge (Wrenbury Schol.; BA Econs, MA; PhD 1992); Open Univ. (BA Maths and Stats). FRSE 2005. University of Cambridge: Research Officer, Dept of Applied Econs, 1978–85; Res. Fellow, Queens' Coll., 1981–83; Fellow and Dir of Studies, Robinson Coll., 1983–85; Sen. Economist, World Bank, Washington, 1985–90; Sen. Economic Advr, Scottish Office, 1990–95; Principal Economist, OECD Develt Centre, Paris, 1995–96; Chief Economist, DFID (formerly ODA), 1996–99. Mem., Adv. Gp, Oxfam Scotland, 2010–; Dir, Scotland Malawi Partnership, 2013–. Hon. DLitt Strathclyde, 2003. *Publications:* articles in learned jls, incl. Econ. Jl, Jl Royal Statistical Soc., Economica, Scottish Jl Political Economy. *Address:* University of Strathclyde, 16 Richmond Street, Glasgow G1 1XQ. *T:* (0141) 552 4400.

GOUDIE, (Thomas) James (Cooper); QC 1984; a Recorder, 1986–2008; a Deputy High Court Judge (Queen's Bench Division), since 1995; *b* 2 June 1942; *s* of late William Cooper Goudie and Mary Isobel Goudie; *m* 1969, Mary Teresa Brick (*see* Baroness Goudie); two *s. Educ:* Dean Close Sch.; London School of Economics (LLB Hons). FCIArb 1991. Solicitor, 1966–70; called to the Bar, Inner Temple, 1970 (Bencher, 1991). A Dep. Chm., 2000–12, Pres., 2007–12, Information Tribunal (for nat. security appeals). Chairman: Law Reform Cttee, Gen. Council of the Bar, 1995–96; Administrative Law Bar Assoc., 1994–96; Soc. of Labour Lawyers, 1994–99; Bar European Gp, 2001–03. Contested (Lab) Brent North, Feb. and Oct. 1974; Leader of Brent Council, 1977–78. Gov., LSE, 2001–. *Publications:* (ed jtly and contrib.) Judicial Review, 1992, 5th edn 2014; (ed with P. Elias, and contrib.) Butterworths Local Government Law, 1998; (ed jtly and contrib.) Local Authorities and the Human Rights Act 1998, 1999. *Address:* 11 King's Bench Walk, Temple, EC4Y 7EQ. *T:* (020) 7583 0610.

See also A. S. Goudie.

GOUGH, family name of **Viscount Gough.**

GOUGH, 5th Viscount *cr* 1849, of Goojerat, of the Punjaub, and Limerick; **Shane Hugh Maryon Gough;** Bt 1842; Baron Gough 1846; Irish Guards, 1961–67; *b* 26 Aug. 1941; *o s* of 4th Viscount Gough and Margaretta Elizabeth (*d* 1977), *o d* of Sir Spencer Maryon-Wilson, 11th Bt; *S* father, 1951. *Educ:* Abberley Hall, Worcs; Winchester Coll. Mem. Queen's Bodyguard for Scotland, Royal Company of Archers. Member: Exec. Council, RNIB; Scottish Lifeboat Council, RNLI. FRGS. *Heir:* none. *Address:* Keppoch Estate Office, Strathpeffer, Ross-shire IV14 9AD. *T:* (01997) 421224; 17 Stanhope Gardens, SW7 5RQ. *Clubs:* Pratt's, White's, MCC.

GOUGH, Rear-Adm. Andrew Bankes, CB 2000; Secretary-General, Order of St John, 2003–12; *b* 22 June 1947; *s* of late Gilbert Bankes Gough and Pauline Gough; *m* 1971, Susanne Jensen, Copenhagen; two *s. Educ:* Bridgnorth Grammar Sch.; Britannia Royal Naval Coll. Joined RN, 1965; flying tours, 1970–76; i/c, HMS Bronington, 1976–78; 824 Naval Air Sqdn, 1978–80; i/c, 737 Naval Air Sqdn, 1980–81; SS Uganda, Falklands Task Force, 1982; HMS Glamorgan, 1982–84; JSDC, 1985; MoD, 1985–87; in command HM Ships: Broadsword, 1987–88; Beaver, 1988; Brave, 1988–89; RCDS, 1990; MoD, 1991–93; Dep. UK Mil. Rep. to NATO, 1993–96; Comdr, Standing Naval Force, Atlantic, 1996–97; ACOS (Policy/Requirements), Supreme HQ Allied Powers in Europe, 1997–2000. Dep. Chief Exec., 2000–02, Man. Dir, 2003, Affinitas Ltd; Man. Dir, AFFAS Ltd, 2003. KStJ 2004. *Recreations:* military history, Bordeaux wine.

GOUGH, Prof. Douglas Owen, PhD; FRS 1997; Professor of Theoretical Astrophysics, University of Cambridge, 1993–2008, now Emeritus; Leverhulme Emeritus Fellow, Institute of Astronomy, Cambridge, 2008–11 (Director, 1999–2004); Fellow, Churchill College, Cambridge, since 1972; *b* 8 Feb. 1941; *s* of Owen Albert John Gough and Doris May Gough (*née* Camera); *m* 1965, Rosanne Penelope Shaw; two *s* two *d. Educ:* Hackney Downs Sch.; St John's Coll., Cambridge (BA 1962; MA 1966; PhD 1966). Res. Associate, Jt Inst. for Lab. Astrophysics, Univ. of Colo, 1966–67; Nat. Acad. of Scis Sen. Postdoctoral Resident Res. Associate, Inst. for Space Studies, NY, 1967–69; Vis. Mem., Courant Inst. of Mathematical Scis, NYU, 1967–69; University of Cambridge: Mem., Grad. Staff, Inst. of Theoretical Astronomy, 1969–73; Lectr in Astronomy and Applied Maths, 1973–85; Reader in Astrophysics, 1985–93; Dep. Dir, Inst. of Astronomy, 1993–99. Astronome Titulaire Associé des Observatoires de France, 1977; SRC Sen. Fellow, 1978–83; Prof. Associé, Univ. of Toulouse, 1984–85; Hon. Prof. of Astronomy, QMW, Univ. of London, later QMUL, 1986–2009; Fellow Adjoint, Jt Inst. for Lab. Astrophysics, Boulder, Colo, 1986–; Scientific Co-ordinator, Inst. for Theoretical Physics, Univ. of Calif, Santa Barbara, 1990; Vis. Prof., 1996–2010, Consulting Prof., 2010–, Stanford Univ.; Vis. Fellow, S African Astronomical Observatory, 2004–10; Associé de recherche, CNRS, Observatoire de Paris-Meudon, 2005–06; Vis. Fellow, 2005, Invitation Fellow, 2005, 2012, Japan Soc. for the Promotion of Sci.; Vis. Scientist, High Altitude Observatory, Boulder, Colo, 2014–. Lectures: James Arthur, Harvard, 1982; Sir Joseph Larmor, Cambridge Philosophical Soc., 1988; Wernher von Braun, Marshall Space Flight Center, 1991; Morris Loeb, Harvard, 1993; Halley, Oxford Univ., 1996; Bishop, Columbia Univ., 1996; R. J. Tayler Meml, RAS, 2000; Colloquium Ehrenfestii, Instituut Lorentz, 2003; Vainu Bappu, Indian Inst. of Astrophysics, 2008. Member, Editorial Board: Solar Physics, 1983–2004; Fundamentals of Cosmic Physics, 1985–93; Inverse Problems, 1997–2003; Advr, Encyclopedia of Astronomy and Astrophysics, Inst. of Physics, 1997–2000. FInstP 1997; Fellow, Nat. Astronomical Observatory of Japan, Tokyo, 2014. For. Mem., Royal Danish Acad. of Scis and Letters, 1998. William Hopkins Prize, Cambridge Philosophical Soc., 1984; George Ellery Hale Prize, Amer. Astronomical Soc., 1994; Eddington Medal, 2000, Gold Medal, 2010, RAS; Pioneer to Life of the Nation, 2003. Mousquetaire d'Armagnac, 2001. *Publications:* mainly res. papers and reviews in scientific jls. *Recreations:* cooking, listening to music, hiking. *Address:* Institute of Astronomy, Madingley Road, Cambridge CB3 0HA. *T:* (01223) 337548.

GOUGH, Rev. Canon Flora Jane Louise; *see* Winfield, Rev. Canon F. J. L.

GOUGH, Janet, MA; *b* 1 Aug. 1940; *d* of Clifford Gough and Sarah (*née* Allen). *Educ:* Ludlow High Sch.; Newnham Coll., Cambridge (BA Hons, MA). St Paul's Girls' Sch., 1964–71; Manchester Grammar Sch., 1972; Worcester High Sch. for Girls, 1973; St Paul's Girls' Sch., 1973–98, High Mistress, 1993–98. Governor: Dulwich Coll., 1999–2008; Oundle Sch., 2002–12; Ludlow Coll., 2009–11. *Recreations:* book collecting, architecture, music. *Address:* 58 Corve Street, Ludlow, Shropshire SY8 1DU.

GOUGH, Janet Frances, (Mrs Jim Lloyd); Director, Cathedral and Church Buildings Division, Archbishop's Council, Church of England, since 2008; fundraiser, moderniser, policy advocate; *b* London, 3 Sept. 1961; *d* of Geoffrey and Caryl Gough (*née* Howard); *m* 2001, Jim Lloyd; one *s* one *d. Educ:* St Margaret's, Bushey; Haileybury; Emmanuel Coll., Cambridge (BA Hist. and Hist. of Art 1983; MA). ACA 1989. Art for Offices, 1984; KPMG, 1985–89; Charterhouse Bank, 1989–91; Sotheby's, 1991–2000, Dir, 1995–2000; Acting Dir, Prince of Wales's Phoenix Trust (UK Building Preservation Trust), 2001–02; V&A tours and Janet Gough Architectural Tours, 2002–08. Trustee: Fulham Palace Trust, 1997–2011; Churches Conservation Trust, 1998–2006; Friends of V&A, 2013–. Mem., Judging Panel, Art and Christianity Enquiry 2015 Award for art in a Christian context. *Publications:* Director's Choice: the Cathedrals of the Church of England, 2015. *Recreations:* historic sites, museums, galleries, exhibitions and collecting, walking, sailing, travel, my family (and dog and cat), entertaining. *Address:* Church House, Great Smith Street, SW1P 3AZ. *T:* (020) 7898 1887. *E:* janet.gough@churchofengland.org.

GOUGH, Rev. Canon Jonathan Robin Blanning; Royal Army Chaplains' Department, since 2005; Deputy Assistant Chaplain General, since 2011; *b* 11 May 1962; *s* of Alec Robin Blanning Gough and Margaret Gough (*née* Elliston); *m* 1985, Rev. Canon Flora Jane Louise Winfield, *qv. Educ:* Exeter Sch.; St David's UC, Lampeter (BA Hons 1983); St Stephen's House, Oxford; Westminster Coll., Oxford (MTh 1996). Ordained deacon, 1985, priest, 1986; Assistant Curate: Braunton, 1985–86; Matson, 1986–89; Royal Army Chaplains' Department, 1989–2001: served: NI, 1990–92 and 2000–01; Bosnia (UN Protection Force), 1993–94 and 1995, (NATO Stabilisation Force), 1997; Kosovo (NATO Kosovo Force), 1999–2000; Archbishop of Canterbury's Sec. for Ecumenism, 2001–05; Iraq, 2005; Sen. Chaplain British Forces, Afghanistan, 2008; Chaplain, RMA Sandhurst, 2009–11. Hon. Canon: Holy Trinity Cathedral, Gibraltar, 2002–05; St Paul's Cathedral, Nicosia, 2006–. *Recreations:* music, history, country pursuits. *Address:* c/o Ministry of Defence Chaplains (Army), HQ Land Forces, 2nd Floor, Zone 6, Ramillies Building, Marlborough Lines, Monxton Road, Andover, Hants SP11 8HJ.

GOUGH, Judith Margaret; *see* Carlisle, J. M.

GOUGH, Judith Mary; HM Diplomatic Service; Ambassador to Ukraine, since 2015; *b* Amersham, 8 Nov. 1972; *d* of Richard and Mary Gough; civil partnership 2011, Nerantzoula, (Julia), Kleiousi; two *s. Educ:* Univ. of Nottingham (BA Jt Hons German and Russian 1995); King's Coll. London (MA War in Modern World 2012). Audit trainee, 1995–96, Asst, later Sen. Consultant, Mgt Consultancy Services, 1996–2001, Ernst & Young; entered FCO, 2001; Gibraltar Desk, 2001–02, Hd, Albania, former Yugoslav Rep. of Macedonia and Balkans Strategic Policy Team, Eastern Adriatic Dept, 2002–04, FCO; Political Counsellor, Seoul, 2004–07; Dep. Dir, Corporate Services Prog., 2007–08; Dep. Hd, Security Policy Gp, 2008–10; Ambassador to Georgia, 2010–12; Dir, Eastern Europe and Central Asia Directorate, FCO, 2013–14; lang. trng, 2014–15. Mem., CIMA 1999. *Recreations:* climbing mountains, cycling, collecting maps, talking. *Address:* c/o Foreign and Commonwealth Office, King Charles Street, SW1A 2AH.

GOUGH, Michael Charles, CEng, FIET, FBCS; information technology and services consultant, since 2014; *b* 21 May 1960; *s* of Cyril John Gough and Evelyn Rose Gough; *m* 1982, Lesley Irene Baglee; three *s. Educ:* Univ. of Liverpool (BSc Hons Computational and Statistical Sci. 1981); MSc Computer Sci. 1987). CITP 2002; CEng 2006; FIET 2006; FBCS 2006; Univ. of Chester (Church Colls Cert. 2009). Computer software engr, Fraser Williams, 1981–87; Project Manager, CAP Gp Plc, 1987–89; IT Dir, CERT Plc, 1989–91; Dir, Technol. Strategy, SEMA Gp Plc, 1991–2000; Chief Exec., National Computing Centre, 2000–08; Hewlett Packard Enterprise Services (formerly Electronic Data Systems): Hd, Information Assce, UK Public Sector, 2008–11; Prog. Leader, 2009–11; Delivery Assce Dir, Application Services EMEA, 2011–14. Director: Dynamic Systems Develt Method Consortium, 1997–2003; AIRTO, 2000–03. Mem., Exec. Cttee, BCS, 2013–. MInstD 1996. *Recreations:* music: teaching, playing and composing, photography, theology, the Methodist Church.

GOUGH, Prof. Michael John, FRCS; Professor of Vascular Surgery, University of Leeds, since 2009; Head, School of Surgery, Yorkshire and Humber Postgraduate and Dental Deanery, since 2009; Consultant Vascular Surgeon, Leeds Teaching Hospitals NHS Trust, since 1990; *b* Birmingham, 18 Feb. 1952; *s* of Henry John Gough and Kathleen June Gough; *m* 1974, Moira Cockerham; two *s* one *d. Educ:* Teignmouth Grammar Sch.; Leeds University Sch. of Medicine (MB ChB 1975; ChM 1984). FRCS 1980. Surgical Registrar, Royal Free Hosp., London, 1980–82; Sen. Surgical Registrar, Yorks RHA, 1982–86; Consultant Surgeon, Bradford Hosps, 1986–90. President: Vascular Soc. (formerly Vascular Surgical Soc.) of GB and Ire., 2007–08 (Mem., 1986–); Moynihan Chirurgical Club, 2009–10 (Mem., 1995–); Member: Assoc. of Surgeons of GB and Ire., 1986–; Eur. Soc. for Vascular Surgery, 1986–. Mem., Court of Examiners (Gen. Surgery), FRCS Intercollegiate Exams Bd, 2002–07. Associate Ed. and Mem. Editl Bd, Eur. Jl of Vascular and Endovascular Surgery, 2009–. *Publications:* over 100 articles in learned jls incl. Lancet, BMJ, Brit. Jl of Surgery, Jl of Vascular Surgery, Eur. Jl of Vascular and Endovascular Surgery, Stroke, Radiology. *Recreations:* golf, tennis, sailing, ski-ing, fly fishing, photography, family, anything outdoors. *Address:* Yorkshire and the Humber Postgraduate Deanery, University of Leeds, Willow Terrace Road, Leeds LS2 9JT. *T:* (0113) 343 1557. *E:* michael.gough@yorksandhumber.nhs.uk.

GOUGH, Piers William, CBE 1998; RA 2001; RIBA; architect; Partner, CZWG Architects, since 1975; *b* 24 April 1946; *s* of late Peter Gough and Daphne Mary Unwin Banks; *m* 1991, Rosemary Elaine Fosbrooke Bates (marr. diss. 2009). *Educ:* Uppingham Sch., Rutland; Architectural Assoc. Sch. of Architecture. Principal works: Phillips West 2, Bayswater, 1976; Lutyens Exhibn, Hayward Gall., 1982; Cochrane Sq., Glasgow, 1987–94; China Wharf, 1988, The Circle, 1990, Bermondsey; Craft, Design and Technol. Bldg, 1988, two boarding houses, 1994, Bryanston Sch.; Street-Porter House, 1988, 1–10 Summers St, 1994, Clerkenwell; Crown St Regeneration Proj., Gorbals, 1991–2004; Westbourne Grove Public Lavatories, 1993; Brindleyplace Café, Birmingham, 1994–97; Bankside Lofts, Southwark, 1994–99; 19th and 20th century galls, 1995–96, Regency galls, 2003, Nat. Portrait Gall.; Soho Lofts, Wardour Street, 1995; Leonardo Centre, Uppingham Sch., 1995; The Glass Building, Camden, 1996–99; Camden Wharf, Camden Lock, 1996–2002; Green Bridge, Mile End Park, 1997–2000; Westferry Studios, Isle of Dogs, 1999–2000; Bankside Central, 2000–02; Allen Jones' Studio, Ledwell, 2000–01; Samworths' Boarding House, Uppingham Sch., 2000–01; Site A, Edinburgh Park, 2000–01; Tunnel Wharf, Rotherhithe, 2001; Fulham Island Site, 2001–02; Ladbroke Green, 2002–; Arsenal Masterplan project, 2002–; Queen Elizabeth Square and Crown Street Corner, Gorbals, 2003–04; Saved Exhibn, Hayward Gall., 2003–04; Fortune Green, 2003–10; Maggie's Centre, Nottingham, 2003–11; Brewery Square, Dorchester, 2003–; Steedman St, SE17, 2006; Bling Bling Building, Liverpool, 2006; Islington Sq., 2006–; One Lansdowne Rd, Croydon, 2008–; Canada Water Library, 2008–11. Commissioner: English Heritage, 2000–07 (Mem., London Adv. Cttee, 1995–2003; Mem., Urban Panel, 1999–2003); CABE, 2007–11. Pres., AA, 1995–97 (Mem. Council, 1970–72, 1991–99; Trustee, 1999–2007). Trustee, Artangel, 1994–2004. Television: (co-writer and presenter) The Shock of the Old (series), Channel 4, 2000. Hon. Fellow, Queen Mary, Univ.

of London, 2001. DUniv Middlesex, 1999. *Publications:* English Extremists, 1988. *Recreation:* swimming. *Address:* CZWG Architects LLP, 17 Bowling Green Lane, EC1R 0QB. *T:* (020) 7253 2523, *Fax:* (020) 7250 0594. *E:* piersgough@czwgarchitects.co.uk.

GOUGH, Rachel Mary; *see* Sandby-Thomas, R. M.

GOULBORN, Caroline Barbara; a District Judge (Magistrates' Courts), 2004–14; *b* 9 Sept. 1949; *d* of Sydney Aubrey Goulborn and Peggy Goulborn (*née* Millhouse). *Educ:* Wycombe High Sch.; Trent Polytech. (BA Hons (Law) 1978). Admitted solicitor, 1981; Assistant Solicitor: Huntsmans, Nottingham, 1981–84; Nelsons, Nottingham, 1985–88; Sen. Partner, Fletcher's Solicitors, 1989–2004. *Recreations:* long-distance Wycombe Wanderers supporter, Sutton Bonington Cricket Club (Vice Pres.), reading, foreign travel.

GOULD, family name of **Baronesses Gould of Potternewton** and **Rebuck**.

GOULD OF POTTERNEWTON, Baroness *cr* 1993 (Life Peer), of Leeds in the Metropolitan County of West Yorkshire; **Joyce Brenda Gould;** a Deputy Speaker, House of Lords, 2002–12; *b* 29 Oct. 1932; *d* of Sydney and Fanny Manson; *m* 1952, Kevin Gould (separated); one *d*. *Educ:* Cowper Street Primary Sch.; Roundhay High Sch. for Girls; Bradford Technical Coll. Dispenser, 1952–65; Labour Party: Mem., 1951–; Asst Regional Organiser, 1969–75; Asst Nat. Agent and Chief Women's Officer, 1975–85; Dir of Organisation, 1985–93. Opposition spokesperson on women's affairs, 1995–97; a Baroness in Waiting (Govt Whip), 1997–98. Chm., All Party Parly Gp on Pro-Choice, 1995–. Member: Council of Europe, 1993–96 (Ldr, Delegn to UN Conf. on Women, Beijing, 1995); WEU, 1993–96; CPA, 1998–; IPU, 1998–; Fellow, Parlt and Industry Trust. Mem., Ind. Commn on Voting Systems, 1998–; Vice-Chm., Hansard Soc., 2002–06. Chairman: Ind. Adv. Cttee for Sexual Health, 2003–; Women's Nat. Commn, 2008– (Interim Chm., 2007–08). Sec., Nat. Jt Cttee of Working Women's Orgns, 1975–85; Vice-Pres., Socialist Internat. Women, 1978–86. President: BEA, 1998–2007; FPA, 1999–; Brighton and Hove Fabian Soc., 2001–; Straight Talking, 2007–. Chm., Mary MacArthur Holiday Trust, 1994–2007. Patron: FORWARD, 1996–; Brighton and Hove Women's Centre, 2000–; Yorks MESMAC, 2008–; HIV Sport, 2010–; Sussex Beacon, 2011–; Vice Patron, Impact's 30th Anniv. Appeal, 2008; Trustee, Age UK, Brighton and Hove, 2011–. Hon. FFSRH (Hon. FFFP 2006); Hon. Fellow, British Assoc. for Sexual Health and HIV, 2007. Hon. Dr: Bradford; Birmingham City; Greenwich. Health Champion, Charity Champion Awards, 2007. *Publications:* (ed) Women and Health, 1979; pamphlets on feminism, socialism and sexism, women's right to work, and on violence in society; articles and reports on women's rights and welfare. *Recreations:* relaxing, sport as a spectator, theatre, cinema, reading. *Address:* 58 Hangleton Way, Hove BN3 8EQ; House of Lords, SW1A 0PW.

GOULD, Dr Alexander Paul, FMedSci; Group Leader, Francis Crick Institute, since 2015; *b* 29 Jan. 1964; *s* of Dr Arthur Gould and Mrs Jean Alison Firth (*née* Brighton); partner, Dr Caroline Vincent. *Educ:* Burleigh Community Coll., Loughborough; King's Coll., Cambridge (BA Hons Natural Scis 1986; MA 1990; PhD Develtl Biol. 1990). Wellcome Trust Res. Associate, Univ. of Cambridge, 1990–91; Jun. Res. Fellow, King's Coll., Cambridge, 1991–95; MRC National Institute for Medical Research: Beit Meml Fellow, 1992–95; MRC Trng Fellow, 1995–97; Gp Leader, 1998–2012; Hd, Div. of Physiol. and Metabolism, 2012–15. Mem., EMBO, 2008–. Wellcome Trust: Mem., Molecules, Genes and Cells Funding Cttee, 2007–11; Mem., Peer Rev. Coll., 2012–. Member: British Soc. for Develtl Biol., 1987; Genetics Soc. of America, 1990; Biochem. Soc., 1998. Mem., Editl Adv. Bd, Develt, 2013–. FMedSci 2013. Francis Perch Bedford Prize for Zool., UCL, 1986; Hooke Medal, British Soc. for Cell Biol., 2011. *Publications:* contrib. articles and reviews to learned jls, incl. Nature, Cell. *Recreations:* keeping fit, gastronomy, travelling, wildlife. *Address:* Francis Crick Institute, The Ridgeway, Mill Hill, NW7 1AA. *T:* (020) 8816 2103. *E:* agould@nimr.mrc.ac.uk.

GOULD, Andrew Frederick James; Chairman, BG-Group plc, since 2012; *b* Walton-on-Thames, 17 Dec. 1946; *s* of James McIntosh Gould and Joan Vivien Gould (*née* Wilson); *m* 1974, Sylvie de Thesut; one *s* two *d*. *Educ:* W Buckland Sch., Barnstaple, Devon; Univ. of Wales Coll. of Cardiff (BA Hons). CA 1969. Schlumberger: financial and mgt positions, Asia, USA and Europe, 1975–2003; Chm. and CEO, 2003–11. Mem., Bd of Dirs, Saudi Aramco, 2013. Mem., Prime Minister's Council for Sci. and Technol., 2004–07. Member: Adv. Bd, King Fahd Univ. Petroleum and Minerals, Daahran, Saudi Arabia, 2007–; Bd of Trustees, King Abdullah Univ. for Sci. and Technol., Jeddah, Saudi Arabia, 2009–. *Recreation:* fly fishing. *Address:* BG-Group plc, Eagle House, 108–110 Jermyn Street, SW1Y 6RP. *T:* (020) 7707 4878, *Fax:* (020) 7707 4858.

See also D. J. Gould.

GOULD, Bryan Charles, CNZM 2005; Vice-Chancellor, Waikato University, New Zealand, 1994–2004; Chair, National Centre for Tertiary Teaching Excellence, since 2007; *b* 11 Feb. 1939; *s* of Charles Terence Gould and Elsie May Driller; *m* 1967, Gillian Anne Harrigan; one *s* one *d*. *Educ:* Auckland Univ. (BA, LLM); Balliol Coll., Oxford (MA, BCL). HM Diplomatic Service: FO, 1964–66; HM Embassy, Brussels, 1966–68; Fellow and Tutor in Law, Worcester Coll., Oxford, 1968–74. MP (Lab): Southampton Test, Oct. 1974–1979; Dagenham, 1983–94; an opposition spokesman on trade, 1983–86, on economy and party campaigns, 1986–87, on Trade and Industry, 1987–89, on the environment, 1989–92, on national heritage, 1992 (Mem. of Shadow Cabinet, 1986–92). Presenter/Reporter, TV Eye, Thames Television, 1979–83. Chm., Eastern Bay Primary Health Alliance, 2011–. Chm., Foundn for Res., Sci. and Technol., 2008–11. Hon. Dr Waikato, 2006. *Publications:* Monetarism or Prosperity?, 1981; Socialism and Freedom, 1985; A Future for Socialism, 1989; Goodbye to All That (memoirs), 1995; The Democracy Sham, 2006; Rescuing The New Zealand Economy, 2008; Myths, Politicians and Money, 2013. *Recreations:* gardening, food, wine. *Address:* 239 Ohiwa Beach Road, Opotiki, New Zealand.

GOULD, David John, CB 2004; General Manager, Submarines, Department of Defence, Australia, 2012–15; *b* 9 April 1949; *s* of James McIntosh Gould and Joan Vivienne Gould; *m* 1st, 1973; two *s* one *d*; 2nd, 2001, Christine Lake. *Educ:* West Buckland Sch., Barnstaple; Univ. of Sussex (Hons, French and European Studies). Joined MoD Naval Weapons Dept, 1973; Materiel Finance (Air), 1978; NATO Defence College, 1980; MoD (Air), 1981; UK Delegn to NATO, 1983; Asst Sec., Materiel Finance (Air), 1987; Head of Resources and Programmes (Air), 1990; Assistant Under-Secretary of State: (Supply and Orgn) (Air), 1992; Policy, 1993; seconded to Cabinet Office, 1993–95; Asst Under-Sec. of State, Fleet Support, 1995–99; Dir Gen., Finance and Business Plans, Defence Logistics Orgn, MoD, 1999–2000; Dep. Chief Exec., Defence Procurement Agency, 2000–07; Chief Operating Officer, Defence Equipment and Support, MoD, 2007–08. Non-exec. Dir, Vega Consulting Services Ltd, 2009–10; Exec. Chm., Selex Systems Integration Ltd, 2010–12. Silver Jubilee Medal, 1977. *Recreations:* fitness, Bath Rugby, fly fishing (Avon and tributaries), music, especially opera and lieder.

See also A. F. J. Gould.

GOULD, Edward John Humphrey, MA; FRGS; Master, Marlborough College, 1993–2004; *b* Lewes, Sussex, 31 Oct. 1943; *s* of Roland and Ruth Gould; *m* 1970, Jennifer Jane, *d* of I. H. Lamb; two *d*. *Educ:* St Edward's Sch., Oxford; St Edmund Hall, Oxford (BA 1966, MA 1970, DipEd 1967). FRGS 1974. Harrow School, 1967–83: Asst Master, 1967–83; Head, Geography Dept, 1974–79; Housemaster, 1979–83; Headmaster, Felsted Sch., 1983–93. Chm., ISC, 2006–07 (Mem., Council, and Policy Cttee (Chm., 2000), 2000–02); Member: Ind. Schs Curriculum Cttee, 1985–92 (Chm., 1990–92); Bd, QCA, 2002–07; Bd, United Learning Trust, 2004–14 (Chm., 2010–14); Bd, ESU, 2004–11 (Dep. Chm., 2005–11); Nat. Council for Educnl Excellence, 2007–10. Chairman: ISIS East, 1989–93; HMC, 2002. Governor: St Edward's Sch., Oxford, 2003–11; Harrow Sch., 2004–; Norwich Sch., 2004–; Gresham's Sch., 2013–; Chm., Harrow Internat. Schs Ltd, 2010–. JP Essex, 1989–93. *Recreations:* Rugby (Oxford Blue, 1963–66), swimming (Half Blue, 1965), rowing (rep. GB, 1967), music, golf, sailing. *Address:* Brette Cottage, Cross Lane, Brancaster, Norfolk PE31 8AE. *Clubs:* East India, Devonshire, Sports and Public Schools; Vincent's (Oxford).

GOULD, Jane Elizabeth; *see* Cannon, J. E.

GOULD, Matthew Steven, CMG 2014; MBE 1998; HM Diplomatic Service; Director of Cyber Security, Cabinet Office, since 2015; *b* 20 Aug. 1971; *s* of Sidney and Jean Gould; *m* 2009, Celia Jane Leaberry; two *d*. *Educ:* Orley Farm Sch., Harrow; St Paul's Sch., Barnes; Peterhouse, Cambridge (BA Theol. 1993). Teacher, Nyarukunda Secondary Sch., Zimbabwe, 1989–90; entered FCO, 1993; Manila, 1994–97; Speech Writer to Foreign Sec., 1997–99; Dep. Hd, Consular Div., FCO, 1999–2001; Political Counsellor, Islamabad, 2002–03; Dep. Hd of Mission, Tehran, 2003–05; Counsellor (Foreign and Security Policy), Washington, 2005–07; Pvte Sec. for For. Affairs to Prime Minister (on secondment), 2007; Principal Private Sec. to Sec. of State for Foreign and Commonwealth Affairs, 2007–10; Ambassador to Israel, 2010–15. *Recreations:* horse-riding, ski-ing, films, cats and dogs, curry. *Address:* c/o Cabinet Office, 70 Whitehall, SW1A 2AS.

GOULD, Patricia, CBE 1978; RRC 1972; Matron-in-Chief, Queen Alexandra's Royal Naval Nursing Service, 1976–80; *b* 27 May 1924; *d* of Arthur Wellesley Gould. *Educ:* Marist Convent, Paignton. Lewisham Gen. Hosp., SRN, 1945; Hackney Hosp., CMB Pt I, 1946; entered QARNNS, as Nursing Sister, 1948; accepted for permanent service, 1954; Matron, 1966; Principal Matron, 1970; Principal Matron Naval Hosps, 1975. QHNS 1976–80. OStJ (Comdr Sister), 1977. *Recreations:* gardening, photography.

GOULD, Peter John Walter; Owner/Director, Gould Advisory Services Ltd, 2007–12; Chief Executive, Northamptonshire County Council, 2000–07; Clerk to Lord-Lieutenant of Northamptonshire, 2000–07; *b* 10 Feb. 1953; *s* of Morris Edwin Gould and Hilda Annette Gould; *m* 1977, June Lesley Sutton; one *s*. *Educ:* Yeovil Sch., Som; NE London Poly. (BScSoc, London Univ.). Res. Fellow, Sch. for Independent Study, NE London Poly., 1976; London Borough of Lambeth, 1977–98: Hd of Strategy, 1995; Dir of Personnel, 1996–98; Corporate Dir, Middlesbrough Unitary Council, 1998–2000. Chair, 78 Derngate Trust, 2008–14. Mem., Eye Town Council, 2014–. FRSA 2007. *Recreations:* music, opera, flute, cooking, literature, social history, woodcarving. *Address:* Brome Park Farm, Brome Avenue, Eye, Suffolk IP23 7HW.

GOULD, Richard; Chief Executive, Surrey County Cricket Club, since 2011; *b* London, 14 March 1970; *s* of Bobby and Margery Gould; *m* 1993, Rebecca Yelland; two *d*. *Educ:* Bristol Grammar Sch.; Royal Mil. Acad., Sandhurst; Army Staff Coll. Jun. Div. and Cranfield Univ.; Harvard Business Sch. (AMP). Served RTR, 1990–2001 (retd as Major). Commercial Dir, Bristol City FC, 2001–05; CEO, Somerset CCC, 2005–11. *Recreation:* cycling. *Address:* The Chestnuts, Hatch Beauchamp, Som TA3 6AE. *T:* (01823) 480592. *E:* rgould@surreycricket.com.

GOULD, Robert; JP; DL; Member, Glasgow City Council, 1994–2003 (Leader, 1994–97); *b* 8 Feb. 1935; *s* of James and Elizabeth Gould; *m* 1953, Helen Wire; two *s* two *d*. *Educ:* Albert Secondary Sch. Formerly with BR. Entered local government, 1970: Glasgow Corp., 1970–74; Mem., Strathclyde Regl Council, 1974–96 (Leader, 1992–96). JP Glasgow; DL Glasgow, 1997. *Recreations:* all sports (spectator), hill-walking. *Address:* Flat 6D, 15 Eccles Street, Springburn, Glasgow G22 6BJ. *T:* (0141) 558 6438.

GOULD, Prof. Warwick Leslie; Professor of English Literature, University of London, 1995–2013, now Emeritus; Founder Director, Institute of English Studies, School of Advanced Study, University of London, 1999–2013, now Senior Research Fellow; *b* 7 April 1947; *s* of Leslie William Gould and Fedora Gould (*née* Green). *Educ:* Brisbane Grammar Sch.; Univ. of Queensland (BA 1st Cl. Hons English Language and Lit. 1969). Royal Holloway College, then Royal Holloway and Bedford New College, University of London: Lectr in English Language and Lit., 1973–86; Sen. Lectr, 1986–91; Reader in English Lit., 1991–95; British Acad. Res. Reader, 1992–94; Prof., 1995–; Dep. Prog. Dir, 1994–97, Prog. Dir, 1997–99, Centre for English Studies, Sch. of Advanced Study, Univ. of London; Dep. Dean, 2000–03, Mem., Bd, 2011–13, Sch. of Advanced Study. Acting Dir, Inst. of Commonwealth Studies, 2009. University of London: Member: Senate, 1990–94; Academic Council, 1990–94; Academic Cttee, 1994–2000; Council, 1995–2000 and 2002–09. FRSL 1997; FRSA 1998; FEA 1999. Cecil Oldman Meml Medal for Bibliography and Textual Criticism, Leeds Univ., 1993; British Acad. Pres.'s Medal, 2012. Editor, Yeats Annual, 1983–. *Publications:* (jtly) Joachim of Fiore and the Myth of the Eternal Evangel, 1987, 2nd edn, as Joachim of Fiore and the Myth of the Eternal Evangel in the Nineteenth and Twentieth Centuries, 2001; (ed jtly) The Secret Rose: stories by W. B. Yeats, 1981, 2nd edn 1992; (ed jtly) The Collected Letters of W. B. Yeats, Vol. II 1896–1900, 1997; (jtly) Gioacchino da Fiore e il mito dell'Evangelo eterno nella cultura europea, 2000; (ed jtly) Mythologies by W. B. Yeats, 2005; (ed) The Living Stream: essays in memory of A. Norman Jeffares, 2013; (ed jtly) Yeats's Mask, 2013. *Recreation:* book collecting. *Address:* Institute of English Studies, Room 239, Senate House, Malet Street, WC1E 7HU. *T:* (020) 7862 8673, *Fax:* (020) 7862 8720. *E:* warwick.gould@sas.ac.uk.

GOULDBOURNE, Rev. Dr Ruth Mary Boyd; Co-Minister, Bloomsbury Central Baptist Church, since 2006; *b* 5 July 1961; *d* of Derek Boyd Murray and Giles Watson Murray; *m* 1984, Ian Duncan Gouldbourne. *Educ:* Drummond High Sch., Edinburgh; St Andrews Univ. (MA 1983); King's Coll. London (BD 1986); Royal Holloway and Bedford New Coll., Univ. of London (PhD 2000); Bristol Univ. (Postgrad. Dip. Counselling 2004). Baptist Minister, Bunyan Meeting Free Ch, 1988–95; Tutor, Bristol Baptist Coll., 1995–2006. *Publications:* Reinventing the Wheel: women and ministry in English Baptist history, 1997; The Flesh and the Feminine: gender and theology in the writings of Caspar Schwenckfeld, 2007; (jtly) On Being the Church, 2008; (ed jtly) Questions of Identity: studies in honour of Brian Haymes, 2011. *Recreations:* reading, live theatre, watching Rugby, wine, being bemused at being in Who's Who, cross-stitch. *Address:* Bloomsbury Central Baptist Church, 235 Shaftesbury Avenue, WC2H 8EP. *T:* (020) 7240 0544, *Fax:* (020) 7836 6843.

GOULDEN, Sir (Peter) John, GCMG 2001 (KCMG 1996; CMG 1989); PhD; HM Diplomatic Service, retired; *b* 21 Feb. 1941; *s* of George Herbert Goulden and Doris Goulden; *m* 1962, Diana Margaret Elizabeth Waite; one *s* one *d*. *Educ:* King Edward VII Sch., Sheffield; Queen's Coll., Oxford (BA 1st Cl. Hons History, 1962); Durham Univ. (PhD Music 2013). HM Diplomatic Service, 1962–2001: Ankara, 1963–67; Manila, 1969–70; Dublin, 1976–79; Head of Personnel Services Dept, 1980–82; Head of News Dept, FCO, 1982–84; Counsellor and Hd of Chancery, Office of the UK Permt Rep. to EEC, Brussels, 1984–87; Asst Under-Sec. of State, FCO, 1988–92; Ambassador to Turkey, 1992–95; Ambassador and UK Perm. Rep. to N Atlantic Council and to Perm. Council of WEU, 1995–2001. *Recreations:* music, theatre, opera, family.

GOULDER, Catharine Anne O.; *see* Otton-Goulder.

GOULDING, Jeremy Wynne Ruthven, MA; Headmaster, Shrewsbury School, 2001–10; *b* 29 Aug. 1950; *s* of Denis Arthur and Doreen Daphne Goulding; *m* 1974, Isobel Mary Fisher; two *s* two *d*. *Educ:* Becket Sch., Nottingham; Magdalen Coll., Oxford (MA, PGCE). Asst

Master and Head of Divinity, Abingdon Sch., 1974–78; Head of Divinity, 1978–83, and Housemaster, Oldham's Hall, 1983–89, Shrewsbury Sch.; Headmaster: Prior Park Coll., 1989–96; Haberdashers' Aske's Sch., 1996–2001. Freeman, 2001, Liveryman, 2012–, Haberdashers' Co. *Recreations:* music-making, hill-walking. *Address:* 2 Chalford Lane, Chipping Norton, Oxon OX7 5GG.

GOULDING, Very Rev. June; *see* Osborne, Very Rev. J.

GOULDING, Sir Lingard; *see* Goulding, Sir W. L. W.

GOULDING, Paul Anthony; QC 2000; *b* 24 May 1960; second *s* of Byron and Audrey Goulding; *m* 1984, June Osborne (*see* Very Rev. J. Osborne); one *s* one *d.* *Educ:* Latymer Sch.; St Edmund Hall, Oxford (BA 1st Cl. Jurisprudence 1981; BCL 1982; MA). Tutor in Law, St Edmund Hall, Oxford, 1982–84; called to the Bar, Middle Temple, 1984, Bencher, 2011; practising barrister, 1985–. Chm., 1998–2000, Vice-Pres., 2000–04, Employment Lawyers Assoc.; Member: Mgt Cttee, Bar Pro Bono Unit, 2000–03; Mgt Bd, European Employment Lawyers Assoc., 2001–05; Specialist Mem., FA Judicial Panel, 2008–. *Publications:* European Employment Law and the UK, 2001; Employee Competition: covenants, confidentiality, and garden leave, 2007, 2nd edn 2011. *Recreations:* football, golf, opera, ballet. *Address:* Blackstone Chambers, Blackstone House, Temple, EC4Y 9BW. *T:* (020) 7583 1770. *Club:* Reform.

GOULDING, Sir (William) Lingard (Walter), 4th Bt *cr* 1904; Headmaster of Headfort Preparatory School, 1977–2000; *b* 11 July 1940; *s* of Sir (William) Basil Goulding, 3rd Bt, and Valerie Hamilton (Senator, Seanad Éireann), *o d* of 1st Viscount Monckton of Brenchley, PC, GCVO, KCMG, MC, QC; *S* father, 1982, but his name does not appear on the Official Roll of the Baronetage. *Educ:* Ludgrove; Winchester College; Trinity College, Dublin (BA, HDipEd). Computer studies for Zinc Corporation and Sulphide Corporation, Conzinc Rio Tinto of Australia, 1963–66; Systems Analyst, Goulding Fertilisers Ltd, 1966–67; Manager and European Sales Officer for Rionore, modern Irish jewellery company, 1968–69; Racing Driver, formulae 5000, 3 and 2, 1967–71; Assistant Master: Brook House School, 1970–74; Headfort School (IAPS prep. school), 1974–76. *Publications:* Your Children are not Your Children: the story of Headfort School, 2012. *Recreations:* squash, cricket, running, bicycling, tennis, music, reading, computers. *Heir: b* Timothy Adam Goulding [*b* 15 May 1945; *m* 1971, Patricia Mohan]. *Address:* The Habitaunce, Headfort Estate, Kells, Co. Meath, Ireland. *T:* (46) 49952.

GOULDSBROUGH, Catherine Mary; *see* Newman, C. M.

GOULTY, Alan Fletcher, CMG 1998; HM Diplomatic Service, retired; Ambassador to Tunisia, 2004–08; *b* 2 July 1947; *s* of late Anthony Edmund Rivers Goulty and Maisie Oliphant Goulty (*née* Stein); *m* 1983, Lillian Craig Harris, OBE; one *s* by former marr. *Educ:* Bootham School, York; Corpus Christi College, Oxford (MA 1972). FCO 1968; MECAS, 1969–71; Beirut, 1971–72; Khartoum, 1972–75; FCO, 1975–77; Cabinet Office, 1977–80; Washington, 1981–85; FCO, 1985–90; Counsellor, 1987; Head of Near East and N Africa Dept, 1987–90; Dep. Head of Mission, Cairo, 1990–95; Ambassador to Sudan, 1995–99; Fellow, Weatherhead Center for Internat. Affairs, Harvard Univ., 1999–2000; Dir, Middle East and N Africa, FCO, 2000–02; UK Special Rep. for Sudan, 2002–04, for Darfur, 2005–06. Sen. Scholar, 2009–13, Global Fellow, 2013–, Woodrow Wilson Internat. Center for Scholars, Washington, DC; Adjunct Prof., Georgetown Univ., 2010–11. Cross of St Augustine, Lambeth, 2002. Grand Cordon du Wissam Alaouite (Morocco), 1987. *Recreations:* Real tennis, chess, bird-watching, gardening. *Clubs:* Travellers, Royal Over-Seas League, MCC.

GOURDAULT-MONTAGNE, Maurice, Hon. CMG 2004; Hon. LVO 1992; Ambassador of France to China, since 2014; *b* Paris, 16 Nov. 1953; *s* of Col Jean Gourdault-Montagne and Colette Nelly Bastide; *m* 1980, Soline de Courrèges d'Agnos; two *s* three *d.* *Educ:* Institut d'Études Politiques, Paris (MA 1975); Faculté de Droit, Paris II (MA 1976); Institut Nat. des Langues et Civilisations Orientales (MA 1977; Dip. Hindi and Urdu 1977). Joined Min. of Foreign Affairs, 1978; Indian Desk, 1978–81; First Sec., New Delhi, 1981–83; Pvte Sec. to Sec. Gen., 1983–86; Advr to Foreign Minister for Parlt and Press, 1986–88; Counsellor, Bonn, 1988–91; Dep., then Actg Spokesman, Min. of Foreign Affairs, 1991–93; Dep. Principal Sec. to the Foreign Minister, 1993–95; Principal Sec., Head of Prime Minister's Office, 1995–97; Ambassador to Japan, 1998–2002; Sen. Diplomatic Advr to President of France and G8 Sherpa, 2002–07; Ambassador: to the Court of St James's, 2007–11; to Germany, 2011–14. Chevalier de l'Ordre national du Mérite, 1998; Officier de la Légion d'Honneur, 2010. *Recreations:* music (opera), history, linguistics, hiking and mountaineering. *Address:* Embassy of France, Faguo Zhuhua Dashiguan, 60 Tianze Lu, 100600 Beijing, China.

GOURGEON, Pierre-Henri; President, 1998–2011 and Chief Executive Officer, 2009–11, Air France (Chief Operating Officer, 1998–2008); President and Chief Executive Officer, Air France-KLM, 2009–11 (Deputy Chief Executive Officer, 2004–08); *b* 28 April 1946; *s* of Henri Gourgeon and Hélène (*née* Deiziani); *m* 1969, Mireille Blanc; one *s* one *d.* *Educ:* Lycée Gautier à Alger, Algeria; Lycée Louis-le-Grand, Paris; Ecole polytechnique, Paris; Ecole nationale supérieure de l'aéronautique; California Inst. of Technol. (MSc). Fighter pilot, French Air Force; engrg posts in aeronautical tech. and prodn depts, MoD, 1971–81; Mem., Prime Minister's staff, 1981–83; Special Tech. Advr to Minister of Labour and Vocational Trng, 1984; Vice-Pres. i/c mil. progs, Soc. nationale d'études et de constructions de moteurs d'avions, 1985–88; Special Advr to Minister of Transport, Equipt and Housing, 1988–90; Dir Gen., Civil Aviation Authorities, 1990–93; Pres., Eur. Civil Aviation Conf., 1993; Air France Group, 1993–2011: Chairman: and CEO, Servair Gp, 1993–96; and CEO, Esterel, 1996–97; Amadeus Internat., 1997–2002; Exec. Vice-Pres. for Corporate Develt and Internat. Affairs, 1997–98. Officier: Ordre national du Mérite; de la Légion d'honneur. *Recreations:* flying, skiing.

GOURGEY, Alan; QC 2003; *b* 27 Oct. 1961; *s* of Zaki and Vilma Gourgey; *m* 1987, Rosalynd Samuels; two *s* one *d.* *Educ:* Epsom Coll.; Bristol Univ. (LLB Hons); Inns of Court Sch. of Law. Called to the Bar, Lincoln's Inn, 1984; in practice, specialising in commercial litigation. *Recreations:* 5-a-side football, golf, Daf Yomi, my family. *Address:* 11 Stone Buildings, Lincoln's Inn, WC2A 3TG. *T:* (020) 7831 6381, *Fax:* (020) 7831 2575. *E:* gourgey@11sb.com.

GOURIET, Gerald William; QC 2006; *b* 31 March 1947; *s* of Geoffrey George Gouriet, CBE and Annie Wallace (*née* Campbell). *Educ:* Royal Coll. of Music (BMus). Called to the Bar, Inner Temple, 1974; in practice at the Bar, 1974–; writing film music, Hollywood, 1991–99: Madame Sousatzka, 1988; A Question of Attribution, 1992; The Innocent, 1994; The Substitute, 1996. *Recreations:* music, film, theatre. *Address:* Francis Taylor Building, Inner Temple, EC4Y 7BY. *T:* (020) 7735 6123. *Clubs:* Travellers, Reform.

GOURLAY, Robert Martin, (Robin); Chairman, awg (formerly Anglian Water) plc, 1994–2003; *b* 21 April 1939; *s* of late Cleland Gourlay and Janice (*née* Martin); *m* 1971, Rosemary Puckle Cooper; one *s* two *d.* *Educ:* Sedbergh Sch.; St Andrews Univ. (BSc). Joined BP, 1958: Gen. Manager, BP of Greece, 1970–74; European Finance and Planning Co-ordinator, 1975–77; Asst Gen. Manager, Corporate Planning, 1978–79; Gen. Manager, Public Affairs, 1979–83; BP Australia: Dir, Refining and Marketing, 1983–86; Chief Exec., 1986–90; Chm., BP PNG, 1986–90; Dir, BP NZ, 1988–90; Chief Exec., BP Nutrition, 1990–94. Chairman: Rugby Gp plc, 1994–2000 (non-exec. Dir, 1994–96); Fundamental Data, 2000–08; Director: Beazer Gp (formerly Beazer Homes) plc, 1995–2001; Astec (BSR) plc, 1996–99. Bd Mem., Australia Staff Coll., Mt Eliza, 1986–90; Chm., BITC, Victoria, 1988–90. Mem. Council, WaterAid, 1995–2002; Chm., Meath Epilepsy Trust, 2004–14. Gov., Sedbergh Sch., 2002–09. *Recreations:* music, gardening, tennis, Greece and Greek affairs. *Club:* Boodle's.

GOURLAY, Sir Simon (Alexander), Kt 1989; President, National Farmers' Union, 1986–91; *b* 15 July 1934; *s* of David and Helga Gourlay; *m* 1st, 1956, Sally Garman; one *s*; 2nd, 1967, Caroline Mary Clegg; three *s.* *Educ:* Winchester; Royal Agricultural College. National Service, Commission 16th/5th Lancers, 1954–55. Farm manager, Cheshire, 1956–58; started farming on own account at Knighton, 1958; Man. Dir, Maryvale Farm Construction Ltd, 1977–85; Dir, Agricl Mortgage Corp., 1991–2002; Vice Chm., Hereford HA, 1996–2000. Chm., BFREM Ltd, 2000–01; Dir, Britannica Fare Ltd, 2000–03. Chm., Guild of Conservation Grade Producers, 1992–2004. Gov., Harper Adams Agricl Coll., 1992–99. *Recreations:* gardening, music, hill walking. *Address:* Hill House Farm, Knighton, Powys LD7 1NA. *T:* (01547) 528542.

GOURLEY, Prof. Brenda Mary; higher education consultant and coach; Vice-Chancellor and President, Open University, 2002–09, now Emeritus; *b* 1 Dec. 1943; *d* of William and Irene Elliott; *m* 1966, James Ednie Gourley; three *s* one *d.* *Educ:* Univ. of Witwatersrand (Cert. Theory of Accountancy); Univ. of S Africa (MBL). Professional Chartered Accountant; Dep. Vice-Chancellor, 1988–93, Vice-Chancellor and Principal, 1994–2001, Univ. of Natal. Non-exec. Dir, SAGE Publications, 2006–11; Ind. non-exec. Dir, AdvTech Ltd, 2008–; Dir, Internat. Assoc. for Digital Publishing, 2009–. Member: Bd, ACU, 1997–2009 (Chm., 1996–97, 2007–09); Bd, Internat. Assoc. of Univs, 2000–08; Unesco Bd of Educn, 2005–06; Bd, Talloires Network, 2007–13 (Mem., Steering Cttee, 2005–11); Bd, Nat. Inst. of Adult Continuing Educn, 2009–11; Council, Univ. of Brighton, 2011–15; Bd, City and Guilds Inst., 2011–15. Trustee, Royal Anniversary Trust, 2011–; Trustee and Chair, Council for Educn in Commonwealth, 2013–. Gov., Univ. of the World, 2012– (Chair). FCGI 2008. Hon. Fellow: Open Univ. of Israel, 2008; Commonwealth of Learning, 2008; Open Univ., 2011; Hon. LLD Nottingham, 1997; Hon. DHL Richmond, Amer. Internat. Univ. in London, 2004; Hon. DEd: Abertay Dundee, 2004; Witwatersrand, 2013; Hon. DPhil: Allama Iqbal, 2007; SA, 2011; Gloucestershire, 2011; Hon. Dr: Québec à Montreal, 2007; Open Univ. of Netherlands, 2009; Open Univ. of Catalonia, 2011; Hon. DCom Pretoria, 2008. Symon's Medal, Assoc. of Commonwealth Univs, 2008; Ind. Prize of Excellence, Internat. Council for Distance Educn, 2008; UK Internat. Public Servant of the Year and Outstanding Achiever of the Year, Women in Public Life Initiative, 2009; Outstanding Educator Award, Univ. of S Africa, 2014. *Publications:* Dancing with History: a cautionary tale, 2010; (contrib.) Turning the University Upside Down: actions for the future, 2011; (contrib.) Higher Education and Civic Engagement, 2012; contrib. The Independent, THES etc. *Recreations:* reading, writing, public speaking, gardening. *Address:* 88 Wayland Avenue, Brighton, E Sussex BN1 5JN. *T:* (01273) 509791. *W:* brendagourley.com.

GOVE, Rt Hon. Michael (Andrew); PC 2010; MP (C) Surrey Heath, since 2005; Lord Chancellor and Secretary of State for Justice, since 2015; *b* 26 Aug. 1967; *s* of Ernest and Christine Gove; *m* 2001, Sarah Vine; one *s* one *d.* *Educ:* Robert Gordon's Coll., Aberdeen; Lady Margaret Hall, Oxford (BA). Reporter, Aberdeen Press and Jl, 1989; researcher/reporter, Scottish TV, 1990–91; reporter, BBC News and Current Affairs, 1991–95; editor, 1995–2005, writer, 1995–2010, The Times. Sec. of State for Educn, 2010–14; Parly Sec. to HM Treasury (Govt Chief Whip), 2014–15. *Publications:* Michael Portillo, 1995; The Price of Peace: a study of the Northern Ireland peace process, 2000; Celsius 7/7, 2006. *Address:* House of Commons, SW1A 0AA. *T:* (020) 7219 3000.

GOVENDER, Very Rev. Rogers Morgan; Dean of Manchester, since 2006; *b* 29 June 1960; *s* of Joseph and Sheila Govender; *m* 1985, Celia; one *s* one *d.* *Educ:* St Paul's Coll., Grahamstown, RSA (DipTh 1985); Univ. of Natal (BTh 1997). Ordained deacon, 1985, priest, 1986; Curate, Christ Church, Overport, S Africa, 1985–87; Rector: St Mary's, Greyville, Durban, SA, 1988–93; St Matthew's, Hayfields, Pietermaritzburg, 1993–97; Archdeacon, Pietermaritzburg, 1997–99; Rector, St Thomas, Berea, Durban, 1999–2000; Priest-in-charge, Christ Church, Didsbury, Manchester, 2000–06; Area Dean, Withington, 2003–06. *Recreations:* fishing, walking, reading, listening to music (esp. rock, classical and folk). *Address:* 1 Booth-Clibborn Court, Park Lane, Salford M7 4PJ. *T:* (0161) 833 2220. *E:* dean@manchestercathedral.org.

GOVENDIR, Ian John; business coach, since 2006; Founder, 2009, and Chief Executive Officer, since 2014, Aids Orphan UK Trust (Chairman, 2009–14); *b* 5 April 1960; *s* of Philip Govendir and Eve Karis Govendir (*née* Cohen). *Educ:* City of London Poly. (HND (Dist.) Business and Finance); Univ. of Lancaster (MA Mktg). MCIM 1990; MInstF 1992. Asst Product Manager, then Showroom Manager, Sony UK Ltd, 1979–83; Direct Marketing Manager, Bull Computers, 1988–92; Head of Direct Marketing/Fundraising, BRCS, 1992–94; Chief Exec., British Lung Foundn, 1994–96; marketing and fundraising consultant, Ian Govendir Marketing, 1997–2000; Marketing Manager, Jewish Care, 2000–02; Chief Exec., Complementary Health Trust, 2002–03; Head of Fundraising, Carers UK, 2003–04; on sabbatical, travelling the world, Sri Lanka tsunami relief, 2004–05; life coach, 2006–; Hd of Big Gifts and Legacies, then of Develt, National Deaf Children's Soc. and Deaf Child Worldwide, 2007–09; Hd of Individual Giving, ABF The Soldiers' Charity, 2010. Part-time Lectr in Marketing, London Guildhall Univ., 1992–95; Fellow, and Lectr in strategic mkting and voluntary sector mgt, MSc prog., South Bank Univ., 2007–. Mem., CSCLeaders progs, 2015–. Sec., UK Coalition Trust, 1996–97; Member, Board: Cara, 2007– (Treas., 2011–12; Chm., 2012–); Home Live Art, 2009–12; Trustee: Jewish AIDS Trust, 1998–2003; Stop Aids, 2000–; UK Consortium on AIDS and Internat. Develt, 2011–; Royal Commonwealth Soc., 2012–15. Interim Dir, Commonwealth Business Council, 2013. FRSA 1996. Halifax Giving Extra Award, 2015. *Recreations:* swimming, travel, cooking, gardening, preservation of national heritage, such as National Trust, architecture old and new, effect of religions on society, Middle Eastern politics, digital photography, interested in what is happening with the fight against AIDS and involved with a number of grass roots orgns. *E:* ian@aidsorphan.net.

GOVETT, William John Romaine; *b* 11 Aug. 1937; *s* of John Romaine Govett and Angela Mostyn (*née* Pritchard); *m* 1st, Mary Hays; two *s* one *d*; 2nd, Penelope Irwin; one *d*; 3rd, 1994, Jacqueline de Brabant. *Educ:* Sandroyd; Gordonstoun. National Service, commnd Royal Scots Greys, 1956–58. Joined John Govett & Co. Ltd, 1961; Chm., 1974–86; Dep. Chm., 1986–90. Director: Legal & General Gp, 1972–96; Govett Oriental Investment Trust, 1972–98; Govett Strategic Investment Trust, 1975–98; Scottish Eastern Investment Trust, 1977–98; Govett Amer. Smaller Cos Trust (formerly Govett Atlantic Investment Trust), 1979–98; Union Jack Oil Co., 1981–94; 3i (formerly Investors in Industry), 1984–98; Coal Investment Nominees NCB Pension Fund, 1985–96; Ranger Oil (UK), 1988–95; Ranger Oil (N Sea), 1995–97; Halifax Financial Services (Hldgs), 1998–2002; Halifax Life, 1998–2002; Halifax Unit Trust Mgt, 1998–2002; Halifax Fund Mgt, 1998–2002; Insight Investment Mgt (formerly Clerical and Medical Investment Mgt) Ltd, 2002–. Chairman: Hungarian Investment Co., 1990–98; 3i Smaller Quoted Cos Trust, 1996–2006; Govett Mexican Horizons Investment Co. Ltd, 1991–96. Advr, Mineworkers' Pension Scheme, 1996–2003. Trustee: NACF, 1985–2008; Tate Gall., 1988–93. *Recreations:* modern art, fishing.

GOW, David James, CBE 2014; FREng; Head, Smart Services, NHS Lothian, since 2009; *b* Dumfries, 15 Jan. 1957; *s* of James Gow and Effie Gow; *m* 2004, Janet Brunton. *Educ:* Annan Acad., Dumfriesshire; Univ. of Edinburgh (BSc Hons); Queen Margaret Univ. (Postgrad. Dip.). CEng 1995; CSci 2004; FIPEM 2009; FREng 2010. Develt Engr, Electro-Optics Gp, Ferranti, Scotland, 1980–81; Res. Associate, Univ. of Edinburgh, 1981–84; NHS Lothian,

1984–: Dir, Rehabilitation Engrg Services, 1993–2009; on pt-time secondment as CEO, Touch Emas Ltd, 2002–04, Dir of Res. and Technol., Touch Bionics, 2004–09. FRSA. MacRobert Award, RAEng, 2008. *Publications:* papers in various jls and patents. *Recreations:* football (watching, videoing and archiving Queen of the South Football Club), cricket, music. *Address:* 33 Fox Spring Rise, Edinburgh EH10 6NE. *T:* (0131) 445 2450. *E:* David.Gow@blueyonder.co.uk; Smart Centre, Astley Ainslie Hospital, 133 Grange Loan, Edinburgh EH9 2HL.

GOW, Dame Jane; *see* Whiteley, Dame J. E.

GOW, John Stobie, PhD; CChem, FRSC; FRSE 1978; Secretary-General, Royal Society of Chemistry, 1986–93; *b* 12 April 1933; *s* of David Gow and Anne Scott; *m* 1955, Elizabeth Henderson; three *s*. *Educ:* Alloa Acad.; Univ. of St Andrews (BSc, PhD). Res. Chemist, ICI, Billingham, 1958; Prodn Man., Chem. Co. of Malaysia, 1966–68; ICI: Res. Man., Agric. Div., 1968–72; Gen. Man. (Catalysts), Agric. Div., 1972–74; Res. Dir, Organics, 1974–79; Dep. Chm., Organics, 1979–84; Man. Dir, Speciality Chemicals, 1984–86. Assessor, SERC, 1988–94; Sec., CSTI, 1995–2001; Chief Exec., Sci. Council, 2001–02; Dir, Sci., Engrg and Manufacturing Technol. Assoc., 2002–05. FRSA 1980. *Publications:* papers and patents in Fertilizer Technology and Biotechnology. *Recreations:* choral music, golf. *Address:* 19 Longcroft Avenue, Harpenden, Herts AL5 2RD. *T:* (01582) 764889.

GOW, Roderick Charles, OBE 2002; Founder, Canongate Partners Ltd, since 2011; *b* 9 Sept. 1947; *s* of Gen. Sir (James) Michael Gow, GCB; *m* 1st, 1977, Anne Bayart (*d* 2000); two *s*; 2nd, 2001, April Riddle. *Educ:* Winchester Coll.; Trinity Coll., Cambridge (BA 1970, MA 1972). ACIB 1982. Capt., Scots Guards, NW Germany, NI and Belgium, 1966–78; ADC to Chm., Mil. Cttee, NATO, Brussels, 1975–77; Instructor, RMA, Sandhurst, 1977–78. Barclays Bank, London and NY, 1978–83 (Vice-Pres., to 1983); Russell Reynolds Associates, London, 1983–91 (Man. Dir, UK, then Man. Dir, Internat., 1986–91); Chief Exec., GKR Gp, London, 1991–93, NY, 1993–95; Exec. Vice Pres. and Co-Hd, Global Financial Services Practice, NY, LAI Worldwide, later TMP, 1995–2000; Chm., Americas, later Dep. Chm., Worldwide, Amrop Internat., 1995–99; Odgers, Ray & Berndtson: London Dir, 2000–02; Chm. Bd, Practice and Financial Services Practice, 2000–02; Founder and Chm., Gow & Partners Gp, later Gow & Partners World Team, 2002–09; Chief Exec., Asia House, 2010–11; Chm. and Founder, Asia Scotland Inst., 2012–. Chm., Adv. Bd, Positive Moves Consulting (UK) Ltd, 2011–; Vice-Chairman: Cubitt Consulting, 2011–; Internat. Prudent Capital Partners, 2012–. Chm., Action Resource Centre, 1991–93. Chm., British American Chamber of Commerce of NY and London, 1999–2001; Chm., Pres. and Vice-Pres., British American Business Council, 2001–03; Mem. Bd, British American Business, 2006. Chm. and Founder, Asia Scotland Inst., 2012–. Mem., Adv. Council, Prince of Wales Business Trust, 2002–03. Mem., Business Adv. Council, Saïd Business Sch., Oxford Univ., 2006–. Mem. Council, Brookings Instn, 2008–09. Member: Adv. Council, LSO (Co-Chm., Amer. Foundn), 2001–09; Adv. Bd, Welsh Nat. Opera, 2012–; Chm., Commonwealth Youth Orch., 2011–12. Mem., Guild of Internat. Bankers, 2001–09. FIPD; FRSA. Fellow, Foreign Policy Assoc., 1994–2000. Mem., Royal Co. of Archers, Queen's Bodyguard for Scotland, 1982–. *Recreations:* shooting, sailing, music, reading. *Address:* 12/1 Cumberland Street, Edinburgh EH3 6SA. *E:* roddy.gow@canongatepartners.com. *Clubs:* Brooks's, Pratt's, Cavalry and Guards; Indian Harbor Yacht (Greenwich, CT); Leash (NYC).

GOWAN, David John, CMG 2005; HM Diplomatic Service, retired; *b* 11 Feb. 1949; *s* of late Prof. Ivor Lyn Gowan and of Gwendoline Alice Gowan (*née* Pearce); *m* 1975, Marna Irene Williams; two *s*. *Educ:* Nottingham High Sch.; Ardwyn Grammar Sch., Aberystwyth; Balliol Coll., Oxford (MA Eng. Lang. and Lit.). Asst Principal, MoD, 1970–73; Home CS, 1973–75; joined HM Diplomatic Service, 1975: Second Sec., FCO, 1975–76; Russian lang. trng, 1976–77; Second, then First Sec., Moscow, 1977–80; First Sec., FCO, 1981–85; Hd of Chancery and Consul, Brasilia, 1985–88; on secondment to Cabinet Office, 1988–89; Asst Hd, Soviet Dept, FCO, 1989–90; on secondment, as Counsellor, Cabinet Office, 1990–91; Counsellor (Commercial and Know How Fund), Moscow, 1992–95; Counsellor and Dep. Hd of Mission, Helsinki, 1995–99; Counsellor, FCO, 1999; Sen. Associate Mem., St Antony's Coll., Oxford, 1999–2000; Minister, Moscow, 2000–03; Ambassador to Serbia and Montenegro, 2003–06. Guest Mem., St Antony's Coll., Oxford, 2007–10; Hon. Sen. Res. Fellow, Univ. of Birmingham, 2008–11. Chm., Russian Booker Cttee, 2012–15. Mem. Council, Keston Inst., 2009–. Mem., Bishop's Council, 2007–, Synod, 2008–, Dio. in Europe. *Publications:* How the EU Can Help Russia, 2000. *Recreations:* reading, walking, travel, music, theatre. *Address:* 8 Blackmore Road, Malvern, Worcs WR14 1QX. *T:* (01684) 565707. *Club:* Athenæum.

GOWANS, Sir James (Learmonth), Kt 1982; CBE 1971; FRCP 1975; FRS 1963; Secretary General, Human Frontier Science Programme, Strasbourg, 1989–93; Secretary, Medical Research Council, 1977–87; *b* 7 May 1924; *s* of John Gowans and Selma Josefina Ljung; *m* 1956, Moyra Leatham; one *s* two *d*. *Educ:* Whitgift Middle Sch., Croydon; King's Coll. Hosp. Med. Sch. (MB BS (Hons) 1947; Fellow, 1979); Lincoln Coll., Oxford (BA (1st cl. Hons Physiology) 1948; MA; DPhil 1953; Hon. Fellow, 1984). MRC Exchange Scholar, Pasteur Institute, Paris, 1952–53; Research Fellow, Exeter Coll., Oxford, 1955–60 (Hon. Fellow, 1983–); Fellow, St Catherine's Coll., Oxford, 1961–87 (Hon. Fellow, 1987); Henry Dale Res. Prof. of Royal Society, 1962–77; Hon. Dir, MRC Cellular Immunology Unit, 1963–77; Dir, 1980–86, Sen. Sci. Advr, 1988–90, Celltech Ltd. Consultant: WHO Global Prog. on AIDS, 1987–88; 3i plc, 1988–92. Member: MRC, 1965–69; Adv. Bd for Res. Councils, 1977–87; Director: Charing Cross Sunley Res. Centre, 1989–91; European Initiative for Communicators of Science, Munich, 1995–99. Royal Society: Mem. Council and a Vice-Pres., 1973–75; Assessor to MRC, 1973–75. Member: Governing Council, Internat. Agency for Res. on Cancer, Lyon, 1980–87; Sci. Cttee, Fondation Louis Jeantet de Médicine, Geneva, 1984–87; Council, St Christopher's Hospice, 1987–98; Res. Progs Adv. Cttee, Nat. MS Soc., NY, 1988–90; Awards Assembly, Gen. Motors Cancer Res. Foundn, NY, 1988–90; Scientific Advr, Motor Neurone Disease Assoc., 1992–2002; Chm., Scientific Adv. Cttee, Lister Inst. of Preventive Medicine, 1994–97. Non-exec. Dir, Tavistock and Portman NHS Trust, 1994–97. Delegate, OUP, 1971–77. Trustee, Spinal Muscular Atrophy Trust, 2006–. FRSA 1994. Founder FMedSci 1998. Vis. Prof., NY Univ. Sch. of Med., 1967; Lectures: Harvey, NY, 1968; William Withering, Birmingham, 1970; Foundation, RCPath, 1970; Dunham, Harvard, 1971; Bayne-Jones, Johns Hopkins, 1973; Langdon Brown, RCP, 1980; Harveian Orator, RCP, 1987. Foreign Associate, Nat. Acad. of Scis, USA, 1985. Mem., Academia Europaea, 1991. Hon. Member: Amer. Assoc. of Immunologists; Soc. of Leukocyte Biol. Hon. ScD Yale, 1966; Hon. DSc: Chicago, 1971; Birmingham, 1978; Rochester, NY, 1987; Hon. MD: Edinburgh, 1979; Sheffield, 2000; Hon. DM Southampton, 1987; Hon. LLD Glasgow, 1988. Gairdner Foundn Award, Toronto, 1968; Paul Ehrlich Ludwig-Darmstaedter Prize, Frankfurt, 1974; Royal Medal, Royal Society, 1976; Feldberg Foundn Award, 1979; Wolf Prize in Medicine, Wolf Foundn, Israel, 1980; Medawar Prize, 1990; Galen Medal, Soc. of Apothecaries, 1991. *Publications:* articles in scientific journals. *Address:* 75 Cumnor Hill, Oxford OX2 9HX. *T:* (01865) 862304.

GOWANS, James Palmer; JP; DL; Lord Provost of Dundee and Lord-Lieutenant of the City of Dundee, 1980–84; *b* 15 Sept. 1930; *s* of Charles Gowans and Sarah Gowans (*née* Palmer); *m* 1950, Davina Barnett (*d* 2000); one *s* three *d* (and one *s* one *d* decd). *Educ:* Rockwell Secondary School, Dundee. With National Cash Register Co., Dundee, 1956–94. Elected to Dundee DC, May 1974; Mem., Dundee City Council, 1975–92. JP 1977; DL Dundee 1984. *Recreations:* golf, motoring. *Address:* 41 Dalmahoy Drive, Dundee DD2 3UT. *T:* (01382) 84918.

GOWAR, Martyn Christopher; Senior Counsel, McDermott Will & Emery UK LLP, since 2014 (Partner, 2009–14); *b* Cheam, Surrey, 11 July 1946; *s* of Thomas Welch Gowar and Maude Annie Gowar (*née* Bower); *m* 1971, Susan Mary Scotchmer; three *s*. *Educ:* King's Coll. Sch., Wimbledon; Magdalen Coll., Oxford (BA). ATII 1976, CTA (Fellow) (FTII 1981). Lawrence Graham & Co.: articled clerk, 1967; admitted as solicitor, 1970; Partner, 1973–2006; Sen. Partner, 1997–2002; Consultant, 2006–08; Consultant, Penningtons, 2008–09. Academician, 1986, Vice Pres. (Europe), 2008–, Internat. Acad. of Estate and Trust Law; Mem., Internat. Cttee, Soc. of Trusts and Estate Practitioners, 1996–; Mem., Exec. Cttee, Inst. of Advanced Legal Studies, 1998–. Chm., Succession Sub-cttee, Chartered Institute of Taxation, 2009–; Mem., Estates Business Gp, 1997–. Internat. Fellow, Amer. Coll. of Trusts and Estate Counsel, 2011–. Gov., St Paul's Cathedral Sch., 1998–2014. Chm., Ashley Family Foundn, 2010– (Trustee, 1995–); Mem., Addington Soc., 1990–. Liveryman: Glaziers' Co., 1979–; Tax Advrs' Co., 2007–. Mem., Lord's Taverners, 1988–. FRSA 1995. *Publications:* (contrib.) Trusts in Prime Jurisdictions, 2010; contribs to Soc. of Trusts and Estate Practitioners Jl, Spear's Wealth Mag. *Recreations:* golf, cricket, gardening. *Address:* McDermott Will & Emery UK LLP, Heron Tower, 110 Bishopsgate, EC2N 4AY. *T:* (020) 7577 6900, *Fax:* (020) 7577 6950. *E:* mgowar@mwe.com. *Clubs:* Naval and Military, MCC; Hankley Common Golf, Rye Golf, London Solicitors' Golfing Society.

GOWAR, Prof. Norman William; Chairman, Office of the Independent Adjudicator for Higher Education, 2003–09; Principal, Royal Holloway (Royal Holloway and Bedford New College), University of London, 1990–2000; Professor Emeritus, University of London, since 2000; *b* 7 Dec. 1940; *s* of Harold James and Constance Dawson-Gowar; *m* 1st, 1963, Diane May Parker (marr. diss.); one *s* one *d*; 2nd, 1981, Prof. Judith Margaret Greene, *d* of Lord Gordon-Walker, PC, CH. *Educ:* Sir George Monoux Grammar Sch.; City Univ. (BSc, MPhil). FIMA. English Electric Co., 1963; Lectr in Maths, City Univ., 1963; Open University: Lectr and Sen. Lectr, 1969; Prof. of Mathematics, 1983; Dir, Centre for Maths Educn, 1983; Pro-Vice-Chancellor, 1977–81; Dep. Vice-Chancellor, 1985–90; Dir, Open Coll., 1986. Vis. Fellow, Keble Coll., Oxford, 1972. Member, Council: CNAA, 1979–83; NCET, 1986–91 (Chm., Trng Cttee); Mem. Bd, CVCP, 1998–2000; Mem., Fulbright Commn, 2001–05. Chm. and Dir, Open Univ. Educational Enterprises Ltd, 1988–90. Dir, Surrey TEC, 1991–93. Mem., London Math. Soc. Governor: South Bank Univ. (formerly Polytechnic), 1992–95; UCS, 1993–2000; Rugby Sch., 1994–2004; Middlesex Univ., 2000–04; Sussex Univ., 2004–08. Mem. Council, IMA, 1993–96. FRSA. Hon. Fellow, Royal Holloway, Univ. of London, 2002. Hon. DSc City, 1994; DUniv Open, 2001. *Publications:* Mathematics for Technology: a new approach, 1968; Basic Mathematical Structures, vol. 1, 1973, vol. 2, 1974; Fourier Series, 1974; Invitation to Mathematics, 1980; articles and TV series. *Address:* 1 Prior Bolton Street, N1 2NX.

GOWDY, David Clive, CB 2001; Permanent Secretary, Department of Health, Social Services and Public Safety, Northern Ireland, 1997–2005; *b* 27 Nov. 1946; *s* of Samuel David Gowdy and Eileen Gowdy (*née* Porter); *m* 1973, Linda Doreen Traub; two *d*. *Educ:* Royal Belfast Academical Instn; Queen's Univ. Belfast (BA, MSc). Min. of Finance, NI, 1970; N Ireland Office, 1976; Exec. Dir, Industrial Develt Bd for NI 1985; Under Sec., Dept of Econ. Develt, NI, 1987; Under Sec., Dept of Health and Social Services, NI, 1990; Dir of Personnel, NICS, 1994. Vis. Prof., Univ. of Ulster, 2006–13. Chm., Unlocking Potential Project, Volunteer Now, 2009–14; Member: Bd, Belfast Charitable Soc., 2006– (Chm., 2010–13); Regl Cttee, Nat. Trust, 2008–10. *Recreations:* exercise and relaxation. *Address:* Bangor, Co. Down.

GOWENLOCK, Prof. Brian Glover, CBE 1986; PhD, DSc; FRSE; FRSC; Professor of Chemistry, 1966–90, Leverhulme Emeritus Fellow, 1990–92, Heriot-Watt University; *b* 9 Feb. 1926; *s* of Harry Hadfield Gowenlock and Hilda (*née* Glover); *m* 1953, Margaret L. Davies (*d* 2013); one *s* two *d*. *Educ:* Hulme Grammar Sch., Oldham; Univ. of Manchester (BSc, MSc, PhD). DSc Birmingham. FRIC 1966; FRSE 1968. Asst Lectr in Chemistry 1948, Lectr 1951, University Coll. of Swansea; Lectr 1955, Sen. Lectr 1964, Univ. of Birmingham; Dean, Faculty of Science, Heriot-Watt Univ., 1969–72, 1987–90. Vis. Scientist, National Res. Council, Ottawa, 1963; Erskine Vis. Fellow, Univ. of Canterbury, NZ, 1976; Hon. Res. Fellow, 1992–2002, Hon. Vis. Prof., 2002–05, Exeter Univ. Mem., UGC, 1976–85, Vice-Chm., 1983–85. Methodist local preacher, 1946–2016. *Publications:* (with Sir Harry Melville) Experimental Methods in Gas Reactions, 1964; (with James C. Blackie) First Year at the University, 1964; (with Alex Anderson) Chemistry in Heriot-Watt 1821–1991, 1998; contribs to scientific jls. *Recreation:* genealogy. *Address:* Riccarton, 5 Roselands, Sidmouth, Devon EX10 8PB. *T:* (01395) 516864.

GOWER; *see* Leveson Gower.

GOWER, David Ivon, OBE 1992; broadcaster and journalist; *b* 1 April 1957; *s* of Richard Hallam Gower and Sylvia Mary Gower (*née* Ford); *m* 1992, Thorunn Ruth Nash; two *d*. *Educ:* King's Sch., Canterbury; University Coll., London. Professional cricketer, 1975–93; Leicestershire, 1975–89; Hampshire, 1990–93; 117 Test matches for England, 1978–92; 8,231 Test runs (3rd highest for England), incl. 18 centuries; captained England 32 times, 1984–86, 1989; retired from 1st class cricket, Nov. 1993. PR consultant (cricket sponsorship), Nat. Westminster Bank, 1993–2000. BBC Cricket Commentator, 1994–99; Presenter: Gower's Cricket Monthly, BBC TV, 1995–98; David Gower's Cricket Weekly, BBC Radio 5, 1995–98; Internat. Cricket, Sky Sports, 1999–; panel mem., They Think It's All Over, BBC TV, 1996–2003. Columnist, Sunday Times, 2002–14. Hon. MA: Southampton Inst. (Nottingham Trent Univ.), 1993; Loughborough, 1994; Hon. DSc Winchester, 2010; Hon. DLitt De Montfort, 2014. Hon. Blue, Heriot-Watt Univ. *Publications:* With Time to Spare, 1979; Heroes and Contemporaries, 1983; A Right Ambition, 1986; On the Rack, 1990; Gower, The Autobiography, 1992; An Endangered Species, 2013. *Recreations:* ski-ing, safari, Cresta Run, tennis. *Address:* c/o Jon Holmes Media, 3 Wine Office Court, EC4A 3BY. *Clubs:* East India, MCC (Mem. Cttee, 2000–03), Home House, Garrick, Groucho; St Moritz Tobogganing.

GOWER, Rear Adm. John Howard James, CB 2014; OBE 1998; Assistant Chief of Defence Staff, Nuclear and Chemical, Biological, 2011–14; *b* Carshalton, 28 July 1960; *s* of late Howard Gower and of Josephine Gower (*née* Smart); *m* 1986, Diana Steven; two *s* one *d*. *Educ:* Solihull Sch.; Salford Univ. (BSc Electrical Engrg Sci. 1982). Joined RN, 1978; sea-going career, 1978–97; Submarine Commands: HMS Unicorn, 1992–94; HMS Trafalgar, 1995–97; Ministry of Defence: Naval Ops, 1997–99 (Comdr); Naval Staff, 1999–2002 (Captain); Asst Naval Attaché to USA, 2002–05; Divl Dir, Staff Coll., 2005–06; Dir Underwater Capability, MoD, 2006–08 (Cdre); Chemical, Biological, Radiological and Nuclear Policy, MoD, 2008–11. *Recreations:* poetry, cycling, refereeing football, theatre. *Club:* Royal Navy of 1765 and 1785.

GOWER, His Honour John Hugh; QC 1967; a Circuit Judge, 1972–96; a Deputy Circuit Judge, 1996–99; *b* 6 Nov. 1925; *s* of Henry John Gower, JP and Edith (*née* Brooks); *m* 1960, Shirley Mameena Darbourne (*d* 2012); one *s* one *d*. *Educ:* Skinners' Sch., Tunbridge Wells. RASC, 1945–48 (Staff Sgt). Called to the Bar, Inner Temple, 1948, Bencher, 1995; Dep. Chm., Kent QS, 1968–71; Resident and Liaison Judge of Crown Courts in E Sussex, 1986–96. Mem., Lord Chancellor's Adv. Cttee on Legal Educn and Conduct, 1991–96 (Vice-Chm., 1994–96). Chm., Kent and Sussex Area Criminal Justice Liaison Cttee, 1992–96; Pres., E Sussex Magistrates' Assoc., 1997–99 (Vice-Pres., 1986–97). Ind. Assessor, UK Govt Review of NI Criminal Justice System, 1998–2000; reviewed and reported on prosecutions conducted by Solicitor's Office of HM Customs and Excise, 2000–01. Pres., Tunbridge Wells Council

of Voluntary Service, 1974–88. Hon. Vice-Pres., Kent Council of Voluntary Service, 1971–86. Pres., Kent Assoc. of Parish Councils, 1963–71. Chm., Southdown and Eridge Hunt, 1985–91. Churchwarden, St Michael and All Angels, Withyham, 2005–07, 2009–11. Freeman, City of London (by purchase), 1960. *Recreations:* tapestry, painting. *Address:* The Coppice, Lye Green, Crowborough, E Sussex TN6 1UY.
See also P. J. de P. Gower.

GOWER, Peter John de Peauly; QC 2006; **His Honour Judge Gower;** a Circuit Judge, since 2012; *b* 30 Nov. 1960; *s* of His Honour John Hugh Gower, *qv*; *m* 1993, Emma Clout; two *s*. *Educ:* Lancing Coll.; Christ Church, Oxford (Classics Schol.; MA Juris.). Called to the Bar, Lincoln's Inn, 1985; in practice specialising in criminal and regulatory law; a Recorder, 2002–12. Standing Counsel to BIS (formerly DTI, later BERR), 1991–2006. Chm., Kent Bar Mess, 2007–10. *Recreations:* spending time with the family, reading, walking, gardening, horses, fishing. *Address:* Croydon Crown Court, The Law Courts, Altyre Road, Croydon, Surrey CR9 5AB.

GOWER ISAAC, Anthony John; *see* Isaac.

GOWERS, Andrew; Global Head of Corporate Affairs, Trafigura, since 2013; *b* 19 Oct. 1957; *s* of Michael and Anne Gowers; *m* 1982, Finola Clarke; one *s* one *d*. *Educ:* Trinity Sch., Croydon; Gonville and Caius Coll., Cambridge (MA 1980). Reuters, London, Brussels and Zurich, 1980–83; Financial Times, 1983–2005: on foreign staff, 1983–84; Agric. Corresp., 1984–85; Commodities Ed., 1985–87; ME Ed., 1987–90; Features Ed., 1990–92; Foreign Ed., 1992–94; Dep. Ed., 1994–97; Actg Ed., 1997–98; Ed.-in-Chief, FT Deutschland, 1998–2001; Editor, 2001–05; Global Co-Hd of Communications, Mkting and Brand Mgt, Lehman Brothers, 2006–08; Hd, External Relns, London Business Sch., 2008–09; Hd of Media Relns, BP plc, 2009–10; Dir, External Relns, Assoc. for Financial Mkts in Europe, 2011–13. Leader, Gowers Review of Intellectual Property, HM Treasury, 2006; Mem., Digital Britain Steering Bd, 2008–09. *Publications:* Arafat: the biography, 1990; Investing in Change: the reform of Europe's financial markets, 2012. *Recreations:* Theatre, food, wine, tennis, film, music.

GOWERS, Sir (William) Timothy, Kt 2012; PhD; FRS 1999; Rouse Ball Professor of Mathematics, University of Cambridge, since 1998; Fellow of Trinity College, Cambridge, since 1995; Royal Society 2010 Anniversary Research Professor, since 2010; *b* 20 Nov. 1963; *s* of late William Patrick Gowers and of Caroline Molesworth Gowers; *m* 1988, Emily Joanna (marr. diss. 2007), *d* of Sir Keith (Vivian) Thomas, *qv*; two *s* one *d*; *m* 2008, Julie, *d* of Alain and Sylvie Barrau; one *s* one *d*. *Educ:* Eton Coll.; Trinity Coll., Cambridge (BA; PhD 1990). Res. Fellow, Trinity Coll., Cambridge, 1989–93; Lectr, 1991–94, Reader, 1994–95, UCL; Lectr, Univ. of Cambridge, 1995–98. Hon. Fellow, UCL, 1999. Hon. DSc St Andrews, 2013. European Mathematical Soc. Prize, 1996; Fields Medal, 1998; Stefan Banach Medal, Polish Acad. of Scis, 2011. *Publications:* Mathematics: a very short introduction, 2002; (ed) The Princeton Companion to Mathematics, 2008; contrib. papers in mathematical jls. *Recreation:* jazz piano. *Address:* Department of Pure Mathematics and Mathematical Statistics, Centre for Mathematical Sciences, Wilberforce Road, Cambridge CB3 0WB. *T:* (01223) 337999.

GOWING, Nicholas Keith, (Nik); Main Presenter, BBC World News, BBC News, 2000–14 (Presenter, 1996–2000); Visiting Professor, King's College London; *b* 13 Jan. 1951; *s* of Donald James Graham Gowing and Margaret Mary Gowing (*née* Elliott); *m* 1982, Judith Wastall Venables; one *s* one *d*. *Educ:* Latymer Upper Sch.; Simon Langton Grammar Sch., Canterbury; Bristol Univ. Reporter, Evening Chronicle, Newcastle upon Tyne, 1973–74; Presenter and Reporter, Granada TV, 1974–78; joined ITN, 1978; Rome Corresp., 1979; Eastern Europe Corresp., Warsaw, 1980–83; Foreign Affairs Corresp., 1983–87, Diplomatic Corresp., 1987–89, Diplomatic Editor, 1989–96, Channel 4 News; presenter, World Debates, 1999–, Dateline London, 1999–2012, The Hub, 2010–12, BBC. Fellow, Shorenstein Center, J. F. Kennedy Sch., Harvard Univ., 1994; Vis. Fellow, Keele Univ., 1998–. Consultant: Carnegie Commn on Preventing Deadly Conflict, 1996–97; on Wars and Information Mgt, EC Humanitarian Office, 1997–98. Vice Chair and Gov., Westminster Foundn for Democracy, 1996–2005; Governor: British Assoc. for Central and Eastern Europe, 1996–2008; Ditchley Foundn, 2000–; Member: IISS 1990; Council, 1998–2004, Exec. Council, 2000–02, RIIA; Adv. Council, Wilton Park, 1998–2012; Adv. Bd, Birmingham Univ. Centre for Studies in Security and Diplomacy, 1999–2011; Cttee, Project on Justice in Times of Transition, 1999–; Steering Cttee, Konigswinter Conf., 1999–; Exec. Cttee and Council, 2005–, Adv. Council, 2011–, RUSI; Council, ODI, 2007–14; Cttee, Rory Peck Trust, 1996–2014; Trustee, Liddell Hart Archive, KCL, 2004–. Fellow, Reuters Inst., Oxford Univ., 2008–09. Hon. Dr: Exeter, 2012; Bristol, 2015. *Publications:* The Wire, 1988; The Loop, 1993; Skyful of Lies and Black Swans, 2009. *Recreations:* cycling, ski-ing, authorship, lecturing, chairing conferences. *Club:* Savile.

GOWRIE, 2nd Earl of, *cr* 1945; **Alexander Patrick Greysteil Hore-Ruthven;** PC 1984; Baron Ruthven of Gowrie, 1919; Baron Gowrie, 1935; Viscount Ruthven of Canberra, 1945; Chairman, The Magdi Yacoub Institute (formerly Harefield Research Foundation), since 2003; Director, Sotheby's Holdings Inc., 1985–98 (Chairman, Sotheby's Europe, 1987–94); *b* Dublin, 26 Nov. 1939; *er s* of late Capt. Hon. Alexander Hardinge Patrick Hore-Ruthven, Rifle Bde, and Pamela Margaret (as Viscountess Ruthven of Canberra, she *m* 1952, Major Derek Cooper, MC, The Life Guards), 2nd *d* of late Rev. A. H. Fletcher; *S* grandfather, 1955; *m* 1st, 1962, Xandra (marr. diss. 1973), *yr d* of Col R. A. G. Bingley, CVO, DSO, OBE; one *s*; 2nd, 1974, Adelheid Gräfin von der Schulenburg, *y d* of late Fritz-Dietlof, Graf von der Schulenburg. *Educ:* Eton; Balliol Coll., Oxford. Visiting Lectr, State Univ. of New York at Buffalo, 1963–64; Tutor, Harvard Univ., 1965–68; Lectr in English and American Literature, UCL, 1969–72. Fine Art consultant, 1974–79. Provost, RCA, 1986–95. Chm., Arts Council of England, 1994–98. Chairman: The Really Useful Gp, 1985–90; Development Securities, 1995–99; Fine Art Fund, 2002–. A Conservative Whip, 1971–72; Parly Rep. to UN, 1971; a Lord in Waiting (Govt Whip), 1972–74; Opposition Spokesman on Economic Affairs, 1974–79; Minister of State: Dept of Employment, 1979–81; NI Office, 1981–83 (Dep. to Sec. of State); Privy Council Office (Management and Personnel), 1983–84; Minister for the Arts, 1983–85; Chancellor, Duchy of Lancaster, 1984–85. FRSL 2003. Freeman, City of London, 1976. Picasso Medal, UNESCO, 1996. *Publications:* A Postcard from Don Giovanni, 1972; (jtly) The Genius of British Painting, 1975; (jtly) The Conservative Opportunity, 1976; (jtly) Derek Hill: an appreciation, 1987; The Domino Hymn: poems from Harefield, 2005; Third Day: new and selected poems, 2008; The Italian Visitor and Other Poems, 2013; Collected Poems, 2014. *Recreation:* Wales. *Heir: s* Viscount Ruthven of Canberra, *qv*. *Address:* The Magdi Yacoub Institute, Heart Science Centre, Harefield, Middlesex UB9 6JH.
See also Hon. M. W. M. K. H. Ruthven.

GOY, David John Lister; QC 1991; *b* 11 May 1949; *s* of late Rev. Leslie Goy and Joan Goy; *m* 1970, Jennifer Anne Symington; three *s*. *Educ:* Haberdashers' Aske's School, Elstree; King's College London. Called to the Bar, Middle Temple, 1973, Bencher, 2007. Chm., Revenue Bar Assoc., 2005–08. *Publications:* VAT on Property, 1989, 2nd edn 1993. *Recreation:* golf and other sports. *Address:* Gray's Inn Tax Chambers, 36 Queen Street, EC4R 1BN. *T:* (020) 7242 2642.

GOYMER, Andrew Alfred; His Honour Judge Goymer; a Circuit Judge, since 1999; *b* 28 July 1947; *s* of late Richard Kirby Goymer and Betty Eileen Goymer (*née* Thompson); *m* 1972, Diana Mary, *d* of late Robert Harry Shipway, MBE and of Sheila Mary Shipway; one *s* one *d*. *Educ:* Dulwich Coll.; Pembroke Coll., Oxford (Hull Schol.; MA). Called to the Bar, Gray's Inn, 1970 (Gerald Moody Entrance Schol., Holker Sen. Exhibnr, Arden Atkin and Mould Prizeman); practised, S Eastern Circuit, 1972–99; admitted to NSW Bar, 1988; Asst Recorder, 1987–91; Recorder, 1991–99. Mem. Cttee, 2009–, Asst Sec., 2012–, Chm., Criminal Sub-Cttee, 2014–, Council of HM Circuit Judges. Mem., Forensic Sci. Adv. Council, 2007–14. *Address:* Southwark Crown Court, 1 English Grounds, SE1 2HU. *T:* (020) 7522 7200.

GOZNEY, Sir Richard Hugh Turton, KCMG 2006 (CMG 1993); CVO 2009; HM Diplomatic Service, retired; Governor and Commander-in-Chief of Bermuda, 2007–12; *b* 21 July 1951; *s* of Thomas Leonard Gozney and Elizabeth Margaret Lilian Gozney (*née* Gardiner); *m* 1982, Diana Edwina Baird; two *s*. *Educ:* Magdalen Coll. Sch., Oxford; St Edmund Hall, Oxford (BA Hons Geol. 1973). Teacher, Tom Mboya Rusinga Secondary Sch., Kenya, 1970; joined FO, 1973; Jakarta, 1974–78; Buenos Aires, 1978–81; FCO, 1981–84; Hd of Chancery, Madrid, 1984–88; Asst Private Sec., later Private Sec., to Foreign Sec., FCO, 1989–93; High Comr, Swaziland, 1993–96; Head of Security Policy Dept, FCO, 1996–97; Chief of Assessments Staff, Jt Intelligence Orgn, Cabinet Office, 1998–2000; Ambassador, Indonesia, 2000–04; High Comr, Nigeria, 2004–07, and Ambassador (non-resident) to Benin, 2005–07, and to Equatorial Guinea, 2006–07. Strategic Advr, Green Park Worldwide; Consultant, Guardian Global Resources. Non-exec. Dir, Asia Resource Minerals plc, 2013–. Vice-Chm., Bermuda Soc., 2012–. Trustee, Orangutan Foundn, 2014–. KStJ 2010. *Publications:* Gibraltar and the EC, 1993; Birds on the Abuja Golf Course, 2007. *Recreations:* bird-watching, walking, sailing, gardening. *Address:* The Old House, North Street, Langham, Holt, Norfolk NR25 7DG; Flat 11, 230 Ferndale Road, SW9 8AT.

GRAAFF, Sir De Villiers, 4th Bt *cr* 1911, of Cape Town; Managing Director, Degrendel Wines (Pty) Ltd, since 2015; *b* Cape Town, 16 July 1970; *s* of Sir David de Villiers Graaf, 3rd Bt and of Winifred Sally Melinda Graaf (*née* Williams); *S* father, 2015; *m* 2000, Gaedry Laurian Kriel; three *s* one *d*. *Educ:* Diocesan Coll., Cape Town; Univ. of Stellenbosch (BAgricAdmin); Univ. of Colorado. Director: Graaff Fruit, 1995; Delecta Fruit, 2000; Waitrose Foundation, 2007; Graaffs Trust, 1995; Milnerton Estates, 2015. *Recreations:* golf, fishing. *Heir: s* David Peter Berkeley de Villiers Graaff, *b* 1 Feb. 2003. *Address:* Degrendel Estate, Plattekloof Road, Panorama, 7500 Western Cape, South Africa. *T:* 5586280, *Fax:* 5586280. *E:* devilliers@degrendel.co.za.

GRABBE, Dr Heather Mary Claire; Director, Open Society European Policy Institute (formerly Open Society Institute - Brussels), since 2009; *b* Pasadena, Calif, 30 Aug. 1970; *m* 1994, Prof. Andrew Ian Wilson, *qv* (marr. diss.); two *d*. *Educ:* Somerville Coll., Oxford (BA Hons PPE 1991); Univ. of Birmingham (PhD 2002). Res. Fellow, Eur. Prog., RIIA, 1996–97; Dep. Dir, Centre for Eur. Reform, 2000–04; Sen. Advr to EU Enlargement Comr, Olli Rehn, 2004–09. Vis. Fellow, Eur. Inst., LSE, 2004–. Member: Eur. Council on Foreign Relns, 2008–; Adv. Bd, Centre for Eur. Reform, 2011–. Mem., Sen. Common Room, St Antony's Coll., Oxford 2004–. *Publications:* The EU's Transformative Power: Europeanisation through conditionality in Central and Eastern Europe, 2006; contrib. Jl Eur. Public Policy, Hommes & Migrations, Internat. Politik, Jl Common Mkt Studies Annual Rev., Internat. Spectator. *Address:* Open Society European Policy Institute, Rue d'Idalie 9–13, 1050 Brussels, Belgium. *T:* (2) 5054646, *Fax:* (2) 5024646. *E:* heather.grabbe@opensocietyfoundations.org.

GRABINER, family name of **Baron Grabiner**.

GRABINER, Baron *cr* 1999 (Life Peer), of Aldwych in the City of Westminster; **Anthony Stephen Grabiner;** QC 1981; Master of Clare College, Cambridge, since 2014; a Deputy High Court Judge, since 1994; *b* 21 March 1945; *e s* of late Ralph Grabiner and Freda Grabiner (*née* Cohen); *m* 1983, Jane, *er d* of late Dr Benjamin Portnoy, TD, JP, MD, PhD, FRCP, Hale, Cheshire; three *s* one *d*. *Educ:* Central Foundn Boys' Grammar Sch., London, EC2; LSE, Univ. of London (LLB 1st Cl. Hons 1966, LLM with Distinction 1967; Hon. Fellow, 2009). Lincoln's Inn: Hardwicke Scholar, 1966; called to the Bar, 1968; Droop Scholar, 1968; Bencher, 1989; Treas., 2013–14. Standing Jun. Counsel to Dept of Trade, Export Credits Guarantee Dept, 1976–81; Jun. Counsel to the Crown, 1978–81; a Recorder, 1990–99. Mem., Financial Markets Law Cttee, Bank of England, 2002–06. Non-executive Director: Next plc, 2002; Goldman Sachs Internat., 2015–; non-exec. Chm., Arcadia Gp, 2002–. Chm., Ct of Govs, LSE, 1998–2007 (Mem., 1991–; Vice-Chm., 1993–98). Mem., Bd of Mgt, Surrey CCC, 2011–. Gov., St Paul's Boys' Sch., 2015–. *Publications:* (ed jtly) Sutton and Shannon on Contracts, 7th edn 1970; contrib. Banking Documents, to Encyclopedia of Forms and Precedents, 5th edn, 1986. *Recreations:* theatre, golf. *Address:* 1 Essex Court, Temple, EC4Y 9AR. *T:* (020) 7583 2000. *E:* agrabiner@oeclaw.co.uk; Master's Lodge, Clare College, Cambridge CB2 1TL. *T:* (01223) 333207. *Clubs:* Garrick, MCC; Wentworth Golf.

GRABINER, Michael, CBE 2012; Partner, Portland Place Advisers LLP, since 2012; *b* 21 Aug. 1950; *s* of Henry Grabiner and Renée (*née* Geller); *m* 1976, Jane Olivia Harris; three *s* one *d*. *Educ:* St Albans Sch.; King's Coll., Cambridge (MA Econ; Pres., Students' Union, 1972–73). Joined Post Office, 1973: Personal Asst to Man. Dir, Telecommunications, 1976–78; London Business Sch. (Sloan Prog.), 1980–81; British Telecommunications: Controller, Commercial Finance Divl HQ, 1982–84; Dep. Dir, Mktg, 1984–85; General Manager: Northern London Dist, 1985–88; City of London Dist, 1988–90; Director: Quality and Orgn, 1990–92; Global Customer Service, Business Communications Div., 1992–94; BT Europe, 1994–95; Chief Executive: Energis Communications Ltd, then Energis plc, 1996–2001; Partner, Apax Partners, 2002–09. Director: BT Telecommunications SA Spain, 1994–95; VIAG InterKom Germany, 1994–95; Telenordia Sweden, 1994–95; Albacom Italy, 1994–95; Chairman: Planet Online, 1998–2000; Spectrum Strategy Consultants, 2003–07; Partnerships for Schs, 2005–11; non-executive Director: Littlewoods plc, 1998–2002; Emblaze Systems, 2000–05; Chelsfield plc, 2002–04; Synetrix Hldgs Ltd, 2004–09; Telewest Global Inc., 2004–06; Tim Hellas Telecommunications SA, 2005–06; Bezeq, 2006–10; Pelephone, 2008–10. Mem. (Lab) Brent BC, 1978–82 (Chm., Devel Cttee, 1980–82). Dir, E London Partnership, 1994–95; non-exec. Dir, Centre for Effective Dispute Resolution, 2012–. Treas., Reform Synagogues of GB, 2002–05. Chairman: UK Jewish Film Fest., 2004–06; UK Movt for Reform Judaism, 2005–08; ResponseAbility, 2009–11; World Union for Progressive Judaism, 2011–15 (Vice Chm., 2009–11); Mem., Jewish Leadership Council, 2005–08. Trustee, Jewish Community Secondary Sch., 2008– (Chm. of Govs, 2009–13). Freeman, City of London, 1995; Mem., Co. of Inf. Technologists, 1995. ACMA 1979. *E:* mike@grabiner.net.
See also S. Grabiner.

GRABINER, Stephen; Chairman: Timewise Foundation, since 2012; Jewish Chronicle, since 2013; Partner: Grabiner LLP, since 2011; Portland Place Advisers LLP, since 2012; *b* 30 Sept. 1958; *s* of Henry and Renée Grabiner (*née* Geller); *m* 1984, Miriam Lœbl; two *s* one *d*. *Educ:* Univ. of Sheffield (BA 1981); Manchester Business Sch. (MBA 1983). Mgt Consultant, Coopers and Lybrand, 1983–86; Telegraph plc: Mktg Dir, 1986–93; Dep. Man. Dir, 1993–94; Man. Dir, 1994–96; Exec. Dir, UK Consumer Publishing, United News and Media plc, 1996–98; Chief Exec., ONdigital, 1998–99; Partner, and Hd of Media and London Office, Apax Partners, 1999–2010. Ind. Nat. Dir, Times Newspaper Hldgs Ltd, 2012–. *Recreations:* family, community. *E:* stephen@grabiner.com.
See also M. Grabiner.

GRACE, Clive Lester, OBE 2013; DPhil; Chairman, UK Shared Business Services Ltd (formerly Research Councils UK Shared Services Centre Ltd), since 2007; *b* 5 Aug. 1950; *s* of Henri Hyams Grace and Mary Madeline Grace; *m* 1982, Vivienne Robins (now V. Robins-Grace); one *s* two *d*. *Educ:* Univ. of Birmingham (BSocSc 1971); Univ. of Calif (MA Govt 1972); Wolfson Coll., Oxford (DPhil Law and Sociol. 1984); Open Univ. (Professional Dip.

in Mgt). Solicitor of the Supreme Court, 1981. Hd of Legal Br., ILEA, 1987–89; Dir of Law and Admin, London Bor. of Southwark, 1989–95; Chief Exec., Torfaen CBC, 1995–2003; Dir-Gen., Audit Commn in Wales, 2003–05; Dep. Auditor Gen. for Wales, 2004–05. Chairman: Internat. Panel, CIPFA, 2006–09; Local Better Regulation Office, 2007–12; BT Wales Bd (formerly Wales Adv. Forum, BT), 2009– (Mem., 2000–); Observer Mem., Financial Reporting Council, 2004–07. Non-exec. Chm., Supporta plc, 2007–10; non-exec. Dir, Nominet, 2008–; Co-Founder and Dir, UK Research and Consultancy Services Ltd, 2013–. Mem., Corporate Governance Cttee (Health and Social Services), Welsh Assembly Govt, later Welsh Govt, 2009–13. Mem., Local Govt Knowledge Navigator Team, 2013–15. Hon. Secretary: SOLACE, 1998–2002; SOLACE Foundn, 1998–2014 (Chm., SOLACE Foundn Imprint, 2005–14). Mem., Morristours, 2005–. Hon. Res. Fellow, Cardiff Business Sch., 2005–. *Publications:* Sociological Inquiry and Legal Phenomena, 1979; Social Workers, Children and the Law, 1986; (ed) Civil Service Reform: experiences of the United Kingdom, India, South Africa, and Nepal, 2012. *Recreations:* ski-ing, walking, golf. *Address:* The Old Rectory, Llanellen Road, Llanfoist, Abergavenny, Monmouthshire NP7 9NF. *T:* (01873) 851289. *E:* clivegrace@hotmail.com. *Club:* Reform.

GRACEY, Howard, OBE 1998; FIA, FIAA, FPMI; consulting actuary; Senior Partner, R. Watson and Sons, 1993–95 (Partner, 1970–95); *b* 21 Feb. 1935; *s* of late Charles Douglas Gracey and Margaret Gertrude (*née* Heggie); *m* 1960, Pamela Jean Bradshaw; one *s* two *d*. *Educ:* Birkenhead Sch. FIA 1959; FIAA 1982; FPMI 1977; ASA 1978. National Service, 1960–61 (2nd Lieut). Royal Insurance Co., 1953–69. Church Comr, 1978–95; Member: Gen. Synod of C of E, 1970–97; C of E Pensions Bd, 1970–97 (Chm., 1980–97); Archbishops' Commn on orgn of C of E; Treasurer, S Amer. Missionary Soc., 1975–93 (Chm., 1994–2004); Pres., Pensions Management Inst., 1983–85; Chm., Assoc. of Consulting Actuaries, 1991–93. Mem. Council, St John's Coll., Nottingham, 1998–2003. *Recreations:* fell-walking, photography. *Address:* Loughrigg, Guildford Road, Fetcham, Surrey KT22 9DY.

GRACIAS, His Eminence Cardinal Oswald; *see* Bombay, Archbishop of, (RC).

GRADE, family name of **Baron Grade of Yarmouth**.

GRADE OF YARMOUTH, Baron *cr* 2011 (Life Peer), of Yarmouth in the County of Isle of Wight; **Michael Ian Grade,** CBE 1998; Chairman, Pinewood-Shepperton (formerly Pinewood Studios) plc, since 2000; Director, WRG Group, since 2011; *b* 8 March 1943; *s* of Leslie Grade and *g s* of Olga Winogradski; *m* 1st, 1967, Penelope Jane (*née* Levinson) (marr. diss. 1981); one *s* one *d*; 2nd, 1982, Hon. Sarah Lawson (marr. diss. 1991), *y d* of 5th Baron Burnham; 3rd, 1998, Francesca Mary (*née* Leahy); one *s*. *Educ:* St Dunstan's Coll., London. Daily Mirror: Trainee Journalist, 1960; Sports Columnist, 1964–66; Theatrical Agent, Grade Organisation, 1966; joined London Management and Representation, 1969, Jt Man. Dir until 1973; London Weekend Television: Dep. Controller of Programmes (Entertainment), 1973; Dir of Programmes and Mem. Bd, 1977–81; Pres., Embassy Television, 1981–84; Controller, BBC1, 1984–86; Dir of Programmes, BBC TV, 1986–87; Chief Exec., Channel Four, 1988–97; First Leisure Corporation: Dir, 1991–2000; non-exec. Chm., 1995–97; Chm., 1997–98; Chief Exec., 1997–2000; Exec. Chm. and Chief Exec., ITV, 2007–09. Chairman: VCI plc, 1995–98; Octopus Publishing Gp, 2000–01; Hemscott plc, 2000–06; Bd of Govs, BBC, 2004–06; James Grant Gp, 2010–12; Ocado, 2006–13; Director: ITN, 1989–93; Delfont Macintosh Theatres Ltd, 1994–99; Charlton Athletic FC, 1997–2008; New Millennium Experience Co., 1997–2001; Camelot Gp, 2000–04 (Chm., 2002–04); Reel Enterprises Ltd, 2002–04; SMG, 2003–04; Television Corp., 2003–04. Chm. Devlt Council, RNT, 1997–2004; Member: Council, LAMDA, 1981–93; Council, RADA, 1996–2004; Council, BAFTA, 1981–82, 1986–88 (Vice-Pres., 2004–); 300 Group; Milton Cttee; British Screen Adv. Council, 1986–97; Council, Cinema and Television Benevolent Fund, 1993–2004; Council, Royal Albert Hall, 1997–2004. Chm., Wkg Gp, Fear of Crime, 1989; Member: Nat. Commn of Inquiry into Prevention of Child Abuse, 1994–96; Panel on Fair Access to the Professions, 2009; Chm., Index on Censorship, 2000–04; Lay Mem., Press Complaints Commn, 2011–14. President: TV and Radio Industries Club, 1987–88; Newspaper Press Fund, 1988–89; Entertainment Charities Fund, 1994–; Vice-Pres., Children's Film Unit, 1993–97; Director: Open Coll., 1989–97; Cities in Schools, 1991–96; Gate Theatre, Dublin, 1990–2004; Internat. Council, Nat. Acad. of Television Arts and Scis, 1991–97; Jewish Film Foundn, 1997–99. Chm., Nat. Media Mus., Bradford, 2012–. Trustee: Science Mus. Gp (formerly Nat. Mus. of Sci. and Industry), 2011–; Band Aid; Samaritans, 2013–; Dep. Chm., Soc. of Stars, 1995–; Hon. Treas., Stars Organisation for Spastics, 1986–92. FRTS 1991 (Pres., 1995–97); Fellow, BAFTA, 1994. Hon. Prof., Thames Valley Univ., 1994. Hon. LLD Nottingham, 1997. *Publications:* It Seemed Like a Good Idea at the Time (autobiog.), 1999. *Recreations:* entertainment, sailing. *Address:* House of Lords, SW1A 0PW. *Club:* Royal Thames Yacht.

GRADIN, Anita Ingegerd; Chairperson, Swedish Council for Working Life and Social Research, 2000–06; *b* 12 Aug. 1933; *d* of Ossian Gradin and Alfhild Gradin; *m* Bertil Kersfelt; one *d*. *Educ:* Grad. Fr. Sch. of Social Work and Public Admin, Stockholm. Journalist in various newspapers, 1950–63; Mem., Social Welfare Planning Cttee, Stockholm, 1963–67; MP, 1968–92; posts include: Chairperson: Council, Cttee on Educn and Financial Affairs; Cttee on Migration, Refugees and Democracy, Council of Europe; Cabinet Minister for Migration and Equality between Women and Men, 1982–86; Minister for Foreign Trade and Eur. Affairs, 1986–91; Swedish Ambassador to Austria, Slovenia and UN, 1992–95; Mem., Commn of EC, 1995–99. Vice-Chairperson, Nat. Fedn of Social Democratic Women, 1975–92; Vice-Pres., Socialist Internat., 1983–92; Pres., Socialist Internat. Women, 1986–92. Member: Bd, Stockholm Sch. of Econs, 2001–; Bd, Center for Gender Medicine, Karolinska Inst., 2002–. FD *hc* Umeå, 2002. Pro Merito Medal, Council of Europe, 1982; Wizo Woman of the Year Award, 1986; Marisa Bellizario European Prize, Italy, 1998; King's Medal, Royal Order of Seraphim, Sweden, 1998. Cavalieri di Gran Croce (Italy), 1991; Order of Merit (Austria) 1995; European of the Year, Swedish Pan-Europa Orgn, 2007. *Recreations:* swimming, walking in the woods, stamps, fishing. *Address:* Fleminggatan 85, 11245 Stockholm, Sweden. *E:* gradin.kersfelt@lelia.com.

GRADY, Prof. Monica Mary, (Mrs I. Wright), CBE 2012; PhD; Professor of Planetary and Space Sciences, since 2005, and Head, Department of Physical Sciences, since 2011, Open University; *b* 15 July 1958; *d* of James and Mary Grady; *m* 1986, Prof. Ian Peter Wright, *qv*; one *s*. *Educ:* Notre Dame Grammar Sch., Leeds; Durham Univ. (BSc); Cambridge Univ. (PhD). Natural History Museum: researcher in meteorites, 1991–97; Hd, Div. of Petrology and Meteoritics, 1997–2005. Hon. Reader in Meteoritics, 2000–04, Hon. Prof., 2004, UCL. Christmas Lectures, Royal Instn, 2003. *Publications:* (ed jtly) Meteorites: their flux with time and impact effects, 1998; The Catalogue of Meteorites, 5th edn 2000; Search for Life, 2001; (with S. S. Russell) Meteorites, 2002; A Voyage in Space and Time, 2003; contrib. numerous papers to peer-reviewed jls. *Recreations:* reading, gardening, crossword puzzles. *Address:* Department of Physical Sciences, Open University, Walton Hall, Milton Keynes MK7 6AA. *T:* (01908) 659251, *Fax:* (01908) 858022. *E:* monica.grady@open.ac.uk.

GRADY, Patrick John; MP (SNP) Glasgow North, since 2015; *b* Inverness, 5 Feb. 1980. *Educ:* Inverness Royal Acad.; Univ. of Strathclyde. Work in London and in Malawi; campaigning and policy posts in charity and public sector. SNP Spokesperson on Internat. Develt, 2015–. Nat. Sec., SNP, 2012–. Contested (SNP) Glasgow N, 2010. *Address:* House of Commons, SW1A 0AA.

GRAEF, Roger Arthur, OBE 2006; writer, director and producer of films; criminologist; Chief Executive, Films of Record, since 1979; *b* NYC, 18 April 1936; UK citizen, 1995; *m* 1st, 1971, Karen Bergemann (marr. diss. 1983); one *s* one *d*; 2nd, 1986, Susan Mary Richards. *Educ:* Horace Mann Sch., NYC; Putney Sch., Vermont; Harvard Univ. (BA Hons). Directed, USA, 26 plays and operas; also directed CBS drama; Observer/Dir, Actors Studio, NYC, 1958–62; resident in England, 1962–; Director, London: Period of Adjustment (Royal Court, Wyndham's); Afternoon Men (Arts); has written, produced and/or directed more than 100 films; *films for television include:* The Life and Times of John Huston, Esq., 1965; (Exec. Producer) 13-part Who Is series, 1966–67 (wrote/dir. films on Pierre Boulez, Jacques Lipchitz, Walter Gropius, Maurice Béjart); Günter Grass' Berlin, 1965; Why Save Florence?, 1968; In the Name of Allah, 1970; The Space between Words, 1971–72; A Law in the Making, 1973; Inside the Brussels HQ, 1975; Is This the Way to Save our Cities?, 1975; Decision series: British Steel, etc, 1976–77, British Communism, 1978 (Royal Television Soc. Award); Pleasure at Her Majesty's, The Secret Policeman's Ball, 1977–78; Inside Europe, 1977–78; Police series, 1980–82 (BAFTA Award); Police: Operation Carter, 1981–82; Nagging Doubt, 1984; The Fifty-Minute Hour, 1984; Maybe Baby, 1985; Comic Relief, 1986; Closing Ranks, 1987; The Secret Life of the Soviet Union, 1990; Turning the Screws, 1993; Look at the State We're In, 1995; In Search of Law and Order (UK), 1995; Breaking the Cycle, 1996; In Search of Law and Order (USA), 1998; Keeping it in the Family, 1998; The Siege of Scotland Yard, 1999; Race Against Crime, 1999; Masters of the Universe, 1999; Police, 2001; executive producer: Looks That Kill, Who's Your Father, 2000; Not Black and White, 2001; Who Cares for Granny?, 2003; September Mourning, Chinatown, Feltham Sings (BAFTA Award), Rail Cops, RailCops 2, Welcome to Potters Bar, The Protectors, Who am I Now?, 2004; Murder Blues, Classroom Chaos, What Killed My Dad?, Malaria: Fever Road/The Vaccine Challenge, What Future for Kurt? (Panorama), 2005; This World: Blood and Land, Property to Die For, Potters Bar: Search for the Truth, 2006; Hold Me Tight, Let Me Go, 2007; Race for the Beach, The Burning Season, 2007; Searching for Madeline, 2008; May Contain Nuts (Panorama), Remember the Secret Policeman's Ball, The Millionaire and the Murder Mansion, The Truth about Crime, Dispatches: Ready for a Riot, The Child Protectors (Panorama), 2009; Requiem for Detroit, Great Ormond Street, Kids in Care (Panorama Special), The Trouble with Pirates, 2010; Storyville: Amnesty! When They Are All Free, Dispatches: Medical Devices, Adoption (Panorama), Sex, Lies and Parkinsons, 2011; producer/director, Police 2001, 2001; Series Editor: Inside Europe, 1977–78; Signals, 1988–89; *radio:* The Illusion of Information, 2000. Mem., Develt Control Review (Dobry Cttee), Chm., Study Gp on Public Participation in Planning, and Mem., Cttee on Control of Demolition, DoE, 1974–76; Member: Commn on Child and Adolescent Mental Health, 1997–98; Prince's Trust Wkg Party on surviving damage in childhood, 1997–98; Fulbright Commn, 2000– (Chm., Police Scholarships Cttee, 1999–); Advr, Oxford Probation Studies Unit, 1997–; Social Affairs Advr, Paul Hamlyn Foundn, 1999–; Advr, Sentencing Council, 2010–. Chm., AIP, 1988–89; Member: Council, ICA, 1970–82; Council, BAFTA, 1976–77; Bd, Channel Four, 1980–85; Governor, BFI, 1974–78. Adviser on broadcasting to Brandt Commn, 1979–80; Media Advisor: Collins Publishing, 1983–88; London Transport (Mem. Bd, LTE, 1976–79; co-designer, new London Bus Map). Pres., Signals Internat. Trust, 1990–; Trustee: Koestler Trust for Prisoners' Art, 1995–; Butler Trust, 1997–2001; Divert Trust, 1999–2000. Chm., Youth Advocate Prog. UK, 2002–. Chairman: Book Aid, 1991; Théâtre de Complicité, 1991–; Bd Mem., Photographers' Gall., 2003. Member: Collège Analytique de Securité Urbaine, 1993–98; British Soc. of Criminology. Visiting Professor: Broadcast Media, Oxford Univ., 1999–2000; Univ. of London, 2001–02; Mannheim Centre for the Study of Criminology and Criminal Justice, LSE (formerly Vis. Fellow); Bournemouth Univ. Media Sch. FRTS 1996; Fellow, BAFTA, 2004. Hon. FRIBA 2014. *Publications:* Talking Blues, 1989; Living Dangerously, 1992; Why Restorative Justice?, 2000; contrib. Daily Telegraph, The Times (media columnist, 1992–94), Sunday Telegraph, Observer, Daily Mail, Mail on Sunday, Evening Standard, Police Review, The Independent, Guardian, Sunday Times, Independent on Sunday. *Recreations:* tennis, flute, photography, Dorset. *Address:* 72 Westbourne Park Villas, W2 5EB. *T:* (020) 7727 7868. *Clubs:* Beefsteak, Groucho, Pilgrims.

GRAF, (Charles) Philip, CBE 2003; Chairman, Gambling Commission, since 2011; *b* 18 Oct. 1946; *s* of Charles Henry Graf and Florence (*née* Mulholland); *m* 1st, 1970, Freda Mary Bain (marr. diss. 2003); three *d*; 2nd, 2004, Kirstan Anne Marnane. *Educ:* Methodist Coll., Belfast; Carlmont High Sch., Calif; Clare Coll., Cambridge (MA). Circulation Mktg Controller, Thomson Regl Newspapers, 1978–83; Asst Man. Dir, Liverpool Daily Post and Echo, 1983–85; Chief Exec., Trinity Paper and Packaging, 1986–90; Corporate Devélt Dir, 1990–93, Chief Exec., 1993–99, Trinity plc; Chief Exec., Trinity Mirror plc, 1999–2002. Dir, TDG plc, 2003–07; Partner, Praesta Partners LLP, 2005–10. Chairman: Press Standards Bd of Finance, 2004–05; Broadband Stakeholders Gp, 2005; Dep. Chm., Ofcom, 2006–11 (Chm., Content Bd, 2006–11). Dir, Archant Ltd, 2006–09. Chair, CfBT Educn Trust, 2011–. Trustee, Crisis, 2004–13. *Recreations:* reading, opera, watching Rugby, soccer and cricket, theatre.

GRAF, Prof. Hans-Friedrich, PhD, DSc; Professor of Environmental Systems Analysis, University of Cambridge, since 2003; Fellow of Clare Hall, Cambridge, since 2003; *b* 6 Jan. 1950; *s* of Dr Hans and Ilse Graf; *m* 1997, Dr Marie-Luise Waguer-Kuschfeldt; two *d*. *Educ:* Humboldt Univ., Berlin (MSc Met. 1974; PhD Met. 1979; Habilitation Dr *scientiae naturalis*, 1989). Scientific Asst, Humboldt Univ., Berlin, 1974–78; Industrial Meteorologist, Kombinat Kraftwerksanlagenbau, Berlin, 1978–79; Scientific Asst, Meteorol Inst., Humboldt Univ., Berlin, 1979–90; Sen. Scientist, Max-Planck-Inst. for Meteorol., Hamburg, 1991–2003. Suehring Medal, Deutsche Meteorologische Gesellschaft, 1989. *Publications:* more than 160 book chapters and papers in jls. *Address:* Department of Geography, University of Cambridge, Cambridge CB2 3EN. *T:* (01223) 330242. *E:* hfg21@cam.ac.uk.

GRAF, Philip; *see* Graf, C. P.

GRAF, Stefanie; German tennis player, 1982–99; Founder, and Chairman, Children for Tomorrow, since 1998; *b* 14 June 1969; *d* of late Peter and Heidi Graf; *m* 2001, André Agassi, *qv*; one *s* one *d*. Has won 107 singles titles, including 22 Grand Slam titles: French Open, 1987–88, 1993, 1995–96, 1999; Australian Open, 1988–90, 1994; Wimbledon, 1988–89, 1991–93, 1995–96; US Open, 1988–89, 1993, 1995–96. Olympic Gold Medal, Seoul, 1988; Olympic Silver Medal, Barcelona, 1992; Olympic Order, 1999. *Publications:* (jtly) Wege zum Erfolg, 1999. *Address:* Stefanie Graf Marketing, Gartenstrasse 1, 68723 Schwetzingen, Germany.

GRAFEN, Prof. Alan, DPhil; FRS 2011; Professor of Theoretical Biology, University of Oxford, since 1999; Fellow, St John's College, Oxford, since 1999; *b* 1956; *m* 1998, Prof. Elizabeth Anne Fallaize, PhD (*d* 2009). *Educ:* Univ. of Oxford (BA Exptl Psychol. 1977; MPhil Econs 1979; DPhil Zool. 1983). Lectr in Quantitative Methods in Biol., Univ. of Oxford. Trustee, Oxford Playhouse, 2010–. *Publications:* (contrib.) Reproductive Success, 1988; (ed) Evolution and its Influence, 1989; (contrib.) Behavioural Ecology, 3rd edn 1991; (contrib.) Phylogenies and the Comparative Method in Animal Behaviour, 1996; (with R. Hails) Modern Statistics for the Life Sciences, 2002; (ed with M. Ridley) Richard Dawkins: how a scientist changed the way we think, 2006; contribs to jls incl. Animal Behaviour, Nature, Jl Theoretical Biol., Parasitol., Proc. Royal Soc., Science, Jl Evolutionary Biol. *Address:* Department of Zoology, South Parks Road, Oxford OX1 3PS.

GRAFF, Laurence, OBE 2013; Founder and Chairman, Graff Diamonds Holdings, since 1960; *b* 13 June 1938; *s* of Harry Graff and Rebecca Graff (*née* Segal); *m* 1962, Anne-Marie Bessiere; two *s* one *d*. *Educ:* St George's Sch., E London. Jeweller apprentice, Hatton Garden,

1953; founded Graff Diamonds, 1960; opened first major retail store in Knightsbridge, 1974; other stores incl. Bond St, London, NY, Monte Carlo, Courchevel, Geneva, Hong Kong, China and Japan. Mem., European Adv. Bd, Christies, 2014–. Member: Internat. Council, Tate, 2004–; Exec. Cttee, Internat. Dir's Council, Guggenheim Mus., 2005–; Internat. Council, Berggruen Mus., Berlin, 2009–; Internat. Bd of Trustees, Mus. of Contemporary Art, LA, 2010–; Bd of Govs, Tel Aviv Mus. of Art, 2010–. Queen's Award to Industry, 1973; Queen's Award for Export Achievement, 1977, 1994; Queen's Award for Enterprise, 2006, 2014. *Recreations:* collector of contemporary and modern art, ski-ing, sailing. *Address:* Graff Diamonds Ltd, 28–29 Albemarle Street, W1S 4JA. *Clubs:* Annabel's, Harry's Bar, George, Mark's, Arts, 5 Hertford Street.

GRAFTON, 12th Duke of, *cr* 1675; **Henry Oliver Charles FitzRoy;** Earl of Euston, Viscount Ipswich, Baron Sudbury 1672; *b* 6 April 1978; *s* of Earl of Euston (*d* 2009) and of Countess of Euston; *S* grandfather, 2011; *m* 2010, Olivia Margaret Hogarth, *d* of Simon Sladen; one *s*. *Educ:* Harrow Sch.; Edinburgh Univ.; RAC, Cirencester. Music business mgt, FBMM, and radio host, Nashville, Tenn, 2002–04; merchandise co-ordinator, Rolling Stones tour, A Bigger Bang, 2005–06. *Heir: s* Earl of Euston, *qv*.

GRAFTON, Fortune, Duchess of; (Ann) Fortune FitzRoy, GCVO 1980 (DCVO 1970; CVO 1965); Mistress of The Robes to the Queen, since 1967; *o d* of Captain Eric Smith, MC, LLD, Lower Ashfold, Slaugham; *m* 1946, Earl of Euston, later 11th Duke of Grafton, KG (*d* 2011); one *s* three *d* (and one *s* decd). Lady of the Bedchamber to the Queen, 1953–66. SRCN Great Ormond Street, 1945; Mem. Bd of Governors, The Hospital for Sick Children, Great Ormond Street, 1952–66; Patron, Nurses' League. President: W Suffolk Mission to the Deaf; W Suffolk Decorative and Fine Arts Soc.; Bury St Edmunds Br., BHF; National Vice Pres., Royal British Legion Women's Section, 2003 (Vice Pres., Suffolk Br., 1970–2009); Vice Pres., Trinity Hospice, Clapham Common, 1951–. Governor: Felixstowe Coll.; Riddlesworth Hall. Patron: Relate, W Suffolk; Guildhall String Ensemble; Clarence River Historical Soc., Grafton, NSW. JP County of London, 1949, W Suffolk, 1970–95. *Address:* 14 Whitelands House, Cheltenham Terrace, SW3 4QX.

See also Jeremy F. E. Smith.

GRAFTON-GREEN, Patrick; Senior Partner, Michael Simkins LLP, since 2006; *b* 30 March 1943; *s* of George Grafton-Green and Brigid Anna Grafton-Green (*née* Maxwell); *m* 1982, Deborah Susan Goodchild; two *s* two *d*. *Educ:* Ampleforth Coll., York; Wadham Coll., Oxford (MA 1965). Joined Theodore Goddard, later Addleshaw Goddard, solicitors, 1966; qualif. as solicitor, 1969; Partner, 1973–2006; Head, Media and Communications Dept, 1993–2006; Sen. Partner, 1997–2003; Chm., 2003–06. *Recreations:* cricket, music, theatre. *Address:* Michael Simkins LLP, Lynton House, 7–12 Tavistock Square, WC1H 9LT. *T:* (020) 7874 5634. *Club:* MCC.

GRAHAM, family name of **Duke of Montrose** and **Baron Graham of Edmonton**.

GRAHAM, Marquis of; James Alexander Norman Graham; *b* 16 Aug. 1973; *s* and *heir* of Duke of Montrose, *qv*; *m* 2004, Cecilia, *d* of late Francesco Manfredi. *Educ:* Eton; Univ. of Edinburgh (BSc); Univ. of Cape Town (MSc). *Address:* Auchmar, Drymen, Glasgow G63 0AG.

GRAHAM OF EDMONTON, Baron *cr* 1983 (Life Peer), of Edmonton in Greater London; **Thomas Edward Graham;** PC 1998; *b* 26 March 1925; *m* 1950, Margaret (*d* 2005), *d* of Frederick Golding; two *s*. *Educ:* elementary sch.; WEA Co-operative College; BA Open Univ., 1976. Newcastle-on-Tyne Co-operative Soc., 1939–52; Organiser, British Fedn of Young Co-operators, 1952–53; Educn Sec., Enfield Highway Co-operative Soc., 1953–62; Sec., Co-operative Union Southern Section, 1962–67; Nat. Sec., Co-operative Party, 1967–74. Mem. and Leader, Enfield Council, 1961–68. Contested (Lab) Enfield W, 1966; MP (Lab and Co-op) Enfield, Edmonton, Feb. 1974–1983; contested (Lab) Edmonton, 1983. PPS to Minister of State, Dept of Prices and Consumer Protection, 1974–76; a Lord Comr of HM Treasury, 1976–79; Opposition spokesman on the environment, 1980–83; Opposition Chief Whip, H of L, 1990–97. Chm., Labour Peers' Gp, 1997–2000. FCMI. *Address:* 2 Clerks Piece, Loughton, Essex IG10 1NR.

GRAHAM, Alastair Carew; Head Master, Mill Hill School, 1979–92; *b* 23 July 1932; *s* of Col J. A. Graham and Mrs Graham (*née* Carew-Hunt); *m* 1969, Penelope Rachel Beaumont; two *d*. *Educ:* Winchester Coll.; Gonville and Caius Coll., Cambridge (1st Cl. Mod. and Med. Langs). Served 1st Bn Argyll and Sutherland Highlanders, 1951–53. Foy, Morgan & Co. (City), 1956–58; Asst Master, 1958–70, House Master, 1970–79, Eton. *Recreations:* education, European travel, DFAS, theatre and opera, music listening. *Address:* Apartment 7, Lawnswood Court, Wellington Square, Cheltenham, Glos GL50 4AB.

GRAHAM, Alexander; television producer; Chief Executive, Wall to Wall Media, 1997–2013; *b* 28 Oct. 1953; *s* of Alexander and Jean Graham; *m* 2000, Maeve Haran; one *s* two *d*. *Educ:* West Coats Primary Sch., Cambuslang; Hamilton Acad.; Glasgow Univ. (MA Hons English Lit. and Sociol.); City Univ. (Dip. Journalism). Reporter, Bradford Telegraph and Argus, 1978–79; researcher and producer, LWT, 1979–83; Editor, Diverse Reports, 1983–86, Media Show, 1987–91, Channel 4; Jt Man. Dir, Wall to Wall Media, 1991–97; Executive Producer: Baby It's You, 1993; Our Boy, 1997; A Rather English Marriage, 1998; The 1900 House, 1999; The 1940s House, 2001; Edwardian Country House, 2003; New Tricks, 2002–13; Who Do You Think You Are?, 2004–13; Who Do You Think You Are? (USA), 2007–. Vis. Fellow, Bournemouth Media Sch., 2004–10; Vis. Prof., Univ. of Lincoln, 2011–. Producers Association for Cinema and Television: Mem. Council, 1991–2008; Vice Chm., 1995–96 and 1999–2000; Chm., 2006–07. Chm., Media Literary Task Force, 2009. Chm., Sheffield Internat. Documentary Fest., 2011–. Chair, The Space, 2014–15. Trustee, The Creative Society (formerly New Deal of the Mind), 2010–; non-exec. Dir, The Scott Trust, 2013–. Ambassador, ActionAid, 2010–. Mem. Bd, Hampstead Th., 2011–. FRSA 2004; FRTS 2006. Hon. DArts City, 2009. *Recreations:* cooking, walking, guitar, piano, Arsenal FC, single malt whisky. *T:* 07940 965104. *E:* alex@bigeck.com. *Club:* Reform.

GRAHAM, Sir Alexander (Michael), GBE 1990; JP; Chairman, Employment Conditions Abroad International Ltd, 1993–2005 (Director, 1992–93); Lord Mayor of London, 1990–91; *b* 27 Sept. 1938; *s* of Dr Walter Graham and Suzanne Graham (*née* Simon); *m* 1964, Carolyn, *d* of Lt-Col Alan Wolryche Stansfeld, MBE; three *d*. *Educ:* Fyvie Village Sch.; Hall Sch., Hampstead; St Paul's Sch. National Service, 1957–59; commnd Gordon Highlanders; TA 1959–67; Chm., Nat. Employers Liaison Cttee for TA and Reserve Forces, 1992–97. Joined Norman Frizzell & Partners Ltd, 1957: Dir, 1967–93; Man. Dir, 1973–90; Dep. Chm., 1990–93; Underwriting Member of Lloyd's, 1978–2000; Director: Folgate Insce Co. Ltd, 1975–2001, 2004–05 (Chm., 1995–2001); Folgate Partnership Ltd, 2002–05; Chairman: FirstCity Insce Brokers, 1993–98; Euclidian plc, 1994–2001. Mercers' Co.: Liveryman, 1971–; Mem., Ct of Assistants, 1980; Master, 1983–84; Mem., Ct of Common Council, City of London, 1978–79; Alderman for Ward of Queenhithe, 1979–2004; Pres., Queenhithe Ward Club, 1979–2004. Sheriff, City of London, 1986–87; HM Lieut, City of London, 1989–2004. Hon. Liveryman, Co. of Chartered Secretaries and Administrators, 1992; Hon. Freeman: Insurers' Co., 1992; Merchant Adventurers of York, 1983. President: CS Motoring Assoc., 1993–2006; British Insurance Law Assoc., 1994–96; Vice-Pres., Insurance Inst. of London, 1978–. Governor: Hall Sch., Hampstead, 1975–93; Christ's Hosp. Sch., 1979–2004; King Edward's Sch., Whitley, 1979–2004; St Paul's Sch., 1980–93, 2003–09 (Chm., 2004–09; Vice Pres., 1988–2000, Dep. Pres., 2000–01, Pres., 2001–03, Old Pauline Club; Chm., Gen. Charitable Trust, 1997–2004); St Paul's Girls' Sch., 1980–93, 2004–09; City of London Boys' Sch., 1983–85; City of London Girls' Sch., 1992–95; Mem. Council, Gresham Coll., 1983–93; Trustee, Morden College, 1988–2013 (Chm., 1995–2013); Chancellor, City Univ., 1990–91; Mem. Court, Univ. of Herts, 2006–. Trustee: United Response, 1988–2002 (Chm., 1993–2002); Lord Mayor's 800th Anniversary Trust, 1989–2000; Temple Bar Trust, 1992–2004; Vice Pres., 1992–, and Hon. Life Mem., 1993, Macmillan Cancer Relief (formerly Cancer Relief Macmillan Fund); Vice Pres., Garden House Hospice, 1992–; Hon. Mem., Ct, HAC, 1979–2004; Mem., Exec. Cttee, Army Benevolent Fund, 1991–98; Chm. Council, Order of St John, Herts, 1993–2001; Mem., Royal Soc. of St George, 1981–; Vice Pres., Royal Soc. of St George, Herts Br., 1999–. Vice Pres., Herts Agricl Show, 1996–2015. Mem., Adv. Council, Herts Community Foundn, 2008–. Gentlemen Usher of the Purple Rod, Order of the British Empire, 2000–13. FCII 1964; FBIIBA 1967; FCIS 1990; FInstD 1975; CCMI (CBIM 1991); FRSA 1980. JP City of London, 1979. Hon. Keeper of the Quaich, 1992; Commandeur de l'Ordre du Tastevin, 1985; Vigneron d'Honneur et Bourgeois de St Emilion, 1999. Hon. DCL City, 1990. KStJ 1990. Silver Medal, City of Helsinki, 1990; Medal, City of Santiago, 1991. Order of Wissam Alouite (Morocco), 1987; Grand Cross Order of Merit (Chile), 1991. *Recreations:* wine, calligraphy, genealogy, music, reading, silver, bridge, golf, swimming, avoiding gardening. *Address:* Walden Abbotts, Whitwell, Hitchin, Herts SG4 8AJ. *T:* and *Fax:* (01438) 871223. *Clubs:* Garrick, City Livery; Royal Worlington and Newmarket Golf, Mid Herts Golf, Lloyd's Golf (Capt. 1994, Pres., 1996).

See also Lt-Gen. Sir P. W. Graham.

GRAHAM, Sir Alistair; *see* Graham, Sir J. A.

GRAHAM, Rt Rev. Andrew Alexander Kenny; an Hon. Assistant Bishop, Diocese of Carlisle, since 1997; *b* 7 Aug. 1929; *o s* of late Andrew Harrison and Magdalene Graham; unmarried. *Educ:* Tonbridge Sch.; St John's Coll., Oxford (Hon. Fellow, 1986); Ely Theological College. Curate of Hove Parish Church, 1955–58; Chaplain and Lectr in Theology, Worcester Coll., Oxford, 1958–70; Fellow and Tutor, 1960–70, Hon. Fellow, 1981; Warden of Lincoln Theological Coll., 1970–77; Canon and Prebendary of Lincoln Cathedral, 1970–77; Bishop Suffragan of Bedford, 1977–81; Bishop of Newcastle, 1981–97. Chairman: ACCM, 1984–87; Doctrine Commn, 1987–95. DD Lambeth, 1995; Hon. DCL Northumbria, 1997. *Address:* Fell End, Butterwick, Penrith, Cumbria CA10 2QQ. *T:* (01931) 713147. *Club:* Oxford and Cambridge.

GRAHAM, Lt Gen. Andrew John Noble, CB 2011; CBE 2002 (MBE 1993); Executive Director, British Exploring Society, since 2014; *b* 21 Oct. 1956; *er s* and heir of Sir John (Alexander Noble) Graham, Bt, *qv*; *m* 1984, Susie Mary Bridget, *er d* of Rear Adm. John Patrick Bruce O'Riordan, *qv*; one *s* three *d*. *Educ:* Eton Coll.; Trinity Coll., Cambridge (MA). Commnd Argyll and Sutherland Highlanders, 1979; served in UK, NI, Hong Kong, Cyprus, S Georgia, MoD, 1979–88; acsc 1988; 1 Argyll and Sutherland Highlanders, Germany, 1989–90; MoD, 1990–92; Directing Staff, Army Staff Coll., 1992–95; CO, 1st Bn, Argyll and Sutherland Highlanders (Princess Louise's), 1995–97; Comdr, 3rd Inf. Bde, 1999–2001; Dir, Army Resources and Plans, MoD, 2001–03; Dep. Comdg Gen., Multinat. Corps, Iraq, 2004; Director General: Army Trng and Recruiting, subseq. Army Recruiting and Trng Div., 2004–07; Defence Academy of the UK, 2008–11. Hd of Doctrine and Strategic Analysis, Gen. Dynamics UK, 2011–13. Non-exec. Dir, DWP, 2015– (Mem., 2013–, Chair, 2015–, Audit and Risk Assurance Cttee). Colonel: Argyll and Sutherland Highlanders (Princess Louise's), 2000–06; Royal Regt of Scotland, 2007–14. Brig., Queen's Body Guard for Scotland (Royal Company of Archers), 2012–. Trustee, Combat Stress, 2012– (Chair, 2013–). Officer, Legion of Merit (USA), 2006. *Recreations:* piping, outdoor sports, destructive gardening, travel/history reading, hobby smallholding, beekeeping.

GRAHAM, Andrew Winston Mawdsley; Master, Balliol College, Oxford, 2001–11 (Hon. Fellow, 2011); Acting Warden, Rhodes House, Oxford, 2012–13; *b* 20 June 1942; *s* of late Winston Mawdsley Graham, OBE, FRSL; *m* 1970, Peggotty Fawssett. *Educ:* Charterhouse; St Edmund Hall, Oxford (MA (PPE); Hon. Fellow, 2002). Economic Assistant: NEDO, 1964; Dept of Economic Affairs, 1964–66; Asst to Economic Adviser to the Cabinet, 1966–68; Economic Adviser to Prime Minister, 1968–69; Balliol College, Oxford: Fellow, 1969–2001; Tutor in Econs, 1969; Estates Bursar, 1978; Investment Bursar, 1979–83; Vice Master, 1988 and 1992–94; Acting Master, 1997–2001; Policy Adviser to Prime Minister (on leave of absence from Balliol), 1974–75; Economic Advr to Shadow Chancellor of Exchequer, 1988–92, to Leader of the Opposition, 1992–94. Tutor, Oxford Univ. Business Summer Sch., 1971, 1972, 1973 and 1976; Acting Dir, Oxford Internet Inst., 2002 (Chm., Adv. Bd, 2001–11; Mem., Adv. Bd, 2011–12; Sen. Fellow, 2011–). Vis. Researcher, SE Asian Central Banks Res. and Trng Centre, Malaysia, 1984; Vis. Fellow, Griffith Univ., Brisbane, 1984; Vis. Scholar, MIT, and Vis. Fellow, Center for Eur. Studies, Harvard, 1994; Sen. Fellow, Gorbachev Foundn of N America, 1999–. Chm., Europaeum Academic Council, 2010–. Founder Mem., Editl Bd, Liby of Political Economy, 1982–. Member: Council of Mgt, Templeton Coll., Oxford, 1990–95; Council, Oxford Univ., 2006–10. Member: Wilson Cttee to Review the Functioning of Financial Institutions, 1977–80; Economics Cttee, SSRC, 1978–80; British Transport Docks Bd, 1979–82; Chm., St James Gp (Economic Forecasting), 1982–84, 1985–92. Mem., ILO/Jobs and Skills Prog. for Africa (JASPA) Mission to Ethiopia, 1982; Hd, Queen Elizabeth House/Food Studies Gp team assisting Govt of Republic of Zambia, 1984. Consultant: BBC, 1989–92; Mammoth Screen, 2014–; Mem. Bd, Channel Four Television Ltd, 1998–2005. Mem., Media Adv. Cttee, IPPR, 1994–97; Trustee: Foundn for Information Policy Res., 1998–2000; Esmée Fairbairn Foundn, 2003–05; Rhodes Trust, 2013–; Dir, Scott Trust Ltd, 2005–15. Hon. DCL Oxford, 2003. *Publications:* (ed) Government and Economies in the Postwar Period, 1990; (jtly) Broadcasting, Society and Policy in the Multimedia Age, 1997. *Recreation:* windsurfing on every possible occasion. *Address:* 8 Leckford Place, Oxford OX2 6JB.

GRAHAM, Anne Silvia, (Lady Graham); Chairman, South Cumbria Health Authority, 1988–94; *b* 1 Aug. 1934; *o d* of late Benjamin Arthur Garcia and Constance Rosa (*née* Journeaux). *Educ:* Francis Holland Sch., SW1; LSE (LLB). Called to the Bar, Inner Temple, 1958; Yarborough-Anderson Scholar, 1959. Joined Min. of Housing and Local Govt, 1960; Dep. Legal Advr, DoE, 1978–86. Mem. Court, Lancaster Univ., 1993–2006. *Recreations:* gardening, arts, music.

GRAHAM, Anthony Ronald, CEng; FRINA; Director, Ships, Defence Equipment and Support, Ministry of Defence, since 2011; *b* Omagh, Co. Tyrone, 13 Aug. 1962; *s* of Ronald George Graham and Bridie Graham; *m* 1993, Catherine Tuck; one *s* one *d*. *Educ:* Bath Tech. Coll. (MoD apprenticeship; Higher Technician Cert. Shipbuilding 1984); Univ. of Glasgow (BEng 1st Cl. Naval Architecture and Ocean Engrg 1987); University Coll. London (MSc Naval Architecture and Marine Engrg 1988; Submarine Design Dip. 1988); Univ. of W of England (MBA 1997). FRINA 2002. Ministry of Defence: Mil. Exchange Officer in Canada, 1997–2000; Hd, Ship Safety Mgt Office, 2000–03; Team Leader: Battlefield Infrastructure Integrated Project, 2003–05; Landing Ship Dock (Auxiliary) Integrated Project, 2005–07; Mil. Afloat Reach and Sustainability Integrated Project, 2007–08; Dir, Afloat Support, 2008; Hd, Capital Ships, 2008–11. Hd, RCNC, 2011–. MAPM. *Recreations:* family, qualified swimming judge Level 2. *Address:* Ministry of Defence, Birch 1c, #3136, Abbey Wood, Bristol BS34 8JH. *T:* (0117) 913 7500. *E:* DESShips-dir@mod.uk.

GRAHAM, Antony Richard Malise; management consultant, retired; Director, Clive & Stokes International, 1985–95; *b* 15 Oct. 1928; *s* of late Col Patrick Ludovic Graham, MC, and Barbara Mary Graham (*née* Jury); *m* 1st, 1958, Gillian Margaret Cook (marr. diss. 1996);

two *s* one *d*; 2nd, 2006, Mrs Alny Mary Younger (*née* Burton) (MBE 2011). *Educ:* Abberley Hall; Nautical Coll., Pangbourne. Merchant Navy, 1945–55 (Master Mariner). Stewarts and Lloyds Ltd, 1955–60; PE Consulting Group Ltd, management consultants, 1960–72 (Regional Dir, 1970–72); Regional Industrial Dir (Under-Sec.), DTI, 1972–76; Dir, Barrow Hepburn Gp, and Maroquinerie Le Tanneur et Tanneries du Bugey SA, 1976–81; Chm., Paton & Sons (Tillicoultry) Ltd, 1981–82; Dir, DTI, 1983–85. Contested (C) Leeds East, 1966. *Recreation:* oil painting. *Address:* Old Bank House, Haddington, E Lothian EH41 3JS. *Club:* New (Edinburgh).

GRAHAM, (Arthur) William; JP; Member (C) South Wales East, National Assembly for Wales, since 1999; *b* 18 Nov. 1949; *s* of late William Douglas Graham and of Eleanor Mary Scott (*née* Searle); *m* 1981, Elizabeth Hannah, *d* of late Joshua Griffiths; one *s* two *d*. *Educ:* Blackfriars; Coll. of Estate Mgt, London. FRICS 1974. Principal, Graham & Co., Chartered Surveyors, 1970–. Newport Harbour Comr, 1990–2005 (Chm., 2001). Member: Gwent CC, 1985–89; Newport County BC, subseq. CC, 1988–2004 (Leader, Conservative Gp, 1992–2004). National Assembly for Wales: Chief Whip, Cons. Gp, 2001–14; opposition spokesman on local govt and housing, 2001–03, on social justice, 2003–07; Shadow Leader of the House, 2007–14; Shadow Minister for Social Services, 2012–14, for Business, Enterprise and Skills, 2014–; Chairman: Educn Cttee, 1999–2001; Constitutional Cttee, 2009–11; Enterprise and Business Cttee, 2014–; First Comr for Assembly Resources, 2007–11. Gov., Rougemont Sch. Trust, 1991–2005 (Chm., 2002–05). JP Newport, 1979. *Recreations:* breeder of pedigree Suffolk sheep, foreign travel. *Address:* The Volland, Lower Machen, Newport NP10 8GY. *T:* (01633) 440419. *Club:* Carlton.

GRAHAM, Billy; *see* Graham, W. F.

GRAHAM, Charles Robert Stephen; QC 2003; *b* 1 April 1961; *s* of Major (Cosmo) Stephen Graham and Mary Graham; *m* 1991, Jane Lindsay; three *s*. *Educ:* Ludgrove Sch., Wokingham; Wellington Coll., Crowthorne; University Coll., Oxford (1st cl. Greats (Lit. Hum.) 1984); City Univ. (Dip Law 1985). Called to the Bar, Middle Temple, 1986; in practice, specialising in commercial law; Mem., SE Circuit. *Address:* One Essex Court, Temple, EC4Y 9AR. *T:* (020) 7583 2000, *Fax:* (020) 7583 0118. *E:* cgraham@oeclaw.co.uk.

GRAHAM, Prof. Christopher Forbes, DPhil; FRS 1981; Professor of Animal Development, and Professorial Fellow, St Catherine's College, University of Oxford, 1985–2007, now Professor Emeritus; *b* 23 Sept. 1940. *Educ:* St Edmund Hall, Oxford (BA 1963); DPhil Oxon 1966. Formerly Junior Beit Memorial Fellow in Med. Research, Sir William Dunn Sch. of Pathology. Lectr, Zoology Dept, Oxford Univ., 1970–85. Member: Brit. Soc. Cell Biology; Brit. Soc. for Developmental Biology; Soc. for Experimental Biology; Genetical Soc. *Publications:* The Developmental Biology of Plants and Animals, 1976, new edn as Developmental Control in Plants and Animals, 1984. *Address:* Department of Zoology, University of Oxford, South Parks Road, Oxford OX1 3PS.

GRAHAM, Christopher Sidney Matthew; Information Commissioner, 2009–June 2016; *b* 21 Sept. 1950; *s* of late David Maurice Graham and Rosemary West Graham; *m* 1st, 1985, Christine Harland (*née* McLean) (marr. diss. 2008); 2nd, 2010, Mary Elizabeth Shevaun Crockett. *Educ:* Canterbury Cathedral Choir Sch.; St Edward's Sch., Oxford (Music Scholar); Univ. of Liverpool (Pres., Guild of Undergrads, 1971–72; BA Hons Hist. 1973). BBC News Trainee, 1973–75; Producer: General Talks, Radio, BBC Manchester, 1976–78; Television Current Affairs, BBC, Lime Grove, 1979–87; A Week in Politics, Channel 4, 1987–88; Dep. Editor, The Money Prog., BBC, 1988–89; Asst Editor, 1989–90, Man. Editor, 1990–93, BBC Television News; Man. Editor, BBC News Progs, 1994–95; Sec., BBC, 1996–99; Dir Gen., Advertising Standards Authy, 2000–09. Chm., European Advertising Standards Alliance, 2003–05. Vice-Chair, Article 29 Wkg Party of Eur. data protection authorities, 2012–14. Non-exec. Dir, Electoral Reform Services Ltd, 2001–09. Lay Mem., Bar Standards Bd, 2006–09. Mem. (L), Liverpool City Council, 1971–74. Contested (L) Wilts N, 1983, 1987. *Recreations:* singing, concerts, opera, theatre, studying late 19th and early 20th century political history. *Address:* Information Commissioner's Office, Wycliffe House, Water Lane, Wilmslow, Cheshire SK9 5AF. *T:* (01625) 545709.

GRAHAM, David; *see* Graham, S. D.

GRAHAM, Sir (David) John, KNZM 2011; CBE 1994; ED 1969; company director; Headmaster, Auckland Grammar School, 1973–93; President, New Zealand Rugby Union, 2005–06; *b* Stratford, NZ, 9 Jan. 1935; *s* of Harold Graham and Florence Cicely Graham (*née* Townend); *m* 1959, Shiela Fergus McGregor; one *s* two *d*. *Educ:* New Plymouth Boys' High Sch.; Auckland University Coll. (MA Hons). Mem., NZ All Black RU football team, 1958, 1960–65, Capt., 1964. Head of Department: Social Studies, Christchurch Boys' High Sch., 1968–70; Social Studies and Hist., Linwood High Sch., 1970–73. Director: Owens Gp Ltd, 1986–2002 (Chm., 1994–99; Dep. Chm., 2000–02); University Bookshop, 1995– (Chm., 1998–2009); Renaissance Ltd, 1996–2007. Manager, NZ Cricket Team, 1997–99. Founder Dir, Foundn for Alcohol and Drug Educn, 1987–91; Mem., NZ Educn Forum, 1991–95; Co-Founder and Chm., 1995–98, Dir, 1998–, Academic Colleges Gp (formerly Sen. College of NZ); Comr, Nga Tapuwae Coll., 1995–2003 (Mem., Bd of Trustees); Chancellor, Univ. of Auckland, 1999–2005 (Mem., Council, 1999–2005). Dep. Chm., NZ Secondary Schs' Rugby Council, 1981–87 (Life Mem.). New Zealand Rugby Union: Chm., Board Selection Cttee, 1996–2001; Mem., Boundaries Commn, 1996–97; Review Cttee, Super 12 Coaches, 1999–2004; Review Cttee, All Black Coaches, 2001–03; Vice-Pres., 2003–04. President: NZ Rugby Foundn, 1996–2014; Auckland Rugby Union, 1996–98; Chm., Ministerial Task Force on Sport, Fitness and Leisure, 2000–01; Dir, Bd, Auckland Cricket Assoc., 2000–. Founder Dir, Maxim Inst., 2001–09. Chairman: NZ Educn Scholarship Trust, 1987–; Parents Inc., 1995–2014; Southern Cross Campus Foundn, 1998–2015. Trustee: Woolf Fisher Trust, 1985–; Project K, 1995–2003; Academy Sport North, 1999–2002; Patron and Trustee, John Drake Meml Scholarship Trust Fund, 2009–. Hon. LittD Auckland, 2005. Blake Medal, Sir Peter Blake Trust, 2012. *Recreations:* follower of all sport, avid reader. *Club:* Northern (Auckland).

See also Sir J. T. Graham.

GRAHAM, Rt Hon. Sir Douglas (Arthur Montrose), KNZM 1999; PC 1998; Minister of Justice, 1990–97, Minister in charge of Treaty of Waitangi Negotiations, 1991–99, and Attorney General, 1997–99, New Zealand; *b* 12 Jan. 1942; *s* of late Robert James Alister Graham and Patricia Kennedy Graham; *m* 1966, Beverley Virginia Cordell; two *s* one *d*. *Educ:* Southwell Preparatory Sch.; Auckland GS; Auckland Univ. (BL 1965). Barrister and solicitor, 1968–84; Sen. Partner, Graham & Co., Solicitors, 1972–84. MP (N) New Zealand, 1984–99, for Remuera, 1984–96; Minister of Cultural Affairs, and of Disarmament and Arms Control, 1990–96. Hon. Dr Waikato, 1998. *Publications:* Trick or Treaty?, 1997. *Recreations:* music, gardening. *Address:* 3A Martin Avenue, Remuera, Auckland, New Zealand. *T:* (9) 5242921. *E:* douglas.graham@xtra.co.nz.

GRAHAM, Duncan Gilmour, CBE 1987; Senior Partner, Duncan Graham Consultants, 1991–2001; *b* 20 Aug. 1936; *s* of Robert Gilmour Graham and Lilias Turnbull Graham (*née* Watson); *m* 1st, 1962, Margaret Gray Graham (*née* Cairns) (marr. diss. 1991); two *s* one *d*; 2nd, 1991, Wendy Margaret Wallace (*d* 2012). *Educ:* Hutchesons', Glasgow; Univ. of Glasgow (MA (Hons) History); Jordanhill Coll. of Education (Teachers' Secondary Cert.). Teacher of History: Whitehill Sec. Sch., Glasgow, 1959–62; Hutcheson's, Glasgow, 1962–65; Lectr in Social Studies, Craigie Coll. of Educn, Ayr, 1965–68; Asst Dir of Educn, Renfrewshire, 1968–70; Sen. Depute Dir of Educn, Renfrewshire, 1970–74, Strathclyde Regl Council, 1974–79; Advr to COSLA and Scottish Teachers' Salaries Cttee, 1974–79; County Educn Officer, Suffolk, 1979–87; Chief Exec., Humberside CC, 1987–88; Chm. and Chief Exec., Nat. Curriculum Council, 1988–91. Advr to ACC, 1982–88; Mem., Burnham Cttee, 1983–87 and of ACAS Ind. Panel, 1986. Sec., Co. Educn Officers Soc., 1985–87; Chm., Assoc. of Educn Officers, 1985; Project Dir, DES Teacher Appraisal Study, 1985–86; Chm., Nat. Steering Gp on Teacher Appraisal, 1987–90. Member: BBC North Adv. Council, 1988–91; Lincs and Humberside Arts Council, 1988–91; Yorks and Humberside Arts, 1991–94; Council of Nat. Foundn for Educnl Res., 1984, and 1989–90; Exec. Council, Industrial Soc., 1988–90; Chm., Nat. Mathematics Wkg Gp, 1988. Mem. Exec., Caravan Club, 1997–2000. Chairman: Eden Rivers Trust, 2000–03; Cumbria Local Access Forum, 2003–10, England Access Forum, 2008–11; Fellrunner Village Bus, 2004–08; Youth Work in Cumbria Partnership, 2005–08. Trustee, S Tynedale Rlwy, 2013–14. FRSA 1981. *Publications:* Those Having Torches, 1985; In the Light of Torches, 1986; Sense, Nonsense and the National Curriculum, 1992; A Lesson For Us All, 1992; Sunset on the Clyde, 1993, 3rd edn 2005; The Education Racket, 1996; Visiting Distilleries, 2001, 2nd edn 2003; many articles in nat. press and educn and local govt jls. *Recreations:* garden railways, walking, fly-fishing, cycling. *Address:* Parkburn, Colby, Appleby, Cumbria CA16 6BD. *T:* (01768) 352920.

GRAHAM, Elizabeth; Director of Education, London Borough of Enfield, 1994–2003; *b* 25 Jan. 1951. *Educ:* Knightswood Secondary Sch., Glasgow; Edinburgh Univ. (MA History); Moray House Coll. of Educn, Edinburgh (PGCE). Teacher, Stirlingshire CC, 1971–73; Head of Dept, Waltham Forest LBC, 1973–81; Professional Asst, Haringey LBC, 1982–84; Asst Educn Officer, Enfield LBC, 1984–89; Asst Dir of Educn, Redbridge LBC, 1989–94. Dir, Forest Acad. Trust, 2011–. *Recreations:* cats, the crusades.

GRAHAM, George; Manager, Tottenham Hotspur Football Club, 1998–2001; *b* Scotland, 30 Nov. 1944; *m* 1998, Sue Schmidt. Professional football player, 1962–77: Aston Villa, 1962–64; Chelsea, 1964–66 (League Cup, 1965); Arsenal, 1966–72 (League and FA Cups, 1971); Manchester United, 1972–74; Portsmouth, 1974–76; Crystal Palace, 1976–77; twelve Scotland caps; coach: Queen's Park Rangers, 1977; Crystal Palace, 1977–82; Manager: Millwall, 1982–86; Arsenal, 1986–95 (League Cup, 1987, 1993; League Champions, 1989, 1991; FA Cup, 1993; European Cup Winners' Cup, 1994); Leeds, 1996–98; Tottenham Hotspur, 1998–2001 (League Cup, 1999).

GRAHAM, (George) Ronald (Gibson), CBE 1986; Partner, 1968–2000, Senior Partner, Maclay, Murray & Spens, Solicitors, Glasgow, Edinburgh, Aberdeen and London; *b* 15 Oct. 1939; *o s* of James Gibson Graham, MD, and Elizabeth Waddell; *m* 1965, Mirren Elizabeth Carnegie; three *s*. *Educ:* Glasgow Academy; Loretto Sch., Musselburgh; Oriel Coll., Oxford (MA); Glasgow Univ. (LLB). Director: Scottish Widows' Fund and Life Assce Soc., 1984–2000; Scottish Widows Bank PLC, 1995–2002; Second Scottish National Trust plc, 2002–04. Co-ordinator of Diploma in Legal Practice, 1979–83; Clerk to Gen. Council, Glasgow Univ., 1990–96, Mem. Ct, 1996–2004. Mem. Council, 1977–89, Pres., 1984–85, Law Soc. of Scotland. Gov., Jordanhill Coll. of Educn, Glasgow, 1991–93; Chm. of Govs, Loretto Sch., 2004–07. *Recreations:* fishing, golf, swimming, walking. *Address:* Carse of South Coldoch, Gargunnock, by Stirling FK8 3DF. *T:* (01786) 860397.

GRAHAM, Gordon; *see* Graham, L. G.

GRAHAM, Ian David; His Honour Judge Graham; a Circuit Judge, since 2008; *b* Alnwick, 9 May 1955; *s* of late David Graham and Elsie Graham. *Educ:* Duke's Sch., Alnwick; Christ Church, Oxford (Open Exhibnr; BA Hons Juris. 1977; MA 1981). Called to the Bar, Middle Temple, 1978 (Harmsworth Exhibnr; Astbury Scholar); barrister, NE Circuit, 1979–2008; Recorder, 2000–08. Chm., Northumbria Club, 2013–. *Recreations:* listening to music, travelling in Europe. *Address:* Basildon Crown Court, The Gore, Basildon, Essex SS14 2BU.

GRAHAM, Ian James Alastair, OBE 1999; FSA; Director, Maya Corpus Program, Peabody Museum of Archaeology, Harvard University, 1993–2004; *b* 12 Nov. 1923; *s* of Captain Lord Alastair Graham, RN, *y s* of 5th Duke of Montrose, and Lady Meriel Olivia Bathurst (*d* 1936), *d* of 7th Earl Bathurst; unmarried. *Educ:* Winchester Coll.; Trinity Coll., Dublin. RNVR (A), 1942–47; TCD 1947–51; Nuffield Foundn Research Scholar at The National Gallery, 1951–54; independent archaeological explorer in Central America, 1959–68; Res. Fellow, 1968–75, Asst Curator, 1975–93, Peabody Mus. of Archaeol., Harvard Univ. Occasional photographer of architecture. Hon. LHD Tulane, 1998; Hon. DLitt Dublin, 2000. MacArthur Foundn Prize Fellowship, 1981; Lifetime Achievement Award, Soc. for Amer. Archaeology, 2004. Order of the Quetzal (Guatemala), 2007. *Publications:* Splendours of the East, 1965; Great Houses of the Western World, 1968; Archaeological Explorations in El Peten, Guatemala, 1967; Corpus of Maya Hieroglyphic Inscriptions, 20 parts, 1975–; Alfred Maudslay, a Biography, 2002; The Road to Ruins (memoir), 2012. *Address:* Chantry Farm, Campsey Ash, Suffolk IP13 0PZ.

GRAHAM, Sir James Bellingham, 11th Bt *cr* 1662; *b* 8 Oct. 1940; *e s* of Sir Richard Bellingham Graham, 10th Bt, OBE, and Beatrice, OBE (*d* 1992), *d* of late Michael Hamilton-Spencer-Smith, DSO, MC; *S* father, 1982; *m* 1986, Halina, *d* of Major Wiktor Grubert, soldier and diplomat and Eleonora Grubert. *Educ:* Eton College; Christ Church, Oxford (MA). Researcher in fine and decorative arts, Cecil Higgins Mus. and Art Gall., Bedford, 1980–96; Curator (with Halina Graham), Norton Conyers and its collections, 1996–. *Publications:* Guide to Norton Conyers, 1976, revised 2004; (with Halina Graham) Cecil Higgins, Collector Extraordinary, 1983; (with Halina Graham) A Guide to the Cecil Higgins Museum and Art Gallery, 1987; reviews of art exhibitions. *Recreations:* travel, visiting historic houses and museums. *Address:* Norton Conyers, Wath, near Ripon, N Yorks HG4 5EQ. *T:* (01765) 640333.

GRAHAM, Sir James (Fergus Surtees), 7th Bt *cr* 1783, of Netherby, Cumberland; farmer; *b* 29 July 1946; *s* of Sir Charles Graham, 6th Bt and Isabel Susan Anne, *d* of Major R. L. Surtees, OBE; *S* father, 1997; *m* 1975, Serena Jane, *yr d* of Ronald Frank Kershaw; one *s* two *d*. *Educ:* Milton Abbey; Royal Agricl Coll., Cirencester. Lloyd's Reinsurance Broker, 1969–90. *Heir:* *s* Robert Charles Thomas Graham, *b* 19 July 1985. *Address:* Crofthead, Longtown, Cumbria CA6 5PA. *T:* (01228) 791262.

GRAHAM, James Lowery, OBE 1991; DL; Deputy Chairman, Border Television Ltd, Carlisle, 2001–06; *b* 29 Oct. 1932; *s* of William and Elizabeth Graham; *m* 1984, Ann Routledge; two *d* by previous marr. *Educ:* Whitehaven Grammar School. Journalist, North West Evening Mail, Barrow, 1955–62; News Editor, Border Television, 1962–67; Producer, BBC, Leeds, 1967–70; BBC: Regional News Editor, North, 1970–75; Regional Television Manager, North East, 1975–80; Head of Secretariat, Broadcasting House, 1980–82; Border Television plc: Man. Dir, 1982–96; Dep. Chm., 1990–96; CEO and Chm., 1996–98; non-exec. Chm., 1999–2001. Sec., BBC Central Music Adv. Council, 1981–82; Jt Sec., Broadcasters' Audience Res. Bd, 1980–82. Dir, Ind. Television Publications, 1982–89. Chairman: Independent Television Facilities Centre Ltd, 1987–2007; Beat 106 FM, Glasgow, 2001–05; Director: Oracle Teletext, 1988–93; Radio Borders, 1989–93; Radio SW Scotland, 1989–93 (Chm., 1990–93); Bay Radio Ltd, 1992–94; Central Scotland Radio, 1993–95; Century (formerly North East) Radio, 1993–2000; Border Radio Holdings, 1997–2000; Century Radio 105, 1998–2000; Sunderland City Radio, 1998–2003; Reliance Security Gp plc, 1999–2002. Pres., Prix Italia, 1998–2002, now Hon. Life Pres. (ITVA rep., 1987–2011). Dir, Educnl Broadcasting Services Trust, 1992–2008. Ombudsman, GM-TV, London,

2008–10. Member: BAFTA; Internat. Council, Nat. Acad. of Television Arts and Scis, NY, 1999–2011 (ITVA rep.); European Movement; Co-operative Internationale de Recherche et d'Action en Matière de Communication (European Producers). Governor: Newcastle Polytechnic, 1975–80; Cumbria Inst. of Art (formerly Coll. of Art and Design), 1995–2007; Mem. Court, Univ. of Central Lancs, 2006–. DL Cumbria 2000–10. FRSA 1987. FRTS 1994. Hon. Fellow: Univ. of Central Lancashire, 2001; Univ. of Cumbria, 2012. Hon. DCL Northumbria, 1999. News Film Award, RTS, 1975; European Flag of Honour, Council of Europe, 1980; Beffroi d'Or, Lille (European regional broadcasting award), 1983; RTS Regl Broadcasting Award, 1989. *Publications:* Whistler Rhymes (poetry), 1998. *Recreations:* hill walking, ski-ing, cycling. *Address:* Carlisle, Cumbria; Whistler, BC, Canada. *Club:* Groucho.

GRAHAM, Sir James (Thompson), Kt 1990; CMG 1986; farmer, since 1946; Director, 1979–89, Chairman, 1982–89, New Zealand Dairy Board, retired; *b* 6 May 1929; *s* of Harold Graham and Florence Cicely Graham; *m* 1955, Ina Isabelle Low (*d* 2002); one *s* two *d*; *m* 2005, Robin. *Educ:* New Plymouth Boys' High Sch. Dir, NZ Co-op Dairy Co., 1974–89 (Chm., 1979–82). *Recreations:* golf, tennis, bowls. *Address:* 12A Sunbrae Grove, Mount Maunganui, Tauranga, New Zealand. *T:* (75) 754043.

GRAHAM, Janice Joanne, (Mrs Anthony Woolley); Artistic Director, English Sinfonia, since 2005 (Leader, since 1995); Leader, English National Opera Orchestra, since 2007; *b* Watford, 21 April 1968; *d* of John and Jean Graham; *m* 1996, Anthony Woolley; one *s* one *d*. *Educ:* Purcell Sch.; Guildhall Sch. (AGSM Dist.; ARCM Hons); Juilliard Sch., NY (Adv. Cert.). Principal 2nd, 1993–95, Asst Leader, 1995–2000, LSO; Leader, BBC Nat. Orch. of Wales, 1997–2002; Guest Leader: LPO; RPO; Royal Opera Hse; BBC SO; BBC Philharmonic Orch.; BBC Scottish Orch.; CBSO; Bournemouth SO; RTE SO. Professor: RCM, 1995–2009; GSM, 2009–. Has made recordings. Gov., Purcell Sch., 2001–. Winner, Shell/LSO Competition, 1990. *Recreations:* family, sailing. *Address:* 1 Causton Road, Highgate, N6 5ES. *E:* Janice.Woolley@me.com.

GRAHAM, Sir John; *see* Graham, Sir D. J.

GRAHAM, Sir John (Alexander Noble), 4th Bt *cr* 1906, of Larbert; GCMG 1986 (KCMG 1979 CMG 1972); HM Diplomatic Service, retired; Registrar, Order of Saint Michael and Saint George, 1987–2001; Director, Ditchley Foundation, 1987–92; *b* 15 July 1926; *s* of Sir John Reginald Noble Graham, 3rd Bt, VC, OBE and Rachel Septima (*d* 1984), *d* of Col Sir Alexander Sprot, 1st and last Bt; *S* father, 1980; *m* 1st, 1956, Marygold Ellinor Gabrielle Austin (*d* 1991); two *s* one *d*; 2nd, 1992, Jane, *widow* of Christopher Howells. *Educ:* Eton Coll. (scholar); Trinity Coll., Cambridge (scholar). Army, 1944–47; Cambridge, 1948–50; HM Foreign Service, 1950; Middle East Centre for Arab Studies, 1951; Third Secretary, Bahrain 1951, Kuwait 1952, Amman 1953; Asst Private Sec. to Sec. of State for Foreign Affairs, 1954–57; First Sec., Belgrade, 1957–60, Benghazi, 1960–61; FO 1961–66; Counsellor and Head of Chancery, Kuwait, 1966–69; Principal Private Sec. to Foreign and Commonwealth Sec., 1969–72; Cllr (later Minister) and Head of Chancery, Washington, 1972–74; Ambassador to Iraq, 1974–77; Dep. Under-Sec. of State, FCO, 1977–79; Ambassador to Iran, 1979–80; Deputy Under-Sec. of State, FCO, 1980–82; Ambassador and UK Permanent Representative to NATO, Brussels, 1982–86. Hon. Air Cdre, RAuxAF Regt, 1990–2001. *Publications:* Ditchley Park: the house and the foundation, 1996. *Heir: s* Lt Gen. Andrew John Noble Graham, *qv*. *Address:* Salisbury Place, Church Street, Shipton under Wychwood, Oxon OX7 6BP. *Club:* Army and Navy.

GRAHAM, Sir (John) Alistair, Kt 2000; Chairman, PhonePayplus, the Premium Rate Services Regulator (formerly Independent Committee for the Supervision of Standards of the Telephone Information Services), 2008–12; Lay Member, Queen's Counsel Selection Panel for England and Wales, since 2011; *b* 6 Aug. 1942; *s* of late Robert Graham and Dorothy Graham; *m* 1967, Dorothy Jean Wallace; one *s* one *d*. *Educ:* Royal Grammar Sch., Newcastle upon Tyne. FCIPD (FITD 1989; FIPM 1989). Clerical Asst, St George's Hosp., Morpeth, 1961; Admin. Trainee, Northern Regional Hosp. Bd, 1963; Higher Clerical Officer, Royal Sussex County Hosp., Brighton, 1964; Legal Dept, TGWU, 1965; The Civil and Public Services Association: Asst Sec., 1966; Asst Gen. Sec., 1975; Dep. Gen. Sec., 1976; Gen. Sec., 1982–86; Chief Executive: Industrial Soc., 1986–91; Calderdale & Kirklees TEC, 1991–96; Leeds TEC, 1996–2000; Chairman: Police Complaints Authy, 2000–04; W Yorks Strategic HA, 2002–03; Northern and Yorks Regl Comr, NHS Appts Commn, 2003–04; British Transport Police Authy, 2004–08; Mem., British Transport Police Cttee, 2004; Mem., 2003–07, Chm., 2004–07, Cttee on Standards in Public Life. Chm., Shareholders' Trust FI Group, 1991–97. Vis. Fellow, Nuffield Coll., Oxford, 1984–92; Vis. Prof., Mgt Sch., Imperial Coll., London Univ., 1989–91. External assessor, teacher trng courses, Univ. of Huddersfield, 1993–96. Chairman: BBC S and E Regl Adv. Council, 1987–90; Training and Develt Lead Body, 1989–94; Member: Personnel Lead Body, 1991–94; BBC Educn Broadcasting Council, 1991–97; Restrictive Practices Court, 1993–99; Bd, Univ. of Huddersfield Trng and Quality Services Certification Div., 1993–96; Overview Gp on producing standards for Teachers, Teacher Trng Agency, 1996–97; Employment Appeal Tribunal, 2003–12; Lay Mem., Fitness to Practise Cttee, General Optical Council, 2005–15. Lay Observer, Council of Chartered Inst. of Taxation, 2011–. Non-exec. Dir, Mgt Bd, Information Comr's Office, 2004–09. Mem., TUC Gen. Council, 1982–84, 1985–86. Mem., 1988–97, Chm., Staff Cttee, 1991–97, OU Council. Trustee, Duke of Edinburgh Study Conf., 1989–92. Mem., Work, Income and Social Policy Cttee, Joseph Rowntree Foundn, 1997–2000. Vice-Pres., Opera North, 2002– (Bd Mem., 1989–2002, Chm. Finance Cttee, 1996–97); Mem. Mgt Cttee, Huddersfield Contemp. Music Fest., 1992–97; Chm., Yorks Youth and Music, 1995–97. Assessor, Guildford and Woolwich Inquiry, 1990–94; Chm., Parades Commn for NI, 1997–2000. Contested (Lab) Brighton Pavilion, 1966. DUniv: Open, 1999; Bradford, 2006. *Recreations:* music, theatre, Durham CCC (non-exec. dir, 2007–). *Address:* Queen's Counsel Selection Panel, 3rd Floor, Totara Park House, 34–36 Gray's Inn Road, WC1X 8HR.

GRAHAM, Prof. (John) Michael (Russell), PhD; FREng; Professor of Unsteady Aerodynamics, Imperial College, University of London, since 1990; *b* 26 April 1942; *s* of George Desmond Graham and Evelyn Ann Graham (*née* Russell); *m* 1966, Philippa Gabrielle Freeman; one *s* one *d*. *Educ:* Epsom Coll., Surrey; Clare Coll., Cambridge (BA Maths, MA); Imperial Coll., Univ. of London (PhD Aeronautical Engrg). Lectr, 1970–90, Head of Dept of Aeronautics, 1999–2003, Imperial Coll., Univ. of London. FRAeS 1999; FCGI 2000; FREng 2006; FRINA 2007. *Recreations:* walking, climbing, grandchildren. *Address:* Department of Aeronautics, Imperial College, SW7 2AZ. *E:* m.graham@imperial.ac.uk.

GRAHAM, Sir John (Moodie), 2nd Bt *cr* 1964; Director, Kinnegar Inns Ltd, since 1981; Chairman, John Graham (Dromore) Ltd, 1966–83; *b* 3 April 1938; *s* of Sir Clarence Graham, 1st Bt, MICE, and Margaret Christina Moodie (*d* 1954); *S* father, 1966; *m* 1970, Valerie Rosemary (marr. diss. 1983), *d* of late Frank Gill, Belfast; three *d*; civil partnership 2006, David Galway. *Educ:* Trinity Coll., Glenalmond; Queen's Univ., Belfast. BSc, Civil Engineering, 1961. Joined family firm of John Graham (Dromore) Ltd, Building and Civil Engineering Contractors, on graduating from University. Director: Electrical Supplies Ltd, 1967–83; Concrete (NI) Ltd, 1967–83; Ulster Quarries Ltd; Graham (Contracts) Ltd, 1971–83; Fieldhouse Plant (NI) Ltd, 1976–83. Chm., Concrete Soc., NI, 1972–74; Senior Vice-Pres., Concrete Soc., 1980; Pres., Northern Ireland Leukaemia Research Fund, 1967. Mem., Lloyd's, 1977–2004. *Recreations:* sailing, photography.

GRAHAM, John Strathie; Chief Executive, Historic Scotland, 2004–09; *b* 27 May 1950; *s* of Sir Norman William Graham, CB and of Catherine Mary Graham (*née* Strathie); *m* 1979, Anne Janet Stenhouse; two *s* one *d*. *Educ:* Edinburgh Academy; Corpus Christi College, Oxford (BA Lit. Hum.). Joined Scottish Office, 1972; Private Sec. to Minister of State, 1975–76; Industrial Develt and Electricity Divs, 1976–82; Private Sec. to Sec. of State, 1983–85; Asst Sec., Planning and Finance Divs, 1985–91; Under Sec. (Local Govt), Envmt Dept, 1991–96; Prin. Finance Officer, 1996–98; Sec. and Head, Scottish Office Agric., Envmt and Fisheries Dept, then Scottish Exec. Rural Affairs Dept, subseq. Scottish Exec. Envmt and Rural Affairs Dept, 1998–2004. *Recreations:* music, hillwalking.

GRAHAM, Rev. Prof. (Lawrence) Gordon, PhD; FRSE; Henry Luce Professor of Philosophy and the Arts, Princeton Theological Seminary, since 2006; Director, Princeton Center for the Study of Scottish Philosophy, since 2007; *b* 15 July 1949; *s* of William Moore Graham and Hyacinth Elizabeth (*née* Donald); *m* 1971; one *s* one *d*; *m* 2003; one *s* one *d*. *Educ:* Univ. of St Andrews (MA); Univ. of Durham (MA; PhD 1975). FRSE 1999. University of St Andrews: Lectr in Moral Philosophy, 1975–88; Reader, 1988–95; Dir of Music, 1991–95; Regius Prof. of Moral Philosophy, Univ. of Aberdeen, 1996–2005; Stanton Lectr, Univ. of Cambridge, 2005. Adjunct Prof. of Sacred Music, Westminster Choir Coll., Rider Univ., 2010–12. Ordained deacon, 2005, priest, 2006, Scottish Episcopal Church. Sec., Scots Philosophical Club, 1987–2001. Founding Editor: Jl of Scottish Philosophy, 2004–; Kuyper Center Rev., 2010–. *Publications:* Historical Explanation Reconsidered, 1983; Politics in its Place, 1986; Contemporary Social Philosophy, 1988, 4th edn 1995; The Idea of Christian Charity, 1990; Living the Good Life, 1990, 2nd edn 1994; The Shape of the Past, 1997; Ethics and International Relations, 1997, 2nd edn 2008; Philosophy of the Arts, 1997, 3rd edn 2005; The Internet: a philosophical inquiry, 1999; Evil and Christian Ethics, 2000; Genes: a philosophical inquiry, 2002; The Case Against the Democratic State, 2002; Universities: the recovery of an idea, 2002, 2nd edn 2008; Eight Theories of Ethics, 2004; The Institution of Intellectual Values, 2005; The Re-enchantment of the World, 2007; Theories of Ethics, 2011; Wittgenstein and Natural Religion, 2014; (ed) Scottish Philosophy in the 19th and 20th centuries, 2015. *Recreations:* music, walking, cookery. *Address:* Princeton Theological Seminary, 64 Mercer Street, Princeton, NJ 08542–0803, USA.

GRAHAM, Michael; *see* Graham, J. M. R.

GRAHAM, Ven. Olivia Josephine; Archdeacon of Berkshire, since 2013; *b* Dartford, 21 June 1956; *d* of Michael William Graham and Rachel Mildred Graham; *m* 1989, Keith Malcolm Glenny; two *s* one *d*. *Educ:* Cobham Hall, Kent; Stake Farm Coll., Kent; Univ. of E Anglia (BA Hons 1st Cl. 1984); St Albans and Oxford Ministry Course (CTh 1997). Teaching, Africa, 1974–81; Co-ord., UN Refugee Educn Prog., World Univ. Service, Djibouti, 1984–86; Dep. Country Dir, Oxfam Somalia, 1986–88; Co-ord., Arid Lands Information Network, Oxfam, 1988–93; ordained deacon, 1997, priest, 1998; non-stipendiary Curate, St Mary's, Garsington, 1997–98; Curate, St Mary's, Princes Risborough, 1998–2001; Vicar, St Peter's, Burnham, 2001–07; Parish Develt Advr, Oxford Archdeaconry, 2007–13. Hon. Canon, Christ Church Cath., Oxford, 2012–. *Recreations:* walking, swimming, reading, inventive cooking, playing with paint, good comedy, music. *Address:* Foxglove House, Love Lane, Donnington, Newbury, Berks RG14 2JG. *T:* (01635) 552820. *E:* archdber@oxford.anglican.org.

GRAHAM, Sir Peter, KCB 1993 (CB 1982); QC 1990; First Parliamentary Counsel, 1991–94; *b* 7 Jan. 1934; *o s* of late Alderman Douglas Graham, CBE, Huddersfield, and Ena May (*née* Jackson); *m* 1st, Judith Mary Dunbar; two *s*; 2nd, Anne Silvia Garcia; 3rd, Janet, *o d* of late Capt. William Eric Walker, TD, Mayfield, Sussex. *Educ:* St Bees Sch., Cumberland (scholar); St John's Coll., Cambridge (scholar, 1st cl. Law Tripos, MA, LLM, McMahon Law Studentship). Served as pilot in Fleet Air Arm, 1952–55, Lieut, RNR. Called to the Bar, Gray's Inn, 1958 (Holker Exhibn; H. C. Richards Prize, Ecclesiastical Law; Bencher, 1992), Lincoln's Inn, 1982; joined Parliamentary Counsel Office, 1959; Parly Counsel, 1972–86; with Law Commn, 1979–81; Second Parly Counsel, 1987–91. External Examr (Legislation), Univ. of Edinburgh, 1977–81; Consultant: in Legislative Drafting, Office of Attorney-Gen., Dublin, 1994–96; to Hassans (formerly J. A. Hassan & Partners), Gibraltar, 1997–; for specific legislative projects incl. Brunei, Hong Kong, Maldives, Malta, Mauritius, Sri Lanka, SA. Mem., Tax Law Review Cttee, Inst. of Fiscal Studies, 1994–2006. Mem., Council, Huddersfield Univ., 1992–96. Hon. Legal Adviser, Historic Vehicle Clubs Cttee, 1967–86. *Recreations:* restoring and enjoying vintage and classic cars, la bonne cuisine. *Address:* Le Petit Château, La Vallette, 87190 Magnac Laval, France. *Club:* Sette of Odd Volumes.

GRAHAM, Dr Peter John; Director, Change Programme, Health and Safety Executive, 2002–03 (Board Member, 1994–2003); *b* 16 Sept. 1943; *s* of John Graham and late Judy Graham; *m* 1968, Janice Head; three *s*. *Educ:* St Joseph's Coll., Stoke-on-Trent; Liverpool Univ. (BSc; PhD Maths 1968). DTI, 1969–79; 1st Sec., UK Perm. Repn, Brussels, 1979–82; DTI, 1982–84; Dept of Employment, 1984–88; Health and Safety Executive: Hazardous Substances Div., 1988–91; General Policy Br., 1991–93; Offshore Safety Div., 1993–94; Dir, Health, 1994–99; Dir, Strategy and Analytical Support, 1999–2002. Lay Mem. Bd, Faculty of Occupational Medicine, 2005–11. Chm., Centre 33, St Albans, 2003–12.

GRAHAM, Lt-Gen. Sir Peter (Walter), KCB 1991; CBE 1981 (OBE 1978; MBE 1972); GOC Scotland and Governor of Edinburgh Castle, 1991–93, retired; *b* 14 March 1937; *s* of Dr Walter Graham and Suzanne Graham (*née* Simon); *m* 1963, Alison Mary, MB ChB, MRCGP, *d* of D. B. Morren, TD; three *s*. *Educ:* Fyvie Village School, Aberdeenshire; Hall Sch., Hampstead; St Paul's Sch.; RMA Sandhurst; psc (Aust), ocds (Can). Commissioned, The Gordon Highlanders, 1956; regtl appts, Dover, BAOR, Scotland, Kenya, 1957–62; HQ Highland Bde, 1962–63; Adjt, 1 Gordons, Kenya, Scotland, Borneo (despatches), 1963–66; Staff Capt., HQ (1 Br) Corps, 1966–67; Aust. Staff Coll., 1968; Co. Comdr, 1 Gordons, BAOR, 1969–70; Bde Maj., 39 Inf. Bde, Ulster, 1970–72; 2nd i/c 1 Gordons, Scotland, Ulster, Singapore, 1972–74; MA to Adjt-Gen., MoD, 1974–75; CO 1 Gordons, Scotland, Ulster, 1976–78; COS HQ 3rd Armd Div., BAOR, 1978–82; Comdr UDR, 1982–84 (despatches); Nat. Defence Coll., Canada, 1984–85; Dep. Mil. Sec., MoD, 1985–87; GOC Eastern Dist, 1987–89; Comdt, RMA Sandhurst, 1989–91. Col, The Gordon Highlanders, 1986–94; Col Comdt, The Scottish Div., 1991–93. Mem., Royal Company of Archers, Queen's Body Guard for Scotland, 1986–. Chm., Gordon Highlanders Regtl Trust Fund, 1986–2004; Vice Patron, The Gordon Highlanders Mus., 2003– (Chm., Mgt Cttee, 1994–2003); Pres., Gordon Highlanders London Assoc., 2009–. Mem., NE Scotland Co-ordination Cttee, Better Together, 2012–14. Hon. Firemaster, Grampian Fire and Rescue Service, 2010–13. Burgess of Guild, City of Aberdeen, 1994. Hon. DLitt Robert Gordon Univ., Aberdeen, 1996. *Publications:* (with Pipe Major B. MacRae) The Gordon Highlanders Pipe Music Collection, Vol. 1, 1983, 3rd edn 1986, Vol. 2, 1985; (contrib.) John Baynes, Soldiers of Scotland, 1988; contrib. to Jl of RUSI. *Recreations:* military history, hill walking, reading, pipe music, amusing grandchildren, gardening under wife's directions. *Address:* c/o Gordon Highlanders Museum, Viewfield Road, Aberdeen AB15 7XH.

See also Sir A. M. Graham.

GRAHAM, Prof. Philip Jeremy; Professor of Child Psychiatry, Institute of Child Health, London University, 1975–94, now Emeritus; Chairman, Association of Child Psychology and Psychiatry, 2002–04; *b* 3 Sept. 1932; *s* of Jacob Rackham Graham and Pauline Graham; *m* 1960, Nori (*née* Burawoy); two *s* one *d*. *Educ:* Perse Sch., Cambridge; Cambridge Univ. (MA); University Coll. Hosp., London. FRCP 1973; FRCPsych 1972. Consultant Psychiatrist: Maudsley Hosp., London, 1966–68; Hosp. for Sick Children, Great Ormond Street, London,

1968–74; Dean, Inst. of Child Health, London Univ., 1985–90; Prof. of Child Psychiatry, Univ. of Oslo, 1994–2000; Lectr, Dept of Develtl Psychiatry, Univ. of Cambridge, 1994–2000; Sen. Mem., Wolfson Coll., Cambridge, 1994–2002. Chm., Nat. Children's Bureau, 1994–2000 (Chm., Child Policy Rev. Gp, 1987–89). Vice-Chair, Dignity and Dying, 2011– (Mem. Bd, 2010–). President: European Soc. for Child and Adolescent Psychiatry, 1987–91; Psychiatry Section, RSM, 1994–95; Vice-Pres., RCPsych, 1996–98. Community Governor: Woodside High Sch., Haringey, 2009–; Riverside School, Haringey, 2012–. Hon. FRCPCH 1993; Hon. FRCPsych 2004. *Publications:* A Neuropsychiatric Study in Childhood (jtly), 1970; (ed) Epidemiological Approaches to Child Psychiatry, 1977; (jtly) Child Psychiatry: a developmental approach, 1986, 4th edn 2007; (jtly) So Young, So Sad, So Listen, 1995, 2nd edn 2005; (ed) Cognitive Behaviour Therapy for Children and Families, 1998, 3rd edn 2012; The End of Adolescence, 2004; Susan Isaacs: freeing the minds of children, 2008; Where There Is No Child Psychiatrist, 2012; various publications on child and adolescent psychiatry. *Recreations:* walking, chess. *Address:* 36 St Alban's Road, NW5 1RD.

GRAHAM, Sir Ralph Stuart, 14th Bt *cr* 1629 (NS), of Esk, Cumberland; *b* 5 Nov. 1950; *s* of Sir Ralph Wolfe Graham, 13th Bt and of Geraldine, *d* of Austin Velour; *S* father, 1988, but his name does not appear on the Official Roll of the Baronetage; *m* 1st, 1972, Roxanne (*d* 1978), *d* of Mrs Lovette Gurzan; 2nd, 1979, Deena Vandergrift; one adopted *s*. *Heir: b* Robert Bruce Graham [*b* 14 Nov. 1953; *m* 1974, Denise, *d* of T. Juranich; two *s*].

GRAHAM, Richard; MP (C) Gloucester, since 2010; *b* Reading, 4 April 1958; *s* of Robin and Judith Graham; *m* 1989, Anthea Knaggs; two *s* one *d*. *Educ:* Eton Coll.; Christ Church, Oxford (BA Hist. 1979); Investment Mgt Cert. 1998. Airline Manager, Cathay Pacific Airways and John Swire & Sons, 1980–86; HM Diplomatic Service, 1986–93: First Sec., Nairobi, Peking; Trade Comr, China, and Consul, Macau, 1989–92; Chief Rep. in China, Barings plc, 1993–95; Dir, ING Barings, 1995–97; Hd, Instnl Business, Baring Asset Mgt, 1997–2010. Director: Greater China Fund Inc., 1994–2004; Care 4 Children, 1999–2001; Chm., British Chamber of Commerce, Shanghai, 1995–97. Prime Minister's Trade Envoy to Indonesia, 2012–. Mem. (C) Cotswold DC, 2003–07. Contested (C) SW England, EP, 2004. PPS to Minister of State, FCO, 2010–14. Mem., Work and Pensions Select Cttee, 2010; Chm., All Party Parly China Gp, 2010–15; Founder Chm., All Party Parly Commonwealth Gp, 2012–13. *Recreations:* cricket, squash, watching Gloucester Rugby, walking. *Address:* House of Commons, SW1A 0AA. *T:* (020) 7219 7077. *E:* richard.graham.mp@parliament.uk. *Clubs:* MCC, Lords and Commons Cricket, Gloucester City Winget Cricket.

GRAHAM, Robert Martin; Chief Executive, British United Provident Association, 1984–91; *b* 20 Sept. 1930; *s* of Francis P. Graham and Margaret M. Graham (*née* Broderick); *m* 1959, Eileen (*née* Hoey); two *s* two *d*. *Educ:* Dublin; ACII. Hibernian Fire and General Insurance Co. Ltd, 1948–57; Voluntary Health Insurance Board, 1957–82 (to Chief Exec.); Dep. Chief Exec., BUPA, 1982–84. Chm., Board of Management, Meath Hosp., 1972–82; Pres., Internat. Fedn of Voluntary Health Service Funds, 1988–90 (Dep. Pres., 1986–88); Vice-Pres., Assoc. Internationale de la Mutualité, 1990– (Mem. Bd of Govs, 1978–91); Mem., Central Council, Federated Voluntary Hosps, Ireland, 1978–82. *Address:* 39 Garratts Lane, Banstead, Surrey SM7 2ED. *Clubs:* Royal Automobile, Rotary Club of London.

GRAHAM, Ronald; *see* Graham, G. R. G.

GRAHAM, Dr Ronald Cairns, CBE 1992; General Manager, Tayside Health Board, 1985–93 (Chief Administrative Medical Officer, 1973–85); *b* 8 Oct. 1931; *s* of Thomas Graham and Helen Cairns; *m* 1959, Christine Fraser Osborne; two *s* one *d*. *Educ:* Airdrie Acad.; Glasgow Univ. MB, ChB Glasgow 1956; DipSocMed Edin. 1968; FFCM 1973; FRCPE 1983. West of Scotland; house jobs, gen. practice and geriatric med., 1956–62; Dep. Med. Supt, Edin. Royal Infirmary, 1962–65; Asst Sen. Admin. MO, SE Regional Hosp. Bd, 1965–69; Dep. and then Sen. Admin. MO, Eastern Regional Hosp. Bd, 1969–73. Mem. Court, Univ. of Dundee, 1994–2003. *Recreations:* fishing, bowling. *Address:* 34 Dalgleish Road, Dundee DD4 7JT. *T:* (01382) 455426.

GRAHAM, Prof. Stephen Douglas Nelson, PhD; Professor of Cities and Society, University of Newcastle, since 2010; *b* Tynemouth, 26 Feb. 1965; *s* of David and Doreen Graham; *m* 1997, Annette Kearney; two *s*. *Educ:* Univ. of Southampton (BSc Hons Geog.); Univ. of Newcastle upon Tyne (MPhil Urban Planning); Univ. of Manchester (PhD Sci. and Technol. Policy 1995). Planning Officer, Sheffield CC, 1989–92; Lectr, 1992–97, Reader, 1997–2000, Prof., 2000–04, Sch. of Architecture, Planning and Landscape, Univ. of Newcastle upon Tyne; Prof. of Human Geog., Univ. of Durham, 2004–10. Vis. Prof. of Urban Planning, MIT, 1999–2000. *Publications:* (with S. Marvin) Telecommunications and the City, 1996; (with S. Marvin) Splintering Urbanism, 2001; Cities, War and Terrorism, 2004; The Cybercities Reader, 2004; Disrupted Cities, 2009; Cities Under Siege: the new military urbanism, 2010; Vertical: the politics of up and down, 2014; (with C. McFarlane) Infrastructural Lives, 2014. *Recreations:* cycling, hill walking, cinema, rock music concerts, history writings. *Address:* School of Architecture, Planning and Landscape, University of Newcastle, Newcastle upon Tyne NE1 7RU. *T:* (0191) 222 8579, *Fax:* (0191) 222 6115. *E:* steve.graham@ncl.ac.uk.

GRAHAM, (Stewart) David; QC 1977; Partner, Cork Gully, 1985–92; *b* 27 Feb. 1934; *s* of late Lewis Graham and of Gertrude Graham; *m* 1959, Corinne Carmona (*d* 2009); two *d*. *Educ:* Leeds Grammar Sch.; St Edmund Hall, Oxford (MA, BCL). Called to the Bar, Middle Temple, 1957; Harmsworth Law Scholar, 1958. Mem. Council, Justice, 1976–96 (Chm., Cttee on Protection of Small Investor, 1989–92; Chm., Cttee on Insolvency, 1993–94); Mem., Insolvency Rules Adv. Cttee, 1984–86; Chm., Law, Parly and Gen. Purposes Cttee, Bd of Deputies of British Jews, 1983–88. Ind. Mem. Council, The Insurance Ombudsman Bureau, 1993–2001; Associate Mem., British and Irish (formerly UK) Ombudsman Assoc., 1994–. Vis. Fellow, Centre for Commercial Law, QMW, London, 1992–; Vis. Prof., Faculty of Business, Centre for Insolvency Law and Policy, Kingston Univ., 2004–. Member Committee: Stanmore Soc., 2001–; Harrow Heritage Trust, 2002–. Chm. Editorial Bd, Insolvency Intelligence, 1988–94. FRSA 1995. *Publications:* (ed jtly) Williams and Muir Hunter on Bankruptcy, 18th edn 1968, 19th edn 1979; (contrib.) Longman's Insolvency, 1986; (contrib.) Muir Hunter on Personal Insolvency, 2002; (contrib.) Oxford DNB, 2005; (ed) legal textbooks; contrib. Internat. Insolvency Review. *Recreations:* biography, music, drama, travel, history of insolvency. *Address:* 6 Grosvenor Lodge, Dennis Lane, Stanmore, Middx HA7 4JE. *T:* (020) 8954 3783.

GRAHAM, Stuart Twentyman, CBE 1981; DFC 1943; FCIS, FCIB; Chairman, Aitken Hume Bank (formerly Aitken Hume) Ltd, 1985–93; *b* 26 Aug. 1921; *s* of late Twentyman Graham; *m* 1948, Betty June Cox (*d* 1999); one *s*. *Educ:* Kilburn Grammar Sch. Served War, 1940–46: commissioned, RAF, 1942. Entered Midland Bank, 1938; Jt Gen. Manager, 1966–70; Asst Chief Gen. Manager, 1970–74; Chief Gen. Manager, 1974–81; Gp Chief Exec., 1981–82; Dir, 1974–85. Chairman: Northern Bank Ltd, 1982–85; International Commodities Clearing House Ltd, 1982–86; Director: Allied Lyons plc, 1981–92; Sheffield Forgemasters Holdings, 1983–85; Aitken Hume International, 1985–93; Scotia (formerly Efamol) Hldgs, 1985–95. *Recreations:* music, reading. *Club:* Royal Air Force.

GRAHAM, Susan Alesta; mezzo soprano; *b* 23 July 1960; *d* of Floyd Ben Graham and Betty Fort. *Educ:* Midland Lee High Sch.; Texas Technical Univ.; Manhattan Sch. of Music. Opera début in Vanessa, St Louis, 1988. Regular performances with NY Metropolitan Opera, 1991–, and at Salzburg Fest.; other appearances include: Royal Opera, 1994–; WNO, 1994–; Glyndebourne; Vienna State Opera; La Scala; Paris Opéra, etc. Rôles include: title rôle, Chérubin; Octavian in Der Rosenkavalier; Dorabella in Così fan tutte; Cherubino in Le Nozze di Figaro; title rôle, Arianna; title rôle, Iphigénie en Tauride; Charlotte in Werther; title rôle, Béatrice et Bénédict; Marguerite in La damnation de Faust; title rôle in world première of Monteverdi's Arianna; Composer in Ariadne auf Naxos; Donna Elvira in Don Giovanni; Iphigénie in Iphigénie en Tauride; Sycorax in The Enchanted Island; *theatre*: The King and I, Théâtre du Châtelet, Paris, 2014. Numerous recitals and recordings. Metropolitan Opera Nat. Council Award, 1988.

GRAHAM, Teresa Colomba, CBE 2008 (OBE 1998); business and government advisor, since 2003; Member, Office of Tax Simplification, HM Revenue and Customs, since 2009; *b* Newcastle upon Tyne, 8 March 1956; *d* of Albert Rea and Anna Rea (*née* Mastroianni). *Educ:* Univ. of Newcastle upon Tyne (BA Eng. Linguistics 1977). FCA 1982. Price Waterhouse, 1977–90; Baker Tilly, 1990–2003. Chm., Salix Finance, 2004–; non-exec. dir of various cos. Seconded to Enterprise and Deregulation Unit, 1986–87; Mem., Deregulation Adv. Panel, 1988–90; Dep. Chm., Better Regulation Task Force, subseq. Better Regulation Commn, 1997–2007 (Chm. gp on report Better Routes to Redress, 2004; Chm. Subgp on report Regulation—Less is More, 2005); leader, independent review of Small Firms Loan Guarantee, 2003–04 (Graham Review of Small Firms Loan Guarantee, 2004); Chm., Admin. Burdens Adv. Bd, HMRC, 2006–. Ind. Regulator, RICS, 2007–09. *Recreations:* walking, travelling, reading, cinema, art. *Address:* Upper Maisonette, 9 Eccleston Square, SW1V 1NP. *T:* 07767 486486, *Fax:* (020) 7630 6264. *E:* teresa@teresagraham.co.uk.

GRAHAM, Thomas; *b* 5 Dec. 1943; *m* Joan Bagley; two *s*. Engineer with Rolls-Royce, 1965–78; Office Manager, Robertson and Ross, solicitors, 1982–87. Mem., Strathclyde Reg. Council, 1978–87. MP Renfrew and Inverclyde, 1987–97, Renfrewshire, 1997–2001 (Lab 1987–98, Ind. 1998–2001). *Address:* 265 Gilmartin Road, Linwood, Paisley PA3 3SU.

GRAHAM, Rear-Adm. Wilfred Jackson, CB 1979; *b* 17 June 1925; *s* of late William Bryce Graham and Jean Hill Graham (*née* Jackson); *m* 1951, Gillian Mary Finlayson (*d* 2004); three *s* one *d*. *Educ:* Rossall Sch., Fleetwood, Lancs. Served War of 1939–45, Royal Navy: Cadet, 1943; specialised in gunnery, 1951; Comdr 1960; Captain 1967; IDC, 1970; Captain, HMS Ark Royal, 1975–76; Flag Officer, Portsmouth, 1976–79, retired. Dir and Sec., RNLI, 1979–87. Mem. Council, Rossall Sch., 1988–95. Gov., E. Hayes Dashwood Foundn, 1994–2004. FNI 1987. *Address:* Yarnfield Cottage, Maiden Bradley, Warminster, Wilts BA12 7HY. *Clubs:* Royal Naval Sailing Association, Royal Yacht Squadron.

GRAHAM, William; *see* Graham, A. W.

GRAHAM, Hon. William Carvel; PC (Can) 2002; QC (Can.); MP (Liberal) Toronto Centre (formerly Rosedale, then Toronto Centre-Rosedale), Canada, 1993–2007; *b* 17 March 1939; *s* of Francis Ronald Graham and Helen Payne Graham (*née* White); *m* 1962, Catherine Elizabeth Curry; one *s* one *d*. *Educ:* Univ. of Toronto (BA 1961; LLB 1964); Univ. of Paris (DJur 1970). Barrister and solicitor, Fasken and Calvin, 1967–80, Partner, 1983; Prof. of Law, 1980–94, and Dir, Centre for Internat. Studies, 1986–88, Univ. of Toronto. Minister of Foreign Affairs, 2002–04, of Nat. Defence, 2004–06; Leader of the Opposition, 2006; Interim Leader, Liberal Party of Canada, 2006. Chancellor, Trinity Coll., Univ. of Toronto, 2007–. Chair: Atlantic Council of Canada, 2007–13; Canadian Internat. Council, 2013– (Co-Vice Chair, 2007–13). Hon. Col, Gov. Gen.'s Horse Guards, 2011– (Hon. Lt-Col, 2008–11). Hon. LLD Royal Mil. Coll. of Canada, 2010; Doctoral Ring, Univ. of Siena, 2010. Chevalier, Legion of Honour (France), 1984; Chevalier, Order of the Pléiade (France), 1999. *Publications:* contrib. to books and jls on internat. trade law and public internat. law. *Address:* 151 Bloor Street West, Suite 1130, Toronto, ON M5S 1S4, Canada.

GRAHAM, William Franklin, (Billy Graham), Hon. KBE 2001; evangelist; *b* Charlotte, NC, 7 Nov. 1918; *s* of late William Franklin Graham and Morrow (*née* Coffey); *m* 1943, Ruth McCue Bell (*d* 2007); two *s* three *d*. *Educ:* Florida Bible Institute, Tampa (ThB); Wheaton Coll., Ill (AB). Ordained to Baptist ministry, 1939; first Vice-Pres., Youth for Christ Internat., 1945–50; Pres., Northwestern Coll., Minneapolis, 1947–52; Evangelistic campaigns, 1946–; world-wide weekly broadcast, 1950–; many evangelistic tours of Great Britain, Europe, the Far East, South America, Australia and Russia. Chairman, Board of World Wide Pictures Inc. Holds numerous honorary degrees in Divinity, Laws, Literature and the Humanities, from American universities and colleges; also varied awards from organisations, 1954–, inc. Templeton Foundn Prize, 1982; President's Medal of Freedom Award, 1983; Congressional Gold Medal, 1996. *Publications include:* Peace with God, 1953; World Aflame, 1965; Jesus Generation, 1971; Angels—God's Secret Agents, 1975; How to be Born Again, 1977; The Holy Spirit, 1978; Till Armageddon, 1981; Approaching Hoofbeats: the four horsemen of the Apocalypse, 1983; A Biblical Standard for Evangelists, 1984; Unto the Hills, 1986; Facing Death and the Life After, 1987; Answers to Life's Problems, 1988; Hope for the Troubled Heart, 1991; Storm Warning, 1992; Just As I Am, 1997; Hope for Each Day, 2002; The Journey, 2006; Nearing Home: thoughts on life, faith and finishing well, 2011. *Recreations:* swimming, walking. *Address:* (office) 1 Billy Graham Parkway, Charlotte, NC 28201, USA. *T:* (704) 4012432.

GRAHAM, Prof. William George, PhD; FInstP; Professor of Physics, since 1995, and Director, Centre for Plasma Physics, 2006–12, Queen's University Belfast; *b* Belfast, 11 June 1949; *s* of Albert and Hazel Graham; *m* 1987, Bernadette Hannigan; two *s*. *Educ:* Annadale Grammar Sch., Belfast; Queen's Univ., Belfast (BSc 1971; PhD 1974). FInstP 1987. Scientist, Lawrence Berkeley Lab., USA, 1974–79; Lectr, Univ. of Ulster, 1979–88; Queen's University, Belfast: Lectr, 1988–90; Reader, 1990–95; Dir, Internat. Centre for Exptl Physics, 2001–05. Ed. in Chief, Plasma Sources Sci. and Technol., 2014– (Associate Ed., 2007–13). Fellow, APS, 1996. MRIA 2006. Hon. Prof., Univ. of Bucharest, 2004. Von Engel and Franklin Prize in Plasma Physics, Internat. Conf. on Phenomena in Ionised Gases, 2013. *Publications:* over 150 articles in physics jls. *Recreations:* hiking, ski-ing, travelling, blues and rock music, beer. *Address:* Centre for Plasma Physics, Queen's University Belfast, Belfast BT7 1NN. *T:* (028) 9097 3564.

GRAHAM, Yvonne Georgette; Headmistress, Clifton High School, Bristol, 1996–97; *b* 31 Aug. 1943; *d* of J. van Gorkom and M. E. van Gorkom-Pas; *m* 1967, Lt-Col I. G. Graham, RE (retd) (*d* 2008); two *s*. *Educ:* Alexander Hegius-Gymnasium-Deventer; Amsterdam Univ. (MA); London Univ. Various teaching posts in England, Germany and Holland, 1965–90; Headmistress, Lavant House Sch., Chichester, 1990–95. *Recreations:* reading, travel, theatre, music. *Address:* 20 Stanton Drive, Chichester, West Sussex PO19 5QN. *T:* (01243) 528111.

GRAHAM-BRYCE, Ian James, CBE 2001; DPhil; Principal and Vice-Chancellor, University of Dundee, 1994–2000, now Principal Emeritus; *b* 20 March 1937; *s* of late Alexander Graham-Bryce, FRCS, and Dame Isabel Graham-Bryce, DBE; *m* 1959, Anne Elisabeth Metcalf; one *s* three *d*. *Educ:* William Hulme's Grammar Sch., Manchester; University Coll., Oxford (Exhibnr). BA, MA, BSc, DPhil (Oxon); FRSC, CChem 1981; FRSE 1996. Research Asst, Univ. of Oxford, 1958–61; Lectr, Dept of Biochemistry and Soil Sci., UCNW, Bangor, 1961–64; Sen. Scientific Officer, Rothamsted Experimental Station, 1964–70; Sen. Res. Officer, ICI Plant Protection Div., Jealott's Hill Res. Station, Bracknell, Berks, 1970–72; Special Lectr in Pesticide Chemistry, Dept of Zoology and Applied Entomology, Imperial Coll. of Science and Technology, 1970–72 (Vis. Prof., 1976–79); Rothamsted Experimental Station: Head, Dept of Insecticides and Fungicides, 1972–79; Dep. Director, 1975–79; Dir, East Malling Res. Stn, Maidstone, Kent, 1979–86 (Trustee, 1986–2010, Chm., 2001–10, Develt and Endowment Fund, subseq. E Malling Trust for Horticl Res.); Cons. Dir, Commonwealth Bureau of Horticulture and Plantation Crops,

1979–86; Hon. Lectr, Dept of Biology, Univ. of Strathclyde, 1977–80; Hd of Envmtl Affairs Div., Shell Internat. Petroleum Maatschappij BV, 1986–94. Pres., British Crop Protection Council, 1996–2000 (Hon. Vice-Pres., 2000–02). Society of Chemical Industry, London: Pres., 1982–84; Mem. Council, 1969–72 and 1974–89; Hon. Sec., Home Affairs, 1977–80; Chm., Pesticides Gp, 1978–80; Sec., Physico-Chemical and Biophysical Panel, 1968–70, Chm., 1973–75; Mem., British Nat. Cttee for Chemistry, 1982–84. President: Assoc. of Applied Biologists, 1988 (Vice-Pres., 1985–87); Scottish Assoc. for Marine Sci., 2000–04. Chm., Agrochemical Planning Gp, IOCD, 1985–88; Mem., Scientific Cttee, Eur. Chemical Industry Ecol. and Toxicol. Centre, 1988–94; Vice-Chm., Environmental Res. Wkg Gp, Industrial R&D Adv. Cttee to EC, 1988–91; Member: NERC, 1989–96 (Chm., Polar Sci. and Technol. Bd, 1995–96); Royal Commn on Envmtl Pollution, 2000–10. Member, Board of Directors: British Council Educnl Counselling Service, 1996–98; Quality Assurance Agency for Higher Educn, 1997–98; Rothamsted Experimental Station, 2000–04; Convener, Cttee of Scottish Higher Educn Principals, 1998–2000; Vice Pres., CVCP, 1999–2000. Governor: Long Ashton Res. Stn, 1979–85; Wye Coll., 1979–86, Imperial Coll., 1985–2001, Univ. of London; Hon. Advr, Zhejiang Wanli Univ., China, 1999–. Member, Editorial Board: Chemico-Biological Interactions, 1973–77; Pesticide Science, 1978–80; Agriculture, Ecosystems and Environment, 1978–87. Mem., Old Members' Trust, University Coll., Oxford, 2004–14 (Chm., 2011–14). E Sussex Ambassador, 2008–; Chm., Rye Arts Fest., 2013–. FRSA 1996. Hon. LLD Dundee, 2001. British Crop Protection Council Medal, 2000. *Publications:* Physical Principles of Pesticide Behaviour, 1980; papers on soil science, plant nutrition, crop protection, and envmtl matters in sci. jls. *Recreations:* music (espec. opera), ski-ing and other sports. *Club:* Athenæum.

GRAHAM-CAMPBELL, Prof. James Alastair, FBA 2001; FSA, FSAScot; FRHistS; Professor of Medieval Archaeology, University of London, at University College, 1991–2002, now Emeritus; *b* 7 Feb. 1947; *s* of David John Graham-Campbell and Joan Sybil Graham-Campbell (*née* Maclean). *Educ:* Eton Coll.; Trinity Coll., Cambridge (MA, PhD); Bergen Univ.; Oslo Univ.; UCL. FSA 1977. Asst Lectr in Archaeology, UC Dublin, 1971–73; University College London: Lectr, 1973–82; Reader in Medieval Archaeology, 1982–91; Fellow, 2003. Vis. Prof., Univ. of Minnesota, 1981; British Acad. Res. Reader, 1988–90; O'Donnell Lectr, Univ. of Wales, 1989; Crabtree Orator, UCL, 1990; Rhind Lectr, Soc. of Antiquaries of Scotland, 1996; Special Prof. of Viking Studies, Nottingham Univ., 2003–12; Hon. Prof., Aarhus Univ., 2004–11. Mem., Ancient Monuments Adv. Cttee, English Heritage, 1992–97. Sec., Soc. for Medieval Archaeology, 1976–82 (Hon. Vice-Pres., 2001–). *Publications:* Viking Artefacts, 1980; The Viking World, 1980, 4th edn 2013; (jtly) The Vikings, 1980; (ed) Cultural Atlas of the Viking World, 1994; The Viking-Age Gold and Silver of Scotland, 1995; (jtly) Vikings in Scotland: an archaeological survey, 1998; (ed with G. Williams) Silver Economy in the Viking Age, 2007; (ed with M. Valor) The Archaeology of Medieval Europe, Vol. 1, 2007; (ed with M. Ryan) Anglo-Saxon/Irish Relations before the Vikings, 2009; (ed with R. Philpott) The Huxley Viking Hoard: Scandinavian settlement in the North West, 2009; (ed jtly) Silver Economies, Monetisation and Society in Scandinavia AD 800–1100, 2011; The Cuerdale Hoard and Related Viking-Age Silver and Gold from Britain and Ireland in the British Museum, 2012; Viking Art, 2013; numerous articles in learned jls. *Recreations:* cooking, gardening. *Address:* Institute of Archaeology (UCL), 31–34 Gordon Square, WC1H 0PY.

GRAHAM-DIXON, Andrew Michael; writer and presenter, BBC Television, since 1992; Chief Art Critic, Sunday Telegraph, since 2004; *b* 26 Dec. 1960; *s* of Anthony Philip Graham-Dixon, QC and Margaret Suzanne Graham-Dixon; *m* 1985, Sabine Marie-Pascale Tilly; one *s* two *d*. *Educ:* Westminster Sch.; Christ Church, Oxford (MA 1st Cl. English); Courtauld Inst. Chief Art Critic, 1986–97, Chief Arts Feature Writer, 1997–99, The Independent; Chief Arts Feature Writer, Sunday Telegraph Mag., 1999–2004. Presenter, The Culture Show, BBC TV, 2010–. Television series include: A History of British Art, 1996; Renaissance, 1999; The Secret of Drawing, 2006; Art of Eternity, 2007; Art of Spain, 2008; The Art of Russia, 2009; Art of Germany, 2010; The High Art in the Low Countries, 2013; Art of China, 2014; Art of Gothic, 2014. BP Arts Journalist of Year, 1988, 1989, 1990; Hawthornden Prize for Art Criticism, 1991; 1st Prize, Reportage Section, Montreal Internat. Fest. of Films, 1994. *Publications:* Howard Hodgkin: paintings, 1994; A History of British Art, 1996; Paper Museum: writings about paintings, mostly, 1996; Renaissance, 1999; In the Picture: the year through art, 2003; Michelangelo and the Sistine Chapel, 2008; Caravaggio: a life sacred and profane, 2010. *Recreations:* golf, horse-racing. *Address:* Sunday Telegraph Magazine, 111 Buckingham Palace Road, SW1W 0DT. *Clubs:* Royal Society of Arts; Muswell Hill Golf.

GRAHAM-HALL, John, (John Leonard Hall); operatic tenor (freelance); *b* Pinner, 23 Nov. 1955; *s* of Leonard Hall and Betty Hall; *m* 1990, Helen Williams; two *d*. *Educ:* Malvern Coll.; King's Coll., Cambridge (BA 1977; MA 1981); Royal Coll. of Music. Major roles include: title role in Albert Herring, Glyndebourne, 1985–90, Royal Opera House, 1989; Kudrjas in Katya Kabanova, Glyndebourne, 1988, 1990; Aschenbach in Death in Venice, Glyndebourne on Tour, 1989, Monnaie Brussels, 2009, La Scala Milan, 2011, ENO 2013; Eisenstein in Die Fledermaus, Scottish Opera, 1989, Glyndebourne on Tour, 2006; title role in Perela, world première, Paris Bastille, 2003; Michel in Juliette, Paris Bastille, 2006; Podesta in Finta Giardiniera, Salzburg Fest., 2006; title role in Adventures of Mr Broucek, Opera North, 2009, Scottish Opera, 2010; title role in Peter Grimes, La Scala, Milan, 2012, Opéra de Nice, 2015; Shuisky in Boris Godunov, Toulouse, 2014; Zivny in Osud, Stuttgart, 2012–13; Kaufmann in Jakob Lenz, Stuttgart, 2014, Brussels Monnaie, 2015; company principal, ENO, 1997–2003, then freelance: roles include: Herod in Salome, 1998, 2005; Sylvester in Silver Tassie, 2000; Alwa in Lulu, 2002; Mime in Ring of the Nibelung, 2002–04; Danilo, 2008; Mayor in Albert Herring, Opera North, 2002, Glyndebourne, 2008, Toulouse, 2013; Basilio in Nozze de Figaro, NY Metropolitan and Aix-en-Provence, 2012; Valzacchi in Rosenkavalier and Triquet, Onegin Metropolitan, 2013. Other roles include: Monostatos in Magic Flute; Bob Boles in Peter Grimes; Tikhon in Katya Kabanova; Tanzmeister in Ariadne auf Naxos; Lysander. Trustee, ENO Benevolent Fund, 1998– (Chm., 2004–08). Numerous recordings, 1986–. *Recreations:* theatre, cooking, bridge. *Address:* c/o Musichall UK, Oast House, Crouch's Farm, Hollow Lane, E Hoathly, E Sussex BN8 6QX. *T:* (01825) 840437. *E:* jgraham.hall@btinternet.com.

GRAHAM-HARRISON, Catherine, (Lady Warren), OBE 2010; adviser and non-executive director; *b* London, 11 Jan. 1949; *d* of Francis Laurence Theodore Graham-Harrison, CB and Carol Mary St John Graham-Harrison, *d* of Sir Francis Stewart, CIE; *m* 1994, Hon. Sir Nicholas Roger Warren, *qv*; two step *s* one step *d*. *Educ:* North London Collegiate Sch.; St Anne's Coll., Oxford (BA Mod. Hist. 1970). Dep. Dir, New Islington and Hackney Housing Assoc., 1978–83; Vice Pres., Citibank, 1983–92; Dir, Paul Hamlyn Foundn, 1992–94. Member, Board: Heritage Lottery Fund, 2002–08; Nat. Heritage Meml Fund, 2002–08; Natural England, 2009–14; Nat. Trust Architectural Panel, 2009– (Chair, 2012–). Chair, Nat. Forest Company, 2011–. Trustee: Joseph Rowntree Foundn, 1998–2006; Womankind Worldwide, 2001–05 (Chm., 2001–05); Foundling Mus., 2008–09; Gov., Coram, 2005–09. *Recreations:* built and natural heritage, arts, walking, gardening. *E:* Catherine@cghassociates.co.uk.

See also R. M. Graham-Harrison.

GRAHAM-HARRISON, Robert Montagu, CMG 2003; Senior Clerk, House of Lords, 2003–08; *b* 16 Feb. 1943; *s* of Francis Laurence Theodore Graham-Harrison, CB and Carol Mary St John, *d* of Sir Francis Stewart, CIE; *m* 1977, Kathleen Patricia, *d* of John and Mary Gladys Maher; two *d*. *Educ:* Eton Coll.; Magdalen Coll., Oxford. VSO India, 1965; GLC, 1966; Min. of Overseas Development, later Overseas Development Administration, then Dept for Internat. Develt, 1967–2003; World Bank, Washington, 1971–73; Private Sec. to Minister for Overseas Development, 1978; Asst Sec., ODA, 1979; Hd, British Develt Div. in E Africa, Nairobi, 1982–86; Hd, E Asia Dept, ODA, 1986–89; Alternate Exec. Dir, World Bank, Washington, 1989–92; UK Exec. Dir, EBRD, 1992–97; Dir, British Develt Co-op Office, New Delhi, 1997–2003. Mem., Remuneration Cttee, EBRD, 2012–. Trustee: CASA Social Care, 2003–12; EveryChild, 2006–; Blenheim CDP, 2012–; PlaNet Finance UK, 2011–14. Mem., Internat. Cttee, Leonard Cheshire Disability, 2006–09. Chm., DFID Alumni Assoc., 2007–13. Ambassador, Paintings in Hospitals, 2007–11. Mem. Cttee, Wine Soc., 2010–13. *Recreations:* hill walking, travel, tennis. *Address:* 122 St George's Avenue, N7 0AH.

See also C. Graham-Harrison.

GRAHAM-MOON, Sir Peter Wilfred Giles; *see* Moon.

GRAHAM-SMITH, Sir Francis; *see* Smith.

GRAHAM-TOLER, family name of **Earl of Norbury**.

GRAHAME, Angela Thomson; QC (Scot.) 2009; *b* Edinburgh, 8 April 1968; *d* of late Joseph Scott Grahame and of Norma Grahame (*née* Thomson); *m* 2004, Kenneth Wilson Cloggie; one *d*. *Educ:* Leith Acad.; Univ. of Aberdeen (LLB Hons, DipLP). Admitted solicitor, 1993; admitted to Faculty of Advocates, 1995; Advocate Depute, 2003–05; Sen. Advocate Depute, 2005–07. Legal Mem., Police Appeals Tribunal, Scotland, 2013–. *Publications:* contribs Juridical Rev., Scottish Law Agents Gazette, Reparation Law Bulletin. *Recreation:* reading murder mysteries. *Address:* Advocates' Library, Parliament House, Edinburgh EH1 1RF. *T:* (0131) 226 5071.

GRAHAME, Christine; Member (SNP) Midlothian South, Tweeddale and Lauderdale, Scottish Parliament, since 2011 (South Scotland, 1999–2011); *b* 9 Sept. 1944; *d* of Christie and Margaret Grahame; *m* (marr. diss.); two *s*. *Educ:* Edinburgh Univ. (MA 1966; DipEd 1967; LLB 1984; DipLP 1985). Schoolteacher, secondary schs, 1967–80; solicitor, 1986–99. Shadow Minister for Social Justice, Scottish Exec., 2004–07. Scottish Parliament: Convenor: Cross Party Gp, Borders Rail; Justice Cttee I, 2001–03; Health Cttee, 2003–04; Health and Sport Cttee, 2007–11; Justice Cttee, 2011–; Policing sub-cttee; Cross Party Gp, Animal Welfare. *Recreations:* cats, trad jazz, and additionally gardening and drinking malt, not necessarily at the same time. *Address:* Scottish Parliament, Edinburgh EH99 1SP. *T:* (0131) 348 5729.

GRAINGE, Lucian Charles, CBE 2010; Chairman and Chief Executive Officer, Universal Music Group, since 2011 (Co-Chief Executive Officer, 2010–11); *b* London, 29 Feb. 1960; *s* of Cecil and Marion Grainge; *m* 2002, Caroline Lewis; one *s* one *d* and one step *d*. *Educ:* Queen Elizabeth Grammar Sch., Barnet, London. Hd, Creative Dept, April Music/CBS UK, 1979–82; Dir and Gen. Manager, RCA Music UK, 1982–85; A&R Dir, MCA UK, 1985–86; Man. Dir, PolyGram Music Publishing UK, 1986–93; Gen. Manager, A&R and Business Affairs, 1993–97, Man. Dir, 1997–99, Polydor Records UK; Dep. Chm., 1999–2001, Chm. and Chief Exec., 2001–05, Universal Music UK; Chm. and Chief Exec., Universal Music Gp Internat., 2005–10. Member, Board: Internat. Fedn of Phonographic Industry, 2005–; Music Industry Trusts' Award, Vivendi 2008, 2010–12; Activision Blizzard, 2011–13. Member, Board of Directors: Northwestern Univ., 2012–; DreamWorks, 2013–. UK Trade Ambassador for global and media entertainment, 2012–. Trustee, American Friends of Royal Foundn of the Duke and Duchess of Cambridge and Prince Harry, 2011–. President's Merit Award, Recording Acad., 2014. Officier des Arts et des Lettres (France), 2011. *Recreations:* soccer, automobiles. *Address:* Universal Music Group, 2220 Colorado Avenue, Santa Monica, CA 90404, USA. *T:* (310) 8651823, *Fax:* (310) 8653230. *E:* lucian.grainge@umusic.com, jackie.steen@umusic.com.

GRAINGER, Ian David; His Honour Judge Grainger; a Circuit Judge, since 2009; *b* Kingston upon Hull, 1 Aug. 1956; *s* of David Grainger and Edna Grainger (*née* Rudrum). *Educ:* Tynemouth High Sch.; Tynemouth Coll.; University Coll., Oxford (MA Juris. 1981); London Univ. (BA Italian (ext.) 2001); University Coll. London (MA Italian Studies 2003). Called to the Bar, Inner Temple, 1978, Bencher, 2008; in commercial practice, 1979–2009; a Recorder, 2003–09. Mem. Council and Chair, Audit Cttee, Roehampton Univ., 2003–09; Mem., Bd of Trustees, Univ. of London, 2008–14. Vice Chm., British-Italian Soc., 2007–09. *Publications:* (with M. Fealy) An Introduction to the New Civil Procedure Rules, 1999, 2nd edn as The Civil Procedure Rules in Action, 2000. *Recreations:* Italy and all things Italian, classical music, reading, walking. *Address:* Reading Crown Court, Old Shire Hall, The Forbury, Reading, Berks RG1 3EH. *T:* (0118) 967 4400, *Fax:* (0118) 967 4444.

GRAINGER, Ian Richard Peregrine L.; *see* Liddell-Grainger.

GRAINGER, John Andrew, CMG 2005; HM Diplomatic Service, retired; Deputy Legal Adviser, Foreign and Commonwealth Office, 2003–14; *b* 27 Aug. 1957; *m* 1998, Katherine Veronica Bregou (*d* 2011); one *s*. Called to the Bar, Lincoln's Inn, 1981. Joined HM Diplomatic Service, 1984; Asst Legal Advr, FCO, 1984–89; First Sec. (Legal Advr), BMG Berlin, 1989–91; Asst Legal Advr, FCO, 1991–94; Legal Counsellor: FCO, 1994–97; UK Mission to UN, NY, 1997–2001; FCO, 2001–03.

GRAINGER, Stephen, MBE 2007; Rugby Development Director, Rugby Football Union, since 2011; *b* Saltburn-by-the-Sea, 5 March 1966; *s* of Malcolm and Patricia Grainger; *m* 1989, Julie Tack; two *d*. *Educ:* Saltscar Sch., Redcar; Sir William Turner's Sixth Form Coll., Redcar; Leeds Poly. (BA Hons). Athletics Manager, Mansfield DC, 1987–89; Principal Officer (Sport), Notts CC, 1989–92; various posts with Nat. Coaching Foundn, 1992–95; Youth Sport Trust: Implementation Dir, 1995–99; Man. Dir, 1999–2004; Chief Exec., 2004–11. *Recreations:* track and field athletics, road running, ski-ing, travel. *Address:* Rugby Football Union, Rugby House, Twickenham Stadium, 200 Whitton Road, Twickenham, Middx TW2 7BA. *E:* stevegrainger@rfu.com.

GRAMMENOS, Prof. Constantinos Theophilos, Hon. CBE 2008 (Hon. OBE 1994); Comdr, Order of Phoenix 2013; DSc; Founding Chairman, Costas Grammenos Centre (formerly Centre, then International Centre) for Shipping, Trade and Finance, since 1984, and Professor of Shipping, since 1986, Cass Business School, City University, London (formerly City University Business School); *b* 23 Feb. 1944; *s* of late Commander Theophilos C. Grammenos and Argyro (*née* Spanakos); *m* 1972, Anna C. Papadimitriou; one *s*. *Educ:* Third State Sch. of Athens; Pantion Univ. (BA); Univ. of Wales (MSc); City University (DSc). National Service, Greek Navy, 1968–70. Nat. Bank of Greece, 1962–74 (shipping finance expert, head office, 1972–74); independent researcher and advr, 1977–82; Vis. Prof., 1982–86, Actg Dean, 2000, Dep. Dean, Cass Undergrad. Sch., 2003–10, Cass Business Sch., City Univ. (formerly City Univ. Business Sch.); Pro Vice-Chancellor, City Univ., London, 1998–2011. Visiting Professor: World Maritime Univ., Malmö, 1990–95; Univ. of Antwerp, 2000–. Pres., Man. Cttee, Internat. Hellenic Univ., Thessaloniki. Founder, 1999, and Chm., 1999–, City of London Biennial Meeting; Pres., Internat. Assoc. of Maritime Economists, 1998–2002; Member: Bd of Dirs, Alexander S. Onassis Public Benefit Foundn, 1995–; American Bureau of Shipping, 1996–; Baltic Exchange, 1997–. Mem., Bd of Trustees, Inst. of Marine Engineers Meml Trust, 2000–12. Vice Chm., Maria Tsakos Foundn, 2011–. Freeman, City of London, 2000; Liveryman, Shipwrights' Co., 2002–. Hon. FIMarEST 2008. Archon of Ecumenical Patriarchate of Constantinople, 1994. FRSA 1996; FCIB 2004. Seatrade Personality of the Year, 1998. *Publications:* Bank Finance for Ship Purchase, 1979;

(ed) The Handbook of Maritime Economics and Business, 2002, 2nd edn 2010. *Recreations:* cooking, music, walking. *Address:* Cass Business School, City University, 106 Bunhill Row, EC1Y 8TZ. *T:* (020) 7040 8670. *Club:* Travellers.

GRAN, Maurice Bernard; scriptwriter, since 1978; *b* 26 Oct. 1949; *s* of Mark and Deborah Gran; *m* 1994, Carol James; one *s* one *d. Educ:* William Ellis Sch., London; University Coll. London (BSc Internat. Relations 1971). Mgt trainee, Dept of Employment, 1971; Manager, Tottenham Employment Exchange, 1974–76; marketing develt advr, 1976–78, Manager, London Employment Intelligence Unit, 1978–80, Dept of Employment. Co-Founder and Company Dir, Alomo Productions, 1988–2001. With Laurence Marks, scriptwriter, 1980–: main *television* credits: Shine on Harvey Moon, 1982–85, 1995; The New Statesman, 1987–91 (BAFTA Award, Best Comedy, 1990); Birds of a Feather, 1989–98 and 2014–15; Love Hurts, 1991–93; Goodnight Sweetheart, 1993–99; Mosley, 1997; *radio:* My Blue Heaven, 2006; Dr Freud Will See You Now, Mr Hitler, 2007; My Blue Wedding, 2007; Von Ribbentrop's Watch, 2008; Grey Expectations, 2009; Love Me Do, 2012; *stage:* Playing God, Stephen Joseph Th., Scarborough, 2005; The New Statesman - Episode 2006, nat. tour, 2006–07; Dreamboats and Petticoats (musical), nat. tour, then Savoy, 2009, transf. Playhouse, 2010, nat. tours, 2010–12 and 2013–14, Wyndham's, 2012; Von Ribbentrop's Watch, nat. tour, 2010; Save the Last Dance for Me (musical), nat. tours, 2012–13; Dreamboats and Miniskirts (musical), nat. tour, 2014–15; Love Me Do, Watford Palace, 2014. BAFTA Councillor, 1994–95. BAFTA Writers Award, 1992. *Publications:* with Laurence Marks: Holding the Fort, 1981; The New Statesman Scripts, 1992; Dorien's Diary, 1993; Shine on Harvey Moon, 1995. *Recreations:* watching football, theatre, film. *Address:* 61 Gratton Road, Cheltenham GL50 2BZ. *Club:* Groucho.

GRANARD, 10th Earl of, *cr* 1684 (Ire.); **Peter Arthur Edward Hastings Forbes;** Bt (NS) 1628; Viscount Granard, Baron Clanehugh (Ire.), 1675; Baron Granard (UK), 1806; *b* 15 March 1957; *s* of Hon. John Forbes (*d* 1982), *yr s* of 8th Earl, and of Joan, *d* of A. Edward Smith; *S* uncle, 1992; *m* 1980, Noreen Mitchell; three *s* one *d. Heir: s* Viscount Forbes, *qv. Address:* Strathallan Cliff House, Strathallan Road, Onchan, Isle of Man IM3 1NN.

GRANATT, Michael Stephen Dreese, CB 2001; Director (formerly Partner), Luther Pendragon, since 2004; Chair, Emergency Aid, since 2014; *b* 27 April 1950; *s* of Arthur Maurice Granatt and Denise Sylvia Granatt (*née* Dreese); *m* 1974, Jane Veronica Bray; one *s* three *d. Educ:* Westminster City Sch.; Queen Mary Coll., London. Sub-ed., subseq. Dep. Chief Sub-ed., Kent & Sussex Courier, 1973–77; Prodn Ed., Industrial Relns Services, 1977–79; Asst Ed., Dept of Employment, 1979–81; Press Officer, Home Office, 1981–83; Sen. Press Officer, 1983–85, Chief Press Officer, 1985–86, Hd of Inf., 1986–89, Dept of Energy; Dir, Public Affairs and Internal Communication, Metropolitan Police Service, 1989–92; Director of Communication: DoE, 1992–94; Home Office, 1995–98; Hd of Profession, Govt Inf. Service, subseq. Govt Inf. and Communication Service, 1997–2003 (Dir-Gen., 2002–03); also Hd of Civil Contingencies Secretariat, Cabinet Office, 2001–02. Vis. Prof., Univ. of Westminster, 2003–06; Sen. Res. Fellow, Inst. for Security and Resilience Studies, UCL, 2011–. Chairman: London Emergency Press Officers' Gp, 1989–92; Nat. Industries Press Officers' Gp, 1992–94; Media Emergency Forum, 1996–2003; UK Press Card Authy, 2004–. Chair, Community Resilience, 2012–14; Controller, Kent County Raynet, 2014–. Bd Mem., Sci. Media Centre, Royal Instn, 2004–11. Co-ordinator, Club of Venice, 2003–14. Gov., Mary Hare Schs, 2004– (Chm. Govs, 2010–). FCIPR (FIPR 2000). Master, City of London Guild of Public Relns Practitioners, 2005–06. *Publications:* (contrib.) Disasters and the Media, 1999; contrib. Jl Communication Mgt, Internat. Jl Emergency. *Recreations:* amateur radio, walking the dogs, photography, reading science fiction, gadgets. *Address:* c/o Luther Pendragon, Priory Court, Pilgrim Street, EC4V 6DR. *T:* (020) 7618 9100. *Club:* Savage.

GRANBY, Marquis of; Charles John Montague Manners; *b* 3 July 1999; *s* and *heir* of Duke of Rutland, *qv.*

GRAND, Stephen Lewis, OBE 2000; independent scientist and writer, since 1999; *b* 12 Feb. 1958; *s* of Dennis and Jean Grand; *m* 1979, Ann Nicholson (marr. diss. 2007); one *s. Educ:* self-taught. Sen. Programmer, Millennium Ltd, 1993–96; Dir of Technology, Cyberlife Technology Ltd, 1996–99; Dir, Cyberlife Research Ltd, 1999–. NESTA Fellow, 2002–03. Hon. Fellow: Cognitive Sci., Univ. of Sussex, 1997–99; Psychology, Univ. of Cardiff, 2001–04; Biomimetics, Univ. of Bath, 2002–04; Res. Fellow, Inst. of Creative Technologies, De Montfort Univ., 2006–07. DUniv Open, 2008. *Publications:* Creation: life and how to make it, 2000; Growing Up With Lucy: how to build an android in twenty easy steps, 2003. *Recreation:* work! *E:* steve@cyberlife-research.net.

GRANDAGE, Michael, CBE 2011; theatre director and producer; *b* 2 May 1962. *Educ:* Humphry Davy Grammar Sch., Cornwall; Central Sch. of Speech and Drama, London (Hon. Fellow). Theatre director, 1995–; Associate Dir, Crucible Th., Sheffield, 2000–05; Artistic Dir, Donmar Warehouse, London, 2002–12. Pres., Royal Central Sch. of Speech and Drama (formerly Central Sch. of Speech and Drama), 2010–. Vis. Prof., Falmouth Univ. (formerly University Coll., Falmouth), 2009–14. *Productions* include: Crucible Theatre, Sheffield: What the Butler Saw, 1997; Twelfth Night, 1998; The Country Wife, As You Like It, transf. Lyric, Hammersmith (Best Director award, Evening Standard, Critics' Circle; award for theatre, South Bank Show), 2000; Edward II, Don Juan, 2001; Richard III, The Tempest, transf. Old Vic, 2002; A Midsummer Night's Dream, 2003; Suddenly Last Summer, 2004; Don Carlos, 2004, transf. Gielgud Th., 2005 (Best Director award, Evening Standard, 2005); Almeida Theatre: The Doctor's Dilemma, 1998; The Jew of Malta, 1999; Donmar Warehouse: Good, 1999; Passion Play, transf. Comedy Th. (Best Director award, Evening Standard, Critics' Circle), Merrily We Roll Along (Best Director award, Critics' Circle; Olivier Award for Best New Musical), 2000; Privates on Parade, 2001; The Vortex, 2002; Caligula (Olivier Award for Best Dir, 2004), After Miss Julie, 2003; Henry IV, Grand Hotel (Olivier Award for Outstanding Musical; Best Director award, Evening Standard, 2005), 2004; Guys and Dolls (at Piccadilly Th.), The Wild Duck, 2005 (Best Director award, Critics' Circle, 2005); The Cut, 2006; Frost/Nixon, 2006, transf. Gielgud, 2006, NY, 2007; John Gabriel Borkman, 2007; Othello, 2007 (Best Director award, Evening Standard, 2008); The Chalk Garden (Best Director award, Evening Standard, 2008), Ivanov, Twelfth Night (at Wyndham's Th.), 2008; Madame de Sade (at Wyndham's Th.), 2009; Hamlet (at Wyndham's Th.), transf. NY, 2009; Red, 2009, transf. NY, 2010 (Tony Award); King Lear, 2010 (Jt Best Director award, Critics' Circle); Luise Miller, 2011; Richard II, 2011; other productions: Evita, Adelphi Th., 2006, transf. NY, 2012; Danton's Death, NT, 2010; Noël Coward Theatre: Privates on Parade, 2012; Peter and Alice, 2013; The Cripple of Inishmaan, 2013; A Midsummer Night's Dream, 2013; Henry V, 2013; Photograph 51, 2015; Dawn French: 30 Million Minutes, solo UK tour, 2014; opera: Billy Budd, Glyndebourne, 2010, 2013; Madama Butterfly, Houston, 2010; Don Giovanni, Met. Opera, NY, 2011; Le nozze di Figaro, Glyndebourne, 2012, 2013; film, Genius, 2014. DUniv: Sheffield Hallam, 2002; Sheffield, 2004; London, 2014. *Address:* Michael Grandage Company, Fourth Floor, Gielgud Theatre, Shaftesbury Avenue, W1D 6AR. *T:* (020) 3582 7210. *E:* mg@michaelgrandagecompany.com.

GRANGE, Sir Kenneth Henry, Kt 2013; CBE 1984; RDI, FCSD; product designer; in private practice, since 1958; *b* 17 July 1929; *s* of Harry Alfred Grange and Hilda Gladys (*née* Long). *Educ:* London. Technical Illustrator, RE, 1948–50; Design Asst, Arcon Chartered Architects, 1948; Bronek Katz & Vaughn, 1950–51; Gordon Bowyer & Partners, 1951–54; Jack Howe & Partners, 1954–58; Founding Partner, Pentagram Design, 1972–91. Retrospective exhibn, Kenneth Grange: Making Britain Modern, Design Mus., 2011. Pres., CSD, 1987–88; Master of Faculty, RDI, 1985–87. RDI 1969; FCSD (FSIAD 1959). Hon. Prof., Heriot-Watt, 1987. Hon. Dr RCA, 1985; DUniv: Heriot-Watt, 1986; De Montfort, 1998; Staffs, 1998; Open, 2003. 10 Design Council Awards; Duke of Edinburgh Award for Elegant Design, 1963; Prince Philip Designers Prize, 2001. *Recreations:* memories of tennis, ski-ing. *Address:* 53 Christchurch Hill, NW3 1LG.

GRANGER, John; Headmaster, Bournemouth School, 1996–2009; *b* Heston, Middx, 5 Aug. 1949; *s* of Raymond and Mary Jane, (Jenny), Granger; *m* 1974, Heather Pyatt; two *d. Educ:* Spring Grove Grammar Sch.; Atlantic Coll.; Univ. of Hull (BSc Hons Applied Physics; PGCE). Sci. teacher, Plymstock Sch., 1973–74; Hd of Physics, 1977–87, Hd of Sci., 1987–96, Dep. Headmaster, 1991–96, Torquay Boys' GS, 1974–96. FRSA. *Recreations:* keeping fit, being with the family, music.

GRANGER, Richard; Director General, NHS Information Technology, and Chief Executive Officer, NHS Connecting for Health, Department of Health, 2002–08; *b* 21 April 1965; *m* 1998, Gabrielle Virag; one *s* two *d. Educ:* Univ. of Bristol (BSc Hons (Geol.) 1987). Geologist, Geoservices SA, Singapore and Australia, 1987–89; Andersen Consulting, 1989–96 (Manager, 1993–96); Prog. Dir, Electronic Data Systems, 1996–98; Partner, Deloitte & Touche, 1998–2002. Hon. DSc City, 2006. *Publications:* articles on electronic govt and electronic health. *Recreations:* family, cycling, walking, books. *Clubs:* Reform, Ronnie Scott's; Cycle Touring.

GRANT; *see* Lyall Grant.

GRANT, family name of **Earl of Dysart** and **Baron Strathspey**.

GRANT, Andrew Robert; educational consultant; Headmaster, St Albans School, 1993–2014; *b* Rochford, 29 April 1953; *s* of Walter Frank Grant and Joan Grant (*née* Bartram); *m* 1977, Hilary Sheena Kerr (*née* Charlton); two *s. Educ:* Southend High Sch.; Corpus Christi Coll., Cambridge (Open Exhibn; BA Hons English 1975; MA 1979; PGCE 1976). Asst Master, Merchant Taylors' Sch., Northwood, 1976–83; Hd of English, Whitgift Sch., Croydon, 1983–90; Second Master, Royal Grammar Sch., Guildford, 1990–93. Chm., HMC, 2009–10 (Chm., London Div., 2006–07); Director: ISC, 2009–11; Minerva Educn, 2014–; Member: HMC/GSA Educn and Academic Policy Cttee, 2000–06 (Chm., 2002–05); Jt Assocs Curriculum Gp, 2000–06; Tomlinson 14–19 Rev. Assessment Gp, 2003–05; QCA 14–19 Adv. Gp, 2004–06; HMC/GSA Univs Cttee, 2005–08; Ind. State Schs Partnership Forum, DCSF, 2006–08. Mem. Court, Univ. of Hertfordshire, 2006–14; Governor: Colfe's Sch., 2012–; Norwich Sch., 2013–; St Mary's Sch., Cambridge, 2014–. FRSA. *Recreations:* theatre, literature, music, cycling, squash, sailing. *E:* abbotwulsin@icloud.com. *Clubs:* East India, Lansdowne; Hawks (Cambridge).

GRANT, Andrew Steven, RDI 2012; landscape architect; Founder and Director, Grant Associates, since 1996; *b* Withernsea, 29 Oct. 1958; *s* of Peter and Joyce Grant; *m* 2010, Caroline Ambrose; two *d*; two *s* by a previous marriage. *Educ:* Edinburgh Coll. of Art, Heriot Watt Univ. (BA Hons Landscape Architecture 1982). CMLI 1992. Landscape architect, Ash Gulf, Doha, 1983–86; Associate, Nicholas Pearson Associates, 1986–95. Vis. Prof., Univ. of Sheffield, 2013–. Hon. FRIBA 2010. *Address:* Grant Associates, 22 Milk Street, Bath BA1 1UT. *T:* (01225) 332664. *E:* ag@grant-associates.uk.com.

GRANT, Andrew Young; Chief Operating Officer (formerly Principal), Grant Leisure Group, 1982–2005; Chief Executive Officer, Grant Leisure Inc., since 2005; Chairman, Real Live Leisure Co. Ltd, 1998–2007; *b* 8 April 1946; *s* of Marshall Grant and Marilyn Greene (*née* Phillips); *m* 1st, 1969, Dietra (marr. diss.); one *d*; 2nd, 1973, Lindy Lang (marr. diss.); one *d*; 3rd, 2005, Debra Gould (marr. diss. 2013). *Educ:* Univ. of Oregon (BSc). Personnel Manager, Universal Studios Tour, Universal City, Calif, 1967–69; Dir of Personnel, Busch Gardens, LA, 1969–71, Ops Dir, 1971–73; Gen. Manager, Squaw Valley Ski Resort, 1973–74; Gen. Manager, Busch Gardens, 1974–76; Dir, Economic Research Associates, LA, 1976–79; Dep. Dir, Zoological Soc., San Diego, 1979–83; Dir, Leeds Castle Enterprises, 1983–88; Director: Granada Studios Tour, 1987–90; Grant Leisure Developments, 1987–; Blackpool Zoo, 2003–; Man. Dir, Zoo Operations Ltd, Zoological Soc., 1988–91; Principal, Internat. Spirit Develt Corp. Ltd (formerly Internat. Spirit Management Co.), 1995–. Member: Internat. Assoc. of Amusement Parks and Attractions, 1975–; Tourism Soc., 1988–; Tourism and Leisure Industries Sector Gp, NEDC, 1990–; Urban Land Inst., 1998–. Member Board: Montecito YMCA, 2006–; Channel Islands YMCA, 2010–; Mem. Adv. Bd, Devereux Foundn, Calif, 2013–. *Publications:* Nearly Human: the gorilla's guide to good living, 2007; Rain Forest Wisdom, 2013. *Recreations:* swimming, fishing, golf. *Address:* Grant Leisure Inc., 2920 Hermosa Road, Santa Barbara, CA 93105, USA. *T:* (805) 4035873. *E:* andy@grant-leisure.com.

GRANT, Ann; Vice Chairman, Africa, Standard Chartered Capital Markets Ltd, 2005–14; *b* 13 Aug. 1948. *Educ:* Univ. of Sussex; SOAS, Univ. of London (MSc 1971). Joined FCO, 1971; Calcutta, 1973–75; Dept of Energy, 1976–79; Head of Chancery and Consul, Maputo, 1981–84; First Sec. (Energy), Office of UK Perm. Rep. to EU, Brussels, 1987–89, resigned; Communications Dir, Oxfam, 1989–91; rejoined FCO, 1991; Counsellor (Econ. and Social Affairs), UK Mission to UN, NY, 1992–96; Counsellor, FCO, 1996–98; Dir, African Dept, FCO, 1998–2000; High Comr, South Africa, 2000–05. Non-exec. Dir, Tullow Oil plc, 2009–. Mem. Council, ODI. Trustee, UK Disasters Emergency Cttee. Chair, Serious Music Trust. *Address:* c/o Tullow Oil plc, 3rd Floor, Building 9, Chiswick Park, 566 Chiswick High Road, W4 5YS.

GRANT, Sir Anthony, Kt 1983; solicitor and company director; *b* May 1925; *m* Sonia Isobel (*d* 2009); one *s* one *d. Educ:* St Paul's Sch.; Brasenose Coll., Oxford. Army 1943–48, Third Dragoon Guards (Capt.). Admitted a solicitor, 1952. MP (C): Harrow Central, 1964–83; Cambs SW, 1983–97. Opposition Whip, 1966–70; Parly Sec., Board of Trade, June–Oct. 1970; Parliamentary Under-Secretary of State: Trade, DTI, 1970–72; Industrial Develt, DTI, 1972–74. Chm., Cons. back bench Trade Cttee, 1979–83; Mem., Foreign Affairs Select Cttee, 1980–83. A Vice-Chm., Conservative Party Organisation, 1974–76; Mem. Exec., 1922 Cttee, 1978–97. Formerly Member: Council of Europe (Chm., Econ. Cttee, 1980–87); WEU. Pres., Guild of Experienced Motorists. Dir, British Human Assoc., 2002–09. Freeman, City of London; Master, Guild of Freemen, 1979–80, 1997–98; Liveryman, Co. of Solicitors. *Recreations:* watching Rugby and cricket, golf. *Address:* Whiteacre, The Chase, Oxshott, Surrey KT22 0HR. *Clubs:* Carlton; Walton Heath Golf.

GRANT of Monymusk, Sir Archibald, 13th Bt *cr* 1705; *b* 2 Sept. 1954; *e s* of Captain Sir Francis Cullen Grant, 12th Bt, and of Lady Grant (Jean Margherita, *d* of Captain Humphrey Douglas Tollemache, RN), who *m* 2nd, 2nd Baron Tweedsmuir, CBE, CD; *S* father, 1966; *m* 1st, 1982, Barbara Elizabeth (marr. diss. 2009), *e d* of A. G. D. Forbes, Druminnor Castle, Rhynie, Aberdeenshire; two *d*; 2nd, 2012, Fiona Mary Julia, *e d* of Sir Duncan Alexander Grant of Dalvey, 13th Bt. *Address:* House of Monymusk, Aberdeenshire AB51 7HL. *T:* (01467) 651220.

See also Sir P. A. B. Grant of Dalvey, Bt.

GRANT, Prof. (Barbara) Rosemary, PhD; FRS 2007; Senior Research Scholar, since 1997, with rank of Professor, 1997–2008, now Emeritus, Department of Ecology and Evolutionary Biology, Princeton University (Research Scholar and Lecturer, 1985–96); *b* Arnside, Cumbria, 8 Oct. 1936; *m* 1962, Peter Raymond Grant, *qv*; two *d. Educ:* Edinburgh Univ. (BSc Hons 1960); Uppsala Univ., Sweden (PhD 1985). Research Associate: Univ. of BC, 1960–64; Yale Univ., 1964–65; McGill Univ., 1973–77; Univ. of Michigan, 1977–85.

Vis. Prof., Univ. of Zurich, 2002, 2003. Mem., Amer. Acad. Arts and Scis, 1997; For. Mem., NAS, 2008. Darwin Medal, Royal Soc., 2002; Darwin-Wallace Medal, Linnean Soc., 2009; with P. R. Grant: Balzan Prize for Population Biol., Internat. Balzan Prize Foundn, 2005; Kyoto Prize, Inamori Foundn, 2009. *Publications:* (with P. R. Grant) Evolutionary Dynamics of a Natural Population: the large cactus finch of the Galapagos, 1989; (with P. R. Grant) How and Why Species Multiply: the radiation of Darwin's finches, 2008; (ed with P. R. Grant) In Search of the Causes of Evolution: from field observations to mechanisms, 2010; 40 Years of Evolution, 2014; contribs to jls incl. Proc. NAS, Oecologia (Berlin), Ecology, Evolution, Proc. Royal Soc. London, Biol Conservation, Science, Nature. *Address:* Department of Ecology and Evolutionary Biology, Princeton University, Princeton, NJ 08544–1003, USA. *E:* rgrant@princeton.edu.

GRANT, Charles Peter, CMG 2013; Co-founder, 1995, and Director, since 1998, Centre for European Reform; *b* 9 Oct. 1958; *s* of Peter Forbes Grant and Elizabeth Ann Grant (*née* Shirreff). *Educ:* Selwyn Coll., Cambridge (BA Hons Hist. 1980); Grenoble Univ. (Dip. French). Journalist, Euromoney, 1981–86; joined The Economist, 1986; financial journalist, 1986–89; Brussels corresp., 1989–93; home news, 1993–94; Defence Ed., 1994–98. Dir and Trustee, British Council, 2002–08; Trustee and Mem. Council of Mgt, Ditchley Foundn, 2013–. Mem. Bd, Moscow Sch. of Civic Educn (formerly Moscow Sch. of Pol Studies), 2002–. Chevalier, Ordre Nat. du Mérite (France), 2004; Bene Merito Medal (Poland), 2015. *Publications:* Delors: inside the house that Jacques built, 1994; Can Britain Lead in Europe?, 1998; EU 2010: an optimistic vision of the future, 2000; Transatlantic Rift: how to bring the two sides together, 2003; What Happens if Britain Votes No?, 2005; Europe's Blurred Boundaries: rethinking enlargement and neighbourhood policy, 2006; European Choices for Gordon Brown, 2007; Preparing for the Multipolar World: European foreign and security policy in 2020, 2007; Can Europe and China Shape a New World Order?, 2008; Is Europe Doomed to Fail as a Power?, 2009; Cameron's Europe: can the Conservatives achieve their EU objectives? 2009; Russia, China and Global Governance, 2012; (jtly) How to Build a Modern EU, 2013. *Recreations:* classical music, hill-walking. *Address:* Centre for European Reform, 14 Great College Street, SW1P 3RX. *T:* (020) 7233 1199, *Fax:* (020) 7233 1117. *E:* charles@cer.org.uk. *Club:* Reform.

GRANT, Dr David, CBE 1997; CEng, FREng, FIET; FLSW; Vice-Chancellor, Cardiff University, 2001–12; *b* 12 Sept. 1947; *s* of Edmund Grant and Isobel Scorer Grant (*née* Rutherford); *m* 1974, Helen Joyce Rutter; one *s* one *d*. *Educ:* Univ. of Durham (PhD 1974). CEng 1975; FIET (FIEE 1984); FREng (FEng 1997). Reyrolle Parsons Gp, 1966–77; United Technologies Corp., 1977–84; Gp Technical Dir, Dowty Gp, 1984–91; Technical Dir, GEC, then Marconi plc, 1991–2001. Non-executive Director: Renishaw plc, 2012–; DSTL, 2012–; Sen. Ind. Dir, IQE plc, 2012–. Member: EPSRC, 2001–06; UK Technol. Strategy Bd, later Innovate UK, 2007–14 (Interim CEO, 2015). Vice-Pres., RAEng, 2007–12; Chair, STEMNET, 2012–. FLSW 2011. Mensforth Internat. Gold Medal, IEE, 1996. *Recreation:* classic cars. *Address:* Cardiff University, Main Building, Park Place, Cardiff CF10 3AT.

GRANT, Helen; MP (C) Maidstone and the Weald, since 2010; *b* London, 28 Sept. 1961; *d* of Dr Julius Okuboye and Dr Gladys Spedding (*née* Butler); *m* 1991, Simon Julian Grant; two *s*. *Educ:* St Aidan's Sch., Carlisle; Trinity Sch., Carlisle; Univ. of Hull (LLB Hons); Guildford Coll. of Law (solicitors finals). Articled clerk, Cartmell Mawson and Maine, Carlisle; admitted solicitor, 1988; Clinical Negligence Solicitor, Hempsons, London, 1987–88; Equity Partner, Fayers & Co., S Wimbledon, 1988–94; Founder and Sen. Partner, Grants Solicitors LLP, 1996–. Non-exec. Dir, Croydon NHS PCT, 2005–07. Member: Family Div., Social Justice Policy Gp, 2006–08, Family Law Reform Commn, 2007–09, Centre for Social Justice; Equality and Diversity Cttee, Law Soc., 2008–09. Parliamentary Under-Secretary of State: (Women and Equalities), MoJ, 2012–13; (Women, Equalities, Sport and Tourism), DCMS, 2013–15. Mem., Justice Select Cttee, 2010–11; Vice Chm., Army Div., All Party Parly Gp for Armed Forces, 2010. Pres., Bd of Trustees, Maidstone Museums' Foundn, 2008–; Patron, Maidstone Br., Tomorrow's People, 2009–; Hon. Vice-Pres., Maidstone MENCAP Trust, 2010–. Hon. MInstRE 2010. *Publications:* contrib. to reports for Social Justice Policy Gp, Centre for Social Justice. *Recreations:* tennis, cinema, major sporting events, family life. *Address:* House of Commons, SW1A 0AA. *T:* (020) 7219 7107. *E:* helen.grant.mp@parliament.uk.

GRANT, Helen Louise; *see* Munn, H. L.

GRANT, Hugh John Mungo; actor; *b* 9 Sept. 1960; *s* of James Murray Grant and late Fynvola Susan Grant (*née* Maclean); one *s* one *d* by Tinglan Hong; one *s* by Anna Eberstein. *Educ:* Latymer Upper Sch., Hammersmith; New Coll., Oxford (BA). Began career in theatre performing in Jockeys of Norfolk (written with Chris Lang and Andy Taylor); actor in theatre, TV and films; co-founder, 1994, and producer for Simian Films. *Films include:* White Mischief, Maurice (Best Actor, jtly with James Wilby, Venice Film Fest.), 1987; Lair of the White Worm, La Nuit Bengali, 1988; Impromptu, 1989; Bitter Moon, 1992; Remains of the Day, 1993; Four Weddings and a Funeral (Golden Globe Award, BAFTA Award, Evening Standard Peter Sellers Award for Comedy, 1995), Sirens, 1994; The Englishman Who Went Up a Hill but Came Down a Mountain, Nine Months, An Awfully Big Adventure, Sense and Sensibility, 1995; Restoration, 1996; Notting Hill, 1999 (Evening Standard Peter Sellers Award for Comedy, Empire Film Awards Best British Actor, 2000); Small Time Crooks, 2000; Bridget Jones's Diary, 2001 (Evening Standard Peter Sellers Award for Comedy, 2002); About A Boy, 2002 (Empire Film Awards Best British Actor, London Critics' Circle Film Awards Best British Actor, 2003); Two Weeks Notice, Love Actually, 2003; Bridget Jones: The Edge of Reason, 2004; American Dreamz, 2006; Music and Lyrics, 2007; Did You Hear About the Morgans?, 2010; Cloud Atlas, 2013; The Rewrite, 2014; The Man from U.N.C.L.E., 2015; Simian Films productions: Extreme Measures, 1996; Mickey Blue Eyes, 1998. Mem. Bd, Hacked Off. Patron: Fynvola Foundn; Pancreatic Cancer Action; DIPEx. Ambassador Marie Curie Cancer Care.

GRANT, Sir Ian (David), Kt 2010; CBE 1988; DL; Chairman, Scottish Exhibition Centre Ltd, 2002–13 (Director, since 1998; Deputy Chairman, 2001–02); *b* Dundee, 28 July 1943; *s* of late Alan H. B. Grant and Florence O. Grant; *m* 1968, Eileen May Louisa Yule; three *d*. *Educ:* Strathallan Sch.; East of Scotland College of Agriculture (Dip.). Vice Pres. 1981–84, Pres. 1984–90, National Farmers' Union of Scotland; Mem., Scottish Council, CBI, 1984–96; Crown Estate Comr for Scotland, 1996–2009; First Crown Estate Comr, later Chm., The Crown Estate, 2002–09. Mem. Bd, 1988–90, Chm., 1990–98, Scottish Tourist Bd; Mem. Bd, BTA, 1990–98. Director: East of Scotland Farmers Ltd, 1978–2002; Clydesdale Bank PLC, 1989–97; NFU Mutual Insce Soc. Ltd, 1990–2008 (Dep. Chm., 2003–08); Scottish and Southern Energy plc (formerly Scottish Hydro Electric PLC), 1992–2003 (Dep. Chm., 2000–03); Chm., Cairngorms Partnership, 1998–2003. Vice Pres., Royal Smithfield Club, 1996. Trustee: NFU Mutual Charitable Trust, 2009–; Queen Elizabeth Castle of Mey Trust, 2010–. FRAgS 1987. DL Perth and Kinross, 2011. Hon. DBA Napier, 1999. *Recreations:* travel, gardening, reading, music. *Address:* Leal House, Loyal Road, Alyth PH11 8JQ.

GRANT, (Ian) Nicholas; Chief Executive Officer, Mediatrack Research Ltd, since 2007 (Managing Director, 1992–2002, Chairman, 2002, Mediatrack); *b* 24 March 1948; *s* of late Hugo and Cara Grant; *m* 1977, Rosalind Louise Pipe; one *s* one *d*. *Educ:* Univ. of London (LLB); Univ. of Warwick (MA, Industrial Relns). Confederation of Health Service Employees: Research Officer, 1972–74; Head of Research and Public Relations, 1974–82; Dir of Communications, Labour Party, 1982–85; Public Affairs Advr, Mirror Group Newspapers and Maxwell Communication Corp., 1985–89. Pres., Internat. Assoc. for the Measurement and Evaluation of Communication (formerly Assoc. of Media Evaluation Cos, then Assoc. for Measurement and Evaluation of Communication), 2011–13 (Dep. Chm., 1997–2005; Chm., 2005–10). Member: Council, London Borough of Lambeth, 1978–84; Lambeth, Southwark and Lewisham AHA, 1978–82; W Lambeth DHA, 1982–83. Contested (Lab) Reigate, 1979. FCIPR. FRSA 2013. *Publications:* contrib. to: Economics of Prosperity, ed D. Blake and P. Ormerod, 1980; Political Communications: the general election campaign of 1983, ed I. Crewe and M. Harrop, 1985. *Recreations:* walking, reading, photography. *Address:* Mediatrack Research Ltd, 123 Pall Mall, SW1Y 5EA. *T:* (020) 7430 0699. *E:* ngrant@mediatrack.com. *Club:* Reform.

GRANT, Prof. Ian Philip, DPhil; FRS 1992; CMath; FIMA, FRAS, FInstP; Professor of Mathematical Physics, University of Oxford, 1992–98, now Emeritus Professor; Tutorial Fellow in Mathematics, Pembroke College, Oxford, 1969–98, now Emeritus Fellow; Visiting Professor, Department of Applied Mathematics and Theoretical Physics, University of Cambridge; *b* 15 Dec. 1930; *er s* of Harold Hyman Grant and Isabella Henrietta Ornstien; *m* 1958, Beryl Cohen; two *s*. *Educ:* St Albans Sch., Herts; Wadham Coll., Oxford (Open Scholar 1948; MA; DPhil 1954). FInstP (FPhysS 1955); FIMA 1965; CMath 1990. SSO, 1957–61, PSO, 1961–64, UKAEA, Aldermaston; Res. Fellow, Atlas Computer Lab., SRC, 1964–69; Lectr in Maths, 1969–90, Reader in Mathematical Physics, 1990–92, Oxford Univ.; Res. Fellow in Maths, 1964–69, Actg Master, 1984–85, Pembroke Coll., Oxford. Visiting Professor: McGill Univ., 1976; Abo Akademi, Finland, 1977; Inst. de Fisica, Univ. Nacional Autónoma de México, 1981; Imperial Coll., London, 2001–08. Governor: Royal Grammar Sch., High Wycombe, 1981–99; St Paul's Schs, 1993–2001. *Publications:* Relativistic Quantum Theory of Atoms and Molecules, 2006; papers in learned jls on relativistic quantum theory in atomic and molecular physics, and on radiative transfer theory in astrophysics and atmospheric science. *Recreations:* walking, music, theatre-going. *Address:* Mathematical Institute, University of Oxford, Andrew Wiles Building, Radcliffe Observatory Quarter, Woodstock Road, Oxford OX2 6GG. *E:* ipg@maths.ox.ac.uk, ipg21@damtp.cam.ac.uk; Apt 46 Abbeyfield Girton Green, Wellbrook Way, Girton, Cambridge CB3 0GQ. *T:* (01223) 276364.

GRANT, Rt Rev. James Alexander, AM 1994; Assistant Bishop, Diocese of Melbourne, 1985–99; Dean of St Paul's Cathedral, Melbourne, 1985–99; *b* 30 Aug. 1931; *s* of late V. G. Grant, Geelong; *m* 1983, Rowena Margaret Armstrong. *Educ:* Trinity College, Univ. of Melbourne (BA Hons); Melbourne College of Divinity (BD). Deacon 1959 (Curate, St Peter's, Murrumbeena), priest 1960; Curate, West Heidelberg 1960, Broadmeadows 1961; Leader Diocesan Task Force, Broadmeadows, 1962; Domestic and Examining Chaplain to Archbishop of Melbourne, 1966–70; Chaplain, Trinity Coll., Univ. of Melbourne, 1970–75, Fellow, 1975; Bishop Coadjutor, dio. of Melbourne, 1970–85; Chairman, Brotherhood of St Laurence, 1971–87 (Director, 1969); Pres., Diocesan Mission to Streets and Lanes, 1987–97. Jubilee Medal, 1977; Centenary Medal, Australia, 2003. *Publications:* (with Geoffrey Serle) The Melbourne Scene, 1957; Perspective of a Century—Trinity College 1872–1972, 1972; Episcopally Led and Synodically Governed: Anglicans in Victoria 1803–1997, 2010; St Paul's Cathedral, Melbourne, 2014. *Recreation:* historical research. *Address:* 151 Park Drive, Parkville, Vic 3052, Australia. *Club:* Melbourne (Melbourne).

GRANT, Janet; *see* Thompson, J.

GRANT, Sir (John) Anthony; *see* Grant, Sir A.

GRANT, Sir John Douglas Kelso, KCMG 2005 (CMG 1999); HM Diplomatic Service, retired; Executive Vice-President, Policy and Corporate Affairs, BG Group plc, since 2009; *b* 17 Oct. 1954; *s* of Douglas Marr Kelso Grant and Audrey Stevenson Grant (*née* Law); *m* 1983, Anna Maria Lindvall; one *s* two *d*. *Educ:* Edinburgh Acad.; St Catharine's Coll., Cambridge (BA 1976). HM Diplomatic Service: W African Dept, FCO, 1976; Stockholm, 1977–80; Russian lang. trng, 1980–81; Moscow, 1982–84; Morgan Grenfell and Co. Ltd, 1985–86; Press Office, FCO, 1986–89; UK Permt Repn to EU, 1989–93 (Press Spokesman, later External Relns) and 1994–97 (Counsellor, External Relns); European Secretariat, Cabinet Office, 1993–94; Principal Private Sec. to Sec. of State for Foreign and Commonwealth Affairs, 1997–99; Ambassador to Sweden, 1999–2003; UK Permanent Rep. to EU, Brussels, 2003–07. Pres., BHP Billiton Europe, 2007–09. *Recreations:* cross-country ski-ing, walking. *Address:* 33 Drummond Place, Edinburgh EH3 6PW.

GRANT, John Stephen; author; business consultant, since 1999; social entrepreneur; *b* Hythe, Kent, 8 Nov. 1964; *s* of Paul and Ursula Grant; one *s*. *Educ:* Emmanuel Coll., Cambridge (BA Hons Natural Scis 1987); Birkbeck Coll., London (MSc Psychodynamics of Infant Develt 2002). Account Rep., J. Walter Thomson, 1987–89; Account Planner, BMP DDB Needham, 1989–94; Planning Dir, Chiat Day, 1994–95; Co-founder, St Luke's Communications, 1995–99. Associate: Demos, 2007–09; Forum for the Future, 2008–12. Non-executive Director: Onzo Ltd, 2007–11; Ecoinomy Ltd, 2009–14. FRSA 2009. *Publications:* The New Marketing Manifesto, 1999; After Image, 2002; The Brand Innovation Manifesto, 2006; The Green Marketing Manifesto, 2007; Coopportunity, 2010; Made With, 2013. *Recreations:* reading, music, cinema, social campaigns. *E:* thejohngrant@btinternet.com.

GRANT, Keith Wallace; Dean, Faculty of Design, Kingston University (formerly Polytechnic), 1988–99; *b* 30 June 1934; *s* of Randolph and Sylvia Grant; *m* 1968, Deanne (*née* Bergsma); one *s* one *d*. *Educ:* Trinity Coll., Glenalmond; Clare Coll., Cambridge (MA). Account Exec., W. S. Crawford Ltd, 1958–62; General Manager: Covent Garden Opera Co., later Royal Opera, 1962–73; English Opera Group, 1962–73; Sec., Royal Soc. of Arts, 1973–77; Dir, Design Council, 1977–88. Called to the Bar, Middle Temple, 2001. Member: Adv. Council, V&A Mus., 1977–83; PO Stamp Adv. Cttee, 1978–89; Exec. Bd, Internat. Council of Socs of Industrial Design, 1983–87; Chm., Nat. Lead Body for Design, 1995–98. Chm., English Music Theatre Co., 1979–92; Mem., Management Cttee, Park Lane Gp, 1988–95; Sec., Peter Pears Award for Singers, 1988–95. Governor: Central Sch. of Art and Design, 1974–77; Birmingham Polytechnic, 1981–86; Edinburgh Coll. of Art, 1982–86; Mem. Ct, Brunel Univ., 1985–89. Hon. Prof., Heriot-Watt Univ., 1987. Hon. Fellow, Birmingham City Univ. (formerly Birmingham Poly., later Univ. of Central England), 1988. Hon. FCSD (Hon. FSIAD, 1983). *Recreations:* music, gardening, voluntary work for the Royal Botanic Gardens, Kew. *Address:* 43 St Dunstan's Road, W6 8RE. *Club:* Garrick.

GRANT, Kenneth Isaac; a District Judge (Magistrates' Courts) (formerly Metropolitan Stipendiary Magistrate), since 1999; *b* 14 Nov. 1951; *s* of late Samuel Grant and Mercia Grant; *m* 1980, Irene Whilton; one *s* one *d*. *Educ:* Haberdashers' Aske's Sch., Elstree; Univ. of Sussex (BA); Coll. of Law. Admitted Solicitor, 1977; Solicitor, Darlington & Parkinson, 1977–99, Sen. Partner, 1990–99. Chm., Area Cttee, Legal Aid Bd, 1994–99 (Chm., Area 14 Regional Cttee, 1997–99). *Recreations:* theatre, opera. *Address:* Hammersmith Magistrates' Court, 181 Talgarth Road, W6 8DN. *T:* (020) 8700 9350. *Club:* Hurlingham.

GRANT, Rev. Canon Malcolm Etheridge; Priest Associate, All Saints', Leighton Buzzard, since 2009; *b* 6 Aug. 1944; *s* of Donald Etheridge Grant and Nellie Florence May Grant (*née* Tuffey); *m* 1984, Katrina Russell Nuttall (*née* Dunnett); one *s* one *d*. *Educ:* Dunfermline High School; Univ. of Edinburgh (Bruce of Grangehill Bursar, 1962; BSc (Hons Chemistry); BD (Hons New Testament); Divinity Fellowship, 1969); Edinburgh Theological College. Deacon 1969, priest 1970; Assistant Curate: St Mary's Cathedral, Glasgow, 1969–72; St Wulfram's, Grantham (in charge of Church of the Epiphany, Earlesfield), 1972; Team Vicar of Earlesfield, Grantham, 1972–78; Priest-in-charge, St Ninian's, Invergordon, 1978–81; Examining Chaplain to Bishop of Moray, Ross and Caithness, 1979–81; Provost and Rector: St Mary's Cathedral, Glasgow, 1981–91; St Andrew's Cathedral, Inverness, 1991–2002 (Hon. Canon,

2002–); Rector, St Paul's, Strathnairn, and Priest i/c, St Mary's-in-the-Fields, Culloden, 1991–97. Vicar of Eaton Bray with Edlesborough, Dio. St Albans, 2002–09; RD of Dunstable, 2004–09; permission to officiate, Dio. St Albans, 2009, Dio. Oxford, 2009. Member, Highland Regional Council Education Cttee, 1979–81. Trustee, Scottish Churches Architectural Heritage Trust, 1991–2011. *Address:* 13 Rock Lane, Leighton Buzzard, Beds LU7 2QQ. *T:* (01525) 372771. *E:* mandkgrant@btinternet.com.

GRANT, Sir Malcolm (John), Kt 2013; CBE 2003; LLD; FAcSS; Chairman, NHS England (formerly NHS Commissioning Board), since 2011; Chancellor, University of York, since 2015; *b* 29 Nov. 1947; *s* of Francis William Grant and Vera Jessica Grant; *m* 1974, Christine (*née* Endersbee); two *s* one *d*. *Educ:* Waitaki Boys' High Sch., NZ; Univ. of Otago (LLB 1970; LLM 1973; LLD 1986). Called to the Bar, Middle Temple, 1998, Bencher, 2004. Lectr, subseq. Sen. Lectr in Law, Southampton Univ., 1972–86; University College London: Sen. Lectr in Law, 1986–88; Prof. of Law, and Vice-Dean, Faculty of Laws, 1988–91; Cambridge University: Prof. of Land Economy, 1991–2003; Pro-Vice-Chancellor, 2002–03; Fellow of Clare Coll., 1991–; Provost and Pres., UCL, 2003–13. Chairman: Local Govt Commn for England, 1996–2002 (Mem., 1992–2002; Dep. Chm., 1995–96); Ind. Panel on Remuneration of Councillors in London, 1999–2004; Agric. and Envmt Biotechnol. Commn, 2000–05; Steering Bd for Nat. Public Debate on Genetic Modification, 2002–03; Member: ESRC, 2008–12; Bd, HEFCE, 2008–14. British Business Ambassador, 2008–. Dir, Genomics England Ltd, 2014–. Mem., 2000–08, Chm., 2004–08, Standards Cttee, GLA. Chm., Russell Gp, 2006–09; Governor: Ditchley Foundn, 2002– (Mem., Council of Mgt, 2003–11); London Business Sch., 2003–13; Royal Instn, 2006–09; Member: Internat. Council, Free Univ. of Berlin, 2006–12; Univ. Grants Cttee, Hong Kong, 2008–; Higher Educn Adv. Council, Russian Fedn, 2013–; Internat. Adv. Bd, Moscow Inst. of Physics and Technol., 2013–. Pres., Council for the Assistance of At-Risk Academics, 2013–. Trustee, Somerset Hse, 2014–. Patron: New London Orch., 2005–; UK Envmtl Law Assoc., 2006–; Envmtl Law Foundn, 2010–. Hon. MRTPI 1993 (Hon. Life Mem., 2014); Hon. MRICS 1995. FAcSS (AcSS 2000). Hon. Life Fellow, Selwyn Coll., Dunedin, NZ, 2013; Montgomery Fellow, Dartmouth Coll., USA, 2014. Hon. LLD: Otago, 2006; UCL, 2013. Gen. Editor, Encyclopedia of Planning Law and Practice, 1981–2005 (Consultant Editor, 2005–); Consultant Editor, Encyclopedia of Environmental Law, 1993–. Officier, Ordre National du Mérite (France), 2004. *Publications:* Planning Law Handbook, 1981; Urban Planning Law, 1982, 2nd Suppl. 1990; Rate Capping and the Law, 1985, 2nd edn 1986; Permitted Development, 1989, 2nd edn 1996; (ed jtly) Concise Lexicon of Environmental Terms, 1995; Singapore Planning Law, 1999. Environmental Court Report, 2000. *Recreations:* opera, woodlands, forestry management, grandchildren, organ music. *Address:* NHS England, Skipton House, 80 London Road, SE1 6LH. *T:* (0113) 825 1104.

GRANT, Margaret; *see* Exley, M.

GRANT, (Martin Alistair) Piers; His Honour Judge Grant; a County Court Judge (peripatetic), Northern Ireland, since 2005; *b* 1 April 1950; *s* of Ranald and Maureen Grant; *m* 1977, Siobhan Bell; three *d*. *Educ:* Queen's Univ., Belfast (LLB Hons 1974). Called to the Bar, 1975; Dep. County Court Judge, 1992–2005. *Recreations:* travel, reading, family, tennis, golf. *Address:* c/o Royal Courts of Justice, Chichester Street, Belfast BT1 3JF. *Clubs:* Army and Navy; Royal Belfast Golf.

GRANT, Martin James; Chief Executive Officer, Park Resorts, 2007–08; *b* 29 June 1949; *s* of James and Barbara Grant; *m* 1979, Helena Kay; two *s*. *Educ:* King Henry VIII, Coventry; Nottingham Univ. (BSc). Marks and Spencer, 1971–74; Grand Metropolitan, 1974–79; Holt Lloyd, 1979–82; Imperial Foods, 1982–83; Whitbread & Co. plc, 1983–90; Allied Lyons, subseq. Allied Domecq, 1990–98: Managing Director: Ansells Ltd, 1990–95; Allied Domecq Leisure, 1995–98; Chief Executive: Vaux Gp, 1998–99; Inn Partnerships, 1999–2002; RoadChef Motorways Hldgs, 2004–07. Mem. Council, Aqa Education, 2012–. Fellow, Mktg Soc., 1995; Chm., BII, 2007–12 (Treas., 2000–07; CBII 2003). *Recreations:* military music, military history.

GRANT, Martin Macdonald, PhD; FREng; Chief Executive Officer, Energy, Atkins plc, since 2012; *b* Inverness, 23 Dec. 1958; *s* of Alistair Grant and Patricia Grant; *m* 1988, Shona Robertson; one *d*. *Educ:* George Heriot's Sch., Edinburgh; Univ. of Edinburgh (BSc 1st Cl. Hons Mech. Engrg 1980); City Univ. (PhD Fluid Mechanics 1984). FREng 2012. Atkins plc: Consultant Engr, 1984–97; Managing Director: Oil and Gas, 1997–2008; Energy, 2008–12. *Recreations:* golf, football, Land Rovers, learning French. *Address:* Atkins plc, Euston Tower, 286 Euston Road, NW1 3AT. *T:* (020) 7121 2000. *E:* martin.grant@atkinsglobal.com.

GRANT, Dame Mavis, DBE 1999; Headteacher, Canning Street Primary School, Newcastle upon Tyne, 1999–2008; *b* 1 Feb. 1948; *d* of Joseph S. Edgar and Edna M. Edgar (*née* Hewson); *m* 1970, Roger M. Grant. *Educ:* Northumberland Coll. of Educn (CertEd and Cert. Advanced Educn Studies). Teaching in primary schools, Herts, Northumberland and Newcastle upon Tyne, 1969–2008: Dep. Headteacher, Cowgate Primary Sch., Newcastle upon Tyne, 1978–84; Headteacher, Mary Trevelyan Primary Sch., Newcastle upon Tyne, 1984–99. *Recreations:* reading, theatre, travel, dining out.

GRANT, Michael John, CEng, FICE, FCT; Partner, Aaronite Partners Ltd, since 2006; *s* of Michael George Grant and Zena Grant; *m* 1979, Maureen Hampson; one *s* two *d*. *Educ:* North East London Poly. (BSc Hons Civil Engrg); City Univ. Business Sch., London (MBA Finance); Harvard Business Sch. (AMP). Trainee engr, Sir Alexander Gibb & Partners Consulting Engrs, 1971–72; Civil Engineer: DoE, 1972–78; BRB, 1978–84; Financial Analyst, Laing & Cruikshank (Stock Brokers), 1985–86; Dir of Corporate Finance and Gp Treas., Eurotunnel plc, 1987–98; Property Dir, Railtrack, 1998–99; Chief Exec., Strategic Rail Authy, 1999–2001; Franchising Dir, OPRAF, 1999–2001; Dir, Cable & Wireless, 2003–06; Chm., Cable & Wireless USA, 2003–06; Strategic Advr, UK Houses of Parlt, 2006–07; Chief Restructuring Officer: Deutsche Woolworth, 2007–09; Investment Dar (Kuwait), 2009–11; Ind. Exec., Energy City Qatar, 2011–12; Chief Restructuring Officer, Al Jaber Gp (Abu Dhabi), 2011–. Director: Eurotunnel Finance & Services, 1987–98; Broadgate Plaza, 1998–99; Railtrack Devlets, 1999; BRB, 1999; non-executive Director: Liverpool Vision, 1999; Great Eastern Telecommunications, Cayman Islands, 2004–06; Monaco Telecom, 2004–05; Mobile One, Singapore, 2004–06; Torexretail plc, 2007. Mem., Inst. for Turnaround. *Recreations:* travel, live music, sport. *Club:* Reform.

GRANT, Nicholas; *see* Grant, I. N.

GRANT of Dalvey, Sir Patrick Alexander Benedict, 14th Bt *cr* 1688 (NS); Chieftain of Clan Donnachy, (Donnachaidh); Managing Director, Grants of Dalvey Ltd, since 1988; *b* 5 Feb. 1953; *e s* of Sir Duncan Alexander Grant, 13th Bt, and Joan Penelope (*d* 1991), *o d* of Captain Sir Denzil Cope, 14th Bt; *S* father, 1961; *m* 1981, Dr Carolyn Elizabeth Highet, MB ChB, DRCOG, MRCGP (marr. diss. 2005), *d* of Dr John Highet, Glasgow; two *s*. *Educ:* St Conleth's Coll., Dublin; The Abbey Sch., Fort Augustus; Univ. of Glasgow (LLB 1981). Former deer-stalker, inshore fisherman. *Recreations:* professional competing piper, deerstalking, shooting. *Heir:* *s* Duncan Archibald Ludovic Grant, *b* 19 April 1982. *Address:* Tomintoul House, Flichity, Inverness-shire IV2 6XD. *Club:* New (Edinburgh).

GRANT, Patrick James; fashion designer and tailor; Director, Norton & Sons, since 2005; Creative Director: E. Tautz, since 2008; Hammond & Co., since 2012; *b* Edinburgh, 1 May 1972; *s* of James Gilbert Turner Grant and Susan Grant (*née* Fitzearle). *Educ:* Univ. of Leeds (BEng Materials Sci. and Engrg); Saïd Business Sch., Oxford Univ. (MBA 2005). Hon. Prof., Sch. of Business and Society, Glasgow Caledonian Univ., 2014. Judge, Great British Sewing Bee, BBC TV, 2013–15. *Publications:* Original Man, 2014. *Address:* c/o Norton & Sons, 16 Savile Row, W1S 3PL. *T:* (020) 7437 0829. *E:* patrick@etautz.com.

GRANT, Prof. Patrick Spencer, DPhil; FREng; Vesuvius (formerly Cookson) Professor of Materials, Oxford University, since 2004; Fellow, St Catherine's College, Oxford, since 2004; *b* 24 Feb. 1966; *s* of Richard Arthur Grant and Ann Dorothy Grant (*née* Reynolds); *m* 1999, Dr Zena Louise Forster; two *s* one *d*. *Educ:* Univ. of Nottingham (BEng Metallurgy and Materials Sci. 1987); St Edmund Hall, Oxford (DPhil Materials 1991). University of Oxford: Department of Materials: Res. Asst, 1990–92; SERC Postdoctoral Fellow, 1992–94; Royal Soc. Res. Fellow, 1994–2002; Lectr, 2002–04; Dir, Oxford Centre for Advanced Materials and Composites, 1999–2004; Jun. Res. Fellow, Jesus Coll., 1993–95; Sen. Res. Fellow, Linacre Coll., 1995–2004. Dir, Faraday Advance, 2000–07. FREng 2010. *Publications:* papers on process-microstructure relationships and modelling of materials processing. *Recreations:* running, guitar. *Address:* Department of Materials, Oxford University, Parks Road, Oxford OX1 3PH. *T:* (01865) 283763, *Fax:* (01865) 848785. *E:* patrick.grant@materials.ox.ac.uk.

GRANT, Sir Paul (Joseph Patrick), Kt 2009; DL; Headteacher, Robert Clack School, since 1997; *b* Liverpool, 16 May 1957; *s* of late Thomas Grant and Teresa Grant (*née* Walsh); *m* 1996, Deniece Jones; three *d*. *Educ:* Salesian Coll., Bootle; Hull Univ. (BA Hons Hist. 1978; Hon. Fellow 2011); Durham Univ. (PGCE 1979); Inst. of Educn, London Univ. (MA Educnl Mgt 1996). Teacher of history, Whitby Sch., 1979–87, exchange teacher, Australia, 1986; Hd of Hist., 1987–90, Hd of Year, 1989–90, Saint Bonaventures Sch.; Hd of Humanities and Sch. Professional Tutor, Robert Clack Sch., 1990–97. Vis. Prof. of Educn, Anglia Ruskin Univ., 2012–. Member: Educn Bd, BITC, 2003–; Nat. Adv. Gp for History in the Curriculum, 2010–; Educn Adv. Gp, FA Premier League, 2013–. Mem., Senate Council, Hull Univ., 2014–; Chair, Hull Univ. Alumni, 2014–. Nat. Leader of Educn, 2014. Freedom of Bor. of Barking and Dagenham, 2009. DL Gtr London, 2009. Hon. LLD Hull, 2011. *Publications:* Changing Times (with Kieran Costello), 1990. *Recreations:* family life, music (popular to classical), hill walking, holidaying in France, reading (historical novels), sports (particularly Everton and Liverpool FC and Lancashire CC). *Address:* Robert Clack School, Gosfield Road, Dagenham RM8 1JU. *T:* (020) 8270 4227. *E:* pgrant@robert-clack.bardaglea.org.uk.

GRANT, Peter; MP (SNP) Glenrothes, since 2015.

GRANT, Peter David; Co-Director, Restored, since 2010; *b* 31 May 1958; *s* of late Desmond John Noel Grant and of Judith Mary Grant; *m* 1985, Stella Elizabeth Lucy Flower; one *s* one *d*. *Educ:* King Edward VI Sch., Birmingham; St John's Coll., Cambridge (BA (Econs) 1980; MA); LSE (MSc Econs). Economist, Govt of Malaŵi (ODI Fellow), 1980–82; Consultant, Coopers & Lybrand Associates, 1983–86; Pricing Strategy Manager, British Telecom Internat., 1986–90; Overseas Development Administration, later Department for International Development: Economist, India, 1990–92; First Sec. (Econ.), Dhaka, 1992–96; Head: Internat. Econs Dept, 1996–98; Econ. Policy and Res. Dept, 1998–2000; Asia Policy Dept, and Dep. Dir, Asia, 2000–02; Dir, Internat., 2002–05; Internat. Dir, Tearfund, 2005–10. Vis. Prof. in Internat. Develt Econs, Richmond Univ., 2014–. Co-Chm., OECD/DAC Poverty Reduction Network, 1999–2001. Mem., Council, Evangelical Alliance, 2008–14. *Publications:* Poor No More, 2008. *Recreations:* theology, travel, running. *Address:* Restored, PO Box 447, 100 Church Road, Teddington, Middx TW11 1AY. *T:* (020) 8943 7706. *E:* peter.grant@restoredrelationships.org.

GRANT, Prof. Peter John, MD; FRCP, FRCPE, FESC, FMedSci; Professor of Medicine, since 2000, and Head, Division of Cardiovascular and Diabetes Research, since 1999, University of Leeds; Honorary Consultant Physician and Diabetologist, Leeds Acute NHS Trust, since 1989; *b* Brighton, 29 July 1952; *s* of John Grant and Joan Grant; *m* 1996, Penny Rice; two *s*, and two step *d*. *Educ:* Univ. of Bristol (MB ChB 1976; MD 1987); FRCP 1995; FRCPE 2003. FESC 2010. Médecin Asst Boursier, Central Hosp., Univ. Vaudois, Lausanne, 1988–89; University of Leeds: Sen. Lectr in Medicine, 1989–96; Prof. of Molecular Vascular Medicine, 1996–2000; Dir of Res., Faculty of Medicine and Health, 2000–04; Dir, Leeds Inst. of Genetics, Health and Therapeutics, 2004–05; Lead, Units of Assessments 1–3, 2001, Unit of Assessments 1, 2008, RAE. Co-Chm., EASD/ESC working party on cardiovascular risk, 2010–. FMedSci 2012. Ed.-in-Chief, Diabetes and Vascular Disease Res., 2004–. *Publications:* over 200 articles in scientific jls incl. Lancet, Circulation, Blood and Diabetes. *Recreations:* tennis, golf, music, walking. *Address:* Division of Cardiovascular and Diabetes Research, LIGHT Laboratories, Clarendon Way, University of Leeds, Leeds LS2 9JT. *T:* (0113) 343 7721, *Fax:* (0113) 343 7738. *E:* p.j.grant@leeds.ac.uk. *Clubs:* Sandmoor Golf, Alwoodley Golf.

GRANT, Prof. Peter Mitchell, OBE 2009; PhD; FRSE; FREng, FIET, FIEEE; Regius Professor of Engineering, University of Edinburgh, 2007–09, now Emeritus; *b* 20 June 1944; *s* of George Mitchell Grant and late Isobel Margaret (*née* Wilkinson); *m* 1974, Marjory Renz; two *d*. *Educ:* Heriot-Watt Univ. (BSc 1966); Univ. of Edinburgh (PhD 1975). FIET (FIEE 1988); FIEEE 1996; FRSE 1997; FREng 1997. Develt Engr, Plessey Co., 1966–70; Sen. Applications Engr, Hughes Microelectronics Ltd, 1970–71; University of Edinburgh: Res. Fellow, 1971–76; Lectr, 1976–82; Reader, 1982–87; Prof. of Electronic Signal Processing, 1987–2007; Hd, Dept of Electronics and Electrical Engrg, 1999–2002; Hd, Sch. of Engrg and Electronics, 2002–08. Vis. Prof., Stanford Univ., 1977–78; Vis. Staff Mem., MIT Lincoln Laboratory, 1985–86. Pres., European Assoc. for Signal Speech and Image Processing, 2000–02. Hon. DEng: Heriot-Watt, 2006; Napier, 2007. Faraday Medal, IEE, 2004. *Publications:* Digital Communications, 1998, 3rd edn 2009; Digital Signal Processing, 1999, 2nd edn 2003. *Address:* School of Engineering, University of Edinburgh, The King's Buildings, Mayfield Road, Edinburgh EH9 3JL. *T:* (0131) 651 7125, *Fax:* (0131) 650 6554. *E:* Peter.Grant@ed.ac.uk.

GRANT, Prof. Peter Raymond, FRS 1987; FRSCan 2003; Class of 1877 Professor of Zoology, Princeton University, 1989–2008, now Emeritus; *b* 26 Oct. 1936; *s* of late Frederick Thomas Charles and Mavis Irene Grant (later Reading); *m* 1962, (Barbara) Rosemary Matchett (*see* Prof. B. R. Grant); two *d*. *Educ:* Whitgift Sch.; Cambridge Univ. (BA Hons); Univ. of British Columbia (PhD). Seessel-Anonymous Postdoctoral Fellow in Biology Dept of Yale Univ., 1964–65; Asst Prof. 1965–68, Associate Prof. 1968–73, Prof. 1973–78, McGill Univ.; Prof., Univ. of Michigan, 1977–85; Prof. of Biology, Princeton Univ., 1985–89. FLS 1986. Hon. PhD: Uppsala, 1986; Zürich, 2008; Hon. DSc: McGill, 2000; San Francisco, Quito, 2005; Ohio Wesleyan, 2012. Kyoto Prize (with B. R. Grant), Inamori Foundn, 2009. *Publications:* Ecology and Evolution of Darwin's Finches, 1986, 2nd ed 1999; with B. R. Grant: Evolutionary Dynamics of a Natural Population, 1989 (Wildlife Soc. Publication Award, 1991); How and Why Species Multiply, 2008; (ed) In Search of the Causes of Evolution: from field observations to mechanisms, 2010; 40 Years of Evolution, 2014; contribs to Science, Nature, Proc. Royal Society, Proc. Nat. Acad. of Scis (USA), etc. *Recreations:* walking, tennis, music. *Address:* Department of Ecology and Evolutionary Biology, Princeton University, Princeton, NJ 08544–1003, USA. *T:* (609) 2585156.

GRANT, Piers; *see* Grant, M. A. P.

GRANT, Rhoda; Member (Lab) Highlands and Islands, Scottish Parliament, 1999–2003 and since 2007; Founder, Positive Politics, political advice consultancy, 2003; *b* 26 June 1963; *d* of Donald and Morag MacCuish; *m* 1989, (Christopher) Mark Grant. *Educ:* Open Univ. (BSc

Hons Social Sci.). Administrator: Highland Regl Council, 1987–93; UNISON, 1993–99. Contested (Lab) Inverness E, Nairn and Lochaber, Scottish Parly elecns, 2003. *Address:* Scottish Parliament, Edinburgh EH99 1SP.

GRANT, Richard E.; actor and writer; *b* 5 May 1957; *né* Richard Grant Esterhuysen; *m* 1986, Joan Washington; one *d. Educ:* Waterford-Kamhlaba, Swaziland; Univ. of Cape Town (BA English). *Films:* Withnail and I, 1986; How to Get Ahead in Advertising, 1988; Warlock, Killing Dad, Henry and June, 1989; LA Story, The Player, Hudson Hawk, 1990; Dracula, The Age of Innocence, 1991; Jack and Sarah, 1993; Prêt-à-Porter, 1994; Twelfth Night, Portrait of a Lady, 1995; Serpent's Kiss, 1996; Keep the Aspidistra Flying, 1997; Cold Light of Day, All for Love, The Match, 1998; Little Vampire, 1999; Gosford Park, 2002; Monsieur Napoleon, Bright Young Things, 2003; Tooth, Colour Me Kubrick, 2004; (writer and dir) Wah-Wah, Penelope, 2006; Filth and Wisdom, 2008; The Nutcracker, Love Hurts, 2009; Jackboots on Whitehall, Cuckoo, Foster, 2010; First Night, Last Fashion Show, Horrid Henry, Iron Lady, Kim and Kinderella, Zambezia, 2011; Dom Hemingway, 2013; Queen and Country, 2015; *television:* Trial and Retribution, Scarlet Pimpernel, 1999; Young Sherlock Holmes, Hildegarde, 2000; Hound of the Baskervilles, 2002; Above and Beyond, 2005; Miss Marple: Nemesis, Dalziel and Pascoe, 2006; Mumbai Calling, 2008; The History of Safari, 2010; The Crimson Petal and the White, Rab C. Nesbitt, Rev, 2011; The Fear, 2012; Hotel Secrets, 2012, 2014; Dr Who, 2012–13; Girls, 2014; Downton Abbey, 2014; Wellington: the Iron Duke Unmasked, 2015; *theatre:* The Play What I Wrote, Wyndhams, 2002; Otherwise Engaged, Criterion, 2005; My Fair Lady, Sydney Opera, 2008; God of Carnage, nat. tour, 2009. *Publications:* With-Nails: film diaries, 1996; By Design: Hollywood novel, 1998; Wah-Wah: film diaries, 2006. *Recreation:* scuba diving. *Address:* c/o ARG, 4a Exmoor Street, W10 6BD. *T:* (020) 7436 6400.

GRANT, Dr Richard Sturge; Chairman, Arts Council of New Zealand, since 2013; *b* 3 Nov. 1945; *s* of Sydney Wallace Grant and Eva Grant; *m* 1973, Cherrilyn Gaye Turnbull; two *d. Educ:* Victoria Univ. of Wellington (MA Hons); Univ. de Clermont-Ferrand (Dr d'Univ.). Department of External Affairs, Wellington, 1968; French Govt Scholar, 1968–70; NZ Embassy, Paris, 1971–75; Min. of Foreign Affairs, 1976–78; Counsellor and Dep. Head of Mission, Vienna, 1978–81; Consul-Gen., Noumea, 1982–85; Head, European Div., Min. of Foreign Affairs, 1985–86; Consul-Gen., Sydney, 1987–90; Ambassador, Bonn, 1990–94; Dir, Australia Div., Min. of Foreign Affairs, 1994–97; High Comr for NZ in the UK, 1997–99; Ambassador for NZ in France, 1999–2002; Dep. Sec., Min. of Foreign Affairs and Trade, NZ, 2002–04; High Comr for NZ in Singapore, 2004–08; Exec. Dir, Asia New Zealand Foundn, 2008–12. Visiting Scholar: John F. Kennedy Sch. of Govt, Harvard Univ., 1999; Oxford Internet Inst., Oxford Univ., 2004. *Recreations:* tennis, cricket, reading. *Address:* (office) Arts Council of New Zealand, PO Box 3806, Wellington 6140, New Zealand.

GRANT, His Honour Rodney Arandall; a Circuit Judge, 1995–2011; *b* 8 May 1944; *s* of Thomas and Olive Grant; *m* 2007, Catherine Jane Grimshaw. *Educ:* Leeds Grammar Sch.; Trinity Coll., Oxford (Minor Scholar; MA Mod. Langs). Called to the Bar, Inner Temple, 1970; NE Circuit, 1970–95; Head of Chambers, 1992–95; a Recorder, 1993–95. Mem., Adv. Panel, Rugby Football League, 2005–. *Recreations:* cookery, travel, jazz, reading, music. *Address:* c/o Circuit Administrator, 17th Floor, West Riding House, Albion Street, Leeds LS1 5AA.

GRANT, Rosemary; *see* Grant, B. R.

GRANT, Lt-Gen. Sir Scott (Carnegie), KCB 1999 (CB 1995); Chief Royal Engineer, 1999–2004; *b* 28 Sept. 1944; *s* of Maurice and Margaret Wotherspoon Gibb Grant; *m* 1973, Catharine Susan Pawsey; one *s* one *d. Educ:* King's Sch., Pontefract; RMA Sandhurst; Clare Coll., Cambridge (MA). Commissioned Royal Engineers, 1965; Regtl duty Aden, Sharjah, BAOR and UK, 1965–73; Instructor, RMA, 1973–74; student, Staff Coll., 1975–76; MoD, 1977–78; Sqn Comdr, BAOR, 1979–80; Instructor, Staff Coll., 1981–82; CO 26 Engineer Regt, 1982–84; MoD, 1985; SHAPE, 1986–87; Comdr, 33 Armoured Brigade, 1988–89; RCDS 1990; Army Member, Prospect Team, 1991; Dir Gen. of Army Trng, 1991–93; Team Leader, Army Command Structure Review, 1993; GOC, UK Support Comd (Germany), 1994–95; Comdt, RCDS, 1996–98; QMG, 1998–2000. Col, The Queen's Lancashire Regt, 1993–99; Colonel Commandant: King's Div., 1997–2001; RE, 1997–2004. Dir, Customer Support, 2001–04, Vice-Pres., Ops, 2004–07, Thales UK; non-exec. Dir, NAAFI, 2001–07 (Dep. Chm., 2006–07). *Recreation:* 20th Century art and literature. *Clubs:* Army and Navy; Hawks (Cambridge).

GRANT, Sharon Margaret, OBE 2014; Health Policy Adviser to Rt Hon. Ann Clwyd, MP, since 2013; *b* 28 Oct. 1952; *d* of Philip Arthur Lawrence and Margaret Theresa Lawrence; *m* 1998, Bernard Alexander Montgomery Grant, MP (*d* 2000). *Educ:* Tonbridge Girls' Grammar Sch.; Univ. of Birmingham (BSocSci Social Admin 1974, MSocSci Comparative Social Policy 1984). Campaigner on social equality issues, 1975–; Sen Lectr in Social Policy, Hatfield Polytechnic, 1977–87; Tutor and Examiner, Open Univ., 1984–87; Parly Sec. to late Bernie Grant, MP, 1987–2000; Chairman: Commn for Patient and Public Involvement in Health, 2003–08; London TravelWatch, 2008–12. Food Standards Agency: Mem., Adv. Cttee on Consumer Engagement, 2007–13; Mem., Food Hygiene Regulation Steering Cttee, 2013–. Councillor, London Bor. of Haringey, 1984–90. Founder and Sec., Bernie Grant Trust, 2000–; Director: Bernie Grant Centre Partnership Ltd, 2002–; Public Voice CIC, 2014–. Mem. Bd, Dignity in Dying, 2008–11. Chairman: Haringey CAB, 2008–; Healthwatch Haringey, 2013–. Mem., Haringey Panel, post-riot enquiry, 2011–13. *Recreations:* gardening, gym, travel, walking.

GRANT, Thomas Paul Wentworth; QC 2013; *b* Colchester, 14 Aug. 1969; *s* of Neville James Henry Grant and Jane Wentworth Grant (*née* Gibbons); *m* 1999, Hester Xanthe Jane, *d* of Rt Hon. Sir Anthony James Denys McCowan, PC; one *s* two *d. Educ:* Colchester Royal Grammar Sch.; Univ. of Bristol (BA 1st Cl. Hons); City Univ. (DipLaw (Dist.)). Called to the Bar, Middle Temple, 1993; in practice as a barrister, 1994–, specialising in commercial chancery, property, professional negligence litigation. *Publications:* (Jt Gen. Ed.) Lender Claims, 2010; (contrib.) Solicitors' Negligence and Liability, 2012; Jeremy Hutchinson's Case Histories, 2015. *Recreations:* the eighteenth century, gossip, hill-running, the 1890s. *Address:* Maitland Chambers, 7 Stone Buildings, Lincoln's Inn, WC2A 3SZ. *T:* (020) 7406 1200. *E:* tgrant@maitlandchambers.com. *Club:* Garrick.

GRANT PETERKIN, Maj. Gen. (Anthony) Peter, CB 2003; OBE 1990; Serjeant at Arms, House of Commons, 2005–07; *b* 6 July 1947; *s* of late Brig. James Grant Peterkin, DSO and of Dorothea Grant Peterkin; *m* 1974, Joanna, *d* of Sir Brian Young, *qv*; one *s* one *d. Educ:* Ampleforth; RMA Sandhurst; Durham Univ. (BA 1971); Madras Univ. (MSc 1980). Commnd Queen's Own Highlanders; ADC to CGS, 1973–74; Indian Staff Coll., 1980; Australian JSSC, 1986; CO, 1st Bn, 1987–89; MA to Mil. Sec., 1989–91; MA, UN Observer Mission, Iraq and Kuwait, 1991; Comdr, 24 Airmobile Bde, 1993–94; rcds, 1995; Dep. Mil. Sec., 1996–98; Sen. Directing Staff, RCDS, 1999; Man. Dir, OSCE Mission, Kosovo, April–Sept. 1999; GOC 5th Div., 2000; Mil. Sec., 2000–03. Chm., ACF, 2005–08. Chm., Global Vetting, 2009–10. Chairman: Saigon Children's Charity, 2000–07; Highlanders' Mus., Fort George, 2009–; Bee House Educn Saigon, 2010–. Chm. Trustees, Queen's Own Highlanders, 2009–. *Recreations:* travelling in Indochina, football, Scottish Victorian art. *Address:* Grange Hall, Forres, Moray IV36 2TR. *Club:* Army and Navy.

GRANT-SUTTIE, Sir James (Edward); *see* Suttie.

GRANTCHESTER, 3rd Baron *cr* 1953; **Christopher John Suenson-Taylor;** *b* 8 April 1951; *e s* (twin) of 2nd Baron Grantchester, CBE, QC and of Betty, *er d* of Sir John Moores, CBE; *S* father, 1995; *m* 1973, Jacqueline (marr. diss.), *d* of Dr Leo Jaffé; two *s* two *d. Educ:* Winchester; LSE (BSc Econ). Elected Mem., H of L, 2003; an Opposition Whip, 2010–. *Heir: s* Hon. Jesse David Suenson-Taylor, *b* 6 June 1977. *Address:* Lower House Farm, Back Coole Lane, Audlem, Crewe, Cheshire CW3 0ER.

GRANTHAM, Bishop Suffragan of; *no new appointment at time of going to press.*

GRANTLEY, 8th Baron *cr* 1782; **Richard William Brinsley Norton;** Baron of Markenfield 1782; a Director, Project and Export Finance, HSBC Bank plc (formerly HSBC Investment Bank), 1997–2005; *b* 30 Jan. 1956; *er s* of 7th Baron Grantley, MC and of Lady Deirdre Freda Mary Hare (who *m* 2001, Ian Bayley Curteis, *qv*), *e d* of Earl of Listowel, GCMG, PC; *S* father, 1995. *Educ:* Ampleforth Coll.; New Coll., Oxford (Open Schol. in Maths; BA (Law), MA). Pres., Oxford Union Soc., 1976. Cons. Res. Dept, 1977–81; Morgan Grenfell & Co. Ltd, 1981–97; Dir, Morgan Grenfell Internat., 1994–97. Contested (C) Wentworth, 1983. Councillor, RBK&C, 1982–86. Leader, UKIP, H of L, 1997. Kt SMO Malta, 1981. *Recreations:* bridge, smoking. *Heir: b* Hon. Francis John Hilary Norton [*b* 30 Sept. 1960; *m* 2004, Eva, *d* of Mr and Mrs Elemér Figder, Budapest]. *Address:* 8 Halsey Street, SW3 2QH. *T:* (home) (020) 7589 7531. *Club:* Pratt's.

GRANVILLE, 6th Earl *cr* 1833; **Granville George Fergus Leveson Gower;** Viscount Granville 1815; Baron Leveson 1833; *b* 10 Sept. 1959; *s* of 5th Earl Granville, MC and Doon Aileen (*née* Plunket); *S* father, 1996; *m* 1997, Anne, *o d* of Bernard Topping; one *s* two *d. Heir: s* Lord Leveson, *qv. Address:* Callernish, Lochmaddy, Isle of N Uist, Western Isles HS6 5BZ.

GRANVILLE-CHAPMAN, Gen. Sir Timothy (John), GBE 2007 (CBE 1991); KCB 2001; Master Gunner, St James's Park, since 2008; *b* 5 Jan. 1947; *s* of Guy Granville-Chapman and Elsa Granville-Chapman (*née* Campbell); *m* 1971, Elizabeth Stevens; one *s* one *d. Educ:* Charterhouse; Christ's Coll., Cambridge (BA Law 1968; MA 1972). VSO, Tanzania, 1965. Commissioned RA, 1968; regtl duties, 1968–77; Staff Coll., 1978–79; MA to Comdr, 1st BR Corps, 1980–82; CO 1st Regt RHA, 1985–88; Higher Command and Staff Course, 1988; Mil. Doctrine Author, 1988; Policy Staff, MoD, 1989–90; Comdr 12th Armd Bde, 1990–93; Dir, Army Staff Duties, MoD, 1994; ACGS, MoD, 1994–96; Comdt, Jt Services Comd and Staff Coll., 1997–99; Adjutant Gen., 2000–03; C-in-C Land Comd, 2003–05; Vice Chief of the Defence Staff, 2005–09; ADC Gen. to the Queen, 2003–09. Col, Dorset Yeomanry, 1997–2008; Pres. and Col Comdt, HAC, 2003–10. Dir, Defence and Nat. Rehabilitation Centre Project, 2009–. Gov., Harrow Sch., 1997–2009. Hon. FKC 2010. *Recreations:* sailing, some country pursuits, architecture, clocks. *Address:* Artillery House, Royal Artillery Barracks, Larkhill, Salisbury, Wilts SP4 8QT.

GRANZIOL, Dr Markus Johannes; non-executive Chairman, Eurex, 2002–06 (non-executive Director, 1997–2006); *b* 21 Jan. 1952; *m* Manuela Fornera; one *s* three *d. Educ:* Univ. of Zurich (MA Econs; PhD Econs 1980). University of Zurich: res. analyst, Inst. for Empirical Res. in Econs, 1976–85; Lectr in Macroecons and Financial Theory, Dept of Juris. and Pol Sci., 1978–90; COS, Dept III, Swiss Nat. Bank, Zurich, 1985–87; Swiss Bank Corporation, 1987–98: Man. Dir and Hd, Securities Dept, 1987–94; Man. Dir, Hong Kong and Global Hd, Equities Business, 1994–95; Jt Global Hd, Equities Business, SBC Warburg, 1995–96 (also Mem. Exec. Bd and Investment Banking Bd); Gen. Manager and Mem., Gp Exec. Bd, 1996–98; Global Hd, Equities and Fixed Income, Warburg Dillon Read, 1998–99; CEO, 1999–2001, Chm., 2000–02, UBS Warburg; Mem., Gp Exec. Bd, UBS AG, 1999–2002. Non-exec. Mem. Bd, Zurich Financial Services, 2002–04; Incentive Asset Mgt, 2005–. Vis. Schol., Grad. Sch. of Business Admin, Univ. of Chicago, 1981–82. *Publications:* contribs to scientific jls. *Recreations:* sports, piano.

GRATTAN, Donald Henry, CBE 1989; Chairman: Adult Continuing Education Development Unit, 1984–91; National Council for Educational Technology (formerly Council for Educational Technology), 1985–91 (Member, 1973–84); *b* St Osyth, Essex, 7 Aug. 1926; *s* of Arthur Henry Grattan and Edith Caroline Saltmarsh; *m* 1950, Valmai Dorothy Morgan; one *s* one *d. Educ:* Harrow Boys Grammar Sch.; King's Coll., Univ. of London. BSc 1st Cl. Hons, Mathematics Dip. in Radio-Physics. Jun. Scientific Officer, TRE, Gt Malvern, 1945–46; Mathematics Teacher, Chiswick Grammar Sch., 1946–50; Sen. Master, Downer Grammar Sch., Middx, 1950–56. BBC: Sch. Television Producer, 1956–60; Asst Head, Sch. Television, 1960–64; Head of Further Educn, Television, 1964–70; Asst Controller, Educnl Broadcasting, 1970–72, Controller, 1972–84. Member: Open Univ. Council, 1972–84 and Univ. Delegacy for Continuing Educn, 1978–84; Vis. Cttee, Open Univ., 1987–92; Adv. Council for Adult and Continuing Educn, 1978–83; European Broadcasting Union Working Party on Educn, 1972–84; Venables' Cttee on Continuing Educn, 1976–78. Chm., Adult Literacy Support Services Fund, 1975–80. Mem., Royal TV Soc., 1982–. Chm., 1993–96, Vice-Pres., 2001–, Marlow Soc. FRSA 1988. DUniv Open, 1985. Burnham Medal of BIM for services to Management Educn, 1969. *Publications:* Science and the Builder, 1963; Mathematics Miscellany (jt, BBC), 1966; numerous articles. *Recreations:* education (formal and informal), planning and organizing, people. *Address:* Delabole, 3 Gossmore Close, Marlow, Bucks SL7 1QG. *T:* (01628) 473571.

GRATTAN-BELLEW, Sir Henry Charles, 5th Bt *cr* 1838; *b* 12 May 1933; *s* of Lt-Col Sir Charles Christopher Grattan-Bellew, 4th Bt, MC, KRRC and Maureen Peyton, *niece* and adopted *d* of late Sir Thomas Segrave, Shenfield, Essex; *S* father, 1948; *m* 1st, 1956, Naomi Ellis (marr. diss. 1966; she *d* 2000); 2nd, 1967, Gillian Hulley (marr. diss. 1973; she *d* 2011); one *s* one *d*; 3rd, 1978, Elzabé Amy (*née* Body) (marr. diss. 1993), *widow* of John Westerveld, Pretoria, Tvl, SA. *Educ:* St Gerard's, Bray, Co. Wicklow; Ampleforth Coll., York. Publisher: Horse and Hound, SA, and Sustagen Supersport, 1977. Sports administrator, leading radio and TV commentator, hotelier, thoroughbred breeder and owner, author. *Publications:* A Pinch of Saltee, 2003; Sundown Safari, 2005; Mountbellew-Moylough: a pictorial memoir, 2010. *Heir: s* Patrick Charles Grattan-Bellew [*b* 7 Dec. 1971; *m* 2000, Liezel Wallis]. *Address:* 14 Ard Lorcain, Stillorgan, Co. Dublin, Ireland.

GRATTON, Paul; Director, Direct Valuations Ltd, since 1989; Executive Chairman: Shepherd Direct Ltd, since 2007; moneyQuest Mortgage Brokers, since 2008; *b* 10 Nov. 1959; *s* of Robert and Audrey Gratton; *m* 1997, Elizabeth; three *s. Educ:* Nottingham High Sch. Various posts incl. mgt posts, Midland Bank plc, 1978–89; Financial Services Dir, First Direct, 1989–96; Ops Dir, Prudential Banking, 1996–98; Chief Operating Officer, Prudential Banking plc/Egg plc, 1998–2000; Dep. Chief Exec., 2000–01, CEO, 2001–06, Egg plc; Exec. Chm., Artilium (formerly Future Internet Technologies) plc, 2006–07 (non-exec. Dir, 2007–08). Non-exec. Dir, borro Ltd, 2010–.

GRATWICKE, Charles James Phillip; His Honour Judge Gratwicke; a Circuit Judge, since 2003; Resident Judge, Chelmsford Crown Court, since 2012; *b* 25 July 1951; *s* of Phillip and Maeve Gratwicke; *m* 1981, Jane Vivien Meyer; two *s* one *d. Educ:* Franciscan Coll., Buckingham; St John's Coll., Southsea; Leeds Univ. (LLB Hons). Called to the Bar, Middle Temple, 1974; in practice as barrister, 1974–2003; a Recorder, 1998–2003; Hon. Recorder of Chelmsford, 2013–. Part-time Chairman, Disciplinary Committee: Potato Mktg Bd, 1990–2003; MMB, 1991–96. *Recreations:* long distance walking, sailing, maritime matters, marine painting, London in all its forms and history, foreign travel. *Address:* The Crown Court, New Street, Chelmsford, Essex CM1 1EL. *Clubs:* National Liberal; Seven Seas.

GRAVENEY, David Anthony, OBE 2006; Vice President, Professional Cricketers' Association, since 2003 (General Secretary, subseq. Chief Executive, 1994–2003); *b* 2 Jan. 1953; *s* of Ken Graveney and late Jeanne Graveney; *m* 1978, Julie Anne Smith Marriott; one *s* one *d*. *Educ:* Millfield Sch., Somerset. Gloucestershire CCC, 1972–90, Captain 1981–88; Somerset CCC, 1991; Durham CCC, 1992–94, Captain 1992–93. Treasurer, Professional Cricketers' Assoc., 1979–94. Manager: England cricket team, South Africa tour, 1990; England A team, Australia tour, 1996; England cricket team, One-Day series, Australia, 1998–99, and World Cup, 1999; Selector, England cricket team, 1995–96, Chm. of Selectors, 1997–2008; Nat. Performance Manager, ECB, 2008–. Mem., Exec. Bd, Gloucestershire CCC, 2013–. *Recreations:* golf, watching Rugby. *Address:* 6 Southover Close, Westbury-on-Trym, Bristol BS9 3NG.

GRAVES, family name of **Baron Graves**.

GRAVES, 10th Baron *cr* 1794 (Ire.); **Timothy Evelyn Graves;** *b* 27 March 1960; *s* of 9th Baron Graves and of Marjorie Ann (*née* Holder), OAM; *S* father, 2002. *Heir:* none.

GRAVES, Christopher James Mitchell; Director, Tudor Trust, since 1986 (Project Officer, 1985–86); *b* 6 April 1956; *s* of Desmond James Turner Graves and late Mary Kathleen Graves, OBE (*née* Mitchell); *m* 1986, Amanda Patricia Mayhew; one *s* two *d*. *Educ:* Westminster Sch.; Queens' Coll., Cambridge (BA 1978, MA 1981, DipArch 1981). RIBA 1983. Architect, Trehearne, Norman, Preston & Partners, 1981–85. *Recreations:* watercolours, opera, singing, watching a failing football team. *Address:* Tudor Trust, 7 Ladbroke Grove, W11 3BD. *T:* (020) 7727 8522.

GRAVES, Rev. Dr Peter Charles; Interim Senior Minister, Centenary United Methodist Church, Winston-Salem, North Carolina, 2009–11; Interim Minister, Histon Methodist Church, Cambridge, 2014–15; *b* 23 March 1943; *s* of Walter and Eileen Graves; *m* 1976, Patricia Mary Campbell; two *s* one *d*. *Educ:* Handsworth Theol Coll., Birmingham; Union Theol Seminary, Virginia (ThM, DMin); London Univ. (Cert Ed). Minister: Enfield Circuit (St John's, Goffs Oak), 1968–69; Highgate Circuit (Holly Park), 1969–72; Chaplain and Associate Lectr, Enfield Coll. of Technol., 1969–72; Chaplain and Sen. Lectr, 1972–77, Sen. Chaplain and Hd of Student Welfare, 1977–79, Middlesex Poly.; Minister: Epsom, 1979–89; Cullercoats, 1989–95; Superintendent Minister, Methodist Central Hall, Westminster, 1995–2000; Minister, Wesley Methodist Ch, Cambridge, and Methodist Chaplain to the Univs in Cambridge, 2000–08. Methodist Tutor, North East Ordination Course, 1990–95; Tutor, Wesley Study Centre, Cranmer Hall, Durham, 1992–95; Chaplain to Methodist MPs and Leader, Methodist Parly Fellowship, 1995–2000. Finch Lectr, High Point Univ., NC, USA, 1997. Vice Pres., Bible Soc., 1998–2008. Chm. Judges, Times Preacher of the Year Award, 1998–2000. Broadcaster, Premier Radio, London, 1997–2008. *Publications:* Living and Praying the Lord's Prayer, 2002; contrib. New Daylight, 1997–2005. *Recreations:* travel, theatre, family life. *Address:* Old Ness Farm, Ness Road, Burwell, Cambridge CB25 0DB.

GRAVES, Rupert; actor; *b* Weston-super-Mare, 30 June 1963; *m* 2001, Susie Lewis; three *s* two *d*. *Educ:* Wyvern Comp. Sch. Early career in a circus; London theatrical début, King's Head, Islington; film actor, 1986–. *Theatre includes:* Torch Song Trilogy, Albery, 1985; The Importance of Being Earnest; Candida, 1988; 'Tis Pity She's a Whore, NT, 1988; A Madhouse in Goa, Lyric, Hammersmith, 1989; Les Enfants du Paradis, Barbican, 1996; Hurlyburly, Old Vic, transf. Queen's, 1997; The Iceman Cometh, Almeida, 1998; Closer, NY, 1999; The Caretaker, Comedy, 2000; The Elephant Man, NY, 2002; Dumb Show, Royal Court, 2004; The Exonerated, Riverside Studios, 2006. *Films include:* A Room with a View, 1986; Maurice, 1987; A Handful of Dust, 1988; Where Angels Fear to Tread, 1991; Damage, 1992; The Madness of King George, 1994; Different for Girls, 1996; Intimate Relations, Mrs Dalloway, 1997; All My Loved Ones, 1999; Extreme Ops, 2003; Rag Tale, 2005; V for Vendetta, 2005; Intervention, 2006; Death at a Funeral, 2006; The Waiting Room, 2008; Made in Dagenham, 2010; Bone in the Throat, 2014. *Television includes:* Fortunes of War, 1987; Open Fire, 1994; The Tenant of Wildfell Hall, 1996; Blonde Bombshell, 1999; The Forsyte Saga, 2002; Charles II: The Power and the Passion, 2003; Clapham Junction, The Dinner Party, 2007; God on Trial, 2008; Garrow's Law, 2009–11; Single Father, 2010; Sherlock (3 series), 2010, 2012–14; Case Sensitive, 2011; Scott & Bailey, 2011; Secret State, 2012; The White Queen, 2013; Turks & Caicos, Salting the Battlefield, 2014; Last Tango in Halifax, 2014. *Address:* c/o United Agents, 12–26 Lexington Street, W1F 0LE.

GRAY; *see* Pereira Gray.

GRAY, 23rd Lord *cr* 1445; **Andrew Godfrey Diarmid Stuart Campbell-Gray;** *b* 3 Sept. 1964; *s* of 22nd Lord Gray and Patricia Margaret (*née* Alexander); *S* father 2003; *m* 1993, Hon. Lucy, *y d* of 2nd Baron Elton, *qv*; one *s* one *d*. *Heir: s* Master of Gray, *qv*.

GRAY, Master of; Hon. Alexander Godfrey Edward Diarmid Campbell-Gray; *b* 7 Oct. 1996; *s* and *heir* of Lord Gray, *qv*.

GRAY, Alasdair James; self-employed verbal and pictorial artist; *b* 28 Dec. 1934; *s* of Alexander Gray and Amy (*née* Fleming); *m* 1st, 1961, Inge Sørensen (marr. diss.); one *s*; 2nd, 1991, Morag McAlpine. *Educ:* Glasgow Sch. of Art (Scottish Educn Dept Dip. in mural painting and design); Jordanhill Teachers' Trng Coll. (CertEd). Part-time teacher and painter, 1958–62; theatrical scene painter, 1962–63; social security scrounger, 1963–64; painter and playwright, 1965–76 (8 one-man exhibns, two retrospective; 17 TV and radio plays broadcast; 4 plays staged); Glasgow's official artist-recorder for People's Palace local history mus., 1977; Writer-in-Residence, 1977–79, Consulting Prof. of Creative Writing, 2001–03, Glasgow Univ.; mural decorator, Oran Mor Leisure Centre, Glasgow, 2003–; one-man show, Talbot Rice Gall., Edinburgh, 2010; exhibition: Alasdair Gray: City Recorder, Gall. of Modern Art, Glasgow, 2011; Spheres of Influence I, Gall. of Modern Art, Glasgow, 2015. Collections of paintings owned by: Collins Gall., Strathclyde Univ.; People's Palace local history mus., Glasgow Green; Hunterian Gall., Glasgow Univ.; personal archives lodged with Nat. Liby of Scotland, Edinburgh. *Publications: novels:* Lanark, 1981; 1982 Janine, 1984; The Fall of Kelvin Walker, 1985; Something Leather, 1990; McGrotty and Ludmilla, 1990; Poor Things, 1992; A History Maker, 1994; Old Men in Love, 2007; *short story collections:* Unlikely Stories Mostly, 1983; (with J. Kelman and A. Owens) Lean Tales, 1985; Ten Tales Tall and True, 1993; Mavis Belfrage, 1996; The Ends of Our Tethers: thirteen sorry stories, 2003; Every Short Story 1952–2012, 2012; *poetry:* Old Negatives, 1989; Sixteen Occasional Poems, 2000; Collected Verse, 2010; *plays:* Working Legs (a play for people without them), 1997; Fleck (verse comedy), 2008; A Gray Play Book, 2009 (collection of plays); *non-fiction:* Saltire Self-Portrait no 4 (autobiog.), 1989; (ed) The Book of Prefaces, 2000; A Short Survey of Classic Scots Writing, 2001; A Life in Pictures, 2010; Some of Me and Others: a life in prose (autobiog.), 2014; *polemics:* Why Scots Should Rule Scotland, 1992; Why Scots Should Rule Scotland, 1997; (with A. Tomkins) How We Should Rule Ourselves, 2005; Independence, 2014.

GRAY, Anthony James; *b* 12 Feb. 1936; *o s* of Prof. Sir James Gray, CBE, MC, FRS; *m* 1st, 1963, Lady Lana Mary Gabrielle Baring (*d* 1974), *d* of 3rd Earl of Cromer, KG, GCMG, MBE, PC; one *s* one *d*; 2nd, 1980, Mrs Maxine Redmayne (*d* 2007), *er d* of Captain and Mrs George Brodrick. *Educ:* Marlborough Coll.; New Coll., Oxford (MA). C. T. Bowring & Co. (Insurance) Ltd, 1960–64; Sen. Investment Analyst, de Zoete & Gorton, 1965–67; Head of Equity Research and Partner, James Capel & Co., 1967–73. Member, London Stock Exchange, 1971–73. Dep. Dir, Industrial Development Unit and Dir, Industry Studies, Dept of Trade and Industry, 1973–75; Special Industrial Advr, Dept of Industry, 1975–76; Assoc., PA Management Consultants Ltd, 1977–81; Chief Exec., Cogent Gp (technol. transfer collaboration with Assoc. of Ind. Contract Res. Orgns), 1982–88; Chm., various advanced technol. cos, 1982–96; Assoc., HSBC Bank plc (Regl Advr), 2000–03. Member: Foundries EDC (NEDO), 1973–75; Hammersmith and Fulham DHA, 1982–85; Research and Manufacturing Cttee, CBI, 1988–90; Science and Industry Cttee, BAAS, 1989–91. Member Council: Charing Cross Hosp. Med. Sch., 1982–84; ERA Technology Ltd (formerly Electrical Res. Assoc.), 1986–89. Governor: Cobham Hall Sch., Kent, 1966–70; British American Drama Acad., 1996–99. Director: Apollo Soc., 1966–73; Nat. Trust Concert Soc., 1966–73. FRSA. *Recreations:* fishing, music. *Address:* The Old Coach House, Reepham, Norfolk. *Club:* Garrick.

GRAY, Sir Bernard Peter, Kt 2015; Chief of Defence Materiel, Ministry of Defence, 2011–15; *b* Redhill, Surrey, 6 Sept. 1960; *s* of Peter and Angela Gray; *m* 2010, Kathryn Anne Rowbotham; one *d*. *Educ:* Hitchin Boys Sch.; Hertford Coll., Oxford (MA Hons). Investment banker, Bankers Trust and Chase Manhattan, 1983–88; FT Group, 1988–97: Dep. Editor, Investors Chronicle, 1989–92; Lex Columnist, FT, 1992–94; Defence Correspondent, FT, 1994–97; Special Advr to Sec. of State for Defence, 1997–99; Strategy Dir, UBM, 1999–2001; CEO, CMP Information, 2001–05; CEO, then Chm., TSL Educn, 2005–11. Non-exec. Dir, Cable & Wireless plc, 2003–06. *Publications:* Beginners' Guide to Investment, 1991, 2nd edn 1993. *Recreations:* cinema, opera, motor sport. *Clubs:* Royal Air Force, Ivy.

GRAY, Brian James; consultant on accounting and audit in the international public sector, since 2012; *b* Wellington, India, 12 March 1946; *s* of John Alan Gray and Doreen Nelly Gray (*née* Service); *m* 1967, Gillian Anne Lydon (marr. diss. 2004); one *s* two *d*; partner, Christina Borchmann; one *s* one *d*. *Educ:* Woking Grammar Sch. FCA 1973. Audit manager, London and Zambia, Deloitte, Haskins and Sells, 1973–78; Auditor, Eur. Court of Auditors, 1978–91; European Commission: Hd, audit of CAP, 1992–99; Dir, Regl Fund resources, 1999–2002; Chief Financial Officer, 2003–09; Dir-Gen., Internal Audit Service, and Internal Auditor, 2009–12. *Publications:* articles in accounting and auditing jls. *Recreations:* horse-riding, ski-ing, bridge, snooker, defending the European Union. *Address:* Avenue des Chalets 5, 1180 Brussels, Belgium. *T:* 47 7284891. *E:* briangray2012@gmail.com.

GRAY, Bryan Mark, CBE 2009 (MBE 2001); DL; Pro Chancellor, Lancaster University, 2003–13; Chairman, Westmorland Ltd, since 2005; *b* 23 June 1953; *s* of late Clifford Benjamin Gray and June Mary Gray; *m* 1976, Lydia Ann Wallbridge; three *s*. *Educ:* Wath-upon-Dearne Grammar Sch.; Univ. of York (BA (Chemistry) 1974). Joined ICI, 1974; commercial appointments: Sales Office, Birmingham; ICI Petrochemicals and Plastics Div., Wilton; ICI Films and ICI Advanced Materials, Welwyn Garden City; Man. Dir, EVC Compounds Ltd, 1989–93; Commercial Dir, 1993, Chief Exec., 1994–2000, Baxi Partnership; Dep. Chm., Baxi Gp Ltd, 2000–04; Chm., Baxi Technologies, 2001–08. Chairman: Urban Splash Hotels, 2006–09; Peel Media Gp Ltd, 2008–11; non-exec. Dir, United Utilities Water plc, 2008–09. Chm., NW Develt Agency, 2002–09. Chairman: NW Reg., CBI, 2000–02; Central Heating Inf. Council, 2000–03; Mem., LSC, 2004–09. Pres., Soc. of British Gas Industries, 2000–01; Vice President: European Heating Industries Assoc., 2002–04; Micropower Council, 2005–08. Founder Chm., Nat. Football Mus., 1995–2001; Board Member: NW Cultural Consortium, 2003–08; Liverpool Culture Co. Ltd, 2003–09; Adv. Bd, Nat. Rlwy Mus., 2011–; Trustee, Nat. Mus. Liverpool, 2004–12; Mem., Lake Dist Nat. Park Authy, 2006–14. Chairman: Churches Trust in Cumbria, 2008–; Lowther Castle and Gardens Trust, 2008–; Cumbria County History Trust, 2010–; Cumbria Bldgs Preservation Trust, 2012–. Chm., Preston Post Grad. Med. Centre, 1996–2004; Gov., Univ. of Central Lancashire, 1999–2002. Hon. Prof., Dept of Built Envmt, Univ. of Nottingham, 2003–. Vice Patron, Deafway, 2002–13. Reader, C of E, various dios, 1981– (Carlisle Dio., 2009–); Lay Canon and Mem. Chapter, Carlisle Cathedral, 2014–. FRSA. DL 2002–10, High Sheriff, 2003–04, Lancs; DL Cumbria, 2010. *Recreations:* heritage, Midland Railway, scrapbooks, Preston North End. *Address:* c/o Westmorland Ltd, Tebay, Cumbria CA10 3SB. *E:* bryangray@bryangray.co.uk. *Club:* Preston North End Football (Chm., 1994–2001, Vice Pres., 2001–).

GRAY, Charles; *see* Gray, J. C. R.

GRAY, Hon. Sir Charles (Antony St John), Kt 1998; a Judge of the High Court, Queen's Bench Division, 1998–2008; *b* 6 July 1942; *s* of late Charles Herbert Gray and Catherine Margaret Gray; *m* 1st, 1968, Rosalind Macleod Whinney (marr. diss. 1990); one *s* one *d*; 2nd, 1995, Susan Astor (*née* Eveleigh) (*d* 1997); 3rd, 2001, Cynthia Elizabeth Selby. *Educ:* Winchester; Trinity College, Oxford (scholar; Hon. Fellow 2003). Called to the Bar, Lincoln's Inn, 1966, Bencher, 1991; QC 1984; a Recorder, 1990–98; arbitrator/mediator, 2008–. Comr, Royal Court of Jersey, 2011–. *Recreations:* travel, music, tennis, ski-ing, gardening. *Address:* The Old Rectory, Puncknowle, Dorchester, Dorset DT2 9BW. *Club:* Brooks's.

GRAY, Sir Charles (Ireland), Kt 2007; CBE 1994; JP; Member, North Lanarkshire Council, 1995–2007 (Chairman, Education Committee, 1995–2007); *b* 25 Jan. 1929; *s* of Timothy Gray and Janet (*née* Brown); *m* 1952, Catherine Creighton Gray; three *s* two *d*. *Educ:* Coatbridge. Dept of Public Affairs, Scotrail, 1946; Mem. (later Chm.), Lanark DC, 1958–64; Mem., Lanark CC, 1964–75; founder Mem., 1975–96, first Vice-Convener, and Leader 1986–92, Strathclyde Regl Council. Leader, UK delegn to Euro Cttee of the Regions, 1994–98. Pres., Convention of Scottish Local Authorities, 1992–94. Member: Scottish Exhibn and Conf. Centre, 1986–91; Scottish Enterprise Bd, 1990–93. Trustee, AgeScotland, 2007–12. FEIS 2005. JP Strathclyde, 1970. *Recreations:* music, reading, politics. *Address:* 9 Moray Place, Chryston G69 9LZ. *T:* (0141) 779 2962.

GRAY, Christopher Mark, FRCO; Director of Music, Truro Cathedral, since 2008; *b* Bangor, NI, 2 June 1978; *s* of Denis and Anne Gray. *Educ:* Pembroke Coll., Univ. of Cambridge (BA 1999); Royal Coll. of Music (Dip. 2000). FRCO 2005. Organ Scholar, Guildford Cathedral, 1999–2000; Asst Dir of Music, Truro Cathedral, 2000–08. *Recreation:* surfing. *Address:* Truro Cathedral, 14 St Mary's Street, Truro, Cornwall TR1 2AF. *T:* (01872) 245004. *E:* christophergray@trurocathedral.org.uk.

GRAY, David; *see* Gray, J. N. D.

GRAY, David John; Chairman, Eversheds International, 2009–13; Pro-Chancellor and Chair of Council, University of Leeds, since 2013; *b* 9 Jan. 1955; *s* of Allan and Vena Gray; *m* 1984, Julie Sergeant. *Educ:* Magdalene Coll., Cambridge (BA (Law) 1976; MA). Admitted solicitor, 1979; Equity Partner, Hepworth and Chadwick, 1982; Eversheds: Hd of Corporate, Leeds and Manchester, 1995–98; Dep. Managing Partner, Leeds and Manchester, and Head of Corporate, 1998–2000; Managing Partner, Leeds and Manchester, 2000–03; Managing Partner, later CEO, 2003–09. Non-exec. Dir, DWF plc, 2013–. *Recreations:* golf, National Hunt racing, football. *Address:* University of Leeds, Leeds LS2 9JT. *Clubs:* Alwoodley Golf; Ganton Golf.

GRAY, Rev. Canon Dr Donald Clifford, CBE 1998; TD 1970; Canon of Westminster and Rector of St Margaret's, Westminster Abbey, 1987–98, Canon Emeritus, since 1998; Chaplain to the Queen, 1982–2000; Chaplain to the Speaker, House of Commons, 1987–98; *b* 21 July 1930; *s* of Henry Hackett Gray and Constance Muriel Gray; *m* 1955, Joyce (*née* Jackson) (*d* 2010); one *s* two *d*. *Educ:* Newton Heath Technical High Sch.; King's Coll., London and Warminster (AKC); Univ. of Liverpool (MPhil); Univ. of Manchester (PhD). Curate, Leigh Parish Church, 1956–60; Vicar: St Peter's, Westleigh, 1960–67; All Saints', Elton, Bury, 1967–74; Rector of Liverpool, 1974–87; RD of Liverpool, 1975–81; Canon

Diocesan of Liverpool, 1982–87. Proctor-in-Convocation for Manchester, 1964–74; Mem., Gen. Synod, 1980–87. President: Soc. for Liturgical Study, 1998– (Chm., 1978–84); Societas Liturgica, 1987–89 (Treas., 1981–87); Mem., Liturgical Commn, 1968–86; Chm., Jt Liturgical Gp, 1989–94 (Mem., 1969–96; Sec., 1980–89); Mem., Cathedrals Fabric Commn, 1991–96. Chairman: Liverpool Luncheon Club, 1981–82; Alcuin Club, 1987–2015. CF (TA), 1958–67; CF (T&AVR), 1967–77; QHC, 1974–77. FRHistS 1988; FSA 2007. KStJ 2003. *Publications:* (contrib.) Worship and the Child, 1975; (contrib.) Getting the Liturgy Right, 1982; (contrib.) Liturgy Reshaped, 1982; (ed) Holy Week Services, 1983; Earth and Altar, 1986; (ed) The Word in Season, 1988; (contrib.) Towards Liturgy 2000, 1989; (contrib.) Liturgy for a New Century, 1990; Chaplain to Mr Speaker, 1991; Ronald Jasper: his life, his work and the ASB, 1997; (contrib.) They Shaped Our Worship, 1998; All Majesty and Power: royal prayers, 2000; Percy Dearmer, 2000; Memorial Services, 2002; (contrib.) Liturgy in a Postmodern World, 2003; (contrib.) St Paul's: the Cathedral Church of London, 2004; (contrib.) Oxford DNB, 2004; (contrib.) Strengthen For Service, 2005; (contrib.) Liturgical Renewal as a Way to Christian Unity, 2005; The 1927–28 Prayer Book Crisis, part i, 2005, part ii, 2006; (contrib.) The Oxford Handbook of English Literature & Theology, 2007; (contrib.) The Collect in the Reformed Tradition, 2010. *Recreations:* watching cricket, reading modern poetry. *Address:* 3 Barn Hill Mews, Stamford, Lincs PE9 2GN. *T:* (01780) 765024. *Clubs:* Army and Navy; Athenæum (Pres., 1983–84), Artists' (Liverpool).

GRAY, Prof. Douglas, FBA 1989; J. R. R. Tolkien Professor of English Literature and Language, University of Oxford, 1980–97, now Emeritus; Professorial Fellow of Lady Margaret Hall, Oxford, 1980–97, now Hon. Fellow; *b* 17 Feb. 1930; *s* of Emmerson and Daisy Gray; *m* 1959, Judith Claire Campbell; one *s*. *Educ:* Wellington College, NZ; Victoria Univ. of Wellington (MA 1952); Merton Coll., Oxford (BA 1956, MA 1960). Asst Lecturer, Victoria Univ. of Wellington, 1952–54; Oxford University: Lectr, Pembroke and Lincoln Colls, 1956–61; Fellow, Pembroke Coll., 1961–80, now Emeritus; University Lectr in English Language, 1976–80. Mem. Council, EETS, 1981–2005; Pres., Soc. for Study of Mediæval Langs and Lit., 1982–86. De Carle Lectr, Univ. of Otago, 1989; M. M. Bhattacharya Lectr, Calcutta Univ., 1991. Hon. LitD Victoria Univ. of Wellington, 1995. *Publications:* (ed) Spenser, The Faerie Queene, Book 1, 1969; Themes and Images in the Medieval English Religious Lyric, 1972; (ed) A Selection of Religious Lyrics, 1975; (part of) A Chaucer Glossary, 1979; Robert Henryson, 1979; (ed with E. G. Stanley): Middle English Studies presented to Norman Davis, 1983; Five Hundred Years of Words and Sounds for E. J. Dobson, 1983; (ed) The Oxford Book of Late Medieval Verse and Prose, 1985; (ed) J. A. W. Bennett, Middle English Literature, 1986; (ed jtly) From Anglo-Saxon to Early Middle English: studies presented to E. G. Stanley, 1994; Selected Poems of Robert Henryson and William Dunbar, 1998; (ed) The Oxford Companion to Chaucer, 2003; Later Medieval English Literature, 2008; From the Norman Conquest to the Black Death, 2011; The Phoenix and the Parrot: Skelton and the language of satire, 2013; Simple Forms, 2015; articles on medieval literature. *Address:* Lady Margaret Hall, Oxford OX2 6QA; 31 Nethercote Road, Tackley, Oxon OX5 3AW.

GRAY, Dr George Gowans, CBE 2000; FIMechE; Chairman, National Physical Laboratory, 1995–2002; *b* 21 Jan. 1938; *s* of Alexander Newlands Gray and Elizabeth Hunter Gray (*née* Gowans); *m* 1959, Grace Alicia Edmondson; one *s* two *d* (and one *s* decd). *Educ:* Linlithgow Acad.; Edinburgh Univ. (BSc Hons 1958); Corpus Christi Coll., Cambridge (PhD 1972). MIMechE 1972, FIMechE 1990. Engineer: Pratt & Whitney (Canada), 1960–63; RCA Ltd (Canada), 1963–69; Researcher, Univ. of Cambridge, 1969–71; Manager, 1972–74, Dir, 1974–87, RCA Ltd (UK); Chm., Serco Gp plc, 1987–99; Director: Misys plc, 1996–2002; Regus Business Centres plc, 1999–2002 (Chm., 2000–02). Member: Security Vetting Appeals Panel, 1997–2008; PPARC, 2003–05. Mem. Court and Council, Imperial Coll. London, 2004–09 (Dep. Chm., 2006–09). *Publications:* papers in engrg jls. *Recreations:* walking, reading, golf, theatre. *Clubs:* Oxford and Cambridge; Wentworth Golf.

GRAY, George Thomas Alexander; First Legislative Counsel for Northern Ireland, 1996–2012; *b* 20 Jan. 1949; *s* of George Gray and Eveline Gray; *m* 1985, Mary Louise Gray; two *s*. *Educ:* Annadale Grammar Sch., Belfast; The Queen's University of Belfast (LLB 1st Cl. Hons). Called to the Bar of N Ireland; Draftsman, 1971–88, Second Legislative Counsel, 1988–96, Office of the Legislative Counsel for NI. *Recreation:* cricket.

GRAY, (Hamish) Martin (Vincent); Chairman: The Evolution Group plc, 2005–11; National Savings & Investments, 2009–11 (Director, 2005–11); *b* 8 June 1946; *s* of Kenneth Dunwell Gray and Helen McGeorge Gray; *m*; two *s*; *m* 2nd, 1992, Alison Margaret Wells. *Educ:* Cockburn High Sch., Leeds; Harvard Business Sch. (AMP 1987). FCIB. Appts with National Westminster Bank, 1963–99; Head of Group Planning, Business Develt Div., 1986–88; Asst Gen. Manager, Group Develt, 1988–89; Gen. Manager, UK Branch Business, 1990–92; Chief Exec., UK Br. Business, later NatWest UK, 1992–98; Exec. Dir, Retail and Commercial Businesses and Main Bd Dir, 1993–99. Mem., Global Bd, Mastercard Inc., 1993–96; Dir, Visa Europe, 1996–99. Chm., Mktg Adv. Cttee, England and Wales Cricket Bd, 2000–03. *Recreations:* walking, gardening, cricket. *Address:* Wethered Park, Marlow, Bucks SL7 2BH.

GRAY, Prof. Hanna Holborn, PhD; President, University of Chicago, 1978–93, now President Emeritus (Harry Pratt Judson Distinguished Service Professor of History, 1993–2000, now Emeritus); *b* 25 Oct. 1930; *d* of Hajo and Annemarie Holborn; *m* 1954, Charles Montgomery Gray (*d* 2011). *Educ:* Bryn Mawr Coll., Pa (BA); Univ. of Oxford (Fulbright Schol.); Univ. of Harvard (PhD). Instructor, Bryn Mawr Coll., 1953–54; Harvard University: Teaching Fellow, 1955–57, Instr, 1957–59, Asst Prof., 1959–60, Vis. Lectr, 1963–64; Asst Prof., Univ. of Chicago, 1961–64, Associate Prof., 1964–72; Dean and Prof., Northwestern, Evanston, Ill, 1972–74; Provost, and Prof. of History, Yale Univ., 1974–78, Acting Pres., 1977–78. Hon. degrees include: LHD: Duke, 1982; Brandeis, 1983; Amer. Coll. of Greece, 1986; Univ. of Chicago, 1996; LLD: Dartmouth Coll., Yale, 1978; Brown, 1979; Rochester, Notre Dame, 1980; Michigan, 1981; Princeton, 1982; Georgetown, 1983; Columbia, 1987; Toronto, 1991; Harvard, 1995; DLaws Pontifical Inst. of Mediaeval Studies, Toronto, 2005; DLitt: Oxford, 1979; Washington, 1985; DSc Rockefeller, 2010. Charles Frankel Prize, 1993; Jefferson Medal, Amer. Philosophical Soc., 1993; Centennial Medal, Harvard Univ., 1994; Dist. Service Award in Educn, Inst. of Internat. Educn, 1994; Fritz Redlich Dist. Alumni Award, Internat. Inst. of Educn, 2004; Gold Medal, Nat. Inst. of Social Scis, 2006; Newberry Liby Award, Chicago, 2006; Chicago History Maker Award, Chicago Hist. Mus., 2008. Medal of Liberty (USA), 1986; Presidential Medal of Freedom (USA), 1991. *Publications:* ed (with Charles M. Gray) Jl Modern History, 1965–70; Searching for Utopia, 2011; articles in professional jls. *Address:* (office) 1126 E 59th Street, Chicago, IL 60637, USA. *T:* (773) 7027799. *Clubs:* Quadrangle (Chicago); Cosmopolitan (New York City).

GRAY, Huon Hamilton, MD; FRCP; National Clinical Director (Cardiac), NHS England, since 2013; *b* Liverpool, 6 Oct. 1954; *s* of late Tom Douglas, (Tony), Gray and of Kathleen Elizabeth Craig Gray; *m* 2004, Marion Slevin; two *s*. *Educ:* Shrewsbury Sch.; St Thomas's Hosp. Med. Sch., Univ. of London (MB BS 1977; MD 1986). FRCP 1994; FESC 1997; FACC 1999. Consultant Cardiologist, Univ. Hosp. of Southampton, 1989–. Dep. Nat. Clin. Dir for Heart Disease, DoH, 2007–13. Hon. Civilian Clin. Advr to Army, 2008–. Hon. Professor: QMUL, 2010–; UCL, 2012–. Pres., British Cardiac Soc., 2003–05. Trustee, Amer. Coll. of Cardiol., 2012–. Trustee, Wessex Heartbeat, 1990–2012. *Publications:* articles in jls on cardiol. and health service delivery. *Recreations:* wine appreciation, ski-ing, sailing. *Address:* c/o Wessex Cardiology, Spire Southampton Hospital, Southampton SO16 6UY. *T:* (023) 8076 4333. *E:* huon@cardiology.co.uk. *Club:* Royal Over-Seas League.

GRAY, Iain Cumming; Member (Lab) East Lothian, Scottish Parliament, since 2007; *b* Edinburgh, 7 June 1957; *s* of Robert and Catherina Gray; *m* 1997, Gillianne (*née* McCormack); one *d*, and two step *d*. *Educ:* Inverness Royal Acad.; Edinburgh Univ. (BSc Hons). Physics teacher: Gracemount High Sch., Edin., 1978–82; Escola Agrária, Chokwe, Mozambique, 1982–83; Inveralmond High Sch., Livingston, 1983–86; Campaigns Manager, OXFAM, Scotland, 1986–99. MSP (Lab) Edinburgh Pentlands, 1999–2003; contested same seat, 2003; Scottish Executive: Deputy Minister: for Community Care, 1999–2000; for Justice, 2000–01; Minister: for Social Justice, 2001–02; for Enterprise, Transport and Lifelong Learning, 2002–03. Leader, Scottish Labour Party, 2008–11. Special Advr to Sec. of State for Scotland, 2003–07. *Recreations:* football (season ticket, Hibernian FC), reading, hill-walking. *Address:* Scottish Parliament, Edinburgh EH99 1SP.

GRAY, Iain Gilmour, CBE 2014; CEng, FREng; FRAeS; FRSE; Director, Aerospace, Cranfield University, since 2015; *b* Manchester, 22 March 1957; *s* of Alexander William and Mary Bulloch Gray; *m* 1980, Rhona May Gammack; three *s* one *d*. *Educ:* Aberdeen Grammar Sch.; Aberdeen Univ. (BSc Eng. Hons); Southampton Univ. (MPhil). CEng 1985; FRAeS 1998; FREng 2008. Engr, British Aerospace, 1979–2007, Man. Dir, Airbus UK, 2004–07; Chief Exec., Technol. Strategy Bd, later Innovate UK, 2007–14. Member, Board: SEMTA (formerly Sector Skills Council for Sci., Engrg and Manuf. Technols), 2005–; EngineeringUK (formerly Engrg and Technol. Bd), 2008–14. Gov., UWE, 2006–; Mem. Council, City Univ. London, 2013–. Chm., Bristol Aero Collection Trust, 2012–. Mem., Co. of Engrs, 2008. FRSE 2011. Hon. Fellow, Cardiff Univ., 2012. Hon. DEng: Bath, 2005; Bristol, 2006; Exeter, 2012; Hon. DSc: Aberdeen, 2007; Aston, 2011. Gold Medal, RAeS, 2007. *Recreations:* walking, ski-ing, stamp collecting, friends and family, travelling. *Address:* Cranfield University, Aerospace Building 83, Cranfield, Beds MK43 0AL. *T:* (01234) 750111. *E:* I.gray@cranfield.ac.uk.

GRAY, Irene Elizabeth; Director, IreneGray.co.uk, since 2012; executive coach, since 2014; *b* 1 Oct. 1954; *d* of Bernard and Eileen Rowlinson; *m* 1984, George Scott (marr. diss.); two *s*; *m* 2009, Malcolm Gray. *Educ:* S Manchester HA (RN); Nottingham Univ. (MSc). Ward Sister, 1976–83, Dep. Dir of Nursing, 1983–86, Withington Hosp., Manchester; Director of Nursing: Christie Hosp., Manchester, 1986–94; Leicester Royal Infirmary, 1994–99; Regl Dir of Nursing, W Midlands NHS Exec., 1999–2001; Dir of Nursing, Guy's Hosp. and St Thomas' Hosp., 2001–04; CEO, Nurse Dirs Assoc. UK, 2004–05; Dir of Nursing, Surrey and Sussex Healthcare NHS Trust, 2005–08; Chief Operating Officer, University Hosps of Bristol NHS Foundn Trust, 2008–10; Dir of Care, Southern Cross Healthcare plc, 2010–11; Interim Dir of Nursing, 2012–13, Professional Advr, 2013–, Weston Area Health NHS Trust. Non-exec. Dir, Forest Healthcare, 2014–; Sen. Associate, IMD Consulting, 2012–. Vis. Prof. of Nursing, De Montfort Univ., 1992–2003; Hon. Professor of Nursing: Wolverhampton Univ., 2000–; South Bank Univ., 2002–; KCL, 2002–. Trustee and Dir, Royal Hosp. for Neurol Diseases, 2001–07. *Publications:* (with W. Bishop) Challenges in Clinical Practice, 2000. *Recreations:* gardening, keep fit, reading for relaxation. *Address:* The Old Vicarage, 2 Queens Road, Weston-super-Mare, N Som BS23 2LG. *E:* irene@irenegray.co.uk.

GRAY, (James Northey) David; Principal, Erskine Stewart's Melville Schools (Stewart's Melville (formerly Daniel Stewart's and Melville) College, and Mary Erskine School), Edinburgh, since 2000; *b* 30 April 1955; *s* of Baron Gray of Contin, PC; *m* (marr. diss.); one *s* two *d*; *m* 2009, Marie-Helene Gray. *Educ:* Fettes Coll.; Univ. of Bristol (BA Hons; PGCE). English teacher, Henbury Sch., Bristol, 1978–80; Partner, Key Lang. Sch., Athens, 1980–85; teacher, English and Modern Greek, Dulwich Coll., 1985–88; Hd of English, Leeds GS, 1988–92; Headmaster, Pocklington Sch., E Yorks, 1992–2000. *Recreations:* cricket, golf, cross-country running, music, Anglo-Saxon literature, Balkan current affairs. *Address:* Erskine Stewart's Melville Schools, Queensferry Road, Edinburgh EH4 3EZ. *T:* (0131) 311 1000, *Fax:* (0131) 311 1099. *E:* principal@esms.org.uk.

GRAY, James Whiteside; MP (C) North Wiltshire, since 1997; *b* 7 Nov. 1954; *s* of Very Rev. John Rodger Gray, VRD, sometime Moderator, Gen. Assembly of C of S, and of Dr Sheila Gray (*née* Whiteside); *m* 1st, 1980, Sarah Ann Beale (marr. diss. 2007); two *s* one *d*; 2nd, 2009, Philippa Gay Mayo (*née* Keeble); one step *s* two step *d*. *Educ:* Hillhead Primary Sch., Glasgow; Glasgow High Sch.; Glasgow Univ. (MA Hons); Christ Church, Oxford. Grad. mgt trainee, P&O, 1977–78; Shipbroker, Anderson Hughes & Co., 1978–84; Mem., Baltic Exchange, 1978–91, 1997–; Dir, Baltic Futures Exchange, 1989–91; Man. Dir, GNI Freight Futures, 1985–92; Special Advr to Sec. of State, DoE, 1992–95; Dir, Westminster Strategy Ltd, 1995–97. Dep. Chm., Wandsworth Tooting Cons. Assoc., 1994–96. Contested (C) Ross, Cromarty and Skye, 1992. An Opposition Whip, 2000–01; Opposition front bench spokesman on defence, 2001–02, on countryside, 2002–05; Shadow Sec. of State for Scotland, 2005. Member, Select Committee: on Envmtl Affairs, 1997–2000; on DEFRA, 2007–10; on Procedure, 2010–15; on Defence, 2013–; on Admin, 2015–; Jt Chm., All-Party Minerals Gp, 1997–2001 and 2009–; Chairman: All-Party Multiple Sclerosis Gp, 2004–11; All-Party Parly Gp for the Army, 2004–10; All-Party Parly Gp for Armed Forces, 2010–; Vice-Chairman: All-Party Parly Gp on Deafness, 2004–07; All-Party Parly Gp for Polar Regions, 2012–; Member: Speakers Panel of Chairmen, 2010–; Commons Finance and Services Cttee, 2010–13; Chm., Cons. Rural Action Gp, 2003–05; Cons. Defence and Foreign Affairs Policy Gp, 2006–07. Mem., UK Delegn, Council of Europe and WEU, 2007–08. Chm., Horse and Pony Taxation Cttee, 1999–2002. Trustee, Armed Forces Parly Trust (formerly Scheme), 2013– (Chm., 2013–) (Graduate, 1997–98, Post-grad. Scheme, 2001, Advanced Post-grad., 2010; rcds, 2003); Vis. Parly Fellow, St Antony's Coll., Oxford, 2005–06. Convenor, Poles Apart Conf., RUSI, 2013. Mem., Cons. Party Bd for SW, 2010–. Served HAC (TA), 1977–84 (Mem., Court of Assts, 2002–07); Vice-Pres., HAC Saddle Club. Vice-Chm., Charitable Properties Assoc., 2002–10; President: Chippenham Br., Multiple Sclerosis Soc., 2000–06 (Patron, Devizes Br., 2007–); Assoc. of British Riding Schs, 2001–; Consultant, British Horse Industry Confedn, 1999–2002. Patron, Mutual Support, 2006–. Freeman, City of London, 1982. *Publications:* Financial Risk Management in the Shipping Industry, 1985; Futures and Options for Shipping, 1987 (Lloyds of London Book Prize); Shipping Futures, 1990; Crown vs Parliament: who decides on going to war? (thesis), 2003; Poles Apart, 2013; (with M. Lomas) Who Takes Britain to War?, 2014. *Recreations:* countryside, riding horses, English local history, Polar regions. *Address:* House of Commons, SW1A 0AA. *T:* (020) 7219 6237. *Clubs:* Pratt's; Chippenham Constitutional (Pres., 1999–); Royal Wootton Bassett Conservative.

See also J. C. R. Gray.

GRAY, Sir (John Armstrong) Muir, Kt 2005; CBE 1998; MD; FRCP, FRCPSGlas; FFPH; Director, National Knowledge Service, NHS (formerly Director of Clinical Knowledge, Process and Safety, Department of Health), 2004–13; Director, Better Value Healthcare Ltd, since 2007; *b* 21 June 1944; *yr s* of late John Gray and Nancie Gray (*née* Armstrong); *m* 1974, Jacqueline Elizabeth Rosenthal; two *d*. *Educ:* Jordanhill Coll. Sch.; Univ. of Glasgow (MB, ChB 1969; MD 1981); Univ. of Bristol (DPH 1973). FFPH (FFPHM 1984); MRCGP 1985; FRCPSGlas 1989; FRCP 1993. House surgeon, Western Infirmary, Glasgow, 1966–70; Sen. House Officer, Aberdeen, 1970–71; SMO, City of Oxford, 1972–74; Public Health Specialist, Oxfordshire HA, 1974–91; Dir, Health Policy and Public Health, Oxford RHA, 1991–94; Dir of R&D, Anglia and Oxford RHA, then Anglia and Oxford Regl Office, NHS Exec., DoH, 1994–98; Dir, Inst. of Health Scis, Univ. of Oxford, 1999–2002; Chief Knowledge Officer, NHS, until 2013. Fellow, Green Coll., Oxford, 1984–94, Fellow Emeritus, 1994. Co-ordinator: Nat. Breast Cancer Screening Prog., 1988–91; Nat. Cervical Screening Prog., 1988–94; Programmes Dir, UK Nat. Screening Cttee, 1995–2008. Dir,

National Campaign for Walking; Campaign for Greener Healthcare. Advr, WHO, 1984–91. Hon. DSc: UEA 1998; City 2006. *Publications:* Man Against Disease, 1979; Take Care of Your Elderly Relative, 1980; Football Injuries, 1981; Prevention of Diseases in the Elderly, 1985; Evidence Based Healthcare, 1996, 3rd edn 2007; The Resourceful Patient, 2002; How to get Better Value Healthcare, 2008; Dr Gray's Walking Cure, 2009; articles in med., epidemiology and public health jls. *Recreations:* reading, linguistics, combating the effects of biological ageing. *Address:* 59 Lakeside, Oxford OX2 8JQ. *T:* (01865) 554066.

GRAY, (John) Charles (Rodger), CMG 2003; LVO 2013; HM Diplomatic Service, retired; HM Marshal of the Diplomatic Corps, 2008–14; *b* 12 March 1953; *s* of Very Rev. John Rodger Gray, VRD, sometime Moderator, Gen. Assembly of C of S, and of Dr Sheila M. Gray (*née* Whiteside); *m* 1988, Anne-Marie Lucienne Suzanne, *d* of Marquis and Marquise de Dax d'Axat, Paris; three *s*. *Educ:* High Sch. of Glasgow; Glasgow Univ. (MA). Entered HM Diplomatic Service, 1974; W Africa Dept, FCO, 1974; Polish lang. trng, 1975; Third, later Second, Sec., Warsaw, 1976–79; Eastern European and Soviet Dept, FCO, 1979–83; First Sec., UK Delegn, OECD, Paris, 1983–87; Seconded Assessments Staff, Cabinet Office, 1987–89; Foreign and Commonwealth Office: Deputy Head: Central African Dept, 1989; Central European Dept, 1989–92; Hd, Eastern Adriatic Dept, 1992–93; Counsellor and Hd of Chancery, Jakarta, 1993–96; Fellow, Centre for Internat. Affairs, Harvard Univ., 1996–97; Counsellor, Washington, 1997–2002; Hd, ME Dept, FCO, 2002–04; Iran Coordinator, FCO, 2004–05; Ambassador to Morocco, 2005–08. Consultant Advr, Prime Minister's Office, Govt of Hungary, 2014. Lectr, Barcelona Inst. of Internat. Affairs, 2014. Mem., Chatham House (RIIA). *Recreations:* history, church music, ecclesiastical architecture, town planning. *Address:* Flat 23, Drayton Court, Drayton Gardens, SW10 9RH. *E:* jcrgray53@gmail.com. *Club:* New (Edinburgh).

See also J. W. Gray.

GRAY, Prof. John Clinton, PhD; Professor of Plant Molecular Biology, University of Cambridge, 1996–2011, now Emeritus; Fellow, Robinson College, Cambridge, since 1977; *b* 9 April 1946; *s* of William John Gray and Edith Grace Gray (*née* Tooke); *m* 1971, Julia Hodgetts; one *s* one *d*. *Educ:* Sir Joseph Williamson's Mathematical Sch., Rochester; Simon Langton Grammar Sch., Canterbury; Univ. of Birmingham (BSc 1967; PhD 1970); MA Cantab 1977. Res. Fellow, Univ. of Birmingham, 1970–73; Res. Biochemist, UCLA, 1973–75; University of Cambridge: SRC Res. Fellow, 1975–76; Demonstrator, 1976–80; Lectr, 1980–90; Reader in Plant Molecular Biol., 1990–96; Hd, Dept of Plant Scis, 2003–09. Nuffield Foundn Sci. Res. Fellow, 1983–84; Royal Soc. Leverhulme Trust Res. Fellow, 1991–92. Non-exec. Dir, Horticulture Res. Internat., 1997–2003. Member: SERC Biol Scis Cttee, 1990–93; EMBO, 1994–; Council, Sainsbury Lab., 1999–2008. Plant Sci. Advr, Gatsby Charitable Foundn, 1996–2008. Trustee, Sci. and Plants for Schs, 1991–2008. Mem., Midlands Assoc. of Mountaineers, 1967–. *Publications:* (ed with R. J. Ellis) Ribulose Bisphosphate Carboxylase-Oxygenase, 1986; (ed with D. L. Hallahan) Plant Trichomes, 2000; papers in scientific and philatelic jls. *Recreations:* growing plants, family history, philately. *Address:* 47 Barrons Way, Comberton, Cambridge CB23 7EQ. *T:* (01223) 263325.

GRAY, Prof. John Michael, DPhil; FBA 2000; Professor of Education, since 2001, and Chairman of Board, Faculty of Education, since 2008, University of Cambridge; Fellow, since 2001, and Vice-Principal, since 2009, Homerton College, Cambridge; *b* 25 March 1948; *s* of Ronald Gray and Patricia Gray (*née* Martin); *m* 1st, 1977, Susan Lendrum (marr. diss. 1985); one *d*; 2nd, 2005, Prof. Jean Rudduck (*d* 2007); 3rd, 2012, Dr Margaret Challis. *Educ:* Exeter Coll., Oxford (BA); Harvard Univ. (EdM); Sussex Univ. (PGCE, DPhil 1976). Asst to Dir, Shelter, 1966–67; Res. Asst, Harvard Univ., 1970–72; teacher, ILEA, 1974–75; Res. Fellow, Edinburgh Univ., 1975–79; Sheffield University: Lectr, 1979–84; Reader, 1984–86; Prof., 1987–93; Jt Dir, Qualitative and Quantitative Studies in Educn Res. Gp, 1988–93; Res. Co-ordinator Social Scis, 1989–93; Dir of Res., Homerton Coll., Cambridge, 1994–2001; Syndic, Cambridge Assessment, 2001–13. Vis. Prof., Inst. of Educn, Univ. of London, 1996–2000. Mem., Res. Adv. Cttee, DfES, 2002–06; Specialist Advr, Children, Schs and Families Select Cttee, 2009–10. Mem. Cttees, 1985–2009, Chm., Wkg Party on Future of Educnl Res., 1992, ESRC. Mem. Bd and Chm., Res. Cttee, TTA, 1997–2000; Chairman: Standards Cttee, Oxford, Cambridge and RSA Exams Bd, 2001–13; Section S4, British Acad., 2012–. *Publications:* jointly: Reconstructions of Secondary Education, 1983; Elton Enquiry into School Discipline, 1989; National Youth Cohort Study of England and Wales (1988–94), Good School, Bad School, 1995; Merging Traditions, 1996; Inspecting Schools, 1996; Gender and Educational Performance, 1998; Improving Schools, 1999; Quality and Equity in European Education, 2004; Schools on the Edge, 2006; The Supportive School, 2011. *Address:* Homerton College, Cambridge CB2 8PH. *T:* (01223) 767649.

GRAY, Prof. John Nicholas, DPhil; Professor of European Thought, London School of Economics and Political Science, 1998–2007; Emeritus Professor, University of London, since 2008; *b* 17 April 1948; *s* of Nicholas Chatt Wardle Gray and Joan Gray (*née* Bushby); *m* 1988, Mieko Kawai. *Educ:* South Shields Grammar-Technical Sch. for Boys; Exeter Coll., Oxford (BA Hons 1971; MA 1976; DPhil 1978). Lectr in Political Theory, Univ. of Essex, 1973–76; Fellow and Tutor in Politics, Jesus Coll., Oxford, 1976–98; Prof. of Politics, Univ. of Oxford, 1996–98. Vis Prof. in Govt, Harvard Univ., 1986; Olmsted Vis. Prof. in Social Philosophy, Yale Univ., 1994. DUniv Open, 2006. *Publications:* Mill on Liberty: a defence, 1983, 2nd edn 1996; Hayek on Liberty, 1984, 3rd edn 1998; Liberalism, 1986, 2nd edn 1995; Liberalisms: essays in political philosophy, 1989; Post-liberalism: studies in political thought, 1993; Beyond the New Right: markets, government and the common culture, 1993; Enlightenment's Wake: politics and culture at the close of the modern age, 1995; Isaiah Berlin, 1995; Endgames: questions in late modern political thought, 1997; Voltaire and Enlightenment, 1998; False Dawn: the delusions of global capitalism, 1998, 3rd edn 2002; Two Faces of Liberalism, 2000; Straw Dogs: thoughts on humans and other animals, 2002; Al Qaeda and What It Means To Be Modern, 2003, 2nd edn 2007; Heresies: against progress and other illusions, 2004; (contrib.) The Political Theory of John Gray, 2007; Black Mass: apocalyptic religion and the death of Utopia, 2007 (Notable Book Award, Lannan Foundn, 2008); Gray's Anatomy: selected writings, 2009; The Immortalization Commission: science and the strange quest to cheat death, 2011; The Silence of Animals: on progress and other modern myths, 2013; Isaiah Berlin: an interpretation of his thought, 2013; The Soul of the Marionette: a short inquiry into human freedom, 2015. *Recreations:* reading, films, music. *Address:* c/o Tracy Bohan, The Wylie Agency, 17 Bedford Square, WC1B 3JA. *E:* tbohan@wylieagency.co.uk.

GRAY, Jonathan; Editor, since 2008, and Creative Director, since 2010, Dancing Times; *b* Newport, S Wales, 3 May 1967; *s* of Douglas John Gray and Judith Gray (*née* Wilson); civil partnership 2006, Robin Francis. *Educ:* Royal Ballet Sch., London; Wycliffe Secondary Sch., Leicester; Wyggeston Collegiate Sixth Form Coll., Leicester; Leicester Poly. (Foundn Cert. Art and Design); Wimbledon Sch. of Art (BA Hons Theatre Design). Archive Asst, 1990–95, Asst Curator, 1995–2005, Theatre Mus.; Associate Ed., Dancing Times, 2005–08. Member: Critics' Circle, 2007–; Costume Soc., 2010–. Trustee: Dance Teachers' Benevolent Fund, 2012–; Voices of British Ballet, 2014–. *Publications:* (with Dr J. Fowler) Unleashing Britain: theatre gets real 1955–1964, 2005; contrib. articles to FT; prog. notes for Royal Ballet and Birmingham Royal Ballet. *Recreations:* travel, theatre, opera, particular interest in historical costume. *Address:* c/o Dancing Times, 45–47 Clerkenwell Green, EC1R 0EB. *T:* (020) 7250 3006, *Fax:* (020) 7253 6679. *E:* jonathan@dancing-times.co.uk.

GRAY, Kenneth Walter, CBE 1992; PhD; FREng; FInstP, FIET; Chairman, Gorilla TV, 2011–14; *b* 20 March 1939; *s* of late Robert W. Gray and Ruby M. Gray; *m* 1st, 1962, Jill Henderson (marr. diss. 2006); two *s* one *d*; 2nd, 2010, Jean Woodley. *Educ:* Blue Coat Sch.; Univ. of Wales (BSc, PhD). FInstP 1991; FIET (FIEE 1992); FREng (FEng 1996). Research on magnetic resonance, as Nat. Res. Council of Canada post-doctoral Fellow, Univ. of British Columbia, Vancouver, 1963–65; research on semiconductor devices and on radiometry, N American Rockwell Science Center, Thousand Oaks, Calif, 1965–70; research on devices and systems at Royal Signals and Radar Estabt, 1971; Supt Solid State Physics and Devices Div., 1976; Head of Physics Group, 1979; RCDS 1981; Royal Signals and Radar Establishment: CSO, MoD, Dep. Dir (Applied Physics), 1982–84; Under Sec., Dep. Dir (Information Systems), 1984; Dir of Res., 1984–86, Technical Dir, 1986–96, THORN EMI plc; Technical Dir, EMI Group plc, Aug.–Dec. 1996; Exec. Chm., Thorn Software, 1987–89; Technical Dir, Thorn Security and Electronics, 1991–93; Man. Dir, Thorn Transaction, 1993–96. Chairman: Scipher plc, 1996–2004; London Biofuels, 2006–08; Ocean Blue Software, 2006–08; DGTL Products, 2008–11; non-exec. Dir, British Steel, 1995–99. Visiting Research Fellow: Univ. of Newcastle, 1972–74; Univ. of Leeds, 1976–90; Vis. Prof., Univ. of Nottingham, 1986–96. Member: DTI Innovation Adv. Bd, 1988–93; SERC, 1991–94; Technology Foresight Steering Cttee, OST, 1993–97; HEFCW, 1996–2002. Hon. DSc Nottingham Trent, 1998. *Publications:* over 30 scientific and technical papers in various learned jls. *Recreations:* bird-watching, theatre, gardening.

GRAY, Kevin Adrian; a District Judge (Magistrates' Courts), Devon and Cornwall, since 2011; *b* 12 Oct. 1947; *s* of Kenneth Thomas Gray and Gladys Gray; *m* 1st, 1971 (marr. diss.); one *s* one *d*; 2nd, 2005, Anita Poole. *Educ:* Portsmouth Southern Grammar Sch.; Kingston Poly. (LLB Hons). Police Officer, Portsmouth City Police, later Hampshire Constabulary, 1964–71; admitted Solicitor, 1976; Sen. Partner, Gray Purdue & Co., 1977–90; sole practitioner, 1990–92; Partner, Gregsons, 1993–94; Acting Metropolitan Stipendiary Magistrate, 1993–95; Stipendiary Magistrate, then District Judge (Magistrates' Courts), Essex, 1995–2011. *Recreation:* enjoying family and good friendships. *Address:* c/o Plymouth Magistrates' Court, St Andrew Street, Plymouth, Devon PL1 2DP. *T:* (office) (01752) 206200.

GRAY, Prof. Kevin John, PhD, LLD, DCL; FBA 1999; Professor of Law, University of Cambridge, 1993–2011, now Emeritus; Fellow, Trinity College, Cambridge, 1981–90 and since 1993 (Dean, 2004–05 and 2006–15); *b* 23 July 1951; *s* of late Bryce Holmes Gray, Belfast, and of Priscilla Margaret Gray (*née* McCullough), Lisburn; *m* 1996, Susan (*d* 2014), *d* of late Arthur Walter David Francis and Helen Francis (*née* Waggott). *Educ:* Trinity Hall, Cambridge (BA 1972 (1st Cl. Law Tripos Parts I and II); MA, PhD 1976; Yorke Prize, 1977; LLD 1991); DCL Oxford, 1994. Called to the Bar, Middle Temple, 1993, Bencher, 2014. University of Cambridge: Jt Coll. Lectr, Queens' and Trinity Colls, 1975–77; Fellow, Queens' Coll., 1975–81; Asst Lectr and Lectr in Law, 1978–90; Univ. Advocate, 1986–88; Res. Fellow, ANU, 1990; Drapers' Prof. of Law, QMW, Univ. of London, 1991–93. Vis. Fellow, ANU, 1979, 1989, 1998, 2005–06; Sen. Vis. Res. Fellow, St John's Coll., Oxford, 1993–94; Leverhulme Trust Major Res. Fellow, 2008–11; Prof. of Law, Nat. Univ. of Singapore, 2008–; Visiting Professor: Grad. Sch. of Law, Univ. of Osaka, 2001; Univ. of NSW, 2003; Univ. of Stellenbosch, 2005 and 2008; Univ. of Tasmania, 2006; Nat. Univ. of Singapore, 2006, 2007. Dist. Gifford Lect., Univ. of Hawaii, 2010; Dist. Visiting Mentor, ANU, 2015. Associate Mem., Acad. Internat. de Droit Comparé, 1995; Overseas Res. Fellow, Nat. Res. Foundn of SA, 2005. Member: Access, Conservation and Envmt Gp (formerly Access and Conservation Cttee), British Mountaineering Council, 2002–06; AHRC (formerly AHRB) Peer Rev. Coll., 2004–07. Fellow, Stellenbosch Inst. for Advanced Study, 2009–. Jun. and sen. internat. athlete, 1968–69. *Publications:* Reallocation of Property on Divorce, 1977; Elements of Land Law, 1987, 5th edn (with S. F. Gray) 2009; (with S. F. Gray) Land Law, 1999, 7th edn 2011; other books and articles on law, legal theory, human rights, and the envmt. *Recreations:* mountaineering, rock climbing, wild country, old churches. *Address:* Trinity College, Cambridge CB2 1TQ. *T:* (01223) 314520.

GRAY, Linda Esther, (Mrs Peter McCrorie); retired as opera singer, now teaching; *b* 29 May 1948; *d* of James and Esther Gray; *m* 1971, Peter McCrorie; one *d*. *Educ:* Greenock Academy; Royal Scottish Academy of Music and Drama. Cinzano Scholarship, 1969; Goldsmith Schol., 1970; James Caird Schol., 1971; Kathleen Ferrier Award, 1972; Christie Award, 1972. London Opera Centre, 1969–71; Glyndebourne Festival Opera, 1972–75; Scottish Opera, 1974–79; Welsh Opera, 1980; English National Opera, 1979; American début, 1981; Royal Opera House: Sieglinde, 1982; Fidelio, 1983. Records: Tristan und Isolde, 1981; Wagner's Die Feen, 1983. Principal rôles: Isolde, Sieglinde, Kundry (Wagner); Tosca (Puccini); Fidelio (Beethoven). *Publications:* A Life Behind Curtains (autobiog.), 2007; (with Caroline Finlayson) Can We All Sing?, 2007; Dame Eva Turner: a life on the high Cs, 2011. *Recreations:* cooking, swimming. *Address:* 35 Green Lane, New Malden, Surrey KT3 5BX.

GRAY, Lindsay; *see* Gray, Peter Lindsay.

GRAY, Martin; *see* Gray, H. M. V.

GRAY, Ven. Martin Clifford; Archdeacon of Lynn, 1999–2009, now Emeritus; *b* 19 Jan. 1944; *s* of John Oscar Gray and Lilian Annie Bertha Gray; *m* 1966, Pauline Jean Loader; three *s*. *Educ:* West Ham Coll. of Technology (DipChemEng; AWHCT 1967); Westcott House, Cambridge. Process Engineer, May & Baker, Norwich, 1968–70; Process Engr, Plant Supt, Project Manager, 1970–78, Dow Chemical, Kings Lynn, Norfolk and Bilbao, Spain. Deacon 1980, priest 1981; Asst Curate, St Faith's, Gaywood, Kings Lynn, 1980–84; Vicar, St Peter's, Sheringham, 1984–94; Rector, Lowestoft St Margaret Team Ministry, Suffolk, 1994–99. *Recreations:* golf, hill-walking. *Address:* 11 Cann's Lane, Hethesett, Norwich NR9 3JE. *E:* mandpgray@btinternet.com.

GRAY, Morag Graham, MBE 2005; Director, Black and White Communication (Scotland) Ltd, since 2004; *b* 12 Oct. 1962; *d* of Bill and Mary Chalmers; *m* 1st, 1993, Nigel Gray (marr. diss. 1998); 2nd, 2012, Angus Crichton-Miller. *Educ:* Lanark Grammar Sch.; Univ. of Strathclyde (BA 1983). Product Manager, British Telecom, 1983–88; Clerk of the Course, Scottish Racing, 1988–90; Planning Exec., 1990–97, Racing Dir, 1997–2000, Racecourse Assoc.; Chief Exec., Hamilton Park Racecourse, 2000–04; Dir, Racecourse Assoc., 2002–04. Ind. Dir, British Horseracing Authy, 2007–14. *Recreations:* horseracing, Scottish Rugby, fitness, food. *E:* morag@blackandwhite.uk.com.

GRAY, Sir Muir; *see* Gray, Sir J. A. M.

GRAY, Muriel Janet, (Mrs H. Barbour); presenter, broadcaster and author; *b* 30 Aug. 1958; *d* of Adam and Elizabeth Gray; *m* 1991, Hamish Barbour; two *s* one *d*. *Educ:* Glasgow Sch. of Art (BA Hons Graphic Design). Asst Hd of Design, Mus. of Antiquities, Edinburgh, 1980–83; presenter and broadcaster, 1982–: *television* includes: The Tube, The Media Show, Design Awards, Art is Dead, The Munro Show, The Snow Show; *radio* includes: Start the Week, Whatever Gets You Through, various progs for Radio Scotland; newspaper and magazine columnist, including: Time Out, Sunday Mirror, Sunday Correspondent, Scotland on Sunday, Sunday Herald. Rector, Edinburgh Univ., 1988–91. Founder and Man. Dir, Gallus Besom Prodns, 1987. Dir, Ideal World and IWC Prodns, 1990–2005. Chair, Bd of Govs, Glasgow Sch. of Art, 2013–. *Publications:* The First Fifty, 1991; The Trickster, 1994; Furnace, 1997; The Ancient, 2001; Kelvingrove: portal to the world, 2006. *Recreations:* growing trees, mountaineering, chess, snow boarding, horror cinema. *Address:* IWC Media, St George's Studios, 93–97 St George's Road, Glasgow G3 6JA. *T:* (0141) 353 3222, *Fax:* (0141) 353 3221.

GRAY, Neil Charles; MP (SNP) Airdrie and Shotts, since 2015; *b* Orkney Isles, 16 March 1986; *m* Karlie; one *d*. *Educ:* Kirkwall Grammar Sch.; Stirling Univ. (BA 1st Cl. Hons Politics and Journalism 2008). Contract producer and reporter, BBC Radio Orkney, 2003–08; press and res. intern, SNP, Scottish Parlt, 2008; work in office of Alex Neil, MSP, 2008–15, Office Manager, 2011–15. *Address:* House of Commons, SW1A 0AA.

GRAY, Paul Alexander; Director General, Health and Social Care, Scottish Government, since 2013; Chief Executive, NHS Scotland, since 2013; *b* Edinburgh, 17 Aug. 1962; *s* of Robert Gray and Rachel Gray; *m* 1982, Fiona Gray; one *s* two *d*. *Educ:* Linlithgow Acad. Scottish Office, later Scottish Executive, then Scottish Government: various posts, 1979–2000; Dir, Inf. and Communications Technol., 2000–03; Dir for Social Justice, 2003–05; Dir, Primary and Community Care and Dir, eHealth, 2005–07; Dir, Change and Corporate Services, 2007–09; Director General: Rural Affairs and Envmt, then Rural Affairs, Envmt and Services, 2009–11; Governance and Communities, 2011–13. *Address:* Scottish Government, Room 1E.08, St Andrews House, Regent Road, Edinburgh EH1 3DG.

GRAY, Paul Edward, ScD; Chairman of the Corporation, 1990–97, Hon. Chairman and President Emeritus, 1997–2003, Massachusetts Institute of Technology; *b* 7 Feb. 1932; *s* of Kenneth Frank Gray and Florence (*née* Gilleo); *m* 1955, Priscilla Wilson King; one *s* three *d*. *Educ:* Massachusetts Inst. of Technol. (SB 1954, SM 1955, ScD 1960). Served Army, 1955–57 (1st Lieut). Massachusetts Institute of Technology: Mem., Faculty of Engrg, 1960–71, 1990–2007; Class of 1922 Prof. of Electrical Engrg, 1968–71; Dean, Sch. of Engrg, 1970–71; Chancellor, 1971–80; Pres., 1980–90; Mem., 1971–2007 (now Life Mem. Emeritus) of Corp. Emeritus Trustee, Museum of Science, Boston; Life Trustee, Wheaton Coll., Mass. Fellow, Amer. Acad. of Arts and Sciences; Member: National Acad. of Engrg (Treas., 1994–2001); Mexican National Acad. of Engrg; Life Fellow, IEEE (Founders Medal, 2009). *Address:* c/o Massachusetts Institute of Technology, 77 Massachusetts Avenue, Cambridge, MA 02139, USA.

GRAY, Paul Herbert Lucas, DPhil; Managing Director, Public Service Solutions Ltd, since 2006; *b* 20 Jan. 1957; *s* of Alfred N. Gray and Doris J. Gray (*née* Hutchens); *m* 1st, 1982, Patricia Ann Wright (marr. diss. 2005); 2nd, 2011, Joanne Bedford; one *s*. *Educ:* Univ. of Durham (BA Hons); Univ. of Birmingham (DPhil). Lectr, 1980–84, Sen. Lectr and Asst Principal, 1984–86, Merseyside; Sen. Educn Officer, Cambs CC, 1986–90; Dep. Chief Educn Officer, Devon CC, 1990–96; Dir of Educn, Surrey CC, 1996–2006. Vis. Prof., Univ. of London, 1997–2002. Chm., QCDA (formerly QCA) Curriculum and Assessment Cttee, 1999–2003. Mem. Bd, Nat. Youth Agency, 1999–2004. Trustee, Exeter CVS, 2013–. Freeman, City of London, 2004. FRSA 1997. *Recreations:* sport, music, literature, sailing, extreme charity fundraising events, wide-ranging voluntary work. *Address:* 36 Bartholomew Street West, Exeter EX4 3BN.

GRAY, Paul Richard Charles, CB 2000; Executive Coach, Praesta Partners LLP, since 2008; Chairman, Social Security Advisory Committee, since 2011; *b* 2 Aug. 1948; *s* of Rev. Sidney Gray and Ina (*née* Maxey); *m* 1972, Lynda Elsie Braby; two *s*. *Educ:* Wyggeston Boys' Sch., Leicester; LSE (BSc Econ 1969). Dept of Econ. Affairs, 1969; HM Treasury, 1969–77; with Booker McConnell Ltd, 1977–79; HM Treasury: Principal, 1979–83; Asst Sec., 1984–87; Econ. Affairs Private Sec. to Prime Minister, 1988–90; Under Sec., Monetary Gp, 1990–93; Dir, Personnel and Support Services, 1994–95; Dir, Budget and Public Finances, 1995–98; Hd of Policy Gp, DSS, 1998–99; Gp Dir, Children, Pensioners and Disabled, DSS, subseq. DWP, 1999–2001; Man. Dir, Pensions and Disability, 2001–04, Second Permanent Sec., 2002, DWP; Dep. Chm., 2004–06, Chm., 2006–07, HMRC. Dir (non-exec.), Laing Management Ltd, 1993–95. *Recreations:* family, walking, sport.

GRAY, Paul Shapter, FRSC; Director, Environment, Climate and Marine Science and Technology Research Programmes, European Commission, 1992–97; *b* 18 Sept. 1932; *s* of Frederick Archibald and Vera Emma Gray; *m* 1958, Diane Lillian Platt; one *s* one *d* (and one *s* decd). *Educ:* St Chad's Coll., Wolverhampton; Birmingham Univ. (BSc Hons; MSc). FRSC (FRIC 1967). Chief Chemist, Midland Tar Distillers, 1954–57; Sen. Research Fellow, Ministry of Power, 1957–59; Head of Div., Reactor Chemistry, UKAEA, Winfrith, 1959–63; Ops Controller, OECD DRAGON (high temp. gas cooled reactor expt), 1963–73; European Commission, 1973–97: Dep. Head of Div., Elimination of Technical Barriers to Trade, 1977–81; Head of Service, Wood, Paper and Construction Industries, 1981–83; Head of Div., Food Law and Food Trade, 1983–91; Advr for industrial aspects of biotechnology, 1991–92. Sci. Advr, European Assoc. for Global Ocean Observing System, 1996–2001; Mem., Sci. Cttee, Royal Inst. for sustainable mgt of natural resources and promotion of clean technols, Belgium, 1997–2010; Royal Society of Chemistry: Member: Council, 2004–05; Prof. Affairs Bd, 2005–07; Pres., Belgium Section, 2005–09. Vis. Prof., Human Ecol., Vrije Universiteit Brussel, 2002–10. Hon. DSc Birmingham, 1999. Mem., St Nicholas, Alcester PCC, 2012–. *Publications:* jointly: Radionuclides in the Food Chain, 1988; Chernobyl, 1991; EU Committees as Influential Policymakers, 1998; International Handbook on Food Safety, 1999; numerous pubns in scientific and economic jls. *Recreations:* music, singing, sailing, playwriting, gardening.

GRAY, Peter Francis; Chairman, Berkeley Capital Ltd, since 2009; *b* 7 Jan. 1937; *s* of Rev. George Francis Selby Gray; *m* 1978, Fiona Bristol; two *s*. *Educ:* Marlborough; Trinity College, Cambridge. MA; FCA. Served Royal Fusiliers, attached 4th Kings African Rifles, Uganda, 1956–58. HM Foreign Service, 1963–64; SG Warburg & Co., 1964–66; Cooper Brothers & Co., 1966–69; Samuel Montagu & Co., 1970–77; Head of Investment Div., Crown Agents for Oversea Govts & Admins, 1977–83; Man. Dir, Touche Remnant & Co., 1983–87; Dep. Chm., Assoc. of Investment Trust Cos, 1985–87. Chairman: Exmoor Dual Investment Trust plc, 1988–98; Aberdeen Lloyd's Insurance Trust plc, 1993–98; Finsbury Income and Growth Investment Trust plc, 1993–2004; Supervisory Bd, Postbank and Savings Bank Corp. (Hungary), 1998; Close Finsbury Euro-Tech Trust plc, 2000–06; Hampden Capital plc, 2001–07; New Europe Property Investments plc, 2007–09; Anglo Japanese Investment Corp. plc, 2006–12; KB Re Ltd, 2010–; Director: TR Industrial and General Trust plc, 1984–88; New Zealand Investment Trust plc, 1988–2003; Gartmore Value Investments plc, 1989–94; Gartmore Distribution Trust plc, 1993–2002; F&C Private Equity Trust plc, 1994–2002; Graphite Enterprise Trust plc, 2002–09; UTI India Pharma Fund, 2005–10; Farida (Europe) Ltd, 2008–. Member, Advisory Board: Mellenthin Corporate Finance, 2004–; Al Farida Investments, 2007–; OMFIF, 2013–. *Recreations:* literature, music. *Address:* 1 Bradbourne Street, SW6 3TF; Berkeley Capital Ltd, 42 Berkeley Square, W1J 5AW. *Club:* Brooks's.

GRAY, (Peter) Lindsay; consultant, adviser and mediator (education, music and charities), since 2012; Director, Royal School of Church Music, 2008–12, now Emeritus; *b* Nottingham, 22 July 1953; *s* of Harold Geoffrey Gray and Mairi Gray (*née* Hay); *m* 1980, Caroline Susan Bick; two *d*. *Educ:* Nottingham High Sch.; King's Coll., Cambridge (BA 1974; Choral Schol.; MA); Durham Univ. (PGCE 1975); ARCO (Dip. 1971). Dir of Music, Grenville Coll., Bideford, 1975–79; Asst Dir of Music, Magdalen College Sch., Oxford, 1979–80; Director of Music: Queen's Coll., Taunton, 1980–86; Cheltenham Coll., 1986–92; Headmaster: Brightlands Sch., Newnham-on-Severn, 1992–94; Cathedral Sch., Llandaff, Cardiff, 1994–2008. Conductor, Bottisham Choral Soc., 1973–74; Organist and Choirmaster: St John's, Neville's Cross, 1974–75; St Peter's, Peterston-super-Ely, 1999–2006; Dir, Somerset Youth Choir, 1984–86; Director and Founder: Llandaff Cathedral Girl Choristers, 1995–2000, 2002–04; Caritas Choir, 2013–. Trustee, Woodard Academies Trust, 2013–14. Gov., Peterston-super-Ely Sch., 2013–; Mem. Council, Clifton Coll., 2014–. FRSCM 2013. *Recreations:* cricket, golf, table tennis, singing, choir directing, organ, rural and coastal walking, socialising, Indian food. *T:* 07823 325844. *E:* plgray227@gmail.com. *Clubs:* Mitres Cricket (Llandaff); Peterston-super-Ely Table Tennis (Vale of Glamorgan).

GRAY, Phillip; Chief Executive, Chartered Society of Physiotherapy, 1998–2014; *b* 30 April 1949; *s* of Paul and Sally Gray; *m* 1979, Pauline Tierney; two *s* three *d*. *Educ:* Liverpool Poly. (grad. IPM 1970); UC, Cardiff (BSc Econs 1st Cl. Hons 1976; Pres., Students' Union, 1976–77); LSE (MSc Industrial Relations 1978). Personnel Officer, Plessey Electronics, Liverpool, 1968–73; Dir of Industrial Relations, Chartered Soc. of Physiotherapy, 1978–90; Dir of Labour Relations, RCN, 1990–98. Chm., Arthritis and Musculoskeletal Alliance, 2013–. Member: NHS Workforce Develt Bd; NHS Older People's Services Taskforce; Primary Care Alliance Exec.; Allied Health Professions Fedn. Hon. FCSP. *Recreations:* squash, walking, football, poetry, collecting books, family and five children.

GRAY, Richard Dennis; proprietor, Hillrise Stonework (formerly Hillrise Walls), since 2007; *b* 19 Sept. 1951; *s* of John Dennis and Betty Gray; *m* 1976, Cherry Elizabeth Allen; two *s*. *Educ:* Carre's Grammar Sch.; Bristol Univ. (BA Hist. and Hist. of Art); Manchester Univ. (Museum Studies). AMA. Asst Keeper and Keeper, Manchester City Art Galls, 1974–89; Director: Manchester City Art Galls, 1989–98; Compton Verney, 1998–2005; Consultant Dir, NE Inst., Newcastle upon Tyne, 2005–10. Member: English Ceramic Circle, 1976–; Glass Circle, 1981–; Cttee, Glass Assoc., 1983–87; Cttee, Northern Ceramic Soc., 1986–89; NW Museums Service Adv. Panel, 1988–98 (Mem., Bd of Management, 1994–98); W Midlands Mus. Policy Forum, 2004–. Ind. Assessor, Reviewing Cttee on Export of Works of Art; Ext. Examr, Manchester Polytechnic, 1989–92. Trustee: Spode Mus., 1989–; Rekonstruktsiya Trust, 1991–93. Professional Mem., Dry Stone Walling Assoc. of GB, 2010–. Silver Gilt Medal (with Christine Cottrell) for Conceptual Garden, RHS Hampton Court Palace Flower Show, 2012. *Publications:* The History of Porcelain, Chapter 1, 1982; catalogues and inventories, Manchester Art Galleries; articles and book reviews for arts jls. *Recreations:* music, fishing, walking. *Address:* 35 Park Street, Bladon, Woodstock, Oxon OX20 1RW.

GRAY, Prof. Richard John, PhD; FBA 1993; Professor of Literature, University of Essex, since 1990; *b* 5 Jan. 1944; *s* of George Ernest Gray and Helen Gray; *m* 1st, 1965, Joyce Mary Gray (marr. diss. 1991); one *s* one *d*; 2nd, 1991, Sheona Catherine Binnie; one *s* one *d*. *Educ:* St Catharine's Coll., Cambridge (BA, MA, PhD). Sen. Res. Schol., St Catharine's Coll., Cambridge, 1966–67; Harkness Fellow, for res. in US Univs, 1967–69; Lectr, Sen. Lectr and Reader in Literature, Univ. of Essex, 1969–90. Robert E. McNair Vis. Prof. in Southern Studies, Univ. of South Carolina, 1993; Barbara Lester Methvin Vis. Dist. Prof. of Southern Studies, Univ. of Georgia, 2009. Lectures: Ecclar Centre, BL, 2004; Sarah Toyphena Phillips, British Acad., 2005; Lamar, USA, 2006; Fullbrook, Bristol, 2008; Methvin, Univ. of Georgia, 2009; De La Warr Pavilion, 2010. Editor, Jl of Amer. Studies, 1997–2001. Research awards of: Amer. Philos. Soc., 1979; Internat. Communications Agency, 1981; Humanities Res. Bd, 1995, 1998; AHRB, 1997, 2000; British Acad., 2006. *Publications:* American Verse of the Nineteenth Century, 1973; American Poetry of the Twentieth Century, 1976; The Literature of Memory: modern writers of the American South, 1977; Robert Penn Warren: essays, 1980; American Fiction: new readings, 1983; Writing the South: ideas of an American region (C. Hugh Holman Award, Soc. for Study of Southern Lit.), 1986, 2nd edn 1997; American Poetry of the Twentieth Century, 1990; (ed) The Complete Poems of Edgar Allan Poe, 1993; The Life of William Faulkner: a critical biography, 1994; (ed) Selected Poems of Edgar Allan Poe, 1996; Southern Aberrations: writers of the American South and the problems of regionalism, 2000; Companion to the Literature and Culture of the American South, 2004; A History of American Literature, 2004, rev. edn 2011; A Web of Words: the great dialogue of Southern literature, 2007; Transatlantic Exchanges: the South in Europe - Europe in the American South, 2007; A Brief History of American Literature, 2011; After the Fall: American literature since 9/11, 2011; A History of American Poetry, 2014. *Recreations:* running, tennis, wine tasting, cycling, cinema, travel, walking, music. *Address:* Department of Literature, University of Essex, Wivenhoe Park, Colchester, Essex CO4 3SQ. *T:* (01206) 872590.

GRAY, Hon. Sir Robert McDowall, (Sir Robin), Kt 1994; *b* 2 July 1931; *s* of Adam Gray and Elsie McDowall; *m* 1957, Mary Thomson (*d* 1981); one *s* two *d*. *Educ:* George Watson's Boys' Coll., Edinburgh. Served 4th/7th Royal Dragoon Guards, 1949–51; immigrated to NZ, as farm labourer, 1952; purchased farm, 1956; entered politics, 1978; MP (Nat.) Clutha, 1978–96; Whip, 1985, Sen. Whip, 1987; Speaker, NZ House of Reps, 1990–93; Minister of State, Associate Minister of For. Affairs and Trade, 1993–96. Chm., Parly Service Commn, 1990–93.

GRAY, Robin; Member, Parliamentary Boundary Commission for England, 1999–2009; management consultant, since 1993; *b* 16 April 1944; *s* of late Robert George and Jeannie Gray; *m* 1971, Kathleen Rosemary Kuhn; two *d*. *Educ:* Woking County Grammar Sch. for Boys; London Univ. (BA Hons). UKAEA, 1962–64; HM Treasury, 1964–70; Asst Sec. to Crowther Cttee on Consumer Credit, 1968–70; Min. of Housing and Local Govt, subseq. DoE, 1970–92; seconded to Water Resources Bd, 1973–75, to W Sussex CC, 1982–83; Sec., London and Metropolitan Govt Staff Commn, 1984–86; PSA, 1986–92; Under Sec., 1988–92; Dir of Civil Projects, 1988–89; Dir, Marketing and Planning, 1990–92; Internat. Dir, 1991–92; Business Develt Dir, PSA Projects Ltd, 1992–93. Mem., Local Govt Commn for England, 1996–2002; Dep. Electoral Comr and Mem., Boundary Cttee for England, 2002–08. Chm., Hampshire Govs Assoc., 2002–. Governor: Oak Farm Community Sch., 1994–2011; The Connaught Sch., 2006–; Samuel Cody Specialist Sports Coll., 2013–; Member, Interim Executive Board: Andover C of E Primary Sch., 2011–13; Cove Secondary Sch., 2014–. *Recreations:* cricket, walking and other outdoor activities, talking.

GRAY, Hon. Robin (Trevor), BAgrSc; farmer, since 2005; Chairman, Botanical Resources Australia Pty Ltd, 1996–2011; *b* 1 March 1940; *s* of late Rev. W. J. Gray; *m* 1965, Judith, *d* of late A. G. Boyd; two *s* one *d*. *Educ:* Box Hill High Sch.; Dookie Agricl Coll., Melbourne Univ. Teacher, 1961–65 (in UK, 1964); agricl consultant, Colac, Vic, 1965, Launceston, Tas, 1965–76; pt-time Lectr in Agricl Econs, Univ. of Tasmania, 1970–76. MHA (L) for Wilmot, Tas, 1976–85, for Lyons, 1985–95; Dep. Leader of the Opposition, Tasmania, 1979–81; Leader of the Opposition, 1981–82 and 1989–91; Premier of Tasmania and Treasurer, 1982–89; Minister: for Racing and Gaming, 1982–84; for Energy, 1982–88; for Forests, 1984–86; for State Develt, 1984–89; for Small Business, 1986–89; for Status of Women, 1989; for Antarctic Affairs, 1989; for Science and Technology, 1989; for Primary Industry, Fisheries and Energy, 1992–95; for the TT-Line, 1993–95. Partner, Evers Gray Consultants, 1996–2004. Director: Evergreen Olive Oil Pty Ltd, 1995–2000; Gunns Ltd, 1996–2010; Fujii Tasmania Pty Ltd, 1996–2000; AMC Search Ltd, 1996–11; Agribusiness Project Mgt Pty Ltd, 1999–; Gunns Plantations Ltd, 2009–11. Trustee, Tasmanian Wool Museum, 1996–. *Address:* 11 Beech Road, Launceston, Tas 7250, Australia.

GRAY, Victor William, MBE 2010; Director, Rothschild Archive, 1993–2004; *b* 27 Oct. 1946; *s* of William Albert Gray and Eva Thirza (*née* Bint); *m* 1967, Jennifer Anne Whittle; one *s* one *d*. *Educ:* King's Coll., Cambridge (BA Hons Eng., MA). County Archivist, Essex, 1978–93. Chm., Nat. Council on Archives, 1996–2001; Member: Lord Chancellor's Adv. Council on Public Records, 1992–98; Royal Commn on Historical Manuscripts, 2000–03; Bd, MLA (formerly Resource: Council for Museums, Archives and Libraries), 2000–04. Pres., Soc. of Archivists, 2005–08 (Chm., 1989–91); Chm., Suffolk Records Soc., 2013– (Vice Chm., 2012–13). FSA 2007. DU Essex, 1993. Ellis Prize for dist. contribs to archival theory and practice, Soc. of Archivists, 2002. *Publications:* Bookmen: London: 250 years of Sotheran bookselling, 2011; numerous articles on archives for prof. jls, esp. Jl of Soc. of Archivists. *Recreations:* reading, walking, collecting dictionaries. *Address:* 8A Station Road, Halesworth, Suffolk IP19 8BZ. *T:* (01986) 872437. *E:* grayvw@globalnet.co.uk.

GRAY, Sir William (Hume), 3rd Bt *cr* 1917; Director: Eggleston Hall Ltd; William Gray Associates; Meals in Fields Ltd; *b* 26 July 1955; *s* of William Talbot Gray (*d* 1971) (*er s* of 2nd Bt), and of Rosemarie Hume Gray, *d* of Air Cdre Charles Hume Elliott-Smith; *S* grandfather, 1978; *m* 1984, Catherine Victoria Willoughby (marr. diss. 1998), *y d* of late John Naylor and of Mrs Jerram, Wadebridge, Cornwall; one *s* two *d*; *m* 2001, Juliet Rachel, *d* of Mr and Mrs D. J. Jackson, Headlam, Co. Durham; one *s* one *d*. *Educ:* Aysgarth School, Bedale, Yorks; Eton College; Polytechnic of Central London BA (Hons) Architecture; DipArch; RIBA. High Sheriff, Durham, 1998–99. *Recreation:* sport. *Heir: s* William John Cresswell Gray, *b* 24 Aug. 1986. *Address:* Eggleston Hall, Barnard Castle, Co. Durham DL12 0AG. *T:* (01833) 650316.

GRAYDON, Air Chief Marshal Sir Michael (James), GCB 1993 (KCB 1989); CBE 1984; FRAeS; *b* 24 Oct. 1938; *s* of James Julian Graydon and Rita Mary Alkan; *m* 1963, Margaret Elizabeth Clark. *Educ:* Wycliffe Coll.; RAF Coll., Cranwell. Qualified Flying Instructor No 1 FTS, Linton-on-Ouse, 1960–62; No 56 Sqn, 1962–64; No 226 OCU, 1965–67 (Queen's Commendation); Flight Comd, No 56 Sqn, 1967–69; RAF Staff Coll., Bracknell, 1970; PSO to Dep. C-in-C Allied Forces Central Region, Brunssum, 1971–73; Operations, Joint Warfare, MoD, 1973–75; NDC, Latimer, 1976; OC No 11 Sqn, Binbrook, 1977–79; MA to CDS, MoD, 1979–81; OC RAF Leuchars, 1981–83; OC RAF Stanley, Falkland Is, 1983; RCDS, 1984; SASO 11 Gp, Bentley Priory, 1985–86; ACOS Policy, SHAPE, 1986–89; AOC-in-C, RAF Support Comd, 1989–91; AOC-in-C, RAF Strike Comd, and C-in-C, UK Air Forces, 1991–92; CAS, and Air ADC to the Queen, 1992–97. Non-exec. Dir, Thales plc, 1999–2011. Vice-Patron, Air Cadet Council, 1999–; Pres., Battle of Britain Meml Trust, 1999–. Chm., Air Sqdn, 2005–10. Mem. Council, Church Schs Co., 1997– (Dep. Chm., 2003–11); Governor: Wycliffe Coll., 1986– (Vice-Chm., 1992–2011; Vice Pres., 2011–); Sutton's Hosp. in Charterhouse, 1998– (Chm., 2006–); ESU, 2012–. Chm., Lincs Br., ESU, 2003–. Chm., United Learning (formerly United Church Schools Gp), 2012–. FRAeS 1993. Freeman, City of London, 1995; Liveryman, Hon. Co. of Air Pilots (formerly GAPAN), 1996–. *Publications:* contrib. to professional jls. *Recreations:* golf, flying, reading. *Address:* c/o Lloyds Bank, Cox and King's Branch, 8–10 Waterloo Place, SW1Y 4BE. *Clubs:* Royal Air Force; Royal & Ancient Golf (St Andrews).

GRAYLING, Prof. Anthony Clifford, DPhil; FRSL; Master, New College of the Humanities, since 2011; *b* 3 April 1949; *s* of Henry Clifford Grayling and Ursula Adelaide Burns; *m* 1970, Gabrielle Yvonne Smyth (marr. diss. 1979); one *s* one *d*; partner, 1999, Katie Hickman; one *d*. *Educ:* Sussex Univ. (BA Hons 1971, MA 1976); London Univ. (BA Hons ext. 1975); Magdalen Coll., Oxford (DPhil 1981). Lectr in Philosophy, St Anne's Coll., Oxford, 1983–91; Lectr in Philosophy, 1991–99, Reader, 1999–2005, Prof. of Philosophy, 2005–11, Birkbeck Coll., Univ. of London. Supernumerary Fellow, St Anne's Coll., Oxford, 1991–; Vis. Prof., Univ. of Tokyo, 1998. A Judge, Man Booker Prize, 2003, Chm. Judges, 2014. FRSA 2004; FRSL 2007. *Publications:* An Introduction to Philosophical Logic, 1982, 3rd edn 1997; The Refutation of Scepticism, 1985; Berkeley: the central arguments, 1986; Wittgenstein, 1988; (jtly, as Li Xiao Jun) The Long March to the Fourth of June, 1990; (with S. Whitfield) A Literary Companion to China, 1994; (ed) Philosophy, vol. 1, A Guide Through the Subject, 1995, vol. 2, Further Through the Subject, 1998; Russell, 1996; Moral Values, 1997; The Quarrel of the Age: the life and times of William Hazlitt, 2000; The Meaning of Things, 2001; The Reason of Things, 2002; What is Good?, 2003; The Mystery of Things, 2003; (ed) Robert Herrick: lyrics of love and desire, 2003; The Heart of Things, 2005; Descartes, 2005; Among the Dead Cities, 2006; The Form of Things, 2006; Against All Gods, 2007; Truth, Meaning and Reality, 2007; Towards the Light, 2007; The Choice of Hercules, 2007; Scepticism and the Possibility of Knowledge, 2008; Ideas That Matter, 2009; Liberty in the Age of Terror, 2009; To Set Prometheus Free, 2009; Thinking of Answers, 2010; The Good Book: a secular Bible, 2011; The God Argument: the case against religion and for humanism, 2013; Friendship, 2013; The Challenge of Things: thinking through troubled times, 2015. *Clubs:* Athenæum, Beefsteak, Groucho, Garrick.

GRAYLING, Rt Hon. Christopher (Stephen); PC 2010; MP (C) Epsom and Ewell, since 2001; Leader of the House of Commons and Lord President of the Council, since 2015; *b* 1 April 1962; *s* of John Terence Grayling and Elizabeth Grayling; *m* 1987, Susan Dillistone; one *s* one *d*. *Educ:* Royal Grammar Sch., High Wycombe; Sidney Sussex Coll., Cambridge (MA Hist.). BBC News producer, 1985–88; producer and editor, Business Daily, Channel 4, 1988–91; Commissioning Editor, BBC Select, 1991–93; Dir, Charterhouse Prodns, 1993; Div. Dir, Workhouse Ltd, 1993–95; Dir, SSVC Gp, 1995–97; Change Consultant and Eur. Mktg Dir, Burson-Marsteller, 1997–2001. An Opposition Whip, 2002; Opposition front bench spokesman on health, 2002–03, on higher and further educn, 2003–05; Shadow Leader, H of C, 2005; Shadow Secretary of State: for Transport, 2005–07; for Work and Pensions, 2007–09; Shadow Home Sec., 2009–10; Minister of State, DWP, 2010–12; Lord Chancellor and Sec. of State for Justice, 2012–15. *Publications:* The Bridgewater Heritage, 1984; A Land Fit for Heroes, 1985; The Story of Joseph Holt, 1985, 2nd edn 1999; (jtly) Just Another Star, 1988. *Recreations:* football, cricket. *Address:* House of Commons, SW1A 0AA. *T:* (020) 7219 8194.

GRAYSON, David Roger, CBE 1999 (OBE 1994); Chair of Corporate Responsibility and Director, Doughty Centre for Corporate Responsibility, Cranfield School of Management, since 2007; *b* 26 May 1955; *s* of late Henry Eric Fitton Grayson and of Patricia Grayson (*née* Clayton). *Educ:* Mount St Mary's Coll.; Downing Coll., Cambridge (MA Law); Free Univ. of Brussels (Wiener Anspach Schol.; MA 1978); Newcastle Univ. (MBA 1985). Brand Mgt, Procter and Gamble, 1978–80; Co-Founder and Dir, Project NE, 1980–86; Jt Man. Dir, Prince's Youth Business Trust, 1986–87; Business in the Community, 1987–2007: Jt Man. Dir, resp. for ops and staff, 1989–92; Man. Dir, Business Strategy Gp, 1992–95; Dir, 1995–2007. Principal, BLU, 2001–06. Visiting Fellow: Sch. of Mgt, Imperial Coll., 1998–2007; Teesside Business Sch., 2004–07; Vis. Prof., London Guildhall Univ., 2000–03; Vis. Sen. Fellow, Kennedy Sch. of Govt, Harvard, 2006–10. Chairman: Business Link Nat. Assessment Panel, DTI, 1993–97; Business Link Nat. Accreditation Bd, 1996–2000; Nat. Disability Council, 1996–2000; UK Small Business Consortium, 2002–10; UnLtd Ageing Challenge Cttee, 2010–; Member: Bd, Strategic Rail Authority (formerly BRB), 2000–05; SustainAbility Faculty, 2008–10; Corporate Responsibility Adv. Panel, Camelot, 2008–; Editl Bd, Ethical Corp., 2009–14. Chm. Judges, UK Capital Enterprise, 2005–06. Ambassador, Nat. AIDS Trust, 2000–; Trustee: Prince of Wales Innovation Trust, 1989–; AbilityNet, 2000–02; Responsibility in Gambling Trust, 2004–08; Chm., Housing 21, 2006–11. Gov., Lilian Baylis Sch., Lambeth, 2000–05. Trustee, Carers UK, 2012– (Chm., 2013–). Patron, SCOPE, 2003–10. FRSA 1991. Hon. LLD London South Bank, 2005. Contrib. Ed., Corporate Citizenship Briefing, 2008–13. *Publications:* (contrib.) Mastering Enterprise, 1996; (contrib.) What If..., 2000; (with A. Hodges) Everybody's Business: managing risks and opportunities in today's global society, 2001; Corporate Social Opportunity, 2004; (contrib.) Entrepreneurship: a catalyst for urban regeneration, 2004; (contrib.) Sustainable Enterprise, 2004; (contrib.) The Accountable Corporation, 2005; (ed jtly) Cranfield on Corporate Sustainability, 2012; (with J. Nelson) Corporate Responsibility Coalitions: the past, present and future of alliances for sustainable capitalism, 2013; (with M. McLaren and H. Spitzeck) Social Intrapreneurism and all that Jazz, 2014. *Recreations:* scuba diving, travel; happiest in, on or underwater, preferably in warm climates. *Address:* Cranfield School of Management, Cranfield, Bedford MK43 0AL. *E:* david.grayson@cranfield.ac.uk. *Club:* Royal Automobile.

GRAYSON, Sir Jeremy (Brian Vincent), 5th Bt *cr* 1922, of Ravenspoint, Co. Anglesey; *b* 30 Jan. 1933; *s* of Brian Harrington Grayson (*d* 1989), 3rd *s* of 1st Bt and of Sofia Maria (*née* Buchanan); *S* uncle, 1991; *m* 1958, Sara Mary, *d* of C. F. Upton; three *s* three *d* (and one *d* decd). *Educ:* Downside. Retired photographer. *Heir: s* Simon Jeremy Grayson, *b* 12 July 1959.

GRAZIANO da SILVA, José, PhD; Director General, Food and Agriculture Organization of the United Nations, since 2012; *b* 17 Nov. 1949; *m* Paola Ligasacchi; two *c*. *Educ:* Univ. of São Paulo (Bachelor's degree Agronomy; Master's degree Rural Econs and Sociol.); State Univ. of Campinas (PhD Econs); University Coll. London (Latin Amer. Studies); Univ. of Calif, Santa Cruz (Envmtl Studies). State University of Campinas: teaching, from 1978; Prof.; Chair, Master's and Doctoral Prog. in Econ. Develt and Envmt, Inst. of Econs; co-ordinated formulation of 'Zero Hunger' Prog. (Fome Zero), Brazil, 2001; Extraordinary Minister of Food Security and the Fight against Hunger, 2003; Regl Rep. for Latin America and Caribbean and Asst Dir-Gen., UNFAO, 2006–11. *Publications:* over 25 books on rural develt, food security and agrarian econs. *Address:* Food and Agriculture Organization of the United Nations, Viale delle Terme di Caracalla, 00153 Rome, Italy.

GREANEY, Paul Richard; QC 2010; *b* Halifax, 5 April 1970; *s* of Patrick Greaney and Anne Lesley Greaney (*née* Filby, now Phillips); *m* 1st, 2003, Pauline Mary Healy (marr. diss. 2006); one *d*; 2nd, 2009, Selina Ruth Cranidge; one *s* one *d*. *Educ:* Bradford Grammar Sch.; Durham Univ. (BA Hons Law 1992); Inns of Court Sch. of Law. Called to the Bar, Inner Temple, 1993; in practice as barrister, specialising in criminal and regulatory law, Leeds, London and Hong Kong. *Address:* New Park Court Chambers, 16 Park Place, Leeds LS1 2SJ.

GREATOREX, Barbara; Headteacher, Wallington High School for Girls, 2002–12; *b* 11 March 1951; *d* of Benjamin John Jackson and Millicent Claire Jackson; two *s* one *d*. *Educ:* Warwick Univ. (BSc Hons); York Univ. (PGCE); Open Univ. (MA). Sen. Teacher, Joseph Rowntree Sch., 1995–97; Dep. Headteacher, Wolverhampton Girls' High Sch., 1997–2002. Master Practitioner, Neuro-Linguistic Programming, 2009–11. *Recreations:* birdwatching, reading, travelling.

GREATOREX, Raymond Edward, FCA; Executive Chairman, Baker Tilly, 2002–06; *b* 28 May 1940; *s* of late Percy Edward and Lilian Alice Greatorex; *m* 1982, Barbara Anne (*née* Booth); one *d*. *Educ:* Westcliff High Sch.; Lewes Co. Grammar Sch. FCA 1975. Sydenham, Snowden Nicholson & Co., chartered accountants, subseq. Sydenham & Co.: Articled Clerk, 1959; Partner, 1970; firm merged into Hodgson Harris, 1980, Hodgson Impey, 1985, Kidsons Impey, 1990, and merged with Baker Tilly, 2002; Mem., Nat. Exec. and Regl Man. Partner, Southern England, 1990–94; Chm., HLB Internat., 1994–99; Nat. Managing Partner, HLB Kidsons, 2000–02. Liveryman and Freeman, City of London; Liveryman, Farriers' Co. (Master, 2002–03). *Recreations:* race horse owner, cricket (watching), gardening, travelling, reading, especially autobiographies. *Address:* Beeches Brook, Strood Green, Wisborough Green, Billingshurst, W Sussex RH14 0HP. *T:* (01403) 700796. *Clubs:* East India, MCC.

GREATREX, Neil; National President and General Secretary, Union of Democratic Mineworkers, 1993–2009; *b* 1 April 1951; *s* of late John Edward and Joyce Irene Greatrex; *m* 1972, Sheila Waterhouse; two *d*. *Educ:* Greenwood Drive Jun. Sch.; Mowlands Intermediate Sch.; Ashfield Comprehensive Sch. Bentinck Colliery, 1965–85. National Union of Mineworkers: Cttee Mem., 1970–74; Branch Treas., 1974–80; Branch Pres., 1980–85; full-time Area Official, 1985–86; Union of Democratic Mineworkers: Area Pres., 1986–88; Nat. Vice-Pres., 1988–93. *Recreations:* Do It Yourself, shooting. *Address:* c/o Miners' Offices, Berry Hill Lane, Mansfield, Notts NG18 4JU. *T:* (01623) 626094.

GREATREX, Thomas James; *b* Ashford, Kent, 30 Sept. 1974; *s* of Simon Greatrex and Brenda Greatrex; *m* 2003, Laura Orrock; two *d*. *Educ:* Judd Sch., Tonbridge; London Sch. of Econs and Pol Sci. (BSc Econs, Govt and Law 1996). Parly Asst, Opposition Whips' Office, 1996–97; Special Advr to Chief Whip, 1997–98, to Minister of Agric., Fisheries and Food, 1998–99; regl organiser, GMB, 1999–2004; Hd, Policy and Public Affairs, E Dunbartonshire Council, 2004–06; Dir, Corporate Affairs, NHS 24, 2006–07; Special Advr to Sec. of State for Scotland, 2007–10. MP (Lab Co-op) Rutherglen and Hamilton W, 2010–15; contested (Lab Co-op) same seat, 2015. Mem., Fulham Supporters' Trust. *Recreations:* football (Fulham FC), cinema. *E:* tomgreatrex1974@gmail.com. *Club:* Blantyre Miners Welfare.

GREAVES, family name of **Baron Greaves**.

GREAVES, Baron *cr* 2000 (Life Peer), of Pendle in the county of Lancashire; **Anthony Robert Greaves;** *b* 27 July 1942; *s* of Geoffrey Greaves and Moyra Greaves (*née* Brookes); *m* 1968, Heather Ann (*née* Baxter); two *d*. *Educ:* Queen Elizabeth GS, Wakefield; Hertford Coll., Oxford (BA Hons Geog.). Teacher/Lectr, 1968–74; Organising Sec., Assoc. of Liberal Councillors, 1977–85; Man. Dir, Hebden Royd Publications Ltd, (Lib Dem publications), 1985–90; second-hand book dealer, Liber Books, 1992–. Member: (L) Colne BC, 1971–74; (L then Lib Dem): Pendle BC, 1973–92, 1994–98, 2004–; Lancs CC, 1973–97. Contested: (L) Nelson and Colne, Feb. and Oct. 1974; (Lib Dem) Pendle, 1997. Vice President: LGA 2011–; Open Spaces Soc. *Publications:* (with Rachael Pitchford) Merger: the inside story, 1988. *Recreations:* climbing, mountain/hill walking, wild flowers, cycling, politics. *Address:* 3 Hartington Street, Winewall, Colne, Lancashire BB8 8DB. *T:* (01282) 864346, *T:* (office) (020) 7219 8620.

GREAVES, James Peter, (Jimmy); TV broadcaster, since 1983; football correspondent, The People; *b* 20 Feb. 1940; *s* of James and Mary Greaves; *m* Irene Barden; two *s* two *d* (and one *s* decd). *Educ:* Kingswood Sch., Hainault. Professional footballer (inside forward), 1957; played for: Chelsea, 1957–61; AC Milan, 1961; Tottenham Hotspur, 1961–70 (FA Cup wins, 1962, 1967); West Ham, 1970–71; scored record 357 goals in First Division, 55 goals in FA Cup ties; played 57 times for England (scored 44 goals). Football correspondent, The Sun. *Publications* include: Greavsie (autobiog.), 2003; (with N. Giller): This one's on me, 1981; It's a funny old life, 1990; The Heart of the Game, 2005. *Address:* c/o Sports Department, The People, 1 Canada Square, Canary Wharf, E14 5AP.

GREAVES, Jeffrey; HM Diplomatic Service, retired; Consul General, Alexandria, 1978–81; *b* 10 Dec. 1926; *s* of Willie and Emily Greaves; *m* 1949, Joyce Mary Farrer; one *s* one *d*. *Educ:* Pudsey Grammar Sch. Served RN, 1945–48. Joined HM Foreign Service, 1948; FO, 1948; Benghazi, 1951; Vice Consul, Tehran, 1953; ME Centre for Arab Studies, 1955; Second Sec. and Vice Consul, Paris, 1960; Vice Consul, Muscat, 1962; Second Sec. and Consul, Athens, 1965; Second Sec. (Commercial), Cairo, 1968; First Sec. and Consul, Muscat, 1970; First Sec. (Com.), Bangkok, 1972; FCO, 1976. *Address:* 17 Queens Drive, Pudsey LS28 7HL. *T:* (0113) 257 7238.

GREAVES, Prof. Malcolm Watson, MD, PhD; FRCP; Consultant Dermatologist, St John's Institute of Dermatology, St Thomas' Hospital, since 2007; Consultant in Dermatology and Allergy, London Allergy Clinic, since 2007; *b* 11 Nov. 1933; *s* of Donald Watson Greaves and Kathleen Evelyn Greaves; *m* 1964, Evelyn Yeo; one *s* one *d*. *Educ:* Epsom College; Charing Cross Med. Sch. MD, PhD London. MRC Clinical Res. Fellow, UCL, 1963–66; Reader in Dermatology, Univ. of Newcastle upon Tyne, 1966–75; Prof. of Dermatology, Univ. of London, 1975–99, now Emeritus; Dean, St John's Inst. of Dermatology, UMDS of Guy's and St Thomas' Hosps, 1989–95. Prof. of Dermatology, Nat. Univ. of Malaysia,

2001–02. Sen. Consultant in Dermatology, Singapore Gen. Hosp., 2003–05; Sen. Consultant Dermatologist, Singapore Nat. Skin Centre, 2005–07; Clinical Prof., Faculty of Medicine, Nat. Univ. of Singapore, 2006–07. Chm., Scientific Cttee and Trustee, Skin Disease Res. Fund, 1980–96; Mem., Cttee on Safety of Medicines, DHSS, 1982–89. President: European Soc. for Dermatol Research, 1984; Sect. of Dermatol., RSM, 1996; Chm., Therapy and Audit Cttee, British Assoc. of Dermatologists, 1994–96. Prog. Dir, American Acad. of Dermatol., 1998–2001. Dean, Internat. Faculty, Regl Conf. on Dermatol., Malaysia, 2010. Internat. Hon. Mem., Amer. Dermatol. Assoc., 1987; Hon. Member: Amer. Soc. for Investigative Dermatol., 1989; Malaysian Dermatol Assoc., 1995; British Assoc. of Dermatologists, 2000; Eur. Soc. for Dermatol Res., 2000. Mem. Management Bd Exec., UMDS, 1990–95; Mem. Governing Body, Sch. of Pharmacy, Univ. of London, 1990–95. FAMS 2005. Sir Archibald Gray Gold Medal, British Assoc. of Dermatologists, 1998; Leo Von Zumbusch Gold Medal, Univ. München, 1998; Cert. of Appreciation, Internat. Cttee of Dermatol., 2001; Dist. Sci. Achievement Award, Eur. Acad. of Allergy and Clin. Immunology, 2002; Dist. Res. Award, Eur. Acad. of Dermatol. and Venereol., 2005; Dist. Res. Award, World Allergy Orgn, 2007; Dist. Academic Achievement Award, Amer. Skin Foundn, 2010; Medal for Contribs to Dermatol Res., British Soc. for Investigative Dermatol., 2012. *Publications:* Pharmacology of the Skin, Vol. I, Pharmacology of Skin Systems and Autocoids in Normal and Inflamed Skin, 1989; Vol. II, Methods, Absorption, Metabolism, Toxicity, Drugs and Diseases, 1989; (ed) Urticaria and Angioedema, 2004, 2nd edn 2009; Itch: basic mechanisms and therapy, 2004; contrib. Immunol. and Allergy Clinics of N America. *Recreations:* swimming, walking. *Address:* Dovecote House, 32/34 Church Street, Guilden Morden, Royston, Herts SG8 0JD; 515 East, County Hall Apartments, Forum Magnum Square, Belvedere Road, SE1 7GN. *W:* www.clinidermsolutions.co.uk.

GREAVES, Mary; *see* Bownes, M.

GREAVES, Prof. Melvyn Francis, FRS 2003; Chairman, Section of Haemato-Oncology, since 2006, and Founding Director, Centre for Evolution and Cancer, since 2013, Institute of Cancer Research; *b* 12 Sept. 1941; *s* of Edward and Violet Greaves; *m* 1966, Josephine Pank; one *s* one *d. Educ:* City of Norwich Grammar Sch.; University Coll. London; Middlesex Hosp. Med. Sch. BSc, PhD London. FRCPath 1997. Vis Scientist, Karolinska Inst., Stockholm, 1968–69; Res. Fellow, Nat. Inst. for Med. Res., London, 1969–72; Res. Scientist, Dept of Zoology, UCL, 1972–76; Hd, Membrane Immunology Dept, Imperial Cancer Res. Fund, 1976–84; Dir, Leukaemia Res. Fund Centre, Inst. of Cancer Res., London, 1984–2005. Hon. MRCP 1987. FMedSci 1999. Paul Martini Prize (Germany), 1977; Peter Debye Prize (Holland), 1981; King Faisal Internat. Prize for Medicine, 1988; José Carreras Prize (Europe), 2001. *Publications:* T and B Lymphocytes, 1973; Cellular Recognition, 1975; Atlas of Blood Cells, 1981, 2nd edn 1988; Monoclonal Antibodies to Receptors, 1984; Cancer: the evolutionary legacy, 2000; White Blood: personal journeys with childhood leukaemia, 2008; contribs to bio-med. jls. *Recreations:* music, cooking, photography, natural history, being grandad. *Address:* Institute of Cancer Research, Sutton, Surrey SM2 5NG.

GREEN, family name of **Barons Green of Deddington** and **Green of Hurstpierpoint**.

GREEN OF DEDDINGTON, Baron *cr* 2014 (Life Peer), of Deddington in the County of Oxfordshire; **Andrew Fleming Green,** KCMG 1998 (CMG 1991); HM Diplomatic Service, retired; Founder Chairman, Migrationwatch UK, since 2001; *b* 6 Aug. 1941; *s* of late Gp Captain J. H. Green, RAF, and Beatrice Mary (*née* Bowditch); *m* 1968, C. Jane Churchill; one *s* one *d. Educ:* Haileybury and ISC; Magdalene Coll., Cambridge (MA). Served as 2nd Lieut, RGJ, 1962–65; joined HM Diplomatic Service, 1965; Middle East Centre for Arab Studies, 1966–68; Aden, 1968–69; Asst Political Agent, Abu Dhabi, 1970–71; First Secretary, FCO, 1972–74; Private Sec. to Minister of State, FCO, 1975, and to Parliamentary Under Sec. of State, 1976; First Secretary, UK Delegn to OECD, Paris, 1977–79; First Sec., FCO, 1980–81; Counsellor, Washington, 1982–85; Counsellor, Hd of Chancery and Consul Gen., Riyadh, 1985–88; Counsellor, FCO, 1988–90; Ambassador to Syria, 1991–94; Asst Under-Sec. of State (Middle East), FCO, 1994–96; Ambassador to Saudi Arabia, 1996–2000. Chm., Med. Aid for Palestinians, 2002–04. *Recreations:* tennis, bridge.

GREEN OF HURSTPIERPOINT, Baron *cr* 2010 (Life Peer), of Hurstpierpoint in the County of West Sussex; **Stephen Keith Green;** *b* 7 Nov. 1948; *s* of late Dudley Keith Green and Dorothy Rosamund Mary Green; *m* 1971, Janian Joy; two *d. Educ:* Lancing Coll.; Exeter Coll., Oxford (BA PPE); MIT (MSc Pol Sci.). ODA, FCO, 1971–77; McKinsey & Co. Inc., 1977–82; Hong Kong & Shanghai Banking Corp. Ltd, 1982–92; HSBC Hldgs plc, 1993–2010: Exec. Dir, Investment Banking and Markets, 1998–2003; Gp Chief Exec., 2003–06; Gp Chm., 2006–10. Director: HSBC Bank plc, 1995–2010 (Chm., 2005–10); PEC Concerts Ltd, 1999–2001. Dep. Pres., CBI, 2010. Minister of State (Minister for Trade and Investment), BIS and FCO, 2011–13. Chm. Trustees, Natural History Mus., 2014–. Ordained deacon 1987; priest 1988. *Publications:* Serving God? Serving Mammon?, 1996; Good Value: reflections on money, morality and an uncertain world, 2009; Reluctant Meister, 2014. *Recreations:* opera, art, European literature, walking. *Address:* House of Lords, SW1A 0PW. *Club:* Athenæum.

GREEN, Sir Albert A.; *see* Aynsley-Green.

GREEN, Sir Allan (David), KCB 1991; QC 1987; *b* 1 March 1935; *s* of late Lionel and Irene Green; *m* 1st, 1967, Eva (*d* 1993), *yr d* of Prof. Artur Attman and Elsa Attman, Gothenburg, Sweden; one *s* one *d*; 2nd, 2004, Anna, *er d* of late Lemuel Harries and Muriel Harries, Gower. *Educ:* Charterhouse; St Catharine's Coll., Cambridge (Open Exhibnr, MA). Served RN, 1953–55. Called to the Bar, Inner Temple, 1959, Bencher, 1985; Jun. Prosecuting Counsel to the Crown, Central Criminal Court, 1977, Sen. Prosecuting Counsel, 1979, First Senior Prosecuting Counsel, 1985; a Recorder, 1979–87; DPP and Hd of Crown Prosecution Service, 1987–91. Mem., Gen. Council of the Bar, 1992. *Recreations:* music, especially opera, admiring calligraphy. *Address:* c/o 2 Hare Court, Temple, EC4Y 7BH. *Clubs:* Athenæum, Garrick.

GREEN, Andrew Curtis; farmer and horticulturist, since 1960; *b* 28 March 1936; *s* of Christopher Green and Marjorie (*née* Bennett); *m* 1966, Julia Margaret (*née* Davidson); two *s. Educ:* Charterhouse; Magdalene Coll., Cambridge. MA (Nat. Scis), Dip. of Agriculture. Commnd RNVR, 1954–56. Farm management, 1960–67; founded Greens of Soham farming and horticultural business, 1967; Director: Elsoms Spalding Seed Co., 1982–2009; Spearhead Internat. Ltd, 1999–2011; Chm., Hassy Ltd, 1983–89. Mem., AFRC, 1984–88. Mem., E England Regl Cttee, NT, 2005–11. Founder, Kingfishers Bridge Wetland Creation Project, 1995. FLS 1978; Hon. FIHort 1986 (Industrial Mem. Council, 1988–94); FRAgS 1995. MInstD 1985. Extra Mem., Court of Skinners' Co., 1994–96. *Recreations:* wildlife conservation, sailing, ski-ing, fishing, shooting. *Address:* Mill House, Tower Road, Burnham Overy Staithe, Kings Lynn, Norfolk PE31 8JB. *Clubs:* Sloane, Farmers; Hawks (Cambridge).
See also P. C. Green.

GREEN, Andrew James; Chairman, IG Group, since 2014; *b* England, 7 Sept. 1955; two *s* one *d*; *m* 2014, Susan Elizabeth Jukes. *Educ:* King Edward's Sch., Edgbaston; Leeds Univ. (BSc Hons Chem. Engrg 1976). Sales and mktg, Shell, 1976–83; Consultant, Deloitte, Haskin & Sells, 1984–86; Bd Mem., BT, 1986–2007; CEO, Logica, 2008–12; Chairman: Dockon Inc., 2012–; NP Gp, 2013–; Connected Digital Catapult, 2013–. Non-executive Director: ARM Hldgs, 2011–; Avanti Communications, 2014–. Pres., UK Space, 2009–. Liveryman, Information Technologists' Co., 2011–. FRSA. *Recreations:* scuba diving, cricket, whisky and wine. *Address:* 24 The Wallpaper Aparrtments, 142 Offord Road, N1 1NS. *T:* 07802 243885. *E:* agreen8@mac.com.

GREEN, Andrew James Dominic; QC 2010; *b* London, 8 Nov. 1965; *s* of Barry and Marilyn Green; *m* 1994, Jennifer Hirschl; one *s* one *d. Educ:* Eton Coll.; London Sch. of Econs (LLB). Called to the Bar, Inner Temple, 1988; in practice as barrister, specialising in commercial law, 1988–. *Recreation:* too few. *Address:* Blackstone Chambers, Blackstone House, Temple, EC4Y 9BW. *T:* (020) 7583 1770. *Clubs:* Athenæum, Garrick.

GREEN, Andrew Michael Walter; Librarian, National Library of Wales, 1998–2013; *b* 30 Sept. 1952; *s* of Harry Green and Ellen Martha Kennedy Green (*née* Allan); *m* 1980, Carys Evans; two *d. Educ:* Hoylandswaine Primary Sch.; Queen Elizabeth Grammar Sch., Wakefield; Gonville and Caius Coll., Cambridge (BA 1973; MA 1975; Wace Medal for Classical Archaeology 1973); Coll. of Librarianship, Wales (Dip. Librarianship 1975). MCLIP (ALA 1977). Asst Librarian, UC, Cardiff, 1975–88; Arts and Social Studies Librarian, UWCC, 1988–89; Sub-Librarian (Services and Collection Develt), Univ. of Sheffield, 1989–92; Librarian, 1992–95, Dir of Library and Information Services, 1996–98, UC, Swansea. Vice-Chm., 2000–02, Chm., 2002–04, SCONUL. Chair, Coleg Cymraeg Cenedlaethol, 2014–. FLSW 2013. Hon. Fellow: Univ. of Wales, Swansea, 2001; NE Wales Inst. of Higher Educn, 2003; Univ. of Wales, Lampeter, 2006. Mem., Gorsedd Beirdd Ynys Prydein, 2009. Hon. DLitt Wales, 2013; Hon. PhD Open, 2015. *Publications:* In the Chair: how to guide groups and manage meetings, 2014; numerous articles on library and information studies; weekly blog. *Recreations:* running, cycling, walking, music, looking out of windows. *Address:* 30 Caswell Drive, Caswell, Swansea SA3 4RJ. *T:* (01792) 361260.

GREEN, Ann Margaret, CBE 2010; Pro-Chancellor and Chairman, Governing Board, York St John University, since 2011; *b* Chester, 28 March 1951; *d* of John Britton and Margaret Britton (*née* Constable). *Educ:* Southport High Sch. for Girls. Nationwide Bldg Soc., 1969–77; Partner, commercial and business insce brokers, 1977–83; Northern Dir, Stock Exchange, 1983–85; Dir, Allied Provincial Securities, 1986–91; Northern Dir, Industrial Soc., 1992–96; self-employed business consultant, 1996–. Non-executive Director: Stag Security Services Ltd, 2006–12; DCMS, 2009–11. Chairman: Hadrian's Wall Heritage Ltd, 2006–; York Th. Royal Trust, 2014–. Trustee, Royal Armouries, 1998–2011 (Chm., 2003–11). *Recreations:* heritage, museums, art, theatre, driving, my home in Canada. *Address:* 89 Postern Close, Bishops Wharf, York YO23 1JF. *T:* 07702 213013. *E:* annmargaretgreen@gmail.com.

GREEN, Anthony Eric Sandall, RA 1977 (ARA 1971); NEAC 2002; Member, London Group, 1964; artist (painter); *b* 30 Sept. 1939; *s* of late Frederick Sandall Green and Marie Madeleine (*née* Dupont); *m* 1961, Mary Louise Cozens-Walker; two *d. Educ:* Highgate Sch., London; Slade Sch. of Fine Art, University Coll. London (Fellow, UCL, 1991). Henry Tonks Prize for drawing, Slade Sch., 1960; French Govt Schol., Paris, 1960; Gulbenkian Purchase Award, 1963; Harkness Fellowship, in USA, 1967–69. Trustee, RA, 2000–08. Has exhibited in: London, New York, Haarlem, Rotterdam, Stuttgart, Hanover, Helsingborg, Malmö, Tokyo, Brussels, W Berlin, Chicago and Sydney. Paintings in various public collections, including: Tate Gallery; Metropolitan Mus. of Art, N York; Olinda Museum, Brazil; Baltimore Mus. of Art, USA; Mus. of Fine Art, Boston, USA; Nat. Mus. of Wales; Gulbenkian Foundn; Arts Council of GB; British Council; Victoria and Albert Mus.; Contemporary Art Soc.; Frans Hals Mus., Holland; Boymans-van Beuningen Mus., Holland; Ulster Mus., Belfast; Ikeda and Niigata Mus., Setagaya Art Mus., Metropolitan, Tokyo; Hiroshima; Fukuoka. Featured Artist, RA Summer Exhibn, 2003. Hon. RBA 1998; Hon. ROI 2004. Hon. Fellow, Wolfson Coll., Cambridge, 2015. DUniv Buckingham, 2011. Exhibit of the Year award, RA, 1977. *Publications:* A Green Part of the World, 1984. *Recreations:* travelling, family life. *Address:* Mole End, 40 High Street, Little Eversden, Cambridge CB23 1HE. *T:* (01223) 262292, *Fax:* (01223) 265656.

GREEN, Prof. Anthony Richard, PhD; FRCP, FRCPath, FMedSci; Professor of Haemato-Oncology, since 1999, and Head, Department of Haematology, since 2000, University of Cambridge; Chair, Department of Haematology, Addenbrooke's Hospital, since 2000; *b* 13 Oct. 1955; *s* of John Richard Green and Jeanne Dorothy Green; *m* 1984, Sarah Frances Rann; one *s* two *d. Educ:* Highgate Sch.; Queens' Coll., Cambridge; University Coll. Hosp., London (PhD 1987). FRCP 1995; FRCPath 1997. Jun. hosp. posts, London, 1980–84; Clinical Res. Fellow, ICRF, 1984–87; Lectr in Haematology, Univ. Hosp. of Wales, Cardiff, 1987–89; CRC Hamilton Fairley Travelling Fellow, Walter & Eliza Hall Inst., Melbourne, 1989–91; Wellcome Trust Sen. Clinical Fellow, Dept of Haematology, Cambridge Univ., 1991–99. FMedSci 2001. *Recreations:* family, friends, hill walking, scuba diving, photography. *Address:* Department of Haematology, Cambridge Institute for Medical Research, Hills Road, Cambridge CB2 0XY.

GREEN, Arthur; Senior Partner, Grant Thornton, 1986–88, retired; President, Institute of Chartered Accountants in England and Wales, 1987–88; *b* 15 June 1928; *s* of Arthur Henry and Elizabeth Burns Green; *m* 1952, Sylvia Myatt; one *s* one *d. Educ:* Liverpool Collegiate. FCA. Qualified Chartered Accountant, 1950; Partner, Bryce Hanmer & Co., Liverpool, 1954 (merged Thornton Baker; later Grant Thornton); Nat. Managing Partner, Thornton Baker, 1975–84; Chm. and Man. Dir, Grant Thornton International, 1984–85. Vice-Pres., 1985–86, Dep. Pres., 1986–87, ICA. *Recreations:* bridge, theatre. *Address:* Up Yonder, Herbert Road, Salcombe, Devon TQ8 8HP. *T:* (01548) 842075.

GREEN, Prof. Ben Joseph, PhD; FRS 2010; Waynflete Professor of Pure Mathematics, University of Oxford, since 2013; Fellow, Magdalen College, Oxford, since 2013; *b* 27 Feb. 1977; *s* of late Robert Norman Green and of Judith Mary Green; *m* 2014, Dr Yvonne Lee. *Educ:* Trinity Coll., Cambridge (BA Hons Maths 1998, MA 2001; PhD 2003). Res. Fellow, Trinity Coll., Cambridge, 2001–05; Prof. of Pure Maths, Univ. of Bristol, 2005–06; Herchel Smith Prof. of Pure Maths, Univ. of Cambridge, 2006–13; Fellow, Trinity Coll., Cambridge, 2006–13. *Publications:* contrib. learned jls. *Recreations:* orienteering, hill-walking, cricket, jazz. *Address:* Mathematical Institute, University of Oxford, Andrew Wiles Building, Radcliffe Observatory Quarter, Woodstock Road, Oxford OX2 6GG. *E:* Ben.green@maths.ox.ac.uk.

GREEN, Brian Russell; QC 1997; *b* 25 July 1956; *s* of late Bertram Green and Dora Green (*née* Rinsler); *m* 1994, Yvonne Mammon; one *s* one *d*, and two step *d. Educ:* Ilford County High Sch. for Boys; St Edmund Hall, Oxford (BA, BCL). Called to the Bar, Middle Temple, 1980; Mem., Lincoln's Inn, 1991. *Recreations:* travel, hill-walking, ski-ing, the arts. *Address:* Wilberforce Chambers, 8 New Square, Lincoln's Inn, WC2A 3QP. *T:* (020) 7306 0102.

GREEN, Prof. Brynmor Hugh, OBE 1995; Sir Cyril Kleinwort Professor of Countryside Management, University of London, Wye College, 1987–96, now Professor Emeritus; *b* 14 Jan. 1941; *s* of Albert Walter Green and Margaret Afona Green (*née* Griffiths); *m* 1965, Jean Armstrong; two *s. Educ:* Dartford Grammar Sch.; Univ. of Nottingham (BSc 1st Cl. Hons Botany, PhD Plant Ecol.). Lectr in Plant Ecology, Dept of Botany, Univ. of Manchester, 1965–68; Dep. Regl Officer (SE) 1968–69, Regl Officer (SE) 1969–75, Nature Conservancy Council; Lectr and Sen. Lectr, Wye Coll., 1975–87. A Countryside Comr, 1984–93. Vice-Pres., Kent Wildlife Trust, 2002–. Churchill Fellow, 1999. *Publications:* Countryside Conservation: landscape ecology, planning and management, 1981, 3rd edn 1996; (jtly) The Diversion of Land: conservation in a period of farming contraction, 1990; (jtly) The Changing Role of the Common Agricultural Policy: the future of farming in Europe, 1991; (jtly) Threatened Landscapes: conserving cultural environments, 2001; Natural Kent: an introduction to the habitats, wildlife and wild places of the county, 2008; numerous chapters in books, conf. reports, sci. jls. *Recreations:* golf, watercolour sketching, bird-watching. *Address:* Heatherbank, 49 Brockhill Road, Saltwood, Hythe, Kent CT21 4AF. *T:* (01303) 261093.

GREEN, Charlotte Rosamund; freelance writer and broadcaster, since 2013; continuity announcer and newsreader, BBC Radio 4, 1985–2013; *b* 4 May 1956; *y d* of Geoffrey Hugh Green, CB and of Ruth Hazel (*née* Mercy). *Educ:* Haberdashers' Aske's Sch. for Girls; Univ. of Kent at Canterbury (BA Hons Eng. and American Lit.). Joined BBC as studio manager, 1978; newsreader, Today, BBC Radio 4, 1986–2013; regular participant in The News Quiz, 1987–2013; producer and presenter, Morning has Broken, BBC Radio 4, 1986–91; presenter, News Speak, BBC World Service, 1999; narrator, Music in Camera, BBC TV, 1989; presenter, Charlotte Green's Great Composers, 2013, Charlotte Green's Culture Club, 2013–, Classic FM; reader of classified football results, Sports Report, BBC Radio 5 Live, 2013–. Trustee, Univ. of Kent Develt Trust, 2003–10. Judge, BBC Frank Gillard Annual Local Radio Awards, 2000–02. DUniv Kent, 2013. Most Attractive Female Voice on the Radio award, Radio Times, 2002; Roberts Radio Special Award for Excellence in Broadcasting, 2009; Radio Broadcaster of the Year Award, Broadcasting Press Guild, 2013. *Publications:* The News is Read (autobiog.), 2014. *Recreations:* theatre, books, art, music, laughing with friends, supporting Tottenham Hotspur FC, gardening. *Address:* c/o Excellent Talent, 118–120 Great Titchfield Street, W1W 6SS. *T:* 0845 210 0111.

GREEN, Chris; MP (C) Bolton West, since 2015; *b* 12 Aug. 1973. Engr, mass spectrometry industry. Contested (C) Manchester Withington, 2010. Mem., Sci. and Technol. Select Cttee, 2015–. *Address:* House of Commons, SW1A 0AA.

GREEN, Christopher Edward Wastie, MA; FCILT; non-executive Director: Dover Harbour Board, 2010–14; Heathrow Express, since 2013; *b* 7 Sept. 1943; *s* of James Wastie Green and Margarita Mensing; *m* 1966, Waltraud Mitzie Petzold; one *s* one *d*. *Educ:* St Paul's School, London; Oriel College, Oxford. MA Mod. Hist. British Rail: Management Trainee, 1965–67; served Birmingham, Nottingham, Hull, Wimbledon; Passenger Operating Manager, HQ, 1979–80; Chief Operating Manager, Scotland, 1980–83; Dep. Gen. Manager, Scotland, 1983–84; Gen. Manager, Scottish Region, 1984–86; Dir, Network SouthEast, 1986–91; Managing Director: InterCity, 1992–94; ScotRail, 1994–95; Chief Exec. and Comr, English Heritage, 1995–96; Director: Gibb Rail Ltd, 1996–99; Gibb Ltd, 1996–99; Chief Exec., Virgin Trains, 1999–2004; Dir, 1999–2004, Chm., 2004–05, Virgin Rail Gp. Director: Eurotunnel, 1995–2004; Connex Rail, 1998–99. Chm., Rail Forum, 2004–07. Non-executive Director: Network Rail, 2005–10; W Herts Hosp. NHS Trust, 2010–13. Chm., Expert Adv. Panel, Crossrail, 2013–. Mem., Regl Council, CBI, 1986. President: Railway Study Assoc., 1989–90, 1997–98; Railway Convalescent Homes, 2002–; Vice Pres., CIT, 1988; Mem., Railway Heritage Trust Adv. Panel, 2003–. Mem. Adv. Bd, Cranfield Univ. Logistics and Transportation Centre, 1996–2002; Trustee, Royal Liverpool Phil. Orch., 2004–08. Hon. DBA IMCB, 2002; DUniv UCE, 2002. *Recreations:* music, reading, walking, canals, architecture. *Address:* 14 Meadway, Berkhamsted, Herts HP4 2PN. *T:* (01442) 862978. *E:* chrisgreen0709@gmail.com.

GREEN, Prof. Christopher Kenneth, PhD; FBA 1999; Professor of History of Art, Courtauld Institute of Art, 1991–2008, now Emeritus; *b* 1943; *m* Charlotte Sebag-Montefiore; one *s* one *d*. *Educ:* Christ's Coll., Cambridge (BA 1966); London Univ. (MA); PhD. Courtauld Institute of Art: successively Asst Lectr, Lectr, and Reader in History of Art; Curator, Juan Gris exhibn, Whitechapel Gall., 1992; Curator, Roger Fry exhibn, Courtauld, 1999; Co-curator, Henri Rousseau exhibn, Tate Modern, Paris and Washington, 2005; Curator, Picasso exhibn, Barcelona, 2008; Co-curator, Modern Antiquity exhibn, J. Paul Getty Museum, LA, 2011; Co-curator, Mondrian/Nicholson exhibn, Courtauld, 2012. Leverhulme Res. Fellow, 1997–98. Trustee, Nat. Museums Liverpool, 2001–10. *Publications:* Léger and the Avant-Garde, 1976; Cubism and its Enemies, 1987; (jtly) Juan Gris, 1992; European Avant-Gardes, 1995; One Man Show (novel), 1995; (ed) Art Made Modern: Roger Fry's vision of art, 1999; Art in France 1900–1940, 2000; Picasso: architecture and vertigo, 2005; (ed) Modern Antiquity: Picasso, de Chirico, Léger, Picabia, 2011; (ed) Mondrian/Nicholson: in parallel, 2012; exhibn catalogues. *Recreation:* finding calm. *Address:* Courtauld Institute of Art, Somerset House, Strand, WC2R 0RN.

GREEN, Colin Raymond; Chairman, Hermes Group Pension Scheme, 2002–13; *b* 16 April 1949; *s* of Gerald and Maisie Green; *m* 1975, Hazel Ruth Lateman; one *s* one *d*. *Educ:* Hampton Grammar Sch.; LSE (LLB Hons); Coll. of Law; WUJS Post-grad. Inst., Israel. Solicitor, 1973; Paisner & Co., 1971–74; Partner, Clintons, 1975–77; Solicitor's Office, Post Office, 1977; British Telecommunications: Solicitor's Office, 1981; Head, Privatisation Div., 1982–84; Head, M&A Div., 1984–85; Dir, Commercial Dept, 1985–89; Solicitor, 1989–94; Chief Legal Adviser, 1989–99; Secretary, 1994–2002; Mem. Exec. Cttee, 1996–2002; Gp Commercial Dir, 1999–2002. Trustee, BT Pension Scheme, 1994–2002. Chm., BT Telecomunicaciones SA, 2001–02; Director: Vio (Worldwide) Ltd, 1998–2001; Airtel SA, 1999–2001; Radware Inc., 2009–10; Sen. non-exec. Dir, ECI Telecom Inc., 2002–07. Chm., Shalom Nursery Ltd, 2007–09. Dir, Centre for Dispute Resolution, 1995–2000. Chm., Green Aid, 2004–. Trustee: Nightingale Hammerson (formerly Nightingale House), 2003–; Refugee Action Kingston, 2013–. Voluntary Advr, CAB, 2002–. *Recreations:* music (playing and composing), walking, reading, theatre, football. *Address:* PO Box 771, Edgware HA8 4QW. *T:* 07447 066569.

GREEN, Rt Hon. Damian (Howard); PC 2012; MP (C) Ashford, since 1997; *b* 17 Jan. 1956; *s* of Howard and late Audrey Green; *m* 1988, Alicia Collinson; two *d*. *Educ:* Reading Sch.; Balliol Coll., Oxford (MA 1st cl. Hons. PPE). Producer, BBC Financial Unit, 1980–82; Business Producer, Channel 4 News, 1982–84; Business News Ed., The Times, 1984–85; Business Ed., Channel 4 News, 1985–87; Presenter and City Ed., Business Daily prog., Channel 4, 1987–92; Prime Minister's Policy Unit, 1992–94; Public Affairs Advr, 1994–97. Opposition spokesman: on employment and higher educn; 1998–99; on the envmt, 1999–2001; Shadow Educn Sec., 2001–03; Shadow Transport Sec., 2003–04; Shadow Minister for Immigration, 2005–10; Minister of State: (Minister for Immigration), Home Office, 2010–12; (Minister for Policing, Criminal Justice and Victims), Home Office and MoJ, 2012–14. Chairman: European Mainstream Gp, 2014–; All-Party BBC Gp. Contested (C) Brent E, 1992. Trustee, Communities Develt Foundn, 1997–2001; Vice-Chm., John Smith Meml Trust, 2004–10. *Publications:* ITN Budget Factbook, annually 1984–86; A Better BBC, 1990; Communities in the Countryside, 1995; The Four Failures of the New Deal, 1998; Better Learning, 2002; More Than Markets, 2003; (with David Davis) Controlling Economic Migration, 2006. *Recreations:* cricket, football, opera, cinema. *Address:* House of Commons, SW1A 0AA. *T:* (020) 7219 3000.

GREEN, Sir David; *see* Green, Sir G. D.

GREEN, David Charles, CBE 2001; *b* 3 June 1943; *s* of Phillip and Eileen Green; *m* 1969, Anne Patricia Ward; one *s* one *d*. *Educ:* Latymer Upper Sch. Exec. Officer, Traders Road Transport Assoc., 1966–71; Freight Transport Association: Regl Controller, 1971–87; Exec. Dir, 1987–93; Dir-Gen., 1993–2000; Exec. Vice-Pres., 2001–03. Pres., Internat. Road Transport Union, 1995–2001. *Publications:* numerous articles and reports on freight transport and logistics. *Recreations:* golf, cricket, modern political history.

GREEN, David George, PhD; Director, Civitas: Institute for the Study of Civil Society, since 2000; *b* 24 Jan. 1951; *s* of George Green and Kathleen Mary (*née* Ellis); *m* 1980, Catherine Walker; one *s* one *d*. *Educ:* Newcastle upon Tyne Univ. (BA Hons 1973; PhD 1980). Pt-time Lectr, Newcastle upon Tyne Poly., 1974–81; Res. Fellow, ANU, 1981–83; Res. Fellow, 1984–86, Dir, Health and Welfare Unit, 1986–2000, Inst. of Economic Affairs. Mem. (Lab), Newcastle upon Tyne CC, 1975–81. *Publications:* Power and Party in an English City, 1981; Mutual Aid or Welfare State, 1984; Working Class Patients and the Medical Establishment, 1985; Challenge to the NHS, 1986; The New Right, 1987; Everyone a Private Patient, 1988; Reinventing Civil Society, 1993; Community without Politics, 1996; From Welfare State to Civil Society, 1996; Benefit Dependency, 1998; An End to Welfare Rights, 1999; Delay, Denial and Dilution, 2000; Stakeholder Health Insurance, 2000; Health Care in France and Germany, 2001; Crime and Civil Society, 2005; We're (Nearly) All Victims Now!, 2007; Individualists Who Co-operate, 2009; Prosperity with Principles, 2010; The Demise of the Free State, 2014. *Recreation:* walking. *Address:* Civitas, 55 Tufton Street, Westminster, SW1P 3QL.

GREEN, Prof. David Headley, AM 2006; FRS 1991; FAA; Director, Research School of Earth Sciences, Australian National University, 1994–2001, now Professor Emeritus; Honorary Research Professor, University of Tasmania, since 2008; *b* 29 Feb. 1936; *s* of Ronald Horace Green and Josephine May Headley; *m* 1959, Helen Mary McIntyre; three *s* three *d*. *Educ:* Univ. of Tasmania (BSc Hons 1957; MSc 1959; DSc 1988); Univ. of Cambridge (PhD 1962). FAA 1974; Fellow, Aust. Inst. of Mining and Metallurgy, 1987. Geologist, Bureau of Mineral Resources, Geology and Geophysics, Canberra, 1957–59; Postgrad. Scholarship, Royal Commn for Exhibn of 1851, 1959–62; Research School of Earth Sciences, Australian National University: Res. Fellow, 1962–65; Fellow, 1965–68; Sen. Fellow, 1968–74; Professorial Fellow, 1974–76; Prof. of Geology, Univ. of Tasmania, 1977–93. Chief Science Advr, Dept of Arts, Sport, Envmt, Tourism and Territories, 1991–93. Hallimond Lect., Mineralogical Soc., 1996. For. Mem., Russian Acad. of Scis, 2003. Fellow: Amer. Geophysical Union, 2004; Mineralogical Soc., 2004. Hon. Fellow: Eur. Union of Geoscis, 1985; Geol Soc. of America, 1986. Hon. DLitt Tasmania, 1994. Edgeworth David Medal, Royal Soc., NSW, 1968; Stillwell Medal, Geol Soc. of Australia, 1977; Mawson Medal, 1982, Jaeger Medal, 1990, Aust. Acad. of Sci.; A. G. Werner Medaille, Deutsche Mineralogische Ges., 1998; Murchison Medal, Geol Soc., 2000; Humboldt Research Prize, 2001; Centenary Medal (Australia), 2002; Internat. Gold Medal, Geol Soc. of Japan, 2007; Medal, Internat. Mineralogical Assoc., 2012. *Publications:* numerous articles in fields of experimental petrology and geochemistry, in learned jls. *Recreation:* music. *Address:* School of Earth Sciences, University of Tasmania, Private Bag 79, Hobart, Tas 7001, Australia. *T:* (3) 62262814. *E:* david.h.green@utas.edu.au.

GREEN, David John Mark, CB 2011; QC 2000; Director, Serious Fraud Office, since 2012; *b* 8 March 1954; *s* of John Geoffrey Green and Margaret Rowena Green (*née* Millican); *m* 1980, Kate Sharkey; one *s* two *d*. *Educ:* Christ's Hosp., Horsham; St Catharine's Coll., Cambridge (MA Hons). Defence Intelligence Staff, MoD, 1975–78; called to the Bar, Inner Temple, 1979, Bencher, 2008; practising barrister, 1979–2004, 2011–12; an Asst Recorder, 1995–2000; Recorder, 2000–; Director: Revenue and Customs (formerly Customs and Excise) Prosecutions Office, 2004–10; Central Fraud Gp, CPS, 2010–11. Liveryman, Co. of Gardeners, 2000– (Mem., Ct of Assts, 2007–). *Recreations:* walking, gardening, cooking. *Address:* Serious Fraud Office, 2–4 Cockspur Street, SW1Y 5BS. *Club:* Garrick.
See also G. S. Green.

GREEN, Prof. David Mino Allen; Vice Chancellor and Chief Executive, and Professor of Economics, University of Worcester (formerly University College Worcester), since 2003; *b* 12 Aug. 1952; *s* of Prof. Mino Green, *qv*; *m* 1999, Catherine Nicole Mortimore; two *d*. *Educ:* Westminster Sch.; St John's Coll., Cambridge (MA, BA Econs 1973). Res./Campaigns Officer, Shelter (Scotland), 1973–74; Founder, Welfare Rights Service, Harlow DC, Essex, 1975–77; Economist, Imres Ltd, 1977–79; South Bank Polytechnic, then South Bank University: Lectr, 1979–84; Sen. Lectr, 1984–89; Principal Lectr and Hd of Econs, 1989–94; Jt Hd of Sch., Business Sch., 1994–98; Prof. of Econs, and Dean of Leeds Business Sch., Leeds Metropolitan Univ., 1998–2001; Pro Vice Chancellor, Thames Valley Univ., 2001–02. Bd Mem., Teaching and Develt Agency for Schs, 2006–12; Mem., Adv. Cttee on Degree Awarding Powers, QAA, 2010–; Chm., Univs W Midlands (formerly W Midlands Higher Educn Assoc.), 2010–11). Chm., Worcester Alliance, 2005–; Member, Board: Worcester Cathedral Council, 2010–; Worcs Local Econ. Partnership, 2011–12. Trustee, Worcester Warriors RFC Community Foundn, 2011–. Pride of Worcs award, Worcs Ambassadors, 2006. *Publications:* Banking and Financial Stability in Central Europe, 2002; contrib. articles to econ. and socio-econ. learned jls; contrib. articles on higher educn policy and issues to UK and US press and broadcast media. *Recreations:* family life, cooking, cricket, tennis, reading, travelling, ski-ing. *Address:* Vice Chancellor's Office, University of Worcester, St John's Campus, Henwick Grove, Worcester WR2 6AJ. *T:* (01905) 855123, *Fax:* (01905) 424638. *E:* vc@worc.ac.uk. *Clubs:* Hurlingham; Worcestershire County Cricket (Mem. Bd, 2010–).

GREEN, Prof. Diana Margaret, (Mrs J. W. Davy), CBE 2007; PhD; DL; leadership, organisational development and change management consultant; Founder and Director, Diana Green Consultancy Ltd, 2008–12; *b* 10 April 1943; *d* of Charles Edward Harris and Joan Harris (*née* Beresford); *m* 1st, 1967, Neville A. Green (marr. diss. 1979); 2nd, 2011, John William Davy. *Educ:* South Park High Sch. for Girls, Lincoln; Reading Univ.; Queen Mary Coll., London (BSc Econ.); London Sch. of Econs (PhD Econ. 1976). HM CS, 1969–76; Lectr, Sen. Lectr and Actg Hd, Dept of Politics and Govt, City of London Poly., 1976–83; University of Central England: Hd of Dept, 1984–87; Asst Dir, 1987–92; Pro Vice-Chancellor, 1992–98; Vice-Chancellor, Sheffield Hallam Univ., 1998–2007. Consultant (part-time), DTI, 1976–81. Key Associate: Leadership Foundn for Higher Educn, 2008–11 (Mem., 2003–07); Active Human Capital Ltd, 2008–11. Member: Quality Assessment Cttee, HEFCE, 1992–96; Higher Educn Innovation Fund Expert Gp, HEFCE/DTI, 2001–; Better Regulation Stakeholder Gp, DfES, 2003–; Chm., SRHE, 1998–99. Member: Black Country Develt Corp., 1992–94; Alexandra NHS Healthcare Trust, 1996–98. Member: W Midlands Regl Council, CBI, 1994–98; W Midlands Council, IoD, 2008–12; Birmingham Chamber of Commerce and Industry, 2008–. Founder Dir, Midlands Excellence, 1996–99; Director: Phoenix Sports UK, 1997–2000; Sheffield TEC, 1998–2001; Sheffield Industrial Mus. Trust, 1998–2002; Sheffield First for Investment, 1999–2002; Sheffield One, 2000–07; UUK, 2001–07; Creative Sheffield, 2006–07; Centre for Cities, 2006–09; non-exec. Dir, Mid Staffordshire NHS Foundn Trust, 2009–11. Trustee: Sheffield Galls and Museums Trust, 2000–08; AGORA, Forum for Culture and Educn, 2007–08; Flying Scholarships for Disabled People Trust, 2007–12; Kings World Trust for Children, 2013–. Hon. Co. of Air Pilots (formerly GAPAN): Trustee, Air Safety Trust, 2006–13; Dir, 9 Warwick Court Ltd, 2009–; Chm., Envmt Cttee, 2010–13. Former Mem. Council, All Party Parly Univ. Gp (now Hon. Mem.). Member: E Surrey Business Club, 2012– (Mem. Cttee, 2014–); Limpsfield Common Local Cttee, NT London and SE Region, 2014–. FRSA. Freeman, City of London, 1998; Freeman, 2005, Liveryman, 2008, GAPAN (Mem., Court of Assts, 2009–15); Freeman, Guild of Educators, 2008–11. DL W Midlands, 2008. *Publications:* articles, chapters, books and reports on industrial change and quality in higher education; contrib. to THES; articles on aspects of aviation in Guild News. *Recreations:* flying light aircraft, music, art, theatre.

GREEN, Ven. Duncan Jamie; Archdeacon of Northolt, since 2013; *b* 30 April 1952; *m* 1975, Janet Mary Orpin; one *s* two *d*. *Educ:* Salisbury and Wells Theol Coll. Sales Dir, Agricultural Engrg firm, Surrey; ordained deacon, 1984, priest, 1985; Asst Curate, Holy Cross, Uckfield, 1984–87; Diocesan Youth Officer, Dio. of Chelmsford, 1987–96; Warden and Chaplain, St Mark's Coll. Res. Youth Centre, Audley End, 1993–96; Team Rector, 1996–2007, Rural Dean, 2000–07, Saffron Walden; C of E Olympic and Paralympic Co-ordinator, 2007–13 (seconded to LOCOG as Faith Advr and Hd, Multi-Chaplaincy Services). Hon. Canon, Chelmsford Cath., 2003–13. *Address:* c/o Willesden Area Office, London Diocesan House, 36 Causton Street, SW1P 4AU. *T:* (020) 7932 1275.

GREEN, Edward Maurice; Director, Green & Frederick Ltd, since 1998; Trustee, National Galleries of Scotland, since 2014; *b* London, 19 Aug. 1952; *s* of late Joseph Green and of Toby Green (later Lawson); *m* 1994, (Elizabeth) Maryla (Helen) Chojecki; one *s*. *Educ:* Haberdashers' Aske's Sch.; Univ. of Strathclyde (BA Hotel and Catering Mgt). Collingwood of Conduit St, 1975–83, Dir, 1977–83; Man. Dir, Mappin & Webb Ltd, 1985–91; Dep. Chm., Garrard the Crown Jewellers, 1986–91; Pres., Asprey United States, 1991–95. FGA 1977 (Diamond Grading Assoc. 1978). *Recreations:* ski-ing, opera, family, art, antiques. *Address:* Innerwick, Ellersly Road, Murrayfield, Edinburgh EH12 6HZ. *T:* (office) (020) 3544 6440. *E:* edwardmgreen@me.com. *Club:* New (Edinburgh).

GREEN, Rev. Canon Dr (Edward) Michael (Bankes); Member, Associate Staff, Wycliffe Hall, Oxford, since 2005 (Senior Research Fellow, 1997–2005; Hon. Fellow); Chaplain and Tutor, Oxford Centre for Christian Apologetics, 2008–10; *b* 20 Aug. 1930; British; *m* 1957, Rosemary Wake (*née* Storr); two *s* two *d*. *Educ:* Clifton Coll.; Oxford and Cambridge Univs. BD Cantab 1966. Exeter Coll., Oxford, 1949–53 (1st cl. Lit. Hum.); Royal Artillery (Lieut, A/Adjt), 1953–55; Queens' Coll., Cambridge, 1955–57 (1st cl. Theol. Tripos Pt III; Carus Greek Testament Prize; Fencing Blue), and Ridley Hall Theol Coll., 1955–57; Curate, Holy Trinity, Eastbourne, 1957–60; Lectr, London Coll. of Divinity, 1960–69; Principal, St John's Coll., Nottingham (until July 1970, London Coll. of Divinity), 1969–75; Canon Theologian of Coventry, 1970–76, Canon Theologian Emeritus, 1978–; Rector of St Aldates, Oxford, 1975–87 (with Holy Trinity, Oxford, 1975–82 and with St Matthew, 1982–87); Prof. of Evangelism at Regent Coll., Vancouver, Univ. of BC, 1987–92; Co-Rector, Holy Trinity, Raleigh, N Carolina, 2005–08. Member: Doctrine Commission of the Church, 1968–77; Church Unity Commn, 1974–. Archbishops' Advr in Evangelism, 1992–2001; leader of missions, overseas and in UK. Hon. DD Toronto, 1992; DD Lambeth, 1996. *Publications:* Called to Serve, 1964; Choose Freedom, 1965; The Meaning of Salvation, 1965; Man Alive, 1967; Runaway World, 1968; Commentary on 2 Peter and Jude, 1968; Evangelism in the Early Church, 1970; Jesus Spells Freedom, 1972; New Life, New Lifestyle, 1973; I Believe in the Holy Spirit, 1975, new edn 1985; You Must Be Joking, 1976; (ed) The Truth of God Incarnate, 1977; Why Bother With Jesus?, 1979; Evangelism—Now and Then, 1979; What is Christianity?, 1981; I Believe in Satan's Downfall, 1981; The Day Death Died, 1982; To Corinth with Love, 1982; World on the Run, 1983; Freed to Serve, 1983; The Empty Cross of Jesus, 1984; Come Follow Me, 1984; Lift Off to Faith, 1985; Baptism, 1987; Matthew for Today, 1988; Ten Myths about Christianity, 1988; Evangelism Through the Local Church, 1990; Reflections from the Lions Den, 1990; Who is this Jesus?, 1991; My God, 1992; On Your Knees, 1992; Good News and How to Share It, 1993; Acts for Today, 1993; (with Alister McGrath) Springboard for Faith, 1993; (with Paul Stevens) New Testament Spirituality, 1994; How Can I Lead a Friend to Christ?, 1995; Critical Choices, 1995; Strange Intelligence, 1997; Evangelism for Amateurs, 1998; After Alpha, 1998; Bible Reading for Amateurs, 1999; Churchgoing for Amateurs, 2000; The Message of Matthew, 2000; Asian Tigers for Christ, 2001; Adventure of Faith (autobiog.), 2001; But don't all religions lead to God?, 2002; Sharing your faith with a friend, 2002; Thirty Years that changed the world, 2002; The Books the Church Suppressed, 2005; Lies, Lies, Lies!, 2009; Compelled by Joy, 2011; Jesus for Sceptics, 2013; When God Breaks In, 2014; contribs to various jls. *Recreations:* family, countryside pursuits, squash, fly fishing. *Address:* Hilltop, Lodge Hill, Abingdon, Oxon OX14 2JD. *T:* (01865) 682350. *E:* embgreen@gmail.com.

GREEN, Sir Edward (Patrick) Lycett, 6th Bt *cr* 1886, of Wakefield, Yorkshire and Ken Hill, Norfolk; *b* 14 Oct. 1950; *s* of late Richard David Rafe Lycett Green and (Marie) Patricia (*née* Maguire); *S* cousin, 2003; *m* 1st, 1971, Cordelia Sarah (marr. diss. 1975), *d* of C. B. Stretton Wilson; 2nd, 1977, Annette Patricia Josephine, *d* of O. P. J. Rochfort; two *d*. *Educ:* Stowe. *Heir: uncle* Rupert William Lycett Green [*b* 24 Oct. 1938; *m* 1963, Candida Betjeman (writer, as Candida Lycett Green; *d* 2014); two *s* three *d*].

GREEN, Felicity, (Mrs Geoffrey Hill), OBE 2012; fashion journalist; *b* Dagenham, 6 June 1926; *d* of Emanuel and Annie Green; *m* 1952, Geoffrey Hill. *Educ:* Clarks Coll., Ilford; Pitmans Coll., Forest Gate (Shorthand Cert.). Fashion Ed., Woman and Beauty mag., 1951–53; Exec. Ed., and est. Press and PR dept, Crawfords, London, 1953–55; Mirror Group Newspapers, 1955–77: Associate Ed., Women's Ed., and Fashion Ed., Women's Sunday Mirror, later Sunday Pictorial, 1955–60; Associate Ed., Women's Ed., and Fashion Ed., Daily Mirror, 1960–73; Press and Publicity Dir, 1973–77; Man. Dir, Vidal Sassoon Europe, and Exec. Vice Pres., Vidal Sassoon Internat., 1977–79; Associate Ed., and consultant, Daily Express, 1980–84; Contributing Ed., Working Woman mag., 1984–87; Sen. Lectr, Fashion Journalism and Promotion, BA degree course, St Martin's Sch. of Art, London, 1984–90; Editl and Mktg Consultant, Daily Telegraph Gp, 1986–96; Creative Consultant, Redwood Gp, 1987–2013 (incl. Launch Ed., Marks & Spencer Mag.); Editl Consultant, Express Newspapers, 1996–99; Editl and Launch Consultant, ONdigital Ind. Television listings mag., ON7, 1998–2001. Mem. Bd, Nat. Film Finance Corp., 1972–77. Member: Cttee, Media Soc.; Internat. Women's Forum, 1995–; BSME, 2002–03. Mem. Cttee, Hugh Cudlipp Trust, 2004–14. Women's Page Journalist of Year, Nat. Press Awards, Internat. Publishing Corp., 1970; Mark Boxer Award for Outstanding Contribn to Journalism, BSME, 1991; Press Gazette Hall of Fame, 2005. *Publications:* (ed jtly) Colour by Quant, 1984; (ed jtly) Jean Muir: beyond fashion, 2007. *Recreations:* walking, theatre, cinema, lecturing on fashion at Central St Martins. *Address:* 78 Nottingham Terrace, York Gate, NW1 4QE. *T:* (020) 7486 3405.

GREEN, Dr Frank Alan, CEng, FIMMM; Principal, Charing Green Associates, since 1983; non-executive Director: 2 GC Active Management Ltd, since 2000; Somerset Health Authority, 2001–02; *b* 29 Oct. 1931; *s* of Frank Green and Winifred Hilda (*née* Payne); *m* 1957, Pauline Eleanor Tayler (*d* 2014); one *s* one *d* (and one *d* decd). *Educ:* Mercers' Sch., London; Univ. of London (BSc, PhD); Univ. of Exeter (MA 2002). CEng 1980; FIMMM (FIM 1978). UKAEA, 1956–57; various appts, Glacier Metal Co. Ltd (Associated Engrg Gp), 1957–65; Technical Dir, Alta Fricción SA, Mexico City, 1965–68; Manufg Dir, Stewart Warner Corp., 1968–72; Marketing Develt Manager, Calor Gp, 1972–74; Manufg Dir, 1974–77, Man. Dir, 1977–81, British Twin Disc Ltd; Industrial Advr (Under-Sec.), DTI, 1981–84. Director: Gen. Technology Systems (Scandinavia), 1989–91; Gen. Technology Systems (Portuguesa), 1989–91; Principal Consultant, General Technology Systems Ltd, 1984–90. Dir, Anglo-Mexican Chamber of Commerce, Mexico City, 1966–68. Member of Council: Inst. of Metals, 1990–91; Inst. of Materials, 1992–94; Chm., W of England Metals and Materials Assoc., 1999–2000. BUniv Surrey, 2011. *Publications:* contrib. technical, medical ethical, historical and managerial books and jls in UK and Mexico. *Recreations:* military history, rough walking. *Address:* Lynedale, Green Lane, Milford, Godalming, Surrey GU8 5BG.

GREEN, Prof. Gary George Reginald, DPhil; Director, York Neuroimaging Centre and Professor of Neuroimaging, since 2004, and Co-Director, Centre for Hyperpolarisation in Magnetic Resonance, since 2013, University of York; *b* 27 May 1951; *s* of Harry Clifford Green and Iris Ellen Green (*née* Asser); *m* 1981, Rose Hilton; one *s* one *d*. *Educ:* Burnt Mill Comp. Sch., Harlow; Hertford Coll., Oxford (MA 1979; DPhil 1976; BM BCh 1979). E. P. Abrahams Fellow, Hertford Coll., Oxford, 1978–80; University of Newcastle upon Tyne: Lectr, 1980–95; Reader, 1995–2004; Dir, Inst. of Neuroscience, 2003–04. Chm., Am Systems Ltd, 1987–95; Dir, YNI Ltd, 2004–15. Mem. Court, RCS, 1994–2000. Vice-Chm., Wellcome Trust Neurosci. and Mental Health Cttee, 2004 (Mem., 2000–04). Trustee, Jesmond Swimming Pool, 2002–04. *Publications:* articles on neurosci., non-linear dynamics, child language and neurological problems in learned jls. *Recreations:* making my wife laugh, gardening, swimming. *Address:* Wanwood House, Front Street, Benton, Newcastle upon Tyne NE7 7XE. *T:* (01904) 435346, *Fax:* (01904) 435356. *E:* gary.green@ynic.york.ac.uk.

GREEN, Geoffrey Stephen; Head of Asia, Ashurst LLP, since 2009; *b* 3 Sept. 1949; *s* of John Geoffrey Green and Margaret Rowena Green (*née* Millican); *m* 1982, Sarah Charlton Chesshire; three *s*. *Educ:* Forest Sch.; St Catharine's Coll., Cambridge (MA). Admitted Solicitor, 1975. Ashurst Morris Crisp, later Ashurst LLP: Solicitor, 1975–; Partner, 1983–; Sen. Partner, 1998–2008. *Recreations:* golf, tennis, riding. *Address:* Ashurst Hong Kong, 11/F Jardine House, 1 Connaught Place, Central, Hong Kong. *T:* 28468989.

See also D. J. M. Green.

GREEN, Gerard Nicholas Valentine; Chairman, HCP Infrastructure UK Ltd (formerly Health Care Projects Ltd) 2010–12 (Executive Director, 1997; Chief Executive, 1999–2010); *b* 6 Aug. 1950; *s* of James Arnold Green and Margarathe Ella Green; *m* 1977, Maralyn Ann Ranger; one *s* one *d*. *Educ:* Highgate Sch.; University Coll., London (BA); Univ. of Warwick (MA); Birkbeck Coll., London (MA). AHSM. Nat. admin. trainee, 1974–75; Dep. Hosp. Sec., St George's Hosp., SW17, 1975–77; Asst Sector Administrator, Cane Hill Hosp., Surrey, 1977–79; Sector Administrator, Farnborough Hosp., Kent, 1979–82; Administrator, KCH, 1982–84; Chief Exec. Officer, Tabuk Military Hosp., Saudi Arabia, 1984–87; Dist Gen. Man., Bromley HA, 1987–89; Regl Gen. Man., SE Thames RHA, 1989–94; Chief Exec., Royal Hosps NHS Trust, 1994–97. Dir, HCP (Defence Projects) Ltd, 2001–08. Non-exec. Dir, Meridian Hosp. Co., 2000–05; Chairman: Derby Healthcare plc, 2003–06; Central Nottinghamshire Hosps plc, 2005–07; HCP (Canada) Ltd, 2006–12; ISL Health (Victoria) Ltd, 2008–11; ISL Health (Fort St John), 2009–11. Mem., UKCC, 1993–98. FRSA 1989. *Recreations:* travel, reading, wine. *Club:* Reform.

GREEN, Sir (Gregory) David, KCMG 2004 (CMG 1999); Director-General, British Council, 1999–2007; *b* 2 Dec. 1948; *s* of Thomas Dixon Green and Mary Mabella Green (*née* Walley); *m* 1977, Corinne Butler; three *d*. *Educ:* Leys Sch., Cambridge; Keswick Hall Coll. of Educn, Norwich (Cert Ed); Trinity Hall, Cambridge (BEd). Volunteer, VSO, Pakistan, 1967–68; teaching, Conisborough and Rotherham, 1972–76; Dir, Children's Relief Internat., 1976–79; Save the Children Fund: Staff Develt and Trng Officer, 1979; Dep. Dir of Personnel, 1982; Dir of Personnel, 1983–88; Dep. Dir-Gen., 1988–90; Dir, VSO, 1990–99. Dir and Council Mem., Council for Colony Holidays for School-children, 1970–80; Mem. Council, VSO, 2000–08. Member: Laurence Olivier Awards Panel, 1984–85; Council, English Stage Co., 2005–; Bd, Finnish Inst., 2015–. Chm., Prince's Sch. of Traditional Arts, 2008–. Governor: Univ. of the Arts London, 2007–; ESU, 2008–10. Chair: Dartington Hall Trust, 2008–15; Dash Arts, 2010–; Soumik Datta Arts, 2012–. FRGS 1991. Freeman, City of London, 2006. Freeman, City of Freetown, Sierra Leone, 2004. Hon. FCT 2006. *Publications:* Chorus, 1977; Drawing on Experience, 2011. *Recreations:* theatre, music, painting, international development, cultural relations.

GREEN, Hon. Sir Guy (Stephen Montague), AC 1994; KBE 1982; CVO 2000; Governor of Tasmania, 1995–2003; *b* 26 July 1937; *s* of Clement Francis Montague Green and Beryl Margaret Jenour Green; *m* 1963, Rosslyn Mary Marshall; two *s* two *d*. *Educ:* Launceston Church Grammar Sch.; Univ. of Tasmania. Alfred Houston Schol. (Philosophy) 1958; LLB (Hons) 1960. Admitted to Bar of Tasmania, 1960; Partner, Ritchie & Parker Alfred Green & Co. (Launceston), 1963–71; Magistrate 1971–73; Chief Justice of Tasmania, 1973–95; University of Tasmania: Mem., Faculty of Law, 1974–85; Chancellor, 1985–95. Lieut-Gov., Tasmania, 1982–95; Adminr, Commonwealth of Australia, May–Aug. 2003. Pres., Tasmanian Bar Assoc., 1968–70; Chm., Council of Law Reporting, 1978–85; Dep. Chm., Australian Inst. of Judicial Admin, 1986–88. Chm., Tasmanian Cttee, Duke of Edinburgh's Award Scheme in Australia, 1975–80; Dir, Winston Churchill Meml Trust, 1975–85 (Dep. Nat. Chm., 1980–85; Chm. Tasmanian Regional Cttee, 1975–80); Chairman: Bd, Ten Days on the Island, 2003–; Trustees, Tasmanian Mus. and Art Gall., 2004–; Tim Hawkins Meml Scholarship Cttee, 2004–. Chm., Internat. Antarctic Inst., 2006– (Chm. Steering Cttee, 2004–06). Member: Bd, Menzies Foundn, 2005–12 (Chm., 2008–12); Menzies Res. Inst., 2005–12; Trustee and Mem., Foundn Council, Constitution Educn Fund Australia, 2004–08. Advr, Arts and Culture Centre, Beijing Normal Univ./Hong Kong Baptist Univ. United Internat. Coll., 2010–; Hon. Pres., Tianjin Modern Vocational Technol. Coll., China, 2012–. Nat. Pres., Order of Australia Assoc., 2004–07. St John Ambulance, Australia: Pres., Tasmanian Council, 1984–92; Priory Exec. Officer, 1984–91; Chancellor, 1991–95; Dep. Prior, 1995–2003. Hon. Antarctic Ambassador for Tasmania, 2005–15. Hon. Prof., Antarctic Climate and Ecosystems Co-operative Res. Centre, Univ. of Tasmania, 2005–15. Hon. LLD Tasmania, 1996. KStJ 1985. *Address:* 13 Marine Terrace, Battery Point, Hobart, Tas 7004, Australia. *Club:* Tasmanian (Hobart).

GREEN, Harriet, OBE 2010; Vice President and General Manager, IBM, since 2015; *b* 12 Dec. 1961; *d* of late Dermot Green and of Nerys Allen; *m* 2004, Graham Clarkson; two step *c*. *Educ:* Univ. of London (BA Hons Medieval Hist. 1983); London Sch. of Econs (Business Psychol. 1985); Harvard Business Sch.; Aspen Inst.; Ashridge Mgt Coll. Man. Dir, Macro Gp, 1985–94; Arrow Electronics Inc.: Vice Pres., Eur. Mktg, 1994–96; Pres., Arrow N Europe and Africa, and Corp. Vice Pres., 1996–2000; Pres., Arrow CMS, N America, 2000–01; Hd, Global Strategy and New Business Develt, 2002; Pres., Asia Pacific, 2002–06; CEO, Premier Farnell plc, 2006–12; CEO, Thomas Cook Gp plc, 2012–14. Non-executive Director: Emerson, 2008–; BAE Systems, 2010–. Former Mem., Young Presidents Assoc. *Recreations:* yoga, reading, theatre, hiking, horse-riding, cycling.

GREEN, Henrietta-Jane; food writer, since 1977; broadcaster; company director, since 1987; food consultant, since 1989; *b* 27 Oct. 1948; *d* of Aubrey and Valerie Green. *Educ:* Sarum Hall Prep. Sch.; Queen's Coll., Harley St; Royal Acad. of Dramatic Art (Dip. Stage Mgt). Free-lance journalist, broadcaster and consultant; Consultancy Dir, Henrietta Green Associates, 2012–. Founder, FoodLoversBritain.com, and organiser of FoodLovers' Fairs; involved with the introduction of Farmers' Markets in the UK and develt of local and regl strategy for Waitrose; launched consumer mkt at Borough Mkt. Mem., London Food Bd, 2004–08; Partner, Independent Hotel Show (annual), 2012–. Trustee, Jane Grigson Trust. *Publications:* Fine Flavoured Food, 1978; The Marinade Cookbook, 1978; RAC Food Routes, 1988; 10 Minute Cuisine, 1991; The Festive Food of England, 1991; Henrietta Green's New Country Kitchen, 1992; A Glorious Harvest, 1994; Fresh From the Garden, 1994; Henrietta Green's Food Lovers' Guide to Britain, 1994, 1996; British Food Finds, 1997; The Food Lovers' Christmas, 1997; Henrietta's Home Cooking, 1997; Recipes from an English Country Garden, 1998; Henrietta Green's Farmers' Market Cookbook, 2001. *Recreations:* walking, talking, shopping, playing with my dog, eating, movies, looking at gardens, gardening, looking at buildings, bird-watching. *Address:* 17 Hopefield Avenue, NW6 6LJ. *T:* (020) 8969 0866. *Club:* Groucho.

GREEN, Ven. John, CB 2010; Archdeacon of Coventry, and Archdeacon Pastor, Diocese of Coventry, since 2012; Associate Minister, St Mary Magdalen's, Coventry, since 2014; *b* 14 Aug. 1953; *s* of Albert Frederick and Lilian Green; *m* 1977, Janette Silvester; two *s*. *Educ:* S W Ham Co. Tech. Sch.; NE London Poly. (Grad. Inst. Physics); Lincoln Theol Coll. (BCS 1983). Project engr, Thorn Lighting Ltd, 1974–80 (Sen. Engr, 1977–80); ordained deacon 1983, priest 1984; Curate: St Michael and All Angels, W Watford, 1983–86; St Stephen's, St Albans, 1986–91; Chaplain, RN, 1991–2010: HMS Sultan, 1991–92; 3rd Destroyer Sqdn, 1992–93; HM Naval Base, Portsmouth, 1993–94; HMS Excellent, 1994–95; Minor Warfare

Vessel Flotilla, 1996–98; Staff Chaplain to Chaplain of the Fleet, 1998–2001; HMS Ark Royal, 2001–03; HMS Collingwood, 2003–06; Dir Gen., Naval Chaplaincy Service, Chaplain of the Fleet and Archdeacon for RN, 2006–10. Chair, Coventry and Warks Br., RSCM, 2014–. QHC 2006–10. *Recreations:* music, inland waterways and boating, photography. *Address:* c/o Cathedral and Diocesan Office, 1 Hill Top, Coventry CV1 5AB. *E:* john.green@covcofe.org.

GREEN, John Edward, PhD; FREng, FRAeS, FAIAA; Consultant and Chief Scientist to Aircraft Research Association Ltd, 1995–2013 (Chief Executive, 1988–95); *b* 26 Aug. 1937; *s* of John Green and Ellen Green (*née* O'Dowd); *m* 1959, Gillian (*née* Jackson); one *s* one *d*. *Educ:* Birkenhead Inst. Grammar Sch.; St John's Coll., Cambridge (Scholar; BA 1959; MA 1963; PhD 1966). CEng 1972; FRAeS 1978. Student Apprentice, Bristol Aircraft Ltd, 1956; De Havilland Engine Co., 1959–61; Royal Aircraft Establishment, 1964–81: Head of Transonic/Supersonic Wind Tunnel Div., 1971; Head of Propulsion Div., 1973; Head of Noise Div., 1974; Head of Aerodynamics Dept, 1978–81; Dir, Project Time and Cost Analysis, MoD (PE), 1981–84; Minister-Counsellor Defence Equipment, and Dep. Head of British Defence Staff, Washington, 1984–85; Dep. Dir (Aircraft), RAE, 1985–87. Vis. Prof., Cranfield Univ., 1996–2004. President: Internat. Council of the Aeronautical Scis, 1996–98 (Mem. Council, 1986–2000; Chm., Prog. Cttee, 1992–96; Life Mem., 2002; Hon. Fellow, 2008); RAeS, 1996–97 (Mem. Council, 1986–2000; Vice Pres., 1992–95; Hon. Treas., 1992–96); Mem. Council, AIRTO, 1988–95. Corresp., L'Académie de l'Air et de l'Espace, 2010. Mem. Court, Cranfield Univ. (formerly Cranfield Inst. of Technol.), 1988–2008 (Mem. Council, 1995–2005). Royal Aeronautical Society: Goldstein Lectr, 1991; Busk Prize, 1992; de Havilland Lectr, 2000; Westland Prize, 2002; Templer Lectr, 2004; Lanchester Lectr, 2005; Wilbur and Orville Wright Lectr, 2006; Hodgson Prize, 2005; Gold Award, 2005; J. D. North Lectr, 2008; R. K. Pierson Lectr, 2008. FREng (FEng 1994); FAIAA 1999. Maurice Roy Medal, Internat. Council of Aeronautical Scis, 2006. *Publications:* contribs to books and learned jls, chiefly on fluid mechanics, aerodynamics and envmtl impact of aviation. *Recreations:* music, mountain walking (Munroist, 1994). *Address:* 1 Leighton Street, Woburn, Beds MK17 9PJ. *T:* (01525) 290631.

GREEN, John Louis, FCA; Chairman, Merchant John East Securities plc (formerly Merchant Securities), 2006–12; *b* 2 March 1945; *s* of Stanley and Rose Green; *m* 1972, Kathleen Whelan; three *s* one *d*. *Educ:* Merchant Taylors' Sch., Northwood; Oriel Coll., Oxford (MA). FCA 1970. Price Waterhouse & Co., 1966–69; Kleinwort Benson, 1969–70; McAnally Montgomery & Co., 1970–79; James Capel, 1979–92; HSBC Investment Bank, 1992–96, Man. Dir, HSBC-Capel UK, 1995–96; Chief Exec., James Capel Investment Mgt, 1996–98. Chairman: Principal Investment Mgt, 2000–08; Inventive Leisure plc, 2000–06; IBG plc, 2008–09; Huntress Group, 2008–09. Dir various cos, 1999–2012. *Recreations:* golf, opera, reading. *Address:* 1 Northcote, Oxshott, Surrey KT22 0HL. *T:* (01483) 282600. *Clubs:* Royal Automobile; Effingham Golf; Wisley Golf; Old Corkscrew Golf (Florida).

GREEN, Dr John Timothy; Chair: Alexander Street Press, since 2009; Astins Ltd, since 2011; *b* 1 Jan. 1944; *s* of Thomas Albert Green and Joan (*née* Chamberlain); *m* 1985, Susan Mary Shattock; one *s*. *Educ:* King Edward's Five Ways Sch., Birmingham; Queens' Coll., Cambridge (BA 1966; MA 1970; PhD Maths 1970). Queens' College, Cambridge: Bye Fellow, 1970–72; Fellow, 1972–93; Lectr in Maths, 1972–93; Dean of Coll., 1972–77; Tutor, 1977–80; Sen. Tutor, 1980–93; Life Fellow, 1993; Chief Exec., RSocMed, 1993–96; Dir, Historic Properties (London), English Heritage, 1997–98; Sec., Faculty of Medicine, 1998–2004, Chief Co-ordinating Officer, 2004–10, Imperial Coll. London. Director: S Leics Garages Ltd, 1985–95; Pennant Hotels Ltd, 1987–95; RSM Press Ltd, 1993–96; Chadwyck-Healey Ltd, 1997–99; Kennedy Inst. of Rheumatology, 1999–2010; NW London Hosps Trust, 2001–10; Imperial Coll. Bioincubator Ltd, 2004–07; MyAction Ltd, 2009–10; Careers Information Services Ltd, 2009–10; myChoice Data Systems Ltd, 2009–; Ind. Dir, 3i plc, 1996–2007. Member: CBI Professions Wkg Gp, 1995–96; London First Medicine, 1995–96. Recruitment Advr, FCO, 1992–99. Dir, Assoc. of Research Managers and Administrators, 2008–10. Trustee: Harpur Trust, Bedford, 1984–87; Project Hope, 1995–2001 (Vice-Chm., 1998–2001). Governor: Hills Rd Sixth Form Coll., Cambridge, 1993–98; Perse Sch., Cambridge, 2001–09. *Publications:* contrib. Jl Fluid Mechanics and others. *Recreations:* opera, music, fell-walking. *Address:* 40 Newton Road, Cambridge CB2 8AL.

GREEN, Katherine Anne, (Kate), OBE 2005; MP (Lab) Stretford and Urmston, since 2010; *b* 2 May 1960; *d* of Maurice Green and Jessie Craig Green (*née* Bruce); *m* 1985, Richard Duncan Mabb (marr. diss. 2006). *Educ:* Currie High Sch., Midlothian; Univ. of Edinburgh (LLB Hons 1982). Barclays Bank, 1982–97; Whitehall and Industry Gp Secondee to Home Office, 1997–99; Dir, NCOPF, 2000–04; Chief Exec., Child Poverty Action Gp, 2004–09. Member: Lord Chancellor's Adv. Cttee, City of London, 2001–09; Nat. Employment Panel, 2001–07; London Child Poverty Commn, 2006–09; Greater Manchester Poverty Commn, 2012–13. Shadow Minister: for Equalities, 2011–13; for Disabled People, 2013–15; for Women and Equalities, 2015–. Dir, Project Fresh Start, 2001–03. Trustee: Family and Parenting (formerly Nat. Family and Parenting) Inst., 2000–07 (Treas., 2006–07); Avenues Youth Project, 2000–05; Inst. for Fiscal Studies, 2004–09; Friends Provident Foundn, 2007–09; Webb Meml Trust, 2011–. JP City of London, 1993–2009. *Recreations:* theatre, swimming. *Address:* House of Commons, SW1A 0AA. *T:* (020) 7219 7162. *E:* kate.green.mp@parliament.uk.

GREEN, Rt Rev. Dr Laurence Alexander, (Laurie); Area Bishop of Bradwell, 1993–2011; Hon. Assistant Bishop, Diocese of Chichester, since 2011; *b* 26 Dec. 1945; *s* of Leonard Alexander and Laura Elizabeth Green; *m* 1969, J. Victoria Bussell; two *d*. *Educ:* King's Coll. London (BD Hons, AKC); New York Theological Seminary, NY State Univ. (STM, DMin); St Augustine's Coll., Canterbury. Curate, St Mark, Kingstanding, Birmingham, 1970–73; Vicar, St Chad, Erdington, Birmingham, 1973–83; Industrial Chaplain, British Steel Corp., 1975–83; Lectr in Urban Studies, Urban Theol. Unit, Sheffield, 1976–82; Principal, Aston Training Scheme, 1983–89; Hon. Curate, Holy Trinity, Birchfield, Handsworth, 1983–89; Team Rector, All Saints, Poplar, 1989–93; Tutor in Urban Theology, Sheffield Univ., 1989–93. Chair: Nat. Estate Churches Network, 1996–; Friends of the Poor in S India, 2007–. Episcopal Visitor, W Malling Abbey, Kent, 2011–. *Publications:* Power to the Powerless, 1987; (jtly) A Thing Called Aston (ed Todd), 1987; Let's Do Theology, 1989, (ed) rev. edn 2009 (trans. Mandarin Chinese, 2012); God in the Inner City, 1993; (jtly) God in the City, 1995; (contrib.) Urban Christ, 1997; (contrib.) Gospel from the City, 1997; (jtly) A Reader in Urban Theology, 1998; The Impact of the Global: an urban theology, 2001 (trans. Japanese, Spanish, Tamil, Portuguese); Urban Ministry and the Kingdom of God, 2003; Building Utopia, 2008; Blessed are the Poor, 2015; contrib. St George's Windsor Review. *Recreations:* folk, jazz and classical guitar, DIY. *Address:* 86 Belle Hill, Bexhill-on-Sea TN40 2AP. *E:* mail@lauriegreen.org. *W:* www.lauriegreen.org.

GREEN, Prof. Leslie, DPhil; Professor of the Philosophy of Law, University of Oxford, since 2007; Fellow of Balliol College, Oxford, since 2007; *b* Bridge of Weir, Scotland, 27 Nov. 1956; *s* of Robert Frederick Green and Elizabeth Laird Mackie; *m* 1980, Prof. Denise Réaume. *Educ:* Queen's Univ., Kingston, Ont (BA 1978); Nuffield Coll., Oxford (MPhil 1980; DPhil 1984). Darby Fellow and Tutor in Pol Theory, Lincoln Coll., Oxford, 1983–85; Prof. of Law and Philos., Osgoode Hall Law Sch., York Univ., Toronto, 1986–2006; Prof. of Law and Distinguished Fellow, Queen's Univ., Canada, 2010–. Visiting Professor: Boalt Hall Sch. of Law, Univ. of Calif, Berkeley, 1995; Sch. of Law, Univ. of Texas, Austin, 2002–06; Hauser Global Law Sch. Prog., NY Univ. Sch. of Law, 2007; Univ. of Chicago Law Sch., 2009; Vis. Fellow, Centre for Law and Philos., Columbia Law Sch., NY, 2003. Jt Ed., Oxford Studies in the Philosophy of Law. *Publications:* The Authority of the State, 1988; Law and the Community, 1989; Kelsen Revisited, 2013; articles in jls incl. Oxford Jl of Legal Studies, Legal Theory, Michigan Law Rev., NYU Law Rev., Philos. Qly, Jl of Pol Philos., Canadian Jl of Law and Jurisprudence, Osgoode Hall Law Jl, Ethics, Current Legal Problems, etc. *Recreation:* music. *Address:* Balliol College, Oxford OX1 3BJ. *T:* (01865) 277777. *E:* leslie.green@law.ox.ac.uk.

GREEN, Prof. Leslie Leonard, CBE 1989; PhD; FInstP; Professor of Experimental Physics, University of Liverpool, 1964–86, now Emeritus; Director, Daresbury Laboratory, 1981–88; *b* 30 March 1925; *s* of Leonard and Victoria Green; *m* 1952, Dr Helen Therese Morgan; one *s* one *d*. *Educ:* Alderman Newton's Sch., Leicester; King's Coll., Cambridge (MA, PhD). FInstP 1966. British Atomic Energy Proj., 1944–46; University of Liverpool: Lectr, 1948–57; Sen. Lectr, 1957–62; Reader, 1962–64; Dean, Faculty of Sciences, 1969–72; Pro-Vice-Chancellor, 1978–81. Mem., SRC Nuclear Physics Bd, 1972–75 and 1979–82. *Publications:* articles on nuclear physics in scientific jls. *Address:* Oakwood House, Eastbury, Hungerford, Berks RG17 7JP.

GREEN, Lucinda Jane, MBE 1978; three-day event rider; *b* 7 Nov. 1953; *d* of Maj.-Gen. George Erroll Prior-Palmer, CB, DSO and Lady Doreen Hersey Winifred Prior-Palmer; *m* 1981, David (marr. diss. 1992), *s* of Burrington Green, Brisbane; one *s* one *d*. *Educ:* St Mary's, Wantage; Idbury Manor, Oxon. Member of winning Junior European Team, 1971; Winner, 3 Day Events: Badminton Horse Trials Championships, 1973, 1976, 1977, 1979, 1983, 1984; Burghley, 1977, 1981; Individual European Championships, 1975, 1977; World Championship, 1982; Member: Olympic Team, Montreal, 1976, Los Angeles, 1984; European Championship Team: Luhmühlen, W Germany, 1975 (team Silver Medallist and individual Gold Medallist); Burghley, 1977 (team Gold Medallist), 1985 (team Gold Medallist), 1987 (team Gold Medallist); European Team, 1979, 1983 (team and individual Silver Medallist); Alternative Olympic Team, 1980; World Championship Team: Kentucky, 1978; Luhmühlen, W Germany, 1982 (team and individual Gold Medallist). Co-presenter, Horses, Channel 4, 1987; Commentator: BBC, Badminton, 1987–2005; BBC, Olympic Games, 1988; Channel 7, Australia, Olympic Games, 1992, 1996, 2000 and 2004; Channel 9, Australia, Olympic Games, 2012; Presenter, Rural Rides, Meridian TV, 1997 and 1998. Selector, British three-day event teams, 2002–08; cross-country coach worldwide. Editorial Consultant, Eventing, 1989–92. Contrib., various equestrian mags. *Publications:* Up, Up and Away, 1978; Four Square, 1980; Regal Realm, 1983; Cross-Country Riding, 1986, 2nd edn 1995; The Young Rider, 1993. *Recreations:* driving, ski-ing, scuba diving, travelling abroad. *Address:* The Tree House, Appleshaw, Andover SP11 9BS.

GREEN, Prof. Sir Malcolm, Kt 2007; DM; FRCP; Vice Principal, Faculty of Medicine, 1997–2006, and Head of National Heart and Lung Institute, 2001–06, Imperial College of Science, Technology and Medicine; Professor of Respiratory Medicine, Imperial College, 1998–2006, now Professor Emeritus; Consultant Physician, Royal Brompton Hospital (formerly Brompton Hospital), 1975–2006; *b* 25 Jan. 1942; *s* of late James Bisdee Malcolm Green and Frances Marjorie Lois Green; *m* 1971, Julieta Caroline Preston; two *s* two *d* (and one *d* decd). *Educ:* Charterhouse Sch. (Foundn Scholar); Trinity Coll., Oxford (Exhibnr; BA 1963; BSc 1965; MA, BM, BCh 1967; DM 1978; Hon. Fellow, 2011); St Thomas's Hosp. Med. Sch. (Scholar). FRCP 1980 (MRCP 1970). Jun. appts, St Thomas' and Brompton Hosps, 1968–71; Lectr, Dept of Medicine, St Thomas' Hosp., 1971–74; Radcliffe Travelling Fellow, Harvard University Med. Sch., 1971–73; Sen. Registrar, Westminster and Brompton Hosps, 1974–75; Consultant Physician and Physician i/c Chest Dept, St Bartholomew's Hosp., 1975–86; Dean, Nat. Heart and Lung Inst., 1988–90 (Mem., Cttee of Management, 1988–95); Dir, BPMF, 1991–96; Campus Dean, St Mary's Hosp., 1997–2001. Member: Supraregl Services Adv. Cttee, 1991–96; NHS Taskforce on Res. (Culyer Cttee), 1993–94; Health of the Nation Wider Health Wkg Gp, 1991–97; NHS Central R&D Cttee, 1995–2002 (Chm., 1999); NHS Exec. Bd, 1999; Chairman: NHS R&D Bd, 1999; NHS London Leading for Health, 2010–11; acting Dir, R&D for NHS, 1999. Chm., Exec. Cttee and Nat. Council, British Lung Foundn, 1984–94 (Pres. and Chm., Council, 1994–2001); Chm. Acad. Steering Gp, BPMF, 1989–90; Member, Committees of Management, Institutes of Child Health, Psychiatry, Neurology, Ophthalmology, Cancer Research, Dental Surgery, and RPMS, 1991–96. Member: Bd of Govs, Nat. Heart and Chest Hosps, 1988–90; Senate, 1998–2004, Council, 1997–2005, Imperial Coll., London. Chm., London Medicine, 1996–2000; Member: Bd, London First Centre, 1996–99, London First, 2000–02; Adv. Bd, Medtel, 2006–08; Adv. Bd, Westover (formerly Brompton Cross) Clinic, 2006–10; Adv. Bd, Greenbrook Healthcare, 2008–. Non-executive Director: St Mary's NHS Trust, 1997–2001; Royal Brompton and Harefield Hosps, 2001–06. Trustee: Heart Disease and Diabetes Res. Trust, 1988–2003; Fledgeling Charity Funds, 1993–98; Nat. Heart and Lung Foundn, 2000–; Chm., Medikidz Foundn, 2010–. Treasurer, 1977–85, Pres., 1992–2001, United Hosps Sailing Club. FMedSci 2000. *Publications:* chapters and articles in med. books and jls on gen. medicine, respiratory medicine and respiratory physiology. *Recreations:* sailing, ski-ing. *Address:* 38 Lansdowne Gardens, SW8 2EF. *T:* (020) 7622 8286. *E:* malcolm@malcolmgreen.net. *Clubs:* Royal Thames Yacht; Itchenor Sailing (Commodore, 2006–09); Royal Yacht Squadron; Imperial Poona Yacht (Hon. Sec., 1985–2010).

GREEN, Prof. Malcolm Leslie Hodder, PhD; FRS 1985; CChem, FRSC; Professor of Inorganic Chemistry, 1989–2003, now Emeritus, and Head of Department, Inorganic Chemistry Laboratory, 1988–2003, University of Oxford; Fellow of St Catherine's College, Oxford, 1988–2003, now Emeritus; *b* 16 April 1936; *s* of late Leslie Ernest Green, MD and Sheila Ethel (*née* Hodder); *m* 1965, Jennifer Clare Bilham; two *s* one *d*. *Educ:* Denstone Coll.; Acton Technical Coll. (BSc); Imperial Coll. of Science and Technol., London Univ. (DIC, PhD 1958); MA Cantab; MA Oxon. CChem, FRSC 1981. Asst Lectr in Inorganic Chem., Univ. of Cambridge, 1960–63; Fellow of Corpus Christi Coll., Cambridge, 1961–63; University of Oxford: Septcentenary Fellow and Tutor in Inorganic Chem., Balliol Coll., 1963–88, now Emeritus Fellow; Deptl Demonstrator, 1963; Lectr, 1965–88; British Gas Royal Soc. Sen. Res. Fellow, 1979–86. A. P. Sloan Vis. Prof., Harvard Univ., 1973; Sherman Fairchild Vis. Scholar, CIT, 1981. Tilden Lectr and Prize, RSC, 1982; Debye Lectr, Cornell Univ., 1985; Sir Edward Frankland Prize Lectr, 1988; Ernest H. Swift Lectr, CIT, 1998. A Founder and Dir, Oxford Catalysts Gp Plc. Dr *hc* Universidade Técnica de Lisboa, 1996. Corday-Morgan Medal and Prize in Inorganic Chem., Chemical Soc., 1974; Medal for Transition Metal Chem., Chemical Soc., 1978; Award for Inorganic Chem., ACS, 1984; RSC Award for Organometallic Chem., 1986; Karl-Ziegler Prize, Ges. Deutscher Chemiker, 1992; Davy Medal, Royal Soc., 1995; Award for Organometallic Chem., ACS, 1997; Sir Geoffrey Wilkinson Medal, RSC, 1999. *Publications:* Organometallic Compounds: Vol. II, The Transition Elements, 1968; (with G. E. Coates, P. Powell and K. Wade) Principles of Organometallic Chemistry, 1968. *Address:* St Catherine's College, Oxford OX1 3UJ.

GREEN, Malcolm Robert, DPhil; Member, City of Glasgow Council, 1995–2007; Lecturer in Roman History, University of Glasgow, 1967–98; *b* 4 Jan. 1943; *m* 1971; one *s* two *d*. *Educ:* Wyggeston Boys' School, Leicester; Magdalen College, Oxford. MA, DPhil. Member: Glasgow Corp., 1973–75; Strathclyde Regional Council, 1975–96 (Chairman: Educn Cttee, 1982–90; Envmt Sub-Cttee, 1990–94; Racial Equality Sub-Cttee, 1994–96); Chm., Educn Cttee, 1996–99, Chief Whip, subseq. Business Manager, 1999–2005, City of Glasgow Council. Chairman: Educn Cttee, Convention of Scottish Local Authorities, 1978–90; Management Side, Scottish Jt Negotiating Cttees for Teaching Staff in Sch. and Further Educn, 1977–90; Nat. Cttee for In-Service Training of Teachers, 1977–86; Scottish Cttee for Staff Develt in Educn, 1987–91. Chair, Scottish Alliance of Regl Equality Councils, 2012–;

Vice-Chair, W of Scotland Regl Equality Council, 2010–. Commissioner, Manpower Services Commn, 1983–85. *Recreation:* talking politics. *Address:* 4A Hughenden Gardens, Glasgow G12 9XW. *T:* (0141) 339 2007.

GREEN, Margaret Beryl; *see* Clunies Ross, M. B.

GREEN, Air Vice-Marshal Mark Colin, CBE 2005; Director, Information Superiority, Ministry of Defence, since 2011; *b* London, 10 May 1959; *s* of Leslie and Sylvia Green; *m* 2001, Jane Louise Trant; one *s* one *d*. *Educ:* Imperial Coll. London (BSc Hons Aeronautical Engrg). Joined RAF, 1977; Stn Comdr, RAF Valley, 2003–05; Team Leader, Jt Combat Aircraft Integrated Project, 2005–09; Dir, Flying Trng, 2009–10; AOC 22 (Trng) Gp, 2010–11. Adm. and Trustee, RAF Sailing Assoc., 2011–. *Recreations:* sailing, ski-ing, running, cycling.

GREEN, Martin, OBE 2012; Chief Executive, Care England, since 2004; *b* Birmingham, 10 Nov. 1959; *s* of Ronald George Green and late Margaret Winifred Green. *Educ:* King Edward VI Sch., Morpeth; Northumbria Univ. (BSc Hons Sociol.). Chief Executive: Age Concern Greenwich, 1984–87; Action for Dysphasic Adults Speakability, 1987–90; Project Dir, Uganda Cooperative Alliance Kampala, Uganda, 1990–92; Chief Executive: Age Concern Wandsworth, 1992–94; Age Concern Lambeth, 1994–99; Counsel and Care, 1999–2004. DoH Ind. Sector Dementia Champion, 2011–. Vis. Prof., Social Care, Bucks New Univ., 2012–. Chm., Internat. Longevity Centre UK, 2011–. Trustee: Nat. AIDS Trust, 2010–; Ind. Age, 2013–. FInstLM 2005; FIAM 2006; FIPEM 2008; FRSA. *Recreations:* theatre, cinema, travel. *Address:* Care England, 40 Artillery Lane, E7 1LS. *E:* mgreen@careengland.org.uk. *Clubs:* National Liberal, Army and Navy.

GREEN, Prof. Martin Andrew, AM 2012; PhD, DEng; FRS 2013; Director, Australian Centre for Advanced Photovoltaics, since 2013, and Scientia Professor, since 1999, UNSW Australia (formerly University of New South Wales); *b* Brisbane, 20 July 1948; *s* of Eric William Green and Gwendolyn Lorraine Green (*née* Horsfall); *m* 1970, Judith Frances Smith; one *s* one *d*. *Educ:* Univ. of Queensland (BEng 1970; MEng Sc 1971); McMaster Univ., Canada (PhD 1974); Univ. of New South Wales (DEng 2010). Grad. engr, AWA Microelectronics, Sydney, 1969–70; Lectr, 1974–78, Sen. Lectr, 1978–82, Univ. of NSW; res. scientist, Hitachi Central Res. Labs, Tokyo, 1977; Associate Prof., 1982–86, Prof., 1996–98, Univ. of NSW; Res. Dir, Pacific Solar Pty Ltd, 1995–2004. Dir, CSG Solar AG, 2004–10. Visiting Professor: Kathlieke Univ., Leuven, Belgium, 1977; Huazhong Univ. of Sci. and Technol., Wuhan, China, 1984; Vis. Consultant, Solar Energy Res. Inst., Golden, USA, 1981. Hon. DSc McMaster, 2010. *Publications:* Solar Cells: operating principles, technology and system application, 1982; High Efficiency Silicon Solar Cells, 1987; (jtly) Applied Photovoltaics, 1993, 3rd edn 2012; Silicon Solar Cells: advanced principles and practice, 1995; Power to the People, 2000; Third Generation Photovoltaics, 2003. *Recreations:* travel, family, jogging, bicycle touring. *Address:* School of Photovoltaic and Renewable Energy Engineering, UNSW Australia, Sydney, NSW 2052, Australia. *T:* (2) 93854018. *Club:* Bronte Surf (Sydney) (Hon. Vice Pres., 1990).

GREEN, Matthew Roger; Planning Consultant since 2005, and Senior Partner, since 2007, Green Planning Solutions LLP (formerly Green Planning Solutions); *b* 12 April 1970; *s* of Roger Hector Green and Pamela Gillian Green; *m* 1999, Sarah Louise Henthorn. *Educ:* Birmingham Univ. (BA (Hons) Medieval Studies). Sales and Marketing Manager, Plaskit Ltd, 1991–96; self employed, working in timber products and PR sectors, 1996–2003. Contested (Lib Dem) Wolverhampton SW, 1997; MP (Lib Dem) Ludlow, 2001–05; contested (Lib Dem) same seat, 2005. *Recreations:* cricket, mountaineering. *Address:* (office) Unit D, Lunesdale Upton Magna Business Park, Shrewsbury SY4 4TT. *E:* mghome@btconnect.com. *Club:* Liberal.

GREEN, Michael; *see* Green, N. M.

GREEN, Rev. Canon Michael; *see* Green, Rev. Canon E. M. B.

GREEN, Michael Anthony; QC 2009; *b* London, 23 Oct. 1964; *s* of late Jeffrey Isaac Green and of Susan Henrietta Green (*née* Bush); *m* 1991, Giselle Serena Finlay; one *s* two *d*. *Educ:* University Coll. Sch., Hampstead; Jesus Coll., Cambridge (BA 1986; MA 1990). Called to the Bar, Lincoln's Inn, 1987; in practice as barrister, 1988–, specialising in commercial, company and insolvency law. Mem., Attorney Gen.'s A Panel of Counsel, 1997–2008. Inspector for Insider Dealing Inquiry, DTI, 1997. Mem., Ind. Monitoring Bd, HM Prison Wormwood Scrubs, 2008–. *Recreations:* ski-ing, squash, cricket, Manchester United, 20th century classical music. *Address:* Fountain Court Chambers, Temple, EC4Y 9DH. *T:* (020) 7583 3335, *Fax:* (020) 7353 0329. *E:* mg@fountaincourt.co.uk.

GREEN, Prof. Michael Boris, FRS 1989; Lucasian Professor of Mathematics, University of Cambridge, 2009–13, now Emeritus; Fellow of Clare Hall, Cambridge, 1993–2010, now Hon. Fellow; *b* 22 May 1946; *s* of late Absalom and Genia Green; *m* 2005, Prof. Joanna Chataway; one *d*. *Educ:* Churchill Coll., Cambridge (BA, PhD; Rayleigh Prize 1969; Hon. Fellow 2010). Res. Fellow, Inst. for Advanced Study, Princeton, NJ, 1970–72; Fellowships in Cambridge, 1972–77; SERC Advanced Fellow, Oxford, 1977–79; Lectr, Queen Mary Coll., London Univ., 1979–85; Prof. of Physics, QMC, later QMW, 1985–93; John Humphrey Plummer Prof. of Theoretical Physics, Univ. of Cambridge, 1993–2009. Vis. Associate, Caltech, Pasadena, for periods during 1981–85; Nuffield Science Fellowship, 1984–86; SERC Sen. Fellowship, 1986–91. Hon. Fellow, Clare Hall, Cambridge, 2009; Hon. FInstP 2013. Hon. DSc QMUL, 2004. Maxwell Medal and Prize, 1987, Dirac Medal and Prize, 2004, Inst. of Physics; Hopkins Prize, Cambridge Philosophical Soc., 1987; Dirac Medal, Internat. Centre for Theoretical Physics, Trieste, 1989; Dannie Heinemann Prize, APS, 2002; Naylor Prize, London Math. Soc., 2008; Fundamental Physics Prize, 2014. *Publications:* Superstring Theory, vols I and II (with J. H. Schwarz and E. Witten), 1987; many contribs to physics and mathematics jls. *Address:* Department of Applied Mathematics and Theoretical Physics, University of Cambridge, Cambridge CB3 0WA.

GREEN, Michael John; Controller, BBC Radio 4, 1986–96; Deputy Managing Director, BBC Network Radio, 1993–96; *b* 28 May 1941; *s* of David Green and Kathleen (*née* Swann); *m* 1965, Christine Margaret Constance Gibson; one *s* one *d*. *Educ:* Repton Sch.; Barnsley Grammar Sch.; New Coll., Oxford (BA Modern Langs). Swiss Broadcasting Corp., 1964–65; Sheffield Star, 1965–67; Producer, BBC Radio Sheffield, 1967–70; Documentary Producer, BBC Manchester, 1970–77; Editor, File on Four, 1977; Head of Network Radio, Manchester, 1978–86. Chm., Radio Acad., 1990–95. Mem., NCC, 1997–2001. *Recreations:* France, cinema, collecting glass.

GREEN, Michael Philip; company director; *s* of Cyril and Irene Green; *m* 1st, 1972, Hon. Janet Frances Wolfson (*see* Hon. Dame J. F. W. de Botton) (marr. diss. 1989); two *d*; 2nd, 1990, Theresa Mary Buckmaster (*see* T. M. Green); three *s* one *d*. *Educ:* Haberdashers' Aske's School; Univ. of Wales (MA); Advanced Dip. Integrative Psychotherapy. Co-Founder and Dir, Tangent Industries Ltd, 1968–. Chairman: Carlton Communications Plc, 1983–2004 (Chief Exec., 1983–91); Carlton Television Ltd, 1991–94; Tangent Communications plc, 2012–; Director: GMTV Ltd, 1992–2004; Reuters Holdings PLC, 1992–99; ITN, 1993–2004 (Chm., 1993–95); Getty Communications plc, 1997–98; Thomson SA, 2001–04. Founder, Tangent Charitable Trust, 1984; Chm., The Media Trust, 1997–2006. Trustee, Sainsbury Centre for Mental Health, 2001–05. Mem., British Assoc. for Counselling and Psychotherapy, 2010–. UKCP registered. Hon. DLitt City, 1999. *Recreations:* reading, bridge. *Address:* 21 South Street, W1K 2XB. *T:* (020) 7663 6464. *Club:* Portland.

GREEN, Prof. Mino, FIET; Professor of Electrical Device Science, Electrical Engineering, 1983–92, now Emeritus, Senior Research Fellow, since 1992, Imperial College of Science and Technology; Founder and Chief Scientist, Nexeon Ltd, since 2006; *b* 10 March 1927; *s* of Alexander and Elizabeth Green; *m* 1951, Diana Mary Allen (*d* 2012); one *s* one *d*. *Educ:* Dulwich Coll.; University Coll., Durham Univ. (BSc, PhD, DSc). Group Leader: Solid State Res., Lincoln Laboratory, MIT, 1951–55; Res., Zenith Radio Corp., USA, 1956–60; Associate Dir, Electrochemistry Lab., Univ. of Pennsylvania, 1960–62; Man. Dir, Zenith Radio Research Corp. (UK) Ltd, 1962–72; Lectr, then Reader, Elec. Engrg Dept, Imperial Coll. of Science and Technology, 1972–83. *Publications:* Solid State Surface Science, vols I, II and III (ed), 1969–73; many pubns (and many patents) on various aspects of semiconductor and optical device science and of nano-science and technol. *Recreations:* walking, art appreciation. *Address:* 55 Gerard Road, SW13 9QH. *T:* (020) 8748 8689. *Club:* Hurlingham.
See also D. M. A. Green.

GREEN, Miranda Jane A.; *see* Aldhouse-Green.

GREEN, Hon. Sir Nicholas (Nigel), Kt 2013; PhD; **Hon. Mr Justice Green;** a Judge of the High Court of Justice, Queen's Bench Division, since 2013; *b* 15 Oct. 1958; *s* of John Reginald Green and Pauline Barbara Green; *m* 1990, Fiona Clare Cramb; one *s* one *d*. *Educ:* King Edward's VI Sch., Camp Hill, Birmingham; Univ. of Leicester (LLB 1980); Univ. of Toronto (LLM 1981); Univ. of Southampton (PhD 1985). Lectr in Law, Univ. of Southampton, 1981–85; pt-time Lectr in Law, UCL, 1985–87; called to the Bar, Inner Temple, 1986 (Bencher, 2002; Exec. Cttee, 2003–06); in practice at the Bar, 1986–2013; QC 1998; a Recorder, 2004–13; Jt Hd of Chambers, Brick Court Chambers, 2011–13. Chm., Bar European Gp, 1999–2001; Bar Council of England and Wales: Vice Chm., Internat. Relns Cttee, 2000–02; Chm., European Cttee, 2003–05; Chm., Legal Services Cttee, 2006–08; Mem., Gen. Mgt Cttee, 2002–10; Vice Chm., 2009; Chm., 2010; Chm., Advocacy Trng Council, 2011–. UK Perm. Rep. of CCBE to European Court of Justice, Court of First Instance and EFTA Court, 2000–02. Vis. Prof. of Law, Univ. of Durham, 2000–07; Hon. Prof. of Law, Univ. of Leicester, 2005–. Mem., BMA Bd of Sci. Ref. Gp on Drugs of Dependence, 2011–12. *Publications:* Commercial Agreements and Competition Law: practice and procedure in the UK and EEC, 1986, 2nd edn (jtly) 1997; (jtly) The Legal Foundations of the Single European Market, 1991; (ed jtly) Competition Litigation, 2009; over 50 articles in legal jls worldwide. *Recreations:* family, swimming (former international, 1976–77), collecting Victorian watercolours. *Address:* Royal Courts of Justice, Strand, WC2A 2LL.

GREEN, Dr (Norman) Michael, FRS 1981; affiliated to Department of Mathematical Biology, National Institute for Medical Research, 1992–2015; *b* 6 April 1926; *s* of Ernest Green and Hilda Margaret Carter; *m* 1953, Iro Paulina Moschouti; two *s* one *d*. *Educ:* Dragon Sch., Oxford; Clifton Coll., Bristol; Magdalen Coll., Oxford (BA; Athletics Blue, Cross Country Blue); UCH Med. Sch., London (PhD). Res. Student, Univ. of Washington, Seattle, 1951–53; Lectr in Biochemistry, Univ. of Sheffield, 1953–55; Res. Fellow and Lectr in Chem. Pathol., St Mary's Hosp. Med. Sch., London, 1956–62; Vis. Scientist, NIH, Maryland, 1962–64; Res. Staff, Divs of Biochem. and Protein Structure, NIMR, 1964–91. *Publications:* research papers on the structure of proteins and of membranes, in scientific jls. *Recreations:* mountain climbing, geometry. *Address:* 57 Hale Lane, Mill Hill, NW7 3PS.

GREEN, Sir Owen (Whitley), Kt 1984; Chairman, BTR plc, 1984–93 (Managing Director, 1967–86); *b* Stockton-on-Tees, 14 May 1925; *m* 1948, Doreen Margaret Spark (*d* 2006); one *s* two *d*. FCA 1950. Served RNVR, 1942–46. BTR, 1956–93. Dir, The Spectator, 1988–93. Trustee, Natural History Mus., 1986–95. Businessman of the Year, 1982; BIM Gold Medal, 1984; Founding Societies' Centenary Award, ICA, 1985. *Recreation:* golf. *Address:* Edgehill, Succombs Hill, Warlingham, Surrey CR6 9JG.

GREEN, Patrick Curtis; QC 2012; *b* Cambridge, 1967; *s* of Andrew Curtis Green, *qv*; *m* 2001, Trisha Leigh Little; one *s* two *d*. *Educ:* Haileybury Coll. (Exhibnr); Magdalene Coll., Cambridge (BA Law 1989). 2nd Lieut, RM SSLC, 1985–86. Called to the Bar, Middle Temple, 1990; in practice as barrister, 1990–, specialising in fields of commercial and employment law and judicial review. Vis. Fellow, LSE, 2005–. Director: ResoLex Ltd, 2000–; ResoLex Hldgs, 2003–; Habeas Film Co., 2011–. *Publications:* The Manual of Employment Appeals, 2008. *Recreations:* Real tennis, tennis, ski-ing, sailing, shooting, art, music, film, theatre and comedy. *Address:* Henderson Chambers, 2 Harcourt Buildings, Temple, EC4Y 9DB. *T:* (020) 7583 9020. *E:* clerks@hendersonchambers.co.uk. *Club:* Brooks's.

GREEN, Patrick G.; *see* Grafton-Green.

GREEN, Dame Pauline, DBE 2003; President, International Co-operative Alliance, since 2009; *b* 8 Dec. 1948; *d* of late Bertram Wiltshire and of Lucy Wiltshire; *m* 1971, Paul Adam Green (marr. diss. 2003); one *s* one *d*. *Educ:* John Kelly Secondary Modern Sch. for Girls, Brent; Kilburn Poly.; Open Univ. (BA); London School of Economics (MSc). Sec., 1981, Chair, 1983, Chipping Barnet Labour Party. MEP (Lab): London N, 1989–99; London Reg., 1999; Leader: European PLP, 1993–94; Gp of Pty of Eur. Socialists, 1994–99; Chief Exec., Co-operative Union Ltd, later Co-operatives UK, 2000–09. Contested (Lab) Arkley ward, Barnet Council elecns, 1986. Parly Asst, Co-operative Movement, 1986–89. Pres., Co-operative Congress, 1997; Vice Pres., Socialist International, 1994–. Mem., NEC, Labour Party, 1998–99. Mem., USDAW. *Recreations:* music, swimming. *Address:* International Co-operative Alliance, Avenue Milcamps 105, 1030 Brussels, Belgium.

GREEN, Prof. Peter James, PhD; FRS 2003; Professorial Research Fellow, University of Bristol, since 2011 (Professor of Statistics, 1989–2011, now Emeritus); Distinguished Professor, University of Technology, Sydney, since 2011; *b* 28 April 1950; *s* of late Frank Green and Joyce (*née* Walder); *m* 1984, Elizabeth Jane Bennett; two *d*. *Educ:* Solihull Sch.; Pembroke Coll., Oxford (BA 1971, MA); Univ. of Sheffield (MSc; PhD 1976). CStat 2000. Lectr in Stats, Univ. of Bath, 1974–78; Lectr, then Sen. Lectr in Stats, Univ. of Durham, 1978–89; Henry Overton Wills Prof. of Maths, Univ. of Bristol, 2003–11. Various vis. appts at foreign univs, 1979–. Pres., Royal Statistical Soc., 2001–03. FIMS 1991. Guy Medals, Bronze, 1987 and Silver, 1999, Royal Statistical Soc.; Royal Soc. Wolfson Res. Merit Award, 2006. *Publications:* (with B. Silverman) Nonparametric Regression and Generalized Linear Models, 1994; (ed with S. Richardson and N. L. Hjort) Highly Structured Stochastic Systems, 2003; contrib. numerous papers to learned jls. *Recreations:* biking, mountains, running. *Address:* School of Mathematics, University of Bristol, Bristol BS8 1TW. *T:* (0117) 928 7967. *E:* P.J.Green@bristol.ac.uk.

GREEN, Prof. Peter Morris; author and translator, since 1953; Professor of Classics, University of Texas at Austin, 1972–97 (James R. Dougherty Jr Centennial Professor of Classics, 1982–84, 1985–97), now Emeritus; Adjunct Professor of Classics, University of Iowa, since 1998; *b* 22 Dec. 1924; *oc* of late Arthur Green, CBE, MC, LLB, and Olive Slaughter; *m* 1st, 1951, Lalage Isobel Pulvertaft (marr. diss.); two *s* one *d*; 2nd, 1975, Carin Margreta, *y d* of late G. N. Christensen, Saratoga, USA. *Educ:* Charterhouse; Trinity Coll., Cambridge. Served in RAFVR, 1943–47: overseas tour in Burma Comd, 1944–46. 1st Cl. Hons, Pts I and II, Classical Tripos, 1949–50; MA and PhD Cantab 1954; Craven Schol. and Student, 1950; Dir of Studies in Classics, 1951–52; Fiction Critic, London Daily Telegraph, 1953–63; Literary Adviser, The Bodley Head, 1957–58; Cons. Editor, Hodder and Stoughton, 1960–63; Television Critic, The Listener, 1961–63; Film Critic, John o'London's, 1961–63; Mem. Book Soc. Cttee, 1959–63. Former Mem. of selection cttees for literary prizes: Heinemann Award, John Llewellyn Rhys, W. H. Smith £1000 Award for Literature. Translator of numerous works from French, Italian, Latin, and classical and modern Greek, including books by Simone de Beauvoir, Fosco Maraini, Joseph Kessel, Yannis Ritsos. FRSL 1956; Mem. Council, Royal Society of Literature, 1958–63 (resigned on emigration). In 1963 resigned all positions and emigrated to Greece as full-time writer (1963–71). Visiting Professor of Classics: Univ. of Texas, 1971–72; UCLA, 1976; Mellon Prof. of Humanities, Tulane Univ., 1986; Vis. Prof. of History, Univ. of Iowa, 1997–98; Sen. Fellow for independent study and res., National Endowment for the Humanities, 1983–84; Vis. Res. Fellow and Writer-in-Residence, Princeton Univ., 2001; King Charles II Dist. Vis. Prof. in Classics and Ancient Hist., 2004, Whichard Dist. Vis. Prof. in the Humanities, 2006, 2009, E Carolina Univ. Editor, Syllecta Classica, 1999–2009, 2013–. *Publications:* The Expanding Eye, 1953; Achilles His Armour, 1955; Cat in Gloves (pseud. Denis Delaney), 1956; The Sword of Pleasure (W. H. Heinemann Award for Literature), 1957; Kenneth Grahame 1859–1932: A Study of his Life, Work and Times, 1959; Essays in Antiquity, 1960; Habeas Corpus and other stories, 1962; Look at the Romans, 1963; The Laughter of Aphrodite, 1965, repr. 1993; Juvenal: The Sixteen Satires (trans.), 1967, 3rd edn 1998; Armada from Athens: The Failure of the Sicilian Expedition 415–413 BC, 1970; Alexander the Great: a biography, 1970; The Year of Salamis 480–479 BC, 1971, rev. as The Greco-Persian Wars, 1996; The Shadow of the Parthenon, 1972; The Parthenon, 1973; A Concise History of Ancient Greece, 1973; Alexander of Macedon 356–323 BC: a historical biography, 1974, repr. 1991; Ovid: The Erotic Poems (trans.), 1982; Beyond the Wild Wood: the world of Kenneth Grahame, 1982; Medium and Message Reconsidered: the changing functions of classical translation, 1986; Classical Bearings: interpreting ancient history and culture, 1989; Alexander to Actium: the historical evolution of the Hellenistic Age, 1990, rev. edn 1993; (ed) Hellenistic History and Culture, 1993; Yannis Ritsos: The Fourth Dimension (trans.), 1993; Ovid: The Poems of Exile (trans.), 1994, rev. edn 2005; Apollonios Rhodios: The Argonautika (trans. and commentary), 1997; From Ikaria to the Stars, 2004; The Poems of Catullus (trans.), 2005; Diodorus Siculus Bks 11–12.37.1: Greek History 480–431 BCE the alternative version, 2006; Alexander the Great and the Hellenistic Age: a short history, 2007; Diodorus Siculus, The Persian Wars to the Fall of Athens: books 11–14.34 (480–401 BCE) (trans.), 2010; Homer's Iliad (trans.), 2015. *Recreations:* reading poetry and fiction, keeping in touch with old friends, avoiding urban life, listening to chamber music. *Address:* 1268 Chamberlain Drive, Iowa City, IA 52240–2922, USA. *T:* (319) 3419805, (319) 6213710. *E:* peter-green-1@uiowa.edu. *Club:* Savile.

GREEN, Peter Richard Austin; Head Master, Rugby School, since 2014; *b* Dumfries, Scotland, 8 Dec. 1964; *s* of Louis and Margaret Green; *m* 1990, Brenda O'Connor; one *s* one *d*. *Educ:* St Joseph's Coll., Dumfries; Edinburgh Univ. (MA Hons 1986); St Andrew's Coll. (PGCE, Cert. RE 1987). Teacher of Geography, St Olave's and St Saviour's Grammar Sch., 1987–89; Teacher of Geography and i/c Rugby, Strathallan Sch., 1989–95; Housemaster, Hd of Geography and i/c Rugby, Uppingham Sch., 1996–2002; Second Master, Ampleforth Coll., 2002–07; Headmaster, Ardingly Coll., 2007–14. Vice Chair, Woodard Heads Assoc., 2011–14. Gov., Belhaven Hill Prep. Sch., 2003–11. Mem., Ampleforth Soc.; St Joseph's Past Pupils. *Recreations:* Rugby, opera, wine tasting, family, theatre, school governor, Church. *Address:* Rugby School, Rugby CV22 5EH. *T:* (01788) 556217, *Fax:* (01788) 578635. *E:* head@rugbyschool.net. *Clubs:* Lansdowne, East India.

GREEN, Sir Philip, Kt 2006; retail executive; *b* 15 March 1952; *m* 1990, Cristina; one *s* one *d*. Took over family property company, 1973; bought: Jean Jeanie, 1985 (sold to Lee Cooper, 1986); Owen Owen, 1994; Olympus Sports, 1995 (merged with Sports Division, 1996; sold to JJB Sports, 1998); Mark One, 1996; Shoe Express, 1997 (sold, 1998); Sears (incl. Miss Selfridge, Wallis, Warehouse, Freemans), 1999; Bhs, 2000 (sold, 2015); Arcadia (incl. Top Shop, Dorothy Perkins, Evans, Burton), 2002; Chm. and Chief Exec., Amber Day, 1988–92. *Address:* Arcadia Group Ltd, Colegrave House, 70 Berners Street, W1T 3NL.

GREEN, Philip Nevill, CBE 2014; non-executive Chairman: BakerCorp. Inc., since 2011; Sentebale, since 2011; Carillion plc, since 2014 (Senior Independent non-executive Director, 2011–14); Chairman Designate, Williams & Glyn Bank Ltd; *b* 12 May 1953; *s* of Harry Green and Sheila Saveker (*née* Emery); *m* 1977, Judy Rippon; two *d*. *Educ:* UC of Swansea, Wales (BA Hons); London Business Sch. (MBA). DHL: Regl Dir, Northern Europe, 1990–94; Chief Operating Officer, Europe and Africa, 1994–99; Divl CEO, 1999–2001, Chief Operating Officer, 2001–03, Reuters Gp Plc; Chief Executive: Royal P&O Nedlloyd, 2003–06; United Utilities plc, 2006–11. Sen. Ind. Dir, Saga plc, 2014–. Adviser to Prime Minister on Corporate Responsibility, 2011–. Trustee: Philharmonia Orch., 2002–14; Bible Soc., 2012– (Chm., 2012–). Patron, Hope Through Action, 2007–. *Recreations:* walking, cricket, Africa, wine, music. *Clubs:* Royal Automobile, MCC.

GREEN, Rodney Alan Rupert, CBE 2015; Prior of England and the Islands, Order of St John, and Chairman, St John Ambulance, since 2010; *b* 7 Feb. 1953; *s* of Timothy Green and Mercy Green (*née* Mathison); *m* 1975, Helen Frances Benjamin; two *s*. *Educ:* Christ's Hosp., Horsham; Emmanuel Coll., Cambridge (MA 1974). Greater London Council: cttee clerk, Dir-Gen.'s Dept, 1974–76; Scientific Br. Staffing Officer, 1976–78; Surrey County Council: Head, Teaching Personnel Section 1978–82; Principal: Schools, 1982–84; Special Needs, 1984–87; Asst Co. Educn Officer, 1987–91; Asst Chief Exec., W Glamorgan CC, 1991–96; Chief Exec., Leicester CC, 1996–2008. Director: Leics TEC, 1998–2001; Nat. Space Centre, 1998–2006; Leicester Regeneration Co., 2001–06; Leicestershire Cares, 2001–08; Member: Adv. Panel on Beacon Scheme, 2005–08; Inst. of Community Cohesion, 2006–08; Migration Impacts Forum, 2007–08. Trustee, A Rocha Internat., 2010–. Non-exec. Dir, British Waterways, 2009–12. Hon. LLD De Montfort, 2003. KStJ 2010. *Publications:* 90,000 Hours: managing the world of work, 2002. *Recreations:* films, theatre, travel, Leicester Tigers Rugby, swimming, Biblical studies, feasting.

GREEN, Prof. Roger, FRCP; Professor of Physiology, University of Manchester, 1981–2005, now Professor Emeritus; *b* 9 Feb. 1942; *s* of Donald Victor and Joyce Green; *m* 1965, Rita Mavis; one *s* two *d*. *Educ:* Univ. of Sheffield (MB ChB 1965); Univ. of Manchester (MSc 1981). FRCP 2002. House Officer posts, Sheffield Royal Hosp., 1965–66; University of Manchester: Asst Lectr, Lectr, Sen. Lectr, then Reader in Physiol., 1966–81; Dean: Undergrad. Med. Studies, 1993–97; Medical Sch., 1997–2003. Hon. DSc: St Andrews, 2004; Keele, 2004; Hon. MD Internat. Med. Univ. Malaysia, 2012. *Publications:* contribs to physiological jls. *Recreation:* brass bands. *Address:* 105 Heaton Park Road, Manchester M9 0QQ. *T:* (0161) 795 9983.

GREEN, Samuel; QC 2015; *b* Ballymena, NI, 30 Dec. 1975; *s* of Rev. Norman Green and Mildred Green (*née* Bond); *m* Anne; one *d*. *Educ:* Trinity Coll., Cambridge (BA 1997). Called to the Bar: Lincoln's Inn, 1998; NI, 2007; in practice as a barrister, 1998–. *Recreations:* cycling, boxing, keeping fit, legal biography, travel, wine. *Address:* New Park Court Chambers, Leeds LS1 2SJ. *T:* (0113) 243 3277. *E:* samuel.green@npc-l.co.uk.

GREEN, Susan Valerie; District Judge (Magistrates' Courts), since 2001; *b* 1 Nov. 1954; *d* of Nat Green and Ettie Green (*née* Blacker); *m* 2004, Haydn Gott, *qv*. *Educ:* Birmingham Univ. (LLB); Coll. of Law, Guildford. Admitted solicitor, 1981; J. P. Malnick and Co., subsequently Malnick & Rance: articled clerk, 1979–81; Asst Solicitor, 1981–82; Partner, 1982–98; Consultant, Traymans, 1998–2000. Legal Mem. and Pres., Mental Health Review Tribunal, then Tribunal Judge, First-tier Tribunal (Mental Health), 2003–. Formerly Sec. and Pres., NE London Law Soc.; Pres., London Criminal Courts Solicitors' Assoc., 1998–99. *Recreations:* sports, cookery, travel, all things Australasian. *Address:* c/o Camberwell Green Magistrates' Court, D'Eynsford Street, SE5 7UP. *T:* (020) 7805 9802.

GREEN, Terence Anthony; Chief Executive, Clothing, Tesco, 2006–10; retail consultant, since 2011; *b* 9 Oct. 1951; *s* of Henry Green and Nora Green (*née* Sayers); *m* 1981, Geraldine A. Daniels (marr. diss. 1996); one *s* two *d*; one *d* by Vanessa Field; partner, Dr Julleanne Parsons. *Educ:* Liverpool Univ. (BSc Maths; BSc (Hons) Maths, Computer Sci. and Stats). Exec. Dir, Burton Gp plc, 1992–98; Chief Executive: Debenhams, 1992–98; Topshop and Top Man, 1995–98; Debenhams plc, 1998–2000 (Debenhams demerged from Burton Gp, 1998); Bhs Ltd, 2000–02; Allders, 2003–05. Non-exec. Dir, First Choice Holidays plc, 1997. FRSA 1997. Hon. DA Hertfordshire, 2010. *Recreations:* food, opera, reading, collecting art and fine wines, writing, painting.

GREEN, Theresa Mary, CBE 2008; Chairman, Royal Marsden NHS Foundation Trust (formerly NHS Trust), 1998–2010; *b* 29 July 1964; *d* of Richard Buckmaster and Jacqueline Buckmaster (*née* Leche); *m* 1990, Michael Philip Green, *qv*; three *s* one *d*. *Educ:* Putney High Sch.; Lady Margaret Hall, Oxford (MA); City Univ. (LLB 1993). Called to the Bar, Middle Temple, 1994. Head of Corporate Communications, Carlton Communications Plc, 1986–90. Non-executive Director: Royal Berkshire and Battle Hosps NHS Trust, 1994–98; Barts Health NHS Trust, 2013–; Pets at Home plc, 2014–. Member: Res. Ethics Cttee, Royal Marsden Hosp., 1994–98 (Chm., 1996); Bd of Trustees, Inst. of Cancer Res., 1998–2010; Assoc. Mem., BUPA, 2013– (Mem., Medical Adv. Panel, 2013–). Trustee: Nat. Portrait Gall., 1999–2002; Royal Botanic Gardens, Kew, 2011–14; Royal Foundn of the Duke and Duchess of Cambridge (formerly of Prince William) and Prince Harry, 2011–.

GREEN-ARMYTAGE, John McDonald; Chairman: JZ International Ltd, since 1996; Star Capital Partners, since 2001; *b* 6 June 1945; *s* of John Whitla Green-Armytage and Elizabeth McDonald Green-Armytage; *m* 1977, Susan Rosemary Le Messurier; one *s* three *d*. *Educ:* McGill Univ., Montreal (BA (Econs) 1966); Columbia Univ., NY (MBA 1970). Joined N. M. Rothschild & Sons Ltd, 1970, exec. Dir, 1977–82, non-exec. Dir, 1988–97; Man. Dir, Guthrie Corp. plc, 1982–88; Jt Chm. and CEO, Kelt Energy plc, 1990–91; William Baird plc: non-exec. Dir, 1992–94; CEO, 1995–96; Dep. Chm., 1996. Non-exec. Chm., AMEC plc, 2004–11 (non-exec. Dir, 1996–2011). *Recreations:* country pursuits, polo, sailing. *Address:* JZ International Ltd, 17a Curzon Street, W1J 5HS. *Clubs:* Brooks's, Turf; Guards Polo (Chm., 2011–).

GREEN-PRICE, Sir Robert (John), 5th Bt *cr* 1874; landowner; Assistant Professor of English, Chiba University of Commerce, 1982–97; *b* 22 Oct. 1940; *o s* of Sir John Green-Price, 4th Bt, and Irene Marion (*d* 1954), *d* of Major Sir (Ernest) Guy Lloyd, 1st Bt, DSO; *S* father, 1964. *Educ:* Shrewsbury. Army Officer, 1961–69; Captain, RCT, retd. ADC to Governor of Bermuda, 1969–72. Lectr in English, Teikyo Univ., 1975–82. Part-time Lecturer: Keio Univ., 1977–97; Waseda Univ., 1986–97; Guest Lectr, NHK Radio, 1978–83. *Heir: cousin* Simon Richard Green-Price, *b* 10 May 1964.

GREENALL, family name of **Baron Daresbury**.

GREENAWAY, Sir David, Kt 2014; DL; Vice Chancellor, since 2008, and Professor of Economics, since 1987, University of Nottingham; *b* 20 March 1952; *s* of David and Agnes Greenaway; *m* 1975, Susan Elizabeth Hallam; two *s*. *Educ:* Henry Mellish Grammar Sch.; Liverpool Poly. (BSc London ext. 1974); Liverpool Univ. (MCom 1975); DLitt Nottingham 1997. Lectr in Econs, Leicester Poly., 1975–78; University of Buckingham: Lectr, 1978–83; Sen. Lectr, 1983–85; Reader, 1985–86; Prof. of Econs, 1986–87; Pro-Vice-Chancellor, Univ. of Nottingham, 1994–2001, 2004–08. Non-executive Director: Nottingham HA, 1994–98; Queen's Med. Centre, Nottingham Univ. Hosp. NHS Trust, 2001–04. Member: Council, 1990–97, Exec., 1991–97, REconS; Acad. Adv. Council, IEA, 1991–2004; Technology Foresight Steering Gp, 1994–95; Council, ESRC, 1997–2001; Armed Forces Pay Review Body, 1997– (Chm., 2004–10); Sen. Salaries Rev. Body, 2004–10; Asia Task Force, 2010–; Chair, Panel for Econs and Econometrics, RAE, HEFCE, 2001 and 2008 (Vice Chair, 1996). Chair, Ind. Review of Postgrad. Med. Educn and Trng, 2012–13. Adviser: UNIDO, 1983; World Bank, 1986, 1988; GATT, 1986; DTI, 1994; UNECE, 1994; Commonwealth Secretariat, 1997; Asian Develt Bank, 1997; Caribbean Regl Negotiating Machinery, 2000; Dept for Transport, 2003–04. Gov., NIESR, 1995–. FRSA 1994; AcSS 2000. Hon. Fellow, Liverpool John Moores Univ., 2012. Hon. Col, E Midlands Univs OTC, 2013–. Hon. Citizen, City of Ningbo, China, 2012. DL Notts, 2009. *Publications:* International Trade Policy, 1983; (jtly) Economics of Intra-Industry Trade, 1986; (jtly) Imperfect Competition and International Trade, 1986; Companion to Contemporary Economic Thought, 1991; (jtly) Evaluating Trade Policy in Developing Countries, 1993; (jtly) Economics of Commodity Markets, 1999; Globalisation and Labour Markets, 2000; Adjusting to Globalisation, 2005; (ed jtly) China and the World Economy, 2010; Palgrave Handbook of International Trade, 2011; (ed jtly) The Globalization of Higher Education, 2012; (ed jtly) The Business Growth Benefits of Higher Education, 2014; papers in learned jls. *Recreations:* golf, tennis, football, wine, reading, cycling. *Address:* Vice-Chancellor's Office, University of Nottingham, University Park, Nottingham NG7 2RD. *T:* (0115) 951 3001; 1 Dormy Close, Bramcote, Nottingham NG9 3DE.

GREENAWAY, Peter, CBE 2007; film director, painter and writer; Professor of Cinema Studies, European Graduate School, Saas-Fee, Switzerland; *b* 5 April 1942; *m*; two *d*. *Educ:* Forest Sch.; Walthamstow Coll. of Art. Film Editor, Central Office of Information, 1965–76. Maker of short films, 1966–, of feature length films, 1978–. *Exhibitions:* Lord's Gall., 1964; The Physical Self, Rotterdam, 1991; 100 Objects to Represent the World, Acad. of Fine Arts, Vienna, 1992; Flying Out of this World, Louvre, 1992; Watching Water, Venice, 1993; Some Organising Principles, Swansea, 1993; The Audience of Macon, Cardiff, 1993; The Stairs, Geneva, 1994, Munich, 1995; Spellbound, London, 1996; Flying Over Water, Barcelona, 1997; *one-man shows:* Canterbury, 1989; Carcassone, Paris, 1989; NY, Melbourne, Liège, Tokyo, Fukoa, Munich, Copenhagen, Oddense, Brussels, 1990; Brentford, Dublin, 1991; Bremen, NY, 1992; Tempe, Ariz, and Salzburg, 1994; Biel-Bienne, Switzerland, New York, and Munich, 1995; Milan, Ghent, and Thessaloniki, 1996; Manchester, 1998; Edinburgh, 1999; *group shows* include: Freezeframe, Lamont Gall., 1996; The Director's Eye, Mus. of Modern Art, Oxford, 1996. *Films:* (writer and director): Train, 1966; Tree, 1966; Five Postcards from Capital Cities, 1967; Revolution, 1967; Intervals, 1969; Erosion, 1971; H is for House, 1973; Windows, 1975; Water Wrackets, 1975; Goole by Numbers, 1976; Dear Phone, 1977; 1–1Co, 1978; A Walk Through H, 1978; Vertical Features Remake, 1978; The Falls, 1980 (Special Award, BFI); Act of God, 1981 (Best short film, Melbourne Film Fest.); Zandra Rhodes, 1981; The Draughtsman's Contract, 1982; Four American Composers, 1983; Making a Splash, 1984; (jtly) A TV Dante-Canto V, 1984; Inside Rooms—The Bathroom, 1985; A Zed and Two Noughts, 1985; The Belly of an Architect, 1986; Fear of Drowning, 1988; Drowning by Numbers, 1988 (Prize for Best Artistic Contribution, Cannes Film Fest.); The Cook, the Thief, his Wife and her Lover, 1989; Prospero's Books, 1990; M is for Man, Music, Mozart, 1991; Rosa, 1992; Darwin, 1992; The Baby of Macon, 1993; The Stairs, Geneva, 1994; The Pillow Book, 1996; The Bridge, 1996; 8½ Women, 1999; Nightwatching, 2007; Goltzius and the Pelican Company, 2012; *operas:* Rosa: a Horse Drama, 1994; Writing to Vermeer, 1999. Officier de l'Ordre des Arts et des Lettres (France), 1998. *Publications:* The Falls, 1993; filmscripts and exhibn catalogues.

GREENBERG, Daniel Isaac; Parliamentary Counsel, Berwin Leighton Paisner LLP, since 2010; *b* 5 Sept. 1965; *s* of Dr Morris Greenberg and Dr Gillian Greenberg; *m* 1988, Julia Sharon Becker; two *s* two *d*. *Educ:* Trinity Coll., Cambridge (BA); Inns of Court Sch. of Law. Legal Advr, Lord Chancellor's Dept, 1988–91; Asst Parly Counsel, 1991–95; Sen. Asst Parly Counsel, 1995–99; Dep. Parly Counsel, 1999–2003; Parly Counsel, 2003–08, pt-time,

2009–10. Gen. Editor, Annotated Statutes (formerly Technical Annotations), Westlaw UK, 2008–; Editor in Chief, Statute Law Review, 2012–. *Publications:* (ed) Stroud's Judicial Dictionary, 6th edn 2000, 8th edn 2012; (ed) Craies on Legislation, 9th edn 2008, 10th edn 2012; How to Become Jewish (and Why Not To), 2009; (ed) Jowitt's Dictionary of English Law, 3rd edn 2010; Laying Down the Law, 2011; contrib. articles on Jewish law and philosophy to Jewish Chronicle. *Recreations:* teaching Jewish law and philosophy, reading. *Address:* 74 North End Road, NW11 7SY. *T:* 07950 491512. *E:* dgreenberg@hotmail.co.uk.

GREENBERG, Joanna Elishever Gabrielle; QC 1994; **Her Honour Judge Greenberg;** a Circuit Judge, since 2014; *b* 28 Nov. 1950; *d* of Ivan Marion Greenberg and Doris Rosalie Greenberg (*née* Sandground). *Educ:* Brondesbury and Kilburn High Sch. for Girls; King's Coll. London (LLB, AKC). Called to the Bar, Gray's Inn, 1972, Bencher, 2002; an Asst Recorder, 1992–95; a Recorder, 1995–2014. Approved Counsel for Internat. Criminal Court, 2007; Approved Lead Counsel for Special Tribunal for Lebanon, 2009. Chm., Police Appeals Tribunals, 1997–2014. *Address:* Inner London Crown Court, Sessions House, Newington Causeway, SE1 6AZ.

GREENBURGH, Matthew Steven; Vice Chairman and Senior Vice President, Merrill Lynch & Co., Inc., 2008–10; *b* London, 6 March 1961; *s* of Raymond Greenburgh and Virginia Greenburgh (*née* Rothman); *m* 1990, Helen Elisabeth Payne; one *s* one *d*. *Educ:* Westminster Sch.; Worcester Coll., Oxford (BA Hons Philos. and Econs). Barclays Merchant Bank/BZW, 1983–87; Enskilda Securities, 1987–91; Baring Brothers, 1991–98, Dir, 1995–98; Merrill Lynch, 1998–2010: Co-Head, Global Financial Instns Gp, 2001–06; Vice Chm., Global Investment Banking, 2006–08. *Recreations:* arboriculture, puericulture, culture.

GREENBURY, Sir Richard, Kt 1992; Chairman, 1991–99, and Chief Executive, 1988–99, Marks & Spencer plc; *b* 31 July 1936; *s* of Richard Oswald Greenbury and Dorothy (*née* Lewis); *m* 1st, 1959, Sian Eames Hughes (marr. diss.); two *s* two *d*; 2nd, 1985, Gabrielle Mary McManus (marr. diss. 1996); remarried, 1996, Sian Eames (*née* Hughes). *Educ:* Ealing County Grammar Sch. Joined Marks & Spencer Ltd as Jun. Management Trainee, 1952; Alternate Dir, 1970; Full Dir, 1972; Jt Man. Dir, 1978–85; Chief Operating Officer, 1986–88. Non-executive Director: British Gas, 1976–87; MB Group (formerly Metal Box), 1985–89; ICI, 1992–93; Lloyds Bank, 1992–97; Zeneca, 1993–99; Electronics Boutique, 2000–03; Mem. Supervisory Bd, Philips Electronics NV, 1998–2010. Trustee, Royal Acad., 1992–97. Patron, Samaritans, 1992–2000. *Recreations:* tennis, reading, music. *Address:* Ambarrow Wood, Ambarrow Lane, Sandhurst, Berks GU47 8JE. *Clubs:* All England Lawn Tennis and Croquet, International Tennis Club of GB.

GREENE, Anthony Hamilton Millard K.; *see* Kirk-Greene.

GREENE, Graham Carleton, CBE 1986; publisher; Chairman, London Merchant Securities plc, 2000–07 (Director, 1996–2007); Chairman of Trustees, British Museum, 1996–2002 (Trustee, 1978–2002, now Trustee Emeritus); *b* 10 June 1936; *s* of Sir Hugh Carleton Greene, KCMG, OBE and Helga Mary Connolly; *m* 1957, Judith Margaret (marr. diss. 1976), *d* of Rt Hon. Lord Gordon-Walker, CH, PC; *m* 1976, Sally Georgina Horton (marr. diss. 1984), *d* of Sidney Wilfred Eaton; one *s*, and one step *s* one step *d*. *Educ:* Eton; University Coll., Oxford (MA). Merchant Banking, Dublin, New York and London, 1957–58; Secker & Warburg Ltd, 1958–62; Jonathan Cape, 1962–90 (Man. Dir, 1966–88). Director: Chatto & Jonathan Cape, subseq. Chatto, Virago, Bodley Head & Jonathan Cape Ltd, 1969–88 (Chm., 1970–88); Jackdaw Publications Ltd (Chm., 1964–88); Cape Goliard Press Ltd, 1967–88; Guinness Mahon Holdings Ltd, 1968–79; Australasian Publishing Co. Pty Ltd, 1969–88 (Chm., 1978–88); Sprint Productions Ltd, 1971–80; Book Reps (New Zealand) Ltd, 1971–88 (Chm., 1984–88); CVBC Services Ltd (Chm., 1972–88); Guinness Peat Group PLC, 1973–87; Grantham Book Storage Ltd (Chm., 1974–88); Triad Paperbacks Ltd, 1975–88; Chatto, Virago, Bodley Head & Jonathan Cape Australia Pty Ltd (Chm., 1977–88); Greene, King PLC, 1979–2004; Statesman & Nation Publishing Co. Ltd, 1980–85 (Chm., 1981–85); Statesman Publishing Co. Ltd, 1980–85 (Chm., 1981–85); Nation Pty Co. Ltd (Chm., 1981–87); New Society Ltd (Chm., 1984–87); Random House Inc., 1987–88; Random House UK Ltd, 1988–90; British Museum Co. (formerly British Museum Publications) Ltd, 1988–2002 (Chm., 1988–96); Merlin Internat. Green, subseq. Jupiter Internat. Green Investment Trust plc, 1989–2001; Henry Sotheran Ltd, 1990–; Ed Victor Ltd, 1991–; Rosemary Sandberg Ltd, 1991–2002; Libra KFT (Budapest), 1991–; Raymond Chandler Ltd, 2005– (Chm., 2012–); Chm., Frontline Club, 2003–10. Pres., Publishers Assoc., 1977–79 (Mem. Council, 1969–88; Trustee, 1995–97); Member: Book Develt Council, 1970–79 (Dep. Chm., 1972–73); Internat. Cttee, Internat. Publishers Assoc., 1977–88 (Exec. Cttee, 1981–88); Groupe des Editeurs de Livres de la CEE, (Fedn of European Publishers), 1977–86 (Pres., 1984–86); Arts Council Working Party Sub-Cttee on Public Lending Right, 1970; Paymaster General's Working Party on Public Lending Right, 1970–72; Bd, British Council, 1977–88; Chairman: Nat. Book League, 1974–76 (Dep. Chm., 1971–74); Nat. Book Cttee, 1994–95; Museums and Galls Commn, 1991–96; Mem. Gen. Cttee, Royal Literary Fund, 1975. Chairman: Friends of Musica nel Chiostro, 1993–2004; Garsington Opera Ltd, 2006–10 (Mem. Adv. Cttee, 1990–96; Dir, 1996–); Mem., Adv. Bd, Mus. of Modern Art, Oxford, 1992–96. Trustee: George Bernard Shaw Estate, 1986–; Trollope Soc., 1989–2004; Han Suyin Trust (formerly Han Suyin Fund for Scientific Exchange), 1989–; Open Coll. of the Arts, 1990–97; Albany, 2010–11. Chm., BM Develt Trust, 1986–93 (Vice Chm., 1993–2004); Pres., BM Foundn Inc., 1989–90; Dir, American Friends of BM, 1990–2002. Vice-Pres., GB-China Centre, 1997– (Chm., 1986–97). Gov., Compton Verney House Trust, 1995–11 (Chm., 2005–11); Member: Bd, Sainsbury Inst. for Study of Japanese Arts and Culture, 1999–; Stiftung Hans Arp und Sophie Tauber Arp, 1999–; Stiftung Temple Gift, 2000–07. Freeman, City of London, 1960; Liveryman, Fishmongers' Co., 1960–. Hon. DLitt: Keele, 2002; Buckingham, 2004; Hon. DCL UEA, 2002. Chevalier de l'Ordre des Arts et des Lettres, France, 1985. *Address:* D2 Albany, Piccadilly, W1J 0AP. *T:* (020) 7734 0270. *E:* grahamc.greene@virgin.net.

GREENE, Jenny, (Mrs Michael Boys-Greene); Editor, Country Life, 1986–93, retired; *b* 9 Feb. 1937; *d* of Captain James Wilson Greene and Mary Emily Greene; *m* 1971, John Gilbert (marr. diss. 1987); *m* 1994, Michael Boys-Greene. *Educ:* Rochelle Sch., Cork; Trinity Coll., Dublin; Univ. of Montpellier, France. Researcher, Campbell-Johnson Ltd, 1963–64; Account-Exec., Central News, 1964–65; Account-Exec., Pemberton Advertising, 1965–66; Publicity Exec., Revlon, 1966–71; Beauty Editor, Woman's Own, 1971–75; Features Writer and Theatre Critic, Manchester Evening News, 1975–77; Asst Editor, Woman's Own, 1977–78; Editor: Homes and Gardens, 1978–86; A La Carte, 1984–85; columnist, Today, 1985–87. Contrib., Country Life and Gardens Illustrated, 1998–. *Recreations:* gardening, trying to entertain the French. *Address:* 21 rue de Grissais, 85200 Fontenay-le-Comte, France.

GREENE, Maurice Alan; His Honour Judge Maurice Greene; a Circuit Judge, since 2012; *b* Salford, 19 April 1960; *s* of late Jack Greene and Freda Greene; *m* 1986, Amanda Ashe; two *d*. *Educ:* Prestwich Jewish Day Sch.; Stand Grammar Sch., Whitefield; Liverpool Poly. (BA Hons Law); Leicester Univ. (Postgrad. Dip Criminal Justice Studies). Called to the Bar, Inner Temple, 1982; in practice as barrister, specialising in crime and regulatory work, Sheffield, 1982–91, Manchester, 1991–2012; a Dep. Dist Judge (Magistrates' Courts), 1999–2012; a Recorder, 2002–12; Liaison Judge, Tameside Magistrates' Court, 2013–. *Recreations:* English and European political history, sport, dog walking. *Address:* Manchester Crown Court, Minshull Street, Manchester M1 3FS. *T:* (0161) 954 7500. *E:* enquiries@manchesterminshullstreet.crowncourt.gsi.gov.uk.

GREENE, Peter Livesey; His Honour Judge Greene; a Circuit Judge, since 2011; a Deputy High Court Judge, since 2012; *b* 21 June 1947; *s* of late George Greene, MBE and Nell Greene; *m* 1986, Linda Rowell; three *d*. *Educ:* Bemrose Grammar Sch., Derby; Manchester Coll. of Commerce (LLB); Guildford Coll. of Law. Admitted solicitor, 1972; Sen. Partner, Greene D'sa, 1977–94, Greene Deavin, 1994–2001, Solicitors, Leicester; Dep. Dist Judge, 1999–2004, Dist Judge, 2004–11, Principal Registry of Family Div.; Designated Family Judge for Cambridge and Peterborough, 2012–. *Recreations:* hill walking, music, theatre. *Address:* Peterborough Combined Court Centre, Crown Buildings, Rivergate, Peterborough PE1 1EJ.

GREENER, Sir Anthony (Armitage), Kt 1999; Chairman, Minton Trust, since 2006; *b* 26 May 1940; *s* of William and Diana Marianne Greener; *m* 1974, Min Ogilvie; one *s* one *d*. *Educ:* Marlborough Coll. FCMA. Marketing Manager, Thames Board Mills, 1969; Retail Controller 1972, Dir 1974, Alfred Dunhill Ltd; Man. Dir, Alfred Dunhill Ltd, subseq. Dunhill Holdings plc, 1975; Man. Dir, United Distillers, 1987–92, Chm., 1996–97; Guinness PLC: Dir, 1986–97; Jt Man. Dir, 1989–91; Chief Exec., 1992–97; Chm., 1993–97; Jt Chm., 1997–98, Chm., 1998–2000, Diageo plc; Dep. Chm., British Telecommunications plc, 2001–06; Chm., University for Industry Ltd, 2000–04. Director: Louis Vuitton Moët Hennessy, 1989–97; Reed International, 1990–98; Reed Elsevier, 1993–98; Nautor's Swan, 2009–12. Chm., QCA, 2002–08; Board Member: United Learning Trust, 2005–; Williams Sonoma, 2007–; WNS Global Services, 2007–. Chm., St Giles Trust, 2008–. *Recreations:* skiing, sailing. *Clubs:* Royal Ocean Racing; Royal Yacht Squadron (Cowes).

GREENER, George Pallister, CBE 2005; PhD; FCIWEM; Chairman, Kellen Investments Ltd, 2006–14; *b* 14 July 1945; *m* 1969, Rosemary Orchard; one *s*. *Educ:* Newcastle upon Tyne Univ. (BSc Hons 1966); PhD Southampton 1969. Joined Mars Gp, 1971; Man. Dir, Mars UK, 1986–91; Dir, BAT Industries, 1991–96; Chief Exec., BAT UK Financial Services, 1993–96; Chm. and Chief Exec., Allied Dunbar Assurance, 1991–96; Chairman: Eagle Star Hldgs, 1993–96; Threadneedle Asset Mgt, 1994–96; Chief Exec., Hillsdown Hldgs, 1996–98; Chairman: Swallow Gp, 1999–2000; British waterways, 1999–2005; Big Food (formerly Iceland) Group plc, 2001–05; SHA for London, 2006–08. Non-executive Director: Reckitt & Coleman, subseq. Reckitt Benckiser, 1996–2006; J. P. Morgan American Investment (formerly Fleming American Investment) Trust, 1999–2008. Chm., HEROS (homing of ex-racehorses charity), 2008–12 (Patron, 2012–). Mem. Ct, Univ. of Newcastle upon Tyne, 2005–07. FRSA. *Recreations:* piano playing, horses. *Address:* 5 Horbury Mews, W11 3NL.

GREENER, Very Rev. Jonathan Desmond Francis; Dean of Wakefield, since 2007; *b* 9 March 1961; *s* of Desmond Walter Kingsley Greener and Maureen Frances (*née* Murden); *m* 2006, Pamela Green. *Educ:* Reigate Grammar Sch.; Trinity Coll., Cambridge (BA 1983, MA 1987); Coll. of the Resurrection, Mirfield. Sales and Export Manager, A & M Hearing Ltd, 1984–89. Ordained deacon, 1991, priest, 1992; Asst Curate, Holy Trinity with St Matthew, Southwark, 1991–94; Bp of Truro's Domestic Chaplain, 1994–96; Vicar, Ch of the Good Shepherd, Brighton, 1996–2003; Archdeacon of Pontefract, 2003–07. Co-ordinator, Archbp of Canterbury's Romania Liaison Gp, 1993–2006; Chm., Nat. Archdeacons' Forum, 2007. A Church Comr, 2011–. Chair of Sponsors, Trinity Acad. Halifax, 2007–. *Publications:* (contrib.) The Fire and the Clay, 1993. *Recreations:* France, icons, ski-ing, photography. *Address:* The Deanery, Cathedral Close, Margaret Street, Wakefield WF1 2DP. *T:* (01924) 239308.

GREENFIELD, Baroness *cr* 2001 (Life Peer), of Ot Moor in the County of Oxfordshire; **Susan Adele Greenfield,** CBE 2000; DPhil; Professor of Pharmacology, Oxford University, 1996–2013; Senior Research Fellow, Lincoln College, Oxford, since 1999 (Fellow, 1985–99); Hon. Research Fellow, St Hilda's College, Oxford, since 1999; Chief Executive Officer, Neuro-Bio, since 2014 (Chief Scientific Officer, 2013–14); *b* 1 Oct. 1950; *d* of Reginald Myer Greenfield and Doris Margaret Winifred Greenfield; *m* 1991, Peter William Atkins, *qv* (marr. diss. 2003). *Educ:* Godolphin and Latymer Sch. for Girls; St Hilda's Coll., Oxford (BA Hons Exp. Psychol. 1973; MA 1978; DPhil 1977; Hon. Fellow, 1999). Dame Catherine Fulford Sen. Scholarship, St Hugh's Coll., Oxford, 1974; MRC Training Fellow, Univ. Lab. of Physiol., Oxford, 1977–81; Collège de France, Paris; Royal Soc. Study Visit Award, 1978; MRC-INSERM French Exchange Fellow, 1979–80; Oxford University: Jun. Res. Fellow, Green Coll., 1981–84; Lectr in Synaptic Pharmacol., 1985–96. Dir, Royal Institution, 1998–2010. Co-founder: Synaptica Ltd, 1997; BrainBoost Ltd, 2002. Gresham Prof. of Physic, Gresham Coll., 1995–99; Vis. Fellow, Inst. of Neuroscience, La Jolla, USA, 1995; Vis. Dist. Scholar, Queen's Univ., Belfast, 1996. Adelaide Thinker in Residence, 2004–06; Chancellor, Heriot-Watt Univ., 2006–12. Mem., Nat. Adv. Cttee on Cultural and Creative Educn, 1998–; Pres., ASE, 2000; Vice-Pres., Assoc. of Women in Sci. and Engrg, 2001. Trustee, Science Mus., 1998–2003. Non-executive Director: Britech Foundn Ltd, 2002–06; Oxford Inspires Ltd, 2002–05; Israel Britain Business Council, 2002; Young Foresight Ltd, 2003; Bank Leumi (UK), 2003–06; Cherwell Capital plc, 2004–06; Enkephala Ltd, 2005–. Presenter, Brain Story, BBC 2, 2000. Dimbleby Lectr, 1999. FRSE 2007; Fellow: Australian Davos Connection, 2007; Sci. Mus., 2010. Hon. Fellow, Cardiff Univ., 2000. Hon. FRCP 2000; Hon. Fellow, Inst. of Risk Mgt, 2012. 31 hon. degrees. Michael Faraday Award, Royal Soc., 1998; Woman of Distinction, Jewish Care, 1998; Hon. Australian of Year, 2006; Sci. and Technol. Award, British Inspiration Awards, 2010; Australian Soc. for Med. Res. Medal, 2010. Chevalier, Légion d'Honneur (France), 2003. *Publications:* (ed with C. B. Blakemore) Mindwaves, 1987; (with G. Ferry) Journey to the Centers of the Brain, 1994; Journey to the Centers of the Mind, 1995; (ed) The Human Mind Explained, 1996; The Human Brain: a guided tour, 1997; (ed) Brain Power, 2000; Private Life of the Brain, 2000; Brain Story, 2000; Tomorrow's People, 2003; ID: the quest for identity in the 21st Century, 2008; You And Me: the neuroscience of identity, 2011; 2121: a tale from the next century, 2013; Mind Change: how digital technologies are leaving their mark on our brains, 2014; contribs to learned jls, press and media. *Recreations:* squash, dance. *Address:* Lincoln College, Turl Street, Oxford OX1 3DR. *T:* (01235) 420083. *W:* www.susangreenfield.com. *Club:* Hospital.

GREENFIELD, Andrew, PhD; Programme Leader, Medical Research Council, Harwell, since 1996; *b* Essex, 15 April 1963; *s* of John Greenfield and Joyce Greenfield (*née* Fitt); *m* 1994, Eila Watson; two *s*. *Educ:* Bedfords Park Comp. Sch.; St John's Coll., Cambridge (BA); St Mary's Hosp. Med. Sch., London (PhD); Birkbeck Coll., Univ. of London (MA). Postdoctoral Researcher, Inst. for Molecular Bioscis, Univ. of Queensland, 1992–96. Member: HFEA, 2009–; Nuffield Council on Bioethics, 2014–. *Publications:* over 50 articles in scientific jls. *Recreations:* youth football coach, stem ambassador (outreach), music, philosophy. *Address:* Mammalian Genetics Unit, Medical Research Council, Harwell, Oxon OX11 0RD. *T:* (01235) 841126. *E:* a.greenfield@har.mrc.ac.uk.

GREENFIELD, Howard; *see* Greenfield, R. H.

GREENFIELD, Peter Charles; a District Judge (Magistrates' Courts), since 2012; *b* Hitchin, Herts, 1 Nov. 1961; *s* of late Lawrence Greenfield and Elisabeth Greenfield (*née* Dyke); *m* 1991, Alyson Lyndsey Florence; three *d*. *Educ:* Kingston Univ. (BA Hons Law 1984); Inns of Court Sch. of Law. Called to the Bar, Middle Temple, 1989; Crown Prosecutor, Hants and Dorset, 1990–93; in practice as barrister, Kings Bench Chambers, Bournemouth, 1994–2012; a Dep. Dist Judge (Magistrates' Courts), 2006–12. Mem., Lord Chancellor's Adv. Cttee, Hants, 2006–12. Mem., Ind. Monitoring Bd, HMP Winchester, 2006–11. Mem. (C), New Forest DC, 1999–2012 (Cabinet Mem. for Housing, 2000–07). *Recreations:* fly fishing, sport, astronomy, family, cricket, golf. *Address:* Chief Magistrate's Office, Westminster Magistrates' Court, 181 Marylebone Road, NW1 5BR. *E:* districtjudgepeter.greenfield@judiciary.gsi.gov.uk. *Clubs:* Naval, Savage.

GREENFIELD, (Robert) Howard, FCA; Project Director, British Gas plc, 1990, retired; *b* 4 Feb. 1927; *s* of James Oswald Greenfield and Doris Burt Greenfield; *m* 1951, Joyce Hedley Wells; one *s* one *d*. *Educ:* Rutherford Coll., Newcastle upon Tyne. FCA 1953. Northern Gas Board, 1956–74; Northern Gas: Dir of Customer Service, 1974; Dir of Marketing, 1976; Dep. Chm., 1977; Chm., N Eastern Reg., 1982–85; Regl Chm., British Gas, N Western, 1985–89. OStJ 1988.

GREENGARD, Prof. Paul, PhD; Vincent Astor Professor and Head, Laboratory of Molecular and Cellular Neuroscience, since 1983, and Director, Fisher Center for Research on Alzheimer's Disease, since 1995, Rockefeller University, New York; *b* 11 Dec. 1925; *m* 1986, Ursula von Rydingsvard; two *s* one *d*. *Educ:* Hamilton Coll., NY (AB 1948); Univ. of Pennsylvania; Johns Hopkins Univ. (PhD Neurophysiol. 1953). Served USNR, 1943–46. Research posts at: Inst. of Psychiatry, Univ. of London, 1953–54; Molteno Inst., Univ. of Cambridge, 1954–55; NIMR, London, 1955–58; Lab. of Clinical Biochem., NIH, 1958–59; Dir, Dept of Biochem., Geigy Res. Labs, NY, 1959–67; Prof. of Pharmacol. and Psychiatry, Yale Univ. Sch. of Medicine, 1968–83. Visiting Professor: Albert Einstein Coll. of Medicine, NY, 1968–70; Depts of Pharmacol. and Microbiol., Vanderbilt Univ. Sch. of Medicine, Nashville, 1968; Henry Bronson Prof. of Pharmacol., Yale Univ. Sch. of Medicine, 1981; Wellcome Vis. Prof. in Basic Med. Scis, Univ. of Iowa, 1986. Founder and Series Editor: Advances in Biochemical Psychopharmacol., 1968–; Advances in Cyclic Nucleotide and Protein Phosphorylation Res., 1971–; mem., numerous editl bds and editl adv. bds. Hon. MD Karolinska Inst., 1987. Holds numerous awards including: Award in the Neuroscis, NAS, 1991; Ralph W. Gerard Prize in Neurosci., Soc. For Neurosci., 1994; Charles A. Dana Award for Pioneering Achievements in Health, 1997; Nobel Prize in Physiol. or Medicine, 2000. *Publications:* Cyclic Nucleotides, Phosphorylated Proteins and Neuronal Function, 1978; (with E. J. Nestler) Protein Phosphorylation in the Nervous System, 1984; contrib. numerous chapters and reviews. *Address:* Laboratory of Molecular and Cellular Neuroscience, Rockefeller University, 1230 York Avenue, New York, NY 10065, USA. *T:* (212) 3278780.

GREENGROSS, family name of **Baroness Greengross**.

GREENGROSS, Baroness *cr* 2000 (Life Peer), of Notting Hill in the Royal Borough of Kensington and Chelsea; **Sally Greengross,** OBE 1993; Chief Executive, International Longevity Centre UK, since 2004 (Chairman, 2000–04); Vice-President, Age Concern England, 2002–09 (Director, then Director General, 1987–2000); *b* 29 June 1935; *m* 1959, Sir Alan Greengross, *qv*; one *s* three *d*. *Educ:* Brighton and Hove High Sch.; LSE. Formerly linguist, executive in industry, lectr and researcher; Asst Dir, 1977–82, Dep. Dir, 1982–87, Age Concern England. Secretary General: Internat. Fedn on Ageing, 1982–87 (Vice-Pres. (Europe), 1987–2001); Eurolink Age, 1989–2001. Jt Chm. Bd, Age Concern Inst. of Gerontology, KCL, 1987–2000. Mem. Bd, Britain in Europe, 1999–2006; House of Lords: Mem., Sub-Cttee F, Select Cttee on EU, 2000–03, Sub-Cttee G, 2004–07; Chair, All Party Gp on Corporate Social Responsibility, on Intergenerational Futures, on Continence Care; Chair, All Party Parly Gp on Dementia; Vice Chair, All Party Gp on Ageing and Older People, 2001–10; Treas., All Party Gp on Equalities. Chm., Experience Corps, 2001–05. Vice-Pres., LGA, 2001–. Independent Member: UN Network on Ageing, 1983–2000; WHO Network on Ageing, 1983–2000; Mem., OFCOM Adv. Gp on Older and Disabled People, 2004–06. Member: HelpAge Internat., 2000–07; Adv. Council, Internat. Assoc. of Homes and Services for the Ageing, 2002–. Mem., Equality and Human Rights Commn, 2006–12. Former Member: Inner London Juvenile Court Panel; Management Bd, Hanover Housing Gp. Gov., Pensions Policy Inst., 2002– (Pres., 2004–); Adviser: Internat. Centre for Health and Soc., UCL, 2000–; Good Corp., 2000–07; Merck Inst. of Ageing and Health, 2001–05; Chm. Adv. Cttee, English Longitudinal Study on Ageing, UCL, 2000–; Co-Chair, Alliance for Health and the Future, 2003–08. Patron: Action on Elder Abuse, 1999–; Groundwork Foundn, 1999–; Pennell Initiative, 1999–; Sheffield Inst. for Studies on Ageing, 1999–; Care and Repair England, 1999–; Ransackers, 2006–; Global Ambassador, Help Age Internat., 2007–; Trustee, Help Age Internat. Sri Lanka, 2008–. Hon. Pres., Women for Europe, 1999–. FRSPH (FRSH 1994); FRSA 1994. Hon. FIA 2001. Hon. DLitt: Ulster, 1994; Brunel, 2002; Keele, 2004; DUniv: Kingston, 1996; Open, 2002; Leeds Metropolitan, 2002; Hon. LLD Exeter, 2000. UK Woman of Europe Award, EC, 1990. *Publications:* (ed) Ageing: an adventure in living, 1985; (ed) The Law and Vulnerable Elderly People, 1986; (jtly) Living, Loving and Ageing, 1989; and others on ageing issues and social policy. *Recreations:* countryside, music. *Address:* House of Lords, SW1A 0PW. *T:* (020) 7219 5494. *Clubs:* Reform, Hurlingham, Royal Society of Medicine.

GREENGROSS, Sir Alan (David), Kt 1986; DL; Chairman and Managing Director, Indusmond (Diamond Tools) Ltd; Director: Blazy & Clement Ltd and associated companies; South West Trains, since 2001; *b* 1929; *m* 1959, Sally (*see* Baroness Greengross); one *s* three *d*. *Educ:* University Coll. Sch.; Trinity Coll., Cambridge (Sen. Schol.; MA). Formerly Member Council, London Borough of Camden (past Alderman). Dep. Traffic Comr, 1968–70. GLC: Member (C), 1977–84; Leader, Planning and Communications Policy, 1979–81; Leader of the Opposition, 1983–84. Director: Port of London Authority, 1979–83; London First Centre, 1994–; Chm., London Regl Passengers Cttee, 1996–2000; Mem., Central Rail Users Consultative Cttee, 1996–2000 (Dep. Chm., 1999–2000). Chm., Bloomsbury and Islington HA, 1990–93. Vis. Prof., City of London Polytechnic, 1988–. Dir, The Roundhouse Black Arts Centre, 1988–89. Chairman: Steering Gp, Inst. for Metropolitan Studies, 1989–; Policy Gp, Bartlett Sch. of the Built Envmt, UCL, 1993–2005; Vice-Chm., Retirement Security Ltd. 2010–; Director: Built Envmt Res. Foundn, 1996–; STEP Foundn, 2005–. Member, Governing Council: UCS, 1987–2005; UCL, 1991–2005 (Vice Chm., 2003–05). DL Greater London, 1986. Hon. Fellow, UCL, 1999. *Clubs:* Hurlingham, Royal Society of Medicine.

GREENHALGH, Prof. Christine Anne, PhD; Professor of Applied Economics, University of Oxford, 2008–09, now Emeritus; Fellow and Tutor in Economics, St Peter's College, Oxford, 1979–2009, now Emeritus Fellow; *b* Crayford, Kent, 16 May 1946; *d* of late John Graham and Vera Graham (*née* Hammond); *m* 1967, Dr Peter Greenhalgh; one *s* one *d*. *Educ:* London Sch. of Econs (BSc 1st Cl. Econs 1967; MSc 1968); Princeton Univ. (PhD 1978). Lecturer: Univ. of Cape Coast, Ghana, 1968–70; Univ. of Ghana, Legon, 1971–72; Univ. of Southampton, 1975–79; University of Oxford: Lectr, 1979–96; Reader in Econs, 1996–2008. Vis. Associate Prof., London Business Sch., 2000–01; Res. Associate, Intellectual Property Res. Inst. of Australia, Univ. of Melbourne, 2004–; Vis. Schol., Stanford Inst. Econ. Policy Res., 2007; Departmental Guest, Industrial Relns Section, Princeton Univ., 2011. Hon. Professorial Fellow, Melbourne Inst. for Applied Econ. and Social Res., 2012–Aug. 2016. *Publications:* (ed jtly) The Causes of Unemployment, 1984; (with M. Rogers) Innovation, Intellectual Property and Economic Growth, 2010; contrib. articles to learned jls on labour econs, innovation and intellectual property; reports to UK Intellectual Property Office on small firms and intellectual property. *Recreations:* travel, concerts. *Address:* 4 The Green, Cuddesdon, Oxford OX44 9JZ. *T:* (01865) 873643, (office) (01865) 350459. *E:* christine.greenhalgh@spc.ox.ac.uk.

GREENHALGH, Colin Ayton, CBE 2003 (OBE 1997); DL; MA; Principal, Hills Road Sixth Form College, Cambridge, 1984–2002; Vice Chairman, 2002–10, and Senior Independent Director, 2006–10, Cambridge University Hospitals NHS Foundation Trust (formerly Addenbrooke's NHS Trust) (non-executive Director, 2001–02); *b* 11 Aug. 1941; *s* of Robert Ayton Greenhalgh and Ethel Mary Henderson (*née* Cattermole); *m* 1966, Vivienne Christine Grocock, MSc, PhD; one *s* two *d*. *Educ:* Gateway Sch., Leicester; St John's Coll., Cambridge (MA); Univ. of Nottingham (PGCE). Teacher of Hist., Bradford Grammar Sch., 1964–70; Hd of Hist., Hd of Upper Sch. and Dep. Hd, Bulmershe Sch., Reading, 1970–76; Dep. Hd and Second Master, St Bartholomew's Sch., Newbury, 1976–84. Non-exec. Dir, Cambs HA, 2000–01. Mem., Cambs LEA Inspectorate, 1991–92; Further Education Funding Council: Mem., Eastern Regl Cttee, 1993–98, Quality Assessment Cttee, 1997–2001; Registered Inspector, 1998–2001; Board Member: Learning and Skills Develt Agency (formerly Further Educn Develt Agency), 1999–2003; Further Educn Cttee, SHA, 1998–2002; Mem., Appeals Panel, 2000–, Malpractice Panel for Internat. Exams, 2004–, Oxford, Cambridge and RSA Exams Bd. Registered OFSTED Inspector, 2001–10; educnl consultant, 2002–. Cambridgeshire Association of Secondary Heads: Sec., 1988–89; Chm., 1989–90. Mem., Univ. of Cambridge Sports Centre Appeal Cttee, 2003–05. Trustee, Cambridge Centre for Sixth Form Studies, 2002–08; Chm. of Trustees, Addenbrooke's Recreational and Develt Trust, 2004–09. Governor: Stapleford Primary Sch., 1992–2007; Grammar Sch. at Leeds, 2005–14; Comberton Village Coll., 2013–; Long Rd Sixth Form Coll., 2013–; Trustee and Dir, Comberton Acad. Trust, 2014–. Patron, Romsey Mill, Cambridge, 2004–. Hon. Sen. Mem., Wolfson Coll., Cambridge, 1990–. Hon. Fellow, Anglia Poly. Univ., 2002. Pres., Johnian Soc., St John's Coll., Cambridge, 2015 (Sec., 1992–99 and 2013; Chm., 1999–2012; Vice Pres., 2014); Mem., Rotary Club, Cambridge, 1988–. Mem., Stapleford Parish Council, 1996–2002. DL Cambs, 1998. *Recreations:* churches and country houses, cinema, collecting books, sport, travel, Venice. *Address:* 9 Finch's Close, Stapleford, Cambridge CB22 5BL. *Clubs:* MCC; Hawks; Rotary (Cambridge); Cambridge University Cricket; Leicestershire County Cricket; Jack Frost Cricket.

GREENHALGH, Prof. Douglas Anthony, PhD; CEng, CPhys, FInstP; Executive Dean and Pro-Vice Chancellor, School of Engineering and Built Environment, Glasgow Caledonian University, 2011–14; collaborative research on combustion, fuels and laser diagnostics, Technical University of Berlin and Imperial College London; *b* Manchester, 26 Sept. 1951; *s* of William Douglas and Josephine Greenhalgh; *m* (marr. diss. 1996); two *s*. *Educ:* William Harvey Grammar Sch., Folkestone; Univ. of Newcastle upon Tyne (BSc; PhD 1977). CPhys 1983; CEng 2001; FInstP 2001. Res. Fellow, Southampton Univ., 1976–78; Govt Scientist, UKAEA Harwell, 1979–89; Prof. and Hd of Dept, Cranfield Univ., 1989–2007; Hd, Sch. of Engrg and Physical Scis, Heriot-Watt Univ., 2007–11. Consultant, Rolls-Royce 1971 plc, 1998–2001. Director: CIM Ltd, 2003–07; iSLI Ltd, 2008–11. Ind. Mem., UK Defence Sci. Adv. Council, 2008–. UK Rep. and Vice-Chair, Exec. Cttee, Task Leaders Gp on Energy Conservation and Emissions Reduction in Combustion, Internat. Energy Agency, 2004–. Dir, Beds Golf Club, 2006–07. FHEA; FIES 2013. *Publications:* contrib. book chapters on laser diagnostics and papers to jls; two patents. *Recreations:* golf, walking, gastronomy and wine. *Clubs:* New Golf (St Andrews), Luffness New Golf.

GREENHALGH, Jack; Vice-Chairman, Cavenham Ltd, 1974–81; retired; *b* 25 July 1926; *s* of Herbert Greenhalgh and Alice May (*née* Clayton); *m* 1951, Kathleen Mary Hammond (*d* 1983); two *s* two *d*. *Educ:* Manchester Grammar Sch.; Trinity Coll., Cambridge (MA Hons). Marketing Dept, Procter & Gamble Ltd, Newcastle upon Tyne, 1950–59; Marketing Dir, Eskimo Foods Ltd, Cleethorpes, 1959–64; Dir of Continental Ops, Compton Advertising Inc., NY, 1964–65; Cavenham Ltd, 1965–81: Man. Dir, 1968–79. FCMI. *Recreations:* golf, sailing.

GREENHALGH, Prof. Patricia Mary, (Trisha), (Mrs Fraser Macfarlane), OBE 2001; MD; FRCP, FRCGP; FRSB; FMedSci; Professor of Primary Health Care Sciences, University of Oxford, since 2015; *b* Newcastle-under-Lyme, 11 March 1959; *d* of Daniel Joseph Greenhalgh and Audrey Mary Greenhalgh; *m* 1987, Fraser Macfarlane; two *s*. *Educ:* Folkestone Grammar Sch.; Clare Coll., Cambridge (BA 1980; MD Diabetes and Endocrinol. 1995); University Coll., Oxford (BM BCh 1983). MRCP 1986, FRCP 1998; MRCGP 1990, FRCGP 2000; FRSB (FSB 2011); FFPH 2012; FMedSci 2014. University College London: Lectr, 1992–96; Sen. Lectr, 1996–2001; Prof., 2001–10; Queen Mary University of London: Prof. of Primary Health Care, 2010–14; Dean for Res. Impact, 2013–14. Mem., Health Cttee on Ethical Aspects of Pandemic Flu, DoH, 2008–14. Dep. Chair, Main Panel for Medicine, UK REF, 2010–14. Mem. Council, RCGP, 2011–. *Publications:* How to Read a Paper: the basics of evidence-based medicine, 1997, 5th edn 2014; Primary Health Care: theory and practice, 2007; What Seems to be the Trouble?: stories in illness and health care, 2007.

GREENHALGH, Paul; Director, Sainsbury Centre for Visual Arts, University of East Anglia, since 2010; *b* 21 Oct. 1955; *s* of William Greenhalgh and Marie Joan Greenhalgh; *m* 1981 (marr. diss.); two *s*. *Educ:* Bolton Smithills Grammar Sch.; Univ. of Reading (BA); Courtauld Inst., Univ. of London (MA). Lectr, Cardiff Inst., 1980–87; Dep. Curator of Ceramics and Glass, V&A Mus., 1988–92; Tutor in Art History, RCA, 1990–92; Hd of Art History, Camberwell Coll. of Arts, 1992–94; Hd of Res., V&A Mus., 1994–2000; Curator, Art Nouveau 1890–1914 exhibn, V&A and Nat. Gall. of Art, Washington, 2000, Metropolitan Mus., Tokyo, 2001; Pres., NSCAD Univ. (formerly Nova Scotia Coll. of Art and Design), 2001–06; Dir and Pres., Corcoran Gall. of Art and Coll. of Art and Design, Washington, 2006–10. Vis. Prof., Brighton Univ., 2009–; Prof. of Art History, UEA, 2011–. Academic Editor, Manchester Univ. Press, 1989–. Chair, Cttee for Art, Design and Art History, REF 2014, 2012–15; Chair, Art Adv. Cttee, Edinburgh Univ., 2012–; Arts Consultant, BBC, 2012–. Mem., Crafts Council Educn Cttee, 1992–. Hon. Fellow, Res. Dept, V&A Mus., 2001. Hon. PhD Brighton, 2007; Hon. DLitt Brighton. *Publications:* Ephemeral Vistas: great exhibitions, expositions universelles and world's fairs 1850–1939, 1988; (ed) Modernism in Design, 1990; Quotations and Sources on Design and the Decorative Arts 1800–1990, 1993; (ed) Art Nouveau 1890–1914, 2000; The Essential Art Nouveau, 2000; The Persistence of Craft, 2002; The Modern Ideal: the rise and collapse of idealism in the visual arts from the enlightenment to postmodernism, 2005; Fair World: a history of expositions from London to Shanghai 1851–2010, 2011; L'Art Nouveau: les artistes de la vie moderne, 2013. *Recreations:* running, football. *Address:* Sainsbury Centre for Visual Arts, University of East Anglia, Norwich NR4 7TJ. *T:* (01603) 592467. *E:* p.greenhalgh@uea.ac.uk.

GREENHALGH, Prof. Roger Malcolm, FRCS; Emeritus Professor of Surgery and Head of Imperial College of Science, Technology and Medicine Vascular Research Group at Charing Cross Hospital, since 2006; Hon. Consultant Surgeon, Charing Cross Hospital, since 1976; *b* 6 Feb. 1941; *s* of John Greenhalgh and Phyllis Poynton; *m* 1964, Karin Maria Gross; one *s* one *d*. *Educ:* Clare Coll., Cambridge; St Thomas' Hosp., London. BA 1963, BChir 1966, MB, MA 1967, MChir 1974, MD 1983 (Cantab); FRCS 1971. Ho. Surg., 1967, Casualty Officer, 1968, St Thomas' Hosp.; Sen. Ho. Officer, Hammersmith Hosp., 1969; Registrar in Surgery, Essex County Hosp., Colchester, 1970–72; Lectr and Sen. Registrar in Surgery, St Bartholomew's Hosp., 1972–76; Sen. Lectr in Surgery, Charing Cross Hosp., 1976–81; Head of Dept of Surgery, 1981–84, Prof. of Surgery, 1982–2006, Chm. of Dept of Surgery, 1989–97, Dean, 1993–97, Charing Cross Hosp. Med. Sch., later Charing Cross and Westminster Med. Sch.; Clinical Dir, 1994–98, Chief of Vascular Surgical Service, 1998–2002, Hammersmith Hosps NHS Trust; Head of Dept of Vascular Surgery, Div. of Surgery, Anaesthetics and Intensive Care, Imperial Coll. London, 1997–2006. Chm., Eur. Examining Bd, Surgery Qualification, 1995–2002; President: Surgery sect., EU of Medical Specialities, 1998–2002; Eur. Bd of Surgery, 2002–06; Eur. Fedn of Surgical Specialties, UEMS, 2004–08. Sometime examiner, Univs of Cambridge, London, Edinburgh, Bristol, Leicester, UCD, Southampton, Birmingham, Hong Kong. Chairman: Charing Cross Internat. Symposium, 1978–; Liaison Cttee, Bioengrg Centre, Roehampton, London, 1985–88; Riverside Med. Council, 1992–93; Member: Scientific Cttee on Tobacco and Health (formerly Ind. Scientific Enquiry into Smoking and Health), 1979–; Coll. of Experts, MRC, 2002–; CMO's Scientific Cttee on Tobacco and Health, 2004–; Abdominal Aortic

Aneurysm Nat. Screening Prog. Adv. Gp (formerly Wkg Party), 2004–; DoH Mem., NICE approval cttee for endovascular aneurysm repair, 2008–. Vice-President: Section of Surgery, RSM, 1986–89; BRCS, 1992–; Sec. Gen. and Chm. Exec. Cttee, Assoc. of Internat. Vascular Surgeons, 1982–2005; Chm. Dirs and Trustees, European Soc. for Vascular Surgery, 1987–2006 (Mem. Council, 1987–93); Mem. Council, Assoc. of Surgeons of GB and Ireland, 1993–2008; Pres., Vascular Soc. of GB and Ire., 1999–2000. Hon. Life Pres., Eur. Bd of Vascular Surgery, 2004. Hon. FRCSE (*ad eundem*) 1999; Hon. FRCSI 2007; Hon. Fellow, British Soc. of Interventional Radiol., 2006; Hon. Member: S African Vascular Surgical Soc., 1989; Canadian Vascular Soc., 1991; Polish Surgical Soc., 1991; German Vascular Soc., 1992; Hellenic Surgical Soc., 1992; Eur. Soc. for Vascular Surgery, 1993 (Dist. Person's Award, 2002); Brazilian Angiology Soc., 1993; Hellenic Vascular Surg. Soc., 1995; Mediterranean League of Vascular Surgeons, 1996; Soc. for Vascular Surgery, 2003 (Corresp. Mem., 1991); Austrian Vascular Soc., 2002; Swiss Vascular Soc., 2003; Eur. Venous Forum, 2007; Internat. Union of Angiol., 2008; Soc. of Clinical Vascular Surgeons, 2011. Moynihan Fellow of Assoc. of Surgeons, 1975; Hunterian Prof., RCS, 1980; Protem Prof., Brigham Hosp., Harvard Med. Sch., 1984; Boone Powell Prof., Baylor Dallas Med. Sch., 1984; Hunter Sweeney Prof., Duke Univ., 1991; Mannick Vis. Prof., Harvard Univ., 1996. Sir Peter Freyer Lect., Univ. of Galway, 1995; Scott Heron Lect., QUB, 1999; Michael van Vloten Lect., Eindhoven, 2003. Hon. Dr: Warsaw Med. Acad., 2003; Athens Univ., 2004. Hon. Citizen, Kranidi, Greece, 2006; Lifetime Achievement Award, Vascular and Endovascular Surgery, Arizona Heart Inst. and Miami Heart Inst., 2011. Chm. Editl Bd, European Jl of Vascular Surgery, 1987–2003; Mem. Editl Bd, Annals of Surgery, 1991–; Ed., Vascular News, 1998–. *Publications:* Progress in Stroke Research, 1, 1979; Smoking and Arterial Disease, 1981; Hormones and Vascular Disease, 1981; Femoro-distal bypass, 1981; Extra-Anatomic and Secondary Arterial Reconstruction, 1982; Progress in Stroke Research, 2, 1983; Vascular Surgical Techniques, 1984, 2nd edn 1989, 3rd edn as Vascular and Endovascular Surgical Techniques, 1994, 4th edn 2001; Diagnostic Techniques and Assessment Procedures in Vascular Surgery, 1985; Vascular Surgery: issues in current practice, 1986; Indications in Vascular Surgery, 1988; Limb Salvage and Amputations for Vascular Disease, 1988; The Cause and Management of Aneurysms, 1990; The Maintenance of Arterial Reconstruction, 1991; Vascular Surgical Emergencies, 1992; Surgery for Stroke, 1993; Vascular Imaging for Surgeons, 1995; Trials and Tribulations of Vascular Surgery, 1996; Clinical Surgery, 1996; Inflammatory and thrombotic problems in vascular surgery, 1997; Indications in Vascular and Endovascular Surgery, 1998; The Durability of Vascular and Endovascular Surgery, 1999; Vascular and Endovascular Opportunities, 2000; The evidence for vascular and endovascular reconstruction, 2002; Vascular and Endovascular Controversies, 2003; Vascular and Endovascular Challenges, 2004; Towards Vascular and Endovascular Consensus, 2005; More Vascular and Endovascular Controversies, 2006; More Vascular and Endovascular Challenges, 2007; More Vascular and Endovascular Consensus, 2008; Vascular and Endovascular Controversies Update, 2009, 2012; Vascular and Endovascular Challenges Update, 2010; Vascular and Endovascular Consensus Update, 2011; Born to be a Surgeon, 2011; Vascular and Endovascular Controversies, 2012; Vascular and Endovascular Challenges Update, 2013; Vascular and Endovascular Consensus Update, 2014. *Recreations:* tennis, ski-ing, swimming, music. *Address:* 271 Sheen Lane, East Sheen, SW14 8RN. *T:* (020) 8878 1110. *Club:* Garrick.

GREENHALGH, Trisha; *see* Greenhalgh, P. M.

GREENHILL, family name of **Baron Greenhill**.

GREENHILL, 3rd Baron *cr* 1950, of Townhead; **Malcolm Greenhill;** retired from Ministry of Defence; *b* 5 May 1924; *s* of 1st Baron Greenhill, OBE and Ida, *d* of late Mark Goodman; *S* brother, 1989. *Educ:* Kelvinside Acad., Glasgow; Glasgow Univ. (BSc). CPA. Ministries of Aircraft Production and Supply, 1944–54; UK Scientific Mission, Washington DC, USA, 1950–51; UKAEA, 1954–73; MoD, 1973–89. *Recreation:* gardening. *Club:* Civil Service.

GREENHOUGH, Kathleen; *see* Soriano, K.

GREENING, Rt Hon. Justine; PC 2011; MP (C) Putney, since 2005; Secretary of State for International Development, since 2012; *b* 30 April 1969. *Educ:* Oakwood Comprehensive Sch., Rotherham; Thomas Rotherham Coll.; Univ. of Southampton (BSc 1990); London Business Sch. (MBA 2000). ACA 1995. Audit Asst, Price Waterhouse, 1991–94; Audit Asst Manager, Revisuisse Price Waterhouse, 1995–96; Finance Manager, SmithKline Beecham, 1996–2001; Business Strategy Manager, GlaxoSmithKline, 2001–02; Sales and Mktg Finance Manager, Centrica, 2002–05. Econ. Sec., HM Treasury, 2010–11; Sec. of State for Transport, 2011–12. Mem. (C), Epping Town Council, 1999. Contested (C) Ealing, Acton and Shepherd's Bush, 2001. *Address:* (office) 3 Summerstown Road, SW17 0BQ; House of Commons, SW1A 0AA. *W:* www.justinegreening.co.uk.

GREENISH, Rear Adm. Philip Duncan, CBE 2003; CEng, FIET; Chief Executive, Royal Academy of Engineering, since 2003; *b* Sept. 1951; *s* of late Comdr Geoffrey Harold Greenish, OBE, RN and Alice Greenish (*née* Thierens); *m* 1972, Wendy Midmer; two *s* one *d*. *Educ:* Cheltenham Coll.; Durham Univ. (BSc Hons Engrg Sci.). CEng 1989; FIET (FIEE 2001). Captain Weapon Trials and Acceptance, 1992–94; MA to Chief of Defence Procurement, 1994–96; rcds 1997; Director: Operational Requirements (Sea Systems), 1997–99; Equipment Capability (Above Water Battlespace), 1999–2000; COS (Corporate Develt) to C-in-C Fleet, 2000–02; COS (Support) to C-in-C Fleet, 2002–03. ADC to the Queen, 1997–2000. Member: CCLRC, 2005–07; STFC, 2007–11; EngineeringUK (formerly Engrg and Technology Bd), 2007–. Mem. Council, Southampton Univ., 2011–. Trustee: Daphne Jackson Trust, 2004–; Sci. Media Centre, 2011–. *Recreations:* tennis, golf, ski-ing, music, gardening. *Address:* Royal Academy of Engineering, 3 Carlton House Terrace, SW1Y 5DG.

See also S. Greenish.

GREENISH, Simon, MBE 2013; Chief Executive Officer and Director, Bletchley Park Trust, 2006–12, Consultant, since 2012; *b* 11 Oct. 1949; *s* of late Comdr Geoffrey Harrold Greenish, OBE, RN and Alice Greenish (*née* Thierens); *m* 1986, Gillian (*née* Wilkinson); two *d*. *Educ:* Durham Univ. (BSc Hons Eng. Sci. 1971). CEng, MICE 1975. Engr, N Beds BC, 1971–80; Prin. Engr, CAA, 1980–95; Develt Manager, 1995–2004, Dir of Collections, 2004–06, RAF Mus. Hon. DSc Bedfordshire, 2012. *Recreation:* music. *Address:* Cartref, Grange Road, Felmersham, Beds MK43 7EU. *T:* (01234) 782559. *E:* simongreenish@btinternet.com.

See also Rear Adm. P. D. Greenish.

GREENO, Edward Patrick; Partner, Quinn Emanuel Urquhart & Sullivan LLP, since 2013; *b* Walton-on-Thames, 10 May 1958; *s* of Edward Greeno and Brenda Greeno; *m* 1987, Fleur van Roosmalen (marr. diss. 2015); two *s* one *d*. *Educ:* Cranleigh Sch.; King's Coll., London (LLB). Admitted solicitor, 1983; Herbert Smith, later Herbert Smith Freehills, 1981–2013: Partner, Litigation and Arbitration Div., 1989–2013; Recruitment Partner, 1993–97; Mem., Partnership Council, 2002–06; Solicitor Advocate, 2006. Mem., Editl Bd, Commercial Dispute Resolution, 2011–. *Recreations:* tennis, golf, music, Rugby, ski-ing, family. *Address:* Quinn Emanuel Urquhart & Sullivan LLP, 1 Fleet Place, EC4M 7RA. *T:* (020) 7653 2030. *E:* tedgreeno@quinnemanuel.com. *Clubs:* Athenæum, Kandahar, 606 Jazz; St George's Hill Tennis, St George's Hill Golf; Harlequin Football.

GREENOAK, Francesca; writer; Alexander Teacher: in private practice, since 1999; Tring Park School for the Performing Arts (formerly Arts Educational School), since 2000; *b* 6 Sept. 1946; *d* of Francis Buchanan Greenoak and Alice Lavinia (*née* Marston); *m* 1981, John Kilpatrick; one *s* one *d*. *Educ:* St Mary's Convent Grammar Sch., Woodford Green; Univ. of Essex (BA Hons); Alexander Re-Educn Centre, Stoke Mandeville. Book Club Associates, 1968; Editor: George Harrap, 1970; Penguin Educn, Penguin Books, 1972; Chameleon Publishing Co-operative, 1974; Gardening Correspondent: She mag., 1978–80; The Times, 1986–94; Gardens Ed., Good Housekeeping, 1993–96; Express Saturday, 1997–99. Member: Garden History Soc., 1999–2009 (Mem. Council, 1999–2002; Ed., Garden History Soc. News, 1999–2002; Mem., Educn and Pubns Cttee, 2000–02); Soc. of Teachers of the Alexander Technique, 1999– (Mem. Council, 2000–05; Dir, 2005–09; Mem., Pubns Cttee, 2000–13). Chair and Founder Trustee, Hardings Wood Trust, 2002–. Ed., Alexander Jl, 2001–13. Leverhulme Res. Award, to study cultural and natural history of churchyards, 1995. *Publications:* Trees, 1976; Guide to Wildflowers, 1977; What Right Have You Got?, 1977; Alone, 1978; Heath and Moorland, 1979; All The Birds of the Air, 1979, 2nd edn as British Birds: their folklore, names and literature, 1997; Forgotten Fruit, 1983; (with R. Mabey) Back to the Roots, 1983; God's Acre, 1985, 2nd edn as Wildlife in Churchyards, 1993; (ed) Journals of Gilbert White, 3 vols, 1989; Glorious Gardens, 1989; Fruit and Vegetable Gardens, 1990; Water in Small Gardens, 1996, 2nd edn as Water Features for Small Gardens, 2002; Natural Style for Gardens, 1998, 2nd edn as The Natural Garden, 2001; Gardens of the National Trust for Scotland, 2005; Hardings Wood, 2009; The Alexander Album: a century of Alexander pupils, 2014. *Recreations:* literature, gardening, botany, music, dance, education and science. *Address:* 3–4 Wood Row, Wigginton, Tring, Herts HP23 6HS. *W:* www.fgreenoak.com.

GREENOCK, Lord; Alan George Cathcart; Director, Spring Garden Eggs Ltd, since 2011; *b* 16 March 1986; *s* and *heir* of Earl Cathcart, *qv*. *Educ:* Stowe. *Address:* Gateley Hall, North Elmham, Dereham, Norfolk NR20 5EF.

GREENSHIELDS, Robert McLaren; HM Diplomatic Service, retired; Counsellor, Foreign and Commonwealth Office, 1985–88; *b* 27 July 1933; *s* of late Brig. James Greenshields, MC, TD, and Mrs James Greenshields; *m* 1960, Jean Alison Anderson; one *s* two *d*. *Educ:* Edinburgh Academy; Lincoln Coll., Oxford (MA Hons); Open Univ. (Dip. German 2009). National Service, 2nd Lieut Highland Light Infantry, 1952–54. District Officer, Tanganyika, HMOCS, 1958–61; Asst Master and Housemaster, Gordonstoun Sch., 1962–68; HM Diplomatic Service, 1969–88. Chm., Berwickshire Br., Cons. Party, 2014–15. *Recreations:* ornithology, conservation, politics.

GREENSLADE, Roy; freelance journalist, broadcaster and author, since 1992, and blogger, since 2006; Professor of Journalism, City University, since 2003; *b* 31 Dec. 1946; *s* of Ernest Frederick William Greenslade and Joan Olive (*née* Stocking); *m* 1984, Noreen Anna Taylor (*née* McElhone); one step *s* one step *d*. *Educ:* Dagenham County High Sch.; Sussex Univ. (BA (Hons) Politics, 1979). Trainee journalist, Barking Advertiser, 1964–66; Sub-Editor: Lancashire Evening Telegraph, 1966–67; Daily Mail, 1967–69; The Sun, 1969–71; researching and writing book, 1973–75; Daily Star, 1979–80; Daily Express, 1980–81; Daily Star, 1981; Asst Editor, The Sun, 1981–87; Man. Editor, Sunday Times, 1987–90; Editor, Daily Mirror, 1990–91; Consultant Editor, Today and Sunday Times, 1991. Columnist: Observer, 1996; Guardian, 1996–2005; Daily Telegraph, 2005–06; Evening Standard, 2006–; blogger, Guardian, 2006–. Dir, Impact Books, 1993–98. Presenter: Mediumwave, Radio 4, 1995–96; Britain Talks Back, TV, 1996–97. Mem. Bd, British Journalism Review, 1994–. FRSA 2004. Hon. DLitt Brighton, 1999. *Publications:* Goodbye to the Working Class, 1975; Maxwell's Fall, 1992; Press Gang, 2003. *Recreation:* reading. *Address:* Brighton BN2 1GA.

GREENSPAN, Alan, Hon. KBE 2002; President, Greenspan Associates LLC, since 2006; Chairman, Board of Governors of the Federal Reserve System, USA, 1987–2006; *b* 6 March 1926; *o s* of late Herbert Greenspan and Rose (*née* Goldsmith); *m* 1997, Andrea Mitchell. *Educ:* New York Univ. (BS 1948; MA 1950; PhD 1977). Pres., 1954–74 and 1977–87, Townsend-Greenspan & Co., NY. Director: Trans World Financial Co., 1962–74; Dreyfus Fund, 1970–74; Gen. Cable Corp., 1973–74, 1977–78; Sun Chemical Corp., 1973–74; Gen. Foods Corp., 1977–85; J. P. Morgan & Co., 1977–87; Mobil Corp., 1977–87; Capital Cities/ABC, 1978–87; ALCOA, 1978–87; ADP, 1980–87. Consultant to Council of Economic Advisers, 1970–74, to US Treasury, 1971–74, to Fed. Reserve Board, 1971–74; Chairman: Council of Economic Advisers, 1974–77; Nat. Commn on Social Security Reform, 1981–83; Dir, Council on Foreign Relations; Presidential Commn on Financial Structure and Regulation, 1971, on an All-Volunteer Armed Force, 1971; Member: President's Econ. Policy Adv. Board, 1981–87; President's Foreign Intell. Adv. Board, 1983–85. Hon. degrees from Edinburgh, Harvard, Leuven, Pennsylvania and Yale univs. Jefferson Award, 1976; William Butler Meml Award, 1977; US Presidential Medal of Freedom, 2005. Commander, French Legion of Honour, 2003. *Publications:* The Age of Turbulence, 2007; The Map and the Territory: risk, human nature, and the future of forecasting, 2013. *Address:* (office) 1133 Connecticut Avenue NW, Suite 810, Washington, DC 20036, USA.

GREENSTOCK, Sir Jeremy (Quentin), GCMG 2003 (KCMG 1998; CMG 1991); HM Diplomatic Service, retired; King of Arms, Most Distinguished Order of St Michael and St George, since 2007; Chairman, UN Association-UK, since 2011; *b* 27 July 1943; *s* of late John Wilfrid Greenstock and Ruth Margaret Logan; *m* 1969, Anne Derryn Ashford Hodges; one *s* two *d*. *Educ:* Harrow Sch.; Worcester Coll., Oxford (MA Lit. Hum.; Hon. Fellow, 2006). Asst Master, Eton Coll., 1966–69; entered HM Diplomatic Service, 1969; MECAS, 1970–72; Dubai, 1972–74; Private Sec. to the Ambassador, Washington, 1974–78; FCO, 1978–83 (Planning Staff, Personnel Ops Dept, N East and N African Dept); Counsellor (Commercial), Jedda, 1983–85, Riyadh, 1985–86; Hd of Chancery, Paris, 1987–90; Asst Under-Sec. of State, FCO, 1990–93; Minister, Washington, 1994–95; Dep. Under Sec. of State, FCO, 1995; Pol Dir, FCO, 1996–98; UK Perm. Rep. to UN, 1998–2003; UK Special Rep. for Iraq, 2003–04. Dir, Ditchley Foundn, 2004–10. Special Advr, BP Gp, 2004–10. Chairman: Gatehouse Advisory Partners Ltd, 2010–; Lambert Energy Advisory Ltd, 2012– (non-exec. Dir, 2010–); non-exec. Dir, De La Rue plc, 2005–13. Member: Adv. Gp, UN Develt Fund for Women, 2005–09; Internat. Adv. Gp, Brookings Instn, 2007–09; Nat. Security Commn, IPPR, 2007–09; Council, RIIA, 2011–; BASIC Trident Commn, 2012–14; Special Consultant, Forward Thinking, 2006–. Trustee, Internat. Rescue Cttee (UK), 2006–12. Mem. Adv. Council, Oxford Philomusica Orchestra, 2007–11. Gov., London Business Sch., 2005–07. Hon. FKC 2006. *Recreations:* family, travel/wildlife, golf, ski-ing, watching sport, music/theatre. *Address:* 3 Cornwall Gardens, SW7 4AJ.

GREENTREE, (William Wayne) Chris; Chief Executive, LASMO Group plc, 1982–93; *b* 6 April 1935; *s* of J. Murray and Grace M. Greentree; *m* 1st, 1956, Patricia Ann Hugo (marr. diss. 1990); four *d* (and one *d* decd); 2nd, 1990, Hilary J. Wilson; one *d*. *Educ:* Moose Jaw Technical High Sch., Saskatoon; Univ. of Alberta (BSc Hons, PEng). Joined Shell Canada, 1957: technical and managerial appts, onshore and offshore exploration; Ranger Oil London, 1972–79: Man. Dir, 1976; Mapco Inc. USA: Sen. Vice Pres. Exploration and Production, 1979–82. Chm., Bd of Govs, Internat. Sch. São Lourenço, Algarve, 2005–12. Ordre National du Mérite (Gabon), 1987. *Recreation:* golf.

GREENWAY, family name of **Baron Greenway**.

GREENWAY, 4th Baron *cr* 1927; **Ambrose Charles Drexel Greenway;** Bt 1919; marine photographer and author; *b* 21 May 1941; *s* of 3rd Baron Greenway and Cordelia Mary, *d* of late Major Humfrey Campbell Stephen; *S* father, 1975; *m* 1985, Mrs Rosalynne Schenk. *Educ:* Winchester. Chairman: Marine Soc., 1994–2000; Sail Trng Assoc., subseq. Tall Ships Youth Trust, 2001–03; World Ship Trust, 2003–. Elected Mem., H of L, 1999. Jt Chm., All-Party Ports and Maritime Gp, 2010–. Elder Brother, Trinity House, 2007–. *Publications:* Soviet Merchant Ships, 1976; Comecon Merchant Ships, 1978; A Century of Cross Channel Passenger Ferries, 1980; A Century of North Sea Passenger Steamers, 1986; Cargo Liners,

2009. *Recreations:* ocean racing and cruising, swimming. *Heir:* *b* Hon. Nigel Paul Greenway [*b* 12 Jan. 1944; *m* 1979, Gabrielle, *e d* of Walter Jean Duchardt; two *s*]. *Address:* c/o House of Lords, SW1A 0PW. *Club:* House of Lords Yacht.

GREENWAY, Prof. Diana Eleanor, PhD; FBA 2001; Professor of Medieval History, University of London, 1998–2003; Hon. Fellow, Institute of Historical Research, University of London, since 2004; *b* 1937; *d* of Charles and Winifred Greenway. *Educ:* Aylesbury Grammar Sch.; Girton Coll., Cambridge (BA Hist. 1959; MA 1963; PhD 1967). Asst Archivist, Lambeth Palace Liby, 1963–64; University of London: Ed., Fasti Ecclesiae Anglicanae 1066–1300 (11 vols, 1968–2011), at Inst. of Historical Res., 1964–2003; teaching hist. and palaeography, 1966–97; Reader in Medieval Hist., 1993–98. Founder and Chair, Univ. of London Palaeography and Diplomatic Teachers' Gp, 1993–98. Gen. Ed., Oxford Medieval Texts, 1974–97. Literary Dir, RHistS, 1982–87. Dir, Summer Insts in Palaeography, Newberry Liby, Chicago, 1985, 1990 and 1994. British Rep., Assembly of Repertorium Fontium Historiae Medii Aevi, 1993–2003. Freeman, City of London, 2011. *Publications:* Charters of the Honour of Mowbray 1107–91, 1972; (ed jtly) Early Yorkshire Families, 1973; (ed jtly) Richard fitzNigel: Dialogus de Scaccario, 1983; (ed jtly) Tradition and Change: essays in honour of Marjorie Chibnall, 1985; (ed jtly) Handbook of British Chronology, 1986; (jtly) The Chronicle of Jocelin of Brakelond, 1989; Henry, Archdeacon of Huntingdon: Historia Anglorum, 1996; (ed jtly) The Book of the Foundation of Walden Monastery, 1999; Saint Osmund, Bishop of Salisbury 1078 to 1099, 1999; Henry of Huntingdon: The History of the English People 1000–1154, 2002; contrib. articles to learned jls. *Recreations:* birdwatching, dragonflies. *Address:* Institute of Historical Research, University of London, Senate House, WC1E 7HU.

GREENWAY, Harry; *b* 4 Oct. 1934; *s* of John Kenneth Greenway and Violet Adelaide (*née* Bell); *m* 1969, Carol Elizabeth Helena, *e d* of late Major John Robert Thomas Hooper, barrister at law and Metropolitan Stipendiary Magistrate, and Dorinda Hooper (*née* de Courcy Ireland); one *s* two *d*. *Educ:* Warwick Sch.; College of St Mark and St John, London; Univ. of Caen, Normandy. Assistant Master, Millbank Sch., 1957–60; successively, Head of English Dept, Sen. Housemaster, Sen. Master, Acting Dep. Head, Sir William Collins Sch., 1960–72; Dep. Headmaster, Sedgehill Sch. (Comprehensive for 2,000 plus pupils), 1972–79. Contested (C) Stepney, 1970, Stepney and Poplar, Feb. and Oct. 1974; MP (C) Ealing North, 1979–97; contested (C) same seat, 1997. Vice-Chm., Greater London Cons. Members, 1981–97; Chairman: All Party Adult Educn Cttee, 1979–97; All Party Parly Friends of Cycling, 1987–95; Member: Parly Select Cttee on Educn, Science and the Arts, 1979–92; Parly Select Cttee on Employment, 1992–95, on Educn and Employment, 1995–97; Vice-Chairman: Cons. Parly Educn Cttee, 1983–87 (Sec., 1981); Cons. Parly Sports Cttee, 1990–97 (Sec., 1986–90); Parly Sec., Cons. National Adv. Cttee on Educn, 1981–94; Sec., Cons. Parly Arts and Heritage Cttee, 1986–87. Parly Sec., Cons. Nat. Educn Soc., 1995–97 (Dep. Pres., 1998–); Chm., Mauritius Parly Gp, 1983–97. Led All Party Parly Delegn to Sri Lanka, 1985, to Gibraltar, 1989, to Zaire, 1990. Pres., Cons. Trade Unionist Teachers, 1982–83; Chm., Educn Cttee, British-Atlantic Cttee, 1971–85; Open University: Mem. Council, 1981–99; Audit Cttee, 1997–99; Grievance Cttee, 1998–99; Mem., Educn Cttee, NACRO, 1985–88. President: Age Concern, Greenford, Northolt and Perivale, 1980–; Ealing Youth Choir, 1985–; Nat. Equine Welfare Council, 1990–; Assoc. of British Riding Schs, 1993–2003; Spencer Hockey Club, 2000–03; Ealing N Cons. Assoc., 2012–; Mem. Council, British Horse Soc., 1973–97 (Trustee, 1998–2006); Mem. Bd of Govs, Horse Rangers Assoc., 2000–02; Founder Trustee, The Greater London Equestrian Centres Trust Ltd; Trustee, Teenage Cancer Trust, 1991–2007. Vice-Pres., Greenford Br., RBL, 1977–. Chm., National Prayer Breakfast, 1995. Freeman: City of London, 1986; London Bor. of Ealing, 2008; Liveryman, Farriers' Co., 1986–2006. DUniv Open, 2001. Award of Merit, 1980, President's Award, 2006, Sefton Award, 2007, British Horse Soc. Kt Comdr's Cross, Order of Merit (Poland), 1998. *Publications:* Adventure in the Saddle, 1971; (ed and compiled) Electing to Bat: tales of glory and disaster from the Palace of Westminster, 1996; regular contributor to educnl and equestrian jls. *Recreations:* riding (Asst Instructor, BHS, 1966), ski-ing, choral music, hockey (Vice-Pres., England Schoolboys' Hockey Assoc.; Founder, Lords and Commons Hockey Club), tennis, cricket, parliamentary parachutist. *Address:* 64 Cambridge Street, Westminster, SW1V 4QQ. *Clubs:* National, MCC, Middlesex CC, Lord's Taverners, Ski Club of Gt Britain; Worcs CC.

GREENWAY, John Robert; *b* 15 Feb. 1946; *s* of Thomas William and Kathleen Greenway; *m* 1st, 1974, Sylvia Ann Gant (marr. diss. 2006); two *s* one *d*; 2nd, 2008, Johanna ten Kate. *Educ:* Sir John Deane's Grammar School, Northwich; London College of Law. Midland Bank, 1964; Metropolitan Police, 1965–69; Equitable Life Assurance Soc., 1970–71; National Provident Instn, 1971–72; own firm of insurance brokers, J. R. Greenway, subseq. Greenway Middleton, & Co. Ltd, York, then Greenway Smart and Cook Ltd, later Smart and Cook Ltd, now part of Bluefin Gp, 1972–. Treasurer, Ryedale Cons. Assoc., 1984–86; Mem., North Yorks CC, 1985–87; Vice-Chm., N Yorks Police Authy, 1986–87. MP (C) Ryedale, 1987–2010. PPS to Minister of State, MAFF, 1991–92; Opposition front bench spokesman on home affairs, 1997–2000, on sport and tourism, 2000–03. Mem., Home Affairs Select Cttee, 1987–97. Chm., Jt Scrutiny Cttee, Draft Gambling Bill, 2003–05; Sec., Cons. backbench Health Cttee, 1988–91; Vice-Chairman: Cons. backbench Agricl Cttee, 1989–97; All Party Football Cttee, 1989–2010; Chairman: All Party Racing and Bloodstock Cttee, 1993–97; All Party Insce and Financial Services Gp, 1992–2010 (Sec., 1991–92); Jt Chm., All Party Opera Gp, 1994–2010. Elected rep. to Council of Europe, 2005–10 (Chm., Rules Cttee, 2008–10; Chm., Migration Cttee, 2010–); Mem., Assembly of WEU, 2005–10. Dir, Responsibility in Gambling Trust, 2006–10. Pres., Inst. of Insce Brokers, 1987–2011; Chm., Fedn of Insce and Investment Intermediary Assocs, 1998–2001; Mem., Insce Brokers Registration Council, 1991–2001. Pres., The Insurance Charities, 2014–15 (Dep. Pres., 2012–14). *Recreations:* opera, football (Pres., York City FC, 1989–2003), wine, travel, home in France.

GREENWELL, (Arthur) Jeffrey, CBE 1991; DL; Chief Executive, Northamptonshire County Council, 1973–96; Independent Adjudicator, Department for Communities and Local Government (formerly Department of the Environment, Transport and the Regions, later Department for Transport, Local Government and the Regions, then Office of the Deputy Prime Minister), 1998–2008; *b* 1 Aug. 1931; *s* of late George Greenwell and of Kate Mary Greenwell (*née* Fleming), Durham; *m* 1958, Margaret Rosemary, *d* of late Sidney David Barnard; one *s* two *d*. *Educ:* Durham Sch.; University Coll., Oxford (MA). FCIS. Solicitor (Hons). Nat. Service, RHA, 1950–51. Articled to Town Clerk, Newcastle upon Tyne, 1955–58; law tutor, Gibson & Weldon, 1958–59; Asst Solicitor, Birmingham Corp., 1959–61; Hants County Council: Asst Solicitor, 1961–64; Asst Clerk, 1964–67; Dep. Clerk of Council, Dep. Clerk of the Peace and Dep. Clerk, Hants River Authy, 1967–73; Clerk of Northants Lieutenancy, 1977–96. Chm., Assoc. of Co. Chief Execs, 1993–94 (Hon. Sec., 1980–84); Hon. Sec., SOLACE, 1984–88 (Pres., 1991–92); President: CIS, 1989; Northants Assoc. of Local Councils, 1974–96. Chm., Home Office Gp on Juvenile Crime, 1987. Vice-Pres., Internat. City Management Assoc., 1990–92; Chm., Northants ACRE, 1998–2002; Vice-Chm., Northants CPRE, 2002–08. Trustee, Central Festival Opera. Gov., UC, Northampton, 1998–2002. Freeman, City of London, 1989 (Pres., Aldgate Ward Club, 2008–09); Liveryman, Chartered Secretaries' and Administrators' Co. (Master, 2005–06). DL Northants, 1996. Freeman, City of Durham, 1992. *Recreations:* bridge, travel, local history, going to meetings. *Address:* 2 Hillside Way, Northampton NN3 3AW. *T:* (01604) 401858.

GREENWELL, Sir Edward (Bernard), 4th Bt *cr* 1906; DL; farmer, since 1975; *b* 10 June 1948; *s* of Sir Peter McClintock Greenwell, 3rd Bt, TD, and Henrietta (who *m* 1985, Hugh Kenneth Haig), 2nd *d* of late Peter and Lady Alexandra Haig-Thomas; *S* father, 1978; *m* 1974, Sarah Louise Gore-Anley (*d* 2010); one *s* three *d*. *Educ:* Eton; Nottingham University (BSc); Cranfield Institute of Technology (MBA). Pres., CLA, 2001–03. DL, 1988, High Sheriff, 2013–14, Suffolk. *Heir:* *s* Alexander Bernard Peter Greenwell, *b* 11 May 1987. *Address:* Gedgrave Hall, Woodbridge, Suffolk IP12 2BX. *T:* (01394) 450440. *Club:* Turf.

GREENWELL, Jeffrey; *see* Greenwell, A. J.

GREENWELL, Joseph, CBE 2011; DL; Chairman, Ford of Britain, 2009–13; *b* Portsmouth, 8 May 1951; *s* of Joseph and Eileen Joyce Florence Greenwell; *m* 1979, Anne Carson; three *d* (one *s* decd). *Educ:* Purbrook Grammar Sch.; Univ. of East Anglia (BA Hons English and American Lit. 1973). Grad. trainee, British Leyland, 1973–82; Jaguar Cars: Mktg Res. Manager, 1983–84; Product Strategy Manager, 1984–88; Public Affairs Manager, 1988–93; Dir, Overseas Sales, 1993–96; Dir, Public Affairs, 1996–99; Public and Govt Affairs Dir, Ford of Europe, 1999–2001; Global Vice Pres., Mktg, Ford Motor Co., USA, 2001–03; Chm. and CEO, Jaguar Land Rover, 2003–05; Vice Pres., Govt Affairs, Ford of Europe, 2005–09. Mem. Bd, SEMTA, Sector Skills Council, 2006–14. Hon. Pres., SMMT, 2009–10. Pres., BEN, 2006–13. Trustee, Nat. Motor Mus., 2009–13. DL Warwicks, 2011. *Recreations:* golf, classic cars, football, tennis, walking, theatre, music, family, history and art history. *Address:* Field House, The Pound, Harbury, Warwicks CV33 9HH. *E:* joegreenwell2003@yahoo.co.uk. *Clubs:* Athenæum, Royal Automobile; Warwick Boat; Leamington and County Golf.

GREENWOOD, Alan Eliezer; His Honour Judge Greenwood; a Circuit Judge, since 2000; *b* 5 June 1947; *s* of Rabbi Hans Isaac Grunewald and Martha Grunewald; *m* 1975, Naomi (*née* Ohayon); two *s* one *d*. *Educ:* University Coll., London (LLB Hons). Called to the Bar, Middle Temple, 1970; in practice at the Bar, 1971–2000. *Recreations:* travel, film, theatre, football, tennis, ski-ing, swimming, cycling. *Address:* Harrow Crown Court, Hailsham Drive, Harrow HA1 4TU.

GREENWOOD, Sir Christopher (John), Kt 2009; CMG 2002; QC 1999; a Judge, International Court of Justice, since 2009; *b* 12 May 1955; *o s* of late Murray Guy Greenwood and Diana Maureen (*née* Barron); *m* 1978, Susan Anthea, *d* of late Geoffrey and Patricia Longbotham; two *d*. *Educ:* Wellingborough Sch.; Magdalene Coll., Cambridge (MA Law 1st Cl. Hons; LLB Internat. Law 1st Cl. Hons; McNair Schol. 1976, Whewell Schol. 1977, in Internat. Law). Pres., Cambridge Union Soc., 1976. Called to the Bar, Middle Temple, 1978, Bencher, 2003; Fellow, Magdalene Coll., Cambridge, 1978–96 (Hon. Fellow, 2009); Asst Lectr in Law, 1981–84, Lectr, 1984–96, Univ. of Cambridge; Prof. of Internat. Law, LSE, 1996–2009. Mem., Panel of Arbitrators: Law of the Sea Convention, 1998–; ICSID, 2004–. Vice-Pres., British Inst. of Internat. and Comparative Law, 2012–. Hon. Fellow, Lauterpacht Centre for Internat. Law, 2009–. Gov., Ditchley Foundn, 2001–. Jt Editor, International Law Reports, 1990–. *Publications:* Essays on War in International Law, 2006; contrib. articles in Brit. Year Book of Internat. Law, Internat. and Comparative Law Qly, Modern Law Rev. and other legal jls. *Recreations:* political biography, the novels of Anthony Trollope, walking. *Address:* International Court of Justice, Peace Palace, Carnegieplein 2, 2517 KJ The Hague, Netherlands. *T:* (70) 3022415. *Clubs:* Athenæum, Oxford and Cambridge; Haagsche, De Witte Society (The Hague).

GREENWOOD, Prof. Geoffrey Wilson, PhD, DMet; FRS 1992; FInstP, FIMMM, FREng; Professor of Metallurgy, University of Sheffield, 1966–94, now Emeritus; *b* 3 Feb. 1929; *s* of Richard Albert Greenwood and Martha Alice (*née* Wilson); *m* 1954, Nancy Cole; two *s* one *d*. *Educ:* Grange Grammar Sch., Bradford; Univ. of Sheffield (BSc, PhD, DMet). FInstP 1966; FIMMM (FIM 1966); FREng (FEng 1990). SO and SSO, UKAEA, Harwell, 1953–60; Head, Fuel Materials Section, Berkeley Nuclear Labs, CEGB, 1960–65; Res. Manager, Scis Div., Electricity Council Res. Centre, 1965–66. Pro-Vice-Chancellor, Univ. of Sheffield, 1979–83. L. B. Pfeil Prize, Inst. Metals and Iron and Steel Inst., 1972; Rosenhain Medal, Metals Soc., 1975; Griffith Medal, Inst. of Materials, 1995. *Publications:* contribs to Metallurgy, Materials Science, Physics and Engrg. *Recreations:* music, variety of outdoor activities. *Address:* Department of Materials Science and Engineering, University of Sheffield, Sir Robert Hadfield Building, Mappin Street, Sheffield S1 3JD. *T:* (0114) 222 5517; 26 Stumperlowe Hall Road, Sheffield S10 3QS. *T:* (0114) 230 3565.

GREENWOOD, Jeffrey Michael; Senior Partner, Nabarro Nathanson, 1987–95; *b* 21 April 1935; *s* of Arthur Greenwood and Ada Greenwood (*née* Gordon); *m* 1964, Naomi Grahame; three *s* one *d*. *Educ:* Raine's Foundation Sch.; LSE; Downing Coll., Cambridge (MA, LLM). Admitted solicitor 1960; Partner, Nabarro Nathanson, 1963–95, Consultant, 1995–2001. Dir, Bank Leumi (UK), 1990–2005; Chairman: Wigmore Property Investment Trust, 1996–2004; Stow Securities, 1997–2007; Dep. Chm., Jewish Chronicle, 1994–2005. Chm., CCETSW, 1993–98. Chairman: Jewish Welfare Bd, 1986–90; Jewish Care, 1990; Council Member: Jewish Historical Soc. of England, 1993–; Anglo Israel Assoc., 2010–; Hampstead Garden Suburb Trust (Law Soc. Appointee), 1984–87; Trustee, Policy Res. Inst. for Ageing and Ethnicity, 2000–09. Founder Mem., Campaign Cttee, ProHelp. *Publications:* articles in learned jls. *Recreations:* conversing with grandchildren, swimming, literature, travel. *Address:* (office) 5 Spencer Walk, Hampstead High Street, NW3 1QZ. *T:* (020) 7794 5281, *Fax:* (020) 7794 0094. *E:* jeff@thegreenwoods.org.

GREENWOOD, Dr Jeremy John Denis, CBE 2008; Director, British Trust for Ornithology, 1988–2007 (Hon. Research Fellow, 2007); *b* 7 Sept. 1942; *s* of Denis Greenwood and Phyllis Marjorie Greenwood (*née* Leat); *m* 1971, Cynthia Anne Jones; two *d*. *Educ:* Royal Grammar Sch., Worcester; St Catherine's Coll., Oxford (BA 1964); Univ. of Manchester (PhD 1972). MRSB (CBiol, MIBiol 1990). Dundee University: Asst Lectr in Zoology, 1967–70; Lectr in Biol Scis, 1970–87; University of East Anglia: Hon. Lectr, 1994–98; Hon. Reader, 1998–2002; Hon. Prof., 2002–08; Hon. Professor: Univ. of Birmingham, 2003–; Univ. of St Andrews, 2007–. Vis. Prof. in Animal Ecology, Univ. of Khartoum, 1976. Natural Environment Research Council: Workshop on Grey Seal Population Biol., 1979–84; Special Cttee on Seals, 1986–96, 2008–13; Terrestrial Life Scis Cttee, 1988–91; Data Adv. Gp, 2000–01. Mem., Scottish Govt Wildlife Penalties Rev. Gp, 2014–. Chairman: Exec. Cttee, European Bird Census Council, 1992–98; Scientific and Tech. Adv. Gp, Langholm Demonstration Project, 2007–11 (Mem., 2007–); Member: Council, RSPB, 1983–88; Adv. Cttee on Birds, NCC, 1988–91; Envmtl Res. Cttee, British Agrochem. Assoc., 1988–93; Grants Cttee, Internat. Council for Bird Preservation, British Section, 1988–92; Council, British Ornith. Union, 1989–93; Sci. Adv. Cttee, Wildfowl & Wetlands Trust, 1989–92; Professional Affairs Cttee, Inst. of Ecology and Envmtl Management, 1991–93; Scottish Wildlife Trust Conservation Cttee, 2007–13; Natural Envmt Panel (formerly Nature Conservation Panel), NT, 2007–13; Vice Pres., 2003–05, Pres., 2005–09, Eur. Ornithologists' Union. Director: West Palaearctic Birds Ltd, 1990–2000; BB 2000 Ltd, 2001–13. Pres., Scottish Ornithologists' Club, 1987. Hon. DSc Birmingham, 2007. Trustee, British Birds Charitable Trust, 2001–. Editor, Bird Study, 1984–87; Member, Editorial Board: Heredity, 1988–92; Biol Conservation, 2001–08. *Publications:* (ed jtly) Joint Biological Expedition to North East Greenland 1974, 1978; (ed jtly) Birds as Monitors of Environmental Change, 1993; papers in learned jls; chapters in books. *Recreations:* birdwatching, walking, gardening. *Address:* Centre for Research into Ecological and Environmental Modelling, University of St Andrews, Fife KY16 9LZ.

GREENWOOD, Lilian Rachel; MP (Lab) Nottingham South, since 2010; *b* Bolton, Lancs, 26 March 1966; *d* of Harry Greenwood and Patricia Greenwood; three *d*; *m* 2008, Ravi Subramanian. *Educ:* Canon Slade Sch., Bolton; St Catharine's Coll., Cambridge (BA Hons 1987); South Bank Poly. (MSc). Research Officer: LACSAB, 1988–89; Civil and Public Services Assoc., 1989–92; Trainee Regl Officer, NUPE, 1992–93; UNISON: Regl Organiser, 1993–98; Regl Educn Officer, 1998–2002; Regl Manager, 2002–10. Shadow Sec. of State for Transport, 2015–. *Recreations:* running, walking, cycling, cinema. *Address:* (office) 12 Regent Street, Nottingham NG1 5BQ. *T:* (0115) 711 7000; House of Commons, SW1A 0AA. *E:* lilian.greenwood.mp@parliament.uk.

GREENWOOD, Margaret; MP (Lab) Wirral West, since 2015; *b* 14 March 1959. Teacher of English in secondary schs, further educn colleges and adult educn centres, Liverpool and Wirral; teacher of literacy to adult learners and adults with special needs; travel writer; website consultant. *Address:* House of Commons, SW1A 0AA.

GREER, Adrian, CMG 2004; Chief Operating Officer, British Council, since 2012; *b* 26 April 1957; *s* of David Smith Greer and Christine Greer (*née* Dawson); *m* 1985, (Mary) Diana Cuddy; one *s* three *d*. *Educ:* Queen Mary's Grammar Sch., Walsall; St Andrews Univ. (MA Eng. Lang. and Lit.). CPFA 1984. Auditor, Nat. Audit Office, 1979–84; joined British Council, 1984; Finance Develt Office, 1984–85; Finance Manager, Japan, 1985–88; Finance Project Manager, 1988–89, Chief Accountant, 1989–91, London; Director: Lesotho and Swaziland, 1991–93; Zambia, 1993–96; Europe (Develt and Trng Services), 1996–98; Asia and Americas (Develt and Trng Services), 1998–2000; Cultural Counsellor and Dir, Russia, 2000–04; Dir of Learning, Creativity and Society, 2004–07; Regl Dir, E Asia, 2007–11; Dir, Global Network, 2011–12. FRSA. *Recreations:* travel, swimming, running, reading. *Address:* c/o British Council, 10 Spring Gardens, SW1A 2BN.

See also K. Greer.

GREER, Bonnie, OBE 2010; writer; *b* Chicago, 16 Nov. 1948; *d* of late Ben Greer and of Willie Mae Greer; naturalised British citizen, 1997; *m* 1993, David Hutchins, solicitor. *Educ:* DePaul Univ., Chicago (BA Hist. 1974). Studied playwriting: with David Mamet, St Nicholas Th., Chicago, 1975–76; with Elia Kazan, Actors Studio, NYC, 1982–86; Arts Council Playwright in Residence: Soho Th., 1990; Black Th. Co-op., 1992. Plays include: 1919, 1977; Diary of a Slave Girl, 1984; Roadhouse, 1985; Zebra Days, 1989; Dancing on Black Water, 1996; Ella, Meet Marilyn, 2006; Equiano, Esclave, Maitre, Survivant, 2006; opera, Yes, 2011; radio plays include Marilyn and Ella Backstage at the Mocambo, 2005, and various adaptations and translations; television: White Men Are Cracking Up, 1996; Reflecting Skin (also co-producer), 2004. Critic, Late Review and Newsnight Review, BBC2, 1998–2005. Chancellor, Kingston Univ., 2013–. Member: Bd, Serpentine Gall., 2013–; Adv. Cttee, 2013–, Cultural Cttee, 2013–, First World War Centenary. Trustee, BM, 2005–09 (Dep. Chm., 2005–13). Mem., Acad. and Artistic Bd, and Mem. Council, 2009–, RADA. Judge: Orange Prize, 2000; Samuel Johnson Prize, 2003; Whitbread First Novel Prize, 2003; Best Play, Sony Radio Awards, 2010. FRSA 2003. DuNouy Prize for Playwriting, Phoenix Th., NYC, 1979; Verity Bargate Award, 1992. *Publications:* So Very English (short stories), 1989; Hanging By Her Teeth (novel), 1994; How Maxine Learned To Like Her Legs (short stories), 1995; (contrib.) Black Plays Three, 1995; Entropy (novel), 2009; Obama Music (memoir), 2009; Langston Hughes, 2011; A Parallel Life, 2014. *Recreations:* reading popular books on theoretical maths esp. Prime Number Theory and the Riemann Hypothesis, collecting studio jewellery, listening and dancing to jazz, soul and funk music, the gym. *Address:* c/o Judith Antell, The Antell Agency, Peckhams, Knowle Lane, Lewes, E Sussex BN8 6PR. *T:* 07736 063726. *E:* judith@theantellagency.co.uk. *Club:* Union.

GREER, Prof. David Clive; Professor of Music, University of Durham, 1986–2001, now Emeritus (Chairman, Music Department, 1986–94); Tutor, University College, Durham, 2008–15; *b* 8 May 1937; *s* of William Mackay Greer and Barbara (*née* Avery); *m* 1st, 1961, Patricia Margaret Regan (*d* 1999); two *s* one *d*; 2nd, 2002, Harriet, *d* of Lt-Col Sir John Marling, 4th Bt, OBE. *Educ:* Dulwich Coll.; Queen's Coll., Oxford (BA 1960; MA 1964); MusD TCD, 1991. Lectr in Music, Birmingham Univ., 1963–72; Hamilton Harty Prof. of Music, QUB, 1972–84; Prof. of Music, Univ. of Newcastle upon Tyne, 1984–86. Mellon Vis. Fellow, 1989, Mayers Foundn Fellow, 1991 and 2007, Huntington Liby, Calif; Folger Vis. Fellow, Folger Shakespeare Liby, Washington, 1994, 1998, 2008 and 2014. Mem. Bd, Arts Council of NI, 1972–84. Chm., Mgt Cttee, and Guest Conductor, Ulster Orch., 1972–84; Mem. Council, Royal Musical Assoc., 1977–90. FRSA 1986. Editor, Proceedings, subseq. Jl, of Royal Musical Assoc., 1977–90. *Publications:* (ed) English Madrigal Verse, 1967; Hamilton Harty: his life and music, 1979, 2nd edn 1980; Hamilton Harty: early memories, 1979; (ed) Collected English Lutenist Partsongs, 2 vols, 1987–89, and other editions of 16th and 17th century music; A Numerous and Fashionable Audience: the story of Elsie Swinton, 1997; (ed) John Dowland, Ayres for four voices, 2000; Musicology and Sister Disciplines: past, present, future, 2000; Musica Transalpina, 2011; (contrib.) New Grove Dictionary of Music and Musicians, Die Musik in Geschichte und Gegenwart; (contrib.) The Canterbury Dictionary of Hymnology, 2013; Manuscript Inscriptions and other Marks of Ownership in Early English Printed Music, 2015; articles in Music and Letters, Music Review, Musical Times, Shakespeare Qly, English Studies, Notes & Queries, Lute Soc. Jl. *Recreations:* reading, cinema, walking. *Address:* 20 Haldane Terrace, Jesmond, Newcastle upon Tyne NE2 3AN. *T:* (0191) 281 6766. *E:* d.c.greer@durham.ac.uk. *Club:* Athenæum.

GREER, Prof. Germaine, PhD; writer and broadcaster; Professor of English and Comparative Studies, Warwick University, 1998–2003; *b* Melbourne, 29 Jan. 1939. *Educ:* Melbourne Univ. (BA 1959); Sydney Univ. (MA 1962); Commonwealth Scholarship, 1964; Cambridge Univ. (PhD 1967). Sen. Tutor in English, Sydney Univ., 1963–64; Asst Lectr, then Lectr in English, Warwick Univ., 1967–72; Lectr, American Program Bureau, 1973–78; Prof. of Modern Letters, Univ. of Tulsa, 1980–83; Founder Dir, Tulsa Centre for Studies in Women's Literature, 1981; Special Lectr and Unofficial Fellow, Newnham Coll., Cambridge, 1989–98. Vis. Prof., Univ. of Tulsa, 1979. Proprietor, Stump Cross Books, 1988–. *Publications:* The Female Eunuch, 1970; The Obstacle Race: the fortunes of women painters and their work, 1979; Sex and Destiny: the politics of human fertility, 1984; Shakespeare, 1986; The Madwoman's Underclothes: selected journalism, 1986; (ed jtly) Kissing the Rod: an anthology of 17th century women's verse, 1988; Daddy, We Hardly Knew You, 1989 (J. R. Ackerly Prize; Premio Internazionale Mondello); (ed) The Uncollected Verse of Aphra Behn, 1989; The Change: women, ageing and the menopause, 1991; Slip-shod Sibyls: recognition, rejection and the woman poet, 1995; (ed jtly) The Surviving Works of Anne Wharton, 1997; The Whole Woman, 1999; (ed) 101 Poems by 101 Women, 2001; The Boy, 2003; (ed) Poems for Gardeners, 2003; Whitefella Jump Up: the shortest way to nationhood, 2004; Shakespeare's Wife, 2007; White Beech: the rainforest years, 2014; contribs to Journalist. *Address:* c/o Aitken Alexander Associates Ltd, 291 Gray's Inn Road, WC1X 8EB.

GREER, Prof. Ian Andrew, MD; FRCP, FRCPE, FRCPGlas, FRCPI, FRCOG, FFSRH, FCCP; FMedSci; Vice President, Dean, Faculty of Medical and Human Sciences, and Director, Manchester Academic Health Science Centre, University of Manchester, since 2015. *Educ:* Univ. of Glasgow (MB ChB 1980; MD 1986). MRCP 1984, FRCP 2001; MRCOG 1987, FRCOG 1999; FRCPGlas 1994; FRCPE 1999; FRCPI 2006; MFFP 1994, FFSRH (FFFP 2008); FCCP 2011. Registrar in Medicine, Glasgow Royal Infirmary, 1983–85; Lectr in Obstetrics and Gynaecol., Univ. of Edinburgh, 1987–90; Clinical Res. Scientist, MRC Reproductive Biol. Unit, Edinburgh, 1990–91; Glasgow University: Muirhead Prof., 1991–2000; Regius Prof., 2000–06; Head, Dept of Obstetrics and Gynaecology, 1991–2006; Depute Dean, 2003–06; Dean, Hull York Med. Sch., 2007–10; Exec. Pro-Vice-Chancellor, 2010–15, Provost, 2013–15, Faculty of Health and Life Scis, Univ. of Liverpool. FMedSci 2006. *Publications:* (jtly) Haemostasis and Thrombosis in Obstetrics and Gynaecology, 1992; Venous Thromboembolism in Obstetrics and Gynaecology, in Baillière's Clinical Obstetrics and Gynaecology, 1997; (jtly) Mosby's Colour Atlas and Text of Obstetrics and Gynaecology, 2000; (with A. J. Thomson) Antenatal Disorders for the MRCOG, 2000; Pregnancy: the inside guide, 2003; Venous Thrombosis in Women, 2003; (jtly) Problem-based Obstetrics and Gynaecology, 2003; (jtly) The Menopause in Practice, 2003; (jtly) Practical Obstetric Haematology, 2005; (jtly) Preterm Labour, 2005; Fertility and Conception, 2007; (jtly) Women's Vascular Health, 2007; (jtly) Maternal Medicine, 2007; (jtly) Textbook of Periconceptional Medicine, 2009; contrib. numerous res. papers and rev. articles on haemostasis and thrombosis, medical disorders in pregnancy and labour and preterm labour. *Address:* Faculty of Medical and Human Sciences, University of Manchester, 46 Grafton Street, Manchester M13 9NT.

GREER, Ian Bramwell; Chairman, Corporate and Government Relations International Ltd, 1998–2012; *b* 5 June 1933; *s* of Bramwell and Janet Greer. *Educ:* Cranbrook Coll., Essex; Victoria Sch., Glasgow. Conservative Central Office and Party Agent, 1956–67; Nat. Dir, Mental Health Trust, 1967–70; Man. Dir, Russell Greer & Associates, 1970–82; Chairman: Ian Greer Associates, 1982–96; Internat. Govt Relations, 1997–2004. Chm., Helderberg Street People's Centre, 2000–; Mem., Bd of Visitors, HMP Wormwood Scrubs, 1992–98. *Publications:* Right to be Heard, 1985; One Man's Word, 1997. *Recreations:* antiques, walking, gardening, dogs. *Address:* The Long House, PO Box 213, Stellenbosch, Western Cape 7599, South Africa. *Club:* Royal Automobile.

GREER, Kenneth; Senior Adviser, Abu Dhabi Education Council, since 2014; *b* 21 Nov. 1953; *s* of David Smith Greer and Christine Greer (*née* Dawson); *m* 1st, 1977, Lorna Margaret Murray (*d* 2001); two *s*; 2nd, 2008, Belinda Margaret Sheehan. *Educ:* St Edmund's Coll., Ware; Univ. of St Andrews (MA Hons English Lang. and Lit.); Moray House Coll. (PGCE); Open Univ. (MA Educn). Teacher: Lanark GS, 1976–78; Whitburn Acad., 1978–80; Buckhaven High Sch., 1980–84; Dunfermline High Sch., 1984–90; Advr in English, Grampian Reg., 1990–94; HM Inspector of Schs, 1994–2003; Sen. Educn Manager, 2003–05, Exec. Dir (Educn), 2005–14, Fife Council. Vice-Pres., Assoc. of Dirs of Educn in Scotland, 2011–13. Trustee, Link Community Develt, Scotland, 2007–. *Recreations:* running, ski-ing, reading. *Address:* Abu Dhabi Education Council, PO Box 36005, Abu Dhabi, United Arab Emirates. *T:* 26150000.

See also A. Greer.

GREGG, Hilary; *see* Manley, H.

GREGG, Prof. Paul James, MD; FRCS; Professor of Orthopaedic Surgical Science, University of Durham, since 2000; Consultant Orthopaedic Surgeon, South Tees Acute Hospitals NHS Trust, 2000–12, now Emeritus Consultant Orthopaedic Surgeon; *b* 26 Nov. 1945; *s* of George Ernest Gregg and Hebe Elizabeth Gregg; *m* 1977, Jennifer Hall; one *d*. *Educ:* St Peter's Sch., York; Med. Sch., Univ. of Newcastle upon Tyne (MB BS 1969; MD 1977). FRCS 1974; FRCSE *ad hominem* 1998. House Physician and House Surgeon, Royal Victoria Infirmary, Newcastle upon Tyne, 1969–70; surgical trng, Newcastle upon Tyne hosps, 1971–74; University of Newcastle upon Tyne: Demonstrator in Anatomy, 1970–71; Sen. Res. Associate, MRC Decompression Sickness Res. Team, 1976–77; Lectr in Orthopaedic Surgery, 1979–83; Sen. Registrar in Orthopaedic Surgery, N Reg. Trng Prog., 1977–79; Clin. Res. Fellow, Massachusetts Gen. Hosp., 1982–83; Sen. Lectr in Orthopaedic Surgery, Univ. of Edinburgh, 1983–85; Foundation Prof. of Orthopaedic Surgery, Univ. of Leicester, 1985–97; Prof. of Trauma and Orthopaedic Surgery, Univ. of Newcastle upon Tyne, 1997–2000. Pres., British Orthopaedic Assoc., 2002–03. *Publications:* Fractures and Dislocations: principles of management, 1995; contribs to books; more than 140 scientific papers. *Recreations:* walking, golf. *Address:* Upper Loads Farm, Upper Loads, Holymoorside, Derbys S42 7HP.

GREGG, Paul Richard; Chairman, Apollo Cinemas, 2003–07; *b* 2 Oct. 1941; *m* 1970, Anita Kim, (Nita), Grehan (*d* 2010); two *s* one *d*. *Educ:* Hull Nautical Coll. ABC Cinema Gp, 1961–65; Star Gp of Cinemas, 1965–67; Pressed Steel Fisher Ltd, 1967–70; Entertainment Dir, Rover Motor Co., 1968–70; Entertainment and Tourist Manager, Southport DC, 1970–77; Chm., Apollo Leisure Gp plc, 1978–2001. Mem., Variety Club of GB (former Pres.; Chief Barker, 1991). *Recreation:* theatre.

GREGOR, Anna, (Mrs Neil Magee), CBE 2005; FRCPE, FRCR; Consultant Oncologist, Lothian Health Board, 1997–2008; *b* Prague, 13 Aug. 1948; *d* of Dr and Mrs J. Drachovsky; *m* 1983, Neil Magee; two *s*. *Educ:* Academic Grammar Sch., Prague; Faculty of Medicine, Charles Univ., Prague; Royal Free Sch. of Medicine, Univ. of London. LRCP, MRCS 1973, MRCP 1975; FRCR 1981; FRCPE 1993. Postgrad. trng, Brompton Hosps, Cardiothoracic Inst. and Royal Marsden Hosps, London, 1974–80; Lectr in Clinical Oncology, Univ. of Edinburgh, 1980–83; Consultant Oncologist, Beatson Oncol. Centre, Glasgow, 1983–87; Sen. Lectr, Univ. of Edinburgh, 1987–97; Clin. Dir, SE Scotland Cancer Network, 2001–08; Lead Cancer Clinician for Scotland, 2001–06. Trustee, Nat Museums of Scotland, 2009–. *Publications:* Lung Cancer: recent results, 1989; Oxford Textbook of Oncology, 1995; Comprehensive Textbook of Thoracic Oncology, 1999; contribs to jls incl. Clin. Oncol., BMJ, Thorax, Annals NY Acad. Sci., Clin. Radiol. *Recreations:* friends, music, food and wine. *Address:* 45 Spylaw Bank Road, Edinburgh EH13 0JF. *T:* (0131) 441 6360. *E:* annagregor@doctors.net.uk. *Club:* New (Edinburgh).

GREGORIADIS, Prof. Gregory, PhD, DSc; Member, Scientific Advisory Board, Xenetic Biosciences plc (formerly Lipoxen plc), since 1998 (Founder, Director of Research and Board Member, 1998–2015); Professor and Head, Centre for Drug Delivery Research, School of Pharmacy, University of London, 1990–2001, now Professor Emeritus; *b* 27 Feb. 1934; *s* of late Christos Gregoriadis and Athina Sakellariou; *m* 1968, Susan Byron-Brown; one *s* one *d*. *Educ:* Univ. of Athens (BSc 1958); McGill Univ. (MSc 1966; PhD 1968); DSc London 2002. Research Fellow: Albert Einstein Coll. of Medicine, 1968–70; Royal Free Hosp. Sch. of Medicine, 1970–72; Sen. Scientist, MRC, 1972–93. Pres., Internat. Liposome Soc., 2003–. Fellow: Amer. Assoc. of Pharmaceutical Scientists, 1998; Acad. of Pharmaceutical Scientists, 2008; Controlled Release Soc., 2010. 15 NATO Scientific Affairs Div. awards, 1980–98; Founder's Award, Controlled Release Soc., 1994; Bangham Award, 1995, Founders Award, 2010, Liposome Res. Days Inc.; Lifetime Achievement Award, Jl of Drug Targeting, 2008. *Publications:* (ed) Drug Carriers in Biology and Medicine, 1979; (ed jtly) Liposomes in Biology and Medicine, 1980; (ed jtly) Targeting of Drugs, 1982, 10th edn 2000; (ed) Liposome Technology, 1984, 3rd edn 2007; (ed) Liposomes as Drug Carriers: recent trends and progress, 1988; (ed jtly) Vaccines, 1989, 5th edn 1997; Still the Cicadas Sing (novel), 2014; over 300 papers on drug and vaccine targeting. *Recreations:* creative writing, history and philosophy of Ancient Athens, politics. *Address:* Crantock, Kewferry Hill, Rickmansworth Road, Northwood, Middx HA6 2RQ.

GREGORIOS, His Eminence The Most Rev. the Archbishop of Thyateira and Great Britain; *see* Theocharous, Archbishop Gregorios.

GREGOROWSKI, Rt Rev. Christopher John; an Assistant Bishop of Cape Town (Bishop of Table Bay), 1998–2005; *b* 19 Feb. 1940; *s* of William Victor Gregorowski and Doris Alice Gregorowski (*née* Skinner); *m* 1964, Margaret Merle Perold; two *d* (and one *d* decd). *Educ:* Diocesan Coll., Rondebosch, S Africa; Univ. of Cape Town (BA, MA); Birmingham Univ. (DPS); Cuddesdon Coll., Oxford. Deacon 1963, priest 1964, Anglican Church of Southern

Africa (formerly Church of Province of S Africa); Rector: St Cuthbert's, Tsolo, 1968–74; St Thomas, Rondebosch, 1974–86; All Saints, Somerset West, 1986–98. *Publications:* Why a Donkey was Chosen, 1975; The Bible for Little Children, 1982; Fly, Eagle, Fly!, 1982, 2nd edn 2000; Angelo at the Waterfront, 2008; Bill Davis, Sculptor: his life and work, 2010. *Recreations:* marathon running, reading, walking, ornithology. *Address:* 15 Starke Road, Bergvliet, 7945, South Africa. *T:* (21) 7125136. *Clubs:* Western Province Cricket, Spartan Harriers Athletic (Cape Town).

GREGORY, Prof. Alan, FCMA; Professor of Corporate Finance, University of Exeter, since 1997; *b* Mountain Ash, S Wales, 19 March 1954; *s* of William Raymond and Margaret Mary Gregory; *m* 2007, Julie Mary Whittaker. *Educ:* St Bartholomew's Grammar Sch., Newbury; London Sch. of Econs and Pol Sci. (MSc). Management Accountant: British Rail; Green Shield Stamps; Professor: of Accounting, Univ. of Glasgow, 1995–96; of Business, Univ. of Wales, Aberystwyth, 1996–97. Man. Dir, AGRF Ltd, 2013–. Mem., Competition, 2002–10. *Publications:* Strategic Valuation of Companies, 2000, 2nd edn 2002; contribs to peer-reviewed jls incl. Econ. Jl, Jl Business Finance & Accounting, Accounting and Business Res., British Jl Mgt, Jl Business Ethics. *Recreations:* painting, sailing, running, ski-ing. *Address:* Xfi Centre, Streatham Campus, University of Exeter, Exeter EX4 4ST. *E:* a.gregory@exeter.ac.uk.

GREGORY, Alan Thomas, CBE 1984; Director, Willis Corroon (formerly Willis Faber) plc, 1987–97; *b* 13 Oct. 1925; *s* of Lloyd Thomas Gregory and Florence Abbott; *m* 1st, 1952, Pamela Douglas Scott (*d* 1986); one *s* two *d*; 2nd, 1988, Mrs Marion Newth (*née* Nash), JP (*d* 2007). *Educ:* Dulwich Coll.; St John's Coll., Cambridge (Classics). Directed into coal mining, coal face worker, 1944; Min. of Power, 1948; JSSC 1957; Chm., NATO Petroleum Planning Cttee, 1967–70; joined British Petroleum, 1971; Gen. Manager, BP Italiana, 1972–73; Dir, Govt and Public Affairs, 1975–85, and Dir, UK and Ireland Region, 1980–85, British Petroleum Co.; Chm., BP Oil Ltd, 1981–85; Director: BP Chemicals International Ltd, 1981–85; National Home Loans Corp., 1985–91. Governor, Queen Mary Coll., London Univ., 1981–87. President, Inst. of Petroleum, 1982–84. Univ. Comr, 1988–95. Churchwarden, St Mary's, Stoke D'Abernon, 1990–92. *Recreations:* books, gardening, theatre. *Address:* 10 Summerhays, Cobham, Surrey KT11 2HQ. *T:* (01932) 864457. *Club:* Travellers.

GREGORY, Rear-Adm. Alexander Michael, OBE 1987; Lord-Lieutenant of Dunbartonshire, since 2008; *b* 15 Dec. 1945; *s* of Vice-Adm. Sir (George) David (Archibald) Gregory, KBE, CB, DSO and Florence Eve Patricia Gregory (*née* Hill); *m* 1970, Jean Charlotte Muir; four *d*. *Educ:* Marlborough; BRNC Dartmouth. Served HM Ships Albion, Aisne, Narwhale, Otter, Warspite, Courageous, Odin (Australia), Finwhale (i/c), Repulse 1965–80; Staff, US 3rd Fleet, Hawaii, 1980–82; HMS Renown (i/c), 1982–85; Comdr 10th SM Sqdn and HMS Resolution (i/c), 1985–86; Jt Services Defence Coll., 1987; Naval Warfare, MoD, 1987–88; HMS Cumberland (i/c), 1988–91; Captain, 10th Submarine Sqdn, 1991–93; Naval Staff Duties, MoD, 1993–94; Naval Attaché, Washington, 1994–97; Flag Officer, Scotland, Northern England and NI, 1997–2000. Chief Executive: Mechanical and Metal Trades Confedn, 2001–04; Energy Industries Council, 2004–07. Dir, Mercy Corps Scotland, 2007–. Pres., Highland RFCA, 2012–. Lt, Queen's Body Guard for Scotland, Royal Company of Archers. *Recreations:* fishing, ski-ing, gardening.

GREGORY, Lt Gen. Andrew Richard, CB 2010; Chief of Defence Personnel, since 2013; *b* 19 Nov. 1957; *s* of Lt Col Richard B. Gregory and Alison Gregory (*née* Egerton); *m* 1986, Sally Ann Sheard; two *s*. *Educ:* Malsis Sch.; Sedbergh Sch.; St John's Coll., Cambridge (BA Eng 1979; MA 1982). Graduate trainee/shift foreman, Metal Box Co. Ltd, 1975–81; Army: jun. officer appts, UK, NI and Germany, 1982–97; CO, 1st Regt RHA, UK and Bosnia, 1997–2000; Dir, Army Jun. Div., JSCSC, 2000–02; Comdr, RA and Dep. Comdr, 1st (UK) Armoured Div., Germany and Iraq, 2002–04; ACOS Comd and Battlespace Mgt, HQ Land Comd, 2004–06; Team Leader, HQ Land Comd and HQ Adjt Gen. Co-location Study, 2006–08; Dir Gen. Personnel and Dir Gen. Service Conditions (Army), MoD, 2008–11; Military Secretary, 2011–13. Hon. Colonel: 106 (Yeomanry) Regt RA (V), 2008–15; 1st Regt RHA, 2012–. *Recreations:* Admiral of Army Sailing, President of Army Golf, Rowing and Netball and of Armed Forces Muslim Association. *Address:* Ministry of Defence, Whitehall, SW1A 2HB.

GREGORY, Rt Rev. Clive Malcolm; *see* Wolverhampton, Bishop Suffragan of.

GREGORY, Conal Robert; wine consultant and financial journalist; *b* 11 March 1947; *s* of Patrick George Murray Gregory and Marjorie Rose Gregory; *m* 1971, Helen Jennifer Craggs; one *s* one *d*. *Educ:* King's College Sch., Wimbledon; Univ. of Sheffield (BA Hons Mod. Hist. and Pol Theory and Instns, 1968). Master of Wine by examination, Vintners' Co., 1979. Manager, Saccone & Speed Vintage Cellar Club, 1971–73; Wine Buyer, Reckitt & Colman, 1973–77; Editor, Internat. Wine and Food Soc.'s Jl, 1980–83; Dir, Standard Fireworks Ltd, 1987–92; Chm., Internat. Wine and Spirit Competition Ltd, 1997–98; Dir, Jackson Prentice Ltd, 1999–2004. Norfolk County Councillor, Thorpe Div., 1977–81; Vice-Pres., Norwich Jun. Chamber of Commerce, 1975–76; Mem., E Anglia Tourist Bd, 1979–81. Chairman: Norwich N Cons. Assoc., 1980–82; Norwich CPC, 1978–81; Vice-Chm., Eastern Area CPC, 1980–83; Member: Cons. Eastern Area Agric. Cttee, 1975–79; Cons. Provincial Council, Eastern Area, 1978–83; Chm. and Founder, Bow Gp of E Anglia, 1975–82; Nat. Vice-Chm., Bow Gp, 1976–77. MP (C) York, 1983–92. Hon. Treas., British/Cyprus CPA Gp, 1987–92; Sec., UK-Manx Parly Gp, 1987–92; Chm., Cons. Parly Food and Drinks Industries Cttee, 1989–92 (Vice-Chm., 1985–89); Vice-Chairman: Cons. Parly Tourism Cttee, 1985–92; Cons. Parly Transport Cttee, 1987–89 and 1990–92 (Sec., 1983–87); All Party Parly Hospice Gp, 1990–92; All Party Parly Tourism Cttee, 1991–92 (Sec., 1983–91); Mem. Cttee, British Atlantic Gp of Young Politicians, 1983–92 (Chm., 1988–89; Pres., 1989–92); Pres., York Young Conservatives, 1982–93; Vice-Pres., York Br., UNA, 1983–92. Parliamentary Consultant: The Market Res. Soc., 1984–91; Consort Hotels Ltd, 1984–91; Consultant: Andry Montgomery Ltd, 1979–97; Smith & Taylor Ltd, 1992–2000; Jackson Nugent Vintners Ltd, 1997–. Fellow, Industry and Parlt Trust, 1984–87. Private Member's Bills on consumer safety, 1985, on smoke alarms, 1991, on cheque fraud, 1992. Member: Wymondham Abbey PCC, 1982–83; Humbleyard Deanery Synod, 1982–83; High Steward's Cttee, York Minster Fund, 1983–89; York Archaeol Trust, 1983–; York Georgian Soc., 1982–92, 2002–; York Civic Trust, 1982–92, 2007–; 20th/21st Century British Art Fair Council, 1992–; ESU, 1994–2014. Governor, Heartsease Sch., Norwich, 1977–83; Member, Court of Governors: Univ. of Sheffield, 1981–90; Univ. of York, 1983–92; Univ. of Hull, 1983–92. Patron, Selby Abbot's Staith Heritage Trust, 2015–. Sen. Judge, Internat. Wine Challenge, 2003–. Wine Corresp., Catering Times, 1979–83. Personal Finance Regional Journalist of the Year: Bradford & Bingley, 2007; BIBA, 2007, 2009; Assoc. of Investment Cos, 2008, 2012. *Publications:* (with W. Knock) Beers of Britain, 1975; (with R. A. Adley) A Policy for Tourism?, 1977; A Caterer's Guide to Drinks, 1979; (with M. Shersby and A. McCurley) Food for a Healthy Britain, 1987; The Cognac Companion, 1997; contribs to The Times, Scotsman, Yorkshire Post, etc. *Address:* c/o Jackson Nugent Vintners Ltd, 30 Homefield Road, Wimbledon Village, SW19 4QF.

GREGORY, David St John Thomas; Chairman, Assured Food Standards Ltd, since 2009; *b* London, 27 Aug. 1953; *s* of Francis Gregory and Margaret Gregory; *m* 1975, Susan Barker; two *s* one *d*. *Educ:* Brunel Univ. (BTech Hons Applied Chem. 1975); North London Coll. (Dip. Envmtl Health 1978); Slough Coll. (Dip. Mgt Studies 1981). FIFST 2002; CSci 2004. Tech. Dir (Foods) Marks & Spencer plc, 1983–2009. Non-executive Director: 2 Sisters Food Gp, Boparan Hldgs Ltd, 2010–; BRC Trading Ltd, 2012–. Mem., BBSRC, 2010–. Chm., Trustees, Brit. Nutrition Foundn, 2012– (Vice Chm., 2007–12); Trustee, Inst. of Food Res., Norwich, 2006–. Vis. Prof., Centre for Food Security, Univ. of Reading, 2010–. *Recreations:* fine food and wine, cycling, photography, family. *E:* dstgregory@googlemail.com. *Club:* Farmers.

GREGORY, Janice; Member (Lab) Ogmore, National Assembly for Wales, since 1999; *b* 10 Jan. 1955; *d* of Sir Raymond Powell, MP and of Marion Grace (*née* Evans); *m* 1977, Michael Gregory; two *d*. Parly Asst to Sir Raymond Powell, MP, 1991–99. National Assembly for Wales: Chair: Social Justice and Regeneration Cttee, 2003–07; Communities and Culture Cttee, 2007–09; Govt Chief Whip, 2009–. Member: Fabian Soc., 1980; Co-op. Party, 1980; Unite the Union (TGWU, 1997; Amicus, 2002). *Address:* National Assembly for Wales, Cardiff Bay, Cardiff CF99 1NA; (constituency office) 44a Penybont Road, Pencoed, Bridgend CF35 5RA.

GREGORY, Prof. Kenneth John, CBE 2007; PhD, DSc; CGeog; Warden, Goldsmiths' College, University of London, 1992–98, now Professor Emeritus and Hon. Fellow; *b* 23 March 1938; *s* of Frederick Arthur Gregory and Marion Gregory; *m* Margaret Christine Wilmot; one *s* two *d*. *Educ:* University College London (BSc Special 1959; PhD 1962; DSc 1982; Fellow 1999). University of Exeter: Lectr in Geography, 1962–72; Reader in Physical Geography, 1972–76; University of Southampton: Prof. of Geography, 1976–92; Head of Geography Dept, 1978–83; Dean of Science, 1984–87; Dep. Vice-Chancellor, 1988–92; Vis. Prof., 1998–. Hon. Res. Fellow, UCL, 1993–; Hon. Prof., Univ. of Birmingham, 1997–2008; Leverhulme Emeritus Fellow, 1998–2001. Vis. Lectr, Univ. of New England, NSW, 1975; Distinguished Visiting Professor, 1987: Univ. Kebangsaan; Arizona State Univ.; Snyder Lectr, Univ. of Toronto, 1990. President: Commn on Global Continental Palaeohydrology, Internat. Assoc. on Union for Quaternary Res., 1999–2004 (Vice-Pres., 1992); British Soc. for Geomorphology, 2009–14. Trustee, Horniman Mus. and Gardens, 1997–2003. Gov., Southampton Solent Univ. (formerly Southampton Inst.), 1998–2007 (Vice Chm., Bd of Govs, 1999–2007); Mem. Council, Brunel Univ., 2010– (Dep. Chm., 2015–). For. Mem., Polish Acad. of Arts and Scis, 1995. Freeman, City of London, 1997; Liveryman, Goldsmiths' Co., 1998– (Freeman, 1997; Mem., Educn Cttee, 1999–2006). Fellow, British Soc. for Geomorphol. 2013. Hon. Fellow, Goldsmiths' Coll., 1998. Hon. FRGS 2015. Hon. DSc: Southampton, 1997; Greenwich, 1997; DUniv Southampton Solent, 2008. Back Award, 1980, Founder's Medal, 1993, RGS; Linton Award, British Geomorphological Res. Gp, 1999; Scottish Geographical Medal, RSGS, 2000. *Publications:* (with A. H. Shorter and W. L. D. Ravenhill) Southwest England, 1969; (with D. E. Walling) Drainage Basin Form and Process, 1973; (jtly) An Advanced Geography of the British Isles, 1974; (with E. Derbyshire and J. R. Hails) Geomorphological Processes, 1979; The Yellow River, 1980; The Nature of Physical Geography, 1985 (trans. Russian and Portuguese); (ed jtly) The Encyclopedic Dictionary of Physical Geography, 1985; (ed) Energetics of Physical Environment, 1987; (ed jtly) Human Activity and Environmental Processes, 1987; (ed jtly) Palaeohydrology in Practice, 1987; (ed jtly) Horizons in Physical Geography, 1988; (ed) The Earth's Natural Forces, 1990; (ed) The Guinness Guide to the Restless Earth, 1991; (ed jtly) Temperate Palaeohydrology, 1991; (ed jtly) Global Continental Palaeohydrology, 1995; (ed jtly) Global Continental Changes: the context of palaeohydrology, 1996; (ed jtly) Evaluating Teacher Quality in High Education, 1996; (ed) Geological Conservation Review Fluvial Geomorphology of Great Britain, 1997; (ed jtly) Palaeohydrology and Environmental Change, 1998; The Changing Nature of Physical Geography, 2000; (ed jtly) Palaeohydrology: understanding global change, 2003; (with P. W. Downs) River Channel Management, 2004; (ed) Physical Geography, 4 vols, 2005; (jtly) Environmental Sciences: a student's companion, 2008; The Earth's Land Surface, 2010; (ed jtly) The Sage Handbook of Geomorphology, 2011; (with J. Lewin) Basics of Geomorphology: the key concepts, 2014. *Recreations:* travel, gardening, reading. *Address:* 9 Poltimore Road, Guildford, Surrey GU2 7PT. *E:* k.j.gregory@ntlworld.com.

GREGORY, Sir Michael (John), Kt 2011; CBE 2003; FREng; Head, Manufacturing and Management Division, Department of Engineering, and Head, Institute of Manufacturing, University of Cambridge; Fellow, Churchill College, Cambridge, since 1985. *Educ:* MA Cantab. Lectr, Engrg Dept, then Prof. of Manufacturing Engrg, 1995–2000, Univ. of Cambridge. Springer Vis. Prof., Univ. of Calif, Berkeley, 2008–09. Mem., UK Govt Stakeholder Gp on Manufg. FREng 2011. *Address:* Department of Engineering, University of Cambridge, Trumpington Street, Cambridge CB2 1PZ.

GREGORY, Prof. Peter John, PhD; FRSB, FRASE, FCIHort; Professor of Global Food Security, University of Reading, since 2011; *b* 19 July 1951; *s* of Joseph Henry Gregory and June Rosamond Gregory; *m* 1973, Jane Sandra Crump; two *s*. *Educ:* Chatham House Grammar Sch.; Univ. of Reading (BSc Soil Sci.); Univ. of Nottingham (PhD Soil Sci. 1977). FRSB (FIBiol 1994). Lectr, Univ. of Reading, 1980–89; Principal Res. Scientist, CSIRO Div. of Plant Industry, Australia, 1990–93; University of Reading: Prof. of Soil Sci., 1994–2005; Pro-Vice-Chancellor, 1998–2003, 2004–05; Dir, Scottish Crop Res. Inst., 2005–11; Chief Exec., East Malling Research, 2011–15. Chair, Global Envmtl Change and Food Systems, 2001–06. Chairman: UK Adv. Cttee on Novel Foods and Processes, 2009–; Sci. Cttee, RHS, 2010– (Mem. Council, 2010–); Recommended List Bd, HGCA, 2014–; Jt Chm., TempAg Internat. Res. Prog., 2014–; Member: Scottish Sci. Adv. Council, 2010–11; Nutrition Cttee Rank Prize Funds, 2011–. Hon. Res. Fellow, Rothamsted Res., 2013–. FRASE 2004; FCIHort 2014. *Publications:* (ed jtly) Root Development and Function, 1987; (ed jtly) Soils in the Urban Environment, 1991; (ed jtly) Crop Production on Duplex Soils, 1992; (ed jtly) Land Resources: on the edge of the Malthusian precipice?, 1997; (ed jtly) Science in the Garden, 2002; Plant Roots: growth, activity and interactions with soil, 2006; (ed jtly) Soil Conditions and Plant Growth, 2013; (ed jtly) Climate Change Impact and Adaptation in Agricultural Systems, 2014; numerous scientific papers on soil/plant interactions in learned jls and books. *Recreations:* gardening, folk dancing. *Address:* School of Agriculture, Poicy and Development, University of Reading, Reading RG6 6AR.

GREGORY, Peter Joseph John; His Honour Judge Peter Gregory; a Circuit Judge, since 2015; *b* Belfast, 18 Sept. 1958; *s* of Patrick Brian Gregory and Sheila Gregory (*née* Kennedy); *m* 1982, Jennifer; four *s* one *d*. *Educ:* St MacNissi's Coll., Garron Tower; Manchester (LLB Hons 1981). Called to the Bar, Gray's Inn, 1982; a Recorder, 2002–15; Jun. Treasury Counsel (Civil), 2007–15. *Publications:* (contrib.) Occupational Illness Litigation. *Recreations:* football, music, reading, beer. *Address:* Liverpool Civil and Family Court, 35 Vernon Street, Liverpool L2 2BX. *T:* (0151) 296 2200. *E:* HHJPeter.Gregory@judiciary.gsi.gov.uk.

GREGORY, Peter Roland; JP; Director, Personnel, Management and Business Services, subsequently Personnel and Accommodation, National Assembly for Wales, 2000–03; *b* 7 Oct. 1946; *s* of Tom and Ruby Gregory; *m* 1978, Frances Margaret Hogan. *Educ:* Sexey's Grammar Sch., Blackford, Som; University College Swansea (BA Hons 1968); Manchester Univ. (PhD 1972). Joined Welsh Office, 1971; Private Sec. to Perm. Sec., 1974–75; Principal, 1976; Asst Sec., 1982; Under Sec., Transport, Planning and Envmt Gp, 1990–94; Dir, Health Dept, 1994–99; Dir, NHS Wales, 1999–2000. JP Somerset, 2006. *Recreations:* walking, theatre, music. *Address:* Littlemoor House, Littlemoor Road, Mark, Somerset TA9 4NG.

GREGORY, Philip John; His Honour Judge Gregory; a Circuit Judge, since 2004; *b* 13 Jan. 1953; *s* of John Godfrey Gregory and late Winifred Gregory; *m* 1979, Deborah Ann (*née* Lane); one *s* two *d*. *Educ:* Moseley Grammar Sch., Birmingham; Pembroke Coll., Oxford

(MA). Called to the Bar, Middle Temple, 1975; in practice as barrister, specialising in personal injury, 1975–2004; Asst Recorder, 1998–2000, Recorder, 2000–04. *Recreations:* golf, tennis, reading. *Address:* Coventry Combined Court, 140 Much Park Street, Coventry CV1 2SN.

GREGORY, Philip William, MBE 2008; Chairman, United Bristol Healthcare NHS Trust, 1998–2006; *b* 30 Sept. 1947; *s* of late Thomas Douglas Gregory and Winifred (*née* Brooks); partner, Rosemary Clarke. *Educ:* Beaminster Comprehensive Sch., Dorset; Southampton Coll. of Technology (Dip. Municipal Admin). Regl Official, NALGO, 1974–82; SW Regl Sec., TUC, 1982–93. Member: Dorset AHA, 1974–79; Somerset AHA, 1979–91. Member Board: South West Electricity, 1985–89; Bristol Develt Corp., 1988–96; DTI Develt Bd for SW, 1988–97; SW Regl Chm., Nat. Training Awards, 1993–97; Chm., Community Foundn Network, 1995–2000; Member: Employment Tribunal, 1975–; Bristol Initiative, 1989–2006. Mem. (Lab Co-op), Lockleaze Ward, Bristol CC, 1992–99. Treas., Lockleaze Neighbourhood Trust, 1996–2006. Sec., Brixham CC, 2012–. Vice Chm. Govs, Torbay Sch., 2013–. *Recreations:* gardening, walking, watching cricket (Somerset), scoring for cricket team (Brixham). *Address:* 2 Oxford Lane, Brixham, Devon TQ5 8PP.

GREGORY, Dr Philippa; author; *b* 9 Jan. 1954; *d* of Arthur Gregory and Elaine Gregory (*née* Wedd); *m* Anthony Mason; one *s* one *d*. *Educ:* Univ. of Sussex (BA 1979); Univ. of Edinburgh (MLitt; PhD 1984). Newspaper journalist, 1971–75; BBC Radio journalist, 1975–; book reviewer, TV presenter, broadcaster and playwright, 1986–. Founder, Gardens for The Gambia, 1993. *Publications:* Wideacre, 1986; The Favoured Child, 1988; Meridon, 1990; Mrs Hartley and the Growth Centre, 1991; The Wise Woman, 1992; Fallen Skies, 1994; The Little House, 1995; A Respectable Trade, 1997 (televised); Earthly Joys, 1999; Virgin Earth, 2000; The Other Boleyn Girl, 2001 (televised 2003, filmed 2008); The Queen's Fool, 2003; The Virgin's Lover, 2004; The Constant Princess, 2005; The Boleyn Inheritance, 2006; The Other Queen, 2008; The White Queen, 2009; The Red Queen, 2010; The Lady of the Rivers, 2011; (jtly) The Women of the Cousins' War, 2011; Changeling, 2012; The Kingmaker's Daughter, 2012; Stormbringers, 2013; The White Princess, 2013; The King's Curse, 2014; The Taming of the Queen, 2015. *Recreations:* child-raising (2 children, 5 step-children), riding, gardening, ski-ing, hiking, loafing. *Address:* c/o Rogers Coleridge & White, 20 Powis Mews, W11 1JN.

GREGORY, Richard John, OBE 2004; Yorkshire Bank Chair, since 2004, and Senior Independent Director and Chair, Risk Committee, Clydesdale Bank plc, since 2012, National Australia Group Europe Ltd; *b* 18 Aug. 1954; *s* of John and Joan Gregory. Trainee, Doncaster Gazette, 1972–75; gen. reporter, Doncaster Evening Post, 1976; labour corresp. and industrial corresp., Sheffield Morning Telegraph, 1977–79; News Ed., Granada TV, 1979–81; Yorkshire Television: News Ed., 1981–82; Producer, 1982–84; Ed., Calendar, 1984–89; Hd of News, 1989–92; Controller, 1992–93; Dir, Regl Progs, 1993–95; Dir of Broadcasting, 1995; Man. Dir, Broadcasting, Yorkshire Tyne Tees, 1996–97; Man. Dir, 1997–2002. Non-executive Director: Yorkshire Bank, 2000–; Clydesdale Bank plc, 2000–; Imagesound plc, 2002–10 (Chm., 2002–05; Sen. Ind. non-exec. Dir, 2005–); Sheffield University Enterprises Ltd, 2005–07. Member: Bd, BITC, 2001–08 (Chm., Yorks and Humber Regl Leadership Team, 2001–08); Yorkshire Forward (formerly Yorks and Humber Regl Develt Agency), 1998–2004 (Dep. Chm., 1999–2004); Chairman: Yorks Initiative, 1997–2001; Yorkshire Innovation (formerly Yorkshire Science), 2006–11; Science City York, 2007–13; Chair, Yorks Internat. Business Convention, 1999–2003. Chair, Chesterfield Royal Hosp. NHS Foundn Trust, 2006–15; Mem. Bd, Foundn Trust Network, 2010–13; Mem., Strategic Adv. Bd, NHS Leadership Acad., 2013–15. Mem., Yorkshire Culture (formerly Yorks Regl Cultural Consortium), 2000–04. Mem. Council, Inst. for Employment Studies, 2003–05. Chm., Sheffield Hallam Univ., 1999–2003 (Gov., 1992–2003). Trustee Dir, Sheffield Galls and Mus Trust, 2002–08. Hon. DLit: Bradford, 1999; Sheffield Hallam, 2003. *Recreations:* Peak District, Kefalonia.

GREGORY, Roger Michael; Deputy Receiver for the Metropolitan Police, 1989–94, retired; *b* 1 June 1939; *s* of Walter James Gregory and Catherine Emma Gregory (*née* Regan); *m* 1961, Johanna Margaret O'Rourke; five *s* two *d*. *Educ:* Gillingham (Kent) Grammar Sch.; Univ. of Herts (BA Hons 2006). Joined Metropolitan Police Civil Staff, 1957; Hd of Operations, Police National Computer Unit, 1976; Dep. Dir of Finance, Metropolitan Police, 1981; Dir of Computing, Metropolitan Police, 1983. *Recreations:* cricket, bridge, gentle gardening. *Address:* Willow Lodge, Poplar Close, Leighton Buzzard, Beds LU7 3BS.

GREGORY-HOOD, Peter Charles Freeman; HM Diplomatic Service, retired; *b* 12 Dec. 1943; *s* of late Col A. M. H. Gregory-Hood, OBE, MC and Diana, *d* of Sir John Gilmour, 2nd Bt (she *m* 2nd, Sir John Beith, KCMG); *m* 1966, Camilla Bethell (*d* 2006); three *d*. *Educ:* Summerfields, St Leonard's; Eton Coll.; Aix-en-Provence Univ.; Trinity Coll., Cambridge (BA Econs and Sociol.); Univ. of Buckingham (MA Biography 2003). Joined FCO, 1965: Third Sec., Dakar, 1967–69; Third, later Second Sec., Tel Aviv, 1969–71; First Secretary: FCO, 1972–76; (Commercial), Paris, 1976–80; FCO, 1980–86; (Inf.), New Delhi, 1986–90; Counsellor and Consul-Gen., Casablanca, 1990–95; Dep. High Comr, Colombo, 1995–98. *Recreations:* tennis, golf, swimming, theatre. *Address:* Loxley Hall, Loxley, Warwick CV35 9JP. *Clubs:* White's, Royal Over-Seas League; Rotary (Stratford-upon-Avon); Tadmarton Heath Golf.

GREGSON, Charles Henry; Chairman, Public Catalogue Foundation, since 2011 (Trustee, 2002–11); *b* 7 June 1947; *s* of Geoffrey and Anne Gregson; *m* 1972, Caroline Blake; two *s*. *Educ:* Harrow; Trinity Hall, Cambridge (MA). Solicitor; Clifford-Turner & Co., 1970–74; Gp Solicitor and Company Sec., Mills & Allen Internat. plc, later MAI plc, subseq. United Business Media, 1974–77, Dir, 1984–2007; Chief Executive: Shepperton Studios Ltd, 1975–79; Harlow Butler/Garban Gp, 1980–98; exec. Chm., 1998–2001, non-exec. Chm., 2001–, ICAP plc (formerly Garban plc, then Garban-Intercapital plc); CEO, 2005–09, Chm., 2010, PR Newswire; non-executive Director: International Personal Finance plc, 2007–12; Caledonia Investments plc, 2009–; Chairman: CPPGroup plc (formerly CPP plc), 2010–14; St James's Place plc, 2011–13 (Dir, 2010–13). *Recreations:* deerstalking, gardening, National Hunt racing. *Address:* Hope House, The Haven, Billingshurst RH14 9BN. *T:* (01403) 822066. *E:* charles.gregson@icap.com. *Club:* Turf.

GREGSON, David John; Chairman: Crime Reduction Initiatives, since 2010; Lawn Tennis Association, since 2013; *b* Walton-on-Thames, 28 June 1956; *s* of Bill and Rosalind Gregson; *m* 1987, Renée Cambier van Nooten; one *s* two *d*. *Educ:* Edinburgh Acad.; St Catharine's Coll., Cambridge (BA Hons Natural Scis 1978); Manchester Business Sch. (MBA 1983). Prodn Controller, Metal Box (Wrexham), 1979–81; Venture Capital Fund Manager, Dartington & Co., 1983–85; Dir, Globe Investment Trust, 1985–90; Phoenix Equity Partners: Co-founder, 1991; Chair, 2001–12; Sen. Advr, 2012–13. Chm., Precise Media Gp, 2006–14; Dir, Letts Filofax, 2007–13. Adviser, Carter Review: of Legal Aid, 2006; of Prison Service in England and Wales, 2008. Chair, Mayor's 2012 Olympic Legacy Bd of Advrs, 2008–09; Dir, Olympic Park Legacy Co., later London Legacy Develt Corp., 2009–. Member: Assoc. of British Sch., Netherlands, 2008–; Steering Bd Cttee, Apeldoorn: British-Dutch Dialogue, 2010–; Green Investment Bank Adv. Gp, 2011–12; Adv. Bd, Educn Endowment Foundn, 2011–. Chair, Jane Goodall Inst. (UK), 2002–06. Trustee: WWF-UK, 2006–12; Climate Gp, 2006–11; Advr, Sutton Trust, 2006–. *Recreations:* tennis, golf, ski-ing, family. *Address:* Lawn Tennis Association, National Tennis Centre, 100 Priory Lane, Roehampton, SW15 5JQ. *T:* (020) 7434 6989, *Fax:* (020) 7434 6999. *E:* david.gregson@lta.org.uk. *Clubs:* Lansdowne, Mosimann's; Royal Wimbledon Golf, Koninklijke Haagsche Golf and Country; Leimonias Lawn Tennis.

GREGSON, Prof. Edward; composer; Principal, Royal Northern College of Music, Manchester, 1996–2008; *b* 23 July 1945; *s* of Edward Gregson and May Elizabeth (*née* Eaves); *m* 1967, Susan Carole Smith; two *s*. *Educ:* Manchester Central Grammar Sch.; Royal Academy of Music (GRSM, LRAM); Goldsmiths' Coll., Univ. of London (BMus Hons). Lectr in Music, Rachel McMillan Coll., London, 1970–76; Sen. Lectr, 1976–89, Reader, 1989–94, and Prof. of Music, 1994–96, Goldsmiths' Coll., Univ. of London. Hon. Prof. of Music, Univ. of Manchester, 1996. Mem., Music Industry Forum, DCMS, 1998–2001; Bd Mem., Cultural Consortium Northwest, 2003–04; Chm., Conservatoires UK, 2004–08. Vice-Chm., Composers' Guild, 1976–78; Chm., Assoc. of Professional Composers, 1989–91; Director: PRS, 1995–2010, 2012–; Associated Bd of Royal Schs of Music, 1996–2008; Hallé Orch., 1998–2006. Gov. and Feoffee, Chetham's Sch. of Music, 1996–. Trustee: Nat. Foundn for Youth Music, 1999–2003; PRS Foundn, 2009–. Companion, RNCM, 2008. Fellow: Dartington Coll. of Arts, 1997; Leeds Coll. of Music, 2008. FRAM 1990; FRNCM 1998; Hon. FLCM 1999; FRCM 2000. Hon. DMus: Sunderland, 1996; Lancaster, 2006; Manchester, 2008; Chester, 2009; Hon. DArts Manchester Metropolitan, 2003; DUniv UCE, 2007. *Compositions include:* Oboe Sonata, 1965; Brass Quintet, 1967; Music for Chamber Orchestra, 1968; Horn Concerto, 1971; Essay for Brass Band, 1971; Tuba Concerto, 1976; Music for the York Cycle of Mystery Plays, 1976 and 1980; Connotations for Brass Band, 1977; Metamorphoses, 1979; Trombone Concerto, 1979; Trumpet Concerto, 1983; Piano Sonata in one movement, 1983; Contrasts for orchestra, 1983, revised 2001 as Contrasts—a concerto for orch.; Dances and Arias, 1984; Festivo, 1985; Missa Brevis Pacem, 1988; RSC History Play Cycles: Plantagenets Trilogy, 1988–89; Henry IV Parts 1 and 2, 1990–91; Celebration, 1991; Of Men and Mountains, 1991; The Sword and the Crown, 1991; Blazon, 1992; Clarinet Concerto, 1994; Concerto for Piano and Wind, 1995; The Kings Go Forth, 1996; Stepping Out, 1996; A Welcome Ode, 1997; …And the Seven Trumpets, 1998; Three Matisse Impressions, 1998; The Dance, forever the Dance, 1999; Violin Concerto, 2000; The Trumpets of the Angels, 2000; An Age of Kings, 2004; Shadow of Paradise, for Oboe and Percussion, 2005; Saxophone Concerto, 2006; A Song for Chris - concerto for cello and chamber orchestra, 2007; Rococo Variations, 2008; Goddess, for string orchestra, 2009; Aztec Dances for recorder (or flute) and piano, 2010; Dream Song for large orch., 2010; Tributes for clarinet and piano, 2010; An Album for my Friends (piano), 2011; Triptych for solo violin, 2011; Symphony in two movements for brass band, 2012; Of Distant Memories (for brass band), 2013; Concerto for flute and ensemble, 2013; Three John Donne Settings for choir, 2013; String Quartet, 2014; Symphony in two movements (for symphonic brass and percussion), 2015; many recordings. *Publications:* music articles in professional jls incl. Musical Opinion, BBC Music Mag. *Recreations:* walking, wine, watching sport. *Address:* c/o Novello Publishing Ltd, 14/15 Berners Street, W1T 3LJ. *E:* promotion@musicsales.co.uk. *W:* www.edwardgregson.com. *Club:* Savile.

GREGSON, Sir Peter (John), Kt 2011; FREng, FIAE; Chief Executive and Vice-Chancellor, Cranfield University, since 2013; *b* 3 Nov. 1957; *s* of Howard Davenport Gregson and Susan Katharine Gregson (*née* Lunn); *m* 1983, Rachael Kathleen McClaughry; three *d*. *Educ:* Imperial Coll., London (BSc Eng 1980 (Bessemer Medal); PhD 1983 (Matthey Prize, 2000)). CEng 1983, FREng 2000; FIMMM (FIM 1998); FIEI 2005; MRIA 2007; FIAE 2007; CCMI 2007. University of Southampton: Lectr in Engrg Materials, 1983–90; Sen. Lectr, 1990–92; Reader, 1992–95; Prof. of Aerospace Materials, 1995–2004; Hd, Engrg Materials, 1995–99; Dir of Res., Faculty of Engrg and Applied Sci., 1993–99; Dep. Hd, Sch. of Engrg Scis, 1999–2000; Dep. Vice-Chancellor, 2000–04; Pres. and Vice-Chancellor, QUB, 2004–13. Academic Director: Luxfer Advanced Technol. Centre, 1999–2001; Defence and Aerospace Res. Partnership in Advanced Metallic Airframes, 1999–2004; DePuy Internat. Univ. Technol. Partnership, 2000–04. Director: Southampton Innovations Ltd, 2000–04; Southampton Asset Mgt Ltd, 2000–04; Photonic Innovations Ltd, 2000–04; Univ. of Southampton Hldgs Ltd, 2000–04; SULIS Innovations, 2002–04; NI Sci. Park, 2004–13; QUBIS Ltd, 2004–13; QUB Bookshop, 2004–13; Rolls Royce Gp plc, 2007–12; Cranfield Ventures Ltd, 2013–; Chm., SETsquared, 2002–04. Sen. Res. Fellow, DERA, 1997–2001; Consultant: Johnson & Johnson/DePuy Internat., 1986–2004; Alcan Internat., 1989–93. Mem., DTI/OST Materials Foresight Panel, 1997–99. Mem. Council, CCLRC, 2003–07. Institute of Materials: Chairman: Alloy Design Cttee, 1991–92; Metals Sci. Cttee, 1992–93; Materials Strategy Commn, 1997–99; Mem. Council, Royal Acad. Engrg, 2005–08. EPSRC: Member: Structural Materials Coll., 1994–2005; Engrg Rev. Panel, 1999; User Panel, 2005–07; Chm., Postgrad. Trng Prog. Panel, 2000. Dir, ACU, 2010–; Sen. Advr, Chongqing Acad. of Sci. and Technol., 2011–. Trustee: Southampton Univ. Develt Trust, 2000–04; Wessex Med. Trust, 2001–04; Windsor Leadership Trust, 2002–. Associate Ed., Jl Materials Letters, 1990–2004. Chm., St Albans Internat. Organ Fest. FCGI 2006. DL Belfast 2007–13. Hon. DSc: Bengal Engrg and Science Univ., 2008; NUI, 2008; Southampton, 2009; Soka, 2010; QUB, 2014. Donald Julius Groen Prize, IMechE, 1994; Rosenhain Medal and Prize, Inst. Materials, 1996; Flax Trust Award, 2010. *Publications:* numerous scientific papers in learned jls, on engrg performance of aerospace materials and computational and experimental modelling of load bearing med. devices. *Recreations:* opera, gardening, tennis, sailing. *Address:* Cranfield University, Cranfield, Beds MK43 0AL. *T:* (01234) 754014. *Club:* Athenæum.

GREGSON, Sir Peter (Lewis), GCB 1996 (KCB 1988; CB 1983); Permanent Secretary, Department of Trade and Industry, 1989–96; *b* 28 June 1936; *s* of late Walter Henry Gregson and Lillian Margaret Gregson. *Educ:* Nottingham High Sch.; Balliol Coll., Oxford. Classical Hon. Mods, class I; Lit. Hum. class I; BA 1959; MA 1962. Nat Service, 1959–61; 2nd Lieut RAEC, attached to Sherwood Foresters. Board of Trade: Asst Principal, 1961; Private Sec. to Minister of State, 1963–65; Principal, 1965; Resident Observer, CS Selection Bd, 1966; London Business Sch., 1967; Private Sec. to the Prime Minister, 1968–72 (Parly Affairs, 1968–70; Econ. and Home Affairs, 1970–72); Asst Sec., DTI, and Sec., Industrial Development Adv. Bd, 1972–74; Under Sec., DoI, and Sec., NEB, 1975–77; Under Sec., Dept of Trade, 1977–80, Dep. Sec. (Civil Aviation and Shipping), 1980–81; Dep. Sec., Cabinet Office, 1981–85; Perm. Under-Sec. of State, Dept of Energy, 1985–89. Sen. Ind. Dir, Scottish Power plc, 1996–2004; Dir, Woolwich plc, 1998–2000; Chm., Woolwich Pension Fund Trust Co. Ltd, 1999–2000. Chairman: Beckenham and Bromley NT Centre, 2003–06; Beckenham Decorative and Fine Arts Soc., 2009–12. CCMI (CBIM 1988; Mem., Bd of Companions, 1996–2002 (Dep. Chm., 1999–2002)); FRSA 1999. *Recreations:* gardening, listening to music. *Address:* 9 Lavender Court, 10 Greenways, Beckenham, Kent BR3 3NG. *T:* (020) 8650 5925.

GREIDER, Prof. Carol W., PhD; Daniel Nathans Professor and Director, Department of Molecular Biology and Genetics, since 2003, and Professor of Oncology, since 2001, Johns Hopkins University School of Medicine; *b* San Diego, Calif, 15 April 1961; *d* of Kenneth Randolph Greider and Jean Foley Greider; *m* (marr. diss.); one *s* one *d*. *Educ:* Univ. of California, Santa Barbara (Regents Scholar 1981; BA Biol. 1983); Univ. of California, Berkeley (PhD Molecular Biol. 1987). Cold Spring Harbor Fellow, 1988–90; Cold Spring Harbor Laboratory: Asst Investigator, 1990–92; Associate Investigator, 1992–94; Investigator, 1994–97; Johns Hopkins University School of Medicine: Associate Prof. of Molecular Biol. and Genetics, 1997–99; Prof. of Molecular Biol. and Genetics, 1999–2003. Member: Inst. of Medicine, 2010–; Royal Acad. of Medicine of Catalonia, 2012–; Alpha Omega Honor Med. Soc., 2013–. MNAS 2003; FAAAS 2003; Fellow: Amer. Acad. of Arts and Scis, 2003; Amer. Acad. of Microbiol. 2004. (Jtly) Wiley Prize in Biomed. Scis, Wiley Foundn, 2006; Dickson Prize in Medicine, Univ. of Pittsburgh, 2007; (jtly) Paul Ehrlich and Ludwig Darmstaedter Prize, 2009; (jtly) Nobel Prize in Physiology or Medicine, 2009. *Publications:* (jtly) Molecular Biology: principles of genome function, 2010; contrib. chapters in books; articles in learned jls. *Address:* Department of Molecular Biology and Genetics, Johns Hopkins University School of Medicine, 603 PCTB, 725 N. Wolfe Street, Baltimore, MD 21205, USA. *T:* (410) 6146506, *Fax:* (410) 9550831. *E:* cgreider@jhmi.edu.

GREIG, Geordie Carron; Editor, Mail on Sunday, since 2012; Director: Mail Newspapers, since 2012; London Evening Standard and Independent Print Ltd, since 2012; *b* 16 Dec. 1960; *s* of Sir (Henry Louis) Carron Greig, KCVO, CBE and of Monica Kathleen Greig; *m* 1995, Kathryn Elizabeth Terry; one *s* twin *d*. *Educ:* Eton Coll.; St Peter's Coll., Oxford (MA English Lit. and Lang.). Reporter: South East London and Kentish Mercury, 1981–83; Daily Mail, 1984–85; Today, 1985–87; Sunday Times: Reporter, 1987–89; Arts Corresp., 1989–91; NY Corresp., 1991–95; Literary Editor, 1995–99; Editor: Tatler, 1999–2009; London Evening Standard (formerly Evening Standard), 2009–10; Editl Dir, London Evening Standard, Independent, Independent on Sunday and i, 2010–12. Trustee: Raisa Gorbachev Foundn, 2006–12; Friends of Nat. Libraries, 2013–. FRSA 2005. *Publications:* Louis and the Prince, 1999; Breakfast with Lucian, 2013. *Address:* Mail on Sunday, Northcliffe House, 2 Derry Street, W8 5TT.

GREIG, Kenneth Muir, PhD; Rector, Hutchesons' Grammar School, Glasgow, since 2005; *b* 30 March 1960; *s* of Walter and Margaret Greig; *m* 1987, Josephine Claire Berenice Taylor; one *s* one *d*. *Educ:* George Heriot's Sch., Edinburgh; Worcester Coll., Oxford (BA 1981, MA); Univ. of Edinburgh (PhD 1984). Exploration geologist, BP, 1984–87; Maths Teacher and Housemaster, Christ's Hosp., 1987–93; Hd of Maths and Dir of Studies, Dollar Acad., 1993–2000; Headmaster, Pangbourne Coll., 2000–05. *Recreations:* natural history, smallholding, beachcombing, watching sport. *Address:* Hutchesons' Grammar School, Beaton Road, Glasgow G41 4NW. *T:* (0141) 423 2933, *Fax:* (0141) 424 0251. *E:* rector@hutchesons.org.

GREIG, Lesley Gillian; *see* Glaister, L. G.

GREIG-SMITH, Peter William, DPhil; Director, Swift Impact Ltd, 2007–13; *b* 17 May 1953; *s* of late Peter Greig-Smith and of Edna (*née* Gonzalez); *m* 1st, 1978, June Ann Fettes (marr. diss. 2000); one *s* one *d*; 2nd, 2001, Lindsay Ann Murray. *Educ:* Aberdeen Univ. (BSc Hons Zoology 1975); Sussex Univ. (DPhil Behavioural Ecology 1980). Joined MAFF, 1980; Res. Scientist, Agricl Sci. Service, 1980–86; Head of Envmtl Res., 1986–90, of Conservation and Envmt Protection, 1990–92, Central Sci. Lab.; Head of Aquatic Envmt Protection, 1992–94, Dir, 1994–97, Directorate of Fisheries Res.; Chief Exec., Centre for Envmt, Fisheries and Aquaculture Sci., 1997–2004; Asst Dir, Special Projects, Envmt and Transport Dept, 2004–05, Actg Dir, Envmt and Regulation, 2005, Cambs CC. *Publications:* edited jointly: Field Margins, 1987; Field Methods for the Study of Environmental Effects of Pesticides, 1988; Pesticides, Cereal Farming and the Environment: the Boxworth project, 1992; Ecotoxicology of Earthworms, 1992; ECOtoxicology: ecological dimensions, 1996; numerous articles in sci. jls. *Recreations:* mountains, golf, DIY. *Address:* Street Farmhouse, Stanway, Colchester, Essex.

GREINER, Hon. Nicholas Frank, (Nick), AC 1994; Chairman, QBE Australia/New Zealand and Asia-Pacific, since 2011; *b* 27 April 1947; *s* of Nicholas and Clare Greiner; *m* 1970, Kathryn Callaghan (AO 2001) (separated); one *s* one *d*. *Educ:* St Ignatius Coll., Riverview; Sydney Univ. (BEc Hons); Harvard Univ. (MBA High Dist.). Asst Vice-Pres., Boise Cascade Corp., USA, 1970–71; NSW Dir and Chief Exec., White River Corp., 1972–80; Chm., Harper & Row (Australasia), 1977–83. Chairman: Baulderstone Hornibrook, 1993–2004; United Utilities Australia Pty Ltd (formerly North West Water), 1993–2010; Natwest Markets, 1993–97 (Dir, 1992–98); IAMA (formerly SBS-IAMA) Ltd, 1994–2000; W. D. & H. O. Wills, 1996–99 (Dir, 1995–99); British American Tobacco Australasia, 1999–2004; BMC Media, 1999–2002; Nuance Australia, 2001–; Bilfinger Berger Australia Pty Ltd, 2003–10; Bradken Resources Pty Ltd, 2004– (Dir, 2002–04); Healthcare Australia Ltd, 2006–10; BlueStar Print Gp, 2007–12; QBE LMI (formerly PMI), 2008–11 (Dir, 2007–08); Citigroup Australia, 2008–11; Australian Adv. Bd, Rothschild Global Financial Adv., 2011–; Adv. Bd, Degremont and SAS Gp of Cos, Australia/NZ, 2011–; Accolade Wines, 2013–; Rearden Capital, 2014–; Adv. Bd, Crosby Textor, 2014–. Co-Chair, Ausflag Ltd, 1996–2000; Deputy Chairman: Stockland Trust Property Gp, 1992–2010; Coles Myer, 1995–96 (Dir, 1992–2000); Castle Harlan Australian Mezzanine Pty Ltd, 2000–. Director: Australian Vintage Pty Ltd (formerly Brian McGuigan Wines, subseq. McGuigan Simeon Wines), 1992–2008; QBE Insce Gp, 1992–2007; Blue Freeway, 2006–09; Consultant: Clayton Utz, 1992–2004; Citigroup, 1997–2008; Deloitte Touche Tohmatsu, 1999–2004; Advr, BDO Australia, 2015–. Prof., Macquarie Grad. Sch. of Management, 1992–2004. Director: Harvard Business Sch. Alumni Assoc. Bd., 2005–08; Harvard Business Sch. Asia-Pacific Adv. Bd, 2011–; Chm., SMART Infrastructure Facility, Univ. of Wollongong 2009–11. Chm., Australian Subscription Television and Radio Assoc., 2003–08. MP (L) Ku-ring-gai, NSW, 1980–92; Shadow Minister for Urban Affairs, June 1981; Shadow Treasurer, and Shadow Minister for Housing and Co-operatives, Oct. 1981; Leader of State Opposition, 1983–88; Shadow Treasurer, and Shadow Minister for Ethnic Affairs, 1983; Premier, Treasurer, and Minister for Ethnic and Aboriginal Affairs, NSW Coalition Govt, 1988–92. Chm., Infrastructure NSW, 2011–13. Mem., GST Distribution Review Panel, Australian Govt, 2011–12. Dir, European-Australian Business Council, 2013– (Mem., Corporate Council, 2002–13). Gov., CEDA, 2005–. Director: Sydney Organising Cttee for Olympic Games, 1993–2000; S Sydney Rugby League Club, 2003–06, now Life Mem. President: Squash Australia, 1998–2000; Soccer Australia, 1996–99. Life Fellow, Australian Inst. of Co. Dirs; Hon. Fellow, CPA Australia; Life Mem., State Council, NSW Div., Liberal Party, 2012–. Centenary Medal (Australia), 2000. *Recreations:* walking, ski-ing, theatre, opera, spectator sports. *Address:* Level 10, 139 Macquarie Street, Sydney, NSW 2000, Australia.

GRENDER, Baroness *cr* 2013 (Life Peer), of Kingston upon Thames, in the London Borough of Kingston upon Thames; **Rosalind Mary, (Olly) Grender,** MBE 1996; *b* 19 Aug. 1962. Res. and Policy Officer to Leader of Liberal Democrats, 1989–92; Communications Director: Lib Dem Party, 1992–95; Shelter, 1995–2000; Sen. Consultant, LLM Communications, 2000–02; Dep. Dir of Communications for Govt, 2011–12. *Address:* House of Lords, SW1A 0PW.

GRENFELL, family name of **Baron Grenfell**.

GRENFELL, 3rd Baron *cr* 1902; **Julian Pascoe Francis St Leger Grenfell;** Baron Grenfell of Kilvey (Life Peer) 2000; *b* 23 May 1935; *o s* of 2nd Baron Grenfell, CBE, TD, and of Elizabeth Sarah Polk, *o d* of late Captain Hon. Alfred Shaughnessy, Montreal, Canada; *S* father, 1976; *m* 1st, 1961, Loretta Maria Reali (marr. diss. 1970), Florence; one *d*; 2nd, 1970, Gabrielle Raab (marr. diss. 1987), Berlin; two *d*; 3rd, 1987, Mrs Elisabeth Porter (marr. diss. 1992), Washington, DC; 4th, 1993, Mrs Dagmar Langbehn Debreil, *yr d* of late Dr Carl Langbehn, Berlin. *Educ:* Eton; King's Coll., Cambridge. BA (Hons), President of the Union, Cambridge, 1959. 2 Lieut, KRRC (60th Rifles), 1954–56; Captain, Queen's Royal Rifles, TA, 1963; Programme Asst, ATV Ltd, 1960–61; frequent appearances and occasional scripts, for ATV religious broadcasting and current affairs series, 1960–64. Joined World Bank, Washington, DC, 1965; Chief of Information and Public Affairs for World Bank Group in Europe, 1970; Dep. Dir, European Office, 1973; Special rep. of World Bank to UN, 1974–81; Special Advr, 1983–87, Sen. Advr, 1987–90; Head of Ext. Affairs, European Office, 1990–95; Sen. Advr, European Office, 1995, retired. UK Delegn to Parly Assemblies of Council of Europe and WEU, 1997–99. A Dep. Speaker, H of L, 2002–08; Chm., Econ. and Financial Subcttee, H of L Select Cttee on EU, 1999 and 2001–02; Principal Dep. Chm. of Cttees and Chm., Select Cttee on EU, 2002–08; retired from H of L, 2014. Pres., Anglo-Belgian Soc. of the UK, 2006–14. Chevalier de la Légion d'Honneur (France), 2005; Médaille d'Honneur du Senat (France), 2008; Comdr, Cross of the Order of Merit (Germany), 2008; Comdr, Order of the Crown (Belgium), 2009; High Order of Merit (Croatia), 2010. *Publications:* Margot (novel), 1984; The Gazelle (novel), 2004. *Recreation:* European history. *Heir: cousin* Richard Arthur St Leger Grenfell [*b* 4 Nov. 1966; *m* 1995, Sally Marie Halstead; one *s*]. *Address:* 24 rue Chaptal, 75009 Paris, France. *Club:* Royal Green Jackets.

GRENFELL, Andrée, (Mrs David Milman); Director: Milman International Australia, since 1990; Mossplum Pty Ltd, since 1995; *b* 14 Jan. 1940; *d* of Stephen Grenfell (writer) and Sybil Grenfell; *m* 1st, 1972, Roy Warden; two step *s*; 2nd, 1984, David Milman; two step *s*. *Educ:* privately. Graduate Diploma in Agric., Hawkesbury Agricl Coll., 1989. Man. Dir, Elizabeth Arden Ltd, UK, 1974–76; Pres., Glemby Internat., UK and Europe, 1976–80; Sen. Vice Pres., Glemby Internat., USA, 1976–80. Chm., Kelly Burrell & Jones, 1988–91; Director: Harvey Nichols Knightsbridge, 1972–74; Peter Robinson Ltd, 1968–72; Non-executive Director: NAAFI, 1981–83; Prince of Wales Res. Inst., Sydney, 1994–2004. Mem. Council, Inst. of Dirs, 1976; FCMI (FBIM 1977). Mem., Cercle des Amis de la Veuve. Business Woman of the Year, FT, 1979. *Recreations:* riding, dressage, swimming, yoga. *Address:* 3/1 Rosemont Avenue, Woollahra, NSW 2025, Australia. *T:* (2) 93275964, *Fax:* (2) 93275964.

GRENFELL, Prof. Bryan Thomas, OBE 2002; DPhil; FRS 2004; Professor of Ecology and Public Affairs, Princeton University, since 2009; *b* 7 Dec. 1954; *s* of Bryan and Gwenda Grenfell; *m* 1996, Catherine Williams. *Educ:* Imperial Coll., London (BSc; ARCS); Univ. of York (MSc; DPhil 1981). Res. Fellow, Dept of Biol., Imperial Coll., London, 1981–86; Lectr, Dept of Animal and Plant Scis, Univ. of Sheffield, 1986–90; Department of Zoology, University of Cambridge: Lectr, 1990–98; Reader, 1998–2002; Prof. of Population Biol., 2002–04; Fellow, Girton Coll., Cambridge, 2001–04; Alumni Prof. of Biol., Pennsylvania State Univ., 2004–09. *Publications:* (ed with A. P. Dobson) Ecology of Infectious Diseases in Natural Populations, 1995; numerous papers in learned jls. *Recreations:* cooking, reading, hiking. *Address:* 211 Eno Hall, Princeton University, Princeton, NJ 08544, USA. *T:* (609) 9240308.

GRENFELL, (Jeremy) Gibson; QC 1994; a Recorder, since 1992; *b* 13 Dec. 1945; *s* of late Edward Gerald James Grenfell and of June (*née* Hunkin). *Educ:* Falmouth Grammar Sch.; Fitzwilliam Coll., Cambridge (Open Exhibnr, MA). Called to the Bar, Middle Temple, 1969 (Harmsworth Schol.; Bencher, 2003). *Address:* c/o 21 College Hill, EC4R 2RP. *T:* (020) 3301 0910.

GRENFELL, Ven. Dr Joanne Woolway; Archdeacon of Portsdown, since 2013; *b* Enfield, 27 May 1972; *d* of John Woolway and Christine Woolway; *m* 1998, Rev. Dr James Grenfell; two *s* one *d*. *Educ:* Oriel Coll., Oxford (BA 1993; DPhil 1997); Univ. of British Columbia (MA English Lit. 1994); Anglia Ruskin Univ. (PGDPT). Advr to Women Students, 1995–98, Lectr, 1997–98, Oriel Coll., Oxford; ordained deacon, 2000, priest, 2001; Curate, Kirkby Team Ministry, 2000–03; Priest-in-charge, Manor Ecumenical Parish, 2003–06; Diocese of Sheffield: Dir of Ordinands and Res. Canon, 2006–13; Dean of Women's Ministry, 2008–13. *Publications:* (contrib.) Literature, Mapping and the Politics of Space in Early Modern Britain, 2001; (contrib.) Women and Men in Scripture and the Church, 2013; (contrib.) Reflections for Daily Prayer, 2014; articles in Early Modern Literary Studies. *Recreations:* poetry, film, cookery. *Address:* 313 Havant Road, Farlington, Portsmouth PO6 1DD. *T:* 07833 430140. *E:* joanne.grenfell@portsmouth.anglican.org.

GRENFELL, Dr Michael Paul; Executive Director, Enforcement, Competition and Markets Authority, since 2015; *b* London, 17 Feb. 1963; *s* of Dr Joseph Grenfell and late Eva Hanna Grenfell; *m* 2006, Sally Sweiry; two *s*. *Educ:* Haberdashers' Aske's Sch., Elstree; Peterhouse, Cambridge (BA Hons Hist. and Law 1985); London Sch. of Econs and Political Sci. (PhD Political Thought 1991). Admitted solicitor, 1988; Associate, Linklaters, 1988–91; Associate, 1991–98, Partner, 1998–2013, Norton Rose, later Norton Rose Fulbright; Sen. Dir, Sector Regulation, CMA, 2014–15. *Publications:* (with Martin Coleman) The Competition Act 1998: law and practice, 1999; (contrib.) The Philosophy, Politics and Religion of British Democracy: Maurice Cowling and conservatism, 2010. *Recreations:* current affairs, history, travel, good conversation. *Address:* Competition and Markets Authority, Victoria House, 37 Southampton Row, WC1B 4AD. *T:* (020) 3738 6000. *E:* michael.grenfell@cma.gsi.gov.uk.

GRENFELL, His Honour Simon Pascoe; commercial, civil and community mediator, since 2011; a Circuit Judge, 1992–2010; Senior Circuit Judge, 2002–10; a Deputy Circuit Judge, 2010–14; *b* 10 July 1942; *s* of late Osborne Pascoe Grenfell and Margaret Grenfell; *m* 1974, Ruth De Jersey Harvard; one *s* three *d*. *Educ:* Fettes College; Emmanuel College, Cambridge (MA). Called to the Bar, Gray's Inn, 1965; practice on NE Circuit; a Recorder, 1985–92; Designated Civil Judge: Bradford Group of Courts, 1998–2000; Leeds Group of Courts, 2000–10. Accredited mediator, 2011; Mediation and Trng Alternatives, RICS, 2011; Member: Assoc. of Northern Mediators; ARCH Mediation Services. Chancellor, Dio. of Ripon and Leeds (formerly Dio. of Ripon), 1992–2014. *Recreations:* music, sailing and messing about in boats, coarse gardening, online information, walking, travelling, good food, young grandchildren.

GRENIER, Rear-Adm. Peter Francis, (Frank), CB 1989; self-employed glass engraver; *b* 27 Aug. 1934; *s* of late Dr F. W. H. Grenier and Mrs M. Grenier; *m* 1957, Jane Susan Bradshaw; two *s* one *d* (and one *s* decd). *Educ:* Montpelier School, Paignton; Blundell's School, Tiverton. Entered RN (Special Entry), 1952; Midshipman, Mediterranean Fleet, 1953; commissioned, 1955; joined Submarine service, 1956; 1st command (HMS Ambush), 1965; final command (HMS Liverpool), 1982; Chief of Staff to C-in-C Naval Home Command, 1985–87; FO Submarines, and Comdr Submarine Forces E Atlantic, 1987–89. Defence Advr, H of C Defence Cttee, 1991–98. Vice-Pres., Royal Naval FA, 1988–. Liveryman, Glass Sellers' Co., 1987. Chm. of Govs, Blundell's Sch., 1991–96 (Gov., 1986–96). FGE 2009 (AFGE 1998). *Recreations:* family, sketching and painting, golf. *Address:* 2 Grange Cottages, North Cadbury, Yeovil, Somerset BA22 7BY. *T:* (01963) 440176, *Fax:* (01963) 440389. *W:* www.frankgrenier.co.uk. *Club:* Army and Navy.

GRENVILLE; *see* Freeman-Grenville, family name of Lady Kinloss.

GRENVILLE, Dr Jane Clare, OBE 2014; FSA; Pro-Vice-Chancellor for Students, University of York, since 2007 (Deputy Vice-Chancellor, 2012–15); Commissioner, English Heritage, 2001–08; *b* 17 June 1958; *d* of Henry William Grenville and Helen Caroline Grenville (*née* Westmacott). *Educ:* Girton Coll., Cambridge (BA Hons Archaeol. and Anthropol., MA 1983); Univ. of York (PhD 2005). MCIfA (MIFA 1993); IHBC 1996; FSA 2002. Caseworker, Listed Buildings Resurvey for Yorkshire and Humberside, 1984–87; Res. Officer, Chester Rows Res. Project, 1987–88; Historic Buildings Officer, Council for British Archaeol., 1988–91; University of York: Lectr, 1991–2000; Sen. Lectr in Archaeol., 2000–; Hd, Dept of Archaeology, 2001–06. Trustee: York Civic Trust, 2006–; York Museums Trust, 2008–11; Chm. Trustees, Council for British Archaeol., 2013–. *Publications:* Medieval Housing, 1997; Managing the Historic Rural Landscape, 1999. *Recreations:* dogs, academic Russian roulette. *Address:* University of York, King's Manor, York YO1 7EP. *T:* (01904) 323903. *E:* jane.grenville@york.ac.uk.

GRENVILLE-GREY, Wilfrid Ernest; Civil Society advocate at United Nations, New York, 1991–2006; *b* 27 May 1930; *s* of late Col Cecil Grenville-Grey, CBE and Monica Grenville-Grey (*née* Morrison-Bell); *m* 1st, 1963, Edith Sibongile Dlamini (marr. diss. 1989), *d* of Rev. Jonathan Dlamini, Johannesburg; two *s* one *d*; 2nd, 2006, Cynthia Elizabeth, *d* of Stanley Goddard, Barbados and NYC. *Educ:* Eton; Worcester College, Oxford (scholar; MA); Yale University (Henry Fellow, 1953–54). 2nd Lieut, KRRC, 1949–50. Overseas Civil Service, Nyasaland, 1956–59; Booker McConnell Ltd, 1960–63; Mindolo Ecumenical Foundn, Zambia, 1963–71 (Dir, 1966–71); Sec., Univ. Study Project on Foreign Investments in S Africa, 1971–72; Dir, Centre for Internat. Briefing, Farnham Castle, 1973–77; Internat. Defence and Aid Fund for Southern Africa, London and UN, 1978–83; Sec. for Public Affairs to Archbishop of Canterbury, 1984–87; British Dir, Global Forum of Spiritual and Parly Leaders on Human Survival, 1987–88; Internat. Develt Dir, Icewalk, 1988–89. DHL Ignatius Univ., Ohio, 2005. *Publications:* All in an African Lifetime, 1969; UN Jigsaw, 2000; anthologies of aphorisms: Sixty Marker Buoys and Anchors, 1990, 1995, 2000, 2005, 2010 and 2015. *Recreations:* gardening, apophthegms. *Address:* 47 Halnaker, Chichester, West Sussex PO18 0NQ. *Club:* Travellers.

GRETTON, family name of **Baron Gretton**.

GRETTON, 4th Baron *cr* 1944, of Stapleford; **John Lysander Gretton;** *b* 17 April 1975; *s* of 3rd Baron Gretton and of Jennifer Ann (*see* Jennifer, Lady Gretton); *S* father, 1989; *m* 2006, Sarah Elizabeth Anne, *er d* of Alfred Attard; one *s* one *d*. *Educ:* Shrewsbury; RAC Cirencester. Dir and Partner, Gretton Bergius (formerly Griffiths Bergius), independent home search agents, 2007–; Partner, Stapleford Farms and Stapleford Estate, 2009–. *Heir: s* Hon. John Frederick Bruce Gretton, *b* 9 June 2008.

GRETTON, Jennifer, Lady; Jennifer Ann Gretton; Lord-Lieutenant of Leicestershire, since 2003; owner, Stapleford Estate; *b* 14 June 1943; *o d* of Edmund Sandford Moore and Emily Joan Moore; *m* 1970, Hon. John Henrik Gretton (later 3rd Baron Gretton; he *d* 1989); one *s* one *d*. *Educ:* York Coll. for Girls. Member: Leics and Rutland CLA Cttee, 1989–2012; Envmt and Water Cttee, CLA, 1994–98. President: Melton Mowbray & District Model Engrg Soc., 1989–; Rural Community Council (Leics and Rutland), 1994–; Leics Orgn for the Relief of Suffering, 1999–; St John Council, Leics, 2003–; Leics and Rutland Cttee, Army Benevolent Fund, 2003–; Leics and Rutland Br., SSAFA, 2008–; Vice-President: Scout Council, Leics, 2003–; E Midlands RFCA, 2003– (Pres., Leics and Rutland County Cttee, 2003–); Leics and Rutland Branch, Magistrates' Assoc., 2004–; Co. Vice Pres., Leicester, Leics and Rutland, Girlguiding, 2011–. Member: Cttee, Somerby PCC, 1991–; Leics Cathedral Council, 2003–12. Patron: Sir Frank Whittle Commem. Gp, 2003–; Heart of the Nat. Forest Foundn, 2003–; Change Ashby Now, 2003–; Leics and Rutland Wildlife Trusts, 2004–; Laura Centre, 2008–; Friends of Leicester Cathedral, 2011–; Radio Leicester Applause Charity, 2011–; Soft Touch Arts, 2013–; Co. Patron, Leics and Rutland, RBL, 2006–. DL 2001, JP 2003, Leics. *Recreations:* sport, music, all aspects of steam. *T:* (01664) 454607.
See also Baron Gretton.

GRETTON, Prof. George Lidderdale, WS; Lord President Reid Professor of Law, University of Edinburgh, since 1994; a Scottish Law Commissioner, 2006–11; *b* 10 Nov. 1950; *s* of David Foster Gretton and Patience Mary Gretton (*née* Lidderdale); *m* 1976, Helen Jessica Morgan; two *s* one *d*. *Educ:* King Edward's Sch., Birmingham; Univ. of Durham (BA); Univ. of Edinburgh (LLB). WS 1980. Lectr, Sen. Lectr, and Reader, Univ. of Edinburgh, 1981–94. FRSE 2002. *Publications:* The Law of Inhibition and Adjudication, 1996; (with K. Reid) Conveyancing (2005), 2005; contribs to books, and jls incl. Edinburgh Law Rev., Scots Law Times, Jl Business Law, Eur. Rev. of Private Law. *Address:* University of Edinburgh, School of Law, Old College, South Bridge, Edinburgh EH8 9YL. *E:* G.Gretton@ed.ac.uk.

GRETTON, Vice Adm. Michael Peter, CB 1998; CVO 2005; Associate, 2020 Delivery, since 2012; Chairman, Winchester and Eastleigh Healthcare NHS Trust, 2007–12; *b* 14 March 1946; *s* of Vice Adm. Sir Peter Gretton, KCB, DSO, OBE, DSC, MA and late Dorothy (*née* Du Vivier); *m* 1973, Stephanie O'Neill; one *s* three *d*. *Educ:* Ampleforth Coll.; BRNC Dartmouth; Trinity Coll., Oxford (BA PPE; MA). Joined RN, 1963; served HMS Torquay, Tiger, Rothesay, Ark Royal and Bacchante; commanded: HMS Bossington, 1972–73; HMS Ambuscade, 1977–80; RCDS, 1987; commanded: HMS Invincible, 1988–90; NATO Standing Naval Force Atlantic, 1990–91; Dir of Naval Staff Duties, MoD, 1991–93; comd UK Task Force and NATO Anti-Submarine Warfare Striking Force, 1993–94; Rep. of SACLANT in Europe, 1994–98. Dir, Duke of Edinburgh's Award, 1998–2005; World Challenge Ltd, 2005–07. Chm., Youth Options (formerly Hants and IoW Youth Options), 2007–. Governor: St Edward's Sch., Oxford, 1985–2008; Farleigh Sch., Red Rice, 1992–2004; St Mary's Sch., Shaftesbury, 1998–2008. Pres., RN RFU, 1993–95. Mem. Council, Tall Ships Youth Trust (formerly Sail Training Assoc.), 1999–2010. Chm., HMS Whimbrel (1942–49) Battle of the Atlantic Meml, 2004–. FNI 1994. *Recreations:* Real Tennis, sightseeing, listening to music. *Clubs:* Naval (Pres., 2005–13); I Zingari.

GREVE, Prof. John; Professor of Social Policy and Administration, University of Leeds, 1974–87, now Emeritus; *b* 23 Nov. 1927; *s* of Steffen A. and Ellen C. Greve; *m* (marr. diss. 1986); one *s* one *d*. *Educ:* elementary and secondary Schs in Cardiff; London Sch. of Economics (BSc(Econ)). Various jobs, incl. Merchant Navy, Youth Employment Service, and insurance, 1946–55; student, 1955–58; research work, then Univ. teaching, 1958–. Has worked in Norway at research institutes. Community Programmes Dept, Home Office, 1969–74; Prof. of Social Admin, Univ. of Southampton, 1969–74. Hon. Vis. Prof., 1987–88, Hon. Sen. Res. Fellow, 1988–2002, Univ. of York. Chm., Care and Support Services Ltd, 1995–97. Mem., Royal Commn on Distribution of Income and Wealth, 1974–79; directed GLC Enquiry into Homelessness in London, 1985–86; Member: Bd, East Thames Housing Group (formerly Mem. Management Cttee, E London Housing Assoc.), 1988–98; York CHC, 1997–2002; Cardiff CHC, 2004–08. *Publications:* The Housing Problem, 1961 (and 1969); London's Homeless, 1964; Private Landlords in England, 1965; (with others) Comparative Social Administration, 1969, 2nd edn 1972; Housing, Planning and Change in Norway, 1970; Voluntary Housing in Scandinavia, 1971; (with others) Homelessness in London, 1971; Low Incomes in Sweden, 1978; (jtly) Sheltered Housing for the Elderly, 1983; Homelessness in Britain, 1990, rev. edn 1991; Poland—the reform of housing, 1994; various articles and papers, mainly on social problems, policies and administration, a few short stories. *Recreations:* walking, painting, listening to music, writing, good company.

GREVILLE, family name of **Earl of Warwick**.

GREWAL, Harnam Singh, CBE 1990; ED 1976; Secretary for the Civil Service, Government Secretariat, Hong Kong, 1987–90, retired; *b* 5 Dec. 1937; *s* of late Joginder Singh Grewal and Ajaib Kaur; *m* 1973, Shiv Pal Kaur Chima; one *s* one *d*. *Educ:* Sir Ellis Kadoorie Sch.; King's Coll., Univ. of Hong Kong (BA Hons 1959; DipEd 1960); Pembroke Coll., Cambridge Univ. (BA 1962; MA 1974). Asst Educn Officer, Hong Kong, 1962; Admin. Officer, 1964; Dist Officer, Tai Po, 1970; Dep. Dir of Urban Services, New Territories, 1976; Dep. Sec. for CS, 1980; Comr of Customs and Excise, 1984; Sec. for Transport, 1986. Royal Hong Kong Regt (The Volunteers), 1963–84, Major (retd); Hon. Col, 1987–90. *Recreation:* lawn bowls. *Address:* 3495 Cadboro Bay Road, Victoria, BC V8R 5K7, Canada.

GREY; *see* De Grey.

GREY, family name of **Earl Grey**.

GREY, 7th Earl *cr* 1806; **Philip Kent Grey;** Bt 1746; Baron Grey, 1801; Viscount Howick, 1806; *b* 11 May 1940; *s* of Albert Harry George Campbell Grey (*d* 1942) and Vera Helen Louise Grey (*née* Harding); *S* brother, 2013; *m* 1968, Ann Catherine, *y d* of Cecil Applegate; one *s* one *d*. *Heir: s* Alexander Edward Grey, Viscount Howick, *b* 20 Dec. 1968.

GREY de WILTON, Viscount; Julian Francis Martin Grosvenor; *b* 8 June 1959; *s* of Earl of Wilton, *qv*; *m* 1987, Danielle (marr. diss. 1989), sixth *d* of Theo Rossi, Sydney, Australia; one *s* (*b* 2006).

GREY OF CODNOR, 6th Baron *cr* 1397 (in abeyance 1496–1989); **Richard Henry Cornwall-Legh;** *b* 14 May 1936; *s* of 5th Baron Grey of Codnor, CBE and Dorothy (*d* 1993), *er d* of J. W. Scott; *S* father, 1996; *m* 1974, Joanna Storm, 7th *d* of Sir Kenelm Cayley, 10th Bt; three *s* one *d*. *Educ:* Stowe. High Sheriff, 1993, DL 1995, Cheshire. *Heir: s* Hon. Richard Stephen Cayley Cornwall-Legh [*b* 24 March 1976; *m* 2005, Annie Helen, *y d* of Frederick Riches; two *s* one *d* (of whom one *s* one *d* are twins)]. *Address:* High Legh House, Knutsford, Cheshire WA16 0QR. *Clubs:* Boodle's, MCC.

GREY, Alan Hartley, OBE 1999; HM Diplomatic Service, retired; Judge, Council of Europe Administrative Tribunal (formerly Member, Council of Europe Appeals Board), 1993–96; *b* 26 June 1925; *s* of William Hartley Grey and Gladys Grey; *m* 1950, Joan Robinson (*d* 1985); one *s* one *d*. *Educ:* Bootle Secondary Sch. for Boys. RAF, 1943–48; Foreign Service (Br. B), 1948; Tel Aviv, 1949; Tabriz and Khorramshahr, 1950–52; 3rd Sec., Belgrade, 1952–54; Vice-Consul, Dakar, 1954–57; Second Sec. (Commercial), Helsinki, 1958–61; FO, 1961–64; Second Sec. (Econ.), Paris, 1964–66; FO (later FCO), 1966–70; Consul (Commercial), Lille, 1970–74; FCO, 1974–82; Ambassador at Libreville, 1982–84; re-employed in FCO (as Staff Assessor), 1985–90. Vice Pres., Lambeth Horticl Soc., 2013– (Vice Chm., 1998–2013). *Recreation:* gardening.

GREY, Sir Anthony (Dysart), 7th Bt *cr* 1814; former Inspector, Department of Industrial Affairs, Government of Western Australia; *b* 19 Oct. 1949; *s* of Edward Elton Grey (*d* 1962) (*o s* of 6th Bt) and of Nancy, *d* of late Francis John Meagher, Perth, WA; *S* grandfather, 1974; *m* 1970 (marr. diss.); *m* 1993, Alison Turner; one *s* three *d*. *Educ:* Guildford Grammar School, WA. *Recreations:* fishing, painting. *Heir: s* Thomas Jasper Grey, *b* 30 April 1998. *Address:* 86 Kingsway Gardens, 38 Kings Park Road, W Perth, WA 6005, Australia.

GREY, Dame Beryl (Elizabeth), DBE 1988 (CBE 1973); a Director, Royal Opera House, 1999–2003; Prima Ballerina, Sadler's Wells Ballet, now Royal Ballet, 1941–57; Artistic Director, London Festival Ballet, 1968–79; *b* London, 11 June 1927; *d* of late Arthur Ernest Groom; *m* 1950, Dr Sven Gustav Svenson (*d* 2008); one *s*. *Educ:* Dame Alice Owen's Girls' Sch., London. Professional training: Madeline Sharp Sch., Sadler's Wells Sch. (Schol.), de Vos Sch. Début Sadler's Wells Co., 1941, with leading Ballerina rôles following same year in Les Sylphides, The Gods Go A'Begging, Le Lac des Cygnes, Act II, Comus. First full-length ballet, Le Lac des Cygnes on 15th birthday, 1942. Has appeared since in leading rôles of many ballets including: Sleeping Beauty, Giselle, Sylvia, Checkmate, Ballet Imperial, Donald of the Burthens, Homage, Birthday Offering, The Lady and the Fool. Film: The Black Swan (3 Dimensional Ballet Film), 1952. Left Royal Ballet, Covent Garden, Spring 1957, to become free-lance ballerina. Regular guest appearances with Royal Ballet at Covent Garden and on European, African, American and Far Eastern Tours. Guest Artist, London's Festival Ballet in London and abroad, 1958–64. First Western ballerina to appear with Bolshoi Ballet: Moscow, Leningrad, Kiev, Tiflis, 1957–58; First Western ballerina to dance with Chinese Ballet Co. in Peking and Shanghai, 1964. Engagements and tours abroad include: Central and S America, Mexico, Rhodesia and S Africa, Canada, NZ, Lebanon, Germany, Norway, Sweden, Denmark, Finland, Belgium, Holland, France, Switzerland, Italy, Portugal, Austria, Czechoslovakia, Poland, Rumania; Producer: Sleeping Beauty, 1967; Swan Lake, 1972, London Fest. Ballet; Giselle, Western Australia Ballet, 1984, 1986; Sleeping Beauty, Royal Swedish Ballet, Stockholm, 1985, 2002. Regular television and broadcasts in England and abroad; concert narrator. Dir-Gen., Arts Educational Trust and Teacher Trng Coll., 1966–68. Vice-Pres., Royal Acad. of Dancing, 1980– (Exec. Mem., 1982–89); Pres., Dance Council of Wales, 1981–2004; Life Pres., ISTD, 2002– (FISTD 1960; Mem. Council, 1966–91; Chm., 1984–91; Pres., 1991–2001; ISTD Imperial Award for Outstanding Service, 1987, Lifetime Achievement Award, 2004); Mem. Bd, BRB, 1995–99; Council for Dance Education and Training: Mem. Council, 1984–96; Mem. Exec., 1995–96; Patron, 2011–. Trustee: London City Ballet, 1978–92; Adeline Genée Theatre, 1982–90; Royal Ballet Benevolent Fund, 1982– (Chm. Trustees, 1992–2011; Patron, 2011–); Dance Critics Circle, 2005–11 (Patron, 2005–); Vice Chm., Dance Teachers Benevolent Fund, 1984–2004 (Trustee, 1981–2004; Pres., 2012–); President: Keep Fit Assoc., 1992–93; E Grinstead Operatic Soc., 1986–2009; English Nat. Ballet, 2005–; British Ballet Orgn, 2010–; Vice-President: Music Therapy Charity, 1980–; British Fedn of Music Festivals, 1985–; London Ballet Circle, 2001–. Governor: Dame Alice Owens Girls' Sch., London, 1960–77; Frances Mary Buss Foundn, 1963–72; Royal Ballet Cos, 1993–2002 (Vice Chm. Govs, 1995–2002). Patron: Lisa Ullman Travelling Scholarship Fund, 1986–; British Sch. of Osteopathy, 1987–; Benesh Inst. of Choreology, 1988–; Dancers' Career Develt (formerly Dancers' Resettlement Trust), 1988–; Nature Cure Clinic, 1988–2005; Tanya Bayona Princess Poutiatine Acad. of Ballet, Malta, 1988–2005; Language of Dance Centre, 1990–; Friends of Sadler's Wells Theatre, 1991–; Pro-Dogs, 1991–2005; Osteopathic Centre for Children, 1992–; Furlong Research Foundn, 1993– (Trustee, 2005–09); AMBER Trust, 1995–; Theatre Design Trust, 1995–; Legat Foundn, 1998–; Sussex Opera and Ballet Soc., 2001–; Discs, 2005– (Trustee, 1993–2005); Early Dance Circle, 2007–; German Shepherd Dog Rescue, 2010–; Internat. Dance Teachers Assoc., 2011–; Vice-Patron, BASE, 2007–. Hon. DMus: Leicester, 1970; Univ. of London, 1996; Hon. DLitt: City, 1974; Buckingham, 1993; Hon. DEd CNAA, 1989; Hon. DArt Bedford, 2010. Queen Elizabeth II Coronation Award, Royal Acad. of Dancing, 1995; Critics' Circle Award for Service to Dance, 2002; Lifetime Achievement Carl Alan Award, Internat. Dance Teachers' Assoc., 2010. *Publications:* Red Curtain Up, 1958; Through the Bamboo Curtain, 1965; My Favourite Ballet Stories, 1981; *relevant publications:* biographical studies (by Gordon Anthony), 1952, (by Pigeon Crowle), 1952; Beryl Grey, Dancers of Today (by Hugh Fisher), 1955; Beryl Grey, a biography (by David Gillard), 1977. *Recreations:* music, opera, reading, swimming. *Address:* Pen-Bré, Beaconsfield Road, Chelwood Gate, E Sussex RH17 7LF.

GREY, Prof. Clare Philomena, DPhil; FRS 2011; Geoffrey Moorhouse Gibson Professor of Chemistry, University of Cambridge, since 2009; Fellow, Pembroke College, Cambridge, since 2011; Professor, Department of Chemistry, Stony Brook University, since 2001. *Educ:* Christ Church, Oxford (BA 1st Cl. Hons Chem. 1987; DPhil 1991). Res. Fellow, Balliol Coll., Oxford, 1990–91; Royal Soc. Postdoctoral Fellow, Univ. of Nijmegen, 1991–92; Vis. Scientist, DuPont CR&D, 1992–94; Stony Brook University: Asst Prof., 1994–97, Associate Prof., 1997–2001, Dept of Chemistry; Associate Dir, NSF Center for Envmtl Molecular Sci., 2002–07. John Jeyes Award, RSC, 2010; Kavli Medal and Lect., 2011, Davy Prize, 2014, Royal Soc. *Publications:* contribs to jls incl. Nature Materials, Jl Amer. Chem. Soc., Chem. Materials, Science. *Address:* Department of Chemistry, University of Cambridge, Lensfield Road, Cambridge CB2 1EW.

GREY, John Egerton, CB 1980; Clerk Assistant and Clerk of Public Bills, House of Lords, 1974–88; *b* 8 Feb. 1929; *s* of late John and Nancy Grey; *m* 1961, Patricia Hanna (*d* 2007); two adopted *s*. *Educ:* Dragon Sch., Oxford; Blundell's; Brasenose Coll., Oxford. MA, BCL. Called to the Bar, Inner Temple, 1954; practised at Chancery Bar, 1954–59. Clerk in Parliament

Office, House of Lords, 1959–88. Adviser, Colchester CAB, 1989–99. *Recreations:* gardening, boating. *Address:* 51 St Peters Road, West Mersea, Colchester, Essex CO5 8LL. *T:* (01206) 383007. *Clubs:* Arts; West Mersea Yacht.

GREY, Maj.-Gen. John St John, CB 1987; *b* 6 June 1934; *s* of late Major Donald John Grey, RM and Doris Mary Grey (*née* Beavan); *m* 1958, Elisabeth Ann (*née* Langley); one *s* one *d*. *Educ:* Christ's Hospital. rcds, ndc, psc(M), osc(US). Commissioned 2/Lt 1952; Commando service, Malta, Egypt, Cyprus, 1955–64; Cruiser HMS Lion as OC RM, 1964–65; Instructor, Army Sch. of Infantry, 1967–69; US Marine Corps, 1970–71; Commando service, 1972–76; Commanded 45 Cdo Gp (incl. tours in N Ireland and Arctic Norway), 1976–78; Mil. Sec. and Col Ops/Plans, MoD, 1979–84; Maj.-Gen. Commando Forces, 1984–87; RM COS, 1987–88, retired. Clerk, Pewterers' Co., 1988–96. Col Comdt RM, 1995–98. Pres., SSAFA, Devon, 1993–2007. President: Exeter and Dist, ESU, 2010–13 (Mem. Council, 2000–10); Topsham br., RBL, 2007–12. Chm. of Trustees, Northcott Devon Foundn, 2010–. *Recreations:* sailing, walking. *Address:* c/o Lloyds Bank plc, Teignmouth Branch, PO Box 99 BX1 1LT. *Clubs:* Army and Navy; Royal Naval Sailing Association (Portsmouth); Royal Marines Sailing.

GREY, Robin Douglas; QC 1979; barrister; a Recorder of the Crown Court, 1979–99; *b* 23 May 1931; *s* of Dr Francis Temple Grey, MA, MB, and Eglantine Grey; *m* 1st, 1972, Berenice Anna Wheatley (marr. diss.); one *s* one *d*; 2nd, 1993, Mrs Annick Regnault. *Educ:* Summer Fields Prep. Sch., Oxford; Eastbourne Coll.; London Univ. (LLB Hons). Called to the Bar, Gray's Inn, 1957. Crown Counsel, Colonial Legal Service, Aden, 1959–63 (Actg Registrar Gen. and Actg Attorney Gen. for short periods); practising barrister, 1963–; Dep. Circuit Judge, 1977. FCO Consultant to Govt of Russian Fedn, 1993–; led FCO team to Moscow on Jury Trials, 1993. Chm., Home Office Police Appeals Tribunals, 1990–2006; Legal Assessor to GMC, 1995–; Legal Advr to GDC, 2010–; Legal Assessor for Health and Care Professions Council, 2012–. Appeal Chm., British Equestrian Fedn, 2010–. Member: Internat. Bar Assoc., 1994; Cttee, Criminal Bar Assoc., 1990–93 (Chm., Internat. Sub-Cttee, 1993); Cttee, European Criminal Bar Assoc., 1998–; British Acad. of Forensic Sciences. *Recreations:* walking, reading, theatre, fishing, six grandsons. *Address:* 184 Bromyard House, Bromyard Avenue, W3 7BN. *T:* (020) 8740 7709. *Clubs:* Hurlingham, New Cavendish.

GREY, Wilfrid Ernest G.; *see* Grenville-Grey.

GREY-THOMPSON, family name of **Baroness Grey-Thompson**.

GREY-THOMPSON, Baroness *cr* 2010 (Life Peer), of Eaglescliffe in the County of Durham; **Carys Davina, (Tanni), Grey-Thompson,** DBE 2005 (OBE 2000; MBE 1993); wheelchair athlete; Board Member: Transport for London, since 2008; London Legacy Development Corporation; Chairman, UK Active, since 2015; *b* 26 July 1969; *d* of Peter Alexander Harvey Grey and Sulwen Davina Grey (*née* Jones); *m* 1999, Dr (Robert) Ian George Thompson; one *d*. *Educ:* Loughborough Univ. (BA Hons Politics & Admin 1991). Develt Officer, UK Athletics, 1996–2000. Member Council: Sports Council for Wales, 1996–2002; UK Sport, 1998–2003; Dep. Chm., UK Lottery Sports Fund, 1998–2002; Vice Chm., Sports Adv. Gp, LOCOG, 2007–13. Member Board: Winston Churchill Meml Trust, 2006–; V, 2006–14. Has represented GB at 100m–800m distances, 1987–2007: competitor: Paralympics, 1988, 1992, 1996, 2000 and 2004 (winner 16 medals, incl. 11 Gold Medals); Olympics, 1992 and 1996 (in exhibn 800m), 2000, 2004; World Championships (winner 11 medals, incl. 5 Gold Medals); has broken over 30 world records; winner, London Marathon, 1992, 1994, 1996, 1998, 2001, 2002. Pro-Vice-Chancellor, Staffordshire Univ., 2004–14. Hon. Fellow: UWCC, 1997; UWIC, Swansea Univ., Coll. of Ripon and York St John, 2001; John Moores Univ., Liverpool, 2004. Hon. MA Loughborough, 1994; Hon. Dr Sport Staffordshire, 1998; Hon. DBA Southampton, 1998; Hon. MSc Manchester Metropolitan, 1998; DUniv: Surrey, 2000; Open, 2004; Sheffield Hallam, 2005; Hon. Master Teesside, 2001; Hon. DTech Loughborough, 2001; Hon. Dr: Leeds Metropolitan, 2001; Wales, 2002; Oxford Brookes, 2005; Glasgow, 2015; Hon. LLD: Exeter, 2003; Heriot-Watt, 2004; Leicester, 2005; Hon. DCL Newcastle, 2005; Hon. DLaws Bath, 2010; Hon. DSc: Hull, 2006, Greenwich, 2013; Oxford, 2013. *Publications:* Seize the Day (autobiog.), 2001; Aim High, 2007. *Address:* c/o Benchmark Sport, 23/24 Henrietta Street, Covent Garden, WC2E 8ND. *T:* (020) 7240 7799, *Fax:* (020) 7240 7703.

GREY-WILSON, Christopher, PhD; VMH 2008; Editor, Alpine Garden Society, 1990–2011; *b* 28 Sept. 1944; *s* of late Vyvyan William Grey-Wilson and Jean Grey-Wilson (*née* Parsley); *m* 1978, Christine Mary Dent; one *d*. *Educ:* Churston Ferrers Grammar Sch.; Wye Coll., Univ. of London (BSc Hort. 1967); Reading Univ. (PhD 1976). Botanist (PSO), Royal Botanic Gardens, Kew, 1968–90. Editor: Curtis's Botanical Magazine, incl. Kew Magazine, 1983–89; The New Plantsman, subseq. The Plantsman, 2001–05. Botanical Scientific expeditions: Iran and Afghanistan, 1971; Nepal, 1973, 1978, 1989; Kenya and Tanzania, 1976, 1979; Sri Lanka, 1978; W China, 1987, 1994. *Publications:* The Alpine Flowers of Britain and Europe, 1979, 2nd edn 1995; Impatiens of Africa, 1980; (jtly) Bulbs, 1981; (jtly) Gardening on Walls, 1983; The Genus Cyclamen, 1988; The Genus Dionysia, 1989; The Illustrated Flora of Britain and Northern Europe, 1989; A Manual of Alpine and Rock Garden Plants, 1989; Poppies, 1993, 2nd edn 2000; Mediterranean Wild Flowers, 1993; The Alpine Garden, 1994; (jtly) Gardening with Climbers, 1997; Cyclamen, 1997, 2nd edn 2002; Clematis: the genus, 2000; How to Identify Wild Flowers, 2000; Alpines: the new plant library, 2001; Wildflowers of Britain and Northern Europe, 2003; The Rock Garden Plant Primer, 2009; A Field Guide to the Bulbs of Greece, 2010; (jtly) Flowers of Western China, 2011; Pasque-flowers, the Genus Pulsatilla, 2014; The Genus Meconopsis: blue poppies and their relatives, 2014; numerous scientific papers in Kew Bulletin, gen. papers in The Garden, Bull. of Alpine Garden Soc., The Alpine Gardener, Gardens News and The New Plantsman. *Recreations:* gardening, walking, drawing, photography, listening to classical music. *Address:* Honeysuckle Cottage, The Green, Redgrave, Suffolk IP22 1RR.

GRIBBIN, John Richard, PhD; writer; Visiting Fellow in Astronomy, University of Sussex, since 1993; *b* 19 March 1946; *s* of William James Gribbin and Lilla (*née* Reed); *m* 1966, Mary Murray; two *s*. *Educ:* Univ. of Sussex (BSc Physics 1966; MSc Astronomy 1967); University Coll., Cambridge (PhD Astrophysics 1971). Asst Editor, Nature, 1970–75; Vis. Fellow, Sci. Policy Res. Unit, 1975–78; Physics Consultant, New Scientist, 1978–98. FRAS 1972; FRMetS 1985; FRSL 1999; FRSA. Lifetime Achievement Award, Assoc. of British Sci. Writers, 2009. *Publications:* (jtly) The Jupiter Effect, 1974; Our Changing Climate, 1975; Forecasts, Famines and Freezes, 1976; Galaxy Formation, 1976; Astronomy for the Amateur, 1976; Our Changing Universe, 1976; Our Changing Planet, 1977; White Holes, 1977; (ed and contrib.) Climatic Change, 1978; The Climatic Threat, 1978 (US edn as What's Wrong with our Weather?); This Shaking Earth, 1978; Timewarps, 1979; Climate and Mankind, 1979; Weather Force, 1979; (jtly) The Sixth Winter (novel), 1979; Future Worlds, 1979; The Strangest Star, 1980 (US edn as The Death of the Sun); Carbon Dioxide, Climate and Man, 1981; Genesis, 1981; (jtly) The Jupiter Effect Reconsidered, 1982; (ed and contrib.) Cosmology Today, 1982; (jtly) The Weather Book, 1982; (jtly) The Monkey Puzzle, 1982; Brother Esau (novel), 1982; Future Weather, 1982; Beyond the Jupiter Effect, 1983; Spacewarps, 1983; (jtly) The Redundant Male, 1984; In Search of Schrödinger's Cat, 1984; In Search of the Double Helix, 1985; (ed and contrib.) The Breathing Planet, 1986; In Search of the Big Bang, 1986, rev. edn 1998; The Omega Point, 1987; The Hole in the Sky, 1988; (jtly) Double Planet (novel), 1991; Father to the Man (novel), 1989; (jtly) Cosmic Coincidences, 1989; (jtly) Winds of Change, 1989; Hothouse Earth, 1990; (jtly) The Cartoon History of Time, 1990; Blinded by the Light, 1991; (jtly) Reunion (novel), 1991; (jtly) Ragnarok (novel), 1991; (jtly) The Matter Myth, 1991; (jtly) Stephen Hawking, 1992; In Search of the Edge of Time, 1992 (US edn as Unveiling the Edge of Time); Innervisions, 1993; In the Beginning, 1993; (jtly) Albert Einstein, 1993; Schrödinger's Kittens and the Search for Reality, 1995; (jtly) Darwin, 1995; (jtly) Origins, 1997; Cosmology, 1998; Watching the Universe, 1998 (US edn as The Case of the Missing Neutrinos); In Search of SUSY, 1998 (US edn as The Search for the Superstrings); (jtly) Empire of the Sun, 1998; (ed and contrib.) A Brief History of Science, 1998; The Birth of Time, 1999; The Little Book of Science, 1999; Dalla scimmia all'universo, 1999; Get a Grip on the New Physics, 1999; (jtly) Deep Space, 1999; (jtly) The First Chimpanzee, 2001; Space, 2001; (jtly) XTL, 2001; (jtly) The Mating Game, 2001; Science: a history, 2002; Quantum Physics, 2002; The Fellowship, 2005; The Origins of the Future, 2006; The Universe: a biography, 2007; Not Fade Away: the life and music of Buddy Holly, 2009; Timeswitch (novel), 2009; In Search of the Multiverse, 2010; The Alice Encounter (novel), 2010; The Reason Why, 2011; From Here to Infinity, 2011; (jtly) Planet Earth, 2012; Erwin Schrödinger and the Quantum Revolution, 2012; Computing with Quantum Cats, 2013; *with Mary Gribbin*: Weather, 1985; The One Per Cent Advantage, 1988; Children of the Ice, 1990; Too Hot to Handle?: the greenhouse effect, 1992; Being Human, 1993; Time and Space, 1994; Companion to the Cosmos, 1996; Fire on Earth, 1996; Watching the Weather, 1996; Richard Feynman, 1997; Time and the Universe, 1997; Curie, Halley, Newton, Darwin, Faraday, Galileo, and Einstein, all in In 90 Minutes series, 1997; Q is for Quantum, 1998; Almost Everyone's Guide to Science, 1998; Chaos and Uncertainty, 1999; Stardust, 2000; Ice Age, 2001; Big Numbers, 2003; How Far is Up?, 2003; FitzRoy, 2003; The Science of Philip Pullman's His Dark Materials, 2003; Deep Simplicity, 2004; Inventing the Future, 2004; Annus Mirabilis: Einstein in 1905, 2005; Flower Hunters, 2008; He Knew He Was Right: the irrepressible life of James Lovelock and Gaia, 2009; Know About Planets, 2009; Know About Stars, 2009; Know About Moons, 2009. *Recreations:* watching Kent CCC, collecting vinyl 45 rpm records, travel, cooking, songwriting. *Address:* Astronomy Group, University of Sussex, Falmer, Brighton BN1 9RH. *E:* j.r.gribbin@sussex.ac.uk.

GRIBBON, Deborah, PhD; Interim Deputy Director for Collections, Education, and Performing Arts, Cleveland Museum of Art, since 2013; *b* 11 June 1948; *d* of late Daniel M. and Jane Gribbon; *m* 1976, Dr Winston Alt; two *d*. *Educ:* Wellesley Coll., Mass (BA Art Hist. 1970); Harvard Univ. (MA Fine Arts 1972; PhD 1982). Teaching Fellow, Dept of Fine Arts, Harvard Univ., 1972–74; Curator, Isabella Stewart Gardner Mus., 1976–84; Instructor, Extension Sch., Harvard Univ., 1982–84; J. Paul Getty Museum: Asst Dir, 1984–87; Associate Dir for Curatorial Affairs, 1987–91; Associate Dir and Chief Curator, 1991–98; Dep. Dir and Chief Curator, 1998–2000; Dir, 2000–04; Interim Dir, Cleveland Mus. of Art, 2009–10. Vice Pres., J. Paul Getty Trust, 2000–04. Mem. Bd, Courtauld Inst., 2001–04. Mem., Internat. Women's Forum, 2003–. Phi Beta Kappa, 1970. *Publications:* Sculpture in the Isabella Stewart Gardner Museum, 1978; (with J. Walsh) The J. Paul Getty Museum and its Collections: a museum for a new century, 1997; contrib. articles to Apollo, Burlington Mag. and Connoisseur.

GRIBBON, Edward John; Under Secretary, Board of Inland Revenue, 1991–2000; Director, Compliance Division, 1996–2000; *b* 10 July 1943; *s* of late Henry Derwent Gribbon and Dorothy Gribbon (*née* Boyd); *m* 1968, Margaret Nanette Flanagan; one *s* two *d*. *Educ:* Coleraine Academical Instn; Univ. of London (LLB). FCA. Qualified as Chartered Accountant, 1965; joined Inland Revenue as HM Inspector of Taxes, 1966; HM Principal Inspector of Taxes, 1981; Dep. Dir of Operations, 1989–90; Dir, Business Profits Div., 1991–96. JP N and E Herts (formerly N Herts), 2002–13. Gov., N Herts Coll., 2004–10. *Recreations:* family, photography, local church, ornithology, philately.

GRICE, Ian Michael; Partner, Newby Management UK Ltd (Chairman, 2010–11); *b* 2 May 1953; *s* of James Frederick and late Joan Grice; *m* Patricia; two *d*. *Educ:* Royal Grammar Sch., High Wycombe; Loughborough Univ. (BSc Hons Civil Engrg). MICE. Engineer: John Laing plc, 1974–76; Mowlem plc, 1976–79; Kier plc, 1979–81; Mowlem plc, 1981–95; Alfred McAlpine plc, 1995–2008, Gp Chief Exec., 2003–08; Chm., Pims Gp, 2008–10. *Recreations:* golf, shooting, watching football, walking. *Address:* Newby Management UK Ltd, 18 The Stables, Newby Hall, Ripon, N Yorks HG4 5AE.

GRICE, Joseph William; Executive Director and Chief Economist, Office for National Statistics, since 2012; *b* Tamworth, Staffs, 25 July 1952; *s* of Stanley John Grice and Emily Grice; *m* 1976, Deborah Mary Wicks; two *s* one *d*. *Educ:* Worcester Coll., Oxford (BA PPE 1972); Univ. of Chicago (AM Econs 1976). Economist, HM Treasury, 1972–81; Asst Dir, Baring Brothers & Co Ltd, 1981–84; HM Treasury: Hd of Monetary and Exchange Rate Policy, 1986–90; Hd of Health Spending, 1991–95; Dir, Macroeconomic Policy, 1996–2000; Chief Economist and Dir, Public Services, 2000–03; Office for National Statistics: Executive Director: Atkinson Review of Measurement of Public Sector Output, 2004–05; Social and Public Sector Analysis and Reporting, 2006–08; Chief Economist and Exec. Dir, Economic, Labour Mkt and Social Analysis, 2008–12; Actg Chief Economist, DfT, 2012–13. Dep. Hd, Govt Econ. Service, 2000–05; Mem., Adv. Bd, UK Secure Data Service, 2010–11; Mem., ONS Bd, UK Stats Authy, 2014. Chm., Wkg Party on Macroeconomic and Structural Policy Issues, OECD, 2002–12. Chairman: EU Econ. Policy Cttee, 2005–08; EU Cttee on Monetary, Financial and Balance of Payments Stats, 2013–15; Mem., EU Council of Econ. and Finance Ministers, 2005–08. Mem. Adv. Council, Green Growth Knowledge Forum, 2012–. Mem. Adv. Bd, Wales Inst. for Social and Econ. Res. Data and Methods, 2010–; Mem. Council, REconS, 2011–. Treas., First Richmond Scout Gp, 1988–2000. *Publications:* Microeconomic Reform in Britain (with Ed Balls and Gus O'Donnell), 2004; various articles in learned jls. *Recreations:* swimming, theatre, ballet. *Address:* Office for National Statistics, Government Buildings, Cardiff Road, Newport NP10 8XG. *E:* joe.grice@ons.gov.uk.

GRICE, Paul Edward; Clerk and Chief Executive, Scottish Parliament, since 1999; *b* 13 Oct. 1961; *s* of Kenneth William Grice and Maureen (*née* Power); *m* 1987, Elaine Rosie; two *d*. *Educ:* Archbishop Holgate's Sch., York; York Coll. of Arts and Technol.; Univ. of Stirling (BSc Econs and Envmtl Sci.). Dept of Transport, 1985–87; DoE, 1987–92; Scottish Office, Edinburgh, 1992–99: Head of Housing and Urban Regeneration Br., 1992–95; Head of Mgt and Change Unit, 1995–97; Head of Division, Constitution Group: Referendum, Scotland Bill, 1997–98; Dir of Implementation, 1998–99. Mem., ESRC, 2009–15. Mem. Ct, Univ. of Stirling, 2005–13. Hon. FRIAS 2006. Trustee, Bank of Scotland Foundn, 2011–. Mem. Council, Edinburgh Internat. Fest., 2013–. *Recreations:* reading, theatre, triathlons. *Address:* Scottish Parliament, Holyrood, Edinburgh EH99 1SP. *T:* (0131) 348 5255.

GRIDLEY, family name of **Baron Gridley**.

GRIDLEY, 3rd Baron *cr* 1955; **Richard David Arnold Gridley;** Senior Lecturer in Travel and Tourism (formerly in Leisure and Tourism and Information Technology), and Teaching Mentor, South Downs College of Further Education, since 1995; *b* 22 Aug. 1956; *o s* of 2nd Baron Gridley and Edna Lesley, *e d* of Richard Wheen; *S* father, 1996; *m* 1st, 1979, Amanda Mackenzie (marr. diss.); 2nd, 1983, Suzanne Elizabeth Hughes (marr. diss.); one *s* one *d*; 3rd, 2008, Marie Hooper. *Educ:* Monkton Combe; Portsmouth Polytech.; Univ. of Brighton (BA). Project manager, construction industry, 1980–92. Patron, Care for the Wild Internat., 1996. *Address:* Little Hollow, 94 The Dale, Widley, Hants PO7 5DF. *E:* lordgrid@yahoo.co.uk.

GRIEF, Alison Sarah; QC 2015; a Recorder, since 2012; *b* Kent, 5 Nov. 1966; *d* of William Kenneth and Sheila Grief; *m* 2001, Martin King; two *s*. *Educ:* Middlesex Poly. (LLB Hons 1988). Called to the Bar, Inner Temple, 1990; in practice as barrister, specialising in family law (children), 1990–; Assistant Coroner: Mid-Kent and Medway, 2008–; Herts, 2012–. *Address:* 4 Paper Buildings, Temple, EC4Y 7EX. *E:* ag@4pb.com.

GRIERSON, Prof. Donald, OBE 2000; PhD, DSc; FRS 2000; FRSB; Professor of Plant Physiology, Nottingham University, 1986–2008, now Emeritus; Guang Biao Professor, Zhejiang University, China, since 2011; *b* 1 Oct. 1945; *s* of John Harvey Grierson and Margaret (*née* Head); *m* 1965, Elizabeth Carole Judson; two *s* two *d*. *Educ:* Univ. of E Anglia (BSc 1967); Univ. of Edinburgh (Ellis Prize in Physiol. 1970; PhD 1971); DSc Nottingham 1999. FRSB (FIBiol 1985). Plant Physiologist, British Sugar Corp. Res. Lab., Norwich, 1967–68; University of Nottingham: Asst Lectr in Plant Physiol., 1971–74; Lectr, 1974–82; Nuffield Foundn Sci. Res. Fellow, 1981–82; Reader, 1982–86; Head: Dept of Physiol. and Envmtl Sci., 1988–91 and 1992–94; Plant Sci. Section, 1988–97; Plant Sci. Div., 1997–2002; Sch. of Bioscis, 2000–02; Pro-Vice-Chancellor for Res. and Industry, 2003–07. EMBO Res. Fellow, Genetics Dept, Univ. of Tubingen, 1975–76; Vis. Prof., Shanxi Agricl Univ., 2014–. Chm., Sainsbury Lab. Council, 2000–04. Hon. DSc l'Institut Nat. Polytechnique de Toulouse, 2000. Res. Medal, RASE, 1990. *Publications:* (with S. N. Covey) Plant Molecular Biology, 1984, 2nd edn 1988 (English, Mandarin Chinese and Spanish edns); edited: (with H. Smith) The Molecular Biology of Plant Development, 1982; (with H. Thomas) Developmental Mutants in Higher Plants, 1987; (with G. W. Lycett) Genetic Engineering of Crop Plants, 1990; (with G. W. Lycett and G. A. Tucker) Mechanisms and Applications of Gene Silencing, 1996; Plant Biotechnology, vol. I, 1991, vol. II, 1991, vol. III, 1993; contrib. numerous refereed scientific papers and articles. *Recreations:* walking, boating, gardening, snorkelling. *Address:* Plant and Crop Sciences Division, School of Biosciences, University of Nottingham, Sutton Bonington Campus, Loughborough LE12 5RD. *T:* (0115) 951 6333.

GRIESE, Sister Carol, CHN; Religious Sister since 1970; *b* 26 Sept. 1945; *d* of Gwendoline and Donald Griese. *Educ:* Merrywood Grammar School, Bristol; King's College London (BA Hons English 1968); Clare Hall, Cambridge (Cert. Theol. 1970). Member, Community of the Holy Name, 1970–; Lay Rep. of Religious in General Synod, 1980–95. Mem., Crown Appointments Commn, 1990–92. *Recreations:* reading, walking. *Address:* Convent of the Holy Name, Morley Road, Oakwood, Derby DE21 4QZ. *T:* (01332) 671716.

GRIEVE, Alan Thomas, CBE 2003; Chairman, Jerwood Foundation, since 1991; *b* 22 Jan. 1928; *s* of late Lewis Miller Grieve and Doris Lilian (*née* Amner); *m* 1st, 1957, Anne, *d* of Dr Lawrence Dulake (marr. diss. 1971); two *s* one *d*; 2nd, 1971, Karen Louise, *d* of late Michael de Sivrac Dunn; one *s* one *d*. *Educ:* Aldenham; Trinity Hall, Cambridge (MA, LLM). Nat. Service, 2nd Lieut, 14/20 King's Hussars; Capt., City of London Yeo., TA. Admitted solicitor, 1953; Senior Partner: Taylor & Humbert, 1979–82; Taylor Garrett, 1982–88; Consultant: Taylor Joynson Garrett, 1988–2002; Taylor Wessing, 2002–09. Director: Baggeridge Brick plc, 1964–2003; Wilson Bowden plc, 1993–96, and other cos; Chm., Reliance Resources Ltd, 1978–97. Mem., Educnl Assets Bd, 1988–90. Chm., Racehorse Owners Award, 1978–99. Mem. Council, Royal Court Th., 2000–. Dir, Med. Insce Agency Charity, 1992–98; Trustee: Hereford Mappa Mundi Trustee Co. Ltd, 1998–2011; Jerwood Space Ltd, 1999–; RCP, 2007–10 (Mem., F and GP Bd, 1986–92); Jerwood Gall. Ltd, 2011–. Pres., Trinity Hall Assoc., Cambridge, 2001–03. Vice Cdre, Sea Cadets Assoc., 2001–. Patron, Brendoncare for the Elderly, 1993–; Ambassador, Samaritans, 1999–. Hon. FTCL 2002; Hon. FRCP 2002. *Publications:* Purchase Tax, 1958; Jerwood: the Foundation and the Founders, 2009. *Recreations:* performing and visual arts, country life, collecting. *Address:* (office) 7 St Stephen's Mews, W2 5QZ. *T:* (020) 7792 1410, *Fax:* (020) 7792 1539; Stoke Lodge, Clee Downton, Ludlow, Salop SY8 3EG. *T:* (01584) 823413, *Fax:* (01584) 823419. *Clubs:* Boodle's; Hawks (Cambridge).

See also Baron Harlech.

GRIEVE, Rt Hon. Dominic (Charles Roberts); PC 2010; QC 2008; MP (C) Beaconsfield, since 1997; *b* Lambeth, London, 24 May 1956; *s* of William Percival Grieve, QC and Evelyn Grieve (*née* Mijouain); *m* 1990, Caroline Hutton; two *s*. *Educ:* Westminster Sch.; Magdalen Coll., Oxford (MA Modern History); Poly. of Central London. Called to the Bar, Middle Temple, 1980, Bencher, 2004. Mem., Hammersmith and Fulham LBC, 1982–86. Contested (C) Norwood, 1987. Opposition front bench spokesman: for Scotland and on constitutional affairs, 1999–2001; on home affairs, 2001–03; on community cohesion, 2003–08; Shadow Attorney Gen., 2003–09; Shadow Home Sec., 2008–09; Shadow Sec. of State for Justice, 2009–10; Attorney Gen., 2010–14. Member: Jt Select Cttee on Statutory Instruments, 1997–2001; Select Cttee on Envmtl Audit, 1997–2001; Intelligence and Security Cttee, 2015–. Chm. Res. Cttee, 1992–95, Chm. Exec. Cttee, 2006–08, Finance and Gen. Purposes Cttee, 2006–, Soc. of Cons. Lawyers. Member: Council, Justice, 1997–; Franco-British Soc., 1997–2010 (Pres., 2011–); Luxembourg Soc., 1997–; Franco-British Council, 2010– (Vice Chm., 2011–). Hon. Recorder, Royal Bor. of Kingston-upon-Thames, 2012–. Lay visitor, police stations, 1990–96. Mem., London Dio. Synod, C of E, 1995–2001; a Dep. Church Warden. Gov., Ditchley Foundn, 2010–. *Recreations:* mountaineering, ski-ing, scuba diving, fell walking, travel, architecture. *Address:* House of Commons, SW1A 0AA. *T:* (020) 7219 6220; 1 Temple Garden Chambers, 1 Harcourt Buildings, Temple, EC4Y 9DA. *T:* (020) 7353 0407. *Club:* Garrick.

GRIEVE, James Robert; Joint Artistic Director, Paines Plough, since 2010; *b* Ashford, Kent, 28 July 1979; *s* of Robert Grieve and Linda Grieve. *Educ:* Harvey Grammar Sch., Folkestone; Univ. of Sheffield (BA Hons Eng. Lit. 2001). Reporter, Kent Regl Newspapers, 1997–98; freelance journalist, 1998–2001; JustGiving: Content Editor, 2001–02; Mktg Manager, 2003–05. Co-Founder and Artistic Dir, nabokov, 2001–10; Associate Dir, Bush Th., 2007–10. *Recreations:* theatre, opera, books, travel, restaurants, cooking, playing golf (badly), Folkestone Invicta FC. *Address:* Paines Plough Ltd, 4th Floor, 43 Aldwych, WC2B 4DN. *T:* (020) 7240 4533. *E:* james@painesplough.com.

GRIEVE, Michael Robertson Crichton; QC 1998; **His Honour Judge Grieve;** a Circuit Judge, since 2011; *b* 12 Aug. 1951; *s* of Hon. Lord Grieve, VRD and Lorna St John Grieve, *y d* of late Engineer Rear-Adm. E. P. St J. Benn, CB; *m* 1983, Nadine Hilary Dyer; one *s*. *Educ:* Edinburgh Acad.; Sedbergh Sch.; New Coll., Oxford (BA PPE 1st cl. Hons 1972). Called to the Bar, Middle Temple, 1975, Bencher, 2008; in practice at the Bar, 1975–2011; Asst Recorder, 1998–2000; Recorder, 2000–11. *Recreations:* playing and watching football, tennis, music. *Address:* Southwark Crown Court, 1 English Grounds, SE1 2HU. *Club:* Queen's Park Rangers Football.

GRIEVES, David, CBE 1988; Vice Chairman, British Steel plc, 1991–94; Chairman, BSC Industry plc, 1995–98 (Deputy Chairman, 1980–95); *b* 10 Jan. 1933; *s* of Joseph and Isabel Grieves; *m* 1960, Evelyn Muriel Attwater; two *s*. *Educ:* Durham Univ. BSc, PhD. Graduate apprentice, United Steel cos, 1957; Labour Manager, Appleby Frodingham Steel Co., 1962; British Steel Corporation: Manager, Industrial Relations, S Wales Group, 1967; Gen. Man., Stocksbridge and Tinsley Park Works, 1971; Personnel Dir, Special Steels Div., 1973; Dir, Indust. Relations, 1975; Man. Dir, Personnel and Social Policy, 1977; Dir, BSC, later British Steel plc, 1983. Chairman: Avesta Sheffield, 1992–94; Xansa plc pension funds, 1995–2004. Mem. (non-exec.), Post Office, 1990–98. Mem., Employment Appeal Tribunal, 1983–2003. *Address:* 6 Collens Road, West Common, Harpenden, Herts AL5 2AJ. *T:* (01582) 259081.

GRIEVES, John Kerr; Senior Partner, Freshfields, 1990–96; *b* 7 Nov. 1935; *s* of Thomas and Nancy Grieves; *m* 1961, Ann Gorrell (*née* Harris); one *s* one *d*. *Educ:* King's Sch., Worcester; Keble Coll., Oxford (MA Law); Harvard Business Sch. (AMP). Articled clerk and asst solicitor, Pinsent & Co., Birmingham, 1958–61; joined Freshfields, 1963; Partner, 1964–96; Deptl Man. Partner, Company Dept, 1974–78; Man. Partner, 1979–85; Head, Corporate Finance Group, 1985–89. Director: British Invisibles, 1992–96; Northern Electric plc, 1996–97; Enterprise Oil plc, 1996–2002; Barclays Private Bank Ltd, 1997–2006; Hillsdown Holdings plc, 1997–98; New Look Group plc, 1998–2004 (Chm., 2001–04); Chairman: First Leisure Corp. plc, 1998–2000; Esporta plc, 2000–02; Advr, Apax Partners, 1996–99. Member: Reporting Financial Review Panel, 1998–2009; Takeover Appeal Bd, 2008–. Trustee: Emmaus UK, 2005–11 (Chm., 2009–11); Acad. of Ancient Music, 2007–. Officer, Order of the Crown (Belgium), 1993. *Recreations:* the arts (especially music), sport. *Address:* 7 Putney Park Avenue, SW15 5QN. *T:* (020) 8876 1207. *Club:* Athenæum.

GRIFFEE, Andrew John; communications, broadcasting and projects consultant, since 2013; owner, Griff Consultancy Ltd; Senior Associate, Marquis Media Partners LLP; *b* 25 Aug. 1961; *s* of John William Griffee and Kathleen Sandra Griffee; *m* 1988, Helen Caroline Emery; one *s* one *d*. *Educ:* Duke of York's Royal Military Sch., Dover; Highbury Coll. of Technol. (NCTJ Proficiency 1981); Univ. of Manchester (BA 1st cl. Hons 1986); Stanford Univ. (Exec. Develt Prog. 2001). Reporter: Poole and Dorset Herald, 1982–86; Northern Echo, 1986–87; Bath Evening Chronicle, 1987–89; Asst News Editor, BBC Bristol, 1989–92; Editor, News and Current Affairs, 1992–96, Head of Regl and Local Progs, 1996–99, BBC South; Controller, BBC English Regions, 1999–2008; Editl Dir, then Dir, W1 Project, BBC, 2008–13. *Address:* Vinney Hill, Kingswood, Stanford Bridge, Worcs WR6 6SB.

GRIFFIN, Avril; *see* MacRory, A.

GRIFFIN, Brian; photographer; *b* Birmingham, 13 April 1948; *s* of James Henry Griffin and Edith Griffin; *m* 2003, Brynja Sverrisdottir; one *s* one *d*. *Educ:* Manchester Poly. (Dip. Photography; Dip. Associateship of Manchester). Freelance photographer and film maker, 1972–. Vis. Prof. of Photography, Univ. of Derby, 2013–. Hon. FRPS. DUniv Birmingham City, 2014. *Publications:* Copyright, 1978; Power, 1980; 'Y', 1983; Open, 1986; Portraits, 1987; Work, 1988; Influences, 2005; The Black Kingdom, 2013. *Recreations:* cycling, speedway racing. *Address:* Flat 22, Canada Wharf, 255 Rotherhithe Street, SE16 5ES. *T:* (020) 7394 7447, 07836 687166. *E:* brian@briangriffin.co.uk.

GRIFFIN, Prof. George Edward, PhD; FRCP, FRCPI, FMedSci; Professor of Infectious Diseases and Medicine, St George's, University of London (formerly St George's Hospital Medical School), 1992–2013, now Emeritus (Chairman, Department of Cellular and Molecular Medicine, 2003–10; Vice Principal for Research, 2004–10); *b* 27 Feb. 1947; *s* of Herbert Griffin and Enid Mary Griffin (*née* Borril); *m* 1972, Daphne Joan Haylor (*d* 1998), Romford; two *s* one *d*. *Educ:* Malet Lambert Grammar Sch., Kingston upon Hull; King's Coll., London (BSc); St George's Hosp. Med. Sch. (MB BS); Univ. of Hull (PhD 1974); Harvard Univ. (Harkness Fellow). MRCP 1979, FRCP 1988; FRCPI 2009. Registrar and Tutor in Medicine, RPMS, 1977–78; St George's Hospital Medical School: Lectr in Medicine, 1978–82; Wellcome Trust Sen. Lectr, 1982–90; Dir, Wellcome Trust Clinical Tropical Unit, 1994–99; Chm., Dept of Internal Medicine, 1994–95; Hon. Cons. Physician, St George's Hosp., 1988–. Vis. Prof. of Medicine, Univ. of Michigan, 1992–. Chairman: Adv. Cttee on Dangerous Pathogens, DoH, 2005– (Mem., 1994–98); Ind. Cttee investigating E. Coli O157 outbreak in Surrey, 2009; Prior Risk Mgt Gp, 2011–; TSE Risk Cttee, 2012–; Chair: Cttee Rev. of Highest Level Containment Facilities in UK, 2008; Cttee on Common Regulatory Regulations for Contained Use of Pathogens, 2009–10; Expert Advr, H of L Select Cttee on Fighting Infection, 2002–03. Wellcome Trust: Member: Infection and Immunity Panel, 1989–94; Tropical Interest Gp, 1991–94; Internat. Interest Gp, 1991–; Medical Research Council: Chm., Cttee for Develt and Implementation of Vaccines, 1994–; Member: Physiological Medicine and Infection Bd, 1994–; AIDS Vaccine Cttee, 1995–; HIV Virucidal Cttee, 1995–; Bd, PHLS, 1995–2002; Adv. Bd, Public Health England, 2013–. Founder FMedSci 1998 (Foreign Sec., 2013–). *Publications:* scientific and clinical papers relating to pathogenesis of infection, vaccines. *Recreations:* walking, gardening, music. *Address:* 8 Buxton Drive, New Malden, Surrey KT3 3UZ. *T:* (020) 8949 4953. *Clubs:* Royal Automobile, MCC, Kennels.

GRIFFIN, Dr Ian Paul; Director, Otago Museum, Dunedin, New Zealand, since 2013; *b* St Mary Cray, Orpington, Kent, 22 Jan. 1966; *s* of late Barry Paul Griffin and Carole Anne Griffin (*née* Armstrong); *m* 1990, Maria Anna Dunphy; one *s* two *d*. *Educ:* St Olave's Sch., Orpington; University Coll. London (BSc 1st Cl. Hons Astronomy 1987); Univ. of London (PhD Astrophys 1991). Director: Armagh Planetarium, Armagh, NI, 1990–94; Astronaut Meml Planetarium and Observatory, Cocoa, Fla, 1994–99; Auckland Observatory, NZ, 1999–2001; Hd, Office of Public Outreach, NASA Space Telescope Sci. Inst., Baltimore, Md, 2001–04; Dir, Mus. of Sci. and Industry, Manchester, 2004–07; CEO, Oxford Trust, 2008–13. Chm., UK Assoc. of Sci. and Discovery Centres, 2011–13. *Publications:* contrib. papers to scientific jls. *Recreations:* stargazing, panoramic photography, playing Aunt Sally. *Address:* c/o Otago Museum, 419 Great King Street, PO Box 6202, Dunedin 9059, New Zealand. *T:* 34747471. *E:* ian.griffin@otagomuseum.nz.

GRIFFIN, Prof. James Patrick, DPhil; White's Professor of Moral Philosophy, University of Oxford, 1996–2000; Fellow, Corpus Christi College, Oxford, 1996–2000, now Emeritus Fellow; *b* 8 July 1933; *s* of Gerald Joseph Griffin and Catherine Griffin (*née* Noonan); *m* 1966, Catherine Maulde von Halban (*d* 1993); one *s* one *d*. *Educ:* Choate Sch., Wallingford, Conn; Yale Univ. (BA 1955); Oxford Univ. (DPhil 1960; MA 1963). University of Oxford: Rhodes Schol., Corpus Christi Coll., 1955–58; Sen. Schol., St Antony's Coll., 1958–60; Lectr, Christ Church, 1960–66; Fellow and Tutor in Philosophy, Keble Coll., 1966–96 (Hon. Fellow, 1996); Lectr in Philosophy, 1964–90; Radcliffe Fellow, 1982–84; Reader, 1990–96. Visiting Professor: Univ. of Wisconsin, 1970, 1978; Univ. of Santiago de Compostela, 1988, 1995; Gtr Philadelphia Philosophy Consortium, 1989; ITAM, Mexico, 1994; UNAM, Mexico, 1995, etc; Adjunct Prof., Centre for Applied Philosophy and Public Ethics, Canberra, 2002–; Dist. Vis. Prof., Rutgers Univ., 2002–; Tang Chun-I Vis. Prof., Chinese Univ. of Hong Kong, 2010. Medal, Nat. Educn Commn, Poland, 1992. Hon. DFil Santiago de Compostela, 2003. Order of Diego de Losada (Venezuela), 1999. *Publications:* Wittgenstein's Logical Atomism, 1964, repr. 1997; Well-Being: its meaning, measurement and moral importance, 1986; (jtly) Values, Conflict and the Environment, 1989, 2nd edn 1996; Value Judgement: improving our ethical beliefs, 1996; On Human Rights, 2008; Griffin on Human Rights, 2014; articles in philosophical jls. *Recreations:* eating, drinking. *Address:* 10 Northmoor Road, Oxford OX2 6UP. *T:* (01865) 554130. *Clubs:* Brooks's, Oxford and Cambridge.

See also N. J. Griffin.

GRIFFIN, Janet Mary, (Mrs Paul Griffin); *see* Turner, Janet M.

GRIFFIN, Prof. Jasper, FBA 1986; Professor of Classical Literature, and Public Orator, Oxford University, 1992–2004; Fellow and Tutor in Classics, Balliol College, Oxford, 1963–2004; *b* 29 May 1937; *s* of Frederick William Griffin and Constance Irene Griffin (*née* Cordwell); *m* 1960, Miriam Tamara Dressler; three *d*. *Educ:* Christ's Hospital; Balliol College, Oxford (1st Cl. Hon. Mods 1958; 1st Cl. Lit. Hum. 1960; Hertford Scholar 1958; Ireland Scholar 1958). Jackson Fellow, Harvard Univ., 1960–61; Oxford University: Dyson Research Fellow, Balliol Coll., 1961–63; Reader in Classical Lit., 1990–92. T. S. Eliot Meml Lectr, Univ. of Kent at Canterbury, 1984. *Publications:* Homer on Life and Death, 1980; Homer, 1980; Snobs, 1982; Latin Poets and Roman Life, 1985; The Mirror of Myth, 1986; (ed with

J. Boardman and O. Murray) The Oxford History of the Classical World, 1986; Virgil, 1986; Homer, The Odyssey, 1987; Homer, Iliad ix, 1995. *Address:* Balliol College, Oxford OX1 3BJ. *T:* (01865) 559507.

GRIFFIN, Dr John Parry, BSc, PhD, MB, BS; FRCP, FRCPath, FFPM; Director, Asklepieion (formerly John Griffin Associates) Ltd, since 1994; *b* 21 May 1938; *o s* of late David J. Griffin and Phyllis M. Griffin; *m* 1962, Margaret, *o d* of late Frank Cooper and Catherine Cooper; one *s* two *d. Educ:* Howardian High Sch., Cardiff; London Hosp. Medical Coll. Lethby and Buxton Prizes, 1958; BSc (1st Cl. Hons) 1959; PhD 1961; George Riddoch Prize in Neurology, 1962; MB BS 1964; LRCP, MRCS 1964; MRCP 1980, FRCP 1990; FRCPath 1986 (MRCPath 1982); FFPM 1989. Ho. Phys., London Hosp. Med. Unit, and Ho. Surg., London Hosp. Accident and Orthopaedic Dept, 1964–65; Lectr in Physiology, King's Coll., London, 1965–67; Head of Clinical Research, 3M Riker Labs (formerly Riker Labs), 1967–71; SMO, Medicines Div., 1971–76; PMO, Medicines Div., and Medical Assessor, Cttee on Safety of Medicines, 1976–77; SPMO and Professional Head of Medicines Div., DHSS, 1977–84; Med. Assessor, Medicines Commn, 1977–84; Dir, Assoc. of the British Pharmaceutical Industry, 1984–94. Hon. Clinical Asst, Royal Brompton Hosp., 1969–75; Hon. Consultant, Lister Hosp., Stevenage, 1973–94. Faculty Mem., Scripps Med. Res. Center, San Diego, 1997–98; Vis. Prof., Univ. of Surrey, 2000–05. Mem., Jt Formulary Cttee for British Nat. Formulary, 1978–84; UK Rep., EEC Cttee on Proprietary Med. Products; Chairman: Cttee on Prop. Med. Products Working Party on Safety Requirements, 1977–84; ICH Working Party on Safety Requirements, 1987–94. Mem. Bd, Faculty of Pharmaceutical Med., RCP, 1993–2005 (Chm., Bd of Examiners, 1997–2003; Mem., Fellowship Cttee, 1998–2005; Acad. Registrar, 2003–06). Ed. in Chief, Adverse Reactions and Toxicology Reviews, 1990–2003. FRSocMed. Thomas Young Lectr and Gold Medallist, St George's Hosp. Med. Sch., 1992. Commemorative Medal, Faculty of Pharm. Med., 2005. *Publications:* (jtly) Iatrogenic Diseases, 1972, 3rd edn 1985; (jtly) Manual of Adverse Drug Interactions, 1975, 5th edn 1997; (jtly) Drug Induced Emergencies, 1980; Medicines: research, regulation and risk, 1989, 2nd edn 1992; International Medicines Regulations, 1989; (jtly) The Textbook of Pharmaceutical Medicine, 1993, 7th edn 2013; Regulation of Medicinal Products, 2003; numerous articles in sci. and med. jls, mainly on aspects of neurophysiology, clinical pharmacology, toxicology and pharmacoeconomics. *Recreations:* gardening, local history. *Address:* Quartermans, Digswell Lane, Digswell, Herts AL6 0SP. *E:* jqmans5@icuknet.co.uk.

GRIFFIN, Keith Broadwell, DPhil; Distinguished Professor of Economics, University of California, Riverside, 1988–2004 (Chairman, Department of Economics, 1988–93); *b* 6 Nov. 1938; *s* of Marcus Samuel Griffin and Elaine Ann Broadwell; *m* 1956, Dixie Beth Griffin; two *d. Educ:* Williams Coll., Williamstown, Mass (BA; Hon DLitt, 1980); Balliol Coll., Oxford (BPhil, DPhil). Fellow and Tutor in Econs, Magdalen Coll., Oxford, 1965–76, Fellow by special election, 1977–79; Warden, Queen Elizabeth House, Oxford, 1978–79 (Actg Warden, 1973 and 1977–78); Dir, Inst. of Commonwealth Studies, Oxford, 1978–79 (Actg Dir, 1973 and 1977–78); Pres., Magdalen Coll., Oxford, 1979–88. Chief, Rural and Urban Employment Policies Br., ILO, 1975–76; Vis. Prof., Inst. of Econs and Planning, Univ. of Chile, 1962–63 and 1964–65; Dist. Vis. Prof., Amer. Univ. in Cairo, 2001; Vis. Fellow, Oxford Centre for Islamic Studies, 1998. Consultant: ILO, 1974, 1982, 1994, 1996, 1997; Internat. Bank for Reconstruction and Develt, 1973; UN Res. Inst. for Social Develt, 1971–72; FAO, 1963–64, 1967, 1978; Inter-Amer. Cttee for Alliance for Progress, 1968; US Agency for Internat. Develt, 1966; UNDP, 1989, 1991–98, 2001–02, 2004. Res. Advr, Pakistan Inst. of Develt Econs, 1965, 1970; Sen. Advr, OECD Develt Centre, Paris, 1986–88; Economic Advr, Govt of Bolivia, 1989–91. Member: Council, UN Univ., 1986–92; UN Cttee for Develt Planning, 1987–94; Chm., UN Res. Inst. for Social Develt, 1988–95. Mem., World Commn on Culture and Develt, 1994–95. Pres., Develt Studies Assoc., 1978–80. FAAAS 1997. *Publications:* (with Ricardo ffrench-Davis) Comercio Internacional y Políticas de Desarrollo Económico, 1967; Underdevelopment in Spanish America, 1969; (with John Enos) Planning Development, 1970; (ed) Financing Development in Latin America, 1971; (ed with Azizur Rahman Khan) Growth and Inequality in Pakistan, 1972; The Political Economy of Agrarian Change, 1974, 2nd edn 1979; (ed with E. A. G. Robinson) The Economic Development of Bangladesh, 1974; Land Concentration and Rural Poverty, 1976, 2nd edn 1981; International Inequality and National Poverty, 1978; (with Ashwani Saith) Growth and Equality in Rural China, 1981; (with Jeffrey James) The Transition to Egalitarian Development, 1981; (ed) Institutional Reform and Economic Development in the Chinese Countryside, 1984; World Hunger and the World Economy, 1987; Alternative Strategies for Economic Development, 1989; (ed with John Knight) Human Development and the International Development Strategy for the 1990s, 1990; (ed) The Economy of Ethiopia, 1992; (ed with Zhao Renwei) The Distribution of Income in China, 1993; (with Terry McKinley) Implementing a Human Development Strategy, 1994; (ed) Poverty and the Transition to a Market Economy in Mongolia, 1995; Studies in Globalization and Economic Transitions, 1996; (ed) Social Policy and Economic Transformation in Uzbekistan, 1996; (ed) Economic Reform in Vietnam, 1998; Studies in Development Strategy and Systemic Transformation, 2000; (ed) Poverty Reduction in Mongolia, 2003. *Recreation:* travel. *Address:* 24870 SW Mountain Road, West Linn, OR 97068, USA.

GRIFFIN, Kenneth James, OBE 1970; Deputy Chairman, Ugland International, 1993–2000; *b* 1 Aug. 1928; *s* of late Albert Griffin and Catherine (*née* Sullivan); *m* 1951, Doreen Cicely Simon (*d* 1992); one *s* one *d* (and one *s* decd). *Educ:* Dynevor Grammar Sch., Swansea; Swansea Technical College. Area Sec., ETU, 1960; Dist Sec., Confedn of Ship Building Engrg Unions, 1961; Sec., Craftsmen Cttee (Steel), 1961; Mem., Welsh Council, 1968; Mem., Crowther Commn on Constitution (Wales), 1969; Joint Sec., No 8 Joint Industrial Council Electrical Supply Industry, 1969; Industrial Adviser, DTI, 1971–72; Co-ordinator of Industrial Advisers, DTI, 1972–74; Special Adviser, Sec. of State for Industry, 1974; part-time Mem., NCB, 1973–82; a Dep. Chm., British Shipbuilders, 1977–83; Chm., Blackwall Engrg, 1983–85; Member: Suppl. Benefits Commn, 1968–80; Solicitors Disciplinary Tribunal, 1982–2002; Tribunal, Inst. of Legal Execs, 1992–2008. Chm., Network Housing Assoc., 1991–97; Vice-Chm., UK Housing Trust, 1989; Mem. Bd, Housing Corp., 1995–2002; Exec. Advr, Mobile Training, 1989–90. *Recreations:* golf, music, reading. *Address:* 214 Cyncoed Road, Cyncoed, Cardiff CF23 6RS. *T:* (029) 2075 2184. *Club:* Reform.

GRIFFIN, Liam; Chief Executive Officer, Addison Lee Ltd, since 2013; *b* Barnet, 9 March 1973; *s* of John Griffin and Janet Griffin; *m* Clare; three *s. Educ:* Loughborough Univ. (BSc Econs and Politics). Ops Dir, 2002–05, Man. Dir, 2005–13, Addison Lee Ltd. *Recreations:* motor racing, golf. *Address:* Addison Lee Ltd, 35–37 William Road, NW1 3ER. *T:* (020) 7387 8888. *E:* mel.bartram@addisonlee.com.

GRIFFIN, Michael; *see* Griffin, S. M.

GRIFFIN, Nicholas John; Member (BNP) North West Region, European Parliament, 2009–14; *b* Barnet, 1 March 1959; *s* of Edgar Griffin and Jean Griffin; *m* 1985, Jacquelene Cook; one *s* three *d. Educ:* Downing Coll., Cambridge (BA Hons Law 1980; boxing blue). Former agricl engr, builder, forestry worker. Editor, Spearhead, 1996–99. Leader, 1999–2014, Pres., 2014, BNP. Contested (BNP): Barking, 2010; NW Reg., EP, 2014. Mem., Editl Bd, Nationalism Today, 1980–89. *Recreations:* walking, reading, cooking, annoying liberals.

GRIFFIN, Nicholas John; QC 2012; *b* Oxford, 14 Feb. 1968; *s* of Prof. James Patrick Griffin, *qv*; *m* 2001, Julia Zagrodnik; one *d. Educ:* Univ. of Bristol (LLB Hons Eur. Legal Studies). Called to the Bar: Inner Temple, 1992; NI, 2011. Assistant Commissioner: Boundary Commn for England, 2011–12; to Dist Electoral Areas Comr for NI, 2013. Trustee, Anti-Slavery Internat., 2015–. *Address:* 5 Paper Buildings, EC4Y 7HB. *T:* (020) 7583 6117.

GRIFFIN, Robert; Headmaster, Exeter School, since 2003; *b* 17 June 1962; *s* of Paschal and Patricia Griffin; *m* 1989, Allison White; one *s* one *d. Educ:* Wallington High Sch. for Boys; Christ Church, Oxford (MA 1st Cl. Mod. Langs 1985; Arteaga prize); Univ. of York (PGCE Mod. Langs 1989). Asst Master, Markham Coll., Lima, 1986–88; Asst Master and Hd of Mod. Langs, Haileybury, Hertford, 1989–98; Second Master, Royal Grammar Sch., Guildford, 1998–2003. Chm., SW Div., HMC, 2010–11. *Recreations:* cycling, walking on Dartmoor, the works of García Márquez and Neruda, United Ushers, visiting National Trust properties. *Address:* Exeter School, Victoria Park Road, Exeter, Devon EX2 4NS. *T:* (01392) 273679. *E:* headmaster@exeterschool.org.uk. *Club:* East India.

GRIFFIN, Prof. (Selwyn) Michael, OBE 2013; MD; FRCS; Professor of Surgery, University of Newcastle upon Tyne, since 1999; Consultant Surgeon, Newcastle upon Tyne Hospitals NHS Trust, since 1998; Head, Northern Oesophagogastric Cancer Unit, Royal Victoria Infirmary, Newcastle upon Tyne, since 1990; *b* Newcastle upon Tyne, 7 Feb. 1955; *s* of late Selwyn Griffin and Joan Campbell Griffin (*née* Dickinson); *m*; one *s* two *d. Educ:* Fettes Coll., Edinburgh; Univ. of Newcastle upon Tyne (MB BS 1978; MD 1989). FRCS 1983. Sen. Registrar in Surgery, northern reg.; Consultant Surgeon: to Newcastle Gen. Hosp., 1990–98; to Royal Victoria Infirmary, 1998–. Mem. Bd, Intercollegiate Examinations, 2010–; Chm., Intercollegiate Bd of Gen. Surgery, 2013–; external examr at univs incl. Edinburgh, Trinity Coll., Dublin, Hong Kong, Cambridge, Southern Calif, Nottingham and London. Member: N of England Surgical Soc., 1990– (Pres., 2008–09); Assoc. of Upper Gastrointestinal Surgeons of GB and Ire., 1996– (Pres., 2004–06); European Soc. of Diseases for the Oesophagus, 2000– (Pres., 2011–13); James IV Assoc. of Surgeons, 2000– (Vice Pres., 2011–); Internat. Soc. for Diseases of the Oesophagus, 2000–. Mem. Council, RCSE, 2009–. Hon. FCSHK 1995; Hon. FRCSE 1997; Hon. FRCSGlas 2015; Hon. FRCSI 2015. Ed., Diseases of the Oesophagus, 2009–. *Publications:* (ed jtly) Oesophagogastric Surgery: a companion to specialist surgical practice, 1997, 5th edn 2012; over 300 articles in med. and surgical jls incl. BMJ, Brit. Jl Surgery. *Recreations:* Rugby Union, cricket, football, fine wine. *Address:* Northern Oesophagogastric Cancer Unit, Ward 36 Office, Royal Victoria Infirmary, Queen Victoria Road, Newcastle upon Tyne NE1 4LP. *T:* (0191) 282 0234, *Fax:* (0191) 282 0237. *E:* michael.griffin@nuth.nhs.uk.

GRIFFIN, Theresa Mary; Member (Lab) North West Region, European Parliament, since 2014; *b* Coventry, 11 Dec. 1962. *Educ:* Bishop Ullathorne Comprehensive Sch.; Lancaster Univ. (BA 1st Cl.; MA). Worked in community theatre; Dir of Communications and Res., North West Arts; Regl Organiser, UNISON, 2009–14. Former Mem. (Lab) Liverpool CC. Mem., NW Political Cttee, UNITE. *Address:* European Parliament, 60 Rue Wiertz, 1047 Brussels, Belgium; (office) Unit 303, Vanilla Factory, 39 Fleet Street, Liverpool L1 4AR.

GRIFFIN, Very Rev. Victor Gilbert Benjamin; Dean of St Patrick's Cathedral, Dublin, 1969–91; *b* 24 May 1924; *s* of Gilbert B. and Violet M. Griffin, Carnew, Co. Wicklow; *m* 1958, Daphne E. Mitchell; two *s. Educ:* Kilkenny Coll.; Mountjoy Sch., and Trinity Coll., Dublin (MA, 1st class Hons in Philosophy). Ordained, 1947; Curacy: St Augustine's, Londonderry, 1947–51; Christ Church, Londonderry, 1951–57; Rector of Christ Church, Londonderry, 1957–69. Lecturer in Philosophy, Magee Univ. Coll., Londonderry, 1950–69. Hon. MRIAI 1992. Hon. DD TCD, 1992. *Publications:* Trends in Theology 1870–1970, 1970; Anglican and Irish, 1976; Pluralism and Ecumenism, 1983; The Mark of Protest: experience of a Southern Protestant in Northern Ireland and the Republic, 1993; The Churches and Sectarianism in Ireland, 1995; Swift and His Hospital, 1995; Swift's Message to Ireland Today, 1996; Enough Religion to Make us Hate: reflections on religion and politics in Ireland, 2002; Holding the Centre: Anglicanism in Ireland, 2007; Basic Christianity: a catechism, 2008; (contrib.) History of St Patrick's Cathedral, Dublin, 2009; contrib. to New Divinity. *Recreations:* music, biography, watching sport on TV. *Address:* 7 Tyler Road, Limavady, N Ireland BT49 0DW. *Clubs:* Friendly Brothers of St Patrick, Kildare Street and University (Dublin).

GRIFFINS, Roy Jason, CB 2003; Chairman, London City Airport, since 2007; *b* 8 May 1946; *s* of Manuel Griffins and Betty Griffins; *m* 1984, Margaret Alison Redfern; one *d. Educ:* Blackpool Grammar Sch.; Bristol Univ. (BA). Barclays Bank Foreign Branches, 1967–68; Systems Analyst, Internat. Computers Ltd, 1968–70; Sen. Systems Analyst, with BBC, 1970–74; Copywriter, Krohn Advertising, Montreal, 1975–76; Principal, Wildlife Conservation, DoE, 1976–77; First Sec. (Envmt), UK Representation to EC, Brussels (on secondment), 1978–80; Sec. to Third London Airport Inquiry, DoE, 1981–83; Department of Transport: Principal (Aviation), then Head, Airports Policy, 1984–87; Principal Private Sec. to Sec. of State for Transport, 1987–89; Counsellor, Washington (on secondment), 1990–93; Asst Sec., Channel Tunnel Rail Link, Dept of Transport, 1993–96; Dir, Railways, DETR, 1996–99; Dir-Gen., Civil Aviation, DETR, subseq. DTLR, then DfT, 1999–2004; UK Public Affairs Dir, Eurotunnel, 2004; Dir-Gen., Airports Council Internat. for Europe, 2004–06; Head, UK Delegn to Channel Tunnel Intergovernmental Commn, 2006–12. Mem., Franco-British Council, 2006– (Treas., 2010–). Non-executive Director: London Ambulance Service, 2006–14 (Vice-Chair, 2010–14); NHS Blood and Transplant, 2012–. *Recreations:* tennis, France, films, food. *Address:* 55 Brookfield, Highgate West Hill, N6 6AT. *Club:* Reform.

GRIFFITH, Rev. (Arthur) Leonard; Lecturer in Homiletics, Wycliffe College, Toronto, 1977–87, retired; *b* 20 March 1920; *s* of Thomas Griffiths and Sarah Jane Taylor; *m* 1947, Anne Merelie Cayford; two *d. Educ:* Public and High Schs, Brockville, Ont; McGill Univ., Montreal (BA, McGill, 1942); United Theological Coll., Montreal (BD 1945; Hon. DD 1962); Mansfield Coll., Oxford, England, 1957–58. Ordained in The United Church of Canada, 1945; Minister: United Church, Arden, Ont, 1945–47; Trinity United Church, Grimsby, Ont, 1947–50; Chalmers United Church, Ottawa, Ont, 1950–60; The City Temple, London, 1960–66; Deer Park United Church, Toronto, 1966–75; ordained in Anglican Church 1976; Minister, St Paul's Church, Bloor St, Toronto, 1975–85 (Hon. Asst, 1995–). Hon. DD Wycliffe Coll., Toronto, 1985. *Publications:* The Roman Letter Today, 1959; God and His People, 1960; Beneath The Cross of Jesus, 1961; What is a Christian?, 1962; Barriers to Christian Belief, 1962; A Pilgrimage to the Holy Land, 1962; The Eternal Legacy, 1963; Pathways to Happiness, 1964; God's Time and Ours, 1964; The Crucial Encounter, 1965; This is Living!, 1966; God in Man's Experience, 1968; Illusions of our Culture, 1969; The Need to Preach, 1971; Hang on to the Lord's Prayer, 1973; We Have This Ministry, 1973; Ephesians: a positive affirmation, 1975; Gospel Characters, 1976; Reactions to God, 1979; Take Hold of the Treasure, 1980; From Sunday to Sunday, 1987. *Recreations:* music, drama, travelling, adult education, bridge.

GRIFFITH, Martin Peter W.; *see* Wyn Griffith.

GRIFFITH, Nia Rhiannon; MP (Lab) Llanelli, since 2005; *b* 4 Dec. 1956; *d* of Prof. T. Gwynfor Griffith and Dr Rhiannon Griffith (*née* Howell); *m* (marr. diss.). *Educ:* Univ. of Oxford (BA 1st cl. Hons Mod. Foreign Langs 1979); UCNW, Bangor (PGCE 1980). Language teacher: Oldham, 1981–83; Queen Elizabeth Cambria Sch., Carmarthen, 1983–85; Hd of Langs Faculty, Gowerton Comp. Sch., Swansea, 1986–92; Advr and Schs Inspector, Estyn, 1992–97; Hd of Langs, Morriston Comp. Sch., Swansea, 1997–2005. Mem. (Lab),

Carmarthen Town Council, 1987–99 (Sheriff, 1998; Dep. Mayor, 1998). Shadow Minister for Business, Innovation and Skills, 2010–11, for Wales, 2011–15; Shadow Sec. of State for Wales, 2015–. *Publications:* Ciao! Book 2: a textbook for teaching Italian, 1990; 100 Ideas for Teaching Languages, 2005. *Address:* (office) 6 Queen Victoria Road, Llanelli SA15 2TL; House of Commons, SW1A 0AA.

GRIFFITH, Prof. Rachel Susan, CBE 2015; PhD; FBA 2009; Professor of Economics, University of Manchester, since 2010; Deputy Research Director, Institute for Fiscal Studies, since 2006; *b* Ithaca, NY, 16 May 1963; *d* of Joe H. Griffith and Patricia Jean Griffith (*née* Jeffries); *m* 2000, James Banks. *Educ:* Univ. of Massachusetts (BSc); City of London Poly. (MSc Econometrics and Forecasting 1991); Keele Univ. (PhD 1999). Hd of Res., EIRIS Services Ltd, London, 1986–93; Lectr (pt-time), City of London Poly., 1991–93; Institute for Fiscal Studies: Sen. Res. Economist, 1993–97; Dir, Productivity and Innovation Res., 1997–2002; Dep. Dir, 2002–06; Sen. Economist, Competition Commn, 2001–02; Hon. Res. Fellow, 1997–2002, Reader in Econs, 2003–07, Prof. of Econs, 2006–10, UCL. Vis. Prof., UCLA, 1999–2000; Res. Associate, Centre for Econ. Policy Res., London, 1999–. Academic Panellist: Competition Commn, 2004–06; HM Treasury Productivity Team, 2005–. Expert Advr to EC on Corporate Taxation and Innovation, 2000–01. Mem., Panel of Experts, Barker Rev. of Land Use Planning, 2006. Mem. Council, REconS, 2006–10 (Prog. Chair, Annual Conf., 2011); Mem., Exec. Cttee and Council, 2005–11, Pres., 2015, Eur. Econ. Assoc. Dep. Chair, HEFCE REF 2014 sub-panel 18, 2011–14. Jt Man. Ed., Fiscal Studies, 1995–99; Bd Mem., 2002–, Dir, 2006–, Rev. of Econ. Studies; Ed., Econ. Jl Conf. Vol., 2004–05; Man. Ed., Econ. Jl, 2011–. *Publications:* (contrib.) Creating a Premier League Economy, 2004; (contrib.) International Handbook of Competition, 2004; (with P. Aghion) Competition and Growth, 2005; contribs to learned jls incl. Amer. Econ. Rev., Qly Jl of Econs, Econ. Jl, Rev. of Econs and Stats, Jl of the Eur. Econ. Assoc., Jl of Public Econs, Fiscal Studies, Oxford Rev. of Econ. Policy. *Recreations:* running, cycling, hiking. *Address:* Institute for Fiscal Studies, 7 Ridgemount Street, WC1E 7AE.

GRIFFITH-JONES, David Eric; QC 2000; **His Honour Judge David Griffith-Jones;** a Circuit Judge, since 2007; *b* Nairobi, 7 March 1953; *s* of Sir Eric Newton Griffith-Jones, KBE, CMG, QC and Mary Patricia Griffith-Jones; *m* 1st, 1978, Deborah Judith Laidlaw Mockeridge (marr. diss. 1983); 2nd, 1984, Virginia Ann Meredith Brown; two *s* one *d*. *Educ:* Marlborough Coll.; Bristol Univ. (LLB 1974). FCIArb 1991. Called to the Bar, Middle Temple, 1975; Asst Recorder, 1992–97; Recorder, 1997–2007. Asst Boundary Comr, 2000–. Part-time Pres., Mental Health Review Tribunal, 2002–08; a Tribunal Judge, First-tier Tribunal (Health, Educn and Social Care Chamber) Mental Health, 2009–; Judicial Mem., Parole Bd, 2009–14. Member: Sports Disputes Resolution Panel, 2000–; Panel of Sports Arbitrators, CIArb, 2002–; Chairman: Drugs Appeal Tribunal, ICC Champions Trophy, 2004, ICC Johnny Walker Series, 2005, ICC Under-19 World Cup, 2006, World Cup, 2007; Appeals Cttee, LTA, 2004–06. CIArb accredited mediator, 2003. *Publications:* Law and the Business of Sport, 1997; (contrib.) Sport: law and practice, 2003, 3rd edn 2014. *Recreations:* sport, the blues, woodturning, skydiving. *Address:* Maidstone Combined Court Centre, The Law Courts, Barker Road, Maidstone, Kent ME16 8EQ. *Clubs:* Sevenoaks Rugby Football, Falconhurst Cricket, Royal Ashdown Forest Golf.

GRIFFITH-JONES, John Guthrie; Chairman, Financial Conduct Authority, since 2013; *b* 11 May 1954; s of Mervyn Griffith-Jones and Joan (*née* Baker); *m* 1990, Cathryn Mary Stone; one *s* one *d*. *Educ:* Eton; Trinity Hall, Cambridge (BA 1975). Peat Marwick Mitchell, subseq. KPMG: joined 1975; Partner, Corporate Finance, 1987–2002; Chief Exec., 2002–06, Chm and Sen. Partner, KPMG UK, 2006–12; Chm., Europe, Middle East, Africa and India Region, 2008–12. Non-exec. Dir and Dep. Chm., FSA, 2012–13. Served TA, Royal Green Jackets, 1975–90. Liveryman, Co. of Skinners, 1997–. *Recreations:* tennis, bridge. *Address:* Financial Conduct Authority, 25 The North Colonnade, Canary Wharf, E14 5HS.

GRIFFITH-JONES, Richard Haydn; His Honour Judge Griffith-Jones; a Circuit Judge, since 1999; Resident Judge, Coventry and Warwick Crown Court, since 2011; *b* 29 June 1951; *s* of Wyn and Mary Griffith-Jones; *m* 1974, Susan Hale; three *s* one *d*. *Educ:* Solihull Sch.; Leeds Univ. (LLB Hons). Called to the Bar, Middle Temple, 1974; a Recorder, 1994–99. Liaison Judge to Birmingham Magistrates and Sutton Coldfield Magistrates, 2006–10. Hon. Recorder of Coventry, 2011–. *Publications:* contrib. to Law Qly Rev. *Recreations:* poultry keeping, watching Association football. *Address:* Warwickshire Justice, Leamington Spa CV32 4EL.

GRIFFITH-JONES, Rev. Robin Guthrie, DLitt; FSA; Master of The Temple, Temple Church, since 1999; *b* 29 May 1956; *s* of Mervyn and Joan Griffith-Jones. *Educ:* Westminster; New Coll., Oxford (MA); Westcott House; Christ's Coll., Cambridge (MA); Univ. of London (DLitt 2014). Christie's (English Drawings and Watercolours), 1978–84; ordained deacon, 1989, priest, 1990; Curate, St Jude, Cantril Farm and Stockbridge Village, Liverpool, 1989–92; Chaplain: Lincoln Coll., Oxford, 1992–99; to Lord Mayor of London, 2002–03. Vis. Lectr, 2008–12, Sen. Lectr, 2012–, KCL. *Publications:* The Four Witnesses, 2000; The Gospel according to St Paul, 2004; The Da Vinci Code and the Secrets of the Temple, 2006; Mary Magdalene, 2008; (ed jtly) The Temple Church, 2010; (ed) Islam and English Law, 2013. *Address:* Master's House, Temple, EC4Y 7BB. *T:* (020) 7353 8559. *Clubs:* Athenæum, Pratt's.

GRIFFITH WILLIAMS, Hon. Sir John, Kt 2007; a Judge of the High Court of Justice, Queen's Bench Division, 2007–14; President and Lay Judge, Provincial Court of Church in Wales, since 2007; Commissioner, Special Immigration Appeals Commission, since 2014; *b* 20 Dec. 1944; *s* of Griffith John Williams, TD and Alison Williams; *m* 1971, Mair Tasker Watkins, *d* of Rt Hon. Sir Tasker Watkins, VC, GBE, PC; two *d*. *Educ:* King's School, Bruton; The Queen's College, Oxford (BA; Hon. Fellow 2014). Served 4th Bn, RWF (TA), 1965–68; Welsh Volunteers (TAVR), 1968–71 (Lieut). Called to the Bar, Gray's Inn, 1968, Bencher, 1994; a Recorder, 1984–2000; QC 1985; a Dep. High Court Judge, 1993–2000; a Circuit Judge, 2000–01; a Sen. Circuit Judge and Hon. Recorder of Cardiff, 2001–07; a Presiding Judge, Wales Circuit, 2010–13. Mem., Criminal Injuries Compensation Bd, 1999–2000. Mem., Bar Council, 1990–93; Leader, Wales and Chester Circuit, 1996–98 (Treas., 1993–95). Asst Comr, Boundary Commn for Wales, 1994–2000. Chancellor, dio. of Llandaff, 1999– (Dep. Chancellor, 1996–99). Hon. Fellow, Cardiff Univ., 2008. Hon. LLD S Wales, 2013. *Recreation:* golf. *Address:* c/o Royal Courts of Justice, Strand, WC2A 2LL. *Clubs:* Cardiff and County (Cardiff); Royal Porthcawl Golf.

GRIFFITHS, family name of **Barons Griffiths of Burry Port** and **Griffiths of Fforestfach**.

GRIFFITHS OF BURRY PORT, Baron *cr* 2004 (Life Peer), of Pembrey and Burry Port in the County of Dyfed; **Rev. Dr Leslie John Griffiths;** Superintendent Minister, Wesley's Chapel, since 1996; President of the Methodist Conference, 1994–95; *b* 15 Feb. 1942; *s* of late Sidney and Olwen Griffiths; *m* 1969, Margaret, *d* of Alfred and Kathleen Rhodes; two *s* one *d*. *Educ:* Llanelli Grammar Sch.; Univ. of Wales (BA); Univ. of Cambridge (MA); Univ. of London (PhD). Junior Res. Fellow, University Coll. of S Wales and Monmouthshire, Cardiff, 1963; Asst Lectr in English, St David's Coll., Lampeter, 1964–67; trained for Methodist Ministry, Wesley Ho., Cambridge, 1967–70; Asst Minister, Wesley Church, Cambridge, 1969–70; Petit Goâve Circuit, Haïti, 1970–71; Port-au-Prince Circuit and Asst Headmaster, Nouveau Collège Bird, 1971–74; Minister, Reading Circuit, 1974–77; Superintendent Minister: Cap Haïtien Circuit, Haïti, 1977–80; Wanstead and Woodford Circuit, 1980–86; W London Mission, 1986–91; Finchley and Hendon Circuit, 1991–96. Hon. Canon, St Paul's Cathedral, 2000– (Mem. Council, 2000–13). Trustee: Addiction Recovery Foundn, 1989–2004; Sir Halley Stewart Trust, 1999–2013; Art and Christianity Enquiry, 1999–2008; One World Trust, 2008–11; Mem., Bd of Dirs, The Abraham Path, Harvard Univ., 2009–11. Dir, Birnbeck Housing Assoc., 1992–96. Gov., Bd of Christian Aid, 1990–98 (Chm., Africa and ME Cttee, 1991–95); Chm., Bd of Govs, Southlands Coll., 1997–2003; Mem. Council, Univ. of Surrey Roehampton (formerly Roehampton Inst.), 1997–2003; Gov. and Trustee, Central Foundn Schs of London, 2000– (Vice Chm., Central Foundn Schs Trust, 2009–11; Chm. of Trustees, 2011–); Trustee, Wesley House, Cambridge, 2002–04 (Chm., F and GP Cttee, 2002–04). Chairman: Methodist Church's European Reference Gp, 1996–99; Churches Adv. Council on Local Broadcasting, 1996–2000; Coll. of Preachers, 2004–11; Methodist Church Heritage Cttee, 2008–11. Pres., Boys' Brigade, 2011–. FLSW 2012. Hon. Fellow: Sarum Coll., 2001; Sion Coll., 2002; Cardiff Univ., 2005; St David's Coll., Lampeter, 2006. Mem., Order of Christopher Columbus (Dominican Republic), 2011. KCSJ 1989. *Publications:* A History of Haïtian Methodism, 1991; Letters Home, 1995; The Aristide Factor, 1997; Touching the Pulse: worship and our diverse world, 1998; Voices from the Desert, 2002; (with J. Potter) World Without End?, 2007; View from the Edge (autobiog.), 2010. *Recreation:* fun and fellowship spiced with occasional moments of solitude. *Address:* Wesley's Chapel, 49 City Road, EC1Y 1AU. *T:* (020) 7253 2262. *Club:* Graduate Centre (Cambridge).

GRIFFITHS OF FFORESTFACH, Baron *cr* 1991 (Life Peer), of Fforestfach in the county of West Glamorgan; **Brian Griffiths;** Vice Chairman, Goldman Sachs (Europe), since 1991; *b* 27 Dec. 1941; *s* of Ivor Winston Griffiths and Phyllis Mary Griffiths (*née* Morgan); *m* 1965, Rachel Jane Jones; one *s* two *d*. *Educ:* Dynevor Grammar School; London School of Economics, Univ. of London. (BSc(Econ), MSc(Econ)). Assistant Lecturer in Economics, LSE, 1965–68, Lecturer in Economics, 1968–76; City University: Prof. of Banking and Internat. Finance, 1977–85; Dir, Centre for Banking and Internat. Finance, 1977–82; Dean, Business Sch., 1982–85; Head of Prime Minister's Policy Unit, 1985–90. Vis. Prof., Univ. of Rochester, USA, 1972–73; Prof. of Ethics, Gresham Coll., 1984–87; Dir, Bank of England, 1984–86 (Mem., Panel of Academic Consultants, 1977–86). Director: Herman Miller, 1991–; Times Newspapers, 1991–; HTV (Wales), 1991–93; Servicemaster, 1992–2007; Telewest, 1994–98; English, Welsh and Scottish Railway, 1996–2007; Chairman: Trillium, 1998–2008; Westminster Health Care, 1999–2002. Chairman: Centre for Policy Studies, 1991–2000; Sch. Exams and Assessment Council, 1991–93; Trustees, Lambeth Fund, 1997–2009. Fellow: Trinity Coll., Carmarthen, 1997; Swansea Inst. of HE, 2003; Sarum Coll., 2006; Univ. of Wales, Swansea, 2006. Hon. DSc City, 1999; Hon. DSc(Econ) Wales, 2004. *Publications:* Is Revolution Change? (ed and contrib.), 1972; Mexican Monetary Policy and Economic Development, 1972; Invisible Barriers to Invisible Trade, 1975; Inflation: The Price of Prosperity, 1976; (ed with G. E. Wood) Monetary Targets, 1980; The Creation of Wealth, 1984; (ed with G. E. Wood) Monetarism in the United Kingdom, 1984; Morality and the Market Place, 1989. *Address:* c/o House of Lords, SW1A 0PW. *Club:* Garrick.

GRIFFITHS, (Albert) John; Member (Lab) Newport East, National Assembly for Wales, since 1999; *b* 19 Dec. 1956; *s* of Albert John Griffiths and Hannah Griffiths (*née* O'Connor); *m* 1978, Alison Kim Hopkins; two *s*. *Educ:* UC, Cardiff (LLB Hons Law); Dip. in Social Studies, 1996. Lectr in Further Educn and Higher Educn, 1988–89; Production Exec., 1989–90; solicitor, 1990–99. National Assembly for Wales: Dep. Minister for Economic Develt, 2001–03, for Health and Social Care, 2003–07, for Educn, Lifelong Learning and Skills (formerly for Skills), 2007–10; Counsel Gen. and Leader of Legislative Prog., 2010–11; Minister for Envmt and Sustainable Develt, 2011–13, for Culture and Sport, 2013–14. Chm., All Party Gp on Internat. Develt, 2004–, on Sport, 2004–. *Recreations:* cricket, tennis, running, circuit training, reading, travel. *Address:* National Assembly for Wales, Cardiff Bay, Cardiff CF99 1NA. *T:* 0300 200 7122; (office) Suite 5, Seventh Floor, Clarence House, Clarence Place, Newport NP19 7AA. *T:* (01633) 222302.

GRIFFITHS, Prof. Allen Phillips; Professor of Philosophy, University of Warwick, 1964–92, now Emeritus; Director, Royal Institute of Philosophy, 1979–94; *b* 11 June 1927; *s* of John Phillips Griffiths and Elsie Maud (*née* Jones); *m* 1st, 1948, Margaret Lock (*d* 1974); one *s* one *d*; 2nd, 1984, Vera Clare (marr. diss. 1990). *Educ:* University Coll., Cardiff (BA; Hon. Fellow 1984); University Coll., Oxford (BPhil). Sgt, Intell. Corps, 1945–48 (despatches). Asst Lectr, Univ. of Wales, 1955–57; Lectr, Birkbeck Coll., Univ. of London, 1957–64. Pro-Vice-Chancellor, Univ. of Warwick, 1970–77. Vis. Professor: Swarthmore Coll., Pa, 1963; Univ. of Calif, 1967; Univ. of Wisconsin, 1965 and 1970; Carleton Coll., Minnesota, 1985. Silver Jubilee Medal, 1977. *Publications:* (ed) Knowledge & Belief, 1967; (ed) Of Liberty, 1983; (ed) Philosophy and Literature, 1984; Philosophy and Practice, 1985; (ed) Contemporary French Philosophy, 1988; (ed) Key Themes in Philosophy, 1989; (ed) Wittgenstein Centenary Essays, 1990; (ed) A. J. Ayer Memorial Essays, 1992; (ed) The Impulse to Philosophise, 1993; articles in learned philosophical jls. *Address:* 6 Brockley Road, West Bridgford, Nottingham NG2 5JY. *T:* (0115) 878 1059. *E:* cyfaill@ntlworld.com. *Club:* West Bridgford Conservative.

GRIFFITHS, Alun Brynmor, MW; International Director, Vats Liquor Chain Store Management Co. Ltd, Beijing, since 2013; *b* 29 Dec. 1953; *s* of Islwyn ap Ifan Griffiths and Olwen Enid Griffiths; *m* 1981, Helen Mary Hayes; two *s*. *Educ:* Glyn Grammar Sch., Epsom; University Coll. of Wales, Aberystwyth (BA Hons French). MW 1991. Manager: Stones of Belgravia, wine merchants, 1976–81; Butlers Wine Bar, London, 1981–83; Sales Exec., Enotria Wines, London, 1983–85; Admin. Manager, Fields Wine Merchants, London, 1985–87; Wine buyer: Fortnum & Mason, 1987–92; Harrods, 1992–94; Gen. Manager Heathrow, 1994–96, Wine Dir, 1996–2012, Berry Bros & Rudd Ltd. Hospitalier de Pomerol, 1989; Jurade de St Emilion, 1990; Comdr de Bontemps du Medoc et du Graves, 1992; Chevalier du Tastevin, 2001. *Recreations:* squash, horse-racing, food and wine, walking, tennis. *E:* alun.griffiths@vatsliquor.com.

GRIFFITHS, Andrew James; MP (C) Burton, since 2010; *b* Wolverhampton, 19 Oct. 1970; *s* of Robert Griffiths and Harriet Griffiths (*née* Du'Rose); *m* 2013, Kate Kniveton. *Educ:* High Arcal Sch., Sedgley. Worked for family engrg business, 1996–2002; Advr to Cons. MEPs, 1999–2004; Chief of Staff: to Shadow Sec. of State for Envmt and Transport, 2004, for Family, 2004–05, for Culture, Media and Sport, 2005–07, for Community and Local Govt, 2007–09; to Chm., Cons. Party, 2009–10; Sec. to Bd, Cons. Party, 2009–10. Contested (C) Dudley N, 2001. *Recreations:* supporting British brewing industry, football, cricket. *Address:* (office) Gothard House, 9 St Paul's Square, Burton on Trent, Staffs DE14 2EF. *T:* (01283) 568894. *E:* andrew.griffiths.mp@parliament.uk. *Clubs:* Carlton; Uttoxeter British Legion; Rolleston Working Men's.

GRIFFITHS, Dame Anne; *see* Griffiths, Dame E. A.

GRIFFITHS, Antony Vaughan, FBA 2000; Keeper, Department of Prints and Drawings, British Museum, 1991–2011; *b* 28 July 1951; *s* of late Richard Cerdin Griffiths and Pamela de Grave Griffiths (*née* Hetherington). *Educ:* Highgate Sch.; Christ Church, Oxford (BA); Courtauld Inst. of Art, London Univ. (MA). Joined Dept of Prints and Drawings, BM, 1976, as Asst Keeper; Dep. Keeper, 1981–91. Slade Prof. of Fine Art, Univ. of Oxford, 2014–15. Chm., Print Quarterly Pubns, 2001–. Chm., Walpole Soc., 2013–. Trustee: Art Fund, 2011–; Henry Moore Foundn, 2014–. *Publications:* Prints and Printmaking, 1980, 2nd edn 1996; (with Reginald Williams) The Department of Prints and Drawings in the British Museum: a user's guide, 1987; (with Frances Carey) German Printmaking in the Age of Goethe, 1994; The Print in Stuart Britain, 1998; Prints for Books: book illustration in France 1760–1800, 2004; British Museum exhibn catalogues; contribs to learned jls, esp. Print Qly. *Address:* 1 Highbury Hill, N5 1SU.

GRIFFITHS, Prof. Christopher Ernest Maitland, MD; FRCP, FMedSci; Foundation Professor of Dermatology, University of Manchester, since 1994 (Head, School of Translational Medicine, 2007–08; Associate Dean for Research, Faculty of Medical and Human Sciences, 2008–10; Director, Manchester Academic Health Science Centre, 2010–11); *b* Dudley, 14 June 1954; *s* of Sir (Ernest) Roy Griffiths and of Winifred Griffiths; *m* 1992, Dr Tamara Wang; two *d*. *Educ:* Dulwich Coll.; St Thomas' Hosp. Med. Sch., Univ. of London (BSc 1st Cl. Hons 1976; MB BS 1979; MD 1991). FRCP 1995; FRCPath 2002; FRCPE 2011. Jun. hosp. doctor posts, London, 1979–85; Wellcome Trust Clin. Res. Trng Fellow, St Mary's Hosp. Med. Sch., London, 1985–87; Sen. Res. Fellow, then Asst Prof. of Dermatol., Univ. of Michigan, 1987–93; Hon. Consultant Dermatologist, Salford Royal NHS Foundn Trust, and Hd, Gtr Manchester Dermatol. Centre, 1994–. Non-exec. Dir, University Hosp. of S Manchester NHS Foundn Trust, 2008–10. Sen. Investigator, NIHR, 2011–. President: British Assoc. of Dermatologists, 2004–05; European Dermatology Forum, 2010–11; Mem., Exec. Bd, Internat. League of Dermatological Socs, 2011–. Co-founder and Hon. Sec., Internat. Psoriasis Council, 2004–13 (Pres., 2014–). FMedSci 2011. *Publications:* (ed jtly) Rook's Textbook of Dermatology, 7th edn 2004, 8th edn 2010; contrib. Lancet, New England Jl Medicine, BMJ and specialist dermatology jls on psoriasis, ageing skin and brain-skin interaction. *Recreations:* natural history, gardening, exploring Welsh hillsides, distance running, cycling. *Address:* Dermatology Centre, Barnes Building, Salford Royal Hospital, Manchester M6 8HD. *T:* (0161) 206 4392, *Fax:* (0161) 206 1095. *E:* Christopher.Griffiths@manchester.ac.uk. *Club:* Royal Automobile.

GRIFFITHS, Hon. Clive Edward, AO 1997; JP; consultant and company director, since 2001; Agent-General for Western Australia, 1997–2001; *b* Perth, WA, 20 Nov. 1928; *s* of T. E. Griffiths and D. M. Beattie; *m* 1st, 1949, Myrtle Holtham (marr. diss. 1995; she *d* 1996); one *d*; 2nd, 1995, Norma Marie Paonessa. *Educ:* Fremantle Boys' High Sch.; Kalgoorlie Sch. of Mines. Electrical Engineer and Contractor, 1953–66. City Councillor, S Perth, 1962–66; MLC (L), WA, 1965–97 (Pres., 1977–97); Parly Sec., Lib Party and Jt Govt Parties, 1974–77; Regl Rep. for Australia and Pacific Region, 1988–90, Chm., Exec. Cttee, 1990–93, Commonwealth Parly Assoc. JP W Australia, 1983. *Recreations:* sailing, football, cricket. *Address:* PO Box 412, Melville, WA 6956, Australia. *T:* (8) 932 99039. *E:* haigroad@linet.net.au. *Club:* Shelley Sailing.

GRIFFITHS, Courtenay Delsdue McVay; QC 1998; a Recorder, since 2000; *b* 10 Oct. 1955; *s* of Wrenford Dacosta Griffiths and Adelaide Tamonda Griffiths; *m* 1985, Angela Maria Hill; three *s*. *Educ:* Bablake Sch., Coventry; LSE, London Univ. (LLB Hons 1979). Called to the Bar, Gray's Inn, 1980, Bencher, 2002; Legal Asst, GLC Police Cttee, 1980–84; Revson Fellow, Urban Legal Studies Prog., City Coll., CUNY, 1984–85; in practice at the Bar, 1985–; an Asst Recorder, 1999–2000; Head of Chambers, Garden Court Chambers, 2002–11. Hon. Lectr in Law, KCL, 1987–. Hon. PhD: Leeds Metropolitan, 2005; Coventry, 2005. *Recreations:* swimming, squash, music (reggae and soul), play piano, drawing and painting.

GRIFFITHS, David Hubert; Clerk/Adviser, House of Commons European Scrutiny Committee (formerly Select Committee on European Legislation), since 1998; *b* 24 Dec. 1940; *s* of late Hubert Griffiths and Margaret Joan Waldron; *m* Mary Abbott; one *s* one *d*. *Educ:* Kingswood School, Bath; St Catharine's College, Cambridge (MA). Joined Ministry of Agriculture, Fisheries and Food as Asst Principal, 1963; Principal, 1968; Asst Secretary, 1975; Under Secretary, 1982–97; Hd, European Communities Gp, 1982–83; Fisheries Sec., 1983–87; Hd, Food, Drink and Marketing Policy Gp, 1987–90; Dir of Establishments, 1990–94; Hd, Arable Crops and Horticulture Gp, 1995–97. Non-exec. Dir, ICI (Paints Div.), 1985–87. *Recreations:* cooking, music. *Address:* (office) 7 Millbank, SW1P 3JA.

GRIFFITHS, His Honour David Laurence; a Circuit Judge, 1989–2009; *b* 3 Aug. 1944; *s* of late Edward Laurence Griffiths and of Mary Middleton Pudge; *m* 1971, Sally Hollis; four *d*. *Educ:* Christ's Hospital; Jesus College, Oxford (MA). Called to the Bar, Lincoln's Inn, 1967; Asst Recorder, 1981; Recorder, 1985. *Recreations:* walking, cycling, watching Rugby and cricket, opera, history, classical music.

GRIFFITHS, Prof. Dorothy Seymour, OBE 2010; Professor of Human Resource Management, since 2002 and Provost's Envoy for Gender Equality, since 2014, Imperial College London (Dean, Imperial College Business School, 2012–13); Chair, Central and North West London NHS Foundation Trust, since 2014; *b* London, 26 May 1947; *d* of Henry Griffiths and Jackie Griffiths (*née* Broderick). *Educ:* Enfield Coll. of Technol.; London Univ. (BSc Sociol. (ext.) 1968); Univ. of Bath (MSc 1970). Imperial College London: Res. Asst, 1969–72; Lectr in Sociol., 1972–87; Sen. Lectr in Sociol., 1987–2001; Dep. Principal and Hd of Progs, Imperial Coll. Business Sch., 2001–12. Non-exec. Dir, 2000–13, Sen. Ind. Dir, 2009–13, Central and NW London NHS Foundn Trust. Chair, Feminist Rev. Trust, 2003–. Governor: Salisbury Sch., 2007–11 (Chm. Govs, 2011–); Queens Park Community Sch., 2008–. *Recreations:* work, cats, tennis when knees permit, watching sport, house in Cyprus, politics. *Address:* Imperial College London, South Kensington Campus, SW7 2AZ. *T:* (020) 7594 9125. *E:* d.griffiths@imperial.ac.uk.

GRIFFITHS, Elaine Mary, (Mrs P. Doyle), FRCS, FRCSEd; Consultant Cardiac Surgeon, Liverpool Heart and Chest Hospital NHS Foundation Trust (formerly Cardiothoracic Centre Liverpool), 1993; *b* 15 Jan. 1955; *d* of Hedley and Kathleen Griffiths; *m* 2000, Dr Peter Doyle; two step *d*. *Educ:* Bullers Wood Sch., Chislehurst; King's College Med. Sch., London (MB BS 1979; AKC 1979). FRCS 1985; FRCSEd 1985. Surgical trng, Southampton, Royal Brompton, Harefield and St George's Hosps; Hon. Dir, Cardiothoracic Studies, Univ. of Liverpool Med. Sch., 1994–2012. Member: DoH Ext. Ref. Gp for Nat. Service Framework for Coronary Heart Disease, 1998–2000; Welsh NHS Ext. Ref. Gp, Welsh Nat. Service Framework for Coronary Heart Disease, 1999–2002; Doctors' Forum, DoH, 2002–; Med. Devices Adv. Gp, H of C, 2005–. Royal College of Surgeons of England: Consultant Appts Assessor, 1998–; Regl Rep., Women in Surgical Trng Scheme, 2005–09; Mem. Council, RCSE, 2006– (Equality and Diversity Lead, 2012–). Lectr on patient level costing, 2010–. Member: Exec., Soc. of Cardiothoracic Surgeons of GB and Ire., 1997–2000; Amer. Soc. of Women in Cardiothoracic Surgery, 1996–. Member: BMA; Hosp. Consultants and Specialists Assoc. Founder Mem. and Advr, Heart of Mersey and Cheshire Charity, 2002–. *Recreations:* foreign travel, ski-ing, gardening, collecting horse sculptures, ancient coins and netsuke, looking after pets: Koi carp, tropical fish, dog and two cats. *T:* 07802 448017. *E:* elainegriffiths@doctors.org.uk.

GRIFFITHS, Dame (Elizabeth) Anne, DCVO 2005 (CVO 1995; LVO 1988; MVO 1960); Librarian and Archivist to The Duke of Edinburgh, since 1983; *b* 2 Nov. 1932; *d* of William Hugh Stevenson and Elizabeth Margaret Stevenson (*née* Wallace); *m* 1960, David Latimer Griffiths (*d* 1982), Dir, McKinsey & Co.; three *s* one *d* (and one *d* decd). *Educ:* St Leonard's Sch., St Andrews. Lady Clerk in the Office of The Duke of Edinburgh, 1952–60. *Recreations:* watching sport, particularly football, cricket, golf and Rugby.
See also R. W. Ellis, Sir H. A. Stevenson.

GRIFFITHS, Prof. Gillian Margaret, PhD; FRS 2013; Professor of Immunology and Cell Biology, since 2007, and Director, Cambridge Institute for Medical Research, since 2012, University of Cambridge; Fellow, King's College, Cambridge, since 2007; *m* Prof. James Frederick Kaufman; two *c*. *Educ:* University Coll. London; Darwin Coll. and King's Coll., Cambridge (PhD 1984). Post-doctoral Fellow, Stanford Univ., 1985–90; Scientific Mem., Basel Inst. for Immunol., 1990–95; Wellcome Trust Senior Fellow: MRC Lab. for Molecular Cell Biol., UCL, 1995–97; Sir William Dunn Sch. of Pathology, Univ. of Oxford, 1997–2007. Mem., Editl bd, Jl Cell Biol. FMedSci 2005. *Publications:* contribs to jls incl. Nature, Proc. NAS, Immunity. *Address:* Cambridge Institute for Medical Research, Wellcome Trust/MRC Building, Cambridge Biomedical Campus, Hills Road, Cambridge CB2 0XY.

GRIFFITHS, Harold Morris; Assistant Secretary, HM Treasury, 1978–86; *b* 17 March 1926; *s* of Rt Hon. James Griffiths, CH; *m* 1st, 1951, Gwyneth Lethby (*d* 1966); three *s* one *d*; 2nd, 1966, Elaine Burge (*née* Walsh); two *s*. *Educ:* Llanelly Grammar Sch.; London Sch. of Economics. Editorial Staff: Glasgow Herald, 1949–55; Guardian, 1955–67; Information Division, HM Treasury: Deputy Head, 1967–68, Head, 1968–72; Asst Sec., HM Treasury, 1972–75; Counsellor (Economic), Washington, 1975–78. *Address:* The Old Coach House, Park Road, Hampton Hill, Middx TW12 1HR. *T:* (020) 8979 1214.

GRIFFITHS, Howard; Command Secretary, RAF Logistics Command, 1994–98; *b* 20 Sept. 1938; *s* of Bernard and Olive Griffiths; *m* 1963, Dorothy Foster (*née* Todd) (*d* 2011); one *s* one *d*. *Educ:* London School of Economics (BScEcon, MScEcon). Ministry of Defence: Research Officer, 1963–69; Principal, Army Dept, 1970–72; Central Staffs, 1972–76; Asst Secretary, Head of Civilian Faculty, National Defence Coll., 1976–78; Procurement Executive, 1978–80; Deputy and Counsellor (Defence), UK Delegn, Mutual and Balanced Force Reductions (Negotiations), Vienna, 1980–84; Asst Sec., Office of Management and Budget, 1984–86; Asst Sec. and Head of Defence Arms Control Unit, 1986–88; Asst Under Sec. of State (Policy), 1988–91; Fellow, Center for Internat. Affairs, Harvard Univ., 1991–92; Assistant Under Secretary of State: (Ordnance), 1992; (Supply and Orgn) (Air), 1993–94. *Address:* 95 Brands Hill Avenue, High Wycombe HP13 5PX.
See also L. Griffiths.

GRIFFITHS, Ian Ward; Group Finance Director, ITV plc, since 2008; *b* St Asaph, N Wales, 26 Sept. 1966; *s* of Glyn and Dorothy Griffiths; *m* 1996, Alison Barbara. *Educ:* Flint High Sch.; Rydal Sch., Colwyn Bay; Fitzwilliam Coll., Cambridge (BA 1988; MA). ACA 1991. Audit and Corporate Finance, Ernst & Young, Cambridge, 1988–94; finance rôles, 1994–2005, Gp Finance Dir, 2005–08, Emap plc. *Recreations:* football, photography, philately, walking. *Address:* ITV plc, London Television Centre, Upper Ground, SE1 9LT. *T:* (020) 7157 3000.

GRIFFITHS, Jane Patricia; Editor, European Court of Human Rights, Strasbourg, since 2007; *b* 17 April 1954; *d* of late John Griffiths and of Patricia Griffiths (*née* Thomas); *m* 1st, 1975, Ralph Spearpoint (marr. diss. 1994); one *s* one *d*; 2nd, 1999, Andrew Tattersall. *Educ:* Univ. of Durham (BA Hons Russian). GCHQ linguist, 1977–84; Editor, BBC Monitoring, 1984–97. Mem. (Lab), Reading BC, 1989–99. MP (Lab) Reading E, 1997–2005. Languages teacher, Riga, Latvia and E London, 2006–07. *Publications:* (with John Newman) Bushido, 1988; The One (political memoir), 2008; Priors Gardens (novel), 2012. *Recreations:* urban living, fancy rats. *Address:* 18 rue de Molsheim, Strasbourg 67000, France.

GRIFFITHS, John; *see* Griffiths, Albert J.

GRIFFITHS, John Calvert, CMG 1983; QC 1972; SC (Hong Kong) 1997; *b* 16 Jan. 1931; *s* of Oswald Hardy Griffiths and Christina Flora Griffiths (*née* Littlejohn); *m* 1958, Jessamy, *er d* of Prof. G. P. Crowden and Jean Crowden; three *d*; *m* 1999, Marie Charlotte Biddulph. *Educ:* St Peter's Sch., York (scholar); Emmanuel Coll., Cambridge (sen. exhibnr) (BA 1st Cl. Hons 1955; MA 1960). Called to the Bar, Middle Temple, 1956 (Bencher, 1983), Hong Kong, 1979; a Recorder, 1972–90. Attorney-General of Hong Kong, 1979–83; Mem. Exec. and Legislative Councils, and Chm. Hong Kong Law Reform Commn, 1979–83. Chm., Telecommns (Competition Provisions) Appeal Bd, HK, 2000–07; Mem., Competition Policy Rev. Cttee, 2005–07. Member: Exec. Cttee, General Council of the Bar, 1967–71, 1983–89 (Treas., 1987); Senate of Inns of Court and the Bar, 1984–86 (Mem., Exec. Cttee, 1973–77); Nat. Council of Social Service, 1974–79; Greater London CAB Exec. Cttee, 1978–79; (co-opted) Develt and Special Projects Cttee, 1977–79; Court, Hong Kong Univ., 1980–84; Exec. Cttee, Prince Philip Cambridge Scholarships, 1980–84. Chm., Middle Temple Soc. (Hong Kong), 2000–. Lieutenant, RE, 1949–50 (Nat. Service). *Recreations:* fishing, reading, gardening. *Address:* Des Voeux Chambers, Floor 38, Gloucester Tower, Landmark, 15 Queen's Road Central, Hong Kong. *T:* 25263071; Brick Court Chambers, 7–8 Essex Street, WC2R 3LD. *T:* (020) 7379 3550. *Clubs:* Flyfishers', Hurlingham; Hong Kong, Foreign Correspondents', Hong Kong Jockey (Hong Kong).

GRIFFITHS, John Charles, FLS; JP; writer; *b* 19 April 1934; *s* of Sir Percival Griffiths, KBE, CIE; *m* 1st, 1956, Ann Timms (marr. diss.); four *s*; 2nd, 1983, Carole Jane Mellor (marr. diss.); one *d*. *Educ:* Uppingham; Peterhouse, Cambridge (MA). Exec. Dir, Nat. Extension Coll., 1965–68; Dep. General Manager, Press Association, 1968–70; PR adviser, British Gas, 1970–74; Chm., MSG Public Relations, 1974–78; Chm. and founder, The Arts Channel, 1983–89; Chairman: Minerva Arts Channel, 1989–98; Minerva Vision, 1989–2009. Chairman: National League of Young Liberals, 1962–64 (Mem., Nat. Exec., 1964–66); Assoc. of Liberals in Small Business and Self Employed, 1980; Pres., Liberal Party, 1982–83. Contested (L): Ludlow, 1964; Wanstead and Woodford, 1966; Bedford, Feb. 1974, Oct. 1974. Develt Dir, Bardsey Island Trust, 1992–96. Chm. Govs, Llangynidr Sch., 1993–95. Trustee, Nat. Asthma Campaign, subseq. Asthma UK, 2002–12 (Vice Chm., 2009–12). FLS 2005. JP Cardiff, 1960. *Publications:* The Survivors, 1964; Afghanistan, 1967; Modern Iceland, 1969; Three Tomorrows, 1980; The Science of Winning Squash, 1981; Afghanistan: key to a continent, 1981; The Queen of Spades, 1983; Flashpoint Afghanistan, 1986; The Third Man: the life and times of William Murdoch, 1992; Nimbus, 1994; Fathercare, 1997; Imperial Call, 1997; Afghanistan: a history of conflict, 2001; Hostage, 2003; Tea, 2006; Afghanistan: land of conflict and beauty, 2009, 2nd edn 2011. *Recreations:* conversation, reading, music, walking. *Address:* Greenbank, Savage Hill, Newland, Glos GL16 8NH.

GRIFFITHS, Sir John N.; *see* Norton-Griffiths.

GRIFFITHS, John Pankhurst, RIBA; Clerk to the Worshipful Company: of Chartered Architects, 1995–2000; of Tylers and Bricklayers, 1996–97; *b* 27 Sept. 1930; *s* of late William Bramwell Griffiths and Ethel Doris Griffiths (*née* Pankhurst); *m* 1959, Helen Elizabeth (*née* Tasker); two *s* one *d*. *Educ:* Torquay Grammar School; King George V School, Southport; School of Architecture, Manchester Univ. Dip Arch. Resident architect, Northern Nigeria, for Maxwell Fry, 1956–58; staff architect, Granada Television, 1959; Founder and first Dir, Manchester Building Centre, 1959–65; Head of Tech. Inf., Min. of Public Buildings and Works, later DoE, 1965–77; formed Building Conservation Assoc. later Building Conservation Trust, 1977, Dir, 1979–93. Mem. Bd of Mgt, Surrey Historic Bldgs Trust, 1996–2000; Trustee, Tylers and Bricklayers Craft Trust, 1993–96. *Publications:* articles in tech. and prof. jls. *Recreations:* looking at buildings, writing, speaking, cooking. *Address:* 19 Watchbell Street, Rye, E Sussex TN31 7HB.

GRIFFITHS, (John) Peter (Gwynne); QC 1995; a Recorder, since 1991; *b* 9 Dec. 1945; *m* 1st (marr. diss.); four *c*; *m* 2nd; two *c*. *Educ:* Bristol Univ. (Civil Engrg); UWIST (LLB Hons). Work in oil exploration industry, 1968–70; called to the Bar, Gray's Inn, 1970; Asst Recorder, 1987–91. Mem., Welsh Arts Council, then Arts Council of Wales, 1992; Chm., Visual Arts Bd for Wales; Vice-Pres., Cywailh Cymru (formerly Welsh Sculpture Trust). *Publications:* (ed jtly) Injuries at Work, 1996. *Recreations:* angling, sailing, ski-ing, the arts. *Address:* 2 Bedford Row, WC1R 4BU. *T:* (020) 7440 8888.

GRIFFITHS, Lawrence; a Recorder of the Crown Court, 1972–93; *b* 16 Aug. 1933; *s* of Bernard Griffiths, CBE and Olive Emily Griffiths (*née* Stokes); *m* 1959, Josephine Ann (*née* Cook), JP (*d* 2012); one *s* two *d*. *Educ:* Gowerton Grammar Sch.; Christ's Coll., Cambridge (MA). Called to the Bar, Inner Temple, 1957; practised Swansea, 1958–99; Mem. Wales and

Chester Circuit; Prosecuting Counsel to Inland Revenue for Wales and Chester Circuit, 1969–93; Standing Counsel to HM Customs and Excise for Wales and Chester Circuit, 1989–93. Mem., Mental Health Review Tribunal for Wales, 1970–91. *Recreations:* wine, walking, travel by sea, snooker. *Address:* 26 Hillside Crescent, Uplands, Swansea SA2 0RD. *T:* (01792) 473513; (chambers) Iscoed Chambers, 86 St Helens Road, Swansea SA1 4BQ. *T:* (01792) 652988. *Club:* Bristol Channel Yacht (Swansea).

See also H. Griffiths.

GRIFFITHS, Lesley; *see* Griffiths, S. L.

GRIFFITHS, Martin Alexander; QC 2006; a Recorder, since 2009; *b* 27 April 1962; *s* of Roy Arnold Griffiths and Susan Reay Gail Griffiths (*née* Landon); *m* 1995, Susan Jane Burden, barrister, only *c* of Kenneth John Burden; two *s* one *d. Educ:* City of London Sch. (Temple Chorister; John Carpenter Schol.); New Coll., Oxford (Open Schol.; BA 1st Cl. Hons Modern Hist. and Modern Langs 1984; MA 1988); City Univ. (Dip. Law 1985); Inns of Court Sch. of Law. Called to the Bar, Inner Temple, 1986 (Duke of Edinburgh Schol., Horace Avory Schol., Inner Temple Award), Bencher, 2013; in practice at the Bar, 1986–; instructed in Cayman Is, 2006–; admitted to the Bar: Eastern Caribbean Supreme Court, 2008; Dubai Internat. Financial Centre Courts, 2008. Volunteer, Waterloo Legal Advice Service, 1988–93; Mem., Mgt Cttee, N Kensington Law Centre, 2007–09; Chm., Professional Conduct Sub-Cttee, London Maritime Arbitrators Assoc., 2007–; Mem. Cttee, Employment Law Bar Assoc., 2008–. Member: Bar Council, 2008–; Advocacy Trng Council, 2012– (Mem., Res. and Develt Cttee). Sponsor: New Coll., Oxford Burden Griffiths Awards, 2001–; Brenda Landon Pye Portrait Prize, Chelsea Coll. of Art, 2006–. *Recreations:* the piano, the library, the gym, Chelsea FC. *Address:* Essex Court Chambers, 24 Lincoln's Inn Fields, WC2A 3EG. *T:* (020) 7813 8000, *Fax:* (020) 7813 8080. *Club:* Travellers.

GRIFFITHS, Sir Michael, Kt 2014; education consultant, SMG Education Ltd, since 2014; Headmaster, Northampton School for Boys, 2001–14; *b* Wednesfield, Wolverhampton, 23 Sept. 1951; *s* of David Wesley Griffiths and Muriel Griffiths (*née* Belfield); *m* 1984, Kathryn Margaret Simister; two *s. Educ:* Wolverhampton Grammar Sch.; Univ. of York (BA Biochem.); Univ. of Sussex (PGCE). NPQH 1999. Teacher of Science: Highfields Sch., Wolverhampton, 1974–86; Moreton Community Coll., Wolverhampton, 1986–89; Sen. Lectr in Sci. Educn, Sheffield City Poly., 1989–91; Sci. Advr, Sefton LEA, 1991–93; Dep. Headteacher, Northampton Sch. for Boys, 1993–99; Headmaster, Wallingford Sch., Oxford, 1999–2001. Ofsted Inspector, 1993–2005. Pres., Assoc. of Sch. and Coll. Leaders, 2012–13 (Mem. Council, 2006–; Hon. Life Mem., 2014). Chair, Strategy Gp, Nat. Sci. Learning Network (formerly Nat. Sci. Learning Centres), 2014–; Mem., Headteacher Bd for NW London and S Central, 2014–. Member, Council: UCAS, 2013–; AQA, 2014–. Trustee, Northants Music and Performing Arts Trust, 2014–. FRSA 2007. *Recreations:* supporting Wolverhampton Wanderers FC, golf, wine, music, travel, politics, education, Abingdon Wind Band. *E:* sir.michael.griffiths@btinternet.com. *Clubs:* East India; Old Wulfrunians, Old Northamptonians.

GRIFFITHS, Nicholas Mark; HM Diplomatic Service; Ambassador to Mali, 2010–12, and to Niger, 2011–12; *b* St Asaph, 20 Nov. 1958; *s* of late Bernard Parry Griffiths and of Jennifer Ann Griffiths (*née* Northall). *Educ:* Monmouth Sch.; Southampton Univ. (LLB). Admitted as solicitor, 1984; entered FCO, 1985; Second Secretary: Moscow, 1988–90; Arms Control and Disarmament Dept, 1990–93; S Asian Dept, 1993–96; First Secretary: UK Delegn, OECD, Paris, 1996–2001; Aviation, Maritime and Energy Dept, 2001–05; Dep. Ambassador to Sweden, 2005–10. *Recreations:* sport, travel. *Address:* c/o Foreign and Commonwealth Office, King Charles Street, SW1A 2AH.

GRIFFITHS, Nigel; Chairman, Queen's Hall, Edinburgh, since 2014; Founder, Leasehold Capital Partners; *b* 20 May 1955; *s* of late Lionel and Elizabeth Griffiths; *m* 1979, Sally, *d* of Hugh and Sally McLaughlin. *Educ:* Hawick High Sch.; Edinburgh Univ. (MA 1977); Moray House Coll. of Education. Joined Labour Party, 1970; Pres., EU Labour Club, 1976–77; Sec., Lothian Devolution Campaign, 1978; Rights Adviser to Mental Handicap Pressure Group, 1979–87. City of Edinburgh: District Councillor, 1980–87 (Chm., 1986–87; Chm., Housing Cttee; Chm., Decentralisation Cttee); Member: Edinburgh Festival Council, 1984–87; Edinburgh Health Council, 1982–87; Exec., Edinburgh Council of Social Service, 1984–87; Wester Hailes Sch. Council, 1981. MP (Lab) Edinburgh S, 1987–2010. Opposition Whip, 1987–89; Opposition front bench spokesman on consumer affairs, 1989–97; Parly Under-Sec. of State, 1997–98, Parly Under-Sec. of State (Minister for Small Business), 2001–05, DTI; Parly Sec., Privy Council Office, and Dep. Leader, H of C, 2005–07. Exec. Mem. and Convenor, Finance Cttee, Scottish Constitutional Convention. Chairman: Enforce Technol.; FuelQC. Vice Pres., Inst. of Trading Standards Admin, 1994. Member: War on Want, SEAD, Amnesty Internat., Anti-apartheid, Friends of the Earth, Nat. Trust, Ramblers' Assoc. *Publications:* Guide to Council Housing in Edinburgh, 1981; Council Housing on the Point of Collapse, 1982; Welfare Rights Survey, 1981; various welfare rights guides. *Recreations:* squash, travel, live entertainment, badminton, hill walking and rock climbing, architecture, reading, politics, helicopter pilot. *Address:* 30 McLaren Road, Edinburgh EH9 2BN. *T:* (0131) 667 1947.

GRIFFITHS, Paul Anthony, OBE 2014; writer; Music Critic of The New Yorker, 1992–96; *b* 24 Nov. 1947; *s* of Fred Griffiths and Jeanne Veronica (*née* George); *m* 1st, 1977; two *s*; 2nd, 1998, Anne Kathryn West. *Educ:* King Edward's Sch., Birmingham; Lincoln Coll., Oxford (BA, MSc). Area Editor for Grove's Dictionary of Music and Musicians, 6th edn, 1973–76; Asst Music Critic, 1979–82, Music Critic, 1982–92, The Times. Fellow, Amer. Acad. of Arts and Scis, 2011. Chevalier, Ordre des Arts et des Lettres (France), 2002. *Publications:* A Concise History of Modern Music, 1978; Boulez, 1978; A Guide to Electronic Music, 1979; Modern Music, 1980; Cage, 1981; Igor Stravinsky: The Rake's Progress, 1982; Peter Maxwell Davies, 1982; The String Quartet, 1983; György Ligeti, 1983, 2nd edn 1997; Bartók, 1984; Olivier Messiaen, 1985; New Sounds, New Personalities, 1985; The Thames & Hudson Encyclopaedia of 20th-Century Music, 1986; Stravinsky, 1992; Modern Music and After, 1995, 2nd edn 2010; The Sea on Fire: Jean Barraqué, 2003; The Penguin Companion to Classical Music, 2004 (repr. as The New Penguin Dictionary of Music, 2006); The Substance of Things Heard: writings about music, 2005; A Concise History of Western Music, 2006; *fiction:* Myself and Marco Polo, 1989; The Lay of Sir Tristram, 1991; let me tell you, 2008; The Tilted Cup, 2013; *libretti:* The Jewel Box, 1991; Marco Polo, 1996; What Next?, 1999; The General, 2007. *Recreation:* swimming. *Address:* Disgwylfa 2, Manorbier SA70 7TE.

GRIFFITHS, Prof. Paul David, MD; Professor of Virology, UCL Medical School (formerly Royal Free Hospital School of Medicine, then Royal Free and University College Medical School), since 1989; *b* 30 Jan. 1953; *s* of George Griffiths and Jean Beckett (formerly Griffiths, *née* Pring); *m* 1979, Brenda Louise Attenborough; three *s. Educ:* St Bartholomew's Hosp. Med. Coll., Univ. of London (BSc 1974; MB BS Hons 1977; MD 1982); DSc (Med) London, 1995. FRCPath 1996. Lawrence Postgrad. Res. Schol., 1979; Lectr, Bart's Med. Coll., 1979–82; Fogarty Internat. Scholar, NIH, USA, 1980–81; Royal Free Hospital School of Medicine, London University: Sen. Lectr in Virology, 1982–86; Reader, 1986–87; Chm., Univ. Div. of Pathology and Communicable Diseases, 1991–95. William Julius Mickle Fellow, London Univ., 1991. Member: UK med. socs; Internat. AIDS Soc.; Fellow, Amer. Soc. for Microbiol., 2003. Editor, Reviews in Medical Virology, 1990–. Ian Howat Prize in Med. Microbiol., 1975, Wheelwright Prize for Paediatrics, 1977, St Bartholomew's Hosp. Med. Coll.; Wellcome Award, European Gp for Rapid Viral Diagnosis, 1988. *Publications:* The Stealth Virus, 2012; Gut Feeling, 2014; papers on viruses, HIV/AIDS, herpes viruses and cytomegalovirus. *Recreations:* family, music, viruses, bridge. *Address:* Centre for Virology, UCL Medical School, Rowland Hill Street, Hampstead, NW3 2PF. *T:* (020) 7794 0500, ext. 33210.

GRIFFITHS, Paul Dennis, CMG 2015; Chief Executive Officer, Dubai Airports, since 2007; *b* London, 16 Oct. 1957; *s* of Dennis Frederick Griffiths and Jean Griffiths; *m* 2001, Joanna Marsh; two *s* one *d* (and one *s* decd). *Educ:* Richard Hale Sch., Hertford. LRAM 1981; ARCM 1982; FRCO 1984; FRAeS 2011. Manager, Mktg and Res., Reed Publishing, 1980–85; Mktg and Planning Manager, Dragonair Hong Kong, 1985–89; Man. Dir, Trinity Aviation Systems, 1989–91; Executive Director: Virgin Atlantic Airways, 1991–2002; Virgin Rail Gp, 2002–04; Chm. and Man. Dir, Gatwick Airport Ltd, 2004–07. Chm., Bd of Trustees, 2000–07, Vice Pres., 2007–, RCO. Organist, Guildford Cath. Singers, 2003–. Trustee, St Albans Cathedral Trust, 2001–07. Hon. PhD Middlesex, 2015. *Recreations:* music, motorsports, theatre, cycling, collecting motorcycles and model trains, commissioning pipe organs. *Address:* Dubai Airports, Dubai International Airport Building, PO Box 2525, Dubai, United Arab Emirates. *T:* (4) 2162727, *Fax:* (4) 2244074. *E:* paul.griffiths@dubaiairports.ae. *Clubs:* Royal Automobile, Home House; Capital (Dubai).

GRIFFITHS, Rev. Paula Whitmore Llewellyn; Associate Priest, Saffron Walden and Villages (formerly Saffron Walden) Team Ministry, since 2013 (Assistant Curate, 2009–13); *b* 30 June 1949; *d* of Rev. John Whitmore Griffiths and Evelyn Doreen Griffiths (*née* Pearson); *m* 1st, 1971 (marr. diss. 1978); two *d*; 2nd, 2006, Roger John Mance. *Educ:* S Hampstead High Sch. (GPDST); Lady Margaret Hall, Oxford (BA (Mod. Hist.) 1971; MA 1975); Westcott House, Cambridge (Cert. Christian Theology, 2009). Departments of the Environment and Transport, 1972 and 1976–92: Principal, 1982; posts incl. Hd, branches in Planning Land Use Policy Directorate, 1983–87, and Heritage Sponsorship Div., 1987–92; English Heritage, 1992–2002: Head: SE Team, 1993–94; Anglia Team, 1994–99; Asst Regl Dir, E of England Region, 1999–2002. Hd, Cathedral and Church Buildings Div. (Secretary: Council for Care of Churches; Cathedrals Fabric Commn for England), Archbishops' Council, 2002–07; ordained deacon, 2009, priest, 2010. FRSA 1985. *Publications:* articles in conservation and church jls. *Recreations:* travel, walking, poetry, travel writing, watching sunlight on fields. *Address:* Greatford Cottage, Stocking Green, Radwinter, Saffron Walden, Essex CB10 2SS.

GRIFFITHS, Peter; *see* Griffiths, J. P. G.

GRIFFITHS, Peter Anthony, CBE 2013; Chairman: Queen Victoria Hospital NHS Foundation Trust, 2005–15; Foundation Trust Network, 2010–13 (Trustee, 2007–08; Vice Chairman, 2008–10); *b* 19 May 1945; *m* 1966, Margaret Harris; two *s. Educ:* Swansea Technical Coll. Regl admin. trainee, Welsh Hosp. Bd, Cardiff Royal Inf., 1963–66; nat. admin. trainee, Birmingham Reg./Nuffield Centre, Leeds, 1966–69; Dep. Hosp. Sec., E Birmingham HMC, 1969–71; Dep. Dist Administrator, Hosp. Sec., Southampton and SW Hampshire Health Dist (Teaching), 1971–76; Dist Administrator, Medway Health Dist, 1976–81; Actg Area Administrator, Kent AHA, 1981–82; Dist Administrator, 1982–84, Dist Gen. Man., 1984–88, Lewisham and N Southwark HA; Regl Gen. Manager, SE Thames RHA, 1988–89; Dep. Chief Exec., NHS Management Exec. for England, 1990–91; Chief Exec., Guy's and Lewisham NHS Trust, 1991–94; Dep. Chief Exec., King's Fund, 1994–97; Chief Exec., The Health Quality Service, 1997–2004. Non-exec. Dir, Sussex Downs and Weald PCT, 2002–05. Chm., NHS Pensioners' Trust, 2005– (Trustee, 2002–); Trustee, 2010–, non-exec. Mem., Corporate Bd, 2010–, NHS Confederation. *Recreation:* golf.

GRIFFITHS, Prof. Peter Denham, CBE 1990; MD, FRCPath, FRCPE; Professor of Biochemical Medicine 1968–89, and Dean, Faculty of Medicine and Dentistry, 1985–89, University of Dundee (Vice-Principal, 1979–85); Hon. Consultant Clinical Chemist, Tayside Health Board, 1966–89; *b* 16 June 1927; *s* of Bernard Millar Griffiths and Florence Marion Fletcher; *m* 1949, Joy Burgess; three *s* one *d. Educ:* King Edward VI Sch., Southampton; Guy's Hosp. Med. Sch., Univ. of London (BSc 1st Cl. Hons, MD). LRCP, MRCS; FRCPath 1978; FRCPE 1998. Served RN, 1946–49. Jun. Lectr in Physiol., Guy's Hosp. Med. Sch., 1957–58; Registrar, then Sen. Registrar in Clin. Path., Guy's and Lewisham Hosps, London, 1958–64; Consultant Pathologist, Harlow Gp of Hosps, Essex, 1964–66; Sen. Lectr in Clin. Chemistry, Univ. of St Andrews and subseq. Univ. of Dundee, 1966–68. Pres., Assoc. of Clin. Biochemists, UK, 1987–89 (Chm. Council, 1973–76); Member: Tayside Health Bd, 1977–85; GMC, 1986–93; various cttees of SHHD and DHSS, 1969–98. Dir, Drug Development (Scotland), 1982–89. Dir, Dundee Rep. Theatre, 1977–90. FCMI; FRSA. Consulting Editor, Clinica Chimica Acta, 1986–96 (Mem. Editl Bd, 1976; Jt Editor-in-Chief, 1979–85). *Publications:* contrib. scientific and med. jls (pathology, clin. chemistry, computing). *Recreations:* music, gardening, walking. *Address:* 52 Albany Road, West Ferry, Dundee DD5 1NW. *T:* (01382) 776772.

GRIFFITHS, Peter John; higher education management consultant, since 2000; *b* 19 April 1944; *s* of Ronald Hugh Griffiths and Emily Vera (*née* Cockshutt); *m* 1968, Lesley Florence (*née* Palmer) (marr. diss. 1993); two *d. Educ:* Battersea Grammar Sch.; Univ. of Leicester (BA Classics); McMaster Univ. (MA Classics). University of London: Asst to Principal, 1968–70; Asst Sec. to Cttee of Enquiry into governance of the university, 1970–72; Special Duties Officer, Vice-Chancellor's and Principal's Office, 1972–78; Dep. Head, Legal and Gen. Div., Court Dept, 1978–82; Asst Clerk of the Court, 1982–85; Dep. Clerk of the Court, 1985–87; Clerk of the Court, 1987–91; Dir of Resources and Planning, 1991–93; Sec. and Chief Admin. Officer, Charing Cross and Westminster Med. Sch., 1993–97; Dep. Sec., Imperial Coll. Sch. of Medicine, 1997–2000. *Recreation:* choral singing. *Address:* Upland House, Upland Road, Sutton, Surrey SM2 5HW. *T:* (020) 8643 3599.

GRIFFITHS, Prof. Ralph Alan, OBE 2005; PhD; DLitt; FRHistS; FLSW; Professor of Medieval History, University of Wales, Swansea, 1982–2002, now Emeritus; Emeritus Leverhulme Fellow, 2003–05; *b* 4 Nov. 1937; *er s* of Thomas Rowland Griffiths and Marion Lovin Griffiths (*née* Jones). *Educ:* Lewis Sch., Pengam, Gwent; Univ. of Bristol (BA 1959; PhD 1963; DLitt 1983). FRHistS 1966. Research Asst, Bd of Celtic Studies, Univ. of Wales, 1961–64; University of Wales, Swansea: Asst Lectr, 1964–66; Lectr, 1966–71; Sen. Lectr, 1971–78; Reader, 1978–82; Dean of Admissions, 1990–2002; Pro-Vice-Chancellor, 1998–2002. Visiting Professor: Dalhousie Univ., Canada, 1964; Ohio Univ., 1977, 1981; Haverford Coll., USA, 1977, 1981; Lectures: James Ford in English Hist., Univ. of Oxford, 1993; Sir John Rhys, British Acad., 2001; Stenton, Reading Univ., 2001; Virgoe, UEA, 2003; Bond, St George's Chapel, Windsor, 2006. Member: Royal Commn on Ancient and Historical Monuments (Wales), 1990–2009 (Chm., 1999–2009); Hist. and Archaeol Panel, Humanities Res. Bd, 1994–96; Adv. Council on Public Records, 1996–2001; Adv. Council, Inst. of Histl Res., 1996–2003 (Hon. Fellow, 2005). Member, Council: RHistS, 1987–91 (Vice-Pres., 1992–96; Hon. Vice-Pres., 2003–); Royal Instn, S Wales, 2004–09. Hon. Sec., Glamorgan Co. History Trust, 1974–2002; Trustee, Glamorgan-Gwent Archaeol Trust, 1985–98; President: S Wales Record Soc., 1994–97, 2004–07; Histl Assoc., Swansea, 2011–. FLSW 2011. Hon. Fellow, Histl Assoc., 2011. *Publications:* The Principality of Wales in the Later Middle Ages, I: South Wales 1277–1536, 1972; The Reign of King Henry VI, 1981, 2nd edn 1998; (with R. S. Thomas) The Making of the Tudor Dynasty, 1985, 2nd rev. edn 2013; (with J. Cannon) The Oxford Illustrated History of the British Monarchy, 1988, 2nd edn 1998; King and Country: England and Wales in the Fifteenth Century, 1990; Sir Rhys ap Thomas and his Family, 1993, rev. edn 2014; Conquerors and Conquered in Medieval Wales, 1994; (with J. Gillingham) Medieval Britain: a very short history, 2000 (trans. Chinese 2006); (ed) The Fourteenth and Fifteenth Centuries, 2003 (trans. Japanese 2010); The Household Book of Sir Edward Don, 2004; (Gen. Ed.) Gwent County History, (5 vols),

2004–13; (with J. E. Law) Rawdon Brown and the Anglo-Venetian Relationship, 2005; (ed jtly) Gwent County History II: age of the marcher lords, 2008; In Conversation with Napoleon Bonaparte: J. H. Vivian's visit to the island of Elba, 2008; (ed jtly) Hidden Histories: discovering the heritage of Wales, 2008; (ed jtly) Wales and the Welsh in the Middle Ages, 2011; contrib. to books and learned jls. *Recreations:* music, painting, Shakespeare. *Address:* Department of History, Swansea University, Swansea SA2 8PP.

GRIFFITHS, Richard Anthony; Senior Partner, Farrer & Co., 1993–2000; *b* 30 Oct. 1936; *s* of Howel Harris Griffiths and Rena Kelford Griffiths; *m* 1964, Sarah Janet Williams (*d* 1964); *m* 1970, Sheila Mary Wallace; two *d*. *Educ:* Denstone Coll.; Trinity Coll., Cambridge (MA). Admitted Solicitor, 1963; Partner, Farrer & Co., 1966–2000. Dir, London Cremation Co. plc, 2000–. Life Trustee, Sir John Soane's Mus., 1994–2014 (Chm., 1997–2008). Mem. Council, ICRF, 1997–2002. Founder Mem., Resolution (formerly Solicitors Family Law Assoc.), 1982–2000. FRSA. *Recreations:* golf, fishing, theatre, travel. *Address:* Wyndham House, Wickham Market, Suffolk IP13 0QU. *Clubs:* Oxford and Cambridge; Aldeburgh Golf.

GRIFFITHS, Richard Perronet, RIBA; Founding Partner, Richard Griffiths Architects, 1993; *b* 21 Feb. 1954; *s* of Richard Cerdin Griffiths and Pamela Griffiths (*née* Hetherington); *m* 1985, Penelope Roskell; one *s* one *d*. *Educ:* Highgate Sch.; Trinity Hall, Cambridge (BA 1976, DipArch); Architectural Assoc. (Grad. Dip. Conservation). RIBA 1983; AABC. Worked with Frederick Burn, Christophe Grillet and Julian Harrap before setting up Richard Griffiths Architects, 1993. Major projects include: Lambeth Palace, 1998–; Sutton House (NT), 1999–2003; St Pancras Hotel, 2003–; Freston Tower (Landmark Trust), 2002–05; Burghley House, 2002–06; Kenilworth Castle (English Heritage), 2005–. Cathedral Architect: Southwark Cathedral, 1997–2012; St Albans Abbey, 2000–; Russian Orthodox Cathedral, London. Member: Cttee, SPAB, 1993–99; Awards Panel, RIBA, 2004–12. Trustee, Churches Conservation Trust, 2000–06. *Publications:* articles in ASCHB Trans, SPAB News, Architects' Jl, Building Design. *Recreation:* music (bassoon). *Address:* c/o Richard Griffiths Architects, 5 Maidstone Mews, 72/76 Borough High Street, SE1 1GN. *T:* (020) 7357 8788. *E:* richard@rgarchitects.com.

GRIFFITHS, Robert; *see* Griffiths, W. R.

GRIFFITHS, Prof. Robert Charles, PhD; FRS 2010; FIMS; Professor of Mathematical Genetics, University of Oxford, 2000–11, now Emeritus; Fellow, Lady Margaret Hall, Oxford, 1998–2011, now Emeritus; *b* Wagga Wagga, Australia, 17 July 1944; *s* of Noel Charles Griffiths and Evelyn Eunice Griffiths; *m* 1977, Yvonne Joy Fripp; one *s* one *d* (and one *s* from previous marriage decd). *Educ:* Yanco Agricl High Sch.; Univ. of Sydney (BSc Hons 1967; PhD 1970). FIMS 1993. Lectr, Dept of Stats, Macquarie Univ., 1970–73; Department of Mathematics, Monash University: Lectr, 1973–79; Sen. Lectr, 1979–88; Reader, 1989–98; Univ. Lectr, Dept of Stats, Univ. of Oxford, 1998–2011. *Publications:* about 100 articles on mathematical genetics in Theoretical Population Biology, Applied Probability and other jls. *Recreations:* photography, music, walking, cycling, yoga. *Address:* Department of Statistics, University of Oxford, 1 South Parks Road, Oxford OX1 3TG. *T:* (01865) 281237, *Fax:* (01865) 272595. *E:* griff@stats.ox.ac.uk.

GRIFFITHS, Prof. Roderic Keith, CBE 2000; Professor of Public Health Practice, University of Birmingham, since 1990; President, Faculty of Public Health Medicine, Royal Colleges of Physicians of the UK, 2004–07; *b* 12 April 1945; *s* of Tom and Olwen Griffiths; *m* 1st, 1967, Margaret Ash (marr. diss. 1993); one *s* two *d*; 2nd, 1995, Lois Parker. *Educ:* Birmingham Univ. (BSc, MB ChB 1969). Lectr in Anatomy, 1970, in Social Medicine, 1978, Birmingham Univ.; GP in Birmingham, 1975; Dir of Public Health, Central Birmingham HA, 1982; Regl Dir of Public Health, W Midlands, DoH (formerly W Midlands RHA), 1993–2004. Chm., Assoc. of CHCs England and Wales, 1979–81. Mem., Birmingham Lunar Soc., 1992–. *Publications:* A Rag Doll Falling (novel), 2010; articles on stress in bones, and public health in UK. *Recreations:* ski-ing, pottery, sailing very occasionally, creative writing. *E:* rod.griff@gmail.com.

GRIFFITHS, Roger Noel Price, MA Cantab; Membership Secretary, The Headmasters' Conference, 1990–97 (Deputy Secretary, The Headmasters' Conference and Secondary Heads' Association, 1986–89); *b* 25 Dec. 1931; *er s* of late William Thomas and of Annie Evelyn Griffiths; *m* 1966, Diana, *y d* of late Capt. J. F. B. Brown, RN; three *d*. *Educ:* Lancing Coll.; King's Coll., Cambridge. Asst Master at Charterhouse, 1956–64; Headmaster, Hurstpierpoint Coll., 1964–86. Governor: Mill Hill Sch., 1987–92; Tormead Sch., 1987–94; Prebendal Sch., Chichester, 1987–2008; Worth Sch., 1990–99. Mem., Management Cttee, Pallant House Trust, Chichester, 1987–92. Asst to Court of Worshipful Co. of Wax Chandlers, 1985, Master, 1990. MA Oxon, by incorporation, 1960. JP Mid Sussex, 1976–86. *Recreations:* music, theatre, bowls. *Address:* Hanbury Cottage, Cocking, near Midhurst, West Sussex GU29 0HF. *T:* (01730) 813503. *Clubs:* East India, Devonshire, Sports and Public Schools; Sussex (Sussex).

GRIFFITHS, Siân Meryl, (Mrs Ian Wylie), OBE 2000; FFPH, FRCP, FHKCCM, FHKAM; JP; Professor of Public Health, 2005–13, Professor Emeritus, 2014, Founding Director, Centre for Global Health, 2013, and Senior Adviser on Academic Development, 2013, Chinese University of Hong Kong (Director, School of Public Health and Primary Care, 2005–13); *b* 20 March 1952; *d* of late John Daniel Griffiths, FRCS and of Rosemary Marjorie Griffiths (*née* Quick); *m* 1st, 1978, Anthony Chu (marr. diss. 1986); two *d*; 2nd, 1987, Ian Martin Wylie, *qv*; one *s*. *Educ:* Felixstowe College; N London Collegiate Sch.; New Hall, Cambridge (MB BChir 1977; MA). MSc London, 1981. DRCOG 1979; FFPH (FFPHM 1991), Hon. FFPH 2011; FRCP 1998; FHKCCM 2006; FHKAM 2009. Clinical MO, KCH, 1979–80; Res. Fellow, NY, 1981; Dist MO, City and Hackney HA, 1985–87; Consultant in Public Health Medicine, Oxford RHA, 1988–90; Dir of Public Health and Health Policy, SW Thames RHA, 1990–93, Oxfordshire HA, 1994–2002; Consultant in Public Health Medicine, Oxford Radcliffe Hosps NHS Trust, 2002–05; Sen. Fellow, Oxford Inst. for Ethics and Communication in Health Care Practice, Oxford Univ., 2002–05. Hon. Sen. Clin. Lectr, Oxford Univ., 1997–; Visiting Professor: Oxford Brookes Univ., 1999–2005; Inst. of Global Health Innovation, Imperial Coll. London, 2015–; Honorary Professor: Cardiff Univ., 2008–; Guangzhou Med. Univ., 2009–. Specialist Advr to Healthcare UK, 2013–; Associate non-exec. Mem. Bd, Public Health England, 2014–. Mem., Health Policy Forum, IPPR, 1998–2000; Advr, Democratic Health Network, 1999–2001. Co-Chair, Assoc. of Public Health, 1995–99; Chairman: Pharmacy Healthlink, 2003–04; NHS Alliance Health Network, 2004–05; Member Board: NAHAT, 1995–98; FPH (formerly FPHM), 1999–2005 (Treas., 1995–99; Vice-Pres., 2000–01; Pres., 2001–04; Chm., Internat. Cttee, 2004–05); New Opportunities Fund, 1998–2004; Postgrad. Med. Educn Trng Bd, 2003–05; HPA, 2003–05; Mem., Nat. Cancer Task Force, 2001–05; Co-Chm., Hong Kong Govt SARS Expert Review, 2003; Convenor, Task Force on concepts for health care reform, Hong Kong Govt, 2009–. Trustee, Thames Valley Partnership, 1999–2001. Member: Adv. Cttee, Common Purpose, 1999–2003; Central Res. Ethics Adv. Gp, Unilever, 2010–15; Nat. Workforce Develt Bd, 2002–04; Nat. Cycling Strategy Bd, 2002–04; Adv. Gp on Physical Activity, 2002–04. Trustee, RSPH, 2015–. JP Hong Kong, 2011. Hon. Fellow, Cardiff Univ., 2012. Hon. Dr UWE. *Publications:* Indicators for Mental Health, 1990; Creating a Common Profile, 1990; (ed jtly) Prevention of Suicide, 1993; (ed) Perspectives in Public Health, 1999; Health of Rough Sleepers, 2002; Change and Development of Specialist Public Health Practice, 2005; New Perspectives on Public Health, 2006; Public Health and Primary Care, 2006; Routledge Handbook on Global Public Health in Asia, 2014; contribs to med. jls. *Recreations:* spending time with family, films, theatre, grandparenting. *Address:* 37A Hawley Road, NW1 8RW. *Clubs:* Athenæum; Jockey (Hong Kong).

GRIFFITHS, Steffan Daniel Anderson; Head Master, Norwich School, since 2011; *b* Lingfield, 22 June 1972; *s* of Brian Griffiths and Jane Griffiths; *m* 2000, Harriet Richmond; two *s* one *d*. *Educ:* Whitgift Sch., Croydon; University Coll., Oxford (BA Lit Hum; Plumptre Exhibnr 1993; Richard Blackwell Schol. 1992–94); Open Univ. (BA 1st Cl. Eng.). Assistant Master: Tonbridge Sch., 1995–99; Eton Coll., 1999–2006; Usher (Dep. Hd), Magdalen College Sch., 2006–11. Mem., Sports Sub-Cttee, HMC, 2012–. Trustee: Swifts Sports Trust, 2009– (Chm., 2014–); Royal Norfolk Agricl Assoc., 2014–. Gov., City Acad., Norwich, 2011–. *Recreations:* theatre, birdwatching, sport (especially hockey and golf). *Address:* Norwich School, 70 The Close, Norwich NR1 4DD.

GRIFFITHS, Stuart Mark, OBE 2015; Programming Director, Ambassador Theatre Group, since 2015; *b* Castleford, Leeds, 23 April 1963; *s* of George Griffiths and Brenda Griffiths; *m* 2006, Daryl Back; two *d*. *Educ:* Univ. of Leicester (BA Hons 1986). Gen. Manager, Beck Th., Hayes, London, 1987–92; Chief Executive Officer: Wycombe Swan Th., High Wycombe, 1992–2001; Birmingham Hippodrome, 2002–15. *Recreations:* theatre, dance, opera, visual arts, The Archers. *Address:* 48 Acre End Street, Eynsham, Oxon OX29 4PA. *T:* (01865) 882849. *E:* stuartgriffiths123@gmail.com.

GRIFFITHS, (Susan) Lesley; Member (Lab) Wrexham, National Assembly for Wales, since 2007; Minister for Communities and Tackling Poverty, since 2014; two *d*. Wrexham Maelor Hosp.; Constituency Asst to Ian Lucas, MP, 2001–07. Dep. Minister for Sci., Innovation and Skills, 2009–11, Minister for Health and Social Services, 2011–13, Minister for Local Govt and Govt Business, 2013–14, Wales. *Address:* National Assembly for Wales, Cardiff Bay, Cardiff CF99 1NA.

GRIFFITHS, Tania Veronica; QC 2006; a Recorder, since 2000; *b* 7 Dec. 1959; *d* of Robert and Vera Griffiths; two *s* two *d*. *Educ:* Our Lady of Lourdes RC Primary Sch., Southport; Christ the King RC Comp. Sch., Southport; Liverpool Poly. (BA Hons Law 1981). Called to the Bar, Gray's Inn, 1982; Treasury Counsel, 2002–. *Recreations:* I love my football (Liverpool FC), my dogs and my kids (not necessarily in that order!). *Address:* Exchange Chambers, Pearl Assurance House, Derby Square, Liverpool L2 9XX. *T:* (0151) 236 7747, *Fax:* (0151) 236 3433. *E:* griffithsqc@exchangechambers.co.uk.

GRIFFITHS, Trevor; playwright; *b* 4 April 1935; *s* of Ernest Griffiths and Anne Connor. *Educ:* Manchester Univ. BA (Hons) Eng. Lang. and Lit. Teaching, 1957–65; Educn Officer, BBC, 1965–72. Writer's Award, BAFTA, 1981. DUniv York, 2013. *Publications:* Occupations, 1972, 3rd edn 1980; Sam Sam, 1972; The Party, 1974, 2nd edn 1978; Comedians, 1976, 2nd edn 1979; All Good Men, and Absolute Beginners, 1977; Through the Night, and Such Impossibilities, 1977; Thermidor and Apricots, 1977; (jtly) Deeds, 1978; (trans.) The Cherry Orchard, 1978; Country, 1981; Reds (screenplay), 1981 (Writers' Guild of America Best Original Screenplay Award); Oi for England, 1982; Sons and Lovers (television version), 1982; Judgement Over the Dead (television screenplays of The Last Place on Earth), 1986; Fatherland (screenplay), and Real Dreams, 1987; Collected Plays for Television, 1988; Piano, 1990; The Gulf Between Us, 1992; Hope in the Year Two, 1994; Thatcher's Children, 1994; Who Shall Be Happy…?, 1996; Collected Stage Plays, Vol. 1, 1996; Food for Ravens (screenplay), 1998 (RTS Best Regl Prog. Award; BAFTA Cymru Gwyn A. Williams Award); Camel Station, 2001; These are the Times: a life of Thomas Paine, 2005 (adapted for stage, 2009); Trevor Griffiths: theatre plays one, 2007; Trevor Griffiths: theatre plays two, 2007; Willie and Maud, 2008; Bill Brand: the screenplays, 2010; March Time, 2012. *Address:* c/o United Agents, 12–26 Lexington Street, W1F 0LE.

GRIFFITHS, William Arthur; Director, Acklea Homes Ltd, since 2004; Chairman, Fremantle Trust, 2004–11; *b* 25 May 1940; *s* of Glyndwr and Alice Rose Griffiths; *m* 1963, Margaret Joan Dodd (marr. diss. 1988); two *s* one *d*. *Educ:* Owen's Sch., London; Queens' Coll., Cambridge; Univ. of Manchester. VSO, 1959–60. Probation Officer, Southampton, 1965–71; Home Office, 1971–76; Chief Probation Officer, N Ireland, 1977–84; Dir, NCVO, 1985–86; mgt consultant, 1986–95; Principal Inspector, Social Services, Bucks CC, 1995–2002; Asst Dir, Nat. Soc. for Epilepsy, 2002–04. Official Visitor, Ministry of Community Develt, Singapore, 1982 and 1985. Mem., Westminster CC, 1990–94. *Recreations:* literature, travel, horseracing.

GRIFFITHS, (William) Robert; QC 1993; SC (NSW) 1999; Joint Head of Chambers, 4–5 Gray's Inn Square, since 2008; *b* 24 Sept. 1948; *s* of late (William) John Griffiths and of Megan Marjorie Griffiths (*née* Green); *m* 1984, Angela May Crawford; one *s* two *d*. *Educ:* Haverfordwest Grammar Sch.; St Edmund Hall, Oxford (Open Schol.; BCL, MA). Called to the Bar, Middle Temple, 1974, Bencher, 2004; Jun. Counsel to the Crown (Common Law), 1989–93; admitted as Legal Practitioner, NSW, 1998, Sen. Counsel, 1999; Special Advocate, 2004. Mem., Trade Mission to Dubai and Abu Dhabi, London Chamber of Commerce and BIS, 2014; Dir and Mem. Bd, LCCI, 2014–. Chairman: Test Match Grounds Consortium, 1998–2002; First Class Forum Internet Working Party, 2000–02; Special Advr, Prince's Regeneration Trust, 2008–. Marylebone Cricket Club: Member: Cttee, 2000–01, 2001–03 (resigned re. Zimbabwe), 2006–11, 2012–; Estates Sub-Cttee, 1996–2004; Cricket Cttee, 2000–04, 2008–; Indoor Sch. and Coaching Sub-Cttee, 2000–10; Chairman: Laws Sub-Cttee, 2008–14; Develt Cttee, 2009–11; Ambassador on cricket tours to Singapore, Malaysia and Dubai, 2014. Freeman, City of London, 1997. *Recreations:* reading, philosophy, collecting modern first editions, British paintings, 18th and 19th century furniture; cricket (Schoolboy Cricket Internat., Wales, 1966–68; rep. Glamorgan CCC (non first-class), 1967–68, OUCC and OUCC (Authentics), 1968–72), Rugby (Schoolboy Internat., Wales, 1965–66), travel. *Address:* 4/5 Gray's Inn Square, Gray's Inn, WC1R 5AY. *T:* (020) 7404 5252; Selborne Wentworth Chambers, 174 Phillip Street, Sydney, NSW 2000, Australia. *T:* (2) 92334081; Lascelles Great House, Holetown, Barbados, WI. *T:* 4321262. *Clubs:* MCC (Mem. Cttee), Garrick, Lord's Taverners (Trustee, 2011–13).

GRIFFITHS, Winston James, OBE 2012; Chairman: Abertawe Bro Morgannwg University Local Health Board, 2009–12 (Chairman, Bro Morgannwg NHS Trust, 2005–08, Abertawe Bro Morgannwg University NHS Trust, 2008–09); Wales Council for Voluntary Action, 2006–14; *b* 11 Feb. 1943; *s* of (Rachel) Elizabeth Griffiths and (Evan) George Griffiths; *m* 1966, (Elizabeth) Ceri Griffiths; one *s* one *d*. *Educ:* State schools in Brecon; University College of South Wales and Monmouthshire, Cardiff. BA Hons, DipEd. Taught in Tanzania, Birmingham, Barry, Cowbridge. Non-exec. Dir, Welsh Biofuels, 2005–07. Mem., Ct of Govs, Nat. Mus. and Galls of Wales, 1998–2005. European Parliament: MEP (Lab) Wales South, 1979–89; Hon. Life Mem., 1989; a Vice Pres., 1984–87; former Chm., Parliamentarians for World Order, then Parliamentarians Global Action for Disarmament, Develt and World Reform; former Mem., delegn to S Asia. MP (Lab) Bridgend, 1987–2005. Opposition front bench spokesman on: envmtl protection, 1990–92, on education, 1992–94; on Welsh affairs, 1994–97; Parly Under-Sec. of State, Welsh Office, 1997–98. Mem., Speaker's Panel of Chairmen, 2001–05; All-Party Parliamentary Groups: Chairman: British Indonesia, 2001–05; Sierra Leone, 2004–05; Co-Chm., Street Children, 2001–05; Vice-Chm., Botswana, 2003–05; Sec., Southern Africa, 2001–05; Co-Sec., Children in Wales, 2001–05. H of C Rep., EU Convention on Charter of Fundamental Rights, 1999–2000. Member: Labour Movt for Europe (Sec., 2002); Labour Campaign for Electoral Reform. Chairman: Wales Non-Emergency Transport Services Review, 2007–10 (Interim Griffiths' Report, 2010), Non-Emergency Patient Transport Review Project, 2010–12 (Griffiths'

Review Report, 2012); Wales NHS Confederation, 2010–12 (Mem., 2005–12); Task and Finish Gp, Access to Justice (Access to Justice guidebook, 2013). Member: Rural Health Implementation Gp, Wales, 2010–12; Wales Learning Disabilities and Criminal Justice Working Gp, 2010–12. Member: Christians on the Left (formerly Christian Socialist Movement); Amnesty International; Fabian Society; Anti-Apartheid Movement; Socialist Educn Assoc.; Socialist Health Assoc.; Exec. Bd, Internat. Islamic Christian Council for Reconciliation and Reconstruction, 2003–; Vice-Chm., British Cttee for Iran Freedom, 2003–; Chm., ABMU Health Bd, Africa Health Links, 2009–12. Trustee for Wales, Action on Hearing Loss, RNID, 2010–. President: Kenfig Hill and Dist Male Voice Choir, 1986–; Porthcawl Choral Soc., 1993–; Cefn Cribwr Boys' and Girls' (formerly Boys') Club, 1987–2007; Boys' Brigade, Wales, 1994–2004 (Hon. Pres., 2005–). Methodist local preacher, 1966–. *Address:* Tŷ Llon, John Street, Y Graig, Cefn Cribwr, Mid Glamorgan CF32 0AB. *T:* (01656) 740526.

GRIGG, family name of **Baron Altrincham**.

GRIGG, Christopher Montague; Chief Executive, British Land Co. plc, since 2009; President, British Property Foundation, 2012–13 (Vice-President, 2011–12); *b* Basingstoke, 6 July 1959; *s* of Colin and Ann Grigg; *m* 1987, Fionna Stirling; one *s* four *d*. *Educ:* King Edward VI Sch., Southampton; Trinity Hall, Cambridge (BA 1st Cl. Econs 1981; MA). With Morgan Grenfell, 1981–85; Goldman Sachs International, 1985–2004: Man. Dir, 1997–2000; Partner, 2000–04; Treas., 2005–07, CEO, 2007–08, Commercial Bank, Barclays Bank plc. Non-exec. Dir, BAE Systems plc, 2013–. Mem. Exec. Bd, European Public Real Estate Assoc., 2010–. *Recreations:* military history, ski-ing, golf, supporter of England's cricket and Rugby teams. *Address:* British Land Co. plc, York House, 45 Seymour Street, W1H 7LX. *T:* (020) 7486 4466.

GRIGG, Prof. Ronald, PhD; FRS 1999; Professor of Medicinal Chemistry, since 2000 (Professor of Organic Chemistry, 1989–2000), and Director, Molecular Innovation Diversity and Automated Synthesis (Midas) Centre, since 1994, University of Leeds; *b* 1935. *Educ:* Univ. of Nottingham (PhD). Lectr, Dept of Chemistry, Univ. of Nottingham, 1965–74; Prof. of Organic Chemistry, QUB, 1974–89. Co-ordinator, Eur. Network on Cascade Combinatorial Chem., 1998. Lectures: Inaugural Schering Plough, 2008; Syngenta, 2008. Yorks Enterprise Fellow, 2009. Royal Society of Chemistry: Chm., Heterocyclic Gp, 1985–87; Heterocyclic Chemistry Medal, 1985; Tilden Medal and Lectr, 1986; Pedler Medal and Lectr, 1998; Medal for Synthesis, 2000. *Publications:* contribs to sci. jls incl. Tetrahedron, Jl of Med. Chem., Chem. Eur. Jl and Chem. Communications. *Address:* School of Chemistry, University of Leeds, Leeds LS2 9JT.

GRIGGS, Prof. David John, PhD; FRMetS, FTSE; Professor of Sustainable Development: Monash University, Australia, since 2015; University of Warwick, since 2015; *b* 14 April 1958; *s* of Robert William Griggs and Barbara Griggs (*née* Musgrave); *m* 1982, Hillarie Jean Paston; one *s* one *d*. *Educ:* Helsby Grammar Sch. for Boys; UMIST (BSc Hons (Physics) 1979; PhD (Atmospheric Physics) 1982). Post Doctoral Fellow: Univ. of Toronto, 1982–84; UMIST, 1984–86; joined Meteorological Office, 1986: Hd, Sensor Develt, 1987–91; Internat. Manager, 1991–96; Hd, Wkg Gp I, Tech. Support Unit, Intergovtl Panel on Climate Change, 1996–2001; Dir, Hadley Centre for Climate Prediction and Res., 2001–06 and Dep. Chief Scientist, 2005–06; Dir, Govt Business, Met Office, 2006–07; Prof. of Math. Scis, 2007–15, Dir, Monash Sustainability Inst., 2007–15, Monash Univ. CEO, ClimateWorks, Australia, 2007–15. Gen. Sec., RMetS, 1993–96. FTSE 2011. Vilho Vaisala Award, WMO, 1992. *Publications:* co-ed and contrib., Reports of Intergovtl Panel on Climate Change, 1997, 1999, 2001; scientific papers on glaciation processes in clouds, sustainability and sustainable develt to jls incl. Nature. *Recreations:* trying to keep fit, sports, music. *Address:* Monash Sustainability Institute, Building 74, Monash University, Clayton Campus, 8 Scenic Boulevard, Vic 3800, Australia. *E:* dave.griggs@monash.edu.

GRIGGS, Rt Rev. Ian Macdonald; Bishop Suffragan of Ludlow, 1987–94; an Hon. Assistant Bishop, Diocese of Carlisle, since 1994; *b* 17 May 1928; *s* of late Donald Nicholson Griggs and Agnes Elizabeth Griggs; *m* 1953, Patricia Margaret Vernon-Browne; two *s* three *d* (and one *s* decd). *Educ:* Brentwood School; Trinity Hall, Cambridge (MA); Westcott House, Cambridge. Curate, St Cuthbert, Copnor, dio. Portsmouth, 1954–59; Domestic Chaplain to Bishop of Sheffield, 1959–64; Diocesan Youth Chaplain (part-time), 1959–64; Vicar of St Cuthbert, Fir Vale, dio. Sheffield, 1964–71; Vicar of Kidderminster, 1971–83; Hon. Canon of Worcester Cathedral, 1977–83; Archdeacon of Ludlow, 1984–87; Priest-in-Charge, St Michael, Tenbury, 1984–88. Mem., Gen. Synod of C of E, 1984–87. Chm., Churches' Council for Health and Healing, 1990–99. Governor: Bedstone Coll., 1987–93; Atlantic Coll., 1988–2002; Chm., Coll. of the Ascension, Selly Oak, 1992–94. *Address:* Rookings, Patterdale, Penrith, Cumbria CA11 0NP. *T:* (017684) 82064. *E:* ian.griggs@virgin.net.

GRIGGS, His Honour Jeremy David; a Circuit Judge, 1995–2010; Designated Civil Judge for Devon and Cornwall, 2006–10; a Deputy Circuit Judge, since 2010; *b* 5 Feb. 1945; *s* of Celadon Augustine Griggs and Ethel Mary Griggs (*née* Anderson); *m* 1st, 1971, Wendy Anne Russell (*née* Culham) (marr. diss. 1982); two *s* one *d*; 2nd, 1985, Patricia Maynard; two step *d*. *Educ:* St Edward's Sch., Oxford; Magdalene Coll., Cambridge (MA). Called to the Bar, Inner Temple, 1968; Mem., Western Circuit, 1968–; a Recorder, 1990–95. Bar Rep., CCBE, 1990–94. Chm., London Choral Soc., 1986–90. *Publications:* A South African Childhood, 2006. *Recreations:* studying history at the OU, keeping honey bees, walking on Dartmoor. *Address:* c/o Crown and County Court, Southernhay Gardens, Exeter EX1 1UH. *Club:* Victory Services.

GRIGOR, (William Alexander) Murray, OBE 2012; film maker, writer and exhibition designer; Director: Viz Ltd, since 1972; Channel Four Television, 1995–99; *b* 20 June 1939; *s* of James McIntosh Grigor and Katharine Grigor (*née* Murray); *m* 1st, 1968, (Joan) Barbara Sternschein (*d* 1994); two *d*; 2nd, 2011, Carol Høgel (*née* Colburn). *Educ:* Loretto Sch.; St Andrews Univ. (BSc). Film Editor, BBC, 1963–67; Dir, Edinburgh Internat. Film Fest., 1967–72 (Hon. Chm., 1991–94). Mem. Production Bd, BFI, 1968–72. *Films* include: Mackintosh, 1968; Space and Light, 1972; Big Banana Feet, 1975; The Architecture of Frank Lloyd Wright, 1981; Eduardo Paolozzi—Sculptor, 1986 (Rodin Prize, Paris Biennale, 1992); Carlo Scarpa, 1996; The Architecture of Alexander 'Greek' Thomson, 1999; Nineveh on the Clyde (Europa Nostra Award), 2000; The Work of Angels, 2001; (jtly) Is Mise an Teanga (I am the Tongue), 2003; Sir John Soane—British Architect—American Legacy, 2005; Infinite Space: The Architecture of John Lautner, 2008; Space and Light Revisited (two screen), 2008; Contemporary Days, 2010; Ever to Excel (documentary to mark 600th anniv. of St Andrews Univ.), 2012; Beatus—The Spanish Apocalypse, 2014; television series: (jtly) Pride of Place (USA), 1986; Face of Russia (USA), 1998. *Exhibitions:* Scotch Myths, Edinburgh Fest., 1981; Scotland Creates, McLellan, Glasgow, 1990; Seeds of Change, Royal Mus. of Scotland, 1992; The Sixties, Barbican, 1992; The Unknown Genius: Alexander Greek Thomson, Glasgow 1999; John Byrne at 60, Paisley Mus. and Art Galls, 2000. UK/US Bicentennial Fellow in the Arts, 1976; Hon. FRIAS 1994; Hon. FRIBA 1999. Hon. DArts Anglia Ruskin, 2010; Hon. DLitt St Andrews, 2012. Reith Award, RTS, 1990. *Publications:* (with Richard Murphy) The Architects' Architect, 1993; (with Sir Sean Connery) Being a Scot, 2008. *Recreation:* travels with my rant. *Address:* (office) 4 Bank Street, Inverkeithing, Fife KY11 1LR. *T:* 07769 716141. *Clubs:* Chelsea Arts; Scottish Arts (Edinburgh).

GRIGSON, Hon. Sir Geoffrey (Douglas), Kt 2000; a Judge of the High Court of Justice, Queen's Bench Division, 2000–09; Presiding Judge, North Eastern Circuit, 2004–05; *b* 28 Oct. 1944; *s* of Frederic Walter Grigson and Nora Marion Grigson; *m* 1967, Jay Sibbring (marr. diss. 1998); two *s* one *d*. *Educ:* Denstone Coll.; Selwyn Coll., Cambridge (MA). Called to the Bar, Gray's Inn, 1968; Midland and Oxford Circuit; a Recorder, 1985–89; a Circuit Judge, 1989–2000; a Permanent Judge, CCC, 1993–2000. A Dep. Sen. Judge, Sovereign Base Area, Cyprus, 1997–2000; Acting Puisne Judge, Gibraltar, 2012–14. *Recreations:* reading newspapers, walking. *Clubs:* Athenæum, Achilles.

GRIGSON, Sophie; freelance food writer and broadcaster, since 1983; Principal, Sophie's Cookery School; *b* 19 June 1959; *d* of late Geoffrey Edward Harvey Grigson and Jane Grigson; *m* 1992, William Black (marr. diss. 2005); one *s* one *d*. *Educ:* UMIST (BSc Hons Maths). Cookery Correspondent: Evening Standard, 1986–93; Independent, 1993–94; Sunday Times Magazine, 1994–96; Restaurant Reviewer, Independent on Sunday, 1997–98. Presenter: television: Grow Your Greens, and, Eat Your Greens, 1993; Travels à la Carte, 1994; Sophie's Meat Course, 1995; Taste of The Times, 1997; Sophie Grigson's Herbs, 1999; Feasts for a Fiver, 1999; Sophie's Sunshine Food, 2000; Sophie's Weekends, 2003; Sophie in the Souk, 2009; Sophie Grigson in the Orient, 2010; Sophie Grigson in the Home Counties, 2011; Sophie Grigson in Thailand, 2012; radio: Curious Cooks, 1994, 1995; The Food Programme: Pears, BBC Radio 4, 2008. Trustee, Jane Grigson Trust, 1991– (Chairperson, 1993–96, 2007–08). Food Writer of the Year, Restaurateurs' Assoc. of GB, 1992; Magazine Writer of the Year, 1998, Cookery Journalist of 2001, Guild of Food Writers. *Publications:* Food For Friends, 1987; (with J. Molyneux) The Carved Angel Cookbook, 1990; Sophie's Table, 1990; Sophie Grigson's Ingredients Book, 1991; The Students' Cookbook, 1992; Eat Your Greens, 1993; (with William Black) Travels à la Carte, 1994; Sophie's Meat Course, 1995; Sophie Grigson's Taste of The Times, 1997; (with William Black) Fish, 1998; Sophie Grigson's Herbs, 1999; Feasts for a Fiver, 1999; Sunshine Food, 2000; The Complete Sophie Grigson Cookbook, 2001; My Favourite Family Recipes, 2003; Sophie's Country Kitchen, 2003; The First-Time Cook, 2004; Vegetables, 2006; Spices, 2011. *Recreations:* travel, reading, eating. *Address:* c/o Borra Garson, Deborah McKenna Ltd, Riverbank House, 1 Putney Bridge Approach, SW6 3BQ. *T:* (020) 8846 0966.

GRILLS, Michael Geoffrey; a Recorder of the Crown Court, 1982–2000; a District Judge, 1991–2000; *b* 23 Feb. 1937; *s* of Frank and Bessie Grills; *m* 1969, Ann Margaret Irene (*née* Pyle); two *d*. *Educ:* Lancaster Royal Grammar Sch.; Merton Coll., Oxford (MA). Admitted Solicitor, 1961; Partner with Crombie Wilkinson & Robinson, York, 1965; County Court and District Registrar, York and Harrogate District Registries, 1973–90. *Recreations:* music, tennis, golf. *Address:* Cobblestones, Skelton, York YO30 1XX. *T:* (01904) 470246.

GRIME, Prof. (John) Philip, PhD; FRS 1998; Director, Buxton Climate Change Impacts Laboratory, Unit of Comparative Plant Ecology, since 1989, and Professor, 1983–98, now Emeritus, University of Sheffield; *b* 30 April 1935; *s* of Robert and Gertrude Grime; *m* 1st, 1966, Jean Carol Sorensen (marr. diss. 1982); one *s*; 2nd, 2000, Sarah Margaret Buckland. *Educ:* Middleton Grammar Sch., Lancs; Sheffield Univ. (BSc; PhD 1960). Postgrad. researcher, Univ. of Sheffield, 1960–63; Ecologist, Connecticut Agricl Expt Stn, 1963–65; University of Sheffield: Res. Ecologist, Nature Conservancy Grassland Res. Unit, 1965–71; Dep. Dir, NERC Unit of Comparative Ecol., 1971–89. Vice Pres., British Ecological Soc., 1989–91. Foreign Mem., Royal Netherlands Acad. Arts and Sci., 1991; Hon. Member: Lund Ecological Soc., 1992; Ecol Soc. of America, 1998. Hon. Dr Univ. of Nijmegen, Netherlands, 1998. Marsh Award for Ecol., British Ecol Soc., 1997. *Publications:* Ecological Atlas of Grassland Plants (with P. S. Lloyd), 1973; Plant Strategies and Ecological Processes, 1979; (jtly) Comparative Plant Ecology: a functional approach to common British species, 1988; Plant Strategies, Vegetation Processes and Ecosystem Properties, 2001; numerous contribs to scientific jls. *Recreation:* league and friendly cricket. *Address:* Department of Animal and Plant Sciences, Alfred Denny Building, University of Sheffield, Western Bank, Sheffield S10 2TN; 24 Delph House Road, Crosspool, Sheffield S10 5NR. *T:* (0114) 267 1214.

GRIME, Mark Stephen Eastburn; QC 1987; *b* 16 March 1948; *s* of late R. T. Grime, ChM, FRCS and M. D. Grime; *m* 1973, Christine Emck; two *d*. *Educ:* Wrekin College; Trinity College, Oxford (Scholar; MA). FCIArb 1997. Called to the Bar, Middle Temple, 1970, Bencher, 1997; practising Northern Circuit, 1970–; Asst Recorder, 1988–90; Recorder, 1990–2003; Technol. and Construction Recorder, 1998–2003. Chairman: Disciplinary Appeal Tribunal, UMIST, 1980–2003; Northern Arbitration Assoc., 1994–98 (Mem. Council, 1990–94); Northern Circuit Med. Law Assoc., 1999–2002. *Recreations:* antiquarian horology, sailing. *Address:* Homestead Farm, Jackson's Edge, Disley, Cheshire SK12 2JR. *T:* (01663) 766976; Deans Court Chambers, 24 St John Street, Manchester M3 4DF. *T:* (0161) 214 6000.

GRIME, Philip; *see* Grime, J. P.

GRIMES, Hon. Roger (Dale); MHA (L) Exploits, 1989–2005; Premier, Newfoundland and Labrador, Canada, 2000–03; *b* 2 May 1950; *s* of late Fred and Winnie Grimes; *m* 1996, Mary Ann Lewis; one *d*. *Educ:* Meml Univ. of Newfoundland (BSc; BEd 1972; MEd 1988). High Sch. teacher, 1972–89. Pres., Newfoundland and Labrador Teachers' Assoc., 1985–87; Dir, Canadian Teachers' Fedn, 1985–87. Parly Asst to Premier of Newfoundland and Labrador, 1989–91; Minister: of Employment and Labour Relns, 1991–93; of Tourism, Culture and Recreation, 1993–96; of Educn, 1996–98; of Mines and Energy, 1998–99; of Health and Community Services, 2000–01; Leader of Opposition, Newfoundland and Labrador, 2003–05. *Recreations:* recreational hockey, jogging, golf, softball, reading.

GRIMLEY, Very Rev. Robert William; Dean of Bristol, 1997–2009, now Dean Emeritus; *b* 26 Sept. 1943; *s* of William Bracebridge Grimley and Gladys Mary (*née* Draper); *m* 1968, Joan Elizabeth Platt; two *s* one *d*. *Educ:* Derby Sch.; Christ's Coll., Cambridge (BA 1966; MA 1970); Wadham Coll., Oxford (BA 1968; Ellerton Theol Essay Prize, 1974; MA 1976); Ripon Hall, Oxford. Ordained deacon 1968, priest 1969; Asst Curate of Radlett, 1968–72; Chaplain, King Edward's Sch., Birmingham and Hon. Curate, St Mary, Moseley, 1972–84; Vicar, St George's, Edgbaston, 1984–97. Examining Chaplain to the Bishop of Birmingham, 1988–97; Bishops' Inspector of Theol Colls, 1998–2009. Chaplain to the High Sheriff of W Midlands, 1988–89. A Church Comr for England, 2006–08 (Mem., Bishoprics and Cathedrals Cttee, 2005–09). Select Preacher, Univ. of Oxford, 2013. Trustee, Bishop's Palace, Wells, 2005–06. Governor: The Queen's Coll., Birmingham, 1974–97; The Foundn of the Schs of King Edward VI in Birmingham, 1991–97; Bristol Cathedral Sch., 1997–2009; Kingswood Sch., 1998–2008; Bristol Cathedral Choir Sch., 2008–09. Hon. DLitt UWE, 2004; Hon. LLD Bristol, 2009. *Recreations:* reading, travel, languages, bread-making. *Address:* 88 Old High Street, Oxford OX3 9HW. *T:* (01865) 308219. *E:* robertgrimley88@gmail.com.

GRIMLEY EVANS, Sir John, Kt 1997; FRCP, FMedSci; Professor of Clinical Geratology (formerly Geriatric Medicine), University of Oxford, 1985–2002, now Emeritus; Fellow of Green College, Oxford, 1985–2002, now Emeritus; Consultant Physician in Geriatric and General Medicine, Oxford Radcliffe Hospitals, 1985–2002; *b* 17 Sept. 1936; *s* of Harry Walter Grimley Evans and Violet Prenter Walker; *m* 1966, Corinne Jane Cavender; two *s* one *d*. *Educ:* King Edward's Sch., Birmingham (Foundn Scholar); St John's Coll., Cambridge (Rolleston Scholar; MA, MD); Balliol Coll., Oxford (DM); FFPH. Res. Asst, Nuffield Dept of Clin. Med., Oxford, 1963–65; Vis. Scientist, Sch. of Public Health, Univ. of Michigan, 1966; Res. Fellow, Med. Unit, Wellington Hosp., NZ, 1966–69; Lectr in Epidemiology, LSHTM, 1970–71; Consultant Physician, Newcastle Gen. Hosp., 1971–73; Prof. of Medicine (Geriatrics), Univ. of Newcastle upon Tyne, 1973–84. Chairman: Specialist Adv. Cttee on Geriatric Medicine, Jt Cttee for Higher Med. Trng, 1979–86; Cttee on Ethical Issues in Medicine, 2000–; Member: WHO Expert Panel on Care of Elderly, 1984– (Rapporteur, 1987); MRC, 1992–95 (Chm., Health Services Res. Cttee, 1989–92; Chm., Health Service and Public Health Res. Bd, 1992–94); Cttee on Med. Aspects of Food Policy, DoH, 1992–2000 (Chm., 1999–2000); GMC, 1994–99; Central R & D Cttee, DoH, 1997–2003; Royal College of Physicians: Chairman: Examining Bd, Dip. in Geriatric Medicine, 1985–90; Geriatric Medicine Cttee, 1989–94; Pro-censor, 1990–91; Censor, 1991–92; Vice-Pres., 1993–95; Harveian Orator, 1997. Founder FMedSci 1998. Editor, Age and Ageing, 1988–95. *Publications:* Care of the Elderly, 1977; (jtly) Advanced Geriatric Medicine (series), 1981–88; (jtly) Improving the Health of Older People: a world view, 1990; (jtly) The Oxford Textbook of Geriatric Medicine, 1992, 2nd edn 2000; papers on geriatric medicine and epidemiology of chronic disease. *Recreations:* fly-fishing, literature. *Address:* Green Templeton College, Oxford OX2 6HG. *Clubs:* Royal Society of Medicine, Oxford and Cambridge.

GRIMMETT, Prof. Geoffrey Richard, DPhil, DSc, ScD; FRS 2014; Professor of Mathematical Statistics, Cambridge University, since 1992; Master, Downing College, Cambridge, since 2013; *b* 20 Dec. 1950; *s* of Benjamin and Patricia Grimmett; *m* 1986, Rosine Bonay; one *s*. *Educ:* King Edward's Sch., Birmingham; Merton Coll., Oxford (BA 1971; MSc 1972; MA, DPhil 1974); DSc (Oxon) 2010; ScD (Cantab) 2010. Jun. Res. Fellow, New Coll., and IBM Res. Fellow, Oxford Univ., 1974–76; Bristol University: Lectr, 1976–85; Reader, 1985–89; Prof. of Maths, 1989–92; Cambridge University: Dir, Statistical Lab., 1994–2000; Hd, Dept of Pure Maths and Math. Stats, 2002–07; Fellow, 1999–2013, Mem. Council, 2000–02, Churchill Coll., Cambridge. Vis. appts at Cornell Univ., Univ. of Arizona, Univ. of Rome II, Univ. of Utah, UCLA, UBC, Univ. of Paris, etc. Managing Editor: Probability Theory and Related Fields, 2000–05; Probability Surveys, 2009–11. Public Schs Foil Champion, 1968; GB Under 20 Foil Champion, 1970; Member: GB Fencing Team, 1973–77; Olympic Foil Team, 1976. Hon. FIA 1999. *Publications:* (with D. R. Stirzaker) Probability and Random Processes, 1982, 3rd edn 2001; (with D. J. A. Welsh) Probability: an introduction, 1986, 2nd edn 2014; Percolation, 1989, 2nd edn 1999; (with D. R. Stirzaker) One Thousand Exercises in Probability, 2001; The Random-Cluster Model, 2006; Probability on Graphs, 2010; contrib. to learned jls. *Recreations:* mountaineering, music. *Address:* Statistical Laboratory, University of Cambridge, Wilberforce Road, Cambridge CB3 0WB. *T:* (01223) 337957. *W:* www.statslab.cam.ac.uk/~grg; Downing College, Cambridge CB2 1DQ. *T:* (01223) 334800. *Clubs:* Alpine; Climbers'.

GRIMMOND, Steven David; Chief Executive, Fife Council, since 2013; *b* Dundee, 12 June 1963; *s* of David Grimmond and Freda Grimmond (*née* Connolly); *m* 1983, Audrey Krawec; one *s* one *d*. *Educ:* Craigie High Sch., Dundee; Dundee Univ. (BA Politics and Social Admin 1985; MBA 1995). Exec. Officer, DHSS, 1985–87; Sen. Housing Officer, Dundee DC, 1987–90; Prin. Officer, 1990–95, Policy Planning Manager, 1995–98, Dundee CC; Area Manager, Aberdeenshire Council, 1998–2000; Dir, Arts and Heritage, 2000–02, Leisure and Arts, 2002–05, Dundee CC; Hd, Community Services, 2005–09, Exec. Dir, 2009–13, Fife Council. Mem. Bd, Creative Scotland, 2012–. *Recreations:* cycling, football, painting. *Address:* Fife Council, Fife House, North Street, Glenrothes, Fife KY7 5LT. *T:* 03451 555555, ext. 444143. *E:* steven.grimmond@fife.gov.uk. *Clubs:* West End Tennis; Royal Tay Yacht.

GRIMSBY, Bishop Suffragan of, since 2014; **Rt Rev. Dr David Court;** *b* Norwich, 16 Oct. 1958; *s* of Eric and Eileen Court; *m* 1984, Ann White; two *s* one *d*. *Educ:* Univ. of Southampton (BSc 1980; PhD 1983; PGCE 1984); Oak Hill Theol Coll. (BA 1991). Teacher of Chemistry and Physics, Prince William Sch., Oundle, Northants, 1984–88; ordained deacon, 1991, priest, 1992; Assistant Curate: St Botolph, Barton Seagrave, 1991–94; St Andrew, Kinson, 1994–97; Priest-in-charge, 1997–99, Vicar, 1999–2003, St Catherine, Mile Cross; Vicar, St Peter and St Paul, Cromer, 2003–14; Rural Dean, Repps, 2010–14. Hon. Canon, Norwich Cathedral, 2010–14. *Recreations:* family, friends, sport, reading, music, theatre, walking. *Address:* c/o The Diocese of Lincoln, Edward King House, Minster Yard, Lincoln LN2 1PU.

GRIMSEY, Elizabeth Jon, CBE 2002; LVO 1977; Director of Judicial Services (formerly of Policy), 2003–07, and of Corporate Diversity, 2006–07, Legal and Judicial Services Group, Ministry of Justice (formerly Department for Constitutional Affairs); *b* 31 May 1947; *d* of Archibald Charles Sermon and Betty Elaine Sermon (*née* Swanborough); *m* 1976, Colin Robert Grimsey (*d* 2002); one *s* one *d*. *Educ:* Old Palace Sch., Croydon; Univ. of Durham (BA Hons 1968). Home Office: Asst Principal, 1968–73; Principal, 1973–77 and 1983–86; Head of Division: Personnel and Immigration Depts, 1986–90; Prison Service, 1990–96; Dir, Corporate Services, 1996–99, Judicial Gp, 1999–2003, LCD. Trustee, Children and Families Across Borders (formerly International Social Service (UK)), 2005–11. *Recreations:* family, reading, music, theatre going, supporting Crystal Palace FC.

GRIMSEY, Inga Margaret Amy, (Mrs G. R. Dunn); Chairman: East England Committee, Heritage Lottery Fund, since 2010; Saxmundham Free School, since 2012; *b* 20 Oct. 1952; *d* of Robert Jessup Grimsey and Annelise Grimsey (*née* Albeck); *m* 2002, Geoffrey Richard Dunn. *Educ:* Gravesend Grammar Sch.; Regent Street Poly. (BA Hons (Finance) Business Studies). Man. Dir, Anonymous (fashion chain), Storehouse plc, 1983–91; Chief Exec., Ski Club of GB, 1991–96; National Trust: Man. Dir, National Trust (Enterprises), 1996–2001; Territory Dir, 2001–05; Hd, Trading, NPG, 2005–06; Dir Gen., RHS, 2006–09. Gov., Seckford Foundn, 2011–. *Recreations:* ski-ing, opera, gardening, countryside.

GRIMSHAW, John Roland, CBE 2008 (MBE 1996); Engineer and Director, 1981–2008, Chief Executive, 1984–2008, Sustrans; *b* 12 July 1945; partner, Sue Learner; two *s* one *d*. *Educ:* Gonville and Caius Coll., Cambridge (BA Engrg 1966). Engr, Taylor Woodrow, 1963–68; VSO, Uganda, 1969–70; engr, MRM (Bristol), 1971–80. Asst Hon. Engr, Cyclebag, 1977–83. Board Member: Railway Paths Ltd, 1997–2009; Cycling England, 2005–08 (Special Advr, 2008–10); Transport Advr to Mayor of Bristol, 2013–. DUniv York, 2000; Hon. Dr: Strathclyde, 2001; Bath, 2008; Hon. MSc Bristol, 2007. *Publications:* Cycling in the South East of England, 2010; Cycling in the South West of England, 2010. *Recreation:* sculpture. *Address:* 58 Bellevue Crescent, Bristol BS8 4TF.

GRIMSHAW, Mark; Chief Executive, Rural Payments Agency, since 2011; *b* Stafford, 13 Jan. 1961; *s* of Antony John and Thelma Jean Grimshaw; *m* 1984, Nicola Jane; three *d*. *Educ:* Manshed Upper Sch.; RAF St Athan Tech. Sch.; INSEAD Euro-Asia Centre. Served RAF, 1979–83. Swan Nat. Car Rental Gp, 1984–89; Dir, Mercury Communications, 1990–95; Customer Service Dir, UK and Europe, and Sen. Vice Pres. for Service Delivery, Cable and Wireless, 1996–2001; Employer Services Dir, Job Centre Plus, 2002–06; Chief Operating Officer, Strategic Prog. Dir and Man. Dir, Child Support Agency, 2006–11. *Recreations:* supporter of Manchester City FC, holder of Private Pilot's Licence. *Address:* Rural Payments Agency, 21–23 Valpy Street, Reading, Berks RG1 1AF. *T:* (0118) 968 7555. *E:* mark.grimshaw@rpa.gsi.gov.uk.

GRIMSHAW, Sir Nicholas (Thomas), Kt 2002; CBE 1993; RA 1994; Chairman, Grimshaw Architects LLP (formerly Nicholas Grimshaw & Partners Ltd), architects, planners and industrial designers, since 1980; President, Royal Academy of Arts, 2004–11; *b* 9 Oct. 1939; *s* of Thomas Cecil Grimshaw and Hannah Joan Dearsley; *m* 1972, Lavinia, *d* of late John Russell, CBE; two *d*. *Educ:* Wellington College; Edinburgh College of Art; Architectural Assoc. Sch. AA Dip. Hons 1965; RIBA 1967; FCSD (FSIAD 1969); numerous prizes and scholarships. Major projects include: Channel Tunnel terminal, Waterloo (Mies van der Rohe Pavilion Award, 1994, RIBA Building of the Year Award, 1994); British Pavilion for Expo '92, Seville, Spain; Financial Times Printing Plant (Royal Fine Art Commn/Sunday Times Building of the Year Award, 1989); Pusan Internat. Rly Terminus, Korea, 1996; Zurich Airport Expansion, 1996; Regl HQ for Orange Telephones, Darlington, 1996; restoration of Paddington Stn, 1996; restoration of existing Spa and new building, Bath, 1997; Caixa Galicia Art Foundn, La Coruña, Spain, 1997; Berlin Stock Exchange and Communications Centre; British Airways Combined Operations Centre, Heathrow; HQ for Igus GmbH, Cologne; RAC Rescue Services HQ; Satellite and Piers, Heathrow Airport; Research Centre for Rank Xerox; BMW HQ, Bracknell; Herman Miller Factory, Bath; Oxford Ice Rink; Gillingham Business Park; J. Sainsbury Superstore, Camden; Head Office and Printing Press for Western Morning News; redevelopment of Terminal One, Manchester Airport, for MA plc; teaching and res. bldg, Univ. of Surrey; head office for Mabeg GmbH, Soest (RIBA Internat. Award), 1999; Eden Project, St Austell, 2000; Exhibn Hall, Frankfurt Fair, 2000; HQ and factory for Pfeiffer Vacuum, Dortmund, 2000; Plant Sci. Centre, St Louis, USA, 2001; Nat. Space Sci. Centre, Leicester, 2001; Ijburg Bridge, Amsterdam, 2001; HQ and assembly plant for Rolls Royce, Goodwood, Sussex, 2001; NE Wing, RCA, 2001; Millennium Point, Birmingham, 2001; UCL Cancer Inst., 2001; HQ for Lloyds TSB, London, 2002; Spine House, Cologne, 2002; London Stock Exchange, 2003; KPMG Berlin HQ, 2003; Southern Cross Stn, Melbourne, 2006 (Lubetkin Award, 2007; Australian Construction Achievement Award, 2007; Victorian Industry Capability Award, 2007; Victorian Arch. Medal, Walter Burley Griffin Award for Urban Design, RAIA, 2007; William Wardle Public Arch. Award, 2007); high-speed rly stn, Bijlmer, Amsterdam, 2007 (Bldg of the Year, Royal Inst. of Dutch Architects, 2008; Brunel Award, Watford Gp, 2008); Newport City Footbridge, Wales, 2007; Experimental Media and Perf. Arts Centre for Rensselaer Poly. Inst., Albany, NY, 2007 (Structl Engrg Award, 2010); Steel Mus., Monterrey, Mexico, 2007 (Nuevo Leon Arch. Chapter 14th Arch. Biennale; Cemex Bldg Awards, 2008; AIA Honor Award for Arch., 2009; American Soc. of Landscape Architects Honor Award, 2009); New Academic Bldg for LSE, 2008 (Camden Bldg Quality Award, 2009); Front Engrg Bldg, UCL, 2008; K2 London Southbank Univ., 2009; Minerva Bldg, St Botolph's, City of London, 2010; ExCel Phase 2 Develt, 2010 (UK Commercial Property Award); Nunawading Stn, Melbourne, 2010; Newport Stn, S Wales, 2010 (Inst. of Civil Engrg Award, 2011); John Lewis Fashion Pavilion, London, 2012; Cutty Sark, Greenwich, 2012; Via Verde, NY, 2012 (Andrew J. Thomas Award for Housing, 2012); Highpoint Retail Centre, Melbourne, 2013; Stoke on Trent City Centre Bus Station, 2013; Peter Doherty Inst., Univ. of Melbourne, 2013; Queens Mus., NY, 2013; Pulkova Airport, St Petersburg, 2013; Terminal 2 Concourse B, Heathrow, 2014; Reading Station, 2014; Queens Mus., NY, 2014; Fulton Center, NY, 2014. Pres. Council, AA, 1999–2001. Assessor for: British Construction Industry Awards; DoE; British Gas; Scottish Develt Agency; Stirling Prize, 2012. Hon. Mem., Bund Deutscher Architekten, 1997. Hon. FAIA 1995; Hon. FRIAS 2002; Hon. Fellow, Politecnico Milano, 2009. Hon. DLitt: South Bank, 1993; Heriot-Watt, 2008; Edinburgh, 2008; UCL, 2011; Hon. DSocSc Edinburgh, 2010. Awards and Commendations include: RIBA, 1975, 1978, 1980, 1983, 1986, 1989, 1990, 1991, 1994, 1995, 1999, 2001, 2002, 2003, 2004, 2008, 2009, 2013, 2014; Financial Times (for Industrial Architecture), 1977, 1980, 1995; Structural Steel Design, 1969, 1977, 1980, 1989, 1993, 1994, 1995, 1999, 2000, 2001, 2002, 2003, 2007, 2013; Civic Trust, 1978, 1982, 1989, 1990, 1991, 1996, 2007; British Construction Industry Awards, 1988, 1989, 1992, 1993, 1995, 1999, 2001, 2010; Royal Fine Art Commn/Sunday Times Bldg of the Year Award, 1989, 1993, 1994, 1999, 2001, 2004; Constructa Preis for Industrial Architecture in Europe, 1990; Quaternario Foundn Internat. Award for Innovative Technol. in Architecture, 1993; AIA/London UK Chapter Design Excellence Award, 1995, 2001, 2005, AIA State Award, 2013; Nat. Heritage Arts Sponsorship Scheme Award, 1995; Design Innovation Award, 1996; British Council for Offices Award, 1996; Internat. Brunel Award, 1996; Leisure Property Award for best regeneration scheme, 2001; European Award for Aluminium in Architecture, 2001; Archtectl Practice of Year, Transport Architect of Year, World Architect of Year, Building Design Awards, 2008; British Construction Industry Award, 2010; Medal and Dip. for IAA Academician, Internat. Acad. Architecture, Sofia, 2012. *Publications:* Nicholas Grimshaw & Partners: product and process, 1988; (jtly) Architecture, Industry and Innovation: the work of Nicholas Grimshaw & Partners 1966–88, 1995; (jtly) Structure, Space & Skin: the work of Nicholas Grimshaw & Partners 1988–93, 1993; Equilibrium: the work of Nicholas Grimshaw & Partners 1993–99, 2000; Capturing the Concept: the sketchbooks of Sir Nicholas Grimshaw, CBE, PRA, from 1987 to 2007, 2009; Grimshaw: Architecture: the first 30 years, 2011; articles for RSA Jl. *Recreations:* sailing, tennis. *Address:* 57 Clerkenwell Road, EC1M 5NG. *T:* (020) 7291 4141.

See also T. Traeger.

GRIMSTON, family name of **Earl of Verulam** and of **Baron Grimston of Westbury**.

GRIMSTON, Viscount; James Walter Grimston; Assistant Portfolio Manager, Odey Asset Management LLP, since 2010; *b* 6 Jan. 1978; *s* and *heir* of Earl of Verulam, *qv*; *m* 2008, Lady Rosanagh Innes-Ker, *d* of Duke of Roxburghe, *qv* and Lady Jane Dawnay, *qv*; two *s* one *d*. *Educ:* Eton; St Edmund Hall, Oxford (MSc). *Heir:* *s* Hon. John Innes Archie Grimston, *b* 10 Aug. 2010.

See also Countess of Verulam.

GRIMSTON OF WESTBURY, 3rd Baron *cr* 1964; **Robert John Sylvester Grimston;** Bt 1952; *b* 30 April 1951; *er s* of 2nd Baron Grimston of Westbury and Hon. June Mary (*d* 2010), *d* of 5th Baron de Mauley; *S* father, 2003; *m* 1984, Emily Margaret, *d* of Major John Shirley; two *d*. *Educ:* Eton; Reading Univ. (BSc). ACA 1985. Commnd, The Royal Hussars (PWO), 1970–81 (Captain 1976). *Heir:* *b* Hon. Gerald Charles Walter Grimston [*b* 4 Sept. 1953; *m* 1980, Katherine Evelyn (*née* Kettle); two *s* one *d*].

GRIMSTONE, Sir Gerald Edgar, (Sir Gerry), Kt 2014; Chairman, Standard Life plc, since 2007; *b* 27 Aug. 1949; *s* of Edgar Wilfred Grimstone and Dorothy Yvonne Grimstone; *m* 1973, Hon. Janet Suenson-Taylor (marr. diss. 1995); one *s* two *d*. *Educ:* Winterbourne Primary Sch.; Whitgift Sch.; Merton Coll., Oxford (MA, MSc). NATO-CCMS Fellow, Wolfson Coll., Oxford. Civil Service, 1972–86, Asst Sec., HM Treasury, 1984–86; J. Henry Schroder Wagg, 1986–99: Head: Internat. Finance Adv. Dept, 1992–94; Investment Banking, Asia Pacific, 1994–97; Investment Banking, N America, 1997–98; Global Vice-Chm., Investment Banking, 1998–99; Mem., Horserace Totalisator Bd, 1999–2006; Chairman: Candover Investments plc, 2006–11; TheCityUK, 2012–15. Ind. non-exec. Dir, Deloitte LLP, 2011–. HM Treasury Operational Efficiency Prog. Advr, 2008–10; UK Business Ambassador, 2009–10; Mem. Bd, Shareholder Exec., BIS, 2009–; Advr, 2010–, Lead non-exec. Dir and Mem., Defence Bd, 2011–, MoD; Bd Advr, Abu Dhabi Commercial Bank, 2013–. Member: RAF Strike Comd Bd, 2000–07; RAF Air Comd Bd, 2007. Trustee, RAF Mus., 2008–. *Publications:* contribs on pollution to learned jls. *Recreations:* travelling, tidying my office, my friends and family. *Address:* Standard Life plc, 30 Lothian Road, Edinburgh EH1 2DH. *Clubs:* Athenæum, Royal Air Force; Hong Kong, China (Hong Kong).

GRIMTHORPE, 5th Baron *cr* 1886; **Edward John Beckett;** Bt 1813; *b* 20 Nov. 1954; *er s* of 4th Baron Grimthorpe, OBE and of Lady Grimthorpe (*see* Elizabeth, Lady Grimthorpe); *S* father, 2003; *m* 1st, 1992, Mrs Carey Elisabeth McEwen (marr. diss. 2009), *yr d* of Robin Graham; one *s*; 2nd, 2013, Mrs Emma Benyon (*née* Villiers). *Educ:* Harrow. Mem., Jockey Club, 2007–. Chm., York Racecourse, 2012–. *Heir:* *s* Hon. Harry Maximillian Beckett, *b* 28 April 1993. *Address:* Brinkley House, Brinkley, Newmarket, Suffolk CB8 0RB.

GRIMTHORPE, Elizabeth, Lady; Elizabeth Beckett, DCVO 1995 (CVO 1983); Lady of the Bedchamber to HM Queen Elizabeth The Queen Mother, 1973–2002; *b* 22 July 1925; 2nd *d* of 11th Earl of Scarbrough, KG, GCSI, GCIE, GCVO, PC and Katharine Isabel, Countess of Scarbrough, DCVO, K-i-H Gold Medal; *m* 1954, Hon. Christopher John Beckett, later 4th Baron Grimthorpe, OBE (*d* 2003); two *s* one *d*. *Address:* Westow Hall, York YO60 7NE. *T:* (01653) 618225.

GRIMWADE, Sir Andrew (Sheppard), Kt 1980; CBE 1977; Australian industrialist, cattle breeder, arts patron and aged care philanthropist; *b* 26 Nov. 1930; *s* of late Frederick and Gwendolen Grimwade; *m* 1st, 1959, Barbara (*d* 1990), *d* of J. B. D. Kater; one *s*; 2nd, 1994, Marsha, *d* of Hon. Dr Reginald John David Turnbull. *Educ:* Melbourne Grammar Sch.; Trinity Coll., Melbourne Univ. (Exhib. Eng.; BSc); Oriel Coll., Oxford (swimming blue; MA). FRACI, FAIM. Principal, Green Valley Cattle Co., 1959–; Man. Dir, Carba Ind. Ltd, 1960–70; Chairman: Kemtron Ltd, 1964–88; Australian Cons. Ind. Ltd, 1975–82; Founding Chm., Beolite Village Ltd, 2005–; Vice-Chm., Nat. Mutual Life Assoc., 1988–92 (Dir, 1970–92); Dep. Chm., Turoa Ski Resort Ltd, 1986–2001; Director: Commonwealth Ind. Gases Ltd, 1960–90 (Dep. Chm., 1987–90); Nat. Aust. Bank, 1965–85; IBM (Aust.) Ltd, 1971–92; Sony (Aust.) Pty Ltd, 1974–92. Member: Bd, Melbourne UP, 1996–2002; Adv. Bd, Deutscher-Menzies Pty Ltd, 1998–; Dep. Chm., Cert. Aust. Angus Beef Pty, 1996–2003. Mem., first Aust. Govt Trade Mission to China, 1973. Member: Australian Govt Remuneration Tribunal, 1974–82; Bd, Rev. of Victorian Govt Salaries and Allowances, 1980. Pres., Walter and Eliza Hall Inst. of Med. Research, 1978–92 (Mem. Bd, 1963–92; Laureate, 2007); Founding and Life Mem., Miegunyah Fund, Melbourne Univ., 1987–; Patron, Miegunyah Press. Chairman: Australian Art Exhibn Corp. (Chinese Exhibn), 1976–77; Australian Govt Official Estabts Trust, 1976–82; Trustee, Victorian Arts Centre, 1980–90; Emeritus Trustee, Nat. Gallery of Vic, 1990– (Trustee, 1964–90; Pres., 1976–90); Dep. Chm., Art Foundn of Victoria, 1976–90; Dep. Pres., Australiana Fund, 1978–82; Chm., Royal Soc. of Victoria Foundn, 2007–08. Member: Council for Order of Australia, 1975–82; Felton Bequests' Cttee, 1973– (Chm., 2004–). Hon. Life Mem., RACI; Hon. Mem., Royal Soc. of Victoria. *Publications:* Involvement: The Portraits of Clifton Pugh and Mark Strizic, 1968; (with Dr G. Vaughan) Great Philanthropists on Trial, 2006; Storied Windows: casting light on the arts, science and life in Australia 1959 to 2011, an anthology, 2011. *Recreations:* ski-ing, Australian art, limericks. *Address:* PO Box 607, Mansfield, Vic 3724, Australia.

GRIMWOOD, Sam Jayne; *see* Baker, Samantha J.

GRINDLEY, Prof. Nigel David Forster, PhD; FRS 2006; Professor of Molecular Biophysics and Biochemistry, Yale University, 1986–2012, now Professor Emeritus and Senior Research Scientist; *b* 24 Nov. 1945; *s* of Eric Edward Grindley and Evelyn Marion Grindley; *m* Catherine Mary Joyce; one *s* one *d*. *Educ:* Gonville and Caius Coll., Cambridge (BA 1967); Univ. of London (PhD 1974). Mem., Scientific Staff, Central Public Health Lab., London, 1967–73; Postdoctoral Fellow: Biol Scis, Carnegie-Mellon Univ., 1973–75; Molecular Biophysics and Biochem., Yale Univ., 1975–78; Asst Prof. of Biol Scis, Univ. of Pittsburgh, 1978–80; Yale University: Asst Prof. of Molecular Biophysics and Biochem., 1980–83, Associate Prof., 1983–86; Chm., Dept of Molecular Biophysics and Biochem., 2003–06. NATO Postdoctoral Fellow, SRC, 1974–76; Guggenheim Fellow, 1987–88; Vis. Fellow, Brasenose Coll., Oxford, 2007–08. FAAAS 2007; Fellow, Amer. Acad. of Microbiol., 2011. Ed., Molecular and Gen. Genetics, 1985–91; Member, Editorial Board: Jl Bacteriol., 1988–93; Molecular Microbiol., 1990–2003 (Mem., Editl Adv. Bd, 2005–09); Mobile DNA, 2009–13. World Health Organisation: Mem., Immunol. of Leprosy Molecular Biol. Subcttee, Geneva, 1987–90 (Mem., Steering Cttee, 1990–92); Immunol. of Mycobacterial Disease Steering Cttee, 1992–96; Mem., NIH Study Section, Microbial Physiol. and Genetics, 1988–92. Merit Award, NIH, 1991–2001. *Publications:* contrib. to learned jls. *Address:* Department of Molecular Biophysics and Biochemistry, Yale University, Bass Center, 260 Whitney Avenue, New Haven, CT 06520–8114, USA. *T:* (203) 4328991. *E:* nigel.grindley@yale.edu.

GRINDROD, David William; Casting Director, David Grindrod Associates, since 1998; *b* Warwick, 2 June 1952; *s* of William Grindrod and Betty Grindrod (*née* Ellis). *Educ:* Feldon Sch., Leamington Spa; London Acad. of Music and Dramatic Art. Stage manager and co. manager for various prodns in UK and overseas, incl. RSC, 1977–80, Really Useful Gp, 1991–98. Associate Artist, Old Vic Th., 2015–. Mem., Casting Dirs' Guild of UK and Ireland, 1999–. Consultant, Andrew Lloyd Webber Foundn, 2011–. Casting credits include: *films:* Phantom of the Opera, 2004; Mamma Mia! (ensemble), 2008; Nine (dancers), 2009; *television:* How Do You Solve a Problem Like Maria?, 2006; Any Dream Will Do, 2007; I'd Do Anything, 2008; Over the Rainbow, 2010; Superstar, 2012; *theatre:* all Andrew Lloyd Webber musicals; Mamma Mia! (worldwide); Matilda; Once; Chicago. *Recreations:* theatre, film, music, walking. *Address:* (office) 4th Floor, Palace Theatre, Shaftesbury Avenue, W1D 5AY. *T:* (020) 7437 2506. *E:* dga@grindrodcasting.co.uk. *Clubs:* Ivy, Union.

GRINDROD, Prof. Peter, CBE 2005; Professor of Mathematics, University of Oxford, since 2013; *b* Oxford, 22 Nov. 1959; *s* of Alan and Alma Grindrod; *m* 1985, Dora Louise Bennett; three *s* one *d*. *Educ:* Bristol Univ. (BSc Hons Maths 1981); Dundee Univ. (PhD Maths 1984). Res. Fellow in Maths, Dundee Univ., 1983–85; Oxford University: Jun. Lectr, 1985–88, SRC Advanced Fellow in Maths, 1988–89, Mathematical Inst.; Jun. Res. Fellow, Brasenose Coll., 1985–88; Dynamical Systems Gp Leader, Intera Inf. Technologies, later QuantSci, Henley-on-Thames, 1989–98; Technical Dir, and Co-founder, Numbercraft Ltd, Oxford, 1998–2007; Prof. of Maths and its Applications, Univ. of Reading, 2007–13. Visiting Professor: in Applied Maths, Univ. of Bath, 2001–; in Applied Industrial Maths, Oxford Univ., 2005–08. Mem., User Panel, 1999– (Chm., 2000–04), Mem. Council, 2000–04, EPSRC; Mem. Council, BBSRC, 2009–. Mem. Council, Inst. of Maths and its Applications, 1996 (Pres., 2006–08). Mem., Bioinformatics Cttee, Wellcome Trust, 1999–2002. *Publications:* Patterns and Waves: theory and applications of reaction-diffusion equations, 1990, 2nd edn 1995; contrib. numerous papers to learned jls. *Recreations:* published poet, guitarist, football fan (Manchester United). *Address:* Mathematical Institute, University of Oxford, Andrew Wiles Building, Radcliffe Observatory Quarter, Woodstock Road, Oxford OX2 6GG. *E:* peter_grindrod@hotmail.com.

GRINLING, Jasper Gibbons, CBE 1978; Chairman, London Jazz Radio plc, 1989–91, retired; *b* 29 Jan. 1924; *s* of late Lt-Col Antony Gibbons Grinling, MBE, MC, and Jean Dorothy Turing Grinling; *m* 1950, Jane Moulsdale; one *s* two *d*. *Educ:* Harrow (Scholar); King's Coll., Cambridge (Exhibnr, BA). Served War, 12th Lancers, 1942–46 (Captain). Joined W. & A. Gilbey Ltd, 1947, Dir 1952; Man. Dir, Gilbeys Ltd, 1964; Man. Dir, International Distillers & Vintners Ltd, 1967; Dir, North British Distillery Co. Ltd, 1968–86; Dir of Corporate Affairs, Grand Metropolitan, 1981–85, Dir of Trade Relations, 1985–86; Chm., The Apple & Pear Devel Council, 1986–89. Pres., EEC Confedn des Industries Agricoles et Alimentaires, 1976–80; Mem. Council, Scotch Whisky Assoc., 1968–86. CCMI (FBIM 1969). Chevalier, Ordre National du Mérite, France, 1983. *Publications:* The Annual Report, 1986. *Recreations:* gardening, jazz drumming, painting. *Address:* The Old Vicarage, Helions Bumpstead, near Haverhill, Suffolk CB9 7AS. *T:* (01440) 730316.

GRINYER, Clive; Director, Customer Experience, Barclays, since 2013; *b* Southampton, 29 July 1960; *s* of Tony and Hazel Grinyer; *m* 1988, Janis; two *s*. *Educ:* Highcliffe Comprehensive Sch., Dorset; Central Sch. of Art and Design (BA Hons Industrial Design). Founder, Tangerine, 1989–94; Hd, Samsung Studio, Palo Alto, Calif, then Eur. Design Hd, Samsung Electronics, 1994–98; Hd, Eur. Product Design, Fitch Design plc, 1998–99; Hd, Product Design, TAG McLaren Audio, 1999–2001; Dir, Design and Innovation, Design Council, 2001–03; Hd, Customer Experience and Design and Usability, Orange and France Telecom, 2003–08; Dir, Customer Experience, CISCO, 2008–13. Vis. Prof., Glasgow Sch. of Art. Trustee: RSA; Policy Connect. *Publications:* Smart Products, 2000, 3rd edn 2005. *Recreations:* musician - guitarist, classic car owner, sailing. *Address:* 122 Dorset Road, SW19 3HD. *T:* (020) 8544 1785. *E:* clive@clivegrinyer.com.

GRINYER, Prof. Peter Hugh; Emeritus Professor, University of St Andrews, since 1993; *b* 3 March 1935; *s* of Sidney George and Grace Elizabeth Grinyer; *m* 1958, Sylvia Joyce Boraston; two *s*. *Educ:* E Ham Grammar Sch.; Balliol Coll., Oxford (BA, subseq. MA, PPE); LSE (PhD in Applied Economics). Unilever Sen. Managerial Trainee, 1957–59; PA to Man. Dir, E. R. Holloway Ltd, 1959–61; Lectr and Sen. Lectr, Hendon Coll. of Tech., 1961–64; Lectr, 1965–69, Sen. Lectr, 1969–72, City Univ.; Reader, 1972–74, Prof. of Business Strategy, 1974–79, City Univ. Business School; Esmée Fairbairn Prof. of Econs (Finance and Investment), Univ. of St Andrews, 1979–93 (Vice-Principal, 1985–87, Actg Principal). Chairman: St Andrews Management Inst., 1989–96; St Andrews Strategic Management Ltd, 1989–96. Visiting Professor: Stern Sch. of Business, New York Univ., 1992, 1996–98; Imperial Coll., London, 2002–04; Erskine Fellow, Univ. of Canterbury, NZ, 1994. Member: Business and Management Studies Sub-Cttee, UGC, 1979–85; Scottish Legal Aid Bd, 1992–2000; Appeal Tribunals Panel, Competition Commn, 2000–03; Competition Appeal Tribunals, 2003–11. Founding Dir, Glenrothes Enterprise Trust, 1983–86; Director: John Brown PLC, 1984–86; Don and Low (Hldgs) Ltd (formerly Don Bros Buist), 1985–91; Ellis and Goldstein (Hldgs) PLC, 1987–88; Chm., McIlroy Coates, 1991–95. *Publications:* (with J. Wooller) Corporate Models Today, 1975, 2nd edn 1979; (with G. D. Vaughan and S. Birley) From Private to Public, 1977; (with J.-C. Spender) Turnaround: the fall and rise of Newton Chambers, 1979; (with D. G. Mayes and P. McKiernan) Sharpbenders, 1988; (with Dr Foo Check Teck) Organizing Strategy: Sun Tzu business warcraft, 1994; some 55 papers in academic jls. *Recreations:* hill walking, golf. *Address:* 60 Buchanan Gardens, St Andrews, Fife KY16 9LX. *Club:* Royal & Ancient Golf (St Andrews).

GRISHAM, John; author; *b* 8 Feb. 1955; *m* Renée Jones; one *s* one *d*. *Educ:* Mississippi State Univ. (BS Accounting); Univ. of Mississippi (JD 1981). Mem., Miss. Bar, 1981; Law practice, Southaven, 1981–91; Mem. (Democrat), Miss. House of Reps, 1984–90. *Publications:* The Firm, 1991; The Pelican Brief, 1992; A Time to Kill, 1992; The Client, 1993; The Chamber, 1994; The Rainmaker, 1995; The Runaway Jury, 1996; The Partner, 1997; The Street Lawyer, 1998; The Testament, 1999; The Brethren, 2000; A Painted House, 2001; The Summons, 2002; The King of Torts, 2003; Bleachers, 2003; The Last Juror, 2004; The Broker, 2005; Playing for Pizza, 2007; The Appeal, 2008; The Associate, 2009; Theodore Boone, 2010; Theodore Boone: the abduction, 2011; The Litigators, 2011; The Racketeer, 2012; Calico Joe, 2012; Gray Mountain, 2014; *non-fiction:* The Innocent Man, 2006. *Recreations:* reading, coaching baseball. *Address:* c/o Doubleday, 1745 Broadway, New York, NY 10019, USA.

GRIST, John Frank; broadcasting consultant; Supervisor of Parliamentary Broadcasting, 1991–93 (Supervisor of Broadcasting, House of Commons, 1989–91); *b* 10 May 1924; *s* of Austin Grist, OBE, MC, and Ada Mary Grist (*née* Ball); *m* Gilian (*d* 2014), *d* of Roger Cranage and Helen Marjorie Rollett; one *s* one *d* (and one *d* decd). *Educ:* Ryde Sch., IoW; London Sch. of Economics and Political Science (BSc Econ); Univ. of Chicago. RAF course, St Edmund Hall, Oxford, 1942; RAF Pilot, 1942–46. BBC External Services, 1951–53; seconded to Nigerian Broadcasting Service, 1953–56; BBC TV Talks and Current Affairs at Lime Grove, 1957–72, producer of political programmes and Editor of Gallery and of Panorama; Hd of Current Affairs Gp, 1967–72; Controller, English Regions BBC, 1972–77; US Rep., BBC, 1978–81; Man. Dir, Services Sound and Vision Corp., 1982–88. Specialist Advr to Select Cttee on Televising of Proceedings of H of C, 1988–89. Observer, Russian Election, 1993; Advr, Ind. Media Commn, S African Elections, 1994. BP Press Fellow, Wolfson Coll., Cambridge, 1988. Gov., Royal Star and Garter Home, 1986–94. FRTS 1986 (Mem. Council, 1984–88). *Publications:* Grace Wyndham Goldie, First Lady of Television, 2006; The Good Years (novel), 2009; Town and Country (novel), 2011; The Long Afternoon (novel), 2013. *Address:* 4 Burlington House, Kings Road, Richmond, Surrey TW10 6NW. *T:* (020) 8940 6351. *Club:* Reform.

GRIST, Maj.-Gen. Robin Digby, CB 1994; OBE 1979; Director, Gloucestershire Enterprise Ltd, 2001–11; Chairman, Quality South West Ltd, 2003–08 (Director, since 2001); *b* 21 Oct. 1940; *s* of late Lt-Col and Mrs Digby Grist; *m* 1971, Louise Littlejohn; one *s* two *d*. *Educ:* Radley Coll.; Royal Military Acad., Sandhurst. Commnd, Gloucestershire Regt, 1960; seconded to Army Air Corps, 1965–69 (despatches, 1968); CO 1st Bn Gloucestershire Regt, 1979–82; Comdr 6 Airmobile Bde, 1985–86; rcds 1987; Mil. Attaché and Comdr Brit. Army Staff, Washington, USA, 1988–89; Dir, AAC, 1989–92; Dir Gen., AGC, 1992–94. Col, The Gloucestershire Regt, 1990–94, The Royal Gloucestershire, Berkshire and Wiltshire Regt, 1994–2001. Chm., Glos Community Foundn, 2000–05. DL Gloucestershire, 1995–2002. *Publications:* Their Laurels are Green: a short history of The Royal Gloucestershire, Berkshire and Wiltshire Regiment, 1997. *Recreations:* fishing, gardening, military history. *Address:* The Rifles, Gloucester Office, Custom House, Gloucester GL1 2HE.

GRISWOLD, Rt Rev. Frank Tracy, III; Presiding Bishop, Episcopal Church in the United States of America, 1998–2006; *b* 18 Sept. 1937; *s* of Frank Tracy Griswold Jr and Louisa Johnson (*née* Whitney); *m* 1965, Phoebe Wetzel; two *d*. *Educ:* Harvard Univ. (BA 1959); Gen. Theol Seminary; Oriel Coll., Oxford (BA 1962; MA 1966). Ordained deacon 1962, priest 1963; Curate, Church of the Redeemer, Bryn Mawr, Penn, 1963–67; Rector: St Andrew's, Yardley, Penn, 1967–74; St Martin-in-the-Fields, Philadelphia, 1974–85; Bishop Coadjutor of Chicago, 1985–87; Bishop of Chicago, 1987–97. Hon. DD: Gen. Theol Seminary, 1985; Seabury-Western Theol Seminary, 1985; Virginia Theological Seminary, 1999; Nashotah House, Wisconsin, 2000; Univ. of the South, 2001; Berkeley Divinity Sch., 2002; Bexley Hall, 2006; Episcopal Divinity Sch., 2006; Church Divinity Sch. of the Pacific, 2007; Hon. LHD: Episcopal Theol Seminary of the Southwest, 2004; Rikkyo, Tokyo, 2005.

GRITTON, Susan; soprano; Principal with English National Opera, 2000–02; *b* 31 Aug. 1965; *m* Stephen Medcalf; two *c*. *Educ:* Univ. of Oxford; Univ. of London; National Opera Studio. Major rôles include: Liù in Turandot and Micaëla in Carmen, Royal Opera, Covent Gdn; Konstanze in Die Entführung aus dem Serail, Deutsche Staatsoper and Bayerische Staatsoper; Vitellia in La Clemenza di Tito, Blanche in Dialogues des Carmelites, Bayerische Staatsoper, Munich; Elettra in Idomeneo, Netherlands Opera; Countess in Le Nozze di Figaro, ENO; Donna Anna in Don Giovanni, Opera de Montréal and Bolshoi; Ellen Orford in Peter Grimes, La Scala, Opera Australia and New Nat. Th., Tokyo; Countess Madeleine in Capriccio, Tatyana in Eugene Onegin, Grange Park Opera; Female Chorus in Rape of Lucretia, Snape Maltings; title rôles include: Theodora, Glyndebourne; Rodelinda, Bayerische Staatsoper, Munich; The Bartered Bride, Royal Opera, Covent Garden; The Cunning Little Vixen, ENO; has performed with Rome Opera, Teatro la Fenice, Venice, Th. des Champs Elysées, Paris and Mostly Mozart Fest., NY. Recitalist at Wigmore Hall (solo début, 1994), Lincoln Centre, NY, and Oxford Lieder Fest.; has performed in concert with many orchestras including BBC orchs, LSO, Orch. of the Age of Enlightenment, Berlin Philharmonic and NY Philharmonic. Has made numerous recordings. Arts Foundn Fellowship, 1994. Kathleen Ferrier Meml Prize, 1994. *Address:* c/o Askonas Holt Ltd, Lincoln House, 300 High Holborn, WC1V 7JH.

GROARKE, Ven. Nicola Jane; Archdeacon of Dudley, since 2014; *b* London, 2 June 1962; *d* of Basil and Thelma Barnett; *m* 1986, Philip Groarke (*d* 1992). *Educ:* Univ. of Lancaster (BA Hons 1984); Ridley Hall, Cambridge (CTM 2000). Sen. Marketing Manager, Elsevier Sci. Publishers, 1985–95; Bereavement Services Co-ord., Sobell House Hospice, 1985–88; ordained deacon, 2000, priest, 2001; Curate/Associate Vicar, Ascension, Balham Hill, 2000–08; Vicar, St Stephen's, Canonbury, 2008–13. *Recreations:* hill-walking, cycling, horse riding, gardening, entertaining. *Address:* 15 Worcester Road, Droitwich, Worcs WR9 8AA. *T:* (01905) 773301. *E:* NGroarke@cofe-worcester.org.uk.

GROBEL, His Honour Peter Denis Alan Christian Joseph; a Circuit Judge, 2001–14; *b* 11 Aug. 1944; *s* of Cyril Peter Grobel and Kathleen (*née* Donaghy); *m* 1975, Susan Twemlow, LRAM; three *s* one *d*. *Educ:* Mt St Mary's Coll.; University Coll. London (LLB Hons). Called to the Bar, Lincoln's Inn, 1967; in practice at common law bar, 1971–2001; a Recorder, SE Circuit, 1991–2001. Chm., Special Educnl Needs Tribunal, 1994–2001. Chm. of Govs, St Teresa's Sch., Effingham, 2002–09.

GROCOCK, Dr (Catherine) Anne; Executive Director, Royal Society of Medicine, 1997–2006; *b* 7 March 1947; *d* of late Arthur Raymond Grocock and Alice Grace Grocock. *Educ:* Westonbirt Sch.; St Anne's Coll., Oxford (BA Zool. 1968; MA, DPhil 1973). University of Oxford: Deptl Demonstrator in Human Anatomy, 1973–79; Deptl Res. Asst, 1979–80 and 1982–85, and ICRF Res. Fellow, 1985–89, Dept of Human Anatomy; Lectr in Anatomy, Merton Coll., Oxford, 1977–80 and 1985–89; Bursar and Official Fellow, St Antony's Coll., Oxford, 1990–97; Asst Registrar, Univ. of Oxford, 2006–10. Chm., Reproduction Res. Inf. Services Ltd, 1988–93. Member: Defence Estates Audit Cttee, 2006–10; Veterinary Labs Agency Owners' Adv. Bd, 2007–11; Defence Storage and Distribution Agency Audit Cttee, 2008–10; Standards Cttee, Gen. Optical Council, 2010–. Non-exec. Dir, Oxford Health NHS Foundn Trust (formerly Oxfordshire and Bucks Mental Health Trust), 2008–. Trustee: Nat. Mus. Sci. and Industry, 1996–2006 (Chm. Audit Cttee, 1997–2006; Dep. Chm. of Trustees, 2002–06); Royal Med. Benevolent Fund, 1998–2004; Nuffield Oxford Hosp. Fund, 2001– (Chm., 2005–). Member: Court, ICSTM, 2001–06; Council, Taunton Sch., 1990–2001; Gov., Westonbirt Sch., 1991–97. Trustee, Oxford Soc., 1995–2003; Pres., ASM, St Anne's Coll., Oxford, 1997–2000. FRSA 2000. *Publications:* contribs to learned jls in reproductive physiology. *Recreations:* gardens, opera, sculpture.

GROCOTT, family name of **Baron Grocott**.

GROCOTT, Baron *cr* 2001 (Life Peer), of Telford in the County of Shropshire; **Bruce Joseph Grocott;** PC 2002; Captain of the Hon. Corps of Gentleman at Arms (Government Chief Whip in the House of Lords), 2002–08; Chancellor, Leicester University, since 2013; *b* 1 Nov. 1940; *s* of Reginald Grocott and Helen Grocott (*née* Stewart); *m* 1965, Sally Barbara Kay Ridgway; two *s*. *Educ:* Hemel Hempstead Grammar Sch.; Leicester and Manchester Univs. BA (Pol), MA (Econ). Admin. Officer, LCC, 1963–64; Lectr in Politics, Manchester Univ., Birmingham Polytechnic, and N Staffs Polytechnic, 1964–74. Television presenter and producer, 1979–87. Chm., Finance Cttee, Bromsgrove UDC, 1972–74. Contested (Lab): SW Herts, 1970; Lichfield and Tamworth, Feb. 1974, 1979; The Wrekin, 1983. MP (Lab): Lichfield and Tamworth, Oct. 1974–1979; The Wrekin, 1987–97; Telford, 1997–2001. Parliamentary Private Secretary: to Minister for Local Govt and Planning, 1975–76; to Minister of Agriculture, 1976–78; Dep. Shadow Leader, H of C, 1987–92; Opposition front bench spokesman on foreign affairs, 1992–93; PPS to Leader of the Opposition, 1994–97, to Prime Minister, 1997–2001; a Lord in Waiting (Govt Whip), 2001–02. Mem., Select Cttee on Nat. Heritage, 1994–95. *Recreations:* sport, steam railways. *Address:* House of Lords, SW1A 0PW. *Club:* Trench Labour.

GROCOTT, Susan; QC 2008; a Recorder, since 2003; Deputy High Court Judge, Family Division, since 2010; *b* Rochdale, 30 March 1963; *d* of late Peter and Joan Grocott. *Educ:* Oulder Hill Community Sch., Rochdale; Exeter Coll., Oxford (BA). Called to the Bar, Middle Temple, 1986. *Recreations:* literature, shopping, fine dining. *Address:* Deans Court Chambers, 24 St John Street, Manchester M3 4DF. *T:* (0161) 214 6000, *Fax:* (0161) 214 6001. *E:* grocott@deanscourt.co.uk.

GRODZINSKI, Samuel Marc; QC 2011; *b* London, 12 Feb. 1968; *s* of Emmanuel Grodzinski and Vera Grodzinski; *m* 1993, Marion Baker; three *s* one *d*. *Educ:* University College Sch., London; St Anne's Coll., Oxford (BA Juris.). Admitted Solicitor, 1993; Solicitor, 1993–95; called to the Bar, Middle Temple, 1996; in practice as a barrister, specialising in public law and tax law, 1996–; Mem., Attorney Gen.'s Panel of Civil Counsel, 1997–2011. *Recreations:* walking, reading, ski-ing. *Address:* Blackstone Chambers, Blackstone House, Temple, EC4Y 9BW. *T:* (020) 7583 1770. *E:* samgrodzinski@blackstonechambers.com.

GROENING, Matthew Abram; cartoonist; *b* Portland, Oregon, 15 Feb. 1954; *s* of late Homer Philip Groening and Margaret Ruth Groening (*née* Wiggum); *m* 1987, Deborah Lee Caplan (marr. diss. 1999); two *s*. *Educ:* Lincoln High Sch., Portland, Oregon; Evergreen State Coll. (BA 1977). Worked at LA Reader, 1979–85; cartoonist, weekly comic strip, Life in Hell, 1980–2012; creator: The Simpsons, interludes on The Tracey Ullman Show, 1987–89; TV series, The Simpsons, 1990– (also Exec. Prod.); TV series, Futurama (also Co-developer), 1999–2003, 2008–; Exec. Prod., TV film, Olive the Other Reindeer, 1999; The Simpsons Movie, 2007. Co-founder, Life in Hell, Inc., 1985; President: Matt Groening Prodns, Inc., 1988–; Bongo Entertainment, Inc., 1993–; Founder and Publisher: Bongo Comics Gp, 1993–; Zongo Comics, 1995. *Publications:* Love is Hell, 1985; Work is Hell, 1986; School is Hell, 1987; Childhood is Hell, 1988; Greetings from Hell, 1989; Akbar and Jeff's Guide to Life, 1989; The Postcards That Ate My Brain, 1990; The Big Book of Hell, 1990; The Simpsons Xmas Book, 1990; Greetings from the Simpsons, 1990; With Love from Hell, 1991; The Simpsons Rainy Day Fun Book, 1991; The Simpsons Uncensored Family Album, 1991; The Simpsons Student Diary, 1991; How to Go to Hell, 1991; Maggie Simpson's Alphabet Book, 1991; Maggie Simpson's Counting Book, 1991; Maggie Simpson's Book of Colors and Shapes, 1991; Maggie Simpson's Book of Animals, 1991; The Road to Hell, 1992; The Simpsons Fun in the Sun Book, 1992; Making Faces with the Simpsons, 1992; Bart Simpson's Guide to Life, 1993; The Simpsons Ultra-Jumbo Rain-Or-Shine Fun Book, 1993; Cartooning with the Simpsons, 1993; Bongo Comics Group Spectacular, 1993; Binky's Guide to Love, 1994; Simpsons Comics Extravaganza, 1994; Simpsons Comics Spectacular, 1994; Bartman: the best of the best, 1994; Simpsons Comics Simps-O-Rama, 1995; Simpsons Comics Strike Back, 1995; Simpsons Comics Wing Ding, 1997; The Huge Book of Hell, 1997; A Little Book of Hell, 2006; The Simpsons Forever - and Beyond!, 2006. *Address:* c/o Fox Broadcasting Company, PO Box 900, Beverly Hills, CA 90213, USA.

GROGAN, John Timothy; *b* 24 Feb. 1961; *s* of late John Martin Grogan and Maureen Grogan (*née* Jennings). *Educ:* St Michael's Coll., Leeds; St John's Coll., Oxford (BA Hons 1982; Pres., Student Union, 1982). Asst to Leader, Wolverhampton Council, 1985–87; Communications Dir, Leeds CC, 1987–94; Press Officer, Eur. Parly Lab. Party, 1994–95; Conf. Organiser, Yorks, 1995–97. Contested (Lab): Selby, 1987, 1992; York, EP elecn, 1989. MP (Lab) Selby, 1997–2010. Contested (Lab) Keighley, 2015. *Recreations:* running, football, keen supporter of Bradford City FC and Yorks CCC. *Club:* Yorks CC.

GRONN, Prof. Peter Christian, PhD; Professor of Education, 2008–15, now Emeritus, and Head, Faculty of Education, 2011–14, University of Cambridge; Fellow of Hughes Hall, Cambridge, 2009–14, now Quondam Fellow; *b* Melbourne, 15 Nov. 1946; *s* of Lorenz Christian Gronn and Ena Winifred Gronn; *m* 1972, Barbara Jean Reith; one *d* (and one *d* decd). *Educ:* Canterbury State Sch.; Camberwell Central Sch.; Camberwell High Sch.; Univ. of Melbourne (BA Hons 1968; DipEd 1969); Monash Univ. (BEd 1973; PhD 1979). Teacher, Educn Dept of Vic, Australia, 1970–73; Lectr in Politics, State Coll. of Vic, Burwood, 1974–79; Faculty of Education, Monash University: Lectr, 1980–84; Sen. Lectr, 1985–94; Associate Prof., 1995–2003; Prof. of Educn, 2003–07; Prof. Emeritus, 2014; Prof. of Public Service, Educnl Leadership and Mgt, Dept of Educnl Studies, Univ. of Glasgow, 2007–08. Fellow, Australian Council of Educnl Leaders, 1997. FRSA 2004. FAcSS (AcSS 2012). *Publications:* The Making of Educational Leaders, 1999; The New Work of Educational Leaders, 2003; contrib. articles to jls, incl. Leadership Qly, Jl Educnl Admin, Australian Jl Educn, Australian Historical Studies. *Recreations:* reading, music, travel, walking, sport, gardening, house renovating.

GRONOW, David Gwilym Colin, MSc, PhD; Central Member, Engineering, Marketing and Research, Electricity Council, 1985–90, retired; *b* Leigh-on-Sea, 13 Jan. 1929; *s* of David Morgan Gronow and Harriet Hannah Gronow; *m* 1st, 1953, Joan Andrew Bowen Jones (marr. diss. 1970); one *s* one *d*; 2nd, 1970, Rosemary Freda Iris Keys. *Educ:* North Street Elem. Sch., Leigh-on-Sea; Grammar Sch., Swansea; University Coll. London (MSc, PhD). Institute of Aviation Medicine, RAF Farnborough, Hants: Jun. Technician, 1951–53; Sci. Officer, then Sen. Sci. Officer, 1953–57; Sen. Sci. Officer, UKAEA, Capenhurst, Cheshire, 1957; Second Asst Engr, then Sen. Asst Engr, CEGB, HQ Operations Dept, London, 1957–64; Asst Commercial Officer/Asst Chief Commercial Officer/Chief Commercial Officer, SSEB, Glasgow, 1964–78; Marketing Advr, 1978–80, Commercial Advr, 1980–85, Electricity Council, London. *Recreations:* travel, bird watching, theatre, horse racing, the stock market, Southampton FC. *Address:* 8 Arundel Way, Highcliffe, Christchurch, Dorset BH23 5DX.

GROOM, Brian William Alfred; writer and editorial consultant; UK Business and Employment Editor, Financial Times, 2009–14; *b* 26 April 1955; *s* of Fred and Muriel Groom; *m* 1980, Carola May Withington; one *s* one *d*. *Educ:* Manchester Grammar Sch.; Balliol Coll., Oxford (BA Hons). Journalist: Goole Times, 1976–78; Financial Times, 1978–88; Dep. Editor, 1988–94, Editor, 1994–97, Scotland on Sunday; Financial Times: British and Regl Affairs Ed., 1997–2000; Political Ed., 2000–02; Ed., European Edn, 2002–05; Ed., Comment and Analysis, 2005–09. *Recreations:* cricket and football, walking, Britain's culture and history. *Address:* Alphin House, 69 Chew Valley Road, Greenfield, Oldham OL3 7JG. *T:* (01457) 878278.

GROOM, Maj.-Gen. John Patrick, CB 1984; CBE 1975 (MBE 1963); Director General, Guide Dogs for the Blind Association, 1983–89; *b* Hagley, Worcs, 9 March 1929; *s* of Samuel Douglas Groom and Gertrude Groom (*née* Clinton); *m* 1951, Jane Mary Miskelly; three *d*. *Educ:* King Charles I Sch., Kidderminster; Royal Military Academy, Sandhurst. Enlisted as Sapper, Dec. 1946; commnd into RE, 1949; regimental service, N Africa, Egypt, Singapore, Malaya, UK, 1949–59; sc Camberley, 1960; War Office, 1961–63; regimental service, UK, Aden, 1963–65 (despatches); Directing Staff, Staff Coll., 1965–68; Regimental Comdr, BAOR, 1968–70; MoD, Military Operations, 1970–71; Dep. Sec., Chiefs of Staff Cttee, 1971–73; HQ Near East Land Forces, Cyprus, 1973–75; RCDS 1976; Comdr, Corps of Royal Engineers, BAOR (Brig.), 1976–79; Chief Engineer, HQ BAOR, 1979–82; Head of Army Trng Rev. Team, MoD (Army), 1982–83. Col Comdt, 1983–91, Rep. Col Comdt, 1986, RE. Chairman: GDBA (Trading Co.) Ltd, 1984–89; GDBA (Recreational Services) Co. Ltd, 1986–89; (non-exec.) BKP Environmental Services Ltd, 1992–99; Dir, GDBA (Pension Fund Trustees) Ltd, 1985–89; Hon. Vice-Pres., Internat. Fedn of Guide Dog Schs, 1989–. Chm., Reach Foundn, 1993–96; Member: Adv. Bd, Talking Newspapers, 1988; Council, Oakhaven Hospice, 1992–96. Governor: Gordon's Sch., Woking, 1982–88; Sandle Manor Sch., Fordingbridge, 1984–88. Vice-Chm., Solent Protection Soc., 1994–99; Chm., Adv. Bd, Yarmouth Harbour Comrs, 1997–2002. Member: RYA, 1982–; ASA, 1982–. FCMI (FBIM 1979); FIPlantE 1976; Fellow, RSPB 1975. Freeman, City of London, 1978; Liveryman, Worshipful Co. of Plumbers, 1978–92. *Recreations:* ocean sailing, country pursuits, the environment. *Address:* Medlar House, 6 Grove Pastures, Lymington, Hants SO41 3RG. *T:* (01590) 675710. *Clubs:* Royal Ocean Racing; Royal Engineer Yacht; Royal Lymington Yacht; British Kiel Yacht (Germany) (Life Mem.); Kieler Yacht (Germany) (Hon. Mem.).

GROOM, Michael John, FCA; President, Institute of Chartered Accountants in England and Wales, 2001–02; *b* 18 July 1942; *s* of Thomas Rowland Groom and Eliza Groom; *m* 1966, Sheila Mary Cartwright; two *d*. *Educ:* St Chad's Grammar Sch., Wolverhampton; Cotton Coll., N Staffs. FCA 1964. Articled, Plevey & Co., Chartered Accountants, 1958–63; Sen. Clerk, Dixon Hopkinson, Chartered Accountants, 1963–65; Sec. and Dir, Thorneville Properties Ltd/Aldridge Builders Ltd, 1965–67; Manager/Partner, Camp Ravenscroft & Co., Chartered Accountants, 1967–71; in practice as chartered accountant, 1971–76, 1981–89; Partner, Tansley Witt/Binder Hamlyn, Chartered Accountants, 1976–81. Mem. Council, ICAEW, 1975–2004. Dep. Chm., Financial Reporting Council, 2001–02; Chm., CCAB, 2001–02; Mem., Takeover Panel, 2001–02. Non-exec. dir of cos; lectr and consultant on strategy formulation in the medium-sized business, the rôle of the non-exec. director, mgt and financial advice, professional practice mgt. Freeman, City of London, 1977; Liveryman, Chartered Accountants' Co., 1977 (Mem., Ct of Assts, 1994–2006); Trustee, Chartered Accountants' Livery Charity, 2004–06. Hon. DBA Wolverhampton, 2003. *Publications:* The Chartac Administration Manual, 1975; Financial Management in the Professional Office, 1977; (jtly) Cash Control in the Smaller Business, 1978; (jtly) Current Cost Accounting the Easy Way, 1980; (jtly) Budgeting and Cash Management, 1981; joint author and series editor, 1975–81: The Chartac Accounting Manual; The Chartac Auditing Manual; The Chartac Taxation Manual; The Chartac Accounting and Auditing Model File. *Recreations:* ballet, theatre, music, photography, travel, food and wine. *Address:* 14 High Meadows, Compton, Wolverhampton WV6 8PH. *T:* (01902) 753816. *Club:* Albert Lawn Tennis (Wolverhampton).

GROOM, Hon. Raymond John, AO 2010; barrister and solicitor; MHA (L) for Denison, Tasmania, 1986–2001; Chairman, Southern Cross Care (Tasmania) Inc., since 2006; *b* 3 Sept. 1944; *s* of Raymond James Groom and Eileen Margaret (*née* Waters); *m* 1967, Gillian M. Crisp; four *s* two *d*. *Educ:* Burnie High Sch., Tasmania; Univ. of Melbourne (LLB 1967). Barrister and Solicitor, Supreme Court, Victoria, 1968, Tasmania, 1970; practised: Melbourne, 1968–69; Burnie, 1969–76; Partner, Hudson and Mann, Tasmania, 1969–76. Sec., Law Liby Cttee, NW Tasmania Law Soc., 1969–75; Mem. Council, Bar Assoc., Tasmania, 1974–75. MHR, Braddon, Tasmania, 1975–84; Federal Minister for: Envmt, Housing, Community Develt, 1977–78; Housing and Construction, 1978–80; Mem., Parly Delegn to Bangladesh, India, Sri Lanka, 1978; Leader, Australian Delegn to ESCAP UN Meeting, Manila (Chm., First Session), 1979; Chm., S Pacific Commonwealth and State Housing Ministers Conf., NZ, 1980; Tasmania: Minister for Forests, Sea Fisheries and Mines, and Minister Assisting the Premier, 1986–89; Dep. Premier, 1988; Dep. Leader, Liberal Party, 1986–91; Shadow Attorney-General and Shadow Minister for Deregulation, 1989–91; Leader of Opposition, Shadow Treas. and Shadow Minister for Commonwealth and State Relns, 1991–92; Premier of Tasmania, 1992–96; Treas. and Minister for Economic Develt, 1992–93; Minister for State Develt and Resources, for Forests, and for Mines, 1993–96; Attorney-General, Minister for Justice, Minister for Tourism and for Workplace Standards, 1996–98; Shadow Minister: for Justice and for Tourism, 1998–99; for Industrial Relns and for Workplace Standards, 1998–2001; for Educn and Trng and for Public Sector Mgt, 1999–2001; for Consumer Affairs, for Justice and Shadow Attorney-Gen., 2001. Chm., Australian Construction Industry Council, 1979–80. Dep. Pres., Administrative Appeals Tribunal (Australia), 2004–. Stolen Generations Assessor, Tasmania, 2007. *Recreations:* family, painting, golf, football. *Address:* 25 Cromwell Street, Battery Point, Tas 7004, Australia. *T:* (3) 62248181. *Clubs:* Melbourne Cricket; Royal Hobart Golf; Royal Yacht (Tasmania).

GROOMBRIDGE, Rev. Jeremy Carl, CB 2008; independent consultant and Director, LCS Services; Curate, All Saints Church, Sanderstead, since 2015; *b* Derby, 10 Oct. 1955; *s* of late Denis Groombridge and of Betty Groombridge; *m* 1983, Sandra Young; three *s*. *Educ:* Spondon Park Grammar Sch.; Wilmorton Coll. Joined DHSS, 1974; Private Sec. to Sec. of State for Health and Social Security, 1988–90; Hd, Policy Develt Unit, Benefits Agency, Leeds, 1990–92; Hd, Unemployment Benefit Policy, 1992–94, Policy Manager, Jobseekers and Incentives, 1994–2001, DSS; Dir, Implementation Prog., 2002–06, Dir, 2006–11, Jobcentre Plus; Dir, Universal Credit Prog., DWP, 2011–13. Ordained deacon, 2015. Chair, European Skills/Competences, Qualifications and Occupations Bd, 2011–. Dir, Reedham Trust, 2013–. Gov., Beaumont Sch., Purley, 2014–. Mem., Scotch Malt Whisky Soc. *Recreations:* family, church organist, training for ordained ministry in C of E, photography, travel, whisky. *Address:* All Saints Church, Onslow Gardens, Sanderstead, Surrey CR2 9AB.

GROOTENHUIS, Prof. Peter, FREng, FIMechE; Professor of Mechanical Engineering Science, Imperial College of Science, Technology and Medicine, 1972–89, now Emeritus Professor and Senior Research Fellow; *b* 31 July 1924; *yr s* of Johannes C. Grootenhuis and Anna C. (*née* van den Bergh); *m* 1954, Sara J. Winchester, *oc* of late Major Charles C. Winchester, MC, The Royal Scots (The Royal Regt), and Margaret I. (*née* de Havilland); one *d* one *s*. *Educ:* Nederlands Lyceum, The Hague; City and Guilds College. BSc MechEng 1944, PhD, DIC, DSc London Univ.; Apprenticeship and Design Office, Bristol Aero Engine Co., 1944–46; Lectr 1949, Reader 1959, Mech. Eng. Dept, Imperial College, research in heat transfer and in dynamics; Dir, Derritron Electronics, 1969–82; Partner, Grootenhuis Allaway Associates, consultants in noise and vibration, 1970–93; Associate Mem., Ordnance Board, 1965–70; Mem. Governing Body, Imperial College, 1974–79. Freeman, City of London, 1984; Liveryman, Engineers' Co., 1985–2014. FCGI 1976; Mem., Inst. of Acoustics; Fellow, Soc. of Environmental Engineers (Pres., 1964–67); FREng (FEng 1982). *Publications:* technical papers to learned jls, and patents. *Recreations:* sailing, gardening.

GROSE, Vice-Adm. Sir Alan, KBE 1989; Group Executive, Security, De Beers Consolidated Mines Ltd, 1993–2000; *b* 24 Sept. 1937; *s* of George William Stanley Grose and Ann May Grose (*née* Stanford); *m* 1961, Gillian Ann (*née* Dryden Dymond); two *s* one *d*. *Educ:* Strode's School; Britannia Royal Naval College, Dartmouth. Served: Mediterranean and S Atlantic, 1957–63; sub-specialised in Navigation, 1964; RAN, 1964–66; Home, W Indies, Med., 1966–72; Comd, HMS Eskimo, 1973–75; Staff of C-in-C, Naval Home Command, 1975–77; MoD, 1977–79; RCDS 1980; Comd, HMS Bristol, 1981–82; RN Presentation Team, 1983–84; Comd, HMS Illustrious, 1984–86; Flag Officer, Sept. 1986; ACDS, Operational Requirements (Sea Systems), MoD, 1986–88; Flag Officer Flotilla Three and Comdr, Anti-Submarine Warfare Striking Force, 1988–90; Flag Officer Plymouth, Naval Base Comdr Devonport, Comdr Central Sub Area Eastern Atlantic, and Comdr Plymouth Sub Area Channel, 1990–92, retired. Hon. Fellow, Liverpool John Moores Univ., 1993. *Recreations:* genealogy, opera, home computers. *Address:* Flat 4, Marwell Court, Oakcroft Road, SE13 7EE. *E:* sagrose@mweb.co.za. *Club:* Cape Town.

GROSS, Prof. David Jonathan, PhD; Director, Kavli Institute for Theoretical Physics, since 1997, and Frederick W. Gluck Professor of Theoretical Physics, since 2002, University of California, Santa Barbara; *b* 19 Feb. 1941; *s* of Bertram Meyer Gross and Nora Gross (*née* Faine); *m* 1st, 1962, Shulamith Toaff; two *d*; 2nd, 2001, Jacquelyn Savani. *Educ:* Hebrew Univ., Jerusalem (BSc 1962); Univ. of Calif, Berkeley (PhD 1966). Princeton University: Asst Prof., 1969–71; Associate Prof., 1971–73; Prof., 1973–86; Eugene Higgins Prof. of Physics, 1986–95; Thomas Jones Prof. of Math. Physics, 1995–97, now Emeritus; Prof., Univ. of Calif, Santa Barbara, 1997–. (Jtly) Nobel Prize in Physics, 2004. *Address:* Kavli Institute for Theoretical Physics, Kohn Hall, University of California, Santa Barbara, CA 93106, USA.

GROSS, Howard Anthony, FCA, FCCA; Founder, 1968, and Chief Executive, since 2001, Gross Klein and Gross Klein Wood; *b* Hoddesdon, Herts, 24 May 1948; *s* of late Harold Gross and Pamela Gross; *m* 1973, Beverley Teff; two *d*. *Educ:* Minchenden Sch.; City of London Coll. FCA 1971; CTA 1972; FCCA 1980. Chartered Accountant, 1968–. Chairman: (Founding) Hartley Computer User Gp, 1979–82; N London Chartered Accountants, 1984–85; Solution 6 Accounts Computer User Gp, 1998–2000. Mem., 1984–, Hon. Treas., 1990–93, Pres., 2001–02, London Soc. of Chartered Accountants; Mem. Council, 2002–, Mem., Main Bd, 2012–, ICAEW (Chairman: Practice Cttee, 2011–12; Members Bd, 2012–); Vice Chm., Soc. of Professional Accountants, 2010–. Exec. Ed., Accountants Digest, 2001–06; Mem., Editl Adv. Bd, Economia, 2012–. Chm., Heathfield Sch. Parents' Assoc., 1985–89. Freeman, City of London. *Recreations:* London Marathon (1989), jogging, football. *Address:* Gross Klein, 6 Breams Buildings, EC4A 1QL. *T:* (020) 7242 2212. *E:* howard@grosskleinnet.com.

GROSS, Miriam Marianna, (Lady Owen); freelance journalist and editor; *b* 12 May 1938; *d* of late Kurt May and of Wera May; *m* 1st, 1965, John Jacob Gross (marr. diss. 1988; he *d* 2011); one *s* one *d*; 2nd, 1993, Sir Geoffrey Owen, *qv*. *Educ:* Dartington Hall Sch.; St Anne's Coll., Oxford (MA). Observer: Dep. Lit. Editor, 1969–81; Woman's Editor, 1981–84; Arts Editor, Daily Telegraph, 1986–91; Literary Editor, Sunday Telegraph, 1991–2005; Sen. Editor, Standpoint Mag., 2008–10. Editor, Book Choice, Channel Four TV, 1986–89. Trustee, Real Action, 2014–. *Publications:* (ed) The World of George Orwell, 1971; (ed) The World of Raymond Chandler, 1976; So Why Can't They Read?, 2010; An Almost English Life: literary, and not so literary recollections, 2012. *Recreations:* painting, tennis. *Address:* 24A St Petersburgh Place, W2 4LB. *T:* (020) 7727 2291.

See also S. Gross.

GROSS, Rt Hon. Sir Peter (Henry), Kt 2001; PC 2010; **Rt Hon. Lord Justice Gross;** a Lord Justice of Appeal, since 2010; *b* 13 Feb. 1952; *s* of late Sam Lewis Gross and Fanny Alice Gross; *m* 1985, Ruth Mary Cullen; two *s*. *Educ:* Herzlia Sch., Cape Town; Univ. of Cape Town (BBusSc, MBusSc); Oriel Coll., Oxford (Rhodes Scholar, MA, BCL, Eldon Scholar). Called to the Bar, Gray's Inn, 1977, Bencher, 2000; admitted to the Bar of NSW, 1986; QC 1992; a Recorder, 1995–2001; a Judge of the High Ct, QBD, 2001–10; Presiding Judge, SE Circuit, 2004–08; Judge in Charge of Commercial Court, 2009–10; Dep. Sen. Presiding Judge of England and Wales, 2011–13; Sen. Presiding Judge of England and Wales, 2013–15. Chairman: London Common Law and Commercial Bar Assoc., 1995–97; Bar Educn and Trng Cttee, 1998–2000; Bar Internat. Relations Cttee, 2001; Judicial Security Cttee, 2009–11. Chm., Adv. Bd, Inst. of Law, City Univ., 2003–05. *Publications:* Legal Aid and its Management, 1976. *Recreations:* jogging, cricket, sailing, cross-country ski-ing. *Address:* Royal Courts of Justice, Strand, WC2A 2LL. *Club:* Oxford and Cambridge.

GROSS, Philip John; poet, novelist and playwright; Professor of Creative Writing, University of South Wales (formerly Glamorgan University), since 2004; *b* Delabole, 27 Feb. 1952; *s* of Juhan Karl Gross and Mary Jessie Alison Gross; *m* 2000, Zélie Marmery; one *s* one *d*. *Educ:* Devonport High Sch. for Boys; Sussex Univ. (BA Hons English 1973); N London Poly. (DipLib 1977). Librarian, London Bor. of Croydon, 1977–84; freelance writer and educator, 1984–; Lectr, Bath Spa UC, 1990–2004. FHEA 2007; FEA 2011; Fellow, Welsh Acad., 2011. Mem., Religious Soc. of Friends (Quakers). *Publications: poetry*: Familiars, 1983; The Ice Factory, 1984; Cat's Whiskers, 1987; (with S. Kantaris) The Air Mines of Mistila, 1988; The Son of the Duke of Nowhere, 1991; I.D., 1994; A Cast of Stones, 1996; The Wasting Game, 1998; Change of Address: poems 1980–98, 2001; Mappa Mundi, 2003; The Egg of Zero, 2006; The Water Table, 2009 (T. S. Eliot Prize); (with S. Denison) I Spy Pinhole Eye, 2009; Deep Field, 2011; Caves, 2013; Later, 2013; (with Valerie Coffin Price) A Fold in the River, 2015; *for children*: Manifold Manor, 1989; The All-Nite Cafe, 1993; Scratch City, 1995; Off Road to Everywhere, 2010; *novels*: The Song of Gail and Fludd, 1991; Plex, 1994; The Wind Gate, 1995; Transformer, 1996; Psylicon Beach, 1998; Facetaker, 1999; Going for Stone, 2002; Marginaliens, 2003; The Lastling, 2004; The Storm Garden, 2006. *W:* www.philipgross.co.uk. *Club:* Penn.

GROSS, Susanna, (Mrs John Preston); Literary Editor, Mail on Sunday, since 1999; *b* 31 July 1968; *d* of late John Jacob Gross, and of Miriam Marianna Gross, *qv*; *m* 2005, John Preston; one *s* one *d*. *Educ:* Godolphin and Latymer Sch., Hammersmith; Univ. of York (BA Philosophy). Obituaries Ed., Daily Mail, 1993–96; Features Ed., Harpers & Queen, 1996–97; Dep. Ed., The Week, 1997–2000; bridge columnist, Spectator, 2000–. *Recreations:* bridge, blackjack, hiking. *Address:* 11 Luxemburg Gardens, W6 7EA; Mail on Sunday, Northcliffe House, 2 Derry Street, W8 5TS. *T:* (020) 3615 3254.

GROSSART, Sir Angus (McFarlane McLeod), Kt 1997; CBE 1990; DL; Managing Director, since 1969, and Chairman, Noble Grossart Ltd, Merchant Bankers, Edinburgh, since 1990; merchant banker; *b* 6 April 1937; 3rd *s* of William John White Grossart and Mary Hay Gardiner; *m* 1978, Mrs Gay Thomson; one *d*. *Educ:* Glasgow Acad.; Glasgow Univ. (MA 1958, LLB 1960). CA 1962; Mem., Faculty of Advocates, 1963. Practised at Scottish Bar, 1963–69. Chm., Scottish Investment Trust PLC, 1975–2003; major directorships include: Edinburgh US Tracker Trust (formerly American Trust), 1973–2007; Royal Bank of Scotland plc, 1982–2005 (Vice Chm., 1996–2005); Alexander & Alexander, 1985–97; Scottish Financial Enterprise, 1987–2001; British Petroleum Scottish Bd, 1990–2005; Trinity Mirror (formerly Mirror Gp) PLC, 1998–2007; Scottish & Newcastle plc, 1998–2008; Chairman: Scotland Internat., 1997–; Lyon and Turnbull, 2000–; Edinburgh Partners, 2006–; Charlotte St Partners, 2014–; Deputy Chairman: Edinburgh Fund Managers PLC, 1991–2002 (Chm., 1983–91); Ronson Capital Partners, 2010–. Mem., Scottish Develt Agency, 1974–78; Dir, St Andrews Management Inst., 1990–97 (Chm. Adv. Council, 1994–97). Chm., Scottish Futures Trust, 2008–. Chairman, Board of Trustees: National Galleries of Scotland, 1988–97 (Trustee, 1986–97); Nat. Museums Scotland, 2006–12; Trustee and Dep. Chm., Nat. Heritage Meml Fund, 1999–2005; Trustee: Heritage Lottery Fund, 1999–2005; Glasgow Life (formerly Culture and Sport Glasgow), 2007–; High Steward of Scotland's Dumfries House Trust, 2007–; Chm., Edinburgh Internat. Cultural Summit, 2014–. Vice Pres., Scottish Opera, 1986–93; Director: Edinburgh Internat. Film Festival, 1994–96; Friends of Royal Scottish Acad., 1989–97; Chairman: Fine Art Soc., 1998–; Burrell Renaissance, 2013–. Formerly: Trustee, Scottish Civic Trust; Dir, Scottish Nat. Orch.; Mem., Scottish Industrial Develt Adv. Bd. Mem., Speculative Soc. Hon. QC (Scot.) 2011. FRSE 1998; FSA (Scot.) 2011. DL Edinburgh, 1996. Livingstone Captain of Industry Award, 1990. Hon. FCIBS 1999. Hon. LLD: Glasgow, 1985; Aberdeen, 2006; Hon. DBA Strathclyde, 1998; Hon. DLitt St Andrews, 2004. Lord Provost of Glasgow Award for public service, 1994; Paolozzi Gold Medal, 1997; Walpole Medal of Excellence, 2003; Nat. Museums of Scotland Gold Medal, 2012. Formerly, Scottish Editor, British Tax Encyc., and British Tax Rev. *Recreations:* golfing (runner-up, British Youths' Golf Championship, 1957; Captain, Scottish Youths' Internat., 1956 and 1957), the applied and decorative arts, Scottish painting, Scottish castle restoration. *Address:* 48 Queen Street, Edinburgh EH2 3NR. *T:* (0131) 226 7011. *Clubs:* New, Honourable Company of Edinburgh Golfers (Edinburgh); Royal and Ancient (St Andrews).

GROSSMAN, Loyd Daniel Gilman, CBE 2015 (OBE 2003); FSA; broadcaster, writer; *b* Boston, Mass, 16 Sept. 1950; *s* of late David K. Grossman and Helen Katherine Grossman (*née* Gilman); *m* 1985, Hon. Deborah Jane (marr. diss. 2005), *d* of Baron Puttnam, *qv*; two *d*. *Educ:* Marblehead High Sch.; Boston Univ. (BA *cum laude*); London School of Economics (MSc Econ.); Magdalene Coll., Cambridge (MPhil; PhD 2014). Design Editor, Harpers and Queen, 1981–84; Contributing Editor: Sunday Times, 1984–86; Condé Nast Traveller, 2006–. *Television* includes: deviser or writer or presenter: Through the Keyhole, 1983–2003; Behind the Headlines; MasterChef, 1990–2000 (Glenfiddich Award, 1996); The Dog's Tale, 1993; Junior MasterChef, 1995–99; Off Your Trolley, 1995; Conspicuous Consumption, 1996; The World on a Plate, 1997; Loyd on Location, 1999–2001; History of British Sculpture, 2003; Build Britain, 2007; Step Up to the Plate, 2008. Presenter, Composers at Home, BBC Radio 3, 2004–. Member: Bd, mda (formerly Museum Documentation Assoc.), 1998–2001; MLA (formerly Museums, Libraries and Archives Council, subseq. Resource: Council for Mus, Archives and Libraries), 1999–2006 (Chm., Designation Challenge Fund, 2001–03); Commissioner: Museums and Galleries Commn, 1996–2000; English Heritage, 1997–2003 (Chairman: Mus. and Collections Adv. Cttee, 1997–2001; Nat. Blue Plaques Panel, 2003–06; Mus and Archives Panel, 2001–03); Royal Commn on Histl Monuments of England, 1999–2003; Chm., 2000, Co-Chm., 2001–08, Museums and Galleries Month; Chairman: Campaign for Mus, 1995–2009; The 24 Hour Mus., 2000–05; Public Monuments and Sculpture Assoc., 2001–07; Nat. Mus Liverpool, 2005–08; Churches Conservation Trust, 2007–June 2016; Heritage Alliance, 2009–; Dep. Chm., Liverpool Culture Co., 2005–07; Vice-Chm., NW Regl Cultural Consortium, 2000–02; Member, Board: Culture Northwest: Cultural Consortium for England's Northwest, 2002–09 (Chm., 2004–09); Assoc. of Leading Visitor Attractions, 2013–. President: British Assoc. of Friends of Mus, 2005–14; NADFAS, 2014–. Trustee: Mus. of Sci. and Industry in Manchester, 1999–2002; St Deiniol's Liby, 2003–08 (Fellow, 2008); Gladstone's Liby, 2014–. Mem., Court of Govs, LSE, 1996–2009 (Mem. Council, 2003–08, Emeritus Gov., 2009); Chm., Univ. for the Creative Arts, 2008–12; Mem. Council, British Sch. at Rome, 2013–; Dep. Chm., Royal Drawing Sch., 2014–; Gov., Building Arts Coll., 2014–. Chm., Conservation Awards, 1998–2003; Chm. of Judges, Gulbenkian Prize for Mus, 2004. Vice-Pres., Sick Children's Trust; Chm., Better Hosp. Food Panel, NHS, 2001–06; Patron: Haslemere Educnl Mus., 2011–; Heritage Open Days, 2012–; Historic Lincoln Trust, 2012–; Cavell Nurses' Trust, 2014–; Amer. Mus. in Britain, 2014–. Hon. Life Mem., Dogs Trust (formerly Nat. Canine Defence League). Middle Warden, Ct of Assts, Arts Scholars' Co. (formerly Co. of Arts Scholars, Dealers and Collectors), 2010–; Hon. Liveryman, Glaziers' Co., 2011–; Freeman: City of London, 2011; Carpenters' Co., 2012– (Liveryman, 2013–). Album with The New Forbidden, Ain't Doin' Nothin', 2010 (songwriter and guitarist); performances at various festivals, incl. Glastonbury, Vintage, Cornbury and Rebellion. Mem., Piscatorial Soc., 2014–. FRSA; FSAScot; FRSocMed 2004. Hon. DLitt Chester, 2007; Hon. DArts Lincoln, 2011; Hon. Dr Essex, 2014. *Publications:* The Social History of Rock Music, 1975; Harpers and Queen Guide to London's 100 Best Restaurants, 1987; The Dog's Tale, 1993; Loyd Grossman's Italian Journey, 1994; (ed) Courvoisier's Book of the Best, 1994–96; The World on a Plate, 1997; The 125 Best Recipes Ever, 1998; Foodstuff, 2002; Benjamin West and the Struggle to be Modern, 2015; articles on architecture, design and food in newspapers and magazines. *Recreations:* fishing, scuba diving (PADI Divemaster), looking at buildings, tennis, chess, the Boston Red Sox, playing Gibson and Gretsch guitars. *Clubs:* Brooks's, Flyfishers', Hurlingham, Chelsea Arts, Oxford and Cambridge.

GROSSMAN, Russell Lawrence; Group Director, Communications, Department for Business, Innovation and Skills (formerly Department for Business, Enterprise and Regulatory Reform), since 2008; *b* Blackpool, 7 April 1961; *s* of David Grossman and Irene Grossman; *m* 1985, Eunice Goodstone; three *s* one *d*. *Educ:* Arnold Sch., Blackpool; Univ. of Manchester (BSc Hons Mgt and Chem. Scis); Univ. of Salford (MSc Transport Engrg and Planning); London Metropolitan Univ. (DipPR); Royal Roads Univ. (ABC). Hd, Transport Communications, London Docklands Develt Corp., 1988–94; PR Manager, Jubilee Line Extension, London Underground, 1994–96; Sen. Consultant, Nichols Associates, 1994–97; Dir, Communications, Royal Mail, London, 1997–99; Hd, Internal Communications, BBC, 1999–2006; Hd, Internal and Change Communications, HMRC, 2006–08. Vis. Fellow, Cass Business Sch., 2011–. FCIM; FRSA; FCIPR. *Recreations:* family, reading, hill walking, music. *Address:* Department for Business, Innovation and Skills, 1 Victoria Street, SW1H 0ET. *T:* (020) 7215 1229. *E:* russell.grossman@hotmail.com.

GROSVELD, Prof. Franklin Gerardus, (Frank), PhD; FRS 1991; Professor of Cell Biology, Erasmus University, Rotterdam, since 1993; *b* 18 Aug. 1948; *m*; two *s*. *Educ:* Univ. of Amsterdam (MSc); McGill Univ. (PhD). Sen. Scientist, NIMR, 1982–93. *Publications:*

papers on human globin genes. *Address:* Department of Cell Biology, Erasmus MC, PO Box 2040, 3000 CA Rotterdam, The Netherlands.

GROSVENOR, family name of **Duke of Westminster** and of **Earl of Wilton**.

GROSVENOR, Earl; Hugh Richard Louis Grosvenor; *b* 29 Jan. 1991; *o s* and *heir* of Duke of Westminster, *qv*.

GROSZ, Stephen Ernest; Partner, 1981–2013, Senior Consultant, since 2013, Bindmans LLP (formerly Bindman & Partners), solicitors; *b* 14 April 1953; *s* of Emil, (Joe), Grosz and Therese Grosz (*née* Baer); *m* 1981, Judith Beale (marr. diss. 1995); *m* 2012, Vicki Chapman. *Educ:* William Ellis Sch.; Clare Coll., Cambridge (BA 1974); Université Libre de Bruxelles (licencié special en droit européen 1976). Joined Bindman & Partners, 1976. Significant cases include: Marshall *v* Southampton & SW Hants AHA, instrumental in changing UK law on equal rights for retirement age and for compensation for discrimination; R *v* Sec. of State for Foreign & Commonwealth Affairs ex parte World Develt Movt, in which the High Court declared unlawful aid for construction of the Pergau Dam in Malaysia; R *v* Lord Chancellor ex parte Witham, quashing changes to court fees as contrary to constitutional rights of access to the courts; R *v* MoD ex parte Lustig-Prean and Lustig-Prean & others *v* UK, concerning the rights of homosexuals & lesbians to serve in the armed forces; Abdulaziz & others *v* UK, instrumental in removing sex discrimination from the immigration rules; Silver & others *v* UK, instrumental in removing restrictions on prisoners' rights to respect for correspondence; Sutherland *v* UK, in which the European Commission of Human Rights ruled unlawful discrimination in the age of consent for gay men; R *v* Sec. of State for Home Dept, ex parte Amnesty Internat. & others, concerning disclosure of med. reports relating to extradition of Augusto Pinochet; Sahin *v* Turkey, concerning ban on headscarves in Turkish univs; Goodwin *v* UK, concerning recognition of transsexuals; Ghaidan *v* Ghodin, concerning succession rights for same-sex partners; R (David Hicks) *v* Sec. of State for Home Dept, concerning power to deny citizenship on public policy grounds; R (RJM) *v* Sec. of State for Work and Pensions, concerning discrimination against homeless people and effects of Human Rights Act 1998. Civil and commercial mediator, 2012. Gov., 1992–2004, Mem. Adv. Bd, 2004–, British Inst. of Human Rights; Chm., Domestic Human Rights Reference Gp, 2004–08, Mem., Human Rights Cttee, 2011– (Chm., 2014), Law Soc.; Member: Mgt Cttee, Public Law Project, 1991–2001; Exec. Bd, Justice, 1999–2014; Council, Liberty, 2001–03; Member Advisory Board: Judicial Review Qly, 1996–; Educn, Public Law and the Individual, 1996. Fellow, Bingham Centre for Rule of Law, 2013–. Mem., Editl Bd, Civil Procedure, 2000–04. Hon. QC 2012. *Publications:* (jtly) Human Rights: the 1998 Act and the European Convention, 2000; (jtly) Human Rights: judicial protection in the United Kingdom, 2008; *contributions to:* Public Interest Law, 1986; Atkin's Court Forms, 1987; Public Interest Perspectives in Environmental Law, 1995; Judicial Rev. in the New Millennium, 2003; articles and reviews in newspapers and legal jls. *Recreations:* cycling, walking, choral singing, eating and drinking, trying to make people laugh. *Address:* (office) 236 Gray's Inn Road, WC1X 8HB. *T:* (020) 8123 7431.

GROTE, Dr John David, OBE 1991; Director, British Council, Egypt, 2001–05; *b* 5 Sept. 1945; *s* of Roy and Dorothy Grote; *m* 1st, 1970, Pauline Bolton (marr. diss. 1979); one *s* one *d*; 2nd, 1979, Barbara Elzbieta Orzechowska (*née* Smigielska). *Educ:* Rydens Co. Secondary Sch.; Southampton Univ. (BSc 1st Cl. Hons Maths 1967; PhD 1971). Temp. Lectr, Maths Dept, Univ. of Southampton, 1970–71; Res. Fellow, Control Theory Centre, Warwick Univ., 1971–74; British Council, 1974–2005: Sci. Advr, 1974–75; Sci. Officer, Poland, 1975–79; Staff Inspector, 1979–82; Dep. Dir, Computer Systems, 1982–83; Science Officer: Germany, 1983–86; Japan, 1987–91; Director: Hungary, 1991–96; Singapore, 1996–2000. Ext. Mem., Audit and Risk Mgt Cttee, Essex Univ., 2008–14. *Recreations:* reading, thinking, wine, walking with my wife. *Address:* Bridgeford House, 68 Belle Vue Road, Wivenhoe, Essex CO7 9LD. *E:* johngrote_99@yahoo.com.

GROTRIAN, Sir Philip Christian Brent, 3rd Bt *cr* 1934; *b* 26 March 1935; *s* of Robert Philip Brent Grotrian (*d* on active service, 1945) (*y s* of 1st Bt), and Elizabeth Mary, *d* of Major Herbert Hardy-Wrigley; *S* uncle, 1984; *m* 1st, 1960, Anne Isabel, *d* of Robert Sieger Whyte, Toronto; one *s*; 2nd, 1979, Sarah Frances, *d* of Reginald Harry Gale, Montreal; one *s* one *d*. *Educ:* Eton; Trinity Coll., Toronto. *Heir: s* Philip Timothy Adam Brent Grotrian, *b* 9 April 1962. *Address:* Calle Ample 2, Regencós, Gerona, Spain.

GROUND, (Reginald) Patrick; QC 1981; *b* 9 Aug. 1932; *s* of late Reginald Ground and Ivy Elizabeth Grace Ground (*née* Irving); *m* 1964, Caroline Dugdale; three *s* one *d*. *Educ:* Beckenham and Penge County Grammar Sch.; Lycée Gay Lussac, Limoges, France; Selwyn Coll., Cambridge (Open Exhibnr; MA Mod. Langs, French and Spanish); Magdalen Coll., Oxford (MLitt, Mod. History). Inner Temple Studentship and Foster Boulton Prize, 1958; called to the Bar, Inner Temple, 1960, Bencher, 1987. National Service, RN, 1954–56: Sub-Lt RNVR; served in Mediterranean Fleet and on staff of C-in-C Mediterranean; rep. RN at hockey and lawn tennis; Lt-Comdr RNR. Worked for FO on staff of Wilton Park European Conf. Centre, 1958–60. Councillor, London Bor. of Hammersmith, 1968–71 (Chm., Cttees responsible for health and social services, 1969–71). Contested (C): Hounslow, Feltham and Heston, Feb. and Oct. 1974, and 1979; Feltham and Heston, 1992 and 1997. MP (C) Feltham and Heston, 1983–92. PPS to the Solicitor General, 1987–92. Treasurer and Pres., Oxford Univ. Cons. Assoc., 1958; Chm., Fulham Soc., 1975–96. Trustee, Daisy Trust, 1981–. *Publications:* articles on housing, security of tenure and paying for justice. *Recreations:* lawn tennis, theatre, music, sailing, travel, forestry. *Address:* 13 Ranelagh Avenue, SW6 3PJ. *T:* (020) 7736 0131. *Clubs:* Brooks's, Carlton, Queen's (Trustee, 2008–10).

GROUNDS, Dr Adrian Thomas, FRCPsych; Hon. Research Fellow, Institute of Criminology, University of Cambridge, since 2010; Fellow, Darwin College, Cambridge, since 1987; *b* Bath, 21 Feb. 1952; *s* of Thomas and Mary Grounds; *m* 1985, Krishna Kumari Singh; one *s*. *Educ:* Monkton Combe Sch.; Univ. of Nottingham (BMedSci 1974; BM BS 1977; DM 1986). MRCPsych 1981, FRCPsych 1996. SHO and Registrar in Psychiatry, Maudsley Hosp., London, 1979–82; Sen. Registrar in Forensic Psychiatry, Broadmoor Hosp. and Bethlem Royal Hosp., 1982–84; Clin. Lectr in Forensic Psychiatry, Inst. of Psychiatry, 1984–87; University of Cambridge: Lectr in Forensic Psychiatry and Hon. Consultant Forensic Psychiatrist, Inst. of Criminol., 1987–2003; Sen. Lectr, 2003–10. Northern Ireland: Sentence Rev. Comr, 1998–; Life Sentence Rev. Comr, 2001–08; Parole Comr, 2008–. Mem., Adv. Cttee, Miscarriages of Justice Support Service, Royal Courts of Justice Advice Bureau, 2004–; Med. Mem., First-tier Tribunal (Mental Health), 2013–. Trustee, Prison Reform Trust, 2001–. *Publications:* contrib. articles on forensic psychiatry and effects of miscarriages of justice. *Address:* Institute of Criminology, Sidgwick Avenue, Cambridge CB3 9DA. *T:* (01223) 335360. *E:* ag113@cam.ac.uk.

GROVE, Dr Andrew Steven; Senior Advisor to Executive Management, Intel Corporation, since 2005 (President, 1979–97; Chief Executive Officer, 1987–98; Chairman, 1997–2005); *b* Budapest, 2 Sept. 1936; *m* 1958, Eva; two *d*. *Educ:* City Coll. of NY (BSc Chem. Engrg); Univ. of Calif, Berkeley (PhD Chem. Engrg). FIEEE. Asst Dir of R&D, Fairchild Semiconductor, 1967–68; joined Intel, 1968. Mem., Nat. Acad. of Engrg. Fellow, Amer. Acad. of Arts & Scis, 1994. Hon. DEng Worcester. Engrg Leadership Recognition Award, 1987; Heinz Foundn Award for Technol. and the Econ., 1995; Time Man of the Year, 1997; IEEE 2000, Medal of Honour, 1998. *Publications:* Physics and Technology of Semiconductor Devices, 1967; High Output Management, 1983; One-on-One With Andy Grove, 1987; Only the Paranoid Survive, 1996. *Address:* Intel Corporation, 2200 Mission College Boulevard, Santa Clara, CA 95052-1549, USA.

GROVE, Sir Charles Gerald, 5th Bt *cr* 1874; *b* 10 Dec. 1929; *s* of Walter Peel Grove (*d* 1944) (3rd *s* of 2nd Bt) and Elena Rebecca, *d* of late Felipe Crosthwaite; *S* brother, 1974, but his name does not appear on the Official Roll of the Baronetage. *Heir: b* Harold Thomas Grove, *b* 6 Dec. 1930.

GROVE, Trevor Charles; JP; journalist; *b* 1 Jan. 1945; *s* of Ronald and Lesley Grove; *m* 1975, Valerie Jenkins (*see* V. Grove); one *s* three *d*. *Educ:* St George's, Buenos Aires; Radley; St Edmund Hall, Oxford. Editorial Staff, Spectator, 1967–70; Leader Writer, then Features Editor, Evening Standard, 1970–78; Asst Editor, Sunday Telegraph, 1978–80; Sen. Asst Editor, Observer, 1980–83; Editor, Observer Magazine, 1983–86; Asst Editor, Daily Telegraph, 1986–89; Editor, Sunday Telegraph, 1989–92; Gp Exec. Ed. and Dep. Ed., Daily Telegraph, 1992–94; Launch Editor, El Periódico de Tucumán, Argentina, 1994; Chm., Inside Time: The Prisoners' Newspaper, 2004–. JP Haringey, 1999. Trustee, Butler Trust, 2006–14. *Publications:* (co-ed) Singlehanded, 1984; (ed) The Queen Observed, 1986; The Juryman's Tale, 1998; The Magistrate's Tale, 2002; One Dog and His Man, 2003. *Recreations:* tennis, cooking, dog-walking, grandchild-minding. *Address:* 14 Avenue Road, Highgate, N6 5DW. *T:* (020) 8348 2621.

GROVE, Valerie; journalist and biographer; feature writer, The Times, 1992–2013; *b* 11 May 1946; *d* of Doug Smith, cartoonist; *m* 1st, 1968, David Brynmor Jenkins (marr. diss. 1975); 2nd, 1975, Trevor Charles Grove, *qv*; one *s* three *d*. *Educ:* South Shields Grammar Sch.; Kingsbury County Grammar Sch.; Girton Coll., Cambridge (MA 1969). Evening Standard, 1968–87; Sunday Times, 1987–92; wireless column, The Oldie, 1992–. *Publications:* (as Valerie Jenkins) Where I Was Young, 1976; (as Valerie Grove): The Compleat Woman, 1987; Dear Dodie: the life of Dodie Smith, 1996; Laurie Lee: the well-loved stranger, 1999, rev. edn as The Life and Loves of Laurie Lee, 2014; A Voyage Round John Mortimer, 2007; So Much to Tell: the life of Kaye Webb, 2010. *Recreations:* tennis, archives, walking Dalmatian, litter-picking. *Address:* 14 Avenue Road, Highgate, N6 5DW. *T:* (020) 8348 2621. *E:* vgrove@dircon.co.uk.

GROVE-WHITE, Prof. Robin Bernard; Professor of Environment and Society, Institute for Environment, Philosophy and Public Policy, Lancaster University, 2000–05, now Emeritus; *b* 17 Feb. 1941; *s* of Charles William Grove-White and Cecile Mary Rabbidge; *m* 1st, 1970, Virginia Harriet Ironside (marr. diss.); one *s*; 2nd, 1979, Helen Elizabeth Smith; two *s* one *d*. *Educ:* Uppingham Sch.; Worcester Coll., Oxford (BA); Bangor Univ. (PhD Welsh History 2013). Freelance writer for TV, radio, press and advertising in UK, Canada and US, 1963–70; McCann-Erickson Ltd, London, 1970; Asst Secretary, 1972–80, Dir, 1981–87, CPRE; Res. Fellow, Centre for Envmtl Technol., Imperial Coll., London, 1987–89; Lancaster University: Sen. Res. Fellow, 1989–91; Dir, Centre for Study of Envmtl Change, 1991–2001. Member: Forestry Commn, 1991–98; Agric. and Envmt Biotechnology Commn, 2000–05; Standards Cttee, Anglesey CC, 2007–11. Chm., Greenpeace UK, 1997–2003; Pres., N Wales Wildlife Trust, 2010–. High Sheriff Anglesey and Gwynedd, 2011. Hon. DSc Bath, 2011. *Publications:* (contrib.) Politics of Physical Resources, 1975; (contrib.) Future Landscapes, 1976; (with Michael Flood) Nuclear Prospects, 1976; contribs to New Scientist, Nature, Times, Independent, and numerous academic jls. *Recreations:* walking, cricket. *Address:* Brynddu, Llanfechell, Ynys Mon LL68 0RT. *T:* (01407) 710245.

GROVENOR, Prof. Christopher Richard Munro, DPhil; FInstP, FIMMM; Professor of Materials, since 2004, and Head, Department of Materials, since 2005, University of Oxford; Fellow, St Anne's College, Oxford, since 1990; *b* 21 Oct. 1955; *s* of late John and Christine Grovenor; *m* 1987, Susan Ruth Ortner; two *d*. *Educ:* Marlborough Coll.; St Catherine's Coll., Oxford (MA, DPhil). FInstP 2004; FIMMM 2008. Lectr in Materials, Univ. of Oxford, 1986–. *Publications:* contribs on relationship between microstructure and properties of functional materials. *Recreations:* cricket, bassoonist. *Address:* Department of Materials, University of Oxford, Parks Road, Oxford OX1 3PH. *T:* (01865) 273737. *E:* chris.grovenor@materials.ox.ac.uk.

GROVER, Derek James Langlands, CB 1999; consultant, 2005–11; Group Director of Distributed Learning, NHSU, Department of Health, 2004–05; *b* 26 Jan. 1949; *s* of late Donald James Grover and Mary Barbara Grover; *m* 1972, Mary Katherine Morgan; one *s*. *Educ:* Hove County Grammar Sch. for Boys; Clare Coll., Cambridge (Foundn Schol. 1970; BA Eng. Lit. 1971, MA 1975; Grene Prize 1971). Various positions, Dept of Employment, 1971–78; Cabinet Office, 1978–80; MSC, 1980–87; Training Agency: Head of Personnel, 1987–89; Dir of Youth Training, 1989; Dir of Systems and Strategy, 1989; Dir of Trng Strategy and Standards, later of Trng Strategy and Infrastructure, 1990–94; Dep. Chief Exec. and Sen. Dir of Operations, Employment Service, 1994–97; Dir of Employment and Adult Trng, DFEE, 1997–98; Dir, Skills and Lifelong Learning, then Adult Learning Gp, DfEE, then DfES, 1998–2002; Dir of Develt, NHSU, 2002–03. Chair: NIACE Enquiry on ESOL, 2005–06; Nat. ESOL Adv. Forum, 2007–11; Sheffield Assoc. for Voluntary Teaching of English, 2012–. Chm. of Govs, Broomhill Sch., Sheffield, 2009–; Gov., Norfolk Park Sch., Sheffield, 2014–. Nat. Leader of Governance, Nat. Coll. for Teaching and Leadership, 2014–. FRSA 1991. MCIPD (MIPM 1993). *Recreations:* music, reading, walking, watching cricket. *Address:* 8 Oakbrook Road, Sheffield S11 7EA.

GROVER, Rajiv, MD; FRCS; Consultant Plastic Surgeon, King Edward VII Hospital, London, since 2002; President, British Association of Aesthetic Plastic Surgeons, 2012–14; *m* 1992, Nikita; two *d*. *Educ:* St Bartholomew's Medical Sch., Univ. of London (BSc 1st Cl. Hons 1986; MB BS (Triple Dist.) 1989; MD 1996). FRCS 1993 (Hallett Prize and Gold Medal); FRCS (Plast) 2000. Hse Surgeon and Hse Physician, St Bartholomew's Hosp., 1989–90; Surgical SHO rotation, University Coll. Hosp., 1991–93; RCS Res. Fellow in Plastic Surgery, 1994–96; Pan Thames Plastic Surgery Rotation, Mt Vernon Hosp., Royal Marsden Hosp. and Gt Ormond St Hosp., 1996–99; RCS Schol. in Plastic Surgery, Harvard Med. Sch., 1999; Consultant Plastic Surgeon, NW London Regl Centre, Mt Vernon Hosp., 2001–06; in private practice, Harley St, 2002–. Hunterian Prof., RCS, 1998–. *Publications:* (with B. Jones) Textbook of Facial Rejuvenation Surgery, 2008; contrib. papers on improving outcome and safety in cosmetic surgery to Amer. and British Jls of Plastic Surgery. *Recreations:* personal fitness, cycling, photography. *Address:* 144 Harley Street, W1G 7LE. *T:* (020) 7486 4301, *Fax:* (020) 7486 4327. *Club:* Arts.

GROVES, His Honour Richard Bebb, TD 1966; RD 1979; a Circuit Judge, 1985–2000; *b* 4 Oct. 1933; *s* of George Thomas Groves and Margaret Anne (*née* Bebb); *m* 1958, Eileen Patricia (*née* Farley); one *s* one *d*. *Educ:* Bancroft's Sch., Woodford Green, Essex; DipFrench Open, 2003. Admitted Solicitor of the Supreme Court, 1960. Partner, H. J. Smith & Co. and Richard Groves & Co., 1962–85. Dep. Circuit Judge, 1978–80; a Recorder, 1980–85. Nijmegen Medal, Royal Netherlands League for Physical Culture, 1965 and 1966. *Recreations:* Royal Naval Reserve, tennis, philately, walking, reading. *Club:* Royal Automobile.

GROVES, Sally Hilary, MBE 2015; Creative Director, Schott Music Ltd, 2011–14 (Director, 2001–14); *b* Manchester, 11 March 1949; *d* of Sir Charles Barnard Groves, CBE and Hilary Hermione Groves; *m* 1992, Dennis Michael Marks (*d* 2015); one *s*. *Educ:* Belvedere Sch., Liverpool; Univ. of Birmingham (BMus Hons 1970). Promotions Manager: Stainer and Bell, 1970–72; Novello, 1972–74; Promotions Manager, 1974–90, Hd of Contemp. Music, 1990–2011, Schott Music Ltd. Consultant, Minerva Search, 2015–. Chm., Bd of Trustees, British Music Inf. Centre, 2000–08. Member: Bd of Govs, Royal Coll. of Music, 1999–2008; Bd, Bournemouth Symphony Orch., 2000–04; Bd, Birmingham Contemporary Music Gp, 2000–04; Bd of Trustees, Sound and Music, 2000–08. Trustee: Vaughan Williams Charitable

Trust, 2012– (Chm., 2015–); RVW Trust, 2014–. Lesley Boosey Award, Royal Philharmonic Soc., 2013. *Recreations:* chamber music, theatre, grandchildren. *E:* sallygroves49@gmail.com, sally@minervasearch.com.

GRUBB, Prof. Andrew, LLD; a Judge of the Upper Tribunal (Immigration and Asylum Chamber) (formerly a Senior Immigration Judge and Training Judge, Asylum and Immigration Tribunal), since 2005; a Recorder, since 2009; a Deputy High Court Judge, since 2013; *b* 24 March 1958; *s* of late Graham Grubb and of Valerie Grubb; *m* 1988, Helga Anne Moore (marr. diss. 2015); two *s* one *d. Educ:* Brynmawr Comprehensive Sch.; Selwyn Coll., Cambridge (BA 1st Cl. Hons 1979; MA 1983); LLD London 1998. Called to the Bar, Inner Temple, 1980 (Scarman Schol., 1980; Certificate of Honour 1980). Cambridge University: Law Fellow, Fitzwilliam Coll., 1981–90; Asst Univ. Lectr, 1984–89, Univ. Lectr, 1989–90, in Law; King's College, London: Sen. Lectr in Law, 1990–92; Reader in Med. Law, 1992–94; Prof. of Health Care Law, 1994–98; acting Dir, 1992–93, Dir, 1993–97, Centre of Med. Law and Ethics; Prof. of Med. Law, 1998–2004, Hd of Sch., 1999–2004, Cardiff Law Sch., Cardiff Univ. (Vis. Prof., 2004–09; Hon. Vis. Prof., 2009–); Trng Immigration Adjudicator, Immigration Appellate Authy, 2004–05. Visiting Professor of Law: Boston Univ. Sch. of Law, 1989; Univ. of New Mexico Sch. of Law, 1989. Member: Ethical Cttee, RCP, 1994–2004; HFEA, 1997–2003; UK Xenotransplantn Regulatory Authy, 2003–04; Nuffield Council on Bioethics, 2003–04; pt-time Immigration Adjudicator, 1996–2004; Chm., Ind. Review Panel (NHS Complaints), Wales, 1998–99. Vice Pres., Wales Medico-Legal Soc., 2000–04. Founder FMedSci 1998. Editor, Medical Law Review, 1993–2004. Ver Heyden de Lancey Medico-Legal Prize, Cambridge Univ., 1991. *Publications:* (with I. Kennedy) Medical Law: cases and materials, 1989, rev. edn, Medical Law: text with materials, 1994, 3rd edn 2000; (with D. Pearl) Blood Testing, AIDS and DNA Profiling: law and policy, 1990; (jtly) Doctors' Views on the Management and Care of Patients in Persistent Vegetative State: a UK study, 1997; (ed) Principles of Medical Law, (with I. Kennedy) 1998, 3rd edn (with J. Laing and J. Mettale) 2010. *Recreations:* music and music trivia, appreciating electric guitars, the Welsh countryside, Welsh Rugby. *Address:* Upper Tribunal (Immigration and Asylum Chamber), Columbus House, Langstone Business Park, Chepstow Road, Langstone, Newport NP18 2LX. *T:* (01633) 416749.

GRUBB, Deborah Mary Hinton; Chair: Gardner Arts Centre, 2001–07; South East Regional Arts Council, 2002–05; *b* 21 Feb. 1946; *d* of Joe Grubb and Winifred Grubb (*née* Axtell); *m* 2000, Peter Guttridge. *Educ:* Haberdashers' Aske's Sch. for Girls; UC Cardiff (BA Hons). Various posts in local govt, theatre and PR; Dir, Arts, Recreation and Tourism, Brighton and Hove CC, 1991–2000. Mem., Arts Council England (formerly Arts Council of England), 2002–05. *Recreations:* theatre, gardening, travel. *E:* deborahgrubb@btinternet.com.

GRUBB, George Darlington Wilson; Lord Lieutenant and Lord Provost of Edinburgh, 2007–12; *b* 5 Dec. 1935; *s* of Robert Birnie Grubb and Georgina Wilson Grubb (*née* Pratt); *m* 1960, Elizabeth Grant; one *s* one *d. Educ:* James Gillespie's Boys' Sch.; Royal High Sch.; Wesley Theol Coll.; Open Univ. (MA 1974; BPhil 1983); Univ. of Edinburgh (BD 1978); San Francisco Theol Seminary (DMin 1993). Nat. Service (Royal Army Ordnance Corps), 1954–56. Ordained, 1962; Sqdn Leader Chaplain, RAF, 1962–70; Parish Minister, Craigsbank Ch, Edinburgh, 1971–2001. Mem. (Lib Dem) Edinburgh CC, 1999– (Chm., Lib Dem Gp, 2000–07). President: Edinburgh Internat. Sci. Fest.; Edinburgh Peace Initiative, 2012; Director and Chairperson: Edinburgh Internat. Fest. Soc.; Edinburgh Mil. Tattoo Ltd; Edinburgh Mil. Tattoo (Charities) Ltd. Dir, Dynamic Earth Charitable Trust, 2007–12; Convener, UN Assoc. Edinburgh, 2012. *Recreations:* running, reading, being with grandchildren; Scottish Schools 880 yards champion 1954, Scottish Junior 880 yards champion 1954.

GRUBB, Prof. Michael John, PhD; Professor of International Energy and Climate Change Policy, University College London, since 2014; Senior Adviser, Sustainable Energy Policy, Office of Gas and Electricity Markets, since 2011; *b* Southall, Middx, 29 Feb. 1960; *s* of Martyn Patrick and Anne Isobel Grubb; *m* 2005, Joanna Depledge; one *s* two *d. Educ:* King's Coll., Cambridge (BA 1982; PhD 1987). Res. Fellow, Electrical Engrg, Imperial Coll., London, 1986–88; Res. Fellow, 1988–92, Hd, Energy and Envmt Prog., 1993–98, RIIA; Prof. of Climate Change and Energy Policy, Imperial Coll., London, 1999–2001; Associate Dir of Policy, 2002–04, Chief Economist, 2005–10, Carbon Trust; Sen. Res. Associate, Cambridge Univ., 2005–14. Chm., Climate Strategies, 2007–12; Mem., UK Climate Change Cttee, 2008–11. Lead Author, Intergovtl Panel on Climate Change: Assessment Reports II 1996, III 2001 and IV 2007; Ed.-in-Chief, Climate Policy Jl, 2000–. *Publications:* Energy Policies and the Greenhouse Effect, vol. 1 1990, vol. 2 (ed) 1991; (ed) Emerging Energy Technologies: impacts and policy implications, 1992; The Earth Summit Agreements: a guide and assessment, 1993; Renewable Energy Strategies for Europe: vol. 1 1995, vol. 2 1997; The Kyoto Protocol: a guide and assessment, 1999; (ed jtly) A Low Carbon Electricity System for the UK: technology, economics and policy, 2008; Planetary Economics: energy, climate change and the three domains of sustainable energy development, 2014. *Recreations:* time with family; music, guitar. *Address:* UCL Institute for Sustainable Resources, Central House, 14 Upper Woburn Place, WC1H 0NN. *E:* m.grubb@ucl.ac.uk.

GRUBB, Parmjit-Kaur, (Bobbie); *see* Cheema, P.-K.

GRUBB, Prof. Peter John, PhD, ScD; Professor of Investigative Plant Ecology, Cambridge University, 2000–01, now Emeritus; Fellow, Magdalene College, Cambridge, 1960–2002, now Emeritus (President, 1991–96); *b* 9 Aug. 1935; *s* of Harold Amos Grubb and Phyllis Gertrude (*née* Hook); *m* 1965, Elizabeth Adelaide Anne, *d* of Charles Edward and Adelaide Gertrude Hall; one *s* one *d. Educ:* Royal Liberty Sch.; Magdalene Coll., Cambridge (Schol.; BA 1957; PhD 1962; ScD 1995). Magdalene College, Cambridge: John Stothert Bye Fellow, 1958–60; Res. Fellow, 1960; Tutor, 1963–74; Jt Dir of Studies in Natural Scis, 1980–96; Cambridge University: Demonstrator in Botany, 1961–64; Lectr, 1964–92; Reader, 1992–2000. Nuffield-Royal Soc. Bursar, Univ. of Adelaide, 1963; Hon. Res. Fellow, ANU, 1970–71; Vis. Prof., Cornell Univ., 1982, 1987; Sen. Vis. Researcher, CSIRO Tropical Forest Res. Centre, Atherton, 1992–2000; Vis. Prof., ICSTM, 1999–2007. Editor: Jl of Ecology, 1972–77; Biol Flora of British Isles, 1978–87. Jt Leader, Cambridge Expedn to Colombian Cordillera Oriental, 1957; Leader, Oxford Univ. Expedn to Ecuador, 1960. President: Brit. Ecol Soc., 1990–91 (Hon. Mem., 2001; first Award for outstanding service to the Soc., 2003); Cambridge Philosophical Soc., 1990–91. Frank Smart Prize in Botany, Cambridge Univ., 1956; Rolleston Meml Essay Prize, Oxford Univ., 1963. *Publications:* (with P. F. Stevens) Forests of Mt Kerigomna, Papua New Guinea, 1985; (ed with J. B. Whittaker) Toward a More Exact Ecology, 1989; (ed with J. B. Whittaker) 100 Influential Papers, 2013; papers in ecol and botanical jls. *Recreations:* history of architecture, biographies, savouring continental cheeses. *Address:* Magdalene College, Cambridge CB3 0AG. *T:* (01223) 332109.

GRUBBS, Prof. Robert Howard, PhD; Victor and Elizabeth Atkins Professor of Chemistry, California Institute of Technology, Pasadena, since 1990 (Professor of Chemistry, 1978–90); *b* 27 Feb. 1942; *s* of Henry Howard Grubbs and Evelyn Faye Grubbs; *m* 1967, Helen M. O'Kane; two *s* one *d. Educ:* Univ. of Florida, Gainesville (BS Chem. 1963, MS Chem. 1965); Columbia Univ., NY (PhD Chem. 1968). NIH Postdoctoral Fellow, Stanford Univ., Calif, 1968–69; Asst Prof., 1969–73, Associate Prof., 1973–78, Michigan State Univ., E Lansing. MACS 1964; MNAS 1989; Fellow, Amer. Acad. of Arts and Scis, 1994; FRCS 2004. Hon. MRIA 1999; Hon. FRSC 2006. Hon. Prof., Shanghai Inst. of Organic Chemistry, Chinese Acad. of Scis, 2001. Camille and Henry Dreyfus Teacher-Scholar Award, 1975; American Chemical Society Awards: Nat. Award in Organometallic Chem., 1988; Arthur C. Cope Scholar, 1990; Polymer Chemistry, 1995; Herman F. Mark Polymer Chemistry, 2000; Herbert C. Brown for Creative Res. in Synthetic Methods, 2001; Arthur C. Cope, 2002; for Creative Res. in Homogenous or Heterogeneous Catalysis, 2003; Richard C. Tolman Medal, 2003; Pauling Award Medal, 2003; Kirkwood Medal, 2005; Nagoya Univ. Medal of Organic Chemistry, 1997; Fluka Prize, Reagent of the Yr, 1998; Benjamin Franklin Medal in Chemistry, Franklin Inst., 2000; Bristol-Myers Squibb Dist. Achievement Award in Organic Synthesis, 2004; August Wilhelm von Hofmann Denkmünze, German Chem. Soc., 2005; (jtly) Nobel Prize in Chemistry, 2005; Havinga Medal, Leiden Univ., 2006. *Publications:* 495 research pubns and 106 patents issued. *Recreations:* rock climbing, walking. *Address:* Chemistry & Chemical Engineering, MC 164–30, California Institute of Technology, Pasadena, CA 91125, USA. *T:* (626) 3956003, *Fax:* (626) 5649297. *E:* rhg@caltech.edu.

GRUBE, Claus, Comdr, First Cl., Order of Dannebrog (Denmark), 2010; Ambassador of Denmark to the Court of St James's, since 2013; *b* Copenhagen, 14 Dec. 1950; *s* of late Willy Grube and Grethe Grube Mikkelsen; *m* 2005, Susanne Fournais; one *s* two *d. Educ:* Copenhagen Univ. (Master in Law 1976). Dep. Judge, Min. of Justice, 1976–77; entered Danish Foreign Service, 1977; Sec., Perm. Mission to EC, Brussels, 1979–83; Hd of Section, Min. of Foreign Affairs, 1983–84; Personal Asst to State Sec. for For. Econ. Affairs, 1984–88; Counsellor (Econ. Affairs), Paris, 1988–93; Dep. Hd, 1993–94, Hd, N Gp 3rd Dept, 1994–97, Min. of Foreign Affairs; Under Sec., N Gp and Ambassador, Min. of Foreign Affairs, 1997–2000; Dep. Perm. Rep., 2000–03, Perm. Rep., 2003–09, EU, Brussels; Perm. Sec. of State, Min. of Foreign Affairs, 2009–13. Grand Cross, Order of Phoenix (Greece), 2009; Grand Cross, Order of Lion (Finland), 2011; Comdr, Order of the Crown (Belgium); Officier, Ordre nat. du Mérite (France). *Recreations:* sailing, outdoor activities. *Address:* Royal Danish Embassy, 55 Sloane Street, SW1X 9SR. *T:* (020) 7333 0202, *Fax:* (020) 7333 0270. *Clubs:* Travellers; Rotary International.

GRUBEN, Baron Thierry de; *see* de Gruben.

GRUDER, Jeffrey Nigel; QC 1997; *b* 18 Sept. 1954; *s* of late Bernard Gruder and Lily Gruder; *m* 1979, Gillian Vera Hyman; one *s* two *d. Educ:* City of London Sch.; Trinity Hall, Cambridge (MA). Called to the Bar, Middle Temple, 1977, Bencher, 2008; in practice at the Bar, 1978–. *Recreations:* reading, theatre, art. *Address:* Essex Court Chambers, 24 Lincoln's Inn Fields, WC2A 3EG. *T:* (020) 7813 8000.

GRÜNBERG, Prof. Peter Andreas; Helmholtz Professor, Forschungszentrum Jülich, Germany, since 2007; *b* Pilsen, 18 May 1939; s of Feodor A. Grünberg and Anna Grünberg; *m* 1966, Helma Prausa; one *s* two *d. Educ:* Johann Wolfgang Goethe Univ., Frankfurt (Intermediate Dip. Physics 1962); Darmstadt Univ. of Technol. (Dip. 1966; Dr 1969); Univ. of Cologne (Privatdozent 1984). Postdoctoral Fellow, NRCC, Carleton Univ., Ottawa, 1969–72; Res. Scientist, Inst. Solid State Res., Forschungszentrum Jülich, 1972–2004. Res. at Argonne Nat. Lab., Ill, 1984–85; Adjunct Prof., Univ. of Cologne, 1992; res. at Univ. of Sendai and Tsukuba Res. Centre, Japan, 1998. Member: Max Planck Soc.; Acad. of Sci. in N Rhine-Westfalia; Gerhard Herzberg Gesellschaft, Darmstadt. Hon. Dr: Ruhr Univ., Bochum, 2002; RWTH Aachen, 2007; Cologne, 2008; Saarland, 2008; Athens, 2009. German Future Prize, Pres. of FRG, 1998; Manfred von Ardenne Prize for Applied Physics, Eur. Soc. of Thin Films, 2004; Eur. Inventor of Year, EC and Eur. Patent Office, 2006; Stern Gerlach Medal, German Physics Soc., 2007; jointly: APS Internat. Prize for New Materials, 1994; Magnetism Award, IUPAP, 1994; Hewlett-Packard Europhysics Prize, 1997; Japan Prize, Sci. and Technol. Foundn of Japan, 2007; Wolf Foundn Prize in Physics, Israel, 2007; Nobel Prize in Physics, 2007. Cross, Order of Merit (Germany), 2008. *Publications:* contrib. jls incl. Physics Rev., Jl Materials Sci. and Engrg, Jl IMMM, Applied Physics, Vacuum. *Recreations:* golf, table tennis, tennis. *Address:* Forschungszentrum Jülich, Institut Peter Grünberg, Wilhelm-Johnen-Straße, 52425 Jülich, Germany.

GRUNDY, David Stanley, CB 1997; Commissioner for Policy and Resources, Forestry Commission, 1992–97; *b* 10 April 1943; *s* of Walter Grundy and Anne Grundy (*née* Pomfret); *m* 1965, Elizabeth Jenny Schadla Hall; one *s. Educ:* De La Salle Coll., Manchester; Jesus Coll., Cambridge (MA); Jesus Coll., Oxford (MPhil). Asst Principal, MOP, 1967–70; Asst Private Sec. to Minister, Min. of Technology, 1970–71; Principal, DTI, 1971–73; Economic Adviser: FCO, 1976–78; DoE, 1978–79; Chief Economic Advr, Govt of Vanuatu, 1979–81; Forestry Commission: Chief Economist, 1982–90; Comr for Finance and Admin, 1990–92. Member: Scottish Ornithologists' Club, 1997–; Scottish Wildlife Trust, 1999– (Vice Chm., 2002–08). *Publications:* (ed) The Birds of Scotland, 2007. *Recreations:* angling, bird watching, gardening, tennis. *Address:* 9 Ann Street, Edinburgh EH4 1PL. *Club:* Dean Tennis (Edinburgh).

GRUNDY, Prof. Emily Marjata Dorothea, PhD; Professor of Demography, London School of Economics and Political Science, since 2013; *b* 24 July 1955; *d* of late John Grundy and Dorothea Grundy (later Sheppard); *m* M. J. Murphy; one *s* one *d* (twins). *Educ:* King's Coll., Cambridge (BA (Hist.) 1976); LSHTM (MSc (Med. Demography) 1979); Univ. of London (PhD Medicine 1989). Res. Officer, Dept of Health Care of Elderly, Univ. of Nottingham, 1981–83; Res. Fellow, Social Stats Res. Unit, City Univ., London, 1983–86; Lectr, then Reader, in Social Gerontology, KCL, 1986–98; Reader in Social Gerontology, 1998–2003, Prof. of Demographic Gerontology, 2003–12, LSHTM; Prof. of Demography, Univ. of Cambridge, 2012–13. Pres., British Soc. for Population Studies, 2008–10. Sec. Gen. and Treas., Internat. Union for the Scientific Study of Population, 2010–14 (Mem. Council, 2014–). *Publications:* Women's Migration, Marriage, Fertility and Divorce, 1989; (jtly) Living Well into Old Age, 1997; (ed jtly) Ageing Well: nutrition, health and social interventions, 2007; approx. 200 papers in learned jls and book chapters. *Recreations:* family and friends, cycling. *Address:* Department of Social Policy, London School of Economics and Political Science, Houghton Street, WC2A 2AE.

GRUNDY, (James) Milton; Founder and Chairman, The Milton Grundy Foundation (formerly Warwick Arts Trust), since 1978; *b* 13 June 1926; civil partnership 2010, Omar Afridi. *Educ:* Cowley Sch.; Sedbergh Sch.; Gonville and Caius Coll., Cambridge (MA). Called to the Bar, Inner Temple, 1954. Founder and Chm., Gemini Trust for the Arts, 1959–66; Founder Mem. and Pres., Internat. Tax Planning Assoc., 1975–; Charter Mem., Peggy Guggenheim Collection, 1980–89; Chm., Internat. Management Trust, 1986–96; Trustee: Nat. Museums and Galls of Merseyside, 1987–96; New End Theatre, Hampstead, 1994–96. *Publications:* Tax and the Family Company, 1956, 3rd edn 1966; Tax Havens, 1968, 8th edn (jtly), as Offshore Business Centres, 2008; Venice, 1971, 6th edn 2007; The World of International Tax Planning, 1984; (jtly) Asset Protection Trusts, 1990, 3rd edn 1997; (with V. I. Atroshenko) Mediterranean Vernacular, 1991; Essays in International Tax Planning, 2001; More Essays in International Tax Planning, 2007; Six Fiscal Fables, 2010. *Recreation:* conversation. *Address:* Gray's Inn Tax Chambers, 36 Queen Street, EC4R 1BN. *T:* (020) 7242 2642.

GRUNDY, Jennifer Anne; JP; Vice Lord-Lieutenant of Merseyside, 2004–10; *b* 29 Sept. 1935; *d* of Edward and Marjorie Denton; *m* 1956, Martin Anthony Wilson Grundy (*d* 2007); one *s* four *d. Educ:* Huyton Coll. JP Knowsley, 1975 (Chm. Bench, 2000–03); DL Merseyside, 1989. *Recreations:* calligraphy, narrow-boating, gardening, traditional canal painting. *Address:* Stanley Cottage, 60 Roby Road, Roby, Liverpool L36 4HF. *T:* (0151) 489 1159. *E:* grundy500@tiscali.co.uk.

GRUNDY, Rev. Canon Dr Malcolm Leslie; Partner, Live-Wires Associates, 2009–12; *b* 22 March 1944; *s* of Arthur James Grundy and Gertrude Alice Grundy; *m* 1972, Wendy Elizabeth Gibson; one *s. Educ:* Sandye Place Sch., Beds; Mander Coll., Bedford; King's Coll.,

London (AKC 1968); Open Univ. (BA 1976); Leeds Univ. (PhD 2014). Ordained deacon 1969, priest 1970; Curate, St George's, Doncaster, 1969–72; Chaplain and Sen. Chaplain, Sheffield Industrial Mission, 1972–80; Dir of Educn, dio. of London, 1980–86; Team Rector of Huntingdon, 1986–91; Dir, Avec, 1991–94; Archdeacon of Craven, 1994–2005; Actg Dean, Bradford Cathedral, 2004–05; Dir, Foundn for Church Leadership, 2005–09. Hon. Canon of Ely, 1988–94; Canon Emeritus, Bradford, 2005. Vis. Fellow, York St John Univ., 2014–. Trustee, Women's Educn Partnership. Mem. Council, Retired Clergy Assoc., 2014–. *Publications:* Light in the City, 1990; An Unholy Conspiracy, 1992; Community Work, 1995; (ed) The Parchmore Partnership, 1995; Management and Ministry, 1996; Understanding Congregations, 1998; (contrib.) Managing, Leading, Ministering, 1999; (jtly) Faith on the Way, 2000; What They Don't Teach You at Theological College, 2003; What's New in Church Leadership, 2007; Leadership and Oversight, 2011; Multi-Congregation Ministry, 2015. *Recreations:* classic cars, gardening, writing. *Address:* 11 Givendale Grove, York YO10 3QF.

GRUNDY, Sir Mark, Kt 2006; Executive Principal, Collegiate Academy Trust and Shireland Collegiate Academy, since 2007; *b* 19 July 1959; *s* of James and Gloria Grundy. *Educ:* Hawtonville Jun. Sch., Newark; Magnus Grammar Sch., Newark; Loughborough Univ. (MSc Human Biol. 1983). Teacher, Forest Comp. Sch., Walsall, 1983–84; Teacher, Darlaston Comp. Sch., Walsall, 1984–87; Sen. Teacher, Thorns Community Coll., Dudley, 1987–92; Dep. Headteacher, Wodensborough Community Technology Coll., Wednesbury, 1992–97; Headteacher, Shireland Lang. Coll., Smethwick, 1997–2007. Exec. Dir, George Salter High Sch., West Bromwich, 2003–11. Consultant Headteacher, DfES, 2001–03. FRSA 2007. *Recreations:* hockey, tennis, watching sport, ICT. *Address:* Shireland Collegiate Academy, Waterloo Road, Smethwick B66 4ND. *T:* (0121) 558 8086, *Fax:* (0121) 558 8377. *E:* m.grundy@collegiateacademy.org.uk.

GRUNDY, Milton; *see* Grundy, J. M.

GRUNDY, Stephanie Christine; legal consultant, legislative drafting; *b* 11 Dec. 1958; *d* of Harry Grundy and June (*née* Hazell). *Educ:* Grange Sch., Oldham; Hertford Coll., Oxford (Schol.; Gibbs Prize; MA, BCL). Called to the Bar, Middle Temple, 1983. Research Asst, Law Commn, 1985; Asst Parly Counsel, 1985–92; on secondment to Law Commn, 1988–90; Legal Advr, Treasury Solicitor's Dept, 1992–2000; Lawyer, FSA, 2000–05; consultancy services to govt depts, IMF, Shearman and Stirling, Bindman and Partners, Lord Lester of Herne Hill, MPs, and others, 2000–. *Recreations:* yoga, walking, conservation. *Address:* 87 Hermitage Road, N4 1LU.

GRUNENBERG, Dr Christoph; Director, Kunsthalle Bremen, since 2011; *b* 28 Oct. 1962; *s* of Johannes and Marlis Grunenberg; *m* 1994, Gina. *Educ:* Johann Wolfgang Goethe Gymnasium, Frankfurt am Main; Courtauld Inst. of Art, Univ. of London (MA 1988; PhD 1993). Res. Asst, Nat. Gall. of Art, Washington, 1990–91; Asst Curator, Kunsthalle Basel, 1993–95; Curator, 1995–99, Actg Dir, 1997–98, Inst. of Contemporary Art, Boston; Curator, Contemporary Art, Collections Div., Tate Gall., London, 1999–2001; Dir, Tate Liverpool, 2001–11. *Publications:* Mark Rothko, 1991; (ed) Gothic: transmutations of horror in late twentieth century art, 1997; (ed) Enterprise: venture and process in contemporary art, 1997; (ed) FRIEZE: wall paintings by Franz Ackerman, John Armleder, Margaret Kilgallen, Sarah Morris and Alexander Scott, 1999; (ed with Victoria Pomery) Marc Quinn, 2002; (ed) Summer of Love: art of the psychedelic era, 2005; (ed with J. Harris) Summer of Love: psychedelic art, social crisis and counterculture in the 1960s, 2005. *Recreations:* books, reading, music, travel. *Address:* Kunsthalle Bremen, Am Wall 207, 28195 Bremen, Germany.

GRUNWALD, Henry Cyril; OBE 2009; QC 1999; *b* 15 Aug. 1949; *s* of Eugen Grunwald and Hetty Grunwald (*née* Steppel); *m* 1976, Alison Appleton; two *s* two *d*. *Educ:* City of London Sch.; University Coll. London (LLB Hons; Fellow, 2006). Called to the Bar, Gray's Inn, 1972, Bencher, 2002. Pres., Bd of Deputies of British Jews, 2003–09 (Vice-Pres., 1997–2000, Sen. Vice-Pres., 2000–03); Warden, Hampstead Synagogue, 1997–2008; Chm., Jewish Leadership Council, 2003–09; Pres., World Jewish Relief, 2009–; Vice-Pres., Council of Christians and Jews, 2009–. Mem., Expert Wkg Gp on Educn, Prime Minister's Holocaust Commn, 2014–. Pres., Relate N London, 2007–09 (Trustee, 1996–2006); Vice-Chm., Holocaust Meml Day Trust, 2005–13; Chairman: Holocaust Centre, Laxton, Nottingham, 2012–; Covenant and Conversation Trust, 2013–. Chm., Shechita UK, 2003–. Patron: Interfaith Youth Trust, 2007–; Drugsline, 2011–; Jewish Heritage UK, 2013–. *Recreations:* family, friends, theatre, reading, travel. *Address:* Charter Chambers, 33 John Street, WC1N 2AT. *T:* (020) 7618 4400. *Club:* Royal Automobile.

GRYBAUSKAITĖ, Dalia, PhD; President of Lithuania, since 2009; *b* Vilnius, 1 March 1956. *Educ:* Leningrad Univ. (degree in Econs 1983); Moscow Acad. of Public Scis (PhD 1988); Foreign Service Sch., Georgetown Univ., Washington. Hd, Dept of Sci., Inst. of Econs, 1990–91; Prog. Dir, Prime Minister's Office, Lithuania, 1991; Director: European Dept, Min. of Internat. Econ. Relns, 1991–93; Econ. Relns Dept, Min. of Foreign Affairs, 1993–94; Envoy and Minister, Lithuanian Mission to EU, Brussels, 1994–95; Minister, Lithuanian Embassy, USA, 1996–99; Deputy Minister: of Finance, 1999–2000; of Foreign Affairs, 2000–01; Minister of Finance, 2001–04; Mem., European Commn, 2004–09. *Address:* (office) S. Daukanto a. 3, Vilnius 01122, Lithuania.

GRYLLS, Edward, (Bear); television presenter and author; Chief Scout, Scout Association, since 2009; *b* 7 June 1974; *s* of Sir (William) Michael (John) Grylls and Sally Grylls; *m* 2000, Shara Cannings Knight; three *s*. *Educ:* Eton Coll.; University Coll. London (BA Hons Spanish). Trooper, E Sqdn, 21 SAS Regt, 1994–99. Ascended summit of Mt Ama Dablam, 1997, summit of Mt Everest, 1998; circumnavigated UK on jetski for RNLI, 2000; crossed Arctic Ocean in open rib for Prince's Trust, 2003; highest open air dinner under hot-air balloon for Duke of Edinburgh Awards, 2005; flew above Mt Everest in powered paraglider for Global Angels, 2007. *Television* series: Escape to the Legion, 2005; Born Survivor, 2006–13; Man vs Wild, 2006–11; Mission Everest, 2008; Bear Grylls: Escape from Hell, 2013; The Island with Bear Grylls, 2014, 2015; Extreme Survival Caught on Camera, 2014; Running Wild, 2014; Bear Grylls: Mission Survive, 2015; Bear Grylls: Breaking Point, 2015; Britain's Biggest Adventures, 2015. Hon. Lt Comdr, RN, 2004; Hon. Lt Col, RM Reserves, 2014. FRGS 1998. *Publications:* Facing Up, 2000; Facing the Frozen Ocean, 2004; Born Survivor, 2007; Bear Grylls' Great Outdoor Adventures, 2008; Mission Survival: gold of the gods, 2008; Mission Survival: way of the wolf, 2008; Mission Survival: sands of the scorpion, tracks of the tiger, 2009; Living Wild, 2009; With Love Papa x, 2009; Mud, Sweat and Tears (autobiog.), 2011; Survival Guide to Life, 2012; To My Sons, 2012; True Grit, 2013; Strike of the Shark, 2013; Claws of the Crocodile, 2013; Rage of the Rhino, 2014; Extreme Food, 2014; Ghost Flight, 2015. *Recreations:* mountaineering, paragliding, sailing, yoga, martial arts, piano. *W:* www.beargrylls.com. *Clubs:* Special Forces, Alpine.

GUARENTE, Catherine Jean; *see* May, C. J.

GUBBAY, Hon. Anthony Roy; SC; Chief Justice of Zimbabwe, 1990–2001; *b* 26 April 1932; *s* of Henry and Gracia Gubbay; *m* 1st, 1962, Alice Wilma Sanger (*d* 2002); two *s*; 2nd, 2006, Suzanne Lesley Cox. *Educ:* Univ. of Witwatersrand, SA (BA); Jesus Coll., Cambridge Univ. (MA, LLM; Hon. Fellow, 1992). Admitted to practice, 1957; emigrated to S Rhodesia, 1958; in private practice as advocate, Bulawayo; SC 1974; Judge: of the High Court, 1977–83; of the Supreme Court, 1983–90. Pres., Valuations Bd, 1974–77; National President: Special Court for Income Tax Appeals, 1974–77; Fiscal Court, 1974–77; Patents Tribunal, 1974–77. Chairman: Legal Practitioners' Disciplinary Tribunal, 1981–87; Law Devolt Commn, 1990–2001; Judicial Service Commn, 1990–2001. Mem., Perm. Court of Arbitration, 1993–. Member: Commonwealth Reference Gp on the promotion of human rights of women and the girl child through the Judiciary, 1996–; Gruber Justice Adv. Bd, 2002–05. Patron, Commonwealth Magistrates' and Judges' Assoc., 1994–2001. Former Pres., Oxford and Cambridge Soc. of Zimbabwe; Mem., Oxford and Cambridge Soc. of Vancouver, 2013–. Hon. Bencher, Lincoln's Inn, 1997. Hon. Mem., Soc. of Legal Scholars, 2004. DU Essex, 1994; Hon. LLD: London, 2002; Witwatersrand, 2005. Peter Gruber Foundn's Annual Justice Award, 2001. Great Cross, Order of Rio Branco (Brazil), 1999. *Recreations:* classical music, philately, tennis, bridge. *Address:* 2802 West One, 1408 Strathmore Mews, Vancouver, BC V6Z 3A9, Canada. *T:* (11) 6046206542. *E:* coxgub@shaw.ca.

GUBBAY, Raymond Jonathan, CBE 2001; Chairman, Raymond Gubbay Ltd, since 2006 (Managing Director, 1966–2006); *b* 2 April 1946; *s* of late David and Ida Gubbay; *m* 1972, Johanna Quirke (marr. diss. 1988); two *d*. *Educ:* University Coll. Sch., Hampstead. Concert promoter, 1966–: regular series of concerts at major London concert halls, including: Royal Festival Hall; Royal Albert Hall; The Barbican (*c* 1,200 concerts, 1982–); also major regl arenas and concert venues; has presented many of the world's greatest artists in concert; The Ratepayers Iolanthe, South Bank and Phoenix Theatre, 1984; The Metropolitan Mikado, South Bank, 1985; also Royal Opera prodn of Turandot, Wembley Arena, 1991; Royal Albert Hall: Centenary prodn of La Bohème, 1996; Carmen, 1997; Swan Lake, 1997; Madam Butterfly, 1998; Romeo and Juliet, 1998; Tosca, 1999; Sleeping Beauty, 2000; Aida, 2001; Cavalleria Rusticana and Pagliacci, 2003; Strictly Gershwin, 2008; The King and I, 2009; Royal Festival Hall: D'Oyly Carte Opera Co., 1998 and 1999 (also Queen's Th., 1998–99, and Savoy Th., 2000, 2001, 2002, 2003); Follies, 2002; On Your Toes, 2003; Carmen Jones, 2007; Bolshoi Ballet, Th. Royal, 2001; Ute Lemper, Queen's Th., 1999, Savoy Th., 2001; Pirates of Penzance, Savoy Th., 2004; Barber of Seville, Marriage of Figaro, Savoy Opera, Savoy Th., 2004; Julie Andrews, Carmen, O2, 2010; Romeo and Juliet, Royal Ballet, O2, 2011; tours and seasons by various visiting ballet cos, incl. Stanislavsky Ballet, RFH, 2001, 2003, 2004; Carl Rosa Gilbert and Sullivan season, Gielgud Th., 2008; Spring Dance Season, incl. NY City Ballet, Carlos Acosta, Sylvie Guillem, Amer. Ballet Th., Cuban Nat. Ballet, Mark Morris, London Coliseum, 2008–10. Founder, City of London Antiques and Fine Art Fair, Barbican Exhibn Halls, 1987–92. Member: Council, Corps of Army Music, 2001–09; Bd of Govs, Central Sch. of Ballet, 2010–; Bd, RPO, 2011–; Bd, Fiery Dragons Ltd, 2011–; Bd, Mousetrap Foundn, 2013–. Hon. FRAM 1988; Hon FTCL 2000. FRSA 2001. *Recreations:* living in Paris and Provence, having six grandchildren. *Address:* Dickens House, 15 Tooks Court, EC4A 1QH. *T:* (020) 7025 3750, *Fax:* (020) 7025 3751. *E:* info@raymondgubbay.co.uk.

GUBBAY, Dr Susan, (Mrs A. R. Davis), FRICS; independent marine consultant working on projects for public sector, private sector, and non-governmental organisations on marine ecology, marine conservation and integrated coastal management, since 1994; *d* of Eldred Gubbay and Flora Gubbay; *m* 1986, Alan Ramsay Davis. *Educ:* Lancaster Univ. (BSc Hons Ecol.); York Univ. (DPhil Marine Ecol.). FRICS. Conservation Officer, 1984–88, Sen. Conservation Officer, 1988–94, Marine Conservation Soc. Buckland Prof. (Marine Protected Areas and Fisheries), Buckland Foundn, 1993. Specialist Advisor: to H of C Envmt Select Cttee inquiry into Coastal Zone Protection and Planning, 1991–94; to Parly Scrutiny Unit Jt Select Cttee inquiry into draft Marine Bill, 2008; Mem., Ministerial Gp reviewing EU Commn Fisheries Policy, 1995–96. Wildlife and Countryside Link: Chair: Jt Marine Wkg Gp, 1993–94; Marine Gp, 1993–96; Member: Action Plan Steering Gp, UK Biodiversity, 1994–95; Cttee, UK Marine Biodiversity, 1997–99; Council, English Nature, 1998–2004; Council, Countryside Council for Wales, 2008–13. Marine and Coastal Biol Diversity expert on Roster of Experts for Convention on Biol Diversity, 1998–. Pres., Eur. Coastal Assoc. of Sci. and Technol. (EUROCOAST), 1994–96. External Examiner: MSc Coastal and Marine Resource Mgt, Univ. of Portsmouth, 1999–2004; Marine Resource Mgt, Univ. of Aberdeen, 2001–05. FRSA 1995. *Publications:* (ed) Marine Protected Areas: principles and techniques for management, 1995; numerous contribs on marine conservation to jls, reports and popular articles. *Recreations:* the great outdoors (above and below sea level), scuba diving, natural history, clarinet, gardening, photography, travel, painting.

GUBBINS, Prof. David, PhD; FRS 1996; CPhys, FInstP; Professor of Geophysics, University of Leeds, 1989–2009, now Emeritus; Research Associate, Institute of Geophysics and Planetary Physics, Scripps Institution of Oceanography, since 2009; Visiting Professor, University of Sydney, since 2011; *b* 31 May 1947; *s* of late Albert Edmund Gubbins and of Joyce Lucy Gubbins; *m* 1972, (Margaret) Stella McCloy; one *s* two *d*. *Educ:* King Edward VI Grammar Sch., Southampton; Trinity Coll., Cambridge (BA, PhD). CPhys, FInstP 1996. Vis. Res. Fellow, Univ. of Colorado, 1972–73; Instructor in Applied Maths, MIT, 1973–74; Asst Prof., Inst. of Geophysics and Planetary Physics, UCLA, 1974–76; Cambridge University: Res. Assistant and Sen. Assistant in Res., Dept of Geodesy and Geophysics, 1976–81; Asst Dir of Res., Dept of Earth Scis, 1981–89; Fellow of Churchill Coll., 1978–90. Fellow, Amer. Geophys. Union, 1985; Foreign Mem., Norwegian Acad. of Arts and Sci., 2005. Murchison Medal, Geol Soc., 1999; Gold Medal, RAS, 2003; John Adam Fleming Medal, Amer. Geophys. Union, 2004; Chree Medal, Inst. of Physics, 2005; Love Medal, 2007, Holmes Medal and Hon. Mem., 2009, Eur. Geoscis Union. *Publications:* Seismology and Plate Tectonics, 1990; Time Series Analysis and Inverse Theory for Geophysicists, 2004; (ed) Encyclopedia of Geomagnetism and Paleomagnetism, 2007; scientific papers. *Recreations:* sailing, swimming. *Address:* School of Earth and Environment, University of Leeds, Leeds LS2 9JT. *T:* (0113) 343 5255. *Club:* Wigtown Bay Sailing.

GUBERT, Walter Alexander; Vice Chairman, since 1988, Chairman, Europe, Middle East and Africa, since 2004, and Member, Executive Committee, since 2005, J. P. Morgan Chase & Co. (formerly J. P. Morgan); *b* Merano, Italy, 15 June 1947; *m* 1974, Caroline Espagno; two *d*. *Educ:* Univ. of Florence (Dr in Law 1970); INSEAD (MBA 1973). Joined J. P. Morgan, Paris, 1973; Hd, Capital Mkts, USA, 1981–87; Leader, J. P. Morgan Securities, EMEA and Asia, 1987–88; Hd, Global Investment Banking, 1988–2000; Sen. Exec. in London, 1989–; Dir, 1995–; Chm., JP Morgan Investment Bank, 2000–. *Recreations:* golf, piano, history, books. *Address:* J. P. Morgan, 1 Boulevard du Roi Albert II, 1210 Brussels, Belgium. *T:* 22088822. *E:* walter.gubert@jpmorgan.com.

GUCKIAN, Dr Noel Joseph, CVO 2010; OBE 2001; HM Diplomatic Service, retired; Ambassador to Oman, 2005–11; *b* 6 March 1955; *s* of William Joseph Guckian and late Mary Patricia Joan Guckian (*née* Kelly); *m* 1990, Lorna Ruth Warren (*d* 2012); one *s* three *d*. *Educ:* Notre Dame Internat. Sch., Rome; New Univ. of Ulster (BA Hons History 1976); UCW, Aberystwyth (MSc Econs, Internat. Politics 1977; PhD Internat. Politics 1985). FCO 1980; Arabic at SOAS, 1983–84; Jedda, 1984–87; 1st Sec., Financial, Paris, 1988; Head, British Interest Section, Tripoli, 1990; Head, Political Section, Kuwait, 1991–92; Counsellor and Dep. Head of Mission, Muscat, 1994–97; Dep. Hd of Mission and Consul-Gen., Tripoli, 1998–2002 (Hd, British Interests Sect., 1998–99, then Chargé d'Affaires *ai* on restoration of diplomatic relns, 1999); Dep. Hd of Mission, Damascus, 2002–04; Consul Gen., Northern Iraq, 2004–05. *Recreations:* fly-fishing, diving, sailing. *Clubs:* Royal Over-Seas League, Travellers; Salisbury and District Angling.

GUDJONSSON, Prof. Gisli Hannes, CBE 2011; PhD; Professor of Forensic Psychology, King's College London, 2000–11, now Emeritus; Hon. Consultant Clinical and Forensic Psychologist, Broadmoor Hospital, since 2012; *b* Reykjavik, Iceland, 26 Oct. 1947; *s* of Gudjon Gudmundsson and Thora Hannesdottir; *m* 1979, Julia Vivienne; two *d*. *Educ:* Brunel Univ. (BSc 1st Cl. Hons Social Scis 1975); Univ. of Surrey (MSc Clin. Psychol. 1977; PhD

1981). Health Professionals Council registered clinical and forensic psychologist. Clin. Psychologist, West Park and Epsom Dist Hosps, 1977–79; Lectr in Psychol., 1980–86, Sen. Lectr in Psychol., 1987–93, Reader in Forensic Psychol., 1993–99, Inst. of Psychiatry, KCL. Consultant in cases for police, prosecution, Criminal Cases Rev. Commn and defence lawyers; also testimony abroad, incl. in USA, Canada, Norway, Israel and The Hague. Hon. DMed Iceland, 2001. JP Croydon, 1990–99. Lifetime Achievement Award: BPsS, 2009; Eur. Assoc. Psychol. and Law, 2012. *Publications:* (with H. Eysenck) The Causes and Cures of Criminality, 1989; The Psychology of Interrogations, Confessions and Testimony, 1992; The Gudjonsson Suggestibility Scales Manual, 1997; (with L. R. C. Haward) Forensic Psychology: a guide to practice, 1998; The Psychology of Interrogations and Confessions: a handbook, 2003; (ed jtly) Witness Testimony: psychological investigative and evidential perspectives, 2006; (ed jtly) Forensic Neuropsychology in Practice: a guide to assessment and legal processes, 2009. *Recreations:* walking, travelling. *Address:* Department of Psychology (PO 78), Institute of Psychiatry, Psychology and Neuroscience, King's College London, De Crespigny Park, Denmark Hill, SE5 8AF. *E:* gisli.gudjonsson@kcl.ac.uk.

GUÉGUINOU, Jean, Hon. GCVO 1996; Commandeur de la Légion d'Honneur (Chevalier 1991; Officier, 2003); Officier de l'Ordre du Mérite, 1995 (Chevalier, 1979); Commandeur, Ordre des Arts et des Lettres, 2007; Ambassadeur de France, 2000; Chairman, French Section, Franco British Council, 2007–10; *b* 17 Oct. 1941. *Educ:* Ecole Nationale d'Administration. Press and Inf. Dept, Min. of Foreign Affairs, Paris, 1967–69; Second Sec., London, 1969–71; Chargé de Mission, Private Office of Ministre d'Etat, Minister of Nat. Defence, 1971–73; Asst Private Sec., then Special Advr to Minister of Foreign Affairs, 1973–76; Principal Private Sec. to Minister of State resp. to Prime Minister, 1976–77; Head of Southern Africa and Indian Ocean Dept, Min. of Foreign Affairs, 1977–82; Consul Gen., Jerusalem, 1982–86; Dir of Press and Inf. Dept, Min. of Foreign Affairs, and Ministry Spokesman, 1986–90; French Ambassador: in Prague, 1990–93 (Czechoslovakia, 1990–92; Czech Republic, 1993); to UK, 1993–98; to the Holy See, 1998–2001; Ambassador and Perm. Deleg. of France to UNESCO, 2002–07. Mem. Governing Body, Agence France Presse, 1986–90. KSG 1976. *Address:* 5 avenue Montespan, 75116 Paris, France.

GUERIN, Orla, Hon. MBE 2005; Egypt Correspondent, BBC News, since 2013; *b* Dublin, 15 May 1966; *d* of late Patrick James Guerin and Monica Guerin; *m* 2003, Michael Georgy. *Educ:* Coll. of Commerce, Dublin (Journalism Cert. 1985); University Coll., Dublin (MA Film Studies 1999). Joined RTE, 1987, E Europe Corresp., 1990–94; BBC: joined as news corresp., 1995; S Europe Corresp., 1996–2000; ME Corresp., 2001–05; Africa Corresp., 2006–08; Pakistan Corresp., 2009–13. DU Essex, 2002; Hon. Dr Dublin Inst. of Technology, 2005; Hon. DLitt Ulster, 2009; DUniv: Open, 2007; QUB, 2009. Broadcaster of the Year, London Press Club, 2002; News and Factual Award, Women in Film and TV, 2003; a Bayeux Prize for War Correspondents, 2007; David Bloom Award, Radio and TV Assoc., 2009.

GUERNSEY, Lord; Heneage James Daniel Finch-Knightley; *b* 29 April 1985; *s* and *heir* of Earl of Aylesford. *Recreations:* ski-ing, archery, field sports. *Heir:* *s* Hon. Alfie Charles Heneage Finch-Knightley, *b* 28 Sept. 2014. *Address:* c/o Packington Hall, Meriden, Warwickshire CV7 7HF.

GUERNSEY, Dean of; *see* Barker, Very Rev. T. R.

GUEST; *see* Haden-Guest.

GUEST, family name of **Viscount Wimborne**.

GUEST, Prof. Anthony Gordon, CBE 1989; QC 1987; FBA 1993; FCIArb; Barrister-at-Law; Professor of English Law, King's College, University of London, 1966–97; *b* 8 Feb. 1930; *o s* of late Gordon Walter Leslie Guest and Marjorie (*née* Hooper), Maidencombe, Devon; unmarried. *Educ:* Colston's Sch., Bristol; St John's Coll., Oxford (MA). Exhibnr and Casberd Schol., Oxford, 1950–54; 1st cl. Final Hon. Sch. of Jurisprudence, 1954. Bacon Schol., Gray's Inn, 1955; Barstow Law Schol., 1955; called to the Bar, Gray's Inn, 1956, Bencher, 1978. University Coll., Oxford: Lectr, 1954–55; Fellow and Prælector in Jurisprudence, 1955–65; Dean, 1963–64; Reader in Common Law to Council of Legal Educn (Inns of Court), 1967–80. Travelling Fellowship to S Africa, 1957; Mem., Lord Chancellor's Law Reform Cttee, 1963–84; Mem., Adv. Cttee on establishment of Law Faculty in University of Hong Kong, 1965; UK Deleg. to UN Commn on Internat. Trade Law, NY, Geneva and Vienna, 1968–84 and 1986–87, to UN Conf. on Limitation of Actions, 1974. Vis. Prof., Univ. of Leuven, 2004–05. Mem., Board of Athlone Press, 1968–73; Mem. Governing Body, Rugby Sch., 1968–88. FKC 1982; FCIArb 1984; FRSA 2004. Served Army and TA, 1948–50 (Lieut RA). *Publications:* (ed) Anson's Principles of the Law of Contract, 21st to 26th edns, 1959–84; Chitty on Contracts: (Asst Editor) 22nd edn 1961, 28th edn to 31st edns, 1999–2012, (Gen. Editor) 23rd to 27th edns, 1968–94; (ed) Oxford Essays in Jurisprudence, 1961; The Law of Hire-Purchase, 1966; (Gen. Editor) Benjamin's Sale of Goods, 1st to 7th edns, 1974–2006; (ed jtly) Encyclopedia of Consumer Credit, 1975; (jtly) Introduction to the Law of Credit and Security, 1978; (ed) Chalmers and Guest on Bills of Exchange, 14th edn to 17th edns, 1991–2009; Only Remember Me (anthology), 1993; The Law of Assignment, 2012; articles in legal jls. *Address:* 17 Ranelagh Grove, SW1W 8PA. *T:* (020) 7730 2799. *Club:* Garrick.

GUEST, Christopher; *see* Haden-Guest, 5th Baron.

GUEST, Ivor Forbes, FRAD 1982; Chairman, 1969–93, Member, 1965–93, Executive Committee, a Vice-President, since 1993, Royal Academy of Dancing; Solicitor; *b* 14 April 1920; *s* of Cecil Marmaduke Guest and Christian Forbes Guest (*née* Tweedie); *m* 1962, Ann Hutchinson; no *c*. *Educ:* Lancing Coll.; Trinity Coll., Cambridge (MA). Admitted a Solicitor, 1949; Partner, A. F. & R. W. Tweedie, 1951–83, Tweedie & Prideaux, 1983–85. Organised National Book League exhibn of books on ballet, 1957–58; Mem. Cttee, Soc. for Theatre Research, 1955–72; Chm., Exec. Cttee, Soc. for Dance Research, 1982–97 (Pres., 1998–); Jt Pres., Dolmetsch Early Dance Soc., 1990–; Member: Exec. Cttee, British Theatre Museum, 1957–77 (Vice-Chm., 1966–77); Cttee, The Theatre Museum, 1984–89 (Mem., Adv. Council, 1974–83). Editorial Adviser to the Dancing Times, 1963–; Trustee: Calvert Trust, 1976–2007; Cecchetti Soc. Trust, 1978–2006; Radcliffe Trust, 1997–2010 (Sec., 1966–96). DUniv Surrey, 1997. Queen Elizabeth II Coronation Award for services to ballet, 1992; Lifetime Achievement Award, Congress on Res. in Dance, 2000. Chevalier, Ordre des Arts et des Lettres (France), 1998. *Publications:* Napoleon III in England, 1952; The Ballet of the Second Empire, 1953–55; The Romantic Ballet in England, 1954; Fanny Cerrito, 1956; Victorian Ballet Girl, 1957; Adeline Genée, 1958; The Alhambra Ballet, 1959; La Fille mal gardée, 1960; The Dancer's Heritage, 1960; The Empire Ballet, 1962; A Gallery of Romantic Ballet, 1963; The Romantic Ballet in Paris, 1966, 2nd edn 2008; Carlotta Zambelli, 1969; Dandies and Dancers, 1969; Two Coppélias, 1970; Fanny Elssler, 1970; The Pas de Quatre, 1970; Le Ballet de l'Opéra de Paris, 1976, 2nd edn 2001, English edn 2006; The Divine Virginia, 1977; Adeline Genée: a pictorial record, 1978; Lettres d'un Maître de ballet, 1978; contrib. Costume and the 19th Century Dancer, in Designing for the Dancer, 1981; Adventures of a Ballet Historian, 1982; Jules Perrot, 1984; Gautier on Dance, 1986; Gautier on Spanish Dancing, 1987; Dr John Radcliffe and his Trust, 1991; Ballet in Leicester Square, 1992; (contrib.) Musica in Scena, 1995; The Ballet of the Enlightenment, 1996; Ballet Under Napoleon, 2002. *Address:* Flat 4, 17 Holland Park, W11 3TD. *T:* (020) 7229 3780. *E:* ahg@lodc.org. *Club:* Garrick.

GUEST, Prof. John Rodney, FRS 1986; Professor of Microbiology, Sheffield University, 1981–2000, now Emeritus; *b* 27 Dec. 1935; *s* of Sidney Ramsey Guest and Dorothy Kathleen Guest (*née* Walker); *m* 1962, Barbara Margaret (*née* Dearsley); one *s* two *d*. *Educ:* Campbell College, Belfast; Leeds Univ. (BSc); Trinity Coll., Oxford Univ. (DPhil). Guinness Fellow, Oxford, 1960–62, 1965; Fulbright Scholar and Research Associate, Stanford, 1963, 1964; Sheffield University: Lectr, Sen. Lectr, Reader in Microbiology, 1965–81. SERC Special Res. Fellow, 1981–86. Marjory Stephenson Prize Lectr, Soc. Gen. Microbiol., 1992; Leeuwenhoek Lectr, Royal Soc., 1995. *Publications:* contribs to Jl of Gen. Microbiol., Biochem. Jl, Microbiol., Molec. Microbiol. *Recreations:* walking in the Peak District, family history. *Address:* Department of Molecular Biology and Biotechnology, Sheffield University, Western Bank, Sheffield S10 2TN. *T:* (0114) 222 4406.

GUEST, Megan Michelle Elaine; *see* Pullum, M. M. E.

GUEST, Melville Richard John, OBE 2007; Chief Executive, Asia House, 1996–2002; *b* 18 Nov. 1943; *s* of late Ernest Melville Charles Guest, DFC and Katherine Mary Guest; *m* 1970, Beatriz Eugenia, (Jenny), Lopez Colombres de Velasco; four *s*. *Educ:* Rugby Sch.; Magdalen Coll., Oxford (MA Jurisprudence). HM Diplomatic Service, 1966–96: Third, later Second, Sec., Tokyo, 1967–72; Pvte Sec. to Parly Under-Sec. of State, FCO, 1973–75; First Sec., Paris, 1975–79; FCO, 1979–80; Prés.-Dir Gén., Soc. Française des Industries Lucas, 1980–85; Dir, Thomson-Lucas SA, 1980–85; Director: Franco-British Chamber of Commerce, 1980–85; Channel Tunnel Gp, 1985–86; Counsellor (Commercial), Tokyo, 1986–89; Counsellor (Political) and Consul General, Stockholm, 1990–93; Head, S Pacific Dept, 1993–94, SE Asian Dept, 1994–96, FCO. Executive Director: UK-Korea Forum for the Future, 1998–2007; UK-Japan 21st Century Gp, 2001–08; Rapporteur, UK-India Round Table, 2000–08. Sen. Adviser, Imperial Coll. London, 2005–13. Mem., Bd of Govs, Ampleforth Coll., 1989–96. Japanese Foreign Minister's Award, 2009. *E:* melvilleguest@hotmail.com. *Clubs:* Hurlingham; Vincent's (Pres., 1965–66; Chm., Vincent's 150, 2011–).

GUETERBOCK, family name of **Baron Berkeley**.

GUGGENHEIM, Her Honour Anna Maeve; QC 2001; a Circuit Judge, 2006–14; *b* 2 Sept. 1959; *d* of Peter Francis Guggenheim and Maura Teresa Guggenheim (*née* McCarthy); *m* 1987, Mark Eban; one *s* one *d*. *Educ:* King Edward VI High Sch. for Girls, Edgbaston; Somerville Coll., Oxford (BA Juris. 1981). Called to the Bar, Gray's Inn, 1982; barrister, 1982–2005; a Recorder, 2002–05. *Recreation:* sailing.

GUILD, Lorna Allison; *see* Drummond, L. A.

GUILD, Rear-Adm. Nigel Charles Forbes, CB 2003; PhD; FIET, FIMarEST, FREng, FIMA, FCGI; Chief Naval Engineer Officer, and Senior Responsible Owner (Carrier Strike), Ministry of Defence, 2003–08; *b* 9 Feb. 1949; *s* of Surg. Capt. William John Forbes Guild and Joan Elizabeth Guild (*née* Innes); *m* 1971, Felicity Jean Wilson; two *s*. *Educ:* Fernden Sch.; Bryanston Sch.; BRNC Dartmouth; Trinity Coll., Cambridge (BA); Univ. of Bristol (PhD 1979; Hon. DEng 2006). MIEE 1980; MIMA 1980; FIMarEST 2001; FIET (FIEE 2002); FREng 2007; FIMA 2008. Joined Royal Navy, 1966; HMS Hermes, 1972–75; Weapons Trials, 1976–78; British Underwater Test and Evaluation Centre Project, 1979–82; HMS Euryalus, 1982–84 and 1986–87; Future Projects (Naval), 1984–85; HMS Beaver, 1987–88; Staff Weapons Engr Officer to FO Sea Trng, 1988–90; MA to Chief of Defence Procurement, 1991–92; CSO (E) Surface Flotilla, 1993–95; Project Dir, PE, MoD, 1996–99; Controller of the Navy, and Exec. Dir 4, Defence Procurement Agency, MoD, 2000–03. Chm., Atlas Elektronik UK Ltd, 2009–. Chm., Engrg Council, 2011–. FCGI 2010. *Publications:* contrib. papers on Fuzzy Logic. *Recreations:* rowing, village pantomime, steam boating. *Address:* 20 Church Street, Modbury, Devon PL21 0QR. *E:* nigel_guild@lineone.net. *Club:* Leander (Henley on Thames).

GUILDFORD, Bishop of, since 2014; **Rt Rev. Andrew John Watson;** *b* Bicester, 16 July 1961; *s* of Angus Watson and Alison Watson; *m* 1986, Beverly Anne Woolcock; two *s* two *d*. *Educ:* MA Cantab 1990. Ordained deacon, 1987, priest, 1988; Curate, St Peter's, Ipsley, Redditch, 1987–91; Curate, subseq. Associate Vicar, St John's & St Peter's, Notting Hill, 1991–96; Vicar, St Stephen's, E Twickenham, 1996–2008; Area Dean of Hampton, 2003–08; Bishop Suffragan of Aston, 2008–14. *Publications:* The Fourfold Leadership of Jesus, 2008; Confidence in the Living God, 2009; The Way of the Desert, 2011. *Recreations:* piano, bassoon, singing, composing, cliff-walking, photography. *Address:* Willow Grange, Woking Road, Guildford, Surrey GU4 7QS. *T:* (01483) 590500. *E:* bishop.andrew@cofeguildford.org.uk.

GUILDFORD, Dean of; *see* Gwilliams, Very Rev. D. L.

GUILFORD, 10th Earl of, *cr* 1752; **Piers Edward Brownlow North;** Baron Guilford 1683; *b* 9 March 1971; *s* of 9th Earl of Guilford and Osyth Vere Napier, *d* of Cyril Napier Leeston Smith; *S* father, 1999; *m* 1994, Michèle Desvaux de Marigny; one *s* one *d*. *Heir:* *s* Lord North, *qv*. *Address:* Waldershare Park, Dover, Kent CT15 5BA. *T:* (01304) 820245.

GUILFOYLE, Hon. Dame Margaret (Georgina Constance), AC 2005; DBE 1980; Chair, Judicial Remuneration Tribunal, 1995–2001; Deputy Chair, Infertility Authority, 1995–2001; *b* 15 May 1926; *d* of William and Elizabeth McCartney; *m* 1952, Stanley M. L. Guilfoyle; one *s* two *d*. *Educ:* ANU (LLB 1990). FCIS; FCPA. Senator for Victoria, 1971–87; Minister: for Education, Commonwealth of Australia, 1975; for Social Security, 1975–80; for Finance, 1980–83. Dep. Chm., Mental Health Res. Inst., 1988–2001; Dir, Aust. Children's TV Foundn, 1989–2002 (Dep. Chm., 1989–2002). Mem., Infertility Treatment Authy, 1996–2003. *Recreations:* reading, gardening. *Address:* 34/2 Malmsbury Street, Kew, Vic 3101, Australia. *Club:* Lyceum (Melbourne).

GUILLAUME, Gilbert Pierre; Judge, International Court of Justice, 1987–2005 (President, 2000–03), now Judge *ad hoc*; *b* 4 Dec. 1930; *s* of Pierre Guillaume and Berthe (*née* Brun); *m* 1961, Marie-Anne Hidden; one *s* two *d*. *Educ:* Univ. of Paris (LLM Law and Econ.); Inst. of Political Scis, Paris (Dip.); Ecole Nat. d'Admin. Mem., Council of State, France, 1957–96; Legal Advr, Secretariat for Civil Aviation, France, 1968–79; Director of Legal Affairs: OECD, 1978–79; Ministry of Foreign Affairs, France, 1979–87. Pres. or Mem., Permanent Court of Arbitration, ICSID and other arbitration tribunals. Mem., Institut de France, 2007. Grand Officier de la Légion d'Honneur (France) 2005. *Publications:* Terrorisme et Droit International, 1989; Les grandes crises internationales et le droit, 1994; La Cour Internationale de Justice à l'Aube du XXIe Siècle, 2003. *Address:* 36 rue Perronet, 92200 Neuilly-sur-Seine, France. *E:* g.ma.guillaume@orange.fr.

GUILLE, Very Rev. John Arthur; Dean of Southwell, 2007–14, now Dean Emeritus; *b* 21 May 1949; *s* of Arthur Leonard Guille and Winifred Maud Guille (*née* Lane); *m* 1976, Susan Stallard; one *s* two *d*. *Educ:* Guernsey GS for Boys; Christ Church Coll., Canterbury (CertEd London 1970); Salisbury and Wells Theol Coll.; BTh Southampton 1979; Univ. of Wales, Lampeter (MA 2008). Teacher of Religious Studies: Stockbridge Co. Secondary Sch., 1970–72; St Sampson's Secondary Sch., 1972–73; ordained deacon 1976, priest 1977; Curate, Chandler's Ford, 1976–80; Priest i/c, St John, Surrey Road, Bournemouth, 1980–84, Vicar, St John with St Michael, 1984–89; Rector, St André de la Pommeraye, Guernsey, 1989–99; Vice Dean, Guernsey, 1996–99; Archdeacon of Basingstoke, 1999–2000; Canon Residentiary, Winchester Cathedral, 1999–2007; Archdeacon of Winchester, 2000–07. *Publications:* A Millennium of Archdeacons, 2003. *Recreations:* walking, gardening, family history.

GUILLEBAUD, Rev. (Jette) Margaret; Associate Chaplain, Sarum College, 2010–13; Chaplain, Church House, Salisbury, since 2011; *b* 24 March 1948; *d* of Justin Brooke and Kirsten (*née* Møller-Larsen); *m* 1st, 1971, Robin Simon, *qv* (marr. diss. 1978); one *s* one *d*; 2nd, 1984, Hugh Guillebaud. *Educ:* Wycombe Abbey Sch. (Head Girl); Exeter Univ. (BA Hons Eng.); Ripon Coll., Cuddesdon. Tutor, Oxford Sch. of English, Verona, Italy, 1971–72; Examr, Oxford Exams Bd, 1972–75; Tutor, Open Univ., 1973–75; Man. Dir, Jobline Employment Agency, 1989–91; Chairman: SW Arts, 1991–97; English Regl Arts Bds, 1993–94; Mem., Arts Council of England, 1994–97. Ordained deacon, 2005, priest, 2006. Curate, later Cathedral Asst Priest, Salisbury Cath., 2005–10. Chm., Glos Ambulance NHS Trust, 1991–93. Non-executive Director: Cheltenham Festivals Ltd, 1991–96; at Bristol (formerly Bristol 2000), 1995–2001; Harbourside Centre, Bristol, 1995–2000; South West Film Commn, 1997–2002. Mem. Bd, Salisbury Internat. Arts Festival, 2006–15. Trustee, Holburne Mus., Bath, 1997–2002. Governor: Bath Spa UC (formerly Bath Coll. of Higher Educn), 1996–98; Wyvern Coll., 2007–11; Sarum Acad., Salisbury, 2011–. Mem., Univ. of Gloucestershire Develt Adv. Bd, 2001–03. JP S Glos, 1988–98. FRSA 1992. Hon. MA UWE, 1998. *Recreations:* opera, theatre, visual arts, fishing, travel. *Address:* 178 The Close, Salisbury SP1 2EZ.

GUILLEM, Sylvie, Hon. CBE 2003; ballet dancer; *b* Paris, 23 Feb. 1965. *Educ:* Ecole de Danse, Paris Opera. With Paris Opera, 1981–89, Etoile, 1984; with Royal Ballet Co., 1989–2006; guest artist with other cos, 1989–2015. Lead roles in: Giselle; Swan Lake; La Bayadère; Cinderella; Sleeping Beauty; Romeo and Juliet; Raymonda; Manon; Don Quixote; Marguerite and Armand; Lilac Garden; Carmen; Winter Dreams. Title role created for her in Sissi, Rudra Béjart Co.; other created roles in: In the Middle, somewhat Elevated; Le Martyre de Saint-Sebastien; Firstext; Rearray, Bye, 2011. Prod Giselle for Nat. Ballet of Finland, 1999, for La Scala, Milan, 2001. Comdr des Arts et des Lettres (France), 1988; Chevalier de la Légion d'Honneur (France), 1994; Officier de l'Ordre du Mérite (France), 1999.

GUILLEMIN, Prof. Roger Charles Louis, MD, PhD; Distinguished Professor, Salk Institute, La Jolla, since 1997 (Interim President, 2007–09); *b* Dijon, France, 11 Jan. 1924; (naturalized US Citizen, 1963); *s* of Raymond Guillemin and Blanche (*née* Rigollot); *m* 1952, Lucienne Jeanne Billard; one *s* five *d*. *Educ:* Univ. of Dijon (BA 1941, BSc 1942); Faculty of Medicine, Lyons (MD 1949); Univ. of Montreal (PhD 1953). Resident Intern, univ. hosps, Dijon, 1949–51; Associate Dir, then Asst Prof., Inst. of Exper. Medicine and Surgery, Univ. of Montreal, 1951–53; Prof. of Physiol. and Dir, Labs for Neuroendocrinology, Baylor Coll. of Med., Houston, 1953–70; Associate Dir, Dept of Exper. Endocrinol., Coll. de France, Paris, 1960–63; Resident Fellow and Res. Prof., and Chm., Labs for Neuroendocrinology, Salk Inst. for Biol Studies, 1970–89; Dist. Prof., Whittier Inst. for Diabetes and Endocrinology, La Jolla, 1989–94 (Dir, 1993–94). Adjunct Professor: of Physiol., Baylor Coll. of Med., 1970–; of Medicine, UCSD, 1970–94. Member: Nat. Acad. of Sciences, USA, 1974; Amer. Acad. Arts and Scis, 1976; Amer. Physiol Soc.; Endocrine Soc. (Pres., 1986); Soc. of Exptl Biol. and Medicine; Internat. Brain Res. Orgn; Internat. Soc. Res. Biol Reprodn. Foreign Associate: Acad. des Sciences, France; Acad. Nat. de Médecine, Paris; Hon. Mem., Swedish Soc. of Med. Scis; Foreign Mem., Acad. Royale de Médecine de Belgique. Mem. Club of Rome. Hon. DSc: Rochester, NY, 1976; Chicago, 1977; Manitoba, 1984; Kyung Hee Univ., Seoul, Korea, 1986; Univ. de Paris VII, 1986; Madrid, 1988; Univ. Claude Bernard, Lyon, 1989; Laval Univ., Quebec, 1990; Sherbrooke Univ., Quebec, 1997; Hon. MD: Ulm, 1978; Montreal, 1979; Univ. Libre de Bruxelles, Belgium, 1979; Turin, 1985; Barcelona, 1988; Univ. Claude Bernard, Lyon I, 1989; Laval Univ., Quebec, 1996; Hon. LMed Baylor Coll. of Med., 1978. Gairdner Internat. Award, 1974; Lasker Award, USA, 1975; Dickson Prize in Medicine, Univ. of Pittsburgh, 1976; Passano Award in Med. Sci., Passano Foundn, Inc., 1976; Schmitt Medal in Neuroscience, Neurosciences Res. Prog., MIT, 1977; National Medal of Science, USA, 1977; (jtly) Nobel Prize in Physiology or Medicine, 1977; Barren Gold Medal, USA, 1979; Dale Medal (Soc. for Endocrinology), UK, 1980; Ellen Browning Scripps Soc. Medal, Scripps Meml Hosps Foundn, San Diego, 1988; Dist. Scientist Award, Nat. Diabetes Res. Coalition, 1996. Officier, Légion d'Honneur, France, 1984. *Publications:* scientific pubns in learned jls. *Recreation:* computer art (one-man shows, Milan, 1991, Houston, 1996, Paris, 1999; jtly with sculptures by son François, Athenaeum, La Jolla, Calif, 2012). *Address:* The Salk Institute, 10010 N Torrey Pines Road, La Jolla, CA 92037–1099, USA.

GUILLERY, Prof. Rainer Walter, PhD; FRS 1983; Professor of Anatomy, Marmara University, 2007–10; Visiting Professor, Department of Anatomy, University of Wisconsin, 1996–2002, now Professor Emeritus; *b* 28 Aug. 1929; *s* of Hermann Guillery and Eva (*née* Hackel); *m* 1954, Margot Cunningham Pepper (marr. diss. 2000); three *s* one *d*. *Educ:* University Coll. London (BSc, PhD; Fellow, 1987). Asst Lectr, subseq. Reader, Anatomy Dept, UCL, 1953–64; Associate Prof., subseq. Prof., Anatomy Dept, Univ. of Wisconsin, Madison, USA, 1964–77; Prof., Dept of Pharmacol and Physiol Sciences, Univ. of Chicago, 1977–84; Dr Lee's Prof. of Anatomy and Fellow of Hertford Coll., Univ. of Oxford, 1984–96. Hon. Emeritus Res. Fellow, MRC Anatomical Neuropharmacol. Unit, Oxford Univ., 2010–. Pres., Anatomical Soc. of GB&I, 1994–96. Editor-in-chief, European Jl of Neuroscience, 1988–92. *Publications:* (jtly) Exploring the Thalamus, 2001, 2nd edn 2006; Functional Connections of Cortical Areas, 2013; contrib. Jl of Anat., Jl of Comp. Neurol., Jl of Neuroscience, and Brain Res. *Address:* 4 Sherwood Place, Oxford OX3 9PR.

GUILLOU, Prof. Pierre John, MD; FRCS, FMedSci; Professor of Surgery, St James's University Hospital, Leeds, 1993–2007, now Emeritus; Dean of the School of Medicine, University of Leeds, 1998–2002; *b* 30 Oct. 1945; *s* of Sarah Anne Guillou (*née* Greenfield) and Yves Guillou; *m* 1998, Patricia Katherine Ollerenshawe; one *s* one *d* from previous marriage. *Educ:* Normanton Grammar Sch.; Univ. of Leeds (BSc; MB ChB 1970; MD 1975). Leeds Gen. Infirmary and St James's Univ. Hosp., 1970–73; S Manchester Univ. Hosp., 1973–74; Surgical Registrar, Leeds Gen. Infirmary, 1974–76; Lectr in Surgery, Univ. of Leeds, 1976–79; MRC Fellow in Immunology, Hôpital Necker, Paris, 1979–80; Sen. Lectr in Surgery, Univ. of Leeds, 1980–88; Prof. of Surgery, Imperial Coll. of Sci., Technology and Medicine and Dir, Academic Surgical Unit, St Mary's Hosp., London, 1988–93. Visiting Professor: Aust. Surgical Res. Soc., 1989, 1992; Univ. of Richmond, Va, 1992; S African Surgical Res. Soc., 1993; Ethicon, Malaysia, 1995; Sir Arthur Sims Commonwealth Prof., 1996; Lectures: Crookshank, Royal Soc. of Radiologists, 1990; Smith, Univ. of WA, 1991; A. B. Mitchell, QUB, 1991; jt meeting of Royal Colls of Surgeons of India and Glasgow, Madras, 1992; G. B. Ong, also Wilson T. S. Wang Internat. Surgical Symposium on Surgical Oncology, Chinese Univ. of Hong Kong, 1992, 1994; Annual Scientific Meeting of the Royal Coll. of Surgeons of Thailand, 1993; Stanford Cade, RCS, 1994; Marjorie Budd, Univ. of Bristol, 1995; 12th Asia Pacific Cancer Conf., Singapore, 1995. Member: James IV Assoc. of Surgeons, 1992–; Eur. Surgical Assoc., 1994–. Founder FMedSci 1998. Ed., British Jl of Surgery, 1994–2003; Ed.-in-Chief, Internat. Jl of Med. Robotics and Computer-Assisted Surgery, 2003–06. *Publications:* (ed) Surgical Oncology, 1991; Clinical Surgery, 1992; numerous papers on immunology, cell biology and surgery in treatment of cancer. *Recreations:* work, golf, fishing, work. *Club:* Royal Society of Medicine.

GUINERY, Paul Trevor; musician; broadcaster; *b* 19 Jan. 1957; *s* of Dennis William Prickett and Eileen Grace Guinery. *Educ:* St Paul's Sch.; Royal Coll. of Music (ARCM 1975); Queen's Coll., Oxford (BA 1979). Joined BBC, 1980: studio manager, 1980–85; announcer and newsreader: World Service, 1985–89; Radio 3, 1989–2002; Presenter: Your Concert Choice, 1990–92; Concert Hall, 1992–98; Sacred and Profane, 1993–98; Choral Voices, 1998; Sounding the Millennium, 1999; Choirworks, 1999–2003. Vice-Chm., Delius Soc., 2001–03. *Publications:* Delius and Fenby (with Lyndon Jenkins), 2004; Delius and his Music, 2014; articles in Delius Soc. Jl. *Recreations:* playing the piano, theatre, collecting sheet music. *Address:* 68 Cambridge Street, SW1V 4QQ.

GUINNESS, family name of **Earl of Iveagh** and **Baron Moyne**.

GUINNESS, Bunny; landscape architect, journalist and broadcaster; Director, Bunny Guinness Landscape Design Ltd, since 1986; *b* Marlborough, 16 Dec. 1955; *d* of late Sqdn Ldr Peter William Ellis, DFC and Barbara Helen Stockitt (*née* Austin); *m* 1976, Kevin Michael Rundell Guinness; one *s* one *d*. *Educ:* Bath High Sch.; Reading Univ. (BSc Hons Horticulture 1977); Birmingham City Univ. (Dip. Landscape Arch. 1981). Assistant landscape architect: Maurice Pickering Associates, 1978–80; Wimpey Gp Services, 1980–82; landscape architect, Lewisham BC, 1982–84; Regl Landscape Architect, McCarthy & Stone plc, 1984–86. Panellist, Gardeners' Question Time, BBC Radio 4, 1999–; presenter and/or contributor to TV progs, incl. Guinness in the Garden, Better Gardens, Small Town Gardens, Great Garden Challenge; gardening columnist, Sunday Telegraph, 2003–. DUniv Birmingham City, 2009. Gold Medals, Chelsea Flower Show, 1994, 1995, 1996, 1998, 1999, 2001; Garden Writer of the Year, LSL Property Press Awards, 2014, 2015. *Publications:* Creating a Family Garden, 1996, 4th edn as Family Gardens, 2008; Garden Transformations, 1999, 2nd edn 2002; Garden Workshop, 2001; Decorative Gardening with Bunny Guinness, 2005; (with J. Knox) Garden Your Way to Health and Fitness, 2008; (with HRH the Prince of Wales) Highgrove: a garden celebrated, 2014. *Recreations:* family, including Jack Russells, extreme gardening, self sufficiency including growing, breeding and eating my own livestock and veg, cooking. *Address:* Sibberton Lodge, Thornhaugh, Peterborough, Cambs PE8 6NH. *E:* bunnyguinness@btconnect.com. *W:* www.bunnyguinness.com.

GUINNESS, Hon. Desmond (Walter); writer; *b* 8 Sept. 1931; *yr s* of 2nd Baron Moyne and Hon. Diana Mitford (later Hon. Lady Mosley) (*d* 2003); *m* 1st, 1954, Marie-Gabrielle von Urach (marr. diss. 1981; she *d* 1989); one *s* one *d*; 2nd, Penelope, *d* of late Graham and Teresa Cuthbertson. *Educ:* Gordonstoun; Christ Church, Oxford (MA). Founder, 1958, and Chm., 1958–91, Irish Georgian Society to work for the study of, and protection of, buildings of architectural merit in Ireland, particularly of the Georgian period. Mem., Friendly Brothers of St Patrick, 1973–. Hon. LLD TCD, 1980. *Publications:* Portrait of Dublin, 1967; Irish Houses and Castles, 1971; Mr Jefferson, Architect, 1973; Palladio, 1976; Georgian Dublin, 1980; The White House: an architectural history, 1981; Newport Preserv'd, 1982; (with Jacqueline O'Brien) Great Irish Houses and Castles, 1992; (with Jacqueline O'Brien) Dublin: a Grand Tour, 1994. *Clubs:* Chelsea Arts; Kildare Street and University, Royal Irish Automobile.

GUINNESS, Sir Howard (Christian Sheldon), Kt 1981; VRD 1953; *b* 3 June 1932; *s* of late Edward Douglas Guinness, CBE and Martha Letière (*née* Sheldon); *m* 1958, Evadne Jane Gibbs; two *s* one *d*. *Educ:* King's Mead, Seaford, Sussex; Eton Coll. National Service, RN (midshipman); Lt-Comdr RNR. Union Discount Co. of London Ltd, 1953; Guinness Mahon & Co. Ltd, 1953–55; S. G. Warburg & Co. Ltd, 1955–85 (Exec. Dir, 1970–85). Dir, Harris & Sheldon Gp Ltd, 1960–81; Dir and Dep. Chm., Youghal Carpets (Holdings) Ltd, 1972–80. Director: Quality Milk Producers Ltd, 1988–2000; Riyad Bank Europe, 1993–99. Chm., N Hampshire Conservative Assoc., 1971–74; Vice-Chm. 1974, Chm. 1975–78, and Treasurer 1978–81, Wessex Area, Cons. Assoc. Mem. Council, English Guernsey Cattle Soc., 1963–72, 1996–99. *Recreations:* ski-ing, tennis. *Address:* The Manor House, Glanvilles Wootton, Sherborne, Dorset DT9 5QF. *T:* (01963) 210217. *Club:* White's.

See also Sir J. R. S. Guinness.

GUINNESS, Sir John (Ralph Sidney), Kt 1999; CB 1985; FSA; Chairman, Trinity Group Finance Ltd, 1999–2003; *b* 23 Dec. 1935; *s* of late Edward Douglas Guinness and Martha Letière (*née* Sheldon); *m* 1967, Valerie Susan North (*d* 2014); one *s* one *d* (and one *s* decd). *Educ:* Rugby Sch.; Trinity Hall, Cambridge (BA Hons History, MA Hons). Union Discount Co. Ltd, 1960–61; Overseas Develt Inst., 1961–62; joined FO, 1962; Econ. Relations Dept, 1962–63; Third Sec., UK Mission to UN, New York, 1963–64; seconded to UN Secretariat as Special Asst to Dep. Under-Sec. and later Under-Sec. for Econ. and Social Affairs, 1964–66; FCO, 1967–69; First Sec. (Econ.), Brit. High Commn, Ottawa, 1969–72; seconded to Central Policy Rev. Staff, Cabinet Office, 1972–75; Counsellor, 1974; Alternate UK Rep. to Law of the Sea Conf., 1975–77; seconded to CPRS, 1977–79; transferred to Home Civil Service, 1980; Under-Sec., 1980–83, Dep. Sec., 1983–91, Permanent Sec., 1991–92, Dept of Energy. Chm., British Nuclear Fuels, 1992–99; Director: Guinness Mahon Hldgs, 1993–99; Ocean Gp, 1993–2000; Mithras Investment Trust, 1994–2006. Governor, Oxford Energy Inst., 1984–92. Chairman: Reviewing Cttee on Export of Works of Art, 1995–2004; Expert Panel, Heritage Lottery Fund, 2005; Expert Panel, NHMF, 2006–13. Member: E Anglia Regl Cttee, NT, 1989–94; Develt Cttee, Nat. Portrait Gall., 1994–99; Council, BITC, 1992–99; Pres. Cttee, CBI, 1997–99 (Mem. Council, 1993–97); Dir, UK-Japan 2000 Gp, 1995–99. Mem., Adv. Council, Business Div., Prince's Trust, 1999–; Trustee: Prince's Youth Business Trust, 1992–99; Royal Collection Trust, 2001–07; Nat. Maritime Mus., 2005–13; Heritage Conservation Trust, 2006–; Gov., Compton Verney House Trust, 2000–03; Mem., Eton Collections Cttee, 2009–. Hon. Freeman, Co. of Fuellers, 1999. FSA 2005. Hon. Fellow: Mgt Sch., Lancaster Univ., 1997; Univ. of Central Lancashire, 1998. *Recreation:* iconography. *Clubs:* Brooks's, Beefsteak.

See also Sir H. C. S. Guinness.

GUINNESS, Sir Kenelm (Edward Lee), 5th Bt *cr* 1867, of Ashford, co. Galway; commercial pilot; *b* Washington, DC, USA, 30 Jan. 1962; *er s* of Sir Kenelm Ernest Lee Guinness, 4th Bt and of Jane Nevin Guinness (*née* Dickson); *S* father, 2011; *m* 2001, Melissa Ann Wheeley; one *s* one *d*. *Educ:* Maret Sch., Washington, DC; Embry-Riddle Aeronautical Univ., USA (BSc). Founder/operator, Bay Seaplane Service, 1988; chief pilot, Safari Air, 1999–2011. *Recreation:* yacht racing. *Heir: s* Kenelm Arthur Lee Guinness, *b* 15 Nov. 2005. *Address:* General Delivery, Hope Town, Elbow Cay, Bahamas. *T:* 6993109. *Clubs:* Cruising Club of America; Quiet Birdmen.

GUINNESS, William Loel Seymour; Chairman, Sibir Energy Plc, 1999–2009; *b* 28 Dec. 1939; *s* of Thomas Loel Evelyn Guinness, OBE and Lady Isabel Guinness (*née* Manners, later Throckmorton), *d* of 9th Duke of Rutland; *m* 1st, 1971, Elizabeth Lynn Day (marr. diss. 1994); two *s* one *d*; 2nd, 2003, Lucia Gomez de Parada. *Educ:* Ludgrove; Eton. Commnd Irish Guards, 1959–61. Non-exec. Dir, Henry Ansbacher, 1983–93, and other cos. Mem. (C), Daventry DC, 1976–83 (Leader, 1977–83). *Recreations:* golf, photography, gardening, travelling. *Address:* Zanroc, Chemin de Ballegue 58, 1066 Epalinges, Switzerland. *T:* (21) 7843427, *Fax:* (21) 7843565. *E:* bguinness@mac.com. *Clubs:* White's, Pratt's; Swinley Forest Golf; Royal West Norfolk Golf (Brancaster); Golf de Lausanne; Corviglia (St Moritz).

GUISE, Sir (Christopher) James, 8th Bt *cr* 1783, of Highnam Court, Glos; *b* 10 July 1930; *s* of Sir Anselm William Edward Guise, 6th Bt and Nina Margaret Sophie, *d* of Sir James Augustus Grant, 1st Bt; *S* brother, 2007; *m* 1969, Mrs Carole Hoskins Benson (*née* Master); one *s* one *d*. *Educ:* Wellesley House; Stowe. Business and banking career in London and S Africa; now retired company Dir. *Recreations:* fishing, shooting, gardening. *Heir: s* Anselm Mark Guise [*b* 7 Feb. 1971; *m* (marr. diss.); *m* 2010, Sarah Whewell; one *s* one *d*]. *Address:* Weir Farm, Elmore, Glos GL2 3NS. *E:* jamie.guise@virgin.net. *Clubs:* Turf, Beefsteak, MCC.

GUIVER, Rev. Fr George Paul Alfred, CR; Superior, Community of the Resurrection, since 2003; *b* 18 Dec. 1945; *s* of Alfred and Doris Guiver. *Educ:* St Chad's Coll., Durham (BA 1968); Cuddesdon Coll., Oxford (Cert. in Theology 1973). Ordained deacon 1973, priest

1974; Curate, Mill End and Heronsgate with West Hyde, St Albans, 1973–76; Priest-in-charge, Bishop's Frome, Castle Frome, Acton Beauchamp and Evesbatch, Hereford, 1976–82; Community of the Resurrection, 1983–; Vice-Principal, Coll. of the Resurrection, 1990–2002. Hon. Lectr, Leeds Univ., 1990–. *Publications:* Company of Voices: daily prayer and the people of God, 1988; Faith in Momentum: the distinctiveness of the church, 1990; (ed) The Fire and the Clay: the priest in today's church, 1993; Everyday God, 1994; Pursuing the Mystery: worship and daily life as presences of God, 1996; (ed) Priests in a People's Church, 2001; Vision Upon Vision: processes of change and renewal in Christian worship, 2009. *Recreations:* cycling and recycling. *Address:* Community of the Resurrection, Mirfield, W Yorks WF14 0BN. *T:* (01924) 483301, *Fax:* (01924) 490489. *E:* GGuiver@mirfield.org.uk.

GULL, Prof. Keith, CBE 2004; PhD; FRS 2003; Professor of Molecular Microbiology, University of Oxford, since 2004, and Principal, St Edmund Hall, Oxford, since 2009; *b* 29 May 1948; *s* of David Gull and Doris Gull (*née* Manging); *m* 1972, Dianne Hilary Leonora Elgar; one *s* one *d*. *Educ:* Queen Elizabeth Coll., Univ. of London (BSc Hons 1969, PhD 1972, Microbiology). University of Kent: Lectr, 1972–82; Sen. Lectr, 1982–84; Reader, 1984–86; Prof. of Cell Biology, 1986–89; Prof. of Molecular Biology, Univ. of Manchester, 1989–2002; Wellcome Trust Principal Res. Fellow, Univ. of Oxford, 2002–09; Sen. Res. Fellow, Lincoln Coll., Oxford, 2002–09. Vis. Sen. Scientist, Sandoz Inst., Vienna, 1978; Vis. Prof., McArdle Lab. for Cancer Res., Univ. of Wisconsin, 1982. Darwin Lectr, BAAS, 1983; Marjory Stephenson Lectr, Soc. for Gen. Microbiology, 1996. Mem., EMBO, 2010. FMedSci 1999; FRSB (FSB 2010). *Publications:* numerous contribs to books and scientific jls. *Recreations:* fly fishing, painting. *Address:* Sir William Dunn School of Pathology, University of Oxford, South Parks Road, Oxford OX1 3RE. *T:* (01865) 285455. *E:* keith.gull@path.ox.ac.uk; St Edmund Hall, Queen's Lane, Oxford OX1 4AR. *T:* (01865) 279076. *E:* keith.gull@seh.ox.ac.uk.

GULL, Sir Rupert (William Cameron), 5th Bt *cr* 1872, of Brook Street; company director; *b* 14 July 1954; *s* of Sir Michael Swinnerton Cameron Gull, 4th Bt and Yvonne (*d* 1975), *o d* of Dr Albert Oliver Macarius Heslop, Cape Town; *S* father, 1989; *m* 1980, Gillian Lee, *d* of Robert MacFarlaine; three *d*. *Educ:* Diocesan Coll., Cape Town; Cape Town Univ. *Heir:* *cousin* Angus William John Gull [*b* 24 Dec. 1963; *m* 1988, Jacqueline Mary, *d* of Gerald Edgar Ford; one *s* two *d* (of whom one *s* one *d* are twins)]. *Address:* 2 Harcourt Road, Claremont, Cape Town, South Africa.

GULLAND, Robert Rainsford M.; *see* Milner-Gulland.

GULLICK, His Honour Stephen John; a Circuit Judge, 1998–2015; *b* 22 Feb. 1948; *s* of late David and Evelyn Gullick; *m* 1973, Lesley Steadman; two *s*. *Educ:* Taunton Sch.; Birmingham Univ. (LLB 1970). Called to the Bar, Gray's Inn, 1971; in practice at the Bar, 1971–98; a Recorder, 1990–98; Standing Counsel, NE Circuit, HM Customs and Excise, 1991–98; Resident Judge, Bradford Crown Court, 2001–09. Hon. Recorder, Bradford, 2002–09. *Recreations:* campanology, watching sport.

GULLIFORD, Rev. Canon William Douglas FitzGerald; Vicar, St Mark's, Regent's Park, since 2012; *b* 23 Sept. 1969; *s* of late Maurice Nicholas Gulliford and of Caroline Mary Louise Gulliford; *m* 1993, Béatrice Priscilla Marie Rambaud; three *d* (one *s* decd). *Educ:* Taunton Sch.; Richard Huish Coll., Taunton; Selwyn Coll., Cambridge (BA 1991; MA 1995); Westcott House, Cambridge. Ordained deacon, 1994, priest, 1995; Asst Curate, All Saints', Banstead, 1994–97; Asst Priest, St Paul's, Knightsbridge, 1997–2000; Vicar, Guild Church of St Dunstan-in-the-West, 2000–12; Rector, St Mary le Strand with St Clement Danes, 2002–08. Dir of Ordinands, Dio. of Europe, 2003–; Canon of Gibraltar, 2012–. Chaplain: GSMD, 1997–2001; to Bishop of London, 2000–02; Courtauld Inst. of Art, 2003–08; to Master Draper, Lady Victoria Leatham, 2012–13. Gen. Sec., Anglican & Eastern Churches Assoc., 2000–04. Hon. Chaplain to: Aldermanic Sheriff of London, 2005–06; Lord Mayor of London, 2006–07. Freedom, City of London, 2001. *Recreations:* domestic ecumenism, theatre, other people's gardening. *Address:* St Mark's Vicarage, 4 Regent's Park Road, NW1 7TX. *T:* and *Fax:* (020) 7485 6340. *E:* william.gulliford@london.anglican.org.

GULLY, family name of **Viscount Selby**.

GUMBEL, Elizabeth-Anne, (Mrs Michael Wainwright); QC 1999; *d* of Walter and Muriel Gumbel; *m* 1984, Michael Wainwright; one *s* one *d*. *Educ:* St Paul's Girls' Sch.; Wycombe Abbey Sch.; Lady Margaret Hall, Oxford (MA). Called to the Bar, Inner Temple, 1974, Bencher, 2002. *Address:* 1 Crown Office Row, EC4Y 7HH.
See also Rev. N. G. P. Gumbel.

GUMBEL, Rev. Nicholas Glyn Paul; Vicar, Holy Trinity, Brompton, since 2005; *b* 28 April 1955; *s* of Walter and Muriel Gumbel; *m* 1978, Philippa Hislop; two *s* one *d*. *Educ:* Trinity Coll., Cambridge (BA Law 1976); Wycliffe Hall, Oxford (MA Theol. 1986). Called to the Bar, Middle Temple, 1977; in practice as barrister, 1977–83; ordained deacon, 1986, priest, 1987; Curate, Holy Trinity, Brompton, 1986–2005. Pioneer of Alpha Course (a practical introduction to Christian faith, running in over 63,000 locations in 169 countries); Alpha Chaplain, 1996–2005. Vice Pres., Tearfund, 2008–. Hon. DPhil Glos, 2007. *Publications:* Questions of Life, 1993, 7th edn 2010; Searching Issues, 1994, 8th edn 2013; How to Run the Alpha Course: telling others, 1994, 5th edn as Telling Others, 2011; A Life Worth Living, 1994, 6th edn 2010; Challenging Lifestyle, 1996, 5th edn as The Jesus Lifestyle, 2010; The Heart of Revival, 1997; 30 Days, 1999, 4th edn 2008; The Da Vinci Code: a response, 2005, 2nd edn 2006; Wilberforce: the challenge for today, 2007; Is God a Delusion?, 2008. *Address:* Holy Trinity Brompton, Brompton Road, SW7 1JA.
See also E.-A. Gumbel.

GUMENDE, António; Ambassador and Permanent Representative of the Republic of Mozambique to the United Nations, since 2011; High Commissioner to Jamaica (non-resident), since 2014; *b* Capezulo, Maputo, 1 Jan. 1961; *s* of Solomone Gumende and Macumbine Tembe; *m* 1992, Simangaliso Gatsi; one *s* three *d*. *Educ:* Sch. of Journalism, Mozambique (Dip. Journalism 1984); Nottingham Trent Univ. (Postgrad. Dip. Mgt Studies 1998; MBA 1999); Open Univ. (Dip. Econs 2004); Birkbeck Coll., London (Postgrad. Cert. Econs 2005); Centre for Financial and Mgt Studies, Sch. of Oriental and African Studies, Univ. of London (MSc Financial Econs 2010). News writer, then reporter, later Business Ed., Mozambique News Agency, Maputo, 1984–90; Staff Writer, then Business Ed., Southern African Economist, Harare, 1990–96; Man. Ed., then Business Ed., Southern African Political Economy Series, SAPES Trust, Harare, 1996–97; Exec. Ed., Southern African Res. and Documentation Centre, Maputo, 1997–2002 (Exec. Ed., Nat. Human Develt Report for Mozambique, 1998, 1999, 2000, 2001); High Comr for Mozambique in UK, 2002–11. Chair, Bd of Govs, Commonwealth Secretariat, 2006–08. Exec. Chm., 1997–2002, Chm. AGM, 2002–, MediaCoop Jornalistas Associados SCRL. Correspondent: Italian News Agency, 1988–90; Southern African Economist, 1988–90; Harare Correspondent: MediaFax, Savana Independent Weekly, Mozambique, 1993–97; Lusa News Agency, Portugal, 1993–97; A Bola newspaper, Portugal, 1994–97; Channel Africa Radio, Portuguese Service, 1994–97. *Recreations:* reading with particular interest in journalism, economics, finance, management, politics and international relations, watching movies and documentaries about nature and history. *Address:* c/o Mozambique Mission to the United Nations, 420 E 50th Street, New York, NY 10022, USA. *E:* agumende15@gmail.com, originarioag@gmail.com.

GUMLEY-MASON, Frances Jane, MA; broadcaster and journalist; Headmistress, St Augustine's Priory, Ealing, 1995–2011; *b* 28 Jan. 1955; *o d* of late Franc Stewart Gumley and Helen Teresa (*née* McNicholas); name changed to Gumley-Mason by statutory declaration, 1995; *m* 1988, Andrew Samuel Mason (now Gumley-Mason); one *s* one *d*. *Educ:* St Augustine's Priory, Ealing; Newnham Coll., Cambridge (MA). Parly research, 1974; Braille transcriber, 1975; Catholic Herald: Editorial Assistant and Assistant Literary Editor, Dec. 1975; Literary Editor and Staff Reporter, 1976–79; Editor, 1979–81; RC Asst to Head of Religious Broadcasting, and sen. producer, religious progs, radio, and producer, religious television, 1981–88; Series Editor, Religious Programmes, C4, 1988–89; guest producer, scriptwriter and presenter, BBC World Service and Radio 4, 1989–94. Mistress of The Keys, Guild of Catholic Writers, 1983–88. ACIEA 2008. *Publications:* (as F. J. Gumley, with Brian Redhead): The Good Book, 1987; The Christian Centuries, 1989; The Pillars of Islam, 1990; Protestors for Paradise, 1993; (jtly) Discovering Turkey, 1995. *Recreation:* playing with children's toys. *Address:* 2 Rathgar Avenue, Ealing, W13 9PL.

GUMMER, family name of **Barons Chadlington** and **Deben**.

GUMMER, Benedict Michael; MP (C) Ipswich, since 2010; Parliamentary Under-Secretary of State, Department of Health, since 2015; *b* London, 19 Feb. 1978; *s* of Baron Deben, *qv*. *Educ:* St Saviour's C of E Prim. Sch.; St John's College Sch., Cambridge; Tonbridge Sch.; Peterhouse, Cambridge (MA Hons). Company Dir, 2001–10; writer. *Publications:* The Scourging Angel: the black death in the British Isles, 2009. *Recreations:* music, reading, visiting Suffolk pubs with my friends. *Address:* House of Commons, SW1A 0AA. *E:* ben@bengummer.com.

GUMMETT, Prof. Philip John, CBE 2013; PhD; Chief Executive, Higher Education Funding Council for Wales, 2004–12; *b* 26 Oct. 1947; *s* of Rev. Philip Charles Gummett and Morfydd Ioli Gummett (*née* Brown); *m* 1969, Karen Hope Thurgood; one *s* one *d*. *Educ:* Univ. of Birmingham (BSc); Univ. of Manchester (MSc; PhD). University of Manchester: Lectr in Sci. and Technol. Policy, 1974–81; Sen. Lectr, 1981–94; Prof. of Govt and Technol. Policy, 1994–2000; Pro-Vice-Chancellor, 1997–2000; Dir, PREST (Prog. of Policy Res. in Engrg, Sci. and Technol.), Manchester, 1997–2000; Dir of Higher Educn, HEFCW, 2000–04. Advr to UK and European Parlts and EC. Trustee, Jisc, 2013–Sept. 2016. *Publications:* Scientists in Whitehall, 1980; (ed with J. Reppy) The Relations Between Defence and Civil Technologies, 1988; (with W. Walker) Nationalism, Internationalism and the European Defence Market, 1993; (ed) Globalisation and Public Policy, 1996; (ed with R. Bud) Cold War Hot Science: applied research in Britain's defence laboratories 1945–1990, 1999. *Recreations:* reading, walking, cycling, music, grandchildren. *E:* phil@gummett.com.

GUMMOW, Hon. William Montague Charles, AC 1997; Non-Permanent Judge, Hong Kong Court of Final Appeal, since 2013; *b* 9 Oct. 1942; *s* of W. C. R. Gummow and A. C. Gummow (*née* Benson). *Educ:* Sydney Grammar Sch.; Univ. of Sydney (BA 1962; LLB 1965; LLM 1970). Admitted Solicitor, Supreme Court of NSW, 1966; Partner, Allen, Allen & Hemsley, 1969–76; admitted to NSW Bar, 1976; in practice at the Bar, 1976–86; QC (NSW) 1986; Judge, Federal Court of Australia, 1986–95; Justice, High Ct of Australia, 1995–2012. Clarendon Law Lectr, Oxford Univ., 1999; WA Lee Equity Lectr, Qld Univ. of Technol., 2002; Sir Maurice Byers Lectr, NSW Bar Assoc., 2005; Prof. of Law, Univ. of Sydney and ANU, 2013–. Mem., Amer. Law Inst., 1997. Hon. LLD Sydney, 1992. *Publications:* Jacobs' Law of Trusts in Australia, 3rd edn 1971 to 6th edn (jtly) 1997; Equity: doctrines and remedies, 1975, 3rd edn (jtly) 1992; Cases and Materials on Equity and Trusts, 1975, 4th edn 1993. *E:* wmcg1@bigpond.com.au. *Club:* Australian (Sydney).

GUNAWARDENA, Jeremy Harin Charles, PhD; Associate Professor of Systems Biology, since 2010, Harvard Medical School, since 2010 (Director, Virtual Cell Program, Department of Systems Biology, 2004); *b* 12 Nov. 1955; *s* of late Charles Gunawardena and of Yvonne Gunawardena (*née* Weerakoon). *Educ:* Imperial Coll., London (BSc); Trinity Coll., Cambridge (MA; PhD 1983). L. E. Dickson Instr, Dept of Mathematics, Univ. of Chicago, 1981–83; Res. Fellow in Mathematics, Trinity Coll., Cambridge, 1983–87; Hewlett-Packard Laboratories: Mem., Technical Staff, 1987–2001; Dir, Basic Res. Inst. in the Mathematical Scis, 1994–2001; Vis. Scientist and Hd of Systems Biol., Bauer Center for Genomics Res., Harvard Univ., 2002–04. Vis. Schol., Dept of Computer Sci., Stanford Univ., 1992–94; Vis. Res. Fellow, Trinity Coll., Cambridge, 1995; Prof. Invitée, Ecole Normale Supérieure, Paris, 2000. Mem., EPSRC, 1999–2002. *Publications:* (ed) Idempotency, 1998. *Recreations:* tennis, cricket, classical music, flying aeroplanes. *Address:* Department of Systems Biology, Harvard Medical School, 200 Longwood Avenue, Boston, MA 02115, USA. *T:* (617) 4324839.

GUNDARA, Prof. Jagdish Singh, PhD; UNESCO Chair in Intercultural Studies and Teacher Education, since 2000, and Director, International Centre for Intercultural Studies, since 2012, Institute of Education, University College London (formerly Institute of Education, University of London); Senior Research Fellow, Institute of Commonwealth Studies, University of London, since 2013; *b* Nairobi, Kenya, 11 Sept. 1938; *s* of Darbar Singh Gundara, MBE and Jagir Kaur Gundara; partner, Sarah Jones. *Educ:* Bowdoin Coll., Brunswick, Maine (BA); McGill Univ., Montreal (MA); Edinburgh Univ. (PhD 1975). Educn Officer, Islington Cttee for Community Relns, 1970–79; Head, Internat. Centre for Intercultural Studies, 1979–2006, Prof. of Educn, Inst. of Educn, Univ. of London, 1989–2006, now Prof. Emeritus. Mem., CRE, 2002–07. Pres., Internat. Assoc. for Intercultural Educn, 2002–. Mem. Council, St George's House, Windsor Castle, 1994–2000. Pres., Jury of Intercultural Awards, Evens Foundn, Antwerp, 1997–2010. Chm., 2000–05, Pres., 2005–11, Bd of Trustees, Scarman Trust; Founding Mem., Bd of Trustees, Internat. Broadcasting Trust, 1979–2012; Mem., Bd of Trustees, UNICEF (UK), 2011–. FRSA. *Publications:* Interculturalism, Education and Inclusion, 2000; (ed jtly) Intercultural Social Policy in Europe, 2000 (trans. Greek 2012); The Case for Intercultural Education in a Multicultural World (essays), 2015. *Recreations:* visual arts, Baroque music, horticulture. *Address:* UCL Institute of Education, 20 Bedford Way, WC1H 0AL. *T:* (020) 7612 6722, *Fax:* (020) 7612 6733. *E:* j.gundara@ioe.ac.uk. *Clubs:* Two Brydges; Middx County Cricket.

GUNEWARDENA, Desmond Anthony Lalith; Chairman and Chief Executive, D&D London (formerly Conran Restaurants), since 2006; *b* Kandy, Sri Lanka, 11 Aug. 1957; *s* of Kingsley and Muriel Gunewardena; *m* 1991, Elisabeth Pask; one *s* one *d*. *Educ:* Wimbledon Coll.; Univ. of Bristol (BSc 1978). ACA 1981. Ernst & Young, 1978–84; Heron Internat., 1984–89; Chief Exec., Conran Hldgs, 1989–2006. Non-executive Director: Fitch plc, 1994–99; Individual Restaurant Co. plc, 2005–08; Conran, 2006–. Non-executive Director: London First, 2002–; Visit London, 2005–09. FRSA 2002. *Recreations:* tennis, ski-ing, chess. *Address:* D&D London, 16 Kirby Street, EC1N 8TS. *T:* (020) 7716 7800. *E:* vicky@danddlondon.com.

GUNN, Prof. John Charles, CBE 1994; MD; FMedSci, FRCPsych; Professor of Forensic Psychiatry, Institute of Psychiatry, 1978–2002, now Emeritus; *b* 6 June 1937; *s* of late Albert Charles Gunn and Lily Hilda Edwards; *m* 1st, 1959, Celia Willis (marr. diss. 1986, she *d* 1989); one *s* one *d*; 2nd, 1989, Pamela Jane Taylor, *qv*. *Educ:* Brighton, Hove and Sussex Grammar Sch.; Reigate Grammar Sch.; Birmingham Univ. (MB ChB 1961; Acad. DPM 1966; MD 1969). MRCPsych 1971, FRCPsych 1980, Hon. FRCPsych 2010. Queen Elizabeth Hosp., Birmingham, 1961–63; Maudsley Hosp., 1963–67; Institute of Psychiatry: Res. Worker, 1967–69; Lectr, 1969–71; Sen. Lectr, 1971–75; Dir, Special Hosps Res. Unit, 1975–78. H. B. Williams Vis. Prof. to Aust. and NZ, 1985. Advisor, H of C Select Cttees on Violence in Marriage, 1975, on Prison Med. Service, 1986; Member: Home Sec's Adv. Bd on Restricted Patients, 1982–91; Royal Commn on Criminal Justice, 1991–93; Parole Bd for England and

Wales, 2006–. WHO Specialist Advisor in Forensic Psychiatry to China, 1987; Consultant, Eur. Cttee for Prevention of Torture, 1993–; Co-organiser, Ghent Gp, 2004–. Royal College of Psychiatrists: Chm., Res. Cttee, 1976–80; Dep. Chief Examr, 1993–95; Mem., Council, 1977–83, 1997–2004; Mem., Ct of Electors, 1985–91, 1993–99, 2003–04; Mem., Exec. Cttee, 1998–2004; Chm., Faculty of Forensic Psychiatry, 2000–04. Founder FMedSci 1998. Editor, Criminal Behaviour and Mental Health, 1991–. *Publications:* Epileptics in Prison, 1977; Psychiatric Aspects of Imprisonment, 1978; Current Research in Forensic Psychiatry and Psychology, vols 1–3, 1982–85; Violence in Human Society, 1983, 2nd edn 2013; (ed with P. J. Taylor) Forensic Psychiatry: clinical, legal and ethical issues, 1993; 118 peer reviewed papers. *Recreations:* theatre, opera, cinema, photography, walking, living with Pamela. *Address:* PO Box 725, Bromley BR2 7WF. *E:* johncgunn@gmail.com. *Clubs:* Athenæum, Royal Society of Medicine.

GUNN, John Humphrey; company director and venture capitalist; Chairman, Rotala plc, since 2005; *b* 15 Jan. 1942; *s* of Francis (Bob) Gunn and Doris Gunn; *m* 1965, Renate Sigrid (*née* Boehme); two *d* (and one *d* decd). *Educ:* Sir John Deane's Grammar School, Northwich; Univ. of Nottingham (BA Hons 1964). Barclays Bank, 1964–68; Astley & Pearce, 1968–85; Chief Executive: Exco International, 1979–85; British & Commonwealth Holdings, 1986–87 and 1990 (Chm., 1987–90). Dir, John Duncan & Co., 1992–2001; Chm., Wengen Ltd, 1994–. Hon. LLD Nottingham, 1989. *Recreations:* golf, ski-ing, mountain walking, classical music, opera. *Address:* Rotala plc, Beacon House, Long Acre, Birmingham B7 5JJ. *T:* (0121) 322 2222. *Clubs:* MCC; Downhill Only (Wengen).

GUNN, Prof. Michael John; Vice Chancellor and Chief Executive, Staffordshire University, since 2011; *b* Wolverhampton, 29 Dec. 1955; *s* of late Eric James Gunn and of Dorothy Mary Gunn (*née* McKnight); *m* 1986, Diane Birch; two *d*. *Educ:* St George's Primary Sch., New Mills; New Mills Grammar Sch.; Chesterfield Grammar Sch.; Univ. of Manchester (LLB 1977). Lectr, then Sen. Lectr in Law, Univ. of Nottingham, 1978–93; Prof. and Hd, Sch. of Law, Univ. of Westminster, 1993–95; Prof. of Mental Health Law, De Montfort Univ., Leicester, 1995–97; Nottingham Trent University: Prof. of Law, 1997–2006; Hd of Dept; Asst Dean, then Dean, Sch. of Law; Pro Vice Chancellor and Prof., Derby Univ., 2006–10. *Publications:* Halsbury's Laws of England, 4th edn, vol. 11(1) and (2), 1990; (jtly) Smith, Bailey and Gunn on the Modern Legal System, 2nd edn 1991 to 4th edn 2002; (contrib.) Blackstone's Criminal Practice, 1991–2006; Blackstone's Guide to the Sexual Offences Act, 2003; over 100 articles, chapters and notes. *Recreations:* family, gardening, watching sport. *Address:* Staffordshire University, Beaconside, Stafford ST18 0AD. *T:* (01785) 353202. *E:* vicechancellor@staffs.ac.uk.

GUNN, Pamela Jane; *see* Taylor, Pamela J.

GUNN-JOHNSON, Ven. David Allan; Archdeacon of Barnstaple, 2003–14; *b* 2 May 1949; *s* of Sidney and Violet Winifred Johnson; *m* 1979, Susan Wells; two *d*. *Educ:* St Stephen's House, Oxford. Ordained deacon 1981, priest 1982; Assistant Curate: Oxhey, 1981–84; Cheshunt, 1984–88; Team Rector, Colyton, 1988–2003; RD, Honiton, 1990–96; Preb., Exeter Cathedral, 1999–2003. STh (Archbp's Schol. of Theol.) 1985, MA 1995, Lambeth. *Recreations:* historical research, theatre (writing, directing and performing), motorcycling. *Address:* 12 Hylton Gardens, Exeter EX4 2QE. *T:* (01392) 496877, 07921 150428. *E:* dgunnjohnson549@btinternet.com.

GUNNELL, Prof. David John, PhD, DSc; FFPHM, FMedSci; Professor of Epidemiology, University of Bristol, since 2003; *b* London, 17 Nov. 1960; *s* of John C. Gunnell and Rosemary P. Gunnell; *m* 1987, Gillian McLeish; two *d*. *Educ:* Univ. of Bristol (MB ChB 1984; PhD Epidemiol. 1996; DSc Epidemiol. 2009); London Sch. of Hygiene and Tropical Medicine, Univ. of London (MSc Med. Statistics (Dist.) 1997). MRCGP 1989; MFPHM 1993, FFPHM 1999. GP trng, Bristol and Weston-Super-Mare, 1986–89; gen. psychiatry trng, Bristol, 1989–91; Registrar, 1991–93, Sen. Registrar, 1993, in Public Health Medicine, Somerset HA; Lectr in Epidemiol. and Public Health, 1993–96, Consultant Sen. Lectr, Dept of Social Medicine, 1997–2003, Univ. of Bristol; Hon. Sen. Registrar, Avon HA, 1993–96; Hon. Consultant in Public Health, N Bristol NHS Trust, 1997–. Mem., Pharmacovigillance Expert Adv. Gp, Medicines and Healthcare Products Regulatory Agency, 2006–13 (Vice Chm., 2012–13). NIHR Sen. Investigator, 2007. FHEA 2007. Res. Prize, Amer. Foundn for Suicide Prevention, 2015; Stengel Res. Award, Internat. Assoc. of Suicide Prevention, 2015. *Publications:* over 400 research articles in jls incl. Lancet, BMJ, Public Liby of Sci. Medicine, Internat. Jl of Epidemiol. *Recreations:* swimming (Trustee, Portishead Pool Community Trust, 2009–10), palaeontology, travel, walking. *Address:* School of Social and Community Medicine, University of Bristol, Canynge Hall, 39 Whatley Road, Clifton, Bristol BS8 2PS. *T:* (0117) 928 7253. *E:* d.j.gunnell@bristol.ac.uk.

GUNNELL, Sally Jane Janet, OBE 1998 (MBE 1993); DL; athlete, retired 1997; television presenter and motivational speaker; *b* 29 July 1966; *m* 1992, Jonathan Bigg; three *s*. *Educ:* Chigwell High School. Life Member, Essex Ladies' Club, 1978; GB Team Captain, 1992–97; 400 m hurdles wins include: Olympic Champion, 1992; World Champion, 1993; World Record Holder, 1993; European Champion, 1994; Commonwealth Champion, 1994; also Commonwealth Champion, 100 m hurdles, 1986, 1990. Mem. Bd, Sport England, 2013–. DL W Sussex, 2011. *Publications:* Running Tall, 1994; Be Your Best, 2001. *W:* www.sallygunnell.com.

GUNNING, Alexander Rupert; QC 2012; *s* of Peter and Jennifer Gunning; *m* Jerusalen Vital; two *s*. *Educ:* Sherborne Sch.; King's Coll. London (LLB Hons; LLM Commercial and Corporate Law). Called to the Bar, Inner Temple, 1994; in practice as a barrister, specialising in internat. arbitration, insurance, reinsurance and energy-related disputes. *Recreation:* Bath Rugby. *Address:* 4 Pump Court, Temple, EC4Y 7AN. *T:* (020) 7842 5555.

GUNNING, Prof. Brian Edgar Scourse, FRS 1980; FAA 1979; Professor of Plant Cell Biology, Australian National University, 1974–97, now Emeritus; *b* 29 Nov. 1934; *s* of William Gunning and Margaret Gunning (*née* Scourse); *m* 1964, Marion Sylvia Forsyth; two *s*. *Educ:* Methodist Coll., Belfast; Queen's Univ., Belfast (BSc (Hons), MSc, PhD); DSc ANU. Lecturer in Botany, 1957–65, Reader in Botany, 1965–74, Queen's Univ., Belfast. Hon. MRIA 1999. *Publications:* Ultrastructure and the Biology of Plant Cells (with Dr M. Steer), 1975; Intercellular Communication in Plants: studies on plasmodesmata (with Dr A. Robards), 1976; (with M. Steer) Plant Cell Biology, 1996; contribs to research jls. *Recreations:* hill walking, photography. *Address:* 50 Cargelligo Street, Duffy, ACT 2611, Australia. *T:* (2) 62812879.

GUNNING, Sir Charles Theodore, 9th Bt *cr* 1778, of Eltham, Kent; CD 1964; RCN retired; engineering consultant, Promaxis Systems Inc., Ottawa; *b* 19 June 1935; *s* of Sir Robert Gunning, 8th Bt and of Helen Nancy, *d* of Vice-Adm. Sir Theodore John Hallett, KBE, CB; *S* father, 1989; *m* 1st, 1969, Sarah (marr. diss. 1982), *d* of Col Patrick Arthur Easton; one *d*; 2nd, 1989, Linda Martin (*née* Kachmar). *Educ:* Canadian Mil. Coll.; RNEC Plymouth; Tech. Univ. of NS. PEng. Royal Commonwealth Soc. Liaison, Nat. Student Commonwealth Forum, 1979–2009; Chm., Nat. Council in Canada, Royal Commonwealth Soc., 1990–93 (Pres., Ottawa Br., 1974–76, 1979–80 and 1983; a Nat. Hon. Chm.). Silver Jubilee Medal, 1977; Golden Jubilee Medal, 2002. *Heir:* *b* John Robert Gunning [*b* 17 Sept. 1944; *m* 1st, 1969, Alina Tylicki (marr. diss. 1995); two *s* one *d*; 2nd, 1999, Diane Grosschmidt]. *Address:* 2940 McCarthy Road, Ottawa, ON K1V 8K6, Canada.

GUNNYEON, William James, CBE 2009; FRCP, FRCPE, FFOM, FRCGP; independent consultant, since 2014; Chief Medical Adviser, Director, Health and Wellbeing, and Chief Scientist, Department for Work and Pensions, 2005–14; *b* 10 June 1953; *s* of late William Campbell Gunnyeon and Muriel Gunnyeon (*née* Dunn, latterly Shearer); *m* 1975, Joan Elizabeth Moorcroft; two *s*. *Educ:* Dundee Univ. (MB ChB 1977). DIH 1984. FFOM 1994; FRCP 1999; FRCGP 2003; FFOMI 2006; FRCPE 2007. House Officer, Stirling Royal Infirmary, 1977–78; MO, RAF, 1978–83; Med. Advr, then Sen. Med. Advr, OMS Ltd, 1983–92; Principal Med. Advr, Grampian Regl Council, 1992–96; Dir, Grampian Occupational Health Service, 1996–97; Liberty Occupational Health: Dir, Occupational Health, 1997–99; Chief Exec., 1999–2000; Med. Dir, Aon, subseq. Capita, Health Solutions, 2000–05. Faculty of Occupational Medicine: Registrar, 1999–2001; Pres., 2002–05; Mem. Council, RCP, 2002–05; Member: Acad. of Med. Royal Colls, 2002–05; Specialist Trng Authy, 2002–05. Chm., Assoc. of Local Authy Med. Advrs, 1995–97. *Publications:* (jtly) Fitness to Teach, 2000. *Recreations:* gardening, hill-walking, travel, reading, classical music. *E:* bill.gunnyeon@btopenworld.com.

GUNSTON, Sir John (Wellesley), 3rd Bt *cr* 1938, of Wickwar, Co. Gloucester; company director; *b* 25 July 1962; *s* of Sir Richard Gunston, 2nd Bt and of Mrs Joan Elizabeth Marie Gunston; *S* father, 1991; *m* 1990, Rosalind (marr. diss. 1998), *y d* of Edward Gordon Eliott; one *s*. *Educ:* Harrow; RMA Sandhurst. BSAP Reserve, Rhodesia, 1979–80. Commnd 1st Bn Irish Guards, 1981. Since 1983 has covered wars, revolutions and foreign travel assignments in: Afghanistan, Albania, Brazil, Burma, Colombia, Egypt, Eritrea, Israel (West Bank and Gaza), Lebanon, Liberia, South Africa, Sudan, Uganda, Ulster (esp. Derry) and also in North America, Eastern Europe and South East Asia. Dir, North-West Frontier Productions, 1995; Man. Dir, Hard News Ltd, 1998. Chm., Rory Peck Trust and Award, 1995–97. Fellow: Soc. of Authors, 1994; RSAA, 1995; FRGS 1988; FRAS 1998. *Recreations:* books, biking and ballistics. *Heir:* *s* Richard St George Gunston, *b* 3 July 1992. *Clubs:* Cavalry and Guards, Special Forces.

GUNTER, John Forsyth; freelance theatre and opera designer, until 2008; Head of Design, Royal National Theatre, 1989–91; *b* 31 Oct. 1938; *s* of late Herbert and Charlotte Gunter; *m* 1969, Micheline McKnight; two *d*. *Educ:* Bryanston Public Sch.; Central Sch. of Art and Design (Dip. with distinction). Started career in rep. theatre in GB; Resident Designer: English Stage Co., 1965–66 (subseq. designed 28 prodns for co.); Zürich Schauspielhaus, 1970–73; freelance design work, 1973, for West End, NT, RSC, Old Vic, Chichester, New York, Sydney, Los Angeles; also for Peter Hall Co. seasons, 1997, 1998 and 2003; designer of operas: for cos in GB, Italy, Germany, Austria, Holland, Australia, USA and Russia; Glyndebourne Fest. Op., 1985–2008; Royal Opera House, Covent Gdn, 1997–2000; ENO; La Scala, Milan, 1988; Salzburg, 2005; Los Angeles, 2005; Baden-Baden, 2008; St Petersburg, 2008. Head, Theatre Dept, Central Sch. of Art and Design, 1974–82. FRSA 1982. Many awards for design of Guys and Dolls, NT, 1982, incl. SWET Award for Best Design 1982, Drama Magazine Best Design Award 1982, Plays and Players Award for Best Design 1983; Plays and Players and Olivier Awards for Best Design 1984, for design of Wild Honey, NT, 1984; Emmy Award, 1994, for set design of Porgy and Bess.

GUPTA, Atul; Director: Zhaikmunai LP, since 2009; Dominion Petroleum Ltd, since 2009; Seven Energy, since 2010; Vetra Energy, since 2012; *b* 15 Dec. 1959; *s* of Satya Pal Gupta and Sarmishta Gupta; *m* 1991, Anjali Garg, MSc; two *d*. *Educ:* Sidney Sussex Coll., Cambridge (BA Hons 1981; MEng Chem. Eng. 1983); Heriot-Watt Univ., Edinburgh (MEng Pet. Eng.). Charterhouse Petroleum plc, 1983–86; Petrofina SA, 1986–90; Monument Oil plc, 1990–99, Gen. Dir Turkmenistan, 1996–99; Chief Operating Officer, 1999–2006, CEO, 2006–07, Burren Energy plc. *Recreations:* football, cricket, art, reading.

GUPTA, Prof. Sunetra, PhD; novelist; Professor of Theoretical Epidemiology, Department of Zoology, University of Oxford, since 2006; *b* Calcutta, 15 March 1965; *d* of Dhruba and Minati Gupta; *m* 1994, Adrian Vivian Sinton Hill, *qv*; two *d*. *Educ:* Princeton Univ. (AB 1987); Univ. of London (PhD 1992). University of Oxford: Jun. Res. Fellow, Merton Coll., 1993–96; Department of Zoology: Wellcome Trust Sen. Res. Fellow, 1995–99; Reader, 1999–2006. Sahitya Akademi Award, 1997; Scientific Medal, Zool Soc. of London, 2008; Rosalind Franklin Award, Royal Soc., 2009; Doubleday Award, 2013. *Publications:* novels: Memories of Rain, 1992; The Glassblower's Breath, 1993; Moonlight into Marzipan, 1995; A Sin of Colour, 1999 (Southern Arts UK Prize for Lit., 2000); So Good in Black, 2009; contrib. scientific articles to Science, Nature, Lancet. *Recreations:* cinema, art, gardening, architecture. *Address:* Department of Zoology, University of Oxford, South Parks Road, Oxford OX1 3PS. *T:* (01865) 281225. *E:* sunetra.gupta@zoo.ox.ac.uk.

GUPTA, Teertha; QC 2012; a Recorder, since 2009; *b* London, 26 Oct. 1966; *s* of Tapan Kumar Gupta and Gairika Gupta; *m* 1995, Joy Katherine Emmett; two *s*. *Educ:* Mill Hill Sch., London; Leeds Univ. (LLB Hons). Called to the Bar, Inner Temple, 1990; in practice as a barrister, specialising in internat. child law, 1990–. *Recreations:* family, playing and coaching football, golf, following international test cricket and Rugby, reading about developments in sports law, theatre (the plays of Tanika Gupta, MBE). *Address:* 4 Paper Buildings, Temple, EC4Y 7EX. *T:* (020) 7583 0816. *E:* clerks@4pb.com.

GURDON, family name of **Baron Cranworth**.

GURDON, Sir John (Bertrand), Kt 1995; DPhil; FRS 1971; research scientist; Chairman, Company of Biologists, Cambridge, 2001–11; Master, Magdalene College, Cambridge, 1995–2002 (Hon. Fellow, 2002); *b* 2 Oct. 1933; *s* of late W. N. Gurdon, DCM, formerly of Assington, Suffolk, and Elsie Marjorie (*née* Byass); *m* 1964, Jean Elizabeth Margaret Curtis; one *s* one *d*. *Educ:* Edgeborough; Eton (Fellow, 1978–93); Christ Church, Oxford (BA 1956; DPhil 1960). Beit Memorial Fellow, 1958–61; Gosney Research Fellow, Calif. Inst. Technol., 1962; Departmental Demonstrator, Dept of Zool., Oxford, 1963–64; Vis. Research Fellow, Carnegie Instn, Baltimore, 1965; Lectr, Dept of Zoology, Oxford, 1965–72; Research Student, Christ Church, 1962–72; Mem. Staff, MRC Lab. of Molecular Biology, Cambridge, 1972–83 (Hd, Cell Biology Div., 1979–83); Fellow, Churchill Coll., Cambridge, 1973–94; John Humphrey Plummer Prof. of Cell Biology, Univ. of Cambridge, 1983–2001; Chm., Wellcome Cancer Res. Campaign Inst., Cambridge, 1991–2001. Fullerian Prof. of Physiology and Comparative Anatomy, Royal Instn, 1985–91. Lectures: Harvey Soc., NY, 1973; Dunham, Harvard, 1974; Croonian, Royal Soc., 1976; Carter-Wallace, Princeton, 1978; Woodhull, Royal Instn, 1980; Florey, Aust., 1988; Fischberg Meml, Geneva, 1989; Rutherford, Royal Soc., 1996; Rodney Porter Meml, Oxford, 1999; Hitchcock, Berkeley, USA, 2006. Pres., Internat. Soc. Develt Biol., 1989–93. Gov., The Wellcome Trust, 1995–2000. Chm., Co. of Biologists, 2001–. Hon. Foreign Member: Amer. Acad. of Arts and Scis, 1978; Foreign Associate: Nat. Acad. of Sciences, USA, 1980; Belgian Royal Acad. of Scis, Letters and Fine Arts, 1984; Foreign Member: Amer. Philos. Soc., 1983; Lombardy Acad. Sci., Italy, 1989; Acad. Les Sciences, France, 1990; Inst. of Medicine, USA, 2004. Hon. Student, Christ Church, Oxford, 1985; Hon. Fellow, Churchill Coll., Cambridge, 2007. Hon. DSc: Chicago, 1978; René Descartes, Paris, 1982; Oxford, 1988; Hull, 1998; Glasgow, 2000; Cambridge, 2007; Vrije Univ. Brussels, 2009; Univ. Libre de Bruxelles, 2009; Rockefeller, 2014. Albert Brachet Prize (Belgian Royal Academy), 1968; Scientific Medal of Zoological Soc., 1968; Feldberg Foundn Award, 1975; Paul Ehrlich Award, 1977; Nessim Habif Prize, Univ. of Geneva, 1979; CIBA Medal, Biochem. Soc., 1980; Comfort Crookshank Award for Cancer Research, 1983; William Bate Hardy Prize, Cambridge Philos. Soc., 1984; Prix Charles Léopold Mayer, Acad. des Scis, France, 1984; Ross Harrison Prize, Internat. Soc. of Develtl Biologists, 1985; Royal Medal, Royal Soc., 1985; Emperor Hirohito

Internat. Prize for Biology, Japan Acad., 1987; Wolf Prize in Medicine, Israel, 1989; Jan Waldenstram Medal, Swedish Oncol. Soc., 1991; Dist. Service Award, Miami, 1992; Edridge Green Medal, RCOphth, 1997; Jean Brachet Meml Prize, Internat. Soc. Differentiation, 2000; Conklin Medal, Soc. Develtl Biol., 2001; Copley Medal, Royal Soc., 2003; Rosenstiel Award, Brandeis Univ., USA, 2009; Albert Lasker Award for Basic Med. Res., Lasker Foundn, USA, 2009; (jtly) Nobel Prize in Physiology or Medicine, 2012. *Publications:* Control of Gene Expression in Animal Development, 1974; articles in scientific jls, especially on nuclear transplantation. *Recreations:* ski-ing, tennis, horticulture, Lepidoptera. *Address:* Whittlesford Grove, Whittlesford, Cambridge CB22 4NZ. *Club:* Eagle Ski.

GURNEY, Nicholas Bruce Jonathan; management consultant, since 2009; *b* 20 Jan. 1945; *s* of Comdr Bruce William George Gurney and Cynthia Joan Watkins Gurney (*née* Winn, later Mason); *m* 1st, 1970, Patricia Wendy Tulip (marr. diss. 1987); two *s* one *d*; 2nd, 1989, Caroline Mary (*née* Bentley). *Educ:* Wimbledon College; Christ's College, Cambridge. BA 1966, MA 1969. Lectr in English, Belize Teachers' Training College, Belize, as part of British Volunteer Programme, 1966–67; MoD 1967; Asst Private Sec., Minister of State for Defence, 1970–72; Civil Service Dept, 1972–74; Private Sec. to Lord Privy Seal and Leader of House of Lords, 1974–77; Civil Service Dept and Management Personnel Office, 1978–83; Grade 3, Cabinet Office, and CS Comr, 1983–88; Dept of Health, 1988–90; Chief Exec., Wokingham DC, 1990–93; City Mgr, subseq. Chief Exec., Portsmouth CC, 1994–2003; Chief Exec., Bristol CC, 2003–08; Chm., N Bristol NHS Trust, 2008–09.

GURNEY, Prof. Robert James, OBE 2001; PhD; Professor of Earth Observation Science (formerly of Physical Geography), University of Reading, since 1990; *b* 31 March 1951; *s* of James William Stratton Gurney and Jeanne Mary Gurney; *m* 1977, Charlotte Mary (*née* Carr); one *s* one *d*. *Educ:* King's Coll. London (BSc Hons); Univ. of Bristol (PhD). Res. Fellow, Inst. of Hydrology, 1975–80; Research Associate: NASA Goddard Space Flight Center, Maryland, 1981–82; Dept of Civil Engrg, Univ. of Maryland, 1983–84; Hd, Hydrological Scis Branch, NASA Goddard Space Flight Center, Maryland, 1984–90; University of Reading: Dir, NERC Envmtl Systems Sci. Centre, 1990–2012; Co-ordinator, Envmtl Inf., NERC, 2013–14. Chm., ReadiBus, 1993–2007. FRMetS 1970. Award and Gold Medal, Remote Sensing and Photogrammetry Soc., 2013. *Publications:* (with E. T. Engman) Remote Sensing in Hydrology, 1991; (ed jtly) Atlas of Satellite Observations Related to Global Climate Change, 1993; (with K. A. Browning) Global Energy and Water Cycles, 1999. *Recreations:* theatre, arts. *Address:* Department of Meteorology, University of Reading, Harry Pitt Building, PO Box 238, 3 Earley Gate, Reading RG6 6AL. *T:* (0118) 378 8741, *Fax:* (0118) 378 6413. *E:* r.j.gurney@reading.ac.uk.

GURNEY, Tim, OBE 2006; HM Diplomatic Service, retired; Deputy High Commissioner, Canberra, 2006–08; *b* 28 April 1955; *s* of Brian and Joy Gurney; *m* 1976, Denise Elizabeth Harker (marr. diss. 2011); one *s* one *d*. Joined FCO, 1973; Istanbul, 1976–79; Karachi, 1979–82; Montreal, 1982–85; Second Secretary: FCO, 1985–88; (Chancery/Inf.), Accra, 1988–90; Dep. Dir, British Inf. Services, NY, 1991–96; First Sec., FCO, 1996–98; Dep. Governor, Bermuda, 1998–2003; Dep. Hd of Mission, Kabul, 2003–05. Sen. Stabilisation Adviser: Nad-e Ali, Helmand, Afghanistan, 2010–11; Marjah and Khaneshin, 2011–12. *Recreations:* scuba diving instructor, soccer referee, photography. *W:* www.timsimages.uk.

GURR, Douglas John, PhD; President, Amazon China, since 2014; *b* Leeds, 9 July 1964; *s* of Prof. Andrew John Gurr and Elizabeth Ann Gurr; *m* 1996, Lucy Makinson; one *s* one *d*. *Educ:* King's Coll., Cambridge (BA 1986; MMath (Cert. Adv. Studies in Maths Pt III 1987)); Univ. of Edinburgh (PhD 1990). Lectr, Univ. of Aarhus, 1990–91; Principal, Dept of Transport, 1992–94; Partner, McKinsey & Co., 1995–2001; Founder and CEO, Blueheath Hldgs plc, 2001–05; Exec. Bd Dir, Asda-Walmart, 2006–11; Vice-Pres., Amazon.com, 2011–14. Trustee: Sci. Mus. Gp (formerly Nat. Mus. of Sci. and Industry), 2004–14 (Chm., 2010–14); Landmark Trust, 2014–; Dir, Nat. Media Mus., 2006–11; Chm., BHF, 2015–. Mem., LMS, 2011. Fellow, Sci. Mus., 2014. *Publications:* Staying Alive Off Piste, 2012; contrib. articles in acad. jls incl. Jl of Pure and Applied Algebra, Logic in Computer Sci. and Information and Computation. *Recreations:* Ironman Triathlon, ski mountaineering including over 20 first ascents (Mem., Bob Graham 24 Hour Club #1649), museums and galleries. *Address:* Amazon China, Ocean International Centre, 56 East 4th Ring Road, Chaoyang District, Beijing 100025, China. *Club:* Calderdale.

GURR, Dr Michael Ian; Maypole Scientific Services, private nutrition consultancy, 1990–99; Partner, Isles of Scilly Specialist Crops, 1999–2006; Secretary, Isles of Scilly Bat Group, since 2006; *b* 10 April 1939; *s* of Henry Ormonde Gurr and Hilda Ruth Gurr; *m* 1963, Elizabeth Anne Mayers; two *s* one *d*. *Educ:* Dunstable Grammar Sch.; Univ. of Birmingham (BSc, PhD). Postdoctoral Fellowship, Harvard Univ., 1964–66; Unilever European Fellowship of Biochem. Soc., State Univ. of Utrecht, 1966–67; Res. Scientist, Unilever Res. Lab., Sharnbrook, Bedford, 1967–78; Hd, Department of Nutrition, Nat. Inst. for Res. in Dairying, Shinfield, Reading, 1978–85; Dir, Reading Lab. of AFRC Inst. of Food Res., 1985–86; Nutrition Consultant and Hd of Nutrition Dept, MMB, 1986–90. Chm., Isles of Scilly Wildlife Trust, 2001–05; Mem., Jt Adv. Cttee. Isles of Scilly Area of Outstanding Beauty, 2008–10. Visiting Professor: Univ. of Reading, 1986–99; Oxford Poly., later Oxford Brookes Univ., 1990–99. Leader, Isles of Scilly U3A Music Appreciation Gp, 2014–. Chairman: Editl Bd, British Jl of Nutrition, 1988–90; Editl Adv. Bd, British Nutrition Foundn, 1994–99; Man. Ed., Nutrition Research Reviews, 1991–99. *Publications:* Lipid Biochemistry: an introduction (jtly), 1971, 6th edn 2015; Role of Fats in Food and Nutrition, 1984, 2nd edn 1992; Anthony Trafford James: a biography, 2014; numerous original pubns and reviews. *Recreations:* sailing, walking, gardening, piano playing, choral singing, hand-bell ringing, nature conservation volunteer (especially studies of bats). *Address:* Vale View Cottage, Maypole, St Mary's, Isles of Scilly TR21 0NU. *T:* (01720) 422224.

GURR, Nicholas Bryan; Deputy Chief Defence Intelligence, Ministry of Defence, since 2011; *b* Barnehurst, Kent, 1 June 1964; *s* of Brian and Patricia Gurr; *m* 1992, Susan Railton; two *d*. *Educ:* Bexley/Erith Tech. Sch. for Boys. Joined CS, 1982; various policy posts, 1983–98, Hd of Communication Planning, 1999–2002, MoD; Mem., RCDS 2002; Dep. Chief of Assessments Staff, Cabinet Office, 2003–06; Dir, Communication Planning, 2006–07, Dir (formerly Dir Gen.) Media and Communications, 2007–11, MoD. *Recreations:* sport, music, travel. *Address:* Ministry of Defence, Whitehall, SW1A 2HB. *T:* (020) 7218 0585. *E:* nick.gurr665@mod.uk.

GURR, Prof. Sarah Jane, PhD; Professor of Food Security, University of Exeter, since 2013; *b* Cuckfield, Sussex, 7 May 1958; *d* of Denis Smith and late Marie Smith; two *d*. *Educ:* King's Sch., Canterbury; Imperial Coll. of Sci., Technol. and Medicine (BSc Hons 1979; ARCS 1979; PhD 1984; DIC); MA Oxon 1992. Postdoctoral Res. Fellow, Univ. of St Andrews, 1984–89; Res. Fellow and Royal Soc. Univ. Res. Fellow, Univ. of Leeds, 1989–92; University of Oxford: Lectr, 1992–2002; Reader, 2002–04; Prof. of Molecular Plant Pathol., 2004–13; Fellow, Somerville Coll., Oxford, 1992–2013. Bd Dir, Rothamsted Res., 1999–2006. Royal Soc. Leverhulme Trust Sen. Res. Fellow, 2002–03; NESTA Fellow, 2004–07. Mem. Cttee, 2008–12, Council, 2012–, BBSRC. Pres., British Soc. for Plant Pathol., 2009–10. Governor: King's Sch., Canterbury, 1999–2012; Stowe Sch., 2005–. Huxley Medal, RAI, 1998. *Publications:* (ed jtly) Molecular Plant Pathology, 2 vols, 1992; contrib. res. articles and papers to jls incl. Nature, Nature Climate Change, Science. *Recreations:* wine, art, reading, plants, progeny. *Address:* BioSciences, University of Exeter, Exeter EX4 4QD. *E:* s.j.gurr@exeter.ac.uk.

GURRÍA TREVIÑO, (José) Angel; Secretary-General, Organisation for Economic Co-operation and Development, since 2006; *b* Tampico, Mexico, 8 May 1950; *s* of Francisco José Gurría Lacroix and Carmen Treviño Humana; *m* 1973, Lulu Ululani Quintana Pali; one *s* two *d*. *Educ:* Univ. Nacional Autónoma de México (BA Econs); Univ. of Leeds (MA Econs). Financial analyst, Federal Power Commn, 1968–70; COS to Dep. Mayor of City of Mexico, 1970; COS to Dep. CEO, then CEO, Nafinsa (Mexico's Develt Bank); Hd, Dept of Negotiations of Foreign Loans, Nafinsa; Dep. Financial Manager, Rural Develt Fund, 1975–76; Perm. Rep. to Internat. Coffee Orgn, London, 1976–78; Treasury posts, 1978–92: Dep. Dir, Public Debt; Dir, Foreign Debt; Gen. Dir, Public Credit; Dep. Sec. for Internat. Affairs; Pres. and CEO, Bancomext (Mexico's Export/Import Bank), 1992–93, Nafinsa, 1993–94; Sec. for Internat. Affairs, Instnl Revolutionary Party (PRI), 1993–94; Minister: of Foreign Affairs Mexico, 1994–97; of Finance and Public Credit, 1998–2000. Holds numerous foreign decorations. *Publications:* Politics of External Debt, 1994; contribs on econs, debt develt and governance. *Address:* Organisation for Economic Co-operation and Development, 2 rue André Pascal, 75775 Paris Cedex 16, France. *E:* secretary.general@oecd.org.

GURU-MURTHY, Krishnan; presenter: Channel 4 News, since 1998; Unreported World, since 2011; *b* 5 April 1970; *s* of Krishnan and Indrani Guru-Murthy; *m* 2005, Lisa Jane Colles; one *s* one *d*. *Educ:* Queen Elizabeth's Grammar Sch., Blackburn; Hertford Coll., Oxford (BA Hons PPE). BBC: presenter: Open to Question, 1988–89; East, 1989–90; presenter/reporter, Newsround, 1991–94; reporter, Newsnight, 1994–97; presenter, News 24, 1997–98; presenter: Channel 4: Powerhouse, 2001–03; News at Noon, 2003–08; Ask the Chancellors, 2010; LBC Radio: The Krishnan Guru-Murthy prog., 2003–05. Columnist: Eastern Eye, 2001–03; Metro, 2002–06. *Recreations:* guitar, piano, travel, cycling. *Address:* Channel 4 News, ITN, 200 Gray's Inn Road, WC1X 8XZ. *T:* (020) 7833 3000. *E:* krishnan.guru-murthy@itn.co.uk. *Clubs:* Groucho, Soho House, Ivy.

GUSTERSON, Prof. Barry Austin, PhD; FRCPath; Professor of Pathology, 2000, Head of Forensic Medicine and Forensic Science, 2006, and Project Director for the Beatson Translational Research Centre, 2008, University of Glasgow (Chairman, Division of Cancer Sciences and Molecular Pathology, 2002–07); *b* Colchester, 24 Oct. 1946; *s* of Joseph Austin Gusterson and Doris Edith (*née* Fairweather); *m* 1972, Ann Josephine Davies; one *s* two *d*. *Educ:* St Bartholomew's Hosp., London (BSc Physiol. 1967; MB BS 1976); Royal Dental Hosp. (BDS 1972); Inst. Cancer Res. (PhD 1980). FRCPath 1995. Sen. Clinical Scientist and Cons., Ludwig Inst. Cancer Res., London, 1983–86; Cons. in Histopathol., Royal Marsden Hosp., 1984–; Prof. of Histopathol., and Chm., Sect. of Cell Biol and Exptl Pathol., Inst. of Cancer Res., London Univ., 1986–2000. Founding Dir, Toby Robins Breast Cancer Res. Centre, London, 1998. Dir, Pathology, Internat. Breast Cancer Study Gp, Berne, 1995–. Oakley Lectr, Pathological Soc. of GB and Ire., 1986. Chm., Pathology Gp, Orgn Eur. Cancer Insts, Geneva, 1992–96 (Mem., Faculty Bd, 1992–96); Mem., Faculty Bd, Eur. Soc. Mastology, Milan, 1994–. Mem., Brit. Soc. Cell Biol. *Publications:* contrib. chapters in books and numerous articles to professional jls. *Recreations:* antique English glass and furniture, gardening, walking, reading.

GUTCH, Richard Evelyn; Associate, Prospectus, 2008–13; freelance consultant, 2008–14; *b* 17 Nov. 1946; *s* of Sir John Gutch, KCMG, OBE, and late Diana Mary Gutch (*née* Worsley); *m* 1971, Rosemary Anne Capel Pike; two *s*. *Educ:* Winchester Coll.; Gonville and Caius Coll., Cambridge (BA); University Coll. London (MPhil). Town planning posts in Camden and S Yorks, 1970–76; Sen. Lectr, Planning Unit, PCL, 1976–80; Asst to Chief Exec., Brent LBC, 1980–85; Asst Dir, NCVO, 1985–92; Chief Exec., Arthritis Care, 1992–2001; Dir for England and Strategic Progs, Community Fund, 2001–04; Chief Exec., Futurebuilders England, 2004–08. FRSA 1992. *Publications:* reports and booklets. *Recreations:* the arts, Venice, the Isle of Wight, walking, carpentry, gardening. *Address:* Carina, Cliff Road, Totland Bay, Isle of Wight PO39 0EH. *T:* (01983) 752180.

GUTERRES, António Manuel de Oliveira; United Nations High Commissioner for Refugees, since 2005; *b* 30 April 1949; *m* (wife decd); one *s* one *d*. *Educ:* Technical Univ. of Lisbon. Electrical engr; Asst Prof., Technical Univ. of Lisbon, 1973–75; Chief of Staff to Sec. of State for Industry, 1974–75. Deputy (Socialist), Portuguese Parlt, 1976–83 and 1985–93; Prime Minister of Portugal, 1995–2002. Mem., Commn for European Integration, 1976–79; Pres., Parly Commn for Economy and Finance, 1977–79, for Territory Admin, Local Power and Envmt, 1985–88; Strategic Develt Dir, State Investment and Participation Agency, 1984–85. Mem., Parly Assembly, Council of Europe, 1981–83. Mem., Municipal Assembly of Fundão, 1979–95 (Pres.). Portuguese Socialist Party: joined 1974; Mem., Nat. Secretariat, 1986–88; Pres., Parly Gp, 1988–91; Sec.-Gen., 1992–2001; Vice Pres., 1992–99, Pres., 1999–2005, Socialist Internat. Founder and Vice Pres., Portuguese Assoc. for Consumer Protection, 1973–74; Mem., Assoc. for Economic and Social Develt, 1970–96. *Publications:* articles in jls. *Address:* (office) 94 Rue de Montbrillant, CP 2500, 1202 Geneva, Switzerland.

GUTFREUND, Prof. Herbert, FRS 1981; Professor of Physical Biochemistry, University of Bristol, 1972–86, now Emeritus; Scientific Member (external), Max-Planck-Institut für medizinische Forschung, Heidelberg, since 1987; Hon. Scientist, Rutherford Appleton Laboratory, Oxfordshire, 2001–09; *b* 21 Oct. 1921; *s* of late Paul Peter Gutfreund and Clara Angela Gutfreund; *m* 1958, Mary Kathelen, *er d* of late Mr and Mrs L. J. Davies, Rugby; two *s* one *d*. *Educ:* Vienna; Univ. of Cambridge (PhD). Research appts at Cambridge Univ., 1947–57; Rockefeller Fellow, Yale Univ., 1951–52; part-time Research Associate, Yale Univ., 1953–58; Principal Scientific Officer, National Inst. for Research in Dairying, Univ. of Reading, 1957–65; Visiting Professor: Univ. of California, 1965; Max Planck Inst., Göttingen, 1966–67; Reader in Biochemistry and Director of Molecular Enzymology Laboratory, Univ. of Bristol, 1967–72. Visiting appointments: Univ. of Leuven, 1972; Univ. of Adelaide, 1979; Univ. of Alberta, 1983. Part-time Scholar in Residence, NIH, Bethesda, 1986–89. Mem., EMBO, 1971. Hon. Member: British Biophysical Soc., 1990; Amer. Soc. for Biochem. and Molecular Biol., 1993; Biochemical Soc., 1996. *Publications:* An Introduction to the Study of Enzymes, 1966; Enzymes: physical principles, 1972; (ed) Chemistry of Macromolecules, 1974; (ed) Biochemical Evolution, 1981; Biothermodynamics, 1983; Kinetics for the Life Sciences, 1995; papers and reviews on many aspects of physical biochemistry. *Recreations:* mountain walking in Austria, cooking, reading general literature and philosophy of science, listening to music and all other good things in life. *Address:* Somerset House, Chilton Road, Upton, Oxon OX11 9JL. *T:* (01235) 851468. *E:* h.gutfreund@bristol.ac.uk. *Club:* Oxford and Cambridge.

GUTFREUND, John Halle; President, Gutfreund & Co. Inc., since 1993; Senior Adviser, Collins Stewart LLC (formerly C. E. Unterberg, Towbin), 2002–08; *b* 14 Sept. 1929; *s* of B. Manuel Gutfreund and Mary Halle Gutfreund; *m* 1st, 1958, Joyce L. Gutfreund; three *s*; 2nd, 1981, Susan K. Gutfreund; one *s*. *Educ:* Oberlin College, Ohio (BA 1951). Served in Army, Korea, 1951–53; Salomon Brothers, 1953–91: Exec. Partner, 1966; Managing Partner, 1978; Chm. and Chief Exec., 1981–91; Chm., Pres. and Chief Exec., Salomon Inc., 1986–91. Vice-Chm., NY Stock Exchange, 1985–87; formerly: Mem., Bd of Dirs, Securities Industry Assoc.; Mem., Bd of Govs and Pres., Bond Club of NY; Chm., Downtown-Lower Manhattan Assoc.; Chm., Wall Street Cttee for Lincoln Center's 1986–87 Corporate Fund Campaign. Member: Council on Foreign Relations; Brookings Instn; past Mem., Tri-Lateral Commn. Director: AXES LLC; Evercel Inc., 2000–; Nutrition 21 Inc. (formerly Ambi Inc.), 2001; LCA-Vision Inc.; Advr, Universal Bond Fund. Dir, Montefiore Medical Center Corp. (Mem. Exec. Cttee, Bd of Trustees; Mem., Financial and Real Estate Cttees); Lifetime Mem., NY Public Library (Vice-Chm., Corporate Congress). Trustee, Aperture Foundn (Chm. Emeritus); Hon. Trustee, Oberlin Coll. Hon. DH Oberlin Coll., 1987.

GUTHARDT, Rev. Dame Phyllis (Myra), DBE 1993; PhD; retired Methodist minister; *b* 1 Aug. 1929; *d* of Johan Detlef Guthardt and Amelia Guthardt. *Educ:* University of New Zealand: Auckland (BA 1957); Canterbury (MA 1959); Newnham Coll., Cambridge (PhD 1963). Primary school teacher, 1950–53; Methodist theol trng, 1954–56; ordained, 1959 (first woman ordained in NZ); active ministry in Methodist and Presbyterian parishes, incl. hosp. and univ. chaplaincy, 1957–90. Pres., Methodist Ch of NZ, 1985–86; Mem. Praesidium, World Methodist Council, 1986–91. Chancellor, Univ. of Canterbury, 1999–2002 (Mem. Council, 1981–2002; Pro-Chancellor, 1992–99). Hon. Dr Waikato, 1986; Hon. LLD Canterbury, 2003. *Publications:* contrib. theol jls. *Recreations:* music, reading, gardening. *Address:* 5 Cholmondeley Lane, Governors Bay, RD1 Lyttelton 8971, New Zealand. *T:* (3) 3299675.

GUTHRIE, family name of **Baron Guthrie of Craigiebank**.

GUTHRIE OF CRAIGIEBANK, Baron *cr* 2001 (Life Peer), of Craigiebank in the City of Dundee; **Field Marshal Charles Ronald Llewelyn Guthrie,** GCB 1994 (KCB 1990); LVO 1977; OBE 1980; DL; Chief of the Defence Staff, 1997–2001; Aide-de-Camp General to the Queen, 1993–2001; *b* 17 Nov. 1938; *s* of late Ronald Guthrie and Nina (*née* Llewelyn); *m* 1971, Catherine (OBE 2010), *er d* of late Lt Col Claude Worrall, MVO, OBE, Coldstream Guards; two *s*. *Educ:* Harrow; RMA Sandhurst. Commnd Welsh Guards, 1959; served: BAOR, Aden; 22 SAS Regt, 1965–69; psc 1972; MA (GSO2) to CGS, MoD, 1973–74; Brigade Major, Household Div., 1976–77; Comdg 1st Bn Welsh Guards, Berlin and N Ireland, 1977–80; Col GS Military Ops, MoD, 1980–82; Commander: British Forces New Hebrides, 1980; 4th Armoured Brigade, 1982–84; Chief of Staff 1st (BR) Corps, 1984–86; GOC NE Dist and Comdr 2nd Infantry Div., 1986–87; ACGS, MoD, 1987–89; Comdr 1 (BR) Corps, 1989–91; Comdr Northern Army Gp, 1992–93; C-in-C BAOR, 1992–94; CGS, 1994–97. Director: N. M. Rothschild & Sons, 2001–10; Petropavlovsk PLC (formerly Peter Hambro Mining), 2008–; Gulf Keystone Petroleum, 2011–. Vis. Prof., Dept of War Studies, KCL, 2002–. Col Comdt, Intelligence Corps, 1986–95; Col, The Life Guards, 1999–; Gold Stick to the Queen, 1999–; Col Comdt, SAS Regt, 2000–09. President: Army Saddle Club, 1991–96; Army LTA, 1991–99; Fedn of London Youth Clubs, 2001–; Action Research, subseq. Action Medical Research, 2001–; Army Benevolent Fund, 2002–11; Weston Spirit, 2003–12; Harrow Assoc., 2011–. Chairman: Liddle Hart Archives, 2002–; Hosp. of St John and St Elizabeth, 2009–; St John's Hospice, 2009–. Mem. Council and Trustee, IISS, 2002–. Chancellor, Liverpool Hope Univ., 2013–. Hon. Bencher, Middle Temple, 2010. Freeman, City of London, 1988; Liveryman, Painter Stainers' Co., 1989. DL Dorset, 2007. Hon. FKC 2002. Kt, SMO Malta, 1999. Comdr, Legion of Merit (USA), 2001. *Publications:* (with Sir Michael Quinlan) Just War: the just war tradition: ethics in modern warfare, 2007. *Recreations:* tennis, opera. *Address:* PO Box 25439, SW1P 1AG. *Clubs:* White's, All England Lawn Tennis and Croquet.

See also J. D. Guthrie.

GUTHRIE, James Dalglish; QC 1993; a Recorder, since 1999; *b* 21 Feb. 1950; *s* of late Ronald Guthrie and Nina Guthrie (*née* Llewelyn); *m* 1981, Lucille Gay Page-Roberts; one *s* one *d*. *Educ:* Harrow; Worcester Coll., Oxford (BA Modern History). Called to the Bar, Inner Temple, 1975, Bencher, 2000; admitted as barrister: Turks and Caicos Is, 1995; St Lucia, 1997; St Vincent and The Grenadines, 1998; Trinidad and Tobago, 2000; St Kitts and Nevis, 2005; Grenada, 2006; Bermuda, 2007; Belize, 2008; Antigua, 2008. *Recreations:* bonefishing, travel, photography. *Address:* 3 Hare Court, Temple, EC4Y 7BJ. *T:* (020) 7415 7800. *Club:* Turf.

See also Baron Guthrie of Craigiebank.

GUTHRIE, Sir Malcolm (Connop), 3rd Bt *cr* 1936; *b* 16 Dec. 1942; *s* of Sir Giles Connop McEacharn Guthrie, 2nd Bt, OBE, DSC, and Rhona, *d* of late Frederic Stileman; *S* father, 1979; *m* 1967, Victoria, *o d* of late Brian Willcock; one *s* one *d*. *Educ:* Millfield. *Heir: s* Giles Malcolm Welcome Guthrie [*b* 16 Oct. 1972; *m* 2000, Susan, *e d* of Bill and Sheila Thompson]. *Address:* Brent Eleigh, Belbroughton, Stourbridge, Worcestershire DY9 0DW.

GUTHRIE, Prof. Peter Moir, OBE 1993; FREng, FICE; Professor of Engineering for Sustainable Development, University of Cambridge, since 2000; *b* La Paz, Bolivia, 21 Feb. 1951; *s* of William Moir Guthrie and Mary Barbara Guthrie; *m* 1979, Lorna Jane Cowcher; one *s* one *d*. *Educ:* Imperial Coll., London (BSc 1973; MSc 1976; DIC 1973). FICE 1992; FREng 1998. VSO, Kaduna, Nigeria, 1974; Engineer: Turriff Taylor, Flotta, 1975, Iran, 1976; Soil Mechanics, 1976–78; Engr, then Dir, Scott Wilson, 1978–2004. Non-exec. Dir, Buro Happold, 2009–. Mem., Scientific Adv. Council, DEFRA, 2004–11. Founder, 1980, and Vice-Pres., RedR, 2005–, Engrs for Disaster Relief. FCGI 1995. FRSA. Hon. LLD. *Publications:* (jtly) Building Roads By Hand, 1990; contrib. papers on sustainable develt to learned jls. *Recreations:* ski-ing, tennis, golf. *Address:* Department of Engineering, University of Cambridge, Trumpington Street, Cambridge CB2 1PZ. *T:* (01223) 765627, *Fax:* (01223) 765625. *E:* pmg31@cam.ac.uk.

GUTHRIE, Robert Bruce, PhD; Principal, Hockerill Anglo-European College, 1996–2008; *b* 16 Jan. 1949; *s* of Robert Guthrie and Edith Guthrie (*née* Wilcock); *m* 1970, Christine Haswell; one *s* one *d*. *Educ:* Sale County Grammar Sch. for Boys; Univ. of Leeds (BSc Hons Phys 1969; PhD Ceramics 1975); Univ. of Durham (MBA Distn 1995). Teacher and House Tutor: Bedstone Coll., 1973–74; Stonyhurst Coll., 1974–79; Housemaster and Hd of Sci., Dover Coll., 1979–90; Hd, St George's Sch., Rome, 1991–94. Chm., State Boarding Schs Assoc., 2000–02. Mem. (Ind), Oakham Town Council, 2011–. Dir, Oakham Town Partnership, 2012–. Chm., Trustees, Harington Sch., 2014–. *Publications:* ceramics patent and papers, 1972; contrib. to educnl books and papers. *Recreations:* Rugby (England Schools, British Universities and Yorkshire), watching Leicester Tigers and Man Utd, stationary rowing, cycling, gardening, reading short poems. *Address:* 4 Catmose Park Road, Oakham, Rutland LE15 6HN. *Club:* Bishop's Stortford Hockey (Vice Pres.).

GUTTERIDGE, Charles Norman, FRCP, FRCPath; Chief Clinical Information Officer, Barts Health NHS Trust, since 2013; *b* 15 March 1952; *s* of Frank and Mary Gutteridge; *m* 1976, Charlotte Lorimer; two *s*. *Educ:* Rugby Sch.; Trinity Hall, Cambridge (BA, MB BChir 1976); London Hosp. Med. Coll. FRCP 1995; FRCPath 1997. Dist MO, Soufrière Dist, St Lucia, WI, 1977–79; training posts in gen. medicine and haematology, 1980–88; Wellcome Res. Training Fellow in Haematology, 1985–88; Sen. Lectr in Haematol., and Hon. Consultant Haematologist, Newham Gen. Hosp., 1988–2002, Actg Chief Exec., 1996–97, Med. Dir, 1997–2001, Newham Healthcare NHS Trust; Med. Dir, Barts and the London NHS Trust, 2002–10; Nat. Clinical Dir for Informatics, DoH, 2010–13. *Address:* Barts Health NHS Trust, Pathology and Pharmacy Building, Royal London Hospital, 80 Newark Street, E1 2ES.

GUTTRIDGE, Deborah Mary Hinton; *see* Grubb, D. M. H.

GUY, Alan James, DPhil; FRHistS, FRAS, FSA; Director, National Army Museum, 2004–10; *b* 13 July 1950; *s* of late James Alfred Guy and Florence Elizabeth Guy (*née* Farr); *m* 1975, Vivien Ruth Wilson; one *s*. *Educ:* Keble Coll., Oxford (MA 1976; DPhil 1983). National Army Museum: Curator, Dept of Weapons, 1977–86; Special Asst to Dir, 1986–88; Asst Dir (Collections), 1988–2000; Asst Dir (Admin), 2000–04. Vis. Fellow, Wolfson Coll., Cambridge, 2010–13. FRHistS 1989; FRAS 1999; FSA 2001. *Publications:* Oeconomy and Discipline: officership and administration in the British Army 1714–1763, 1985; Colonel Samuel Bagshawe and the Army of George II, 1990; (with P. B. Boyden) Soldiers of the Raj: the Indian Army 1660–1947, 1997; (with P. B. Boyden and M. Harding) Ashes and Blood: the British Army in South Africa 1795–1914, 1999; (with A. W. Massie) Captain L. E. Nolan, 15th Hussars: expedition to the Crimea 1854, 2010. *Recreation:* bel canto opera and its substitutes. *Club:* Travellers.

GUY, Diana; a Deputy Chairman, Competition Commission, 2004–10 (Member, 2001–04); *b* 27 March 1943; *d* of late Charles Stanley Eade and Vera Dorothy Eade (*née* Manwaring); *m* 1968, John Robert Clare Guy; two *s*. *Educ:* Lady Margaret Hall, Oxford (MA Juris.). Admitted solicitor; Partner, 1973–95, Consultant, 1995–2001, Theodore Goddard. *Publications:* (with G. I. F. Leigh) The EEC and Intellectual Property, 1981. *Recreations:* reading, walking, spending time at our house in France.

GUY, Frances Mary; HM Diplomatic Service, retired; Head, Middle East Region, Christian Aid, since 2015; *b* 1 Feb. 1959; *d* of David Guy and Elizabeth Guy (*née* Hendry); *m* 1989, Guy Raybaudo; one *s* two *d*. *Educ:* Aberdeen Univ. (MA Hons); Johns Hopkins Univ., Bologna (Dip.); Carleton Univ., Ottawa (MA Internat. Relns). Entered FCO, 1985: lang. trng, 1987; Second Sec. (Chancery), Khartoum, 1988–91; First Secretary: FCO, 1991–95; and Hd, Pol Section, Bangkok, 1995–96; Dep. Hd of Mission, Addis Ababa, 1997–2001; Ambassador to the Yemen, 2001–04; Hd, Engaging the Islamic World Gp, FCO, 2004–06; Ambassador to Lebanon, 2006–11; Advr on ME to Sec. of State for Foreign Affairs, 2011–12; Rep., UN Women, Iraq, 2012–14. *Recreations:* swimming, running.

GUY, Geoffrey William; Founder, and Executive Chairman, GW Pharmaceuticals plc, since 1998; *b* 30 Sept. 1954; *m* 1986, Katherine Mary Husk. *Educ:* St Bartholomew's Hosp. Med. Coll., Univ. of London (BSc Pharmacol. 1976; MB BS 1979). MRCS, LRCP 1979; LMSSA 1979; Dip. Pharmaceutical Medicine, RCP, 1984. Various hosp. appts, incl. St Bartholomew's, Southampton Gen. Hosp. and New Addenbrooke's Hosp., Cambridge, 1979–81; Internat. Clin. Res. Co-ordinator, Pierre Fabre Labs, France, 1981–83; Dir, Clin. Develt, Napp Labs, 1983–85; Founder, 1985, Chief Exec., 1985–97, Ethical Hldgs Plc; Founder, 1989, Chm., 1989–97, Phytopharm Plc (floated on NASDAQ; listed on London Stock Exchange, 1996). Vis. Prof., Sch. of Sci. and Medicine, Univ. of Buckingham, 2011–. Mem. Ct of Benefactors, RSocMed, 2008–. Chm. Bd, Weldmar Hospice Care Trust, 2006–14; Patron, Mji wa Neema, Kenya Orphanage Charity, 2008–. Liveryman, Soc. of Apothecaries. Venturer of Year Award, 3i, 1997; Deloitte Dir of Year Award, Pharmaceuticals and Healthcare, 2011. *Publications:* (ed jtly) The Medicinal Uses of Cannabis and Cannabinoids, 2004; contrib. various scientific papers on drug develt, drug delivery, pharmacokinetics, narcotics, cannabis and cannabinoids. *Recreations:* Real tennis, boating, horse breeding. *Address:* c/o GW Pharmaceuticals plc, 1 Cavendish Place, W1G 0QF.

GUY, Dr John Alexander; historian, author and broadcaster; Fellow in History, Clare College, Cambridge, since 2003; *b* Warragul, Vic, Australia, 16 Jan. 1949; *s* of Frank and Marjorie Guy; *m* 2005, Julia Fox; one *s* one *d*. *Educ:* King Edward VII Sch., Lytham, Lancs; Clare Coll., Cambridge (BA 1970); Selwyn Coll., Cambridge (PhD 1973). Res. Fellow, Selwyn Coll., Cambridge, 1970–73; Asst Keeper of Public Records, PRO, 1973–78; Lectr in Modern British Hist., 1978–82, Reader in British Hist., 1982–90, Univ. of Bristol; Prof. of Modern Hist., Univ. of St Andrews, 1992–2002. Vis. Lectr, Univ. of Calif, Berkeley, 1977; John Hinkley Vis. Prof., Johns Hopkins Univ., 1990; Richard L. Turner Prof. of Humanities and Prof. of Hist., Univ. of Rochester, NY, 1990–92; Hon. Res. Prof., Univ. of St Andrews, 2002–09; Guest Prof., Yale-in-London prog., Paul Mellon Centre for Studies in British Art, London, 2012–14; Vis. Fellow, Clare Coll., Cambridge, 2002–03. Television documentaries: presenter: The King's Servant, 2001; Renaissance Secrets series, 2001; contributor: Wolsey's Lost Palace of Hampton Court, 2002; Royal Deaths and Diseases series, 2003; Tudor histl expert, Time Team, 2004, 2005, 2006; histl consultant, The Tudors, 2008. *Publications:* The Cardinal's Court, 1977; The Public Career of Sir Thomas More, 1980; Law and Social Change in British History, 1984; The Court of Star Chamber and its Records to the Reign of Elizabeth I, 1985; Christopher St German on Chancery and Statute, 1985; (with A. Fox) Reassessing the Henrician Age, 1986; Tudor England, 1988; (with J. Morrill) The Tudors and Stuarts, 1992; The Reign of Elizabeth I: court and culture in the last decade, 1995; The Tudor Monarchy, 1997; Cardinal Wolsey, 1998; Politics, Law and Counsel in Tudor and Early-Stuart England, 2000; Thomas More, 2000; The Tudors: a very short introduction, 2000, 2nd edn 2013; My Heart is My Own: the life of Mary Queen of Scots, 2004 (Whitbread Biography Award); A Daughter's Love: Thomas and Margaret More, 2008 (TV adaptation 2011); Thomas Becket: warrior, priest, rebel, victim - a 900-year-old story retold, 2012; The Children of Henry VIII, 2013; Henry VIII: the quest for fame, 2014; contrib. articles to learned histl jls. *Recreations:* opera, art, theatre, animals, watching the steamers on Lake Geneva. *Address:* Clare College, Trinity Lane, Cambridge CB2 1TL. *T:* (01223) 333237, *Fax:* (01223) 333219. *E:* jag64@cam.ac.uk.

GUY, John Westgarth, OBE 1986; HM Diplomatic Service, retired; Consul General, St Petersburg, 1996–2000; *b* 17 July 1941; *s* of late John Westgarth Guy and Stella (*née* Sanderson); *m* 1st, 1961, Sylvia Kathleen Stokes (*d* 2002); one *s* one *d*; 2nd, 2005, Thelma Georgina Barbieri (*née* Larter). *Educ:* Queen Mary's Sch. for Boys, Basingstoke. CRO, 1960; Karachi, 1961–63; Calcutta, 1964–67; Vice Consul, New York, 1968–70; FCO, 1970–72; Third Secretary: Moscow, 1972–73; Jakarta, 1974; Second Sec., São Paulo, 1975–77; FCO, 1977–79; DTI, 1979–80; First Secretary: Yaoundé, 1981–84; Maputo, 1984–87; FCO, 1987–91; High Comr, PNG, 1991–94; RCDS, 1995. *Recreation:* sailing. *Address:* Hampshire.

GUY, Captain Robert Lincoln, LVO 1980; RN; Executive Director, Hong Kong Association and Hong Kong Society, since 2002; *b* 4 Sept. 1947; *s* of late John and Susan Guy; *m* 1981, Rosemary Ann Walker; two *d*. *Educ:* Radley Coll. Entered BRNC Dartmouth, 1966; ADC to Governor and Commander-in-Chief, Gibraltar, 1973; commanded: HMS Ashton, 1974; HMS Kedleston, 1975; HMS Sirius, 1984–85. Equerry to the Queen, 1977–80; First Lieut, HMS Antelope (sunk in action 1982), 1981–82. Lieut 1971; Lt-Comdr 1979; Comdr 1983; Captain 1991. Exec. Dir, Japan Soc., 1997–2007. *Recreations:* polo, ski-ing, shooting. *Address:* The Barn House, Lees Hill, South Warnborough, Hook, Hants RG29 1RQ. *Club:* White's.

GUYTON, Marjorie A.; *see* Allthorpe-Guyton.

GWILLIAM, John Albert, MA Cantab; Headmaster of Birkenhead School, 1963–88; *b* 28 Feb. 1923; *s* of Thomas Albert and Adela Audrey Gwilliam; *m* 1949, Pegi Lloyd George; three *s* two *d*. *Educ:* Monmouth Sch.; Trinity Coll., Cambridge. Assistant Master: Trinity Coll., Glenalmond, 1949–52; Bromsgrove Sch., 1952–56; Head of Lower Sch., Dulwich Coll., 1956–63. *Address:* Araulfan, 13 The Close, Llanfairfechan, Gwynedd LL33 0AG.

GWILLIAM, Kenneth Mason; Principal Transport Economist, then Economic Adviser, Transport, World Bank, Washington, 1993–2002; *b* 27 June 1937; *s* of John and Marjorie Gwilliam; *m* 1987, Sandra Wilson; two *s* by former *m*. *Educ:* Magdalen Coll., Oxford (BA 1st Cl. Hons PPE). Res. Asst, Fisons Ltd, 1960–61; Lecturer: Univ. of Nottingham, 1961–65; Univ. of E Anglia, 1965–67; Prof. of Transport Economics, Univ. of Leeds, 1967–89; Prof. of Econs of Transport and Logistics, Erasmus Univ., Rotterdam, 1989–93. Director: Nat. Bus Co., 1978–82; Yorkshire Rider, 1986–88. Editor, Jl of Transport Economics and Policy, 1977–87. *Publications:* Transport and Public Policy, 1964; Economics and Transport Policy, 1975; (jtly) Deregulating the Bus Industry, 1984; Cities on the Move, 2002; Africa's Transport Infrastructure: mainstreaming maintenance and management, 2011. *Recreations:* golf, detective fiction, cruising. *Address:* 12720 Grand Traverse Drive, Dade City, FL 33525, USA.

GWILLIAM, Michael Colin; Planning and Transport Director, South East England Regional Assembly, 2001–06; *b* 4 Jan. 1948; *s* of late Alfred and Grace Gwilliam; *m* 1st, 1970, Mary (marr. diss. 1995); two *d*; 2nd, 1996, Janice; two step *d*. *Educ:* Keble Coll., Oxford (MA Hist.); University Coll. London (DipTP); De Montfort Univ., Leicester (DMS). Chief Planner, Leics CC, 1985–88; Co. Planning Officer, Bedfordshire CC, 1988–96; Dir, The Civic Trust, 1996–2000. Vice-Pres., County Planning Officers' Soc., 1995–96. FRSA 1989. Hon. RICS 1999. *Publications:* Sustainable Renewal of Suburban Areas, 1999; Small Town Vitality, 2000; (jtly) Abraham's Children, 2013. *Recreations:* hill-walking, woodland management, supporting Palestine, fair trade.

GWILLIAM, Robert John; Senior Associate Solicitor, British Telecommunications PLC, 1990–96; *b* 6 Jan. 1943; *s* of Benjamin Harold Gwilliam and Dora Gwilliam; *m* 1966, Linda Mary Ellway; two *s*. *Educ:* Lydney Grammar Sch.; Nottingham Univ. (BA Hons Law); Cambridge Univ. (Dip. Criminology); College of Law. Admitted Solicitor, 1969; practised in Local Govt Prosecuting Depts, 1969–83; Chief Prosecuting Solicitor for Hampshire, 1983–86; Chief Crown Prosecutor, Crown Prosecution Service: London South/Surrey Area, 1986; Inner London Area, 1987; London and SE Regl Dir, Grade 3, 1987–89. *Recreations:* member of Harlequins RFC, dog walking in Purbeck, swimming and keep-fit. *Address:* 1 The Downs, Seymer Road, Swanage, Dorset BH19 2AL.

GWILLIAMS, Very Rev. Dianna Lynn; Dean of Guildford, since 2013; *b* Colorado, 1957; *m* Martin; one *s* one *d* (and one *d* decd). *Educ:* California Univ. (BA 1978); King's Coll. London (MA Youth Ministry and Theol Educn 2001). Sound Engr; ordained deacon, 1992, priest, 1994; non-stipendiary Minister, St Saviour, Peckham, 1992–97; Asst Curate, 1997–99, Vicar, 1999–2013, St Barnabas, Dulwich; Area Dean, Dulwich, 2005–12; Priest-in-charge, St Saviour, Peckham, 2007–11; Dean of Women's Ministry, Dio. of Southwark, 2009–12. Chaplain, Alleyn's Foundn, 1999–2013. Hon. Canon, Southwark Cath., 2006–13. *Address:* The Deanery, Cathedral Close, Guildford GU2 7TL. *T:* (01483) 547861, *Fax:* (01483) 303350.

GWILT, George David, FFA; General Manager, 1979–84, Managing Director and Actuary, 1984–88, Standard Life Assurance Company; *b* 11 Nov. 1927; *s* of Richard Lloyd Gwilt and Marjory Gwilt (*née* Mair); *m* 1956, Ann Dalton Sylvester; three *s*. *Educ:* Sedbergh Sch.; St John's Coll., Cambridge (MA). FFA 1952; FBCS. Joined Standard Life Assurance Co., 1949: Asst Official, 1956; Asst Actuary, 1957; Statistician, 1962; Mechanisation Manager, 1964; Systems Manager, 1969; Dep. Pensions Manager, 1972; Pensions Actuary, 1973; Asst General Manager and Pensions Manager, 1977; Asst Gen. Man. (Finance), 1978. Dep. Chm., Associated Scottish Life Offices, 1986–88. Special Advr in Scotland, Citicorp, 1989–91; Director: Hammerson Property Investment and Develt Corp., 1979–94; Scottish Mortgage and Trust, 1983–98; European Assets Trust NV, 1979–2000; Hodgson Martin, 1989–2000. Trustee, TSB of South of Scotland, 1966–83. Member: Younger Cttee on Privacy, 1970–72; Monopolies and Mergers Commn, 1983–87. Pres., Faculty of Actuaries, 1981–83. Convener, Scottish Poetry Library, 1988–2001. *Recreation:* flute playing. *Address:* 39 Oxgangs Road, Edinburgh EH10 7BE. *T:* (0131) 445 1266. *Clubs:* Royal Air Force; New (Edinburgh).

GWILT, Michael Peter; Motor Risk Manager, HDI-Gerling Insurance, since 2012; *b* 29 April 1957; *s* of Geoffrey and Joy Gwilt; *m* 1984, Cheryl Harrison; one *s*. *Educ:* Bishop Perowne C of E Sch., Worcester; King's Sch., Worcester. Family business, R. & G. Gwilt Engineering, 1975–82; Uniweld Ltd, 1983–84; joined Interleasing (UK) Ltd, 1984: Sales and Mktg Dir, 1988–94; Managing Director: Interleasing North, 1994–97; Cowie Interleasing, 1997; Gp Man. Dir, Arriva plc, 1998; Gp Man. Dir, Onlyfair Denmark ApS, subseq. CEO, Fleet Logistics Internat. NV, 1999–2006; Man. Dir, Europe, Drive Cam Inc., 2006–09; Sales Dir, GreenRoad, 2010–11. *Recreations:* ski-ing, travelling, theatre, house renovation.

GWYER, Ven. Judith; *see* Rose, Ven. K. J.

GWYN, Alison Frances M.; *see* Moore-Gwyn.

GWYNEDD, Viscount; William Alexander Lloyd George; *b* 16 May 1986; *er s* and *heir* of Earl Lloyd-George of Dwyfor, *qv*. *Educ:* Eton; Sch. of Oriental and African Studies, Univ. of London.

GWYNN, Dominic Leigh Denys; Partner, Martin Goetze and Dominic Gwynn, Organ Builders, since 1979; *b* 18 Aug. 1953; *s* of Kenneth Leigh Maxwell Gwynn and Elisabeth (*née* Molenaar); *m* 1976, Antonia Rosamund Cordy; two *d*. *Educ:* Christ's Hosp.; St John's Coll., Oxford (BA Hons; MA). Major projects include: reconstructions: 1716 Handel organ, St Lawrence Whitchurch, Little Stanmore, 1994; 1743 organ, St Helen Bishopsgate, London, 1995; new organs: Handel House Mus., 1998; Magdalene Coll., Cambridge, 2000; reconstruction, two early Tudor organs, Early English Organ Project, 2000–01; restoration, 1829 organ, St James Bermondsey, London, 2002. Pres., Inst. of British Organ Building, 2009–. *Publications:* (contrib.) Performing Purcell's Music, 1995; Historic Organ Conservation, 2001; contribs to Jl British Inst. of Organ Studies, Organ Yearbook and Organists Review. *Recreations:* choral singing, early modern church, social and cultural history. *Address:* 12 Burcott Road, Wells, Somerset BA5 2EQ. *T:* (01749) 675955, *T:* (office) (01909) 485635.

GWYNNE, Andrew John; MP (Lab) Denton and Reddish, since 2005; *b* 4 June 1974; *s* of Richard John Gwynne and Margaret Elisabeth Gwynne (*née* Ridgway); *m* 2003, Allison Louise Dennis; two *s* one *d*. *Educ:* Univ. of Salford (BA Hons Politics and Contemp. Hist.); NE Wales Inst. of Higher Educn (HND Business and Finance). Asst to EDS Prog. Manager, ICL, Manchester, 1990–92; Mem., Year 2000 Team, Nat. Computing Centre, 1999–2000; European Co-ordinator, office of Arlene McCarthy, MEP, 2000–01; researcher, office of Andrew Bennett, MP, 2000–05. PPS to Minister of State, Home Office, 2005–07, to Home Sec., 2007–09, to Secretary of State, Children, Schs and Families, 2009–10; Shadow Minister: of Transport, 2010–11; for Health, 2011–15. Mem. (Lab) Tameside MBC, 1996–2008. *Recreations:* history, reading, computing, spending time with family. *Address:* House of Commons, SW1A 0AA. *T:* (020) 7219 4708. *E:* gwynnea@parliament.uk; (constituency office) Town Hall, Market Street, Denton M34 2AP. *T:* (0161) 320 1504, *Fax:* (0161) 320 1503.

GWYNNE, Emily; *see* Maitlis, E.

GWYNNE JONES, family name of **Baron Chalfont**.

GWYTHER, Christine; Member (Lab) Carmarthen West and South Pembrokeshire, National Assembly for Wales, 1999–2007; Member, Pembrokeshire Coast National Park Authority, since 2007; *b* 9 Aug. 1959; *d* of Ivor George Gwyther and Marjorie Gwyther (*née* Doidge). *Educ:* Pembroke Sch.; UC, Cardiff. Milford Haven Waterway Enterprise Zone, 1986; local govt officer, S Pembrokeshire DC, 1987–96, Pembrokeshire CC, 1996–99. National Assembly for Wales: Sec. for Agric. and Rural Develt, 1999–2000; Chm., Econ. Develt and Transport Cttee, 2003–07. Contested (Lab): Carmarthen W and S Pembs, Nat. Assembly for Wales, 2007, 2011; Carmarthen E and Dinefwr, 2010. Welsh Chair, Interreg III Prog. Monitoring Cttee, 2002. Mem., Pembrokeshire Business Club. Mem., RSPB.

GYIMAH, Samuel Phillip; MP (C) East Surrey, since 2010; Parliamentary Under-Secretary of State, Department for Education, since 2014; *b* Beaconsfield, Bucks, 10 Aug. 1976; *m* 2012, Dr Nicky Black. *Educ:* Achimota Secondary Sch., Ghana; Freman Coll., Herts; Somerville Coll., Oxford (BA PPE). Pres., Oxford Union, 1997. Investment Banker, Internat. Equities and Investment Banking Div., Goldman Sachs, 1999–2003; entrepreneur in trng, employment and Internet sectors, 2003–10. PPS to the Prime Minister, 2012–13; a Lord Comr of HM Treasury (Govt Whip), 2013–14; Parly Sec., Cabinet Office, 2014–15. Chm., Bow Gp, 2007. Gov., Haverstock Sch., 2004–07. *Publications:* (ed) From the Ashes…: the future of the Conservative Party, 2005; (jtly) Beyond the Banks, 2011. *Address:* House of Commons, SW1A 0AA. *T:* (020) 7219 3504. *E:* sam@samgyimah.com.

GYLE, Rev. Alan Gordon; Vicar, St Paul's, Knightsbridge, since 2003 (Priest-in-charge, 2001–03); *b* Aberdeen, 27 June 1965; *s* of late Ernest Gordon Gyle and of Janet May Cochrane (*née* Cunningham). *Educ:* Univ. of Aberdeen (MA 1987); St Stephen's House, Oxford (MA 1996); Univ. of E London (MA 2008). Ordained deacon, 1992, priest, 1993; Asst Curate, Acton Green, 1992–94; Minor Canon (Succentor & Dean's Vicar), St George's Chapel, Windsor Castle, 1994–99; Chaplain: Imperial Coll. London, 1999–2004; Royal Coll. of Art, 1999–2004; Dir of Trng and Develt (Two Cities), Dio. of London, 2008–12. Examining Chaplain to the Bishop of London, 2007–; Priest Vicar, Westminster Abbey, 2008–. Hon. Chaplain, Royal Thames Yacht Club, 2001–. Hon. Fellow, St George's House, Windsor, 1999–2001. FRSA 1999. *Recreations:* music, cookery. *Address:* The Vicarage, 32 Wilton Place, SW1X 8SH. *T:* (020) 7201 9999. *E:* alangyle@me.com. *Clubs:* Athenæum, Caledonian.

GYLLENHAMMAR, Dr Pehr Gustaf; Vice Chairman, Europe, Rothschild, since 2003; *b* 28 April 1935; *s* of Pehr Gustaf Victor Gyllenhammar and Aina Dagny Kaplan; *m* 1959, Eva Christina (*d* 2008), *d* of Gunnar Ludvig Engellau; one *s* three *d*; *m* 2010, Christel Behrmann (marr. diss. 2013); *m* 2013, Lee Welton Croll. *Educ:* University of Lund. LLB. Mannheimer & Zetterlöf, solicitors, 1959; Haight, Gardner, Poor & Havens, NY, 1960; Amphion Insurance Co., Gothenburg, 1961–64; Skandia Insurance Co., 1965, Exec. Vice-Pres., 1968, Pres. and Chief Exec. Officer, 1970; AB Volvo, Gothenburg, 1970, Man. Dir and Chief Exec. Officer, 1971; Chm. and Chief Exec. Officer, 1983–90, Exec. Chm. Bd of Dirs, 1990–93, Volvo; Dep. Chm., Commercial Union plc, 1997–98; Chm., CGU, subseq. CGNU, then Aviva, plc, 1998–2005. Chairman: MC European Capital (Holdings), SA, 1994–96; Lazard AB, 1999–2003; Thomson Reuters (formerly Reuters) Founders Share Co. Ltd, 1999–2012; Investment AB Kinnevik, 2004–07; Majid Al Futtaim Hldg LLC, 2004–09; Arise Windpower AB, 2007–14; Sen. Advr, Lazard Frères & Co., 1996–2003; Dir of companies in Sweden, Netherlands, UK and USA. Member: Internat. Adv. Cttee, Chase Manhattan Bank, NA, NY, 1972–95; Bd, Cttee of Common Market Automobile Constructors, 1977–91; Bd, Assoc. des Constructeurs Européens d'Automobiles, 1991–93; Bd, Fedn of Swedish Industries, 1979–93; Roundtable of European Industrialists, 1982–93; Chm., European Financial Services Round Table, 2001–06. Mem. Bd Trustees, Rockefeller Univ., NY, 1991–96; Chm. Bd Trustees, LPO, 2006–. Lethaby Prof., Royal Coll. of Art, London, 1977; Mem., Royal Swedish Acad. of Engineering Scis, 1974. Hon. DM Gothenburg Univ., 1981; Hon. DTech Brunel, 1987; Hon. DEng Technical Univ., NS, 1988; Hon. DSocSc Helsinki, 1990; Hon. DEc Gothenburg, 2003. Golden Award, City of Gothenburg, 1981. Officer, Royal Order of Vasa, 1973; King's Medal, with Ribbon of Order of Seraphim, 1981; Commander: Order of Lion of Finland, 1977 (Comdr 1st Class 1986); Ordre National du Mérite, France, 1980; St Olav's Order, Norway, 1984; Légion d'honneur, France, 1987; Order of Leopold, Belgium, 1989; Kt Grand Officer, Order of Merit, Italy, 1987. *Publications:* Mot sekelskiftet på måfå (Toward the Turn of the Century, at Random), 1970; Jag tror på Sverige (I Believe in Sweden), 1973; People at Work (US), 1977; En industripolitik för människan (Industrial policy for human beings), 1979; Fortsättning följer… (To Be Continued…), 2000; Oberoende ar stark (Independence is Strong), 2014. *Recreations:* golf, music. *Address:* New Court, St Swithin's Lane, EC4N 8AL.

GYPPS, His Honour Godfrey Howard; a Circuit Judge, 2003–08; Designated Family Judge for the County of Essex, and Chairman, Essex Family Justice Council, 2005–08; *b* 24 March 1947; *s* of Jack and Hilda Gypps; *m* 1974, Judith Wendy Falkner; two *d*. *Educ:* Colchester Royal Grammar Sch.; Queen Mary Coll., Univ. of London (LLB Hons 1969). Admitted solicitor, 1972; on teaching staff, Coll. of Law, 1972–90; Dist Judge, 1991–2003; on secondment to staff of Hd of Civil Justice, 1998 and 2000. Vis. Fellow, Dept of Law, Univ. of Essex, 1998–. Member: Civil Procedure Rule Cttee, 1997–2001; Civil Justice Council, 2002–03. *Publications:* contribs to various legal pubns and periodicals. *Recreations:* the countryside, dogs, radio. *Address:* c/o HM Court Service, Priory Place, Chelmsford CM2 0PP. *Clubs:* Colchester Garrison Officers', Old Colcestrians.

H

HAAG, Jessica Margaret Poppaea; *see* Simor, J. M. P.

HAAKONSSEN, Prof. Knud, Dr phil, PhD; FBA 2012; FRSE; FRHistS; Professor of Intellectual History and Director, Sussex Centre for Intellectual History, University of Sussex, 2005–11, now Professor Emeritus; Long-term Fellow, Max-Weber-Kolleg, University of Erfurt, since 2012; Professor of Intellectual History, University of St Andrews, since 2015; *b* Tingsted, Falster, Denmark, 9 July 1947; *s* of Helmer Daniel Haakonssen and Laura Eline Haakonssen; *m* 2001, Åsa Marie Söderman; one *s*. *Educ:* Nykøbing Realskole; Nykøbing Katedralskole; Univ. of Copenhagen (Cand.Art.; MA; Dr phil 1996); Univ. of Aarhus (Gold Medal in Philosophy); Univ. of Edinburgh (PhD 1978). FRHistS 2005. Sen. Tutor, Dept of Philosophy, Monash Univ., 1976–79; Lectr, Sch. of Pol Sci., Victoria Univ. of Wellington, 1979–82; Res. Fellow, Sen. Res. Fellow, Fellow, then Sen. Fellow, Hist. of Ideas Unit, Res. Sch. of Social Scis, ANU, 1982–94; Prof., Dept of Philosophy, Boston Univ., 1995–2004. Fellow, Woodrow Wilson Center, Washington, 1988. Visiting Professor: Dept of Philosophy, McGill Univ., 1992–93; Martin-Luther-Univ. Halle-Wittenberg, 2011; Torgny Segerstedt Prof., Univ. of Uppsala, 2001; Hon. Prof. of Hist., UCL, 2012–; Lim Chong Yah Prof., 2012, Vis Prof., 2013–14, of Pol Sci., NUS; Sen. Scholar, Univ. of Bergen, 2013–14. FASSA 1992; FRSE 2002; Fellow, Japan Soc. for Promotion of Sci., 2000. Corresp. Fellow, Royal Danish Acad. of Sci. and Letters, 1995. *Publications:* The Science of a Legislator, 1981 (trans. French, 1998, Japanese, 2001, Chinese, 2010); Thomas Reid on Practical Ethics, 1990, 2007; (ed jtly) A Culture of Rights: the Bill of Rights in philosophy, politics and Law, 1791 and 1991, 1991; Natural Law and Moral Philosophy: from Grotius to the Scottish Enlightenment, 1996 (trans. Chinese 2010); (ed) Enlightenment and Religion: rational dissent in eighteenth-century Britain, 1996; (ed) The Cambridge History of Eighteenth-Century Philosophy, 2 vols, 2006 (trans. Chinese 2016); (ed) Cambridge Companion to Adam Smith, 2006 (trans. Chinese, 2015); (ed jtly) Northern Antiquities and National Identities: perceptions of Denmark and the North in the eighteenth century, 2008; Enlightenments and Religions, 2010; General Editor: The Edinburgh Edition of Thomas Reid, 10 vols, 1994–; Natural Law and Enlightenment Classics, 44 vols, 2001–. *Recreations:* opera, reading, hiking. *E:* k.haakonssen@gmail.com.

HAAVISTO, Heikki Johannes; Chairman Board of Directors, Raisio Group, 1997–2001 (Chairman, Administrative Council, 1977–96); *b* Turku, Finland, 20 Aug. 1935; *s* of Urho and Alli Haavisto; *m* 1964, Maija Rihko; three *s*. *Educ:* Univ. of Helsinki (MSc, LLM). Hd of Dept, Oy Vehnä Ab, 1963–66; Sec.-Gen., Central Union of Agricl Producers and Forest Owners, 1966–75 (Pres., 1976–94); Member, Administrative Council: Osuuskunta Metsäliitto, Helsinki, 1976–93 (Vice-Chm. and Pres., 1976–93); Central Union Co-op. Banks, Helsinki, 1985–93; Minister of For. Affairs, Finland, 1993–95. Chm., Delegn, Finnish Co-operative Pellervo, Helsinki, 1979–2001. Mem., Internat. Policy Council on Agric. and Trade, Washington, 1988–2000. Mem., Centre Party, Finland. Hon. PhD Turku; Hon. Dr Agr. & For., Hon. DVM Helsinki, 1995. *Address:* Hintsantie 2, 21200 Raisio, Finland.

HABERFELD, Dame Gwyneth; *see* Jones, Dame G.

HABERMAN, Prof. Steven, PhD; FIA; Professor of Actuarial Science, since 1985, and Dean, Cass Business School, since 2012, City University London; *b* London, 26 June 1951; *s* of Louis and Lily Haberman; *m* 1976, Mandy Brecker; one *s* two *d*. *Educ:* Trinity Coll., Cambridge (BA Maths 1972); City Univ. (PhD 1982; DSc 2000). FIA 1975. Trainee actuary, Prudential Assce Co. Ltd, 1972–74; Actuary (pt-time), Govt Actuary's Dept, 1977–97; City University: Lectr in Actuarial Sci., 1974–80; Sen. Lectr, 1980–85; Hd, Dept of Actuarial Sci. and Stats, 1987–95; Dean, Sch. of Maths, 1995–2002; Dep. Dean, Cass Business Sch., 2003–12. *Publications:* Pensions: the problem of today and tomorrow, 1987; History of Actuarial Science, 1995; Modern Actuarial Theory and Practice, 1999; Actuarial Models for Disability Insurance, 1999, 2nd edn 2005; Modelling Longevity Dynamics for Pensions and Annuity Business, 2009. *Recreations:* theatre, cinema, opera, walking, hiking, playing with grandchildren. *Address:* Cass Business School, 106 Bunhill Row, EC1Y 8TZ. *T:* (020) 7040 8601, *Fax:* (020) 7040 8899. *E:* S.Haberman@city.ac.uk.

HABGOOD, family name of **Baron Habgood**.

HABGOOD, Baron *cr* 1995 (Life Peer), of Calverton in the county of Buckinghamshire; **Rt Rev. and Rt Hon. John Stapylton Habgood;** PC 1983; MA, PhD; Archbishop of York, 1983–95; *b* 23 June 1927; *s* of Arthur Henry Habgood, DSO, MB, BCh, and Vera (*née* Chetwynd-Stapylton); *m* 1961, Rosalie Mary Anne Boston; two *s* two *d*. *Educ:* Eton; King's Coll., Cambridge (Hon. Fellow, 1986); Cuddesdon Coll., Oxford. Univ. Demonstrator in Pharmacology, Cambridge, 1950–53; Fellow of King's Coll., Cambridge, 1952–55; Curate of St Mary Abbots, Kensington, 1954–56; Vice-Principal of Westcott House, Cambridge, 1956–62; Rector of St John's Church, Jedburgh, 1962–67; Principal of Queen's College, Birmingham, 1967–73; Bishop of Durham, 1973–83. Retired from H of L, 2011. Hulsean Preacher, Cambridge Univ., 1987–88; first Athenæum Lectr, 1998; Bampton Lectr, Oxford Univ., 1999; Gifford Lectr, Aberdeen Univ., 2000. Moderator, Church and Society Sub-Unit, WCC, 1983–91. Pro-Chancellor, Univ. of York, 1985–90. Chm., UK Xenotransplantation Interim Regulatory Authy, 1997–2003. Hon. Bencher, Inner Temple, 2000. Hon. DD: Durham, 1975; Cambridge, 1984; Aberdeen, 1988; Huron, 1990; Hull, 1991; Oxford, Manchester, and York, 1996; London, 2005; Hon. DHL York Coll., Pa, 1995. *Publications:* Religion and Science, 1964; A Working Faith, 1980; Church and Nation in a Secular Age, 1983; Confessions of a Conservative Liberal, 1988; Making Sense, 1993; Faith and Uncertainty, 1997; Being a Person, 1998; Varieties of Unbelief, 2000; The Concept of Nature, 2002; (ed jtly) Glory Descending: Michael Ramsey and his writings, 2005. *Recreations:* painting, carpentry. *Address:* 18 The Mount, Malton, N Yorks YO17 7ND. *Club:* Athenæum.

HABGOOD, Anthony John; Chairman: Whitbread Group plc, 2005–14; RELX Group (formerly Reed Elsevier), since 2009; Preqin, since 2011; Norwich Research Park LLP, since 2013; Court of Directors, Bank of England, since 2014; *b* 8 Nov. 1946; *s* of John Michael Habgood and Margaret Diana Middleton Habgood (*née* Dalby); *m* 1974, Nancy Atkinson; two *s* one *d*. *Educ:* Gonville and Caius Coll., Cambridge (MA Econ 1972); Carnegie Mellon Univ., Pittsburgh (MS Indust. Admin 1970). Boston Consulting Gp, 1970–86: Director, 1976; Management Cttee, 1979; Exec. Cttee, 1981; Tootal Group, 1986–91: Director, 1986; Chief Exec., 1991; Chief Exec., 1991–96, Chm., 1996–2009, Bunzl plc. Director: Geest, 1988–93; Powergen, 1993–2001; SVG Capital (formerly Schroder Ventures Internat. Investment Trust), 1995–2009; NatWest Gp, 1998–2000; Marks and Spencer, 2004–05; Norfolk and Norwich Univ. Hosp. Trust, 2006–13; Chm., Mölnlycke Health Care, 2006–07. Vis. Fellow, Univ. of Oxford, 2008–. *Recreation:* country pursuits. *Address:* RELX Group, 1–3 Strand, WC2N 5JR. *Clubs:* Brooks's; Royal Norfolk and Suffolk Yacht.

HACKER, Rt Rev. George Lanyon; an Hon. Assistant Bishop, Diocese of Carlisle, since 1994; Bishop Suffragan of Penrith, 1979–94; *b* 27 Dec. 1928; *s* of Edward Sidney Hacker and Carla Lanyon; *m* 1969, June Margaret Erica Smart; one *s* one *d*. *Educ:* Kelly College, Tavistock; Exeter College, Oxford (BA 1952, MA 1956); Cuddesdon College, Oxford. Deacon 1954, priest 1955, Bristol; Curate of St Mary Redcliffe, Bristol, 1954–59; Chaplain, King's College London at St Boniface Coll., Warminster, 1959–64; Perpetual Curate, Church of the Good Shepherd, Bishopwearmouth, 1964–71; Rector of Tilehurst, Reading, 1971–79. Pres., Rural Theol. Assoc., 1989–94; Pres., Age Concern Cumbria, 1991–2007 (Chm., 1987–91); Chm., Age Concern Eden, 1994–2000; Episcopal Advr, Anglican Young People's Assoc., 1987–94. Editor, Chrism, 1996–2008. *Publications:* The Healing Stream: Catholic insights into the ministry of healing, 1998. *Recreations:* gardening, writing poetry. *Address:* Keld House, Milburn, Penrith, Cumbria CA10 1TW. *T:* (01768) 361506. *E:* bishhack@mypostoffice.co.uk.

HACKER, Peter Michael Stephen, DPhil; Fellow and Tutor in Philosophy, 1966–2006, now Emeritus Research Fellow, and Librarian, 1986–2006, St John's College, Oxford; Professor of Philosophy, University of Kent at Canterbury, 2013–Oct. 2016; *b* 15 July 1939; *s* of Emeric Hacker and Thea Hacker (*née* Mendel); *m* 1963, Sylvia Dolores Imhoff; two *s* one *d*. *Educ:* Queen's Coll., Oxford (MA; Hon. Fellow 2010); St Antony's Coll., Oxford (DPhil). Jun. Res. Fellow, Balliol Coll., Oxford, 1965–66; British Acad. Res. Reader, 1985–87; Leverhulme Res. Fellow, 1991–94. Visiting Professor: Swarthmore Coll., Pa, 1973, 1986; Univ. of Michigan, Ann Arbor, 1974; Queen's Univ., Ont, 1985; Vis. Fellow, Rockefeller Foundn, Bellagio, 2006; Vis. Sen. Res. Fellow, Univ. of Bologna, 2009. *Publications:* Insight and Illusion, 1972, 2nd edn 1986; Appearance and Reality, 1987; (ed) The Renaissance of Gravure: the art of S. W. Hayter, 1988; Wittgenstein: meaning and mind, 1990; (ed) Gravure and Grace: the engravings of Roger Vieillard, 1993; Wittgenstein: mind and will, 1996; Wittgenstein's Place in Twentieth Century Analytic Philosophy, 1996; Wittgenstein: connections and controversies, 2001; (with M. R. Bennett) Philosophical Foundations of Neuroscience, 2003; (jtly) Neuroscience and Philosophy, 2007; Human Nature: the categorial framework, 2007; (with M. R. Bennett) A History of Cognitive Neuroscience, 2008; (ed with J. R. Cottingham) Mind, Method and Morality: essays in honour of Anthony Kenny, 2009; (ed with J. Schulte) Wittgenstein: philosophical investigations, 4th edn 2009; with G. P. Baker: Wittgenstein: understanding and meaning, 1980, 2nd edn 2004; Frege: logical excavations, 1984; Language, Sense and Nonsense, 1984; Scepticism, Rules and Language, 1984; Wittgenstein: rules, grammar and necessity, 1985, 2nd edn 2009; *festschrift:* Wittgenstein and Analytic Philosophy: essays for P. M. S. Hacker, ed H.-J. Glock and J. Hyman, 2009; The Intellectual Powers: a study of human nature, 2013; Wittgenstein: comparisons and contexts, 2013. *Recreations:* art history, music. *Address:* St John's College, Oxford OX1 3JP.

HACKER, Richard Daniel; QC 1998; *b* 1954; *s* of Samuel Hacker and Lilli Hacker; *m* 1988, Sarah Anne, *d* of R. J. Millar, Bath; one *d*. *Educ:* Haberdashers' Aske's Sch.; Downing Coll., Cambridge (Wiener Anspach Schol., 1976; BA Law 1976; MA 1979); Univ. Libre de Bruxelles (Licence Spéciale en Droit Européen (Distinction) 1978). Called to the Bar: Lincoln's Inn, 1977 (Hardwicke Schol.; Student of the Year Prize), *ad eundem* Gray's Inn, 1989; British Virgin Islands, 2003; in practice at the Bar, 1979–. Asst Parly Boundary Comr, 2000–; Chm., Inquiry into Herts Parly Constituency Boundaries, 2000. *Recreations:* travel, food, family life. *Address:* 3–4 South Square, Gray's Inn, WC1R 5HP. *T:* (020) 7696 9900, *Fax:* (020) 7696 9911. *E:* contact@hacker.plus.com.

HACKETT, Dennis William; journalist; publishing and communications consultant; Director, Media Search & Selection Ltd, 1988–98; *b* 5 Feb. 1929; *s* of James Joseph Hackett and Sarah Ellen Hackett (*née* Bedford); *m* 1st, 1953, Agnes Mary Collins; two *s* one *d*; 2nd, 1974, Jacqueline Margaret Totterdell; one *d*. *Educ:* De La Salle College, Sheffield. Served with RN, 1947–49. Sheffield Telegraph, 1945–47 and 1949–54; Daily Herald, 1954; Odhams Press, 1954; Deputy Editor, Illustrated, 1955–58; Daily Express, 1958–60; Daily Mail, 1960; Art Editor, Observer, 1961–62; Deputy Editor, 1962, Editor, 1964–65, Queen; Editor, Nova, 1965–69; Publisher, Twentieth Century Magazine, 1965–72; Editorial Dir, George Newnes Ltd, 1966–69; Dir, IPC Newspapers, 1969–71; Associate Editor, Daily Express, 1973–74; TV critic: The Times, 1981–85; Tablet, 1984–92; Editorial Consultant, You, The Mail on Sunday magazine, 1982–86; Exec. Editor, 1986–87, Editor-in-chief, 1987, Today; Editor-in-Chief, M, The Observer Magazine, 1987–88; Editor, Management Today, 1992–94. Chm., Design and Art Directors' Assoc., 1967–68. *Publications:* The History of the Future: Bemrose Corporation 1826–1976, 1976; The Big Idea: the story of Ford in Europe, 1978. *Recreations:* reading, walking. *Address:* 7 Foster Drive, Broadway Grange, Leamington Road, Broadway WR12 7EA. *Club:* Royal Automobile.

HACKETT, John Wilkings, CMG 1989; Director, Financial, Fiscal and Enterprise Affairs, Organisation for Economic Co-operation and Development, Paris, 1979–89; *b* 21 Jan. 1924; *s* of Albert and Bertha Hackett; *m* 1952, Anne-Marie Le Brun. *Educ:* LSE (BSc(Econ) 1950); Institut d'Etudes Politiques, Paris (Diplôme 1952); Univ. of Paris (Dr d'état ès sciences économiques 1957). Served RN, 1942–46. Economic research, 1952–57; OECD, 1958–89. FRSA 1986. *Publications:* Economic Planning in France (with A.-M. Hackett), 1963; L'Economie Britannique—problèmes et perspectives, 1966; (with A.-M. Hackett) The British Economy, 1967; articles on economic subjects in British and French economic jls. *Recreations:* music, painting, reading. *Address:* 48 rue de la Bienfaisance, 75008 Paris, France. *Clubs:* Royal Over-Seas League; Cercle de l'Union Interalliée (Paris).

HACKETT, Peter, OBE 1990; DL; PhD; FREng; Director, 1993–94, and Principal, 1970–94, Camborne School of Mines (first Fellow, 1990); Adviser on Cornwall, Exeter University, 1994–98; *b* 1 Nov. 1933; *s* of Christopher and Evelyn Hackett; *m* 1958, Esmé Doreen (*née* Lloyd); one *s* one *d*. *Educ:* Mundella Grammar Sch.; Nottingham Univ. (BSc 1st Cl. Hons Mining Engrg; PhD). FIMM 1971, Hon. FIMMM (Hon. FIMM 1993); FREng (FEng 1983). Lecturer, Nottingham Univ., 1958–70; Vis. Lectr, Univ. of Minnesota, 1969; Vis. Professor, Univ. of California at Berkeley, 1979. Pres., IMM, 1989–90. Chm., Port of Falmouth Sailing Assoc., 1997–2002. DL Cornwall, 1993. *Recreations:* sailing, classic vehicles. *Club:* Royal Cornwall Yacht (Falmouth).

HACKING, family name of **Baron Hacking**.

HACKING, 3rd Baron *cr* 1945, of Chorley; **Douglas David Hacking;** Bt 1938; International Arbitrator and Mediator; Solicitor of Supreme Court of England and Wales, 1977–99; Attorney and Counselor-at-Law of State of New York, since 1975; Barrister-at-law, 1963–76 and since 1999; Chartered Arbitrator, since 1999; *b* 17 April 1938; *er s* of 2nd Baron Hacking, and Daphne Violet (*d* 1998), *e d* of late R. L. Finnis; *S* father, 1971; *m* 1st, 1965, Rosemary Anne, *e d* of late Francis P. Forrest, FRCSE; two *s* one *d*; 2nd, 1982, Dr Tessa M. Hunt, MB, MRCP, FRCA, *er d* of late Roland C. C. Hunt, CMG; three *s*. *Educ:* Aldro School, Shackleford; Charterhouse School; Clare College, Cambridge (BA 1961, MA 1968). Served in RN, 1956–58; Ordinary Seaman, 1956; Midshipman, 1957; served in HMS Ark Royal (N Atlantic), 1957; HMS Hardy (Portland) and HMS Brocklesby (Portland and Gibraltar), 1958; transferred RNR as Sub-Lt, 1958, on completion of National Service; transf. List 3 RNR, HMS President, 1961; Lieut 1962; retired RNR, 1964. Called to the Bar, Middle Temple, Nov. 1963 (Astbury and Harmsworth Scholarships). With Simpson, Thacher and Bartlett, NYC, 1975–76; with Lovell, White and King, 1976–79; Partner: Lane & Partners, 1979–81; Richards Butler, 1981–94; Sonnenscheins, 1994–99; Mem., Littleton Chambers, 2000–. Mem., H of L Select Cttee on the European Community, 1989–93, 1995–99. Chm. Steering Cttee, London Internat. Arbitration Trust, 1980–81. Trustee, Carthusian Trust, 1971–2001. Gov., Charlotte Sharman Sch., Southwark, 1996–97. Member: Amer. Bar Assoc.; Bar Assoc. of City of New York; Indian Council of Arbitration, 1997–; Swiss Arbitration Assoc., 2000–. Fellow: Singapore Inst. of Arbitration, 2004–; Malaysian Inst. of Arbitration, 2004–. Pres., Assoc. of Lancastrians in London, 1971–72, 1998. Apprenticed to Merchant Taylors' Co., 1955, admitted to Freedom, 1962; Freedom, City of London, 1962. FCIArb 1979. *Recreations:* reading biographies, mountain walking. *Heir: s* Hon. Douglas Francis Hacking [*b* 8 Aug. 1968; *m* 2000, Dr Jodie McVernon; two *d*]. *Address:* 27 West Square, Kennington, SE11 4SP. *T:* (020) 7735 4400. *E:* david.hacking@london-arbitration.com; Littleton Chambers, 3 King's Bench Walk, Temple, EC4Y 7HR. *T:* (020) 7797 8600, *Fax:* (020) 7797 8699. *E:* dhacking@littletonchambers.co.uk. *Clubs:* Reform, MCC.

HACKING, Anthony Stephen; QC 1983; *b* 12 Jan. 1941; *s* of late John and Joan Hacking, Warwick; *m* 1969, Carin, *d* of late Dr Svante and of Brita Holmdahl, Gothenburg; one *d* three *s*. *Educ:* Warwick Sch.; Lincoln Coll., Oxford (MA Jurisprudence). Called to the Bar, Inner Temple, 1965, Bencher, 1993; a Recorder, 1985–2006; a Dep. High Ct Judge (QBD), 1993–2001. Hd of Chambers, 1 King's Bench Walk, 1999–2005. *Clubs:* The Richmond Golf; 1 KBW Cricket (Pres.); Sheepscombe Cricket (Pres.).

HACKING, Prof. Ian MacDougall, CC 2004; PhD; FRSC; University Professor, University of Toronto, 1991–2003, now University Professor Emeritus (Professor, Department of Philosophy, 1981–2003); Chair de philosophie et histoire des concepts scientifiques, Collège de France, 2000–06, now Professeur honoraire; *b* 18 Feb. 1936; *s* of Harold Eldridge Hacking and Margaret Elinore Hacking (née MacDougall); *m* 1983, Judith Baker; one *s* two *d*. *Educ:* Univ. of British Columbia (BA 1956); Trinity Coll., Cambridge (BA 1958, MA 1962; PhD 1962; Hon. Fellow, 2000). Res. Fellow, Peterhouse, Cambridge, 1962–64; Asst Prof., then Associate Prof. of Philos., Univ. of British Columbia, 1964–69, seconded to Makerere UC, by External Aid, Canada, 1967–69; Univ. Lectr in Philos., Univ. of Cambridge and Fellow, Peterhouse, Cambridge, 1969–74 (Hon. Fellow, 2005); Stanford University: Fellow, Center for Advanced Study in the Behavioral Scis, 1974–75; Prof., 1975–82; Henry Waldegrave Stuart Prof. of Philos., 1981–82. FRSC 1986; Fellow Amer. Acad. of Arts and Scis, 1991; Corresp. FBA, 1995. Hon. Dr: British Columbia, 2001; Cordoba, 2007; McMaster, 2008; Toronto, 2010; Carleton, 2012. Gold Medal for Achievement in Res., Social Scis and Humanities Res. Council, Canada, 2008; Ludvig Holberg Internat. Meml Prize, 2009; Austrian Decoration of Honour for Sci. and Arts, 2012. *Publications:* Logic of Statistical Inference, 1965; A Concise Introduction to Logic, 1972; Why Does Language Matter to Philosophy?, 1975; The Emergence of Probability, 1975, 2nd edn 2006; Representing and Intervening, 1983; The Taming of Chance, 1990; Le Plus pur nominalisme: L'énigme de Goodman: 'vleu' et usages de 'vleu', 1993; Rewriting the Soul: multiple personality and the sciences of memory, 1995; Mad Travelers: reflections on the reality of transient mental illnesses, 1998; The Social Construction of What?, 1999; Probability and Inductive Logic, 2001; Historical Ontology, 2002. *Recreations:* canoeing, mountain hiking. *E:* ihack@chass.utoronto.ca.

HACKITT, Judith Elizabeth, (Mrs D. J. Lea), CBE 2006; FIChemE; FCGI; FREng; Chair, Health and Safety Executive (formerly Health and Safety Commission), since 2007 (Member, 2002–06); *b* 1 Dec. 1954; *d* of Kenneth G. Hackitt and Kathleen Rhoda Hackitt (*née* Jeffcott); *m* 1977, David John Lea; two *d*. *Educ:* Queen Elizabeth Grammar Sch., Atherstone, Warwicks; Imperial Coll., London (BSc (Eng) 1975). ACGI 1972, FCGI 2008; FIChemE 2001; FREng 2010. Eur. Pigments Ops Dir, 1990–96, Gp Risk Manager, 1996–98, Elementis plc; Dir, Business and Envmt, 1998–2002, Dir Gen., 2002–06, CIA; Dir of Implementation, CEFIC, Brussels, 2006–07. Non-exec. Dir, Oxon HA, 1995–98. Co-Chair, EU Chemicals Policy Strategy Gp, 2002–05. Member: Chemistry Leadership Council, 2003–05; Bd, Energy Saving Trust, 2009–; Bd, High Value Manufacturing Catapult, 2014–. Mem. Council, IChemE, 2008– (Pres., 2013–14). *Recreations:* music (ageing rock stars), walking, ski-ing, good food and wine. *Address:* Health and Safety Executive, Westminster Office, 7th Floor, Caxton House, Tothill Street, SW1H 9NA. *T:* (020) 7227 3820. *E:* chair@hse.gsi.gov.uk.

HACKLAND, Brian Anthony; Director, Government Office Network Closure Programmes, Department for Communities and Local Government, 2011; *b* 3 March 1951; *s* of Alan Keith Hackland and Catherine Mary Hackland; *m* 1978, Sarah Ann Spencer, *qv*; two *s*. *Educ:* Univ. of Natal (BSc Hons Botany and Entomology 1974); Balliol Coll., Oxford (Rhodes Schol.; BA Hons Pol, Philos. and Econs 1977); DPhil Pol Sci. Oxon 1984. Parly Asst to Shadow Sec. of State for NI, 1985–88; Investigator with Local Govt Ombudsman, 1988–90; on secondment as Ombudsman, Bedfordshire CC, 1990; Department of the Environment: Team Leader, Housing Action Trusts Prog., 1991–93, Central Finance, 1993–95; Private Sec. to Minister for Local Govt, Housing and Regeneration, 1995–97; Hd, Air and Envmt Quality Div., 1997–99; Sen. Policy Advr (Envmt and Transport), Prime Minister's Policy Directorate, 1999–2001; Dir, Town and Country Planning, ODPM, 2002–05; Regl Dir, Govt Office for the E of England, 2005–08; Dir, Regl Coordination Unit and Govt Office Network, later Govt Office Network Centre and Services, DCLG, 2008–10. Dir, Eur. Regl Develt Fund, 2000–06. *Publications:* (with Gwyneth Williams) Dictionary of Contemporary Southern African Politics, 1985. *Recreations:* gardening, walking, cycling.

HACKLAND, Sarah Ann; *see* Spencer, S. A.

HACKNEY, Archdeacon of; *see* Adekunle, Rev. E.

HACKNEY, Roderick Peter, PhD; PPRIBA; Managing Director, Rod Hackney & Associates, since 1972; Co-founder and Director, Kansara Hackney Ltd, architectural consultancy, since 2009; *b* 3 March 1942; *s* of William Hackney and Rose (*née* Morris); *m* 1964, Christine Thornton; one *s*. *Educ:* John Bright Grammar School, Llandudno; Sch. of Architecture, Manchester Univ. (BAArch 1966, MA 1969, PhD 1979). ARIBA 1969; FCIArb 1977; ASAI; FFB 1987; MCIOB 1987. Job Architect, EXPO '67, Montreal, for Monorail Stations; Housing Architect, Libyan Govt, Tripoli, 1967–68; Asst to Arne Jacobsen, Copenhagen, working on Kuwait Central Bank, 1968–71. Established: Castward Ltd, building and develt firm, 1983 (Sec., 1983–92). Royal Institute of British Architects: Pres., 1987–89; Mem. Council, 1978–84 (Vice-Pres., Public Affairs, and Overseas Affairs, 1981–83), and 1991–99 (Vice-Pres., Internat. Affairs, 1992–94); Hon. Librarian, 1998–99; Chairman: Discipline Hearings Cttee, 2001–03; Discipline Cttee, 2003–07; Mem., Conservation Cttee, 2010–; Sen. Conservation Architect, 2010–; Dir, RIBAC Cos, 1996–2001. Mem. Council, Internat. Union of Architects, 1981–85, and 1991–, First Vice-Pres., 1985–87, Pres., 1987–90. Vis. Prof., Paris, 1984; Special Prof., Nottingham Univ., 1987–90; Vis. Prof., Xian Univ., China, 1999; has lectured in Europe, N and S America, Asia, Middle East, Australia and Africa. Chm., Times/RIBA Community Enterprise Scheme, 1985–89; Mem. Council, Nat. Historical Bldg Crafts Inst., 1989–; Advr on regeneration and inner city problems in Sweden, Italy, Brazil, USA, Russia, Dubai, China and Germany, 1990–; Internat. Advr, Centre for Internat. Architectl Studies, Univ. of Manchester Sch. of Architecture, 1992–; Jury Mem., overseas housing develts; Juror for internat. competitions in Netherlands and China, 1992–; Mem., Adv. Gp, UN World Habitat Awards, 2003–; Chm., UN Good Practice Awards, 2004; Pres., UN Cttee on Housing for the Elderly, 2010–; Co-Architectl Advr to Samba Bank HQ, Saudi Arabia, 2010–; deleg., UK and overseas confs. Chairman: Trustees, Inner City Trust, 1986–97; British Architectl Liby Trust, 1999–2001. President: Snowdonia (formerly Snowdonia Nat. Park) Soc., 1987–2005; N Wales Centre, NT, 1990–2008. Patron: Llandudno Mus. and Art Gall., 1988–2007; Dome Project, Buxton, 2000–07. Hon. FAIA 1988; Hon. FRAIC 1990; Hon. Fellow: United Architects of Philippines, 1988; Fedn of Colls of Architects, Mexico, 1988; Indian Inst. of Architecture, 1990; Hon. Member: Superior Council of Colls of Architects of Spain, 1987; Architectural Soc. of China, 2003. Hon. DLitt Keele, 1989. Awards and prizes include: DoE Award for Good Design in Housing (1st Prize), 1975; 1st Prize, St Ann's Hospice Arch. Comp., 1976; RICS Conservation Award, 1980; Sir Robert Matthew Prize, IUA, 1981; PA Consulting Gp Award for Innovation in Bldg Design and Construction (for Colquhoun St, Stirling), 1988; Award for work and leader of Community Arch. Movt, Charleston, USA, 1989; The Times, BITC, and Housing and Homeless Award, 1993. *Television:* Build Yourself a House, 1974; Community Architecture, 1977; BBC Omnibus, 1987; consultant, Europe by Design, BBC, 1991; *radio:* The Listener, 1986; Third Ear, 1990; Call to Account, 1992; Woman's Hour, 1992; Common Ground, 1996. Consultant, World Architecture Review Agency, China, 1992; Advr, Habitat Center News Jl, India, 1992–. *Publications:* Highfield Hall: a community project, 1982; The Good the Bad and the Ugly, 1990, re-issue 2014; Good Golly Miss Molly (music play), 1991; articles in UK and foreign architectural jls. *Recreations:* outdoor pursuits, walking, photography, travelling, looking at buildings, speaking at conferences. *Address:* St Peter's House, Windmill Street, Macclesfield, Cheshire SK11 7HS.

HACKSTON, Fiona C.; *see* Clarke-Hackston.

HACKWOOD, Ven. Paul Colin; Residentiary Canon, Leicester Cathedral, since 2007; *b* 1961; *m* Josie; two *s*. *Educ:* Bradford Coll. of Educn (DipHE 1982); Huddersfield Polytech. (BSc 1984); Birmingham Univ. (DipTh 1988); Queen's Coll., Birmingham; Bradford Business Sch. (MBA 2005). Ordained deacon, 1989, priest, 1990; Curate, Horton, 1989–93; Social Responsibility Advr, Dio. St Albans, 1993–97; Vicar, Thornbury, 1997–2005; Archdeacon of Loughborough, 2005–09. Chair, Trustees, Church Urban Fund, 2009– (Trustee, 2005–).

HADAWAY, Lisa; *see* Armstrong, Lisa.

HADDACKS, Vice-Adm. Sir Paul (Kenneth), KCB 2000; Lieutenant-Governor, Isle of Man, 2005–11; *b* 27 Oct. 1946; *s* of late Kenneth Alexander Haddacks and of Edith Lillian Haddacks (*née* Peardon); *m* 1970, Penny Anne Robertson; one *s*. *Educ:* Plymouth Coll.; Kingswood Sch., Bath; BRNC; RN Staff Coll., RCDS. Joined RN 1964; commanded HM Ships: Scimitar, 1971–72; Cleopatra, 1981–82; Naiad, 1982–83; Intrepid, 1986–88; US Naval Acad., 1979–80; Asst Dir, Navy Plans, 1984–86; Dep. Dir, Naval Warfare, 1988–89; Comdr, RN Task Force, Gulf, 1990; Captain of the Fleet, 1991–94; Asst COS (Policy) to SACEUR, 1994–97; UK Mil. Rep., HQ NATO, 1997–2000; Dir, NATO Internat. Mil. Staff, 2001–04. Chm. Govs, Chichester Coll., 2014–. KStJ 2010 (CStJ 2006). *Recreations:* family, travel. *Clubs:* Army and Navy; Royal Naval Sailing Association.

HADDINGTON, 13th Earl of, *cr* 1619; **John George Baillie-Hamilton;** Lord Binning, 1613; Lord Binning and Byres, 1619; *b* 21 Dec. 1941; *o s* of 12th Earl of Haddington, KT, MC, TD, and Sarah (*d* 1995), *y d* of G. W. Cook, Montreal; *S* father, 1986; *m* 1st, 1975, Prudence Elizabeth (marr. diss. 1981), *d* of A. Rutherford Hayles; 2nd, 1984, Susan Jane Antonia, 2nd *d* of John Heyworth; one *s* two *d*. *Educ:* Ampleforth. *Heir: s* Lord Binning, *qv*. *Address:* Mellerstain, Gordon, Berwickshire TD3 6LG. *Clubs:* Turf, Chelsea Arts; New (Edinburgh).

HADDO, Earl of; George Ian Alastair Gordon; *b* 4 May 1983; *s* and *heir* of Marquess of Aberdeen and Temair, *qv*; *m* 2009, Isabelle Anna Nancy Coaten; two *s*. *Educ:* Harrow; Oxford Brookes Univ. (BSc Hons Real Est. Mgt 2005). With Knight Frank LLP, 2005–06; Rutley Capital Partners LLP (Knight Frank Gp), 2007–09; Cording Real Estate Gp, 2009–14; FORE Partnership, 2011–14; LJ Gp, 2015–. *Heir: s* Viscount Formantine, *qv*.

HADDON, Kenneth William, FCA; Chairman, Axa Reinsurance UK plc, 1994–99 (Chief Executive Officer, 1987–98); *b* 30 April 1938; *s* of William Percy Haddon and Constance Margaret Haddon; *m* 1966, Jarmaine (*née* Cook); one *s* one *d*. *Educ:* Minchenden Grammar Sch. FCA 1960. Nat. Service, RAF, 1960–62. Chartered Accountant, Thomson McLintock, 1962–64; London Reinsurance Co., later Netherlands Reinsurance Gp, then NRG London Reinsurance Co.: Sec. and Accountant, 1964; various posts, 1964–82; Gen. Manager, 1983–87. Chairman: London Underwriting Centre, 1995–98, and 1999–2001; London Processing Centre, 1997–99; London Internat. Insce and Reinsce Mkt Assoc., 1997–98. FRSA. *Recreations:* golf, gardening. *Clubs:* City of London, Langbourn Ward; Brookmans Park Golf.

HADDON-CAVE, Hon. Sir Charles (Anthony), Kt 2011; **Hon. Mr Justice Haddon-Cave;** a Judge of the High Court of Justice, Queen's Bench Division, since 2011; a Presiding Judge, Midland Circuit, since 2014; *b* 20 March 1956; *s* of Sir (Charles) Philip Haddon-Cave, KBE, CMG; *m* 1980, Amanda Charlotte Law; two *d*. *Educ:* King's Sch., Canterbury; Pembroke Coll., Cambridge (MA). Called to the Bar, Gray's Inn, 1978, Bencher, 2003; in practice as barrister, London and Hong Kong, 1980–2011; QC 1999; a Recorder, 2000–11. FRAeS. *Recreations:* art, music, running. *Address:* Royal Courts of Justice, Strand, WC2A 2LL. *Club:* Garrick.

HADDRILL, Stephen Howard; Chief Executive, Financial Reporting Council, since 2009; *b* 12 Jan. 1956; *s* of Albert George and Pauline Haddrill; *m* 1983, Joanne Foakes; two *s*. *Educ:* Trinity Sch., Croydon; New Coll., Oxford (BA Modern Hist. and Econs). Joined Department of Energy, 1978: Private Sec. to Sec. of State, 1987–89; Asst Sec., Nuclear Power Policy, 1989–90; Mem., Governor's Central Policy Unit, Hong Kong Govt, 1991–94; Department of Trade and Industry, 1994–2005: Dep. Dir, Competitiveness Unit, 1994–98; Dir, Consumer Affairs, 1998–2000; Dir, Employment Relns, 2000–02; Dir Gen., Fair Markets, 2002–05; Dir Gen., Assoc. of British Insurers, 2005–09. *Recreations:* gardening, sailing. *Address:* Financial Reporting Council, 5th floor, Aldwych House, 71–91 Aldwych, WC2B 4HN.

HADEN-GUEST, family name of **Baron Haden-Guest**.

HADEN-GUEST, 5th Baron *cr* 1950, of Saling, Essex; **Christopher Haden-Guest;** film director, writer, actor and musician (as Christopher Guest); *b* 5 Feb. 1948; *s* of 4th Baron Haden-Guest and of Jean Haden-Guest (*née* Hindes); *S* father, 1996; *m* 1984, Jamie Lee Curtis; one *s* one *d* (both adopted). *Educ:* The Stockbridge Sch.; New York Univ. *Films:* (writer, director and actor): Waiting for Guffman, 1997; Best in Show, 2000; For Your Consideration, 2006; (writer and director): The Big Picture, 1989; Mighty Wind, 2004; (writer and actor) This is Spinal Tap, 1984; (dir) Almost Heroes, 1998; (actor): Mrs Henderson Presents, 2005; Night at the Museum 2, The Invention of Lying, 2009; (exec. prod.) Her Master's Voice (TV film), 2012; (writer, dir and prod.) Family Tree (TV series), 2013. Scriptwriter for TV and radio progs. *Recreations:* fly-fishing, ski-ing. *Heir: b* Hon. Nicholas Haden-Guest [*b* 5 May 1951; *m* 1st, 1980, Jill Denby (marr. diss. 1988); one *d*; 2nd, 1989, Pamela Rack; one *d*]. *Address:* 212 26th Street #300, Santa Monica, CA 90402, USA.

HADFIELD, Antony; Deputy Chairman, NHS Redditch and Bromsgrove Clinical Commissioning Group, since 2013; Senior Partner, Hadfield Associates, 1997–2005; *b* 9 Sept. 1936; *s* of Thomas Henry Hadfield and Edna (*née* Cooke); *m* 1959, Dorothy Fay Osman; one *s*. *Educ:* Sheffield; Brighton; Middx Poly. (BA). CEng 1966; FIET (FIEE 1975). Design engr, Plessey, 1958–62; design and project engr, Metal Industries Gp, 1962–65; design engr, CEGB, 1965–67; Sen. Engr and Manager, Eastern Electricity, 1967–77; Area Manager, Yorks Electricity, 1977–79; Dir of Engrg, Midlands Electricity, 1979–85; Chief Exec. and Dep. Chm., NI Electricity (formerly NI Electricity Service), 1985–91; Man. Dir, 1991–94, Chief Exec., 1994–97, Northern Electric plc; Chief Exec., Teesside Power Ltd, 1998–2000 (Dir, 1991–97). Chairman: Northern Inf. Systems Ltd, 1994–97; NEDL Ltd, 1994–97; Northern Utility Services Ltd, 1994–97; Sovereign Exploration Ltd, 1996–97; Dep. Chm., BCN Data Systems Ltd, 1998–2000. Non-exec. Dir, NHS Worcestershire, 2008–13. Associate, PB Power Ltd, 1997–2004. Mem., Competition (formerly Monopolies and Mergers) Commn, 1998–2005. Chm., Power Div., IEE, 1992–93. Chm., BITC, Tyneside, 1993–97. CCMI (CIMgt 1987); FRSA 1993. *Recreations:* mountaineering, sailing.

HADFIELD, Mark; a District Judge (Magistrates' Courts), since 2005; *b* 6 July 1960; *s* of late William Hadfield and Marie Helen Hadfield; *m* 1993, Denise Ferns; one *d*. *Educ:* St Augustine's Grammar Sch., Manchester; Liverpool Poly. (BA Hons Law). Admitted solicitor, 1985; in private practice with Colin Watson Solicitors, Warrington, 1985–2005; Solicitor Advocate, 1995. *Recreations:* golf, supporting Manchester City FC. *Address:* Manchester City Magistrates' Court, Crown Square, Manchester M60 1PR.

HADID, Dame Zaha (Mohammad), DBE 2012 (CBE 2002); RA 2005; architectural designer; *b* Baghdad, 31 Oct. 1950. *Educ:* Sch. of Architecture, Architectural Assoc., London (Diploma Prize). Lectr, AA, 1977, 1980; Vis. Design Critic, Harvard Grad. Sch. of Design, 1986; Vis. Prof., 1987, Kenzo Tange Prof., 1994, Columbia Univ., NY; Sullivan Prof., Univ. of Illinois, 1997; Guest Prof., Hochschule für Bildende Kunst, Hamburg, 1997. *Projects* include: 59 Eaton Place, SW1, 1980 (RIBA, Gold Medal, 1982); Hamburg Docklands Bauforum 1, 1985, Bauforum 2, 1989; Tomigaya and Azabu-Jyuban, Tokyo, 1987; Monsoon Restaurant, Sapporo, Japan, 1989 (completed 1990); Bordeaux Docklands, 1989; Osaka Folly, 1989 (completed 1990); Vitra Fire Station, Weil am Rhein, 1990 (completed 1993); Hotel Billie Strauss, Stuttgart, 1992–95; Kunst und Medienzentrum Rheinhafen, Düsseldorf, 1993; Cardiff Bay Opera House, 1994–96 (Opera House Trust First Prize, 1994; Special Award, Royal Acad. Summer Exhibn, 1995); Spittelau Viaduct Mixed Use Project, Vienna, 1994–97; Contemporary Arts Center, Cincinnati, 1998 (completed 2003); MAXXI Mus. of 21st Century Arts, Rome, 1998 (completed 2009) (RIBA Stirling Prize, 2010); Science Centre, Wolfsburg; Bridge Structure, Abu Dhabi; Tram station, Strasbourg; Guangzhou Opera House, China, 2003 (completed 2010); Maggie's Centre, Victoria Hosp., Fife, 2006; Evelyn Grace Acad., Brixton, 2010 (RIBA Stirling Prize, 2011); Heydar Aliyev Cultural Centre, Baku; Aquatics Centre, London 2012 Olympics (completed 2011); Serpentine Sackler Gall., 2013; Middle East Centre, Oxford Univ., 2015. Has exhibited in Europe, Japan, and USA; has lectured in Europe, USA, Australia, Brazil, Canada, China, Hong Kong, Jordan, Lebanon, Mexico, Taiwan, Thailand, and UAE. Pritzker Architecture Prize, 2004; Praemium Imperiale, Japan Art Assoc., 2009; Royal Gold Medal for Architecture, RIBA, 2016. *Publications:* articles in newspapers, magazines and architectl and design jls. *Address:* (office) Studio London, 10 Bowling Green Lane, EC1R 0BQ. *T:* (020) 7253 5147, *Fax:* (020) 7251 8322.

HADKISS, Christopher; Chief Executive, Animal and Plant Health Agency (formerly Animal Health and Veterinary Laboratories Agency), since 2012; *b* Erith, Kent, 28 Jan. 1960; *s* of Ronald Leonard Hadkiss and Rosemary Hadkiss; *m* 1985, Kim Denise Oram; one *s* one *d*. *Educ:* Bromley Coll. of Technol. (HNC Applied Biol. 1980); Univ. of London (BSc Hons Applied Biol. 1983). Forensic Science Service: Operational Forensic Scientist, 1979–2003; Gen. Manager, 2003–04; Regl Gen. Manager, 2004–07; Ops Dir, 2007–08; Exec. Dir, 2008–12; Advr on Forensic Sci., Home Office, 2012; Consultant Forensic Scientist, Optimal Forensics Ltd, 2012. *Publications:* contribs to Jl of Forensic Sci. Soc., Interpol Jl. *Recreations:* model engineering, motorsport racing. *Address:* Animal and Plant Health Agency, Woodham Lane, New Haw, Addlestone, Surrey KT15 3NB. *T:* (01932) 357235, *Fax:* (01932) 357214. *E:* chris.hadkiss@apha.gsi.gov.uk.

HADLEE, Sir Richard (John), Kt 1990; MBE 1980; New Zealand cricketer, retired; *b* 3 July 1951; *s* of late Walter Hadlee, CBE; *m* 1973, Karen Ann Marsh; two *s*; *m* 1999, Dianne Taylor. *Educ:* Christchurch Boys' High Sch. Played for: Canterbury, 1972–89; Nottinghamshire (UK), 1978–87 (made 1000 runs and took 100 wickets in English season, 1984); Tasmania, 1979–80; Test début for NZ, 1973; toured: Australia, 1972–73, 1973–74, 1980–81, 1985–86; England, 1973, 1978, 1983, 1986, 1990; India, 1976, 1988; Pakistan, 1976; Sri Lanka, 1983–84, 1987; West Indies, 1984–85. Held world record of 431 Test wickets, 1990 (passed previous record of 373 in 1988). NZ Selector, 2000–08 (Chm., NZ Bd Selectors, 2001–04). Est. Sir Richard Hadlee Sports Trust, 1990. *Publications:* Rhythm and Swing (autobiog.), 1989; Changing Pace: a memoir, 2009. *Address:* PO Box 29186, Christchurch 8540, New Zealand. *W:* www.hadlee.co.nz. *Club:* MCC (Hon. Life Mem.).

HADLEY, David Allen, CB 1991; Deputy Secretary (Agricultural Commodities, Trade and Food Production), Ministry of Agriculture, Fisheries and Food, 1993–96; *b* 18 Feb. 1936; *s* of Sydney and Gwendoline Hadley; *m* 1965, Veronica Ann Hopkins; one *s*. *Educ:* Wyggeston Grammar Sch., Leicester; Merton Coll., Oxford. MA. Joined MAFF, 1959; Asst Sec., 1971; HM Treas., 1975–78; Under Sec., 1981–87, Dep. Sec., 1987–89, MAFF; Dep. Sec., Cabinet Office, 1989–93. *Recreations:* gardening, music. *Address:* Old Mousers, Dormansland, Lingfield, Surrey RH7 6PP.

HADLEY, Gareth Morgan; Chairman, General Optical Council, since 2013; *b* 22 April 1951; *s* of Ronald Hadley and late Gweneth Doreen Hadley (*née* Morgan). *Educ:* Harrow Weald Grammar Sch.; University Coll. London (BSc); Henley Mgt Coll. (MA). FCIPD. Greater London Council, 1972–86: Asst to Hd of Industrial Relns, 1980–81; Head: Central Recruitment, 1981–83; craft, operative manual and fire service employee relns, 1983–86; Asst Dir of Personnel, ILEA, 1986–89; British Railways Board, 1989–97: Gp Employee Relns Manager, 1989–94; Director: Employee Relns, 1994–97; Human Resources, N and W Passenger Ops, 1994–97; Principal, Gareth Hadley Associates, 1997–99; Dir of Personnel, HM Prison Service, 1999–2006; Comr responsible for E of England and E Midlands regions, 2007–12, London, 2011–12, Appointments Commission. Chairman: British Transport Police Pension Fund, 1992–97; ScotRail Railways Ltd, 1996–97. Human Resources Advr, Nat. Offender Mgt Service, 2004–05. Dir, Skills for Justice (Justice Sector Skills Council), 2004–06. Mem., Inf. and Consultation Taskforce, 2002–04, Employee Relations Panel, 2003–08, CIPD; Member: Adv. Bd, SW London Academic Network, Inst. of Mgt and Leadership in Health, 2008–11; Ext. Adv. Bd, Centre for Better Managed Health and Social Care, Cass Business Sch., City Univ., 2010–. Vis. Fellow, Kingston Univ., 2005–. Gov., Notts Healthcare NHS Trust, 2014–. MInstD 1997. Liveryman, Spectacle Makers' Co., 2014. *Recreations:* opera, food and drink. *Address:* General Optical Council, 41 Harley Street, W1G 8DJ. *T:* (020) 7307 3468. *E:* ghadley@optical.org; 29 Bemish Road, Putney, SW15 1DG. *E:* gareth.hadley@lowerputney.demon.co.uk. *Club:* Savile.

HADLEY, Graham Hunter; economic and business management consultant, 2007–12; Member, Competition (formerly Monopolies and Mergers) Commission, 1998–2007; *b* 12 April 1944; *s* of late Dr A. L. Hadley and Mrs L. E. Hadley; *m* 1971, Lesley Ann Smith; one *s*. *Educ:* Eltham Coll., London; Jesus Coll., Cambridge (BA Hons Mod. Hist.); Harvard Business Sch. (AMP 1991). Entered Civil Service (Min. of Aviation), 1966; Dept of Energy, 1974; seconded to: Civil Service Commn, 1976–77; British Aerospace, 1980–81; Under-Sec., Dept of Energy, 1983; Sec., CEGB, 1983–90; Exec. Dir, 1990–95, and Man. Dir, Internat. Business Develt, 1992–95, National Power. Sen. Advr, Nat. Econ. Res. Associates, 1996–2007. Dir, de Havilland Aircraft Heritage Centre (formerly Mus. Trust), 1990–2010; Trustee and Vice Chm., Cirencester Brewery Arts, 2006–. *Recreations:* include cricket, long-distance walking, theatre, architecture, aviation. *Address:* 129 The Hill, Burford, Oxon OX18 4RE.

HADLEY, Dr Tessa Jane, FRSL; novelist and short story writer; Professor of Creative Writing, Bath Spa University, since 2012; *b* Bristol, 28 Feb. 1956; *d* of Geoffrey and Mary Nichols; *m* 1982, Eric Hadley; three *s*. *Educ:* Ashton Park Comprehensive Sch., Bristol; Clare Coll., Cambridge (BA Hons English 1978); Bath Spa Univ. (MA 1994; PhD 1997). Sen. Lectr in English and Creative Writing, Bath Spa Univ., 1997–2012. Fellow, Welsh Acad.; FRSL 2009. *Publications:* Accidents in the Home, 2002; Henry James and the Imagination of Pleasure, 2002; Everything Will Be All Right, 2004; Sunstroke and Other Stories, 2004; The Master Bedroom, 2007; The London Train, 2011; Married Love and Other Stories, 2012; Clever Girl, 2013; The Past, 2015; contrib. short stories to New Yorker. *Recreations:* reading, cinema, paintings. *Address:* Bath Spa University, Corsham Court, Corsham, Chippenham, Wilts SN13 0BZ. *E:* t.hadley@bathspa.ac.uk.

HADOW, Rupert Nigel Pendrill, (Pen); explorer; Director, Pen Hadow Consultancy Ltd, since 2004; *b* Perth, Scotland, 26 Feb. 1962; *s* of late Nigel Phillip Ian Hadow and of Anne Pendrill Hadow (*née* Callingham); *m* 1995, Mary Frances Nicholson (marr. diss. 2013); one *s* one *d*. *Educ:* Temple Grove Prep. Sch.; Harrow Sch.; University Coll. London (BA Hons Geog. 1984). Agent, Internat. Management Gp, 1985–88; Founder and Director: Polar Travel Co. Ltd, 1995–2004; Geo Mission Ltd, 2009–14. Expeditions: first person solo without resupply from Canada to North Geographic Pole, 2003; first Briton without resupply from continental coasts to North and South Geographic Poles, 2004. Hon. Vice-Pres., RSGS, 2009; Hon. Vice-Patron, British Exploring Soc., 2009. Member: RGS (Hon. Fellow, 2009); Harrow Assoc. Hon. LLD Exeter, 2004; Hon. DSc Plymouth, 2009. World Technol. Award - Envmt, World Technol. Network, 2009. *Publications:* Solo: alone and unsupported to the North Pole, 2004, 4th edn 2014; Catlin Arctic Survey 2009: the story of a pioneering scientific mission to the Arctic Ocean, 2010; Catlin Survey 2009–2011: investigating the changing Arctic Ocean environment, 2013. *Recreations:* classic shrub roses, ornamental wildfowl, surfing, mountaineering, Rugby, cricket, writing. *Address:* 34 Dymock Street, SW6 3HA. *T:* 07970 619161. *E:* pen@penhadow.com. *Clubs:* Frontline, MCC.

HADRILL, Andrew Frederic W.; *see* Wallace-Hadrill.

HAENDEL, Ida, CBE 1991; violinist; *b* Poland, 15 Dec. 1928; Polish parentage; adopted British nationality. Began to play at age of 3½; amazing gift discovered when she picked up her sister's violin and started to play. Her father, a great connoisseur of music, recognised her unusual talent and abandoned his own career as an artist (painter) to devote himself to his daughter; studied at Warsaw Conservatoire and gained gold medal at age of seven; also studied with such masters as Carl Flesch and Georges Enesco. British début, Queen's Hall, with Sir Henry Wood, playing Brahms' Violin Concerto. Gave concerts for British and US troops and in factories, War of 1939–45; after War, career developed to take in North and South America, USSR and Far East, as well as Europe; has accompanied British orchestras such as London Philharmonic, BBC Symphony and English Chamber on foreign tours including Hong Kong, China, Australia and Mexico; performs with major orchestras worldwide, incl. Berlin Philharmonic, Boston Symphony, and Concertgebouw. Has performed with conductors such as Beecham, Klemperer, Szell, Celibidache, Mata, Pritchard, Rattle, Haitink, Ashkenazy; performances include appearances at BBC Prom. A major interpreter of Sibelius, Brahms and Beethoven. Concerts, Edinburgh Fest., masterclasses. Hon. DMus McGill, 2008. Huberman Prize; Sibelius Medal, Sibelius Soc. of Finland, 1982. *Publications:* Woman with Violin (autobiog.), 1970. *Address:* c/o Ernest Gilbert Association, 109 Wheeler Avenue, Pleasantville, NY 10570, USA.

HAFFENDEN, Prof. John Charles Robert, DPhil; FBA 2007; FRSL; Senior Research Fellow, since 2009 and Principal Investigator, T. S. Eliot Research Project, 2009–14, Institute of English Studies, School of Advanced Study, University of London; *b* 19 Aug. 1945; *s* of Donald Haffenden and Sheila McCulloch Haffenden; *m* 1973, Susan Bellville (marr. diss. 1977). *Educ:* Trinity Coll., Dublin (MA 1970); St Peter's Coll., Oxford (DPhil 1977). Educn Officer, Oxford Prison, 1970–73; Lectr in English, Univ. of Exeter, 1973–74; University of Sheffield: Lectr, 1975; Sen. Lectr, 1985; Reader, 1988; Prof. of English Literature, 1994–2004, now Emeritus; Res. Prof., 2004–. British Acad. Res. Reader, 1989–91; Leverhulme Res. Fellow, 1995–96. Vis. Fellow Commoner, Trinity Coll., Cambridge, 1995–96; Vis. Scholar, St John's Coll., Oxford, 1997; Vis. Fellow, Magdalen Coll., Oxford, 1998. Mem., Soc. of Authors; FEA. Gen. Editor, Letters of T. S. Eliot, 2009. *Publications:* (ed) Henry's Fate and Other Poems 1967–1972 by John Berryman, 1978; John Berryman: a critical commentary, 1980; Viewpoints: poets in conversation, 1981; The Life of John Berryman, 1982; (ed) W. H. Auden: the critical heritage, 1983; Novelists in Interview, 1985; (ed) The Royal Beasts and Other Works by William Empson, 1988; (ed) Argufying: essays on literature and culture by William Empson, 1988; (ed) Essays on Renaissance Literature, vol. 1, Donne and the New Philosophy by William Empson, 1993, vol. 2, The Drama by William Empson, 1994; (ed) The Strength of Shakespeare's Shrew: essays, memoirs and reviews by William Empson, 1996; (ed) Berryman's Shakespeare, 1999; (ed) The Complete Poems of William Empson, 2000; William Empson: among the Mandarins (Award for Biog. and Autobiog., Assoc. of Amer. Publishers), 2005; William Empson: against the Christians, 2006; (ed) Selected Letters of William Empson, 2006; General Editor: Letters of T. S. Eliot, vol. 1: 1898–1922, 2009, vol. 2: 1923–1925, 2009; Editor with Valerie Eliot: Letters of T. S. Eliot, vol. 3: 1925–1928, 2012, vol. 4: 1928–1929, 2013, vol. 5: 1930–31, 2014; contrib. to periodicals incl. London Rev. of Books, Essays in Criticism and PN Rev. *Recreations:* country walking, travel, art and architecture, filleting research libraries.

HAGARD, Dr Spencer; international consultant in health promotion and public health, since 1989; *b* 25 Oct. 1942; *s* of Maurice (Bozzie) Markham (killed in action, 11 June 1944) and Eva Markham (*née* Mearns, subseq. Hagard) and, by adoption, of late Noel Hagard; *m* 1968, Michele Dominique, *d* of late Stanislas and Madeleine Aquarone; two *s* one *d*. *Educ:* Varndean Grammar Sch., Brighton; Univ. of St Andrews (MB ChB 1968); Univ. of Glasgow (PhD 1977); MA Cantab 1977. DPH 1972; FFPH (FFCM 1981). Jun. med. appts, Arbroath, London and Dorking; MO and Med. Supt, Kawolo Hosp., Lugazi, Uganda, 1971–72; MO, Health Dept, Glasgow, 1972–74; Trainee in Community Med., Greater Glasgow Health Bd, 1974–77; Specialist in Comm. Med., Cambs AHA, 1977–82; Dist MO, Cambridge HA, 1982–87; Chief Exec., HEA, 1987–94; Sen. Lectr, 1999–2005, Course Organiser, MSc (Health Promotion Scis), 2001–03, Hd, Health Promotion Res. Unit, 2002–04, and Distance Learning Tutor, 2007–, LSHTM. Associate Lectr, Univ. of Cambridge Sch. of Clinical Med., 1977–87; Vis. Prof., 2001–02, Thesis Evaluator, 2009–, Univ. of Bergen. Hon. Consultant, Camden PCT (formerly Camden and Islington Community Health Services Trust), 1996–2005; Consultant: WHO, 1991–; DFID, 1999–2004; World Bank, 2000–05; Health Policy Advr, Hungarian Govt, 1996–2000. National Association for the Education of Sick Children: Mem. Council, 1995–2002; Trustee, 1997–2005; Chm. of Trustees, 2000–05. Sec., Eur. Cttee for Health Promotion Develt, 1995–2004; Mem., EU Health Policy Forum, 2006–; Mem., Bd of Trustees, Internat. Union for Health Promotion and Educn, 1991–2007 (Pres., 1996–2001; Mem., Regl Cttee for Europe, 2007–08). FRSA 1997. *Publications:* Health, Society and Medicine (with Roy Acheson), 1984; papers in BMJ and other learned jls. *Recreations:* marriage, family, studying human beings, politics, gardening, reading, photography, appreciation of art, music, sporting new dawns (Brighton & Hove Albion, Sussex CCC). *Address:* 396 Milton Road, Cambridge CB4 1SU. *T:* (01223) 563774, *Fax:* (01223) 423970. *E:* spencer@hagard.net.

HAGART-ALEXANDER, Sir Claud; *see* Alexander.

HAGEN, Martin John, FCA; President, Institute of Chartered Accountants in England and Wales, 2009–10 (Deputy President, 2008–09); *b* Leeds, 20 Sept. 1951; *s* of Christopher and Nancy Hagen; *m* 1978, Hilary Channell; three *s*. *Educ:* Herringthorpe Primary Sch., Rotherham; Rotherham Grammar Sch.; Thomas Rotherham Coll.; Sheffield Poly. FCA 1973. With Knox Franklin & Co., Sheffield, 1969–73; with Spicer and Pegler, London, 1974–81, Bristol, 1981–90; Touche Ross, Bristol, 1990–93; Deloitte & Touche, Bristol, 1993–2005; Consultant, Deloitte, 2007–10. Dep. Chm., Regulatory Decisions Cttee, FSA, 2008–13 (Mem., 2005–13), Financial Conduct Authy, 2013–15. Mem., Takeover Panel, 2009–10. Chm., CCAB, 2009–10. Ind. Mem., Audit and Risk Assurance Cttee, DWP, 2014–. Non-executive Director: Oxonica plc, 2006–08; South West Water Ltd, 2010–; Swallowfield plc, 2011–14. Mem. Bd, CIPFA, 2010–11. Trustee, Fleet Air Arm Mus., 2010–. Gov., UWE, 2010–. Freeman, City of London, 2004; Liveryman, Chartered Accountants' Co., 2004. Hon. DBA UWE, 2010. *Recreations:* playing acoustic guitar, Bristol City Football Club, wine, all things French, travel. *Address:* Sunny Brae, 2 Belmont Road, Winscombe, N Somerset BS25 1LE. *Club:* East India.

HAGERTY, William John Gell, (Bill); writer and broadcaster; Chairman, British Journalism Review, since 2012 (Editor, 2002–12); *b* 23 April 1939; *s* of William (Steve) Hagerty and Doris Hagerty (*née* Gell); *m* 1st, 1965, Lynda Beresford (marr. diss. 1990); one *s* one *d* (and one *d* decd); 2nd, 1991, Elizabeth Vercoe (*née* Latta); one *s*. *Educ:* Beal Grammar Sch., Ilford. Local newspapers, East London, 1955–58; RAF Nat. Service, 1958–60; local newspapers, Sunday Citizen, Daily Sketch, 1960–67; Daily Mirror, 1967–81; Sunday Mirror and Sunday People, 1981–85; Managing Editor (Features), Today, 1986; Editor, Sunday Today, 1987; Deputy Editor: Sunday Mirror, 1988–90; Daily Mirror, 1990–91; Editor, The People, 1991–92; Theatre Critic, 1993–95, Film Critic, 1994–95, Today; Theatre Critic: various pubns, 1996–2003; The Sun, 2004–09. Consultant, Tribune, 1993–2004, 2007–. Mem., BAFTA. Mem. Council, 2002–, Chm., 2011–12, Journalists' Charity (formerly Newspaper Press Fund); Dir, London Press Club, 2008–. *Publications:* Flash, Bang, Wallop! (with Kent Gavin), 1978; Read All About It, 2003; (ed with Alastair Campbell) The Alastair Campbell Diaries, vol. 1, prelude to power 1994–1997, 2010, vol. 2, power and the people 1997–99, 2011, vol. 3, power and responsibility 1999–2001, 2011, vol. 4, the pressures of power 2001–03, 2012. *Recreations:* jazz, watching cricket, lunch (thanks to Keith Waterhouse). *Address:* Bull Cottage, 10/11 Strand-on-the-Green, Chiswick, W4 3PQ. *Clubs:* Victory Services, Gerry's, Acts and Actors.

HAGESTADT, John Valentine; adviser on international investment to OECD, World Bank and EU, 1997–2007; *b* 11 Oct. 1938; *s* of late Leonard and Constance Hagestadt; *m* 1963, Betty Tebbs; three *d*. *Educ:* Dulwich Coll.; Worcester Coll., Oxford (BA). Asst Principal, Min. of Aviation, 1963; Principal, BoT, 1967; Nuffield Travelling Fellow, 1973–74; Asst Sec., Vehicles Div., Dept of Industry, 1976; Asst Sec., Overseas Trade Div. (Middle East and Latin America), Dept of Trade, 1980; Dir, British Trade Develt Office, NY 1982; Dir, Invest in Britain Bureau, NY, 1984–87; Head, N Amer. Br., DTI, 1987–93; Dir, Govt Office for London, 1994; Dir, Invest in Britain Bureau, DTI, 1995–96. *Address:* 7 Elm House, 50 Holmesdale Road TW11 9NE.

HAGGAN, Nicholas Somerset; QC 2003; a Recorder, since 2000; *b* 25 Aug. 1955; *s* of David Anthony Haggan and Hope Haggan; *m* 1993, Julie Carolyn Owen. *Educ:* Monkton Combe Sch., Bath; Coll. of Law, London. Called to the Bar: Middle Temple, 1977; NI, 1986; in practice, specialising in crime and regulatory offences, particularly in relation to compliance issues in the field of consumer law and health and safety at work; Asst Recorder, 1997–2000. *Recreations:* running, food and wine, cooking, gardening, travel. *Address:* 12 College Place, Fauvelle Buildings, Southampton, Hants SO15 2FE. *T:* (023) 8032 0320, *Fax:* (023) 8032 0321.

HAGGARD, Prof. Mark Peregrine, CBE 2001; PhD; FMedSci; Medical Research Council External Staff, Cambridge, 2002–08; founder Director, Medical Research Council Institute of Hearing Research, 1977–2002; *b* 26 Dec. 1942; *m* 1962, Liz (*née* Houston); two *s*. *Educ:* Edinburgh Univ. (MA Psych, 1st cl. hons); Corpus Christi Coll., Cambridge (PhD Psych 1967). Univ. Demonstrator in Experimental Psychology, Univ. of Cambridge, 1967–71; Prof. of Psychology and Head of Dept, QUB, 1971–76; sabbatical, 1975–76; Special Prof. in Audiological Scis, Nottingham Univ., 1980. Trustee, Deafness Research UK, 1986 (former Chm., Vice Pres. and Chief Scientific Advr). Founder FMedSci 1998. Hon. FRCSE 2001. *Publications:* Screening Children's Hearing, 1991; Research in the Development of Effective Services for Hearing-impaired People, 1993; contribs to learned jls. *Recreations:* ski-ing, choral music. *Club:* Royal Society of Medicine.

HAGGARD, Prof. Patrick Neville, PhD; FBA 2014; Professor of Cognitive Neuroscience, Department of Psychology, and Deputy Director, Institute of Cognitive Neuroscience, University College London. *Educ:* Trinity Hall, Cambridge (BA Hons 1987; PhD 1991). Harkness Fellow, Yale Univ., 1987–88; Wellcome Trust Prize Fellow, Physiol. Dept, Univ. of Oxford, and Jun. Res. Fellow, Christ Church, Oxford, 1991–94; Psychology Department, University College London: Lectr, 1995–98; Sen. Lectr, 1998–2002; Reader in Cognitive Neurosci., 2002. Leverhulme Res. Fellow, 2001–03. Chm., Steering Cttee, Study of Cognition, Adolescents and Mobile Phones, 2014–. *Publications:* (ed jtly) Hand and Brain: the neurophysiology and psychology of hand movements, 1996; (ed jtly) Sensorimotor Foundations of Higher Cognition: attention and performance, 2007; (ed jtly) Mental Processes in the Human Brain, 2008; contribs to learned jls incl. Exptl Brain Res., Jl Psychosomatic Res., Neuropsychologia, Psychol Sci., Jl Neurosci. *Address:* Institute of Cognitive Neuroscience, University College London, 17 Queen Square, WC1N 3AR.

HAGGART, Mary Elizabeth; *see* Scholes, M. E.

HAGGETT, Prof. Peter, CBE 1993; FBA 1992; Professor of Urban and Regional Geography, 1966–98, now Emeritus Professor, and Acting Vice-Chancellor, 1984–85, University of Bristol; *b* 24 Jan. 1933; *s* of Charles and Elizabeth Haggett, Pawlett, Somerset; *m* 1956, Brenda Woodley; two *s* two *d*. *Educ:* Dr Morgan's Sch., Bridgwater; St Catharine's Coll., Cambridge (Exhib. and Scholar; MA 1958; PhD 1970; ScD 1985). Asst Lectr, University Coll. London, 1955–57; Demonstrator and University Lectr, Cambridge, 1957–66, and Fellow, Fitzwilliam Coll., 1963–66 (Hon. Fellow, 1994). Leverhulme Research Fellow (Brazil), 1959; Canada Council Fellow, 1977; Erskine Fellow (NZ), 1979; Res. Fellow, Res. Sch. of Pacific Studies, ANU, 1983. Visiting Professor: Berkeley; Monash; Pennsylvania State; McMaster; Toronto; Western Ontario; Wisconsin; Hill Prof., Minnesota, 1994. Provost, Inst. for Advanced Studies, Bristol Univ., 1996–99. Member, SW Economic Planning Council, 1967–72. Governor, Centre for Environmental Studies, 1975–78; Member: Council, RGS, 1972–73, 1977–80; UGC, 1985–89; Nat. Radiological Protection Bd, 1986–93; Chm., Hist. of Med. Grants Panel, Wellcome Trust, 1994–2000. Vice-Pres., British Acad., 1995–97. Hon. Fellow, Bristol Univ., 1998. Hon. Foreign Mem., Amer. Acad. of Arts and Sci., 2006; Foreign Associate, NAS, 2008. Hon. DSc: York, Canada, 1983; Durham, 1989; Copenhagen, 1999; UWE, 2004; UCL, 2008; Hon. LLD Bristol, 1986; Hon. FilDr Helsinki, 2003. Cullum Medal of American Geographical Soc., 1969; Meritorious Contribution Award, Assoc. of American Geographers, 1973; Patron's Medal, RGS, 1986; Prix Internationale de Géographie, 1991; Lauréat d'Honneur, IGU, 1992; Scottish Medal, RSGS, 1993; Anders Retzius Gold Medal, Sweden, 1994. *Publications:* Locational Analysis in Human Geography, 1965; Geography: a modern synthesis, 1972, 4th edn, 1983; The Geographer's Art, 1990; Geographical Structure of Epidemics, 2000; Geography: a global synthesis, 2001; The Quantocks, 2012; *jointly:* (with R. J. Chorley): Models in Geography, 1967; Network Analysis in Geography, 1969; (with M. D. I. Chisholm) Regional Forecasting, 1971; (with A. D. Cliff and others): Elements of Spatial Structure, 1975; Spatial Diffusion, 1981; Spatial Aspects of Influenza Epidemics, 1986; Atlas of Disease Distributions, 1988; Atlas of AIDS, 1992; Measles: an historical geography, 1993; Deciphering Global Epidemics, 1998; Island Epidemics, 2000; World Atlas of Epidemic Diseases, 2004; Emerging Diseases: a geographical analysis, 2009; research papers on related geographical topics. *Recreations:* Somerset history, cricket. *Address:* 5 Tun Bridge Close, Chew Magna, Somerset BS40 8SU. *Club:* Oxford and Cambridge.

HAGGETT, Stuart John, MA; Headmaster, English School, Nicosia, 2003–09; *b* 11 April 1947; *s* of William Francis and Doreen Ada Haggett; *m* 1971, Hilary Joy Hammond; two *d*. *Educ:* Dauntsey's Sch., West Lavington, Wilts; Downing Coll., Cambridge (MA 1972); PGCE London (ext.), 1970. Canford Sch., Wimborne, Dorset, 1970–83: Head of Modern Languages, 1973–83; Housemaster, 1975–83; Second Master, King's Sch., Rochester, 1983–88; Headmaster, Birkenhead Sch., 1988–2003. *Recreations:* France (travel and culture), sport, theatre, architecture, cooking.

HAGGIE, Dr Paul; HM Diplomatic Service, retired; Deputy Director (Africa), Foreign and Commonwealth Office, 2001–04; *b* 30 Aug. 1949; *s* of George Henry Haggie and Eva Haggie (*née* Hawke); *m* 1979, Rev. Deborah (marr. diss. 2000), *d* of Douglas Graham Frazer, CBE; one *s* one *d*. *Educ:* Royal Grammar Sch., Newcastle upon Tyne; Manchester Univ. (BA; PhD 1974). Joined HM Diplomatic Service, 1974: Second, later First Sec., Bangkok, 1976–80; First Secretary: FCO, 1980–82; Islamabad, 1982–86; FCO, 1986–89; Pretoria, 1989–93; Counsellor, FCO, 1993–94; on secondment to Cabinet Office as Sec., Requirements and Resources, 1994–96; FCO, 1996–98; Counsellor and UK Perm. Rep. to ESCAP, Bangkok, 1998–2001. Licensed Lay Minister, Dio. of Rochester, 2012–. *Publications:* Britannia at Bay: the defence of the British Empire against Japan 1931–1941, 1981; contrib. various articles to historical jls. *Recreations:* sailing, scuba, music, history (esp. maritime). *Address:* 2 Marc Brunel Way, Historic Dockyard, Chatham, Kent ME4 4BH. *Club:* Royal Automobile.

HAGUE, Prof. Clifford Bertram; freelance consultant; Professor, School of the Built Environment, Heriot-Watt University, 2002–06, now Emeritus (Professor, School of Planning and Housing, Edinburgh College of Art, Heriot-Watt University, 1995–2002); *b* 22 Aug. 1944; *s* of Bertram Hague and Kathleen Mary Hague; *m* 1966, Irene Williamson; one *s* three *d*. *Educ:* Magdalene Coll., Cambridge (MA); Univ. of Manchester (DipTP). MRTPI 1973. Planning Asst, Glasgow Corp., 1968–69; Edinburgh College of Art, Heriot-Watt University: Lectr, 1969–73; Sen. Lectr, 1973–90; Head, Sch. of Planning and Housing, 1990–95. Mem., Permanent Internat. Wkg Party, European Biennial of Towns and Town Planning, 1996–2011; UK National Contact: European Spatial Planning Observation Network, 2001–06; Eur. Observation Network for Territorial Develt and Cohesion, 2008–14 (Consultant, 2012–). Project Consultant: EU INTERREG projects: NoordXXI, 1998–2000; PIPE, 2004; Innovation Circle, 2005–06; SusSET, 2006; CoUrbit, 2006; Trans-in-Form, 2010–12; EU INTERACT project, CULTPLAN, 2007; ESPON Projects: INTERSTRAT, 2010–12; USESPON, 2012–13; ESPON on the Road, 2014; EU ERASMUS+ project, Young Eyes, 2015; UN-Habitat on Planning in Area C, West Bank, 2015; also UK govt projects. Chairman: Commonwealth Expert Gp on Urbanisation, 2011; Built Envmt Forum Scotland, 2011–14; Member: Strategic Historic Envmt Forum for Scotland, 2014; Strategic Historic Envmt Operational Gp, Scotland, 2014. Member: Jury, Internat. Urban Planning and Design Competition for the banks of Huangpu River, 2001; Internat. Jury, Detailed Construction Plan, Qingdao Olympic Sailing, 2003; Jury, planning of Olympic Central Green and Forest Park, Beijing, 2003. Pres., RTPI, 1996–97; Pres. and CEO, 2000–06, Sec. Gen., 2006–10, Commonwealth Assoc. of Planners. Patron, Planning Aid for Scotland, 2013–. FAcSS; Fellow, Higher Educn Acad., 2004. Series Ed., RTPI Library Series, 2000–08. Centenary Medal, Technical Univ. of Brno, 2000. *Publications:* The Development of Planning Thought: a critical perspective, 1984; (ed with P. Jenkins) Place Identity, Participation and Planning, 2005; (jtly) Making Planning Work: a guide to approaches and skills, 2006; (jtly) Regional and Local Economic Development, 2011; articles in Town Planning Rev., Town and Country Planning, Planning, etc. *Recreations:* Manchester United, cricket, theatre, films. *W:* www.cliffhague.com, www.twitter.com/cliffhague.

HAGUE, Ffion Llywelyn; author; Founder and Principal Consultant, Independent Board Evaluation, since 2008; *b* 21 Feb. 1968; *d* of (John) Emyr Jenkins, *qv*, and Myra (*née* Samuel); *m* 1997, William Jefferson Hague, *qv*. *Educ:* Jesus Coll., Oxford (BA English Lit. 1989); UCW, Aberystwyth (MPhil Welsh Lit. 1993). Joined CS, 1991; Private Sec. to Sec. of State for Wales, 1994–97; Dir of Policy and Planning, Arts & Business (formerly Dir of Ops, ABSA), 1997–2000; Director: Leonard Hull Internat., 2000–02; Hanson Green, 2003–08. Mem., Barclays Wealth Adv. Cttee, 2007–12. Presenter/Exec. Producer (S4C): Dwy Wraig Lloyd George, 2009; Mamwlad, 2012, 2013. Mem. Bd, British Council, 1999–2002. Mem. Adv. Council, LSO, 1998–2008; Trustee: Voices Foundn, 1998–2005; Action on Addiction, 2001–04; Outward Bound Trust, 2002–12; ENO, 2009–14. Hon. Fellow, Harris Manchester Coll., Oxford, 2010. *Publications:* The Pain and the Privilege: the women in Lloyd George's life, 2008. *Address:* BM Box 1983, London, WC1N 3XX.

See also M. B. Antoniazzi.

HAGUE, Rt Hon. William (Jefferson), FRSL; PC 1995; Chairman, Royal United Services Institute, since 2015; *b* 26 March 1961; *s* of Timothy Nigel Hague and Stella Hague; *m* 1997, Ffion Llywelyn Jenkins (*see* F. L. Hague). *Educ:* Wath-upon-Dearne Comprehensive School; Magdalen College, Oxford (MA); Insead (MBA). Pres., Oxford Union, 1981; Pres., Oxford Univ. Cons. Assoc., 1981. Management Consultant, McKinsey & Co., 1983–88. Political Adviser, HM Treasury, 1983. Contested (C) Wentworth, S Yorks, 1987. MP (C) Richmond, Yorks, Feb. 1989–2015. PPS to Chancellor of the Exchequer, 1990–93; Parly Under-Sec. of State, DSS, 1993–94; Minister for Social Security and Disabled People, DSS, 1994–95; Sec. of State for Wales, 1995–97; Leader, Cons. Party and Leader of the Opposition, 1997–2001; Shadow Foreign Sec., 2005–10; Sec. of State for Foreign and Commonwealth Affairs, 2010–14; First Sec. of State and Leader of the H of C, 2014–15; Prime Minister's Special Representative on Preventing Sexual Violence in Conflict, 2014–15. FRSL 2009. *Publications:* William Pitt the Younger, 2004 (History Book of the Year, British Book Awards, 2005); William Wilberforce, 2007. *Clubs:* Beefsteak, Carlton, Buck's, Pratt's, Budokwai, Groucho.
[Created a Baron (Life Peer) 2015 but title not yet gazetted at time of going to press.]

HAHN, Carl Horst, Dr rer. pol.; German business executive; *b* 1 July 1926; *m* 1960, Marisa Traina (*d* 2013); three *s* one *d.* Chm. Bd, Continental Gummi-Werke AG, 1973–81; Chm. Mgt Bd, Volkswagen AG, 1981–92, now Chm. Emeritus. Member, Supervisory Board: Hanseatisches Wein und Sekt Kontor, Hamburg; Perot Systems, Dallas; Member, International Advisory Board: Instituto de Empresa, Madrid; Textron Inc., Providence; Indesit Co. (formerly Merloni Electrodomestic), Fabriano. Board Member: Mayo Clinic Stiftung, Frankfurt; Global Consumer Acquisition Corp., NY; Lauder Inst., Wharton Sch., Philadelphia; Mem. Internat. Adv. Cttee, Salk Inst., La Jolla, Calif. *Address:* Hollerplatz 1, 38440 Wolfsburg, Germany. *T:* (5361) 26680, *Fax:* (5361) 266815.

HAIG, family name of **Earl Haig**.

HAIG, 3rd Earl *cr* 1919; **Alexander Douglas Derrick Haig;** Viscount Dawick 1919; Baron Haig 1919; 31st Laird of Bemersyde; farmer; *b* 30 June 1961; *o s* of 2nd Earl Haig, OBE and Adrienne Thérèse, *d* of Derrick Morley; *S* father, 2009; *m* 2003, Jane Hartree Risk, *widow* of Michael Risk and *d* of late Donald Grassick Crieff. *Educ:* Stowe School; Royal Agricl Coll., Cirencester. *Heir:* none. *Address:* Findas Farm, Chance Inn, Cupar, Fife KY15 5PQ. *Club:* New (Edinburgh).

HAIG, David, MBE 2013; actor and writer; *m* Jane Galloway; five *c. Theatre includes:* seasons with RSC, 1983, 1986; Tom and Viv, Royal Court, 1984, NY, 1985; Our Country's Good (Olivier Award for best actor in a new play), Royal Court, 1988; Berenice, RNT, 1990; Dead Funny, Vaudeville, 1994; Fair Ladies at a Game of Poem Cards, RNT, 1996; Art, Wyndham's, 1997, NY, 1998; My Boy Jack (also writer), Hampstead, 1997; House and Garden, RNT, 2000; Gasping (tour), 2000; Life x 3, Savoy, 2002; Hitchcock Blonde, Royal Court, transf. Lyric, 2003; Journey's End, Comedy, 2004; Mary Poppins, Prince Edward, 2004; Donkey's Years, Comedy, 2006; The Country Wife, Haymarket, 2007; The Sea, Haymarket, 2007; Loot, Tricycle, 2008; Yes, Prime Minister, Chichester Fest. Th., transf. Gielgud, 2010; The Madness of George III, Th. Royal, Bath, 2011, transf. Apollo, 2012; King Lear, Th. Royal, Bath, 2013; Someone Who'll Watch Over Me, Chichester, 2015; writer, The Good Samaritan, Hampstead, 2000; writer and actor, Pressure, Royal Lyceum, Edinburgh, transf. Chichester, 2014. *Films include:* The Moon Stallion, 1978; Dark Enemy, 1984; Morons from Outer Space, 1985; Four Weddings and a Funeral, 1994; Two Weeks Notice, 2002; *television includes:* Portrait of a Marriage, 1990; Soldier, Soldier, 1991; Love on a Branch Line, 1993; Nice Day at the Office, 1994; The Thin Blue Line (series), 1995; Keeping Mum, 1997; Talking Heads 2, 1998; Station Jim, 2001; Crime and Punishment, 2002; Hustle, 2004; My Boy Jack (also writer), 2007; Mo, 2010; Yes, Prime Minister, 2013; The Wright Way, 2013. *Address:* c/o United Agents, 12–26 Lexington Street, W1F 0LE.

HAIGH, Andrew Michael; Executive Director, Coutts & Co., since 2001; *b* Manchester, 28 Oct. 1958; *s* of Colin and Audrey Haigh. *Educ:* Hipperholme Grammar Sch.; Univ. of Hull (BA Jt Hons). Finance Dir, Internat. Businesses, NatWest, 1993–96; Chief Operating Officer, NatWest Offshore, 1996–99; Chief Corporate Officer, N America, NatWest, 1999–2000. Mem. Council, RCM, 2010–. Trustee: Chisenhale Gall., 2008–; Photographers' Gall., 2009–. FRSA 1999. *Recreations:* visual and performing arts, gardening, cooking. *Address:* Coutts & Co., 440 Strand, WC2R 0QS.

HAIGH, Edward; Assistant General Secretary, Transport and General Workers' Union, 1985–91; *b* 7 Nov. 1935; *s* of Edward and Sarah Ellen Haigh; *m* 1st, 1958, Patricia (marr. diss. 1982); one *s* two *d*; 2nd, 1982, Margaret; two step *d. Educ:* St Patrick's RC Sch., Birstall; St Mary's RC Sch., Batley, W Yorks. Carpet weaver, 1956–69; shop steward, 1960–69; National Union of Dyers, Bleachers and Textile Workers: Dist Organiser, 1969–73; Dist Sec., 1973–77; Nat. Organiser/Negotiator, 1977–79; Asst Gen. Sec., 1979–82; Nat. Sec., Textile Gp, TGWU, 1982–85. Mem., Labour Party NEC, 1982–91. JP Batley, W Yorks, 1971–85. *Recreations:* politics (Labour Party), Rugby League football, cricket. *Club:* Birstall Irish Democratic League (W Yorks).

HAIGH, Prof. Joanna Dorothy, CBE 2013; DPhil; FRS 2013; Professor of Atmospheric Physics, since 2001, and Co-director, Grantham Institute - Climate Change and Environment, since 2014, Imperial College London; *b* London, 7 May 1954; *d* of Adrian Haigh and Sanda Haigh; *m* 1981, Paul Julian Fouracre; one *s* two *d. Educ:* Hitchin Girls' Grammar Sch.; Somerville Coll., Oxford (MA Phys 1975); Imperial Coll. London (MSc Meteorol. 1977); St Cross Coll., Oxford (DPhil Phys 1980). Post-doctoral Res. Asst, Atmospheric Phys, Univ. of Oxford, 1980–84; Imperial College London: Lectr in Remote Sensing, 1984–90; Lectr, 1990–97, Reader, 1997–2001, Atmospheric Phys; Hd, Dept of Phys, 2009–14. Pres., RMetS, 2012–14. *Address:* Grantham Institute - Climate Change and Environment, Imperial College London, SW7 2AZ. *T:* (020) 7594 5798. *E:* j.haigh@imperial.ac.uk.

HAIGH, Louise Margaret; MP (Lab) Sheffield Heeley, since 2015; *b* Sheffield; 22 July 1987. *Educ:* Sheffield High Sch.; Nottingham Univ. Call centre worker; council youth services; Co-ordinator, All Party Parly Gp on Internat. Corporate Responsibility; Corporate Governance Policy Manager, Aviva plc. *Address:* House of Commons, SW1A 0AA.

HAILEY, Prof. John Martin, PhD; Co-Founder, International NGO Training and Research Centre, Oxford, 1992–2012; Professor, Cass Business School, City University London, since 2003; *b* Oxford, 31 Aug. 1952; *s* of Peter and Rowena Hailey; *m* 1995, Prof. Veronica Hope Hailey, *qv*; two *d* and three step *d. Educ:* Douai Abbey Sch.; Exeter Univ. (BA); City Univ. (MBA); Queensland Univ. (PhD 1990). Lectr, Univ. of S Pacific, Fiji, 1980–85; Res. Fellow, East-West Center, Hawaii, 1986–88; Lectr, Cranfield Sch. of Mgt, 1988–98; Dept Dir, Oxford Brookes Univ. Business Sch., 1998–2003. *Recreations:* dog walking, tennis, theatre, film, sailing, Bath Rugby. *Address:* Cass Business School, 106 Bunhill Row, EC1Y 8TZ. *T:* (020) 7040 8600. *E:* john.hailey.2@city.ac.uk.

HAILEY, Veronica H.; *see* Hope Hailey.

HAILSHAM, 3rd Viscount *cr* 1929, of Hailsham, co. Sussex; **Douglas Martin Hogg;** PC 1992; QC 1990; Baron 1928; *b* 5 Feb. 1945; *er s* of Baron Hailsham of Saint Marylebone (Life Peer), PC, KG, CH, FRS (who disclaimed his hereditary peerages for life, 1963); *S* father, 2001; *m* 1968, Sarah Boyd-Carpenter (*see* Baroness Hogg); one *s* one *d. Educ:* Eton (Oppidan Schol.); Christ Church, Oxford (Schol.; Pres., Oxford Union). Called to the Bar, Lincoln's Inn, 1968 (Kennedy Law Schol.). MP (C) Grantham, 1979–97, Sleaford and N Hykeham, 1997–2010. Mem., Agric. Select Cttees, 1979–82; PPS to Chief Sec., HM Treasury, 1982–83; an Asst Govt Whip, 1983–84; Parly Under-Sec. of State, Home Office, 1986–89; Minister of State (Minister for Industry and Enterprise), DTI, 1989–90; Minister of State, FCO, 1990–95; Minister of Agriculture, Fisheries and Food, 1995–97. *Heir: s* Hon. Quintin John Neil Martin Hogg [*b* 12 Oct. 1973; *m* 2006, Elizabeth Sophia Anne Heneage].
See also Hon. C. M. Hogg, Hon. Dame M. C. Hogg.
[Created a Baron (Life Peer) 2015 but title not yet gazetted at time of going to press.]

HAILSHAM, Viscountess; *see* Hogg, Baroness.

HAIN, Rt Hon. Peter (Gerald); PC 2001; *b* 16 Feb. 1950; *s* of Walter and Adelaine Hain; *m* 1st, 1975, Patricia Western (marr. diss. 2002); two *s*; 2nd, 2003, Dr Elizabeth Haywood. *Educ:* Queen Mary College, London (BSc Econ 1st cl. hons); Univ. of Sussex (MPhil). Brought up in S Africa, until family forced to leave in 1966, due to anti-apartheid activity, since when lived in UK. Union of Communication Workers: Asst Research Officer, 1976–87; Head of Research, 1987–91. Chm., Stop the Seventy Tour campaign, 1969–70; Nat. Chm., Young Liberals, 1971–73; Press Officer, Anti-Nazi League, 1977–80. Contested (Lab) Putney, 1983, 1987. MP (Lab) Neath, April 1991–2015. An Opposition Whip, 1995–96; an Opposition Spokesman on employment, 1996–97; Parly Under-Sec. of State, Welsh Office, 1997–99; Minister of State, FCO, 1999–2000 and 2001–02; Minister of State, DTI, Jan.–June 2001; Sec. of State for Wales, 2002–08 and 2009–10; Leader, H of C, 2003–05; Sec. of State for NI, 2005–07, for Work and Pensions, 2007–08; Shadow Sec. of State for Wales, 2010–12. *Publications:* Don't Play with Apartheid, 1971; Community Politics, 1976; Mistaken Identity, 1976; (ed) Policing the Police, vol. I, 1978, vol. II, 1980; Neighbourhood Participation, 1980; Crisis and Future of the Left, 1980; Political Trials in Britain, 1984; Political Strikes, 1986; A Putney Plot?, 1987; The Peking Connection (novel), 1995; Ayes to the Left, 1995; Sing the Beloved Country, 1996; Mandela, 2010; Outside In, 2012; Ad & Wal, 2014; Back to the Future of Socialism, 2015. *Recreations:* soccer, cricket, Rugby, motor racing, fan of Chelsea, Neath Athletic and Swansea FCs, Ospreys and Neath RFCs, rock and folk music fan. *Address:* 39 Windsor Road, Neath SA11 1NB. *T:* (01639) 630152. *Clubs:* Neath Workingmen's; Neath Rugby; Resolven Rugby; Ynysygerwn Cricket.
[Created a Baron (Life Peer) 2015 but title not yet gazetted at time of going to press.]

HAINER, Herbert; Chief Executive Officer and Chairman, Executive Board, adidas AG (formerly adidas-Salomon AG), since 2001; *b* Dingolfing, Germany, 3 June 1954; *m* Angela; two *d. Educ:* Univ. of Landshut (degree in Business Studies 1979). Div. Manager, Sales and Mktg Germany, Procter & Gamble GmbH, 1979–87; adidas Germany: Sales Dir Hardware (Bags, Rackets, Balls), 1987–89; Sales Dir Field (Footwear, Textiles, Hardware), 1989–91; Nat. Sales Dir, 1991–93; Man. Dir (Sales and Logistics), 1993–95; adidas AG, then adidas-Salomon AG: Sen. Vice Pres. (Sales and Logistics), Europe, Africa, Middle East Reg., 1996–97; Mem., 1997–, Dep. Chm., 2001, Exec. Bd. Member Supervisory Board: Bayerische Versicherungsbank AG, Munich; Engelhorn KGaA, Mannheim; Dep. Chm. Supervisory Bd, FC Bayern München AG, Munich. *Address:* adidas AG, Adi-Dassler-Str. 1, 91074 Herzogenaurach, Germany.

HAINES, Andrew; Chief Executive Officer, Civil Aviation Authority, since 2009; *b* Merthyr Tydfil, 21 April 1964; *s* of Eric and Megan Haines; *m* 1986, Caroline Fletcher; one *s* one *d. Educ:* Cyfarthfa High Sch.; King's Coll. London (BA Hons Hist. 1985); Kingston Univ. (MBA 1995). South West Trains: Ops Dir, 1999–2000; Man. Dir, 2000–05; Man. Dir, Rail Div., FirstGroup, 2005–08; Chief Operating Officer, First Great Western, 2007–08. Non-exec. Dir, Eversholt Rail Ltd, 2013–. Chm., Balsam Family Project, 2009–. Gov., Oxford Acad., 2010–13. FIRO; FCILT; FRAeS; FRSA. Hon. DLitt Kingston, 2013. *Recreations:* keeping fit, classical music, gardening, cooking. *Address:* Civil Aviation Authority, CAA House, 45–59 Kingsway, WC2B 6TE. *T:* (020) 7453 6002, *Fax:* (020) 7453 6011. *E:* andrew.haines@caa.co.uk.

HAINES, Sir Andrew (Paul), Kt 2005; MD; FRCP, FRCGP, FFPH; FMedSci; Professor of Public Health and Primary Care, London School of Hygiene and Tropical Medicine, University of London, since 2001 (Director (formerly Dean), 2001–10); *b* 26 Feb. 1947; *s* of Charles George Thomas Haines and Lilian Emily Haines; *m* 1st, 1982, June Marie Power (marr. diss. 1987); 2nd, 1998, Dr Anita Berlin; two *s. Educ:* King's Coll., London (MB BS 1969; MD Epidemiology 1985; Hon. Fellow 2009). MRCP 1971, FRCP 1993; MRCGP 1976, FRCGP 1991; MFCM 1987, FFPH (FFPHM 1992; Hon. FFPH 2009). Mem. Scientific Staff, MRC Epidemiology and Med. Care Unit, 1974–87; part-time Sen. Lectr in General Practice, Middlesex Hosp. Med. Sch., 1980–84, St Mary's Hosp. Med. Sch., 1984–87; on secondment as Dir, R&D, NE Thames RHA, subseq. N Thames Reg., NHS Exec., 1993–96; Prof. of Primary Health Care, UCL, 1987–2000; Head, Dept of Primary Care and Population Scis, Royal Free and UC Med. Sch., 1998–2000. Medical Research Council: Mem., 1996–98; Mem., Strategy Bd, 2008–12; Chm., Global Health Gp, 2008–12. Chm., Health Services and Public Health Bd, 1996–98; Mem. Bd, Univs UK, 2007–10 (Chm., Health and Social Care Policy Cttee, 2007–09); Mem., Scientific Adv. Cttee, AMRC, 1998–2004; Mem., Res. Strategy Cttee, Multiple Sclerosis Soc., 2010– (Chm., 2011–); Chm., Res. Strategy Cttee, Marie Curie Cancer Care. Mem., UN Intergovernmental Panel on Climate Change, 1993–96, 1998–2001 (Rev. Ed., Health Chapter, Working Gp II, AR5, 2011–14); Consultant, 1998, Mem., Adv. Cttee on Health Res., 2004–08, WHO; Chairman: WHO Task Force on Evidence for Health Systems Strengthening, 2010–11; Scientific Adv. Panel, WHO World Health Report 2013. Chm., Tropical Health Educn Trust, 2010–; Trustee: UK Biobank, 2010–; Med. Res. Foundn, 2014–; RSocMed, 2014–. Founder FMedSci 1998; FRGS 2012. Hon. Fellow, UCL, 2006; Hon. Fellow, Philippines Acad. of Family Physicians, 2011. For. Associate Mem., Inst. of Medicine, USA, 2008; Hon. Mem., Nat. Acad. of Medicine, Mexico, 2012. *Publications:* (ed jtly) Climate Change and Human Health, 1996; (ed jtly) Evidence Based Practice in Primary Care, 1998; (ed jtly) Getting Research Findings into Practice, 1998; numerous articles in medical and scientific jls; ed series of articles on climate change mitigation and public health in Lancet, 2009. *Recreations:* swimming, environmental issues. *Address:* London School of Hygiene and Tropical Medicine, Keppel Street, WC1E 7HT. *T:* (020) 7927 2938.

HAINES, Christopher John Minton; Chairman, Harlequin Football Club, 1998–2004; *b* 14 April 1939; *m* 1967, Christine Cobbold; two *s* two *d. Educ:* Stowe. The Rifle Brigade, 1957–68; sugar trade, 1968–89; Chm., James Budgett & Son, 1984–89. Non-executive Director: Devonshire Arms (Bolton Abbey), 1995–2003; SPG Media (formerly Sterling Publg Gp) plc, 1996–2008 (Chm., 1996–2001). Chief Exec., The Jockey Club, 1989–93. *Recreations:* music, gardening, racing. *Club:* Turf.
See also M. Haines.

HAINES, Joseph Thomas William; Assistant Editor, The Daily Mirror, 1984–90; Group Political Editor, Mirror Group Newspapers, 1984–90; *b* 29 Jan. 1928; *s* of Joseph and Elizabeth Haines; *m* 1955, Irene Betty Lambert; no *c. Educ:* Elementary Schools, Rotherhithe, SE16. Parly Correspondent, The Bulletin (Glasgow) 1954–58, Political Correspondent, 1958–60; Political Correspondent: Scottish Daily Mail, 1960–64; The Sun, 1964–68; Dep. Press Sec. to Prime Minister, Jan.–June 1969; Chief Press Sec. to Prime Minister, 1969–70 and 1974–76, and to Leader of the Opposition, 1970–74; Feature Writer, 1977–78, Chief Leader Writer, 1978–90, The Daily Mirror. Political Columnist, Today, 1994–95. Director: Mirror Gp Newspapers (1986) Ltd, 1986–92; Scottish Daily Record & Sunday Mail Ltd, 1986–92. Mem. Tonbridge UDC, 1963–69, 1971–74. Mem., Royal Commn on Legal Services, 1976–79. *Publications:* The Politics of Power, 1977; (co-editor) Malice In

Wonderland, 1986; Maxwell, 1988; Glimmers of Twilight (memoir), 2003. *Recreations:* heresy, watching football. *Address:* 1 South Frith, London Road, Southborough, Tunbridge Wells, Kent TN4 0UQ. *T:* (01732) 365919.

HAINES, Margaret Patricia Joyce, FCLIP; University Librarian, Carleton University, Ottawa, 2006–14; *b* Ottawa, 28 May 1950; *d* of Ernest and Mary Haines; *m* 1st, Roderick Stewart Taylor (marr. diss. 1989); 2nd, 1991, Ian Cordery (marr. diss. 2007); one step *d. Educ:* Carleton Univ. (BA Psychol. 1970); Univ. of Toronto (MLS 1975). Librarian, Health Scis Educn Centre, Mohawk Coll., Hamilton, Canada, 1975–78; Dir, Liby Services, Children's Hosp. of Eastern Ontario, Ottawa, 1978–88; Associate Instructor (Inf. Sci.), Univ. of Toronto, 1988–89; Dir, Inf. Resources, Kings' Fund, London, 1989–94; NHS Liby Advr, DoH, 1995–96; Chief Exec., Liby and Inf. Commn, 1996–2000; Dir, Res. and Knowledge Mgt, NHS SE London, 2000–02; Actg Dir, Knowledge Mgt, NHS Modernisation Agency, 2002–03; Dir, Inf. Services and Systems, KCL, 2003–06. Pres., CLIP, 2004–05. Pres., Ontario Hosp. Libraries Assoc., 1987. Hon. FCLIP 2006 (FCLIP 2004). Barnard Prize, LA, 1996. *Publications:* contrib. numerous articles to liby and information jls and chapters in books, including: Health Care Librarianship and Information Work, 2nd edn 1995; (jtly) Getting Research Findings into Practice, 1998; (jtly) Challenge and Change in the Information Society, 2003. *Recreations:* gardening, travelling, reading. *Address:* 37 Shandon Avenue, Nepean, ON K2J 4E3, Canada. *T:* (613) 8259615. *E:* mpjhaines@aol.com.

HAINES, Miranda, (Mrs Luke Taylor); writer; Consultant Editor, Geographical magazine, 2002–05 (Editor, 1999–2002); *b* 15 Oct. 1968; *d* of Christopher Haines, *qv*; *m* 1998, Luke Taylor; one *s* one *d. Educ:* Manchester Coll., Oxford (BA Hons English Lit.). International Herald Tribune, 1993–96; freelance writer, London, 1996–97; Editor, Traveller magazine, 1997–98. *Publications:* (ed jtly) The Traveller's Handbook, 1998; (ed jtly) The Traveller's Health Book, 1998; (contrib.) A Pilgrimage to Mecca, 2008. *Recreation:* travelling. *Address:* 2 Souldern Road, W14 0JE.

HAINES, Patricia, (Trish); Chief Executive, Worcestershire County Council, 2008–14; *d* of David and Roberta Calvert; *m* 1991, Terence Haines; two *s*, and one step *s* three step *d. Educ:* Belfast Royal Acad.; Univ. of Bradford (BA Hons, CQSW 1979); Henley Mgt Coll. (MBA 1994). Case worker, Manchester Law Centre, 1979–80; Intake Social Worker, Bradford MBC, 1980–83; Fostering and Adoption Social Worker, Kirklees MBC, 1983–86; Sen. Social Worker, Bradford MBC, 1986–87; Prin. Social Worker, Social Services, Berks CC, 1987–92; Prin. Staff Officer, Suffolk Social Services, 1992–96; Asst Dir, Social Services, Hereford and Worcs CC, 1996–97; Dir of Social Services, Warwicks CC, 1997–2002; Chief Exec., Reading BC, 2002–08. Pres., SOLACE, 2008–09 (Vice-Pres., 2006–08). Mem. Bd, Malvern Theatres Trust, 2012–; Trustee, New Coll., Worcester, 2012–. Lay Mem., Governing Body, S Worcs CCG, 2014–. *Recreations:* enjoying family life, going to the races, clay pigeon shooting.

HAINES, Ronald William Terence, FICE, FIStructE; Director of Construction Services, HM Prison Service, 1993–96; *b* 19 Dec. 1937; *s* of John William Haines and Mary Agnes Power; *m* 1957, Linda, *d* of Sidney and Lilian Hampton; one *s* two *d. Educ:* South East London Tech. Coll.; Regent Street Poly.; City Univ. MCIWEM. Design Engineer: William Harbrow & Co., 1954–56; Liverpool Reinforced Concrete Co., 1956–58; Civil and Structl Engr, Min. of Works and MPBW, 1958–67; Chief Civil and Structl Engr, Home Office, 1967–87; Dep. Dir of Works, HM Prison Service, Home Office, 1987–93. *Recreations:* organic farming, walking, theatre. *Address:* Barklye Farm, Swife Lane, Broad Oak, Heathfield, E Sussex TN21 8UR.

HAINES, Timothy Michael; Creative Director, Drama, ITV, since 2013; *b* 14 Oct. 1960; *s* of Douglas and Ann Haines; *m* 1989, Clare Worgan; three *s* two *d. Educ:* Tonbridge Sch., Kent; University Coll. of N Wales, Bangor (BSc Hons Zool.; Hon. Fellow 2004). Medical journalist, Doctor newspaper, 1981–85; Producer: BBC Radio, 1986–88; BBC TV Sci. and Features, 1989–2001; Creative Dir and Founder, Impossible Pictures Ltd, 2002–13; Creator and Producer, Walking with Dinosaurs, 1999; Executive Producer: Ballad of Big Al, 2000; Walking with Beasts, 2001; Lost World, 2001; Space Odyssey, 2004; Walking with Monsters, 2005; Ocean Odyssey, 2006; Sinbad, 2012; Co-creator and Exec. Producer, Primeval, 2007–11. Consultant, Walking with Dinosaurs, Live Arena Experience, 2009. *Publications:* Walking with Dinosaurs, 1999; Walking with Beasts, 2001; Space Odyssey, 2004; Complete Guide to Prehistoric Life, 2005. *Recreations:* watching film and TV, gardening, walking. *Address:* ITV, Upper Ground, SE1 9LT.

HAIRD, Susan Margaret, CB 2007; European Trade and Investment Representative for British Columbia, since 2012; *b* 10 Oct. 1952; *d* of late Douglas Haird and Myrah Haird; one *s* one *d. Educ:* Dollar Acad.; St Andrews Univ. (MA Hons Hist. and Econs); Coll. of Europe, Bruges (Cert. and Dip. in Advanced Eur. Studies). Stage at EC, 1976; joined Department of Trade and Industry, 1976: Private Secretary: to Perm. Sec., 1978; to Parly Under-Sec., 1979; Commercial Relns and Exports Div., 1980–84; Personnel Div., 1985–89; Industrial Materials Div., 1989; Equal Opportunities Div., Cabinet Office (on loan), 1989–92; Atomic Energy Div., 1992–96; Office of Manpower Econs, 1996–99; Director: Export Control, 1999–2000; Export Control and Non-Proliferation, 2000–02; UK Gov., IAEA and UK Mem., Exec. Council, Orgn for Prohibition of Chemical Weapons, 2000–02; Dir, Human Resources and Change Mgt, DTI, 2002–04; Dep. Chief Exec., UK Trade & Investment, 2004–12. Dir, Canada-UK Chamber of Commerce, 2013–; non-exec. Dir, Engrg Employers Fedn, 2012–; Mem., Adv. Council, British Expertise, 2012–. *Recreations:* family, travel, swimming.

HAIRE, William David Adams, CB 2015; Permanent Secretary, Department for Social Development, Northern Ireland, 2010–15; *b* 14 April 1956; *s* of Prof. James Haire and Dr Margaret Haire; *m* 1984, Bronwen Jess; two *d. Educ:* Queens' Coll., Cambridge (BA 1979); Univ. of Ulster (MSc). Joined Dept of Manpower Services, NI, 1980; on secondment, UKRep, Brussels, 1990–93; Director: Equality and Industrial Relns, Dept of Econ. Develt, 1993–97; Internat. Mktg, Industrial Develt Bd for NI, 1997–2000; Dir, Econ. Policy Unit, 2000–02, Second Perm. Sec., 2002–04, Office of First and Dep. First Minister; Permanent Secretary: Dept for Employment and Learning, 2004–06; Dept of Educn, 2006–10. Trustee, Joseph Rowntree Foundn, 2014–. *Recreations:* gardening, walking, reading.

HAIRER, Prof. Martin, PhD; FRS 2014; Professor, since 2010, and Regius Professor of Mathematics, since 2014, University of Warwick; *b* Geneva, 14 Nov. 1975; *s* of Ernst and Evi Hairer; *m* 2003, Xue-Mei Li. *Educ:* Univ. of Geneva (BSc Maths; MSc Physics; PhD Physics 2001). Asst Prof., 2004–06, Associate Prof., 2006–09, Univ. of Warwick; Associate Prof., New York Univ., 2009. *Publications:* (with P. Friz) A Course on Rough Paths, 2014. *Address:* Mathematics Department, University of Warwick, Coventry CV4 7AL. *T:* (024) 7652 8335. *E:* m.hairer@warwick.ac.uk, martin@hairer.org.

HAITES, Prof. Neva Elizabeth, OBE 2006; PhD; FRCPE; FRCPath; FMedSci; Professor of Medical Genetics, since 1996, and Vice-Principal for Development, since 2011, University of Aberdeen (Vice-Principal and Head of College of Life Sciences and Medicine, 2004–11); *b* 4 June 1947; *d* of Jack Kingsbury and Neva (*née* Gartside); *m* 1971, (Binnert) Roy Haites; two *d. Educ:* Somerville House, Brisbane; Univ. of Queensland (BSc; PhD 1974); Univ. of Aberdeen (MB ChB 1980). MRCPath 1996; FRCPE 1997. Lectr in Med. Genetics, Univ. of Aberdeen, 1986–96; Hon. Consultant Clinical Geneticist, 1991–, and non-exec. Bd Mem., NHS Grampian (formerly Aberdeen Royal Hosps NHS Trust). Mem., HFEA, 2003–. FMedSci 2000. *Publications:* (ed jtly) Familial Breast and Ovarian Cancer: genetics, screening and management, 2002. *Address:* College of Life Sciences and Medicine, University of Aberdeen, Polwarth Building, Foresterhill, Aberdeen AB25 2ZD; 32 Cairn Road, Bieldside, Aberdeen AB15 9AL.

HAITINK, Bernard, Hon. CH 2002; Hon. KBE 1977; Commander, Order of Orange Nassau, 1988; Principal Conductor, Chicago Symphony Orchestra, 2006–10; Music Director: Royal Opera House, Covent Garden, 1987–2002; Dresden Staatskapelle, 2002–04; *b* Amsterdam, 4 March 1929. *Educ:* Amsterdam Conservatory. Studied conducting under Felix Hupke, but started his career as a violinist with the Netherlands Radio Philharmonic; in 1954 and 1955 attended annual conductors' course (org. by Netherlands Radio Union) under Ferdinand Leitner; became 2nd Conductor with Radio Union at Hilversum with co-responsibility for 4 radio orchs and conducted the Radio Philharmonic in public during the Holland Fest., in The Hague, 1956; conducted the Concertgebouw Orch., Oct. 1956; then followed guest engagements with this and other orchs in the Netherlands and elsewhere. Debut in USA, with Los Angeles Symph. Orch., 1958; 5 week season with Concertgebouw Orch., 1958–59, and toured Britain with it, 1959; apptd (with Eugen Jochum) as the Orchestra's permanent conductor, Sept. 1961; sole artistic dir and permanent conductor of the orch., 1964–88; toured Japan, USSR, USA and Europe; 1974; début at Royal Opera House, Covent Garden, 1977. London Philharmonic Orchestra: Principal Conductor, Artistic Dir, 1967–79; toured: Japan, 1969; USA, 1970, 1971, 1976; Berlin, 1972; Holland, Germany, Austria, 1973; USSR, 1975. Musical Dir, Glyndebourne Opera, 1978–88; conducted Figaro for rebuilt opera house of Glyndebourne (60th anniversary), 1994; Music Dir, EU Youth Orch., 1994–99; Principal Guest Conductor, Boston Symph. Orch., 1995–2004, now Conductor Emeritus. Appearances at BBC Promenade Concerts and at Tanglewood, Salzburg, Edinburgh and Lucerne Festivals. Hon. RAM 1973. Hon. DMus: Oxford, 1988; Leeds, 1988; RCM, 2004. Bruckner Medal of Honour, 1970; Gold Medal, Internat. Gustav Mahler Soc., 1971; Erasmus Prize, Netherlands, 1991. Chevalier de L'Ordre des Arts et des Lettres, 1972; Officer, Order of the Crown (Belgium), 1977. *Address:* c/o Askonas Holt Ltd, Lincoln House, 300 High Holborn, WC1V 7JH.

HAJDUCKI, Andrew Michael; QC (Scot.) 1994; FSAScot; *b* London, 12 Nov. 1952; *s* of Henryk Hajducki, civil engineer, and Catherine Maxwell Moore, teacher; *m* 1st, 1980, Gayle Shepherd (marr. diss. 1998); two *s* one *d* (and one *s* decd); 2nd, 2002, Katharine Lilli Dodd. *Educ:* Dulwich Coll.; Downing Coll., Cambridge (BA 1975; MA 1979). FSAScot 1990. Called to the Bar, Gray's Inn, 1976; Advocate at Scots Bar, 1979–; Tutor, Edinburgh Univ., 1979–81; reporter, Session Cases, 1980; temp. Sheriff, 1987–99. Safeguarder: Lothian Reg. Children's Panel, 1987–96; Edinburgh and E Lothian Children's Panels, 1996–98; Reporter, Scottish Legal Aid Bd, 1999–; Arbitrator, Motor Insurers' Bureau (Untraced Drivers) scheme, 2000–03. Agent for Scottish Liberal Party and contested (Scottish L), local govt elections, 1979–85. Chm. of Trustees, Edinburgh Gestalt Inst., 2010–. *Publications:* Scottish Civic Government Licensing Law, 1994, 3rd edn 2009; Civil Jury Trials, 1998, 2nd edn 2005; (contrib.) Scottish Licensing Handbook, 1999; (contrib.) Renton & Brown's Statutory Offences, 1999; *railway history*: The North Berwick & Gullane Branch Lines, 1992; The Haddington, Macmerry & Gifford Branch Lines, 1994; The Lauder Light Railway, 1996; The St Andrews Railway, 2008; The Anstruther and St Andrews Railway, 2009; The Railways of Beckenham, 2011; The Leven and East of Fife Railway, 2013; articles in Scots Law Times and other legal, local history and railway jls. *Recreations:* reading, travel, local history and topography. *Address:* Advocates' Library, Parliament House, Edinburgh EH1 1RF. *T:* (0131) 226 2881.

HAJI-IOANNOU, Sir Stelios, Kt 2006; Founder, and Chairman, easyGroup, since 1998; Honorary General Consul for Republic of Cyprus in Principality of Monaco, since 2009; *b* 14 Feb. 1967; *s* of late Loucas Haji-Ioannou. *Educ:* London Sch. of Econs and Pol Sci. (BSc Econs); City of London Business Sch. (MSc Shipping, Trade and Finance). Joined Troodos Maritime, 1988; Founder: Stelmar Tankers, based in Athens and London, 1992 (floated NY Stock Exchange 2001, sold 2005); easyJet budget airline, 1995 (floated London Stock Exchange 2000) (Chm., 1995–2002; non-exec. Dir, 2005–10); easyCar, 2000; easyBus, 2004; easyHotel, 2005 (floated London Stock Exchange 2014); easyVan, 2006; easyOffice, 2007; easyGym, 2010; easyProperty, 2014. Founder: Cyprus Marine Envmt Protection Assoc., 1992; Stelios Philanthropic Foundn, 2006; Stelios Philanthropic Foundn (UK), 2011. Hon. Dr: Liverpool John Moores; Newcastle Business Sch.; Cranfield; Cass Business Sch. *Recreations:* yachting, philanthropy. *Address:* easyGroup Ltd, 10 Sydney Place, South Kensington, SW7 3NL.

HAKESLEY-BROWN, Roswyn Ann, CBE 2007; author; consultant in healthcare education, since 1996; *b* 2 Aug. 1945; *d* of Hector Redvers Hakesley; *m* 1968, Alan Graham Brown; one *s* one *d. Educ:* SE Staffs Co. Commercial Secondary Sch., Wednesbury; Univ. of Birmingham (Cert Ed); Open Univ. (BA Social Studies); Univ. of Warwick (MPhil Sociol.); Royal Hosp., Wolverhampton (RGN 1966); New Cross Hosp., Wolverhampton (RM 1967); London Univ. (DipN 1970). Nurse Tutor, Queen Elizabeth Hosp., Birmingham, 1973–84; Principal Lectr, Birmingham Poly., later UCE, Birmingham, 1984–96. Florence Nightingale Schol., 1995. Pres., RCN, 2000–02. Member: Refugee Healthcare Professionals' Steering Gp, DoH, 2002–06; Council, Grubb Inst., 2007–; PLAB Review Working Gp, GMC, 2012–14; Chairman: Refugee Nurses' Task Force, 2003–04; Allied Health Professionals Patients' Forum, 2009–14; Acad. of Nursing, Midwifery and Health Visiting Res. (UK), 2012–. Trustee, ExtraCare Charitable Trust for Older People, 1997–2006. FRSPH (FRSH 1990). Member: Soc. of Authors, 1992; Sigma Theta Tau Internat., 1996; Honour Sch. of Nursing. World of Difference 100 Award, Internat. Alliance for Women, 2009. Commng Ed., reviewer and mem., editl bds. *Publications:* Individualised Care: the role of the ward sister, 1989; Portfolios and Profiling for Nurses, 1992, 2nd edn 1995; (with B. Hawkesley) Learning Skills, Studying Styles and Profiling, 1996; chapters, reviews, prefaces and articles. *Recreations:* antique collecting, the National Trust, partying, picnics, having fun, reading, watching films, ballet, plays, listening to classical music. *Address:* c/o Royal College of Nursing, 20 Cavendish Square, W1G 0RN. *Club:* New Cavendish.

HAKIM, Prof. Nadey, MD, PhD; FRCS, FRCSI, FACS; Consultant General and Bariatric Surgeon, Imperial College Healthcare NHS Trust, since 2005 (Surgical Director, Transplant Unit, 2005); Professor of Transplantation Surgery, Imperial College London, since 2013 (Reader, 2010–12); Transplantation Tutor, London School of Surgery, since 2009; Max Thorek Professor of Surgery, International College of Surgeons, Chicago, since 2008; *b* 9 April 1958; *s* of Subhy Elias A. Hakim and Katy Hakim (*née* Namur); *m* 1992, Nicole Abounader; one *s* three *d. Educ:* René Descartes Univ., Paris (MD 1983); University Coll. London (PhD 1991). FRCSI 1987; FRCS 1988. Fellow in Surgery: Mayo Clinic, Rochester, Minn, 1987–89; Univ. of Minnesota, 1993–95; Consultant Surgeon, 1995–2005 and Surgical Dir, Transplant Unit, 1996–2005, St Mary's Hosp., London. Hon. Consultant Paediatric Transplant Surgeon, Gt Ormond St Hosp., 1996–2001; Hon. Consultant Transplant Surgeon: Royal Free Hosp., 1996–2001; Hammersmith Hosp., 1998–2005; Harefield Hosp., 2000–. Hon. Professor of Surgery: Univ. of São Paulo, 1999; Baskent Univ., Ankara, 2006–; Lima Univ., Peru, 2006–; Lyon Univ., 2007–; Visiting Professor: Harvard Univ., 2007; Cleveland Clinic, 2011. Editor in Chief: Internat. Surgery, 2001–11, Emeritus, 2012; Introductory Series in Medicine, Imperial Coll. Press, 2012–. First Vice-Pres., 2000–02, Pres., 2004–06, Internat. Coll. Surgeons; Mem. Council, RSM, 2009– (Hon. Sec., 2011–14; Pres., Transplant Sect., 2001–03; Vice Pres., 2014–16); Gov., Amer. Coll. of Surgeons, 2015–. Non-exec. Dir, Medicsight, 2003–05. Hon. Scientific Chm., Roads for Life, 2015–. FACS 1998; FICS 1987. Internat. Fellow, Amer. Soc. for Metabolic and Bariatric Surgery, 2008. Hon. Fellow:

Internat. Napoleonic Soc., 2008; Internat. Med. Scis Assoc., 2009; Assoc. of Surgeons of India, 2010. Hon. Dr: Charles Univ., Prague, 1998; Aden, 2003; Lima, 2007. Laureate, Faculty of Medicine, Paris, 1994; Prize of Excellence in Medicine, Makhzoum Foundn, 1998; J. Wesley Alexander Award for outstanding res. in transplantation, 2007. GCStJ 2010 (KStJ 1998; KCJSJ 2007); Bailiff OStJ 2010. *Publications:* (jtly) Enteric Physiology of Transplanted Intestine, 1994; (ed) Introduction to Organ Transplantation, 1997; British Symposium Pancreas Transplantation, 1998; Access Surgery, 2001; joint editor: Transplantation Surgery, 2001; Pancreas and Islet Transplantation, 2002; History of Organ and Cell Transplantation, 2003; Hernias Update, 2005; Composite Tissue Allograft, 2005; Haemostasis in Surgery, 2005; Living Related Transplants, 2005; Surgical Complications, 2008; Artificial Organs, 2009; Pancreas, Islets and Stem Cell Transplantation for the Cure of Diabetes, 2010; Bariatric Surgery, 2011; Atlas of Transplantation, 2012; Ethics and Legal Issues in Modern Surgery, 2015. *Recreations:* sculpture (sculpture of HM Queen Elizabeth in Royal Collection Trust, 2009; sculpture of Rt Hon. David Cameron exhibited at Carlton Club and Conservative HQ, 2014), clarinet (six recordings), languages. *Address:* 34 Hocroft Road, NW2 2BL.

See also N. S. P. I. Hakim.

HAKIM, Naji Subhy Paul Irénée; organist and composer; Professor of Musical Analysis, Conservatoire à Rayonnement Régional de Boulogne-Billancourt, since 1988; *b* Beirut, 31 Oct. 1955; *s* of Subhy Elias A. Hakim and Katy Hakim; *m* 1980, Marie-Bernadette Dufourcet; one *s* one *d*. *Educ:* Ecole Nationale Supérieure des Télécommunications, Paris (Ingénieur); Conservatoire National Supérieur de Musique, Paris. Organist: Basilique du Sacré-Coeur, Paris, 1985–93; Eglise de la Trinité, Paris, 1993–2008. Vis. Prof., RAM, 1993–. Mem., Consociatio Internat. Musicae Sacrae, Rome. Dr *hc* Saint-Esprit, Lebanon, 2002. Prix André Caplet, Académie des Beaux-Arts, 1991; first prizes at internat. organ, improvisation and composition competitions. Papal honour, Augustae crucis insigne pro Ecclesia et Pontifice, 2007. *Compositions* include: works for organ, violin, flute, oboe, guitar, trumpet; Fantasy for Piano and Orchestra, Concerto for Violin and String Orchestra, four concertos for organ, an oratorio, symphony, Les Noces de l'Agneau, a symphonic poem, Hymne de l'Univers, Augsburger Symphonie; three Masses; two Magnificats. *Publications:* Guide Pratique d'Analyse Musicale, 1991, 8th edn 2012; Anthologie Musicale pour l'Analyse de la Forme, 1995; The Improvisation Companion, 2000. *Address:* Conservatoire de Boulogne-Billancourt, 22 Rue de la Belle Feuille, 92100 Boulogne-Billancourt, France. *E:* mail@najihakim.com. *W:* www.najihakim.com.

See also N. Hakim.

HAKIN, Dame Barbara (Ann), DBE 2009 (OBE 2001); National Director, Commissioning Operations (formerly Chief Operating Officer and Deputy Chief Executive), NHS England, 2013–15. *Educ:* Univ. of Leeds (MB ChB 1975). MRCP 1977; MRCGP 1980. GP, Bradford, 1980–2000; Chief Exec., Bradford S and W PCT, 2000–06; Interim Dir Gen., Commng, DoH; Dir, Primary Care Modernisation Agency; Chief Exec., E Midlands SHA, 2006–10; Nat. Man. Dir, Commng Devel t, DoH, 2010–13; Interim Dep. Chief Exec. and Chief Operating Officer, NHS Commng Bd, 2013.

HÄKKINEN, Mika; former racing driver; Brand Ambassador and Driver Manager with Aces Management Group, since 2008; *b* Helsinki, 28 Sept. 1968; two *s* three *d*. Driver in: Go-karts, 1974–86 (five times Finnish champion); Formula Ford 1600, 1987 (Finnish, Swedish and Nordic champion); Opel Lotus Euroseries Championship, 1988; Formula 3, 1989–90 (British champion, 1990) and 2005–07; Formula 1: Lotus team, 1991–93; McLaren team, 1993–2001. Grand Prix wins: European, 1997; Australia, 1998; Brazil, 1998, 1999; Spain, 1998, 1999, 2000; Monaco, 1998; Austria, 1998, 2000; Germany, 1998; Luxembourg, 1998; Japan, 1998, 1999; Hungary, 1999, 2000; Canada, 1999; Belgium, 2000; USA, 2001; Britain, 2001; Drivers' World Champion, 1998, 1999.

HALBERG, Sir Murray (Gordon), ONZ 2008; Kt 1988; MBE 1961; *b* 7 July 1933; *s* of Raymond Halberg; *m* 1959, Phyllis, *d* of Alex Korff; two *s* one *d*. *Educ:* Avondale College. Started internat. distance running, Commonwealth Games, 1954; Commonwealth Gold Medals, 3 miles, 1958, 1962; Olympic Gold Medal, 5,000 metres, Rome, 1960; world records at 2 miles and 3 miles, 1961, participant in 4x1 mile record. Founder, Halberg Trust (to honour sporting excellence and to support children with disabilities), 1963. Blake Medal, Sir Peter Blake Trust, 2008.

HALBERT, His Honour Derek Rowland; a Circuit Judge, 1995–2015; *b* 25 March 1948; *s* of Ronald Halbert and Freda Mabel Halbert (*née* Impett); *m* 1972, Heather Rose Ashe; two *d*. *Educ:* King's Sch., Chester; Selwyn Coll., Cambridge (MA Law 1974); Open Univ. (BA Technol. 1984). Called to the Bar, Inner Temple, 1971; Mem., Wales and Chester Circuit, 1971–; a Recorder, 1991–95; Designated Civil Judge: Chester and N Wales, 2003–07; Cheshire, 2007–15. Hon. LLD Chester, 2012. *Recreations:* walking, tennis. *Club:* Leander (Henley).

HALDANE, Prof. (Frederick) Duncan (Michael), PhD; FRS 1996; Eugene Higgins Professor of Physics, Princeton University, since 1999 (Professor of Physics, 1990–99); *b* 14 Sept. 1951; *s* of Frederick Paterson Haldane and Ljudmila Haldane (*née* Renko); *m* 1981, Odile Marie Elisabeth Belmont; one *s* one *d*. *Educ:* St Paul's Sch.; Christ's Coll., Cambridge (BA 1973; MA; PhD 1978). FInstP. Physicist, Inst. Laue-Langevin, Grenoble, 1977–81; Asst Prof., Univ. of Southern California, 1981–85; Mem. Technical Staff, AT&T Bell Labs, 1985–87; Prof. of Physics, Univ. of California, San Diego, 1987–90. Fellow: Amer. Phys. Soc. (Oliver E. Buckley Prize in Condensed-Matter Physics, 1993); Amer. Acad. of Arts and Scis; FAAAS 2001. *Publications:* contribs to Jl of Physics, Physical Review and other learned jls. *Address:* 74 Maclean Circle, Princeton, NJ 08540, USA. *T:* (609) 9211531.

HALDANE, Prof. John Joseph, PhD; FRSE; Professor of Philosophy, since 1994, and Director, Centre for Ethics, Philosophy and Public Affairs, 1988–2000 and since 2002, St Andrews University; *b* London, 19 Feb. 1954; *s* of James Haldane and Hilda Haldane (*née* Dunne); *m* 1980, Hilda Budas; two *s* two *d*. *Educ:* St Aloysius Coll., Glasgow; Wimbledon Coll. of Art (BA Fine Art 1975); Inst. of Educn, Univ. of London (PGCE 1976); Birkbeck Coll., Univ. of London (BA Philosophy 1980; PhD Philosophy 1984). Art Master, St Joseph's Convent Sch., Abbey Wood, 1976–79; University of St Andrews: Lectr in Philosophy, 1983–90; Reader in Moral Philosophy, 1990–94. Royden Davis Prof. of Humanities, Georgetown Univ., 2001–02. Stanton Lectr in Philosophy and Religion, Univ. of Cambridge, 1999–2002; Gifford Fellow and Gifford Lectr, Univ. of Aberdeen, 2004–05; Sen. Fellow, Witherspoon Inst., Princeton, 2007–; McDonald Lectr, Univ. of Oxford, 2011; Remick Senior Fellow, Center for Ethics and Culture, Univ. of Notre Dame, Indiana, 2013–; Hon. Prof., Sch. of Educn, Univ. of Birmingham, 2014–; J. Newton Rayzor Sr Dist. Prof. of Philosophy, Baylor Univ., 2015–. Chm., Royal Inst. of Philos., 2011–. Consultor, Pontifical Council for Culture, Vatican 2005–. FRSE 1995. Corresp. Member: Pontifical Acad. of St Thomas Aquinas, Vatican, 2010; Pontifical Acad. of Life, Vatican, 2015. KCHS 2011 (KHS 2004). *Publications:* (with J. J. C. Smart) Atheism and Theism, 1996, 2nd edn 2002; An Intelligent Person's Guide to Religion, 2003; Faithful Reason, 2004; Seeking Meaning and Making Sense, 2008; The Church and the World, 2008; Practical Philosophy: ethics, culture and society, 2009; Reasonable Faith, 2010; edited vols on art, educn and philosophy; contribs to jls incl. Amer. Philosophical Qly, Analysis, Jl Applied Philosophy, Jl Architecture, Jl Scottish Philosophy, Monist, New Blackfriars, Philosophical Papers, Philosophical Investigations, Philosophical Rev., Philosophy, Proc. Aristotelian Soc., Ratio, Rev. of Metaphysics, Scottish Jl Theol.; contrib. articles and reviews to Art Book, Burlington Mag., Catholic Herald, Catholic Times, First Things, Herald, Modern Painters, Scotland on Sunday, Scotsman, Sunday Herald, Tablet, The Times, TES, THE. *Recreations:* gardening, visiting art exhibitions, music. *Address:* Department of Philosophy, University of St Andrews, Fife KY16 9AL. *T:* (01334) 462488. *E:* jjh1@st-and.ac.uk. *Club:* Travellers.

HALDENBY, Andrew John; Director, Reform, since 2005; *b* London, 4 Jan. 1972; *s* of Gerald Haldenby and Elizabeth Haldenby; *m* 2003, Simone Macey; one *s* one *d*. *Educ:* Burnham Grammar Sch.; Corpus Christi, Cambridge (BA Hons Hist. 1993); Birkbeck, Univ. of London (MSc Econs 2008). Conservative Res. Dept, 1995–97; Dir of Studies, Centre for Policy Studies, 1998–99; Dir of Communications, Business for Sterling, 2000–01; Co-founder and Dir of Res., Reform, 2001–05. *Recreations:* family, chess, reading, house music. *Address:* Reform, 45 Great Peter Street, SW1P 3LT. *T:* (020) 7799 6699. *E:* andrew.haldenby@reform.co.uk.

HALE OF RICHMOND, Baroness *cr* 2004 (Life Peer), of Easby in the County of North Yorkshire; **Brenda Marjorie Hale,** DBE 1994; PC 1999; a Justice, since 2009, and Deputy President, since 2013, Supreme Court of the United Kingdom (a Lord of Appeal in Ordinary, 2004–09); *b* 31 Jan. 1945; *d* of Cecil Frederick Hale and Marjorie Hale (*née* Godfrey); *m* 1st, 1968, Anthony John Christopher Hoggett, *qv* (marr. diss. 1992); one *d*; 2nd, 1992, Julian Thomas Farrand, *qv*. *Educ:* Richmond High School for Girls, Yorks; Girton College, Cambridge (MA; Hon. Fellow, 1996). University of Manchester: Asst Lectr in Law, 1966; Lectr, 1968; Sen. Lectr, 1976; Reader, 1981; Prof., 1986–89. Vis. Prof., KCL, 1990–; Vis. Fellow, Nuffield Coll., Oxford, 1997–2005. Called to the Bar, Gray's Inn, 1969 (Vice-Treas., 2016); Barrister, Northern Circuit, 1969–72; Law Comr, 1984–93; QC 1989; an Asst Recorder, 1983–89; a Recorder, 1989–94; a Judge of the High Court, Family Div., 1994–99; Family Div. Liaison Judge for London, 1997–99; a Lord Justice of Appeal, 1999–2004. Legal Mem., Mental Health Review Tribunal for NW Region, 1979–80; Member: Council on Tribunals, 1980–84; Civil and Family Cttee, Judicial Studies Bd, 1990–94; Human Fertilisation and Embryology Authy, 1990–93. Chm., Mgt Cttee, Royal Courts of Justice Advice Bureau, 2002–03. Man. Trustee, Nuffield Foundn, 1987–2002; Governor, Centre for Policy on Ageing, 1990–93. President: Nat. Family Mediation, 1994– (Chm., Nat. Family Conciliation Council, then Nat. Assoc. of Family Mediation and Conciliation Services, 1989–93); Assoc. of Women Barristers, 1998–2005; UK Assoc. of Women Judges, 2004–; Internat. Assoc. of Women Judges, 2010–12. Chancellor, Bristol Univ., 2004–; Visitor, Girton Coll., Cambridge, 2004–. Editor, Jl of Social Welfare Law, 1978–84. Hon. FBA 2004; Hon. FRCPsych 2007. Hon. LLD: Sheffield, 1989; London Guildhall, 1996; Manchester, 1997; Bristol, 2002; Cambridge, 2005; Hull, 2006; KCL, 2007; Oxford, 2007; City, 2007; Reading, 2007; College of Law, 2008; UWE, 2009; Huddersfield, 2009; Sussex, 2009; Georgetown, Washington, DC, 2010; Salford, 2010; Glasgow, 2011; Kent, 2011; Westminster, 2011; Liverpool, 2013; Swansea, 2014; York, 2015; LSE, 2015; DUniv Essex, 2005. *Publications:* Mental Health Law, 1976, 5th edn 2010; Parents and Children, 1977, 4th edn 1993; (jtly) The Family Law and Society: Cases and Materials, 1983, 6th edn 2008; (with S. Atkins) Women and the Law, 1984; Mental Health Law, in Halsbury's Laws of England, 4th edn 1992; From the Test Tube to the Coffin: choice and regulation in private life (Hamlyn Lectures), 1996; many contribs to legal periodicals and other texts. *Recreations:* domesticity, drama, duplicate bridge. *Address:* Supreme Court of the United Kingdom, Parliament Square, SW1P 3BD. *Club:* Athenæum.

HALE, Charles Stanley; QC 2014; *b* Bournemouth; *s* of Roland and Sandra Hale; *m* 2006, Emily; three *d*. *Educ:* Winton Boys' Sch., Bournemouth; Kingston Univ. (LLB Hons); Council of Legal Educn. Called to the Bar, Middle Temple, 1992. Mem., Bar Council, 2001–13. Fellow, Internat. Acad. of Matrimonial Lawyers, 2012–. *Publications:* contrib. Counsel Mag. *Recreations:* sport, fine wine, food, friends and family. *Address:* 4 Paper Buildings, Temple, EC4Y 7EX. *T:* (020) 7583 0816. *E:* csh@4pb.com. *W:* www.twitter.com/twitbarrister. *Club:* Refreshers Cricket.

HALE, His Honour David John; a Circuit Judge, 1994–2013; *b* 18 June 1948; *s* of John and Kathleen Hale; *m* 1st, 1974, Lynn Thomas (*d* 1998); 2nd, 1999, Mrs Eileen Rafferty (*née* Hawthornthwaite). *Educ:* Calday Grange GS, West Kirby; Liverpool Univ. (LLB (Hons)). Called to the Bar, Gray's Inn, 1970; in practice, 1970–94.

HALE, Prof. Geoffrey, PhD; consultant scientist and entrepreneur, since 2011; Chairman, Native Antigen Co., since 2011; Visiting Professor, Sir William Dunn School of Pathology, University of Oxford, since 2007; *b* 2 Sept. 1953; *s* of Harold and Christine Hale; *m* 1977, Gillian Hutson; one *s* two *d*. *Educ:* Fitzwilliam Coll., Cambridge (MA; PhD 1977). University of Cambridge: Research Asst, Dept of Biochem., 1977–80; Sen. Res. Associate, Dept of Pathology, 1980–95; University of Oxford: Res. Lectr, Sir William Dunn Sch. of Pathol., 1995–98; Res. Dir, Therapeutic Antibody Centre, 1995–2007; Reader in Therapeutic Immunol., 1998–2000; Prof. of Therapeutic Immunol., 2000–07; Founder and CEO, BioAnalab Ltd, 2002–09; Man. Dir, 2009–10, Chief Scientist, 2010–11, Millipore Biopharma Services. *Publications:* numerous contribs on protein chemistry and therapeutic uses of monoclonal antibodies in various jls. *Recreations:* playing the piano, watching the garden grow.

HALE, Norman Morgan, CB 1992; Under Secretary, Department of Health (formerly of Health and Social Security), 1975–93; *b* 28 June 1933; *s* of late Thomas Norman Hale and Ada Emily Hale, Evesham, Worcs; *m* 1965, Sybil Jean (*née* Maton); one *s* one *d*. *Educ:* Prince Henry's Grammar Sch., Evesham; St John's Coll., Oxford (MA). Min. of Pensions and National Insurance, 1955; Asst Sec., Nat. Assistance Bd, 1966; Min. of Social Security, 1966; CSD, 1970–72. Consultant: MoD, 1994; Medicines Control Agency, 1994–2003; National Trust, 1995–97. Churchwarden Emeritus, St Mary the Virgin, Ewell (Churchwarden, 1993–97). Chm. of Govs, Ewell Grove Infant Sch., 1998–2005. *Recreations:* gardening, historical geography. *Address:* 64 Castle Avenue, Ewell, Epsom, Surrey KT17 2PH. *T:* (020) 8393 3507. *Club:* Oxford and Cambridge.

HALE, Raymond, CPFA; County Treasurer, Leicestershire County Council, 1977–97; *b* 4 July 1936; *s* of Tom Raymond Hale and Mary Jane (*née* Higgin); *m* 1959, Ann Elvidge; one *s*. *Educ:* Baines Grammar Sch., Poulton-le-Fylde. Lancashire CC, 1952–54; served Royal Air Force, 1954–56; Lancashire CC, 1956–61; Nottinghamshire CC, 1961–65; Leicestershire CC, 1965–97. Treasurer: Leics Police Authy, 1977–97; Leicester Univ. Med. Sch. and Associated Leics Teaching Hosps Jt Trust (Medisearch), 1988–; Access Cttee for England, 1997–99; Chm., Hind Sisters Homes Charity, 1993–; Treas. and Co. Sec., Mosaic - Shaping Disability Services (formerly Leics Guild of Disabled), 1999– (Vice-Chm., 1990–97). *Recreations:* Rugby, cricket, gardening. *Address:* The Stables, Main Street, Nailstone, Nuneaton, Warwicks CV13 0QB. *T:* (01530) 264174.

HALE, Rt Rev. Stephen John; Senior Minister, St Hilary's Kew/North Balwyn, since 2009; *b* Sydney, 26 June 1955; *s* of William James and Patricia Edna Hale; *m* 1986, Karen (*née* Ellis); one *s* one *d*. *Educ:* Univ. of Sydney (BA 1975; DipEd 1976); Moore Theol Coll., Sydney (BTh 1983; DipArts (Theol.) 1984). Secondary teacher, NSW Dept of Educn, 1977–80; ordained deacon 1985, priest 1985, Sydney; Curate, St Paul's, Castle Hill, NSW, 1985–88; Youth Dir, dio. Melbourne, 1988–96; Vicar, St John's, Diamond Creek, Vic, 1996–2001; an Asst Bishop, Dio. of Melbourne (Bishop of the Eastern Region), 2001–09. Chm. Council, ACCESS ministries (formerly Christian Educn in Schs), 2006– (Mem. Council, 2002–); Chm., Anglican Diocesan Schs Commn, Vic, 2002–09. Chm., Arrow Leadership Aust. Inc., 1994–; Mem. Bd, Benetas Vic, 2005–07. *Recreations:* swimming, surfing, theatre, golf, travel, tennis. *Address:* 1/38 Melrose Street, Mont Albert North, Vic 3129, Australia; St Hilary's Kew/North Balwyn, 12 John Street, Kew, Vic 3101, Australia. *T:* (3) 98167100, *Fax:* (3) 98171078. *E:* stephenh@sthils.com.

HALE, Stephen Maynard, OBE 2011; Chief Executive, Refugee Action, since 2015; *b* London, 5 Sept. 1971; *s* of Richard Hale and Jean Hale; *m* 2005, Zoë Parks; one *s* one *d*. *Educ:* Sevenoaks Sch.; Manchester Univ. (BA Econ.); Middlesex Univ. (MProf). Senior Consultant: GPC, 1997–99; ERM, 1999–2002; Special Advr, DEFRA, 2002–06; Dir, Green Alliance, 2006–10; Dep. Advocacy and Campaigns Dir, Oxfam Internat., 2010–14. Trustee, Christian Aid, 2007–10. *Recreations:* cycling, Crystal Palace Football Club. *Address:* Refugee Action, Victoria Charity Centre, Belgrave Road, SW1V 1RB. *T:* (020) 7952 1511. *E:* stephenhale@refugee-action.org.uk.

HALES, Antony John, CBE 2008; Chairman, Canal and River Trust (formerly British Waterways), since 2005; *b* 25 May 1948; *s* of Sidney Alfred Hales and Margaret Joan (*née* Wood); *m* 1975, Linda Churchlow; three *s* one *d*. *Educ:* Repton; Bristol Univ. (BSc Chem). With Cadbury Schweppes, 1969–79; Mkting Dir, Joshua Tetley & Son, 1979–83; Managing Director: Halls Oxford & West Brewery Co., 1983–85; Ind Coope-Taylor Walker, 1985–87; Retail Dir, Allied Breweries, 1987; Man. Dir, Ansells, 1987–89; Chief Exec., J. Lyons & Co., 1989–91; Dir, 1989–99, Chief Exec., 1991–99, Allied Lyons, then Allied Domecq; Chairman: Allied Domecq Spirits & Wine Ltd (formerly Hiram Walker Gp), 1992–99; Allied Domecq (formerly Allied Lyons) Retail, 1992–99. Director: Hyder PLC (formerly Welsh Water), 1993–97; Aston Villa plc, 1997–2006; non-executive Director: HSBC (formerly Midland) Bank, 1994–2001; David Halsall Internat., 2000–05; Tempo Hldgs, 2000–01; Reliance Security Gp, 2001–05; SIS Hldgs, 2002–10; IPF Gp plc (formerly Provident Financial plc), 2006–; Capital and Regional plc, 2011–; Chm., Workspace Gp plc, 2002–11. Chairman: Navy, Army, Air Force Institutes Ltd, 2001–08; NAAFI Pension Trustees, 2010–; Trustees, Greenwich Foundn, 2014–. Director: SSVC Corp., 2010–; WNO, 2010–. Chm., Nat. Manufg Council, CBI, 1993–95. Hon. Governor, RSC, 2000–.

HALES, Prof. Frederick David, FREng, FIMechE, FIMA; Professor of Surface Transport, Loughborough University of Technology, 1968–93, now Professor Emeritus; *b* 19 Dec. 1930; *s* of Christina Frances and Frederick David Hales; *m* 1955, Pamela Hilary Warner (*d* 2009); one *s* one *d* (and one *d* decd). *Educ:* Kingswood Grammar Sch.; Bristol Univ. (BSc Hons Maths, PhD). Sigma Xi. Asst Chief Aerodynamicist, Bristol Aircraft, 1953–60; Group Research Head, MIRA, 1960–67; Vis. Scientist, Stevens Inst., Hoboken, 1967–68; Loughborough University: Hd of Dept of Transport Technology, 1982–89; Pro-Vice-Chancellor, 1984–85, Sen. Pro-Vice-Chancellor, 1985–87; acting Vice-Chancellor, 1987–88; Dean of Engrg, 1989–92. Mem., Tech. Adv. Council to Ford Motor Co., 1985–93; Scientific Visitor to Dept of Transport, 1986–90. FREng (FEng 1990). Hon. DSc Loughborough, 2000. *Publications:* papers on dynamics and vehicle control and stability. *Recreations:* sailing, photography, wine, wood carving, painting. *Address:* 14 Kenilworth Avenue, Loughborough, Leics LE11 4SL. *T:* (01509) 261767. *Club:* Rutland Sailing.

HALES, Sally-Ann, (Mrs C. E. Children); QC 2012; a Recorder, since 2010; *b* Estevan, Canada, 18 July 1965; *d* of Peter Jeffrey Skinner and Patricia Ann Skinner (now Mrs Thomas David Hales); *m* 2011, Charles Edward Children; two *d*. *Educ:* Macclesfield Co. High Sch. for Girls; De Montfort Univ. (LLB Hons 1987). Called to the Bar, Gray's Inn, 1988; in practice as a barrister, specialising in criminal law, 1988–. *Recreations:* family and friends, cooking, fine dining. *Address:* 18 Red Lion Court, EC4A 3EB. *E:* clerks@18rlc.co.uk.

HALEY, Prof. Keith Brian, PhD; Professor of Operational Research, Birmingham University, 1968–99, now Emeritus; *b* 17 Nov. 1933; *s* of Arthur Leslie Haley and Gladys Mary Haley; *m* 1960, Diana Elizabeth Mason; one *s*. *Educ:* King Edward VI, Five Ways, Birmingham; Birmingham Univ. (BSc, PhD). FIMA 1970; FIEE 1980; CompOR 1997. OR Scientist, NCB, 1957–59; Birmingham University: Lectr, 1959–63; Sen. Lectr, 1963–68; Head, Dept of Engrg Prodn, 1981–89; Head, Centre for Ergonomics and OR, 1990–91; Dir, Centre of Applied Gerontology, 1991–95; Hd, Sch. of Manufg and Mech. Engrg, 1994–96. President: ORS, 1982–83 (Mem. Council, 2007–09; Chm., Pubns Cttee, 1999–2010); IFORS, 1992–94 (Vice-Pres., 1983–86); Editor, Jl of ORS, 1972–80. Governor, 1968–2008, a Vice Pres., 2008–, Bromsgrove Sch. Beale Medal, ORS, 2010. *Publications:* Mathematical Programming for Business and Industry, 1966; Operational Research '75, 1976; Operational Research '78, 1979; Search Theory and Applications, 1980; Applied Operations Research in Fishing, 1981; many articles. *Recreations:* badminton, bridge. *Address:* 22 Eymore Close, Selly Oak, Birmingham B29 4LB. *T:* (0121) 475 3331.

HALFON, Rt Hon. Robert; PC 2015; MP (C) Harlow, since 2010; Minister of State (Minister without Portfolio), Cabinet Office, since 2015. *Educ:* Highgate Sch.; Exeter Univ. (BA Politics 1991; MA Russian and E Eur. Politics 1992). Formerly: res. and policy analyst to public affairs consultancies; freelance consultancy work; COS to Oliver Letwin, MP, 2001–05. Mem., Adv. Bd, Centre for Social Justice. Political Consultant to Cons. Friends of Israel, 2005–10. Member: Public Admin Select Cttee, 2010–14; Exec., 1922 Cttee, 2010–. Chair: Western Area Cons. Students, 1987–90; Exeter Univ. Cons. Assoc., 1989–90; Dep. Chair, Vauxhall Cons. Assoc., 1998–2000; Mem., Cons. Way Forward. Contested (C) Harlow, 2001, 2005. Mem. (C) Roydon PC, 2005–11. Trustee, Harlow Employability. Formerly: Gov., Passmores Sch.; Patron, Harlow Homeless Centre. *Publications:* contrib. articles to nat. newspapers. *Recreations:* reading, watches, Chelsea Football, countryside. *Address:* House of Commons, SW1A 0AA. *T:* (020) 7219 7223. *E:* Halfon4harlow@roberthalfon.com.

HALFORD, Alison Monica; Member (C), Flintshire County Council, since 2008; *b* 8 May 1940; *d* of William Charles Halford and Yvonne (*née* Bastien). *Educ:* Notre Dame Grammar Sch., Norwich. Metropolitan Police, 1962–83; Asst Chief Constable (most senior post for woman in UK), Merseyside Police, 1983–92. Mem. (Lab) Delyn, Nat. Assembly for Wales, 1999–2003. Flintshire County Council: Mem. (Lab), 1995–99; Member of Committees, 2008–: Community and Housing; Planning; Audit; Mem., Hawarden Community Council, 2008–. Mem., Cons. Party, 2006–. Gov., Hawarden High Sch., 2011–. Police Long Service and Good Conduct Medal, 1984. Following police tapping her telephone in sex discrimination case, brought action in which Court of Human Rights ruled, 1997, that statutory warning required; resulted in introduction of Regulation of Statutory Powers Act 2000. *Publications:* No Way up the Greasy Pole (autobiog.), 1993; Leaks from the Back Benches (autobiog.), 2007. *Recreations:* birdwatching, serving the community, theatre, painting, gardening, music, charity work.

HALFORD, John Gordon; Solicitor, since 2002, and Partner, since 2006, Bindmans LLP; *b* Newcastle upon Tyne, 28 May 1967; *s* of Gordon and Mary Halford. *Educ:* Abraham Darby Sch.; Marlwood Comprehensive Sch.; Essex Univ. (LLB Hons); Southampton Univ. (LLM). Manager and Legal Advr, Immigration Rights Centre, Bristol, 1990–91; Solicitor, Humberside Law Centre, 1992–98; admitted Solicitor, 1996; Project Solicitor, Public Law Project, 1998–2002. *Publications:* Butterworths' Health Services Law and Practice, 2001; contrib. articles to Judicial Rev., Legal Action. *Recreations:* spending time with my family, hill-walking, reading, looking out for injustices I might be able to challenge. *Address:* Bindmans LLP, 236 Gray's Inn Road, WC1X 8HB. *T:* (020) 7833 4433, *Fax:* (020) 7837 9792. *E:* j.halford@bindmans.com.

HALFORD, Prof. Stephen Edgar, PhD; FRS 2004; Professor of Biochemistry, University of Bristol, 1995–2011, now Emeritus; *b* 22 Sept. 1945; *s* of Walter R. Halford and Jessie M. Halford (*née* Edgar). *Educ:* Univ. of Bristol (BSc 1967; PhD 1970). Department of Biochemistry, University of Bristol: Lectr, 1976–89; Reader, 1989–95. *Publications:* numerous scientific papers. *Recreations:* turf, jazz, wine. *Address:* Department of Biochemistry, School of Medical Sciences, University of Bristol, University Walk, Bristol BS8 1TD. *E:* s.halford@bristol.ac.uk.

HALFPENNY, Ven. Brian Norman, CB 1990; Team Rector of the Parish of the Ridge, Redditch, 1991–2001; Hon. Assistant Priest, St Lawrence, Bourton-on-the-Water, since 2001; *b* 7 June 1936; *s* of Alfred Ernest Halfpenny and Fanny Doris Halfpenny (*née* Harman); *m* 1961, Hazel Beatrice Cross; three *d*. *Educ:* George Dixon Grammar Sch., Birmingham; St John's Coll., Oxford (BA 1960; MA 1964); Wells Theol Coll. Curate, Melksham, 1962–65; Chaplain, RAF, 1965–91; served RAF Stations Cosford, Wildenrath, Leeming, Hong Kong, Brize Norton, Halton, Akrotiri; RAF Coll., Cranwell, 1982–83; Asst Chaplain-in-Chief, Support Comd, 1983–85, Strike Comd, 1985–88; QHC 1985–91; Chaplain-in-Chief and Archdeacon, RAF, 1988–91; Priest i/c St Clement Danes, 1988–91; Canon and Prebendary, Lincoln Cathedral, 1989–91; permission to officiate, dio. Gloucester, 2001–. Co. Chaplain, RBL, Worcs, 1994–2001. Mem., Gen. Synod of C of E, 1988–91. Vice-Pres., Clergy Orphan Corp., 1988–91. Mem. Council, RAF Benevolent Fund, 1988–91; Visitor, Soldiers' and Airmen's Scripture Readers Assoc., 1988–91. *Recreations:* music, theatre, running. *Address:* 80 Roman Way, Bourton-on-the-Water, Cheltenham, Glos GL54 2EW. *T:* (01451) 821589. *Clubs:* Royal Air Force; Oxford Union Society.

HALFPENNY, Prof. Peter John, PhD; Professor of Sociology, University of Manchester, 1993–2010, now Emeritus; *b* Whitehaven, 1 March 1945; *s* of Arthur and Joan Halfpenny; *m* 1968, Daphne Taylorson; two *s*. *Educ:* Whitehaven Grammar Sch.; Magdalen Coll., Oxford (BA Hons Natural Sci.; MA); Univ. of Essex (MA; PhD Sociol. 1976). University of Manchester: Lectr in Sociol., 1971–83; Sen. Lectr, 1983–92; Hd, Dept of Sociol., 1993–96; Dir, Centre for Applied Social Res., 1985–2004; Dean, Faculty of Social Scis and Law, 2003–04; Hd, Sch. of Social Scis, 2003–06; Exec. Dir, Nat. Centre for e-Social Science, 2004–09; Dep. Dir, Manchester Informatics, 2007–10. Chm. Trustees, Voluntary Sector Studies Network, 2003–09. Ed., Voluntary Sector Rev., 2009–14. *Publications:* Positivism and Sociology: explaining social life, 1982, 3rd edn 2014; (ed with P. McMylor) Positivist Sociology and its Critics, 3 vols, 1994; contrib. jl articles, chapters, reports and conf. presentations. *Recreations:* computer applications, crossing disciplinary boundaries, modern literary novels, gardening. *Address:* Sociology, School of Social Sciences, University of Manchester, Manchester M13 9PL. *E:* p.halfpenny@manchester.ac.uk.

HALIFAX, 3rd Earl of, *cr* 1944; **Charles Edward Peter Neil Wood;** JP; DL; Bt 1784; Viscount Halifax, 1866; Baron Irwin, 1925; Vice Lord-Lieutenant, East Riding of Yorkshire, 1996–2006; *b* 14 March 1944; *s* of 2nd Earl of Halifax and Ruth (*d* 1989), *d* of late Captain Rt Hon. Neil James Archibald Primrose, MC, sometime MP; *S* father, 1980; *m* 1976, Camilla, *d* of late C. F. J. Younger, DSO, TD; one *s* one *d*. *Educ:* Eton; Christ Church, Oxford. Contested (C) Dearne Valley, Feb. and Oct. 1974. High Steward of York Minster, 1988–. JP Wilton Beacon, 1986, Bridlington, 2001; DL Humberside, 1983–96, 2005. KStJ 1994. *Heir:* *s* Lord Irwin, *qv*. *Address:* Garrowby, York YO41 1QD. *Clubs:* White's, Pratt's.

HALIFAX, Archdeacon of; *see* Dawtry, Ven. Dr A. F.

HALL, family name of **Baron Hall of Birkenhead**.

HALL OF BIRKENHEAD, Baron *cr* 2010 (Life Peer), of Birkenhead in the County of Cheshire; **Anthony William, (Tony), Hall,** CBE 2006; Director-General, BBC, since 2013; *b* 3 March 1951; *s* of late Donald William Hall and of Mary Joyce Hall; *m* 1977, Cynthia Lesley Hall (*née* Davis); one *s* one *d*. *Educ:* King Edward's Sch., Birmingham; Birkenhead Sch., Merseyside; Keble Coll., Oxford (Exhibnr; MA). Joined BBC as News trainee, 1973; Producer: World Tonight, 1976; New York (Radio), 1977; Sen. Producer, World at One, 1978; Output Editor, Newsnight, 1980; Sen. Producer, Six O'Clock News, 1984; Asst Editor, Nine O'Clock News, 1985; Editor: News and Election '87, 1987; News and Current Affairs, BBC TV, 1988–90; Dir, 1990–93, Man. Dir, 1993–96, News and Current Affairs, BBC; Chief Exec., BBC News, 1996–2001; Exec. Dir, later Chief Exec., Royal Opera House, Covent Gdn, 2001–13. Non-exec. Dir, HM Customs and Excise, 2002–05; Dep. Chm., Channel 4, 2012 (non-exec. Dir, 2005–12). Mem., King's Healthcare Expert Reference Gp, 1995–96. Mem., Steering Cttee, Regeneration through Heritage, BITC, 1999–2000; Chairman: Strategic Skills Council, Creative and Cultural Industries, 2004–09; Music and Dance Adv. Gp, DFES, 2004–07; Member: Olympics Cultural Adv. Bd, DCMS, 2006–13; LOCOG, 2009–13 (Chm. Bd, Cultural Olympiad, 2009–13). Chm., Theatre Royal, Stratford, 2001–09 (Dir, 1999–2009). Member: Mgt Cttee, Clore Leadership Prog., 2005–11; Bd, Paul Hamlyn Foundn, 2011–. Trustee, British Council, 2008–12. Non-exec. Dir, Univ. for Industry, 2003–06. Hon. Vis. Fellow, City Univ., 1999–2000. Mem. Council, Brunel Univ., 1999–2003. Patron, Newsworld, 1999; Gov. for Media, World Econ. Forum, 2000. Mem. Cttee, Race for Opportunity, 1999–2001 (as Race Champion led BBC's campaign on diversity and race issues). Liveryman, Painter Stainers' Co., 1989–. FRTS 1994 (Chm., 1998–2000); FRSA 1997. *Publications:* King Coal: a history of the miners, 1981; Nuclear Politics, 1984; articles in various periodicals. *Recreations:* architecture, opera, ballet, walking, gardening, my family. *Address:* BBC Broadcasting House, Portland Place, W1A 1AA; House of Lords, SW1A 0PW.

HALL, Alexandra Mary H.; *see* Hall Hall.

HALL, Andrew; Chief Executive, AQA Education (formerly Assessment and Qualifications Alliance), since 2010; *b* Bournemouth, 13 June 1956; *s* of John Hall and Esther Ina Hall; *m* 1980, Susan Jacqueline Evans; two *d*. *Educ:* King Edward's Sch., Witley; St Paul's Coll., Cheltenham; Univ. of Bristol (BEd Hons). ACA 1981, FCA 1991. Ernst & Young, 1983–87; TRW Valves, 1983–87; Finance Dir, 1987–90, Man. Dir, 1990–94, Bomford Turner; Chief Exec., Eliza Tinsley Gp plc, 1994–2006; Chief Exec. and Dir, QCA, 2006–10. *Recreations:* tennis, travel, family time. *Address:* AQA Education, Argyle House, 29–31 Euston Road, NW1 2SD. *E:* ahall@aqa.org.uk.

HALL, Sir Andrew (James), Kt 2013; PhD; Professor of Epidemiology, London School of Hygiene and Tropical Medicine, University of London, 2000–13; *b* 9 Feb. 1951. *Educ:* Guy's Hosp. Med. Sch., London Univ. (MB BS 1973); London Sch. of Hygiene and Tropical Medicine (MSc 1982); Southampton Univ. (PhD 1986). MRCP 1976, FRCP 1994; MFPHM 1990; FFPH 1996. Epidemiologist, Internat. Agency for Res. on Cancer, WHO, 1986–90; Sen. Lectr in Epidemiol., 1990–96, Reader in Epidemiol., 1996–2000, LSHTM. Mem., cttees of WHO, MRC and DoH. Member: Bd, PHLS, 1997–2004; Bd, HPA, 2003–13; Chm., Jt Cttee on Vaccines and Immunisation, 2006–13 (Mem., 2002–06). *Publications:* (with D. J. P. Barker) Practical Epidemiology, 2nd edn 1991; numerous contribs to scientific literature. *Recreations:* live music, cooking and baking, gardening, hill walking, photography. *E:* andrewjhall1@icloud.com.

HALL, Andrew Joseph; QC 2002; *b* 17 Feb. 1953; *s* of James Clement Hall and Jane Hall. *Educ:* Marist Coll.; Univ. of Birmingham (LLB); Inst. of Criminol., Univ. of Sheffield (MA). Admitted solicitor, 1980; in practice as solicitor, 1980–90, Partner, Hodge, Jones & Allen, London, 1982–90; called to the Bar, Gray's Inn, 1991, Bencher, 2005; in practice as barrister, 1991–. Member: Gen. Council of the Bar, 1998–; Criminal Bar Assoc., 1998– (Chm., 2006–07); Bar Human Rights Cttee, 1999–. Chm., Kalisher Scholarship Trust, 2011–. Mem., Editl Bd, Internat. Jl Evidence and Proof, 1998–. *Publications:* Emergency Procedures Handbook, 1986; Criminal Justice in Crisis, 1993; Confidentiality and Mental Health, 2001;

Guide to the Proceeds of Crime Act, 2002. *Recreations:* African skies, Spanish mountains. *Address:* Doughty Street Chambers, 53–54 Doughty Street, WC1N 2LS. *T:* (020) 7404 1313, *Fax:* (020) 7404 2283.

HALL, Andrew Rotely, OBE 1994; HM Diplomatic Service, retired; Ambassador to Nepal, 2006–10; *b* 3 May 1950; *s* of David and Sheila Hall; *m* 1973, Kathie Wright; two *d. Educ:* Univ. of Keele (BA Hons); Sch. of Oriental and African Studies, Univ. of London (PhD 1982). Joined HM Diplomatic Service, 1980; First Secretary: New Delhi, 1984–87; FCO, 1987–91; Dep. Hd of Mission and Consul, Kathmandu, 1991–95; FCO, 1995–2003; Dep. High Comr in Eastern India, Kolkata, 2003–06. *Club:* Tollygunge (Kolkata).

HALL, Anthony Stewart, (Tony); Director, Central Council for Education and Training in Social Work, 1986–97; *b* 26 Oct. 1945; *s* of Dora Rose Ellen Hall (*née* Rundle) and Albert Hall; *m* 1968, Phoebe Katharine Souster; one *s* one *d. Educ:* Gillingham Grammar School; London Sch. of Economics (BScSoc). Research Student, LSE, 1968–71; Lectr in Management and Organisation Studies, Nat. Inst. for Social Work, 1971–73; Lectr in Social Admin, Univ. of Bristol, 1973–78; Dir, Assoc. of British Adoption and Fostering Agencies, 1978–80; Dir and Sec., British Agencies for Adoption and Fostering, 1980–86; Dep. Man. Dir, Retirement Security Ltd, 1997. *Publications:* A Management Game for the Social Service (with J. Algie), 1974; The Point of Entry: a study of client reception in the social services, 1975; (ed) Access to Birth Records: the impact of S.26 of the Children Act 1975, 1980; (with Phoebe Hall) Part-time Social Work, 1980; (series editor) Child Care Policy and Practice, 1982–86; chapters in books and articles in professional and learned jls. *Recreations:* photography, genealogy, watching sport and old films, music, collecting British stamps and cribbage boards, computers and computer games, cricket, Bob Dylan, looking after grandchildren. *Address:* 115 Babington Road, Streatham, SW16 6AN. *T:* (020) 8480 9045. *E:* tony_hall@dsl.pipex.com. *Club:* Surrey CC.

HALL, Rev. Bernard, SJ; Spiritual Director, Infirmary of the Roman Delegation, Society of Jesus, since 2004 (Director, 2001–04); *b* 17 Oct. 1921. *Educ:* St Michael's Coll., Leeds; Heythrop Coll., Oxford. LicPhil, STL. Captain RA, 1941–46. Entered Society of Jesus, 1946; ordained priest, 1955; Provincial of the English Province, Society of Jesus, 1970–76; Rector, Collegio San Roberto Bellarmino, Rome, 1976–82 and 1989–94; English Asst to Father General, SJ, Rome, 1982–88; Superior, Jesuit Hse of Writers, Rome, 1994–2001. *Address:* Residenza di San Pietro Canisio, via dei Penitenzieri 20, 00193 Rome, Italy.

HALL, Betty, CBE 1977; Regional Nursing Officer, West Midlands Regional Health Authority, 1974–81; *b* 6 June 1921; *d* of John Hall and Jane (*née* Massey), Eagley, Lancs. *Educ:* Bolton Sch.; Royal Infirm., Edinburgh (RGN); Radcliffe Infirm., Oxford and St Mary's Hosp., Manchester (SCM); Royal Coll. of Nursing (RNT). Nursed tuberculous patients from concentration camps, Rollier Clinic, Leysin, 1948–49; Ward Sister, Salford Royal Hosp., 1949–51; Sister Tutor, Royal Masonic Hosp., London, 1952–54; Principal Tutor, St Luke's Hosp., Bradford, 1954–61 (Mem. Leeds Area Nurse Trng Cttee); King Edward's Hosp. Fund Admin. Staff Coll., 1961–62; Work Study Officer to United Bristol Hosps, 1961–64; Asst Nursing Officer to Birmingham Regional Hosp. Bd, 1964–65, Regional Nursing Officer, 1966–81. Mem., Exec. Cttee, Grange-over-Sands Abbeyfield Soc., 1982–93. Hon. Sec., Grange-over-Sands RUKBA, 1987–2001. *Recreations:* reading, tapestry making, cricket. *Address:* Chailey, Ash Mount Road, Grange-over-Sands, Cumbria LA11 6BX. *Club:* Naval and Military.

HALL, Brian; *see* Hall, F. B.

HALL, Prof. Bronwyn Hughes, PhD; Professor, Graduate School, University of California at Berkeley, since 2005 (Professor of Economics, 1999–2005, now Emeritus); Professor of Economics of Technology, University of Maastricht, since 2005; *b* 1 March 1945; *d* of Richard Roberts Hughes and Elizabeth Flandreau Hughes; *m* 1966, Robert Ernest Hall (marr. diss. 1983); one *s* one *d. Educ:* Wellesley Coll., Mass (BA 1966); Stanford Univ. (PhD 1988); MA Oxon 1997. Programmer: Lawrence Berkeley Lab., Berkeley, Calif, 1963–66; Lyman Lab. of Physics, Harvard Univ., 1966–67; Lawrence Berkeley Lab., 1967–70; Sen. Programmer, Harvard Inst. of Econ. Res., 1971–77; National Bureau of Economic Research, Cambridge, Massachusetts: Research Economist, 1977–88; Res. Associate, 1988–; Asst Prof., 1987–94, Assoc. Prof., 1994–99, Univ. of Calif, Berkeley; Internat. Res. Associate, Inst. for Fiscal Studies, London, 1995–; Prof. of Econs, and Fellow of Nuffield Coll., Oxford Univ., 1996–2001. Sloan Dissertation Fellow, 1985–86; Hoover Instn Nat. Fellow, 1992–93; Professorial Res. Fellow, UNU-MERIT, Netherlands, 2005–; Vis. Res. Fellow, NIESR, 2013–. Mem., Sci. Technol. and Econ. Policy Bd, Nat. Res. Council, Washington, 1999–2005. Owner and Partner, TSP Internat., Palo Alto, Calif, 1977–. Mem., Sigma Xi Soc., 1966. Associate Editor: Econs of Innovation and New Technol., 1994– (Mem. Editl Bd, 1989–94); Jl of Economic Behavior and Organization, 2001–07; Industrial and Corporate Change, 2009–; Mem. Adv. Bd, Internat. Finance jl, 1997–2005; Mem., Editl Bd, Res. Policy, 2006–13. *Publications:* TSP 4.3 User's Manual, 1977, rev. edn, version 5.1, 2009; TSP 4.3 Reference Manual, 1977, rev. edn, version 5.1, 2009; (ed jtly) Handbook of Economics of Innovation; contrib. articles to Amer. Econ. Rev., Econometrica, Jl Industrial Econs, Jl Econometrics, Brookings Papers on Econ. Activity, Econs of Innovation and New Technol., Rand Jl of Econs, Industrial and Corp. Change, Rev. of Econs and Stats, Small Business Econs Jl. *Recreations:* travel, walking, opera, painting. *Address:* Department of Economics, University of California at Berkeley, Berkeley, CA 94720, USA.

HALL, Christopher Myles; Editor of The Countryman, 1981–96; *b* 21 July 1932; *s* of Gilbert and Muriel Hall; *m* 1957, Jennifer Bevan Keech (marr. diss. 1980); one *s* one *d*; lives with Kate Ashbrook, *qv. Educ:* Berkhamsted Sch.; New Coll., Oxford (2nd cl. Hons PPE); Kellogg Coll., Oxford (MSt English Local History, with distinction, 1996). Reporter and Feature-writer, Daily Express, 1955–58; Sub-editor and Leader-writer, Daily Mirror, 1958–61; Feature-writer and Leader-writer, Daily Herald/Sun, 1961–65; Special Asst (Information): to Minister of Overseas Develt, 1965–66; to Minister of Transport, 1966–68; Chief Information Officer, MoT, 1968; Ramblers' Association: Sec., 1969–74; Mem. Exec. Cttee, 1982–84; Vice-Chm., 1984–87; Chm., 1987–90; Pres., 1990–93; Vice-Pres., 1993–; Chm., Oxfordshire Area, 1984–87, 1994–97, 2002–07, Footpaths and Publicity Sec., 1997–98; Dir, Council for Protection of Rural England, 1974–80. Pres., The Holiday Fellowship, 1974–77; Vice-Chm., S Reg. Council of Sport and Recreation, 1976–82; Member: DoT Cttee of Inquiry into Operators' Licensing, 1977–79; Common Land Forum, 1984–86; Countryside Access Forum, Oxon CC, 2003–06; Hon. Sec., Chiltern Soc., 1965–68; Chm., Oxfordshire Local Hist. Assoc., 2001–11. Columnist, Rambling Today, 1993–96; Editor, Oxfordshire Local History, 1997–; Sub-ed., ad familiares (Jl of Friends of Classics), 2008–. Publishing Award, British Assoc. for Local Hist., 2011. *Publications:* How to Run a Pressure Group, 1974; (jtly) The Countryside We Want, 1988; The Countryman's Yesterday, 1989; Scenes from The Countryman, 1992; contributions to: Motorways in London, 1969; No Through Road, 1975; The Countryman's Britain, 1976; Book of British Villages, 1980; Sunday Times Book of the Countryside, 1981; Walker's Britain, 1982; Britain on Backroads, 1985; Making Tracks, 1985; (with John Tookey) The Cotswolds, 1990; pamphlets; contrib. to Oxford DNB, Vole, The Countryman, New Statesman, New Scientist, The Geographical Magazine, Country Living, The Guardian and various jls. *Recreations:* local history, walking in the countryside. *Address:* Telfer's Cottage, Turville, Henley-on-Thames RG9 6QL. *T:* (01491) 638396. *Club:* Oxford and Cambridge.

HALL, David, CBE 1983; QPM 1977; consultant in security and personnel management; Chief Constable of Humberside Police, 1976–91; *b* 29 Dec. 1930; *s* of Arthur Thomas Hall and Dorothy May Charman; *m* 1952, Molly Patricia Knight; two *s. Educ:* Richmond and East Sheen Grammar School for Boys. Joined Metropolitan Police and rose through ranks from PC to Chief Supt, 1950–68; Staff Officer to Chief Inspector of Constabulary, Col Sir Eric St Johnson, 1968; Asst Chief Constable, 1970, Dep. Chief Constable, 1976, Staffordshire Police. Vice-Pres., Assoc. of Chief Police Officers of England, Wales and NI, 1982–83, Pres. 1983–84. CCMI (CBIM 1988). Freeman, City of London, 1987. OStJ 1980. *Recreations:* gardening, walking, playing the piano. *Address:* Fairlands, 1 Copper Beech Close, West Leys Park, Kemp Road, Swanland, North Ferriby HU14 3LR.

HALL, Sir David (Christopher), 4th Bt *cr* 1923, of Grafham, co. Surrey; *b* 30 Dec. 1937; *yr s* of Sir Frederick Henry Hall, 2nd Bt and Olwen Irene (*née* Collis); *S* brother, 2013; *m* 1st, 1962, Irene Duncan (marr. diss. 1987; she *d* 2014); one *s* one *d*; 2nd, 1991, Annie Madelaine Renée Olivier, adopted *d* of late Bottemanne Raouald. *Heir: s* John Christopher Hall, *b* 22 May 1965.

HALL, Prof. Sir David (Michael Baldock), Kt 2003; FRCP, FRCPCH; Hon. Professor of Community Paediatrics, University of Cape Town, since 2007; Professor of Community Paediatrics, University of Sheffield, 1993–2005, now Emeritus; President, Royal College of Paediatrics and Child Health, 2000–03; *b* 4 Aug. 1945; *s* of Ronald Hall and Ethel Gwen Hall (*née* Baldock); *m* 1966, Susan M. Luck; two *d. Educ:* Reigate Grammar Sch.; St George's Hosp., London Univ. (MB BS; BSc; Univ. Gold Medal). FRCP 1986; FRCPCH 1996. SMO, Baragwanath Hosp., Johannesburg, 1973–76; Sen. Registrar, Charing Cross Hosp., 1976–78; Consultant Paediatrician, St George's Hosp., 1978–93. Hon. FRCPE 2003. Mem., Breede River Winelands Rotary Club (former Pres.). *Publications:* Health for All Children, 1989, rev. 4th edn 2006; Child Surveillance Handbook, 1990, 3rd edn 2009; Child with a Disability, 1996; contrib. numerous papers to jls, etc. *Recreation:* travel. *Address:* Storrs House Farm, Storrs Lane, Stannington, Sheffield S6 6GY. *E:* d.hall@sheffield.ac.uk.

HALL, Col David Stevenson, CBE 1993; TD 1971 (and bars 1977, 1983, 1989); Chairman: Meadowcroft Management Ltd, since 1985; NHS Logistics Agency, 2000–02; *b* 29 March 1938; *s* of late Robert Hall and Maude Hall; *m* 1962, Marion Esmé Blundstone; one *s* one *d. Educ:* Scarborough Coll. Nat. Service, RAOC, 1956–58. Man. Dir, UDS Tailoring Ltd, 1979–81; Chm. and Man. Dir, Collier Holdings plc, 1982–85. Non-executive Director: Sharp and Law plc, 1989–90; Toye plc, 1994–95. Chairman: United Leeds Teaching Hosps NHS Trust, 1995–98; NHS Supplies, 1998–2000. Trustee, RAOC Charitable Trust, 1993–2000. RAOC (TA), 1958–93; Col, 1985–89; ADC, 1986–91; TA Col Logistics MoD/UKLF, 1989–93; Hon. Col, RAOC Specialist Units, 1991–93; Combat Services Support Group, RLC(V), 1995–2000. Freeman, City of London, 1993. *Recreations:* cricket, reading. *Address:* Courtways, Potterton Court, Barwick in Elmet, Leeds LS15 4HP. *T:* (0113) 281 3587. *Clubs:* Army and Navy (Vice-Chm., 2003–05), MCC; Yorkshire County Cricket (Chm., Archives Cttee, 2005–10; Vice Pres., 2011–).

HALL, Duncan; Managing Director, Duncan Hall Associates Ltd, since 1998; *b* 2 Sept. 1947; *s* of Leslie and Joan Elizabeth Hall; two *s* one *d*; *m* 2004, Fiona Mary Blackwell. *Educ:* Acklam Hall Grammar Sch.; LLB Hons. Articled Clerk and Senior Legal Assistant, Wellingborough UDC, 1970–74; Corby District Council: PA to Chief Exec., 1974–75; Asst Chief Exec., 1975–78; Housing and Property Controller, 1978–79; Chief Exec., 1980–87; Chief Exec., Teesside Develt Corp., 1987–98. FRSA. *Recreations:* reading, travel, music, theatre. *Address:* Duncan Hall Associates Ltd, Ivor House, 1 South Green, Staindrop, Darlington, Co. Durham DL2 3LD. *T:* (01833) 660077.

HALL, Edward Peter; theatre director; *b* 27 Nov. 1966; *s* of Sir Peter Reginald Frederick Hall, *qv* and Jacqueline Hall; *m* 2000, Issy van Randwyck; two *d. Educ:* Bedales Sch.; Univ. of Leeds; Mountview Theatre Sch. Associate, NT, 2004–; Associate Director: Watermill Th. Co., 2006–; Old Vic, 2006–; Founder and Artistic Dir, Propeller Th. Co., 1997–; Artistic Dir, Hampstead Th., 2010–. Watermill Theatre productions: Othello, 1995; Propeller Theatre Co. productions include: Henry V, 1997; The Comedy of Errors, 1998; Twelfth Night, 1999; Rose Rage (adaptation of Shakespeare's Henry VI trilogy), 2001, transf. Th. Royal, Haymarket, 2002; A Midsummer Night's Dream, transf. Comedy Th., 2003; The Winter's Tale, 2005; The Taming of the Shrew, and Twelfth Night, 2006, transf. Old Vic, 2007; For Services Rendered, 2007; Merchant of Venice, 2009; Richard III, and The Comedy of Errors, 2011 (Best Touring Production, TMA Awards, 2011); Henry V, The Winter's Tale, 2012; A Midsummer Night's Dream, 2013; The Comedy of Errors, 2014; Hampstead Theatre productions: Enlightenment, 2010; Loyalty, No Naughty Bits, 2011; Chariots of Fire, 2012, transf. Gielgud Th.; Raving, 2013; Sunny Afternoon, transf. Harold Pinter Th., 2014; Wonderland, 2014; other productions include: Two Gentlemen of Verona, Henry V, 2000; Julius Caesar, RSC, 2001; Edmond, 2003, A Funny Thing Happened on the Way to the Forum, 2004, Once in a Lifetime, 2005, NT; A Streetcar Named Desire, Roundabout Th., NY, 2005; The Deep Blue Sea, Vaudeville, 2008; Two Men of Florence, Boston, 2009; (co-dir) Tantalus, Denver, 2000, UK tour and Barbican, 2001; The Constant Wife, Apollo, 2002; Macbeth, Albery, 2002; Calico, Duke of York's, 2004. Director: Into Exile, Dear Exile, Radio 4; Restless, BBC TV/Sundance; episodes of TV series, Miss Marple, Trial and Retribution, Kingdom, Spooks, Strike Back, Downton Abbey, Partners in Crime. *Publications:* Rose Rage, 2001; (ed) A Midsummer Night's Dream, 2003. *Address:* c/o Casarotto Ramsay & Associates Ltd, Waverley House, 7–12 Noel Street, W1F 8GQ.

HALL, Prof. Elizabeth Anne Howlett, (Lisa), CBE 2015; PhD; CChem, FRSC; Professor of Analytical Biotechnology, Institute of Biotechnology, since 2003, and Deputy Head (Research), Department of Chemical Engineering and Biotechnology, since 2010, University of Cambridge; Fellow, since 1988, and Vice President, since 2013, Queens' College, Cambridge; *b* Bromley, Kent, 28 Nov. 1952; *d* of Philip Sydney Hall and Joan Howlett; *m* 2013, Dr John Robert Saffell; one step *s* one step *d. Educ:* Stratford Hse Sch., Kent; Queen Mary Coll., Univ. of London (BSc Chem. 1974; PhD 1977); Queens' Coll., Cambridge (MA 1988). CChem 1983; FRSC 2005. Asst de Récherche, Univ. of Clermont, France, 1977–78; Res. Associate, Johannes Gutenberg Univ., Mainz, Germany, 1978–80; Sen. Analyst, Bernard Dyer and Partners (1948) Ltd, London, 1980–81; Res. Fellow, Nuffield Dept of Anaesthetics, Univ. of Oxford, 1981–85; New Blood Lectr, 1985–99, Reader, 1999–2003, Inst. of Biotechnol., Univ. of Cambridge. Queen Eugene Vis. Prof., Complutense Univ. of Madrid, 2005–06. Chm., Editl Bd, Analyst, 2006–10. Co-Founder and Dir, CamBridgeSens, 2008–. Mem., Diagnostics Adv. Cttee, NICE, 2010–12. Vice Pres., Analytical Div., RSC, 2006–08. Chm., Disability Snowsport UK, 1993–. *Publications:* contrib. articles to learned sci. and engrg jls. *Recreations:* ski-ing, adaptive snowsport, sailing, woodcrafts, DIY. *Address:* Queens' College, Silver Street, Cambridge CB3 9ET. *E:* lisa.hall@biotech.cam.ac.uk.

HALL, Sir Ernest, Kt 1993; OBE 1986; DL; pianist and composer, since 1954; property developer, since 1971; Chairman, Dean Clough Business, Arts and Education Centre, 1983–2007; *b* 19 March 1930; *s* of Ernest and Mary Elizabeth Hall; *m* 1st, 1951, June (*née* Annable) (*d* 1994); two *s* two *d*; 2nd, 1975, Sarah (*née* Wellby); one *s. Educ:* Bolton County Grammar Sch.; Royal Manchester Coll. of Music (ARMCM (teacher and performer) 1950–51; Royal Patron's Fund Prize for Composition, 1951). Textile manufr, 1961–71. Dep. Chm., Eureka! Children's Museum, 1989–2000; Mem., Arts Council of England (formerly of GB), 1990–97; Chm., Yorks and Humberside Arts Bd, 1991–97; Pres., Yorks Business in the Arts, 1990–; Vice-Pres., RSA, 1994–99. Trustee: Yorkshire Sculpture Park, 1989–2003; Henry Moore Foundn, 1999–2002. Founder, Camel House Concerts, Lanzarote, 2010.

Chancellor, Univ. of Huddersfield, 1996–2003. DL W Yorks, 1991. Hon. Fellow: Huddersfield Polytechnic, 1989; Leeds Polytechnic, 1991; Bolton Inst., 1994. DUniv: York, 1986; Leeds Metropolitan, 1996; Hon. DLitt Bradford, 1990; Hon. DArt Bristol Poly., 1991; Hon. LLD Leeds, 1996. Envmt Award, Business and Industry Panel, RSA, 1988; Guildhall Helping Hand, Nat. Fedn of Self-Employed and Small Businesses, 1989; Special Free Enterprise Award, Aims of Industry, 1989; Best Practice Award, BURA, 1992; Lifetime Achievement Award, Inst. for Social Inventions, 1992; Albert Medal, RSA, 1994; Montblanc de la Culture UK Award, Fondation d'Enterprise, France, 1996; Goodman Award, ABSA, 1997. *Publications:* How to be a Failure and Succeed (autobiog.), 2008. *Recreations:* gardening, art collecting, theatre, languages. *T:* (Lanzarote) (928) 834150.

HALL, Fiona Jane, MBE 2013; advisor; Member (Lib Dem) North East Region, European Parliament, 2004–14; Leader, Liberal Democrat European Parliamentary Party, 2009–14; *b* 15 July 1955; *d* of Edward and Dorothy Cutts; *m* 1975, Michael Hall (marr. diss. 2009); two *d*. *Educ:* St Hugh's Coll., Oxford (MA Mod. Langs 1976); Oxford Poly. (PGCE). Teacher in self-help sch., Naledi, Gaborone, Botswana, 1977–79; pt-time, supply teacher, tutor, 1986–95; Asst to Newcastle City Councillors, 1994–97; Press Officer to Lembit Öpik, MP and Richard Livsey, MP, 1997–99; Researcher and Organiser to Rt Hon. Alan Beith, MP, 1999–2004. *Address:* The School House, Whittingham, Alnwick, Northumberland NE66 4UP. *T:* (01665) 574383.

HALL, (Frederick) Brian; Master (Care and Protection), Supreme Court of Judicature of Northern Ireland, 1986–2006; *b* 2 Oct. 1934; *s* of Frederick Hall and late Mary Hall (*née* Kernahan); *m* 1965, Isobel Frances Deirdre Boyce; two *d*. *Educ:* Coleraine Academical Instn; Queen's Univ. Belfast (LLB). Admitted Solicitor, NI, 1958; Legal Adviser, Min. of Home Affairs, 1972; Asst Solicitor, NI Office, 1973; Dep. Dir, NI Court Service, 1979; Official Solicitor to Supreme Court, NI, 1982. Mem., Sec. of State's Cttee on County Courts and Magistrates' Courts, 1974. *Recreations:* golf, travel, reading. *Club:* Royal Belfast Golf.

HALL, Gareth John; on secondment from Welsh Government to promote proposed nuclear new build project and other major energy generation projects on Anglesey, since 2011; *b* 26 June 1956; *s* of late Trevor John Grenville Hall and Margaret Gwendoline Hall (*née* Jones); *m* 1986, Moira Ann Llewellyn. *Educ:* Brecon Boys' Grammar Sch.; Bristol Poly. (BSc 1977); Univ. of Reading (MSc 1981); Cardiff Univ. (MBA 1989). MRICS 1980. Valuation Office, SE London, 1977–80; Defence Land Agent, Wales, MoD, 1981–91; jsdc, 1991; Welsh Development Agency: Sen. Manager on land reclamation, property and regeneration projects, 1991–97; Regl Dir, SW Wales, Strategy Develt, 1997–2004; Chief Exec., 2004–06; Dir, then Dir Gen., Dept for Enterprise, Innovation and Networks, later for Econ. and Transport, 2006–11, Welsh Assembly Govt. Chm., Wales European Centre, Brussels, 2003–15. Vis. Lectr, Sch. of Planning and Geography (formerly Dept of City and Regl Planning), Cardiff Univ., 1995–. Mem., Nat. and Regl Gp, LOCOG, 1997–2011. Gov., Swansea Coll., 1998–2000. *Recreation:* sawing logs for wood burning stove. *T:* 07788 185430. *E:* gareth.hall@wales.gsi.gov.uk.

HALL, Sir Geoffrey, Kt 2012; Chair, Information Authority, 2011–13; *b* Sutton Coldfield, 26 Jan. 1951; *s* of late Leonard and Florence Hall; *m* 1976, Fionnuala Mary; one *s* one *d*. *Educ:* Bishop Vesey's Grammar Sch., Sutton Coldfield; Liverpool Univ. (BA Hons 1972); Manchester Poly. (Dip. Mgt Educn 1982). Further Educn Officer, Birmingham LEA, 1984–88; Dir of Educn, London Bor. of Bexley, 1988–93; Director: FEFC, 1993–2000; LSC, 2000–02; Dep. Chief Exec., 2002–03, Principal and Chief Exec., 2004–11, New Coll. Nottingham. *Publications:* (contrib.) British Politics Today, 1976; Managing and Changing Further Education, 1988; (contrib.) Unfinished Business in Widening Participation, 2008; (contrib.) Global Development of Community Colleges, 2008. *Recreations:* walking our two setters, current affairs, watching Rugby Union.

HALL, Prof. George Martin, PhD, DSc; FRCA; Foundation Professor of Anaesthesia, St George's, University of London (formerly St George's Hospital Medical School), since 1992; *b* 14 May 1944; *s* of George Vincent Hall and Dora Hortensia Hall; *m* 1964, Marion Edith Burgin; one *d*. *Educ:* University Coll. Hosp. Med. Sch. (MB BS 1967; PhD 1976); DSc London, 1999. FRCA 1971. Royal Postgraduate Medical School: Sen. Lectr in Anaesthesia, 1977–85; Reader, 1985–89; Prof. of Clinical Anaesthesia, 1989–92. Hunterian Prof., RCS, 1983–84. *Publications:* How to Write a Paper, 1994, 5th edn 2012; How to Survive in Anaesthesia, 1997, 4th edn 2012; Short Practice of Anaesthesia, 1997; Diabetes: emergency and hospital management, 1999; Perioperative Care of the Eye Patient, 2000; How to Present at Meetings, 2001, 3rd edn 2012; res. papers on anaesthesia and physiology. *Recreations:* running, cycling, supporting Staffordshire. *Address:* Department of Anaesthesia and Intensive Care Medicine, St George's, University of London, SW17 0RE. *T:* (020) 8725 2836. *Club:* Farmers.

HALL, Rev. Canon George Rumney, CVO 2003 (LVO 1999); Rector of the Sandringham Group of Parishes, and Domestic Chaplain to the Queen, 1987–2003; Chaplain to the Queen, 1989–2007; *b* 7 Nov. 1937; *s* of John Hall; *m* 1965, Diana Lesley Brunning; one *s* one *d*. *Educ:* Brasted Place, Kent; Westcott House, Cambridge. Deacon 1962, priest 1963; Assistant Curate: St Philip's, Camberwell, 1962–65; Holy Trinity, Waltham Cross, 1965–67; Rector of Buckenham, Hassingham, Strumpshaw, dio. Norwich, 1967–74; Chaplain: St Andrew's Psychiatric Hosp., Norwich, 1967–72; HM Prison, Norwich, 1972–74; Vicar of Wymondham, 1974–87; RD of Humbleyard, 1986–87; Hon. Canon, Norwich Cathedral, 1987–2003, now Canon Emeritus; RD of Heacham and Rising, 1989–2001. Founder Mem., Wymondham Branch of Mind Day Centre; Mem. Bd, Cotman Housing Assoc., Norwich. *Recreations:* walking, reading, theatre, music. *Address:* Town Farm Cottage, Lynn Road, Bircham, King's Lynn, Norfolk PE31 6RJ. *T:* (01485) 576134. *E:* george_hall@btinternet.com.

HALL, Sir Graham (Joseph), Kt 2003; Chairman, Leeds Bradford International Airport, 2007–08; *b* 12 Oct. 1943; *s* of Herbert and Phyllis Hall; *m* 1963, Pamela Wilmot; one *s* one *d*. *Educ:* Doncaster Technical Coll.; Rotherham Coll. of Technol. (DipEE 1967); Blackburn Coll. of Technol. CEng 1977; FIET (FIEE 1988). Commercial Dir, 1984–89, Divl Dir, Energy Supply, 1989–91, Yorkshire Electricity Bd; Gp Exec. Dir, 1991–97, Gp Ops Dir, 1997, Chief Exec., 1998–2001, Yorkshire Electricity Gp plc. Chm., Regl Develt Agency for Yorkshire and the Humber (Yorkshire Forward), 1998–2003. Mem. Ct Dirs, Bank of England, 2001–07. Chm., Yorks and the Humber Regl Council, CBI, 1997–99. CCMI 2002 (FIMgt 1987). Hon. DEng Bradford, 1999. *Recreations:* gardening, golf, international travel.

HALL, Prof. Henry Edgar, FRS 1982; Emeritus Professor of Physics, University of Manchester, since 1995; *b* 1928; *s* of John Ainger Hall; *m* 1962, Patricia Anne Broadbent; two *s* one *d*. *Educ:* Latymer Upper Sch., Hammersmith; Emmanuel Coll., Cambridge. BA 1952; PhD 1956. At Royal Society Mond Laboratory, Cambridge, 1952–58; Senior Student, Royal Commission for the Exhibition of 1851, 1955–57; Research Fellow of Emmanuel Coll., 1955–58; Lecturer in Physics, 1958–61, Prof. of Physics, 1961–95, Univ. of Manchester. Visiting Professor: Univ. of Western Australia, 1964; Univ. of Oregon, 1967–68; Cornell Univ., 1974, 1982–83; Univ. of Tokyo, 1985. Simon Memorial Prize (with W. F. Vinen), 1963; Guthrie Medal and Prize, 2004. *Publications:* Solid State Physics, 1974; papers in scientific journals. *Recreation:* mountain walking. *Address:* The Schuster Laboratory, The University, Manchester M13 9PL.

HALL, Air Vice-Marshal Hubert Desmond, CB 1979; CMG 2003; CBE 1972; AFC 1963; FRAeS; RAF retd; *b* 3 June 1925; *s* of Charles William and Violet Victoria Kate Hall; *m* 1951, Mavis Dorothea (*née* Hopkins). *Educ:* Portsmouth Municipal Coll. Commissioned RAF, 1945; RAF Coll., Cranwell QFI, 1951–55; Flt Comdr, 9 Sqdn, 1955–56; 232 OCU Gaydon, Sqdn Ldr, Medium Bomber Force; Instructor, Wing Comdr 1962; 3 Group Headquarters (Training), 1963–65; Air Warfare Coll., 1965; commanded No 57 Sqdn (Victors), 1966–68; Gp Captain Nuclear Operations SHAPE HQ, 1968–71; comd RAF Waddington, 1971–73; Overseas Coll. of Defence Studies India, 1974; MoD: Director (Air Cdre) of Establishments, RAF, 1975–77; Air Comdr Malta, 1977–79; Air Vice-Marshal 1979; Defence Advr, Canberra, 1980–82. Pres., ACT, Australian-Britain Soc., 1993–2003. Mem., Lord's Taverners, ACT, 1989– (Foundg Chm., 1985–88). Mem., St John Council, ACT, 1983–. KStJ 1992. Queen's Commendation, 1957. *Recreations:* gardening, reading. *Clubs:* Royal Air Force; Commonwealth (Canberra).

HALL, Sir Iain (Robert), Kt 2002; education consultant; Chief Executive, Great Schools for All Children, since 2012; Executive Principal: King's Leadership Academy, Warrington, since 2012; Hawthornes' Free School, Bootle, since 2012; *b* 13 Feb. 1943; *s* of Edward and Annie Hall; three *s* from former *m*. *Educ:* Liverpool Collegiate Sch.; Liverpool Univ. (BSc). Physics teacher, Liverpool Inst., 1965–72; Hd of Sci., Brookfield Sch., Kirkby, 1972–78; Dep. Headteacher, Glenburn High Sch., Lancs, 1978–82; Headteacher: Breckfield Sch., Liverpool, 1982–91; Parrs Wood Technol. Coll., Manchester, 1991–2003. Mem., Gov. Council, Nat. Coll. of Sch. Leadership, 2002. Associate Dir, Schools Network, 2002–12. Advr, Oasis Community Learning, 2012–; Educn Advr, Oasis Academies, 2012– (Principal, Oasis Acad., Oldham, 2011–12); Leadership Advr, Teach First, 2009–12. *Publications:* Nuffield Physics, 1985; contribs to various educnl mags. *Recreations:* cooking, supporter of Liverpool FC. *E:* IainRHall@btconnect.com.

HALL, James Douglas Ellis; Chairman: Carbon Clear Ltd, since 2011; Save Britain's Heritage, since 2012; *b* 9 Oct. 1954; *s* of (William) Douglas Hall and (Helen) Elizabeth Hall; *m* 1980, Carol; two *d*. *Educ:* Edinburgh Acad.; Univ. of Aberdeen (MA Hons Pol Studies). Accenture, 1976–2006: UK Man. Partner, 1994–2000; Global Man. Partner, Technol. and Systems Integration, 2001–05; Chief Exec., Identity and Passport Service, 2006–10; Registrar Gen. for England and Wales, 2008–10. Commn on Public Policy and British Business, 1996–97. Mem. Court, Univ. of Aberdeen, 2011–. *Recreations:* camera, rod and gun. *Address:* Barlaston Hall, Staffordshire ST12 9AT.

HALL, Prof. James William, PhD; FREng, FICE; Professor of Climate and Environmental Risks, and Director, Environmental Change Institute, University of Oxford, since 2011; Fellow of Linacre College, Oxford, since 2011; *b* Sidcup, Kent, 6 May 1968; *s* of Dr David Sunderland Hall and Gillian Mary Hall; *m* 1999, Laura Madurini; one *s* two *d*. *Educ:* Eltham Coll.; Univ. of Bristol (BEng 1st Cl. Civil Engrg 1990; PhD 1999); MA Oxon 2011. CEng 1996; MICE 1996, FICE 2005; FREng 2011. Engineer: VSO, Guyana, 1991–93; HR Wallingford, 1993–95; Lectr, 1998–2004, Reader, 2004, Univ. of Bristol; Prof., Newcastle Univ., 2004–11. Mem., Adaptation Sub-Cttee, Cttee on Climate Change, 2009–. Fellow, Royal Statistical Soc., 2004. Associate Ed., Jl of Flood Risk Mgt, 2007–. *Publications:* Flood Risk Management in Europe, 2007; Applied Uncertainty Analysis for Flood Risk Management, 2014; The Future of National Infrastructure Systems, 2015. *Recreation:* mountaineering. *Address:* Oxford University Centre for the Environment, South Parks Road, Oxford OX1 3QY. *T:* (01865) 275846, *Fax:* (01865) 275850. *E:* jim.hall@eci.ox.ac.uk. *Club:* Alpine.

HALL, Janice Elizabeth, (Jan), OBE 1996; Partner, JCA Group, since 2005; *b* 1 June 1957; *d* of John Brian Hall and late Jean Hall; one *s*. *Educ:* St Anne's Coll., Oxford (MA Hons). Mktg Manager, ICI, 1979–83; Chm. and Chief Exec., Coley Porter Bell, 1983–93; Eur. Chief Exec., GGT Gp, 1994–97; Partner, Spencer Stuart, 1997–2005. Sen. non-exec. Dir, First Choice Holidays, 1994–2003. Hon. Prof., Warwick Business Sch., 1995–2008 (Mem., Bd, 1993–). Mem. Council, IoD, 1991–2005. Mem. Adv. Bd, Saïd Business Sch., Univ. of Oxford, 2009–. *Publications:* Dementia Essentials, 2013. *Address:* 37 St John's Wood Road, NW8 8RA.

HALL, Jean Morag; *see* Rankine, J. M.

HALL, Joan Valerie, CBE 1990; Member, Central Transport Consultative Committee, 1981–86; *b* 31 Aug. 1935; *d* of late Robert Percy Hall and Winifred Emily Umbers. *Educ:* Queen Margaret's Sch., Escrick, York; Ashridge House of Citizenship. Contested (C) Barnsley, 1964 and 1966. MP (C) Keighley, 1970–Feb. 1974; PPS to Minister of State for Agriculture, Fisheries and Food, 1972–74. Vice-Chm., Greater London Young Conservatives, 1964. Chm., Sudan Studies Soc. of UK, 1989–92. Mem. Council, Univ. of Buckingham (formerly University Coll. Buckingham), 1977–. *Address:* 7 Greenland, High Hoyland, Barnsley, South Yorks S75 4AZ.

HALL, John; *see* Hall, W. J.

HALL, Sir John, Kt 1991; DL; Chairman: Cameron Hall Developments Ltd, 1973–93; Newcastle United Football Club, 1992–97; a Director, Bank of England, 1996–98; *b* 21 March 1933; *m* Mae; one *s* one *d*. *Educ:* Bedlington Grammar Sch. Chartered surveyor. Developed MetroCentre (shopping and leisure complex), Gateshead, 1985. Mem., Millennium Commn, 1994–2000. Gordon Grand Fellow, Yale Univ., 1991. DL Co. Durham, 2007. Hon. DCL: Newcastle upon Tyne, 1988; Durham, 1995. NE Business Man of the Year, 1987. *Address:* Wynyard Hall, Billingham, Cleveland TS22 5NF.

HALL, Ven. John Barrie; Archdeacon of Salop, 1998–2011, now Archdeacon Emeritus; *b* 27 May 1941; *s* of Arthur Cyril Hall and Beatrice Hall (*née* Clark); *m* 1963, Kay Deakin; three *s*. *Educ:* Salisbury and Wells Theol Coll. Self-employed in garage and caravan sales until 1982; ordained deacon 1984, priest 1985; Curate, St Edward, Cheddleton, 1984–88; Vicar, Rocester, then Rocester and Croxden with Hollington, 1988–98. Mem., Gen. Synod of C of E, 2002–10. Hon. Canon of Lichfield Cathedral, 1999. Lichfield Diocese: Chairman: Redundant Church Users' Cttee, 2001–11; Child Protection Cttee, 2002–11; Pastoral Cttee, 2006–11; Adv. Cttee on care of churches, 2014–; Vice Chm., Bd of Finance, 2007–11. Mem., C of E Inter-Diocesan Finance Forum, 2007–11. Pres., Adv. Cttee, Telford Christian Council, 2007–11. Chairman: Shropshire Historical Churches Trust, 1998–2011; Staffs Historic Churches Trust, 2013–. *Recreations:* reading, a little walking, most sports (now watching only), cooking, building a model railway. *Address:* 16 Mill House Drive, Cheadle, Stoke-on-Trent ST10 1XL.

HALL, Sir John (Bernard), 3rd Bt *cr* 1919; Chairman, The Nikko Bank (UK) plc, 1992–95 (Managing Director, 1990–92); *b* 20 March 1932; *s* of Lieut-Col Sir Douglas Montgomery Bernard Hall, DSO, 2nd Bt, and Ina Nancie Walton (Nancie Lady Hall), *d* of late Col John Edward Mellor, CB (she *m* 2nd, 1962, Col Peter J. Bradford, DSO, MC, TD, who *d* 1990; she *d* 1998); *S* father, 1962; *m* 1957, Delia Mary (*d* 1997), *d* of late Lieut-Col J. A. Innes, DSO; one *s* two *d*; *m* 1998, Diana Joan Tower, *d* of late Surg.-Comdr E. R. Sorley and *widow* of Peter Ravenshear. *Educ:* Eton; Trinity Coll., Oxford (MA). FCIB 1976. Lieut, Royal Fusiliers (RARO). J. Henry Schroder Wagg & Co. Ltd, formerly J. Henry Schröder & Co., 1955–73 (Dir, 1967–73); Director: The Antofagasta (Chili) and Bolivia Rly Co. Ltd, 1967–73; Bank of America International, 1974–82; Man. Dir, European Brazilian Bank, subseq. Eurobraz, 1983–89 (Dir, 1976–89); a Vice-Pres., Bank of America NT & SA, 1982–90; Chm., Assoc. of British Consortium Banks, 1985–86. Chm., Anglo-Colombian Soc., 1978–81. Mem., St

Alban's Diocesan Synod and Bd of Finance, 1992–2000. Pres., Blindaid (formerly Metropolitan Soc. for the Blind), 2004–12. FRGS 1988; FRSA 1989–2013. Mem., Lord Mayor of London's No 1 Cttee, 1993–95; Liveryman: Clothworkers' Co., 1957 (Mem., Court of Assts, 1987–2007, Asst Emeritus, 2007; Master, 1999–2000); Co. of Internat. Bankers, 2007–13. Mem. Court, Univ. of Leeds, 1994–2000. *Recreations:* travel, fishing. *Heir: s* David Bernard Hall, *b* 12 May 1961. *Address:* Deanery Lodge, Church Walk, Hadleigh, Ipswich, Suffolk IP7 5ED. *T:* (01473) 828966. *Clubs:* Boodle's, Lansdowne.

HALL, Sir John Douglas Hoste, 15th Bt *cr* 1687 (NS), of Dunglass, Haddingtonshire; Professor of Performance Writing, Falmouth University (formerly University College Falmouth), since 2010; *b* 7 Jan. 1945; *s* of Sir Douglas Basil Hall, 14th Bt, KCMG and Rachel Marion Gartside-Tippinge; *S* father, 2004; *m* 1972, Angela Margaret, *d* of George Keys (marr. diss. 2009); two *s*. *Educ:* Dover Coll.; Gonville and Caius Coll., Cambridge (BA); Southampton Univ. (Cert Ed); Dartington Coll. of Arts, Plymouth (PhD). Dartington College of Arts, later University College Falmouth: Vice-Principal (Academic), 1990–2002; Associate Dir of Res., 2002–10. *Publications:* (*poems*): Between the Cities, 1968; Days, 1972; Meaning Insomnia, 1978; Malo-lactic Ferment, 1978; Couch Grass, 1978; Else Here: selected poems, 1999; Couldn't You?, 2007; The Week's Bad Groan, 2008; (with Peter Hughes) Interscriptions, 2011; Keepsache, 2013; (*novel*) Apricot Pages, 2005; (*essays*): Thirteen Ways of Talking about Performance Writing, 2008; Essays on Performance Writing, Poetics and Poetry, 2013: vol. 1, On Performance Writing, with Pedagogical Sketches; vol. 2, Writings towards Writing and Reading: on Poetics, with implicated readings. *Heir: s* Thomas James Hall, *b* 10 Dec. 1975.

HALL, John Leonard; *see* Graham-Hall.

HALL, Dr John Lewis; Senior Fellow, National Institute of Standards and Technology, USA, Emeritus since 2004; *b* Aug. 1934; *s* of John Ernest Hall and Elizabeth Rae Hall (*née* Long); *m* 1958, Marilyn Charlene Robinson; two *s* one *d*. *Educ:* Carnegie Mellon Univ., Pittsburgh (BS 1956, MS 1958; PhD Physics 1961). National Bureau of Standards, later National Institute of Standards and Technology, USA: Postdoctoral Res. Associate, Washington, 1961–62; Physicist, Boulder, Colo, 1962–75; Sen. Scientist, 1975–2004; Lectr, 1997, Prof. Adjoint, 2007–, Dept of Physics, Univ. of Colorado. Adv. Prof., E China Normal Univ., Shanghai, 1995. Mem., NAS. Hon. Dr: Paris Nord, 1989; Carnegie-Mellon, 2006; Glasgow, 2007; Ohio State, 2008. (Jtly) Nobel Prize for Physics, 2005. Légion d'Honneur (France), 2004. *Publications:* (ed) Laser Spectroscopy III, 1977; 235 papers in jls; 11 US patents. *Recreations:* music, electronic hobbies, reading, travel. *Address:* JILA, University of Colorado, Boulder, CO 80309–0440, USA. *T:* (303) 4927843, *Fax:* (303) 4925235. *E:* jhall@jila.colorado.edu.

HALL, John Peirs; Chief Executive (formerly Managing Director), Brewin Dolphin Holdings PLC, 1987–2007; *b* 26 June 1940; *s* of Robert Noel Hall and Doreen Cecelia Hall (*née* Russell); *m* 1965, Sarah Gillian Page; three *s* (and one *s* decd). *Educ:* Stowe. Read Hurst-Brown, Stockbrokers, 1959–65; joined Wontner Renwick & Francis, 1965, which became Wontner Dolphin & Francis, 1970, then Brewin Dolphin Hldgs PLC, 1974; Partner, 1967; Chm., Mgt Cttee, 1980. Chm., Strategic Protection Ltd, 2014–. Chm., Assoc. of Private Client Investment Managers and Stockbrokers, 2006–12. Freeman, City of London, 1970; Mem., Ct of Assts, Co. of Merchant Taylors, 1993– (Master, 2005–06). *Recreations:* sailing, golf, breeding British White cattle, Suffolk horse breeding. *Address:* Chalkhouse Green Farm, Kidmore End, near Reading RG4 9AL. *T:* (0118) 972 3631. *Clubs:* City of London; Royal Yacht Squadron, Island Sailing; Huntercombe Golf.

HALL, Very Rev. John Robert; Dean of Westminster, since 2006; Dean of the Order of the Bath, since 2006; *b* 13 March 1949; *e s* of late Ronald John Hall, FCIB, FCIS and Katie Margaret Brock Hall (*née* Walker). *Educ:* St Dunstan's Coll.; St Chad's Coll., Durham (BA Hons Theol.; Hon. Fellow 2009); Cuddesdon Theol Coll. Head of RE, Malet Lambert High Sch., Hull, 1971–73; ordained deacon 1975, priest 1976; Curate, St John the Divine, Kennington, 1975–78; Priest-in-charge, All Saints', S Wimbledon, 1978–84; Vicar, St Peter's, Streatham, 1984–92; Dir of Educn, Dio. Blackburn, 1992–98; Residentiary Canon, Blackburn Cathedral, 1994–98, Canon Emeritus, 2000 (Hon. Canon, 1992–94, 1998–2000); Gen. Sec., C of E Bd of Educn, subseq. Chief Educn Officer, C of E, and Gen. Sec., Nat. Soc. for Promoting Religious Educn, 1998–2006; Hon. Curate, St Alban's, S Norwood, 2003–06; Hon. Pres., Coll. of St Barnabas Lingfield, 2013–. Examng Chaplain to Bp of Southwark, 1988–92. Member: Gen. Synod of C of E, 1984–92; C of E Bd of Educn, 1991–92; Lancs Educn Cttee, 1992–98; Council, National Soc., 1997–98; Gen. Teaching Council, 2000–04. Chm., Standards Cttee, City of Westminster, 2008–12. Chm., Fedn of Catholic Priests, 1991–94. Mem. Council, Sch. of St Mary and St Anne, Abbots Bromley, 1992–2002; Governor: St Martin's Coll., Lancaster, 1992–98; St Dunstan's Coll., 2002–11; Sutton Valence Sch., 2013–; Chairman of Governors: Westminster Sch., 2006–; Harris Westminster Sixth Form, 2014–; Member, Governing Body: Urban Learning Foundn, 1998–2002; Canterbury Christ Church Univ. (formerly University Coll.), 1999–2006 (Hon. Fellow, 2007); Pro Chancellor, Roehampton Univ., 2011–. Trustee: St Gabriel's Trust, 1998–2006; King James Bible Trust (formerly 2011 Trust), 2008–11. Pres., Westminster Soc., 2006–; Vice Pres., The London Soc., 2006–. Fellow, Woodard Corp., 1992–. FRSA 2002; FSA 2014. Hon. FCollT 2009. Hon. Liveryman, Educators' Co., 2015. Hon. Fellow, Univ. of Wales Trinity St David, 2015. Hon. DD Roehampton, 2007; Hon. DTheol Chester, 2008; Hon. DLitt Westminster, 2014. *Publications:* (contrib.) Distinctiveness in Church Schools, 1998; (jtly) Governing and Managing Church Schools, 2nd edn 2003; Queen Elizabeth II and Her Church: Royal Service at Westminster Abbey, 2012; contrib. Church Times, TES, Parly Brief, Guardian, C of E Newspaper, Tablet, etc. *Recreations:* music, British political history. *Address:* The Deanery, Westminster Abbey, SW1P 3PA. *Clubs:* Athenæum, Royal Over-Seas League (Vice Pres.), Beefsteak.

HALL, John Thridgould; education sector lawyer, 1988; Chair, Education Group, Eversheds LLP, 2006–13; *b* Pinner, Middx, 23 Dec. 1948; *s* of Stanley Dennis Hall and Kathleen Joan Hall; *m* 1982, Julie Charlotte Arnold; two *s* one *d*. *Educ:* St John's Sch., Pinner; University Coll. Sch., London; Wadham Coll., Oxford (BA 1971; MA 1973). Admitted as solicitor, 1975; Asst Solicitor, 1975–78, Partner, 1978–93, Wedlake Saint; Partner, Eversheds LLP, 1994–2008. Chm., London Young Solicitors Gp, 1982–83. Mem. Bd, E-ACT, 2009–13. Mem., London Diocesan Synod, 2012–. Member: Bd, Barnet Coll., 1992–2002; Council, RCM, 1999–2009; Bd, Lochinver Hse Sch., 2000–14; Chm., Crest Academies, London, 2009–14. Mem., Internat. Adv. Council, Centre for Excellence in HE Law and Policy, Stetson Univ., Florida, 2008–. Hon. RCM 2010. Hon. Fellow, Brunel Univ., 2012. FRSA 1996. Church Warden and Trustee, St Paul's Ch, Hadley Wood, 2002–. *Publications:* (also Gen. Ed.) Purposive Governance: an annotated guidance for further education colleges, 1999, 14th edn 2013; Model Code of Conduct for Further Education Colleges, 1999, 11th edn 2013. *Recreations:* music, history, art, Mallorca, walking, family, Bible exposition. *Address:* 31 Lancaster Avenue, Hadley Wood, Barnet, Herts EN4 0EP. *T:* (020) 8440 1820, 07767 304361. *E:* johnthridhall@hotmail.co.uk.

HALL, Dr John Tristan Dalton; University Librarian, University of Durham, 1989–2009, now Librarian Emeritus; *b* 28 Oct. 1945; *m* 1970, Inge Lise Lindqvist; one *s* two *d*. *Educ:* Lady Lumley's Sch., Pickering; Univ. of Manchester (BA 1968; PhD 1977); MA Cantab 1989. Asst Librarian, John Rylands Univ. Library of Manchester, 1971–78; Sub-Librarian (Special Collections), Edinburgh Univ. Library, 1978–86; Dep. Librarian, Cambridge Univ. Library, 1986–89; Fellow, Darwin Coll., Cambridge, 1987–89. *Publications:* Manuscript Treasures in Edinburgh University Library: an album of illustrations, 1980; The Tounis College: an anthology of Edinburgh University student journals 1823–1923, 1985; articles and reviews in learned jls. *Recreations:* music, pottery, gardening.

HALL, Jonathan David D.; *see* Durham Hall.

HALL, Maj.-Gen. Jonathan Michael Francis Cooper, CB 1998; OBE 1987; DL; Lieutenant Governor, Royal Hospital, Chelsea, 1997–2005; *b* 10 Aug. 1944; *s* of Charles Richard Hall and Rosemary Hall (*née* Beckwith); *m* 1968, Sarah Linda Hudson; two *d*. *Educ:* Taunton Sch.; RMA Sandhurst. Commissioned 3rd Carabiniers, 1965; Staff Coll., 1977; commanded Royal Scots Dragoon Guards, 1984–86 and 12th Armd Bde, 1988–90; Higher Command and Staff Course, 1988; Mem., RCDS, 1991; Dep. Mil. Sec., MoD(A), 1992–93; DRAC, 1994; GOC Scotland, and Gov., Edinburgh Castle, 1995–97. Colonel Commandant: RAVC, 1995–2001; Scottish Div., 1995–97; Col, Royal Scots Dragoon Guards, 1998–2003. Mem., 1999–2012, Standard Bearer, 2012–14, HM Body Guard of Hon. Corps of Gentlemen-at-Arms. Trustee: RACWM Benevolent Fund, 1998–2011; VC and GC Assoc. Benevolent Fund, 2004–; Army Mus Ogilby Trust, 2004–14. Mem., Ethical Review Process, Imperial Coll., London, 2003–09; Designated Mem., Ethics and Welfare Gp, BVA, 2007–10. Managing Consultant, Compton Fundraising Ltd, 2006–. Gov., Blind Veterans UK (formerly St Dunstan's), 2011–. Vice President: ABF Dorset, 2008–; Soc. of Dorset Men, 2010–14; Vice Patron, Nat. Assoc. of Almshouses 65th Anniv. Appeal, 2012–13. Mem., Sherborne Abbey PCC, 2006–16. Chm. and Mem. Council, Order of St John, Dorset, 2008–11. Gov., Taunton Sch., 2007–. FCMI (FIMgt 1997). Hon. Associate Mem., BVA, 1996. Freeman, City of London, 2006; Liveryman, Farriers' Co., 2006–. DL Dorset, 2010. Kt Comdr, Order of Francis I, 2014; OStJ 1998. *Recreations:* country, music, travel. *Address:* Orchard House, Nether Compton, Sherborne, Dorset DT9 4QA. *Clubs:* Cavalry and Guards (Mem. Adv. Council; Trustee, 2007–14), MCC, Pratt's; Woodroffe's.

HALL, Jonathan Rupert; QC 2014; a Recorder, since 2012; *b* Brighton, 23 July 1971; *s* of Stephen Hall and Dr Rosemary Hall; *m* 2000, Michelle Dyson; two *s* one *d*. *Educ:* Tonbridge Sch., Kent; Christ Church, Oxford (BA English Lang. and Lit.). Called to the Bar, Inner Temple, 1994; in practice as barrister, 1994–. *Recreations:* family, squash, reading novels, cycling, under 10s football. *Address:* 6KBW College Hill, 21 College Hill, EC4R 2RP. *T:* (020) 3301 0946. *E:* jonathan.hall@6kbw.com.

HALL, His Honour Julian; a Circuit Judge, 1986–2010; Resident Judge, Oxford Combined Court Centre, 2002–10; authorised to sit in the Court of Appeal (Criminal Division), 2007–10; *b* 13 Jan. 1939; *s* of late Dr Stephen Hall, FRCP and Dr Mary Hall, Boarstall Tower, Bucks; *m* 1st, 1968, M. Rosalind Perry (marr. diss. 1988); one *s* one *d*; 2nd, 1989, Ingrid Cecilia, *er d* of late Rev. Canon Ronald Lunt, MC. *Educ:* Eton (Scholar); Christ Church, Oxford (Scholar; MA); Trinity Coll., Dublin (LLB). ARCM (flute). Industrial Chemist, Shell Internat. Chemical Co., 1961–63. Called to the Bar, Gray's Inn, 1966, Bencher, 2002; in practice in Common Law Chambers on Northern Circuit, Manchester, 1966–86; Standing Prosecuting Counsel to Inland Revenue, Northern Circuit, 1985–86; a Recorder, 1982–86; Resident Judge, Northampton Combined Court Centre, 2000–02; Hon. Recorder of Oxford, 2002–10. A Judge of Appeal, Oxford Univ. Student Disciplinary Panel, 2010–. Mem., Adv. Panel, HM Prison Grendon, 2008–. Tutor judge, Judicial Studies Bd, 1989–93. Chm., Northants Family Mediation Service, 1995–2000; Pres., Mental Health Rev. Tribunals, 1997–2011. Shrieval Remembrancer for Oxon, 2010–. Trustee, Oxford Lieder Festival, 2012–. *Recreations:* making music, in orchestras, choirs and at home, photography, bread and jam making. *Address:* c/o Oxford Crown Court, St Aldate's, Oxford OX1 1TL.

See also C. E. Henderson.

HALL, Katja Anneli; Deputy Director-General, Confederation of British Industry, 2014–15; *b* Sweden, 24 Sept. 1972; *d* of Kjell Klasson and Riitta Harkola; *m* 2002, Chris Hall; two *d*. *Educ:* Univ. of York (BA Hons Econs and Politics 1995); Univ. of Nottingham (MA Internat. Relns 1996). Policy Advr, Sen. Policy Advr, then Hd, Employee Relns, CBI, 1996–2002; Sen. Manager, HR Policy and Employee Relns, BBC, 2002–05; Hd, Employee Relns, 2006–08, Dir, Employment Policy, 2008–11, Chief Policy Dir, 2011–14, CBI. *Recreations:* ski-ing, reading.

HALL, Sir Kenneth Octavius, ON 2006; GCMG 2007; OJ 2004; PhD; Governor-General of Jamaica, 2006–09; Hon. Distinguished Research Fellow, University of West Indies, Mona, since 2009; *b* Lucea, Hanover, Jamaica; *m* Rheima Holding. *Educ:* Univ. of W Indies, Mona (BA 1966); Univ. of W Indies, Trinidad (Dip. Internat. Relns 1967); Queen's Univ., Ontario (MA Hist. 1967; PhD 1971). Teacher, Rusea's High Sch., Jamaica, 1961–63; Admin. Officer, Min. of Agric., Govt of Jamaica, 1966; teaching asst, Div. of Social Scis, Univ. of WI, St Augustine, Trinidad and Tobago, 1966–67; Instructor, Hist. Dept, Queen's Univ., Ontario, 1969–71; Asst Prof. of Hist., SUNY, 1971–73; Lectr, Hist. Dept, Univ. of WI, Mona, Jamaica, 1972–73; Faculty Res. Associate, Foreign and Comparative Studies, Syracuse Univ., NY, 1973–84; State University of New York: Oswego: Associate Prof. of Hist., 1973–84; Asst Provost, 1982–84; Prof. of Hist., 1984–86; Central Administration, Albany: Asst Vice-Chancellor for Acad. Progs, 1984–88; Asst Provost for Acad. Progs, 1988–89; Vice Pres. for Acad. Affairs and Dean of Faculty, SUNY at Old Westbury, 1990–94; Principal, Univ. of WI, Mona, Jamaica, 1996–2006. Chancellor, University Coll. of the Caribbean, 2011–12. Caribbean Community Secretariat, Guyana: Chief, Res. and Conf. Section, 1975–76; Dir, Gen. Services and Admin, 1976–77; Dep. Sec.-Gen., 1994–96. *Publications:* (ed) Education and the Black Experience, 1979; The Group of 77: strengthening its negotiating capacity, 1979; Imperial Proconsul: Sir Hercules Robinson and South Africa, 1881 to 1889, 1980; (ed) Makers of the Twentieth Century, 1982; (with D. Benn) Globalisation: a calculus of inequality, perspectives from the South, 2000; (with D. Benn) Contending with Destiny: the Caribbean in the 21st Century, 2000; CARICOM: unity in adversity, 2000; The Caribbean Community: beyond survival, 2001; Reinventing CARICOM: the road to a new integration, 2002; Integrate or Perish!: perspectives of leaders of the integration movement 1963–1999, 1999, 2nd edn 2003; (with D. Benn) Caribbean Imperatives: regional governance and integrated development, 2005; Rex N: Rex Nettleford, selected speeches, 2006; (with D. Benn) Production Integration in CARICOM: from theory to action, 2006; (with Rheima Holding) Tourism: the driver of change in the Jamaican economy?, 2006; (ed with Myrtle Chuck-A-Sang): Integration: CARICOM's key to prosperity, 2006; CARICOM Single Market and Economy: genesis and prognosis, 2007; CARICOM Single Market and Economy: challenges, benefits prospects, 2007; Confronting Challenges, Maximising Opportunities: a new diplomacy for market access, 2007; Intervention Border and Maritime Issues in CARICOM, 2007; The Caribbean Integration Process: a people-centred approach, 2007; CARICOM Policy Options for International Engagement, 2010; contrib. chapters in books and articles in jls and papers on history and current issues in the Caribbean.

HALL, Lee; dramatist; *b* 20 Sept. 1966; *s* of Peter and Sylvia Hall; *m* 2003, Beeban Kidron (*see* Baroness Kidron). *Educ:* Benfield Comprehensive Sch., Newcastle; Fitzwilliam Coll., Cambridge (BA English Lit.). Writer in Residence: Live Th., Newcastle upon Tyne, 1997–98; RSC, 1998–99. *Plays:* I Luv You Jimmy Spud (radio), 1995 (Sony Award); Spoonface Steinberg (radio), 1996; The Student Prince (TV), 1996; Mr Puntila and his Man Matti (trans.), Almeida, 1997; Cooking with Elvis, Live Th., transf. Whitehall, 2000; A Servant to Two Masters, RSC at Young Vic, 2000; The Good Hope, NT, 2001; Two's Company/Child of the Snow, Bristol Old Vic, 2005; Billy Elliot—the Musical, Victoria Palace, 2005, NY, 2008; The Pitmen Painters, Live Th., Newcastle, 2007, RNT UK tour, 2009–10, NY, 2010; Shakespeare in Love, Noël Coward Th., 2014; Our Ladies of Perpetual

Succour, Traverse Th., Edinburgh, 2015; *films:* Billy Elliot, 2000; (with R. Curtis) War Horse, 2012; *television:* The Wind in the Willows, 2006; Toast, 2010. *Publications:* Spoonface Steinberg and other plays, 1996; Cooking with Elvis, 1999; A Servant to Two Masters (new adaptation), 2000; Pinocchio (new adaptation), 2000; Billy Elliot (screenplay), 2001; The Good Hope (new adaptation), 2001; Plays 1, 2002; Plays 2, 2003. *Recreations:* cooking, reading, sleeping. *Address:* c/o Judy Daish Associates, 2 St Charles Place, W10 6EG.

HALL, Lisa; *see* Hall, E. A. H.

HALL, Luke Anthony; MP (C) Thornbury and Yate, since 2015; *b* S Glos, 8 July 1986. Shop worker, then Store Manager, Lidl, Yate; Area Manager, Farmfoods, until 2015. *Address:* House of Commons, SW1A 0AA.

HALL, Margaret Dorothy, OBE 1973; RDI 1974; Head of Design, British Museum, 1964–2001; *b* 22 Jan. 1936; *d* of Thomas Robson Hall and Millicent (*née* Britton). *Educ:* Bromley County Grammar Sch.; Bromley College of Art; Royal College of Art (DesRCA). Design Assistant: Casson, Condor & Partners, 1960–61; Westwood Piet & Partners, 1961–63; Dennis Lennon & Partners, 1963–64; British Museum, 1964–2001: exhibitions designed include: Masterpieces of Glass, 1968; Museum of Mankind, 1970; Treasures of Tutankhamun, 1972; Nomad and City, 1976; Captain Cook in the South Seas, 1979. Designer, Manuscripts and Men, National Portrait Gallery, 1969. Chm., Gp of Designers/Interpreters in Museums, 1978–81; Mem. Council, RSA, 1984–89. FCSD (FSIAD 1975–90; MSIAD 1968) (Chm., SIAD Salaried Designers Cttee, 1979–81). Chm., Wynkyn de Worde Soc., 1982. Governor, Ravensbourne College of Art, 1973–78. FRSA 1974; FMA 1983. *Publications:* On Display: a grammar of museum exhibition design, 1987. *Club:* Double Crown (Pres., 1998).

HALL, Prof. Martin; Vice-Chancellor, University of Salford, since 2009; Chairman, Jisc, since 2014; *b* Guildford; *m* Prof. Brenda Cooper; three *c*. *Educ:* Peterhouse, Cambridge (BA 1973). Worked in museums in S Africa; University of Cape Town, 1983–2009: Head: Centre for African Studies; Dept of Archaeol.; Dean, Higher Educn Develt, 1999–2002; Dep. Vice-Chancellor, 2003–09. Pres., World Archaeol Congress, 1999–2003; former Gen. Sec., S African Archaeol Soc. *Publications:* The Changing Past, 1987, 2nd edn 1990; (with C. Malherbe) Changes in the Land, 1988; The Iron Age: an illustrated dictionary of South African history, 1994; Slaves, Rings and Rubbish, 1995; Archaeology Africa, 1996; The Smuts Hall Windows, 1997; (jtly) Writing from the Edge: historical archaeology, 1999; (with R. Steffof) Great Zimbabwe, 2006; (ed jtly) Desire Lines: memory and identity in the post-apartheid city, 2007; contribs to jls incl. Jl African Hist., S African Jl Sci., British Archaeol Reports, Annals of Natal Mus., S African Archaeol Soc., Social Dynamics, Jl Social Archaeol., Studies in Higher Educn, Histl Archaeol. *Address:* University of Salford, Salford M5 4WT.

HALL, Melanie Ruth; QC 2002; *b* 29 Dec. 1959; *m* 1991, Martin Harold Hall; one *s* two *d*. *Educ:* Durham Univ. (BA). Called to the Bar, Inner Temple, 1982. Non-exec. Dir, Home Housing Ltd, 1995–99. Ed., Tax Jl, 2008–. *Address:* Monckton Chambers, Gray's Inn, WC1R 5NR. *T:* (020) 7405 7211, *Fax:* (020) 7405 2084.

HALL, Dr Michael George, FRS 1993; scientific consultant, since 1991; *b* 16 Oct. 1931; *s* of George Albert Victor Hall and Mabel Hall (*née* Gittins); *m* 1964, Merete Blatz; one *s* one *d*. *Educ:* Sydney Grammar Sch.; Univ. of Sydney (BSc, BE, MEngSc, PhD). Research in Fluid Dynamics at Aerodynamics Dept, RAE, 1958–91, retired 1991; sabbatical at Dept of Mechanics, Johns Hopkins Univ., 1966–67. Founder-Director, Hall C. F. D. Ltd, 1991–2003. *Publications:* contribs on fluid dynamics to sci. and tech. jls. *Address:* 8 Dene Lane, Farnham, Surrey GU10 3PW.

HALL, Michael Harold Webster, FSA; art historian; *b* 6 July 1957; *s* of late Dr L. W. Hall and Barbara Hall. *Educ:* Cambridgeshire High Sch. for Boys; Trinity Hall, Cambridge (BA 1980); Birkbeck Coll., London (MA). Ed., Thames and Hudson, 1982–89; Country Life: architectural writer, 1989–94; architectural ed., 1994–98; Dep. Ed., 1998–2004; Ed., Apollo, 2004–10. Contrib. Ed., Visual Arts, Country Life, 2010–. FSA 2003. Trustee: Emery Walker Trust, 1999–; Victorian Soc., 2000–06; Marc Fitch Fund, 2007–; Mem. Cttee, William Morris Soc., 2013–. *Publications:* The English Country House: from the archives of Country Life, 1994, repr. 2001; Waddesdon Manor, 2002, 3rd edn 2012; (ed) Gothic Architecture and its Meanings 1550–1830, 2002; The Victorian Country House, 2009; George Frederick Bodley and the Later Gothic Revival in Britain and America, 2014; contrib. articles to Country Life, Architectural Hist., Jl Soc. of Architectural Historians, Furniture Hist., Jl British Inst. of Organ Studies, etc. *E:* michael@michaelhwhall.com.

HALL, Michael Thomas; *b* 20 Sept. 1952; *s* of late Thomas and Veronica Hall; *m* 1975, Lesley Evelyn Gosling; one *s*. *Educ:* Padgate Coll. of Higher Educn (Teachers' Cert. 1977); N Cheshire Coll., Victoria Univ., Manchester (BEd Hons 1987). Scientific Asst, ICI Ltd, 1969–73; teaching history and physical educn, Bolton, 1977–85; support teacher, Halton Community Assessment Team, 1985–92. Councillor, Warrington Borough Council, 1979–93: Chairman: Envmtl Health Cttee, 1981–84; Finance Sub-Cttee, 1984–85; Policy and Resources Cttee, 1985–92; Dep. Leader of Council, 1984–85, Leader 1985–92. Member, Parish Council: Great Sankey, 1979–83; Birchwood and Croft, 1983–87; Poulton with Fearnhead, 1987–93. MP (Lab) Warrington S, 1992–97, Weaver Vale, 1997–2010. PPS to Ldr of the House of Commons and Pres. of the Council, 1997–98; an Asst Govt Whip, 1998–2001; PPS to Sec. of State for Health, 2001–05, to Lord Chancellor and Sec. of State for Justice, 2008–10. Member: Modernisation Select Cttee, 1997–98; Culture, Media and Sports Select Cttee, 2005–10. Mem., Public Accounts Cttee, 1992–97; Chm., Labour Party Back Bench Educn Cttee, 1996–97. *Recreations:* tennis, reading, cooking, dog walking, World War I.

HALL, Nigel John, RA 2003; sculptor; *b* 30 Aug. 1943; *s* of Herbert John Hall and Gwendoline Mary Hall (*née* Olsen); *m* 1986, Manijeh Yadegar. *Educ:* Bristol Grammar Sch.; West of England Coll. of Art; Royal Coll. of Art (MA). Harkness Fellow, USA, 1967–69; Tutor, RCA, 1971–74; Principal Lectr, Chelsea Sch. of Art, 1974–81. Ext. Examr, RCA, Goldsmiths Coll., Brighton Univ., Reading Univ., Middlesex Univ., Central Sch. of Art, W Surrey Coll. of Art. Mem. Faculty, British Sch. at Rome, 1979–83. Member: CNAA, 1975–76; Bursaries Cttee, 1975, Exhibns Cttee, 1983, Arts Council. First solo exhibn, Galerie Givaudan, Paris, 1967. *Solo exhibitions include:* Robert Elkon, NY, 1974, 1977, 1979, 1983; Annely Juda Fine Art, London, 1978, 1981, 1985, 1987, 1991, 1996, 2000, 2003, 2005, 2011; Galerie Maeght, Paris, 1981, 1983; Staatliche Kunsthalle, Baden-Baden, 1982; Nishimura Gall., Tokyo, 1980, 1984, 1988; Garry Anderson Gall., Sydney, 1987, 1990; Hans Mayer Gall., Düsseldorf, 1989, 1999; Fondation Veranneman, Kruishoutem, Belgium, 1987, 1995, 1997; Galerie Ziegler, Zurich, 1986, 1988, 1995; Park Gall., Seoul, 1997, 2000, 2005, 2008; Galerie Konstruktiv Tendens, Stockholm, 2000; Schoenthal Monastery, Switzerland, 2001; Galerie Scheffel, Bad Homburg, 2004, 2007, 2011, 2015; Kunsthalle, Mannheim, 2004; Galleri C. Hjärne, Helsingborg, 2004; Centre Cultural Contemporani Pelaires, Palma de Mallorca, 2007, 2009; Yorks Sculpture Park, 2008; Galerie Andres Thalmann, Zurich, 2010, 2012, 2014; Oklahoma City Art Center, 2010; Royal Acad., 2011; Churchill Coll., Cambridge, 2013; Galerie Alvaro Alcazar, Madrid, 2015; *group exhibitions include:* Kassel, 1977; Whitechapel Gall., 1981; Tokyo Metropolitan Mus., 1982; Le Havre Mus. of Fine Art, 1988; MOMA, NY, 1993; Fogg Art Mus., Harvard Univ., 1994; Schloss Ambras, Innsbruck, 1998; British Council touring exhibn, Pakistan, S Africa, Zimbabwe, 1997–99; York City Art Gall. and tour, 2001–02; Bad Homburg, Germany, 2003; Beaufort Triennial, Ostend, 2006; Rhode Island Sch. of Design, Providence, 2011; Inst. of Contemporary Arts, Singapore, 2012; Mus. Biedermann, Donaueschingen, 2015. *Commissions:* Australian Nat. Gall., Canberra, 1982; IBM, London, 1983; Airbus Industrie, Toulouse, 1984; Mus. of Contemp. Art, Hiroshima, 1985; Olympic Park, Seoul, 1988; Clifford Chance, London, 1992; Glaxo Wellcome Res., Stevenage, 1994; NTT, Tokyo, 1996; Bank of America, London, 2003; Saïd Business Sch., Univ. of Oxford, 2005; Bank for Internat. Settlements, Basel, 2007. *Work in collections including:* Tate Gall.; BM; Musée Nat. d'Art Moderne, Paris; Nat. Gall., Berlin; MOMA, NY; Australian Nat. Gall., Canberra; Art Inst. of Chicago; Kunsthaus, Zurich; Tokyo Metropolitan Mus.; Musée d'Art Moderne, Brussels; Louisiana Mus., Denmark; Nat. Mus. of Art, Osaka; Mus. of Contemp. Art, Sydney; Dallas Mus. of Fine Art; Tel Aviv Mus.; Los Angeles Co. Mus.; Nat. Mus. of Contemp. Art, Seoul. *Relevant publications:* Nigel Hall: sculpture and works on paper, by A. Lambirth, 2008; Nigel Hall: other voices, other rooms, by A. Lambirth, 2012. *Address:* 11 Kensington Park Gardens, W11 3HD. *T:* (020) 7727 3162. *E:* nigelhallra@gmail.com.

HALL, Patrick; *b* 20 Oct. 1951; *m* 2004, Claudia Caggiula. *Educ:* Bedford Modern Sch.; Birmingham Univ.; Oxford Poly. Local Govt Planning Officer, Bedford, 1975–91; Bedford Town Centre Co-ordinator, 1991–97. Mem., Bedfordshire CC, 1989–97. Contested (Lab) Bedfordshire N, 1992. MP (Lab) Bedford, 1997–2010; contested (Lab) same seat, 2010, 2015.

HALL, Sir Peter (Edward), KBE 1993; CMG 1987; HM Diplomatic Service, retired; *b* 26 July 1938; *s* of late Bernard Hall and Monica Hall (*née* Blackbourn); *m* 1972, Marnie Kay; one *s* one *d*. *Educ:* Portsmouth Grammar Sch.; HM Services (Jt Services Sch. for Linguists); Pembroke Coll., Cambridge (Scholar; 1st Cl. parts I and II, Mediaeval and Modern Langs Tripos). Foreign Office, 1961–63; 3rd Sec., Warsaw, 1963–66; 2nd Sec., New Delhi, 1966–69; FCO (European Integration Dept), 1969–72; 1st Sec., UK Permanent Representation to EEC, 1972–76; Asst Head, Financial Relations Dept, FCO, 1976–77; Counsellor, Caracas, 1977–78; Hd of British Information Services, NY, 1978–83 and Counsellor, British Embassy, Washington, 1981–83; Dir of Res., FCO, 1983–86; Under Sec., Cabinet Office, 1986–88; Vis. Schol., Stanford Univ., 1988–89; Ambassador to Yugoslavia, 1989–92; Advr to Lord Carrington, 1992, Lord Owen, 1992–93, Peace Conf. on Yugoslavia; Ambassador to Argentina, 1993–97. *Recreations:* reading (A. Powell, Byron), music (Rolling Stones, Mozart). *Address:* 13 Raby Place, Bath BA2 4EH.

HALL, Prof. Peter Gavin, AO 2013; DPhil; FRS 2000; FAA; Professor of Statistics and Australian Research Council Federation Fellow, University of Melbourne, 2006–12, now Laureate Fellow; *b* 20 Nov. 1951; *s* of William Holman Hall and Ruby Violet (*née* Payne-Scott); *m* 1977, Jeannie Jean Chien Loh. *Educ:* Univ. of Sydney (BSc 1st Cl. Hons); Australian Nat. Univ. (MSc 1976); Brasenose Coll., Oxford (DPhil 1976). Lectr in Stats, Univ. of Melbourne, 1976–78; Australian National University: Lectr in Stats, 1978–82; Sen. Lectr, 1983–85; Reader, 1986–88; Prof. of Stats, 1988–2006. FIMS 1984; FAA 1987; Fellow, Amer. Statistical Assoc., 1996; Corresp. FRSE, 2002; Foreign Associate, NAS, 2014. Dr *hc* Univ. Catholique de Louvain, 1997; Hon. DSc Glasgow, 2005; DSc *hc* Sydney, 2009. Medal, 1986, George Szekeres Medal, 2010, Australian Mathematical Soc.; Rollo Davison Prize, Cambridge Univ., 1986; Lyle Medal, 1989, Hannan Medal, 1995, Australian Acad. of Sci.; Pitman Medal, Statistical Soc. of Australia, 1990; Guy Medal in Silver, Royal Statistical Soc., 2011. *Publications:* (with C. C. Heyde) Martingale Limit Theory and its Applications, 1980; Rates of Convergence in the Central Limit Theorem, 1982; Introduction to the Theory of Coverage Processes, 1988; The Bootstrap and Edgeworth Expansion, 1992; contrib. numerous papers. *Recreations:* photography, interests in railway and aviation. *Address:* Department of Mathematics and Statistics, University of Melbourne, Melbourne, Vic 3010, Australia.

HALL, Sir Peter (Reginald Frederick), Kt 1977; CBE 1963; director of plays, films and operas; own producing company, Peter Hall Co., formed 1988; Artistic Director, Old Vic, 1997; *b* Bury St Edmunds, Suffolk, 22 Nov. 1930; *s* of late Reginald Edward Arthur Hall and Grace Pamment; *m* 1956, Leslie Caron (marr. diss. 1965); one *s* one *d*; *m* 1965, Jacqueline Taylor (marr. diss. 1981); one *s* one *d*; *m* 1982, Maria Louise Ewing, *qv* (marr. diss. 1990); one *d*; *m* 1990, Nicola Frei; one *d*. *Educ:* Perse Sch., Cambridge; St Catharine's Coll., Cambridge (MA Hons; Hon. Fellow, 1964). Professional début directing The Letter, Th. Royal, Windsor, 1953; Director: Oxford Playhouse, 1954–55; Arts Theatre, London, 1955–57 (directed several plays incl. first productions of Waiting for Godot (new prodn, Old Vic, 1997), South, Waltz of the Toreadors); formed own producing company, International Playwrights' Theatre, 1957, and directed their first production, Camino Real; at Sadler's Wells, directed his first opera, The Moon and Sixpence, 1957. First productions at Stratford: Love's Labour's Lost, 1956; Cymbeline, 1957; first prod. on Broadway, The Rope Dancers, Nov. 1957. Plays in London, 1956–58: Summertime, Gigi, Cat on a Hot Tin Roof, Brouhaha, Shadow of Heroes; Madame de…, Traveller Without Luggage, A Midsummer Night's Dream and Coriolanus (Stratford), The Wrong Side of the Park, 1959; apptd Dir of Shakespeare Fest., Stratford upon Avon, Jan. 1960, founded RSC as a permanent ensemble, and responsible for its move to Aldwych Theatre, 1960; Man. Dir at Stratford-on-Avon and Aldwych Theatre, London, 1960–68; Associate Dir, RSC, 1968–73; Dir, Nat. Theatre, 1973–88; Artistic Dir, Glyndebourne Fest., 1984–90; Founder Dir, Rose Th., Kingston, 2003–08, now Dir Emeritus. Plays produced/directed for *Royal Shakespeare Company:* Two Gentlemen of Verona, Twelfth Night, Troilus and Cressida, 1960; Ondine, Becket, Romeo and Juliet, 1961; The Collection, Troilus and Cressida, A Midsummer Night's Dream, 1962; The Wars of the Roses (adaptation of Henry VI Parts 1, 2 and 3, and Richard III), 1963 (televised for BBC, 1965); Sequence of Shakespeare's histories for Shakespeare's 400th anniversary at Stratford: Richard II, Henry IV Parts 1 & 2, Henry V, Henry VI, Edward IV, Richard III, 1964; The Homecoming, Hamlet, 1965; The Government Inspector, Staircase, 1966; The Homecoming (NY) (Tony Award for Best Dir), 1966; Macbeth, 1967; A Delicate Balance, Silence, Landscape, 1969; The Battle of the Shrivings, 1970; Old Times, 1971 (NY, 1971, Vienna, 1972; Th. Royal, Bath and tour, 2007); All Over, Via Galactica (NY), 1972; Julius Caesar, 1995; plays produced/directed for *National Theatre:* The Tempest, 1973; John Gabriel Borkman, Happy Days, 1974; No Man's Land, Hamlet, 1975; Tamburlaine the Great, 1976; No Man's Land (NY), Volpone, Bedroom Farce, The Country Wife, 1977; The Cherry Orchard, Macbeth, Betrayal, 1978; Amadeus, 1979, NY 1981 (Tony Award for Best Director); Othello, 1980; Family Voices, The Oresteia, 1981, 1986 (Evening Standard Award for Best Director, 1981); Importance of Being Earnest, 1982; Other Places, 1982; Jean Seberg, 1983; Animal Farm, Coriolanus, 1984; Martine, Yonadab, 1985; The Petition, Coming into Land, 1986; Antony and Cleopatra (Evening Standard Award for Best Director), Entertaining Strangers, 1987; The Tempest, Cymbeline, Winter's Tale, 1988; The Oedipus Plays, 1996; The Bacchai, 2002; Twelfth Night, 2011; plays produced/directed for *Peter Hall Company:* Orpheus Descending, NY, 1988; Merchant of Venice, 1989; The Wild Duck, Phoenix, 1990; The Homecoming, Comedy, 1990; Twelfth Night, The Rose Tattoo, Tartuffe, Playhouse, 1991; Four Baboons Adoring the Sun, NY, 1992; Sienna Red, 1992; All's Well That Ends Well, RSC, 1992; An Ideal Husband, Globe, 1992, Haymarket, Old Vic, 1996; The Gift of the Gorgon, Wyndham's, 1993; Separate Tables, Albery, 1993; Lysistrata, Old Vic and Wyndhams, 1993; She Stoops to Conquer, Queen's, 1993; Piaf, Piccadilly, 1993; An Absolute Turkey, Globe, 1994; On Approval, Playhouse, 1994; Hamlet, Gielgud, 1994; The Master Builder, 1995, Mind Millie for Me, 1996, A Streetcar Named Desire, 1997, Haymarket; Waste, The Seagull, King Lear, Waiting for Godot, Old Vic, 1997; The Misanthrope, Major Barbara, Filumena, Kafka's Dick, Piccadilly, 1998; Mrs Warren's Profession, Strand, 2002; Betrayal, Design for Living, As You Like It, Where There's a Will, Th. Royal, Bath, 2003; Galileo's Daughter, Man and Superman, Th. Royal, Bath, 2004; The Dresser, Duke of York's, 2005; Much Ado About Nothing, Private Lives, You Never Can Tell, Waiting for Godot, Th. Royal, Bath, 2005, transf. New Ambassadors, 2006; Measure for Measure, Habeas

Corpus, Th. Royal, Bath, 2006; Pygmalion, Th. Royal, Bath, 2007, transf. Old Vic, 2008; Little Nell, Animal Farm, Th. Royal, Bath, 2007; The Portrait of a Lady, A Doll's House, Th. Royal, Bath, 2008; The Apple Cart, The Browning Version/Swansong, Th. Royal, Bath, 2009; The Rivals, Th. Royal, Bath, 2010, transf. Haymarket, 2010; Henry IV Parts 1 & 2, Th. Royal, Bath, 2011; plays produced/directed for *Rose Theatre, Kingston:* As You Like It, 2004, US tour 2005; Uncle Vanya, 2008; Love's Labour's Lost, 2008, Where There's a Will, Bedroom Farce, 2009, transf. Duke of York's, 2010, A Midsummer Night's Dream, 2010; *other productions:* Amadeus, Old Vic, 1998; Lenny, Queen's, 1999; Cuckoos, Gate, Notting Hill, 2000; Tantalus, Denver, 2000, UK tour and Barbican, 2001; Japes, The Royal Family, 2001, Lady Windermere's Fan, 2002, Th. Royal, Haymarket; Betrayal, Duchess, 2003; Happy Days, Arts, 2003; Whose Life Is It Anyway?, Comedy, 2005; Hay Fever, Th. Royal, Haymarket, 2006; Amy's View, Garrick, 2006; The Vortex, Apollo, 2008. *Films:* Work is a Four Letter Word, 1968; A Midsummer Night's Dream, Three into Two Won't Go, 1969; Perfect Friday, 1971; The Homecoming, 1973; Akenfield, 1974; She's Been Away, 1989; Orpheus Descending, 1991; Final Passage, 1996. *Opera:* at Covent Garden: Moses and Aaron, 1965; The Magic Flute, 1966; The Knot Garden, 1970; Eugene Onegin, Tristan and Isolde, 1971; Salome, 1988; Albert Herring, 1989; at Glyndebourne: La Calisto, 1970; Il Ritorno d'Ulisse in Patria, 1972; The Marriage of Figaro, 1973, 1989; Don Giovanni, 1977; Così Fan Tutte, 1978, 1988; Fidelio, 1979; A Midsummer Night's Dream, 1981, 2001; Orfeo ed Euridice, 1982; L'Incoronazione di Poppea, 1984, 1986; Carmen, 1985; Albert Herring, 1985, 1986, 2002, 2008; Simon Boccanegra, 1986, 1998; La Traviata, 1987; Falstaff, 1988; Otello, 2001; La Cenerentola, 2005, 2007; at Metropolitan Opera, NY: Macbeth, 1982; Carmen, 1986; at Bayreuth: The Ring, 1983; at Geneva: Figaro, 1983; at Los Angeles: Salome, 1986; Così Fan Tutte, 1988; The Magic Flute, 1992; at Chicago: Figaro, 1987; Salome, 1988; Otello, 2001; The Midsummer Marriage, 2005; at Houston: New Year (world première), 1989. *Television:* Presenter, Aquarius (LWT), 1975–77; Carmen, 1985; Oresteia (C4), L'Incoronazione di Poppea, Albert Herring, 1986; La Traviata, 1987; The Marriage of Figaro, 1989; (series) The Camomile Lawn (C4), 1992. Associate Prof. of Drama, Warwick Univ., 1964–67. Mem., Arts Council, 1969–73; Founder Mem., Theatre Dirs' Guild of GB, 1983–. Wortham Prof. of Performing Arts, Houston Univ., 1999–2004; Chancellor, Kingston Univ., 2000–13. DUniv York, 1966; Hon. DLitt: Reading, 1973; Essex, 1993; Hon. LittD: Liverpool, 1974; Leicester, 1977; Cambridge, 2003; Bath, 2005; London, 2007. Freedom, City of London, 2010. Mem., Athens Acad. for Services to Greek Drama, 2004. Hamburg Univ. Shakespeare Prize, 1967; Standard Special Award, 1979; Standard Award for outstanding achievement in Opera, 1981; Lifetime Achievement Award, South Bank Show, 1998; Olivier Special Award for Lifetime Achievement, 1999; NY Shakespeare Soc. Lifetime Achievement Award, 2003; Lifetime Achievement Award, NY Theater Hall of Fame, 2006; Moscow Art Theatre Golden Seagull Award for Lifetime Achievement, Evening Standard Awards, 2010; Spirit of Shakespeare Award, Lifetime Achievement, Chicago Shakespeare Th., 2011; TMA/UK Theatre Awards, Lifetime Achievement 2011. Chevalier de l'Ordre des Arts et des Lettres, 1965. *Publications:* (with John Barton) The Wars of the Roses, 1970; (with Inga-Stina Ewbank) John Gabriel Borkman, an English version, 1975; Peter Hall's Diaries (ed John Goodwin), 1983; Animal Farm, a stage adaptation, 1986; (with Inga-Stina Ewbank) The Wild Duck, an English adaptation, 1990; Making an Exhibition of Myself (autobiog.), 1993; (with Nicki Frei) trans. Feydeau, An Absolute Turkey, 1994; (with Inga-Stina Ewbank) The Master Builder, an English version, 1995; The Necessary Theatre, 1999; Exposed by the Mask, 2000; Shakespeare's Advice to the Players, 2003. *Recreation:* music. *Club:* Garrick.

See also E. P. Hall.

HALL, Prof. Philip, PhD; Professor of Applied Mathematics, Imperial College London, since 1996; Head, School of Mathematical Sciences, Monash University, since 2014; *b* 21 Feb. 1950; *s* of John Thomas Hall and Pamela Hall; *m* 1973, Eileen Haig; two *d. Educ:* Goole Grammar Sch.; Imperial Coll., London (BSc 1971; PhD 1973). Reader in Maths, Imperial Coll., London, 1984–85; Prof. of Maths, Exeter Univ., 1985–90; Beyer Prof. of Maths, Manchester Univ., 1990–96; Hd, Dept of Maths, ICSTM, 1998–2003. Sen. Fellow, EPSRC, 1990–95. *Publications:* about 120 articles on fluid dynamics, mostly with relevance to aerodynamics and transition to turbulence. *Recreations:* golf, reading, theatre, travelling. *Address:* Department of Mathematics, 180 Queen's Gate, S Kensington Campus, Imperial College London, SW7 2AZ. *T:* (020) 7594 8480, *Fax:* (020) 7594 8517. *E:* phil.hall@ic.ac.uk.

HALL, Philip David; Chairman, PHA Media (formerly Phil Hall Associates), since 2005; *b* 8 Jan. 1955; *s* of Norman Philip Hall and Olive Jean Hall; *m* 1997, Marina Thomson, patent attorney; one *s* two *d. Educ:* Beal Grammar Sch., Ilford. Reporter: Dagenham Post, 1974–77; Ilford Recorder, 1977–80; Sub-editor: Newham Recorder, 1980–84; Weekend Magazine, 1984–85; The People: Reporter, 1985–86; Chief Reporter, 1986–89; News Editor, 1989–92; News Editor, Sunday Express, 1992–93; News of the World: Asst Editor (Features), 1993–94; Dep. Editor, 1994–95; Editor, 1995–2000; with Max Clifford Associates, 2000; Ed.-in-chief, Hello! magazine, 2001–02; Man. Dir, Contract Publg Div., Press Assoc., 2002–03; Dir of Editorial Develt, Trinity Mirror, 2003–05. Mem., Press Complaints Commn, 1998–2000, 2002–03. Member: Guild of Editors; PPA, 2001–02. *Recreations:* golf, cinema, theatre. *Address:* PHA Media, Hammer House, 117 Wardour Street, W1F 0UN. *T:* (020) 7025 1350. *Club:* Stoke Park.

HALL, Raymond Walter, CBE 1993; FREng; Chief Executive, Magnox Electric plc, 1996–98; *b* 24 Sept. 1933; *s* of Alfred Henry Hall and Elsie Frieda Hall; *m* 1955, Diane Batten; one *s* three *d. Educ:* Portsmouth, Grays Thurrock, and Gravesend Colls of Technology. FIMechE 1981; FIET (FIEE 1983); FNucI (FINucE 1983); FREng (FEng 1993). Engineering and managerial positions, CEGB, 1975–89: Station Manager: Trawsfynydd Nuclear Power Station, 1975–77; Hinkley Point A & B Nuclear Power Stations, 1978–82; Corporate Trng Manager, 1983–85; Corporate Dir of Personnel, 1986–87; Divl Dir of Generation, 1988–89; Exec. Dir, Operations, Nuclear Electric plc, 1990–95. World Association of Nuclear Operators: Gov., Main Bd, 1993–97; Chm., Paris Centre, 1993–97; Chairman: Orgn Producteurs d'Energie Nucléaire, 1994–97; British Nuclear Industry Forum, 1997–2002 (Mem. Bd, 1996–2002). Trustee, Bristol Exploratory, 1992–2000. FRSA 1980; FCMI (FIMgt 1980); FIPD 1988. Freeman: City of London, 1996; Worshipful Co. of Engrs, 1996 (Liveryman, 1997–). *Publications:* contribs to learned jls on nuclear engrg matters. *Recreations:* music, gardening, walking, golf, travel. *Address:* Kingsthorn, Trull, Taunton, Somerset TA3 7HA. *T:* (01823) 252325. *E:* hall.r15@sky.com.

HALL, Rev. Canon Roger John, MBE 1999; QHC 2006; Chaplain of the Chapel Royal of St Peter ad Vincula, HM Tower of London, since 2007; a Deputy Priest in Ordinary to the Queen, since 2007; Canon of the Chapels Royal within the Tower of London, since 2012; *b* 1 Dec. 1953; *s* of Sydney and Patricia Hall; *m* 1979, Barbara Mary Hutchinson; one *s* two *d. Educ:* Wolsingham Sch., Co. Durham; Lincoln Theological Coll. Ordained deacon, 1984, priest, 1985; Asst Curate, St Giles, Shrewsbury with St Eata's, Atcham, 1984–87; Regtl Chaplain, 1987–90; Brigade Sen. Chaplain, 1990–95; Amport House: Asst Warden, 1996–98; Warden, 1998–2000; Dep. Asst Chaplain Gen., Germany, 2000–01; Sen. Chaplain, Guard's Chapel, 2001–03; Asst Chaplain Gen., 2003–07. Mem., Forces Synod, 1993–; Dir of Ordinands, 1996–2001; Warden of Readers, 1998–. Nat. Chaplain, BLESMA, 2001–; Chaplain, MoD Main Bldg, 2007–; Sch. Chaplain, Bacon's Acad., 2007–; Hon. Chaplain: Co. of City of London Solicitors, 2007–; Co. of Builders Merchants, 2007–; Guild of Arts Scholars, Dealers and Collectors, 2007–; Co. of Security Professionals, 2007–. Member: Family Support Working Pty, SSAFA, 1998–; Scottish Veterans Housing Assoc., 2003–; Trustee, Chapter 1 Charity (formerly Christian Alliance Housing Assoc.), 2007–. Mem., Stone Masons' Co., 2007–; Mem., Anglo-German Soc. QCVS 1995. *Recreations:* music, art, reading, travel, ski-ing, shooting, café culture. *Address:* Chaplain's Residence, HM Tower of London, EC3N 4AB. *T:* (020) 3166 6796. *E:* roger.hall@hrp.org.uk. *Clubs:* Army and Navy, East India.

HALL, Ruth, CB 2004; FRCP, FRCPCH, FFPH; Director, Health Protection Agency South West, 2006–09; *b* 8 Feb. 1948; *d* of Robert and Molly Dobson; *m* 1971, William Hall; two *s* two *d. Educ:* Sch. of St Helen and St Katharine, Abingdon; King's Coll. Hosp. Med. Sch., London (MB BS 1970). LRCP, MRCS 1970; FFPH (FFPHM 1994); FRCPCH 1997; FRCP 2000. Posts in London, 1970–71, Chester, 1971–73, and N Wales, 1973–97; Dir of Public Health, N Wales HA, 1995–97; CMO, Welsh Office, then Welsh Assembly Govt, 1997–2005; Dir of Public Health, Avon, Glos and Wilts Strategic HA, 2005–06. Member: MRC, 1997–2005; Public Health Interventions Adv. Cttee, NICE, 2005–; Future Regulatory Adv. Panel, Ofwat, 2010–13; all-Wales Partnership, Canal and River Trust, 2013–; non-executive Director: Envmt Agency, 2005–12; Natural Resources Wales, 2012–. Career Mentor, Office of Public Appts, Cabinet Office, 2009–. Vis. Prof., Faculty of Health and Social Care, UWE, 2006–; Ext. Examiner, Univ. of Surrey, 2012. Gov., Public Policy Inst. for Wales, 2013–. Liveryman, Apothecaries' Soc., 2009; Freeman, City of London, 2008.

HALL, Sasha; *see* Wass, S.

HALL, Simon Robert Dawson, MA; Warden of Glenalmond College, 1987–91; *b* 24 April 1938; *s* of late Wilfrid Dawson Hall and Elizabeth Helen Hall (*née* Wheeler); *m* 1961, Jennifer Harverson; two *s. Educ:* Tonbridge School; University College, Oxford. 2nd Lieut, 7th Royal Tank Regt, 1956–58; Asst Master, Gordonstoun School, 1961–65; Joint Headmaster, Dunrobin School, 1965–68; Haileybury: Asst Master, 1969–79; Senior Modern Languages Master, 1970–76; Housemaster, Lawrence, 1972–79; Second Master, 1976–79; Headmaster, Milton Abbey School, 1979–87. 21st SAS Regt (TA), 1958–61; Intelligence Corps (V), 1968–71. *Recreations:* reading, music, motoring, sailing, hill-walking. *Address:* 2 Stone Hill, Bloxham, Banbury, Oxon OX15 4PT.

HALL, Prof. the Rev. Stuart George; Priest-in-Charge, St Michael's, Elie, and St John's, Pittenweem, 1990–98; Professor of Ecclesiastical History, King's College, University of London, 1978–90; *b* 7 June 1928; *s* of George Edward Hall and May Catherine Hall; *m* 1953, Brenda Mary Henderson; two *s* two *d. Educ:* University Coll. Sch., Hampstead; New Coll., and Ripon Hall, Oxford (BA 1952, MA 1955, BD 1973). National Service, Army, 1947–48. Deacon 1954, priest 1955; Asst Curate, Newark-on-Trent Parish Church, 1954–58; Tutor, Queen's Coll., Birmingham, 1958–62; Lectr in Theology, Univ. of Nottingham, 1962–73, Sen. Lectr, 1973–78. Pres., Acad. Internat. des Scis Religieuses, 2006–11. Editor for early church material, Theologische Realenzyklopädie. *Publications:* Melito of Sardis On Pascha and fragments: (ed) texts and translations, 1979, rev. edn 2013; (contrib.) The Easter Sermons of Gregory of Nyssa, 1981; (contrib.) El "Contra Eunomium 1" en la producción literaria de Gregorio de Nisa, 1988; Doctrine and Practice in the Early Church, 1991, 2nd edn 2005; (ed) Gregory of Nyssa, Homilies on Ecclesiastes, 1993; (ed with Averil Cameron) Eusebius, Life of Constantine, 1999; (ed jtly) Gregory of Nyssa, Homilies of the Beatitudes, 2000; Heritage and Hope: the Episcopal churches in the East Neuk of Fife 1805–2005, 2004; (ed jtly) Decoding Early Christianity: truth and legend in the Early Church, 2007; (ed jtly) Gregory of Nyssa, Contra Eunomium II, 2007; (ed) Jesus Christ Today, 2009; contrib. to vols of Procs of Acad. Internat. des Scis Religieuses, 1986–2011; contrib. to Cambridge History of Christianity, Cambridge Ancient History, Expository Times, Heythrop Jl, Jl of Eccles. History, Jl of Theol Studies, Religious Studies, Studia Evangelica, Studia Patristica, Theology and Theologische Realenzyklopädie. *Recreations:* gardening, choral music. *Address:* 15 High Street, Elie, Leven, Fife KY9 1BY. *T:* (01333) 330216.

HALL, Susan Margaret; *see* Standring, S. M.

HALL, Suzanne; Headmistress, Rugby High School, 1998–2006; *b* 5 Jan. 1946; *d* of John and Louise Keats; *m* 1971, Eric Lonsdale Hall; two *s. Educ:* Braintree Grammar Sch.; Univ. of Wales (BSc Hons Chem. 1969); Univ. of Southampton (PhD research). Cancer res., ICRF, 1966; Information Scientist, 1970; teacher, 1975; Dep. Hd, Chelmsford Co. High Sch., 1993–98. *Publications:* papers on x-ray crystallography in Jl of Chemical Soc. *Recreations:* reading, crosswords, Scrabble, gardening. *Address:* The Old Rectory, Main Street, Sedgeberrow, Worcs WR11 7UE. *T:* (01386) 881261.

HALL, Col Thomas Armitage, CVO 1998; OBE 1966; HM Body Guard of Honourable Corps of Gentlemen at Arms, 1980–98 (Lieutenant, 1994–98); *b* 13 April 1928; *s* of Athelstan Argyle Hall and Nancy Armitage Hall (*née* Dyson); *m* 1954, Mariette Hornby; two *s* four *d. Educ:* Heatherdown Sch.; Eton Coll. Commissioned, 11th Hussars, 1947, Berlin; ADC to CIGS, 1952–53; Adjutant, 11 H Malayan Emergency, 1953–56 (despatches); Army Staff Coll., 1960–61; Sqdn Leader 11 H, Aden, Gulf, Kenya, Kuwait, 1961–62; Instr, RN Staff Coll., Greenwich, 1962–64; CO 11 H, Germany, 1965–66; Equerry to King of Thailand, 1966; Regtl Col, Royal Hussars, 1974–83; Advr to Crown Prince of Japan, 1983–85. Regl Dir, Lloyds Bank, 1983–85. Chm., Internat. Lang. Centres, 1971–88. High Sheriff, Oxon, 1981–82. FRSA. *Recreations:* ski-ing, shooting, travel, architecture. *Address:* Marylands Farm, Chiselhampton, Oxford OX44 7XD. *T:* (01865) 890350. *Club:* Cavalry and Guards (Chm., 1990–96; Vice Pres., 2007–13).

HALL, Thomas William; Under-Secretary, Department of Transport, 1976–79 and 1981–87; retired; *b* 8 April 1931; *s* of Thomas William and Euphemia Jane Hall; *m* 1961, Anne Rosemary Hellier Davis; two *d. Educ:* Hitchin Grammar Sch.; St John's Coll., Oxford (MA); King's Coll., London (MA). Asst Principal, Min. of Supply, 1954; Principal: War Office, Min. of Public Building and Works, Cabinet Office, 1958–68; Asst Sec., Min. of Public Building and Works, later DoE, 1968–76; Under Sec., Depts of Environment and Transport, 1979–81. Member: Road Traffic Law Review, 1985–88; Transport Tribunal, 1990–99. *Recreations:* literature, gardening, walking. *Address:* 43 Bridge Road, Epsom, Surrey KT17 4AN. *T:* (01372) 725900.

HALL, Veronica Jane, (Ronni); *see* Ancona, V. J.

HALL, His Honour Victor Edwin; a Circuit Judge, 1994–2013; Family Mediator and Arbitrator, Trinity Family Mediation and Arbitration, since 2013; *b* 2 March 1948; *s* of Robert Arthur Victor James Hall and Gwladys (*née* Fukes); *m* 1974, Rosemarie Berdina Jenkinson; two *s*; *m* 2009, Anita Elaine Everill. *Educ:* Univ. of Hull (LLB 1969). Lectr in Law, Kettering Tech. Coll., 1969–71; called to the Bar, Inner Temple, 1971; an Asst Recorder, 1983–88; a Recorder, 1988–94. Designated Family Judge, Leicester County Court, 1996–2003. Asst Parly Boundary Comr, 1991–93; Mem./Pres., Mental Health Review Tribunals, 1997–2003. Member: Cttee, Council of Circuit Judges, 1997–2002 (Treas., 1999–2001); Family Rules Cttee, 2001–04; Jt Course Dir, Family Seminars, 2002–03, Dir of Studies, 2004–06, Judicial Studies Bd. Lectr in Dispute Resolution, Univ. of Derby, 2014–. Mem. Adv. Cttee, Commonwealth Judicial Educn Inst., 2004–06; Sec.-Gen., 2008–11, Mem., Linguistics Prog., 2014–, European Judicial Trng Network, Brussels. Member, Board of Trustees: European Acad. of Law, Trier, 2008–; Internat. Orgn for Judicial Trng, 2009– (Mem. Bd, 2004–06; European Vice Pres., 2004–09). External Examr in Family Law, City Univ., Hong Kong, 2010– (Adjunct Prof. of Law, 2005–08). *Recreations:* sailing (and dreaming about being on the water!), cookery, fell walking, gardening, cricket.

HALL, (Wallace) John; Regional Director, DTI East (Cambridge), Department of Trade and Industry, 1989–94; *b* 5 Oct. 1934; *s* of Claude Corbett Hall and Dulcie Hall (*née* Brinkworth); *m* 1962, Janet Bowen (*d* 2010); three *d*. *Educ:* Crypt Sch., Gloucester; Hertford Grammar Sch.; Downing Coll., Cambridge (MA Classics). National Service, RAF, 1953–55. Pirelli-General Cable Works Ltd, 1958–62; Sales Manager, D. Meredew Ltd, 1962–67; Principal, Min. of Technology, 1967–70; Dept of Trade and Industry, Civil Aviation Policy, 1970–72; Consul (Commercial), São Paulo, Brazil, 1972–76; Asst Secretary, Dept of Trade, Shipping Policy, 1976–79; Counsellor (Economic), Brasilia, 1979–81; Consul-Gen., São Paulo, 1981–83; Assistant Secretary, DTI: Internat. Trade Policy, 1983–85; Overseas Trade (E Asia), 1985–89. *Recreations:* bridge, croquet, walking. *Address:* 10 Greenway, Letchworth Garden City, Herts SG6 3UG.

HALL, Dame Wendy, (Dame Wendy Chandler), DBE 2009 (CBE 2000); PhD; FRS 2009; FREng; Professor of Computer Science, since 1994 and Executive Director, Web Science Institute, since 2014, University of Southampton; *b* 25 Oct. 1952; *d* of Kenneth D. Hall and Elizabeth Hall; *m* 1980, Dr Peter E. Chandler. *Educ:* Ealing Grammar Sch. for Girls; Univ. of Southampton (BSc Maths 1974; PhD 1977); City Univ. (MSc Computer Sci. 1986). CEng 1990; FIET (FIEE 1998). Lecturer: in Engrg, Oxford Poly., 1977–78; La Sainte Union Coll. of Higher Educn, 1978–84; University of Southampton: Lectr, 1984–90, Sen. Lectr, 1990–94, Dept of Electronics and Computer Sci.; Hd, Sch. of Electronics and Computer Sci., 2002–07; Dean, Faculty of Physical and Applied Scis, subseq. Faculty of Physical Scis and Engrg, 2010–14. Mem., EPSRC, 1997–2002 (Sen. Fellow, 1996–2001). Member: Prime Minister's Council for Sci. and Technol., 2004–10; Scientific Council, European Res. Council, 2005–10; Bd, British Library, 2007–15; Bd, DSTL, 2012–; Council, Royal Soc., 2013–; Bd, Digital Catapult, 2014–; Global Commn on Internet Governance, 2014–; Chm., Educn Cttee, British Council, 2014–. Non-exec. Dir, Idox plc. Pres., ACM, 2008–10. FBCS 1996 (Pres., 2003–04); FREng 2000 (Sen. Vice Pres., 2005–08); FCGI 2002; FACM 2011. Hon. Fellow, Cardiff Univ., 2004. Hon. DSc: Oxford Brookes, 2002; Glamorgan, 2005; Loughborough, 2008; Glasgow, 2009; QUB, 2012; Birmingham, 2012; Sussex, 2013; Hon. PhD Pretoria, 2007; Hon. LLD Dalhousie, 2012; Hon. Dr Aristotle Univ. of Thessaloniki, 2010; Hon. DSc City, 2013; Hon. DSc(Eng) UCL, 2014. *Publications:* (jtly) Rethinking Hypermedia: the microcosm approach, 1996; (jtly) Hypermedia and the Web: an engineering approach, 1999; (jtly) A Framework for Web Science, 2006; articles in jls, conf. proceedings. *Recreations:* going to the gym and swimming, walking with my husband, particularly in the New Forest; fine wines and dining, travelling, theatre; favourite form of relaxation is reading a good book on a sunny beach or shopping! *Address:* Web Science Institute, University of Southampton, Southampton SO17 1BJ. *T:* (023) 8059 2388.

HALL, Sir William (Joseph), KCVO 2009; JP; Lord-Lieutenant of Co. Down, 1996–2009; *b* 1 Aug. 1934; *s* of late Capt. Roger Hall and Marie Hall; *m* 1964, Jennifer Mary Corbett (*d* 2008); one *s* one *d*; *m* 2012, Catharine Dorinda Okuno (*née* Clements). *Educ:* Ampleforth Coll., York. SSC, Irish Guards, 1952–56. With W. C. Pitfield & Hugh McKay, investment mgt co., then with Shell Oil, Canada, 1956–62; dir of own wine wholesale business, also sheep farmer and commercial narcissus bulb grower, 1962–90, retired. Chm., Rostrevor and Warrenpoint Bee Keepers Assoc., 2010–. Mem., Lord Chancellor's Adv. Cttee on JPs, 1975–2009 (Chm., Ards Div., 1996–2009). County Down: JP 1973; DL 1975–93; High Sheriff, 1983; Vice Lord Lieutenant, 1993–96. NI ACF, 1967–79 (Hon. Major, 1980; Pres., NI ACFA, 1999–2002); President: RFCA NI, 2000–05; Ulster Br., Irish Guards Assoc., 2009– (Chm., 1979–2009). Hon. Col, 1st Bn (NI), ACF, 2003–05. Vice Pres., RBL, NI, 2005–. KStJ 2011 (CStJ 1997), Kt Comdr, Commandery of Ards (Order of St John), 2011. *Recreations:* field sports in general, bridge, travel abroad when time allows! *Address:* The Mill House, Narrow Water, Warrenpoint, Co. Down, Northern Ireland BT34 3LW. *T:* (028) 4175 4904. *Clubs:* Army and Navy; Down Hunt (Downpatrick).

HALL HALL, Alexandra Mary, (Mrs D. C. Twining); HM Diplomatic Service; Ambassador to Georgia, since 2013; *b* 1 Feb. 1964; *d* of late Francis Alleyne Hall Hall and Mary Hall Hall (*née* Whittaker); *m* 2002, Daniel Charles Twining; two *s*. *Educ:* Durham Univ. (BA Jt Hons Politics and Econs 1986); Sch. of Oriental and African Studies, Univ. of London (Advanced Thai); FCO Advanced Thai Dip. 1999. Entered FCO, 1986; Desk Officer, SE Asian Dept, FCO, 1987–88; Second Sec., Political and Inf. Officer, Bangkok, 1989–93; Hd, Humanitarian Section, UN Dept, FCO, 1993–95; European Secretariat, Cabinet Office (on secondment), 1995–97; Hd, ME Peace Process Section, FCO, 1997–98; First Sec. (Political), Washington, 1999–2001; Counsellor, on secondment to US State Dept, Washington, 2002–04; Hd of Human Rights, Democracy and Good Governance Gp, FCO, 2004–06; Political Counsellor, New Delhi, 2006–07; Dep. Hd of Mission, British Embassy, Bogota, 2009–11. *Recreations:* travel, tennis, ski-ing, archery, dogs, hard labour to convert a scrap of wilderness in W Virginia, USA into the American answer to Sissinghurst, Kent. *Address:* c/o Foreign and Commonwealth Office, King Charles Street, SW1A 2AH.

HALL-MATTHEWS, Rt Rev. Dr Anthony Francis Berners; Bishop of Carpentaria, 1984–96, Emeritus, 2011; Chaplain and Welfare Officer, Honourable Company of Air Pilots (formerly Guild of Air Pilots and Air Navigators), Australian Region, since 2010; *b* 14 Nov. 1940; *s* of Rev. Cecil Berners Hall and Barbara (who *m* 1944, Rt Rev. Seering John Matthews); *m* 1966, Valerie Joan Cecil; two *s* three *d*. *Educ:* Sanctuary School, Walsingham, Norfolk; Southport School, Queensland; St Francis Theol Coll., Milton, Brisbane; James Cook Univ., Qld (Graduate Dip. of Arts, 1997; PhD 2005). ThL Aust. Coll. of Theology, 1962. Asst Curate at Darwin, 1963–66; Chaplain, Carpentaria Aerial Mission, 1966–84, and Rector of Normanton, 1966–76; Hon. Canon of Carpentaria, 1970–76; Archdeacon of Cape York Peninsula, 1976–84; Priest-in-charge of Cooktown, Dio. Carpentaria, 1976–84; Bishop Resident in Mareeba, Dio. N Qld, 1999–2000. Liaison Officer for PNG, Third Order of Soc. of St Francis (Provincial Chaplain, 2003–09). Principal, Carpentaria Consulting Services, 1997–2006. Centenary Medal (Australia), 2001. *Publications:* From Village to Mission then Community, 2004; A Remarkable Venture of Faith, 2007. *Recreations:* flying, reading, composting. *Address:* 5 Wattle Close, Yungaburra, Queensland 4884, Australia. *T:* (7) 40953188.

HALL-SMITH, Vanessa Frances, MBE 2009; Director, British Institute of Florence, 2004–11; *b* 30 April 1951; *d* of late Patrick Hall-Smith and Angela Hall-Smith; two *d*. *Educ:* Roedean Sch., Brighton; Univ. of Exeter (LLB); Johannes Gutenberg Univ. Mainz; Univ. d'Aix-Marseilles. Called to the Bar, Inner Temple, 1976; Sec., Internat. Law Assoc., 1976–79; admitted solicitor, 1993; Partner: Simkins Partnership, Solicitors, 1996–2000; Harrison Curtis Solicitors, 2001–03. Trustee, Estorick Collection of Modern Italian Art, 2011–. Co-ed., Rivista, Mag. of British Italian Soc., 2013–. *Publications:* (contrib. ed) Butterworths Encyclopaedia of Forms and Precedents, Advertising vol., 5th edn 1993. *Recreations:* theatre, music, cinema, cooking.

HALLAM, Bishop of, (RC), since 2014; **Rt Rev. Ralph Heskett,** CSSR; *b* Sunderland, 3 March 1953. Ordained priest, 1976; Superior and Dir of Missions, Redemptorist Community at Kinnoull, Perth, 1987–90; Superior, Redemptorist Community and Parish of Our Lady of the Annunciation, Bishop Eton, Liverpool, 1990–96; Parish Priest, St Mary's, Clapham, 1999–2008; Bishop of Gibraltar, (RC), 2010–14. *Address:* Bishop's House, 75 Norfolk Road, Sheffield S2 2SZ.

HALLAM, David John Alfred; communications specialist; Managing Director, Horizon Glen Ltd, since 2003; *b* 13 June 1948; *s* of Arthur Ernest Hallam and Marjorie Ethel Hallam (*née* Gibbs); *m* 1988, Claire Vanstone; two *s* one *d*. *Educ:* Upton House Secondary Modern Sch., London; Univ. of Sussex (BA). Res. Asst, Sussex CC, 1971–73; Information Officer, Birmingham Social Services Dept, 1973–80; Public Relations Officer, Nat. Children's Home, 1984–89; Dir of Communications, Birmingham Heartlands and Solihull NHS Trust, 2000–02. Mem., Sandwell BC, W Midlands, 1976–79. MEP (Lab) Hereford and Shropshire, 1994–99; contested (Lab) W Midlands Reg., 1999. Mem., Agricl Cttee, 1994–99, Substitute Mem., Budget Cttee, 1997–99, Eur. Parlt; Mem., Slovak Delegn, 1995–99; Substitute Mem. of Israel Delegn and to EU African, Caribbean and Pacific Parly Assembly, 1994–99. Contested (Lab): Shropshire and Staffordshire, European parly elections, 1984, 1989; Hereford, 2001. MCIM; MCIPR. Methodist local preacher. Editor, The Potter, newspaper, 1982–94. *Publications:* Eliza Asbury: her cottage and her son, 2003. *T:* (0121) 429 4207. *E:* davidhallam5@aol.com. *W:* www.davidhallam.com.

HALLAM, Prof. Susan, MBE 2015; PhD; CPsychol; Professor of Education and Music Psychology (formerly Professor of Education), Institute of Education, University of London, 2003–14, now Emerita (Dean, Faculty of Policy and Society, 2007–13); *b* Leicester, 9 April 1949; *d* of Thomas and Gwendoline Whetstone; *m* 1971, Richard John Hallam; one *s*. *Educ:* Hinckley Grammar Sch., Leics; Royal Acad. of Music (LRAM, ARAM 2006); Univ. of London (BA Psychol. (ext.)); City of Birmingham Poly. (Cert Ed); Inst. of Educn, Univ. of London (MSc, PhD 1992). CPsychol 1994. Principal 2nd violin, Midland Light Orch., 1971–77; peripatetic violin teacher: Sandwell Educn Authy, 1978–80; Oxon Local Authy, 1980–82; Thame Area Music School: Dir, 1982–88; Sen. Instrumental Teacher, 1983–88; Hd of Strings, 1988–90; Lectr in Psychol., City of Westminster Coll., 1991; Course Tutor, Open Univ., 1991–95; Lectr, then Sen. Lectr, Inst. of Educn, Univ. of London, 1991–2000; Prof. of Educn (Teaching and Learning) and Hd, Curriculum Acad. Div., Westminster Inst. of Educn, Oxford Brookes Univ., 2000–01; Institute of Education, University of London: Sen. Lectr, 2001, Reader, 2001–03, in Educn and Chair, Learning and Teaching Cttee; Hd, Sch. of Lifelong Educn and Internat. Devlt, 2004–07. Subject Reviewer for Educn, 2000–01, Instnl Auditor, 2001–, QAA. British Psychological Society: Sec., Educn Section, 1998–99; Chair, Psychol. of Educn Section, 1999–2001, 2004–06 and 2011–; British Educational Research Association: Mem. Council, 2000–02; Treas., 2002–08; Mem., Advocacy Cttee, Internat. Soc. for Music Educn, 2006–. Jt Ed., British Psychol Soc. Educn Section Rev., 1996–99; Ed., Psychol. of Music, 2002–07. AFBPsS 1995; FHEA 2001; FAcSS (AcSS 2003). FRSA 1996. *Publications:* (with C. Roaf) Here Today, Here Tomorrow: helping schools to promote attendance, 1995; Improving School Attendance, 1996; Instrumental Teaching: a practical guide to better teaching and learning, 1998; (with J. Ireson) Ability Grouping in Education, 2001; (jtly) Effective Pupil Grouping in the Primary School: a practical guide, 2002; Ability Grouping in Schools: a literature review, 2002; Homework: the evidence, 2004; Music Psychology in Education, 2006; (with L. Rogers) Improving Behaviour and Attendance at School, 2008; (ed jtly) Oxford Handbook of Music Psychology, 2008; (ed jtly) Music Education in the 21st Century in the United Kingdom: achievements, analysis and aspirations, 2010; (with Helena Grant) Preparing for Success: a practical guide for young musicians, 2012; (jtly) Active Ageing with Music: supporting wellbeing in the third and fourth ages, 2014; contrib. chapters to books and articles to jls. *Recreations:* reading, films, walking. *Address:* UCL Institute of Education, 20 Bedford Way, WC1H 0AL. *T:* (01908) 522850, *Fax:* (020) 7612 6632. *E:* s.hallam@ioe.ac.uk.

HALLAM SMITH, Elizabeth, PhD; FSA, FRHistS; Director of Information Services and Librarian, House of Lords, since 2006; *b* 5 Nov. 1950; *d* of Edwin William Lewis Hallam and Barbara Mary Hallam; *m* 1975, Terence Stephen Smith (marr. diss. 2004); one *s* one *d*. *Educ:* Bath High Sch. for Girls; Westfield Coll., London (BA Hons Hist.; PhD Hist.). FRHistS 1980; FSA 1982. Tutorial Fellow, Univ. of Reading, 1975–76; Public Record Office: Asst Keeper, 1976–88; Hd, Publishing and Publicity, 1988–94; Dir, Public Services, 1994–2003; Dir, Nat. Adv. and Public Services, National Archives, 2003–06. Chm., Nat. Council on Archives, 2005–06. Vis. Prof., Sch. of Liby, Archives and Information, UCL, 2007–. Mem., Westminster Abbey Fabric Commn, 2009–. Chairman: Adv. Bd, Victoria County History, 2012–15; Adv. Bd, St Stephen's Chapel Westminster Proj., 2013–. Vice Pres., Soc. of Antiquaries of London, 1998–2002; Hon. Vice Pres., Soc. of Genealogists, 1999–2014. FRSA 1999. *Publications:* Capetian France 987–1328, 1980, 2nd edn 2001 (with Judith Everard); Itinerary of Edward II and his Household, 1307–1328, 1984; Domesday Book through Nine Centuries, 1986; The Domesday Project Book, 1986; (ed) The Plantagenet Chronicles, 1986; (ed) Chronicles of the Age of Chivalry, 1987; (ed) Chronicles of the Wars of the Roses, 1988; (ed) Chronicles of the Crusades, 1989; (ed) Saints: over 200 Patron Saints for today, 1994; (ed) Gods and Goddesses, 1996; (ed with Andrew Prescott) The British Inheritance: a treasury of historic documents, 1999; Domesday Souvenir Guide, 2000; (ed with D. Bates) Domesday Book, 2001; articles on inf. sci. and hist. in learned jls. *Recreations:* travel, walking, music, gardens, historical research. *Address:* House of Lords, SW1A 0PW. *T:* (020) 7219 3240. *E:* hallamsmithe@parliament.uk.

HALLATT, Rt Rev. David Marrison; an Assistant Bishop, Diocese of Salisbury, since 2011; *b* 15 July 1937; *s* of John Vincent Hallatt and Edith Elliott Hallatt; *m* 1967, Margaret Smitton; two *s*. *Educ:* Birkenhead School; Southampton Univ. (BA Hons Geography 1959); St Catherine's Coll., Oxford (BA Theology 1962; MA 1966). Curate, St Andrew's, Maghull, Liverpool, 1963–67; Vicar, All Saints, Totley, dio. Sheffield, 1967–75; Team Rector, St James & Emmanuel, Didsbury, Manchester, 1975–89; Archdeacon of Halifax, 1989–94; Bishop Suffragan of Shrewsbury, 1994–2001; an Asst Bishop, Dio. of Sheffield, 2001–10. FRGS 2009. *Recreations:* walking, birdwatching, music, crosswords, golf. *Address:* St Nicholas Hospital, St Nicholas Road, Salisbury, Wilts SP1 2SW. *T:* (01722) 413360. *E:* david.hallatt@btopenworld.com.

HALLCHURCH, David Thomas, TD 1965; Chief Justice, Turks and Caicos Islands, West Indies, 1996–98; *b* 4 April 1929; *s* of Walter William Hallchurch and Marjorie Pretoria Mary Hallchurch (*née* Cooper); *m* 1st, 1954, Gillian Mary Jagger (marr. diss. 1972); three *s*; 2nd, 1972, Susan Kathryn Mather Brennan; one step *s* one step *d*. *Educ:* Bromsgrove Sch.; Trinity Coll., Oxford (MA Hons). Called to the Bar, Gray's Inn, 1953; Whitehead Travelling Scholarship, Canada and USA, 1953–54; practised as barrister-at-law on Midland and Oxford Circuit, 1954–60 and 1964–96; a Recorder, 1980–97. Puisne Judge, Botswana, 1986–88; Actg Chief Justice, Turks and Caicos Is, 1993. Pt-time Immigration Adjudicator, 1990–96; Asst Comr, Parly Boundary Commn for England, 1992. Legal Mem., Mental Health Review Tribunal for the West Midlands, 1979–86. Major, Staffs Yeomanry (Queen's Own Royal Regiment), TA, 1953–66. *Publications:* The Law is Not a Bore, 2008. *Recreations:* cricket, drawing (cartoons). *Address:* Neachley House, Tong, Shifnal, Shropshire TF11 8PH. *Club:* Vincent's (Oxford).

HALLETT; *see* Hughes-Hallett and Hughes Hallett.

HALLETT, Anthony Philip; Chairman, CE Facilities Services Ltd (formerly Cleanevent Group Ltd), since 2012; Director, Richmond Football Club, since 2000; Chairman: Richmond Athletic Association, since 2011; Richmond Rugby Redevelopment Group, since 2012; *b* 11 Feb. 1945; *s* of late Maurice George Hallett and Ann Halliwell Bailey; *m* 1972, Faith Mary Holland-Martin; three *s*. *Educ:* Ipswich Sch.; Britannia RN Coll. Joined RN 1963; served in HM Ships Victorious and Hermes; Flag Lieut, Hong Kong; HMS Eskimo; RNC Greenwich; BRNC, 1975–77; MoD, 1978–79; HMS Invincible, 1979–81; served C-in-C Fleet, 1982–83; HMS Illustrious, 1983–85; MoD, 1986–90; RNSC Greenwich, 1990–91; Sec. to Chief of Fleet Support, 1992–94; Captain, RN, retd 1995. Rugby Football: Navy Captain, 1969; 11 caps; played for US Portsmouth, Banbury, Blackheath, Richmond, Oxfordshire, S Counties, Combined Services, Hong Kong *v* England 1971. Rugby Football

Union: Mem., 1979–97; Privilege Mem., 1997–; Chm., Ground Cttee, 1979–95; Chm., Twickenham Stadium Redevelt, 1991–95; Sec., 1995–97; Chief Exec., 1997; Selector and Chm., RN RU, 1985–94. Richmond Football Club: Chm., 1991–95 and 1999–2004; Chief Exec., 1998–99; Pres., 2004–07. *Recreations:* gardening (Mem., Nat. Gardens Scheme), contemporary art, all sports. *Address:* Whitcombe, Overbury, Tewkesbury GL20 7NZ. *T:* (01386) 725206. *Clubs:* Turf, East India, MCC, Lord's Taverners; Royal Mid-Surrey Golf; Wooden Spoon (Whitstable).

HALLETT, Prof. Christine Margaret, PhD; FRSE; Professor of Social Policy, 1995–2010, and Principal and Vice-Chancellor, 2004–10, University of Stirling; *b* 4 May 1949; *d* of Richard William Hallett and Gwendoline Hallett (*née* Owen). *Educ:* Newnham Coll., Cambridge (BA 1970); Loughborough Univ. (PhD Social Policy 1994). Civil servant, DHSS, 1970–74; research and teaching posts: Oxford Univ., 1974–76; Keele Univ., 1976–83; Univ. of WA, 1983–84; Univ. of Leicester, 1984–89; University of Stirling: Reader in Social Policy, 1989–95; Sen. Dep. Principal, 2001–03. A Civil Service Comr, 2008–13. Trustee, UKCISA, 2007– (Chm., 2007–11). Mem. Bd, Bournemouth Univ., 2010–12. FRSE 2002. *Publications:* (with O. Stevenson) Child Abuse: aspects of interprofessional co-operation, 1979; The Personal Social Services in Local Government, 1982; (ed) Women and Social Services Department, 1989; (with E. Birchall) Co-ordination and Child Protection, 1992; Interagency Co-ordination in Child Protection, 1995; (with E. Birchall) Working Together in Child Protection, 1995; (ed) Women and Social Policy: an introduction, 1996; (ed jtly) Social Exclusion and Social Work, 1998; (ed jtly) Hearing the Voices of Children: social policy for a new century, 2003; monographs; contrib. learned jls. *Recreations:* golf, walking, tennis, music.

HALLETT, Rt Hon. Dame Heather (Carol), DBE 1999; PC 2005; **Rt Hon. Lady Justice Hallett;** a Lord Justice of Appeal, since 2005; Vice-President, Court of Appeal (Criminal Division), since 2013; *b* 16 Dec. 1949; *d* of late Hugh Hallett, QPM and Doris Hallett; *m* 1974, Nigel Wilkinson, *qv*; two *s*. *Educ:* St Hugh's Coll., Oxford (MA; Hon. Fellow, 1999). Called to the Bar, Inner Temple, 1972, Bencher, 1993 (Treasurer, 2011); QC 1989; a Recorder, 1989–99; a Dep. High Court Judge, 1995–99; a Judge of the High Court of Justice, QBD, 1999–2005. Leader, S Eastern Circuit, 1995–97; Presiding Judge, Western Circuit, 2001–04; Vice Pres., QBD, 2012–14. Mem., Judicial Appts Commn, 2006–10 (Vice-Chm., 2007–10); Chm., Judicial College (formerly Judicial Studies Bd), 2010–14 (Mem., 2000–04). Chm., Gen. Council of the Bar, 1998 (Vice Chm., 1997). Hon. LLD: Derby, 2000; UCL, 2012; Portsmouth, 2012; DUniv Open, 2004. *Recreations:* theatre, music, games. *Address:* Royal Courts of Justice, Strand, WC2A 2LL.

HALLETT, Prof. Mark Louis, PhD; Director of Studies, Paul Mellon Centre for Studies in British Art, since 2012; *b* Worcester, 11 March 1965; *s* of Roger Hallett and Linda Hallett; *m* 2005, Lynda Murphy; one *d*. *Educ:* Tregaron Secondary Sch., Dyfed; Pembroke Coll., Cambridge (BA Hons Hist. 1986); Courtauld Inst. of Art (MA Hons Hist. of Art 1989; PhD Hist. of Art 1995). University of York: Lectr, 1994–2001, Sen. Lectr, 2001–04, Reader, 2004–06, in Hist. of Art; Prof. of History of Art, 2006–12; Hd, Dept of Hist. of Art, 2007–12. Andrew W. Mellon Fellow, Yale Univ., 1990–91. Co-Curator: Hogarth Exhibn, Musée du Louvre, Tate Britain and Caixa Forum, Barcelona, 2006–07; William Etty: art and controversy, York Art Gall., 2011–12; Joshua Reynolds: Experiments in Paint, Wallace Collection, 2015. Vis. Scholar, Pembroke Coll., Cambridge, 2013–14; Vis. Prof., Courtauld Inst. of Art, 2014–15. *Publications:* The Spectacle of Difference: graphic satire in the age of Hogarth, 1999; Hogarth, 2000; (ed with Jane Rendall) Eighteenth-Century York: culture, space and society, 2003; Faces in a Library: Sir Joshua Reynolds's 'Streatham Worthies', 2012; (ed jtly) Living with the Royal Academy: artistic ideals and experiences in England, 1768–1848, 2013; Reynolds: portraiture in action, 2014; exhibition catalogues. *Recreations:* reading short stories and The New York Review of Books, watching films and football. *Address:* Paul Mellon Centre for Studies in British Art, 16 Bedford Square, WC1B 3JA. *T:* (020) 7580 0311. *E:* mhallett@paul-mellon-centre.ac.uk.

HALLETT, Rob Leonard; Chief Executive Officer: Robomagic Live Ltd, since 2015; Robomagic 360; Robomagic Capital; *b* London, 9 March 1958; *s* of Vernon Harold Leonard Hallett and Alma Victoria Hallett (*née* Braham); *m* Yvette Isha Allen; one *s*. *Educ:* Holy Cross Primary Sch., Uckfield; Uckfield Sch.; Lewes Tertiary Coll. Dir, DBA Artist Agency, 1980–84; Man. Dir, Performance and Trident Studios, 1984–90; Director: Marshall Arts Ltd, 1990–2000; Mean Fiddler plc, 2000–04; Sen. Vice Pres., 2004–07, Pres., 2007–14, AEG Live; CEO, AEG Live UK, 2012–14. Member: Cttee, Julie's Bicycle, 2007–; Bd, Fund for Tolerance, Reconciliation and Peace, 2009–; Bd, Revox Internat. AG, 2012–; Bd, Tickets for Troops, 2014–. Fundraising Ambassador, Community Links, 2013–. *Recreations:* watching Chelsea FC, food, wine, not accepting universal alibi. *E:* rob@robomagiclive.com.

HALLGARTEN, His Honour Anthony Bernard Richard; QC 1978; a Circuit Judge, 1993–2004; Mercantile List Judge, Central London County Court, 1996–2004; arbitrator, since 2004; *b* 16 June 1937; *s* of late Fritz and Friedel Hallgarten; *m* 1962, Katherine Borchard (marr. diss. 1996); one *s* three *d*; *m* 1998, Theresa Carlson (*née* Tower). *Educ:* Merchant Taylors' Sch., Northwood; Downing Coll., Cambridge (BA). Called to the Bar, Middle Temple, 1961 (Barstow Scholar, Inns of Court, 1961); Bencher, 1987 (Reader, Lent 2006); a Recorder, 1990–93. Chm., Bar/Inns' Councils Jt Regulations Cttee, 1990–93. Mem., London Maritime Arbitrators' Assoc., 2008. Chair, Management Cttee, Camden Victim Support, 1989–93. *Recreations:* ski-ing, SW France, cycling. *Address:* 20 Essex Street, WC2R 3AL. *Clubs:* Garrick, MCC.

HALLIDAY, Prof. Alexander Norman, PhD; FRS 2000; Professor of Geochemistry, since 2004 and Head, Mathematical, Physical and Life Sciences Division, 2007–15, University of Oxford; Fellow of Wadham College, Oxford, since 2012 (Fellow of St Hugh's College, 2004–12); *b* 11 Aug. 1952; *s* of Ronald James Rivers Halliday and Kathleen Elizabeth Halliday; *m* 1986, Christine Craig Young; two *s*. *Educ:* Univ. of Newcastle upon Tyne (BSc Hons Geol.; PhD Physics). Postdoctoral Fellow, 1976–81, Lectr, 1981–86, Scottish Univs Res. and Reactor Centre, E Kilbride; Department of Geological Sciences, University of Michigan: Associate Prof., 1986–91; Prof., 1991–98; Adjunct Prof., 1998–2000; Prof., ETH, Zürich, 1998–2004. Member: NERC, 2004–11; Panel, UK RAE, 2005–08; Council, Royal Soc., 2011– (Physical Sec. and Vice-Pres., 2014–). Trustee, Natural History Mus., 2006–14. President: Geochemical Soc., 1995–97 (Fellow, 2001); European Assoc. for Geochemistry, 2007–08 (Urey Medal, 2012). Fellow, Amer. Geophysical Union, 2000 (Bowen Award, 1998; Pres. Volcanology, Geochemistry and Petrology sect., 2008–10); Foreign Associate, US Nat. Acad. of Scis, 2015. Murchison Medal, Geol Soc., 2003; Oxburgh Medal, Inst. of Measurement and Control, 2015. *Publications:* over 360 articles in sci. jls. *Recreation:* cycling. *Address:* Department of Earth Sciences, Oxford University, South Parks Road, Oxford OX1 3AN.

HALLIDAY, Charlotte Mary Irvine, NEAC 1961; RWS 1976 (ARWS 1971); topographical artist; Keeper, New English Art Club, since 1989; *b* 5 Sept. 1935; *d* of late Edward Halliday, CBE, RP, RBA and Dorothy Halliday. *Educ:* Francis Holland Sch.; Royal Academy Sch. *Commissions* include: construction of the Shell Centre, 1957–59; head offices of many City banks and insurance cos, incl. Willis Faber, Nat West Tower; clubs, colleges, major ecclesiastical buildings, incl. St Paul's and Salisbury Cathedrals; numerous stately and private homes. *Publications:* (illus.) A. Stuart Gray, Edwardian Architecture, 1985; (with A. Stuart Gray) Fanlights, a visual architectural history, 1990. *Recreations:* choral singing, walking in the Downs, cats. *Address:* 36A Abercorn Place, St John's Wood, NW8 9XP. *T:* (020) 7289 1924; St Magnus Cottage, Houghton, near Arundel, W Sussex.

HALLIDAY, Prof. Ian Gibson, CBE 2009; PhD; FRSE, FLSW; Chief Executive, Scottish Universities Physics Alliance, 2005–09; Professor, University of Edinburgh, 2005–09, now Emeritus; *b* 5 Feb. 1940; *s* of John Alexander Halliday and Gladys (*née* Taylor); *m* 1965, Ellenor Gardiner Hervey Wilson; one *s* one *d*. *Educ:* Kelso High Sch.; Perth Acad.; Edinburgh Univ. (MA 1961; MSc 1962); Clare Coll., Cambridge (PhD 1964). Instructor, Princeton Univ., 1964–66; Fellow, Christ's Coll., Cambridge, 1966–67; Imperial College, University of London: Lectr, 1967–75; Reader, 1975–90; Prof., 1990–92; University of Wales, Swansea: Prof. of Physics and Hd of Dept, 1992–98; Dean of Graduate Sch., 1993–96; Hon. Prof., 2002–; Hon. Fellow, 2005; Chief Exec., PPARC, 1998–2005. Chm., Prior Options Review of Royal Observatories, 1995. Member: PPARC, 1994–98; European Res. Adv. Bd, 2001–07; Reconfiguration and Collaboration Panel, 1998–2013, Res. Libraries Review, 2001–02, HEFCE. Member: Bd, World Premier Inst., Min. of Educn, Culture, Sports, Sci. and Technol., Japan, 1998–; Governing Bd, Fermi Res. Alliance, Fermi Nat. Accelerator Lab., Chicago, 2007–13; Internat. Review, Korean Nat. Res. Foundn, 2012. Pres., European Sci. Foundn, 2006–11. FLSW 2011. Hon. FInstP 2012. Hon. DSc: Edinburgh, 2005; Wales, 2006; Glasgow, 2006. *Publications:* numerous papers on theoretical particle physics in Nuclear Physics, Physics Letters. *Recreations:* catching Tweed salmon, golf, tennis. *Address:* Derwent House, Walkley Hill, Rodborough, Stroud GL5 3TX. *E:* Ian.Halliday@e-halliday.org.

HALLIDAY, Dr John Dixon; Rector, High School of Dundee, since 2008; *b* Wantage, 24 June 1955; *s* of Dixon and Audrey Halliday; *m* 1988, Anna Salvesen; two *s* one *d*. *Educ:* Abingdon Sch., Oxon; Univ. of Exeter (BA Hons German and Linguistics); Robinson Coll., Cambridge (PhD German and Austrian Satire 1986). Lectr in English, Univ. of Passau, Germany, 1982–85; freelance translator, Cambridge, 1985–87; Head of German, Merchiston Castle Sch., Edinburgh, 1987–91; Head of Modern Langs, 1991–95, Housemaster, 1993–96, Dir of Studies (Middle Sch.), 1996–97, Sedbergh Sch.; Headmaster, Rannoch Sch., Perthshire, 1997–2001; teacher of French and German, Dollar Acad., 2001–02; Headmaster, Albyn Sch., Aberdeen, 2002–08. Burgess: City of Aberdeen; Guildry, Dundee. *Publications:* Karl Kraus, Franz Pfemfert and the First World war, 1986; contrib. articles on German literary hist., censorship and the GDR. *Recreations:* sport - participating, coaching, refereeing; music - viola, fiddle, singing; reading - history, politics. *Address:* High School of Dundee, Euclid Crescent, Dundee DD1 1HU. *Club:* Rotary (Dundee).

HALLIDAY, John Frederick, CB 1994; Deputy Under Secretary of State, Home Office, 1990–2001; *b* 19 Sept. 1942; *s* of E. Halliday; *m* 1970, Alison Burgess; four *s*. *Educ:* Whitgift School, Croydon; St John's College, Cambridge (MA). Teacher, under VSO, Aitchison College, Lahore, 1964–66; Home Office, 1966; Principal Private Sec. to Home Sec., 1980; Asst Under-Sec. of State, Home Office, 1983–87; Under Sec., DHSS, then Dept of Health, 1987–90, on secondment. *Publications:* Making Punishments Work (Govt report), 2001. *Recreations:* music, gardening, theatre.

HALLIDAY, Prof. Michael Alexander Kirkwood; Professor of Linguistics in the University of Sydney, 1976–87, Emeritus Professor, since 1988; *b* 13 April 1925; *s* of late Wilfrid J. Halliday and Winifred Halliday (*née* Kirkwood). *Educ:* Rugby School; SOAS, University of London (BA); MA, PhD, Cambridge. Served Army, 1944–47. Asst Lectr in Chinese, Cambridge Univ., 1954–58; Lectr in General Linguistics, Edinburgh Univ., 1958–60; Reader in General Linguistics, Edinburgh Univ., 1960–63; Dir, Communication Res. Centre, UCL, 1963–65; Linguistic Soc. of America Prof., Indiana Univ., 1964; Prof. of General Linguistics, UCL, 1965–71; Fellow, Center for Advanced Study in the Behavioral Sciences, Stanford, Calif., 1972–73; Prof. of Linguistics, Univ. of Illinois, 1973–74; Prof. of Language and Linguistics, Essex Univ., 1974–75. Visiting Professor of Linguistics: Yale, 1967; Brown, 1971; Nairobi, 1972; Nat. Univ. of Singapore, 1990–91; Internat. Christian Univ., Tokyo, 1992; Lee Kuan Yew Distinguished Visitor, Nat. Univ. of Singapore, 1986; Hon. Sen. Res. Fellow, Birmingham Univ., 1991; Dist. Vis. Prof., Univ. of HK, 2003–04. FAHA 1979. Corresp. FBA 1989; For. Mem., Academia Europaea, 1994. Guest Prof., Peking Univ., 1995. Hon. Fellow: Univ. of Wales, Cardiff, 1998; Central Inst. of English and For. Langs, Hyderabad, India, 1999. Dr *hc* Nancy, 1968; Hon. DLitt: Birmingham, 1987; York (Canada), 1988; Athens, 1995; Macquarie, 1996; Lingnan, Hong Kong, 1999; DUniv Open, 2002; Hon. LLD British Columbia, 2007; Hon. DPhil Southern Denmark, 2011. *Publications:* The Language of the Chinese 'Secret History of the Mongols', 1959; (with A. McIntosh and P. Strevens) The Linguistic Sciences and Language Teaching, 1964; (with A. McIntosh) Patterns of Language, 1966; Intonation and Grammar in British English, 1967; A Course in Spoken English: Intonation, 1970; Explorations in the Functions of Language, 1973; Learning How To Mean, 1975; (with R. Hasan) Cohesion in English, 1976; System and Function in Language, ed G. Kress, 1976; Language as Social Semiotic, 1978; An Introduction to Functional Grammar, 1985; Spoken and Written Language, 1985; (with J. Martin) Writing Science, 1993; (with C. Matthiessen) Construing Experience through Meaning, 1999; (with W. Greaves) Intonation in the Grammar of English, 2008; Complementarities in Language, 2008; Collected Papers, vols 1 and 2, 2002, vol. 3, 2003, vols 4 and 5, 2004, vols 6 and 7, 2005, vol. 8, 2006, vols 9 and 10, 2007, vol. 11, 2013; articles in Jl of Linguistics, Word, Trans of Philological Soc., Functions of Lang., Functional Linguistics, etc. *Address:* Box 46, 145 Sydney Road, Fairlight, NSW 2094, Australia.

HALLIDAY, Norman Pryde; Senior Principal Medical Officer (Under Secretary), Department of Health and Social Security, later Department of Health, 1977–92; *b* 28 March 1932; *s* of late James and Jessie Thomson Hunter Halliday; *m* 1st, 1953, Eleanor Smith (marr. diss. 2012); three *s* one *d*; 2nd, 2012, Eithne Keaveney; one *s* one *d*. *Educ:* Woodside, Glasgow; King's Coll., London; King's Coll. Hosp. Med. Sch. SRN 1955; MB BS, MRCS, LRCP 1964; DCH RCPGlas 1969; MBA: Warwick, 1991; Open Univ., 1992. Various posts in clinical medicine, incl. Registrar (Paediatrics), KCH, London; SMO, DHSS, 1972. Gen. Man., Eur. Dialysis and Transplant Assoc., 1994–95; Consultant Advr to Minister of Health, Saudi Arabia, 1996–2000; Consultant to UN in Abu Dhabi, 2001. Tutor: Open Univ., 1992–96; Warwick Univ., 1992–96. QHP 1990–93. *Publications:* articles on medical subjects in professional journals. *Recreations:* photography, sub aqua diving, fashion, DIY, cross-bow shooting. *Address:* Gurrs Farm, Crowborough Hill, Crowborough, E Sussex TN6 2SD. *T:* (01892) 669132.

HALLIDAY, Rt Rev. Robert Taylor; Bishop of Brechin, 1990–96; *b* 7 May 1932; *s* of James Halliday and Agnes Logan Halliday (*née* Scott); *m* 1960, Georgina Mabel, (Gena) (*née* Chadwin) (*d* 2013); one *d*. *Educ:* High Sch. of Glasgow; Univ. of Glasgow (MA, BD); Episcopal Theol Coll., Edinburgh. Deacon 1957; priest 1958. Assistant Curate: St Andrew's, St Andrews, 1957–60; St Margaret's, Newlands, Glasgow, 1960–63; Rector, Church of the Holy Cross, Davidson's Mains, Edinburgh, 1963–83; External Lectr in New Testament, Episcopal Theol Coll., Edin., 1963–74; Canon of St Mary's Cathedral, Edinburgh, 1973–83; Rector of St Andrew's, St Andrews, 1983–90; Tutor in Biblical Studies, Univ. of St Andrews, 1984–90; warrant, dio. of Edinburgh, 1997–. Hon. Canon, Trinity Cathedral, Davenport, Iowa, 1990. *Recreations:* walking, reading, visiting gardens, shredding appeals from Uganda. *Address:* 28 Forbes Road, Edinburgh EH10 4ED. *T:* (0131) 221 1490.

HALLIDAY, Sandra Pauline, CEng; Founder and Principal, Gaia Research, since 1996. *Educ:* Warwick Univ. (BSc Hons Engrg Design and Appropriate Technology); Reading Univ. (MPhil 1999). MCIBSE 1994. Research at Univs of Bath and Reading, 1986–91; Founder, then Head of Centre for Construction Ecology, BSRIA, 1990–95. Current research projects incl. solar design, innovative building membranes, daylighting, low allergy housing, teaching, research and guidance in sustainable building design, model briefs for sustainable develt of schs, communities. Royal Acad. of Engrg Vis. Prof. in Sustainable Engrg Design, Univ. of Strathclyde, 2003–08. FRSA. *Publications:* Green Guide to the Architects' Job Book, 2000, 2nd edn 2007; Anarchi: animal architecture, 2003; Sustainable Construction, 2008; papers, articles, technical reports and conf. proceedings. *Recreations:* squash, Go, walking, cycling, ecology.

HALLIDAY, Prof. Timothy Richard, DPhil; Professor in Biology, The Open University, 1991–2009; *b* 11 Sept. 1945; *s* of Jack and Edna Halliday; *m* 1970, Carolyn Bridget Wheeler; one *s* two *d*. *Educ:* Marlborough Coll.; New Coll., Oxford (MA, DPhil); King's Coll., Cambridge (CertEd). Lectr, Sen. Lectr and Reader, 1977–91, Open Univ. Internat. Dir, IUCN/SSC Declining Amphibian Populations Task Force, 1994–2006. Chm., Conservation and Consultancy Bd, Zool Soc. of London, 1993–96. *Publications:* Vanishing Birds, 1978; Sexual Strategy, 1980; (with K. Adler) The Encyclopedia of Reptiles and Amphibians, 1986 (numerous foreign language edns); (with K. Adler) The New Encyclopedia of Reptiles and Amphibians, 2002; The Book of Frogs, 2015. *Recreations:* biological illustration, gardening, travel. *Address:* 21 Farndon Road, Oxford OX2 6RT. *T:* (01865) 512163.

HALLIGAN, Prof. Aidan William Francis, MD; FRCP, FRCOG; Director, Well North, since 2014; Principal, NHS Staff College, since 2007; *b* Dublin, 17 Sept. 1957; *s* of Michael and Maureen Halligan; *m* 1985, Dr Carol Mary Sarah Furlong; three *d*. *Educ:* Templeogue Coll., Dublin; Trinity Coll., Dublin (MB BCh BAO, MA); MD. MRCOG 1991, FRCOG 2004; MRCPI 1996; FFPH (FFPHM 2003); FRCP 2004. SHO, Royal City of Dublin Hosp., St James's and Rotunda Hosps, Dublin, 1986–88; Registrar, Rotunda Hosp., then Mater Misericordiae Hosp., Dublin, 1989–90; Res. Registrar, Rotunda Hosp., Dublin, 1991–93; Lectr, 1993–94, Sen. Lectr, 1994–97, in Obstetrics and Gynaecology, Leicester Univ.; Consultant Obstetrician and Gynaecol., Leicester Royal Infirmary, 1994–97; Prof. of Fetal Maternal Medicine, Leicester Univ. and Univ. Hosps of Leicester NHS Trust, 1997–99; Postgrad. Dir, Training, Obstetrics and Gynaecol., 1995–99, Hd, Obstetric Service, 1998–99, Univ. Hosps of Leicester NHS Trust; Prog. Trng Dir, Obstetrics and Gynaecol., S Trent, 1995–99; Hd, NHS Clinical Governance Support Team, 1999–2002; Dep. CMO, DoH, 2003–05; Dir of Clinical Governance for NHS, 1999–2006; Chief Exec., Elision Health Ltd, 2006–08; Dir, Educn, UCL Hosp., 2007–13; Chief of Safety, Brighton and Sussex Univ. Hosps NHS Trust, 2008–13. Visiting Professor: Dept of Surgical Oncology and Technol., Imperial Coll. London, 2005–10; Postgrad. Med. Sch., Univ. of Surrey, 2007–09. Chm., London Pathway Homeless Health Service, 2009–. *Publications:* articles in Br. Jl of Obstetrics and Gynaecol., BMJ, Lancet, Jl of Hypertension, Obstetrics and Gynecol., Hypertension in Pregnancy, Amer. Jl of Obstetrics and Gynecol., Br. Jl of Clinical Governance, Jl of RSocMed, and other learned jls. *Recreations:* reading, walking. *Address:* Well North, Manchester Academic Science Centre, University of Manchester, Core Technology Facility, Grafton Street, Manchester M13 9NT. *T:* (0161) 275 0180. *E:* aidan.halligan@manchester.ac.uk.

HALLIGAN, Liam James; Managing Director, New Sparta Media, since 2013; Business Section columnist, Sunday Telegraph, since 2001; Editor-at-Large, Business New Europe, since 2013; *b* 29 April 1969; *s* of Martin Thomas Halligan and Evelyn Halligan (*née* Thorp); partner, Lucy Ward; one *s* two *d*. *Educ:* John Lyon Sch., Harrow (entrance schol., head boy); Univ. of Warwick (BSc 1st Cl. Hons Econs 1991); St Antony's Coll., Oxford (MPhil Econs 1994). Economics Intern: Internat. Food Policy Res. Inst., 1991; IMF, 1992; Hd of Res., Social Mkt Foundn, 1993; Res. Economist, and author, Russian Econ. Trends, LSE, 1994–95; Moscow Reporter, The Economist, 1995–96; columnist, Moscow Times, 1995–96; Political Corresp., FT, 1996–98; Econs Corresp., Channel 4 News, 1998–2006; Econs Ed., Sunday Telegraph, 2006–07; columnist, Sunday Business, 2000–01; Financial Columnist, GQ Mag., 2007–10; Chief Economist, Prosperity Capital Mgt, 2007–13. Wincott Business Broadcaster of Year, Harold Wincott Foundn, 1999; Business Journalist of Year (Broadcast), World Leadership Forum, 2004, 2005; Business and Finance Journalist of Year, British Press Awards, 2007; Columnist of Year, Workworld, 2007. *Publications:* (with Frank Field) Europe Isn't Working, 1994; contrib. numerous articles for Economist Intelligence Unit and Wall St Jl. *Recreations:* family, sailing, rowing, guitar, double bass, Saffron Walden Choral Society, football, roller-skating, film. *Address:* Bridge House, 15 Bridge Street, Saffron Walden, Essex CB10 1BT. *E:* liam.halligan@telegraph.co.uk.

HALLINAN, Mary Alethea; *see* Parry Evans, M. A.

HALLIWELL, Prof. (Francis) Stephen, DPhil; FBA 2014; FRSE; Professor of Greek, since 1995, and Wardlaw Professor of Classics, since 2014, University of St Andrews; *b* Wigan, 18 Oct. 1953; *s* of Francis Halliwell and Joyce Halliwell (*née* Casey); *m* 1978, Helen Ruth Gainford (marr. diss. 2010); two *s*. *Educ:* St Francis Xavier's Coll., Liverpool; Worcester Coll., Oxford (Schol.; BA 1st Cl. Lit. Hum. 1976 (Passmore Edwards Prize 1976); DPhil 1981). Lecturer: in Classics, Jesus Coll., Oxford, 1979–80; in Classics and Drama, Westfield Coll., London, 1980–82; Fellow, Corpus Christi Coll., Cambridge, 1982–84; Birmingham University: Lectr in Classics, 1984–90; Sen. Lectr, 1990–94; Reader, 1994–95. Visiting Professor: of Classics, Chicago Univ., 1990; of Aesthetics, Univ. of Rome (Roma Tre), 1998; H. L. Hooker Dist. Vis. Prof., McMaster Univ., 2009; Chaire Cardinal Mercier, Univ. of Louvain, 2010; Townsend Vis. Prof., Cornell Univ., 2012; Vis. Faculty Fellow, Center for Ideas and Society, Univ. of Calif, Riverside, 1993. FRSE 2011. *Publications:* Aristotle's Poetics, 1986, 2nd edn 1998; The Poetics of Aristotle, 1987; Plato Republic 10, 1988; Plato Republic 5, 1993; Aristotle Poetics (Loeb Classical Liby edn), 1995; Aristophanes: Birds, Lysistrata, Assembly-Women, Wealth, 1997; The Aesthetics of Mimesis, 2002 (Premio Europeo d'Estetica, Società Italiana d'Estetica, 2008); Greek Laughter, 2008 (Criticos Prize, Hellenic Soc. of London); Between Ecstasy and Truth, 2011. *Recreation:* music. *Address:* School of Classics, University of St Andrews, St Andrews, Fife KY16 9AL. *T:* (01334) 462617. *E:* fsh@st-andrews.ac.uk.

HALLIWELL, Prof. Richard Edward Winter; William Dick Professor of Veterinary Clinical Studies, Royal (Dick) School of Veterinary Studies, University of Edinburgh, 1988–2002, now Emeritus (Dean, Faculty of Veterinary Medicine, 1990–94 and 2000–02); *b* 16 June 1937; *s* of Arthur Clare Halliwell and Winifred Dorothea Goode; *m* 1963, Jenifer Helen Roper; two *d*. *Educ:* St Edward's Sch., Oxford; Gonville and Caius Coll., Cambridge (MA, VetMB, PhD); MRCVS. Jun. Fellow in Vet. Surgery, Univ. of Bristol, 1961–63; private vet. practice, London, 1963–68; Vis. Fellow in Dermatology, Univ. of Pennsylvania Sch. of Vet. Med., 1968–70; Wellcome Vet. Fellowship Univ. of Cambridge, 1970–73; Asst Prof. of Dermatology, Univ. of Pennsylvania Sch. of Vet. Med., 1973–77; Prof. and Chm., Dept of Med. Scis, Univ. of Florida Coll. of Vet. Med., 1977–88; Prof., Dept of Med. Microbiol., Univ. of Florida Coll. of Med., 1977–88. Part-time Prof., Sch. of Veterinary Medicine, St George's Univ., Grenada, 2008–12. UK Rep., EC Adv. Cttee on Vet. Trng, 1994–98. President: Amer. Acad. of Veterinary Allergy, 1978–80; Amer. Assoc. of Veterinary Immunologists, 1984; Amer. Coll. of Veterinary Dermatology, 1984–86; Eur. Assoc. of Estabs for Vet. Educn, 1994–98 (Hon. Life Pres., 2002); Eur. Coll. of Vet. Dermatology, 1996–98; World Congress of Vet. Dermatology Assoc., 1999–2010; Royal College of Veterinary Surgeons: Treas., 2001–02; Jun. Vice-Pres., 2002–03; Pres., 2003–04; Sen. Vice-Pres., 2004–05. FMedSci 1999. Dr *hc* Warsaw Agricl Univ., 2003. Lifetime Career Achievement Award, Eur. Coll. of Veterinary Dermatol., 2004; Internat. Award for Scientific Achievement, World Small Animal Veterinary Assoc., 2012; Schindelka Award, World Assoc. for Veterinary Dermatology, 2012. *Publications:* (with N. T. Gorman) Veterinary Clinical Immunology, 1989; (with C. von Tscharner) Advances in Veterinary Dermatology, 1990; numerous pubns in area of clin. immunology and vet. dermatology. *Recreations:* wine, music, travelling. *Address:* 2A Ainslie Place, Edinburgh EH3 6AR. *T:* (0131) 225 8765.

HALLIWELL, Stephen; *see* Halliwell, F. S.

HALLS, Andrew David, MA; Head Master, King's College School, Wimbledon, since 2008; *b* 29 Jan. 1959; *s* of Gerald and Barbara Halls; *m* 1987, Véronique Le Droff; two *d*. *Educ:* Shenley Court Sch., Birmingham; Gonville and Caius Coll., Cambridge (Schol.; BA Double 1st Cl. Hons English 1981; MA). English teacher: Chigwell Sch., 1981–84; Whitgift Sch., 1984–89; Hd of English, Bristol GS, 1989–95; Dep. Headmaster, Trinity Sch., 1995–98; Master, Magdalen Coll. Sch., 1998–2007. *Recreations:* family, reading, theatre, running. *Address:* King's College School, Wimbledon, SW19 4TT.

HALLS, David John; Director of Music, Salisbury Cathedral, since 2005; *b* 14 Jan. 1963; *s* of William and Sally Halls; *m* 1986, Nicola Holman; three *s* two *d*. *Educ:* Worcester Coll., Oxford (BA Hons Music 1984, MA); Winchester (PGCE 1985). FRCO 1985. Organ Scholar, Winchester Cath., 1984; Salisbury Cathedral: Asst Organist, 1985–2000; Asst Dir of Music, 2000–05. *Recreations:* reading, wine, football, cricket. *Address:* Wyndham House, 65 The Close, Salisbury SP1 2EN. *T:* (01722) 555125, *Fax:* (01722) 555117. *E:* d.halls@salcath.co.uk.

HALONEN, Tarja Kaarina; President of Finland, 2000–12; Drylands Ambassador, UN Convention to Combat Desertification, since 2014; *b* Helsinki, 24 Dec. 1943; *m* (marr. diss.); one *d*; *m* 2000, Pentti Arajarvi. *Educ:* Univ. of Helsinki (ML). Lawyer, Lainvalvonta Oy, 1967–68; Social Affairs Sec. and Gen. Sec., Nat. Union of Finnish Students, 1969–70; Lawyer, Cultural Orgn of Finnish Trade Unions, 1970–74; lawyer, 1975–79. Prime Minister's Parly Sec., 1974–75; Mem., Helsinki CC, 1977–96. MP (SDP), Finland, 1979–2000; Chm., Parly Social Affairs Cttee, 1984–87; Minister, Min. of Social Affairs and Health, 1987–90; Minister: for Nordic Co-operation, 1989–91; of Justice, 1990–91; for Foreign Affairs, 1995–2000.

HALPERN, David Anthony; QC 2006; a Recorder, since 2009; a Deputy High Court Judge, Chancery Division, since 2013; *b* 23 May 1956; *s* of Cecil and Audrey Halpern; *m* 1981, Dr Helen Kahn; two *s* one *d*. *Educ:* St Paul's Sch., London; Magdalen Coll., Oxford (Exhibnr; MA Juris). Called to the Bar, Gray's Inn, 1978, Bencher, 2009; in practice as barrister, 1979–, specialising in commercial chancery work and professional negligence. *Publications:* (contrib.) Jackson & Powell on Professional Liability, 6th edn 2006, 7th edn 2012. *Recreations:* piano, cycling, travel, cold-water swimming. *Address:* (chambers) 4 New Square, Lincoln's Inn, WC2A 3RJ. *T:* (020) 7822 2000. *E:* d.halpern@4newsquare.com.

HALPERN, Prof. Jack, FRS 1974; FRS(Can) 2005; Louis Block Distinguished Service Professor of Chemistry, University of Chicago, since 1984; *b* Poland, 19 Jan. 1925; (moved to Canada, 1929; USA 1962); *s* of Philip Halpern and Anna Sass; *m* 1949, Helen Peritz; two *d*. *Educ:* McGill Univ., Montreal. BSc 1946, PhD 1949. NRC Postdoc. Fellow, Univ. of Manchester, 1949–50; Prof. of Chem., Univ. of Brit. Columbia, 1950–62 (Nuffield Foundn Travelling Fellow, Cambridge Univ., 1959–60); Prof. of Chem., Univ. of Chicago, 1962–71, Louis Block Prof., 1971–84. Visiting Professor: Univ. of Minnesota, 1962; Harvard Univ., 1966–67; CIT, 1969; Princeton Univ., 1970–71; Copenhagen Univ., 1978; Firth Vis. Prof., Sheffield, 1982; Sherman Fairchild Dist. Scholar, CIT, 1979; Guest Scholar, Kyoto Univ., 1981; Phi Beta Kappa Vis. Scholar, 1990; R. B. Woodward Vis. Prof., Harvard Univ., 1991; External Sci. Mem., Max Planck Institut für Kohlenforschung, Mulheim, 1983–; Lectureships: 3M, Univ. of Minnesota, 1968; FMC, Princeton Univ., 1969; Du Pont, Univ. of Calif., Berkeley, 1970; Frontier of Chemistry, Case Western Reserve Univ., 1971, 1989; Venable, Univ. of N Carolina, 1973; Ritter Meml, Miami Univ., 1980; University, Univ. of Western Ontario, F. J. Toole, Univ. of New Brunswick, 1981; Werner, Univ. of Kansas, Lansdowne, Univ. of Victoria, 1982; Welch, Univ. of Texas, 1983; Kilpatrick, Illinois Inst. of Tech., 1984; Dow, Univ. of Ottawa, Boomer, Univ. of Alberta, 1985; Bailar, Univ. of Illinois, 1986; Priestley, Penn State Univ., 1987; Taube, Stanford Univ., 1988; Res. Schol., Drew Univ., Liebig. Univ. of Colorado, 1989; Kennedy, Washington Univ., Karcher, Univ. of Oklahoma, Nieuland, Notre Dame, Swift, CIT, Hutchison, Univ. of Rochester, 1992; Rhone-Poulenc, Scripps Res. Inst., Basolo, Northwestern Univ., 1993; Patrick, Kansas State Univ., Jonassen, Tulane Univ., 1995. Associate Editor: Jl of Amer. Chem. Soc.; Inorganica Chimica Acta; Procs of Nat. Acad. of Scis; Mem. Editorial Bds: Accounts of Chemical Research; Jl of Catalysis; Catalysis Reviews; Jl of Coordination Chem.; Inorganic Syntheses; Jl of Molecular Catalysis; Jl of Organometallic Chemistry; Amer. Chem. Soc. Advances in Chemistry series; Gazzetta Chimica Italiana; Organometallics; Catalysis Letters; Reaction Kinetics and Catalysis Letters; Co-editor, OUP International Series of Monographs in Chemistry. Member: Nat. Sci. Foundn Chemistry Adv. Panel, 1967–70; MIT Chemistry Vis. Cttee, 1968–70; Argonne Nat. Lab. Chemistry Vis. Cttee, 1970–73; Amer. Chem. Soc. Petroleum Res. Fund Adv. Bd, 1972–74; NIH Medicinal Chem. Study Sect., 1975–78 (Chm., 1976–78); Princeton Univ. Chem. Adv. Council, 1982–85; Chemistry Adv. Cttee, CIT, 1991–95; Trans-Atlantic Sci. and Humanities Prog. Adv. Bd, Humboldt Foundn, 2001–; Encyclopaedia Britannica Univ. Adv. Cttee, 1985–. Mem., Bd of Trustees and Council, Gordon Research Confs, 1968–70; Chm., Gordon Conf. on Inorganic Chem., 1969; Chm., Amer. Chemical Soc. Div. of Inorganic Chem., 1971; Mem., 1985–, Mem., Council, 1990–, Chm., Chem. Sect., Vice-Pres., 1993–2001, Nat. Acad. of Scis (For. Mem., 1984–85). Chm., German-Amer. Acad. Council, 1993–96, Chm. Bd of Trustees, 1996–99. Member: Bd of Dirs, Renaissance Soc., 1984–87; Bd of Govs, Smart Mus., Univ. of Chicago, 1988–; Adv. Bd, Court Theatre, Univ. of Chicago, 1989–; Dir, Amer. Friends of Royal Soc., 2000–. Fellow, Amer. Acad. of Arts and Sciences, 1967; Sci. Mem., Max Planck Soc., 1983. Hon. FRSC 1987. Hon. DSc: Univ. of British Columbia, 1986; McGill Univ., 1997. Holds numerous honours and awards, including: Amer. Chem. Soc. Award in Inorganic Chem., 1968; Chem. Soc. Award, 1976; Humboldt Award, 1977; Kokes Award, Johns Hopkins Univ., 1978; Amer. Chem. Soc. Award for Distinguished Service in the Advancement of Inorganic Chemistry, 1985; Willard Gibbs Medal, 1986; Bailar Medal, Univ. of Illinois, 1986; Hoffman Medal, German Chem. Soc., 1988; Chemical Pioneer Award, Amer. Inst. of Chemists, 1991; Paracelsus Prize, Swiss Chem. Soc., 1992; Basolo Medal, Northwestern Univ., 1993; Robert A. Welch Award in Chemistry, 1994; Amer. Chem. Soc. Award in Organometallic Chemistry, 1995; Henry Alberts Award, Internat. Precious Metals Inst., 1995. Cross of Merit (Germany), 1996. *Publications:* Editor (with F. Basolo and J. Bunnett) Collected Accounts of Transition Metal Chemistry, vol. I, 1973, vol. II, 1977; contrib. articles on Catalysis and on Coordination Compounds to Encyclopaedia Britannica; numerous articles to Jl of Amer. Chemical Soc. and other scientific jls. *Recreations:* art, music, theatre. *Address:* Department of Chemistry, University of Chicago, 929 East 57th Street, Chicago, IL 60637, USA. *T:* (773) 6436837. *Club:* Quadrangle (Chicago).

HALPERN, Sir Ralph (Mark), Kt 1986; Chairman, Halpern (formerly Halpern Associates), 1994–2005; Chairman, 1981–90, and Chief Executive, 1978–90, Burton Group plc (Managing Director, 1978); Halpern Consulting, since 1992; *b* 24 Oct. 1938; *m* (marr. diss.); one *d*; *m* 2003, Laura (marr. diss. 2007); one *s*. *Educ:* St Christopher School, Letchworth. Started career as trainee, Selfridges; joined Burton Group, 1961; founder, Top Shop, 1970. Member: President's Cttee, CBI, 1984–90; President's Cttee, Business in the Community, 1991–92; Adv. Council, Prince's Youth Business Trust, 1991. Chm., British Fashion Council, 1990–94. Formerly: Local Councillor, Surrey; Chm., E Surrey Rural Police and Community Partnership Gp. FInstD; CCMI.

HALSALL, Hazel Anne; *see* Blears, Rt Hon. H. A.

HALSEY, Rev. John Walter Brooke, 4th Bt *cr* 1920 (but uses designation Brother John Halsey); *b* 26 Dec. 1933; *s* of Sir Thomas Edgar Halsey, 3rd Bt, DSO, and of Jean Margaret Palmer, *d* of late Bertram Willes Dayrell Brooke; *S* father, 1970. *Educ:* Eton; Magdalene College, Cambridge (BA 1957). Deacon 1961, priest 1962, Diocese of York; Curate of Stocksbridge, 1961–65; Brother in Community of the Transfiguration, 1965–. *Heir: cousin* Nicholas Guy Halsey, TD [*b* 14 June 1948; *m* 1976, Viola Georgina Juliet, *d* of Maj. George Thorne, MC, DL; one *s*]. *Address:* The Hermitage, 70E Clerk Street, Loanhead, Midlothian EH20 9RG. *T:* (0131) 440 3028.

HALSEY, Philip Hugh, CB 1986; LVO 1972; Deputy Secretary, Department of Education and Science, 1982–88; *b* 9 May 1928; *s* of Sidney Robert Halsey and Edith Mary Halsey; *m* 1956, Hilda Mary Biggerstaff; two *s*. *Educ:* University Coll. London (BSc; Fellow, 1992). Headmaster, Hampstead Sch., 1961; Principal, DES, 1966; Under-Sec., 1977. Chm. and Chief Exec., Sch. Exams and Assessment Council, 1988–91; Mem., Sch. Teachers' Review Body, 1991–96.

HALSEY, Simon Patrick, CBE 2015; Chorus Director: City of Birmingham Symphony Orchestra, since 1983; London Symphony Orchestra, since 2012; Director, BBC Proms Youth Chorus, since 2012; Chief Conductor, Rundfunkchor Berlin, 2001–15, now Conductor Laureate; Artistic Director, Berlin Philharmonic Youth Choral Programme, since 2012; Professor and Director of Choral Activities, University of Birmingham, since 2012; *b* 8 March 1958; *s* of Louis Arthur Owen Halsey and Evelyn Elisabeth (*née* Calder); *m* 1986, Lucy Jane Lunt; one *s* one *d*. *Educ:* chorister, New Coll., Oxford; Winchester Coll.; King's Coll., Cambridge (Choral Schol.; BA 1979; MA 1983); Royal Coll. Music (Schol.). Conductor, Scottish Opera (Opera-Go-Round), 1979; Dir of Music, Univ. of Warwick, 1980–88; Principal Conductor, City of Birmingham Touring Opera, 1987–2000; Chorus Dir, De Vlaamse Opera, Antwerp, 1991–94; Founder and Artistic Dir, BBC Nat. Chorus of Wales, 1995–2000; Founding Conductor, European Voices, 1999–; Chief Conductor, Netherlands Radio Choir, 2002–08 (Chief Guest Conductor, 1995–2002); Principal Conductor, Choral Programme, Northern Sinfonia, 2004–12. Chief Guest Conductor, Sydney Philharmonia Choirs, 1997–2001; frequent Guest Conductor of choruses, Châtelet Th., Paris, 1996–, and Salzburg Fest., 1998–; Chorus Dir, Sydney Olympic Games, 2000; Artistic Advr, Choir Acad., Schleswig-Holstein Music Fest., 2014–. Consultant Ed., Choral Prog. Series, Faber Music, 1986–, Faber Music, 1994–. Internat. Chair of Choral Conducting, RWCMD, Cardiff, 2008–14. Hon. Dr UCE, 2000; Hon. MA Warwick, 2007; Hon. DMus Birmingham, 2009. Recording awards include: Gramophone Record of Year, Gramophone Magazine (many); Deutsche Schallplatten Kritik Preis (many); Grammy, 2008, 2009, 2011. Queen's Medal for Music, 2015. Bundesverdienstkreuz, 1st Cl. (Germany), 2011. *Publications:* Ed., 30 vols of choral music, 1995–; Schott Master Class Chorleitung - Vom Konzept zum Konzert, 2011. *Recreations:* reading, walking. *Address:* c/o Intermusica Artists' Management, 36 Graham Street, N1 8GJ.

HALSTEAD, Sir Ronald, Kt 1985; CBE 1976; Deputy Chairman, British Steel plc (formerly British Steel Corporation), 1986–94; *b* 17 May 1927; *s* of Richard and Bessie Harrison Halstead; *m* 1st, 1968, Yvonne Cecile de Monchaux (*d* 1978); two *s*; 2nd, 2000, Eugenie Susanne Stoessl (*d* 2013). *Educ:* Lancaster Royal Grammar Sch.; Queens' Coll., Cambridge (Hon. Fellow, 1985). MA, FRSC. Research Chemist, H. P. Bulmer & Co., 1948–53; Manufg Manager, Macleans Ltd, 1954–55; Factory Manager, Beecham Products Inc. (USA), 1955–60; Asst Managing Dir, Beecham Research Labs, 1960–62; Vice-Pres. (Marketing), Beecham Products Inc. (USA), 1962–64; Pres., Beecham Research Labs Inc. (USA), 1962–64; Chairman: Food and Drink Div., Beecham Group Ltd, 1964–67; Beecham Products, 1967–84; Man. Dir (Consumer Products) Beecham Gp, 1973–84; Chm. and Chief Exec., Beecham Gp, 1984–85. Dir, Otis Elevator Co. Ltd (UK), 1978–83; non-executive Director: BSC, later British Steel, 1979–94; The Burmah Oil PLC, 1983–89; Amer. Cyanamid Co. (USA), 1986–94; Davy Corp. plc, 1986–91; Gestetner Holdings PLC, 1986–95; Laurentian Financial Gp, 1991–95. Mem. Egg Re-organisation Commn, 1967–68; Pres., Incorp. Soc. of Brit. Advertisers, 1971–73; Chairman: British Nutrition Foundn, 1970–73; Knitting Sector Gp (formerly Knitting Sector Working Party), NEDO, 1978–90; Bd for Food Studies, Reading Univ., 1983–86; Garment and Textile Sector Gp, NEDO, 1991–93; CAB Internat., 1995–98; Cons. Foreign and Commonwealth Council, 1995–. Vice-Chairman: Proprietary Assoc. of GB, 1968–77; Advertising Assoc., 1973–81; Food and Drink Industries Council, 1973–76; Member: Council and Exec. Cttee, Food Manufrs' Fedn Inc., 1966–85 (Pres., 1974–76); Council, British Nutrition Foundn, 1967–79; Cambridge Univ. Appts Bd, 1969–73; Council, CBI, 1970–86; Council, BIM, 1972–77; Council, Univ. of Buckingham (formerly University Coll. at Buckingham), 1973–95; Council, Nat. Coll. of Food Technol., 1977–78 (Chm. Bd, 1978–83); Council, Univ. of Reading, 1978–98; AFRC, 1978–84; Council, Trade Policy Res. Centre, 1985–89; Monopolies and Mergers Commn, 1993–99 (Mem., Newspaper Panel, 1980–92); Industrial Develt Adv. Bd, 1984–93 (Chm., 1985–93); Council and Exec. Cttee, Imperial Soc. of Knights Bachelor, 1986–2002; Pres., EIA, 1991. Dir and Hon. Treas., Centre for Policy Studies, 1984–93. Trustee, Inst. of Economic Affairs, 1980–93. Governor, Ashridge Management Coll., 1970–2006 (Vice-Chm., 1977–2006); President: Nat. Advertising Benevolent Soc., 1978–80; Inst. of Packaging, 1981–82 (a Vice-Pres., 1979–81). Fellow, Marketing Soc., 1981; FCMI; FInstM; FRSA; FRSC. Hon. Fellow, Inst. of Food Sci. and Technol., 1983–84. Hon. DSc: Reading, 1982; Lancaster, 1987. *Recreations:* sailing, squash racquets, ski-ing. *Address:* 37 Edwardes Square, W8 6HH. *T:* (020) 7603 9010. *Clubs:* Athenæum, Brooks's, Hurlingham, Carlton, Royal Thames Yacht.

HALTON, Prof. David John, EdD; Vice Chancellor, University of Glamorgan, 2005–10, now Professor Emeritus; *b* 23 June 1949; *s* of late Kenneth Robert Depledge Halton and Margaret Alice (*née* Searle); *m* 1973, Yvonne Geneste Ambrose; three *d*. *Educ:* Beckenham and Penge Grammar Sch. for Boys; Thames Poly. (BA 1972); Roehampton Inst. (PGCE 1973); Aston Univ. (MSc 1976); Univ. of Leicester (EdD 1998). Teacher, Hurlingham Comprehensive Sch., 1973–76; Lectr, N Tyneside Coll. of Further Educn, 1977–80; Hd of Dept of Business and Marketing, Coll. for Distributive Trade, 1980–86; Dean, Business Sch., N London Poly., 1987–90; Dep. Rector, Nene Coll., Northampton, 1990–99; Dep. Vice-Chancellor, Dep. Chief Exec., and Prof. of Higher Educn, UWE, Bristol, 1999–2004, Prof. Emeritus, 2004. Chm. Council, Bristol Old Vic Th. Sch., 2012–; Interim CEO, Conservatoire for Dance and Drama, 2014. Hon. LLD Roehampton, 2010; DUniv Glamorgan, 2011. Hon. FRWCMD 2010. *Publications:* Theories of Education Management in Practice, 1998; Pricing Toolkit for Higher Education, 2001. *Recreations:* playing blues piano, running, ornithology. *Address:* 45 High Street, Saltford, Bristol BS31 3EJ.

HALUSA, Dr Martin Charles; Chairman, Apax Partners, since 2014 (Chief Executive Officer, 2003–14); *b* Bangkok, 12 Feb. 1955; *s* of Dr Arno Halusa, sometime Ambassador, and Constance Halusa (*née* Monro); *m* 1986, Angelika Scheerbath (marr. diss. 2004); four *s*. *Educ:* Schule Schloss Salem; Georgetown Univ. (BA); Harvard Univ. (MBA); Univ. of Innsbruck (Dr oec.). Partner, Boston Consulting Gp, 1979–86; Dir, Daniel Swarovski, 1986–90; Co-Founder and Man. Dir, Apax Partners, Germany, 1990–2003. Mem. Bd, Russian Direct Investment Fund, 2011–. Mem., Internat. Business Council, World Econ. Forum, 2009–. Gov., Courtauld Inst. of Art, 2009–; Mem., Eur. Adv. Bd, Harvard Business Sch., 2009–; Co-Chm., London City Alliance, Georgetown Univ., 2009–. Mem. Bd, Schwab Foundn for Social Entrepreneurship, 2010–. *Recreations:* mountains, art, classic cars. *Address:* Apax Partners, 33 Jermyn Street, SW1Y 6DN. *T:* (020) 7872 6300, *Fax:* (020) 7666 6525. *E:* martin.halusa@apax.com.

HALVERSON, Hon. Robert George, OBE 1978; Ambassador for Australia to Ireland and the Holy See, 1999–2003; *b* 22 Oct. 1937; *m* 1958, Margaret Charlton; three *s* one *d*. *Educ:* Swinburne Tech. Coll.; Canberra Coll. of Advanced Education. Joined RAAF, 1956; commnd, 1957; Australian Jt Services Staff Coll., 1979; retired in rank of Gp Capt., 1981; with Robertson Thompson Partners, 1981–84. MP (L) Casey, Victoria, 1984–98; Chief Opposition Whip, 1994–96; Speaker, House of Reps, Australia, 1996–98. Knight, Order of Pius IX, 2003. *Address:* PO Box 19, Holbrook, NSW 2644, Australia.

HAM, Prof. Christopher John, CBE 2004; DL; PhD; Chief Executive, The King's Fund, since 2010; Professor of Health Policy and Management, University of Birmingham, 1992–2014, now Emeritus; *b* 15 May 1951; *s* of Raymond Percival Thomas Ham and Agnes Anne Ham (*née* Evans); *m* 1980, Ioanna Burnell; two *s* one *d*. *Educ:* Cardiff High Sch.; Univ. of Kent (BA MPhil); Univ. of Bristol (PhD 1983). Research Asst, Univ. of Leeds, 1975–77; Lectr in Health Policy, Univ. of Bristol, 1977–86; Fellow, King's Fund Coll. and King's Fund Inst., 1986–92; Dir, Health Services Mgt Centre, Univ. of Birmingham, 1992–2000; Policy Analyst, 2000–01, Dir, Strategy Unit, 2001–04, DoH (on secondment). Vis. Prof., Univ. of Surrey, 2009–12; Hon. Prof., LSHTM, 2011–. Sen. Associate, Nuffield Trust, 2008–10. Non-exec. Dir, Heart of England NHS Foundn Trust, 2007–10 (Gov., 2005–07); Gov., Health Foundn, 2006–10; Trustee, Canadian Health Services Res. Foundn, 2006–09. Advr to World Bank, WHO, Audit Commn, NAO, BMA, RCP, etc. FRSocMed; Founder FMedSci 1998. Hon. FRCP 2004; Hon. FRCGP 2008. Hon. DLitt Kent, 2012. DL W Midlands, 2013. Homenot Internat. Award, Avedis Donabedian Foundn, 2013. *Publications:* Policy Making in the NHS, 1981; Health Policy in Britain, 1982, 6th edn 2009; (with M. J. Hill) The Policy Process in the Modern Capitalist State, 1984; Managing Health Services, 1986; (jtly) Health Check: health care reforms in an international context, 1990; The New NHS: organisation and management, 1991; (jtly) Priority Setting Processes for Healthcare, 1995; Public, Private or Community: what next for the NHS?, 1996; Management and Competition in the NHS, 1994, 2nd edn 1997; (ed) Health Care Reform, 1997; (with S. Pickard) Tragic Choices in Health Care: the case of Child B, 1998; (with A. Coulter) The Global Challenge of Health Care Rationing, 2000; The Politics of NHS Reform 1988–1997, 2000; (with S. McIver) Contested Decisions, 2000; (with G. Robert) Reasonable Rationing, 2003; (with J. Ellins) NHS Mutual, 2009; (jtly) Medical Leadership: from the dark side to centre stage, 2012. *Recreations:* sport, music, theatre, reading, travel. *Address:* The King's Fund, 11-13 Cavendish Square, W1G 0AN. *T:* (020) 7307 2487.

HAM, Sir David Kenneth R.; *see* Rowe-Ham.

HÄMÄLÄINEN-LINDFORS, Sirkka Aune-Marjatta, DSc; Member of Supervisory Board, European Central Bank, since 2014; Chairman, Finnish National Opera, since 2007; *b* 8 May 1939; *m* Bo Lindfors; two *c*. *Educ:* Helsinki Sch. of Econs (DSc 1981). Economics Department, Bank of Finland: Economist, 1961–72; Head of Office, 1972–79; acting Head of Econs Dept, 1979–81; Dir, Econs Dept, Finnish Min. of Finance, 1981–82; Bank of Finland: Dir resp. for macroeconomic analysis and monetary and exchange rate policy, 1982–91; Mem. of Bd, 1991–92; Gov. and Chm. of Bd, 1992–98; Mem., Exec. Bd, European Central Bank, 1998–2003. Docent and Adjunct Prof. in Econs, Helsinki Sch. of Econs and Business Admin, 1991–2006. Member: Council, European Monetary Inst., 1992–98; Economic Council of Finland, 1992–98; Nat. Bd of Economic Defence, 1992–98; Internat. Adv. Council, CEPS, 1993–98; Bd, Foundn for Economic Educn, 1996–2007; Develt Prog. of Nat. Strategy, 1996–98; Chm., Bd of Financial Supervision Authy, 1996–97. Director: Investor AB, 2004–11; Sanoma Corp. (formerly SanomaWSOY), 2004–13; KONE Corp., 2004–15 (Vice Chm., 2004–12). Member: Bd, Finnish Nat. Theatre, 1992–98; Supervisory Bd, Finnish Cultural Foundn, 1996–2005; Chm., The Raging Roses, theatre gp, 1997–99. Foreign Academician, Real Academia de Ciencias Económicas y Financieras, Spain, 2010. Hon. Dr Turku Sch. of Econs, 1995. Comdr, 1st Cl., Order of White Rose (Finland); Merit Medal, 1st Cl., Order of White Star (Estonia). *Publications:* numerous articles on economics and monetary policy.

HAMANN, Paul; Managing Director and Creative Director, Wild Pictures Ltd, since 2006; *b* 9 Nov. 1948; *s* of Leonard Hamann and Anita Hamann (*née* Davies); *m* 1st, 1971, Kay Allen (marr. diss. 1981); (one *d* decd); 2nd, 1981, Marilyn Wheatcroft (marr. diss. 1999); one *s* one *d*. Dir and Prod., over 50 documentaries for BBC TV, 1976–88: incl. Your Life in Their Files, Sister Genevieve, Pushers, I Call It Murder, The Survivalists, At the Edge of the Union, A Company, Transmit and be Damned, Africa's Last Colony, Phantom, Lest We Forget, The Duty Men (Best Factual Series Award, BAFTA, 1987), Fourteen Days in May (Grierson Award, BFI, 1988); Editor, BBC 1 Documentaries, 1989–93: series incl. Inside Story, Rough Justice, Children's Hospital; Head of Documentaries, 1994–97, Chair, Factual Bd, 1996–99, Head of Documentaries and Hist. and of Community Prog. Unit, 1997–2000, BBC TV; Creative Director, Factual Progs, Shine Ltd, 2000–05: progs incl. Macintyre's Millions, Warrior School, Snatched, The Day I'll Never Forget, The Death Belt, My Shakespeare with Baz Luhrmann. Exec. Prod., feature film, Bullet Boy, 2005; Creative Director: Putin's Palace, 2006; Execution of a Teenage Girl, 2007 (Amnesty Documentary of the Year, 2007); Romanov: King of Hearts, 2007; World's Tallest Man, 2007; The Slaves in the Cellar, 2008; In the Line of Fire, 2009; Holloway, 2009; Wormwood Scrubs, 2010; The Zoo, 2010, 2012, 2013; Smugglers, 2011; Strangeways, 2011; Baby Hospital, 2011; Fraud Squad, 2011, 2012, 2013, 2015; The Factory, 2011; The Real Thumbelina, 2012; Death Row Dogs, 2012; Britain's Hidden Alcoholics, 2012; My Dad is a Woman, 2012; Smugglers Special, 2012; Dirty Britain, 2012, 2013; Pensioners Behind Bars, 2012; Trouble Abroad, 2013; Allotment Wars, 2013; Her Majesty's Prison: Aylesbury, 2013; Brady and Hindley: possession, 2013; Dangerous Dogs, 2014; The Betrayers, 2014; Kids Behind Bars, 2014; Last Chance Academy, 2014; Hit and Run, 2014; The Billion Dollar Chicken Shop, 2015. Mem. Council, BAFTA, 1993–96. Chm., Reprieve, 2000–10 (Trustee, 2000–). *Publications:* (with Peter Gillman) The Duty Men, 1987; contrib. professional jls. *Recreations:* family, popular culture, reading, opera, Italy. *T:* (020) 7428 5622. *E:* paul@wildpictures.co.uk.

HAMBIDGE, Most Rev. Douglas Walter, DD; Principal, St Mark's Theological College, and Assistant Bishop, Dar es Salaam, 1993–95; *b* London, England, 6 March 1927; *s* of Douglas Hambidge and Florence (*née* Driscoll); *m* 1956, Denise Colvill Lown; two *s* one *d*. *Educ:* London Univ.; London Coll. of Divinity. BD, ALCD; DD, Anglican Theol. Coll. of BC, 1970. Asst Curate, St Mark's, Dalston, 1953–56; Rector: All Saints, Cassiar, BC, 1956–58; St James, Smithers, BC, 1958–64; Vicar, St Martin, Fort St John, BC, 1964–69; Canon, St Andrew's Cathedral, Caledonia, 1965–69; Bishop of Caledonia, 1969–80; Bishop of New Westminster, 1980; Archbishop of New Westminster and Metropolitan of Province of BC, 1981–93. Mem., ACC, 1987–93 (Mem., Standing Cttee, 1990–93). Pres., Missions to Seamen, 1980–93. Chancellor, Vancouver Sch. of Theology, 1999–2007 (Mem. Bd of Governors, 1980–85). *Publications:* The 'S' Word, 2009. *Address:* 1621 Golf Club Drive, Delta, BC V4M 4E6, Canada. *E:* douglashambidge@gmail.com.

HAMBLEDEN, 5th Viscount *cr* 1891; **William Henry Bernard Smith;** *b* 18 Nov. 1955; *e s* of 4th Viscount Hambleden and of Donna Maria Carmela Attolico di Adelfia; *S* father, 2012; *m* 1983, Sarah Suzanne Anlauf; two *d*. *Heir: b* Hon. Bernardo James Smith, *b* 17 May 1957. *Address:* The Manor House, Hambleden, Henley-on-Thames, Oxon RG9 6SG.

HAMBLEN, Prof. David Lawrence, CBE 2001; FRCSE, FRCS, FRCSGlas; Professor of Orthopaedic Surgery, University of Glasgow, 1972–99, now Emeritus; Hon. Consultant Orthopaedic Surgeon, 1972–2002, and Chairman, 1997–2002, Greater Glasgow Health Board; *b* 31 Aug. 1934; *s* of Reginald John Hamblen and Bessie Hamblen (*née* Williams); *m*

1968, Gillian Frances Bradley; one *s* two *d*. *Educ:* Roan Sch., Greenwich; Univ. of London (MB BS 1957); PhD Edinburgh 1975. FRCSE 1962; FRCS 1963; FRCSGlas 1976. Fulbright Fellow, Harvard; Fellow, Massachusetts Gen. Hosp., 1966–67; Lectr in Orthopaedics, Nuffield Orthopaedic Centre, Univ. of Oxford, 1967–68; Sen. Lectr in Orthopaedic Surgery, Univ. of Edinburgh and Hon. Consultant Orthopaedic Surgeon to SE Regl Hosp. Bd, Scotland, 1968–72. Hon. Consultant in Orthopaedic Surgery to the Army in Scotland, 1976–99. Vis. Prof., Univ. of Strathclyde (Nat. Centre for Trng and Educn in Prosthetics and Orthotics), 1981–2008. Non-exec. Dir, W Glasgow Hosps Univ. NHS Trust, 1994–97. Chm. Council, Jl of Bone and Joint Surgery, 1995–2001. Pres., British Orthopaedic Assoc., 1990–91 (Hon. Fellow, 2002); Member: British Hip Soc. (Pres., 2001–02); European Hip Soc. Mem. Council and Trustee, St Andrew's Ambulance Assoc., 1998–2014; Mem., Merchants House of Glasgow, 2009–. Hon. DSc: Strathclyde, 2003; Glasgow, 2003. *Publications:* (ed with J. C. Adams): Outline of Fractures, 10th edn 1992 to 12th edn 2007; Outline of Orthopaedics, 11th edn 1990 to 14th edn 2009. *Recreations:* golf, music, reading, curling. *Address:* 3 Russell Drive, Bearsden, Glasgow G61 3BB. *T:* (0141) 942 1823. *Club:* Royal Society of Medicine.

HAMBLEN, Rt Hon. Sir Nicholas Archibald, Kt 2008; PC 2015; **Rt Hon. Lord Justice Hamblen;** a Lord Justice of Appeal, since 2015; *b* 23 Sept. 1957; *s* of Derek Ivens Archibald Hamblen, CB, OBE; *m* 1985, Kate Hayden; one *s* one *d*. *Educ:* Westminster Sch.; St John's Coll., Oxford (MA); Harvard Law Sch. (LLM). Called to the Bar, Lincoln's Inn, 1981; QC 1997; Asst Recorder, 1999–2000; Recorder, 2000–08; a Judge of the High Court, QBD, 2008–15. *Address:* Royal Courts of Justice, Strand, WC2A 2LL.

HAMBLETON, Prof. Kenneth George, FREng; Professor of Defence Engineering, University College London, 1991–2001, now Emeritus; *b* 15 Jan. 1937; *s* of George William Hambleton and Gertrude Nellie Hambleton (*née* Brighouse); *m* 1959, Glenys Patricia Smith; one *s* one *d*. *Educ:* Chesterfield Grammar Sch.; Queens' Coll., Cambridge (MA). CEng, FIET; FREng (FEng 1994). Services Electronics Res. Lab., Baldock, 1958–73; ASWE, Portsdown, 1973–81; a Dep. Dir, ASWE, 1981–82; Dir, Strategic Electronics-Radar, MoD PE, 1982–85; Asst Chief Scientific Advr (Projects and Res.), MoD, 1985–86; Dir Gen., Air Weapons and Electronic Systems, 1986–90, Air 3, 1990–91, MoD. *Publications:* numerous articles and letters in nat. and internat. physics and electronic jls. *Recreations:* chess, bridge, golf, music—especially jazz.

HAMBLIN, Jeffrey John, OBE 1999; Chief Executive, British Tourist Authority, 1999–2002; *b* 11 April 1945; *s* of late John Birkbeck Hamblin and Florence Hamblin; *m* 1968, Valerie Whitehead. *Educ:* Northern Counties Coll.; Univ. of Newcastle upon Tyne. Geography teacher, Newcastle, 1966–72; Develt Officer, Northumbria Tourist Bd, 1972–78; Dir, E Midlands Tourist Bd, 1978–85; British Tourist Authority: Manager, Canada, 1985–88; General Manager: Northern Europe, 1988–91; Europe, 1991–93; The Americas, 1993–98. Member Board: Hamilton Community Care Access Centre, Ont, 2005–06; Hamilton, Niagara, Haldimand, Brant Community Care Access Centre, Ont, 2006–09; Mem., Tourism Adv. Cttee, 2013–15, Vice-Chm., Cultural Roundtable, 2014–, Hamilton CC, Ont. *Recreations:* golf, philately, gardening, reading. *Address:* 1460 Limeridge Road East, Hamilton, ON L8W 3J9, Canada.

HAMBLING, Sir (Herbert) Peter (Hugh), 4th Bt *cr* 1924, of Yoxford, co. Suffolk; *b* 6 Sept. 1953; *o s* of Sir (Herbert) Hugh Hambling, 3rd Bt, and Anne Page Oswald (*d* 1990), Spokane, Washington, USA; *S* father, 2010; *m* 1991, Lorayn Louise, *d* of late Frank Joseph Koson; three *s*. *Educ:* Univ. of Washington (BSc); Von Karman Inst. (Dip.); Yale Univ. Sch. of Management (MBA). Co-Founder, and Pres., Digital Control Inc., WA. *Heir: s* Colin Hugh Hambling, *b* 1991.

HAMBLING, Maggi, CBE 2010 (OBE 1995); artist; *b* 23 Oct. 1945; *d* of late Harry Hambling and Marjorie Hambling (*née* Harris). *Educ:* Hadleigh Hall Sch., Suffolk; Amberfield Sch., Suffolk; Ipswich Sch. of Art; Camberwell Sch. of Art (DipAD 1967); Slade Sch. of Fine Art (HDFA 1969). Boise Travel Award, NY, 1969; first Artist in Residence, Nat. Gall., London, 1980–81; Tutor in Painting and Drawing, Morley Coll. *One-man exhibitions include:* Paintings and Drawings, Morley Gall., London, 1973; New Oil Paintings, Warehouse Gall., London, 1977; Drawings and Paintings on View, Nat. Gall., 1981; Pictures of Max Wall, Nat. Portrait Gall., 1983 (and tour); Maggi Hambling, Serpentine Gall., 1987 (and tour); An Eye Through a Decade, Yale Center for British Art, Newhaven, Conn, 1991; Towards Laughter, Northern Centre for Contemporary Art, 1993–94 (and tour); Maggi Hambling, Marlborough Fine Art, London, 1996; A Matter of Life and Death, Yorkshire Sculpture Park, 1997; also exhibn, A Statue for Oscar Wilde, Nat. Portrait Gall., and Hugh Lane Gall. of Modern Art, Dublin, 1997; statue, A Conversation with Oscar Wilde, bronze and granite, Adelaide Street, London, 1998; Good Friday paintings, drawings and sculpture, Gainsborough's House, Sudbury, Suffolk, 2000, LMH, Oxford, 2001; Henrietta Moraes, Marlborough Fine Art, London, 2001; Father, Morley Gall., London, 2001; The Very Special Brew Series, Sotheby's, 2003; North Sea Painting, Aldeburgh Fest., 2003; Scallop, Aldeburgh beach, 2003; Portraits of People and the Sea, Marlborough Fine Art, 2006; No Straight Lines, Fitzwilliam Mus., Cambridge and tour, 2007; Waves Breaking, Marlborough Fine Art, 2007; Waves and Waterfalls, Abbot Hall Art Gall., Kendal, Marlborough Fine Art, London, 2008; George Always: portraits of George Melly, Walker Art Gall., Liverpool, 2009; The Sea, Lowry, Manchester, 2009; Maggi Hambling: The Wave, Fitzwilliam Mus., Cambridge, New Sea Sculpture, Marlborough Fine Art, 2010; The Brixton Heron, 2010; The North Sea, Europe House, 2010; Wall of Water, Hermitage Mus., St Petersburg, 2013; The Winchester Tapestries, Winchester Cathedral, 2013; Walls of Water, Nat. Gall., 2014; Walls of Water: the monotypes, Marlborough Fine Art, 2014; War Requiem & Aftermath, KCL, 2015; *participating artist*: Snap, Aldeburgh Fest., 2012, 2013; *public collections include*: Arts Council; Ashmolean Mus., Oxford; Australian Nat. Gall.; Birmingham City Art Gall.; British Council; BM; Contemporary Art Soc.; Fitzwilliam Mus., Cambridge; Gulbenkian Foundn, Lisbon; Harris Mus. and Art Gall., Preston; Imperial War Mus.; Nat. Gall.; Nat. Portrait Gall.; Rugby Collection; Scottish Nat. Gall. of Modern Art, Edinburgh; Scottish Nat. Portrait Gall., Edinburgh; Southampton Art Gall.; Swindon Art Gall.; Tate Gall.; V&A Mus.; Wakefield Art Gall.; Whitworth Art Gall.; Yale Center for British Art. Hon. Fellow: New Hall, Cambridge, 2004; Univ. of the Arts, London, 2004; London South Bank Univ., 2011. *Publications:* (with John Berger) Maggi & Henrietta, 2001; (with Andrew Lambirth) Maggi Hambling: the works, 2006; The Aldeburgh Scallop, 2010; (with James Cahill) War Requiem & Aftermath, 2015. *Recreation:* tennis. *Address:* Morley College, Westminster Bridge Road, SE1 7HT. *Club:* Chelsea Arts.

HAMBLING, Sir Peter; *see* Hambling, Sir H. P. H.

HAMBLY, Christl Ann; *see* Donnelly, C. A.

HAMBRO, James Daryl; Chairman: J. O. Hambro Capital Management Ltd, since 1994; James Hambro & Partners LLP, since 2010; *b* 22 March 1949; *s* of late Jocelyn Hambro, MC and Ann Silvia Hambro (*née* Muir); *m* 1981, Diana Cherry; three *d*. *Educ:* Eton College; Harvard Business Sch. Hambros Bank, 1970–85 (Exec. Dir, 1982–85); J. O. Hambro & Co., subseq. J. O. Hambro Ltd, 1986–99. Chairman: Ashtenne Hldgs, 1997–2005; ViCTory (formerly Singer & Friedlander) AIM VCT, 2000–11; Hansteen Holdings plc, 2005–; Wiltons (St James's) Ltd, 2008– (Dir, 1992). Director: Vodafone plc, 1982–85; Primary Health Properties, 1996–; Capital Opportunities Trust, 1997–2003; Enterprise Capital Trust, 1997–2004; Biocompatibles Internat., 2002–03. Dep. Chm., Peabody Trust, 1998–2005; Chairman: Internat. Students' Trust, 1988–; Henry Smith's Charity, 2007–. *Recreations:* shooting, golf, farming, painting. *Address:* James Hambro & Partners, Ryder Court, 14 Ryder Street, SW1Y 6QB; 15 Elm Park Road, SW3 6BP; Manor Farm, Kimberley, Wymondham, Norfolk NR9 4DT. *Clubs:* White's; Royal West Norfolk.

See also R. N. Hambro.

HAMBRO, Peter Charles Percival; Executive Chairman, Petropavlovsk PLC (formerly Peter Hambro Mining Plc), since 1994; *b* 18 Jan. 1945; *s* of late Lt Col Everard Hambro and Mary Hambro; *m* 1968, Karen Brodrick; three *s*. *Educ:* Eton Coll. Founder, Peter Hambro Ltd, 1990. Chm., Sundeala Ltd. *Recreation:* painting. *Clubs:* White's, Pratt's.

HAMBRO, Rupert Nicholas, CBE 2014; Chairman: J O Hambro Ltd, since 1986 (Group Managing Director, 1986–94); Robinson Hambro, since 2010; *b* 27 June 1943; *s* of late Jocelyn Olaf Hambro, MC and Ann Silvia (*née* Muir); *m* 1970, Mary Robinson Boyer; one *s* one *d*. *Educ:* Eton; Aix-en-Provence. Peat Marwick Mitchell & Co., 1962–64; joined Hambros Bank, 1964, Director, 1969, Dep. Chm., 1980, Chm., 1983–86; Chm., J. O. Hambro Magan Ltd, 1988–96. Director: Anglo American Corporation of South Africa, 1981–97; Chatsworth House Trust Ltd, 1982–2004; Racecourse Hldgs Trust Ltd, 1985–94; Telegraph Group Ltd (formerly Daily Telegraph PLC, then The Telegraph plc), 1986–2003; Sedgwick Group plc, 1987–92; Triton Europe plc, 1987–90; Pioneer Concrete Hldgs PLC, 1989–99; Hamleys plc, 1988–96 (Chm., 1989–94); KBC Peel Hunt Ltd (formerly Peel Hunt plc), 2000–03; Business for Sterling, 2002–07; Open Europe Ltd, 2006–07; Mem. Supervisory Bd, Bank Gutmann AG, 2000–; Chairman: Wilton's (St James's) Ltd, 1987–2003; Mayflower Corp. Plc, 1988–2004; Internat. Adv. Bd, Montana AG, Vienna, 1988–2000; Fenchurch plc, 1993–97; CTR Group plc, 1990–97; Longshot plc, 1996–2007; Woburn Golf & Country Club Ltd, 1998–2008; Third Space Gp Ltd, 1999–2007; Jermyn Street Assoc. Ltd, 2000–03; Roland Berger & Partners Ltd, 2000–02; Walpole Cttee Ltd, 2000–05; Cazenove & Loyd Ltd, 2004–; Lovedean Ltd, 2008–10; Sipsmith Ltd, 2009–; Woburn Enterprises Ltd, 2008–11; Theo Fennell plc, 2009–14. Chairman: Assoc. of International Bond Dealers, 1979–82; Soc. of Merchants Trading to the Continent, 1995–2009. Mem., SE Econ. Planning Council, 1971–74. Treas., NACF, 1991–2003; Chm. Govs, Mus. of London, 1998–2005; Co. Chm., Mus. in Docklands, 2003–05; Chm. Develt Strategy Bd, ZSL, 2011–; Patron, RBS, 1997–. Chm. Council, Univ. of Bath in Swindon, 2000–07; Member, Council: Univ. of Bath, 2004–10; RCA, 2010–. Vice-Chm., 1991–96, Dep. Pres., 2001–11, Clubs for Young People (formerly NAYC); Chairman of Trustees: Boys' Club Trust, 1991–2000; Chiswick House & Gardens Trust, 2005–11; Silver Trust, 1987–; Trustee, Wallace Collection, 2013–; Mem., English Heritage Blue Plaques Panel, 2014–; Patron, 2005–08, Pres., 2008–, British Assoc. of Adoption and Fostering; Patron, Assoc. of British Designer Silversmiths, 2006–. Dep. Pres., Anglo-Danish Soc., 1987–. Freeman, Fishmongers' Co., 1969–; Liveryman, Goldsmiths' Co., 1994– (Mem. Ct of Assts, 1998–; Prime Warden, 2009–10). Hon. Fellow, Univ. of Bath, 1998. Walpole Award for British excellence, 2005. Knight of the Falcon (Iceland), 1986. *Recreation:* country pursuits. *Address:* J O Hambro Ltd, 1 Queen Anne's Gate Building, 21 Dartmouth Street, SW1H 9BP. *T:* (020) 7399 9986. *Clubs:* White's, Walbrook, Groucho; Jupiter Island (Florida).

See also J. D. Hambro.

HAMEED, Baron *cr* 2007 (Life Peer), of Hampstead in the London Borough of Camden; **Khalid Hameed,** CBE 2004; DL; Chairman, Alpha Hospital Group, since 2003; Chairman and Chief Executive, London International Hospital, since 2006; *s* of late Prof. M. Abdul Hameed and Rashida Abdul Hameed; *m* 1989, Dr Ghazala Hameed; two *s* two *d* and one step *s* one step *d*. *Educ:* Lucknow Univ., India (BSc; DPA; MB BS; DSc); London Univ. (DTM&H). FRCP 2006. CEO, Cromwell Hosp., London, 1990–2005. Chm., Commonwealth Youth Exchange Council, 1999–; Trustee, Political Council for Co-existence, 2006–; Chm., Woolf Inst., 2007–; Gov., Internat. Students Hall, 2007–. Vice Pres., Friends of BL. Pres., Little Foundn, 2007–. Patron, Three Faiths Forum, 2006–. Freedom, City of London, 2011. High Sheriff, 2006–07, DL 2007, Greater London. Hon. DLitt Middlesex, 2008; Hon. DSc London Metropolitan. Sternberg Award for Interfaith Work, 2006; Ambassador of Peace Award, Universal Peace Fedn, 2007; Asian of the Year Award, 2011. *Recreations:* chess, cricket, poetry, polo, bridge. *Address:* House of Lords, SW1A 0PW. *E:* hameed@parliament.uk. *Clubs:* Athenæum, Mosimann's, Mark's, MCC; Guards Polo.

HAMER, Christopher John; Property Ombudsman (formerly Ombudsman for Estate Agents), 2006–15; *b* 26 Dec. 1952; *s* of late Ronald and Olive Hamer; *m* 1975, Sarah Anne Preston; three *s*. *Educ:* Thornbury Grammar Sch., Glos; Dorset Inst. of Higher Educn (HNC Business Studies). HM Customs & Excise, Dover, Southampton and London, 1974–84; Private Sec. to Parly Comr for Admin, 1984–85; Mem., Mgt and Efficiency Unit, Cabinet Office, 1985–88; Dir of Services, Insurance Ombudsman Bureau, 1988–96; Gen. Manager, Personal Investment Authy Ombudsman Bureau, 1996–2000; Hd, Product Risk, HSBC Insce, 2000–06. *Recreations:* motoring, First and Second World Wars.

HAMER, John Alan, OBE 2011; Chairman, AlphaPlus Consultancy Ltd, since 2012 (Vice-Chairman, 2000–12); *b* Manchester, 24 Jan. 1940; *s* of Frank Hamer and Mary Hamer; *m* 1965, Rachel Hamilton; one *s* one *d*. *Educ:* Manchester Grammar Sch.; Hatfield Coll., Durham Univ. (BA Hons Mod. Hist. 1962); Pembroke Coll., Oxford (DipEd 1965); Inst. of Educn, London Univ. (Advanced Dip. Educn 1972; MA Educn 1974). Primary sch. teacher, Manchester LEA, 1962–63; Asst Teacher, Jun. High Sch., Montreal, 1963–64; Asst Teacher, 1965–67, Hd of Hist., 1967–79, Collyer's Grammar Sch., Horsham; Asst Vice Principal, Collyer's Sixth Form Coll., Horsham, 1979–83; HM Inspector of Schs, 1984–97; Educn Policy Advr, Heritage Lottery Fund, 1997–2000. Hon. Lectr (formerly Special Lectr), Sch. of Educn, Nottingham Univ., 2000–14. Educn Consultant, Council of Europe, 2000–. Trustee: Heritage Educn Trust, 2000– (Chm., 2008–); Historic Royal Palaces, 2005–11; Mem. Council, Nat. Trust, 2002–05; Educn Advr, Historic Houses Assoc., 2005–10. Governor: Farlington Sch., Horsham, 2003–14; Tanbridge House Sch., Horsham, 2003–10; Frewen Coll., Northiam, 2005–. Mem., Warnham Parish Council, 2007–. FRSA. *Publications:* History in the Making: the twentieth century, 1980, 2nd edn 1992; contribs to various UK and Council of Europe pubns on aspects of history and heritage educn. *Recreations:* local history, travel, golf, walking. *Address:* The Banks, Bailing Hill, Warnham, W Sussex RH12 3RT. *T:* (01403) 265088, *Fax:* (01403) 259988. *E:* j.a.hamer@btinternet.com.

HAMEROW, Prof. Helena Francisca, DPhil; Professor of Early Medieval Archaeology, University of Oxford, since 1996; Fellow, St Cross College, Oxford, since 1996; *b* Madison, Wisconsin, 18 Sept. 1961; *d* of Theodore S. Hamerow and Margareta Lotter Hamerow; partner, Eric R. Brown; one *s* one *d*. *Educ:* Univ. of Wisconsin-Madison (BA Hons Anthropol. 1983); Lincoln Coll., Oxford (DPhil Archaeol. 1988). Mary Somerville Res. Fellow, Somerville Coll., Oxford, 1988–90; Lectr in Early Medieval Archaeol., Durham Univ., 1990–96. Hon. Ed., 1999–2002, Vice Pres. and Mem. Council, 2012–, Royal Archaeol Inst.; Pres., Soc. for Medieval Archaeol., 2014–. Trustee, Oxford Archaeol., 2011–. FSA 1996. *Publications:* Mucking Excavations, vol. 2, The Anglo-Saxon Settlement, 1993; Early Medieval Settlements: the archaeology of rural communities in Northwest Europe, AD 400–900, 2002; Rural Settlements and Society in Anglo-Saxon England, 2012. *Recreations:* music, travel. *Address:* Institute of Archaeology, University of Oxford, 34–36 Beaumont Street, Oxford OX1 2PG. *T:* (01865) 278240. *E:* Helena.hamerow@arch.ox.ac.uk.

HAMES, Christopher William; QC 2015; *b* Brentwood, Essex, 11 Jan. 1964; *s* of Peter Hames and Sheila Hames (*née* Hickman, now Markwick); *m* 1989, Megan Veronica Butler, *qv*; one *s* one *d*. *Educ:* Eastbourne Grammar Sch.; Univ. of Sheffield (LLB Hons). Called to the Bar, Inner Temple, 1987; in practice as a barrister, specialising in internat. children law and matrimonial finance, 1987–; 4 Paper Buildings, 2000–. Mem. Cttee, Child Abduction Lawyers Assoc., 2015–. *Publications:* articles in Family Law and Family Law Week. *Recreations:* running, tennis, cycling, archaeology and history, opera, travel, Chelsea FC. *Address:* 4 Paper Buildings, Temple, EC4Y 7EX. *T:* (020) 7427 5200, *Fax:* (020) 7353 4979. *E:* ch@4pb.com.

HAMES, Duncan John; *b* Herts, 16 June 1977; *m* 2011, Jo Swinson, *qv*; one *s*. *Educ:* Watford Boys' Grammar Sch.; New Coll., Oxford (BA PPE 1998). Business consultant, Deloitte Consulting, 1998–2004; Dir, Chippenham Consultants Ltd, 2005–10. Mem. Bd, 2003–09, Chm., Audit Cttee, 2008–09, SW England RDA; Mem. Bd, Culture SW, 2006–08. Mem. (Lib Dem) W Wilts DC, 2003–07. Contested (Lib Dem): Tottenham, June 2000; Watford, 2001; Westbury, 2005. MP (Lib Dem) Chippenham, 2010–15; contested (Lib Dem) same seat, 2015. PPS: to Minister of State for Children and Families, 2010–11; to Sec. of State for Energy and Climate Change, 2011–12; to Dep. Prime Minister, 2012–13. Member: Policy Adv. Bd, Social Market Foundn, 2010; Bd, Great Britain-China Centre, 2011–.

HAMES, Megan Veronica; *see* Butler, M. V.

HAMID, Rt Rev. David; *see* Gibraltar in Europe, Suffragan Bishop of.

HAMID, David; Partner, OpCapita LLP (formerly Merchant Equity Partners), since 2006; Chairman: Ideal Shopping Ltd, since 2011; Game Digital plc (formerly Game Retail Ltd), since 2012; *b* 11 Dec. 1951; *s* of Osman and Doreen Hamid; *m* 1984, Gillian Joy; three *s* one *d*. *Educ:* Alleyne's Grammar Sch., Stevenage; Univ. of Bradford (BSc Hons Industrial Technol. and Mgt). Marketing Director: Jewellery Div., Alfred Dunhill, 1985–86; Supasnaps, 1987; Managing Director: Dixons Financial Services, 1988–90; Mastercare Ltd, 1990–95; Commercial Service Dir, Dixons Gp plc, 1995–98; Gp Man. Dir, PC World, 1998–2001; Chief Operating Officer, Dixons Gp plc, 2001–03; CEO, Halfords Gp plc, 2003–05; Partner, MEP Mayflower Hldgs, 2006–08; Chm., Nationwide Autocentres, 2006–10. Non-exec. Dir, Homeserve Membership, 2006–11; Dep. Chm., MVideo OAO (Russia), 2011– (Dir, 2005–). Chm., Music for Youth, 2008–. *Recreations:* field hockey, playing in a rock band, golf. *Address:* OpCapita LLP, 173–176 Sloane Street, SW1X 9QG. *Club:* Royal Automobile.

HAMILL, Keith, OBE 2012; FCA; Chairman, Horsforth Holdings Ltd, since 2012; *b* 7 Dec. 1952; *s* of Gerard Hamill and Edith Hamill; *m* 1975, Angela Sylvia Green; three *s*. *Educ:* Cambridge Grammar Sch. for Boys; Univ. of Nottingham (BA Politics). FCA 1989. Price Waterhouse, 1975–98 (Partner, 1987–88); Dir, Financial Control, Guinness PLC, 1988–91; Finance Director: United Distillers plc, 1991–93; Forte plc, 1993–96; W H Smith plc, 1996–2000; Chairman: W H Smith N America, 1996–2000; Collins Stewart, then Collins Stewart Tullett, later Tullett Prebon plc, 2000–13. Chairman: Alterian plc, 2000–11; Go Ltd, 2001–02; Luminar plc, 2001–06; Moss Bros Gp PLC, 2001–08; Bertram Books Ltd, 2001–07; Travelodge, 2003–10 and 2012 (Dep. Chm., 2010–12); Heath Lambert Gp Ltd, 2005–11; Fundsmith, 2010–12; Avant Homes Ltd (formerly Gladedale Ltd), 2013–14; Deputy Chairman: Collins Stewart plc, 2006–10; Dir, Newmarket Racecourse Ltd, 2002–11; non-executive Director: Electrocomponents plc, 1999–2008; William Hill PLC, 2000–01; Tempus Gp PLC, 2000–01; TDG plc, 2001–05; Cadmus Communications Corp., 2002–07; EasyJet, 2009–; Max Property plc, 2009–14; Samsonite, 2010–. Mem., Urgent Issues Task Force, Accounting Standards Bd, 1992–98; Chm., Financial Reporting Cttee, CBI, 1993–97. Treas., 1997–2003, Pro-Chancellor, 2003–11, Univ. of Nottingham. Dir, Greenwich and Bexley Hospice, 1999–2008. Trustee, British Internat. Sch. in Rome, 2014–. Hon. LLD Nottingham, 2012. *Recreations:* opera, horse racing, soccer, golf. *Address:* Horsforth Holdings Ltd, LDH House, Si Two, St Ives Business Park, Cambs PE27 4EE. *T:* (01480) 484250. *Clubs:* Royal Automobile; Royal Ascot Racing; Chislehurst Golf.

HAMILTON; *see* Baillie-Hamilton, family name of Earl of Haddington.

HAMILTON; *see* Douglas-Hamilton.

HAMILTON, family name of **Duke of Abercorn,** of **Lord Belhaven,** and of **Barons Hamilton of Dalzell, Hamilton of Epsom** and **HolmPatrick**.

HAMILTON, 16th Duke of, *cr* 1643 (Scot.), **AND BRANDON,** 13th Duke of, *cr* 1711 (GB); **Alexander Douglas-Hamilton;** Marquess of Douglas 1633; Lord Abernethy and Jedburgh Forest 1633; Marquess of Clydesdale 1643; Earl of Angus; Earl of Arran, Lanark and Cambridge; Lord Aven and Innerdale 1643; Lord Machanshire and Polmont; Baron Dutton (GB) 1711; Premier Peer of Scotland; Hereditary Keeper of Holyrood Palace; *b* 31 March 1978; *er s* of 15th Duke of Hamilton and Sarah (*d* 1994), *d* of Sir Walter Scott, 4th Bt; *S* father, 2010; *m* 2011, Sophie Ann Rutherford; two *s*. *Heir: s* Marquess of Douglas and Clydesdale, *qv*.

HAMILTON, Marquess of; James Harold Charles Hamilton; *b* 19 Aug. 1969; *s* and *heir* of Duke of Abercorn, *qv*; *m* 2004, Tanya, *d* of late Douglas Nation; two *s*. A Page of Honour to the Queen, 1982–84. *Heir: s* Viscount Strabane, *qv*. *Address:* Barons Court, Omagh, Co. Tyrone BT78 4EZ.

HAMILTON OF DALZELL, 5th Baron *cr* 1886; **Gavin Goulburn Hamilton;** DL; *b* 8 Oct. 1968; *s* of 4th Baron Hamilton of Dalzell and (Ann Anastasia) Corinna (Helena) Hamilton (*née* Dixon); *S* father, 2006; *m* 1997, Harriet Louise, *yr d* of Thomas Roskill; one *s* three *d* (of whom two *d* are twins). *Educ:* Eton Coll.; Buckingham Univ. (BSc). ACA 1994. Smith & Williamson, chartered accountants, 1990–95; DHL International (UK) Ltd, 1995–2007. Director: Apley Estate, Goulburn Farms, 2007–; Apley Farm Shop, 2011–. Chm., County Priory Gp (formerly Chm. Council), St John Ambulance Shropshire, 2008–14. DL Shropshire, 2011. *Recreation:* shooting. *Heir: s* Hon. Francis Alexander James Goulburn Hamilton, *b* 20 Oct. 2009. *Address:* Harrington Hall, Shifnal, Shropshire TF11 9DR. *T:* (01952) 730870. *E:* gavin.hamilton@ukgateway.net. *Clubs:* Boodle's, Pratts.

HAMILTON OF EPSOM, Baron *cr* 2005 (Life Peer), of West Anstey in the county of Devon; **Archibald Gavin Hamilton,** Kt 1994; PC 1991; *b* 30 Dec. 1941; *yr s* of 3rd Baron Hamilton of Dalzell, GCVO, MC; *m* 1968, Anne Catharine Napier; three *d*. *Educ:* Eton Coll. Borough Councillor, Kensington and Chelsea, 1968–71. Contested (C) Dagenham, Feb. and Oct., 1974. MP (C) Epsom and Ewell, April 1978–2001; PPS to Sec. of State for Energy, 1979–81, to Sec. of State for Transport, 1981–82; an Asst Govt Whip, 1982–84; a Lord Comr of HM Treasury (Govt Whip), 1984–86; Parly Under-Sec. of State for Defence Procurement, MoD, 1986–87; PPS to Prime Minister, 1987–88; Minister of State, MoD, 1988–93. Member: Intelligence and Security Cttee, 1994–97; Select Cttee on Standards in Public Life, 1995; Select Cttee on Members' Interests, 1995. Chm., 1922 Cttee, 1997–2001 (Exec. Mem., 1995–97). Mem., NATO Parly Assembly, 2012–. Pres., European-Atlantic Gp, 2014–. Gov., Westminster Foundn for Democracy, 1993–99. Mem. Council, Nat. Army Mus., 2013–. Mem., Garden Soc. *Address:* House of Lords, SW1A 0PW. *Clubs:* White's, Pratt's.

HAMILTON, Rt Hon. Lord; Arthur Campbell Hamilton; PC 2002; Lord Justice General of Scotland and Lord President of the Court of Session, 2005–12; Member of the Supplementary Panel of the Supreme Court of the United Kingdom, since 2012; a Judge of the Court of Appeal, Botswana, since 2012; arbitrator, since 2014; *b* 10 June 1942; *s* of James Whitehead Hamilton and Isobel Walker Hamilton (*née* McConnell); *m* 1970, Christine Ann Croll; one *d*. *Educ:* The High School of Glasgow; Glasgow Univ.; Worcester Coll., Oxford (BA; Hon. Fellow, 2003); Edinburgh Univ. (LLB). Admitted member, Faculty of Advocates, 1968; QC (Scot.) 1982; Standing Junior Counsel: to Scottish Development Dept, 1975–78; to Board of Inland Revenue (Scotland), 1978–82; Advocate Depute, 1982–85; Judge, Courts of Appeal, Jersey and Guernsey, 1988–95; Pres., Pensions Appeal Tribunals for Scotland, 1992–95; a Senator of the Coll. of Justice in Scotland, 1995–2005. Hon. Bencher, Inner Temple, 2006. *Recreations:* music, history. *Address:* 8 Heriot Row, Edinburgh EH3 6HU. *T:* (0131) 556 4663. *Club:* New (Edinburgh).

HAMILTON (NZ), Bishop of, (RC), since 1994; **Most Rev. Denis George Browne,** CNZM 2001; *b* 21 Sept. 1937; *s* of Neville John Browne and Catherine Anne Browne (*née* Moroney). *Educ:* Holy Name Seminary, Christchurch, NZ; Holy Cross College, Mosgiel, NZ. Assistant Priest: Gisborne, 1963–67; Papatoetoe, 1968–71; Remuera, 1972–74; Missionary in Tonga, 1975–77; Bishop of Rarotonga, 1977–83; Bishop of Auckland, 1983–94. Hon. DD. *Recreation:* golf. *Address:* Chanel Centre, PO Box 4353, Hamilton East 2032, New Zealand.

HAMILTON, Adrian Walter; QC 1973; commercial arbitrator and mediator, retired; a Recorder of the Crown Court, 1974–95; *b* 11 March 1923; *er s* of late W. G. M. Hamilton, banker, Fletching, Sussex and of late Mrs S. E. Hamilton; *m* 1966, Jill, *d* of S. R. Brimblecombe, Eastbourne; two *d*. *Educ:* Highgate Sch.; Balliol Coll., Oxford (BA 1st cl. Jurisprudence 1948; MA 1954; Jenkyns Law Prize; Paton Meml Student, 1948–49). Served with RN, 1942–46 (N Atlantic, Mediterranean, English Channel, Far East): Ord. Seaman, 1942; Sub-Lt RNVR, 1943, Lieut 1946. Cassel Scholar, Lincoln's Inn, 1949; called to Bar, Lincoln's Inn, 1949 (Bencher 1979), Middle Temple and Inner Temple; Dep. High Court Judge, 1982–95. Mem., Senate of Inns of Court and the Bar, 1976–82, Treas., 1979–82; Mem. Council, Inns of Court, 1987–91. Mem., Council of Legal Educn, 1977–87. Chairman: Appellate Cttee for Exam. Irregularities, London Univ., 1985–; Mental Health Review Tribunals, 1986–95; Lautro Disciplinary Cttees, 1991–94. Inspector, Peek Foods Ltd, 1977. *Recreations:* family, travelling, history. *Address:* 63 Abbotsbury Road, W14 8EL. *T:* (020) 7603 0185. *Club:* Garrick.

HAMILTON, Alfred William, (Wilfred); Deputy Secretary, Department of Enterprise, Trade and Investment, Northern Ireland, 2001–08; *b* 13 June 1948; *s* of Albert George Hamilton and Anna Hamilton (*née* Christie); *m* 1972, Sandra Magill; one *s* one *d*. *Educ:* Boys' Model Sch., Belfast. Dip. Admin and Mgt. Northern Ireland Civil Service: posts in mgt services, Rayner Scrutinies, NI Econ. Council and Eur. Div., Dept of Health and Social Services, 1967–91; Asst Sec., 1991; Head of Finance Div., 1991–95, Head of Finance, EU and Efficiency Div., 1995–2001, Dept of Econ. Develt. Chm., Ulster-Scots Acad. Project Steering Gp, 2010–. *Recreations:* golf, sport in general, reading. *Address:* c/o Department of Enterprise, Trade and Investment, Netherleigh, Massey Avenue, Belfast BT4 2JP.

HAMILTON, Sir Andrew Caradoc, 10th Bt *cr* 1646, of Silverton Hill, Lanarkshire; *b* 23 Sept. 1953; *s* of Sir Richard Hamilton, 9th Bt and Elizabeth Vidal Barton; *S* father, 2001; *m* 1984, Anthea Jane Huntingford; three *d*. *Educ:* Charterhouse; St Peter's Coll., Oxford (BA). *Heir: cousin* Paul Howden Hamilton [*b* 24 Dec. 1951; *m* 1980, Elizabeth Anne Harrison; two *d*].

HAMILTON, Prof. Andrew David, PhD; FRS 2004; Vice-Chancellor, University of Oxford, 2009–Dec. 2015; President, New York University, from Jan. 2016; *b* 3 Nov. 1952; *m* 1981, Jennifer Letton; two *s* one *d*. *Educ:* Univ. of Exeter (BSc 1974); Univ. of British Columbia (MSc 1976); Univ. of Cambridge (PhD 1980). Asst Prof. of Chem., Princeton Univ., 1981–88; University of Pittsburgh: Associate Prof., 1988–92; Prof. of Chem., 1992–97; Hd, Dept of Chem., 1994–97; Yale University: Irénée duPont Prof. of Chem., 1997–2004; Prof. of Molecular Biophysics and Biochem., 1998–2009; Hd, Dept of Chemistry, 1999–2003; Dep. Provost for Sci. and Technol., 2003–04; Benjamin Silliman Prof. of Chemistry and Provost, 2004–09. Mem., EPSRC, 2011–15. *Publications:* articles in learned jls. *Address:* New York University, 70 Washington Square South, New York, NY 10012, USA.

HAMILTON, Andrew Ninian Roberts; His Honour Judge Andrew Hamilton; a Circuit Judge, Midland Circuit, since 2001; *b* 7 Jan. 1947; *s* of Robert Bousfield Hamilton and Margery Wensley Iowerth Hamilton (*née* Roberts); *m* 1982, Isobel Louise Goode; one *s* one *d*. *Educ:* Cheltenham Coll.; Birmingham Univ. (LLB). Called to the Bar, Gray's Inn, 1970; in practice, Midland and Oxford Circuit; Asst Recorder, 1993–99; a Recorder, 1999–2001. Mem. (C) Nottingham CC, 1973–91 (Chairman: Transport Cttee, 1976; Archaeology Cttee, 1987–91; Vice-Chm., Leisure Services Cttee, 1987–88; Hon. Alderman, 1991). Chairman: Nottingham Civic Soc., 1978–83 (Vice-Pres., 1983–); Nottingham Civic Soc. Sales Ltd, 1988–2001; Nottingham Park Conservation Trust, 1992–; Nottingham Caves Forum, 2010–; Wollaton Histl and Conservation Soc., 2011–; Dir, Nottingham and Notts United Services Club, 1994–2001. Chm., Nottingham Bar Mess, 1995–2001. External examiner, BVC, Nottingham Trent Univ., 1997–2000. Contested (C) Ilkeston, Oct. 1974. *Publications:* Nottingham's Royal Castle and Ducal Palace, 1976, 5th edn 1999; Nottingham, City of Caves, 1978, 3rd edn 2004; Historic Walks in Nottingham, 1978, 2nd edn 1985. *Recreations:* tennis, ski-ing, golf, walking, local history. *Address:* Nottingham Crown Court, 60 Canal Street, Nottingham NG1 7EL. *Club:* Nottingham and Notts United Services.

HAMILTON, Angus Warnock; a District Judge (Magistrates' Courts), since 2005; *b* 1 June 1957; *s* of Sir James Arnot Hamilton, KCB, MBE. *Educ:* Univ. of Leicester (LLB 1979); Univ. of Sheffield (MA Socio-Legal Studies 1980); Guildford Coll. of Law. Trainee solicitor, 1981–83; admitted solicitor, 1983; solicitor in private practice, 1983–97; solicitor/sole Principal, Hamiltons Solicitors, 1997–2005; a Dep. Dist Judge, 1998–2005; Dist Judge, E London Family Court, 2014–. Member: Gambling Appeals Tribunal, 2007–; Information Rights Tribunal, 2010–. Mem., Equal Treatment Adv. Cttee, Judicial Studies Bd, 2008–11. Tutor, Judicial Coll., 2013–. *Publications:* (with Rosemary Jay) Data Protection Law and Practice: a guide to the Data Protection Act 1998, 1999, 2nd edn 2003; *contributions to:* Liberating Cyberspace, 1998; Staying Legal, 1999; Advising HIV+ Clients: a guide for lawyers, 1999; Advising Gay and Lesbian Clients: a guide for lawyers, 1999. *Recreations:* travel, photography, cinema, live music, weight training, scuba-diving, directing pop promo videos. *E:* angus.hamilton@mac.com. *Clubs:* Athenæum, The Hospital.

HAMILTON, Arthur Campbell; *see* Hamilton, Rt Hon. Lord.

HAMILTON, Arthur Richard C.; *see* Cole-Hamilton.

HAMILTON, Christina Mary; *see* Slade, C. M.

HAMILTON, David; *b* 24 Oct. 1950; *s* of Agnes and David Hamilton; *m* 1969, Jean Macrae; two *d*. *Educ:* Dalkeith High Sch. Coalminer, 1965–84; Landscape Supervisor, Midlothian DC, 1987–89; Training Officer and Placement Officer, Craigmillar Fest. Soc., 1989–92; Chief Exec., Craigmillar Opportunities Trust, 1992–2000. Mem., Midlothian Council, 1995–2001. MP (Lab) Midlothian, 2001–15. Scottish Whip, 2011–15. Chm., Midlothian Innovation Technol. Trust, 2001–; Director: Lothian Miners Convalescent Home, 2004–; Scottish Mining Mus., 2008–11. Hon. Pres., Midlothian Community Artists, 1995. *Recreations:* films, current affairs, grandchildren.

HAMILTON, Derek Jack; Sheriff of North Strathclyde at Greenock, since 2012; *b* Airdrie, 30 May 1961; *s* of Jack Hughes Hamilton and Janet Hamilton (*née* Shilliday); *m* 1986, Marion Ann Sutherland; one *s* two *d*. *Educ:* Airdrie Acad.; Univ. of Glasgow (LLB 1981; DipLP 1982). Admitted as solicitor, 1983; Partner: Bonnar & Co., Airdrie, 1986–98; Hamilton Ross, Airdrie, 1999–2009; Hon. Sheriff, 2006–12; Immigration Judge (pt-time), 2006–12; Duty Immigration Judge (pt-time), 2010–12; Convener (pt-time), 2007–12, In-house Convener (pt-time), 2008–12, Mental Health Tribunal for Scotland; Judge (pt-time), Social Entitlement

Chamber, 2011–12. Legal Advr, GDC, 2010–12. *Recreations:* cycling, mountain biking, tennis. *Address:* Greenock Sheriff Court, Sheriff Court House, Nelson Street, Greenock PA15 1TR. *T:* (01475) 787073. *E:* sheriffdhamilton@scotcourts.gov.uk.

HAMILTON, His Honour Donald Rankin Douglas; a Circuit Judge, 1994–2012; *b* 15 June 1946; *s* of Allister McNicoll Hamilton and Mary Glen Hamilton (*née* Rankin); *m* 1974, (Margaret) Ruth Perrens; one *s* one *d.* *Educ:* Rugby Sch.; Balliol Coll., Oxford (BA). Called to the Bar, Gray's Inn, 1969 (Atkin Schol. 1970); pupillage in Birmingham, 1970–71; practised in Birmingham, 1971–94; Designated Family Judge, Birmingham, 1996–2008. Mem., Council of Mgt, CBSO, 1974–80; Dir, CBSO Soc. Ltd, 1984–99; former Trustee: City of Birmingham Orchestral Endowment Fund; CBSO Benevolent Fund. Patron: Eve Brook Fund; Solihull Child Contact Centre. *Recreation:* music.

HAMILTON, Douglas Owens; Senior Partner, Norton Rose (formerly Norton, Rose, Botterell & Roche), 1982–94; *b* 20 April 1931; *s* of Oswald Hamilton and Edith Hamilton; *m* 1962, Judith Mary Wood; three *s.* *Educ:* John Fisher Sch., Purley, Surrey; Univ. of London (LLB). Admitted Solicitor, 1953; joined Botterell & Roche, 1955, Partner, 1959; Exec. Partner, Norton, Rose, Botterell & Roche, 1976–82. Mem., Chancellor's Court of Benefactors, Oxford Univ., 1990–94. Chm., Thames Nautical Trng Trust Ltd, 1995–98; Vice-Chm., Marine Soc., 1993–99; Hon. Treasurer: British Maritime Charitable Foundn, 1987–97; British Polish Legal Assoc., 1989–93. *Address:* Mariteau House, Winchelsea, East Sussex TN36 4ES.

HAMILTON, Duncan Graeme; Advocate at Scottish Bar; *b* 3 Oct. 1973; *s* of Rev. David Gentles Hamilton and Elsa Catherine Hamilton (*née* Nicolson); *m* 2003, Susan De Brun; two *s* one *d.* *Educ:* Glasgow Univ. (MA 1st Cl. Hons Hist.); Edinburgh Univ. (LLB Scots Law; DipLP); Kennedy Sch. of Govt, Harvard Univ. (Kennedy Schol.). Asst Brand Manager, Proctor & Gamble, 1995; Aide and advr to Alex Salmond, MP, 1997–99. MSP (SNP) Highlands and Is, 1999–2003; Mem., Health and Community Care Cttee, 1999–2000, Enterprise and Life Long Learning Cttee, 2000–03, Justice Cttee, 2001–03, Scottish Parlt. Mem., SNP, 1994–; Asst to SNP Chief Exec., 1998–99. Bar trainee, Simpson & Marwick Solicitors, Edinburgh, 2004–05; devilling at Scottish Bar, 2005–06; called to Scottish Bar, 2006. Political advr to First Minister, Scottish Exec., later Scottish Govt, 2007–08; Standing Jun. Counsel to Scottish Govt, 2013–. Mem. Council, London Information Network on Conflict and State-building, 2003– (spokesman for Caucasus Caspian Commn, 2007–08). Columnist: Scotsman, 2003–07; Scotland on Sunday, 2009–12. *Recreations:* football, reading, friends. *Address:* c/o Faculty of Advocates, Parliament House, Edinburgh EH1 1RF.

HAMILTON, Dundas; *see* Hamilton, J. D.

HAMILTON, Eben William; QC 1981; *b* 12 June 1937; *s* of late Rev. John Edmund Hamilton, MC and Hon. Lilias Hamilton, *e d* of 1st Baron Maclay of Glasgow; *m* 1st, 1973, Catherine Harvey (marr. diss. 1977); 2nd, 1985, Themy Rusi Bilimoria, *y d* of late Brig. Rusi Bilimoria. *Educ:* Winchester; Trinity Coll., Cambridge. Nat. Service: 4/7 Royal Dragoon Guards, 1955–57; Fife and Forfar Yeomanry/Scottish Horse, TA, 1958–66. Called to the Bar: Inner Temple, 1962, Bencher, 1985; (*ad eundem*) Lincoln's Inn, 1966; admitted (*ad hoc*): Hong Kong Bar, 1978; Singapore Bar, 1982; Cayman Bar, 2001. Dep. High Court Judge, Chancery Div., 1990–2005. Mem., Inst. of Conveyancers, 1981– (Pres., 1995–96). Jt DTI Inspector, Atlantic Computers plc, 1990–94. Trustee, Royal Scottish Corp., 2008–. FRSA 1988. *Address:* 3rd Floor South, 6 Stone Buildings, Lincoln's Inn, WC2A 3XT. *T:* (020) 7242 7650. *Club:* Garrick.

HAMILTON, Rt Hon. Dame Eleanor (Warwick); *see* King, Rt Hon. Dame E. W.

HAMILTON, Fabian; MP (Lab) Leeds North East, since 1997; *b* 12 April 1955; *s* of late Mario Uziell-Hamilton and Her Honour Adrianne Uziell-Hamilton; *m* 1980, Rosemary Ratcliffe; one *s* two *d.* *Educ:* Brentwood Sch., Essex; Univ. of York (BA Hons). Graphic designer (own company), 1979–94; computer systems consultant, 1994–97. Leeds City Council: Mem. (Lab), 1987–97; Chm., Employment and Econ. Develt Cttee, 1994–96; Chm., Educn Cttee, 1996–98. Mem., Select Cttee on Foreign Affairs, 2001–10, on Political and Constitutional Reform, 2010–15. Contested (Lab) Leeds NE, 1992. Trustee, Heart Research UK (formerly Nat. Heart Res. Fund), 1999–2012. Gov., Northern Sch. of Contemporary Dance. *Recreations:* film, theatre, opera, photography, cycling. *Address:* House of Commons, SW1A 0AA. *T:* (020) 7219 3493.

HAMILTON, Prof. George, MD; FRCS; Professor of Vascular Surgery, UCL Medical School (formerly Royal Free and University College School of Medicine), University of London, since 2003; Consultant in Vascular and General Surgery, since 1987 and Divisional Director of Surgery and Associated Services, since 2011, Royal Free London NHS Foundation (formerly Royal Free Hampstead NHS) Trust; Consultant Vascular Surgeon, Great Ormond Street Hospital for Sick Children NHS Trust, since 1998; Serjeant Surgeon to the Queen, since 2010 (Surgeon to the Queen, 2007–10); *b* 2 Sept. 1947; *s* of George Hamilton and Ginetta Lucaccini Hamilton; *m* 1980, Margaret Handyside; one *s* two *d.* *Educ:* St Modan's High Sch., Stirling; Univ. of Glasgow Sch. of Medicine (MB ChB 1971; MD 2002). DObstRCOG 1974; FRCS 1977; FRCSGlas *ad eundem* 2007. Charing Cross Hosp., London; Surg. Registrar, Basildon Hosp.; Royal Free Hospital, subseq. Royal Free and University College, School of Medicine: Surg. Res. Fellow, 1980; Lectr in Surgery, 1981–87; Hon. Sen. Lectr, 1987–2003; Clin. Sub-Dean, 1997–2005; Faculty (formerly Site) Tutor, Royal Free Campus, 2000–05. Clin. Res. Fellow, Mass Gen. Hosp. and Harvard Sch. of Medicine, 1985–86. Surgeon to the Royal Household, 2001–07. President: Vascular Soc. of GB and Ireland, 2006–07; European Soc. for Vascular Surgery, 2012–13. Mem., British Fulbright Scholars' Assoc. *Publications:* (ed jtly) Renal Vascular Disease, 1995; contribs to learned jls of surgery and vascular surgery and disease. *Recreations:* family, good food and wine, travel, cinema, theatre, water sports, walking, ski-ing. *Address:* University Department of Surgery, Royal Free Hospital, Pond Street, NW3 2QG. *T:* (020) 7830 2163; 34 Circus Road, NW8 9SG. *T:* (020) 7586 9180, *Fax:* (020) 7586 9458.

HAMILTON, George, QPM 2015; Chief Constable, Police Service of Northern Ireland, since 2014; *b* Newtownards, Co. Down, 27 June 1967; *s* of Robert Hamilton and Elsie Hamilton; *m* 1989, Ruth Rainey; one *s* three *d.* *Educ:* Gransha High Sch., Bangor, Co. Down; Open Univ. (BA Politics and Econs); Univ. of Ulster (MBA Dist.). Various roles up to Detective Chief Insp., RUC, 1985–2001, to Chief Supt, Police Service of NI, 2001–07; Asst Chief Constable, Crime and Public Protection, Strathclyde Police, 2007–11; Asst Chief Constable, Criminal Justice, 2011–13, Rural Reg., 2013–14, Police Service of NI. *Address:* Chief Constable's Private Office, Police Service of Northern Ireland Headquarters, Brooklyn, 65 Knock Road, Belfast BT5 6LE. *T:* (028) 9056 1613. *E:* zcomsec1@psni.pnn.police.uk.

HAMILTON, His Honour Iain McCormick, CBE 2015; a Circuit Judge, 2000–14; Designated Family Judge for Greater Manchester, 2005–14; a Senior Circuit Judge, 2010–14; *b* 11 Nov. 1948; *s* of James Hamilton and Mary Isabella Hamilton; *m* 1975, Marilyn Tomlinson; one *s* two *d.* *Educ:* Heversham Grammar Sch.; Manchester Poly. (BA Hons Law). Admitted solicitor, 1974; Walls, Johnston & Co., Stockport, 1974–94; Jones Maidment Wilson, Manchester, 1994–2000; Asst Recorder, 1992–96; Recorder, 1996–2000. Pres., Stockport Law Soc., 1990–91. Chm., 1992–93 and 1996–99, Patron, 2001–, Child Concern. Hon. DH Manchester Metropolitan, 2010. *Recreations:* music, reading, cooking, watching sport, bird watching.

HAMILTON, Ian Lethame; Chief Executive, St George's Healthcare NHS Trust, 1999–2003; *b* 24 July 1951; *s* of Robert Hamilton and Margaret Henderson (*née* McKay). *Educ:* Larkhall Acad.; Glasgow Coll. of Technol. CIPFA 1974. Supervisory accountant, 1975–78, Asst Chief Accountant, 1978–81, Strathclyde Regl Council; Regl Finance Officer, Housing Corp., 1981–83; Dep. Dir of Finance, Wandsworth HA, 1983–88; Project Manager, King's Fund Centre for Health Services Develt, 1988–89 (on secondment); Resource Mgt Project Manager, Wandsworth HA, 1989–91; Dir of Service Develt, 1991–98, Dep. Chief Exec., 1998–99, St George's Healthcare NHS Trust. *Recreations:* gardening, reading, country walks. *Address:* 20 Artesian Road, W2 5AR.

HAMILTON, Ian Robertson; QC (Scot.) 1980; *b* Paisley, Scotland, 13 Sept. 1925; *s* of John Harris Hamilton and Martha Robertson; *m* 1974, Jeannette Patricia Mari Stewart, Connel, Argyll; one *s*, and one *s* two *d* by former marriage. *Educ:* John Neilson Sch., Paisley; Allan Glen's Sch., Glasgow; Glasgow and Edinburgh Univs (BL). Served RAFVR, 1943–48. Called to the Scottish Bar, 1954 and to the Albertan Bar, 1982. Advocate Depute, 1962; Dir of Civil Litigation, Republic of Zambia, 1964–66; Hon. Sheriff of Lanarks, 1967; retd from practice to work for National Trust for Scotland and later to farm in Argyll, 1969; returned to practice, 1974; Sheriff of Glasgow and Strathkelvin, May–Dec. 1984; resigned commn Dec. 1984; returned to practice. Founder, Castle Wynd Printers, Edinburgh, 1955 (published four paperback vols of Hugh MacDiarmid's poetry, 1955–56). Founder and first Chm., The Whichway Trust, to provide adventure training for young offenders, 1988. Chief Pilot, Scottish Parachute Club, 1978–80. Student Pres., Heriot-Watt Univ., 1990–96; Rector, Aberdeen Univ., 1994–96. Hon. Research Fellow, 1997, Hon. LLD 1997, Aberdeen. Hon. Brother, Sir William Wallace Free Colliers, 1997. *Publications:* No Stone Unturned, 1952 (also New York); The Tinkers of the World, 1957 (Foyle award-winning play); The Taking of the Stone of Destiny, 1991; *autobiography:* A Touch of Treason, 1990; A Touch More Treason, 1994; contrib. various jls. *Recreations:* motor biking, neophobia. *Address:* Lochnabeithe, North Connel, Oban, Argyll PA37 1QX. *T:* (01631) 710427.

HAMILTON, (James) Dundas, CBE 1985; Chairman: Wates City of London Properties plc, 1984–94; LWT Pension Trustees Ltd, 1992–94; *b* 11 June 1919; *o s* of late Arthur Douglas Hamilton and Jean Scott Hamilton; *m* 1954, Linda Jean (*d* 2008), *d* of late Sinclair Frank Ditcham and Helen Fraser Ditcham; two *d.* *Educ:* Rugby; Clare Coll., Cambridge. Served War, Army (Lt-Col RA), 1939–46. Member, Stock Exchange, 1948, Mem. Council, 1972–78 (Dep. Chm., 1973–76). Partner, 1951–86, Sen. Partner, 1977–85, Fielding, Newson-Smith & Co. Chairman: TSB Commercial Holdings (formerly UDT Holdings), 1985–90 (Dir, 1983–90); United Dominions Trust Ltd, 1985–89; Director: Richard Clay plc, 1971–84 (Vice-Chm., 1981–84); LWT (Holdings) plc, 1981–91; Datastream Hldgs Ltd, 1982–86; TSB Gp plc, 1985–90; TSB Investment Management Ltd, 1986–88; Archival Facsimiles Ltd, 1986–89; WIB Publications Ltd, 1987–98 (Chm., 1990–98); Camp Hopson & Co., 1991–2002 (Chm., 2002). Dep. Chm., British Invisible Exports Council, 1976–86; Member: Exec. Cttee, City Communications Centre, 1976–88; City and Industrial Liaison Council, 1987–98 (Chm., 1970–73 and 1991–95). Governor, Pasold Res. Fund, 1976–90 (Chm., 1978–86). Member: Council of Industrial Soc., 1959–78 (Exec. Cttee, 1963–68; Life Mem., 1978); Adv. Bd, RCDS, 1980–87. Plays performed, GBS Th., RADA: Teatime for a Triangle, 2011; Who Does She Think Who She Is?, 2011. Contested (C) East Ham North, 1951. FRSA 1988. *Publications:* The Erl King (radio play), 1949; Lorenzo Smiles on Fortune (novel), 1953; Three on a Honeymoon (TV series), 1956; Six Months Grace (play, jointly with Robert Morley), 1957; Stockbroking Today, 1968, 2nd edn 1979; Stockbroking Tomorrow, 1986; 21 Years to Christmas (short stories and verse), 1994. *Recreations:* writing, swimming, golf, watching tennis. *Address:* 45 Melbury Court, W8 6NH. *T:* (020) 7602 3157. *Clubs:* City of London, Hurlingham; All England Lawn Tennis and Croquet; Royal and Ancient Golf (St Andrews); Hankley Common; Worplesdon; Kandahar Ski.

HAMILTON, His Honour John; a Circuit Judge, 1987–2006; *b* 27 Jan. 1941; *s* of late John Ian Hamilton and Mrs Margaret Walker; *m* 1965, Patricia Ann Hamilton (*née* Henman); two *s* one *d.* *Educ:* Durlston Court Prep. Sch., New Milton, Hants; Harrow (schol.); Hertford Coll., Oxford (schol.; MA Jurisp.). Called to the Bar, Gray's Inn, 1965; a Recorder, 1985. KStJ 1982. *Recreations:* golf, bridge, gardening. *Address:* Red Stack, Anstey, near Buntingford, Herts SG9 0BN. *T:* (01763) 848536.

HAMILTON, John Robert Anderson; QC (Scot.) 2011; *b* Glasgow, 14 Jan. 1969; *s* of John Anthony Hamilton, FRCSE and Edith Mary Allardice Anderson (or Hamilton); *m* 1995, Ruth Hamilton, PhD; one *s* one *d.* *Educ:* Kelvinside Acad.; Aberdeen Univ. (LLB 1990; DipLP 1991). Admitted as solicitor, 1993; in practice as solicitor, 1993–97; admitted to Faculty of Advocates, 1998; Tutor, Glasgow Law Sch., 2002–03; Advocate Depute, 2003–06; Dir, Trng and Educn, Faculty of Advocates, 2009–12. Convenor, Mental Health Tribunal Scotland, 2008–; Judge of First-tier Tribunal (Social Entitlement Chamber), 2014–. Mem., Parole Bd for Scotland, 2014–. *Recreation:* curling. *Address:* Advocates Library, Parliament House, Edinburgh EH1 1RF. *T:* (0131) 226 5071. *E:* john.hamilton@advocates.org.uk. *Clubs:* Reform Curling, Partick Curling.

HAMILTON, Kirstie Louise, (Mrs Charles Stewart-Smith); Director, Newsfury, since 2010; *b* 5 April 1963; *d* of Elizabeth Kate Marie Hamilton and Mark Robert Hamilton; *m* 1998, Charles Stewart-Smith; two *s.* *Educ:* Hillcrest High Sch., Hamilton, NZ. Columnist, National Business Review, NZ, 1988–89; Business Correspondent, Evening Standard, 1989–92; Business Correspondent, 1992–95, Dep. City Editor, 1995–96, Sunday Times; City Editor, The Express and Sunday Express, 1996–97; City Editor, Sunday Times, 1997–2002; Partner, Tulchan Communications, 2002–07. *Recreations:* riding, ski-ing. *Address:* 37 Stockwell Park Crescent, SW9 0DQ.

HAMILTON, Sir Malcolm William Bruce S.; *see* Stirling-Hamilton.

HAMILTON, (Mostyn) Neil; Chairman, Sheila Childs Recruitment Ltd, since 2004; legal consultant, broadcaster, writer, entertainer, actor; *b* 9 March 1949; *s* of Ronald and Norma Hamilton; *m* 1983, (Mary) Christine Holman. *Educ:* Amman Valley Grammar School; University College of Wales, Aberystwyth (BSc Econs, MSc Econs); Corpus Christi College, Cambridge (LLM). Called to the Bar, Middle Temple, 1979. MP (C) Tatton, 1983–97; contested (C) same seat, 1997. PPS to Minister of State for Transport, 1986–87; an Asst Govt Whip, 1990–92; Parly Under-Sec. of State, DTI, 1992–94. Mem., Select Cttee on Treasury and Civil Service, 1987–90; Vice-Chm., Conservative backbench Trade and Industry Cttee, 1984–90 (Sec., 1983 and 1994–97); Secretary: Cons. backbench Finance Cttee, 1987–90 and 1995–97; UK-ANZAC Parly Gp, 1984–97; Chm., All Party Anglo-Togo Parly Gp, 1988–97. Mem., Nat. Exec. Cttee, UKIP, 2011– (Dep. Chm., 2013–); Chm., UKIP Wilts, 2012–. Columnist, Sunday Express, 2007–. Vice-Pres., Small Business Bureau, 1985–97. Vice-Pres., Cheshire Agricl Soc., 1986–. Actor: Jack and the Beanstalk, Yvonne Arnaud Th., Guildford, 2002–03; Cinderella, Lighthouse Th., Kettering, 2011; narrator, Rocky Horror Show, 30th anniversary tour, 2002–03; actor/performer, Lunch with the Hamiltons, 2006, 2007, 2008, High Jinks with the Hamiltons, 2011, Edinburgh Fest. *Publications:* UK/US Double Taxation, 1980; The European Community—a Policy for Reform, 1983; (ed) Land Development Encyclopaedia, 1981–; (jtly) No Turning Back, 1985; Great Political Eccentrics, 1999; pamphlets on state industry, schools and the NHS. *Recreations:* campaigning to restore Parliamentary sovereignty, gardening, opera, the arts, architecture and conservation, country pursuits, silence. *Address:* Bradfield Manor, Hullavington, Wilts SN14 6EU.

HAMILTON, Sir Nigel, KCB 2008; Head of Northern Ireland Civil Service, 2002–08; Vice Lord-Lieutenant, Belfast, since 2009; *b* 19 March 1948; *s* of James and Jean Hamilton; *m* 1974, Lorna Woods; two *s*. *Educ:* Queen's Univ., Belfast (BSc Hons); Henley Mgt Coll.; Federal Exec. Inst., Virginia; Univ. of Ulster. Joined NICS, 1970; Under Sec., Central Community Relns, Urban Regeneration, 1990–98; Permanent Secretary: Dept of Educn, 1998–2001; Dept for Regl Develt, 2001–02. Non-executive Director: Ulster Bank, 2009–; Belfast City Airport, 2009–13. Chairman: Council, Prince's Trust, NI, 2008–; Bryson Charitable Gp, 2008–12; New Irish Arts, 2014–. Patron, Tiny Life, 2008–. DUniv Ulster, 2008. *Recreations:* Rugby (Pres., Ulster Referees Soc., 1996–97; Pres., Ulster Br., Irish RFU, 2010–11), golf.

HAMILTON, Nigel John Mawdesley; QC 1981; *b* 13 Jan. 1938; *s* of late Archibald Dearman Hamilton and Joan Worsley Hamilton (*née* Mawdesley); *m* 1963, Leone Morag Elizabeth Gordon (*d* 2006); two *s*. *Educ:* St Edward's Sch., Oxford; Queens' Coll., Cambridge. Nat. Service, 2nd Lieut, RE, Survey Dept, 1956–58. Assistant Master: St Edward's Sch., Oxford, 1962–63; King's Sch., Canterbury, 1963–65. Called to the Bar, Inner Temple, 1965, Bencher, 1989. Mem., Gen. Council of the Bar, 1989–94. Mem. (C) for Chew Valley, Avon CC, 1989–93. *Recreation:* fishing. *Address:* New Bailey Chambers, 4th Floor, Corn Exchange, Fenwick Street, Liverpool L2 7QS. *Club:* Flyfishers'.

HAMILTON, Peter Bryan, MA; Head Master of Haberdashers' Aske's School, since 2002; *b* 28 Aug. 1956; *s* of Brian George Hamilton and Clara Hamilton (*née* Marchi); *m* 1st, 1981, Danièle Lahaye (marr. diss. 1987); one *d*; 2nd, 1993, Sylvie (*née* Vulliet); one *d*. *Educ:* King Edward VI Grammar Sch., Southampton; Christ Church, Oxford (1st Cl. Hons Modern Foreign Languages 1979; MA). Head of French, Radley Coll., 1981–89; Head of Modern Langs and Housemaster of Wren's, Westminster Sch., 1989–96; Head Master, King Edward VI Sch., Southampton, 1996–2002. Examr in French, Oxford and Cambridge Schs Exam. Bd, 1992–97. Governor: Stroud Sch., 1997–2002; Princes' Mead, 1997–2002; Durlston Court Sch., 1999–2002; Reddiford Sch., 2003–; Lochinver House, 2004–; Krishna Avanti Sch., 2009–; Bushey Acad., 2009–14. *Recreations:* canoeing, horse-riding, hill walking, karate, sailing, ski-ing, squash, wind surfing, comparative literature, European cinema, opera, classical music, study of Arabic. *Address:* Haberdashers' Aske's School, Butterfly Lane, Elstree, Borehamwood, Herts WD6 3AF.

HAMILTON, Reeta; *see* Chakrabarti, R.

HAMILTON, His Honour Richard Graham; a Circuit Judge, 1986–97; Chancellor, Diocese of Liverpool, 1976–2002; *b* 26 Aug. 1932; *s* of late Henry Augustus Rupert Hamilton and Frances Mary Graham Hamilton; *m* 1960, Patricia Craghill Hamilton (*née* Ashburner) (*d* 2008); one *s* one *d*; partner, Mrs Sonia Abrahamson (*d* 2014). *Educ:* Charterhouse; University Coll., Oxford (MA); MA Screenwriting, Liverpool John Moores Univ., 1999. Called to the Bar, Middle Temple, 1956; a Recorder, 1974–86. Regular broadcasting work for Radio Merseyside, inc. scripts: Van Gogh in England, 1981; Voices from Babylon, 1983; A Longing for Dynamite, 1984; Dark Night, 1988 (winner of first prize for a short religious play, RADIUS); Murder Court productions (dramatised trials), Liverpool: The Maybrick Case, 1989; The Veronica Mutiny, 1990; Threatening Behaviour, 2006. *Publications:* Foul Bills and Dagger Money, 1979; All Jangle and Riot, 1986; A Good Wigging, 1988. *Recreations:* reading, walking, films. *Club:* Athenæum (Liverpool).

HAMILTON, Dr Russell Douglas, CBE 2010; FFPH; Director of Research and Development, Department of Health, since 2007; *b* 6 Sept. 1955; *s* of Ronald Adrian Hamilton and June Grace Hamilton; *m* 1993, Angela Carole Shore; two *d*. *Educ:* Pimlico High Sch.; James Cook Univ. (BSc Hons 1976); Univ. of London (PhD Physiol. 1990); Brunel Univ./Henley Mgt Coll. (MBA 1993). DipM 1993; FFPH 2003. Tutor, James Cook Univ., 1976; SO in Respiratory Medicine, Flinders Med. Centre, Adelaide, 1977–79; SO, then Principal Clinical Scientist, Acad. Dept of Medicine, Charing Cross Hosp., 1980–93; Regl R&D Manager, SW RHA and NHS Exec. S and W, 1993–98; Department of Health: Regl Dir, R&D, then Hd of R&D Div. S, 1998–2003; Hd, Res. Policy and Strategy, then Dep. Dir of R&D, 2003–07. Director, National NHS R&D Programmes: in Asthma, 1998–2003; in Complex Disability, 1998–2003; in Cancer, 1998–2007. Mem., Govt Chief Scientific Advr's Cttee, 2004–13. Member: various sci. and professional adv. cttees, 1991–; Consumers in NHS Res., 1999–2004; Res. for Patient Benefits Wkg Party, 2003–04. HEFCE Panel Member: RAE 2001; RAE 2008 Main Panel A; REF 2014 Main Panel A. Member, Board: NCRI (formerly Nat. Cancer Res. Funders Forum), 2000–; UK Clinical Res. Collaboration, 2004–; Office for Strategic Coordination of Health Res., 2007–. Hon. DSc Exeter, 2012. *Publications:* contrib. papers esp. on research strategy and respiratory physiology in health and disease. *Recreations:* family, sailing, hill walking, music. *Address:* Department of Health, Richmond House, 79 Whitehall, SW1A 2NS. *T:* (020) 7210 5786. *Club:* North Curry Cricket.

HAMILTON, Simon Terence; Member (DemU) Strangford, Northern Ireland Assembly, since 2007; *b* Newtownards, Co. Down, 17 March 1977; *s* of Frank and Muriel Hamilton; *m* 2003, Nicola Karen McAvoy; two *s*. *Educ:* Comber Primary Sch.; Regent Hse Sch., Newtownards; Queen's Univ. Belfast (BA Hons Modern Hist. and Politics 1999; BLegS Hons Law 2001). Auditor, PricewaterhouseCoopers, 2001–03; Press Officer, DUP, 2003–07. Mem. (DemU) Ards BC, 2005–10. Northern Ireland Assembly: Private Sec. to Minister of Finance and Personnel, 2011–13; Minister of Finance and Personnel, 2013–15; Minister for Health, Social Services and Public Safety, 2015; Deputy Chairman: Cttee on Finance and Personnel, 2008–09; Cttee for the Envmt, 2011–13; Chm., Cttee for Social Develt, 2009–11. Member: Orange Order; Royal Black Instn. *Recreations:* reading, walking, travelling. *Address:* 7 The Square, Comber, Co. Down BT23 5DX. *T:* (028) 9187 0900. *E:* simonhamilton@dup.org.uk.

HAMILTON, Her Honour Susan, (Mrs Eric Kelly); QC 1993; a Circuit Judge, 1998–2007; *m* 1977, Dr Eric Peter Kelly; two *s*. *Educ:* Hove Grammar Sch. for Girls. Called to the Bar, Middle Temple, 1975; a Recorder, 1996–98. *Publications:* The Modern Law of Highways, 1981; (contrib.) Halsbury's Laws of England, vol. 21, 4th edn, 1995, vol. 39(1), 4th edn, 1998; (contrib.) Encyclopaedia of Forms and Precedents, 5th edn, 1986. *Recreations:* sailing, gardening, tapestry, travelling. *Club:* Royal Southern Yacht.

HAMILTON, Wilfred; *see* Hamilton, Alfred W.

HAMILTON, William Francis Forbes, CA; Chairman, Macrae & Dick Ltd, since 1994; Vice Lord-Lieutenant, Inverness, 2002–15; *b* 19 April 1940; *s* of late Col William Hamilton, OBE, CA and of Amy Constance Hamilton (*née* Forbes); *m* 1971, Anne Davison, MB BS; one *s*. *Educ:* Inverness Royal Acad.; Edinburgh Univ. (BCom 1961). CA 1967. Macrae & Dick Ltd: Co. Sec., 1968–80; Finance Dir, 1971–80; Man. Dir, 1980–2003. Dir, Highlands & Islands Airports Ltd, 1995–2001; Chm., Menzies BMW, 1998–. Mem., Distributor Council, BL Cars, 1977–78. Member, Highland Committee: Scottish Council Develt and Ind., 1971–2007; Police Dependants' Trust, 1998–2008. Director: Highland Hospice, 1992–95; Highland Hospice Trading Co., 1995–2008. Trustee, Fresson Trust, 1991–. DL Inverness, 2000. *Recreations:* sailing, travel. *Address:* Craigrory, North Kessock, Inverness IV1 3XH. *T:* (01463) 230430, *Fax:* (01463) 668990. *E:* wffhamilton@macraeanddick.co.uk. *Club:* Royal Highland Yacht.

HAMILTON-DALRYMPLE, Sir Hew; *see* Dalrymple.

HAMILTON-RUSSELL, family name of **Viscount Boyne**.

HAMILTON-SMITH, family name of **Baron Colwyn**.

HAMLIN, Prof. Michael John, CBE 1994; FICE, FREng; FRSE; consulting water engineer, since 1984; Principal and Vice Chancellor of the University of Dundee, 1987–94; *b* 11 May 1930; *s* of late Dr Ernest John Hamlin and Dorothy Janet Hamlin; *m* 1951, Augusta Louise, *d* of late William Thomas Tippins and Rose Louise Tippins; three *s*. *Educ:* St John's Coll., Johannesburg; Dauntsey's Sch.; Bristol Univ. (BSc); Imperial Coll. of Science and Technol., London (DIC). FIWEM (FIWES 1973); FICE 1981; FREng (FEng 1985); FRSE 1990. Asst Engineer, Lemon & Blizard, Southampton, 1951–53; Engineer: Anglo-American Corp., Johannesburg, 1954–55; Stewart, Sviridov & Oliver, Johannesburg, 1955; Partner, Rowe & Hamlin, Johannesburg, 1956–58; Univ. of Witwatersrand, 1959–60; University of Birmingham, 1961–87: Prof. of Water Engrg, 1970–87; Hd of Dept of Civil Engrg, 1980–87; Pro Vice-Chancellor, 1985–86; Vice-Principal, 1986–87. Chm., Aquatic and Atmospheric Phys. Scis Grants Cttee, NERC, 1975–79; Member: Severn Trent Water Authority, 1974–79; British National Cttee for Geodesy and Geophysics, 1979–84 (Chm., Hydrology Sub-Cttee, 1979–84); Scottish Econ. Council, 1989–93; Internat. Relns Cttee, 1992–95, Scientific Unions Cttee, 1995–99, Royal Soc. President: Internat. Commn on Water Resource Systems of the Internat. Assoc. of Hydrological Scis (IAHS), 1983–87; British Hydrological Soc., 1995–97. International Union of Geodesy and Geophysics: Mem., Council, 1992–2000; Mem., 1991–2007, Chm., 2003–07, Finance Cttee. Chm., Scottish Centre for Children with Motor Impairment, 1991–94. Hon. Life Mem., Guild of Students, Birmingham Univ., 1980; Hon. Mem., Students' Assoc., Dundee Univ., 1994–. FRCPS (Glas) 1992; Hon. FRCGP 1993. Dist. Fellow, Internat. Med. Univ., Kuala Lumpur, 1999. Hon. LLD: St Andrews, 1989; Dundee, 1996; Hon. DEng: Birmingham, 1995; Bristol, 2000; Hon. DLitt Southern Queensland, 2003. President's Premium, IWES, 1972. OStJ 1991. *Publications:* contribs on public health engrg and water resources engrg in learned jls. *Recreations:* walking, gardening. *Address:* The Coombes, Hope Bagot, Ludlow, Shropshire SY8 3AQ.

HAMLYN, Claire; *see* Jakens, C.

HAMLYN, Jane Sarah; Director, Frith Street Gallery, London, since 1988; Chair, Paul Hamlyn Foundation, since 2003 (Trustee, since 1987); *b* London, 17 April 1958; *d* of Baron Hamlyn, CBE and late Eileen Margaret, (Bobbie), Hamlyn; partner, 1988, James Lingwood, *qv*; one *s* two *d*. *Educ:* King Alfred Sch., London; Brighton Sch. of Art (Foundn course); City and Guilds Sch. of Art (BA 1st Cl. with Dist. Illustrative Arts); London Coll. of Printing (Postgrad. Dip. Book Prodn and Design). Asst Book Designer, John Roberts Press, 1983–85; Asst Art Editor, Folio Soc., 1985–88; freelance work with publishers, and teaching, 1987–89. Sen. Advisory Counsel, India Inst., KCL, 2012–. Hon. Dir, Royal Opera House, Covent Gdn, 2012–. *Recreations:* contemporary art, architecture and design, music and opera, India, travel. *Address:* c/o Paul Hamlyn Foundation, 5–11 Leeke Street, WC1X 9HY.

HAMLYN, Peter John, MD; FRCS; Hon. Consultant Neurosurgeon, University College London Hospital, since 2007; Director of Education, Institute of Sport Exercise and Health, University College Hospital, London, since 2009; *b* 10 Aug. 1957; *s* of David William Hamlyn and Paula Anne Hamlyn (*née* Bowker); *m* 1994, Geraldine Marie Frances Shepherd; three *s*. *Educ:* N Cestrian Grammar Sch.; Solihull Sixth Form Coll.; University Coll. London (BSc 1st Cl. Hons Neurosci. 1979; MB BS 1982; MD 1994 (Rogers Prize)). FRCS 1986; FInstLM (FISM 1995). Consultant Neurological and Spinal Surgeon: St Bartholomew's Hosp., 1990–2007; The Royal London Hosp., 1996–2007. Dir, Sport and Exercise Medicine, Queen Mary, Univ. of London, 2003–07. Chm., Ministerial Wkg Gp on Safety and Medicine in Sport, DCMS, 2001. Corresp. in sports medicine, Daily Telegraph, 1993. Founder, 1992, and Vice-Chm., 1997–, British Brain and Spine Foundn. Med. Advr, London 2012 Olympic Bid, 2004–05; Mem., London Specialist Trng Cttee in Sport and Exercise Medicine, 2005–07. *Publications:* Neurovascular Compression of the Cranial Nerves in Neurological and Systematic Disease, 1999. *Recreation:* sculpture.

HAMM, John (Frederick), OC 2009; MD; Chairman, Assisted Human Reproduction Canada, 2006; Premier of Nova Scotia, Canada, 1999–2006; *b* 8 April 1938; *m* 1964, Genesta Hartling; two *s* one *d*. *Educ:* Univ. of King's Coll., Halifax (BSc 1958); Dalhousie Med. Sch. (MD 1963). Family physician, 1963–93. MLA (PC) Pictou Centre, Nova Scotia, 1993–2006; Leader of Opposition, NS, 1995–98. Leader, PC Party of NS, 1995–2006. Mem., Provincial Med. Bd, NS, 1963–96. President: Coll. of Family Physicians, NS; Pictou Co. Med. Soc., 1971–73; Med. Soc. of NS, 1977. Pres., Aberdeen Hosp. Med. Staff, 1986–88; Chm., Aberdeen Hosp. Foundn, 1990–92. Former Warden, St George's Ch. *Recreations:* hockey, running, wood working.

HAMMARBERG, Thomas; international human rights adviser; Commissioner for Human Rights, Council of Europe, 2006–12; Chairman, Swedish Commission for Roma Rights; *b* 2 Jan. 1942; *s* of Harald and Naima Hammarberg; *m* 1997, Alfhild Petren; one *s*. *Educ:* Stockholm Sch. of Econs (BS). Foreign Editor, daily Expressen, then Swedish broadcasting, 1970–80; Secretary General: Amnesty Internat., 1980–86; Save the Children—Sweden, 1986–92; Ambassador and Special Advr to the Foreign Minister, 1994–2002; Sec. Gen., Olof Palme Internat. Center, Stockholm, 2002–06. Vice Chm., UN Cttee on the Rights of the Child, 1991–96; Special Rep. of the UN Sec. Gen. in Cambodia, 1996–2000. DJur *hc*, Stockholm, 2010; Hon. Dr PolSci Göteborg, 2013. King of Sweden Hon. Medal, 2005; Stockholm Human Rights Award, 2012; Geuzenpenning, 2014. *Publications:* books in Swedish and English on media reporting and human rights matters. *Recreation:* ski-ing. *Address:* Tistelvagen 22, 12134 Enskededalen, Sweden.

HAMMER, James Dominic George, CB 1983; Chairman, Certification Management Council, Zurich (formerly Eagle Star) Certification Ltd, 1996–2001; *b* 21 April 1929; *s* of E. A. G. and E. L. G. Hammer; *m* 1955, Margaret Eileen Halse; two *s* one *d*. *Educ:* Dulwich Coll.; Corpus Christi Coll., Cambridge. BA Hons Mod. Langs. Joined HM Factory Inspectorate, 1953; Chief Inspector of Factories, 1975–84; Dep. Dir Gen., HSE, 1985–89. Dir, UK SKILLS, 1990–2000. Pres., Internat. Assoc. of Labour Inspection, 1984–93; Chairman: Nat. Certification Scheme for In-Service Inspection Bodies, 1990–92; Nat. Steering Cttee, Eur. Year of Safety, Health and Hygiene at Work 1992, 1991–93; NACCB, 1992–95; Nat. Exam. Bd in Occupational Safety and Health, 1992–95. Vice Chm., Camberwell HA, 1982–91; Associate Mem., King's Healthcare, 1992–97. FIOSH 1992. *Address:* 10 Allison Grove, Dulwich, SE21 7ER. *T:* (020) 8693 2977.

HAMMERBECK, Brig. Christopher John Anthony, CB 1991; CBE 2007; Executive Director, British Chamber of Commerce in Hong Kong, 1994–2015; *b* 14 March 1943; *s* of Sqn Leader O. R. W. Hammerbeck and I. M. Hammerbeck; *m* 1974, Alison Mary Felice (marr. diss. 1996); one *s* two *d*. *Educ:* Mayfield Coll., Sussex. Commnd, 1965; 2nd RTR, 1965–70; Air Adjt, Parachute Sqn, RAC, 1970–72; GSO3 (Ops), HQ 20 Armoured Bde, 1972–74; psc, 1975; DAA&QMG, HQ 12 Mechanised Bde, 1976–78; Sqn Comdr, 4th RTR, 1978–80; DAAG(O), MoD, 1980–82; Directing Staff, Army Staff Coll., 1982–84; CO, 2nd RTR, 1984–87; Col, Tactical Doctrine/Op. Requirement 1 (BR) Corps, 1987–88; RCDS, 1989; Comdr, 4th Armoured Brigade, 1990–92; Dep. Comdr, British Forces Hong Kong, 1992–94. Senior Advisor: Guangzhou Foreign Trade and Investment Bureau, 2008–; Guangzhou Regl Sub-Council, China Council for Promotion of Internat. Trade, 2008–; Vermilion Partners Ltd, 2006–15; Steve Vickers Associates Ltd, 2010–. Pres., Inst. of Export (HK), 2004–; Sen. Advr to European Chamber of Commerce, Hong Kong, 2015. President: Hong Kong Br., RBL, 1995–; HK Ex-Servicemen's Assoc., 1995–. Trustee, Locally Enlisted Personnel Trust, 1997–. Member: Hong Kong Inst. of Dirs, 2001–; Hong Kong Sea Cadets

Council, 2004–. MCMI. Hon. Citizen, Xiamen City, China, 2006. *Recreations:* golf, ski-ing, reading, travel, hiking. *Clubs:* Army and Navy, Royal Over-Seas League; Shek O, Hong Kong (Hong Kong).

HAMMERSLEY, (Constance) Ann; *see* Cryer, C. A.

HAMMERSLEY, Rear-Adm. Peter Gerald, CB 1982; OBE 1965; *b* 18 May 1928; *s* of late Robert Stevens Hammersley and Norah Hammersley (*née* Kirkham); *m* 1959, Audrey Cynthia Henderson Bolton; one *s* one *d*. *Educ:* Denstone Coll.; RNEC Manadon; Imperial Coll., London (DIC). Served RN, 1946–82; Long Engrg Course, RNEC Manadon, 1946–50; HMS Liverpool, 1950–51; Advanced Marine Engrg Course, RNC Greenwich, 1951–53; HMS Ocean, 1953–54; joined Submarine Service, 1954; HMS Alaric, HMS Tiptoe, 1954–58; Nuclear Engrg Course, Imperial Coll., 1958–59; First Marine Engineer Officer, first RN Nuclear Submarine, HMS Dreadnought, 1960–64; DG Ships Staff, 1965–68; Base Engineer Officer, Clyde Submarine Base, 1968–70; Naval Staff, 1970–72; Asst Director, S/M Project Team, DG Ships, 1973–76; CO, HMS Defiance, 1976–78; Captain, RNEC Manadon, 1978–80; CSO (engrg) to C-in-C Fleet, 1980–82. Comdr 1964; Captain 1971; Rear-Adm. 1980; Chief Exec., British Internal Combustion Engine Manufacturers' Assoc., 1982–85; Dir, British Marine Equipment Council, 1985–92. Fellow, Woodard Schs Corp., 1992–98 (Hon. Fellow, 1998). Gov., Denstone Coll., 1986–98 (Chm., 1994–98). Founder Liveryman, Engineers' Co., 1983 (Master, 1988–89). *Recreations:* walking, gardening, golf. *Address:* Wistaria Cottage, Linersh Wood, Bramley, near Guildford GU5 0EE. *Clubs:* Army and Navy; Bramley Golf.

HAMMERSLEY, Philip Tom, CBE 2000 (OBE 1989); CEng; Chairman, University Hospitals of Leicester NHS Trust, 2000–06; *b* 10 Feb. 1931; *s* of Tom Andrew Hammersley and Winifred Hammersley (*née* Moyns); *m* 1954, Lesley Ann Millage; two *s* one *d*. *Educ:* Bancroft's Sch.; Imperial Coll., Univ. of London (BSc Eng.). CEng 1965; MIMechE 1965. Tech. Officer, ICI Plastics Div., 1954–65; Clarks Ltd: Chief Engr, 1965–68; Prodn Services Manager, 1968–71; Dir, Children's Div., 1971–79; Pres., Striderite Footwear, Boston, Mass, 1979–81; British Shoe Corporation, Leicester: Factories Dir, 1981–87; Man. Dir, Freeman, Hardy & Willis, 1987–89; Commercial Dir, 1989–90; non-exec. Dir, BSS Gp PLC, 1991–99 (Dep. Chm., 1995; Chm., 1995–99). Vice-Chm., Leics HA, 1990–92; Chm., Leicester Royal Infirmary NHS Trust, 1992–97; Regl Chm., Trent, NHS Exec., DoH, 1997–99. Chm. Council, Shoe & Allied Trades Res. Assoc., 1983–86; Pres., Brit. Footwear Manufacturers Fedn, 1986–87; Chm., E Midlands Regl Council, CBI, 1988–90. Chm., Nat. Space Centre (Ops) Ltd, 2001–09; Trustee, Nat. Space Centre, 1997–2001, 2006–09. Freeman, City of London, 1983; Mem., Patten Makers' Co., 1983–. Hon. DBA De Montfort, 1999; Hon. LLD Leicester, 2008. *Recreations:* golf, theatre, music. *Address:* 3 Holywell, Hook Heath Road, Woking, Surrey GU22 0LA. *T:* (01483) 493191. *Clubs:* East India, MCC.

HAMMERSLEY, Stephen John, CBE 2012; Chief Executive, UK Community Foundations (formerly Community Foundation Network), since 2004; *b* Ipswich, 23 Dec. 1961; *s* of John and Janet Hammersley; *m* 1987, Susan Elizabeth; three *c*. *Educ:* Bramcote Hills Grammar Sch.; Durham Univ. (BSc Maths). Barclays Bank, 1983–2000; Tearfund, 2000–04. Chair, TLMT Trading Ltd, 2010–. *Recreation:* outdoor pursuits. *Address:* UK Community Foundations, 12 Angel Gate, 320–328 City Road, EC1Y 2PT. *T:* 07717 221653. *E:* sjh_123@btinternet.com.

HAMMERTON, Alastair Rolf; His Honour Judge Alastair Hammerton; a Circuit Judge, since 2014; *b* Sussex, 3 Nov. 1960; *s* of His Honour Rolf Eric Hammerton and of Thelma Hammerton; *m* 1991, Vanessa Rumboll; one *s* two *d*. *Educ:* Winchester Coll.; Queens' Coll., Cambridge (BA 1982); Univ. of Virginia Sch. of Law (LLM 1984). Called to the Bar, Inner Temple, 1983, Bencher, 2004; a Recorder, 2004–14. *Recreations:* theatre, cooking, gardening. *Address:* Snaresbrook Crown Court, 75 Hollybush Hill, Snaresbrook, E11 1QW.

See also V. L. Hammerton.

HAMMERTON, Veronica Lesley; Her Honour Judge Hammerton; a Circuit Judge, since 2005; *b* 1 Oct. 1954; *d* of His Honour Rolf Eric Hammerton; *m* 1981, David John Knight; one *s* one *d*. *Educ:* Cheltenham Ladies' Coll.; Girton Coll., Cambridge (BA 1976). Called to the Bar, Inner Temple, 1977; Asst Recorder, 1996–2000; a Recorder, 2000–05. Legal Mem., Mental Health Rev. Tribunal, 2003–. *Recreations:* embroidery, sailing, tennis, theatre-going. *Address:* Tunbridge Wells County Court, Merevale House, 42–46 London Road, Tunbridge Wells, Kent TN1 1DP.

See also A. R. Hammerton.

HAMMETT, Ven. Barry Keith, CB 2006; Chaplain of the Fleet, Archdeacon for the Royal Navy and Director General, Naval Chaplaincy Service, 2002–06; *b* 9 Oct. 1947; *s* of George and Irene Hammett. *Educ:* Eltham Coll.; Magdalen Coll., Oxford (BA 1971, MA 1974); St Stephen's House, Oxford; Ven. English Coll., Rome (exchange student). Ordained deacon 1974, priest 1975; Asst Curate, St Peter's, Plymouth, 1974–77; Chaplain, RN, 1977–2006: Staff Chaplain, MoD, 1986–90; Principal, Armed Forces' Chaplaincy Centre, 1996–2000. QHC 1999–2006. Hon. Canon: Portsmouth Cathedral, 2002–06, Hon. Canon Emeritus, 2006; Cathedral Chapter, Dio. in Europe (Gibraltar), 2003–06. *Recreations:* travel, historic houses, gardening, motoring, photography, genealogy. *Address:* 1 de Port Heights, Corhampton, Hants SO32 3DA.

HAMMICK, Sir Jeremy (Charles), 6th Bt *cr* 1834, of Cavendish Square, London; landscape artist; *b* 3 Feb. 1956; *s* of Sir Stephen George Hammick, 5th Bt, OBE and Gillian Elizabeth Hammick (*née* Inchbald); *S* father 2014; *m* 1997, Mrs Melanie Louise Stock (marr. diss. 2014); two *s*. *Educ:* Bournemouth Coll. of Art. *Heir:* *s* George Frederick Love Hammick, *b* 16 Feb. 1998.

HAMMOND, Sir Anthony (Hilgrove), KCB 2000 (CB 1992); Standing Counsel to General Synod of the Church of England, 2000–13; *b* 27 July 1940; *s* of late Colonel Charles William Hilgrove Hammond and Jessie Eugenia Hammond (*née* Francis); *m* 1988, Avril Collinson. *Educ:* Malvern Coll.; Emmanuel Coll., Cambridge (BA, MA, LLM). Admitted Solicitor of Supreme Court, 1965. Articled with LCC, 1962; Solicitor, GLC, 1965–68; Home Office: Legal Assistant, 1968; Sen. Legal Assistant, 1970; Asst Legal Advr, 1974; Principal Asst Legal Advr, 1980–88, Legal Advr, 1988–92, Home Office and NI Office; Solicitor and Dep. Sec., then Dir Gen. Legal Services, DTI, 1992–97; HM Procurator Gen., Treasury Solicitor and Queen's Proctor, 1997–2000; Legal Counsel to Hakluyt & Co. Ltd, 2001–05. Mem. Bd, Inst. of Advanced Legal Studies, 1997–. Fellow, Soc. of Advanced Legal Studies, 1997. Freeman, City of London, 1991; Liveryman, Glass Sellers' Co., 1991– (Master, 2007). Hon. QC 1997. *Recreations:* bridge, music, opera, walking, birdwatching.

HAMMOND, Christopher Mark; Founder and Director, MOT International (formerly MOT), since 2002; *b* Glasgow, 29 May 1968; *s* of Michael Hammond and Marjorie Hammond; partner, Una Murtagh; two *d*. *Educ:* Wimbledon Sch. of Art. Lectr in Curating, Goldsmiths, Univ. of London. *Address:* MOT International, 72 New Bond Street, W1S 1RR; (from 2016) MOT International, 15 Babmaes Street, SW1Y 6HD; MOT International, Avenue Louise, Brussels, B-1000, Belgium. *Club:* Soho House.

HAMMOND, Prof. Gerald, PhD; FBA 1998; John Edward Taylor Professor of English Literature, University of Manchester, 1993–2006, now Emeritus; *b* 3 Nov. 1945; *s* of Frank George Hammond and Ruth Hammond (*née* Wallen); *m* 1971, Patsy Talat Naheed Khaliq; one *s* one *d*. *Educ:* University Coll. London (BA 1968; PhD 1974). University of Manchester: Lectr, 1971–83, Sen. Lectr, 1983–90, Reader, 1990–93, in English; Dean: Faculty of Arts, 1999–2002; Internat. and Grad. Educn, 2002–03; Faculty of Engrg and Physical Scis, 2003–04; Associate Vice Pres., Grad. Educn, 2005–06. Res. Posts Co-ordinator, British Acad., 2002–05. Distinguished Vis. Humanities Prof., Auburn Univ., Alabama, 1987; Nat. Sci. Council of Taiwan Res. Fellow, 1997–98. Chatterton Lecture, 1985, Warton Lecture, 1995, British Acad. *Publications:* (ed) The Metaphysical Poets, 1974; (ed) John Skelton: poems, 1980; The Reader and Shakespeare's Young Man Sonnets, 1981; The Making of the English Bible, 1984; (ed) Sir Walter Ralegh, 1984; (ed) Elizabethan Poetry, Lyrical and Narrative, 1984; (ed) Richard Lovelace: poems, 1987; Fleeting Things: English poets and poems 1616–1660, 1990; Horseracing: a book of words, 1992; articles in learned jls, reviews. *Recreation:* horseracing. *Address:* 29 Belfield Road, Manchester M20 6BJ. *T:* (0161) 445 2399.

HAMMOND, Hon. Sir Grant; *see* Hammond, Hon. Sir R. G.

HAMMOND, His Honour James Anthony; a Circuit Judge, 1986–2010; *b* 25 July 1936; *s* of James Hammond and Phyllis Eileen Hammond; *m* 1963, Sheila Mary Hammond, JP (*née* Stafford); three *d*. *Educ:* Wigan Grammar Sch.; St Catherine's Coll., Oxford (MA). Called to the Bar, Lincoln's Inn, 1959; National Service, 1959–61; a Recorder, 1980–86. Mem. (pt-time), Parole Bd, 2010–. Councillor: Up Holland UDC, 1962–66; Skelmersdale and Holland UDC, 1970–72. Chairman: NW Branch, Society of Labour Lawyers, 1975–86; W Lancs CAB, 1982–86; Pres., NW Branch, Inst. for Study and Treatment of Delinquency, 1987–98. *Recreation:* walking. *Clubs:* Wigan Hockey (Vice Pres., 1983–); Broughton Park Rugby Union Football.

HAMMOND, (John) Martin; Headmaster, Tonbridge School, 1990–2005; *b* 15 Nov. 1944; *s* of late Thomas Chatterton Hammond and Joan Cruse; *m* 1974, Meredith Jane Shier; one *s* one *d*. *Educ:* Winchester Coll. (Scholar); Balliol Coll., Oxford (Domus Scholar; Hertford Scholar and (1st) de Paravicini Scholar, (2nd) Craven Scholar, 1st Cl. Hons Mods, 1963; Chancellor's Latin Prose Prize, Chancellor's Latin Verse Prize, Ireland Scholar, 1964; Gaisford Greek Prose Prize, Gaisford Greek Verse Prize (jtly), 1965; 2nd Cl. Lit. Hum. 1966). Asst Master, St Paul's Sch., 1966–71; Teacher, Anargyrios Sch., Spetsai, Greece, 1972–73; Asst Master, Harrow Sch., 1973–74; Head of Classics, 1974–80, and Master in College, 1980–84, Eton Coll.; Headmaster, City of London Sch., 1984–90. Mem., Gen. Adv. Council of BBC, 1987–91. *Publications:* Homer, The Iliad (trans.), 1987; Homer, The Odyssey (trans.), 2000; Marcus Aurelius (trans. and notes), 2006; Thucydides, The Peloponnesian War (trans.), 2009; Arrian, Alexander the Great (trans.), 2013. *Address:* Shepherds' Hey, Hundon Road, Barnardiston, Haverhill, Suffolk CB9 7TJ. *T:* (01440) 786441.

HAMMOND, (Jonathan) Mark; Chief Executive, Equality and Human Rights Commission, since 2011; *b* 8 Aug. 1961; *s* of Rev. Leslie Hammond and Sherry Hammond; *m* 1993, Susan Margaret Postle; one *s*. *Educ:* Kingswood Sch., Bath; Magdalene Coll., Cambridge (BA Hons Hist. 1983). Department of the Environment, 1985–93: Private Sec. to Sir Gordon Manzie, 1987–89; Global Atmosphere Div., 1989–93; First Sec., Washington, 1993–97; Hd of Econ. and Envmt Policy, Surrey CC, 1997–2000; Dir, Envmt and Develt, 2000–04, Chief Exec., 2004–10, W Sussex CC. Vis. Prof. in Public Admin, Canterbury Christchurch Univ., 2011–. Trustee, Council for At-Risk (formerly Assisting Refugee) Academics, 2012–. Mem., Adv. Bd, Office of the Children's Comr, 2014–. *Recreations:* golf, reading, crosswords. *Address:* Equality and Human Rights Commission, Fleetbank House, 2–6 Salisbury Square, EC4Y 8JX. *Club:* Goodwood Golf.

HAMMOND, Julia Jessica; *see* Eccleshare, J. J.

HAMMOND, Karen Ann; a District Judge (Magistrates' Courts), since 2013; *b* London, 9 June 1962; *d* of Brian William Hammond and Dorothy Catherine Hammond (*née* Parker); *m* 2000, Michael Patrick Collins; two *d*. *Educ:* Archbishop Tenison's Grammar Sch., Croydon; Croydon Tech. Coll. (OND 1980); Univ. of Nottingham (LLB Hons 1983); Inns of Court Sch. of Law. Called to the Bar, Middle Temple, 1985; in practice as barrister, 1985–98; Lecturer: Coll. of Law, 1998–2000; Nottingham Law Sch., 2000–05; BPP UC, 2005–13; a Dep. Dist Judge (Magistrates' Courts), 2003–13. *Recreations:* family, friends, ski-ing, film and theatre, beach-hutting. *Address:* Camberwell Green Magistrates' Court, D'Eynsford Road, SE5 7UP. *E:* DistrictJudgeKarenAnn.Hammond@judiciary.gsi.gov.uk.

HAMMOND, Mark; *see* Hammond, Jonathan M.

HAMMOND, Martin; *see* Hammond, John M.

HAMMOND, Mary Elaine, (Mrs P. C. Vel), FRAM; freelance singing teacher; Sondheim Professor of Musical Theatre Vocal Studies, Royal Academy of Music (Head of Musical Theatre, 1992–2012); *b* Bristol, 16 Nov. 1940; *d* of Herbert Leslie Hammond and Winifred Elsie Hammond; *m* 1962, Peter Charles Vel; two *s*. *Educ:* Colston's Girls' Sch., Bristol; Royal Acad. of Music (LRAM 1961). FRAM 1998. Extensive work as a session singer encompassing wide range of music incl. opera, pop/rock, TV, film, radio and live concerts, 1962–87; singing consultant on 27 West End shows with companies incl. Cameron Mackintosh Ltd, Really Useful Gp, Bill Kenwright, NT, Donmar, Menière and RSC; coach of singers in TV, radio and pop and rock gps. Member Board: British Voice Assoc., 1993–; Actors Centre, London, 1996–. *Publications:* Thank You, That's All We Need for Today, 2009. *Recreation:* visiting antique fairs and car boot sales. *Address:* 164 Camden Road, NW1 9HJ. *T:* (020) 7267 3418. *E:* vox@maryhammond.co.uk.

HAMMOND, Michael Harry Frank, CBE 1990; DL; Chief Executive and Town Clerk, Nottingham City Council, 1974–90; *b* 5 June 1933; *s* of late Edward Cecil Hammond and Kate Hammond; *m* 1965, Jenny Campbell (*d* 2014); two *s* one *d*. *Educ:* Leatherhead; Law Society Sch. of Law; Nottingham Univ. (LLM Internat. Law 1996). Admitted solicitor, 1958; Asst Solicitor in Town Clerk's office, Nottingham, 1961–63; Prosecuting Solicitor, 1963–66; Asst Town Clerk, 1966–69; Dep. Town Clerk, Newport, Mon, 1969–71; Dep. Town Clerk, Nottingham, 1971–74. Hon. Secretary: Major City Councils Gp, 1977–88; Notts County Br., Assoc. of District Councils, 1974–88; Chairman: Assoc. of Local Authority Chief Execs, 1984–85; E Midlands Br., Soc. of Local Authority Chief Execs, 1988–90; Pres., Notts Law Soc., 1989–90 (Vice-Pres., 1988–89). Mem., Nat. Forest Adv. Bd, 1991–95; Ambassador, Nat. Forest, 2005–. Member: Midlands Regl Cttee, N British Housing Assoc., 1992–97; Develt Steering Gp, St John's Coll., Nottingham, 1995–2000; URC E Midlands Province Listed Bldgs Adv. Cttee, 1995–2000; Notts Valuation Tribunal, 1998–2005 (Chm., 2001–05). Trustee, Hillsborough Disaster Appeal Fund, 1989–96; Chm., E Midlands Chair in Stroke Medicine Appeal, 1991–92. British Red Cross Society: Pres., 1995–2002, Notts Br. (Trustee, 1992–97; Dep. Pres., 1994); Nat. Trustee, 1998–2000; Mem., Midlands Reg. Council, 1998–2002; Trustee, Nottingham Almshouse and Nottingham Annuity Charities, 1994–2008. Governor, Nottingham High Sch., 1990–2003. An Elections Supervisor, Rhodesia/Zimbabwe Independence Elections, 1980. Mem., Magdala Debating Soc., 1990–94. Mem., RAI, 1993. DL Notts, 1990. Rhodesia Medal, 1980; Zimbabwe Independence Medal, 1980. *Recreations:* bowls, gardening, travel. *Address:* 15 Crow Park Drive, Burton Joyce, Nottingham NG14 5AS. *T:* (0115) 931 4180. *Clubs:* Nottingham and Notts United Services (Nottingham); Southwell Burgage Probus (Pres., 2013–14); Queen Anne's Bowling Green (Pres., 1999–2000); Nottingham Rugby (Mem. Cttee, 1994–97); Notts CC.

HAMMOND, Prof. Norman David Curle, FSA; FBA 1998; Archaeology Correspondent, The Times, since 1967; Professor of Archaeology, Boston University, 1988–2010, now Emeritus; Associate in Maya Archaeology, Peabody Museum, Harvard University, since 1988; Senior Fellow, McDonald Institute, Cambridge University, since 2009; *b* 10 July 1944; *er s* of late William Hammond and Kathleen Jessie Hammond (*née* Howes); *m* 1972, Jean, *er d* of late A. H. Wilson and Beryl Wilson; one *s* one *d*. *Educ:* Varndean GS; Peterhouse, Cambridge (Trevelyan Schol.; Leaf Studentship 1964; BA 1966; Dip. Classical Archaeol. 1967; MA 1970; PhD 1972; ScD 1987). FSA 1974 (Mem. Council, 1996–99). Centre of Latin American Studies, Cambridge: Res. Fellow, 1967–71; Leverhulme Res. Fellow, 1972–75; Res. Fellow, Fitzwilliam Coll., Cambridge, 1973–75; Sen. Lectr, Univ. of Bradford, 1975–77; Rutgers University: Vis. Prof., 1977–78; Associate Prof., 1978–84; Prof. of Archaeol., 1984–88; Distinguished Prof. of Archaeol., 1987–88; Chm., Dept of Archaeol., Boston Univ., 2005–07 (Acting Chm., 1989–91, 2002–03). Irvine Chair of Anthropol., Calif. Acad. of Scis, 1984–85; Fellow in Pre-Columbian Studies, Dumbarton Oaks, Washington, 1988; Rockefeller Foundn Scholar, Bellagio, 1997. Visiting Professor: Univ. of California, Berkeley, 1977; Jilin Univ., Changchun, 1981; Univ. of Paris, Sorbonne, 1987; Univ. of Bonn, 1994; de Carle Dist. Prof., Univ. of Otago, NZ, 2013; Visiting Fellow: Worcester Coll., Oxford, 1989; Peterhouse, Cambridge, 1991, 1996–97; McDonald Inst., Cambridge Univ., 1997, 2004; All Souls Coll., Oxford, 2004; Clare Hall, Cambridge, 2004. Lectures: Curl, RAI, 1985; Bushnell, Cambridge Univ., 1997; Willey, Harvard Univ., 2000; Brunswick Distinguished, MMA, 2001; Taft, Univ. of Cincinnati, 2006; Reckitt, British Acad., 2006; Holleyman, Sussex Univ., 2006; Aronui, Royal Soc. of NZ, 2011; de Carle, Univ. of Otago, 2013. Acad. Trustee, Archaeol. Inst. of America, 1990–93. Hon. Mem., Phi Beta Kappa, 1989. Mem. editl bds, archaeol. jls, USA, UK, 1984–; Editor, Afghan Studies, 1976–79; Consulting Editor, Liby of Congress, 1977–89; Archaeol. Consultant, Scientific American, 1979–95; Archaeol. Editor, TLS, 2009–11. Excavations and surveys: Libya and Tunisia, 1964; Afghanistan, 1966; Belize, 1970–2002 (Lubaantun, Nohmul, Cuello, La Milpa); Ecuador, 1972–84. Hon. DSc Bradford, 1999. Press Award, British Archaeol. Awards, 1994, (jtly) 1998; Soc. of Antiquaries Medal, 2001. *Publications:* (ed) South Asian Archaeology, 1973; (ed) Mesoamerican Archaeology, 1974; Lubaantun: a Classic Maya realm, 1975; (ed) Social Process in Maya Prehistory, 1977; (ed with F. R. Allchin) The Archaeology of Afghanistan, 1978; (ed with G. R. Willey) Maya Archaeology and Ethnohistory, 1979; Ancient Maya Civilisation, 1982, 5th edn 1994, numerous foreign edns; (gen. editor) Archaeology Procs, 44th Congress of Americanists, 1982–84; (ed) Nohmul: excavations 1973–83, 1985; (ed) Cuello: an early Maya community in Belize, 1991; The Maya, 2000; contribs to learned and unlearned jls. *Recreations:* heraldry, genealogy, serendipity. *Address:* Wholeway, Harlton, Cambridge CB23 1ET. *T:* (01223) 262376. *Clubs:* Athenæum; Tavern (Boston).

HAMMOND, Prof. Paul Francis, FBA 2002; Professor of Seventeenth-Century English Literature, University of Leeds, since 1996; *b* 1953; *s* of Ronald Francis Hammond and Maureen Margaret Hammond. *Educ:* Peter Symonds' Sch., Winchester; Trinity Coll., Cambridge (BA, MA; PhD 1979; LittD 1996). Fellow, Trinity Coll., Cambridge, 1978–82; University of Leeds: Lectr in English, 1978–89; Sen. Lectr, 1989–95; Reader in Seventeenth-Century Literature, 1995–96. Vis. Fellow Commoner, Trinity Coll., Cambridge, 2007; Leverhulme Trust Res. Fellow, 2007–08. An Associate Ed., New, later Oxford, DNB, 1998–2002. *Publications:* John Oldham and the Renewal of Classical Culture, 1983; (ed) Selected Prose of Alexander Pope, 1987; John Dryden: a literary life, 1991; (ed jtly) The Poems of John Dryden, 5 vols, 1995–2005; Love Between Men in English Literature, 1996; Dryden and the Traces of Classical Rome, 1999; (ed jtly) John Dryden: Tercentenary Essays, 2000; (ed) Restoration Literature: an anthology, 2002; Figuring Sex between Men from Shakespeare to Rochester, 2002; (ed jtly) Shakespeare and Renaissance Europe, 2004; The Making of Restoration Poetry, 2006; The Strangeness of Tragedy, 2009; (ed jtly) John Milton: life, writings, reputation, 2010; (ed) Shakespeare's Sonnets: an original spelling edition, 2012; Milton and the People, 2014; articles on seventeenth century English literature in scholarly jls. *Recreations:* France and Germany. *Address:* School of English, University of Leeds, Leeds LS2 9JT. *T:* (0113) 343 4739.

HAMMOND, Prof. Peter Jackson, PhD; FBA 2009; Professor of Economics, University of Warwick, since 2007 (Marie Curie Professor, 2007–10); *b* Marple, Cheshire, 9 May 1945; *s* of Fred and Elsie Hammond; *m* 1979, Mrudula Patel. *Educ:* Trinity Hall, Cambridge (BA Hons Maths 1967; PhD Econs 1974). Jun. Res. Fellow, Nuffield Coll., Oxford, 1969–71; Lectr in Econs, 1971–76, Prof. of Econs, 1976–79, Univ. of Essex; Professor of Economics: Stanford Univ., Calif, 1979–2007, now Emeritus; European University Inst., 1989–91. John Simon Guggenheim Fellow, USA, 1987–88; Humboldt Res. Award, Germany, 1993–94. *Publications:* (jtly) Mathematics for Economic Analysis, 1995, 4th edn as Essential Mathematics for Economic Analysis, 2012; (ed jtly) Handbook of Utility Theory, vol. 1, 1998, vol. 2, 2004; (jtly) Further Mathematics for Economic Analysis, 2005, 2nd edn 2008. *Recreations:* admiring, sometimes critically, those near the frontiers of human endeavour, reinforcing memories of active participation in sport, especially cricket and chess. *Address:* Department of Economics, University of Warwick, Gibbet Hill Road, Coventry CV4 7AL. *T:* (024) 7652 3052, *Fax:* (024) 7652 3032. *E:* p.j.hammond@warwick.ac.uk.

HAMMOND, Rt Hon. Philip; PC 2010; MP (C) Runnymede and Weybridge, since 1997; Secretary of State for Foreign and Commonwealth Affairs, since 2014; *b* 4 Dec. 1955; *s* of Bernard Lawrence Hammond and Doris Rose Hammond; *m* 1991, Susan Carolyn, *d* of E. Williams-Walker; one *s* two *d*. *Educ:* Shenfield Sch., Brentwood; University Coll., Oxford (Open Scholar, 1st cl. PPE, MA). Various posts, Speywood Labs Ltd, 1977–81; Dir, Speywood Medical Ltd, 1981–83; established and ran medical equipment distribution co., and dir, medical equipment manufg cos, 1983–94; Partner, CMA Consultants, 1993–95; Director: Castlemead Ltd, 1984–; Castlemead Homes Ltd, 1994–; Consort Resources Ltd, 2000–03. Consultant, Govt of Malawi, 1995–97. Contested (C) Newham NE, June 1994. Opposition spokesman on health and social services, 1998–2001, on trade and industry, 2001–02; on local and devolved govt, 2002–05; Shadow Chief Sec. to HM Treasury, 2005 and 2007–10; Shadow Sec. of State for Work and Pensions, 2005–07; Secretary of State: for Transport, 2010–11; for Defence, 2011–14. Mem., Select Cttee on Envmt, Transport and the Regions, 1997–98, on Trade and Industry, 2002. Sec., Cons. Parly Health Cttee, 1997–98. *Recreations:* reading, cinema, walking. *Address:* House of Commons, SW1A 0AA. *T:* (020) 7219 4055.

HAMMOND, Richard Mark; television presenter and journalist, since 1990; *b* 19 Dec. 1969; *s* of Alan and Eileen Hammond; *m* 2002, Amanda Etheridge; two *d*. *Educ:* Solihull Boys' Sch.; Ripon Grammar Sch.; Harrogate Coll. of Art and Technol. Presenter and producer: BBC Radio York, 1989–92; BBC Radio Stations: Leeds, Newcastle, Cleveland, Cumbria and Lancs; presenter: Men and Motors; Livetime; Top Gear, 2002–15; Brainiac: Science Abuse, 2003–06; Should I Worry About?, 2003–05; Richard Hammond's Engineering Connections, 2008–11; Richard Hammond's Invisible Worlds, 2010; Richard Hammond's Journey to the Bottom of the Ocean, 2011; Planet Earth Live, 2012; Richard Hammond's Crash Course, 2012; Richard Hammond's Miracles of Nature, 2012; Richard Hammond's Secret Service, 2013; Richard Hammond Builds a Planet, 2013; Wild Weather, 2014; Richard Hammond's Jungle Quest, 2015; columnist, Daily Mirror, 2005–. *Publications:* What Not to Drive, 2005; Richard Hammond's Car Confidential, 2006; Can You Feel the Force?, 2006; On the Edge: my story, 2007; As You Do…: adventures with Evel, Oliver and the Vice-president of Botswana, 2008; A Short History of Caravans in the UK, 2009; Or Is That Just Me?, 2009; On the Road: growing up in eight journeys - my early years, 2013. *Recreations:* motorcycling, writing, painting, photography, horse-riding, cycling, running.

HAMMOND, Hon. Sir (Robert) Grant, KNZM 2011; President, New Zealand Law Commission, since 2010; *b* Waipawa, NZ; *s* of Geoffrey Robert Hammond, QSM and Adeline Joy Hammond (*née* Worthington); *m* 1989, Nanette Alice Moreau; two *d*. *Educ:* Univ. of Auckland (LLB Hons; MJur 1st Cl. Hons); Univ. of Illinois (LLM). Judge of High Court of NZ, 1992; Judge, Court of Appeal: of NZ, 2004; of Samoa, 2011. Prof. of Law, Auckland Univ., 1992. Vis. Prof., Cornell Univ., 1993; Robert S. Campbell Fellow, Magdalen Coll., Oxford, 2007. LLD Waikato, 2014. *Publications:* Personal Property, 1990; Judicial Recusal, 2009. *Recreations:* golf, fly fishing. *Address:* 8 Flers Street, Karori, Wellington, New Zealand. *T:* (4) 4760215. *E:* lamothe@xtra.co.nz. *Clubs:* Wellington; Paraparaumu Beach Golf.

HAMMOND, Roy John William; Director, City of Birmingham Polytechnic, 1979–85; *b* 3 Oct. 1928; *s* of John James Hammond and Edith May Hammond; *m* 1st, 1949, Audrey Cecilia Dagmar Avello (*d* 1988); three *d*; 2nd, 1990, Dorothy Forder. *Educ:* East Ham Grammar Sch.; University College of the South West, Exeter; Sorbonne, Paris. BA Hons, 1st Cl. French and Latin, London. Royal Air Force Education Branch, 1952–56; Asst Lectr, Blackburn Municipal Technical Coll. and School of Art, 1956–59; Hd of Dept, Herefordshire Technical Coll., 1960–66; Hd, Dept of Professional and Gen. Studies, Leeds Poly., 1966–71; Asst Dir, City of Birmingham Poly., 1971–79. Hon. Fellow, Birmingham City Univ. (formerly City of Birmingham Poly., later Univ. of Central England), 1985. FRSA. *Recreations:* cricket, theatre, music, walking, golf. *Club:* Aston Wood Golf (Pres., 2001–05).

HAMMOND, Simon Tristram; His Honour Judge Simon Hammond; a Circuit Judge, since 1993; *b* 5 Jan. 1944; *s* of Philip J. Hammond and Sylvia D. (*née* Sillem); *m* 1976, Louise (*née* Weir); one *s* two *d*. *Educ:* Eastbourne Coll.; Coll. of Law. Articled to Philip J. Hammond, Leicester; admitted Solicitor, 1967; Solicitor, later Partner, Victor J. Lissack, London, 1968–76; Partner, Philip J. Hammond & Sons, Leicester, 1977–93. An Asst Recorder, 1985–90; a Recorder, 1990–93; Diversity and Community Relns Judge for Leicester, 2002–. Asst Comr to Parly Boundary Commn for England, 1992. Mem., Probation Bd, Leics and Rutland, 2003–14. Member: Law Soc.'s Standing Cttee on Criminal Law, 1982–91; Crown Court Rules Cttee, 1988–93; Enforcement Sub-cttee, Home Office Rev. of Magistrates Court Procedure, 1989–90; Equal Treatment Adv. Cttee, Judicial Studies Bd, 2006–10. Churchwarden, 1990–. *Recreations:* horses, ski-ing, vegetable gardening, bread making. *Address:* c/o Circuit Administrator's Office, Midland Circuit, The Priory Courts, 33 Bull Street, Birmingham B4 6DW.

HAMMOND, Stephen William; MP (C) Wimbledon, since 2005; *b* 4 Feb. 1962; *s* of Bryan Norman Walter and Janice Eve Hammond; *m* 1991, Sally Patricia Brodie; one *d*. *Educ:* King Edward VI Sch., Southampton; Queen Mary Coll., London (BSc Econ Hons). Reed Stenhouse Investment Services, 1983–85; Canada Life, 1985–87; UBS Phillips & Drew, 1987–91; Dir, Kleinwort Benson Securities, 1991–98; Commerzbank, 1998–2003, Dir of Res., 1999–2001. Mem., Merton BC, 2002–06. Contested (C): Warwickshire North, 1997; Wimbledon, 2001. Shadow Minister for Transport, 2005–10; PPS to Sec. of State for Communities and Local Govt, 2010–12; Parly Under-Sec. of State, DfT, 2012–14. Chm., All Party Parly Gp for Wholesale Financial Markets, 2010–12. Chm. Cons. Friends of India, 2010–12. *Address:* House of Commons, SW1A 0AA. *T:* (020) 7219 1029. *E:* hammonds@parliament.uk. *Clubs:* Royal Wimbledon Golf, Wimbledon Hockey, Wimbledon Civic Forum (Pres.), Wimbledon Society.

HAMMOND BOOTH, Jonothan; Managing Director, Catapult Group, since 1994; mentor and coach, since 1994; *b* Chepstow, Gwent, 27 Aug. 1958; *s* of Alan Parry Booth and Mary Lynn Booth; *m* 1985, Beverley Close; one *s* two *d*. *Educ:* Holme Valley Grammar Sch. Trainee surveyor and auctioneer, 1977–79; European disc jockey, 1980–82; commercial radio presenter, 1983–87; BBC presenter and producer, 1987–95; television presenter, BBC and independent, 1987–94. Dir, 2003–11, Vice-Pres., 2011–, Northern Ballet. Dir, Frazier Hist. Mus., Louisville, Ky, 2011–12. Trustee, Royal Armouries, 2004–12. Gov., York St John Univ., 2013–. MInstD 1999. *Publications:* Pond Life: creating the ripple effect in everything you say and do, 2006. *Recreations:* family, theatre, dance, travel, history, writing. *Address:* Catapult Group, The Old Stables, Holmfirth, W Yorks HD9 7TH. *T:* (01484) 680444. *E:* jon@thecatapultgroup.co.uk.

HAMMOND-CHAMBERS, (Robert) Alexander; Chairman, Ivory & Sime, 1985–91; Chairman, Dobbies Garden Centres plc, 1994–2007; *b* 20 Oct. 1942; *s* of late Robert Rupert Hammond-Chambers and of Leonie Elise Noble (*née* Andrews); *m* 1968, Sarah Louisa Madeline (*née* Fanshawe); two *s* one *d*. *Educ:* Wellington College; Magdalene College, Cambridge (Hons Economics). Ivory & Sime: joined 1964; Partner, 1969; Director, 1975, upon incorporation; Dep. Chm., 1982. Chairman: Fidelity Special Values plc, 1994–2010; Hunter Property Fund Management, 2003–13; Hansa Trust, 2004– (Dir, 2002–); Sandstorm Internat. Ltd, 2008–; Director: Internat. Biotechnology Trust plc, 2001–12; Montanaro European Smaller Companies plc, 2004–, and other cos. Chm., Assoc. of Investment Trust Cos, 2003–05 (Dep. Chm., 2002–03); Overseas Governor, Nat. Assoc. of Securities Dealers Inc., 1984–87. Chm., Edinburgh Green Belt Trust, 1991–2001. *Recreations:* tennis, photography, golf, writing. *Address:* The Old White House, 3 Liberton Tower Lane, Edinburgh EH16 6TQ. *T:* (0131) 672 1697. *Clubs:* Caledonian, Pilgrims; New, Hon. Co. of Edinburgh Golfers (Edinburgh).

HAMNETT, Prof. Andrew, DPhil; FRSC; FRSE; Principal and Vice-Chancellor, University of Strathclyde, 2001–09; *b* 12 Nov. 1947; *s* of Albert Edward Hamnett and Dorothy Grace Hamnett (*née* Stewart); *m* 1976, Suzanne Marie Parkin; three *d*. *Educ:* William Hulme's Grammar Sch., Manchester; University Coll., Oxford (Open Schol.; BA Hons Chem. 1970); St John's Coll., Oxford (Sen. Schol.; DPhil 1973). CChem, FRSC 1991; FRSE 2002. Jun. Res. Fellow in Chemistry, Queen's Coll., Oxford, 1972–77; Deptl Res. Asst, then Lectr in Inorganic Chemistry, Oxford Univ., 1977–89; Fellow by Special Election, then Tutorial Fellow, St Catherine's Coll., Oxford, 1980–89; University of Newcastle upon Tyne: Prof. of Physical Chemistry, 1989–2000; Pro-Vice-Chancellor, 1993–2000. Killam Fellow, Univ. of BC, 1974–76. Pres., Scottish Assoc. of Marine Sci., 2010–13. Chm., Newcastle and Dist Soc. of Organists, 2013–. Sec., URC Northern Synod Trust, 2012–. DL Glasgow City, 2004–09. Hon. Fellow, Univ. of Strathclyde 2009. Hon. DSc Technical Univ. Lodz, Poland, 2005; DUniv Strathclyde, 2009; Hon. DCL Newcastle, 2010. *Publications:* (with P. A. Christensen) Techniques and Mechanism in Electrochemistry, 1994; (ed with R. G. Compton) Novel Methods of Studying the Electrode-Electrolyte Interface, 1989; (jtly) Electrochemistry, 1998, 2nd rev. edn 2007 (trans. Chinese); numerous papers and review articles on physical and inorganic chemistry. *Recreations:* music, languages, mathematics. *Address:* c/o University of Strathclyde, 16 Richmond Street, Glasgow G1 1XQ. *Clubs:* Rotary; Northern Counties (Newcastle upon Tyne).

HAMNETT, Katharine, CBE 2011; fashion designer; *b* 16 Aug. 1947; *d* of Gp Capt. James Appleton. *Educ:* Cheltenham Ladies' Coll.; St Martin's Sch. of Art. Set up Tuttabankem (with Anne Buck), 1969–75; freelance designer in London, Paris, Milan, New York and Hong Kong, 1975–79; established Katharine Hamnett Ltd, 1979, and subseq. launched men's and women's collections, Asia, Europe, USA; transf. production to Italy, 1989, moving from manufacturing to licensing base. Vis. Prof., UAL (formerly London Inst.), 1997–. Numerous awards include British Fashion Designer of the Year, 1984. *Publications:* contribs to fashion magazines and newspapers. *Recreations:* gardening, agriculture, photography, archaeology, travel. *E:* info@katharinehamnett.com.

HAMON, Francis Charles, OBE 2000; Deputy Bailiff, Jersey, 1995–2000; Chairman, Channel Television, 2000–05; *b* 30 July 1939; *s* of Clifford Charles Hamon and Lily Kathleen (*née* Le Gentil); *m* 1963, Sonia Muriel Parslow; one *s* one *d*. *Educ:* Victoria Coll., Jersey. First staff announcer, Channel TV, 1962–64; Asst Land Officer, States of Jersey, 1964–66; called to the Bar: Middle Temple, 1966; Jersey, 1968; in private practice in Jersey, 1968–87; Sen.

Partner, Crill, Cubitt-Sowden & Tomes, 1985–87; Comr (Judge), Royal Court, Jersey, 1988–95, 2001–09. Director: Royal Bank of Scotland (Jersey) Ltd, 1982–95 (Dep. Chm., 1986–95); Media Hldgs Ltd, 2000–01; Channel Television (Hldgs) Ltd, 2001–06. Comr, Jersey Financial Services Commn, 2000–03. Chm., Jersey Arts Trust, 1992–95. Founder Member: Good Theatre Co.; Jersey Fencing Club; Jersey Rugby Fives Assoc. Gov., Victoria Coll., 1987–97. *Publications:* The Phoenix Too Frequent: the story of Jersey's Opera House, 2004. *Recreations:* theatre, bird-watching, travel, Rugby fives, reading. *Address:* La Maison du Sud, Rue de la Pièce Mauger, Trinity, Jersey JE3 5HW. *T:* (01534) 863199.

HAMPDEN; *see* Hobart-Hampden.

HAMPDEN, 7th Viscount *cr* 1884, of Glynde, co. Sussex; **Francis Anthony Brand;** *b* London, 17 Sept. 1970; *s* of 6th Viscount Hampden and of Cara Brand (*née* Proby); *S* father, 2008; *m* 2004, Dr Caroline Pryor, *d* of His Honour Robert Charles Pryor, *qv*; one *s* two *d*. *Educ:* Windlesham House Sch.; Millfield Sch.; Edinburgh Univ.; Cranfield Sch. of Mgt. *Address:* The Estate Office, Glynde Place, Glynde, East Sussex BN8 6SX. *T:* (01273) 858224.

HAMPEL, Rev. Canon Michael Hans Joachim; Residentiary Canon and Precentor, St Paul's Cathedral, since 2011; *b* Kendal, 11 Oct. 1967; *s* of Heinz and Barbara Hampel. *Educ:* King Edward VI Sch., Stratford-upon-Avon; University Coll., Durham (BA 1989); St Chad's Coll., Durham (MA 2002); Westcott House, Cambridge (CTM 1993). Ordained deacon, 1993, priest, 1994; Asst Curate, Whitworth with St Paul, Spennymoor, 1993–97; Minor Canon, Precentor and Sacrist, Durham Cathedral, 1997–2002; Sen. Tutor and Dir of Develt, St Chad's Coll., Durham, 2002–04; Res. Canon and Precentor, 2004–11, Sub-Dean, 2009–11, St Edmundsbury Cathedral. Chaplain, 1407 (Newton Aycliffe) Sqdn, ATC, 1995–2004. Vice-Chair of Governors: King Edward VI Upper Sch., Bury St Edmunds, 2004–11; St Paul's Cathedral Sch., 2011–. FRSA 2002. *Publications:* contribs to books and learned jls; lyric writer for sacred anthems and songs. *Recreations:* constitutional history, art history, collecting Vanity Fair prints, reading, music, theatre, cinema, food and wine, family and friends. *Address:* 1 Amen Court, EC4M 7BU. *E:* precentor@stpaulscathedral.org.uk.

HAMPEL, Sir Ronald (Claus), Kt 1995; Chairman: ICI plc, 1995–99; United Business Media (formerly United News & Media), 1999–2002; *b* 31 May 1932; *s* of Karl Victor Hugo Hampel and Rutgard Emil Klothilde Hauck; *m* 1957, Jane Bristed Hewson; three *s* one *d*. *Educ:* Canford Sch., Wimborne; Corpus Christi Coll., Cambridge (MA Mod. Lang. and Law; Hon. Fellow, 1996). Nat. service, 2nd Lt, 3rd RHA, 1951–52. Joined ICI, 1955; Vice-Pres., ICI US, 1973–77; Gen. Manager, Commercial, 1977–80; Chairman: ICI Paints, 1980–83; ICI Agrochemicals, 1983–85; Dir, ICI, 1985–99; Chief Operating Officer, 1991–93, Dep. Chm. and Chief Exec., 1993–95, ICI plc. Non-executive Director: Powell Duffryn, 1984–88; Commercial Union, 1988–95; BAE Systems (formerly British Aerospace), 1989–2002; ALCOA, USA, 1995–2005; Templeton Emerging Markets Investment Trust, 2003–07 (Chm., 2004–07); TI Automotive, 2007–09; Internat. Stadia Gp, 2010– (Chm., 2010–); Geeknet Inc., 2011–; Adv. Dir, Teijin, Japan, 2000–04. Dir, Amer. Chamber of Commerce, 1986–91; Chm., Cttee on Corporate Governance, 1995–98; Member: Listed Cos Adv. Cttee, Stock Exchange, 1996–99; Nomination Cttee, NY Stock Exchange, 1996–98; Adv. Cttee, Karlpreis Aachen, 1997–2001. Mem. Exec. Cttee, British North America Cttee, 1989–95. Mem., European Round Table, 1995–99. Chm. Trustees, Eden Project, 2000–07. CCMI (CBIM 1985). *Recreations:* tennis, golf, ski-ing, music. *Clubs:* MCC, All England Lawn Tennis; Royal & Ancient.

HAMPSHER-MONK, Dame Susan Catherine; *see* Leather, Dame S. C.

HAMPSHIRE, Prof. Michael John, CBE 1987; Research Professor of Electronic Information Technology, University of Salford, 1990–2004; *b* 13 Oct. 1939; *s* of Jack and Hilda May Hampshire; *m* 1962, Mavis (*née* Oakes); one *d*. *Educ:* Heckmondwike Grammar Sch.; Univ. of Birmingham (BSc Physics, PhD Elec. Engrg). University of Salford: Lectr, 1964; Sen. Lectr, 1972; Prof. of Solid State Electronics, 1978–85, of Electronic IT, 1985–90; Chm., Dept of Electronic and Electrical Engrg, 1981–89; Asst Man. Dir, 1989–95, Dir, 1989–98, Salford Univ. Business Services Ltd. Consultant: Ferranti, 1970–74; Volex Gp, 1977–99 (Chm., R&D Cttee, 1987–92); Thorn EMI Flow Measurement, 1980–88. Founder and Chm., Vertec (Electronics), 1982–92 (Dir, 1992–98). Commendation EPIC Award, 1982; Academic Enterprise Award, 1982; Techmart Technology Transfer Trophy, 1984. Hon. FIED 2001 (Hon. MIED 1982). *Publications:* Electron Physics and Devices, 1969; 80 pubns and patents on solid state electronics and electronic systems, vehicle multiplexing, innovation. *Recreation:* music. *Address:* 3 Brookfield, Upper Hopton, Mirfield, West Yorks WF14 8HL.

HAMPSHIRE, Nancy Lynn Delaney, (Lady Hampshire); *see* Cartwright, N. L. D.

HAMPSHIRE, Susan, OBE 1995; actress; *b* 12 May; *d* of George Kenneth Hampshire and June Hampshire; *m* 1st, 1967, Pierre Granier-Deferre (marr. diss. 1974); one *s* (one *d* decd); 2nd, 1981, Sir Eddie Kulukundis, *qv*. *Educ:* Hampshire Sch., Knightsbridge. *Stage:* Expresso Bongo, Saville, tour, 1959; 'that girl' in Follow That Girl, Vaudeville, 1960; Fairy Tales of New York, Comedy, 1961; Marion Dangerfield in Ginger Man, Royal Court, 1963; Past Imperfect, St Martin's and Savoy, 1964; Kate Hardcastle in She Stoops to Conquer, tour, 1966; On Approval, tour, 1966; Mary in The Sleeping Prince, St Martin's, tour, 1968; Nora in A Doll's House, Greenwich, 1972; Katharina in The Taming of the Shrew, Shaw, 1974; Peter in Peter Pan, Coliseum, 1974; Jeannette in Romeo and Jeannette, tour, 1975; Rosalind in As You Like It, Shaw, 1975; title rôle in Miss Julie, Greenwich, 1975; Elizabeth in The Circle, Haymarket, 1976; Ann Whitefield in Man and Superman, Savoy, 1978; Siri Von Essen in Tribades, Hampstead, 1978; Victorine in An Audience Called Edouard, Greenwich, 1978; Irene in The Crucifer of Blood, Haymarket, 1979; Ruth Carson in Night and Day, Phoenix, 1979; Elizabeth in The Revolt, New End, 1980; Stella Drury in House Guest, Savoy, 1981; Elvira in Blithe Spirit, Vaudeville, 1986; Marie Stopes in Married Love, Wyndhams, 1988; Countess in A Little Night Music, Piccadilly, 1989; Mrs Anna in The King and I, Sadler's Wells, 1990; Gertrude Lawrence in Noel and Gertie, Duke of York's, 1991; Felicity, Countess of Marshwood in Relative Values, Savoy, 1993; Suzanna in Suzanna Andler, Battersea, 1995; Alicia in Black Chiffon (tour), 1996; Sheila in Relatively Speaking (tour), 2000; Felicity, Countess of Marshwood in Relative Values (tour), 2002; Miss Shepherd in The Lady in the Van (tour), 2004–05; Fairy Godmother in Cinderella, Wimbledon, 2005, Woking, 2006; The Bargain (tour), 2007; Kitty in The Circle, Chichester, 2008; Mrs Bennet in Pride and Prejudice, Th. Royal, Bath (and tour), 2009; *TV Serials:* Katy in What Katy Did; Andromeda (title rôle), Fleur Forsyte in The Forsyte Saga (Emmy Award for Best Actress, 1970), Becky Sharp in Vanity Fair (Emmy Award for Best Actress, 1973), Sarah Churchill, Duchess of Marlborough, in The First Churchills (Emmy Award for Best Actress, 1971), Glencora Palliser in The Pallisers; Lady Melfont in Dick Turpin; Signora Neroni in The Barchester Chronicles; Martha in Leaving, 2 series; Going to Pot, 3 series; Don't tell Father; Esme Harkness in The Grand, 2 series; Coming Home; Monarch of the Glen, 7 series; Sparkling Cyanide; The Royal; Casualty, 2010, 2013. *Films include:* During One Night, The Three Lives of Thomasina, Night Must Fall, Wonderful Life, Paris in August, The Fighting Prince of Donegal, Monte Carlo or Bust, Rogan, David Copperfield, Living Free, A Time for Loving, Malpertius (E. Poe Prizes du Film Fantastique, Best Actress, 1972), Neither the Sea Nor the Sand, Roses and Green Peppers, Bang. Dir, Conservation Foundn, 1995–; Mem. Exec. Cttee, Population Concern; Pres., Dyslexia Inst.; Vice-Pres., Internat. Tree Foundn. Hon. DLitt: London, 1981; City, 1984; St Andrews, 1986; Exeter, 2001; Hon. DEd Kingston, 1994; Hon. DArts Pine Manor Coll., Boston, USA, 1994. *Publications:* Susan's Story, 1981; The Maternal Instinct, 1984; Lucy Jane at the Ballet, 1989; Lucy Jane on Television, 1989; Trouble Free Gardening, 1989; Every Letter Counts, 1990; Lucy Jane and the Dancing Competition, 1991; Easy Gardening, 1991; Lucy Jane and the Russian Ballet, 1993; Rosie's First Ballet Lesson, 1996. *Recreations:* gardening, music, the study of antique furniture. *Address:* c/o Chatto & Linnit Ltd, Worlds End Studios, 132–134 Lots Road, SW10 0RJ. *T:* (020) 7349 7222.

HAMPSON, Christopher, CBE 1994; Chairman: RMC Group, 1996–2002; British Biotech plc, 1998–2002; *b* 6 Sept. 1931; *s* of Harold Ralph Hampson and Geraldine Mary Hampson; *m* 1954, Joan Margaret Cassils Evans; two *s* three *d*. *Educ:* McGill Univ. (BEng Chem. 1952). Vice-Pres., 1956–78 and Sen. Vice-Pres., 1982–84, Canadian Industries, Canada; Imperial Chemical Industries: Gen. Manager, Planning, 1978–82; Man. Dir and Chief Exec. Officer, ICI Australia, 1984–87; Exec. Dir, ICI, 1987–94; Chm., Yorkshire Electricity Gp, 1994–97. Non-executive Director: SNC-Lavalin Group, 1992–2002; TransAlta Corp., 1993–2003; BG plc, 1997–2000; Lattice Gp plc, 2000–02. Mem. Bd, 1996–99, Dep. Chm., 1999–2000, Environment Agency. *Recreations:* tennis, ski-ing. *Address:* 77 Kensington Court, W8 5DT. *Clubs:* Boodle's, Hurlingham; York (Toronto).

See also H. A. Hampson.

HAMPSON, Christopher; choreographer; Artistic Director, Scottish Ballet, since 2012; *b* 31 March 1973; *s* of Geoffrey and Janice Hampson. *Educ:* Royal Ballet Schs, White Lodge and Upper Sch. Soloist with English Nat. Ballet, 1992–99; rôles include: principal role in Square Dance; Drosselmeyer in Nutcracker; Headmistress in Graduation Ball; Dancing Master in Cinderella; also created soloist role in Symphonic Dances, and Caterpillar in Alice in Wonderland; Ballet Master, London City Ballet and Royal NZ Ballet, 1999–2000; guest teacher/coach: English Nat. Ballet; Royal Swedish Ballet; Royal NZ Ballet; Atlanta Ballet; National Th., Prague; Royal Acad. of Dance; English Nat. Ballet Sch.; Nat. Ballet of Canada; Matthew Bourne's New Adventures; Hong Kong Ballet; Genée Internat. Ballet Competition; Northern Ballet Th. Created ballets: for English National Ballet: Perpetuum Mobile, 1997; Country Garden, 1998; Concerto Grosso, 1999; Double Concerto, 2000; Nutcracker, 2002; Trapeze, 2003; for London City Ballet: Dinaresade, Canciones, 1999; for Royal New Zealand Ballet: Saltarello, 2001; Romeo and Juliet, 2002; Esquisses, 2005; Cinderella, 2007 (filmed for TVNZ, 2008); Silhouette, 2010; for National Theatre, Prague: Giselle, 2004; for Atlanta Ballet, USA: Sinfonietta Giocosa, 2005; Rite of Spring, 2011; for Royal Festival Hall: A Christmas Carol, 2000; for Royal Academy of Dance: La Vision, Caprice, 2003; for Royal Ballet: Dear Norman, 2009; for Ballet Black: Sextet, 2010; Storyville, 2012; for Scottish Ballet: Hansel and Gretel, 2013. Dir, Johann Strauss Gala (annually), 2005–. Co-founder, Internat. Ballet Masterclasses, Prague, 2003. Award for Best Classical Choreog., Critics' Circle, 2002; Award for Outstanding Achievement in Dance, Barclays Th., 2002. *Recreations:* music, theatre, wine, marathon running, knitting. *Address:* Scottish Ballet, Tramway, 25 Albert Drive, Glasgow G41 2PE. *E:* chris.hampson@scottishballet.co.uk.

HAMPSON, Harold Arthur; Managing Director, Head of Financial Sponsor Coverage, Investment Banking, J P Morgan Europe, since 2012; *b* Montreal, 14 April 1965; *s* of Christopher Hampson, *qv*; *m* 1991, Rachel Mary Gibson; two *s* two *d*. *Educ:* St Paul's Sch., London; Trinity Coll., Cambridge (BA 1987; MA Hons; MEng). Joined J P Morgan, 1988; Equity Syndicate Manager, 1991–95; Hd, Equity Capital Mkts, 1995–99; Hd, Media Investment Banking, Europe, 2000–09; Hd of Telecom, Media, Technology, Investment Banking Europe, 2009–12. *Recreations:* ski-ing, running, biking, opera. *Clubs:* Buck's, Walbrook, 5 Hertford Street; Leander (Henley-on-Thames).

HAMPSON, Dr Keith; *b* 14 Aug. 1943; *s* of Bertie Hampson and Mary Elizabeth Noble; *m* 1st, 1975, Frances Pauline (*d* 1975), *d* of late Mathieu Donald Einhorn and of Ellen-Ruth Einhorn; 2nd, 1979, Susan, *d* of Mr and Mrs John Wilkie Cameron. *Educ:* King James I Grammar Sch., Bishop Auckland, Co. Durham; Univ. of Bristol; Harvard Univ. BA, CertEd, PhD. Personal Asst to Edward Heath, 1966 and 1970 Gen. Elections and in his House of Commons office, 1968; Lectr in American History, Edinburgh Univ., 1968–74. MP (C) Ripon, Feb. 1974–1983, Leeds North West, 1983–97; contested (C) Leeds North West, 1997. PPS: to Minister for Local Govt, 1979–83; to Sec. of State for Environment, 1983; to Sec. of State for Defence, 1983–84. Member: Select Cttee on Trade and Industry, 1987–97; Public Accounts Commn, 1992–97; Vice Chairman: Cons. Parly Educn Cttee, 1975–79; Cons. Parly Defence Cttee, 1988–89 (Sec., 1984–88). Mem., Educn Adv. Cttee of UK Commn for UNESCO, 1980–84. Mem., Gen. Adv. Council, IBA, 1980–88. Vice President: WEA, 1978–97; Assoc. of Business Executives, 1979–; Vice-Chm., Youthaid, 1979–83. UK Project Manager, DFID and FCO funds for democracy progs in Russia, 1998–2003; Sec., Internat. Adv. Bd, Moscow Sch. of Pol Studies, 2003–. *Recreations:* DIY, music, gardening. *Club:* Carlton.

HAMPSON, Peter, CBE 2003; QPM 1998; Director General, National Criminal Intelligence Service, 2003–06; *b* 8 Jan. 1947; *s* of Maj. Ronald Hampson, MBE and Edith Hampson; *m* 1971, Pamela Mary Cotes; one *s* two *d*. *Educ:* Sandford Orleigh Sch., Newton Abbot; King's Coll. London (LLB 1982; AKC). Joined Metropolitan Police Service, 1967: Constable, 1967–71; Chief Superintendent, 1991–94; Asst Chief Constable, Surrey Police, 1994–96; Asst Inspector of Constabulary, Home Office, 1996–99; Chief Constable, W Mercia Constabulary, 1999–2003. Trustee: Surrey Community Foundn, 2006–; Police Rehabilitation Trust, 2007–. Gov., Treloar Coll., Alton, 2008–. FRSA 1992. OStJ 1998. *Recreations:* family and friends, reading, theatre, cycling, music, St John Ambulance, National Trust, Surrey Community Foundn, Police Rehabilitation Trust, Treloar School and College.

HAMPSON, Roger; Chief Executive, London Borough of Redbridge, since 2000; *b* Gosforth, Northumberland, 1950; *s* of William Hampson and Betty Hampson; *m* 1st, 1972, Caroline St John-Brooks (*d* 2003); one *s* one *d*; 2nd, 2008, Esther Wallington; two *d*. *Educ:* Univ. of Ulster (BA Hons 1973); Univ. of Bristol (DipSocAdmin 1978). Res. Fellow, Personal Social Services Res. Unit, Univ. of Kent, 1983–86; Chief Social Services Officer, London Bor. of Bexley, 1988–94; Dir, Social Services and Housing, London Bor. of Redbridge, 1994–2000. FRSA. *Publications:* (jtly) Care in the Community: the first steps, 1988; (jtly) Directing Social Services, 1999; articles on local govt services and others. *Address:* London Borough of Redbridge, Town Hall, High Road, Ilford, Essex IG1 1DD. *T:* (020) 8708 2100. *E:* rh@redbridge.gov.uk.

HAMPSON, Stephen Fazackerley; Under Secretary, Scottish Executive (formerly Scottish Office), 1993–2002; *b* 27 Oct. 1945; *s* of Frank Hampson and Helen (*née* Ellis); *m* 1970, Gunilla Brunk; one *s* one *d*. *Educ:* University Coll., Oxford (BPhil; MA). Lectr, Aberdeen Univ., 1969–71; Economist, NEDO, 1971–75; various posts, Scottish Office, 1975–78, and at Scottish Office, then Scottish Executive, 1981–2002 (Head: Envmt Gp, 1993–2000; Enterprise and Industrial Affairs Gp, 2000–02); First Sec., FCO, New Delhi, 1978–81. Member, Board: British Trade Internat., 2000–02; Mercy Corps Scotland, 2008–10. Mem., Council, WWF Scotland, 2002–08. Hon. FCIWEM 1998. *Address:* Glenelg, Park Road, Kilmacolm PA13 4EE. *T:* (01505) 872615.

HAMPSON, Sir Stuart, Kt 1998; DL; Chairman, The Crown Estate, since 2010; *b* 7 Jan. 1947; *s* of Kenneth and Mary Hampson; *m* 1973, Angela McLaren; one *s* one *d*. *Educ:* Royal Masonic Sch., Bushey; St John's Coll., Oxford (BA Mod. Langs, MA; Hon. Fellow, 2001). Board of Trade, 1969–72; FCO UKMIS to UN, Geneva, 1972–74; Dept of Prices and Consumer Protection, 1974–79; Dept of Trade, 1979–82; John Lewis Partnership, 1982–2007: Dir of Research and Expansion, 1986; Dep. Chm., 1989; Chm., 1993–07. Dep. Chm., London First, 1992–97; Chm., Centre for Tomorrow's Company, 1998–99. Chm., RSA, 1999–2001 (Treas., 1997–98; Dep. Chm., 1998–99, 2001–02). President: Royal Agricl

Soc. of England, 2005–06; Employee Ownership Assoc. (formerly Job Ownership Ltd), 2005–11. High Sheriff, Bucks, 2013–14; DL Bucks, 2015. Hon. FCGI 2002. Hon. DBA: Kingston, 1998; Southampton Inst., 2001; Middlesex 2007; Hon. DSc Buckingham, 2010; Hon. LLD Warwick, 2010.

HAMPSON, (Walter) Thomas; singer; *b* Elkhart, Indiana, 28 June 1955; *s* of Walter Hampson and Ruthye Hampson; one *d*. *Educ:* Eastern Washington Univ. (BA Govt); Fort Wright Coll.; Music Acad. of West. Début in Hansel and Gretel, 1974; with Düsseldorf Ensemble, 1981–84; title rôle in Der Prinz von Homburg, Darmstadt, 1982; débuts: Cologne, Munich, Santa Fé, 1982–84; Metropolitan Opera, NY, Vienna Staatsoper, Covent Garden, 1986; La Scala Milan, Deutsche Oper, Berlin, 1989; Carnegie Hall, San Francisco Opera, 1990; rôles include: Marcello in La Bohème; Guglielmo in Così fan tutte; Figaro in Il Barbiere di Siviglia; Count in Le Nozze di Figaro; Ulisse in Il Ritorno d'Ulisse in Patria; Lescaut in Manon; Count in La Traviata; Vicomte de Valmont in Dangerous Liaisons (world première, 1996); Marquis de Posa in Don Carlos; Riccardo in I Puritani; Wolfram in Tannhäuser; Oreste in Iphigénie en Tauride; Amfortas in Parsifal; Mandryka in Arabella; Renato in Un Ballo in Maschera; Athanael in Thais; Lago in Otello; title rôles: Don Giovanni; Der Prinz von Homburg; Billy Budd; Hamlet; Eugene Onegin; William Tell; Werther (seldom-performed baritone version); Doktor Faust; Der Riese vom Steinfeld (world première, 2002); Macbeth; Simon Boccanegra; Wozzeck. Has performed with Wiener Philharmoniker, NY Philharmonic (Artist-in-Residence, 2009–10), LPO and Chicago Symphony orchs. Recital repertoire includes Schumann, Mahler and American Art Song. Has made numerous recordings. Founded Hampsong Foundn, 2003. Hon. RAM 1996; Hon. Mem., Wiener Konzerthaus, 2004; Mem., Amer. Acad. of Arts and Scis, 2010. Hon. Dr: San Francisco Conservatory of Music; Whitworth Coll., USA. Awards include: Gold Medal, Internat. Mahler Soc.; Lotte Lehman Medal, Music Acad. of West, 1979; Edison Prize, Netherlands, 1990 and 1992; Grand Prix du Disque, 1990, 1996, Echo Klassik, 1995, Deutsche Schallplattenpreis; Cannes Classical Award, 1994; Citation of Merit, Nat. Arts Club, 1997; Vienna Kammersänger, 1999; Austrian Medal of Honour in Arts and Scis, 2004; Edison Life Achievement Award, 2005. Commandeur de l'Ordre des Arts et des Lettres (France), 2010. *Publications:* (ed jtly) Mahler Songs: critical edition, 1993; (ed jtly) Schumann/Heine 20 Lieder und Gesänge: critical edition. *Address:* 1841 Broadway, Suite 1204, New York, NY 10023, USA; c/o Centre Stage Management, Stralauer Allee 1, 10245 Berlin, Germany.

HAMPSTEAD, Archdeacon of; *see* Hawkins, Ven. J. E. I.

HAMPTON, 7th Baron *cr* 1874; **John Humphrey Arnott Pakington;** Bt 1846; owner, Johnnie Pakington Photography, since 2010; *b* 24 Dec. 1964; *s* of 6th Baron Hampton and Jane Elizabeth Farquharson Pakington (*née* Arnott); *S* father, 2003; *m* 1996, Siena, *yr d* of Remo Caldato; one *s* one *d*. *Educ:* Exeter Coll. of Art and Design (BA Hons). Creative Dir, Band & Brown Communications, London, 1995–2010. Mem., ECB Coaches Assoc., 2010– (UK Coaching Cert. Level 2 Cricket Coach). Member: Friends of Worcester Record Office, 2001–; British Italian Soc., 2004–. *Recreations:* gardening, sport, photography. *Heir: s* Hon. Charles Richard Caldato Pakington, *b* 2 May 2005. *Clubs:* King's Head Members; Stoke Newington Cricket, Saracens Amateur Rugby Football.

HAMPTON, Alison Wendy; Her Honour Judge Hampton; a Circuit Judge, since 2002; Designated Civil Judge, Leicester and Northampton; *b* 14 March 1955; *d* of Wing Comdr Gordon Hampton, OBE, DFC and Eve Hampton; *m* 1977, Nigel Haynes. *Educ:* Abbeydale Girls' Grammar Sch., Sheffield; Leicester Univ. (LLB Hons). Called to the Bar, Gray's Inn, 1977; Circuit Jun., Midland and Oxford Circuit, 1987–88. Mem., WI, 1995–. *Recreations:* fine arts, fine food, cycling, walking, scuba diving, ski-ing, cats. *Address:* Leicester County Court, Wellington Street, Leicester LE1 6HG.

HAMPTON, Christopher James, CBE 1999; FRSL; playwright; *b* 26 Jan. 1946; *s* of Bernard Patrick Hampton and Dorothy Patience Hampton (*née* Herrington); *m* 1971, Laura Margaret de Holesch; two *d*. *Educ:* Lancing Coll.; New Coll., Oxford (MA; Hon. Fellow, 1997). First play: When Did You Last See My Mother?, 1964 (perf. Royal Court Theatre, 1966; transf. Comedy Theatre; prod. at Sheridan Square Playhouse, New York, 1967, Trafalgar Studios, 2011). Resident Dramatist, Royal Court Theatre, Aug. 1968–70. FRSL 1976 (Mem. Council, 1984–90). Officier, l'Ordre des Arts et des Lettres (France), 1997. *Plays:* Total Eclipse, prod. Royal Court, 1968; The Philanthropist, Royal Court and Mayfair, 1970 (Evening Standard Best Comedy Award, 1970; Plays & Players London Theatre Critics Best Play, 1970), NY, 1971, Chichester, 1985, Donmar, 2005, NY, 2009; Savages, Royal Court, 1973, Comedy, 1973, LA, 1974 (Plays & Players London Theatre Critics Best Play, Jt Winner, 1973; Los Angeles Drama Critics Circle Award for Distinguished Playwriting, 1974); Treats, Royal Court, 1976, Mayfair, 1976, Garrick, 2007; Able's Will, BBC TV, 1977; After Mercer, NT, 1980; The History Man (from Malcolm Bradbury) BBC TV, 1981; Total Eclipse (rev. version) Lyric, Hammersmith, 1981; The Portage to San Cristobal of A. H. (from George Steiner), Mermaid, 1982; Tales from Hollywood, LA, 1982, NT 1983 (Standard Best Comedy Award, 1983), Donmar, 2001; Les Liaisons Dangereuses (from Laclos), RSC, 1985, transf. Ambassadors Th., 1986, NY, 1987, 2008 (Plays & Players London Theatre Critics Best Play, Jt Winner, 1985; Time Out Best Production Award, 1986; London Standard Best Play Award, 1986; Laurence Olivier Best Play Award, 1986; NY Drama Critics' Circle Best For. Play Award, 1987); Hotel du Lac (from Anita Brookner), BBC TV, 1986 (BAFTA Best TV Film Award, 1987); The Ginger Tree (from Oswald Wynd), BBC TV, 1989; White Chameleon, NT, 1991; Alice's Adventures Under Ground, NT, 1994; The Talking Cure, NT, 2002, Theater in der Josefstadt, Vienna, 2014; Embers (from Sándor Márai), Duke of York's, 2006; Youth Without God (from Horváth), Theater in der Josefstadt, Vienna, 2009; Appomattox, Guthrie Th., Minneapolis, 2012; The Thirteenth Tale (from Diane Setterfield), BBC TV, 2013; *musicals:* Sunset Boulevard (book and lyrics with Don Black), Apollo, 1992, LA, 1993, NY, 1994 (Tony Award: Best Original Score, 1995; Best Book of a Musical, 1995), Comedy, 2008; Dracula (book and lyrics with Don Black), La Jolla, 2001, NY, 2004; Stephen Ward (book and lyrics with Don Black), Aldwych, 2013; *opera:* Waiting for the Barbarians (libretto, based on novel by J. M. Coetzee; music by Philip Glass), Erfurt, 2005, Austin, Texas, 2007; Appomattox (libretto; music by Philip Glass), San Francisco, 2007, (rev. version) Nat. Opera, Washington, 2015; The Trial (libretto based on novel by Kafka; music by Philip Glass), ROH, 2014; *translations:* Marya, by Isaac Babel, Royal Court, 1967; Uncle Vanya, by Chekhov, Royal Court, 1970, Vaudeville, 2012; Hedda Gabler, by Ibsen, Fest. Theatre, Stratford, Ont, 1970, Almeida, Islington, 1984, rev. version, NT, 1989; A Doll's House, by Ibsen, NY, 1971, Criterion, 1973, NY, 1975, W Yorks Playhouse, 2005; Don Juan, by Molière, Bristol Old Vic, 1972; Tales from the Vienna Woods, by Horváth, NT, 1977; Don Juan Comes Back from the War, by Horváth, NT, 1978; Ghosts, by Ibsen, Actors' Co., 1978; The Wild Duck, by Ibsen, NT, 1979; The Prague Trial, by Chéreau and Mnouchkine, Paris Studio, 1980; Tartuffe, by Molière, RSC, 1983; Faith, Hope and Charity, by Horváth, Lyric, Hammersmith, 1989, Southwark Playhouse, 2011; Art, by Yasmina Reza, Wyndhams, 1996 (Standard Best Comedy Award and Laurence Olivier Best Comedy Award, 1997), NY (Tony Award, Best Play), 1998; An Enemy of the People, by Ibsen, RNT, 1997, Crucible, Sheffield, 2010; The Unexpected Man, by Yasmina Reza, RSC, 1998, NY, 2000; Conversations After a Burial, by Yasmina Reza, Almeida, 2000; Life x 3, by Yasmina Reza, RNT, transf. Old Vic, 2000, NY 2003; Three Sisters, by Chekhov, Playhouse, 2003, Lyric Hammersmith, 2010; The Seagull, by Chekhov, Royal Court, 2007, NY, 2008; God of Carnage, by Yasmina Reza, Gielgud, 2008 (Laurence Olivier Best Comedy Award), NY (Tony Award, Best Play), 2009; Judgment Day, by Horváth, Almeida, 2009; The Father, by Florian Zeller, Ustinov Studio, Th. Royal, Bath, 2014, transf. Tricycle Th., 2015; The Mother, by Florian Zeller, Th. Royal Bath, 2015; *screenplays:* A Doll's House, 1973; Tales From the Vienna Woods, 1979; The Honorary Consul, 1983; The Good Father, 1986 (Prix Italia 1988); Wolf at the Door, 1986; Dangerous Liaisons, 1988 (Academy Award, and Writers Guild of America Award, for best adapted screenplay; Critics' Circle Award for best screenplay, 1989; BAFTA best screenplay award, 1990); Total Eclipse, 1995; Mary Reilly, 1996; The Quiet American, 2002; Atonement, 2007 (Hollywood Screenwriter of the Year, 2007; Richard Attenborough Screenwriter of the Year, 2008; Best Literary Adaptation, Forum Internat. Cinéma et Littérature, Monaco, 2008); Chéri, 2009; A Dangerous Method, 2012; Perfect Mothers (aka Adore), 2013; (*also directed*): Carrington, 1995 (Special Jury Prize, Cannes Fest., 1995); The Secret Agent, 1996; Imagining Argentina, 2003. *Publications:* When Did You Last See My Mother?, 1967; Total Eclipse, 1969, rev. version, 1981; The Philanthropist, 1970, 3rd edn 2005, The Philanthropist and other plays, 1991; Savages, 1974; Treats, 1976, rev. version, 2007; Able's Will, 1979; Tales from Hollywood, 1983, 2nd edn 2001; The Portage to San Cristobal of A. H. (George Steiner), 1983; Les Liaisons Dangereuses, 1985; Dangerous Liaisons: the film, 1989; The Ginger Tree, 1989; White Chameleon, 1991; (with Don Black) Sunset Boulevard, 1993; Alice's Adventures Under Ground, 1995; Carrington, 1995; Total Eclipse: the film, 1996; Plays One, 1997; The Secret Agent and Nostromo (Conrad), 1997; Collected Screenplays, 2002; The Talking Cure, 2002; Hampton on Hampton, ed Alastair Owen, 2005; Embers, 2006; Atonement: the shooting script, 2007; Appomattox, 2012; *translations:* Isaac Babel, Marya, 1969; Chekhov, Uncle Vanya, 1971, 2nd edn 2012; Ibsen, Hedda Gabler, 1972, rev. version 1989; Ibsen, A Doll's House, 1972, 2nd edn 1989; Molière, Don Juan, 1972; Horváth, Tales from the Vienna Woods, 1977, 2nd edn 2000; Horváth, Don Juan Comes Back from the War, 1978; Ibsen, The Wild Duck, 1980; Ibsen, Ghosts, 1983; Molière, Tartuffe, 1984, 2nd edn 1991; Horváth, Faith, Hope and Charity, 1989; Yasmina Reza, Art (Scott Moncrieff Trans. Prize, Translators' Assoc.), 1997; Ibsen, An Enemy of the People, 1997; Yasmina Reza, The Unexpected Man, 1998; Yasmina Reza, Conversations After a Burial, 2000; Yasmina Reza, Life x 3, 2000; Chekhov, Three Sisters, 2004; Yasmina Reza, Plays One, 2005; Chekhov, The Seagull, 2007; Yasmina Reza, God of Carnage, 2008; Horváth, Judgment Day, 2009. *Recreations:* travel, cinema. *Address:* 2 Kensington Park Gardens, W11 3HB. *Club:* Dramatists'.

HAMPTON, Sir Geoffrey; *see* Hampton, Sir L. G.

HAMPTON, John; a Recorder of the Crown Court, 1983–98; *b* 13 Nov. 1926; *e s* of late Thomas Victor Hampton and Alice Maud (*née* Sturgeon), Oulton Broad; *m* 1954, Laura Jessie, *d* of Ronald Mylne Ford and Margaret Jessie Ford (*née* Coghill), Newcastle-under-Lyme; three *d*. *Educ:* Bradford Grammar School; University College London (LLB). Served Royal Navy, 1945–47. Called to the Bar, Inner Temple, 1952; NE Circuit; Solicitor General and Attorney General; Dep. Circuit Judge, 1975–82. Dep. Chm., Agricultural Land Tribunal, Yorks and Lancs Area, 1980–82, Yorks and Humberside Area, 1982–99; Dep. Traffic Comr, NE Traffic Area, 1988–94. *Recreations:* mountaineering, sailing. *E:* jlhampton@bigpond.com.

HAMPTON, Prof. Kay; Member, Scottish Human Rights Commission, since 2007; consultant, KK Consulting, since 2011; Lead Commissioner, 2002–07, and Chairman, 2006–07, Commission for Racial Equality (Deputy Chairman, 2003–06); *b* 25 Dec. 1957; *m* Russell Hampton; two *d*. *Educ:* Univ. of Durban-Westville, SA (BA Hons 1985; MA (Sociol.) *cum laude* 1987). Res. Asst, 1978–79, Researcher, 1980–89, Inst. for Social and Econ. Res., Univ. of Durban-Westville, SA; Researcher, Strategic Planning Dept, City of Durban Municipality, 1990–93; Glasgow Caledonian University: Res. Fellow, 1994–96, Res. Dir, 1996–2000, Scottish Ethnic Minorities Res. Unit; Lectr in Sociol., 2000–06, Prof. of Communities and Race Relns, 2006–11, Sch. of Law and Social Scis. Observer, Exec. Cttee, West of Scotland Community Relns Council, 1994–98; Mem. Adv. Cttee, Scottish Poverty Information Unit, 1996–99; Member Committee: SCVO Race Equality Adv. Gp, 1996–2002; Apna Ghar (Scotland's first black-led housing assoc.), 1997–99; Board Member: Nat. Lottery Charities Bd, subseq. Community Fund, 1998–2004 (Chm. Scotland Cttee, 1998–2004); Meridian, Black and Ethnic Minority Women's Information and Resource Centre, 2000–01; Res. Advr, Black and Ethnic Minority Infrastructure in Scotland (BEMIS), 1998–99; Member: Regulatory Cttee, Law Soc. of Scotland, 2011–; Adjudicating Panel, Gen. Teaching Council for Scotland, 2012–; Scottish Solicitors Disciplinary Tribunal, 2013–; Public Appts Assessor, Commn for Ethical Standards in Public Life in Scotland, 2012–; non-executive Director: Positive Action in Housing, 1999–2002; Scottish Refugee Council, 2003; Chm., Saheliya, Women's Mental Health Project, 1999–2000. Trustee, Scottish Assoc. for Mental Health, 2010–14. Mem. Editl Bd, Scottish Youth Issues Jl, 2000–04. ILTM. Mem. AUT. Bronze Medal for Scientific Achievement, SA Assoc. for Advancement in Scis, 1988. *Publications:* (contrib. chapter) Ageing in South Africa, 1989; articles in Scottish Youth Issues Jl, Internat. Jl of Health Promotion and Educn, SA Jl of Sociol., Jl of Scottish Anti-racist Fedn in Community Develt and Social Work, Scottish Ethnic Minorities Res. Unit occasional papers series. *Recreation:* attempting to make a difference by promoting fairness and justice!

HAMPTON, Sir (Leslie) Geoffrey, Kt 1998; Director, Midlands Leadership Centre, since 1999, and KPMG Professor of Education Leadership, since 2005, University of Wolverhampton (Dean of Education, 2000–06; Pro Vice Chancellor, 2006–09; Deputy Vice-Chancellor, 2009–13); Chief Executive, Education Central, since 2013; *b* 2 Aug. 1952; *s* of Leslie and Irene Hampton; *m* 1975, Christine Joyce Bickley; two *s*. *Educ:* King Alfred's Coll., Winchester (Cert Ed); Southampton Univ. (BEd); Birmingham Univ. (MEd). Teacher of Technology, Pensnett Sch., Dudley, W Midlands, 1973–86 (Dep. Head, 1985–86); Dep. Head, Buckpool Sch., Dudley, 1986–93; Headteacher, Northicote Sch., Wolverhampton, 1993–99. Co-Dir, Nat. ICT Res. Centre, 2001–03. Chief Advr to Minister for Sch. Standards, Black Country Challenge Prog., 2007–10. Member: Nat. Adv. Gp, Basic Skills Agency, 2002–07; Bd, Black Country Partnership for Learning, 2006–; Adv. Bd, Nat. Educn Business Partnerships, 2007–08; Nat. Challenge Expert Advisers Gp, DCSF, then DFE, 2008–. Associate Dir, Specialist Schs and Academies Trust, 2005–; Leader, Educn and Skills, Black Country Consortium, 2006–. Chairman: Walsall Educn Bd, 2003–08; Wolverhampton Local Educn Partnership, 2010–. Hon. DEd King Alfred's Coll., Winchester, 2003. *Publications:* (contrib.) Developing Quality Systems in Education, ed G. Doherty, 1994; (jtly) Transforming Northicote, 2000; (jtly) A Guide to Teacher Professional Development, 2004. *Recreations:* DIY, cycling, gardening. *Address:* University of Wolverhampton, Executive Suite, Wulfruna Street, Wolverhampton WV1 1LY.

HAMPTON, Sir Philip (Roy), Kt 2007; Chairman, GlaxoSmithKline plc, since 2015; *b* 5 Oct. 1953; *m* 1983, Amanda Lowe; two *s*. *Educ:* Lincoln Coll., Oxford (MA English 1975; Hon. Fellow 2010); INSEAD, Fontainebleau (MBA 1980). ACA 1978. Lazard Brothers, 1981–89: corporate finance rôles, 1981–86; Exec. Dir, 1987–89; Group Finance Director: British Steel, 1990–96; British Gas, then BG, 1996–2000; BT Gp, 2000–02; Gp Finance Dir, Lloyds TSB Gp plc, 2002–04; Chairman: J. Sainsbury plc, 2004–09; Royal Bank of Scotland Gp, 2009–15. Chm., UK Financial Investments Ltd, 2008–09. Non-executive Director: Belgacom, 2004–10; Anglo American plc, 2009–. *Recreations:* history, sailing, ski-ing. *Address:* GlaxoSmithKline plc, 980 Great West Road, Brentford, Middx TW8 9GS. *Club:* Royal Thames Yacht.

HAMWEE, Baroness *cr* 1991 (Life Peer), of Richmond upon Thames; **Sally Rachel Hamwee;** Member (Lib Dem), London Assembly, Greater London Authority, 2000–08 (Chairman, 2001–02, 2003–04, 2005–06 and 2007–08; Deputy Chairman, 2000–01, 2002–03, 2004–05 and 2006–07); Consultant, Clintons, solicitors (Partner, 1984–2000); *b* 12 Jan. 1947; *d* of late Alec Hamwee and Dorothy (*née* Saunders). *Educ:* Manchester High Sch. for Girls; Girton Coll., Cambridge (MA). Admitted as solicitor, 1972. Councillor, London

Borough of Richmond upon Thames, 1978–98 (Chm., Planning Cttee, 1983–94; Vice Chm., Policy and Resources Cttee, 1987–91); Chair, London Planning Adv. Cttee, 1986–94. Vice Chm., Assoc. of Liberal Democrat Councillors, 1988–99; Member: Nat. Exec., Liberal Party, 1987–88; Federal Exec., Liberal Democrats, 1989–91; Lib Dem spokesman on local govt, 1991–98, on planning and housing, 1993–98, on transport and the regions, 1997–2001, and on ODPM, subseq. DCLG, 2001–09, on Home Affairs, 2009–10, H of L; Co-Chair, Lib Dem Policy Cttee on Home Affairs, Justice and Equality, 2010–; Member: Select Cttee on Econ. Affairs, 2008–10, on Adoption Legislation, 2012–13, on Inquiries Act 2005, 2013–14, H of L; Leader's Group on H of L Code of Conduct, 2009, on working practices of H of L, 2010–11; Secondary Legislation Scrutiny (formerly Merits of Statutory Instruments) Cttee, 2010–. Member: Adv. Council, London First, 1996–98 (Dir, 1993–96); Council, Parents for Children, 1977–86; Council of Mgt, Refuge (formerly Chiswick Family Rescue), 1991–2005; Adv. Bd, Centre for Public Scrutiny. Chm., Xfm Ltd, 1996–98. Member, Board: Arts Council London, 2006–08; Rose Th., Kingston, 2009– (Trustee, Kingston Th. Trust, 2009–). Vice-President: TCPA, 2002– (Pres., 1995–2002); Chartered Inst. of Envmtl Health; Jt Pres., London Councils, 2005–. *Address:* 101A Mortlake High Street, SW14 8HQ.

HANAN, Dame Elizabeth (Ann), DNZM 1998; CRSNZ 2006; Deputy Mayor, Dunedin City, 1998–2004 (City Councillor, 1986–2004); *b* 21 Aug. 1937; *d* of Sir John Patrick Walsh, KBE; *m* 1966, John Murray Hanan; one *s* two *d*. *Educ:* Columba Coll.; Otago Girls' High Sch.; Otago and Canterbury Univs (BSc Univ. of NZ 1961; Dip. Recreation and Sport 1983). Secondary School Teacher, Christchurch, London and Dunedin, 1960–66, 1984–88; Supervisor and Demonstrator, Chemistry, Univ. of Otago, 1975–86; Tutor, Otago Poly., 1982–85. Member: NZ Council, 1986–88, Bd, 1989–98, Consumers' Inst. of NZ; Electrical Workers' Registration Bd, 1993–98 (Presiding Mem., 1993–97). Member: Otago Br., Fedn of Graduate Women (formerly Fedn of University Women), 1961– (Pres., 1990–92); Nat. Exec., Plunket Soc., 1972–74; Bd, Otago Mus. Trust, 1986–2001 (Chair, 1987–99); Otago Theatre Trust, 1986–2001; Friends of Otago Mus. (Patron); Fortune Theatre (Mem., Bd of Mgt, 1995–2006; Pres., 2003–06); Discovery World, 1989–98; Mgt Cttee, Theomin Gall., 2001–07; Arrowtown Village Assoc. Chair, Assoc. of Science and Technology Centres, 1994–96; Pres., NZ Internat. Science Fest., Dunedin, 1996–2004 (Mem. Cttee, 2004–15; Life Mem., 2010). Commemoration Medal, 1990, Suffrage Centennial Medal, 1993, NZ. *Publications:* Playgrounds and Play, 1981 (trans. Japanese 1993); The Clans From Newton Hall: a family history Wallace Morris, 2002; The Hanan Journey, 2009; Pioneers: Walsh family history, 2012; Elsie Hanan *née* Nimmo, 2013; The Legend of Lorenzo Resta, Macetown Miner and the Story of His House at 82 McDonnell Road, Arrowtown, 2014. *Recreations:* walking, reading, computers, genealogy, theatre, travel. *Address:* 159 Highgate, Dunedin 9010, New Zealand. *T:* 027 2211739, *T:* and *Fax:* (3) 4774388. *Club:* University (Dunedin).

HANBURY, Heather Gail; Head Mistress, Lady Eleanor Holles School, Hampton, since 2014; *b* Belfast, 20 Sept. 1960; *d* of Douglas Adams and Jane Adams; *m* 1993, Roland Hanbury. *Educ:* Princess Gardens Sch., Belfast; Univ. of Edinburgh (MA Geog. 1983); Wolfson Coll., Cambridge (MSc Land Economy 1986); Inst. of Educn, Univ. of London (PGCE 1996). Mkt Analyst, Planning, Research and Systems plc, 1986–88; Sen. Consultant, Touche Ross Mgt Consultants, 1988–93; Hd, Corporate Fundraising, VSO, 1993–95; Teacher of Geog., Hd of Upper Sch., then Hd of Sixth Form, Blackheath High Sch., 1996–2001; Hd of Sixth Form, Haberdashers' Aske's Sch. for Girls, 2001–03; Dep. Hd, Latymer Upper Sch., 2003–08; Headmistress, Wimbledon High Sch., 2008–14. *Recreations:* bridge, cooking and entertaining, theatre, travel. *Address:* Lady Eleanor Holles School, Hanworth Road, Hampton, Middx TW12 3HF. *T:* (020) 8979 1601.

HANBURY-TENISON, (Airling) Robin, OBE 1981; DL; MA, FLS, FRGS; farmer; President, Survival International (Chairman, since 1969); *b* 7 May 1936; *s* of late Major Gerald Evan Farquhar Tenison, Lough Bawn, Co. Monaghan, Ireland, and Ruth, *o* surv. *c* of late John Capel Hanbury, JP, DL, Pontypool Park, Monmouthshire; *m* 1st, 1959, Marika Hopkinson (*d* 1982); one *s* one *d*; 2nd, 1983, Mrs Louella Edwards (High Sheriff of Cornwall, 2006–07), *d* of Lt Col G. T. G. Williams, DL, and late Mrs Williams, Menkee, St Mabyn, Cornwall; one *s*. *Educ:* Eton; Magdalen Coll., Oxford (MA). Made first land crossing of South America at its widest point, 1958 (Mrs Patrick Ness Award, RGS, 1961); explored Tassili N'Ajjer, Tibesti and Aïr mountains in Southern Sahara, 1962–66; crossed S America in a small boat from the Orinoco to Buenos Aires, 1964–65; Geographical Magazine Amazonas Expedn, by Hovercraft, 1968; Trans-African Hovercraft Expedn (Dep. Leader), 1969; visited 33 Indian tribes as guest of Brazilian Govt, 1971; Winston Churchill Memorial Fellow, 1971; British Trans Americas Expedn, 1972; explored Outer Islands of Indonesia, 1973; Eastern Sulawesi, 1974; Sabah, Brunei, Sarawak, 1976; RGS Mulu (Sarawak) Expedn (Leader), 1977–78; expedns to Ecuador, Brazil and Venezuela, 1980–81; rode across France, 1984; rode along Great Wall of China, 1986; rode through New Zealand, 1988; led mission for IUCN, Friends of the Earth and Survival Internat. to Malaysia to investigate imprisonment of envmtl protesters, 1988; rode as pilgrim to Santiago de Compostela, 1989; rode across Spain driving 300 cattle on Trans Humance, 1991; visited tribal peoples of E Siberia for Survival Internat., 1992 and 1994; rode route of proposed Pennine Bridleway, 1994; visited: tribal people of Arunachal Pradesh, NE India, 1995; Innu of Labrador, 1997; Tuareg of Ténéré desert, S Sahara, 1999, 2002, 2003; Bushmen of the Kalahari, 2005; Kimberley, Australia rock art, 2006; rode through Albania, 2007; climbed Mt Roraima, Venezuela, 2008; Maya forest res., 2009; Gran Chaco, Paraguay, 2012; return to Mulu for circuit of Mt Api, 2014. Mulu (film for C4), 1999. Chief Executive: BFSS, 1995–97; Countryside Alliance (BFSS, Countryside Business Gp and Countryside Movt), 1997–98 (Patron, 2003); organised Countryside Rally, 1997, Countryside March, 1998. Comr of Income Tax, 1965–95; Mem., SW Regl Panel, MAFF, 1993–96; Mem. of Lloyd's, 1976–95. Mem., Invest in Britain (formerly Think British) Campaign, 1987–; Trustee, Ecological Foundn, 1988–2004; President: Cornwall Wildlife Trust, 1988–95; Rain Forest Club, 2001–05; Patron: Cornwall Heritage Trust, 1994–; Countryside Alliance, 2003–. DL Cornwall, 2003. Hon. Consul of Cornwall in Kosovo, 2014. Mem. Council, RGS, 1968–70, 1971–76, 1979–82 (Vice-Pres., 1982–86); Patron's Medal, RGS, 1979; Krug Award of Excellence, 1980; Farmers Club Cup, 1998; Personality of the Year, Internat. Council for Game and Wildlife Conservation, 1998; Contribution to Countryside Award, CLA, 2000; Medal of Italian Chamber of Deputies, Pio Manzù Centre, 2000; Mungo Park Medal, RSGS, 2001. Dr *hc* Mons-Hainaut, 1992; Hon. DSc Plymouth, 2012. *Publications:* The Rough and the Smooth, 1969, 2nd edn 2005; Report of a Visit to the Indians of Brazil, 1971; A Question of Survival, 1973, 2nd edn 2005; A Pattern of Peoples, 1975, 2nd edn 2005; Mulu: the rain forest, 1980, 3rd edn 2005; Aborigines of the Amazon Rain Forest: the Yanomami, 1982; Worlds Apart (autobiog.), 1984, 3rd edn 2005; White Horses Over France, 1985, 2nd edn 2005; A Ride along the Great Wall, 1987, 2nd edn 2005; Fragile Eden: a ride through New Zealand, 1989, 2nd edn 2005; Spanish Pilgrimage: a canter to St James, 1990, 2nd edn 2005; (ed) The Oxford Book of Exploration, 1993, 3rd edn 2010; Worlds Within, 2005; (ed) The Seventy Great Journeys in History, 2006; Land of Eagles: riding through Europe's forgotten country, 2009, 2nd edn 2013; The Great Explorers, 2010; Echoes of a Vanished World: a lifetime in pictures, 2012; Beauty Freely Given, 2012; The Modern Explorers, 2013; *for children:* Jake's Escape, 1996, 2nd edn 2013; Jake's Treasure, 1998, 2nd edn 2013; Jake's Safari, 1998, 2nd edn 2013; articles in: The Times, Telegraph, Spectator, Daily Mail, Sunday Express, etc; articles and reviews in Geographical Magazine (numerous), Geographical Jl, Ecologist, Literary Review, TLS, New Scientist, Traveller, Country Life, Field, etc. *Recreations:* travelling, riding across countries. *Address:* Cabilla Manor, Bodmin, Cornwall PL30 4DW. *T:* (01208) 821224. *E:* robin@cabilla.co.uk. *W:* www.cabilla.co.uk, www.robinsbooks.co.uk. *Clubs:* Travellers, Pratt's, Geographical.

See also Sir R. Hanbury-Tenison.

HANBURY-TENISON, Sir Richard, KCVO 1995; JP; Lord-Lieutenant of Gwent, 1979–2000; *b* 3 Jan. 1925; *e s* of late Major G. E. F. Tenison, Lough Bawn, Co. Monaghan, Ireland, and Ruth, *oc* of late J. C. Hanbury, JP, DL, Pontypool Park, Monmouthshire; *m* 1955, Euphan Mary (*d* 2012), *er d* of late Major A. B. Wardlaw-Ramsay, 21st of Whitehill, Midlothian; three *s* two *d*. *Educ:* Eton; Magdalen Coll., Oxford. Served Irish Guards, 1943–47 (Captain, wounded). Entered HM Foreign Service, 1949: 1st Sec., Vienna, 1956–58; 1st Sec. (and sometime Chargé d'Affaires), Phnom Penh, 1961–63, and Bucharest, 1966–68; Counsellor, Bonn, 1968–70; Head of Aviation and Telecommunications Dept, FCO, 1970–71; Counsellor, Brussels, 1971–75; retired from Diplomatic Service, 1975. South Wales Regional Dir, Lloyds Bank, 1980–91 (Chm., 1987–91). Dir, Gwent TEC, 1991–99. Mem. Court and Council, Nat. Museum of Wales, 1980–2002 (Chm., Art Cttee, 1986–90). President: Gwent Assoc. of Vol. Orgns (formerly Monmouthshire Rural Community Council), 1959–2000; Internat. Tree Foundn, Wales; St David's Assoc. Hospice Care, 1998–; Gwent Local Hist. Council, 1979–; Gwent County History Assoc., 1998–; Gwent County Scout Council, 1979–2000. President: TA&VRA for Wales, 1985–90; S Wales Regl Cttee, TA&VRA, 1990–2000. Hon. Col, 3rd (V) Bn, The Royal Regt of Wales, 1982–90. DL 1973, High Sheriff 1977, JP 1979, Gwent. Hon. Fellow, UCW, Newport, 1997. KStJ 1990 (CStJ 1980). Dulverton Flagon, Timber Growers (UK), 1990. Foundn Mem., Order of St Woolos, 2006 (for service to dio. of Monmouth). *Publications:* The Hanburys of Monmouthshire, 1995; The Sheriffs of Monmouthshire and Gwent, 2008. *Recreations:* reading history, forestry. *Address:* Clytha Park, Abergavenny NP7 9BW. *Clubs:* Boodle's; Kildare Street and University (Dublin).

See also A. R. Hanbury-Tenison.

HANBURY-TENISON, Robin; *see* Hanbury-Tenison, A. R.

HANBURY-TRACY, family name of **Baron Sudeley**.

HANCOCK, Prof. Barry William, OBE 2009; MD; FRCP, FRCPE, FRCR; Yorkshire Cancer Research Professor of Clinical Oncology, University of Sheffield, 1988–2009, now Emeritus; *b* 25 Jan. 1946; *s* of George Llewellyn Hancock and Sarah Hancock; *m* 1969, (Christine Diana) Helen Spray; one *s* one *d*. *Educ:* Univ. of Sheffield Med. Sch. (MB ChB 1969; MD 1977); Univ. of London (DCH 1971). FRCP 1985; FRCPE 1995; FRCR 1995. Lectr, 1974–78, Sen. Lectr, 1978–86, Reader, 1986–88, in Medicine, Univ. of Sheffield; Dir of Supraregl Gestational Trophoblastic Tumour Service (N of England and Wales), 1991–2009; Yorks Cancer Res. Dir of Cancer Res., 2000–09. Chm., Renal Clinical Studies Gp, NCRI, 2001–08. Pres., Internat. Soc. for Study of Trophoblastic Diseases, 2007–09 (Gold Medal, 2009). New Year Hons Award, Lord Mayor of Sheffield, 1999; Sheffield Community Hero Award (Health), 2002; Centenary Achievement Medal, Sheffield Univ., 2005; Excellence in Oncology Lifetime Achievement Award, Pfizer/British Oncol. Assoc., 2008; Sheffield Legends Award, Sheffield CC, 2010. *Publications:* (ed) Assessment of Tumour Response, 1982; (ed jtly) Immunological Aspects of Cancer, 1985; (ed jtly) Lymphoreticular Disease, 1985; (jtly) Lecture Notes in Clinical Oncology, 1986; (ed) Cancer Care in the Community, 1996; (ed) Cancer Care in the Hospital, 1996; (ed jtly) Gestational Trophoblastic Disease, 1997, 4th edn 2015; (ed jtly) Malignant Lymphoma, 2000; over 250 articles in med. jls. *Recreations:* railways, ornithology, philately, tennis. *Address:* (home) Treetops, 253 Dobcroft Road, Ecclesall, Sheffield S11 9LG. *T:* (0114) 235 1433; Academic Unit of Clinical Oncology, Weston Park Hospital, Whitham Road, Sheffield S10 2SJ. *E:* b.w.hancock@sheffield.ac.uk.

HANCOCK, Brian John; Director, PRIME Partners, since 2003; Telecommunication and Media Advisor, 2010, and Team Manager, 2012, Firstsource (formerly Conduit); *b* 8 Aug. 1950; *s* of John and Joan Hancock; *m*; one *s* one *d*. *Educ:* Poly. of Wales (BSc Chem. Engrg 1974); Aston Univ. (Post Grad. Dip. Occupnl Safety and Health, 1986); Cardiff Univ. Business Sch. (Post Grad. Cert. in Sustainable Profitable Growth and Leadership, 2007). Registered Safety Practitioner, 1994; MIOSH 1992; AMIChemE. Chemical Project Engr, Monsanto Ltd, 1974–76; Shift Prodn Supervisor, 1976–80, Asst Plant Manager, 1980–85, ReChem International Ltd; Chemical Specialist Inspector of Factories, Health and Safety Inspectorate, 1985–88; Health, Safety and Envmt Supt, BP Chemicals, 1988–92; health, safety and envmt consultant and advr, and Dir of own consultancy, 1992–2000. National Assembly for Wales: Mem., (Plaid Cymru) Islwyn, 1999–2003; contested (Plaid Cymru): Islwyn, 2003; Newport West, 2007. Governor: primary and secondary schs, 1985–2000; Ysgol Gyfun Gwynllyn, 2004– (Chm., 2011–14). Chair, Alexis Enterprises Ltd, 2003–05; Gen. Manager, Phoenix Community Transport, 2003–06; Employment Liaison Officer, Dash Trng Ltd, 2007–08; Family Job Liaison Officer, A4e, 2008–09; Volunteer, Workers' Educn Assoc., 2009–10. Mem., Risca West Community Council, 2012–. Chair, Plaid Cymru Cangen De Islwyn South Br., 2005–08. Chm., Pontywaun Boat Club. Mem., CAMRA. *Recreations:* athletics (Newport Harriers AC), Rugby, DIY. *T:* (01633) 601934. *Clubs:* Newport Harriers Athletic; Risca Rugby Football.

HANCOCK, Christine; Founder and Director, C3 Collaborating for Health, since 2009. *Educ:* London School of Economics (BScEcons). RGN. Formerly: Chief Nursing Officer, Bloomsbury Health Authority; General Manager, Waltham Forest Health Authority; Gen. Sec., RCN, 1989–2001; Pres., Internat. Council of Nurses, 2001–05; Eur. Dir, Oxford Health Alliance, 2006–09. Gov., De Montfort Univ., 2006–. *Address:* C3 Collaborating for Health, 1st Floor, 28 Margaret Street, W1W 8RZ.

HANCOCK, Very Rev. Christopher David, PhD; Director, Oxford House Consultancy (formerly Institute for Religion and Society in Asia, then Oxford House Research Ltd), since 2010; *b* 18 Feb. 1954; *s* of late Rev. Dr Ronald and of Vera Hancock; *m* 1975, Suzie Nichols; one *s* one *d*. *Educ:* Highgate Sch.; Queen's Coll., Oxford (BA 1975, MA 1980); Cranmer Hall, Durham (BA 1978); St John's Coll., Durham (PhD 1984). Ordained deacon 1982, priest 1983; Curate, Holy Trinity with St John, Leicester, 1982–85; Chaplain, Magdalene Coll., Cambridge, 1985–88; Lectr, Divinity Faculty, Univ. of Cambridge, 1985–88; Asst, 1988–91, Associate Prof., 1991–94, Virginia Theol Seminary, USA; Vicar, Holy Trinity, Cambridge, 1994–2002; Dean of Bradford, 2002–04; Dir, Centre for the Study of Christianity in China, KCL (formerly at Oxford), 2005–09. Chaplain (part-time), St Peter's Coll., Oxford, 2012–14; Vis. Scholar, Wolfson Coll., Oxford, 2012–14. Vis. Prof., S Asia Inst. of Advanced Christian Studies, Bangalore, 1996–. Exec. Dir, AMO Global, 2005–. Hon. Fellow, Wycliffe Hall, Oxford, 2010. *Recreations:* music, sport, woodwork, walking, fishing, bird-watching, films, family. *Address:* 3 College Farm Cottages, Garford, Abingdon, Oxon OX13 5PF; 13 Westmoreland Terrace, SW1V 4AG. *Club:* Oxford and Cambridge.

HANCOCK, Christopher Patrick; QC 2000; a Recorder, since 2004; Deputy High Court Judge, since 2008; *b* 7 June 1960; *s* of Alan Hancock and Dr (Rosemary) Ann Turner; *m* 1985, Diane Galloway; two *s*. *Educ:* Perse Sch. for Boys, Cambridge; Trinity Coll., Cambridge (MA Hons); Harvard Law Sch. (LLM). Called to the Bar, Middle Temple, 1983, Bencher, 2011; in practice at the Bar, 1985–. Gov., Hatfield Heath Community Primary Sch., 2012–. *Recreations:* golf, music, watching football, family, Cub Scout leader and Group Contact. *Address:* 20 Essex Street, WC2R 3AL. *T:* (020) 7583 9294.

HANCOCK, Elisabeth Joy; Head, Old Palace School, Croydon, 2000–04; *b* 2 Dec. 1947; *d* of Reginald Arthur Lord and Evelyn Maud Mary Lord; *m* 1970, Barry Steuart Hancock; one *d*. *Educ:* Queen's Coll., Harley Street; Nottingham Univ. (BA Hons); Univ. of Sussex

(PGCE). GB East Europe Centre, 1969; Nevill Sch., Hove, 1969–72; Brighton and Hove High Sch. (GPDST), 1972–89, Dep. Hd, 1986–89; Head, Bromley High Sch. (GDST), 1989–2000. FRSA 1988. *Publications:* Teaching History, 1970. *Recreations:* theatre, opera, watching cricket. *Address:* c/o Old Palace School, Old Palace Road, Croydon CR0 1AX.

HANCOCK, Group Captain Ethnea Mary, RRC 1990; Director and Matron-in-Chief, Princess Mary's Royal Air Force Nursing Service, and Deputy Director, Defence Nursing Services (Organisation), 1991–94; *b* 5 April 1937; *d* of late Sydney Ludwig Hancock and Catherine Teresa Hancock (*née* O'Dea). *Educ:* Convent of the Cross, Boscombe; University Coll. Hosp., London; RGN 1958; Southlands Hosp., Shoreham; Whittington Hosp., London; RM 1960; BA Hons Open Univ. 2003. Joined PMRAFNS, 1961–65; Columbia Presbyterian Medical Center, NY, 1966–67; rejoined PMRAFNS, 1967; served RAF Hosps and Units, UK, N Africa, Cyprus, Singapore, Germany; appts include Sen. Matron, RAF Hosp., Ely, 1985–87; MoD, 1987–88; Principal Nursing Officer, PMRAFNS, 1988–91. QHNS, 1991–94. *Recreations:* home and garden, music and the arts, travelling, golf. *Address:* Nationwide Building Society, PO Box 8888, Swindon SN3 1TS. *Club:* Royal Air Force.

HANCOCK, Frances Winifred; *see* Done, F. W.

HANCOCK, Prof. Gus, PhD; Professor of Chemistry, University of Oxford, 1996–2012, now Emeritus (Head, Physical and Theoretical Chemistry Laboratory, 2005–10); Fellow, Trinity College, Oxford, since 1976; *b* Chell, 17 Nov. 1944; *s* of Reginald and Mary Hancock; *m* 1971, Rosemary Margaret Norfolk Brown; one *s* one *d*. *Educ:* Bangor Grammar Sch., Co. Down; Trinity Coll., Dublin (Louis Claude Purser Schol. and Foundn Schol.; BA Hons Natural Scis; MA); Peterhouse, Cambridge (PhD Physical Chem. 1971). Res. Asst, Univ. of Calif, San Diego, 1971–73; Wissenschaftlicher Angestellte, Univ. Bielefeld, 1973–76; Lectr in Physical Chem., Oxford Univ., 1976–96. Vis. Prof. of Chem., Stanford Univ., 1989. Corday Morgan Medal and Prize, 1982, Reaction Kinetics Award, 1995, Polanyi Medal, Gas Kinetics Gp, 2002, Chemical Dynamics Award, 2010, RSC; Italgas Prize for Sci. and Technol. for the Envmt, 2000. *Publications:* contrib. jls and books. *Address:* 124 Divinity Road, Oxford OX4 1LW. *T:* (01865) 275439. *E:* gus.hancock@chem.ox.ac.uk.

HANCOCK, Heather Jane, LVO 2013; Deputy Chairman, World Athletics Championships 2017, since 2013; Director, Amerdale Group, since 2014; *b* Colne, Lancs, 27 Aug. 1965; *d* of Colin and Pamela Margaret Wilkinson; *m* 1992, Mark Edward Hancock; two *s*. *Educ:* Colne Park High Sch.; Nelson and Colne Further Educn Coll.; St John's Coll., Cambridge (BA 1st Cl. Land Econ.). Land Agent, Carter Jonas, 1987–88; Economist, Home Office, 1988–90; Private Secretary: to Home Sec., 1990–92; to Perm. Sec., DNH, 1992–93; Hd, Millennium Commn Unit, 1993–94; Chief Exec., 1994–95, Dep. Chief Exec., 1995–96, Millennium Commn; Mgt Consultant, Deloitte and Touche, 1996–98; Chief Exec., Yorks Dales Nat. Park Authy, 1998–2000; Exec. Dir, Yorks Forward, 2000–03; Deloitte LLP: Partner, 2003–14; Mem. Bd, 2006–08; Man. Partner, Talent, Innovation and Brand, 2008–12, Talent and Brand, 2012–13, Client Experience, 2013–14; Global Man. Dir, Communications and Brand, Deloitte Touche Tohmatsu Ltd, 2011–13. Non-exec. Chair, Wavelength Ltd, 2015–. Dep. Chm., Food Standards Agency, 2015–. Chm., Football League Wkg Party on Structure of Football, 1997–98. Trustee: Prince's Trust, 2000–12 (Chair: Yorks and Humber Regl Council, 1999–2007; Audit Cttee, 2007–12); Internat. Business Leaders Forum, 2011–. Chm., Rural Affairs Cttee, BBC, 2003–10. Hon. Sec., 1995–97, Pres., 2003–04, Land Soc. Founder Trustee, Yorks Dales Millennium Trust, 1996–2003; Trustee, Waterways Trust, 1998–2002. Vice-Pres., Upper Wharfedale Agricl Soc., 1999–. Vice-Pres., Johnian Soc., 2012–13; Chair, Develt Cttee, St John's Coll., Cambridge, 2013–. Gov., Giggleswick Sch., 2007– (Chm. of Trustees and Govs, 2013–). *Recreations:* rural affairs, grouse, gardening. *Address:* The Old Vicarage, Arncliffe, N Yorks BD23 5QD.

HANCOCK, Herbert Jeffrey, (Herbie); jazz pianist and composer; *b* Chicago, 12 April 1940; *s* of Wayman Edward Hancock and Winnie Hancock (*née* Griffin); *m* 1968, Gudrun Meixner; one *d*. *Educ:* Grinnell Coll., Iowa; Roosevelt Univ., Chicago; Manhattan Sch. of Music; New Sch. for Social Res. Owner and publisher, Hancock Music Co., 1962–; founder, Hancock and Joe Prodns, 1989–. Pres., Harlem Jazz Music Center Inc.; Institute Chm., Thelonious Monk Inst. of Jazz, 2004–; Creative Chair of Jazz, LA Philharmonic, 2010–; Norton Prof. of Poetry, Harvard Univ., 2014. Performances with: Chicago SO, 1952; Coleman Hawkins, Chicago, 1960; Donald Byrd, 1960–63; Miles Davis Quintet, 1963–68. Composer of music for films: Blow Up, 1966; The Spook Who Sat by the Door, 1973; Death Wish, 1974; A Soldier's Story, 1984; Jo Jo Dancer, Your Life is Calling, 1986; Action Jackson, 1988; Colors, 1988; Harlem Nights, 1989; Livin' Large, 1991; writer of score and actor in film, 'Round Midnight, 1986 (Acad. Award for best original score, 1986). Numerous awards. *Albums include:* Takin' Off, 1963; Succotash, 1964; Speak Like a Child, 1968; Fat Albert Rotunda, 1969; Mwandishi, 1971; Crossings, 1972; Sextant, 1972; Headhunters, 1973; Thrust, 1974; Man-Child, 1975; The Quintet, 1977; V. S. O. P., 1977; Sunlight, 1978; An Evening with Herbie Hancock and Chick Corea in Concert, 1979; Feets Don't Fail Me Now, 1979; Monster, 1980; Lite Me Up, 1982; Future Shock, 1983; Sound System, 1984; (with Foday Musa Suso) Village Life, 1985; (with Dexter Gordon) The Other Side of 'Round Midnight, 1987; Perfect Machine, 1988; Jamming, 1992; Cantaloupe Island, 1994; Tribute to Miles, 1994; Dis Is Da Drum, 1995; The New Standard, 1996; (with Wayne Shorter) 1 + 1, 1997; Gershwin's World, 1998; Return of the Headhunters, 1998; future 2 future, 2001; Possibilities, 2005; River: the Joni letters, 2007 (Grammy Award, 2008); The Imagine Project, 2010. *Publications:* (with Lisa Dickey) Herbie Hancock: possibilities (memoir), 2014. *Address:* Hancock Music Co., Suite 1600, 1880 Century Park East, Los Angeles, CA 90067, USA.

HANCOCK, Janet Catherine, LVO 2005; FRGS; HM Diplomatic Service, retired; Deputy High Commissioner, Malta, 2005–09; *b* 5 Jan. 1949; *d* of Joseph Paul Knox and Alice Cecælia (*née* Ouzman); *m* 1973, Roger Arnold Hancock (marr. diss. 1976); *m* 2007, David Kemp. *Educ:* Convent of Jesus and Mary, Felixstowe and Ipswich; St Anne's Coll., Oxford (MA); Birkbeck Coll., London (MA). Entered FCO, 1971: res. analyst, 1971–94; Beirut, 1985, 1986, 1987; Hd, ME and N Africa Res. Gp, 1994–2000; Actg Dep. Head of Mission, Jerusalem, 1998; Dep. Hd of Mission, Tunis, 2000–04. FRGS 1998. Trustee, SWORDE-Teppa, Tajikistan, 2009–. Mem. Editl Bd, Asian Affairs, 2011–. *Publications:* contrib. articles to Mediterranean Politics, Jl Royal Soc. for Asian Affairs, etc. *Recreations:* plants and birds, dalmatians, cats (Mem. Cttee, Southend and Dist. Br., Cats Protection), trying to compensate for woeful lack of classical education by studying Greek and Roman history.

HANCOCK, Prof. Keith Jackson, AO 1987; Vice-Chancellor, The Flinders University of South Australia, 1980–87; Senior Deputy President, Australian Industrial Relations Commission (formerly Australian Conciliation and Arbitration Commission), 1992–97 (Deputy President, 1987–92); *b* 4 Jan. 1935; *s* of late A. S. Hancock and Mrs R. D. Hancock; three *s* one *d*. *Educ:* Univ. of Melbourne (BA); Univ. of London (PhD). Tutor in Economic History, Univ. of Melbourne, 1956–57; Lectr in Economics, Univ. of Adelaide, 1959–63; Professor of Economics, 1964–87, now Emeritus, and Pro-Vice-Chancellor, 1975–79, Flinders Univ. of SA. Hon. Vis. Fellow, Univ. of Adelaide, 1998–; Professorial Fellow, Nat. Inst. of Labour Studies, 1998–. Chairman: Cttee of Inquiry into S Australian Racing Industry, 1972–74; Nat. Superannuation Cttee of Inquiry, 1973–77; Cttee of Review of Aust. Industrial Relns Law and Systems, 1983–85; Mem., Review Gp on Aust. Financial Instns, 1983. Chm., Energy Industry Ombudsman (SA) Ltd, 2000–09. Pres., Acad. of Social Sciences in Australia, 1981–84. FASSA 1968. Hon. Fellow, LSE, 1982. Hon. DLitt Flinders, 1987; Hon. DCom Melbourne, 2013. *Publications:* The National Income and Social Welfare, 1965; (with P. A. Samuelson and R. H. Wallace) Economics (Australian edn), 1969, 2nd edn 1975; (ed jtly) Applied Economics: readings for Australian students, 1975; Incomes Policy in Australia, 1981; (ed jtly) Japanese and Australian Labour Markets: a comparative study, 1983; (ed) Australian Society, 1989; Australian Wage Policy: infancy and adolescence, 2013; contrib. to various racing industry, superannuation, and financial and industrial law systems reports in Australia; articles in Economic Jl, Economica, Amer. Econ. Rev. and other jls. *Recreations:* bridge, sailing, music. *Address:* 6 Maturin Road, Glenelg, SA 5045, Australia. *T:* (8) 82948667. *Clubs:* Adelaide (Adelaide); Royal South Australian Yacht Squadron (Treas., 2008–).

HANCOCK, Rt Hon. Matthew (John David); PC 2014; MP (C) West Suffolk, since 2010; Minister for the Cabinet Office and Paymaster General, since 2015; *b* Chester, 2 Oct. 1978; *s* of Michael Hancock and Shirley Hills (now Carter); *m* 2006, Martha Hoyer Millar; two *s* one *d*. *Educ:* Farndon Co. Prim. Sch.; King's Sch., Chester; W Cheshire Coll.; Exeter Coll., Oxford (BA 1st Cl. PPE 1999); Christ's Coll., Cambridge (MPhil Econ 2003). Economist, Bank of England, 2000–05; COS to George Osborne, MP, 2005–10. Parly Under-Sec. of State for Skills, 2012–13, Minister of State (Minister for Skills and Enterprise), 2013–14, BIS and DfE; Minister of State (Minister for Business, Enterprise and Energy), BIS and DECC, 2014–15. Member: Public Accounts Cttee, 2010–12; Cttee on Standards and Privileges, 2010–12. *Publications:* (with N. Zahawi) Masters of Nothing, 2011. *Recreations:* cricket, cooking, racing, walking with family. *Address:* House of Commons, SW1A 0AA. *T:* (020) 7219 7186. *E:* matthew.hancock.mp@parliament.uk.

HANCOCK, Michael Thomas, CBE 1992; *b* 9 April 1946; *m* 1967, Jacqueline, *d* of Sidney and Gwen Elliott; one *s* one *d*. *Educ:* well. Member: Portsmouth City Council, 1971–2014 (for Fratton Ward, 1973–2014; Leader, Lib Dem Gp, 1989–97; Chm., Planning and Econ. Develt Cttee, 1991–94; Exec. Mem., Planning, Econ. Develt, Tourism and Property, 2003–14); Hampshire County Council, 1973–97 (Leader of the Opposition, 1977–81, 1989–93; Leader, Lib Dem Gp, 1989–97; Leader of Council, 1993–97). Joined SDP, 1981 (Mem., Nat. Cttee, 1984); contested Portsmouth S (SDP) 1983. MP (SDP) Portsmouth S, June 1984–1987; contested (SDP/Alliance) same seat, 1987. MP Portsmouth S, 1997–2015 (Lib Dem 1997–2014, Ind, 2014–15); contested (Ind) same seat, 2015. Lib Dem parly spokesman on defence, 1997–2001. Member: Public Admin Cttee, 1997–99; Select Cttee on Defence, 1998–2011; Panel of Chairmen, 2000–15; UK Parly Delegn to Council of Europe, 1997–2015 (Mem. Bd, Lib Dems; Chm., Youth and Support Cttee); WEU Parly Assembly (Leader, Liberal Gp); NATO Parly Assembly (Dep. Leader, Liberal Gp). Contested (Lib Dem) Wight and Hampshire South, Eur. Parly elecns, 1994. Dist Officer for Hants, IoW and CI, Mencap, 1989–97. Vice Chairman: Portsmouth Operating Co., 1992–95; Portsmouth Docks, 1992–2002. Dir, Daytime Club, BBC, 1987–90. Bd of Dirs, Drug Rehabilitation Unit, Alpha Drug Clinic, Alpha House, Droxford, 1971–. Trustee, Royal Marine Museum, 1993. Hon. Alderman, Hants, 1997. Hon. award for contrib. to Anglo-German relations, Homborn, W Germany, 1981. *Publications:* contribs to various jls. *Recreations:* people, living life to the full. *Club:* too many to mention.

HANCOCK, Rt Rev. Peter; *see* Bath and Wells, Bishop of.

HANCOCK, Sheila, CBE 2011 (OBE 1974); actor, director and writer; *d* of late Enrico Hancock and Ivy Woodward; *m* 1st, 1955, Alexander Ross (*d* 1971); one *d*; 2nd, 1973, John Thaw, CBE (*d* 2002); one *d*. *Educ:* Dartford County Grammar Sch.; Royal Academy of Dramatic Art. Acted in Repertory, Theatre Workshop, Stratford East, for 8 years. Associate Dir, Cambridge Theatre Co., 1980–82; Artistic Dir, RSC Regional Tour, 1983–84; acted and directed, NT, 1985–86. Dir, The Actors Centre, 1978–. Starring roles in: Rattle of a Simple Man, 1962; The Anniversary, 1966, 2005; A Delicate Balance (RSC), 1969; So What About Love?, 1969; Absurd Person Singular, 1973; Déjà Revue, 1974; The Bed Before Yesterday, 1976; Annie, 1978; Sweeney Todd, 1980; The Winter's Tale, RSC, Stratford 1981, Barbican 1982; Peter Pan, Barbican, 1982–83; The Cherry Orchard, The Duchess of Malfi, National, 1985–86; Greenland, Royal Court, 1988; Prin, Lyric, Hammersmith, 1989, Lyric, Shaftesbury Avenue, 1990; A Judgement in Stone, The Way of the World, Lyric, Hammersmith, 1992; Gypsy, W Yorkshire Playhouse, 1994 (Best Actress, Theatre Awards UK, TMA); Harry and Me, Royal Court, 1996; Lock Up Your Daughters, Chichester, 1996; Then Again…, Lyric, Hammersmith, 1997; Vassa, Albery, 1999; Under the Blue Sky, Royal Court, 2000; In Extremis, RNT, 2000; Arab-Israeli Cookbook, Gate, 2004; The Anniversary, Garrick, 2005; Cabaret, Lyric, 2006 (Olivier and Clarence Derwent Awards for best supporting role); The Birthday Party, Lyric, Hammersmith, 2008; Sister Act, Palladium, 2009; The Last of the Duchess, Hampstead Th., 2011; Barking in Essex, Wyndham's Th., 2013. Has starred in several successful revues; appeared on Broadway in Entertaining Mr Sloane. Directed: The Soldier's Fortune, Lyric, Hammersmith, 1981; A Midsummer Night's Dream, RSC, 1983; The Critic, National, 1986. *Films:* The Love Child, 1987; Making Waves, 1987; Hawks, 1988; Buster, 1988; Three Men and a Little Lady, 1990; Hold Back the Night, 1999; Love and Death on Long Island, 2000; Yes, 2005; Boy in the Striped Pyjamas, 2008. *Television:* many successes, including The Rag Trade, Jumping the Queue, The Rivals, and several comedy series, incl. Gone to the Dogs, 1991, Gone to Seed, 1992, Brighton Belles, 1993; other appearances include: The Buccaneers, 1994; Dangerous Lady, 1994; Close Relations, 1998; Eastenders, Love or Money, The Russian Bride, 2001; Bedtime, 2001, 2002, 2003; Bait, 2002; 40 Something, 2003; Grumpy Old Women, 2003, 2004, 2005; Feather Boy, 2004; Bleak House, 2005; After Thomas, 2006; The Last Word, 2008; My Life in Verse (documentary), 2009; Suffragette City (documentary), 2010; Over the Rainbow, 2010; The Art of Water Colours (documentary), 2011; Hustle, 2012; Perspectives: the Brontes (documentary), 2013; wrote and acted in Royal Enclosure, 1990. Chancellor, Univ. of Portsmouth, 2008–12. Awards: Variety Club, London Critics, Whitbread Trophy (for best Actress on Broadway); Carmen Silvera Award, Grand Order of Lady Ratlings, 2010; Lifetime Achievement Award, Women in Film and TV, 2011. *Publications:* Ramblings of an Actress, 1987; The Two of Us, 2004 (Author of the Year, British Book Awards, 2005); Just Me, 2008; Miss Carter's War (novel), 2014. *Recreations:* reading, music. *Address:* c/o Independent Talent Group Ltd, 40 Whitfield Street, W1T 2RH.

See also M. J. Byam Shaw.

HAND, Prof. David John, OBE 2013; PhD; FBA 2003; Professor of Statistics, Imperial College London, 1999–2011, now Emeritus Professor of Mathematics; Chief Scientific Advisor, Winton Capital Management, since 2010; *b* 30 June 1950; *s* of Peter Hand and Margaret Hand; *m* 1993, Dr Shelley Channon; two *d*. *Educ:* Christ Church, Oxford (BA Maths 1972); Southampton Univ. (MSc Stats 1974; PhD Pattern Recognition 1977). CStat 1993; FIMA 2011. Statistician, Inst. of Psychiatry, 1977–88; Prof. of Statistics, Open Univ., 1988–99. Non-exec. Dir, UK Statistics Authy, 2013–. Pres., Royal Statistical Soc., 2008–09, 2010. Hon. FIA 1999. Guy Medal in Silver, Royal Statistical Soc., 2002. *Publications:* Discrimination and Classification, 1981; Finite Mixture Distributions, 1981; Kernel Discriminant Analysis, 1982; Artificial Intelligence and Psychiatry, 1985; Multivariate Analysis of Variance and Repeated Measures, 1987; (ed) The Statistical Consultant in Action, 1987; Analysis of Repeated Measures, 1990; (ed) Artificial Intelligence Frontiers in Statistics, 1993; (ed) AI and Computer Power: the impact on statistics, 1994; (ed) A Handbook of Small Data Sets, 1994; Elements of Statistics, 1995; Biplots, 1996; Practical Longitudinal Data Analysis, 1996; Construction and Assessment of Classification Rules, 1997; (ed) Statistics in Finance, 1998; Intelligent Data Analysis, 1999; Advances in Intelligent Data Analysis, IDA–99, 1999; Principles of Data Mining, 2001; (ed) Advances in Intelligent Data Analysis, IDA 2001, 2001; Pattern Detection and Discovery, 2002; Methods and Models in Statistics, 2004; Measurement Theory and Practice, 2004; (ed) Selected Papers of Sir David Cox, 2005; Information Generation, 2007; Statistics: a very short introduction, 2008; ROC Curves for

Continuous Data, 2009; The Improbability Principle, 2014; The Wellbeing of Nations, 2014; over 300 scientific articles. *Address:* Department of Mathematics, Imperial College London, 180 Queen's Gate, SW7 2AZ. *T:* (020) 7594 2843. *E:* d.j.hand@imperial.ac.uk.

HAND, Prof. Geoffrey Joseph Philip, DPhil; Barber Professor of Jurisprudence in the University of Birmingham, 1980–92, now Professor Emeritus; *b* 25 June 1931; *s* of Joseph and Mary Macaulay Hand. *Educ:* Blackrock Coll.; University Coll., Dublin (MA); New Coll., Oxford (DPhil); King's Inns, Dublin. Called to Irish Bar, 1961. Lecturer: Univ. of Edinburgh, 1960; Univ. of Southampton, 1961; University Coll., Dublin, 1965; Professor: University Coll., Dublin, 1972–76; European University Inst., Fiesole, 1976–80; Dean of Faculty of Law, University Coll., Dublin, 1970–75. Chairman: Arts Council of Ireland, 1974–75; Irish Manuscripts Commn, 1998. Mem. Council, RIA, 1994–98 (Vice Pres., 1996–97). Gold Medal, Irish Legal History Soc., 2010. *Publications:* English Law in Ireland 1290–1324, 1967; Report of the Irish Boundary Commission 1925, 1969; (with Lord Cross of Chelsea) Radcliffe and Cross's English Legal System, 5th edn 1971, 6th edn 1977; (with J. Georgel, C. Sasse) European Election Systems Handbook, 1979; Towards a Uniform System of Direct Elections, 1981; (ed with J. McBride) Droit sans Frontières, 1991; numerous periodicals. *Recreations:* listening to classical music, playing chess. *Address:* 72 Granitefield, Dun Laoghaire, Republic of Ireland. *Clubs:* Oxford and Cambridge; Royal Irish Yacht (Dun Laoghaire); Casino Maltese (Valletta).

HAND, Graham Stewart; Director, GSH Consulting, since 2013; Co-ordinator, UK Anti-Corruption Forum, since 2010; *b* 3 Nov. 1948; *s* of Ronald Charles Hand and Mary Fraser Hand (*née* Stewart); *m* 1973, Anne Mary Seton Campbell; one *s* one *d* (and one *s* decd). *Educ:* RMA Sandhurst; St John's Coll., Cambridge (MA 1979). Regular Army, 1969–80; FCO, 1980–2004: served UN Dept, 1980–82; Dakar, 1982–84; News Dept, FCO, 1984–87; Head of Chancery, Helsinki, 1987–90; Aid Policy Dept, ODA, 1991–92; Head of Human Rights Policy Dept, FCO, 1992–94; Dep. High Comr, Nigeria, 1994–96; RCDS, 1997; Ambassador to Bosnia and Herzegovina, 1998–2001; Chargé d'Affaires, Tajikistan, 2002; Ambassador to Algeria, 2002–04; Chief Exec., British Expertise (formerly British Consultants & Construction Bureau), 2004–13. *Recreations:* opera, choral singing, sailing, golf, cooking. *E:* graham.hand@talktalk.net.

HAND, Jessica Mary; HM Diplomatic Service; Head of Arms Export Policy Department, Foreign and Commonwealth Office, since 2014; *b* 1 Sept. 1957; *d* of William Evan Pearce and Mary Elizabeth Pearce (*née* Pimm); *m* 1999, Lt Col Robert Wayne Hand, US Army (retd). *Educ:* Aberdeen Univ. (MA Jt Hons, French and Internat. Relations). PA to Dir, NERC Research Vessel Base, Barry, 1976–78; sales co-ordinator for wine co., Cardiff, 1983–85; joined FCO, 1985; Second Sec., FCO, 1985–87; Dakar, Senegal, 1987–90; First Sec., UN Dept, 1990–92, African Dept (Southern), 1992–94, FCO; lang. trng, 1994–95; Ambassador to Belarus, 1996–99; Dep. Hd, Non-Proliferation Dept, FCO, 1999–2001; UK Pol Advr, Allied Forces North, 2002–04; Counsellor (Mgt), later Dir, Ops and Business Change, and Consul-Gen., Moscow, 2004–08; Dir, UK Trade & Investment, Turkey and Consul-Gen., Istanbul, 2008–12; FCO, 2012–14. *Recreations:* campanology, walking, reading, cooking, music (classical, jazz and anything to dance to). *Address:* c/o Foreign and Commonwealth Office, Old Admiralty Building, The Mall, SW1A 2PA.

HAND, John Lester; QC 1988; **His Honour Judge Hand;** a Circuit Judge, since 2008; *b* 16 June 1947; *s* of John James and Violet Hand; *m* 1st, 1972, Helen Andrea McWatt (marr. diss.); 2nd, 1990, Lynda Ray Ferrigno; one *d*. *Educ:* Huddersfield New College; Univ. of Nottingham (LLB 1969). Called to the Bar, Gray's Inn, 1972, Bencher, 1996; Northern Circuit, 1972; Recorder, 1991–2008. Mem., Employment Appeal Tribunal, 2002–04. *Recreations:* motorcycling, windsurfing. *E:* jlh@johnhandqc.co.uk.

HANDCOCK, family name of **Baron Castlemaine**.

HANDFORD, Rt Rev. (George) Clive, CMG 2007; Bishop in Cyprus and the Gulf, 1996–2007; President Bishop, Episcopal Church in Jerusalem and the Middle East, 2002–07; an Honorary Assistant Bishop, Diocese of West Yorkshire and the Dales, since 2014 (an Honorary Assistant Bishop, Diocese of Ripon and Leeds, 2007–14); *b* 17 April 1937; *s* of Cyril Percy Dawson Handford and Alice Ethel Handford; *m* 1962, Anne Elizabeth Jane Atherley; one *d*. *Educ:* Hatfield Coll., Durham (BA); Queen's Coll., Birmingham and Univ. of Birmingham (DipTh). Curate, Mansfield Parish Church, 1963–66; Chaplain: Baghdad, 1967; Beirut, 1967–73; Dean, St George's Cathedral, Jerusalem, 1974–78; Archdeacon in the Gulf and Chaplain in Abu Dhabi and Qatar, 1978–83; Vicar of Kneesall with Laxton, and Wellow and Rufford, 1983–84; RD of Tuxford and Norwell, 1983–84; Archdeacon of Nottingham, 1984–90; Suffragan Bishop of Warwick, 1990–96. ChStJ 1976. *Address:* Wayside, 1 The Terrace, Kirby Hill, Boroughbridge, York YO51 9DQ. *T:* (01423) 325406.

HANDLEY, Ven. (Anthony) Michael; Archdeacon of Norfolk, 1993–2002, now Emeritus; *b* 3 June 1936; *s* of Eric Harvey Handley and Janet Handley; *m* 1962, Christine May Adlington; two *s* one *d*. *Educ:* Spalding Grammar School; Selwyn Coll., Cambridge (MA Hons); Chichester Theol Coll. Asst Curate, Thorpe St Andrew, 1962–66; Anglican Priest on Fairstead Estate, 1966–72; Vicar of Hellesdon, 1972–81; RD of Norwich North, 1979–81; Archdeacon of Norwich, 1981–93. Proctor in Convocation, 1980–85; Mem., General Synod, 1990–95. Research Project, The Use of Colour, Shape, and Line Drawings as Experiential Training Resources, 1976. *Publications:* A Parish Prayer Card, 1980. *Recreations:* visiting islands, painting, bird watching. *Address:* 25 New Street, Sheringham, Norfolk NR26 8EE. *T:* (01263) 820928.

HANDLEY, Mrs Carol Margaret; Headmistress, Camden School for Girls, 1971–85; *b* 17 Oct. 1929; *d* of Claude Hilary Taylor and Margaret Eleanor Taylor (*née* Peebles); *m* 1952, Prof. Eric Walter Handley, CBE, FBA (*d* 2013). *Educ:* St Paul's Girls' Sch.; University Coll. London (BA; Fellow 1977). Asst Classics Mistress: North Foreland Lodge Sch., 1952; Queen's Gate Sch., 1952; Head of Classics Dept, Camden Sch. for Girls, 1956; Deputy Headmistress, Camden Sch. for Girls, 1964. Dir, Reading Classical Greek Courses, Inst. of Continuing Educn, Univ. of Cambridge, 1990–2006. Sen. Mem., Wolfson Coll., Cambridge, 1989–. Member Council: RHC, then RHBNC, 1977–95; Middx Hosp. Med. Sch., 1980–84; Mem. Governors and Council, Bedford Coll., 1981–85; Community (formerly Partnership) Gov., Comberton Village Coll., 2004– (Chm., 2006–10); Mem., Comberton Acad. Trust, 2011–; Community Gov., Cambourne Village Coll., 2012–. Pres., Classical Assoc., 1996–97. *Publications:* (jtly) An Independent Study Guide to Reading Greek, 1995, 2nd edn 2008; (jtly) A Greek Anthology, 2002. *Recreation:* gardening. *Address:* Colt House, 44 High Street, Little Eversden, Cambs CB23 1HE.

HANDLEY, David Thomas, CMG 2000; HM Diplomatic Service, retired; Managing Director, Veracity Worldwide, 2012–14; *b* 31 Aug. 1945; *s* of late Leslie Thomas Handley and Frances Handley (*née* Harrison); *m* 1st, 1967, Lilian Duff (marr. diss. 1977); one *s* one *d*; 2nd, 1978, Susan Elizabeth Beal; two *s* one *d* (and one *d* decd). *Educ:* Univ. of Newcastle upon Tyne (BA Jt Hons Politics and Econs). British Leyland Motor Corp., 1967–72; joined FCO, 1972: language studies, MECAS, Lebanon, 1974–76; First Sec., Budapest, 1978–81; Hd of British Interests Sect. and Chargé d'Affaires, Guatemala City, 1984–87; Counsellor: Cairo, 1990–93; FCO, 1993–2000. Hd, Gp Strategic Analysis, BAE Systems, 2000–12. Co-Chair, Bd of Govs, Bedales Sch., 2005–08. *Recreations:* family, friends, fitness, fun. *Address:* The Red House, Froxfield, Hants GU23 1BB. *T:* (01730) 827039.

HANDLEY, Ven. Michael; *see* Handley, Ven. A. M.

HANDLEY, Paul; Editor, Church Times, since 1995; *b* 29 May 1958; *s* of Arnold Terence Handley and Margaret Hardy; *m* 1980, Terence MacMath; two *s* two *d*. *Educ:* Colchester Royal Grammar Sch.; Goldsmiths' Coll., Univ. of London (BA English 1980). News Editor, Church of England Newspaper, 1981–85; freelance publisher, writer, 1986–88; Reporter, Church Times, 1988–90; Press Sec. to Archbishop of Canterbury, 1990–92; freelance writer, 1992–94; News Editor, Church Times, 1994. Trustee, Sandford St Martin Trust, 2004–15. Mem. Cttee, Bloxham Faith and Literature Fest., 2012–. *Recreations:* evensong, walking. *Address:* c/o Church Times, 108–114 Golden Lane, EC1Y 0TG. *T:* (020) 7776 1060. *E:* editor@churchtimes.co.uk.

HANDOVER, Richard Gordon, CBE 2008; DL; Chairman, Power to Change Trust, since 2014; *b* 13 April 1946; *s* of Gordon Handover and Hilda Handover (*née* Dyke); *m* 1972, Veronica Joan Woodhead; one *s* two *d*. *Educ:* Blundell's Sch. W H Smith, 1964–2005: various jun. managerial appts, 1964–74; sen. mgt appts, 1974–89; Man. Dir, Our Price Music, 1989–95; joined main co. bd, 1995; Man. Dir, W H Smith News, 1995–97; Gp Chief Exec., W H Smith Gp plc, subseq. W H Smith PLC, 1997–2003; Chm., 2003–05. Chm., Alexon Gp plc, 2008–11; non-executive Director: Nationwide Bldg Soc., 2000–07; Royal Mail, 2002–11. Chm., Adult Learning Inspectorate, 2002–07. Chm., Age Concern Enterprises Ltd, 1992–99; Dir, BITC, 1999–2005; Vice Chm., Kids Company, 2005–15. Chm. Govs, Dauntsey's Sch., 2005–. Chm., Wilts and Swindon Community Foundn, 2005–14. DL Wilts, 2011. *Recreations:* tennis, golf, painting. *Address:* Power to Change Trust, Chandlery Business Centre, 50 Westminster Bridge Road, SE1 7QY.

HANDS, Rt Hon. Gregory (William); PC 2014; MP (C) Chelsea and Fulham, since 2010 (Hammersmith and Fulham, 2005–10); Chief Secretary to the Treasury, since 2015; *b* 14 Nov. 1965; *s* of Edward and Mavis Hands; *m* 2005, Irina Hundt; one *s* one *d*. *Educ:* Dr Challoner's Grammar Sch.; Robinson Coll., Cambridge (BA 1989). Banker, 1989–97. Mem. (C), Hammersmith and Fulham BC, 1998–2006. An Asst Govt Whip, 2011–13; Treas. of HM Household (Dep. Chief Whip), 2013–15. *Address:* House of Commons, SW1A 0AA.

HANDS, Guy; Group Chairman and Chief Investment Officer, Terra Firma Capital Partners, since 2008 (Chairman and Chief Executive Officer, 2002–08); *b* 27 Aug. 1959; *s* of Christopher and Sally Hands; *m* 1984, Julia Caroline Ablethorpe; two *s* two *d*. *Educ:* Judd Sch., Tonbridge; Mansfield Coll., Oxford (BA Hons PPE, MA; Bancroft Fellow 2000). Hd of Eurobond Trading, Goldman Sachs, 1982–94 (Trading, 1986; Hd, Global Asset Structuring Gp, 1990); Founder and Man. Dir, Principal Finance Gp, Nomura Internat. plc, 1994–2001. Mem., Chancellor's Court of Benefactors, Univ. of Oxford, 2000–. Fellow, Duke of Edinburgh Award Scheme, 2001–. *Recreations:* films, wine, fine art. *Address:* Terra Firma Capital Management Ltd, Royal Chambers, St Julian's Avenue, St Peter Port, Guernsey GY1 3RE. *T:* (01481) 754660.

HANDS, Terence David, (Terry), CBE 2007; theatre and opera director; Director, Clwyd Theatr Cymru (formerly Theatr Clwyd), since 1997 (Artistic Consultant, 1996–97); *b* 9 Jan. 1941; *s* of Joseph Ronald Hands and Luise Berthe Kohler; *m* 1st, 1964, Josephine Barstow (marr. diss. 1967); 2nd, 1974, Ludmila Mikael (marr. diss. 1980); one *d*; partner, 1988–96, Julia Lintott; two *s*; 3rd, 2002, Emma (*née* Lucia). *Educ:* Woking Grammar Sch.; Birmingham Univ. (BA Hons Eng. Lang. and Lit.); RADA (Hons Dip.). Founder-Artistic Dir, Liverpool Everyman Theatre, 1964–66 (Hon. Dir, 1996); Artistic Dir, RSC Theatregoround, 1966–67; Associate Dir, 1967–77, Jt Artistic Dir, 1978–86, Chief Exec. and Artistic Dir, 1986–91, Director Emeritus, 1991–, RSC; Consultant Dir, Comédie Française, 1975–80. Vis. Prof., ATRiuM, Univ. of S Wales (formerly Univ. of Glamorgan), 2007–. Associate Mem., RADA; Hon. Fellow, Shakespeare Inst. Jt Pres., Arvon Foundn, 1990–; Hon. FRWCMD (Hon. FWCMD 2002); Hon. Fellow: NE Wales Inst. of HE, 2002; Bangor Univ., 2013. Hon. DLitt: Birmingham, 1988; Liverpool, 2006; Hon. Dr Middlesex, 1997. Chevalier des Arts et des Lettres, 1973. *Director* (for Liverpool Everyman Theatre, 1964–66): The Importance of Being Earnest; Look Back in Anger; Richard III; The Four Seasons; Fando and Lis; *Artistic Director* (for RSC Theatregoround): The Proposal, 1966; The Second Shepherds' Play, 1966; The Dumb Waiter, 1967; Under Milk Wood, 1967; *directed for RSC:* The Criminals, 1967; Pleasure and Repentance, 1967; The Latent Heterosexual, 1968; The Merry Wives of Windsor, 1968, Japan tour, 1970; Bartholomew Fair, 1969; Pericles, 1969; Women Beware Women, 1969; Richard III, 1970, 1980; Balcony, 1971, 1987; Man of Mode, 1971; The Merchant of Venice, 1971; Murder in the Cathedral, 1972; Cries from Casement, 1973; Romeo and Juliet, 1973, 1989; The Bewitched, 1974; The Actor, 1974; Henry IV, Parts 1 and 2, 1975; Henry V, 1975, USA and European Tour, 1976; Old World, 1976; Henry VI parts 1, 2 and 3 (SWET Award, Dir of the Year, Plays and Players, Best Production, 1978), Coriolanus, 1977, European tour, 1979; The Changeling, 1978; Twelfth Night, The Children of the Sun, 1979; As You Like It, Richard II, 1980; Troilus and Cressida, 1981; Arden of Faversham, Much Ado About Nothing, 1982 (European tour and Broadway, 1984), Poppy, 1982; Cyrano de Bergerac, 1983 (SWET Best Dir award), Broadway, 1984 (televised, 1984); Red Noses, 1985; Othello, 1985; The Winter's Tale, 1986; Scenes from a Marriage, 1986; Julius Caesar, 1987; Carrie (Stratford and Broadway), 1988; (with John Barton) Coriolanus, 1989; Romeo and Juliet, 1989; Singer, 1989; Love's Labours Lost, 1990; The Seagull, 1990; Tamburlaine the Great, 1992 (Evening Standard Award, London Drama Critics Award, 1993); *directed for Royal National Theatre:* The Merry Wives of Windsor, 1995; *directed for Chichester Festival Theatre:* Hadrian VII, 1995; The Visit, 1995; *directed for Birmingham Rep.:* The Importance of Being Earnest, 1995 (transf. Old Vic, 1995); *directed for Theatr Clwyd/Clwyd Theatr Cymru:* The Importance of Being Earnest, (also Birmingham and Toronto), Equus, A Christmas Carol, 1997; The Journey of Mary Kelly, The Norman Conquests, 1998; Twelfth Night, Macbeth, Under Milk Wood, 1999; Private Lives, 2000; King Lear, Bedroom Farce, The Rabbit, 2001; Rosencrantz and Guildenstern are Dead, Betrayal, Romeo and Juliet, The Four Seasons, 2002; Blithe Spirit, The Crucible, Pleasure and Repentance, 2003; One Flew Over the Cuckoo's Nest, 2004; Troilus and Cressida, Night Must Fall, 2005; A Chorus of Disapproval, Memory, 2006; Arcadia, 2007; Cherry Orchard, 2007; Macbeth, 2008; Noises Off, 2009; Mary Stuart, 2009; Pygmalion, 2009; Arden of Faversham, 2010; A Small Family Business, 2010; The Taming of the Shrew, 2011; As You Like It, 2012; Boeing Boeing, 2012; The Winslow Boy, 2013; Under Milk Wood, 2014; Hamlet, 2015; *directed for Comédie Française:* Richard III, 1972 (Meilleur Spectacle de l'Année award); Pericles, 1974; Twelfth Night, 1976 (Meilleur Spectacle de l'Année award); Le Cid, 1977; Murder in the Cathedral, 1978; *directed for Paris Opéra:* Verdi's Otello, 1976 (televised 1978); *directed for Burg Theatre, Vienna:* Troilus and Cressida, 1977; As You Like It, 1979; *directed for Royal Opera:* Parsifal, 1979; *directed for Teatro Stabile di Genova, Italy:* Women Beware Women, 1981; *directed for Schauspielhaus, Zürich:* Arden of Faversham, 1992; *directed for Recklinghausen:* Buffalo Bill, 1992; *directed for Bremen:* Simon Boccanegra, 1992; *directed for National Theatre, Oslo:* Merry Wives of Windsor, 1995; The Pretenders, 1996; The Seagull, 1998; Sag Mir Wo Die Blumen Sind, Berlin, 1993; Hamlet, Marigny Theatre, Paris, 1994; Royal Hunt of the Sun, Tokyo, 1996; *recording:* Murder in the Cathedral, 1976; *television:* Cyrano de Bergerac, 1984. *Publications:* trans. (with Barbara Wright) Genet, The Balcony, 1971; Pleasure and Repentance, 1976; (ed Sally Beauman) Henry V, 1976; Hamlet (French trans.), 1994; contribs to Theatre 72, Playback. *Address:* c/o Clwyd Theatr Cymru, Mold, Flintshire CH7 1YA.

HANDS, Dr Timothy Roderick; Master, Magdalen College School, Oxford, since 2008; *b* 30 March 1956; *s* of late Rory Hands and Catherine Hands (*née* Walker); *m* 1988, Jane, *er d* of Ian and late Ann Smart; two *s*. *Educ:* Emanuel Sch., Battersea; Guildhall Sch. of Music and Drama; King's Coll. London (BA 1st Cl. English Lang. and Lit.; William Stebbing Prize, 1976, J. S. Brewer Prize, 1977, EETS and L. M. Faithfull Prizes, 1978; AKC with Credit; 1st Leathes

Prizeman, 1978; Coll. Jelf Medallist); St Catherine's Coll., Oxford (Sen. Schol.); Oriel Coll., Oxford (R. W. B. Burton Sen. Schol.; DPhil 1984). Stipendiary Lectr, Oriel Coll., Oxford, 1985–86; Asst Master, King's Sch., Canterbury, 1986–94 (Housemaster, Galpin's, 1990–94); Second Master, Whitgift Sch., 1994–97; Headmaster, Portsmouth Grammar Sch., 1997–2007. Conductor, Schola Cantorum of Oxford, 1982–85. Mem., Editl Bd, Conf. and Common Room, 2000–13. Member: Admiralty Interview Bd, 1998–2004; Ind. State Sch. Partnership Forum, DFES, 2002–04. Mem., ISC Wkg Gp on Access to Ind. Educn, 2000–03. Mem., Ext. Adv. Bd, Oxford Univ. Faculty of English, 2006–. Headmasters' and Headmistresses' Conference: Sec., 2003–04, Chm., 2004–05, S Central Div.; Mem. Cttee, 2003–; Mem., 2003–12, Co-Chair, 2005–12, HMC/GSA Univs Cttee; Chm., 2013–14. Bishop's Rep., Portsmouth Cathedral Council, 2001–05. Founding Chm., Portsmouth Festivities, 2000–07 (Chm., Trustees and Bd of Dirs, 2006–07; Patron, 2007–). Trustee: Portsmouth Cathedral, 1999–2005; HMS Warrior 1860, 2003–08; Schola Cantorum, Oxford, 2008–. Governor: Alleyn's Sch., 2005–09; St Mary's Calne, 2010–; Bedales, 2010–; Mem. Council, Cheltenham Ladies' Coll., 2009. *Publications:* A George Eliot Chronology, 1989; Thomas Hardy: distracted preacher, 1989; A Hardy Chronology, 1992; (contrib.) New Perspectives on Thomas Hardy, 1994; Thomas Hardy: writers in their time, 1995; (contrib.) The Achievement of Thomas Hardy, 2000; (contrib.) Oxford Reader's Companion to Hardy, 2000; Ideas to Assemble, 2006; Heads: expert advice for changing times, 2007; (contrib.) Ashgate Research Companion to Thomas Hardy, 2010; literary and musical articles, editions and reviews. *Recreations:* classical music, sport, especially Rugby and cricket, writing. *Address:* Magdalen College School, Oxford OX4 1DZ. *T:* (01865) 242191. *Club:* East India.

HANDY, Charles Brian, CBE 2000; author; *b* 25 July 1932; *s* of Archdeacon Brian Leslie Handy and Joan Kathleen Herbert Handy (*née* Scott); *m* 1962, Elizabeth Ann Hill; one *s* one *d*. *Educ:* Oriel Coll., Oxford (BA 1956; MA 1966; Hon. Fellow, 1998); MIT (SM 1967). Shell Internat. Petroleum Co., 1956–65; Charter Consolidated Ltd, 1965–66; Sloan Sch. of Management, MIT (Internat. Faculty Fellow), 1967–68; London Business School, 1968–94; Prof., 1972–77; Vis. Prof., 1977–94; Fellow, 1994; Warden, St George's House, Windsor Castle, 1977–81. Chm., Royal Soc. for Encouragement of Arts, Manufactures and Commerce, 1987–89. FCGI 2000. Hon. Fellow: Inst. of Educn, London Univ., 1999; St Mary's Coll., Twickenham, 1999. Hon. DLitt: Bristol Poly., 1988; Open Univ., 1989; UEA, 1993; QUB, 1998; Middlesex, 1998; Exeter, 1999; Essex, Hull, Durham, 2000; Roehampton, 2014; Hon. LLD Dublin, 2006. *Publications:* Understanding Organizations, 1976, 4th edn 1999; Gods of Management, 1978, 2nd edn 1991; Future of Work, 1982; Understanding Schools as Organizations, 1986; Understanding Voluntary Organizations, 1988; The Age of Unreason, 1989; Inside Organizations, 1990; Waiting for the Mountain to Move, 1991; The Empty Raincoat, 1994; Beyond Certainty (essays), 1995; The Hungry Spirit, 1997; The New Alchemists, 1999; Thoughts for the Day, 1999; The Elephant and the Flea, 2001; Reinvented Lives, 2002; Myself and Other More Important Matters, 2006; The New Philanthropists, 2006; The Second Curve, 2015. *Address:* Flat 2, 73 Putney Hill, SW15 3NT. *T:* (020) 8788 1610; Old Hall Cottages, Bressingham, Diss, Norfolk IP22 2AG. *T:* (01379) 687546. *E:* candehandy@aol.com.

HANDYSIDE, Richard Neil; QC 2009; *b* Cardiff, 27 Sept. 1968; *s* of Robert Handyside and Rhona Handyside (now Aldridge); *m* 1999, Philippa Betts; two *s*. *Educ:* Marlborough; Univ. of Bristol (LLB); Brasenose Coll., Oxford (BCL). Called to the Bar, Lincoln's Inn, 1993; in practice as a barrister, specialising in commercial law. *Recreations:* tennis, travel, watching Rugby. *Address:* Fountain Court, Temple, EC4Y 9DH. *T:* (020) 7583 3335, *Fax:* (020) 7353 0329.

HANGARTNER, John Robert Wilfred; Principal Director, Brett Cook Consulting Ltd, since 2000; Consultant Pathologist, Guy's and St Thomas' Hospitals, since 2002; *b* 5 Feb. 1955; *s* of John Hangartner and Ita Patricia (*née* Brett); *m* 1980, Jillian Mary Ansell; one *s* one *d*. *Educ:* Merchant Taylors' Sch., Northwood; Guy's Hosp. Med. Sch., Univ. of London (BSc Hons 1976; MB BS 1979); Open Univ. (MBA 1995). MRCS, LRCP 1979; MRCPath 1988, FRCPath 1997. Clin. Lectr in Histopathology, St George's Hosp. Med. Sch., 1983–88; Department of Health: SMO, 1988–91; Temp. PMO, 1991–93; PMO, 1993; Under Sec., and SPMO, 1993–97; CMO, Guardian Health Ltd, 1997–2000; Sen. Med. Advr, PPP healthcare, 1999–2000; Gp Med. Advr, Capio Healthcare (UK), 2001–03; Bd Med. Advr, CS Healthcare, 2004–13; Clin. Dir, Diagnostic and Therapeutic Services Directorate, 2004–05, Divisional Dir, Core Clinical Services Div., 2004–06, Guy's and St Thomas' NHS Foundn Trust; Clin. Dir, GSTS Pathology LLP, 2009–14. Chm., Hosp. Jun. Staff Cttee, BMA, 1984–85. FRSA 1994. *Recreations:* photography, singing, sailing. *Address:* Brett Cook Consulting Ltd, 11 Annesley Road, Blackheath, SE3 0JX. *T:* (020) 8319 3164, 07773 335608.

HANHAM, family name of **Baroness Hanham**.

HANHAM, Baroness *cr* 1999 (Life Peer), of Kensington in the Royal Borough of Kensington and Chelsea; **Joan Brownlow Hanham,** CBE 1997; *b* 23 Sept. 1939; *d* of Alfred Spark and Mary (*née* Mitchell); *m* 1964, Dr Iain William Ferguson Hanham (*d* 2011); one *s* one *d*. *Educ:* Hillcourt Sch., Dublin. Royal Borough of Kensington and Chelsea: Mem. (C), 1970–2010; Mayor, 1983–84; Leader of Council, 1989–2000; Chairman: Town Planning Cttee, 1984–86; Social Services Cttee, 1987–89; Policy and Resources Cttee, 1989–2000. Chm., Policy Cttee, London Boroughs Assoc., 1991–95. An Opposition Whip, H of L, 2000–08; Opposition spokesman for local govt, housing, planning and the regions, 2002–07, Scotland, 2003–07, transport, 2005–07, home affairs, 2007–10; Parly Under-Sec. of State, DCLG, 2010–13. Mem., Mental Health Act Commn, 1983–90; non-exec. Mem., NW Thames RHA, 1983–94; non-exec. Dir, Chelsea and Westminster Health Care NHS Trust, 1994–2000; Chairman: St Mary's Hosp. NHS Trust, 2000–07; NHS Monitor, 2014–15. Vice-Pres., Commonwealth Inst., 1998–2000. Pres., Volunteering England, 2008–10. JP City of London Commn 1984–2009, and Inner London Family Proceedings Court, 1992–2009. Freeman: City of London, 1984; Royal Bor. of Kensington and Chelsea, 2011. *Recreations:* music, travel. *Address:* House of Lords, SW1A 0PW. *Club:* Hurlingham.

HANHAM, Prof. Harold John; Vice-Chancellor, University of Lancaster, 1985–95; *b* Auckland, New Zealand, 16 June 1928; *s* of John Newman Hanham and Ellie Malone; *m* 1973, Ruth Soulé Arnon, *d* of Prof. Daniel I. Arnon, Univ. of Calif, Berkeley. *Educ:* Mount Albert Grammar Sch.; Auckland UC (now Univ. of Auckland); Univ. of New Zealand (BA 1948, MA 1950); Selwyn Coll., Cambridge (PhD 1954). FRHistS 1960; FAAAS 1974. Asst Lectr to Sen. Lectr, in Govt, Univ. of Manchester, 1954–63; Prof. and Head of Dept of Politics, Univ. of Edinburgh, 1963–68; Prof. of History, 1968–73 and Fellow of Lowell House, 1970–73, Harvard Univ.; Prof. of History and Political Science, 1972–85 and Dean, Sch. of Humanities and Social Sci., 1973–84, MIT; Hon. Prof. of History, Univ. of Lancaster, 1985–. Mem., ESRC, 1986. Guggenheim Fellow, 1972–73. Hon. AM Harvard, 1968; Hon. DSc Lancaster, 1995. John H. Jenkins Prize for Bibliography, Union Coll., 1978. *Publications:* Elections and Party Management, 1969, 2nd edn 1978; The Nineteenth-Century Constitution, 1969; Scottish Nationalism, 1969; Bibliography of British History 1851–1914, 1976. *Recreations:* discovering Canada, squash. *Clubs:* Oxford and Cambridge; St Botolph (Boston).

HANHAM, Sir William (John Edward), 13th Bt *cr* 1667, of Wimborne, Dorsetshire; landowner, Dorset, since 2007; *b* Nairobi, Kenya, 4 Sept. 1957; *o s* of Sir Michael William Hanham, 12th Bt, DFC and Margaret Jane Hanham (*née* Thomas); *S* father, 2009; *m* 2011, Alison (Christina), *d* of John Birch and Sylvia (*née* MacNair). *Educ:* Winchester Coll.; Courtauld Inst. of Art (BA Hons History of Art). Press and PR Officer, Christie's Auctioneers, London, 1983–91; Art Dealer in Old Master Paintings, London, 1993–2007. *Recreations:* art history, gardening, bee-keeping, astronomy, sailing. *Address:* c/o Deans Court Estate Office, 2 Deans Court Lane, Wimborne, Dorset BH21 1EE. *Club:* Garrick.

HANKES, Sir Claude, KCVO 2006; macro-strategist and adviser; *b* 8 March 1949. *Educ:* Grey. With Manufacturers Hanover, 1968–72; Robert Fleming & Co. Ltd, 1972–77, Director 1974–77; Chm., Management Cttee, Price Waterhouse and Partners, 1983–89. Advr to Bd, (Corange) Boehringer Mannheim, 1988–94; Dep. Chm., Leutwiler and Partners Ltd, 1992–96; Chm., Shaw & Bradley Ltd, 1993–; Interim Chm., Roland Berger Strategy Consultants Ltd, 2003–05. Masterminded resolution to S African debt crisis, 1985–86; Chm., Adv. Cttee to Kingdom of Jordan on Strategic Economic Policy Issues, 1993–94; Advisor: to Iraq, 2003, to Iraq Governing Council, 2003–04, to Iraq on macro strategic issues, 2005–06; Trade Bank of Iraq, 2007–11. Testified to US Congress on UN Oil for Food scandal, 2004. Trustee: Windsor Leadership Trust, 1998– (Chm., 2000–07); Hawthornden Internat. Retreat for Writers, 2008–10. Hon. Fellow and Life Mem. Council, St George's House, Windsor Castle, 2006 (Trustee and Advr, 2000–06; Lect., 2014); Hon. Mem., Coll. of St George, Windsor Castle, 2006 (Hon. Fellow and Advr, 2002–06). Hon. Fellow, Corpus Christi Coll., Oxford. *Publications:* Nobel Industrier report, Stockholm, 1991. *Recreations:* gardening, art. *E:* officesirclaude@gmail.com. *Club:* Turf.

HANKES-DRIELSMA, Sir Claude Dunbar; *see* Hankes, Sir Claude.

HANKEY, family name of **Baron Hankey**.

HANKEY, 3rd Baron *cr* 1939, of The Chart, Surrey; **Donald Robin Alers Hankey;** *b* 12 June 1938; *s* of 2nd Baron Hankey, KCMG, KCVO and Frances Bevyl Stuart-Monteth (*d* 1957); *S* father, 1996; *m* 1st, 1963, Margaretha Thorndahl (marr. diss. 1974); 2nd, 1974, Eileen Désirée (marr. diss. 1994), *yr d* of Maj.-Gen. Stuart Battye, CB; two *d*; 3rd, 1994, June, *d* of late Dr Leonard Taboroff. *Educ:* Rugby; University Coll. London (DipArch). RIBA. Founder, 1973, Chm., 1973–2006, Consultant, 2006–, Gilmore Hankey Kirke Ltd, architects, planners, engineers and conservation specialists (part of the GHK Group of cos incl. engrg, econs, sociols and mgt); founder, Gilmore Hankey Kirke SA, Paris (consultants to Commercial Union, Bovis Investissements SA, Givenchy, Mayor of Nemours). Pres., ICOMOS (UK), 2006–12 (Vice-Chm., 1997–2002; Vice Pres., 2002–06); Vice-Chm., Historic Bldgs Adv. Gp, MoD, 1999–2004. Founder and former Chm., All Party Gp on Architecture and Planning. Consultant to: World Bank; IADB in Jamaica; USAID in Jordan; EU; Yemen; Pakistan; China; World Heritage sites; specialising in conservation, design upgrading and re-use of the cultural and historic envmt, legal and admin. systems and cities mgt. FRSA; FSA; FRAI. *Recreations:* piano, the arts, cultural anthropology, tennis, ski-ing. *Heir:* *b* Hon. Alexander Maurice Alers Hankey, PhD [*b* 18 Aug. 1947; *m* 1970, Deborah Benson (marr. diss. 1990)]. *Address:* 8 Sunset Road, SE5 8EA.

HANKIN, Jonas Keith; QC 2013; *b* Birmingham, 6 Aug. 1969; *s* of Roderick and Jacqueline Hankin; *m* 2006, Hannah Cartledge; two *s*. *Educ:* King Edward's Sch., Birmingham; King's Coll. London (BA Hons Hist.); Birmingham Univ. (CPE); Inns of Court Sch. of Law (BVC). Called to the Bar, Middle Temple, 1994; in practice as a barrister, specialising in crime. *Recreations:* family, mountains, music, film, wine. *Address:* St Philips Chambers, 55 Temple Row, Birmingham B2 5LS. *T:* (0121) 246 7000. *E:* jhankin@st-philips.com.

HANKINS, (Frederick) Geoffrey; Chairman, Fitch Lovell plc, 1983–90 (Chief Executive, 1982–89); Director, Booker plc, 1990–97; *b* 9 Dec. 1926; *s* of Frederick Aubrey Hankins and Elizabeth (*née* Stockton); *m* 1951, Iris Esther Perkins; two *d*. *Educ:* St Dunstan's College. Commissioned Army, 1946–48; J. Sainsbury management trainee, 1949–51, manufacturing management, 1951–55; Production/Gen. Manager, Allied Suppliers, 1955–62; Production Dir, Brains Food Products, 1962–69; Kraft Foods, 1966–69; Gen. Man., Millers, Poole, 1970–72, Man. Dir, 1972–82, Chm., 1975–86; Fitch Lovell: Dir, 1975–90; Chm., Manufacturing Div., 1975–84; Chairman: Robirch, 1975–84; Jus Rol, 1976–85; Blue Cap Frozen Food Services, 1975–84; Newforge Foods, 1979–84; Bells Bacon (Evesham), 1980–83; L. Noel, 1982–84; Dir, Salaison Le Vexin, 1980–90. Liveryman, Poulters' Co., 1982–. *Recreations:* genealogy, antiques, practical pursuits. *Address:* 15 Little Fosters, Chaddesley Glen, Canford Cliffs, Poole, Dorset BH13 7PB.

HANKS, Patrick Wyndham, PhD; lexicographer, corpus linguist and onomastician; *b* 24 March 1940; *s* of Wyndham George Hanks and Elizabeth Mary (*née* Rudd); *m* 1st, 1961, Helga Gertrud Ingeborg Lietz (marr. diss. 1968); one *s* one *d*; 2nd, 1979, Julie Eyre (marr. diss. 1996); two *d*. *Educ:* Ardingly Coll., Sussex; University Coll., Oxford (BA, MA); Masaryk Univ., Brno (PhD). Editor, Dictionaries and Reference Books, Hamlyn Group, 1964–70; Man. Dir, Laurence Urdang Associates, 1970–79; Dir, Surnames Res. Project, Univ. of Essex, 1980–83; Project Manager, Cobuild, Univ. of Birmingham, 1983–87; Chief Editor, Collins English Dictionaries, 1987–90; Manager, then Chief Editor, Current English Dictionaries, OUP, 1990–2000. Adjunct Prof., Dept of Computer Sci., Brandeis Univ., 2002–06; Associate Prof., Faculty of Informatics, Masaryk Univ., Brno, 2005–08; Vis. Prof., UWE, 2007– (res. project, Family Names of UK, 2010–); Sen. Researcher and Vis. Prof., Inst. of Formal and Applied Linguistics, Charles Univ., Prague, 2008–10; Vis. Prof. of Computational Lexicography, 2009, Prof. in Lexicography, 2012– (res. project, Disambiguation of Verbs by Collocation), Res. Inst. for Information and Language Processing, Univ. of Wolverhampton. Vis. Scientist (corpus lexicography), AT&T Bell Labs, 1988–90; Chief Investigator, Hector project in corpus analysis, Systems Res. Center, Digital Equipment Corp., Palo Alto, CA, 1991–92. Consultant: Electronic Dictionary of the German Lang., Berlin-Brandenburg Acad. of Scis, 2003–06; Patakis Publishers, Athens, 2006–09; Inst. for the Czech Lang., Prague, 2008–09. *Publications:* (ed) Hamlyn Encyclopedic World Dictionary, 1971; (ed) Collins English Dictionary, 1979; (with J. Corbett) Business Listening Tasks, 1986; (managing editor) Collins Cobuild English Language Dictionary, 1987; (with F. Hodges) Dictionary of Surnames, 1988; (with F. Hodges) Oxford Dictionary of First Names, 1990, 2nd edn 2006; (ed jtly) New Oxford Dictionary of English, 1998; (ed) New Oxford Thesaurus of English, 2000; Dictionary of American Family Names, 2003; (ed) Lexicology: critical concepts in Linguistics, 2008; (ed with R. Giora) Metaphor and Figurative Language: critical concepts in linguistics, 2012; Lexical Analysis: norms and exploitations, 2013; articles in Computational Linguistics, Internat. Jl Corpus Linguistics, Computing and the Humanities, Internat. Jl of Lexicography, Onoma, Names, and other jls; *festschrift:* A Way with Words, 2010. *Recreations:* onomastics, philology, bridge, punting. *E:* patrick.w.hanks@gmail.com.

HANKS, Tom; actor and producer; *b* 9 July 1956; *s* of Amos Hanks and Janet; *m* 1st, 1978, Samantha Lewes (marr. diss. 1985); one *s* one *d*; 2nd, 1988, Rita Wilson; two *s*. *Educ:* Calif State Univ. *Films* include: Splash, 1984; Bachelor Party, 1984; The Money Pit, 1986; Dragnet, 1987; Big, 1988; Punchline, 1988; Turner and Hooch, 1989; The Bonfire of the Vanities, 1990; A League of their Own, 1992; Sleepless in Seattle, 1993; Philadelphia, 1994 (Best Actor Award, Berlin Film Fest.; Acad. Award for Best Actor); Forrest Gump, 1995 (Acad. Award for Best Actor); Apollo 13, 1995; Toy Story, 1996; (also writer and dir) That Thing You Do!, 1997; Saving Private Ryan, 1998; You've Got Mail, 1999; The Green Mile, Toy Story 2, 2000; Cast Away, 2001; Road to Perdition, 2002; Catch Me If You Can, 2003; The Ladykillers, The Terminal, 2004; The Da Vinci Code, 2006; Charlie Wilson's War, 2007; Angels and Demons, 2009; Toy Story 3, 2010; (also writer and dir) Larry Crowne, 2011; Extremely Loud and Incredibly Close, 2012; Cloud Atlas, Captain Phillips, Saving Mr Banks, 2013; *television* includes: Bosom Buddies, 1980–82; co-prod., Band of Brothers, 2001; executive producer: The Pacific, 2010; The Sixties, 2014; *theatre:* Lucky Guy, NY, 2013. *Address:* c/o Creative Artists Agency, 2000 Avenue of the Stars, Los Angeles, CA 90067, USA.

HANLEY, Rt Hon. Sir Jeremy (James), KCMG 1997; PC 1994; chartered accountant, company director, lecturer and broadcaster; *b* 17 Nov. 1945; *s* of late Jimmy Hanley and Dinah Sheridan; *m* 1973, Verna, Viscountess Villiers (*née* Stott); one *s*, one step *d*, and one *s* by previous marriage. *Educ:* Rugby. FCA 1969; FCCA 1980; FCIS 1980. Peat Marwick Mitchell & Co., 1963–66; Lectr in law, taxation and accountancy, Anderson Thomas Frankel, 1969, Dir 1969; Man. Dir, ATF (Jersey and Ireland), 1970–73; Dep. Chm., The Financial Training Co. Ltd, 1973–90; Sec., Park Place PLC, 1977–83; Chm., Fraser Green Ltd, 1986–90. Non-executive Director: ITE Gp, 1997–2009; Brass Tacks Publishing, 1997–2000; GTECH Hldgs Corp., 2001–07; Eur. Adv. Bd, Credit Lyonnais, 2000–05; NYMEX Europe, 2005–07; Willis Hldgs Inc., 2006–; Langbar Internat., 2006–14; Blue Hackle Ltd, 2006–10; Lottomatica SpA, 2007–; CSS Stellar plc, 2007–08; Nymex London, 2008–09; Mountfield Gp, 2008–09; Willis Ltd, 2008–; London Asia Capital plc, 2011–14; Chairman: Internat. Trade and Investment Missions, 1997–2002; AdVal Gp plc, 1998–2003; Braingames Network plc, 2000–02; Falcon Fund Mgt Ltd, 2000–03; Onslow Suffolk Ltd, 2007–09. Sen. Consultant, Kroll Associates, 2003–04; Mem. Adv. Bd, Talal Abu-Ghazaleh Internat., 2004–05. Dir, Arab-British Chamber of Commerce, 1998–2011. Parly Advr to ICA, 1986–90. Contested (C) Lambeth Central, April 1978, 1979. MP (C) Richmond and Barnes, 1983–97; contested (C) Richmond Park, 1997. PPS to Minister of State, Privy Council Office (Minister for CS and the Arts), 1987–90, to Sec. of State for Envmt, 1990; Parly Under-Sec. of State, NI Office, 1990–93 (Minister for Health, Social Security and Agric., 1990–92, for Pol Develt, Community Relns and Educn, 1992–93); Minister of State for the Armed Forces, MoD, 1993–94; Chm. of Cons. Party and in Cabinet as Minister without Portfolio, 1994–95; Minister of State, FCO, 1995–97. Mem., H of C Select Cttee on Home Affairs, 1983–87 (Mem., Subcttee on Race Relns and Immigration, 1983–87); Jt Vice-Chm., Cons. Backbench Trade and Industry Cttee, 1983–87. Member: British-American Parly Gp, 1983–97; Anglo-French Parly Gp, 1983–97; British-Irish Interparly Body, 1990; Life Member: CPA, 1983; IPU, 1983; Chm., Cons Candidates Assoc., 1982–83. Member: Bow Gp, 1974– (Chm., Home Affairs Cttee); European Movt, 1974–97; Mensa, 1968–. Vice-Pres., British-Iranian Chamber of Commerce, 2002–06 (Chm., 2000–02). Freeman, City of London, 1989; Liveryman: Chartered Accountants' Co., 1993– (Mem., Ct of Assts, 1996–2011; Master, 2005–06); Dyers' Co., 2011–. *Recreations:* cookery, chess, cricket, languages, theatre, cinema, music. *Address:* 6 Buttsmead, Northwood, Middlesex HA6 2TL. *T:* (01923) 826675; Berry Head House, Victoria Road, Brixham, Devon TQ5 9AR. *Clubs:* Garrick, Pilgrims, Lord's Taverners; Brixham Rotary, Brixham Yacht.

HANLEY, Lynsey Emma; author; writer for The Guardian, since 2007; *b* Birmingham, 12 April 1976; *d* of Lloyd Hanley and Christine Hanley; *m* 2003, Jamie Robert Thomas O'Brien; one *s* one *d*. *Educ:* Queen Mary and Westfield Coll., London (BA Pols and Hist. 1997). Freelance journalist and reviewer, The Guardian, The Observer, New Statesman, Prospect, TLS, Daily Telegraph, 1996–. Hon. Res. Fellow, Lancaster Univ., 2009–12; Vis. Fellow, Liverpool John Moores Univ., 2013–. Hon. Res. Fellow, Lancaster Univ., 2014–. FRSA 2008. *Publications:* Estates: an intimate history, 2007, 3rd edn 2012. *Recreations:* walking, listening to music, friends and family, reading, cooking, concerts, sitting quietly. *Address:* c/o Caroline Dawnay, United Agents, 12–26 Lexington Street, W1F 0LE. *T:* (020) 3812 0800. *E:* sscard@unitedagents.co.uk.

HANMER, Sir (Wyndham Richard) Guy, 9th Bt *cr* 1774, of Hanmer, Flintshire; farmer and landowner; *b* 27 Nov. 1955; *s* of Sir John Wyndham Edward Hanmer, 8th Bt, and of Audrey Melissa, *d* of Major A. C. J. Congreve; *S* father, 2008; *m* 1986, Elizabeth Ann, *yr d* of Neil Taylor; two *s* one *d*. *Educ:* Wellington Coll. Army, Blues and Royals, 1975–81. *Recreation:* shooting. *Heir:* *s* Thomas Wyndham William Hanmer, *b* 10 May 1989. *Address:* The Stables, Bettisfield Park, Whitchurch, Shropshire SY13 2JZ. *T:* (01948) 710634.

HANNA, Brian Petrie, CBE 2000; *b* 15 Dec. 1941; *m* 1968, Sylvia Campbell; one *d*. *Educ:* Royal Belfast Academical Instn; Belfast Coll. of Technol.; Ulster Coll., NI Poly. (DMS). FCIEH. Belfast Corporation: Clerical Asst, City Treasurer's Dept, 1959; Health Department: Clerical Officer, 1960–61; Pupil Public Health Inspector, 1961–65; Public Health Inspector, 1965–73; Sen. Trng Advr, Food and Drink ITB, 1974–75; Principal Public Health Inspector, Eastern Gp Public Health Cttee, Castlereagh BC, 1975–77; Belfast City Council: Dep. Dir, 1978–84, Dir, 1984–92, Envmtl Health Services; Dir, Health and Envmtl Services, 1992–94; Chief Exec., 1994–2002. Royal Acad. of Engrg Vis. Prof. on Sustainable Develt, Ulster Univ., 2003–05. Member: UK Sustainable Develt Commn, 2000–04; NI Public Service Commn, 2007–10 and 2013–; Chm., NI Local Govt Staff Commn, 2005–10 and 2013–. Non-exec. Dir, Ivy Wood Properties Ltd, 2005–. Dep. Chm., NI Science Park, 2008–14. Pres., 2002–05, Vice-Pres., 2005–, Chartered Inst. of Envmtl Health; Vice Pres., Envmt Protection UK, 2007–11. Gov., Royal Belfast Academical Instn, 2001–; Mem. Senate, QUB, 2002–09; Chm. Bd, Envmtl Sustainability and Health Inst. (formerly Envmtl Health Sci. Inst.), Dublin Inst. of Technol., 2011–. Chm., NI Adv. Cttee, 2004–12, Trustee, 2009–11, British Council. CCMI (CIMgt 2001). Hon. FRSPH 2005. Hon. DSc (Econ) QUB, 2001. *Recreations:* apart from my family, the sport of hockey (Past Pres., Irish Hockey Union).

HANNA, Carmel; Member (SDLP) South Belfast, Northern Ireland Assembly, 1998–2010; *b* 26 April 1946; *d* of John and Mary McAleenan; *m* 1973, Eamon Hanna; one *s* three *d*. *Educ:* Our Lady's Grammar Sch., Newry; Belfast City Hosp. (SRN); Royal Maternity Hosp. (SCM). Staff nurse in hosps in Belfast (Accident and Emergency), Guernsey, and Dublin, 1967–73; Staff Nurse, Musgrave Park Hosp., 1984–93; Social Services, South and East Belfast HSS Trust, 1993–98. Mem. (SDLP) Belfast CC, 1997–2008. Northern Ireland Assembly: Minister for Employment and Learning, 2001–02; SDLP health spokesperson; Chair, Cttee on Standards and Privileges, 2007–10; Member: Health Cttee, 1998–10; Assembly and Exec. Review Cttee, 2007–10. Chm., All-Party Gp on Internat. Develt, 2000. *Recreations:* gardening, travel, Irish history, cooking. *Address:* 12 Bawnmore Road, Belfast BT9 6LA. *T:* (028) 9066 7577.

HANNA, Prof. David Colin, PhD; FRS 1998; Professor of Physics, 1988–2007, now Emeritus, and Deputy Director, Optoelectronics Research Centre, 1989–2007, University of Southampton; *b* 10 April 1941; *s* of James Morgan Hanna and Vera Elizabeth Hanna (*née* Hopkins); *m* 1968, Sarah Veronica Jane Heigham; two *s*. *Educ:* Nottingham High Sch.; Jesus Coll., Cambridge (BA 1962); Southampton Univ. (PhD 1967). University of Southampton: Lectr, Dept of Electronics, 1967–78; Sen. Lectr, 1978–84; Reader, Dept of Physics, 1984–88. Fellow, Winchester Coll., 2001–09. Consiglio Nazionale della Ricerca Vis. Fellow, Politecnico di Milano, 1971; Alexander von Humboldt Fellow, Univ. of Munich, 1978–79. Dir-at-Large, 1996, Fellow, 1998, Optical Soc. of America. Max Born Medal and Prize, German Physical Soc., 1993; Quantum Electronics and Optics Prize, Eur. Physical Soc., 2000; Alexander von Humboldt Res. Award, Alexander von Humboldt Foundn, 2000; Charles Hard Townes Award, Optical Soc. of Amer., 2003. *Publications:* Nonlinear Optics of Free Atoms and Molecules, 1979; more than 250 papers in learned jls on lasers and nonlinear optics. *Recreations:* walking, climbing, gardening, cooking, sailing, music, theatre, travel. *Address:* Optoelectronics Research Centre, University of Southampton, Southampton SO17 1BJ. *T:* (023) 8059 2150.

HANNAH, Prof. Leslie; Visiting Professor, London School of Economics, since 2007; *b* 15 June 1947; *s* of Arthur Hannah and Marie (*née* Lancashire); *m* 1984, Nuala Barbara Zahedieh (*née* Hockton) (marr. diss. 1998), *e d* of Thomas and Deirdre Hockton; one *s*, and two step *d*. *Educ:* Manchester Grammar Sch.; St John's and Nuffield Colleges, Oxford. MA, PhD, DPhil. Research Fellow, St John's Coll., Oxford, 1969–73; Lectr in economics, Univ. of Essex, 1973–75; Lectr in recent British economic and social history, Univ. of Cambridge, and Fellow and Financial Tutor, Emmanuel Coll., Cambridge, 1976–78; London School of Economics: Dir, Business History Unit, 1978–88; Prof. of Business Hist., 1982–97; Pro-Dir, 1995–97; Acting Dir, 1996–97; Dean, City Univ. Business Sch., subseq. Sir John Cass Business Sch., City of London, 1997–2000, Vis. Prof., 2000–03; Chief Exec., Ashridge Mgt Coll., 2000–03; Prof. of Economics, Univ. of Tokyo, 2004–07, 2012–13; Dir d'Etudes Associé, Ecole des Hautes Etudes en Scis Sociales, Paris, 2007. Vis. Prof., Harvard Univ., 1984–85. Director: NRG London Reinsurance, 1986–93; London Econs Ltd, 1991–2000. *Publications:* Rise of the Corporate Economy, 1976, 2nd edn 1983; (ed) Management Strategy and Business Development, 1976; (with J. A. Kay) Concentration in Modern Industry, 1977; Electricity before Nationalisation, 1979; Engineers, Managers and Politicians, 1982; Entrepreneurs and the Social Sciences, 1983; Inventing Retirement, 1986; (with M. Ackrill) Barclays, 2001; (with K. Wada) Invisible Hand Strikes Back, 2001; contribs to jls. *Recreation:* England. *Address:* 332 Lauderdale Tower, Barbican, EC2Y 8NA. *Club:* Reform.

HANNAH, His Honour William; a Circuit Judge, 1988–95; *b* 31 March 1929; *s* of William Bond Hannah and Elizabeth Alexandra Hannah; *m* 1950, Alma June Marshall; one *s* one *d*. *Educ:* Everton School, Notts. RAF 1947–52; Police Officer, 1952–77. Called to the Bar, Gray's Inn, 1970; in practice, NE Circuit, 1977–88; a Recorder, 1987–88; Resident Judge, Teesside, 1993–96; Dep. Chief Justice, Supreme Ct of St Helena, S Atlantic, 1996–2001. *Recreations:* golf, swimming, walking, theatre. *Address:* c/o New Court Chambers, 3 Broad Chare, Newcastle upon Tyne NE1 3DQ. *Club:* South Shields Golf.

HANNAM, Sir John (Gordon), Kt 1992; *b* 2 Aug. 1929; *s* of Thomas William and Selina Hannam; *m* 1st, 1956, Wendy Macartney; two *d*; 2nd, 1983, Mrs Vanessa Wauchope (*née* Anson). *Educ:* Yeovil Grammar Sch. Studied Agriculture, 1945–46. Served in: Royal Tank Regt (commissioned), 1947–48; Somerset LI (TA), 1949–51. Studied Hotel industry, 1950–52; Managing Dir, Hotels and Restaurant Co., 1952–61; Developed Motels, 1961–70; Chm., British Motels Fedn, 1967–74, Pres. 1974–80; Mem. Council, BTA, 1968–69; Mem. Economic Research Council, 1967–85. MP (C) Exeter, 1970–97. PPS to: Minister for Industry, 1972–74; Chief Sec., Treasury, 1974. Mem., Select Cttee on Procedure, 1993–97; Secretary: Cons. Parly Trade Cttee, 1971–72; All-Party Disablement Gp, 1974–92 (Co-Chm., 1992–97); 1922 Cttee, 1987–97; Mem., Govt Adv. Cttee on Transport for Disabled, 1983–97; Chairman: Anglo-Swiss Parly Gp, 1987–97; West Country Cons. Cttee, 1973–74, 1979–81; Cons. Party Energy Cttee, 1979–92; Arts and Leisure Standing Cttee, Bow Group, 1975–84; Vice-Chairman: Arts and Heritage Cttee, 1974–79; British Cttee of Internat. Rehabilitation, 1979–92; Parly Gp on Energy Studies, 1992–97 (Hon. Mem., 1997–). Captain: Lords and Commons Tennis Club, 1975–97; Lords and Commons Ski Club, 1977–82; Cdre, House of Commons Yacht Club, 1975. Mem., Snowdon Working Party on the Disabled, 1975–76; Chm. Trustees, Snowdon Awards Scheme, 1997–2012. Vice-President: Disablement Income Gp; Alzheimer's Soc.; Council, Action Medical Research (formerly Action Research for Crippling Diseases); Disabled Motorists Gp; Disabled Drivers Assoc.; Rehabilitation UK, 2005– (Bd Mem., 1995–2005). Member: Bd, Nat. Theatre, 1979–92; Glyndebourne Festival Soc.; Council, British Youth Opera, 1989–2008 (Chm., 1997–2008; Vice-Pres., 2008–). Hon. MA Open, 1986. *Recreations:* music (opera), theatre, sailing (anything), ski-ing (fast), Cresta tobogganing (foolish), gardening; county tennis and hockey (Somerset tennis champion, 1953), croquet. *Address:* 85 Bromfelde Road, SW4 6PP. *Clubs:* All England Lawn Tennis, International Lawn Tennis, Veterans Lawn Tennis Club of GB.

HANNAN, Daniel John; Member (C) South East Region, England, European Parliament, since 1999; *b* 1 Sept. 1971; *s* of late Hugh R. Hannan and Lavinia M. Hannan (*née* Moffat); *m* 2000, Sara Maynard; two *d*. *Educ:* Marlborough; Oriel Coll., Oxford (MA). Leader writer, Daily Telegraph, 1996–2008. Dir, European Res. Gp, 1994–99. *Publications:* Time for a Fresh Start in Europe, 1993; Britain in a Multi-Speed Europe, 1994; The Challenge of the East, 1996; A Guide to the Amsterdam Treaty, 1997; What if we vote No?, 2004; The Case for EFTA, 2005; Direct Democracy, 2006; (with D. Carswell) The Plan: twelve months to renew Britain, 2008; The New Road to Serfdom, 2010; Why America Shouldn't Copy Europe, 2011; A Doomed Marriage: Britain and the EU, 2012; How We Invented Freedom & Why It Matters, 2013. *Recreation:* Shakespeare. *Address:* (office) PO Box 99, Hassocks BN6 0DY. *Clubs:* Garrick, Pratt's.

HANNAN, Menna; *see* Richards, Menna.

HANNAY, family name of **Baron Hannay of Chiswick**.

HANNAY OF CHISWICK, Baron *cr* 2001 (Life Peer), of Bedford Park in the London Borough of Ealing; **David Hugh Alexander Hannay,** GCMG 1995 (KCMG 1986; CMG 1981); CH 2003; *b* 28 Sept. 1935; *s* of late Julian Hannay; *m* 1961, Gillian Rex; four *s*. *Educ:* Winchester; New Coll., Oxford (Hon. Fellow 2001). Foreign Office, 1959–60; Tehran, 1960–61; 3rd Sec., Kabul, 1961–63; 2nd Sec., FO, 1963–65; 2nd, later 1st Sec., UK Delegn to European Communities, Brussels, 1965–70; 1st Sec., UK Negotiating Team with European Communities, 1970–72; Chef de Cabinet to Sir Christopher Soames, Vice President of EEC, 1973–77; Head of Energy, Science and Space Dept, FCO, 1977–79; Head of Middle East Dept, FCO, 1979; Asst Under-Sec. of State (European Community), FCO, 1979–84; Minister, Washington, 1984–85; Ambassador and UK Permanent Rep. to Eur. Communities, Brussels, 1985–90; British Perm. Rep. to UN, 1990–95; retd from Diplomatic Service, 1995. British Govt Special Rep. for Cyprus, 1996–2003; Prime Minister's Personal Envoy to Turkey, 1998; EU Presidency Special Rep. for Cyprus, 1998. Member: EU Select Cttee, H of L, 2002–06, 2008–14 (Chm., Sub-Cttee for Home Affairs, 2010–14); Intergovtl Orgns Cttee, H of L, 2007–08; Cttee on the Arctic, H of L, 2014–15; Chm., All Party Parly Gp on UN, 2012– (Vice-Chm., 2005–11); Vice-Chm., All Party Parly Gp on EU, 2006–; Jt Convenor, All Party Parly Gp on Global Security and Non-Proliferation, 2008–; Mem. Exec., British-American Parly Gp, 2008–12; Member: Top Level Gp of Parliamentarians for Multilateral Nuclear Disarmament and Non-Proliferation, 2011–; European Leadership Network for Nuclear Disarmament and Non-Proliferation, 2013–. Mem., UN Sec.-General's High Level Panel on Threats, Challenges and Change, 2003–04. Chm., UNA of UK, 2006–11. Non-executive Director: Chime Communications, 1996–2006; Aegis, 2000–03; Mem., Ind. Adv. Panel, Tangguh, 2002–09; Mem., Bd, Salzburg Seminar, 2002–05; Mem., Adv. Bd, GPW, 2011–. Mem., Bd, Centre for European Reform, 1997–; Mem., Council of Britain in Europe, 1999–2005; Mem., Sen. European Experts Gp, 1999– (Chm., 2014–). Chm., Internat. Adv. Bd, EDHEC Business Sch., 2003–09; Mem., Internat. Adv. Bd, Judge Business Sch., Univ. of Cambridge, 2004–10. Gov., Ditchley Foundn, 2005–. Mem. Court and Council, 1998–, Pro-Chancellor, 2001–06, Birmingham Univ.; Mem. Council, Univ. of Kent, 2009–15. Patron, Wyndham Place Charlemagne Trust, 2009–. Hon. DLitt Birmingham, 2003. *Publications:* Cyprus: the search for a solution, 2004; New World Disorder: the UN after the Cold War – an insider's view, 2008; Britain's Quest for a Role: a diplomatic memoir from Europe to the UN, 2012. *Recreations:* travel, gardening, photography. *Address:* 3 The Orchard, W4 1JZ. *Club:* Travellers.

HANNAY, Prof. David Rainsford, MD, PhD; FRCGP, FFPH; Vice Lord-Lieutenant, District of Wigtown, Dumfries and Galloway, 2009–14; *b* London, 3 Jan. 1939; *s* of Ramsay and Margaret Rainsford Hannay; *m* 1963, Janet Mary Gilliat; three *s*. *Educ:* Winchester Coll.; Trinity Coll., Cambridge (BChir 1964; MB 1965; MA; MD 1982); Univ. of Glasgow (PhD 1975). FRCGP 1988. Glasgow University: Lectr, Dept of Community Medicine, 1968–75; Sen. Lectr, Dept of Gen. Practice, 1975–84; Principal in Gen. Practice, Newton Stewart, Wigtownshire, 1984–86; Prof. of Gen. Practice, Univ. of Sheffield, 1986–96, Prof. Emeritus,

1997; Principal in Gen. Practice, Newton Stewart, 1997–2004. Dir, Primary Care Res. Network, Dumfries and Galloway, 2000–03. Non-exec. Dir, Dumfries and Galloway NHS Bd, 2010–14. FFPH 1982. *Publications:* The Symptom Iceberg: a study of community health, 1979; Lecture Notes on Medical Sociology, 1988; contrib. papers to learned jls. *Recreations:* playing bagpipes, sailing. *Address:* Cuddyfield, Carsluith, Newton Stewart, Wigtownshire DG8 7DS.

HANNAY, Elizabeth Anne Scott; *see* Prescott-Decie, E. A. S.

HANNETT, John; General Secretary, Union of Shop, Distributive and Allied Workers, since 2004; *b* 23 June 1953; *s* of John and Mary Hannett; *m* 1979, Linda Sargeant; one *s* one *d*. *Educ:* St George's RC High Sch., Liverpool. Union of Shop, Distributive and Allied Workers: Area Organiser, 1985–90; Nat. Officer, 1990–97; Dep. Gen. Sec., 1997–2004. Member: Low Pay Commn, 2007–; Council, ACAS, 2010–. *Recreation:* football. *Address:* USDAW, 188 Wilmslow Road, Manchester M14 6LJ. *T:* (0161) 224 2804, *Fax:* (0161) 257 2566.

HANNIGAN, Robert Peter, CMG 2013; Director, Government Communications Headquarters, since 2014; *b* 1965. *Educ:* Wadham Coll., Oxford (MA). Northern Ireland Office: Dep. Dir of Communications, 2000–01; Dir of Communications, 2001–04; Associate Pol Dir, 2004–05; Dir Gen., Political, 2005–07; Security Advr to Prime Minister, and Hd of Security, Intelligence and Resilience, Cabinet Office, 2007–10; Dir Gen., Defence and Intelligence, FCO, 2010–14. *Address:* Government Communications Headquarters, Hubble Road, Cheltenham, Glos GL51 0EX.

HANNINGFIELD, Baron *cr* 1998 (Life Peer), of Chelmsford in the co. of Essex; **Paul Edward Winston White;** DL; farmer; Member (C), 1970–2011, and Leader, 1998–99 and 2001–10, Essex County Council; *b* 16 Sept. 1940; *s* of Edward Ernest William White and Irene Joyce Gertrude White (*née* Williamson). *Educ:* King Edward VI Grammar Sch., Chelmsford (Nuffield Scholarship). Chm., 1989–92, Leader, Cons. Gp, 2001–10, Essex CC. Chairman: Council, Local Educn Authorities, 1990–92; Eastern Area, FEFC, 1992–97. Dep. Chm., LGA, 1997–2001. Mem., EU Cttee of the Regions (Vice Pres., European People's Party, 1998; Vice Pres., Transport and Information Soc. Commn, 1998–2000). Mem. Ct, Essex Univ., 1980. DL Essex, 1991. *Publications:* many contribs to local govt jls. *Recreations:* gardening, wine and food, travel, walking the dog. *Address:* Pippins Place, Helmons Lane, West Hanningfield, Chelmsford, Essex CM2 8UW. *T:* (01245) 400229.

HANNON, Rt Rev. Brian Desmond Anthony; Bishop of Clogher, 1986–2001; *b* 5 Oct. 1936; *s* of late Ven. Arthur Gordon Hannon and of Hilda Catherine Stewart-Moore Hannon (*née* Denny); *m* 1964, Maeve Geraldine Audley (*née* Butler); three *s*. *Educ:* Mourne Grange Prep. School, Co. Down; St Columba's Coll., Co. Dublin; Trinity Coll., Dublin (BA Hons 1959, 1st Class Divinity Testimonium 1961). Deacon 1961, priest 1962; Diocese of Derry: Curate-Assistant, All Saints, Clooney, Londonderry, 1961–64; Rector of Desertmartin, 1964–69; Rector of Christ Church, Londonderry, 1969–82; RD of Londonderry, 1977–82; Diocese of Clogher: Rector of St Macartin's Cathedral, Enniskillen, 1982–86; Canon of Cathedral Chapter, 1983; Dean of Clogher, 1985. Chm., Council for Mission in Ireland, C of I, 1987–99. Pres., CMS (Ireland), 1990–96; Chm., Irish Council of Churches, 1992–94; Co-Chm., Irish Inter-Church Meeting, 1992–94; Mem., WCC Central Cttee, 1983–92. Chm. of Western (NI) Education and Library Bd, 1985–87 and 1989–91 (Vice-Chm., 1987–89 and 1991–93). Hon. MA TCD, 1962. *Publications:* (editor/author) Christ Church, Londonderry—1830 to 1980—Milestones, Ministers, Memories, 1980. *Recreations:* walking, music, travel, sport. *Address:* Drumconnis Top, 202 Mullaghmeen Road, Ballinamallard, Co. Fermanagh, N Ireland BT94 2DZ. *T:* (028) 6638 8557. *E:* bdah@btinternet.com.

HANNON, Richard Michael; racehorse trainer, 1970–2013; *b* 30 May 1945; *m* 1966, Josephine Ann McCarthy; two *s* four *d* (of whom two *s* one *d* are triplets). First trainer's licence, 1970; wins include: 2000 Guineas, 1973 (Mon Fils), 1987 (Don't Forget Me), 1990 (Tirol); Irish 2000 Guineas, 1987 (Don't Forget Me), 1990 (Tirol); leading Flat trainer, 1992, 2010, 2011, 2013; trained record number of winners (182), 1993 season. *Address:* East Everleigh Stables, Marlborough, Wilts SN8 3EY.

HANNS, Raquel; *see* Agnello, R.

HANRATTY, James Robert Anthony, RD 1987; Immigration Judge (formerly Adjudicator), 1997–2014; *b* 6 Feb. 1946; *s* of late Dr J. F. Hanratty, OBE, KSG, and Irene Hanratty (*née* Belton); *m* 1975, Pamela Hoare; one *s* two *d*. *Educ:* Stonyhurst Coll.; Coll. of Law. Admitted solicitor, UK 1970, Hong Kong 1982. Criminal Appeal Office, Royal Courts of Justice, 1971–74; Lawyer, LCD, H of L, 1974–81; Sen. Crown Counsel, Attorney Gen.'s Chambers, Hong Kong, 1981–85; Asst Sec., Hd, Judicial Appts Div., LCD, 1985–88; Administrator and Chief Exec., Royal Courts of Justice, 1988–91; Dep. Legal Advr, then Legal Advr, to British Side of Sino-British Liaison Gp on Handover of Hong Kong to China, Hong Kong, 1991–97. Marking Examr in Criminal Law, Law Soc., 1971–81. Pres., Council of Immigration Judges for Eng., Wales and Scotland, 2001–03. Mem. Cttee, Hong Kong Soc., 2008–13. Joined RNR as ordinary seaman, 1971; Lieut Comdr, 1994, retd. Member: RYA, 1990–; RNSA, 2002–. Pres., Stonyhurst Assoc., 2013–14. *Publications:* contrib. various articles to legal jls on internat. law aspects of the Hong Kong Handover and Immigration Law. *Recreations:* sailing, tennis, watching cricket, club life, family, standing on bridges and waving at trains. *E:* jrhanratty@btinternet.com. *Clubs:* Athenæum, Hurlingham (Cttee 2000–03); Royal Yacht Squadron; RNVR Yacht (Cdre, 2002–04); Royal Southampton Yacht; Royal Hong Kong Yacht; Deauville Yacht.

HANRATTY, Judith Christine, CVO 2008; OBE 2002; Chairman, Commonwealth Education Trust, since 2007 (Chairman, Commonwealth Institute, 2002–07); Director, Partner Re Ltd, since 2005; *b* Wellington, NZ, 16 Aug. 1943; *d* of late John Edward Hanratty and Joyce Hanratty. *Educ:* Chilton St James Sch., NZ; St Hilda's Collegiate Sch., NZ; Victoria Univ. of Wellington, NZ (LLB; LLM; LLD). Barrister: High Court of NZ, 1966; Supreme Court of Vic, Australia, 1980; Inner Temple, 1987. Co. Sec., BP plc, 1994–2003. Non-executive Director: BP Pension Trustees, 1992–2004; London Electricity plc, 1995–97; Charles Taylor plc, 2000–12; Partnerships UK plc, 2001–05; BSI, 2002–05. Non-exec. Dir, England Golf, 2011–. Member: Insce Brokers' Registration Council, 1993–98; Competition (formerly Monopolies and Mergers) Commn, 1997–2003; Takeover Panel, 1997–2003; Council, Lloyd's of London, 1998–2009; Gas and Electricity Mkts Authy, 2004–10. Fellow, Lucy Cavendish Coll., Cambridge, 1998. FRSA 1994. *Recreations:* golf, croquet. *Address:* 36 Sloane Court West, SW3 4TB. *E:* judith@sloanecourtwest.com; 341 Fergusson Drive, Upper Hutt 5018, New Zealand. *Clubs:* Athenæum, Wellington, Roehampton; Royal Wimbledon Golf; Royal Wellington Golf.

HANRATTY, Mary Bridget, CBE 2003; Director of Nursing and Midwifery Education, Beeches Management Centre, Dungannon, Northern Ireland, 1997–2006; *b* 15 Nov. 1943; *d* of Edward Holland and late Rose Anne Holland; *m* 1967, (Malachy) Oliver Hanratty; two *s*. *Educ:* BA, MSc. RGN; RMN; RNT. Dir, Nurse Educn, 1991–97; involved in professional regulation of nurses, midwives and health visitors. Mem., 1989–2002, Vice-Pres., 1998–2002, UKCC; Mem., NMC, 2001 (Vice-Pres., 2001–05). *Recreations:* foreign travel, crosswords, entertaining.

HANRETTY, Gerald Francis; QC (Scot.) 2002; *b* 13 April 1958; *s* of Peter Hanretty and Margaret Hanretty (*née* Soutar); *m* 1979, Moira Walker; two *s* one *d*. *Educ:* St Mirin's Acad., Paisley; Univ. of Glasgow (LLB). Solicitor, 1980–89; admitted Advocate, 1990; Advocate Depute, 2001–03; Chairman (part-time): Mental Health Tribunal for Scotland, 2005–; Police Appeals Tribunal, 2010–13. *Recreations:* family interests, reading, Formula One racing. *Address:* c/o Advocates' Library, Parliament House, Edinburgh EH1 1RF.

HÄNSCH, Dr Klaus; Member (SPD), European Parliament, 1979–2009 (President, 1994–97); *b* Sprottau, Silesia, 15 Dec. 1938; *s* of Willi Hänsch and Erna (*née* Sander); *m* 1969, Ilse Hoof. *Educ:* Univ. of Cologne (degree in Pol Sci. 1965); Univ. of Paris; Univ. of Berlin (PhD 1969). Escaped from Silesia to Schleswig-Holstein, 1945. Mil. Service, 1959–60. Res. Asst, Otto Suhr Inst., Free Univ. of Berlin, 1966–68; Ed., Dokumente, 1968–69; Advr to Rep. of FRG under Franco-German Treaty, 1969–70; Press Officer, 1970–79 and expert advr, 1977–79, to Minister for Sci. and Res., N Rhine/Westphalia; Lectr, Duisburg Univ., 1976–94 (Hon. Prof., 1994). European Parliament: Member: Foreign Affairs and Security and other cttees, 1979–94; For. Affairs, Human Rights, Common Security and Defence Policy Cttee, 1997; Vice-Chm., Party of Eur. Socialists Gp, 1997; Adv. Mem., Bundestag Cttee on EC issues, 1985–95; Chm., Delegn for relns with US, 1987–89. Member: SPD, 1964–; ÖTV (Union of Tspt and Public Service Workers). *Publications:* Kontinent der Hoffnungen: mein europäisches leben, 2010; pamphlets, contribs to books, and many articles on politics and society in France and on issues relating to unification of Europe and European security policy.

HÄNSCH, Prof. Theodor Wolfgang, PhD; Director, Department of Laserspectroscopy, Max Planck Institute for Quantum Optics, since 1986; Carl Friedrich von Siemens Professor of Physics, Ludwig Maximilians University, Munich, since 2007 (Professor of Physics, since 1986); *b* Heidelberg, 30 Oct. 1941. *Educ:* Helmholtz Gymnasium, Heidelberg; Univ. of Heidelberg (Physics Dip. 1966; PhD summa cum laude 1969). Asst Prof., Inst. of Applied Physics, Univ. of Heidelberg, 1969–70; Stanford University: NATO Postdoctoral Fellow, 1970–72; Associate Prof. of Physics, 1972–75; Prof. of Physics, 1975–86; Consulting Prof., 1988–; Exec. Dir, Max Planck Inst. for Quantum Optics, 1993–96 and 2003–04; Chm., Physics Dept, Ludwig Maximilians Univ., 2001–02. Visiting Professor: Coll. de France, 1978; Univ. of Kyoto, 1979; Univ. of Florence, 1979, 1995–; Fudan Univ., Shanghai, 1982; Ecole Normale Supérieure, Paris, 1992; Gordon Moore Dist. Schol., CIT, Pasadena, 2001. Hon. Professor: Nat. Chiang Tung Univ., HsinChu, Taiwan, 2010; Univ. System of Taiwan, 2010. Member, Editorial Board: Applied Physics B, 1983–; Physics in Perspective, 1997–; Springer Series in Optical Scis, 1998–; Laser Physics Rev., 2004–; Mem., Adv. Cttee, Physics Today, 1985–95. Fellow: APS, 1973; Optical Soc. of America, 1973. Member: Amer. Acad. Arts and Scis, 1983; Bavarian Acad. Arts and Scis, 1991; Berlin-Brandenburg Acad. Scis, 2005. Hon. Dr rer. nat. Free Univ., Berlin, 2006; Hon. Dr Bar Ilan Univ., Tel Aviv, 2008; Hon. DSc St Andrews, 2006. Awards include: Alexander von Humboldt Sen. US Scientist Award, 1977; Michelson Medal, Franklin Inst., Philadelphia, 1986; Einstein Medal for Laser Sci., 1995; Arthur L. Schawlow Prize for Laser Sci., APS, 1996; Arthur L. Schawlow Award and Life Mem., Laser Inst. of America, 2000; Quantum Electronics and Optics Prize, Eur. Physical Soc., 2001; Alfried Krupp Prize for Sci., 2002; I. I. Rabi Award, IEEE, 2005; Frederic Ives Medal, Optical Soc. of America, 2005; Otto-Hahn Prize for Chemistry and Physics, 2005; (jtly) Nobel Prize in Physics, 2005; Carl Friedrich von Siemens Prize and Chair, 2006; Ioannes Marcus Marci Medal, Czech Spectroscopic Soc., 2006; Rudolf Diesel Gold Medal, German Inst. of Interventions, 2006; Großes Bundesverdienstkreuz mit Stern, 2006; Medal, Acad. of Scis of Czech Republic, 2007; James Joyce Award, UCD, 2009; Sayling Wen Excellent Lect. Award, Nat. Central Univ., Taiwan, 2010; Wilhelm Exner Medal, Wilhelm Exner Foundn, Vienna, 2012; Fitzpatrick Pioneer Award, Duke Univ., 2015. Hon. Citizen, Florence, Italy, 2006. Order of Merit: Germany, 2003; Bavaria, 2003 (Maximiliansorden, Constitutional Medal in Gold, 2010); Italy, 2006 (Grand Officer Cross); for Sciences and Arts (Germany), 2008. *Publications:* approx. 580 articles. *Address:* c/o Gabriele Gschwendtner (Manager and Personal Consultant), Faculty of Physics, Ludwig Maximilians University, Schellingstrasse 4/III, H327/H 328, 80799 Munich, Germany. *T:* (89) 21803212; (mobile) 01741 1931522, *Fax:* (89) 285192. *E:* t.w.haensch@physik.uni.muenchen.de, t.w.haensch@lmu.de.

HANSELL, Prof. David Matthew, MD; FRCP, FRCR; FRSM; Professor of Thoracic Imaging, Imperial College School of Medicine, since 1998; Consultant Radiologist, Royal Brompton Hospital, since 1989 (Director, Department of Radiology, 1992–95 and 2004–14); *b* London, 3 April 1957; *s* of Peter Hansell and Jean Hansell (*née* Nicol); *m* 1981, Mary Anne Gadsden; three *d*. *Educ:* Framlingham Coll.; King's Coll., London and Westminster Hosp. Med. Sch. (MB BS 1981; MD 1997). MRCP 1984, FRCP 1999; FRCR 1987. FRSM 2011 (DipABRSM 2004, LRSM 2006). Registrar and Sen. Registrar in Diagnostic Radiol., Westminster Hosp., 1984–88. Vis. Asst Prof., Dept of Radiological Scis, UCLA, 1989. Academic Hd, Lung Imaging Res. Team, Nat. Heart and Lung Inst., 1994–96. Sen. Investigator, NIHR, 2013–. Pres., Eur. Soc. of Thoracic Imaging, 2005; Pres., Fleischner Soc., 2012–13. Ed., Clinical Radiology, 2002–06; Associate Ed., Radiology (USA), 2000–03. RCR Gold Medal, 2015. *Publications:* (jtly) Imaging of Diseases of the Chest, 1990, 5th edn 2010; numerous chapters and over 300 papers on all aspects of thoracic imaging; contrib. to N Amer. and Eur. guidelines on diffuse lung diseases. *Recreations:* baroque recorders and traverso flute, looking at London plane trees. *Address:* Department of Radiology, Royal Brompton Hospital, Sydney Street, SW3 6NP. *T:* (020) 7351 8034. *E:* davidhansell@rbht.nhs.uk. *Club:* Athenæum.

HANSEN, Alan David; football pundit, BBC, 1992–2014; *b* 13 June 1955; *s* of John and Anne Hansen; *m* 1980, Janette Rhymes; one *s* one *d*. *Educ:* Lornshill Acad. Professional footballer, Liverpool FC, 1977–91: League Champions, 1979, 1980, 1982, 1983, 1984, 1986, 1988, 1990; Capt., FA Cup winning team, 1986, 1988; winners: European Cup, 1978, 1981, 1984; League Cup, 1981, 1982, 1983, 1984. Presenter: Football's Dream Factory, BBC, 2001; Club or Country, BBC, 2003; Life After Football, BBC, 2005. Football columnist, Daily Telegraph, 2002–. *Publications:* Tall, Dark and Hansen, 1988; Matter of Opinion, 1999. *Address:* c/o Jon Holmes Media Ltd, 3 Wine Office Court, EC4A 3BY. *Clubs:* Hillside Golf; Southport and Birkdale Cricket.

HANSEN, Diana Jill; Director, Somerset House Trust, 2002–05; *b* 24 March 1948. *Educ:* Univ. of Sussex (MA 2010). HM Treasury, 1969–89; Dir, VAT Control, and a Comr, HM Customs and Excise, 1989–91; Asst Under-Sec. of State, Air, 1992, Finance, 1993, MoD (PE), Programmes, 1994, MoD; Comd Sec., HQ Land Comd, 1998–2002.

HANSEN, Prof. Jean-Pierre, DèS; FRS 2002; Professor of Theoretical Chemistry, 1997–2007, now Emeritus, and Fellow of Corpus Christi College, since 1997, University of Cambridge; *b* 10 May 1942; *s* of late Georges Hansen and Simone Flohr; *m* 1971, Martine Bechet; one *d*. *Educ:* Athénée Grand-Ducal de Luxembourg; Univ. de Liège (Licence en Sciences Physiques, 1964); Univ. de Paris (DèS 1969). CChem, FRSC 1998. Chargé de recherche, CNRS, France, 1967–73; Prof. of Physics, Univ. Pierre et Marie Curie, Paris, 1973–87; Directeur Adjoint, 1987–93, Prof. and Hd of Dept of Physics, 1987–97, Ecole Normale Supérieure, Lyons. Miller Prof., Univ. of Calif at Berkeley, 1992. Mem., Inst. Universitaire de France, 1992–97. Hon. Dr Liège, 2008. Grand Prix de l'Etat, Académie des Sciences, Paris, 1990; Prix Spécial, Soc. Française de Physique, 1998; Liquid Matter Prize, Eur. Physical Soc., 2005; Rumford Medal, Royal Soc., 2006; Grand Prix des Scis Physiques, Institut Grand-Ducal, Luxembourg, 2010; Berni J. Alder Prize, CECAM, 2013. Chevalier de l'Ordre de la Couronne de Chêne (Luxembourg), 1997. *Publications:* (jtly) Theory of Simple Liquids, 1976, 4th edn 2013; (ed jtly) Liquids, Freezing and the Glass Transition, 1991; (jtly) Basic Concepts for Simple and Complex Liquids, 2003; papers in internat. jls. *Recreations:* history of art, classical music, hill walking. *Address:* Department of Chemistry, Lensfield Road, Cambridge CB2 1EW. *T:* (01223) 336377.

HANSEN, Hon. Sir John (William), KNZM 2009 (DCNZM 2008); a Judge, High Court of New Zealand, 1995–2008; Executive Judge, South Island, 1997–2008; Senior Puisne Judge, 2005–08; *b* Fairlie, NZ, 11 May 1944; *s* of William John and Jane Hansen; *m* 1966, Ann Porter; one *s* one *d*. *Educ:* Wakari Prim. Sch., Dunedin; Dunedin North Intermediate Sch., Dunedin; Otago Boys' High Sch., Dunedin; Univ. of Otago (LLB 1968). Admitted solicitor, 1966, called to the Bar, 1967, Supreme Court of NZ, admitted solicitor and called to the Bar, Supreme Court of WA, 1985; Clerk, Collier & Taylor, Dunedin, 1966; Solicitor, Aspinall, Joel & Co., Dunedin, 1967; Barrister and Solicitor, John E. Farry, Dunedin, 1969; Partner, John E. Farry & Hansen, Dunedin, 1969–79; Hong Kong Judiciary, 1979–88: variously Magistrate, Coroner, Dist Court Judge, Family Court Judge, Master of the Supreme Court; High Court of New Zealand: Master, 1988; Temp. Judge, 1993–95; Ct of Appeals Judge, Solomon Is and Western Samoa, 2010–. Associate Mem., Shortland Chambers, 2010–. Mem., Rulings Panel, Gas Industry Co. Ltd, 2009–; Chm., Legal Services Agency, 2009–11; Consultant, Legal Issues Centre, Otago Univ., 2010–. Chm., Dunedin (formerly Dunedin Venues) Mgt Ltd, 2010–. Foundn Pres., Otago Br., NZ Legal Assoc. Trustee: Canterbury Youth Develt Trust, 2009–; Christchurch Casino Charitable Trust, 2009–; Canterbury Cricket Trust, 2009–. Chair, Red Cross Christchurch Earthquake Commn, 2011–. Manager: Hong Kong Cricket XI to Malaysia and Singapore, 1983, to ICC Associate Mems Trophy, UK, 1986; NZ Team, Hong Kong Internat. Cricket Sixes Tournament, 2003; Member: Code of Conduct Commn, ICC, 2007–10; Bd, NZ Cricket, 2009–. Internat. Rugby Bd Appeals Officer, 2009–; Mem., NZ RFU Appeals Council, 2009–. Capt. of Cricket, Kowloon Cricket Club, Hong Kong; Pres., Willows Cricket Club, Christchurch, 2003–. Former music reviewer, South China Morning Post, Hong Kong; book reviewer, Christchurch Press. NZ Medal, 1990. *Publications:* contribs to various legal jls. *Recreations:* Rugby, cricket, hiking, reading, book reviewing, music, poetry, law reform, cooking, wine. *Address:* Totara, Wolffs Road, RD6, Rangiora 7476, New Zealand. *T:* (3) 3125843. *E:* totaraa@xtra.co.nz. *Clubs:* MCC, London New Zealand Cricket; Valley Peace Cricket, The Willows Cricket (Christchurch, NZ).

HANSENNE, Michel; Member (Christian Social Party), European Parliament, 1999–2004; *b* 23 March 1940; *s* of Henri and Charlier Georgette Hansenne; *m* 1978, Mme Gabrielle Vanlandschoot; one *s* one *d*. *Educ:* Liège Univ. (Dr Law 1962; degree in Econs and Finance, 1967). Research work, Univ. of Liège, 1962–72. Mem. Belgian Parliament, 1974–89; Minister: for French Culture, 1979–81; for Employment and Labour, 1981–88; for Civil Service, 1988–89; Dir-Gen., ILO, 1989–99. Mem., EPP Gp, EP, 1999–2004. *Publications:* Emploi, les scénarios du possible, 1985; Un garde-fou pour la mondialisation: le BIT dans l'après-guerre froide, 1999; articles in national and international jls. *Address:* 28 rue des Deux Eglises, 4120 Rotheux-Rimière, Neupré, Belgium.

HANSFORD, John Edgar, CB 1982; Under-Secretary, Defence Policy and Matériel Group, HM Treasury, 1976–82, retired; *b* 1 May 1922; *s* of Samuel George Hansford, ISO, MBE, and Winifred Louise Hansford; *m* 1947, Evelyn Agnes Whitehorn (*d* 2005); one *s*. *Educ:* Whitgift Middle Sch., Croydon. Clerical Officer, Treasury, 1939. Served War of 1939–45: Private, Royal Sussex Regt, 1940; Lieutenant, Royal Fusiliers, 1943; served in: Africa, Mauritius, Ceylon, India, Burma, on secondment to King's African Rifles; demobilised, 1946. Exec. Officer, Treasury, 1946–50; Higher Exec. Officer, Regional Bd for Industry, Leeds, 1950–52; Exchange Control, Treasury, 1952–54; Agricultural Policy, Treasury, 1954–57; Sen. Exec. Officer, and Principal, Defence Div., Treasury, 1957–61; Principal, Social Security Div., Treasury, 1961–66; Public Enterprises Div., 1966–67; Overseas Develt Div., 1967–70; Asst Sec., Defence Policy and Matériel Div., Treasury, 1970–76; Under-Sec. in charge of Gp, 1976. *Recreations:* gardening, motoring.

HANSFORD, Peter George, CEng, FREng, FICE; FAPM; President, Institution of Civil Engineers, 2010–11; Chief Construction Adviser to UK Government, since 2012; *b* Basingstoke, 4 March 1954; *s* of Leonard George Hansford and Avis Maud Hansford; *m* 1977, Pamela Wendy Baker; one *s* one *d*. *Educ:* Queen Mary's Sch., Basingstoke; Univ. of Nottingham (BSc Civil Engrg 1975); Cranfield Sch. of Mgt (MBA 1986). CEng 1980; FICE 1992; FAPM 2006; FREng 2013. Sen. Engr, Amey Roadstone Construction, 1975–81; Resident Engr, Maunsell Consultants Asia, 1981–85; Man. Dir, Nichols Gp, 1986–99; Exec. Dir, Infrastructure, Strategic Rail Authy, 2000–02; Partner, Gardiner & Theobald, 2003–04; Exec. Dir, Nichols Gp, 2004–12. Non-exec. Chm., Thomas Telford Ltd, 2008–09. Chm., Engrs Without Borders, 2012– (Trustee, 2010–). Mem., Expert Witness Inst., 2009. FRSA 2004; MInstD; CCMI 2011. Hon. FICES 2014. Hon. LLD Nottingham, 2014. *Recreations:* golf, watching Rugby, active in village community. *Address:* Institution of Civil Engineers, One Great George Street, Westminster, SW1P 3AA. *T:* (020) 7222 7722, *Fax:* (020) 7222 7500.

HANSJEE, Anil; Partner, mojo.capital, since 2015; *b* London, 6 Sept. 1967; *s* of Raman Hansjee and Lillian Hansjee; *m* 2008, Carina Christiansen; one *s*. *Educ:* Rygaards Internat. Sch., Copenhagen; Gammel Hellerup Gymnasium; Univ. of Edinburgh (BSc Hons Computer Sci. and Artificial Intelligence 1990); London Business Sch. (MSc Finance 1997). Consultant, Price Waterhouse, 1990–91; software engr, Swiss Bank Corp., 1992–94; Vice Pres., IT, 1994–97, Associate, 1997–2000, Chase Manhattan; Vice Pres., Bear Stearns, 2000–01; Principal, IDG Ventures, 2002–06; Dir, GP Bullhound, 2006; Hd, Corporate Develt, EMEA, Google, 2006–11; Sen. Industrial Advr, EQT, 2011–13; Co-founder and Partner, Firestartr.co, 2012–; Chief Digital Investment Officer, Modern Times Gp, 2013–15. Member, Board: Shazam, 2005–06; Fon, 2006–11; Sine Wave Co., 2011–13; StoryBricks, 2011–14; Culture Label, 2011–14; RollUp Media, 2011–13; Zattikka, 2012–13; Splay Sverige AB, 2013–15; Investinor, 2013–. Advisor: Seedcamp, 2008–13; Badoo, 2011–13; Bookingbug, 2011–; Digital Vega, 2011–; Worldwide Computer Co., 2011–14; Creandum, 2011–13; Lepe Partners, 2011–13; MCI Funds, 2011–12; Peak Labs, 2012–14; ClusterHQ, 2012–14; Trustev, 2013–. Mem. Bd, Policy and Public Affairs, BCS, 2010–12. FBCS 2007. Hon. Dr Computing Kingston, 2011. *Recreations:* running, football, film, art, French cuisine. *E:* anil@hansjee.net. *Club:* Chelsea Football.

HANSON, Brian John Taylor, CBE 1996; Joint Secretary, Panel of Reference of the Anglican Communion, 2005–08; Registrar and Legal Adviser to General Synod of Church of England, 1975–2001; Joint Principal Registrar, Provinces of Canterbury and York, 1980–2001; Registrar, Convocation of Canterbury, 1982–2001; *b* 23 Jan. 1939; *o s* of Benjamin John Hanson and Gwendoline Ada Hanson (*née* Taylor); *m* 1972, Deborah Mary Hazel, *yr d* of Lt-Col R. S. P. Dawson, OBE; two *s* three *d*. *Educ:* Hounslow Coll.; Law Society's Coll. of Law; Univ. of Wales (LLM 1994). Solicitor (admitted 1963) and ecclesiastical notary; in private practice, Wilson Houlder & Co., 1963–65; Solicitor with Church Comrs, 1965–99; Asst Legal Advr to General Synod, 1970–75; Dir of Legal Services, Archbishops' Council, 1999–2001. Reviewer, Commn for Health Improvement, 2001–04; Mem., Healthcare Commn Appeals Panel, 2005–09. Mem., Notaries Public Disciplinary Tribunal, 2001–. An Assessor to Archbp of Canterbury under the Clergy Discipline Measure, 2011–. Member: Legal Adv. Commn of General Synod, 1980–2001 (Sec., 1970–86); Gen. Council, Ecclesiastical Law Soc., 1987–2003. Chm., Chichester Dio. Bd of Patronage, 1998–2013; Vice-Pres., Chichester Diocesan Synod, 2001–. Lay Canon, 2003–12, Lay Canon Emeritus, 2012–, Gibraltar Cathedral, Dio. in Europe. Pres., Soc. for Maintenance of the Faith, 1999–. Guardian, Nat. Shrine of Our Lady of Walsingham, 1984–; Fellow, Corp. of SS Mary and Nicholas (Woodard Schools), 1987–; Member Council: St Luke's Hosp. for the Clergy, 1985–2001 (Archbishop's Nominee, St Luke's Res. Foundn, 1998–2006); Chichester Cath., 2000–. Governor: St Michael's Sch., Burton Park, 1987–94; Pusey House, Oxford, 1993–2005 (Vice-Pres., 2005–); Quainton Hall Sch., 1994–2005. Warden of the Lower Liberty, St Andrew, Holborn, 2002–13, now Churchwarden Emeritus. Freeman, City of London, 1991; Liveryman, Co. of Glaziers and Painters of Glass, 1992–. FRSA 1996; FInstD 1998. DCL Lambeth, 2001. *Publications:* (ed) The Canons of the Church of England, 2nd edn 1975, 5th edn 1993; (ed) The Opinions of the Legal Advisory Commission, 6th edn 1985; (ed) Atkin's Court Forms, ecclesiastical vol., 1992, 2nd edn 1996; (jtly) Moore's Introduction to English Canon Law, 3rd edn 1992. *Recreations:* the family, gardening, genealogy. *Address:* Garden Cottage, Wappingthorn Farm Lane, Steyning, W Sussex BN44 3AG. *T:* (01903) 812214.

HANSON, Sir (Charles) Rupert (Patrick), 4th Bt *cr* 1918, of Fowey, Cornwall; Revenue Assistant, HM Inspector of Taxes, 1993–2010; *b* 25 June 1945; *s* of Sir Charles John Hanson, 3rd Bt and late Patricia Helen (*née* Brind; subseq. Mrs Miéville); *S* father, 1996; *m* 1977, Wanda Julia, *d* of Don Arturo Larrain, Santiago, Chile; one *s*. *Educ:* Eton Coll.; Polytech. of Central London. BA (CNAA) Modern Langs; Dip. in Technical and Specialised Trans. Technical, legal and commercial translator, 1977–83; TEFL (part-time), 1981–83; voluntary charity worker, 1984–85; Inland Revenue, then HMRC, 1986–2010. *Recreations:* classical music, writing poetry, tennis, walking. *Heir:* *s* Alexis Charles Hanson, *b* 25 March 1978.

HANSON, Christopher John; a Deputy District Judge (Civil), since 1998; a Judge of the Upper Tribunal (Immigration and Asylum Chamber) (formerly Senior Immigration Judge, Asylum and Immigration Tribunal), since 2009; *b* Fulford, York, 17 Sept. 1960; *m* 1985, Moira Tonkins; one *s* one *d*. *Educ:* Gravesend Co. Grammar Sch. for Boys; Poly. of Wales (BA Hons Law). Admitted as solicitor, 1987; in practice as solicitor, 1987–2002; Immigration Judge, 2002–08; Designated Immigration Judge, Asylum and Immigration Tribunal, 2008–09. *Recreations:* walking, cycling, athletics, spending time with my family. *Address:* Upper Tribunal (Immigration and Asylum Chamber), Field House, 15 Bream's Buildings, EC4A 1DZ. *E:* christopher.hanson@judiciary.gsi.gov.uk.

HANSON, Rt Hon. David (George); PC 2007; MP (Lab) Delyn, since 1992; *b* 5 July 1957; *s* of late Brian George Hanson and of Glenda Doreen (*née* Jones); *m* 1986, Margaret Rose Mitchell; two *s* two *d*. *Educ:* Verdin Comprehensive, Winsford, Ches.; Hull Univ. (BA Hons, PGCE). Vice-Pres., Hull Univ. Students' Union, 1978–79. Management trainee, Co-op. Union/Plymouth Co-op. Soc., 1980–82; with Spastics Soc., 1982–89; Dir, RE-SOLV (Soc. for Prevention of Solvent Abuse), 1989–92. Councillor: Vale Royal BC, 1983–91 (Leader, Lab Gp and Council, 1989–91); Northwich Town Council, 1987–91. Contested (Lab): Eddisbury, 1983; Delyn, 1987; Cheshire W (European Parlt), 1984. PPS to Chief Sec. to HM Treasury, 1997–98; an Asst Govt Whip, 1998–99; Parly Under-Sec. of State, Wales Office, 1999–2001; PPS to the Prime Minister, 2001–05; Minister of State: NI Office, 2005–07; MoJ, 2007–09; Home Office, 2009–10; Shadow Treasury Minister, 2010–11; Shadow Minister for Police, 2011–13, for Immigration, 2013–15. *Recreations:* football, family, cinema. *Address:* House of Commons, SW1A 0AA. *T:* (020) 7219 5064; (constituency office) 64 Chester Street, Flint, Flintshire CH6 5DH. *T:* (01352) 763159.

HANSON, Sir John (Gilbert), KCMG 1995; CBE 1979; Warden, Green College, Oxford, 1998–2006; *b* 16 Nov. 1938; *s* of Gilbert Fretwell Hanson and Gladys Margaret (*née* Kay); *m* 1962, Margaret Clark (*d* 2003); two *s* (and one *s* decd). *Educ:* Manchester Grammar Sch.; Wadham Coll., Oxford (BA Lit. Hum. 1961, MA 1964; Hon. Fellow, 1997). Asst Principal, WO, 1961–63; British Council: Madras, India, 1963–66; ME Centre for Arab Studies, Lebanon, 1966–68; Rep., Bahrain, 1968–72; Dep. Controller, Educn and Science Div., 1972–75; Representative, Iran, and Counsellor (Cultural) British Embassy, Tehran, 1975–79; Controller, Finance Div., 1979–82; RCDS, 1983; Head, British Council Div. and Minister (Cultural Affairs), British High Commn, New Delhi, 1984–88; Dep. Dir-Gen., 1988–92; Dir-Gen., 1992–98. Patron, GAP, 1989–98. Chm., Supervisory Bd, Eur. Care Gp, 2008–11. Member: Franco-British Council, 1992–98; UK-Japan 2000 Gp, 1993–98; Council, VSO, 1993–98; Chm., Bahrain-British Foundn, 1997–2005. Pres., British Skin Foundn, 1997–2002. Member Governing Council: Soc. for S Asian Studies, 1989–93; SOAS, 1991–99; Univ. of London, 1996–99. Trustee: Charles Wallace (India) Trust, 1998–2000; Research in Specialist and Elderly Care, 2008–12. FRSA 1993; CCMI (CIMgt 1993). Hon. Freeman, Girdlers' Co., 2010. Hon. Fellow: St Edmund's Coll., Cambridge, 1998; Green Coll., Oxford, 2006; Green Templeton Coll., Oxford, 2008. Hon. DLitt Oxford Brookes, 1995; Hon. Dr: Humberside, 1996; Greenwich, 1996. *Recreations:* books, music, sport, travel. *Address:* c/o Green Templeton College, Oxford OX2 6HG. *Clubs:* MCC; Gymkhana (Chennai).

HANSON, Sir Rupert; *see* Hanson, Sir C. R. P.

HANSON, Samantha; *see* Bond, S.

HANWORTH, 3rd Viscount *cr* 1936, of Hanworth, co. Middlesex; **(David) Stephen (Geoffrey) Pollock;** Bt 1922; Baron Hanworth 1926; Professor of Econometrics and Computational Statistics, University of Leicester, since 2007; *b* 16 Feb. 1946; *er s* of 2nd Viscount Hanworth and Isolda Rosamond, *yr d* of Geoffrey Parker; *S* father, 1996; *m* 1968, Elizabeth Liberty, *e d* of Lawrence Vambe, MBE; two *d*. *Educ:* Wellington Coll.; Guildford Tech. Coll.; Sussex Univ. (BA); Univ. of Southampton (MSc); Univ. of Amsterdam (DEcon). Lectr, Dept of Economics, 1971–92, Reader in Econometrics, 1992–2007, QMC, then QMW, later QMUL. Elected Mem. (Lab), H of L, 2011. *Heir:* *nephew* Harold William Charles Pollock, *b* 30 April 1988.

HAPGOOD, Mark Bernard; QC 1994; *b* 2 April 1951; *m* 1978, Linda Fieldsend; two *d*; *m* 2008, Arzu Kebes; two *s*. *Educ:* Nottingham Univ. (LLB). Called to the Bar, Gray's Inn, 1979, Bencher, 2003. *Publications:* (ed) Paget's Law of Banking, 10th edn 1989 to 13th edn 2007; (contrib.) Halsbury's Laws of England, vol. 3 (1): Banking, reissue, 2005; Bills of Exchange, vol. 4 (1), reissue, 2002. *Recreations:* running, 16th/17th century financial documents. *Address:* Brick Court Chambers, 7–8 Essex Street, WC2R 3LD. *Club:* St Enedoc Golf.

HAPPÉ, Prof. Francesca Gabrielle, PhD; FBA 2014; Professor of Cognitive Neuroscience, since 2008, and Director and Head of Department, MRC Social, Genetic and Developmental Psychiatry Centre, since 2012, Institute of Psychiatry, Psychology and Neuroscience (formerly Institute of Psychiatry), King's College London; *b* Cambridge, 2 June 1967; *d* of Peter Bernard Happé and Gabrielle Happé (*née* Forrest); partner, Daniel Richard Gordon; two *s* one *d*. *Educ:* Burgess Hill Sch.; Corpus Christi Coll., Oxford (BA 1st Cl. Hons Exptl Psychol. 1988); University Coll. London (PhD Psychol. 1991). MRC Studentship, 1988–91, Res. Scientist, 1991–95, MRC Cognitive Develt Unit, London; Temp. Lectr in Develtl Psychol., Cambridge Univ., 1993 and 2001; Human Frontiers Sci. Prog. Fellow, Dept of Psychol. and Aphasia Res. Centre, Boston Coll., 1995–96; Sen. Scientist in Cognitive Psychol., 1996–2000, Reader in Cognitive Neurosci., 2000–08, MRC Social, Genetic and Develtl Psychiatry Centre, Inst. of Psychiatry, KCL. Co-founder, Nat. Forum for Neurosci. and Special Educn, 2012–. Pres., Internat. Soc. for Autism Res., 2013–15 (Mem. Bd, 2012–). Member: BPsS 1989; Assoc. for Child and Adolescent Mental Health, 1990–; EPsS 1992. Spearman Medal, BPsS, 1998; EPsS Prize, 1999; Rosalind Franklin Award, Royal Soc., 2011. *Publications:* Autism: an introduction to psychological theory, 1994, 2nd edn 2007 (US edn 1995; trans. Danish, 1995, Japanese, 1997, Spanish, 1998, Greek, 2003, Russian, 2006); (ed with Uta Frith) Autism and Talent, 2010; contrib. peer-reviewed papers to learned jls. *Recreation:* making things. *Address:* MRC Social, Genetic and Developmental Psychiatry

Centre, Institute of Psychiatry, Psychology and Neuroscience (PO80), De Crespigny Park, Denmark Hill, SE5 8AF. *T:* (020) 7848 0873, *Fax:* (020) 7848 0866. *E:* francesca.happe@kcl.ac.uk.

HAPPÉ, Rhiannon; *see* Jones, R.

HAQUE, Muhammed Luthful; QC 2015; *b* Loughborough, 26 July 1973; *s* of Serajul and Dilwara Hoque; *m* 2006, Emma Louise Peacock; one *s* two *d*. *Educ:* Loughborough Grammar Sch.; Hertford Coll., Oxford (BA Hons; MA); City Univ., London (MA Law). Called to the Bar, Lincoln's Inn, 1997; in practice as barrister specialising in common and commercial law, 1997–. *Recreations:* golf, cricket, the history of typography. *Address:* Crown Office Chambers, 2 Crown Office Row, Temple, EC4Y 7HJ. *T:* (020) 7797 8100. *E:* haque@crownofficechambers.com.

HARBAGE, William John Hirons; QC 2003; a Recorder, since 2000; *b* 7 Feb. 1960; *s* of late Thomas William (John) Harbage, solicitor, and of Patricia Margaret Harbage (*née* Amis); *m* 1986, Julia Mary Herschel Dunkerley; one *s* two *d*. *Educ:* Haileybury Coll.; St John's Coll., Cambridge (BA Hons Law 1982, MA 1986). Short Service Limited Commn, 7th Duke of Edinburgh's Own Gurkha Rifles, 1979. Called to the Bar, Middle Temple, 1983; in practice as barrister, specialising in criminal law, 1983–; Asst Recorder, 1999–2000. Chm. Appeal Bd, Prescription Medicines Code of Practice Authy, 2006–. *Address:* 36 Bedford Row, WC1R 4JH. *T:* (020) 7421 8000. *E:* wharbage@36bedfordrow.co.uk. *Club:* Luffenham Heath Golf.

HARBERD, Prof. Nicholas Paul, PhD; FRS 2009; Sibthorpian Professor of Plant Science, University of Oxford, since 2008; Fellow, St John's College, Oxford, since 2008; *b* 15 July 1956; *s* of David and Muriel Harberd; *m* 1993, Jessica Ruth Harris; one *s* one *d*. *Educ:* Christ's Coll., Cambridge (MA; PhD 1981). Res. Project Leader, John Innes Centre, Norwich, 1990–2007. Hon. Prof., UEA, 2004–07. *Publications:* Seed to Seed, 2006; papers in learned jls incl. Nature, Science, Proc. NAS, Genes and Develt, Current Biol., Plant Cell. *Recreations:* music (playing piano, organ and Javanese gamelan music), walking. *Address:* Department of Plant Sciences, University of Oxford, South Parks Road, Oxford OX1 3RB.

HARBERTON, 11th Viscount *cr* 1791 (Ire.); **Henry Robert Pomeroy;** Baron Harberton 1783; Director, CHASE Africa, since 2013; *b* 23 April 1958; *s* of late Major Hon. Robert William Pomeroy and (Winifred) Anne (*née* Colegate); *S* uncle, 2004; *m* 1990, Caroline Mary, *d* of Jeremy Grindle; two *s*. *Educ:* Eton; RAC Cirencester; Univ. of Reading (MA Tropical Agricl Develt 1993). Chartered Surveyor: Portman Estate, 1981–88; P&O Properties, 1988–92; internat. develt aid in Africa and UK, 1994–; Country Dir, Rwanda and Grants Co-ordinator, Send a Cow, 2005–13. Lay Reader, C of E, 2002–. *Heir: s* Hon. Patrick Christopher Pomeroy, *b* 10 May 1995.

HARBIDGE, Ven. Adrian Guy; Rector, Seale, Puttenham and Wanborough, since 2015 (Priest-in-Charge, 2010–15); *b* 10 Nov. 1948; *s* of John and Pat Harbidge; *m* 1975, Bridget West-Watson; one *s* one *d*. *Educ:* Marling Sch., Stroud; St John's Coll., Durham (BA); Cuddesdon Coll., Oxford. Purser, Mercantile Marine, 1970–73. Deacon 1975, priest 1976; Curate, Romsey Abbey, 1975–80; Vicar: St Andrew's, Bennett Road, Bournemouth, 1980–86; Chandler's Ford, 1986–99; RD of Eastleigh, 1993–99; Archdeacon of Winchester, 1999–2000; Archdeacon of Bournemouth, 2000–10. Hon. Canon, St Peter's Cathedral, Tororo, Uganda, 2000. *Publications:* Those whom DDO hath joined together…, 1996. *Recreations:* landscape gardening, walking, cycling. *Address:* The Rectory, Elstead Road, Seale, Farnham, Surrey GU10 1JA. *T:* (01252) 783057. *E:* rector@spw.org.uk.

HARBISON, Dame Joan (Irene), DBE 2004 (CBE 1992); *b* 21 Jan. 1938; *d* of Tom and Jane McAllister; *m* 1966, Jeremy Harbison; one *d*. *Educ:* Victoria Coll., Belfast; QUB (BA 1960; MSc (Educnl Psychol.) 1972). Sen. Lectr, Stranmillis Coll., Belfast, 1972–97. Deputy Chm., Eastern Health and Social Services Bd, NI, 1984–89; Chair, CRE (NI), 1997–99; Chief Comr, Equality Commn for NI, 1999–2005; Mem., NI Judicial Appts Commn, 2005–09; Older People's Advocate for NI, 2008–11. Member: GDC, 1990–99; HFEA, 1990–96; Standing Adv. Commn on Human Rights, 1989–96; Regulation and Quality Improvement Authy, 2005–09; a Civil Service Comr, 2006–09. Chair, Age Concern NI. Hon. LLD Ulster, 2005. *Publications:* (with Jeremy Harbison) A Society Under Stress: children and young people in NI, 1980; (ed) Children of the Troubles, 1983; (ed) Growing Up in Northern Ireland, 1989. *Recreations:* travel, food and wine.

See also *J. B. McAllister.*

HARBISON, Dr Samuel Alexander, CB 1998; international health and safety consultant; HM Chief Inspector of Nuclear Installations, Health and Safety Executive, 1991–98; *b* 9 May 1941; *s* of Adam Harbison and Maude Harbison (*née* Adams); *m* 1st, 1964, Joyce Margaret Buick (marr. diss. 1991); three *d*; 2nd, 1991, Margaret Gail (*née* Vale) (*d* 2005). *Educ:* Queen's Univ., Belfast (Hons BSc); Univ. of California, Los Angeles (MSc); Univ. of London (PhD). Reactor Physicist, UKAEA, Windscale, 1962–64; Research and Teaching Asst, UCLA, 1964–66; Research at Rutherford High Energy Lab., Harwell, 1966–69; Sen. Lectr, Royal Naval Coll., Greenwich, 1969–74; Nuclear Installations Inspectorate, HSE, 1974–98. Chm., Defence Nuclear Safety Cttee, 2001–06. *Publications:* An Introduction to Radiation Protection (jtly), 1972, 6th edn 2012; numerous sci. and tech. papers in learned jls. *Recreations:* golf, music, walking. *Address:* Winnats, Whitehill Road, Meopham, Kent DA13 0NS.

HARBISON, Air Vice-Marshal William, CB 1977; CBE 1965; AFC 1956; RAF, retired; Vice-President, British Aerospace Inc., Washington, DC, 1979–92; *b* 11 April 1922; *s* of W. Harbison; *m* 1950, Helen, *d* of late William B. Geneva, Bloomington, Illinois; two *s*. *Educ:* Ballymena Academy, N Ireland. Joined RAF, 1941; 118 Sqdn Fighter Comd, 1943–46; 263, 257 and 64 Sqdns, 1946–48; Exchange Officer with 1st Fighter Group USAF, 1948–50; Central Fighter Estabt, 1950–51; 4th Fighter Group USAF, Korea, 1952; 2nd ATAF Germany: comd No 67 Sqdn, 1952–55; HQ No 2 Group, 1955; psc 1956; Air Min. and All Weather OCU, 1957; comd No 29 All Weather Sqdn Fighter Comd, Acklington and Leuchars, 1958–59; British Defence Staffs, Washington, 1959–62; jssc 1962; comd RAF Leuchars Fighter Comd, 1963–65; ndc 1965–66; Gp Capt. Ops: HQ Fighter Comd, 1967–68; No 11 Group Strike Comd, 1968; Dir of Control (Ops), NATCS, 1968–72; Comdr RAF Staff, and Air Attaché, Washington, 1972–75; AOC 11 Group, RAF, 1975–77. *Recreations:* flying, motoring. *Address:* 3292 Annandale Road, Falls Church, VA 22042–3800, USA.

HARBORD, Clare Mary Petre; Corporate Affairs Director, BAA, since 2011; *b* London, 25 Jan. 1957; *d* of late Captain Thomas Hornsby and of Hon. Patricia Mary Hornsby (*née* Dent, now Bence); *m* 1984, Robert Harbord (marr. diss. 2005); two *s* one *d*. *Educ:* Woldingham Sch., Surrey; Southampton Univ. (BA Hons Archaeol.). Journalist, IPC Mags, 1980–85; Sen. Account Manager, Valin Pollen, 1986–88; PR Manager, Corporate Communications, Eagle Star, 1988–99; Dir, Countrywide, Porter Novelli, 1999–2003; Hd of Communications, E.ON UK, 2004–07; Dir of Communications, MoJ, 2007–11. FCIPR 2007. *Recreations:* archaeology, travelling, theatre, films, swimming. *Address:* BAA Airports Ltd, Compass Centre, Nelson Road, London Heathrow Airport, Hounslow TW6 2GW. *E:* clare_harbord@baa.com.

HARBORD-HAMOND, family name of **Baron Suffield**.

HARBORNE, Peter Gale; HM Diplomatic Service, retired; Clerk Adviser to the European Scrutiny Committee, House of Commons, since 2004; *b* 29 June 1945; *s* of late Leslie Herbert and Marie Mildred Edith Harborne; *m* 1976, Tessa Elizabeth Henri; two *s*. *Educ:* King Edward's Sch., Birmingham; Birmingham Univ. (BCom). Dept of Health, 1966–72; FCO, 1972–74; First Sec., Ottawa, 1974–75; First Sec., Commercial, Mexico City, 1975–78; Lloyd's Bank Internat., 1979–81; FCO, 1981–83; Head of Chancery, Helsinki, 1983–87; Dep. Head of Mission, Budapest, 1988–91; Counsellor, FCO, 1991–95; Ambassador, Slovak Republic, 1995–98; High Comr, Trinidad and Tobago, 1999–2004. *Recreations:* watching cricket, playing tennis, the arts. *Address:* House of Commons, 7 Millbank, SW1P 3JA. *Club:* MCC.

HARBOUR, Ivan William; architect; Senior Partner, Rogers Stirk Harbour + Partners LLP, since 2011; *b* Irvine, Scotland, 3 June 1962; *s* of John Harbour and Celia Harbour (*née* Whitehead); *m* 1993, Roxanne Stacey; one *s* one *d*. *Educ:* Bartlett Sch. of Architecture and Planning, University Coll. London (BSc Hons, DipArch). Richard Rogers Partnership, later Rogers Stirk Harbour + Partners, 1985–, Sen. Dir, 1993–2011; *major projects include:* Parc Bit Masterplan, Mallorca, 1994; ECHR, Strasbourg, 1995; VR Techno Plaza, Gifu, Japan, 1995; South Bank Masterplan, London, 1996; Bordeaux Law Courts, 1999; Amano Res. Labs, Gifu, 1999; Shin-Puh-Kan Shopping Centre, Kyoto, Japan, 2001; Minami Yamashiro Sch., Kyoto Prefecture, 2003; Silvercup Studios, NY, 2003; Nippon TV HQ, Tokyo, 2004; Mossbourne Community Acad., London, 2004; Nat. Assembly for Wales, Cardiff, 2005; Berkeley Hotel, London, 2005; Antwerp Law Courts, 2006; Terminal 4, Barajas Airport, Madrid, 2006 (Stirling Prize, RIBA, 2006); E Darling Harbour Masterplan Competition, Sydney, Australia, 2006; R9 Metro Station, Kaohsiung, Taiwan, 2007; Ching Fu HQ, Kaohsiung, 2007; Maggie's Centre, London, 2008 (Stirling Prize, RIBA, 2009); Jacob K Javits Convention Centre, NY, 2008; Design for Manufacture/Oxley Woods, Milton Keynes, 2009 (Manser Medal 2008); Port Authy Bus Terminal, NY, 2010; Parc 1, Seoul, 2014; 1201 K St, Washington, 2014; 8 Chifley Sq., Sydney, 2015; *current projects:* 360 London, 2004–; Barangaroo Masterplan, Sydney, 2009–. *Recreations:* building, cycling, drawing. *Address:* Rogers Stirk Harbour + Partners, Thames Wharf Studios, Rainville Road, W6 9HA. *T:* (020) 7385 1235, *Fax:* (020) 7385 8409. *E:* enquiries@rsh-p.com.

HARBOUR, Malcolm John Charles, CBE 2013; Member (C) West Midlands, European Parliament, 1999–2014; *b* 19 Feb. 1947; *s* of John and Bobby Harbour; *m* 1969, Penny Johnson; two *d*. *Educ:* Bedford Sch.; Trinity Coll., Cambridge (MA Mech Eng); Aston Univ. Business Sch. (Dip. Mgt Studies). CEng, MIMechE, 1975; FIMI 1984. Engr Apprentice, BMC Longbridge, 1967–69; Design and Develt Engr, BMC, 1969–72; Product Planning Manager, Rover-Triumph, 1972–76; Project Manager, Medium Cars, BL Cars, 1976–80; Austin-Rover: Director: Business Planning, 1980–82; Mkting, 1982–84; Sales, UK and Ireland, 1984–86; Overseas Sales, 1986–89; Founder Partner, Harbour Wade Brown, motor industry consultants, 1989–99; Founder Dir, Internat. Car Distribn Prog., 1993–2006; Project Dir, 3 Day Car Prog., 1998–99. European Parliament: Cons. spokesman on internal market, 1999–2009; Member: Cttee for Legal Affairs and Internal Market, 1999–2004; Cttee for Industry, External Trade, Res. and Energy, 1999–2004; Cons. Delegn Bureau, 1999–2003; Delegn to Japan, 1999–2014; Cttee for Internal Mkt and Consumer Protection, 2004–14 (Chm., 2009–14); Cttee for Industry, Technol., Res. and Energy, 2004–09; Cttee Co-ordinator, EPP-ED Gp, 2004–09; Vice-Pres., Sci. and Technol. Panel, 2002–14; Co-Chm., Eur. Forum for the Automobile and Soc., 2000–09; Chairman: Ceramics Industry Forum, 2000–14; Cons. Technol. Forum, 2004–10; Eur. Manufg Forum, 2009–14; Rapporteur: Eur. Commn Reform, 2000; Universal Service in Electronic Communications, 2001–14; Internal Market Strategy, 2003; Motor Vehicle Type Approval, 2007; Innovative Procurement, 2008; Recreational Craft, 2011. Vice Pres., Trading Standards Inst., 2011–. Guardian, Birmingham Assay Office, 2007–. Mem. Bd, Birmingham Sci. City, 2010–. Mem. Council, Univ. of Birmingham, 2014–. Gov., Eur. Internet Foundn, 2003–14. Hon. DSc Aston, 2008. *Publications:* reports on the car industry for DTI, OECD, etc. *Recreations:* choral singing, motor sport, travel, cooking. *Address:* The Cottage, Nutlands Farm, Oldberrow Lane, Henley in Arden, Warwickshire B95 5NH. *T:* (01564) 637387. *E:* Harbournutlands@sky.com.

HARCOURT; *see* Vernon-Harcourt, family name of Baron Vernon.

HARCOURT, Prof. Geoffrey Colin, AO 1994; PhD, LittD; FASSA; FAcSS; Fellow and College Lecturer in Economics, Jesus College, Cambridge, 1982–98, now Emeritus Fellow (President, 1988–89 and 1990–92); Reader (*ad hominem*) in the History of Economic Theory, Cambridge University, 1990–98, now Emeritus; *b* 27 June 1931; *s* of Kenneth Kopel Harcourt and Marjorie Rahel (*née* Gans); *m* 1955, Joan Margaret Bartrop; two *s* two *d*. *Educ:* Malvern Grammar Sch.; Wesley Coll., Melbourne; Queen's Coll., Univ. of Melbourne (BCom (Hons) 1954; MCom 1956; Hon. Fellow, 1998); King's Coll., Cambridge. PhD 1960, LittD 1988, Cantab. University of Adelaide: Lectr in Econs, 1958–62; Sen. Lectr, 1963–65; Reader, 1965–67; Prof. of Econs (Personal Chair), 1967–85, Prof. Emeritus 1988; Cambridge University: Lectr in Econs and Politics, 1964–66, 1982–90; Fellow and Dir of Studies in Econs, Trinity Hall, 1964–66. Leverhulme Exchange Fellow, Keio Univ., Tokyo, 1969–70; Visiting Fellow: Clare Hall, Cambridge, 1972–73; ANU, 1997; Sugden Fellow, Queen's Coll., Univ. of Melbourne, 2002; Vis. Professorial Fellow, Univ. of NSW, 2008, 2009, 2010–Aug. 2016; Visiting Professor: Scarborough Coll., Univ. of Toronto, 1977, 1980; Univ. of Melbourne, 2002; Hon. Prof., Univ. of NSW, 1997, 1999. Howard League for Penal Reform, SA Branch: Sec., 1959–63; Vice-Pres., 1967–74; Pres., 1974–80. Mem., Exec. Cttee, Campaign for Peace in Vietnam, 1967–75 (Chm., 1970–72). Mem., Aust. Labor Party Nat. Cttee of Enquiry, 1978–79. Pres., Econ. Soc. of Aust. and NZ, 1974–77; Mem. Council, Roy. Econ. Soc., 1990–95. FASSA 1971 (Exec. Cttee Mem., 1974–77). Lectures: Wellington-Burnham, Tufts Univ., USA, 1975; Edward Shann Meml, Univ. of WA, 1975; Newcastle, in Pol Economy, Univ. of Newcastle, NSW, 1977; Academy, Acad. of Social Scis in Aust., 1978; G. L. Wood Meml, Univ. of Melbourne, 1982; John Curtin Meml, ANU, 1982; Special Lectr in Econs, Manchester Univ., 1983–84; Nobel Conf., Minnesota, USA, 1986; Laws, Univ. of Tennessee at Knoxville, USA, 1991; Second Donald Horne Address, Melbourne, 1992; Sir Halford Cook, Queen's Coll., Melbourne, 1995; Kingsley Martin Meml, Cambridge, 1996; Annual Colin Clark, Univ. of Qld, 1997; Bernard Haskell, Univ. of Missouri, 2006. FAcSS (AcSS 2003). Hon. Mem., European Soc. for Hist. of Economic Thought, 2004. Distinguished Fellow: Economic Soc. of Australia, 1996; Hist. of Econs Soc., 2004; Hist. of Economic Thought Soc. of Australia, 2012. Hon. LittD De Montfort, 1997; Hon. DCom Melbourne, 2003; Hon Dr rer. pol Fribourg, 2003. (Jtly) Veblen-Commons Award, Assoc. for Evolutionary Econs, USA, 2010. *Publications:* (with P. H. Karmel and R. H. Wallace) Economic Activity, 1967 (trans. Italian 1969); (ed jtly) Readings in the Concept and Measurement of Income, 1969, 2nd edn 1986; (ed with N. F. Laing) Capital and Growth: Selected Readings, 1971 (trans. Spanish 1977); Some Cambridge Controversies in the Theory of Capital, 1972 (trans. Italian 1973, Polish and Spanish 1975, Japanese 1980); Theoretical Controversy and Social Significance: an evaluation of the Cambridge controversies (Edward Shann Meml Lecture), 1975; (ed) The Microeconomic Foundations of Macroeconomics, 1977; The Social Science Imperialists: selected essays (ed Prue Kerr), 1982; (ed) Keynes and his Contemporaries, 1985; (ed with Jon Cohen) International Monetary Problems and Supply-Side Economics: Essays in Honour of Lorie Tarshis, 1986; Controversies in Political Economy (selected essays, ed O. F. Hamouda), 1986; On Political Economists and Modern Political Economy (selected essays, ed C. Sardoni), 1992; Markets, Madness and a Middle Way (Second Annual Donald Horne Address), 1992; Post-Keynesian Essays in Biography: portraits of Twentieth Century political economists, 1993; (ed jtly) The Dynamics of the Wealth of Nations, Growth, Distribution and Structural Change: essays in honour of Luigi Pasinetti, 1993; (ed jtly) Income and Employment in Theory and Practice: essays in memory of Athanasios Asimakopulos, 1994; Capitalism, Socialism and Post-Keynesianism: selected essays, 1995; (ed with P. A. Riach) A 'Second Edition' of The General Theory, 2 vols, 1997 (trans.

Japanese, 2004); 50 Years a Keynesian and other essays, 2001; Selected Essays on Economic Policy, 2001; (ed) L'Économie Rebelle de Joan Robinson, 2001; (ed jtly) Editing Economics: essays in honour of Mark Perlman, 2002; (with Prue Kerr) Joan Robinson: critical assessments of leading economists, 5 vols, 2002; (ed jtly) Capital Theory, 3 vols, 2005; The Structure of Post-Keynesian Economics: the core contributions of the pioneers, 2006; (with Prue Kerr) Joan Robinson, 2009; On Skidelsky's Keynes and Other Essays, 2012; The Making of a Post-Keynesian Economist, 2012; (ed with P. Kriesler) The Oxford Handbook of Post-Keynesian Economics, 2 vols, 2013; (ed with J. Pixley) Financial Crises and the Nature of Capitalist Money: mutual developments from the work of Geoffrey Ingham, 2013; many articles and reviews in learned jls and chapters in edited books. *Recreations:* cricket, Australian rules football, running (not jogging), bike riding, reading, politics. *Address:* School of Economics, University of New South Wales, Sydney, NSW 2052, Australia; 42/67 St Marks Road, Randwick, Sydney, NSW 2031, Australia. *Clubs:* Melbourne Cricket, South Australian Cricket Association.

HARCOURT, Geoffrey David, RDI 1978; DesRCA; freelance consultant designer, since 1962; painter in oils and watercolours, since 2005; *b* 9 Aug. 1935; *s* of William and Barbara Harcourt; *m* 1965, Jean Mary Vaughan Pryce-Jones (*d* 2009); one *s* one *d*. *Educ:* High Wycombe Sch. of Art; Royal Coll. of Art; DesRCA, Silver Medal 1960. FSIAD 1968. Designer: Latham, Tyler, Jensen, Chicago, 1960–61; Jacob Jensen, Copenhagen, 1961; Andrew Pegram Ltd, London, 1961–62; consultant, Artifort, Holland, 1962–95 (domestic and business furniture designer; many models still in prodn including RCA Silver Medal chair of 1960 in Italy). Visiting Lecturer: High Wycombe Coll. of Art and Design, 1963–74; Leicester Polytechnic, 1982–93; Ext. Assessor for BA Hons degrees, Kingston Polytechnic, 1974–77, Loughborough Coll. of Art and Design, 1978–81, Belfast Polytechnic, 1977–81 and Buckinghamshire Coll. of Higher Educn, 1982–85; Ext. Examr, RCA, 1996–98. Chair design for Artifort awarded first prize for creativity, Brussels, 1978; Member: Design Awards Cttee, Design Council, 1979–80; Furniture Design Wkg Party, EDC, 1986–87; Chm., RSA Bursaries Cttee (Furniture Design Section, 1982–86, Ceramics Section, 1989–91, Woven Textiles, 1992–94, Footwear, 1996–97); approved consultant, Design Council 'Support for Design' initiative. Work exhibited: permanent collection, Stedelijk Mus., Amsterdam, 1967; Prague Mus. of Decorative Arts, 1972; Science Mus., London, 1972; Design Council, London and Glasgow, 1976 and 1981; Eye for Industry Exhibn, V&A, 1987; Nederlands Textielmuseum, 1988; Manchester Prize exhibn, City Art Gall., 1988; St George's Hall, Windsor Exhibn, Architecture Foundn, London, 1993; RCA Centennial Exhibn, 1996; RCA 175th year Exhibn, Design for Industry section, 2012. Painter in oils and watercolours; exhibited Oxfordshire Artsweek, 2011–15, Henley Royal Regatta, 2013, 2014. Master, Faculty of RDI, 2003–05. Chm., Adv. Panel to Lord Lieutenant of Oxfordshire, 1998–2000. FRSA 1979. Freeman, City of London; Liveryman, Worshipful Co. of Furniture Makers, 1975–2009 (Chm., Design Awards Cttee, 1994–97). JP Thame and Henley, 1981–2000 (Chm., Youth Court Panel, 1993–95; Chm. Bench, 1996–98). *Recreations:* painting, bridge, cooking, golf. *Address:* The Old Vicarage, Benson, Oxfordshire OX10 6SF. *W:* GeoffreyHarcourt.com. *Clubs:* Leander (Assoc. Mem.); Goring and Streatley Golf.

HARCOURT, Michael Franklin, OC 2012; Associate Director, Continuing Studies Centre for Sustainability, University of British Columbia, since 2009; Premier of British Columbia, 1991–96; *b* Edmonton, Alta, 6 Jan. 1943; *e s* of Frank and Stella Louise Harcourt; *m* 1971, Beckie Salo; one *s*. *Educ:* Sir Winston Churchill High Sch., Vancouver; University of British Columbia (LLB 1968). Lawyer, Vancouver, 1968–72. Alderman, 1972–80, Mayor, 1980–86, City of Vancouver. MLA (NDP) Vancouver Centre, 1986–91, Vancouver-Mt Pleasant, 1991–96; Leader of the Opposition, BC, 1987–92. Sen. Associate, Sustainable Develt Res. Inst., later Sustainable Develt Res. Initiative, UBC, 1996–2009. Director: Vancouver Port Authy, 1998–2006; Vancouver Airport Authy, 1998. Exec. Mem., Nat. Roundtable on Envmt and Economy, 1996–2005. *Publications:* (with John Lekich) Plan B: one man's journey from tragedy to triumph (autobiog.), 2004; City Making in Paradise, 2007. *Recreations:* tennis, golf, ski-ing, watching basketball and football.

HARCOURT-SMITH, Air Chief Marshal Sir David, GBE 1989; KCB 1984; DFC 1957; aviation consultant; Chairman, Chelworth Defence Ltd, 1991–96; Controller Aircraft, Ministry of Defence, Procurement Executive, 1986–89, retired; *b* 14 Oct. 1931; *s* of late Air Vice-Marshal G. Harcourt-Smith, CB, CBE, MVO, and of M. Harcourt-Smith; *m* 1957, Mary (*née* Entwistle); two *s* one *d*. *Educ:* Felsted Sch.; RAF College. Commnd 1952; flying appts with Nos 11, 8 and 54 Squadrons; Staff Coll., 1962; OC No 54 Squadron, 1963–65; PSO to AOC-in-C, Tech. Training Comd, 1965–67; Defence Planning Staff, 1967–68; OC No 6 Squadron, 1969–70; Central Tactics and Trials Organisation, 1970–72; OC RAF Brüggen, 1972–74; Dir of Op. Requirements, 1974–76; RCDS, 1977; Comdt, RAF Coll., Cranwell, 1978–80; Asst Chief of Air Staff (Op. Reqs), 1980–84; AOC-in-C, RAF Support Command, 1984–85. Dir, DESC, 1991–97. Gov., Downe House, 1993–96. *Recreations:* walking, golf. *Club:* Royal Air Force.

HARDAKER, Paul James, PhD; FRMetS, FInstP, CMet; Chief Executive, Institute of Physics, since 2012; *b* 14 Sept. 1966; *s* of late Jack Hardaker and Judith Mary Bolton (*née* James); *m* 2001, Lynwen Davies. *Educ:* Univ. of Essex (BSc 1st Cl. Hons 1988; PhD Maths 1992); Univ. of Portsmouth (Dip Mgt Studies 1998). FRMetS 1993; CMet 2001; CEnv 2005–12; FInstP 2012. Sen. Res. Fellow, Dept of Maths, Essex Univ., 1989–93; Meteorological Office, subseq. Met Office, 1993–2006; Sen. Scientist, then Hd of Internat. Business Unit, 1993–96; Weather Radar Prog. Manager and UK Hydrology Advr, 1996–99; Hd, Remote Sensing and Observations Develt, 1999–2002; Gp Hd, New Products and Services, 2002–04; Chief Govt Advr, 2004–06; Chief Exec., Royal Meteorological Soc., 2006–12. Visiting Professor: Envmtl Scis, Salford Univ., 1999–2011; Sch. of Maths, Physics and Meteorol., Univ. of Reading, 2006–. Chm., Flood Risk from Extreme Events prog., NERC, 2005–11. Non-executive Director: WeatherXChange, 2002–05; Reading PCT, 2005–07; Dep. Chm., NHS Berks West (formerly Berks West PCT), 2007–10. Interim Man. Dir, EcoConnect Ltd, 2004. Member: Bd, Soc. for the Envmt, 2006–11; Bd, Sense about Sci., 2009– (Chm., 2012–); Bd, Sci. Council, 2009–14; Adv. Council on Standards Quality, PAA\VQ-SET, 2008–12. Guest Presenter, BBC Radio Berkshire, 2008–10. Trustee, RMetS, 1996–2006. Ed., Atmospheric Sci. Letters, 1998–2006. *Publications:* contributor to: Hydrometeorology and Climatology, 1997; Weather Radar Technology for Water Resources Management, 1997; Weather Radar: principle advances and applications, 2004; Known Risk, 2005; numerous contribns to learned jls. *Recreations:* tennis, ballroom dancing, music. *Address:* Institute of Physics, 76 Portland Place, W1B 1NT. *T:* (020) 7470 4800. *E:* paul.hardaker@iop.org.

HARDCASTLE, Prof. Jack Donald, CBE 1998; MChir (Cantab); FRCP, FRCS; Lead Clinician, Mid Trent Cancer Network, 1998–2005; Professor of Surgery, University of Nottingham, 1970–98, then Emeritus; *b* 3 April 1933; *s* of Albert Hardcastle and Bertha (*née* Ellison); *m* 1965, Rosemary Hay-Shunker; one *s* one *d*. *Educ:* St Bartholomew's Grammar Sch., Newbury; Emmanuel Coll., Cambridge (Senior Scholar 1954; BA, MA; Windsor Postgrad. Schol.); London Hospital (Open Scholarship 1955; MB, BChir, MChir (Distinction)). MRCP 1961; FRCS 1962; FRCP 1984. House Phys./Surg., Resident Accoucheur, London Hosp., 1959–60; Ho. Surg. to Prof. Aird, Hammersmith Postgraduate Hosp., 1961–62; London Hospital: Research Asst, 1962; Lectr in Surgery, 1963; Registrar in Surgery, 1964; Registrar in Surgery, Thoracic Unit, 1965; Sen. Registrar in Surgery, 1965; Sen. Registrar, St Mark's Hosp., London, 1968; Sen. Lectr in Surgery, London Hosp., 1968. Sir Arthur Sims Commonwealth Travelling Prof., RCS, 1985; Mayne Vis. Prof., Univ. of Brisbane, 1987. Member Council: RCS, 1987–99 (Dir, Raven Dept of Educn, 1994–99; Vice-Pres., 1995–97); Med. Protection Soc., 1995–2003 (Dir). Founder FMedSci 1998. Hon. FRCSGlas. Hunterian Orator, 1999, Gold Medal, 2000, RCS. *Publications:* Isolated Organ Perfusion (with H. D. Ritchie), 1973; various scientific papers. *Recreations:* ski-ing, walking, golf. *Address:* Field House, 32 Marlock Close, Fiskerton, Notts NG25 0UB.

HARDCASTLE, (Jesse) Leslie, OBE 1974; exhibition and museum consultant, since 1996; *b* 8 Dec. 1926; *s* of Francis Ernest Hardcastle and Dorothy Schofield; *m* 1968, Vivienne Mansel Richards; two *s*. *Educ:* St Joseph's College, Croydon. British Lion Film Productions, 1943–44; Royal Navy, 1944–47. British Film Inst., 1947–94; Telekinema Festival of Britain, 1951; London Film Fest. admin, 1958–91; Controller, NFT, 1968–91; Museum of the Moving Image: originator, 1981–88; Curator, 1988–94. A Governor, BFI, 2004–. Sec., Projected Picture Trust, 1994–99; Consultant, London Film Mus., 2009– (exhibns include Charles Chaplin; Ray Harryhausen; Magnum Photographers on Set: Lights, Camera, London; Bond in Action). Pres., The Soho Soc.; Founder Mem., Soho Housing Assoc. *Recreations:* community work, theatre, music, cinema. *Address:* 37c Great Pulteney Street, W1F 9NT.

HARDCASTLE, Prof. William John, PhD; FBA 2004; FRSE; Professor of Speech Sciences and Director, Speech Science Research Centre (formerly Scottish Centre for Speech and Communication Science Research), Queen Margaret University (formerly Queen Margaret University College), Edinburgh, 2003–10, now Professor Emeritus; *b* 28 Sept. 1943; *s* of late Gilbert William Hardcastle and Gwendolen Rose Hardcastle (*née* Barber); *m* 1969, Francesca MacDonald; two *s* one *d*. *Educ:* Brisbane Grammar Sch.; Univ. of Queensland (BA 1966; MA 1967); Univ. of Edinburgh (Dip. Phonetics 1968; PhD 1971). Lectr, Inst. für Phonetik, Univ. Kiel, 1972–74; University of Reading: Lectr, Dept of Linguistic Sci., 1974–81; Reader, 1981–89; Prof. of Speech Scis, 1989–93; Queen Margaret University College, Edinburgh: Hd, Dept of Speech and Lang. Scis, 1993–99; Dean: Health Scis, 1999–2002; Res., 2002–03. Vis. Lectr, Sch. of English and Linguistics, Macquarie Univ., Sydney, 1978–79. Member: Acad. Accreditation Panel, Royal Coll. of Speech and Lang. Therapists, 1988; Res. and Commercialisation Cttee, Univs Scotland, 1996–2007; Res. Policy and Adv. Cttee, SHEFC, 1999–2004; Linguistics Panel (sub-panel Phonetics), RAE 2001, 2001; Linguistics Panel, RAE 2008, 2005–. Member Editorial Board: Speech Communication, 1982–92; Clinical Linguistics and Phonetics, 1992–; Internat. Jl Lang. and Communication Disorders, 2001–. Consultant, Lawrence Erlbaum publishers, 2000–. Pres., Internat. Clinical Phonetics and Linguistics Assoc., 1991–2001. Fellow, Inst. Acoustics, 1996–2002; FRSA 1997; FRSE 2007. Mem., Norwegian Acad. of Sci. and Letters, 2007. Hon. FRCSLT 2003. Hon. DSc Napier, 2007; Hon. DLitt Queen Margaret, 2009. *Publications:* Physiology of Speech Production, 1976; (with P. Dalton) Disorders of Fluency and their Effects on Communication, 1977, 2nd edn 1989; (ed with A. Marchal) Speech Production and Speech Modelling, 1990; (ed with J. Laver) Handbook of Phonetic Sciences, 1997, (ed with J. Laver and F. Gibbon) 2nd edn, 2010; (ed with N. Hewlett) Coarticulation: theory, data and techniques, 1999; contribs to conf. procs and vols of studies, res. papers in phonetic, linguistic and speech therapy jls. *Recreations:* walking the Scottish hills, badminton, golf, gardening. *Address:* Queen Margaret University, Musselburgh EH21 6UU. *T:* (0131) 474 0000.

HARDEN, Peter William Mason; Publisher, Harden's, since 1991; Managing Director, York Press, since 2011; *b* 1 June 1966; *s* of late John Harden and of Susan Harden; *m* 1996, Francesca Elizabeth Freeman; three *s* one *d*. *Educ:* King's Sch., Chester; Trinity Coll., Cambridge (BA 1987). Saudi International Bank, 1987–90; publishing, mkt res. and restaurant reviewing, 1991–. FRSA. *Publications:* Harden's London Restaurants, annually, 1992–; Harden's UK Restaurants, annually, 1999–. *Recreations:* gym, tennis. *Address:* Harden's Ltd, The Brew, Victoria House, Paul Street, EC2A 4NA. *T:* (020) 7839 4763. *E:* ph@hardens.com. *Club:* Hawks (Cambridge).

See also R. J. M. Harden.

HARDEN, Richard John Mason; independent management consultant, since 2014; Publisher, Harden's, 1991–2014; *b* 26 July 1959; *s* of late John Harden and of Susan Harden; *m* 2000, Jeanette Elizabeth Holland; two *d*. *Educ:* King's Sch., Chester; Christ's Coll., Cambridge (BA 1981). Called to the Bar, Middle Temple, 1982; Baring Brothers, 1983–84; Samuel Montagu, 1984–91; publishing, mkt res., restaurant reviewing and journalism, 1991–2014. *Publications:* Harden's London Restaurants, annually, 1992–2015; Harden's UK Restaurants, annually, 1999–2015. *Recreation:* wandering around cities. *Address:* 30 Vincent Square, SW1P 2NW. *T:* (020) 7233 7277. *E:* rh@hardenuk.com.

See also P. W. M. Harden.

HARDENBERGER, (Ulf) Håkan; musician; international trumpet soloist; *b* 27 Oct. 1961; *s* of Åke and Mona Hardenberger; *m* 1986, Heidi Thomassen; two *s*. *Educ:* Paris Conservatory. Concerts as soloist with orchestras including LA Philharmonic, Chicago Symphony, Vienna Phil., London Phil., London Symphony, Philharmonia, Orch. des Bayerische Rundfunk, Accademia Nazionale di Santa Cecilia, NHK Symphony; festivals include Lucerne, Salzburg, BBC Proms. Prof. of Trumpet, Malmö Acad. of Music; Internat. Chair in Brass Studies, RNCM, Manchester; Prince Consort Prof. of Trumpet, Royal Coll. of Music. Hon. RAM 1992. *Address:* c/o KDS UK Ltd, 40 St Martin's Lane, WC2N 4ER.

HARDIE, family name of **Baron Hardie**.

HARDIE, Baron *cr* 1997 (Life Peer), of Blackford in the City of Edinburgh; **Andrew Rutherford Hardie;** PC 1997; a Senator of the College of Justice in Scotland and Lord of Session, 2000–12; *b* 8 Jan. 1946; *s* of late Andrew Rutherford Hardie and Elizabeth Currie Lowe; *m* 1971, Catherine Storrar Elgin; two *s* one *d*. *Educ:* St Mungo's Primary Sch., Alloa; St Modan's High Sch., Stirling; Edinburgh Univ. (MA, LLB Hons). Enrolled Solicitor, 1971; Mem., Faculty of Advocates, 1973; Advocate Depute, 1979–83; QC (Scot.) 1985; Lord Advocate, UK, 1997–99, Scotland, 1999–2000. Treasurer, 1989–94, Dean, 1994–97, Faculty of Advocates. Hon. Pres., Capability Scotland, 2012–. Hon. Bencher, Lincoln's Inn, 1998. *Address:* 4 Oswald Road, Edinburgh EH9 2HF. *T:* (0131) 667 7542.

HARDIE, Dr Alexander, OBE 1990; political consultant, since 2012; *b* 5 March 1947; *s* of Alexander Merrie Hardie and Phyllis A. I. Hardie; *m* 1971, Jillian Hester Rowlands (marr. diss. 2004); one *s* two *d*. *Educ:* Aberdeen Grammar Sch.; Bristol Grammar Sch.; Univ. of Edinburgh (MA); Corpus Christi Coll., Oxford (DPhil). Jun. Research Fellow, Univ. of Bristol, 1972–73; HM Diplomatic Service, 1973–2001: FCO, 1973–77; First Secretary: Budapest, 1977–78; Bucharest, 1979–81; FCO, 1981–86; Lusaka, 1986–90; FCO, 1990–93; Counsellor, Pretoria, 1993–97; FCO, 1997–2001. Consultant in Security Sector Reform, FCO, 2005–12. Hon. Res. Associate in Classics, Royal Holloway, London Univ., 1998–2001; Fellow and Bursar, Oriel Coll., Oxford, 2001–04; Hon. Res. Fellow in Classics, Edinburgh Univ., 2007–. *Publications:* Statius and the Silvae, 1983. *Recreation:* classical studies. *Address:* The Old School House, Clava, Culloden, Inverness-shire IV2 5EL. *E:* ahardie5@virginmedia.com. *Club:* Travellers.

HARDIE, (Charles) Jeremy (Mawdesley), CBE 1983; Research Associate, Centre for Philosophy of Natural and Social Sciences, London School of Economics, since 2000; *b* 9 June 1938; *s* of Sir Charles Hardie, CBE; *m* 1st, 1962, Susan Chamberlain (marr. diss. 1976); two *d* two *s*; 2nd, 1978, Xandra, Countess of Gowrie (marr. diss. 1994), *d* of late Col R. A. G. Bingley, CVO, DSO, OBE; one *d*; 3rd, 1994, Kirsteen Margaret Tait. *Educ:* Winchester Coll.; New Coll., Oxford (2nd Cl. Hon. Mods, 1st Cl. Lit. Hum.); Nuffield Coll., Oxford (BPhil Econs). ACA 1965, Peat, Marwick, Mitchell & Co.; Nuffield Coll., Oxford, 1966–67; Jun. Res. Fellow, Trinity Coll., Oxford, 1967–68; Fellow and Tutor in Econs, Keble Coll.,

Oxford, 1968–75 (Hon. Fellow, 1998). Partner, Dixon Wilson & Co., 1975–82. Chairman: Nat. Provident Instn, 1980–89 (Dir, 1972–89, Dep. Chm., 1977); Alexander Syndicate Management Ltd, 1982–95; Radio Broadland Ltd, 1983–85 (Dir, 1983–90); D. P. Mann Underwriting Agency Ltd, 1983–99; W. H. Smith Gp, 1994–99 (Dir, 1988–99; Dep. Chm., 1992–94); Touch Clarity Ltd, 2001–04; Loch Fyne Restaurants Ltd, 2002–05; Brasserie Blanc plc, 2006–11. Director: Alexanders Discount Co. Ltd, 1978–87 (Dep. Chm., 1981–84; Chm., 1984–86); John Swire & Sons Ltd, 1982–98; Amdahl (UK) Ltd, 1983–86; Mercantile House Holdings Ltd, 1984–87; Additional Underwriting Agencies (No 3) Ltd, 1985–2007; Alexanders Laing & Cruickshank Gilts Ltd, 1986–87 (Chm., 1986); Northdoor Hldgs, 1989–93. Chm., Centre for Economic Policy Res., 1984–89; Treas., REconS, 1987–93; Dep. Chm., NAAFI, 1986–92 (Dir, 1981–). Member: Monopolies and Mergers Commn, 1976–83 (Dep. Chm., 1980–83); Council, Oxford Centre for Management Studies, 1978–85; Hammersmith Health Authority, 1982–83; Arts Council of GB, 1984–86; Peacock Cttee on Financing of BBC, 1985–86. Mem. Council, KCL, 1992–2004 (Dep. Chm., 1997–2004; FKC 2004). Chair: Open Foundn, 2004–09; China Dialogue, 2014–; Flipside, 2015–; Mem., Adv. Bd, Evidence Campaign, 2014–. Fellow, Centre for Social Policy, 2014–. Contested Norwich South, (SDP) 1983, (SDP/Alliance) 1987. Trustee: Esmée Fairbairn Foundn, 1972–2008 (Chm., 2003–07); Butler Trust, 1985–87; IPPR, 2000–09; Somerset Hse Trust, 2001–; Internat. Hse, 2007–09; Early Intervention Foundn, 2014–. *Recreations:* sailing, ski-ing, tennis, walking. *Address:* 23 Arlington Road, NW1 7ER. *T:* (020) 7387 1697.

HARDIE, Prof. (David) Grahame, PhD; FRS 2007; FRSE; FMedSci; Professor of Cellular Signalling, University of Dundee, since 1994; *b* 25 April 1950; *s* of Grahame McLean Hardie and Bertha Tyson Hardie; *m* 1977, Linda Margaret; four *s*. *Educ:* Downing Coll., Cambridge (BA 1971); Heriot-Watt Univ. (PhD). University of Dundee: Lectr, 1977–87; Sen. Lectr, 1987–90; Reader, 1990–94. Member: Physiol Medicine and Infections Bd, MRC, 1997–2001; Molecular and Cell Panel, Wellcome Trust, 2001–04; Internat. Conf. Grant and Short Visits Panel, Royal Soc., 2008–10; Chairs and Prog. Grants Cttee, BHF, 2008–12; Advanced Investigator Panel, Eur. Res. Council, 2011–. FRSE 1998; FMedSci 2002. *Publications:* Biochemical Messengers, 1991; over 300 reviews, chapters and peer-reviewed scientific papers. *Recreations:* sailing, hill walking. *Address:* Division of Cell Signalling and Immunology, College of Life Sciences, University of Dundee, Dundee DD1 5EH. *T:* (01382) 384253. *E:* d.g.hardie@dundee.ac.uk.

HARDIE, Brig. Donald David Graeme, CVO 2008; TD 1968; JP; FIMMM; Lord-Lieutenant, Dunbartonshire (formerly Strathclyde Region, Districts of Dumbarton, Clydebank, Bearsden and Milngavie, Strathkelvin, Cumbernauld and Kilsyth), 1990–2007; Keeper of Dumbarton Castle, since 1996; *b* 23 Jan. 1936; *m* 1st, 1961, Rosalind Allan Ker (marr. diss. 1998); two *s*; 2nd, 1999, Sheena Roome. *Educ:* Larchfield, Blairmore and Merchiston Castle Schools. U.T.R. Management Trainee, 1956–59; F. W. Allen & Ker, 1960–61; with J. & G. Hardie & Co., 1961–2001, Dir, 1966–2001, Chm., 1990–2001; Man. Dir, 2001–05, Chm., 2005–10, Preston Stretchform Ltd (formerly Hardie Mgt Consultants, then Hardie Internat. Sales); Director: Gilbert Plastics, 1973–76; Hardie Polymers, 1976–2001; Hardie Polymers (England), 1989–2001; Ronaash, 1988–2000; Tullochan Trust Ltd (Trustee, 1996). Commissioned 41st Field Regt RA, 1955; Battery Comdr, 277 (Argyll & Sutherland Highlanders) Regt, RA TA, 1966; CO GSV OTC, 1973; TA Colonel: Lowlands, 1976; DES, 1980; Scotland, 1985; Hon. Colonel: Glasgow and Lanarks Bn, ACF, 1990–2000; 105 Air Defence Regt, RA(V), 1992–99; ACF Brig. Scotland, 1983–87; Chm., RA Council for Scotland, 1996–2001. President: Dunbartonshire SSAFA, 1992–2007; Dunbartonshire Scout Council, and Girl Guides, 1994–2007; Boys Bde, Argyll and Lennox, 1999–2007; Highland RFCA, 2005–07; Vice-Pres., Nat. Artillery Assoc., 2002–. Hon. Col Comdt, RA, 2003–07. Patron: Cornerstone, 1999–2009; Craighalbert Centre, 1999–2009. Chieftain, Loch Lomond Games, 1996–2009. JP Dumbarton, 1990. FIMMM (FPRI 1984). KStJ 1997. *Recreations:* ski-ing, sailing, shooting, fishing. *Address:* East Lodge, Arden, Dunbartonshire G83 8RD. *T:* (01389) 850790. *Clubs:* Royal Scots (Edinburgh); Royal Northern and Clyde Yacht.

HARDIE, Grahame; *see* Hardie, D. G.

HARDIE, Jeremy; *see* Hardie, C. J. M.

HARDIE, John Macdonald; Chief Executive Officer, ITN Ltd, since 2009; *b* Glasgow, 7 Jan. 1962; *s* of Donald and Mary Hardie; *m* 2005, Nicola Swash; two *s*. *Educ:* Glasgow Univ. (MA Hons English and Philosophy). Procter and Gamble: brand asst, 1983–86; Brand Manager, 1986–89; Associate Advertising Manager, 1989–91; Advertising Dir, 1991–94; Man. Dir, 1994–97; Mktg and Commercial Dir, ITV Ltd, 1997–2001; Walt Disney Co.: Man. Dir and Sen. Vice Pres., 2001–04; Man. Dir and Exec. Vice Pres., 2005–09; non-exec. Chm., Super RTL, 2008–09; CEO, Jetix NV, 2009. Chm., RTS, 2011–. Liveryman, Marketors' Co., 2007–. *Recreations:* piano, guitar, golf, TV and cinema, writing. *Address:* ITN Ltd, 200 Gray's Inn Road, WC1X 8XZ. *T:* (020) 7430 4332. *E:* john.hardie@itn.co.uk. *Clubs:* Caledonian, Marketing Group of GB (Chm., 2012–13), Soho House, Thirty.

HARDIE, Philip Russell, PhD; FBA 2000; Hon. Professor of Latin Literature, Cambridge University and Senior Research Fellow, Trinity College, Cambridge, since 2006; *b* 13 July 1952; *s* of late Miles Clayton Hardie, OBE and Pauline Le Gros (*née* Clark); partner, Susan Elizabeth Griffith; one *s* (and one *s* decd). *Educ:* St Paul's Sch., London; Corpus Christi Coll., Oxford (MA); MPhil London; PhD Cantab 1990. Editl Asst, Oxford Dictionaries, 1977–80; P. S. Allen Jun. Res. Fellow, Corpus Christi Coll., Oxford, 1980–84; Guest Faculty appt in Classical Hist., Sarah Lawrence Coll., NY, 1984–85; Cambridge University: Fellow and Coll. Lectr in Classics, Magdalene Coll., 1986–90; Fellow, 1990–2002, Emeritus Fellow, 2005, New Hall; Reader in Latin Lit., 1998–2002; Corpus Christi Prof. of Latin Lang. and Lit., and Fellow of Corpus Christi Coll., Oxford, 2002–06. Hon. FAHA 2014. *Publications:* Virgil's Aeneid: cosmos and imperium, 1986; The Epic Successors of Virgil, 1993; (ed) Virgil Aeneid 9, 1994; Virgil, 1998; Ovid's Poetics of Illusion, 2002; (ed) The Cambridge Companion to Ovid, 2002; (ed) The Cambridge Companion to Lucretius, 2007; Lucretian Receptions, 2009; Rumour and Renown, 2012; The Last Trojan Hero: a cultural history of Virgil's Aeneid, 2014; Ovidio Metamorfosi, vol. 5 Libri XIII–XV, 2015. *Recreations:* walking, music. *Address:* Trinity College, Cambridge CB2 1TQ. *T:* (01223) 338400.

HARDIE, Prof. Roger Clayton, PhD; FRS 2010; Professor of Cellular Neuroscience, University of Cambridge, since 2006; *b* 1953. *Educ:* Emmanuel Coll., Cambridge (BA 1974); Australian Nat. Univ. (PhD 1979). Max-Planck Inst. of Biol Cybernetics, 1979–85; Dept of Zool., 1985–95, Dept of Anatomy, 1995–2006, Univ. of Cambridge. Rank Prize for Opto-electronics, 2012. *Publications:* contribs to jls incl. Nature, Current Biol., Cell, Neuron, Jl Neurosci. *Address:* Department of Physiology, Development and Neuroscience, University of Cambridge, Downing Street, Cambridge CB2 3EG.

HARDIE BOYS, Rt Hon. Sir Michael, GNZM 1996; GCMG 1996; QSO 2001; PC 1989; Governor General of New Zealand, 1996–2001; *b* Wellington, 6 Oct. 1931; *s* of Hon. Mr Justice Reginald Hardie Boys and Edith May (*née* Bennett); *m* 1957, Edith Mary Zohrab; two *s* two *d*. *Educ:* Wellington Coll.; Victoria Univ. (BA, LLB). Admitted Barrister and Solicitor, 1954; Partner, Scott Hardie Boys & Morrison, 1955–80; Chm., Legal Aid Bd, 1978–80; Judge of NZ High Court, 1980–89; Judge of the Court of Appeal, NZ, 1989–96. Pres., Wellington Dist Law Soc., 1979; Treas., NZ Law Soc., 1980. Hon. Bencher, Gray's Inn, 1994. Hon. Fellow, Wolfson Coll., Cambridge, 1995. Hon. LLD Victoria Univ. of Wellington, 1997.

HARDING, family name of **Baron Harding of Petherton**.

HARDING OF PETHERTON, 2nd Baron *cr* 1958, of Nether Compton; **John Charles Harding;** farmer, 1968–90; *b* 12 Feb. 1928; *s* of Field Marshal 1st Baron Harding of Petherton, GCB, CBE, DSO, MC, and Mary Gertrude Mabel (*d* 1983), *er d* of late Joseph Wilson Rooke, JP; *S* father, 1989; *m* 1966, Harriet (*d* 2012), *d* of Maj.-Gen. James Francis Hare, CB, DSO; two *s* one *d*. *Educ:* Marlborough College; Worcester Coll., Oxford (BA). National Service, 1945–48; 2nd Lieut, 11th Hussars (PAO), 1947; demobilised, 1948; Oxford Univ., 1948–51; Regular Commn, 11th Hussars (PAO), 1953; retired from Army, 1968. *Recreations:* hunting, racing. *Heir:* *s* Hon. William Allan John Harding [*b* 5 July 1969; *m* 2000, Susannah, *o d* of Richard Ratcliff; two *s* one *d*]. *Address:* Myrtle Cottage, Lamyatt, near Shepton Mallet, Somerset BA4 6NP. *T:* (01749) 812292.

See also Baroness Harding of Winscombe.

HARDING OF WINSCOMBE, Baroness *cr* 2014 (Life Peer), of Nether Compton in the County of Dorset; **Hon. Diana Mary, (Dido) Harding;** Chief Executive Officer, TalkTalk Telecom Group plc, since 2010; *b* Germany, 9 Nov. 1967; *d* of Baron Harding of Petherton, *qv*; *m* 1995, John David Penrose, *qv*; two *d*. *Educ:* Univ. of Oxford (BA 1st Cl. Hons PPE); Harvard Univ. (MBA 1992). McKinsey & Co., 1988–90, 1992–95; Mktg Dir, Thomas Cook, 1995–98; Global Sourcing Dir, Kingfisher plc, 1998–99; Commercial Dir, Woolworths plc, 1999–2000; various posts, Tesco plc, 2000–08; Convenience Dir, Sainsbury plc, 2008–10. Non-executive Director: British Land, 2010–; Cheltenham Racecourse; Bank of England, 2014–. *Publications:* Cool Dawn: my National Velvet, 1998. *Recreations:* horse racing, looking after my children. *Address:* c/o TalkTalk Telecom Group plc, 11 Evesham Street, W11 4AR. *E:* Dido.Harding@talktalkplc.com.

HARDING, Prof. Alan Paul, DPhil; Professor of Public Policy and Director, Heseltine Institute for Public Policy and Practice, University of Liverpool Management School, since 2012; *b* 14 Sept. 1958; *s* of late Alan Harding and of Ada Harding; *m* 2006, Karen Kauffman; one *s* one *d* (twins). *Educ:* Andrew Marvell Sen. High Sch., Hull; Middx Univ. (BA Humanities); LSE (MSc Econ); Nuffield Coll., Oxford (DPhil Politics). Res. Associate, Centre for Urban Studies, Univ. of Liverpool, 1988–92; Sen. Res. Fellow, 1992–94, Prof. of Urban Policy and Politics, 1994–99, European Inst. for Urban Affairs, Liverpool John Moores Univ.; Prof. of Urban and Regl Governance and Co-Dir, Centre for Sustainable Urban and Regl Futures, Univ. of Salford, 1999–2007; Prof. of Urban and Regl Governance and Dir (formerly Co-Dir), Inst. for Political and Economic Governance, Univ. of Manchester, 2007–12. *Publications:* European Cities Towards 2000, 1994; Regional Government in Britain: an economic solution?, 1996; Is There a 'Missing Middle' in English Governance?, 2000; Changing Cities, 2005; Bright Satanic Mills, 2007; articles in Internat. Jl of Urban and Regl Res., Urban Studies, Urban Affairs Rev., British Jl of Political Sci., W European Politics, Govt and Policy, etc. *Recreations:* family driving holidays, flying alone, Thai food, pre-post-modern music, enduring the beautiful madness that goes with being a Hull City Supporter. *Address:* University of Liverpool Management School, Chatham Street, Liverpool L69 7ZH. *E:* alan.harding@liverpool.ac.uk.

HARDING, Andrew William John; Africa Correspondent, BBC News, since 2009; *b* Epsom, 14 May 1967; *s* of John and Barbara Harding; *m* 1996, Jenny Hodgson; three *s*. *Educ:* King's Sch., Canterbury; Emmanuel Coll., Cambridge (BA Hons English Lit. 1989); City Univ. (Dip. Journalism). Moscow Corresp., Ind. Radio News and Monitor Radio, 1991–94; BBC News: Caucasus Corresp., 1994–96; Moscow Corresp., 1996–2000; E Africa Corresp., 2000–04; Asia Corresp., 2004–09. *Recreations:* books, boats. *Address:* c/o BBC News, 1 Park Road, Richmond 2092, Johannesburg, South Africa. *T:* 114822305, *Fax:* 114823400. *E:* andrew.harding@bbc.co.uk.

HARDING, Prof. Anthony Filmer, PhD; FBA 2001; FSA; Anniversary Professor of Archaeology, University of Exeter, since 2004; *b* 20 Nov. 1946; *s* of Edward Filmer Harding and Enid (*née* Price). *Educ:* Corpus Christi Coll., Cambridge (MA, PhD 1973). FSA 1983. Durham University: Lectr in Archaeol., 1973–88; Sen. Lectr, 1988–90; Prof. of Archaeol., 1990–2004. Pres., European Assoc. of Archaeologists, 2003–09. *Publications:* (with J. M. Coles) The Bronze Age in Europe, 1979; The Mycenaeans and Europe, 1984; Henge Monuments and Related Sites of Great Britain, 1987; Die Schwerter im ehemaligen Jugoslawien, 1995; European Societies in the Bronze Age, 2000; (with J. Ostoja-Zagórski and others) Sobiejuchy: a fortified site of the Early Iron Age in Poland, 2004; (with R. Šumberová and others) Velim: violence and death in Bronze Age Bohemia, 2007; Warriors and Weapons in Bronze Age Europe, 2007; Explorations in Salt Archaeology in the Carpathian Zone, 2013; Salt in Prehistoric Europe, 2013; (ed with H. Fokkens) The Oxford Handbook of the European Bronze Age, 2013. *Recreations:* music, gardening, walking. *Address:* Department of Archaeology, University of Exeter, North Park Road, Exeter EX4 4QE. *T:* (01392) 264520.

HARDING, Brian John; Director, Food and Farming Group, Department for Environment, Food and Rural Affairs, 2007–12; *b* 24 Sept. 1952; *s* of Edwin Ernest Harding and Hilda Mary Harding; *m* 1975, Pamela Bliss; one *s* one *d*. *Educ:* Queen Elizabeth's Sch., Crediton; UCL (BA Geog.). Ministry of Agriculture, Fisheries and Food, subseq. Department for Environment, Food and Rural Affairs: admin trainee, 1974–78; Private Sec. to Minister of State, 1978–80; Sec. to Zuckerman Rev. of Badgers and Bovine TB, 1980–81; Hd of Branch, Food Standards Div., 1981–84; Desk Officer (Agric.), European Secretariat, Cabinet Office, 1984–85 (on secondment); First Sec. (Agric. and Commercial), Washington, 1985–89 (on secondment); Head: Regl Mgt Div., 1990–92; Milk Div., 1992–96; Financial Policy Div., 1996–2000; Director: Policy and Corporate Strategy Unit, 2000–03; Wildlife, Countryside and Land Use, 2003–06; Sustainable Food Chain, 2006–07. *Recreations:* walking, reading, gardening, painting in water colours.

HARDING, Daniel John; conductor; Music Director: Swedish Radio Symphony Orchestra, since 2007; Orchestre de Paris, since 2016; *b* 31 Aug. 1975; *s* of Dr John Harding and Caroline Harding (*née* Cameron); *m* 2000, Beatrice Muthelet; one *s* one *d*. *Educ:* Chetham's Sch. of Music, Manchester; Trinity Hall, Cambridge. Assistant to Music Director: CBSO, 1993–94; Berlin Philharmonic Orch., 1995–96; Principal Conductor, Trondheim SO, 1997–2000; Music Director: die Deutsche Kammerphilharmonie, Bremen, 1999–2003; Mahler Chamber Orchestra, 2003–11, now Conductor Laureate; Principal Guest Conductor, LSO, 2006–; Music Partner, New Japan Philharmonic, 2010–. Débuts: BBC Proms, 1996; Berlin Philharmonic Orch., 1996; Royal Opera Hse, Covent Garden, 2002. Has made numerous recordings. Chevalier, Ordre des Arts et des Lettres (France), 2002. *Recreations:* match-going Manchester United supporter, playing Championship Manager. *Address:* c/o Askonas Holt Ltd, Lincoln House, 300 High Holborn, WC1V 7JH. *T:* (020) 7400 1700, *Fax:* (020) 7400 1799.

HARDING, Prof. Dennis William, MA, DPhil; FRSE; Abercromby Professor of Archaeology, University of Edinburgh, 1977–2007; *b* 11 April 1940; *s* of Charles Royston Harding and Marjorie Doris Harding. *Educ:* Keble Coll., Oxford (BA, MA, DPhil). Assistant Keeper, Dept of Antiquities, Ashmolean Museum, Oxford, 1965–66; Lecturer in Celtic Archaeology, 1966, Sen. Lectr, 1975–77, Univ. of Durham; University of Edinburgh: Dean, Faculty of Arts, 1983–86; Vice-Principal, 1988–91. Member: Board of Trustees, National Museum of Antiquities of Scotland, 1977–85; Ancient Monuments Board for Scotland, 1979–83; Scottish Postgrad. Studentships Awards Cttee, 1981–2001 (Chm., 1997–2001). FRSE 1986. *Publications:* The Iron Age in the Upper Thames Basin, 1972; The Iron Age in Lowland Britain, 1974, repr. 2014; (with A. J. Challis) Later Prehistory from the Trent to the Tyne, 1975; ed and contrib., Archaeology in the North: Report of the Northern Archaeological Survey, 1976; ed and contrib., Hillforts: later prehistoric earthworks in Britain and Ireland, 1976; Prehistoric Europe, 1978; (with I. M. Blake and P. J. Reynolds) An Iron Age Settlement in Dorset: excavation and reconstruction, 1993; (with T. N. Dixon) Dun Bharabhat, Cnip: an Iron Age settlement in West Lewis, 2000; (with S. M. D. Gilmour) The Iron Age Settlement at Beirgh, Riof, Isle of Lewis, 2000; The Iron Age in Northern Britain, 2004; The Archaeology of Celtic Art, 2007; The Iron Age Round-house: later prehistoric building in Britain and beyond, 2009; Iron Age Hillforts in Britain and Beyond, 2012; Death and Burial in Iron Age Britain, 2015.

HARDING, Sir (George) William, KCMG 1983 (CMG 1977); CVO 1972; HM Diplomatic Service, retired; *b* 18 Jan. 1927; *s* of late Lt Col G. R. Harding, DSO, MBE, and Grace Henley (*née* Darby); *m* 1955, Sheila Margaret Ormond Riddel (*d* 2002); four *s*. *Educ:* Aldenham Sch.; St John's College, Cambridge (Exhibnr; MA Hons). Royal Marines, 1945–48. Entered HM Foreign Service, 1950; served (other than in London) in Singapore, 1951–52; Burma, 1952–55; Paris, 1956–59; Santo Domingo, 1960–63; Mexico City, 1967–70; Paris, 1970–74; Ambassador to Peru, 1977–79; Asst Under-Sec. of State, FCO, 1979–81; Ambassador to Brazil, 1981–84; Dep. Under-Sec. of State, FCO, 1984–86. Mem., Trilateral Commn, 1988–93. Vis. Fellow, Harvard Centre for Internat. Affairs, 1986. Chairman: First Spanish Investment Trust, 1987–96; Thai-Euro Fund, 1988–97; British Thai Business Gp, 1995–97; Dir, Lloyds Bank Plc, 1988–93. Chairman: Margaret Mee Amazon Trust, 1988–94; Anglo-Peruvian Soc., 1987–89; Brazilian Chamber of Commerce in Britain, 1988–91. Vice-Pres., RGS, 1991–93; Mem. Council, RIIA, 1988–94. *Address:* La Dreyrie, 24510 Pezuls, France.

HARDING, Hazel, CBE 2006; DL; Chairman, East Lancashire Hospitals NHS Trust, 2009–13; *b* 17 Dec. 1946; *d* of Trevlyn William Sanderson and Florence Ward Sanderson; *m* 1975, Steven Harding (marr. diss. 2002); four *d*. Member (Lab): Lancashire CC, 1985–2009 (Chm., 1997–98; Chm., Lancs Educn Authy, 1998–2001; Leader, 2001–09); Rossendale BC, 1990–94, 1995–99. Board Member: Burnley Healthcare Trust, 1997–2002; Lancs LSC, 2000–06. Local Government Association: Member: Educn Exec., 1998–2005; Children's Bd, 2005. Founder Mem., Gen. Teaching Council of England, 2000; Chm., Rochdale Local Educn Partnership, 2010–. DL Lancs, 2009. *Recreations:* voluntary work, playing with grandchildren. *Address:* 21 Hawthorne Meadows, Crawshawbooth, Rossendale, Lancs BB4 8BF. *T:* (01706) 215767.

HARDING, Rev. James Owen Glyn; Director and Chief Executive, National Society for the Prevention of Cruelty to Children, 1995–2000, Vice-President, since 2001; *b* 18 Oct. 1942; *s* of Walter James Harding and Elizabeth May Harding; *m* 1965, Sally Goldie; one *s* two *d*. *Educ:* Pinner Grammar Sch.; Univ. of Sussex (BA); Univ. of Exeter (Home Office Letter of Recognition in Child Care); NE Oecumenical Course. Royal Borough of Kensington and Chelsea: Child Care Officer and Sen. Child Care Officer, Children's Dept, 1968–71; Area Officer and Asst Dir, Social Services Dept, 1971–85; National Society for the Prevention of Cruelty to Children: Dir, Child Care, 1986–89; Dep. Chief Exec. and Dir of Children's Services, 1989–95. Mem., Commn of Inquiry on death of Kimberley Carlisle, 1987. Ordained deacon, 2006, priest, 2007; non-stipendiary Asst Curate, Holy Redeemer, Acomb and York Workplace Chaplaincy, 2006–12; permission to officiate and Asst Dir of Ordinands, dio. York, 2012–. Patron, Nat. Assoc. of People Abused as Children. *Publications:* (jtly) A Child in Mind, 1987; The Parentalk Guide to Being a Grandparent, 2001; contrib. to various jls on social work and children's issues. *Recreations:* writing, literature, walking, sport, the theatre. *Address:* Strathmore, 63 Station Road, Upper Poppleton, York YO26 6PZ.

HARDING, Keith; Member (C) Mid Scotland and Fife, Scottish Parliament, 1999–2003; *b* 21 Nov. 1938; *s* of late Cyril Dennis Harding and Ella Evelyn Harding; *m* 1974, Elizabeth Anne Fowler; one *s* one *d*. *Educ:* Chipping Norton GS; Oxford Coll. of Further Educn. Newsagent and banker. Mem (C) Stirling DC, then Stirling Council, 1986–99 (Leader, 1993–96; Opposition Leader, 1996–99). Contested (Scottish People's Alliance) Stirling, Scottish Parly elecns, 2003.

HARDING, Rt Rev. Malcolm Alfred Warden; Assisting Bishop, Anglican Network in Canada, since 2009 (Bishop Suffragan, 2007–09); *b* 28 June 1936; *s* of Henry Warden Harding and Grace (*née* Walker); *m* 1962, Marylou (*née* Richards); one *s* two *d*. *Educ:* Univ. of Western Ontario (BA 1959); Huron Coll. (LTh 1962); Univ. of Manitoba (BSW 1965, MSW 1966). Ordained deacon, 1962; i/c of five rural parishes, dio. of Fredericton, 1962–63; Child Welfare Worker, Children's Aid Soc., Ont., 1963–64; Social Worker, 1966–68, Supervisor, 1968–73, Manitoba Dept of Health and Social Develt; ordained priest, 1973; Priest-in-charge, Birtle, Solsgirth, 1973–78; Rector, St George's, Brandon, 1978–92; Archdeacon of Brandon, 1986–92; Diocesan Administrator, Brandon, 1992; Bishop of Brandon, 1992–2001. Ambassador for Anglican Renewal Ministries, Canada, 2001–06. Hon. DD Huron, 1993. *Recreations:* model railroad, fishing, reading, railway enthusiast. *Address:* c/o Anglican Network in Canada, Box 1013, Burlington, ON L7R 4L8, Canada.

HARDING, Marshal of the Royal Air Force Sir Peter (Robin), GCB 1988 (KCB 1983; CB 1980); FRAeS; Chairman and Chief Executive, Merlyn International Associates, 1997–2006; *b* 2 Dec. 1933; *s* of late Peter Harding and Elizabeth Clear; *m* 1955, Sheila Rosemary May; two *s* one *d* (and one *s* decd). *Educ:* Chingford High Sch. Joined RAF, 1952; Pilot, 12 Sqdn, 1954–57; QFI and Flt Comdr, RAF Coll., Cranwell, 1957–60; Pilot, 1 Sqdn, RAAF, 1960–62; sc 1963; Air Secretary's Dept, MoD, 1964–66; OC, 18 Sqdn, Gutersloh and Acklington, 1966–69; jssc, Latimer, 1969–70; Defence Policy Staff, MoD, 1970–71; Director, Air Staff, Briefing, MoD, 1971–74; Station Comdr, RAF Brüggen, 1974–76; ADC to the Queen, 1975; Dir of Defence Policy, MoD, 1976–78; Asst Chief of Staff (Plans and Policy), SHAPE, 1978–80; AOC No 11 Group, 1981–82; VCAS, 1982–84; VCDS, 1985; AOC-in-C, RAF Strike Comd, and C-in-C, UK Air Forces, 1985–88; Chief of Air Staff, 1988–92; Chief of the Defence Staff, 1992–94. Dep. Chm., GEC Marconi Ltd, 1995–98; Chm., Thorlock Internat. Ltd, 1999–2000. Member: Partnership Korea, 1995–99; Anglo Korean Forum, 1995–99. FRAeS 1983, Hon. CRAeS 1989; FRSA 1988 (Life Fellow 2008). Liveryman, Hon. Co. of Air Pilots (formerly GAPAN), 1989–. Member: Council, Winston Churchill Meml Trust, 1990–2008; Leonard Cheshire Conflict Recovery Centre, 1998–2005. Vice Pres., Guild of Aviation Artists, 1994–. Hon. DSc Cranfield, 1990. Comdr, Legion of Merit (USA), 1992. *Publications:* articles for professional jls, magazines and books. *Recreations:* pianoforte, bridge, birdwatching, fishing. *Club:* Garrick.

HARDING, Philip Douglas; journalist, broadcaster and international media consultant, since 2007; *b* London, 28 April 1947; *s* of Douglas Harding and Leonora Harding; *m* 1979, Margo Blythman; one *d*. *Educ:* Harrow Co. Sch. for Boys; Univ. of York (BA Hons); Wharton Business Sch. (AMP). BBC: News trainee, 1969–70; News writer, BBC Radio News, 1970–72; Producer, TV Current Affairs, 1972–81; Dep. Ed., Panorama, 1981; Dep. Ed., Nationwide, 1981–83; Ed., London Plus, 1983–84; Hd, London and SE Regl TV, 1984–85; Asst Hd, Current Affairs TV, 1985–87; Editor, Today prog., Radio 4, 1987–92; Proj. Dir, then Founding Editor, News Progs, Radio Five Live, 1993–95; Chief Political Advr, 1995–96; Controller, Editl Policy, 1996–2001; Dir, English Networks and News, World Service, 2001–07. Progs and interviews for broadcast media. Editl Trustee, Press Assoc., 2008–; Trustee: One World Media, 2007–; CPU Media Trust, 2007–. Fellow: Radio Acad., 2000–; Soc. of Editors, 2007–. *Publications:* articles in newspapers. *Recreations:* watching football, supporting QPR, walking, travelling, listening to music from across the world. *E:* phil@hardingmedia.com. *Clubs:* Frontline, Hospital.

HARDING, Rear Adm. Russell George, CBE 2015 (OBE 2002); Rear Admiral Fleet Air Arm and Assistant Chief of Naval Staff (Aviation, Amphibious Capability and Carriers) (formerly Assistant Chief of Naval Staff (Aviation and Carriers)), 2012–15; *b* Perth, 13 May 1960; *s* of George and Anne Harding; *m* 1983, Suzanne Pugh; two *d*. *Educ:* BRNC Dartmouth; Edinburgh Univ. (BSc Electrical Engrg 1982). Joined RN, 1978; Watchkeeper, HMS Hermione, 1983–85; flying trng, RNAS Culdrose, 1985–86; 814 Naval Air Sqn, HM Illustrious, 1987–88; 750 Naval Air Sqn as Navigation Systems Instructor, RNAS Culdrose, 1988–89; in command: HMS Brereton, 1989–91; HMS Alderney, 1991; Flight Comdr, HMS Cumberland, 1992–93; Exec. Officer and 2nd in comd, HMS Brilliant, 1993–95; Trng Way Ahead Study, MoD, 1995–96; in comd HMS Brave, 1996–98; Trng Comdr, Britannia RN Coll., Dartmouth, 1998–2000; Air Warfare Desk Officer, Directorate of Navy Resources and Plans, 2000–02, Dep. Dir, Above Water Capability area, 2003–05, MoD; Dep. to Cdre Fleet Air Arm, Navy Comd H1 Portsmouth, 2005–06; in comd HMS Ocean, 2006–07; Hd of Air and Littoral Manoeuvre Capability, MoD, 2008–11; Dep. Comdr, Strike Force NATO, 2011–12 (Dep. Comdr, NATO Libya Operation Unified Protector, 2011). *Recreations:* running, sailing.

HARDING, Stephen Mark; Attorney General, Isle of Man, since 2011; *b* Liverpool, 11 Nov. 1961; *s* of Bryan Wilfrid Harding and Beatrice Nancy Deeming (*née* Moore); *m* 1997, Frances Tracey Dean; one *s* one *d*. *Educ:* Onchan Primary Sch., IOM; King William's Coll., Castletown; Douglas High Sch.; Lancaster Univ. (BA Hons Orgn Studies). Called to the Manx Bar, 1992; NP, 1996; admitted solicitor, England, 1998; Govt Advocate, IOM, 2002–11. *Recreations:* walking, mountain biking. *Address:* Attorney General's Chambers, 3rd Floor, St Mary's Court, Hill Street, Douglas, Isle of Man IM1 1EU. *T:* (01624) 685452.

HARDING, Sir William; *see* Harding, Sir G. W.

HARDINGE, family name of **Viscount Hardinge** and **Baron Hardinge of Penshurst**.

HARDINGE, 8th Viscount *cr* 1846, of Lahore and King's Newton, Derbyshire; **Thomas Henry de Montarville Hardinge;** Bt 1801; *b* Carshalton, Surrey, 19 June 1993; s of 7th Viscount Hardinge and of Sophia Mary Hardinge (*née* Bagnell); *S* father, 2014. *Educ:* Stowe Sch.; Brunel Univ. (engrg). *Recreations:* shooting, tennis. *Heir: b* Hon. Jamie Alexander David Hardinge, *b* 4 Nov. 1996. *Address:* 20 Niton Street, SW6 6NJ. *Club:* East India.

HARDINGE OF PENSHURST, 4th Baron *cr* 1910; **Julian Alexander Hardinge;** Chairman, Mallory International, since 2002; *b* 23 Aug. 1945; *s* of 3rd Baron Hardinge of Penshurst and Janet Christine Goschen (*d* 1970), *d* of late Lt-Col Francis Cecil Campbell Balfour, CIE, CVO, CBE, MC; *S* father, 1997; *m* 1st, 1972, Anthea June West (marr. diss. 1993); two *d*; 2nd, 2001, Ulrike Adolph. *Educ:* Eton; Trinity Coll., Cambridge. A Page of Honour to HM the Queen, 1959–62. Booksellers' Association: Dir, Book Tokens Ltd, 1984–2004; Chairman: Coll. and Univ. Booksellers Gp, 1985–87; Export Booksellers Gp, 1993–95; Batch.co.uk, 2002–06 (Dir, 1998–2006); Baobab Ebook Services Ltd, 2013–; Hon. Vice Pres. Director: John Smith & Son, Booksellers, 1998–2001; ESQN Ltd, 2002–11; Hardinge Simpole Publishing, 2001–12. Chm., Mind Sports Olympiad, 1998–2002. *Heir: b* Hon. Hugh Francis Hardinge, *b* 9 April 1948. *Address:* Upper Yewdale, 7 Links Road, Budleigh Salterton, Devon EX9 6DF.

HARDMAN, Rt Rev. Christine Elizabeth; *see* Newcastle, Bishop of.

HARDMAN, John Nimrod, FCA; Chairman: ASDA Group PLC (formerly ASDA-MFI), 1988–91 (Deputy Chairman, 1986–87; Director, 1984–91); Dewhurst Butchers, 1996–2006; *b* 8 Oct. 1939; *s* of late Harry John Hardman and of Florence Gladys Sybil Anne Hardman (*née* Dolby); *m* 1966, Joan McHugh (*d* 2009); one *s* one *d*. *Educ:* Quarry Bank High Sch., Liverpool; Liverpool Univ. (BComm Hons). FIGD. Duncan Watson & Short, Chartered Accts, 1962–66; RCA Corp., 1967–69; Finance Dir, Thorn Colour Tubes Ltd, 1969–75; Dir, Europe, Africa and Far East, RCA Corp. Picture Tube Div., 1976–80; Finance Director: Oriel Foods, 1981; ASDA Stores, 1981–84 (Man. Dir, 1984–89); Director: Maples Stores plc, 1995–98; Adderley Featherstone plc, 1991–2007. Director: Leeds Develt Corp., 1988–92; Yorks Electricity Bd, 1989–97. CCMI; FRSA. *Recreations:* golf, tennis, shooting, cricket. *Address:* Hillside, Spofforth Hill, Wetherby, Yorks LS22 4SF. *Clubs:* Lord's Taverners; Liverpool Artists, Royal Liverpool Golf, Liverpool Racquets (Liverpool); Pannal Golf (Harrogate).

HARDMAN, Richard Frederick Paynter, CBE 1998; CGeol, FGS; consultant explorationist, since 2002; Director, Atlantic Petroleum Ltd, since 1994; Director and Technical Adviser, FX Energy Inc., since 2003; *b* 2 May 1936; *s* of late Dr Charles Ramsay Hardman and of Mary Hardman (*née* Barnsley); *m* 1st, 1960, Janet Quintrell Treloar (marr. diss.); two *s* two *d*; 2nd, 1982, Marilyn Merryweather (marr. diss.); one *d*; 3rd, 1995, Elizabeth Jane Atkinson (*d* 2008); 4th, 2009, Alice Deschampsneufs. *Educ:* Arnold Sch., Blackpool; Corpus Christi Coll., Oxford (MA). FGS 1959; CGeol 1991. Nat. Service, RN, 1954–56. Geologist with BP, in UK, Libya, Kuwait, Colombia, 1959–69; Exploration Manager with Amoco, Superior Oil and Amerada Hess, based in London and Norway, 1969–88; Exploration Dir, Amerada Hess Ltd, 1989–98; Amerada Hess International Ltd: Vice-Pres., NW Europe, 1996–98; Dir and Vice-Pres., Exploration, 1998–2001; Exploration Dir, Regal Petroleum, 2005–06. Dir, DENERCO OIL A/S, 1997–2001. Mem., Programme Bd, Brit. Geol Survey, 1993–95. Mem., NERC, 1998–2003 (Chm., Sci and Innovation Strategy Bd, 2001–03); Chm., Industrial Liaison Panel, Eur. Consortium for Ocean Res. Drilling, 2010–12. Geological Society: Chm., Petroleum Gp, 1987–90; Pres., 1996–98. Chm., Petroleum Exploration Soc. of GB, 1985–86; Pres., Earth Sci. Teachers Assoc., 1993–95. Chm., Artsline, 2001–03. Chair, Friends of Southwark Cathedral, 2002–06. Petroleum Gp Silver Medal, 2002, William Smith Medal, 2003, Geol Soc.; Lifetime Achievement Award, Petroleum Gp of Geol Soc. *Publications:* (ed jtly) Tectonic Events Responsible for Britain's Oil and Gas Reserves, 1990; (ed) Exploration Britain: geological insights for the next decade, 1992; papers on chalk as an oil and gas reservoir. *Recreations:* geology, jam making, theatre, music, ski-ing, wide open spaces. *Address:* Long Barn, Treen, St Levan, Penzance TR19 6LG. *T:* (01736) 810991. *Club:* Athenæum.

HARDMAN MOORE, John Halstead; *see* Moore, J. H. H.

HARDSTAFF, Veronica Mary; Member (Lab), Sheffield City Council, 1971–78 and 2002–07; *b* 23 Oct. 1941; *d* of Rev. Ernest Tutt and Mary Tutt; *m* 1st, 1964 (marr. diss. 1977); one *s* one *d*; 2nd, 2007, Rev. Canon Dr Alan Roy Billings, *qv*. *Educ:* Manchester Univ. (BA Hons German); Cologne Univ. Teacher of German and French: High Storrs Girls' GS, Sheffield, 1963–66; St Peter's Sec. Mod. Sch., Sheffield, 1969–70; Knottingley High Sch., 1977–79; Frecheville Sch., Sheffield, 1979–86; Birley Sch., Sheffield, 1986–94. Mem. (Lab), Sheffield CC, 1971–78. MEP (Lab) Lincs and Humberside S, 1994–99; contested (Lab) Yorks and Humber Reg., 1999. Vice-Chm., Jt Parly Cttee, EP-Poland, 1995–99. *Recreations:* reading, walking, classical music, playing flute, local activism! *Address:* 43 Northfield Court, Sheffield S10 1QR. *T:* (0114) 267 6549.

HARDWICK, Very Rev. Christopher George, PhD; Vicar, Tavistock, Gulworthy and Brent Tor, since 2015; *b* 7 Oct. 1957; *s* of Keith Hardwick and Vera Elizabeth Hardwick; *m* 1st, 1982, Linda Dorothy Hicks (marr. diss. 2010); one *s* one *d*; 2nd, 2011, Sarah Katherine Louise White. *Educ:* King Edward VI Sch., Lichfield; Ripon Coll., Cuddesdon; Open Univ. (BA 1994); Birmingham Univ. (MA 1996; PhD 2000). ACIB 1979. Ordained deacon, 1992, priest, 1993; Asst Curate, Worcester SE Team, 1992–95; Chaplain (part-time): St Richard's Hospice, Worcester, 1992–95; RNIB (New Coll.) Worcester, 1992–95; Rector: Ripple,

Earls Croome with Hill Croome and Strensham, 1995–2005; Upton upon Severn and Church of the Good Shepherd, Hook Common, 2000–05; Dean of Truro, 2005–11; Priest-in-charge, Pyworthy, Pancrasweek and Bridgerule, 2011–15. RD Upton, 1997–2005; Hon. Canon, Worcester Cathedral, 2003–05. Chm., Worcester Diocesan House of Clergy, 2002–05; Proctor in Convocation, Gen. Synod, 2004–05. A Church Comr, 2007–11. *Recreations:* choral music, current affairs, reading, cooking, entertaining, sailing. *Address:* The Vicarage, 5A Plymouth Road, Tavistock, Devon PL19 8AU.

HARDWICK, Matthew Richard; QC 2014; *b* Haslemere, Surrey, 14 March 1969; *s* of Dr Richard Gerald Hardwick and Mrs Richard Hardwick; *m* 2002, Philippa Anne; two *s* two *d.* *Educ:* Marlborough Coll.; Trinity Coll., Cambridge (BA Classics and Law 1991); Université Libre de Bruxelles (Licence spéciale en droit européen 1993). Called to the Bar, Gray's Inn, 1994. Member: Commercial Bar Assoc.; Chancery Bar Assoc. *Recreations:* family walks and bike rides, Lakeland swims, chaotic sailing trips with family (and two dogs), chopping and stacking wood with my sons and daughters, singing (croakily). *Address:* Springhead, Marley Lane, near Haslemere, W Sussex GU27 3RE. *T:* 07788 743472. *E:* mhardwick@3vb.com.

HARDWICK, Nicholas Lionel, CBE 2010; HM Chief Inspector of Prisons for England and Wales, 2010–Jan. 2016; *b* 19 July 1957; *s* of Lionel and Nancy Hardwick; one *d*; *m* 1985, Susan Heaven; one *s*. *Educ:* Epsom Coll.; Hull Univ. (BA Hons English Lit. 1979). Youth Training Manager, NACRO, 1980–85; Dep. Chief Exec., Soc. Voluntary Associates, 1986; Chief Executive: Centrepoint, 1986–95; British Refugee Council, subseq. Refugee Council, 1995–2003; Shadow Chm., 2003–04, Chm., 2004–10, Ind. Police Complaints Commn. Special Advr, Rough Sleeping, DoE, 1991. Chm., Housing Ombudsman Service, 2010–13. Chm., European Council for Refugees and Exiles, 1999–2003. Chm., Gtr London Radio Adv. Council, 1993–95; Mem., BBC SE Regl Adv. Cttee, 1993–95. Member: Social Security Adv. Cttee, 1994–99; Holocaust Meml Day Steering Gp, 2001–05. Bd Mem., Stonebridge HAT, 1994–97. Trustee: Youth Hostel Assoc., 2007–09; New Horizon Youth Centre, 2009–. FRSA 1995. Hon. Fellow, Dept of Criminology, Univ. of Leicester, 2013. Hon. DSSc Wolverhampton, 2002; Hon. DLitt Hull, 2011. *Recreations:* walking, Spain, Queens Park Rangers FC.

HARDWICKE, 10th Earl of, *cr* 1754; **Joseph Philip Sebastian Yorke;** Baron Hardwicke 1733; Viscount Royston 1754; *b* 3 Feb. 1971; *s* of Philip Simon Prospero Rupert Lindley, Viscount Royston (*d* 1973) and Virginia Anne (*d* 1988), *d* of Geoffrey Lyon; *S* grandfather, 1974; *m* 2008, Siobhan Loftus; one *s*. *Heir: s* Viscount Royston, *qv*.

HARDY; *see* Gathorne-Hardy, family name of Earl of Cranbrook.

HARDY, Alan; Member (C) for Brent North, Greater London Council, 1967–86 (Chairman, Finance and Establishment Committee, 1977–81); *b* 24 March 1932; *s* of late John Robert Hardy and Emily Hardy; *m* 1972, Betty Howe (*d* 2010), *d* of late Walter and Hilda Howe. *Educ:* Hookergate Grammar Sch.; Univ. of Manchester; Inst. of Historical Res., Univ. of London (MA). Res. Asst to Sir Lewis Namier, History of Parliament Trust, 1955–56; Res. Officer and Dep. Dir, London Municipal Soc., 1956–63; Mem. British Secretariat, Council of European Municipalities, 1963–64. Member: Local Authorities' Conditions of Service Adv. Bd, 1977–81; Nat. Jt Council for Local Authorities' Services (Manual Workers), 1977–81. Mem. Bd, Harlow Develt Corp., 1968–80. Hon. Life Pres., Brent North Conservative Assoc., 1986. Contested (C) Islington SW, 1966. *Publications:* Queen Victoria Was Amused, 1976; The Kings' Mistresses, 1980. *Recreation:* admiring old things. *Address:* The Old Garden, 20 Ledger Lane, Outwood, Wakefield WF1 2PH. *T:* (01924) 823771. *Club:* Naval.

HARDY, Amanda Jane; QC 2015; *b* Hornchurch, Essex, 12 Dec. 1969; *d* of late V. W. M. Richards and M. V. Richards; *m* 1994, Matthew David Hardy; three *d*. *Educ:* City of London Sch. for Girls; King's Coll. London (LLB Hons; LLM Tax; AKC). Called to the Bar, Middle Temple, 1993. Chair, Chancery Bar Litigants in Person Scheme, 2013–. Mem., Main Cttee, 2012–, Chair, Pro Bono Sub-cttee, 2013–, Chancery Bar Assoc. *Publications:* (with R. Venables) Inheritance Tax Planning, 3rd edn 1997; International Taxation of Trusts, 2004, 2014. *Recreations:* my family, reading, theatre. *Address:* 15 Old Square, Lincoln's Inn, WC2A 3UE. *T:* (020) 7242 2744, *Fax:* (020) 7831 8095. *E:* taxchambers@15oldsquare.co.uk.

HARDY, Anna Gwenllian; *see* Somers Cocks, Hon. A. G.

HARDY, Prof. Barbara Gladys, FBA 2006; FRSL; Professor of English Literature, Birkbeck College, University of London, 1970–89, now Emeritus; teacher and author; *b* 27 June 1924; *d* of Maurice and Gladys Nathan; *m* Ernest Dawson Hardy (decd); two *d*. *Educ:* Swansea High Sch. for Girls; University Coll. London (BA, MA). Subsequently on staff of English Dept of Birkbeck Coll., London; Prof. of English, Royal Holloway Coll., Univ. of London, 1965–70. Dir, Yeats Summer School, 1990–91. Pres., Dickens Soc., 1987–88; Vice-Pres., Thomas Hardy Soc., 1991–. Hon. Prof. of English, UC Swansea, 1991. Fellow, Welsh Acad., 1982; FRSL 1997. Hon. Mem., MLA. Hon. Fellow: Birkbeck Coll., London, 1991; RHBNC, 1992; Univ. of Wales, Swansea, 1998. DUniv Open, 1981. *Publications:* The Novels of George Eliot, 1959 (Rose Mary Crawshay Prize); The Appropriate Form, 1964; (ed) George Eliot: Daniel Deronda, 1967; (ed) Middlemarch: Critical Approaches to the Novel, 1967; The Moral Art of Dickens, 1970; (ed) Critical Essays on George Eliot, 1970; The Exposure of Luxury: radical themes in Thackeray, 1972; (ed) Thomas Hardy: The Trumpet-Major, 1974; Tellers and Listeners: the narrative imagination, 1975; (ed) Thomas Hardy: A Laodicean, 1975; A Reading of Jane Austen, 1975; The Advantage of Lyric, 1977; Particularities: readings in George Eliot, 1982; Forms of Feeling in Victorian Fiction, 1985; Narrators and Novelists: collected essays, 1987; Swansea Girl, 1993; London Lovers (novel), 1996 (Sagittarius Prize, 1997); Henry James: the later writing, 1996; Shakespeare's Storytellers, 1997; Thomas Hardy: imagining imagination, 2000; Dylan Thomas: an original language, 2000; Severn Bridge: new and selected poems, 2001; George Eliot: a critic's biography, 2006; The Yellow Carpet: new and selected poems, 2006; Dickens and Creativity, 2008; (ed with Kate Hardy) London Rivers, 2011; Dorothea's Daughter and other nineteenth-century postscripts, 2012; Dante's Ghosts, 2013; The Novels of Ivy Compton-Burnett, 2016. *Address:* c/o Birkbeck College, Malet Street, WC1E 7HX.

HARDY, Rev. Canon Brian Albert; Rector, All Saints, St Andrews, 1991–96; *b* 3 July 1931; *s* of Albert Charles Hardy and Edith Maude Sarah Mabe. *Educ:* City Boys' School, Leicester; St John's Coll., Oxford (MA, DipTheol); Westcott House, Cambridge. Curate, Rugeley, Staffs, 1957–62; Chaplain, Downing Coll., Cambridge, 1962–66; Livingston (West Lothian) Ecumenical Team Ministry, 1966–74; Churches' Planning Officer for Telford, Salop, 1974–78; Chaplain, Coates Hall Theological Coll., Edinburgh, 1978–82; Rector, St Columba's by the Castle Episcopal Church, Edinburgh, 1982–91; Episcopalian Chaplain, Royal Infirmary of Edinburgh and Royal Edinburgh Hosp., 1982–86; Dean of the dio. of Edinburgh, 1986–91. Hon. Canon, Edinburgh Cathedral, 1991. *Recreations:* music, especially choral and piano; cycling. *Address:* 3/3 Starbank Road, Newhaven, Edinburgh EH5 3BN. *T:* (0131) 551 6783.

HARDY, David Ian Brooker; Director, Distance Education International, since 2007; *b* 28 Sept. 1950; *s* of late Leslie Hardy and of Ruth Eveline Hardy (*née* Brooker); *m* 1979, Christine Mary Wilson; two *d*. *Educ:* Bradford Grammar Sch.; Univ. of London (BSc Hons); Univ. of Leeds (Grad. Cert Ed). Chartered FCIPD. Dept of Educn, Leeds City Council, 1979–85; Department of Education and Science: Yorks and Humberside, 1985–86; Nat. Manager, Post Experience Vocational Educn, 1986–90; Asst Sec., 1990; Chief Exec., 1990–2000, Hon. Pres., 2000–01, Open Poly., then Open Learning Foundn; Chief Exec., Open Learning Internat., 2002–07. Chm., European Open Univ. Network BV, 1996–2001. Moderator, BTEC, 1982–85; Member: UGC/NAB Standing Cttee on Continuing Educn, 1986–90; Inter-Ministerial Rev. of Highly Qualified Manpower, 1989–90; CNAA, 1991–92; Bd, Eur. Assoc. Distance Teaching Univs, 1993–2001 (Pres., 1999–2001); Eur. Open and Distance Learning Liaison Cttee, 1999–2002. Vice Pres. (Europe), Internat. Council for Open and Distance Educn, 1999–2002. Advr on educn reform to govts of Kazakhstan, Kyrgyzstan, Georgia, Azerbaijan, Russian Fedn, Turkey and Romania, 2002–. Vis. Lectr, Immanuel Kant State Univ. of Russia, 2007–08. Hon. Mem., Central Asian Business Women's Assoc., 2007–. Mem. Council, Bradford Chamber of Commerce, 1982–86. Mem., RIIA, 2012–. MInstD 2014. *Publications:* (jtly) Onchocerciasis in Zaire, 1977; articles in learned jls on post-secondary education reform. *Recreations:* Central Asia, swimming, fell walking, travel. *E:* d.hardy@mailbox.ulcc.ac.uk.

HARDY, David Malcolm; Director, PowerPlay Golf Holdings Limited, since 2008; *b* 16 July 1955; *s* of Roy Hardy and late Mary (*née* Ebsworth); *m* 1981 (marr. diss. 1994); one *s* one *d*; *m* 1995, Marion Dorothy Brazier. *Educ:* Westcliff High Sch. ACIB; FCT. Barclays Bank, 1973–81; Barclays Merchant Bank, 1981–85; LCH.Clearnet (formerly London Clearing House), 1985–2006, Gp Chief Exec., 1987–2006; Hd, Strategic Mkt Develt, MF Global, 2007–08. Director: London Commodity Exchange (1986) Ltd, 1991–96; Internat. Petroleum Exchange of London Ltd, 1993–99; Futures and Options Assoc., 1993–2006; Inst. of Financial Markets, US, 2000–10; GCSA LLC (US), 2012– (Chm., 2013–); Co-Chm., SBL Network, 2014–. Mem., Adv. Bd, Cleartrade Exchange Pte Ltd, 2011–. Member: FSA Practitioner Panel, 2001–06. FRSA. Freeman, City of London, 1994; Liveryman, Co. of World Traders, 1993; Mem., Internat. Bankers' Co., 2005–10. Member: Futures Industry Hall of Fame, 2009; Securities Services Hall of Fame, 2009. *Recreations:* golf, photography. *E:* oak.park@mac.com. *Clubs:* Royal Automobile; West Byfleet Golf.

HARDY, Sir David (William), Kt 1992; Chairman, Transport Research Laboratory, 1996–2007; Chairman of Trustees, National Maritime Museum, 1995–2005 (Trustee, since 1992); *b* 14 July 1930; 3rd *s* of late Brig. John H. Hardy, CBE, MC; *m* 1957, Rosemary, *d* of late Sir Godfrey F. S. Collins, KCIE, CSI, OBE; one *s* one *d*. *Educ:* Wellington Coll.; Harvard Business School (AMP). Chartered Accountant. Served 2nd RHA, 2/Lt, 1953–54. Funch Edye & Co. Inc., NY, New Orleans and Norfolk, Va, 1954–64 (Dir, 1960); Vice Pres. Finance and Admin, Imperial Tobacco, USA, 1964–70; HM Govt Co-ordinator of Industrial Advrs, 1970–72; Gp Finance Dir, Tate & Lyle Ltd, 1972–77; Dir, Ocean Transport & Trading PLC, 1977–83; Chairman: Ocean Inchcape, 1980–83; London Park Hotels, 1983–87; Globe Investment Trust, 1983–90 (Dir, 1976–90); Docklands Light Railway, 1984–87; Swan Hunter, 1986–88; MGM Assurance, 1986–2000 (Dep. Chm., 1985–86; Dir, 1985–2000); Europa Minerals, 1991–94; Bankers Trust Investment Management, 1992–94; Burmine Ltd, 1992–96; Y. J. Lovell, 1994–99; Colliers Capital UK, 2004–07; Committed Capital UK, 2004–; 100 Group Chartered Accountants, 1986–88; LDDC, 1988–92 (Dep. Chm., 1988); Deputy Chairman: LRT, 1984–87; Agricultural Mortgage Corp., 1985–92 (Dir, 1973–); Director: Sturge Holdings PLC, 1985–95; Waterford Wedgwood plc (formerly Waterford Glass), 1984–90; Paragon Group, 1985–88; Aberfoyle Holdings, 1986–91; Chelsea Harbour Ltd, 1986–90; Electra Kingsway Managers Hldgs Ltd, 1990–91; Tootal Gp, 1990–91; CIBA-GEIGY, 1991–96; Hanson, 1991–2001; J. A. Devenish, 1991–93; Stirling-Lloyd Holdings, 1992–; James Fisher & Sons, 1993–2003 (Chm., 1993–94); Milner Estates (formerly Conrad Ritblat) plc, 1996–99; Imperial Tobacco Gp, 1996–2001; Sons of Gwalia, 1996–99; Milner Consultancies, 2000–01; Fitzhardinge, 2001–04; Colliers CRE, 2004–07; Adv. Dir, HSBC Investment Banking, 1995–97. Chm., Engrg Marketing Adv. Cttee, DTI, 1989–90; Member: NEDC Cttee for Agriculture, 1970–72; Export Credit Guarantees Adv. Council, 1973–78; Industrial Develt Adv. Bd, DTI, 1992–96; Co-opted Council of Inst. of Chartered Accountants, 1974–78; Economic and Fiscal Policy Cttee, CBI, 1981–88; Council, BIM, 1974–78 (CCMI (CBIM 1975)). Mem., Develt Cttee, NACF, 1988–98; Vice Chm., St Katherine and Shadwell Trust, 2000– (Mem., 1990–); Founder Mem., Royal Albert Dock Trust, 1992–; Dir, Greenwich Millennium Trust, 1996–2001; Trustee: Mary Rose Trust, 2000–; Sir John Fisher Charitable Foundn, 2008–. Pres., Poplar, Blackwall and Dist Rowing Club, 1992–; Patron, Pitlochry Angling Club, 1994–. Gov., Chelsea Open Air Nursery Sch., 1992–2004 (Dep. Chm., 1994–2004). Hon. British Consul, Norfolk, Va, 1960–62. Member: Co. of Chartered Accountants, 1976; Co. of Shipwrights, 1990. Younger Brother, Trinity House, 1996. FCILT (FCIT 1988). Hon. LLD Greenwich, 2003. *E:* seahardy@aol.com. *Clubs:* Brooks's, Beefsteak, MCC, Flyfishers', HAC.

HARDY, Sir James (Gilbert), Kt 1981; OBE 1975; Consultant, Accolade Wines Australia (formerly Hardy Wine Company, then Constellation Wines Australia), since 2003; Senior Partner, Leadership, CMLpartners Ltd Executive Search, 2011–13; *b* 20 Nov. 1932; *s* of Tom Mayfield Hardy and Eileen C. Hardy; *m* 1st, 1956, Anne Christine Jackson (marr. diss. 1991); two *s*; 2nd, 1991, Joan Margaret McInnes. *Educ:* St Peter's Coll., Adelaide, SA; S Australian Sch. of Mines; S Australian Inst. of Technol. (Dip. in Accountancy). FCPA; FAICD. National Service, 13th Field Artillery Regt, Adelaide, 1951. Elder Smith & Co. Ltd, 1951; J. C. Correll & Co., 1952; Thomas Hardy & Sons Pty Ltd, Winemakers, Adelaide, 1953–92: Shipping Clerk, Sales Rep., Sales Supervisor and Lab. Asst, 1953–62; Dir and Manager, Sydney Br., 1962–77; Regional Dir, Eastern Australia, 1977–81; Chm. of Dirs, 1981–92; Chm. of Dirs, Houghton Wines Pty Ltd, 1981–92; Dir, BRL Hardy Ltd, 1992–2002. Director: S Australian Film Corp., 1981–87; America's Cup Challenge 1983 Ltd, 1981–85; Advertiser Newspapers Ltd, 1983–88; Lorna Hodgkinson Sunshine Home Ltd, 1993–2003. Dep. Chm., Racing Rules Cttee, Yachting Fedn, 1969–81; Dir of Sailing/Captain, S Australian Challenge for the Defence of America's Cup 1984–87. Vice Pres., Internat. 12 Metre Assoc., 1986–92. Treasurer, Liquor Trade Supervisory Council of NSW, 1965–70; Fellow, Catering Inst. of Australia, 1972; Pres., Wine and Brandy Assoc. of NSW, 1980–83. NSW Chm., Aust. National Travel Assoc., 1976; Vice Pres., Royal Blind Soc. of NSW, 1980–88 (Mem. Council, 1967–91); Pres., NSW Aust. Football League and Sydney Football League, 1982–83; Pres., "One and All" Sailing Ship Assoc. of SA Inc., 1981–90; Chm., Adelaide 1998 Commonwealth Games Bid, 1990–92; Mem., Bd of Advice, Rothmans Nat. Sport Foundn, 1985–87; Trustee: Rothmans Foundn, 1987–93; Sydney Cricket and Sports Ground Trust, 1990–95; Mem., Council, Australian Nat. Maritime Mus., 1992–97; Dir/Trustee, HM Bark Endeavour Foundn, 1996–2003. Chairman: Adv. Cttee, Life Educn Centre of SA, 1988–91; Landcare Australia Ltd Foundn, 1994–98; Adv. Cttee, Natural Heritage Trust, 1998–2009. Member: Exec. Cttee, Neurosurgical Res. Foundn of SA, 1988–2004; Adv. Bd, John Curtin Sch. of Medical Res., ANU, Canberra, 1982–87. Dep. Grand Master, United Grand Lodge of NSW, 1977–80. Australian Yachtsman of the Year, 1981; inducted into America's Cup Hall of Fame, 1994. *Relevant publication:* Sir James Hardy: an adventurous life, by Rob Mundle, 1993. *Recreation:* yachting (skipper or helmsman in America's Cup and Admiral's Cup races). *Address:* Accolade Wines Australia, PO Box 96, Botany, NSW 1455, Australia. *T:* (2) 96665855, *Fax:* (2) 93169738. *Clubs:* Royal Ocean Racing; Australian, Tattersalls, Royal Sydney Yacht Squadron (Sydney); Cruising Yacht of Australia (NSW); Royal Perth Yacht; Royal Queensland Yacht; Fort Worth Boat (Texas, USA).

HARDY, Joanna; independent jewellery consultant and broadcaster; *b* London, 9 Nov. 1961; *d* of Albert Edward John Hardy and Julia Hardy; *m* 1996, Craig Emerson; one *s* one *d*. *Educ:* Littlefields Sch.; Bedales Sch.; W Surrey Sch. of Art and Design; Sir John Cass Sch. of Art and Design (Diamond Dip. 1983). FGA 1982. Rough diamond sorter/valuer, De Beers Diamond Trading Co., London, 1982–84; Asst Manager, Polished Diamond Buying Office, J C Ginder Pty Ltd, Antwerp, 1985–86; Diamond Dealer, J C Ginder Ltd, Diamond Merchants, London,

1986–89; Diamond Specialist and Antique Jewellery Valuer and Cataloguer, Phillips Fine Art Auctioneers, London, 1989–92; travelled overland through SE Asia to Australia, 1992–94; Sen. Jewellery Specialist, Dir and Auctioneer, Sotheby's, 1995–2009. Jewellery Specialist, BBC Antiques Roadshow, 2007–. FRSA 2010. Freeman, City of London, 2006; Liveryman, Goldsmiths' Co., 2013. *Publications:* Collect Contemporary Jewellery, 2012; (with J. Self) Emerald, 2013; contribs to jewellery mags and to newspapers. *Recreations:* music, golf, arts, travel, gardening, photography, opera, theatre. *Address:* London, SW19. *E:* joanna@joannahardy.com. *Club:* Royal Over-Seas League.

HARDY, Prof. John, PhD; FMedSci; FRS 2009; Professor of Neuroscience, since 2007, Chair of Molecular Biology of Neurological Disease, and Head of Department of Molecular Neuroscience, University College London. *Educ:* Univ. of Leeds (BSc 1976); Imperial Coll. London (PhD). Postdoctoral Fellow, MRC Neuropathogenesis Unit, Newcastle upon Tyne, 1979–83; Asst Prof., Swedish Brain Bank, Umeå, 1983–84; Asst Prof., 1984–89, Associate Prof., 1989–92, Dept of Biochemistry and Molecular Genetics, St Mary's Hospital Med. Sch., Imperial Coll. London; Pfeiffer Prof. of Alzheimer's Res., Univ. of S Florida, 1992–96; Consultant and Prof. of Neuroscience, Mayo Clinic, Jacksonville, Fla, 1996–2001 (Vis. Scientist, 2001–04); Sen. Investigator and Chief, Lab. of Neurogenetics, Nat. Inst. of Ageing, Bethesda, 2001–07. FMedSci 2008. *Publications:* contrib. articles to jls. *Address:* UCL Institute of Neurology, Queen Square, WC1N 3BG.

HARDY, Maj.-Gen. John Campbell, CB 1985; LVO 1978; Administrator, Sion College, 1993–2000; *b* 13 Oct. 1933; *s* of late General Sir Campbell Hardy, KCB, CBE, DSO; *m* 1961, Jennifer Mary Kempton; one *s* one *d. Educ:* Sherborne Sch. Joined Royal Marines, 1952; 45 Commando, 1954; HMS Superb, 1956; Instructor, NCOs' School, Plymouth, 1957; 42 Commando, 1959; 43 Commando, 1962; Adjt, Jt Service Amphibious Warfare Centre, 1964; Company Comdr, 45 Commando, 1965; sc Bracknell, 1966; Instr, RNC Greenwich, 1967; Extra Equerry to Prince Philip, 1968–69; SO, Dept of CGRM, 1969; Rifle Company Comdr, 41 Commando, 1971; ndc Latimer, 1972; Staff of Chief of Defence Staff, 1973; Staff Officer HQ Commando Forces, 1975; CO RM Poole, 1977; COS and Asst Defence Attaché, British Defence Staff Washington, 1979; ADC to the Queen, 1981–82; Chief of Staff to Comdt Gen. RM, 1982–84; DCS (Support) to C-in-C Allied Forces N Europe, 1984–87. Col Comdt, RM, 1990–94. Dir, British Digestive Foundn, 1987–92. Gen. Comr of Taxes, 1989–2008. Gov., Dashwood Foundn, 1998–. *Address:* c/o National Westminster Bank plc, 31 High Street, Deal, Kent CT14 6EW. *Club:* Army and Navy.

HARDY, John Sydney; QC 2008; a Recorder, since 2002; *b* London, 12 Dec. 1953; *s* of Sydney and Margaret Hardy; *m* 1990, Claire McCririck; one *s* one *d. Educ:* Christ's Hosp.; Magdalen Coll., Oxford (BA Hons Modern Hist.). Teacher, Priory Sch., Banstead, Surrey, 1977–86. Called to the Bar, Gray's Inn, 1988, Bencher, 2014; in practice as barrister specialising in extradition and serious fraud. *Recreations:* music and opera, Rugby Union, cricket, golf, food and wine, travel. *Address:* 3 Raymond Buildings, Gray's Inn, WC1R 5BH.

HARDY, Prof. Michael Christopher, CMG 2010; OBE 2001; Professor of Intercultural Relations and Director, Human Security Grand Challenge Initiative, since 2011, and Executive Director, Centre for Trust, Peace and Social Relations, since 2014, Coventry University (Director, Centre for Social Relations (formerly Institute of Community Cohesion), 2011–14); *b* 24 April 1949; *s* of Wilfred Alexander Hardy and Barbara Linington Hardy; *m* 1973, Dorothy Marjorie Skinner; one *s* one *d. Educ:* London Univ. (BSc Hons Econs ext. 1971); Univ. of London Inst. of Educn (Cert. Further and Higher Educn 1972); Brunel Univ. (MA Econs 1976). Lectr in Econs, Orpington Coll., 1973–77; Sen. Lectr in Econs, 1977–87, Hd, Sch. of Econs and Public Policy, 1986–87, Leeds Metropolitan Univ.; Hd, Sch. of Econs, 1987–95, Prof. of Internat. Business, 1990–95, Lancs Polytechnic, subseq. Univ. of Central Lancs, now Prof. Emeritus; British Council: Dir, Private Sector Develt, 1995–97; Regl Dir for Develt Services, ME, Cairo, 1997–2001; Mem., Sen. Mgt Team and Dir, Develt Services, 2001–04; Dir, Indonesia, 2004–08; Prog. Leader, Intercultural Dialogue, 2008–11; Sen. Advr to Min. of Culture and Tourism, Govt of Azerbaijan, UN Alliance of Civilisations, 2012–. Life FRSA. *Publications:* (jtly) Controversies in Applied Economics, 1987; (ed jtly) Controversy in Applied Economics, 1989; (contrib.) Management Development in Poland: building management training capacity with foreign partnerships, 1998; articles in jls. *Recreations:* cooking, family, gadgets, trying to keep up with my grandson William James. *Address:* Centre for Trust, Peace and Social Relations, Coventry University, Priory Street, Coventry CV1 5FB. *T:* (024) 7679 5765, *Fax:* (024) 7679 5761. *E:* mike.hardy@coventry.ac.uk.

HARDY, Michael James Langley; Director for Telecommunications Policy and Postal Services, Directorate-General for Information Technologies and Industries, and Telecommunications, Commission of the European Communities, 1992–93; *b* 30 Jan. 1933; *s* of James Hardy and Rosina (*née* Langley); *m* 1959, Dr Swana Metger; one *s* two *d. Educ:* Beckenham Grammar Sch.; Magdalen Coll., Oxford (Exhibnr; BA 1956; MA 1959); Magdalene Coll., Cambridge (LLB 1957; LLM 1963); Exeter Sch. of Art and Design, Univ. of Plymouth (BA (Fine Art) 1996, MA 2002). Called to the Bar, Gray's Inn, 1957. Asst Lecturer, Law Faculty: Manchester Univ., 1958–59; KCL, 1959–60; Legal Officer, later Sen. Legal Officer, Legal Service, UN, 1960–73; Legal Adviser, Govt of Nepal, 1968–69 (on leave of absence from UN); Commn of the European Communities, 1973–93: Legal Adviser, Legal Service, 1973–77; Head of Div., Japan, Australia and NZ, Directorate-General for External Relations, 1978–82; Head of Commn Delegn, New York, 1982–87; Dir for Gen. Affairs, Directorate-Gen. for Telecommunications, Information Industries and Innovation, 1987–92. *Publications:* Blood Feuds and the Payment of Blood Money in the Middle East, 1963; Modern Diplomatic Law, 1968; (with T. Grumley-Grennan) Gidleigh: a Dartmoor village past and present, 2000; articles in legal and political science jls. *Recreations:* walking, talking. *Address:* Castle House, Gidleigh, Devon TQ13 8HR. *T:* (01647) 433567.

HARDY, Sir Richard (Charles Chandos), 5th Bt *cr* 1876, of Dunstall Hall, co. Stafford; *b* 6 Feb. 1945; *o s* of Sir Rupert Hardy, 4th Bt and of Hon. Diana Joan Allsopp, *er d* of 3rd Baron Hindlip; *S* father, 1997; *m* 1972, Venetia, *d* of late Simon Wingfield Digby, TD; four *d. Educ:* Eton. *Heir: cousin* Gerald Alan Hardy [*b* 4 April 1926; *m* 1953, Carolyn, *d* of Maj.-Gen. Arthur Charles Tarver Evanson, CB, MC; two *d*]. *Address:* Springfield House, Gillingham, Dorset SP8 5RD.

HARDY, Robert; *see* Hardy, T. S. R.

HARDY, His Honour Robert James; a Circuit Judge, 1979–94; *b* 12 July 1924; *s* of James Frederick and Ann Hardy; *m* 1951, Maureen Scott; one *s* one *d. Educ:* Mostyn House Sch.; Wrekin Coll.; University Coll., London (LLB). Served, 1942–46, Royal Navy, as Pilot, Fleet Air Arm. Called to the Bar, 1950; a Recorder of the Crown Court, 1972–79. *Recreation:* reading. *Address:* 12 Bollin Mews, Prestbury, Cheshire SK10 4DP. *T:* (01625) 820026; Betlem, Mallorca.

HARDY, Rt Rev. Robert Maynard, CBE 2001; an Hon. Assistant Bishop, Diocese of Carlisle, since 2002; *b* 5 Oct. 1936; *s* of Harold and Monica Mavie Hardy; *m* 1970, Isobel Mary, *d* of Charles and Ella Burch; two *s* one *d. Educ:* Queen Elizabeth Grammar School, Wakefield; Clare College, Cambridge (MA). Deacon 1962, priest 1963; Assistant Curate, All Saints and Martyrs, Langley, Manchester, 1962; Fellow and Chaplain, Selwyn College, Cambridge, 1965 (Hon. Fellow, 1986); Vicar of All Saints, Borehamwood, 1972; Priest-in-charge, Aspley Guise, 1975; Course Director, St Albans Diocese Ministerial Training Scheme, 1975; Incumbent of United Benefice of Aspley Guise with Husborne Crawley and Ridgmont, 1980; Bishop Suffragan of Maidstone, 1980–86; Bishop of Lincoln, 1986–2001; Bishop to HM Prisons, 1985–2001. Hon. DD Hull, 1992; Hon. DLitt Lincoln, 2002. *Recreations:* walking, gardening, reading. *Address:* Carleton House, Back Lane, Langwathby, Penrith, Cumbria CA10 1NB. *T:* (01768) 881210.

HARDY, Russell; Chairman, South Warwickshire NHS Foundation Trust, since 2015; *b* London, 29 Sept. 1960; *s* of Arthur Hardy and Olive Hardy (*née* Carter); *m* 2000, Kim Mitchell; one *s* one *d. Educ:* Fryerns Sch., Basildon; Warwick Univ. (BA Hons; MA Econs). Economist, Unilever plc, 1982–85; Sen. Manager, Deloitte Haskins & Sells, 1985–88; Kingfisher plc, 1988–92; Trading Dir, Safeway, 1992–95; Chm. and Chief Exec., Dolland & Aitchison, 1995–2005; Gp CEO, Blacks Leisure plc, 2005–07; Chairman: Hunters Moor Ltd, 2008–13; Fosse Healthcare, 2014–. Chm., Robert Jones and Agnes Hunt Orthopaedic and Dist Hosp. NHS Trust, 2009–15. Gov., Nuffield Health, 2010– (Chm., 2012–). Chm., Multiple Sclerosis Trust, 1993–2014; Trustee, UK Acquired Brain Injury Forum. CIMA 1985. *E:* russell.hardy2909@btinternet.com.

HARDY, (Timothy Sydney) Robert, CBE 1981; FSA; actor and writer; *b* 29 Oct. 1925; *s* of late Major Henry Harrison Hardy, CBE, and Edith Jocelyn Dugdale; *m* 1st, 1952, Elizabeth (marr. diss.), *d* of late Sir Lionel Fox and Lady Fox; one *s*; 2nd, 1961, Sally (marr. diss. 1986), *d* of Sir Neville Pearson, 2nd Bt, and Dame Gladys Cooper, DBE; two *d. Educ:* Rugby Sch.; Magdalen Coll., Oxford (Hons degree, Eng. Lit.). *Stage:* Shakespeare Meml Theatre, 1949–51; London, West End, 1951–53; Old Vic Theatre, 1953–54; USA, 1954 and 1956–58 (plays incl. Hamlet and Henry V); Shakespeare Meml 1959 Centenary Season; Rosmersholm, Comedy, 1960; The Rehearsal, Globe, 1961; A Severed Head, Criterion, 1963; The Constant Couple, New, 1967; I've Seen You Cut Lemons, Fortune, 1969; Habeas Corpus, Lyric, 1974; Dear Liar, Mermaid, 1982; Winnie, Victoria Palace, 1988; Body and Soul, Albery, 1992; Churchill, in Celui qui a dit non, Paris, 1999; *films include:* The Far Pavilions, 1983; The Shooting Party, 1985; Jenny's War, 1985; Paris by Night, 1988; War and Remembrance, 1988; Mary Shelley's Frankenstein, 1994; A Feast at Midnight, 1995; Sense and Sensibility, 1996; Mrs Dalloway, 1997; The Tichborne Claimant, 1998; The Barber of Siberia, 1998; My Life So Far, 1998; An Ideal Husband, 1999; Harry Potter and the Chamber of Secrets, 2002; Harry Potter and the Prisoner of Azkaban, 2004; Harry Potter and the Goblet of Fire, 2005; Harry Potter and the Order of the Phoenix, 2007; *television:* David Copperfield; Age of Kings, 1960; Trouble-shooters, 1966–67; Elizabeth R, 1970; Manhunt, 1970; Edward VII, 1973; All Creatures Great and Small, 1978–80, 1983, 1985, 1987–90; Speed King; Fothergill; Winston Churchill—The Wilderness Years, 1981; Paying Guests, 1986; Make and Break, 1986; Churchill in the USA, 1986; Hot Metal, 1987, 1988; Northanger Abbey, 1987; Marcus Welby in Paris (film), 1988; Sherlock Holmes, 1991; Inspector Morse, 1992; Middlemarch, 1993; Castle Ghosts, 1995, 1996 and 1997; Gulliver's Travels (film), Bramwell, 1996; Nancherrow, 1998; Midsomer Murders, Tenth Kingdom, 1999; Justice in Wonderland, 2000; Bertie and Elizabeth, 2002; Lucky Jim, Death in Holy Orders, 2003; Margaret, Little Dorrit, 2008. Author of TV documentaries: Picardy Affair, 1962; The Longbow, 1972; Horses in our Blood, 1977; Gordon of Khartoum, 1982. Consultant, Mary Rose Trust, 1979– (Trustee, 1991–); Trustee: WWF (UK), 1983–89; Battlefields Trust (Patron, 2010–; Pres., 2011–); Member: Bd of Trustees of the Royal Armouries, 1984–95; Battlefields Panel, English Heritage; Chm., Berkshire, Buckinghamshire and Oxfordshire Naturalists' Trust Appeal, 1984–90. FSA 1996. Master, Court of Worshipful Co. of Bowyers, 1988–90; Mem., Co. of Woodmen of Arden, 1981–. Hon. DLitt: Reading, 1990; Durham, 1997; Portsmouth, 2007. *Publications:* Longbow, 1976, 4th edn 2012; The Great War-Bow, 2004, 2nd edn 2011. *Recreations:* archery, bowyery. *Address:* c/o Chatto & Linnit, Worlds End Studios, 132–134 Lots Road, SW10 0RJ. *Clubs:* Buck's, Royal Toxophilite, British Longbow.

HARE, family name of **Viscount Blakenham** and **Earl of Listowel**.

HARE, Sir David, Kt 1998; FRSL 1985; playwright; *b* 5 June 1947; *s* of Clifford Theodore Rippon Hare and Agnes Cockburn Hare; *m* 1st, 1970, Margaret Matheson (marr. diss. 1980); two *s* one *d*; 2nd, 1992, Nicole Farhi, *qv. Educ:* Lancing Coll.; Jesus Coll., Cambridge (MA Hons; Hon. Fellow, 2001). Founded Portable Theatre, 1968; Literary Manager and Resident Dramatist, Royal Court, 1969–71; Resident Dramatist, Nottingham Playhouse, 1973; founded Joint Stock Theatre Group, 1975; US/UK Bicentennial Fellowship, 1977; founded Greenpoint Films, 1982; Associate Dir, Nat. Theatre, 1984–88, 1989–97. Chm. Jury, BFI London Film Fest., 2012. Mem., Amer. Acad. of Arts and Scis, 2012. Hon. DLit: Tel Aviv, 2001; Cambridge, 2005; UEA, 2010. Officier, l'Ordre des Arts et des Lettres (France), 1997. *Author of plays:* Slag, Hampstead, 1970, Royal Court, then NY, 1971; The Great Exhibition, Hampstead, 1972; Knuckle (televised, 1989), Comedy, 1974; Fanshen, Joint Stock, 1975, NT 1992; The Secret Rapture, NT, 1988, NY, 1989 (dir, NY only), Lyric, 2003; Racing Demon, NT, 1990, NY, 1995; Murmuring Judges, NT, 1991; The Absence of War, NT, 1993 (televised, 1996); Skylight, NT, 1995, NY and Wyndhams, 1996, Vaudeville, 1997, Wyndhams, 2014, Broadway, 2015; Amy's View, NT, transf. Aldwych, 1997, NY 1999, Garrick, 2006; The Judas Kiss, Playhouse, then NY, 1998, Hampstead, 2012, Duke of York's, 2013; Via Dolorosa, Royal Court, 1998 (also actor), NY, 1999, Duchess Th., 2002; The Breath of Life, Haymarket, 2002; The Permanent Way, Out of Joint Th. Co., NT, 2004; Stuff Happens, NT, 2004, NY 2006; The Vertical Hour, NY, 2006, Royal Court, 2008; Gethsemane, NT, 2008; Berlin/Wall, NT, Royal Court and NY, 2009 (also actor); The Power of Yes, NT, 2009; South Downs, Chichester, 2011, trans. Pinter, 2012; Behind the Beautiful Forevers, NT, 2014; *author and director of plays:* Brassneck (with Howard Brenton), Nottingham Playhouse, 1973; Teeth 'n' Smiles, Royal Court, 1975, Wyndhams, 1976; Plenty, NT, 1978, NY, 1983, Albery (dir. J. Kent), 1999; A Map of the World, Adelaide Fest., 1982, NT, 1983, NY, 1985; (with Howard Brenton) Pravda, NT, 1985; The Bay at Nice, and Wrecked Eggs, NT, 1986; My Zinc Bed, Royal Court, 2000; The Moderate Soprano, Hampstead, 2015; *opera libretto:* The Knife, NY Shakespeare Fest., 1987 (also directed); *TV films:* Man Above Men, 1973; Licking Hitler, 1978 (also directed); Dreams of Leaving, 1980 (also directed); Saigon—Year of the Cat, 1983; Heading Home, 1991; My Zinc Bed, 2008; Page Eight, 2011 (also directed); Turks & Caicos, 2014 (also directed); Salting the Battlefield, 2014 (also directed). *Directed:* The Party, NT, 1974; Weapons of Happiness, NT, 1976; Total Eclipse, Lyric, Hammersmith, 1981; King Lear, NT, 1986; The Designated Mourner, NT, 1996; Heartbreak House, Almeida, 1997; The Year of Magical Thinking, NY, 2007, NT, 2008. *Adapted:* Pirandello, The Rules of the Game, NT, 1971, Almeida, 1992; Brecht, Life of Galileo, Almeida, 1994, NT, 2006; Brecht, Mother Courage and her Children, NT, 1995; Chekhov, Ivanov, Almeida, 1997, Chichester, 2015; Schnitzler (La Ronde), The Blue Room, Donmar Warehouse, 1998, NY 1999, Th. Royal, Haymarket, 2000; Chekhov, Platonov, Almeida, 2001, Chichester, 2015; Lorca, The House of Bernarda Alba, NT, 2005; Gorky, Enemies, Almeida, 2006; Craig Murray, Murder in Samarkand (radio play), 2010; Chekhov, The Seagull, Chichester, 2015. *Films:* wrote and directed: Wetherby, 1985; Paris by Night, 1988; Strapless, 1989; (screenplay) Plenty, 1985; Damage (adapted from novel by Josephine Hart), 1992; The Secret Rapture, 1994; directed, The Designated Mourner, 1997; wrote and acted, Via Dolorosa, 2000; (screenplay) The Hours (adapted from novel by Michael Cunningham), 2002; (screenplay) The Reader (adapted from novel by Bernard Schlink), 2008; (screenplay) Wall (animation), 2015. *Publications:* Slag, 1970; The Great Exhibition, 1972; Knuckle, 1974; Brassneck, 1974; Fanshen, 1976; Teeth 'n' Smiles, 1976; Plenty, 1978; Licking Hitler, 1978; Dreams of Leaving, 1980; A Map of the World, 1982; Saigon, 1983; Pravda, 1985; Wetherby, 1985; The Bay at Nice and Wrecked Eggs, 1986; The Secret Rapture, 1988; Paris By Night, 1989; Strapless, 1990; Racing Demon, 1990; Writing Lefthanded, 1991; Heading Home, 1991; Murmuring Judges, 1991; The Absence of War, 1993; Asking Around, 1993; Rules of the Game, 1994; Skylight, 1995; Mother Courage,

1995; Plays One, 1996; Plays Two, 1996; Amy's View, 1997; Ivanov, 1997; The Judas Kiss, 1998; The Blue Room, 1998; Via Dolorosa, 1998; Acting Up, 1999; My Zinc Bed, 2000; Platonov, 2001; The Hours, 2002; The Breath of Life, 2002; Collected Screenplays, 2002; The Permanent Way, 2003; Stuff Happens, 2004; The House of Bernarda Alba, 2005; Obedience, Struggle and Revolt, 2005; Enemies, 2006; The Vertical Hour, 2006; Plays Three, 2008; Gethsemane, 2008; The Reader, 2008; Berlin/Wall, 2009; The Power of Yes, 2009; Lee Miller, 2010; South Downs, 2011; Behind the Beautiful Forevers, 2014; The Blue Touch Paper (memoir), 2015; Young Checkhov—Platonov, Ivanov and The Seagull, 2015; The Moderate Soprano, 2015.

HARE, Ewan Nigel Christian, (Nick); Canadian Diplomat, retired; Deputy Secretary-General (Development Co-operation) of the Commonwealth, 1993–99; *b* 11 May 1939; *m* 1985, Raina Ho; one *s* two *d*. *Educ:* Earlham Coll. (BA); Carleton Univ. (DPA). First Sec., Canadian High Commn, Accra, 1969–72; Canadian International Development Agency: Regl Dir, Asia SE, 1972–76; Regl Dir, Central and S Africa, 1976–78; Dir-Gen., Resources Br., 1978–80; Dir-Gen., UN Progs, 1980–84; Ambassador of Canada to Zaire, Rwanda, Burundi and Congo, 1984–87; Dir, Africa Trade Div., Dept of Foreign Affairs, Ottawa, 1987–88; Dir-Gen., Industrial Co-operation Prog., Canadian Internat. Develt Agency, 1988–91; Canadian High Comr to Nigeria and Ambassador to Benin, 1991–93. Internat. Electoral Observer, 2011–. Chm., Canadian Hunger Foundn—Partners in Rural Develt, 2001–08; Chair, Internat. Cttee, Canadian Comprehensive Audit Foundn, 2002–10. Board Member: Retired Hds of Mission Assoc., 2003–09; Pearson Peacekeeping Centre, 2004–10; North-South Inst., 2008–; Canadian Executive Service Orgn, 2010–. Mem., Canadian Council for Internat. Co-operation, 2011–. *Recreations:* ski-ing, canoeing, jogging, sailing. *Clubs:* Canadian Kennel; Leonberger (Ontario).

HARE, Prof. Lisa Anne; *see* Jardine, L. A.

HARE, Margaret Flora, (Mrs David Hare); *see* Spittle, M. F.

HARE, Sir Nicholas (Patrick), 7th Bt *cr* 1818, of Stow Hall, Norfolk; *b* 27 Aug. 1955; *o s* of Sir Philip Hare, 6th Bt and Anne Lisle Hare (*née* Nicholson); *S* father, 2000; *m* 1982, Caroline Keith, *d* of T. P. K. Allan; two *s*. *Educ:* Bryanston. *Heir: s* Thomas Hare, *b* 7 Aug. 1986. *Address:* Tavern House, Sopworth, Chippenham, Wilts SN14 6PR.

HARE, Nick; *see* Hare, E. N. C.

HARE, Nicole, (Lady Hare); *see* Farhi, N.

HARE, Paul Webster, LVO 1985; HM Diplomatic Service, retired; Project Director, Shanghai World EXPO 2010, UK Trade and Investment, 2005–08; Lecturer and Fellow, Center for International Affairs, Boston University, since 2009; *b* 20 July 1951; *s* of Maurice Leslie Hare and Anne Dorothy Hare (*née* Webster); *m* 1978, Lynda Carol Henderson, *d* of Ian Stuart McWalter Henderson, CBE, GM, KPM and Marie Beatrice Henderson (*née* Green); three *s* three *d*. *Educ:* Leeds Grammar Sch. (Foundn Schol.); Trinity Coll., Oxford (Open Schol., MA 1st Cl. Hons PPE 1972); Coll. of Law, London. Qualified as solicitor, with Herbert Smith & Co., London, 1973–75; TEFL, Biella and Genoa, Italy, 1976; Corporate Finance Dept, J. Henry Schroder Wagg & Co., London, 1976–78; entered HM Diplomatic Service, 1978: Private Sec. to Ambassador to EC, Brussels, 1979–80; First Sec. and Hd of Chancery, Lisbon, 1981–85; FCO, 1985–88; Consul and Dep. Dir, Investment, USA, NY, 1988–94; Dep. Hd of Mission and Counsellor (Commercial and Economic), Caracas, 1994–97; Hd, Non-Proliferation Dept, FCO, 1997–2001; Ambassador to Republic of Cuba, 2001–04; Vis. Fellow, Weatherhead Center for Internat. Relations, Harvard Univ., 2004–05. Mem., Cuba Policy Gp, Brookings Instn, Washington, 2008–. Pres., Baseball Softball UK, 2000–01. Online Cuba Topics expert, New York Times, 2009–. Order of Prince Henry the Navigator (Portugal), 1985; Order of 5 May 1810, Barinas (Venezuela), 1995. *Publications:* Moncada - a Cuban Story (novel), 2010; Making Diplomacy Work: intelligent responses to the hopes and fears of the modern world, 2015; articles for Miami Herald, Brookings Instn, Poder 360 mag., Cuban Affairs. *Recreations:* family, music, sport. *Address:* c/o International Relations, Boston University, 152 Bay State Road, Boston, MA 02215, USA.

HARE, Timothy James Pitt; Vice Lord-Lieutenant of West Yorkshire, since 2012; *b* Wetherby, 7 June 1948; *s* of Clifford Ronald Pitt Hare and Hazel Mary Hare; *m* 1977, Diana Marion Trigg; one *s* two *d* (and one *d* decd). *Educ:* Uppingham Sch. Director: James Hare Ltd, 1973–; Harecroft Estates Ltd, 1973–; Merchanting Div., Illingworth Morris, 1977–79; Sales Dir, Salts of Saltaire, 1982–83; Partner, N Deighton Farms, 1986–. High Sheriff, 2005–06, DL 2007, W Yorks. *Recreations:* country pursuits, gardening, golf, classic cars, breeding alpacas, wine, travel. *Address:* The Old Hall, The Green, North Deighton, Wetherby, N Yorks LS22 4EN. *T:* (01937) 580775. *E:* tim.hare@james-hare.com. *Club:* Sloane.

HAREN, Sir Patrick (Hugh), Kt 2008; PhD; FREng, FIET; Chairman, Viridian Group Ltd, 2009–12 (Deputy Chairman, 2007–09; Chief Executive, 1998–2007); *b* 4 Aug. 1950; *s* of James Joseph Haren and Sarah Haren; *m* 1971, Anne Elizabeth McNally; two *s*. *Educ:* Queen's Univ. Belfast (BSc 1971; PhD 1976); University Coll., Dublin (MBA 1986). FIET (FIEE 1990); FREng (FEng 1998). Power Systems Engrg, Electricity Supply Bd, Dublin, 1971–73; Engr, Superconducting Magnet Prog., CERN, Geneva, 1976–78; Electricity Supply Board, Dublin: engrg appts, 1978–84; Divl Manager, Strategic Planning, 1985–87; Regl Accountant, 1987–88; Manager, Business Ventures, 1988–89; Dir, 1989–92; Dir, Hoermann Electronics Ltd, 1990–91; Chief Exec., 1992–98, Chm., 1999–2008, NI Electricity. Mem. Study Cttee, Power System Operation and Control, CIGRE, 1982–86. Non-executive Director: Bank of Ireland, 2012–; Bank of Ireland (UK) plc, 2012–. *Publications:* technical papers in power system operation and computer control. *Recreations:* ski-ing, walking, languages. *Address:* 57 Ringdufferin Road, Toye, Downpatrick BT30 9PH. *T:* (028) 4482 8584.

HAREWOOD, 8th Earl of, *cr* 1812; **David Henry George Lascelles;** Baron Harewood 1796; Viscount Lascelles 1812; freelance film and television producer; *b* 21 Oct. 1950; *s* of 7th Earl of Harewood, KBE, Hon. AM and Maria, (Marion), Donata (*née* Stein, later Thorpe), CBE; *S* father, 2011; *m* 1979, Margaret Rosalind Messenger; three *s* one *d*; *m* 1990, Diane Jane Howse. *Educ:* The Hall Sch.; Westminster; Bristol Univ. Productions include: *films:* Tibet - a Buddhist Trilogy, 1977; Richard III, 1995; The Wisdom of Crocodiles, 1998; *television:* Inspector Morse IV and V, 1989–90 (BAFTA Best TV Series award); Wide-Eyed & Legless, 1992; Moll Flanders, 1996; Second Sight, 1999; *stage:* Carnival Messiah, Harewood, 2007. Chairman: Harewood House Trust Ltd, 1993–; Alchemy, 2008–; Orient Foundn (Trustee, 1983–); Trustee: Bradford City of Film, 2010–; York Minster Mystery Plays, 2014–; Co-Founder, Geraldine Connor Foundn, 2012; Patron: Kala Sangam, 2004–; Leeds W Indian Centre; Yorks CCC. *Heir: s* Viscount Lascelles, *qv*. *Address:* Harewood House, Harewood, Leeds, West Yorks LS17 9LG.

HARFORD, Sir Mark (John), 4th Bt *cr* 1934, of Falcondale, co. Cardigan; *b* 6 Aug. 1964; *er s* of Sir (John) Timothy Harford, 3rd Bt, and of Carolyn Jane Mullens; *S* father, 2010; *m* 1999, Louise Rosamond, *d* of Robert Langford, of Tadworth, Surrey; three *d*. *Heir: b* Simon Guy Harford [*b* 24 Sept. 1966; *m* 1998, Alexandra (marr. diss. 2015), *d* of Frederick Gans; two *s*].

HARGREAVES, Andrew Raikes; Member, Supervisory Board, Thyssen Petroleum, since 2014; *b* 15 May 1955; *s* of Col and Mrs D. W. Hargreaves; *m* 1978, Fiona Susan, *o d* of G. W. Dottridge; two *s*. *Educ:* Eton; St Edmund Hall, Oxford (MA Hons). Auctioneer and valuation expert, Christies, 1977–81; executive, Hill Samuel & Co. Ltd, 1981–83; Asst Dir, Sanwa Internat. Ltd, 1983–85; Asst Dir J. Henry Schroder Wagg & Co. Ltd, 1985–87; Consultant: Schroders plc, 1987–92; Midlands Electricity plc, 1989–97; UK Man. Dir, Daimler-Benz, subseq. DaimlerChrysler, Aerospace AG, 1997–2000; UK Chm., 2000–04, Sen. Advr and Gp Dir, Govt Affairs, 2004–12, EADS UK Ltd; Managing Director: Securisys Mgt Ltd, 2014–; Securisys Hldgs and Securisys Information Ltd, 2012–13. Contested (C) Blyth Valley, 1983. MP (C) Birmingham, Hall Green, 1987–97; contested (C) same seat, 1997. PPS to Ministers of State, FCO, 1992–97. Member: Select Cttee on Information, 1992–97; Select Cttee for Parly Comr for Admin, 1993–97; Secretary: back bench Urban and Inner Cities Cttee, 1987–91 (Chm., 1992–94); back bench Defence Cttee, 1992–94 (Vice-Chm., 1994–97). Mem., Bow Gp. *Recreations:* fishing, gardening, walking, antiques, art. *Club:* Boodle's.

HARGREAVES, David Harold, PhD; Fellow, Wolfson College, Cambridge, 1988–2006, now Emeritus; *b* 31 Aug. 1939; *s* of Clifford and Marion Hargreaves. *Educ:* Bolton School; Christ's College, Cambridge (MA, PhD). Asst Master, Hull Grammar Sch., 1961–64; Research Associate, Dept of Sociology and Social Anthropology, Univ. of Manchester, 1964–65; Lectr, Senior Lectr then Reader, Dept of Education, Univ. of Manchester, 1965–79; Reader in Education and Fellow of Jesus College, Oxford, 1979–84; Chief Inspector, ILEA, 1984–88; University of Cambridge: Prof. of Educn, 1988–2000; Member: Gen. Bd of the Faculties, 1989–92; Local Exams Syndicate, 1990–92; Bd of Grad. Studies, 1990–92; Chairman: Council, Sch. of Humanities and Soc. Scis, 1990–92; Cttee on the Training and Develt of Univ. Teachers, 1990–92; Needs Cttee, 1991–92. Chief Executive, QCA, 2000–01. Vis. Prof., Univ. of Manchester, 2003–08. Member: Educn Res. Bd, SSRC, 1979–82; Educn Adv. Council, Royal Opera House, Covent Garden, 1985–90; Educn Adv. Council, IBA, 1988–90; ESRC, 1991–95 (Chm., Res. Centres Bd, 1992–94); Res. Cttee, Teacher Trng Agency, 1995–97; Educn Cttee, NESTA, 1999–2003; Nat. Educnl Res. Forum, 1999–2004; Jt Vice-Chm., Sec. of State for Educn and Employment's Standards Task Force, 1997–2000; Policy Advr to Sec. of State for Educn and Skills, 2001–02; Bd Mem., 1999–2000, Chm., 2002–05, British Educnl Communications and Technol. Agency. Chairman: Eastern Arts Bd, 1991–94; Internat. Adv. Council on Quality of Educn, NSW, 1993–95. Non-exec. Dir, W Suffolk Hosps NHS Trust, 1998–2000. Sen. Associate, Demos, 2003. Consultant: Lifelong Learning Foundn, 2002–04; Paul Hamlyn Foundn, 2002–07; Specialist Schs Trust, 2003–09 (Associate Dir, Develt and Res.); (on self-improving sch. systems) Nat. Coll. for Sch. Leadership, 2010–12. Trustee, Villiers Park Educnl Trust, 2004–07. Mem., Educn Cttee, LSO, 2002–05. FRSA 1984; FAcSS (Founding AcSS, 1999). Hon. FCT 2001. Hon. EdD Wolverhampton, 2002. *Publications:* Social Relations in a Secondary School, 1967; Interpersonal Relations and Education, 1972; (jtly) Deviance in Classrooms, 1975; The Challenge for the Comprehensive School, 1982; (jtly) Planning for School Development, 1990; (jtly) The Empowered School, 1991; The Mosaic of Learning, 1994; (jtly) On-the-Job Training for Surgeons, 1997; (jtly) On-the-Job Training for Physicians, 1997; Creative Professionalism, 1998; Education Epidemic, 2003; Learning for Life, 2004. *Recreation:* the arts.

HARGREAVES, Prof. Ian Richard, CBE 2012; Professor of Digital Economy, University of Wales, Cardiff, since 2010 (Professor of Journalism, 1998–2010); *b* 18 June 1951; *s* of Ronald and Edna Hargreaves; *m* 1st, 1972, Elizabeth Anne Crago (marr. diss. 1991); one *s* one *d*; 2nd, 1993, Adele Esther Blakebrough, *d* of Rev. E. and M. Blakebrough; two *d*. *Educ:* Burnley Grammar Sch.; Altrincham Grammar Sch.; Queens' Coll., Cambridge (MA). Community worker, Kaleidoscope Project, 1972–73; Reporter, Keighley News, 1973–74; Journalist, Bradford Telegraph & Argus, 1974–76; Financial Times, 1976–87: Industrial Corresp.; Transport Corresp.; New York Corresp.; Social Affairs Ed.; Resources Ed.; Features Ed.; Man. Ed., 1987–88, Controller, 1988–89, Dir, 1989–90, News and Current Affairs, BBC; Dep. Editor, The Financial Times, 1990–94; Editor: Independent, 1994–96; New Statesman & Soc., then New Statesman, 1996–98; Gp Dir, Corporate and Public Affairs, BAA plc, 2003–06; Strategic Communications Dir, FCO, 2008–10. Mem. Bd, S London and Maudsley NHS Trust, 2000–03. Chm., Demos, 1997–2002. Member Board: New Statesman, 1996–2003; Greenpeace UK, 1997–2002; Presentable, 2001–03; OFCOM, 2002–08 (Sen. Partner, 2007–08); Alacrity, 2013–; Nat. Theatre of Wales, 2013–. Res. Fellow, NESTA, 2012–13; Sen. Fellow, Lisbon Council, 2013–. Trustee, Centre Forum, 2012–. *Publications:* Sharper Vision: the BBC and the communications revolution, 1993; (with Ian Christie) Tomorrow's Politics: the third way and beyond, 1998; Who's Misunderstanding Whom?: science and the media, 2000; Journalism: truth or dare?, 2003; A Very Short Intro to Journalism, 2005, 2nd edn 2014; The Heart of Digital Wales: a review for the Welsh Assembly Government, 2010; Digital Opportunity: review of intellectual property and growth, 2011; A Manifesto for the UK Creative Economy, 2013. *Recreations:* walking, tennis, football, music, poetry. *Address:* Cardiff School of Journalism, Media and Cultural Studies, Bute Building, King Edward VII Avenue, Cardiff CF10 3NB. *T:* 07909 534545.

HARGREAVES, Dr Jonathan Watson, CBE 2008; Chairman, North East Regional Flood and Coastal Committee, since 2014; Chief Executive Officer, Scottish Water, 2002–07; *b* 10 March 1950; *m* 1974, Hilary; two *d*. *Educ:* Hatfield Poly. (BSc); Durham Univ. (PhD). MRSB; FICE 2005. Business Develt Manager, Northumbrian Water Gp, 1990–91; Managing Director: Entec Europe Ltd, 1991–93; Northumbrian Water Ltd, and Dir, Northumbrian Water Gp plc, 1993–96; Northumbrian Lyonnaise Internat. Div., Suez Lyonnaise, 1996–2000; CEO, E of Scotland Water, 2000–02. Mem. Bd, British Waterways, 2008–12; Chm. Bd, Scottish Canals, 2012–14. Member, Board: Baltic Centre for Contemporary Arts Trust and Trading Co. (formerly Trustee, Baltic Centre for Contemporary Art, Gateshead), 2008–14; Port of Tyne Trust, 2010–. *Recreations:* gardening, theatre, DIY. *Address:* c/o Regional Flood and Coastal Committee Secretariat, Environment Agency, Tyneside House, Skinnerburn Road, Newcastle upon Tyne NE4 7AR.

HARGREAVES, Simon John Robert; QC 2009; *b* Rochdale, 15 Jan. 1968; *s* of Edward Hargreaves and Christina Hargreaves; *m* 2001, Catherine Morgan; three *d*. *Educ:* Shrewsbury Sch.; Worcester Coll., Oxford (BA Juris. 1989). Called to the Bar, Inner Temple, 1991; in practice as a barrister, specialising in construction, engrg and IT law, 1991–; Mem., Attorney-Gen.'s Panel of Counsel, 2003–08. *Recreations:* ski-ing, scuba diving. *Address:* Keating Chambers, 15 Essex Street, WC2R 3AA. *T:* (020) 7544 2600, *Fax:* (020) 7544 2700. *E:* shargreaves@keatingchambers.com.

HARINGTON, Michael Kenneth; His Honour Judge Harington; a Circuit Judge, since 2000; *b* 9 Aug. 1951; *s* of late Kenneth Douglas Evelyn Herbert Harington, and Maureen Helen (*née* McCalmont); *m* 1984, Deirdre Christine Kehoe; one *s* two *d*. *Educ:* Eton Coll.; Christ Church, Oxford (MA). Called to the Bar, Inner Temple, 1974; a Recorder, 1998. *Recreations:* golf, shooting. *Address:* Gloucester County Court, Kimbrose Way, Gloucester GL1 2DE. *Club:* MCC.

HARINGTON, Sir Nicholas (John), 14th Bt *cr* 1611; Legal Adviser, Export Credits Guarantee Department, 1988–2002; *b* 14 May 1942; *s* of His Honour John Charles Dundas Harington, QC (*d* 1980) (*yr s* of 12th Bt) and Lavender Cecilia Harington (*d* 1982), *d* of late Major E. W. Denny, Garboldisham Manor, Diss; *S* uncle, 1981. *Educ:* Eton; Christ Church, Oxford (MA Jurisprudence). Called to the Bar, 1969. Employed in Persian Gulf, 1971–72. With Civil Service, 1972–2002. *Recreation:* numerous. *Heir: b* David Richard Harington [*b* 25 June 1944; *m* 1983, Deborah (*née* Catesby); two *s*]. *Address:* The Ring o'Bells, Whitbourne, Worcester WR6 5RT. *T:* (01886) 821819.

HARKER, Lisa Marie; Director of Strategy, Policy and Evidence, National Society for the Prevention of Cruelty to Children, since 2014 (Head of Strategy Unit, later Head of Strategy and Development, 2011–14); *b* Farnborough, Kent, 3 May 1969; *d* of Dr Paul Harker and Jacqueline Harker; *m* 1999, Mark Norman; one *s* one *d*. *Educ:* Lord Digby's Sch., Sherborne; Bristol Univ. (BSc Hons Psychol.); London Sch. of Econs (MSc Social Policy and Planning). Policy Officer, Daycare Trust, 1992–95; Campaign Team Co-ordinator, Child Poverty Action Gp, 1995–97; Social Affairs Specialist, BBC News, 1997–99; UK Advocacy Co-ordinator, Save the Children UK, 1999–2000; Dep. Dir, IPPR, 2000–03; Ind. Policy Advr, 2003–07; Co-Dir, IPPR, 2007–10. Vis. Fellow, Nuffield Coll., Oxford, 2015–. Mem., London Child Poverty Commn, 2006–08. Chm., Daycare Trust, 2001–06; Trustee: Aspire Oxfordshire, 2002–11; NACRO, 2006–09; KPMG Foundn, 2009–. *Publications:* Poverty: the facts, 1996; (ed) From Welfare to Wellbeing: the future of social care, 2002; An Equal Start, 2003; Delivering on Child Poverty: what would it take?, 2006; How Safe Are Our Children?, 2013. *Recreations:* cooking for friends, snowboarding, exploring Italy by Vespa. *Address:* National Society for the Prevention of Cruelty to Children, Weston House, 42 Curtain Road, EC2A 3NH. *T:* (020) 3772 9102, *Fax:* (020) 7596 3737. *E:* lharker@nspcc.org.uk.

HARKNESS, Very Rev. James, KCVO 2005; CB 1993; OBE 1978; Moderator of the General Assembly of The Church of Scotland, 1995–96; a Chaplain to the Queen in Scotland, 1996–2006 (an Extra Chaplain, 1995–96 and since 2006); Dean of the Chapel Royal in Scotland, 1996–2006; *b* 20 Oct. 1935; *s* of James and Jane Harkness; *m* 1960, Elizabeth Anne Tolmie; one *s* one *d*. *Educ:* Univ. of Edinburgh (MA). Asst Minister, North Morningside Parish Church, Edinburgh, 1959–61; joined RAChD, 1961: Chaplain: 1 KOSB, 1961–65; 1 Queen's Own Highlanders, 1965–69; Singapore, 1969–70; Dep. Warden, RAChD Centre, 1970–74; Senior Chaplain: N Ireland, 1974–75; 4th Div., 1975–78; Asst Chaplain Gen., Scotland, 1980–81; Senior Chaplain: 1st British Corps, 1981–82; BAOR, 1982–84; Dep. Chaplain Gen. to the Forces, 1985–86, Chaplain Gen., 1987–95. QHC 1982–95. Chaplain, BLESMA, 1995–2002; Nat. Chaplain, 1995–2002, Pres., 2001–06, RBL, Scotland. Chm., Bd of Dirs, Carberry, 1998–2001. Mem., Pensions Appeal Tribunals, Scotland, 1999–2005. Chm., Veterans Scotland, 2003–06. Member: Scot. Adv. Cttee, ICRF, 1995–2000; Bd, Mercy Corps, Scotland, 2001–08; Pres., Soc. of Friends, St Andrew's, Jerusalem, 1998–2005. President: ACFA, Scotland, 1996–2004; Earl Haig Fund Scotland, 2001–06; Officers' Assoc. Scotland, 2001–06. Trustee: Nat. Prayer Breakfast for Scotland, 1996–2012; Liberating Scots Trust, 1998–2001; Anglo Israel Assoc., 2001–11 (Mem., Exec. Cttee, 1995–2001); Scottish Nat. War Meml, 2003–15; Gen. Trustee, Church of Scotland, 1996–2011. Gov., Fettes Coll., 1999–2009. Patron, St Mary's Music Sch., Edinburgh, 1995–2000. FRSA 1992. DD Aberdeen, 2000. KStJ 2012 (OStJ 1988; ChStJ 1999; Dean, Order of St John, Scotland, 2005–11). *Recreation:* general pursuits. *Address:* 13 Saxe Coburg Place, Edinburgh EH3 5BR. *Clubs:* New, Royal Scots (Edinburgh).

HARKNESS, John Diamond; First Scottish Parliamentary Counsel to the United Kingdom, 2000–02; *b* 14 July 1944; *s* of Jack Harkness and Isabel Harkness. *Educ:* High Sch. of Glasgow; Univ. of Glasgow (MA, LLB). Legal Asst, then Sen. Legal Asst, Office of Solicitor to Sec. of State for Scotland, 1971–79; Asst, then Depute Scottish Parliamentary Counsel, 1979–2000; Asst Legal Sec. to Lord Advocate, 1979–99. *Recreations:* reading, music, travel. *Address:* 10 The Limes, Linden Gardens, W2 4ET.

HARLE, John Crofton, FGS; saxophonist, composer, conductor, record producer; Professor of Saxophone (formerly of Saxophone, Performance and Music History), Guildhall School of Music and Drama, since 1988; *b* 20 Sept. 1956; *s* of Jack Harle and Joyce Harle (*née* Crofton); *m* 1st, 1985, Julia Jane Eisner (marr. diss. 2004); two *s*; 2nd, 2010, Riccarda Anne Kane. *Educ:* Newcastle Royal Grammar Sch.; Royal Military Sch. of Music, Kneller Hall (Cousins Meml Medal for Best Army Musician 1975); Royal Coll. of Music (Foundn Schol.; ARCM (Hons) 1980; Dannreuther Concerto Prize 1980); French govt scholarship for study with Daniel Deffayet, Paris Conservatoire, 1981–82. FGS (FGSM 1990). Began career as clarinettist; served as solo clarinettist, Band of Coldstream Guards; Leader of Myrha Saxophone Quartet, 1977–82; formed duo with pianist John Lenehan, 1979; actor/musician, RNT, London, 1979–85; saxophone soloist, 1980–, with major internat. orchs, incl. LSO, English Chamber Orch., LPO, Amsterdam Concertgebouw, New World Symphony; Principal Saxophone, London Sinfonietta, 1987–97; founder Mem., Michael Nyman Band, 1980; formed: Berliner Band, 1980); John Harle Band, 1988; also worked with Nash Ensemble and the Fires of London. Compositions for several ensembles, 1983–, incl. London Brass and LSO. Frequent composer and soloist on TV (incl. BBC series, Silent Witness (RTS Award for best TV theme music, 1998), BBC2 documentary, Lucien Freud—A Painted Life (RTS Best Original Music Award, 2012), and History of Britain) and feature films (incl. Prick Up Your Ears (Cannes Film Fest. Award for Best Artistic Achievement in a Feature Film); regular broadcaster on BBC Radio; featured in One Man and his Sax, BBC2 TV, 1988. Has made many recordings. Major works written for him by Dominic Muldowney, Ned Rorem, Richard Rodney Bennett, Luciano Berio, Michael Nyman, Gavin Bryars, Mike Westbrook, Stanley Myers, Harrison Birtwistle, Michael Torke, John Tavener, Sally Beamish. Artistic Dir, Green Hall, Tokyo, 1986–88; Founder and Man. Dir, Harle Records, 2005–13; producer, EMI Classics, Tokyo, 2011–12; Artistic Dir and Producer, Sospiro Records, 2013–. Founder, Sospiro Leadership Masterclasses, 2007–; speaker and lectr on leadership and music, 2007–. GLAA Young Musician, 1979, 1980. *Publications:* John Harle's Saxophone Album, 1986, reissued as John Harle's Sax Album, 1998; Rachmaninov Vocalise, 2001. *Recreations:* nostalgia, New Wave British films of the 1960s, fogeydom, Viz. *Address:* The Old Malthouse, Goodnestone, Kent CT3 1PB. *T:* 07711 223313. *E:* john@sospiro.com. *Clubs:* East India; Wingham Lawn Tennis.

HARLECH, 6th Baron *cr* 1876; **Francis David Ormsby Gore;** *b* 13 March 1954; *s* of 5th Baron Harlech, KCMG, PC, and Sylvia (*d* 1967), *d* of Hugh Lloyd Thomas, CMG, CVO; *S* father, 1985; *m* 1986, Amanda Jane (marr. diss. 1998), *d* of Alan T. Grieve, *qv*; one *s* one *d*. *Educ:* Worth. *Heir:* *s* Hon. Jasset David Cody Ormsby Gore, *b* 1 July 1986. *Address:* Glyn Hall, Talsarnau, Harlech, Gwynedd LL47 6TE. *Club:* Brooks's.

HARLECH, Pamela, Lady; journalist and producer; *b* 18 Dec. 1934; *d* of Ralph Frederick Colin and Georgia Talmey; *m* 1969, 5th Baron Harlech, KCMG, PC (*d* 1985); one *d*. *Educ:* Smith Coll., Northampton, Mass; Finch Coll. (BA). London Editor, (American) Vogue, 1964–69; Food Editor, (British) Vogue, 1971–82; freelance journalist, 1972–; prodn work for special events, 1986–87; Commissioning Editor, Thames and Hudson, Publishers, 1987–89. Chairman: Women's Playhouse Trust, 1984–94; V&A Enterprises, 1987–94; English Nat. Ballet, 1990–2000; Council, British Amer. Arts Assoc., 1990–92; Bath Shakespeare Festival, 2004–06; Trustee, V&A Mus., 1986–94; Member: Welsh Arts Council, 1981–85; Arts Council of GB, 1986–90; South Bank Bd, 1986–94; Council, Managing Bd, Crusaid, 1987–96; Council, ABSA, 1988–95 (Chm., Judging Panel for Awards, 1989–90); Bd, Th. Royal, Bath, 2001–08; Bd, Wales Millennium Centre, 2002–07. Pres., Bath Cancer Support, 1998–. *Publications:* Feast without Fuss, 1976; Pamela Harlech's Complete Guide to Cooking, Entertainment and Household Management, 1981; Vogue Book of Menus, 1985. *Recreations:* music, cooking, laughing.

HARLEN, Prof. Wynne, OBE 1991; PhD; Director, Scottish Council for Research in Education, 1990–99; *b* 12 Jan. 1937; *d* of Arthur Mitchell and Edith (*née* Radcliffe); *m* 1958, Frank Harlen (*d* 1987); one *s* one *d*. *Educ:* St Hilda's Coll., Oxford (BA 1958; MA 1961); Univ. of Bristol (PhD 1974). Asst teacher, Cheltenham Ladies' Coll., 1959–60; Lectr, St Mary's Coll. of Educn and Glos Coll. of Art, 1960–66; Research Fellow: Univ. of Bristol, 1966–73; Univ. of Reading, 1973–77; Sen. Res. Fellow, KCL, 1977–84; Sidney Jones Prof. of Science Educn, Univ. of Liverpool, 1985–90. Visiting Professor: Univ. of Liverpool, 1990–2001; Bristol Univ., 2000–; Project Dir, Univ. of Cambridge, 2003–06. Bernard Osher Fellow, Exploratorium, San Francisco, 1995. Chair, Sci. Expert Gp, OECD Student Assessment Project, 1998–2003. President: British Educnl Res. Assoc., 1993–94; Educn Sect., BAAS, 2001–02; ASE, 2009–10. FEIS 1999. Editor, Primary Sci. Rev., 1999–2004. Purkwa Prize for contribs to sci. and educn, 2008; recognised by INNOVEC (Mexico) for contrib. to sci. educn, 2011. *Publications:* Science 5/13: a formative evaluation, 1977; Guides to Assessment: Science, 1983; New Trends in Primary Science Education, 1983; Teaching and Learning Primary Science, 1985, 2nd edn 1994; Primary Science: taking the plunge, 1985, 2nd edn 2001; The Teaching of Science, 1992, 6th edn as The Teaching of Science in Primary Schools, 2014; Enhancing Quality in Assessment, 1994; Developing Primary Science, 1997; Effective Teaching of Science: a review of research, 1999; Teaching, Learning and Assessing Science: 5–12, 2000, 4th edn 2006; Assessment of Learning, 2007; Student Assessment and Testing, 2008; Developing Teacher Assessment, 2010; Principles and Big Ideas of Science Education 2010; Assessment and Inquiry-Based Science Education: issues in policy and practice, 2013; numerous articles in jls incl. Internat. Jl Sci. Educn, Studies in Educnl Evaluation, Cambridge Jl Educn, Curriculum Jl, Brit. Educnl Res. Jl, Res. Papers in Educn, Jl Curriculum Studies, Assessment in Educn, Studies in Sci. Educn. *Recreations:* opera, orchestral music, hill-walking, gardening, bee-keeping. *Address:* Haymount Coach House, Bridgend, Duns, Berwickshire TD11 3DJ.

HARLEY, Gen. Sir Alexander (George Hamilton), KBE 1996 (OBE 1981); CB 1991; Master Gunner, St James's Park, 2001–08; Senior Military Adviser, Thales Defence Systems, 2003–12; *b* India, 3 May 1941; *s* of late Lt-Col William Hamilton Coughtrie Harley, 1st Punjab Regt and later Royal Indian Engineers, and Eleanor Blanche (*née* Jarvis); *m* 1967, Christina Valentine, *d* of late Edmund Noel Butler-Cole and Kathleen Mary (*née* Thompson); two *s*. *Educ:* Caterham Sch.; RMA Sandhurst. Commissioned RA 1962; 1962–73: 7 Para Regt RHA; Staff Capt. MoD; Adjutant; Canadian Staff Coll.; Mil. Asst to Chief of Jt Intelligence, MoD, 1974–75; Battery Comdr, 1975–78 (despatches); Directing Staff, Staff Coll., 1978–79; CO 19 Field Regt RA (The Highland Gunners), 1979–82; Col Defence Staff, and Operations Centre, Falklands War, MoD, 1983–85; Comdr 33 Armd Brigade, 1985–87; Chief of Ops, Northern Army Group, 1988–90; Asst Chief Jt Ops, Overseas and Gulf War, MoD, 1990–93; Administrator, Sovereign Base Areas, and Comdr British Forces Cyprus, 1993–95; DCDS Ops, and Dir Jt Ops, MoD, 1995–97. Adjt Gen., 1997–2000; ADC Gen. to the Queen, 1998–2000. Col Comdt, HAC, RHA, 1998–2003. Chm., Purple International, 2001–03. Pres., Combined Services Hockey, 1995–2000 (Hon. Vice-Pres., 2001–11); Patron: The Nordics Hockey Club, 1992–; Dan's Fund for Burns, 2003–. Hon. Vice President: Raleigh Internat., 1998–2008; Army Hockey Assoc., 2001–. Gov., King's Sch., Bruton, 2001–12; Pres., Caterham Sch., 2009–13. Visitor/Trustee, Bishop Sexey's Hosp., Bruton, 2013–. FCMI (FBIM 1982). Freeman: City of London, 2002; Wheelwrights' Co., 2002. *Clubs:* Naval and Military, Honourable Artillery Company.

HARLEY, David Charles Mount-Stephen, CMG 2011; Visiting Practitioner Fellow, Aston Centre for Europe, since 2010; Chairman, Burson-Marsteller, Brussels, since 2011; *b* Hartfield, 10 Dec. 1948; *s* of Richard and Rose Harley; *m* 2008, Susanne Oberhauser; one *s* one *d*. *Educ:* Queens' Coll., Cambridge (BA 1971). EU official, 1975–2010, Dep. Sec.-Gen., EP, 2007–10; Sen. Advr, Burson-Marsteller, Brussels, 2010–11. Dir, Hartfield Consulting Ltd, 2010–. *Recreations:* theatre, literature. *E:* dcmsharley@btinternet.com. *Club:* Groucho.

HARLEY, Ian, FCA, FCIB; Chief Executive, Abbey National plc, 1998–2002; *b* 30 April 1950; *s* of Michael Harley and Mary Harley (*née* Looker); *m* 1975, Rosalind Caroline Smith; three *s*. *Educ:* Falkirk High Sch.; Edinburgh Univ. (MA 1972). FCA 1982; FCIB 1998. Articled Clerk, Touche Ross, 1972–76; Corporate Planning Team, Morgan Crucible, 1976; joined Abbey National, 1977. Dir, Dah Sing Financial Hldgs, Hong Kong, 1998–2002; non-executive Director: Rentokil Initial plc, 1999–2007; British Energy plc, 2002–09; Remploy Ltd, 2004–10; John Menzies plc, 2009–; Chm., Rentokil Initial Pension Trustee Ltd, 2007–. Pres., CIB, 2001–02. Chm., Ct of Govs, Whitgift Foundn, 2007– (Gov., 2002–). *Recreations:* reading, walking, cycling, golf. *Club:* Oriental.

HARLEY, Ven. Michael; Archdeacon of Winchester, 2009–15, now Archdeacon Emeritus; *b* Ivybridge, Devon, 4 Sept. 1950; *s* of Ian Peter Harley and Joan Agnes Mabel Harley; *m* 1974, Deborah Mary Whillock; three *d*. *Educ:* Queen Elizabeth's Sch., Crediton; King's Coll., London (AKC 1973); Christ Church Coll., Canterbury (CertEd 1974); St Augustine's Coll., Canterbury; Lambeth Diploma (STh 1992); Univ. of Kent (MPhil 1995). Ordained deacon, 1975, priest, 1976; Curate, St William's, Walderslade, Chatham, 1975–78; Curate-in-charge, St Barnabas, Weeke, 1978–81; Vicar: St Mary Extra, Southampton, 1981–86; Hurstbourne Tarrant Benefice, 1986–99; Rural Dean, Andover, 1995–99; Vicar, Chandlers Ford, Winchester, 1999–2009; Master, St Cross Hosp., and Priest-in-charge, Winchester St Cross and St Faith, 2009–11. Chair, House of Clergy, 2004–09; Mem., Gen. Synod, 2005–. Acora Link Officer, Dio. of Winchester, 1991–94; Diocesan Rural Officer, Winchester, 1994–97. Hon. Canon, Winchester Cathedral, 2007–15, now Canon Emeritus. *Recreations:* reading, music, films, theatre, cooking, history, current affairs.

HARLING, Christopher Charles, (Kit), CBE 2010; FRCP, FFOM, FFPH; Consultant Occupational Physician, Derriford Hospital, Plymouth, 2006–11; Director (part-time), NHS Plus, 2002–11; *b* 12 Jan. 1951; *s* of Robert and Dorothy Harling; *m* 1976, Philippa Ann Capper; two *s*. *Educ:* Leeds GS; Manchester GS; Keble Coll., Oxford (MA); University Coll. Hosp. Med. Sch. (MB BS); Univ. of Plymouth (MRes Marine Biol., 2013). DAvMed 1988; FFOM 1991; FRCP 1995; FFPH (FFPHM 1999). Res. Fellow and Hon. Registrar, Inst. Envmtl and Offshore Medicine, Univ. of Aberdeen, 1979–80; Area MO, NCB, 1981–84; Consultant Occupational Physician: Sheffield HA, 1984–88; Bristol Royal Infirmary, 1988–2005; Sen. Lectr in Occupl Medicine, Univ. of Bristol, 1988–2005. Civilian Consultant Advr in Occupational Medicine to RN, 1993–2012; Hon. Advr in Occupational Medicine to RNLI, 2005–13 (Mem., Med. and Survival Sub-cttee, 2005–13). MO, RNR, 1988–95 (PMO, HMS Flying Fox, 1994–95). Hon. Sec., Specialist Trng Authy of Med. Royal Colls, 1999–2008 (Mem., 1996–98; Vice-Chm., 1998–99); Sec., 1987–90, Chm., 1990–93, Assoc. NHS Occupational Physicians; Mem. Council, 1982–84, Mem., NHS Work Gp, 1985–87, SOM; Faculty of Occupational Medicine, Royal College of Physicians: Examr, 1990–99, Dep. Chief Examr, 1993–94; Vice-Dean, 1994–96; Dean, later Pres., 1996–99; Chm., Ethics Cttee, 1999–2007. Mem., Nat. DNA Database Ethics Gp, Home Office, 2014–. Vice Chm., Salcombe Harbour Bd, 2006–. Mem., RNSA, 1988–. *Publications:* papers on ethics, occupational medicine and health care workers. *Recreations:* sailing, flying, polar bears, penguins. *Club:* Salcombe Yacht.

HARLOE, Prof. Michael Howard, PhD; FAcSS; Vice-Chancellor, University of Salford, 1997–2009, now Emeritus Professor; Visiting Professor, London School of Economics, since 2009; Visiting Fellow, Kellogg College, Oxford, since 2014; *b* 11 Oct. 1943; *s* of Maurice Edward and May Cecilia Harloe; *m* 1976, Judy Rosilyn Philip; one *s* two *d*. *Educ:* Watford Boys' GS; Worcester Coll., Oxford (MA 1970); PhD Essex 1984. Res. Asst, Borough of Swindon, 1967–69; Res. Officer, LSE, 1969–72; PSO, Centre for Envmtl Studies, London, 1972–80; University of Essex: Lectr, 1980–84, Sen. Lectr, 1984–87, Reader, 1987–90, Prof., 1990–97, Dept of Sociology; Dean of Social Scis, 1988–91; Pro-Vice-Chancellor, 1992–97. FAcSS (AcSS 2000). Hon. DLitt Salford, 2010. *Publications:* (jtly) The Organisation of Housing: public and private enterprise in London, 1974; Swindon, A Town in Transition: a study in urban development and overspill policy, 1975; (ed) Captive Cities: studies in the political economy of cities and regions, 1977; (ed) New Perspectives in Urban Change and

Conflict, 1981; (ed with E. Lebas) City, Class and Capital, 1981 (US edn 1982); Private Rented Housing in the United States and Europe, 1985; (jtly) Housing and Social Change in Europe and the USA, 1988; (ed and contrib.) Place, Policy and Politics, 1990; (with M. Martens) New Ideas for Housing: the experience of three countries, 1990; (ed jtly) Divided Cities: New York and London in the contemporary world, 1992; The People's Home: social rented housing in Europe and America, 1995; (ed) Sociology of Urban Communities, Vols I–III, 1996; (ed jtly) Cities After Socialism: urban and regional change and conflict in post-Socialist societies, 1996; (jtly) Working Capital: life and labour in contemporary London, 2002. *Recreations:* gardening, travel, reading, sociology, yoga. *Club:* Oxford and Cambridge.

HARLOW, Archdeacon of; *see* Webster, Ven. M. D.

HARLOW, Prof. Carol R., PhD; FBA 1999; Professor of Public Law, London School of Economics, University of London, 1989–2002, now Emeritus (Hon. Fellow, 2007); *b* 28 Aug. 1935; *d* of late Prof. Charles Harold Williams and Clare Williams (*née* Pollak); *m*; one *s* one *d*. *Educ:* King's Coll., London (LLB 1956; LLM 1970); LSE (PhD 1980). Lectr, Kingston Poly., 1972–76; Lectr, 1976–86, Reader, 1986–89, LSE. Jean Monnet Prof., European Univ. Inst., 1995, 1996. Bencher, Middle Temple, 2009. Hon. QC 1996. *Publications:* Compensation and Government Torts, 1982; (jtly) Law and Administration, 1984, 3rd edn 2008; Understanding Tort Law, 1986, 3rd edn 2005; (jtly) Pressure Through Law, 1992; Accountability in the European Union, 2002; Tort Law and Beyond (Clarendon Lectures), 2004; (ed jtly) Administrative Law in a Changing State, 2009; (jtly) Process and Procedure in EU Administration, 2014. *Recreations:* theatre, gardening, walking, painting. *Address:* Law Department, London School of Economics, Houghton Street, WC2A 2AE. *E:* c.harlow@lse.ac.uk.

HARMAN, Rt Hon. Harriet; PC 1997; QC 2001; MP (Lab) Camberwell and Peckham, since 1997 (Peckham, Oct. 1982–1997); *b* 30 July 1950; *d* of late John Bishop Harman, FRCS, FRCP, and of Anna Charlotte Harman; *m* 1982, Jack Dromey, *qv*; two *s* one *d*. *Educ:* St Paul's Girls' Sch.; York Univ. Brent Community Law Centre, 1974–78; Legal Officer, NCCL, 1978–82. Opposition Chief Sec. to the Treasury, 1992–94; opposition front bench spokesman: on employment, 1994–95; on health, 1995–96; on social security, 1996–97; Sec. of State for Social Security, 1997–98; Solicitor-Gen., 2001–05; Minister of State, DCA, subseq. MoJ, 2005–07; Lord Privy Seal and Leader of the House of Commons, and Minister for Women and for Equality, 2007–10; Dep. Leader and Chair of Labour Party, 2007–15; Shadow Sec. of State for Internat. Develt, 2010–11, for Culture, Media and Sport, 2011–15; Shadow Dep. Prime Minister, 2011–15. Mem., NEC, Labour Party, 1993–98. *Publications:* Sex Discrimination in Schools, 1977; Justice Deserted: the subversion of the jury, 1979; The Century Gap, 1993. *Address:* House of Commons, SW1A 0AA.

HARMAN, Sir Jeremiah (LeRoy), Kt 1982; a Justice of the High Court, Chancery Division, 1982–98; *b* 13 April 1930; *er s* of late Rt Hon. Sir Charles Eustace Harman, PC; *m* 1960, Erica Jane (marr. diss. 1986), *e d* of late Hon. Sir Maurice Richard Bridgeman, KBE; two *s* one *d*; *m* 1987, Katharine Frances Goddard Pulay (*d* 2002), *d* of late Rt Hon. Sir Eric Sachs and *widow* of George Pulay. *Educ:* Horris Hill Sch.; Eton Coll. Served Coldstream Guards and Parachute Regt, 1948–51; Parachute Regt (TA), 1951–55. Called to the Bar, Lincoln's Inn, 1954, Bencher, 1977, Treas., 2000; QC 1968; called to Hong Kong Bar, 1978, Singapore Bar, 1980; Mem., Bar Council, 1963–67. Dir, Dunford & Elliott Ltd, 1972–79. *Recreations:* fishing, watching birds, reading, listening to music. *Address:* c/o Treasury Office, Lincoln's Inn, WC2A 3TL.

HARMAN, Sir John (Andrew), Kt 1997; DL; Chairman, Institute for European Environment Policy, since 2010 (Director, 2008–10); *b* 30 July 1950; *s* of John E. Harman and Patricia J. Harman (*née* Mullins); *m* 1971, Susan Elizabeth Crowther; one *s* three *d*. *Educ:* St George's Coll., Weybridge; Manchester Univ. (BSc Hons Maths); Huddersfield Coll. of Educn (Technical) (PGCE). Maths teacher, Greenhead Coll., Huddersfield, 1973–79; Head of Maths, Barnsley 6th Form Coll., 1979–90; Sen. Lectr in Maths, Barnsley Coll., 1990–97. Joined Labour Party, 1977: various posts, incl. Br. Sec., Co-ordinating Cttee Chm. and Constituency Vice-Chm.; Mem., Policy Commns on Envmt, 1995–96, and Local Govt, 1995–. Member (Lab): W Yorks CC, 1981–86 (Vice-Chm. 1982–85, Chm. 1985–86, Finance Cttee); Kirklees MDC, 1986–2000 (Leader, Council, and Labour Gp, 1986–99); Lead Comr for Intervention, Doncaster MBC, 2010–12. Dep. Chm. 1988–92, Vice-Chm. 1992–97, AMA; Local Government Association: Dep. Leader, Labour Gp, 1997–2000; Chm., Urban Commn, 1997–2000. Mem., Sec. of State's New Deal Task Force, 1997–2001; Mem., UK Delegn to Earth Summit, Rio de Janeiro, 1992. Chm., Kirklees Stadium Develt Ltd, 1993–. Mem. Bd, 1995–2008, Chm., 2000–08, Envmt Agency. Director: Energy Saving Trust, 1997–2012; Aldersgate Gp, 2007–; Nat. House Builders Council, 2009–; Mem. Bd, Centre for Low Carbon Futures, 2010–14; Chm., One Community Foundn Ltd, 2010–. Trustee: Nat. Coal Mining Mus., 2004–; Forum for the Future, 2007–14. Contested (Lab) Colne Valley, 1987, 1992. DL W Yorks, 2012. Hon. FICE 2000; Hon. FIWM 2002; Hon. FIWEM 2002; Hon. FSE 2005. Hon. DCL Huddersfield, 2000. *Recreations:* music, reading, gardening, Huddersfield Town AFC. *Address:* 82A New North Road, Huddersfield HD1 5NE.

HARMAN, Richard Stuart; Headmaster, Uppingham School, since 2006; *b* 11 March 1959; *s* of late Donald George Harman and of Jean Patricia Harman (*née* Harrison); *m* 1989, Dr Karin Voth (Rev. Dr Karin Harman); one *d*. *Educ:* Trinity Coll., Cambridge (BA English Lit. 1981); Exeter Univ. (PGCE). Sales Exec., Acad. Press/Harcourt Brace Internat. (Publishers), 1981–83; teacher of English and Drama, Marlborough Coll., 1984–88; Eastbourne College: Hd of English, 1988–91; Housemaster, 1991–95; Co-educn Co-ordinator, 1995–97; Registrar and Dir of Drama, 1997–2000; Headmaster, Aldenham Sch., Elstree, 2000–06. Chm., Boarding Schs' Assoc., 2011–12; Chm., HMC, 2014–15. *Recreations:* sports, theatre, music, travel. *Address:* Uppingham School, Rutland LE15 9QE. *Clubs:* East India, Lansdowne.

HARMAN, Robert Donald; QC 1974; a Recorder of the Crown Court, 1972–97; a Judge of the Courts of Appeal of Jersey, 1986–98, and of Guernsey, 1986–99; *b* 26 Sept. 1928; *o s* of late Herbert Donald Harman, MC and Dorothy (*née* Fleming); *m* 1st, 1960, Sarah Elizabeth (*d* 1965), *o d* of late G. C. Cleverly; two *s*; 2nd, 1968, Rosamond Geraldine, 2nd *d* of late Comdr G. T. A. Scott, RN; two *d*. *Educ:* privately; St Paul's Sch.; Magdalen Coll., Oxford. Called to the Bar, Gray's Inn, 1954, Bencher, 1984; South-Eastern Circuit; a Junior Prosecuting Counsel to the Crown at Central Criminal Court, 1967–72; a Senior Treasury Counsel, 1972–74. Mem., Senate of the Inns of Court and the Bar, 1985–87. Appeal Steward, BBB of C, 1981–98. Liveryman, Goldsmiths' Co. *Address:* 2 Harcourt Buildings, Temple, EC4Y 9DA. *T:* (020) 7353 2112; The Clock House, near Sparsholt, Winchester, Hants SO21 2LX. *T:* (01962) 776461. *Clubs:* Garrick; Swinley Forest Golf.

HARMAN, Stephen Richard; Chairman, British Horseracing Authority, since 2013; *b* Durham, 20 June 1956; *s* of Alec and Gill Harman; *m* 1983, Patricia Robigo; twin *s* one *d*. *Educ:* Durham Univ. (BA); Warwick Univ. (MBA). Dowty Mining, 1978–80; Shell: various UK posts, 1980–87; Dir, HK and China, 1987–93; Chief Exec., Eur. Liquefied Petroleum Gas, 1994–98; Chief Exec., Shell Marine, 1999–2002; Vice-Pres., Downstream, 2003–05; CEO, Pennzoil, 2006–10; Vice-Pres., Downstream Jt Ventures, 2010–13. Sen. Ind. Dir, UPOL, 2014–. Chm., Ustinov Coll. Council, Durham Univ., 2013–. Trustee/Dir, Help for Heroes, 2010–. *Recreations:* horseracing, golf, tennis, cricket, Rugby, historical fiction, mentoring, Cornwall, mining art. *E:* srh.harman@googlemail.com. *Clubs:* Lensbury (Teddington); Royal Cinque Ports Golf, Mullion Golf.

HARMER, David John; Chairman, Shaftesbury Society, 2005–07; Chief Executive, John Grooms Housing Association, 1988–2005; *b* 14 May 1940; *s* of Stanley James Arthur Harmer and Eileen Joan (*née* Callaghan); *m* 1971, Janet Arnott Dodds; one *s* one *d*; one *s* one *d* from previous *m*. *Educ:* Dulwich Coll.; Spurgeon's Coll. Surveyor, Portman Family Settled Estates, 1957–61; Ministerial Assistant, W Ham Central Mission, 1961–62; Church Pastor, Shaftesbury Soc., 1964–71; Founder, 1971, Dep. Dir, 1971–88, Shaftesbury Soc. Housing Assoc. Member: Exec., Christian Alliance Housing Assoc., 1987–90; Regl Exec., Nat. Housing Fedn, 1987–95 (Chm., 1990–93); Chm., Nat. Wheelchair Housing Assoc. Gp, 1992–95. Livability (formerly Shaftesbury Society, then Grooms-Shaftesbury): Member: Council, 1995–2010; Urban Action Cttee, 1995–99 (Chm., 1997–99); Audit Cttee, 2001–10; Pay Review Panel, 2002; Chief Exec.'s Appts Panel, 2002, 2010; Chairman: Grooms-Shaftesbury Merger Project Gp, 2006–07; Fundraising and Marketing Cttee, 2007–10; Vice Chm., Bd of Trustees, 2007–10; voluntary helper for Publicity and Fundraising; Vice Pres., 2013–. Mem., West Ham Central Mission Wkg Gp, 2000–01. Link Trustee, Nash Coll., Bromley, 2003–10 (Mem., Resources Cttee; Chm. Govs, 2005–10). Mem., John Grooms Disability Enquiry, 2003. Mem., Inst. of Advanced Motorists, 2006–. Freeman, City of London, 2002. Diaconate Mem., Woodmansterne Baptist Ch., 2010–. *Recreations:* housing and disability issues, Church and Christian activities, exhibition budgerigars (Sec., 2000–, Pres., 2008, Croydon Budgerigar Soc.; Mem. Council, 2009–, Chm., 2011–, London and Southern Counties Budgerigar Soc.), fuchsias, family tree, Christian preaching. *Address:* Remrah, 146 Hayes Lane, Kenley, Surrey CR8 5HQ.

HARMES, Stephen Douglas; a District Judge (Magistrates' Courts), since 2014; *b* St Asaph, N Wales, 29 May 1959; *s* of Frank and Irene Harmes; *m* 1997, Tracey Lynne Hopkins; one *s* one *d*. *Educ:* Deeside High Sch., Queensferry, Flintshire; Univ. of Wales Inst. Sci. and Technol., Cardiff (BSc Hons Econs 1980); Inns of Court Sch. of Law. Called to the Bar, Gray's Inn, 1993; Crown Prosecutor, 1994–99; Crown Advocate, 1999–2014; First-tier Tribunal Judge (Immigration and Asylum), 2006–13. *Recreations:* tennis, Rugby. *Address:* Teesside Magistrates' Court, Victoria Square, Middlesbrough, Teesside TS1 2AS. *T:* (01642) 240301. *E:* DistrictJudges.Harmes@judiciary.gsi.gov.uk. *Club:* Cardiff Castle Lawn Tennis.

HARMSWORTH, family name of **Viscount Rothermere** and **Baron Harmsworth**.

HARMSWORTH, 3rd Baron *cr* 1939, of Egham; **Thomas Harold Raymond Harmsworth;** publisher; *b* 20 July 1939; *s* of Hon. Eric Beauchamp Northcliffe Harmsworth (*d* 1988) and Hélène Marie (*d* 1962), *d* of Col Jules Raymond Dehove; *S* uncle, 1990; *m* 1971, Patricia Palmer, *d* of late M. P. Horsley; two *s* three *d*. *Educ:* Eton; Christ Church, Oxford (MA). Nat. Service, Royal Horse Guards (The Blues), 1957–59 (2nd Lieut). Stockbroker, 1962–74; DHSS, 1974–88. Chm., Dr Johnson's House Trust. *Publications:* Gastronomic Dictionary: French-English, 2003; Gastronomic Dictionary: Spanish-English, 2004; Gastronomic Dictionary: Italian-English, 2005; Gastronomic Dictionary: Portuguese-English, 2008. *Recreations:* sundry, including music. *Heir:* *s* Hon. Dominic Michael Eric Harmsworth [*b* 18 Sept. 1973; *m* 1999, Veronica Patricia, *d* of Luis and Veronica Ausset, San Fernando, Chile; three *s* two *d* (of whom one *s* one *d* are twins)]. *Address:* The Old Rectory, Stoke Abbott, Beaminster, Dorset DT8 3JT. *T:* (01308) 868139. *Clubs:* Carlton, Brooks's.

HARMSWORTH, Sir Hildebrand Harold, 3rd Bt *cr* 1922; gardening writer; *b* 5 June 1931; *s* of Sir Hildebrand Alfred Beresford Harmsworth, 2nd Bt, and Elen, *d* of Nicolaj Billenstein, Randers, Denmark; *S* father, 1977, but his name does not appear on the Official Roll of the Baronetage; *m* 1960, Gillian Andrea (*d* 2005), *o d* of William John Lewis; one *s* two *d*. *Educ:* Harrow; Trinity College, Dublin. *Heir:* *s* Hildebrand Esmond Miles Harmsworth [*b* 1 Sept. 1964; *m* 1988, Ruth Denise, *d* of Dennis Miles; one *s* two *d*]. *Address:* Ewlyn Villa, 42 Leckhampton Road, Cheltenham GL53 0BB.

HARNDEN, Prof. David Gilbert, PhD; FRCPath; FRSE 1982; FRSB; Chairman, South Manchester University Hospitals NHS Trust, 1997–2002; *b* 22 June 1932; *s* of William Alfred Harnden and Anne McKenzie Wilson; *m* 1955, Thora Margaret Seatter; three *s*. *Educ:* George Heriot's School, Edinburgh; University of Edinburgh. BSc. Lectr, Univ. of Edinburgh, 1956–57; Sci. Mem., Radiobiology Unit, MRC, Harwell, 1957–59; Sci. Mem., Clinical and Population Cytogenetics Unit, MRC, Edinburgh, 1959–69; Prof. of Cancer Studies, Univ. of Birmingham, 1969–83; Dir, Paterson Labs, later Paterson Inst. for Cancer Res., Christie Hosp. and Holt Radium Inst., later Christie Hosp. NHS Trust, 1983–97; Hon. Prof. of Experimental Oncology, 1983–97, Prof. Emeritus, 1998–, Univ. of Manchester; Emeritus Fellow, CRC, 1997. Chairman: Educn Cttee, Cancer Res. Campaign, 1987–92; NW Regl Adv. Cttee on Oncology Services, 1991–95. Dir, Christie Hosp. (NHS) Trust, 1991–97. Trustee: New Heart/New Start, Wythenshawe Hosp. Transplant Fund, 1998–2002; Gray Lab. Cancer Res. Trust, 2000–06; Chm., Trustees, Friends of Rosie, Children's Cancer Res. Fund, 1999–2011. Hon. MRCP 1987. Chm., Editorial Bd, British Jl of Cancer, 1983–98. Mem., NRPB, 1995–99. *Publications:* papers on cancer research and human genetics in learned jls. *Recreation:* sketching people and places. *Address:* Tanglewood, Ladybrook Road, Bramhall, Stockport SK7 3NE. *T:* (0161) 485 3214. *E:* dgharnden@btinternet.com.

HARNEY, Mary; Leader, Progressive Democrats, Ireland, 1993–2006 and 2007–08; *b* March 1953; *m* 2001, Brian Geoghegan. *Educ:* Convent of Mercy, Inchicore, Dublin; Presentation Convent, Clondalkin, Co. Dublin; Trinity Coll., Dublin (BA). Contested (FF) Dublin SE, 1977. Mem. Dublin CC, 1979–91. Senator, 1977–81; TD Dublin SW, then Dublin Mid West: FF, 1981–85; Prog. Dem., 1985–2008, Ind., 2008–11; Minister: of Envmtl Protection, 1989–92; for Enterprise, Trade and Employment, 1997–2004; for Health and Children, 2004–11; Tánaiste, 1997–2006. Progressive Democrats: Co-Founder, 1985; Dep. Leader, and Spokesperson on Justice, Equality and Law Reform, 1993. Non-executive Director: Biocon Ltd, 2012–; Euro Insurances, 2012–; Ward Biotech, 2012–.

HAROCHE, Prof. Serge, PhD; Professor, since 2001, and Chair of Quantum Physics and Director, since 2012, Collège de France; *b* Casablanca, Morocco, 11 Sept. 1944; *m* 1965, Claudine Zeligson; one *s* one *d*. *Educ:* Lycée Carnot, Paris; École Normale Supérieure, Paris (PhD 1971). Postdoctoral Fellow, Stanford Univ., 1972–73; Lectr, École Normale Supérieure, Paris, 1973–84; Maître du Conference, École Polytechnique, 1974–84; Prof., Paris VI Univ., 1975–2001 (Chm., Physics Dept, École Normale Supérieure, 1994–2000); Prof. (pt-time), Yale Univ., 1984–93. Vis. Prof., Harvard Univ., 1981. Mem., Inst. Universitaire de France, 1991–2000. Mem., French Acad. Scis, 1994; Foreign Mem., NAS, USA. Grand Prix Jean Ricard, French Physical Soc., 1983; Einstein Prize for Laser Sci., 1988; Humboldt Award, Humboldt Foundn, 1992; Michelson Medal, Franklin Inst., 1993; Tomassoni Award, La Sapienza Univ., Rome, 2001; Quantum Electronics Prize, Eur. Physical Soc., 2002; Townes Award, Optical Soc. of America, 2009; Gold Medal, Centre Nat. de la Recherche Scientifique, 2009; (jtly) Nobel Prize in Physics, 2012. Comdr, Légion d'Honneur (France), 2013. *Publications:* (with J.-M. Raimond) Exploring the Quantum: atoms, cavities and photons, 2006; contrib. papers to learned jls. *Address:* Département de Physique de l'École Normale Supérieure, 24 rue Lhomond, 75005 Paris, France.

HARPER, Rt Rev. Alan Edwin Thomas, OBE 1996; FRGS; Archbishop of Armagh, and Primate of All Ireland, 2007–12; *b* Tamworth, 20 March 1944; *m* 1967, Helen Louise McLean; one *s* three *d*. *Educ:* Leeds Univ. (BA 1965); C of I Theol Coll. Sen. Insp. of Historic Monuments, Archaeol Survey of NI, 1966–74; Asst Prin. Planning Officer, Staffs CC, 1974–75. Ordained deacon, 1978, priest, 1979; Curate Asst, Ballywillan, 1978–80; Incumbent: Moville with Greencastle, 1980–82; Christ Church, Londonderry, 1982–86; St John's, Malone, 1986–2002; Precentor, Belfast Cathedral, 1996–2002; Archdeacon of Connor, 1996–2002; Bishop of Connor, 2002–07. Preb. of St Audoen, Nat. Cathedral and

Collegiate Church of St Patrick, Dublin, 1990–2001. Founder Trustee and first Chm., Ulster Historic Churches Trust, 1995–2000; Mem., 1980–95, Chm., 1988–95, Historic Monuments Council for NI. FRGS 2012. *Address:* Forth Cottage, 67 Lisnacroppin Road, Rathfriland, Newry, Co. Down BT34 5NZ. *T:* (028) 4065 1649. *E:* a.e.t.harper@gmx.com.

HARPER, Dr Caroline Anne, OBE 2000; Chief Executive, Sightsavers International, since 2005; *b* 4 May 1960; *d* of Douglas and Barbara Harper. *Educ:* Bristol Univ. (BSc); Churchill Coll., Cambridge (PhD 1986). British Gas, 1985–91; Amerada Hess, 1991–2002 (Man. Dir, Amerada Hess Gas); CEO, Harper & Associates, 2002–05. Hon. DSc Bristol, 2013. *Recreations:* ski-ing, travel. *Address:* 4A Wellington Close, W11 2AN. *T:* (020) 7467 0515. *E:* harper_ca@hotmail.com.

HARPER, Air Marshal Sir Christopher (Nigel), KBE 2011 (CBE 2002); Director General, NATO International Military Staff, HQ NATO, since 2013; *b* 25 March 1957; *s* of late Denis Alan Harper and Cynthia Nancy Harper; *m* 1980, Janet Elizabeth Edwards; one *s* (and one *s* decd). *Educ:* Alleyn's Sch., Dulwich; King's Coll., London (MA Defence Studies). Joined RAF, 1976; officer trng, RAF Henlow, 1976 (Sword of Honour); with 41 (Fighter) Sqdn, 1979–81; with Nos 31 and 14 Sqdns, 1982–85; Jaguar Qualified Weapons Instructor, 1984; Exchange tour, Canadian Air Force flying CF-18 Hornet with 421 Sqdn, 1986–89; Eurofighter Project Officer, MoD, 1989–92; RAF Staff Coll., Bracknell, 1992; MA to Minister (Armed Forces), MoD, 1992–94; OC No 41 (F) Sqdn, 1994–97; hcsc, 1997; Exec. Officer to Comdr AAFCE, 1997–99; Stn Comdr, RAF Coltishall, 1999–2001 (dispatches, Iraq, 2002); Air Cdre Typhoon, HQ 1 Gp, 2002–04; Dir, Jt Commitments, MoD, 2004–05; COS Ops, HQ Strike Comd, 2005–07; AOC No 1 Gp, 2007–09; Dep. Comdr, Jt Force Comd Brunssum, 2009–11; UK Mil. Rep. to NATO and EU, 2011–13. Pres., RAF Flying Clubs' Assoc., 2005–; Hon. Pres., No 1475 Sqdn ATC, 2003–. Vice Pres., RAF Charitable Trust, 2013–. Pres., Edward Alleyn Club, 2010–11. FCMI (FIMgt 1997), CCMI 2012. *Recreations:* flying, motorcycling, shooting, running, ski-ing, golf, cooking, fine wine. *Address:* NATO HQ, Boulevard Leopold III, 1110 Brussels, Belgium. *Clubs:* Royal Air Force (Vice Pres., 2013–); Air Squadron; Strangers' (Norwich).

HARPER, Prof. David Alexander Taylor, PhD, DSc; CGeol, FGS; Professor of Palaeontology, and Principal, Van Mildert College, Durham University, since 2011; *b* 29 Sept. 1953; *s* of David and Jessie Harper; *m* 1981, Dr Maureen McCorry; two *s* one *d*. *Educ:* George Watson's Boys' Coll., Edinburgh; Walbottle Grammar Sch., Throckley; Imperial Coll. London (BSc); Queen's Univ., Belfast (PhD 1979; DSc 2005). ARSM 1975; EurGeol. Lectr, 1984–97, Reader, 1997–98, University Coll. Galway; Prof., Univ. of Copenhagen, 1998–2011. Einstein Prof., Chinese Acad. of Scis, 2008; Vis. Prof., Lund Univ., 2014–. Foreign Member: Royal Danish Acad. Scis and Letters, 2004; Royal Swedish Physiographic Soc., 2014. *Publications:* (with P. J. Brenchley) Palaeoecology: ecosystems, environments and evolution, 1998; (with Ø. Hammer) Palaeontological Data Analysis, 2006; (with M. J. Benton) Introduction to Palaeobiology and Fossil Record, 2009; contrib. peer-reviewed papers to learned jls. *Recreations:* hill walking, opera, enjoying malt whisky. *Address:* Principal's House, Van Mildert College, Durham University, Durham DH1 3LQ. *E:* david.harper@durham.ac.uk.

HARPER, David Ross, CBE 2002; FFPH; CBiol, FRSB; Managing Director, Harper Public Health Consulting Ltd, since 2014; *b* 6 June 1955; *s* of Frank Harper and Louise Harper (*née* Mason); *m* 1978, Lorraine Chadwick; two *s* one *d*. *Educ:* Univ. of Dundee (BSc Hons Microbiol. 1977); Univ. of Birmingham (PhD Microbial Biochem. 1982). CBiol, FRSB (FIBiol 1995); FFPH 2006. Hd, Microbiol. Unit, Metropolitan Police Forensic Sci. Lab., 1981–89; Department of Health: Head: Microbiol. Pathology Services, 1989–91; Food Microbiol. Sci. Unit, 1991–94; Dangerous Pathogens, Biotechnol. and Envmtl Microbiol. Unit, 1994–2000; Envmt Br., 2000–03; Dir Gen. for Health Protection, Internat. Health and Scientific Develt, 2003–08; Chief Scientist and Hd of Profession for Scientists, 1996–2013, Dir Gen. of Health Improvement and Protection, 2008–13; Dir Gen. and Chief Scientist, Dept of Health, WHO (on secondment), 2012–13. Vis. Prof., Cranfield Univ., 2012–. Hon. Prof., Univ. of Dundee, 2007. Hon. FRSPH 2011. Hon. DSc Cranfield, 2010. *Publications:* articles in jls. *Recreations:* music, sport, motorcycles. *Address:* 30 Mycenae Road, SE3 7SG. *T:* 07872 492717. *E:* david@harperz.com.

HARPER, Donald John; Chief Scientist, Royal Air Force, 1980–83; aerospace consultant, 1983–93; *b* 6 Aug. 1923; *s* of Harry Tonkin and Caroline Irene Harper; *m* 1947, Joyce Beryl Kite-Powell; two *d*. *Educ:* Purley County Grammar Sch. for Boys; Queen Mary Coll., London (1st cl. BSc (Eng) 1943). CEng, FRAeS. Joined Aero Dept, RAE Farnborough, 1943; Scientific Officer, Spinning Tunnel, 1947–49; High Speed and Transonic Tunnel, 1950–59; Sen. Scientific Officer; Principal Scientific Officer, 1955; Dep. Head of Tunnel, 1958–59; Space Dept RAE, Satellite Launching Vehicles, 1960–62; Senior Principal Scientific Officer, MoD, Central Staff, 1963–65; Head of Assessment Div., Weapons Dept, RAE, 1966–68; Dir of Project Time and Cost Analysis, MoD (PE), 1968–71; Dir-Gen., Performance and Cost Analysis, MoD (PE), 1972–77; Dir-Gen. Research C, MoD (PE), 1978–83. Mem. Council, RAeS, 1990–92. *Publications:* contrib. Aeronautical Res. Council reports and memoranda and tech. press. *Recreations:* music, especially (in the past) choral singing; gardening, home improvement, family history research, formerly fell-walking.

HARPER, Dame Elizabeth (Margaret Way), DBE 1995; farmer, retired; *b* 20 June 1937; *d* of Jack Horsford Horrell and Margaret Faith Horrell (*née* Rickard); *m* 1956, Charles John Harper; one *s* (and one *s* one *d* decd). *Educ:* Lagmhor Sch., Mid-Canterbury, NZ; Ashburton High Sch.; Craighead Diocesan Sch., Timaru. Save the Children: Br. Sec., 1970–84; Pres., Ashburton Br., 1984–87; S Island Vice-Pres., 1987–89; NZ Pres., 1990–93. Red Cross volunteer, Dist Nursing Service, 1984–; night sitter volunteer for terminally ill, 1987–. Mem. Bd, Ashburton Benevolent Trust, 1998–. Save the Children Award for Dist. and Meritorious Service, 1994. *Recreations:* golf, sewing, knitting.

HARPER, Sir Ewan William, Kt 2003; CBE 1997; JP; Chief Executive: United Church Schools Trust (formerly The Church Schools Company), 1990–2011; United Learning Trust, 2002–11 (Governor, 2002–11); *b* 21 June 1939; *s* of Leonard Robert Harper and Enid Harper (*née* Redman); *m* 1965, Jennifer Margaret Hoare-Scott; one *s* three *d*. *Educ:* Marlborough Coll.; Trinity Hall, Cambridge (Open Exhibnr; MA Hist.; Hon. Fellow, 2013). Man. Dir, 1972–87, Chm., 1985–87, Harper and Tunstall Ltd; Dir, Restoration of Lambeth Palace Chapel, 1987–88; Sec., Archbishops' Commn on Rural Areas, 1988–90. Mem., Hurd Commn on Office of Archbishop of Canterbury, 2000. Chm., Northants Industry Year, 1986; Vice Chm., Bd of Visitors, Wellingborough Borstal, 1970–82. Lay Mem., Chapter of Peterborough Cath., 2002–07. Governor: Benenden Sch., 1983–92 (Chm., Benenden Sch. Trust); Oundle Sch., 1992–2003; Maidwell Hall, 1993–2000; UC Northampton, 1997–2002. Trustee: Lambeth Fund, 1983–2014 (Chm., 2011–14); Academy Sponsors Trust, 2004–06. JP Northants, 1973. Kt Comdr, Royal Order of Francis I, 2011. *Recreations:* gardening, golf, tennis, watercolours, history. *Clubs:* Athenæum, MCC.

HARPER, Prof. Fred, PhD; educational consultant, Central and Eastern Europe, since 1997; Dean, Seale-Hayne Faculty of Agriculture, Food and Land Use, University of Plymouth (formerly Plymouth Polytechnic), 1989–97, now Emeritus Professor of Agriculture; *b* 7 June 1947; *s* of Frederick and Queenie Elizabeth Harper; *m* 1971, Moyna Carole Hunter (marr. diss. 1996); one *d*. *Educ:* Univ. of Nottingham (BSc Hons Agric., PhD). Lecturer: Writtle Agricl Coll., Chelmsford, 1971–75; and Dir of Studies, Univ. of Edinburgh, 1975–82; Vice-Principal and Dir of Studies, Harper Adams Agricl Coll., Shropshire, 1983–88; Principal, Seale-Hayne Coll., Devon, 1988–89. ARAgS, 1993. *Publications:* The Principles of Arable Crop Production, 1983; numerous pubns on crop physiology and production, agricl educn and overseas agriculture. *Recreations:* walking, travel, observing wildlife, watching sport. *Address:* 11 The Village, Shobrooke, Crediton, Exeter EX17 1AU. *T:* (01363) 776105.

HARPER, Heather Mary, (Mrs E. J. Benarroch), CBE 1965; soprano; Professor of Singing and Consultant, Royal College of Music, 1985–93; Director of Singing Studies, Britten-Pears School, Aldeburgh, 1986; *b* 8 May 1930; *d* of late Hugh Harper, Belfast; *m* 1973, Eduardo J. Benarroch. *Educ:* Trinity Coll. of Music, London. Has sung many principal roles incl. Arabella, Ariadne, Marschallin, Chrysothemis, Elsa and Kaiserin, at Covent Garden, Glyndebourne, Sadler's Wells, Bayreuth, Teatro Colon (Buenos Aires), Edinburgh Fest., La Scala, NY Met, San Francisco, Deutsche Oper (Berlin), Frankfurt, Netherlands Opera, Canadian Opera Co., Toronto, and sang at every Promenade Concert season, 1957–90; created the soprano role in Benjamin Britten's War Requiem in Coventry Cathedral in 1962; soloist at opening concerts: Maltings, Snape, 1967; Queen Elizabeth Hall, 1967. Toured USA, 1965, and USSR, 1967, with BBC SO; toured USA annually, 1967–91, and appeared regularly at European music fests; toured: Japan and S Korea as Principal Soloist Soprano with Royal Opera Co., 1979; Australia and Hong Kong with BBC Symph. Orch., 1982; has also sung in Asia, Middle East, Australia and S America; Principal Soloist Soprano with Royal Opera House Co., visit to Los Angeles Olympic Games, 1984; Principal Soloist with BBC Philharmonic Orch.'s first South American tour, 1989. Has made many recordings, incl. works of Britten, Beethoven, Berg, Mahler, Mozart, Strauss and Verdi; broadcasts frequently throughout the world, and appears frequently on TV; Masterclasses for advanced students and young professionals, Britten-Pears Sch.; retired from operatic stage, 1984, from concert stage, 1991. Member: BBC Music Panel, 1989; RSA Music Panel, 1989. FTCL; FRCM 1988; Hon. RAM 1972. Hon. DMus Queen's Univ., Belfast, 1966; Hon. DLitt Ulster, 1992. Edison Award, 1971; Grammy Nomination, 1973; Grammy Award, 1979, 1984, 1991; Best vocal performance for Ravel's Shéhérazade; Grand Prix du Disque, 1979. *Recreations:* gardening, cooking.

HARPER, Prof. John Martin, DMus; FLSW; Director, International Centre for Sacred Music Studies, Bangor University, 2008–14, now Emeritus; Honorary Professor of Liturgy and Music, University of Birmingham, since 2014; *b* 11 July 1947; *s* of late Geoffrey Martin and Kathleen Harper; *m* 1970, Cynthia Margaret Dean (marr. diss.); three *s*; *m* 1991, Sally Elizabeth Roper. *Educ:* King's Coll. Sch., Cambridge; Clifton Coll., Bristol; Selwyn Coll., Cambridge (Organ Scholar; MA); Birmingham Univ. (PhD 1976); MA Oxon. Dir, Edington Music Fest., 1971–78; Dir of Music, St Chad's Cathedral, Birmingham, 1972–78; Lectr in Music, Birmingham Univ., 1974–75, 1976–81; Asst Dir of Music, King Edward's Sch., Birmingham, 1975–76; Fellow, Organist, Informator Choristarum and Tutor in Music, Magdalen Coll., and Univ. Lectr in Music, Oxford, 1981–90; University College of North Wales, then University of Wales, Bangor, subseq. Bangor University: Prof. of Music, 1991–98; Res. Prof., 1998–; Dir Gen., RSCM, 1998–2007 (Emeritus Dir, 2008). Leverhulme Fellow, 1997–98; Vis. Scholar, Sarum Coll., 2005–. Founder Dir, Centre for Advanced Welsh Music Studies, 1994–2003. Vice-Pres., Plainsong and Medieval Music Soc., 2008–. FRCO(CHM) 1972; FRSCM 2007; FLSW 2012. DMus Lambeth, 2010. Hon. FGCM 1996. Benemerenti Papal award, 1978. *Publications:* choral compositions, 1974–; (ed) Orlando Gibbons: consort music, 1982; The Forms and Orders of Western Liturgy, 1991; (ed) Hymns for Prayer and Praise, 1996, 2nd edn 2011; (ed) Music for Common Worship (7 vols), 2000–06; (ed) The Light of Life, 2002; The Spirit of the Lord, 2004; (ed jtly) Psallam, 2006; contribs to: New Grove Dictionary of Music and Musicians, 1980, 2000; Oxford DNB; Sarum Customary Online; articles and reviews in music jls and papers. *Address:* Bethania, Llangoed, Beaumaris, Anglesey LL58 8PH.

HARPER, (John) Michael; Deputy Chairman, QinetiQ plc, since 2012 (non-executive Director, since 2011); *b* 2 Jan. 1945; *s* of Mark and Kathleen Harper; *m* 1st, 1968, Julia Carey (marr. diss. 1979); one *s* one *d*; 2nd, 1979, Judith Soesan; two *s* one *d*. *Educ:* King's Coll., London (BSc Eng, AKC, 1966); Imperial Coll., London (MSc 1967). Managing Director: Vickers S. Marston, 1975–80; BAJ Vickers, 1980–84; Graviner Ltd, 1984–88; Divl Man. Dir, 1988–99, Dir, 1999–2000, Williams plc; Chief Exec., Kidde plc, 2000–05. Chairman: Vitec Gp plc, 2004–12; BBA Aviation plc, 2007–14; Ricardo plc, 2009–14 (non-exec. Dir, 2003–14). Non-executive Director: Catlin Gp plc, 2005–10; Aerospace Technology Inst., 2014–. Trustee, Tring Park Sch., 2010–. Freeman, City of London, 2003. Liveryman, Firefighters' Co., 2004– (Master, 2012–13). *Recreations:* sport generally, particularly cricket, football, Rugby; ballet, opera. *Address:* Claridges, High Street, Eggington, Beds LU7 9PQ. *Clubs:* Travellers, MCC.

HARPER, Prof. (John) Ross, CBE 1986; Founder, 1961, and Senior Partner, 1961–2001, Ross Harper & Murphy, Solicitors; Consultant, Harper Macleod, since 2001 (Senior Partner, 1991–2001); Professor of Law, Strathclyde University, 1986–2002, now Emeritus; *b* 20 March 1935; *s* of late Rev. Thomas Harper, BD, STM, PhD and Margaret Simpson Harper (later Clarkson); *m* 1963, Ursula Helga Renate Gathman; two *s* one *d*. *Educ:* Hutchesons' Boys' Grammar School; Glasgow Univ. (MA, LLB), Pres., Students Rep. Council, 1955. Pres., Scottish Union of Students, 1956–58; Chm., Internat. Students' Conf., 1958. Asst Solicitor, McGettigan & Co., Glasgow, 1959; founded Ross Harper & Murphy, 1961. Temp. Sheriff, 1979–89; a Parly Comr, 1992–. Pres., Law Soc. of Scotland, 1988–89 (Vice-Pres., 1987–88). Pres., Glasgow Bar Assoc., 1975–78; International Bar Association: Chm., Criminal Law Div., 1983–87; Chm., Gen. Practice Section, 1990–92 (Sec. and Treas., 1988–90); Vice-Pres., 1992–94; Pres., 1994–96. Chairman: Mining (Scotland), 1997–2007 (Jt Chm., 1993–95); Scottish Coal, 1997–2007; Alarm Protection Ltd, 2000–; Eur. Scanning Clinic Ltd, 2004–07; Admiralty Resources NL (Australia), 2005–. Chm., Finance Cttee, Greater Glasgow Health Board, 1984–87; Non-exec. Dir, Scottish Prison Service, 1993–96. Consultant, Makanyane Safari Lodge, SA, 2001–. Trustee, Nat. Galls of Scotland, 1996–99. Contested (C): Hamilton, 1970; W Renfrewshire, Feb. and Oct. 1974. Founder Chm., Soc. of Scottish Cons. Lawyers, 1982–86; Pres., Scottish Cons. & Unionist Assoc., 1989 (Hon. Sec., 1986–89). *Publications:* A Practitioner's Guide to the Criminal Courts, 1985; Glasgow Rape Case, 1985; Fingertip Criminal Law, 1986; Global Law in Practice, 1997; pamphlets on devolution, referendums, etc. *Recreations:* bridge, angling. *Address:* 3 Bungalow Court, Peppermint Grove, Perth, WA 6011, Australia. *Club:* Caledonian.

HARPER, Joseph Charles; QC 1992; *b* 21 March 1939; *e s* of Frederick Charles Harper and Kitty (*née* Judah); *m* 1st, 1984, Sylvia Helen Turner (marr. diss. 1994); two *d*; 2nd, 2012, Susannah Deighton. *Educ:* Charterhouse; LSE (BA, LLB, LLM). ARCM 1960. Lectr, later Hd, Dept of Law, Kingston Poly., 1965–70; called to the Bar: Gray's Inn, 1970 (Bencher, 2000); Antigua, 1985. Mem. Council, Justice, 1979–91. *Publications:* (Specialist Editor) Hill and Redman, Law of Landlord and Tenant (looseleaf), 17th edn 1982, 18th edn 1988–2013; (ed and contrib.) Halsbury's Laws of England, vol. 8(I) Compulsory Acquisition of Land, vol. 46 Town and Country Planning; (ed) Planning Encyclopedia, 2006–13. *Recreations:* music (especially playing the French horn), bibliomania. *Address:* Landmark Chambers, 180 Fleet Street, EC4A 2HG. *T:* (020) 7430 1221. *Clubs:* Garrick, Chelsea Arts.

HARPER, Rt Hon. Mark; PC 2015; MP (C) Forest of Dean, since 2005; Parliamentary Secretary to HM Treasury (Government Chief Whip), since 2015; *b* 26 Feb. 1970; *m* 1999, Margaret Whelan. *Educ:* Headlands Sch., Swindon; Swindon Coll.; Brasenose Coll., Oxford (BA 1991). Auditor, KPMG, 1991–95; Intel Corporation (UK) Ltd: Sen. Finance Analyst, 1995–97; Finance Manager, 1997–2000; Ops Manager, 2000–02; own accountancy practice, Forest of Dean, 2002–06. Contested (C) Forest of Dean, 2001. Shadow Minister: for Defence, 2005–07; for Disabled People, 2007–10; Parly Sec., Cabinet Office, 2010–12; Minister of

State (Minister for Immigration), Home Office, 2012–14; Minister of State, DWP, 2014–15. *Address:* (office) 35 High Street, Cinderford, Glos GL14 2SL; House of Commons, SW1A 0AA.

HARPER, Michael; *see* Harper, J. M.

HARPER, Monica Celia, CMG 2004; HM Diplomatic Service, retired; Head of International Relations, Shakespeare's Globe, 2005–06; *b* 18 Aug. 1944; *d* of late Frank Ernest Harper and Renee Alice Harper. *Educ:* Reading Univ. and Sorbonne (BA Hons); City of London Coll. (Dip. Business Studies). Entered HM Diplomatic Service, 1967; FCO, 1967–69; on secondment to internat. staff of SEATO, Bangkok, 1969–72; attached to Ecole Nat. d'Admin, Paris, 1973–74; Third Sec., BMG, Berlin, 1974–77; Second Secretary: Bonn, 1977–79; Personnel Ops Dept, FCO, 1979–82; Mexico City, 1982–84; Press and Inf. Officer, UK Delegn to NATO, 1984–88; First Sec., Western European Dept (Germany), 1989–94; Dep. Hd of Mission, Luxembourg, 1994–98; Consul Gen., Lille, 1998–2004; Counsellor, FCO, 2004. *Recreations:* music, theatre, cinema, food. *Address:* 51 Tudor Way, Church Crookham, Hants GU52 6LX.

HARPER, Prof. Peter Stanley, Kt 2004; CBE 1995; DM; FRCP; University Research Professor in Human Genetics, Cardiff University, 2004–08, now Professor Emeritus; *b* 28 April 1939; *m*; two *s* three *d*. *Educ:* Exeter Coll., Oxford (BA 1961; MA, BM BS 1964; DM 1972). With Sir Cyril Clarke, Nuffield Inst. for Med. Genetics, Liverpool, 1967–69; with Dr Victor McKusick, Div. of Med. Genetics, Johns Hopkins Hosp., Baltimore, 1969–71; UWCM, Cardiff, 1971–2004, Prof. of Med. Genetics, 1981–2004. *Publications:* Myotonic Dystrophy, 1979, 3rd edn 2001; Practical Genetic Counselling, 1981, 7th edn 2010; (ed) Huntington's Disease, 1991, 3rd edn 2002; Landmarks in Medical Genetics, 2004; A Short History of Medical Genetics, 2008. *Recreations:* natural history, music. *Address:* Institute of Medical Genetics, Cardiff University, Heath Park, Cardiff CF14 4XN. *T:* (029) 2074 4057. *E:* HarperPS@cf.ac.uk.

HARPER, Richard Saul; His Honour Judge Harper; a Circuit Judge, since 2015; *b* 19 June 1953; *s* of Alfred and Netta Harper; *m* 1988, Amanda Louise Price; two *s* one *d*. *Educ:* Magdalen Coll., Oxford (MA). Called to the Bar, Gray's Inn, 1975; practising barrister, 1976–94; District Judge, Principal Registry of the Family Div., 1994–2015; nominated to sit in Court of Protection, 2008–. *Publications:* Child Care Law: a basic guide for practitioners, 1991; Medical Treatment and the Law: the protection of adults and minors in the Family Division, 1999; Medical Treatment and the Law: Issues of Consent: the protection of the vulnerable: children and adults lacking capacity, 2014. *Recreations:* international affairs, reading, sport, music. *Address:* Manchester Civil Justice Centre, HM Courts and Tribunals Service, 1 Bridge Street West, Manchester M60 1TE. *T:* (0161) 240 5813.

HARPER, Robin Charles Moreton; Member (Green) Lothians, Scottish Parliament, 1999–2011; *b* 4 Aug. 1940; *s* of late Comdr C. H. A. Harper, OBE, RN and Jessicca Harper; *m* 1994, Jennifer Helen Carter (*née* Brown); one step *s*. *Educ:* Aberdeen Univ. (MA); Edinburgh Univ. (Dip. Guidance & Curriculum). Teacher: Braehead Sch., Fife, 1964–68, 1970–71; Kolanya Sch., Kenya, 1968; Amukura Sch., Kenya, 1969; teacher: English, Newbattle High Sch., 1971–72; Modern Studies, Boroughmuir High Sch., 1972–99. Rector: Edinburgh Univ., 2000–03; Aberdeen Univ., 2005–08. Co-convener, Scottish Green Party, 1999–2009. Contested (Green) Edinburgh E, 2010. Trustee: Nat. Trust Scotland, 2011–; Scottish Wildlife Trust, 2011–. Patron: Play Scotland, 2011–; Scottish Ecol Design Assoc., 2011–. FEIS; FRSA; FRSSA (Pres., 2009–11). Hon. FRIAS, 2008. *Recreation:* music.

HARPER, Ross; *see* Harper, J. R.

HARPER, Stephen Joseph; PC (Can.) 2004; MP (Alliance, then C) Calgary Southwest, since 2002; Prime Minister of Canada, since 2006; *b* 30 April 1959; *s* of late Joseph Harper and Margaret Johnstone; *m* 1993, Laureen Teskey; one *s* one *d*. *Educ:* Richview Collegiate Inst.; Univ. of Calgary. Chief Aide to Jim Hawkes, MP, 1985; Exec. Asst, then Chief Advr and Speech Writer to Deborah Grey, MP, 1989–93. Vice-Pres., 1997, Pres., 1997–2001, Nat. Citizens' Coalition. Contested (Reform) Calgary W, 1988. MP (Reform), Calgary W, 1993–97; Leader of the Opposition, 2002–04, 2004–06. Founding Mem., Reform Party, 1993; Leader, Canadian Alliance, 2002–03; Co-founder, 2003, Leader, 2004–, Cons. Party of Canada. *Address:* (office) 80 Wellington Street, Ottawa, ON K1A 0A2, Canada.

HARPER, William Ronald; a Director, Thames Water, 1982–97; *b* 5 June 1944; *s* of William and Dorothy Harper; *m* 1969, Susan Penelope (*née* Rider); two *s* two *d*. *Educ:* Barton Peveril Grammar Sch., Eastleigh, Hants. IPFA 1965. Hampshire CC, 1960–64; Eastbourne CBC, 1964–68; Chartered Inst. of Public Finance and Accountancy, 1968–70; Greenwich London BC, 1970–74; Thames Water Authority: joined 1974; Dir of Finance, 1982; Dir of Corporate Strategy, 1984; Man. Dir, 1986; Dep. Chm., Thames Water Utilities, 1989; Thames Water PLC: Bd Mem., 1989–97; Gp Dir, Corporate Activities, 1992; Divl Dir, Products, 1994; Strategy Dir, 1996–97. Chm., Foundn for Water Res., 1989–94. Member: Council, Water Services Assoc., 1990–94; Bd of Management, Water Training, 1991–99 (Chm., 1993–99). CEN Rapporteur-Water, 1998–2013. *Address:* 37 Kidmore End Road, Reading, Berks RG4 8SN. *T:* (0118) 947 0895.

HARPHAM, (Robert) Harry; MP (Lab) Sheffield, Brightside and Hillsborough, since 2015; *b* 21 Feb. 1954; *m* Gill Furniss. *Educ:* Northern Coll.; Univ. of Sheffield. NUM Mem. and rep., Clipstone Colliery, Nottingham. Mem. (Lab), Sheffield CC, 2000–15 (Dep. Leader, 2012; Cabinet Mem. for Homes and Neighbourhoods). *Address:* House of Commons, SW1A 0AA.

HARPIN, Richard David; Chief Executive, HomeServe plc, since 1999 (Managing Director, Homeserve GB Ltd, 1993–99); Founder, Enterprise Trust, 2009; *b* Huddersfield, 10 Sept. 1964; *s* of David and Philippa Harpin; *m* 1997, Kate; two *s* one *d*. *Educ:* Royal Grammar Sch., Newcastle upon Tyne; York Univ. (BA Hons Econs). Brand Manager, Procter and Gamble, 1986–90; Harpin Ltd, 1988–; Sen. Consultant, Deloitte, 1990–91; Franchisee, Mortgage Advice Shop, Middlesbrough, 1991–92. Non-executive Chairman: Heating Components and Equipt Ltd, 1998–2004; Amsys Rapid Prototype and Tooling Ltd, 1999–2001; non-executive Director: Professional Properties Ltd, 1990–99; Baker Tilly Consulting, 1992–97; Mortgage Advice Bureau, 1997–2000. Mem., Leaders Gp, Cons. Party, 2009–. Mem., Nat. Apprenticeship Ambassadors Network, 2009–; Chm., W Midlands Apprenticeship Network, 2009–11. Enterprise Fellow, Prince's Trust, 2009–; created Scouting Entrepreneur Badge, Scout Assoc., 2010; Scouting Ambassador, 2011–. Ernst & Young Entrepreneur of the Year, 2008; PLC Awards Entrepreneur of the Year, 2011. *Recreations:* off piste and heliski-ing, swimming, private pilot's license, helicopter license. *Address:* HomeServe plc, Cable Drive, off Green Lane, Walsall WS2 7BN. *T:* (01922) 659701. *E:* richard.harpin@homeserve.com.

HARPUM, Charles, LLD; barrister; Fellow, Downing College, Cambridge, 1977–2001, now Emeritus; *b* 29 March 1953; *s* of Dr John Richard Harpum and Beatrice Doreen Harpum (*née* Harper). *Educ:* Queen Elizabeth Grammar Sch., Penrith; Cheltenham Grammar Sch.; Downing Coll., Cambridge (BA 1st Cl. Hons with Dist. 1975; LLB 1st Cl. Hons with Dist. 1977; Chancellor's Medal; MA 1979; LLD 2003). Called to the Bar, Lincoln's Inn, 1976, Bencher, 2001. Asst Lectr in Law, 1979–84, Lectr, 1984–98, Cambridge Univ.; a Law Comr, 1994–2001. Vis. Schol., Sch. of Law, Univ. of Va, Charlottesville, USA, 1991. *Publications:* (jtly) Megarry and Wade's Law of Real Property, 7th edn 2008 to 8th edn 2012; (jtly) Registered Land, 2002; (jtly) Registered Land: law and practice under the Land Registration Act 2002, 2004; numerous articles on property law in learned jls. *Recreations:* travelling, listening to classical music, drinking single island malts. *Address:* Falcon Chambers, Falcon Court, EC4Y 1AA. *T:* (020) 7353 2484.

HARRAP, Prof. Kenneth Reginald, CBE 1998; PhD, DSc; CChem, FRSC; Partner, Weston & Harrap Consulting, 1997–2014; Professor of Biochemical Pharmacology, Institute of Cancer Research, 1984–97, now Emeritus; *b* 20 Nov. 1931; *s* of George Ernest Harrap and Lilian Florence Olive Harrap (*née* Critchley); *m* 1st, 1954, Kathleen Ann Gotts (marr. diss. 1980); two *d*; 2nd, 1983, Beverley Jane Weston. *Educ:* George Green Sch.; London Univ. (BSc 1955; PhD 1961; DCC 1963; DSc 1977). CChem 1975; FRSC 1980. Institute of Cancer Research, Royal Marsden Hospital: Lectr, subseq. Sen. Lectr, in Chemistry, 1954–64; Head, Leukaemia Biochemistry Gp, 1964–70; Head of Department: Applied Biochemistry, 1970–77; Biochemical Pharmacology, 1977–82; Chm., Drug Develt Section, 1982–94; Dir, CRC Centre for Cancer Therapeutics, 1994–97; Vis. Scientist, 1997–2005; Fellow, 1997–; Emeritus Fellow, and Award of Distinction, CRC, 1998; Fellow, Inst. of Cancer Res., 2005. Bruce F. Cain Meml Award, Amer. Assoc. of Cancer Res., 1995, NZ Cancer Soc., 1996; Barnett Rosenberg Award, Internat. Symposium on Platinum Compounds in Cancer Chemotherapy, 1995. *Publications:* 400 papers in learned jls, contribs to books, reviews etc. *Recreations:* yachting and off-shore cruising, wildlife, concert music, opera. *Address:* Little Orchard, Wonham Way, Peaslake, Surrey GU5 9PA. *Club:* Sussex Yacht.

HARREL, David Terence Digby; independent consultant; Consultant, King & Wood Mallesons SJ Berwin (formerly S. J. Berwin), Solicitors, since 2007 (Partner, 1982–2007; Senior Partner, 1992–2006); *b* 23 June 1948; *s* of late Capt. H. T. Harrel, RN; *m* 1974, Julia Mary Reeves; two *s* one *d*. *Educ:* Marlborough Coll.; Bristol Univ. (LLB). William Charles Crocker: articled clerk, 1971–74; Asst Solicitor, 1974–77; Partner, 1977–79; Partner, Burton & Ramsden, 1979–81. Chairman: Kyte Gp Ltd, 2008–11; CPA Global, 2011–12; Savile Gp plc, 2011–13; Fairpoint plc, 2013–; non-executive Director: Wichford plc, 2007–11; Rathbone Brothers plc, 2007–. Mem. Bd, ENO, 2005–. Trustee, Clore Duffield Foundn, 1985–. *Recreations:* golf, tennis, fishing, shooting, walking, reading. *Clubs:* Swinley Forest Golf; Royal St George's Golf.

HARRELL, Lynn Morris; 'cellist; *b* 30 Jan. 1944; *s* of Mack Harrell, Metropolitan Opera baritone and Marjorie Harrell (*née* Fulton), violinist. *Educ:* Juilliard Sch. of Music; Curtis Inst. of Music. Principal 'Cellist, Cleveland Orch., 1963–71; Professor: College Conservatory of Music, Cincinatti, 1971–77; Juilliard Sch. of Music, 1977–86; Internat. Chair of 'Cello Studies, RAM, 1987–95; Piatigorsky Chair, Sch. of Music, USC, 1987–93; Artistic Dir, Los Angeles Philharmonic Inst., 1988–92; Principal, RAM, 1993–95; Prof. of Cello, Shepherd Sch. of Music, Rice Univ., Houston, 2002–09; Prof., Musikhochschule Lübeck, 2002–. Numerous awards and Grammys. *Recreations:* fishing, golf, chess. *Address:* c/o Columbia Artists Management Inc., 5 Columbus Circle, 1790 Broadway, New York, NY 10019–1412, USA.

HARRHY, Eiddwen Mair; soprano; Professor of Vocal Studies, Royal College of Music, since 2001; *b* 14 April 1949; *d* of David and Emily Harrhy; *m* Greg Strange, journalist and broadcaster; one *d*. *Educ:* St Winefride's Convent, Swansea; Royal Manchester College of Music (Gold Medal Opera Prize); Paris (Miriam Licette Prize). Welsh Nat. Opera Chorus, 1970–71; Glyndebourne Festival Opera Chorus, 1971–73; début at Royal Opera House, Covent Garden, Wagner Ring Cycle, 1974; début, ENO, 1975; performances: Welsh Nat. Opera; La Scala Milan; Teatro Colon Buenos Aires; ENO; Glyndebourne; Opera North; Scottish Opera; UK and overseas orchestras; BBC promenade concerts; Australia, NZ, Hong Kong, S America, Europe, Scandinavia, USA; numerous recordings. Visiting Professor: at Conservatoires in Vienna, Stockholm, Prague, Utrecht, Vilnius; Jacobs Sch. of Music, Indiana Univ., 2009; Helsinki, 2012; Nanyang Acad. of Fine Arts and Yong Siew Toh Conservatory of Music, Univ. of Singapore, 2013; Vocal Coach: Jacob's Sch. of Music, Indiana Univ., 2013–; Nat. Opera Studio, London, 2013–. Hon. DMus Swansea, 2015. FRWCMD (FWCMD 2002); FRCM 2012. FRSA 2003. *Recreations:* chamber music, ski-ing, golf. *Address:* c/o Royal College of Music, Prince Consort Road, SW7 2BS.

HARRI, Guto; Director of Communications, News UK (formerly News International), since 2012; *b* Caerdydd, Wales, 8 July 1966; *s* of Harri Elwyn and Lenna Ogwen Pritchard-Jones; *m* 2000, Shireen Louise Jilla; two *s* one *d*. *Educ:* Queen's Coll., Oxford (BA); Centre for Journalism Studies, Cardiff Univ. (Dip. Journalism). Corresp., BBC Wales, 1989–96; reporter and presenter, The World at One, BBC Radio 4, 1996–99; Political corresp., BBC News, 1999–2002; Chief Political corresp., BBC News 24, 2002–04; Rome corresp., 2004–05, N America Business corresp., 2005–07, BBC News; Political corresp., Six O'Clock News, 2007–08; Sen. Policy Advr, Fleishman-Hillard, 2008; Dir of Ext. Affairs and Spokesman for Mayor of London, 2008–12. Hon. Fellow, Bangor Univ., 2008. *Recreations:* travel, sailing, ski-ing, food and friends. *Address:* News UK, 1 London Bridge Street, SE1 9GF.

HARRIES, family name of **Baron Harries of Pentregarth**.

HARRIES OF PENTREGARTH, Baron *cr* 2006 (Life Peer), of Ceinewydd in the County of Dyfed; **Rt Rev. Richard Douglas Harries;** Bishop of Oxford, 1987–2006; an Hon. Assistant Bishop, Diocese of Southwark, since 2006; Gresham Professor of Divinity, 2008–12; *b* 2 June 1936; *s* of late Brig. W. D. J. Harries, CBE and Mrs G. M. B. Harries; *m* 1963, Josephine Bottomley, MA, MB, BChir, DCH; one *s* one *d*. *Educ:* Wellington Coll.; RMA, Sandhurst; Selwyn Coll., Cambridge (MA 1965; Hon. Fellow, 1998); Cuddesdon Coll., Oxford. Lieut, Royal Corps of Signals, 1955–58. Curate, Hampstead Parish Church, 1963–69; Chaplain, Westfield Coll., 1966–69; Lectr, Wells Theol Coll., 1969–72; Warden of Wells, Salisbury and Wells Theol Coll., 1971–72; Vicar, All Saints, Fulham, 1972–81; Dean, King's Coll., London, 1981–87. GOE examr in Christian Ethics, 1972–76; Dir, Post Ordination Trng for Kensington Jurisdiction, 1973–79. Chm., C of E Bd for Social Responsibility, 1996–2001; Vice-Chairman: Council of Christian Action, 1979–87; Council for Arms Control, 1982–87; Member: Home Office Adv. Cttee for reform of law on sexual offences, 1981–85; ACC, 1994–2003; Bd, Christian Aid, 1994–2002; Royal Commn on H of L reform, 1999; Nuffield Council on Bioethics, 2002–07; HFEA, 2002–09. Chairman: Southwark Ordination Course, 1982–87; Shalom; ELTSA (End Loans to Southern Africa), 1982–87; CCJ, 1992–2001; H of L Select Cttee on Stem Cell Res., 2001–02. Pres., Johnson Soc., 1988–89. Consultant to Archbishops of Canterbury and York on Interfaith Relns, with special resp. for Jewish Christian relns, 1986–92 (Sir Sigmund Sternberg Award, 1989). Founder, Oxford Abrahamic Gp, 1992. Radio and TV work. Vis. Prof., Liverpool Hope UC, 2002; Hon. Prof. of Theol., KCL, 2006–. Lectures: Hockerill, and Drawbridge, London, 1982; Stockton, London Business Sch., 1992; Pall Mall, Inst. of Dirs, 1993; Theological, QUB, 1993; Heslington, York, 1994; Drummond, Stirling, 2007; Sarum Theol, Sarum Coll., 2009; Sir D. J. James, Cardiff, 2011; Sir D. O. Evans, Aberystwyth, 2011. FKC 1983; FRSL 1996; FLSW 2012. Hon. FMedSci 2004; Hon. FIBiol 2009. Hon. Fellow, St Anne's Coll., Oxford, 2006. Hon. DD London, 1994; DUniv: Oxford Brookes, 2001; Open, 2006; Hon. DCL Huddersfield, 2008. President's Medal, British Acad., 2012. *Publications:* Prayers of Hope, 1975; Turning to Prayer, 1978; Prayers of Grief and Glory, 1979; Being a Christian, 1981; Should Christians Support Guerillas?, 1982; The Authority of Divine Love, 1983; Praying Round the Clock, 1983; Prayer and the Pursuit of Happiness, 1985; Morning has Broken, 1985; Christianity and War in a Nuclear Age, 1986; C. S. Lewis: the man and his God, 1987; Christ is Risen, 1988; Is There a Gospel for the Rich?, 1992; Art and the Beauty of God, 1993; The Real God, 1994; Questioning Belief, 1995; A Gallery of Reflections: the Nativity of Christ, 1995; In the Gladness of Today, 1999; God Outside the Box: why spiritual people object to Christianity, 2002; After the evil: Christianity and Judaism in the shadow of the holocaust, 2003; The Passion in Art, 2004; Praying the Eucharist, 2004; The Re-enchantment of Morality: wisdom for a troubled world, 2008; Faith in Politics?: rediscovering the Christian roots of our political values, 2010; Issues of Life and Death: Christian faith and medical intervention, 2010; The Image of Christ in Modern Art, 2013; *edited:* (jtly) Seasons of the Spirit, 1984; The One Genius; Through the Year with Austin Farrer, 1987; (jtly) Two Cheers for Secularism, 1998; (jtly) Christianity: two thousand years, 2001; (jtly) Abraham's Children: Jews, Christians and Muslims in conversation, 2006; *edited and contributed:* What Hope in an Armed World?, 1982; Reinhold Niebuhr and the Issues of Our Time, 1986; (jtly) Reinhold Niebuhr and Contemporary Politics, 2010; *contributed to:* Stewards of the Mysteries of God, 1979; Unholy Warfare, 1983; The Cross and the Bomb, 1983; Dropping the Bomb, 1985; Julian, Woman of our Time, 1985; If Christ be not raised, 1986; The Reality of God, 1986; A Necessary End, 1991; The Straits of War: Gallipoli remembered, 2000; That Second Bottle: essays on John Wilmot, Earl of Rochester, 2000; A Companion to English Renaissance Literature and Culture, 2000; Runcie: on reflection, 2002; Comparative Theology: essays for Keith Ward, 2003; Jesus in History, Thought and Culture, 2003; The Ethics of War, 2006; Britain's Next Bomb: what next?, 2006; The Price of Peace: just war in the twenty-first century, 2007; What makes us Human?, 2007; Does God Believe in Human Rights?, 2007; Intelligent Faith, 2009; British Foreign Policy and the Anglican Church, 2008; The Oxford Handbook of the Reception History of the Bible, 2011; articles in Theology, The Times, The Observer and various other periodicals. *Recreations:* theatre, literature, walking, lecturing on cruises. *Address:* House of Lords, SW1A 0PW.

HARRIES, Prof. John Edward, PhD; CPhys, FInstP; FRMetS; FLSW; Professor of Earth Observation, Imperial College London (formerly Imperial College of Science, Technology and Medicine), 1994–2013, Emeritus Professor of Physics and Senior Research Fellow, since 2013; on secondment as Chief Scientific Adviser to Welsh Government (formerly Welsh Assembly Government), 2010–13; *b* 26 March 1946; *s* of Brynmor and Marion Harries; *m* 1968, Sheila Margaret Basford; two *s* one *d. Educ:* Univ. of Birmingham (BSc Hons Physics 1967); King's Coll., London (PhD Physics 1971). Nat. Physical Lab., 1967–80; SO, later SSO, then PSO; Hd, Envmtl Standards Gp, 1976–80; Rutherford Appleton Laboratory, 1980–93; SPSO and Hd, Geophysics and Radio Div., 1980–84; DCSO, 1984; Associate Dir and Hd of Space Science Dept, 1984–93. Mem., NERC, 1995–97. President: Internat. Radiation Commn, 1992–96; RMetS, 1994–96. FLSW 2011. Fellow, Aberystwyth Univ., 2014. Hon. DSc Glamorgan, 2012. Dist. Public Service Medal, NASA, 2011; Mason Gold Medal, RMetS 2014. *Publications:* Earthwatch: the climate from space, 1991; more than 100 articles in books, jls and magazines. *Recreations:* walking, reading, music, supporting Welsh Rugby. *Address:* Spring Cottage, 129 Plymouth Road, Penarth, Vale of Glamorgan CF64 5DG. *E:* j.harries@imperial.ac.uk.

HARRINGTON, 12th Earl of, *cr* 1742; **Charles Henry Leicester Stanhope;** Viscount Stanhope of Mahon and Baron Stanhope of Elvaston, 1717; Baron Harrington, 1729; Viscount Petersham, 1742; *b* 20 July 1945; *s* of 11th Earl of Harrington and Eileen, *o d* of Sir John Foley Grey, 8th Bt; *S* father, 2009; *m* 1966, Virginia Alleyne Freeman Jackson, Mallow (marr. diss. 1983); one *s* one *d*; *m* 1984, Anita Countess of Suffolk and Berkshire. *Educ:* Eton. *Heir: s* Viscount Petersham, *qv. Address:* c/o 2 Astell House, Astell Street, SW3 3RX.

See also Viscount Linley.

HARRINGTON, Illtyd; JP; DL; *b* 14 July 1931; *s* of Timothy Harrington and Sarah (*née* Burchell); unmarried. *Educ:* St Illtyd's RC Sch., Dowlais; Merthyr County Sch.; Trinity Coll., Caermarthen. Member: Paddington Borough Council, 1959–64; Westminster City Council, 1964–68 and 1971–78, Leader, Lab. Gp, 1972–74; GLC, 1964–67 and for Brent S, 1973–86: Alderman, 1970–73; Chairman, Policy and Resources Cttee, 1973–77, Special Cttee, 1985–86; Dep. Leader, 1973–77, 1981–84; Dep. Leader of the Opposition, 1977–81; Chm. of the Council, 1984–85. Special Advr to Chm. and Leader of ILEA, 1988–90; Waterways Advr to Mayor of London, 2001–. JP Willesden 1968. First Chairman, Inland Waterways Amenity Adv. Council, 1968–71; Chm., London Canals Consultative Cttee, 1965–67, 1981–; Vice Pres., IWA, 1990–; Member: British Waterways Bd, 1974–82; BTA, 1976–80. Member: Bd, Theatre Royal, Stratford E, 1978–; Bd, Wiltons Music Hall, 1979–; Nat. Theatre Bd, 1975–77; Bd, National Youth Theatre, 1976–; Globe Theatre Trust, 1986–2001; Chm., Half Moon Theatre, 1978–90; Director: Soho Poly Theatre, 1981–2001; The Young Vic, 1981–2001. Chm., Nat. Millennium Maritime Fest., 1997–2000; Mem., London Dockland Mgt Adv. Gp, 1997–. President: Grand Union Canal Soc., 1974–; Islington Boat Club, 1985–; SE Region, IWA, 1986–; Immunity (Legal aid facility for AIDS victims), 1986–; Chairman: Kilburn Skills, 1977–2001; Battersea Park Peace Pagoda, 1984–; Limehouse Basin Users Gp, 1986–; Vice Pres., Coventry Canal Soc., 1970–. Gov., London Marathon, 1980–91. Trustee: Kew Bridge Pumping Mus., 1976–; Queen's Jubilee Walkway, 1977–; Chiswick Family Rescue, 1978–2001; Arthur Koestler Awards for Prisoners, 1987–; CARE, 1987–; Dominica Overseas Student Fund, 1987–; Mem., Montgomery Canal Trust, 1988–; Managing Trustee, Mutual Municipal Insurance Co., 1985–96. Governor, Brunel Univ., 1981–87. Patron: Westminster Cathedral Appeal, 1977–; Abandoned and Destitute Children Appeal (India), 2006–. DL Greater London, 1986. Contributor, The Guardian, 1982–; Literary Ed., Camden Jl gp of papers, 1995–. *Recreations:* defender of local government; laughing, singing and incredulity. *Address:* 44 Belbourne Court, Bread Street, Brighton BN1 1TT. *T:* (01273) 732693. *Club:* Savile.

HARRINGTON, Prof. (John) Malcolm, CBE 1992; MD; FRCP, FFOM, FFOMI, FMedSci, FFPH; Foundation Professor of Occupational Health, now Emeritus, and Director, Institute of Occupational Health, University of Birmingham, 1981–2000; *b* 6 April 1942; *s* of John Roy Harrington and Veda Naomi Harrington; *m* 1967, Madeline Mary Davies; one *d. Educ:* King's Coll., London (BSc, MSc); Westminster Hosp. Med. Sch. MD 1976; FFOM 1981; FRCP 1982; FFOMI 1994; MFPHM 1996, FFPH 2006. Hospital appointments, 1966–69; Lectr in Occupational Medicine, LSHTM, 1969–75; Vis. Scientist, Centers for Disease Control, Atlanta, US Public Health Service, 1975–77; Sen. Lectr in Occupational Medicine, LSHTM, 1977–80. Chm., Ind. Injuries Adv. Council, 1982–96. Ind. Review Lead, Work Capability Assessment, DWP, 2010–13. Gov., 2007–10, Lead Gov., 2009–10, Royal Devon and Exeter NHS Foundn Trust. Founder FMedSci 1998; Hon. FRSocMed 2004. *Publications:* (ed jtly) Occupational Hygiene, 1980, 3rd edn 2005; (with F. S. Gill) Occupational Health, 1983, 6th edn 2015; (ed) Recent Advances in Occupational Health, Vol. 2 1984, Vol. 3 1987; (ed jtly) Hunter's Diseases of Occupation, 10th edn 2010; papers in scientific professional jls. *Recreations:* music, gardening, cricket, reading biographies, theatre. *Address:* 1 The Cliff, Budleigh Salterton, Devon EX9 6JU. *Clubs:* Athenæum, Royal Society of Medicine.

HARRINGTON, Dr Michael John, CEng, FICE, FCIWEM; consultant, since 2011; Director, Michael Harrington Associates Ltd, since 2011; *b* Neath, W Glamorgan, 6 Jan. 1953; *s* of late James Henry Harrington and of Kathleen Harrington (*née* Stitson); one *d. Educ:* Univ. of Wales, Cardiff (BEng 1st Cl 1976; PhD 2003); Harvard Business Sch. (AMP); Henley Management Sch. (Top Mgt Prog. 1990). CEng 1979; FICE 1996. Various construction and gen. mgt positions, 1976–95; Dir, Welsh Water, 1995–97; Managing Director: Hyder Infrastructure Services, 1997–99; Hyder Services, 1999–2001; Partner, Harrington Associates, 2001–03; Chief Information Officer and Dir, Corporate Services, Welsh Assembly Govt, 2003–11. FCIWEM (FIWEM 1996). *Recreations:* fine wine, cinema, keeping fit, theatre. *E:* back.bay@tesco.net. *Club:* Cardiff and County.

HARRINGTON, Patrick John; QC 1993; a Recorder, since 1991; *b* 23 June 1949; *s* of Murtagh Joseph Harrington and Eileen Mary Harrington (*née* Kelly); *m* 1975, Susan Jane, *o c* of Captain K. W. Bradley, RN; one *s* one *d. Educ:* Ebbw Vale Grammar Sch.; Birmingham Coll. of Commerce (LLB Hons (London) 1972); Univ. of Wales (MA Eng. Lit. 2007). Called to the Bar, Gray's Inn, 1973, Bencher, 2001; Leader, Wales and Chester Circuit, 2000–03; Hd of Chambers, 2005–. Chm., Gwent Health Research Ethics Cttee, 1993–97. Sometime Lectr on advocacy, Univ. of Florida. Protector: Millennium Awards Trust, 2003–; Legacy Trust, 2006–14. Mem., Nat. Anti-Doping Panel, 2008–14 (Vice Pres., 2008–09). Pres., Ebbw Vale Male Choir, 2010–. *Publications:* A Nutshell on Evidence, 1974; (with Bobby Graham) The Session Man, 2004. *Recreations:* playing and listening to music, tennis, ski-ing, classic motoring, horse racing, collecting books. *Address:* Farrar's Building, Temple, EC4Y 7BD; Broom House, Raglan, Monmouthshire NP15 2HW. *Clubs:* Cardiff and County; Ebbw Vale Rugby Football.

HARRINGTON, Richard; MP (C) Watford, since 2010; Parliamentary Under Secretary of State, Home Office, Department for Communities and Local Government and Department for International Development, since 2015; *b* Leeds, 4 Nov. 1957; *s* of John Harrington and Alma Harrington; *m* 1982, Jessie Benardette; two *s. Educ:* Leeds Grammar Sch.; Keble Coll., Oxford (MA Juris.). Graduate trainee, John Lewis Partnership, 1980–83; Co-Founder and Dir, Harvington Properties, 1983–; CEO, LSI Gp Hldgs plc, 1992–97. Non-exec. Dir, Eden Financial Ltd (formerly Eden Gp plc), 2005–. Vice Chm., Target Seats, Cons. Party, 2012–. *Recreations:* cinema, reading, taunting, citrology. *Address:* House of Commons, SW1A 0AA. *T:* (020) 7219 7180. *E:* richard.harrington.mp@parliament.uk. *Clubs:* Oriental; Oxhey Conservative; Town and Country (Watford).

HARRIS, family name of **Earl of Malmesbury** and of **Barons Harris, Harris of Haringey** and **Harris of Peckham**.

HARRIS, 8th Baron *cr* 1815, of Seringapatan and Mysore and of Belmont, Kent; **Anthony Harris;** *b* 8 March 1942; *s* of 7th Baron Harris and Laura Cecilia (*née* McCausland); *S* father, 1996; *m* 1966, Anstice (*d* 2007), *d* of Alfred Winter; two *d. Heir: cousin* Rear-Adm. Michael George Temple Harris, *qv.*

HARRIS OF HARINGEY, Baron *cr* 1998 (Life Peer), of Hornsey in the London Borough of Haringey; **(Jonathan) Toby Harris;** *b* 11 Oct. 1953; *s* of Prof. Harry Harris, FRS and of Muriel Hargest; *m* 1979, Ann Sarah Herbert; two *s* one *d. Educ:* Haberdashers' Aske's Sch., Elstree; Trinity Coll., Cambridge (BA Hons NatScis and Econ). Chair, Cambridge Univ. Labour Club, 1973; Pres., Cambridge Union Soc., 1974. Economics Div., Bank of England, 1975–79; Electricity Consumers' Council, 1979–86, Dep. Dir, 1983; Dir, Assoc. of CHCs for England and Wales, 1987–98. Chm., Toby Harris Associates, 1998–. Vis. Prof., London South Bank Univ., 2009–14. Non-exec. Dir, London Ambulance Service NHS Trust, 1998–2005. Chm., Nat. Trading Standards Bd, 2013–; Mem., Trading Standards Inst., 2013–. Consultant Advr, KPMG, 1999–2013; Trng Advr, Infolog Ltd, 1998–2005; Sen. Associate, King's Fund, 1999–2004; Special Advr to the Bd, Transport for London, 2004–08; Mem., Public Sector Adv. Council, Anite, 2005–06. Mem., Haringey BC, 1978–2002 (Chair, Social Services Cttee, 1982–87; Leader, 1987–99). Mem. (Lab) Brent and Harrow, London Assembly, GLA, 2000–04 (Leader, Labour Gp, 2000–04); Member: Adv. Cabinet, Mayor of London, 2000–04; Metropolitan Police Authy, 2004–12 (Chm., 2000–04). Dep. Chair, AMA, 1991–96 (Chair, Social Services Cttee, 1986–93); Chair: Assoc. of London Authorities, 1993–95 (Dep. Chair, 1990–93; Chair, Social Services Cttee, 1984–88); Assoc. of London Govt, 1995–2000; LBTC-Training for Care, 1986–94; Local Govt Anti-Poverty Unit, 1994–97; Local Government Association: Chairman: Labour Gp, 1996–2004; Community Safety Panel, 1997–98; Mem., Exec., 1999–2003; Vice-Pres., 2005–10. Nat. Chair, Young Fabian Gp, 1976–77; Chair, Hornsey Labour Party, 1978, 1979, 1980; Mem., Labour Party Nat. Policy Forum, 1992–2004; Co-opted Mem., Lab. Party Local Govt Cttee, 1993–2004. Chm., Labour Peers' Gp, 2012– (Vice-Chm., 2009–12). Chm., All-Party Parly Gp on Policing, 2005–; Treas., Parly Inf. and Communications Technol. Forum (formerly Parly IT Cttee), 2005–; Member: H of L Select Cttee Inquiry on Personal Internet Security, 2006–07; Jt Cttee on Nat. Security Strategy, 2010–14; Chm., H of L Cttee on Olympic and Paralympic Legacy, 2013. Chair, Adv. Bd, City Security and Resilience Network, 2011–; Dep. Chair, Nat. Fuel Poverty Forum, 1981–86; Member: London Drug Policy Forum, 1990–98; Jt London Adv. Panel, 1996–97. Jt Chair: London Pride Partnership, 1995–98; London Waste Action, 1997–2000; Founding Chair, Inst. of Commissioning Professionals, 2007–08; Member: King's Fund Orgnl Audit Adv. Council, 1991–98; Exec. Cttee, RADAR, 1991–93; Nat. Nursery Exam. Bd, 1992–94; Home Office Adv. Council on Race Relations, 1992–97; Bd, London First, 1993–2002; Exec. Council, RNIB, 1993–94; Cttee of Regns of EU, 1994–2002; NHS Charter Advisor's Gp, 1997–98; London Pension Funds Authority, 1998–2000; Metropolitan Police Cttee, 1998–2000; Bd, London Develt Partnership, 1998–2000; Police Counter-Terrorism Bd, 2007–12; Police Counter-Terrorism Ministerial Adv. Gp, 2007–10; Chairman: Ind. Adv. Panel on Deaths in Custody, 2009–15; Audit Panel, Metropolitan Police, 2012; Indep. Review into Deaths of Young People in Prison Custody, 2014–15. Non-exec. Dir, Cyber Security Challenge UK, 2011–. Chair: Wembley Nat. Stadium Trust, 1997–; Freedom Charity, 2009–15. Trustee: Evening Standard Blitz Meml Appeal, 1995–99; Help for Health Trust, 1995–97; The Learning Agency, 1996–98; Safer London Foundn, 2005–08; Bilimankwhe Arts, 2008–14. London Ambassador, CSV, 2005–12. Mem. Adv. Bd, Three Faiths Forum, 2003–08. Patron, The Larches, 2002–. Mem. Court, Middx Univ., 1995–. Governor: Nat. Inst. for Social Work, 1986–94; Sch. of St David and St Katherine, 1978–96; St Mary's Schs, Hornsey, 1978–96. FRSA 1993; FBCS 2011. Freeman, City of London, 1998. DUniv Middx, 1999. *Publications:* (with Nick Butler and Neil Kinnock) Why Vote Labour?, 1979; (contrib.) Economics of Prosperity, 1980; (ed with Jonathan Bradshaw) Energy and Social Policy, 1983; (contrib.) Rationing in Action, 1993; (contrib.) Whistleblowing in the Health Service: accountability, law, and professional practice, 1994. *Recreations:* reading, theatre, classical music, opera. *Address:* House of Lords, SW1A 0PW. *W:* www.lordtobyharris.org.uk, www.twitter.com/LordTobySays.

HARRIS OF PECKHAM, Baron *cr* 1995 (Life Peer), of Peckham in the London Borough of Southwark; **Philip Charles Harris,** Kt 1985; Chairman: Harris Ventures Ltd, since 1988; Carpetright plc, 1993–2014 (Chief Executive, 1988–2012); *b* 15 Sept. 1942; *s* of Charles William Harris, MC and Ruth Ellen (*née* Ward); *m* 1960, Pauline Norma Chumley (*see* Dame P. N. Harris); three *s* one *d. Educ:* Streatham Grammar School. Chm., 1964–88, Chief Exec., 1987–88, Harris Queensway Plc; Chm., C. W. Harris Properties Ltd, 1988–97. Dir, Harveys Hldgs, 1986–2000; non-executive Director: Great Universal Stores, 1986–2004; Fisons Plc, 1986–94; Molyneux Estates, 1990–95; Matalan plc, 2004–06; Arsenal FC, 2005–. Mem., British Show Jumping Assoc., 1974–. Chm., Guy's and Lewisham NHS Trust, 1991–93; Vice-Chm., Lewisham Hospital NHS Trust, 1993–97; Member: Council of Governors, UMDS of Guy's and St Thomas' Hosps, 1984–98 (Hon. Fellow, 1992); Court of Patrons, RCOG, 1984–98; Chm., Generation Trust, 1984–; Dir, Outward Bound Trust, 2001–03; Lead Sponsor, Harris Fedn of S London Schools, 2007–. Dep. Chm., Cons. Party Bd of Treasurers, 1993–97. Dep. Chm., Nat. Appeal Bd, NSPCC, 1998–2007. Trustee, RA, 1998–2005. Freeman, City of London, 1992. Hon. Fellow, Oriel Coll., Oxford, 1989; FGCL 1995; Hon. FRCR 1993. Hon. DEc Richmond Coll., London, 1996; Hon. LLD South Bank, 1998. Hambro Business Man of the Year, 1983; Ernst & Young UK Entrepreneur of the Year, 2007. *Recreations:* football, cricket, show jumping, tennis. *Address:* Harris Ventures Ltd, Philip Harris House, 1A Spur Road, Orpington, Kent BR6 0PH.

HARRIS OF RICHMOND, Baroness *cr* 1999 (Life Peer), of Richmond in the county of North Yorkshire; **Angela Felicity Harris;** DL; *b* 4 Jan. 1944; *d* of late Rev. George Henry Hamilton Richards and Eva Richards; *m* 1st, 1965, Philip Martin Bowles (marr. diss. 1975); one *s*; 2nd, 1976, John Philip Roger Harris. *Educ:* Canon Slade Grammar Sch., Bolton, Lancs. Careers Advr and Employment Asst, 1974–76. Member (L, then Lib Dem): Richmond Town Council, 1978–81 and 1991–99; Richmondshire DC, 1978–89; N Yorks CC, 1981–2001. Chm., N Yorks Police Authy, 1995–2001. Dep. Chm., Assoc. of Police Authorities, 1997–2001; Chm. Adv. Cttee to the Constables' Central Cttee, Police Fedn of England and Wales, 2014–. Chm., EU Select Sub-Cttee F, H of L, 2000–04; Spokesperson, Police, 2003–10; Dep. spokesperson, NI, 2003–; Dep. Speaker, H of L, 2008–. Chm., Industry and Parliament Trust, 2010–14 (Dep. Chm., 2007–10); Pres., Nat. Assoc. of Chaplains to the Police, 2003–; Trustee, Police Rehabilitation Centre, 2004–. High Steward, Ripon Cathedral, 2011. DL N Yorks, 1994. *Address:* House of Lords, SW1A 0PW.

HARRIS, Prof. Adrian Llewellyn, FRCP; Cancer Research UK (formerly ICRF) Professor of Medical (formerly Clinical) Oncology, Oxford University, since 1988; Fellow of St Hugh's College, Oxford; *b* 10 Aug. 1950; *m* 1975, Margaret Susan Denman; one *s* one *d*. *Educ:* Univ. of Liverpool (BSc Hons Biochem. 1970; MB ChB Hons 1973); DPhil Oxon 1978. MRCP 1975, FRCP 1985. Hosp. appts, Liverpool, 1973–74; Clinical Scientist, MRC Clinical Pharmacology Unit, Radcliffe Infirmary, Oxford and Nuffield Dept of Medicine, 1975–78; Registrar in Academic Unit, Royal Free Hosp., 1978–80; Lectr and Sen. Registrar, Inst. for Cancer Res., Royal Marsden Hosp., 1980–82; Vis. Researcher, Imp. Cancer Res. Fund Mutagenesis Lab., London, 1982–83; Prof. of Clinical Oncology, Newcastle upon Tyne Univ., 1983–88. *Publications:* papers on growth factors in cancer, mechanisms by which cancers become resistant to treatment, hormone and drug treatment of cancer. *Recreations:* swimming, modern dance, science fiction. *Address:* Cancer Research UK Laboratories, Weatherall Institute of Molecular Medicine, John Radcliffe Hospital, Oxford OX3 9DS.

HARRIS, Hon. Dame Anna Evelyn Hamilton; *see* Pauffley, Hon. Dame A. E. H.

HARRIS, Anthony David, CMG 1995; LVO 1979; HM Diplomatic Service, retired; Senior Executive Officer, RFIB Middle East, Dubai, since 2006; Director, RFIB Saudi Arabia Ltd, Riyadh, since 2014 (General Manager, 2011–14); *b* 13 Oct. 1941; *s* of Reginald William Harris and Kathleen Mary Harris (*née* Daw); *m* 1st, 1970, Patricia Ann Over (marr. diss. 1988); one *s*; 2nd, 1988, Sophie Kisling (marr. diss. 2009); two *s* one *d*; 3rd, 2009, Erminia De Marco. *Educ:* Plymouth College; Exeter College, Oxford (BA 2nd cl. Hons Lit. Hum.; MA). Third Sec., Commonwealth Relations Office, 1964; Middle East Centre for Arab Studies, Lebanon, 1965; Third, later Second Sec., and Vice-Consul, Jedda, 1967; Second Sec. (Inf.), Khartoum, 1969; First Sec., FCO, 1972; First Sec., Head of Chancery and Consul, Abu Dhabi, 1975; First Sec., UK Mission to UN, Geneva, 1979; Counsellor, FCO, 1982; seconded to MoD as Regl Marketing Dir 1 (Arabian Peninsula and Pakistan), 1983; Dep. Head of Mission, Cairo, 1986; Head of Information Dept, FCO, 1990–93; Scrutiny of Security in FCO, 1993–94; Ambassador to UAE, 1994–98. Dir, Robert Fleming and Co. Ltd, 1999–2000; Advr, Technocraft Motor Corp., Iran, 2001–03; estabd Gemini Consultants, Dubai, 2001, in association with Jefferson Waterman Internat., Washington (Man. Partner, 2001–03); PR Manager, Ilyas and Mustafa Galadari Gp, Dubai, 2003–05; estabd Dubai branch, RFIB Middle East, 2006, set up RFIB Saudi Arabia Ltd, 2011. Regl Advr, Brunswick Gp, 2007–10; Middle East Consultant, M Communications, 2010–13. Mem. Council, RSAA, 1999–2001. Dep. Chm. (Gulf Affairs), Next Century Foundn, 1999–. *Recreations:* shooting (HM the Queen's Prize, Bisley, 1964; British team to Canada, 1974), ski-ing, climbing, diving, Neolithic studies, Oriental, particularly Caucasian carpets. *Address:* RFIB Middle East, Gate Village 7 Office 108, DIFC, PO Box 506670, Dubai, UAE. *Club:* Reform.

HARRIS, Anthony Geoffrey S.; *see* Stoughton-Harris.

HARRIS, Anthony George, CBE 2005 (OBE 1991); Principal, Harper Adams Agricultural College, 1977–94, retired; *b* 29 July 1929; *s* of John and Emily Kate Harris; *m* 1955, Sylvia Pyle; one *s* one *d* (and two *s* decd). *Educ:* Seale-Hayne Agricl Coll. (NDA, CDA Hons). FRSB, FRAgS. Lectr in Agric., Dorset Coll. of Agric., 1953–55; Lectr in Crop Production, Harper Adams Agricl Coll., 1955–58; Vice-Principal, Walford Coll. of Agric., 1958–66; Principal, Merrist Wood Agric. Coll., 1967–77. Chm., W Midlands Rural Affairs Forum, 2002–05. Hon. FRASE 1999. Hon. Nuffield Schol., 2007. DUniv Open 1996. BCPC Medal, 1998. *Publications:* Crop Husbandry, 1961; Farm Machinery, 1965, 2nd edn 1974. *Recreations:* walking, reading. *Club:* Farmers.

HARRIS, Rt Rev. Mgr Anthony John, SCA; priest, Our Lady of the Visitation, Greenford, 1994–2004; former Assistant Priest, St Thomas More, Barking; *b* 6 May 1940; *s* of Philip John Harris and Eileen (*née* Kelly). *Educ:* St Patrick's Seminary, Thurles, Co. Tipperary (graduated in Phil. and Theol.). Ordained as Pallottine Priest, 1965; Dean of Discipline, 1965; Assistant Priest: Clerkenwell, 1965–68; Hastings, 1968–73; joined Chaplains' Br., RAF, 1973; served in UK, Germany, Cyprus and Ascension Island; Asst Principal Chaplain, 1986–92; Prin. RC Chaplain to RAF, 1992–94; VG, RAF, 1992–94. Prelate of Honour, 1992. *Recreations:* walking, swimming. *Address:* 6 Three Corners, Barnehurst, Kent DA7 6HF. *Clubs:* Royal Air Force; Essex.

HARRIS, Prof. Anthony Leonard, CGeol; FRSE, FGS; Professor of Geology, University of Liverpool, 1987–2001, now Emeritus; Distinguished Visiting Fellow, Cardiff University, since 2002; *b* 11 May 1935; *s* of Thomas Haydn Harris and Dora Harris (*née* Wilkinson); *m* 1959, Noreen Jones; one *s* one *d*. *Educ:* Cardiff High Sch.; University College of Wales, Aberystwyth (BSc, PhD). Geologist and Principal Geologist, British Geol Survey, 1959–71; Liverpool University: Lectr, Sen. Lectr, then Reader, 1971–87; Head, Dept of Earth Scis, 1983–94; Dean, Faculty of Science, 1994–2000. Hon. Res. Associate, 2004–10, Hon. Res. Fellow, 2010–, Nat. Mus. of Wales; Hon. Prof. in Geol., Aberystwyth Univ., 2010–. Pres., Geol Soc., 1990–92. Fellow, Geol Soc. of Amer., 1978. Sometime Captain Men's Hockey: UCW; Univ. of Wales; Edinburgh Civil Service. Major John Coke Medal, Geol Soc., 1985; C. T. Clough Meml Medal, Geol Soc. of Edinburgh, 1989; Silver Medal, Liverpool Geol Soc., 2003. *Publications:* (ed and contrib.) Caledonides of the British Isles, 1979; The Caledonian-Appalachian Orogen, 1988; papers in learned jls. *Recreations:* music, ornithology. *Address:* Department of Earth Sciences, Cardiff University, Cathays Park, Cardiff CF10 3YE; Pentwyn, St Andrews Major, Vale of Glamorgan CF64 4HD. *Clubs:* Geological Society; Rotary (Dinas Powys), Probus (Dinas Powys).

HARRIS, Ven. Brian; *see* Harris, Ven. R. B.

HARRIS, Brian Nicholas, FRICS; Consultant, CBRE (formerly Richard Ellis, then Richard Ellis St Quintin, subseq. CB Richard Ellis), Chartered Surveyors and International Property Consultants, since 1996 (Chairman of Partnership, 1984–93; Partner, 1961–96); *b* 12 Dec. 1931; *s* of Claude Harris and Dorothy (*née* Harris); *m* 1961, Rosalyn Marion Caines; two *d*. *Educ:* King Alfred's Sch., Wantage; College of Estate Management. Chartered Surveyor. Chm., City of London Br. of RICS, 1984–85; Member of Council: London Chamber of Commerce, 1985– (Dep. Chm., 1990–92; Pres., 1992–94; Bd Mem., 1989–96); ABCC, 1992–98 (Mem. Bd, 1994–98; Chm., Southern Reg., 1994–96); Australian British Chamber of Commerce (UK), 1988–2000; Mem., Aust. and NZ Trade Adv. Cttee, 1991–98. Chairman: Heathrow Airport Support Gp, 1993–99; Priority Sites Ltd, 2001–03; Educn Develt Internat. plc, 2003–05; Bann System Ltd, 2005–10; Bd Mem., London First, 1993–94. Hon. Property Advr, Order of St John, 1996–2001. Chairman: London Chamber of Commerce Educnl Trust, 2000–05; Britain Australia Soc., 2002–03. Gov., Woldingham Sch., 1986–93 (Dep. Chm., 1991–93). Mem., Court of Common Council, City of London, 1996–; Sheriff, City of London, 1998–99; Mem. Ct of Assts, Co. of Glaziers and Painters of Glass, 1990– (Master, 2003); Liveryman, Co. of World Traders, 1989–. *Recreations:* flyfishing, gardening, golf. *Address:* Grants Paddock, Grants Lane, Limpsfield, Surrey RH8 0RQ. *T:* (01883) 723215. *Clubs:* Carlton, City of London, Flyfishers'; Tandridge Golf.

HARRIS, Brian Thomas, OBE 1983; QC 1982; *b* 14 Aug. 1932; *s* of Thomas and Eleanor Harris; *m* 1957, Janet Rosina Harris (*née* Hodgson); one *s* one *d*. *Educ:* Henry Thornton Grammar Sch.; King's Coll., Univ. of London. LLB (Hons). Called to the Bar, Gray's Inn, 1960; joined London Magistrates' Courts, 1963; Clerk to the Justices, Poole, 1967–85; Dir, Professional Conduct Dept, 1985–94, Sec., Exec. Cttee, Jt Disciplinary Scheme, 1986–94, ICAEW. Member: Juvenile Courts Committee, Magistrates' Assoc., 1973–85; NACRO Juvenile Crime Adv. Cttee, 1982–85; former member: CCETSW working party on legal trng of social workers (report, 1974); NACRO cttee on diversion (Zander report, 1975); HO/DHSS working party on operation of Children and Young Persons' Act 1969 (report, 1978); ABAFA working party on care proceedings (report, 1979). Chairman: Membership and Disciplinary Tribunal, PIA, 1994–2002; Disciplinary Tribunal, SFA, 1994–2002; Appeals Tribunal, Assoc. of Accounting Technicians, 1996–2002. Reviewer of Complaints: ICAS, 2001–10; Assoc. of Accounting Technicians, 2002–10. Pres., Justices' Clerks Soc., 1981–82. Editor: Justice of the Peace Review, 1982–85 (Legal Editor, 1973; Jt Editor, 1978–85); The Regulator and Professional Conduct Qly, 1994–98. *Publications:* Criminal Jurisdiction of Magistrates, 1969, 11th edn 1988; Warrants of Search and Entry, 1973; The Courts, the Press and the Public, 1976; The Rehabilitation of Offenders, 1976, 3rd edn 1999; New Law of Family Proceedings in Magistrates' Courts, 1979; (ed jtly) Clarke Hall and Morrison on Children, 1985; The Law and Practice of Disciplinary and Regulatory Proceedings, 1995, 7th edn 2013; The Tribunal Member, 1995; The Literature of the Law, 1998; Injustice, 2006; Intolerance, 2008; Passion, Poison and Power, 2010; The Calm Retreat: a short history of Olney, 2012; Tales from the Courtroom, 2013; (ed) entry on Magistrates in Halsbury's Laws of England, 4th edn 1979; The Surprising Mr Kipling, 2014. *Recreation:* the contemplation of verse. *Address:* 24 Coneygere, Olney, Bucks MK46 4AF. *T:* (01234) 712932. *E:* brianharris2@mac.com.

HARRIS, Carolyn; MP (Lab) Swansea East, since 2015; *b* Swansea; *d* of Don and Pauline Marvelly; three *s*. *Educ:* Swansea Univ. Project Manager, Guiding Hands charity, 1998–2000; Wales Regl Dir, Community Logistics, 2000–03; Wales Regl Manager, children's cancer charity, 2003–05; Sen. Parly Asst and Constituency Manager, Office of Siân James, MP, 2005–15. *Address:* (office) 485 Llangyfelach Road, Brynhyfryd, Swansea SA5 8EA. *T:* (01792) 462059. *E:* carolyn.harris.mp@parliament.uk.

HARRIS, Cecil Rhodes, FCIS, FSCA; Deputy Chairman, Trade Indemnity PLC, 1986–93; Chief Executive, Commercial Union Assurance Company Ltd, 1982–85; *b* 4 May 1923; *s* of Frederick William Harris and Dorothy Violet Plum; *m* 1946, Gwenyth Evans; one *s* two *d*. *Educ:* private schools. FCIS 1950; FSCA 1951. Joined Employers Liability Assurance, 1949, Asst Sec., 1961–64, Overseas Manager, Northern & Employers, 1965–68; Commercial Union Assurance Co. Ltd: Asst Gen. Man., 1969–73; Dep. Gen. Man., 1974; Dir and Sec., 1975–78; Exec. Dir, 1979; Dep. Chief Gen. Man., 1980–82. *Recreations:* tennis, study of the Scriptures.

HARRIS, Charles; *see* Harris, G. C. W.

HARRIS, Christine Elizabeth; *see* Holt, C. E.

HARRIS, Christopher H.; *see* Heaton-Harris.

HARRIS, Prof. Christopher John, DPhil; Professor of Economics, University of Cambridge, since 1995; Fellow, King's College, Cambridge, 1995, now Emeritus; *b* 22 Sept. 1960; *s* of Colin Christopher Harris and Barbara Kay (*née* Hall); *m* 1993, Qun Li. *Educ:* Oundle Sch.; Corpus Christi Coll., Oxford (BA Maths 1981); Nuffield Coll., Oxford (MPhil Econ 1983; DPhil Econ 1984). Prize Research Fellow, Nuffield Coll., Oxford, 1983–84; Univ. Lectr in Econs, Univ. of Oxford and Fellow of Nuffield Coll., 1984–94. Vis. Prof., MIT, 1990–91; Vis. Fellow, Princeton Univ., 2000–01; British Acad. Res. Prof., 2000–03. Richard B. Fisher Mem., IAS, 2001–02. *Publications:* articles on dynamic games and theory of industrial organisation in Econometrica, Rev. of Econ. Studies, Jl of Econ. Theory, etc. *Recreations:* walking, running, swimming. *Address:* Faculty of Economics, Austin Robinson Building, Sidgwick Avenue, Cambridge CB3 9DD.

HARRIS, Prof. Christopher John, PhD, DSc; FIMA, FREng, FIET; Lucas Professor of Aerospace Systems Engineering, 1987–96, Professor of Computational Intelligence, 1996–2003, now Professor Emeritus, University of Southampton (Head, Department of Electronic and Computer Science, 1999–2002); *b* 23 Dec. 1945; *s* of George Harris and Hilda Harris; *m* 1965, Ruth Joy Harris; one *s* two *d*. *Educ:* Univ. of Leicester (BSc); MA Oxon; Univ. of Southampton (PhD 1972; DSc 2002). FIMA 1979; CEng 1979; FIET (FIEE 1991); FREng (FEng 1996). Lecturer: Hull Univ., 1967–72; UMIST, 1972–76; Oxford Univ., 1976–80; Fellow, St Edmund Hall, Oxford, 1976–80; Dep. Chief Scientist, MoD, 1980–84; Prof., Cranfield Inst. of Technol., 1984–86; Dir, Nat. Defence Technol. Centre in Data and Information Fusion, MoD, 2002–04. Hon. Professor: Univ. Hong Kong, 1991; Huazhong Univ., China, 1991. Achievement Medal, 1998, Faraday Medal, 2001, IEE. *Publications:* (with J. F. Miles) Stability of Linear Systems, 1980, 2nd edn 1985; (with J. M. Valenca) Stability of Input-output Dynamic Systems, 1983, 2nd edn 1987; (ed) Applications of Artificial Intelligence to C^2 Systems, 1988; (jtly) Intelligent Control: aspects of fuzzy logic and neural nets, 1993; (with M. Brown) Neurofuzzy Adaptive Modelling and Control, 1994; (jtly) Advanced Adaptive Control, 1995; Adaptive Neural Network Control of Robotic Manipulators, 1998; Data Based Modelling, Estimation and Control, 2002. *Recreations:* painting, scuba diving, gardening, fly fishing. *Address:* 14 Beechwood Rise, West End, Southampton, Hants SO18 3PW. *T:* (023) 8047 2363.

HARRIS, Sir Christopher (John Ashford), 3rd Bt *cr* 1932, of Bethnal Green, co. London; Chief Executive Officer, North Pacific Securities Ltd, since 1980; *b* Wellington, NZ, 26 Aug. 1934; *er s* of Sir Jack Wolfred Ashford Harris, 2nd Bt and Patricia, *o d* of A. P. Penman, Wahroonga, Sydney, NSW; *S* father, 2009; *m* 1957, Anna, *d* of F. H. T. de Malmanche, Auckland, NZ; one *s* two *d*. *Educ:* Wanganui Collegiate Sch., NZ. Former Mem. Bd of ten cos. *Recreations:* sailing, athletics, golf. *Heir:* *s* Andrew Frederick Ashford Harris [*b* 17 March 1958; *m* 1st, 1990, Terena Ann (marr. diss. 1999); one *d*; 2nd, 2004, Gabriele Schaefer]. *Address:* 21 Anne Street, Wadestown, Wellington, New Zealand. *T:* (4) 4723212. *Clubs:* Wellington, Royal Wellington Golf (Wellington, NZ).

HARRIS, Colleen Lorraine, MVO 2004; DL; Director, Colleen Harris Associates, since 2007; *b* 24 Sept. 1955; *d* of late Gladstone Meertins and Sheila Meertins; *m* 1976, Wayne Harris; two *s*. Press Officer to Prime Minister, 1987–88; various Govt PR roles, 1988–97; Hd, Media Planning for Dep. Prime Minister, 1997–98; Dep. Press Sec., 1998–2000, Press Sec., 2000–03, to Prince of Wales; Strategy and Communications Dir, CRE, 2003–06; Interim Dir of Communications, Equality and Human Rights Commn, 2007; Dir, Dignity Mgt Consultancy, 2007–09. Chm., Caribbean Bd, 2002–08. Member: CRUK, 2003–; Press Complaints Commn, 2006–09. FRSA 2006; MCIPR 2008. Member: Council, Royal Albert Hall, 2004–14; Bd, Hackney Empire, 2008–14. Trustee: YMCA Central, 2010–; Dulwich Picture Gall., 2011–. Gov., City Lit. Inst., 2011–12. DL Gtr London, 2015. *Recreations:* music, dance, drama, radio. *Club:* Soho House.

HARRIS, David Anthony; *b* 1 Nov. 1937; *s* of late E. C. Harris and Betty Harris; *m* 1st, 1962, Diana Joan Hansford (*d* 1996); one *s* one *d*; 2nd, 1998, Mrs Alison Bunker. *Educ:* Mount Radford Sch., Exeter. Jun. Reporter, Express and Echo, Exeter, 1954–58. Nat. Service, commnd Devonshire and Dorset Regt, 1958; Staff Captain (Public Relns) GHQ, MELF, 1959. Reporter, Western Morning News, 1960–61; joined Daily Telegraph, Westminster Staff, 1961; Political Correspondent, Daily Telegraph, 1976–79; MEP (C) Cornwall and Plymouth, 1979–84. Chm., Parly Lobby Journalists, 1977–78. Mem. (C) Bromley, and Bromley, Ravensbourne, GLC, 1968–77; Chm. Thamesmead Cttee, 1971–73. Contested (C) Mitcham and Morden, Feb. 1974. MP (C) St Ives, 1983–97. PPS to Minister of State for Foreign and Commonwealth Affairs, 1987–88, to Sec. of State for Foreign and Commonwealth Affairs, 1988–89, to Dep. Prime Minister and Leader of Commons, 1989–90. Member, Select Committee: on Agriculture, 1983–87; on Broadcasting, 1988–97; on Foreign Affairs, 1991–97; on Social Security, 1991–92. Chairman: Cons. Fisheries Cttee, 1987–97; W Country Cons. MPs, 1991–92. Leading Cons. spokesman for Cornwall, 1997–2001. Chm., Seafood Cornwall, 2004–12. Mem. Council, Royal Nat. Mission to Deep Sea Fishermen, 1993–2013 (Chm., 2009–12). Churchwarden, St Piran's, Perran-ar-Worthal, 2001–05. *Recreations:* gardening, reading obituaries. *Address:* Trewedna Farm, Perranwell Station, near Truro, Cornwall TR3 7PQ.

HARRIS, David John, CMG 1999; PhD; Professor of Public International Law, 1981–2003, now Emeritus, and Co-Director, Human Rights Law Centre, since 1993, University of Nottingham; *b* 3 July 1938; *s* of Sidney and May Harris; *m* 1963, Sandra Jean Nelson; two *s*. *Educ:* Sutton High Sch., Plymouth; KCL (LLB 1959); LSE (LLM 1961; PhD 1977). Ford Foundn Res. Fellow, Univ. of Michigan Law Sch., 1961–62; Asst Lectr, QUB, 1962–63; University of Nottingham: Asst Lectr, 1963–64; Lectr, 1964–73; Sen. Lectr in Law, 1973–81; Head, Law Dept, 1987–90. Mem., Cttee of Ind. Experts, European Social Charter, 1990–96. *Publications:* (ed) Garner's Environmental Law, 5 vols, 1973–2005; Cases and Materials on International Law, 1973, 8th edn (with S. Sivakumaran) 2015; (with S. Bailey and B. Jones) Civil Liberties: cases and materials, 1980, 5th edn 2001; The European Social Charter, 1984, 2nd edn (with J. Darcy) 2001; (with M. O'Boyle and C. Warbrick) The Law of the European Convention on Human Rights, 1995, 3rd edn (with M. O'Boyle, E. Bates and C. Warbrick) 2014; (with S. Joseph) The International Covenant on Civil and Political Rights and United Kingdom Law, 1995; (with S. Livingstone) The Inter-American System of Human Rights, 1998; (consultant ed.) Moeckli, Sivakumaran and Shah, International Human Rights Law, 2nd edn 2013. *Recreations:* travelling, walking. *Address:* School of Law, The University, Nottingham NG7 2RD. *T:* (0115) 951 5701.

HARRIS, His Honour David Michael; QC 1989; a Circuit Judge, 2001–12; *b* 7 Feb. 1943; *s* of Maurice and Doris Harris; *m* 1970, Emma Lucia Calma; two *s* one *d*. *Educ:* Liverpool Institute High School for Boys; Lincoln Coll., Oxford (BA 1964; MA 1967); Trinity Hall, Cambridge (PhD 1969). Asst Lectr in Law, Manchester Univ., 1967–69. Called to the Bar, Middle Temple, 1969, Bencher, 1997; Asst Recorder, 1984–88; Recorder, 1988–2001; Dep. High Ct Judge, 1993–12. *Publications:* (ed jtly) Winfield and Jolowicz on Tort, 9th edn, 1971; (ed jtly) Supplement to Bingham's Modern Cases on Negligence, 3rd edn, 1985. *Recreations:* the Arts, travel, sport.

HARRIS, Evan; Associate Director, Hacked Off; *b* 21 Oct. 1965; *s* of Prof. Frank Harris, *qv*. *Educ:* Blue Coat Sch., Liverpool; Wadham Coll., Oxford (BA Hons Physiol.); Oxford Univ. Med. Sch. (BM BCh 1991). House Officer, John Radcliffe Hosp. and Royal Liverpool Univ. Hosp., 1991–92; Sen. House Officer (Medicine), Central Oxford Hosps, 1992–94; Hon. Registrar in Public Health, and Regl Task Force MO, Oxford Regl Postgrad. Dept of Med. Educn and Oxfordshire HA, 1994–97. Mem. Council, BMA, 1994–97 (Mem., Med. Ethics Cttee, 1999). MP (Lib Dem) Oxford W and Abingdon, 1997–2010; contested (Lib Dem) same seat, 2010. Parly Lib Dem spokesman on: NHS, 1997–99; higher educn and women's issues, 1999–2001; health, 2001–03; science, 2005–10. Chm., All Party Kidney Gp, 1999–2010; Officer, All Party Gps on Refugees, and on AIDS, 1997–2010; Member: Sci. and Technol. Select Cttee, 2003–10; Jt Select Cttee on Human Rights, 2005–10. *Publications:* contribs to med. jls. *Recreations:* chess, bridge, squash, television. *Address:* 32A North Hinksey Village, Oxford OX2 0NA. *T:* (01865) 250424. *Club:* Oxford Rotary.

HARRIS, Prof. Frank, CBE 1996; FMedSci; Dean, Faculty of Medicine and Biological Sciences (formerly of Medicine) and Professor of Paediatrics, University of Leicester, 1990–2000, now Professor Emeritus; Hon. Consultant Paediatrician, Leicester Royal Infirmary, 1990–2000; *b* 6 Oct. 1934; *s* of David and Miriam Harris; *m* 1963, Brenda van Embden; two *s*. *Educ:* Univ. of Cape Town (MB ChB 1957; MMed (Paed), 1963; MD 1964); CertHE Oxon 2006. FRCPE 1975; FRCP 1982; FRCPCH 1997 (Hon. FRCPCH 2000). Groote Schuur and Red Cross War Memorial Children's Hosp., Cape Town; CSIR Res. Fellow, Dept of Medicine, Univ. of Cape Town; Lectr and Sen. Lectr in Child Health, Univ. of Sheffield, 1965–74; University of Liverpool: Prof. of Child Health and Dir, Inst. of Child Health, 1974–89; Pro-Vice-Chancellor, 1981–84; Dean, Faculty of Medicine, 1985–89; Hon. Cons. Paediatrician to Royal Liverpool Children's Hosps at Myrtle Street and Alder Hey. Exec. Sec., Council of Deans of UK Med. Schs and Faculties, 1992–96. Member: Liverpool AHA and DHA, 1977–84; Mersey RHA, 1983–89; Trent RHA, 1990; Vice-Chm., Leics HA, 1993–97, 1998–2000 (non-exec. Dir, 1990–). Member: Cttee on Review of Medicines, 1981–90; Cttee on Safety of Medicines, 1990–92; Joint Planning Adv. Cttee, DoH, 1990–94; GMC, 1990–99 (Overseas Review Bd, 1992–96; Educn Cttee, 1994–99; Preliminary Proceedings Cttee, 1994–99; Registration Cttee, 1997–99; Overseas Cttee, 1997–98); NAHAT Wkg Gp on Teaching, Res. and Audit, 1992–93; Scientific Cttee, EU Alban Prog., 2003–06. Member: Exec., Univ. Hosps Assoc., 1991–98; Exec. Cttee, Assoc. of Med. Schs in Europe, 1993–99; Adv. Cttee on Med. Trng, EC, 1994–2001 (Chm., 1999–2001). Examr for RCP and Univs, UK and overseas. Founder FMedSci 1998. *Publications:* Paediatric Fluid Therapy, 1973; chapters in med. books; contribs to med. jls. *Recreations:* bridge, history. *Address:* 39 Frenchay Road, Oxford OX2 6TG.

See also E. Harris.

HARRIS, (Geoffrey) Charles (Wesson); QC 1989; **His Honour Judge Charles Harris;** a Circuit Judge, since 1993; a Senior Circuit Judge, since 2014; *b* 17 Jan. 1945; *s* of late G. Hardy Harris and M. J. P. Harris (*née* Wesson); *m* 1970, Carol Ann Alston; two *s* one *d*. *Educ:* Repton; Univ. of Birmingham (LLB). Called to the Bar, Inner Temple, 1967, Bencher, 2009; practice on Midland and Oxford Circuit and in London, 1967–93; a Recorder, 1990–93; Designated Civil Judge: Oxford and Northampton, 1998–2001; Oxford/Thames Valley, 2001–13; Oxfordshire, Bucks, Berks, Beds and Herts, 2014–. Member: Parole Bd, 1995–2000; Crown Court Rule Cttee, 1997–2005; Council of Circuit Judges: Mem. Cttee, 2002–11; Vice-Pres., 2009; Pres., 2010. Contested (C) Penistone, Yorks, Oct. 1974. *Publications:* contrib. to Halsbury's Laws of England, 4th edn 1976, and other legal publications; magazine articles on stalking and ballooning. *Recreations:* history, architecture, deer stalking, ski-ing, mountain walking, travel. *Address:* c/o Oxford Combined Court, St Aldates, Oxford. *Clubs:* Travellers, Kandahar.

HARRIS, Hugh Christopher Emlyn, CBE 2009; Consultant, London First, since 2011 (Director of Operations, 1995–99; Director, Global Network, 1999–2011); *b* 25 March 1936; *s* of Thomas Emlyn Harris and Martha Anne (*née* Davies); *m* 1968, Pamela Susan Woollard; one *s* one *d*. *Educ:* The Leys Sch., Cambridge; Trinity Coll., Cambridge (BA 1959; MA). FCIPD (FIPM 1990, FIPD). Bank of England, 1959–94: Chief of Corporate Services, 1984–88; Associate Dir, 1988–94; Comr, CRE, 1995–2000 (Dep. Chm., 1996–2000). Director: BE Services Ltd, 1984–94; BE Museum Ltd, 1989–94; BE Property Holdings Ltd, 1989–94; Securities Management Trust Ltd, 1987–94; Solefield School Educational Trust Ltd, Sevenoaks, 1986–2001. Dir, London Film Commn, 1996–2000. Member: Business Leaders Team, BITC Race for Opportunity Campaign, 1994–98; Windsor Fellowship Adv. Council, 1988–94; Council, London Civic Forum, 2001–09. Vice Pres., Bankers Benevolent Fund, 1990–2011. Gov., Newham Coll. of Further Educn, 2004–14. Trustee, Learning Revolution Trust, 2014–. Chm., Broad St Ward Club, 2002–03; Liveryman, Turners' Co., 1993–. Hon. Treas., Kemsing Br., RBL, 1971–2014. FRSA. *Recreations:* tennis, watching Rugby, films, opera, ballet. *Address:* London First, Middlesex House, 34–42 Cleveland Street, W1T 4JE. *T:* (020) 7665 1570. *E:* hharris@londonfirst.co.uk.

HARRIS, Air Cdre Irene Joyce, (Joy), CB 1984; RRC 1976; SRN, SCM; Director, Nursing Services (RAF), and Matron-in-Chief, Princess Mary's Royal Air Force Nursing Service, 1981–84; *b* 26 Sept. 1926; *d* of late Robert John Harris and Annie Martha Harris (*née* Breed). *Educ:* Southgate County Sch.; Charing Cross Hosp.; The London Hosp.; Queen Mary's Maternity Home, Hampstead. SRN 1947, SCM 1950. Joined Princess Mary's RAF Nursing Service, 1950; gen. nursing and midwifery duties in UK, Singapore, Germany and Cyprus; Dep. Matron, 1970; Sen. Matron, 1975; Principal Matron, 1978; Dep. Dir, Nursing Services (RAF), 1981. QHNS 1981–84. *Recreations:* travel, ornithology, music, archaeology, gardening. *Address:* 51 Station Road, Haddenham, Ely, Cambs CB6 3XD. *Club:* Royal Air Force.

HARRIS, Dr Jane; author; *b* Belfast, 1961; *m* 1993, Tom Shankland. *Educ:* Univ. of Glasgow (MA 1984); Univ. of E Anglia (MA Creative Writing 1992; PhD Creative and Critical Writing 1997). Arts Council Writer in Residence, HMP Durham, 1992–94; script and novel reader for film cos and The Literary Consultancy; script ed.; teacher of creative writing, UEA; film script writer, incl. Bait, 1999, Going Down, 2000. *Publications:* The Observations, 2006; Gillespie and I, 2011. *E:* janeharrisinfo@gmail.com. *W:* www.janeharris.com.

HARRIS, Jane Rosalind; *see* Rogers, J. R.

HARRIS, Jeffery Francis, FCA; Chairman: Essentra (formerly Filtrona), since 2005; Cookson Group plc, 2010–12; *b* 8 April 1948; *s* of Ernest and Kathleen Veronica Harris; *m* 1976, Elizabeth Helen Hancock; two *s*. *Educ:* Rendcomb Coll., Cirencester; Southampton Univ. (BSc Hons 1970). FCA 1979. Trainee chartered accountant, 1970; with Barton Mayhew & Co., later Ernst & Young, 1980–85; UniChem, subseq. Alliance UniChem, 1985–2005: Gp Chief Accountant, 1985–86; Finance Dir, 1986–91; Dep. Chief Exec., 1991–92; Chief Exec., 1992–2001; Chm., 2001–05. Board Member: ANZAG AG (Germany), 1999–2007; Bunzl plc, 2000–09; Associated British Foods plc, 2003–07. Chm., British Assoc. of Pharmaceutical Wholesalers, 1996–98; Pres., GIRP-European Assoc. of Pharmaceutical Wholesalers, 2003–04. Chm. of Trustees, Richmond Parish Lands Charity, 2002–12. Hon. DBA Kingston Univ., 2003. *Recreations:* walking, ski-ing, cycling, gardening, opera. *Address:* Essentra, Avebury House, 201–249 Avebury Boulevard, Milton Keynes MK9 1AU. *T:* (01908) 359100.

HARRIS, Jeremy Michael; Director of Public Affairs, University of Oxford, since 2005; Fellow of New College, Oxford, since 2006; *b* 31 Oct. 1950; *s* of late David Arnold Harris and of Beryl May Harris (*née* Howe); *m* 1983, Susan Lynn Roberts (marr. diss. 2011); one *s* one *d*; *m* 2014, Jennifer Butler. *Educ:* Sevenoaks Sch., Kent; Clare Coll., Cambridge (MA Hons); Nottingham Univ. (PGCE 1972). BBC News: Reporter, BBC Radio News, 1978–82; Madrid Corresp., 1982–86; Moscow Corresp., 1986–89; Foreign Affairs Corresp., 1989–90; Washington Corresp., 1990–95; Radio Presenter, BBC Current Affairs Progs incl. World Tonight, and Today, 1995–99; Archbishop of Canterbury's Sec. for Public Affairs, and Dep. Chief of Staff, Lambeth Palace, 1999–2005. Mem. Bd, Oxford Playhouse, 2005–. *Recreations:* theatre, maps, walking. *Address:* University of Oxford, Wellington Square OX1 2JD.

HARRIS, Joanne Michèle Sylvie, MBE 2013; author; *b* 3 July 1964; *d* of Robert Ian Short and Jeannette Payen-Short; *m* 1988, Kevin Steven Harris; one *d*. *Educ:* St Catharine's Coll., Cambridge (BA Mod. and Mediaeval Langs; MA 1985; Hon. Fellow, 2012); Sheffield Univ. (PGCE 1987). Hon. DLit: Huddersfield, 2003; Sheffield, 2004. *Publications:* The Evil Seed, 1992; Sleep, Pale Sister, 1994; Chocolat, 1999; Blackberry Wine, 2000; Five Quarters of the Orange, 2001; Coastliners, 2002; (with F. Warde) The French Kitchen, 2002; Holy Fools, 2003; Jigs and Reels, 2004; Gentlemen and Players, 2005; (with F. Warde) The French Market, 2005; The Lollipop Shoes, 2007; Runemarks, 2007; Blueeyedboy, 2010; Runelight, 2011; Peaches for Monsieur le Curé, 2012; A Cat, A Hat and a Piece of String, 2012; The Gospel of Loki, 2014; The Little Book of Chocolat, 2014. *Recreations:* mooching, lounging, strutting, strumming, priest-baiting and quiet subversion of the system. *Address:* c/o Eldon House, Sharp Lane, Almondbury, Huddersfield HD5 8XL.

HARRIS, Very Rev. John; Dean of Brecon, and Vicar of Brecon St Mary with Battle and Llanddew, 1993–98; *b* 12 March 1932; *s* of Richard and Ivy Harris; *m* 1956, Beryl June Roberts; two *s* one *d*. *Educ:* St David's Coll., Lampeter (BA 1955); Salisbury Theol Coll. Ordained deacon 1957, priest 1958; Curate: Pontnewynydd, 1957–60; Bassaleg, 1960–63; Vicar: Penmaen, 1963–69; St Paul, Newport, 1969–84; Maindee, 1984–93; RD of Newport, 1977–93. Canon, St Woolos Cath., 1984–93. *Recreations:* classical archæology, music, ballet, natural history. *Address:* 40 Mounton Drive, Chepstow, Monmouthshire NP16 5EH.

HARRIS, Prof. John Buchanan, PhD; CBiol, FRSB; Professor of Experimental Neurology, Faculty of Medical Sciences, Newcastle University, 1980–2007, now Emeritus (Director of International Postgraduate Studies, 2002–05); Head of Neurotoxicology, Chemicals Division, Health Protection Agency, Newcastle upon Tyne, 2004–07; *b* 18 Jan. 1940; *s* of John Benjamin Sargent Harris and Mary Isobel Harris; *m* 1965, Christine Margaret Holt; one *s* one *d* (and one *s* decd). *Educ:* Tiffin Sch.; Bradford Inst. of Technol.; Univ. of Bradford (PhD 1967); BPharm (London ext. 1963). MRPharmS 1964; FRSB (FIBiol 1981); CBiol 1990. Research Asst, Univ. of Bradford, 1963–67; Newcastle upon Tyne University: Sen. Res. Associate, 1967–72; Principal Res. Associate, 1972–74; Sen. Lectr, 1974–80. Wellcome Fellow, Univ. of Lund, Sweden, 1970–71; MRC/NIH Fellow, UCLA, 1977–78; Wellcome/Ramaciotti Fellow, Monash Univ., Melbourne, 1980. *Publications:* (ed) Muscular Dystrophy and Other Inherited Diseases of Skeletal Muscle in Animals, 1979; (ed jtly) Natural Toxins: animal, plant and microbial, 1986; (ed jtly) Muscle Metabolism, Vol. 4 (3) of Baillière's Endocrinology and Metabolism, 1990; (ed jtly) Medical Neurotoxicology, 1999; over 200 refereed pubns. *Address:* Institute of Neurosciences and Medical Toxicology Centre, Faculty of Medical Sciences, Newcastle University, Framlington Place, Newcastle upon Tyne NE2 4HH. *T:* (0191) 222 8046, *Fax:* (0191) 222 5772. *E:* j.b.harris@ncl.ac.uk.

HARRIS, John Charles, CBE 2007; solicitor; International Management and Legal Consultant, John Harris Consultancy and Associates, since 1986; *b* 25 April 1936; *s* of Sir Charles Joseph William Harris, KBE and Lady Harris (Emily (*née* Thompson)); *m* 1961, Alison Beryl Sturley; one *s* one *d*. *Educ:* Dulwich College (LCC scholarship); Clare College, Cambridge. MA, LLM. 2nd Lieut, Intelligence Corps, 1954–56. UKAEA (seconded to OECD), 1959–63; articled to Town Clerk, Poole, 1963–66; Asst Sol., then Senior Asst Sol., Poole BC, 1966–67; Asst Sol., then Principal Asst to Chief Exec. and Town Clerk, 1967–71, Dep. Town Clerk, 1972–73, County Borough of Bournemouth; County Sec., 1973–83, Chief Exec. and County Clerk, 1983–86, S Yorks CC; Dir, S Yorks Passenger Transport Exec., 1984–86; Sec. to Yorkshire and Humberside County Councils Assoc., 1984–86; Dir, S Yorks Residuary Body, 1985–86; Clerk to Lord Lieutenant of S Yorks, 1984–86; Public Sector Adviser/Associate Consultant: PA Consulting Gp, 1986–91; Daniel Bates Partnership,

1991–95; Executive Director: Solace Internat. (1992) Ltd, 1992–2000; Solace Internat. Southern Africa Pty Ltd, 1993–2001. Chair: Coal Authy, 1999–2007; Coal Forum, 2007–13. Adviser to AMA Police and Fire Cttee, 1976–86; Member: Home Office Tripartite Working Party on Police Act 1964, 1983–86; Rampton SHSA Cttee, 1989–96; Arts Council Touring Bd, 1989–92; Pontefract HA, 1990–93; Council, Local Govt Internat. Bureau, 1993–96. Mem., Exec. Council, Solace, 1984–86; Dir, Trustee, and Mem. Bd, Homeless Internat. Ltd, 1998–2000; Dir, South Africa Housing Network Trust Ltd, 1998–2001; Jt Chm., Ivory Park/ Wakefield Educn Partnership, 2002–07; Chair: Northern Counties Housing Assoc. Ltd, 1994–2000 (Mem. Bd, 1990–2009, Vice Chm., 1994, 2002–03); Northern Counties Specialised Housing Assoc. Ltd, 1994–2007; Mid Yorks Hospitals NHS Trust, 2008–09 (non-exec. Dir, 2007–08); Rossington Eco-Town Partnership, 2008–10; Little Red Bus (HDCT) Ltd, 2011–13. Chair, Guinness Northern Counties, NE Region, 2007–11; Mem. Bd, Guinness Trust Partnership, 2007–08. Director: Stray Services Ltd, 2010–; Hatfield Colliery EBT Co. Ltd, 2014–. Chm., Soc. of County Secretaries, 1983–84; Mem., Law Society. Independent Member: W Yorks Police Authy, 1994–99; Police Cttee, AMA, 1995; MoD Police Cttee, 2003–07; MoD Police and Guarding Agency: Chm., Audit Cttee, 2004–12; Mem., Owner's Adv. Bd, 2007–12; non-exec. Mem., Mgt Bd, 2011–13. Hon. PR Officer, S Yorks and Humberside Region, Riding for Disabled Assoc., 1983–92 (Mem., Nat. Publications Cttee, 1987–90); Chair, Bd of Trustees, Art House, Wakefield, 2009–; Trustee: S Yorks Charity Inf. Service, 1977–87; Housing Assocs Charitable Trust, 1994–96; Harrogate Homeless Project, 2014–. Founder Mem./Sec., Barnsley Rockley Rotary Club, 1976–79 (Hon. Sec.); Vice-Chm. and Sec., Friends of Opera North, 1979–86; Mem., Council/Co., and Develt Cttee, Opera North, 1980–95; Trustee, Harrogate (White Rose) Theatre Trust Ltd, and Chair, Friends of Harrogate Th., 2011–; Trustee and Hon. Administrator, Harrogate Royal Hall Restoration Trust, 2013–. Guild of Freemen, City of London, 1967; Justice; European Movement; Actsa. Governor, Wakefield Dist Community Sch. (formerly Ackworth Moor Top, then Felkirk Community Special Sch.), 1996–2009 (Chm., 1998–2009). DL S Yorks, 1986. FRSA 1984. *Recreations:* being with family and friends, theatre and opera, foreign travel, visiting South Africa. *Address:* 7 Stray Towers, Victoria Road, Harrogate HG2 0LJ. *T:* (01423) 398847. *E:* jcharris7stray@gmail.com.

HARRIS, John Frederick, OBE 1986; FSA; Curator, British Architectural Library's Drawing Collection and Heinz Gallery, 1960–86; Consultant: to Collection, Canadian Centre for Architecture, 1986–88 (Member Advisory Board, 1983–88); Heinz Architectural Center, Carnegie, 1991–94; Victoria and Albert Museum Primary Galleries Project, 1996–2001; *b* 13 Aug. 1931; *s* of Frederick Harris and Maud (*née* Sellwood); *m* 1960, Eileen Spiegel, New York; one *s* one *d*. *Educ:* Cowley C of E School. Itinerant before 1956; Library of Royal Inst. of Architects, 1956. Mem., Mr Paul Mellon's Adv. Bd, 1966–78; Trustee, Amer. Mus. in Britain, 1974–88; Chm., Colnaghi & Co., 1982–92. President: Internat. Confedn on Architectural Museums, 1981–84 (Chm., 1979–81; Hon. Life Pres., 1984); Marylebone Soc., 1978–80; Twentieth Century Soc. (formerly Thirties Soc.), 1986– (Mem. Cttee, 1979–); Member: Council, Drawing Soc. of America, 1962–68; Council, Victorian Soc., 1974–; Nat. Council, Internat. Council of Monuments and Sites, 1976–83; Soc. of Dilettanti, 1977–; Member Committee: Soc. of Architectural Historians of GB, 1958–66; Georgian Gp, 1970–74, 1986–89; Save Britain's Heritage, 1970–; Stowe Landscape, 1980–2001 (Patron, Stowe Gardens Buildings Trust, 1986–92); Bldg Museum Proj., 1980–86; Garden History, 1980–84; Jl of Garden History, 1980–89. Member: Adv. Council, Drawings Center, NY, 1983–89; Management Cttee, Courtauld Inst. of Art, 1983–87; Somerset House Building Cttee, 1986–89; Council, Royal Archaeol. Inst., 1984–86; Adv. Cttees, Historic Bldgs and Monuments Commn, 1984–88; Ashton Meml Steering Gp, 1984–86; GLC Historic Buildings Panel, 1984–86; Ambrose Congreve Award, 1980–82; Ashmole Archive Cttee, 1985–87; Adv. Bd, Irish Architectural Archive, 1988–91; Appeal Cttee, Painshill Park Trust, 1988–89; Spencer House Restoration Cttee, 1986–95; Nat. Trust Arts Panel, 1996–; Council, Georgian Gp, 2007–; Trustee: Architecture Foundn, 1991–94; Save Europe's Heritage, 1996–; Holburne Mus., Bath, 2000–06. Andrew W. Mellon Lectr in Fine Arts, Nat. Gall., Washington, 1981; Slade Prof. of Fine Art, Univ. of Oxford, 1982–83. Exhibitions Organizer: The King's Arcadia, 1973; The Destruction of the Country House (with Marcus Binney), 1974; The Garden, 1979; Dir, British Country House Exhibn, Nat. Gall., Washington, 1982–83; many exhibns in Heinz Gall.; travelling exhibns and catalogues: Italian Architectural Drawings, 1966; Sir Christopher Wren, 1970; Designs of the British Country House, 1985. FSA 1968; FRSA 1975; Hon. FRIBA 1972; Hon. MA Oxon, 1982; Hon. Brother Art Workers' Guild, 1972. Harris Testimonial Medal, 1999. Editor, Studies in Architecture, 1976–99. *Publications:* English Decorative Ironwork, 1960; Regency Furniture Designs, 1961; (ed), The Prideaux Collection of Topographical Drawings, 1963; (jtly) Lincolnshire, 1964; (contrib.) The Making of Stamford, 1965; (jtly) Illustrated Glossary of Architecture, 1966, 2nd edn 1969; (jtly) Buckingham Palace, 1968; Georgian Country Houses, 1968; (contrib.) Concerning Architecture, 1968; Sir William Chambers, Knight of the Polar Star, 1970 (Hitchcock Medallion 1971); (ed) The Rise and Progress of the Present State of Planting, 1970; (ed jtly) The Country Seat, 1970; Catalogue of British Drawings for Architecture, Decoration, Sculpture and Landscape Gardening in American Collections, 1971; A Country House Index, 1971, 2nd edn 1979; Catalogue of the Drawings Collection RIBA: Inigo Jones and John Webb, 1972; (contrib.) Guide to Vitruvius Britannicus, 1972; (jtly) The King's Arcadia: Inigo Jones and The Stuart Court, 1973; Catalogue of the Drawings Collection RIBA: Colin Campbell, 1973; Headfort House and Robert Adam, 1973; (jtly) The Destruction of the Country House, 1974; Gardens of Delight, The Art of Thomas Robins, 1976; Gardens of Delight, The Rococo English Landscape of Thomas Robins, 1978; (jtly) Catalogue of Drawings by Inigo Jones, John Webb and Isaac de Caus in Worcester College, Oxford, 1979; A Garden Alphabet, 1979; (ed) The Garden Show, 1979; The Artist and the Country House, 1979 (Sir Banister Fletcher prize, 1979), 2nd edn 1986; (contrib.) Village England, 1980; (contrib.) Lost Houses of Scotland, 1980; The English Garden 1530–1840: a contemporary view, 1981; (contrib.) John Claudius Loudon and the Early Nineteenth Century in Great Britain, Washington, 1980; (jtly) Interiors, 1981; The Palladians, 1981; Die Hauser der Lords und Gentlemen, 1982; William Talman, Maverick Architect, 1982; (contrib.) SAVE Gibraltar's Heritage, 1982; Architectural Drawings in the Cooper Hewitt Museum, New York, 1982; (contrib.) Vanishing Houses of England, 1982; (contrib.) Macmillan Encyclopedia of Architecture, 1982; (contrib.) Great Drawings from the Collection of Royal Institute of British Architects, 1983; (jtly) Britannia Illustrata Knyff & Kip, 1984; The Design of the British Country House, 1985; (jtly) Inigo Jones—Complete Architectural Drawings, 1989; (contrib.) In Honor of Paul Mellon, Collector and Benefactor, 1986; (contrib.) Canadian Centre for Architecture Building and Gardens, 1989; (contrib.) The Fashioning and Functioning of the British Country House, 1989; (jtly) Jamaica's Heritage: an untapped resource, 1991; (contrib.) Writers and their Houses, 1993; The Palladian Revival: Lord Burlington, his villa and garden at Chiswick, 1994; The Artist and the Country House, 1995; (ed jtly and contrib.) Sir William Chambers: architect to George III, 1996; (contrib.) Chambers and Adelcranz, 1997; No Voice from the Hall: early memories of a country house snooper, 1998; (contrib.) Summerson and Hitchcock, 2002; Echoing Voices: more memories of a country house snooper, 2002; (contrib.) Kinaslott, 2002; (contrib.) Description of the Idea and General-Plan for an English Park, 2004; (contrib.) L'Art anglais dans les collections de l'Institut de France, 2004; Moving Rooms: the trade in architectural salvages, 2007 (William M. B. Berger Prize, 2009); The Duke of Beaufort his House, 2007; (jtly) A Passion for Building: the amateur architect in England 1650–1850, 2007; (contrib.) John Talman: an early-eighteenth-century connoisseur, 2008; (contrib.) The Persistence of the Classical, 2008; (contrib.) Chatsworth: the attic sale, 2010; (contrib.) William Kent: designing Georgian Britain, 2013; articles in Georgian Gp Jl, Annali di Architettura, and other jls. *Recreation:* flinting.

HARRIS, John Howard; management consultant in children's services and education, since 2011; Director, John Harris Consulting Ltd, since 2011; *b* 27 Sept. 1956; *s* of late James Edward Harris and Mary Mildred Harris; *m* 1982, Pauline Donnelly; one *d*. *Educ:* St Catharine's Coll., Cambridge (BA Hons Hist. 1979); Univ. of London Inst. of Educn (PGCE (Dist.); Storey Miller Prize); Essex Inst. of Higher Educn (Dip. Professional Studies in Educn (Dist.) 1986). London Borough of Newham: teacher: Langdon Sch., 1980–82; Forest Gate Community Sch., 1982–87; Advr for Tech. and Vocational Educn Initiative, 1987–90; Essex County Council: Sen. Co. Inspector, 14–19 Curriculum, 1990–91; Principal Co. Inspector, 1991–92; Service Manager, Community Educn and Post-16 Liaison, 1992–95; Sen. Educn Officer, 1995–96; Asst Dir, Educn, 1996–99, Dir of Educn, 1999–2003, Westminster CC; Sen. Educn Exec., CAPITA Strategic Educn Services, 2003; Dir, Children, Schools and Families, Herts CC, 2003–11. Independent Chair: Doncaster and Sandwell Local Safeguarding Children Bds, 2014–; Hounslow Learning Partnership, 2014–. Trustee, Nat. Foundn for Educnl Res. Chm., W Herts Community Free Sch., Trust, 2013–. *Recreations:* reading, film, travel, cycling, running (ran Paris Marathon), football (supporting Leyton Orient FC).

HARRIS, Air Marshal Sir John (Hulme), (Win), KCB 1992 (CB 1991); CBE 1982; FRAeS; Air Officer Commanding No 18 Group (RAF Strike Command) and Commander Maritime Air Eastern Atlantic and Allied Forces Northwestern Europe (formerly Channel), 1992–96; *b* 3 June 1938; *s* of late George W. H. Harris and Dorothy Harris (*née* Hulme); *m* 1962, Williamina (*née* Murray); two *s*. *Educ:* English Sch., Cairo; King Edward VII Sch., King's Lynn. FRAeS 2008. No 224 Sqn, RAF, 1960–62; RAF Leeming, Flying Instructor, 1963–67; Exchange Officer, US Navy Air Test and Evaluation Sqn, Florida, 1968–70; Central Tactics and Trials Organisation, 1970–73; OC No 201 Sqn, 1973–75; Nat. Defence Coll., 1975–76; OPCON (CCIS) Project Team, Northwood, 1976–78; SASO, RAF Pitreavie Castle, 1979; OC RAF Kinloss, 1979–81; MA to Dir, Internat. Mil. Staff, Brussels, 1982–83; RCDS, 1984; Dir Training (Flying), RAF, 1985–87; Comdt Gen. RAF Regiment and Dir Gen. of Security (RAF), 1987–89; ACDS (Logistics), 1990–91; COS, HQ No 18 Gp (RAF Strike Comd), 1991–92. ADC to the Queen, 1979–81. *Recreations:* fly fishing for salmon, trout and navigators, gardening, travel. *Club:* Royal Air Force.

HARRIS, Prof. John Morley, DPhil; FMedSci; Lord (formerly Sir David) Alliance Professor of Bioethics, since 1997, and Director, Institute for Science, Ethics and Innovation, since 2007, University of Manchester; *b* 21 Aug. 1945; *s* of Albert Harris and Ruth Harris; *m* 1978, Sita Williams; one *s*. *Educ:* University of Kent at Canterbury (BA 1966); Balliol Coll., Oxford (DPhil 1976). Lectr in Philosophy, 1974–77, Sen. Lectr, 1977–79, City of Birmingham Poly.; Associate Lectr in Philosophy, Brunel Univ., 1977–79; University of Manchester: Lectr in Philosophy, 1979–84, Sen. Lectr, 1984–88, Dept of Educn; Res. Dir, Centre for Social Ethics and Policy, 1986–; Reader in Applied Philosophy, Sch. of Educn, 1988–90; Prof. of Bioethics and Applied Philosophy, 1990–97; Dir, Inst. of Medicine, Law and Bioethics, 1996–. Series Ed., Social Ethics and Policy, 1985–; Founder and a Gen. Ed., Issues in Biomedical Ethics series, 1994–. Member: Adv. Cttee on Genetic Testing, 1997–99; Human Genetics Commn, 1999–; Ethics Cttee, BMA, 1991–97 and 1999–. Chm., Values and Attitudes Wkg Party, Age Concern, 1996–99. Mem., Romanian Acad. Med. Scis, 1994–; MAE 2011. FMedSci 2001; FRSA. Hon. DLitt Kent, 2010. *Publications:* Violence and Responsibility, 1980; The Value of Life, 1985; (ed with S. Hirsch) Consent and the Incompetent Patient, 1988; (ed with A. Dyson) Experiments on Embryos, 1990; Wonderwoman and Superman: ethics and human biotechnology, 1992; (ed with A. Dyson) Ethics and Biotechnology, 1994; Clones, Genes and Immortality, 1998; (ed jtly) AIDS: ethics, justice and European policy, 1998; (ed with S. Holm) The Future of Human Reproduction, 1998; (ed jtly) A Companion to Genethics: philosophy and the genetic revolution, 2001; (ed.) Bioethics, 2001; On Cloning, 2004; Enhancing Evolution, 2007. *Recreations:* cooking, walking, driving, argument, Italy, Manchester United. *Address:* Institute for Science, Ethics and Innovation, Faculty of Life Sciences, Stopford Building, University of Manchester, Manchester M13 9PL. *T:* (0161) 275 7704.

HARRIS, His Honour John Percival, DSC 1945; QC 1974; a Circuit Judge, 1980–95; *b* 16 Feb. 1925; *o s* of late Thomas Percival Harris and Nora May Harris; *m* 1959, Janet Valerie Douglas; one *s* two *d*. *Educ:* Wells Cathedral Sch.; Pembroke Coll., Cambridge. BA 1947. Served in RN, 1943–46: Midshipman, RNVR, 1944, Sub-Lt 1945. Called to the Bar, Middle Temple, 1949, Bencher 1970. A Recorder of the Crown Court, 1972–80; Dep. Sen. Judge, Sovereign Base Areas, Cyprus, 1983–2000 (Acting Sen. Judge, 1995). *Recreations:* golf, reading, Victorian pictures. *Address:* Tudor Court, Fairmile Park Road, Cobham, Surrey KT11 2PP. *T:* (01932) 864756. *Club:* Royal St George's Golf (Sandwich).

HARRIS, (John Robert) William, FRCP, FRCPI; Consultant in Genito-Urinary Medicine, Imperial College Healthcare NHS Trust (formerly St Mary's Hospital NHS Trust), since 1976; *b* 25 Sept. 1943; *s* of William James Smyth Harris and Anne (*née* Glass); *m* 1st, 1968, Mary Elizabeth Keating (marr. diss. 1992; remarried 1994); one *s* one *d*. *Educ:* Ballymena Acad.; Queen's Univ., Belfast (MB). FRCP 1985; FRCPI 1996. Postgrad. trng, Royal Victoria Hosp., Belfast and Liverpool Sch. of Tropical Medicine, 1968–72; Consultant and Hon. Sen. Lectr, Sheffield Royal Infirmary, 1972–74; Consultant, King's Coll. Hosp., 1974–75; Med. Dir, St Mary's Hosp. NHS Trust, 1991–97. Lock Lectr, RCPSG, 1993. Internat. Health Award, 1973; Scott-Heron Medal, Royal Victoria Hosp., Belfast, 1985. *Publications:* Recent Advances in Sexually Transmitted Diseases, 1975, 4th edn 1991; papers on sexually transmitted diseases, AIDS and prostatitis. *Recreations:* walking, cinema, travel. *Address:* 75 Harley Street, W1G 8QL. *T:* (020) 7486 4166. *Club:* Athenæum.

HARRIS, Jonathan David, CBE 2002 (OBE 1993); chartered surveyor; consultant; President, Royal Institution of Chartered Surveyors, 2000–01; *b* 28 Sept. 1941; *s* of Wilfred Harris and Ann Harris (*née* Godel); *m* 1964, Jeniffer Cecilia Fass; one *s* three *d*. *Educ:* Haberdashers' Aske's Sch. FRICS 1964. Pepper Angliss & Yarwood, Chartered Surveyors, 1959–94 (Sen. Partner, 1974–94); Director: Cardinal Group, 1973–; Carlisle Gp, 1987–99; Cressida Gp, 1996–; Babraham Bioscience Technologies Ltd, 2002–04. Mem. Bd, Plymouth Develt Corp., 1993–96; Dep. Chm., UN Real Estate Adv. Gp, 2001–06; Chair, Total Place Asset Mgt Bd, Kent CC, 2010. Committee Member: Sackville Property Unit Trust, 1974–99; Langbourn Income Growth & Property Unit Trust, 1984–2010. Member: Property Adv. Gp, Bank of England, 1999–2001; Professions Wkg Gp, Council for Excellence in Mgt and Leadership, 2000–02. Founder and Pres., Educational Foundn for Life-Long Learning (formerly Continuing Professional Develt Foundn), 1980–; Founder, Inst. of Continuing Professional Develt, 1997. Treas., Prison Reform Trust, 1998–2001. Trustee: Enterprise Education Trust (formerly Understanding Industry, subseq. businessdynamics), 1997– (Dep. Chm., 2006–); LPO Trust, 1996–; Chm. of Trustees, Resource (formerly Employment Resource Centre), 2004–13; Vice Patron, Commonwealth Housing Trust, 2014–. Governor: Univ. of Westminster (formerly Poly. of Central London), 1988–99; Manor Lodge Sch., 2002–13 (Trustee). Mem., Counselors of Real Estate, USA, 2005– (White Landau Meml Prize, 2009). Liveryman: Co. of Chartered Surveyors, 1977; Co. of Basketmakers, 1962. Hon. DLitt Westminster, 1998. *Recreations:* bridge, grandchildren. *Address:* 24 Hays Mews, W1J 5PY. *T:* (020) 7495 3132.

HARRIS, Prof. Jose Ferial, PhD; FBA 1993; Professor of Modern History, University of Oxford, 1996–2008, now Emeritus; Fellow, St Catherine's College, Oxford, 1978, now Emeritus (Vice-Master, 2003–05); *d* of Leonard Cecil Chambers and Freda Ellen Chambers (*née* Brown); *m* 1968, Prof. James William Harris, FBA (*d* 2004); one *s*. *Educ:* Dame Alice Harpur Sch., Bedford; Newnham Coll., Cambridge (MA, PhD). Res. Fellow, Nuffield Coll., Oxford, 1966–69; Lectr, 1969–74, Sen. Lectr, 1974–78, Dept of Social Sci. and Admin, LSE; Reader in Modern History, Oxford Univ., 1990–96. Vis. Res. Fellow, Princeton, 1985–86. Ford Lectr in English History, Oxford Univ., 1996–97; Leverhulme Res. Prof., Oxford Univ., 1998–2002. Vis. Res. Prof., Sch. of Advanced Studies, Univ. of London, 2006–07; Hon. Vis. Prof., Birkbeck, Univ. of London, 2007–10; Vis. Res. Fellow, Harry Ransom Center, Univ. of Texas, 2010. *Publications:* Unemployment and Politics: a study in English social policy, 1972, 2nd edn 1984; William Beveridge: a biography, 1977, 2nd edn 1997; Private Lives, Public Spirit: a social history of Britain 1870–1914, 1993, 2nd edn 1994; Ferdinand Tönnies: community and civil society, 2001; Civil Society in British History, 2003; Le Rapport Beveridge: le text fondateur de l'état providence, 2012. *Recreations:* painting, walking, river boats, family life. *Address:* 5 Belbroughton Road, Oxford OX2 6UZ.

HARRIS, Joseph Hugh; Vice Lord-Lieutenant of Cumbria, 1994–2007; *b* 3 June 1932; *s* of late John Frederick Harris and of Gwendolen Arden Harris; *m* 1957, Anne, *d* of Brig. Leslie Harrison McRobert, CBE. *Educ:* Aysgarth Sch.; Harrow; Royal Agricl Coll. (MRAC). Lieut, 11th Hussars, PAO. Chairman: Cumbrian Newspapers Ltd, 1987–2002; Grasmere Sports (Dir, 1977–2008). Member: Northern Regl Panel, MAFF, 1977–83; Rural Develt Commn, 1989–2000. Royal Agricultural Society: Sen. Steward, 1960–77; Dep. Pres., 1987; Trustee, 1992–2009; Hon. Dir, Royal Show, 1978–82. High Sheriff of Cumbria, 1976–77; DL 1984, JP 1971–2002, Cumbria. Chm., Penrith and Alston Bench, 1991–95. Chm. of Govs, Aysgarth Sch., 1975–78; Gov., RAC, Cirencester, 1987–90. Liveryman, Farmers' Co., 1973–. *Recreations:* shooting, country sports, conservation. *Address:* West View, Bowscar, Penrith, Cumbria CA11 9PG. *T:* and *Fax:* (01768) 885661.

HARRIS, Air Cdre Joy; *see* Harris, I. J.

HARRIS, Dr Keith Murray, CBiol, FRSB, FRES; Director, International (formerly Commonwealth) Institute of Entomology, 1985–92; *b* 26 Nov. 1932; *s* of Clifford Murray Harris and Doris (*née* Cottam); *m* 1957, Elizabeth Harrison; one *s* one *d*. *Educ:* Lewis Sch., Pengam; Univ. of Wales, Aberystwyth (BSc, DSc); Selwyn Coll., Cambridge (DipAgricSci); Imperial Coll. of Tropical Agric., Trinidad (DipTA). FRES 1960; FRSB (FIBiol 1985). Entomologist, then Sen. Entomologist, Federal Dept of Agricl Res., Nigeria, 1955–62; Sen. Res. Fellow, BM (Natural History), 1962–66; Entomologist and Sen. Scientist, RHS, Wisley, 1966–74; Principal Taxonomist, Commonwealth Inst. of Entomology, 1974–85. *Publications:* (jtly) Collins Guide to the Pests, Diseases and Disorders of Garden Plants, 1981, 4th edn (as Collins Photoguide to the Pests, Diseases and Disorders of Garden Plants), 2014; scientific research papers and articles on pests of cultivated plants, esp. pests of African cereal crops, and on taxonomy and biol. of gall midges. *Recreations:* walking, cycling, gardening, music. *Address:* 81 Linden Way, Ripley, Woking, Surrey GU23 6LP. *T:* (01483) 224963.

HARRIS, Laura; Her Honour Judge Laura Harris; a Circuit Judge, since 2008; *b* London, 3 July 1954; *d* of Emanuel and Patricia Harris; one *s* by Paul Krempel. *Educ:* Henrietta Barnett Sch.; Lady Margaret Hall, Oxford (BA Hons). Called to the Bar, Middle Temple, 1977; in practice as a barrister, specialising in family law, 1977–2008; Dep. Dist Judge, Principal Registry, Family Div., 1990–2008; Recorder, 2003–08. *Recreations:* travel, theatre, visual arts, cinema, reading, walking. *Address:* Principal Registry Family Division, First Avenue House, 422-49 High Holborn, WC1V 6NP.

HARRIS, Leonard John; Commissioner, and Director, VAT Policy (formerly Internal Taxes), Customs and Excise, 1991–96; *b* 4 July 1941; *s* of Leonard and May Harris; *m* 1st, 1965, Jill Christine Tompkins (marr. diss.); one *s* two *d*; 2nd, 1986, Jennifer Dilys Biddiscombe (*née* Barker). *Educ:* Westminster City Sch.; St John's Coll., Cambridge. BA 1964 (Eng. Lit.), MA 1967. HM Customs and Excise: Asst Principal, 1964; Private Sec. to Chairman, 1966–68; Principal, 1969; CS Selection Bd, 1970; HM Customs and Excise, 1971; Cabinet Office, 1971–74; First Sec., UK Rep. to EEC, 1974–76, Counsellor, 1976–77; Asst Sec., HM Customs and Excise, 1977–80, Cabinet Office, 1980–83; Under Sec., 1983; Comr of Customs and Excise, 1983–87; Under Sec., MPO, 1987; Under Sec., HM Treasury, 1987–91. *Recreations:* cooking, music, naturism. *Address:* 2 Greens Row, Laundry Lane, Aston, Oxon OX18 2DG. *Club:* Oxford Naturist (Oxford).

HARRIS, Louise Anne; *see* Bloom, L. A. H.

HARRIS, Mark; Assistant Treasury Solicitor, Department for Education (formerly Education and Science), 1988–94; *b* 23 Feb. 1943; *s* of late Solomon Harris and Eva (*née* Lazarus); *m* 1972, Sharon Frances Colin; one *d*. *Educ:* Central Foundation Boys' Grammar Sch., London; London School of Economics and Political Science, London Univ. (LLB Hons). Solicitor of the Supreme Court, 1967. Entered Solicitor's Office, Dept of Employment, as Legal Asst, 1968; Sen. Legal Asst, 1973; Asst Solicitor, 1978; Legal Advr, 1987–88. Vol. mem. mgt cttee, dep. ed. and journalist, Essex Jewish News, 1996–. Vol. Mem., Mgt Cttee, and Publicity Officer, Cambridge Jewish Residents' Assoc., 2010–. *Publications:* The Shtetl and Other Jewish Stories, 2009; The Chorister and Other Jewish Stories, 2011; The Music Makers and Other Jewish Stories, 2012; numerous short stories, magazine and newspaper articles. *Recreations:* travel, walking, short-story writing, theatre, choral singing (first tenor, London Jewish Male Choir, 1988–2008, London Cantorial Singers, 2009–).

HARRIS, Mark Philip Allen; Executive Director and Member, National Lottery Committee, Gambling Commission, since 2013; *b* 29 July 1961; *s* of Roy Allen Harris and Vivienne Harris; *m* 1993, Patricia Mary Allen; one *s* one *d*. *Educ:* Bishop's Stortford Coll.; Nottingham Univ. (LLB Hons). CPFA 1987. Audit Examr, 1983–88, Manager, 1988–91, Sen. Manager, 1991–94, District Audit; Associate Controller, Audit Commn, 1994–97; Exec. Consultant, Hammersmith Hosps NHS Trust, 1997–98; Associate Dir (Strategic Develt), Audit Commn, 1998–99; Chief Exec., Nat. Lottery Commn, 1999–2013. Mem., Alumni Council, 2005–10, Chair, 2008–10, Ashridge Business Sch. Trustee: Responsibility in Gambling Trust, 2007–09; Responsible Gambling Fund, 2009–12. *Recreations:* family, driving, hill walking, mountaineering literature. *Address:* Gambling Commission, Victoria Square House, Victoria Square, Birmingham B2 4BP. *T:* (0121) 230 6733.

HARRIS, Prof. Sir Martin (Best), Kt 2000; CBE 1992; DL; Chairman, Universities Superannuation Scheme Ltd, 2006–15 (Director, 1991–2015; Deputy Chairman, 2004–06); President, Clare Hall, Cambridge, 2008–13 (Hon. Fellow, 2013); *b* 28 June 1944; *s* of William Best Harris and Betty Evelyn (*née* Martin); *m* 1966, Barbara Mary (*née* Daniels); two *s*. *Educ:* Devonport High Sch. for Boys, Plymouth; Queens' Coll., Cambridge (BA, MA; Hon. Fellow, 1992); Sch. of Oriental and African Studies, London (PhD). Lecturer in French Linguistics, Univ. of Leicester, 1967; University of Salford: Sen. Lectr in French Linguistics, 1974; Prof. of Romance Ling., 1976–87; Dean of Social Sciences and Arts, 1978–81; Pro-Vice-Chancellor, 1981–87; Vice-Chancellor: Essex Univ., 1987–92; Manchester Univ., 1992–2004; Dir, Office for Fair Access, 2004–12. Chancellor, Univ. of Salford, 2004–09. Chairman: CVCP, 1997–99 (Vice-Chm., 1995–97); NW Univs Assoc., 1999–2000; Cambridge Commonwealth Trust, 2011–14; Cambridge Overseas Trust, 2011–14. Member: Internat. Cttee for Historical Linguistics, 1979–86; UGC, 1984–87; HEFCE Review of Univ. Libraries, 1992–93; Chairman: NI Sub Cttee, UFC (formerly UGC), 1985–91; Nat. Curriculum Wkg Gp for Modern Foreign Langs, 1989–90; HEFCE/CVCP Review of Postgrad. Educn, 1995–96; Clinical Standards Adv. Gp, 1996–99; DfEE Careers Review, 2000. Member: Commn for Health Improvement, 1999–2002; NW Develt Agency Bd, 2001–08 (Dep. Chm., 2002–08). Chm., Manchester: Knowledge Capital, 2004–08. Mem. Council, Philological Soc., 1979–86, 1988–92. Chm. of Govs, Centre for Inf. on Lang. Teaching, 1990–96; Vice Chm. of Governors, Parrs Wood High Sch., 1982–86; Gov., Colchester Sixth Form Coll., 1988–92; Member Governing Body: Anglia Polytechnic Univ. (formerly Anglia Poly.), 1989–93; Plymouth Univ., 2004–09; Dep. Chm. of Govs, SOAS, Univ. of London, 2014– (Mem. Governing Body, 1990–93). Mem. High Council, Eur. Univ. Inst., 1992–96. Mem. Editorial Board: Journal Linguistics, 1982–91; Diachronica, 1983–92; French Studies, 1987–93; Jt Gen. Editor, Longman Linguistics Library, 1982–96. MAE 1991; AcSS 2001. DL Greater Manchester, 1998. Hon. Fellow: Bolton Inst., 1996; Univ. of Central Lancashire, 1999; Hon. RNCM 1996; Hon. FRCP 2005; Hon. FRCSE 2005. Hon. LLD QUB, 1992; DUniv: Essex, 1993; Keele, 2006; Hon. DLitt: Salford, 1995; Manchester Metropolitan, 2000; Leicester, Lincoln, 2003; Ulster, Manchester, UMIST, 2004; Exeter, 2008; Plymouth, 2009; London, 2013. *Publications:* (ed) Romance Syntax: synchronic and diachronic perspectives, 1976; The Evolution of French Syntax: a comparative approach, 1978; (ed with N. Vincent) Studies in the Romance Verb, 1982; (ed with P. Ramat) Historical Development of Auxiliaries, 1987; (ed with N. Vincent) The Romance Languages, 1988; about 35 articles in appropriate jls and collections. *Recreations:* gardening, travel, wine. *Address:* Chairman's Office, School of Oriental and African Studies, University of London, Thornhaugh Street, WC1H 0XG. *T:* (020) 7898 4014.

HARRIS, Martin Fergus, OBE 2010; HM Diplomatic Service; Minister and Deputy Head of Mission, Moscow, since 2014; *b* Edinburgh, 17 May 1969; *s* of Rev. W. Fergus Harris and Ruth Harris; *m* 1993, Linda MacLachlan; three *d*. *Educ:* George Watson's Coll., Edinburgh; Glenalmond Coll.; Corpus Christi Coll., Cambridge (BA 1991; MA 1995; Pres., Cambridge Union, 1990); Open Univ. (MPA 2008). Joined FCO, 1991; Second Sec., UK Delegn to OSCE, 1992–96; S Asia Dept, FCO, 1997–98; First Sec., Moscow, 1999–2003; Dep. Hd of Mission, Kiev, 2003–08; Dep. Dir, Cabinet Office (on secondment), 2008–10; Ambassador to Romania, 2010–14. *Recreations:* opera, church music, history. *Address:* c/o Foreign and Commonwealth Office, King Charles Street, SW1A 2AH.

HARRIS, Mervyn Leslie Richard; a District Judge (Magistrates' Courts) (formerly Stipendiary Magistrate), Nottinghamshire, 1991–2010; *b* 9 Aug. 1942; *s* of Albert Leslie Harris and Gladys Mary (*née* Plummer); *m* 1967, Marcia Jane Tomblin; one *s* one *d*. *Educ:* King Henry VIII Sch., Coventry; University Coll. London (LLB 1964). Admitted solicitor, 1969; Partner, Hughes & Masser, solicitors, Coventry, 1969–91. Chm. (part-time), Social Security Appeals Tribunal, 1985–91; Actg Stipendiary Magistrate, 1987–91. Clerk to local charities in Coventry and Atherstone. *Recreations:* walking, railways, railway history, watching football, Rugby and cricket.

HARRIS, Michael David, FRCO; Organist and Master of the Music, St Giles' Cathedral, Edinburgh, since 1996; organ recitalist, conductor and adjudicator; *b* 29 Dec. 1958; *s* of David John Harris and Muriel Harris (*née* Pearson); *m* 1987, Brigitte Johanne Hannelore Schröder; one *d*. *Educ:* King's Sch., Gloucester; Reading Sch.; St Peter's Coll., Oxford (MA); Royal Coll. of Music (ARCM); FRCO 1980. Sub Organist, Leeds Parish Church, 1982–86; Asst Dir of Music, Leeds Grammar Sch., 1982–86; Asst Organist, Canterbury Cathedral, 1986–96; Organist, King's Sch., Canterbury, 1986–96; Lectr in Music, Edinburgh Napier (formerly Napier) Univ., 1996–; Director: Scottish Chamber Choir, 1997–2010; Edinburgh Organ Acad., 1998–2010; Cantica Alba, 2010–. Organ recitals in UK, Germany, Belgium, Italy, Poland, Australia, NZ and USA. Recordings and broadcasts with choirs of Canterbury Cathedral and St Giles' Cathedral, Edinburgh. *Recreations:* railways, cooking. *Address:* St Giles' Cathedral, Edinburgh EH1 1RE.

HARRIS, Michael Deane; Senior Business Advisor, Fasken Martineau DuMoulin LLP, since 2013; consultant and advisor to various Canadian companies, since 2002; Premier of Ontario, 1995–2002; *b* 23 Jan. 1945; *s* of Sidney Deane Harris and Hope Gooding Harris (*née* Robinson). *Educ:* Algonquin High Sch.; North Bay Teachers' Coll. ICD.D 2005. Formerly: entrepreneur (owned and operated ventures incl. tourist resort and ski center); sch. teacher (Trustee, 1975–81, Chm., 1977–81, Nipissing Bd of Educn). MPP (PC) for Nipissing, Ontario, 1981; Parly Asst to Minister of the Envmt; Minister of Natural Resources and Minister of Energy, 1985. House Leader, 1986–89, Leader, 1990–2002, Ontario Progressive Conservative Party. Senior Business Adviser: Goodmans LLP, 2002–10; Cassels Brock & Blackwell LLP, 2010–13; Director: Canaccord Genuity Gp (formerly Capital, then Cannacord Financial Inc.), 2004–; FirstService Corp., 2006–; Element Financial Corp., 2011–; Luminato, 2014–; Chairman: Route1 Inc., 2009–; Magna Internat. Inc., 2011–12 (Lead Dir, 2003–11). Chm. of Trustees, Chartwell Retirement Residences (formerly Chartwell Seniors Housing Real Estate Investment Trust), 2003–; Dir, Tim Horton Children's Foundn, 2002–14. Sen. Fellow, Fraser Institute, 2002. Freedom Medal, Nat. Citizens Coalition, Canada, 1996; E. P. Taylor Award of Merit, Jockey Club of Canada, 2000; Cam Fella Award, Standardbred Canada, 2000. *Address:* Fasken Martineau DuMoulin LLP, 333 Bay Street, Suite 2400, Bay Adelaide Centre, Box 20, Toronto, ON M5H 2T6, Canada.

HARRIS, His Honour Sir Michael (Frank), Kt 2008; a Circuit Judge, 1992–2007; *b* 11 Jan. 1942; *s* of Joseph Frank Harris and Edna Harris; *m* 1969, Veronica Brend; one *s* one *d*. *Educ:* St Bartholomew's Grammar Sch., Newbury; Merton Coll., Oxford (BA). Called to the Bar, Middle Temple, 1965, Bencher, 2003; a Recorder, 1990–92. Chief Social Security Comr and Chief Child Support Comr, 2001–03. President: Social Security, Medical, Disability and Child Support Appeal Tribunals, 1998–99; The Appeals Service, 1999–2007. *Recreations:* piano playing, amateur dramatics, walking, music, theatre, travel, reading.

HARRIS, Rear-Adm. Michael George Temple; JP; Clerk to the Clothworkers' Co. of the City of London and Secretary to the Clothworkers' Foundation, 1992–2001; *b* 5 July 1941; *s* of late Comdr Antony John Temple Harris, OBE, RN and Doris Drake Harris; *heir-pres.* to Baron Harris, *qv*; *m* 1970, Katrina Chichester; three *d*. *Educ:* Pangbourne Coll.; RNC Dartmouth; Open Univ. (BA, Dip. Spanish 2004). FRGS 1978–2002; FNI 1988–2002. Qualified Submarines, 1963, TAS 1968; commanded HM Submarines: Osiris, 1970–72; Sovereign, 1975–77 (N Pole, 1976); 3rd Submarine Sqn, 1982–85; commanded HM Ships: Cardiff, 1980–82 (Falkland Is, 1982); Ark Royal, 1987–89; ACDS (NATO/UK), 1989–92. Exchange service with USN, 3rd Fleet Staff, 1972–75. Younger Brother of Trinity House, 1989–. Trustee, 1984–2014, Chm., 1995–2014, Belmont House, Kent; Trustee, Emmaus Hampshire, 2005–14. Mem., Ancient Soc. of Coll. Youths, 1995–. Liveryman, Clothworkers' Co., 1997– (Mem., Ct of Assistants, 2001–). Gov., Pangbourne Coll., 1997–2007. JP NW Hants, 2002–11. Churchwarden, All Hallows, Whitchurch, Hants, 2011–13. *Recreations:* fishing, bell-ringing, monumental brasses, historical and biographical research. *Address:* c/o Clothworkers' Hall, Dunster Court, Mincing Lane, EC3R 7AH. *Club:* Band of Brothers.

HARRIS, Michael John; Owner, Find Your Lightbulb Ltd, since 2009; *b* 10 March 1949; *s* of John Melton and Ivy May Harris; *m* 1971, Susan Cooper; one *s* one *d*. *Educ:* Dudley Grammar Sch.; University Coll. London (BSc Chemistry). Variety of positions in IT, incl. Head of Systems Develt for Retail Bank, Midland Bank, 1972–86; Dir, Space-Time Systems, 1986–88; Chief Executive: Firstdirect, 1988–91; Mercury Communications Ltd, 1991–95; Prudential Banking, then Egg, 1995–2000; Vice Chm., Egg plc, 2000–05; Chm., Gp

Innovation, Royal Bank of Scotland, 2006–09; Co-founder and Chm., Garlik, 2006–11. *Publications:* Find Your Lightbulb: how to make millions from apparently impossible ideas, 2008. *Recreations:* tennis, walking, theatre, photography, watching Aston Villa.

HARRIS, Rear Adm. Nicholas Henry Linton, CB 2006; MBE 1987; Clerk to Merchant Taylors' Company, since 2006; *b* 26 Feb. 1952; *s* of Peter N. Harris and Theodora M. F. Harris (*née* Patterson); *m* 1974, Jennifer Mary Peebles; two *d. Educ:* Malvern Coll.; BRNC Dartmouth. Joined RN, 1969; CO, HMS Oberon, 1985–86, HMS Sovereign, 1988–90; US Naval War Coll., 1991–92; Naval Staff, Washington, 1992–94; on staff, MoD, 1994–97; Captain, Second Submarine Sqdn, 1997–99; Dep. Flag Officer, Submarines, 1999–2000; Naval Attaché, Washington, 2000–03; FO Scotland, Northern England and NI, 2003–06. *Recreations:* cricket, golf. *Address:* c/o Merchant Taylors' Hall, 30 Threadneedle Street, EC2R 8JB. *T:* (020) 7450 4442. *Clubs:* Royal Navy of 1765 and 1785, City Naval (Chm., 2011–); RN Cricket; Broadhalfpenny Brigands Cricket (Hambledon) (Chm., 2012–); Hartley Wintney Golf.

HARRIS, Canon Patricia Ann, (Mrs J. N. K. Harris); Central President, The Mothers' Union, 1989–94 (Vice-President, 1986–88); *b* 29 May 1939; *m* 1963, Rev. James Nigel Kingsley Harris, BA; one *s* one *d. Educ:* Trinity Coll., Carmarthen (Hon. Fellow, 1995). Teaching Dip. Teacher, 1959–63; pt-time special needs teacher, 1963–88; vol. teacher, Gloucester Prison, 1978–85. Member: Glos Dio. Synod, 1980–2001; C of E General Synod, 1985–2000 (Mem. Exec., 1991–2001, Vice Chm., 1996–2001, Chm., Trust Funds, 1996–2001, Bd of Mission); Bishops' Council, 1985–2001; Cttee, Partnership for World Mission, 1993–2000; Women's Nat. Commn, 1994–96; USPG Council, 1994–96; Cttee, Black Anglican Concerns, 1995–96; Council, 1996–, Publications Cttee, 1997–, Bible Reading Fellowship. Mothers' Union: Young Wives Leader, 1963–65; Enrolling Mem., 1967–76; Presiding Mem., 1969–74; Diocesan Social Concern Chm., 1974–80; Pres., Glos dio., 1980–85; Mem., Worldwide Council, 1995–. Hon. Lay Canon, Gloucester Cathedral, 2001–. Mem., Archbishops' Bd of Examiners, 1996–99. Paul Harris Fellow, Rotary Internat., 1995. Cross of St Augustine, 1995. *Recreations:* family, watching Rugby, cooking, craft work, gym. *Address:* 14 Shalford Close, Cirencester, Glos GL7 1WG. *T:* (01285) 885641.

HARRIS, Rt Rev. Patrick Burnet; Hon. Assistant Bishop, Diocese of Europe, since 1999; Hon. Assistant Bishop, Diocese of Gloucester, since 2005; *b* 30 Sept. 1934; *s* of Edward James Burnet Harris and Astrid Kendall; *m* 1968, Valerie Margaret Pilbrow; two *s* one *d. Educ:* St Albans School; Keble Coll., Oxford (MA); Clifton Theol Coll. Asst Curate, St Ebbe's, Oxford, 1960–63; Missionary with S American Missionary Soc., 1963–73; Archdeacon of Salta, Argentina, 1969–73; Diocesan Bishop of Northern Argentina, 1973–80; Rector of Kirkheaton and Asst Bishop, Dio. Wakefield, 1981–85; Sec., Partnership for World Mission, 1986–88; Asst Bishop, Dio. Oxford, 1986–88; Bishop of Southwell, 1988–99. Asst Bp, Dio. Lincoln, 1999–2005. Mem., South Atlantic Council, 1986–2011. Chairman: Bible Reading Fellowship, 1995–98; Council, Ridley Hall, 1994–2003; Internat. Anglican Family Network, 2007–12; Pres., S Amer. Mission Soc., 1993–2010; Vice-Pres., TEAR Fund, 1994–2003. Mem., H of L, 1996–99. *Recreations:* ornithology, S American Indian culture, music, harvesting. *Address:* Apt B, Ireton House, Pavilion Gardens, The Park, Cheltenham, Glos GL50 2SP.

HARRIS, Prof. Paul; Professor of Screen Media, and Dean, Duncan of Jordanstone College of Art and Design, University of Dundee, since 2014; *b* Birmingham, 4 June 1959; *s* of John Leonard Harris and Ethel Rose Harris; *m* 1986, Denise Hazel Bruno. *Educ:* Yardley Grammar Sch.; Birmingham Coll. of Art and Design (DA Photography 1980). Various broadcast television posts, Channel 4, BBC, ITV and freelance, 1980–92; Depute Dir, Media Centre, Dundee Inst. of Technol., 1992–94; freelance producer and lectr, 1994–96; Hd, Dept of Film and Television, Edinburgh Coll. of Art, 1996–2002; University of Abertay, Dundee: Sen. Lectr in Computer Arts and Vis. Prof., 2002–04; Prof. of Screen Media, 2004–10 (Vis. Prof. of Screen Media, 2010–); Creative Dir, Inst. of Arts, Media and Computer Games, 2009–10; Prof. of Screen Media, and Hd, Gray's Sch. of Art, Robert Gordon Univ., Aberdeen, 2010–14. Project Dir, 2001–02, Exec. Chm., 2002–07, Angus Digital Media Centre. Chairman: Lottery and Investment Panel, Scottish Screen, 2005–07; Regional Screen Scotland, 2014–; Member: Bd, Learning and Teaching Scotland, 2010–12; Bd, sound, Scotland's Fest. of New Music, 2012–. Specialist Expert in Film and Digital Media, Hong Kong Council for Accreditation of Acad. and Vocational Quals, 2014–. FRSA 2008. *Publications:* articles in Jl of Media Practice, Internat. Jl of Educn Through Art, Jl of Audience and Reception Studies. *Recreations:* travel, good food, fine wines, art, photography, cycling, driving, motorcycling. *Address:* Duncan of Jordanstone College of Art and Design, University of Dundee, Perth Road, Dundee DD1 4HT. *T:* (01382) 388820, *Fax:* (01382) 388305. *E:* p.harris@dundee.ac.uk.

HARRIS, Prof. Paul Lansley, DPhil; FBA 1998; Professor of Education, Harvard University, since 2001; *b* 14 May 1946; *s* of Joseph and Betty Harris; *m* Pascale Torracinta; three *s. Educ:* Chippenham Grammar Sch.; Sussex Univ. (BA Psychol.); Linacre Coll., Oxford (DPhil Psychol. 1971). Research Fellow: Center for Cognitive Studies, Harvard Univ., 1971–72; in Exptl Psychol., Oxford Univ., 1972–73; Lectr, Dept of Psychol., Lancaster Univ., 1973–76; Reader, Free Univ., Amsterdam, 1976–79; Lectr, Dept of Social Psychology, LSE, 1979–81; Oxford University: Lectr in Exptl Psychol., 1981–96; Reader, 1996–98; Prof. of Develtl Psychol., 1998–2001; Fellow, St John's Coll., 1981–2001, now Emeritus. Fellow, Center for Advanced Study in Behavioral Scis, Stanford, USA, 1992–93; John Simon Guggenheim Meml Foundn Fellow, 2005. Foreign Mem., Norwegian Acad. of Sci. and Letters, 2006–. Hon. Fellow, Cardiff Univ., 2011–. Dr *hc* Lausanne, 2009. Preyer Award, European Soc. for Develtl Psychol., 2009; Cognitive Develt Soc. Book Award, 2013; Eleanor Maccoby Book Award, Amer. Psychol Assoc., 2015; Mentor Award in Develtl Psychol., Amer. Psychol Assoc., 2015. *Publications:* Children and Emotion, 1989; The Work of the Imagination, 2000; Trusting What You're Told: how children learn from others, 2012; articles in learned jls, incl. Child Development, Philosophical Trans. of Royal Soc. and Psychological Sci. *Recreations:* cooking, writing. *Address:* 503A Larsen Hall, Harvard Graduate School of Education, Appian Way, Cambridge, MA 02138, USA.

HARRIS, Dame Pauline (Norma), DBE 2004; DL; company director; *b* 5 Jan. 1942; *d* of Bertie William Chumley and Constance Chumley (*née* Woolett); *m* 1960, Philip Charles Harris (*see* Baron Harris of Peckham); three *s* one *d. Educ:* St Helen's Sch., Streatham. Chairman: Organising Cttee, Children's Royal Variety Performance, 1985–88; Appeal Cttee, Birthright, 1988–91; Kingdom Appeal, Foetal Res. Unit, KCH, 1991–93; Co-Chm., Mencap Opera, 1993–96; Vice President: Friends of Guy's Hosp., 1991–; Mencap, 1995–; Pres., Harris HospisCare, 1997–. Dir and Mem., Special Educnl Needs Sub-cttee, Harris City Technol. Coll., Croydon, 1988–; Mem. Council, Harris Manchester Coll., Oxford, 1994–; Dir and Gov., Harris Girls' Acad., E Dulwich, 2006–; Dir, Harris Fedn of S London Schs, 2007–. Hon. Fellow: Oriel Coll., Oxford, 1994; RVC, S Mimms, 1994; Harris Manchester Coll., Oxford, 1996; Lucy Cavendish Coll., Cambridge, 1996. Trustee: Dyslexia Educn Trust, 1986–; Bacon City Technol. Coll., Bermondsey, 1990–; Mem. Cttee, Specialist Schs Trust, 2001–06; Trustee and Gov., Acad. of Peckham, 2002–. Gov., Kemnal Technol. Coll., Sidcup, 1994–. Patron: Nat. Eczema Soc., 1989–; Lewisham Children's Hosp., 1992–. Mem., British Showjumping Assoc., 1958–. DL Kent, 2005. Hon. DHL Richmond, London, 2002. *Recreations:* historic car rallying, dressage. *Address:* c/o Philip Harris House, 1A Spur Road, Orpington, Kent BR6 0PH. *T:* (01689) 886886, *Fax:* (01689) 886887. *E:* judy.willett@harrisventures.co.uk.

HARRIS, Group Captain Peter Langridge, CBE 1988; AE 1961 (Clasp 1971); CEng, FIET; ADC to the Queen, 1984–88; Inspector, Royal Auxiliary Air Force, 1983–88; *b* 6 Sept. 1929; *s* of Arthur Langridge Harris and Doris Mabel (*née* Offen); *m* 1955, (Yvonne) Patricia Stone (*d* 2003); two *d. Educ:* St Edward's Sch., Oxford; Univ. of Birmingham (BSc). CEng, FIET (FIEE 1976). Served: RAF, 1947–49; RAFVR, 1949–60; RAuxAF, 1960–78 and 1982–88; commanded 1 (Co. Hertford) Maritime HQ Unit, 1973–78; Air Force Mem., 1978–94, Vice-Chm. (Air), 1988–94, TA&VRA for Greater London; Gp Captain 1983. Elliott Bros (London) Ltd, 1952–55; Decca Navigator Co. Ltd, 1955–59; GEC plc, 1959–89; retired, 1989. Mem. Bd, Milton Keynes Business Venture, 1983–89. Mem. Bd of Management, 1990–2003, Mem., Adv. Bd, 2003–05, Princess Marina House, Rustington. Chm., Hatfield Dist IEE, 1979–80. Mem., Council, Reserve Forces Assoc., 1989–95. Pres., 1 Maritime HQ Unit Old Comrades Assoc., 1990–. Patron, Cerebral Palsy Centre, Portsmouth, 2003–10. Liveryman, Hon. Co. of Air Pilots (formerly GAPAN), 2005– (Freeman, 1987). DL Greater London, 1986–98. GCMJ 2014 (Chevalier, OSMTH, 1994; Grand Chancellor, NATO Grand Priory, 2005–07; Prior, NATO UK Priory, 2015). *Recreation:* travel. *Address:* 10 Dolphin Court, St Helens Parade, Southsea, Hants PO4 0QL. *T:* (023) 9281 7602. *E:* plharris-southsea@supanet.com. *Clubs:* Royal Air Force; Royal Naval and Royal Albert Yacht (Portsmouth).

HARRIS, Peter Michael; Official Solicitor to the Supreme Court, 1993–99; *b* 13 April 1937; *m* 1963, Bridget Burke; one *s* two *d. Educ:* Cirencester Grammar School; Britannia Royal Naval College, Dartmouth. Cadet, RN, 1953; Lieut Comdr 1967; retired from RN 1972. Called to the Bar, Gray's Inn, 1971; Lord Chancellor's Department: Legal Asst, 1974; Circuit Administrator, Northern Circuit, 1986–93. Chm. and Trustee, Dorothy Pamela Smith Trust, 1999; Chm., Grandparents' Assoc., 2003–11 (Vice Pres., 2011–). *Publications:* The Children Act 1989: a procedural handbook, 1991; The Expert Witness Pack, 1997. *Recreations:* reading, walking, gardening. *Address:* 23 Rook Wood Way, Little Kingshill, Great Missenden, Bucks HP16 0DF.

HARRIS, Dame Philippa Jill Olivier, (Dame Pippa), DBE 2015; film and television producer; Co-Founder and Director, Neal Street Productions, since 2003; *b* Oxford, 27 March 1967; *d* of Dr Anthony Harris and Angela M. O. Harris (*née* Richards); *m* 1997, Richard McBrien; one *d. Educ:* Oxford High Sch.; Robinson Coll., Cambridge (BA Hons English 1989). Prodn asst, Jacaranda Prodns, 1989–91; Drama Ed., Carlton TV, 1993–97; BBC: Develt Exec., Films, 1997–99; Exec. Producer, Drama Serials, 1999–2001; Hd, Drama Commng, TV, 2001–03; producer/executive producer: Warriors, 1999 (BAFTA and RTS Awards); Care, 2000 (BAFTA and Prix Italia Awards); Other People's Children, 2000; The Sleeper, 2000; Love in a Cold Climate, 2001; The Cazalets, 2001; The Way We Live Now, 2001 (BAFTA and BPG Awards); The Inspector Lynley Mysteries, 2001–02; The Key, 2003; The Young Visiters, 2003; Jarhead, 2006; Starter for Ten, 2006; Stuart A Life Backwards, 2007 (Banff World TV and RTS Awards; Best TV Film, Reims Internat. TV Fest.); Things We Lost in the Fire, 2007; Revolutionary Road, 2008; Away We Go, 2009; Call the Midwife, 2012 (TRIC Best Drama Prog. of Year; TV Choice Best New Drama; Christopher Award); The Hollow Crown, 2012 (RTS and BPG Best Single Drama Awards); Blood, 2013; Penny Dreadful, 2014; We Are Many, 2015. Mem., Council, 2008–, Film Cttee, 2008– (Dep. Chair), BAFTA; Gov., Royal Central Sch. of Speech and Drama (formerly Central Sch. of Speech and Drama), 2010–. Trustee, Creative Soc. (formerly New Deal of the Mind), 2009–. Mem., Charleston Appeal Cttee, 2013–. *Publications:* Song of Love: the letters of Rupert Brooke and Noel Olivier, 1991. *Recreations:* theatre, cinema, reading, contemporary art. *Address:* Neal Street Productions, 26–28 Neal Street, WC2H 9QQ. *T:* (020) 7240 8890. *E:* post@nealstreetproductions.com.

HARRIS, Phillip, FRCSE, FRCPE, FRCSGlas; FRSE; former Consultant Neurosurgeon; formerly Deputy Director, Department of Surgical Neurology, Royal Infirmary and Western General Hospital, Edinburgh; Senior Lecturer, Edinburgh University, 1955–87; Member, MRC Brain Metabolism Unit, University of Edinburgh, 1952–80; Editor, Paraplegia, later Spinal Cord, 1980–97, now Emeritus Editor; *b* Edinburgh, 28 March 1922; *s* of late Simon Harris, Edinburgh; *m* 1949, Sheelagh Shèna (*née* Coutts); one *s* one *d. Educ:* Royal High Sch., Edinburgh; Edinburgh Univ.; Sch. of Med. of Royal Colls, Edinburgh. Medallist in Anatomy, Physiol., Physics, Materia Medica and Therapeutics, Med., Midwifery and Gynaec., and Surgery. LRCP and LRCSE, LRCPSGlas 1944; FRCSE 1948; MRCPE 1954; FRCPE 1959; FRCSGlas 1964 (*ad eundem*). Capt., RAMC, 1945–48. Past Chm., Sch. of Occupational Therapy, Edinburgh. Sometime Vis. Prof./Guest Chief in Neurosurg., USA, Canada, Europe, S America, Far East, Middle East and Russia; Lectures: Sydney Watson-Smith, RCPE, 1967; Honyman-Gillespie, Edinburgh Univ., 1968. Mem., WHO Cttee for Prevention of Neurotrauma, 1985. Past Chm., Professional and Linguistics Assessments Bd, GMC. World Federation of Neurosurgical Societies: past Sen. UK Deleg. in Neurosurg.; Hon. Vice-Pres., 1977–94; Mem. Exec., Neurotraumatol. Cttee and Archivist and Historian; Founder, Internat. Conf. of Recent Advances in Neurotraumatol.; Founder and Past Chairman: Epilepsy Soc., SE Scotland; Scottish Assoc. of Neurol Scis; Scottish Sports Assoc. for Disabled (Hon. Pres.); Past Member of Council: Soc. of British Neurol Surgs; Neurol Sect., RSocMed; Past Pres., British Cervical Spine Soc. Past Director, Epilepsy Internat.; Dir and Trustee, Scottish Trust for Physically Disabled; Mem. Council, Thistle Foundn. President: Royal High Sch. FP Club, 1978; Edinburgh Rotary Club, 1991–92. Inventor of neurosurg. instruments and apparatus. Medal, Internat. Med. Soc. of Paraplegia, 1985; Dr A. S. Lakshumpathi Medal and Prize, Madras, 1986. *Publications:* (ed jtly) Epilepsy, 1971; (ed jtly) Head Injuries, 1971; chapters in books on neurological surgery; over 100 papers in scientific jls on various neurosurgical topics. *Recreations:* sport, music, travel. *Address:* 4/5 Fettes Rise, Edinburgh EH4 1QH. *T:* (0131) 552 8900. *Club:* New (Edinburgh).

HARRIS, Rebecca Elizabeth; MP (C) Castle Point, since 2010; *b* Windsor, 22 Dec. 1967; *d* of Philip and Louise Harris; *m* Frank; one *s. Educ:* London Sch. of Econs and Pol Sci. (BSc). Mktg Dir, Phillimore & Co. Ltd (publishers), 1997–2007. Special Advr to Tim Yeo, MP, 2003–10. Mem. (C) Chichester DC, 1999–2003. Mem., Select Cttee for Business, Innovation and Skills, 2010–15, for Regulatory Reform, 2012–15. *Recreation:* gardening. *Address:* House of Commons, SW1A 0AA. *T:* (020) 7219 7602. *E:* rebecca.harris.mp@parliament.uk.

HARRIS, Ven. (Reginald) Brian; Archdeacon of Manchester, 1980–98; a Residentiary Canon of Manchester Cathedral, 1980–98, Sub-Dean 1986–98; *b* 14 Aug. 1934; *s* of Reginald and Ruby Harris; *m* 1959, Anne Patricia Hughes; one *s* one *d. Educ:* Eltham College; Christ's College, Cambridge (MA); Ridley Hall, Cambridge. Curate of Wednesbury, 1959–61; Curate of Uttoxeter, 1961–64; Vicar of St Peter, Bury, 1964–70; Vicar of Walmsley, Bolton, 1970–80; RD of Walmsley, 1970–80. *Recreations:* walking, painting, music. *Address:* 9 Cote Lane, Hayfield, High Peak SK22 2HL. *T:* (01663) 746321.

HARRIS, Rhian Sara; Director, V&A Museum of Childhood, since 2008; *b* 4 Dec. 1967; *m* 2001, Jonathan Hourigan; one *s* one *d. Educ:* Essex Univ. (BA Hons Art Hist. and Theory); City Univ. (MA Mus. and Gall. Mgt). Res. Asst, 1990–93, Sen. Picture Cataloguer, 1993–95, Wellcome Inst. for Hist. of Medicine; Curator, 1995–2001, Dir, 2001–08, Foundling Mus. Member, Advisory Committee: Hogarth Gp, 2004–; Arts Forum; Homerton Foundn Hosp., 2008–; Nat. Toy Council, 2008–; London Children's Mus., 2011–; Trustee: Little Angel Th., 2011–; 19 Princelet St (Mus. of Immigration), 2011–; Betty Cadbury Trust, 2011–. *Publications:* (ed jtly and contrib.) Enlightened Self-Interest, 1997; (ed) The Foundling Museum Guidebook, 2004; (contrib.) Children, Childhood and Cultural Heritage, 2012; contrib. articles to Art Quarterly, Christies Mag., LTS Newsletter, BBC History Online,

Museums Jl, Outlook (Children England). *Recreations:* art, contemporary Welsh art, childhood studies, cinema, dance, music, travelling, pilates, gardening. *Address:* V&A Museum of Childhood, Cambridge Heath Road, E2 9PA. *T:* (020) 8983 5222, *Fax:* (020) 8983 5225.

HARRIS, Robert Dennis; author; *b* 7 March 1957; *s* of late Dennis Harris and Audrey (*née* Hardy); *m* 1988, Gillian, *d* of Sir Derek Peter Hornby and Margaret (*née* Withers); two *s* two *d*. *Educ:* King Edward VII Sch., Melton Mowbray; Selwyn Coll., Cambridge (BA Hons English; Hon. Fellow 2013). Pres., Cambridge Union, 1978. Joined BBC TV Current Affairs Dept, 1978; Reporter, Newsnight, 1981–85, Panorama, 1985–87; Political Editor, Observer, 1987–89; Political Columnist, Sunday Times, 1989–92, 1996–97; Columnist, Daily Telegraph, 2001–02; book reviewer, Sunday Times, 2009–. Patron, Bletchley Park Trust, 2001–. Pres., Classical Assoc., 2007–08. Mem., BAFTA, 2002. FRSL 1996. Hon. DLitt Nottingham, 2012. Columnist of the Year, British Press Awards, 2003. *Publications: novels:* Fatherland, 1992 (filmed 1994); Enigma, 1995 (filmed 2001); Archangel, 1998 (televised 2005); Pompeii, 2003; Imperium, 2006; The Ghost, 2007 (filmed 2010; writer of screenplay with Roman Polanski (Eur. Film Award, César and Lumière Prizes for best adapted screenplay)); Lustrum, 2009; The Fear Index, 2011; An Officer and a Spy, 2013 (Popular Fiction Book of Yr, Nat. Book Awards, 2013; Walter Scott Prize, 2014; Ian Fleming Steel Dagger Award, CWA, 2014); *non-fiction:* (with Jeremy Paxman) A Higher Form of Killing: the history of gas and germ warfare, 1982; Gotcha! the media, the government and the Falklands crisis, 1983; The Making of Neil Kinnock, 1984; Selling Hitler: the story of the Hitler diaries, 1986 (televised, 1991); Good and Faithful Servant: the unauthorized biography of Bernard Ingham, 1990; The Media Trilogy, 1994. *Recreations:* collecting books, walking, dove-keeping. *Address:* The Old Vicarage, Kintbury, Berks RG17 9TR. *T:* (01488) 658073. *Club:* Garrick.

HARRIS, Robert K.; *see* Kirby-Harris.

HARRIS, Robert Malcolm; HM Diplomatic Service, retired; Governor of Anguilla, 1997–2000 (Acting Governor, 1996–97); *b* 9 Feb. 1941; *m* 1984, Mary Lavinia Allmark (*née* Taggart). Joined Foreign Office, 1960, Archives Clerk, 1960–62; Istanbul, 1962–63; Cento, Ankara, 1963–65; Blantyre, 1965–69; FCO, 1969; Moscow, 1970–72; FCO, 1972–75; Second Sec., Dublin, 1975–79; Nat. Defence Coll., Latimer, 1979–80; First Sec., FCO, 1980–84; Hd of Chancery, Brunei, 1984–89; Consul, Lyon, 1989–90; First Sec., FCO, 1990–92; Chargé d'Affaires, Almaty, 1992–93; First Sec., FCO, 1993–96. *Recreations:* golf, music, gardening. *Address:* Le Bourg, 46500 Miers, France. *Club:* Golf de Montal.

HARRIS, Robert William, CEng, FREng, FIOA; Director, Arts and Culture UKMEA, Arup, since 2009; *b* London, 6 Dec. 1954; *s* of William Harris and Mabel Harris; *m* 1981, Susan-Jayne Ashton; one *s* one *d*. *Educ:* Warwick Univ. (BSc Hons Physics 1975); Univ. of Southampton (MSc Sound and Vibration 1977). CEng 1995; FREng 2009. Acoustic Consultant, Acoustic Technology Ltd, 1977–82; Acoustic Consultant, 1983–89, Principal, 1990–97, Arup Acoustics; Dir, Acoustics, Arup, 1998–. Internat. auditorium acoustic designer; projects include: Glyndebourne Opera House, 1994; Bridgewater Hall, Manchester, 1996; Royal Opera House, London, 2000; City Recital Hall, Sydney, 2002; Concertgebouw, Bruges, 2002; Copenhagen Opera House, 2004; Oslo Opera House, 2008; Kings Place recital hall, London, 2008. Theatre consultant. FIOA 1990. *Publications:* numerous papers in professional jls and conf. procs on auditorium design and sound system design. *Recreations:* cycling, photography, travel, performing arts, sailing, powerboating. *Address:* Arup, Parkin House, 8 St Thomas Street, Winchester SO23 9HE. *T:* (01962) 829906, *Fax:* (01962) 867270. *E:* rob.harris@arup.com.

HARRIS, Robin (David Ronald), CBE 1988; writer; *b* 22 June 1952; *s* of Ronald Desmond Harris and Isabella Jamieson Harris. *Educ:* Canford Sch.; Exeter Coll., Oxford (Stapeldon Schol., MA History, DPhil). Desk Officer, Conservative Res. Dept, 1978–81; Special Adviser: to Financial Sec. to the Treasury, 1981–83; to Home Secretary, 1983–85; Dir, Conservative Res. Dept, 1985–89; Mem., Prime Minister's Policy Unit, 1989–90; Advr to Baroness Thatcher, 1990–2003. Consultant Dir, Politeia, 2003–11. Sen. Vis. Fellow, Heritage Foundn, 2009–13. Order of the Morning Star (Croatia), 2008. *Publications:* Valois Guyenne: a study of politics, government and society in medieval France, 1994; (ed) Margaret Thatcher: the collected speeches, 1997; Dubrovnik: a history, 2003; Beyond Friendship: the future of Anglo-American relations, 2006; Talleyrand: betrayer and saviour of France, 2007; The Conservatives: a history, 2011; Not for Turning: the life of Margaret Thatcher, 2013. *Recreations:* reading, travel. *Club:* Oxford and Cambridge.

HARRIS, Rolf; entertainer; *b* 30 March 1930; *s* of C. G. Harris and A. M. Harris (*née* Robbins); *m* 1958, Alwen Hughes, sculptress; one *d*. *Educ:* Bassendean State Sch.; Perth Modern Sch.; Univ. of WA; Claremont Teachers' Coll. Jun. backstroke champion, Australia, 1946; teacher, Perth; paintings exhibited: RA, London, 1954, 1955; Nat. Gall., London, 2002; 80th birthday portrait of HM Queen, 2005; Clarendon Gall., Mayfair, 2011; Walker Art Gall., Liverpool, 2012; *television* includes: Rolf Harris Show, 1967–71; Rolf on Saturday-OK, 1977–79; Cartoon Time, 1984–89; Rolf's Cartoon Club, 1989–93; Animal Hospital, 1994–2004; Rolf's Amazing Animals, 1998; Rolf on Art, 2001; Rolf's Golden Jubilee, 2003; Rolf Harris' Star Portraits, 2004–07; Rolf Harris Paints His Dream, 2010; *recordings* include: Tie Me Kangaroo Down Sport, 1960; Sun Arise, 1962; Two Little Boys, 1969; Stairway to Heaven, 1993. *Publications:* Write Your Own Pop Song, 1968; Rolf Goes Bush, 1975; Picture Book of Cats, 1978; Looking at Pictures, 1978; Instant Music, 1980; Your Cartoon Time, 1986; Catalogue of Comic Verse, 1988; Every Picture Tells a Story, 1989; Win or Die: the making of a King, 1989; Your Animation Time, 1991; Personality Cats, 1992; Me and You and Poems Too, 1993; Can You Tell What it is Yet? (autobiog.), 2001; Rolf on Art, 2002; Tie Me Kangaroo Down, Sport, 2009; True Animal Tales, 2011.

HARRIS, Rosemary Jeanne; author; *b* 20 Feb. 1923; *yr d* of Marshal of the RAF Sir Arthur Harris, 1st Bt, GCB, OBE, AFC, LLD, and of Barbara Kyrle Money. *Educ:* privately; Thorneloe Sch., Weymouth; St Martin's, Central and Chelsea Schs of Art. Red Cross Nursing Auxiliary, London, Westminster Div., from 1941. Student, 1945–48; picture restorer, 1949; student at Courtauld Inst. (Dept of Technology), 1950; Reader, MGM, 1951–52; subseq. full-time writer. Reviewer of children's books for The Times, 1970–73. Television plays: Peronik, 1976; The Unknown Enchantment, 1981. *Publications:* The Summer-House, 1956; Voyage to Cythera, 1958; Venus with Sparrows, 1961; All My Enemies, 1967; The Nice Girl's Story, 1968; A Wicked Pack of Cards, 1969; The Double Snare, 1975; Three Candles for the Dark, 1976; *for children:* The Moon in the Cloud, 1968 (Carnegie Medal); The Shadow on the Sun, 1970; The Seal-Singing, 1971; The Child in the Bamboo Grove, 1971; The Bright and Morning Star, 1972; The King's White Elephant, 1973; The Lotus and the Grail, 1974; The Flying Ship, 1974; The Little Dog of Fo, 1976; I Want to be a Fish, 1977; A Quest for Orion, 1978; Beauty and the Beast, 1979; Greenfinger House, 1979; Tower of the Stars, 1980; The Enchanted Horse, 1981; Janni's Stork, 1982; Zed, 1982; (adapted) Heidi, by Johanna Spyri, 1983; Summers of the Wild Rose, 1987; (ed) Poetry Anthology: Love and the Merry-Go-Round, 1988; Colm of the Islands, 1989; Ticket to Freedom, 1991; The Wildcat Strike, 1995; The Haunting of Joey M'basa, 1996. *Recreations:* music, theatre, reading.

HARRIS, Russell James; QC 2003; *b* 10 Nov. 1961; *s* of late Donald Harris and of Jean Harris (*née* Hall); *m* 1999, Nicola Richards; one *s* two *d*. *Educ:* Heolddu Comprehensive Sch., Bargoed; St John's Coll., Cambridge (MacMahon Schol., Pres. JCR, Lamour Prize, MA 1984); City Univ. (Dip Law 1985). Called to the Bar, Gray's Inn, 1986, Bencher, 2009 (Trustee, 2013); in practice as a barrister, specialising in planning and public law, 1986–; Special Advocate, 2009–. Mem. Wales Council, Prince's Trust, 2013–. Series advr, The Welsh in London (BBC Wales TV), 2006. Rugby coach, WRU Exiles squad, 2013–. *Publications:* (jtly) Environmental Law, 2001; various articles in Jl of Planning and Envmtl Law. *Recreations:* family, Wales (especially Ramsey Sound and the Farmer's Arms, St Davids). *Address:* Landmark Chambers, 180 Fleet Street, EC4A 2HG. *T:* (020) 7430 1221. *E:* russellharrisqc@Mortonhouse.co.uk. *Clubs:* London Welsh Rugby Football; St Davids Rugby Football (Vice-Pres., 2006–).

HARRIS, Prof. Ruth, DPhil; FBA 2011; Professor of Modern History, University of Oxford, since 2011; Fellow, New College, Oxford, since 1990; *b* 25 Dec. 1958; *m* 1985, Dr Iain George Pears, *qv*; two *s*. *Educ:* Univ. of Pennsylvania (BA, MA); DPhil. Jun. Res. Fellow, St John's Coll., Oxford, 1983; Associate Prof., Smith Coll., Northampton, Mass; Lectr in Modern Hist., Univ. of Oxford, 1990. *Publications:* Murders and Madness, 1989; (ed jtly and contrib.) Clinical Diseases of the Nervous System, 1990; Lourdes: body and spirit in the secular age, 1999; The Man on Devil's Island: Alfred Dreyfus and the affair that divided France, 2010 (Wolfson History Prize 2011); Dreyfus: politics, emotion and the scandal of the century, 2011. *Address:* New College, Oxford OX1 3BN.

HARRIS, Sheila Lesley; *see* Scales, S. L.

HARRIS, (Terence) Victor; Keeper of Japanese Antiquities, British Museum, 1997–2003, now Keeper Emeritus; *b* 3 Aug. 1942; *s* of William Victor Clayton Harris and Theresa Harris (*née* Bingham); *m* 1974, Kazuko Yanagawa; one *d*. *Educ:* Bancroft's Sch., Essex (Drapers' Co. Schol.); Birmingham Univ. (BSc Mech. Engrg). Lectr, Komazawa Univ., Tokyo, 1968–71; self-employed, Japanese Engineering Translation and Consultancy, 1971–78; British Museum: Res. Asst, Dept of Oriental Antiquities, 1978–87; Asst Keeper of Japanese Antiquities, 1987–97. Vis. Prof., Meiji Univ., Tokyo, 2005. Consultant, Japanese Dept, Christie's, 2005. Pres., Tokenkai of GB, 1999; Past Pres., Eur. Kendo Fedn; Past Vice Pres., Internat. Kendo Fedn. Trustee, Chiddingstone Castle until 2002. Mem., HAC. Metropolitan Special Constable, 1980–2003. Hon. Librarian, Japan Soc., 2006; Hon. Curator, Khalili collection of Japanese Art, 2006. Jubilee Medal; Japanese Foreign Minister's Commendation, 2008. *Publications:* A Book of Five Rings, 1974 (trans. several languages); Swords of the Samurai, 1990; Kamakura: the renaissance of Japanese sculpture, 1991; Japanese Imperial Craftsmen, 1994; Netsuke: the Hull Grundy collection, 1987; (jtly) Masterpieces of Japanese Art, 1991; (ed) Shinto: the sacred art of ancient Japan, 2001; (jtly) William Gowland: the father of Japanese archeology (Japanese/English), 2002; Cutting Edge: Japanese swords in the British Museum collection, 2004; Art of the Samurai, 2009. *Recreation:* Kendo-Japanese sword-fencing. *Club:* Nenriki Kendo (Pres.).

HARRIS, Sir (Theodore) Wilson, Kt 2010; CCH 1991; *b* 24 March 1921; *m* 1st, 1945, Cecily Carew; 2nd, 1959, Margaret Whitaker (*née* Burns). *Educ:* Queen's Coll., Georgetown, British Guiana. Studied land surveying, British Guiana, 1939, and subseq. qualified to practice; led many survey parties (mapping and geomorphological research) in the interior; Senior Surveyor, Projects, for Govt of British Guiana, 1955–58. Came to live in London, 1959. Writer in Residence, Univ. of West Indies and Univ. of Toronto, 1970; Commonwealth Fellow, Leeds Univ., 1971; Vis. Prof., Univ. of Texas at Austin, 1972; Guggenheim Fellow, 1973; Henfield Fellow, UEA, 1974; Southern Arts Writer's Fellowship, 1976; Guest Lectr, Univ. of Mysore, 1978; Vis. Lectr, Yale Univ., 1979; Writer in Residence: Univ. of Newcastle, Australia, 1979; Univ. of Qld, Australia, 1986; Vis. Prof., Univ. of Texas at Austin, 1981–82; Regents' Lectr, Univ. of California, 1983. Hon. DLit Univ. of West Indies, 1984; Hon. DLitt: Kent at Canterbury, 1988; Essex, 1996; Macerata (Italy), 1999; Liège, 2001. Guyana Prize for Fiction, 1985–87; Premio Mondello dei Cinque Continenti, 1992. *Publications:* Eternity to Season (poems, privately printed), 1954; Palace of the Peacock, 1960, 4th edn 1998; The Far Journey of Oudin, 1961; The Whole Armour, 1962; The Secret Ladder, 1963; Heartland, 1964; The Eye of the Scarecrow, 1965; The Waiting Room, 1967; Tradition, the Writer and Society: Critical Essays, 1967; Tumatumari, 1968; Ascent to Omai, 1970; The Sleepers of Roraima (a Carib Trilogy), 1970; The Age of the Rainmakers, 1971; Black Marsden, 1972; Companions of the Day and Night, 1975; Da Silva da Silva's Cultivated Wilderness (filmed, 1987), and Genesis of the Clowns, 1977; The Tree of the Sun, 1978; Explorations (essays), 1981; The Angel at the Gate, 1982; The Womb of Space: the cross-cultural imagination, 1983; Carnival, 1985; The Infinite Rehearsal, 1987; The Four Banks of the River of Space, 1990; The Radical Imagination (essays), 1992; Resurrection at Sorrow Hill, 1993; Jonestown, 1996; Selected Essays, 1999; The Dark Jester, 2001; The Mask of the Beggar, 2003; The Ghost of Memory, 2006. *Address:* c/o Faber and Faber, Bloomsbury House, 74–77 Great Russell Street, WC1B 3DA.

HARRIS, Thomas, (Tom); *b* 20 Feb. 1964; *s* of Tom Harris and Rita Harris (*née* Ralston); *m* 1998. *Educ:* Garnock Acad., Kilbirnie, Ayrshire; Napier Coll., Edinburgh (SHND Journalism). Trainee Reporter, E Kilbride News, 1986–88; Reporter, Paisley Daily Express, 1988–90; Press Officer: Labour Party in Scotland, 1990–92; Strathclyde Regl Council, 1993–96; Sen. Media Officer, Glasgow CC, 1996; PR Manager, E Ayrshire Council, 1996–98; Chief PR and Marketing Officer, Strathclyde PTE, 1998–2001. MP (Lab) Glasgow, Cathcart, 2001–05, Glasgow S, 2005–15; contested (Lab) same seat, 2015. Parly Under-Sec. of State, DfT, 2006–08; Shadow Minister for Envmt, Food and Rural Affairs, 2012–13. Mem., Select Cttee on Transport, 2010–12 and 2013–15, on Admin, 2010 and 2013–15. *Recreations:* tennis, astronomy, hill walking, cinema.

HARRIS, Sir Thomas (George), KBE 2002; CMG 1995; HM Diplomatic Service, retired; Chairman, European Services Forum, since 2010; *b* 6 Feb. 1945; *s* of late Kenneth James Harris and of Dorothy Harris; *m* 1967, Mei-Ling Hwang; three *s*. *Educ:* Haberdashers' Aske's School; Gonville and Caius College, Cambridge. MA. Board of Trade, 1966–69; British Embassy, Tokyo, 1969–71; Asst Private Sec. to Minister for Aerospace, 1971–72; Dept of Trade, 1972–76; Cabinet Office, 1976–78; Principal Private Sec. to Sec. of State for Trade, 1978–79; Asst Sec., Dept of Trade, 1979–83; HM Diplomatic Service: Counsellor (Commercial), British Embassy, Washington, 1983–88; Head of Chancery, Lagos, 1988–90; Dep. High Comr, Nigeria, 1990–91; Head, East African Dept, 1991–92, African Dept (Equatorial), 1992–94, FCO; Ambassador, Repub. of Korea, 1994–97; Dir-Gen., Export Promotion, DTI, 1997–99 (on secondment); Dir-Gen., Trade and Investment in the US, and Consul-Gen., NY, 1999–2004. Vice-Chm., Standard Chartered Bank Ltd, 2004–14. Special Advr, Center for Strategic and Internat. Studies, Washington, 2004–08. Chairman: Pakistan Britain Trade and Investment Forum, 2006–12; Taiwan Britain Business Council, 2007–13; Trade Policy Adv. Gp, British Bankers' Assoc., 2007–13. Member: Internat. Adv. Bd, BritishAmerican Business, 2004–; Indonesian British Business Council, 2004–12; UK-Korea Forum for the Future, 2004–14; Philippine-British Business Council, 2004–15; Korea Britain Business Council, 2007–12; Saudi British Jt Business Council, 2005–12; Singapore British Business Council, 2005–12; Transatlantic Task Force on Trade and Investment, 2011–12. Non-executive Director: Biocompatibles plc, 2005–11; ISFL Ltd, 2007–10; Johnson Matthey plc, 2009–12; SC First Bank, Korea, 2009–14; City UK Ltd, 2010–14. Trustee: Imperial War Mus., 2005–09; Asia House, London, 2005–10; Confucius Business Inst., LSE, 2011–14; Imperial War Mus. Develt Trust, 2012–. *Publications:* (contrib.) Conflict and Consensus, 1985; (contrib.) Reforming the City: responses to the global financial crisis, 2009; contribs to Jl of Korean Hist. of Sci. Society, Thunderbird Internat. Business Rev., Asian Affairs. *Address:* 8 Oakeshott Avenue, Highgate, N6 6NS. *Club:* Oxford and Cambridge.

HARRIS, Victor; *see* Harris, T. V.

HARRIS, William; *see* Harris, J. R. W.

HARRIS, Prof. William Anthony, PhD; FRS 2007; Professor of Anatomy, since 1997 and Head, Department of Physiology, Development and Neuroscience, since 2006, Cambridge University; Fellow, Clare College, Cambridge, since 1997; *b* 26 Nov. 1950; *s* of Louis Jacob Harris and Helen Gallendar Harris; *m* 1983, Christine Elizabeth Holt, *qv*; one *s* one *d*. *Educ:* Univ. of Calif, Berkeley (BA); California Inst. of Technol. (PhD 1976). Jun. Fellow, Harvard Univ., 1977–80; Faculty Mem., Univ. of Calif, San Diego, 1980–97; engaged in res. on genetic and molecular basis of neural develt. Co-founder, DanioLabs, 2002–. FMedSci 2007. Hd Coach, Cambridge Univ. Ice Hockey Club. *Publications:* Genetic Neurobiology, 1982; Development of the Nervous System, 2000, 3rd edn 2012. *Recreations:* ice-hockey, painting. *Address:* Department of Physiology, Development and Neuroscience, Cambridge University, Downing Street, Cambridge CB2 3DY. *T:* (01223) 766137.

HARRIS, Sir Wilson; *see* Harris, Sir T. W.

HARRIS, Winifred Anne Charlotte, (Lady Normington), CBE 2007; Director, Joint International Unit, Department for Work and Pensions, Department for Business, Innovation and Skills (formerly Department for Innovation, Universities and Skills), and Department for Children, Schools and Families (formerly Department for Education and Skills), 2006–09; *b* 1 Jan. 1947; *d* of Leslie Frank Harris and Winifred Maisie Bissett Harris (*née* Wilson); *m* 1985, David John Normington (*see* Sir D. J. Normington). *Educ:* Univ. of Aberdeen (MA Hons Hist. 1969). Private Sec. to Sec. of State for Employment, 1974; First Sec. (Labour), British Embassy, Brussels, 1980–84; Area Manager (W London), MSC, 1985–86; Dir, Individual Conciliation, ACAS, 1986–88; Hd, Financial Mgt Services, 1988–91, Regl Dir, London, 1992–96, Dept for Employment; Hd, EU Div., DFEE, 1997–2003; Dep. Dir, Internat., Home Office, 2003–06. Mem., Educn Adv. Bd, Dulwich Picture Gall., 2010–. Gov., Hackney Community Coll., 2010–; Mem., Bd of Govs, Univ. of Winchester, 2011– (Vice Chm., 2012–). MCIPD 1987. *Recreations:* opera, ballet, music, walking, gardening, reading, collecting antique fans.

HARRISON; *see* Graham-Harrison.

HARRISON, family name of **Baron Harrison**.

HARRISON, Baron *cr* 1999 (Life Peer), of Chester in the county of Cheshire; **Lyndon Henry Arthur Harrison;** *b* 28 Sept. 1947; *s* of late Charles William Harrison and Edith (*née* Johnson); *m* 1980, Hilary Anne Plank; one *s* one *d*. *Educ:* Oxford Sch.; Univ. of Warwick (BA Hons 1970); Univ. of Sussex (MA 1971); Univ. of Keele (MA 1978). Part time Lectr, N Staffs Polytechnic, 1973–75; Research Officer, Students' Union, UMIST, 1975–78; Union Manager, NE Wales Inst. of Higher Educn, Wrexham, 1978–89. Cheshire County Councillor, 1981–90 (Chairman: Libraries and Countryside Cttee, 1982, 1984–89; Further Educn, 1984–89; Tourism, 1985–89). Dep. Chm., NW Tourist Bd, 1987–89. MEP (Lab) Cheshire W, 1989–94, Cheshire W and Wirral, 1994–99. European Parliament: Lab spokesman on monetary union, and on ASEAN and Korea, 1994–99; Vice-President: Tourism Intergp, 1995–99; Small and Med. Size Enterprises Intergp, 1995–99. Vice Chm., ACC, 1990–97. Liaison Peer, NI Office, 2000–02; Mem., H of L Cttee on Common Foreign and Security Policy, 2000–03, on Social Policy, 2003–07, on Hybrid Instruments, 2003–, on EU, 2004–; Chm., H of L Cttee on Econ. and Financial Affairs (formerly on Econ. and Financial Affairs and Internat. Trade), 2010–. H of L Rep. on internat. trade affairs to IPU and Delegate to Parly Assembly of WTO, 2012–14. *Recreations:* chess, bridge, the arts, sport. *Address:* House of Lords, SW1A 0PW.

HARRISON, Prof. Alan, TD 1983 (Bar 1989, 2nd Bar 1995); PhD; FDSRCS; FDSRCSE; Professor of Dental Care of the Elderly, University of Bristol, 1987–2004, now Emeritus; *b* 24 July 1944; *s* of Lt-Col John Thomas West Harrison and Mona Evelyn (*née* Gee); *m* 1st, 1967, Pauline Lilian (*née* Rendell) (marr. diss. 1980); one *s* one *d*; 2nd, 1982, Margaret Ann (*née* Frost); two *d*. *Educ:* Rydal Sch., Colwyn Bay; Univ. of Wales (BDS, PhD). FDS RCS; FDSRCSE *ad hominem*; FADM. Lectr, Dental Sch. Cardiff, 1970–78; Sen. Lectr and Hon. Consultant, Univ. of Leeds, 1978–87. Vis. Asst Prof., Univ. of South Carolina, 1974–75. Mem., Inst. for Learning and Teaching in Higher Educn, 2002–. OC 390 Field Dental Team (V), 1971–73; CO 308 Evacuation Hosp. RAMC(V), 1989–94; CO 306 Field Hosp. RAMC(V), 1994–95; Hon. Col Comdt RADC, 1996–2001; Col RADC(V), 1989–2005. QHDS 1996–99. Hon. Fellow, Cardiff Univ., 2006. *Publications:* Overdentures in General Dental Practice, 1988, 3rd edn 1993; Complete Dentures: problem solving, 1999; over 160 publications in scientific jls. *Recreations:* walking, woodworking, digital photography. *E:* alan.harrison@bristol.ac.uk.

HARRISON, Alistair; *see* Harrison, W. A.

HARRISON, Prof. Andrew, DPhil; FRSE; Chief Executive Officer, Diamond Light Source Ltd, since 2014; *b* Oxford, 3 Oct. 1959; *s* of Prof. Martin Harrison and Wendy Harrison; *m* 1988, Alison Charlotte; three *d*. *Educ:* Newcastle-under-Lyme High Sch.; St John's Coll., Oxford (BA; DPhil). Royal Soc. Univ. Res. Fellow, Univ. of Oxford, 1988–92; Lectr, then Reader, 1992–99, Prof. of Solid State Chem., 1999–2006, Univ. of Edinburgh; Associate Dir, 2006–11, Dir Gen., 2011–13, Institut Laue Langevin. Res. Fellow, McMaster Univ., 1989. FRSE 2002. *Publications:* Fractals in Chemistry, 1995; over 100 articles in learned jls. *Recreations:* ski-ing, snowboarding, cycling on and off road, hillwalking. *Address:* Diamond Light Source Ltd, Diamond House, Harwell Science and Innovation Campus, Didcot, Oxon OX11 0DE. *T:* (01235) 778811, *Fax:* (01235) 778499. *E:* andrew.harrison@diamond.ac.uk.

HARRISON, (Anne) Victoria, (Lady Harrison), DPhil; Executive Secretary (Chief Executive), Wolfson Foundation, 1997–2006; *d* of Lawrence Greggain and Amy Isabel Greggain (*née* Briggs); *m* 1967, Brian Howard Harrison (*see* Sir Brian Harrison). *Educ:* Workington GS; Milham Ford Sch., Oxford; St Anne's Coll., Oxford (BA 1st Cl. Hons Animal Physiology 1965; Theodore Williams Schol. 1965; MA 1970; DPhil 1970). Exec. Editor, Internat. Abstracts of Biological Scis, 1971–72; MRC HQ Office, 1972–83, PSO, 1974; seconded to Science and Technology Secretariat, Cabinet Office, 1983–85, Dep. to Chief Scientific Advr, 1984–85; Head of Secretariat, MRC, 1985–89; Head of Policy Div., AFRC, 1989–94; Dir of Policy and Assessment, BBSRC, 1994–97; Consultant, DIPEx Charity, 2007–10. Mem. Bd, Inst. of Sports and Exercise Medicine, 2007–13. Trustee: Comparative Clinical Sci. Foundn, 2007–; UCL Hosps Charity, 2007– (Chm., 2015–); Hearing Dogs for Deaf People, 2011–. *Recreations:* phoning friends from the bath, armchair gardening. *Address:* The Book House, Yarnells Hill, Oxford OX2 9BG. *Clubs:* Athenæum, Royal Society of Medicine.

HARRISON, Air Vice-Marshal Anthony John, CB 1997; CBE 1992 (OBE 1986); JP; Executive Vice-President and General Manager, Singapore, BAE SYSTEMS (formerly British Aerospace) plc, 1998–2005; *b* 9 Nov. 1943; *s* of Jack and Jean Harrison; *m* 1965, Glynn Dene Hyland-Smith; one *s* one *d*. *Educ:* Woodbridge Sch., Suffolk. Commnd RAF, 1963; Commanding Officer: 617 Sqdn (The Dambusters), 1982–85; RAF Bruggen, 1989–92; Dir, Jt Warfare, MoD, 1992–94; ACDS (Ops), MoD, 1994–97. Upper Freeman, GAPAN, 1985. Pres., Woodbridge RAF Assoc., 1994. FRAeS. JP Devon, 2007. *Recreations:* golf, tennis, aviation history. *Address:* Chudleigh Knighton, Devon. *Club:* Royal Air Force.

HARRISON, Sir Brian (Howard), Kt 2005; DPhil; FBA 2005; FRHistS; Emeritus Fellow of Corpus Christi College, Oxford, since 2004; Titular Professor of Modern History, University of Oxford, 1996–2004; *b* 9 July 1937; *s* of Howard Harrison and Mary Elizabeth (*née* Savill); *m* 1967, Anne Victoria Greggain (*see* A. V. Harrison). *Educ:* Merchant Taylors' Sch., Northwood; St John's Coll., Oxford (BA 1st Cl. Hons Mod. Hist. 1961; MA 1966; DPhil 1966; Hon. Fellow, 2010). FRHistS 1973. Nat. Service, 2nd Lieut, Malta Signal Sqdn, 1956–58. Oxford University: Sen. Schol., St Antony's Coll., 1961–64; Jun. Res. Fellow, Nuffield Coll., 1964–67; Fellow and Tutor in Modern Hist. and Pols, 1967–2000, Official Fellow, 2000–04, Sen. Tutor, 1984–86 and 1988–90, Vice-Pres., 1992, 1993 and 1996–98, CCC; Univ. Reader in Modern British History, 1990–2000. Editor, Oxford DNB, 2000–04. Visiting Professor: Univ. of Michigan (Ann Arbor), 1970–71; Harvard Univ., 1973–74; Visiting Fellow: Melbourne Univ., 1975; ANU, 1995. *Publications:* Drink and the Victorians, 1971, 2nd edn 1994; Separate Spheres: the opposition to women's suffrage in Britain, 1978; (ed with P. Hollis) Robert Lowery: Chartist and lecturer, 1979; Peaceable Kingdom: stability and change in modern Britain, 1982; (with C. Ford) A Hundred Years Ago: Britain in the 1880s in words and photographs, 1983; Prudent Revolutionaries: portraits of British feminists between the wars, 1987; (ed and contrib.) The History of the University of Oxford, Vol. 8: The Twentieth Century, 1994; (ed) Corpuscles: a history of Corpus Christi College, Oxford, 1994; The Transformation of British Politics 1860–1995, 1996; (ed jtly and contrib.) Civil Histories: essays presented to Sir Keith Thomas, 2000; New Oxford History of England series: Seeking a Role: the United Kingdom 1951–1970, 2009; Finding a Role?: the United Kingdom 1970–1990, 2010. *Recreations:* looking at architecture, cooking, listening to classical music. *Address:* The Book House, Yarnells Hill, Oxford OX2 9BG.

HARRISON, Prof. Bryan Desmond, CBE 1990; PhD; FRS 1987; FRSE; Professor of Plant Virology, University of Dundee, 1991–96, now Professor Emeritus; *b* 16 June 1931; *s* of John William and Norah Harrison; *m* 1968, Elizabeth Ann Latham-Warde; two *s* one *d*. *Educ:* Whitgift Sch., Croydon; Reading Univ. (BSc Hons Agric. Bot. 1952); London Univ. (PhD 1955). FRSE 1979. Postgraduate student, ARC, 1952; Scottish Hort. Res. Inst., Dundee, 1954; Rothamsted Exp. Station, 1957; Head, Virology Section, 1966, Dep. Dir, 1979, Scottish Hort. Res. Inst.; Head, Virology Dept, Scottish Crop Res. Inst., 1981–91. Visiting Professor: Japan Soc. for Promotion of Science, 1970; Organization of American States, Venezuela, 1973; Hon. Prof., Univ. of St Andrews, 1986–99; Hon. Vis. Prof., Univ. of Dundee, 1988–91; Hon. Res. Fellow (formerly Hon. Res. Prof.), James Hutton Inst. (formerly Scottish Crop Res. Inst.), 1991–; Vis. Prof., Univ. of Zhejiang, China, 2001–. Pres., Assoc. of Applied Biologists, 1980–81. Life Mem., Internat. Cttee for Taxonomy of Viruses, 1997. Hon. Member: Assoc. of Applied Biologists, 1989; Soc. for Gen. Microbiol., 1990; Phytopathological Soc. of Japan, 1992; For. Associate, US Nat. Acad. of Scis, 1998. Hon. DAgrFor Univ. of Helsinki, 1990. *Publications:* Plant Virology: the principles (with A. J. Gibbs), 1976 (trans. Russian and Chinese); research papers and reviews on plant viruses and virus diseases. *Recreations:* growing garden crops, foreign travel. *Address:* James Hutton Institute, Invergowrie, Dundee DD2 5DA. *T:* (01382) 562731, *Fax:* (01382) 562426.

HARRISON, Bryan James; management consultant, 2001–12; *b* 30 Oct. 1947; *s* of late James Harrison and Doris Harrison (*née* Burnham); *m* 1st, 1973 (marr. diss. 1988); two *d*; 2nd, 1990, Valerie Mayo; one *d*. *Educ:* Southmoor Sch., Sunderland; Exeter Univ. (BA Politics). DHSS, 1971–81; seconded to Camden and Islington AHA, 1981–82; Dist Administrator, Islington HA, 1982–84; District General Manager: Islington HA, 1984–88; Bloomsbury HA, 1988–90; Bloomsbury and Islington HA, 1990–92; Regl Gen. Manager, NE Thames RHA, 1992–94; Chief Exec., Forest Healthcare NHS Trust, 1995–99; Special Advr, Workforce and Develt, NHS Exec., 1999–2001. Non-exec. Dir, Barnet PCT, 2004–11. Trustee and Mem. Council, Marie Curie Cancer Care, 2002–08. *Recreations:* golf, reading, music, soccer, art.

HARRISON, Rev. Cameron Elias; international consultant on education policy; Director, Harrison Leimon Associates, since 2002; *b* 27 Aug. 1945; *s* of Elias Harrison and Herries Harrison; *m* 1968, Pearl Leimon; one *s* one *d*. *Educ:* Cumnock Acad.; Strathclyde Univ. (BSc Hons Physics); Stirling Univ. (MEd). Physics Teacher, Greenock Acad., 1968–71; Head of Physics, Graeme High Sch., 1971–79; Depute Rector, Kirkcudbright Acad., 1979–82; Rector, The Gordon Schools, 1982–91; Chief Exec., Scottish Consultative Council on the Curriculum, 1991–98. Sec.-Gen., Consortium of Instns for Develt & Res. in Educn in Europe, 1993–97; Dir, Inst. for Educnl Policy, Open Soc. Inst., Budapest, 1998–2002. Ordained, C of S, 2006; Assoc. Minister, Church of the Holy Trinity, St Andrews, 2008–. FRSA. *Publications:* Managing Change, 1989. *Recreations:* walking, singing, talking, listening, teaching, learning. *Address:* St Andrews, Fife.

HARRISON, Caroline Mary Alice; QC 2013; *b* Haslingden, Lancs, 31 Dec. 1961; *d* of Peter Harrison and Patricia Harrison. *Educ:* Regent's Park Coll., Oxford (BA Philos. and Theol.); City Univ., London (DipLaw); King's Coll. London (MA Med. Law and Ethics). Called to the Bar, Lincoln's Inn, 1986; barrister in ind. practice, 1986–. Member: Gene Therapy Adv. Cttee, 1999–2009; Human Genetics Commn, 2004–12; Nat. Res. Ethics Expert Adv. Panel, 2010–12. *Recreations:* music (especially opera and early church music), art (especially portraits), wine, fly fishing, running. *Address:* 2 Temple Gardens, EC4Y 9AY. *T:* (020) 7822 1200, *Fax:* (020) 7822 1300. *E:* charrison@2tg.co.uk. *Club:* Royal Automobile.

HARRISON, Charles Rupert; Organist and Master of the Choristers, Chichester Cathedral, since 2014; *b* Nottingham, 21 March 1974; *s* of Richard and Valerie Harrison. *Educ:* Minster Sch., Southwell; Jesus Coll., Cambridge (BA 1995; MA 2000). Asst Organist, Carlisle Cathedral, 1995–99; Dir of Music, St George's Church, Belfast, 2000–03; Tutor, QUB, 2000–03; Asst Dir of Music and Sub Organist, Lincoln Cathedral, 2003–14. *Recreations:* theatre, travel, walking, wine, flying, art. *Address:* The Royal Chantry, Cathedral Cloisters, Chichester PO19 1PX. *T:* (01243) 782595, *Fax:* (01243) 812499. *E:* organist@chichestercathedral.org.uk.

HARRISON, Sir Colin; *see* Harrison, Sir R. C.

HARRISON, Rev. Fr Crispin; *see* Harrison, Rev. Fr M. B. C.

HARRISON, Sir David, Kt 1997; CBE 1990; FREng; Fellow, since 1957, and Master, 1994–2000, Selwyn College, Cambridge; *b* 3 May 1930; *s* of Harold David Harrison and Lavinia Wilson; *m* 1962, Sheila Rachel Debes; one *s* one *d* (and one *s* decd). *Educ:* Bede Sch., Sunderland; Clacton County High Sch.; Selwyn Coll., Cambridge (1st Cl. Pts I and II Natural Sciences Tripos, BA 1953, PhD 1956, MA 1957, ScD 1979). CEng, FREng (FEng 1987); FRSC (FRIC 1961), FIChemE 1968. 2nd Lieut, REME, 1949. Cambridge University: Research student, Dept of Physical Chemistry, 1953–56; Univ. Asst Lectr in Chem. Engrg, 1956–61; Univ. Lectr, 1961–79; Sen. Tutor, Selwyn Coll., 1967–79; Mem., Council of the Senate, 1967–75; Mem., Univ. Council, 1995–2000; Dep. Vice-Chancellor, 1995–2000; Pro-Vice-Chancellor, 1997; Chm., Faculty Bd of Educn, 1976–78, of Engrg, 1994–2001; Vice-Chancellor: Univ. of Keele, 1979–84; Univ. of Exeter, 1984–94. Visiting Professor of Chemical Engineering: Univ. of Delaware, USA, 1967; Univ. of Sydney, 1976. Chm., Adv. Cttee on Safety in Nuclear Installations, 1993–99; Mem., Engineering Council, 1994–96. Hon. Editor, Trans Instn of Chemical Engrs, 1972–78; Member Council: Lancing Coll., 1970–82; Haileybury, 1974–84; St Edward's, Oxford, 1977–89; Bolton Girls' Sch., 1981–84; Shrewsbury Sch., 1983–2003 (Chm., 1989–2003); Taunton Sch., 1986–89; Fellow, Woodard Corporation of Schools, 1972–94; Chairman: Bd of Trustees, Homerton Coll., Cambridge, 1979–2010; UCCA, 1984–91; Voluntary Sector Consultative Council, 1984–88; Southern Univs Jt Bd, 1986–88; Church and Associated Colls Adv. Cttee, PCFC, 1988–91; CVCP, 1991–93; Bd of Management, Northcott Theatre, 1984–94; Eastern Arts Bd, 1994–98 (Mem., Arts Council of England, 1996–98); Council, RSCM, 1996–2005; Ely Cathedral Council, 2000–. Pres., IChemE, 1991–92 (Vice-Pres., 1989–91); Dir, Salters' Inst. of Industrial Chemistry, 1993–2015. Mem., Marshall Aid Commemoration Commn, 1982–89. FRSA 1985; FRSCM 2005; CCMI (CBIM 1990). Freeman, City of London, 1998; Liveryman, Salters' Co., 1998. DUniv: Keele, 1992; York, 2008; Hon. DSc Exeter, 1995. George E.

Davis Medal, IChemE, 2001. *Publications:* (with J. F. Davidson) Fluidised Particles, 1963; (also with J. F. Davidson) Fluidization, 1971, rev. edn (with J. F. Davidson and R. Clift) 1985; numerous articles in scientific and technological jls. *Recreations:* music, tennis, hill walking, good food. *Address:* 7 Gough Way, Cambridge CB3 9LN. *T:* (01223) 359315. *E:* sirdavidharrison@gmail.com. *Clubs:* Athenæum, Oxford and Cambridge; Federation House (Stoke-on-Trent).

HARRISON, Prof. David James, MD; FRCPath, FRCPE, FRCSE; John Reid Professor of Pathology, University of St Andrews, since 2012; Head of Specialty Pathology, NHS Lothian, since 2009; Honorary Consultant in Histopathology, Royal Infirmary of Edinburgh, since 1991; *b* Belfast, 24 March 1959. *Educ:* Campbell Coll., Belfast; Univ. of Edinburgh (BSc Hons 1980; MB ChB 1983; MD 1990). FRCPath 1998; FRCPE 2003; FRCSE 2003. University of Edinburgh: Lectr, 1986–91, Sen. Lectr, 1991–97, Reader, 1997–98, in Pathol.; Prof. of Pathol., 1998–2012; Hd, Div. of Pathol., 1998–2012; Dir, Cancer Res. Centre, 2005–08; Dir, Breakthrough Breast Cancer Res. Unit, 2007–12; Hon. Prof., Coll. of Medicine and Veterinary Medicine, 2012–; Clin. Dir, Pathol. Directorate, Lothian Univ. Hosps Div., 2001–04. Adjunct Professor: in Medicinal Chemistry, Univ. of Florida, Gainesville, 2003–; of Pathol. and Forensic Educn, Univ. of Canberra, 2004–. Chm., Med. Res. Scotland, 2009– (Mem., Scientific Adv. Bd, 2007–); Member: Biomed. and Therapeutics Res. Cttee, Chief Scientist Office, Scotland, 1998–2008 (Dep. Chm.); DoH Gene Therapy Adv. Cttee, 2000–09 (Vice-Chm., 2006–09); DoH Cttee on Carcinogenicity of Chemicals in Food, Consumer Products and the Envmt, 2000–09; Food Standards Agency/DoH Cttee on Toxicity of Chemicals in Food, Consumer Products and the Envmt, 2007–. MRC Coll. of Experts Physiological Systems and Clin. Scis Bd, 2004–; Member: CRUK Strat. Adv. Gp, 2006–; Scientific Adv. Cttee, Yorks Cancer Research, 2007–. Trustee, Melville Trust for Care and Cure of Cancer, 2008. *Publications:* (ed jtly) Muir's Textbook of Pathology, 14th edn 2008; contrib. chapters in books and jls. *Recreations:* EMMS Nazareth charity (Chm. 2002–) which operates a hospital and nursing school in the Middle East, music, hill walking. *Address:* Medical and Biological Sciences Building, University of St Andrews, North Haugh, St Andrews, Fife KY16 9TF.

HARRISON, Denis Byrne; Local Government Ombudsman, 1974–81 and Vice-Chairman, Commission for Local Administration, 1975–81; *b* 11 July 1917; *y s* of late Arthur and Priscilla Harrison; *m* 1956, Alice Marion Vickers (*d* 1989), *e d* of late Hedley Vickers. *Educ:* Birkenhead Sch.; Liverpool Univ. (LLM). Legal Associate Mem. RTPI, 1949. Articled to E. W. Tame, OBE (Town Clerk of Birkenhead); admitted Solicitor, 1939. Served War, 1939–46: 75th Shropshire Yeo. (Medium Regt) RA; 168 Field Regt RA; Combined Ops Bombardment Unit; took part in Normandy campaign landing on D-Day with Queen's Own Rifles of Canada; an assault bn of 3rd Canadian Div. and in battle for mouth of River Scheldt landing with 41 RM Commando on Walcheren; Staff Captain at HQ of OC, Cyprus. First Asst Solicitor, Wolverhampton Co. Borough, 1946–49; Dep. Town Clerk of Co. Boroughs: Warrington, 1949–57; Bolton, 1957–63; Sheffield, 1963–66; Town Clerk and CEO, Sheffield, 1966–74. Member: Advisory Council on Noise, 1970–79; Cttee on the use of valuers in the public service, 1972–73. Mem. Council, 1975–82, Pro-Chancellor, 1980–82, Univ. of Sheffield. Hon. Sec., Trustees, building of Crucible Theatre. JP City of London, 1976–86. *Recreations:* reading, music, walking (London-Ventimiglia, 1989, London-Milan, 1990). *Address:* 2 Leicester Close, Henley-on-Thames, Oxon RG9 2LD. *T:* (01491) 572782.

HARRISON, (Desmond) Roger (Wingate); Chairman, Toynbee Hall, 1990–2002; Deputy Chairman, Capital Radio, 1991–2000 (Director, 1975–2000); *b* 9 April 1933; *s* of late Maj.-Gen. Desmond Harrison, CB, DSO and Kathleen Harrison (*née* Hazley); *m* 1965, Victoria Lee-Barber, MVO, *d* of Rear-Adm. John Lee-Barber, CB, DSO; three *d* (and one *s* one *d* decd). *Educ:* Rugby School; Worcester College, Oxford (MA); Harvard Univ. Business Sch. Writing freelance, principally for The Times, 1951–57; joined staff of The Times, 1957–67; The Observer: joined 1967; Dir, 1970–92; Jt Managing Dir, 1977–84; Chief Exec., 1984–87. Dir, The Oak Foundn, 1987–89. Chairman: Greater Manchester Cablevision, 1990–93; Sterling Publishing, 1993–96; Director: LWT and LWT (Holdings), 1976–94; Sableknight, 1981–; Trinity International Holdings, 1991–2003. Chairman: Asylum Aid, 1991–98; Royal Acad. of Dancing, 1993–2006. Governor, Sadler's Wells, 1984–95. Vice Pres., Hampshire Wildlife Trust, 2011–. *Recreations:* theatre, environment issues, tennis. *Address:* Itchen Stoke Mill, Alresford SO24 0RA. *Clubs:* Beefsteak, Flyfishers'.

See also H. K. Harrison.

HARRISON, Edward Peter Graham, (Ted), PhD; writer, painter, cartoonist, television producer and broadcaster; *b* 14 April 1948; *s* of Rev. Peter Harrison and Joan Harrison; *m* 1968, Helen Grace Waters; one *s* one *d*. *Educ:* Grenville Coll., Bideford, Devon; University of Kent at Canterbury (BA 1968; PhD Theol. 1998); Univ. for the Creative Arts (MA Fine Art 2010). Graduate trainee, Kent Messenger, 1968–72; Reporter: Morgan-Grampian Magazines, 1972; Southern Television, 1970–73; BBC World Service, Radio 4 You and Yours, 1972–80; BBC Radio 4 Sunday, 1972–88; BBC TV Scotland Current Account, 1981–83; Presenter and Reporter, BBC Radio Scotland News and Current Affairs, 1980–85; Reporter: BBC Radio 4 World Tonight, 1981–83; BBC Radio 4 World at One and PM, 1983–87; Presenter: Radio 4 Opinions, 1986–87; Radio 4 Sunday, 1986–88 and Soundings, 1985–88; ITV series The Human Factor, 1986–92; Channel 4 series on Lambeth Conf., 1988; BBC Religious Affairs Corresp., 1988–89; presenter, Does He Take Sugar?, Radio 4, 1991–95; series ed., Ultimate Questions, ITV, 2000; dir, animation series, Wise and Wonderful, 2002; producer: Redcoats, ITV, 2003–04; Essentials of Faith, ITV, 2005; Mosque, ITV, 2005. Dir, Pilgrim Productions, Canterbury, 1992–2008; Founder, Unst Animation Studio, 2000. Contested (L) gen. elections: Bexley, 1970; Maidstone, Feb. 1974. London exhibition of caricatures, 1977; exhibition of watercolours, Oxford, Canterbury, 1981; exhibn of cartoons and paintings, Rutherford Coll., Canterbury, 2010; art installation, Innocence Betrayed, St Paul's Cathedral, 2011; Cherry Tree, artwork to honour organ donors, Guy's Hosp., 2015; exhibitions: Stations of the Cross: Forces of Creation, Norwich Cathedral, 2013; North, South-East, George's Hse Gall., Folkestone, 2013; Stations of the Cross and The Twelve Apostles, St David's Cathedral, 2014; Unst Modern, Shetland, 2014; Llandaff Cathedral, 2015. *Publications:* Modern Elizabethans, 1977; (jtly) McIndoe's Army, 1978; Marks of the Cross, 1981; Commissioner Catherine, 1983; Much Beloved Daughter, 1984; The Durham Phenomenon, 1985; Living with kidney failure, 1990; Kriss Akabusi—on track, 1991; The Elvis People, 1992; Members Only, 1994; Stigmata: a medieval mystery for a modern age, 1994; Letters to a friend I never knew, 1995; Disability: rights and wrongs, 1995; Tanni, 1996; Defender of the Faith, 1996; Diana: icon and sacrifice, 1998; Beyond Dying, 2000; Will the next Archbishop please stand up?, 2002; Diana: myth and reality, 2006; King Clone, 2010; From the Ridiculous to the Sublime, 2010; Remembrance Today, 2012; Apocalypse When?, 2012; (with R. Coles) Lives of the Improbable Saints, 2012; (with R. Coles) Legends of the Improbable Saints, 2013; Tales of Three Popes, 2014. *Recreation:* drawing caricatures of friends and foes.

HARRISON, George; *see* Harrison, S. G.

HARRISON, (George) Michael (Antony), CBE 1980; Chief Education Officer, City of Sheffield, 1967–85; *b* 7 April 1925; *s* of George and Kathleen Harrison; *m* 1951, Pauline (*née* Roberts); two *s* one *d*. *Educ:* Manchester Grammar Sch.; Brasenose Coll., Oxford. MA (Lit. Hum.); DipEd. Military service, Lieut, 3rd Recce and Parachute Regt, 1947. Asst Master, Bedford Modern Sch., 1951–53; Admin. Asst, W Riding CC, Education Dept, 1953–55; Asst Educn Officer, Cumberland CC Educn Dept, 1955–64; Dep. Educn Officer, Sheffield, 1965–67. Advr, Educn and NVQ Programmes, Dept of Employment, 1985–96. Hon. Research Fellow, Leeds Univ., 1985–89; Associate Prof., Sheffield Univ., 1991–95. Member various cttees, incl.: Taylor Cttee of Enquiry on Govt in Schools, 1975–77; UK Nat. Commn for Unesco Educn Adv. Cttee, 1977–83; Yorkshire and Humberside Econ. Planning Council, 1978–79; Technician Educn Council, 1979–83; Engineering Council, 1982–87; Board, Nat. Adv. Body on Local Authority Higher Educn, 1981–83. Pres., Soc. of Educn Officers, 1976; Vice-Pres., Standing Conf. on Schools' Science and Technology, 1980– (Chm. 1975–79). Vice-Pres., St William's Foundn, York, 1992–95. Hon. LLD Sheffield, 1988. *Recreation:* foreign travel. *Address:* 7 Eaveslea, New Road, Kirkby Lonsdale, Cumbria LA6 2AB. *T:* (015242) 73834. *E:* gmah070425@gmail.com. *W:* www.educando.co.uk.

HARRISON, Prof. Henrietta Katherine, DPhil; FBA 2014; Professor of Modern Chinese Studies, University of Oxford, since 2012; Fellow, St Cross College, Oxford, since 2012; *b* London, 1967; *d* of (Desmond) Roger (Wingate) Harrison, *qv*. *Educ:* St Paul's Sch., Hammersmith; Newnham Coll., Cambridge (BA Classics 1989); Harvard Univ. (MA Regl Studies East Asia 1992); Univ. of Oxford (DPhil Oriental Studies 1996). Fulford Jun. Res. Fellow, St Anne's Coll., Oxford, 1996–98; Lectr in Chinese, Univ. of Leeds, 1999–2006; Prof. of Hist., Harvard Univ., 2006–12. *Publications:* China: inventing the nation, 2001; The Making of the Republican Citizen: ceremonies and symbols in China 1911–1929, 2000; The Man Awakened from Dreams: one man's life in a North China village 1857–1942, 2005; The Missionary's Curse and Other Tales from a Chinese Catholic Village, 2013. *Recreation:* needlework. *Address:* University of Oxford China Centre, Dickson Poon Building, Canterbury Road, Oxford OX2 6LU. *E:* henrietta.harrison@orinst.ox.ac.uk.

HARRISON, John Clive, LVO 1971; HM Diplomatic Service, retired; High Commissioner, Mauritius, 1993–97; *b* 12 July 1937; *s* of Sir Geoffrey Harrison, GCMG, KCVO; *m* 1967, Jennifer Heather Burston; one *s* two *d*. *Educ:* Winchester Coll.; Jesus Coll., Oxford. BA. Entered Foreign Office, 1960; Rangoon, 1961; Vientiane, 1964; FO, 1964; Second, later First, Sec. (Information), Addis Ababa, 1967; Ankara, 1971; seconded to Cabinet Office, 1973; First Sec., FCO, 1976; First Sec., Head of Chancery and Consul, Luxembourg, 1978; Counsellor and Head of Chancery, Lagos, 1981–84; Counsellor, attached to Protocol Dept, FCO, 1984; Hd of Consular Dept, FCO, 1985–89; Dep. High Comr, Islamabad, 1989–93. *Recreations:* gardening, tennis, golf, family holidays. *Address:* Wymering, Sheet Common, Petersfield, Hants GU31 5AT. *Clubs:* Royal Over-Seas League; Petersfield Golf.

HARRISON, Prof. John Fletcher Clews, PhD; Emeritus Professor of History, University of Sussex, since 1985 (Professor of History, 1970–82; Hon. Professor of History, 1982–85); *b* 28 Feb. 1921; *s* of William Harrison and Mary (*née* Fletcher); *m* 1945, Margaret Ruth Marsh; one *s* one *d*. *Educ:* City Boys' Sch., Leicester; Selwyn Coll., Cambridge (Schol. and Prizeman; Goldsmiths' Open Exhibnr in History, BA 1st Cl. Hons 1942, MA 1946); PhD Leeds. Served Army, 1941–45 (overseas 1942–45): commnd, Leics Regt and seconded to KAR, 1942; Captain and Adjt, 17th Bn, KAR, 1943–44; Staff Captain, GSO3, E Africa Comd, 1944–45. Lectr, Dept of Adult Educn and Extra-Mural Studies, Univ. of Leeds, 1947–58; Dep. Dir, Extra-Mural Studies and Dep. Head of Dept, Univ. of Leeds, 1958–61; Prof. of History, Univ. of Wisconsin, USA, 1961–70. Research and teaching (Fulbright Award), Univ. of Wisconsin, 1957–58; Faculty Res. Fellow, SSRC, USA, 1963–64; Vis. Professorial Res. Fellow, ANU, 1968–69 and 1977; Res. Fellow, Harvard Univ., 1972–73; Social Sci. Res. Fellow, Nuffield Foundn, 1975; Vice-Chancellor's Cttee Visitor, NZ, 1977; Herbert F. Johnson Res. Prof., Univ. of Wisconsin, 1977–78; Hon. Prof. of History, Warwick Univ., 1987–92. Vice-Pres., Soc. for Study of Labour History, 1984– (Sec., 1960–61; Chm., 1974–81); Mem., Adv. and Editorial Bds, Victorian Studies, 1963–. Hon. Mem., Phi Beta Kappa, Wisconsin, 1978. *Publications:* A History of the Working Men's College 1854–1954, 1954; Social Reform in Victorian Leeds: The Work of James Hole 1820–1895, 1954; Learning and Living 1790–1960: A Study in the History of the English Adult Education Movement, 1961, Toronto 1961; (ed) Society and Politics in England 1780–1960, NY 1965; (ed) Utopianism and Education: Robert Owen and the Owenites, NY 1968; Quest for the New Moral World: Robert Owen and the Owenites in Britain and America, 1969, NY 1969 (Walter D. Love Meml Prize, USA, 1969); The Early Victorians 1832–1851, 1971, NY 1971; The Birth and Growth of Industrial England 1714–1867, 1973; (ed) Eminently Victorian, 1974; (with Dorothy Thompson) Bibliography of the Chartist Movement 1837–1976, 1978; The Second Coming: Popular Millenarianism 1780–1850, 1979, NJ 1979; The Common People, 1984; Late Victorian Britain 1875–1901, 1990; Scholarship Boy: a personal history of the mid-twentieth century, 1995; *festschriften:* New Views of Co-operation, ed S. Yeo, 1988; Living and Learning, ed I. Dyck and M. Chase, 1996; articles and reviews in Victorian Studies, TLS and usual academic history jls. *Recreations:* walking, gardening, book collecting.

HARRISON, John Seymour H.; *see* Heslop-Harrison.

HARRISON, Kate Elizabeth; Founder Partner, Harrison Grant Solicitors, since 2004; *b* Durham, 25 Nov. 1955; *d* of Jonathan Harrison and Jean Harrison (*née* Bradbury); one *s* one *d*. *Educ:* Nottingham Girls' High Sch.; New Hall, Cambridge (BA 1978); London Sch. of Econs and Pol Sci. (LLM). Admitted solicitor, 1981; solicitor, Lawford & Co., Gordon & James Morton, and Tooting and Balham Law Centre, 1981–85; Senior Lecturer: North East London Poly., 1985–88; Bristol Poly., 1988–92; Hd, Law, Mind (Nat. Assoc. for Mental Health), 1992–97; solicitor, Scott-Moncrieff & Co., 1997–2001; Lawyer, Greenpeace, 2001–03. *Recreations:* music, film, walking. *Address:* Harrison Grant Solicitors, 45 Beech Street, EC2Y 8AD. *T:* (020) 7826 8520. *E:* kateharrison@hglaw.co.uk.

HARRISON, Kaye Barbara; Headteacher, Sutton Coldfield Grammar School for Girls, 2000–10; *b* Romiley, Cheshire, 13 Sept. 1950; *d* of Henry James and Ada Patricia Morris; *m*; marr. diss. *Educ:* York Univ. (BA Maths and Educn 1971; PGCE 1972); Wolverhampton Poly. (MEd 1987). Hd of Maths, Haunton Hall, Tamworth, 1972–75; Teacher of Maths, Woodhouse Sch., Tamworth, 1975–83; Curriculum Co-ordinator and Hd of Maths, Queen Mary's High Sch., Walsall, 1983–92; Headteacher, Newport Girls' High Sch., Shropshire, 1992–2000. Member: Inland Waterways Assoc.; Shropshire Union Canal Soc.; Nat. Women's Register. *Recreations:* theatre, inland waterways, photography, walking.

HARRISON, Kristina, (Mrs J. Pattinson); a District Judge (Magistrates' Courts), since 2005; *b* 5 June 1957; *d* of late John, (Jack), Harrison and of Sybil Mary Harrison; *m* 1985, John Pattinson; one *s* two *d*. *Educ:* Manchester Poly. (BA Hons Law, 1978). Founded Kristina Harrison, Solicitors, Manchester, 1985, specialising in criminal law. *Recreations:* endlessly renovating old houses, all aspects of interior design, collecting handbags. *Address:* Teesside Magistrates' Court, Victoria Square, Middlesbrough TS1 2AS.

HARRISON, Michael; *see* Harrison, G. M. A.

HARRISON, Dr Michael; JP; Chairman and Medical Director, Midlands Health Consultancy Network Ltd, since 1996; *b* 1 March 1939; *s* of Frank Harrison and Ruby Wilhelmina (*née* Proctor); *m* 1962, Ann Haiser; two *d*. *Educ:* Leamington Coll.; Univ. of London (St Mary's Hosp.) (MB BS, BA). LRCP, MRCS, DPH, FFPH, MHSM, FRSPH. Hosp. med. appts, 1964–66; health MO appts, 1966–70; Birmingham RHB, 1971–74; specialist in community medicine, W Midlands RHA, 1974–76; Area MO, Sandwell AHA, 1976–83; Dist MO, 1983–88, Dist Gen. Manager, 1985–88, Sandwell HA; Sen. Clinical Lectr, Univ. of Birmingham, 1988; Regl Dir of Public Health and Regl MO, 1988–93, Exec. Dir, 1990–94, Dep. Chief Exec., 1993–94, West Midlands RHA. Cons. Advr, WHO, 1989. Pres., Assoc. for Industrial Archaeology, 1998. Pres., Droitwich Spa Saltway Rotary Club,

2001–02. FCMI. SBStJ. JP Birmingham, 1980. *Recreations:* sailing, photography, industrial archaeology. *Address:* 19 Sandles Close, Droitwich Spa, Worcs WR9 8RB. *T:* (01905) 798308.

HARRISON, Rev. Fr (Michael Burt) Crispin, CR; Superior of the Community of the Resurrection, Mirfield, 1998–2003; *b* 26 April 1936. *Educ:* Univ. of Leeds (BA Phil. with Hist. 1959); Trinity Coll., Oxford (BA Theol. 1962; MA 1966); Coll. of the Resurrection, Mirfield. Ordained deacon 1963, priest 1964; Curate: St Aidan, W Hartlepool, 1963–64; All Saints, Middlesbrough, 1964–66; licensed to officiate: Dio. Wakefield, 1966–69, 1978–87 and 1998–; Dio. Christ the King, SA, 2003–06; professed, CR, 1968; Tutor, St Peter's Coll. and Lectr, Federal Theol Seminary, S Africa, 1970–77; Tutor, Coll. of the Resurrection, 1978–84, Vice-Principal, 1984–87; Provincial and Prior, St Peter's Priory, Johannesburg, 1987–97; Canon Theologian, Dio. of Christ the King, S Africa, 1990–97. *Address:* House of the Resurrection, Mirfield, W Yorks WF14 0BN. *T:* (01924) 483337, *Fax:* (01924) 490489.

HARRISON, Hon. Sir Michael (Guy Vicat), Kt 1993; a Judge of the High Court of Justice, Queen's Bench Division, 1993–2004; *b* 28 Sept. 1939; *s* of late Hugh Francis Guy Harrison and Elizabeth Alban Harrison (*née* Jones); *m* 1966, Judith (*née* Gist); one *s* one *d. Educ:* Charterhouse; Trinity Hall, Cambridge (MA). Called to the Bar, Gray's Inn, 1965, Bencher, 1993; QC 1983; a Recorder, 1989–93. Dep. Chm., Parly Boundary Commn for England, 1996–2004 (Asst Comr, 1981–93). Chm., Panel for Examination of Structure Plans, Somerset, 1981, Isles of Scilly, 1982, W Sussex, 1986. Trustee, Butler Trust, 2010–. *Recreations:* tennis, sailing, fishing.

HARRISON, Prof. Michael Jackson; Vice-Chancellor, University of Wolverhampton, 1992–98 (Director, Wolverhampton Polytechnic (formerly The Polytechnic, Wolverhampton), 1985–92); *b* 18 Dec. 1941; *s* of Jackson Harrison and Norah (*née* Lees); *m* 1974, Marie Ghislaine Félix. *Educ:* Guildford Tech. Coll.; Univ. of Leicester (BA, MA). Lecturer in Sociology: Enfield Coll. of Technol., 1966–67; Univ. of Leeds, 1967–68; Sen. Lectr, Enfield Coll. of Technol., 1968–72; Principal Lectr, Sheffield City Polytechnic, 1972–76; Head of Dept, Hull Coll. of Higher Educn, 1976–81; Asst Dir, 1982–84, Dep. Dir, 1985, The Polytechnic, Wolverhampton. Vis. Lectr, Univ. of Oregon, 1971. Governor: Bilston Community Coll.; Thomas Telford CTC. FCMI (FBIM 1983). *Publications:* (jtly) A Sociology of Industrialisation, 1978; contribs to learned jls. *Recreations:* cinema, travelling, music. *Address:* 34 Mount Road, Penn, Wolverhampton WV4 5SW. *T:* (01902) 338807.

HARRISON, Sir Michael James Harwood, 2nd Bt *cr* 1961, of Bugbrooke; JP; *b* 28 March 1936; *s* of Sir (James) Harwood Harrison, 1st Bt, TD, MP (C) Eye, Suffolk 1951–79, and Peggy Alberta Mary (*d* 1993), *d* of late Lt-Col V. D. Stenhouse, TD; *S* father, 1980; *m* 1967, Rosamund Louise, *d* of Edward Clive; two *s* two *d. Educ:* Rugby. Served with 17th/21st Lancers, 1955–56. Member of Lloyd's. Mem. Council, Sail Training Assoc., 1966–2005; Vice-Pres., Assoc. of Combined Youth Clubs, 1976–99. Patron and Lord of the Manor, Bugbrooke, Northampton, 1980–. Master, Mercers' Co., 1986–87; Freeman of the City of London. JP London, 1993. *Recreation:* sailing. *Heir: s* Edwin Michael Harwood Harrison, *b* 29 May 1981. *Address:* Rise Cottage, Hasketon, near Woodbridge, Suffolk IP13 6JA. *T:* (01394) 382352. *Club:* Boodle's.

HARRISON, Dr Michelle; Chief Executive Officer, TNS BMRB, since 2009, and Government and Public Sector Practice, since 2013, WPP; *b* Coventry, 1968; *m* 1999, Nicholas Bull; two *s* one *d. Educ:* Higham Lane Comprehensive Sch., Nuneaton; Univ. of Liverpool (PhD Social Sci. 1994). Res. Asst, Dept of Geog., Univ. of Liverpool, 1989–90; post-doctoral research, Univ. of Cardiff, 1994–97; Consultant, 1997–2003, Consultant to Bd Dir, 2003–07, Henley Centre for Forecasting, then Henley Centre, later Henley Centre Headlight Vision; Chm., Inst. for Insight in the Public Services, 2007–12; Man. Dir, Govt and Public Affairs, BMRB, 2008–09. Associate Lectr, Internat. Develt, Open Univ., 1998; Hon. Res. Fellow, Sch. of Geog., Univ. of Birmingham, 2000–. Member: Green Fiscal Commn, 2007–10; Mem., Food Ethics Council, 2011. Associate, Demos, 2002–09; Trustee: Involve, 2005–11; NESTA, 2012–. *Publications:* (jtly) Consuming Interests: the social provision of foods, 2000; King Sugar: Jamaica, the Caribbean and the world sugar economy, 2001. *Recreations:* current affairs, horses and Riding for Disabled Association. *Address:* TNS BMRB, 6 More London Place, SE1 2QY. *T:* (020) 7656 5739. *E:* mharrison@wpp.com.

HARRISON, Norman, CChem, FRSC, FNI; Director of Strategic Development, Babcock International Group, 2010–14; *b* 25 Jan. 1952; *s* of Robert and Elsie Harrison; *m* 1973, Jacqueline Ogden. *Educ:* John Dalton Poly. Coll., Manchester; Blackburn Tech. Coll. (DMS). CChem, 1981; MRSC 1981, FRSC 2012; FNI 2010. British Energy plc (formerly Central Electricity Generating Board, then Nuclear Electric plc): Commng Team Mem., Heysham 1 Nuclear Power Stn, 1981–85; Control Room Supervisor, Heysham 2 Nuclear Power Stn, 1985–93; Shift Manager, 1993–95, Tech. and Safety Manager, 1995–96, Hartlepool Nuclear Power Stn; Ops Manager, 1996–99, Dir, 1999–2000, Heysham 1 Nuclear Power Stn; Dir, Sizewell B Nuclear Power Stn, 2000–03; Dir, Dounreay Div., 2003–07, CEO, 2007–09, UKAEA. Sen. Advr to Exec., Culham Centre for Fusion Energy, 2014–; Strategic Advr, Amec Foster Wheeler, 2014–. Member: Nuclear Liabilities Funding Adv. Bd, 2009–; Bd, Nuclear Industries Assoc., 2011–14; Nuclear Liabilities Fund, 2011–. Pres., Nuclear Inst., 2011–13. Ind. Gov., Manchester Metropolitan Univ., 2008– (Dep. Chm., 2014–). FRSA 2007. *Recreations:* travel, opera, gardening.

HARRISON, Dame Patricia (Mary), DNZM 2009 (DCNZM 2001); QSO 1987; Member, Otago Regional Council, 1996–2004; *b* 6 Sept. 1932; *d* of Hugh and Catherine Thomson; *m* 1957, Arthur Keith Harrison; one *s* two *d. Educ:* Otago Girls' High Sch.; Dunedin Teachers' Coll.; Otago Univ. (MA Hons Philosophy; James Clark Meml Prize in Philosophy 1955). Hd of English, Burnside High Sch., 1973–75; Principal, Queen's High Sch., Dunedin, 1975–94. Chm., Otago Youth Wellness Trust, 1996–2008 (Trustee, 2009–). Chm., Otago Regl Access Employment Council, 1985–87. Mem. Council, Univ. of Otago, 1985–96. Board Member: YWCA, 1970–80; Southern Th. Trust, 1987–90. Volunteer, Victim Support, 2010–. Commemoration Medal (NZ), 1990; Suffrage Medal (NZ), 1993. *Publications:* Magic, Myth and Legends: a supplementary English text, 1974. *Recreations:* gardening, bridge, walking. *Address:* 31 Gladstone Road, Dalmore, Dunedin North, New Zealand. *T:* (3) 4738606.

HARRISON, Patrick Kennard, CBE 1982; Secretary, Royal Institute of British Architects, 1968–87; *b* 8 July 1928; *e s* of late Richard Harrison and Sheila Griffin; *m* 1955, Mary Wilson, *y d* of late Captain G. C. C. Damant, CBE, RN; one *d. Educ:* Lord Williams's Sch., Thame; Downing Coll., Cambridge (Exhbnr in English). Wireless Fitter, RAFVR, 1947–49; Asst Principal, Dept of Health for Scotland, 1953; Private Sec. to Deptl Sec. and to Parly Secs, Scottish Office, 1958–60; Principal, Scottish Develt Dept and Regional Develt Div., Scottish Office, 1960–68. Dir, Building Mus. Project, 1990–97. Hon. Mem., Amer. Inst. of Architects, 1978. Hon. FRIAS, 1987; Hon. FRIBA, 1988. *Recreations:* gardening, travel, reading, music. *Address:* 28B Moray Place, Edinburgh EH3 6BX. *T:* (0131) 225 5342. *Clubs:* Reform; New (Edinburgh).

HARRISON, Prof. Paul Jeffrey, FRCPsych; Professor of Psychiatry, University of Oxford, since 2000; Fellow, Wolfson College, Oxford, since 1997; *b* 18 Oct. 1960; *s* of Walford John Harrison and Bridget Ann Harrison; *m* 1984, Sandra Hallett; three *d. Educ:* City of London Sch.; Balliol Coll., Oxford (BA 1982; BM BCh 1985; MA 1987); DM Oxon 1991. MRCPsych 1989, FRCPsych 2001. MRC Trng Fellow, St Mary's Hosp. Med. Sch., 1988; University of Oxford: Clinical Lectr in Psychiatry, 1991–94; Wellcome Trust Sen. Res. Fellow, 1995–97; Clinical Reader in Psychiatry, 1997–2000. Collegium Internationale Neuro-Psychopharmacologicum Schizophrenia Award, 1998; Sen. Clinical Prize, Brit. Assoc. for Psychopharmacol., 1999; A. E. Bennett Award, Soc. for Biol Psychiatry, 2004; Joel Elkes Award, Amer. Coll. of Neuropsychopharmacol., 2005; Clin. Neurosci. Award, Collegium Internat. Neuro-Psychopharmacol., 2010; Clin. Neuropsychopharmacol. Award, Eur. Coll. Neuropsychopharmacol., 2012. *Publications:* Lecture Notes on Psychiatry, 8th edn 1998 to 10th edn 2010; The Neuropathology of Schizophrenia, 2000; Shorter Oxford Textbook of Psychiatry, 6th edn 2012; Schizophrenia, 3rd edn 2011; articles on schizophrenia, depression and Alzheimer's disease. *Recreations:* sport, music. *Address:* University Department of Psychiatry, Warneford Hospital, Oxford OX3 7JX. *T:* (01865) 223730.

HARRISON, Prof. Peter Duncan, PhD; Director, Institute for Advanced Studies in the Humanities (formerly Centre for the History of European Discourses), University of Queensland, since 2011; Senior Research Fellow, Ian Ramsey Centre, University of Oxford, since 2011; Australian Laureate Fellow, since 2015; *b* 29 Nov. 1955; *s* of Duncan and Jean Harrison; *m* 1994, Carol Taylor; one *s* one *d. Educ:* Yeronga Infants Sch.; Bundaberg State High Sch.; Univ. of Queensland (BSc; BA Hons; PhD 1989); Yale Univ. (MA); Univ. of Oxford (MA; DLitt). Bond University: Asst Prof., 1989–93, Associate Prof., 1994–2000, of Philos.; Prof. of Hist. and Philos., 2001–06; Andreas Idreos Prof. of Sci. and Religion, and Dir, Ian Ramsey Centre, Univ. of Oxford, 2007–11; Fellow, Harris Manchester Coll., Oxford, 2007–11. Hon. Res. Consultant, Dept of Studies in Religion, Univ. of Queensland, 1990–2010. Gifford Lectr, Edinburgh, 2011. FAHA 1998. Centenary Medal (Australia), 2001. *Publications:* Religion and the Religions in the English Enlightenment, 1990, 2nd edn 2002; The Bible, Protestantism and the Rise of Natural Science, 1998, 2nd edn 2002; The Fall of Man and the Foundations of Science, 2007; The Cambridge Companion to Science and Religion, 2010; (ed jtly) Wrestling with Nature: from omens to science, 2011; The Territories of Science and Religion, 2015. *Address:* Institute for Advanced Studies in the Humanities, Level 5 Forgan Smith Building, University of Queensland, Qld 4072, Australia.

HARRISON, Ven. Peter Reginald Wallace; Archdeacon of the East Riding, 1999–2006; *b* 22 June 1939; *s* of Gilbert V. W. Harrison and Mary L. W. Harrison (*née* Blair); *m* 1970, Elizabeth Mary Byzia; one *s* one *d. Educ:* Charterhouse; Selwyn Coll., Cambridge (BA Theol 1962); Ridley Hall, Cambridge. Ordained deacon 1964, priest 1965; Curate, St Luke's, Barton Hill, Bristol, 1964–69; Youth Worker and Chaplain, Greenhouse Trust, London, 1969–77; Dir, Northorpe Hall Trust, Mirfield, 1977–84; Team Rector, Drypool Team Ministry, Hull, 1984–98. *Recreations:* reading, voluntary community work. *Address:* 10 Priestgate, Church Street, Sutton, Hull HU7 4QR. *T:* (01482) 797110.

HARRISON, Philippa Mary, (Mrs Anthony McConnell); Chairman, Investment Committee, Book Tokens Ltd, since 2009 (Director, 1996–2014; Chairman, 2011–14); Editorial Director, Ed Victor Literary Agency, since 2002; *b* 25 Nov. 1942; *d* of Charles Kershaw Whitfield and Alexina Margaret Whitfield; *m* 1st, 1968 (marr. diss. 1976); 2nd, 2011, Anthony McConnell. *Educ:* Walthamstow Hall; Bristol Univ. (BA Hons); Courtauld Inst. Promotions Organiser, Associated Book Publishers, 1963–66; reader and editor, Jonathan Cape, 1967–73; Editl Dir, Hutchinson, 1974–78; Jt Editor-in-Chief, Penguin, 1979–80; Editl Dir, Michael Joseph, 1980–85; Man. Dir and Publisher, Macmillan London, 1986–88; Man. Dir, V&A Enterprises, 1990–91; Man. Dir and Publisher, Macdonald & Co., subseq. Little, Brown & Co. (UK), 1991–96; Chief Exec. and Publisher, 1996–2000, non-exec. Chm., 2000–01, Little, Brown & Co. (UK). Director: Royal Acad. of Arts Enterprise Bd, 1999–2014; British Mus. Co., 2002–09. Member: Bd, Book Marketing Council, 1983–88; Booker Mgt Cttee, 1987–89; Literature Panel, Arts Council, 1988–92. Mem. Council, Publishers' Assoc., 1995–2002 (Pres., 1998–99). Trustee: Eric & Salome Estorick Foundn, 1996–99; Cumbria Bldgs Preservation Trust, 2011–. CCMI (CIMgt 1987; Mem. Bd, 1999–2005); FRSA 1992. *Recreations:* walking, gardening, theatre, politics, looking at pictures, friends. *Address:* 3B Connaught House, Clifton Gardens, W9 1AL. *T:* (020) 7289 8808. *Club:* Groucho.

HARRISON, Richard Tristan; QC 2012; *b* Santiago, Chile, 13 Nov. 1968; *s* of Peter Alan Harrison, OBE and Maria-Luisa Harrison; *m* 2003, Sarah Katharine Whitten; three *s* one *d. Educ:* Cranleigh Sch.; Emmanuel Coll., Cambridge (BA Modern and Medieval Langs 1991); City Univ. (DipLaw). Called to the Bar, Inner Temple, 1993; in practice as a barrister, specialising in divorce and internat. family law, 1994–. Consultant Ed., Hersham and McFarlane Child Law and Practice, 2007–. *Recreations:* family, food, Spain. *Address:* 1 King's Bench Walk, Temple, EC4Y 7DB. *T:* (020) 7936 1500. *E:* rharrison@1kbw.co.uk.

HARRISON, Sir (Robert) Colin, 4th Bt *cr* 1922; *b* 25 May 1938; *s* of Sir John Fowler Harrison, 2nd Bt, and Kathleen (*d* 1993), *yr d* of late Robert Livingston, The Gables, Eaglescliffe, Co. Durham; *S* brother, 1955; *m* 1963, Maureen, *er d* of late E. Leonard Chiverton, Garth Corner, Kirkbymoorside, York; one *s* two *d. Educ:* St Peter's Coll., Radley; St John's Coll., Cambridge. Commissioned with Fifth Royal Northumberland Fusiliers (National Service), 1957–59. Chm., John Harrison (Stockton) Ltd, 1963–2006. Chm., Young Master Printers Nat. Cttee, 1972–73. *Heir: s* John Wyndham Fowler Harrison, *b* 14 Dec. 1972. *Address:* Dinsdale House, 6 Uppleby, Easingwold, York YO61 3BB.

HARRISON, Roger; *see* Harrison, D. R. W.

HARRISON, Prof. Roy Michael, OBE 2004; PhD, DSc; FRSC, FRMetS; Queen Elizabeth II Birmingham Centenary Professor of Environmental Health, since 1991, and Head, Division of Environmental Health & Risk Management, since 1999, University of Birmingham; *b* 14 Oct. 1948; *s* of Wilfred Harrison and Rosa (*née* Cotton); *m* 1st, 1981, Angela Copeman (marr. diss.); one *s* one *d*; 2nd, 1989, Susan Sturt; one *s. Educ:* Henley Grammar Sch.; Univ. of Birmingham (BSc; PhD 1972; DSc 1988). FRMetS 1982; FRSC 1988. Res. Asst, Imperial Coll., Univ. of London, 1972–74; Lectr, Lancaster Univ., 1974–84; Reader, Univ. of Essex, 1984–91. Dist. Adjunct Prof., King Abdulaziz Univ., Jeddah, 2011–. Margary Lectr, RMetS, 1994; John Jeyes Lectr, RSC, 1995. Department of the Environment: Mem., Photochem. Oxidants Rev. Gp, 1986–97; Chairman: Quality of Urban Air Rev. Gp, 1991–97; Airborne Particles Expert Gp, 1997–99; Vice-Chm., Expert Panel on Air Quality Standards, 2003– (Mem., 1992–2002); Member: Adv. Cttee on Hazardous Substances, 2001–06; Air Quality Expert Gp, 2002–; Department of Health: Member: Cttee on Med. Effects of Air Pollution, 1993–2003, 2006–; Health Adv. Gp on Chem. Contamination Incidents, 1994–; Mem., Sci. Adv. Council, DEFRA, 2009–. Hon. Consulting Envmtl Toxicologist, Nat. Poisons Inf. Service, Birmingham Centre and W Midlands Poisons Unit, 1994–99. Mem., HEFCE Panel, 2001, 2008 and 2014 RAEs. Chm., Envmt Gp, RSC, 1990–91; Theme Leader for Envmt, Pollution and Human Health, NERC, 2007–12. Hon. FFOM 1998; Hon. MFPHM 1997; Hon. Mem., Chartered Inst. Envmtl Health, 2010. Fitzroy Prize, RMetS, 2012. *Publications:* (with D. P. H. Laxen) Lead Pollution: causes and control, 1981; Pollution: causes, effects and control, 1983, 5th edn 2014; (with R. Perry) Handbook of Air Pollution Analysis, 2nd edn 1986; (jtly) Acid Rain: scientific and technical advances, 1987; (with S. Rapsomanikis) Environmental Analysis using Chromatography Interfaced with Atomic Spectroscopy, 1989; (jtly) Introductory Chemistry for the Environmental Sciences, 1991, 2nd edn (with S. J. de Mora) 1996; (with R. S. Hamilton) Highway Pollution, 1991; (jtly) Handbook for Urban Air Improvement, 1992; Understanding Our Environment: an introduction to environmental chemistry and pollution, 1992, 3rd edn 1999; (with M. Radojevic) Atmospheric Acidity: sources, consequences and abatement, 1992; (with F. E. Warner) Radioecology after Chernobyl: biogeochemical pathways of artificial radionuclides, SCOPE 50, 1993; (jtly) Urban Air Quality in the United Kingdom, 1993; (jtly)

Diesel Vehicle Emissions and Urban Air Quality, 1993; (with R. E. Hester) Issues in Environmental Science and Technology, vol. 1, 1994 to vol. 40, 2015; (jtly) Airborne Particulate Matter in the United Kingdom, 1996; (with R. Van Grieken) Atmospheric Particles, 1998; (jtly) Source Apportionment of Airborne Particulate Matter in the United Kingdom, 1999; An Introduction to Pollution Science, 2006; Principles of Environmental Chemistry, 2007; many papers to learned jls. *Recreation:* mowing and other outdoor pursuits. *Address:* Division of Environmental Health & Risk Management, University of Birmingham, Edgbaston, Birmingham B15 2TT. *T:* (0121) 414 3494.

HARRISON, Sally, (Mrs R. D. Norton); QC 2010; *b* Cheshire, 4 Nov. 1968; *d* of (Stanley) George Harrison, *qv*; *m* 1997, Richard Damian Norton; one *s* one *d*. *Educ:* Howell's Sch., Denbigh (Drapers' Schol.); Reading Univ. (BSc Hons); City Univ. (CPE). Called to the Bar, Gray's Inn, 1992; in practice as barrister, specialising in family and matrimonial law, 1992–; Hd of Chambers, St John's Bldgs, Manchester, 2013–. *Recreations:* cycling, open water swimming, reading, music. *Address:* St John's Buildings, 24A–28 St John Street, Manchester M3 4DJ. *T:* (0161) 214 1500, *Fax:* (0161) 835 3929. *E:* sally.harrison@stjohnbuildings.co.uk.

HARRISON, Shirley Margaret; non-executive Director, Sheffield Teaching Hospitals NHS Foundation Trust, since 2007; *b* 26 March 1949; *d* of Colin and Ena Gunn; *m* 1990, Robert Harrison; one *s*. *Educ:* Univ. of Kent (BA Philosophy 1970); Univ. of Sheffield (MBA 1989). Mktg exec. and advertising copywriter, 1970–73; homelessness worker, 1973–76; student welfare officer, 1976–82; conf./event mktg exec., 1982–86; Chief Officer (PR Dir), Sheffield CC, 1986–92; Lectr, Leeds Business Sch., 1992–2001. Chair: S Yorks Probation Bd, 2005–07; Human Tissue Authy, 2006–09; HFEA, 2007. Patient rep., Cancer Res. Networks, 2001–. Public Appts Ambassador, 2010–. Consumer rep., CRUK, 2010–. Non-exec. Mem. Bd, NCRI, 2012–. JP Sheffield, 1998–2014. *Publications:* Public Relations: an introduction, 1995, 2nd edn 2000; Disasters and the Media, 1999; contrib. chapters in books; articles in acad. jls on PR and communications, business ethics, etc. *Recreations:* walking the dog, learning the piano, going to the pictures, gardening, cooking and eating. *Address:* c/o Sheffield Teaching Hospitals NHS Foundation Trust, Clock Tower, Herries Road, Sheffield S5 7ZZ. *E:* shirley.harrison@sth.nhs.uk.

HARRISON, (Stanley) George, CBE 2003; a District Judge, Chester County Court and District Registry of High Court, 1985–2008; *b* 16 Aug. 1937; *s* of Stanley George Harrison and Elizabeth Avril Meff (*née* Walker); *m* 1963, Jennifer Lorna Harrow (*d* 2013); one *s* one *d*. *Educ:* Wellington Coll.; Univ. of Manchester (LLB Hons). Commnd Lancs Regt (2nd Lt), 1956–58. Admitted solicitor, 1964; Partner, Wayman Hales, Chester, 1967–82; Registrar, Liverpool Co. Court, 1982–85. Mem., Lord Chancellor's Adv. Cttee on Delay in Public Law, 2002. Sec., 1985–2000, Pres., 2002, Assoc. of Dist Judges. Chm., Muir Housing Gp Assoc., 1986–2002. Dir, CLS Care Services, 1991–2001. *Recreations:* fishing, cricket, grass. *Address:* Boothsdale House, Willington, Tarporley, Cheshire CW6 0NH.

See also S. Harrison.

HARRISON, Ted; *see* Harrison, E. P. G.

HARRISON, Sir Terence, Kt 1995; DL; FREng; FIMechE, FIMarEST; Chairman, Alfred McAlpine plc, 1996–2002 (Director, 1995–2002); *b* 7 April 1933; *s* of late Roland Harrison and of Doris (*née* Wardle); *m* 1956, June (*née* Forster); two *s*. *Educ:* A. J. Dawson Grammar Sch., Co. Durham; West Hartlepool and Sunderland Tech. Colls. BSc(Eng) Durham. CEng 1964; FIMechE 1984; FIMarEST (FIMarE 1973); FREng (FEng 1988). Marine engrg apprenticeship, Richardson's Westgarth, Hartlepool, 1949–53; commnd REME, service in Nigeria, 1955–57; Clarke Chapman, Gateshead (Marine Division): Res. Engr, 1957; Chief Mechanical Engr, 1967; Man. Dir, 1969; Man. Dir, Clarke Chapman Ltd, Gateshead, 1976; Northern Engineering Industries plc: Dir, 1977; Man. Dir, UK Ops, 1980–83; Chief Exec., 1983–86; Exec. Chm., 1986–93; Rolls-Royce: Dir, 1989; Chief Exec., 1992–96. Director: Barclays Bank (Regl Bd), 1986–98; T&N, 1995–98. Member: ACOST, 1987; Engrg Council, 1990–93. Pres., BEAMA, 1989–90. Pres., NEC Inst., 1988. DL Tyne and Wear, 1989. Hon. DEng Newcastle, 1991; Hon. DTech Sunderland, 1995; Hon. DSc Durham, 1996. *Publications:* technical papers to mechanical, marine and mining societies. *Recreations:* golf, fell walking. *Address:* 2 The Garden Houses, Whalton, Northumberland NE61 3UZ. *T:* (01670) 775400.

HARRISON, Tony; poet; *b* 30 April 1937; *s* of Harry Ashton Harrison and Florrie (*née* Wilkinson-Horner). *Publications:* Earthworks, 1964; Aikin Mata, 1966; Newcastle is Peru, 1969; The Loiners (Geoffrey Faber Meml Prize), 1970; The Misanthrope, 1973; Phaedra Britannica, 1975; Palladas: poems, 1975; The Passion, 1977; Bow Down, 1977; From The School of Eloquence and other poems, 1978; The Bartered Bride, 1978; Continuous, 1981; A Kumquat for John Keats, 1981; US Martial, 1981; The Oresteia, 1981; Selected Poems, 1984, expanded edn 1987; The Mysteries, 1985; Dramatic Verse 1973–85, 1985; v., 1985; The Fire-Gap, 1985; Theatre Works 1973–85, 1986; The Trackers of Oxyrhynchus, 1990; v. and other poems, 1990; A Cold Coming: Gulf War poems, 1991; The Common Chorus, 1992; The Gaze of the Gorgon (Whitbread Award for Poetry), 1992; Square Rounds, 1992; Black Daisies for the Bride, 1993; Poetry or Bust, 1993; A Maybe Day in Kazakhstan, 1994; The Shadow of Hiroshima, 1995; Permanently Bard, 1995; Plays Three: The Kaisers of Carnuntum, The Labourers of Herakles, Poetry or Bust, 1996; The Prince's Play, 1996; Prometheus, 1998 (also Dir, film, 1999); Plays One: The Mysteries, 1999; Laureate's Block and Other Poems, 2000; Plays Two: The Oresteia, The Common Chorus, The Trojan Women, 2001; Plays Four: The Misanthrope, Phaedra Britannica, The Prince's Play, 2001; Plays Five: The Trackers of Oxyrhynchus, Square Rounds, 2004; Hecuba, 2005; Under the Clock: new poems, 2005; Collected Poems, 2007; Collected Film Poetry, 2007; Fram, 2008.

HARRISON, Valerie, (Mrs D. M. Harrison); *see* Caton, V.

HARRISON, Victoria; *see* Harrison, A. V.

HARRISON, (William) Alistair, CMG 2012; CVO 1996; HM Diplomatic Service, retired; HM Marshal of the Diplomatic Corps, since 2014; *b* 14 Nov. 1954; *s* of late William Kent Harrison and Alice Rita Harrison; *m* 1st, 1981, Theresa Mary Morrison (marr. diss. 1991); 2nd, 1996, Sarah Judith Wood; one *s* two *d*. *Educ:* Newcastle Royal Grammar Sch.; University Coll., Oxford (BA 1977; MA 1980); Birkbeck Coll., London (DipEcon 1995); Open Univ. (BSc Maths 2012). Joined FCO, 1977: Third, later Second Sec., Warsaw, 1979–82; First Sec., FCO, 1982–84; Private Sec. to Parly Under-Sec., FCO, 1984–86; First Sec., UK Mission to UN, NY, 1987–92; Deputy Head: ME Dept, FCO, 1992–95; of Mission, Warsaw, 1995–98; Foreign Policy Advr to Dir-Gen. for External Relations, EC, Brussels, 1998–2000; Hd of Chancery and Pol Counsellor, UKMIS to UN, NY, 2000–03; Hd, UN (later Internat. Orgns) Dept, FCO, 2003–05; High Comr to Zambia, 2005–08; Gov. of Anguilla, 2009–13. *Recreations:* music, bridge, ski-ing, golf. *Address:* Ambassador's Court, St James's Palace, SW1A 1BL.

HARRISSON, Georgina Jane, (Mrs James Fern); Deputy Secretary, Department of Family and Community Services, New South Wales, since 2014; *b* Norwich, 17 Jan. 1978; *d* of Hugh Geoffrey and Jennifer Harrisson; *m* 2007, James Fern; one *d*. *Educ:* Univ. of Birmingham (BSc Biol Scis (Genetics) 2000). Account Manager, Prime Minister's Delivery Unit, Cabinet Office, 2002–05; Policy Advr to Premier of NSW, Australia, 2005–07 (on secondment); Hd, Performance and Delivery, DCLG, 2007–08; Actg Dir of Strategy and Performance, DCSF, 2009; Dep. Dir, Schools Directorate, DCSF, later DfE, 2009–11; Exec. Co-ordinator, Domestic Policy, Dept of Prime Minister and Cabinet, Australia, 2011–12; Exec. Dir, Strategic Initiatives, Dept of Premier and Cabinet, NSW, 2012–14. *Recreations:* tennis, sailing, live music.

HARROD, Dr Tanya Olivia; design historian; *b* 7 July 1951; *d* of Peter Kingsmill Ledger and Maria Martha Ledger (*née* Sax); *m* 1977, Henry Mark Harrod; one *s* one *d*, and two step *s*. *Educ:* St Felix Sch., Southwold; Univ. of York (BA Hist.); St Hilda's Coll., Oxford (DPhil 1978). Tutor, Open Univ., 1978–88; Architecture and Design corresp., Independent on Sunday, 1989–94; Vis. Fellow, Sch. of World Art and Museology, UEA, 1995–97. Vis. Prof., Sch. of Humanities, RCA, 2000–10. Member, Advisory Board: Jl Design History, 1996–2009; Interpreting Ceramics, 2003–; Burlington Magazine, 2006–. Trustee: Heritage Crafts Assoc., 2011–13; Contemporary Applied Art, 2014–. Mem., Internat. Assoc. of Art Critics, 1992–. Brother, Art Workers' Guild, 2011. Jt Editor, Jl of Modern Craft, 2008–. *Publications:* (ed) Obscure Objects of Desire: reviewing the crafts in the Twentieth Century, 1997; The Crafts in Britain in the 20th Century, 1999; (contrib.) Contemporary Art and the Home, 2002; (contrib.) Out of the Ordinary: spectacular craft, 2007; (contrib.) Neocraft: modernity and the crafts, 2007; (contrib.) Craft, Space and Interior Design, 1855–2005, 2008; (ed) Ann Stokes: artists' potter, 2009; (contrib.) Contemporary British Studio Ceramics: the Grainer Collection, 2010; (contrib.) Anne Dunn, 2010; The Last Sane Man: Michael Cardew, modern pots, colonialism and the counter culture, 2012 (James Tait Black Biography Prize, 2013); The Real Thing: essays on making in the modern world, 2015; contribs to Philosophical Trans Royal Soc., Burlington Mag., TLS, Spectator. *Recreations:* lake, river and sea bathing. *Address:* 51 Campden Hill Square, W8 7JR. *T:* (020) 7727 8485.

HARROLD, Roy Mealham; farmer, 1947–91; *b* 13 Aug. 1928; *s* of John Frederick Harrold and Ellen Selena Harrold (*née* Mealham); *m* 1968, Barbara Mary, *yr d* of William and Florence Andrews; one *s* one *d*. *Educ:* Stoke Holy Cross Primary Sch.; Bracondale Sch., Norwich. County Chm., Norfolk Fedn of Young Farmers' Clubs, 1956–57; Mem., Nat. Council of Young Farmers, 1957–60; Mem. Council, Royal Norfolk Agric. Assoc., 1972–75, 1980–83, 1987–89; Mem., Press Council, 1976–83. Mem., UK Shareholders Assoc., 1993–. Lay Chm., Norwich East Deanery Synod, 1970–79; Member: Norwich Dio. Synod, 1970–96; Norwich Dio. Bd of Patronage, 1970–82; Norwich Dio. Bd of Finance, 1983–96; Pastoral Asst, St Peter Mancroft, Norwich, 1991– (Church Warden, 1978–82, 1988–92). *Recreations:* music, opera, ballet. *Address:* Milkwood, 122 Norwich Road, Stoke Holy Cross, Norwich NR14 8QJ. *T:* (01508) 492322.

HARROP, Andrew Jonathan Gilbert; General Secretary, Fabian Society, since 2011; *b* Wandsworth, 27 Nov. 1976; *s* of Sir Peter John Harrop, *qv*; partner, Katie Sushila Ratna Ghose, *qv*; one *d*. *Educ:* St Paul's Sch.; Gonville and Caius Coll., Cambridge (BA Hons 1998); London Sch. of Econs and Pol Sci. (MSc 1999); London Business Sch. (MBA 2009). Res. asst to Anne Campbell, MP, 1998–99; researcher, New Policy Inst., 1999–2003; Policy Officer, 2003–06, Hd of Policy, 2006–09, Age Concern England; Dir of Policy and Public Affairs, Age UK, 2009–11. Contested (Lab) NE Herts, 2005. *Publications:* Age Discrimination Handbook, 2006. *Recreations:* walking, cycling. *E:* andrew.harrop@fabians.org.uk.

HARROP, Sir Peter (John), KCB 1984 (CB 1980); Second Permanent Secretary, Department of the Environment, 1981–86; *b* 18 March 1926; *s* of late Gilbert Harrop, OBE; *m* 1975, Margaret Joan, *d* of E. U. E. Elliott-Binns, CB; two *s*. *Educ:* King Edward VII Sch., Lytham, Lancs; Peterhouse, Cambridge. MA (Hist. Tripos). Served RNVR, 1945–48 (Sub-Lt). Min. of Town and Country Planning, 1949; Min. of Housing and Local Govt, 1951; Dept of the Environment, 1970 (Chm., Yorks and Humberside Economic Planning Bd, and Regional Dir, 1971–73); Under-Sec., HM Treasury, 1973–76; Deputy Secretary: DoE, 1977–79, 1980–81; Cabinet Office, 1979–80. Chm., National Bus Co., 1988–91; non-executive Director: Nat. Home Loans Hldgs plc, 1987–92; Municipal Mutual Insurance Ltd, 1988–2001; Thames Water plc, 1989–95 (Mem., Thames Water Authority, 1986–89). Chm., UK Cttee, European Year of the Environment, 1986–88. Chairman: Richmond upon Thames Housing Trust, 1990–96; River Thames Boat Project, 2001–06. Chm. of Govs, Richmond upon Thames Coll., 1993–96. Hon. Trustee, British Mus., 1987–97. *Recreation:* golf. *Address:* 19 Berwyn Road, Richmond, Surrey TW10 5BP. *Clubs:* Oxford and Cambridge, Roehampton.

See also A. J. G. Harrop.

HARROW, John Michael; His Honour Judge Harrow; a Circuit Judge, since 2003; *b* 30 March 1946; *s* of Henry John and Edith Harrow; *m* 2000, Maria Liddle; two *s* one *d*. *Educ:* Hemsworth Grammar Sch.; Coll. of Law, Guildford. Admitted solicitor, 1969; a Recorder, 1996–2003. Chm. (pt-time), 1986–96, Dist Chm., 1996–2003, Appeals Service. *Publications:* (contrib.) Butterworth's Road Traffic Service, annually 1991–94. *Recreations:* walking, film, war history. *Address:* Courts of Justice, Deansleigh Road, Bournemouth BH7 7DS. *T:* (01202) 502800. *E:* HHJudge.Harrow@judiciary.gsi.gov.uk.

HARROWBY, 8th Earl of, *cr* 1809; **Dudley Adrian Conroy Ryder;** Baron Harrowby, 1776; Viscount Sandon, 1809; chartered surveyor; *b* 18 March 1951; *s* of 7th Earl of Harrowby, TD and Jeanette Rosalthé (*née* Johnston-Saint); *S* father, 2007; *m* 1st, 1977, Sarah Nichola Hobhouse Payne (*d* 1994), *d* of Captain Anthony Payne; three *s* one *d*; 2nd, 1998, Mrs Caroline J. Coram James (*née* Marks). *Educ:* Eton; Univ. of Newcastle upon Tyne; Magdalene Coll., Cambridge (MA). FRICS 1992. Exec. Dir, Compton Street Securities Ltd, 1988–. Mem., Governing Council, Goldsmiths Coll., Univ. of London, 2003–09 (Mem., Finance and Resources Cttee, 2004–09; Mem., Audit Cttee, 2009–14); Governor: John Archer Sch., Wandsworth, 1986–88; Dean Close Sch., Cheltenham, 2004–. President: Staffordshire Soc., 1995–97; Stafford Historical and Civic Soc., 2008–; Vice Pres., Glos Co. Br., CPRE, 2008–; Mem. Cttee, Glos Br., CLA, 2011–. Mem., NFU, 1975–. Patron: Guild of Handicraft Trust, 1991–; N Staffs Co. RBL, 2008–13; Oak Tree Farm Rural Project, 2014–; Trustee, Bathtub 2 Boardroom charity, 2010–. Mem., Assoc. of Conservative Peers, 2009–. Liveryman, Co. of Goldsmiths, 1997. *Recreations:* travel, fell walking, music, study of fine art and architecture. *Heir: s* Viscount Sandon, *qv*. *Address:* Sandon Estate Office, Sandon, Stafford ST18 0DA.

HARROWER, Rt Rev. John Douglas, OAM 2000; Bishop of Tasmania, 2000–15; *b* 16 Oct. 1947; *s* of John Lawrence Harrower and Enid Dorothy Harrower; *m* 1970, Gayelene Melva Harrower; two *s*. *Educ:* Melbourne Univ. (BE 1970, BA 1973); Ridley Coll., ACT (ThL 1992); Bible Col. of Vict., ACT (MA (Theol.) 1996, Adv. Dip. Missiol Studies 1996). CEng 1976; MIChemE 1976. Process Engr, Petroleum Refineries (Aust.) P/L, Melbourne, 1970–72; Project Officer, Tariff Bd, Melbourne, 1972–74; Director: Industry Studies Br., Industries Assistance Commn, 1975; IMPACT Project, Melbourne, 1975–78; Univ. Chaplain, Buenos Aires, 1979–81; Missionary, CMS, Argentina, 1979–88; Exec Chm., CERTEZA-ABUA, Buenos Aires, 1981–87; Gen. Sec., Argentine Univs Bible Assoc., 1981–86; ordained deacon, 1984, priest, 1986, Buenos Aires; Asst Minister, Iglesia Anglicana de San Salvador, Buenos Aires, 1984–88; Vicar: St Paul's, Glen Waverley, Vic, Aust., 1989–95; St Barnabas Anglican Ch, Glen Waverley, 1995–2000; Area Dean, Waverley-Knox, 1992–94; Archdeacon of Kew, Dio. Melbourne, 1994–2000. Dir, World Vision, Australia, 2006–. MAICD 2007, FAICD 2009. Centenary Medal, Australia, 2003. *Publications:* all in Spanish: Personal Evangelism, 1985, new edn 1996; (with Silvia Chaves) Spiritual Gifts: a body in mission, 1985, new edn 1989; 30 Days with Jeremiah, 1989, new edn 1998; (in English) Cry of Hope, 2001. *Recreations:* reading, pottering in the garden. *Address:* c/o Diocese of Melbourne, The Anglican Centre, 209 Flinders Lane, Melbourne, Vic 3000, Australia. *E:* john.harrower@gmail.com. *Club:* Athenæum.

HARSENT, David, FRSL, FEA; poet, novelist, dramatist, librettist; Professor of Creative Writing, University of Roehampton, since 2013; *b* 9 Dec. 1942; *s* of Albert and Mary Harsent; *m* 1989, Julia Watson; one *d*, and two *s* one *d* from former marriage. *Educ:* trifling! Hon. Res. Fellow, Royal Holloway, Univ. of London, 2005–07; Dist. Writing Fellow, 2005–08, Vis Prof., 2009–, Sheffield Hallam Univ.; Prof. of Creative Writing, Bath Spa Univ., 2012–13. Commns from Royal Opera House and Proms; performances at S Bank Centre, Kammeroper, Vienna, Carnegie Hall, NY, Aldeburgh Fest., Wales Millennium Centre, Salzburg Fest.; *words for music:* music by Harrison Birtwistle: Gawain, opera libretto, 1991; The Woman and the Hare, song cycle, 1999; The Ring Dance of the Nazarene, song setting, 2003; The Minotaur, opera libretto, 2008; Serenade the Silkie, music by Julian Grant, 1994; When She Died, opera libretto, music by Jonathan Dove, 2002; Crime Fiction, music by Huw Watkins, 2009; The Corridor, opera libretto, music by Harrison Birtwistle, 2009; In the Locked Room, opera libretto, music by Huw Watkins, Edinburgh Internat. Fest., 2012; Songs from the Same Earth, song cycle, music by Harrison Birtwistle, Aldeburgh, 2013; The Cure, opera libretto, music by Harrison Birtwistle, Aldeburgh, 2015. FRSL 1999; FEA 2012. Hon. DLitt Roehampton, 2013. *Publications: fiction:* From an Inland Sea, 1985; *poetry:* Truce, 1973; After Dark, 1973; Dreams of the Dead, 1977; A Violent Country, 1979; Mister Punch, 1984; Selected Poems, 1989; Gawain: a libretto, 1991; Storybook Hero, 1992; News From the Front, 1993; The Sorrow of Sarajevo: versions of poems by Goran Simic, 1996; The Potted Priest, 1997; Sprinting from the Graveyard: versions of poems by Goran Simic, 1997; A Bird's Idea of Flight, 1998; Marriage, 2002; Legion (Forward Prize for best poetry collection), 2005; Selected Poems 1969–2005, 2007; Night, 2011 (Griffin Internat. Poetry Prize, Griffin Trust for Excellence in Poetry, 2012); Poetry: In Secret (versions of Yannis Ritsos), 2012; Songs from the Same Earth, 2013; Fire Songs, 2014 (T. S. Eliot Prize, Poetry Book Soc.); *editor:* (with M. Susko) Savramena Britanska Poezija, 1988; Another Round at the Pillars: Festschrift for Ian Hamilton Cargo, 1999; Raising the Iron, 2004. *Recreation:* re-inventing the past for future use. *Address:* c/o United Agents, 12–26 Lexington Street, W1F 0LE.

HARSTON, Julian John Robert Clive; HM Diplomatic Service, retired; Assistant Secretary General, United Nations, 2007–09; Director, Harston Consulting, since 2009; *b* 20 Oct. 1942; *s* of late Col Clive Harston, ERD, and of Kathleen Harston; *m* 1st, 1966, Karen Howard Oake (*née* Longfield) (marr. diss. 2000); one *s*; 2nd, 2008, Marina Vasic (*née* Bareta); two step *d*. *Educ:* King's Sch., Canterbury; Univ. of London (BSc); Univ. of Rhodesia and Nyasaland. British Tourist Authority, 1965–70; FCO, 1970; Consul, Hanoi, 1973; 1st Secretary: Blantyre, 1975; Lisbon, 1982; Counsellor, Harare, 1984–88; FCO, 1988–91; Counsellor, UK Mission, Geneva, 1991–95; Head, Political and Civil Affairs, UN Peace Forces, Zagreb, former Yugoslavia, 1995–96; Dir, UN Liaison Office, Belgrade, Fed. Repub. of Yugoslavia, 1996; Rep. of Sec.-Gen. and Hd of Mission, UN Civilian Police Mission, Haiti, 1998–99; Dep. Special Rep. of UN Sec.-Gen. to Bosnia Herzegovina, 1999–2001; Dir, UN Dept of Peace Keeping, NY, 2001–04; Dir, UN, Belgrade, 2004–07; Hd of Mission for the Referendum in W Sahara and Special Rep. of the Sec.-Gen. in W Sahara, UN, 2007–09; Rep. of the Sec.-Gen. in Belgrade, 2009. Founder Mem., Adv. Panel to UK Defence Coll., 2013–. *Recreations:* photography, travel. *Address:* Toplicin Venac 19, Apt 19, 11000 Belgrade, Serbia. *Clubs:* East India, Special Forces.

HART, family name of **Baron Hart of Chilton**.

HART OF CHILTON, Baron *cr* 2004 (Life Peer), of Chilton in the County of Suffolk; **Garry Richard Rushby Hart;** Special Adviser to Secretary of State for Justice (formerly for Constitutional Affairs) and Lord Chancellor, 1998–2007; *b* 29 June 1940; *s* of late Dennis George Hart and of Evelyn Mary Hart; *m* 1st, 1966, Paula Lesley Shepherd (marr. diss. 1986); two *s* one *d*; 2nd, 1986, Valerie Elen Mary Davies; twin *d*. *Educ:* Northgate Grammar Sch., Ipswich; University Coll. London (LLB; Fellow 2001). Admitted solicitor (Hons) 1966; Herbert Smith: Articled Clerk, 1962–65; Solicitor, 1966–70; Partner, 1970–98; Hd, Property Dept, 1988–97. Member: Partnership Council, 1988–97; Law Soc. (Mem., Specialist Planning Panel). House of Lords: Member: Select Cttee on Merits of Statutory Instruments, 2008–13, on the Constitution, 2009–14, on Extradition Law, 2014–15; Jt Cttee with H of C on Draft Constitutional Bill Session, 2007–08; Leaders Gp on Code of Conduct for Members of H of L, 2009–; Appts Commn, 2010–. Freeman, City of London, 1981; Liveryman, Solicitors' Co., 1981–. Trustee: Architecture Foundn, 1996–2005 (Dep. Chm., 1997–2005); British Architectural Liby Trust, 2001–10. Member: Almeida Develt Bd, 2007– (Trustee, 1997–2005, Chm., 1997–2002, Almeida Th.); Buildings Strategy Cttee, V & A Mus., 2007–. Mem. Council, UCL, 2004–10; Chancellor, Univ. of Greenwich, 2008–14. Vice-Patron, Ipswich Soc. for the Blind, 2008–. FRSA 1998. Hon. FRIBA 2000. Hon. LLD Greenwich, 2014. *Publications:* (ed jtly) Blundell & Dobry's Planning Applications Appeals and Proceedings, 4th edn 1990, 5th edn 1996. *Recreations:* conservation, theatre, talking. *Address:* House of Lords, SW1A 0PW. *Clubs:* Garrick, Beefsteak.

HART, Alan; broadcasting consultant, since 1991; Director, Global AMG, 1995–2000; Executive Director, Eurosport Consortium, 1997–2004 (Trustee, 2004–09); *b* 17 April 1935; *s* of late Reginald Thomas Hart and Lillian Hart; *m* 1961, Celia Mary Vine; two *s* one *d*. *Educ:* Pinnerwood Primary Sch.; University College Sch., Hampstead. Reporter: Willesden Chronicle and Kilburn Times, 1952–58; Newcastle Evening Chronicle, 1958; London Evening News, 1958–59; Editorial Asst, BBC Sportsview, 1959–61; Television Sports Producer, BBC Manchester, 1962–64; Asst Editor, Sportsview, 1964–65; Editor, Sportsview, 1965–68; Editor, Grandstand, 1968–77; Head of Sport, BBC Television, 1977–81; Controller, BBC1 Television, 1981–84; Special Asst to Dir Gen., BBC, 1985; Controller, Internat. Relations, BBC, 1986–91. Dir, Eurosport, 1991–97 (Chm., 1989–91); Chm., British Eurosport, 1997–99. Advr on management of E European broadcasting services, EBU, 1991–93; Trustee, EBU sub-licence scheme, 2005–13. Chm., Inventure Trust, 2003–07; Dir, Give Them a Sporting Chance, 2003–. Gov., S Devon Coll., 2004–13; Chm., Friends of S Devon Coll., 2008–. FRTS 1983. Hon. DEd Plymouth, 2014. *Recreations:* sport, music, walking. *Address:* Cutwellwalls, Avonwick, near South Brent, Devon TQ10 9HA.

HART, Anelay Colton Wright; Partner in Appleby, Hope & Matthews, 1963–95; *b* 6 March 1934; *s* of Anelay Thomas Bayston Hart and Phyllis Marian Hart; *m* 1979, Margaret Gardner (*née* Dewing). *Educ:* Stamford Sch.; King's Coll., London (LLB). Solicitor, retd. Advisory Director, World Society for the Protection of Animals, 1982–2003; RSPCA: Mem. Council, 1969–95; Hon. Treasurer, 1974–81; Chm. of Council, 1981–83, 1985–86, 1988–90; Vice-Chm. Council, 1983–84, 1986–88; Queen Victoria Silver Medal, 1984. President, Rotary Club of South Bank and Eston, 1972–73. *Recreation:* walking. *Club:* Royal Over-Seas League.

HART, Anthony; *see* Hart, T. A. A.

HART, Anthony John, OBE 1995; DSC 1945; JP; Chairman, Cunningham Hart & Co. Ltd, 1985–87 (Senior Partner, 1972–85), retired; *b* 27 Dec. 1923; *s* of Cecil Victor Hart and Kate Winifred Hart (*née* Boncey); *m* 1st, 1947, E. Penelope Morris (*d* 2001); one *s* one *d*; 2nd, 2003, Mrs Mary Eggleton (*d* 2012). *Educ:* King's College Sch., Wimbledon; Dauntsey's Sch. ACII, FCILA. RN, 1942–46 (Ordinary Seaman to Lieut). Joined Hart & Co., 1946, Partner 1952, Senior Partner 1969; on merger name changed to Cunningham Hart & Co. Mem. Council, CILA, 1964, Pres., 1970–71. Chm., Medic Alert Foundn in UK, 1971–83; Governor, Dauntsey's Sch., 1982–93; Mem. Council, Mansfield House University Settlement, 1975–90. Liveryman, 1960, Master, 1976–77, Broderers' Co.; Liveryman, 1979, Mem. Court, 1986, Insurers' Co. Alderman, Ward of Cheap, City of London, 1977–84. FRSA. JP City of London, 1977 (Vice-Chm. of Bench, 1991–93). *Recreation:* golf. *Address:* Dove Barn, Chapel Lane, Minchinhampton, Stroud, Glos GL6 9DL. *T:* (01453) 882154. *Club:* Minchinhampton Golf.

HART, Hon. Sir Anthony (Ronald), Kt 2005; a Judge of the High Court, Northern Ireland, 2005–12; *b* 30 April 1946; *s* of Basil and Hazel Hart; *m* 1971, Mary Morehan; two *s* two *d*. *Educ:* Portora Royal Sch., Enniskillen; Trinity Coll., Dublin (BA Mod.); Queen's Univ., Belfast. Called to the Bar of NI, 1969, Bencher 1995, Treas. 2007; called to the Bar, Gray's Inn, 1975; QC (NI) 1983. Jun. Crown Counsel for Co. Londonderry, 1973–75 and for Co. Down, 1975–79; Asst Boundary Comr, 1980–81; part-time Chm. of Industrial Tribunals, 1980–83; Dep. County Court Judge, 1983–85; County Court Judge, 1985–2005; Recorder of Londonderry, 1985–90; Recorder of Belfast, 1997–2005; Presiding Judge, County Courts, NI, 2002–05. Chm., Inquiry into Histl Instnl Abuse in NI, 2012–. Member: Council of Legal Educn (NI), 1977–83; Review Cttee on Professional Legal Educn in NI, 1984–85; Standing Adv. Commn on Human Rights, 1984–85; Judicial Studies Bd for NI, 1993–97; Criminal Justice Issues (formerly Criminal Justice Consultative) Gp for NI, 1993–99; Civil Justice Reform Gp, 1998–99; Chairman: Council of HM Co. Court Judges in NI, 1995–98 (Hon. Sec., 1989–95); County Court Rules Cttee (NI), 1997–2005. Chancellor, Dio. Clogher, C of I, 1990–. Pres., Irish Legal History Soc., 1991–94 (Gold Medal, 2012). *Publications:* A History of the King's Serjeants at Law in Ireland: honour rather than advantage?, 2000; (Consultant Ed.) Valentine on Criminal Procedure in Northern Ireland, 1989; (contrib.) Brehons, Serjeants and Attorneys: studies in the history of the Irish legal profession, 1990; (contrib.) Explorations in Law and History: Irish legal history society discourses 1989–1994, 1995; A History of the Bar of Northern Ireland, 2013; (contrib.) Lawyers, the Law and History, 2013; contribs on Irish legal history to various pubns. *Recreation:* reading. *Address:* Royal Courts of Justice, Chichester Street, Belfast BT1 3JF.

HART, David Timothy Nelson; QC 2003; *b* 18 Nov. 1958; *s* of late Timothy Norman Hart and Margaret Jane Hart; *m* Rosalind Catherine English; one *s* one *d*. *Educ:* Oundle Sch.; Trinity Coll., Cambridge (BA Classics and Law 1981). Called to the Bar, Middle Temple, 1982; in practice as barrister, 1983–. Mem., Area Cttee, Legal Aid Bd/Legal Services Commn, 1995–; Appeals Officer: EU Emission Trading Scheme, 2005–; Carbon Reduction Commitment, 2010–. Mem., Res. Ethics Cttee, St Thomas' Hosp., 2002–12. *Publications:* (contrib.) Introduction to Human Rights and the Common Law, ed English and Havers; (cons. ed. and contrib.) Burnett-Hall on Environmental Law, 2nd edn 2008 to 3rd edn 2012; numerous contribs on envmtl law issues, esp. human rights. *Recreations:* walking over saltmarshes, sailing, ski-ing, conversation, frequent blogger on environmental issues. *Address:* Lapwing House, Glebe Lane, Burnham Overy Staithe, Norfolk PE31 8JQ. *E:* david.hart@1cor.com. *Clubs:* Overy Staithe Sailing; Downhill Only (Wengen).

HART, Most Rev. Denis James; *see* Melbourne, Archbishop of, (RC).

HART, Edwina, MBE 1998; Member (Lab) Gower, National Assembly for Wales, since 1999; Minister for Economy, Science and Transport (formerly for Business, Enterprise, Technology and Science, and for Transport), since 2013; *b* 26 April 1957; *d* of late Eric G. Thomas and Hannah J. Thomas; *m* 1986, Robert B. Hart; one *d*. Member: Employment Appeal Tribunal, 1992–99; Broadcasting Council for Wales, 1995–99; Adv. Cttee Wales, EOC, 1998–99. Nat. Pres., BIFU, 1992–94; Chair, Wales TUC, 1997–98. National Assembly for Wales: Sec. for Finance, 1999–2000; Minister for Finance, Local Govt and Communities, 2000–03, for Social Justice and Regeneration, 2003–07, for Health and Social Services, 2007–11. Chm., Equal Opportunity Cttee, 2000–02; Mem., SW Wales Regl Cttee, 1999–2007. Non-executive Director: Chwarae Teg, 1994–99; Wales Millennium Centre, 1997–99. Mem., Council, 1998–99, Ct of Govs, 2000–11, Univ. of Wales, Swansea. CStJ 2013. *Recreations:* reading, music, cookery. *Address:* National Assembly for Wales, Tŷ Hywel, Cardiff CF99 1NA. *T:* 0300 200 7112.

HART, Dr (Everard) Peter, CChem, FRSC; Rector, Sunderland Polytechnic, 1981–90; *b* 16 Sept. 1925; *s* of Robert Daniel Hart and Margaret Stokes; *m* Enid Mary Scott; three *s* one *d*. *Educ:* Wyggeston Grammar Sch., Leicester; Loughborough Coll.; London Univ. (BSc, PhD). Asst Lectr, Lectr and Sen. Lectr, Nottingham and Dist Technical Coll., 1951–57; Sunderland Technical College, later Sunderland Polytechnic: Head of Dept of Chemistry and Biology, 1958–69; Vice-Principal, 1963–69; Dep. Rector, 1969–80. Member: Cttee for Sci. and Technol., CNAA, 1974–77; Gen. Council, Northern Arts, 1982–90. Royal Institute of Chemistry: Mem. Council, 1963–65, 1970–73; Vice-Pres., 1973–75. FRSA 1985. Hon. DCL Sunderland, 1994. *Recreations:* music, opera, theatre, travel. *Address:* Redesdale, The Oval, North End, Durham City DH1 4NE. *T:* (0191) 384 8305.

HART, Sir Graham (Allan), KCB 1996 (CB 1987); PhD; Permanent Secretary, Department of Health, 1992–97; *b* 13 March 1940; *s* of Frederick and Winifred Hart; *m* 1964, Margaret Aline Powell; two *s*. *Educ:* Brentwood Sch.; Pembroke Coll., Oxford (Hon. Fellow 1997); Univ. of Essex (MA 2008; PhD 2015). Assistant Principal, 1962, Principal, 1967, Ministry of Health; Asst Registrar, General Medical Council, 1969–71; Principal Private Sec. to Secretary of State for Social Services, 1972–74; Asst Sec., 1974, Under Sec., 1979, DHSS; Under Sec., Central Policy Review Staff, 1982–83; Dep. Sec., DHSS, then DoH, 1984–89; Sec., Home and Health Dept, Scottish Office, 1990–92. Chairman: King's Fund, 1998–2004; Citizens Advice (formerly NACAB), 1999–2004 (Chm., Governance Rev. Gp, 1998–99); Pharmacy Practice Res. Trust, 1999–2005; Appts Cttee, GDC, 2002–08; NI Hospice Review Team, 2003; Mem., Audit Commn, 1999–2004. Dir, NHBC, 2004–12. Trustee, British Lung Foundn, 2006–12; Treas., Hist. of Parlt Trust, 2011–. *Address:* 1 Priory Lodge, Priory Park, SE3 9UY. *T:* (020) 8297 6537.

HART, Prof. Graham John, PhD; FMedSci; Professor of Sexual Health and HIV Research, since 2006, and Dean, Faculty of Population Health Sciences, since 2011, University College London; *b* Middlesbrough, 7 June 1957; *s* of late Trevor Hart and of Doris Hart; civil partnership 2006, Christopher James Thow. *Educ:* Whinney Banks Secondary Modern Sch.; Univ. of Leicester (BA 1st Cl. Hons 1978); Univ. of Kent (PhD 1982). Lectr in Med. Sociol., Middx Hosp. Med. Sch., 1986–93; Sen. Lectr, UCL, 1993–94; Associate Dir, MRC Social and Public Health Scis Unit, Univ. of Glasgow, 1994–2005. *Publications:* (Co-Ed.) Social Aspects of AIDS book series, 1989–99; (Gen. Ed.) Health, Risk and Society book series, 1994–2002; contrib. papers to BMJ, AIDS, Jl AIDS, Archives Internal Medicine, AIDS Care, Sexually Transmitted Infections, Social Sci. and Medicine, Jl Adolescence. *Recreations:* novels, theatre, art, gardens, dogs, walking, running, gym. *Address:* School of Life and Medical Sciences, University College London, Gower Street, WC1E 6BT. *T:* (020) 7679 6814. *E:* g.hart@ucl.ac.uk.

HART, Guy William Pulbrook, OBE 1985; HM Diplomatic Service, retired; *b* 24 Dec. 1931; *s* of late Ernest Guy Hart and Muriel Hart (*née* Walkington); *m* 1954, Elizabeth Marjorie (*née* Bennett) (*d* 2013); one *s* one *d* (and one *d* decd). *Educ:* Cranleigh School. Commissioned, Intelligence Corps, 1951–60. British Cellophane Ltd, 1960–62; CRO, 1962; Consular Officer, Kuala Lumpur, 1963–67; Hungarian Language Course, 1967; Second Sec. (Inf.), Budapest, 1968–71; News Dept, FCO, 1971–74; Second Sec. (Econ.), later First Sec. (Inf.), British Mil. Govt, Berlin, 1974–78; First Sec. (Comm.), Port of Spain, 1978–82, Budapest, 1982–85; Asst Head, Inf. Dept, FCO, 1986; Ambassador to the Mongolian People's Republic, 1987–89; High Comr to Seychelles, 1989–91; Head of British delegn, EC monitor mission, Zagreb, 1993–94; Mem., UN Observer mission, SA election; CSCE observer, election in former Yugoslav republic of Macedonia, 1994. *Publications:* White Month's Return: Mongolia comes of age, 1993. *Recreations:* Alpine sports, shooting, painting. *Address:* 1 Marsh Mill, Wargrave Road, Henley on Thames, Oxon RG9 3JD.

HART, Dr James Maurice, CBE 2007; QPM 1999; Commissioner, City of London Police, 2002–06; law enforcement and security consultant; *b* 10 Sept. 1947; *s* of late Lewis Hart and Beatrice Withington; *m* 1993, Julie Anne Russell; two *s*. *Educ:* Wayneflete Sch., Esher; Kingston Coll.; City Univ. (BSc Hons Systems and Mgt; PhD 1995). Joined Surrey Police, 1966; transf. to Metropolitan Police, as Chief Inspector, 1983; posts at Heathrow Airport, New Scotland Yard and Notting Hill; Chief Superintendent, 1989; Divl Comdr, Wandsworth, 1990–94; Hd, Diplomatic Protection Br., 1994; Asst Chief Constable, Surrey Police, 1994–98: Head: Support Services, 1994–95; Territorial Policing, 1995–96; Specialist Ops, 1997–98; City of London Police: Asst Comr, 1998–2002; Dep. to Comr and Operational Hd, 1998–99; Head, Support Services, 2000–01. Association of Chief Police Officers: Chm., Firearms Licensing Cttee, 1999–2002; Chm., Econ. Crime Cttee, 2002–06. CCMI 2006 (FIMgt 1998). Hon. DSc City, 2004. *Publications:* (jtly) Neighbourhood Policing: theoretical basis for community sector policing, 1981. *Recreations:* ski-ing, creating home and garden, walking, cooking and eating.

HART, Matthew Jason; dancer, choreographer, singer and actor; *b* 13 July 1972; *s* of Colin Dennis Hart and Susan Jean Hart (now Rose). *Educ:* Arts Educational Sch., London; Royal Ballet Sch., London. Dancer: London Fest. Ballet, 1984–87; Royal Ballet soloist, 1991–96; Rambert Dance Co., 1996–2000; George Piper Dances, 2001–03; freelance, 2003–; choreographer: Nat. Youth Dance, 1990; Royal Ballet, 1991–2000; Royal Ballet Sch., 1992–98, 2010, 2012; Birmingham Royal Ballet, 1993; London City Ballet, 1995–96; English Nat. Ballet, 1996; Dance Umbrella, 1996; English Nat. Ballet Sch., 1999, 2012; Ballet Deutsche Oper am Rhein, 2000; Hong Kong Ballet, 2001; London Studio Centre, 2002, 2007, 2011; George Piper Dances, 2002; K Ballet Co., Tokyo, 2003; Millennium Dance, 2000, 2005, 2006, 2013; Central Sch. of Ballet, 2009, 2012; London Children's Ballet, 2010; Sarasota Ballet, Fla, 2011, 2012, 2013; ENB2, 2012. Created rôles as: (for Royal Opera House 2): Toad, in Wind in the Willows, 2002; The Devil, in The Soldier's Tale, 2004, 2005, 2009; Oswald Alving, in Ghosts, 2005; Pinocchio (title rôle), 2005; The King of the Mountains, in The Thief of Baghdad, 2008; (for Arc Dance Co.) The Prince, in The Anatomy of a Storyteller, 2004; (for Royal Opera House 2) Tom Rakewell, in Pleasure's Progress, 2010; other appearances include: On Your Toes (musical), 2004; Mrs Henderson Presents (film), 2005; Riot at the Rite (film for BBC2), 2006; Babes in Arms (musical), Chichester Fest. Th., 2007; Viva La Diva, 2007; A Midsummer Night's Dream, 2008, Romeo and Juliet, 2008, Regent's Park; Margot (film for BBC2), 2009; dance appearances include: Betrothal in a Monastery (opera), Glyndebourne, 2006; The Prince in Matthew Bourne's Swan Lake, 2006. Dance coach and critic, Strictly Dance Fever, BBC, 2006. *Address:* c/o Conway Van Gelder Grant Ltd, 8–12 Broadwick Street, W1F 8HW. *T:* (020) 7287 0077.

HART, Michael, CBE 1990; MA; Education Consultant, European Commission, 1990–93; *b* 1 May 1928; *yr s* of late Dr F. C. Hardt; *m* 1956, Lida Dabney Adams, PhD (Wisconsin Univ.). *Educ:* Collège Français, Berlin; Landerziehungsheim Schondorf; Keble Coll., Oxford (Exhib.; 1st Cl. Hons History, 1951). Administrative Asst, UNRRA, 1945–47; Asst Master and Head of History, Sherborne Sch., 1951–56; Head of History, 1956–61, and Housemaster of School House, 1961–67, Shrewsbury Sch.; Headmaster of Mill Hill Sch., 1967–74; HM Inspector of Schs, DES, 1974–76; Headmaster, European Sch., Mol, Belgium, 1976–80; Headmaster, European Sch., Luxembourg, 1980–89; Dir, European Classes, Alden Biesen, Belgium, 1989–92. FRSA. Commandeur de l'Ordre de Mérite (Luxembourg), 1989. *Publications:* The EEC and Secondary Education in the UK, 1974; The European Dimension in Primary and Secondary Education, 1992; contrib. to Reader's Digest World Atlas and Atlas of British Isles. *Recreations:* dogs, history, music, bridge. *Address:* 13 St Luke's Court, Hyde Lane, Marlborough, Wilts SN8 1YU.

HART, Prof. Michael, CBE 1993; FRS 1982; FInstP; Professor of Physics, University of Manchester, 1984–93, now Emeritus; Chairman, National Synchrotron Light Source, Brookhaven National Laboratory, 1995–2000; *b* 4 Nov. 1938; *s* of Reuben Harold Victor Hart and Phyllis Mary (*née* White); *m* 1963, Susan Margaret (*née* Powell); three *d*. *Educ:* Cotham Grammar Sch., Bristol; Bristol Univ. (BSc, PhD, DSc). FInstP 1971. Research Associate: Dept of Materials Science and Engrg, Cornell Univ., 1963–65; Dept of Physics, Bristol Univ., 1965–67; Lectr in Physics, 1967–72, Reader in Physics, 1972–76, Bristol Univ.; Sen. Resident Res. Associate of Nat. Research Council, NASA Electronics Research Center, Boston, Mass, 1969–70; Special Advisor, Central Policy Review Staff, Cabinet Office, 1975–77; Wheatstone Prof. of Physics and Head of Physics Dept, KCL, 1976–84; Science Programme Co-ordinator (part-time, on secondment), Daresbury Lab., SERC, 1985–88. Prof. of Applied Physics, De Montfort Univ., 1993–98; Hon. Prof. in Engrg, Warwick Univ., 1993–98; Vis. Prof. in Physics, Bristol Univ., 2000–05. Amer. Crystallographic Assoc.'s Bertram Eugene Warren Award for Diffraction Physics (jtly with Dr U. Bonse), 1970; Charles Vernon Boys Prize of Inst. of Physics, 1971. *Publications:* numerous contribs to learned jls on x-ray optics, defects in crystals and synchrotron radiation. *Recreations:* tennis, cookery, flying kites. *Address:* 2 Challoner Court, Merchants Landing, Bristol BS1 4RG. *T:* (0117) 921 5291. *E:* michael_hart@blueyonder.co.uk.

HART, Michael, FCII; non-executive Chairman, Furness Building Society, 2005–09 (Director, 2000–09); *b* 28 Sept. 1937; *s* of William and Kathleen Hart; *m* (separated); two *s* two *d*. FCII 1971. Man. Dir, 1987–94, Chm., 1994–95, Provincial Insurance plc; Chief Exec., Sun Life and Provincial (Hldgs) plc, 1995–97, retired. Non-exec. Chm., Flemings European Fledgeling Investment Trust plc, 1998–2006; Director: Inter American Insurance Ltd, 1998–2001; Active Languages Ltd, 1999–2008; Time Group Ltd, 2001–04; PremierLine Ltd, 2003–06; Home & Legacy Holdings Ltd, 2003–06. Mem. Council, Lancaster Univ., 1998–2006. Chm. Trustees, Brewery Arts Centre, 1997–2011. *Recreations:* walking, wine. *Address:* 17 Whinlatter Drive, Kendal LA9 7HE. *T:* (01539) 736586.

HART, Miranda Katherine; actress, comedienne and writer; *b* Torquay, 14 Dec. 1972; *d* of Captain David Hart Dyke, *qv*. *Educ:* Downe House Sch., Berks; Univ. of West of England (BA Hons Politics); Acad. of Live and Recorded Arts. PA/Office Manager, Macmillan Cancer Support, 1998–2001; PA, Comic Relief, 2001–03; actress in television series: Vicar of Dibley, 2004; Absolutely Fabulous, 2004; Smack the Pony, 2004; Nighty Night, 2005; Hyperdrive, 2006–07; Not Going Out, 2006–09; Angelo's, 2007; Monday, Monday, 2009; Miranda (also writer), 2009–14; Call the Midwife, 2012–; actress in film, Spy, 2015. Stand-up show, My, What I Call Live, Show, UK tour, 2014. Hon. Trustee, Comic Relief, 2010–; Patron, Spear, 2011–. *Publications:* Is it Just Me?, 2012. *Recreations:* theatre, musicals, tennis, walking, animals, travel. *Address:* c/o Troika Talent, 10A Christina Street, EC2A 4PA.

HART, Prof. Oliver Simon D'Arcy, PhD; Professor of Economics, since 1993, and Andrew E. Furer Professor, since 1997, Harvard University; *b* 9 Oct. 1948; *s* of late Philip Montagu D'Arcy Hart, CBE and Ruth Hart; *m* 1974, Rita Goldberg (who retains maiden name); two *s*. *Educ:* University Coll. Sch.; Univ. of Cambridge (BA 1969); Univ. of Warwick (MA 1972); Princeton Univ. (PhD 1974). Lectr in Econs, Univ. of Essex, 1974–75; Asst Lectr in Econs, subseq. Lectr, Univ. of Cambridge, 1975–81; Fellow of Churchill Coll., Cambridge, 1975–81; Prof. of Economics, LSE, 1982–85; Prog. Dir, Centre for Economic Policy Res., 1983–84; Prof. of Economics, MIT, 1985–93. Centennial Vis. Prof., LSE, 1997–. Sec.-Treas., Amer. Law and Econs Assoc., 2004–05 (Pres., 2006–07); Vice-Pres., AEA, 2006–07. Fellow: Econometric Soc., 1979 (Mem. Council, 1983–89, 1994–99); Amer. Acad. of Arts and Scis, 1988; Eur. Corporate Governance Inst., 2002. Corresp. FBA 2000. Editor, Review of Economic Studies, 1979–83. Dr *hc*: Free Univ. of Brussels, 1992; Univ. of Basel, 1994; Univ. of Paris-Dauphine, 2009; Copenhagen Business Sch., 2009; Hon. DSc (Econ) London Business Sch., 2011; Hon. LLD Warwick, 2012. *Publications:* Firms, Contracts, and Financial Structure, 1995; articles in Jl of Pol Economy, Qly Jl of Econs, Amer. Econ. Rev., Econometrica. *Recreations:* playing the piano, watching tennis. *Address:* Department of Economics, Harvard University, Cambridge, MA 02138, USA.

HART, Peter; *see* Hart, E. P.

HART, Roger Dudley, CMG 1998; HM Diplomatic Service, retired; Ambassador to Peru, 1999–2003; *b* 29 Dec. 1943; *s* of Alfred John Hart and Emma Jane Hart; *m* 1968, Maria de Los Angeles (Angela) de Santiago Jimenez; two *s*. *Educ:* St Olave's Grammar Sch., London; Univ. of Birmingham (BA 1965). Entered FO 1965; served British Mil. Govt W Berlin, Bahrain and FCO; First Sec. (Aid), Nairobi, 1975–78; First Sec. (Commercial), Lisbon, 1978–83; FCO, 1983–85; RCDS 1985; BNSC, 1986; Consul-Gen., Rio de Janeiro, 1986–90; Dep. Hd of Mission, Mexico City, 1990–93; Head of Nationality, Treaty and Claims Dept, FCO, 1993–95; Ambassador to Angola, and (non-resident) to São Tomé and Príncipe, 1995–98. Citizen, 1989, Pedro Ernesto Medal, 1990, Rio de Janeiro. *Recreations:* travel, classical music, old silver. *Address:* 7 Rosscourt Mansions, 4 Palace Street, SW1E 5HZ. *Club:* Canning.

HART, Simon Anthony; MP (C) Carmarthen West and Pembrokeshire South, since 2010; *b* 15 Aug. 1963; *s* of Anthony Hart and Judith Hart (*née* Christie); *m* 1998, Abigail Kate Holland; one *s* one *d*. *Educ:* Radley Coll., Oxon; RAC Cirencester (Rural Estate Mgt). MRICS (ARICS 1985–99). Llewellyn Humphreys, Chartered Surveyors, 1988–98; Balfour, Burd & Benson, Chartered Surveyors, 1998–99; Regl Public Relns Officer, 1999, Dir of Campaign for Hunting, 1999–2003, Chief Exec., 2003–10, Countryside Alliance. Member: Pol and Constitutional Select Cttee, 2010–12; Welsh Affairs Select Cttee, 2012–15; Envmt, Food and Rural Affairs Select Cttee, 2015–. Master and Huntsman, S Pembrokeshire Hunt, 1988–99. Trustee, Sundorne Estate, 1995–. *Recreations:* all aspects of country sports, cricket. *Address:* House of Commons, SW1A 0AA. *Clubs:* Farmers; Cresselly Cricket.

HART, Prof. Stephen Malcolm, PhD; Professor of Latin American Film, Literature and Culture, since 2002, and Director, Economic and Social Research Council Doctoral Training Centre, since 2014, University College London; *b* London, 25 Aug. 1959; *s* of Bryan Hart and Barbara Hart; *m* 1978, Danielle Elizabeth Degaute; one *s* three *d*. *Educ:* Downing Coll., Cambridge (BA 1980; PhD 1985). Lectr, Westfield Coll., London, 1984–91; Associate Prof., Univ. of Kentucky, 1991–98; Sen. Lectr, 1998–2000, Reader, 2000–02, UCL. Gen. Ed., Tamesis, 1999–. Corresp. Mem., Peruvian Acad. of Language, 2013. Order of Merit (Peru), 2004. *Publications:* Gabriel García Márquez, 2010; César Vallejo: a literary biography, 2013; Latin American Cinema, 2014. *Recreations:* jogging, cinema, theatre, art. *Address:* Department of Spanish, Portuguese and Latin American Studies, School of European Languages, Culture and Society, 305 Foster Court, University College London, Gower Street, WC1E 6BT. *T:* (020) 7679 3036. *E:* stephen.malcolm.hart@ucl.ac.uk.

HART, Prof. Susan Jane Ritchie, PhD; FRSE; Professor of Marketing, since 1998, Dean, Strathclyde Business School, since 2008, and Executive Dean, Internationalisation, since 2011, Strathclyde University; *b* Edinburgh, 18 July 1960; *d* of Thomas Hart and Jean Sutherland McDonald Forbes Hart; one *s* one *d*. *Educ:* Bearsden Acad.; Strathclyde Univ. (BA Hons 1982; PhD 1987); Mktg Res. Soc., Strathclyde (Dip. 1985). Lectr, Dept of Mktg, Strathclyde Univ., 1987–92; Professor of Marketing: Heriot-Watt Univ., 1993–95; Stirling Univ., 1995–98; Hd, Dept of Mktg, 2002–04, Vice Dean, Strathclyde Business School, 2005–08, Strathclyde Univ. Ed., Jl Mktg Mgt, 2000–. FRSE 2009; Fellow, Leadership Trust Foundn, 2010. Mem. Bd, Assoc. to Advance Collegiate Schs of Business, 2011–. *Publications:* Marketing Changes, 2003; New Product Development, 1996; Product Strategy and Management, 2007. *Recreations:* cycling, ski-ing. *Address:* Strathclyde Business School, University of Strathclyde, Room 321, Level 3, 199 Cathedral Street, Glasgow G4 0QU.

HART, (Thomas) Anthony (Alfred), MA; Headmaster, Cranleigh School, 1984–97; *b* 4 March 1940; *er s* of Rev. Arthur Reginald Hart and Florence Ivy Hart; *m* 1971, Daintre Margaret Withiel (*née* Thomas); one *s* one *d*. *Educ:* City of Bath Sch.; New Coll., Oxford (2nd Cl. Hons PPE; MA); Pres., Oxford Union, 1963. Served with VSO, Mzuzu Secondary Sch., Nyasaland, 1959–60. Asst Principal and Principal, Min. of Transport, 1964–69; seconded to Govt of Malaŵi as Transport Adviser, 1969–70; Principal, DoE and CSD, 1970–73; Head, Voluntary Services Unit, Home Office, 1973–75; Asst Sec., CSD and HM Treasury, 1975–84. *Recreation:* enjoying Cyprus. *Address:* PO Box 59340, Pissouri, 4607, Cyprus. *T:* (25) 222802. *E:* daintrecyprus@cytanet.com.cy.

HART, Prof. Vaughan Anthony, PhD; Professor of Architecture, since 2005, and Director, Centre for Advanced Studies in Architecture, 1994–2001 and 2010–14, University of Bath; *b* Belfast, 23 Oct. 1960; *s* of Ronald Hart and Mary Hart (*née* Glass); *m* 1999, Charlotte Courtman-Davies; one *s*. *Educ:* Univ. of Bath (BSc 1983; BArch 1985); Trinity Hall, Cambridge (MPhil 1987; PhD 1991). University of Bath: Res. Officer, 1991–93; Lectr in Architecture, 1993–95; Sen. Lectr, 1995–97; Reader in Architectural Hist., 1997–2005; Hd, Dept of Architecture and Civil Engrg, 2008–10; Member: Senate, 2010–11; Court, 2011–. Vis. Prof. of Architecture, Univ. of Kent, 2010–. Sen. Fellow, Paul Mellon Centre for Studies in British Art, London, 2005; Vis. Fellow, St John's Coll., Oxford, 2005; Sen. Vis. Fellow, Centre for Advanced Study in Visual Arts, Nat. Gall. of Art, Washington, 2009. Mem., Adv. Bd, Helsinki Collegium for Advanced Studies, Univ. Helsinki, 2012–. Exhibitions curated: Paper Palaces, Fitzwilliam Mus., Cambridge, 1997; Palladio's Rome, British Sch. at Rome, 2008; Virtual Reality, Sorbonne, Paris, 2009. Work displayed in Royal Acad. Summer Exhibns, 1986 (winner, student prize), 1993, 1995. Trustee, Holburne Mus., Bath, 2011–; Trustee and Mem. Council, Oriental Ceramics Soc., 2014–. *Publications:* Art and Magic in the Court of the Stuarts, 1994; (trans. jtly) Sebastiano Serlio on Architecture, vol. 1, 1996, vol. 2, 2001, 2nd edn (2 vols) 2005; St Paul's Cathedral: Christopher Wren, 1995, 2nd edn 1999; Paper Palaces: the rise of the Renaissance architectural treatise, 1998; Nicholas Hawksmoor: rebuilding ancient wonders, 2002, 2nd edn 2007 (Best Book on British Art Prize, Amer. Coll. Art Assoc., 2005); (trans. jtly) Palladio's Rome, 2006, 2nd edn 2009 (Japanese edn 2011); Sir John Vanbrugh: storyteller in stone, 2008; Inigo Jones: the architect of kings, 2011. *Recreations:* swimming, collecting Chinese porcelain, playing chess with Christopher, supporting Fulham FC. *Address:* c/o Department of Architecture and Civil Engineering, University of Bath, Bath BA2 7AY. *T:* (01225) 386361, *Fax:* (01225) 386691. *E:* v.hart@bath.ac.uk.

HART-DAVIS, Dr Adam John; freelance writer, since 1994; *b* 4 July 1943; *yr s* of Sir Rupert Hart-Davis; *m* 1st, 1965, Adrienne Alpin (marr. diss. 1995); two *s*; 2nd, 2010, Susan Blackmore. *Educ:* Eton; Merton Coll., Oxford (BA 1st Cl. Hons Chemistry 1966; Hon. Fellow 2006); York Univ. (DPhil 1968). Post-doctoral Research: Univ. of Alberta, Edmonton, 1969–71; Univ. of Oxford, 1971; College Science Editor, Clarendon Press (OUP), 1971–77; Researcher, 1977–83, Producer, 1983–94, Yorkshire Television. Presenter: TV series: Local Heroes, 1992–2000; Hart-Davis on History, 1998, 1999; Secret City, 2000; What the Romans Did for Us, 2000; What the Victorians Did for Us, 2001; Science Shack, 2001, 2003; Adam Hart-Davis says Come to Your Senses, 2001; Tomorrow's World, 2002; What the Tudors Did for Us, 2002; What the Stuarts Did for Us, 2002; Industrial Nation, 2003; What the Ancients Did for Us, 2005; How London Was Built, 2005, 2006, 2007; The Cosmos: a beginner's guide, 2007; Just Another Day, 2007; How Britain Was Built, 2008; radio series: Inventors Imperfect, 1999–2003; High Resolution, 2001; Elements of Surprise,

2001; Engineering Solutions, 2004, 2006, 2007; Eureka Years, 2004, 2005, 2007, 2008. Mem., ASME, 2014–15. Pres., Tavistock Fest. of Music and Arts, 2013–. Member: Newcomen Soc.; Assoc. of Polelathe Turners; Patron: Wrexham Science Fest., 1998; Cycle West, 2000; Brede Steam Engine Soc., 2002; Theatre Odyssey, 2002; The Garden Sci. Trust, 2003; Museum of Sci. and Industry, Manchester, 2003; ACT, 2003; Ideas 21; Assoc. of Lighthouse Keepers, 2003; Bognor Birdman, 2004; Holgate Windmill Preservation Soc., 2004; Crank It Up, 2004; Transplant Links Community, 2008; Engineering Explained, 2008; Life Pres., Ellenroad Trust, 2004. Hon. Member: British Toilet Assoc.; Associates of Discovery Museum, 2003; S Hams Soc., 2009; Hon. MRI 2005. Comp ILE 2005. Hon. Fellow: Soc. of Dyers and Colourists, 2005; British Sci. Assoc., 2010; Hon. FRSC 2007; Hon. FRPS 2007. DUniv: York, 2000; Brunel, 2007; Open, 2009; Hon DTech: Loughborough, 2001; UWE, 2005; Hon. DSc: Sheffield, Bradford, 2001; Birmingham, 2002; Bristol, Sheffield Hallam, Leicester, 2003; QUB, 2004; Hon. DCL Northumbria, 2002; Hon. DLitt Bath, 2004. Gerald Frewer Meml Trophy, Instn of Engrg Designers, 1999; first medal for public promotion of engrg, Royal Acad. of Engrg, 2002; Sir Henry Royce Meml Medal, IIE, 2003; Judges' Award for Educnl TV, RTS, 2003; ASME Ralph Coats Roe Medal, 2014. *Publications:* Don't Just Sit There!, 1980; (with Hilary Lawson) Where There's Life…, 1982; Scientific Eye, 1986; Mathematical Eye, 1989; World's Weirdest "True" Ghost Stories, 1991; (with Susan Blackmore) Test Your Psychic Powers, 1995; Thunder, Flush and Thomas Crapper, 1997; Science Tricks, 1997; (with Paul Bader) The Local Heroes Book of British Ingenuity, 1997; (with Paul Bader) More Local Heroes, 1998; Amazing Math Puzzles, 1998; Eurekaaargh!, 1999; (with Paul Bader) The Local Heroes Book of DIY Science, 2000; Chain Reactions, 2000; What the Victorians Did for Us, 2001; (with Emily Troscianko) Henry Winstanley and the Eddystone Lighthouse, 2002; What the Tudors and Stuarts Did for Us, 2002; Talking Science, 2004; What the Past Did for Us, 2004; Why Does a Ball Bounce?, 2005; (with Emily Troscianko) Taking the Piss, 2006; Just Another Day, 2006; (with Paul Bader) The Cosmos: a beginner's guide, 2007; (ed) History: the definitive visual guide, 2007; String: unravel the secrets of a little ball of twine, 2009; (ed) Science: the definitive visual guide, 2009; The Book of Time, 2011; (ed) Engineers, 2012; Inventions, 2012; The Science Book, 2014. *Recreations:* green woodwork, drinking wine, chess, growing vegetables, drawing, watercolour painting.

See also P. D. Hart-Davis.

HART-DAVIS, (Peter) Duff; author and journalist; *b* 3 June 1936; *er s* of Sir Rupert Hart-Davis; *m* 1961, Phyllida Barstow; one *s* one *d*. *Educ:* Eton; Worcester Coll., Oxford (BA 1960). Nat. Service, Coldstream Guards, 1955–57. Joined Sunday Telegraph, 1961; Editor, News Background page, 1966–70; feature writer, 1971–75; Literary Editor, 1975–76; Asst Editor, 1976–78. Country Columnist, Independent, 1986–2001. *Publications:* Ascension, 1972; Peter Fleming, 1974; Monarchs of the Glen, 1978; Hitler's Games, 1986; (ed) The Letters and Journals of Sir Alan Lascelles: Vol. 1, End of an Era, 1986; Vol. 2, In Royal Service, 1989; Armada, 1988; Country Matters, 1989; The House the Berrys Built, 1990; Wildings: the secret garden of Eileen Soper, 1991; Further Country Matters, 1992; When the Country Went to Town, 1997; Raoul Millais, 1998; Fauna Britannica, 2002; Audubon's Elephant, 2003; (ed) Pavilions of Splendour, 2004; Honorary Tiger, 2005; (ed) King's Counsellor, 2006; Philip de László: his life and art, 2010; The War that Never Was: the true story of the men who fought Britain's most secret battle, 2011; Among the Deer, 2011; Man of War, 2012; Our Land at War, 2015; *fiction:* The Megacull, 1968; The Gold of St Matthew, 1970; Spider in the Morning, 1972; The Heights of Rimring, 1980; Level Five, 1982; Fire Falcon, 1983; The Man-eater of Jassapur, 1985; Horses of War, 1991. *Recreations:* opera, wine, cutting and splitting firewood, deer. *Address:* Owlpen Farm, Uley, Glos GL11 5BZ. *T:* (01453) 860239.

See also A. J. Hart-Davis.

HART DYKE, Captain David, CBE 1990; LVO 1980; RN; Clerk to Worshipful Company of Skinners, 1990–2003; *b* 3 Oct. 1938; *s* of late Comdr Rev. Eric Hart Dyke and Mary Hart Dyke; *m* 1967, Diana Margaret, *d* of Sir William Luce, GBE, KCMG; two *d*. *Educ:* St Lawrence College, Ramsgate; BRNC Dartmouth. RN 1958; served Far East and Middle East; navigation specialist; Exec. Officer, HMS Hampshire, 1974–76; Staff, RN Staff Coll., 1976–78; Comdr, HM Yacht Britannia, 1978–80; Captain HMS Coventry; action in Falklands, 1982; ACOS to C-in-C Fleet, 1982–84; Asst Naval Attaché, Washington, 1985–87; Dir, Naval Recruiting, 1987–89. ADC to the Queen, 1988–89. *Publications:* Four Weeks in May: the loss of HMS Coventry - a captain's story, 2007. *Recreations:* water-colouring, garden design, military history, tennis. *Address:* Hambledon House, Hambledon, Hants PO7 4RU. *T:* (023) 9263 2380.

See also M. K. Hart.

HART DYKE, Sir David (William), 10th Bt *cr* 1677, of Horeham, Sussex; journalist; *b* 5 Jan. 1955; *s* of Sir Derek William Hart Dyke, 9th Bt and Dorothy Moses; *S* father, 1987. *Educ:* Ryerson Polytechnical Institute (BA). Presenter, Scientists in School, 2012–. Member, Board of Directors: Ontario Envmt Network, 2009–; Earth Day Hamilton-Burlington, 2010–. Contested (Green Party) Hamilton E-Stoney Creek, 2008, 2011. *Recreations:* portage camping, ice hockey, reading. *Heir: uncle* (Oliver) Guy Hart Dyke [*b* 9 Feb. 1928; *m* 1974, Sarah Alexander, *d* of late Rev. Eric Hart Dyke; one *s* one *d*]. *Address:* 28 King Street West, Apt 14B, Stoney Creek, ON L8G 1H4, Canada.

HART DYKE, Miranda Katherine; *see* Hart, M. K.

HART-LEVERTON, Colin Allen; QC 1979; a Recorder of the Crown Court, 1979–2001; *b* 10 May 1936; *s* of Monty Hart-Leverton and Betty (*née* Simmonds); one *s*; *m* 1990, Kathi Jo, *d* of Hal and Jan Davidson. *Educ:* Stowe; self-taught thereafter. Mem., Inst. of Taxation, 1957 (youngest to have ever qualified); called to the Bar, Middle Temple, 1957 (youngest to have ever qual.). Contested (L): Bristol West, 1959 (youngest cand.); Walthamstow West, 1964. Prosecuting Counsel, Central Criminal Court, 1974–79; Dep. Circuit Judge, 1975; Attorney-at-Law, Turks and Caicos Islands, Caribbean, 1976. Occasional television and radio broadcasts. Professional pianist with various well-known jazz bands. *Recreations:* table-tennis, jazz. *Address:* 1MCB, Third Floor, 15 New Bridge Street, EC4V 6AU. *T:* (020) 7452 8900.

HARTE, (Catherine) Miriam; DL; owner and Director, culture heritage and project management consultancy, since 2007; *b* 3 Aug. 1960; *d* of Joseph and Mary Harte. *Educ:* Trinity Coll., Dublin (BA Law 1981). Chartered Accountant, 1985; FCA 1995. Trainee, Arthur Andersen & Co., 1981–86; Finance Manager, UK and Europe/US, Procter & Gamble, 1986–97; freelance trng/consulting, 1997–98; Director: Bede's World, 1998–2001; Beamish, North of England Open Air Mus., 2001–07; Interim Manager, Hancock Project, Gt North Mus., 2008–09. Board Member: MLA NE (formerly NE MLAC), 2001–07; NE Tourism Adv. Bd, 2004–07. Dir, Audiences NE, 2004–. Non-exec. Dir, Sunderland City Hosps Trust, 2007–. DL Co. Durham, 2007. *Recreations:* walking, cooking, theatre, travelling. *Address:* Thorn Cottage, 125 Kells Lane, Low Fell NE9 5XY. *T:* (0191) 487 9258. *E:* miriamharte@gmail.com.

HARTE, Julia Kathleen; *see* McKenzie, J. K.

HARTE, Miriam; *see* Harte, C. M.

HARTER, Dr Andrew Charles, FREng, FIET; FBCS; Founder and Chief Executive Officer, RealVNC Ltd, since 2002; Fellow, St Edmund's College, Cambridge, since 2002; *b* Yorks, 5 April 1961; *s* of late Roy Harter and Jean Dorothy Harter (*née* Brook); *m* 2004, Lily Bacon; two *s*. *Educ:* Queen Elizabeth Grammar Sch., Wakefield; Fitzwilliam Coll., Cambridge (BA 1983); Corpus Christi Coll., Cambridge (PhD 1990). CEng 2002; FIET 2002; FREng 2011. Principal Res. Engr, Olivetti and Oracle Res. Lab., 1990–99; Dir of Res. and Engrg, AT&T Labs Res., 1999–2002. Vis. Fellow, Univ. of Cambridge Computer Lab., 2002–. Chm., Cambridge Network, 2014–. Trustee: RAEng, 2013–; Britten Sinfonia, 2013–; Centre for Computing Hist., 2013–; IET, 2014–. FLCM 1979; FBCS 2007. FRSA 2014. Hon. DSc Anglia Ruskin, 2015. Silver Medal, 2010, MacRobert Award, 2013, RAEng. *Publications:* Three-dimensional Integrated Circuit Layout, 1991, 2nd edn 2009; patents and papers on computer systems. *Recreations:* golf, ski-ing, Rugby, flying, music, opera, theatre, badgers. *Address:* 15 Tenison Avenue, Cambridge CB1 2DX. *T:* 07734 251812. *E:* ach3@cam.ac.uk.

HARTER, Caryl, (Mrs David Harter); *see* Churchill, C.

HARTILL, Edward Theodore, OBE 2004; FRICS; Business Development Advisor, Corderoy, international chartered quantity surveyors and cost consultants, 2008–09; City Surveyor, City of London Corporation (formerly Corporation of London), 1985–2008; *b* 23 Jan. 1943; *s* of late Clement Augustus Hartill and Florence Margarita Hartill; *m* 1975, Gillian Ruth Todd; two *s*, and two *s* from previous marr. *Educ:* Priory Sch. for Boys, Shrewsbury; Coll. of Estate Management, London Univ. BSc (Estate Management); FRICS 1978. Joined Messrs Burd and Evans, Land Agents, Shrewsbury, 1963; Estates Dept, Legal and Gen. Assce Soc., 1964–73; Property Investment Dept, Guardian Royal Exchange Assce Gp, 1973–85 (Hd Office Manager, 1980–85). Vis. Lectr in Law of Town Planning and Compulsory Purchase, Hammersmith and W London Coll. of Advanced Business Studies, 1968–78. Royal Institution of Chartered Surveyors: Member: Gen. Practice Divl Council, 1989–97 (Pres., 1992–93); Governing Council, 1990–2004; Hon. Treas., 2000–04. Mem., Assoc. of Chief Estates Surveyors and Property Managers in Local Govt (formerly Local Authority Valuers Assoc.), 1985–2007 (Mem., Nat. Council, 1988–2007; Pres., 1996–97; Hon. Mem., 2007); Mem., Govt Study Team on Professional Liability, 1988–89; Mem. Steering Gp, 1992–99, and Chm., Property Services Sub-Gp, 1992–99, Construction Industry Standing Conf.; Founder Mem. and Chm., Property Services NTO, 1999–2004; Vice-Chm., Asset Skills, 2004–07 (Chm., 2003). University of London: Member: Council, 2004–08; Bd of Trustees, 2008–15; Estates Cttee, 2004–08 (Dep. Chm., 2006–08); Investments Cttee, 2008–15 (Dep. Chm., 2009–15); Chm., Senate House Project Bd, 2006–12; Dep. Chm., Univ. Marine Biol Station, 2009–13 (Mem., Bd of Trustees, 2008–13); Chm., Safety Cttee, 2009–15. Gov. and Trustee, Coram (formerly Coram Family), 2006–14 (Vice Chm., 2007–08; Chm., 2008–14; Hon. Vice Pres., 2014). Hon. Mem., Investment Property Forum, 1995. Hon. Associate, Czech Chamber of Appraisers, 1992. Mem., British Schs Exploring Soc. Life Fellow, RSA (FRSA 1993). Liveryman, Chartered Surveyors' Co., 1985– (Mem., Court of Assistants, 1991–2009; Master, 2003–04). *Recreations:* hill walking, travel, cars, watching GT racing. *Address:* 215 Sheen Lane, East Sheen, SW14 8LE. *T:* (020) 8878 4494.

See also R. J. Hartill.

HARTILL, Rosemary Jane; journalist and facilitator, Alternatives to Violence Project, Britain, since 1996 (Trustee, 1997–2000); *b* 11 Aug. 1949; *d* of late Clement Augustus Hartill and Florence Margarita Ford. *Educ:* Wellington Girls' High Sch., Salop; Bristol Univ. (BA (Hons) English). Editor: Tom Stacey (Publishing) Ltd, 1970–73; David and Charles Ltd, 1973–75; Sen. Non-fiction Editor, Hamish Hamilton Children's Books Ltd, 1975–76; freelance journalist and broadcaster, 1976–82; freelance book and ballet reviewer, TES, 1976–80; Religious Affairs Reporter, 1979–82, Religious Affairs Corresp., 1982–88, BBC; Reporter: BBC Everyman Prog., 1987; ITV Human Factor series, 1989–92; Presenter: BBC Woman's Hour (NE edns), 1989–90; Meridian Books (BBC World Service), and numerous other progs. Founder, Rosemary Hartill & Associates, 1996; Co-Founder, Voyager TV Ltd, 1997; non-executive Director: Shared Interest, 1996–2005; Ethical Investment Res. Service, 1997–2001. Board Member: Nat. Probation Service, Northumbria, 2001–07; (non-exec.) Northumberland Tyne and Wear Strategic HA, 2002–05; Courts Bd, Northumbria, 2004–07; Youth Justice Bd for England and Wales, 2004–08. Trustee, The Friend, 2004–10; Facilitator, Barter Books book gp, Alnwick, 2003–; Mem. mgt gp, Newcastle Conflict Resolution Network, 2005–13. Mem., Soc. of Friends (Mem., Former Yugoslavia Project Mgt Gp, 2000–02; Mem., Central Cttee, Quaker Communications, 2010–12). FRSA 2001. Hon. DLitt: Hull, 1995; Bristol, 2000. Sandford St Martin Trust personal award for outstanding contrib. to religious broadcasting, 1994, and other awards. *Publications:* (ed) Emily Brontë: poems, 1973; Wild Animals, 1978; In Perspective, 1988; Writers Revealed, 1989; Were You There?, 1995; (ed) Florence Nightingale, 1996. *Recreations:* being in Northumberland, wildlife, theatre, music, film, books, exploring modern art and architecture. *Address:* 101b/17 St Stephen Street, Edinburgh EH3 5AB.

See also E. T. Hartill.

HARTING, Henry Maria Robert Egmont M.; *see* Mayr-Harting.

HARTINGTON, Marquess of; courtesy title of heir of Duke of Devonshire, not used by current heir.

HARTLAND, Michael; *see* James, M. L.

HARTLAND-SWANN, Julian Dana Nimmo, CMG 1992; HM Diplomatic Service, retired; Thai-Europe business consultant, since 1997; *b* 18 Feb. 1936; *s* of late Prof. J. J. Hartland-Swann and of Mrs Kenlis Hartland-Swann (*née* Taylour); *m* 1st, 1960, Ann Deirdre Green (*d* 2000); one *s* one *d*; 2nd, 2004, Julie Katherine Ryan. *Educ:* Stowe; Lincoln Coll., Oxford (History). HM Forces, 1955–57. Entered HM Diplomatic Service, 1960; 3rd Sec., Brit. Embassy, Bangkok, 1961–65; 2nd, later 1st Sec., FO, 1965–68; 1st Sec., Berlin, 1968–71; 1st Sec. and Head of Chancery, Vienna, 1971–74; FCO, 1975–77; Counsellor, 1977; Ambassador to Mongolian People's Republic, 1977–79; Counsellor and Dep. Head of Mission, Brussels, 1979–83; Head of SE Asian Dept, FCO, 1983–85; Consul Gen., Frankfurt, 1986–90; Ambassador to Burma (Myanmar), 1990–95; Exec. Dir, Eur. Business Inf. Centre, Delegn of the EC to Thailand, 1995–97. *Recreations:* French food, sailing, restoring ruins. *Address:* Résidence Hof Ten Berg, Clos Hof Ten Berg 30, 1200 Brussels, Belgium.

HARTLEY, Prof. Brian Selby, PhD; FRS 1971; Professor of Biochemistry, Imperial College, University of London, 1974–91, now Emeritus; Director, 1982–91, Senior Research Fellow, 1991–94, Centre for Biotechnology; *b* 16 April 1926; *s* of Norman and Hilda Hartley; *m* 1949, Kathleen Maude Vaughan; three *s* one *d*. *Educ:* Queens' Coll., Cambridge (BA 1947, MA 1952); Univ. of Leeds (PhD 1952). ICI Fellow, Univ. of Cambridge, 1952; Helen Hay Whitney Fellow, Univ. of Washington, Seattle, USA, 1958; Fellow and Lectr in Biochemistry, Trinity Coll., Cambridge, 1964; Scientific Staff, MRC Laboratory of Molecular Biology, 1961–74. Chairman: Agrol Ltd, 1993–2000; BioConversion Technologies Ltd, 2006–09; Biocaldol Ltd, 2009–10 (Sen. Scientific Advr, 2010–12); Chm. and Res. Dir, E3 Biotechnology Ltd, 2012–. Mem. Council: EMBO (European Centre for Molecular Biology), 1978–84; Royal Soc., 1982–84. Hon. Mem., Amer. Soc. of Biological Chemists, 1977. British Drug Houses Medal for Analytical Biochemistry, 1969. *Publications:* over 150 papers and articles in scientific jls and books. *Recreations:* gardening, genealogy. *Address:* Grove Cottage, 21 Smith Street, Elsworth, Cambridge CB23 4HY.

HARTLEY, Caroline Mary; *see* Rookes, C. M.

HARTLEY, David Fielding, PhD; CEng; FBCS, CITP; Museum Director, National Museum of Computing, 2012–13; Fellow, Clare College, Cambridge, since 1986 (Steward, 2002–05); *b* 14 Sept. 1937; *s* of late Robert M. Hartley and Sheila E. Hartley, LRAM; *m* 1960, Joanna Mary (*d* 1998), *d* of late Stanley and Constance Bolton; one *s* two *d*. *Educ:* Rydal Sch.;

Clare Coll., Cambridge (MA, PhD 1963). FBCS 1968; CEng 1990; CITP 2004. University of Cambridge: Sen. Asst in Research, Mathematical Lab., 1964–65; Asst Dir of Research, 1966–67; Univ. Lectr, 1967–70; Dir, Univ. Computing Service, 1970–94; Jun. Research Fellow, Churchill Coll., Cambridge, 1964–67; Fellow, Darwin Coll., Cambridge, 1969–86; Chief Exec., UK Educn and Res. Networking Assoc., 1994–97; Exec. Dir, Cambridge Crystallographic Data Centre, 1997–2002. British Computer Society: Mem. Council, 1970–73, 1977–80, 1985–90, 1998–2002; Vice Pres. (Technical), 1985–87, (External Relns), 1987–90; Dep. Pres., 1998–99; Pres., 1999–2000. Mem., Computer Conservation Soc., 2007– (Chm., 2007–11; Hon. Treas., 2013–). Chm., Inter-University Cttee on Computing, 1972–74; Mem., Computer Bd for Univs and Research Councils, 1979–83. Mem. Council of Management, Numerical Algorithms Gp Ltd, 1979–2006 (Chm., 1986–97); adviser to Prime Minister, Information Technology Adv. Panel, 1981–86; DTI Hon. Adviser in Information Technology (on sabbatical leave), 1983; Mem. various Govt, Res. Council and Industry cttees and consultancies. Mem., BBC Science Consultative Gp, 1984–87. Hon. Mem., Univ. of Cambridge Computer Lab., 2011–. Dir, CADCentre Ltd, 1983–94. Sec., Clare Alumni Assoc., 2003–. Governor, Rydal Sch., 1982–88. Medal of Merits, Nicholas Copernicus Univ., Poland, 1984. Mem., Editl Bd, Computer Jl, 2010–12. *Publications:* papers in scientific jls on operating systems, programming languages, computing service management. *Address:* Clare College, Cambridge CB2 1TN.

HARTLEY, Prof. Frank Robinson; DL; CChem, FRSC; Vice-Chancellor, Cranfield University (formerly Cranfield Institute of Technology), 1989–2006; *b* 29 Jan. 1942; *s* of Sir Frank Hartley, CBE; *m* 1st, 1964, Valerie Peel (*d* 2005); three *d*; 2nd, 2009, Charmaine Harvey. *Educ:* King's College Sch., Wimbledon (Sambrooke Schol.; Fellow, 2003); Magdalen Coll., Oxford (Demy; BA, MA, DPhil, DSc). FRAeS 1996. Post-doctoral Fellow, Commonwealth Scientific and Industrial Research Organisation, Div. of Protein Chemistry, Melbourne, Aust., 1966–69; Imperial Chemical Industries Research Fellow and Tutor in Physical Chemistry, University Coll. London, 1969–70; Lectr in Inorganic Chemistry, Univ. of Southampton, 1970–75; Professor of Chemistry and Head of Dept of Chemistry and Metallurgy, 1975–82, Acting Dean, 1982–84, Principal and Dean, 1984–89, RMCS, Shrivenham. Chm., Cranfield IT Inst., 1989–90 (Dir, 1986–89); Man. Dir, CIT (Holdings) Ltd, 1993–2006 (Dir, 1989–93); Chm., CIM Inst., 1990–2006; Dir, Cranfield Ventures Ltd, 1990–2006 (Man. Dir, 2000–06); non-executive Director: T & N, 1989–98; Eastern Regl Adv. Bd, National Westminster Bank, 1990–92; Kalon, 1994–99; Kenwood, 1995–99; Hunting-BRAE Ltd, 1999–2000; Bedfordshire TEC, 1994–96. Sen. Travelling Fellow, ACU, 1986. Special Advr to Prime Minister on defence systems, 1988–91; Special Advr to H of L Select Cttee on Sci. and Technol., 1994–95; Mem., Parly Scientific Cttee, 1986– (Mem. Council and Gen. Purposes Cttee, 1992–98; Vice-Pres., 1995–98). Member: Internat. Adv. Bd, Kanagawa Acad. of Sci. and Technol., Japan, 1989–98; Bd, Internat. Foundn for Artificial Intelligence, 1990–98. Chm., Lorch Foundn, 1995–2006; Dir, Shuttleworth Trust, 1994–97. Member: Council, IoD, 2000–; Eastern Regl Bd, CBI, 2000–06. Chairman: Sen. Council for Devon, Teignmouth Br., 2008–13; Teignmouth and Dawlish Ramblers, 2010–. Gov., Welbeck Coll., 1984–89; Mem. Court, Bath Univ., 1982–89. DL Beds, 2005. Mem., Oxford Union. FRSA 1988. Editor-in-Chief, Brassey's New Battlefield Weapons Systems and Technology series, 1988–. *Publications:* The Chemistry of Platinum and Palladium (Applied Science), 1973; Elements of Organometallic Chemistry (Chemical Soc.), 1974, Japanese edn 1981, Chinese edn 1989; (with C. Burgess and R. M. Alcock) Solution Equilibria, 1980, Russian edn 1983; (with S. Patai) The Chemistry of the Metal—Carbon Bond, vol. 1 1983, vol. 2 1984, vol. 3 1985, vol. 4 1987, vol. 5 1989; Supported Metal Complexes, 1985, Russian edn 1987; The Chemistry of Organophosphorus Compounds, vol. 1, 1990, vol. 2, 1992, vol. 3, 1994, vol. 4, 1996; Chemistry of the Platinum Group Metals, 1991; papers in inorganic, coordination and organometallic chemistry in major English, Amer. and Aust. chemical jls. *Recreations:* gardening, swimming, rambling, reading. *Club:* Shrivenham.

HARTLEY, Rt Rev. Helen-Ann Macleod; *see* Waikato, Bishop of.

HARTLEY, John Robert; Headteacher, Saffron Walden County High School, since 2004; Chief Executive, Saffron Academy Trust, since 2012; *b* 4 Oct. 1955; *s* of Peter and Josephine Hartley; *m* 1982, Susanna Newton; two *s* one *d*. *Educ:* Oundle Sch.; St Catharine's Coll., Cambridge (BA 1977, PGCE). Physics teacher, Aylesbury GS, 1978–83; Sen. Physicist, Hazelwick Sch., Crawley, 1983–87; Hd of Sci., St Joseph's RC Comprehensive Sch., Swindon, 1988–90; Dep. Headteacher, Moulsham High Sch., Chelmsford, 1991–97; Headteacher, Notley High Sch., Braintree, 1997–2003. Nat. Leader of Educn, 2011–. *Recreations:* fell-walking, cycling, local and social history. *Address:* Saffron Walden County High School, Audley End Road, Saffron Walden, Essex CB11 4UH. *T:* (01799) 513030, *Fax:* (01799) 513031. *E:* headspa@swchs.net.

HARTLEY, Julian Matthew Frederick; Chief Executive, Leeds Teaching Hospitals NHS Trust, since 2013; *b* Keighley, W Yorks, 24 Feb. 1967; *s* of Max and Rosalind Hartley; *m* 1997, Karina Wood; one *s* one *d*. *Educ:* Bingley Grammar Sch.; Durham Univ. (BA Hons; MBA); King's Coll., Cambridge (PGCE). Chief Executive: Tameside and Glossop PCT, 2002–05; Blackpool Teaching Hosps, 2005–09; University Hosp. of S Manchester, 2009–12; Man. Dir, NHS Improving Quality, 2012–13. *Publications:* Leadership in the NHS: connecting for the future NHS Confederation, 2005; Placing Ladders, 2008. *Recreations:* tennis, theatre, Manchester United. *Address:* Leeds Teaching Hospitals NHS Trust, St James' Hospital, Beckett Street, Leeds LS9 7TF. *E:* julian.hartley@leedsth.nhs.uk.

HARTLEY, Prof. Keith; Professor of Economics, 1987–2008, now Emeritus, and Director, Centre for Defence Economics, 1990–2008, University of York; *b* 14 July 1940; *s* of Walter and Ivy Hartley; *m* 1966, Winifred Kealy; one *s* two *d*. *Educ:* Univ. of Hull (BSc Econs; PhD 1974). Dir, Inst. for Res. in Social Scis, Univ. of York, 1982–94. NATO Res. Fellow, 1977–79 and 1986–87; QinetiQ Vis. Fellow, 2009. *Publications:* Political Economy of NATO, 1999; (with T. Sandler) Economics of Defense, 2001; (with T. Sandler) Economics of Conflict, 2003; (with T. Sandler) Handbook of Defense Economics, vol. 2, 2007; (with C. Tisdell) Microeconomic Policy, 2008; Economics of Defence Policy, 2011; (with D. Braddon) Handbook of the Economics of Conflict, 2011; The Political Economy of Aerospace Industries, 2014. *Recreations:* walking, angling, football, reading. *Address:* Economics Department, University of York, York YO10 5DD. *T:* (01904) 433753. *E:* kh2@york.ac.uk.

HARTLEY, Richard Anthony; QC 2008; a Recorder, since 2002; *b* Crewe, 7 Nov. 1962; *s* of Dr Tony Hartley and Renée Hartley; *m* 1987, Clare Meeke; two *s* two *d*. *Educ:* Haslington Co. Primary Sch.; Sandbach Sch.; Liverpool Univ. (LLB Hons 1984). Called to the Bar, Middle Temple, 1985; in practice as barrister, Manchester, specialising in personal injury, sports law and clinical negligence cases, 1985–. *Recreations:* football (Manchester City), squash, snowboarding, cycling, classic cars and motorbikes, hill walking, a pint with friends. *Address:* Cobden House Chambers, 19 Quay Street, Manchester M3 3HN. *T:* (0161) 833 6000.

HARTLEY, Richard Leslie Clifford; QC 1976; *b* 31 May 1932; *s* of late Arthur Clifford Hartley, CBE and Nina Hartley. *Educ:* Marlborough Coll.; Sidney Sussex Coll., Cambridge (MA). Called to the Bar, Gray's Inn, 1956, Bencher, 1986. Former Chairman: Appeal Bd, Jockey Club; Appeal Bd, HRA. *Recreations:* golf, tennis, horse racing. *Address:* 15 Chesham Street, SW1X 8ND. *T:* (020) 7235 2420. *Clubs:* Garrick, MCC; Woking Golf; Rye Golf; St Enodoc Golf; New Zealand Golf (Weybridge).

HARTMANN, Dr Peter, Hon. KBE 1992; Ambassador of Germany to France, 1998–2001; *b* 9 Oct. 1935; *m* Baroness Lonny von Blomberg-Hartmann (*d* 2008). *Educ:* Frankfurt; Rome (LPH); Cologne; Fribourg Univ. (DPhil). Foreign Service, 1965; Washington, 1966; Karachi, 1968; EC Brussels, 1971; Buenos Aires, 1978; Head, Foreign Relations Office, CDU, 1981–84; Federal Chancellery: Head, European Policy, 1984–87; Asst Under-Sec., Foreign, Security and Develt Policy, 1987–90; Dep. Under-Sec., Foreign Security Policy, and Advr to Federal Chancellor, 1991–93; Ambassador to UK, 1993–95; Under Sec. of State, Foreign Min., Germany, 1995–98. *Address:* 14163 Berlin, Beuckestrasse 6, Germany.

HARTNACK, Paul Richard Samuel, CB 1999; Comptroller General and Chief Executive, The Patent Office, 1990–99; *b* 17 Nov. 1942; *s* of Carl Samuel and Maud Godden Hartnack; *m* 1966, Marion Quirk; two *s*. *Educ:* Hastings Grammar Sch. Clerical and Exec. posts, BoT, 1961–67; Asst Sec., Cttee of Enquiry into Civil Air Transport, 1967–68; Second Sec., British Embassy, Paris, 1969–71; Exec. posts, DTI, 1972–78; Asst Sec., NEB, 1978–80; Sec., Brit. Technology Gp, 1981–85; Asst Sec., Finance and Resource Management Div., DTI, 1985–89. *Recreation:* gardening. *Address:* 24 Benslow Rise, Hitchin, Herts SG4 9QX. *T:* (01462) 457312.

HARTNETT, David Anthony, CB 2003; a Commissioner, 2000–12, and Permanent Secretary for Tax, 2008–12, HM Revenue and Customs (a Deputy Chairman, 2003–05; Director-General, 2005–08; Acting Chairman and Permanent Secretary, 2007–08); *b* 25 Feb. 1951; *s* of late George Peter Hartnett and Mary Christine Hartnett (*née* O'Donoghue); *m* 1977, Aileen Patricia Mary O'Dempsey; two *s* one *d*. *Educ:* Hampton Sch.; Birmingham Univ. (BA Hons Latin). Inland Revenue, 1976–2005: Inspector of Taxes, 1976–86; Investigation Manager, 1986–91; Dir, Financial Intermediaries and Claims Office, 1991–96; Asst Dir, Personal Tax Div., 1996–98; Dir, Savings and Investment and Capital and Valuation Divs, 1998–99; Dir, Capital and Savings Div., 1999–2000. Vice-Chm., OECD Forum on Tax Admin., 2009–12. *Recreation:* Marcus Tullius Cicero.

HARTNOLL, Mary Charmian, CBE 1990; Director of Social Work, Glasgow City Council, 1996–98; *b* 31 May 1939; *d* of Rev. Sydney W. Hartnoll and Margaret Hartnoll. *Educ:* Colston's Girls' Grammar Sch., Bristol; Bedford Coll., Univ. of London (BA Hons); Univ. of Liverpool (HO Cert. in Child Care). Child Care Officer, Dorset CC, 1961–63; various posts, County Borough of Reading, 1963–74; Asst Dir, Berks CC, 1974–75; Divl Officer, Reading, 1975–77; Dir of Social Work: Grampian Regl Council, 1978–93; Strathclyde Regl Council, 1993–96. Chm., E Park, Glasgow, 2000–01; Convener, Scottish Commn for Regulation of Care, 2001–06. Hon. LLD Robert Gordon Univ., 1993. *Recreations:* natural history, walking, music, theatre going. *Address:* 36 Norfolk Road, Aberdeen AB10 6JR.

HARTOP, Barry; Chief Executive, Telenor Business Solutions (formerly Nextra (UK) Ltd), 2001–03; *b* 15 Aug. 1942; *s* of Philip William Hartop and Constance Winifred (*née* Drew); *m* 1966, Sandra Swan; one *s* one *d*. *Educ:* Durham Univ. (BSc Hons Chem. Engrg). Prodn and technical mgt, Lever Bros Ltd, 1965–72; Unilever PLC: Chm., Cost Reduction and R&D, 1972–80; Man. Dir, European Business Centre, 1980–83; Chm. and Man. Dir, Lever Industrial Ltd, 1983–89; Man. Dir, Gestetner Hldgs, 1989–92; Chief Executive: WDA, 1994–96; Millennium Exhibn, 1996; Man. Dir, Norsk Data, 1997–2001. Chairman: Hammicks Bookshops Ltd, 1994–98; Locum Gp Ltd, 1997–2002; Reed Health Gp plc, 2003–06. Chief Consultant, Business Relns (Defence) 2e2 Ltd, 2003–13. Gov., Royal Grammar Sch., Guildford, 1991– (Chm., RGS Foundn, 2004–11). *Recreations:* keep fit, gardening, travel. *Address:* Linton House, Snowdenham Links Road, Bramley, Guildford, Surrey GU5 0BX. *T:* (01483) 890612. *Club:* County (Guildford).

HARTRIDGE, David Charles, CMG 2001; Senior Trade Advisor, White & Case LLP (formerly Senior Director, White & Case International Trade), Geneva, since 2002; *b* 22 April 1939; *s* of Sidney George Hartridge and Mabel Kate (*née* Hunt); *m* 1965, Dorothy Ann Ling (marr. diss. 1997; remarried 2014); two *d*. *Educ:* Windsor Grammar Sch.; Oriel Coll., Oxford (MA). BoT, 1961–71; First Sec., UK Mission, Geneva, 1971–75; Asst Sec., DTI, 1977–79; Counsellor, UK Repn to EEC, Brussels, 1979–80; Chef de Cabinet, GATT, 1980–85; Dir, GATT and WTO, 1985–2001, Dir, Services Div., 1993–2001, Dir-in-Charge, May–Sept. 1999; Special Advr to DG, WTO, 2001–02. *Recreations:* bird watching, music, history. *Address:* Hollow Stones, Nailsworth Hill, Nailsworth, Stroud, Glos GL6 0AW. *T:* (01453) 836884; 23 Route de Sauverny, Grilly 01220, France. *T:* (4) 50201993.

HARTWELL, Sir (Francis) Anthony (Charles Peter), 6th Bt *cr* 1805, of Dale Hall, Essex; marine consultant; Director, International Diamond Drilling, West Africa, since 1999; survey and inspection assignments, oil, gas and shipping services, Lagos, Nigeria, since 2000; Marine Superintendent/Consultant, Peacegate Oil and Gas Ltd, Lagos, Nigeria, since 2008; *b* 1 June 1940; *o s* of Sir Brodrick William Charles Elwin Hartwell, 5th Bt and of his 1st wife, Marie Josephine Hartwell, *d* of S. P. Mullins; *S* father, 1993; *m* 1968, Barbara Phyllis Rae (marr. diss. 1989), *d* of H. Rae Green; one *s*. *Educ:* Thames Nautical Coll., HMS Worcester. Cadet, RNR. Master's Foreign Going (Cl. 1) Cert. MNI, MRIN. Captain (Master Mariner), 1972. Sea Service Navigating Officer, Asst Nautical Inspector, then Cargo Supt (Overseas Containers Ltd) London, P&O Group, 1958–71; Chief Officer/Master, North Sea ops, Ocean Inchcape Ltd, 1972–73; P&O Cadet Trng Officer, 1973–75; overseas port management, Nigeria, Papua New Guinea and Saudi Arabia, 1975–87; Branch Manager, Lloyds Agency, Dammam, Saudi Arabia, 1987–89; marine surveyor and nautical consultant, Saudi Arabia, The Maldives, Nigeria, Cyprus, 1989–93; Man. Dir, Universal UKI Ltd, Nigeria, 1999. *Recreations:* ocean sailing, scuba diving, photography. *Heir:* *s* Timothy Peter Michael Charles Hartwell [*b* 8 July 1970; *m* 2002, Diana Katherine, *d* of Ronald McKelvie Sinclair, Edinburgh; one *s*]. *Clubs:* Cachalots-Southampton Master Mariners'; Old Worcester's Association.

HARTWELL, Prof. Leland Harrison, PhD; Virginia G. Piper Professor of Personalized Medicine and Chief Scientist, Center for Sustainable Health, Biodesign Institute, Arizona State University, since 2010; *b* Los Angeles, 30 Oct. 1939; *s* of Marjorie Hartwell (*née* Taylor); *m* Theresa Naujack. *Educ:* CIT (BS 1961); MIT (PhD 1964). Fellow, Salk Inst., 1964–65; Asst Prof., 1965–67, Associate Prof., 1967–68, Univ. of Calif, Irvine; Associate Prof., 1968–73, Prof. of Genome Scis, 1973–2010, now Emeritus, Univ. of Washington, Seattle; Pres. and Dir, Fred Hutchinson Cancer Res. Center, Seattle, 1997–2010, now Dir Emeritus. Res. Prof., American Cancer Soc., 1990–. (Jtly) Nobel Prize for Physiol. or Medicine, 2001. *Publications:* articles in learned jls. *Address:* Center for Sustainable Health, Biodesign Institute, Arizona State University, PO Box 876701, Tempe, AZ 85287–6701, USA.

HARTY, Bernard Peter, CBE 1998; Chairman, Imerys (UK) Pension Fund (formerly English China Clay Pension Fund), 2000–08; *b* 1 May 1943; *s* of William Harty and Eileen Nora (*née* Canavan); *m* 1965, Glenys Elaine Simpson; one *d*. *Educ:* St Richards Coll., Droitwich; Ullathorne Grammar Sch., Coventry. CPFA 1966. Accountant, Coventry CBC, 1961–69; Forward Budget Planning Officer, Derbyshire CC, 1969–72; Chief Accountant, Bradford CBC, 1972–74; Chief Finance Officer, Bradford MDC, 1973–76; County Treasurer, Oxfordshire CC, 1976–83; Chamberlain, 1983–99, and Town Clerk, 1996–99, City of London Corp.; Man. Dir, Barbican Centre, 1994–95. Chm., London Pension Fund Authy, 1999–2001. Dir, Dexia Public Finance Bank, 1994–2000; Chairman: London Processing Centre Pension Fund, 2001–03; Alstom Pension Trust, 2004–05. Mem. Nat. Cttee, Information Technol. Year 1982 (IT82); Chm., IT82 Local Govt Cttee, 1982. Chm., Foundn for IT in Local Govt, 1988–91. Chm., Treasury Management Panel, 1991–94, Superannuation Investments Panel, 1994–95, CIPFA; Member: Local Govt Sub Gp, Financial

Law Panel, 1993–95; HM Treasury Cttee on Local Authy Borrowing, 1994–95. Chm., Charlton Kings Parish Council, Cheltenham, 2008–10. Freeman, City of London, 1983; Liveryman, Worshipful Co. of Tallow Chandlers, 1984; Founder Mem., Co. of Information Technologists (Hon. Liveryman, 1997). Hon. DPhil London Guildhall Univ., 1997. Commander, Nat. Order of Merit (France), 1996. *Publications:* papers in professional jls. *Recreations:* theatre, music, National Trust, sport. *E:* bernardharty@aol.com.

HARVERSON, Patrick Richard, LVO 2013; Managing Partner, Milltown Partners LLP, since 2013; *b* 8 Nov. 1962; *s* of late John and Quinn Harverson. *Educ:* London Sch. of Econs (BSc (Econ) Internat. Relns). Financial Times, 1988–2000: stockmarket reporter; economics writer; NY Correspondent; Sports Correspondent; Dir of Communications, Manchester United FC, 2000–04; Communications Sec. to the Prince of Wales, 2004–13, and to the Duchess of Cornwall, 2005–13. *Recreation:* football.

HARVEY, family name of **Baron Harvey of Tasburgh**.

HARVEY OF TASBURGH, 3rd Baron *cr* 1954, of Tasburgh, Norfolk; **Charles John Giuseppe Harvey;** Bt 1868; *b* 4 Feb. 1951; *s* of late Hon. John Wynn Harvey (*d* 1989) (*yr s* of 1st Baron Harvey of Tasburgh) and of Elena Maria-Teresa, *yr d* of late Giambattista, Marchese Curtopassi; *S* uncle, 2010; *m* 1979, Margaret, *d* of Cecil Walter Brown; one *s* three *d*. *Educ:* Eton; Trinity Coll., Oxford. *Heir: s* Hon. John Harvey, *b* 11 May 1993.

HARVEY, Alan James, (Tim), RDI 1991; production designer, film and television; *b* 14 Oct. 1936; *s* of Ernest Harvey and Ida Harvey; *m* 1958, Sheila Todd; one *s* one *d*. *Educ:* Hampton Grammar Sch.; Manchester Univ. (BA Hons Architecture). Designer: BBC TV N Region, 1960–64; Telefis Eireann, 1964–66; BBC Scotland, 1966–69; BBC London, 1969–88; freelance film designer, 1988–; *films* include: Henry V, 1989; Much Ado About Nothing, 1993; Mary Shelley's Frankenstein, 1994; Othello, 1995; Hamlet, 1996; The Magic Flute, 2006; Sleuth, 2007. US Emmy Award, 1974, 1976; BAFTA Design Awards, 1976, 1985, 1987; Design Award, RTS, 1982. *Recreations:* football, Italian language and culture, family. *Address:* 2 Cambridge Court, Clevedon Road, Twickenham, Middx TW1 2HT.

HARVEY, Prof. Andrew Charles, FBA 1999; Professor of Econometrics, University of Cambridge, 1996–2014, now Emeritus; Fellow, Corpus Christi College, Cambridge, since 1996; *b* 10 Sept. 1947; *s* of Richard Arthur Harvey and Margaret Frances Harvey (*née* Clark); *m* 1969, Lavinia Mary Young; one *s* one *d*. *Educ:* Leeds Modern Sch.; Univ. of York (BA); LSE (MSc). Economist and statistician, Central Bureau of Stats, Nairobi, 1969–71; Lectr, Univ. of Kent at Canterbury, 1971–77; Vis. Prof., Univ. of British Columbia, 1977–78; London School of Economics: Sen. Lectr, 1978–81; Reader, 1981–84; Prof. of Econometrics, 1984–96. Fellow, Econometric Soc., 1990. *Publications:* The Econometric Analysis of Time Series, 1981, 2nd edn 1990; Time Series Models, 1981, 2nd edn 1993; Forecasting, Structural Time Series Models and the Kalman Filter, 1989; Dynamic Models for Volatility and Heavy Tails, 2013. *Recreations:* football, opera, hill-walking. *Address:* Faculty of Economics, Sidgwick Avenue, Cambridge CB3 9DD.

HARVEY, Rev. Canon Anthony Ernest, DD; Canon of Westminster, 1982–99, and Sub-Dean, 1987–99, Canon Emeritus, 1999; *b* 1 May 1930; *s* of Cyril Harvey, QC, and Nina (*née* Darley); *m* 1957, Julian Elizabeth McMaster; four *d*. *Educ:* Dragon Sch., Oxford; Eton Coll.; Worcester Coll., Oxford (BA, MA, DD 1983); Westcott House, Cambridge. Curate, Christ Church, Chelsea, 1958–62; Research Student, Christ Church, Oxford, 1962–69; Warden, St Augustine's Coll., Canterbury, 1969–76; Univ. Lectr in Theology and Fellow of Wolfson Coll., Oxford, 1976–82; Chaplain, The Queen's Coll., 1977–82; Librarian, Westminster Abbey, 1983–98. Examining Chaplain to Archbishop of Canterbury, 1975–90; Six Preacher, Canterbury Cathedral, 1977–82; Bampton Lectr, 1980. Member: Gen. Synod Doctrine Commn, 1977–86; Archbishop's Commn on Urban Priority Areas, 1983–85; Worcester Cathedral Fabric Adv. Cttee, 2001–06. Chairman: Jedidiah Foundn, 2004–09; Aid for Children of El Salvador, 2014–. Fellow, George Bell Inst., 1997–. *Publications:* Companion to the New Testament (New English Bible), 1970, 2nd edn 2004; Priest or President?, 1975; Jesus on Trial, 1976; Something Overheard, 1977; (ed) God Incarnate: story and belief, 1981; Jesus and the Constraints of History, 1982; Believing and Belonging, 1984; (ed) Alternative Approaches to New Testament Study, 1985; (ed) Theology in the City, 1989; Strenuous Commands, 1990, 2nd edn 1992; Retaliation, 1992; Promise or Pretence?: a Christian's guide to sexual morals, 1994; (ed) The Funeral Effigies of Westminster Abbey, 1994; Renewal through Suffering: a study of 2 Corinthians, 1996; Marriage, Divorce and the Church, 1997; Demanding Peace: Christian responses to war and violence, 1999; By What Authority?: the churches and social concern, 2001; Asylum in Britain: a question of conscience, 2009; Is Scripture Still 'Holy'?: coming of age with the New Testament, 2012; Impelled Three Ways: a ministry, a profession and a marriage, 2016; articles in classical and theological jls. *Recreations:* music, walking. *Address:* Mendelssohn Cottage, Broadway Road, Willersey, Broadway, Worcs WR12 7PH. *T:* (01386) 859260.

HARVEY, Anthony Peter; Chairman, The Broad Oak Consultancy, since 1991; *b* 21 May 1940; *s* of late Frederick William Henry Harvey and Fanny Evelyn Harvey (*née* Dixon); *m* 1963, Margaret Hayward; three *s* one *d*. *Educ:* Hertford Grammar Sch. MCLIP. Dept of Oriental Printed Books, British Museum, 1958–60; British Museum (Natural History): Dept of Palaeontology, 1960–75; Librarian, 1963–75; Head, Dept of Library Services, 1981–88; Co-ordinator of Planning and Development, 1985–88; Head of Marketing and Develt, 1988–91. Director: Natural History Mus. Develt Trust, 1990–91; BM (Natural Hist.) Internat. Foundn, 1990–91. Chm., Heathfield Partnership, 1997–99; Director: Welshpool Partnership, 2002–06; Welshpool Projects, 2007–10. Chm., Geology Inf. Gp, 1975–78, Liby Cttee, 1981–84, Geol Soc.; Chm., N Powys DFAS, 2005–08 and 2012– (Prog. Sec., 2000–03; Vice Chm., 2002–05; Trustee, 2005–08); Member: Printing Hist. Soc., 1965–; Garden Hist. Soc., 1988–; Soc. for Hist. of Natural Hist., 1963– (Treas., 1964–2004; Hon. Mem., 2004–). Trustee: Britain Australia Bicentennial Trust, 1988–; Montgomery Co. Regeneration Assoc., 2002–; Oriel Davies Gall., 2003–10 (Chm., 2005–10); Montgomeryshire Wildlife Trust, 2004–08 (Sec., 2006); Trustee and Dir, Gwasg Gregynog (Gregynog Press), 2006– (Hon. Treas., 2007–). Councillor, Welshpool Town Council, 2004–12 (Chm., Finance and Gen. Purposes Cttee, 2007–10, Vice Chm., 2010–11). Mem., Governing Body, Ch in Wales, 2010–12. Freeman, City of London, 1985; Liveryman, Co. of Marketors, 1991–. *Publications:* (ed) Secrets of the Earth, 1967; (ed) Directory of Scientific Directories, 1969, 4th edn 1986; Prehistoric Man, 1972; Guide to World Science, vol. 1, 1974; (ed) Encyclopedia of Prehistoric Life, 1979; European Sources of Scientific and Technical Information, 1981, 7th edn 1986; numerous contribs to learned jls, ref. works and periodicals. *Recreations:* garden history and design, transport history, bibliography. *Address:* Oak Cottage, 23 High Street, Welshpool, Powys SY21 7JP. *T:* (01938) 559087.

HARVEY, Barbara Fitzgerald, CBE 1997; FSA 1964; FBA 1982; Fellow of Somerville College, Oxford, 1956–93, now Emeritus Fellow; Reader (*ad hominem*) in Medieval History, Oxford University, 1990–93; *b* 21 Jan. 1928; *d* of Richard Henry Harvey and Anne Fitzgerald (*née* Julian). *Educ:* Teignmouth Grammar Sch.; Bishop Blackall Sch., Exeter; Somerville Coll., Oxford (Schol.). First Cl. Final Honour Sch. of Modern History, Oxford, 1949; Bryce Student, Oxford Univ., 1950–51; BLitt Oxon 1953. Assistant, Dept of Scottish History, Edinburgh Univ., 1951–52; Asst Lectr, subseq. Lectr, Queen Mary Coll., London Univ., 1952–55; Tutor, Somerville Coll., Oxford, 1955–93; Vice-Principal, 1976–79, 1981–83. Assessor, Oxford Univ., 1968–69. Ford's Lectr, Oxford, 1989. Mem., Royal Commn on Historical MSS, 1991–97. Pres., Henry Bradshaw Soc., 1997–2007. Hon. Vice-Pres., RHistS, 2003–. Gen. Editor, Oxford Medieval Texts, 1987–99. *Publications:* Documents Illustrating the Rule of Walter de Wenlok, Abbot of Westminster 1283–1307, 1965; Westminster Abbey and its Estates in the Middle Ages, 1977; (ed with L. C. Hector) The Westminster Chronicle 1381–94, 1982; Living and Dying in England 1100–1540: the monastic experience, (jtly, Wolfson Foundn History Prize), 1993; (ed) The Twelfth and Thirteenth Centuries: short Oxford history of the British Isles, 2001; The Obedientiaries of Westminster Abbey and their Financial Records *c* 1275 to 1540, 2002; contribs to Economic History Rev., Trans Royal Historical Soc., Bulletin of Inst. of Historical Research, etc. *Address:* 6 Ritchie Court, 380 Banbury Road, Oxford OX2 7PW. *T:* (01865) 554766.

HARVEY, Caroline; *see* Trollope, Joanna.

HARVEY, Prof. Charles Richard Musgrave, (3rd Bt *cr* 1933, but does not use the title); retired economic consultant; *b* 7 April 1937; *s* of Sir Richard Musgrave Harvey, 2nd Bt, and Frances Estelle (*d* 1986), *er d* of late Lindsay Crompton Lawford, Montreal; *S* father, 1978; *m* 1967, Celia Vivien, *d* of late George Henry Hodson; one *s* one *d*. *Educ:* Marlborough; Pembroke Coll., Cambridge (BA 1960, MA 1964). Fellow, Institute of Development Studies, Sussex, 1972–2002; Sen. Res. Fellow, Botswana Institute for Development Policy Analysis, Gaborone, 1996–2001. *Heir: s* Paul Richard Harvey [*b* 2 June 1971; *m* 2004, Prudence Ruth Daniels; one *s* one *d*].

HARVEY, Christopher John, (Kit), H.; *see* Hesketh Harvey.

HARVEY, (Christopher) Paul (Duncan), CMG 2004; HM Diplomatic Service, retired; *b* 21 July 1956; *s* of late Prof. William John Harvey and of Margaret Anne Harvey; *m* 1989, Anasaini Kamakorewa; one *s* one *d*. *Educ:* Royal Belfast Academical Instn; University Coll., Oxford (MA); Downing Coll., Cambridge. Tutor in Geog., Cambridge Centre for 6th Form Studies, 1982–85; joined FCO, 1986: 2nd Sec., Suva, 1988–90; 1st Sec., Brussels, 1990–94; FCO, 1995–98; UK Rep. to Sierra Leone Peace Talks, Lomé, 1999; UK Special Rep. for Peace in Sierra Leone, 1999–2000; Deputy High Comr, Kenya, 2000–03; on secondment to Coalition Provisional Authy, Iraq, 2003–04; liaison officer, Operation Bracknell, 2005; Internat. Security Directorate, FCO, 2005–08. *Recreations:* books, organic gardening.

HARVEY, Clare; *see* Harvey, M. F. C.

HARVEY, Prof. David William, PhD; Distinguished Professor of Anthropology, since 2001 and Director, Center for Place, Culture and Politics, 2008–13, Graduate Center, City University of New York; *b* 31 Oct. 1935; *s* of Frederick and Doris Harvey. *Educ:* St John's Coll., Cambridge (BA (Hons), MA, PhD). Lectr, Univ. of Bristol, 1961–69; Prof. of Geography, Johns Hopkins Univ., 1969–86; Oxford University: Halford Mackinder Prof. of Geography, 1987–93; Fellow, St Peter's Coll., 1987–93; Supernumerary Res. Fellow, St John's Coll., 2001–; Prof. of Geography, Johns Hopkins Univ., 1993–2001. Guggenheim Meml Fellow, 1976–77. Corresp. FBA 1998. Dr (*hc*): Buenos Aires, 1997; Roskilde, 1997; Uppsala, 2000. Outstanding Contributor Award, Assoc. of Amer. Geographers, 1980; Gill Meml Award, RGS, 1982; Anders Retzius Gold Medal, Swedish Soc. for Anthropology and Geography, 1989; Patron's Medal, RGS, 1995; Vautrin Lud Internat. Prize in Geography, 1995. *Publications:* Explanation in Geography, 1969, 4th edn 1978; Social Justice and the City, 1973, 3rd edn 1989; The Limits to Capital, 1982, 2nd edn 1984; The Urbanisation of Capital, 1985; Consciousness and the Urban Experience, 1985; The Urban Experience, 1989; The Condition of Postmodernity, 1989; Justice, Nature and the Geography of Difference, 1996; Spaces of Hope, 2000; Spaces of Capital, 2001; Paris, Capital of Modernity, 2003; The New Imperialism, 2003; A Brief History of Neoliberalism, 2005; Spaces of Global Capitalism, 2006; The Enigma of Capital and the Crises of Capitalism, 2010; Rebel Cities: from right to the city to the urban revolution, 2012; Seventeen Contradictions and the End of Capitalism, 2014. *Address:* PhD Program in Anthropology, Graduate Center, City University of New York, 365 Fifth Avenue, New York, NY 10016, USA.

HARVEY, Dame DeAnne Shirley; *see* Julius, Dame D. S.

HARVEY, Diane Catherine; *see* Redgrave, D. C.

HARVEY, Rt Rev. Donald Frederick; Bishop of Eastern Newfoundland and Labrador, 1993–2004; Moderator, Anglican Network in Canada, 2004–14; Dean, Anglican Church in North America, 2010–14; Episcopal Vicar, since 2015; *b* St John's, Newfoundland, 13 Sept. 1939; *s* of Robert Joseph and Elsie May Harvey (*née* Vaters); *m* 1964, Gertrude, *d* of George and Jessie Hiscock. *Educ:* St Michael's Sch., 1956; Memorial Univ. (BA 1985; MA 1987); Queen's Theol Coll. (MDiv 1986). Sch. teacher, 1956–57; ordained deacon, 1963, priest, 1964; served in parishes: Portugal Cove, 1963–64, 1973–76; Twillingate, 1965; King's Cove, 1965–68; Happy Valley, Labrador, 1968–73; St Michael & All Angels, St John's, 1976–83; Anglican Chaplain, Meml Univ. of Newfoundland, 1984–87; Rector, and Dean, Cathedral of St John the Baptist, St John's, 1989–92. Rural Dean of Labrador, 1968–73. Lectr in Pastoral Theol., Queen's Coll., 1984–94; Sessional Lectr, English, Meml Univ. of Newfoundland, 1985–89. Hon. DD: Huron Coll., 1996; Nashotah Hse, 2009. *Address:* 501–7 Tiffany Lane, St John's, NL A1A 4B7, Canada.

HARVEY, Estella Jacqueline, (Mrs J. G. Harvey); *see* Hindley, E. J.

HARVEY, Dr Felicity Ann Hope, (Mrs G. D. Royce), CBE 2008; Director General for Public and International Health, Department of Health, since 2012; *b* London, 6 June 1956; *d* of Charles Harvey and Audrey Harvey (*née* Haslett, now Livingston Booth); *m* 1986, George David Royce; two *s*. *Educ:* Richmond Co. Sch. for Girls, Surrey; St Bartholomew's Med. Coll., London (MB BS 1980); London Hosp. Med. Coll., London Univ. (Postgrad. Dip. Clin. Microbiol. 1983); Henley Mgt Coll. (MBA 1997). MRCPath; FFPH 2003. Hse surgeon, Essex Co. Hosp., Colchester, and hse physician, St Bartholomew's Hosp., London, 1980–81; Lectr, Dept of Med. Microbiol., Royal London Hosp. Med. Coll., 1981–83; Lectr and Hon. Sen. Registrar in Med. Microbiol., King's Coll. Sch. of Medicine and Dentistry, 1983–90; Department of Health: SMO, 1990–94; Private Sec. to CMO, 1994–96; Hd, Quality Mgt, NHS Exec., 1997–2000; Dir, Prison Health, HM Prison Service and DoH, 2000–02; Dir and Hd, Medicines Pharmacy and Industry, DoH, 2003–09; HM Treasury: Director: Prime Minister's Delivery Unit, 2009–10; Performance and Reform Unit, 2011–12; Prime Minister's Implementation Unit, Cabinet Office, 2012. Member: BMA, 1980; British Infection Soc., 2000. *Recreations:* Scottish country dancing, singing, acting, family pursuits. *Address:* Department of Health, Richmond House, 79 Whitehall, SW1A 2NS. *T:* (020) 7210 5252/5522. *E:* felicity.harvey@dh.gsi.gov.uk. *Club:* Reform.

HARVEY, Dr Helen Lesley; Headmistress, St Swithun's School, 1995–2010; *b* 7 April 1950; *d* of George Frederick Cox and Olive Cox; *m* 1975, Dr H. Hale Harvey (marr. diss. 1999); one *s* one *d*. *Educ:* Lordswood Sch., Birmingham; Bedford Coll., Univ. of London (BSc); Chester Beatty Cancer Res. Inst., Surrey (PhD). Asst Mistress, Greylands Coll., IoW, 1975–76; Asst Mistress, 1976–89, Dep. Headmistress, 1989–90, Headmistress, 1990–94, Upper Chine Sch., Shanklin, IoW. *Recreations:* sailing, walking.

HARVEY, Jack; *see* Rankin, I. J.

HARVEY, Prof. Jake Burns, RSA 1989 (ARSA 1977); Professor of Sculpture, Edinburgh College of Art, 2001–11, now Emeritus (Head, School of Sculpture, 1998); *b* 3 June 1948; *s* of George and Nan Harvey; *m* 1971, Penelope F. Proctor; one *s* two *d*. *Educ:* Edinburgh Coll. of Art (DA). *Recreation:* fishing. *Address:* Maxton Cross, Maxton, Melrose, Roxburghshire TD6 0RL. *T:* and *Fax:* (01835) 822650.

HARVEY, John Barton; author; *b* London, 21 Dec. 1938; *s* of Thomas Harvey and Helen Harvey (*née* White); partner, Sarah Boiling; one *d*; one *s* one *d* by a previous marriage. *Educ:* St Aloysius Coll., London; Goldsmiths' Coll., Univ. of London (Cert. Teacher Trng); Hatfield Poly. (BA English); Univ. of Nottingham (MA American Studies); Birkbeck Coll., Univ. of London (CertHE Hist. of Art). Teacher of English and drama: Heanor-Aldercar Secondary Sch., 1964–68; Harrow Way Community Sch., 1968–72; Stevenage Girls' Sch., 1972–75. Adaptations for radio: The End of the Affair by Graham Greene, 1998 (Sony Radio Drama Silver Award, 1999); The Heart of the Matter by Graham Greene, 2001; The Frederica Quartet by A. S. Byatt, 2002; (with Shelley Silas) The Raj Quartet by Paul Scott, 2005; adaptations for television: Anna of the Five Towns by Arnold Bennett, 1985; The Old Wives' Tale (as Sophia and Constance) by Arnold Bennett, 1988; The Secret House of Death by Ruth Rendell, 1996. Member: Crime Writers' Assoc., 1990; Mystery Writers of America, 1990; Private Eye Writers of America, 2000; Soc. of Authors, 2008. Hon. DLitt: Nottingham, 2009; Herts, 2013. Cartier Diamond Dagger for Sustained Excellence in Crime Writing, 2007, Short Story Dagger, 2014, CWA. *Publications: fiction*: Lonely Hearts, 1989 (adapted for TV, 1992); Rough Treatment, 1990 (adapted for TV, 1993); Cutting Edge, 1991; Off Minor, 1992; Wasted Years, 1993; Cold Light, 1994 (Grand Prix du Roman Noir Etranger du Cognac, 2000)); Living Proof, 1995; Easy Meat, 1996; Still Water, 1997; Last Rites, 1998 (Sherlock Award for Best British Detective, 1999); Now's the Time, 1999; In a True Light, 2001; Flesh & Blood, 2004 (Silver Dagger for Fiction, CWA); Ash & Bone, 2005 (Prix du Polar Européen, 2007); Darkness & Light, 2006; Gone to Ground, 2007; Cold in Hand, 2008; Nick's Blues, 2008; Minor Key, 2009; Far Cry, 2009; A Darker Shade of Blue, 2010; Good Bait, 2012; Darkness, Darkness, 2014; *editor*: Blue Lightning, 1998; Men from Boys, 2003; *poetry*: Ghosts of a Chance, 1992; Bluer than This, 1998; Out of Silence, 2014. *Recreations:* reading, walking, listening to music, looking at art, going to the cinema, watching Notts County and Spurs, being forever in search of a perfect flat white. *E:* john@mellotone.co.uk. *Clubs:* Detection; Notts County FC Supporters (Hon. Life Mem.).

HARVEY, Kenneth George, CBE 2011; Chairman, Pennon Group (formerly South West Water) plc, 1997–2015; *b* 22 July 1940; *s* of George Harvey and Nellie Harvey (*née* Gilmore); *m* 1st, 1963, Wendy Youldon (*d* 1982); one *s* one *d*; 2nd, 1990, Anne Model. *Educ:* Urmston Grammar Sch., Manchester; City Univ. (BSc, 1st Cl. Hons Elec. Eng). Student Apprentice, Westinghouse, 1958–63; Southern and London Electricity Boards, 1963–81; London Electricity Board: Engineering Dir, 1981–84; Dep. Chm., 1984–89; Chm. and Chief Exec., NORWEB plc (formerly North Western Electricity Bd), 1989–95. Chairman: Greater Manchester Buses South Ltd, 1993–95; Intercare Gp plc, 1996–2004; Comax plc, 1997–99; Beaufort Group plc, 1998–2004; non-executive Director: Lattice Gp, 2000–02; Nat. Grid plc (formerly Nat. Grid Transco), 2002– (Sen. Ind. Dir, 2006–). Pres., Electricity Assoc., 1992–93. Chm., Royal Exchange Theatre Co., Manchester, 1994–98. *Recreations:* sport, gardening, DIY, theatre.

HARVEY, Prof. Leonard Patrick; Fellow, 1994–2001, Senior Research Associate, 2002–11, Oxford Centre for Islamic Studies; Cervantes Professor of Spanish, King's College, University of London, 1973–84, now Professor Emeritus; *b* 25 Feb. 1929; *s* of Francis Thomas Harvey and Eva Harvey; *m* 1954, June Rawcliffe; two *s*. *Educ:* Alleyn's Sch., Dulwich; Magdalen Coll., Oxford. 1st cl. hons BA Mod. Langs 1952; 2nd cl. Oriental Studies 1954; MA 1956; DPhil 1958. Lectr in Spanish, Univ. of Oxford, 1957–58; Univ. of Southampton, 1958–60; Queen Mary Coll., Univ. of London: Lectr, 1960–63; Reader and Head of Dept, 1963; Prof. of Spanish, 1967–73; Dean of Faculty of Arts, 1970–73; Dean of Faculty of Arts, KCL, 1979–81; FKC 1992. Vis. Prof., Univ. of Victoria, BC, 1966; Vis. Fellow, Oxford Centre for Islamic Studies, 1993–94. Mem. UGC, 1979–83. Chm., Educn Cttee, Hispanic and Luso-Brazilian Council, 1984–87. *Publications:* Islamic Spain 1250–1500, 1990; Muslims in Spain, 1500 to 1614, 2005; Ibn Battuta, 2007; articles in Al-Andalus, Bulletin of Hispanic Studies, Nueva Revista de Filología Española, Al-Masāq, Al-Qantara, etc. *Address:* 24 Breton Grove, Kingston, Wellington 6021, New Zealand.

HARVEY, (Mary Frances) Clare, (Mrs D. R. Feaver), MA; Headmistress, St Mary's Hall, Brighton, 1981–88; *b* 24 Aug. 1927; *e d* of late Rev. Oliver Douglas Harvey and Frances Hilda Harvey (*née* Howes); *m* 1988, Rt Rev. Douglas Russell Feaver (*d* 1997). *Educ:* St Mary's Sch., Colchester; St Hugh's Coll., Oxford (BA, Final Honour Sch. of Mod. Hist., 1950; Diploma in Educn, 1951; MA 1954). History Mistress, St Albans High Sch., 1951; Head of History Dept, Portsmouth High Sch., GPDST, 1956; Headmistress: Sch. of St Clare, Penzance, 1962–69; Badminton Sch., Westbury on Trym, Bristol, 1969–81. Governor, Bristol Cathedral Sch., 1978–81; Foundn Gov. and Trustee, Sexey's Sch., Bruton, 1994–95. *Recreations:* music, travel, reading, needlework. *Address:* Blackman House, Canon Lane, Chichester, West Sussex PO19 1PX.

HARVEY, Michael Llewellyn Tucker; QC 1982; a Recorder, since 1986; a Deputy High Court Judge, since 1995; *b* 22 May 1943; *s* of late Rev. Victor Llewellyn Tucker Harvey and Pauline Harvey (*née* Wybrow); *m* 1972, Denise Madeleine Neary; one *s* one *d*. *Educ:* St John's Sch., Leatherhead; Christ's Coll., Cambridge (BA Hons Law, LLB, MA). Called to the Bar, Gray's Inn, 1966 (Uthwatt Schol. 1965, James Mould Schol. 1966; Bencher, 1991). *Publications:* joint contributor of title 'Damages' in Halsbury's Laws of England, 4th edn 1975. *Recreations:* shooting, golf. *Address:* 2 Crown Office Row, Temple, EC4Y 7HJ. *T:* (020) 7797 8100. *Clubs:* Athenæum; Hawks (Cambridge); Burhill Golf.

HARVEY, Sir Nicholas (Barton), Kt 2012; *b* 3 Aug. 1961; *s* of Frederick Barton Harvey and Christine Diana Rosalind (*née* Gildea); *m* 2003, Kate Fox; one *s* one *d*. *Educ:* Queen's Coll., Taunton; Middlesex Poly. (BA Hons). Communications and Marketing Consultant: Profile Public Relns, 1984–86; Dewe Rogerson Ltd, 1986–91; Westminster Consortium, 1991–92. MP (Lib Dem) N Devon, 1992–2015; contested (Lib Dem) same seat, 2015. Lib Dem spokesman: on transport, 1992–94; on trade and industry, 1994–97; on regions, 1997–99; on health, 1999–2001; on culture, media and sport, 2001–03; on defence, 2006–10; Minister of State (Minister for the Armed Forces), MoD, 2010–12. Chair, Lib Dem Campaigns and Communications, 1994–99. Mem., Parly Assembly, Council of Europe, 2005–07. *Recreations:* travelling, walking, playing piano, soccer enthusiast.

HARVEY, Paul; *see* Harvey, C. P. D.

HARVEY, Prof. Paul Dean Adshead, FBA 2003; FSA, FRHistS; Professor Emeritus, University of Durham, since 1985; *b* 7 May 1930; *s* of John Dean Monroe Harvey and Gwendolen Mabel Darlington (*née* Adshead); *m* 1968, Yvonne Crossman (*d* 2014). *Educ:* Bishop Feild Coll., St John's, Newfoundland; Warwick Sch.; St John's Coll., Oxford (BA 1953; MA; DPhil 1960); FRHistS 1961, FSA 1963. Asst Archivist, Warwick County Record Office, 1954–56; Asst Keeper, Dept of Manuscripts, British Museum, 1957–66; Lectr, 1966–70, Sen. Lectr, 1970–78, Dept of History, Univ. of Southampton; Prof. of Mediaeval Hist., Univ. of Durham, 1978–85. Mem., Adv. Council on Public Records, 1984–89. Vice-President: Surtees Soc., 1978–; British Records Assoc., 2005– (Chm., 1995–2000); Dugdale Soc., 2007–. Hon. Fellow, Portsmouth Polytechnic, 1987. Jt Gen. Editor, Southampton Records Series, 1966–78; Gen. Editor, Portsmouth Record Series, 1969–2002. *Publications:* (with H. Thorpe) The printed maps of Warwickshire 1576–1900, 1959; A medieval Oxfordshire village: Cuxham 1240–1400, 1965; (ed with W. Albert) Portsmouth and Sheet Turnpike Commissioners' minute book 1711–1754, 1973; (ed) Manorial records of Cuxham, Oxfordshire, circa 1200–1359, 1976; The history of topographical maps: symbols, pictures and surveys, 1980; (ed) The peasant land market in medieval England, 1984; Manorial records, 1984; (ed with R. A. Skelton) Local maps and plans from medieval England, 1986; Medieval maps, 1991; Maps in Tudor England, 1993; (with A. McGuinness) A guide to British medieval seals, 1996; Editing historical records, 2001; Manors and Maps in Rural England: from the tenth century to the seventeenth, 2010; Medieval Maps of the Holy Land, 2012; contribs to: The Victoria History of the County of Oxford, vol. 10, 1972; History of Cartography, vol. 1, 1987; Agrarian History of England and Wales, vol. 3, 1991; articles in learned jls and periodicals. *Recreation:* British topography and topographical writings. *Address:* Lyndhurst, Farnley Hey Road, Durham DH1 4EA. *T:* (0191) 3869396. *Club:* Athenæum.

HARVEY, Prof. Paul H., CBE 2008; DPhil, DSc; FRS 1992; Professor in Zoology, University of Oxford, 1996–2014, now Emeritus; Fellow of Jesus College, Oxford, 1996–2014, now Emeritus; *b* 19 Jan. 1947; *s* of Edward Walter Harvey and Eileen Joan (*née* Pagett); *m*; two *s*. *Educ:* Queen Elizabeth's Grammar Sch., Hartlebury; Univ. of York (BA 1st Cl. Hons, DPhil); Univ. of Oxford (MA, DSc). Lectr in Biology, Univ. of Wales, Swansea, 1971–73; University of Sussex: Lectr in Biology, 1973–84; Reader, 1984–85; University of Oxford: Lectr in Zoology, 1985–89; Reader, 1989–96; Hd, Dept of Zoology, 1998–2011; Fellow, Merton Coll., Oxford, 1985–96. Vis. Lectr in Biology, Harvard Univ., 1978–79; Visiting Professor: Harvard Univ., 1980; Univ. of Washington, Seattle, 1982; Princeton Univ., 1984–85; Imperial Coll. London, 1995–. Sec., Zoological Soc. of London, 2000–11. MAE 2007. Scientific Medal, Zool Soc., 1986; J. Murray Luck Award, Nat. Acad. of Scis, USA, 1997; Frink Medal, Zool Soc., 2011. *Publications:* The Comparative Method in Evolutionary Biology, 1991; edited books; scientific papers. *Recreations:* walking, cooking. *Address:* Department of Zoology, University of Oxford, South Parks Road, Oxford OX1 3PS. *T:* (01865) 271260.

HARVEY, Peter Kent; DL; Chairman, Poole Hospital NHS Foundation Trust, 2001–10; Pro-Chancellor, Bournemouth University, since 2011; *b* 1 Feb. 1946; *s* of late John Alan Harvey and Joan Harvey; *m* 1976, Wendy Anne Wills; one *d*. *Educ:* Bishop Wordsworth's Sch., Salisbury; Liverpool Univ. (LLB Hons). Articled Clerk, 1968–71, Asst Solicitor, 1971, IoW CC; Asst Solicitor, Bournemouth BC, 1971–73; Dorset County Council: Sen. Asst Solicitor, 1973; Actg Asst Clerk, 1973–74; Dep. County Solicitor, 1974–85; County Solicitor and Dep. Chief Exec., 1985–91; Chief Exec., and Clerk to the Dorset Lieutenancy, 1991–99. Clerk to Dorset Fire Authy, 1991–99, to Dorset Police Authy, 1991–2006. Director: Dorset TEC, 1991–99; Dorset Business Link, 1997–99; Chairman: Dorset Strategic Bd of Young Enterprise, 1996–99; Poole Bay Primary Care Trust, 2000; Fitness to Practise Panel, 2012–, Disciplinary Panels, 2012–, NMC. Trustee: Dorset Health Trust, 2000–08 (Chm., 2000–06); Caxton Foundn, 2011–13. Trustee and Sec., Police Partnership Trust, 1997–2005. DL Dorset, 1999. *Recreations:* golf, sailing, gardening. *Address:* White Cottage, Dogdean, Wimborne, Dorset BH21 4HA.

HARVEY, Richard John, FIA; Chairman, PZ Cussons, since 2010; *b* 11 July 1950; *s* of Lester Harvey and Jean Rose Harvey; *m* 1971, Karen Vowles; one *s* two *d*. *Educ:* Univ. of Manchester (BSc Hons Maths). FIA 1975. Personal Pensions Manager, Phoenix Assurance, 1983–85; Mkting Manager, Sun Alliance, 1985–87; Gen. Manager, Sun Alliance Life (NZ), 1987–92; Chief Exec., Norwich Union Hldgs (NZ), 1992–93; Norwich Union: Gen. Manager (Finance), 1993–94; Actuary, 1994; Gp Finance Dir, 1995–97; Dep. Gp Chief Exec., 1997; Gp Chief Exec., 1998–2000; Dep. Gp Chief Exec., 2000–01, Gp Chief Exec., 2001–07, CGNU, later Aviva plc. Chm., ABI, 2003–05. Advocate, 2007–08, Patron, 2008–, Concern Universal. *Recreations:* theatre, ski-ing, squash.

HARVEY, Robert Lambart; author and journalist; *b* 21 Aug. 1953; *s* of Hon. John and Elena Harvey; *m* 1981, Jane Roper; one *s*. *Educ:* Eton; Christ Church, Oxford (BA 1974, MA 1978). Staff Correspondent, The Economist, 1974–81, Asst Editor, 1981–83; Columnist and Leader Writer, Daily Telegraph, 1987–91. MP (C) SW Clwyd, 1983–87. Mem., House of Commons Select Cttee on Foreign Affairs, 1984–87. Mem., Wilton Park Council, 1984–88; For. Sec.'s Rep., Adv. Bd for Woodrow Wilson Chair of Internat. Politics, 1985–92. Pres., Montgomery Cons. Assoc., 2005–08. *Publications:* Portugal: birth of a democracy, 1978; Fire Down Below: a study of Latin America, 1988; (ed) Blueprint 2000, 1989; The Undefeated: a study of modern Japan, 1994; The Return of the Strong: the drift to global disorder, 1995; Clive: the life and death of a British Emperor, 1998; Liberators: Latin America's struggle for independence 1810–1830, 2000; Cochrane: the life and exploits of a fighting captain, 2000; A Few Bloody Noses: the American War of Independence, 2001; The Fall of Apartheid, 2002; Comrades: the rise and fall of world Communism, 2003; Global Disorder, 2003; The War of Wars: the epic struggle between Britain and France 1789–1815, 2007; (ed) The World Crisis, 2007; The Mavericks: the military commanders who changed the course of history, 2008; Simon Bolivar, 2011. *Recreations:* the arts, films, music, swimming, walking. *Clubs:* Brooks's, Lansdowne.

HARVEY, Sheila Elizabeth; *see* Healy, S. E.

HARVEY, Stephen Frank; QC 2006; *b* 2 Nov. 1951; *s* of Frank George Harvey and Muriel Irene Harvey (*née* Stancombe); *m* 1973, Felicity Anne Murphy (marr. diss. 2000); one *s* two *d*. *Educ:* University Coll. London (LLB Hons); Inns of Court Sch. of Law. ACIArb. Mech. engrg industry, 1968–70; NHS, 1970–72; legal dept, local authy, 1972–76; financial services, 1976–78; called to the Bar, Gray's Inn, 1979; Asst Prosecutor, Essex CC, 1979–82; in private practice as a barrister, 1982–; Hd of Chambers, 1 Gray's Inn Square, 2013–. *Recreations:* sailing, fishing. *Address:* 1 Gray's Inn Square, Gray's Inn, WC1R 5AA. *T:* (020) 7405 0001, *Fax:* (020) 7405 0002.

HARVEY, Tim; *see* Harvey, A. J.

HARVEY, William Graeme; naturalist; *b* 15 Jan. 1947; *s* of late Jack Harvey and Grace (*née* Wilson); *m* 1st, 1970, Pamela Garnham (marr. diss. 1989); one *s* two *d*; 2nd, 1999, Pauline Maria Hayes (CBE 2013). *Educ:* Simon Langton Grammar Sch., Canterbury; University Coll., Oxford (BA Geography; MA). British Council, 1969–2000: Tanzania, 1970–73; Indonesia, 1974–76; Personnel, 1976–80; Madras, 1980–83; Educnl Contracts, 1983–86; Rep., Bangladesh, 1986–90; Gen. Manager, Tech. Co-operation Trng, 1990–92; Regl Dir, Eastern and Central Africa, and Dir, Kenya, 1993–98; Dir, Internat. Partnerships, 1998–2000. MBOU. *Publications:* Birds in Bangladesh, 1990; A Photographic Guide to the Birds of India, 2002; Tails of Dilli (children's stories), 2004; Atlas of the Birds of Delhi and Haryana, 2006; contrib. UK, African and Asian ornithol and conservation jls and books. *Recreations:* bird watching, conservation, gardening, poetry, pop music, Coronation Street. *Address:* Pound Farm, Blackham, Tunbridge Wells TN3 9TY. *E:* billharvey08@gmail.com. *Club:* Madras (Chennai) (Life Mem.).

HARVIE, Amanda; Managing Director, The Harvie Consultancy, since 2009; *b* Glasgow, 5 Jan. 1965; *d* of James Harvie and Dawn Harvie; *m* 2015, Gavin Wallace Hewitt, *qv*. *Educ:* Craigholme Sch., Glasgow; Royal Holloway and Bedford New Coll., Univ. of London (BA Hons). MCIPR 1992. Arts mktg consultant, 1986–88; PR consultant, 1988–95; Regl Manager, Prince's Scottish Youth Business Trust, 1995–99; Chief Executive: Aberdeen and Grampian Chamber of Commerce, 1999–2003; Scottish Financial Enterprise, 2003–07; sabbatical, 2007–08; independent business consultant, 2008–09. Non-exec. Dir, horsescotland, 2012–14. Member: Financial Services Strategy Gp, then Financial Services Implementation Gp, Scottish Govt, 2003–07; Financial Services Sector Adv. Bd, UK Trade and Investment, 2006–07; Shadow Chancellor's Financial Services Implementation Adv. Gp, 2009–10. Contested (C) Aberdeen S, 2010. Member: Scottish Conservatives Commn, 2010; Scottish Exec., Scottish Conservative and Unionist Party, 2011–12. Mem., Guild of Public

Relns Practitioners, 2006–15. Trustee, Reform Scotland, 2008–10. Burgess, City of Aberdeen, 2002. *Recreations:* equestrian sports, the countryside, art, literature, music, wine, travel. *T:* 07710 786807. *E:* amanda@theharvieconsultancy.com. *Club:* Western (Glasgow).

HARVIE, Prof. Christopher, PhD; Member (SNP) Scotland Mid and Fife, Scottish Parliament, 2007–11; *b* 21 Sept. 1944; *s* of George Harvie and Isobel Harvie (*née* Russell); *m* 1980, Virginia Roundell (*d* 2005); one *d. Educ:* Kelso High Sch.; Royal High Sch., Edinburgh; Univ. of Edinburgh (MA 1st Cl. Hons Hist. 1966; PhD 1972). Lectr, then Sen. Lectr in Hist., Open Univ., 1969–80; Prof. of British and Irish Studies, Eberhard-Karls Univ., Tübingen, 1980–2007, now Emeritus. Hon. Professor: of Politics, Univ. of Wales, Aberystwyth, 1996; of Hist., Strathclyde Univ., 1999–2009. Global Horizons Guest Lectr, Nat. Geographic Soc., 2015. Has made broadcasts and TV films. Bundesverdienstkreuz (Germany), 2012. *Publications:* The Lights of Liberalism, 1976; Scotland and Nationalism, 1977, 4th edn 2004; Scotland since 1914, 1981, 4th edn 2015; The Centre of Things: British political fiction, 1991; Cultural Weapons, 1992; The Rise of Regional Europe, 1993; Fool's Gold: the story of North Sea oil, 1993; Travelling Scot, 1999; The Oxford Short History of Scotland, 2002, 2nd edn 2014; Scotland's Transport, 2002; Mending Scotland, 2004; Floating Commonwealth: the Atlantic world, 2008; Broonland: the last days of Gordon Brown, 2010; Scotland the Brief, 2011; 1814 Year of Waverley, 2013; Dalriada: a novel of the Clyde at war, 2015; articles in learned jls, Scotsman, Guardian, etc; *festschrift:* View from Zollernblick, 2013. *Recreations:* walking, painting, music, travel by train and ship. *Address:* West Avenel, 50 High Cross Avenue, Melrose TD6 9SU.

HARVIE, Sir John (Smith), (Sir Jack), Kt 1997; CBE 1992; Senior Partner, J. S. Harvie & Co., since 1993; *b* 9 Aug. 1936; *s* of Alexander Wood Harvie and Margaret Isabella Smith Harvie; *m* 1958, Elizabeth Maxwell; one *s* two *d. Educ:* Ibrox Secondary Sch., Glasgow. Served HLI, 1954–57; Founder, J. S. Harvie & Co., 1959; Chairman: Central Building Contractors (CBC) Ltd, 1971–; Hugh Muirhead & Son Ltd, 1972–; T. W. Scott Ltd, 1974–; City Link Developments (Glasgow) Ltd, 1984–. *Recreations:* travel, reading. *Address:* Auchencraig, Mugdock, Milngavie, Glasgow G62 8EJ.

HARVIE, Jonathan Alexander; QC 1992; *b* 21 March 1950; *s* of late Anthony Bedford Harvie and of Winifred Jean Harvie (*née* Treliving); *m* 1981, Antonia Mary Lea, *d* of late Rev. His Honour Christopher Gerald Lea, MC; two *s* one *d. Educ:* King's Sch., Canterbury; Brasenose Coll., Oxford (BA Jurisprudence). Called to the Bar: Middle Temple, 1973 (Bencher, 2003); Bahamas, 2004. An Asst Recorder, 1994–2000; a Recorder, 2000–02. Life Mem., Internat. Soc. of Dendrologists. *Recreations:* gardening, racing, golf, music. *Address:* Blackstone Chambers, Blackstone House, Temple, EC4Y 9BW. *T:* (020) 7583 1770; 1 Garden Court, Temple, EC4Y 9BJ. *Clubs:* White's, Pratt's; Swinley Forest Golf; Vincent's (Oxford).

HARVIE, Patrick; Member (Green) Glasgow, Scottish Parliament, since 2003; *b* 18 March 1973; *s* of Dave and Rose Harvie. *Educ:* Dumbarton Acad.; Manchester Metropolitan Univ. Youth Worker, then Develt Worker, PHACE West, subseq. PHACE Scotland, 1997–2003. *Recreations:* computing, reading, cinema, food and drink. *Address:* Scottish Parliament, Edinburgh EH99 1SP. *T:* (0131) 348 6363. *E:* patrick.harvie.msp@scottish.parliament.uk.

HARVIE-WATT, Sir James, 2nd Bt *cr* 1945, of Bathgate, Co. Lothian; FCA; company director; *b* 25 Aug. 1940; *s* of Sir George Harvie-Watt, 1st Bt, QC, TD and Bettie, *o d* of Paymaster-Capt. Archibald Taylor, OBE, RN; *S* father, 1989; *m* 1966, Roseline, *d* of late Baron Louis de Chollet, Fribourg, Switzerland, and Frances Tate, Royal Oak, Maryland, USA; one *s* one *d. Educ:* Eton; Christ Church, Oxford (MA). FCA 1975 (ACA 1965). Lieut London Scottish (TA), 1959–67. With Coopers & Lybrand, 1962–70; Executive, British Electric Traction Co. Ltd, and Director of subsid. companies, 1970–78; Man. Dir, Wembley Stadium Ltd, 1973–78; Chairman: Cannons Sports & Leisure Ltd, 1990–93; A H Ball Gp, then Langley & Johnson, then Medi@Invest, 1995–2002; Oliver & Saunders Gp, 1997–2011. Director: Lake & Elliot Industries Ltd, 1988–93; Penna Consulting plc, 1995–2013; US Smaller Companies Investment Trust PLC, 1998–2000; Wellington Mgt Portfolios (Ire.), 2000–02, and other cos. Mem. Executive Cttee, London Tourist Board, 1977–80; Member: Sports Council, 1980–88 (Vice-Chm., 1985–88; Mem. Sports Council enquiries into: Financing of Athletics in UK, 1983; Karate, 1986); Indoor Tennis Initiative Bd, 1986–89. Chm., Crystal Palace Nat. Sports Centre, 1984–88; Dir, National Centres Bd, 1987–88. Member Management Cttee: Nat. Coaching Foundn, 1984–88; Holme Pierrepont Nat. Water Sports Centre, 1985–88; Mem., Stella Artois Tournament Cttee, 1990–94; International Tennis Hall of Fame: Dir, 1996–2005 and 2006–14; Mem., Exec. Cttee, 1997–2005 and 2006–14 (Chm., 2001–05); Chm., Internat. Council, 2006–11. Mem. Council, NPFA, 1985–90. FRSA 1978. OStJ 1964, and Mem. London Council of the Order, 1975–84. *Recreations:* shooting, tennis, golf, photography, walking. *Heir: s* Mark Louis Harvie-Watt [*b* 19 Aug. 1969; *m* 1996, Miranda, *d* of Martin Thompson; two *s* one *d*]. *Address:* 18 St Mary Abbots Terrace, W14 8NX. *T:* (office) (020) 7602 7353. *E:* harviewattjames@gmail.com. *Clubs:* White's, Pratt's, All England Lawn Tennis and Croquet, Queen's (Vice-Chm., 1987–90; Chm., 1990–93; Dir, 1987–2006); Swinley Forest Golf.

HARWERTH, Noël, JD; Chairman: Sumitomo Mitsui Bank Europe (Deputy Chairman, 2003); GE Capital Bank Ltd; *b* 16 Dec. 1947; *d* of Ben and Ira Vida Harwerth; *m* 1976, Seth Melhado. *Educ:* Univ. of Texas (BS); Univ. of Texas Sch. of Law (JD). Chief Tax Officer: Kennecott Copper Co., 1978–82; Dun & Bradstreet, NY, 1982–88; Citigroup, NY, 1988–98; Chief Operating Officer, Citibank Internat. plc, London, 1998–2003. Partnership Dir, London Underground, 2003–08; non-executive Director: RSA (formerly Royal & SunAlliance) plc, 2004–13; Corus Gp, 2005–07; Logica Gp, 2007–12; Impellam Gp, 2008–11; Alent, 2012–; Standard Life, 2012–; London Metal Exchange, 2012–; Sirius Minerals, 2015–. Dir, Dominion Diamond Corp. (formerly Harry Winston Diamond Corp.), 2008–. Non-executive Member: Horserace Totalisator Bd, 2006–11; Bd, British Horseracing Authy, 2014–. Fulbright Comr. *Recreations:* golf, horse-racing, shooting, opera. *Address:* Sumitomo Mitsui Bank Europe, 99 Queen Victoria Street, EC4V 4EH. *Clubs:* University, Cosmopolitan (New York); Wentworth Golf; Millbrook Golf (New York); Saratoga Golf and Polo.

HARWOOD, John Warwick; Vice Lord-Lieutenant of Oxfordshire, since 2009; *b* 10 Dec. 1946; *s* of late Dennis G. and Mrs W. G. Harwood; *m* 1967, Diana, *d* of late Harford Thomas; one *s* one *d. Educ:* Univ. of Kent at Canterbury (BA Hons); Univ. of London (MA). Admin. Officer, GLC, 1968–73; Private Sec. to Leader of ILEA, 1973–77; Head of Chief Exec.'s Office, London Bor. of Hammersmith and Fulham, 1977–79; Asst Chief Exec., London Bor. of Hammersmith and Fulham, 1979–82; Chief Exec., London Bor. of Lewisham, 1982–89; Hon. Clerk, S London Consortium, 1983–89; Chief Exec., Oxfordshire CC, 1989–2000; Clerk, Lieutenancy for Oxfordshire, 1989–2001; Chief Exec., Learning and Skills Council, 2000–03; Interim Chief Exec., Cumbria CC, 2004; Chm., CfBT Educn Trust (formerly CFBT), 2004–12. Sen. Associate Fellow, Warwick Business Sch., Univ. of Warwick, 2004–07. Chief Exec., Food Standards Agency, 2006–08. Director: N Oxfordshire Business Venture Ltd, 1989–98; Thames Business Advice Centre Ltd, 1989–99; Heart of England TEC, 1990–2001 (Chm., 2000–01); South East Regional Investment Ltd, 1998–2000. Member: Commn on Future of Voluntary Sector, 1995–96; Business Link Accreditation Adv. Bd, 1996–2000; Care Quality Commn, 2010–14. Chair, Local Authorities Race Relations Information Exchange, 1990–2000; Mem. Exec. Cttee, TCPA, 1981–89. Chm., Parrott & Lee Foundn, 1998–; Pres., Oxon CPRE, 2013–; Trustee: Oxfordshire Community Foundn, 1996–2004; Oxfordshire Victoria County History Trust Appeal, 1997–; Northmoor Trust, 2003–10 (Chm., 2005–10); Oxfordshire Youth (formerly Assoc. for Young People), 2011–; Cogges Heritage Trust, 2011–; Marriott Trust, 2013–; Young Dementia UK Homes, 2013–. Mem. Ct, Oxford Brookes Univ., 1999–2010. DL Oxfordshire, 2001. Hon. MA Kent, 1995. *Publications:* (contrib.) The Renaissance of Local Government, 1995; (contrib.) Understanding British Institutions, 1998. *Recreations:* walking, cooking, gardening. *Address:* West End House, Wootton, Oxon OX20 1DL. *T:* (01993) 810471. *E:* jharwood.cqc@gmail.com. *Club:* Reform.

HARWOOD, Air Vice-Marshal Michael John, CB 2012; CBE 2004 (MBE 1995); QCVS 1991; Head, British Defence Staff United States, and Defence Attaché, Washington, DC, 2008–12; Director, Matrix Blue Ltd, since 2012; *b* Buenos Aires, 29 Oct. 1958; *s* of (John) Alan (Douglas) Harwood and Mavis Verna Harwood; *m* 1981, Cheryl Kay South; two *d. Educ:* Merchant Taylors' Sch., Northwood; King's Coll. London (MA Defence Studies 1996). No 4 Adv. Flying Trng Sch. and Standards Sqn, RAF Valley, 1980–83; No 63 Sqn, RAF Chivenor, 1983–84; No IV (Army Cooperation) Sqn, RAF Gütersloh, 1985–87; Strike Attack Operational Evaluation Unit, A&AEE, 1987–92; OC Night, then Sqn Exec. Officer, No 1 (Fighter) Sqn (Harriers), RAF Wittering, 1992–95; Directorate of Public Relns, MoD, London, 1995–96; COS's Outer Office, PJHQ (UK), Northwood, 1996–98; OC No 20 Sqn (Harrier Operational Conversion Unit), RAF Wittering, 1998–2000; Comdr British Forces Operation Bolton, Saudi Arabia, 2000; Station Comdr and Harrier Force Comdr, RAF Cottesmore, 2001–03; ACOS (Operational Trng), RAF Strike Command, 2003–05; Dir HCSC and Asst Comdt (Air), Shrivenham, 2005–07; UK Air Component Comdr and AOC 83 Expeditionary Air Gp, Qatar, 2008; British Rep. to UN Mil. Staff Cttee, 2011. Dir, Military Mutual, 2014–. Air Experience Flight pilot, RAF Air Cadet Orgn, 2014–. *Recreations:* family, bookshops, walking and talking. *E:* Michael.Harwood@post.com. *Club:* Royal Air Force.

HARWOOD, Richard John, OBE 2014; QC 2013; *b* Sutton-in-Ashfield, 30 Aug. 1970; *s* of John and Frances Harwood; *m* 2005, Grainne O'Rourke; one *s* one *d* and one step *s. Educ:* Nottingham High Sch.; Jesus Coll., Cambridge (BA 1991; LLM 1992); Inns of Court Sch. of Law. Called to the Bar, Middle Temple, 1993; in practice as barrister, 1993–. Dep. Chm., Adv. Panel on Standards for Planning Inspectorate, 2007–10. Mem. (C) Merton LBC, 1998–2006. Contested (C) Bolsover, 1997. Case Ed., Jl Planning and Envmt Law, 2000–. *Publications:* Planning Enforcement, 1996, 2nd edn 2013; Historic Environment Law, 2012. *Recreations:* astronomy, art, clocks, history. *Address:* 39 Essex Street, WC2R 3AT. *T:* (020) 7832 1111. *E:* clerks@39essex.com.

HARWOOD, Sir Ronald, Kt 2010; CBE 1999; FRSL; writer; *b* 9 Nov. 1934; *s* of late Isaac Horwitz and Isobel Pepper; *m* 1959, Natasha Riehle (*d* 2013); one *s* two *d. Educ:* Sea Point Boys' High Sch., Cape Town; RADA. FRSL 1974. Actor, 1953–60. Artistic Dir, Cheltenham Festival of Literature, 1975; Presenter: Kaleidoscope, BBC, 1973; Read All About It, BBC TV, 1978–79. Visitor in Theatre, Balliol Coll., Oxford, 1986. TV plays include: The Barber of Stamford Hill, 1960; (with Casper Wrede) Private Potter, 1961; The Guests, 1972; Breakthrough at Reykjavik, 1987; Countdown to War, 1989; adapted several of Roald Dahl's Tales of the Unexpected for TV, 1979–80; TV series, All the World's a Stage, 1984; screenplays include: A High Wind in Jamaica, 1965; One Day in the Life of Ivan Denisovich, 1971; Evita Perón, 1981; The Dresser, 1983; Mandela, 1987; The Browning Version, 1994; Cry, The Beloved Country, 1995; Taking Sides, 2002; The Pianist, 2002 (Academy Award, 2003); Being Julia, 2004; The Diving Bell and the Butterfly, 2007 (BAFTA Award, 2008; Humanitas Prize, 2008; Prix Jacques Prévert Du Scénario, 2008); Love in the Time of Cholera, 2007; Quartet, 2012. Directed: The Odd Couple, 1989, Poison Pen, 1993, Royal Exchange, Manchester; Another Time, Steppenwolf Theatre, Chicago, 1991. Chairman: Writers Guild of GB, 1969; Council, RSL, 2001–04 (Mem., 1998–2001); Yvonne Arnaud Th., 2009–13; Member: Lit. Panel, Arts Council of GB, 1973–78; Cttee, Royal Literary Fund, 1995–2005 (Pres., 2005–); Cttee, English PEN, 1987–93 (Pres., 1989–93); Pres., Internat. PEN, 1993–97. Gov., Central Sch. of Speech and Drama, 1993–98. Trustee, Booker Foundn, 2002. Hon. DLitt: Keele, 2002; Aberdeen, 2013; Dr *hc* Nat. Acad. for Theatre and Film Arts, Sofia, 2007; Hon. Fellow: Central Sch. of Speech and Drama, 2007; Univ. of Chichester, 2009. Stefan Mitrov Ljubiša Prize, Budra Festival, Montenegro, for services to European literature and human rights, 2000; Nat. Jewish Th. Lifetime Achievement Award, 2014. Chevalier, Nat. Order of Arts and Letters (France), 1996. *Publications: novels:* All the Same Shadows, 1961; The Guilt Merchants, 1963; The Girl in Melanie Klein, 1969; Articles of Faith, 1973; The Genoa Ferry, 1976; Cesar and Augusta, 1978; Home, 1993 (Jewish Qly prize for fiction, 1994); *short stories:* One. Interior. Day.—adventures in the film trade, 1978; (co-ed) New Stories 3, 1978; *biography:* Sir Donald Wolfit, CBE—his life and work in the unfashionable theatre, 1971; (ed) The Ages of Gielgud, 1984; (ed) Dear Alec: Guinness at seventy-five, 1989; *essays:* (ed) A Night at the Theatre, 1983; (ed) The Faber Book of Theatre, 1993; *plays:* Country Matters, 1969; The Ordeal of Gilbert Pinfold (from Evelyn Waugh), 1977; A Family, 1978; The Dresser, 1980 (New Standard Drama Award; Drama Critics Award); After the Lions, 1982; Tramway Road, 1984; The Deliberate Death of a Polish Priest, 1985; Interpreters, 1985; J. J. Farr, 1987; Ivanov (from Chekhov), 1989; Another Time, 1989; Reflected Glory, 1992; Poison Pen, 1993; The Collected Plays of Ronald Harwood, 1993; Ronald Harwood: Plays 2, 1995; Taking Sides, 1995; The Handyman, 1996; Goodbye Kiss, 1997; Equally Divided, 1998; Quartet, 1999 (screenplay, 2012); Mahler's Conversion, 2001; An English Tragedy, 2008; Collaboration, 2008; Heavenly Ivy, 2010; *screenplays:* The Pianist, and Taking Sides, 2002; *musical libretto:* The Good Companions, 1974; *historical:* All the World's a Stage, 1983. *Recreation:* watching cricket. *Address:* c/o Judy Daish Associates, 2 St Charles Place, W10 6EG. *T:* (020) 8964 8811. *Clubs:* Garrick, MCC.

HASAN, Wajid Shamsul; High Commissioner for Pakistan in the United Kingdom, 1994–97 and 2008–13; *b* 5 Jan. 1941; *s* of late Syed Shamsul Hasan and Ameer Begum; *m* Zarina Wajid Hasan; one *s. Educ:* Karachi Univ. (LLB 1964); Master in Internat. Relations 1962. Freelance journalist, 1960; joined Jang Group of Newspapers, 1962; Editor, The News (English lang. daily), 1969; Founding Editor, MAG (English Weekly), 1981. Chm., Nat. Press Trust, 1989–90. Press Adviser, 1991–94, Adviser, 1997–2007, to Hon. Benazir Bhutto. TV commentator on S Asia and Middle East. *Publications:* contrib. articles to all major newspapers of Pakistan. *Recreation:* reading. *Clubs:* Royal Over-Seas League, Travellers.

HASELER, Prof. Stephen Michael Alan, PhD; author; Director, Global Policy Institute, since 2007, and Professor of Government, since 1986, London Metropolitan University (formerly City of London Polytechnic, then London Guildhall University); *b* 9 Jan. 1942; *m* 1967, Roberta Alexander. *Educ:* London School of Economics (BSc(Econ), PhD). Contested (Lab): Saffron Walden, 1966; Maldon, 1970. Chm., Labour Political Studies Centre, 1973–78. Mem. GLC, 1973–77, Chm. General Purposes Cttee, 1973–75. Founder Mem., SDP, 1981. Sen. Res. Fellow, Federal Trust, London, 2002–. Visiting Professor: Georgetown Univ., Washington DC, 1978; Johns Hopkins Univ., 1984; Maryland Univ., 1984–. Founder and Co-Chm., Radical Soc., 1988–; Chm., Republic, 1992–; Dir, Euro Res. Forum, 1997–2006. MInstD 1987. *Publications:* The Gaitskellites, 1969; Social-Democracy—Beyond Revisionism, 1971; The Death of British Democracy, 1976; Eurocommunism: implications for East and West, 1978; The Tragedy of Labour, 1980; Anti-Americanism, 1985; Battle for Britain: Thatcher and the New Liberals, 1989; The Politics of Giving, 1992; The End of the House of Windsor: Birth of a British Republic, 1993; The English Tribe: identity, nation and Europe, 1996; The Super-Rich: the unequal world of global capitalism, 2000; Super-State: the new Europe and its challenge to America, 2004; Sidekick: British global strategy from

Churchill to Blair, 2007; Meltdown, 2008; The Grand Delusion: Britain after sixty years of Elizabeth II, 2012. *Recreations:* cricket, American politics. *Address:* 2 Thackeray House, Ansdell Street, W8 5HA. *T:* (020) 7937 3976, (office) (020) 7320 1152.

HASELGROVE, Prof. Colin Cliff, PhD; FBA 2009; FSA; Professor of Archaeology, since 2005 and Head, School of Archaeology and Ancient History, 2006–12, University of Leicester; *b* London, 1951; *s* of Dennis Haselgrove and Evelyn Haselgrove; *m* 1998, Pamela Lowther. *Educ:* Westminster Sch.; Univ. of Sussex (BSc Hons Biochem.); Trinity Coll., Cambridge (BA Hons Archaeol. and Anthropol. 1974; PhD Archaeol. 1987). FSA 1989. Department of Archaeology, University of Durham: Lectr, 1977–89; Sen. Lectr, 1989–93; Reader, 1993–95; Prof., 1995–2004. Visiting Professor: Ecole Normale Supérieure, Paris, 1997; JW Goethe Univ., Frankfurt, 2003. Mem., Unité Mixte Recherche 8546 CNRS, 1999–; Corresp. Mem., German Archaeol Inst., 2005–. *Publications:* Iron Age Coinage in South-East England, 1987; Reconstructing Iron Age Societies, 1997; Iron Age Coinage and Ritual Practice, 2005; Les mutations de la fin de l'age du fer, 2006; The Earlier Iron Age in Britain and the Near Continent, 2007; The Later Iron Age in Britain and Beyond, 2007; The Traprain Environs Project, 2009. *Recreations:* gardening novice, French food, wine and markets, reading. *Address:* School of Archaeology and Ancient History, University of Leicester, University Road, Leicester LE1 7RH. *T:* (0116) 252 2611, *Fax:* (0116) 252 5005. *E:* cch7@le.ac.uk.

HASELHURST, Rt Hon. Sir Alan (Gordon Barraclough), Kt 1995; PC 1999; MP (C) Saffron Walden, since July 1977; *b* 23 June 1937; *s* of late John Haselhurst and Alyse (*née* Barraclough); *m* 1977, Angela (*née* Bailey); two *s* one *d*. *Educ:* King Edward VI Sch., Birmingham; Cheltenham Coll.; Oriel Coll., Oxford. Pres., Oxford Univ. Conservative Assoc., 1958; Sec., Treas. and Librarian, Oxford Union Soc., 1959–60; Nat. Chm., Young Conservatives, 1966–68. MP (C) Middleton and Prestwich, 1970–Feb. 1974. PPS to Sec. of State for Educn, 1979–82. Chairman: of Ways and Means and a Dep. Speaker, H of C, 1997–2010; Admin Cttee, 2010–15; Member: Financial Services Cttee, 2010–; Audit Cttee, 2010–; Liaison Cttee, 2010–15; Ecclesiastical Cttee, 2010–15. Mem., H of C Select Cttee on European Legislation, 1982–97, on Catering, 1991–97, on Transport, 1992–97; Chm., All Party Parly Cricket Gp, 2010– (Hon. Sec. 1993–2010). Chm., Rights of Way Review Cttee, 1983–93. Commonwealth Parliamentary Association: Chm., UK Br., 2010–; Chm., Exec. Cttee, 2011–14. Chairman: Manchester Youth and Community Service, 1974–77; Commonwealth Youth Exchange Council, 1978–81; Chm. Trustees, Community Development (formerly Projects) Foundn, 1986–97. *Publications:* Occasionally Cricket, 1999; Eventually Cricket, 2001; Incidentally Cricket, 2003; Accidentally Cricket, 2009; Unusually Cricket, 2010; Fatally Cricket, 2013. *Recreations:* gardening, theatre, music, watching cricket. *Address:* House of Commons, SW1A 0AA. *E:* alan.haselhurst.mp@parliament.uk. *Clubs:* MCC; Essex CC (Mem., Exec. Cttee, 1996–2008); Yorkshire CC; Middlesex CC.

HASELOCK, Rev. Canon Jeremy Matthew, FSA; Residentiary Canon and Precentor, since 1998, Vice Dean, since 2004, Norwich Cathedral; Chaplain to the Queen, since 2013; *b* 20 Sept. 1951; *s* of late Kenneth Pool Haselock and of Pamela Haselock (*née* Bolus). *Educ:* Univ. of York (BA Hons History 1973); Univ. of York Centre for Mediaeval Studies (BPhil 1974); St Stephen's House, Oxford (BA Theol. 1982, MA 1985). Deacon 1983, priest 1984; Asst Curate, St Gabriel, Pimlico, 1983–86; Asst Priest, St John, Lafayette Sq., Washington, 1985; Asst Curate, St James, Paddington, 1986–88; Domestic Chaplain to Bp of Chichester, 1988–91; Vicar of Boxgrove, 1991–98; Chichester Dio. Liturgical Advr, 1991–98; Preb. of Fittleworth and Canon of Chichester Cathedral, 1994–2000. Proctor in Convocation and Mem., Gen. Synod, 1995–. Chm., Norwich Dio. Liturgical Cttee, 1998–2006; Member: C of E Liturgical Commn, 1996–2006; C of E Liturgical Publishing Gp, 2001–03; Chichester DAC for Care of Churches, 1991–98; Norwich DAC for Care of Churches, 1998–; Pubns Cttee, 1988–93, Archaeol Working Party, 1997–99, Council for Care of Churches; Cathedrals Fabric Commn for England, 2003–11; Bishoprics and Cathedrals Cttee, Church Comrs, 2006–13; Council, Guild of Church Musicians, 2001– (Sub-Warden, 2005–11; Warden, 2011–). Vis. Prof. in Liturgics, 2010–11, Adj. Prof. in Liturgics, 2013–, Nashota House. Chm. of Govs, Boxgrove Sch., 1991–98; Gov., Norwich Sch., 1998–. Chaplain Gen., 2001–04, Chancellor, 2005–08, Bailiff, 2008–11, now Bailiff Emeritus, Order of St Lazarus of Jerusalem (Dep. Ecclesiastical Grand Prior, 2011–13); EGCLJ 2009. FSA 2007. Hon. FGCM 2008. Hon. DMus Nashotah Hse, 2013. *Publications:* (with Roger Greenacre) The Sacrament of Easter, 1989, 3rd edn 1995; (with P. Hurst) Norfolk Rood Screens, 2012; chapters in works on history, art and architecture of English cathedrals; articles, reviews and papers on liturgical and artistic matters. *Recreations:* foreign travel, collecting Oriental porcelain, music and theatre, especially opera, reading, church crawling, conversation, cooking and entertaining, wine. *Address:* 34 The Close, Norwich NR1 4DZ. *T:* (01603) 218314. *Club:* Athenæum.

HASKARD, Sir Cosmo (Dugal Patrick Thomas), KCMG 1965 (CMG 1960); MBE 1945; *b* 25 Nov. 1916; *oc* of late Brig.-Gen. J. McD. Haskard, CMG, DSO and Alicia, *d* of S. N. Hutchins, Ardnagashel, Bantry, Co. Cork; *m* 1957, Phillada, *oc* of late Sir Robert Stanley, KBE, CMG and Lady Stanley (*née* Ursula Cracknell); one *s*. *Educ:* Cheltenham; RMC Sandhurst; Pembroke Coll., Cambridge (MA). Served War of 1939–45 (MBE); 2nd Lieut, TA (Gen. List), 1938; emergency Commn, Royal Irish Fusiliers, 1939; seconded KAR, 1941; served 2nd Bn, E Africa, Ceylon, Burma; Major 1944. Apptd Colonial Service cadet, Tanganyika, 1940, but due to war service did not take up duties until 1946 in which yr transf. to Nyasaland; Dist Comr, 1948; served on Nyasaland-Mozambique Boundary Commn, 1951–52; Provincial Commissioner, 1955; acting Secretary for African Affairs, 1957–58; Sec. successively for Labour and Social Development, for Local Government, and for Natural Resources, 1961–64; Governor and C-in-C, Falkland Islands, and High Comr for the British Antarctic Territory, 1964–70. Trustee, Beit Trust, 1976–2003. *Address:* Tragariff, Bantry, Co. Cork, Ireland.

HASKARD, Prof. Dorian Oliver, DM; FRCP, FMedSci; British Heart Foundation Sir John McMichael Professor of Cardiovascular Medicine, since 1995, Head of Vascular Sciences, National Heart and Lung Institute, since 2004, and Head of Immunology and Inflammation, Department of Medicine, since 2010, Imperial College London (formerly Royal Postgraduate Medical School, then Imperial College School of Medicine) at Hammersmith Hospital; *b* 8 July 1951; *s* of Oliver Patrick Miller Haskard and Anna Caroline (*née* Worthington); *m* 1980, Kathleen Ann Keitzman; three *s*. *Educ:* Eton Coll.; St Edmund Hall, Oxford (MA; DM 1989); Middlesex Hosp. Med. Sch. FRCP 1994. Res. Fellow, Southwestern Med. Sch., Dallas, 1984–86; Wellcome Trust Sen. Res. Fellow in Clinical Sci., UMDS, Guy's Hosp., 1987–90; Royal Postgraduate Medical School, Hammersmith Hospital: Sen. Lectr in Rheumatology, 1990–94; Reader, 1994. FMedSci 2001. *Publications:* papers on rôle of blood vessels in inflammation. *Recreation:* gardening. *Address:* National Heart and Lung Institute, Imperial College London, Hammersmith Hospital, Du Cane Road, W12 0NN. *T:* (020) 8383 3064.

HASKEL, family name of **Baron Haskel**.

HASKEL, Baron *cr* 1993 (Life Peer), of Higher Broughton in the Metropolitan County of Greater Manchester; **Simon Haskel;** *b* Kaunas, Lithuania, 9 Oct. 1934; *s* of late Isaac and Julia Haskel; *m* 1962, Carole Lewis, New York, USA; one *s* one *d*. *Educ:* Salford Coll. of Advanced Technol. (BSc Textile Technol.). ATI. Nat Service commn, RA, 1959. Joined Perrotts Ltd, 1961; Chm., Perrotts Gp and associated cos, 1973–97. An opposition whip, H of L, 1994–97; an opposition spokesman on trade and industry, 1995–97; a Lord in Waiting (Govt Whip), 1997–98; front bench spokesman on trade and industry, on treasury, and on social security, 1997–98. Mem., Select Cttee on Sci. and Technol., 1995–97, 1999–2003, 2007–10; Dep. Chm. of Cttees, H of L, 2002–; Dep. Speaker, H of L, 2002–. Labour Party: Sec., 1972 Industry Gp, 1976–81; Sec., 1981–90, Chm., 1990–96, Finance and Industry Gp. Chm., Thames Concerts Soc., 1982–90; Pres., Inst. of Jewish Policy Res. (formerly Inst. of Jewish Affairs), 1998–. Chm. Trustees, The Smith Inst., 1999–2009. Hon. President: Envmtl Industries Commn, 2000–14; Technitex Faraday, 2002–; Materials UK, 2006–. Patron: Soc. of Ops Engrs, 2000–04; Chronic Disease Res. Foundn, 2000–05. FRSA 1979. DUniv Bolton, 2007. *Recreations:* music, cycling. *Address:* House of Lords, SW1A 0PW. *T:* (020) 7219 4076.
See also J. E. Haskel.

HASKEL, Prof. Jonathan Edward, PhD; Professor of Economics, Imperial College Business School, since 2008; *b* London, 13 Aug. 1963; *s* of Baron Haskel, *qv*; *m* 1997, Sue Alexander; two *d*. *Educ:* King's Coll. Sch., Wimbledon; Univ. of Bristol (BSc Econs 1984); London Sch. of Econs and Pol Sci. (MSc Econs 1985; PhD Econs 1990). Temp. Lectr, Univ. of Bristol, 1987–88; Res. Officer, Centre for Business Strategy, London Business Sch., 1988–90; Lectr, 1990–97, Reader, 1997–98, Prof., 1998–2008, Hd of Econs Dept, 2003–08, QMW, later QMUL. Res. Fellow, Labour Econs Prog., Centre for Econ. Policy Res., 1999–; Res. Associate, IZA, Bonn, 2001–. Visiting Professor: Stern Sch. of Business, NY Univ., 1997; Tuck Sch. of Business, Dartmouth Coll., 2012–; Vis. Res. Schol., ANU, 1995. Mem., Reporting Panel, Competition Commn, 2001–09. Mem. Council, REconS, 2012–. Mem., Editl Bd, Economica, 1998–. *Publications:* contribs to learned jls incl. Amer. Econ. Rev., Econ. Jl, Jl Econ. Perspectives, Rev. Econs and Stats, Canadian Jl Econs, Internat. Jl Industrial Orgn, Jl Industrial Econs, Rev. Income and Wealth, Oxford Bull. Econs and Stats, Economica, Oxford Econ. Papers, Eur. Econ. Rev., Scandinavian Jl Econs. *Recreations:* running, cycling. *Address:* Imperial College Business School, Tanaka Building, Room 296, South Kensington Campus, SW7 2AZ. *T:* (020) 7594 8563, *Fax:* (020) 7594 5915. *E:* j.haskel@imperial.ac.uk.

HASKINS, family name of **Baron Haskins**.

HASKINS, Baron *cr* 1998 (Life Peer), of Skidby in the co. of the East Riding of Yorkshire; **Christopher Robin Haskins;** Chairman: Northern Foods, 1986–2002; Express Dairies plc, 1998–2002; *b* 30 May 1937; *s* of Robin and Margaret Haskins; *m* 1959, Gilda Horsley; three *s* two *d*. *Educ:* Trinity Coll., Dublin (BA Mod). Ford Motor Co., Dagenham, 1960–62; Northern Foods, formerly Northern Dairies, 1962–2002. Chm., Better Regulation Task Force, 1997–2002; Member: New Deal Task Force, 1997–2001; Efficiency and Reform Bd, Cabinet Office, 2010–. Mem. Bd, Yorks and Humber Regl Develt Agency, 1998–2008; Chm., Humber Local Enterprise Partnership, 2011–. Member: Culliton Irish Industrial Policy Review Gp, 1991–92; Commn for Social Justice, 1992–94; UK Round Table on Sustainable Develt, 1995–98; Hampel Cttee on Corporate Governance, 1996–97. Member: H of L Europe Sub-Cttee D, 2003–06, Sub-Cttee A, 2007–12; Select Cttee on Small and Med. Sized Enterprises Exports, 2012–13; Chm., European Movement, 2004–06. Trustee: Runnymede Trust, 1989–98; Demos, 1993–2000; Civil Liberties Trust, 1997–99; Legal Assistance Trust, 1998–2004; Lawes Agricl Trust, 1999–. Pro-Chancellor, Open Univ., 2005–14. Hon. LLD: Hull, 1999; Dublin, 2000; Nottingham, Huddersfield, 2002; DU: Leeds Metropolitan, 1998; Essex, 2000; Hon. DSc: Cranfield, 2000; Lincoln, 2003; Bradford, 2005. *Recreations:* writing, only-in-emergency harvest tractor-driver, cricket, Hull City FC. *Address:* Quarryside Farm, Main Street, Skidby, near Cottingham, East Yorks HU16 5TG. *T:* (01482) 842692.

HASLAM, Christopher Peter de Landre; HM Diplomatic Service, retired; Ambassador (non-resident) to Marshall Islands, Micronesia and Palau, 2000–03; Deputy High Commissioner to Fiji Islands, Tuvalu, Kiribati and Nauru, 2000–03; *b* 22 March 1943; *s* of late Jack Harold Haslam and Molly Patricia Haslam; *m* 1969, Lana Whitley; two *s*. *Educ:* Ashley Co. Secondary, Hants. Admiralty, 1960–66; joined HM Diplomatic Service, 1966: Jakarta, 1969–72; Attaché, Sofia, 1972–74; FCO, 1974–78; Canberra, 1978–82; Second Sec. (Commercial), Lagos, 1982–86; FCO, 1986–89; First Sec. (Commercial), Copenhagen, 1989–93; FCO Inspectorate, 1993–96; First Sec. (Commercial and Econ.), Colombo, 1996–99. *Recreations:* reading, lobbying MP and local authorities on current issues, amateur novelist.

HASLAM, David Antony, CBE 2004; Chair, National Institute for Health and Care Excellence, since 2013; *b* 4 July 1949; *s* of Norman and Mary Haslam; *m* 1974, Barbara Flannery; one *s* one *d*. *Educ:* Monkton Combe Sch.; Birmingham Univ. (MB ChB 1972). DObstRCOG 1974; MRCGP (Dist.) 1976, FRCGP 1989; DFFP 1998; FFPH 2003; FRCP 2004. GP, Ramsey Health Centre, Huntingdon, 1976–2011. Nat. Clin. Advr, Healthcare Commn, 2005–09; Nat. Professional Advr, Care Quality Commn, 2009–13. Vis. Prof. in Primary Health Care, De Montfort Univ., Leicester, 2000–; Prof. of Gen. Practice, Univ. of Nicosia, 2014–. Chm. of Council, 2001–04, Pres., 2006–09, RCGP. Mem., Postgrad. Medical Educn and Trng Bd, 2003–10; Co-Chm., Modernising Med. Careers Prog. Bd, 2007–09; Chm., NHS Evidence Adv. Cttee, 2008–13; Member: Nat. Quality Bd for NHS, 2009–; NHS Future Forum, 2011–12. Pres., BMA, 2011–12. FAcadMed 2010. *Publications:* Sleepless Children, 1984 (also US, Dutch, German, Spanish, Finnish, Swedish, Indonesian, Hebrew, Hungarian, Chinese and Bulgarian edns); Eat It Up, 1986 (also Dutch and Hungarian edns); Travelling With Children, 1987 (also Dutch edn); Parent Stress, 1989 (also Dutch, Finnish and Polish edns); The Expectant Father, 1990, 2nd edn 1998; Bulimia: a guide for sufferers and their families, 1994 (also US and Czech edns); Food Fights, 1995 (also US, German and Chinese edns); Coping with a Termination, 1996; Your Child's Symptoms Explained, 1997 (also Czech, Polish, Romanian and Greek edns); Stress Free Parenting, 1998 (also Bulgarian and Russian edns); A–Z Guide to Children's Health, 1999; (ed) The Guide to Your Child's Symptoms, 1999; (ed) Not Another Guide to Stress in General Practice, 2000; contrib. numerous articles and papers to med. jls. *Recreations:* music, photography, travel; ran London Marathon, 2006. *Address:* 35 Biggin Lane, Ramsey, Huntingdon, Cambs PE26 1NB. *T:* (01487) 813033. *E:* davidhaslam@hotmail.com.

HASLAM, (Gordon) Edward; Chairman, Talvivaara Mining Company plc, 2007–12; Chief Executive Officer, Lonmin plc, 1999–2004; *b* 17 April 1944; *s* of Eric and Marjorie Haslam; *m* 1972, Caroline Rosemary Harrington; three *s*. *Educ:* King Edward VII Grammar Sch., Sheffield. Man. Dir, Western Platinum Ltd, SA, 1997–99. Pres., Internat. Platinum Assoc., 1990. FInstD 1995; CCMI 2002. *Publications:* Platinum Group Metals and the Quality of Life, 1989. *Recreations:* aviation (holds Private Pilot's Licence), sailing (qualified Yachtmaster).

HASLAM, Rev. Gregory Paul; Minister, Westminster Chapel, since 2002; *b* Liverpool, 13 June 1953; *s* of late Wilfred Haslam and Jean Elizabeth Haslam (*née* Stackhouse); *m* 1975, Ruth Carson Munro; three *s*. *Educ:* Bootle Grammar Sch., Liverpool; Newton-le-Willows Grammar Sch., Merseyside; Bede Coll., Durham Univ. (BA 1975); Padgate Coll. (PGCE 1976); London Theol Seminary. Religious Educn Teacher, Hindley High Sch., Wigan, 1976–78; Minister, Winchester Family Church, Hants, 1980–2002. *Publications:* Chosen for Good, 1986; Could You Fall Away?, 1988; Elisha - a sign and a wonder, 1995; Preach the Word!, 2006; Let My People Grow, 2006; A Radical Encounter with God, 2007; Moving in the Prophetic, 2009; The Man Who Wrestled With God, 2009; Should Christians Embrace Evolution?, 2010; The Jonah Complex, 2012; Proclaiming Christmas, 2012; If I Had Only One Sermon to Preach, 2013; articles in Evangelicals Now, New Frontiers, Christianity, Cover to Cover Every Day, Closer to God, Daily Bread. *Recreations:* reading, cinema, cycling, motor cycling, walking, apologetics. *Address:* c/o Westminster Chapel, Buckingham Gate, SW1E 6BS. *T:* (020) 7834 1731. *E:* office@westminsterchapel.org.uk.

HASLAM, Rev. John Gordon; non-stipendiary Church of England priest; a Chaplain to the Queen, 1989–2002; *b* 15 July 1932; *s* of Ernest Henry Haslam and Constance Mabel (*née* Moore); *m* 1st, 1957, Margaret Anne Couse (*d* 1985); two *s* one *d*; 2nd, 1987, Marian Kidson

Clarke. *Educ:* King Edward's Sch., Birmingham; Birmingham Univ. (LLB); Queen's Coll., Birmingham. National Service, RA, 1956–58 (2nd Lieut). Solicitor's Articled Clerk, Johnson & Co., Birmingham, 1953–56; Asst Solicitor, 1958–62, Partner, 1962–75, Pinsent & Co., Solicitors, Birmingham; a Chm. of Industrial Tribunals, 1976–92, Regl Chm., 1992–96, part-time Chm., 1996–2001. Ordained deacon and priest, Birmingham dio., 1977; Hon. Curate: St Michael's, Bartley Green, Birmingham, 1977–79; St Mary's, Moseley, Birmingham, 1980–96; Hon. Hosp. Chaplain, 1980–88; temp. service as priest in many Birmingham parishes, 1983–96; licensed to officiate, Hereford dio., 1996–. *Recreations:* gardening, steam railways, fell walking. *Address:* 16 Mill Street, Ludlow, Salop SY8 1BE. *T:* (01584) 876663.

HASLAM, Jonathan, CBE 1997; FRGS; Managing Director, Haslamedia Ltd, since 2005; *b* 2 Oct. 1952; *s* of Arthur and Irene Florence; *m* 1981, Dawn Rachel Saunders; two *s*. *Educ:* Cowbridge Grammar Sch., Glam; Plymouth Poly. (BSc Hons Geog. 1975); Croydon Coll. of Art and Technol. (HNC Business Studies). MCIPR 1997. FRGS 2010. Mgt Trainee, National Westminster Bank, 1975–79; Information Officer: COI, 1979–82; Dept of Industry, 1982–84; Sen. Inf. Officer, Home Office, 1984–86; Chief Press Officer, then Dep. Hd of Inf., Dept of Employment, 1986–89; Dep. Dir of Inf., Home Office, 1989–91; Dep. Press Sec. to Prime Minister, 1991–95; Head of Inf. and Press Sec. to Minister, Min. of Agriculture, 1995–96; Chief Press Sec. to Prime Minister, 1996–97; Dir of Communications, DFEE, 1997; Dir of Corporate Affairs, London Metal Exchange, 1997–2003; Gp Dir of Communications, Jarvis plc, 2003–05; Chm., The Spokesman, 2003–06. Dir, MIP Communications Ltd, 2008–. Sen. Advr, Smith Square Partners LLP, 2010–. Chm., Friends of Dulwich Coll., 2007–10 (Dep. Chm., 2006–07); Gov., Bishop Challoner Sch., 2007–. *Recreations:* long walks, photography, travel, reading, golf, music.

HASLAM, Prof. Jonathan George, FBA 2009; Professor of the History of International Relations, University of Cambridge, 2004–15, now Emeritus; Fellow, Corpus Christi College, Cambridge, since 1993; George F. Kennan Professor, School of Historical Studies, Institute for Advanced Study, Princeton, since 2015; *b* Copthorne, Sussex, 15 Jan. 1951; *s* of Edgar Alfred Haslam and Marjorie May Haslam; *m* 2006, Karina Urbach; one *s*. *Educ:* London Sch. of Econs (BSc (Econ.) 1972); Trinity Coll., Cambridge (MLitt 1978). Lectr, Univ. of Birmingham, 1975–84; Associate Prof., Johns Hopkins Univ., 1984–86; Visiting Associate Professor: Stanford Univ., 1986–87; Univ. of Calif, Berkeley, 1987–88; University of Cambridge: Sen. Res. Fellow, King's Coll., 1988–92; Asst Dir of Studies, 1991–2000; Reader, 2000–04. Visiting Professor: Stanford Univ., 1994 and 2005; Yale Univ., 1996; Harvard Univ., 2001. Member: Inst. for Advanced Study, Princeton, 1998; Soc. of Scholars, Johns Hopkins Univ., 2010–. *Publications:* Soviet Foreign Policy, 1930–33: the impact of the Depression, 1983; The Soviet Union and the Struggle for Collective Security in Europe, 1933–39, 1984; The Soviet Union and the Politics of Nuclear Weapons in Europe, 1969–87, 1990; The Soviet Union and the Threat from the East, 1933–41, 1992; The Vices of Integrity: E. H. Carr, 1892–1982, 1999; No Virtue Like Necessity: realist thought in international relations since Machiavelli, 2002; The Nixon Administration and the Death of Allende's Chile: a case of assisted suicide, 2005; Russia's Cold War: from the October Revolution to the Fall of the Wall, 2011; Near and Distant Neighbors: a new history of Soviet intelligence, 2015. *Recreations:* foreign languages, music, study of the martial arts, gardening. *Address:* Institute for Advanced Study, Einstein Drive, Princeton, NJ 08540, USA. *Club:* Athenæum.

HASLAM, Mark Stanley Culloden; Partner, BCL Burton Copeland, since 1998; *b* Nairobi, 16 June 1957; *s* of Nigel Haslam and Daphne Haslam; *m* 1996, Helen Fiona Copsey; three step *s*. *Educ:* Wellington Coll.; Pembroke Coll., Cambridge (BA Law 1978). Admitted solicitor, 1981; Partner: Claude Hornby & Cox, 1985–95; Magrath & Co., 1995–98. Pres., London Criminal Courts Solicitors' Assoc., 2001. *Recreations:* Rugby, cricket, horseracing, theatre. *Address:* Brook Place, 23 Brook Farm Road, Cobham, Surrey KT11 3AX. *T:* (01932) 864735, (office) (020) 7430 2277, 07976 294270, *Fax:* (office) (020) 7430 1101. *E:* mhaslam@bcl.com. *Clubs:* Brook Cricket, Jersey Rugby, Esher Rugby.

HASLAM, Michael Trevor, TD 1991; MD; retired consultant psychiatrist and medical director; *b* 7 Feb. 1934; *s* of Gerald Haslam and Edna Beatrice Haslam (*née* Oldfield); *m* 1959, Shirley Dunstan Jefferies; one *s* two *d*. *Educ:* Sedbergh Sch.; St John's Coll., Cambridge (MA 1960, MD 1971); St Bartholomew's Hosp.; Univ. of Leeds (MA (Theol) 2003). FRCP(Glas.) 1979; FRCPsych 1980. Captain, RAMC, 1960–62; hosp. posts, York, 1962–64, Newcastle upon Tyne, 1964–67; Consultant Psychiatrist: Doncaster, 1967–70; York, 1970–89; Medical Director: Harrogate Clinic, 1989–91; SW Durham Mental Health NHS Trust, 1993–96; S Durham Health Care NHS Trust, 1996–98. Hon. Sec., Hon. Treas. and former Chm., Soc. of Clinical Psychiatrists; former Cttee Chm., RCP. Freeman: City of London, 1973; City of Glasgow, 2011; Liveryman, Soc. of Apothecaries, 1973. *Publications:* Psychiatric Illness in Adolescence, 1975; Sexual Disorders, 1978 (trans. Spanish 1980); Psychosexual Disorders, 1979; Psychiatry Made Simple, 1982, 2nd edn 1990 (trans. Polish 1997); Transvestism, 1993; (ed) Psychiatry in the New Millennium, 2003; Clifton Hospital: an era, 1997; Close to the Wind, 2006; Shrink in the Clink, 2008; Alzheimer, 2009; A History of the Society of Clinical Psychiatrists, 2014; articles in learned jls. *Recreations:* writing, music, fives, squash, croquet, travel. *Address:* Chapel Garth, Crayke, York YO61 4TE. *T:* (01347) 823042.

HASLAM, Miranda Jayne; *see* Moore, Miranda J.

HASLAM, Nicholas Ponsonby; Founder, and Chief Executive Officer, NH Design (formerly Director, Nicholas Haslam), since 1972; *b* Gt Missenden, Bucks, 27 Sept. 1939; *s* of William Heywood Haslam and Diamond Louise Constance, (Diana), Haslam (*née* Ponsonby). *Educ:* Eton. Asst Art Dir, American Vogue, Condé Nast, USA, 1962–64; Art Dir, Show Mag., NY, 1964–66; owner, Arabian horse ranch, Phoenix, Arizona, 1965–70; worked in film business, LA, 1970–72. *Publications:* Sheer Opulence, 2002, 2nd edn 2010; Redeeming Features (autobiog.), 2009; Folly de Grandeur, 2013; A Designer's Life, 2014. *Recreations:* history, biography, painting. *Address:* NH Design, 76–78 Holland Park Avenue, W11 3RB. *T:* (020) 7730 0808, *Fax:* (020) 7730 0888. *E:* nickyhaslam@nh-design.co.uk. *Club:* Travellers.

HASLAM, Richard Michael, FSA; writer on architecture; buildings consultant; painter; *b* 27 Sept. 1944; *s* of Cecil Henry Cobden Haslam and Sylvia Lois Haslam (*née* Assheton); *m* 1980, Charlotte Sophia Dorrien Smith (*d* 1997); two *s* one *d*. *Educ:* Eton Coll. (Oppidan Schol.); New Coll., Oxford (BA 1966, MA 1967); Courtauld Inst. of Art (MA 1969). FSA 1987. Res. Asst to Sir Nikolaus Pevsner, 1969–71; Statistician, 1971–72, and Mem., Lloyd's. Curator, Clough Williams-Ellis exhibn, Heinz Gall., RIBA, 1997. National Trust: Member: Architectl Panel, 1979–; Cttee for Wales, 1980–88; Properties Cttee, 1985–2005; Council, 2005–11; Member: Historic Buildings Council for Wales, 1980–98; Royal Commn on Ancient and Historical Monuments of Wales, 1986–98; Prize Jury, Premio Dedalo Minosse for commng a building, 1998– (Chm., 2008–11). Trustee, Venice in Peril Fund, 1992– (Hon. Sec., 2011–). Brother, Art Workers' Guild, 2011–. *Publications:* The Buildings of Wales: Powys, 1979; From Decay to Splendour: the repair of church treasures, 1985; Clough Williams-Ellis's Drawings, 1996; (jtly) The Buildings of Wales: Gwynedd, 2009; articles on English, Welsh and Italian subjects in Country Life, Garden History, Arte Lombarda, Perspectives on Architecture and other jls. *Recreations:* walking, ski-ing, family life. *Address:* Bramley Grange, Bramley, Tadley, Hants RG26 5DJ; Parc, Llanfrothen, Gwynedd LL48 6SP.

HASLETT, Prof. Christopher, OBE 2004; FRCP, FRCPE, FMedSci; FRSE; Sir John Crofton Professor of Respiratory Medicine (formerly Professor of Respiratory Medicine) and Director, Rayne Laboratories, since 1990 and Director, Queen's Medical Research Institute, since 2005, University of Edinburgh; Hon. Consultant Physician, Lothian Acute Hospitals Trust, since 1990; *b* 2 April 1953; *s* of James and Elizabeth Haslett; *m* 1973, Jean Margaret Hale; one *s* one *d*. *Educ:* Wirral Grammar Sch.; Univ. of Edinburgh Med. Sch. (BSc 1st Cl. Hons Pathology 1974; MB ChB Hons 1974; Ettles Schol.; Leslie Gold Medal for most distinguished grad. 1977). MRCP 1979, FRCP 1991; FRCPE 1988. Jun. med. posts, Edinburgh, 1977–79; Rotating Med. Registrar, Ealing Hosp. and Hammersmith Hosp., 1980–82; MRC Travelling Fellow, Nat. Jewish Hosp., Denver, 1982–85; MRC Sen. Clin. Fellow and Sen. Lectr, Dept of Medicine, RPMS, Hammersmith Hosp., 1986–90; University of Edinburgh: Associate Dean (Res.), 1996–2001; Head, Div. of Clin. Sci. and Community Health, 1998–2001; Dir, MRC/Univ. of Edinburgh Centre for Inflammation Res., Queen's Med. Res. Inst., 2002–09. Vice-Chairman: Res. Cttee, Nat. Asthma Campaign, 1990–94; MRC Molecular and Cellular Medicine Bd, 1994–98; Mem., MRC Systems A Grants Cttee, 1990–92; Chairman: Lung Injury Section, European Respiratory Soc., 1994–98 (Sec., 1991–94); MRC ROPA Infection and Immunity Panel, 1995, 1996. Medal and Prize for Sci., Saltire Soc., 1996; Gilston Lecture and Medal, Intensive Care Soc., 1998; Sir James Black Medal, RSE, 2014; numerous lectures in UK and abroad. FMedSci 1998. *Publications:* (Sen. Ed.) Davidson's Textbook of Medicine, 17th edn 1995, 18th edn 1999; (ed jtly) ARDS—Acute Respiratory Distress Syndrome in Adults, 1997; numerous articles in learned jls concerning inflammatory cell biology and inflammatory lung disease. *Recreations:* Rugby Union (spectating only, these days), contemporary fiction, cooking, eating and drinking (not necessarily in that order), collecting fine wines. *Address:* Queen's Medical Research Institute, 47 Little France Crescent, Edinburgh EH16 4TJ. *T:* (0131) 242 6561. *E:* C.Haslett@ed.ac.uk.

HASSALL, Prof. Cedric Herbert, FRS 1985; CChem, FRSC; Hon. Visiting Professor, London Metropolitan University (formerly University of North London), since 1999; *b* 6 Dec. 1919; *s* of late H. Hassall, Auckland, NZ; *m* 1st, 1946, H. E. Cotti (marr. diss. 1982); one *d* (and one *s* decd); 2nd, 1984, J. A. Mitchelmore. *Educ:* Auckland Grammar Sch., NZ; Auckland Univ. (MSc); Univ. of Cambridge (PhD, ScD). Lectr, Univ. of Otago, NZ, 1943–45; Sen. studentship, Royal Commn for 1851, Cambridge, 1946–48; Foundn Prof. of Chem., Univ. of WI, 1948–56; Carnegie and Rockefeller Fellowships in USA, 1950, 1956; Head, Dept of Chemistry, Univ. Coll., of Swansea, UCW, 1957–71; Dir of Research, Roche Products Ltd, 1971–84. Comr, Royal Univ. of Malta, 1964–71; Planning Adviser: Univ. of Jordan, 1965–71; Univ. of Aleppo, 1965; Abdul Aziz Univ., Jedda, 1966, 1968. Visiting Professor: Univ. of Kuwait, 1969, 1979, 1997; Aligarh Univ., India (Royal Soc.), 1969–70; Univ. of Liverpool, 1971–79; UCL, 1979–85; Warwick Univ., 1985–95; Hon. Visiting Professor: UC, Cardiff, 1985–92; Imperial Coll., London, 1989–97. Pres., Chem. Section of British Assoc., 1987; Member: various cttees of Royal Soc. Chem., 1959– (Pres., Perkin Div., 1985–87); Council, British Technol. Gp, 1986–92; various Govt cttees relating to sci. affairs; Co-ordinator, Molecular Recognition Initiative, SERC, 1987–90; ODA Advr on science, technology and educn in India, China and Indonesia, 1989–. Chm., Steering Cttee, Oxford Centre for Molecular Scis, 1988–92. Chm., Mother and Child Foundn, 1995–2001; Dir, IMET 2000, 2001–07. Hon. Fellow, UC of Swansea, 1986. Hon. DSc West Indies, 1975. *Publications:* papers on aspects of organic chemistry, largely in Jl of Chemical Soc. *Recreation:* travel. *Address:* 2 Chestnut Close, Westoning, Beds MK45 5LR. *T:* (01525) 712909, *Fax:* (01525) 752550. *E:* cedrichassall@btinternet.com.

HASSALL, Craig Steven; Chief Executive, Opera Australia, since 2013; *b* Australia, 2 Dec. 1964; *s* of Frank Hassall and Brenda Hassall (*née* Zell, now Millan). *Educ:* Univ. of Sydney (BEc). Corporate Inf. Manager, 1987–90, Planning Manager, 1990–92, Opera Australia; Man. Dir, Bell Shakespeare Co., 1993–94; Mktg Dir, Opera Australia, 1995–97; Hd, Cultural Olympiad, Sydney 2000 Olympic Games, 1997–2001; Dep. Gen. Manager, Sydney Theatre Co., 2002–05; Man. Dir, English National Ballet, 2005–12; Chief Operating Officer, Raymond Gubbay Ltd, 2012–13. Artistic Advr, London 2012 Olympic Games, 2010–12. *Recreations:* theatre, music, heritage. *Address:* Opera Australia, The Opera Centre - Sydney, 480 Elizabeth Street, Surry Hills, NSW 2010, Australia.

HASSALL, Eric Ronald, CBE 1999; FIMMM, FRICS; Deputy Chairman, Coal Authority, 1997–2000; Chairman, British Geological Survey Board, 1994–2001; *b* 16 Nov. 1930; *s* of George Arthur Hassall and Margaret Hassall; *m* 1953, Joan Wilson; two *s* three *d*. *Educ:* Leigh Grammar Sch.; Wigan Mining Coll.; Coll. of Estates Management, Manchester Business Sch. CEng. National Coal Bd, 1947–72; Wardell Armstrong: Partner, 1972–81; Sen. Partner, 1981–91; Chairman, 1991–94. Crown Mineral Agent, 1988–92. Mem., NERC, 1993–98. Dep. Pro-Chancellor, Keele Univ., 2003–08. Pres., IMinE, 1997–99. Hon. DSc Staffordshire, 1995; DUniv Keele, 2009. *Publications:* contribs on mining technology. *Recreations:* golf, sport, reading, engineering, science, painting, family, local history. *Address:* 32 Repton Drive, Newcastle under Lyme, Staffs ST5 3JF. *T:* (01782) 619835. *E:* erhjh@hotmail.co.uk. *Clubs:* Newcastle under Lyme Golf; Little Aston Golf.

HASSALL, Tom Grafton, OBE 1999; FSA; archaeologist; Fellow, St Cross College, Oxford, since 1974; *b* 3 Dec. 1943; *s* of late William Owen Hassall and Averil Grafton Beaves; *m* 1967, Angela Rosaleen Goldsmith; three *s*. *Educ:* Dragon Sch., Oxford; Lord Williams's Grammar Sch., Thame; Corpus Christi Coll., Oxford (BA History). FSA 1971. Asst local ed., Victoria County History of Oxford, 1966–67; Director: Oxford Archaeological Excavation Cttee, 1967–73; Oxfordshire Archaeological Unit, 1973–85; Associate Staff Tutor, Oxford Univ. Dept for External Studies, 1978–85; Sec. and Chief Exec., RCHME, 1986–99; archaeological consultant, 1999–; Res. Associate, Inst. of Archaeol., Oxford, 1999–2005. Vis. Fellow, Kellogg Coll., Oxford, 1999–2007. Trustee, Oxford Preservation Trust, 1973–; Chairman: Standing Conf. of Archaeol Unit Managers, 1980–83; British Archaeological Awards, 1983–88; Victoria History of Oxfordshire Trust, 1997–2003; Kelmscott Mgt Cttee, 2000–05; Adv. Cttee on Historic Wreck Sites, 2002–11; Historic Wrecks Panel, English Heritage, 2011–; President: Council for British Archaeology, 1983–86; Oxfordshire Architectural and Historical Soc., 1984–92; ICOMOS, UK, 1997–2003 (Chm., World Heritage Cttee, 2002–07); Mem., Ancient Monuments Adv. Cttee, Historic Buildings and Monuments Commn, 1984–93. Guest Lectr, Swan Hellenic Cruises, 1981–99. Crew mem., Athenian Trireme, 1987. Hon. MCIfA (Hon. MIFA 1999). *Publications:* Oxford: the city beneath your feet, 1972; specialist articles on archaeology. *Recreation:* boating. *Address:* 4 Whitefriars, Back Lane, Blakeney, Norfolk NR25 7NR. *T:* (01263) 741369. *Club:* Athenæum.

HASSAN, Dame Anna (Patricia Lucy), DBE 2006; education consultant, advisor, coach and mentor to head teachers and school leaders, since 2009; Headteacher, 1993–2008, Executive Headteacher, 2008–09, Millfields Community School, Hackney; Executive Headteacher, Daubeney Primary School, Hackney, 2008–09; *b* 16 March 1946; *d* of Angelo Fusco and Rosa orte, Banbridge, Co. Down; *m* 1971, Nevzat Hassan; one *s*. *Educ:* St Patrick's Primary Sch., Banbridge; Santa Giovanna Anita, Sora, Italy; Assumption Convent, Ballynahinch, Co. Down; Coloma Teacher Trng Coll. (Teaching Cert.); NE London Poly. (BEd); London Univ. Inst. of Educn (NPQH). St Joseph's Primary Sch., Rotherhithe, 1969–72; restaurateur, 1973–79; teacher: St Mary's Primary Sch., Banbridge, 1976–79; Baden Powell Sch., Hackney, 1980–85; Headteacher, Grasmere Primary Sch., Hackney, 1987–93. Tutor, NPQH course, London Univ. Inst. of Educn, 2001–. London Challenge Advr, Aspiring Head Teachers' Wave Prog., Nat. Coll. for Leadership of Schs and Children's Services. Advr to educators in NI, Italy, China, India and Emirates. Hon. Fellow, Gloucestershire Univ., 2005. Member: London Diocesan Bd for Schs, 2012–; Nida Trust, 2012–. Chair, Outstanding for All, Haringey Educn Commn, 2012–13; Mem. Bd, Standing Adv. Council for Religious Educn, Hackney, 2004–14. Gov., Hackney Community Coll., 2003–14; Chm. Bd, Oak Community Acads Trust, 2013–. *Publications:* (contrib.) Improving

Schools, Improve Communities, 2003; contrib. educnl jls and pubns. *Recreations:* trained classical singer, going to opera and theatre, enjoys listening to most types of music, reads historical novels and mystery/detective stories, enjoys all types of puzzles.

HASSAN, Mamoun Hamid; producer, director and writer; Dean (formerly Director) of Editing, International Film and Television School, Cuba, 1997–2002; *b* Jedda, 12 Dec. 1937; *s* of late Dr Hamid Hassan and of Fatma Hassan (*née* Sadat); *m* 1966, Moya Jacqueline Gillespie, MA Oxon; two *s*. Formerly script writer, editor and director; Head of Production Board, British Film Inst., 1971–74; Head of Films Branch, UNRWA, Lebanon, 1974–76; Bd Mem., 1978–84, Man. Dir, 1979–84, Nat. Film Finance Corp. Member: Cinematograph Films Council, 1977–78; Scottish Film Production Fund, 1983–87; Advr, European Script Fund, 1989–90; Sen. Consultant for UNESCO, Harare, Zimbabwe, 1991–93; Hd of Editing, Nat. Film and Television Sch., 1993–97 (Gov., 1983–92). Visiting Lecturer: UCLA; California Inst. of the Arts; Eur. Film Coll.; Satyajit Ray Inst. of Film & Television, Calcutta. Films produced include: No Surrender, 1985; co-writer and co-prod., Machuca, 2004; writer, co-prod. and supervising ed., La Buena Vida, 2008; Editing Consultant, My Brother the Devil, 2012. Producer and presenter, Movie Masterclass, C4 series, 1988, 2nd series, 1990. *Publications:* articles in THES. *Address:* 9 South Hill Park Gardens, Hampstead, NW3 2TD.

HASSELL, Barry Frank; Chief Executive, Independent Healthcare Consultants Ltd, since 2004; *b* 26 Sept. 1944; *s* of late Edgar Frank Hassell and of Rosetta Ethel Hassell; *m* 1971, Sylvia Booth; two step *s*. *Educ:* Swanscombe County Secondary Sch. (Head Boy); London Business Sch. (London Exec. Prog.). FCMI. Accounting, marketing and directors appts, UK, Scandinavia, Africa, 1959–73; Management Consultant, 1973–85; Special Projects Exec., Spastics Soc., 1980–85; Chief Exec., Tadworth Court Trust, 1983–92; Chief Exec., Ind. Healthcare Assoc., 1992–2003. Dir, Project Bombay, 1983–88. Vice Pres., Union of European Private Hosps, 1997, 2000 (Hon. Sec., 1993–97). Gov., Nat. Inst. for Social Work, 1998–2004. FRGS. *Publications:* articles on health and social care issues. *Recreations:* travel, photography, ski-ing.

HASSELL, Julia Elizabeth; *see* Simpson, J. E.

HASSELL, Prof. Michael Patrick, CBE 2002; FRS 1987; Professor of Insect Ecology, 1979–2007, Honorary Principal Research Fellow, since 2007, Imperial College London; *b* 2 Aug. 1942; *s* of Albert Marmaduke Hassell and Gertrude Hassell (*née* Loeser); *m* 1st, 1966, Glynis Mary Everett (marr. diss. 1981); two *s*; 2nd, 1982, Victoria Anne Taylor; one *s* one *d*. *Educ:* Whitgift School; Clare College, Cambridge (BA 1964, MA); Oriel College, Oxford (DPhil 1967); DSc Oxford 1980. NERC Research Fellow, Hope Dept of Entomology, Oxford, 1968–70; Imperial College London: Lectr, 1970–75, Reader, 1975–79, Dept of Zoology and Applied Entomology; Dep. Head, 1984–92, Head, 1993–2001, Dept of Biology; Dir, Silwood Park, 1988–2004; Principal, 2001–04, Dean, 2004–07, Faculty of Life Scis. Vis. Lectr, Univ. of California, Berkeley, 1967–68; Storer Life Sciences Lectr, Univ. of California, Davis, 1985. Non-exec. Dir, Ealing, Hammersmith and Hounslow HA, 1996–98. Mem., NERC, 1991–94. Trustee, Natural Hist. Mus., 1999–2008; Chm., Nat. Biodiversity Network Trust, 2012–. Pres., British Ecological Soc., 1998–2000. MAE 1998. Scientific Medal, Zoological Soc., 1981; Gold Medal, 1994, Award, 2010, British Ecol Soc.; Wheldon Prize, Oxford Univ., 1995. *Publications:* Insect Population Ecology (with G. C. Varley and G. R. Gradwell), 1973; The Dynamics of Competition and Predation, 1975; The Dynamics of Arthropod Predator-Prey Systems, 1978; The Spatial and Temporal Dynamics of Host-Parasitoid Interactions, 2000; research papers and review articles on dynamics of animal populations, esp. insects. *Recreations:* natural history, hill walking. *Address:* Barnside, Buckland Brewer, Bideford, Devon EX39 5NF.

HASSELL, Hon. William Ralph Boucher, AM 2000; JP; Proprietor, Hassell Advisory Services, consultants and advisers on community issues and campaigns, 1992–94, and since 1997; *b* 6 June 1943; *s* of John Boucher Hassell and Dorothy Leslie Hassell (*née* Wright); *m* 1974, Susan Vicki Long; one *s* two *d*. *Educ:* Western Australian govt schs; Hale Sch., Perth; Univ. of Western Australia (LLB); Univ. of Reading, UK (MA; Rotary Foundn Graduate Fellow, 1967–68). Barrister and Solicitor; Partner in law firm, Lohrmann, Tindal and Guthrie, WA, 1968–80. MP (L) Cottesloe, WA, 1977–90; Minister for Police and Traffic, 1980–83, for Community Welfare, 1980–82, for Employment and Trng, 1982–83; Leader of the Opposition, 1984–86. Agent Gen. for WA, London, 1994–97; Official Rep., Britain and Europe, Govt of WA, 1997. Dir, Govt Employees Superannuation Bd, WA, 2000–03. Dir, Antares Energy Ltd, 2004–09. Member: Commonwealth Superannuation Complaints Tribunal, 2003–08; Innovation Australia (formerly Commonwealth Industry R&D Bd), 2005–09 (Mem., Engrg and Manufg Cttee, 2000–06; Chm., Automotive Cttee, 2005–09; Chm., Innovation Grants Cttee, 2008–09); Quality Review Cttee, Inst. of Chartered Accountants in Australia, 2008–. Chm., Liberal Party of Western Australia Pty Ltd, 2006–11. Member: Appeal Cttee, Archbp's Appeal for Anglicare, 1987–94 and 1997– (Chm., 1991–94); Bd, Multiple Sclerosis Soc. of WA (Vice-Pres.), 1990–94 and 1997–; Adv. Bd, Constitutional Centre of WA, 1997–2014 (Chm., 2011–14); Nat. Bd, Multiple Sclerosis Australia, 2013–. Councillor, 2011–, Dep. Mayor, 2013–, City of Nedlands, WA. Pres., W Australian-German Business Assoc., 2010–14. Hon. Consul for Germany, WA, 1998–2010. JP WA, 1994–. Centenary Medal, Australia, 2003; Cross, Order of Merit (Germany), 2009. *Publications:* Parliamentary newsletter, 1987–90; various articles. *Recreations:* bridge, tennis, reading. *Address:* 20 Loneragan Street, Nedlands, WA 6009, Australia. *T:* (8) 93809991. *E:* hassell@arach.net.au. *Clubs:* Weld (Perth); Dalkeith Tennis.

HASTE, Norman David, OBE 1997; FREng; FICE; Executive Director, Nuclear New Build, Lang O'Rourke, 2011–12; non-executive Director, C. Spencer Ltd (Hull), since 2013; *b* 4 Nov. 1944; *s* of Jack Haste and Edith Eleanor Haste (*née* Jarvis); *m* 1968, Judith Ann Graham; two *d*. *Educ:* Royal Coll. of Advanced Technol., Salford. FICE 1984; FREng (FEng 1996); FCIHT (FIHT 1996). Contracts Manager, McConnell Dowell SE Asia (Singapore), 1981–84; John Laing Construction Ltd: Dir, Special Projects, 1984–85; Project Director: Main Civil Engrg Works, Sizewell B Power Station, 1985–90; Second Severn Crossing, 1990–95; Terminal 5, Heathrow Airport, 1996–2002; Chief Exec., Cross London Rail Links, 2002–05; Ops Dir, High-Point Rendel, 2005–06; Chief Operating Officer, Laing O'Rourke Middle E and S Asia, 2006–09; Advr on Nuclear New Build, Laing O'Rourke, 2009–11. Chm., Severn River Crossing PLC, 2000–06. Dir, Transnet, South Africa, 2006–10. Hon. DEng West of England, 1997; Hon. DSc: Salford, 1998; Hull, 2013. *Recreations:* golf, music, theatre.

HASTIE, Prof. Nicholas Dixon, CBE 2006; PhD; FMedSci; FRS 2002; FRSE; Member, Scientific Staff, since 1982, Director, since 1994, Medical Research Council Human Genetics Unit, Edinburgh; Director, Edinburgh Institute of Genetics and Molecular Medicine, since 2007; *b* 29 March 1947; *s* of Duncan Sidney Hastie and Eleanor Stella Hastie; *m* 1975, Alison Clayton Todd; one *s* one *d*. *Educ:* Colwyn Bay Grammar Sch.; Univ. of Liverpool (BSc 1969); King's Coll., Cambridge (PhD 1973). FRSE 1993. Res. Fellow, Edinburgh Univ., 1973–75; Cancer Res. Scientist and Associate Res. Prof., Roswell Park Meml Inst., Buffalo, USA, 1975–82. Hon. Prof., Univ. of Edinburgh, 1993; Internat. Res. Schol., Howard Hughes Med. Inst., 1992–97. Eur. Ed., Genes & Develt, 1991–97. Mem., EMBO, 1990. Member: Scientific Adv. Bd, Inst. of Molecular Pathol., Vienna, 1993–2000; Molecular and Cellular Medicine Bd, 1996–2000, Strategy Develt Gp, 1996–99, MRC; Scientific Adv. Cttee, Lister Inst., 1997–; Internat. Scientific Adv. Bd, Develtl Genetics Prog., Sheffield, 2000–; Cancer Res. UK Scientific Exec. Bd, 2002–; Chairman, Scientific Advisory Board: Wellcome Trust Centre for Human Genetics, Oxford, 2000–; Wellcome Trust, Sanger Inst., 2004–; Chm., Adv. Bd, Cambridge Inst. of Medical Res., 2000–. Numerous distinguished lectures. Charter Fellow, Molecular Medicine Soc., 1996; FMedSci 1998. Gov., Beatson Cancer Res. Inst., 1999–. Hon. DSc Edinburgh, 2005. Genetics Soc. Medal, 2008. *Publications:* contrib. numerous papers to various internat. jls incl. Nature, Cell and Science. *Recreations:* reading, gardening, cooking, travelling, walking, gym. *Address:* MRC Human Genetics Unit, Western General Hospital, Crewe Road, Edinburgh EH4 2XU. *T:* (0131) 467 8401.

HASTIE, Sir Robert (Cameron), KCVO 2008; CBE 1983; RD 1968 (Bar 1978); JP; Chairman, Bernard Hastie & Co. Ltd, UK and Australia, 1973–2008; Lord-Lieutenant, West Glamorgan, 1995–2008 (Vice Lord-Lieutenant, 1991–95); *b* Swansea, 24 May 1933; *s* of B. H. C. Hastie and M. H. Hastie; *m* 1961, Mary Griffiths; two *s* one *d*. *Educ:* Bromsgrove Sch. Joined RN, National Service, 1951; Midshipman 1953; qual. RNR Ocean comd, 1963; progressive ranks to Captain RNR, 1974, in comd HMS Cambria, 1974–77; Aide-de-Camp to the Queen, 1977; Commodore RNR 1979–82. Pres., Swansea Unit Sea Cadet Corps, 1982–96. Chairman: Mumbles Lifeboat Station Cttee, 1987–95; Milford Haven Port Authy, 1994–2000. Mem., W Wales Cttee, CBI, 1982–96; Vice Pres., RNLI, 1999– (Mem. Council, 1991–2006; Trustee and Dep. Treas., 1999–2004). President: Glam W Area Scout Council, 1995–2008 (Chm., 1989–96); RFCA Wales, 2005–08. DL West Glamorgan, 1974; JP Swansea, 1989; High Sheriff of W Glamorgan County, 1977–78. KStJ 2006 (CStJ 1996). *Recreations:* farming, sailing, shooting. *Address:* Upper Hareslade Farm, Bishopston, Swansea SA3 3BU. *T:* (01792) 232957. *Clubs:* Naval; Royal Naval Sailing Association (Portsmouth); Bristol Channel Yacht (Swansea); Royal Sydney Yacht Squadron (Sydney, Aust.).

HASTIE-SMITH, Richard Maybury, CB 1984; FIPD 1986; Chairman: Incorporated Froebel Educational Institute, 1993–2003; Templeton Estates Ltd, 1994–2003; *b* 13 Oct. 1931; *s* of Engr-Comdr D. Hastie-Smith and H. I. Hastie-Smith; *m* 1956, Bridget Noel Cox; one *s* two *d*. *Educ:* Cranleigh Sch. (Schol.); Magdalene Coll., Cambridge (Schol.; MA). HM Forces, commnd Queen's Royal Regt, 1950–51. Entered Administrative Class, Home CS, War Office, 1955; Private Sec. to Permanent Under-Sec., 1957; Asst Private Sec. to Sec. of State, 1958; Principal, 1960; Asst Private Sec. to Sec. of State for Defence, 1965; Private Sec. to Minister of Defence (Equipment), 1968; Asst Sec., 1969; RCDS, 1974; Under-Sec., MoD, 1975, Cabinet Office, 1979–81; Dep. Under-Sec. of State, MoD, 1981–91. Mem., Civil Service Appeal Bd, 1992–99; Non-Service Mem., Home Office Assessment Consultancy Unit for police, prison and fire services, 1992–2003. Chm. Council, Cranleigh and Bramley Schs, 1993–99; Mem. Council, Surrey Univ. Roehampton (formerly Roehampton Inst.), 1993–2003. Chm., 1983–94, Vice-Pres., 1994–, Magdalene Coll. Assoc. *Address:* 18 York Avenue, East Sheen, SW14 7LG. *T:* (020) 8876 4597.

See also Rev. T. M. Hastie-Smith.

HASTIE-SMITH, Rev. Timothy Maybury; Team Vicar, Barnsley and Bibury with Winson, Gloucestershire, since 2014; National Director, Scripture Union, since 2010; *b* London, 8 March 1962; *s* of Richard Maybury Hastie-Smith, *qv*; *m* 1987, Joanne Elizabeth, *e d* of David and Marion Ide; one *s* two *d*. *Educ:* Cranleigh Sch. (St Nicholas Scholar); Magdalene Coll., Cambridge (BA 1984); Wycliffe Hall, Oxford (Cert. Theol. 1988). Lay Chaplain, Felsted Sch., 1984–85; ordained deacon, 1988, priest, 1989; Asst Curate, St Ebbe's with Holy Trinity and St Peter-le-Bailey, Oxford, 1988–91; Sen. Chaplain and Admissions Tutor, Stowe Sch., 1991–98; Headmaster, Dean Close Sch., Cheltenham, 1998–2008; Vicar of Kempsford, Glos, 2009–14. Prin. Consultant, Perrett Laver, 2009–10. Dir, Knockout Ltd, 1987–90. Chairman: TISCA, 2001–07; HMC West, 2007–08; HMC, 2008. Trustee: Havelock Trust, 2009–14; David Ross Educnl Trust, 2010–14. Governor: St Hugh's Sch., Woodhall Spa, 1995–2001; Orwell Park Sch., 1997–2003; Aldro Sch., 1997–2011; Hatherop Castle Sch., 1998–2011; Blue Coat Sch., Birmingham, 1999–2006; Beachborough Sch., 2000–07; Swanbourne House Sch., 2000–14; Winterfold House, 2004–08; Bibury C of E Primary Sch., 2015–. Fellow, Univ. of Gloucestershire, 1998. Freeman, Haberdashers' Co., 2012–. *Recreations:* theatre, reading, psephology, cinema, chicken husbandry, Gloucester RUFC, travel, politics, Tottenham Hotspur. *Address:* The Vicarage, Bibury, Cirencester, Glos GL7 5NT. *T:* (01285) 740301. *E:* tim.hastie-smith@hotmail.com; Scripture Union, 207–209 Queensway, Bletchley, Milton Keynes MK2 2EB. *T:* (01908) 856005. *E:* timhs@scriptureunion.org.uk. *Clubs:* Lansdowne, Coningsby, East India.

HASTILOW, Michael Alexander; Director, Glynwed Ltd, 1969–81; *b* 21 Sept. 1923; *s* of late Cyril Alexander Frederick Hastilow, CBE, MSc, BCom, FRIC, and Doreen Madge, MA; *m* 1953, Sheila Mary Tipper (*née* Barker); one *s* one *d* (and one *d* decd). *Educ:* Mill Hill Sch.; Birmingham Univ. (Pres., Guild of Undergrads; BSc Civil Engrg, BCom). Served in Fleet Air Arm, RNVR, 1944–46. Commercial Manager, J. H. Lavender & Co. Ltd, 1948–54; Birmid Industries Ltd, 1954–57: Asst Gen. Man., Birmidal Developments Ltd, 1956–57; Commercial Man., Birmetals Ltd, 1957; Commercial and Gen. Sales Man., Bilston Foundries Ltd, 1957–63; Dir, Cotswold Buildings Ltd, 1963–64; Glynwed Ltd, 1964–81: Dir, The Wednesbury Tube Co. Ltd, 1966–81 (Man. Dir, 1968–74; Chm., 1973–76); dir or chm. of various Glynwed divs and subsids. British Non-Ferrous Metals Federation: Mem. Council, 1973–81; Vice Pres., 1975–79; Pres., 1979–80; Chm., Tube Gp, 1975–77. National Home Improvement Council: Mem. Council, 1975–84; Mem. Bd, 1975–84; Vice Chm., 1979–80; Chm., 1980–81. Member: Commn for New Towns, 1978–86; Construction Exports Adv. Bd, 1975–78; Exec. Cttee, 1973–84, and Council, 1974–84, Nat. Council for Bldg Material Producers; EDC for Building, 1980–82. Hon. Treasurer, Midlands Club Cricket Conf., 1970–81, Pres., 1981–82. *Recreations:* cricket, railways. *Address:* The Mount, 3 Kendal End Road, Rednal, Birmingham B45 8PX. *T:* (0121) 445 2007. *Clubs:* MCC, Old Millhillians.

See also N. G. Hastilow.

HASTILOW, Nigel Graham; Director of Enterprise, Institute of Chartered Accountants, since 2011; Columnist, Wolverhampton Express & Star, since 2004; *b* 22 Feb. 1956; *s* of Michael Alexander Hastilow, *qv*; *m* 1980, Fiona Mary Findlay. *Educ:* Mill Hill Sch.; Birmingham Univ. (BA 2nd Cl. Hons Eng. Lang. and Lit.). Reporter: Solihull News, 1978–80; Evening Mail, Birmingham, 1980–85; Mktg Manager, Birmingham Post & Mail Ltd, 1985–87; Birmingham Post: Political Editor, 1987–90; Asst Editor, 1990–91; Dep. Editor, 1991–92; Exec. Editor, 1992–93; Editor, 1993–99; W Midlands Dir, Inst. of Dirs, 2000–01; W Midlands Regl Dir, Inst. of Chartered Accts, 2001–11; Editl Dir, Heart Media Gp, 2003–05. Contested (C), Birmingham, Edgbaston, 2001. *Publications:* The Last of England, 2004; Tomorrow's England, 2008; The Smoking Gun, 2011; Murder on the Brussels Express, 2014. *Recreations:* usual sporting and cultural interests, air guitar. *Address:* Corner Cottage, Manor Road, Wickhamford, Worcs WR11 7SA.

HASTINGS; *see* Abney-Hastings, family name of Earl of Loudoun.

HASTINGS, family name of **Baron Hastings of Scarisbrick**.

HASTINGS, 23rd Baron *cr* 1290; **Delaval Thomas Harold Astley;** Bt 1660; *b* 25 April 1960; *er s* of 22nd Baron Hastings and Catherine Rosaline Ratcliffe (*née* Hinton); *S* father, 2007; *m* 1987, Veronica, *er d* of Richard Smart; one *s* two *d*. *Educ:* Radley; Durham Univ. *Heir: s* Hon. Jacob Astley, *b* 5 Sept. 1991.

HASTINGS OF SCARISBRICK, Baron *cr* 2005 (Life Peer), of Scarisbrick in the County of Lancashire; **Michael John Hastings,** CBE 2002; Global Head of Corporate Citizenship and Diversity, KPMG, since 2006; *b* 29 Jan. 1958; *s* of Petain and Olive Hastings; *m* 1990, Jane; one *s* two *d*. *Educ:* Scarisbrick Hall Sch., Lancs; London Bible Coll. (BA (Hons)); Westminster Coll., Oxford (PGCE). Teacher (Hd of Religious Studies), 1981–85; Govt Policy Consultant, 1985–90; presenter and reporter: TV AM and GMTV, 1990–94; BBC SE, 1994–95; Hd of

Public Affairs, 1996–2003, Hd of Corporate Social Responsibility, 2003–06, BBC; Hd of Corporate Social Responsibility, KPMG, 2006. Non-exec. Dir, British Telecom (Community Support Cttee), 2004– (Mem., Responsible Business Bd). Comr, CRE, 1993–2001. Vice Pres., UNICEF UK. Chm., Millennium Promise UK. Trustee: Crime Concern, 1988–2008 (Chm., 1995–2008); Vodafone Gp Foundn, 2008–. Patron: Springboard for Children, 2005– (Chm., 1992–98); ZANE, 2005–. *Recreations:* cycling, country walking, cinema, friends. *Address:* House of Lords, SW1A 0PW.

HASTINGS, Archdeacon of; *see* Jones, Ven. P. H.

HASTINGS, Alfred James, CB 1999; Clerk of the Journals, House of Commons, 1991–2001; *b* 10 Feb. 1938; *s* of William Hastings and Letitia (*née* Loveridge); *m* 1972, Susan Edge; three *s*. *Educ:* Leamington College; New College, Oxford (MA). A Clerk of the House of Commons, 1960–2001: Registrar of Members' Interests, 1987–91; Clerk of the Cttee of Privileges, and subseq. of the Cttee on Standards and Privileges, 1991–97; Commons Clerk, Jt Cttee on Parly Privilege, 1997–99. *Recreations:* music, high fidelity sound reproduction. *Address:* 26 Feilden Grove, Headington, Oxford OX3 0DU.

HASTINGS, Alison Jane; media consultant, since 2002; Vice President, British Board of Film Classification, since 2008; Specialist Partner, Alder Media; *b* 14 Aug. 1965; *d* of Len and Jackie Hastings; one *d*; *m* 2007, Dr David Fleming, *qv*; one *d*, and two step *s* one step *d*. *Educ:* Folkestone Girls' Grammar Sch.; Canterbury Coll.; Harlow Coll. (Nat. Council for Trng in Journalism). Hd, Editl Staff Devlt, Thomson Regl newspapers, 1994–95; Dep. Ed., 1995–96, Ed., 1996–2002, Newcastle Evening Chronicle. Member: Press Complaints Commn, 1998–2002; Gambling Commn, 2015–. Non-exec. Dir, Clatterbridge Cancer Centre, 2012–. Mem., Adv. Bd, Pagefield Communications. Mem. Council, Durham Univ., 2015–. Trustee, BBC Trust, 2006–14. *Recreations:* time with family, travelling, reading, watching films. *E:* alisonhastingsmedia@gmail.com.

HASTINGS, Sir Max (Macdonald), Kt 2002; FRSL; author and journalist; *b* 28 Dec. 1945; *s* of late Macdonald Hastings and Anne Scott James, author and journalist; *m* 1st, 1972, Patricia Mary Edmondson (marr. diss. 1994); one *s* one *d* (and one *s* decd); 2nd, 1999, Mrs Penny Grade. *Educ:* Charterhouse (Scholar); University Coll., Oxford (Exhibnr). Researcher, BBC TV Great War series, 1963–64; Reporter, Evening Standard, 1965–67; Fellow, US World Press Inst., 1967–68; Roving Correspondent, Evening Standard, 1968–70; Reporter, BBC TV Current Affairs, 1970–73; Editor, Evening Standard Londoner's Diary, 1976–77; Columnist, Daily Express, 1981–83; contributor, Sunday Times, 1985–86; Editor, The Daily Telegraph, 1986–95; Dir, 1989–95, Editor-in-Chief, 1990–95, The Daily Telegraph plc; Editor, The Evening Standard, 1996–2002; contributor, Daily Mail, 2002–; Contrib. Ed., Financial Times, 2009–13. As War Correspondent, covered Middle East, Indochina, Angola, India-Pakistan, Cyprus, Rhodesia and S Atlantic. Mem., Press Complaints Commn, 1991–92. Churchill Fellow, Westminster Coll., Fulton, Mo, 2011. TV documentaries: Ping-Pong in Peking, 1971; The War about Peace, 1983; Alarums and Excursions, 1984; Cold Comfort Farm, 1985; The War in Korea (series), 1988; We Are All Green Now, 1990; Spies, in series Cold War, CNN, 1998; Hitler's Germany, 2000; The Falklands: reluctant heroes, 2002; Winston's War, 2003; The Falklands Legacy, 2012; The Necessary War, 2014. A Vice Pres., Game Conservancy, 1992–; President: CPRE, 2002–07; Sir Walter Scott Soc. of Edinburgh, 2012–13. Trustee: Nat. Portrait Gall., 1995–2004; Game Conservancy, 2014–. Liddell-Hart Lecture, KCL, 1994; Mountbatten Lecture, Edinburgh Univ., 2004; Leonard Stein Lectures, Oxford Univ., 2009. FRHistS 1988; FRSL 1996. Hon FKC, 2004. Hon. DLitt: Leicester, 1992; Nottingham, 2005. Journalist of the Year, British Press Awards, 1982 (cited 1973 and 1980); What The Papers Say, Granada TV: Reporter of the Year, 1982; Editor of the Year, 1988; Duke of Westminster Medal for military literature, RUSI, 2008; Literary Award for Lifetime Achievement, Chicago Pritzker Library, 2012; Friuladria Prize, Gorizia Internat. Hist. Fest., 2014. *Publications:* America 1968: the fire this time, 1968; Ulster 1969: the struggle for civil rights in Northern Ireland, 1970; Montrose: the King's champion, 1977; Yoni: the hero of Entebbe, 1979; Bomber Command, 1979 (Somerset Maugham Award for Non-Fiction, 1980); (with Len Deighton) The Battle of Britain, 1980; Das Reich, 1981; (with Simon Jenkins) The Battle for The Falklands, 1983 (Yorkshire Post Book of the Year Award); Overlord: D-Day and the battle for Normandy, 1984 (Yorkshire Post Book of the Year Award); Victory in Europe, 1985; (ed) Oxford Book of Military Anecdotes, 1985; The Korean War, 1987; Outside Days, 1989; Scattered Shots, 1999; Going to the Wars, 2000; Editor, 2002; Armageddon, 2004; Warriors, 2005; Country Fair, 2005; Nemesis, 2007; Finest Years, 2009; Did You Really Shoot the Television?: a family fable, 2010; All Hell Let Loose, 2011 (RUSI Duke of Westminster Medal for Military Literature, 2012); Catastrophe: Europe goes to war 1914, 2013; The Secret War, 2015. *Recreations:* shooting, fishing. *Address:* c/o PFD, Drury House, 34–43 Russell Street, WC2B 5HA. *Club:* Brooks's.

HASTINGS, Dr Michael Harvey, FRS 2010; FMedSci; Research Scientist and Group Leader in Circadian Neurobiology, since 2001, and Joint Head, Division of Neurobiology, since 2013, Medical Research Council Laboratory of Molecular Biology; *b* Sheffield, 10 June 1956; *s* of Harvey Hastings and Susan Hastings (*née* Binks); *m* 1986, Angela Charlotte Roberts; one *s* two *d*. *Educ:* Abbeydale Boys' Grammar Sch., Sheffield; Univ. of Liverpool (BSc Marine Biol. 1977; PhD Marine Biol. 1980); Univ. of Manchester (PGCE 1981). University of Cambridge: post-doctoral res. asst, Dept of Anatomy, 1981–84; Demonstrator in Anatomy, 1984–88; Lectr in Anatomy, 1988–98; Reader in Neurosci., 1998–2001; Fellow and Coll. Lectr, Queens' Coll., Cambridge, 1987–90. FMedSci 2008. *Publications:* contrib. res. papers, reviews and commentaries. *Recreations:* birdwatching, African safaris, reading, family holidays. *Address:* MRC Laboratory of Molecular Biology, MRC Centre, Francis Crick Avenue, Cambridge CB2 0QH. *T:* (01223) 267045. *E:* mha@mrc-lmb.cam.ac.uk.

HASTINGS, Lady Selina (Shirley); writer; *b* 5 March 1945; *d* of 16th Earl of Huntingdon and Countess of Huntingdon, (Margaret Lane). *Educ:* St Paul's Girls' Sch.; St Hugh's Coll., Oxford (MA). Daily Telegraph, 1968–82; Literary Ed., Harper's & Queen, 1987–95. *Publications:* Nancy Mitford: a biography, 1985; Evelyn Waugh, 1994; Rosamond Lehmann, 2002; The Secret Lives of Somerset Maugham, 2009; The Red Earl: the extraordinary life of the 16th Earl of Huntingdon, 2014. *Address:* c/o Rogers, Coleridge & White, 20 Powis Mews, W11 1JN. *T:* (020) 7221 3717.

HASTINGS, Sir William (George), Kt 2009; CBE 1999 (OBE 1987); JP; Chairman, Hastings Hotels Ltd, since 1990; *b* Belfast, 17 Oct. 1928; *s* of late William Hastings and Jessie Hastings; *m* 1960, Kathleen Joyce, (Joy), Hamilton; one *s* three *d*. *Educ:* Royal Belfast Academical Instn. Founder, Hastings Hotels Gp, 1967. Director: NI Railways, 1978–90; Bank of Ireland Ltd (NI), 1984–97; Northern Ireland Venture Capital, 1984–96 (Chm.); Queen's University Business and Industrial Services; Bass Ireland Ltd, 1986–88; Merrion Hotel, Dublin, 1997; Landmark Ltd, 1997. Dir, NI Tourist Bd, 1986–92. Former President: NI Chamber of Commerce; NI Licensed Vintners Assoc.; NI Hotels and Caterers Assoc.; CIM. Former Chairman: Help the Aged NI; Crimestoppers NI (Patron); St Patrick's Visitor Centre, Downpatrick (Mem. Bd); Ulster Youth Orch.; Prince's Trust Volunteers; President: NI Chest Heart Stroke Assoc.; NI Polio Fellowship; Mem. Bd, Men Against Cancer. FInstD; Fellow: Hotel and Catering Instnl Mgt Assoc.; Irish Mgt Inst. Hon. Fellow, Irish Hotel and Catering Inst.; Hon. FCIM. Former Mem., Belfast CC. JP NI 1960. Hon. DLitt Ulster, 1982. *Recreation:* golf. *Address:* Hastings Hotels Ltd, 1066 House, 587 Upper Newtownards Road, Belfast BT4 3LP. *T:* (028) 9047 1066. *E:* sirwilliam@hastingshotels.com. *Clubs:* Royal Co. Down Golf, Malone Golf; Belfast East Rotary.

HASTINGS BASS, family name of **Earl of Huntingdon**.

HASZELDINE, Dr Robert Neville, ScD; FRS 1968; CChem, FRSC; scientific consultant; Professor of Chemistry, 1957–82, Head of Department of Chemistry, 1957–76, and Principal, 1976–82, University of Manchester Institute of Science and Technology (Faculty of Technology, The University of Manchester); *b* Manchester, 3 May 1925; *s* of late Walter Haszeldine and Hilda Haszeldine (*née* Webster); *m* 1954, Pauline Elvina Goodwin (*d* 1987); two *s* two *d*. *Educ:* Stockport Grammar Sch.; University of Birmingham (John Watt Meml Schol., 1942; PhD 1947; DSc 1955); Sidney Sussex Coll., Cambridge (MA, PhD 1949); Queens' Coll., Cambridge (ScD 1957). University of Cambridge: Asst in Research in Organic Chemistry, 1949; University Demonstrator in Organic and Inorganic Chemistry, 1951; Asst Dir of Research, 1956; Fellow and Dir of Studies, Queens' Coll., 1954–57, Hon. Fellow, 1976. Chm., Chemical and Biol Defence Bd, Mem., Defence Scientific Adv. Cttee, and mem. of various govt and other cttees, 1957–89. Tilden Lectr, 1968; Vis. Lectr at universities and laboratories in the USA, Russia, Switzerland, Austria, Germany, Japan, China, Israel, S America and France. Chm., Langdales Soc., 1987–93 (Pres., 1998); Lord of the Manor of Langdale, 1988. Meldola Medal, 1953; Corday-Morgan Medal and Prize, 1960; Prix Henri Moissan, 1994. *Publications:* numerous scientific publications in chemical jls. *Recreations:* mountaineering, gardening, natural history, good food, wine, wilderness travel. *Address:* Copt Howe, Chapel Stile, Great Langdale, Cumbria LA22 9JR. *T:* (01539) 437685.

HATCH, Prof. David John, FRCA; Professional Standards Advisor, Royal College of Anaesthetists, 2001–09; Professor of Paediatric Anaesthesia (first chair), University of London, 1991–2002, now Emeritus; *b* 11 April 1937; *s* of James Frederick Hatch and Marguerite Fanny (*née* Forge); *m* 1960, Rita Goulter; two *s* two *d*. *Educ:* Caterham Sch.; University Coll. London (MB BS 1961). MRCS, LRCP 1960; FRCA 1965. Fellow in Anesthesiology, Mayo Clinic, USA, 1968–69; Consultant in Anaesthesia and Respiratory Measurement, Gt Ormond St Children's Hosp., 1969–91. Pres., Assoc. Paediatric Anaesthetists, 1993–95; Vice-Pres., RCAnaes, 1991–93; Member: Med. Soc. of London, 1990–2002; GMC, 1994–2003 (Chm., Cttee on Professional Performance, 1999–2004; Chm., Assessment Gp, 2003–). Hewitt Lectr, RCAnaes, 1999. Hon. FRCPCH 2010. John Snow Medal, Assoc. of Anaesthetists of GB and Ire., 2001; Gold Medal, RCAnaes, 2003. *Publications:* (with E. Sumner) Neonatal Anaesthesia and Intensive Care, 1981, 3rd edn 1995; Paediatric Anaesthesia, 1989, 2nd edn 1999; contribs on paediatric anaesthesia, intensive care and professional self-regulation. *Recreations:* sailing, badminton, magic (Member: Fellowship of Christian Magicians, 2007– (Sec., 2011–15); Magic Circle, 2009– (Welfare Officer, 2012–)).

HATCH, Lionel; Co-founder and Creative Director, The Chase, since 1986; *b* 20 Aug. 1949; *s* of Douglas Hatch and Clarice Hatch (*née* Aldred); *m* Vivien Smith (marr. diss. 1984); one *s*. *Educ:* Bolton Coll. of Art and Design. Jun. Art Dir, Royds, 1970–71; Art Director: Rileys, 1971–72; Cogent Elliott, 1972–73; Stowe Bowden, 1973–75; McDonalds, 1975–77; Yeoward Taylor Bonner, 1977–79; Creative Gp Hd, J Walter Thompson, 1979–80; graphic design consultant, 1980–86. Conducted Graphic Design Student Workshops, Staffordshire Univ., 2010. Projects, drawings and design effectiveness studies exhibited internationally; exhibitions include: Twelve International Lettering Artists, 1983; New York Type Directors Club, 1984. Best in Show, The Roses Awards, 1987, 2009; Grand Global Award, NY Advertising Fest., 1994; DBA Design Effectiveness Award, 2003; Best in Show, 2010, Gold Award, 2012, Fresh Awards; Bronze Award, Cannes Advertising Fest., 2010; Writing for Design, Book D&AD Awards, 2011. *Publications:* The Chase by The Chase: how a design consultancy thinks it thinks, 1993; Fifty Designers' Current Favourite Typefaces, 2010; artworks, design projects and design effectiveness studies in books, jls and other pubns. *Recreations:* garden design and implementation, writing, landscape art, keeping a curious mind. *Address:* The Chase, 1 North Parade, Parsonage Gardens, Manchester M3 2NH. *T:* (0161) 832 5575. *E:* line.thepod@yahoo.co.uk.

HATCH, Dr Marshall Davidson, AM 1981; FRS 1980; FAA 1975; Chief Research Scientist, 1970–97, Hon. Research Fellow, 1997–2006, Division of Plant Industry, CSIRO, Canberra; *b* 24 Dec. 1932; *s* of Lloyd Davidson Hatch and Alice Endesby Hatch (*née* Dalziel); *m* 1st (marr. diss.); two *s*; 2nd, 1983, Lyndall P. Clarke. *Educ:* Newington Coll., Sydney; Univ. of Sydney (BSc, PhD). FAA 1975. Res. Scientist, Div. of Food Res., CSIRO, 1955–59; Post Doctoral Res. Fellow, Univ. of Calif., Davis, 1959–61; Res. Scientist, Colonial Sugar Refining Co. Ltd, Brisbane, 1961–66 and 1968–69 (Reader in Plant Biochemistry, Univ. of Queensland, Brisbane, 1967). Foreign Associate, Nat. Acad. of Sciences, USA, 1990. Rank Prize, Rank Foundn, UK, 1981; Internat. Prize for Biology, Japan Soc. for Promotion of Science, 1991. *Publications:* 164 papers, reviews and chaps in scientific jls and text books in field of photosynthesis and other areas of plant biochemistry. *Recreations:* ski-ing, cycling, reading. *Address:* PO Box 480, Jamison, ACT 2614, Australia. *T:* (2) 62515159.

HATCHER, Prof. (Melvyn) John, PhD, LittD; FAcSS; Professor of Economic and Social History, University of Cambridge, since 1995 (Chairman, Faculty of History, 2005–08); Fellow, Corpus Christi College, Cambridge, since 1976 (Vice-Master, 2000–06); *b* 7 Jan. 1942; *s* of John Edward Hatcher and Lilian Florence Hatcher (*née* Lepper); *m* 1967, Janice Miriam Ranson; two *d*. *Educ:* Owen's GS, Islington; London School of Economics, London Univ. (BSc(Econ), PhD); MA, LittD 1994, Cantab. Salesman, Reckitt and Coleman Ltd, 1960–63; Res. Fellow, Inst. of Historical Research, London, 1966–67; Lectr, 1967–74, Sen. Lectr, 1974–75, in History, Univ. of Kent; Vis. Prof., Univ. of Colorado at Boulder, USA, 1975–76; Lectr in History, 1976–86, Reader in Economic and Social History, 1986–95, Univ. of Cambridge. Vice-Chm., ESRC Econ. Affairs Cttee, 1979–84. Fellow, Huntington Liby, Calif, USA, 1986; Sen. Vis. Fellow, Stanford Univ. Humanities Center, 2008–09. FAcSS (AcSS 2001). Editor, Economic History Review, 1996–2001. *Publications:* Rural Economy and Society in the Duchy of Cornwall 1300–1500, 1970; English Tin Production and Trade before 1550, 1973; A History of British Pewter, 1974; Plague, Population and the English Economy 1348–1530, 1977; (jtly) Medieval England: rural society and economic change 1086–1348, 1978; (contrib.) The Agrarian History of England and Wales, vol. II 1042–1350, 1988; The History of the British Coal Industry: before 1700, 1993; (jtly) Medieval England: towns, commerce and crafts 1086–1348, 1995; (jtly) Modelling the Middle Ages, 2001; The Black Death: an intimate history, 2008; articles in learned jls. *Recreations:* jazz, football. *Address:* Corpus Christi College, Cambridge CB2 1RH. *T:* (01223) 338000. *E:* mjh1001@cam.ac.uk.

HATENDI, Rt Rev. Ralph Peter; Bishop of Harare, 1981–95; Interim Bishop of Manicaland, 2008–09; *b* 9 April 1927; *s* of Fabian and Amelia Hatendi; *m* 1954, Jane Mary Chikumbu; two *s* three *d*. *Educ:* St Peter's Coll., Rosettenville, S Africa (LTh); King's Coll. London (DD; AKC). School teacher, 1952–; clergyman, 1957–; Seminary Tutor, 1968–72; Executive Secretary, 1973–75; Distribution Consultant, 1976–78; Suffragan Bishop of Mashonaland, 1979–80. Chm., Electoral Supervisory Commn, 1998–2000. *Publications:* Sex and Society, 1971; Shona Marriage and the Christian Churches, in Christianity South of the Zambezi, 1973. *Recreation:* poultry. *Address:* 16 Kenny Road, Avondale, Harare, Zimbabwe. *Club:* Harare (Zimbabwe).

HATFIELD, Richard Paul, CB 2012; CBE 1991; Director-General, International, Strategy (formerly Networks) and Environment Group, Department for Transport, 2009–12; *b* 8 Feb. 1953; *m* 1982, Penelope Charlotte Bratton. *Educ:* Whitgift Sch., Croydon; University Coll., Oxford (MA). Admin. trainee, MoD, 1974; Private Secretary to: Under Sec. of State (Army), 1978–80; Cabinet Sec., 1982–85; Ministry of Defence: Asst Private Sec. to Defence Sec., 1986; Head: Defence Lands, 1986–88; Overseas Div., 1988–91; Programme and Policy Div., 1991–93; Dir Gen., Mgt and Orgn, 1993–96; Dep. Under Sec. of State (Policy), subseq. Policy Dir, 1996–2001; Personnel Dir, 2001–08; Dir Gen., Safety, Service Delivery and

Logistics, DfT, 2008–09. Non-exec. Trustee, Charity for Civil Servants (formerly Civil Service Benevolent Fund), 2007–13. Member: Finance and Develt Cttee, Nat. Mus. of RN; Bd, HMS Trincomalee.

HATFIELD, Sally Anne, (Mrs Nicholas Simpson); QC 2013; a Recorder, since 2004; Assistant Coroner (formerly Assistant Deputy Coroner), Manchester, Central, since 2010; *b* Portsmouth, 3 May 1964; *d* of Michael and Anne Hatfield; *m* 1992, Nicholas Simpson; one *s* two *d*. *Educ:* Portsmouth High Sch.; Lincoln Coll., Oxford (BA 1st Cl. Hons Juris. 1986); Inns of Court Sch. of Law. Called to the Bar, Inner Temple, 1988; in practice as barrister, Doughty St Chambers, London, 1989– and Byrom St Chambers, Manchester, 2008–. Gov., Kingsway Sch., Stockport, 2006–. *Publications:* (jtly) Butterworth's Guide to the Mental Capacity Act 2005, 2007. *Recreations:* cooking, birdwatching, school governing, the arts, fair trade, family and friends. *Address:* Byrom Street Chambers, 12 Byrom Street, Manchester M3 4PP. *T:* (0161) 829 2100. *E:* sally.hatfield@byromstreet.com.

HATFULL, Martin Alan; Director, International Public Affairs, Diageo plc, since 2014; *b* 7 June 1957; *s* of late Alan Frederick Hatfull; *m* 1980, Phyllis Julia Mary Morshead; two *s*. *Educ:* Dulwich Coll.; Worcester Coll., Oxford (BA Lit.Hum. 1980). Joined Foreign and Commonwealth Office, 1980; Second, later First, Sec., Tokyo, 1982–86; EU Dept (External), FCO, 1987–88; Private Sec. to Parly Under Sec. of State, FCO, 1988–91; First Sec., UK Rep. to EU, Brussels, 1991–95; Dep. Head, EU Dept (External), FCO, 1995–96; Head, Commonwealth Co-ordination Dept, FCO, 1996–98; Counsellor (Economic and Commercial), Rome, 1998–2002; Minister, Tokyo, 2003–08; Ambassador to Indonesia, 2008–11; Internat. Trade Advr to Diageo plc (on secondment from FCO), 2011–12; Director: EU Balance of Competences, FCO, 2012–13; Govt Relns, Diageo plc, 2013–14.

HATHERTON, 8th Baron *cr* 1835; **Edward Charles Littleton;** agronomist with Del Monte Fresh Produce Inc., Costa Rica; *b* 24 May 1950; *s* of Mervyn Cecil Littleton (*d* 1970) (*g s* of 3rd Baron) and Margaret Ann (*d* 2000), *d* of Frank Sheehy; *S* cousin, 1985; *m* 1974, Hilda Maria, *d* of Rodolfo Robert; one *s* two *d*. *Heir: s* Hon. Thomas Edward Littleton, *b* 7 March 1977. *Address:* PO Box 1341–2150, Moravia, Costa Rica.

HATLEY, Tim; set and costume designer for theatre and film, since 1989; *b* Lincoln, 28 Feb. 1967; *s* of Edward Hatley and Maggie Hatley; partner, Rasshied Din. *Educ:* Bearwood Coll., Berks; Central St Martins Sch. of Art and Design, London (BA 1st Cl. Hons 1989). *Theatre* productions include: National Theatre: Out of a house walked a man (with Complicite), 1995; Stanley, 1996; The Caucasian Chalk Circle, 1997; Flight, 1997; Darker Face of the Earth, 1998; Sleep with Me, 1998; Hamlet, 2000; Humble Boy, 2001; The Talking Cure, 2002; Vincent in Brixton, 2003; Henry V, 2003; Present Laughter, 2007; Rafta Rafta, 2007; Welcome to Thebes, 2010; Timon of Athens, 2012; A Small Family Business, 2014; Great Britain, 2014; 3 Winters, 2015; other productions: Chatsky, Almeida, 1994; The Three Lives of Lucie Cabrol, Complicite, West End, 1995; Suddenly Last Summer, Comedy, 1999; Private Lives, Albery, transf. NY, 2001 (Tony Award for Best Set Design, 2002); Spamalot, NY, 2004; Shrek the Musical, NY, 2008 (Tony Award for Best Costume Design, 2009); Mrs Klein, Almeida, 2009; My Fair Lady, Châtelet, Paris, 2010; Betty Blue Eyes, 2012; The Bodyguard, 2012; Quatermaine's Terms, Wyndham's, 2013; Ghosts, Almeida, transf. NY, 2014; The Pajama Game, Chichester, transf. West End, 2014; Singing in the Rain, Châtelet, Paris, 2015; Mr Footes Other Leg, Hampstead, 2015; Temple, Donmar, 2015; Carmen, Royal Ballet, 2015. *Films:* Stage Beauty, 2003; Closer, 2004; Notes on a Scandal, 2006. *Exhibitions:* Vivienne Westwood - a London Fashion, Mus. of London, 1999; Diaghilev and the Ballet Russes, V&A, 2010. Olivier Award for best set design: for Stanley, 1997; for Humble Boy and Private Lives, 2002. *T:* (020) 8964 8811. *E:* judy@judydaish.com.

HATT, Anthony Faun; Vice President, Immigration Appeal Tribunal, 1996–2001; *b* 23 Aug. 1931; *m* 1954, Norma Irene Stotesbury; one *s* one *d*. *Educ:* Chiswick Grammar Sch.; Westminster Coll. of Commerce. Nat. Service and TA, 1949–62, retd with rank of Captain, transf. to RARO. Admitted solicitor, 1965; solicitor in private practice, 1965–88; Immigration Appeal Adjudicator, part-time 1980–88, full-time 1988–93, Regl Adjudicator, 1993–96; Dep. Metropolitan Stipendiary Magistrate, 1983–85; part-time Legal Chairman: Social Security Appeal Tribunal, 1985–93; Disability Appeal Tribunal, 1992–93; Legal Chm., Immigration Appeal Tribunal, 1995–96; Legal Mem., Special Immigration Appeals Commn, 1998–2001. Mem., Internat. Assoc. of Refugee Law Judges, 1998–2001. British Forces Campaign Medal, 2013. *Clubs:* Royal Automobile; Royal Automobile Country (Epsom).

HATT, Paul William David; Secretary, Royal Hospital Chelsea, since 2007; *b* 21 Nov. 1949; *s* of late William Oliver Hatt and Henrietta Hatt (*née* McGregor); *m* 1975, Cecilia Anne Freeman; two *s* two *d*. *Educ:* Sir Joseph Williamson's Sch., Rochester; Lincoln Coll., Oxford (Schol., BA Hons English Lang. and Lit., PGCE, MA); Nat. Defence Coll. Joined Ministry of Defence, 1973: Principal, 1980–85; on secondment to FCO, as First Sec., UK Delegn to NATO, Brussels, 1985–89; Asst Sec., 1990; Head, Defence Lands, 1990–92; Dir, Proliferation and Arms Control Secretariat, 1992–97; Head, Resources and Programmes (Army), 1997–98; Asst Under Sec., 1998; Comd Sec., RAF Logistics Comd, 1998–2000; Fellow, Center for Internat. Affairs, Harvard Univ., 2000–01; Comd Sec. to Second Sea Lord and C-in-C Naval Home Comd, and Asst Under-Sec. of State (Naval Personnel), MoD, 2001–06; Project Dir, Royal Naval Museum, 2006. *Recreations:* sedentary pursuits, including family, literature and music. *Address:* c/o Royal Hospital Chelsea, SW3 4SR.

HATTER, Sir Maurice, Kt 1999; Chairman, IMO Precision Controls Ltd, since 1970; *b* 6 Nov. 1929; *s* of Ralph and Sarah Hatter; *m* 1999, Irene Noach. Royal Signals, 1949. Formed an electronics manufacturer sold to Thorn, 1968. Pres., World ORT, 2004–08, Pres. Emeritus, 2008. Founded Hatter Inst. of Cardiology, at UCH, 1990. Hon. Life Pres., Charlton Athletic FC, 2000. Hon. Fellow, UCL, 1995. Hon. PhD Haifa, Israel, 1996. *Recreations:* tennis, boating, underwater archaeology. *Address:* IMO Precision Controls Ltd, 1000 North Circular Road, Staples Corner, NW2 7JP.

HATTERSLEY, Baron *cr* 1997 (Life Peer), of Sparkbrook in the co. of West Midlands; **Roy Sydney George Hattersley;** PC 1975; Deputy Leader of the Labour Party, 1983–92; *b* 28 Dec. 1932; *s* of Frederick Roy Hattersley, Sheffield; *m* 1956, Molly Hattersley, *qv* (marr. diss. 2013); *m* 2013, Maggie Pearlstine. *Educ:* Sheffield City Grammar Sch.; Univ. of Hull (BSc (Econ). Journalist and Health Service Executive, 1956–64; Mem. Sheffield City Council, 1957–65 (Chm. Housing Cttee and Public Works Cttee). MP (Lab) Birmingham, Sparkbrook, 1964–97. PPS to Minister of Pensions and National Insurance, 1964–67; Jt Parly Sec., DEP (formerly Min. of Labour), 1967–69; Minister of Defence for Administration, 1969–70; Labour Party spokesman: on Defence, 1972; on Educn and Sci., 1972–74; Minister of State, FCO, 1974–76; Sec. of State for Prices and Consumer Protection, 1976–79; principal opposition spokesman on environment, 1979–80, on home affairs, 1980–83, on Treasury and economic affairs, 1983–87, on home affairs, 1987–92. Visiting Fellow: Inst. of Politics, Univ. of Harvard, 1971, 1972; Nuffield Coll., Oxford, 1984–. Dir, Campaign for a European Political Community, 1966–67. Columnist: Punch; The Guardian; The Listener, 1979–82; Columnist of the Year, Granada, 1982. Hon. DSc Sheffield Hallam; Hon. DCL: Hull; West Midlands. *Publications:* Nelson, 1974; Goodbye to Yorkshire (essays), 1976; Politics Apart, 1982; Press Gang, 1983; A Yorkshire Boyhood, 1983; Choose Freedom: the future for Democratic Socialism, 1987; Economic Priorities for a Labour Government, 1987; Who Goes Home? 1995; 50 Years On, 1997; Blood & Fire, 1999; A Brand from the Burning: the life of John Wesley, 2002; The Edwardians, 2004; Campbell-Bannerman, 2007; Borrowed Time: the story of Britain between the wars, 2007; In Search of England, 2009; David Lloyd George: the great outsider, 2010; The Devonshires: the story of a family and a nation, 2013; *novels:* The Maker's Mark, 1990; In That Quiet Earth, 1991; Skylark Song, 1994; Between Ourselves, 1994; Buster's Diaries, 1998; Buster's Secret Diaries, 2007. *Clubs:* Reform, Garrick.

HATTERSLEY, Prof. Andrew Tym, DM; FRS 2010; FRCP; Professor of Molecular Medicine, University of Exeter Medical School (formerly Peninsula Medical School); Consultant Physician, Royal Devon and Exeter NHS Foundation Trust, since 1995. *Educ:* Emmanuel Coll., Cambridge (BA 1981); Univ. of Oxford (BM BCh 1984; DM 1998). MRCP 1987; FRCP 1999. Registrar in Medicine, Hammersmith Hosp.; MRC Res. Fellow, Diabetes Res. Lab., Radcliffe Infirmary, Oxford; Lectr in Medicine, Queen Elizabeth Hospital, Birmingham. Lectures include: Dorothy Hodgkin Prize, Diabetes UK, 2007; William Osler Prize, Assoc. of Physicians, 2007; Sir Stanley Davidson, RCP, 2008. FMedSci 2004. *Publications:* contribs to jls incl. Science, Nature Genetics, New England jl Medicine, Lancet. *Address:* University of Exeter Medical School, Barrack Road, Exeter EX2 5AX.

HATTERSLEY, Edith Mary, (Molly); Molly, Lady Hattersley; educational consultant, 1990; Visiting Fellow, Institute of Education, University of London (Management Development Centre), 1990–97; *b* 5 Feb. 1931; *d* of Michael and Sally Loughran; *m* 1956, Roy Sydney George Hattersley (*see* Baron Hattersley) (marr. diss. 2013). *Educ:* Consett Grammar Sch.; University College of Hull. BA Hons English (London), CertEd (Hull). Assistant Mistress at schools in Surrey and Yorkshire, 1953–61; Sen. Mistress, Myers Grove Sch., Sheffield, 1961–64; Dep. Headmistress, Kidbrooke Sch., SE3, 1965–69; Headmistress, Hurlingham Sch., SW6, 1969–74; Headmistress, Creighton Sch., N10, 1974–82; Asst Educn Officer, then Dep. Dir of Educn, ILEA, 1983–90. Advr on educnl matters to Trustees of BM, 1978–86. Chairman of Cttee, Assoc. of Head Mistresses, 1975–77; Pres., Secondary Heads Assoc., 1980–81; Chm., Soc. of Educn Consultants, 1994–96. Mem. Ct of Governors, LSE, 1970–99. FRSA 1982–2010. *Recreation:* reading.

HATTON; *see* Finch Hatton, family name of Earl of Winchilsea.

HATTON, Alison Lee; *see* Booth, A. L.

HATTON, Andrew John; His Honour Judge Andrew Hatton; a Circuit Judge, since 2012; *b* Bolton, 15 Sept. 1964; *s* of Thomas William and Margery Hatton; *m* 1990, Caroline Sarah Ann Headley; one *s* one *d*. *Educ:* Bolton Sch.; Leeds Poly. (LLB Hons 1986); Inns of Court Sch. of Law; Liverpool John Moores Univ. (LLM 2015). Called to the Bar, Gray's Inn, 1987; in practice as barrister, 1987–2012; a Dep. Dist Judge (Magistrates' Courts), 2005–12; a Recorder, 2009–12; Internat. Criminal Judge, EU Mission in Kosovo, 2011–12; UN apptd Judge of Residual Special Ct for Sierra Leone, 2013–. Mem., Honourable Soc. of Gray's Inn, 1986. *Recreations:* ski-ing, golf, theatre. *Address:* Crown Court at Liverpool, Queen Elizabeth II Law Courts, Derby Square, Liverpool L2 1XA. *T:* (0151) 473 7373.

HATTON, Prof. Angela Dawn, PhD; FRSB; Associate Director for Research, Scottish Association for Marine Science, Scottish Marine Institute, since 2014; *b* Knutsford, 1969; *d* of John Hatton and Irene Hatton; *m* 2000, Stephen Teape; one *s* one *d*. *Educ:* Liverpool Poly. (BSc Hons Applied Biol. 1991); Univ. of East Anglia (PhD Marine Biogeochem. 1995). Postdoctoral Res. Associate, UEA, 1995–97; Scottish Association for Marine Science: NERC Res. Fellow, 1997–2003; Lectr, 2003–06; Sen. Lectr, 2006–12; Prof., 2012–14; Leader, Dynamic Ocean Theme, 2012–14. Chm., Sci. and Innovation Strategy Bd, NERC, 2015–. FRSB (FSB 2011). *Address:* Scottish Association for Marine Science, Scottish Marine Insitute, Oban, Argyll PA37 1QA. *E:* angela.hatton@sams.ac.uk.

HATTON, David William; QC 1996; **His Honour Judge Hatton;** a Circuit Judge, since 2012; *b* 29 May 1953; *s* of Thomas William Hatton and Margery Hatton; *m* 1994, Janet Elizabeth Bossons; one *s* one *d*. *Educ:* Bolton Sch.; Univ. of Bristol (LLB Hons). Called to the Bar, Gray's Inn, 1976, Bencher, 2005. Recorder, 1994–2012. *Recreations:* reading, music, walking, football. *Club:* Bolton Wanderers Football.

HAUGH, Leslie John; independent consultant, since 2002; Principal Finance Officer, Home Office, 2000–02; *b* 20 Aug. 1947; *s* of John Lamont Haugh and Robina Speed Haugh (*née* Stenhouse); one *s* one *d*. *Educ:* Buckhaven High Sch. ACMA 1980; FCCA 1998. HM Treasury, 1964; MPBW, 1965–67; BoT, then DTI, 1967–76; Dept of Employment, 1976–84; Dep. Accountant and Comptroller Gen., HM Customs and Excise, 1984–92; Accounting Advr, Home Office, 1992–98; seconded to Systems Union, 1998–2000. *Recreations:* golf (badly), bridge (badly), saying no. *Club:* Crail Golfing Society.

HAUGHEY, family name of **Baron Haughey**.

HAUGHEY, Baron *cr* 2013 (Life Peer), of Hutchesontown in the City of Glasgow; **William Haughey,** Kt 2012; OBE 2003; Joint Owner and Executive Chairman, City Refrigeration Holdings (UK) Ltd, since 1985; *b* Glasgow, 2 July 1956; *s* of Thomas Haughey and Margaret Haughey (*née* Morton); *m* 1978, Susan Moore; one *s*. *Educ:* Holyrood Sen. Secondary Sch., Glasgow; Springburn Coll., Glasgow. Engrg supervisor, Turner Refrigeration Ltd, 1973–83; Hd of Engrg, UTS Carrier (USA), UAE, 1983–85. Former Chm., Scottish Enterprise Glasgow. Former non-exec. Dir, Celtic FC. Est. City Charitable Trust, 2010. Hon. DTech Glasgow Caledonian, 2005. Loving Cup, 2001, St Mungo Prize, 2007, City of Glasgow. *Address:* City Refrigeration Holdings (UK) Ltd, Caledonia House, 2 Lawmoor Street, Glasgow G5 0US.

HAUGHEY, Denis; Member (SDLP) Ulster Mid, Northern Ireland Assembly, 1998–2003; *b* 3 Oct. 1944; *s* of Henry Haughey and Elizabeth Falls; *m* 1970, Maureen McCarron; one *s* two *d*. *Educ:* St Patrick's Coll., Armagh; Queen's Univ., Belfast (BA Hons Modern History and Pol Sci.). Mem., Northern Ireland Assembly, 1982–86; Minister, Office of First and Dep. First Ministers, NI Assembly, 1999–2000, 2001–02. Mem., Cttee of the Regions, EU, 1994–2002. Social Democratic and Labour Party: Founder Mem., 1970; Vice-Chair, 1971–73; Chair, 1973–78; Internat. Sec., 1978–2001. *Recreations:* reading (history, biography), music, travel. *Address:* 66 Fairhill Road, Cookstown, Co. Tyrone BT80 8DE. *T:* (028) 8676 3349.

HAUSER, Dr Hermann Maria, Hon. KBE 2015 (Hon. CBE 2002); FRS 2012; Founder Director, Amadeus Capital Partners Ltd, since 1997; Director, Globespan-Virata Inc. (formerly ATM Ltd, later Virata), 2001–03 (Chairman, 1992–2001); *b* 23 Oct. 1948; *s* of Hermann Hauser and Gerti Pizl; *m* 1982, Pamela Raspe; one *s* one *d*. *Educ:* Vienna Univ. (MA Physics); Cavendish Lab., Univ. of Cambridge (PhD Physics 1977). Co-founder, Acorn (BBC) Computers, 1978 (500,000 BBC micro computers sold by 1984); Founder, IQ (Bio) Ltd, 1982; Vice-Pres. Research, Olivetti, Italy, 1986–88; Dir, Harlequin Ltd, 1986–99; Founder, IXI Ltd, 1987; formation of ARM Ltd (jt venture between Acorn and Apple), 1987; Founder and Chm., Active Book Co., 1988; Co-Chm., CTO of EO Inc., 1991; Founder: Vocalis Ltd, 1992; Electronic Share Information Ltd, 1993; Advanced Rendering Technology Ltd, 1995; Founder/Chairman: SynGenix Ltd, 1993; Advanced Displays Ltd, 1993–94; Advanced Telecommunications Modules Ltd, 1993; UK Online Ltd, 1994; Entertainment Online Ltd, 1995. Hon. DSc Bath, 1990; Hon. DSc Loughborough, 1998. *Recreations:* tennis, squash, ski-ing, swimming, piano. *Address:* (office) Mount Pleasant House, 2 Mount Pleasant, Cambridge CB3 0RN. *T:* (01223) 707000.

HAUSER, Wolfhart Gunnar; Chairman, FirstGroup plc, since 2015; *b* 5 Dec. 1949; *s* of Josef Hauser and Eva Bargenda; *m* 1981, Dr Susanne Sandhagen; two *s*. *Educ:* Ludwig Maximilians Univ., Munich (MD 1978). Chief Executive Officer: TÜV Product Service GmbH,

1988–97; TÜV Süd AG, 1998–2002; Bd Dir, 2002–15, Chief Exec., 2005–15, Intertek Gp plc. *Recreations:* ski-ing, tennis, golf. *Address:* FirstGroup plc, 395 King Street, Aberdeen AB24 5RP. *Club:* Rotary (Munich).

HAVARD, Dai; *b* 7 Feb. 1950; *m* 1986, Julia Watts (marr. diss.). *Educ:* Univ. of Warwick (MA). Union studies tutor, 1971–75; researcher, 1975–79; Educn Officer, 1975–82; Official, MSF, 1989–2001. MP (Lab) Merthyr Tydfil and Rhymney, 2001–15.

HAVELANGE, Dr Jean Marie Faustin Godefroid, (João); President, Fédération Internationale de Football Association, 1974–98 (Hon. President, 1998–2013); Member, International Olympic Committee, 1963–2011; *b* 8 May 1916; *m* Anna Maria; one *d. Educ:* Univ. of Rio de Janeiro (Dr jur). Has practised law, 1936–. Pres., COMETA SA, Brazil; Man. Dir, several cos in Brazil. Olympic Games participant, swimming, 1936, and water polo, 1952. Hon. Citizen, Chicago, 1994. Order of Special Merit in Sports (Brazil), 1973; Kt, Order of Vasa (Sweden), 1959; Commandeur de l'Ordre du Lion (Senegal), 1973; Gran Cruz de Isabel la Católica (Spain), 1982; Commendatore dell' Ordine dell Repubblica Italiana (Italy), 1980; Commandeur de la Légion d'Honneur (France), 1991. *Recreation:* swimming. *Address:* Avenida Rio Branco 89–B, conbine 602 Centro, 20040–004 Rio de Janeiro RJ, Brazil.

HAVELOCK-ALLAN, Alison Lee Caroline, (Lady Havelock-Allan); *see* Foster, A. L. C.

HAVELOCK-ALLAN, Sir (Anthony) Mark (David), 5th Bt *cr* 1858, of Lucknow; QC 1993; **His Honour Judge Havelock-Allan;** a Senior Circuit Judge, Bristol Mercantile Court, since 2001; a Deputy High Court Judge, Commercial Court and Admiralty Court, since 2002; Principal Judge, Bristol Technology and Construction Court, since 2005; *b* 4 April 1951; *s* of Sir Anthony James Allan Havelock-Allan, 4th Bt and Valerie Babette Louise Hobson, actress (who *m* 2nd, J. D. Profumo, CBE; she *d* 1998); *S* father, 2003; *m* 1st, 1976, Lucy Clare (marr. diss. 1984), *y d* of late Alexander Mitchell-Innes; 2nd, 1986, Alison Lee Caroline Foster, *qv*; one *s* two *d. Educ:* Eton; Durham Univ. (BA Hons Law 1972); Trinity Coll., Cambridge (LLB 1974; Dip. in Internat. Law, 1976). Called to the Bar, Inner Temple, 1974, Bencher, 1995; Asst Recorder, 1993–96; a Recorder, 1997–2001. FCIArb 1991. *Recreation:* salmon fishing and foreign travel (preferably combined). *Heir: s* Henry Caspar Francis Havelock-Allan, *b* 6 Oct. 1994. *Address:* Bristol Civil Justice Centre, 2 Redcliff Street, Bristol BS1 6GR. *T:* (0117) 366 4800. *Clubs:* Garrick, Royal Automobile.

HAVENHAND, Martin Stephen; Chairman, Rotherham NHS Foundation Trust, since 2014; *b* 14 Oct. 1950; *s* of Mark Havenhand and Jessie Brough; *m*; two *s* one *d. Educ:* Sheffield Business Sch.; Centre for Managing Change, London (MSc Managing Change). Asst Chief Officer (Recreation, Culture and Health), S Yorks MCC, 1980–85; Dir of Leisure Services, then of Envmt, Trafford MBC, 1985–93; Chief Executive: Bassetlaw DC, 1993–99; Yorkshire Forward, 1999–2006. Chairman: Advance Gp Hldgs, 2006–13; Nat. Metals Technol. Centre, 2006–13. Exec. Chm., Yorkshire 2012, 2006–10. Non-exec. Dir, Yorks Water, 2008–. Hon. Dr Bradford Business Sch. *Recreations:* sport, lifelong learning. *Address:* Rotherham NHS Foundation Trust, Rotherham Hospital, Moorgate Road, Rotherham, S Yorks S60 2UD.

HAVERGAL, Giles Pollock, CBE 2002 (OBE 1987); director and actor; Director, Citizens' Theatre Glasgow, 1969–2003; *b* 9 June 1938; *s* of Henry McLeod Havergal and Margaret Graham Hyacinth Havergal (*née* Chitty). *Educ:* Harrow Sch.; Christ Church, Oxford (MA). Trainee Dir, Oldham Repertory, 1963; Director: Her Majesty's Theatre, Barrow-in-Furness, 1964; Palace Theatre, Watford, 1965–69. FRSAMD 1988; FRSE 1994. Hon. DLitt: Glasgow, 1987; Strathclyde, 1996. DDra RSAMD, 1997. St Mungo Prize, City of Glasgow, 1995. *Address:* c/o Alan Brodie Representation Ltd, Paddock Suite, The Courtyard, 55 Charterhouse Street, EC1M 6HA. *T:* (020) 7253 6226.

HAVERS, Hon. Nigel (Allan); actor; *b* 6 Nov. 1951; *yr s* of Baron Havers, PC, and of Carol Elizabeth (who *m* 1993, Charles Frederick Hughesdon, AFC); *m* 1st, 1974, Carolyn Cox (marr. diss. 1989; she *d* 2011); one *d*; 2nd, 1989, Polly Bloomfield (*d* 2004); 3rd, 2007, Georgiana Bronfman. *Educ:* Arts Educational Sch. Researcher, Jimmy Young Programme, BBC Radio 2. *Television* includes: The Glittering Prizes; Nicholas Nickleby; A Horseman Riding By; Upstairs Downstairs; Don't Wait Up, 1983–90; Strangers and Brothers, 1984; The Charmer, 1987; Proof, 1987; A Perfect Hero, 1991; Sleepers, The Good Guys, 1992; The Heart Surgeon, 1997; Dangerfield, 1998 and 1999; The Gentleman Thief, 2001; Manchild, 2002, 2003; Coronation Street, 2009–; Downton Abbey, 2011; *films* include: Chariots of Fire, 1981; A Passage to India, 1985; The Whistle Blower; Empire of the Sun, 1988; *theatre* includes: The Importance of Being Earnest, NT, 1982, Harold Pinter Th., 2014; Art, 2001; See You Next Tuesday, Albery, 2003; Rebecca, nat. tour, 2004–05; Single Spies, nat. tour, 2008; *radio* includes, Mrs Dale's Diary. *Publications:* Playing with Fire (autobiog.), 2006. *Address:* 28 Bramham Gardens, SW5 0HE. *Club:* Garrick.

See also Hon. P. N. Havers.

HAVERS, Hon. Philip Nigel; QC 1995; *b* 16 June 1950; *s* of Baron Havers, PC and of Carol Elizabeth (*née* Lay) (who *m* 1993, Charles Frederick Hughesdon, AFC); *m* 1976, Patricia Frances Searle; one *s* one *d. Educ:* Eton Coll.; Corpus Christi Coll., Cambridge. Called to the Bar, Inner Temple, 1974, Bencher, 2001. A Recorder, 1990–2000; a Dep. High Ct Judge, 2002–. *Recreations:* tennis, music, wine, gardening, travel. *Address:* 1 Crown Office Row, Temple, EC4Y 7HH. *T:* (020) 7797 7500. *Club:* Garrick.

See also Hon. N. A. Havers.

HAVERY, His Honour Richard Orbell; QC 1980; a Judge of the Technology and Construction Court of the High Court, 1998–2007; *b* 7 Feb. 1934; *s* of late Joseph Horton Havery and Constance Eleanor (*née* Orbell). *Educ:* St Paul's; Magdalen Coll., Oxford (MA 1961); Imperial Coll. London (MSc 2010). Called to the Bar, Middle Temple, 1962, Bencher, 1989; an Asst Recorder, 1982–86; a Recorder, 1986–93; a Circuit Judge and Official Referee, 1993–98. Pres., Madrigal Soc., 2009–11. *Publications:* (with D. A. McI. Kemp and M. S. Kemp) The Quantum of Damages: personal injury claims, 3rd edn, 1967; (Gen. Ed.) History of the Middle Temple, 2011. *Recreations:* music, croquet, steam locomotives. *Clubs:* Athenæum, Garrick, Hurlingham; Leander (Henley-on-Thames).

HAVILLAND; *see* de Havilland.

HAWARD, Birkin Anthony Christopher, RIBA; Consultant, van Heyningen and Haward Architects, since 2010 (Joint Principal, 1982–2010); *b* 28 Sept. 1939; *s* of Birkin Haward and Muriel Haward (*née* Wright); *m* 1st, 1963, Rose Hargreaves Heap (marr. diss. 1975; she *d* 1993); one *s* one *d*; 2nd, 1977, Joanna van Heyningen, *qv*; one *s* one *d. Educ:* Northgate Grammar Sch., Ipswich; Architectural Assoc. RIBA 1969. Dir, Foster Associates, 1969–83; formed van Heyningen and Haward Architects, 1982. Studio teacher: Cambridge Univ. Sch. of Architecture, 1969–75; Bartlett Sch. of Architecture, 1976–81; RCA, 1981–84. Vis. critic, Univ. of Pennsylvania, 1976, and most UK architectural schs. Award-winning buildings include: Haward House, London, 1976; Newnham Coll. Rare Books Liby, Cambridge, 1981; 2nd Haward House, London, 1986; Clovelly Visitor Centre, 1989; Wilson Court, Cambridge, 1994; Jacqueline du Pré Music Bldg, Oxford, 1995; King Alfred's Sch., London, 1997; Gateway to the White Cliffs (NT), Dover, 1999; West Ham Station, Jubilee Line Extension, 1999; Nat. Centre for Early Music, York, 2000; Polhill Inf. Centre, Bedford, 2000; Khoan and Michael Sullivan Chinese Painting Gall., Ashmolean Mus., Oxford, 2001; Sutton Hoo Visitor Centre (NT), 2002; Music Res. Centre, Univ. of York, 2004; Trinity Centre, Ipswich, 2005; Kaleidoscope, Lewisham, 2006; RSPB Centre, Rainham Marshes, 2007; Stelios Ioannou Centre for Classical and Byzantine Studies, Oxford, 2008; Performing Arts Centre, Latymer Upper Sch., London, 2008; Lerner Ct, Clare Coll., Cambridge, 2009. Ext. Examr, 1984–87, Mem., Steering Cttee, 1991–96, RIBA. Member: Architectural Panel, NT, 1995–; Council, AA, 2000–03; Fabric Adv. Cttee, St Paul's Cathedral, 2003–. Assessor, Heritage Lottery Fund, 1996–99; Architectural Advr, Arts Council Lottery Panel, 1996–2001. Trustee, William Morris Gall., 2003–. Exhibitions: Kent Design, Maidstone, 2000; University Challenge: buildings for higher educn, Building Centre, 2001; New Connections, Municipal Arts Soc. of NY, 2001; Winning Designs, Bristol Arch. Centre, RIBA, London and Cube Gall., Manchester, 2002; Diverse City, RIBA, London, 2003; Celebration of Architectural Competitions, Cube Gall., Manchester, 2003, RIAS, Edinburgh, 2004; one man exhibn, Beardsmore Gall., 2012, 2014. *Publications:* contribs to major newspaper and architectural jls. *Recreations:* drawing, painting, theatre, church-crawling, 19th and 20th century stained glass, gardening. *Address:* c/o van Heyningen and Haward Architects, 1a Harmood Street, NW1 8DN. *T:* (020) 3362 4488.

HAWARD, Joanna; *see* van Heyningen, J.

HAWARD, John Anthony William; interim management and consultant, since 1999; *b* 8 Feb. 1958; *s* of Anthony Ivor Haward and Joan Haward; partner, Janie Wilson; one *d. Educ:* City of London Sch. Joined: DoE, 1977; Spastics Soc., 1987; Mgt Advr and Hd of Chief Exec.'s Office, Berks CC, 1988; Dir of Corporate Strategy, Southwark Council, 1994; Advr, UN Mission to Kosovo, 1999; Chm., Local Govt Modernisation Team, DETR, subseq. ODPM, 2000–03; Dir of Local Govt Practice SE, ODPM, then DCLG, 2004–07. Expert Adviser: to Govt of Kosovo, 2011–14; to Govt of Macedonia, 2014–. Proprietor, Le Puget, 2008–. *Publications:* Impact of Advanced Information Systems, 1984; Devolved Management, 1989; Project Management, 1991. *Recreations:* walking, reading, history, cooking, wine. *Address:* Le Domaine de Puget, 11270 Gaja La Selve, Aude, France. *E:* john@lepuget.com.

HAWARDEN, 9th Viscount *cr* 1793 (Ire.); **Robert Connan Wyndham Leslie Maude;** Bt 1705; Baron de Montalt 1785; *b* 23 May 1961; *s* of 8th Viscount and Susannah Caroline Hyde, *d* of late Maj. Charles Phillips Gardner; *S* father, 1991; *m* 1995, Judith Anne, *y d* of late John Bates; one *s* two *d. Educ:* St Edmund's Sch., Canterbury; RAC Cirencester. *Heir: s* Hon. Varian John Connan Eustace Maude, *b* 1 Sept. 1997. *Address:* Great Bossington Farm House, Bossington, Adisham, near Canterbury, Kent CT3 3LN.

HAWES, Ven. Arthur John; Archdeacon of Lincoln, 1995–2008, now Archdeacon Emeritus; Canon and Prebendary of Lincoln Cathedral, 1995–2008; *b* 31 Aug. 1943; *s* of late John and Sylvia Hawes; *m* 1969, Melanie Harris; one *s* one *d. Educ:* City of Oxford High Sch. for Boys; Chichester Theol Coll.; Richmond Fellowship (Cert. in Human Relns, 1968); Univ. of Birmingham (Dip. in Pastoral Studies, 1972; Dip. in Liturgy and Architecture, 1975); Univ. of E Anglia (BA Hons 1986). Ordained deacon 1968, priest 1969; Asst Curate, St John the Baptist, Kidderminster, 1968–72; Priest-in-charge, St Richard's, Droitwich, 1972–76; Rector: Alderford with Attlebridge and Swannington, 1976–92; St Faith's, Gaywood, King's Lynn, 1992–95. Chaplain, Hellesdon and David Rice Hosps, Yare Clinic, 1976–92; Rural Dean of Sparham, 1981–91; Hon. Canon of Norwich Cathedral, 1988–95. Mem., General Synod, 2000–08 (Mem., Mission and Public Affairs Council, 2000–09; Chm., Mental Health Adv. Cttee, 1995–2009). Chm., Norwich Diocesan Bd for Social Responsibility, 1990–95. Mental Health Act Comr, 1986–94. Pres., Lincs Rural Housing Assoc., 1998–2007; Chm., East Midlands Develt Centre, 2003–05; non-exec. Dir, Lincolnshire Partnership Trust, 2002–06; Mental Health Act Advr to Lincolnshire Partnership Foundn Trust, 2006–08; Training Consultant, Lincolnshire Partnership Trust, 2008–12. Vice Pres., British Assoc. for Study of Spirituality, 2010–. Chaplaincy Co-ordinator for Saga Cruises, 2009–. Co-Chair, Nat. Spirituality and Mental Health Forum, 2009–11. Vis. Fellow, Staffordshire Univ., 2010–13. Patron, MIND, 1995–2008. *Publications:* (ed jtly) The Ann French Memorial Lectures, 1996; (contrib.) Jewels for the Journey, 2007; (contrib.) Spirituality and Mental Health, 2011; (contrib.) Spirituality and End of Life Care, 2013; (ed) Crossing the River: the contribution of spirituality to humanity and its future, 2014; contribs to theol jls. *Recreations:* golf, medieval art and architecture, theatre, music, grandchildren. *Address:* Sunnyside Farmhouse, 29 Market Street, Shipdham, Thetford, Norfolk IP25 7LY. *T:* (01362) 822441. *E:* arthur.hawes@yahoo.co.uk.

HAWES, Patrick Thomas, FRCO; composer and conductor, since 1989; *b* Grimsby, 5 Dec. 1958; *s* of John William Alfred Hawes and Catherine Agnes Hawes; civil partnership 2011, Andrew Berry. *Educ:* De Aston Sch., Market Rasen; Durham Univ. (MA 1981). FRCO 1984. Asst Dir, Music, Pangbourne Coll., 1981–90; Composer in Residence: Charterhouse, 1990–97; Classic FM, 2006–08. *Compositions:* Quanta Qualia, 2004; Bluebird Variations, 2004; O Lord Our Governor, 2005; Towards the Light, 2006; When Israel Was a Child, 2007; Song of Songs, 2008; Lazarus Requiem, 2008; Highgrove Suite, 2010; Angel, 2014. *Recreations:* horse racing, theatre, ballet, opera, running, cooking. *W:* www.patrickhawes.com.

HAWKE, family name of **Baron Hawke**.

HAWKE, 12th Baron *cr* 1776, of Towton; **William Martin Theodore Hawke;** *b* 23 June 1995; *s* of 11th Baron Hawke and of Bronwen, *d* of William James, MRCVS; *S* father, 2009.

HAWKE, Hon. Robert James Lee, AC 1979; business consultant; Adjunct Professor, Research School of Pacific Studies and Social Sciences, Australian National University, 1992–95; Prime Minister of Australia, 1983–91; *b* 9 Dec. 1929; *m* 1st, 1956, Hazel Masterson (marr. diss. 1995; she *d* 2013); one *s* two *d* (and one *s* decd); 2nd, 1995, Blanche d'Alpuget. *Educ:* Univ. of Western Australia (LLB, BA(Econ)); Oxford Univ. (BLitt; Hon. Fellow, University Coll., 1984). Research Officer and Advocate for Aust. Council of Trade Unions, 1958–69. Pres., ACTU, 1970–80. MP (Lab) Wills, Melbourne, 1980–92; Australian Labor Party: Mem., Nat. Exec., 1971–91; Pres., 1973–78; Leader, 1983–91. Leader of the Opposition, Feb.–March 1983. Member: Governing Body of Internat. Labour Office, 1972–80; Board, Reserve Bank of Australia, 1973–80; Aust. Population and Immigration Council, 1976–80; Aust. Manufacturing Council, 1977–80. Chm., Cttee of Experts on Membership of Educn Internat., 1993. Hon. Vis. Prof., Univ. of Sydney, 1992–97. Member: Adv. Bd, Inst. for Internat. Studies, Stanford Univ.; Bd of Govs, Cttee of Economic Devel t of Australia. Hon. DLitt W Australia, 1984; Hon. Dr Nanjing, 1986; Hon. DPhil Hebrew Univ. of Jerusalem, 1987; Hon. LLD Univ. of NSW, 1987. *Publications:* The Hawke Memoirs, 1994. *Recreations:* tennis, cricket, reading, golf, horse racing, snooker.

HAWKER, Ven. Alan Fort; Archdeacon of Malmesbury, 1999–2010, now Archdeacon Emeritus; *b* 23 March 1944; *s* of Albert Hawker and Florence Lilian Hawker (*née* Fort); *m* 1968, Jeanette Dorothy Law; one *s* three *d. Educ:* Buckhurst Hill County High Sch.; Hull Univ. (BA Hons Soc. Studies 1965); Clifton Theol Coll. (DipTh 1968). PACTA 1973. Asst Curate, St Leonard and St Mary, Bootle, 1968–71; Asst Curate (with charge), St Paul, Fazakerley, 1971–73; Vicar, St Paul, Goose Green, 1973–81; Team Rector, St Mary, Southgate (Crawley), 1981–98; Canon and Prebendary, Chichester Cathedral, 1991–98; Proctor in Convocation, 1990–2010; RD of E Grinstead, 1993–98; Archdeacon of Swindon, 1998–99. Chm., Gen. Synod Working Party on Clergy Discipline and Reform of Ecclesiastical Courts, 1994–2001; Member: Gen. Synod Standing Cttee, 1995–98; Gen. Synod Business Cttee, 2000–10; C of E Clergy Discipline Commn, 2003–10. CEDR Accredited Mediator. Vice Chair, Council, Glos Univ., 2002–08. *Publications:* Under Authority, 1996. *Recreations:* walking, railways, theatre, reading, music. *Address:* 21 Paddocks Close, Wolston, Warwicks CV8 3GW. *T:* (024) 7654 4021. *E:* alanandjen68@gmail.com.

HAWKER, Prof. Craig Jon, PhD; FRS 2010; FRSC; Professor of Materials, Chemistry and Biochemistry, and Director of Materials Research Laboratory, since 2004, Ruth and Alan J. Heeger Chair in Interdisciplinary Science, since 2010, Director, Dow Materials Institute, since 2011, and Clarke Professor and Director, California Nanosystems Institute, since 2013, University of California, Santa Barbara; *b* Toowoomba, Australia, 11 Jan. 1964. *Educ:* Univ. of Queensland (BSc 1st Cl. Hons 1984); Wolfson Coll., Cambridge (Ribbands Schol.; PhD 1988). FRSC 2013. Post-doctoral Res. Associate, Cornell Univ., 1988–90; Queen Elizabeth II Res. Fellow, Univ. of Queensland, 1990–93; Mem., res. staff, IBM Almaden Res. Center, 1993–2004. Hon. Prof. of Chemistry, Univ. of Queensland, 2001–; Prof., King Fahd Univ. of Petroleum and Minerals, Saudi Arabia, 2011–. Consultant to: Hitachi Data Systems, 2002–05; Mitsubishi Chem. Co., 2004–; Eastman Kodak, 2005–06; Ciba Speciality Chemicals, 2005–06; BASF, 2006–08; Allergan, 2006–; Promerus, 2006. Member, Scientific Advisory Board: NSEC, Univ. of Wisconsin, Madison, 2003–; Australian Inst. Bioengrg and Nanotechnol., 2004–; MIT Inst. for Soldier Nanotechnologies, 2004–; Molecular Foundry, Lawrence Berkeley Nat. Lab., 2005–; Materials Res. Lab., Univ. of Illinois, 2006–. Mem., RACI. *Publications:* contribs to jls incl. Jl Amer. Chem. Soc., Adv. Materials, Jl Polymer Sci., Polymer Chem., Chem. Sci., Macromolecules. *Address:* Department of Chemistry and Biochemistry, University of California, Santa Barbara, Santa Barbara, CA 93106–9510, USA.

HAWKER, David Gordon; international education consultant; *b* 11 Feb. 1954; *s* of Gordon Hawker and Peggy Hawker (*née* Lewis); *m* 1987, Judy Tongue; one *s* one *d*. *Educ:* Whitgift Sch., Croydon; Northampton Grammar Sch.; Wadham Coll., Oxford (BA Hons French and German; PGCE). Teacher, 1976–85; Exams Officer, Oxford Schs Exams Bd, 1985–86; Exams Sec., Inst. of Linguists, 1986–89; Schs Advr, Calderdale MBC, 1989–92; Sen. Professional Officer, Sch. Exams and Assessment Council, 1992–93; Asst Chief Exec., SCAA, 1994–97; Hd, Curriculum and Assessment, QCA, 1997–99; Dir of Educn, 1999–2002, Dir of Children's Services, 2002–07, Brighton & Hove City Council; Dep. Chief Exec., Westminster City Council, 2007–08; Dir Gen. for Children, Educn, Lifelong Learning and Skills, Welsh Assembly Govt, 2008–10; Dir Gen., Arms Length Body Reform Prog., DfE, 2010–11. Hon. Prof., Durham Univ., 2012–. Chm., Assoc. of Dirs of Educn and Children's Services, 2004–07 (Chm., Standards, Performance and Inspection Cttee, 2007–08). Consultant to OECD, World Bank and British Council on educnl evaluation and assessment, 2000–; Mem., Gen. Educn Sub-Bd, Open Soc. Inst., 2007–13. Prof., College of Teachers, 2007–; Vis. Res. Fellow, Univ. of Sussex, 2011–14; Vis. Professorial Fellow, Inst. of Educn, London, 2012–. Trustee: 4Children, 2006–08; CfBT Educl Trust, 2011–; CfBT Schs Trust, 2013–. *Publications:* Core Skills Framework for Modern Languages, 1990; Review of Assessment and Testing, 1995; A Higher Vision for LEAs, 2001; Methodological Recommendations for a Quality Monitoring Framework for the Russian Education System, 2002; (contrib.) Contemporary Issues in the Early Years, 5th edn 2009; (contrib.) Parents, Personalities and Power: Welsh medium schools in South East Wales, 2013; Baseline Assessment in an International Context, 2014; (contrib.) Handbook of International Development and Education, 2015. *Recreations:* music, squash, travel. *Address:* Brooklands, Southover High Street, Lewes, E Sussex BN7 1HU. *T:* 07970 909891. *E:* davidandjudyhawker@gmail.com.

HAWKER, Hon. David Peter Maxwell, AO 2012; MP (L) Wannon, Vic, 1983–2010; Deputy Chairman, Joint Standing Committee on Foreign Affairs, Defence and Trade, Australia, 2008–10; *b* Adelaide, 1 May 1949; *s* of David Hawker and Pamela Gavin Hawker (*née* Anderson); *m* 1973, Penelope Ann Ahern; three *s* one *d*. *Educ:* Geelong Grammar Sch.; Univ. of Melbourne (BEng). Man. Dir, Newlands Pty Ltd (agricl business), 1973–. Shadow Minister for Land Transport, 1990–93; Opposition Whip, 1994–96; Mem., Speaker's panel, 1998–2004; Speaker, House of Reps, 2004–08. House of Representatives Standing Committees: Dep. Chm., Industry, Sci. and Technol., 1989–90; Chairman: Finance, Admin and Public Admin, 1996–98; Econs, Finance and Public Affairs, 1998–2004; Chm., Defence Sub-cttee, Jt Standing Cttee on Foreign Affairs, Defence and Trade, 1999–2001; Mem., Jt Select Cttee on Republic Referendum, 1999, on Intelligence Services, 2001–02; Chm., Govt Members Wool Cttee, 1996–2004. Chm., Liberal Party Fed. Rural Cttee, 1987–90. Dir, Abbeyfield Australia Ltd, 2011–. Chairman: Heart Morass Cttee of Govs, 2011–; Motorcycle Adv. Gp, VicRoads, 2011–; Victorian Shooting Sports Facilities Prog., 2014–; Mem., Victorian Hunting Adv. Cttee, 2013–14. Patron, Field and Game Australia, 2008–. Life Gov., Brauer Coll. Alumni Assoc., 2007–. *Publications:* Who Reaps the Benefits?: a chronicle of the wheat debate, 1989; (jtly) The Heart of Liberalism, 1994; Striking a Balance: the lack of adequate and comparable services for regional Australia, 1996. *Recreations:* shooting, golf, cycling. *Address:* PO Box 33, Apsley, Vic 3319, Australia. *Clubs:* Melbourne, Adelaide; Royal Melbourne Golf.

HAWKER, Graham Alfred, CBE 1999; DL; Chief Executive, Hyder (formerly Welsh Water) plc, 1991–2000 (Director of Finance, 1989–91); *b* 12 May 1947; *s* of Alfred Hawker and Sarah Rebecca (*née* Bowen); *m* 1967, Sandra Ann Evans; one *s* one *d*. *Educ:* Bedwellty Grammar Sch. CIPFA 1969; FCCA 1981. Trainee Acct, Caerphilly DC, 1964–66; Abercarn District Council: Acct, 1966–67; Chief Acct, 1967–68; Dep. Treas., 1968–70; Chief Auditor, Taf Fechan Water Bd, 1970–74; Welsh Water Authority: Audit Manager, 1974–78; Div. Finance Manager, 1978–84; Chief Acct, 1984–86; Dir, Planning and Develt, 1986–87; Dir, Finance, 1987–89. A Dir, Bank of England, 1998–2000. Chairman: Dŵr Cymru Ltd, 1993–2000; Hyder Consulting (formerly Acer), 1993–2000; Swalec, 1996–2000. Dep. Chm., 1998–2000, Chief Exec., 2000–04, Welsh Develt Agency. Chairman: BITC (Wales), 1994–2000; New Deal Task Force Adv. Cttee (Wales), 1997–98; Member: CBI Council for Wales, 1994–97; New Deal Adv. Cttee (UK), 1997–98; Prince of Wales' Review Cttee on Queen's Awards, 1999. Prince of Wales Ambassador's Award for Corporate Social Responsibility, 1999. CCMI. DL Gwent, 1998. Hon. Fellow, Univ. of Wales, Cardiff, 1999. Hon. Dr Glamorgan, 1996. *Recreations:* family, walking, wine. *Address:* St Teilo House, Llantilio Pertholey, Abergavenny NP7 6NY.

HAWKER, Stephen, CB 2005; FIET; FICPEM; Senior Civil Servant, Ministry of Defence, retired 2006; company director; *b* 1948; *s* of Derek Hawker and Pamela Hawker (*née* Holland); *m* 1989; one *s* one *d*. *Educ:* Worksop Coll.; Pembroke Coll., Oxford (MA 1970); Univ. of Nottingham (PGCE 1971). FIET (FIEE 2004); FICPEM 2009. Hd of Dept, King James's Coll. of Henley, 1971–78; MoD, 1978–2006; on secondment: to NI Office, 1981–83 and 1998–2000; to Cabinet Office, 1989–92. Nat. Security Advr, Defence Strategy and Solutions, 2006–08. Man. Dir, SHD Consulting Ltd, 2006–. Cityforum Associate, 2014–. Chm., Critical-Link Ltd, 2014–. Non-exec. Dir, FCO Services, 2009–. Mem. Adv. Bd, BAE Systems Applied Intelligence (formerly Detica, then BAE Systems Detica), 2007–14; Bd Advr, Edson Tiger Ltd, 2014–; Member: Lord Chancellor's Adv. Council on Nat. Records and Archives, 2011–; Security Vetting Appeals Panel, 2015–. Vis. Prof., Cranfield Univ., 2006–12. Mem., Audit Cttee, EPSRC, 2013–. Lay Mem. Council, Reading Univ., 2007–. *E:* stephen.hawker@tiscali.co.uk.

HAWKES, Prof. David John, PhD; FREng; CPhys, FInstP; FIPEM; FMedSci; Professor of Computational Imaging Science, and Director, Centre of Medical Image Computing, University College London, since 2005; *b* 16 Jan. 1953; *s* of Roy and Joyce Hawkes; *m* 1978, Elizabeth Anne Nicholson; two *d*. *Educ:* Christ Church, Oxford (BA 2nd cl. Hons Natural Scis (Physics)); Univ. of Birmingham (MSc Radiobiol.); Univ. of Surrey (PhD 1982). FIPEM 1993; CPhys, FInstP 1997. Principal Physicist and Hd, Imaging and Med. Physics, St George's Hosp., London, 1984–88; Sen. Lectr, 1988–93, Reader in Radiol Scis, 1993–98, Guy's Hosp.; Prof. of Computational Imaging Sci., 1998–2004, and Chm., Div. of Imaging Scis, Sch. of Medicine, 2002–04, KCL. Dir, Interdisciplinary Res. Collaboration in Med. Images and Signals, 2003–07. Sen. Investigator, NIHR, 2010. Hon. Consultant Physicist, Guy's and St Thomas' NHS Trust, 1989–. FREng 2003; FBIR 2007; Fellow, Soc. of Med. Image Computing and Computer Assisted Interventions, 2009; FMedSci 2011. Business Fellow, London Technol. Network, 2003. William Roentgen Hon. Lect., Eur. Congress of Radiol., Vienna, 2006; Crookshank Lect. and Medal, RCR, 2008. *Publications:* (ed with A. Colchester) Information Processing in Medical Imaging, 1991; (ed jtly) Medical Image Registration, 2000; over 270 peer reviewed papers on med. imaging. *Recreations:* sailing, ski-ing, windsurfing, hill-climbing, trekking, mountain biking, musician. *Address:* Centre of Medical Image Computing, Department of Medical Physics, University College London, Gower Street, WC1E 6BT.

HAWKES, Sir (John) Garry, Kt 2009; CBE 1999; company director; Chief Executive, Gardner Merchant, 1978–98; Director, Trusthouse Forte, 1983–93; *b* 26 Aug. 1939; *s* of John and Joyce Hawkes; *m* 1963, Peggy Lee; one *d*. *Educ:* Rowlinson Sch., Sheffield; Huddersfield Coll. of Technology. Joined Gardner Merchant, 1963; Regl Dir, 1972–76; European Man. Dir, 1976; Man. Dir, Gardner Merchant Ltd, 1977–95. Directeur Général, Sodexho SA, 1995–98; Chm., Cheese Cellar Co., 2000–07; Vice-Chm., Accord plc, 2005–07 (Dir, 2000–07); Dir, Investors in People, 2000–06; non-exec. Dir, Internat. Skills Standards Orgn. Chairman: Nat. Council, NTO, 1997–2001; British Trng Internat., 1997–2001; ARAMARK UK, 2000–04; Edexcel, 2000–05; Basic Skills Agency, 2002–07; Guidance Accreditation Bd, 2002–05; Vice Chm., London Qualifications, 2003–05. Pres., Hospitality Action, 1996–2004. Pres., Edge Foundn, 2009– (Chm., 2004–09). FIH (FHCIMA 1982). Hon. Fellow: Huddersfield Univ., 1996; Oxford Brookes Univ., 1997. *Recreations:* theatre, modern design, travel. *Address:* Coalpit, Rookery Way, Haywards Heath, W Sussex RH16 4RE.

HAWKES, Michael John; Deputy Chairman, Kleinwort, Benson Group plc, 1988–90; *b* 7 May 1929; *s* of Wilfred Arthur Hawkes and Anne Maria Hawkes; *m* 1st, 1957, Gillian Mary Watts; two *s* two *d*; 2nd, 1973, Elizabeth Anne Gurton. *Educ:* Bedford School; New College, Oxford (Exhibnr; MA); Gray's Inn. Kleinwort Sons & Co. Ltd, 1954; Kleinwort, Benson Ltd: Director, 1967; Vice Chm., 1974; Dep. Chm., 1982; Chm., 1983–87; Director, Kleinwort, Benson, Lonsdale plc, 1974–88; Chairman: Sharps Pixley Ltd, 1971–89; Kleinwort Benson Investment Trust, 1984–89. Mem., Management Bd, Sovereign (formerly W Berks) Housing Assoc., 1988–97. Gov., The Willink Sch., 1988–96. *Recreations:* long distance walking, gardening. *Address:* Brookfield House, Burghfield Common, Berks RG7 3BD. *T:* (0118) 983 2912; White Bays, Daymer Lane, Trebetherick, N Cornwall PL27 6SA. *T:* (01208) 862280. *Club:* Leander (Henley on Thames).

HAWKES, Nigel John Mytton, CBE 1999; Director, Straight Statistics, 2008–11; *b* 1 Sept. 1943; *s* of late R. W. Hawkes, MBE and K. M. Hawkes; *m* 1971, Jo Beresford; two *s* one *d*. *Educ:* Sedbergh Sch.; St Catherine's Coll., Oxford (MA). Mem., editl staff, Nature, 1966–69; Sci. Editor, Science Jl, 1969–70; Associate Editor, Telegraph Mag., 1970–72; The Observer: Sci. Corresp., 1972–81; Foreign News Editor, 1981–83; Diplomatic Corresp., 1983–87; Diplomatic Editor, 1987–90; The Times: Science Editor, 1990–2000; Health Editor, 2000–08. Columnist, BMJ, 2007–. Mem., Adv. Bd, Ultrasis plc, 2008–14. Gov., British Nutrition Foundn, 1999–2006 (British Nutrition Foundn Award, 1992). Chm., Friends of Woodchurch Windmill, 2002–06. Health Journalist Award, MJA, 2007; Freelance Journalist Award, MJA, 2011. *Publications:* The Computer Revolution, 1971; Early Scientific Instruments, 1978; (ed and contrib.) Tearing Down the Curtain, 1989; Structures, 1991; Man on the Move, 1992; numerous science and technology titles for children and teenagers. *Recreations:* walking, opera. *Address:* Well House, Front Road, Woodchurch, Kent TN26 3QE. *T:* (01233) 860518.

HAWKES, Richard Charles; Chief Executive, Scope, since 2010; *b* Wolverhampton, 1 Dec. 1964; *s* of Geoffrey Lawrence Hawkes and Vivienne Wendy Hawkes; *m* 1996, Emily Catto; one *s* two *d*. *Educ:* Wolverhampton Grammar Sch.; Univ. of Manchester (BA Econs 1987). Pres., Univ. of Manchester Students' Union, 1988; Nat. Sec., NUS, 1989–90; Consultant, UN, 1990–92; Internat. Dir, Austrian NUS, 1992–94; Chief Exec., Sense International, 1994–2006; Internat. Dir, VSO, 2006–09. Chm., Bond, 2004–08; Member: Progs Bd, Sightsavers, 2007–; BBC Charity Appeals Adv. Cttee, 2009–; Trustee: iPartner India, 2006– (Chm., 2009–); Skills—Third Sector, 2009–; Voluntary Organisations Disability Gp, 2011–. *Recreations:* family, sport, politics. *Address:* 49 Jerome Drive, St Albans AL3 4LT. *T:* (01727) 750246. *E:* richard.hawkes@scope.org.uk.

HAWKESBURY, Viscount; Luke Marmaduke Peter Savile Foljambe; Director, Savills PLC, since 2012; *b* 25 March 1972; *s* and *heir* of 5th Earl of Liverpool, *qv*; *m* 2013, Katharine, *d* of Jeffrey and Sandra Davis. *Educ:* Ampleforth; Roehampton Inst. With Property Vision Ltd, 1999–2001; with Savills PLC (formerly FPDSavills Ltd), 2001–: Associate Dir, 2009–12. *Recreations:* golf, shooting, fishing. *Clubs:* Turf, Quo Vadis, 5 Hertford Street.

HAWKESWORTH, Prof. Christopher John, DPhil; FRS 2002; FRSE; Wardlaw Professor of Earth Sciences, and Deputy Principal and Vice-Principal (Research), University of St Andrews, 2009–14, now Professor Emeritus; Senior Research Fellow, University of Bristol, since 2014; *b* 18 Dec. 1947; *s* of Desmond and Ann Hawkesworth; *m* 1972, Elizabeth Celia Williams; one *d*. *Educ:* Trinity Coll., Dublin (BA Hons); St Edmund Hall, Oxford (DPhil). NERC Res. Fellow, Univ. of Leeds, 1975–78; Open University: Lectr, 1978–83; Sen. Lectr, 1983–88; Prof., 1988–2000; Prof. of Earth Scis, Bristol Univ., 2000–09. Internat. Sec., Geochemical Soc., 1995–97; Member: NERC Earth Scis and Technology Bd, 1996–99; Res. and Knowledge Exchange Cttee, SFC, 2011–15. Pres., European Assoc. for Geochemistry, 1997–98; Sci. Sec., Geol Soc. of London, 1999–2002; Vice-Pres., European Union of Geosciences, 2001–03. Fellow: American Geophysical Union, 2000; Geochemical Soc., 2001; FRSE 2012. Hon. DSc Copenhagen, 2000. Maj. John Coke Medal, Geol Soc. of London, 1996; Schlumberger Medal, Mineralog. Soc., 2002; Wolfson Merit Award, Royal Soc., 2008; Wollaston Medal, Geol Soc. of London, 2012; Robert Bunsen Medal, Eur. Geoscis Union, 2014. *Publications:* (ed jtly) The Early Earth: physical, chemical and biological development, 2002; edited jointly: Continental Basalts and Mantle Xenoliths, 1983; Mantle Metasomatism, 1987; Understanding the Earth, II, 1992; Chemical Geology, festschrift for A. W. Hofmann, 1997; 320 scientific papers. *Recreations:* hill walking, sports, photography, reading predominantly non-fiction, gardening. *Address:* Woodbine Cottage, Kirtlington, Oxon OX5 3HA. *T:* (01869) 350304. *E:* c.j.hawkesworth@bristol.ac.uk.

HAWKESWORTH, Gareth; *see* Hawkesworth, W. G.

HAWKESWORTH, His Honour (Thomas) Simon (Ashwell); QC 1982; a Circuit Judge, 1999–2011; *b* 15 Nov. 1943; *s* of late Charles Peter Elmhirst Hawkesworth and Felicity Hawkesworth; *m* 1st, 1970, Jennifer Lewis (marr. diss. 1989); two *s*; 2nd, 1990, Dr May Bamber, MD, MRCP; twin *s*. *Educ:* Rugby Sch.; The Queen's Coll., Oxford (MA). Called to the Bar, Gray's Inn, 1967, Bencher 1990; a Recorder, 1982–99. Mem., Mental Health Tribunal, 2009–13.

See also W. G. Hawkesworth.

HAWKESWORTH, (Walter) Gareth; His Honour Judge Gareth Hawkesworth; a Circuit Judge, since 1999; *b* 29 Dec. 1949; *s* of late Charles Peter Elmhirst Hawkesworth and of Felicity Hawkesworth (*née* Ashwell); *m* 1982, Barbara Joyce Tapper; one *s* one *d*, and one step *d*. *Educ:* Rugby Sch.; Magdalene Coll., Cambridge (Schol.; BA 2nd Cl. Hons Law, MA); Council of Legal Educn. Called to the Bar, Gray's Inn, 1972; joined Fenners Chambers,

Cambridge, 1974; a Recorder, 1995–99; Resident Judge, Cambridge Crown Court, 2007–15; Hon. Recorder, City of Cambridge, 2013–15. *Recreations:* gardening, theatre, travel. *See also T. S. A. Hawkesworth.*

HAWKEY, Prof. Peter Michael, MD, DSc; FRCPath; Professor of Clinical and Public Health Bacteriology, Medical School, University of Birmingham, since 2001; Honorary Consultant, Heart of England Hospital, since 2001; West Midlands Lead Public Health Microbiologist (formerly West Midlands Regional Microbiologist), Public Health England (formerly Health Protection Agency), since 2005; *b* London, 21 Feb. 1951; *s* of Reginald Hawkey and Joan Hawkey; *m* 2006, Susan Fiona Cole; two *d* and one step *s* two step *d. Educ:* Univ. of East Anglia (BSc Hons Plant and Gen. Microbiol. 1972); King's Coll. Hosp., Univ. of London (MB BS 1978); Univ. of Bristol (MD 1983); Univ. of Leeds (DSc 2002). FRCPath 1984. Lectr and Hon. Sen. Registrar, Univ. of Bristol, 1979–85; University of Leeds: Lectr, 1985–88; Sen. Lectr, 1988–90; Reader, 1990–93; Prof. of Med. Microbiol., 1993–2001; Hon. Consultant, 1985–2001. Chairman: DoH Cttee on controlling Clostridium difficile infection, 2007–14; Scientific Cttee, Nat. External Quality Assessment Service, 2010–. *Publications:* (ed with D. Lewis) Medical Bacteriology: a practical approach, 1989, 2nd edn 2004; (ed with S. H. Gillespie) Medical Parasitology: a practical approach, 1995; (ed jtly) Principles and Practice of Clinical Bacteriology, 1997, 2nd edn 2006; over 250 articles on antibiotic resistance and hospital infection. *Recreations:* motor racing, restoring old sporting cars, gardening, ski-ing, horse riding, breeding Burmese cats. *Address:* West Midlands Public Health Laboratory, Heart of England NHS Foundation Trust, Birmingham B9 5SS. *T:* (0121) 424 1240, *Fax:* (0121) 772 6229. *E:* peter.hawkey@heartofengland.nhs.uk. *Club:* Farmers.

HAWKHEAD, Sir Anthony Gerard, (Sir Tony), Kt 2011; CBE 2003; Chief Executive, Action for Children, since 2014; *b* 7 Oct. 1957; *s* of late Harry and of Mary Hawkhead; *m* 1981, Marion Small; one *d* (one *s* decd). *Educ:* Whitefriars Sch., Cheltenham. Various policy and finance jobs, MoD, 1978–87; HEOD, Inner Cities Unit, DTI, 1987–88; Leader, Govt's N Peckham Task Force, 1988–89; Hd, Business and Econ. Develt, LDDC, 1989–91; Chief Executive: E London Partnership, 1991–96; Groundwork UK, 1996–2014. Mem., non-exec. Bd, DEFRA, 2011–. Chm., W Warks Develt Trust, 2011–14. FRSA. Hon. FCIWEM 2005; Hon. Fellow, Inst. of Employability Professionals, 2013. *Recreations:* tennis, cricket, music, wine, France. *Address:* Action for Children. 3 The Boulevard, Ascot Road, Watford WD18 8AG. *T:* (01923) 361500. *E:* ask.us@actionforchildren.org.uk. *Clubs:* Mandarins Cricket; W Warks Sports.

HAWKING, Prof. Stephen William, CH 1989; CBE 1982; FRS 1974; Fellow of Gonville and Caius College, Cambridge; Lucasian Professor of Mathematics, Cambridge University, 1979–2009, now Emeritus; *b* Oxford, 8 Jan. 1942; *s* of Dr F. and Mrs E. I. Hawking; *m* 1st, 1965, Jane Wilde (marr. diss. 1995); two *s* one *d*; 2nd, 1995, Elaine Mason (marr. diss. 2007). *Educ:* St Albans Sch.; University Coll., Oxford (BA), Hon. Fellow 1977; Trinity Hall, Cambridge (PhD), Hon. Fellow 1984. Research Fellow, Gonville and Caius Coll., 1965–69; Fellow for distinction in science, 1969–; Mem. Inst. of Theoretical Astronomy, Cambridge, 1968–72; Research Asst, Inst. of Astronomy, Cambridge, 1972–73; Cambridge University: Research Asst, Dept of Applied Maths and Theoretical Physics, 1973–75; Reader in Gravitational Physics, 1975–77, Professor, 1977–79. Fairchild Distinguished Schol., Calif Inst. of Technol., 1974–75. Reith Lectr, 2015. Mem., Pontifical Acad. of Scis, 1986–; Foreign Mem., Amer. Acad. of Arts and Scis, 1984; Internat. Mem. (formerly Foreign Mem.), Amer. Philosophical Soc., 1985. Hon. Mem., RAS (Can), 1985. Hon. DSc: Oxon, 1978; Newcastle, Leeds, 1987; Cambridge, 1989; hon. degrees: Chicago, 1981; Leicester, New York, Notre Dame, Princeton, 1982; Tufts, Yale, 1989; Harvard, 1990. (Jtly) Eddington Medal, RAS, 1975; Pius XI Gold Medal, Pontifical Acad. of Scis, 1975; Dannie Heinemann Prize for Math. Phys., Amer. Phys. Soc. and Amer. Inst. of Physics, 1976; William Hopkins Prize, Cambridge Philosoph. Soc., 1976; Maxwell Medal, Inst. of Physics, 1976; Hughes Medal, Royal Soc., 1976; Albert Einstein Award, 1978; Albert Einstein Medal, Albert Einstein Soc., Berne, 1979; Franklin Medal, Franklin Inst., USA, 1981; Gold Medal, RAS, 1985; Paul Dirac Medal and Prize, Inst. of Physics, 1987; (jtly) Wolf Foundn Prize for Physics, 1988; Britannica Award, 1989; Prince of Asturias Foundn Award, Spain, 1989; Julius Edgar Lilienfeld Prize, 1999; Klein Medal, Nobel Inst., 2003; Michelson Award, Case Western Univ., 2003; James Smithson Bicentennial Medal, Smithsonian Inst., Washington, 2005; Copley Medal, Royal Soc., 2006; Fonseca Prize, Univ. of Santiago de Compostela, Spain, 2008; US Presidential Medal of Freedom, 2009; Cosmos Award for outstanding public presentation of Science, Planetary Soc., 2010; Special Fundamental Physics Prize, Fundamental Physics Prize Foundn, 2012. *Publications:* (with G. F. R. Ellis) The Large Scale Structure of Space-Time, 1973; (ed W. W. Israel) General Relativity: an Einstein centenary survey, 1979; (ed with M. Roček) Superspace and Supergravity, 1981; (ed jtly) The Very Early Universe, 1983; (with W. Israel) 300 Years of Gravitation, 1987; A Brief History of Time, 1988; Black Holes and Baby Universes, 1993; The Universe in a Nutshell, 2001 (Aventis Prize for Sci. Bks, 2002); A Briefer History of Time, 2005; (with Lucy Hawking) George's Secret Key to the Universe (for children), 2007; (ed) A Stubbornly Persistent Illusion: the essential writings of Albert Einstein, 2008; The Grand Design, 2010; (with Lucy Hawking) George's Cosmic Treasure Hunt (for children), 2009; My Brief History, 2013. *Address:* Department of Applied Mathematics and Theoretical Physics, Centre for Mathematical Sciences, Wilberforce Road, Cambridge CB3 0WA. *T:* (01223) 337843.

HAWKINS, Very Rev. Alun John; Dean of Bangor, 2004–11; *b* 28 May 1944; *m* 1971, Ann Deborah Williams, HMI; two *s. Educ:* King's Coll. London (BA, AKC 1966); Univ. of Wales, Bangor (BD 1981); St Deiniol's, Hawarden. Lecturer: in English and Drama, St Mary's Coll. of Educn, Bangor, 1969–77; in Educn, UCNW, Bangor, 1977–79; Chief Examiner, Drama and Th. Arts, Associated Examg Bd, 1971–76. Ordained deacon, 1981, priest, 1982; Curate, Dwygyfylchi, 1981–84; Rector, Llanberis, 1984–89; Tutor, Diocesan NSM Course, 1985–90, Dir of Ordinands, 1986–90, Dio. Bangor; Vicar, Knighton and Norton, 1989–93; Canon Residentiary and Missioner, Bangor Cathedral, and Vicar in Bangor Rectorial Benefice, 1993–2000; Archdeacon of Bangor, 2000–04. Chaplain, Knighton Hosp., 1989–93. Chm., Governing Body, Church in Wales, 2007–11. Archbishop's Commissary, 2004. *Address:* Carreg Wen, 9 Cil y Graig, Llanfairpwll, Anglesey LL61 5NZ. *T:* (01248) 717403.

HAWKINS, Prof. Anthony Donald, CBE 2000; PhD; FRSE; Managing Director, Loughine Ltd, since 2002; Director, Aquatic Noise Trust, since 2011; *b* 25 March 1942; *s* of Kenneth St David Hawkins and Marjorie Lillian Hawkins; *m* 1966, Susan Mary Fulker; one *s. Educ:* Poole Grammar Sch.; Bristol Univ. (BSc 1st Cl. Hons Zoology, 1963; PhD 1968). Dept of Agriculture and Fisheries for Scotland: Scientific Officer, Marine Lab., Aberdeen, 1965, Chief Scientific Officer, 1987; Dir of Fisheries Res., Scottish Office Agriculture and Fisheries Dept, subseq. Dir of Fisheries Res. Services, Scottish Exec., 1987–2002; Hon. Res. Prof., 1987–, Prof. of Marine Resource Mgt, 2002–06, Univ. of Aberdeen; Chm., N Sea Commn Fisheries Partnership, 2002–05. Consultant to FAO, Peru, 1975; Hon. Lectr, Univ. of St Andrews, 1983. Rapporteur, North Sea Regl Adv. Council, 2004–. FRSE 1988. A. B. Wood Medal and Prize, Inst. of Acoustics, 1978. *Publications:* (ed and contrib.) Sound Reception in Fish, 1976; (ed and contrib.) Aquarium Systems, 1981; pubns on marine science, fish physiology and salmon biology. *Recreations:* angling, whippet breeding. *Address:* Kincraig, Blairs, Aberdeen AB12 5YT. *T:* (01224) 868984. *E:* a.hawkins@btconnect.com.

HAWKINS, Catherine Eileen, CBE 1992; World Health Organisation Consultant to Middle Eastern Sector, since 1993; debt consultant; *b* 16 Jan. 1939; *d* of Stanley Richard Hawkins and Mary-Kate Hawkins. *Educ:* La Retraite High Sch., Clifton. SRN, CMB (Pt 1), HVCert, DN London, Queen's Inst. of Nursing Cert, IRCert, DipIT. General nursing, student, 1956–59; Staff Nursing, Charing Cross Hosp., SRN, 1960–61; Pt 1 midwifery, St Thomas' Hosp., 1961; Health Visitor Student, LCC, RCN, 1961–62; LCC Health Visitor, 1962–63; Bristol CC HV, 1963–64; Project Leader, Bahrain Public Health Service, 1964–66; Field Work Teacher, HV, 1966–68; Health Centre Administrator, 1968–71; Administrator, Res. Div., Health Educn Council, 1971–72; Sen. Nursing Officer, Community Services, 1972–74; Area Nurse Service Capital Planning, Avon AHA, 1974–79; Dist Nursing Officer, Bristol and Weston DHA, 1979–82; Chief Nursing Officer, Southmead DHA, 1982–84; Regional Nursing Officer, 1984, Regl Gen. Manager, 1984–93, SW RHA. Non-exec. Dir, N Bristol NHS Trust, 1999–2003. *Address:* Dun An Octa, Haggard, Ramsgrange, Co. Wexford, Eire.

HAWKINS, Christopher James; Deputy Chairman, Black Country Development Corporation, 1992–98; non-executive chairman of a number of cos, 1988–99; *b* 26 Nov. 1937; *s* of Alec Desmond Hawkins and Christina Barbara; *m* Susan Ann Hawkins; two *d. Educ:* Bristol Grammar Sch.; Bristol Univ. BA (Hons) Economics. Joined Courtaulds Ltd, Head Office Economics Dept, 1959; seconded to UK aid financed industrial and economic survey of Northern Nigeria, 1960; similar mission to Tunisia to work on 5 year plan, 1961; Research Div. Economist, Courtaulds Ltd, 1961–66, Building Develt Manager, 1965–66; Lectr in Economics, 1966, Sen. Lectr, 1973–83, Univ. of Southampton. MP (C) High Peak, 1983–92. *Publications:* Capital Investment Appraisal, 1971; Theory of the Firm, 1973; The British Economy: what will our children think?, 1982; Britain's Economic Future: an immediate programme for revival, 1983; articles in Jl of Industrial Economics, Amer. Economic Review. *Recreations:* reading, music, sailing.

HAWKINS, Rt Rev. David John Leader; Area Bishop of Barking, 2002–14; *b* 30 March 1949; *s* of John Mitchell and Monica Mary Hawkins; *m* 1973, Carole Gladwin; three *d. Educ:* Kingsmead Sch.; Wrekin Coll.; London Coll. of Divinity (ALCD 1973); St John's Coll., Nottingham; Nottingham Univ. (BTh, LTh 1973). Teacher, Mbiruri Secondary Sch., Embu, Kenya, 1968–69. Ordained deacon, 1973, priest, 1974; Curate, St Andrew's, Bebington, 1973–76; Founding Warden, Bida Bible Trng Centre, Northern Nigeria, 1976–82; Vicar, St John's, Bida, and Acting Archdeacon, Bida Archdeaconry, 1979–82; Priest i/c, St Matthew's with St Luke's, Oxford, 1983–86; Vicar, 1986–99, Team Rector, 1999–2002, St George's, Leeds. Diocese of Chelmsford: Hd Bishop for Mission and Parish Develt, 2004–14; Hd Bishop for Youth, 2005–14; Archbp's Advr for Black Majority Churches, 2006–14; Lead Bishop: Global Christian Forum, 2005–; for 2012 Olympic and Paralympic Games, 2006–13. Canon Emeritus, Kaduna, Nigeria, 1982. Chaplain, Yorks CCC, 1986–2002. Dir, Ashlar House, 1986–2001; Exec. Trustee, St George's Crypt, 1986–2002; Chair, Leeds Faith in Schs, 1993–2002; Pres., Global Day of Prayer, London, 2012– (Chm., 2007–12). Patron: Commn for Mission; Haven Hse, Woodford, 2012–. Life Pres., Bardsey Bird and Field Observatory, 2008. *Recreations:* painting, music, bird watching, mountain walking, sailing, running, poetry.

HAWKINS, Air Vice-Marshal David Richard; *see* Hawkins-Leth.

HAWKINS, Air Vice-Marshal Desmond Ernest, CB 1971; CBE 1967; DFC and Bar, 1942; *b* 27 Dec. 1919; *s* of Ernest and Lilian Hawkins; *m* 1947, Joan Audrey (*née* Munro); one *s*, and one step *s. Educ:* Bancroft's Sch. Commissioned in RAF, 1938. Served War of 1939–45: Coastal Command and Far East, commanding 36, 230 and 240 Sqdns, 1940–46 (despatches). Commanded RAF Pembroke Dock, 1946–47 (despatches). Staff appts, 1947–50; RAF Staff Coll., 1950; Staff appts, 1951–55; commanded 38 Sqdn, OC Flg, RAF Luqa, 1955–57; jssc, 1957; Staff appts, 1958–61; SASO 19 Gp, 1961–63; commanded RAF Tengah, 1963–66; idc 1967; commanded RAF Lyneham, 1968; SASO, HQ, RAF Strike Command, 1969–71; Dir-Gen., Personal Services (RAF), MoD, 1971–74; Dep. Man. Dir, Services Kinema Corp., 1974–80. *Recreation:* sailing. *Club:* Royal Cruising.

HAWKINS, James Bruce, MA; Head Master, Harrow School, since 2011; *b* Sussex, 10 Dec. 1965; *s* of Dr Philip John Clare Hawkins and José Phyllis Hawkins (*née* Thorneloe); *m* 1999, Zoë Antonia Neeves; one *d. Educ:* King Edward VI Sch., Camp Hill, Birmingham; Brasenose Coll., Oxford (MA Maths; PGCE). Asst Master, Radley Coll., 1988–92; Hd of Maths, Forest Sch., 1992–97; Dep. Hd, Chigwell Sch., 1997–2002; Head Master, Norwich Sch., 2002–11. Vice-Pres., Internat. Boys' Sch. Coalition, 2014–. Trustee: Compassion UK, 2002–11; Norman's Foundn, 2003–11. Governor: Old Sch., Henstead, 2003–11; The Open Acad., Norwich, 2008–11; City Acad., Norwich, 2009–11; John Lyon Sch., 2011–; Orley Farm Sch., 2011–; Aysgarth Sch., 2011–; Wellesley House, 2011–. *Recreations:* music, films, cafés, crosswords. *Address:* Harrow School, Harrow-on-the-Hill, Middx HA1 3HT. *T:* (020) 8872 8000. *Clubs:* East India, Lansdowne.

HAWKINS, Dr John, OBE 2001; Programme (formerly Project) Manager, Knowledge and Learning Centres, British Council, 2001–04; *b* 13 Oct. 1944; *s* of Maurice and Anna Hawkins; *m* 1968, Pamela June Donnelly; one *s* one *d. Educ:* Reading Univ. (BSc Physical Properties of Materials; PhD); Univ. of East Anglia (MA Develt Studies, 1994). Joined British Council, 1971; served Lahore, Islamabad, Bogotá, and Buenos Aires; Budget Department: Management Accountant, 1980–85; Dir, 1985–91; Manager, HQ Relocation Project, 1991–92; Head, Accommodation Services, 1992–93; Regl Dir, W Africa, 1994–97; Dir, Africa and S Asia, 1997–2000; Acting Dir of Finance, 2000; Special Projects, 2000–01. Voluntary work for charities, DISCET UK and Kings Church, Wokingham, 2004–. JP Reading, 2006–14. *Recreations:* running, walking, carpentry. *Address:* 50 Gipsy Lane, Earley, Reading RG6 7HD.

HAWKINS, Prof. John Alan, PhD; Professor of English and Applied Linguistics, University of Cambridge, 2004–13, now Emeritus; Professor of Linguistics, University of California, Davis, since 2007. *Educ:* Trinity Hall, Cambridge (BA 1970; PhD 1975). Lectr, Univ. of Essex, 1973–77; Univ. of Southern Calif, 1977–2004, latterly as Prof. of Linguistics; Max Planck Inst. for Psycholinguistics, Nijmegen, 1982–85. *Publications:* Definiteness and Indefiniteness, 1978; Word Order Universals, 1983; A Comparative Typology of English and German, 1986; A Performance Theory of Order and Constituency, 1994; Efficiency and Complexity in Grammars, 2004. *Address:* Research Centre for English and Applied Linguistics, University of Cambridge, 9 West Road, Cambridge CB3 9DP.

HAWKINS, Prof. John David, FBA 1993; Professor of Ancient Anatolian Languages, School of Oriental and African Studies, University of London, 1993–2005, now Emeritus; *b* 11 Sept. 1940; *s* of John and Audrey Hawkins. *Educ:* Bradfield Coll.; University Coll., Oxford (BA 1962; MA 1965); Inst. of Archaeol., Univ. of London (Postgrad. Dip. 1964). School of Oriental and African Studies, University of London: Res. Fellow, 1964–67; Lectr, then Sen. Lectr, 1967–93. *Publications:* The Hieroglyphic Inscription of the Sacred Pool Complex at Boğazköy-Hattusa, 1995; Corpus of Hieroglyphic Luwian Inscriptions, vol. I, parts 1–3, 2000. *Recreations:* gardening, political cartoons, caricature. *Address:* School of Oriental and African Studies, University of London, Thornhaugh Street, WC1H 0XG. *T:* (020) 7734 5409.

HAWKINS, Ven. John Edward Inskipp; Archdeacon of Hampstead, since 2015; *b* 6 June 1963; *s* of Jeremy and Elizabeth Hawkins; *m* 1st, 1986, Emma Woodhead (*d* 1990); 2nd, 1999, Desiree Shakes; two step *d. Educ:* King's Coll. London (BD 1985); Queen's Coll., Birmingham. Ordained deacon, 1988, priest, 1989; Curate, Holy Trinity, Birchfield, 1988–92; Curate, 1992–93, Team Vicar, 1993–99, All Saints, Poplar; Vicar, St John, W Hendon, 1999–2015; Area Dean, W Barnet, 2004–09; Priest-in-charge, St Matthias, Colindale, 2007–15; Preb., St Paul's Cathedral, 2013–15.

HAWKINS, John Mark; HM Diplomatic Service, retired; Ambassador to Qatar, 2008–12; *b* 30 April 1960; *s* of John Clement Hawkins and Diana Margaret Hawkins (*née* Townsend); *m* 1991, Rosemarie Anne Kleynhans; two *s. Educ:* Bedford Sch.; New Coll., Oxford (MA

Modern Hist.). Mgt trainee, J. Sainsbury plc, 1981–82; joined HM Diplomatic Service, 1982; FCO, 1982–84; Third, later Second, Sec. (Chancery), Pretoria/Cape Town, 1984–88; FCO, 1989–93; First Sec. (Commercial), New Delhi, 1993–96; Internat. Dir, Invest in Britain Bureau, 1997–99; Counsellor and Dir, Trade and Investment Promotion for Spain, Madrid, 2000–04; Consul Gen., Dubai, 2004–08; Fellow, Sheikh Nasser bin Muhammed Al Sabah Prog., Durham Univ., 2012; special unpaid leave, HM Diplomatic Service, 2012–15. Mem., Adv. Bd, Delancey Real Estate Mgt, 2013–; Sen. Advr, ME, Jockey Club and Ascot Racecourse, 2015–. *Recreations:* travel, family, sport, especially horseracing. *Club:* Mandarins Cricket.

HAWKINS, Dr Kevin Howard, OBE 2004; Director General, British Retail Consortium, 2004–08; *b* 25 Aug. 1947; *s* of Jack and Mary Hawkins; *m* 1972, Doreen Margaret Duff. *Educ:* Keighley Boys' Grammar Sch.; Gonville and Caius Coll., Cambridge (BA 1968, MA 1972); Univ. of Bradford (MSc 1970; PhD 1981); Nuffield Coll., Oxford (BLitt 1971). Lectr in Industrial Relns, Univ. of Bradford Mgt Centre, 1970–82; Director: CBI W Midlands, 1982–84; Public Affairs, Lucas Industries plc, 1984–89; Corporate Affairs, WH Smith Gp plc, 1989–95; Dir of Communications, Safeway plc, 1995–2004. Member: MLC, 2002–08; Better Regulation Commn (formerly Task Force), 2002–06; Scottish Food and Health Council, 2004–06; Retail Policy Forum, DTI, 2004–08; Food Industry Better Regulation Gp, 2006–08, Food Industry Sustainability Strategy Gp, 2006–08, DEFRA; Nat. Retail Crime Steering Gp, 2007–08. Chm., Retail Industry Business Engagement Adv. Gp, 2009–. Non-exec. Dir, Internat. Food Exhibn, 2009–. *Publications:* Unemployment, 1978, 3rd edn 1987; The Management of Industrial Relations, 1978; Trade Unions, 1980; Case Studies in Industrial Relations, 1982. *Recreations:* golf, military history, keep fit, local choral society. *Address:* c/o British Retail Consortium, 21 Dartmouth Street, SW1H 9BP.

HAWKINS, Neil Grant; Principal, Concord College, since 2005; *b* Aldershot, 5 Nov. 1965; *s* of Philip and Mary Hawkins; *m* 1989, Vanessa Pond; one *s*. *Educ:* Brentwood Sch.; Robinson Coll., Cambridge (BA Hist. 1988; PGCE). Teacher of History: Norwich Sch., 1989–92; Cranleigh Sch., 1992–94; Head of History: Cranleigh Sch., 1994–98; Sevenoaks Sch., 1998–2000; Dir of Studies, Leys Sch., 2000–05. Mem., Soc. of Heads, 2005–. *Recreations:* running, philosophy, reading, chatting, watching sport. *Address:* Concord College, Acton Burnell, Shrewsbury, Shropshire SY5 7PF. *T:* (01694) 731631. *E:* theprincipal@concordcollegeuk.com. *Club:* Rotary (Shrewsbury) (Hon. Mem.).

HAWKINS, Nicholas John; Chief Executive, LJM and AEPP (UK) Ltd, since 2015; *b* 27 March 1957; *s* of late Arthur Ernest Hawkins, PhD, FInstP, CPhys and of Patricia Jean Hawkins, BSc, BA (*née* Papworth); *m* 1st, 1979, Angela Margaret Turner, MA Oxon, CPFA (marr. diss. 2000); two *s* one *d*; 2nd, 2001, Jenny Cassar; one step *s* one step *d*. *Educ:* Bedford Modern Sch.; Lincoln Coll., Oxford (MA); Inns of Court Sch. of Law. ACIArb. Called to the Bar, Middle Temple, 1979 (Harmsworth Sen. Scholar). Practised from chambers in Birmingham and Northampton, 1979–86; worked in construction and recruitment, 1986–87; Company Legal Advr, Access, 1987–89; Gp Legal Advr, Lloyds Abbey Life plc, 1989–92; Corporate Lawyer, AMJ internat. law firm, Sultanate of Oman, 2005–06; Barrister: Harris Hagan, Solicitors, 2006–07; Gambling Governance, 2006–07; Advr, Plus Mkts, 2006–07; Consultant Hd of Gambling Law, Halliwells LLP, Solicitors, 2007; Legal Dir, 2007–11, Co. Sec., 2008–11, Danoptra Hldgs Ltd, later Danoptra Ltd; Hd of Legislation, Sport and Gambling Law, Spring Law Solicitors, 2011–12; Chief Exec., Acoustic Sensing Technology (UK) Ltd, 2012–14. Mem., Bar Council, 1988–95; Chm., Bar Assoc. for Commerce, Finance and Industry, 1994–95. Contested (C) Huddersfield, 1987. MP (C) Blackpool S, 1992–97, Surrey Heath, 1997–2005. PPS to Ministers of State, MoD, 1995–96, to Sec. of State for Nat. Heritage, 1996–97; opposition frontbench spokesman: on legal affairs, 1999–2001, 2002–03; on home affairs, 2000–03; on internat. develt, 2001–02. Member: Transport Select Cttee, 1993–95; Home Affairs Select Cttee, 1998–99; DCMS Select Cttee, 2004–05; Sec., Cons. backbench Educn Cttee, 1993–95; Vice Chairman: Cons. backbench Culture, Media and Sport (formerly Nat. Heritage) Cttee, 1997–2005; Cons. backbench Home Affairs Cttee, 1997–2005; Chm., Cons. backbench Sports Cttee, 1994–2005; Vice-Chairman: All-Party Sports Cttee, 1997–2005; All-Party Gp on Insurance and Financial Services, 1995–2005. Chm., W Lancs Support Gp, Marie Curie Cancer Care, 1992–96. *Publications:* booklets and articles on Conservative policy, transport hist., sport, legal and employment matters, and on gambling and sports law. *Recreations:* cricket, music, theatre, transport history, Rugby, soccer, swimming. *Address:* c/o The Corner House, 18 Mill Pightle, Aylsham, Norfolk NR11 6LX. *Clubs:* MCC; Lord's Taverners.

HAWKINS, Prof. Philip Nigel, PhD; FRCP, FRCPath; FMedSci; Professor of Medicine, and Head, Centre for Amyloidosis and Acute Phase Proteins, University College London, since 1999; Head, NHS National Amyloidosis Centre, Royal Free Hospital, London, since 1999; *b* London, 1959; *s* of Dr Warren Hawkins and Dr Margaret Hawkins (*née* Segar); *m* Dr Libi Deller; one *s*. *Educ:* Haberdashers' Aske's Sch., Elstree; Univ. of London (MB BS Hons 1982; PhD 1990). FRCP 1994; FRCPath 2004. Trng posts at St George's Hosp. Med. Sch., 1982–84 and RPMS, Hammersmith Hosp., 1984–89; Sen. Lectr in Medicine, 1990–94, Reader, 1994–99, RPMS, Hammersmith Hosp. MRC Trng Fellow, 1987–89. Goulstonian Lectr, 1995. Mem., Assoc. Physicians of GB and Ireland, 1993. FMedSci 2004. Wellcome Trust Univ. Award, 1997. *Publications:* contrib. papers on amyloidosis and inherited inflammatory disorders to learned jls. *Recreations:* thinking outside the box, sailing, windsurfing, walking on the beach, vehicle technology. *Address:* National Amyloidosis Centre, UCL Medical School, Royal Free Hospital, Rowland Hill Street, NW3 2PF. *T:* (020) 7433 2815. *E:* p.hawkins@ucl.ac.uk. *Club:* Hayling Island Sailing.

HAWKINS, Sir Richard Caesar, 9th Bt *cr* 1778, of Kelston, Somerset; *b* 29 Dec. 1958; *yr s* of Sir Humphry Hawkins, 7th Bt and of Anita, *d* of C. H. Funkey; *S* brother, 1999; *m* 1992, Ernestine Ehrensperger; one *s*. *Educ:* Hilton Coll., Natal; Witwatersrand Univ. Chartered Accountant (SA). Manager, 7 casinos and hotels, Sun International, SA, 2001–. Gov., Pridwin Prep. Sch., 2002–. *Heir: s* Jonathan Caesar Hawkins, *b* 23 June 1992. *Address:* PO Box 410838, Craighall Park, Johannesburg 2024, South Africa.

HAWKINS, His Honour Richard Graeme; QC 1984; a Circuit Judge, 1989–2012; *b* 23 Feb. 1941; *s* of late Denis William Hawkins and Norah Mary (*née* Beckingsale); *m* 1969, Anne Elizabeth, *d* of late Dr and Mrs Glyn Edwards, The Boltons, Bournemouth; one *s* one *d*. *Educ:* Hendon County Sch.; University College London (LLB Hons 1962). Called to the Bar, Gray's Inn, 1963, Bencher, 2003. A Recorder, 1985–89. Mem., Hon. Soc. of Gray's Inn, 1959–. Liveryman, Curriers' Co., 1995–. *Recreations:* sailing, University of the Third Age. *Club:* Garrick.

HAWKINS, Rt Rev. Richard Stephen; Suffragan Bishop of Crediton, 1996–2004; an Honorary Assistant Bishop, Diocese of Exeter, since 2005; *b* 2 April 1939; *s* of late Ven. Canon John Stanley Hawkins and Elsie Hawkins (*née* Briggs); *m* 1966, Valerie Ann Herneman; one *s* one *d* (and one *s* one *d* decd). *Educ:* Exeter School; Exeter Coll., Oxford; St Stephen's House, Oxford. MA (Oxon); BPhil (Exeter Univ.); CQSW. Asst Curate, St Thomas, Exeter, 1963–66; Team Vicar of Clyst St Mary, Clyst Valley Team Ministry, 1966–78; Bishop's Officer for Ministry and Joint Director, Exeter-Truro Ministry Training Scheme, 1978–81; Team Vicar, Central Exeter Team Ministry, 1978–81; Diocesan Director of Ordinands, Exeter, 1979–81; Priest-in-charge, Whitestone with Oldridge, 1981–87; Archdeacon of Totnes, 1981–88; Suffragan Bishop of Plymouth, 1988–96; Chapter Canon, Exeter Cathedral, 2006–09. *Address:* 3 Westbrook Close, Whipton, Exeter EX4 8BS. *T:* (01392) 462622.

HAWKINS, Prof. Robert Edward, PhD; FRCP; Cancer Research UK Professor, and Director of Medical Oncology, Christie Hospital NHS Trust, Manchester, and University of Manchester, since 1998; *b* 10 Nov. 1955; *s* of George Edward Russell Hawkins and Rosemary Anne Hawkins; *m* 1989, Gek Kee Lim; one *s*. *Educ:* Trinity Coll., Cambridge (BA (Maths) 1977); UCL (MB BS 1984); MRC Lab. of Molecular Biol., Cambridge (PhD 1994). MRCP 1988, FRCP 1999. MRC Trng Fellow, 1989–92, CRC Sen. Res. Fellow, 1992–96, MRC Lab. of Molecular Biol., Cambridge; Prof. of Oncology, Univ. of Bristol, 1996–98; Hon. Consultant, Christie Hosp. NHS Trust, Manchester, 1998–. Co-ordinator: EU Framework Prog. 6: ATTACK (Adoptive engineered T-cell Targeting to Activate Cancer Killing) Project, 2006–11; EU Framework Prog. 7: ATTRACT (Advanced Teaching and Training for Adoptive Cell Therapy), 2010–13; ATTACK clinical trial network, 2013–; NIHR/Efficacy and Mechanisms Evaluation Prog./MRC METILDA trial in metastatic melanoma, 2013–. Dir, Cellular Therapeutics Ltd, 2010–. Member: MRC Molecular and Cellular Medicine Bd, 2012–; World Immunotherapy Council, 2012–. Pres., Soc. for Cellular Therapy of Cancer, 2012–. Clinical Ed., British Jl of Cancer, 1996–2003. *Publications:* over 140 papers on cancer res. with emphasis on renal cancer, antibody technology, gene and immunotherapy. *Recreation:* golf. *Address:* Medical Oncology, Paterson Institute for Cancer Research, Wilmslow Road, Manchester M20 4BX. *T:* (0161) 446 3208, *Fax:* (0161) 446 3269. *E:* robert.hawkins@ics.manchester.ac.uk.

HAWKINS, Sally; actress; *b* Lewisham, London, 27 April 1976; *d* of Colin Hawkins and Jacqui Hawkins. *Educ:* James Allen Girls' Sch.; RADA. *Theatre* includes: As You Like It, Buckingham Palace Gala; Romeo and Juliet, The Cherry Orchard, Th. Royal, York, 1999; Much Ado About Nothing, A Midsummer Night's Dream, Regents Park, 2000; Country Music, Royal Court, 2004; House of Bernarda Alba, RNT, 2005; The Winterling, Royal Court, 2006; Mrs Warren's Profession, NY, 2010; Constellations, Royal Court, transf. Duke of York's, 2012; *films* include: All Or Nothing, 2002; Layer Cake, 2004; Vera Drake, 2005; Waz, 2007; Cassandra's Dream, Happy-Go-Lucky (Best Actress, LA Film Critics, NY Film Critics, Boston Film Critics, 2008, Amer. Nat. Soc. of Film Critics, 2009; Peter Sellers award for Comedy, Evening Standard Film Awards, Golden Globe for Best Actress in a Comedy or Musical, 2009), 2008; An Education, Desert Flower, 2009; Happy Ever Afters, It's a Wonderful Afterlife, Made in Dagenham, 2010; Never Let Me Go, Submarine, Love Birds, Jane Eyre, 2011; Great Expectations, 2012; Blue Jasmine, 2013; The Phone Call (short), 2013; The Double, 2014; Godzilla, 2014; Paddington, 2014; X + Y, 2015; *television* includes: Tipping the Velvet, 2002; The Young Visiters, 2003; Byron, 2003; Promoted to Glory, 2003; Little Britain, 2003–05; Bunk Bed Boys, 2004; Fingersmith, 2005; 20,000 Streets Under the Sky, 2005; Shiny Shiny Bright New Hole in My Heart, 2006; Man to Man with Dean Learner, 2006; Persuasion, 2007 (Best Actress, RTS, 2008); Little Crackers, 2011; Room on the Broom, 2012; How and Why, 2014. *Recreations:* painting, writing, cycling, walking, meditating, playing with young nieces and nephews. *Address:* c/o Conway van Gelder Grant Ltd, 8–12 Broadwick Street, W1F 8HW. *T:* (020) 7287 0077. *E:* elaine@conwayvg.co.uk.

HAWKINS, Prof. Stephen John, PhD, DSc; CBiol, FRSB; Dean, Faculty of Natural and Environmental Sciences, Southampton University, since 2010; *b* 12 Jan. 1956; *s* of Kenneth and Marjorie Hawkins; *m* 1997, Dr Elspeth Jack. *Educ:* Univ. of Liverpool (BSc Marine Biology 1976; PhD 1980; DSc 2008). MIBiol 1980, FRSB (FIBiol 2009). NERC Post-doctoral Fellow, Marine Biological Assoc., Plymouth, 1979–80; Lectr in Zoology, Univ. of Manchester, 1980–87; Lectr, 1987–90, Sen. Lectr, 1990–95, in Marine Biology, Univ. of Liverpool; University of Southampton: Dir, Centre for Envmtl Scis, 1995–99; Hd, Biodiversity and Ecology Div., 1996–99; Prof. of Envmtl Biology, 1995–2006 (pt-time, 1999–2006); Dir and Sec., Marine Biol Assoc. of UK, 1999–2007 (Vice-Pres., 2010–); Prof. of Marine Biol., Univ. of Plymouth, 2006–07; Prof. of Natural Scis, and Head, Coll. of Natural Scis, 2007–10, Actg Pro-Vice Chancellor, Res. and Enterprise, 2010, Bangor Univ. Partnership for the Observation of Global Oceans Vis. Prof., Argentina, 2010. Pres., Bioadapt Panel, Agence Nat. de la Recherche, France, 2011–13; Chm., Living Earth Panel, 2014–. Vice-Pres., European Marine Res. Stations Network, 2000–07. Mem., Sci. Adv. Council, DEFRA, 2009–11; Chm., Welsh Govt Technical Adv. Gp on Marine Conservation Zones, 2009–. Mem., Adv. Bd, Biodiversity Res. Centre Academia Sinica, Taiwan, 2010–. Trustee: Nat. Biodiversity Network, 2000–04; Nat. Marine Aquarium, Plymouth, 2000–04; Freshwater Biol Assoc., 2014–. *Publications:* (with H. D. Jones) Marine Field Course Guide: Rocky Shores, 1992; (with D. Raffaelli) Intertidal Ecology, 1996, 2nd edn 1999; 270 peer-reviewed papers and book chapters. *Recreations:* cricket, ski-ing, fishing, sailing, occasional fieldwork, watching Rugby. *Address:* Faculty of Natural and Environmental Sciences, Building 27 (Chemistry), Highfield Campus, University Road, Southampton SO17 1BJ. *Clubs:* Braunton Cricket (Vice-Pres., 1995–); Barnstaple Rugby Football.

HAWKINS-LETH, Air Vice-Marshal David Richard, CB 1992; LVO 2007; MBE 1975; DL; Director, Military Affairs, WDSL Aerospace Ltd, since 2009; Head, Defence and Government Relations, Coltraco Ultrasonics Ltd, since 2013; Extra Gentleman Usher to the Queen, since 2007 (Gentleman Usher, 1994–2007); *b* 5 April 1937; 2nd *s* of late Gp Capt. Charles Richard John Hawkins, OBE, AFC and Norah (*née* Terry); *m* 1st, 1965, Wendy Elizabeth Harris (marr. diss. 1981); one *s* one *d*; 2nd, 1982, Elaine Kay Nelson (marr. diss. 1997); 3rd, 1998, Dr Karen Hansen-d'Leth. *Educ:* Worth; Downside Sch.; RMA Sandhurst. Commnd RAF Regt, 1959; Flt Comdr Cyprus and Singapore, 1960–62; ADC to CAS, Air Chief Marshal Sir Charles Elworthy, 1963–65; jun. RAF Regt instructor, RAF Coll., Cranwell, 1965–68; 2nd i/c 63 Sqdn, Singapore, 1968–69; Sqdn Ldr, 1969; Jt Thai/US Mil. R&D Centre as airfield defence specialist, Bangkok, 1969–71; CO, 37 Sqdn, UK, NI and Belize, 1971–74; CO, Queen's Colour Sqdn of RAF, 1974–76; Wing Comdr, on staff of Comdt-Gen., RAF Regt, MoD, 1976–79; Chief, Survivability Br., HQ AAFCE, 1979–82; Sen. Comd RAF Regt Officer, HQ Strike Comd/HQ UK Air, 1982–86; Gp Capt., 1982; CO, RAF Catterick, RAF Regt Depot, 1986–88; NATO Defence Coll., Rome, 1988–89; Dir, RAF Personal Services 1, MoD, 1989–90; Air Cdre, 1989; Dir, RAF Regt, MoD, 1990–91; Comdt-Gen., RAF Regt, and Dir-Gen., RAF Security, 1991–93; Yeoman Usher of the Black Rod and Dep. Serjeant-at-Arms, H of L, 1994–99. Co-Founder and Chief Exec., Safe Waste and Power Ltd, 2003–14. Non-exec. Chm. and Dir, DBeye Ltd, 2005–10. Parachute Wings: UK, 1969; Thai Army (Master), 1970; Thai Police (Master), 1970; US Army (1st class), 1971. Vice-Chm. (Air), TA&VRA, Gtr London, 1994–2003. Life Vice-Pres., Battle of Britain Meml Trust, 2009– (Trustee, 1998–2009). Freeman, City of London, 1992. DL Gtr London, 1994. *Recreations:* golf, ski-ing, walking, shooting. *Clubs:* Royal Air Force, Royal Over-Seas League.

HAWKSLEY, (Philip) Warren; Director, Society for the Prevention of Solvent and Volatile Substance Abuse, 1998–2008; *b* 10 March 1943; *s* of late Bradshaw Warren Hawksley and Monica Augusta Hawksley; *m* 1999, Kathleen Margaret (*née* Lloyd). *Educ:* Denstone Coll., Uttoxeter. Employed by Lloyd's Bank after leaving school. Dir, Edderton Hall, 1989–97. Member: Salop County Council, 1970–81; West Mercia Police Authority, 1977–81. MP (C) The Wrekin, 1979–87; contested (C) same seat, 1987; MP (C) Halesowen and Stourbridge, 1992–97; contested (C) Stourbridge, 1997. Member: Select Cttee on Employment, 1986–87 and 1994–97; Home Affairs Select Cttee, 1996–97; Jt Sec., Cons. Back bench Cttee for New Town and Urban Affairs, 1984–87; Sec., W Midlands Cons. Parly Gp, 1992–97. Hon. Pres., Catering Industries Liaison Council, 1992–98. *Recreations:* collecting political memorabilia, shooting, good food and wines.

HAWKSWORTH, Prof. David Leslie, CBE 1996; DSc; CBiol, FRSB, FLS; mycologist, systematist, and environmental and forensic biologist; Research Professor, Universidad Complutense de Madrid, since 2001; Scientific Associate, Natural History Museum, London, since 2006; *b* Sheffield, 5 June 1946; *e s* of late Leslie Hawksworth and Freda Mary (*née* Dolamore); *m* 1st, 1968, Madeleine Una Ford (marr. diss. 1998); one *s* one *d*; 2nd, 1999 (marr. diss. 2008); 3rd, 2009, Patricia E. J. Wiltshire. *Educ:* Herbert Strutt Grammar Sch., Belper; Univ. of Leicester (BSc 1967; PhD 1970; DSc 1980). FLS 1969; FRSB (FIBiol 1982); CBiol 1986. Mycologist, Commonwealth Mycological Inst., Kew, 1969–81; sci. asst to Exec. Dir, CAB, 1981–83; Dir, Internat. Mycol Inst., CAB Internat., 1983–97. Visiting Professor: Univ. of Riyadh, 1978; Univ. of Reading, 1984–; Univ. of Assiut, 1985; Univ. of Kent, 1990–; Royal Holloway, Univ. of London, 1992–; Univ. Complutense, Madrid, 2000–01; Birkbeck, Univ. of London, 2012–; Prof. of Biology, 2007–09, Prof. of Ecology, 2013–14, Univ. of Gloucestershire. Hon. Res. Associate, Royal Botanic Gdns, Kew, 2013–. Mem. Council, English Nature, 1996–99. President: British Lichen Soc., 1986–87 (Hon. Mem., 1997); Eur. Congress of Mycologists, 1989; Br. Mycol Soc., 1990 (Centenary Fellow, 1996); Internat. Mycol Assoc., 1990–94 (Sec.-Gen., 1977–90; Hon. Pres., 1994–); Internat. Union of Biol Sci., 1994–97; Professional Mem., Chartered Forensic Sci. Soc. (formerly Forensic Sci. Soc.), 2011. Vice-Pres., Linnean Soc., 1985–88; Treasurer and Editor-in-Chief, Systematics Assoc., 1972–86; Treas., Internat. Congress of Systematic and Evolutionary Biol., 1989–96; Chairman: Internat. Commn on Taxonomy of Fungi, 1982–2002; Ruislip-Northwood Woods Adv. Working Party, 1979–82; Internat. Cttee on Bionomenclature, 1994–2012; Chief Rapp., CAB Internat. Review Confs, 1985, 1990, 1993, 1996. Dir, MycoNova, 1998–2003. FRSA 1997. Hon. Member: Soc. Lichenologica Italiana, 1989; Ukrainian Botanical Soc., 1992; Mycol Soc. of America, 1994; Assoc. Latinoamericana de Micología, 1996; Japanese Soc. for Lichenology, 2002. Editor: The Lichenologist, 1970–90; Systema Ascomycetum, 1986–98; Mycosystema, 1987–2008; Sen. (formerly Exec.) Editor, Mycological Research, 2000–08; Editor-in-Chief: Biodiversity and Conservation, 2006–; IMA Fungus, 2010–. FD *hc* Umeå, 1996. First Bicent. Medal, Linnean Soc., 1978; Acharius Medal, Internat. Assoc. for Lichenology, 2002; Josef Adolf von Arx Award, KNAW-CBS Fungal Biodiversity Centre, Utrecht, 2011; Ainsworth Medal, Internat. Mycol Assoc., 2014. *Publications:* (jtly) Dictionary of the Fungi, 6th edn 1971 to 8th edn 1995; (ed jtly) Air Pollution and Lichens, 1973; Mycologist's Handbook, 1974; (ed) The Changing Flora and Fauna of Britain, 1974; (jtly) Lichens as Pollution Monitors, 1976; (ed jtly) Lichenology: progress and problems, 1976; (jtly) Lichenology in the British Isles 1568–1975, 1977; (jtly) Key Works to the Fauna and Flora of the British Isles and Northwestern Europe, 4th edn 1978, 5th edn 1988; (ed) Advancing Agricultural Production in Africa, 1984; (jtly) The Lichen-Forming Fungi, 1984; (jtly) The British Ascomycotina, 1985; (ed jtly) Coevolution and Systematics, 1986; (ed jtly) Coevolution of Fungi with Plants and Animals, 1988; (ed jtly) Living Resources for Biotechnology, 1988; (ed) Prospects in Systematics, 1988; (jtly) International Mycological Directory, 1990; (ed) Frontiers in Mycology, 1991; (ed) Improving the Stability of Names, 1991; (ed) The Biodiversity of Microorganisms and Invertebrates: their role in sustainable agriculture, 1991; (jtly) Lichen Flora of Great Britain and Ireland, 1992; (jtly) Biodiversity and Biosystematic Priorities: microorganisms and invertebrates, 1993; (jtly) IMI: retrospect and prospect, 1993; (ed) Identification and Characterization of Pest Organisms, 1994; Glossary of Terms Used in Bionomenclature, 1994; (ed) Ascomycete Systematics: problems and perspectives in the nineties, 1994; (jtly) The Biodiversity of Microorganisms and the Role of Microbial Resource Centres, 1994; (ed jtly) Microbial Diversity and Ecosystem Function, 1995; (ed jtly) Biodiversity Information: needs and options, 1997; (ed) The Changing Wildlife of Great Britain and Ireland, 2001; (ed jtly) International Code of Botanical Nomenclature (Vienna Code), 2006; (ed jtly) Arthropod Diversity and Conservation, 2006; (ed jtly) Forest Diversity and Management, 2006; (ed jtly) Human Exploitation and Biodiversity, 2006; (ed jtly) Marine, Freshwater and Wetlands Biodiversity Conservation, 2006; (ed jtly) Vertebrate Conservation and Biodiversity, 2007; Plant Conservation and Biodiversity, 2007; Biodiversity and Conservation in Europe, 2008; (ed jtly) Plantation Forests and Biodiversity: oxymoron or opportunity, 2009; (ed jtly) Protist Diversity and Geographical Distribution, 2009; (ed) Management and Conservation of Biodiversity, 2010; (ed) Methods and Practice in Biodiversity and Conservation, 2010; Terms used in Bionomenclature: the naming of organisms (and plant communities), 2010; (ed jtly) International Code of Nomenclature for algae, fungi and plants, 2012; numerous papers on biodiversity, biol nomenclature, fungi (including lichens), forensic mycology. *Recreations:* bibliography, Huxley family, natural history, second-hand books. *Address:* Milford House, The Mead, Ashtead, Surrey KT21 2LZ. *E:* d.hawksworth@nhm.ac.uk.

HAWLEY, Prof. Christine Elizabeth, CBE 2008; RIBA; Professor of Architectural Studies, since 1993, and Dean and Head of The Bartlett, Faculty of the Built Environment, 1999–2009, University College London; *b* 3 Aug. 1949; *d* of John and Margaret Hawley; *m* 1973, Clyde; two *s* one *d*. *Educ:* City of London Sch. for Girls; Architectural Assoc. (AADipl 1975). Lectr, AA, 1978–86; Hd, Sch. of Architecture, Univ. of East London, 1986–93. Visiting Professor: Univ. of Lund, Sweden, 2008; Chinese Univ. of Hong Kong, 2009, 2011; Chisholm Fellowship, Univ. of Western Australia, 2012. Recent built work includes: social housing for Internat. Bauausstellung, Berlin, 1989; Kantine, Städel Acad., Frankfurt, 1992; exhibn pavilions, Osaka and Nagoya Expo, 1993; social housing for Gifu, Japan; mus. for Roman remains at Camuntum, Lower Austria, 1997. Advr, CABE, 2001–04. FRSA. *Publications:* articles in a number of prof. jls inc. GA, Architecture and Urbanism and Architects' Jl. *Recreations:* swimming, reading, film. *Address:* The Bartlett, Faculty of the Built Environment, University College London, Gower Street, WC1E 6BT.

HAWLEY, Sir James (Appleton), KCVO 2010; TD 1969; Lord-Lieutenant of Staffordshire, 1993–2012; *b* 28 March 1937; *s* of late John J. Hawley and Mary Hawley, JP; *m* 1961, Susan, *d* of Alan Stott, JP, DL; one *s* two *d*. *Educ:* Uppingham; St Edmund Hall, Oxford (MA Jurisp.). Called to the Bar, Middle Temple, 1961. Nat. Service, 2nd Lieut South Staffs Regt, Cyprus; Lieut to Major, Staffs Yeomanry Regt (QORR). Chairman: John James Hawley (Speciality Works) Ltd, 1961–98; J. W. Wilkinson & Co., 1970–98; Dir, Stafford Railway Building Soc., 1985–2003. Pres., Made-Up Textiles Assoc., 1984–85; Chm., Camping Trade Assoc., 1977–78. President: Staffs and Birmingham Agricl Soc., 2004–05; Walsall Soc. for the Blind, 2001– (Chm., 1977–92); Lichfield Fest., 2006–; RFCA W Midlands, 1998–2004; Trustee, Armed Forces Meml, 2003–; formerly Patron, President or Trustee of many other organisations in Staffs. Freeman: City of London, 1986; Newcastle-under-Lyme, 2011; Co. of Staffs, 2012. Liveryman, Saddlers' Co., 1986–. JP Staffs 1969; High Sheriff, Staffs, 1976–77; DL Staffs 1978. DUniv: Staffordshire, 2003; Keele, 2009. KStJ 1993. *Recreations:* family, Staffordshire, outdoor pursuits. *Address:* Hoo Mill, Ingestre, Stafford ST18 0RG. *Clubs:* Oxford and Cambridge; Walsall.

HAWLEY, Ven. John Andrew; Archdeacon of Blackburn, 2002–15; *b* 27 April 1950; *s* of Willie and Constance May Hawley. *Educ:* Stannington County Jun. Sch.; Ecclesfield Grammar Sch.; King's Coll., London (BD, AKC 1971); Wycliffe Hall, Oxford. Ordained deacon, 1974, priest, 1975; Asst Curate, Holy Trinity, Hull, 1974–77; Sen. Curate, Bradford Cathedral, 1977–80; Vicar, All Saints, Woodlands, Doncaster, 1980–91; Team Rector, Dewsbury, 1991–2002; Actg Archdeacon of Lancaster, 2010–11. Proctor in Convocation, 1996–2002; Bishop's Adviser: on Urban Priority Areas, 2002–; on Hosp. and Hospice Chaplaincy, 2013–; Chm., Wakefield Diocesan House of Clergy, 2000–02. Hon. Canon, Wakefield Cathedral, 1998. Member: Nat. Archdeacons' Forum, 2010–; Pastoral Measure Rev. Gp, C of E, 2000–03; House for Duty Wkg Gp, C of E, 2010–12. *Recreations:* cricket, golf, fell walking, quiet holidays in Scotland, studying St Paulinus of York. *Address:* 35 Woodland Avenue, Goole, E Yorks DN14 6QT. *T:* (01405) 762678.

HAWLEY, Dr Robert, CBE 1997; FREng, FIET, FIMechE, FInstP; FRSE; Chairman: Engineering Council, 1999–2002; Particle Physics and Astronomy Research Council, 1998–2001; *b* 23 July 1936; *s* of William and Eva Hawley; *m* 1st, Valerie (*née* Clarke) (marr. diss. 2002); one *s* one *d*; *m* 2nd, 2002, Pamela Elizabeth (*née* Neesham). *Educ:* Wallasey Grammar Sch.; Wallasey Technical Coll.; Birkenhead Technical Coll.; Durham Univ. (BSc 1959; PhD 1963); Newcastle upon Tyne Univ. (DSc 1976). FIET (FIEE 1970); FREng (FEng 1979); FIMechE 1987; FInstP 1971. FRSE 1997. Student apprentice, BICC, Prescot, 1952–55; C. A. Parsons & Co. Ltd: Head of Res. Team, 1961–64; Chief Elec. Engr, 1970–74; Dir of Prodn and Engrg, 1974–76; Man. Dir, NEI Parsons Ltd, 1976–84; NEI plc: Man. Dir, Power Engrg Gp, 1984–89; Man. Dir, 1989–92; Chm., NEI ABB Gas Turbines Ltd, 1990–92; Chief Executive: Nuclear Electric plc, 1992–96; British Energy plc, 1995–97. Mem. Bd, Rolls-Royce plc, 1989–92. Non-executive Chairman: Rotork plc, 1997–98; INBIS Group plc, 1997–2000; ERAtech Ltd, 1997–2000; Taylor Woodrow plc, 1999–2003; Rocktron, 2001–05; Berkeley Resources Ltd, 2006–; Lister Petter Investment Hldgs Ltd, 2006–; Carron Acquisition Co. Ltd, 2006–09; non-executive Director: W. S. Atkins Ltd, 1994–97; Tricorder Technology, 1997–2001; Colt Telecom Gp, 1998–2010; Rutland Trust, 2001–07; Consultant, ABB Ltd, 1993–97; Advr, SEMA Gp, 1995–97; Adv. Dir, HSBC Investment Bank, 1998–2004. Member: NE Indust. Develt Bd, DTI, 1989–92; Bd, Northern Develt Co., 1989–92; Industrial Develt Adv. Bd, DTI, 1994–2000; Pres., Partnership Korea, DTI, 1995–2002. Chairman: Hawley Cttee on Corporate Governance Information Management, 1993–98; Hawley Gp on Engrg Profession, DTI and Engrg Council, 1999–2001. Mem., Annual Review Sub-group, and Chm., Energy Wkg Pty, 1986–87, ACARD; Member: DFEE Women's Issues Wkg Gp, 1996–97; Mgt and Leadership in the Professions, DFEE, 2000–. Institution of Electrical Engineers: Vice Pres., 1991–95; Dep. Pres., 1995–96; Pres., 1996–97. Member Council: Fellowship of Engrg, 1981–84; Foundn for Sci. and Technol., 1999–2001 (Dep. Chm., 2002–); Royal Instn, 2000–; Mem., Nat. Centre for Univs and Business (formerly Council for Industry and Higher Educn), 2000–. Pres., Energy Industries Club, 1989–91. Mem., Boat and Shoreworks Cttee, RNLI, 1992–95. Trustee, Daphne Jackson Trust, 2000–. Chm., 2002–07, Pres., 2007–, Anglo-Korean Soc. Lectures include: C. A. Parsons Meml, IEE and Royal Soc., 1977; Hunter Meml, IEE, 1990; Blackadder, NEC Inst., 1992; Wilson Campbell Meml, Univ. of Newcastle upon Tyne, 1994; Bowden, UMIST, 1994; J. G. Collier Meml, Univ. of Brunel, 1997; Higginson, 1998, Temple Chevallier, 2001, Durham; Armstrong, 2001, Newcastle upon Tyne; Royce, IIE, 2001; Mountbatten, IEE, 2002; Bridge, Engineers' Co., 2002; Blumein, IEE, 2005. Member: Court, Univ. of Newcastle upon Tyne, 1979–; Bd of Advrs, Elec. Engrg, Univ. of London, 1982–86; Court, Loughborough Univ., 2003–; Chm., Council, Univ. of Durham, 1997–2002; Vice-Chancellor, World Nuclear Univ., 2006–. Freeman, City of London, 1985; Master, Engrs' Co., 2005–06. Mem., Nat. Acad. of Engrg of Korea, 2001. FRSE 1997; FCGI 2003. Hon. FINucE 1994; Hon. FIEE 2003. Hon. Fellow, Liverpool John Moores Univ., 2002. Hon. DSc: Durham, 1996; City, 1998; Cranfield, 2002; Hon. DEng: South Bank, 1997; West of England, 1997; Newcastle upon Tyne, 2002; UMIST, 2002; Hon. DTech: Staffordshire 2000; Abertay Dundee, 2001; Robert Gordon, Aberdeen, 2002. DUniv Surrey, 2002. Waverley Gold Medal, RSA, 1960; Achievement Medal, for outstanding contribs to power engrg, IEE, 1989. Premio Vicente Lecuna Medal, Venezuela, 1997; Order of Diplomatic Service Kwongda Medal, Korea, 1999. *Publications:* (with A. Maitland) Vacuum as an Insulator, 1967; (with A. A. Zaky): Dielectric Solids, 1970; Conduction and Breakdown in Mineral Oil, 1973; Fundamentals of Electromagnetic Field Theory, 1974; technical papers on electrical breakdown in vacuum, liquids and solids, electrical machine design and power generation. *Recreations:* gardening, writing, philately. *Address:* Summerfield, Rendcomb, near Cirencester, Glos GL7 7HB. *T:* (01285) 831610, *Fax:* (01285) 831801. *Club:* Athenæum.

HAWORTH, Baron *cr* 2004 (Life Peer), of Fisherfield in Ross and Cromarty; **Alan Robert Haworth;** Secretary, Parliamentary Labour Party, 1992–2004; *b* 26 April 1948; *s* of late John Haworth and Hilma Haworth (*née* Westhead); *m* 1st, 1973, Gill Cole; 2nd, 1991, Maggie Rae. *Educ:* Barking Regl Coll. of Technol. (BScSoc London Univ. ext.). Cttee Officer, 1975–85, Sen. Cttee Officer, 1985–92, Parly Labour Party. *Publications:* (ed jtly) Men Who Made Labour, 2006. *Recreations:* hill walking, mountaineering. *Address:* House of Lords, SW1A 0PW.

HAWORTH, Glennis; *see* Haworth, S. G.

HAWORTH, Graham Thomas, RIBA; Director, Haworth Tompkins Architects, since 1991; *b* 15 Jan. 1960; *m* 2008, Lottie Cole; one *d*, and two *s* one *d* from a previous relationship. *Educ:* Univ. of Nottingham (BArch); Jesus Coll., Cambridge (DipArch). RIBA 1989. Architect: Skidmore Owings Merrill, 1986–87; Bennetts Associates, 1988–90. Projects include: Royal Court Th., 2000; Coin Street Housing, 2001; Hayward Gall. extension, 2003; Young Vic Th., London Liby, 2005; Liverpool 1, 2007; Royal Coll. of Art, 2008. *Recreations:* contemporary arts, theatre, walking, fishing, painting. *Address:* Haworth Tompkins, 33 Greenwood Place, NW5 1LB. *E:* graham.haworth@haworthtompkins.com.

HAWORTH, John Leigh W.; *see* Walker-Haworth.

HAWORTH, (John) Martin, PhD; Headmaster, Wallington County Grammar School, 1990–2010; *b* 22 Jan. 1949; *s* of Reginald and Hilda Haworth; *m* 1973, Brenda Dawe; two *d*. *Educ:* London Bible Coll. (BD 1972); Univ. of Birmingham (MA 1973; PhD 1982); Univ. of Warwick (MEd 1984). RE teacher, Plymstock Sch., 1973–77; Hd, RE and Hd, 6th Form, Coundon Court Sch., 1977–84; Dep. Hd, Wisewood Sch., 1985–90. FRSA. *Recreations:* karate (1st Dan), running, church, theatre, concerts, opera. *E:* JMartinHaworth@gmail.com.

HAWORTH, Jonathan Mayo; His Honour Judge Jonathan Haworth; a Circuit Judge, since 1996; *b* 5 Oct. 1948; *s* of George Henry Haworth and Elsa Sophia Haworth; *m* 1973, Brigitte Ilse Müller; one *s* one *d*. *Educ:* King Edward VII Grammar Sch., Sheffield; King's Coll., London (LLB Hons). Called to the Bar, Middle Temple, 1971; practised from Fenners Chambers, Cambridge, 1973–96. *Recreations:* reading, computers, music, cricket. *Address:* c/o Cambridge Crown Court, 83 East Road, Cambridge CB1 1BT.

HAWORTH, Martin; *see* Haworth, J. M.

HAWORTH, Peter; Master of the Senior (formerly Supreme) Court Costs Office, since 2006; *b* 27 March 1951; *s* of Arthur Haworth and Mary Haworth (*née* Aynge); *m* 1975, Margaret Elaine Knowles; three *d*. *Educ:* Towneley High Sch., Burnley; Univ. of Liverpool (LLB 1972). Admitted as solicitor, 1975; Partner, Southerns Solicitors, 1978–2003; a Dep. District Judge, Northern Circuit, 1992–; Solicitor Advocate, 1998; Dep. Master and Costs Judge, 2002–06. Mem., Civil Procedure Rule Cttee, 1996–99; Solicitor Mem. and Chm., Solicitors' Disciplinary Tribunal, 1999–2006. A Lieut Bailiff of Guernsey, 2003–. *Recreations:* yachting, ski-ing, hot air ballooning, fell walking, theatre. *Address:* Senior Court Costs Office, Thomas More Building, Royal Courts of Justice, Strand, WC2A 2LL. *E:* master.haworth@judiciary.gsi.gov.uk. *Clubs:* Royal London Yacht; Royal Ocean Racing.

HAWORTH, Sir Philip, 3rd Bt *cr* 1911, of Dunham Massey, Co. Chester; farmer; *b* 17 Jan. 1927; *s* of Sir Arthur Geoffrey Haworth, 2nd Bt, and Emily Dorothea, (Dorothy) (*d* 1980), *er d* of H. E. Gaddum; *S* father, 1987; *m* 1951, Joan Helen, *d* of late S. P. Clark, Ipswich; four *s* one *d*. *Educ:* Dauntsey's; Reading Univ. BSc (Agric.) 1948. *Recreations:* music, art, ornithology. *Heir:* s Christopher Haworth [*b* 6 Nov. 1951; *m* 1994, Susan Rachel, *d* of David Ives and *widow* of Jonathan Dent; one *s* one *d*, and two step *s*]. *Address:* Free Green Farm, Over Peover, Knutsford, Cheshire WA16 9QX. *Club:* Farmers.

HAWORTH, Prof. (Sheila) Glennis, (Mrs L. F. H. Busk), CBE 2007; MD; FRCP, FRCPath; FRCPCH; FMedSci; Professor of Developmental Cardiology, Institute of Child Health, 1991–2009, and British Heart Foundation Professor of Developmental Cardiology, 1991–2004, University College London, now Professor Emeritus; Founder, 2001, and Lead Clinician, 2001–09, UK Pulmonary Hypertension Service for Children; *b* 31 May 1939; *d* of Richard and Elizabeth Haworth; *m* 1st, 1970, Prof. T. J. McElwain (*d* 1990); 2nd, 1993, Maj.-Gen. Leslie Francis Harry Busk, *qv*. *Educ:* Royal Free Hosp. Sch. of Medicine, Univ. of London (MB BS 1964; MD 1976). FRCP 1981; FRCPath 1991; FRCPCH 1997. Fellow in Fetal Physiol. and Neonatol., Columbia Univ., NY, 1967–69; Med. Registrar, RPMS, 1970; Registrar, then Sen. Lectr, Royal Brompton Hosp., London, 1971–76; Hospital for Sick Children, Great Ormond Street: Hon. Consultant in Paediatric Cardiol., 1976–2009; Sen. Lectr, 1976–82; Reader, 1982–88; Prof. of Paediatric Cardiol., 1989–90; Sub-Dean, Inst. of Child Health, 1982–85. Pres., Pulmonary Vascular Res. Inst., 2014–15. Involved with practice of medicine overseas for over 30 years, incl. improvement of pulmonary hypertension care. FACC 1986; FMedSci 1999. *Publications:* clinical and basic science papers on the develt of the pulmonary circulation, the pathogenesis and treatment of pulmonary hypertension in childhood and paediatric cardiology. *Recreations:* playing the piano, opera, travel. *Address:* Bushwood, Witheridge Hill Bottom, Highmoor, Henley-on-Thames, Oxon RG9 5PE. *T:* (01491) 641223. *E:* s.haworth@ich.ucl.ac.uk.

HAWTHORN, Ven. Christopher John; Archdeacon of Cleveland, 1991–2001, now Archdeacon Emeritus; *b* 29 April 1936; *s* of late Rev. John Christopher Hawthorn and Susan Mary Hawthorn; *m* 1964, Elizabeth Margaret Lowe; three *s* one *d*. *Educ:* Marlborough Coll.; Queens' Coll., Cambridge (MA Hons); Ripon Hall, Oxford. Deacon 1962, priest 1963; Asst Curate, Sutton-in-Holderness, 1962–66; Vicar: St Nicholas, Hull, 1966–72; Christ Church, Coatham, 1972–79; St Martin's-on-the-Hill, Scarborough, 1979–91; RD Scarborough, 1982–91. Proctor in Convocation, 1987–90; Canon of York, 1987–2001, now Canon Emeritus. *Recreations:* gardening, fell walking, sport. *Address:* 11 Holly Tree Lane, Haxby, York YO32 3YJ. *T:* (01904) 591008.

HAWTHORN, Prof. Geoffrey Patrick; Professor of International Politics, University of Cambridge, 1998–2007, now Emeritus; Fellow, Clare Hall, Cambridge, 1982–2007, now Emeritus; *b* 28 Feb. 1941; *s* of Kathleen Mary Hawthorn (*née* Candy); *m* 1st, 1969, Ruth Legg (marr. diss. 1986); two *s*; 2nd, 1987, Gloria Carnevali; one *s*. *Educ:* Jesus Coll., Oxford (BA); London Sch. of Economics. Lectr in Sociology, Univ. of Essex, 1964–70; University of Cambridge: Lectr in Sociology, 1970–85; Reader in Sociology and Politics, 1985–98; Fellow, Churchill Coll., 1970–76. Vis. Prof. of Sociology, Harvard Univ., 1973–74, 1989–90; Vis. Mem., IAS, Princeton, 1979–80. *Publications:* The Sociology of Fertility, 1970; Enlightenment and Despair, 1976, 2nd edn 1987; (ed) Population and Development, 1977; (ed) The Standard of Living, 1987; Plausible Worlds, 1991; The Future of Asia and the Pacific, 1998; Thucydides on Politics, 2014; articles and reviews in learned jls and other periodicals. *Recreations:* ornithology, music. *Address:* 19 St Luke's Street, Cambridge CB4 3DA.

HAWTHORNE, Prof. John P., PhD; FBA 2013; Professor of Philosophy, University of Southern California, since 2015 (part-time, 2013–15). *Educ:* Univ. of Manchester (BA 1985); Syracuse Univ. (PhD 1991); MA Oxon. Former positions at Univ. of NSW, ANU, Arizona State Univ. and Syracuse Univ.; Waynflete Prof. of Metaphysical Philosophy, Univ. of Oxford, 2006–15; Fellow, Magdalen Coll., Oxford, until 2015. Visiting Professor: Rutgers Univ.; Princeton Univ., 2009–13. *Publications:* Knowledge and Lotteries, 2004; Metaphysical Essays, 2006; (with Herman Cappelen) Relativism and Monadic Truth, 2009; (with David Manley) The Reference Book, 2012. *Address:* School of Philosophy, University of Southern California, Mudd Hall of Philosophy, 3709 Trousdale Parkway, Los Angeles, CA 90089–0451, USA.

HAWTIN, Brian Richard, CB 1997; Deputy Director General, Technical Secretariat, Organisation for the Prohibition of Chemical Weapons, 2003–06; *b* 31 May 1946; *s* of late Dick Hawtin and Jean (*née* Middleton); *m* 1969, Anthea Fry; two *d*. *Educ:* Portsmouth Grammar Sch.; Christ Church, Oxford (MA). Ministry of Defence, 1967–2002: Asst Private Sec. to Permt Under Sec. of State, 1970; seconded to FCO as First Sec., UK Delegn to NATO, Brussels, 1978–80; Asst Sec., 1981; RCDS 1987; Private Sec. to Sec. of State for Defence, 1987–89; Asst Under Sec. of State (material/naval), 1989–92, (Progs), 1992–94, (Home and Overseas), 1994–96, (Policy), 1997–99; Fellow, Center for Internat. Affairs, Harvard Univ., 1996–97; Dir Gen., Internat. Security Policy, 1999–2002; Chm., MoD Grievance Appeal Panel, 2007–14. *Recreations:* walking, antiques, grandchildren.

HAWTIN, Rt Rev. David Christopher; Bishop Suffragan of Repton, 1999–2006; an Assistant Bishop, Diocese of Sheffield, since 2007; *b* 7 June 1943; *m* 1968, Elizabeth Ann (*née* Uden) (*d* 2010); one *s* two *d*. *Educ:* King Edward VII Sch., Lytham St Annes; Keble Coll., Oxford (BA 1965; MA 1970); William Temple Coll., Rugby; Cuddesdon Coll., Oxford. Ordained deacon, 1967, priest 1968; Curate: St Thomas, Pennywell, Sunderland, 1967–71; St Peter's, Stockton, 1971–74; Priest in charge, St Andrew's, Leam Lane, Gateshead, 1974–79; Rector, Washington (incl. LEP), 1979–88; Diocesan Ecumenical Officer, Durham, 1988–92; Archdeacon of Newark, 1992–99. Gen. Synod Rep. for E Midlands Ministry Trng Course, 1997–99. Member: Gen. Synod, 1983–99 (Mem., Bd for Mission and Unity, 1986–91); BCC, 1987–90; Churches Together in England, 1990–2006 (Enabling Gp, 1991–99; Dep. Moderator, CTE Forum, 1995–99); Council of Churches for Britain and Ireland, 1990–2006; Chairman: Diocesan Bd of Educn, Southwell, 1993–99; E Midlands Consortium for Educn and Trng for Ministry, 1996–2001; Derby Diocesan Council for Mission and Unity, 1999–2001; Derby Diocesan Pastoral Cttee, 1999–2006; E Midlands Ministry Trng Course, 2002–06. Churches Project Co-ordinator, Nat. Garden Fest., Gateshead, 1988–91. Local Unity Advr, Durham Ecumenical Relations Gp, 1991–92; Consultant, Council for Christian Unity, 1991–96; Member: CCU Local Unity Panel, 1999–2009 (Chm., 2003–06); Churches Together in England Gp for Local Unity, 2001–06; Methodist/Anglican Panel for Unity in Mission, 2009–. Member: N Notts and N Derbys Coalfield Alliance Bd, 1999–2003; Derbys Partnership, 2001. *Address:* 162 Greenhill Avenue, Greenhill, Sheffield S8 7TF.

HAWTIN, Michael Victor; Secretary, TALK, since 2012 (Chairman, 2009–12); *b* 7 Sept. 1942; *s* of Guy and Constance Hawtin; *m* 1966, Judith Mary Eeley; one *s* one *d*. *Educ:* Bournemouth Sch.; St John's Coll., Cambridge (MA); Univ. of Calif, Berkeley (MA). Asst Principal, 1964–69, Principal, 1969–77, HM Treasury; seconded to Barclays Bank, 1969–71; Asst Sec., HM Treasury, 1977–83, Under Sec. (Principal Finance Officer), PSA, 1983–86; Under Sec., HM Treasury, 1986–88; Dir, Resource Management Gp and Principal Establishment and Finance Officer, ECGD, 1988–92; Dir, Underwriting Gp, ECGD, 1992–95; consultancy work for EU and IMF, 1996–2001. Chm., Relate W Surrey, 2000–09. *Recreations:* music, travel.

HAWTON, Prof. Keith Edward, DSc, DM; FRCPsych, FMedSci; Consultant Psychiatrist, Oxford Health NHS Foundation Trust (formerly Oxfordshire Mental Healthcare Unit, then Oxfordshire Mental Healthcare NHS Trust, later Oxfordshire and Buckinghamshire Mental Health NHS Foundation Trust), since 1984; Professor of Psychiatry, since 1996, and Director, Centre for Suicide Research, since 1998, University of Oxford; *b* 23 Dec. 1942; *s* of Leslie William Hawton and Eliza Hawton; *m* 1978, Joan Kirk; two *d*. *Educ:* Balliol Coll., and Med. Sch., Oxford (MB 2001; BChir 1969; DM 1980; DSc 2001); St John's Coll., Cambridge (MA 1970). FRCPsych 1990. Trng in psychiatry, 1970–73; Res. Psychiatrist, Clin. Lectr and Clin. Tutor in Psychiatry, Dept of Psychiatry, Oxford Univ., 1974–84. Boerhaave Vis. Prof., Leiden Univ., 1990–91. Sen. Investigator, Nat. Inst. for Health Res., 2009–. FMedSci 2013. Stengel Res. Award, Internat. Assoc. for Suicide Prevention, 1995; Dublin Award, Amer. Assoc. Suicidology, 2001; Res. Award, American Foundn for Suicide Prevention, 2002; Morselli Medal, Internat. Assoc. Suicide Res., 2013. *Publications:* Attempted Suicide: a practical guide, 1982, 2nd edn 1987; Sex Therapy: a practical guide, 1985; Cognitive Behaviour Therapy for Psychiatric Problems, 1989; Suicide and Stress in Farmers, 1998; The International Handbook of Suicide and Attempted Suicide, 2000; Prevention and Treatment of Suicidal Behaviour: from science to practice, 2005; By Their Own Young Hand: deliberate self-harm and suicidal ideas in adolescents, 2006; Suicide, 2013. *Recreations:* fishing, cricket, wines, golf. *Address:* Centre for Suicide Research, University Department of Psychiatry, Warneford Hospital, Oxford OX3 7JX. *T:* (01865) 738585.

HAY, family name of **Marquis of Tweeddale, Earls of Erroll** and **Kinnoull,** and of **Baron Hay of Ballyore**.

HAY, Lord; Harry Thomas William Hay; *b* 8 Aug. 1984; *s* and *heir* of Earl of Erroll, *qv*.

HAY OF BALLYORE, Baron *cr* 2014 (Life Peer), of Ballyore in the City of Londonderry; **William Alexander Hay;** Member for Foyle, 1998–2014 (DemU, 1998–2007, when elected Speaker), and Speaker, 2007–14, Northern Ireland Assembly; *b* 16 April 1950; *m* (marr. diss.); three *s* two *d*. *Educ:* Newbuildings Primary Sch.; Faughen Valley High Sch. Mem. (DemU), Derry CC, 1981–2010. Contested (DemU) Foyle, 2001, 2005.

HAY, Alasdair George, QFSM 2011; Chief Officer, Scottish Fire and Rescue Service, since 2012; *b* Edinburgh, 24 Dec. 1961; *s* of Alistair and Zandra Hay; *m* 1983, Caroline Lees; three *s*. *Educ:* Gracemount High Sch., Edinburgh; Univ. of Abertay, Dundee (MBA); Dundee Coll. (Post Grad. Dip. HR Mgt). MIFireE 1994. Fire officer, Essex Co. Fire and Rescue Service, 1983–92; Sen. Instructor, Scottish Fire Service Trng Sch., 1992–94; Tayside Fire and Rescue: Station Officer, 1994–95; T/Asst Divl Officer, 1995–97; T/Divl Officer III, Dep. Comdr Tech. Services, 1997; Asst Divl Officer, 1997–99; Divl Officer III, Dep. Divl Comdr Ops, 1999–2002; Divl Officer I, Comdr Tech. Services, 2002–04; Area Mgr B, Hd of Personnel, 2004–07; Asst Chief Fire Officer, 2007–08; Dep. Chief Fire Officer, 2008–11; Chief Fire Officer, 2012; Advr, Scottish Fire and Rescue Service Adv. Unit, 2011–12. Has undertaken courses on Exec. Mentoring, Safety for Sen. Execs and Task Orientated Negotiation. Mem. Bd, Chief Fire Officers Assoc., 2012–. *Recreations:* family, playing tennis, watching Rugby and football, reading, history. *Address:* Scottish Fire and Rescue Service Headquarters, 5 Whitefriars Crescent, Perth PH2 0PA. *T:* (01738) 475260.

HAY, Prof. Allan Stuart, PhD; FRS 1981; Tomlinson Professor of Chemistry, McGill University, Montreal, 1997–2000, now Emeritus (Professor of Polymer Chemistry, 1987–97); *b* 23 July 1929; *s* of Stuart Lumsden and Verna Emila Hay; *m* 1956, Janet Mary Keck; two *s* two *d*. *Educ:* Univ. of Alberta (BSc Hons, MSc); Univ. of Illinois (PhD). General Electric Research and Development Center, Schenectady, NY: Research Associate, 1955; Manager, Chemical Laboratory, 1968; Research and Develt Manager, Chemical Labs, 1980–87. Adjunct Professor, Polymer Science and Engineering Dept, Univ. of Massachusetts, 1975. Hon. DSc Alberta, 1987. Soc. of Plastics Engrs Internat. award in Plastics Science and Engineering, 1975; Achievement award, Industrial Res. Inst., 1984; Chemical Pioneer, Amer. Inst. of Chemists, 1985; Carothers Award, ACS, 1985; Macromolecular Sci. and Engrg Award, Canadian Inst. of Chem., 1998. *Publications:* numerous papers and contribs to learned jls. *Recreations:* philately, reading, swimming. *Address:* 5015 Glencairn Avenue, Montreal, QC H3W 2B3, Canada.

HAY, Dame Barbara (Logan), DCMG 2008 (CMG 1998); LVO 2008; MBE 1991; HM Diplomatic Service; Consul-General, Los Angeles, 2009–13; *b* 20 Jan. 1953; *d* of late Alfred Hay and Isa Hay (*née* Burgon). *Educ:* Boroughmuir Sen. Secondary Sch., Edinburgh. Joined Diplomatic Service, 1971; Russian language training, 1974–75; served Moscow and Johannesburg, 1975–80; Asst Private Sec. to Perm. Under-Sec. and Head of Diplomatic Service, 1981–83; FCO and Montreal, 1983–88; First Sec. (Inf.), Moscow, 1988–91; Consul-Gen., St Petersburg, 1991–92; Jt Assistance Unit (Central Europe), FCO, 1992–94; Ambassador, Republic of Uzbekistan and (non-res.), Republic of Tajikistan, 1995–99; Counsellor, FCO, 1999–2000; Consul-Gen., St Petersburg, 2000–04; Consul-Gen., and Dir of Trade and Investment Promotion, Istanbul, 2004–09. *Recreations:* theatre, travel, music, keeping in touch with friends.

HAY, Charles John, MVO 1996; HM Diplomatic Service; Ambassador to Republic of Korea, since 2015; *b* Aberdeen, 22 Sept. 1965; *s* of John Hay and Avril Hay; *m* 2001, Pascale Sutherland; two *d*. *Educ:* Univ. of Southampton (BA Hons 1987); Open Univ. (MBA 1999). Commnd Gordon Highlanders, 1988; Platoon Comdr, 1988–91; ADC to D Comd British Forces, Cyprus, 1992; joined FCO, 1993; Second Sec. (Political), Prague, 1994–97; First Secretary: FCO, 1998–99; Econ. and Finance, UK Perm. Repn to EU, Brussels, 1999–2003; Hd, G8 Presidency Team, 2004–05; Counsellor (Political) and Dep. Hd of Mission, Madrid, 2006–09; Asst Dir, HR, FCO, 2009–11; Dir, Consular Services, FCO, 2011–14. *Recreations:* P. G. Wodehouse, crime fiction, walking, sending gloating tasteless postcards to friends when travelling, trying to keep up my languages. *Address:* c/o Foreign and Commonwealth Office, King Charles Street, SW1A 2AH. *T:* (Republic of Korea) (2) 3210 5512, *Fax:* (2) 3210 5515. *E:* charles.hay@fco.gov.uk.

HAY, Sir David (Russell), Kt 1991; CBE 1981; FRCP; FRACP; (first) Medical Director, National Heart Foundation of New Zealand, 1977–92; Cardiologist, Canterbury Hospital (formerly North Canterbury Hospital) Board, 1964–89; Hon. Consulting Physician, Canterbury District Health Board, since 1990; *b* 8 Dec. 1927; twin *s* of Sir James Lawrence Hay, OBE, and Lady (Davidina Mertel) Hay; *m* 1958, Dr Jocelyn Valerie Bell; two *d*. *Educ:* St Andrew's Coll., Christchurch; Otago Univ., Univ. of New Zealand (MB, ChB; MD). FRACP 1965; FRCP 1971. Resident appts, Christchurch, Royal South Hants, Hammersmith, Brompton and National Heart Hosps, 1951–55; Sen. Registrar, Dunedin and Christchurch Hosps, 1956–59; Physician, N Canterbury Hosp. Bd, 1959–64; Head of Dept of Cardiology, 1969–78; Chm. of Medical Services and Hd of Dept of Medicine, 1978–84. Chm., Christchurch Hosps Med. Staff Assoc., 1983–85; Clin. Lectr, Christchurch Clinical Sch., Univ. of Otago, 1973–80; Clin. Reader, 1980–88. Pres., Nat. Heart Foundn of NZ, 1996–99 (Councillor, 1968–92, 1996–99; Mem. Scientific Cttee, 1968–92); Vice-Pres., RACP, 1988–92 (Councillor, 1964–66, 1987–88; Examiner, 1974–75; Censor, 1975–79, and 1990–92); Mem. Specialist Adv. Cttee on Cardiology, 1980–90; Chm., Central Specialists Cttee of BMA, 1967–68; Pres., Canterbury Div. of BMA, 1972. Cardiac Society of Australia and New Zealand: Chm., NZ Reg. and Councillor, 1977–81; Life Mem., 1992; Fellow, 2004. Overseas Regl Advr, 1987–2000, Emeritus Internat. Advr, 2000, RCP. Member: Resuscitation Cttee of Nat. Cttee on Emergency Care, 1979–87; Health Promotion Forum of NZ, 1984–91; NZ Govt Adv. Cttee on Prevention of Cardiovascular Disease, 1985–86; NZ Govt Adv. Cttee on Smoking and Health, 1974–88; Ethics Cttee, Southern Regl HA, Canterbury, 1994–97; WHO Expert Adv. Panel on Tobacco or Health, 1977–2003; WHO Working Gp on Tobacco or Health in Western Pacific Reg., Manila, 1994; Hypertension Task Force, 1988–89; Life Mem., Nat. Heart Foundn, 1992. Speaker: World Conf. on Smoking and Health, Stockholm, 1979; Internat. Soc. and Fedn of Cardiology Workshop, Jakarta, 1982; Internat. Congress on Preventive Cardiology, Washington, 1989; World Congress of Cardiology, Manila, 1990. Nat. Heart Foundn Lecture, 1992; Charles Burns Oration, 1992. Trustee: J. L. Hay Charitable Trust, 1959–2004; W. H. Nicholls Charitable

Trust, 1975–2003; Edna and Winifred White-Parsons Charitable Trust, 1986–2003; Keith Laugesen Charitable Trust, 1991–2002. College Medal, RACP, 1993; WHO Tobacco or Health Medal, 1995; Sir David Hay Medal, NZ Resuscitation Council, 2003. Commemoration Medal, NZ, 1990. *Publications:* (ed) Coronary Heart Disease: prevention and control in NZ, 1983; Heart Sounds, 2005; 100 sci. papers in various med. jls, mostly on smoking and health and preventive cardiology. *Recreations:* golf, writing. *Address:* 20 Greers Road, Christchurch 8041, New Zealand. *T:* 3585482. *Club:* Christchurch Golf.

See also Dame M. L. Salas.

HAY, Rt Rev. Mgr George Adam; Canon, Plymouth Cathedral Chapter, since 1994; *b* 14 Nov. 1930; *s* of late Sir William Rupert Hay, KCMG, KCIE, CSI, and late Sybil Ethel, *d* of Sir Stewart Abram. *Educ:* Ampleforth College, York; New Coll., Oxford (BA History, MA); Venerable English Coll., Rome (STL). National Service as Midshipman RNVR, 1949–50; student, Oxford, 1950–53; Venerable English Coll., Rome, 1953–60. Ordained priest at Rome, 1959; Curate, Sacred Heart Church, Exeter, and part-time RC Chaplain to students at Exeter Univ., 1960; Chaplain to students at Exeter Univ. and Priest-in-charge, Crediton, 1966–78; Rector, Venerable English Coll., Rome, 1978–84; Parish Priest: St John the Baptist, Dartmouth, 1984; Sacred Heart and St Teresa, Paignton, 1984–91; St Boniface, Okehampton and Holy Family, Chagford, 1991–97; Our Lady and St Denis, St Marychurch, Torquay, 1997–2003; Church of the Holy Spirit, Bovey Tracey, 2003–09. *Recreations:* fly fishing, mountain walking. *Address:* 30 The Roundway, Kingskerswell TQ12 5BW.

HAY, Lady (Helen) Olga; *see* Maitland, Lady H. O.

HAY, John Anthony, AC 2004; Vice-Chancellor and President, University of Queensland, 1996–2007, now Professor Emeritus; *b* Perth, 21 Sept. 1942; *s* of John Ernest and Neva Moy Ellis Hay; *m* 1965, Barbara McKenna; three *s* one *d* (incl. twin *s*). *Educ:* Perth Modern Sch.; Univ. Western Australia (BA Hons 1964; PhD 1976); Pembroke Coll., Cambridge (BA 1966; MA 1969). University of Western Australia: Lectr, Sen. Lectr and Prof. of English, 1967–87; Dep. Chm., Acad. Bd, 1985; Monash University: Dean, Faculty of Arts, 1987–88; Sen. Dep. Vice-Chancellor, 1988–91; Vice-Chancellor and Pres., Deakin Univ., 1992–95. Editor, Aumla, Jl of Australasian Univs Lang. and Lit. Assoc., 1985–92. Chairman: Carrick Inst. for Learning and Teaching in Higher Educn, 2000–03; Australian Learning and Teaching Council, 2004–; R. L. Martin Inst., 2007–; Queensland Inst. for Med. Res., 2009–. Dep. Chm. Council, Nat. Liby of Australia, 2005–; Chm. Council, Order of Australia, 2009–. Chm., Springfield Health City, 2008–. Mem. Bd, Obesity Australia, 2011–. Chm. of Trustees, Qld Art Gall. and Gall. of Modern Art, 2008–. Dir, Australian Davos Connection Bd, 2007–. Mem., Bd of Trustees, Brisbane Girls Grammar Sch., 2008–. Hon. LittD Deakin, 1995; DUniv Queensland Univ. of Technol., 2004; Hon. DLitt Western Australia, 2005; Hon. LLD Queensland, 2007. *Publications:* Spectrum I, II & III, 1971–79; Directions in Australian Secondary English, 1975; Testing English Comprehension, 1979; Western Australian Literature: a bibliography, 1981; K. S. Pritchard, 1984; European Relations, 1985; Perspectives I, 1985, Perspectives II, 1987; The Early Imprints at New Norcia, 1986; Australian Studies in Tertiary Institutions, 1987; Western Australian Writing, 1990; Narrative Issues, 1990; Bibliography of Australian Literature, I & II, 1995; Bibliography of Australian Literature, vol. I (A-E) 2001, vol. II (F-J) 2004, vol. III (K-O) 2007, vol. IV (P-Z) 2008. *Recreations:* walking, cinema, reading, art museums, architecture. *Address:* 37 Laurel Avenue, Chelmer, Qld 4068, Australia; c/o University Librarian's Office, University of Queensland, Qld 4072, Australia. *Club:* Queensland.

HAY, Sir John (Erroll Audley), 11th Bt *cr* 1663 (NS) of Park, Wigtownshire; *b* 3 Dec. 1935; *o s* of Sir Arthur Thomas Erroll Hay, 10th Bt, ISO, ARIBA and his 1st wife, Hertha Hedwig Paula Louise (*d* 1994), *d* of Ludwig Stölzle, Nagelberg, Austria; *S* father, 1993. *Educ:* Gordonstoun; St Andrews Univ. (MA). *Heir:* none.

HAY, Sir Malcolm John Robert D.; *see* Dalrymple-Hay.

HAY, Peter, CBE 2012; Strategic Director, Adults and Communities (formerly Social Care and Health), Birmingham City Council, since 2003; *b* 17 July 1962; *s* of Martin and Ann Hay; *m* 1989, Carmel Corrigan; one *s* two *d* (and one *s* decd). *Educ:* UC, Swansea (BA Hons 1983); Univ. of Exeter (BPhil 1985); Open Univ. (MBA 1995). CQSW 1985. Humberside County Council: Social worker, 1985–88; Team Ldr Assessment, Grimsby, 1988–89; Prin. Practitioner, Scunthorpe, 1989–92; Area Manager, Grimsby, 1992–96; North East Lincolnshire Council: Asst Dir, Child Care, 1996–97; Acting Dir of Social Services, 1997–98, Dir, 1998–2002; Dir of Community Care, 2002–03. Pres., ADASS, 2011–12 (Vice Pres., 2010–11). Chm., Res. in Practice for Adults, 2011–. *Recreations:* family life, gardening, a good book, a whole range of music, watching sport - preferably a winning Worcester Warriors Rugby team. *Address:* Birmingham City Council, Louisa Ryland House, 44 Newhall Street, Birmingham B3 3PN. *T:* (0121) 303 2992, *Fax:* (0121) 303 4383. *E:* peter.hay@birmingham.gov.uk.

HAY, Rev. Richard, CMG 1992; Vicar, St Paul's, Addlestone, 1999–2007; Rural Dean of Runnymede, 2002–07; *b* 4 May 1942; *s* of Prof. Denys Hay, FBA, FRSE and Sarah Gwyneth Morley; *m* 1969, Miriam Marguerite Alvin England; two *s*. *Educ:* George Watson's Coll., Edinburgh; Edinburgh Univ.; Balliol Coll., Oxford (BA Hons, Mod. Hist.); Cranmer Hall, Durham. Assistant Principal, HM Treasury, 1963–68; Secretary, West Midlands Economic Planning Council, 1966–67; Private Sec. to Financial Sec., Treasury, 1967–68; Principal, Treasury, 1968–73; European Commission: Member, Cabinet of Sir Christopher (later Lord) Soames, Vice-Pres., 1973–75; Dep. Chef de Cabinet, 1975–77; Chef de Cabinet to Mr Christopher (now Lord) Tugendhat, Member, 1977–79; Dir, Economic Structures and Community Interventions, Directorate-Gen. for Economic and Financial Affairs, 1979–81; Dep. Dir-Gen., 1981–86, Dir-Gen., 1986–91, Directorate-General for Personnel and Admin, EC; Special Advr, EC, 1991. Consultant, Sharing of Ministries Abroad, 1992–94. Ordained deacon, 1996, priest, 1997; Curate, St Clement and All Saints, Hastings, 1996–99. Hon. Asst Minister, St Paul's, Woking, 2008–. Chairman: AIACE-UK, 2009– (Dep. Chm., 2009); AIACE-Internat., 2011–15. Trustee, Walsingham, 2008–13 (Chm. of Trustees, 2010–13). *Address:* 15 Fox Close, Pyrford, Surrey GU22 8LP.

HAY, Robert Colquhoun, CBE 1988; WS; Sheriff Principal of North Strathclyde, 1989–98; *b* 1933; *s* of late J. B. Hay, dental surgeon, Stirling and Mrs J. Y. Hay; *m* 1958, Olive Black; two *s* two *d*. *Educ:* Univ. of Edinburgh (MA, LLB). Legal practice, 1957–63, 1968–76; Depute Procurator Fiscal, Edinburgh, 1963–68; Temp. Sheriff, 1984–89; Chm., 1976–81, Pres., 1981–89, Industrial Tribunals for Scotland. Mem., Sheriff Court Rules Council, 1989–95 (Chm., 1993–95). Comr, Northern Lighthouse Bd, 1989–98 (Vice-Chm., 1991–92; Chm., 1992–93). Hon. Sheriff, Dumbarton, 1999. Comr for Clan Hay, 1995–2002. *Publications:* contrib. Laws of Scotland: Stair Memorial Encyclopedia, 1988.

HAY, Robin William Patrick Hamilton; a Recorder, 1985–2005; barrister; *b* 1 Nov. 1939; *s* of William R. Hay and Dora Hay; *m* 1969, Lady Olga Maitland, *qv*; two *s* one *d*. *Educ:* Eltham; Selwyn Coll., Cambridge (MA, LLB). Called to the Bar, Inner Temple, 1964. Legal Advisor: Disciplinary Panel, Inst. and Faculty of Actuaries, 2006–; Statutory Cttees, RPSGB, 2006–. Legal Mem., Res. Ethics Cttee, Nat. Hosp. for Neurology and Neurosurgery, 2001–; Chm., Appeal Panel, Postgrad. Med. Educn and Trng Bd, 2005–09; Legal Assessor: GMC, 2002–; NMC, 2007–; GCC, 2009–; GDC, 2010–. Lay Panellist, ACCA, 2010–. Chm., Nat. (formerly Young) Musicians Symphony Orchestra, 1990–2001. *Recreations:* church tasting, gastronomy, choral singing. *Address:* Lamb Chambers, Lamb Building, Temple, EC4Y 7AS. *Club:* Garrick.

HAY, Prof. Roderick James, DM; FRCP, FRCPath, FMedSci; Professor of Dermatology, Queen's University Belfast, 2002–07, now Emeritus; Chairman, International Foundation for Dermatology, since 2002; Consultant Dermatologist, King's College Hospital NHS Trust, since 2008; Professor of Cutaneous Infection, King's College London, since 2009; *b* 13 April 1947; *s* of Kenneth Stuart Hay and Margery Geidt (*née* Winterbotham); *m* 1973, Delyth Price; two *d*. *Educ:* Wellington Coll.; Merton Coll., Oxford (BA 1968; BM BCh 1971; MA 1979; DM 1980); Guy's Hosp. Med. Sch. MRCP 1974, FRCP 1981; MRCPath 1981, FRCPath 1992. House physician and surgeon, SHO and Dermatol. Registrar, Guy's Hosp., 1971–75; London School of Hygiene and Tropical Medicine: Wellcome Res. Fellow, 1975–77; Lectr, 1977–79; Sen. Lectr, 1979–83; Reader in Clinical Mycology, 1983–89; Hon. Prof., 2000–; Hon. Cons Dermatologist, 1979–2002, Dean, 1993–2000, St John's Inst. of Dermatol.; Prof., UMDS, later Guy's, King's and St Thomas' Hosps' Med. Sch. of KCL, 1989–2002; Mary Dunhill Prof. of Cutaneous Medicine, London Univ., 1990–2002; Clinical Dir, Dermatology, Guy's and St Thomas' NHS Trust, 1996–2000; Dean for Ext. Affairs, GKT, 1998–2002; Queen's University Belfast: Dean, Fac. of Medicine and Health Scis, 2002–05; Hd, Sch. of Medicine and Dentistry (formerly Sch. of Medicine), 2002–07. Inaugural René Touraine Lectr, Eur. Acad. Dermatol., 2012; Gerald Levene Oration, RSocMed, 2014. Non-exec. Dir, Eastern Health and Social Services Bd, 2002–10. Chm. and Trustee, Grants and Res. Cttee, Dunhill Med. Trust, 2015–. FMedSci 2000. Clarence Livingood Award, Amer. Acad. of Dermatology, 2008; Sir Archibald Grey Medal, British Assoc. of Dermatologists, 2011. *Publications:* A Clinician's Guide to Fungal Disease, 1981; Medical Mycology, 1996; contribs to med. and scientific jls on immunology and treatment of fungal infections and epidemiology of skin disease. *Recreations:* gardening, music. *Address:* International Foundation for Dermatology, Willan House, 4 Fitzroy Square, W1T 5HQ. *T:* (020) 7388 6515; Hunters Moon, Plum Lane, Shipton under Wychwood, Oxon OX7 6DZ.

HAY, Sir Ronald Frederick Hamilton, 12th Bt *cr* 1703, of Alderston; *b* 1941; *s* of Sir Ronald Nelson Hay, 11th Bt and Rita, *d* of John Munyard; *S* father, 1988, but his name does not appear on the Official Roll of the Baronetage; *m* 1978, Kathleen, *d* of John Thake; two *s* one *d*. *Heir: s* Alexander James Hay, *b* 1979.

HAY, Prof. Ronald Thomas, PhD; FRS 2010; FRSE; Professor of Molecular Biology, College of Life Sciences, University of Dundee, since 2005; *b* Dundee. *Educ:* Heriot-Watt Univ. (BSc Biochem. 1975); MRC Virol. Unit, Glasgow (PhD 1979). Damon Runyon-Walter Winchell Cancer Fund Postdoctoral Fellow, Harvard Med. Sch., 1979–82; Staff Scientist, MRC Virol. Unit, Glasgow, 1982–85; University of St Andrews: Lectr, then Reader, later Prof. of Molecular Biol., 1985–2005; Dep. Dir, Centre for Biomolecular Scis. Mem., EMBO, 2009. FRSE 1996; FMedSci 2005. *Publications:* contribs to jls incl. Nat. Cell Biol., EMBO Jl, Nat. Structural Molecular Biol., Molecular Cell, Nature, Genes and Develt, Cancer Res., Oncogene, Jl Hepatol., Trends Cell Biol. *Address:* College of Life Sciences, University of Dundee, Dundee DD1 5EH.

HAY, Prof. Simon Iain, DPhil, DSc; FRCPE; FMedSci; Professor of Global Health, University of Washington, since 2015; Professor of Epidemiology, University of Oxford, since 2012; Research Fellow, St John's College, Oxford, since 2012; *b* Rinteln, Germany, 15 Jan. 1971; *s* of Robert Hay and Julia Hay (*née* Harmsworth, now Perry); *m* 2002, Sarah Tomlin; one *s* one *d*. *Educ:* Univ. of Bristol (BSc Hons 1992); Univ. of Oxford (DPhil 1996; DSc 2014). FRCPE 2014. University of Oxford: Postgrad. Res. Asst, 1993–96; Postdoctoral Res. Officer, 1996–99; Sen. Res. Fellow, 1999–2008; Reader of Infectious Disease Epidemiol., 2008–12; Sen. Res. Fellow, Wellcome Trust, 2006–. Pres., RSTM&H, 2013–15. FMedSci 2015. *Publications:* over 250 articles in learned jls. *Recreations:* gardening, music, reading, travel, natural history. *Address:* Institute for Health Metrics and Evaluation, Department for Global Health, University of Washington, 2301 Fifth Avenue, Suite 600, Seattle, WA 98121, USA. *T:* (206) 8972878. *E:* sihay@uw.edu; Wellcome Trust Centre for Human Genetics, Nuffield Department of Medicine, University of Oxford, Roosevelt Drive, Oxford OX3 7BN.

HAY-CAMPBELL, (Thomas) Ian, LVO 1994; HM Diplomatic Service, retired; Deputy Head of Mission, Oslo, 2001–05; *b* 19 May 1945; *s* of Thomas Neil Hay-Campbell and Anthea Joan Hay-Campbell (*née* Carey); *m* 1970, Margaret Lorraine (*née* Hoadley); four *s*. *Educ:* Wanganui Collegiate Sch., NZ; Victoria Univ. of Wellington (BA Hons History). Radio Journalist, NZBC, Wellington, 1969–72; Radio Producer, subseq. Editor, BBC World Service, 1972–84; joined FCO, 1984; First Sec., FCO, 1984–87; Dep. Head of Mission, Kinshasa, 1987–90; FCO, 1990–94; Head of Press and Public Affairs Section, Moscow, 1994–97; Dep. High Comr, Harare, 1998–2001. Chm., Friends of Nat. Archives. *Recreations:* modern history, family history research, reading, tennis, trams. *Address:* High House, Bucknell, Shropshire SY7 0AA. *T:* (01547) 530750.

HAY DAVISON, Ian Frederic; *see* Davison.

HAY-PLUMB, Paula Maria; Finance Director, Rosling King LLP, since 2011; *b* 18 March 1960; *d* of Henry Sephton Green and Eileen Green (*née* Millburn); *m* 1984, Martin Hay-Plumb; one *s* one *d*. *Educ:* Univ. of Exeter (BSc Hons 1980). ACA 1983; MCT 1989. Qualified as chartered accountant with Peat, Marwick, Mitchell; Marks and Spencer plc, 1984–88; Olympia & York Canary Wharf Ltd, 1989–93; Finance Dir, 1994–96, Man. Dir (Ops), 1996–99, Chief Exec., 1999–2002, English Partnerships; Corporate Finance and Gp Reporting Dir, Marks and Spencer plc, 2003–05. Chairman: DETR Coalfields Task Force, 1997–98 (reported 1998); Nat. Australia Gp Common Investment Fund Trustee Ltd, 2007–10; non-executive Director: Skipton Building Soc., 2006–10; Forensic Science Service Ltd, 2006–12; Nat. Audit Office, 2010–14; Hyde Housing Assoc., 2012–; Aberforth Smaller Companies Trust plc, 2014–. A Crown Estate Comr, 2015–. Trustee, Coalfields Regeneration Trust, 1999–2008. *Recreations:* music, theatre.

HAYASHI, Keiichi; Ambassador from Japan to the Court of St James's, since 2011; *b* 8 Feb. 1951. *Educ:* Kyoto Univ. (BA Law); Stanford Univ. (MA Political Scis). Joined Min. of Foreign Affairs, Japan, 1974; Director: 2nd SE Asia Div., 1991–93; Treaties Div., 1993–96; Counsellor, London, 1996–99; Deputy Director-General: N American Affairs Bureau, 1999–2000; Treaties Bureau, 2000–02; Dir-Gen., Internat. Legal Affairs Bureau, 2002–05; Ambassador to Ireland, 2005–08; Dep. Vice-Minister for Foreign Affairs, 2008; Asst Cabinet Sec., 2008–10. *Publications:* If You Know about Ireland, You Will Better Understand Japan, 2009. *Address:* Embassy of Japan, 101–104 Piccadilly, W1J 7JT.

HAYCOCKS, Myra Anne; *see* Kinghorn, M. A.

HAYDAY, Anthony Victor; HM Diplomatic Service, retired; Ambassador to Madagascar, 1987–90; *b* 1 June 1930; *s* of Charles Leslie Victor Hayday and Catherine (*née* McCarthy); *m* 1966, Anne Heather Moffat (*d* 1995); one *s* one *d*. *Educ:* Beckenham and Penge Grammar School. Royal Air Force, 1949–50; HM Foreign (later Diplomatic) Service, 1950; Brazzaville, 1953; British Information Services, New York, 1955; FO, 1958; Vice Consul, Houston, 1961; 2nd Secretary, Algiers, 1962; FO (later FCO), 1966; 1st Secretary, New Delhi, 1969; Head of Chancery, Freetown, 1973; on secondment to Commonwealth Secretariat, 1976–80; Dep. High Comr, Calcutta, 1981–85; Consul-Gen., Cleveland, 1985–87. *Recreations:* birdwatching, athletics. *Address:* Meadow Cottage, Swillbrook, Minety, Malmesbury, Wilts SN16 9QA. *Clubs:* Blackheath Harriers; Bengal (Calcutta).

HAYDEN, Ven. David Frank; Archdeacon of Norfolk, 2002–12; *b* 25 Jan. 1947; *s* of Donald and Margaret Hayden; *m* 1968, Ruby Cowles; two *d*. *Educ:* Tyndale Hall, Bristol (DipTh 1969, BD 1971); London Univ. Ordained deacon, 1971, priest, 1972; Curate: St Matthew's, Silverhill, 1971; Galleywood Common, 1975; Rector, Redgrave cum Botesdale with Rickinghall, 1979–84; RD, Hartismere, 1981–84; Vicar, Cromer, 1984–2002; Hosp. Chaplain (pt-time), 1984–2000; RD, Repps, 1995–2002. Hon. Canon, Norwich Cathedral, 1996–2002. *Recreations:* spending time with wife, children and grandchildren; being on, in, or near water. *Address:* Church Farm House, Church Lane, Oulton Broad, Lowestoft, Suffolk NR32 3JN.

HAYDEN, Prof. Jacqueline, (Mrs. E. M. Dunbar), CBE 2013; Dean, Postgraduate Medical Studies, Health Education North West and Universities of Manchester and Lancashire, since 1997; *b* Croydon, 4 Dec. 1950; *d* of late Robert Leslie James Hayden and Dorothy Blanche Hayden; *m* 1976, Edward Milne Dunbar; two *s*. *Educ:* Croydon High Sch. GPDST; St George's Hosp. Med. Sch., Univ. of London (MB BS 1974; DSc (Med) 2013). MRCP 1976, FRCP 1996; DCH 1977; MRCGP 1979, FRCGP 1987; DRCOG 1979; FRCPE 2012. Preregistration House Officer: St James' Hosp., Balham, 1974–75; Ashford Hosp., Middx, 1975; Postregistration Hse Officer, Medicine Oxford, 1975–76; Gen. Practice Trng Scheme, Oxford, 1976–79; Principal, Unsworth Medical Centre, Bury, 1979–2010. Regl Advr in Gen. Practice, North West RHA and Univ. of Manchester, 1991–96. Associate, GMC, 2005–. FAcadMed 2011. *Publications:* (jtly) A Guide for New Principals, 1996; *contributor:* The Medical Annual, 1987; The Practice Receptionist, 1989; The Child Surveillance Handbook, 1990, 2nd edn 1994; Change and Teamwork in Primary Care, 1993; Professional Development in General Practice, 1996; The Very Stuff of General Practice, 1999; Medical Management, 2012; over 30 jl articles and editorials. *Address:* Health Education North West, Three Piccadilly Place, Manchester M1 3BN. *T:* (0161) 625 7641. *E:* jacky.hayden@nw.hee.nhs.uk; 12 Mercers Road, Heywood, Lancs OL10 2NP. *T:* (01706) 625470; 2 Cliff Terrace, Devonport Hill, Kingsand, Cornwall PL10 1NJ. *T:* 07976 247104. *E:* jackyhayden@aol.com.

HAYDEN, Hon. William George, AC 1989; cattle farmer, Brisbane Valley; Governor-General of Australia, 1989–96; *b* Brisbane, 23 Jan. 1933; *s* of G. Hayden, Oakland, Calif, USA; *m* 1960, Dallas, *d* of W. Broadfoot; one *s* two *d* (and one *d* decd). *Educ:* Brisbane State High Sch.; Univ. of Qld (BEcon). Public Service, Qld, 1950–52; Police Constable, Qld Police Force, 1953–61. MHR (Lab) for Oxley, Qld, 1961–88. Parly Spokesman on Health and Welfare, 1969–72; Minister for Social Security, Australian Govt, 1972–75; Federal Treasurer, June–Nov. 1975; Leader of Australian Labor Party and the Opposition, 1977–83; spokesman on defence, 1976–77 and on economic management, 1976–83; Minister for Foreign Affairs, 1983–87, and for Trade, 1987–88. Adjunct Prof. of Humanities, Qld Univ. of Technol., Brisbane, 1996. Chm., Editl Cttee, Quadrant Jl, 1998–2004. Res. Vis. Fellow, Jane Franklin Hall, Univ. of Tasmania, 2000. Patron: (Qld Br.) Australian Inst. Internat. Affairs; (Qld Br.) Australian Fabian Soc.; Member: Gen. Sir John Monash Foundn; Assoc. of Former Mems of Parlt of Australia. Hon. FRACP 1995. Hon. Dr: Griffith Univ., 1990; Univ. of Central Qld, 1992; Hon. LLD Univ. of Qld, 1990; Hon. DLitt Univ. of S Qld, 1997. Australian Humanist of the Year, 1996. Kt, Order of St John in Australia, 1989. Gwanghwa Medal, Order of Diplomatic Merit, Korea. Commander, Order of Three Stars (Latvia). *Publications:* Hayden: an autobiography, 1996. *Address:* PO Box 7829, Waterfront Place, Brisbane, Qld 4001, Australia.

HAYDEN, William Joseph, CBE 1976; Chairman and Chief Executive, Jaguar plc, 1990–92; *b* 19 Jan. 1929; *s* of George Hayden and Mary Ann Hayden (*née* Overhead); *m* 1954, Mavis Ballard (*d* 2003); two *s* two *d*. *Educ:* Romford Tech. College. Served Army, 1947–49. Ford Motor Co.: Briggs Motor Bodies, Dagenham, 1950–57; financial staff, Dagenham, 1957–63; Div. Controller, Ford Chassis, Transmission and Engine Div., Dagenham, 1963–67; Gen. Ops Manager, Transmission, Chassis and Truck Mfg Ops, 1967–71; Vice-President: Truck Mfg Ops, 1971; Power Train Ops, 1972; Mfg Ford of Europe, Inc., 1974–90. Director (non-executive): Hawtell Whiting, 1992–96; Trans Tec. 1993–96. *Recreations:* golf, gardening, soccer. *Clubs:* Thorndon Park Golf; Stratford on Avon Golf.

HAYDER, Mo; writer of crime fiction; *b* UK, 1962; one *d*. *Educ:* American Univ., Washington (MA Film Making): Bath Spa Univ. (MA Creative Writing). *Publications:* Birdman, 2000; The Treatment, 2001; Tokyo, 2003; Ritual, 2008; Skin, 2009; Pig Island, 2010; Gone, 2010; Hanging Hill, 2011; Poppet, 2013; Wolf, 2014. *Address:* c/o Gregory & Company, 3 Barb Mews, W6 7PA.

HAYDON, Francis Edmund Walter; HM Diplomatic Service, retired; *b* 23 Dec. 1928; *s* of late Surgeon Captain Walter T. Haydon, RN and Maria Christina Haydon (*née* Delahoyde); *m* 1959, Isabel Dorothy Kitchin; two *s* two *d*. *Educ:* Downside School; Magdalen College, Oxford. BA (1st cl. Modern History) 1949. Asst London diplomatic correspondent, Agence France-Presse, 1951–52; Asst diplomatic correspondent, Reuters, 1952–55; joined Foreign Office, 1955; Second Sec., Benghazi, 1959, Beirut, 1962; First Sec., Blantyre, 1969, Ankara, 1978; Counsellor, FCO, 1981–87. *Recreations:* lawn tennis, cricket, bridge, travel, enjoying the countryside. *Address:* Le Picachon, La Rue des Bouillons, Trinity, Jersey JE3 5BB. *T:* (01534) 863155.

HAYE, Colvyn Hugh, CBE 1983; Commissioner for Hong Kong, 1984–87; *b* 7 Dec. 1925; 3rd *s* of Colvyn Hugh Haye and Avis Rose Kelly; *m* 1949, Gloria Mary Stansbury; two *d*. *Educ:* Sherwood Coll.; Univ. of Melbourne (BA, Teachers' Cert.); Christ Church Coll., Oxford (Overseas Service Trng Course). Served War, RNVR, Midshipman and Sub-Lt, 1944–46. Victorian State Educn Service, 1947–52; joined Colonial Service, now HMOCS, Hong Kong Government: Educn Officer, 1953; Sen. Educn Officer, 1962 (world tour, educnl estabs, and trng at Centre for Educnl Television Overseas, London, 1964); Asst Dir and Head of Educnl Television Service, 1969; Dep. Dir, 1975; Dir of Educn and Official Mem., Legislative Council, 1980; Sec., Administrative Service and Comr, London Office, 1984. Jardine Educn Foundn Visitor, Univs of Oxford and Cambridge, 1990–97. Mem. Council, Overseas Service Pensioners' Assoc., 1988–97. JP Hong Kong, 1971–87. *Recreations:* reading, writing, talking, walking. *Club:* Hong Kong (Hong Kong).

HAYES, Sir Brian, Kt 1998; CBE 1992; QPM 1985; security consultant, since 1998; Deputy Commissioner of Metropolitan Police, 1995–98; *b* 25 Jan. 1940; 2nd *s* of James and Jessie Hayes; *m* 1960, Priscilla Rose Bishop; one *s* three *d*. *Educ:* Plaistow County Grammar Sch.; Sheffield Univ. (BA Hons 1st Cl. Mod. Langs). Metropolitan Police, 1959–77; seconded Northern Ireland, 1971–72; Police Adviser, Mexico, 1975 and 1976, Colombia, 1977 and 1993; British Police representative, EEC, 1976–77; Asst Chief Constable, Surrey Constabulary, 1977–81; Dep. Chief Constable, Wiltshire Constabulary, 1981–82; Chief Constable, Surrey Constabulary, 1982–91; Inspector of Constabulary for SE England, 1991–95. Vice-Pres., ACPO, 1990–91. Chm., Police Athletic Assoc., 1989–91 (Nat. Sec., 1984–88); Pres., Union Sportive des Polices d'Europe, 1990–92. Special Advr on Security to FA, 1997–2002; Security Consultant, TRI-MEX Internat. Ltd, 1999–2002. Freeman, City of London, 1998. OStJ 1987. Police Long Service and Good Conduct Medal, 1981; Cruz al Mérito Policial (Spain), 1998. *Recreations:* karate, rowing, cycling, swimming, golf.

HAYES, Sir Brian (David), GCB 1988 (KCB 1980; CB 1976); Permanent Secretary, Department of Trade and Industry, 1985–89, retired (Joint Permanent Secretary, 1983–85); *b* 5 May 1929; *s* of late Charles and Flora Hayes, Bramerton, Norfolk; *m* 1958, Audrey Jenkins (*d* 2014); one *s* one *d*. *Educ:* Norwich Sch.; Corpus Christi Coll., Cambridge. BA (Hist.) 1952, PhD (Cambridge) 1956. RASC, 1947–49. Joined Min. of Agriculture, Fisheries and Food, 1956; Asst Private Sec. to the Minister, 1958; Asst Sec., 1967; Under-Sec., Milk and Poultry Gp, 1970–73; Dep. Sec., 1973–78; Permanent Sec., 1979–83. Director: Guardian Royal Exchange, 1989–99; Tate & Lyle, 1989–98; Adv. Dir, Unilever plc, 1990–99. Chm., CBI Educn Foundn, 1991–96. Dir, SANE, 1990–2007. Lloyd's Members' Ombudsman, 1994–2007. *Recreations:* reading, television, opera.

HAYES, Christine; *see* Farnish, C.

HAYES, Christine Isobel, (Kirsty); HM Diplomatic Service; Ambassador to Portugal, since 2014; *b* Aberdeen, 2 Feb. 1977; *d* of Robert Colin and Rowena Antoinette Paton; *m* 2002, Peter Richard Hayes, *qv*; one *s* one *d*. *Educ:* Dame Alice Harpur Sch.; Inst. of Archaeol., University Coll. London (BA Hons Archaeol.); Sch. of Oriental and African Studies, Univ. of London (MA Internat. Studies and Diplomacy); Kingston Business Sch. (MA HR Strategy). Inst. of Archaeol., 1998–99; entered FCO, 1999; Dept of Envmt Policy, FCO, 1999–2000; Vice-Consul (Pol and Econ.), Hong Kong, 2000–01; Private Sec. to Ambassador, Washington, 2001–05; EU Dept, FCO, 2005–07; Human Resources Dept, FCO, 2007–08; Consultant, UNDP Regl Centre, Colombo, Sri Lanka, 2009–10; Head: Corporate Communications, FCO, 2010; Internat. Orgns Dept, 2011–13. *Recreations:* eventing, show jumping, yoga, scuba diving, swimming. *Address:* British Embassy Lisbon, Rua da São Bernardo, 33, 1249–082 Lisbon, Portugal. *T:* 213924000. *E:* Kirsty.hayes@fco.gov.uk. *Club:* Farmers.

HAYES, Helen Elizabeth; MP (Lab) Dulwich and West Norwood, since 2015; *b* 8 Aug. 1974. *Educ:* Balliol Coll., Oxford (BA Hons PPE); London Sch. of Econs and Pol Sci. (MSc Social Policy and Admin). MRTPI. Jt Man. Dir, Town Centres Ltd, subseq. Urban Practitioners, 1998–2012; Partner, Allies and Morrison, 2011–15. Mem. (Lab) Southwark LBC, 2010–15. *Address:* House of Commons, SW1A 0AA.

HAYES, Most Rev. James Martin; Archbishop (RC) of Halifax (NS), 1967–90, now Archbishop Emeritus; *b* 27 May 1924; *s* of late L. J. Hayes. *Educ:* St Mary's Univ., Halifax; Holy Heart Seminary, Halifax; Angelicum Univ., Rome. Asst, St Mary's Basilica, 1947–54; Chancellor and Sec. of Archdiocese of Halifax, 1957–65; Rector, St Mary's Basilica, 1963–65; Aux. Bp of Halifax, 1965–66; Apostolic Administrator of Archdiocese of Halifax, 1966–67. Pres., Canadian Conf. of Catholic Bishops, 1987–89. Hon. DLitt St Anne's Coll., Church Point, NS, 1966; Hon. DTh King's Coll., Halifax, NS, 1967; Hon. DHL Mount St Vincent Univ., Halifax, 1985; Hon. LLD: St Mary's Univ., Halifax, 1985; St Thomas Univ., 1989; Hon. DD Atlantic Sch. of Theol., Halifax, 1986. *Address:* Catholic Pastoral Centre, Archdiocese of Halifax, PO Box 1527, 1531 Grafton Street, Halifax, NS B3J 2Y3, Canada.

HAYES, Jeremy Joseph James; barrister; freelance journalist and broadcaster; *b* 20 April 1953; *s* of Peter and Daye Hayes; *m* 1979, Alison Gail Mansfield; one *s* one *d*. *Educ:* Oratory Sch.; Chelmer Inst. LLB London. Called to the Bar, Middle Temple, 1977; leading counsel in high profile criminal trials. Formerly Political Ed., Punch mag.; freelance columnist and restaurant reviewer, London Paper, 2006–; paper reviewer, Stephen Nolan Show, BBC Radio 5 Live, 2013–. MP (C) Harlow, 1983–97; contested (C) same seat, 1997. PPS to Minister of State, NI Office, 1992–94, DoE, 1994–97. Member, Select Committee: on Social Services, 1987–90; on Health, 1990–91; on National Heritage, 1996–97; formerly: Member: All Party Parly Gp on Human Rights; All Party Parly Gp on Race Relations; Vice Chm., All Party AIDS Cttee; Chm., All Party ASH Gp. Promoter: Parents' Aid (No 2) Bill; Sexual Offences Bill; Sponsor: Video Recordings Act; Protection of Children against Tobacco Act; Freedom of Information (Medical Records) Act. Mem., Amnesty Internat. Fellow: Industry and Parliament Trust; All Party Armed Forces Trust. Hon. Dir, State Legislative Leaders Foundn, USA. Vice Pres., Wendens Ambo Cricket Club. Freeman, City of London. Lord of the Manor, High Easter, 2002–. *Publications:* An Unexpected MP, 2014. *Recreations:* banker and taxi driver for my children, dining at the Savile, propping up the bar at El Vino, Fleet Street. *Address:* Goldsmith Chambers, Goldsmith Building, Temple, EC4Y 7BL. *W:* jerryhayes.co.uk, www.twitter.com/jerryhayes1. *Clubs:* Savile; Essex.

HAYES, Rt Hon. John Henry; PC 2013; MP (C) South Holland and The Deepings, since 1997; Senior Parliamentary Adviser to the Prime Minister, since 2013; Minister of State, Home Office, since 2015; *b* 23 June 1958; *s* of late Henry John Hayes and Lily Hayes; *m* 1997, Susan Jane Hopewell; two *s*. *Educ:* Colfe's Grammar Sch., London; Univ. of Nottingham (BA Hons, PGCE). Joined The Data Base Ltd, 1983, Dir, 1986–99. Mem., Nottinghamshire CC, 1985–98. Contested (C) Derbyshire NE, 1987, 1992. Shadow Schools Minister, 2000–01; Opposition Pairing Whip, 2001–02; Shadow Agriculture and Fisheries Minister, 2002–03; Shadow Housing and Planning Minister, 2003–05; Shadow Transport Minister, 2005; Shadow Minister: for Vocational Educn and Skills, 2005–07; for Lifelong Learning, Further and Higher Educn, 2007–10; Minister of State: for Further Educn Skills and Lifelong Learning, BIS and DFE, 2010–12; for Energy, DECC, 2012–13; (Minister without Portfolio), Cabinet Office, 2013–14; DfT, 2014–15. Member, Select Committee: Agriculture, 1997–99; Educn and Employment, 1998–99; Administration, 2001–02; Mem., Cttee of Selection, 2001–02. A Vice-Chm., Cons. Party, 1999–2000. Adjunct Associate Prof., Richmond, The American Internat. Univ. in London, 2002–10. *Recreations:* the arts (particularly English painting, poetry and prose), good food and wine, many sports (including darts and boxing), gardening, making jam, antiques, architecture, aesthetics. *Address:* House of Commons, SW1A 0AA. *T:* (020) 7219 1389. *Clubs:* Carlton; Spalding, Spalding Gentlemen's Soc. (Lincs).

HAYES, John William, CBE 1995; Chairman, Law Society Pension Scheme, 2002–13 (Director, Law Society Pensions Archive and Communications Forum); *b* 10 Feb. 1945; *s* of late Dick Hayes and Bridget Isobel Hayes; *m* 1970, Jennifer Hayes (*née* Harvey); two *s* one *d*. *Educ:* Nottingham High Sch.; Morecambe Grammar Sch.; Victoria Univ. of Manchester (LLB). Solicitor. Articled Thomas Foord, 1966–69; Worthing Borough Council, 1966–69; Nottingham County Borough Council, 1969–71; Somerset CC, 1971–74; Asst, Dep. Clerk and Dep. Chief Exec., Notts CC, 1974–80; Clerk and Chief Exec., Warwicks CC, 1980–86; Sec.-Gen., Law Soc., 1987–96; Chm., OPRA, 1996–2001. Chm., Local Govt Gp, Law Soc., 1981–82; Sec., Warwicks Probation Cttee, 1983–86; Clerk to Warwicks Magistrates' Courts' Cttee, 1983–86; Clerk to Lord Lieut of Warwicks, 1980–86. Chm., Ind. Inquiry into River Vessel Safety, 1992. Chairman: Disciplinary Appeals Cttee, CIPFA, 2001–10; Actuarial Profession Disciplinary Bd, 2004–09. Chm., Coventry Dio. Church Urban Fund, 1989–91; Member: Bishop of Coventry's Board of Social Responsibility, 1981–86; Inner Cities' Task Force, 1985–86. Mem., Ind. Remuneration Panel, 2001–04, Ind. Mem., Standards Cttee, 2001– (Chm., 2006–09), W Sussex CC. Legal Assessor, British Council of Osteopathy, 1998–2003. Mem. Council, Warwick Univ., 1980–90; Gov., Univ. of Chichester (formerly UC Chichester), 2001–07. Gov., Kingsley School, 1986–92; Foundn Gov., All Saints C of E Primary Sch., IoW, 2013– (Chm., 2014–). Hon. LLD De Montfort, 1996. *Recreations:* cricket, music, idleness.

HAYES, Kirsty Isobel; *see* Hayes, C. I.

HAYES, Patricia Jane; Director of Aviation, Department for Transport, since 2013; *b* 9 June 1966; *d* of William and Emily Rennie; *m* 1992, Andrew Hayes; three *s*. *Educ:* Armagh Girls' High Sch.; Pembroke Coll., Oxford (BA PPE 1987, MA). Various posts, Dept of Transport and DETR, 1987–96; First Sec., Transport, British Embassy, Washington, 1996–99; Sec., Sustainable Devlt Commn, 2000–02; Department for Transport: Hd, Charging and Local Transport Div., 2002–04; Hd, NW East Midlands Div., 2004–06; Hd, Talent Mgt and People

Develt, 2006–07; Dir, Road and Vehicle Safety and Standards, 2007–11; Dir of Roads, 2011–13; Dir, Motoring, Freight and London, 2013. *Address:* Department for Transport, Great Minster House, 33 Horseferry Road, SW1P 4DR. *T:* (020) 7944 5212.

HAYES, Dr Peter Richard; HM Diplomatic Service; Director, Overseas Territories, Foreign and Commonwealth Office, since 2012; Commissioner: of the British Antarctic Territory, since 2012; of the British Indian Ocean Territory, since 2012; *b* 11 April 1963; *s* of late Jasper Terrence Hayes and of Greta Louvaine Hayes; *m* 2002, Christine, (Kirsty), Isobel Paton (*see* C. I. Hayes); one *s* one *d. Educ:* County Sch., Ashford, Surrey; Univ. of Surrey (BSc Physics); King's Coll. London (PhD 1989). Post-doctoral res. associate, KCL, 1989–90; SSO, NPL, 1990–93; Team Leader, Mgt and Technology Services, DTI, 1993–94; Head of Competition Issues, Cabinet Office, 1994–96; Asst Dir, Internat., OST, 1997–98; Dep. Hd, Envmt, Sci. and Energy, FCO, 1998–2000; Dir, Nuclear Decommng, DTI, 2000–01; Counsellor, then Consul Gen., Washington, 2001–05; Principal Private Sec. to Sec. of State for Foreign and Commonwealth Affairs, 2005–07; High Comr, Sri Lanka and non-resident to Maldives, 2008–10; Hd of Public Affairs, London Stock Exchange Gp (on secondment), 2011–12; Hd, Counter Proliferation, FCO, 2012. *Publications:* contrib. to acad. physics pubns and jls. *Recreation:* family. *Address:* Foreign and Commonwealth Office, King Charles Street, SW1A 2AH. *Club:* Farmers.

HAYES, Dr William; President, St John's College, University of Oxford, 1987–2001 (Hon. Fellow, 2001); Senior Research Fellow, Clarendon Laboratory, Oxford University, since 1987; Pro-Vice-Chancellor, University of Oxford, 1990–2001; *b* 12 Nov. 1930; *s* of Robert Hayes and Eileen Tobin; *m* 1962, Joan Ferriss (*d* 1996); two *s* one *d. Educ:* University Coll., Dublin (MSc, PhD); Oxford Univ. (MA, DPhil). FInstP 1960. St John's College, Oxford: 1851 Overseas Schol., 1955–57; Official Fellow and Tutor, 1960–87; Principal Bursar, 1977–87; University Lectr, 1962–85, Prof., 1985–87, Oxford Univ.; Dir and Head of Clarendon Lab., Oxford, 1985–87. Oxford University: Mem., Gen. Bd of the Faculties, 1985–88; Mem., Hebdomadal Council, 1989–2000; Chm., Curators of Univ. Chest, 1992–2000; Delegate, OUP, 1991–2001. Temporary research appointments at: Argonne Nat. Lab., 1957–58; Purdue Univ., 1963–64; RCA Labs, Princeton, 1968; Univ. of Illinois, 1971; Bell Labs, 1974. Mem., Physics Cttee, SERC, 1982–85. Sen. Foreign Fellow, American Nat. Sci. Foundn, 1963–64; Fellow, American Physical Soc., 1990. Hon. MRIA 1998. Hon. DSc: NUI, 1988; Purdue Univ., 1996. *Publications:* (ed) Crystals with the Fluorite Structure, 1974; (with R. Loudon) Scattering of Light by Crystals, 1978; (with A. M. Stoneham) Defects and Defect Processes in non-metallic Solids, 1985; contribs to Procs of Royal Soc., Jl of Physics, Physical Rev., etc. *Recreations:* walking, reading, listening to music. *Address:* St John's College, Oxford OX1 3JP. *T:* (01865) 277300.

HAYES, William; General Secretary, Communication Workers Union, 2001–15; *b* 8 June 1953; *s* of William and Margaret Hayes; *m* 1995, Dian Lee; one *s* one *d. Educ:* St Swithin's Secondary Modern; Univ. of Liverpool (Dip. Trade Union Studies). Fitter-welder, 1968–71; factory worker, 1971–73; unemployed, 1973–74; joined Post Office, 1974, Postman; Lay Official, Union of Post Office Workers, subseq. UCW, then CWU, 1992; Nat. Official, CWU, 1992–2001. *Recreations:* films, music, books, Liverpool FC. *Address:* Communication Workers Union, 150 The Broadway, Wimbledon, SW19 1RX.

HAYFORD; *see* Casely-Hayford.

HAYHOE, Thomas Edward George; Chairman, West Middlesex University Hospital NHS Trust, since 2010; *b* Wickham, Hants, 3 March 1956; *s* of Capt. George Hayhoe, RN and Carenza Hayhoe (*née* Lee); *m* 1st, 1978, Helen Kendal (marr. diss. 1998); one *d*; 2nd, 1999, Natalie Jobling. *Educ:* Corpus Christi Coll., Cambridge (BA Hons Hist. 1977); Graduate Sch. of Business, Stanford Univ. (MBA 1980). Pres., Cambridge Students Union, 1977–78; Harkness Fellow, 1978–80. Mgt consultant, McKinsey & Co., 1980–85; Gp Planning and Develt Manager, 1985–88, Gen. Manager, Stationery and Cards, 1988–92, WH Smith plc; mgt consultant and entrepreneur, Brackenbury Gp, subseq. The Chambers, 1992–2010. Chm., Gamestation Ltd, 2000–02. Dir and Dep. Chm., Ealing, Hammersmith and Hounslow HA, 1985–2000; Chm., W London Pathol. Consortium, 2000–04. Chm., Building Better Health W London Ltd, 2005–10; Dir, Medihome Ltd, 2005–09. Chm., Fitness to Practise Panel, Nursing and Midwifery Council, 2012–. Trustee, Arthritis Res. UK, 2012–. Contested (SDP) Wycombe, 1987. Cdre, Ranelagh Sailing Club, 1991–92. *Recreations:* sailing, cycling, singing, urban beekeeping, opera, ballet. *Address:* 21 Tabor Road, W6 0BN. *E:* tom@hayhoe.net. *Club:* Royal Ocean Racing (Rear Cdre, 2007–08; Vice Cdre, 2008–10).

HAYMAN, family name of **Baroness Hayman**.

HAYMAN, Baroness *cr* 1995 (Life Peer), of Dartmouth Park in the London Borough of Camden; **Helene Valerie Hayman,** GBE 2012; PC 2001; Lord Speaker, House of Lords, 2006–11; *b* 26 March 1949; *d* of late Maurice Middleweek and Maude Middleweek; *m* 1974, Martin Hayman; four *s. Educ:* Wolverhampton Girls' High Sch.; Newnham Coll., Cambridge (MA; Hon. Fellow 2008). Pres., Cambridge Union, 1969. Worked with Shelter, Nat. Campaign for the Homeless, 1969; Camden Council Social Services Dept, 1971; Dep. Dir, Nat. Council for One Parent Families, 1974. Vice-Chairman: Bloomsbury HA, 1988–90 (Mem., 1985–90); Bloomsbury and Islington HA, 1991–92 (Mem., 1990–91); Chm., Whittington Hosp. NHS Trust, 1992–97. Contested (Lab) Wolverhampton SW, Feb. 1974; MP (Lab) Welwyn and Hatfield, Oct. 1974–1979. Parliamentary Under-Secretary of State: DETR, 1997–98; DoH, 1998–99; Minister of State, MAFF, 1999–2001. Member: Select Cttee on the Assisted Dying for the Terminally Ill Bill, 2004–05; Constitution Cttee, 2005–06. Chairman: Cancer Res. UK, 2001–05; Human Tissue Authy, 2005–06. Member: Human Fertilisation and Embryology Authy, 2005–06; GMC, 2013–. Member: RCOG Ethics Cttee, 1982–96; UCL/UCH Cttee on Ethics of Clinical Investigation, 1987–96 (Vice-Chm., 1990–96); Council, UCL, 1992–97; Review Cttee, Anti-Terrorism, Crime and Security Act, 2002–03; Bd, Roadsafe, 2002–06. Jt Pres., Hansard Soc., 2010–11. Hon. Joint President: UK Br., CPA, 2006–11; IPU, 2006–11. Trustee: Royal Botanical Gardens, Kew, 2002–06; Tropical Health and Educn Trust, 2005–06; Sabin Vaccine Inst., 2011–; Malaria Consortium, 2013–; Disasters Emergency Cttee, 2014–. Hon. Dr: Middx; N London; Brunel, 2012; Hon. DSc Herts, 1999; Hon. LLD Wolverhampton, 2007. *Address:* House of Lords, SW1A 0PW. *T:* (020) 7219 5083.

HAYMAN, Andrew Christopher, CBE 2006; QPM 2004; security commentator, analyst and strategic adviser, since 2008; Assistant Commissioner, Special Operations, in charge of counter terrorism, royalty and diplomatic protection and security of London, 2005–08; *b* 31 July 1959; *s* of Geoffrey and Valerie Hayman; *m* 1993, Jane Nicola Corbett; two *d. Educ:* Exeter Univ. (MA); Fitzwilliam Coll., Cambridge (Postgrad. Dip. in Applied Criminology). Joined Essex Police, 1978; Chief Inspector, Ops, 1993–95; Divl Comdr, Supt and Chief Supt, 1995–98; Metropolitan Police: Comdr, i/c Drugs and Crime, 1998–2001; Dep. Asst Comr, Anti Corruption, and Dep. to Dep. Comr, 2001–02; Chief Constable, Norfolk Constabulary, 2002–05. Security commentator, ITV, NBC and The Times, 2008–11. Mem., Adv. Council on Misuse of Drugs, 2001–06; Chm., Drugs Cttee, 2001–06, Terrorism Cttee, 2006–08, Security Advr, 2008–, ACPO. Broadcaster, Policing Britain, BBC Radio 4, 2009. Ext. Examr, Cambridge Univ., 2001–08. Anglia Ruskin (formerly Anglia Polytechnic) University: Gov., 2000–11 (Chm., Appeals Cttee, 2010–11); Vis. Fellow, 2011–. Chm. of Govs, St Mary's Kelvedon Primary Sch., 2009–. *Publications:* (with M. Gilmore) The Terrorist Hunters, 2009. *Recreations:* gardening, theatre, reading, keeping fit.

HAYMAN, (Anne) Carolyn, OBE 2003; Co-founder, Peace Direct, 2004; *b* 23 April 1951; *d* of Walter Kurt Hayman, *qv* and late Margaret Riley Crann; *m* 1980, Peter John Bury (marr. diss. 2012); two *d. Educ:* Putney High Sch. for Girls; Newnham Coll., Cambridge (BA Classics and Philosophy); Sch. of Oriental and African Studies (MSc Econ). Admin. Trainee, ODM, 1975–78; Advr, Central Policy Review Staff, 1978–80; Senior Consultant, Office Automation: EOSYS, 1980–82; Coopers & Lybrand, 1982–83; Jt Man. Dir, Korda & Co., 1983–95; Exec. Dir, Rutherford Ventures, 1995–96; Chief Exec., Foyer Fedn, 1996–2004. Co. Sec., Sri Lanka Campaign for Peace and Justice, 2010–; Dir, Network for Social Change, 2015–. Chairman: Cambridge Animation Systems, 1990–96; Atraverda, 1992–97. Dir, Technology & Law, 1982–85. Member: Commonwealth Develt Corp., 1994–99; Working Gp on 14–19 Reform, 2003–04. Member: Council, Pitcom, 1981–83; Council for Industry and Higher Educn, 1992–97; Board, Industrial Res. and Tech. Unit, 1995–97; Quaker UN Cttee, 2006–11. Editor, Work and Society, 1984–86. Trustee, Solar Aid, 2008–11. *Recreations:* music, swimming, cycling. *Address:* 36A Lawford Road, NW5 2LN. *T:* (020) 7916 2689.

HAYMAN, His Honour John David Woodburn; a Circuit Judge, 1976–92; *b* 24 Aug. 1918; *m* Jane (*née* Davison) (*d* 2015); two *s* four *d. Educ:* King Edward VII Sch., Johannesburg; St John's Coll., Cambridge (MA, LLM). Served with S African Forces, 1940–42. Called to the Bar, Middle Temple, 1945. Sometime Lecturer in Law: University Coll. of Wales, Aberystwyth; Leeds Univ.; Cambridge Univ.

HAYMAN, Susan Mary; MP (Lab) Workington, since 2015; *b* Upper Bucklebury, 28 July 1962; *d* of John Bentley and Rita Bentley; *m* 1997, Ross Hayman; one *s* one *d*, and one step *s* one step *d. Educ:* St Bartholomew's Comp. Sch., Newbury; Anglia Ruskin Univ. (BA Hons Eng. Lit.). Bookseller, Heffers Bookshop, 1984–86; proof-reader and copy editor, Goodfellow and Egan, 1986–88; self-employed proof-reader and copy editor, 1988–97; Asst to Tess Kingham, MP, 1997–2001, to Michael Foster, MP, 2001–05; Communications Consultant, Copper Consultancy, 2005–14; self-employed communications consultant, 2014–15. Mem. (Lab) Cumbria CC, 2013–15. *Recreations:* music, theatre, gardening, walking the dog, fell walking. *Address:* House of Commons, SW1A 0AA. *T:* (020) 7219 4554. *E:* sue.hayman.mp@parliament.uk.

HAYMAN, Prof. Walter Kurt, MA; ScD (Cambridge); FRS 1956; FIC; Professor of Pure Mathematics, University of York, 1985–93, now Emeritus; Senior Research Fellow, Imperial College, London, since 1995; *b* 6 Jan. 1926; *s* of late Franz Samuel Haymann and Ruth Therese (*née* Hensel); *m* 1st, 1947, Margaret Riley Crann, MA Cantab (*d* 1994), *d* of Thomas Crann, New Earswick, York; three *d*; 2nd, 1995, Dr Waficka Katifi (*d* 2001); 3rd, 2007, Marie Jennings, MBE (*d* 2015). *Educ:* Gordonstoun Sch.; St John's Coll., Cambridge. Lecturer at King's Coll., Newcastle upon Tyne, 1947, and Fellow of St John's Coll., Cambridge, 1947–50; Lecturer, 1947, and Reader, 1953–56, Exeter; Prof. of Pure Maths, 1956–85, and Dean of RCS, 1978–81, Imperial Coll., London (FIC 1989). Visiting Lecturer at Brown Univ., USA, 1949–50, at Stanford Univ., USA (summer) 1950 and 1955, and to the American Mathematical Soc., 1961. Co-founder with Mrs Hayman of British Mathematical Olympiad; Vice-Pres., London Mathematical Soc., 1982–84. Foreign Member: Finnish Acad. of Science and Letters; Accademia Nazionale dei Lincei, Rome; Corresp. Mem., Bavarian Acad. of Science. Hon. DSc: Exeter, 1981; Birmingham, 1985; NUI, 1997; Hon. Dr rer. nat. Giessen, 1992; Hon. DPhil Uppsala, 1992. 1st Smiths Prize, 1948, shared Adams Prize, 1949, Cambridge Univ.; Jun. Berwick Prize, 1955, Sen. Berwick Prize, 1964, de Morgan Medal, 1995, London Mathematical Soc. *Publications:* Multivalent Functions (Cambridge, 1958, 2nd edn 1994) Meromorphic Functions (Oxford, 1964); Research Problems in Function Theory (London, 1967); Subharmonic Functions, vol. I, 1976, vol. II, 1989; papers in various mathematical journals. *Recreations:* music, travel, television. *Address:* Department of Mathematics, Imperial College London, SW7 2AZ; Cadogan Grange, Bisley, Stroud, Glos GL6 7AT.

See also A. C. Hayman.

HAYMAN-JOYCE, Lt-Gen. Sir Robert (John), KCB 1996; CBE 1989 (OBE 1979); DL; Chairman, Raytheon Systems Ltd, 2000–12; *b* 16 Oct. 1940; *s* of late Major T. F. Hayman-Joyce and B. C. Bruford; *m* 1968, Diana Livingstone-Bussell; two *s. Educ:* Radley Coll.; Magdalene Coll., Cambridge (MA). Commnd 11th Hussars (PAO), 1963; CO Royal Hussars (PWO), 1980–82; Comdr RAC, 1 (BR) Corps, 1983–85; Dir, UK Tank Programme, 1988; Dir Gen., Fighting Vehicles and Engr Equipment, later Land Fighting Systems, MoD (PE), 1989–92; Dir, RAC, 1992–94; Military Sec., MoD, 1994–95; MGO, 1995–98, and Dep. Chief of Defence Procurement (Ops), 1996–98. Non-executive Director: Alvis plc, 1999–2004; Disarmco Ltd, 2009. Chm., March Security Ltd, 2006–09. Col Comdt RAC, 1995–99; Hon. Col, Royal Yeomanry, 2002–10. Chairman: Trustees, Tank Mus., 1995–2002; Monmouthshire Hunt, 1998–2002; London Internat. Horse Show, 2010–. Patron: Retired Officers Assoc., 2000–09; Soc. for Welfare of Horses and Ponies, 2003–; Firing Line (Mus. of the Welsh Soldier), 2011–; Arts Alive, 2011–. DL Gwent, 1997. FCIPS 1997. Hon. DSc Cranfield, 1998. *Recreations:* ski-ing, horses. *Address:* Ty Isha, Mamhilad, Pontypool, Monmouthshire NP4 0JE. *Clubs:* Cavalry and Guards; Leander (Henley-on-Thames).

HAYMES, Rev. Dr Brian; Minister, Bloomsbury Central Baptist Church, 2000–05; *b* 8 Dec. 1940; *s* of Reginald and Ella Haymes; *m* 1965, Jennifer Christine Frankland; two *d. Educ:* King's Coll. Sch., Wimbledon; Univ. of Bristol (BA 1965); Univ. of Exeter (MA 1973; PhD 1976). Baptist Minister: St George, Bristol, 1965–69; South Street, Exeter, 1969–77; Mansfield Road, Nottingham, 1977–81; Tutor, 1981–85, Principal, 1985–94, Northern Baptist Coll., Manchester; Principal, Bristol Baptist Coll., 1994–2000. Lecturer (part-time) in Christian Ethics: Univ. of Manchester, 1983–93; Univ. of Bristol, 1996–2000. Pres., Baptist Union of GB, 1993–94. *Publications:* The Concept of the Knowledge of God, 1986; (jtly) On Being the Church, 2008; (jtly) The Communion of Saints, 2014; (jtly) God after Christendom?, 2015. *Recreations:* reading, watching cricket and Rugby. *Address:* 1 Colville Grove, Timperley, Altrincham, Cheshire WA15 6NA. *T:* (0161) 374 0813.

HAYNES, Alison Wendy; *see* Hampton, A. W.

HAYNES, Dana Rebecca; *see* Arnold, D. R.

HAYNES, Ernest Anthony, (Tony), CIGEM; Regional Chairman, British Gas plc, East Midlands, 1983–87; *b* 8 May 1922; *s* of Joseph Ernest Haynes and Ethel Rose (*née* Toomer); *m* 1946, Sheila Theresa (*née* Blane); two *s* two *d. Educ:* King Edward VI Grammar Sch., Totnes, S Devon. Joined Devonshire Regt, 1940; RMC Sandhurst, 1941; commnd Hampshire Regt, 1941; served in N Africa, Italy and NW Europe; Captain, 1945. Govt rehabilitation course for ex-officers, 1947–48; joined Torquay and Paignton Gas Co., 1949; appts with: West Midlands and Northern Gas Boards; Gas Council; Eastern; Dep. Chm., North Eastern, 1977–78; Dep. Chm., North Thames Gas, 1979–82. Vice-Pres., Internat. Colloquium about Gas Marketing, 1983–84. Silver Medal, IGasE, for paper, Energy Conservation—a marketing opportunity. *Recreations:* golf, flyfishing.

HAYNES, John Harold, OBE 1995; Chairman, Haynes Publishing Group plc, 1979–2010, now Founder Director (Chief Executive, 1960–79); *b* 25 March 1938; *s* of Harold and Violet Haynes; *m* 1963, Annette Constance Coleman-Brown; three *s. Educ:* Sutton Valence Sch. Nat. Service, Flt Lieut, RAF, 1957. Wrote first car manual, Building an Austin 750 Special, at age of 16; founded J. Haynes & Co., 1960; Haynes Publishing Group plc, floated on London Stock Exchange, 1979. Founder, Haynes Motor Mus., Sparkford. Mem., Guild of

Motoring Writers, 1974. *Publications:* numerous books on motors and motoring, incl. Haynes Owners Workshop Manuals. *Recreations:* reading, walking, motor car rallying, Haynes Motor Museum, opened 1985. *Address:* Haynes Publishing Group plc, Sparkford, near Yeovil, Som BA22 7JJ. *T:* (01963) 440635. *Club:* Royal Automobile.

HAYNES, Lawrence John; President, Land and Sea Division, Rolls-Royce plc, since 2014; Chairman, Rolls-Royce Power Systems, since 2014; *b* 6 Dec. 1952; *s* of Donald H. Haynes and Irene E. Haynes (*née* Langford); *m* 1978, Carol Anne Nelson; one *d*, and two step *d*. *Educ:* Heriot-Watt Univ. (BA Hons Business Law 1983). FCIHT (FIHT 1995); FCILT (FCIT 1996). RAF technician, 1969–78; Head of Contracts, British Aerospace (Space Systems), 1983–89; Legal Dir, 1989–90, Man. Dir, 1990–91, Microtel Communications; Man. Dir, British Aerospace Communications, 1991–92; Project Dir, British Aerospace, 1992–94; Chief Exec., Highways Agency, 1994–99; Partner and Hd of Ops, Eur. BPO, PricewaterhouseCoopers, 1999–2000; Chief Executive: 186k Ltd, 2000–02; Govt Services Gp, British Nuclear Fuels plc, 2003–04; British Nuclear Gp, 2004–07; Dir, BNFL plc, 2005–07; Chief Exec., White Young Green Plc, 2007–09; Pres. of Nuclear, 2009–13, Pres. of Marine and Nuclear, 2013–14, Rolls-Royce plc. Non-exec. Dir, Network Rail Ltd, 2010–14. Chm., RAF Benevolent Fund, 2014–. FRSA 1994. Hon. DEng Heriot-Watt, 2010. *Recreations:* sailing, ski-ing. *Address:* Rolls-Royce plc, 62 Buckingham Gate, SW1E 6AT.

HAYNES, Very Rev. Peter; Dean of Hereford, 1982–92, now Dean Emeritus; Vicar, St John Baptist, Hereford, 1983–92; *b* 24 April 1925; *s* of Francis Harold Stanley Haynes and Winifred Annie Haynes; *m* 1952, Ruth (*d* 2004), *d* of late Dr Charles Edward Stainthorpe, MRCS, LRCP, Brunton Park, Newcastle upon Tyne; two *s*. *Educ:* St Brendan's Coll., Clifton; Selwyn Coll., Cambridge (MA); Cuddesdon Theol Coll., Oxford. Staff of Barclays Bank, 1941–43; RAF, 1943–47. Deacon 1952, Priest 1953. Asst Curate, Stokesley, 1952–54; Hessle, 1954–58; Vicar, St John's Drypool, Hull, 1958–63; Bishop's Chaplain for Youth and Asst Dir of Religious Educn, Dio. Bath and Wells, 1963–70; Vicar of Glastonbury, 1970–74 (with Godney from 1972); Archdeacon of Wells, Canon Residentiary and Prebendary of Huish and Brent in Wells Cathedral, 1974–82. Proctor in Convocation, 1976–82. Mem., Dioceses Commn, 1978–86. *Recreations:* sailing, model engineering. *Address:* 5 St John Street, Hereford HR1 2NB. *T:* (01432) 266753.

HAYNES, Prof. Peter Howard, PhD; Professor of Applied Mathematics, since 2001, and Head, Department of Applied Mathematics and Theoretical Physics, since 2005, University of Cambridge; Fellow, Queens' College, Cambridge, since 1986; *b* 23 July 1958; *s* of late Bernard Archibald Haynes and of Stella Iris Haynes (*née* Whitehead); *m* 1989, Kathleen Mary Crease; two *s*. *Educ:* Royal Grammar Sch., Guildford; Queens' Coll., Cambridge (BA 1979, MA 1983, PhD 1984). Res. Associate, Dept of Atmospheric Scis, Univ. of Washington, 1984–85; University of Cambridge: Royal Soc. Meteorol Office Res. Fellow, 1986–90; Asst Dir of Res., 1991; Lectr, 1991–99, Reader in Atmospheric Sci., 1999–2001. Mem., Atmospheric Scis Peer Review Cttee, NERC, 1997–2001. Mem. and Chm. Steering Cttee, Prog. on Transport in Atmosphere and Ocean, ESF, 1996–2000; Mem., Scientific Steering Cttee, Stratospheric Processes and Climate Project, World Climate Res. Prog., 2005–10. MAE 1998. *Publications:* contribs to Jl Fluid Mechanics, Jl Atmospheric Scis, Jl Geophysical Res., Qly Jl Royal Meteorol Soc. *Recreations:* orienteering, running, reading, family. *Address:* Department of Applied Mathematics and Theoretical Physics, Centre for Mathematical Sciences, Wilberforce Road, Cambridge CB3 0WA. *T:* (01223) 337862, *Fax:* (01223) 765900. *E:* phh@damtp.cam.ac.uk.

HAYNES, Timothy Hugh Penzer; Headmaster, Tonbridge School, since 2005; *b* 2 April 1955; *s* of Barry and Felicia Haynes. *Educ:* Shrewsbury Sch.; Univ. of Reading (BA Hist.); Pembroke Coll., Cambridge (PGCE). Assistant Master: Hampton Sch., 1980–82; St Paul's Sch., London, 1982–95 (Surmaster, 1992–95); Headmaster, Monmouth Sch., 1995–2005. *Address:* Tonbridge School, Tonbridge, Kent TN9 1JP. *Clubs:* East India, Lansdowne.

HAYS, Irene; *see* Lucas, I.

HAYTER, 4th Baron *cr* 1927, of Chislehurst, Kent; **George William Michael Chubb;** Bt 1900; *b* 9 Oct. 1943; *s* of 3rd Baron Hayter, KCVO, CBE and Elizabeth Anne Chubb (*née* Rumbold); *S* father, 2003; *m* 1983, Waltraud, *yr d* of J. Flackl, Sydney; one *s*. *Educ:* Marlborough; Nottingham Univ. (BSc). Managing Director: Chubb Malaysia, 1972–79; Chubb Australia, 1979–82; Dir, Business Develt for Physical Security, Chubb Security plc, 1982–89; Managing Director: Uniqey Ltd, 1989–90; William Chubb Associates, 1991–2005; Dir, UELS Ltd, 1996–. Liveryman, Weavers' Co. (Mem., Ct of Assts; Upper Bailiff, 1999–2000). *Heir: s* Hon. Thomas Frederik Flackl Chubb, *b* 23 July 1986.

HAYTER OF KENTISH TOWN, Baroness *cr* 2010 (Life Peer), of Kentish Town in the London Borough of Camden; **Dianne Hayter;** an Opposition Whip, House of Lords, since 2011; Shadow Minister for the Cabinet Office and for Consumer Affairs, Department for Business, Innovation and Skills, since 2012; *b* 7 Sept. 1949; *d* of late Alec Hayter and late Nancy Hayter; *m* 1994, Prof. (Anthony) David Caplin. *Educ:* Trevelyan Coll., Durham Univ. (BA Hons Sociology and Social Admin); Univ. of London (PhD 2004). Research Assistant: General and Municipal Workers Union, 1970–72; European Trade Union Confedn (ETUC), Brussels, 1973; Research Officer, Trade Union Adv. Cttee to OECD (TUAC-OECD), Paris, 1973–74; Fabian Society: Asst Gen. Sec., 1974–76; Gen. Sec., 1976–82; Mem. Exec. Cttee, 1986–95; Chm., 1992–93; Journalist, A Week in Politics, Channel Four, 1982–84; Dir, Alcohol Concern, 1984–90; Chief Exec., European PLP, 1990–96; Dir of Corporate Affairs, Wellcome Trust, 1996–99; Chief Exec., Pelican Centre, 1999–2001. Res. Student, QMW, 2001–04. Member: Royal Commn on Criminal Procedure, 1978–80; Bd, Nat. Patient Safety Agency, 2001–04; Dr Foster Ethics Cttee, 2001–10; Financial Services Consumer Panel, 2001–05 (Vice Chm., 2003–05); Bd, NCC, 2001–08; Determinations Panel, Pensions Regulator, 2005–10; Insolvency Practices Council, 2006–10; Bd for Actuarial Standards, Financial Reporting Council, 2006–11; Surveyors Ombudsman Service Bd, 2007–08; NEST Corporation, 2010; Chair: Consumer Panel, Bar Standards Bd, 2006–09; Property Standards Bd, 2008–10; Legal Services Consumer Panel, 2009–11. Vis. Prof., Univ. of Westminster, 2011–. Chair, Camden Alcoholics Support Assoc., 1996–2003, Mem., 2003–12. Member: Exec. Cttee, London Labour Party, 1977–83; Nat. Constitution Cttee, Labour Party, 1987–98; Labour Party NEC, 1998–2010 (Vice-Chm., 2006–07; Chm., 2007–08); Chm., Holborn & St Pancras Labour Party, 1990–93. Member: Labour Party; Soc. of Labour Lawyers; Socialist Health Assoc.; GMB; Jewish Labour Movt; Co-op. Party; Labour Arab Gp; Socialist Educn Assoc. JP Inner London, 1976–90. *Publications:* The Labour Party: crisis and prospects (Fabian Soc.), 1977; (contrib.) Labour in the Eighties, 1980; (contrib.) Prime Minister Portillo and Other Things that Never Happened, 2003; Fightback: Labour's Traditional Right in the 80s, 2005; (ed jtly) Men Who Made Labour, 2006; (contrib.) From the Workhouse to Welfare, 2009; (contrib.) The Prime Ministers Who Never Were, 2011. *Recreations:* reading, politics. *Address:* House of Lords, SW1A 0PW. *E:* hayterd@parliament.uk. *W:* www.twitter.com/HayteratLords.

HAYTER, Sir Paul (David Grenville), KCB 2007; LVO 1992; Clerk of the Parliaments, House of Lords, 2003–07; *b* 4 Nov. 1942; *s* of late Rev. Canon Michael George Hayter and Katherine Patricia Hayter (*née* Schofield); *m* 1973, Hon. Deborah Gervaise, *d* of Baron Maude of Stratford-upon-Avon, TD, PC; two *s* one *d*. *Educ:* Eton (King's Scholar); Christ Church, Oxford (MA). Clerk, Parlt Office, House of Lords, 1964; seconded as Private Sec. to Leader of House and Chief Whip, House of Lords, 1974–77; Clerk of Cttees, 1977; Principal Clerk of Cttees, 1985–90; Prin. Finance Officer, 1991–94; Reading Clerk, 1991–97; Principal Clerk of Public Bills, subseq. Clerk of Legislation, 1994–2003; Clerk Asst, 1997–2003. Sec., Assoc. of Lord-Lieutenants, 1977–91. Chm., CPRE Northants, 2007–. *Recreations:* music, gardening, botanising, local history, archery, painting. *Address:* Walnut House, Charlton, Banbury OX17 3DR.

HAYTHORNE, John; *see* Parsons, Sir R. E. C. F.

HAYTHORNTHWAITE, Richard Neil; Chairman: MasterCard Inc., since 2006; Centrica, since 2014; *b* 17 Dec. 1956; *s* of Christopher Scott Haythornthwaite and Angela Mary Haythornthwaite (*née* Painter); *m* 1979, Janeen Marie Dennis; one *s* one *d*. *Educ:* Colston's Sch., Bristol; Queen's Coll., Oxford (MA Geol.); Massachusetts Inst. of Technol. (SM Mgt). With BP, 1978–95, Pres., BP Venezuela, 1993–95; Commercial Dir, Premier Oil, 1995–97; Blue Circle Industries: Chief Exec., Heavy Bldgs Materials, Europe and Asia, 1997–99; Gp CEO, 1999–2001; Chief Exec., Invensys plc, 2001–05; Man. Dir, 2006–08, Sen. Adviser, 2008–, Star Capital Partners Ltd. Non-executive Director: Cookson Gp plc, 1999–2003; ICI plc, 2001–08; Lafarge SA, 2001–03; Chm., Network Rail, 2009–12. Chief Operating Officer, 2008–12, Exec. Chm. of Operating Businesses, 2013–, PSI. Chair: Better Regulation Commn, 2006–08; Risk and Regulation Adv. Council, 2008–09. Chairman: Centre for Creative Communities, 1996–2006; Almeida Theatre, 2001–08; South Bank Centre, 2008–. Trustee: NMSI, 2002–07; British Council, 2003–08. *Recreations:* cycling, travel, arts. *Club:* Royal Automobile.

HAYTON, Hon. David John; Justice of the Caribbean Court of Justice, since 2005; *b* 13 July 1944; *s* of Arthur Hayton and Beatrice (*née* Thompson); *m* 1979, Linda Patricia Rae; one *s*. *Educ:* Newcastle Royal GS; Univ. of Newcastle upon Tyne (LLB 1st Cl. Hons 1966; LLD 1980); MA 1973, LLD 2006, Cantab. Called to the Bar, Inner Temple, 1968, and Lincoln's Inn *aeg* (Bencher, 2004). Lectr, Sheffield Univ., 1966–69; private practice, Lincoln's Inn, 1970–2005; Lectr, QMC, London, 1970–73; Lectr, Univ. of Cambridge and Fellow of Jesus Coll., 1973–87; Prof. of Law, 1987–2005, Dean, Law Faculty, 1988–90, KCL; FKC 2005; Chm., London Univ. Bd of Studies in Law, 1992–95. Vis. Lectr, Inns of Court Sch. of Law, 1971–84, Hon. Reader, 1984–96. An Asst Recorder, 1984–92; a Recorder, 1992–2000; Actg Justice, Supreme Ct, Bahamas, 2000, 2001. Dep. Chm., Trust Law Cttee, 1994–2005; Mem., Law Panel, 2001 RAE, HEFCE. Chm., Council, Pension Trustees Forum, 1992–95. Hon. Sec., SPTL, 1996–2001. Head of UK Delegns to The Hague Confs on Private Internat. Law, 1984, 1988. *Publications:* Registered Land, 1973, 3rd edn 1981; Hayton & Tiley: Capital Transfer Tax, 1975, 2nd edn 1978; Hayton & Marshall: Cases & Commentary on Trusts, 6th edn 1975 to 12th edn 2005; Underhill & Hayton: Law of Trusts and Trustees, 13th edn 1979 to 18th edn 2010; Law of Trusts, 1989, 4th edn 2003; Hayton Report on Financial Services and Trust Law, 1990; (ed) European Succession Laws, 1991, 3rd edn 2002; (ed) Principles of European Trust Law, 1999; (ed) Modern International Developments in Trust Law, 1999; (ed) Extending the Boundaries of Trust and Similar Ring-fenced Funds, 2002; (ed) Towards an EU Directive on Protected Funds, 2009; (ed) The International Trust, 3rd edn 2011; (contrib.) Halsbury's Laws of England, vol. 98, Trusts and Powers, 5th edn 2013; contribs to chapters in books on trusts, tax and estate planning; articles in learned jls. *Recreations:* health club, watching Rugby and cricket, reading novels, wine tasting. *Address:* Caribbean Court of Justice, 134 Henry Street, Port of Spain, Trinidad, West Indies. *T:* 6259118. *Clubs:* Athenæum, MCC, Queen's Park Cricket (Trinidad), Tranquility Tennis (Trinidad).

HAYTON, Michael Pearson; QC 2013; a Recorder, since 2012; *b* Preston, Lancs, 3 Nov. 1970; *s* of Michael Derek Hayton and Dylis Barbara Hayton; *m* 2004, Victoria Jayne Simmons; one *s*. *Educ:* Queen Elizabeth's Grammar Sch., Blackburn; St Anne's Coll., Oxford (MA Juris.). Called to the Bar, Lincoln's Inn, 1993; in practice as barrister, specialising in regulatory crime and crime, 1993–. *Recreations:* Rugby Union, golf, olive oil production. *Address:* Deans Court Chambers, 24 St John Street, Manchester M3 4DF. *T:* (0161) 214 6000, *Fax:* (0161) 214 6001. *E:* hayton@deanscourt.co.uk. *Clubs:* Vincent's (Oxford); Royal Birkdale Golf.

HAYTON, Philip John; Newscaster, BBC TV News, 1985–2005; *b* 2 Nov. 1947; *s* of Austin and Jennie Hayton; *m* 1972, Thelma Gant; one *s* one *d*. *Educ:* at various schs in USA and UK. Pirate radio disc jockey, 1967; joined BBC, 1968; reporter: Radio Leeds, 1968–71; and newscaster, TV Leeds, 1971–74; TV News: reporter, 1974–80; Foreign Corresp., 1980–83; reporter and newscaster, 1983–2005, Six O'clock and Nine O'clock News, World News and News 24. *Recreations:* theatre, walking, investment, foreign travel. *E:* hayton@talk21.com.

HAYWARD, Baron *cr* 2015 (Life Peer), of Cumnor in the County of Oxfordshire; **Robert Antony Hayward,** OBE 1991; Chief Executive, British Beer and Pub Association (formerly Brewers and Licensed Retailers), 1999–2009; *b* 11 March 1949; *s* of late Ralph and of Mary Hayward. *Educ:* Abingdon Sch.; Maidenhead Grammar Sch.; University Coll. of Rhodesia; BSc Econ Hons London (external). Personnel Officer, Esso Petroleum, 1971–75; Personnel Manager: Coca Cola Bottlers (S & N) Ltd, 1975–79; GEC Large Machines, 1979–82; Dir Gen., British Soft Drinks Assoc., 1993–99. MP (C) Kingswood, 1983–92; contested (C): Kingswood, 1992, Christchurch, July 1993. PPS to Minister for Corporate and Consumer Affairs, 1985–87, to Minister for Industry, 1986–87, to Sec. of State for Transport, 1987–89. Mem., Commons Select Cttee on Energy, 1983–85. Advr to Chm., Cons. Party, 2009–10; Chm., Govt Review of Equality Legislation, 2013. Adviser: Terrence Higgins Trust, 2012–14; Dignity in Dying, 2012– (Treas., 2014–). Chm., Trade Assoc. Forum, CBI, 2007–08. Dir, Stonewall Gp, 1997–2003. Trustee: Central YMCA, 2011– (Dep. Chm., 2014–); YMCA Training, 2014–. Pres., King's Cross Steelers RFC, 1999–2003. *Recreations:* Rugby, psephology. *Address:* 11 Grosvenor Park, SE5 0NQ.

HAYWARD, Alexander; Director of Collections, Research and Lifelong Learning, Queensland Museum, since 2015; *b* 26 Nov. 1960; *s* of Peter and Nikki Hayward; *m* 1990, Rosy Nicholson; one *s* one *d*. *Educ:* Univ. of Sydney (BA 1982, MA 1986); Univ. of Leicester (MSc 1989). LTCL 1982; AMA 1993, FMA 2010. Curator, Science Mus., London, 1990–98; Suffolk County Council: Mus Officer, 1998–2001; Hd of Heritage, 2001–05; Keeper of Sci. and Technol., Nat. Museums of Scotland, 2005–15. Expert Advr, Heritage Lottery Fund, 2000–04; Scottish Rep., UK Science, Technology and Industry Subject Specialist Network, 2005–15; Founding Chm., Scottish Technology and Industry Collections Knowledge Network, 2006–11 (Mem. Cttee, 2012–15); Founding Mem., Dounreay Heritage Adv. Panel, 2010–15; Member: BT Connected Earth Consulting Gp, 2006–07; Cttee, Museums Galleries Scotland (formerly Scottish Museums Council) Collections Recognition (formerly Significance) Scheme, 2006–13; Council, Royal Scottish Soc. of Arts, 2009–15 (Vice Pres., 2010–13); Council, Newcomen Soc., 2013–. FRSSA 2007. *Publications:* The Traction Engine in Scotland, 2011. *Recreations:* enjoying the history of technology, music of G. F. Handel and British dance bands of 1920s. *Address:* Queensland Museum, PO Box 3300, South Brisbane, Qld 4101, Australia.

HAYWARD, Anthony Bryan, PhD; FRSE; Founder, and Chairman, since 2015, Genel Energy plc (Chief Executive Officer, 2011–15); Chairman, Glencore Xstrata (formerly Glencore), since 2014 (Senior Independent Director, 2011–13; interim Chairman, 2013–14); *b* Slough, 21 May 1957; *s* of Bryan and Mary Hayward; *m* 1985, Maureen Fulton (marr. diss. 2013); one *s* one *d*. *Educ:* Univ. of Aston in Birmingham (BSc); Univ. of Edinburgh (PhD Geol 1982). Joined BP, 1982; BP Exploration, 1982–99: various tech. and commercial posts, London, Aberdeen, France, China and Glasgow; Exploration Manager, Colombia; Pres., Venezuela, 1995–97; Gp Vice Pres. and Mem. Upstream Exec. Cttee, 1997–2000; Gp Treas., 2000–02; Exec. Dir and Chief Exec., Exploration and Prodn, 2003–07; Gp Chief Exec., BP plc, 2007–10. Partner and Mem. Adv. Bd, AEA Capital, 2007–; founder, Vallares plc, 2011. Mem. Bd, TNK-BP, 2003–08, 2010–11; Chm., CompactGTL, 2013–. Member: Business

Council for Britain, 2007–10; US Business Council, 2007–12; World Econ. Forum Community of Chairmen, 2014–. Chm., GLOBE CEO Forum for Climate Change, 2007–09. *Recreations:* sailing, ski-ing, triathlons, watching sport.

HAYWARD, Prof. Geoffrey Francis; Professor of Education and Head, Faculty of Education, University of Cambridge, since 2014; *b* Wendover, Bucks, 1955; *s* of Harry Robin Hayward and Patricia Vivien Hayward (*née* Turner); partner, Jill Johnson; two *s*. *Educ:* Lord Williams Sch., Thame; New Coll., Oxford (BA Zool.; DPhil 1983). Postdoctoral Res. Fellow, Univ. of Liverpool, 1980–81; Lecturer: Wakefield Dist Coll., 1982–87; Liverpool Inst. of Higher Educn, 1987–89; Lectr, 1989–2008, Reader in Educn, 2008–10, Univ. of Oxford; Prof. of Educn, Univ. of Leeds, 2011–14. *Publications:* Applied Genetics, 1992; Applied Ecology, 1992; Getting to Grips with GNVQs: a handbook for teachers, 1995; Higher Education in Crisis: the corporate eclipse of the university, 2001; Balancing the Skills Equation: key issues for policy and practice, 2004; Education for All, 2008; Improving Learning by Widening Participation in Higher Education, 2009; contribs to jls and chapters in books. *Recreations:* gardening, fishing, walking. *Address:* Faculty of Education, University of Cambridge, 184 Hills Road, Cambridge CB2 8PQ. *T:* (01223) 767713. *E:* gfh22@cam.ac.uk.

HAYWARD, Gerald William; HM Diplomatic Service, retired; *b* 18 Nov. 1927; *s* of late Frederick William Hayward and Annie Louise (*née* Glasscock); *m* 1956, Patricia Rhonwen (*née* Foster Hall); one *s* three *d*. *Educ:* Tottenham Grammar School; London and Hong Kong Univs. HM Forces, 1946–57. Joined HM Foreign (subseq. HM Diplomatic) Service, 1957; served Bangkok, Hong Kong, Copenhagen, Kuala Lumpur; FCO, 1980–82; (part-time), Cabinet Office, 1984–92. *Address:* Fosters, 9 Ashley Road, Sevenoaks, Kent TN13 3AW. *T:* (01732) 451227.

HAYWARD, Guy Alexander; Global Chief Executive Officer, KBS+, since 2015; *b* London, 18 Feb. 1964; *s* of I. A. C. Hayward and S. E. A. Hayward; three *d*; *m* 2012, Astrid Boesze. *Educ:* St Edward's Sch., Oxford; Christ Church, Oxford (BA Hons Modern Langs). Joined J Walter Thompson Co., later JWT Gp as grad. trainee, 1987; Account Director: JWT Barcelona, then London, 1990–92; WCRS, London, 1992–94; Wieden + Kennedy, Amsterdam, 1994–97; Founding Partner, 180, Amsterdam, 1998–2009; CEO, JWT UK Gp, 2009–11; Global Business Develt Dir, BETC Worldwide, 2011–14. *Address:* 83 Avenue Victor Hugo, 75116 Paris, France. *E:* guy.hayward@rocketmail.com. *Clubs:* Every House; Vincent's (Oxford).

HAYWARD, Prof. Jack Ernest Shalom, FBA 1990; Research Professor of Politics, University of Hull, since 1999; *b* 18 Aug. 1931; *s* of Menahem and Stella Hayward; *m* 1965, Margaret Joy Glenn; one *s* one *d*. *Educ:* LSE (BSc Econ 1952; PhD 1958). Asst Lectr and Lectr, Univ. of Sheffield, 1959–63; Lectr and Sen. Lectr, Univ. of Keele, 1963–73; Prof. of Politics, Univ. of Hull, 1973–92; Prof. of Politics and Dir, European Studies Inst. and Centre for European Politics, Econs and Soc., Univ. of Oxford, and Fellow, St Antony's Coll., Oxford, 1993–98, now Prof. and Fellow Emeritus. Sen. Res. Fellow, Nuffield Coll., Oxford, 1968–69; Vis. Prof., Univ. of Paris III, 1979–80; Elie Halévy Vis. Prof., Inst. d'Etudes Politiques, Paris, 1990–91. Political Studies Association: Chm., 1975–77; Pres., 1979–81; Vice-Pres., 1981–. Editor, Political Studies, 1987–93. DLitt Hull, 2013. Chevalier de l'Ordre National du Mérite (France), 1980; Chevalier de la Légion d'Honneur (France), 1996. *Publications:* Private Interests and Public Policy, 1966; The One and Indivisible French Republic, 1973; The State and the Market Economy, 1986; After the French Revolution, 1991; De Gaulle to Mitterrand, 1993; Industrial Enterprise and European Integration, 1995; Governing the New Europe, 1995; The Crisis of Representation in Europe, 1995; Elitism, Populism and European Politics, 1996; The British Study of Politics in the Twentieth Century, 1999; Governing From the Centre, 2002; Governing Europe, 2003; Etre gouverné, 2003; Fragmented France: two centuries of disputed identity, 2007; Leaderless Europe, 2008; Regression: the withering of the welfare state, 2012; (ed jtly) European Disunion: between sovereignty and solidarity, 2012. *Recreations:* music, reading, walking. *Address:* Hurstwood, 17C Church Lane, Kirk Ella, Hull HU10 7TA.

HAYWARD, Richard Michael; His Honour Judge Hayward; a Circuit Judge, since 1996; *b* 12 July 1946; *s* of George Michael Hayward and Esmé Mary Florence Hayward (*née* Howard); *m* 1969, Laura Louise Buchan; two *s* one *d*. *Educ:* Highgate Sch.; Inns of Court Sch. of Law. Called to the Bar, Middle Temple, 1969; in practice at the Bar, 1970–96; Asst Recorder, 1990–94; Recorder, 1994–96. *Recreations:* golf, painting, horses, gardening. *Clubs:* Rye Golf; Royal & Ancient Golf (St Andrews).

HAYWARD SMITH, His Honour Rodger; QC 1988; a Circuit Judge, 2002–13; *b* 25 Feb. 1943; *s* of late Frederick Ernest Smith and Heather Hayward (*née* Rodgers); *m* 1975, Gillian Sheila (*née* Johnson); one *s* one *d*. *Educ:* Brentwood Sch.; St Edmund Hall, Oxford (MA). Called to the Bar, Gray's Inn, 1967; a Recorder, 1986–2002 (Asst Recorder, 1981–86); a Deputy High Ct Judge, 1990–2002. A Legal Assessor, GMC, 2000–02. *Publications:* (ed jtly and contrib.) Jackson's Matrimonial Finance and Taxation, 5th edn 1992 to 7th edn 2002. *Recreations:* amateur dramatics, walking. *Address:* 1 King's Bench Walk, Temple, EC4Y 7DB.

HAYWOOD, (June) Sandra T.; *see* Tyler-Haywood.

HAYWOOD, Nigel Robert, CVO 2006; HM Diplomatic Service, retired; Governor of the Falkland Islands and Commissioner for South Georgia and the South Sandwich Islands, 2010–14; *b* 17 March 1955; *yr s* of Leslie and Peggy Haywood; *m* 1979, (Mary) Louise Smith; three *s*. *Educ:* Truro Sch.; New Coll., Oxford (MA English, MPhil Comparative Philology); RMA Sandhurst; Bournemouth Univ. (MSc Biodiversity Conservation). MCIL (MIL 1988). Lt, RAEC, 1977–80. Joined HM Diplomatic Service, 1983: Second, later First Sec., Budapest, 1985–89; FCO, 1989–92; Dep. Consul-Gen., Johannesburg, 1992–96; Counsellor and Dep. Head, UK Delegn to OSCE, Vienna, 1996–2000; Asst Dir (Personnel), FCO, 2000–03; Ambassador to Estonia, 2003–07; Consul-Gen., Basra, 2008–09. Director: S Atlantic Envmtl Res. Inst., 2013–; Angling Trust, 2014–; UK Overseas Territories Conservation Forum, 2014–; Falkland Islands Trust, 2015–. Member: Philological Soc., 1981–; Golden Scale Club, 1982– (Hon. Pres., 2002–); British Ecol Soc., 2010–; Cttee, Piddle, Frome and W Dorset Fisheries Assoc., 2014–. Research student in conservation biol., Bournemouth Univ., 2015–. Bard of Cornish Gorsedd, 1976. *Publications:* (contrib.) The One That Got Away, 1991; occasional articles and reviews in angling press. *Recreations:* fishing (especially saltwater fly fishing), marathon running, butterfly and moth conservation, archery, recorders, renaissance lute, bassoon. *Address:* 6 Tom's Mead, Corfe Castle, Dorset BH20 5HH. *Clubs:* Oxford and Cambridge, Flyfishers'; Purbeck Runners.

HAZAREESINGH, Dr Sudhir Kumar, FBA 2006; Lecturer in Politics, University of Oxford, since 1990; Fellow and Tutor in Politics, Balliol College, Oxford, since 1990; *b* 18 Oct. 1961; *s* of late Kissoonsingh Hazareesingh and of Thara Hazareesingh; partner, Dr Karma Nabulsi, Fellow of St Edmund Hall, Oxford. *Educ:* Balliol Coll., Oxford (BA 1st Cl. Hons Politics and Phil. 1984; MPhil Internat. Relns 1986); DPhil Politics Oxon 1990. University of Oxford: Open Prize Res. Fellow, Nuffield Coll., 1987–90; Lectr in Politics, Exeter Coll., 1989–90; Sen. Tutor, Balliol Coll., 1997–2001. Prof. Invité, Inst. des Etudes Politiques, Paris, 2006; British Acad. Res. Reader, 2001–03; Acad. Visitor, Dept of Pol Sci., Princeton Univ., 2002; Dir d'Etudes Invité, Ecole des Hautes Etudes en Scis Sociales, Paris, 2003; Vis. Fellow, Remarque Inst., NY Univ., 2004; Enseignant, Ecole Doctorale, Institut d'Etudes Politiques, Paris, 2009–10. Maître de Conférences, Ecole Pratique des Hautes Etudes, Paris (Section 4), 2000. Chevalier, Ordre des Palmes Académiques (France), 2003; Grand Prix du Mémorial and Medal of Honour, Ajaccio (France), 2006; Prix d'Histoire du Sénat (France), 2011. *Publications:* Intellectuals and the French Communist Party: disillusion and decline, 1991; Political Traditions in Modern France, 1994; From Subject to Citizen: the Second Empire and the emergence of modern French democracy, 1998; (with V. Wright) Francs-Maçons sous le Second Empire: le Grand Orient de France à la veille de la Troisième République, 2001; Intellectual Founders of the Republic: five studies in Nineteenth-Century French political thought, 2001; (ed and contrib.) The Jacobin Legacy in Modern France, 2002; The Saint-Napoleon: celebrations of sovereignty in 19th century France, 2004 (trans. French 2007); The Legend of Napoleon, 2004 (trans. French 2006); (with E. Anceau and V. Wright) Les Préfets de Gambetta, 2007; Le Mythe Gaullien, 2010; In the Shadow of the General, 2012; How The French Think, 2015. *Recreations:* swimming, cinema, reading, listening to music. *Address:* Balliol College, Oxford OX1 3BJ. *T:* (01865) 277758, *Fax:* (01865) 277803. *E:* sudhir.hazareesingh@balliol.ox.ac.uk.

HAZEL, George McLean, OBE 2005; PhD; CEng; Independent Consultant, George Hazel Consultancy, since 2012; *b* 27 Jan. 1949; *s* of George McLean Hazel and Agnes Steven Hazel (*née* Willins); *m* 1974, Fiona Isabella Gault; one *s* two *d*. *Educ:* Heriot-Watt Univ. (BSc Civil Engrg; MSc Transportation); Cranfield Inst. of Technol. (PhD 1986). CEng 1975, MICE 1975. Transportation engr, Lothian Regl Council and Edinburgh CC, 1971–79; Prof. and Hd of Civil Engrg, Napier Univ., 1979–89; Dir, Oscar Faber Ltd (transport consultancy), 1989–93; Dir of Transportation, 1993–96, of City Develt, 1996–2000, Edinburgh CC; Dir, later Chm., McLean Hazel Ltd, later MRC McLean Hazel Ltd, 2000–11. Vis. Prof., Robert Gordon Univ., 2000–09; Adjunct Prof., Queensland Univ. of Technol., 2008–. Pres., Instn of Highways and Transportation, 2003–04. FIHT 1976; FILT 1978. Mem., Triumph TR6 Owners Club. *Publications:* (with Roger Parry) Making Cities Work, 2004. *Recreations:* ski-ing, gardening, restoring vintage cars. *Address:* George Hazel Consultancy, 3 Hill Street, Edinburgh EH2 3JP. *T:* (office) 07974 235209, (home) (0131) 446 0539. *E:* george@georgehazel.com.

HAZELL, Ven. Frederick Roy; Archdeacon of Croydon, 1978–93; *b* 12 Aug. 1930; *s* of John Murdoch and Ruth Hazell; *m* 1st, 1956, Gwendoline Edna Armstrong (*née* Vare) (*d* 1993), *widow* of Major J. W. D. Armstrong; (one step *s* decd); 2nd, 1994, Norma Irene Palmer (*née* Gardner). *Educ:* Hutton Grammar School, near Preston; Fitzwilliam Coll., Cambridge (MA); Cuddesdon Coll., Oxford. HM Forces, 1948–50. Asst Master, Kingham Hill School, 1953–54; Asst Curate, Ilkeston Parish Church, 1956–59; Priest-in-charge, All Saints', Marlpool, 1959–62; First Vicar of Marlpool, 1962–63; Chaplain, Univ. of the West Indies, 1963–66; Asst Priest, St Martin-in-the-Fields, 1966–68; Vicar of Holy Saviour, Croydon, 1968–84; Rural Dean of Croydon, 1972–78; Priest-in-charge: Chard Furnham with Chaffcombe, Knowle St Giles and Cricket Malherbie, 1995–99; St Bartholomew, Tardebigge, 2000–04; Advr in Pastoral Care and Counselling, Dio. of Bath and Wells, 1994–99. Hon. Canon: of Canterbury, 1973–84; of Southwark, 1984–93. *Recreations:* music, history. *Address:* Flat 27 Ramsay Hall, 9–13 Byron Road, Worthing, W Sussex BN11 3HN.

HAZELL, Malcolm John, CVO 1988; AM 2009; consultant to government and business, since 2008; Official Secretary to the Governor-General of Australia, 2003–08; Secretary, Order of Australia, 2003–08; an Extra Equerry to the Queen, since 2010; *b* 17 Dec. 1948; *s* of Neville John and Joan Nell Hazell; *m* 1976, Rhondda Leonie Scells; two *s*. *Educ:* C of E Grammar Sch., Brisbane; Univ. of Qld (BA Hons); Templeton Coll., Oxford; Graduate, Australian Inst. of Co. Dirs, 2009. Admin. Trainee, Public Service Bd, 1972; Exec. Officer to Comr, Nat. Capital Develt Commn, 1973–74; Private Sec., then Sen. Private Sec., to Prime Minister, Aust., 1975–79, 1980–81; Sen. Private Sec. to Minister for Aviation and Minister Assisting Prime Minister, 1982–83; various sen. mgt positions, Dept of Prime Minister and Cabinet, Canberra, 1982–85; Commonwealth Dir, Bicentennial Royal Visits to Aust., 1986–89; Asst Sec. and Hd, Internat. Div., Office of Security and Intelligence Coordination, 1989–94; Hd, S Pacific Forum Task Force, 1994; Asst Sec. and Hd, Cabinet Secretariat, Dept of Prime Minister and Cabinet, 1994–98; Sen. Advr to Prime Minister, 1998–2003. Secretary: Official Estabts Trust, 1985–87, 1995–96; Australian Bravery Decorations Council, 2003–08. Chm., ACT Block Grant Authy, 2009. Dir, Constitution Educn Fund Australia, 2012–. Hon. Sec., Royal Australian Inst. of Public Admin, 1973–75. Member: Australian Inst. Company Dirs, 2007– (Fellow 2009); Ind. Communications Cttee, Australian Govt, 2015–. Mem., Selection Cttee, Winston Churchill Memorial Trust, 2009–. Mem., Commonwealth Day Celebration Cttee, ACT, 2010–. Vice Pres., Canberra Grammar Sch. Foundn, 1993–96; Dir, Canberra Grammar Sch., 1994–2006 (Vice Chm., 2005–06). Dir, Southern Highlands Internat. Piano Comp., 2010–. Foundn Chm., Anglican Dio. Canberra and Goulburn, Diocesan Schs Council, 1998–2002. Hon. Lay Canon, St Saviour's Cathedral, Goulburn, 2002. FAICD 2009. KStJ 2008 (CStJ 2004). Tenth Anniversary of Independence Medal (PNG), 1987. *Recreations:* music, cricket, family. *Address:* 46 Gledden Street, Chifley, ACT 2606, Australia. *T:* (2) 62822274. *E:* malcolm.hazell@netspeed.com.au. *Club:* Commonwealth (Canberra).

HAZELL, Peter Frank; Chairman, Argent Group plc, since 2001; *b* 4 Aug. 1948; *s* of Frank Henry Hazell and Kathleen Hazell; *m* 1972, Maureen Pamela Church; one *s* one *d*. *Educ:* Hertford Coll., Oxford (MA PPE 1969; BPhil Econs 1971). Partner: Deloitte Haskins & Sells, 1980–90; Coopers & Lybrand, 1990–98; UK Managing Partner, PricewaterhouseCoopers, 1998–2000. Non-executive Director: UK Coal, 2003–11; Smith & Williamson, 2004–; Brit Insce, 2004–12; Axa UK, 2013–; Axa Ireland, 2014–; Canopius Managing Agents, 2014–. Member: Competition Commn, 2002–10; NERC, 2004–11. Mem. Court, Univ. of Greenwich, 2010–. *Recreations:* cricket, Rugby, opera, ballet, theatre, hill walking. *Address:* Argent Group plc, 4 Stable Street, N1C 4AB. *T:* (020) 3664 0200. *Club:* MCC.

HAZELL, Prof. Robert John Davidge, CBE 2006; Founder and Director, Constitution Unit, since 1995, and Professor of Government and the Constitution, since 1998, University College London; *b* 30 April 1948; *s* of Peter Hazell and Elizabeth Complin Fowler; *m* 1981, Alison Sophia Mordaunt Richards; two *s*. *Educ:* Eton (King's Schol.); Wadham Coll., Oxford (Minor Schol.; MA Hons). Called to the Bar, Middle Temple, 1973, Bencher, 2012; Barrister, 1973–75; Lay Magistrate, Highbury Corner, 1978–96. Home Office, 1975–89, working in Immigration Dept, Policy Planning Unit, Gaming Bd, Race Relns, Broadcasting, Police and Prison Depts; CS travelling fellowship to investigate freedom of inf. in Australia, Canada, NZ, 1986–87; Dir, Nuffield Foundn, 1989–95. Sen. Fellow, Inst. for Govt, 2010–. Vice-Chm., Assoc. of Charitable Foundns, 1992–95. Mem. Council, Hansard Soc., 1997– (Vice-Chm., Commn on Scrutiny Role of Parlt, 1999–2001). Vice-Chm., Ind. Commn on Proportional Repn, 2002–03. Trustee, Citizenship Foundn, 1991–2000; Mem. Council, Justice, 1995–. FAcSS (AcSS 2011). FRSA 1991. Haldane Medal, RIPA, 1978. *Publications:* Conspiracy and Civil Liberties, 1974; (ed) The Bar on Trial, 1978; An Assembly for Wales, 1996; (ed) Constitutional Futures, 1999; (ed) The State and the Nations, 2000; (ed) The State of the Nations 2003, 2003; (ed) Devolution, Law Making and the Constitution, 2005; (ed) The English Question, 2006; (ed) Constitutional Futures Revisited, 2008; Hung Parliaments: the challenges for Westminster and Whitehall, 2009; Does Freedom of Information Work?: the impact of FOI on central government in the UK, 2010; The Conservative-Lib Dem Agenda for Constitutional Reform, 2010; The Politics of Coalition: how the Conservative-Liberal Democrat coalition works, 2012; Special Advisers: who they are, what they do and why they matter, 2014; The Politics of Judicial Independence in the UK's Changing Constitution, 2015; articles in legal and govt jls. *Recreations:* bird-watching, badgers, opera, canoeing, sailing. *Address:* 94 Constantine Road, NW3 2LS. *T:* (020) 7267 4881; (office) The Constitution Unit, School of Public Policy, University College London, 29 Tavistock Square, WC1H 9QU. *T:* (020) 7679 4971, *Fax:* (020) 7679 4978. *E:* r.hazell@ucl.ac.uk.

HAZLERIGG, family name of **Baron Hazlerigg**.

HAZLERIGG, 3rd Baron *cr* 1945, of Noseley; **Arthur Grey Hazlerigg;** Bt 1622; *b* 5 May 1951; *s* of 2nd Baron Hazlerigg, MC, TD and Patricia, *d* of John Pullar; *S* father, 2002; *m* 1999, Shan (*née* McIndoe); one *s* three *d* (incl. twin *d*) by previous marriage. *Heir: s* Hon. Arthur William Grey Hazlerigg, *b* 13 May 1987. *Address:* Noseley Hall, Billesdon, Leics LE7 9EH. *T:* (0116) 259 6487, *Fax:* (0116) 259 6989. *E:* arthur@noseley.demon.co.uk. *Clubs:* MCC; Leicester Tigers Rugby Football.

HAZLEWOOD, Prof. Arthur Dennis; Research Professor in Commonwealth Studies, Oxford University, 1986–88, now Emeritus; Professorial Fellow, Pembroke College, Oxford, 1979–88, now Emeritus; *b* 24 April 1921; *s* of Harry Arthur Sinclair Hazlewood and Miriam Esther Maltby; *m* 1954, Tamara Oszpicyn (*d* 1998); one *d. Educ:* Finchley County Sch.; LSE (BSc Econ 1948); The Queen's Coll., Oxford (BPhil 1950; MA 1954). Post Office engineer, 1938–48 (RAF radar stations, 1940–44); Oxford University, 1950–88: Tutor to Colonial Service courses, 1950–56; research staff, Inst. of Economics and Statistics, 1956–79; Pembroke College: tutorial fellow, 1961–79; Domestic Bursar, 1970–79; Vicegerent, 1978–79; Warden, Queen Elizabeth House, Dir, Inst. of Commonwealth Studies, 1979–86. Adviser, Nyasaland Govt on Central African Fedn, 1962; Mem., UK Economic Mission to Malawi, 1965; Dir, Common Market Secretariat, President's Office, Kenya, 1965–66; Dir, Trade and Finance Div., Commonwealth Secretariat and Special Adviser, Commonwealth Fund for Technical Co-operation, 1975–76. *Publications:* (jtly) Nyasaland: the economics of federation, 1960; The Economy of Africa, 1961; (jtly) An Econometric Model of the UK, 1961; Rail and Road in East Africa, 1964; (ed) African Integration and Disintegration, 1967; Economic Integration: the East African experience, 1975; (jtly) Aid and Inequality in Kenya, 1976; The Economy of Kenya, 1979; (jtly) Irrigation Economics in Poor Countries, 1982; Education, Work, and Pay in East Africa, 1989; articles in jls and symposia. *Address:* 14 Fyfield Road, Oxford OX2 6QE. *T:* (01865) 559119.

HAZLEWOOD, Charles Matthew Egerton; conductor; *b* 14 Nov. 1966; *s* of Rev. Canon Ian Hazlewood and Helen Hazlewood; *m* 1993, Henrietta Lang; three *s* one *d. Educ:* Christ's Hosp.; Keble Coll., Oxford (Organ Schol.; BA Hons). ARCO 1985. Founder and Music Dir, Excellent Device! (formerly Eos), 1991–; Music Director: Broomhill Opera, 1993–2001; Wiltons Music Hall, 1999–2003; and Co-founder, Dimpho di Kopane, 2000–08 (composer and Music Dir, The Mysteries, Beggar's Opera, The Snow Queen); and Founder, Army of Generals (formerly Harmonieband), 2002–; Principal Guest Conductor, BBC Concert Orch., 2005–09; Founder, Charles Hazlewood All Stars, 2008–; Founder Artistic Director: Orch. in a Field, 2009–; British Paraorch., 2011–; Founder, Soweto Messiah Project, Johannesburg, 2012–. Débuts: Carnegie Hall, 2003; BBC Proms, 2006; Royal Concertgebouw Orch., 2009; Orch. of the Age of Enlightenment, 2009; Malmo SO, 2009; Gothenberg SO, 2010; Philharmonia, 2010; Copenhagen Philharmonic, 2015; Swedish Radio SO, 2015. Author, conductor and presenter of television films: Vivaldi Unmasked, 2001; The Genius of Mozart, 2003; Beethoven, 2005; Stripping Pop, 2005; Tchaikovsky, 2007; How Pop Songs Work, 2008; The Birth of British Music, 2009; Come Clog Dancing, 2010; Come Bell Ringing, 2011; Scrapheap Orchestra, 2011; music dir and conductor of film, U-Carmen E-Khayelitsha, 2005 (Golden Bear for best film, Berlin Film Fest.); conductor and presenter, BBC radio programmes: Discovering Music; The Charles Hazlewood Show. Composer, Dead Dog in a Suitcase (new version of The Beggar's Opera for Kneehigh Th.), 2014. First Prize, Conducting Comp., EBU, 1995; Sony Radio Academy Award, 2005, 2006, 2008. *Recreations:* cooking, film. *Address:* c/o Intermusica, 36 Graham Street, N1 8GJ. *T:* (020) 7608 9900. *E:* annie@charleshazlewood.com, smcleod@intermusica.co.uk. *W:* www.charleshazlewood.com.

HEAD, family name of **Viscount Head**.

HEAD, 2nd Viscount *cr* 1960, of Throope; **Richard Antony Head;** *b* 27 Feb. 1937; *s* of 1st Viscount Head, GCMG, CBE, MC, PC, and Dorothea, Viscountess Head (*d* 1987), *d* of 9th Earl of Shaftesbury, KP, GCVO, CBE, PC; *S* father, 1983; *m* 1974, Alicia Brigid, *er d* of Julian Salmond; two *s* one *d. Educ:* Eton; RMA Sandhurst. The Life Guards, 1957–66 (Captain), retd. Trainer of racehorses, 1968–83. *Recreations:* shooting, golf. *Heir: s* Hon. Henry Julian Head, *b* 30 March 1980. *Address:* Throope Manor, Bishopstone, Salisbury, Wilts SP5 4BA. *T:* (01722) 718318.

HEAD, (John) Philip (Trevelyan); His Honour Judge Head; a Circuit Judge, since 2004; *b* 6 July 1953; *s* of Walter Raleigh Trevelyan Head and Rosemary Constance Beatrice Head (*née* Borwick); *m* 1983, Erica Lesley Cox; one *s* one *d. Educ:* Marlborough Coll.; Merton Coll., Oxford (MA); Univ. of Virginia (LLM). Fulbright Schol., 1974–75. Called to the Bar, Middle Temple, 1976; Asst Recorder, 1996–2000, Recorder, 2000–04. Mem., Parole Bd for Eng. and Wales, 2006–09; Judicial Mem., Restricted Patients Panel, 2011–12. Oxford Univ. Hockey Blue, 1974. *Recreations:* travel, books. *Address:* Leicester Crown Court, 90 Wellington Street, Leicester LE1 6HG. *Clubs:* Savile, Sette of Odd Volumes.

HEAD, Michael Edward, CVO 1991; UK Member, European Commission on Racism and Intolerance (Council of Europe), 1996–2013 (Chairman, 2001–05); *b* 17 March 1936; *s* of Alexander Edward Head and Wilhelmina Head; *m* 1963, Wendy Elizabeth, *d* of R. J. Davies; two *s* two *d. Educ:* Leeds, Kingston, and Woking Grammar Schools; University College London (BA; Pollard Prize for History); Univ. of Michigan (MA). 2nd Lieut, Royal Artillery (Nat. Service), 1958–60. Home Office, 1960; Private Sec. to Parly Under Secs of State, 1964–66; Sec., Deptl Cttee on Liquor Licensing (Erroll), 1971–72; Asst Sec., 1974–84: Probation and After Care Dept; Community Programmes and Equal Opportunities Dept; Criminal Dept; Asst Under Sec. of State, General Dept, 1984, Criminal Justice and Constitutional Dept (Registrar of the Baronetage), 1986, Broadcasting Dept, 1991, Equal Opportunities and Gen. Dept, 1991 (Head of Dept, 1991–96). Dir, Rehab UK, 1996–2005. Member: Surrey Probation Cttee, 1997–2001; Surrey Probation Bd, 2001–07. Vice Chm., Woking Community Leisure Ltd, 1996–98. Mem., Mayford Decorative and Fine Arts Soc. *Recreations:* theatre, reading. *Address:* Rustlings, Castle Road, Horsell, Woking, Surrey GU21 4ET. *T:* and *Fax:* (01483) 772929. *E:* mhead90120@btinternet.com. *Clubs:* County (Guildford); Rotary (Woking Dist).

HEAD, Peter Richard, CBE 2011 (OBE 1998); FREng, FICE, FIStructE; Chief Executive Officer, Ecological Sequestration Trust, since 2014 (Chairman, 2011–14); *b* 27 Feb. 1947; *s* of Robert Cyril Head and Vera Alice (*née* Kent); *m* 1970, Susan Florence East; one *s* one *d. Educ:* Tiffin Boys' Sch., Kingston-upon-Thames; Imperial Coll., London (BSc 1st Cl. Hons Eng 1969). FREng (FEng 1996); FICE 1995; FIStructE 1995; FCIHT (FIHT 1995). Freeman Fox & Partners, 1969–80: team leader for design of: Avonmouth Bridge, M5, 1971–74; Myton Swing Bridge, Hull, 1974–75 (Dep. Resident Engr, construction of Myton Bridge, 1977–80); Section Engr, construction of Friarton Bridge, Perth, 1975–77; G. Maunsell & Partners subseq. Maunsell, later part of AECOM Gp, then FaberMaunsell, 1980–2004: designer of bridges over docks on Dockland Light Rly, London, 1981–84; Project Director: Second Severn Crossing, 1984–96; design and construction, Kap Shui Mun Bridge, Hong Kong, 1994–96; Dir responsible for studies and choice of bridge for third crossing of Forth Estuary, 1993–2004; Man. Dir, 1995–97; Chief Exec., Europe, 1997–2002; Corporate Develt Dir, 2002–04; Dir for supervision of construction, Rion Antirion Bridge, Greece, 1997–2004; Dir and Leader of Global Planning, 2004–11, Consultant, 2011–12, Arup; Proj. Dir, Dongtan Eco-city, Shanghai, 2005–08; Maunsell Structural Plastics Ltd, 1984–97: Dir and designer, Aberfeldy Bridge, 1992 and Bonds Mill Bridge, Stonehouse, Glos, 1994; inventor, Advanced Composite Construction System and Spaces bridge concept. Chm., London First Sustainability Unit, 2000; Comr, GLA Sustainable Develt Commn, 2002–09; Chm., Steel Construction Inst., 2003–06 (Dep. Chm., 1999–2003); Vice-Pres., Construction Industry Res. Assoc., 1999–2004; Mem., 2012 Olympics Construction Task Force, 2005–10; Dir, London Bd, Groundwork Trust, 2008–; Chm., Trust Bd, Inst. for Sustainability, 2009–15. Visiting Professor: Univ. of Surrey, 2000–05; Univ. of Bristol, 2008–; Univ. of Westminster, 2011–14; Hood Fellow, Univ. of Auckland, 2010–11. Innovation Champion, Thames Gateway, 2008–10. Internat. Brunel Lecture Series, ICE, 2008–09. FCGI 2001; FRSA 2008. Hon. DEng Bristol, 2008. Premier Gold Award/PRW Award for Excellence in Design, 1993; Silver Medal, Royal Acad. Engrg, 1995; Laureate Award of Merit Internat. Assoc. of Bridge and Structural Engrg, 1998; Telford Prize, ICE, 2006; Frank Whittle Medal, RAEng, 2008. *Publications:* numerous papers in learned jls and conf. proc. covering sustainability, major bridge projects and pioneering work in advanced composite materials, sustainable cities and low carbon urban develt. *Recreations:* hill-walking, gardening, painting, grandchildren. *Address:* Ecological Sequestration Trust, 10 Queen Street Place, EC4R 1BE. *T:* 07917 231655. *E:* peter.head@ecosequestrust.org; Parkside, 11 Manor Way, Beckenham, Kent BR3 3LH. *T:* (020) 8658 2901.

HEAD, Philip; *see* Head, J. P. T.

HEAD, Philip John, FRICS; programme and project management consultant, since 2012; *b* 24 Nov. 1951; *s* of Dennis George Head and Marjorie Head; *m* 1974, Barbara Fox; two *s. Educ:* Surbiton Grammar Sch.; Herefordshire Tech. Coll.; Univ. of Reading (BSc Hons Estate Management). FRICS 1985. Estates Surveyor, 1973–77, Sen. Commercial Surveyor, 1977–78, Milton Keynes Develt Corp.; Welsh Development Agency, 1978–93: Develt and Funding Manager, 1981–83; Dep. Commercial Dir, 1983–84; Commercial Dir, 1984–87; Exec. Dir, Property and Regional Services, 1987–91; Chief Exec., 1991–93; Hd of Property Services, 1994–98, Asst Dir, 1998–2001, FEFCE; Asst Dir, 2001–02, Dir, Infrastructure and Property Services, 2002–10, LSC; Dir of Capital, Skills Funding Agency, 2010–12. *Recreations:* member of Rotary Club of Cardiff West (Hon. Sec.), gardening, family. *E:* philipjhead@btinternet.com.

HEAD, Sir Richard (Douglas Somerville), 6th Bt *cr* 1838, of Rochester, Kent; Assistant Gardener, RHS Garden, Wisley, 1979–2009; *b* 16 Jan. 1951; *s* of Major Sir Francis Head, 5th Bt, and of Susan, Lady Head (*née* Ramsay); *S* father, 2005; *m* 1991, Edwina Mansell (marr. diss. 1999). *Educ:* Eton; Bristol Poly. (BA Fine Arts 1974); London Univ. Inst. of Educn (PGCE 1975); RA Schs (David Murray Landscape Studentship). Artist in pen and ink, gouache, oil paint, drypoint. Mixed exhibitions: Michael Parkin Fine Arts, 1988; Christie's 20th Century Old Etonian Artists, 1990; Sally Hunter Fine Arts, 1997; Russell Gallery Mixed Christmas Show, 2007, 2008, 2009; solo exhibition, The First Gallery, Southampton, 2005. *Recreations:* music, painting, drawing, garden volunteer at Clandon Park. *Heir: cousin* Patrick John Somerville Head [*b* 4 Oct. 1943; *m* 1st, 1971, Karen Carla Schaufele (marr. diss. 1986); two *d*; 2nd, 1995, Joan Fay Crawford]. *Address:* 6 Viscount Gardens, West Byfleet, Surrey KT14 6HE.

HEAD, Sandra Anne; *see* Phinbow, S. A.

HEADFORT, 7th Marquis of, *cr* 1800; **Thomas Michael Ronald Christopher Taylour;** Bt 1704; Baron Headfort, 1760; Viscount Headfort, 1762; Earl of Bective, 1766; Baron Kenlis (UK), 1831; Senior Consultant, Sotheby's International Realty, since 2011; *b* 10 Feb. 1959; *o s* of 6th Marquis of Headfort and of Hon. Elizabeth Nall-Cain, *d* of 2nd Baron Brocket; *S* father, 2005; *m* 1987, Susan Jane (*d* 2008), *er d* of late C. A. Vandervell and of Mrs Vandervell; two *s* two *d. Educ:* Harrow; RAC Cirencester. Estate agent with John D. Wood & Co., London, 1981–87; property consultant, 1995–2003, Dir, 2003–11, Bective Davidson, later Bective Leslie Marsh Ltd, London; Dir, Central London Estate Agents Ltd. Mem., Irish Peers Assoc. *Heir: s* Earl of Bective, *qv*. *Address:* Shipton Manor, Shipton on Cherwell, Oxon OX5 1JL; (office) 26A Conduit Street, W1S 2XY. *Clubs:* Lansdowne; Royal Dublin Society (Dublin).

HEAL, Prof. (Barbara) Jane, PhD; FBA 1997; Professor of Philosophy, University of Cambridge, 1999–2012, now Emeritus; Fellow, St John's College, Cambridge, since 1986 (President, 1999–2003); *b* 21 Oct. 1946; *d* of William Calvert Kneale and Martha Kneale (*née* Hurst); *m* 1968, John Gauntlett Benedict Heal (marr. diss. 1987); one *s* one *d. Educ:* Oxford High Sch. for Girls; New Hall, Cambridge (BA 1968; PhD 1973). Sarah Smithson Res. Fellow, Newnham Coll., Cambridge, 1971–74; Harkness Fellow, Commonwealth Fund of NY, and Vis. Fellow, Princeton Univ. and Univ. of Calif at Berkeley, 1974–76; Lectr in Philosophy, Univ. of Newcastle upon Tyne, 1976–86; Univ. Asst Lectr, 1986–91, Lectr, 1991–96, Reader, 1996–99, in Philosophy, Univ. of Cambridge. *Publications:* Fact and Meaning, 1989; Mind, Reason and Imagination, 2003; articles in Mind, Philosophical Qly, etc. *Recreations:* reading, walking. *Address:* St John's College, Cambridge CB2 1TP. *T:* (01223) 338668.

HEAL, Dr Felicity Margaret, FBA 2015; Lecturer in History, University of Oxford, 1980–2011, now Emeritus; Fellow, Jesus College, Oxford, 1980–2011 now Emeritus; *b* Hemel Hempstead, 24 Sept. 1945; *d* of John and Winifred Chandler; *m* 1988, Dr Clive Holmes; one *d* and two step *s. Educ:* Lewes Girls' Grammar Sch., Sussex; Newnham Coll., Cambridge (BA Hist. 1967; PhD Hist. 1970). Res. Fellow, Newnham Coll., Cambridge, 1970–73; Staff Tutor, Open Univ., 1976–78; Lectr in Hist., Sussex Univ., 1977–79; University of Oxford: Chair, Faculty of Hist., 1999–2001; Dep. Hd, Humanities Div., 2009–11. Vis. Fellow, Univs of Yale and Stanford, 1975–76. Consultant Ed., Oxford DNB, 1995–. *Publications:* Of Prelates and Princes: a study of the economic and social position of the Tudor Episcopate, 1980; Hospitality in Early Modern England, 1990; (with C. Holmes) The Gentry in England and Wales 1500–1700, 1994; Reformation in Britain and Ireland, 2003; The Power of Gifts: gift-exchange in early modern England, 2014. *Recreations:* music, especially of the Baroque, travel, gardening. *Address:* Jesus College, Turl Street, Oxford OX1 3DW. *T:* (01865) 510068. *E:* felicity.heal@jesus.ox.ac.uk.

HEAL, Oliver Standerwick, PhD; furniture restorer, since 2004; *b* 18 April 1949; *s* of late Anthony Standerwick Heal; *m* 1990, Annik Coatalen; one *s. Educ:* Leighton Park Sch., Reading; Bucks Chiltern UC (BA Hons (Furniture Conservation and Restoration) 2004); Brunel Univ. (PhD 2009). Joined Heal's, 1970; Dir, Heal & Son Ltd, 1974–83, Chm., 1977–83; Chm., Heal & Son Holdings PLC, 1981–83 (Dir, 1975–83); Dir, Staples & Co. Ltd, 1981–84; Chm., Heal Textil GmbH, 1984–90; VRP multi-carte, France, 1990–91; Commercial Dir, Faïenceries de Quimper, France, 1992–94; sales agent, furnishing fabrics, France, 1994–2000. *Publications:* Sir Ambrose Heal and the Heal Cabinet Factory 1897–1939, 2014; article in Jl of Furniture History Soc. *Recreation:* vintage cars. *Club:* Vintage Sports Car (Chipping Norton).

HEAL, Sharon; Director, Museums Association, since 2014; *b* Leeds, 27 Oct. 1967; *d* of John Heal and Josephine Heal; *m* 1996, Alexander Shanks; one *d. Educ:* Roundhay High Sch., Leeds; London Coll. of Printing. Editor, Museums Jl, 2005–10; Hd, Pubns and Events, Mus Assoc., 2010–14. *Publications:* (contrib.) Museums and Public Value, 2013. *Recreations:* horse riding, book club. *Address:* Museums Association, 42 Clerkenwell Close, EC1R 0AZ. *T:* (020) 7566 7800. *E:* sharon@museumsassociation.org.

HEAL, Sylvia Lloyd; JP; *b* 20 July 1942; *d* of late John Lloyd Fox and Ruby Fox; *m* 1965, Keith Heal; one *s* one *d. Educ:* Elfed Secondary Modern School, Buckley, N Wales; Coleg Harlech; University College Swansea (BSc Econ 1968). Social worker, health service and

Dept of Employment, 1968–70 and 1980–90; Nat. Officer, Carers Nat. Assoc., 1992–97. MP (Lab) Mid Staffordshire, March 1990–1992; contested (Lab) Mid Staffordshire, 1992; MP (Lab) Halesowen and Rowley Regis, 1997–2010. PPS to Sec. of State for Defence, 1997–2000; First Dep. Chm. of Ways and Means and a Dep. Speaker, H of C, 2000–10. Mem., Select Cttee on Educn, Sci. and Arts, 1990–92; opposition spokesperson on health and women's issues, 1991–92. Mem. Council, ASA, 1992–97; Mem., Exec. Council, SSAFA, 1990–91. Hon. Fellow, Univ. of Wales, 2003. JP Surrey, 1973. *Recreations:* walking, theatre, listening to male voice choirs, gardening. *Address:* Meadlake, 15 Vicarage Avenue, Egham, Surrey TW20 8NW.

HEALD, Bill; *see* Heald, R. J.

HEALD, Sir Oliver, Kt 2014; QC 2012; MP (C) North East Hertfordshire, since 1997 (North Hertfordshire, 1992–97); *b* 15 Dec. 1954; *s* of late John Anthony Heald and Joyce Heald; *m* 1979, Christine Whittle; one *s* two *d.* *Educ:* Reading Sch.; Pembroke Coll., Cambridge. Called to the Bar, Middle Temple, 1977, Bencher, 2013; practice in E Anglia and London, 1977–95 and 1997–2001. Contested (C) Southwark and Bermondsey, 1987. PPS to Minister of Agric., Fisheries and Food, 1994–95; Parly Under-Sec. of State, DSS, 1995–97; an Opposition Whip, 1997–2000; Opposition spokesman: on home affairs, 2000–01; on health, 2001–02; on work and pensions, 2002–03; Shadow Leader, H of C, 2003–05; Shadow Sec. of State for Constitutional Affairs, and Shadow Chancellor of Duchy of Lancaster, 2005–07; Solicitor General, 2012–14. Member: Employment Select Cttee, 1992–94; Admin Select Cttee, 1998–2000; Select Cttee on Modernisation of H of C, 2003–05; Select Cttee on Work and Pensions, 2007–12; Cttee on Standards in Public Life, 2008–12; Cttee of Selection, 2009–10; Cttee on Standards and Privileges, 2010–12; Ecclesiastical Cttee, 2010–12; Governance Select Cttee, 2014–15. Vice-Chm., Rules Cttee, Council of Europe, 2012. Chm. of Exec., Soc. of Conservative Lawyers, 2007–12. *Recreations:* sports, family. *Address:* House of Commons, SW1A 0AA.

HEALD, Prof. Richard John, (Bill), CBE 2012 (OBE 1998); FRCS, FRCSE; Surgical Director, Pelican Cancer Foundation, Basingstoke, since 2000; *b* 11 May 1936; *o s* of late Jack and Muriel Heald, St Albans; *m* 1969, Denise (*née* Boncey); three *d.* *Educ:* Gonville and Caius Coll., Cambridge (BA 1st Cl. Hons 1957 (Coll. Prize); MA 1960; MB 1960, MChir 1965); Guy's Hosp., London. FRCSE 1964; FRCS 1965. Consultant Surgeon: N Hants Hosp., Basingstoke, 1973–; specialist in colorectal cancer surgery and internat. teacher of surgical technique. Personal Chair, Univ. of Southampton, 1998–. B. V. Petrovsky Hon. Prof., Nat. Res. Centre of Surgery, Russia, 2011. Sir Peter Freyer Meml Lect., NUI, 2011. Mem. Council, RCS, 1989–2001 (Vice-Pres., 1996–98); Pres., Sections of Coloproctol. and of Surgery, RSocMed; Pres., Internat. Colon and Rectal Club—Surgical Dir, TIC, Shanghai, 2005; Colostomy Assoc., 2008. Israel Soc. of Colon and Rectal Surgery, 2007. Hon. Member: Swiss Surgical Soc., 2000; Polish Soc. of Surgical Oncol., 2008 (Gold Medal, 2008). Hon. FRSocMed 2001; Hon. Fellow: Assoc. of Coloproctol. of GB and Ireland, 2001; German Surgical Soc., 2004; Austrian Surgical Soc., 2004; Assoc. Française de Chirurgie, 2005; Amer. Soc. of Colon and Rectal Surgeons, 2012; Surgical Soc. of Rome, 2012; Hon. FACS 2013; Hon. FRCSI 2014. Hon. Dr Linkoping, Sweden, 1997. Gold Medal in Surgery, Assoc. of Surgery of Netherlands, 2001; Centenary Medal, French Cancer Soc., 2005; Herczel Award (Bronze Placket), Hungarian Coloproctology Assoc., 2011. *Publications:* contrib. papers on rectal cancer surgery, particularly total mesorectal excision for rectal cancer to jls incl. Jl RSocMed, Lancet. *Recreation:* sailing. *Address:* Pelican Cancer Foundation, The Ark, Dinwoodie Drive, Basingstoke, Hants RG24 9NN. *T:* (01256) 314848. *Club:* Royal Southampton Yacht.

See also T. H. Henman.

HEALD, His Honour Thomas Routledge; a Circuit Judge (formerly County Court Judge), 1970–95; *b* 19 Aug. 1923; *s* of late John Arthur Heald and Nora Marion Heald; *m* 1950, Jean, *d* of James Campbell Henderson; two *s* one *d* (and one *d* decd). *Educ:* Merchant Taylors' Sch.; St John's Coll., Oxford (Fish Schol., 1941; BA (Jurisprudence) 1947; MA 1949). Lieut, RAC, 1943–45. Called to Bar, Middle Temple, 1948; Midland Circuit; Prosecuting Counsel to Inland Revenue (Midland Circuit), 1965–70; Deputy Chairman, QS: Lindsey, 1965–71; Notts, 1969–71; Notts designated Family Judge, 1991–96. Council of HM Circuit Judges: Asst Sec., 1980–83; Sec., 1984–85; Vice-Pres., 1986–87; Pres., 1988–89; Member: Matrimonial Rules Cttee, 1980–83; President's Cttee on Adoption, 1983–95; President's Family Cttee, 1984–93. Mem., Senate of Inns of Court, 1984–86. Chairman: Notts Children's and Families Mediation Service, 1995–2000; Notts Guardian *Ad Litem*/Reporting Officers Panel, 1995–98. Mem. Council, Nottingham Univ., 1974–93 (Chm., Physical Recreation Adv. Cttee, 1979–85; Chm., Law Adv. Cttee, 1976–84; Chm., Estates and Buildings Cttee, 1985–89); Chm., Law Adv. Cttee, Trent Polytechnic, 1979–84. *Recreations:* golf, local history, family history. *Club:* Notts Golf.

HEALD, Timothy Villiers, FRSL; writer and freelance journalist, since 1972; *b* 28 Jan. 1944; *s* of Villiers Archer John Heald, CVO, DSO, MBE, MC and late Catherine Eleanor Jean Heald (*née* Vaughan); *m* 1st, 1968, Alison Martina Leslie (marr. diss. 1997); two *s* two *d*; 2nd, 1999, Penelope Byrne. *Educ:* Sherborne Sch.; Balliol Coll., Oxford (MA). Atticus column, Sunday Times, 1965–67; Features Ed., Town Mag., 1967; feature writer, Daily Express, 1967–72; Associate Ed., Weekend Mag., Toronto, 1977–78; Pendennis, The Observer, 1990. Chm., Crime Writers' Assoc., 1987–88. FRSL 2000. Pres., Old Shirburnian Soc., 2000–04. *Publications: fiction:* Unbecoming Habits, 1973; Blue Blood Will Out, 1974; Deadline, 1975; Let Sleeping Dogs Die, 1976; Just Desserts, 1977; Caroline R, 1980; Murder at Moose Jaw, 1981; Masterstroke, 1982; Red Herrings, 1983; Class Distinctions, 1984; Brought to Book, 1988; (ed) The Rigby File, 1989; Business Unusual, 1989; (ed) A Classic English Crime, 1990; (ed) A Classic Christmas Crime, 1995; Stop Press, 1998; Death and the Visiting Fellow, 2004; Death and the D'Urbervilles, 2005; A Death on the Ocean Wave, 2007; Death in the Opening Chapter, 2011; Poison at the Pueblo, 2011; Yet Another Death in Venice, 2014; *non-fiction:* It's a Dog's Life, 1971; The Making of Space 1999, 1976; John Steed: the authorised biography, vol. 1, 1977; (with Mayo Mohs) HRH The Man Who Would be King, 1979; Networks (who we know and how we use them), 1983; The Character of Cricket, 1986; (ed) The Newest London Spy, 1988; By Appointment: 150 years of the Royal Warrant and its holders, 1990; (ed) My Lord's, 1990; The Duke: a portrait of Prince Philip, 1991; Honourable Estates, 1992; A Life of Love: the biography of Barbara Cartland, 1994; Denis: the authorised biography of the incomparable Compton, 1994, revd edn as Denis Compton: life of a sporting hero, 2006; Brian Johnston: the authorised biography, 1995; Beating Retreat: Hong Kong under the last Governor, 1997; A Peerage for Trade, 2001; Village Cricket, 2004; Princess Margaret: a life unravelled, 2007; Palmers: the story of a Dorset brewer, 2008; (ed with C. Braun) Tom Foolery: writings of Thomas Braun, 2010; Jardine's Last Tour: India 1933–34, 2011; My Dear Hugh: letters of Richard Cobb, 2011. *Recreations:* talking, wine, food. *Address:* Roselands, Blind Lane, Bower Hinton, Martock, Som TA12 6LG. *T:* (01935) 826059. *E:* tim@timheald.com. *Clubs:* MCC, Army and Navy, Frontline, Groucho, Detection; Real Tennis (Walditch, Dorset).

HEALE, Simon John Newton; Chief Executive, London Metal Exchange, 2001–06; *b* 27 April 1953; *s* of James Newton Heale and Ruth Elizabeth Heale; *m* 1982, Catriona Jean, *d* of Lt-Gen. Sir Robin Macdonald Carnegie, KCB, OBE; one *s* two *d.* *Educ:* Winchester Coll.; Oriel Coll., Oxford (BA 1975). Chartered Accountant, 1978. Finance Dir, Swire Japan, 1982–85; Pres., Oceanroutes Inc., 1985–88; Gen. Manager Cargo, Cathay Pacific, 1988–90; Chief Operating Officer, Dragonair, 1990–94; Dep. Man. Dir, Cathay Pacific Airways, 1994–97; Jardine Fleming: Gp Finance Dir, 1997–99; Chief Operating Officer, 1999–2001. Non-executive Director: LCH.Clearnet Gp Ltd, 2003–06; Morgan Advanced Materials (formerly Morgan Crucible Co.) plc, 2005–14; KAZ Minerals (formerly Kazakhmys) plc, 2007– (Chm., 2013–); Coats plc, 2011–14 (Sen. Ind. Dir, 2013–14); Sen. Ind. Dir, Panmure Gordon & Co. plc, 2010–11 (non-exec. Dir, 2007–11; Interim Chm., 2009–10); Marex Financial, 2007–; PZ Cussons, 2008–13; Sen. Ind. Dir, Coats plc, 2013–; Chm., GMS, 2014–. Chief Exec., China Now Fest., 2007–08. Trustee, Macmillan Cancer Support, 2010– (Treas.). *Recreations:* travel, reading, walking, labradors.

HEALEY, family name of **Baron Healey**.

HEALEY, Baron *cr* 1992 (Life Peer), of Riddlesden in the County of West Yorkshire; **Denis Winston Healey,** CH 1979; MBE 1945; PC 1964; *b* 30 Aug. 1917; *s* of late William Healey, Keighley, Yorks; *m* 1945, Edna May Edmunds (Lady Healey, writer, *d* 2010); one *s* two *d.* *Educ:* Bradford Grammar Sch.; Balliol Coll., Oxford (Hon. Fellow, 1979). First Cl. Hons Mods 1938; Jenkyns Exhib. 1939; Harmsworth Sen. Schol., First Cl. Lit. Hum., BA 1940; MA 1945. War of 1939–45; entered Army, 1940; served N Africa, Italy. Major RE 1944 (despatches). Contested (Lab) Pudsey and Otley Div., 1945; Sec., International Dept, Labour Party, 1945–52. MP (Lab) SE Leeds, Feb. 1952–1955, Leeds E, 1955–92; Shadow Cabinet, 1959–64, 1970–74, 1979–87; Secretary of State for Defence, 1964–70; Chancellor of the Exchequer, 1974–79; opposition spokesman on Foreign and Commonwealth Affairs, 1980–87; Dep. Leader of Labour Party, 1980–83. Mem. Brit. Delegn to Commonwealth Relations Conf., Canada, 1949; British Delegate to: Consultative Assembly, Council of Europe, 1952–54; Inter Parly Union Conf., Washington, 1953; Western European Union and Council of Europe, 1953–55. Chm., IMF Interim Cttee, 1977–79. Mem. Exec. Fabian Soc., 1954–61. Mem., Labour Party Nat. Exec. Cttee, 1970–75. Councillor: RIIA, 1948–60; Inst. of Strategic Studies, 1958–61. Pres., Birkbeck Coll., 1993–99. Pres., Corelli Ensemble, 2011–. Freeman, City of Leeds, 1992. FRSL 1993. Hon. Fellow, Leeds Polytechnic, 1987. Hon. DLitt Bradford, 1983; Hon. LLD Sussex, 1991. Grand Cross of Order of Merit, Germany, 1979. *Publications:* The Curtain Falls, 1951; New Fabian Essays, 1952; Neutralism, 1955; Fabian International Essays, 1956; A Neutral Belt in Europe, 1958; NATO and American Security, 1959; The Race Against the H Bomb, 1960; Labour Britain and the World, 1963; Healey's Eye, 1980; Labour and a World Society, 1985; Beyond Nuclear Deterrence, 1986; The Time of My Life (autobiog.), 1989; When Shrimps Learn to Whistle (essays), 1990; My Secret Planet, 1992; Denis Healey's Yorkshire Dales, 1995; Healey's World, 2002. *Recreations:* travel, photography, music, painting. *Address:* Pingles Place, Alfriston, East Sussex BN26 5TT.

HEALEY, Sir Charles Edward C.; *see* Chadwyck-Healey.

HEALEY, Rt Hon. John; PC 2008; MP (Lab) Wentworth and Dearne, since 2010 (Wentworth, 1997–2010); *b* 13 Feb. 1960; *s* of Aidan Healey, OBE and Jean Healey; *m* 1993, Jackie Bate; one *s.* *Educ:* Christ's Coll., Cambridge (schol., BA 1982). Charity campaigner, 1984–90; Campaigns Manager, Issue Communications, 1990–92; Head of Communications, MSF, 1992–94; Campaigns Dir, TUC, 1994–97. PPS to Chancellor of the Exchequer, 1999–2001; Parly Under-Sec. of State, DFES, 2001–02; Econ. Sec., 2002–05, Financial Sec., 2005–07, HM Treasury; Minister of State (Minister for Local Govt), 2007–09, (Minister for Housing), 2009–10, DCLG; Shadow Minister for Housing, 2010; Shadow Sec. of State for Health, 2010–11; Shadow Minister for Housing and Planning, 2015–. Contested (Lab) Ryedale, 1992. *Address:* House of Commons, SW1A 0AA. *E:* john.healey.mp@parliament.uk.

HEALEY, Prof. John Francis, PhD; FBA 2011; Professor of Semitic Studies, University of Manchester, 1997–2013, now Emeritus; *b* Leeds, 10 Feb. 1948; *s* of George Healey and Frances Healey; *m* 1972, Elizabeth Anne Warman; one *s* one *d.* *Educ:* St Michael's Coll., Leeds; University Coll., Dublin, NUI (BA, MA Semitic Langs and Greek); Sch. of Oriental and African Studies, Univ. of London (PhD 1977). Lectr in Semitic Langs, University Coll., Cardiff, 1974–80; Lectr in Hebrew and Semitic Philol., Univ. of Durham, 1981–89; University of Manchester: Lectr, 1989–92; Sen. Lectr, 1992–95; Reader, 1995–97. *Publications:* Leshono Suryoyo: first studies in Syriac, 1980, 2nd edn 2005; The Early Alphabet, 1990; The Nabataean Tomb Inscriptions of Mada'in Salih, 1993; (with H. J. W. Drijvers) The Old Syriac Inscriptions of Edessa and Osrhoene, 1999; The Religion of the Nabataeans: a conspectus, 2001; (with G. R. Smith) A Brief Introduction to the Arabic Alphabet, 2009; Aramaic Inscriptions and Documents of the Roman Period, 2009; Law and Religion between Petra and Edessa: studies in Aramaic epigraphy on the Roman frontier, 2011; approx. 120 learned articles and contribs to edited works. *Recreations:* travel in the Middle East where possible, The Guardian, The Tablet. *Address:* School of Arts, Languages and Cultures, Faculty of Humanities, University of Manchester, Oxford Road, Manchester M13 9PL. *T:* (0161) 275 3248. *E:* john.healey@manchester.ac.uk.

HEALEY, Prof. Patsy, OBE 1999; PhD; FBA 2009; Professor, School of Architecture, Planning and Landscape, University of Newcastle upon Tyne, 1988–2002, now Emeritus; *b* Loughborough, Leics, 1 Jan. 1940; *d* of late Cecil Terence Ingold, CMG and Leonora Mary Ingold (*née* Kemp); *m* 1st, 1961, Ian Nevill Healey (*d* 1972); 2nd, 1977, David Reiach Hunter (*d* 1979). *Educ:* Walthamstow Hall, Sevenoaks; University Coll., London (BA Geog.); Regent St Poly. (DipTP); London Sch. of Econs (PhD Urban and Regl Planning). MRTPI 1973. Teacher, Llwyn-y-bryn Grammar Sch. for Girls, then Eltham Green Comp. Sch., 1962–65; Planning Officer, Lewisham LBC, then GLC, 1965–69; Res. Fellow, 1969–72; Kingston Poly., 1972–74; Principal Lectr and Dean of Faculty, Oxford Poly., 1974–87. Chair, Glendale Gateway Trust, 2012–. Member: ESRC cttees; Joseph Rowntree Housing and Neighbourhood Res. Cttee; RTPI cttees; HEFCE; RAE Panel 2001. Mem. Bd, Tyne and Wear Develt Corp., 1990–98. FAcSS (AcSS 1999). Gold Medal, RTPI, 2007. *Publications:* (ed jtly) Planning Theory: prospects for the 1980s, 1982; Local Plans in British Land Use Planning, 1983; (ed jtly) Land Policy: problems and alternatives, 1985; (jtly) The Political Economy of Land: urban development in an oil economy, 1985; (jtly) Land Use Planning and the Mediation of Urban Change, 1988; (ed jtly) Rebuilding the City: property-led urban regeneration, 1992; (ed jtly) Managing Cities: the new urban context, 1995; (jtly) Negotiating Development, 1995; (ed jtly) Making Strategic Spatial Plans: innovation in Europe, 1997; Collaborative Planning: shaping places in fragmented societies, 1997, 2nd edn 2006; (jtly) Planning, Governance and Spacial Strategy in Britain, 2000; (ed jtly) The Governance of Place, 2001; (ed jtly) Urban Governance, Institutional Capacity and Social Milieux, 2002; Urban Complexity and Spatial Strategies: towards a relational planning for our times, 2007; (ed jtly) Critical Readings in Planning Theory (3 vols), 2008; Making Better Places: the planning project in the twenty-first century, 2010; (ed jtly) Crossing Borders: international exchange and planning practices, 2010; contrib. papers to learned jls. *Recreations:* gardening, walking, history and archaeology, literature. *Address:* School of Architecture, Planning and Landscape, Newcastle upon Tyne University, Newcastle upon Tyne NE1 7RU. *E:* Patsy.Healey@newcastle.ac.uk.

See also T. Ingold.

HEALY OF PRIMROSE HILL, Baroness *cr* 2010 (Life Peer), of Primrose Hill in the London Borough of Camden; **Anna Mary Healy;** *b* London, 10 May 1955; *d* of late Martin Michael Healy and Kathleen Elizabeth Healy; *m* 1992, Jon Cruddas, *qv*; one *s.* *Educ:* St Aloysius Convent Grammar Sch., London; Royal Holloway Coll., London Univ. (BA Hons Modern Hist., Econ. Hist. and Politics 1976); Birkbeck Coll., London (MSc (Econ) Politics 1982); City Univ. (Postgrad. Dip. Periodical Journalism 1982). Labour Party: PA to Hd of Internat. Dept, 1978–81; PA to Dir of Communications, 1981–82; journalist on various pubns incl. Internat. Broadcasting, 1982–85; Campaigns Press Officer, 1985–88; Parly Press Sec., H of C,

1988–96; Press Officer to Leader of Opposition, 1996–97; Special Adviser: to Sec. of State for NI, 1997–98; to Sec. of State, Cabinet Office, 1998–99; to Minister for Transport, 2000–01; to Minister for Cabinet Office, 2001–03; Hd, Office of Jon Cruddas, MP, 2003–07; Special Advr to Leader of H of C, 2007–10; COS to Leader of the Opposition, H of C, May–Sept. 2010. *Recreations:* music, film, literature. *Address:* House of Lords, SW1A 0PW. *T:* (020) 7219 8912, 07946 524824. *E:* healyab@parliament.uk.

HEALY, Alexandra; QC 2011; *b* 18 Nov. 1968; *d* of Alexander Patrick Healy, III and Janet Mary Healy; *m* 1999, Ken Millett; one *s* one *d*. *Educ:* Ward Freman Sch., Buntingford; Trinity Hall, Cambridge (BA 1991). Called to the Bar, Gray's Inn, 1992, Bencher, 2015; in practice as barrister, specialising in criminal fraud. Sec., Criminal Bar Assoc., 2007–08; Mem., Bar Remuneration Cttee, 2008–. Dir, Bar Mutual Indemnity Fund, 2010–. *Recreations:* family, walking, singing (while walking). *Address:* 9–12 Bell Yard, WC2A 2JR. *T:* (020) 7400 1800. *E:* a.healy@9-12bellyard.com.

HEALY, Maurice Eugene, OBE 2001; Director, National Consumer Council, 1987–91; *b* 27 Nov. 1933; *s* of late Thomas Healy and Emily Healy (*née* O'Mahoney); *m* 1958, Jose Barbara Speller Dewdney; two *d* (and one *d* decd). *Educ:* Downside School; Peterhouse, Cambridge (BA Classics). Nat. service, Royal Artillery, 1954–56. BoT, 1956–60; Consumers' Assoc., working on Which?, 1960–76; Head of Editl Dept and Editor of Which?, 1973–76; Nat. Consumer Council, 1977–91. Chairman, Consumer Policy Committee: BSI, 1993–98; ISO, 1996–98; Member: Council, Bureau Européen des Unions de Consommateurs, 1977–91; Council, Insurance Ombudsman Bureau, 1991–2001 (Chm., 1996–2001); Code of Banking Practice Review Cttee, 1991–99; Ind. Management Cttee, Optical Consumer Complaints Service, 1992–99; Bd, Jazz Services Ltd, 1992–2001; Consumer Panel, PIA, 1993–98; Council, Funeral Ombudsman Service, 2001–03; Assessor to Auld Cttee on reform of shop hours, 1984. Chm., Patients' Assoc., 1991–93. Trustee, European Res. Inst. for Consumer Affairs, 1990–2007. Chm. of Governors, Highgate Wood School, 1983–86. Chm., Friends of Queens Wood, 2000–08. Bereavement counsellor: Cruse, 2006–11; N London Hospice, 2012–14. FRSA. Hon. Mem., Inst. of Consumer Affairs. *Publications:* contribs to Which? and Nat. Consumer Council and other jls and conf. papers. *Recreations:* jazz, Irish music, Shona sculpture. *Address:* 15 Onslow Gardens, Muswell Hill, N10 3JT. *T:* (020) 8883 8955.

HEALY, Sheila Elizabeth; Director, H & H Horizons, since 2009; Member, Arts Council England, and Chair, South West Regional Arts Council, since 2010; *b* 20 Oct. 1954; *m* 2007, Richard Harvey; one *s*, and one step *s* one step *d*. *Educ:* Trinity Coll., Dublin (BA Hons, MA Econs and Social Studies). Residential Social Worker, Brent LBC, 1978–80; Community Worker, Pensioners' Link, 1980–83; Policy Officer, GLC, 1983–85; Hd, Urban Prog., and Hd, Policy and Performance, Wolverhampton MBC, 1985–90; Asst City Sec., Quality and Business Services, Nottingham CC, 1990–92; Chief Exec., City Challenge and Dir of Envmt, Walsall MBC, 1992–97; Corporate Dir, Envmt and Econ., 1997–2000, Community Governance, 2000–03, Bor. of Telford & Wrekin; Regl Associate, W Midlands, IDeA, 2003–04; Regl Dir, Local Govt, ODPM, 2004–06; Chief Exec., Cornwall CC, 2006–08; Interim Chief Exec., Shropshire CC, 2008–09. Dir and Vice-Chm., Ikon Gall., Birmingham, 2000–04. Chair, Audiences Central, W Midlands, 2000–06. Member: Friends of Hall for Cornwall; Tate St Ives Adv. Council, 2006–; Leading Museums Gp, 2009–; Bd, Kneehigh Th. Co., 2011–. *Recreations:* walking, theatre, reading, cinema, travel, contemporary and modern art.

HEALY, Siobán Mary; QC 2010; *b* Leamington Spa, 6 Aug. 1965; *d* of Dr Peter Healy and Dr Mary Healy (*née* Daly). *Educ:* Trinity Sch., Leamington Spa; Brasenose Coll., Oxford (BA Hons Juris.); Northwestern Univ., Chicago (LLM). Admitted solicitor, 1990; called to the Bar, Inner Temple, 1993; in practice as barrister, specialising in commercial law, particularly insce and reinsce, internat. trade and professional negligence. *Recreations:* ski-ing, ski touring, hiking in the Alps and S American volcanoes. *Address:* 7 King's Bench Walk, Temple, EC4Y 7DS. *T:* (020) 7910 8300, *Fax:* (020) 7910 8400.

HEALY, Prof. Thomas Edward John, MD; FRCA; Professor of Anaesthesia, 1981–97, now Emeritus, and Head, School of Surgical Sciences, 1991–95, University of Manchester; *b* 11 Dec. 1935; *s* of late Thomas Healy and Gladys May Healy; *m* 1966, Lesley Edwina Sheppard; one *s* three *d*. *Educ:* St Brendan's Coll., Bristol; Guy's Hosp. Med. Sch., London Univ. (BSc 1st Cl. Hons 1961; MB BS 1964; MD 1975); Manchester Univ. (MSc 1982); Cardiff Univ. (LLM 1999). LRCP 1963; MRCS 1963; DA 1967; FRCA (FFARCS 1968). Consultant Anaesthetist i/c Intensive Care, Gen. Hosp., then Queen's Med. Centre, Nottingham, 1971–81; established Dept of Anaesthetic Studies, 1971, designed and commissioned Intensive Care Unit, 1972 at Gen. Hosp., Nottingham and at Queen's Med. Centre, Nottingham, 1975; Reader in Anaesthesia, Univ. of Nottingham, 1974–81. Dep. Regl Educnl Advr, 1977–80, Regl Educnl Advr, 1980–81, Faculty of Anaesthetists, RCS. Co-Ed.-in-Chief, Monographs in Anaesthesiology, 1982–90; Member, Editorial Board: Jl of Japanese Anesthesiology Reviews, 1982–87; Post Grad. Med. Jl, 1985–88; Jl Evaluation in Clinical Practice, 1995–99; Jl of RSocMed, 1996–97; Ed.-in-Chief, European Jl Anaesthesiology, 1994–99. Mem., Med. Adv. Bd, Med. Litigation, 2000–08. Mem., S Manchester HA, 1981–89. Mem. and Chm., tribunal and appeals cttees. Royal College of Anaesthetists: examr for Fellowship exam, 1976–89; Mem. Council, 1989–97; Chm., Trng Methods Cttee, 1992–94; First Chm., Professional Standards Cttee, 1994–97; Section of Anaesthesia, Royal Society of Medicine: Mem. Council, 1985–97; Hon. Sec., 1986–88; Pres., 1996–97; Member Council: Assoc. Anaesthetists GB and Ireland, 1973–76; Anaesthetic Res. Soc., 1978–81; Postgrad. Med. Fellowship, 1991–94; Academician, 1980, Mem., Senate and Exec. Cttee, 1984–2005, European Acad. Anaesthesiology. Vis. Prof. at Michigan, Philadelphia, Arizona (Phoenix and Tucson Med. Schs) and Vancouver Univs, Mahidol Univ., Thailand and univs across Europe. Special Visitor, Shanghai Med. Coll., 1993. Expert witness for the Crown, GMC, defendants and claimants, UK and Canada. Gov., Linacre Centre for Health Care Ethics, 1999–2005. Hon. Mem., Romanian Soc. Anaesthesiology, 1995. Eisenhower People to People Ambassador to Hong Kong, Changhai, Nanjing, Beijing, 1988. Chm., Fundraising Cttee, ReachOut, 1998–. Gov., Becket Sch., Nottingham, 1973–75. Mem., Stanton-on-the-Wolds Parish Council, 1979. Freeman, City of London, 1978. *Publications:* Aids to Anaesthesia 1: the basic sciences, 1980 (trans. Spanish, Italian), 3rd edn 1991; Aids to Anaesthesia 2: clinical practice, 1984, 2nd edn 1999; (ed) Anaesthesia for Day Case Surgery, 1990; (ed) Wylie and Churchill-Davidson's A Practice of Anaesthesia, 6th edn 1995 (BMA best textbook in a surgical subject, 1995–96), 7th edn 2003; *chapters in:* Adverse Reactions to Anaesthetic Drugs, 1981; Anaesthesia: innovations in management, 1985; The Year Book of the European Academy of Anaesthesiology, 1985; Aspects of Recovery from Anaesthesia, 1987; Textbook of Anaesthesia, 1989; Innovations in Physiological Anaesthesia and Monitoring, 1989; Applied Neuromuscular Pharmacology, 1994; The Handbook of Clinical Anaesthesia, 1996; Medicine for Lawyers, 2005; over 115 scientific papers. *Recreations:* walking, cycling, reading, keeping fit. *Address:* Department of Anaesthesia, Manchester Royal Infirmary, Oxford Road, Manchester M13 9WL.

HEALY, Tim T.; *see* Traverse-Healy.

HEANEY, Albert Lawrence; Director, Social Services and Integration, Welsh Government, since 2013; *b* Co. Armagh, NI, 1964; *s* of Laurence and Elizabeth Heaney; *m* Heather; one *s*. *Educ:* Portadown Coll. Grammar Sch.; Univ. of Glamorgan (BA Hons Sociol. with Professional Studies; MBA; Cert. in Using Systemic Family Therapy). CQSW 1988; CMS 1995; DMS 1996. Sen. Residential Social Worker, 1988–89; Social Worker, Mid Glamorgan CC, 1989–91; Social Work Therapist, Brynfynnon, 1991–94; Team Manager, Merthyr Tydfil CB, 1994–99; Service Mgr, 1999–2001, Area Manager, S and W Wales, 2001–05, NSPCC; Asst Dir, Social Services, 2005–08, Corporate Dir, Social Services, 2008–13, Caerphilly CBC. Chm., Dance Sport Wales, 2011–13. Pres., Assoc. of Dirs of Social Services Wales, 2012. *Recreations:* dance sport, reading. *Address:* Welsh Government, Cathays Park, Cardiff CF10 3NQ. *T:* (029) 2082 3219. *E:* Albert.Heaney@wales.gsi.gov.uk.

HEAP, Sir Brian; *see* Heap, Sir R. B.

HEAP, Sir Peter (William), KCMG 1995 (CMG 1987); HM Diplomatic Service, retired; *b* 13 April 1935; *s* of Roger and Dora Heap; *m* 1st, Helen Wilmerding; two *s* two *d*; 2nd, Dorrit Breitenstein; 3rd, 1986, Ann Johnson; one step *s* one step *d*. *Educ:* Bristol Cathedral Sch.; Merton Coll., Oxford. 2nd Lt Glos Regt and RWAFF, 1954–56. Joined Diplomatic Service, 1959; Third Sec., Dublin, 1960; Second Sec., Ottawa, 1960; First Sec., Colombo, 1963–66; seconded to MoD, 1966–68; FO, 1968–71; Dep. Dir-Gen., British Information Services, New York, 1971–76; Counsellor, Caracas, 1976–80; Head of Energy, Science and Space Dept, FCO, 1980–83; High Comr to the Bahamas, 1983–86; Minister and Dep. High Comr, Lagos, 1986–89; British Trade Comr, Hong Kong, and Consul-Gen., Macau, 1989–92; Ambassador to Brazil, 1992–95. Advr to Bd, HSBC Investment Bank, 1995–98; Mem., Adv. Bd, Tetra Strategy, 2010–14; Consultant: Amerada Hess plc, 1996–2006; BOC Gp, 1997–2001; Adv. Bd, CFS Partners, 2001–10; Internat. Business Consultant, Nabas Legal, 2010–14; Dep. Chm., RCM Gp, 2001–05; non-exec. Dir, D. S. Wolf Internat., 1998–99; non-executive Chairman: Regal Petroleum plc, 2005–06; Moorgate Capital, 2010–. Chairman: Brazilian Chamber of Commerce in GB, 1996–2010, now Chm. Emeritus; Britain Brazil Business Forum, 1998–2003; Labour Finance and Industry Gp, 2003–09; Commonwealth Countries League, 2015–. Mem., Internat. Cttee, CBI, 1997–2002. Member, Council: Anglo Brazil Soc., 1999–; Friends of the Bahamas, 2000–; Chm., Friends of Sri Lanka Assoc., 2011–. Chm., Maria Nobrega Charitable Trust (UK), 2003–10. Gov., Greycoat Hosp. Sch., 2001–12. Freeman, City of London, 2001. *Address:* (home) 6 Carlisle Mansions, Carlisle Place, SW1P 1HX.

HEAP, Sir (Robert) Brian, Kt 2001; CBE 1994; FRS 1989; FRSC; FRSB; Master, St Edmund's College, Cambridge, 1996–2004 (Hon. Fellow, since 2004); Research Associate, Centre for Development Studies, University of Cambridge, since 2012; *b* 27 Feb. 1935; *s* of late Bertram Heap and Eva Mary Heap (*née* Melling); *m* 1961, Marion Patricia Grant; two *s* one *d*. *Educ:* New Mills Grammar Sch.; Univ. of Nottingham (BSc, PhD); King's Coll., Cambridge (MA, ScD). FRSB (FIBiol 1973). FRSC 1987. Univ. Demonstrator, Cambridge, 1960; Lalor Res. Fellow, ARC Babraham, Cambridge, 1963; Staff Mem., AFRC Babraham, 1964–95: Hd, Dept of Physiology, 1976; Hd, Cambridge Res. Station, 1986; Dir, Inst. of Animal Physiol. and Genetics Res., Cambridge and Edinburgh, 1989–93; Dir of Science, AFRC, 1991–94; Dir, AFRC, subseq. BBSRC Babraham Inst., 1993–94. Vis. Prof., Univ. of Nairobi, 1974; Vis. Res. Fellow, Murdoch Univ., 1976; Special Prof., 1988–2010, Hon. Prof., 2011–, Univ. of Nottingham; Vis. Prof., Univ. of Guelph, 1990; Vis. Sen. Fellow, Sch. of Clin. Medicine, Univ. of Cambridge, 1994–2001; Res. Associate, Faraday Inst., St Edmund's Coll., Cambridge, 2006–. Mem., Scientific Adv. Bd, Merck, Sharp and Dohme, 1990–98; Consultant: R. W. Johnson Pharmaceutical Res. Inst., NJ, 1993–98; Ligand Pharmaceuticals, La Jolla, San Diego, 1994–97; Principal Scientific Advr, ZyGEM, NZ, 2005–10; Chief Scientific Advr, Cambridge Malaysian Commonwealth Studies Centre, 2014–. UK Rep. NATO Sci. Cttee, Brussels, 1998–2005. Member: Exec. Council, ESF, 1994–97; Council, Royal Soc., 1994–2001 (Foreign Sec. and Vice-Pres., 1996–2001); Nuffield Council on Bioethics, 1997–2001; Bd, Eur. Advanced Translational Res. Infrastructure in Medicine, 2008–11; Bd, African Technol. Policy Studies Network Bd, 2008–13; Chair: Governing Council, Cambridge Theological Fedn, 2006–10; Cambridge Genetics Knowledge Park, 2002–07; Public Health Genomics, Cambridge, 2008–12; Vice-Chm., 2004–10, Pres., 2010–13, European Acads Sci. Adv. Council. Specialist Advr, Select Cttee on sci. and engrg at heart of govt policy, 2009. Member Committee: Soc. for Study of Fertility, 1967–72; Jls of Reproduction and Fertility Ltd; Bibliography of Reproduction, 1967–70; Soc. and Jl of Endocrinology, 1980–84; Placenta; Oxford Reviews of Reproductive Biology, 1981–94; Exec. Editor, Philosophical Trans of Royal Soc., 2004–07. Consultant: WHO, Geneva, 1975–82; China, 1981–85. Chairman: Ciba Foundn Symposium, 1978; Harden Conf., 1984. President: Inst. of Biol., 1996–98; Internat. Soc. Sci. and Religion, 2006–08. Judge: Templeton Prize, 2001–04; Kilby Awards, 2002. Member, Advisory Board: John Templeton Foundn, 2004–06, 2008–11; Faraday Inst. of Sci. and Religion, 2006–; Edinburgh Global Acads, 2013–; Sen. Scientific Advr, Cambridge Malaysian Commonwealth Studies Centre, 2014–; Trustee: Cambridge Overseas Trust, 2002–08; European Trust, 2002–08; Commonwealth Trust, 2003–08; Sino-British Fellowship Trust, 2004–; Sense about Science, 2004–10; Cambridge Malaysian Educn and Develt Trust, 2010–13 (Chief Scientific Advr, 2014–); Cambridge China Develt Trust, 2010–; Mahathir Sci. Award Foundn, 2012–; Chm. Trustees, Academia Europaea, 2003–10. Vice-Pres., Queen Mother Meml Fund, 2003–04. Lectures: Hammond, Soc. for Study of Fertility, 1986; Linacre, Oxford Univ., 1993; Annual, RASE, 1995; Robinson Meml, Univ. of Nottingham, 1997; Rutherford Meml, South Africa, 1999. Fellow, World Acad. of Sci., 2009. Hon. FRASE 1995; Hon. FZS 2007; Hon. Foreign Fellow, Korean Acad. of Sci. and Technol., 1998. Hon. Fellow, Green Templeton (formerly Green) Coll., Oxford, 1997. Hon. DSc: Nottingham, 1994; York, 2001; St Andrews, 2007. Research Medallist, RASE, 1976; Inventor's Award, AFRC, 1980; Marshall Medal, Soc. for Study of Reproduction, 2000. *Publications:* sci. papers on reproductive biology, endocrinology, biotechnology, sustainability, science advice and policy, in various biol and med. jls. *Recreations:* music, hiking, kite flying. *Address:* St Edmund's College, Cambridge CB3 0BN.

HEAPHY, Clive Andrew; Director of Finance Operations, High Speed Two Ltd, since 2013; *b* Burton upon Trent, 16 June 1961; *s* of Daniel Joseph Heaphy and Amelda Heaphy; *m* 1985, Deborah Ann Jones; one *s* one *d*. *Educ:* Portsmouth Poly. (BSc Hons Engrg Geology and Geotechnics 1982). CIPFA 1986. Trainee Accountant, Westminster CC, 1982–83; various roles, Coventry CC, 1983–91; Finance Manager (Housing), Milton Keynes BC, 1991–94; Man. Consultant, Chapman Hendy Associates, 1994–97; Dir, Resources, S Oxon Housing Assoc., 1997–2000; Director of Finance: English Churches Housing Gp, 2000–03; Sport England, 2003–06; FCO Services, 2006–08; Dir, Finance and Corp. Resources, Central Beds Council, 2008–10; interim Dir, Finance, OFSTED, 2010; Dir, Finance and Corp. Services, London Borough of Brent, 2010–13; Dir, i-Max Solutions Ltd, 2013–. MInstD. Trustee, Inst. of Cancer Res., 2012–. *Recreations:* golf, current affairs, reading, cycling, walking. *Address:* High Speed Two Ltd, 1 Canada Square, Canary Wharf, E14 5AB. *T:* (020) 7944 0128. *E:* clive.heaphy@hs2.org.uk.

HEAPPEY, James Stephen; MP (C) Wells, since 2015; *b* Nuneaton, 30 Jan. 1981; *s* of Stephen and Anita Heappey; *m* 2009, Kate; one *s* one *d*. *Educ:* Queen Elizabeth's Hosp., Bristol; Univ. of Birmingham (BA Hons Pol Sci.); RMA, Sandhurst. Platoon Comdr, 1st Bn, Royal Glos, Berks and Wilts Regt, 2004–06; ADC to GOC, NI, 2006–07; The Rifles: Regtl Signals Officer, 4th Bn, 2007–09; Adjt, 2nd Bn, 2009–11; Exec. Officer, Army Gen. Staff, 2011–12. Parly Asst to Rt Hon. Dr Liam Fox, MP, 2012–13; consultant project manager, 2013–14. *Recreations:* cooking, cricket, golf, Rugby, tennis, family. *Address:* House of Commons, SW1A 0AA. *T:* (020) 7219 4289; 5 Cathedral View Offices, Wookey Hole Road, Wells, Som BA5 2BT. *T:* (01749) 343255. *E:* james.heappey.mp@parliament.uk.

HEAPS, Jeremy David P.; *see* Pickett-Heaps.

HEAPS, John Edward; Chief Executive, Britannia Building Society, 1993–99; *b* 24 Feb. 1939; *m* 1985, Shirley (*née* Jones); two *d*; one *s* one *d* from previous marr. *Educ:* Calday Grange Grammar Sch., W Kirby; Oldershaw Grammar Sch., Wallasey; Univ. of Liverpool. FCIB (FCBSI 1992). Colne Building Society: Sec., 1972; Chief Exec., 1972–80; Chief Exec. and Dir, 1980–83; Britannia Building Society: Dep. Gen. Manager, 1983–87; Gen. Manager, 1987–91; Inf. Systems Dir, 1991; Dep. Man. Dir, 1991–93. Chm., BSA, 1998–99 (Mem. Council, 1994; Dep. Chm., 1996–98); Dir, Bldg Socs Trust, 1997–99. Non-exec. Dir, Police Mutual Assurance Soc., 2001–08. Dir, Staffs TEC, 1996–99. Trustee, Keele Develt Trust, 1996–2001. Mem. Court, Univ. of Keele, 1994–2008. MCMI. *Recreation:* family pursuits. *Address:* The Mistals, Dodsleigh, Stoke on Trent, Staffs ST10 4QA.

HEAPS, John Robert; Chairman, Yorkshire Building Society, since 2015; Partner, Eversheds LLP, 1985–2015 (Head of Litigation, 1999–2008; Chairman, 2010–14); *b* Ilkley, W Yorks, 8 July 1953; *s* of Dennis Heaps and Madeleine Heaps (*née* Coburn); *m* 1981, Vivienne Anne Smith; two *s*. *Educ:* St Thomas Aquinas Grammar Sch., Leeds; Ratcliffe Coll., Leics; Univ. of Liverpool (LLB 1975). Admitted solicitor, 1978; solicitor, Freshfields, 1978–84. Mem., Business and Oversight Bd, Law Society, 2013–. International Bar Association: Mem. Council, Legal Practice Div., 2006–08; Co. Chm., World Orgns Cttee, 2009–12. Mem. Bd, CPR Inst., 2012–. Mem. Bd, Garden Bridge Trust, 2013–. *Publications:* (contrib.) Privilege and Confidentiality: an international handbook, 2006, 2nd edn 2012. *Recreations:* golf, fishing, family, cricket, opera, theatre. *Address:* Yorkshire Building Society, Broadgate, The Headrow, Leeds LS1 8EQ. *T:* (01274) 472262. *Clubs:* Reform; Pannal Golf.

HEARN, Barry Maurice William, FCA; Chairman: World Snooker Ltd, since 2010; Matchroom Sport (formerly Matchroom) Ltd, since 1982; *b* 19 June 1948; *s* of George Sydney and Barbara Winifred Hearn; *m* 1970, Susan Clark; one *s* one *d*. *Educ:* Buckhurst Hill Grammar School. Owner and Chm., Leyton Orient FC, 1995–2014. Chm., Professional Darts Corp., 2001–. *Publications:* The Business, 1990. *Recreations:* football, fishing, poker, golf. *Address:* Matchroom Sport Ltd, Mascalls, Mascalls Lane, Brentwood, Essex CM14 5LJ. *T:* (01277) 359900.

HEARN, David Anthony; General Secretary, Broadcasting Entertainment Cinematograph Theatre Union, 1991–93 (General Secretary, 1987–90, Joint General Secretary, 1984–87, Broadcasting and Entertainment Trades Alliance); Chairman, Litho and Digital Impressions Ltd, since 1997; *b* 4 March 1929; *s* of James Wilfrid Laurier Hearn and Clara (*née* Barlow); *m* 1952, Anne Beveridge; two *s*. *Educ:* Trinity Coll., Oxford (MA). Asst to Gen. Sec., Assoc. of Broadcasting Staff, 1955; subseq. Asst Gen. Sec., then Dep. Gen. Sec.; Gen. Sec., Assoc. of Broadcasting and Allied Staffs, 1972–84. Dir, Nat. Campaign for the Arts Ltd, 1986–93. Chm., Film and Electronic Media Cttee, Fedn of Entertainment Unions, 1991–93; Mem., British Screen Adv. Council, 1987; President: Internat. Fedn of Audio Visual Unions, 1991–93 (Gen. Sec., W European Sect., 1984–91); Eur. Cttee of Trade Unions in Arts, Mass Media and Entertainment, 1992–93. Sen. Res. Fellow, Nuffield Coll., Oxford, 1970–71. *Address:* 4 Stocks Tree Close, Yarnton, Kidlington, Oxon OX5 1LU. *T:* (01865) 374613.

HEARN, Donald Peter; Bursar and Fellow of Clare College, Cambridge, 2001–13, now Emeritus Fellow; *b* 2 Nov. 1947; *s* of late Peter James Hearn and Anita Margaret Hearn; *m* 1973, Rachel Mary Arnold; two *d*. *Educ:* Clifton College; Selwyn College, Cambridge (MA). FCA. Ernst & Whinney, 1969–79; Group Financial Controller, Saga Holidays, 1979–83; Chief Financial Officer, Lee Valley Water Co., 1983–86; Finance Dir, 1986–2001, Sec., 1989–2001, RHS; Gen. Comr for Taxes, 1990–2008. Mem., F and GP Cttee, RPMS, Univ. of London, 1991–97; Imperial College: Chm., Audit Cttee, 1996–2005; Mem. Court, 1998–2005; Chm., House Cttee, 1998–2001; Gov., 2001–05; Member: Selwyn Coll. Assoc. Cttee, 1997–2001; Cambridge Univ. Audit Cttee, 2002–07; Trustee, Cambridge Univ. Staff Pension Scheme, 2002– (Chm., Investments Cttee, 2002–). Director: Fitzwilliam Museum Enterprise, 2003–; Cambridge Colleges Funding plc, 2014–. Trustee: Chelsea Physic Gdn, 2002– (Treas., 2003–); Cambridge Univ. Botanic Gdn, 2003–; Chm., Cambridge Univ. Farm, 2008–. Treas., Cambridge Past, Present and Future, 2013–. Governor, Woldingham Sch., 1990–93. Hon. FRHS. *Recreation:* gardening. *Address:* 60 St Barnabas Road, Cambridge CB1 2DE.

HEARN, Rt Rev. George Arthur; Bishop of Rockhampton, 1981–96; Vicar of Canterbury, diocese of Melbourne, 1996–2001; *b* 17 Nov. 1935; *s* of Albert Frederick and Edith Maxham Hearn; *m* 1957, Adele Taylor (*d* 2006); two *s* one *d*. *Educ:* Northcote High School; University High School; La Trobe Univ., Melbourne. BA, ThL 1965, DipRE, ThSchol Aust. Coll. of Theology; MACE. Deacon 1964, priest 1965, Diocese of Gippsland; Curate of Traralgon, 1964–66; Vicar of Omeo, 1966–69; Rector of Wonthaggi, 1969–73; Rector of Kyabram, dio. Bendigo, 1973–77; Field Officer, Dept of Christian Education, Diocese of Melbourne, 1977–79; Dir, Gen. Bd of Religious Education, 1978–81. *Recreations:* gardening, reading, golf, music. *Address:* 2 Arthur Street, Doncaster, Vic 3108, Australia.

HEARN, Prof. John Patrick, PhD; Professor of Physiology, University of Sydney Medical School, since 2004; Executive Director, Worldwide Universities Network, since 2009; Chairman, Australia Africa Universities Network, since 2010; *b* Limbdi, India, 24 Feb. 1943; *s* of late Lt-Col Hugh Patrick Hearn, Barrister, and Cynthia Ellen (*née* Nicholson); *m* 1967, Margaret Ruth Patricia McNair; four *s* one *d*. *Educ:* Crusaders' Sch., Headley, Hants; St Mary's Sch., Nairobi, Kenya; University Coll., Dublin (BSc, MSc); ANU, Canberra (PhD). Lectr in Zool., 1967–69, and Dean of Science, 1968–69, Strathmore Coll., Nairobi; Res. Scholar, ANU, 1969–72; scientist, MRC Reproductive Biology Unit, Edinburgh, 1972–79; Consultant Scientist, WHO Special Prog. of Res. in Human Reproduction, Geneva, 1978–79; Zoological Society of London: Dir, Wellcome Labs of Comparative Physiology, 1979–80; Dir of Science and Dir, Inst. of Zool., 1980–87; Dep. Sec., AFRC, 1987–90; Dir, MRC/AFRC Comparative Physiology Res. Gp, 1983–89; Dir, Wisconsin Regl Primate Res. Center and Prof. in Physiol., Med. Sch., Univ. of Wisconsin-Madison, 1989–96; Consultant Scientist, WHO Res. Prog. in Family and Reproductive Health, Geneva, 1996–98; Australian National University: Dir, Res. Sch. of Biol Scis, 1998–2001; Dep. Vice-Chancellor (Res.), 2001–04; Dep. Vice-Chancellor (Academic and Internat.), then Vice Pres. (Internat.), Univ. of Sydney, 2004–13. Exec. Chm., Hearn International Pty Ltd, 2013–. Rapporteur and Chm., WHO Asia Pacific Regl Panel in Reproductive Health, 1999–2005; Member: Futures Gp on Bioecon. 2020, OECD, 2008–10; Expert Gp on Internationalisation in Higher Educn, OECD, 2011–13; Innovation, Higher Educn and Res. in Develt Gp, OECD, 2011–15; Educn Adv. Gp, British Council, 2014–. Chm., Australian Biotechnol. Adv. Council, 2001–04; Mem. Bd, Australian Nuclear Sci. and Technol. Orgn, 2008–12. Mem. Bd, Sports Knowledge Australia, 2004–10; Chm., Sydney Confucius Inst., 2008–13. Vis. Prof. in Biology (formerly in Zoology), UCL, 1979–93; Vis. Prof., New England Primate Res. Center, Harvard Univ. Med. Sch., 1989–91; Hon. Res. Fellow, CSIRO Wildlife and Ecology, 1997–99. Pres., Internat. Primatological Soc., 1984–88; Chm., Soc. for Reproductive Biology, 2000–04. Scientific Medal, Zool Soc. London, 1983; Osman Hill Medal, Primate Soc. of GB, 1986; Australian Centenary Medal, 2001. *Publications:* (ed with H. Rothe and H. Wolters) The Biology and Behaviour of Marmosets, 1978; (ed) Immunological Aspects of Reproduction and Fertility Control, 1980; (ed) Reproduction in New World Primates, 1982; (ed) Advances in Animal Conservation, 1985; (ed) Reproduction and Disease in Captive and Wild Animals, 1988; (ed) Conservation of Primate Species studied in Biomedical Research, 1994; papers on develtl and reproductive physiol. in scientific jls. *Recreations:* running, swimming (Mem., Bronte Surf and Life Saving Club). *Address:* 207A Old Teachers College A22, University of Sydney, NSW 2006, Australia. *T:* (4) 23783287, *Fax:* (2) 93514462. *E:* john.hearn@sydney.edu.au. *Club:* Athenæum.

HEARN, Sarah Penelope; *see* Chambers, S. P.

HEARNDEN, Dr Arthur George, OBE 1990; education consultant; General Secretary, Independent Schools Joint Council, 1985–97; *b* 15 Dec. 1931; *s* of Hugh and Violet Hearnden; *m* 1962, Josephine McNeill; one *s* two *d*. *Educ:* Methodist Coll., Belfast; Christ's Coll., Cambridge (MA); Wadham Coll., Oxford (DPhil). Teacher, Friends' Sch., Lisburn, 1952–55; NI short service commn, Royal Signals, 1955–57; CCF, 1957–65; teacher, various schs, incl. Aldenham (1959–67), and in exchange posts, Lycée d'Aix-les-Bains and Bunsengymnasium, Heidelberg, 1957–68; Res. Officer, Oxford Univ., 1969–71; Lectr in Comparative Education, Inst. of Education, Univ. of London, 1972–74; Secretary: Standing Conf. on Univ. Entrance, 1975–84; Overseas Res. Students Awards Scheme, 1982–84. Chairman: Internat. Cttee, Soc. for Res. in Higher Educn, 1977–81; Internat. Baccalaureate Feasibility Study, 1979–80. Member: DES Adv. Cttee on AS level, 1985–91; Hanover Univ./VW Commn on German Univ. Hist., 1985–91; Sch. Exams and Assessment Council, 1988–91; Funding Agency for Schs, 1994–98 (Chm. of Finance, 1997–98); Press Complaints Commn, 1999–2005. Educnl Advr, Royal Ballet Sch., 2001–03. Pres., Ind. Schs Assoc., 1997–2002; Hon. Vice Pres., Council of British Internat. Schs (formerly Indep. Schs in EC), 1997–2010; Chm., HSBC Bursary Fund, 1998–2002; Trustee: Hall Sch. Charitable Trust, 1988–2009 (Chm, 1997–2009); Youth for Britain-Worldwide Volunteering, 1993–2000 (Chm., 1995–2000); Millwood Educn Trust, 2002–11 (Chm., 2007–11). Governor: Wychwood Sch., 1983–90; Abbotsholme, 1985–92; Oxford High Sch., 1985–92; Abingdon Sch., 1988–99; Dunottar Sch., 1990–92; Newton Prep. Sch., 1992–2014; Alpha Plus Schs, 2010–. Sec., Hethe PCC, 1998–2007, 2009–12; Mem., Hethe Parish Council, 2003–05. *Publications:* Paths to University, 1973; Bildungspolitik in der BRD und DDR, 1973 (trans. Education in the Two Germanies, 1974); Education, Culture and Politics in West Germany, 1974; Methods of Establishing Equivalences, 1976; (ed) The British in Germany, 1978; (ed) From School to University, 1980; Red Robert, a Life of Robert Birley, 1984; A Flying Start: the story of The Manor, 2007; reports and articles in learned jls. *Recreations:* family, theatre, coarse gardening. *Address:* Hethe House, Hethe, Bicester, Oxon OX27 8ES. *T:* (01869) 277985. *Club:* Athenæum.

HEARNE, Sir Graham (James), Kt 1998; CBE 1990; Chairman: Catlin Group Ltd, 2003–12; Enterprise Oil plc, 1991–2002 (Chief Executive, 1984–91); *b* 23 Nov. 1937; *s* of Frank Hearne and Emily (*née* Shakespeare); *m* 1961, Carol Jean (*née* Brown); one *s* two *d* (and one *d* decd). *Educ:* George Dixon Grammar Sch., Birmingham. Admitted solicitor, 1959: Pinsent & Co., Solicitors, 1959–63; Fried, Frank, Harris, Shriver & Jacobson, Attorneys, NYC, 1963–66; Herbert Smith & Co., Solicitors, 1966–67; IRC, 1967–68; N. M. Rothschild & Sons Ltd, 1968–77; Finance Dir, Courtaulds Ltd, 1977–81; Chief Exec., Tricentrol, 1981–83; Gp Man. Dir, Carless, Capel and Leonard, 1983–84. Non-executive Director: N. M. Rothschild & Sons Ltd, 1970–2010; Northern Foods, Ltd, 1976–82; BPB Industries, 1982–91; Reckitt & Colman, 1990–97; Courtaulds, 1991–98; Wellcome, 1991–95; The Wellcome Foundn, 1991–95; Gallaher Gp plc, 1997–2007 (Dep. Chm., 1997–2007); BTR plc, 1998–99; Invensys (formerly BTR Siebe) plc, 1999–2003; Braemar Shipping Services (formerly Seascope Shipping Hldgs plc, then Seascope Gp plc), 1999– (Chm., 2002–); Wellstream Hldgs plc (formerly Wellstream Internat. Ltd), 2003–11; Stratic Energy Corp., 2005–10 (Chm., 2005–10); Bumi plc (formerly Vallar plc), 2010–13; Genel Energy plc (formerly Vallares), 2011–. Chairman: Caradon, then Novar, plc, 1999–2005; Rowan Cos plc (formerly Inc.), 2004–; part-time Member: British National Oil Corp., 1975–78; Dover Harbour Bd, 1976–78. Chm., Brindex (Assoc. of British Indep. Oil Exploration Cos), 1986–88. Trustee: Philharmonia Orch. Trust, 1982–2008; Chichester Fest. Theatre Trust, 1988–98; Hayward Foundn, 1992–2002. High Sheriff, Greater London, 1995. *Address:* 5 Crescent Place, SW3 2EA. *Clubs:* Reform, Brooks's, MCC; Brook (New York).

HEARTY, Michael John; Director General, Finance and Corporate Services (formerly Strategic Planning, Finance and Performance), Welsh Government (formerly Welsh Assembly Government), 2010–15; *b* Blackpool; *s* of Patrick Brian and Joan Hearty; *m* 1990, Janet Holden; one *d*. *Educ:* Holy Family Prim. Sch.; St Thomas of Canterbury Sec. Mod. Sch.; Victoria Univ. of Manchester (BA Hons Econs 1983); Liverpool John Moores Univ. (CPFA 1994). Department of Health and Social Security, subseq. Department of Social Security, later Benefits Agency, then Department for Work and Pensions: Clerical grades, 1975–77; Exec. Officer, 1984–90; Higher Exec. Officer (Trainee Accountant), 1990–94; Sen. Exec. Officer (Accountant), 1994–99; Prin. Accountant, 1999–2002; Head: Accounting Gp, 2002–04; Finance, Planning and Performance, 2004–05; Business Mgt Div., 2005–06; Dep. Dir, Gp Finance Directorate, 2005–06; Dep. Dir, Financial Accounting, 2006–07, Dir of Finance, 2007–10, DCSF, later DFE. Non-executive Director: Audit Cttee, DoH, 2007–; Treasury Solicitors' Dept, 2008–10. Mem. Bd, CIPFA, 2012–. Chm. of Govs, Carr Head Prim. Sch., Poulton-le-Fylde, 2006–10. *Recreations:* season ticket holder of Everton FC (with daughter, Rachael), playing guitar.

HEASLIP, Rear-Adm. Richard George, CB 1987; Director-General, English-Speaking Union, 1987–90; *b* 30 April 1932; *s* of Eric Arthur Heaslip and Vera Margaret (*née* Bailey); *m* 1959, Lorna Jean Grayston, Halifax, NS, Canada; three *s* one *d* (incl. twin *s* and *d*). *Educ:* Royal Naval Coll., Dartmouth. CO HMS Sea Devil, 1961–62; Exec. Officer, HMS Dreadnought (1st British nuclear submarine), 1965–66; CO HMS Conqueror (nuclear submarine), 1971–72; CO Second Submarine Sqdn, 1975–77; Staff, SACLANT, 1980–82; Staff, CDS, 1982–84; Dep. Asst COS (Ops), Staff of SACEUR, 1984; Flag Officer Submarines, and NATO Comdr Submarine Forces Eastern Atlantic, 1984–87. ADC 1984–85. Member: European Atlantic Gp Cttee, 1988–89; Bureau, Standing Conf. of Atlantic Orgns, 1988–89. Chm., RN Football Assoc., 1976–84; President: London Submarine Old Comrades Assoc., 1987–2007; Conqueror Assoc., 2003–. Mem., Ferndown Town Council, 2006–08. Vice-Pres., Dorset CPRE, 2015– (Vice-Chm., 2010–14; Chm., 2014–15). Chm., W Parley Parish Council, 2011–13. *Publications:* End to End, 2007. *Recreations:* walking (Land's End to John O'Groats, 2002); music, gardening. *Address:* 2 Longfield Drive, West Parley, Dorset BH22 8TY. *E:* rgheaslip@hotmail.com.

HEATH, Allister Georges Freund; Deputy Director of Content and Deputy Editor, The Telegraph, since 2014; *b* Mulhouse, France, 1977; *s* of Alexander and Sylviane Heath; *m* 2002, Neda; one *d*. *Educ:* Coll. Emile Zola, Kingersheim, France; Lycée Lambert, Mulhouse; London Sch. of Econs and Pol Sci. (BSc Econs 1998); Hertford Coll., Oxford (MPhil Econs 2000). Ed., European Jl and Hd of Res., Eur. Foundn, 2000–02; Associate Ed., 2006–08, Contributing Ed., 2008–11, Spectator; Econs Corresp., 2002, Econs Ed. and Leader Writer, 2002–05, Dep. Ed., 2005–06, Ed., 2007–08, The Business; Ed., City A. M., 2008–14. Columnist, Daily Telegraph, 2012–14. Wincott Vis. Prof. of Business Journalism, Univ. of Buckingham, 2005–07. Chm., 2020 Tax Commn, 2011–12 (author, The Single Income Tax: Final Report of the 2020 Tax Commn, 2012). *Publications:* Flat Tax: towards a British model, 2006; (with D. B. Smith) At a Price: the true cost of public spending, 2006. *Recreation:* family. *Address:* The Telegraph, 111 Buckingham Palace Road, SW1W 0DT. *E:* allister_heath@yahoo.co.uk.

HEATH, Angela; *see* Heath, L. A.

HEATH, Prof. Anthony Francis, CBE 2013; PhD; FBA 1992; Professor of Sociology, University of Oxford, 1999–2010, now Emeritus; Official Fellow, 1987–99, Fellow, 1999–2010, Nuffield College, Oxford, now Emeritus; Professor of Sociology, University of Manchester, since 2010; *b* 15 Dec. 1942; *s* of Ronald John Heath and Cicely Florence (*née* Roberts); *m* 1983, Dr Mary-Jane Pearce, MRCGP, FRCPsych; two *s* one *d*. *Educ:* Merchant

Taylors', Crosby; Trinity Coll., Cambridge (BA 1st cl. Classics pt I, 1st cl. Econs pt II; PhD 1971). Asst Principal, HM Treasury, 1965–66; Fellow of Churchill Coll., 1967–70, Asst Lectr, Faculty of Econs, 1968–70, Cambridge Univ.; Univ. Lectr and Fellow of Jesus Coll., Oxford, 1970–86. Dir, 1983, 1987, 1992 and 1997 British Election Studies, ESRC. *Publications:* Rational Choice and Social Change, 1976; (jtly) Origins and Destinations, 1980; Social Mobility, 1981; (jtly) How Britain Votes, 1985; (jtly) Understanding Political Change, 1991; (jtly) Labour's Last Chance, 1994; (jtly) The Rise of New Labour, 2001; (jtly) Unequal Chances: ethnic minorities in Western labour markets, 2007; (jtly) The Political Integration of Ethnic Minorities in Britain, 2013; contribs to Jl of Royal Stat. Soc., Amer. Jl of Sociol., Ethnic and Racial Studies, Eur. Sociol Rev., Eur. Jl of Sociol., Eur. Jl of Pol Res., Sociology, British Jl of Pol Sci., British Jl of Sociol., Electoral Studies, Acta Sociologica, Oxford Rev. of Educn. *Recreations:* piano playing, cross-country running. *Address:* 72 Lonsdale Road, Oxford OX2 7EP. *T:* (01865) 553512. *Clubs:* Achilles; Hawks (Cambridge).

HEATH, Rt Hon. David (William St John), CBE 1989; PC 2015; Chairman, Western Region, Consumer Council for Water, since 2015; *b* 16 March 1954; *s* of Eric Heath and Pamela Heath; *m* 1987, Caroline Netherton; one *s* one *d*. *Educ:* Millfield Sch.; St John's Coll., Oxford (MA Physiological Scis); City Univ. FADO 1979. In practice as optician, 1979–86. Somerset County Council: Councillor (Lib Dem), 1985–97; Leader, 1985–89; Chm., Educn Cttee, 1996–97. Vice Chm., Assoc. of County Councils, 1993–97. Chm., Avon & Somerset Police Authy, 1993–96; Vice Chm., Cttee of Local Police Authorities, 1993–97. Mem., Audit Commn, 1995–97. Contested (Lib Dem) Somerton and Frome, 1992. MP (Lib Dem) Somerton and Frome, 1997–2015. Lib Dem spokesman on European affairs, 1997–98, on foreign affairs, 1999–2001, on work, family and pensions, 2001–03, on home and legal affairs, 2003–05; on constitutional affairs, and shadow to Leader of the House, 2005–07 and 2009–10; shadow to Sec. of State for Justice and Lord Chancellor, 2007–09; Parly Sec. (Dep. Leader), Office of the Leader of the H of C, 2010–12; Minister of State, DEFRA, 2012–13. Leader, Liberal Gp, OSCE Parly Assembly, 2009–10. Mem., Academic Council, Wilton Park, 2007–10. Lay Mem. Bd, Solicitors Regulation Authy, 2015–. Mem., Witham Friary Friendly Soc., 1984–. FRSA 1995. *Recreations:* cricket, Rugby football, pig breeding until recently. *Address:* The Yard, Witham Friary, near Frome, Somerset BA11 5HF. *T:* (01749) 850458.

HEATH, Prof. John Baldwin; management consultant; Secretary General, International Council for Peace, Reconciliation and Recovery, 1996–99; *b* 25 Sept. 1924; *s* of late Thomas Arthur Heath and late Dorothy Meallin; *m* 1st, 1953, Wendy Julia Betts (marr. diss. 1995); two *s* one *d*; 2nd, 2000, Chris Michell. *Educ:* Merchant Taylors' Sch.; St Andrews Univ.; Cambridge Univ. RNVR, 1942–46. Spicers Ltd, 1946–50; Lecturer in Economics, Univ. of Manchester, 1956–64; Rockefeller Foundation Fellowship, 1961–62; Dir, Economic Research Unit, Bd of Trade, 1964–67; Dir, Economic Services Div., BoT, 1967–70; Prof. of Economics, London Business Sch., 1970–86; Dir, London Sloan Fellowship Programme, 1983–86. Chm., EXE Ltd, 1982–93; Dir, Health Policy Unit, 1994–95. Member: Mechanical Engrg EDC, 1971–76; British Airports Authy, 1980–86; Economic Adviser, CAA, 1972–78. *Publications:* Public Enterprise at the Crossroads, 1990; Revitalizing Socialist Enterprise, 1993; Tibet and China in the 21st Century, 2005; articles in many learned jls on competition and monopoly, productivity, cost-benefit analysis. *Recreations:* music, walking.

HEATH, (Lettyce) Angela; non-executive Director, The North West London Hospitals (formerly Northwick Park and St Mark's) NHS Trust, 1996–2002; *b* 27 May 1944; *d* of late Frank Buchanan Ryde and Emily Rose Ryde (*née* Davies); *m* 1st, 1966, Gareth Thomas (marr. diss. 1975); 2nd, 1985, Roger Heath; two step *d*. *Educ:* Birmingham Univ. (BA 1966; MA 1968); Birkbeck Coll., London (MSc 1999). Department of the Environment, 1971–96: Admin. Trainee, 1971; Private Sec. to Minister of Housing, 1979; Asst Sec., 1983; Central Policy Planning Unit, 1983–85; Local Govt Div., 1985–87; Personnel Management, 1987–90; Housing Corp. Finance, 1990–91; Under-Sec., 1992; Regl Dir for London, 1992–94; Dir, Regeneration Progs, Govt Office for London, 1994–95; Dir, Local Govt, 1995–96. Vis. Sen. Fellow, Sch. of Public Policy, Univ. of Birmingham, 1997–99. JP Middlesex, 1997–2003. FRSA 1995. *Address:* 36 St John Street, Wirksworth, Derbyshire DE4 4DS.

HEATH, Michael John, MBE 2001; freelance cartoonist, since 1956; Cartoons Editor, The Spectator, since 1989; *b* 13 Oct. 1935; *s* of George Heath and Alice (Queenie) Stewert Morrison Bremner; *m* 1st, 1959, Hanne Sternkopf (marr. diss. 1992); two *d*; 2nd, 2003, Martha Swift (marr. diss. 2012); two *d*. *Educ:* no education to speak of (Devon, Hampstead and Brighton); Brighton Art Coll. Trained as animator, Rank Screen Services, 1955; started placing cartoons in Melody Maker, 1955; contributed to: Lilliput; Tatler; John Bull; Man about Town; Men Only; Honey; Punch, 1958–89; Spectator, 1958–; Private Eye, 1964– (strips include The Gays, The Regulars, Great Bores of Today, Baby); Sunday Times, 1967–; London Standard, 1976–86, 1995–96; Mail on Sunday, 1985–; The Independent, 1986–97 (Political Cartoonist, 1991–96), 2003–; London Daily News, 1987. Pocket Cartoonist of the Year, Cartoonist Club of GB, 1977; Glen Grant Cartoonist of the Year, 1978; What the Papers Say Cartoonist of the Year, 1982; Pont Award for drawing the British Character, 2001; Lifetime Achievement Award, Cartoon Fedn of GB, 2010. *Publications:* Private Eye Cartoon Library, 1973, 2nd edn 1975; The Punch Cartoons of Michael Heath, 1976; Book of Bores, No 1, 1976, No 2, Star Bores, 1979, No 3, Bores Three, 1983; Love All, 1982; Best of Heath (foreword by Malcolm Muggeridge), 1984; Welcome to America, 1985; Heath's Nineties, 1997. *Recreations:* listening to Charlie Parker and Thelonious Monk, walking, ballet.

HEATH, Michael John; His Honour Judge Heath; a Circuit Judge, since 1995; Resident Judge, Lincoln Combined Court Centre, 2000–10; *b* Grimsby, 12 June 1948; *s* of late Norman Heath and Dorothy Heath; *m* 1972, Heather, *d* of late Christopher Croft and of Mrs D. Croft, Hetton-le-Hole; two *s*. *Educ:* Barcroft County Sch., Wintringham; Grammar Sch., Grimsby; Leeds Univ. (Lindsey Sen. Scholar 1966; LLB). FCIArb. Asst Solicitor, R. A. C. Symes and Co., Scunthorpe, 1975, Partner, 1977; Dep. Dist Judge, 1987–95; a Recorder, 1993–95; Solicitor Advocate (All Courts), 1994; Ethnic Minorities Liaison Judge, Lincolnshire, 1995–2008; Resident Judge, Grimsby Crown Court, 1999–2001; Magistrates' Liaison Judge, 2004–10. Chm., Humberside Area Criminal Justice Strategy Cttee, 2000–03; Member: Courts Bd, Lincolnshire, 2004–06; Lincolnshire Probation Bd, 2004–06. Hon. Recorder, City of Lincoln, 2001–10. *Recreations:* soccer, cricket, foreign languages. *Address:* Lincoln Combined Court Centre, 360 High Street, Lincoln LN5 7RL. *T:* (01522) 525222.

HEATH, Maj.-Gen. Michael Stuart, CB 1994; CBE 1991; CEng, FIET; Director of Corporate Strategy, NXT plc, 2000–01; *b* 7 Sept. 1940; *s* of late Bernard Stuart Heath and of Blanche Dorothy Ellen Heath (*née* Fairey); *m* 1965, Frances Wood; one *s* one *d*. *Educ:* St Albans Sch.; Welbeck Coll.; Royal Military Coll. of Science (BSc Eng Upper 2nd cl. Hons London). Commissioned REME, 1961; served Malaya, BAOR, Edinburgh, to 1971; RMCS and Staff Coll., 1972–73; Armour Sch., Bovington, 1974–75; Comd 7 Field Workshop, BAOR, 1976–77; Nat. Defence Coll., 1978; Berlin Field Force, 1978–80; Comd Maint., HQ 2 Armd Div., BAOR, 1981–82; MoD, 1982–85; RCDS, 1986; Dir, Support Planning (Army), MoD, 1987–89; Comd Maint., HQ BAOR, 1990–91; Dir Gen., Electrical and Mechanical Engrg, subseq. Equipment Support (Army), MoD, 1991–93; Team Leader, Army Costs Study Team, 1994. Dir Gen., Engrg Council, 1995–98. Chm., 20/20 Speech Ltd, 1999–2000. *Recreations:* walking, music, photography, web design. *Address:* c/o Barclays Bank, 167 High Street, Bromley, Kent BR1 1NL.

HEATH, Samantha Louise; Chief Executive Officer, London Sustainability Exchange, since 2006; *b* 6 June 1960; *d* of Harvey and Gillian Heath; one *s*. *Educ:* Heriot-Watt Univ. (BSc Hons); Univ. of Greenwich (PGCE 1999). Civil engineer, Sir Robert McAlpine & Sons Ltd, 1982–92; Sen. Lectr in Construction, Univ. of Greenwich, 1992–2000. Mem. (Lab) Wandsworth BC, 1994–2000; Mem. (Lab), 2000–04 and Dep. Chm., 2003–04, London Assembly, GLA (Chm., Envmt Cttee, 2000–04). London Sustainable Development Commission: Mem., 2002–15; Co-Chair, 2004–06; Mayor's Rep. on Energy Taskforce, 2002–04. Dep. Chm., Sustainable Energy Action, 2004–09; Member: London Waste Action, 2003–06; London Energy Partnership, 2004–08 (Chm., London Renewables, 2004–); London Climate Change Partnership, 2005–; Water Action Task Gp, 2009–; London Anti-Social Behaviour Gp, 2009–; Thames Water Customer Challenge Gp, 2012–. Mem. Ct, South Bank Univ., 2011–. *Recreations:* reading, music, gardening and now blogging. *Address:* c/o London Sustainability Exchange, 84 Long Lane, SE1 4AU.

HEATH-BROWN, Prof. David Rodney, (Roger), PhD; FRS 1993; Professor of Pure Mathematics, and Fellow of Worcester College, University of Oxford, since 1999; *b* 12 Oct. 1952; *s* of Basil Heath-Brown and Phyllis Joan (*née* Watson); *m* 1992, Ann Louise Sharpley; two *d*. *Educ:* Welwyn Garden City Grammar Sch.; Trinity Coll., Cambridge (BA, MA, PhD). Jun. Res. Fellow, Trinity Coll., Cambridge, 1977–79; Oxford University: Fellow and Tutor in Pure Maths, Magdalen Coll., 1979–98, Emeritus Fellow, 1999; Reader in Pure Maths, 1990–98. Corresp. Mem., Akad. der Wissenschaften, Göttingen, 1999. Jun. Berwick Prize, 1981, Sen. Berwick Prize, 1996, Pólya Prize, 2009, London Math. Soc. *Publications:* numerous mathematical papers in learned jls. *Recreations:* field botany, bridge, gardening. *Address:* Mathematical Institute, Radcliffe Observatory Quarter, Woodstock Road, Oxford OX2 6GG. *T:* (01865) 273535.

HEATHCOAT-AMORY, Rt Hon. David (Philip); PC 1996; FCA; *b* 21 March 1949; *s* of late Roderick and Sonia Heathcoat-Amory; *m* 1978, Linda Adams; one *s* one *d* (and one *s* decd). *Educ:* Eton Coll.; Oxford Univ. (MA PPE). Qual. as Chartered Accountant with Price Waterhouse & Co., 1974; FCA 1980. Worked in industry, becoming Asst Finance Dir of British Technology Gp, until 1983 when resigned to fight Gen. Election. MP (C) Wells, 1983–2010; contested (C) same seat, 2010. PPS to the Financial Sec. to the Treasury, 1985–87, to the Home Secretary, 1987–88; an Asst Govt Whip, 1988–89; a Lord Comr of HM Treasury, 1989; Parly Under Sec. of State, DoE, 1989–90, Dept of Energy, 1990–92; Dep. Govt Chief Whip and Treasurer, HM Household, 1992–93; Minister of State, FCO, 1993–94; HM Paymaster General, 1994–96; Shadow Chief Sec. to HM Treasury, 1997–2000. Trustee, Nat. Heritage Meml Fund, 2014–. *Recreations:* fishing, shooting, music, growing trees. *Address:* 12 Lower Addison Gardens, W14 8BQ. *T:* (020) 7603 3083. *Clubs:* Beefsteak, Portland.

HEATHCOAT AMORY, Sir Ian, 6th Bt *cr* 1874; DL; *b* 3 Feb. 1942; *s* of Sir William Heathcoat Amory, 5th Bt, DSO, and Margaret Isabel Dorothy Evelyn (*d* 1997), *yr d* of Sir Arthur Havelock James Doyle, 4th Bt; *S* father, 1982; *m* 1972, Frances Louise, *d* of J. F. B. Pomeroy; four *s*. *Educ:* Eton. Chairman: Lowman Manufacturing Co. Ltd, 1976–; DevonAir Radio Ltd, 1983–90; Dir, Watts Blake Bearne & Co. PLC, 1984–88. Mem., Devon CC, 1973–85. JP Devon, 1980–93; DL Devon, 1981. *Heir: s* William Francis Heathcoat Amory [*b* 19 July 1975; *m* 2011, Tatiana Rose Sloane; two *s*]. *Address:* Calverleigh Court, Tiverton, Devon EX16 8BB.

HEATHCOTE, Dr (Frederic) Roger, CBE 2005; Chief Executive, Employment Tribunals Service, 2000–04; *b* 19 March 1944; *s* of late Frederic William Trevor Heathcote and Kathleen Annie Heathcote; *m* 1st, 1970, Geraldine Nixon (marr. diss. 1986); 2nd, 1986, Mary Campbell Syme Dickson; one *s* one step *d*. *Educ:* Bromsgrove Sch.; Birmingham Univ. (BSc (Hons) Physics, PhD). Res. Associate, Birmingham Univ., 1969–70; joined CS as Asst Principal, Min. of Technology (later DTI), 1970; Private Secretary to: Secretary (Industrial Develt), 1973; Permanent Under Sec. of State, Dept of Energy, 1974; Department of Energy: Principal, 1974; Asst Sec., 1978; Dir of Resource Management (Grade 4), 1988; Under Sec., Coal Div., 1989–91; Prin. Estabt and Finance Officer, 1991–92; Hd of Services Mgt Div., DTI, 1992–96; Dir, Export Control and Non-Proliferation, DTI, 1996–2000; UK Gov., IAEA, and UK Rep., Exec. Council of Orgn for the Prohibition of Chemical Weapons, 1996–2000. Non-exec. Dir, Trafalgar House Property Ltd, 1988–94. Gov., British Coll. of Osteopathic Medicine, 2004– (Chm., 2006–). *Recreations:* reading, gardening, lapidary, painting. *Address:* 8B The Crescent, Surbiton, Surrey KT6 4BN.

HEATHCOTE, Sir Mark Simon Robert, 10th Bt *cr* 1733, of London; OBE 1988; *b* 1 March 1941; *o s* of Brig. Sir Gilbert Simon Heathcote, 9th Bt, CBE and Patricia Margaret Heathcote (*née* Leslie); *S* father 2014; *m* 1975, Susan Mary, *d* of Lt-Col George Ashley; two *s*. *Educ:* Eton; Magdalene Coll., Cambridge (BA 1963; MA 1981). P & O Orient Lines, 1963–70; Counsellor, FO, 1971–94; BP plc, 1994–2000; FCO, 2000–05. *Heir: s* Alastair Robert Heathcote, *b* 18 Aug. 1977.

HEATHCOTE, Roger; *see* Heathcote, F. R.

HEATHCOTE, Sir Timothy Gilbert, 12th Bt *cr* 1733, of Hursley, Hampshire; *b* 25 May 1957; *er s* of Sir Michael Heathcote, 11th Bt and Victoria (*née* Wilford); *S* father, 2007. Is in remainder to Earldom of Macclesfield. *Heir: b* George Benjamin Heathcote [*b* 2 Feb. 1965; *m* 1999, Dr Kate Rogers; two *s* one *d*].

HEATHCOTE-DRUMMOND-WILLOUGHBY, family name of **Baroness Willoughby de Eresby**.

HEATHERWICK, Thomas Alexander, CBE 2013; RA 2013; RDI 2004; Founder and Principal, Heatherwick (formerly Thomas Heatherwick) Studio, since 1994; *b* 17 Feb. 1970; *s* of Hugh Heatherwick and Stefany (*née* Tomalin). *Educ:* Manchester Metropolitan Univ. (BA Hons Three Dimensional Design 1992); Royal Coll. of Art (MA Furniture 1994). Founded Thomas Heatherwick Studio to combine architecture, product design and sculpture in single practice; projects include: Rolling Bridge, Paddington Basin, 2005; Longchamp flagship store, NY, 2006; East Beach Café, Littlehampton, 2007; UK Pavilion, Shanghai Expo 2010, 2010 (Lubetkin Prize, RIBA, 2010); new Routemaster bus for London, 2010; London 2012 Olympic Flame Cauldron, 2012. Ext. Examr, RCA, 2003–05. Sen. FRCA 2004. Hon. FRIBA 2008. DUniv: Sheffield Hallam, 2005; Brighton, 2008; Hon. Dr Manchester Metropolitan, 2007; Hon. LLD Dundee, 2007. *Address:* Heatherwick Studio, 356–364 Gray's Inn Road, WC1X 8BH. *T:* (020) 7833 8800. *E:* studio@heatherwick.com.

HEATHFIELD, Ven. Simon David; Archdeacon of Aston, since 2014; *b* 1967; *m* Rachel; two *c*. *Educ:* Birmingham Univ. (BMus 1988); Fitzwilliam Coll., Cambridge (BTh 1999); Ridley Hall, Cambridge. RAF Officer; Insurance Manager; Auxiliary Nurse; Church and Community Youth Worker, N Kent and Oxford; ordained deacon, 1999, priest, 2000; Curate, Church of the Good Shepherd, Heswall, 1999–2002; Vocation and Ministry Advr, Church Pastoral Aid Soc., 2002–05; Team Rector, Walthamstow, 2006–14; Area Dean, Waltham Forest, 2012–14. *Address:* 34 Chattock Avenue, Solihull B91 2QX.

HEATHWAITE, Prof. (Ann) Louise, (Mrs A. G. Mackie), PhD; FRSB; FRSE; Professor of Land and Water Systems Science, Lancaster Environment Centre, Lancaster University, since 2004; Chief Scientific Adviser, Rural Affairs and Environment, Scottish Government, since 2012; *b* Huddersfield, 1961; *d* of Ron Heathwaite and Eileen Heathwaite (*née* Throup); *m* 1994, Alistair G. Mackie. *Educ:* Boston Spa Comprehensive Sch.; Univ. of E Anglia (BSc 1st Cl. Hons Envmtl Sci. 1982); Univ. of Bristol (PhD 1987). Res. Officer, MAFF and

Scientific Officer, Soil Survey of England and Wales, 1982–83; NERC Postdoctoral Res. Asst, Dept of Geography, Oxford Univ., 1987–88; Envmtl Hydrologist, Higher Scientific Officer, Chief Scientist's Directorate, NCC, 1988–89; Department of Geography, University of Sheffield: Lectr, 1989–95; Sen. Lectr, 1996–97; Prof., 1998–2004. Theme Leader, Sustainable Use of Natural Resources, NERC, 2008–12 (Mem. Council, 2013–). Member: Sci. Adv. Council, DEFRA, 2011–; Steering Bd, UK Collaborative on Develt Sci., 2012–. FRSB (FSB 2010); FRSE 2015. *Publications:* (ed jtly) Nitrate: processes, patterns and management, 1993; (with K. Göttlich) Mires: process, exploitation and conservation, 1993; (ed with J. M. R. Hughes) The Hydrology and Hydrochemistry of British Wetlands, 1995; The Impact of Land Use Change on Nutrient Loads from Diffuse Sources, 1999; (jtly) Wetland Ecology and Eco-Hydrology, 2004; (ed jtly) Nutrient Mobility within River Basins: a European perspective, 2005; (ed jtly) Dynamics and Biogeochemistry of River Corridors and Wetlands, 2005; over 150 pubns in internat. peer-reviewed jls. *Recreation:* fell running. *Address:* Lancaster Environment Centre, Lancaster University, Lancaster LA1 4YQ. *T:* (01524) 510225. *E:* louise.heathwaite@lancs.ac.uk.

HEATLEY, Brian Antony; Secretary, Green House (green think tank), 2011–14; *b* 20 April 1947; *s* of Thomas Russell Heatley and Margaret Ross (*née* Deacon); *m*; one *d*. *Educ:* Sheen Grammar Sch.; St John's Coll., Cambridge (BA); Balliol Coll., Oxford; Warwick Univ. (MPhil). Volunteer teacher, Ethiopia, 1969–71; Department of Trade and Industry, 1974–89: appts include Financial Services, Consumer Protection and Radio Communications; Head, Small Firms and Enterprise Br., 1989–90, Head, Resource Planning Br., 1990–93, Dept of Employment; Head of Adults and Trng Strategy, Dept of Employment, then DFEE, 1993–96. Student teacher, Sheffield Univ., 1996–97; Maths teacher, Graveney Sch., Tooting, 1997–2001. Policy Co-ordinator and Mem., Nat. Exec., 2004–09, Mem., Policy Cttee, 2009–10, Green Party; co-author, Green Party Gen. Election Manifesto, 2010, 2015. *Recreations:* walking, history, photography, food. *Address:* Lorton Barn, Lorton Lane, Weymouth, Dorset DT3 5QH.

HEATLY, Sir Peter, Kt 1990; CBE 1971; DL; Chairman, Commonwealth Games Federation, 1982–90; *b* 9 June 1924; *s* of Robert Heatly and Margaret Ann Heatly; *m* 1st, 1948, Jean Robertha Hermiston (*d* 1979); two *s* two *d*; 2nd, 1984, Mae Calder Cochrane (*d* 2003). *Educ:* Leith Academy; Edinburgh Univ. (BSc). CEng, FICE. Chm., Scottish Sports Council, 1975–87. DL City of Edinburgh, 1984. Dr *hc* Edinburgh, 1992; Hon. DLitt Queen Margaret Coll., 1994; DUniv Stirling, 1998. *Recreation:* swimming.

HEATON, Clive William; QC 2006; **His Honour Judge Heaton;** a Circuit Judge, since 2011; *b* 20 July 1957; *s* of William and Dilys Heaton; *m* 1980, Susan Margaret Taylor (*d* 2007); two *s*; *m* 2012, Angela Catherine Finnerty, *qv*. *Educ:* Huddersfield New Coll.; Keble Coll., Oxford (MA); Chester Coll. of Law. Admitted solicitor, 1982; called to the Bar, Gray's Inn, 1992; in practice, specialising in family and child care law; Recorder, 2003–11; Dep. High Ct Judge, Family Div., 2009–; authorised to sit in Admin. Ct, 2012. Mem., Standards Cttee, Bar Standards Bd, 2008–11; Chm., Leeds Family Law Bar Assoc., 2011. *Publications:* (with Heather Swindells) Adoption: the modern procedure, 2006; (with L. McCallum and R. Joghi) The Forced Marriage Act, 2009. *Address:* Leeds Combined Court Centre, 1 Oxford Row, Leeds LS1 3BG.

HEATON, David, OBE 1993; Consultant, Museums and Galleries Commission, 1984–93; *b* 22 Sept. 1923; *s* of Dr Trevor Braby Heaton, OBE, MD and Constance Irene Heaton (*née* Wheeler-Bennett); *m* 1961, Joan, *d* of Group Captain E. J. Lainé, CBE, DFC and Phyllis Lainé (*née* Taudevin); two *s* one *d*. *Educ:* Rugby Sch. Served RNVR, 1942–46. Ghana, 1948–58; Cabinet Office, 1961–69; Home Office, 1969–83; Under Sec. of State, 1976–83. *Address:* 53 Murray Road, SW19 4PF. *T:* (020) 8947 0375.

See also R. N. Heaton.

HEATON, Frances Anne; Chairman: Lazards London Directors' Pension Scheme, 2006–15 (Director, 2002–15); Schroder Pension Trustee Ltd, 2008–14; *b* 11 Aug. 1944; *d* of John Ferris Whidborne and Marjorie Annie (*née* Maltby); *m* 1969, Martin Heaton; two *s*. *Educ:* Queen Anne's, Caversham; Trinity Coll., Dublin (BA, LLB). Called to the Bar, Inner Temple, 1967. Dept of Econ. Affairs, 1967–70; HM Treasury, 1970–80; seconded to S. G. Warburg & Co. Ltd, 1977–79; Lazard Brothers & Co. Ltd, 1980–2001, Dir, 1987–2001; seconded as Dir Gen., Panel on Takeovers and Mergers, 1992–94. Director: W. S. Atkins, 1990–2003 (Dep. Chm., 1996–2003); Bank of England, 1993–2001; Elementis plc (formerly Harrisons & Crosfield), 1994–99; Commercial Union, 1994–98; BUPA, 1998–2001; Legal & General Gp plc, 2001–10; AWG plc, 2002–07; Jupiter Primadona Growth Trust, 2005–; BMT Gp, 2007–. Mem., Cttee on Standards in Public Life, 1997–2003. *Recreations:* riding, gardening, bridge.

HEATON, John; *see* Heaton, W. J.

HEATON, Richard Nicholas, CB 2011; Permanent Secretary, Ministry of Justice, since 2015; Clerk of the Crown in Chancery, since 2015; *b* 5 Oct. 1965; *s* of David Heaton, *qv*. *Educ:* Rugby Sch.; Worcester Coll., Oxford (BA 1987). Called to the Bar, Inner Temple, 1988, Bencher, 2013. Home Office, 1991–96; Legal Secretariat to the Law Officers, 1996–98; Home Office, 1998–2000; Cabinet Office, 2000–01; Lord Chancellor's Dept, subseq. DCA, 2001–06, Legal Advr, 2004–06; Dir-Gen., Legal Gp, DWP, and Solicitor to DWP and DoH, 2007–09; Dir-Gen., Strategy, Information and Pensions, DWP, 2009–12; First Parliamentary Counsel, 2012–15; Permanent Sec., Cabinet Office, 2012–15. Chm. of Trustees, United St Saviour's Charity, 2014–. *Recreations:* India, pictures. *Address:* Ministry of Justice, 102 Petty France, SW1H 9AJ.

HEATON, (William) John; consultant to the betting industry, since 2004; Chief Executive, Betting & Gaming Consultancy Ltd, since 2004; *b* 12 Jan. 1954; *s* of Ronald and Hilda Heaton; one *s* two *d*; *m* 2011, Karen Macdonald. *Educ:* Wigan Grammar Sch.; Sheffield Univ. (LLB); Admitted Solicitor, 1975. Principal Solicitor, Manchester CC, 1976–83; Horserace Totalisator Board: Co. Sec. and Solicitor, 1983–96; Chief Exec., 1997–2004. Chm., Scotbet Ltd, 2011–. *Recreations:* Rugby, golf. *Address:* 3 Vicarage Drive, SW14 8RX. *E:* john@heaton.co.uk. *Clubs:* Richmond Rugby (Pres.); Royal Mid Surrey Golf.

HEATON, Sir Yvo (Robert) Henniker-, 4th Bt *cr* 1912; *b* 24 April 1954; *s* of Sir (John Victor) Peregrine Henniker-Heaton, 3rd Bt, and of Margaret Patricia, *d* of late Lieut Percy Wright, Canadian Mounted Rifles; *S* father, 1971; *m* 1978, Freda, *d* of B. Jones; one *s* one *d*. Mem., North West Leics DC, 1987–95. Chm., Kegworth Cons. Assoc., 1988–94. Gov., Ashby Willesley Sch., 1996–2000. *Publications:* Corporate Computer Insurance, 1990. *Heir:* *s* Alastair (John) Henniker-Heaton, *b* 4 May 1990.

HEATON-HARRIS, Christopher; MP (C) Daventry, since 2010; *b* 28 Nov. 1967; *s* of David Barry Heaton-Harris and Ann Geraldine Heaton-Harris; *m* 1990, Jayne Yvonne Carlow; two *d*. *Educ:* Tiffin Grammar Sch. for Boys, Kingston upon Thames. Dir, What 4 Ltd, 1995–2003. Contested (C) Leicester South, 1997, July 2004. MEP (C) East Midlands, 1999–2009. Pres., EU Sports Platform, 2009–10. *Recreation:* grade 5 soccer referee. *Address:* (office) 78 St George's Avenue, Northampton NN2 6JF; House of Commons, SW1A 0AA.

HEATON-JONES, Peter; MP (C) North Devon, since 2015; *b* Kingston upon Thames, 2 Aug. 1963; *s* of Richard Howard Heaton-Jones and Eileen Heaton-Jones (*née* Lewis). *Educ:* Esher Grammar Sch.; Southlands Coll. (BA Hons Sociol. and Geog. Univ. of London); London Coll. of Printing (CNAA Dip. Journalism). Sen. Broadcast Journalist, BBC, 1986–97; Hd, Mktg, ABC, Australia, 1998–2000; freelance broadcaster and media consultant, 2000–06; Press Sec., NSW Parlt, 2007–08; Agent, Cons. Party, 2008–10; Sen. Parly Asst, 2010–15. Mem. (C) Swindon BC, 2010–14. *Address:* House of Commons, SW1A 0AA. *E:* peter.heatonjones.mp@parliament.uk.

HEAVEN, Derick R.; Chief Executive Officer, Sugar Industry Authority, Jamaica, since 2002; *b* 19 Dec. 1940; *m* 1966, Thyra Reid; two *s* one *d*. *Educ:* Cornwall Coll.; Jamaica Sch. of Agriculture. Mem., St Catherine Parish Council, 1974–76; MP for South St Catherine, 1976–80; Parly Sec., Min. of Foreign Affairs, then Minister of Trade and Commerce, 1980; involved in farming and business interests, 1980–89; Consul-General, New York, 1989–92; Ambassador to Japan and (non-resident) to People's Republic of China and Republic of Korea, 1992–94; High Comr for Jamaica in London, 1994–99, and Ambassador (non-resident) to Scandinavia, Spain and Portugal; CEO, Sugar Co. of Jamaica Ltd, 1999–2002. Chm., Commonwealth Fund for Tech. Co-operation, 1996–99. *Recreations:* reading, travelling, sports.

HEBBLETHWAITE, Rev. Dr Brian Leslie; University Lecturer in Divinity, Cambridge, 1977–99, and Life Fellow of Queens' College, since 1994; *b* 3 Jan. 1939; *s* of Alderman Cyril Hebblethwaite and Sarah Anne Hebblethwaite; *m* 1991, Emma Sian (marr. diss. 2003), *d* of John Ivor Disley, *qv*; one *d*. *Educ:* Clifton Coll.; Magdalen Coll., Oxford (BA LitHum 1961; MA 1967); Magdalene Coll., Cambridge (BA Theol 1963; MA 1968; BD 1984; DD 2006); Westcott House, Cambridge; Univ. of Heidelberg. Curate, All Saints', Elton, Bury, 1965–68; Cambridge University: Bye-Fellow and Chaplain, 1968, Fellow and Dean of Chapel, 1969–94, Queens' Coll.; Univ. Asst Lectr in Divinity, 1973–77; Sen. Proctor, 1998–99; Examng Chaplain to Bishop of Manchester, 1977–98; Canon Theologian, Leicester Cathedral, 1982–2001. Pres., Soc. for Study of Theology, 1989–91. Lectures: Teape, Delhi, Calcutta and Bangalore, 1983–84; (jtly) Gifford, Glasgow, 2001; Hensley Henson, Oxford, 2002. Editor for Ethics, Theologische Realenzyklopädie, 1980–2007. *Publications:* Evil, Suffering and Religion, 1976, rev. edn 2000; The Problems of Theology, 1980; (ed jtly) Christianity and Other Religions, 1980, rev. edn 2001; The Adequacy of Christian Ethics, 1981; (ed jtly) The Philosophical Frontiers of Christian Theology, 1982; The Christian Hope, 1984, rev. edn 2010; Preaching Through the Christian Year 10, 1985; The Incarnation, 1987; The Ocean of Truth, 1988; (ed jtly) Divine Action, 1990; The Essence of Christianity, 1996; Ethics and Religion in a Pluralistic Age, 1997; Philosophical Theology and Christian Doctrine, 2004; In Defence of Christianity, 2005; (ed jtly) The Human Person in God's World, 2006; The Philosophical Theology of Austin Farrer, 2007; *festschrift:* Truth, Religious Dialogue and Dynamic Orthodoxy, ed by J. J. Lipner, 2005. *Recreations:* watching cricket, walking, architecture, books. *Address:* The Old Barn, 32 High Street, Stretham, Ely, Cambs CB6 3JQ. *T:* (01353) 648279. *Club:* Athenæum.

HEBDITCH, Maxwell Graham, CBE 1994; Director, Museum of London, 1977–97; *b* 22 Aug. 1937; *s* of late Harold Hebditch, motor engr, Yeovil, and Lily (*née* Bartle); *m* 1963, Felicity Davies; two *s* one *d*. *Educ:* Yeovil Sch.; Magdalene Coll., Cambridge (MA). FSA, FMA. Nat. Service, RAF, 1956–58. Field Archaeologist, Leicester Museums, 1961–64; Asst Curator in Archaeology, later Curator in Agricultural and Social History, City Museum, Bristol, 1965–71; Dir, Guildhall Mus., London, 1971–74; Dep. Dir, Mus. of London, 1974–77. Hon. Curator, Lyme Regis Mus., 2000–08 (Trustee, 2008–14). Chm., Mus. Trng Inst., subseq. Cultural Heritage NTO, 1997–2004 (Bd Mem., 1990–). Co-Dir, Mus. Leadership Prog., UEA, 1994–2000. Mem., EC Cttee of Cultural Consultants, 1990–92. Chm., UK Nat. Cttee, ICOM, 1981–87; Pres., Museums Assoc., 1990–92 (Vice-Pres., 1988–90); Chm., Taunton Cultural Consortium, 2004–13. Trustee: Mus. in Docklands, 1997–2005; Lyme Regis Mus., 2008–15; Weymouth Mus. Trust, 2011–; Dorset County Mus., 2014–. Hon. DLitt City, 1992. *Publications:* contribs to archaeological and museological jls and books. *Recreation:* museums and monuments. *Address:* 4 St John Way, Dorchester, Dorset DT1 2FG.

HEBER-PERCY, Sir Algernon (Eustace Hugh), KCVO 2014; Lord-Lieutenant for Shropshire, since 1996 (Vice Lord-Lieutenant, 1990–96); *b* 2 Jan. 1944; *s* of Brig. A. G. W. Heber-Percy, DSO and Daphne Wilma Kenyon (*née* Parker Bowles); *m* 1966, Hon. Margaret Jane Lever, *y d* of 3rd Viscount Leverhulme, KG, TD; one *s* three *d*. *Educ:* Harrow; Mons OTC. Lieut Grenadier Guards, 1962–66. Farmer and landowner. Chm., Mercia Regional Cttee, Nat. Trust, 1990–99; Trustee, Nat. Gardens Scheme, 1990–2005. Pres., Shropshire and Mid Wales Hospice, 1988–; Chm., Walker Trust Cttee, 1990– (Mem., 1990–). Hon. Colonel: 5th Bn, Shropshire and Herefordshire LI (Vol.), 1998–99; W Midlands Regt, 1999–2005. Gov., Shrewsbury Sch., 2004–14. DL Shropshire, 1986; High Sheriff of Shropshire, 1987. *Recreations:* gardening, country sports. *Address:* Hodnet Hall, Hodnet, Market Drayton, Shropshire TF9 3NN. *T:* (01630) 685202. *Club:* Cavalry and Guards.

HECHT, Samuel, RDI 2008; Co-founder and Partner, Industrial Facility UK, since 2002; *b* London, 7 Aug. 1969; *s* of Jack and Maureen Hecht; *m* 2001, Kim Colin. *Educ:* Mill Hill Sch., London; Central St Martin's, London (BA Hons Industrial Design with dist.); Royal Coll. of Art (MA Industrial Design). IDEO: industrial designer, San Francisco, 1994–96; Sen. Designer, Tokyo, 1996–99; Hd of Design, London, 1999–2002; Creative Dir, Muji Europe, 2004–07. Creative Advisor: Muji Japan, 2002–; Herman Miller Inc., 2008–. Sen. Tutor, RCA, 2007–10. Vis. Prof., Karlsruhe HFG, Germany, 2011–. FRSA 2012. *Publications:* (jtly) Things That Go Unseen, 2002; (jtly) Product as Landscape, 2004; (contrib.) Phaidon Design Classics, 2007; (jtly) Usefulness in Small Things, 2011. *Address:* Industrial Facility, Clerks Well House, 20 Britton Street, EC1M 5UA. *E:* mail@industrialfacility.co.uk.

HECK, Prof. Richard Fred, PhD; Willis F. Harrington Professor, University of Delaware, until 1989, now Professor Emeritus; *b* Springfield, Mass, 15 Aug. 1931; *m* 1979, Socorro. *Educ:* Univ. of Calif, Los Angeles (BS Chem. 1952; PhD 1954). Nat. Sci. Foundn Postdoctoral Fellow, Federal Inst. of Technol., Zurich, 1954–55; UCLA, 1955–56; Hercules Powder Co., Wilmington, Delaware, 1956–71; Univ. of Delaware, 1971–89. Vis. Prof., Queen's Univ., Canada, 2006. Hon. Dr Uppsala, 2010. Wallace H. Carothers Award, 2005, Herbert C. Brown Award, 2006, Amer. Chemical Soc.; (jtly) Nobel Prize in Chemistry, 2010. *Publications:* over 200 scientific papers. *Address:* c/o Department of Chemistry and Biochemistry, University of Delaware, Newark, DE 19716, USA.

HECKMAN, Prof. James Joseph, PhD; Henry Schultz Distinguished Service Professor, University of Chicago, since 1994 (Henry Schultz Professor, 1985–94); *b* 19 April 1944; *s* of John Jacob Heckman and Bernice Irene Medley Heckman; *m* 1st, 1964, Sally Lentz (marr. diss. 1971); 2nd, 1979, Lynne Pettler; one *s* one *d*. *Educ:* Colorado Coll. (BA Math 1965); Princeton (MA Econ 1968; PhD Econ 1971). Instructor-Associate Prof., Columbia Univ., 1970–74; Associate Prof., 1973–77, Prof. of Econs, 1977–, Univ. of Chicago; Yale Univ. (on leave), 1988–90. Guggenheim Fellow, 1977–78; Fellow, Center for Advanced Study in Behavioral Sci., 1977–78. Member: Amer. Acad., 1985–; NAS, 1992–; Resident Mem., Amer. Philosophical Soc., 2008–; Fellow: Econometric Soc., 1980; American Statistical Assoc., 2001; Soc. of Labor Economics, 2004; Amer. Assoc. for the Advancement of Science, 2009; Nat. Acad. of Educn, USA, 2010. Hon. MA Yale, 1989; Hon. PhD Colorado Coll., 2001; Hon. LLD: Chile, 2002; Univ. Autónoma del Estado de México, 2003; Montreal, Bard Coll., 2004; Hon. Dr Catholic Univ. of Chile, 2009; Hon. DSc (Econ) UCL, 2013. John Bates Clark Medal, American Econ. Soc., 1983; Nobel Prize for Economics, 2000; Jacob Mincer Award for Lifetime Achievement, Soc. of Labor Economics, 2005; Ulysses Medal, UC Dublin, 2006. President's Gold Medal (Italy), 2008. *Publications:* Longitudinal Analysis of Labor Market Data, 1985; Inequality in America: what role for human capital policies?, 2003; (with E. Leamer) Handbook of Econometrics, vol. 5 2001, vol. 6A 2007 and vol. 6B 2007;

(ed jtly) Global Perspectives on the Rule of Law, 2009; Giving Kids a Fair Chance, 2012; (ed jtly) The Myth of Achievement Tests: the GED and the role of character in American life, 2014; other books and over 200 articles. *Recreations:* hiking, bicycling, reading, music. *Address:* Department of Economics, University of Chicago, 1126 E 59th Street, Chicago, IL 60637, USA.

HECTOR, Alistair Gordon; Headmaster, George Heriot's School, Edinburgh, 1998–2013; *b* 5 Oct. 1955; *s* of Gordon Matthews Hector, CMG, CBE; *m* 1980, Rosemary Ann Craig; two *s* one *d.* *Educ:* Edinburgh Acad.; Univ. of St Andrews (MA); Univ. of Erlangen, Germany. Lektor in English, Univ. of Erlangen, 1978–80; Head of German, Merchiston Castle Sch., Edinburgh, 1980–85; Head of Dept, German, 1986–89, Modern Langs, 1989–95, King Edward's Sch., Bath; Dep. Headmaster, Warwick Sch., 1995–97. *Recreations:* sport, walking, music, travel, family.

HEDEGAARD, Connie, Silver Cross, Order of Dannebrog, 2005; Chair, KR Foundation, since 2015; *b* Copenhagen, 15 Sept. 1960; *d* of Knud Hedegaard Koksbang and Elinor Hedegaard Koksbang; *m* 1992, Jacob Andersen; two *s.* *Educ:* Univ. of Copenhagen (MA Lit. and Hist.). Journalist, Hd of Radio News and columnist, Danish TV, 1990–2004. MP, Denmark, 1984–90 and 2005–09; Minister: for Envmt, 2004–07, and for Nordic Cooperation, 2005–07; for Climate and Energy, 2007–09; for UN Climate Change Conf., Copenhagen, 2009. Mem., EC, 2010–14. *Publications:* The 20th Century: the 100 most influential people in Denmark (with C. Hagen Pedersen), 1999; Da Klimaet blev Hot, 2008. *Address:* KR Foundation, Havnegade 39, 1058 Copenhagen, Denmark.

HEDGER, John Clive, CB 1998; Chairman, Berkshire Healthcare NHS Foundation Trust, since 2009; *b* 17 Dec. 1942; *s* of late Leslie John Keith Hedger and Iris Hedger (*née* Friedlos); *m* 1966, Jean Ann Felstead; two *s* one *d.* *Educ:* Quirister Sch., Winchester; Victoria Coll., Jersey; Univ. of Sussex (BA 1965; MA 1966). Dept of Educn and Science, 1966; Asst Private Sec., 1970; Sec., Cttee of Enquiry on Educn of Handicapped, 1974–76; Under Sec., DES, 1988–92; Dep. Sec., Dept for Educn, 1992–95; Dir of Ops, DFEE, 1995–2000. Chm., Sector Skills Council for Lifelong Learning, later Lifelong Learning UK, 2005–07; Trustee, Rathbone (formerly Rathbone Training), 2000–09; Trustee and non-exec. Dir, Nat. Foundn for Educnl Research, 2004–12. Mem. Council, Radley Coll., 1998–2007; Gov., Mary Hare Sch., 2006–; Dir, Langley Acad. Trust, 2012–. *Recreations:* walking, gardening, grandchildren, messing about on the Thames. *Address:* 8 Cliveden Gages, Taplow, Berks SL6 0GA. *T:* 07801 276648.

HEDGES, Anthony (John); Reader in Composition, University of Hull, 1978–95; *b* 5 March 1931; *s* of late S. G. Hedges; *m* 1957, Delia Joy Marsden; two *s* two *d.* *Educ:* Bicester Grammar Sch.; Keble Coll., Oxford. MA, BMus, LRAM. National Service as solo pianist and arranger Royal Signals Band, 1955–57. Teacher and Lecturer, Royal Scottish Academy of Music, 1957–63. During this period became a regular contributor to Scotsman, Glasgow Herald, Guardian, Musical Times, etc. Lecturer in Music, Univ. of Hull, 1963, Sen. Lectr, 1968. The Composers' Guild of Great Britain: Chm., Northern Br., 1966–67; Mem. Exec. Cttee of Guild, 1969–73, 1977–81, 1982–87; Chm. of Guild, 1972, Jt Chm., 1973. Member: Council, Central Music Library, Westminster, 1970; Council, Soc. for Promotion of New Music, 1974–81; Music Bd, CNAA, 1974–77; Music Panel, Yorks Arts Assoc., 1974–75, Lincs and Humberside Arts Assoc., 1975–78; Founder-conductor, The Humberside Sinfonia, 1978–81. Hon. DMus Hull, 1997. Wrote regularly for Yorkshire Post, 1963–78, and contributed to many jls, incl. Composer, Current Musicology, etc, and also broadcast on musical subjects. *Publications: (works): orchestral:* Comedy Overture, 1962 (rev. 1967); Overture, October '62, 1962 (rev. 1968); Sinfonia Semplice, 1963; Expressions for Orchestra, 1964; Prelude, Romance and Rondo, strings, 1965; Concertante Music, 1965; Four Miniature Dances, 1967; A Holiday Overture, 1968; Variations on a theme of Rameau, 1969; Kingston Sketches, 1969; An Ayrshire Serenade, 1969; Four Diversions, strings, 1971; Celebrations, 1973; Symphony no 1, 1972–73; Festival Dances, 1976; Overture, Heigham Sound, 1978; Four Breton Sketches, 1980; Sinfonia Concertante, 1980; Scenes from the Humber, 1981; A Cleveland Overture, 1984; Concertino for Horn and String Orchestra, 1987; Sinfonia Giovanile, 1992; Showpiece, 1995; Symphony no 2, 1997; Trumpet Concerto, 2000; Fiddler's Green, 2001; *choral:* Gloria, unaccompanied, 1965; Epithalamium, chorus and orch. (Spencer), 1969; To Music, chorus and orch. (various texts), 1972; Psalm 104, 1973; A Manchester Mass, chorus, orch. and brass band, 1974; A Humberside Cantata, 1976; Songs of David, 1978; The Temple of Solomon, 1979; I Sing the Birth: canticles for Christmas, 1985; I'll make me a world, 1990; The Lamp of Liberty, 2005; *chamber music:* Five Preludes, piano, 1959; Four Pieces, piano, 1966; Rondo Concertante, violin, clarinet, horn, violoncello, 1967; Sonata for violin and harpsichord, 1967; Three Songs of Love, soprano, piano (from Song of Songs), 1968; String Quartet, 1970; Rhapsody, violin, piano, 1971, revd 1988; piano sonata, 1974; Song Cycle, 1977; Piano Trio, 1977; Fantasy for Violin and Piano, 1981; Sonatinas for Flute, Viola, Cello, 1982; Wind Quintet, 1984; Flute Trios, 1985, 1989; Fantasy Sonata for bassoon and piano, 1986; Clarinet Quintet, 1987; Flute Sonata, 1988; Five Aphorisms, piano, 1990; In such a night, string quartet, 1990; Bassoon Quintet, 1991; Piano Quartet, 1992; Trombone Sonata, 1994; Six Song Cycles, 1997–2006; Ten Bagatelles, piano, 2006; Piccolo Divertimento (flute, bassoon, piano), 2010; Three Humours (clarinet, bassoon, piano), 2011; *opera:* Shadows in the Sun (lib. Jim Hawkins), 1976; *musical:* Minotaur (lib. Jim Hawkins), 1978; *miscellaneous:* many anthems, partsongs, albums of music for children; music for television, film and stage. *Recreations:* reading, crosswords, walking. *Address:* Malt Shovel Cottage, 76 Walkergate, Beverley HU17 9ER. *T:* (01482) 860580. *W:* www.westfieldmusic-anthonyhedges.co.uk.

HEDGES, Very Rev. Jane Barbara; Dean of Norwich, since 2014; *b* 6 April 1955; *d* of John William Henry Taylor and Elizabeth Taylor; *m* 1982, Christopher Hedges; two *s.* *Educ:* Durham Univ. (BA Hons). Ordained deaconess, 1980, deacon 1987, priest 1994; Deaconess, Holy Trinity with St Columba, Fareham, 1980–83; Team Vicar, Southampton City Centre Team, 1983–88; Stewardship Advr, Portsmouth Dio., 1988–93; Residentiary Canon, Portsmouth Cathedral, 1993–2001; Team Rector, Honiton Team Ministry, 2001–06; Canon Steward, 2006–14, and Archdeacon, 2006–09, 2011–14, Westminster Abbey. Hon. LLD Portsmouth, 2006. *Recreations:* walking, listening to classical music, animal welfare, sporting events with sons, touring abroad/pilgrimages. *Address:* The Deanery, The Close, Norwich NR1 4EG. *T:* (01603) 280300. *E:* dean@cathedral.org.uk.

HEDGES, (Jonathan) Mark; Editor, Country Life, since 2006; *b* 24 Feb. 1964; *s* of John and Mary Hedges; *m* 1989, Stacey Ann Estella; two *s* one *d.* *Educ:* Radley Coll., Abingdon; Univ. of Durham (BSc Geol. 1985). Tattersalls, Newmarket, 1985–88; Ed., Shooting Times, 1998–2000; Publisher, The Field, Shooting Times, Sporting Gun and Anglers' Mail, 2000–02; Ed., Horse & Hound, 2002–03, 2004; Editor-in-Chief, Country and Leisure Media, IPC, 2002–06. *Publications:* Dog, 2000. *Recreations:* shooting, fly fishing, leaning on a fork, the countryside. *Address:* Country Life, Blue Fin Building, 110 Southwark Street, SE1 0SU. *T:* (020) 3148 4420. *E:* mark.hedges@timeinc.com.

HEDGES, Michael Irving Ian, CBE 2005; QPM 1995; Chief Constable, South Yorkshire Police, 1998–2004; *b* 27 Jan. 1948; *s* of Arthur and Helen Hedges; *m* 1968, Beryl Janet Smith; one *s.* *Educ:* Holyrood Sch., Chard, Som.; King's College, London (LLB). Constable, Somerset and Bath Police, 1967–72; transf. to Metropolitan Police, 1972–87; Chief Superintendent, Thames Valley Police, 1987–88; Asst Chief Constable, Avon and Somerset Police, 1988–93; Dep. Chief Constable, South Yorkshire Police, 1993–98. RHS Medal for Gallantry, 1968. *Recreations:* swimming, reading, golf, fly fishing, gardening; an active Rotarian.

HEDGES, Michael John; Member (Lab) Swansea, National Assembly for Wales, since 2011; *b* Swansea, 8 July 1956; *s* of William John Hedges and Rosemary June Hedges; *m* 1996, Anne Rachel Hopkins; two *d.* *Educ:* Swansea Univ. (BSc Hons Materials Sci. and Technol.); Cardiff Univ. (PGCE). Researcher, BSC, 1978–81; Researcher and Lectr in Computing, 1981–83; Lectr in Computing, Coleg Morgannwg, 1983–2011. Mem. (Lab), Swansea Council, 1989– (Leader, 1997–2001). *Recreations:* football, cricket, Rugby. *Address:* 4 Glyncollen Drive, Ynysforgan, Swansea SA6 6RR. *T:* (01792) 791774. *E:* mike.hedges@assembly.wales. *Clubs:* Morriston Working Men's; Ynystawe Cricket and Football, Morriston Rugby, Morriston Golf, Glais Rugby.

HEDLEY, Prof. Anthony Johnson, MD; JP; FRCPE, FRCPGlas, FRCP, FFPH; Honorary Clinical Professor of Community Medicine, School of Public Health, University of Hong Kong, 2010, now Professor Emeritus (Chair Professor of Community Medicine, 1988–2010); *b* 8 April 1941; *s* of Thomas Johnson Hedley and Winifred Duncan; *m* 1st, 1967, Elizabeth-Anne Walsh (marr. diss. 1992); 2nd, 1996, Andrea Marilyn Miller (marr. diss. 2007); 3rd, 2008, Sarah Morag Harrigan McGhee. *Educ:* Rydal Sch.; Aberdeen Univ. (MB, ChB 1965; MD 1972); Edinburgh Univ. (Dip. Soc. Med. 1973). MRCP 1973; FRCPE 1981; FRCPGlas, 1985; FRCP 1987; FFPH (FFCM 1981; MFCM 1975). Lectr in Community Medicine, Univ. of Aberdeen, 1974–76; Sen. Lectr in Community Health, Univ. of Nottingham, 1976–83; Titular Prof. in Community Medicine, 1983–84, Henry Mechan Prof. of Public Health, 1984–88, Univ. of Glasgow. Med. Adviser (Thailand), ODA, 1977–83. Chm., HK Council on Smoking and Health, 1997–2002. Hon. Dir, Hedley Envmtl Index, 2009–. JP Hong Kong, 1998. Hon. MD Khon Kaen Univ., 1983. WHO Medal for services to public health, 1999. Bronze Bauhinia Star, HKSAR, 2000; Dist. Service Award, Food and Health Bureau, HKSAR, 2007. *Publications:* papers and chapters on endocrine disease, surveillance of chronic disease, air pollution, tobacco control and on med. educn. *Recreations:* long-distance running, photography, rifle shooting, flying (private pilot's licence, 1992). *Address:* Four Winds, Kirkpatrick, Isle of Man IM5 3AH. *E:* hrmrajh@gmail.com. *Clubs:* Aberdeen Boat, Foreign Correspondents', Hong Kong Aviation (Hong Kong).

HEDLEY, Rev. Charles John Wykeham, PhD; Rector, St James's, Piccadilly, 1999–2009; English language teacher, Beijing and Chengdu, 2009–12; *b* 26 June 1947; *s* of Harry and Elisabeth Hedley. *Educ:* Christ's Hospital, Horsham; Royal Holloway Coll., Univ. of London (BSc; PhD 1973); Fitzwilliam Coll., Cambridge (MA); Westcott House, Cambridge. Deacon 1976, priest 1977; Asst Curate, St Anne's, Chingford, 1976–79; Curate, St Martin-in-the-Fields, 1979–86; Chaplain, Christ's Coll., Cambridge, 1986–90; Team Rector of Gleadless, Sheffield, 1990–99. *Recreations:* walking, classical music. *E:* chequal@gmail.com.

HEDLEY, Sir Mark, Kt 2002; DL; a Judge of the High Court, Family Division, 2002–13; *b* 23 Aug. 1946; *s* of late Peter and Eve Hedley; *m* 1973, Erica Britton; three *s* one *d.* *Educ:* Framlingham College; Univ. of Liverpool (LLB Hons). Called to the Bar, Gray's Inn, 1969, Bencher, 2002; VSO, Sudan, 1969–70; practice at Liverpool Bar, 1971–92; Head of Chambers, 1983–92; a Recorder, 1988–92; a Circuit Judge, 1992–2001. Vis. Prof., Liverpool Hope Univ., 2013–. Chancellor, Dio. Liverpool, 2002–. Reader in C of E, 1975–. Hon. LLD Liverpool, 2003; Hon. Fellow, Liverpool John Moores Univ., 2005. DL Merseyside, 2015. *Recreations:* cricket, railways. *Address:* 55 Everton Road, Liverpool L6 2EH.

HEDWORTH, (Alan) Toby; QC 1996; a Recorder, since 1995; *b* 23 April 1952; *s* of late John William Swaddle Hedworth and Margaret Ena Hedworth (*née* Dodds); *m* 1987, Kathleen Mary (*née* Luke); two *d.* *Educ:* King's Sch., Tynemouth; Royal Grammar Sch., Newcastle upon Tyne; St Catharine's Coll., Cambridge (MA). Called to the Bar, Inner Temple, 1975, NI 2012; Head, Trinity Chambers, Newcastle upon Tyne, 1999–. Vice Chm., Northumberland and Newcastle Soc., 1997–. *Recreations:* Newcastle United, the English Lake District, motoring, the built environment. *Address:* The Custom House, Quayside, Newcastle upon Tyne NE1 3DE. *T:* (0191) 232 1927. *Club:* Northern Counties (Newcastle upon Tyne).

HEEGER, Prof. Alan Jay, PhD; Presidential Chair, since 2003, and Professor of Physics, since 1982, and Professor of Materials, since 1987, University of California, Santa Barbara; *b* 22 Jan. 1936; *s* of Peter Jacob Heeger and Alice Minkin Heeger; *m* 1957, Ruth Chudacroft; two *s.* *Educ:* Univ. of Nebraska (BS 1957); Univ. of Calif, Berkeley (PhD 1961). University of Pennsylvania: Prof. of Physics, 1962–82; Director: Lab. for Res. on Structure of Matter, 1974–80; Inst. for Polymers and Organic Solids, 1983–99. Founder, 1990, Chm., 1990–99, Uniax Corp. Member: NAS; NAE. Holds numerous hon. degrees. Buckley Prize, APS, 1983; Balzan Foundn Prize, 1995; Nobel Prize in Chem., 2000. *Recreations:* ski-ing, walking. *Address:* Department of Physics, University of California at Santa Barbara, Santa Barbara, CA 93106, USA. *T:* (805) 8933184, *Fax:* (805) 8934755. *E:* ajhe@physics.ucsb.edu.

HEFFER, Simon James, PhD; columnist, Daily Telegraph and Sunday Telegraph, since 2015; *b* 18 July 1960; *er s* of late James Heffer and of Joyce Mary Heffer (*née* Clements); *m* 1987, Diana Caroline, *d* of Sqdn Ldr P. A. Clee; two *s.* *Educ:* King Edward VI Sch., Chelmsford; Corpus Christi Coll., Cambridge (BA 1982; MA 1986; PhD 2009). Medical journalist, 1983–86; Leader Writer and Parly Sketch Writer, Daily Telegraph, 1986–91; Dep. Ed. and Political Corresp., Spectator, 1991–94; Dep. Ed., Daily Telegraph, 1994–95; columnist, Daily Mail, 1993–94 and 1995–2005; Associate Ed. and columnist, Daily Telegraph, 2005–11; columnist, Daily Mail, 2011–15. Member, Board: Britten Sinfonia, 2005–09; Elgar Foundn and Birthplace Trust, 2009–; New Queen's Hall Orchestra, 2013–. Fellow Commoner, Corpus Christi Coll., Cambridge, 2010. *Publications:* Moral Desperado: a life of Thomas Carlyle, 1995; Power and Place: the political consequences of King Edward VII, 1998; Like the Roman: the life of Enoch Powell, 1998; Nor Shall My Sword: the reinvention of England, 1999; Vaughan Williams, 2000; Great British Speeches, 2007; Strictly English, 2010; A Short History of Power, 2011; High Minds: the Victorians and the birth of modern Britain, 2013; Simply English, 2014. *Recreations:* cricket, music, bibliophily, my family. *Address:* The Daily Telegraph, 111 Buckingham Palace Road, SW1W 0DT. *Clubs:* Beefsteak, Garrick, MCC, Pratt's.

HEFFERNAN, Margaret Anne Windham; author; *b* Corpus Christi, Texas, 15 June 1955; *d* of Jack Edward Windham and Sally Anne Windham; *m* 1st, 1983, Michael Francis Heffernan (*d* 1985); 2nd, 1991, Lindsay Boyd Nicholson; one *s* one *d.* *Educ:* Girton Coll., Cambridge (BA 1977). Producer, BBC TV, 1983–91; Man. Dir, IPPA, 1991–93; Consultant, Boston, MA, 1993; Chief Executive Officer: InfoMation Corp., 1996–97; ZineZone Corp., 1997–99; iCast Corp., 1999–2002. Non-executive Director: Bath Consultancy Gp, 2009–11; RADA Enterprises, 2014–; Merryck and Co., 2015–. Vis. Prof., Simmons Coll., Boston, 2004–08. Mem., Adv. Bd, Sch. of Mgt, 2008–, Vis. Lectr, 2009–, Univ. of Bath. Mem. Council, RADA, 2003–14. Trustee: Bath Festivals, 2010–; London Liby, 2013–. *Plays:* Eve Blinked, 2006; Power Play, 2009; Wilful Blindness, 2009; Mrs Updike, 2011. Hon. DBA Bath, 2011. *Publications:* The Naked Truth: a working woman's manifesto, 2004; How She Does It, 2007; Women on Top, 2008; Wilful Blindness, 2011; A Bigger Prize: why competition isn't everything and how we do better, 2014; Beyond Measure: the big impact of small change, 2015. *Recreations:* singing, earwigging, mowing, arguing, turnarounds. *E:* margaret@mheffernan.com.

HEGARTY, Frances; *see* Fyfield, F.

HEGARTY, Dr John, FInstP; Provost of Trinity College Dublin, 2001–11; Director, Innovation Advisory Partners, since 2012; *b* Mayo, 17 April 1948; *s* of John and Delia Hegarty; *m* 1975, Neasa Ní Chinnéide; two *s.* *Educ:* National Univ. of Ireland, Maynooth (BSc 1969; Higher DipEd 1971); National Univ. of Ireland, Galway (PhD 1976); Trinity

Coll. Dublin (DSc 2001). FInstP 1986. Res. Associate, Univ. of Wisconsin-Madison, 1977–80; Res. Scientist, Bell Labs, Murray Hill, NJ, 1980–86; Prof. of Laser Physics, TCD, 1986–2001. Founder and Dir, Optronics Ireland, 1989–2000. Coordinator, Eur. Consortium on Microcavities, 1993–2000. Member: Bd, Nat. Res. Support Fund, Ireland, 1995–98; Higher Educn Authy, Ireland, 1998–2001; Tech. Adv. Panel on Information and Communications Technol., Sci. Foundn Ireland, 2000–01. Chm., Deans and Vice Presidents for Res. under CHIU, 2000. Fellow, TCD. MRIA. Hon. LLD QUB, 2008; Hon. DSc UCD, 2013. *Publications:* contribs to jls incl. Physical Rev., Optical and Quantum Electronics, IEEE Jl Quantum Electronics, Applied Physics Letters, Jl Luminescence, Jl Crystal Growth, Optics Letters, Electronics Letters. *Recreations:* reader of all forms of literature from biography to novels which enrich the soul and ease me to sleep at night, sailing and a love of the power and unpredictability of the sea, cycling for leisure, especially around W Kerry. *Address:* Provost's Office, Trinity College, Dublin 2, Ireland. *T:* (1) 8961558, *Fax:* (1) 8962303.

HEGARTY, Sir John (Kevin), Kt 2007; Founding Director, Bartle Bogle Hegarty Ltd, since 1982 (Worldwide Creative Director, 1982–2012, and Group Chairman, 1991–2012); *b* 20 May 1944; *s* of Matthew and Anne Hegarty; *m* (separated); one *s* one *d. Educ:* Challoner Grammar Sch.; Hornsey Sch. of Art; London Coll. of Printing. Junior Art Dir, Benton & Bowles, 1965–66; Art Director: John Collings and Partners, 1966–67; Cramer Saatchi, 1967–70; Saatchi & Saatchi: Founding Shareholder, 1970; Dep. Creative Dir, 1971–73; Founding Partner and Creative Dir, TBWA, London, 1973–82. Hon. Prof., London Inst., 1998. FRSA 1992. Wine maker, Domaine de Chamans. *Publications:* Hegarty on Advertising: turning intelligence into magic, 2011; Hegarty on Creativity: there are no rules, 2014. *Recreations:* tennis, ski-ing. *Address:* (office) 60 Kingly Street, W1B 5DS. *Clubs:* Groucho; Century.

HEGARTY, Kevin John; QC 2010; a Recorder, since 2003; *b* London, 9 Jan. 1960; *s* of John Hegarty and Josephine Hegarty; *m* 1984, Alison Day; one *s* two *d. Educ:* St Michael's Sch., Stevenage; Univ. of Newcastle upon Tyne (LLB Hons); Salford Univ. (MA). Called to the Bar, Middle Temple, 1982; in practice as a barrister, Manchester, then Birmingham, specialising in crime and regulatory law, 1990–; Hd, St Philips Chambers, 2011–14. *Recreations:* squash, classical guitar, gardening. *Address:* St Philips Chambers, 55 Temple Row, Birmingham B2 5LS. *Clubs:* Sloane; Stratford upon Avon Squash.

HEGARTY, Most Rev. Séamus; Bishop of Derry, (RC), 1994–2011; *b* 26 Jan. 1940; *s* of James Hegarty and Mary O'Donnell. *Educ:* Kilcar National School; St Eunan's Coll., Letterkenny; St Patrick's Coll., Maynooth; University Coll., Dublin. Priest, 1966; post-grad. studies, University Coll., Dublin, 1966–67; Dean of Studies 1967–71, President 1971–82, Holy Cross College, Falcarragh; Bishop of Raphoe, 1982–94. *Publications:* contribs to works on school administration and student assessment. *Recreations:* bridge, angling.

HEGARTY, Seamus, PhD; researcher and academic; Director, National Foundation for Educational Research, 1994–2005; *b* 19 Oct. 1945; *s* of James Hegarty and Mary Hegarty; *m* 1972, Carol Halls; two *s* one *d. Educ:* St Colman's Coll., Fermoy; University Coll., Dublin (BSc, HDipEd); Univ. of London Inst. of Educn (PhD 1975). Mgt trng, 1969–70; teaching, 1970–75; research, 1975–94. Visiting Professor: Reading Univ., 1996; Inst. of Educn, Univ. of London, 1996–98; Univ. of Aberystwyth (formerly Univ. of Wales, Aberystwyth), 2004–08; Univ. of Warwick, 2005–; Manchester Metropolitan Univ., 2005–09; QUB, 2005–09. Pres., Consortium of Instns for Develt and Res. in Educn in Europe, 2000–02; Chairman: Internat. Assoc. for the Evaluation of Educnl Achievement, 2005–12; Learning Standards Gp, Learning Metrics Task Force, 2012–13. Hon. Dr: Free Univ. of Brussels, 1997; Oxford Brookes, 2001; London, 2006; DUniv York, 1999. MInstD 1994. Ed., Educnl Res., 1983–2005; Founder Ed., European Jl Special Needs Educn, 1986–. *Publications:* Able to Learn?: the pursuit of culture-fair assessment, 1978; Educating Pupils with Special Needs in the Ordinary School, 1981; Integration in Action, 1982; Recent Curriculum Development in Special Education, 1982; The Making of a Profession, 1983; Training for Management in Schools, 1983; Research and Evaluation Methods in Special Education, 1985; Meeting Special Needs in Ordinary Schools, 1987, 2nd edn 1993; Developing Expertise: INSET for special educational needs, 1988; Review of the Present Situation of Special Education, 1988; Boosting Educational Achievement, 1989; Educating Children and Young People with Disabilities: principles and the review of practice, 1993; New Perspectives in Special Education: a six-country study of integration, 1994; Review of the Present Situation in Special Needs Education, 1995; The Role of Research in Mature Education Systems, 1997; (with M. Alur) Education and Children with Special Needs: from segregation to inclusion, 2002. *Recreations:* contemporary fiction, music, board games, golf, walking. *Club:* West Middlesex Golf.

HEGARTY, His Honour Thomas Brendan; QC 1992; a Circuit Judge, 1996–2013; *b* 6 June 1943; *s* of Thomas Hegarty and Louise (*née* Conlan); *m* 1972, Irene Letitia Hall; one *s* one *d. Educ:* St Joseph's Coll., Dumfries; St John's Coll., Cambridge (BA 1964; LLB 1965; MA 1970). Called to the Bar, Middle Temple, 1970; a Recorder, 1988–96. *Club:* Manchester Tennis and Racquet.

HEGDE, Mridul, (Mrs P. J. Tansley), CB 2013; Executive Director, Strategy, Financial Reporting Council, 2012–14; *b* Mangalore, India, 24 March 1967; *d* of Taranath Hegde and Kasturi Hegde (*née* Bhat); *m* 1st, 1994, Brian Brivati (marr. diss.); one *s* one *d*; 2nd, 2009, Philip J. Tansley; one *d. Educ:* Ravenspark Acad.; Balliol Coll., Oxford (BA PPE); Birkbeck Coll., Univ. of London (MSc Econs). AEU, 1988–89; HM Treasury, 1990–94, Speechwriter to the Chancellor, 1992–94; Policy Advr, Policy and Planning Directorate, BBC, 1996–97; DCMS, 1997–2002; HM Treasury: Team Leader, Public Services, 2002–04; Director: Public Spending, 2004–08; Financial Stability, 2008–12.

HEGGESSEY, Lorraine Sylvia; public/motivational speaker and media consultant, since 2010; Adviser, Channel 4 Growth Fund, since 2015; *b* 16 Nov. 1956; *d* of Sam and Doris Heggessey; *m* 1985, Ronald de Jong, musician and composer; two *d. Educ:* Durham Univ. (BA Hons English Lang. and Lit.). BBC: News Trainee and Sub Editor, 1979–83; Producer: Panorama, 1983–86; This Week, 1986–91; Editor, Biteback, 1991–92; Series Producer, The Underworld, 1992–94; Exec. Producer, BBC Science (QED, Animal Hospital, The Human Body, Minders), 1994–97; Head of Children's Programmes, 1997–99; Dep. Chief Exec., BBC Productions, 1999–2000; Controller, BBC1, 2000–05; Chief Exec., talkbackThames, 2005–10; Exec. Chair, Boom Pictures, 2012–14. Chm., Grierson Trust, 2014–. *Recreations:* ski-ing, yoga, open water swimming, hiking, having fun with my family and friends, theatre, cinema.

HEGGS, Geoffrey Ellis; Chairman of Industrial Tribunals, 1977–97, Regional Chairman, London North, 1990–97; a Recorder of the Crown Court, 1983–97; *b* 23 Oct. 1928; *s* of George Heggs, MBE and Winifred Grace Heggs; *m* 1953, Renée Fanny Madeleine Calderan (*see* R. F. M. Heggs); two *s* one *d. Educ:* Elizabeth Coll., Guernsey; LLB London. Admitted Solicitor, 1952. Rotary Foundn Fellow, Yale Univ., 1953–54; LLM Yale; Asst Sec., Law Soc., 1956–58; practised as solicitor in London, 1958–77. Liveryman, City of London Solicitors' Co. *Recreations:* military history, music, painting, sailing. *Address:* 12 Audley Road, Ealing, W5 3ET. *T:* (020) 8997 0305. *E:* g.heggs@ntlworld.com. *Club:* Royal Over-Seas League.

HEGGS, Renée Fanny Madeleine, (Miguette); a Social Security Commissioner, 1981–2002; a Child Support Commissioner, 1993–2002; *b* 29 Nov. 1929; *d* of Emilio and Graziella Calderan; *m* 1953, Geoffrey Ellis Heggs, *qv*; two *s* one *d. Educ:* Notting Hill and Ealing High Sch., GPDST; LLB (London) 1952. Admitted Solicitor, 1955; practising Solicitor, 1955–81. Chm., Nat. Insce Local Tribunal, 1976–81; pt-time Chm. of Industrial Tribunals, 1978–81; Pres., Appeal Tribunal under London Building Acts, 1979–81; Legal Mem., 1985–2000, Dep. Regl Chm., 1995–2000, Mental Health Review Tribunal. Mem., UK Assoc. of Women Judges, 2004–. Liveryman, City of London Solicitors' Co., 2005–. *Recreations:* music, travelling. *Address:* 12 Audley Road, Ealing, W5 3ET. *T:* (020) 8997 0305. *Club:* Royal Over-Seas League.

HEGINBOTHAM, Prof. Christopher John, OBE 2009; healthcare consultant; Chief Executive, Institute of Social Commissioning, 2011–13; Director, Values Based Commissioning Ltd, since 2011; *b* 25 March 1948; *s* of late Joseph William Heginbotham and Marjorie Heginbotham; *m* 1st, 1988, Barbara Joyce, *d* of Charles and Lois-Ella Gill, Cincinnati, Ohio (marr. diss. 2008); two *d*; 2nd, 2011, Christine Sconce, *d* of Roland and Mary Sanderson, Preston, Lancs. *Educ:* Univ. of Birmingham (BSc Hons 1969); Univ. of Essex (MSc 1972); MA Wales 1989; MPhil Cambridge 2001. Area Manager, Circle Thirty Three Housing Trust, 1977–80; Assistant Borough Housing Officer, London Borough of Haringey, 1980–82; Nat. Dir, MIND (Nat. Assoc. for Mental Health), 1982–88; Fellow in Health Services Management, King's Fund Coll., London, 1989–93; Chief Executive: Riverside Mental Health NHS Trust, 1993–96; E and N Herts HA, 1996–2000; Chm. and Chief Exec., Eastern Region Specialised Commissioning Gp, 2000–01; Chief Exec., S Warwicks Gen. Hosps NHS Trust, 2001–03; Chief Exec., Mental Health Act Commn, 2003–08; University of Central Lancashire: Prof. of Mental Health Policy and Mgt, 2005–11, now Emeritus; Co-Dir, Inst. for Philosophy, Diversity and Mental Health, 2006–10; Dep. Hd, 2008–10, Actg Hd, 2010, Internat. Sch. for Communities, Rights and Inclusion. Member: Hampstead DHA, 1981–87; Waltham Forest DHA, 1989–92 (Vice-Chm., 1991–92); Chm., Redbridge and Waltham Forest FHSA, 1992–93; non-exec. Dir, Lancs Care NHS Foundn Trust, 2008–. Member: Nat. Adv. Council on Employment of Disabled People, 1983–90; Bd, World Fedn for Mental Health, 1985–89 (rep., UN Commn on Human Rights, 1985–91); Bd, Internat. Acad. of Law and Mental Health, 1987–89; Bd, Global Health Equity Foundn, Geneva, 2011–. Vis. Res. Fellow, Univ. of Glasgow Inst. of Law and Ethics in Medicine, 1987–91; Vis. Sen. Fellow, Health Services Mgt Centre, Univ. of Birmingham, 1994–2001; Hon. Prof., Inst. of Clin. Educn, Med. Sch., Univ. of Warwick, 2005–; Vis. Prof., Univ. of Cumbria, 2012–. *Publications:* Housing Projects for Mentally Handicapped People, 1981; Promoting Residential Services for Mentally Handicapped People, 1982; Webs and Mazes: approaches to community care, 1984; The Rights of Mentally Ill People, 1987; Return to Community, 1990; (with T. Campbell) Mental Illness: prejudice, discrimination and the law, 1990; (with C. Ham) Purchasing Dilemmas, 1992; Philosophy, Psychiatry and Psychopathy, 2000; Values-based Commissioning of Health and Social Care, 2012; (with K. Newbigging) Commissioning Health and Wellbeing, 2013. *Recreations:* medieval history, art history, walking, cycling. *Address:* Bankfield House, Whitebeck Lane, Priest Hutton, Carnforth, Lancs LA6 1JL.

HEGINBOTHAM, Prof. Wilfred Brooks, OBE 1978; FREng; Director General, Production Engineering Research Association of Great Britain (PERA), Melton Mowbray, 1979–84; *b* 9 April 1924; *s* of Fred and Alice Heginbotham; *m* 1957, Marjorie Pixton; three *d. Educ:* Manchester Univ. (UMIST). BScTech 1949; MScTech 1950; PhD (Manchester) 1956; DSc (Manchester) 1979. FIProdE; MIMechE; FREng (FEng 1985); FRSA. Started in industry as wood pattern maker; part-time courses to HNC, 1938–46; Walter Preston Schol., Manchester Coll. of Tech., 1946; joined staff, 1951; Lectr in Production Engineering subjects, UMIST, 1951–58; industrial experience for 10 years; Nottingham University: Sen. Lectr, 1958; started first BSc course in Prodn Engrg in UK, 1961; Head of Dept of Prodn Engrg and Prodn Management, 1961–63; Cripps Prof., 1963–79; Dean, Faculty of Applied Science, 1967–71; Special Prof. of Prodn Engrg, 1983–86; Prof. Emeritus, 1990. Hon. Prof., Dept of Engrg, Univ. of Warwick, 1984–89; Vis. Prof., Univ. of RI, USA, 1987; Vis. Sen. Res. Fellow, Dept of Mech. Engrg, Univ. of Birmingham, 1989–. Developed group to study Automatic Assembly Systems and Industrial Robot devices, including computer vision and tactile sense, and co-operated with industry in development of advanced automation equipment. Chm. Org. Cttee for establishment of Brit. Robot Assoc., 1977, Chm. of Council, 1977–80, Pres., 1980–84. Editor-in-Chief: The Industrial Robot; Assembly Automation; Advanced Manufacturing Technology Journal. Hon. DTech Scis Eindhoven, 1981; Hon. DSc Aston, 1983. Engelberger Award, Robot Inst. of America, 1983. *Publications:* Programmable Assembly, 1984; (ed with D. T. Pham) Robot Grippers, 1986; contribs to Encyc. Brit. on Robot Devices and to prof. pubns on metal cutting, automated assembly, industrial robots, artificial intelligence and production processes. *Recreations:* gliding, model aircraft construction and operation (radio controlled). *Address:* 7 Paddocks View, Eaton Grange, Long Eaton, Notts NG10 3QF. *T:* (0115) 946 3250.

HEGLEY, John Richard; freelance poet and performer; *b* 1 Oct. 1953; *s* of René Robert Hegley and Joan Hegley; one *d. Educ:* Univ. of Bradford (BSc Hons Social Scis (European Lit./Hist. of Ideas)). Actor/musician: Inter-action Prof. Dogg's Troup, 1978; Soapbox Children's Th., 1979; John Peel Radio sessions, 1983–84; presenter, Word of Mouth, TV poetry series, 1990; BBC on-line Poet-in-Residence, 1998; played Vernon Hines in Pyjama Game, 1999; Hearing with Hegley, BBC Radio series, 1997–99; performed, 21st Edinburgh Fest., 2004; Keats House Poet-in-Residence, 2012. Hon. LLD Luton 2000. *Publications:* Glad to Wear Glasses, 1990; Can I Come Down Now, Dad?, 1992; Five Sugars, Please, 1993; Love Cuts, 1995; The Family Pack, 1997; Beyond Our Kennel, 1998; Dog, 2000; My Dog is a Carrot, 2002; The Sound of Paint Drying, 2003; Uncut Confetti, 2006; Stanley's Stick, 2012; Peace, Love and Potatoes, 2012; I am a Poetato, 2013; New and Selected Potatoes, 2013. *Address:* Troika, 10a Christina Street, EC2A 4PA.

HEIDEN, Paul; Chairman, Intelligent Energy plc, since 2012; *b* 3 Feb. 1957; *s* of Ronald Joseph and Hilda Primrose Heiden; *m* 1979, Susan; one *s* one *d. Educ:* Stratford Grammar Sch.; Imperial Coll., London (BSc 1st cl. Hons Biol.). ARCS; ACA. Accountant, Peat Marwick Mitchell, 1979–84; Financial Controller: Mercury Communications, 1984–88; Hanson plc, 1988–92; Rolls-Royce: Finance Dir, Aerospace, 1992–97; Bd Dir, 1997–2002; Man. Dir, Industrial Businesses, 1997–99; Finance Dir, 1999–2002; Chief Exec., FKI plc, 2003–08; Chm., Talaris Ltd, 2008–12. Non-executive Director: Bunzl, 1999–2005; Filtrona, 2005–06; United Utilities plc, 2006–13; London Stock Exchange Gp plc, 2010–; Meggitt plc, 2010–. *Recreations:* golf, ski-ing, spectator sports. *Clubs:* Nottingham Golf (Hollinwell); Ratcliffe on Trent Golf; Loch Lomond Golf.

HEIGL, Peter Richard; HM Diplomatic Service, retired; Resident Deputy High Commissioner, Republic of Kiribati, 2004–06; *b* 21 Feb. 1943; *s* of late Joseph William Heigl and Violet Heigl (*née* Gatti); *m* 1965, Sally Lupton; three *s* one *d. Educ:* Worthing Technical High Sch. Min. of Power, 1963–66; Min. of Technology, 1966–70; DTI, 1970–74; FCO, 1974; served: Kuala Lumpur, 1974–78; Accra, 1978–81; FCO, 1981–84; 1st Sec., Riyadh, 1984–86; Consul (Commercial), Jedda, 1986–89; FCO, 1989–91; Dep. Head of Mission, Khartoum, 1991–93; Chargé, Phnom Penh, 1994; Dep. Head of Mission, Kathmandu, 1994–99; High Comr to the Bahamas, 1999–2003. *Recreations:* family, travel, swimming, reading, local history. *Address:* c/o Foreign and Commonwealth Office, King Charles Street, SW1A 2AH.

HEILBRON, Hilary Nora Burstein; QC 1987; *b* 2 Jan. 1949; *d* of Dr Nathaniel Burstein and Dame Rose Heilbron, DBE. *Educ:* Huyton College; Lady Margaret Hall, Oxford (MA). Called to the Bar, Gray's Inn, 1971; Bencher, 1995. DTI Inspector into Blue Arrow plc, 1989–91. Chairman: London Common Law and Commercial Bar Assoc., 1992–93; Jt Gen. Council of Bar and Law Soc. indep. working party into civil justice, 1993. Dir, The City

Disputes Panel Ltd, 1994–2007 (Chm., 2006–07). Vice-Chm., Marshall Aid Commemoration Commn, 1998–2002; Member: Adv. Council, Centre for Dispute Resolution, 1996–2002; Civil Justice Council, 1998–2002; Bar Assoc. of NSW. Vice-Pres., Assoc. of Lancastrians in London, 2011–. *Publications:* A Practical Guide to International Arbitration in London, 2008; Rose Heilbron, Legal Pioneer of the 20th Century: inspiring advocate who became England's first woman judge, 2012. *Recreations:* travel, gardening. *Address:* Brick Court Chambers, 7–8 Essex Street, WC2R 3LD. *T:* (020) 7379 3550.

HEIM, Paul Emil, CMG 1988; Chairman, Taxation Disciplinary Board (formerly Tribunal), 2000–04 (Vice Chairman, Appeal Committee, 2004–08); *b* 23 May 1932; *s* of George Heim and Hedy Heim (*née* Herz); *m* 1962, Elizabeth, *er d* of late Lt-Col G. M. Allen, MBE; one *s* two *d*. *Educ:* Prince of Wales School, Nairobi; King's Coll., Univ. of Durham (LLB). Called to the Bar, Lincoln's Inn, 1955, Bencher, 1986. Dep. Registrar, Supreme Court of Kenya, then Sen. Dep. Registrar, Magistrate and Acting Registrar (HMOCS), 1954–65; admitted Advocate, Supreme Court, 1959; Administrator, European Court of Human Rights, Strasbourg, 1965, European Commn of Human Rights, Strasbourg, 1966; Principal Administrator, Political Directorate, Council of Europe, 1967, Dep. Head, Private Office, 1969; Head of Div., then Dir, European Parlt, 1973–81; Registrar, European Court of Justice, 1982–88; Pres., Heads of Admin of EC Instns, 1986–88; Special Advr, European Court of Justice, 1988–89; a Chairman: Financial Services Tribunal, 1988–2002; Value Added Tax Tribunal, 1989–2003; Pres., FIMBRA Appeal Tribunals, 1990–2001; a Dep. Chm., PIA Appeal Tribunal, 1994–2002. Vis. Prof., Leicester Univ., 1988–2000; Hon. Res. Fellow, Univ. of Exeter, 1988–. Chm., George Heim Meml Trust, 1998–; Dep. Chm., 1999–2009, Chm., 2009–14, Luxembourg Soc.; Chm., Langport Area Develt Trust (formerly Langport Forum), 2007–09 (Dep. Chm., 2001–06). Treas., Somerset Anne Frank Awards, 2013–. Grand Officer, Order of Merit (Luxembourg), 1998. *Address:* Wearne Wyche, Langport, Somerset TA10 9AA.

HEIN, Prof. Jotun John; Professor of Bioinformatics, University of Oxford, and Fellow of University College, Oxford, since 2001; *b* Denmark, 19 July 1956; *s* of Piet Hein and Gerd Erikson; two *d*. *Educ:* Aarhus Univ. (Licentiate in Sci. 1990). Asst Prof., 1990–94, Associate Prof., 1994–2001, Aarhus Univ. *Recreations:* reading, golf, tennis, badminton. *Address:* Department of Statistics, University of Oxford, 1 South Parks Road, Oxford OX1 3TG. *T:* (01865) 272860.

HEINE, Prof. Volker, FRS 1974; Professor of Theoretical Physics, University of Cambridge, 1976–97; Fellow of Clare College, Cambridge, since 1960; *b* 19 Sept. 1930; *m* 1955, M. Daphne Hines; one *s* two *d*. *Educ:* Otago Univ. (MSc, DipHons); Cambridge Univ. (PhD). FInstP. Demonstrator, Cambridge Univ., 1958–63, Lectr 1963–70; Reader in Theoretical Physics, 1970–76. Vis. Prof., Univ. of Chicago, 1965–66; Vis. Scientist, Bell Labs, USA, 1970–71. For. Mem., Max-Planck Inst., Stuttgart, 1980–. Fellow, Amer. Phys. Soc., 1987. Maxwell Medal, Inst. of Physics, 1972; Royal Medal, Royal Soc., 1993; Paul Dirac Medal, Inst. of Physics, 1993; Max Born Medal, Inst. of Physics and German Physical Soc., 2001. *Publications:* Group Theory in Quantum Mechanics, 1960; (jtly) Solid State Physics Vol. 24, 1970, Vol. 35, 1980; articles in Proc. Royal Soc., Jl Physics, Physical Review, etc. *Address:* Cavendish Laboratory, 19 J. J. Thomson Avenue, Cambridge CB3 0HE.

HEINEY, Paul; freelance writer and broadcaster; *b* 20 April 1949; *s* of Norbert Wisniewski and Evelyn Mardlin; name changed to Heiney by Deed Poll, 1971; *m* 1980, Elizabeth Mary Purves, *qv*; one *d* (one *s* decd). *Educ:* Parson Cross Primary Sch., Sheffield; High Storrs Grammar Sch. for Boys. Stagehand, Birmingham Rep. Th., 1968; electrician, Mermaid Th., 1969; BBC: asst film recordist, 1969–71; Radio Humberside, 1971–74; television presenter, programmes include: That's Life!, 1978–82; In at the Deep End, 1982–85; Travel Show, 1984–87; Food and Drink, 1991; Watchdog, 2001–09; Trading Places, ITV, 1988–2000; Victorian Farming Year, ITV, 2002–05; Countrywise and Countrywise Kitchen, ITV, 2009–; BBC Radio, includes: reporter: Newsbeat, Radio 1, 1974–76; Today, Radio 4, 1976–78; Radio 2 (occasionally), 1984–96; End of the Line, Radio 4, 1993–94; A Year in Harness, Radio 4, 1996; Home Truths, 2005. Patron, Wolverstone Project, 2006–. Hon. DCL East Anglia, 2006. *Publications:* The Sailing Weekend Book, 1984 (Best Book of the Sea, King George's Fund for Sailors); The English and their Horses, 1987; In at the Deep End, 1989; Farming Times, 1993; Second Crop, 1994; George Soper's Horses, 1997; Ham and Pigs, 1998; Domino's Effect (novel), 1999; Golden Apples (novel), 1999; The Nuts and Bolts of Life, 2003; The Traditional Farming Year, 2004; Can Cows Walk Upstairs?, 2005; Maritime Britain, 2005; Do Cats Have Belly Buttons?, 2007; Farm Fatale, 2012; Can Crocodiles Cry, 2015; One Wild Song: a voyage in a lost son's wake, 2015. *Recreations:* sailing, ploughing with Suffolk Punches. *Address:* c/o Jo Gurnett, 7 Old Park Lane, W1K 1QR. *T:* (020) 7440 1850. *E:* pheiney@me.com. *Clubs:* Royal Cruising (Vice Cdre, 2014–); Suffolk Horse Society.

HEIS, Richard; Restructuring and Insolvency Partner, KPMG, since 1997; *b* Manchester, 26 May 1962; *s* of Jan and Valerie Ann Heis; *m* 1993, Elizabeth Anne Hill; two *s* one *d*. *Educ:* Stockport Grammar Sch.; Birmingham Univ. (LLB). Joined KPMG, 1983; auditor, London and Hong Kong, 1983–89; Restructuring and Insolvency Manager, London, 1989–97. Chair, Tech. Cttee, R3, 2007–10. Mem., Banking Liaison Panel, HM Treasury, 2009–. Liquidator: Barings Bank, 2001–; New Millennium Experience Co., 2001–; Supervisor, Marconi plc scheme, 2003–; Administrator: Connaught plc, 2010–; MF Global UK, 2011–. *Recreations:* golf, cycling, tennis, Listener crossword, Cornwall. *Address:* KPMG, 8 Salisbury Square, EC4Y 8BB. *T:* (020) 7694 3429. *E:* richard.heis@kpmg.co.uk. *Clubs:* Wildernesse Golf, St Enodoc Golf.

HEISBOURG, François; Special Adviser, Fondation pour la Recherche Stratégique, Paris, since 2005 (Director, 2001–05); *b* 24 June 1949; *s* of late Georges Heisbourg and of Hélène Heisbourg (*née* Pinet); *m* 1989, Elyette, *d* of Georges Levy; two *s*. *Educ:* Landon School, Bethesda, Maryland; Collège Stanislas, Paris; Inst. d'Etudes Politiques, Paris; Ecole Nationale d'Administration, Paris. French Foreign Ministry: Asst to Head of Economics Dept, 1978; Mem., Policy Planning Staff, 1979; 1st Sec., French Mission to UN, NY, 1979–81; Diplomatic Adviser to Minister of Defence, 1981–84. Vice-Pres., Thomson SA, Paris, 1984–87; Dir, IISS, 1987–92; Sen. Vice-Pres., Matra Défense-Espace, Paris, 1992–98; Hd, French Interministerial gp on study of internat. relations and strategic affairs, 1999–2000; Prof., Inst. d'Etudes Politiques, Paris, 1999–2001. Chairman: Geneva Centre for Security Policy, 1998–; IISS, 2001–. Member: Presidential White Paper Commn on Defence and Nat. Security, 2007–08, 2012–13; Internat. Commn on Nuclear Non-proliferation and Disarmament, 2008–10. Numerous foreign orders. *Publications:* Emiliano Zapata et la Révolution mexicaine, 1978; (with P. Boniface) La Puce, les Hommes et la Bombe, 1986; (contrib.) The Conventional Defence of Europe, 1986; (contrib.) Conventional Arms Control and East-West Security, 1989; (ed) The Changing Strategic Landscape, 1989; (ed) The Strategic Implications of Change in the Soviet Union, 1990; (contrib.) The Shape of the New Europe, 1992; (contrib.) Western Europe and the Gulf War, 1992; Les Volontaires de l'An 2000, 1995; Warfare, 1997; European Defence: making it work, 2000; Hyperterrorisme: la nouvelle guerre, 2001; La Fin de l'Occident? L'Amérique, l'Europe et le Moyen-Orient, 2005; (with J. L. Marret) Le Terrorisme en France Aujourd'hui, 2006; L'Épaisseur du Monde, 2007; Iran: le choix des armes?, 2007; Après Al Qaida, 2009; Vainqueurs et Vaincus, 2010; (ed) Les armes nucléaires ont-elles un avenir?, 2011; Espionnage et renseignement: le vrai dossier, 2012; La Fin du Rêve Européen, 2013; contribs to internat. jls. *Recreations:* hiking, old atlas collecting. *E:* f.heisbourg@frstrategie.org. *Club:* Travellers (Paris).

HEISER, Sir Terence Michael, (Sir Terry), GCB 1992 (KCB 1987; CB 1984); Permanent Secretary, Department of the Environment, 1985–92; *b* 24 May 1932; *s* of David and Daisy Heiser; *m* 1957, Kathleen Mary Waddle; one *s* two *d*. *Educ:* Grafton Road Primary Sch., Dagenham; London Evacuee Sch., Sunninghill, Berks; Windsor County Boys' Sch., Berks; Birkbeck Coll., Univ. of London; BA (Hons English). Served in RAF, 1950–52; joined Civil Service 1949, served with Colonial Office, Min. of Works, Min. of Housing and Local Govt; Principal Private Sec. to Sec. of State for the Environment, 1975–76; Under Secretary: Housing Directorate, 1976–79; Local Govt Finance Directorate, 1979–81; Dep. Sec., DoE, 1981–85. Non-exec. Director: Abbey National plc, 1992–2001; Sainsbury plc, 1992–2000; Wessex Water plc, 1993–98. Mem. Bd, PIA, 1994–2000; Mem., Senior Salaries Review Bd, Office of Manpower Econs, 1998–2003. Chm., Gen. Adv. Council, BBC, 1992–96. Mem., Adv. Panel on Spoliation, DCMS, 2000–. Mem., Exec. Cttee, 1993–2002, Southern Region Cttee, 2003–04, Nat. Trust; Mem., V&A Theatre Mus. Cttee, 2004–06 (Trustee, V&A Mus., 1993–2003); Trustee, Prince of Wales Phoenix Trust, 1996–2001. Governor, Birkbeck Coll., London, 1990–2002; Mem. Council, Sussex Univ., 1999–2008. Freeman, City of London, 1990. Hon. Fellow, Birkbeck Coll., London, 1988. Hon. DLitt Bradford, 1988. *Recreations:* reading, walking, talking. *Club:* Garrick.

HELAISSI, Sheikh Abdulrahman Al-, Hon. GCVO; retired; Saudi Arabian Ambassador to the Court of St James's, 1966–76; *b* 24 July 1922. *Educ:* Universities of Cairo and London. Secretary to Embassy, London, 1947–54; Under-Sec., Min. of Agriculture, 1954–57; Head of Delegn to FAO, 1955–61; Ambassador to Sudan, 1957–60; Representative to UN, and to various confs concerned with health and agriculture; Delegate to Conf. of Non-aligned Nations, Belgrade, 1961; Ambassador: Italy and Austria, 1961–66; UK and Denmark (concurrently), 1966–76. Versed in Islamic Religious Law. *Publications:* The Rehabilitation of the Bedouins, 1959. *Address:* PO Box No 8062, Riyadh-11482, Saudi Arabia.

HELD, Prof. David Jonathan Andrew, PhD; Master, University College, and Professor, School of Government and International Relations, Durham University, since 2012; *b* London, 27 Aug. 1951; *s* of Peter Held and Gisela Held; three *s* one *d*. *Educ:* Univ. of Manchester Inst. of Sci. and Technol. (BSc 1st Cl. Hons Mgt Scis 1973); Massachusetts Inst. of Technol. (Kennedy Schol.; MSc 1975; PhD 1976); King's Coll., Cambridge. Jun. Res. Fellow, Wolfson Coll., Oxford, 1977–79; Fellow in Pols and Sociol., Univ. of Wales, Cardiff, 1977–79; Lectr in Politics, Univ. of York, 1979–82; Open University: Lectr, 1982–84, Sen. Lectr, 1984–91, in Social Scis; Prof. of Politics and Sociol., 1991–2000; London School of Economics and Political Science: Graham Wallas Prof. of Pol Sci., 2000–11 (Vis. Prof. of Pol Sci., 1999–2000); Co-Dir, LSE Global Governance, 2004–11. Dir, Polity Press, 1984–. Visiting Professor: Sciences Po, Paris, 2007–09; of Global Policy, Central European Univ., 2010–11; of Philos., LUISS Univ. Rome, 2011–. Gen. Editor, Global Policy Jl, 2009–. *Publications:* (ed jtly) Habermas: critical debates, 1982; (ed jtly) States and Societies, 1983; (ed jtly) State and Society in Contemporary Britain, 1984; (ed jtly) New Forms of Democracy, 1986; Models of Democracy, 1987, 3rd edn 2006; Introduction to Critical Theory: Horkheimer to Habermas, 1989; Political Theory and the Modern State, 1989; (ed jtly) Social Theory of Modern Societies, 1989; (ed) Political Theory Today, 1991; (ed jtly) Modernity and its Futures, 1992; (ed) Prospects for Democracy: north, south, east, west, 1993; Democracy and the Global Order: from the modern state to cosmopolitan governance, 1995; (ed jtly) Cosmopolitan Democracy: an agenda for a new world order, 1995; (ed jtly) Re-imagining Political Community, 1998; (jtly) Global Transformations: politics, economics and culture, 1999; (ed jtly) The Global Transformations Reader, 2000; (jtly) Globalization/Anti-Globalization, 2002, 2nd edn 2007; (ed jtly) Governing Globalization: power, authority and global governance, 2002; (ed) Taming Globalization, 2003; Global Covenant: the social democratic alternative to the Washington consensus, 2004; (ed jtly) American Power in the 21st Century, 2004; (jtly) Debating Globalization, 2005; (ed jtly) Global Governance and Public Accountability, 2005; (ed jtly) Global Inequality: patterns and explanations, 2007; (ed jtly) Globalization Theory: concepts and theories, 2007; (ed jtly) Progressive Foreign Policy, 2007; (ed jtly) Cultural Politics in a Global Age, 2008; Cosmopolitanism: ideals and realities, 2010; (ed jtly) The Cosmopolitan Reader, 2010; (ed jtly) Democracy and the Climate Change, 2011; (ed jtly) Handbook of Transnational Governance Innovations, 2011; (ed jtly) The Transformation of the Gulf, 2011; (jtly) Gridlock: why global cooperation is failing, 2013; (jtly) Climate Change Governance in Developing Countries, 2013; (jtly) The End of the American Century: from 9/11 to the Arab Spring, 2015; articles in learned jls incl. Political Studies, Media, Culture and Society, Parliamentary Affairs. *Recreations:* gym, running, music, arts. *Address:* University College, Durham University, Durham Castle, Palace Green, Durham DH1 3RW. *E:* david.held@durham.ac.uk.

HELE, Desmond George K.; *see* King-Hele.

HELIĆ, Baroness *cr* 2014 (Life Peer), of Millbank in the City of Westminster; **Arminka Helić;** Chief of Staff, 2006–15 and Senior Special Adviser, 2010–15 to Rt Hon. William Hague, MP; *b* Bosnia-Herzegovina; adopted British nationality, 2002. Expert on foreign, defence and security policy. Architect of Preventing Sexual Violence Initiative, 2012–. *Address:* House of Lords, SW1A 0PW.

HELLARD, Rebecca Jane; Director of Finance and Resources, Liverpool City Council, since 2012; *b* 11 July 1966; *d* of Hugh Somerled Matheson Macdonald and Sarah Jane Macdonald (*née* Tuffs); one *s* one *d*. *Educ:* Cambridge Coll. of Arts and Technol. (BA Hons Econs). ACCA 1995. Philips Financial Services, 1991–94; Manager, PricewaterhouseCoopers, 1994–97; Breckland Council: Finance and Performance Manager, 1997–99; Finance Dir, 1999–2002; Dep. Chief Exec., 2002–04; Chief Exec., 2004–06; Strategic Dir Corporate Services, Bradford CC, 2007–12. *Recreations:* sports - gym, running, swimming. *Address:* Liverpool City Council, Municipal Building, Dale Street, Liverpool L2 2DH.

HELLAWELL, Keith, QPM 1990; writer and broadcaster; Expert Adviser to Home Secretary on international drugs issues, 2001–02; Director, Huddersfield Rugby League Club, since 2002; *b* 18 May 1942; *s* of Douglas Hellawell and Ada Alice Hellawell (*née* Battye); *m* 1963, Brenda Hey; one *s* two *d*. *Educ:* Kirkburton Sec. Mod. Sch.; Dewsbury Tech. Coll.; Barnsley Coll. of Mining; Inst. of Criminol., Cambridge Univ.; London Univ. (LLB 1972); Cranfield Inst. of Tech. (MSc 1982); Police Staff Coll. Huddersfield Borough Police, 1962; seconded to Home Office, 1975–78, incl. service in NI; Asst Chief Constable, W Yorks Police, 1983; Dep. Chief Constable, Humberside Police, 1985; Chief Constable: Cleveland Police, 1990; W Yorks Police, 1993–98; UK Anti-Drugs Co-ordinator, 1998–2001. Advr, Crimestoppers Trust, 1994–. Chairman: Catapult Presentation plc, 2001; Sterience Ltd; Howells Associates; Goldshield Gp plc, 2006–09; Sports Direct, 2009–; non-executive Director: Evans of Leeds plc, 1998–99; Universal Vehicles Gp plc, 2001; Dalkia plc, 2002–06. Member: Adv. Council on Misuse of Drugs, 1994–98; Bd, Northern Counties Housing Assoc. Ltd, 1996–98; St John's Council, W Yorks, 1983–85 and 1993–; Council, NSPCC (Trustee, 1993–2000; Chm., Services to Children's Cttee, 1996–); Trustee, Children in Crisis. Mem., Editl Bd, Forensic Medicine Jl, 1996–. Hon. LLD Bradford, 1998; Hon. DSSc Leeds, 1998; Hon. DCL Huddersfield, 1998. OStJ 1996. *Publications:* The Outsider (autobiog.), 2002. *Recreations:* design, gardening, reading, sport.

HELLER, Angela Mary; *see* Flowers, A. M.

HELLER, Lucy Lauris; Chief Executive Officer, ARK, since 2012 (Managing Director, ARK Schools, since 2004); *b* London, 8 Feb. 1959; *d* of late Lukas Heller and Caroline Carter; *m* 1990, Sir Charles (Abraham Grierson) Elton, Bt, *qv* (marr. diss. 2007); one *s* one *d*; partner,

Sir Adrian (Frederick Melhuish) Smith, *qv*. *Educ:* Hampstead Comp. Sch.; Lady Margaret Hall, Oxford (BA Hons PPE). Banker, Bankers Trust, 1981–87; Man. Dir, Capital Mkts Gp, Manufacturers Hanover, 1987–90; Gp Treas., Booker, 1990–95; Exec. Chm., Verso, 1995–98; Gen. Manager, The Observer, Guardian Media Gp, 1998–99; Jt Man. Dir, TSL Education, 2000–03. Mem., Marshall Aid Commn, 2002–09. Mem. Bd, Bush Th., 1989–2005. Trustee: Centre for London; Promoting Equality in African Schs. *Publications:* Euro Commercial Paper, 1988. *Address:* ARK, 65 Kingsway, WC2B 6TD. *T:* (020) 3116 0710. *E:* lucy.heller@arkonline.org.

HELLER, Sir Michael Aron, Kt 2013; FCA; Chairman: London & Associated Properties plc, since 1977 (Director, since 1971); Bisichi Mining plc, since 1981 (Director, since 1972); non-executive Chairman, Electronic Data Processing plc, since 1977 (non-executive Director, since 1965); *b* London, 15 July 1936; *s* of Simon and Nettie Heller; *m* 1965, Morven Livingstone; two *s* one *d*. *Educ:* Harrogate Grammar Sch.; St Catharine's Coll., Cambridge (BA 1958; MA 1963; Fellow Commoner). ACA 1961, FCA 1971. Exec. Dir, Kenyon Son & Craven Ltd, 1961–68; Exec. Dir, 1968–70, non-exec. Dir, 1971–91, United Biscuit (Hldgs) plc. Dep. Chm., Centre for Policy Studies, 1993–. Hon. Fellow, UCL, 2007. Hon. Dr: Technion, Haifa, 2010; Sheffield Hallam, 2010. *Recreations:* walking, collecting modern British and French post-Impressionist paintings, opera, ballet. *Address:* 24 Bruton Place, W1J 6NE. *T:* (020) 7415 5000. *E:* M.Heller@lap.co.uk. *Club:* Royal Automobile.

HELLINGA, Dr Lotte, FBA 1990; Secretary, Consortium of European Research Libraries, 1994–2002; a Deputy Keeper, Humanities and Social Sciences, British Library, 1985–95; *b* 9 Sept. 1932; *d* of Arie Querido and Catharina Geertruida Querido (*née* Nagtegaal); *m* Wytze Hellinga (*d* 1985); one *s*. *Educ:* Univ. of Amsterdam. Lectr, then Sen. Lectr, Univ. of Amsterdam, 1967–76; Asst Keeper, British Liby, 1976–85. Vice Pres., Bibliographical Soc., 1996–2010. Correspondent, Royal Netherlands Acad. of Scis, 1989–. Gutenberg Preis, Mainz, 1989; Gold Medal, Bibliographical Soc., 2009; Bernard Breslauer Prize, Internat. League of Antiquarian Booksellers, 2010. *Publications:* The Fifteenth Century Printing Types of the Low Countries, 1966; Caxton in Focus, 1982; (ed jtly) The Cambridge History of the Book in Britain, vol. III, 1999; Impresores, editores, correctores y cajistas Siglo XV, 2006; Catalogue of Books printed in the XVth century now in the British Library, vol. XI (England), 2007; Printing in England in the Fifteenth Century, 2009; William Caxton and Early Printing in England, 2010; Texts in Transit: manuscripts to proof and print in the fifteenth century, 2014; numerous articles in learned jls. *Address:* 40A Canonbury Square, N1 2AW. *T:* (020) 7359 2083.

HELLIWELL, Prof. John Richard, DPhil, DSc; FInstP, FRSC, FRSB; Professor of Structural Chemistry, University of Manchester, 1989–2012, now Emeritus; *b* 19 Sept. 1953; *s* of Henry Smith Helliwell and Amy (*née* Southam); *m* 1978, Madeleine Berry; one *s* one *d* (and one *s* decd). *Educ:* Ossett Sch.; Univ. of York (BSc 1st cl. Hons Physics 1974; DSc 1996); Balliol Coll., Univ. of Oxford (DPhil Molecular Biophysics 1978). CPhys, FInstP 1986; CChem, FRSC 1995; CBiol, FRSB (FIBiol 1998). MRC Res. Asst and Jun. Res. Fellow, Linacre Coll., Oxford, 1978; Lectr in Biophysics, Keele Univ., jtly with SERC Daresbury Lab., 1979–83; SSO, then PSO, SERC Daresbury Lab., 1983–85; Lectr in Physics, York Univ., 1985–88; part-time with SERC, subseq. CCLRC, then STFC, Daresbury Lab., 1985–93, 2001–06, Hon. Scientist, 2007–; CCLRC Dir of Synchrotron Radiation Sci., Daresbury Lab., 2002. Vis. Res. Scholar, Cornell Univ., 1994; Visiting Professor: Univ. of Chicago, 1994; of Crystallography, Birkbeck Coll., London Univ., 2002–. Pres., Eur. Crystallographic Assoc., 2006–09. Leader, UK Delegn, World Congress of Biophysics, New Delhi, 1999; Internat. Union of Crystallography Rep. to Internat. Council of Scientific and Tech. Inf., 2005–14, and to Cttee on Data for Sci. and Technol., 2012–; Chm. and Mem., Sci. Adv. Cttee, Spanish Nat. Synchrotron 'ALBA', 2010–14; Chairman: ALBA Beamtime Panel, 2011–14; Eur. Spallation Neutron Source Neutron Macromolecular Crystallography Sci. and Tech. Adv. Panel, 2013–. Conference Lectures: Yugoslav-Italian Crystallographic Assoc., 1989; Soc. of Crystallographers of Australia, 1994 (1987 Fellow (Hon.), 1994); British Crystallographic Assoc., 1995; 2nd Internat. Conf. on Life Science, Japan, 1996; Dame Kathleen Lonsdale Meml, British Crystallographic Assoc., 2011; other Lectures: Ilyas Haneef Meml, Univ. of Leeds, 1993; Herzenberg Symposium, Yale Univ., 1995; Chem. Dept Dedication, Univ. of Toledo, 1998; K. Banerjee Meml, and Silver Medal, Indian Assoc. for Cultivation of Sci., Calcutta, 2000; 150th Anniv. W. L. Bragg, Univ. of Manchester, 2001; Weizmann Inst., Israel, 2002; Royal Instn, 2004; US Nat. Liby of Medicine, Bethesda, 2006. Transactions Symposium Orgnr, Amer. Crystallographic Assoc., 1999; Chm. of Prog. Cttee, British Crystallographic Assoc. Annual Conf. 2015. Mem., Gen. Assembly, Univ. of Manchester, 2004– (Mem. Court, UMIST, 1996–2004). Hon. Mem., Nat. Inst. of Chem., Slovenia, 1997–. Jt Main Ed., Jl Synchrotron Radiation, 1994–99; Editor-in-Chief, Internat. Union of Crystallography's Jls, 1996–2005; Co-Editor: Jl Applied Crystallography, 1995–2014; Crystallography Reviews, 2006–. Patterson Award, Amer. Crystallographic Assoc., 2014. *Publications:* Macromolecular Crystallography with Synchrotron Radiation, 1992; (ed jtly) Time-resolved Macromolecular Crystallography, 1992; (ed jtly) Synchrotron Radiation in the Biosciences, 1994; (ed jtly) Time-resolved Diffraction, 1997; (jtly) Macromolecular Crystallization and Crystal Perfection, 2010; original res. papers and reviews in scientific jls. *Recreations:* family, cycling (Mem., Cycle Touring Club). *Address:* c/o School of Chemistry, University of Manchester, Oxford Road, Manchester M13 9PL. *T:* (0161) 275 4970, *Fax:* (0161) 275 4598. *E:* john.helliwell@manchester.ac.uk.

HELLYER, Hon. Paul Theodore; PC (Canada) 1957; FRSA 1973; Syndicated Columnist, Toronto Sun, 1974–84; *b* Waterford, Ont, Canada, 6 Aug. 1923; *s* of A. S. Hellyer and Lulla M. Anderson; *m* 1st, 1945, Ellen Jean (*d* 2004), *d* of Henry Ralph, Toronto, Ont; two *s* one *d*; 2nd, 2005, Sandra Dorothy Bussiere. *Educ:* Waterford High Sch., Ont; Curtiss-Wright Techn. Inst. of Aeronautics, Glendale, Calif; University of Toronto (BA). Fleet Aircraft Mfg Co., Fort Erie, Ont. Wartime service, RCAF and Cdn Army. Propr Mari-Jane Fashions, Toronto, 1945–56; Treas., Curran Hall Ltd, Toronto, 1950 (Pres., 1951–62). Elected to House of Commons, 1949; re-elected, 1953; Parly Asst to Hon. Ralph Campney, Minister of Nat. Defence, 1956; Associate Minister of Nat. Defence, 1957; defeated in gen. elections of June 1957 and March 1958; re-elected to House of Commons in by-election Dec. 1958 and again re-elected June 1962, April 1963, Nov. 1965, June 1968, and Oct. 1972; defeated gen. election July 1974; Minister of National Defence, 1963–67; Minister of Transport, 1967–69, and Minister i/c Housing, 1968–69; resigned 1969 on question of principle relating to housing. Chm., Federal Task Force on Housing and Urban Develt, 1968. Served as a Parly Rep. to NATO under both L and C administrations. Joined Parly Press Gallery, Oct. 1974. Distinguished visitor, York Univ., 1969–70. Founder and Leader, Action Canada party, 1971; joined Progressive Cons. Party, 1972; Candidate for leadership of Progressive Cons. Party, Feb. 1976; re-joined Liberal Party, Nov. 1982, resigned Dec. 1996; Leader, Canadian Action Party, 1997–2004. Exec. Dir, The Canada Uni Assoc., 1991–92. *Publications:* Agenda: a Plan for Action, 1971; Exit Inflation, 1981; Jobs for All—Capitalism on Trial, 1984; Canada at the Crossroads, 1990; Damn the Torpedoes, 1990; Funny Money: a common sense alternative to mainline economics, 1994; Surviving the Global Financial Crisis: the economics of hope for Generation X, 1996; Arundel Lodge: a little bit of old Muskoka, 1996; The Evil Empire: globalization's darker side, 1997; Stop: think, 1999; Goodbye Canada, 2001; One Big Party: to keep Canada independent, 2003; Light at the End of the Tunnel: a survival plan for the human species, 2010; A Miracle in Waiting: economics that make sense, 2010; The Money Mafia: a world in crisis, 2014. *Recreations:* philately, music. *Address:* Suite 506, 65 Harbour Square, Toronto, ON M5J 2L4, Canada. *Club:* National.

HELM, James Ernest; Director of Communications, Department for International Development, since 2010; *b* Guisborough, N Yorks, 3 Sept. 1968; *s* of Ernest Helm and Marion Helm; *m* 2000, Charlotte Coleman-Smith; three *s*. *Educ:* Stokesley Sch., N Yorks; Trinity Hall, Cambridge (BA Social and Pol Sci. 1991; MA). Voluntary teacher, South Africa, 1992; reporter, Newcastle Evening Chronicle, 1992–94; BBC News: correspondent, producer, presenter, 1994–2007; Dublin Corresp., 2002–07; PR consultant, Blue Rubicon, and freelance writer, 2007–09; Client Dir, COI, 2009–10. Mem., Stokesley Agricl Soc. *Recreations:* family time, playing and watching sport esp. Middlesbrough FC, walking, all news and current affairs. *Address:* Department for International Development, 22 Whitehall, SW1A 2EG. *E:* j-helm@dfid.gov.uk. *W:* www.twitter.com/jameshelm1.

HELM, Marie Theresa C.; *see* Conte-Helm.

HELME, Nicola Margaret; *see* Padfield, N. M.

HELME, Philippa Ann; Principal Clerk, Table Office, House of Commons, since 2014; *b* Binfield, Berks, 27 Aug. 1960; *d* of late Wing Comdr James Michael Helme, DFC, AFC and Diana Wentworth Helme (*née* Howitt); *m* 1988, Robin Stephen Galliver; two *s* three *d*. *Educ:* Sherborne Sch. for Girls; St Anne's Coll., Oxford (BA 1981). House of Commons, 1983–: Sec. to Chm. of Ways and Means, 1992–95; Clerk: Welsh Affairs Cttee, 1995–2000; Sci. and Technol. Cttee, 2000–02; on secondment as Parly Advr, Cabinet Office, 2002–05; Clerk, Defence Cttee, 2005–07; Hd, Office of the Chief Exec., 2008–10; Deputy Hd, Cttee Office, 2010–14. *Address:* House of Commons, SW1A 0AA. *T:* (020) 7219 3312. *E:* helmep@parliament.uk.

See also N. M. Padfield.

HELMER, Roger; Member for East Midlands, European Parliament, since 1999 (C, 1999–2012, UK Ind, since 2012); *b* 25 Jan. 1944; *s* of Charles Henry Helmer and Nellie Ethel Helmer; *m* 1st, 1967, Veronica Logan (marr. diss. 1984); one *s* one *d*; 2nd, 1987, Sara Thomas (*née* Winterbottom). *Educ:* King Edward VI Sch., Southampton; Churchill Coll., Cambridge (BA, MA). Various mkting and gen. mgt posts with major multinationals, Procter & Gamble, Readers' Digest, and Guinness Plc, UK and overseas, especially E and SE Asia, 1965–98. Hon. Chm., Freedom Assoc., 2007–. *Recreation:* walking the dog. *Address:* 21 Manor Walk, Coventry Road, Market Harborough, Leics LE16 9BP.

HELMORE, Roy Lionel, CBE 1980; Principal, Cambridgeshire College of Arts and Technology, 1977–86; Fellow of Hughes Hall, Cambridge, 1982–94, now Emeritus Fellow; *b* 8 June 1926; *s* of Lionel Helmore and Ellen Helmore (*née* Gibbins); *m* 1969, Margaret Lilian Martin. *Educ:* Montrose Academy; Edinburgh Univ. (BScEng); MA (Cantab). FIET. Crompton Parkinson Ltd, 1947–49; Asst Lectr, Peterborough Techn. Coll., 1949–53; Lectr, subseq. Sen. Lectr, Shrewsbury Techn. Coll., 1953–57; Head of Electrical Engrg and Science, Exeter Techn. Coll., 1957–61; Principal, St Albans Coll. of Further Education, 1961–77. Association of Principals of Colleges: Hon. Sec., 1968–71; Pres., 1972–73; Hon. Treasurer, 1983–86; Chm., of Council, Assoc. of Colls of Further and Higher Educn, 1987–88. Member: BBC Further Educn Adv. Council, 1967–73; Air Transport and Travel ITB, 1967–73; Technician Educn Council, 1973–79 (Vice-Chm.); Manpower Services Commn, 1974–82; RAF Trng and Educn Adv. Cttee, 1976–79; Chm., Trng and Further Educn Cons. Gp, 1977–82. JP St Albans, 1964–78. Hon. DEd Anglia Ruskin, 2008. *Publications:* CCAT—a brief history, 1989. *Recreations:* gardening, watercolours, bowls. *Address:* 31 Saffron Lodge, Radwinter Road, Saffron Walden, Essex CB11 3UZ. *T:* (01799) 523981.

HELTAY, Laszlo Istvan; Founder and Music Director, Academy of St Martin in the Fields Chorus, 1975–99; *b* Budapest, 5 Jan. 1930; *s* of Laszlo Heltay and Gizella Somogy; *m* 1964, Hilary Nicholson. *Educ:* Franz Liszt Acad. of Music, Budapest (MA); Merton Coll., Oxford (MLitt; Hon. Fellow, 1997). Associate Conductor, NZBC Symphony Orchestra and Dir, NZ Opera Co., 1964–67; Conductor, Phoenix Opera Co., 1970–73; Founder and Music Dir, Brighton Fest. Chorus, 1968–95; Dir of Music, Royal Choral Soc., 1985–95; Music Dir, Chorus of Radio Televisión Española SA, Madrid, 1997–2002. Has conducted major orchestras including: Philharmonia, Royal Philharmonic, London Philharmonic, Dresden Philharmonic, Dallas Symphony, Budapest Philharmonic; also radio orchestras and choirs. Choral music for film, Amadeus, 1984. Has made recordings. Hon. DMus Sussex, 1995. Internat. Kodaly Medal, 1982. *Recreations:* chess, reading, dog-walking.

HELY-HUTCHINSON, family name of **Earl of Donoughmore**.

HELY HUTCHINSON, Hon. Timothy Mark; Group Chief Executive, Hachette UK (formerly Chief Executive, Hachette Livre UK), since 2004; *b* 26 Oct. 1953; *s* of Earl of Donoughmore, *qv* and late Sheila (*née* Parsons). *Educ:* Eton Coll. (Oppidan Schol.); Magdalen Coll., Oxford (William Doncaster Schol.; MA Mod. Langs and Phil.). Various appts, Macmillan Publishers, 1975–82; Managing Director: Macdonald & Co. (Publishers) Ltd, 1982–86; Headline Book Publishing PLC, 1986–93; Chief Exec., Hodder Headline Ltd, 1993–2004. Director: WH Smith plc, 1999–2004; Inflexion plc, 2000–03; Chm., WH Smith News, 2001–04. Dir, Publishers Assoc., 1998–2004. Venturer of the Year Award, Brit. Venture Capital Assoc., 1990. *Recreations:* opera, horse-racing, bridge, scuba diving. *Address:* Hachette UK Ltd, Carmelite House, 50 Victoria Embankment, EC4 0DZ. *Club:* Athenæum.

HEMANS, Simon Nicholas Peter, CMG 1992; CVO 1983; HM Diplomatic Service, retired; Partner, Cranmore Co., 1997–2001; *b* 19 Sept. 1940; *s* of late Brig. Peter Rupert Hemans, CBE, and Margaret Estelle Hemans (*née* Melsome); *m* 1970, Ursula Martha Naef; three *s* one *d*. *Educ:* Sherborne; London School of Economics (BScEcon). Joined Foreign Office, 1964; British Embassy, Moscow, 1966–68; FO, 1968–69; Dep. Commissioner, Anguilla, March–Oct. 1969; FO, 1969–71; UK Mission to UN, New York, 1971–75; British Embassy, Budapest, 1975–79; FO, 1979–81; Dep. High Comr, Nairobi, 1981–84; Head of Chancery, Moscow, 1985–87; Head of Soviet Dept, FCO, 1987–90; Asst Under-Sec. of State (Africa), FCO, 1990–92; Ambassador, Ukraine, 1992–95; High Comr to Kenya, 1995–97. *Publications:* trans., Savchuk, The Streets of Kiev, 1996. *Recreations:* travel, guide at two National Trust houses in Hampshire and at London Bus Museum at Brooklands. *Address:* 73 Cranmore Lane, Aldershot, Hants GU11 3AP.

HEMERY, David Peter, CBE 2003 (MBE 1969); Founder and Co-Director, 21st Century Legacy, since 2007; *b* 18 July 1944; *s* of Peter Ronald Bentley Hemery and Eileen Beatrice Price; *m* 1981, Vivian Mary Bruford; two *s*. *Educ:* Boston Univ. (BSc Internat. Business 1968; DEd Social Psychology 1984); St Catherine's Coll., Oxford (CertEd 1970); Harvard Univ. (MEd 1972). Commonwealth Games: Gold Medal, 110m Hurdles, 1966, 1970; Captain, England Team, 1970; Olympic Games: Gold Medal, 400m Hurdles, 1968 (World Record); Bronze Medal, 400m Hurdles, 1972; Silver Medal, 4x400m, 1972. Teacher, Coach and Housemaster, Millfield Sch., 1970–71 and 1972–73; Dir, Sobell Sports Centre, 1973–75; Teacher and Coach, Boston Univ., 1976–83; coaching course for Nat. Coaching Foundn, 1983–85; mgt trng. Mem., Nat. Cttee, 1999–, and Exec., 2001– (Vice Chm., 2004–), BOA; Pres., UK Athletics, 1998–2002; Chm., Confedn of British Sport, 2006–08. Dir, Developing Potential Ltd, 1997–2010; Dep. Chm., Performance Consultants Internat. Ltd, 2006–11. Pres., Marlborough Jr AC, 2003–. Coach and Advr, sch. to internat. level; wrote prog. for schs, Be the Best You Can Be!, secondary version, 2008, primary version, 2011. Patron, British Assoc. of Sport and Exercise Medicine, 2009–. Eur. Olympic Laurel Award, Eur. Olympic Cttee, 2011. *Publications:* Another Hurdle (autobiog.), 1975; The Pursuit of Sporting Excellence, 1986, 2nd edn as Sporting Excellence: what makes a champion, 1991; Athletics in Action, 1987; Winning without Drugs, 1989; How to Help Children Find the Champion

Within Themselves, 2005. *Recreations:* family, sport, walking and running, films, reading on spiritual potential. *Address:* White Acre, Fyfield, Marlborough, Wilts SN8 1PX. *T:* (01672) 861676.

HEMINGFORD, 3rd Baron *cr* 1943, of Watford; **Dennis Nicholas Herbert;** Deputy Chief Executive, Westminster Press, 1992–95 (Editorial Director, 1974–92); *b* 25 July 1934; *s* of 2nd Baron Hemingford and Elizabeth McClare (*d* 1979), *d* of Col J. M. Clark, Haltwhistle, Northumberland; *S* father, 1982; known professionally as Nicholas Herbert; *m* 1958, Jennifer Mary Toresen Bailey (OBE 1997), DL, *d* of F. W. Bailey, Harrogate; one *s* three *d*. *Educ:* Oundle Sch.; Clare Coll., Cambridge (MA). Reuters Ltd, 1956–61; The Times: Asst Washington Corresp., 1961–65; Middle East Corresp., 1965–68; Dep. Features Editor, 1968–70; Editor, Cambridge Evening News, 1970–74. Vice-Pres., Guild of British Newspaper Editors, 1979, Pres., 1980–81. Mem. Bd, Assoc. of British Editors (Hon. Sec., 1985–95), 1985–95. Member: Council, Europa Nostra, 1999–2005; Culture Cttee, UK Commn, UNESCO, 2000–04; Council, Friends of British Library, 2005–11; Council, U3A, Cambridge, 2010–12; Chm., East Anglia Regl Cttee, Nat. Trust, 1990–2000. Pres., Huntingdonshire Family History Soc., 1985–2013. Trustee: Bell Educnl Trust, 1985–90; Ely Cathedral Restoration Trust, 1993–2014. (Jtly) Self Publisher of Year Award, 2010. *Publications:* Successive Journeys: a family in four continents, 2008 (First Prize, non-fiction, Self Publishing Awards, David St John Thomas Charitable Trust and Writing Mag., 2010). *Heir: s* Hon. Christopher Dennis Charles Herbert [*b* 4 July 1973; *m* 2009, Chey Louise Fabing, *o d* of Mrs Anne Fabing; one *s* one *d*]. *Address:* The Coach House, 4 Common Lane, Hemingford Abbots, Huntingdon PE28 9AN. *T:* (01480) 466234.

See also Lady Goodhart, H. T. Moggridge.

HEMINGWAY, Prof. Janet, CBE 2012; PhD; FRS 2011; FMedSci; Professor of Insect Molecular Biology and Director, Liverpool School of Tropical Medicine, University of Liverpool, since 2001; Chief Executive Officer, Gates Foundation Innovative Vector Control Consortium, since 2005; *b* 13 June 1957; *d* of Brian Hemingway and Mollie Hemingway; one *d*. *Educ:* Sheffield Univ. (BSc 1st cl. Genetics); LSHTM, London Univ. (PhD). Lectr, Univ. of California, Riverside, 1981–82; MRC Res. Fellow, 1982–84, Royal Soc. Jun. Res. Fellow and Sen. Lectr, 1984–94, LSHTM; Prof. of Molecular Entomology, Cardiff Univ., 1994–2001. Foreign Mem., NAS, USA, 2009. FMedSci 2006. Hon. FRCP 2008. Hon. DSc Sheffield, 2009. Sci. and Technol. Award, Welsh Woman of the Year, 2000; Public service, BT Merseyside Woman of the Year 2003. *Publications:* over 200 articles in scientific jls. *Recreations:* breaking and riding Arabian horses, squash, tennis, ski-ing, reading. *Address:* Liverpool School of Tropical Medicine, Pembroke Place, Liverpool L3 5QA. *E:* hemingway@liverpool.ac.uk.

HEMINGWAY, Peter, FCA; Director and Chief General Manager, Leeds Permanent Building Society, 1982–87; *b* 19 Jan. 1926; *s* of William Edward and Florence Hemingway; *m* 1952, June Maureen, *d* of Maurice and Lilian A. Senior. *Educ:* Leeds College of Commerce. With John Gordon, Walton & Co., Chartered Accountants, Leeds, 1941–62, Partner 1959–62; Director, Provincial Registrars Ltd, 1955–62; joined Leeds Permanent Bldg Soc. as Secretary, 1962. Local Dir (Leeds), Royal Insurance (UK) Ltd, 1983–93; Dir, Homeowners Friendly Soc., 1983–86. Hon. Sec. 1970–82, Vice-Chm. 1982–84, Chm. 1984–86, Yorkshire and North Western Assoc. of Building Societies; Vice Pres., Northern Assoc. of Building Socs, 1988–96; Mem. Council: Building Societies Assoc., 1981–87; Chartered Building Societies Inst., 1982–87. *Recreations:* travel, motor racing, music, gardening. *Address:* Old Barn Cottage, Kearby, near Wetherby, Yorks LS22 4BU. *T:* (0113) 288 6380.

HEMINGWAY, Wayne Andrew, MBE 2006; Co-Founder and Partner, HemingwayDesign, since 1999; Co-Founder, Vintage Festival, since 2009; *b* 19 Jan. 1961; *s* of Billy Two Rivers and Maureen Hemingway; *m* 1982, Gerardine Astin (MBE 2006); two *s* two *d*. *Educ:* University Coll. London (BSc Hons Geog. and Town Planning); Surrey Univ. (MA Fashion). Co-Founder (with Gerardine Hemingway), Red or Dead, 1982, sold, 1999 (Designer of the Year, 1996, 1997, 1998). Mem., Trustee Bd, Design Council CABE, 2010–. Vis. Prof. of Urban Studies, Northumberland Univ., 2004–. Hon. DA Wolverhampton, 2005. *Publications:* Just Above the Mantelpiece, 1998; Mass Market Classics - The Home, 2000. *Recreations:* running, general sport, my kids. *Address:* HemingwayDesign, 15 Wembley Park Drive, Wembley HA9 8HD. *T:* and *Fax:* (020) 8903 1074. *E:* info@hemingwaydesign.co.uk.

HEMINSLEY, Stephen John; Director of Finance, Planning and Performance, Employment and Wellbeing Groups, Department for Work and Pensions, 2009–10; *b* 19 Dec. 1951; *s* of John and Joyce Margaret Heminsley; *m* 1980, Yvonne Lesley Stephenson; one *s* one *d*. *Educ:* Joseph Leckie Sch., Walsall. CIPFA 1986. Department of Health and Social Security, later Department of Social Security: Office Supervisor, 1972–77; Internal Auditor, 1977–88; Project Manager, DSS Financial Systems Strategy, 1988–90; Director of: Finance (Contributions Agency), 1990–95; Business Planning (CSA), 1995–97; Strategy and Planning (Benefits Agency), 1997–2000; Pensions, subseq. Children and Pensioners, 2000–01; Dir, Nat. Services, 2001–04, Acting Dir Gen., Service Delivery, 2004, Bd of Inland Revenue; Dir, Orgnl Design, subseq. Orgnl Develt, 2004–07, Dir, Finance Transformation, 2007–08, HMRC; Dir, Corporate Services, then Dir of Finance and Corporate Services, Healthcare Commn, later Care Quality Commn, 2008–09. Mem., Central Govt Panel, CIPFA, 1997–. Trustee: Newbrough Town Hall, 2012–14; Dementia Care, Newcastle, 2014–. Mem., Warden Parish Council, Northumberland, 2013–. *Recreations:* walking, Rugby Union, family. *E:* steveheminsley@gmail.com. *Club:* Handsworth Rugby Union Football.

HEMM, Amanda Jane; *see* Roocroft, A. J.

HEMMING, John Alexander Melvin; *b* 16 March 1960; *s* of Melvin John and Doreen Hemming; *m* 1981, Christine Margaret (*née* Richards); one *s* two *d*; one *s* one *d* by Emily Rohaise Cox. *Educ:* King Edward's Sch., Birmingham; Magdalen Coll., Oxford (MA Physics 1981). Founded: John Hemming & Co., subseq. JHC plc, 1983; MarketNet, 1994; Music Mercia International, 1997. Mem., Birmingham CC, 1990–2008 (Dep. Leader, 2004–05; Leader, 1998–2005, Chm., 2005–, Lib Dem Gp). Contested: (L) Birmingham Hall Green, 1983; (L/All) Birmingham Small Heath, 1987; (Lib Dem) Birmingham Yardley, 1992, 1997, 2001. MP (Lib Dem) Birmingham Yardley, 2005–15; contested (Lib Dem) same seat, 2015. *Recreation:* jazz piano in John Hemming and the Sisters of Jazz.

HEMMING, John Henry, CMG 1994; DLitt; FRGS, FSA, FRSL; Chairman, Hemming Group Ltd (formerly Municipal Publications Ltd), 2011–15 (Director, since 1962; Deputy Chairman, 1967–76; Joint Chairman, 1976–2011); Director and Secretary, Royal Geographical Society, 1975–96; *b* 5 Jan. 1935; *s* of late Henry Harold Hemming, OBE, MC, and Alice Louisa Weaver, OBE; *m* 1979, Sukie, *d* of late M. J. Babington Smith, CBE; one *s* one *d*. *Educ:* Eton Coll.; McGill Univ.; Magdalen Coll., Oxford (Hon. Fellow, 2004); DLitt Oxon 1981. FSA 1998. Chairman: Brintex Ltd, 1979– (Man. Dir, 1963–70, Dep. Chm. 1976–78); Newman Books, 1979–. Member, Iriri River Expedition, Brazil, 1961; Leader, Maracá Rainforest Project, Brazil, 1987–88; Co-Chm., Jordan Badia R&D Prog., 1992–2004. Member Bd, British Council, 1993–2002; Member Council: Anglo-Brazilian Soc., 1963–2006; Pro Natura Internat., 1991–2007; Hakluyt Soc., 1996–. Corresp. Mem., Academia Nacional de la Historia, Venezuela. Dep. Chm., Lepra, 1998–2011; Founding Trustee, Survival International, 1969–2003; Trustee: Gilchrist Educnl Trust, 1988–; Anglo-Peruvian Soc., 1996– (Chm. Trustees, 1996–2007); Rainforest Foundn, 1997–; John Ellerman Foundn, 1998–2010; Global Diversity Foundn, 1999–; Cusichaca Trust, 1999–; Earthwatch Trust, 2004–; Chairman: British Empire and Commonwealth Mus. Trust, 1990–99; Rainforest Club, 1997–2002; Greencard Trust, 1997–2009 (Mem. Council, 1989–2009); Amazon Charitable Trust, 2008–; Patron: Earth Love Fund, 1996–; Wilderness Trust, 2003–. FRGS 1962; FRSL 2013. Hon. DLitt Warwick, 1989; DUniv Stirling, 1991. Mungo Park Medal, RSGS, 1988; Founder's Medal, RGS, 1990; Washburn Medal, Boston Mus. of Sci., 1990; Citation of Merit, Explorers' Club, NY, 1997; Special Award, Instituto Nacional de Cultura, Peru, 1997. Grand Cross, Orden al Mérito (Peru), 2007 (Officer, 1986); Gran Oficial, Order of the Sun (Peru), 2010; Comendador, Order of Cruzeiro do Sul (Brazil), 1998. *Publications:* The Conquest of the Incas, 1970 (Robert Pitman Literary Prize, 1970, Christopher Award, NY, 1971), rev. edn 1993 (US rev. edn 2012); (jt) Tribes of the Amazon Basin in Brazil, 1972; Red Gold: The Conquest of the Brazilian Indians, 1978; The Search for El Dorado, 1978; Machu Picchu, 1981; Monuments of the Incas, 1982, 3rd rev. edn 2010; The New Incas, 1983; (ed) Change in the Amazon Basin (2 vols), 1985; Amazon Frontier: the defeat of the Brazilian Indians, 1987; Maracá, 1988; Roraima: Brazil's northernmost frontier, 1990; Maracá Rainforest Island, 1993; (ed) The Rainforest Edge, 1994; The Golden Age of Discovery, 1998; Die If You Must, 2003; Tree of Rivers: the story of the Amazon, 2008; Naturalists in Paradise: Wallace, Bates and Spruce in the Amazon, 2015. *Recreations:* writing, travel. *Address:* 10 Edwardes Square, W8 6HE. *T:* (020) 7602 6697. *Clubs:* Boodle's, Beefsteak (Chm., 2002–04), Geographical.

See also L. A. Service.

HEMMING, Lindy; costume designer for theatre, since 1970 and cinema, since 1983; *b* Haverfordwest, Wales, 21 Aug. 1948; *d* of Alan Hemming and Jean Hemming (*née* Alexander); one *s* one *d*; partner, Robert A. Starrett, cartoonist. *Educ:* Llandovery Coll., Carmarthenshire; Robert Jones and Agnes Hunt Orthopaedic Hosp.; Royal Acad. of Dramatic Art. Costume designer: *theatre:* Hampstead Th. Club; Open Space Th.; NT/RSC (Barbican and Stratford upon Avon); West End theatres; *films* include: My Beautiful Launderette, 1985; Life is Sweet, 1990; Naked, 1993; Four Weddings and a Funeral, 1994; Funny Bones, 1995; GoldenEye, 1995; Tomorrow Never Dies, 1997; The World is Not Enough, 1999; Topsy Turvy, 1999 (Acad. Award, 2000); Tomb Raiders 1, 2001; Die Another Day, 2002; Tomb Raiders 2, 2003; Batman Begins, 2005; Casino Royale, 2006; Dark Knight, 2008 (Designers' Guild Award, 2009); Clash of the Titans, 2010; The Dark Knight Rises, 2012; Paddington, 2014. Guest Curator, Designing Bond, 50th Anniversary, Barbican, 2012. Member: British Film Designers' Guild; BAFTA; Acad. of Motion Pictures, USA. Woman of Year, Media Craft Awards, 1996. *Publications:* contrib. articles and features to newspapers and mags. *Recreations:* eating good food, people watching, travelling, caring for some very needy olive trees in Italy. *Address:* 105 Willoughby House, Barbican, EC2Y 8BL; Casa Lorenzino, Fertigliana no 12, 54010 Bigliolo. Aulla, Italy. *T:* 0187412078. *E:* LindyHmm@aol.com.

HEMMING, Martin John, CB 2003; Deputy Legal Adviser, Foreign and Commonwealth Office, 2009–13; *b* 29 May 1949; *s* of late Albert Reuben Hemming and Constance Rosaline Hemming; *m* 1976, Kathleen Siân Davies; one *s* one *d*. *Educ:* Tudor Grange Grammar Sch., Solihull; Fitzwilliam Coll., Cambridge (BA 1971; MA 1976); London School of Economics and Political Science (LLM 1973). Called to the Bar, Gray's Inn, 1972, Bencher, 2006; practising barrister, 1974–82; Sen. Legal Asst, Treasury Solicitor's Dept, 1982–85; Legal Advr (Grade 6), MoD, 1985–88; Asst Treasury Solicitor, 1988–98; Dir Gen. Legal Services and Legal Advr, MoD, 1998–2009. Associate Fellow, RUSI, 2013. *E:* martin.hemming@gmail.com. *Club:* Oxford and Cambridge.

HEMMINGS, Dr Brian Arthur, PhD; FRS 2009; Senior Scientist, Friedrich Miescher Institute for Biomedical Research, Basel, since 1990 (Junior Group Leader, 1983–89). *Educ:* Univ. of Nottingham (BSc 1972); Univ. of East Anglia (PhD 1975). Res. Fellow, Biochemisches Institut der Universität, Freiburg, 1975–77; Fogarty Vis. Fellow, NIH, Bethesda, 1977–80; MRC Res. Fellow, Med. Scis Inst., Univ. of Dundee, 1980–82; FMI Res. Associate, Rockefeller Univ., NY, 1982–83. Vis. Prof., Faculty of Medicine, Katholieke Universiteit, Leuven, 2000. Mem., Scientific Cttee, Swiss Cancer League, 2001–12. *Publications:* contrib. articles in jls. *Address:* Friedrich Miescher Institute for Biomedical Research, Maulbeerstrasse 66, 4058 Basel, Switzerland.

HEMPHILL, 6th Baron *cr* 1906, of Rathkenny and Cashel; **Charles Andrew Martyn Martyn-Hemphill;** Director, Waverton Investment Management (formerly J. O. Hambro Investment Management), since 2011; *b* Dublin, 8 Oct. 1954; *s* of 5th Baron Hemphill and (Olivia) Anne, *d* of late Major Robert Francis Ruttledge, MC; *S* father, 2012; *m* 1985, Sarah Jane Frances Lumley; two *s* three *d*. *Educ:* Downside Sch., St Benet's Hall, Oxford (BA History; MA). With Deutsche Asset Mgt (formerly Morgan Grenfell Asset Mgt), 1979–2005; Spencer Hse Capital Mgt, 2006–11. Chm. of Governors, St Mary's Sch., Ascot. Trustee: Dulverton Trust; UCL Hosp. Charitable Trust. *Recreations:* ski-ing, golf. *Heir: s* Hon. Richard Patrick Lumley Martyn-Hemphill, *b* 17 May 1990. *Address:* 66 Manville Road, SW17 8JL; Dunkelin, Kiltulla, Athenry, Co. Galway, Ireland. *Clubs:* White's, Hurlingham; New Zealand.

HEMPLEMAN-ADAMS, David Kim, LVO 2007; OBE 1998 (MBE 1994); DL; company director; explorer and mountaineer; *b* 10 Oct. 1956; *m* Claire; three *d*. *Educ:* Writhlington Comp. Sch.; Manchester Univ.; Bristol Poly (post-grad. Business Studies). Ascents: Mt McKinley, Alaska Range, 1980; Kilimanjaro, Tanzania, 1981; Mt Everest, Himalayas, 1993; Vinson Massif, Antarctica, 1994; Aconcagua, Andes, 1994; Mt Carstensz, Indonesia, 1995. Arctic/Antarctic expeditions: first solo unsupported expedition to magnetic North Pole, 1984; leader of first unsupported gp expedition to geomagnetic North Pole, 1992; first Briton to walk solo and unsupported to South Pole, 1996; first person to climb highest peaks of all seven continents and trek to magnetic and geographic North and South Poles, 1998; first person to walk solo and unaided by new route to geomagnetic North Pole, 2003; has reached the Poles 14 times. Hot-air balloon flights: first to cross Andes, 1998; first to cross North-West Passage, 1999; first to fly solo to North Pole, 2000; first to fly solo across Arctic Ocean, 2000; first to cross Atlantic in open wicker-basket, 2003. Director: Hempleman Investments; Global Resins; Ultimate Adventures. Founder, Mitchemp Trust. Trustee, Duke of Edinburgh Award, 2006–. DL Wilts, 2004. Member: RGS; RSGS; Hon. Co. of Air Pilots (formerly GAPAN); Royal Soc. Hon. DSc Leicester, 1998. CStJ 2011. 42 FAI Aviation world records; Fifty awards. Polar Medal and Clasp, 2013. *Publications:* Race Against Time: North Geomagnetic Pole expedition, 1993; Toughing it Out, 1996; Walking on Thin Ice, 1998; At the Mercy of the Winds, 2000; (jtly) At the Heart of the Great Alone, 2009. *Clubs:* Royal Automobile, Alpine, Travellers; Explorers (New York).

HEMPSALL, Dr David Stuart, MA; Headmaster, Queen Elizabeth's Grammar School, Blackburn, 1995–2007; *b* 4 Jan. 1947; *s* of Harold and Freda Hempsall; *m* 1st, 1969, Patricia Land (*d* 2004); one *s* one *d*; 2nd, 2006, Diane Ewart-Jones. *Educ:* Manchester GS; Sidney Sussex Coll., Cambridge (MA); Univ. of Kent (PhD). Assistant Master: Sir William Nottidge Sch., Whitstable, 1971–72; Rugby Sch., 1973–85 (Head of History, 1977–85); Headmaster, Scarborough Coll., 1985–95. Hon. Treas., HMC, 2002–07. Chm. of Govs, The King's Sch., Chester, 2009–12. Hon. Sec., Limey Valley Residents' Assoc., 2009–. FRSA. Sec., Christ Ch Walshaw PCC, 2010–. *Publications:* articles in hist. and educnl learned jls. *Recreations:* do-it-yourself, hill-walking, music, sport, reading. *Address:* c/o Queen Elizabeth's Grammar School, West Park Road, Blackburn BB2 6DF. *T:* (01254) 686300.

HEMSLEY, Oliver Alexander; Chief Executive Officer, Numis Corporation plc, since 2000; *b* Oakham, Rutland, 27 Sept. 1962; *s* of Archie and Valerie Hemsley; *m* 1995, Charlotte Baddeley; two *s* one *d*. *Educ:* Stamford Sch., Lincs. Marine Underwriter, Alston Brockbank Underwriting Ltd, 1981–89; Chief Executive Officer: Hemsley & Co. Securities Ltd,

1990–92; Raphael Zorn Hemsley Ltd, 1992–2000. *Recreations:* hunting, kitchen gardening, flora and fauna, reading. *Address:* Numis Securities, 10 Paternoster Square, EC4M 7LT. *T:* (020) 7260 1000. *E:* o.hemsley@numis.com. *Clubs:* Garrick, City of London.

HEMSLEY, Stephen Glen, FCA; non-executive Chairman, Domino's Pizza Group (formerly Domino's Pizza UK and Ireland) plc, since 2010 (Executive Chairman, 2008–10); Chairman, Franchise Brands Worldwide Ltd, since 2008; *b* Bromley, 3 Aug. 1957. *Educ:* Bromley Grammar Sch. for Boys; Univ. of Kent at Canterbury (BA Hons). FCA 1982. Stoy Hayward & Co., Chartered Accountants, 1978–83; Corp. Finance Manager, Sarasin Internat. Securities, 1983–84; Investment Controller, 1984–88, Sen. Investment Controller, 1988–89, Investment Dir, 1989–92, 3i plc; Domino's Pizza plc: Chief Financial Officer, 1998–2000; CEO, 2000–07. *Recreations:* motor boating, sailing, ski-ing, shooting. *Address:* Domino's Pizza Group plc, 1 Thornbury, West Ashland, Milton Keynes MK6 4BB. *T:* (01908) 580604. *E:* stephenhemsley@hotmail.com. *Clubs:* Royal Thames Yacht, Royal Solent Yacht, Royal Lymington Yacht.

HENDERSON, family name of **Baron Faringdon**.

HENDERSON, Andrew David Forbes; HM Diplomatic Service; Director, Trade and Investment, South Africa, since 2011, and Regional Director, Southern Africa, since 2014; *b* 12 July 1952; *s* of James Porteous Henderson and Patricia Margaret Henderson; *m* 1987, Julia Margaret King; two *d*. *Educ:* Crypt Sch., Gloucester. Entered FCO, 1971; Latin American Floater, 1975–77; Vice Consul, Rio de Janeiro, 1977–80; Second Sec. (Political), Oslo, 1980–84; Asst Private Sec. to Minister of State, 1985–87; Consul (Political), NY, 1987–88; First Sec. (Political), Washington, 1988–91; Dep. Hd of Mission, Luanda, 1992–94; First Sec. (Aid/Econ.), later Hd, Commercial Section, Cairo, 1994–98; Hd, Parly Relns Dept, FCO, 1998–99; Consul-Gen., Jeddah, 2000–03; Consul-Gen., São Paulo, and Dir, Trade and Investment, Brazil, 2003–07; Ambassador to Algeria, 2007–10. *Recreations:* golf, Rugby, cricket, music, travel. *Address:* UKTI Johannesburg, BFPO 5341, HA4 6EP. *E:* Andrew.Henderson@fco.gov.uk.

HENDERSON, Anne Frances; *see* Milton, Rt Hon. A. F.

HENDERSON, Barry; *see* Henderson, J. S. B.

HENDERSON, Bernard Vere, CBE 1987; Chairman: Anglian Water, 1981–94; British Waterways Board, 1994–99; *b* 8 July 1928; *s* of late Percy Cecil and Ruth Elizabeth Henderson; *m* 1952, Valerie Jane Cairns; two *s* one *d*. *Educ:* Ampleforth Coll.; Harvard Business Sch. Served Army, RE, 1946–48. P. C. Henderson Group, 1949–80 (Man. Dir, 1958–80). Chm., Water Services Assoc., 1990–91. Chm., Australia and NZ Trade Adv. Cttee, 1994–95. Pres., Pipeline Industry Guild, 1992–94. *Recreations:* countryside, cruising. *Address:* Lessudden Bank, St Boswells, Melrose TD6 0DU.

HENDERSON, Charles Edward, CB 1992; FIA; Chairman: Total Holding UK (formerly Total Oil Holdings, then TotalFinaElf Holding UK), 1998–2005; Total Exploration and Production UK (formerly Total Oil Marine, then TotalFinaElf Exploration UK), 1998–2005; *b* 19 Sept. 1939; *s* of late David Henderson and of Giorgiana Leggatt Henderson; *m* 1966, Rachel Hilary Hall, *d* of late Dr Stephen Hall, FRCP and Dr Mary Hall; one *d* one *s*. *Educ:* Charterhouse; Pembroke Coll., Cambridge (MA). FIA 1965. Actuarial Trainee, subseq. Asst Investment Sec., Equity & Law Life Assurance Soc., 1960–70; ECGD, 1971–73; DTI, 1973–74; Dept of Energy, 1974–88: Asst Sec., 1975; Under Sec., 1982; Atomic Energy Div., 1982; Oil Div., 1985; Prin. Estabt and Finance Officer, 1986–88; Head, Office of Arts and Libraries, 1989–92; Dep. Sec., DTI, 1992–96. Mem., Competition (formerly Monopolies and Mergers) Commn, 1998–2007. Dir, Aluminium Corp. Ltd, 1981–84. Sen. Associate, Cambridge Energy Res. Associates, 1998–2002. President: Soc. for Underwater Technology, 1999–2001; Inst. of Petroleum, 2000–02. *Recreations:* making and listening to music, mountaineering, golf. *Address:* 17 Sydney House, Woodstock Road, W4 1DP. *T:* (020) 8994 1345.

See also Julian Hall.

HENDERSON, David; *see* Henderson, P. D.

HENDERSON, Sir Denys (Hartley), Kt 1989; Chairman: Imperial Chemical Industries PLC, 1987–95; ZENECA Group plc, 1993–95; The Rank Group Plc (formerly Rank Organisation), 1995–2001; Chairman and First Crown Estate Commissioner, 1995–2002; *b* 11 Oct. 1932; *o s* of John Hartley Henderson and Nellie Henderson (*née* Gordon); *m* 1957, Doreen Mathewson Glashan, *o d* of Robert and Mary Glashan; two *d*. *Educ:* Aberdeen Grammar School; Univ. of Aberdeen (MA, LLB). Solicitor; Mem., Law Soc. of Scotland. Joined ICI as lawyer in Secretary's Dept, London, 1957; Chm., ICI Paints Div., 1977; ICI Main Bd Dir, 1980; Dep. Chm., 1986–87. Non-executive Director: Dalgety plc, 1981–87 and 1996–98 (Chm., 1997–98); Barclays Bank, 1983–97; RTZ Corp., 1990–96; MORI, 1995–2001; Schlumberger Ltd, 1995–2001; QinetiQ plc, 2003–05; Mem., Eur. Adv. Bd, Carlyle Gp, 1997–2005. Member: CBI President's Cttee, 1987–96; Adv. Council, Prince's Youth Business Trust, 1986–99; Adv. Cttee on Business Appointments, 1994–2001; Greenbury Cttee on Directors' Remuneration, 1994–95. Mem., European Round Table, 1992–94. Pres., Soc. of Business Economists, 1990–94. Pres. and Chm. Bd, British Quality Foundn, 1993–97. Trustee, Natural Hist. Mus., 1989–98. Chancellor, Bath Univ., 1993–98; Mem. Court of Governors, Henley Management Coll., 1986–96 (Chm., 1989–96); Chm., Univ. of Aberdeen Quincentenary Appeal Cttee, 1993–96. Hon. Vice-Pres., Chartered Inst. of Marketing, 1989–95. CCMI (CBIM 1981); FInstM 1987. Hon. FCGI 1990. DUniv: Brunel, 1987; Strathclyde, 1993; Hon. LLD: Aberdeen, 1987; Nottingham, 1990; Manchester, 1991; Bath, 1993; Hon. DSc: Cranfield Inst. of Technol., 1989; Teesside, 1993. Centenary Medal, SCI, 1993. *Recreations:* family life, reading, travel.

HENDERSON, Douglas John; Partner, Harley Street Hearing, since 2010; Director: Ossian Services Ltd, since 2009; North West Hearing, since 2014; *b* 9 June 1949; *s* of John and Joy Henderson; *m* 1st, 1974, Janet Margaret Graham (marr. diss.); one *s*; 2nd, 2002, Geraldine Daly; one *d*. *Educ:* Waid Academy, Anstruther, Fife; Central Coll., Glasgow; Univ. of Strathclyde. Apprentice, Rolls Royce, 1966–68; Clerk, British Rail, 1969; Research Officer, GMWU, 1973–75; Regional Organiser, GMWU, then GMB, 1975–87. Mem. Exec., Scottish Council, Labour Party, 1979–87 (Chm., 1984–85). MP (Lab) Newcastle upon Tyne N, 1987–2010. Opposition spokesman on trade and industry, 1988–92, on local govt, 1992–94, on public service, 1994–95, on home affairs, 1995–97; Minister of State: (Europe), FCO, 1997–98; (Minister for the Armed Forces), MoD, 1998–99. Sec., All Party Athletes Gp, 2002–10; Chairman: Northern Gp of Lab MPs, 2000–01; GMB Party Gp, 2002–10 (Sec., 1987–97); Mem. UK Delegn to Council of Europe and WEU, 2005–10; Chm., Defence Cttee, Eur. Security and Defence Assembly, 2009–10. Chm., Falkirk FC, 2015– (Dir, 2013–). *Recreations:* athletics, mountaineering. *Clubs:* Elswick Harriers, Lemington Labour, Newburn Memorial, Dinnington, Union Jack (Newcastle).

HENDERSON, Fergus, MBE 2005; Chef and Owner, St John Restaurant, London, since 1994 (Michelin Star, 2009); *b* 31 July 1963; *s* of Brian and Elizabeth Henderson; *m* 1993, Margot Clayton; one *s* two *d*. *Educ:* King Alfred's Sch.; Architectural Assoc. RIBA pt 2. Chef, French House Dining Room, 1992–94. *Publications:* Nose to Tail Eating: a kind of British cooking, 1999, 4th edn 2004; (jtly) Beyond Nose to Tail, 2007; Complete Nose to Tail, 2012. *Recreation:* cooking. *Address:* St John Restaurant, 26 St John Street, EC1M 4AY. *T:* (020) 7553 9842, *Fax:* (020) 7251 4090. *E:* kitty@stjohnrestaurant.com. *Club:* Groucho.

HENDERSON, Prof. Gavin Douglas, CBE 2004; Principal, Royal Central School of Speech and Drama (formerly Central School of Speech and Drama), University of London, since 2007; *b* 3 Feb. 1948; *s* of Magnus Reg Henderson and Sybil (*née* Horton); *m* 1st, 1973, Jane Williams (marr. diss. 1977); 2nd, 1983, Carole Becker (marr. diss. 1992); two *s*; 3rd, 1992, Mary Jane Walsh. *Educ:* Brighton Coll.; Brighton Coll. of Art; Kingston Art Coll.; University Coll. London; Slade Sch. of Fine Art. Solo trumpet, St Bartholomew's Church, Brighton, 1963–2014; Leader and Dir, Henderson Brass Consort, 1968–75; Principal Trumpet, Worthing Municipal and Concert Orchs, 1969–70; Dep. Front of House and Publicity Manager, Victoria Theatre, Stoke-on-Trent, 1970–71; Founder and Dir, Crawley Fest., 1971–73; Artistic Director: York Fest. Mystery Plays, 1972–76; Portsmouth Fest., 1974–76; Chief Exec., New Philharmonia and Philharmonia Orchs, 1975–78; Dir, S Hill Park Arts Centre and Founder, Wilde Theatre, Bracknell, 1979–84; Artistic Director: Brighton Internat. Fest., 1983–94; Dartington Internat. Summer Sch., 1985–2010; Court in the Act, Royal Acad. of Arts, 1993; Mem., Adv. Bd, London Contemporary Dance Trust, 1986–87; Pres. and Artistic Advr, Bournemouth Fest., 1996–98 (Artistic Dir, 1994–96); Principal, Trinity Coll. of Music, 1994–2005; Principal and Chief Exec., Trinity Laban, 2005–06. Chairman: Clarion Concert Agency, 1972–75; Palindrome Prodns Ltd, 1994–2003; World Circuit Arts, 1995–2004; Nat. Foundn for Youth Music (formerly Youth Music Trust), 1998–2007. Writer and presenter, A View of …, BBC TV Series, 1983. Member: Music Panel and Opera Cttee, 1973–75, Regl Cttee, 1981–84, Arts Council of GB; Arts Council of England, 1994–98 (Chm., Music Panel, 1994–2003); Arts Cttee, RSA, 1991–94; Chairman: British Arts Fests Assoc., 1994–2002 (Dep. Chm., 1987–94); Brighton Youth Orch. Trust, 1998–2005; Regency Soc., 1999–2006; Member: Exec. Cttee, SE Arts Assoc., 1982–89 (Chm., Festival Panel, 1986–89); Exec. Bd, European Fests Assoc., 1988–94 (Vice Pres., 1994–2003, Pres., 2003–05); Southern Arts Bd, 1990–93; Arts Initiative in Mgt Cttee, Gulbenkian Foundn, 1982–83. Trustee: Electro-Acoustic Music Soc., 1984–90; Brighton Early Music Fest., 2005–; Theatres Trust, 2014–. Judge: Prudential Awards, 1992; Audi Young Musician of the Year, 1993; Barclays New Stages, 1994; British Gas Working for Cities, 1995; Olivier Awards, 2001–02; Chm., Royal Over-Seas League Music Competition, 2007–. External Examiner: UEA, 2008–13; Middlesex Univ., 2014. Pres., Nat. Piers Soc., 1986–. One-man exhibitions: Gall. 185, Brighton, 1968; Mulberry Gall., Lancaster, 1969. Mem. Bd, Trinity Coll., London, 1994–2008; Governor: Brighton Univ. (formerly Poly.), 1987–95; Chetham's Sch., Manchester, 1994–2011; Feoffee, Chetham's Hosp., 2007–14. Pres., ISM, 2010–11. Mem., Royal Soc. of Musicians, 1996–. Liveryman, Musicians' Co., 1995. Freeman, City of London, 1995. Hon. Fellow: Univ. of Sussex, 1991; Univ. of Brighton, 1993; Laban, 2000; Hon. FTCL 1998; Hon. FRCM 2002; Hon. FRNCM 2003; Hon. FBC 2010; Hon. CTL 2007. Hon. MA Sussex, 1992. Europe Award, E Sussex CC, 1992; Sir Charles Groves Award, 2005; BACS Gold Award, 2007. *Publications:* Picasso and the Theatre, 1982; articles for Resurgence, Classical Music, Tempo, Musical Times, Stage, and Listener. *Recreations:* seaside pierage, cooking seafood, vintage motor-racing. *Address:* Royal Central School of Speech and Drama, University of London, Eton Avenue, NW3 3HY. *Clubs:* Beefsteak, Garrick, Savile, Royal Over-Seas League (Hon. Mem.), Academy, Acts and Actors.

HENDERSON, Prof. George David Smith, FSA; Professor of Medieval Art, Cambridge, 1986–96, then Emeritus; Fellow of Downing College, Cambridge, 1974–94; *b* 7 May 1931; *yr s* of late Very Rev. Prof. George David Henderson, DLitt, DTh, DD and Jenny Holmes McCulloch Henderson (*née* Smith); *m* 1957, Isabel Bisset Murray, OBE, Hon. FSAScot; one *s* one *d*. *Educ:* Aberdeen Grammar Sch.; Univ. of Aberdeen (MA 1953); Courtauld Inst., Univ. of London (BA 1956); Trinity Coll., Cambridge (MA, PhD 1961). Research Fellow, Barber Inst. of Art, Univ. of Birmingham, 1959–60; Graham Robertson Research Fellow, Downing Coll., Cambridge, 1960–63; University of Manchester: Asst Lectr in History of Art, 1962–64; Lectr, 1964–66; University of Edinburgh: Lectr in Fine Arts, 1966–71; Reader in Fine Arts, 1971–73; University of Cambridge: Lectr in History of Art, 1974–79; Head of Dept, 1974–88; Reader in Medieval Art, 1979–86; a Syndic, Fitzwilliam Museum, 1974–98. Mem., Ely Cathedral Fabric Adv. Cttee, 1990–98. *Publications:* Gothic, 1967; Chartres, 1968; Early Medieval, 1972, repr. 1993; (ed with Giles Robertson) Studies in Memory of David Talbot Rice, 1975; Bede and the Visual Arts (Jarrow Lect.), 1980; Losses and Lacunae in Early Insular Art (Garmonsway Lect.), 1982; Studies in English Bible Illustration, 1985; From Durrow to Kells, 1987; (contrib.) The Eadwine Psalter, 1992; (contrib.) Emulation and Innovation in Carolingian Culture, 1993; Vision and Image in Early Christian England, 1999; (with Isabel Henderson) The Art of the Picts: sculpture and metalwork in early medieval Scotland, 2004 (a Historians of British Art Book Prize, 2006); articles in UK and Amer. jls and papers in procs of internat. confs; *Festschrift:* New Offerings, Ancient Treasures: studies in medieval art for George Henderson, ed. P. Binski and W. Noel, 2001. *Recreations:* listening to Wagner, porphyrology, looking for agates. *Address:* The Old Manse, Nigg by Tain, Ross and Cromarty IV19 1QR.

HENDERSON, Prof. Gideon Mark, PhD; FRS 2013; Professor of Earth Sciences, since 2006, and Head, Department of Earth Sciences, since 2013, University of Oxford; Fellow of University College, Oxford, since 1999; *b* Glasgow, 29 July 1968; *s* of Prof. Paul Henderson, *qv*; *m* 2000, Catherine Mary Wheatley; two *s*. *Educ:* Altwood Comp., Maidenhead; Hertford Coll., Oxford (BA Earth Scis 1989); St John's Coll., Cambridge (PhD Geochem. 1994). Post-doctoral Fellow, 1994–96, Associate Res. Scientist, 1996–99, Lamont-Doherty Earth Observatory, Columbia Univ.; Lectr, Univ. of Oxford, 1999–2006. *Publications:* The Cambridge Handbook of Earth Science Data (with P. Henderson), 2009; articles in scientific jls. *Address:* Department of Earth Sciences, University of Oxford, South Parks Road, Oxford OX1 3AN. *T:* (01865) 272000. *E:* gideonh@earth.ox.ac.uk.

HENDERSON, Giles Ian, CBE 1992; Master, Pembroke College, Oxford, 2001–13, now Honorary Fellow; *b* 20 April 1942; *s* of late Charles David Henderson and Joan K. Firmin; *m* 1971, Lynne Fyfield; two *s* one *d*. *Educ:* Michaelhouse, Natal; Univ. of Witwatersrand (BA); Magdalen Coll., Oxford (Sen. Mackinnon Scholar; MA, BCL). Fulbright Award, 1966–67. Associate in Law, Univ. of California at Berkeley, 1966–67; joined Slaughter and May, 1968; admitted Solicitor, 1970; Partner, Slaughter and May, 1975, Sen. Partner, 1993–2001. Member: Hampel Cttee on Corporate Governance, 1995–98; Financial Reporting Council, 1998–2001; Chm., Law Gp, UK-China Forum, 1997–2000. Non-executive Director: Land Securities plc, 2000–02; Standard Life Assurance Co., 2001–03. Chairman: Nuffield Med. Trust, 2003–; Conf. of Oxford Colls, 2007–09; Dir, Cumberland Lodge, 2007–08. Mem. Council, Univ. of Oxford, 2007–13. *Recreations:* sport, opera, ballet. *Address:* The Old Rectory, Fifield, Chipping Norton, Oxon OX7 6HF.

See also M. G. F. Henderson.

HENDERSON, Gordon; MP (C) Sittingbourne and Sheppey, since 2010; *b* Gillingham, Kent, 27 Jan. 1948; *s* of William John Butler Henderson and Pauline Henderson (*née* Pullen); *m* 1993, Louise Claire Crowder; one *s* two *d*. *Educ:* Fort Luton Secondary Sch. for Boys. Woolworths, 1964–79; restaurateur, 1979–83; Agent, Cons. Party, 1983–85; GEC Marconi, 1985–93; Unwins Wine Gp, 1993–2003; Beams UK Ltd, 2003–08; mgt consultant, 2008–10. Mem. (C) Kent CC, 1989–93. Contested (C): Luton S, 2001; Sittingbourne and Sheppey, 2005. *Recreations:* reading, writing. *Address:* House of Commons, SW1A 0AA. *T:* (020) 7219 7144; (office) Top Floor, Unit 10, Periwinkle Court, Church Street, Milton Regis, Sittingbourne, Kent ME10 2JZ. *E:* gordon.henderson.mp@parliament.uk.

HENDERSON, Prof. Graham, CBE 2011; DL; Vice-Chancellor and Chief Executive, Teesside University, 2003–15; *b* 23 Aug. 1952; *s* of Thomas and Elizabeth Henderson; *m* 1987, Joan Younger; two *s* one *d*. *Educ:* Heaton Grammar Sch.; Lanchester Poly. (BSc Hons); City Univ. (MSc with Dist.); Nene Coll. (FE Teachers' Cert.). Trainee Accountant, 1970–71, Trainee Operational Res. Scientist, 1973–74, NCB; Lectr, Sch. of Maths, Mgt and Business Studies, Nene Coll., Northampton, 1975–79; Lectr, then Sen. Lectr, then Prin. Lectr, Sch. of Business Analysis, Newcastle Poly., 1979–89; Asst Dir, Newcastle Poly., later Newcastle Business Sch., Univ. of Northumbria, 1989–97; Dir, Sunderland Business Sch., Univ. of Sunderland, 1997–99; Dep. Vice-Chancellor, Univ. of Teesside, 1999–2003. Member: CBI Regl Council, 2003–09, 2012–; Bd, Univs for the NE, 2003– (Chm., 2005–09); Bd, NE Chamber of Commerce, 2005–10 (Mem. Council, 2009–); Nat. Exec., Million+ (formerly Campaign for Mainstream Univs), 2005–10; Bd, Universities UK, 2010– (Member: Business and Ind. Policy Network (formerly Employability Business and Ind. Policy Cttee), 2008–; Student Quality and Participation Policy Network (formerly Student Experience Policy Cttee), 2008–); Chairman: Regl Council, NE Higher Skills Network, 2006–09; Regl Sci., Technol., Engrg and Maths NE Bd, 2009–11; Membership Adv. Gp, Leadership Foundn for Higher Educn, 2010–. Member, Corporation Board: Hartlepool Coll., 1999–2004; Laurence Jackson Sch., 1999–2003; Darlington Coll. of Technology, 1999–2006; Mem. Bd, Univ. Alliance, 2011–. Vice-Chm., Transparent Approach to Costing Develt and Implementation Gp, HEFCE, 2008–13. Director: Middlesbrough Town Centre Co., 2003–06; Durham and Tees Valley LSC, 2005–07; NE Regl LSC, 2007–10; Mem. Bd, Tees Valley Unlimited, 2006–. Pres., Guisborough RU Club, 2013–. Trustee: Capt. Cook Birthplace Trust, 2003–; Trincomalee Trust, 2003–07; Patron: Community Campus, 2013–; Middlesbrough Older Persons' Forum, 2011–. CCMI 2010. FSS 1977; FRSA 2000. DL N Yorks 2012. *Recreations:* Rugby Union and football (spectator), walking, ballroom dancing, golf.

HENDERSON, Rear Adm. Iain Robert, CB 2001; CBE 1991; DL; Registrar and Secretary, Order of the Bath, since 2006 (Gentleman Usher of the Scarlet Rod, 2002–06); *b* 1 April 1948; *s* of John and Christina Henderson; *m* 1976, Rosalind Margaret Arkell; two *s* two *d*. *Educ:* Epsom Coll. BRNC 1965; qualified as: rotary wing pilot, 1971; fixed wing pilot, 1974; Exec. Officer, HMS Plymouth, 1980–82; CO, HMS Ariadne, 1984–85, HMS Charybdis, 1985; Trng Comdr, BRNC, 1986–87; Directorate of Naval Officer Appointments (Seaman) (Air), 1988–90; CO, HMS London, 1990–91; AD Warfare Directorate of Naval Plans, 1991–93; CO, RNAS Yeovilton, 1993–96; Comdr, Naval Base, Portsmouth, 1996–98; FONA, 1998–2000; AOC No 3 Gp and FOMA, 2000–01. ADC to the Queen, 1996–98. Chief Exec., Sue Ryder Care, 2001–07. Freeman, City of London, 1992; Liveryman, Co. of Upholders, 1996–; Mem., Ct of Assts, Guild of Freemen, City of London, 1997–2003. DL Hants, 2006. *Recreation:* equestrian and country pursuits.

HENDERSON, Ian James, CBE 2001; FRICS; farmer, since 2007; Deputy Chairman, Capital & Counties Properties plc, since 2010; *b* 18 July 1943; *s* of Robert and Sheila Henderson; *m* 1972, Sheila Sturrock; one *s* one *d*. *Educ:* BSc (Estate Mgt). FRICS 1978. Joined Land Securities, 1971; Chief Exec., Land Securities Gp PLC, 1997–2004. Chm., New West End Co. Ltd, 2000–08; Vice-Chm., London Regl Bd, Royal & Sun Alliance, 1998–; Mem., President's Cttee, London First, 2002–. Chm., London Mayoral Commn into W End Central Retail Area Planning and Develt Policy, 2006–07. Non-executive Chairman: Treveria plc (formerly Dawnay Day Treveria), 2005–09; Ishaan Real Estate PLC, 2006–13; Evans Mgt Ltd, 2008–12; non-exec. Dir, Capital Shopping Centres Gp plc, 2010–12 (non-exec. Dir, Liberty Internat. PLC, 2005–10); consultant, Quintain Estates and Development plc, 2005–08. Chm., St Martin-in-the-Fields Develt Trust, 2005–11; Vice Chm., Bd of Mgt, Central and Cecil Housing Trust, 1992–2007 (Vice Pres., 2007–). Pres., British Property Fedn, 2002–03. Comr, Commonwealth War Graves Commn, 2002–10. Trustee, Natural Hist. Mus., 2005–13 (Chm., Estates Adv. Bd., 2013–); Council Mem., Royal Albert Hall, 2005–; Chm. Govs, Dolphin Square Charitable Foundn, 2005–. Pres., Lighthouse Club, 2005–08. *Clubs:* Brooks's, Naval and Military.

HENDERSON, Ivan John; public affairs consultant, Ivan Henderson Consultancy, since 2008; Member (Lab), Essex County Council, since 2013; *b* 7 June 1958; *s* of Margaret Bloice and step *s* of late Michael Bloice; *m* 1992, Jo'anne Atkinson; two *s*; one *s* one *d* from a previous marriage. *Educ:* Sir Anthony Deane Comprehensive Sch., Harwich. British Rail, Sealink, 1975–97: dock operative; Union Orgnr, Docks, and Exec. Officer, RMT, 1991–94. Member (Lab): Harwich Town Council, 1986–97 and 2011–; Tendring DC, 1995–97 and 2011–. MP (Lab) Harwich, 1997–2005; contested (Lab) same seat, 2005; contested (Lab) Clacton, 2010. PPS to Minister of State: Home Office, 2001–02; ODPM, 2002–03; PPS to Sec. of State, DWP, 2003–04; PPS to Paymaster-General, HM Treasury, 2004–05. Member: All Party Cancer Gp; All Party Maritime Gp; All Party Town Centre Mgt Gp; All Party Gp against Drug Abuse; All Party China Gp; All Party India Gp; All Party Gp on Animal Welfare; All Party Gp on Child Abduction; Labour Parly TU Gp; Seaside Gp, Labour MPs; Chm., All Party Parly Sea Cadets Gp, 2004–05; Vice Chm., All Party Parly Gp Ports and Shipping, 2001–05. Parly Spokesman for Clacton, 2006. Mem. Bd, Harwich Haven Authy, 2007–. Mem., Essex Wildlife Trust, 2001–. *Recreations:* football (Parly football team), golf. *Address:* Harwich, Essex. *T:* 07889 367822. *E:* ivanhenderson4labour@yahoo.co.uk. *Club:* Harwich and Dovercourt Cricket (Vice Pres., 1997).

HENDERSON, James Brodie; Chief Executive, Bell Pottinger, since 2013; *b* São Paulo, Brazil, 30 Dec. 1964; *s* of Ian and Veronica Henderson; *m* 1991, Alexandra Fisher; one *s* three *d*. *Educ:* Haileybury; Buckingham Univ. (LLB). Partner, College Hill PR, 1989–2004; Founder, 2004, Man. Dir, 2004–10, Pelham PR; Man. Dir, Pelham Bell Pottinger, 2010–12. Trustee, Children In Crisis, 2013–. *Recreations:* theatre, travel, running, family. *Address:* 80 Nightingale Lane, Wandsworth, SW12 8NR. *T:* 07774 444163. *E:* jhenderson@bellpottinger.com. *Club:* Brooks's.

HENDERSON, James Frowyke; a District Judge (Magistrates' Courts), since 2004; *b* 17 Dec. 1954; *s* of James Murray Henderson and Myrtle Elizabeth Jean Henderson; *m* 1989, Jane Elisabeth; one *s*. *Educ:* King's Sch., Tynemouth; Univ. of Newcastle upon Tyne (LLB); Univ. of Northumbria (LLM 2006; Sutherland Prize, 2006); Univ. of Cambridge (Postgrad. Dip. Applied Criminol. 2011; MSt 2012; Inst. of Criminol. Annual Prize, 2012). Called to the Bar, Middle Temple, 1984; Tutorial Studentship, 1980–83, Lectr in Laws, 1984–86, KCL; barrister in criminal practice, 1986–2004; Actg Stipendiary Magistrate, 1999–2000; Dep. Dist Judge (Magistrates' Courts), 2000–04. Occasional Lectr, British Acad. of Forensic Sci., 1980–83; Lectr (pt-time), PCL, 1983–84. FRSA 2008. *Publications:* contrib. numerous academic articles on criminal law and evidence to King's Coll. Law Jl, Criminal Bar Assoc. Newsletter, 4 Brick Court Chambers Law Review. *Recreations:* playing mandolin and guitar and various sized recorders, 4th Dan Black Belt in Goshin-Do (a modern Ju-Jitsu style), member of Heraldry Soc. of Scotland and of Scotch Malt Whisky Soc. *Address:* Lavender Hill Magistrates' Court, 176a Lavender Hill, Battersea, SW11 1JU. *Club:* Oxford and Cambridge.

HENDERSON, (James Stewart) Barry; management consultant; *b* 29 April 1936; *s* of James Henderson, CBE and Jane Stewart Henderson (*née* McLaren); *m* 1961, Janet Helen Sprot Todd; two *s*. *Educ:* Lathallan Sch.; Stowe Sch. Nat. Service, Scots Guards, 1954–56; electronics and computer industries, 1957–65; Scottish Conservative Central Office, 1966–70; computer industry, 1971–74; management consultant, 1975–86; paper industry, 1987–90; Dir, British Paper and Board Industry Fedn, 1990–92; Partner, Henderson Consulting, 1993–. Contested (C): E Edinburgh, 1966; E Dunbartonshire, 1970; Fife NE, 1987. MP (C): East Dunbartonshire, Feb.–Sept. 1974; E Fife, 1979–83; Fife NE, 1983–87. PPS to Economic Sec. to HM Treasury, 1984–87. Member: Select Cttee on Scottish Affairs, 1979–87; H of C Chairmen's Panel, 1981–83; Chm., Scottish Cons. Back Bench Cttee, 1983–84; Vice-Chm., PITCOM, 1986–87. Mem., ODPM Right to Manage review, 2001–04. Area Bd Mem., CityWest Homes, 2003–05. Comr, Strathclyde Tram Public Inquiry, 1996. Trustee, St Andrews Links Trust, 1979–87. Comr, Gen. Assembly of Church of Scotland, 1986. Sec., 1997–2000, Vice-Chm., 2000–02, Pimlico Village Housing Co-op; Chm., Westminster Soc., 2004–08. *Publications:* pamphlets on Scottish, European and environmental issues. *Address:* 107 Palladian, Victoria Bridge Road, Bath BA2 3FL.

HENDERSON, Jane Elisabeth, CB 2004; Chairman, Board of Governors, Bath Spa University, since 2013 (Member of Board, since 2011; Deputy Chairman, 2012–13); *b* 2 May 1952; *m* 1979, Clive Abbott; one *s* one *d*. *Educ:* Tunbridge Wells Grammar Sch.; Somerville Coll., Oxford (BA 1973; BPhil 1975; MA); Birkbeck Coll., Univ. of London (MSc 1983). Joined NI Office, 1975, Pvte Sec. to Perm. Sec., 1977–79; HM Treasury, 1979–81; CSSB, 1984–85; Industrial Econs Div., HM Treasury, 1985–86; Dept of Employment, 1986–88; SW Regl Dir, Employment Service, 1988–92; Trng, Enterprise and Educn Directorate, Dept of Employment, 1992–94; Dir of Finance and Funding, HEFCE, 1994–96; Dir of Resources, Rural Develt Commn, 1996–97; Regl Dir, Govt Office for the SW, 1998–2005; Strategic Advr on Sustainable Communities, IDeA, 2005–06; Chief Exec., SW of England Regl Develt Agency, 2006–12. Non-exec. Bd Mem., Yeovil District Hosp. Foundn Trust, 2013–. Trustee, Dementia UK, 2011–13. Hon. LLD Exeter, 2005; Hon. DBus Plymouth, 2010.

HENDERSON, Very Rev. Janet, (Mrs D. M. Challoner); Spiritual and Pastoral Care Manager, St Michael's Hospice, Harrogate, since 2013 (Trustee, 2008–13); *b* 12 May 1957; *d* of John Wilson Henderson and Megan (*née* Williams); *m* 1996, David Michael Challoner. *Educ:* Addenbrooke's Sch. of Nursing, Cambridge (RGN 1982); Durham Univ. (BA Hons 1988). Staff Nurse, Cambridge AHA, 1982–85; ordained deacon, 1988, priest, 1994; Asst Curate, St Peter and St Paul, Wisbech, 1988–90; Parish Deacon, Bestwood Team Ministry, Nottingham, 1990–93; Lectr, St John's Coll., Nottingham, 1993–97; Associate Priest NSM, St Michael and All Angels, Bramcote, Nottingham, 1994–97; Lectr, Cambridge Theol Fedn, and Tutor, Ridley Hall Theol Coll., 1997–2001; Dean, Women's Ministry, Dio. of Southwell, 2001–07; Priest-in-Charge, St Patrick's, Nuthall, 2001–07; Residentiary Canon, Ripon Cath., 2007–11; Archdeacon of Richmond, 2007–13; Hon. Canon, and Diocesan Advr on Non-stip. Ministry, Dio. of Ripon and Leeds, 2011–13; Dean of Llandaff, 2013. Dir, 2008–13, Tutor, 2014–, St John's Coll., Durham Univ. *Publications:* (ed jtly) Pastoral Prayers, 1996; articles in British Jl of Theological Educn, Anvil. *Recreations:* playing the double bass and piano, walking. *Address:* St Michael's Hospice, Crimple House, Hornbeam Park Avenue, Harrogate HG2 8QL.

HENDERSON, Dame Joan; *see* Kelleher, Dame J.

HENDERSON, Rt Rev. Julian Tudor; *see* Blackburn, Bishop of.

HENDERSON, Hon. Sir Launcelot (Dinadan James), Kt 2007; **Hon. Mr Justice Henderson;** a Judge of the High Court of Justice, Chancery Division, since 2007; *b* 20 Nov. 1951; *er s* of Baron Henderson of Brompton, KCB; *m* 1989, Elaine Elizabeth Webb; two *s* one *d*. *Educ:* Westminster Sch.; Balliol Coll., Oxford (MA). Fellow of All Souls Coll., Oxford, 1974–81, 1982–89 and 2008–. Called to the Bar, Lincoln's Inn, 1977, Bencher, 2004; practised as Barrister (Chancery), 1978–2006; Standing Junior Counsel: to Inland Revenue (Chancery), 1987–91; to Inland Revenue, 1991–95; QC 1995; a Dep. High Court Judge, Chancery Div., 2001–07. Trustee, Samuel Courtauld Trust, 2005–13. *Recreations:* botany, art, music, books. *Address:* Royal Courts of Justice, Rolls Building, Fetter Lane, EC4A 1NL.
See also Rt Rev. R. C. A. Henderson.

HENDERSON, Mark; lighting designer, since 1981; *b* 26 Sept. 1957; *s* of Gordon Henderson and Margaret Henderson (*née* Moakes); two *s*. *Educ:* Sherwood Hall Tech. Grammar Sch., Mansfield. Chief electrician for Kent Opera, English Music Th., London Contemporary Dance, Sadler's Wells and Opera North, 1978–; lighting designs for: *theatre:* numerous West End productions including: Grease, Follies, Carmen Jones, Rowan Atkinson in Revue, Home, Design for Living; Passion, 1996; West Side Story, 1998; Spend, Spend, Spend, 1999; The Real Thing, 2000; Sunset Boulevard, 2001; A Few Good Men, 2005; The Sound of Music, 2006; RNT productions include: Cat on a Hot Tin Roof (also Broadway), 1988; Hamlet, 1989; The Oedipus Plays, 1996; Amy's View, Copenhagen, Antony and Cleopatra, 1998; Battle Royal, 1999; All My Sons, 2001; The History Boys, 2004 (also NY; Tony Award for Lighting Design (Play), 2006); The Alchemist, 2006; RSC productions include: Macbeth, Kiss Me Kate, The Lion, the Witch and the Wardrobe; Almeida Theatre productions include: Phèdre, The Ice Man Cometh, 1998; Vassa, Plenty, 1999; Richard II, Coriolanus, 2000; Lulu, 2001; *opera* productions include: The Flying Dutchman (Royal Opera); Anna Karenina, The Silver Tassie, 2000, ENO; Othello, Glyndebourne, 2001; Tosca, ROH, 2006; *dance* productions include: Agora, Shadows in the Sun (London Contemp. Dance Th.); Quicksilver (Rambert Dance Co.); Tales of Beatrix Potter, The Judas Tree, Daphnis and Chloë, Sleeping Beauty (Royal Ballet); The Nutcracker, 1999; *films* include: The Tall Guy, 1988; Under Milk Wood, 1992. Olivier Awards: Lighting Designer of the Year, 1992; Best Lighting Designer, 1995, 2000, 2002. *Address:* c/o PBJ Management, 22 Rathbone Street, W1T 1LG.

HENDERSON, Mark; Chief Executive, Home Group Ltd, since 2008; *b* 12 Oct. 1962; *s* of Ralph and Mary Henderson; *m* 1987, Lindsey Robertson; one *s* one *d*. *Educ:* Univ. of Dundee (BSc Hons). Planning Technician: Dunfermline DC, 1979–87; Dundee DC, 1987–91; Strategic Policy Manager, Clackmannanshire, 1994–96; Partnership Funding Officer, Angus Council, 1996–97; Asst Dir (Regeneration), N Lincs Council, 1997–2000; Dir of Ops, One Northeast, 2000–03; Chief Exec., Northumberland CC, 2003–08. Mem., Dundee DC, 1992–96. *Recreations:* motorsports, family activities, following Dunfermline Athletic FC and Newcastle United FC. *Address:* Home Group Ltd, 2 Gosforth Park Way, Gosforth Business Park, Newcastle-upon-Tyne NE12 8ET.

HENDERSON, Mark Giles Fyfield; Head of Communications, Wellcome Trust, since 2012; *b* Lambeth, 22 Aug. 1974; *s* of Giles Ian Henderson, *qv*; *m* 2009, Niki Vivien; one *s* one *d*. *Educ:* Winchester Coll.; Balliol Coll., Oxford (BA 1st Cl. Hons Modern Hist. 1996). The Times, 1996–2011: sci. corresp., 2000–06; Sci. Ed., 2006–11. Award for Statistical Excellence in Journalism, Royal Statistical Soc.; Med. Journalists' Assoc. awards; Eur. Best Cancer Reporter, Eur. Sch. of Oncol. *Publications:* 50 Genetics Ideas You Really Need to Know, 2009; The Geek Manifesto: why science matters, 2012. *Recreations:* ski-ing, popular science, cricket, football, Twitter. *Address:* Wellcome Trust, 215 Euston Road, NW1 2BE. *T:* (020) 7611 8540. *E:* m.henderson@wellcome.ac.uk. *Club:* Queens Park Rangers Football.

HENDERSON, Michael John Glidden, FCA; Chairman: Advisory Board, Quexco Inc. (USA), since 2005 (Executive Vice-Chairman, 2002–05); Sweett Group PLC (formerly Cyril Sweett Ltd, then Cyril Sweett Group PLC), since 2010 (non-executive Director, since 1998); *b* 19 Aug. 1938; *s* of William Glidden Henderson and Aileen Judith Henderson (*née* Molloy); *m* 1965, Stephanie Maria Dyer; four *s*. *Educ:* St Benedict's Sch., Ealing. FCA 1971. Took articles with William Dyson Jones & Co., 1956; qual. as chartered accountant, 1961; Whinney Smith & Whinney & Co., 1963; Goodlass Wall & Lead Industries, later Cookson Group plc, 1965; Cookson Group: Dir, 1975; Man. Dir, 1979; Chief Exec., 1984–90; Chm. and Chief Exec., 1990–91; Exec. Dir, Ronar Services Ltd, 1991–2006. Chm., Henderson Crossthwaite, subseq. Investec Henderson Crossthwaite, Hldgs Ltd, 1995–2000; Dir, Tioxide Gp, 1987–90; non-executive Director: Guinness Mahon Holdings, 1988–2000; Three Counties Financial Mgt Services Ltd, 1991–2009; ECO-BAT Technologies, 1999–2002. Mem., Innovation Adv. Bd, DTI, 1988–93. Trustee, Natural History Mus. Develt Trust, 1990–2000. Mem.

Council, St Augustine's Soc., 2007–. Mem., Catholic Union, 2008– (Mem. Council, 2012–; Chm., Membership and Commns Cttee, 2013–). Chm., Exec. Cttee and Trustee, Catholic Union Charitable Trust Ltd, 2014–. FRSA 1989. Governor: St George's Coll., Weybridge, 1990–2011 (Dep. Chm., 2002–11; Chm., F and GP Cttee, 1991–2011); Cranmore Sch., W Horsley, 1992– (Chm., 2012–; Dep. Chm., 1998–2012; Chm., F and GP Cttee, 1992–2012); St Teresa's Convent, Effingham, 2002–14 (Chm., F and GP Cttee, 2003–11; Vice Chm., 2011–14). Mem., Effingham and Fetcham Pastoral Council, 2012–. KCHS 2010 (KHS 2005) (Mem. Council and Treas., S Section, 2007–). *Recreations:* tennis, golf, watching all sports, reading, music, visiting and being involved with family including 16 grandchildren. *Address:* Langdale, Woodland Drive, East Horsley, Surrey KT24 5AN. *T:* (01483) 283844. *E:* mike.henderson3@btopenworld.com. *Clubs:* MCC, Queen's; Wisley Golf (Dir, 2002–07; Dep. Chm., 2004–07); Horsley Sports; Sussex Cricket; Surrey Cricket; Thurlestone Golf; Salcombe Yacht; Kingsbridge Tennis.

HENDERSON, Nicholas John; National Hunt racehorse trainer, since 1978; *b* 10 Dec. 1950; *s* of late John Ronald Henderson, CVO, OBE; *m* 1978, Diana Amanda Thorne; three *d*. *Educ:* Eton. Amateur rider, 1970–78 (rode 75 winners, incl. Imperial Cup, Sandown and Liverpool Foxhunters); Asst Trainer to Fred Winter, 1973–78. Trained over 1,000 winners, incl. See You Then (Champion Hurdle, 1985, 1986, 1987), Brown Windsor (Whitbread Gold Cup, 1989), Remittance Man (Champion Chase, 1992), Punjabi (Champion Hurdle, 2009), Binocular (Champion Hurdle, 2010). Leading Nat. Hunt trainer, 1986–87, 1987–88; Piper Heidsieck Trainer of the Year, 1986, 1987, 1988. *Address:* Seven Barrows, Lambourn, Hungerford, Berks RG17 8UH.

HENDERSON, (Patrick) David, CMG 1992; economist, author and consultant; Visiting Professor, Westminster Business School, 2009–12; *b* 10 April 1927; *s* of late David Thomson Henderson and late Eleanor Henderson; *m* 1960, Marcella Kodicek (*d* 2011); one *s* one *d*. *Educ:* Ellesmere Coll., Shropshire; Corpus Christi Coll., Oxford. Fellow and Tutor in Economics, Lincoln Coll., Oxford, 1948–65 (Hon. Fellow, 1991); Univ. Lectr in Economics, Oxford, 1950–65; Commonwealth Fund Fellow (Harvard), 1952–53; Junior Proctor, Oxford Univ., 1955–56; Economic Adviser, HM Treasury, 1957–58; Chief Economist, Min. of Aviation, 1965–67; Adviser Harvard Development Advisory Service (Athens and Kuala Lumpur), 1967–68; Vis. Lectr, World Bank, 1968–69; Economist, World Bank, 1969–75, Dir of Economics Dept 1971–72; Prof. of Political Economy, UCL, 1975–83; Hd of Econs and Stats Dept, OECD, 1984–92. Mem., Commn on Environmental Pollution, 1977–80; Special Adviser, Sec. of State for Wales, 1978–79; Member: Nat. Ports Council, 1979–81; Bd, Commonwealth Develt Corp., 1980–83; Academic Adv. Council, Global Warming Policy Foundn, 2009– (Chm., 2009–14). Formerly Visiting Fellow or Professor: OECD Develt Centre, Paris; Centre for Eur. Policy Studies, Brussels; Fondation Nationale des Sciences Politiques, Paris; Monash Univ., Melb.; Univ. of Melb.; NZ Business Roundtable; Melb. Business Sch. Reith Lectr, BBC, 1985; Copland Meml Address, 1989; Shapiro Lectr, LSE, 1993; Downing Oration, Melbourne Univ., 1995; Hibberd Lectr, Melb. Business Sch., 1997; Wincott Lecture, 2000; Lang Hancock Lecture, 2002. *Publications:* India: the energy sector, 1975; Innocence and Design: the influence of economic ideas on policy, 1986; The Changing Fortunes of Economic Liberalism, 1998; Misguided Virtue, 2001; The Role of Business in the Modern World, 2004; (jointly) Nyasaland: The Economics of Federation, 1960; ed and contrib.: Economic Growth in Britain, 1965; contributed: The British Economy in the 1950's, 1962; Public Enterprise, 1968; Public Economics, 1969; Unfashionable Economics, 1970; The World Bank, Multilateral Aid and the 1970's, 1973; The Economic Development of Yugoslavia, 1975; Contemporary Problems of Economic Policy, 1983; Protectionism and Growth, 1985; Economic Policies for the 1990s, 1991; (ed jtly) Trade Blocs: the future of regional integration, 1994; articles in economic and other jls.

HENDERSON, Prof. Paul, CBE 2003; DPhil; Director of Science, Natural History Museum, 1995–2003; *b* 7 Nov. 1940; *s* of Thomas William Henderson and Dorothy Violet (*née* Marriner); *m* 1966, Elizabeth Kathryn Ankerson; one *s* one *d*. *Educ:* King's Coll. Sch., Wimbledon; Univ. of London (BSc 1963); Univ. of Oxford (DPhil 1966). FGS 1990; CGeol 1990; FLS 1997. Asst Lectr in Chemistry, Glasgow Univ., 1967–68; Lectr in Geochem., Chelsea Coll., Univ. of London, 1968–76; British Museum (Natural History), subseq. Natural History Museum: PSO, 1977, Grade 6, 1984, Dep. Keeper, 1987, Keeper, 1989–95, Dept of Mineralogy; Associate Dir, Earth Scis, 1992–95. Visiting Professor: Univ. of Bern, Switzerland, 1989; UCL, 1990–98 (Hon. Prof., 1999–). Pres., Mineralogical Soc., 1989–91 (Mem. Council, 1974–76 and 1986–89); Vice-Pres., Geol Soc., 2002–08; Member Council: Eur. Assoc. for Geochem., 1986–94; Internat. Mineralog. Assoc., 1989–94. Member: Sci. Adv. Bd, 1994–99, Expert Commn, 2001–02, Museum für Naturkunde, Berlin; Sci. Adv. Cttee, 2000–01, Conseil Scientifique, 2002–06, Muséum Nat. d'Histoire Naturelle, Paris. Trustee, Horniman Mus. and Public Park Trust, 2004–12. Fourmarier Medal, Belgian Geol Soc., 1989. *Publications:* Inorganic Geochemistry, 1982; (ed) Rare Earth Element Geochemistry, 1984; (with G. M. Henderson) Cambridge Handbook of Earth Science Data, 2009; James Sowerby: the enlightenment's natural historian, 2015; contribs to jls on geochem. and mineral chem. *Recreations:* music, mineralogy, history, Paris, wine. *Address:* Department of Earth Sciences, University College London, Gower Street, WC1E 6BT. *E:* p.henderson@ucl.ac.uk.

See also G. M. Henderson.

HENDERSON, Air Vice-Marshal Peter William, CB 2000; MBE 1982; CEng, FRAeS; aerospace consultant; *b* 5 Nov. 1945. *Educ:* King's Sch., Macclesfield; RAF Coll. Cranwell (BSc CNAA). Inspectorate of Flight Safety, 1975; RAF Germany, 1978; RAF Staff Coll., 1982; RAF Abingdon, 1982–84; Dept of Air Mem. for Supply and Orgn, 1984–87; Mem., Ordnance Bd, 1987; Stn Comdr, Abingdon, 1990–92; Logistic Comd Project Sponsor, HQ RAF Support Comd, 1992–95; Dir 1995–97, Dir Gen., 1997–99, RAF Support Mgt; Dir Gen., Equipment Support (Air), Mem., Defence Logistics Mgt Bd, and Mem., Air Force Bd, Defence Council, 1999–2000, retd. *Recreations:* gardening, motoring, sailing. *Club:* Royal Air Force.

HENDERSON, Dr Richard, FRS 1983; Member of the Scientific Staff, Medical Research Council Laboratory of Molecular Biology, Cambridge, since 1973 (Director, 1996–2006); Fellow of Darwin College, Cambridge, 1981–2012, now Emeritus Fellow; *b* 19 July 1945; *s* of late John and Grace Henderson; *m* 1st, 1969, Penelope FitzGerald (marr. diss. 1988); one *s* one *d* (and one *d* decd); 2nd, 1995, Jade Li. *Educ:* Hawick High Sch.; Boroughmuir Secondary Sch.; Edinburgh Univ. (BSc); Corpus Christi Coll., Cambridge (Hon. Fellow, 2003); PhD Cantab 1970. Helen Hay Whitney Fellow, Yale Univ., 1970–73. Mem., MRC, 2008–14. Founder FMedSci 1998. Foreign Associate, Acad. of Sci., USA, 1998. Hon. DSc Edinburgh, 2008. William Bate Hardy Prize, Cambridge Phil Soc., 1978; Ernst Ruska Prize for Electron Microscopy, Ernst Ruska Foundn, 1981; Lewis S. Rosenstiel Award, Brandeis Univ., 1991; Louis Jeantet Award, Jeantet Foundn, Geneva, 1993; Gregori Aminoff Prize, Royal Swedish Acad. of Scis, 1999. *Publications:* research pubns and reviews in scientific jls. *Recreations:* canoeing, wine-tasting. *Address:* MRC Laboratory of Molecular Biology, Francis Crick Avenue, Cambridge CB2 0QH. *T:* (01223) 267000.

HENDERSON, Rt Rev. Richard Crosbie Aitken, DPhil; Team Vicar, Heart of Eden Team Ministry, 2011–12; an Honorary Assistant Bishop, Diocese of Carlisle, 2011–14; *b* 27 March 1957; *s* of Baron Henderson of Brompton, KBE; *m* 1985, Anita Julia Whiting; one *s* two *d*. *Educ:* Westminster Sch.; Magdalen Coll., Oxford (MA, DPhil 1984); St John's Coll., Nottingham (DipTh Univ. of Nottingham 1984; Dip Pastoral Studies 1986). Ordained deacon, 1986, priest, 1987; Curate, Chinnor with Emmington and Sydenham, Dio. Oxford, 1986–89; Diocese of Cork, Cloyne and Ross: Incumbent, Abbeystrewry Union, 1989–95; Ross Union, 1995–98; Canon, Cork and Ross Cathedrals, 1993–95; Prebendary of Cork, 1995–98; Dean of Ross, 1995–98; Bishop of Tuam, Killala and Achonry, 1998–2011. *Publications:* The Jealousy of Jonah, 2006. *Recreations:* woodwork, metalwork, horticulture.

See also Hon. Sir L. D. J. Henderson.

HENDERSON, Richard Mitchell, CB 2007; WS; Solicitor to the Scottish Executive, and Head of the Government Legal Service for Scotland, 1999–2007; President, Law Society of Scotland, 2007–09 (Vice-President, May–Aug. 2007); *b* 17 April 1947; *s* of Thomas Alex Henderson and Hester Susan England Henderson (*née* Mitchell); *m* 1970, Frances Lesley Eadie; one *s* one *d*. *Educ:* Cellardyke Primary Sch., Anstruther; Strathallan Sch.; Univ. of Edinburgh (LIB Hons 1969). Admitted Solicitor, 1971; WS 2006; Solicitor to the Sec. of State for Scotland, 1998. Chm., Scottish Cttee, Admin. Justice and Tribunals Council, 2009–13. *Recreations:* golf (occasional and erratic), walking, being in the fresh air.

HENDERSON, Sir Richard (Yates), KCVO 2006; TD 1966; JP; Lord-Lieutenant of Ayrshire and Arran, 1991–2006; *b* 7 July 1931; *s* of late John Wishart Henderson and Dorothy (*née* Yates); *m* 1957, Frances Elizabeth Chrystal; two *s* one *d* (and one *s* decd). *Educ:* Rugby; Hertford Coll., Oxford (BA); Glasgow Univ. (LLB). Served Royal Scots Greys, 1950–52; Ayrshire Yeomanry TA, 1953–69. Partner, Mitchells Roberton, Solicitors, Glasgow, 1958–90; Trustee, TSB, Glasgow, 1966–74; Dir, West of Scotland TSB, 1974–83. Hon. Sheriff, S Strathclyde, Dumfries and Galloway at Ayr, 1997. Ensign, Royal Company of Archers, Queen's Body Guard for Scotland, 2004–. Hon. Col, Ayrshire Yeo. Sqn, Scottish Yeo., 1992–97; Pres., Lowlands TAVRA, 1996–2000. DL Ayrshire, 1970–90. *Recreations:* shooting, tennis, golf. *Address:* Blairston, by Ayr KA7 4EF. *T:* (01292) 441601. *Club:* Western (Glasgow).

HENDERSON, Roger Anthony; QC 1980; a Recorder of the Crown Court, 1983–2012; a Deputy High Court Judge, 1987–2012; *b* 21 April 1943; *s* of late Dr Peter Wallace Henderson, MC and Dr Stella Dolores Henderson; *m* 1968, Catherine Margaret Williams (*d* 2013); three *d* (and one *d* decd). *Educ:* Radley Coll.; St Catharine's Coll., Cambridge (Scholar; 1st Cl. Hons degree in Law, MA; Adderley Prize for Law, 1964). Inner Temple: Duke of Edinburgh Award, 1962; Major Scholarship, 1964; called to the Bar, 1964; Bencher, 1985. Counsel to King's Cross Inquiry, 1988. Mem., Bar Council, 1988–91; Chm., Public Affairs Cttee of Bar, 1989–90. Chm., Civil Service Arbitration Tribunal, 1994–; Member: Exec. Council, British Acad. of Forensic Sciences, 1977–90 (Pres., 1986–87); Council of Legal Educn, 1983–90. Chm., Assoc. of Regulatory and Disciplinary Lawyers, 2003–09; Vice Pres., Health and Safety Lawyers' Assoc., 2005–. Gov., London Hosp. Med. Coll., 1989–96 (Chm., Council, 1993–96); Chm., Special Cttee, St Peter's Hosps, 1989–92; Mem. Council, QMW, 1993–2005; Mem. Council, Southampton Univ., 2009–12; Chm., Med. Coll. of St Bartholomew's Hosp. Trust, 2012–. FRSA 1994. Hon. Fellow, QMC, London, 2006. *Recreations:* fly-fishing, gardening, shooting. *Address:* Holbury Mill, Lockerley, Romsey, Hants SO51 0JR. *T:* (01794) 340583; 7A Berkeley Gardens, W8 4AP. *Club:* Boodle's.

HENDERSON, Victor Joseph, CMG 2000; HM Diplomatic Service, retired; Senior Consultant, MEC International Ltd, since 2001; *b* 10 Jan. 1941; *s* of Frederick Ilwyn Henderson and Mary Elizabeth Henderson; *m* 1966, Heather Winifred Steed; one *s* one *d*. *Educ:* Rhondda Co. Grammar Sch. for Boys; King's Coll., London (BA Hons Spanish 1961). Joined HM Diplomatic Service, 1966: MECAS, Lebanon, 1967–69; Third Sec. (Commercial), Jedda, 1969–72; Second Sec. (Commercial), Bahrain, 1972–75; FCO, 1975–78; Second, later First Sec., Caracas, 1978–82; Consul, Jerusalem, 1982–87; FCO, 1987–90; First Sec. (Political, later Commercial), Helsinki, 1990–94; Dep. Head, Jt Export Promotion Directorate, FCO/DTI, 1995–97; Ambassador to the Yemen, 1997–2001. Analyst (pt-time), BBC Monitoring Services, 2006–. Chm., British Yemeni Soc., 2006–08. *Recreations:* watching cricket, reading, listening to music (especially jazz). *Address:* c/o MEC International Ltd, Granville House, 132-135 Sloane Street, SW1X 9AX.

HENDERSON-SELLERS, Prof. Ann, PhD, DSc; Professor, Department of Environment and Geography (formerly Physical Geography), Macquarie University, 2008–12, now Emeritus; *b* 7 March 1952; *d* of Thomas William Futtit and Ruth Forester Fielding; *m* 1974, Prof. Brian Henderson-Sellers. *Educ:* Sheffield Girls' High Sch.; Pate's, Cheltenham; Univ. of Bristol (BSc Hons Maths); Univ. of Leicester (PhD 1976, DSc 1999). University of Liverpool: Lectr, 1977–82; Sen. Lectr, 1982–86; Reader, 1986–88; Personal Chair in Physical Geography, 1988; Prof. of Physical Geog., and Dir, Climatic Impacts Centre, Macquarie Univ., 1988–96; Dep. Vice-Chancellor, R&D, RMIT, 1996–98; Dir, Envmt, Australian Nuclear Sci. and Technol. Orgn, 1998–2005; Dir, World Climate Res. Prog., WMO, 2006–07. Vis. Lectr, Univ. of Witwatersrand, S Africa, 1979; Vis. Res. Fellow, NASA Goddard Inst. for Space Studies, 1981–82; Vis. Prof., Univ. of Louvain-la-Neuve, Belgium, 1983; Vis. Scientist, Nat. Center for Atmospheric Res., USA, 1985–2003. Hon. DSc Bristol, 2011. *Publications:* (jtly) Atmospheric Pollution, 4th edn 1981; The Origin and Evolution of Planetary Atmospheres, 1983; Satellite Sensing of a Cloudy Atmosphere, 1984; (jtly) Contemporary Climatology, 1986, 2nd edn 1999; (jtly) The Climate Modelling Primer, 1987, 4th edn 2013; (jtly) The Greenhouse Effect: living in a warmer Australia, 1989; (ed jtly) Vegetation and Climate Interactions in Semi-Arid Regions, 1991; (ed jtly) Climate Change Atlas, 1995; (ed) Future Climates of the World: a modelling perspective, 1995, 2nd edn as Future of the World's Climate, 2012; (ed jtly) Climate Change: developing Southern Hemisphere perspectives, 1996; (ed jtly) Assessing Climate Change, 1997; (jtly) The Great North Walk Companion, 2009; 453 articles in tech. jls. *Recreation:* collecting Winnie the Pooh books in different languages.

HENDERSON-STEWART, Sir David (James), 2nd Bt *cr* 1957; *b* 3 July 1941; *s* of Sir James Henderson-Stewart, 1st Bt, MP, and of Anna Margaret (*née* Greenwell); *S* father, 1961; *m* 1972, Anne, *d* of Count Serge de Pahlen; three *s* one *d*. *Educ:* Eton Coll.; Trinity Coll., Oxford. *Heir: s* David Henderson-Stewart [*b* 2 Feb. 1973; *m* 1997, Xenia Yagello; two *s* two *d* (of whom one *s* one *d* are twins)]. *Address:* 90 Oxford Gardens, W10 5UW. *T:* (020) 8964 4356.

HENDON, David Anthony, CBE 2006; FREng, FIET; Director, Information Economy and Life Sciences, Department for Business, Innovation and Skills, 2010–11; Senior Advisor, Ofcom, since 2011; Director, Hendon Communications Strategy Ltd, since 2011; *b* 19 Oct. 1949; *s* of Anthony Leonard Hendon and Constance Audrey Hendon (*née* Clayton); *m* 1976, Gillian Anne Iles; one *s* two *d*. *Educ:* Royal Grammar Sch., Guildford; Southampton Univ. (BSc Eng 1972). FIET (FIEE 2000); CEng 1978; FREng 2002. MoD, 1973–84 (Principal, 1981–84); Asst Dir (Engrg), Home Office, 1984–88; Dep. Dir, 1988–92, Dir, 1992–98, Technol., Policy, Communications and Inf., Industries Directorate, DTI; Chief Exec., Radiocommunications Agency, 1998–2002; Hd of Communications and Inf. Industries Directorate, DTI, 2002–03; Dir, Business Relns, then Inf. Economy, DTI, later BERR, subseq. BIS, 2003–10. Chm. Bd, Eur. Telecommunications Standards Inst., 1995–99. Chm., Radio Spectrum Internat. Consulting Ltd, 1998–2002. Chair: 4G/TV Co-existence Oversight Bd, DCMS, 2013–; Strategic Adv. Bd, 5G Innovation Centre, Univ. of Surrey, 2013–. Non-executive Director: Multiple Access Communications Ltd, 2012–; Continuum Bridge Ltd, 2013–. Member: PPARC, 2002–06; EPSRC, 2006–09. Vis. Prof., Univ. of Surrey, 2013–. Trustee, Radio Communications Foundn, 2003– (Vice-Chm., 2009–). Spastics Society, later Scope: Mem. Council, 1987–96; Vice-Chm., 1991–93; Chm., Audit

Cttee, 1993–98; Hon. Life Mem., 1996. Chm., White Lodge Centre, Chertsey, 1980–85. Gov., Guildford Co. Sch., 1994–98. *Recreations:* grandchildren, food and wine, Maine Coon cats. *Address:* 2 Ellis Avenue, Onslow Village, Guildford GU2 7SR. *T:* (01483) 823108.

HENDRICK, Mark Phillip, CEng; MP (Lab and Co-op) Preston, since Nov. 2000; *b* 2 Nov. 1958; *s* of Brian Francis Hendrick and Jennifer (*née* Chapman); *m* 2008, Yannan Yu. *Educ:* Liverpool Poly. (BSc Hons Electrical and Electronic Engrg); Univ. of Manchester (MSc Computer Sci.; Cert Ed). CEng 1987. Trainee Technician, Signal and Telecommunications, BR, 1975–78; Student Engr, 1979–81; RSRE Malvern, MoD, 1979; Special Systems Unit, STC plc, 1980; AEG Telefunken, Seligenstadt, Germany, 1981; Design Engr, Daresbury Lab., SERC, 1982–84 and 1985–88; Lectr, Stockport Coll., 1989–94. MEP (Lab and Co-op) Lancashire Central, 1994–99; contested (Lab) NW Reg., 1999. PPS to Sec. of State, DEFRA, 2003–06, FCO, 2006–07, to Minister of Justice, 2007–08. Member: Internat. Develt Select Cttee, 2008–10; Foreign Affairs Select Cttee, 2012–; Chm., All Party Parly China Gp, 2010–12. *Recreations:* football supporter (Manchester City and Preston North End), travel, chess, German and French. *Address:* c/o House of Commons, SW1A 0AA; (constituency office) PTMC, Marsh Lane, Preston PR1 8UQ. *T:* (01772) 883575. *Clubs:* Parkfield Labour; Lonsdale (Preston).

HENDRICKS, Barbara; American soprano; *b* 20 Nov. 1948; *d* of Rev. M. L. Hendricks and Della Hendricks; *m*; one *s* one *d*. *Educ:* Univ. of Nebraska (BS Chem. and Math. 1969); Juilliard Sch. of Music, NY (Schol.; BM); studied under Jennie Tourel. Début, l'Incoronazione di Poppea, San Francisco Opera, 1976; has appeared with opera cos of Berlin, Boston, Florence, Glyndebourne, Hamburg, La Scala, Milan, LA, Royal Opera, Covent Garden, etc; concert performances with major orchestras; numerous recordings. Launched own record label, Arte Verum, 2005. Goodwill Ambassador, UN High Commn for Refugees, 1987. Hon. Dr Juilliard, NY, 2000. Prince of Asturias Prize, 2000. Commandeur des Arts et des Lettres (France), 1986; Chevalier de la Légion d'Honneur (France), 1993; St George's Cross (Catalonia, Spain), 2006.

HENDRICKS, Rt Rev. Paul Joseph; Auxiliary Bishop in Southwark, (RC), since 2006; *b* 18 March 1956; *s* of Gerald Hendricks and Grace Hendricks (*née* Deacon). *Educ:* Holy Innocents Primary Sch., Orpington; St Mary's Grammar Sch., Sidcup; Corpus Christi Coll., Oxford (BA Physics 1977, MA); Gregorian Univ., Rome (PhL 1985). Ordained deacon, 1983, priest, 1984; Asst Priest, St Boniface Church, Tooting, 1985–89; Lectr in Philosophy, St John's Seminary, Wonersh, 1989–99; Parish Priest, Our Lady of Sorrows, Peckham, 1999–2006. *Recreations:* reading, walking, cats, model helicopters, music (playing clarinet and piano). *Address:* 95 Carshalton Road, Sutton SM1 4LL. *T:* (020) 8643 8007. *E:* bishop.hendricks@gmail.com.

HENDRIE, Dr Gerald Mills; musicologist, composer, harpsichordist and organist; Professor of Music, The Open University, 1969–90; *b* 28 Oct. 1935; *s* of James Harold Hendrie and Florence Mary MacPherson; *m* 1st, 1962, Dinah Florence Barsham, BMus, PhD (*d* 1985); two *s*; 2nd, 1986, Dr Lynette Anne Maddern, MB, BS. *Educ:* Framlingham Coll., Suffolk; Royal Coll. of Music; Selwyn Coll., Cambridge (MA, MusB, PhD). FRCO, ARCM. Director of Music, Homerton Coll., Cambridge, 1962–63; Lectr in the History of Music, Univ. of Manchester, 1963–67; Prof. and Chm., Dept of Music, Univ. of Victoria, BC, Canada, 1967–69; Reader in Music, subseq. Prof., The Open Univ., 1969–90; Dir of Studies in Music, St John's Coll., Cambridge, 1981–84, Supervisor, 1977–84. Vis. Fellow in Music, Univ. of WA, 1985. *Publications:* Musica Britannica XX, Orlando Gibbons: Keyboard Music, 1962, 3rd rev. edn 2010; G. F. Handel: Anthems für Cannons, 3 vols, 1985, 1987, 1991; Anthems für die Chapel Royal, 1992; Utrecht Te Deum und Jubilate, 1998; articles for Die Musik in Geschichte und Gegenwart; musical compositions include: Five Bagatelles for piano, 1980; Four Excursions for piano, 1983; Three Pieces for flute and piano, 1985; Specula Petro for organ, 1988; Quintet for Brass, 1988; Choral: Hommage à César Franck for organ, 1990; Le Tombeau de Marcel Dupré (for organ): Toccata and Fugue, 1991; Prelude and Fugue, 1991; Prelude and Fugue on the name BACH, 1992; Two Sketches on the name BACH, 1993; Sonata No 1, In Praise of St Asaph, for organ, 1994; Four Consolations (after Boethius) for unaccompanied choir, 1996; Requiem, for soprano, chorus, organ, 1997; Sonata No 2, In Praise of Reconciliation, for organ, 1998, for piano, 1998; Premier Livre d'Orgue, 1999; Deuxième Livre d'Orgue, 2000; Missa Aquitaniae, for soprano, chorus, organ, 2003; Sounats Campanetos/Ring out, Sing out, Noël Gascon, for SATB accompanied, 2005; Sonata No 3, Sonate en Trio, for organ, 2006; A Handful of Rags for piano, 2013; Another Handful of Rags for piano, 2014; Five New Rags for piano, 2015; much church music. *Recreations:* walking, gardening. *Address:* Au Village, 32190 Caillavet, France. *T:* 562644104.

HENDRIE, Robert Andrew Michie; HM Diplomatic Service, retired; Ambassador to Uruguay, 1994–98; *b* 4 May 1938; *s* of John Hendrie, Edinburgh and Effie Campbell (*née* Mackay); *m* 1964, Consuelo Liaño Solórzano; two *d*. *Educ:* Bradford Grammar Sch.; Trinity Hall, Cambridge (BA, MA). Joined HM Diplomatic Service, 1961; MECAS, Beirut, 1961–62; Political Residency, Bahrain, 1962–65; Tehran, 1965–68; Tripoli, 1968–69; Latin America Dept, FCO, 1969–73; Lima, 1973–75; Buenos Aires, 1975–80; Asst Hd, Central Africa Dept, ME Dept and Inf. Dept, FCO, 1980–86; Consul-General: Lille, 1986–90; Dubai, UAE, 1990–94. Mem., S Atlantic Council, 2001–; Vice Pres., British Uruguayan Soc., 2012–. Mem., RSAA, 2003–. MCIL (MIL 1987). Freeman, City of London, 2012. *Recreations:* reading, walking, watching Rugby, languages. *Address:* c/o Foreign and Commonwealth Office, King Charles Street, SW1A 2AH. *Clubs:* Canning, Roehampton.

HENDRON, Joseph Gerard; Member (SDLP) Belfast West, Northern Ireland Assembly, 1998–2003; *b* 12 Nov. 1932; *m* 1974, Sally (*née* Lennon); three *s* one *d*. *Educ:* St Malachy's Coll.; Queen's Univ., Belfast (MB 1957). FRCGP 1987. GP, W Belfast. Mem. (SDLP) Belfast CC, 1981–93. MP (SDLP) Belfast W, 1992–97; contested (SDLP) same seat, 1983, 1987, 1997. Chm., Health, Social Services and Public Safety Cttee, NI Assembly. Mem., Parades Commn, 2006–10.

HENDRY, Andrew Egan Henderson, (Drew); MP (SNP) Inverness, Nairn, Badenoch and Strathspey, since 2015; *b* 31 May 1964; *m* Jackie; four c. Shop worker, latterly Dir, multinat. appliance manufr; Founder and Chm., Teclan Ltd, 1999–. Mem. (SNP), Highland Council, 2007–15 (Leader, SNP Gp, 2011–15; Leader of Council, 2012–15). Vice Pres., Conf. of Maritime Peripheral Regions, 2012–. *Address:* House of Commons, SW1A 0AA.

HENDRY, Rt Hon. Charles; PC 2015; *b* 6 May 1959; *s* of late Charles William Righton Hendry and Margaret Anne Hendry; *m* 1995, Mrs Sallie A. Moores; two *s*, and one step *s* one step *d*. *Educ:* Rugby Sch.; Univ. of Edinburgh (BCom Hons 1981). Account Dir, Ogilvy and Mather PR, 1983–86; Burson-Marsteller: Associate Dir (PR), 1986–88; Sen. Counsellor, Public Affairs, 1990–92. Non-executive Chairman: Agenda Gp Ltd, 2001–05 (Dir and Chief Exec., 1999–2001); IncrediBull Ideas Ltd, 2003–04. Special Adviser to: Rt Hon. John Moore, 1988; Rt Hon. Anthony Newton, 1988–89; Chief of Staff to Leader of Cons. Party, 1997; Hd of Business Liaison, Cons. Party, 1997–99. Vice-Chm., Battersea Cons. Assoc., 1981–83. Contested (C): Clackmannan, 1983; Mansfield, 1987; MP (C) High Peak, 1992–97; contested (C) same seat, 1997; MP (C) Wealden, 2001–15. PPS to Sec. of State for Educn and Employment, 1995; a Vice Chm., Cons. Party, 1995–97; an Opposition Whip, 2001–02; Shadow Minister: for youth affairs, 2002–05; for industry and enterprise, 2005; for energy, science and technology, 2005–07; for Energy, Industry and Postal Affairs, 2007–08; for Energy, 2008–10; Minister of State, DECC, 2010–12; Prime Minister's Trade Envoy to Azerbaijan, Kazakhstan and Turkmenistan, 2012–15. Dep. Chm., Cons. Party, 2003–05. Member, Select Committee: on Procedure, 1992–94; on NI Affairs, 1994–97; on Culture, Media and Sport, 2003–04; on Energy and Climate Change, 2009–10. Secretary: Conservative Back bench Social Services Cttee, 1992–94; Cons. Back bench Home Improvement Sub-Cttee, 1993–94; Cons. Back bench Urban Affairs Cttee, 1994; Jt Chm., All-Party Parly Gp on Homelessness, 1992–96; Vice Chm., All Party Parly Internet Gp, 2005–08; Chm., British-Swiss Parly Gp, 2007–10. Sec., E Midlands Area Cons. MPs, 1992–97. Chm., Forewind Ltd, 2013–. Vis. Prof., Univ. of Edinburgh, 2012–. President: British Youth Council, 1992–97; Nat. Energy Action, 2013–15; BIEE, 2014–; Trustee: Drive for Youth, 1989–99; Friends of NACAB, 1992–95; Big Issue Foundn, 1995–97 (Patron, 1997–2010); British Youth Parlt, 2003–10. Hon. Fellow, Energy Inst., 2013. *Recreations:* family, opera, ski-ing.

HENDRY, Sir David (Forbes), Kt 2009; PhD; FBA 1987; FRSE; FAcSS; Professor of Economics, since 1982, and Director, Economic Modelling, Institute for New Economic Thinking (formerly Institute for Economic Modelling) at Oxford Martin School, since 2010, University of Oxford; Fellow, Nuffield College, Oxford, since 1982; *b* 6 March 1944; *s* of Robert Ernest Hendry and Catherine Helen (*née* Mackenzie); *m* 1966, Evelyn Rosemary (*née* Vass); one *d*. *Educ:* Aberdeen Univ. (MA 1st Cl. Hons); LSE (MSc Distinction, PhD). Fellow, Econometric Soc., 1975; FRSE 2002. London School of Economics: Lectr, 1969; Reader, 1973; Prof. of Econometrics, 1977–82; Leverhulme Personal Res. Prof. of Econs, Univ. of Oxford, 1995–2000. Vis. Professor: Yale Univ., 1975; Univ. of Calif, Berkeley, 1976; Catholic Univ. of Louvain, 1980; Univ. of Calif, San Diego, 1981, 1989–90; Vis. Research Prof., Duke Univ., 1987–91. Chm., Res. Assessment Panel in Econs, HEFC, 1996. Pres., Royal Economic Soc., 1992–95 (Hon. Vice Pres., 1995–). Fellow, Jl of Econometrics, 1997. Hon. Fellow, Internat. Inst. of Forecasters, 2001. Hon. Foreign Member: Amer. Economic Assoc., 1991; Amer. Acad. of Arts and Scis, 1994; Hon. Mem., Argentine Assoc. of Political Econ., 2010. Hon. LLD: Aberdeen, 1987; St Andrews, 2002; Hon. DSc Nottingham, 1998; Hon. DPhil: Norwegian Univ. of Sci. and Technol., 2001; Lund, 2006; Hon. Dr Oec: St Gallen, 2001; Aarhus, 2013; Dr *hc* Carlos III, 2009. FAcSS (AcSS 2012). Guy Medal in Bronze, Royal Statistical Soc., 1986; Thomson Reuters Citation Laureate, 2013; Lifetime Achievement Award, ESRC, 2014. Editor: Rev. of Econ. Studies, 1971–75; Econ. Jl, 1976–80; Oxford Bulletin of Economics and Statistics, 1983–. *Publications:* (ed with K. F. Wallis) Econometrics and Quantitative Economics, 1984; PC-GIVE, 1989; (with A. J. Neale and N. R. Ericsson) PC-NAIVE, 1991; Econometrics: alchemy or science?, 1993, 2nd edn 2000; (jtly) Cointegration, Error Correction and the Econometric Analysis of Non-stationary Data, 1993; Dynamic Econometrics, 1995; (ed with M. S. Morgan) The Foundations of Econometric Analysis, 1995; (with J. A. Doornik) Empirical Econometric Modelling, 1996; (with J. A. Doornik) An Interface to Empirical Modelling, 1996; (with J. A. Doornik) Modelling Dynamic Systems using PcFiml, 1997; (with M. P. Clements) Forecasting Economic Time Series, 1998; (with M. P. Clements) Forecasting Non-Stationary Economic Time Series, 1999; (ed with N. R. Ericsson) Understanding Economic Forecasts, 2001; (with H. M. Krolzig) Automatic Econometric Model Selection, 2001; (with J. A. Doornik) Econometric Modelling Using PcGive (3 vols), 2001; (with J. A. Doornik) Interactive Monte Carlo Experimentation in Econometrics Using PcNaive, 2001; (ed with M. P. Clements) Companion to Economic Forecasting, 2002; (with B. Nielson) Econometric Modelling: a likelihood approach, 2007; (ed with M. P. Clements) Oxford Handbook of Economic Forecasting, 2011; (with J. A. Doornik) Empirical Model Discovery and Theory Evaluation, 2014; papers in econometrics, statistics and economics jls. *Recreation:* golf. *Address:* Nuffield College, Oxford OX1 1NF; 26 Northmoor Road, Oxford OX2 6UR. *T:* (01865) 515588.

HENDRY, Drew; *see* Hendry, A. E. H.

HENDRY, Ian Duncan, CMG 1996; HM Diplomatic Service, retired; Deputy Legal Adviser, Foreign and Commonwealth Office, 1999–2005; Constitutional Adviser, Overseas Territories Directorate (formerly Overseas Territories Department), Foreign and Commonwealth Office, since 2005; *b* 2 April 1948; *s* of Duncan William Hendry and Edna Beatrice Hendry (*née* Woodley); *m* 1st, 1973, Elizabeth Anne Southall (marr. diss.); one *s* one *d*; 2nd, 1991, Sally Annabel Hill. *Educ:* Uppingham Sch.; King's Coll., London (LLB, LLM). Called to the Bar, Gray's Inn, 1971; Asst Legal Advr, FCO, 1971–82 and 1985–86; Legal Advr, BMG, Berlin, 1982–85; Legal Counsellor: FCO, 1986–91; UK Perm. Representation to EC, 1991–95; FCO, 1995–99. *Publications:* (with M. C. Wood) The Legal Status of Berlin, 1986; (jtly) The External Relations of the European Communities, 1996; (with S. Dickson) British Overseas Territories Law, 2011; articles in Internat. and Comparative Law Qly and German Yearbook of Internat. Law. *Recreations:* travel, gardening, swimming, percussion, the exotic. *Address:* Woodlands Cottage, Sturmer, Haverhill, Suffolk CB9 7UW.

HENDRY, Prof. Martin Anthony, MBE 2015; PhD; FRSE, FInstP; Professor of Gravitational Astrophysics and Cosmology, since 2011, and Head, School of Physics and Astronomy, since 2012, University of Glasgow; *b* Glasgow, 13 Nov. 1967; *s* of William Hendry and Anne Hendry; *m* 2001, Ruth Wilkinson; one *d*. *Educ:* Univ. of Glasgow (BSc Hons 1st Cl. Maths and Astronomy 1988; PhD Cosmology 1992). Res. Fellow, Univ. of Sussex, 1992–96; University of Glasgow: Res. Associate, 1996–98; Lectr in Astronomy, 1998–2003; Sen. Lectr in Phys and Astronomy, 2003–11. Science in Society Fellow, STFC, 2010–12. FRSE 2011; FInstP 2012. *Publications:* over 100 scientific articles in astrophysics and cosmology. *Recreations:* classical music and choral singing, walking, hill climbing, cinema going, watching sports. *Address:* School of Physics and Astronomy, University of Glasgow, Glasgow G12 8QQ. *T:* (0141) 330 5685, *Fax:* (0141) 330 5299. *E:* martin.hendry@glasgow.ac.uk.

HENDRY, Stephen Gordon, MBE 1993; professional snooker player, 1986–2012; *b* 13 Jan. 1969; *s* of Gordon John Hendry and Irene Agnes (*née* Anthony); *m* 1995, Amanda Elizabeth Theresa Tart; two *s*. *Educ:* Inverkeithing High Sch. Embassy World Champion, 1990, 1992, 1993, 1994, 1995, 1996, 1999 (record number of wins); Benson & Hedges Masters Champion, 1989, 1990, 1991, 1992, 1993, 1996; UK Professional Champion, 1989, 1990, 1994, 1995, 1996; World Doubles Champion, 1987. *Publications:* Remember My Name, 1989. *Recreations:* golf, music, cars. *Club:* Lord's Taverners (Scotland).

HENDY, Christopher Rupert, FREng, CEng, FICE, Eur Ing; Technical Director for Highways and Transportation, Atkins Consultants UK, since 2012; *b* Cambridge, 31 July 1970; *s* of Philip Robert Hendy and Anne Hendy; *m* 1994, Wendy Joan Edwin; two *s*. *Educ:* Winchester Coll.; Selwyn Coll., Cambridge (BA Engrg 1992; MA 1995). CEng 1998; FREng 2013; FICE 2006. W S Atkins plc: Engr, 1992–2001; Gp Engr, 2001–06; Chief Engr, 2006–07; Tech. Dir for Bridge Engrg, 2007–12; Chair, Bridge Engrg, 2009–. Chairman: UK Steel Bridge Gp, Steel Construction Inst., 2006–; UK Bridge Cttee, BSI, 2013–. Eur Ing 1998. *Publications:* Designers' Guide to EN 1994-2, Steel and Concrete Composite Bridges, 2006; Designers' Guide to EN 1992-2, Concrete Bridges, 2007; Designers' Guide to EN 1993-2, Steel Bridges, 2007; contrib. papers to ICE Jls. *Recreations:* family, golf, tennis, cricket, walking, watching Rugby, geocaching, juggling. *Address:* Atkins, Woodcote Grove, Ashley Road, Epsom KT18 5BW. *T:* (01372) 756307. *E:* chris.hendy@atkinsglobal.com.

HENDY, John Giles; QC 1987; *b* 11 April 1948; *s* of late Jack Hendy and Hon. Mary Hendy; *m*; three *d*. *Educ:* Ealing Technical Coll. (LLB London Univ. ext.); Queen's Univ., Belfast (DipLL, LLM). Called to the Bar, Gray's Inn, 1972; Bencher, 1995. Dir, Newham Rights Centre, 1973–76; Lectr, Middlesex Polytechnic, 1976–77; Barrister, 1977–. Hon. Prof., Faculty of Law, UCL, 2014–. Chairman: Inst. of Employment Rights, 1989–; Employment Law Bar Assoc., 2003–05. Pres., Internat. Centre for Trade Union Rights, 2011–; Vice-Pres., Campaign for Trade Union Freedom, 2014–. *Publications:* (jtly) Personal Injury Practice, 2nd edn 1993, 3rd edn 1999; Redgrave's Health and Safety, 2nd edn 1994, 3rd edn 1998; (jtly) Munkman on Employer's Liability, 12th edn 1995 to 15th edn 2009; (jtly) The Right to Strike: from the Trade Disputes Act 1906 to a Trade Union Freedom Bill 2006, 2006; (contrib. with K. D. Ewing) Constitutional Labour Rights in Canada: farm workers and the Fraser Case, 2012; contrib. articles on employment law, esp. right to strike to jls incl. Industrial Law Jl, Clin. Risk. *Address:* Old Square Chambers, 10–11 Bedford Row, WC1R 4BU. *T:* (020) 7269 0300, *Fax:* (020) 7405 1387.

See also Sir P. G. Hendy.

HENDY, Sir Peter (Gerard), Kt 2013; CBE 2006; Chairman, Network Rail, since 2015; *b* 19 March 1953; *s* of late Jack Hendy and Hon. Mary Hendy; *m* 1999, Sue Pendle; one *s* one *d. Educ:* Latymer Upper Sch.; Univ. of Leeds (BA Econs and Geog.). London Transport, 1975–89, Dist Ops Manager, 1986–89; Man. Dir, Centre W London Buses Ltd, 1989–98; Divl Dir, First Gp, 1997–98; Dir, New World First Bus, Hong Kong, 1998–99; Dep. Dir, UK Bus for First Gp plc, 1998–2001; Man. Dir, Surface Transport, 2001–06, Comr, 2006–15, Transport for London. Chair, Commn for Integrated Transport, 2005–10 (Mem., 2004–05). Member: Industrial Tribunals, 1993–98; Council, Confedn of Passenger Transport, 1994–2000. President: CILT, 2011–12 (Vice-Pres., 2008–); UITP, 2013–15. FCILT (FCIT 1985); FIHT 2005. Hon. DSc City, 2010; Hon. DEng Bath, 2013. *Recreations:* bus driving, cycling, travel, reading, my family. *Address:* Network Rail, 1 Eversholt Street, NW1 2DN. *Clubs:* Groucho; Widcombe Social.

See also J. G. Hendy.

HENEAGE, James Arthur; Managing Director, Ottakar's plc, 1988–2006; *b* 31 Oct. 1957; *s* of Simon and Elizabeth Heneage; *m* 1987, Charlotte Shott; two *s* two *d. Educ:* Worth Abbey. Commnd Grenadier Guards, 1977–82. Advertising Executive: D'Arcy Macmanus Masius, 1982–84; Ogilvy & Mather, 1984–87; founded Ottakar's, 1987. Chm., Cheltenham Lit. Fest., 2006–. Dir, Prince's Rainforest Project, 2007–09. *Recreations:* history, cartooning, playing piano in a band, Tintin. *Address:* Buddens House, Bowerchalke, Salisbury, Wilts SP5 5BN.

HENES, John Derek; Head, UK Delegation to UK/French Channel Tunnel Intergovernmental Commission, 1997–2006; *b* 8 June 1937; *s* of Frederick William Kingaby Henes and Joan Elizabeth Henes (*née* Colbourne); *m* 1981, Virginia Elizabeth Evans (*d* 2011); one *s* one *d. Educ:* Christ's Hospital; Gonville and Caius College, Cambridge (MA). Ministry of Aviation, 1963; Dept of Trade, 1971; Private Sec. to Christopher Chataway, 1973–74, to Lord Beswick, 1974–75; Asst Sec., 1975; Dept of Transport, 1983–96; Under Sec., 1989. *Recreations:* reading, music. *Address:* 1e Cambridge Road, Twickenham, Middx TW1 2HN.

HENFREY, Claire; *see* Dove, C.

HENIG, family name of **Baroness Henig**.

HENIG, Baroness *cr* 2004 (Life Peer), of Lancaster in the County of Lancashire; **Ruth Beatrice Henig,** CBE 2000; DL; PhD; Chairman, Security Industry Authority, 2007–13; *b* 10 Nov. 1943; *d* of Kurt and Elfriede Munzer; *m* 1st, 1966, Stanley Henig, *qv* (marr. diss. 1993); two *s*; 2nd, 1994, Jack Johnstone (*d* 2013). *Educ:* Wyggeston Girls' Grammar Sch., Leicester; Bedford Coll., London (BA Hons 1st cl. (Hist.) 1965); Lancaster Univ. (PhD 1978). Lancaster University: Lectr, then Sen. Lectr, in Hist., 1968–2002; Hd, Hist. Dept, 1995–97; Dean, Arts and Humanities, 1997–2000. Mem. (Lab) Lancaster E, 1981–2005, Chm., 1999–2000, Lancs CC. Chm., Lancs Police Authy, 1995–2005. Mem., EU External Affairs Sub Cttee, 2012–15, EU Cttee, 2014–15, H of L. Parly Patron: Be Your Best Foundn/Rock Challenge UK, 2006–; Seashell Trust, 2007–. Chm., Assoc. Police Authorities, 1997–2005. Chairman: Adult Coll., Lancaster, 1981–91; Bd, Duke's Playhouse Theatre, Lancaster, 1987–95; Bd, Storey Creative Industries Centre, Lancaster, 2007–11. JP Lancaster, 1984–2004 (Mem., Lancs Adv. Cttee for Appt of Justices, 2000–04); DL Lancs, 2002. *Publications:* The League of Nations, 1973; Versailles and After, 1984, 2nd edn 1995; Origins of the Second World War, 1985; Origins of the First World War, 1989, 3rd edn 2002; (with Chris Culpin) Europe 1870–1945, 1997; The Weimar Republic, 1998; (with Simon Henig) Women and Political Power, 2000; A History of the League of Nations, 2010. *Recreations:* bridge, fell-walking, real ale, wine appreciation, gardening, travel. *Address:* House of Lords, SW1A 0PW. *E:* ruthhenig@gmail.com.

HENIG, Prof. Stanley; Professor of European Politics, 1982–97 and Head of Department of European Studies, 1990–97, University of Central Lancashire (formerly Preston, then Lancashire, Polytechnic); Deputy Pro-Chancellor, University of Lancaster, 2006–11; *b* 7 July 1939; *s* of Sir Mark Henig and Grace (*née* Cohen); *m* 1st, 1966, Ruth Beatrice Munzer (*see* Baroness Henig) (marr. diss. 1993); two *s*; 2nd, 2002, Christine Carole Swann. *Educ:* Wyggeston Grammar Sch.; Corpus Christi Coll., Oxford. BA 1st Cl. Hons, 1961; MA 1965 Oxon. Teaching Asst, Dept of Politics, Univ. of Minnesota, 1961; Research Student, Nuffield Coll., 1962; Lecturer in Politics, Lancaster Univ., 1964–66; MP (Lab) Lancaster, 1966–70; Lectr in Politics, Warwick Univ., 1970–71; Lectr, Civil Service Coll., 1972–75; Preston, subseq. Lancashire, Polytechnic: Head of Div. of Social Admin, later Sch. of Social Studies, 1976–85; Dean, Faculty of Social Studies, 1985–90. Sen. Res. Fellow, Federal Trust, 2001–. Mem., Lancaster CC, 1981–99 (Leader, 1991–99); Dep. Ldr, Lab. Gp, ADC, 1995–97; Sec., Lab. Gp, LGA, 1997–99. Governor, British Inst. of Recorded Sound, 1975–80. Sec., later Man. Dir, Historic Masters Ltd, 1983–2011; Sec., Historic Singers Trust, 1985–2011. Mem. Cttee, Internat. Ernest Bloch Soc., 2011– (Ed., Newsletter, 2011–). Chm., Court, RNCM, 1986–89. Asst Editor, Jl of Common Market Studies, 1964–72, Editor, 1973–76. *Publications:* (ed) European Political Parties, 1969; External Relations of the European Community, 1971; (ed) Political Parties in the European Community, 1979; Power and Decision in Europe, 1980; Uniting of Europe, 1997; (jtly) Enrico Caruso—Recollections and Retrospective, 1999; (ed) The Kosovo Crisis, 2001; (ed) Modernizing Britain: central, devolved, federal, 2002; Modernising British Government: constitutional challenges and federal solutions, 2006; Federalism and the British, 2008; (contrib.) The First Lives of Alfredo Catalani, 2011; articles and reviews on opera and opera singers in numerous jls. *Recreation:* collector of old gramophone records and operatic memorabilia. *Address:* 10 Yealand Drive, Lancaster LA1 4EW. *T:* (01524) 69624.

HENLEY, 8th Baron *cr* 1799 (Ire.); **Oliver Michael Robert Eden;** PC 2013; Baron Northington (UK) 1885; *b* 22 Nov. 1953; *er s* of 7th Baron Henley and of Nancy Mary, *d* of Stanley Walton, Gilsland, Cumbria; *S* father, 1977; *m* 1984, Caroline Patricia, *d* of A. G. Sharp, Mackney, Oxon; three *s* one *d. Educ:* Clifton; Durham Univ. (BA 1975). Called to the Bar, Middle Temple, 1977. A Lord in Waiting (Govt Whip), 1989; Parliamentary Under-Secretary of State: DSS, 1989–93; Dept of Employment, 1993–94; MoD, 1994–95; Minister of State, DFEE, 1995–97; Opposition spokesman on home affairs, 1997–98, on legal affairs, 2005–10; Parly Under-Sec. of State, DEFRA, 2010–11; Minister of State, Home Office, 2011–12. Opposition Chief Whip, H of L, 1998–2001; elected Mem., H of L, 1999. Mem., Cumbria CC, 1986–89. Chm., Penrith and the Border Conservative Assoc., 1987–89. Pres., Cumbria Assoc. of Local Councils, 1981–89. Pres., Cumbria Trust for Nature Conservation, 1988–89. *Heir: s* Hon. John Michael Oliver Eden, *b* 30 June 1988. *Address:* Scaleby Castle, Carlisle, Cumbria CA6 4LN. *Clubs:* Brooks's; Pratt's.

HENLEY, Darren Richard, OBE 2013; Chief Executive, Arts Council England, since 2015; *b* 16 Feb. 1973. *Educ:* Univ. of Hull (BA Hons Politics 1994). Freelance radio journalist for stations incl. Invicta, LBC, IRN, Classic FM and BBC GLR, 1989–94; Sen. Broadcast Journalist, ITN Radio, 1994–95; Classic FM: Prog. Editor, Classic Newsnight, 1995–96; News Manager, 1996–99; News and Prog. Manager, 1999–2000; Man. Editor, 2000–04; Station Manager, 2004–06; Man. Dir, 2006–15; Managing Director: theJazz, 2006–08; Xfm, 2008; Choice FM, 2008; Launch Dir, Global Television, 2012. Dir, Independent Radio News Ltd, 2008–12. Member: Broadcast Journalism Trng Council, 2000–03; SE Regl Arts Council, 2002–04; Adv. Council, 2005–07, Business Develt Cttee, 2007–11, Philharmonia Orch.; DFE (formerly DCSF)/DCMS Music Prog. Bd, 2007–10; Media Bd, Prince's Foundn for Children and the Arts, 2007–12; Steering Gp, In Harmony, 2009–11; Creative and Cultural Industries Task Force, 2009; Adv. Bd, City Music Foundn, 2012–15; Cultural Adv. Gp, Birmingham City Univ., 2012–15; Mem. and Chm., In Tune Nat. Year of Music Legacy Gp (formerly Steering Gp, Nat. Year of Music), 2009–10; Bd Dir, Canterbury Fest. and Th. Trust, 2001–15 (Vice Chm., 2007–09; Vice Pres., 2009–15); Chairman: Music Manifesto Partnership and Advocacy Gp, 2007–10; Henley Review of Funding and Delivery of Music Educn, DfE/DCMS, 2010–11 (report publd 2011); Henley Review of Cultural Educn, DfE/DCMS, 2011 (report publd 2012); Communities in Tune Adv. Gp, DCLG, 2012–15; Mayor of London's Music Educn Adv. Gp, 2013–15; Co-Chm., Cultural Educn Bd, 2013–15; Member: Monitoring Bd, Nat. Plan for Music Educn, DfE/DCMS, 2012–13; Scottish Govt Instrumental Music Gp, 2013. Comr, Univ. of Warwick Commn on Future of Cultural Value, 2013–15. Trustee: Future Talent, 2006–10; Associated Bd, Royal Schs of Music, 2013–15; Global Charities, 2013–15. Patron, Mayor of London's Fund for Young Musicians, 2011–15. Fellow: Radio Acad., 2011; London Coll. of Music, 2012. FRSA 1998. Hon. Fellow: Canterbury Christ Church Univ., 2010; Trinity Laban Conservatoire of Music and Dance, 2011; Liverpool John Moores Univ., 2015; Honorary Member: RNCM, 2012; ISM, 2013. CCMI 2010. Hon. DLitt Hull, 2014; Hon. DUniv: Birmingham City, 2014; Buckinghamshire New, 2014. Gold Medal, Arts and Culture, 2000, Gold Medal, Best Music Prog., 2007, NY Internat. Radio Fest.; Chm.'s Award, 2007, Programmer of the Yr, 2009, Gold Award, 2012, Arqiva Commercial Radio Awards; Gold Award, Music Programming, Sony Radio Acad. Awards, 2009; Making Music Sir Charles Groves Prize, 2012. *Publications:* The Story of Classical Music, 2004; (with Aled Jones) Aled: the autobiography, 2005; Famous Composers, 2005; G4: the official book, 2005; (with John Suchet) The Classic FM Friendly Guide to Beethoven, 2006; The Classic FM Friendly Guide to Music, 2006; More Famous Composers, 2007; (with Hayley Westenra) Hayley Westenra: in her own voice, 2007; The Classic FM Friendly Music Quiz Book, 2007; The Incredible Story of Classical Music, 2008; (with V. McKernan) The Original Liverpool Sound: the Royal Liverpool Philharmonic story, 2009; (with S. Jackson and T. Lihoreau) The Classic FM Hall of Fame, 2011; (with S. Jackson) Everything you Ever Wanted to Know about Classical Music… but were too afraid to ask, 2012; (with S. Jackson) 50 Moments that Rocked the Classical Music World, 2014; *with T. Lihoreau:* The Classic FM Pocket Book of Music, 2003; The Classic FM Book of Quotes, 2004; The Classic FM Book of Trivia, 2004; The Classic FM Friendly Guide to Mozart, 2005; Classic Ephemera, 2005; The Classic FM Friendly Guide to Elgar, 2007; Classic FM 101 Questions & Answers About Classical Music, 2008; Classic Ephemera: a musical miscellany, 2009; The A to Z of Classic FM Music, 2010; The Classic FM Quiz Book, 2012; (with S. Jackson and T. Lihoreau) The Big Book of Classical Music, 2014; (with T. Lihoreau and D. Ross) Charting the Classics, 2014; (with J. Sorrell and P. Roberts) The Virtuous Circle: why creative and cultural education count, 2014; The Classic FM Handy Guide to the Orchestra, 2015; The Classic FM Handy Guide to Everything You Ever Wanted To Know About Classical Music, 2015. *Recreations:* arts and culture, train travel. *Address:* Arts Council England, 21 Bloomsbury Street, WC1B 3HF. *T:* 0845 300 6200. *E:* chief.executive@artscouncil.org.uk. *Club:* Gillingham Football.

HENMAN, Timothy Henry, OBE 2004; professional tennis player, 1993–2007; *b* 6 Sept. 1974; *s* of Anthony and Jane Henman; *m* 1999, Lucy, *d* of Prof. Richard John, (Bill), Heald, *qv*; three *d. Educ:* Reed's Sch., Cobham. Mem., British Davis Cup Team, 1995–2004, 2007. Winner: Nat. Championships, 1995, 1996, 1997, (doubles) 1999; Silver Medal (doubles), Olympic Games, 1996; Sydney Internat. Tournament, 1997; President's Cup, Tashkent, 1997, 1998; Swiss Indoor Championships, (doubles) 1997, 1998, 2001; Monte Carlo Open, (doubles) 1999, 2004; CA Trophy, Vienna, 2000; Samsung Open, Brighton, 2000; Copenhagen Open, 2001; Australian Hardcourt Championships, 2002; Legg Mason Classic, Washington, 2003; BNP Paribas Masters, Paris, 2003. Mem. Bd, AELTC (Chm., Tennis sub-cttee, 2015–). Most Improved Player of the Year Award, ATP, 1996. *Address:* c/o IMG, McCormack House, Burlington Lane, W4 2TH.

HENNESSY, family name of **Barons Hennessy of Nympsfield** and **Windlesham**.

HENNESSY OF NYMPSFIELD, Baron *cr* 2010 (Life Peer), of Nympsfield in the County of Gloucestershire; **Peter John Hennessy,** FBA 2003; FRHistS; FAcSS; Attlee Professor of Contemporary British History, since 2001, and Patron, Mile End Institute of Contemporary British Government, Intelligence and Society, since 2015 (Director, 2006–11), Queen Mary University of London; *b* 28 March 1947; *s* of William Gerald and Edith Hennessy; *m* 1969, Enid Mary Candler; two *d. Educ:* Marling Sch., Stroud; St John's Coll., Cambridge (BA 1969; Hon. Fellow, 2010), PhD Cantab 1990; LittD Cantab 2009; LSE (Hon. Fellow, 2000); Harvard, 1971–72 (Kennedy Meml Scholar). FRHistS 1993. Reporter, THES, 1972–74, The Times, 1974–76; Lobby corresp., Financial Times, 1976; Whitehall corresp., The Times, 1976–82; journalist, The Economist, 1982; home leader writer and columnist, The Times, 1982–84; columnist: New Statesman, 1986–87; The Independent, 1987–91; Director, 1989–93; The Tablet, 2003–11; Prof. of Contemporary History, QMW, Univ. of London, 1992–2000; Chm., Kennedy Meml Trust, 1995–2000. Co-Founder and Co-Dir, 1986–89, Mem. Bd, 1989–98, Inst. of Contemporary British Hist. (Hon. Fellow, 1995). Vis. Prof. of Govt, Strathclyde Univ., 1989–2004; Gresham Prof. of Rhetoric, 1994–97; Vis. Lectr, Dept of Politics, Univ. of Strathclyde, 1983–84 (Hon. Res. Fellow, 1985–89); Visiting Fellow: Policy Studies Inst., 1986–91 (Sen. Fellow, 1984–85; Council Mem., 1991–97); Univ. Depts of Politics, Reading 1988–94, Nottingham 1989–95; RIPA, 1989–92; Hon. Res. Fellow, Dept of Politics and Sociology, Birkbeck Coll., London, 1990–91; Vis. Scholar, Centre for Australian Public Sector Management, Griffith Univ., Brisbane, 1991; Associate, Cold War Studies Prog., LSE, 2010–. Member: Steering Gp, Sharman Review of Audit and Accountability for Central Govt, 2000–01; Cabinet Office Adv. Gp on Security and Intelligence Records, 2004–10; Joint H of C—H of L Cttee on H of L Reform Bill, 2011–12; Chief of Defence Staff's Strategic Adv. Panel, 2011–; BASIC Trident Commn, 2011–14; Sen. Advisory Gp, RCDS, 2013–; FCO Diplomatic Excellence External Panel, 2013–; No 10 History Steering Gp, 2014–; H of L Select Cttee on Sci. and Technol., 2014–; RUSI Surveillance Review, 2014–. Vice-President: Politics Assoc., 1985–90; RHistS, 1996–2000; Pres., Johnian Soc., 1995. Trustee: Attlee Foundn, 1985–98 (Patron, 1998–); Geffrye Mus., 2002–04; Orwell Meml Trust, 2002–04. Patron: Bletchley Park Trust, 2011–; Mile End Gp, 2011–13. Mem. Bd, Inst. of Histl Res., 1992–97; Member: Council, Gresham Coll., 1996–97 (Fellow, 1997); Council of Reference, Westminster Abbey Inst., 2013–; Gov., 2001–11, Mem., Council of Mgt, 2011–, Ditchley Foundn. Member: Advisory Board: Global Strategy Forum, 2015–; Cambridge Security Initiative, 2015–. Dir, The Tablet, 2003–11. FRSA 1992. FAcSS (Founding AcSS 1999). Presenter: Under Fire, TV, 1985–87; Radio 4 Analysis programme, 1986–92; writer and presenter, What Has Become of Us, TV, 1994; numerous other radio and TV productions. Curator, Secret State exhibn, Nat. Archives, 2004. Hon. Vis. Prof., Strategy and Security Inst., Univ. of Exeter, 2012–; Hon. Prof., QUB, 2013–. Hon. Fellow, St Benet's Hall, Oxford, 2008. Hon. DLitt: Univ. of W England, 1995; Univ. of Westminster, 1996; Kingston, 1998; Strathclyde, 2005; Reading, 2011; Glos, 2012; DUniv Open, 2009. Hon. Bencher, Middle Temple, 2012. Times Higher Educn Lifetime Achievement Award, 2008; Norton Medlicott Medal, Historical Assoc., 2010; Diamond Jubilee Award for Pol Studies Communication, Pol Studies Assoc., 2010. *Publications:* (with

Keith Jeffery) States of Emergency, 1983; (with Michael Cockerell and David Walker) Sources Close to the Prime Minister, 1984; What the Papers Never Said, 1985; Cabinet, 1986; (ed with Anthony Seldon) Ruling Performance, 1987; Whitehall, 1989, rev. edn 2001; Never Again: Britain, 1945–51, 1992 (Duff Cooper Prize, 1993; NCR Book Award for Non-Fiction, 1993); The Hidden Wiring: unearthing the British Constitution, 1995; Muddling Through: power, politics and the quality of government in postwar Britain, 1996; The Prime Minister: the office and its holders since 1945, 2000; The Secret State, 2002, 2nd edn 2010; Having It So Good: Britain in the fifties (Orwell Prize for Political Writing), 2006; (ed) The New Protective State: government, intelligence and terrorism, 2007; Cabinets and the Bomb, 2007; Distilling the Frenzy: writing the history of one's own times, 2012; Establishment and Meritocracy, 2014; The Kingdom to Come: thoughts on the union before and after the Scottish referendum, 2015; (with James Jinks) The Silent Deep: the Royal Navy submarine service since 1945, 2015. *Recreations:* reading, listening to music, searching for the British Constitution. *Address:* House of Lords, SW1A 0PW. *T:* (020) 7219 3000. *Clubs:* Savile, Grillions, Naval.

HENNESSY, Sir James (Patrick Ivan), KBE 1982 (OBE 1968; MBE 1959); CMG 1975; HM Diplomatic Service, retired; *b* 26 Sept. 1923; *s* of late Richard George Hennessy, DSO, MC; *m* 1947, Patricia (*d* 2015), *o d* of late Wing Comdr F. H. Unwin, OBE; five *d* (one *s* decd). *Educ:* Bedford Sch.; King's Coll., Newcastle; Sidney Sussex Coll., Cambridge; LSE. Served RA, 1942–44; seconded IA, 1944–46, Adjt and Battery Comdr, 6th Indian Field Regt. Apptd to HM Overseas Service, Basutoland, District Officer, 1948; Judicial Comr, 1953; Dist Comr, 1954–56; Jt Sec., Constitutional Commn, 1957–59; Supervisor of Elections, 1959; Sec. to Exec. Council, 1960; seconded to Office of High Comr, Cape Town/Pretoria, 1961–63; Perm. Sec. for local govt, 1964; MLC, 1965; Sec. for External Affairs, Defence and Internal Security, 1967; Prime Minister's Office, 1968. Retired, later apptd to HM Diplomatic Service; FO, 1968–70; Chargé d'Affaires, Montevideo, 1971–72; High Comr to Uganda and Ambassador (non-resident), Rwanda, 1973–76; Consul-Gen., Cape Town, 1977–80; Governor and C-in-C, Belize, 1980–81; HM Chief Inspector of Prisons for England and Wales, 1982–87. Mem., Parole Bd, 1988–91. Trustee, Butler Trust, 1988–98. *Address:* Slogarie House, by Castle Douglas, Scotland DG7 2NL.

HENNESSY, Brig. Mary Brigid Teresa, (Rita), CBE 1988 (MBE 1967); RRC 1982; Matron-in-Chief, Queen Alexandra's Royal Army Nursing Corps, 1985–89 and Director of Defence Nursing Service, 1986–89; *b* 27 Jan. 1933; *d* of late Bartholomew and Nora Agnes Hennessy. *Educ:* Convent of Mercy, Ennis, Co. Clare; Whittington Hosp., Highgate, London; Victoria Maternity Hosp., Barnet. SRN; SCM. Joined QARANC, 1959; service in Britain, Singapore, Malaya, Germany; various hosp. appts, 1959–74; seconded to office of Chargé d'affaires, Peking, 1965–67; Dep. Matron, Hongkong, 1976; Lt-Col 1979; Col 1982; Brig., Matron-in-Chief and Dir of Army Nursing Services, 1985. QHNS 1985–89. *Recreations:* music, theatre, gardening.

HENNESSY, Patrick James; Deputy Director of Communications, Labour Party, since 2013; *b* 10 July 1963; *s* of late Thomas Michael Hennessy and of Elizabeth Anne Hennessy; *m* 2000, Kate Giemre; one *s* one *d*. *Educ:* Colet Court Sch.; Eton Coll.; Lady Margaret Hall, Oxford (BA Hons 1985). Reporter: Express and Echo, Exeter, 1985–88; The Sun, 1988–92; Political Corresp., Daily Express, 1992–96; Dep. Political Ed., Evening Standard, 1996–2004; Political Ed., Sunday Telegraph, 2004–13. Judge, Spectator Parliamentarian of Year Awards, 2006–. *Recreations:* football, music, reading. *Address:* c/o Labour Party, One Brewer's Green, SW1H 0RH. *Club:* Chelsea Football.

HENNESSY, Richard Patrick, FCA; Chief Financial Officer, The Really Useful Group Ltd, 2004–06; *b* 16 Nov. 1953; *s* of Graham Harold Hennessy and Dolores Hennessy (*née* Ellul); *m* 1979, Angela Carthew; one *s* one *d*. *Educ:* Newcastle Univ. (BA Hons Econs and Accounting). FCA 1979. Manager, Peat Marwick Mitchell, London, 1976–80; Sen. Manager, Peat Marwick Mitchell & Co., Hong Kong, 1980–82; Gp Financial Accountant, Hongkong & Shanghai Banking Corp. Ltd, 1982–84; Financial Controller, Saudi British Bank, 1984–88; Sen. Gp Financial Accountant, Hongkong & Shanghai Banking Corp. Ltd, 1988–92; Gp Chief Accountant, HSBC Holdings plc, 1992–95; Chief Financial Officer, Midland, subseq. HSBC, Bank plc, 1996–2003. Mem. Banking Sub-Cttee, ICAEW, 1993–2003. Events Chm., Arts and Crafts Movement in Surrey, 2012–. Mem., Soc. of London Theatre, 2004–06. Trustee, Iwokrama Internat. Centre for Rain Forest Conservation and Develt, 2006–12. *Recreations:* family, motor sport, music, walking, swimming, painting and stained glass. *Address:* Oak Meadows, 65 Park Road, Woking, Surrey GU22 7BZ.

HENNIKER, 9th Baron *cr* 1800 (Ire.); **Mark Ian Philip Chandos Henniker-Major;** Bt 1765; Baron Hartismere (UK) 1866; *b* 29 Sept. 1947; *s* of 8th Baron Henniker and Margaret Osla (*née* Benning); *S* father, 2004; *m* 1st, 1973, Lesley Antoinette Masterton-Smith (*née* Foskett) (marr. diss. 1996); one *s* three *d* (and one *s* decd); 2nd, 1996, Bente Toft (*née* Petersen) (marr. diss. 2015); one *s*. *Educ:* Eton; Trinity Coll., Cambridge (MA); LLM (London); London Inst. of World Affairs (Dip.). FCIArb; AMRAeS. Solicitor (retired/non-practising). *Heir: s* Hon. Edward George Major Henniker-Major, *b* 22 April 1985. *Address:* 217 Bull Road, Thornham Parva, Eye, Suffolk IP23 8ES. *T:* (01379) 783854. *E:* mhenniker_anglab@btinternet.com.

HENNIKER, Sir Adrian Chandos, 9th Bt *cr* 1813, of Newton Hall, Essex; *b* 18 Oct. 1946; *s* of Brig. Sir Mark Chandos Auberon Henniker, 8th Bt, CBE, DSO, MC and Kathleen Denys (*d* 1998), *d* of John Anderson; *S* father, 1991, but his name does not appear on the Official Roll of the Baronetage; *m* 1971, Ann, *d* of Stuart Britton; twin *d*. *Educ:* Marlborough. *Heir:* none. *Address:* The Coach House, Llwyndu, Abergavenny, Gwent NP7 7HG.

HENNIKER HEATON, Sir Yvo Robert; *see* Heaton.

HENNIKER-MAJOR, family name of **Baron Henniker**.

HENNING, (William) Brian; Chairman, Sport Northern Ireland, since 2012; Director: UK Sport, since 2012; Beulah Business Solutions, since 2012; *b* City of Armagh, 14 July 1954; *s* of William John Henning and Jane Elizabeth Henning; *m* 2006, Yvonne Anna Palnoch (*née* Magowan); two *s* one *d*. *Educ:* Newry Grammar Sch.; Univ. of Ulster. Sen. Quantity Surveyor, Bruce Shaw Partnership, 1978–84; Sen. Surveyor, Farrans Construction, 1984–86; Man. Dir, Cresta Building Services (NI) Ltd, 1988–92; Property and Develt Dir, Crestacare plc, 1992–98; Chief Executive: Cusp Gp, 1998–2007; Lotus Gp, 2008–12. Chm., Lisburn City Centre Mgt, 2002–06. Vice Chm., NI Council for Integrated Educn, 1991. Mem., Cinemagic (Ireland) Ltd, 2007–. Trustee, Age NI, 2013–. *Recreations:* active interest in all sports esp. athletics, Rugby Union (Manager, Ulster Rugby Under 18, 2005–06), soccer, golf, ski-ing, resistance training and yoga, landscape management, family and friends. *Address:* Beulah, 33 Newry Road, Banbridge BT32 3HP. *T:* (028) 4062 8214. *E:* brianhenning@sportni.net.

HENRIQUES, Hon. Sir Richard (Henry Quixano), Kt 2000; a Judge of the High Court of Justice, Queen's Bench Division, 2000–13; Presiding Judge, North Eastern Circuit, 2001–04; *b* 27 Oct. 1943; *s* of late Cecil Quixano Henriques and Doreen Mary Henriques; *m* Joan Hilary, (Toni), (*née* Senior); one *s* and one step *s*. *Educ:* Bradfield Coll., Berks; Worcester Coll., Oxford (BA). Called to the Bar, Inner Temple, 1967; Bencher, 1994. A Recorder, 1983–2000; QC 1986; Mem., Northern Circuit (Leader, 1995–98). Member: Gen. Council of the Bar, 1993–98; Criminal Justice Liaison Cttee, 1993–95; Northern Circuit Exec. Cttee, 1993–98. Council Mem., Rossall Sch., 1985–95. *Recreations:* bridge, golf, the Turf. *Address:* c/o Royal Courts of Justice, Strand, WC2A 2LL. *Clubs:* Royal Lytham and St Anne's Golf, Poulton-le-Fylde Golf.

HENRY, Claire Louise, MBE 2013; Chief Executive: National Council for Palliative Care, since 2014; Dying Matters Coalition, since 2014; *b* Leicester, 29 April 1965; *d* of Victor Henry and Burnice Henry; *m* 2005, Lionel Cunnington. *Educ:* Casterton Community Coll.; Rutland Sixth Form Coll.; Bournemouth Univ. (BSc Hons). RGN; Royal Marsden Hosp. (Postgrad. Dip. Cancer Care). Staff Nurse, 1987–92, Sen. Staff Nurse, 1992–93, Boston, Lincs; Macmillan nurse, 1993–2000; Proj. Manager, Cancer Services Collaborative Improvement Partnership, 2000–01; Nat. Associate Dir, 2001–04, Nat. Prog. Dir, 2005–13. End of Life Care Prog., NHS; Hd, Progs for Long-term Conditions and End of Life Care, NHS Improving Quality, 2013–14. *Publications:* (contrib.) Nursing in Primary Care: a handbook for students, 2001; (contrib.) Advance Care Planning in End of Life Care, 2011; (jtly) Pathways Through Care at the End of Life, 2013. *Recreations:* walking, history, season ticket holder at Leicester Tigers Rugby. *Address:* National Council for Palliative Care, Hospice House, 34–44 Britannia Street, WC1X 9JG. *T:* (020) 7697 1520. *E:* c.henry@ncpc.org.uk.

HENRY, Colin Glen; Chief Executive, Jaeger Ltd, since 2013; *b* Aberdeen, 18 Jan. 1965; *s* of Fulton Henry and Joan Henry; partner, 2005, Ian Macdonald. *Educ:* Uddington Grammar Sch. Merchandiser, Marks and Spencer plc, 1984–97; Man. Dir, Coats Viyella plc, 1997–2000; Sen. Vice Pres., Polo Ralph Lauren Inc., 2000–03; Sen. Vice Pres., Umbro plc, 2003–09; Chief Product Officer, Esprit GmbH, 2010–12. Hon. FRCA 2008. *Recreations:* oenophilia, St Emilion, Wolfie the Jack Russell. *Address:* Jaeger Ltd, 57 Broadwick Street, W1F 9QS. *T:* 07747 289654. *E:* colin.henry@jaeger.co.uk. *Club:* Soho House.

HENRY, Prof. (Diana) Kristin, (Mrs G. G. Blakey), FRCP, FRCPath; Professor of Pathology, Imperial College School of Medicine (formerly Charing Cross and Westminster Medical School), London University, 1987–98, now Emeritus Professor, Imperial College London; *d* of late Colin Neil Thorburn Henry and of Vera (*née* Christensen); *m* 1st, 1960, Charles Michael Yates (marr. diss.); 2nd, 1967, George Gavin Blakey (*d* 2013); one *s* one *d*. *Educ:* Malvern Girls' Coll.; St Thomas's Hosp. Med. Sch. (MB BS). FRCP 1982; FRCPath 1977. Junior appts at Chelsea Hosp. for Women and Brompton Hosp., 1960–64; Res. Registrar, Bd of Governors, Hosp. of Diseases of the Chest, 1964–66; MRC Fellow in Immunology, Middx Hosp., 1966–69; Lectr, RPMS, 1969–74; Reader, 1974–82, Prof. of Histopathology, 1982–84, Westminster Med. Sch., London Univ.; Prof. of Histopathology, Charing Cross & Westminster Med. Sch., 1984–87. Mem., Editl Bd, Histopathology, 1975–2003; Founding Ed., Current Diagnostic Pathology, 1993–; Asst Ed., Internat. Jl of Surgical Pathology, 1999–. British Council Lectr and Foundn Lectr to Coll. of Pathologists, Sri Lanka, 1987; First Daphne Attegale Meml Oration and Gold Medal, 1987, First Cooray Meml Oration and Gold Medal, 1998, Sri Lanka. Member: Thymic Tumour Panel, MRC, 1974–79; Pathology Panel, Brit. Nat. Lymphoma Investigation, MRC, 1975–87 (Expert Pathologist representing BNLI in Nat. Cancer Inst. (USA) study of lymphomas, 1976–81 (report pub. 1982)). Mem., Kettering Prize Award Cttee, Gen. Motors Cancer Res. Foundn, 1981–82. Co-founder, British Lymphoma Pathology Gp, 1974–; founder Mem., Eur. Bone Marrow Pathology Gp, 1992–; Member: Eur. Assoc. Haematopathology, 1986–; Melanoma Study Gp, 1989–. Treas., 1981–94, Pres., 1994–96, Cunningham Gold Medal, British Div., Internat. Acad. of Pathology; Pres., Internat. Acad. of Pathology, 2010–12 (Vice-Pres. for Europe, 1998–2008; Chm., Educn Cttee, 2000–; Gold Medal, 1996); Founder, Arab British Sch. of Pathology, 2001. *Publications:* Systematic Pathology, vol. 7: 3rd edn, The Thymus, Lymph Nodes, Spleen and Lymphatics (ed with W. St C. Symmers and contrib.), 1992; (with G. Farrer-Brown) A Colour Atlas of Thymus and Lymph Node Pathology with Ultrastructure, 1981; (contrib.) The Human Thymus in Disease, 1981; (contrib.) Ultrastructure of the Small Intestine, 1982; (contrib.) Bone Marrow Transplantation in Mucopolysaccharidoses, 1984; numerous contribs to learned jls in field of haematopathology (incl. Lymphoma Study Gp pubns), malignant melanoma and oncology. *Recreations:* painting, driving, animal welfare. *Address:* Imperial College London at Charing Cross Hospital, Fulham Palace Road, W6 8RF. *T:* (020) 8846 7133. *Club:* Royal Over-Seas League.

HENRY, Hugh; Member (Lab) Renfrewshire South, Scottish Parliament, since 2011 (Paisley South, 1999–2011); *b* 12 Feb. 1952; *s* of Joseph and Mary Henry; *m* Jacqueline (*née* Muldoon); one *s* two *d*. *Educ:* Glasgow Univ. (BAcc). Worked in accountancy, teaching and social work. Member (Lab): Renfrew DC, 1985–96; Renfrewshire Council, 1995–99 (Leader, 1995–99). Scottish Executive: Dep. Minister for Health and Community Care, 2001–02, for Social Justice, 2002–03, for Justice, 2003–07; Minister for Educn and Young People, 2007; Convenor, European Cttee, Scottish Parlt, 1999–. Mem., Cttee of the Regions, EU. *Address:* Scottish Parliament, Edinburgh EH99 1SP.

HENRY, John Philip; Chairman, Cheltenham Civic Society, 2001–09; Vice-Chairman, Gloucestershire Hospitals NHS Trust, 2002–10 (non-executive Director, 2002–10); *b* 8 Oct. 1946; *s* of late L. Henry, MD, FRCS and P. M. Henry, MB, ChB; *m* 1992, Gillian Mary Richardson; one *s* one *d*. *Educ:* Cheltenham Coll.; Queen's Coll., Oxford (MA). Psychologist, Road Research Lab., 1968; Admin Trainee, DoE, 1972; Principal, 1976; Private Sec., Minister for Housing and Construction, 1981–83; Asst Sec., 1983–89; Regl Dir, Yorks and Humberside Regl Office, Depts of the Envmt and Transport, 1990–94; Prin. Finance Officer, Property Hldgs, DoE, 1994–95; Hd of Agencies Gp, OPS, Cabinet Office, 1995–96. Non-exec. Dir, E Glos NHS Trust, 2000–02. Chm., Holst Birthplace Trust, 1999–2001. Chm. Govs, St James' Primary Sch., Cheltenham, 2001–14; Governor: Arthur Dye Primary Sch., Cheltenham, 2009–; Pate's Grammar Sch., Cheltenham, 2010–. *Recreations:* arts, architecture, literature. *Address:* 19 Montpellier Terrace, Cheltenham, Glos GL50 1UX.

HENRY, Rt Hon. Sir John (Steele), KNZM 2009 (DCNZM 2001); PC 1996; Judge, Court of Appeal, New Zealand, 1995–2000; *b* 3 July 1932; *s* of Hon. Sir Trevor Ernest Henry and Audrey Kate (*née* Sheriff); *m* 1957, Jennefer Lynne Stevenson; one *s* two *d*. *Educ:* King's Coll., Auckland; Auckland Univ. (LLB 1955). QC (NZ) 1980; High Court Judge, 1984–95; Acting Judge, Supreme Court, NZ, 2002–07. Commemoration Medal (NZ), 1990. *Recreations:* fishing, tramping, golf. *Address:* 310 Riddell Road, Glendowie, Auckland 1071, New Zealand. *T:* (9) 5758526. *Club:* Northern (Auckland).

HENRY, Keith Nicholas, FREng; Chairman: Regal Petroleum plc, since 2008; Greenko Group plc, since 2013 (non-executive Director, since 2012); *b* 3 March 1945; *s* of Kenneth G. Henry and Barbara Henry; *m* 1974, Susan Mary Horsburgh; two *d*. *Educ:* Bedford Sch.; London Univ. (BSc Hons Civil Engrg (ext.) 1967); Birmingham Univ. (MSc Foundn Engrg 1969). With Internat. Mgt and Engrg Gp Ltd, 1969–71; Project Engr, then Manager, Brown & Root, 1971–77; Engrg Manager, Brown & Root Far East, 1977–80; Brown & Root (UK) Ltd: Engrg Manager, 1980–84; Commercial Dir, 1984–85; Technical Dir and Chief Engr, 1985–88; Managing Director: Brown & Root Vickers Ltd, 1987–89; Brown & Root Marine, 1989; Chief Executive: Brown & Root Ltd, 1990–95; Nat. Power plc, 1995–99; Gp Exec. Vice-Pres. and Chief Exec., Engrg and Construction, Kvaerner E&C PLC, 2000–03; Dep. Chm., Petroleum-Geo Services ASA, 2003–06; Chairman: Burren Energy plc, 2006–08 (Dir, 2005–08); Petrojarl ASA, 2006; Helius Energy plc, 2009–11; Mediterranean Oil & Gas plc, 2012–14. Non-executive Director: Enterprise Oil, 1995–2002; Emerald Energy plc, 2004–09; South East Water Ltd, 2005–07; High Point-Rendel Ltd, 2006–; First Calgary Petroleums Ltd, 2008; Sterling Energy plc, 2009–; KSK Power Ventur plc, 2014–. FREng (FEng 1988). *Recreation:* shooting. *Address:* (office) Regal Petroleum plc, 16 Old Queen Street, SW1H 9HP. *E:* keithhenry@btinternet.com. *Club:* Royal Automobile.

HENRY, Dr Kenneth Ross, AC 2007; Secretary to the Treasury, Department of the Treasury, Australia, 2001–11; Special Adviser to the Prime Minister of Australia, 2011–12; *b* 27 Nov. 1957; *s* of John Desmond Henry and Heather Audrey McKay; *m* 1979, Naomi Jayne Smith; one *s* one *d.* *Educ:* Chatham High Sch., Taree; Univ. of New South Wales (BCom Hons); Univ. of Canterbury, NZ (PhD Econs). Res. Officer, Australian Bureau of Stats, 1979–80; Asst Lectr, 1980–81, Lectr, 1982–84, Univ. of Canterbury, NZ; Department of the Treasury, Australia: Sen. Finance Officer, 1984–85, Chief Finance Officer, 1985–86, Taxation Policy Div.; Private Sec., Office of Treas., 1986–89; Sen. Advr to Treas., 1989–91; Principal Advr, 1991–92; Minister (Econ. and Financial Affairs), Australian Delegn to OECD, Paris, 1992–93; First Asst Sec., Taxation Policy Div., 1994–97; Chair, Taxation Taskforce, 1997–98; Exec. Dir, Econ. Gp, 1998–2001. Non-executive Director: Nat. Australia Bank, 2011–; Australian Securities Exchange, 2013–. Mem., Econ. Soc. of Australia, 1999. *Recreations:* care of native fauna, reading, music. *Club:* Commonwealth (Canberra).

HENRY, Kristin; *see* Henry, D. K.

HENRY, Sir Lenworth George, (Sir Lenny), Kt 2015; CBE 1999; stand-up comedian, since 1975; actor; *b* 29 Aug. 1958; *s* of late Winston Henry and Winifred Henry; *m* 1984, Dawn R. French (marr. diss. 2010); one adopted *d.* *Educ:* Blue Coat Secondary Mod. Sch.; W. R. Tewson Sch.; Preston Coll.; Open Univ. (BA); Royal Holloway, Univ. of London (MA). Trustee, Comic Relief, 1987–. Won New Faces Talent Show, 1975; stand-up show, Have You Seen This Man, tour, 2001–02; So Much Things To Say, Wyndhams, 2003; Where You From?, tour, 2007; Cradle to Rave, tour, 2011; *TV appearances* include: Fosters, 1976–77; Tiswas, 1978–81; 3 of a Kind, 1981–84; The Lenny Henry Show, 1984, 1985, 1987, 1988, 1995, 2004; Lenny Henry Tonight, 1986; Xmas Specials, 1987, 1988, 1994, 1995; Chef, 1992, 1994, 1996; Lenny's Big Amazon Adventure, 1997; Lenny Goes to Town, 1998; Hope and Glory, 1999, 2000; Lenny's Big Atlantic Adventure, 2000; Lenny Henry in Pieces, 2002, 2003; This Is My Life, 2003; Lenny's Britain, Lenny Henry: So Much Things to Say, 2007; The Syndicate, Danny and the Human Zoo, 2015; *radio drama series:* Bad Faith, 2008, 2010, 2011; *films:* Coast to Coast, 1984; Work Experience, 1989; Alive and Kicking, 1990; True Identity, 1990; *theatre:* Othello, W Yorks Playhouse, transf. Rose Th., Kingston, then Trafalgar Studios, 2009; The Comedy of Errors, NT, 2011; Fences, Th. Royal, Bath, transf. Duchess Th., 2013 (Best Actor, Critics' Circle Th. Awards, 2014); Rudy's Rare Records, Birmingham Rep., 2014; Educating Rita, Chichester Festival Th., 2015. Lifetime Achievement Award, British Comedy Awards, 2003. *Publications:* Quest for the Big Woof; Charlie and the Big Chill, 1995; (jtly) Charlie, Queen of the Desert, 1996. *Recreations:* huge fan of R'n'B, hiphop, funk, avid reader, tennis, comics, enjoying my family. *Address:* c/o PBJ Management Ltd, 22 Rathbone Street, W1T 1LG. *T:* (020) 7287 1112. *Clubs:* Groucho, Soho House.

HENRY, Patricia; *see* Robertson, P.

HENRY, Sir Patrick (Denis), 3rd Bt *cr* 1923, of Cahore, co. Londonderry; businessman; *b* 20 Dec. 1957; *s* of Denis Valentine Henry (*d* 1983), *yr s* of 1st Bt, and Elizabeth Henry (*née* Walker); *S* uncle, 1997, but his name does not appear on the Official Roll of the Baronetage; *m* 1997, Georgina Ravenscroft (marr. diss.). *Educ:* Corpus Christi Coll., Oxford (BA (Hons) Modern History 1978). *Club:* Blackburn Rovers.

HENRY, Peter Clifford; His Honour Judge Henry; a Circuit Judge, since 2009; *b* Johannesburg, 28 Oct. 1954; *s* of Ian Clifford Henry and Pamela Joan Henry; *m* 1980, Elisabeth Stephens; one *s* one *d.* *Educ:* Uppingham Sch.; Exeter Univ. (LLB Hons). Called to the Bar, Inner Temple, 1977; in practice as barrister, specialising in criminal law; a Recorder, 2001–09; Legal Assessor to GMC, 2007–09. *Recreations:* motorsport, flying, painting, cycling, cricket. *Address:* Courts of Justice, London Road, Southampton, Hants SO15 2XQ. *T:* (023) 8021 3200, *Fax:* (023) 8021 3234. *Clubs:* Vintage Sports Car; Linkenholt Cricket.

HENRY, Simon Peter; Chief Financial Officer and Executive Director, Royal Dutch Shell plc, since 2009; *b* Eckington, Derbyshire, 13 July 1961; *s* of Peter Garland Henry and Marina Henry (*née* Moore); *m* 1986, Jonquil Ruth Porter; two *s* one *d.* *Educ:* King Ecgbert Comprehensive Sch., Sheffield; Churchill Coll., Cambridge (BA 1st Cl. Hons Maths 1982; MA 1986). CIMA 1989, FCMA 2009. Joined Shell, 1982: engr, Stanlow Refinery, 1982; various manufg, internal audit and finance appts, Shell UK Ltd, 1982–92; Finance Manager of Mktg, Egypt, 1992–94; Controller, Upstream business, Egypt, 1994–96; Oil Products Finance Advr, Asia Pacific, 1996–98; Finance Dir, Mekong Cluster, 1998–99; Gen. Manager, Finance, SE Asian Retail business, 1999–2001; Hd, Investor Relns, 2000–04; Chief Financial Officer, Exploration and Prodn, 2004–09. Non-exec. Dir, Lloyds Banking Gp, 2014–. Member: Cttee, 100 Gp of UK Finance Directors, 2010–; Adv. Cttee, Centre for Eur. Reform, 2011–. Chair, Eur. Round Table Chief Financial Officer Taskforce, 2012–. *Recreations:* sport, still playing football at 50, travel, family. *Address:* Royal Dutch Shell plc, Carel van Bylandtlaan 16, 2596 HR The Hague, Netherlands.

HENRY, Wendy Ann; Foster Dog Co-ordinator, Mayhew Animal Home, 2009; *d* of Bernard and Elsa Henry; *m* 1980, Tim Miles; one *d.* *Educ:* Queen Mary School, Lytham. Reporter, Daily Mail, Manchester, 1975–76, News of the World, 1976–79; Features Editor, Woman Magazine, 1979–81; Asst Editor, The Sun, 1981–85; Editor: Sunday Magazine, 1985–86; The News of the World, 1986–88; Dep. Editor, The Sun, 1988; Editor, The People, 1988–89; Ed.-in-Chief, The Globe, Florida, 1990–93; Man. Ed., current affairs TV Prog., 1993–95; Ed., weekend section, Daily News, NY, 1995–97; Ed.-in-Chief, Successful Slimming, and Editl Dir, New Publications, Globe Communications, USA, 1997–99; Ed., Real Homes mag., 1999–2001; Launch Ed., Parkhill Publishing, 2001–09. Foster Dog Co-ordinator, Battersea Dogs' and Cats' Home, 2003–08. Mem., Women in Journalism. *Recreations:* husband, dogs, sleeping.

HENSCHEL, Ruth Mary; *see* Ashton, R. M.

HENSHALL, Dr Christopher Harry; independent consultant in health, research and innovation policy, since 2010; Associate Professor, Health Economics Research Group, Brunel University London, since 2010; *b* 16 Feb. 1954; *s* of late Henry James Henshall and Edna Geraldine Henshall (*née* Watkins). *Educ:* Barnard Castle Sch., Co. Durham; Gonville and Caius Coll., Cambridge (BA Natural Sciences 1975; PhD 1983); Univ. of Nottingham (MA in Child Development 1976). Lectr in Psychol., Univ. of Warwick, 1981–84; Res. Fellow, Univ. of Southampton, 1984–85; Prog. Dir, Health Promotion Res. Trust, 1985–88; Sec., Health Services Res. Cttee, MRC, 1988–91; Research and Development Division, Department of Health: Sen. Principal, 1991; Asst Sec., 1993; Dep. Dir, R&D, 1996–2001; Dir, Sci. and Engrg Base Gp, OST, DTI, 2001–04. Hon. Prof., Dept of Public Health and Policy, LSHTM, 2001–05; Pro Vice-Chancellor for Ext. Relns, Univ. of York, 2005–10. Mem., Internat. Adv. Gp, Initiative to Improve Health in Asia, NUS, 2010–. Pres., 2003–05, Chm., Policy Forum, 2004–07 and 2010–June 2016, Health Technology Assessment Internat. Mem. Bd, Alberta Res. and Innovation Authy, 2009–14; Bd Dir, Alberta Innovates Health Solutions, 2014–. Hon. Fellow, Centre for Health Econs, Univ. of York, 2010–13. *Recreations:* hill walking (Munroist number 3053), opera, music, wine. *Address:* 13 St Mary's Grove, N1 2NT. *T:* 07769 931610. *E:* consulting@chrishenshall.co.uk.

HENSHALL, Rt Rev. Michael; Bishop Suffragan of Warrington, 1976–96; an Hon. Assistant Bishop, Diocese of York, since 1999; *b* 29 Feb. 1928; *m* Ann Elizabeth (*née* Stephenson); two *s* one *d.* *Educ:* Manchester Grammar Sch.; St Chad's Coll., Durham (BA 1954, DipTh 1956). Deacon 1956, priest 1957, Dio. of York; Curate of Holy Trinity, Bridlington and of Sewerby, 1956–59; Priest-in-charge, All Saints, Conventional District of Micklehurst, 1959–62; Vicar, 1962–63; Vicar of Altrincham, 1963–75; Proctor in Convocation, 1964–75; Mem., Terms of Ministry Cttee, General Synod, 1970–75; Hon. Canon of Chester, 1972–75; Secretary, Chester Diocesan Advisory Board for Ministry, 1968–75; Canon Emeritus of Chester Cathedral, 1979. Chairman: Northern Ordination Course Council, 1985–96; Churches Gp NW, Industry Year, 1985–90; Council, St Chad's Coll., Univ. of Durham, 1992–2000; Vice-Chm., National Soc., 1994–96; Mem. Council, Coll. of Preachers, 1989– (Ed., Journal, 1998–2003). *Publications:* Dear Nicholas, 1989. *Recreations:* military history, old battlefields, etc. *Address:* Brackenfield, 28 Hermitage Way, Eskdaleside, Sleights, Whitby, N Yorks YO22 5HG. *T:* (01947) 811233.

See also Very Rev. N. J. Henshall.

HENSHALL, Very Rev. Nicholas James; Dean of Chelmsford, since 2014; *b* Mossley, Lancs, 6 April 1962; *s* of Rt Rev. Michael Henshall, *qv*; *m* 1991, Christine Margaret Goodacre; one *s* two *d.* *Educ:* Manchester Grammar Sch.; British Sch. of Archaeology, Athens; Wadham Coll., Oxford (BA 1985; MA 1988); Ripon Coll., Cuddesdon. Ordained deacon, 1988, priest, 1989; Curate, St Mary's, Blyth, Northumberland, 1988–92; Vicar, St Margaret's, Scotswood, Newcastle, 1992–2002; Canon Precentor, Derby Cathedral, 2002–08; Vicar, Christ Church, Harrogate, 2008–14; Acting Archdeacon of Richmond, 2013–14. *Publications:* regular articles in The Tablet. *Recreations:* walking, cooking. *Address:* Chelmsford Cathedral, 53 New Street, Chelmsford CM1 1TY. *T:* (01245) 294492. *E:* dean@chelmsfordcathedral.org.uk.

HENSHALL, Valentine Ruth, (Ruthie); actress, singer and dancer; *b* 7 March 1967; *d* of David Henshall and Gloria Diana Mary Henshall; *m* 2004, Timothy Michael Howar (marr. diss. 2011); two *d.* *Educ:* Bullers Wood Grammar Sch. for Girls; Laine Theatre Arts, Epsom. *Theatre:* Chorus Line (tour), 1986; West End début, Cats, New London Th., 1987–88; Miss Saigon, Th. Royal, Drury Lane, 1990, NY 2000; Children of Eden, Prince Edward Th., 1991; The Sisterhood, Henry VIII, Valentine's Day, Chichester Fest., 1992; Fantine in Les Miserables, Palace Th., 1993–94, 10th anniv. concert, Royal Albert Hall, 1995; She Loves Me, Savoy, 1994 (Best Actress in a Musical, Laurence Olivier Awards, 1995); Crazy for You, Prince Edward Th., 1995; Oliver!, Palladium Th., 1996; Divorce Me, Darling, Chichester Fest., 1997; Chicago, Adelphi, 1998, NY, 1999, Cambridge Th., 2010; Ziegfeld Follies of 1936, NY, 1999; Vagina Monologues, NY, 1999, Arts Th., London, 2002; Putting it Together, NY, 1999; Peggy Sue Got Married, Shaftesbury, 2001; Woman in White, Palace Th., 2005; The Other Woman, NY, 2006; Stair Way to Paradise, NY, 2007; Marguerite, Th. Royal Haymarket, 2008; Blithe Spirit, Th. Royal Bath, transf. Apollo, 2011; An Intimate Evening with Ruthie Henshall (tour), 2013; Billy Elliot, Victoria Palace, 2014; Follies, Royal Albert Hall, 2015. *Television:* a Judge, Dancing on Ice, 2008–09; The Case, 2011; Curb Your Enthusiasm, HBO, 2011; *film:* A Christmas Carol, 2004; *album:* I've Loved These Days, 2013. Many cast recordings. *Recreations:* I'm a mother of two small children—recreation, what's that? *Address:* 7 Pond Cottages, Manningtree Road, Stutton, Ipswich, Suffolk IP9 2TG. *T:* (01473) 328159. *W:* www.ruthiehenshall.com. *Club:* Soho House.

HENSHAW, Andrew Raywood; QC 2013; *b* Towcester, Northants, 22 April 1962; *s* of Raywood and Patricia Henshaw; *m* 1998, Claire O'Connor; two *s* one *d.* *Educ:* Sponne Sch., Towcester; Downing Coll., Cambridge (BA Hons 1983). Admitted solicitor, 1986; Solicitor, Linklaters & Paines, 1986–2000; called to the Bar, Inner Temple, 2000; in practice as barrister, specialising in commercial, public and EU law, 2000–. *Recreations:* music, bridge, ski-ing. *Address:* Brick Court Chambers, 7–8 Essex Street, WC2R 3LD. *T:* (020) 7379 3550. *E:* andrew.henshaw@brickcourt.co.uk.

HENSHAW, Sir David (George), Kt 2004; Chief Executive, Liverpool City Council, 1999–2006; Chairman: Sir David Henshaw Partnership Ltd, since 2010; Alder Hey Children's NHS Foundation Trust, since 2011; *b* 7 March 1949; *s* of George Ronald Henshaw and Ethel Irene Henshaw; *m* 1st 1978, Rosemary St C. Herbert (marr. diss. 2000); two *s*; 2nd, 2000, Alison Joy Jones. *Educ:* Sheffield Poly. (BA Public Admin 1973); Univ. of Birmingham (MScSoc 1975). Corporate Planning Officer, S Yorks MCC, 1974–84; Prin. Asst County Clerk, then Asst Chief Exec., Essex CC, 1984–89; Chief Exec., Knowsley MBC, 1989–99. Clerk to Merseyside Police Authy, 1989–2000. Dir and Dep. Chm., Mersey Partnership, 1993–2006; Mem. Bd, Improvement and Develt Agency for Local Govt, 2001–03. Non-executive Director: Albany Investment Trust plc, 2004–12; Hedra plc, 2006–08. Dep. Chm., Nat. Task Force on Crime Reduction, 2000–02; non-exec. Dir, Home Office Correctional Services Bd, 2002–05; Hd, Redesign of CSA, 2006–07; Member: Independent Rev. of Higher Educn Pay and Conditions, 1999; Strategy Gp, Civil Service Mgt Bd, 2002–03; Bd, Council for Museums, Libraries and Archives, 2004–06; Public Services Productivity Panel, HM Treasury, 2005–07. Chairman: NW Strategic Health Authy, 2006–11; Bd, NESTA Public Services Innovation Lab., 2008–12; Manchester Acad. of Health Scis, 2009–12; Our Life North West, 2009–11; Interim Chairman: Morecambe Bay Univ. Hosps Foundn Trust, 2012–13; Dorset Healthcare Univ. NHS Foundn Trust, 2013–14. Advr, Prime Minister's Delivery Unit, 2001–04; Public Service Reform Advr, States of Jersey Govt, 2014–. Jt Chm., SOLACE Enterprises, 1998–2005; Pres., SOLACE, 2000–01. Trustee: North West Heritage Trust, 2008–; NESTA, 2010–12; Alder Hey Charitable Trust, 2011–. Chm., Faenol Festival Trust, 2007–10. Gov., Liverpool John Moores Univ., 2009–12 (Hon. Fellow, 2004). Fellow, Liverpool Univ., 1998; Vis. Fellow, Royal Inst. of Technol., Melbourne, Aust., 1997–2002. FRSA 2005. DUniv Sheffield Hallam, 2006. *Recreations:* golf, opera, walking, tennis, active member morris tours. *Clubs:* Royal Automobile; Royal Liverpool Golf; Royal St Davids Golf (Harlech).

HENSHAW, Prof. Denis Lee, PhD; Professor of Physics, University of Bristol, 1995–2011, now Emeritus Professor of Human Radiation Effects; *b* 4 May 1946; *s* of late Frederick Henshaw and Evelyne May (*née* Fox); *m* 1994, Wassana. *Educ:* Westfield Coll., Univ. of London (BSc 1969); Univ. of Nottingham (PhD 1974). Teacher, Mundella GS, 1969–70; University of Bristol: Res. Associate, 1973–82; Res. Fellow, 1982–90; Sen. Res. Fellow, 1990–95. Dir, Track Analysis Systems Ltd, Bristol, 1984–. Trustee, Children with Leukaemia, 2004–11; Dir of Res., Children with Cancer UK, 2011–. Associate Ed., Internat. Jl Radiation Biol., 1995–. *Publications:* over 250 scientific pubns. *Recreation:* Italian language and culture. *Address:* Atmospheric Chemistry Group, School of Chemistry, University of Bristol, Cantocks Close, Bristol BS8 1TS. *T:* (0117) 926 0353.

HENSHAW, Frank Charles, CBE 1993; DL; FRICS; General Manager, Milton Keynes Development Corporation, 1980–92; *b* 28 Aug. 1930; *s* of Frank and Edith Annie Henshaw; *m* 1966, Patricia Jane McDonald; one *s* one *d.* *Educ:* Towcester Grammar Sch.; Coll. of Estate Management. FRICS 1959. Nat. service, RAF, 1948–50. Quantity Surveyor: Northants CC, 1947–53; Coventry City Council, 1953–63; Prin. Quantity Surveyor, Midlands Housing Consortium, 1963–65; Chief Quantity Surveyor: Runcorn Develt Corp., 1965–70; Sheffield City Council, 1970–71; Milton Keynes Development Corporation: Chief Quantity Surveyor, 1971–74; Exec. Dir, 1974–78; Dep. Gen. Manager, 1978–80. Chm., Milton Keynes Housing Assoc., 1985–88; Dep. Chm., Central Milton Keynes Shopping Mgt Co., 1978–89. Pres., Milton Keynes and N Bucks TEC, 1992–95 (Dir, 1990–92). DL Bucks, 1995. Hon. Fellow, De Montfort Univ., 1993. DUniv Open, 1994. OON 1989. *Recreations:* golf, travel. *Club:* Woburn Golf and Country.

HENSHER, Dr Philip Michael, FRSL; novelist; *b* 20 Feb. 1965; *s* of R. J. Hensher and M. Hensher. *Educ:* Tapton Sch., Sheffield; Lady Margaret Hall, Oxford (BA); Jesus Coll., Cambridge (PhD 1992). Clerk, H of C, 1990–96. Chief Book Reviewer, Spectator, 1994–; Art Critic, Mail on Sunday, 1996–; columnist, The Independent. Associate Prof. of English,

Univ. of Exeter, 2005–12; Prof. of Creative Writing, Univ. of Bath Spa, 2013–. Mem., Booker Prize Jury, 2001. FRSL 1998 (Mem. Council, 2000–05). *Publications:* Other Lulus, 1994; Kitchen Venom, 1996 (Somerset Maugham Award); Pleasured, 1998; The Bedroom of the Mister's Wife (short stories), 1999; The Mulberry Empire, 2002; The Fit, 2004; The Northern Clemency, 2008; King of the Badgers, 2011; Scenes from Early Life, 2012; The Missing Ink (essays), 2012; The Emperor Waltz, 2014. *Recreation:* ceramics. *Address:* 83A Tennyson Street, SW8 3TH.

HENSMAN, Claire Theresa; Lord-Lieutenant of Cumbria, since 2013; *b* 5 July 1948; *d* of Dr Peter Wallace Henderson and Dr Stella Dolores Henderson; *m* 1973, Peter Richard Wavell Hensman; one *s* two *d. Educ:* Sherborne Sch. for Girls; London Sch. of Econs and Pol Sci. (BA Laws). Investment Exec., Hill Samuel, 1970–73; Investment Analyst, M&G Investment Mgt, 1973–76; Pension Fund Advr, NM Rothschild, 1976–78; Gen. Comr of Income Tax, 1987–2000. Non-executive Director: Westmorland Hosp. NHS Trust, 1992–98; Univ. of Cumbria, 2010–. Mem. Council, High Sheriffs' Assoc., 2007–13. Mem. Council, Lancaster Univ., 1993–2006 (Dep. Pro-Chancellor, 2001–06; Hon. Fellow, 2007). High Sheriff, Cumbria, 2007–08. Trustee: Bendrigg Trust, 1980–96 and 1998–2010 (Chair, 1988–92 and 1998–2001); Frieda Scott Ch Trust, 2004–13; Chair, Lakeland Arts Support Trust, 2011–. President: Cumbria Alcohol and Drug Adv. Service, 2009–; Cumbria Community Foundn, 2013–; Young Cumbria, 2013–; Cumbria Scouts, 2013–; SSAFA (Cumbria), 2013–; Vice-Pres., NW of Eng. and IoM RFCA, 2013–. Gov., Sedbergh Sch., 2013–; St Bees Sch., 2013–. FRSA. *Recreations:* gardening, music, ski-ing. *Address:* Hill Top, Crosthwaite, Kendal, Cumbria LA8 8JB. *E:* c.hensman@hilltop.uk.com. *Club:* Down Hill Only.

HENSON, Christine Ruth; QC 2015; **Her Honour Judge Henson;** a Circuit Judge, since 2015. *Educ:* Univ. of Warwick (BA 1992). Called to the Bar, Middle Temple, 1994; a Recorder, 2013–15.

HENSON, Judith Rosalind; *see* Mackrell, J. R.

HENSON, Marguerite Ann, (Mrs Nicky Henson); *see* Porter, M. A.

HENSON, Nicholas Victor Leslie, (Nicky); actor; *b* 12 May 1945; *s* of Leslie Henson and Billie Collins; *m* 1st, 1968, Una Stubbs (marr. diss.); two *s*; 2nd, 1986, Marguerite Porter, *qv*; one *s. Educ:* St Bede's, Eastbourne; Charterhouse. Formerly popular song writer; Founder Mem., Young Vic; first stage appearance, 1962; *London stage:* All Square, Vaudeville, 1963; Camelot, Drury Lane, 1964; Passion Flower Hotel, Prince of Wales, 1965; Canterbury Tales, Phoenix, 1968; Ride Across Lake Constance, Mayfair, 1973; Hamlet, Greenwich, 1973; Midsummer Night's Dream, Regent's Park, 1973; Cinderella, Casino, 1973; Mardi Gras, Prince of Wales, 1976; Rookery Nook, Her Majesty's, 1980; Noises Off, Savoy, 1982; The Relapse, Lyric, 1983; Sufficient Carbohydrate, Albery, 1984; Journey's End, Whitehall, 1986; The Three Sisters, Royal Court, 1990; Matador, Queen's, 1991; Reflected Glory, Vaudeville, 1992; An Ideal Husband, Globe, 1993, NY, 1996, Australia, 1997; Rage, Bush, 1994; Enter the Guardsman, Donmar, 1997; Alarms and Excursions, Gielgud, 1998; Passion Play, Comedy, 2000; Frame 312, Donmar, 2002; Jumpers, Piccadilly, 2003, NY, 2004; *Young Vic:* Scapino, Waiting for Godot, She Stoops to Conquer, Taming of the Shrew, Measure for Measure, Soldier's Tale, Oedipus, Romeo and Juliet, The Maids, Look Back in Anger, Rosencrantz and Guildenstern are Dead, Charley's Aunt; *National Theatre:* Cherry Orchard, Macbeth, The Woman, The Double Dealer, A Fair Quarrel, Browning Version, Provok'd Wife, Elephant Man, Mandragola; *Royal Shakespeare Co.:* Man and Superman, Merry Wives of Windsor, As You Like It, Twelfth Night; *television series:* Life of Balzac, 1976; Seagull Island, 1981; Happy Apple, 1983; Thin Air, 1988; The Green Man, 1990; The Healer, 1994; Preston Front, 1994; Shine on Harvey Moon, 1994; Blue Dove, 2002; Downton Abbey, 2009–13; 30 films, incl. Vera Drake, 2004, Syriana, 2005, Blitz, 2010; Truth or Dare, 2011. *Recreation:* music. *Address:* c/o Richard Stone Partnership, Suite 3, De Walden Court, 85 New Cavendish Street, W1W 6XD. *T:* (020) 7497 0849. *W:* www.nickyhenson.me.uk.

HENTON, (Margaret) Patricia, FRSE; FCIWEM, FCIWM; CGeol, FGS; Director of Environment and Business (formerly Environment Protection), Environment Agency, 2005–10; *b* 30 Oct. 1949; *d* of Robert Stuart Sanderson and Lois Lindsay Sanderson; *m* 1971, Richard George Henton; one *s* one *d. Educ:* George Watson's Coll., Edinburgh; Univ. of Manchester (BSc Hons Geol./Geog. 1970). FGS 1974; FCIWEM 1979; FCIWM 2006 (MInstWM 1981); CGeol 1990. Geologist, Associated Portland Cement Manufacturers, 1970–71; Hydrogeologist, Clyde River Purification Bd, 1972–75; Geologist, NCB Opencast Exec., 1975; Inspector, 1975–79, Hydrologist, 1979–83, Forth River Purification Bd; Associate, 1983–85, Sen. Associate, 1985–90, Dir, Scotland and NI, 1990–95, Aspinwall & Co. Ltd; Dir, Envmtl Strategy, 1995–2000, Chief Exec., 2000–02, SEPA. Dir, Scotland and NI Forum for Envmtl Res., 1996–2002; non-exec. Dir, Coal Authy, 2010–. Chm., Ind. Regulatory Challenge Panel, HSE, 2012–. Member: Sec. of State for Scotland's Adv. Gp on Sustainable Devel t, 1993–98; Regulatory Agencies Strategy Bd, DEFRA, 2003–05 (Chm., 2004–05). Chm., Adv. Panel, Forestry Commn, 2003–05; Mem. Council, NERC, 1999–2001; Additional Mem., Water Panel, Competition Commn, 1998–2000. Member: Adv. Cttee for Scotland, 2000–08, Council, 2003–09, RSPB; Bd, British Geol Survey, 2009–11; Council, Geol Soc. of London, 2011–15; Bd, UK Carbon Capture and Storage Res. Centre, 2012–; Trustee: Royal Botanic Garden, Edinburgh, 2010–; British Trust for Ornithology, 2010–14; Inst. for Eur. Envmtl Policy, 2011–. Pres., CIWEM, 1995–96. Mem., Audit Cttee, Heriot-Watt Univ., 2003–05. FRSE 2002. *Recreations:* travel, bird watching, the Levant, hill-walking, gardens. *Address:* 4 Jeffrey Avenue, Edinburgh EH4 3RW.

HENTY, Jonathan Maurice; Commissioner of Social Security and Child Support, 1993–2006; *b* 22 Dec. 1933; *s* of Richard Iltid Henty and Lettice Ellen (*née* Moore Gwyn); *m* 1st, 1956, Margaret Louise Sadler (*d* 1972); one *s* one *d* (and one *s* decd); 2nd, 1977, Veronica Mary Francis Miller; two *d. Educ:* Eton; New Coll., Oxford (MA). Called to the Bar, Lincoln's Inn, 1957, Bencher, 1989. Chancellor, Dio. Hereford, 1977–2000; Deputy Chancellor: Dio. Lincoln, 1994–98; Dio. Chelmsford, 1997–2000; Dio. London, 1997–2000. *Recreations:* books, art and architecture. *Address:* Fisher Hill House, Northchapel, Petworth, W Sussex GU28 9EJ. *Club:* Athenæum.

HENWOOD, John Philip, MBE 1998; Chairman: Byerley Ltd, since 2000; Jersey Tourism Board, since 2013; Visit Jersey Ltd, since 2014; *b* 27 Aug. 1945; *s* of late Snowdon William Henwood and Amy Doris Henwood (*née* Stickley); *m* 1970, Sheila Patricia Renault (marr. diss. 1994). *Educ:* St Lawrence Sch.; Victoria Coll., Jersey. Joined Channel Television Ltd, later Channel Television Group, then ComProp Ltd, 1962: ops trainee, 1962–64; cameraman, 1964–65; Hd of Studio, 1965–66; Dep. Ops Manager, 1966–70; Producer/Dir (setting up commercial prodn unit), 1970–77; Hd, News and Features, 1977–83; Programme Controller, 1983–86; Dir of Progs, 1986–87; Chief Exec. and Man. Dir, 1987–2000; Dir, 1986–2004. Chairman: Jersey Telecom Gp Ltd, 2002–09; G4S Secure Solutions (Jersey) Ltd, 2010–; Director: ITV Network, 1987–99; Jersey Finance, 2001–09 (Vice-Chm.); Kleinwort Benson Channel Islands Hldgs, 2003–12; Kleinwort Benson Bank, 2007–12; Flying Brands Ltd, 2007–; Bailiwick Investments Ltd, 2008–; LFH Internat., 2009–. Chm., Producers' Industrial Relns Service Ltd, 1997–2000. Mem., States of Jersey Review Panel of Machinery of Govt, 1999–2001. Sen. Steward, CI Racing and Hunt Club, 1998 and 2009; Pres., Jersey Race Club, 1998–2001; Mem., Horserace Writers and Photographers Assoc. President, Jersey Branch: CIM; IoD, 2005–08 (Chm., 2001–02). Trustee: ITV Retirement Benefits Scheme, 1997–2000; Durrell Wildlife Conservation Trust, 2006–12; St John Youth and Community Trust, 2009–. *Recreations:* the turf - horse racing and the thoroughbred, writing, current affairs, ski-ing, old cars.

HENWOOD, Stephen Hugh, CBE 2013; TD 1985; FRGS; Chairman: Nuclear Decommissioning Authority, since 2008; Aerospace Technology Institute, since 2014; *b* Newcastle upon Tyne, 11 June 1953; *s* of Hugh Henwood and Cicely Henwood (*née* Gordin); *m* 1981, Gill Rennie; one *s* two *d. Educ:* Leeds Grammar Sch.; Liverpool Univ. (BA Hons Econs); Harvard Business Sch. (Advanced Mgt Prog.). Tate & Lyle plc: financial and operational roles, 1977–85; Strategic Planner and Asst to UK Man. Dir, 1985–87; Man. Dir, Tate & Lyle Distribution Services, 1987–89; Divl Dir, Finance and Planning, Tate & Lyle Sugars, 1989–92; BAE Systems plc: Finance Dir, Mil. Aircraft Div., 1992–96; Man. Dir, Royal Ordnance, 1996–99; Gp Financial Controller, 1999–2000; Gp Man. Dir, Progs, 2000–02, Internat. Partnerships, 2002–06; Chm., NP Aerospace, 2006–07. Hon. Treas. and Mem. Council, RGS, 2008–14 (FRGS 2008; Hon. Fellow 2014). FCMA 1989; FRAeS 2000–10. Trustee, Army Mus Ogilby Trust, 2002–. Regtl Col, London Scottish, 2000–07; Dep. Hon. Col, London Regt, 2000–07. Chm. Bd, Univ. of Cumbria, 2010–14. *Recreations:* walking, bird-watching. *Address:* Woodlands Farm, Hothersall Lane, Hothersall, Preston PR3 2XB. *E:* stephen.henwood@mesuri.com. *Club:* Army and Navy.

HEPBURN, James Douglas; Member (SNP) Cumbernauld and Kilsyth, Scottish Parliament, since 2011 (Scotland Central, 2007–11); Minister for Sport, Health Improvement and Mental Health, since 2014; *b* 21 May 1979; *s* of Iain Hepburn and Mary (*née* Irvine, now Hunter); *m* 2006, Julie Shackleton; one *s* one *d. Educ:* Univ. of Glasgow (MA 2002; Sen. Vice-Pres., Students' Rep. Council, 1999–2000). Front of house asst, Citizens' Th., Glasgow, 2001–02; temp. data processor, Scottish Power, 2002; Res. Asst to Alex Neil, MSP, 2002–07. *Recreations:* football, reading, writing, cinema. *Address:* Scottish Parliament, Holyrood, Edinburgh EH99 1SP. *T:* (0131) 348 6574, *Fax:* (0131) 348 6979.

HEPBURN, Jane Katherine; *see* Lemon, J. K.

HEPBURN, Sir John Alastair Trant Kidd B.; *see* Buchan-Hepburn.

HEPBURN, Stephen; MP (Lab) Jarrow, since 1997; *b* 6 Dec. 1959; *s* of Peter and Margaret Hepburn. *Educ:* Springfield Comprehensive Sch., Jarrow; Newcastle Univ. Former Res. Asst to Donald Dixon, MP. Mem. (Lab) S Tyneside MBC, 1985–97 (Chair: Finance Cttee, 1989–90; Tyne & Wear Pensions, 1989–97; Dep. Leader, 1990–97). Member: Defence Select Cttee, 2000–01; NI Affairs Select Cttee, 2004–; Scottish Affairs Select Cttee, 2015–; Vice Chm., All Party Parly Shipbuilding and Ship Repair Gp; Secretary: All Party Football Gp; All Party Football Team. President: Bilton Hall Boxing Club; Jarrovians RFC; Jarrow FC. *Recreation:* sports. *Address:* House of Commons, SW1A 0AA. *T:* (constituency office) (0191) 420 0648. *Clubs:* Neon (Jarrow); Iona (Hebburn).

HEPBURNE SCOTT, family name of **Lord Polwarth**.

HEPHER, Michael Leslie; Chief Executive, 1996–98, and Chairman, 1997–98, Charterhouse plc; *b* 17 Jan. 1944; *s* of Leslie and Edna Hepher; *m* 1st, 1971, Janice Morton (marr. diss. 2004); one *s* two *d*; 2nd, 2006, Raissa Chtcherbakova. *Educ:* Kingston Grammar School. FIA; Associate, Soc. of Actuaries; FLIA. Provident Life Assoc., UK, 1961–67; Commercial Life Assurance, Canada, 1967–70; Maritime Life Assurance Co., Canada, 1970–79; Chm. and Man. Dir, Abbey Life Group, UK, subseq. Lloyds Abbey Life, 1980–91; Gp Man. Dir, BT, 1991–95. Non-executive Chairman: HambroFraserSmith, 1999–2000; Telecity plc, 2000–05; Lane Clark and Peacock LLP, 2003–05; non-executive Director: Kingfisher, 1997–2010; Canada Life Assurance Co., 1999–; Catlin Gp Ltd, 2003–10; Great-West Life, 2006–; Chartis UK, 2010–12. *Recreations:* reading, golf. *Address:* (office) 35 Piccadilly, W1J 0DW.

HEPPELL, John; *b* 3 Nov. 1948; *m* 1974, Eileen Golding; two *s* one *d. Educ:* Rutherford Grammar Sch.; SE Northumberland Technical Coll.; Ashington Technical Coll. Fitter: NCB, 1964–70; various cos, 1970–75; diesel fitter, 1975–78, workshop supervisor, 1978–89, British Rail. Mem. (Lab) Nottinghamshire CC, 1981–93. MP (Lab) Nottingham E, 1992–2010. PPS to Leader of House of Lords, 1997–98; PPS to Dep. Prime Minister and Sec. of State for Envmt, Transport and the Regions, 1998–2001; a Lord Comr of HM Treasury (Govt Whip), 2001–05; Vice-Chamberlain of HM Household, 2005–07; an Asst Govt Whip, 2009–10. Member: Cttee of Selection, 1997–2007; Children, Schs and Families Select Cttee, 2007–09.

HEPPELL, Prof. Stephen John; Felipe Segovia Professor of Learning Innovation, Universidad Camilo José Cela, Madrid, since 2014; Professor of New Media Environments, Bournemouth University, since 2007; Emeritus Professor, Anglia Ruskin University (formerly Anglia Polytechnic University), since 2004; *b* Chalfont St Peter, 10 Aug. 1950; *s* of Donald Albert William Heppell and Brenda Mary Heppell; *m* 1974, Carole Lynda Chapman; one *s* two *d. Educ:* Chenies Co. Primary Sch.; Dr Challoner's Grammar Sch., Amersham; Univ. of Reading (BA Hons Econs); Univ. of East London (PGCE); South Bank Univ. (MSc). Secondary sch. teacher, E London, Essex and S London, 1974–83; Essex Inst. of Higher Educn, then Anglia Higher Education College, later Anglia Polytechnic, subseq. Anglia Polytechnic University: Lectr, 1983–87; Dir, Learning Technology Res. Centre, later Ultralab, 1985–2004; Prof., 1987–2004. CEO, Learning Possibilities Plus, 2009–. Vis. Prof., Universidad Camilo José Cela, Madrid, 2011–14. Trustee: Creative Skillset, 2008–14; BAFTA, 2011– (Mem. Council, 2009–); Mem., Adv. Bd, Educurious, 2011–. *Publications:* Help your Child with Computers at Home, 1994; papers and jls on technol. in learning, design of learning envmts and educnl policy. *Recreations:* a lifetime of competitive sailing from club to world championship level, currently (with Carole) owns and races a 1907 Oyster Smack 'My Alice' and a 1933 Brightlingsea One Design 'Aina', very fond of fish and chips, and silicon chips. *Address:* Heppell.net Ltd, 41 Belmont Close, Wickford, Essex SS12 0HR. *T:* 07929 621295, *Fax:* (01268) 475435. *W:* www.heppell.net, www.twitter.com/ stephenheppell. *Clubs:* Little Ship; Colne Yacht.

HEPPELL, (Thomas) Strachan, CB 1986; Consultant, Department of Health, 1995–2000; Chairman, Management Board, European Medicines Evaluation Agency, 1994–2000; *b* 15 Aug. 1935; *s* of late Leslie Thomas Davidson Heppell and Doris Abbey Heppell (*née* Potts); *m* 1963, Felicity Ann Rice; two *s. Educ:* Acklam Hall Grammar Sch., Middlesbrough; The Queen's Coll., Oxford. National Assistance Board, Ministry of Social Security/DHSS: Asst Principal, 1958; Principal, 1963–73 (seconded to Cabinet Office, 1967–69); Asst Director of Social Welfare, Hong Kong, 1971–73; Asst Sec., DHSS, 1973–78 (Social Security Adviser, Hong Kong Govt, 1977); Under Sec., DHSS, 1979–83; Dep. Sec., DHSS, later DoH, 1983–95. Chm., Family Fund Trust, 1997–2003; Mem., Broadcasting Standards Commn, 1996–2003; Expert Mem., Fairness Cttee, OFCOM, 2003–04; Mem., Adv. Bd, Institut des Sciences de la Santé, 2004–06; Chair: Audit Adv. Cttee, EMEA, 2004–12; Eur. Inst. for Health, 2006–10. Vis. Fellow, LSE, 1997–2000. *Publications:* contribs on health, social welfare and regulatory affairs. *Recreations:* gardening, travelling.

HEPPLEWHITE, Rosalind Mary Joy, (Ros); Chair, Leicestershire and Rutland Probation Board, 2001–04; *b* 20 Dec. 1952; *d* of Anne and Anthony Phillips; *m* 1971, Julian Hepplewhite; one *s* one *d. Educ:* University College London (BA Hons). Asst House Governor, 1980–83, and Hosp. Sec., 1983–84, Bethlem Royal and Maudsley Hosps; Unit Administrator (Mental Health), Hammersmith and Fulham HA, 1984–85; Unit Gen. Manager (Mental Health and Mental Handicap), 1985–88, Dir, Corporate Devel t, 1988–89, Brighton HA; Nat. Dir, MIND (Nat. Assoc. of Mental Health), 1989–91; Chief Exec., CSA, 1992–94; Chief Exec. and Registrar, GDC, 1996–2000. Mem., Council on Tribunals, 2002–05. JP Leicester, 2002–05. *Recreation:* home and family.

HEPWORTH, Noel Peers, OBE 1980; international public financial management consultant, since 2008; Chairman, Croydon Almshouse and Relief in Need Charities, since 1996; *b* 22 Dec. 1934; *m* 1963, Jean Margaret Aldcroft; one *s* three *d*. *Educ:* Crewe County Grammar Sch.; London Univ. CPFA (IPFA 1958); DPA 1963. Nat. Service, RAF, 1953–55. NW Gas Bd, 1951–58; Asst City Treasurer, Manchester, 1965–72; Dir of Finance, Croydon, 1972–80; Dir, CIPFA, 1980–96. Chairman: Inst. of Public Finance Ltd, 1996–2002; CIPFA Internat., 2002–08. Financial Advr to London Boroughs Assoc. and AMA, 1972–80; Mem., London Treasurers' Adv. Body, 1972–80; Member: Dept of Envmt Property Adv. Group, 1980–88; Audit Commn, 1983–91; Adv. Bd, Treasury Solicitor Agency, 1996–99. Pres., Internat. Consortium on Governmental Financial Management, 1987–92; Proj. Dir, Eur. Fedn of Accountants single Eur. currency project, 1996–2001. Chm., FEE Public Sector Cttee, 1988–2003. FRSA 1985. Freeman, City of London, 1991. Hon. DSc (Econ) Hull; Hon. LLD Brighton; Hon. DSc City. *Publications:* Finance of Local Government, 1970, 7th edn 1984, Japanese edn 1983; Housing Rents, Costs and Subsidies, 1978, 2nd edn 1981; contribs to technical and financial jls, local govt press and nat. and internat. press. *Recreations:* gardening, walking.

HERALD, John Pearson; Sheriff of North Strathclyde, 1992–2012; *b* 12 July 1946; *s* of Andrew James Herald and Martha Wilson or Herald; *m* 1969, Catriona McDougall Anderson; one *d*. *Educ:* Hillhead High Sch., Glasgow; Univ. of Glasgow (LLB). Partner, Carlton Gilruth, Dundee, 1971–91; Dir, William Halley & Sons, Dundee, 1988–91. Depute Town Clerk, Newport-on-Tay, 1970–75; Temp. Sheriff, 1984–91; Chm., Industrial Tribunals, 1984–91. Sec., Angus Legal Aid Cttee, 1979–87; Mem., Legal Aid Central Cttee, 1981–87; Chm., Dundee CAB, 1972–79 and 1982–91. *Recreations:* reading, soccer.

HERBECQ, Sir John (Edward), KCB 1977; a Church Commissioner, 1982–96; *b* 29 May 1922; *s* of late Joseph Edward and Rosina Elizabeth Herbecq; *m* 1947, Pamela Filby (*d* 2009); one *d*. *Educ:* High Sch. for Boys, Chichester. Clerical Officer, Colonial Office, 1939; Asst Principal, Treasury, 1950; Private Sec. to Chm., UK Atomic Energy Authority, 1960–62; Asst Sec., Treasury, 1964; Asst Sec., 1968, Under Sec., 1970, Dep. Sec., 1973, Second Permanent Sec., 1975–81, CSD. Dep. Chm., Review Body for Nursing Staff, Midwives, Health Visitors and Professions Allied to Medicine, 1986–91 (Mem., 1983–91); Chm., Malaŵi Civil Service Review Commn, 1984–85. Member: C of E Pensions Bd, 1985–89; Chichester Diocesan Bd of Finance, 1983–97 (Chm., 1989–97). *Recreations:* was Scottish country dancing (ISTD Supreme Award with Hons), now walking, watching cricket, reading. *Address:* 2 The Stables, Mill Lane, Prestbury, Cheltenham, Glos GL52 3NE. *T:* (01242) 571291.

HERBERG, Javan William; QC 2011; *b* London, 22 Nov. 1965; *s* of Dr Lewis Jacob Herberg and Mary Herberg; partner, Dr Jessica Boyd; four *s* one *d*. *Educ:* University College Sch.; University Coll. London (LLB); Merton Coll., Oxford (BCL). Called to the Bar, Lincoln's Inn, 1992; in practice as a barrister, specialising in commercial law, financial services, public law and human rights, Blackstone Chambers, 1992–. Chair, Constitutional and Administrative Law Bar Assoc., 2012–14. *Publications:* (contrib.) Human Rights Law and Practice, 1999, (ed jtly) 3rd edn 2009. *Recreations:* chamber music, opera, playing 2nd violin, fell walking. *Address:* Blackstone Chambers, Blackstone House, Temple, EC4Y 9BW. *E:* javanherberg@blackstonechambers.com.

HERBERT, family name of **Earls of Carnarvon, Pembroke,** and **Powis,** and **Baron Hemingford**.

HERBERT, 19th Baron *cr* 1461; **David John Seyfried Herbert;** Director, David Seyfried Ltd; *b* 3 March 1952; *s* of late John Beeton Seyfried and Lady Cathleen Blanche Lily Eliot, *d* of 6th Earl of St Germans and *gd* of 9th Duke of Beaufort; Herbert Barony, in abeyance since death of 10th Duke of Beaufort, 1984, called out of abeyance in his favour, 2002; *co-heir* to Barony of Botetourt 1305; assumed additional surname of Herbert by Royal Licence, 2002; *m* 1975, Jane, *d* of Dr Ian Francis Bishop; one *s* one *d*. *Educ:* Harrow. *Heir: s* Dr the Hon. Oliver Richard Seyfried Herbert, MB BS, FRCA [*b* 17 June 1976; *m* 2003, Sarah, (Sally), *d* of Ian Fergusson, FRCS; one *s* two *d*].

HERBERT, Lord; Reginald Michael Henry Herbert; *b* 21 Oct. 2012; *s* and *heir* of Earl of Pembroke and Montgomery, *qv*.

HERBERT, Dr Andrew James, OBE 2010; FBCS; FREng; Distinguished Engineer, 2005–11, and Chairman, 2010–11, Microsoft Research, Cambridge; Fellow, Wolfson College, Cambridge, 2001–11, now Emeritus Fellow; Project Manager (part-time), EDSAC Replica Project, National Museum of Computing, Bletchley Park, since 2012; *b* 30 March 1954; *s* of Edward James Herbert and Catherine Beatrice Herbert (*née* Blaxley); *m* 1976, Jane Elizabeth Cherry; two *s* one *d*. *Educ:* Gillingham Grammar Sch.; Univ. of Leeds (BSc Hons 1st cl. (Computational Sci.) 1975); St John's Coll., Cambridge (PhD (Computer Sci.) 1978). Asst Lectr, 1978–83, Lectr 1983–85, Computer Lab., Cambridge Univ.; Technical Dir, APM Ltd, Cambridge, 1985–98; Chief Architect, ANSA Project, 1985–98; Chief Tech. Officer, Digitivity Inc., 1996–98; Dir, Advanced Technol., Citrix Systems Inc., 1998–2000; Asst Dir, 2001–03, Man. Dir, 2003–10, Microsoft Research, Cambridge. Mem., EPSRC, 2006–11. Vis. Prof., UCL. FBCS 2005; FREng 2007. *Publications:* (with R. M. Needham) The Cambridge Distributed Computing System, 1982; (ed with K. Spärk Jones) Computer Systems: theory, technology and applications, 2004. *Recreations:* restoring and flying vintage aircraft (private pilot's licence and IMC rating), computer and software conservation. *Address:* 17 Latham Road, Cambridge CB2 7EG.

HERBERT, Brian Douglas; Director of Performance Review, East Anglian Regional Health Authority, 1989–91; *b* 29 May 1930; *s* of Stanley and Kathleen Herbert; *m* 1st, 1952, Linda (marr. diss.); two *s* one *d*; 2nd, 1973, Lila; one *d*. *Educ:* Ipswich School. IPFA. Local Govt Finance, 1946–63; Health Service: Asst Treasurer, NW Metropolitan RHB, 1963; Group Treasurer, SW Middlesex HMC, 1967; Area Treasurer, Ealing, Hammersmith and Hounslow AHA(T), 1973; Regional Treasurer, 1981, Dir of Finance and Administration, 1985, E Anglian RHA. *Address:* 3 Dane Drive, Cambridge CB3 9LP. *T:* (01223) 574305.

HERBERT, Rt Rev. Christopher William; Bishop of St Albans, 1995–2009; an Honorary Assistant Bishop: Diocese of Guildford, since 2009; Diocese of Winchester, since 2010; Diocese of Chichester, 2010–14; Diocese of Salisbury, and Archbishop's Delegate, 2011; *b* 7 Jan. 1944; *s* of Walter Meredith Herbert (who *m* 1950, Dorothy Margaret Curnock) and late Hilda Lucy (*née* Dibbin); *m* 1968, Janet Elizabeth Turner; two *s*. *Educ:* Monmouth School; St David's Coll., Lampeter (BA); Univ. of Bristol (PGCE); Wells Theol Coll.; Univ. of Leicester (MPhil 2002; PhD 2008). Asst Curate, Tupsley, Hereford, 1967–71; Asst Master, Bishop's Sch., Hereford, 1967–71; Adv. in Religious Educn, 1971–76, Dir of Educn, 1976–81, Dio. of Hereford; Vicar, St Thomas on the Bourne, Farnham, Surrey, 1981–90; Archdeacon of Dorking, 1990–95. Dir, Post-ordination Training, Dio. of Guildford, 1984–90; Hon. Canon of Guildford, 1984–95. Lectr, NADFAS, 2009–. Dir and Trustee, Abbeyfield Soc., 2009–. Hon. DLitt Hertfordshire, 2003; Hon. DArts, Bedfordshire, 2008. Hon. Citizen, Fano, Italy, 2008. *Publications:* The New Creation, 1971; A Place to Dream, 1976; St Paul's: A Place to Dream, 1981; The Edge of Wonder, 1981; Listening to Children, 1983; On the Road, 1984; Be Thou My Vision, 1985; This Most Amazing Day, 1986; The Question of Jesus, 1987; Alive to God, 1987; Ways into Prayer, 1987; Help in your Bereavement, 1988; Prayers for Children, 1993; Pocket Prayers, 1993; The Prayer Garden, 1994; Words of Comfort, 1994; Pocket Prayers for Children, 1999; Pocket Words of Comfort, 2004; Seeing and Believing, 2008; Pocket Prayers for Commuters, 2009; Health, 2012. *Recreations:* walking, cycling, reading, gardening, writing unpublished novels. *Address:* 1 Beacon Close, Boundstone, Farnham, Surrey GU10 4PA. *T:* (01252) 795600. *W:* www.threeabbeys.me.uk.

HERBERT, David Richard; QC 2013; a Recorder, since 2009; *b* Leicester, 1 March 1968; *s* of Richard and Dorothy Herbert; *m* 1997, Rebecca; one *s* one *d*. *Educ:* Rugby Sch.; Southampton Univ. (BA Hons Hist. 1990); City Univ. (CPE 1991). Called to the Bar, Gray's Inn, 1992. *Recreations:* ski-ing, Rugby, cycling, medieval and ancient history, eating chocolate, family. *Address:* 36 Bedford Row, WC1R 4JH. *T:* (020) 7421 8000. *E:* dherbert@36bedfordrow.co.uk.

HERBERT, (Elizabeth) Jane; Director: Live Well at Home; Kylemore; *d* of Reginald John Herbert and Elsa Herbert (*née* Drake). *Educ:* Durham Univ. (BSc 1977); Bath Univ. (MBA 1991). Factory Manager, Clarks Shoes, 1986–91; Unit Gen. Manager, Greater Glasgow Health Bd, 1991–92; Chief Executive: W Glasgow Hosps Univ. NHS Trust, 1993–98; S Manchester Univ. Hosps NHS Trust, 1998–2002; Beds and Herts HA, 2002–03; Dir, Frontline Consultants, 2004–09; on secondment as Interim Chief Executive: Queen Elizabeth Hosp., King's Lynn, 2005; Hinchingbrooke Healthcare NHS Trust, 2007; Princess Alexandra Hosp., 2010–11; Dir of Strategy, Hertfordshire PCTs, 2009–10; Dir, ejhuk ltd, 2010–13. Non-exec. Dir, Guinness Care and Support, 2012–. *Recreations:* sailing, ornithology, music.

HERBERT, Jeffrey William, FREng, FIMechE; EurIng; engineer and industrialist; *b* 21 July 1942; *s* of Alexander William John Herbert and Amy (*née* Whitwell); *m* 1965, Sheila Heane; one *s* two *d*. *Educ:* Loughborough Univ. (DLC, BEng Mech. and Prodn Engrg). MIET (MIEE 1968); FIMechE 1992; CEng, FREng (FEng 1993). Managing Director: Rover-Triumph Cars Ltd, 1976–81; GEC Diesels Ltd, 1981–85; Exec. Dir, Industry, Charter Consolidated PLC, 1985–89; Chief Exec., 1990–96, Chm., 1996–2001, Charter plc. Chairman: Cape plc, 1985–96; Anderson Gp plc, 1987–95; Esab AB, 1994–2001; British South Africa Co., 1996–2001; Howden Gp plc, 1997–2001; Howden Africa Hldgs Ltd, 1997–2001; Claverham Ltd, 1998–2000; Concentric Gp, 1999–2004; Deputy Chairman: Vickers plc, 1997–2000 (non-exec. Dir, 1991–2000); House of Fraser plc, 2001–06; non-executive Director: M & G Investment Trust, 1992–2002; F. T. Everard & Sons, 2002–07; Veolia Water East Ltd (formerly Tendring Hundred Water Services Ltd), 2003– (Chm., 2005–); Affinity Water Ltd, 2012–. Mem. Council, 1995–2003, Hon. Treas., 1997–2003, Royal Acad. of Engrg. Trustee, Thrombosis Res. Inst., 2004–. CCMI; FRSA 1993. Freeman, City of London, 1993; Liveryman, Wheelwrights' Co., 1993. Hon. DTech Loughborough, 1999; Hon. BSc Loughborough, 2011. *Recreations:* shooting, walking, wine, veteran and classic cars, living in Portugal. *Address:* Baytrees, Long Road West, Dedham, Colchester, Essex CO7 6EL.

HERBERT, Mark Jeremy; QC 1995; Commissioner, Royal Court of Jersey, since 2013; *b* 12 Nov. 1948; *yr s* of late Kenneth Falkner Herbert and Kathleen Ellis Herbert; *m* 1977, Shiranikha Pullenayegum. *Educ:* Lancing Coll.; King's Coll., London (BA). Called to the Bar, Lincoln's Inn, 1974, Bencher, 2004; in practice at Chancery Bar, 1975–; a Dep. High Ct Judge, 2004–15. *Publications:* (contrib.) Whiteman on Capital Gains Tax, 4th edn 1988; Drafting and Variation of Wills, 1989. *Recreations:* bell-ringing, theatre, travel, Italy. *Address:* 5 Stone Buildings, Lincoln's Inn, WC2A 3XT. *T:* (020) 7242 6201.

HERBERT, Nicholas; *see* Hemingford, 3rd Baron.

HERBERT, Rt Hon. Nicholas Le Quesne, (Rt Hon. Nick); PC 2010; MP (C) Arundel and South Downs, since 2005; *b* 7 April 1963; civil partnership 2008, Jason Eades. *Educ:* Haileybury; Magdalene Coll., Cambridge (BA Hons 1985). British Field Sports Soc., 1990–96, latterly Dir of Political Affairs; Chief Exec., Business for Sterling, 1998–2000; Dir, Reform, 2002–05. Contested (C) Berwick-upon-Tweed, 1997. Shadow Sec. of State for Justice, 2007–09, for Envmt, Food and Rural Affairs, 2009–10; Minister of State, MoJ and Home Office, 2010–12. *Address:* House of Commons, SW1A 0AA.

HERBERT, Adm. Sir Peter (Geoffrey Marshall), KCB 1983; OBE 1969; *b* 28 Feb. 1929; *s* of A. G. S. Herbert and P. K. M. Herbert; *m* 1953, Ann Maureen (*née* McKeown) (*d* 2012); one *s* one *d*. *Educ:* Dunchurch Hall; RN Coll., Dartmouth. Specialised in submarines, 1949; served in submarines, 1950–68: Comd HM Submarines Scythian, Porpoise and Excalibur, 1956–60; Submarine Staff, 1960–62; Comd nuclear submarine, HMS Valiant, 1963–68; Comd HMS Venus, 1964; Dep. Dir, Naval Equipment, 1969; Comd 10th (Polaris) Submarine Squadron, 1970–72; COS to Flag Officer Submarines, 1972–74; Comd HMS Blake, 1974–75; Dep. Chief, Polaris Exec., 1976–78; Flag Officer Carriers and Amphibious Ships, 1978–79; Dir Gen., Naval Manpower and Training, 1980–81; Flag Officer Submarines and Comdr Submarines Eastern Atlantic, 1981–83; VCDS (Personnel and Logistics), 1983–85. Non-exec. Dir, Radamec Gp plc, 1985–2004. Chm., SSAFA, 1985–93; President: Glos Br., Seafarers UK (formerly King George's Fund for Sailors), 1990–2011; North Cotswold RNLI, 1990–2004. Governor: Cheam School, 1987–2000 (Chm., 1992–2000); Cheltenham Ladies' Coll., 1993–2001. CCMI; MNucI. *Recreations:* woodwork, gardening. *Club:* Army and Navy.

HERBERT, Prof. Robert Louis, PhD; Alumnae Foundation Professor of Art, 1990–96, Andrew W. Mellon Professor of Humanities, 1996–97, now Emeritus, Mount Holyoke College, Mass; *b* 21 April 1929; *s* of John Newman Herbert and Rosalia Harr Herbert; *m* 1953, Eugenia Randall Warren; one *s* two *d*. *Educ:* Wesleyan Univ., Middletown, Conn (BA 1951); Yale Univ. (MA 1954, PhD 1957). Fulbright Scholar, Paris, 1951–52; Faculty, Yale Univ., 1956–90: Associate Prof., 1963; Prof., 1966; Departmental Chm., 1965–68; Robert Lehman Prof. of Hist. of Art, 1974–90. Guggenheim Fellow, 1971–72; Slade Prof. of Fine Art, Oxford, 1978. Organizer of exhibitions: Barbizon Revisited, Boston Museum of Fine Arts and others, 1962–63; Neo-Impressionism, Solomon R. Guggenheim Mus., 1968; J. F. Millet, Musées Nationaux, Paris, and Arts Council, London, 1975–76; Léger's Le Grand Déjeuner, Minneapolis Inst. of Arts and Detroit Inst. of Arts, 1980; Seurat, Musées Nationaux, Paris and Metropolitan Mus., NY, 1991; Peasants and 'Primitivism': French prints from Millet to Gauguin, Mount Holyoke Coll., RI Sch. of Design, and Univ. of Chicago, 1995–96; Seurat and the Making of La Grande Jatte, Art Inst. of Chicago, 2004. Fellow, Amer. Acad. of Arts and Sciences, 1978; Mem., Amer. Philosophical Soc., 1993. Chevalier, 1976, Officier, 1990, Ordre des Arts et des Lettres. *Publications:* Barbizon Revisited, 1962–63; Seurat's Drawings, 1963; The Art Criticism of John Ruskin, 1964; Modern Artists on Art, 1964, rev. edn 2000; Neo-Impressionism, 1968; David, Voltaire, 'Brutus' and the French Revolution, 1972; J. F. Millet, 1975; (ed jtly) Société Anonyme and Dreier Bequest at Yale University: a catalogue raisonné, 1984; Impressionism: art, leisure and Parisian society, 1988; Monet on the Normandy Coast, 1994; Nature's Workshop: Renoir's writings on the decorative arts, 2000; Seurat: Drawings and Paintings, 2001; From Millet to Léger, 2002; Seurat and the Making of "La Grande Jatte", 2004; A Woman of Amherst, 2008; articles in learned jls.

HERBERT, Robin Arthur Elidyr, CBE 1994; DL; JP; President Emeritus, Royal Horticultural Society, since 1994; Chairman, Leopold Joseph Holdings PLC, 1978–2004; *b* 5 March 1934; *s* of late Sir John Arthur Herbert, GCIE and Lady Mary Herbert; *m* 1st, 1960, Margaret Griswold Lewis (marr. diss. 1988); two *s* two *d*; 2nd, 1988, Philippa Harriet King. *Educ:* Eton; Christ Church, Oxford (MA); Harvard Business School (MBA). MRICS. 2nd Lieut Royal Horse Guards, 1953–54; Captain Royal Monmouthshire RE, 1962–68. Chairman: Union Discount Co. of London, later Union PLC, 1990–96 (Director, 1989–96); Lands Improvement Holdings PLC; Foreign & Colonial Income Growth Investment Trust, 1994–2004; Director: Nat. Westminster Bank, 1972–92; Agricl Mortgage Corp., 1985–93;

Marks & Spencer, 1986–91; Consolidated Gold Fields, 1986–89 (Dep. Chm., 1988–89); F&C Smaller Companies Investment Trust, 1985–2001; Federated Aggregates, 1991–95; SWOAC Holdings, 1990–98. Financial Advisor: Water Superannuation Fund, 1986–89; Nat. Rivers Authy, 1989–96. Mem. Council, BBA, 1992–98. Dep. Chm., Countryside Commn, 1971–80; Member: Council, National Trust, 1969–87 (Mem., Exec. Cttee, 1969–84; Chm. Cttee for Wales, 1969–84); Nat. Water Council, 1980–83; Welsh Develt Agency, 1980–86; Darwin Initiative Adv. Cttee, 1993–99; Royal Parks Agency Adv. Gp, 1993–2000. Chm., Global Heritage Fund UK, 2011–. Royal Horticultural Society: Mem. Council, 1971–74 and 1979–94; Pres. and Chm. Council, 1984–94. Pres., Welsh Historic Gardens Trust, 2011–13; Trustee: Royal Botanic Gardens, Kew, 1987–97 (Chm., 1991–97); Nat. Botanic Gdn of Wales, 1994–2007; Botanic Gdns Conservation Internat., 1991–2012. Chm., Flowers & Plants Assoc., 1998–2006. DL 1968, JP 1964, High Sheriff 1972, Monmouthshire. *Recreations:* dendrology, walking. *Address:* Neuadd, Llanbedr, Crickhowell, Powys NP8 1SP. *T:* (01873) 812164. *Clubs:* Brooks's, Pratt's, Beefsteak.

HERBERT, William Penry Millwarden; Member, Cardiff City Council, 1970–96; Lord Mayor of Cardiff, 1988–89; *b* 31 March 1921; *s* of William John Herbert and Esabella Marinda Francis; *m* 1945, Ellen Vera McCarthy (*d* 2004); two *d* (one *s* decd). *Educ:* Argoed Elementary Sch., Blackwood, Monmouthshire. Cert. of Professional Competence, Transport, 1977. Miner, 1934–37; Railwayman, 1937–45. Served RE, 1945–47. 1947–78: Guest Keen Iron and Steel Works; Guest Keen and Baldwins British Steel Corp.; Plant Supervisor, Traffic Foreman, Transport Manager. *Recreations:* dancing, gardening, reading, travel. *Address:* 27 Wellwood Avenue, Llanedeyrn, Cardiff, South Glamorgan CF23 9JP. *Club:* City Social (Cathays, Cardiff).

HERBISON, Nancy Maureen; *see* Argenta, N. M.

HERDAN, Bernard Laurence, CB 2007; *b* 23 Nov. 1947; *s* of Dr Gustav Herdan and late Estelle Muriel Innes Herdan (*née* Jackson); *m* 1971, Janet Elizabeth Hughes; one *d* (and one *d* decd). *Educ:* Bristol Grammar Sch.; Churchill Coll., Cambridge (BA Hons 1969, MA); Bath Univ. (DMS 1972). Systems Designer, BAe, 1969–73; Prog. Manager, ESA, 1973–84; Managing Consultant, BIS Mackintosh, 1984–85; Man. Dir, Defence Technology Enterprises, 1985–89; Commercial Dir, Meteorological Office, 1990–95; Chief Executive: Driving Standards Agency, 1995–99; UK Passport Agency and Criminal Records Bureau, subseq. Passport and Records Agency, then UK Passport Service, 1999–2006; Exec. Dir for Service Planning and Delivery, Identity and Passport Service, 2006–08; interim Chief Exec., SIA, 2008–09; Chief Exec., Nat. Fraud Authy, 2009–11. Advr to Comr, City of London Police, 2011–. Non-exec. Dir, MoD, 2012–13; Non-exec. Bd Mem., Disclosure and Barring Service, 2012–. Chair, Fitness to Practise Panels, GMC, 2014– (Mem., 2012–13); Mem., Barristers Disciplinary Tribunal Panels, Bar Standards Bd, 2013–. Associate, Univ. of Birmingham Business Sch., 2009. Dep. Chm., Bedford Hosp. NHS Trust, 2004–09. Trustee: Victim Support, 2010–; Bedford CAB, 2010–12; Corporate Alliance Against Domestic Violence, 2011–14; Fostering Network, 2012–14; Alzheimer's Soc., 2013–. MInstD 1986. Hon. DBA Bedfordshire, 2008. Editor-in-Chief, Space Communication and Broadcasting, 1982–86. *Publications:* papers in professional jls. *Recreations:* horse riding, foreign travel, theatre, the arts. *Address:* The Old Rectory, Swineshead, Beds MK44 2AA. *T:* 07881 500877.

HERDON, Christopher de Lancy, OBE 1971; HM Diplomatic Service, retired; freelance journalist, since 1983; news editor, The Tablet, 1986–2004; *b* 24 May 1928; *s* of late Wilfrid Herdon and Clotilde (*née* Parsons); *m* 1953, Virginia Grace; two *s* two *d* (and one *s* decd). *Educ:* Ampleforth; Magdalen Coll., Oxford. Foreign Office, 1951; Vienna, 1953; 2nd Sec., Baghdad, 1957; Beirut, 1961; 1st Sec., Amman, 1962; FO, 1965; Aden, 1967; FCO, 1970; Counsellor: Rome, 1973; FCO, 1977; retired 1983. RC Observer, BCC, 1984–90; Mem., Assembly of Council of Churches for Britain and Ireland, 1990–94. *Recreations:* painting, music, sailing, long-distance walking. *Address:* Broomhill Cottage, Lodsworth, W Sussex GU28 9DG. *T:* (01798) 861701. *Club:* Reform.

HEREFORD, 19th Viscount *cr* 1550; **Charles Robin de Bohun Devereux;** Bt 1611; Premier Viscount of England; *b* 11 Aug. 1975; *s* of 18th Viscount Hereford and Susan Mary, *oc* of Major Maurice Godley; *m* 2010, Louisa Jane, *y d* of William Knight, Holland Park; one *s* one *d*. *Educ:* Stowe; UEA (BA Hons Hist. of Art and Architecture). Valuer, 1998–, Departmental Dir, 2007–, UK Dir, 2010–, Bonhams Auctioneers. *Heir: s* Hon. Henry Walter de Bohun Devereux, *b* 11 Feb. 2015. *Address:* 98 Elms Crescent, SW4 8QT. *Club:* White's.

HEREFORD, Bishop of, since 2014; **Rt Rev. Richard Michael Cokayne Frith;** *b* 8 April 1949; *s* of Roger Cokayne Frith and Joan Agnes Frith; *m* 1st, 1975, Jill Richardson (marr. diss. 2000); two *s* two *d*; 2nd, 2006, Kay Gledhill. *Educ:* Marlborough Coll., Wiltshire; Fitzwilliam Coll., Cambridge (BA 1972; MA 1976); St John's Coll., Nottingham. Ordained deacon, 1974, priest 1975; Asst Curate, Mortlake with East Sheen, Southwark, 1974–78; Team Vicar, Thamesmead, Southwark, 1978–83; Team Rector, Keynsham, Bath and Wells, 1983–92; Archdeacon of Taunton, 1992–98; Bishop Suffragan of Hull, 1998–2014. *Recreations:* cricket, squash, theatre. *Address:* The Bishop's House, The Palace, Hereford HR4 9BN. *T:* (01432) 271355. *E:* bishop.richard@hereford.anglican.org. *Club:* MCC.

HEREFORD, Dean of; *see* Tavinor, Very Rev. M. E.

HEREFORD, Archdeacon of; *see* Benson, Ven. G. P.

HERFT, Most Rev. Roger Adrian; *see* Perth (Australia), Archbishop of.

HERMAN, David Joseph; Consultant on Eastern Europe, General Motors Corporation, 2002; Vice President, Russia and the Commonwealth of Independent States, General Motors, 1998–2002; Chairman, Sollers OJSC, since 2007; *b* 14 Jan. 1946; *m* Isabel Roehrenbach; two *d*. *Educ:* New York Univ. (BA Govt Affairs 1967); LSE; Harvard Univ. Grad. Sch. (JD 1971). Attorney, Legal Staff, General Motors, NY, 1973; Manager, Sales Develt (USSR), GM Internat. Ops, 1976; Special Asst to Man. Dir, GM España, 1979–82; Managing Director: GM Chile, Santiago, 1982; GM Colombia, 1984–86; GM Continental, Antwerp, 1986–88; Exec. Dir, Eur. Parts & Accessories, GM Europe, 1988–89; Pres. and Chief Exec. Officer, SAAB Automobile, 1989–92; Chm. and Man. Dir, Adam Opel AG, 1992–98. Vice Pres., Gen. Motors Corp., 1992–2002. Dir, Golden Telecom, 2002–. *Recreations:* golf, opera, bridge.

HERMANN, Alexander Henry Baxter; HM Diplomatic Service, retired; *b* 28 Dec. 1917; *m* Rita Rosalind Fernandes. Joined Foreign Service, 1939; served 1942–55; Peking, Ahwaz, Chengtu, Chungking, Shanghai, Quito, Panama, Tamsui; Foreign Office, 1956; Commercial Counsellor and Consul-General, Rangoon, 1957–61; HM Consul-General at Marseilles, also to Monaco, 1961–65; Diplomatic Service Inspector, 1965–66; Counsellor, Hong Kong Affairs, Washington, 1967–70, 1974–77; Consul-General, Osaka, 1971–73. *Address:* 32 Old Place, Aldwick, Sussex PO21 3AX.

HERMER, Richard Simon; QC 2009; *b* Cardiff, 1968; *m*; two *d*. *Educ:* Cardiff High Sch.; Manchester Univ. (BA Hons). Called to the Bar, Middle Temple, 1993. *Address:* Matrix Chambers, Griffin Building, Gray's Inn, WC1R 5LN. *E:* richardhermer@matrixlaw.co.uk.

HERMITAGE, Peter Andrew, QPM 1996; management consultant on security, government and police matters, since 2000; *b* 26 Sept. 1948; *s* of late Thomas Henry Hermitage and Freda Helen Hermitage; *m* 1971, Brenda Howard; one *s* one *d*. *Educ:* Chatham House GS, Ramsgate. Joined Kent Constabulary, 1968: numerous operational, investigative and organisational roles, incl. Dir, Jun. Comd Course, Police Staff Coll., Bramshill, 1986–87; Asst Chief Constable, Kent, 1990–94; Asst Inspector of Constabulary, Home Office, 1994–96; Dir, Nat. Police Training (with rank of Chief Constable), 1996–99. Mem. Bd, Security Industry Authy, 2003–06 (Acting Chm., 2003–04; Chm., 2004–06). Dir, Office of Ind. Adjudicator, 2010–. Non-exec. Dir, Perpetuity Res. and Consultancy Internat., 2006–10. Chm., E Kent Hosps NHS Trust, 2000–03. Ed., Police Jl, 1997–99. Vice-Pres., Police Mutual Assce Soc., 1997–99. Gov., Canterbury Christ Church Univ. (formerly UC), 1999– (Vice Chm., 2003–; Dep. Pro-Chancellor, 2005–09; Pro-Chancellor, 2009–13; Hon. Fellow, 2014). MRSPH (MRSH 1992); FCIPD (FIPD 1997); MInstD 1999. FRSA 2010. *Recreations:* Rugby, fly fishing, painting water colours, family. *Address:* 4 Ealham Close, Canterbury, Kent CT4 7BW.

HERMON, Peter Michael Robert; Head of Information Systems, CL-Alexanders Laing and Cruickshank Holdings Ltd, 1989–90; *b* 13 Nov. 1928; British; *m* 1954, Norma Stuart Brealey; two *s* two *d*. *Educ:* Nottingham High Sch.; St John's Coll., Oxford (1st cl. hons Maths; Univ. Maths Prize, 1953); Merton Coll., Oxford. Leo Computers Ltd, 1955–59; Manager, Management and Computer Divs, Dunlop Co., 1959–65; Information Handling Dir, BOAC, 1965–68; Management Services Dir, BOAC, and Mem. Bd of Management, 1968–72; Mem. of Board, BOAC, 1972; British Airways: Gp Management Services Dir, 1972–78; Board Mem., 1978–83; Management Services Dir, 1978–82; Man. Dir, European Services Div., 1982–83. Man. Dir, Tandem Computers Ltd, 1983–84; Dir, Tandem UK, 1983–85; Head of Systems and Communications, Lloyd's of London, 1984–86; Information Systems Dir, Harris Queensway, 1986–88. Mem. Bd of Dirs, Internat. Aeradio Ltd, 1966–83, Chm., 1982–83; Chm., Internat. Aeradio (Caribbean) Ltd, 1967–83; Mem. Bd, SITA, 1972–83, Chm., 1981–83. *Publications:* Hill Walking in Wales, 1991; (jtly) User-Driven Innovation: the world's first business computer, 1996; Lifting the Veil: a plain language guide to the Bible, 2006. *Recreations:* hill walking, music, cats. *Address:* White Flints, Quentin Way, Wentworth, Virginia Water, Surrey GU25 4PS.

HERMON, Sylvia, (Lady Hermon); MP North Down, since 2001 (UU, 2001–10; Ind, since 2010); *b* 11 Aug. 1955; *d* of Robert and Mary Paisley; *m* 1988, Sir John (Charles) Hermon, OBE, QPM (*d* 2008); two *s*. *Educ:* UCW, Aberystwyth (LLB 1st Cl. Hons); Coll. of Law, Chester. Lectr in Law, QUB, 1978–88; PR Consultant, 1993–96. *Publications:* A Guide to EEC Law in Northern Ireland, 1986. *Recreations:* swimming, ornithology. *Address:* House of Commons, SW1A 0AA.

HERMON-TAYLOR, Prof. John, FRCS; Professor of Surgery, St George's Hospital Medical School, 1976–2002, now Professor Emeritus; Visiting Professor, Division of Diabetes and Nutritional Sciences, School of Medicine, King's College London, since 2008; *b* 16 Oct. 1936; *s* of late Hermon Taylor, FRCS; *m* 1971, Eleanor Ann Pheteplace, of Davenport, Iowa; one *s* one *d*. *Educ:* Harrow Sch. (Shepherd-Churchill Open Major Entrance Schol.); St John's Coll., Cambridge (travelling schol., 1955; BA 1957, MB BChir 1960, MChir 1968); London Hosp. Med. Coll. (Open Entrance Schol., 1957, prizes in Med., Path., and Obst.). FRCS 1963 (Hallett Prize, 1962). Training in surgery, 1962–68; MRC Travelling Fellow to Mayo Clinic, USA, 1968–69 (Vis. Prof., 1980, 1985); Senior Lectr, 1970, Reader in Surgery, 1971–76, London Hosp. Med. Coll. Pearce-Gould Vis. Prof., Middlesex Hosp., 1982; Vis. Prof., Pakistan Inst. of Med. Scis, Islamabad, 1989. Hon. Consultant in Gen. Surgery to RN, 1989–2002. Mem. Council, Assoc. of Surgeons of GB and Ireland, 1981–84; Dir, James IV Assoc. of Surgeons, 1983–86. Member: Council, Action Research, 1988–97; Scientific Cttee, British Digestive Foundn, 1991–95; Medical Adv. Cttee, British Liver Trust, 1995–96; Health Services Res. and Clin. Epidemiol. Adv. Cttee, Wellcome Trust, 1996–2001 (Mem., Clinical Panel, 1985–88); wkg gp on Crohn's disease and paratuberculosis, Scientific Cttee on Animal Health and Animal Welfare, EC, 1998–2000. Director: BioScience Internat. Inc., 1987–2013; HAV Vaccines Ltd, 2009–. Mem., numerous professional bodies, UK and overseas. Innovator of the Year award, Times Newspaper/Barclays Bank, 1988. *Publications:* scientific papers on purification and biochem. of enteropeptidase, diseases of pancreas, peptide chem., enzyme activation in gastric disorders, on causation and specific treatment of Crohn's disease, mycobacterial genetics, epidemiology of breast cancer, biol res. on common solid tumours, a novel virally vectored T-cell vaccine to treat Mycobacterium avium subspecies paratuberculosis infection in Crohn's disease. *Recreations:* fishing, sailing, shooting, growing soft fruit and vegetables. *Address:* Division of Diabetes and Nutritional Sciences, School of Medicine, Franklin-Wilkins Building, King's College London, Stamford Street, SE1 9NH. *T:* (020) 7848 3919. *E:* j.hermon@kcl.ac.uk.

HERN, Jane Carolyn; Registrar, Royal College of Veterinary Surgeons, 1997–2011; *b* 22 Sept. 1954; *d* of George Kenneth Hern and Elizabeth Ellen Hern (*née* Byford). *Educ:* Girton Coll., Cambridge (BA Hons Law 1976; MA). Articles with Lovell, White & King, 1977–79; admitted as solicitor, 1979; LCD, 1979–87, Law Commn, 1981–86; Law Soc., 1987–96: Asst Sec.-Gen., 1992–95; Dir, Management and Planning Directorate, 1995–96; Actg Sec.-Gen., 1996. Chairman: UK Inter-Professional Gp, 2005–15; Skills for Justice Appeals Cttee, 2005–; Audit Cttee, Gen. Osteopathic Council, 2010–15. Mem. Bd, QAA, 2010–. *Recreations:* eating, drinking, reading crime thrillers, visiting places of historic interest.

HERNANDEZ, David Anthony; His Honour Judge Hernandez; a Circuit Judge, since 2004; *b* 15 Sept. 1953; *s* of Andrew and Daphne Hernandez; *m* 1987, Lesley Newton, *qv*; one *s* one *d*. *Educ:* Bury Grammar Sch.; St Catherine's Coll., Oxford (MA Jurisprudence). Called to the Bar: Lincoln's Inn, 1976; Trinidad and Tobago, 1981; barrister, practising family law, 1976–2004; Jt Head, Young Street Chambers, Manchester, 2001–04. Asst Recorder, 1996–2000, Recorder, 2000–04. Chm., Rent Assessment Cttee (Northern Panel), 1984–2004. *Recreations:* Tai Chi, listening to jazz, travel. *Address:* Manchester Crown Court, Courts of Justice, Crown Square, Manchester M3 3FL. *T:* (0161) 954 1800.

HERON, Sir Conrad (Frederick), KCB 1974 (CB 1969); OBE 1953; Permanent Secretary, Department of Employment, 1973–76; *b* 21 Feb. 1916; *s* of Richard Foster Heron and Ida Fredrika Heron; *m* 1948, Envye Linnéa Gustafsson (*d* 2014); two *d*. *Educ:* South Shields High Sch.; Trinity Hall, Cambridge. Entered Ministry of Labour, 1938; Principal Private Secretary to Minister of Labour, 1953–56; Under-Secretary, Industrial Relations Dept, 1963–64 and 1965–68, Overseas Dept, 1964–65; Dep. Under-Sec. of State, Dept of Employment, 1968–71; Dep. Chm., Commn on Industrial Relations, 1971–72; Second Permanent Sec., Dept of Employment, 1973. *Address:* Old Orchards, West Lydford, Somerton, Somerset TA11 7DG. *T:* (01963) 240387.

HERON, Mark Nicholas B.; *see* Bryant-Heron.

HERON, Raymond, CBE 1984; retired; Deputy Director, Propellants, Explosives and Rocket Motor Establishment, Ministry of Defence (Procurement Executive), 1977–84; *b* 10 April 1924; *s* of Lewis and Doris Heron; *m* 1948, Elizabeth MacGathan (*d* 2006); one *s* one *d*. *Educ:* Heath Grammar Sch., Halifax; Queen's Coll., Oxford (BA Physics). Shell Refining and Marketing Co., 1944–47; RN, Instructor Branch, 1947–52; Rocket Propulsion Estabt, Min. of Supply (later Min. of Technology), 1952–67; Cabinet Office, 1967; Asst Dir, Min. of Technology, 1967–73; Dep. Dir, Explosives Research and Development Estabt, MoD, 1973; Special Asst to Sec. (Procurement Exec.), MoD, 1973–74; Head of Rocket Motor Exec. and Dep. Dir/2, Rocket Propulsion Estabt, MoD (PE), 1974–76. *Publications:* articles in scientific and technical jls. *Recreations:* music, hill walking, golf. *Address:* 9 Grange Gardens, Wendover, Aylesbury, Bucks HP22 6HB. *T:* (01296) 622921. *Club:* Ashridge Golf.

HERON-MAXWELL, Sir Nigel (Mellor), 10th Bt *cr* 1683; *b* 30 Jan. 1944; *s* of Sir Patrick Ivor Heron-Maxwell, 9th Bt and D. Geraldine E., *yr d* of late Claud Paget Mellor; *S* father, 1982; *m* 1972, Mary Elizabeth Angela (*d* 2010), *o d* of late W. Ewing, Co. Donegal; one *s* one *d. Educ:* Milton Abbey. Volunteer Watchkeeper, Charlestown Lookout, Nat. Coastwatch Instn, 2012–. *Heir: s* David Mellor Heron-Maxwell [*b* 22 May 1975; *m* 2012, Emma Louise Ranger; one *d*].

HERRIDGE, Michael Eric James; HM Diplomatic Service, retired; Deputy High Commissioner to South India, 1999–2003; *b* 23 Sept. 1946; *s* of late Robert James Herridge and Mary Herridge (*née* Beckitt); *m* 1968, Margaret Elizabeth Bramble; one *d*. *Educ:* Ashley Sch., Hampshire; Bournemouth Coll. Joined HM Diplomatic Service, 1966; Prague, 1969–72; Nairobi, 1972–75; FCO, 1975–79; Second Sec., Lagos, 1979–82; Second, then First, Sec., UKMIS NY, 1982–86; FCO, 1986–90; First Sec., Madrid, 1990–95; FCO, 1995–99. *Recreations:* genealogy, gardening, country pursuits. *Address:* Cheddar, Somerset.

HERRIES OF TERREGLES, Lady, (15th in line, of the Lordship *cr* 1490); **Mary Katharine Mumford,** DCVO 1995 (CVO 1982); Lady-in-Waiting to HRH Princess Alexandra, since 1964; *b* 14 Aug. 1940; 2nd *d* of 16th Duke of Norfolk, KG, GCVO, GBE, TD, PC and Lavinia, Duchess of Norfolk, LG, CBE; *S* sister, 2014; *m* 1986, Gp Captain Anthony Mumford, CVO, OBE (*d* 2006). *Heir: sister* Lady (Theresa) Jane Kerr, Marchioness of Lothian [*b* 24 Jan. 1945; *m* 1975, Earl of Ancram (*see* Marquess of Lothian); two *d*]. *Address:* North Stoke Cottage, North Stoke, Arundel, West Sussex BN18 9LS. *T:* (01798) 831203; Lantonside, Glencaple, Dumfries DG1 4RQ. *T:* (01387) 770260. *E:* marymumford2014@gmail.com.

HERRINGTON, Air Vice-Marshal Walter John, CB 1982; Royal Air Force, retired; *b* 18 May 1928; *s* of Major H. Herrington, MBE, MM and Daisy Restal Gardiner; *m* 1958, Joyce Maureen Cherryman; two *s*. *Educ:* Woking Grammar Sch.; RAF Coll., Cranwell. Commnd RAF, 1949, Pilot; 1950–69: Long Range Transp. Sqdns 24, 53, 99; ADC to C-in-C Bomber Comd; Reconnaissance Sqdns; RAF Staff Coll.; Exchange Officer, USAF Acad., Colo; Comd 100 Sqdn; Jt Services Staff Coll.; Air Sec.'s Dept; Stn Comdr RAF Honnington, 1969–71; Ops Dept, MoD, 1971–73; RCDS (student) 1974; Defence Attaché, Paris, 1975–77. Hon. ADC to the Queen, 1971–74; Senior RAF Mem., Directing Staff, RCDS, 1978–80; Dir of Service Intelligence, 1980–82. Aviation Advr, Internat. Mil. Services, 1982–89; aviation and security consultant, 1989–95. Member: European Security Study Gp, 1982–83; Central Council, TA&VRA, 1984–90; Council, Officers Pensions Soc., 1983–89. *Publications:* The Future for the Defence Industry, 1991; text books for courses on air power for USAF Academy. *Recreations:* reading, international affairs, sport. *Club:* Royal Air Force.

HERRMANN, Georgina, OBE 2001; DPhil; FBA 1999; Reader in the Archaeology of Western Asia, University College London, 1994–2002, Visiting Hon. Research Professor, since 2002; *b* 20 Oct. 1937; *d* of John Walker Thompson and Gladys Elaine Thompson; *m* 1965, Prof. Luke John Herrmann; two *s*. *Educ:* Inst. of Archaeology, Univ. of London (post-grad. dip. 1963); St Hugh's Coll., Oxford (DPhil 1966). FSA 1968. Sec., Foreign Office, 1956–61; J. R. MacIver Jun. Res. Fellow, Oxford, 1966–68; Calouste Gulbenkian Fellow, Cambridge, 1974–76; Regents' Prof., Univ. of Calif at Berkeley, 1986; Leverhulme Res. Fellow, 1989–91; part-time Lecturer: Inst. of Archaeology, London Univ., 1985–91; in Mesopotamian Archaeology, UCL, 1991–93. Dir, excavations at Merv, Turkmenistan, 1992–2001. Hon. Foreign Mem., Amer. Inst. of Archaeology, 1997. Editor, Iran (jl of British Inst. of Persian Studies), 1966–81. Laureate, Rolex Award for Enterprise, 1996. *Publications:* Ivories from Nimrud, III (with M. Mallowan), 1974, IV, 1986, V, 1992, VI (with S. Laidlaw), 2009, VII (with S. Laidlaw), 2013; The Iranian Revival, 1977; Iranische Denkmaler (recording Sasanian rock reliefs), 8–11, 1977–83, and 13, 1989; (ed) Furniture of Western Asia, Ancient and Traditional, 1996; Monuments of Merv I, 1999; (ed jtly) After Alexander: Central Asia before Islam, 2007. *Recreations:* planting trees, labradors, walking. *Address:* The Old Vicarage, Penrhos, Raglan, Usk, Mon NP15 2LE. *T:* (01600) 780524. *Club:* Athenæum.

HERROD, His Honour Donald; QC 1972; a Circuit Judge, 1978–95; *b* 7 Aug. 1930; *o s* of Wilfred and Phyllis Herrod, Doncaster; *m* 1959, Kathleen Elaine Merrington, MB, ChB; two *d*. *Educ:* grammar schs, Doncaster and Leeds. Called to the Bar, 1956. A Recorder of the Crown Court, 1972–78. Member: Parole Bd, 1978–81; Judicial Studies Bd, 1982–86. *Recreation:* golf.

HERRON, Michael; Director, Information Management, 2008–10, and Chief Information Officer, 2010, Department for Transport; *b* 7 Jan. 1954; *s* of John Herron and Eileen Herron (*née* Mann); *m* 1989, Tessa Garland; two *s*. *Educ:* North East London Polytech. (BA Hons). Mgt trainee, Aérospatiale, 1978; Sales Manager, MM Electronics, 1979–80; Gen. Manager, York Mill Ltd, 1981–86; DTI, 1986–95; Cabinet Office, 1995–2004; Dir, Business Delivery Services, DfT, 2004–08. *Recreations:* cooking, wine, motor-cycling, rock 'n roll music, skiing. *Address:* 9 Ropemakers Fields, E14 8BX. *Club:* Royal Automobile.

HERSCHBACH, Prof. Dudley Robert; Baird Professor of Science, Harvard University, 1976–2003, now Baird Professor Emeritus; Professor of Physics, Texas A&M University, since 2005; *b* 18 June 1932; *s* of Robert D. Herschbach and Dorothy E. Herschbach; *m* 1964, Georgene L. Botyos; two *d*. *Educ:* Campbell High School; Stanford Univ. (BS Math 1954, MS Chem. 1955); Harvard Univ. (AM Physics 1956, PhD Chem. Phys 1958). Junior Fellow, Soc. of Fellows, Harvard, 1957–59; Asst Prof., 1959–61, Associate Prof., 1961–63, Univ. of California, Berkeley; Prof. of Chemistry, Harvard Univ., 1963–76. Hon. DSc: Univ. of Toronto, 1977; Dartmouth Coll., 1992; Charles Univ., Prague, 1993; Wheaton Coll., 1995; Franklin & Marshall Coll., 1998; Harvard Univ., 2011. (Jtly) Nobel Prize for Chemistry, 1986; US Nat. Medal of Sci., 1991; Heyrovský Medal, Czech Acad. of Scis, 1992; Walker Prize, Boston Mus. of Sci., 1994; Gold Medal, Amer. Inst. of Chemists, 2011. *Publications:* over 400 research papers, chiefly on quantum mechanics, chemical kinetics, reaction dynamics, molecular spectroscopy, collision theory, in Jl of Chemical Physics, Jl of Phys. Chemistry, Molecular Physics, Phys. Review. *Recreations:* tennis, biking, hiking, kayaking, chess, poetry. *Address:* 116 Conant Road, Lincoln, MA 01773, USA. *T:* (617) 6949850, (office) (617) 4953218.

HERSEY, David Kenneth; lighting designer; founder Chairman, DH Design Ltd, since 1972; *b* 30 Nov. 1939; *s* of Ella Morgan Decker and C. Kenneth Hersey; *m* Demetra Maraslis; one *s* two *d*. *Educ:* Oberlin Coll., Ohio. Left NY for London, 1968; lighting designer for theatre, opera and ballet cos, incl. Royal Opera House, ENO, Glyndebourne, Ballet Rambert, London Contemporary Dance, Scottish Ballet; lighting consultant to Nat. Theatre, 1974–84; many productions for RSC. Chm., Assoc. of Lighting Designers, 1984–86. *Designs include:* Evita, 1978 (Tony award, 1980); Nicholas Nickleby, 1980; Cats, 1981 (Tony and Drama Desk awards, 1983); Song and Dance, 1982; Guys and Dolls, 1982; Starlight Express, 1984; Les Misérables, 1985 (Tony award, 1987); Porgy and Bess, 1986; Chess, 1986; Miss Saigon, 1989 (Drama Desk award, 1991); Oliver, 1995; Martin Guerre, Jesus Christ Superstar, 1996; My Fair Lady, 2001; South Pacific, The Coast of Utopia, Anything Goes, 2002; Love's Labours Lost, 2003; The Dark, 2004; Porgy and Bess, 2006; Equus, 2007, Broadway, 2008; Measure for Measure, 2010. Hon. Dr Middx, 2002. Olivier Award for best lighting designer, 1995. *Recreation:* sailing (Millennium Odyssey Round the World Yacht Rally, 1998–2000). *Address:* DH Design Ltd, 64 New Cavendish Street, W1G 8TB.

HERSHAM, Lisa; *see* Cameron, L.

HERSHKO, Avram, PhD, MD; Distinguished Professor, Department of Biochemistry, Technion - Israel Institute of Technology, since 1998 (Associate Professor, 1972–80; Professor, 1980); *b* 31 Dec. 1937; *s* of Moshe Hershko and Shoshana Hershko; *m* 1963, Judith Leibowitz; three *s*. *Educ:* Hebrew Univ., Jerusalem (MD 1965; PhD 1969). Physician, Israel Defence Forces, 1965–67. Post-doctoral Fellow, Univ. of San Francisco, 1969–72. Mem., Israel Acad. of Scis, 2000; Foreign Associate, NAS, 2003. Israel Prize for Biochemistry, 1994; Gairdner Award, Gairdner Foundn, 1999; Lasker Prize for Basic Medical Res., 2000; Wolf Foundn Prize in Medicine, 2001; Louisa Gross Horwitz Award, 2001; (jtly) Nobel Prize in Chemistry, 2004. *Publications:* articles in learned jls. *Address:* Department of Biochemistry, Ruth and Bruce Rappaport Faculty of Medicine, Technion - Israel Institute of Technology, PO Box 9649, Haifa 31096, Israel.

HERSOV, Gregory Adam; Artistic Director, Royal Exchange Theatre, Manchester, 1987–2014; *b* 4 May 1956; *s* of Dr Lionel Hersov and Zoe (*née* Henell). *Educ:* Bryanston; Mansfield Coll., Oxford (MA). Regl dirs trainee, Thames TV, Redgrave Th., Farnham, 1976–78; Royal Exchange Theatre: asst dir, 1980–83; Associate Dir, 1983–85; Associate Artistic Dir, 1985–87; productions include: One Flew Over the Cuckoo's Nest, 1982; Death of a Salesman, 1985; A Doll's House, 1987; The Alchemist, 1987; All My Sons, 1988; The Voysey Inheritance, 1989; The Crucible, 1990; Blues for Mr Charlie, 1992; Romeo and Juliet, 1992; Venice Preserv'd, 1994; Animal Crackers, Royal Exchange Th. Internat. Fest. and Lyric, 1995–99; King Lear, 1999; Uncle Vanya, 2001; The Seagull, 2003; Harvey, 2005; Cyrano de Bergerac, 2006; The Tempest, 2007; Antigone, 2008; Palace of the End, 2009; Pygmalion, 2010; As You Like It, 2011; A Doll's House, 2013; Look Back in Anger, RNT, 1999. *E:* greg.hersov@icloud.com.

HERTFORD, 9th Marquess of, *cr* 1793; **Henry Jocelyn Seymour;** Baron Conway of Ragley 1703; Baron Conway of Killultagh 1712; Earl of Hertford, Viscount Beauchamp 1750; Earl of Yarmouth 1793; DL; *b* 6 July 1958; *s* of 8th Marquess of Hertford and of Comtesse Louise de Caraman Chimay; *S* father, 1997; *m* 1990, Beatriz, *d* of Jorge Karam; two *s* two *d*. DL Warwicks, 2012. *Heir: s* Earl of Yarmouth, *qv*. *Club:* Sloane.

HERTFORD, Bishop Suffragan of, since 2015; **Rt Rev. Noel Michael Roy Beasley;** *b* 1968; *m* Lizzie; one *s* one *d*. *Educ:* Imperial Coll. London (BSc 1991); Oriel Coll., Oxford (DPhil 1995); Cranmer Hall, Durham; St John's Coll., Durham (BA 1998). Ordained deacon, 1999, priest, 2000; Curate, St Nicholas, Newport, with Longford, Chetwynd and Forton, Dio. of Lichfield, 1999–2003; Chaplain, 2003–07, Tutor in Mission and Vice Principal, 2007–10, Westcott House, Cambridge; Dir, Partnership for Child Develt, Dept of Infectious Disease Epidemiology, Imperial Coll. London, 2003–10; Dir of Mission, Dio. of Oxford, 2010–15. Hon. Canon, Christ Church, Oxford, 2014–15. *Address:* Bishopswood, 3 Stobarts Close, Knebworth SG3 6ND.

HERTFORD, Archdeacon of; *see* Jones, Ven. T. P.

HERTRICH, Rainer; Co-Chief Executive Officer, European Aeronautic Defence and Space Company, 2000–05; *b* 6 Dec. 1949. *Educ:* apprenticeship and business training, Siemens AG; Technical Univ. of Berlin; Univ. of Nuremberg (Bachelor of Commerce). Messerschmitt-Bölkow-Blohm GmbH: Information Processing Supervisor, Controlling Dept, Mil. Aircraft Div., 1977; Hd, Controlling Dept, 1978, CFO, 1983, Service Div. (Ottobrunn); Hd, Controlling and Finance Dept, Dynamics Div., 1984; CFO and Mem. Div. Mgt, Marine and Special Products Div., 1987; DaimlerBenz Aerospace, subseq. DaimlerChrysler Aerospace AG: Hd of Divl Controlling, Central Controlling Section, Deutsche Aerospace AG, 1990; Sen. Vice Pres., Corporate Controlling, 1991; Hd, Aeroengines business unit, 1996; Mem., Exec. Cttee, 1996; Pres. and CEO, 2000; President and CEO, Motoren und Turbinen Union München GmbH, 1996.

HERTZ, Prof. Noreena Tamar, PhD; writer, academic, broadcaster, campaigner, corporate and political adviser; Honorary Professor, University College London, since 2014; Fellow, Judge Business School, University of Cambridge, since 2009 (Associate Director, Centre for International Business and Management, 2003–13); Director, Global Reach International, since 2001; *b* London, 24 Sept. 1967; *d* of Jonathan Hertz and Leah Hertz (*née* Treiser); *m* 2012, Daniel Cohen, *qv*. *Educ:* N London Collegiate Sch.; Westminster Sch.; University Coll. London (BA Philos. and Econs 1987; Hon. Fellow, 2010); Wharton Sch., Univ. of Pennsylvania (MBA Finance and Mktg 1991); King's Coll., Cambridge (PhD Mgt and Econs 1996). Hd, Strategy and Res., Centre for ME Competitive Strategy, 1996–97; Lectr in Internat. Business and Sen. Res. Fellow, Econs Strategy Gp, 1997–2001, Sen. Associate, 2001–07, Judge Business Sch., Univ. of Cambridge; Miliband Fellow, Dept of Govt, LSE, 2002–03; Prof. of Global Political Econ., Dept of Econs, Utrecht Univ., 2005–06; Fellow, Centre for Global Governance, LSE, 2007–09; Prof. of Globalisation, Sustainability and Mgt, Duisenberg Sch. of Finance and Erasmus Univ., 2009–13. Vis. Prof., Rotterdam Sch. of Mgt, Erasmus Univ., 2008–09. Consultant: to clients operating in Russia, incl. IFC, Russian Govt, Municipality of Yaroslavl, St Petersburg Stock Exchange, Credit Suisse First Boston, KPMG, Access Industries, 1991–2000; to multinat. corps, 2000–; to Govts, incl. Norwegian, Tanzanian, Dutch, Israeli, Palestinian and Jordanian; to Africa Commn, Dutch Central Bank; to NGOs, incl. Project (RED), Make Poverty History Coalition, Jubilee Debt Campaign. Member: Bd, Global Strategy Gp, Rights and Humanity, 2004–07; Econs and Politics Adv. Bd, Citigroup, 2007–09; Adv. Bd, Edelman, 2009–12; Bd, Warner Music Gp, 2014–. Presenter and creator of television programmes: The End of Politics, 2002; Noreena's Agenda, 2005; The Million Pound Footballers Giveaway, 2007. Trustee, IPPR, 2011–. *Publications:* Russian Business Relationships in the Wake of Reform, 1997; The Silent Takeover: global capitalism and the death of democracy, 2001; IOU: the debt threat and why we must defuse it, 2004; Eyes Wide Open: how to make smart decisions in a confusing world, 2013; contribs to acad. jls on business ethics, sustainability, business-govt-society nexus, globalisation, consumer power, risk mgt, equality and women's rights; contribs to newspapers incl. The Times, Guardian, Washington Post, FT, Daily Beast, Handelsblatt, La Repubblica, Der Spiegel, Die Welt, S China Morning Post, Wall Street Jl. *Recreations:* acting, contemporary art, feminist literature, current affairs, contemporary dance, ballet, giraffes. *Address:* University College London, 2 Taviton Street, WC1H 0BT. *T:* (020) 7679 8580, *Fax:* (020) 7679 8552. *E:* nh@noreena.com.

HERTZBERGER, Herman; Kt, Order of Orange-Nassau (Netherlands) 1991; Companion, Order of Dutch Lion (Netherlands) 1999; architect; owner of architectural practice, Architectuurstudio HH, since 1958; *b* Amsterdam, 6 July 1932; *s* of Herman Hertzberger and Margareta Johanna Alberta Hertzberger (*née* Prins); *m* 1958, Johanna van Seters; one *s* two *d*. *Educ:* Technical Univ., Delft (Bouwkundig ingenieur). Jt Ed., Forum (Dutch mag.), 1959–63; teacher, Acad. of Architecture, Amsterdam, 1965–69; Professor: Technical Univ., Delft, 1970–99; Univ. of Geneva, 1986–93; teacher, Berlage Inst., Amsterdam, 1999–2000; guest teacher, Acad. of Architecture, Amsterdam, 2000–09. Visiting Professor: American and Canadian univs, 1966–81, 1987, 1993, 1996; Univ. of Geneva, 1982–86. Chm., Berlage Inst., Amsterdam, 1990–95. Hon. FRIBA 1991; Hon. FRIAS 1996; Hon. FAIA 2004. Hon. Member: Acad. Royale de Belgique, 1975; Bund Deutscher Architekten, 1983; Akademie der Künste Berlin, 1993; Academie delle Arti del Disegno, Florence, 1995; Acad. d'Architecture de France, 1997; Royal Inst. Dutch Architects, 2002. Projects include: *schools*: Delft Montessori, 1966; Amsterdam Montessori and Willemspark, Amsterdam, 1983; De Evemaar, Amsterdam, 1986; Polygoon, Almere, 1992; Anne Franksch., Papendrecht, 1994; De Koperwiek, Venlo, 1997; Montessori Coll. Oost, Amsterdam, 2000; Stedelijk Dalton Lyceum, Dordrecht, 2008; Municipal Grammar, Leiden, 2009; Istituto Comprensivo Raffaello, Rome, 2012; De Bron, Amersfoort, 2012; *residential developments*: Kassel, Germany, 1982; Het Gein, Amersfoort-Schothorst, 1989; Papendrecht, 1996; Düren, Germany, 1996; Paradijssel, Capelle aan den IJssel, 2000; Ypenburg, 2005; *other projects*: urban renewal, Haarlemmer Houttuinen, Amsterdam, 1982; office buildings, Min. of Social Welfare and

Employment, 1990, Benelux Trademarks Office, 1993, The Hague; Public Liby and Centre for Art and Music, Breda, 1993; urban design/masterplan for Stralauer Halbinsel, Berlin, 1998; exhibn design, Fresh Facts, Dutch Pavilion, Venice 8th Internat. Architecture Biennale, 2002 (Leone d'Oro Award for Best Foreign Pavilion); office complex with studios and housing, Mediapark, Cologne, 2004; theatre and congress centre, Apeldoorn, 2004; office bldg, HQ Waternet, Amsterdam, 2005; Faculty of Sci., Univ. of Amsterdam, 2009; NHL Univ., Leeuwarden, 2010; Faculty of Sci., Univ. of Utrecht, 2011. Dr *hc* Geneva, 2001. Awards include: Berliner Architekturpreis, 1989; Premio Europa Architettura Fondazione Tetraktis Award, 1991; Premios Vitruvio Trayectoria Internacional, 1998; Oeuvre Award for Architecture, Netherlands Foundn for Visual Arts, Design and Architecture, 2004; Gold Medal, RIBA, 2012. *Publications:* Lessons for Students in Architecture, 1991, 6th edn 2009 (Japanese edn 1995, German edn 1995, Dutch, Italian, Portuguese and Chinese edns 1996, Persian edn 1998, Greek edn 2002, Korean and French edns 2010); Herman Hertzberger: projects, 1995; Chassé Theater, 1995; Space and the Architect: lessons in architecture 2, 2000, 2nd edn 2008 (Dutch edn 1999; Chinese edn 1999, 2nd edn 2000); Articulations, 2002; Shelter for Culture: Herman Hertzberger and Apeldoorn, 2004; The Theatres of Herman Hertzberger, 2005; Waternet Double Tower, 2006; Space and Learning: lessons in architecture 3, 2008 (Dutch edn 2008); The Schools of Herman Hertzberger, 2009; NHL University, 2011; contribs to jls incl. Forum, World Architecture, Harvard Educnl Rev., RIBA Jl, Building Ideas, Summarios, Spazio e Società, L'Architecture d'Aujourd'hui, Techniques & Architecture, Archithese, Berlage Cahiers, AIT; *relevant publications:* Hertzberger's Amsterdam, ed by Maarten Kloos, 2007; Herman Hertzberger, by Robert McCarter, 2015. *Address:* Architectuurstudio HH, PO Box 74665, 1070 BR Amsterdam, The Netherlands. *T:* 206765888, *Fax:* 206735510. *E:* office@ahh.nl.

HERTZELL, David John; a Law Commissioner, 2007–14; Consultant, BLM, since 2015; *b* London, 26 Nov. 1955; *s* of Clifford and Barbara Hertzell; *m* 1984, Anne Tootill; one *s* two *d. Educ:* George Abbot Sch., Guildford; Brasenose Coll., Oxford (BA Mod. Hist.); Guildford Coll. of Law. Davies Arnold Cooper Solicitors: trainee, 1981; admitted solicitor, 1983; Partner, 1989–2007; Man. Partner, 1992–96, 2000–06. *Recreations:* squash, cycling, sailing (anything).

HERVEY, family name of **Marquess of Bristol**.

HERVEY, Rear Adm. John Bethell, CB 1982; OBE 1970; independent naval consultant; *b* 14 May 1928; *s* of late Captain Maurice William Bethell Hervey, RN, and Mrs Joan Hervey (*née* Hanbury); *m* 1950, (Audrey) Elizabeth Mote (*d* 2015); two *s* one *d. Educ:* Marlborough Coll., Wilts. Joined RN, 1946; specialised in submarines, 1950, nuclear submarines, 1968; command appointments: HMS Miner VI, 1956; HMS Aeneas, 1956–57; HMS Ambush, 1959–62; HMS Oracle, 1962–64; Sixth Submarine Div., 1964–66; HMS Cavalier, 1966–67; HMS Warspite, 1968–69; Second Submarine Sqdn, 1973–75; HMS Kent, 1975–76; staff appointments: Course Officer, Royal Naval Petty Officers Leadership Sch., 1957–59; Submarine Staff Officer to Canadian Maritime Comdr, Halifax, NS, 1964–66; Ops Officer to Flag Officer Submarines, 1970–71; Def. Op. Requirements Staff, 1971–73; Dep. Chief of Allied Staff to C-in-C Channel and C-in-C Eastern Atlantic (as Cdre), 1976–80; Comdr British Navy Staff, and British Naval Attaché, Washington, and UK Nat. Liaison Rep. to SACLANT, 1980–82, retired. Comdr 1964, Captain 1970, Rear Adm. 1980. Marketing Vice-Pres., Western Hemisphere, MEL, 1982–86. Pres., HMS Cavalier Assoc., 1995–2010; Chm., Friends of RN Submarine Mus., 1995–99. FCMI (FBIM 1983). *Publications:* Submarines, 1994. *Recreations:* walking, talking, reading. *Address:* c/o National Westminster Bank, 208 Piccadilly, W1A 2DG. *Clubs:* Army and Navy, Royal Navy of 1765 and 1785, Anchorites (Pres., 1988).

HERVEY, Sir Roger Blaise Ramsay, KCVO 1991; CMG 1980; HM Diplomatic Service; Ambassador to Mexico, 1992–94; *b* 3 Oct. 1934. HM Forces, 1953–55. Joined Diplomatic Service, 1958; Bonn, 1958; FO, 1961; Prague, 1963; First Sec., FO, 1965; Office of Political Advr, Singapore, 1968; FCO, 1970; First Sec. and Head of Chancery, Bogotá, 1974; Counsellor, FCO, 1976; Counsellor, The Hague, 1979; Minister, Madrid, 1982; Asst Under Sec. of State (Protocol) and Vice Marshal of Diplomatic Corps, 1986. *Address:* c/o Foreign and Commonwealth Office, SW1A 2AH.

HERVEY-BATHURST, Sir Frederick (William John), 8th Bt *cr* 1818, of Lainston, Hants; *b* London, 18 Sept. 1965; *s* of Sir Frederick John Charles Gordon Hervey-Bathurst, 7th Bt and of Caroline Hervey-Bathurst, *d* of Sir William Randle Starkey, 2nd Bt; *S* father, 2011; *m* 1991, Annabel Peta Warburg; one *s* one *d. Educ:* Harrow Sch.; Univ. of Buckingham (BA Hons). Chartered Financial Planner. Director: Chestergate Financial Planning Ltd, 1996–2011; Clarendon Financial Planning Ltd, 2011–. *Recreations:* fly fishing, reading, walking, carpentry, bonfires, deer park. *Heir: s* Frederick Benjamin Guy Hervey-Bathurst, *b* 9 March 1998. *Address:* Somborne Park, Stockbridge, Hants SO20 6QT. *T:* 07899 845610, (office) (01794) 388594. *E:* fhb@clarendonfp.co.uk.

HERZ, Robert Henry, FCA; Chairman, Financial Accounting Standards Board, 2002–10; *b* New York City, 18 June 1953; *s* of James and Susan Herz; *m* 1978, Louise; one *s* one *d. Educ:* Univ. of Manchester (BA (Econ) 1st Cl. Hons 1974). FCA 1977; CPA 1979 (Gold Medal); CGMA. Partner, Coopers & Lybrand, 1985–98; Partner and Mem., US and Global Bds, PricewaterhouseCoopers, 1998–2002. Mem., Internat. Accounting Standards Bd, 2001–02. Director: Fannie Mae, 2011–; Morgan Stanley, 2012–; Sen. Advr, WebFilings, 2011–. Chairman: Transnat. Auditors Cttee, 2000–02; SEC Resolutions Cttee, AICPA; Mem., Internat. Central Mkts Cttee, NY Stock Exchange. Mem., Adv. Bd, Manchester Business Sch., 2008–; Exec.-in-Residence, Columbia Business Sch., 2010–. Pres., Coopers & Lybrand Foundn, later PricewaterhouseCoopers Foundn, 1994–2002. Trustee and Chair, Finance Cttee, Kessler Foundn, 2003–. Hon. LLD Manchester, 2007. Elijah Watt Sells Award, AICPA, 1979. *Publications:* (jtly) Foreign Currency Translation, 1982; (jtly) The Coopers & Lybrand SEC Manual, 1993; (jtly) The Value Reporting Revolution, 2000; Accounting Changes: chronicles of convergence, crisis and complexity in financial reporting, 2013. *Recreations:* travel, golf, softball, volleyball.

HERZBERG, Charles Francis; consultant; Chairman, Unique Business Services Ltd (formerly Newcastle upon Tyne Polytechnic Products Ltd), 1988–95; *b* 26 Jan. 1924; *s* of Dr Franz Moritz Herzberg and Mrs Marie Louise Palache; *m* 1956, Ann Linette Hoare (*d* 2013); one *s* two *d. Educ:* Fettes Coll., Edinburgh; Sidney Sussex Coll., Cambridge (MA). CEng 1954; FIMechE 1964; MIGEM (MIGasE 1967). Alfred Herbert Ltd, 1947–51; Chief Engr and Dir, Hornflowa Ltd, Maryport, 1951–55; Chief Engr, Commercial Plastics Gp of Cos, and Dir, Commercial Plastics Engrg Co. at Wallsend on Tyne, North Shields, and Cramlington, Northumberland, 1955–66; Corporate Planning Dir, Appliance Div., United Gas Industries, and Works Dir, Robinson Willey Ltd, Liverpool, 1966–70; Man. Dir and Chief Exec., Churchill Gear Machines Ltd, Blaydon on Tyne, 1970–72; Regional Industrial Director, Dept of Industry, N Region, 1972–75; Dir of Corporate Devélt, Clarke Chapman Ltd, 1975–77; Gp Industrial Planning Adviser, 1977–84, Dir Industrial Planning, 1984–88, Northern Engineering Industries plc; Dir, Northern Investors Co. Ltd, 1984–89; Pres., Tyne & Wear Chamber of Commerce and Industry, 1989–90 (Vice-Pres., 1986–89). Gov., Univ. of Northumbria (formerly Newcastle upon Tyne Poly.), 1986–96 (Hon. Fellow, 1991). *Recreations:* shooting, gardening. *Address:* Kirkwood Court, Kirkwood Drive, Newcastle upon Tyne NE3 3AX. *T:* (0191) 285 5202. *Club:* East India, Devonshire, Sports and Public Schools.

HERZOG, Roman, Hon. GCB 1998; President of the Federal Republic of Germany, 1994–99; *b* 5 April 1934; *m* 1958, Christiane Krauss (*d* 2000); two *s*; *m* Alexandra Freifrau von Berlichingen. *Educ:* Munich, Berlin and Tübingen Univs. DJur. Lecturer: in Law, Munich Univ., 1958–66; in Law and Politics, Free Univ. of Berlin, 1966–69 (Dean, Faculty of Law, 1967–68); Prof. of Politics, 1969–73, Rector, 1971–73, Postgrad. Sch. of Admin. Scis, Speyer. Rep. of Rhineland-Palatinate, Bundestag, 1973–78; Minister for Culture and Sport, 1978–80, for the Interior, 1980–83, Baden-Württemberg; Vice-Pres., 1983–87, Pres., 1987–94, Federal Constitutional Court. Mem. Federal Cttee, CDU, 1979–83. Chm., Bd of Trustees, Konrad Adenauer Foundn, 2000–. DCL Oxon, 1997. *Publications:* (jtly) Kommentar zur Grundgesetz, 1966, 3rd edn 1987; Allgemeine Staatslehre, 1971; Staaten der Frühzeit, 1988; Ursprünge und Herr-schaftsformen, 1988; Staat und Recht im Wandel, 1993; Preventing the Clash of Civilizations: a peace strategy for the 21st century, 1999; vols of collected speeches. *Address:* (office) Im Stahlbühl 20, 74074 Heilbronn, Germany.

HESELTINE, family name of **Baron Heseltine**.

HESELTINE, Baron *cr* 2001 (Life Peer), of Thenford in the County of Northamptonshire; **Michael Ray Dibdin Heseltine,** CH 1997; PC 1979; Chairman, Haymarket Publishing Group, since 1999 (Director, since 1997); *b* 21 March 1933; *s* of late Col R. D. Heseltine, Swansea, Glamorgan; *m* 1962, Anne Harding Williams (*see* Lady Heseltine); one *s* two *d. Educ:* Shrewsbury Sch.; Pembroke Coll., Oxford (BA PPE; Hon. Fellow 1986). Pres. Oxford Union, 1954. National Service (commissioned), Welsh Guards, 1959. Director of Bow Publications, 1961–65; Chm., Haymarket Press, 1966–70. Contested (C): Gower, 1959; Coventry North, 1964. MP (C): Tavistock, 1966–74; Henley, 1974–2001. Vice-Chm., Cons. Parly Transport Cttee, 1968; Opposition Spokesman on Transport, 1969; Parly Sec., Min. of Transport, June–Oct. 1970; Parly Under-Sec. of State, DoE, 1970–72; Minister for Aerospace and Shipping, DTI, 1972–74; Opposition Spokesman on: Industry, 1974–76; Environment, 1976–79; Sec. of State for the Environment, 1979–83 and 1990–92, for Defence, 1983–86; Pres., BoT, 1992–95; First Sec. of State and Dep. Prime Minister, 1995–97. Pres., Assoc. of Conservative Clubs, 1978; Vice-Pres., 1978, Pres., 1982–84, Nat. Young Conservatives; Pres., Conservative Gp for Europe, 2001. Chm., Ind. Adv. Panel, Regl Growth Fund, 2010–; author of report, No Stone Unturned in Pursuit of Growth, 2012. Mem. Council, Zoological Soc. of London, 1987–90; Vice-Pres., RHS, 2009–. Patron, Nat. Centre for Competitiveness, Univ. of Luton, 2001. Freeman: City of Liverpool, 2012; City of London, 2012. Hon. Fellow: Leeds Polytechnic, 1988; Univ. of Wales, Swansea, 2001. Hon. FRIBA 1991; Hon. FCIM 1998 (Pres., 2006–08); Hon. Fellow: Marketing Soc., 2011; Liverpool John Moores Univ., 2013; Univ. of Northampton, 2013. Hon. LLD Liverpool, 1990; Hon. Dr Univ. of S Wales, 2013; hon. degree, Aston Univ., 2013. *Publications:* Reviving the Inner Cities, 1983; Where There's a Will, 1987; The Challenge of Europe, 1989; Life in the Jungle (memoirs), 2000. *Address:* c/o House of Lords, SW1A 0PW. *Clubs:* Brooks's, Carlton, Pratt's, White's, Beefsteak.

See also R. W. D. Heseltine.

HESELTINE, Lady; Anne Edna Harding Heseltine; a Trustee, National Gallery, since 2008; *b* London, 23 Oct. 1934; *d* of William and Edna Williams; *m* 1962, Michael Ray Dibdin Heseltine (*see* Baron Heseltine); one *s* two *d. Educ:* Bedford Coll., Univ. of London (BA Hons 1956). Career in publishing and art dealing at Victor Gollancz Ltd, Crane Kalman Gall. and Bury St Gall. Mem., Bd of Visitors, Ashmolean Mus., Oxford, 1987–2006, Fellow, 2006; Chm. Adv. Bd, Oxford Univ. Mus. of Natural History, 2009–12; Distinguished Friend, Univ. of Oxford, 1999; Trustee: Imperial War Mus., 1990–97; V & A Mus., 1997–2002; Burlington Mag., 2003–; former Mem. Council, Attingham Foundn. Hon. Fellow, Royal Holloway, Univ. of London, 2011. *Recreations:* travelling, art history, collecting, gardens, fox and stag hunting. *Address:* Thenford House, near Banbury, Oxon OX17 2BX.

See also R. W. D. Heseltine.

HESELTINE, Rupert William Dibdin; Executive Chairman, Haymarket Media Group, since 2009; *b* London, 9 July 1967; *s* of Baron Heseltine, *qv* and Lady Heseltine, *qv*; *m* 2000, Sarah Caroline Fitch; two *s* one *d. Educ:* Harrow; Oxford Poly. With Peter Isaacson Pubns, Australia, 1989; Maxwell Business Communications; joined Haymarket Gp, 1994; consumer mags div., Car Hi-Fi; Wine & Spirit Internat., Wilmington plc; Haymarket Group: Advertising Dir, PR Week; Associate Publisher, Gramophone; Publisher, What Hi-Fi? Sound & Vision; Dir, Haymarket Gp Ltd, 2001–; Deputy Chairman: Haymarket Exhibns, 2004–05; Haymarket Media Gp, 2005–09. *Address:* Haymarket Media Group, Teddington Studios, Broom Road, Teddington, Middx TW11 9BE. *T:* (020) 8267 5000.

HESELTINE, Rt Hon. Sir William (Frederick Payne), GCB 1990 (KCB 1986; CB 1978); GCVO 1988 (KCVO 1982; CVO 1969; MVO 1961); AC 1988; QSO 1990; PC 1986; Deputy Chairman, P & O Australia Ltd, 1998–2001 (Director, 1990–2001); *b* E Fremantle, W Australia, 17 July 1930; *s* of late H. W. Heseltine; *m* 1st, Ann Elizabeth (*d* 1957), *d* of late L. F. Turner, Melbourne; 2nd, Audrey Margaret (*d* 2013), *d* of late S. Nolan, Sydney; one *s* one *d. Educ:* Christ Church Grammar Sch., Claremont, WA; University of Western Australia (1st class hons, History). Prime Minister's dept, Canberra, 1951–62; Private Secretary to Prime Minister, 1955–59; Asst Information Officer to The Queen, 1960–61; Acting Official Secretary to Governor-General of Australia, 1962; Asst Federal Director of Liberal Party of Australia, 1962–64; attached to Household of Princess Marina for visit to Australia, 1964; attached to Melbourne Age, 1964; Asst Press Secretary to the Queen, 1965–67, Press Secretary, 1968–72; Assistant Private Secretary to the Queen, 1972–77, Dep. Private Secretary, 1977–86, Private Sec., and Keeper of the Queen's Archives, 1986–90. Chm., NZI Insurance Australia Ltd, 1992–98 (Dep. Chm., 1991–92); Director: West Coast Telecasters Ltd, 1991–96; NZI Insurance NZ, 1996–98. Pres., Royal Western Australian Histl Soc., 1998–2001. Senator, Murdoch Univ., 2000–06. *Address:* PO Box 35, York, WA 6302, Australia. *Club:* Weld (Perth).

HESFORD, Stephen; Visiting Lecturer in Politics, University of Chester, since 2010; *b* 27 May 1957; *s* of late Bernard Hesford and of Nellie Hesford; *m* 1984, Elizabeth Anne Henshall; two *s. Educ:* Univ. of Bradford (BScSoc Econs/Politics 1978); Poly. of Central London (Postgrad. Dip. in Law 1980). Called to the Bar, Gray's Inn, 1981. Contested (Lab) S Suffolk, 1992. MP (Lab) Wirral W, 1997–2010. PPS to Leader of H of L, 2005–07, to Solicitor Gen. and to Minister of State, MoJ, 2007–09. Mem., Health Select Cttee, 1999–2001. Founder: and Sec., All-Party Parly Gp on Primary Care and Public Health, 1998–2010; and Vice-Chm., All-Party Parly Gp on Autism. Mem. Bd, Mind, 1998–2001. Trustee, Alcohol Concern, 2012–. Mem. Bd and Gov., Edge Hill Univ., 2013–. FRSPH (FRIPHH 1998); Fellow, Soc. of Public Health; FRSA 2006. *Recreations:* watching football, reading. *Club:* Lancashire County Cricket (Life Mem.).

HESKETH, 3rd Baron *cr* 1935, of Hesketh; **Thomas Alexander Fermor-Hesketh,** KBE 1997; PC 1991; Bt 1761; Executive Chairman: Towcester Racecourse, since 1995; British Mediterranean Airways, 1994–2007; *b* 28 Oct. 1950; *s* of 2nd Baron and Christian Mary, OBE 1984, *o d* of Sir John McEwen, 1st Bt of Marchmont, DL, JP; *S* father, 1955; *m* 1977, Hon. Claire, *e d* of 3rd Baron Manton; one *s* two *d. Educ:* Ampleforth. A Lord in Waiting (Govt Whip), 1986–89; Parly Under-Sec. of State, DoE, 1989–90; Minister of State, DTI, 1990–91; Capt. of Gentlemen-at-Arms (Govt Chief Whip in H of L), 1991–93. Chm., Cons. Party Foundn, 2003–10; Treas., Cons. Party, 2003–05. Non-executive Deputy Chairman: Babcock Internat., 1993–2010; Freestream Aircraft Ltd, 2009–; ind. Dir, Air Astana JSC, 2007–; non-exec. Dir, BAE Systems, 1993–2005. President: British Racing Drivers' Club, 1994–99; Remote Sensing and Photogrammetry Soc., 1995–2002. Hon. FSE; Hon. FIET 1982. *Heir:*

s Hon. Frederick Hatton Fermor-Hesketh, *b* 13 Oct. 1988. *Address:* c/o Towcester Racecourse, London Road, Towcester, Northants NN12 6LB. *Clubs:* White's, Turf, Pratt's.
See also J. Goodwin.

HESKETH, Ven. Ronald David, CB 2004; Chaplain-in-Chief and Archdeacon, Royal Air Force, 2001–06; *b* 16 June 1947; *s* of William Ronald Hesketh and Mary Hagar Hesketh; *m* 1971, Vera Ruth Taylor; one *s* one *d*. *Educ:* King David Sch., Liverpool; Bede Coll., Univ. of Durham (BA Hons 1968); Ridley Hall, Cambridge; St Michael's Coll., Llandaff (DPS 1971); Dip in Reformation Studies, Open Univ., 1977. Ordained deacon, 1971, priest, 1972; Curate, Southport, 1971–73; Asst Chaplain, Mersey Mission to Seamen, 1973–75; RAF Chaplain, 1975–98; Command Chaplain, 1998–2001; Canon, Lincoln Cathedral, 2001–06; Vocations Officer, Worcester Dio., 2006–11; Force Chaplain, West Mercia Police, 2009–. Mem., Gen. Synod of C of E, 2001–05. QHC 2001–06. Mem. Council, RAF Benevolent Fund, 2001–04; Chm., Naval, Military and Air Force Bible Soc., 2006–14. Vice Pres., Friends of St Clement Danes, 2001–. FRGS 2002; FCMI 2006. *Recreations:* theatre, travel, philately, antiquarian books. *Address:* Whistledown, Twyning Green, Twyning GL20 6DQ. *T:* (01684) 299773. *E:* ron@hesketh.org.uk. *Club:* Royal Air Force.

HESKETH HARVEY, Christopher John, (Kit); writer, broadcaster and cabaret performer; *b* Zomba, Nyasaland, 30 April 1957; *s* of Noel Harvey and Susan Mary Harvey (*née* Ford); *m* 1986, Catherine, (Kate), Rabett; one *s* one *d*. *Educ:* Cathedral Choir Sch., Canterbury; Tonbridge Sch.; Clare Coll., Cambridge (BA English Lit. 1978); St Catherine's Coll., Oxford (Postgrad. Th. Studies). Staff producer, Music and Arts, BBC TV, 1980–85; *lyricist and star:* (at Vaudeville Th.): Kit and the Widow: Lavishly Mounted, 1991; January Sale, 1994; Salad Days, 1996; Meat on the Bone, 1998; Tom Foolery; starred with Joan Rivers, Haymarket Th. and London Palladium, 2002 and 2006; Cowardy Custard (UK tour), 2011; Abanazar in Aladdin, Guildford, 2012; *plays:* Five O'clock Angel, Hampstead Th., 1998; The Caribbean Tempest, Barbados, 2000; *screenwriter:* Maurice, 1986; Birkin, 1994; Hans Christian Andersen, 2000; *opera translations* include: Bartered Bride, Royal Opera, 2001; Il Turco in Italia, 2002, La Belle Hélène, 2006, ENO; Bluebeard, 2007; Véronique, 2009; The Merry Widow, Grand, Leeds, 2010; The Magic Flute, Scottish Opera, 2012; *librettist* (with James Connel): Orlando, Barbican, 1988 (Vivian Ellis Award); Killing Rasputin, Bridewell, 1998; *television* includes: co-writer, Vicar of Dibley, 1994; Lavishly Mounted; Mounting the Hustings; *radio* includes: Cocktails; panellist, Just a Minute, 1996–. *Recreations:* mushrooming, surfing, playing the piano execrably. *Address:* Park House, Stoke Ferry, King's Lynn, Norfolk PE33 9SF; c/o PBJ Management, 22 Rathbone Street, W1T 1LG. *T:* (020) 7287 1112. *Clubs:* Garrick, Saints and Sinners.

HESKETT, Rt Rev. Ralph; *see* Hallam, Bishop of, (RC).

HESLAM, (Mary) Noelle, (Mrs David Heslam); *see* Walsh, M. N.

HESLOP, David Thomas, OBE 1987; CIGEM; Regional Chairman, British Gas plc Southern, 1988–94; *b* Sept. 1932; *s* of late John Heslop and Frances Mary (*née* Brooks); *m* 1952, Barbara Mary Seddon; one *s* one *d*. *Educ:* Henley Management Coll. (GMC 1974); Harvard Business Sch. (AMP 1981). CIGEM (CompIGasE 1990). Commercial Sales Officer, Scottish Gas, 1960; Marketing Develt Man., West Midlands Gas, 1965; Sales Man., South Eastern Gas, 1972; Dir of Sales, North Western Gas, 1976; HQ Dir of Sales, British Gas, 1982. Pres., Internat. Gas Marketing Colloquium, 1986–89. FCIM 1977; CCMI (CBIM 1990). *Recreations:* church activities, golf. *Address:* Prestolee, Rhinefield Road, Brockenhurst, Hants SO42 7SR.

HESLOP, Martin Sydney; QC 1995; a Recorder of the Crown Court, since 1993; *b* 6 Aug. 1948; *s* of late Sydney Heslop and of Patricia (*née* Day); *m* 1994, Aurea Jane (*née* Boyle). *Educ:* St George's Coll., Weybridge; Bristol Univ. LLB Hons 1971. Called to the Bar, Lincoln's Inn, 1972; Jun. Treasury Counsel, 1987; First Jun. Treasury Counsel, 1992–93; Sen. Treasury Counsel, 1993–95. An Asst Recorder, 1989–93. *Recreations:* sailing, travel, photography, fine wine and food. *Address:* 2 Hare Court, Temple, EC4Y 7BH. *T:* (020) 7353 5324. *Clubs:* Naval, Royal London Yacht, Bar Yacht.

HESLOP, Sean Martin, MA; Executive Principal, Folkestone Academy and Marlowe Academy, 2013–15 (Principal, Folkestone Academy, 2009–13); *b* 31 Oct. 1967; *s* of late Roy Heslop and of Eileen Heslop; *m* 2005, Céline Gagnon. *Educ:* Queens' Coll., Cambridge (BA 1989); King's Coll., London (PGCE); Inst. of Educn, Univ. of London (MA Dist.). Teacher of English, Queen Elizabeth's Sch., Barnet, 1994–97; Hd of English, St Olave's Sch., Orpington, 1997–2000; Dep. Headteacher, Ravens Wood Sch., Bromley, 2000–04; Headmaster, Tiffin Sch., Kingston, 2004–09. Res. Associate, Nat. Coll. of Sch. Leadership, 2003–. Consultant, Thinking & Learning Schs Alliance, 2002–04. FRSA 2007. *Publications:* contrib. articles on social capital, knowledge capital and change process to educn mgt jls. *Recreations:* walking, reading, bird-watching.

HESLOP-HARRISON, Prof. John Seymour, (Pat), PhD; Professor of Molecular Cytogenetics and Cell Biology, University of Leicester, since 2000; *b* Belfast, NI, 14 March 1959; *s* of Prof. John Heslop-Harrison, FRS and Yolande Heslop-Harrison; *m* 1995, Trude Schwarzacher; two *s*. *Educ:* Univ. of Massachusetts; University Coll. of Wales, Aberystwyth (BSc 1980); Peterhouse, Cambridge (PhD 1983). Stone Res. Fellow, Peterhouse, Cambridge, 1982–85; Scientific Officer: Plant Breeding Inst., Cambridge, 1985–90; John Innes Centre, Norwich, 1990–2000. Associate Ed., Chromosome Res., 1994–2012, now Emeritus Ed.; Chief Ed., Annals of Botany, 2008–. Member: Cttee, Global Musa Genomics Consortium, 2001–; Sub-panel, UK REF 2014. Vice-Pres., 2007–09, Pres., 2009–11, Soc. for Exptl Biol.; Mem. Bd, Eur. Cytogeneticists Assoc., 2004–. Reviewer and assessor for grants, res. progs/site visits. *Publications:* contribs to acad. jls. *Recreations:* enjoying the natural and built environment, walking, photography, technology and art. *Address:* Department of Biology, University of Leicester, Leicester LE1 7RH. *T:* (0116) 252 3381. *E:* phh@molcyt.com.

HESS, Edward John Watkin; His Honour Judge Hess; a Circuit Judge, since 2015; *b* Rochdale, 29 Oct. 1962; *s* of John and Valerie Hess; *m* 1988, Elizabeth Bannan; two *s* one *d*. *Educ:* Rugby Sch.; Peterhouse, Cambridge (BA 1984; MA). Called to the Bar, Middle Temple, 1985; barrister, Harcourt Chambers, 1985–2010 (Treas., 1998–2010); Dep. Dist Judge, Co. Courts, 2002–04; Principal Registry of Family Div., 2004–10; a Recorder, 2009–15; Dist Judge (Principal Registry of the Family Div., sitting at Central Family Ct), 2010–15. Mem. Council (C), RBKC, 1988–98 (Mayor, 1997–98; Chm., Housing and Social Services Cttee, 1993–96). Contested (C) Wigan, 1992. Chm., Cambridge Univ. Cons. Assoc., 1984; Treas., Cambridge Union, 1983–84; Chm., Coningsby Club, 1992. Chm., Holton Players, 2012–. *Publications:* (jtly) Pensions on Divorce: a practitioner's handbook, 2008, 2nd edn 2013; (ed) The Collected Works of Kit Arnold, 2011; (jtly) Dictionary of Financial Remedies (annually), 2014–; Wheatley Manor, Its Owners and Occupants: 956–2015, 2015. *Recreations:* lawn tennis, Real tennis, cricket, amateur dramatics. *Address:* Portsmouth Combined Court Centre, Winston Churchill Avenue, Portsmouth PO1 2EB. *E:* HHJEdward.Hess@judiciary.gsi.gov.uk. *Clubs:* Travellers, MCC.

HESS, Nigel John; composer for television, film, theatre and concert hall; *b* 22 July 1953; *s* of John and Sheila Hess; *m* 1996, Lisa Claire Telford; one *d*. *Educ:* Weston-super-Mare Grammar Sch. for Boys; St Catharine's Coll., Cambridge (MA). Composed scores for: *theatre,* including: Troilus and Cressida, Julius Caesar, Much Ado About Nothing and Cyrano de Bergerac (NY Drama Desk Award, 1985), Comedy of Errors, Hamlet, Love's Labour's Lost, Love's Labour's Won, Othello, The Winter's Tale, The Swan Down Gloves, A Christmas Carol, Twelfth Night (all for Royal Shakespeare Company); The Merry Wives of Windsor, Romeo and Juliet, Henry VIII, The Knight of the Burning Pestle, Nell Gwynn (all for Shakespeare's Globe); The Secret of Sherlock Holmes; *television,* including: A Woman of Substance; Deceptions; Anna of the Five Towns; All Passion Spent; Vanity Fair; Campion; Testament (Novello Award for Best TV Theme, 1988); Summer's Lease (TRIC Award for Best TV Theme, 1989); The London Embassy; The One Game; Titmuss Regained; Maigret; Growing Pains; Classic Adventure; Dangerfield; Just William; Wycliffe; Hetty Wainthropp Investigates (Novello Award for Best TV Theme, 1997); Badger; Ballykissangel; New Tricks; Stick with Me Kid; *films,* including: An Ideal Husband, 1999; Ladies in Lavender, 2004; *concert music* includes: Thames Journey; East Coast Pictures, 1985; The Way of Light, 1985; Global Variations, 1990; Stephenson's Rocket, 1991; The Winds of Power, 1993; Scramble!, 1994; To the Stars!, 1996; The TV Detectives, 1998; Monck's March, 2002; New London Pictures, 2003; The Food of Love, 2005; Piano Concerto (commnd by Prince of Wales), 2007; Shakespeare Pictures, 2008; A Christmas Overture, 2007; Jubilate Deo, 2010; March Barnes Wallis, 2013; Chansons de Normandie, 2014; A Celebration Overture, 2015; *ballet,* The Old Man of Lochnagar, 2007; devised Admission: One Shilling—the story of Dame Myra Hess and her wartime concerts, for Nat. Gall., 2009. Has made numerous recordings. Mem., British Acad. Composers and Songwriters, 1985–. *Recreations:* travel, food. *Address:* c/o Bucks Music Ltd, Onward House, 11 Uxbridge Street, W8 7TQ. *T:* (020) 7221 4275, *Fax:* (020) 7229 6893. *E:* nigel@myramusic.co.uk.

HESSAYON, Dr David Gerald, OBE 2007; gardening author; Chairman: Expert Publications Ltd, since 1988; Hessayon Books, since 1993; *b* 13 Feb. 1928; *s* of Jack and Lena Hessayon; *m* 1951, Joan Parker Gray (*d* 2001); two *d*. *Educ:* Salford Grammar Sch.; Leeds Univ. (BSc 1950); Manchester Univ. (PhD 1954). CBiol; FRSB (FIBiol 1971); FCIHort (FIHort 1986). Res. Fellow, UC of Gold Coast, 1953. Pan Britannica Industries Ltd: Technical Man., 1955–60; Tech. Dir, 1960–64; Man. Dir, 1964–91; Chm., 1972–93; Chm., Turbair Ltd, 1972–93. Chm., British Agrochemicals Assoc., 1980–81. Patron, Essex Gardens Trust, 1996–. FCMI (FBIM 1972). Hon. DSc: CNAA, 1990; Hertfordshire, 1994; Leeds, 2008. Lifetime Achievement Trophy, Nat. British Book Awards, 1992; Veitch Gold Meml Medal, RHS, 1992; Lifetime Achievement Award, Garden Writers' Guild, 2005; Outstanding Achievement Award, Romantic Novelists' Assoc., 2014. *Publications:* Be Your Own Gardening Expert, 1959, rev. edn 1977; Be Your Own House Plant Expert, 1960; Potato Growers Handbook, 1961; Silage Makers Handbook, 1961; Be Your Own Lawn Expert, 1962, rev. edn 1979; Be Your Own Rose Expert, 1964, rev. edn 1977; (with J. P. Hessayon) The Garden Book of Europe, 1973; Vegetable Plotter, 1976; Be Your Own House Plant Spotter, 1977; Be Your Own Vegetable Doctor, 1978; Be Your Own Garden Doctor, 1978; The House Plant Expert, 1980, rev. edn 1991; The Rose Expert, 1981, rev. edn 1996; The Lawn Expert, 1982, rev. edn 1997; The Cereal Disease Expert, 1982; The Tree and Shrub Expert, 1983; The Armchair Book of the Garden, 1983; The Flower Expert, 1984, rev. edn 1999; The Vegetable Expert, 1985; The Indoor Plant Spotter, 1985; The Garden Expert, 1986; The Gold Plated House Plant Expert, 1987; The Home Expert, 1987; Vegetable Jotter, 1989; Rose Jotter, 1989; House Plant Jotter, 1989; The Fruit Expert, 1990; Be Your Own Greenhouse Expert, 1990; The Bio Friendly Gardening Guide, 1990; The Bedding Plant Expert, 1991, rev. edn 1996; The Garden DIY Expert, 1992; The Rock and Water Garden Expert, 1993; The Flowering Shrub Expert, 1994; The Greenhouse Expert, 1994; The Flower Arranging Expert, 1994; The Container Expert, 1995; The Bulb Expert, 1995; The Easy-care Gardening Expert, 1995; The Vegetable & Herb Expert, 1997, rev. edn as The New Vegetable & Herb Expert, 2014; The Evergreen Expert, 1998; The Pocket Flower Expert, 2001; The Pocket Tree & Shrub Expert, 2001; The Pocket Garden Troubles Expert, 2001; The Pocket House Plant Expert, 2002; The Pocket Vegetable Expert, 2002; The Garden Revival Expert, 2004; The House Plant Expert Book 2, 2005; The Pest & Weed Expert, 2007; The Orchid Expert, 2008; The Bedside Book of the Garden, 2008; The Green Garden Expert, 2009; The Expert Vegetable Notebook, 2009; The Best of Experts, 2010; The Cat Expert, 2010; The Dog Expert, 2010; The Garden to Kitchen Expert, 2011; The Complete Garden Expert, 2012; The Indoor Plant & Flower Expert, 2013. *Recreations:* American folk music, The Times crossword. *Address:* c/o Transworld Publishers, 61–63 Uxbridge Road, W5 5SA.

HESSE, Prof. Joachim Jens, PhD; Founding Director, European Centre for Comparative Government and Public Policy, Berlin, 1997–2001; Professor of Political Science and Public Administration, Otto Suhr Institute of Political Science, Free University of Berlin, since 1997; Chairman, International Institute for Comparative Government and European Policy, Berlin, since 2001; *b* 20 Nov. 1942; *s* of Joachim Hesse and Frieda Hesse (*née* Madrowski); *m* 1981, Irmgart Wethmar-von Hagen; one *s* one *d*. *Educ:* Schadow Gymnasium, Berlin; Univ. of Goettingen; Univ. of Kiel; Univ. of Berlin (Dipl. Volkswirt. 1967); NY Univ. and Harvard Univ.; Univ. of Cologne (PhD Econs 1972); MA Oxon. Res. Associate, German Inst. of Urbanism, Berlin, 1968–73; Professor of: Pol and Admin. Scis, Univ. of Constance, 1973–77; Pol Sci. and Comparative Govt, Duisburg, 1978–83; Exec. Dir, Rhine-Ruhr Inst. for Social Res. and Public Policy Studies, 1980–84; Prof. of Pol and Admin. Scis, German Post-Grad. Sch. of Admin. Scis, Speyer, 1984–90; Prof. of Eur. Politics and Comparative Govt, and Fellow of Nuffield College, Oxford Univ., 1991–97. Vis. Prof., Coll. of Europe, Bruges, 1987–90; Guest Prof., Tokyo Univ., 2004–05; Visiting Scholar: Harvard Univ., 1984–85; Oxford Univ., 1988–89. Consultant: OECD, 1970–; EU (formerly EEC), 1988–; UN, 1991–; ILO, 1992–; World Bank, 1995–. Fellow, Institute of Advanced Study: Budapest; Kyoto; Wassenaar; Freiburg. Managing Editor: Staatswissenschaften und Staatspraxis, 1990–98; Zeitschrift für Staats und Europawissenschaften, 2003–; Internat. Editor, Public Admin, 1992–95; General Editor: Jahrbuch zur Staatswissenschaft und Staatspraxis, 1987–; European Yearbook on Comparative Govt and Public Admin., 1994–; Staatsreform in Deutschland und Europa; Abhandlungen zur Staats; Europawissenschaft; Member, Editorial Board: German Politics; Jl Contingencies; Australian Jl Public Admin. Hon. Dr Masaryk, 2008; Dr rer. soc. Brno. Univ. Medal, Univ. of Constance. *Publications:* include: (with A. Benz) Die Modernisierung der Staatsorganisation, 1990; (ed) Administrative Transformation in Central and Eastern Europe, 1993; (with T. Ellwein) Der überforderte Staat, 1994, 2nd edn 1997; (ed with N. Johnson) Constitutional Policy and Change in Europe, 1995; (ed with V. Wright) Federalizing Europe?: the costs and benefits of federal political systems, 1996; (ed) Regions in Europe, 2 vols, 1996–97; (jtly) Zur Neuordnung der Europäischen Union: die Regierungskonferenz 1996/97, 1997; (ed with C. Hood and B. G. Peters) Paradoxes in Public Sector Reform, 2003; (with T. Ellwein) Das Regierungssystem der Bundesrepublik Deutschland (2 vols), 9th edn, 2004, 10th edn, 2012; (with F. Grotz) Europa professionalisieren, 2004; Vom Werden Europas, 2007; (ed jtly) The Public Sector in Transition: East Asia and the European Union compared, 2007; Verwaltung erfolgreich modernisieren, 2008; Arbeits und Sozialverwaltung im Bundesstaat, 2009; Die Internationalisierung der Wissenschaftspolitik, 2011. *Address:* International Institute for Comparative Government and European Policy, Matterhornstraße 90, 14129 Berlin - Zehlendorf, Germany.

HESSE, Mary Brenda, MA, MSc, PhD; FBA 1971; Professor of Philosophy of Science, University of Cambridge, 1975–85; Fellow of Wolfson College (formerly University College), Cambridge, 1965–92, subseq. Hon. Fellow; *b* 15 Oct. 1924; *d* of Ethelbert Thomas Hesse and Brenda Nellie Hesse (*née* Pelling). *Educ:* Imperial Coll., London; University Coll., London. MSc, PhD (London); DIC; MA (Cantab). Lecturer: in Mathematics, Univ. of Leeds, 1951–55; in Hist. and Philosophy of Science, UCL, 1955–59; in Philosophy of Science, Univ. of Cambridge, 1960–68; Reader in Philosophy of Sci., Cambridge Univ., 1968–75; Vice-

Pres., Wolfson Coll., 1976–80. Member: Council, British Acad., 1979–82; UGC, 1980–85. Visiting Professor: Yale Univ., 1961; Univ. of Minnesota, 1966; Univ. of Chicago, 1968. Stanton Lectr, Cambridge, 1977–80; Joint Gifford Lectr, Edinburgh, 1983. Pres., Cambridge Antiquarian Soc., 1996–98. Mem., Academia Europaea, 1989. Hon. DSc: Hull, 1984; Guelph, Ontario, 1987; Hon. ScD Cantab, 2002. Editor, Brit. Jl for the Philosophy of Science, 1965–69. *Publications:* Science and the Human Imagination, 1954; Forces and Fields, 1961; Models and Analogies in Science, 1963; The Structure of Scientific Inference, 1974; Revolutions and Reconstructions in the Philosophy of Science, 1980; (jtly) The Construction of Reality, 1987; articles in jls of philosophy and of the history and philosophy of science. *Recreations:* walking, landscape history and archaeology. *Address:* 49 Gretton Court, High Street, Girton, Cambridge CB3 0QN.

HESSELL TILTMAN, Sir John, KCVO 2003 (LVO 1997); Director of Property Services, HM Household, 1996–2003 (Deputy Director, 1991–96); *b* 27 Aug. 1942; *s* of Henry Hessell Tiltman and Rita Florence Hessell Tiltman; *m* 1969, Monique Yvonne Françoise Louge; one *s* one *d*. *Educ:* Brighton Coll.; Brighton Coll. of Art (DipArch 1965). ARIBA 1968. Project Architect, GLC, 1965–68; Property Services Agency, Department of the Environment, 1969–90: Project Architect, 1969–76; Project Manager: PO and BT works, 1976–82; RN works, 1982–85; Chief Architect, work in RN Trng Estabts, 1985–88; Hd of Royal Palaces Gp, 1988–90; Project Dir, reconstruction of fire-damaged areas of Windsor Castle, 1993–97; Dir, Time and Space Project, Nat. Maritime Mus., Greenwich, 2004–06; Mem., Parly Estate Bd, 2006–09. *Recreations:* overseas travel, bridge, French, classical concerts and opera. *Address:* 18 rue Sainte Anne, 31000 Toulouse, France.

HESTER, Prof. Ronald Ernest, DSc, PhD; CChem, FRSC; Professor of Chemistry, University of York, 1983–2001, now Emeritus; *b* 8 March 1936; *s* of Ernest and Rhoda Hester; *m* 1958, Bridget Ann Maddin; two *s* two *d*. *Educ:* Royal Grammar Sch., High Wycombe; London Univ. (BSc; DSc 1979); Cornell Univ. (PhD 1962). CChem 1975; FRSC 1971. Res. Fellow, Cambridge Univ., 1962–63; Asst Prof., Cornell Univ., 1963–65; University of York: Lectr, 1965–71; Sen. Lectr, 1971–76; Reader, 1976–83. Science and Engineering Research Council: Chm., Chemistry Cttee, 1988–90; Mem., Science Bd, 1988–90; Mem., Council, 1990–94. Chm., Envmt Group, RSC, 1982–85. European Editor, BioSpectroscopy, 1994–2003; Mem., Editorial Bd, Biopolymers, 2004–06. *Publications:* (jtly) Inorganic Chemistry, 1965; (ed with R. J. H. Clark) Advances in Infrared and Raman Spectroscopy, 12 vols, 1975–85; (ed with R. J. H. Clark) Advances in Spectroscopy, 14 vols, 1986–98; (ed with R. M. Harrison) Issues in Environmental Science and Technology, 41 vols, 1994–2015; 350 research papers. *Recreations:* tennis, golf, ski-ing, travel. *Address:* Department of Chemistry, University of York, York YO10 5DD. *T:* (01904) 432557.

See also S. A. M. Hester.

HESTER, Stephen Alan Michael; Chief Executive, RSA Insurance Group, since 2014; *b* 14 Dec. 1960; one *s* one *d*. *Educ:* Lady Margaret Hall, Oxford (BA PPE). Credit Suisse First Boston, 1982–2001: various posts, including: Co-Hd, European Investment Banking, 1993–96; Mem. Exec. Bd, 1996–2001; Chief Financial Officer, 1996–2000; Hd, Fixed Income Div., 2000–01; Abbey National plc: Finance Dir, 2002; Chief Operating Officer, 2003–04; Chief Executive: British Land Co. plc, 2004–08; Royal Bank of Scotland Group plc, 2008–13. Non-exec. Dep. Chm., Northern Rock, 2008. *Recreations:* ski-ing, country sports, horticulture.

HETHERINGTON, Prof. Alistair MacCulloch, PhD; Melville Wills Professor of Botany, University of Bristol, since 2006; *b* Glasgow, 3 Feb. 1957; *s* of James Kilmurry Hetherington and Jessie Flora Hetherington (*née* McCulloch); *m* 1984, Nichola Jane Conolly; two *s* one *d*. *Educ:* Atholl Prep. Sch., Milngavie; Aberdour Primary Sch., Aberdour; Woodmill High Sch., Dunfermline; Univ. of St Andrews (BSc; PhD 1983). Res. Fellow, Univ. of Edinburgh, 1982–84; University of Lancaster: Lectr, 1984–91; Sen. Lectr, 1991–94; Prof., 1994–2006. Vis. Prof., UCD, 2004–; Hon. Prof., Tianjin Agricl Univ., China, 2009–; Christensen Vis. Fellow, St Catherine's Coll., Oxford, 2001–02; Vis. Fellow, Magdalen Coll., Oxford, 2013. Mem., Scientific Adv. Council, DEFRA, 2009–11. Chair, Integrative and Systems Biol. Strategy Cttee, BBSRC, 2010–14; Mem. Governing Council, Marine Biol Assoc. of UK, 2011–14. Trustee, New Phytologist Trust, 2006–; Dir (Trustee), Nat. Gdn of Wales, 2008–10. Ed. in Chief, New Phytologist, 2012–. *Publications:* (ed jtly) Post-translational Modifications in Plants, 1993; (ed with C. Grierson) Practical Systems Biology, 2007; contribs to scientific jls. *Recreation:* hill walking. *Address:* Life Sciences Building, University of Bristol, 24 Tyndall Avenue, Bristol BS8 1TQ. *T:* (0117) 394 1188. *E:* Alistair.Hetherington@bristol.ac.uk.

HETHERINGTON, Roger Rooke; His Honour Judge Hetherington; a Circuit Judge, since 2003; Resident Judge, Portsmouth and Newport (Isle of Wight) Crown Courts, since 2011; *b* 2 April 1951; *s* of Dr Stephen Hetherington and Jeanette Hetherington; *m* 1976, Charlotte Elizabeth Bourne; one *s* two *d*. *Educ:* Sherborne Sch.; Trinity Coll., Cambridge (BA Hons). Called to the Bar, Middle Temple, 1973; in practice as barrister, 1973–2003; Asst Recorder, Western Circuit, 1997–2000; Recorder, 2000–03. Hon. Recorder, City of Portsmouth, 2011–. *Recreations:* golf, National Hunt racing. *Address:* Portsmouth Combined Court Centre, Courts of Justice, Winston Churchill Avenue, Portsmouth PO1 2EB. *Clubs:* Royal Naval (Portsmouth); Huntercombe Golf.

HETHERINGTON, Stephen, PhD; Chairman, HQ Theatres Trust, since 2013 (Chairman, HQ Theatres, 2007–13); *b* 20 May 1949; *s* of Jack Hetherington and Constance Alice, (Billie), Hetherington (*née* Harper); three *d*. *Educ:* Northern Sch. of Music; Royal Acad. of Music; Warwick Univ. (MA); Birmingham Univ. (PhD 2014). Trumpeter, with symphony orchs, 1969–75. Formed Hetherington Seelig (with J. Seelig), 1981; Dir, Hetherington Seelig Theatres Ltd, 1981–2007: co. presented opera, ballet, theatre and music worldwide; consultant to govts and cultural instns; formed business plans for Lowry Project (Nat. Landmark Millennium Project for the Arts), 1995, Chief Exec., 1996–2001; led Birmingham CC's bid to become European Capital of Culture 2008; Chm., Southend's bid for city status as part of Queen's Jubilee celebrations, 2011–12. Founder and Trustee, OHMI Trust, 2011–. Hon. Fellow, Exeter Univ., 2013. *Recreations:* sailing, flying. *E:* stephen@hetherington.biz.

HEWES, Robin Anthony Charles; Chief Executive, New Millennium Experience Co., 2001 (Finance Director, 2000–01); *b* 15 April 1945; *s* of late Leslie Augustus Hewes and Lily Violet Hewes (*née* Norfolk); *m* 1967, Christine Diane Stonebridge; one *s* two *d*. *Educ:* Colchester Royal Grammar School; Bristol Univ. (LLB Hons 1966). Inspector of Taxes, 1966; Department of Industry, 1974; Cabinet Office (Management and Personnel Office), 1985–87; Dir, Enterprise and Deregulation Unit, DTI, 1987–88; Lloyd's of London: Head, later Dir, Regulatory Services, 1988–94 (nominated Member, Council of Lloyd's and Lloyd's Regulatory Bd, 1993–94); Dir, Finance and Mem., Lloyd's Mkt Bd, 1994–2000. Non-exec. Dir, Comforto-Vickers (formerly Vickers Business Equipment Div.), 1984–88. Hereditary Freeman, Bor. of Colchester, 1967. Lloyd's Silver Medal, 1996; Queen's Diamond Jubilee Medal, 2012. *Address:* 38 Plovers Mead, Wyatts Green, Brentwood, Essex CM15 0PS. *T:* (01277) 822891.

HEWETSON, Ven. Christopher; Archdeacon of Chester, 1994–2002, now Archdeacon Emeritus; *b* 1 June 1937; *s* of Edward and Mary Hewetson; *m* 1963, Alison Mary Croft; four *d*. *Educ:* Shrewsbury Sch.; Trinity Coll., Oxford (MA); Chichester Theol Coll. Assistant Master: Dragon Sch., Oxford, 1960–64 and 1966–67; The Craig, Windermere, 1964–66. Ordained deacon, 1969, priest, 1970; Assistant Curate: SS Peter and Paul, Leckhampton, 1969–71; All Saints, Wokingham, 1971–73; Vicar, St Peter's, Didcot, 1973–82; Rector, All Saints, Ascot Heath, 1982–90; Chaplain, St George's Sch., Ascot, 1985–88; RD, Bracknell, 1986–90; Priest i/c, Holy Trinity, Headington Quarry, 1990–94; Hon. Canon, Christ Church, Oxford, 1992–94; RD, Cowley, 1994. Mem., Chester Cath. Chapter, 2001–02. Bishop's Advr for Spirituality, dio. Exeter, 2003–07. *Address:* 1 Swan Hill Court, Shrewsbury SY1 1NP.

HEWETSON, Sir Christopher (Raynor), Kt 1984; TD 1967; DL; Partner, Lace Mawer (formerly Laces), Solicitors, Liverpool, 1961–95; President, Law Society, 1983–84; *b* 26 Dec. 1929; *s* of Harry Raynor Hewetson and Emma Hewetson; *m* 1962, Alison May Downie, *d* of late Prof. A. W. Downie, FRCP, FRS; two *s* one *d*. *Educ:* Sedbergh Sch.; Peterhouse, Cambridge (MA). National Service, 2nd Lieut 4th RHA, 1951–53; Territorial Service, 1953–68: Lt-Col commanding 359 Medium Regt, RA, TA, 1965–68. Qualified as solicitor, 1956. Mem. Council, Law Society, 1966–87; Vice-Pres., 1982–83; President, Liverpool Law Society, 1976. Gov., Coll. of Law, 1969–94 (Chm., 1977–82). Hon. Col, 33 Signal Regt (V), 1992–94. DL Merseyside, 1986, High Sheriff, Merseyside, 1998. *Recreations:* golf, walking, music. *Address:* 24c Westcliffe Road, Birkdale, Southport, Merseyside PR8 2BU. *T:* (01704) 567179. *Clubs:* Army and Navy; Athenæum (Pres., 1997–98) (Liverpool); Royal Birkdale Golf (Capt., 1993–94) (Southport).

HEWETT, Prof. Paul Charles, PhD; Professor of Observational Cosmology and Astrophysics, University of Cambridge, since 2007; Fellow of Corpus Christi College, Cambridge, since 1984; *b* London, 4 Dec. 1956; *s* of Henry Charles John Hewett and Iris Joyce Hewett. *Educ:* St Dunstan's Coll., Catford, London; Univ. of Edinburgh (BSc Astrophys 1979; PhD Astrophys 1983); Corpus Christi Coll., Cambridge (MA 1993). Institute of Astronomy, University of Cambridge: SERC Fellow, 1982–84; Res. Fellow, 1984–87; Royal Soc. Univ. Res. Fellow, 1987–90; Sen. Asst in Res., 1990–92; Asst Dir of Res., 1992–2000; John Couch Adams Astronomer, 1995–2000; Reader in Observational Astrophys, 2000–07; Dep. Dir, 2008–11; Dir, 2012–13. *Publications:* over 250 articles on cosmology and astrophys in learned jls. *Recreations:* reading, wine (Wine Steward, Corpus Christi College, Cambridge, 2000–). *Address:* Corpus Christi College, Cambridge CB2 1RH. *T:* (01223) 338000, *Fax:* (01223) 338061. *E:* phewett@ast.cam.ac.uk.

HEWETT, Sir Richard Mark John, 7th Bt *cr* 1813, of Nether Seale, Leicestershire; computer programmer; freelance website developer, since 2012; *b* 15 Nov. 1958; *er s* of Sir Peter John Smithson Hewett, 6th Bt, MM and of Jennifer Ann Cooper Hewett (*née* Jones); *S* father, 2001. *Educ:* Bradfield Coll.; Jesus Coll., Cambridge (BA Nat. Scis 1980). Career in geophysical software develt; Seismograph Service Ltd, 1980–91; Schlumberger Geco-Prakla, 1991–2000; WesternGeco, 2000–09. *Recreations:* filk music, SF, choral singing, folk harp, astronomy, amateur radio. *Heir: b* David Patrick John Hewett [*b* 24 June 1968; *m* 1997, Kate Elizabeth Ormand; two *s* one *d*]. *Address:* Orpington, Kent.

HEWETT, Major Richard William; Senior Vice President and Director, International Operations, Reader's Digest Association Inc., USA, 1986–88; *b* 22 Oct. 1923; *s* of late Brig. W. G. Hewett, OBE, MC and Bar, and Louise S. Hewett (*née* Wolfe); *m* 1954, Rosemary Cridland; two *d*. *Educ:* Wellington Coll., Berks. Enlisted RA, 1941; commnd RA, 1943; regular commn 1944: served Normandy, India, UK, Malaya (dispatches); regtl duty, Air OP, Instr, OCTU, Mons, 1947–54; flying duties, 1948–52; TA Adjt, City of Glasgow Artillery, 1952–53; sc 1955; Staff and regtl duties, Germany, 1956–59; Mil. Mission, USA, 1959–61. Joined Reader's Digest Assoc. Ltd, 1962; Dir 1976; Man. Dir, 1981–84; Chm. and Man. Dir, London, 1984–86. *Recreations:* tennis, fishing, travelling.

HEWISH, Prof. Antony, MA, PhD; FRS 1968; FInstP; Professor of Radioastronomy, University of Cambridge, 1971–89, now Emeritus (Reader, 1969–71); Fellow of Churchill College, since 1961; *b* 11 May 1924; *s* of late Ernest William Hewish and Frances Grace Lanyon Pinch; *m* 1950, Marjorie Elizabeth Catherine Richards; one *s* (one *d* decd). *Educ:* King's Coll., Taunton; Gonville and Caius Coll., Cambridge (BA 1948, MA 1950, PhD 1952; Hamilton Prize, Isaac Newton Student, 1952; Hon. Fellow, 1976). FInstP 1998. RAE Farnborough, 1943–46; Research Fellow, Gonville and Caius Coll., 1952–54; Asst Dir of Research, 1954–62; Fellow, Gonville and Caius Coll., 1955–61; Lectr in Physics, Univ. of Cambridge, 1962–69. Dir, Mullard Radio Astronomy Observatory, Cambridge, 1982–87. Visiting Prof. in Astronomy, Yale, 1963; Prof. of the Royal Instn, 1977; Vikram Sarabhai Prof., Physical Res. Lab., Ahmedabad, India, 1988. Lectures: Karl Schwarzschild, Bonn, 1971; Lindsay Meml, Maryland, 1972; Larmor, Cambridge, 1973; Harland, Exeter, 1974; Kelvin, IEE, 1975; Halley, Oxford, 1979; Selby, Cardiff, 1983; Krishnan Meml, New Delhi, 1989; Gold, Cornell, 1992; Saha Meml, Calcutta, 1993; Birla Meml, Hyderabad, 1993; Waynick Meml, Penn State, 2000. Fellow, Science Mus., London, 2009. MAE 1993. Foreign Mem., Belgian Royal Acad., 1990; Foreign Hon. Mem., Amer. Acad. of Arts and Sciences; Foreign Fellow, Indian Nat. Sci. Acad., 1982; Hon. Fellow: Instn of Electronics and Telecommunication Engrs, India, 1985; Tata Inst. of Fundamental Sci., Bombay, 1996. Hon. DSc: Leicester, 1976; Exeter, 1977; Manchester, 1989; Santa Maria, Brazil, 1989; Univ. Teknologi Malaysia, 1997; Hon. ScD Cambridge, 1996. Eddington Medal, Royal Astronomical Soc., 1969; Charles Vernon Boys Prize, Inst. of Physics and Physical Soc., 1970; Dellinger Gold Medal, Internat. Union of Radio Science, 1972; Michelson Medal, Franklin Inst., 1973; Hopkins Prize, Cambridge Phil Soc., 1973; Holweck Medal and Prize, Soc. Française de Physique, 1974; Nobel Prize for Physics (jtly), 1974; Hughes Medal, Royal Soc., 1977; Vainu Bappu Prize, Indian Nat. Sci. Acad., 1996. Hon. Citizen, Kwangju, S Korea, 1995. *Publications:* Papers in Proc. Royal Society, Phys. Soc., Mon. Not. Royal Astr. Soc., etc. *Recreations:* music, gardening, cliff-walking. *Address:* 1 Redwood Lodge, Grange Road, Cambridge CB3 9AR. *T:* (01223) 350736. *E:* ah120@mrao.cam.ac.uk.

HEWISON, Erica Jane; *see* Bolton, Erica J.

HEWISON, Prof. Robert Alwyn Petrie, DLitt; cultural historian; Theatre Critic, Sunday Times, since 1981; Professor of Cultural Policy and Leadership Studies, City University, 2006–12; *b* 2 June 1943; *s* of Robert John Petrie Hewison and Nancy Courtenay (*née* Henderson); *m* 1st, 1981, Jackie Staples (marr. diss. 1986); one *d*; 2nd, 1986, Erica Jane Bolton, *qv*; two *d*. *Educ:* Bedford Sch.; Ravensbourne Coll. of Art and Design; Brasenose Coll., Oxford (BA 1965; MA 1970; MLitt 1972; DLitt 1989). Grad. trainee, Southern Television, 1966; independent writer and critic, 1967–. Guest Curator: J. B. Speed Art Mus., Louisville, Ky, 1978; Museo Correr, Venice, 1983; Ashmolean Mus., Oxford, 1996; Tate Gall., London, 2000. Vis. Prof., De Montfort Univ., 1993–95; Prof. in Literary and Cultural Studies, 1995–2000, pt-time Prof., Dept of English, 2001, Hon. Prof., 2002, Univ. of Lancaster; Slade Prof. of Fine Art, Oxford Univ., 1999–2000. Associate Prod., film, Effie Gray, 2014. Mem., Writers' Guild of GB, 1968–. Associate, Demos think-tank, 2003–. *Publications:* John Ruskin: the argument of the eye, 1976; Under Siege: literary life in London 1939–45, 1977, rev. edn 1988; Ruskin and Venice, 1978; Irreverence, Scurrility, Profanity, Vilification and Licentious Abuse: Monty Python, the case against, 1981, 2nd edn 1990; (ed) New Approaches to Ruskin: 13 essays, 1981; In Anger: culture in the Cold War 1945–60, 1981, rev. edn 1988; (ed) The Ruskin Art Collection at Oxford: the rudimentary series, 1984; Footlights!: a hundred years of Cambridge comedy, 1986; The Heritage Industry: Britain in a climate of decline, 1987; Too Much: art and society in the Sixties 1960–75, 1988; Future Tense: a new art for the Nineties, 1990; Culture and Consensus: England, art and politics since 1940, 1995, rev. edn 1997; Ruskin and Oxford: the art of education, 1996; (ed) Ruskin's Artists: studies in the Victorian visual economy, 2000; (jtly) Ruskin, Turner and the Pre-Raphaelites, 2000; Ruskin's Venice, 2000; (with John Holden) Experience and Experiment: the UK branch of the Gulbenkian Foundation 1956–2006, 2006; John Ruskin, 2007; Ruskin on Venice: 'The

Paradise of Cities', 2009; John Byrne: art and life, 2011; (with John Holden) The Cultural Leadership Handbook, 2011; (with Chris Orr) Chris Orr: the making of things, 2013; Cultural Capital: the rise and fall of creative Britain, 2014. *Recreation:* gardening. *Address:* 120 The Vale, Acton Park, W3 7JT.

HEWITT, family name of **Viscount Lifford**.

HEWITT, (Alison) Claire; Head Mistress, Manchester High School for Girls, since 2009; *b* Barnsley, 1964; *d* of Jack Thickett and Una Thickett; *m* 1987, Richard Hewitt. *Educ:* Wakefield Girls' High Sch.; Sheffield Univ. (BSc Chem. 1985; PGCE 1986; NPQH 2004). Chemistry teacher, Harrogate Ladies' Coll., 1986–91; Hd of Chemistry, Fulneck Sch., 1991–94; Hd of Chemistry, then Dir of Studies, later Dep. Hd, Sheffield High Sch., 1994–2005; Headteacher, King Edward VI Grammar Sch., Louth, 2005–08. *Recreations:* walking, cycling, puzzles, listening to a wide range of classical and contemporary music. *Address:* Manchester High School for Girls, Grangethorpe Road, Manchester M14 6HS. *T:* (0161) 224 0447, *Fax:* (0161) 224 6192. *E:* admin@mhsg.manchester.sch.uk.

HEWITT, Angela Mary, OC 2000; OBE 2006; FRSC 2006; concert pianist; Artistic Director, Trasimeno Music Festival, since 2005; *b* 26 July 1958; *d* of Godfrey Hewitt and Marion Hewitt (*née* Hogg). *Educ:* Royal Conservatory of Music, Toronto (ARCT 1972); Univ. of Ottawa (BMus 1977). First recital at age 9; American début, Kennedy Center, Washington, 1976; Wigmore Hall début, 1985; Proms début, 1990; recitals and concerto appearances throughout N America, Europe, Far East, Australia, NZ, Mexico, etc; numerous radio and TV broadcasts, UK and overseas; has made numerous recordings, incl. all the major keyboard works of J. S. Bach. Winner of competitions, in N America and Europe, incl. First Prize, Toronto Internat. Bach Piano Comp., 1985. Hon. Fellow, Peterhouse, Cambridge, 2014. Hon. DMus Ottawa, 1995; Hon. LLD: Queen's, Kingston, 2002; Toronto, 2009; DUniv Open, 2006. Juno Award, Canada, for Best Instrumental Recording of Year, 1999, 2001, 2004; Governor Gen.'s Award for Performing Arts, Canada, 2002; Listeners' Award, BBC Radio 3, 2003; Artist of the Year, Gramophone Awards, 2006; Instrumentalist of the Year, MIDEM, Cannes, 2010. *Recreations:* travelling, cooking wheat-free meals, seeing friends. *Address:* c/o HarrisonParrott, 5–6 Albion Court, Albion Place, W6 0QT. *T:* (020) 7313 3502, *Fax:* (020) 7221 5042. *E:* info@harrisonparrott.co.uk.

HEWITT, Prof. (Brian) George, PhD; FBA 1997; Professor of Caucasian Languages, School of Oriental and African Studies, London University, since 1996; *b* 11 Nov. 1949; *s* of late Thomas Douglas Hewitt and Joan (*née* Cousins); *m* 1976, Zaira Kiazimovna Khiba; two *d*. *Educ:* Doncaster Grammar Sch. for Boys; St John's Coll., Cambridge (BA 1972; Dip. in Linguistics 1973; MA 1976; PhD 1982). Open Henry Arthur Thomas Schol. in Classics, 1969–72; John Stewart of Rannoch Univ. Schol. and Coll. Graves Prize, 1971; Warr Classical Student, 1972–73; British Council Exchange Postgrad. Student, Tbilisi, Georgia, 1975–76, 1979–80; Marjory Wardrop Scholar for Georgian Studies, 1978–81. Lectr in Linguistics, Hull Univ., 1981–88; Lectr in Linguistics and Caucasian Langs, 1988–92, Reader in Caucasian Langs, 1992–96, SOAS. Member, Editorial Board: Revue des Etudes Géorgiennes et Caucasiennes, 1985–; Central Asian Survey, 1993–2015. Mem. Council, Philological Soc., 1985–90; First Pres., Societas Caucasologica Europaea, 1986–88 and 1988–90. Hon. Rep. for Republic of Abkhazia in UK, 1993–. Hon. Member: Internat. Cherkess Acad. of Scis, 1997–; Abkhazian Acad. of Scis, 1997; Writers' Union of Abkhazia, 2003–. Mem. Bd of Managers, Marjory Wardrop Fund, Oxford, 1983–. Honour and Glory of Abkhazia Medal, 2004; Medal for Services, Foreign Ministry of Abkhazia, 2013. *Publications:* Lingua Descriptive Studies 2: Abkhaz, 1979; Typology of Subordination in Georgian and Abkhaz, 1987; (ed and contrib.) Indigenous Languages of the Caucasus 2: North West Caucasus, 1989; (ed and contrib.) Caucasian Perspectives, 1992; (ed and contrib. jtly) Subject, Voice and Ergativity: selected essays, 1995; Georgian: a learner's grammar, 1995, 2nd edn 2005; Georgian: a structural reference grammar, 1995; A Georgian Reader, 1996; (with Zaira Khiba) Abkhaz Newspaper Reader (with supplements), 1998; (ed and contrib.) The Abkhazians: a handbook, 1998; The Languages of the Caucasus: scope for study and survival (inaugural lecture), 1998; Introduction to the Study of the Languages of the Caucasus, 2004; Abkhazian Folktales, 2005; (with Zurab Dzhopua) Pages from Abkhazian Folklore, 2008; Abkhaz: a comprehensive self-tutor, 2010; Discordant Neighbours: a reassessment of the Georgian-Abkhazian and Georgian-South Ossetian conflicts, 2013; articles on Caucasian langs and politics in encycs, Central Asian Survey, Bedi Kartlisa, Revue des Etudes Géorgiennes et Caucasiennes and online, incl. www.opendemocracy.net. *Recreation:* classical music. *Address:* Department of Near and Middle East, School of Oriental and African Studies, Thornhaugh Street, Russell Square, WC1H 0XG. *T:* (020) 7898 4332. *E:* gh2@soas.ac.uk.

HEWITT, Prof. (Charles) Nicholas, PhD; CSci; FRSC; CChem; Professor of Atmospheric Chemistry, Lancaster University, since 1993; *b* 23 Sept. 1953; *s* of Peter Hewitt and Amanda Hewitt (*née* Rodwell); *m*; one *s* one *d*. *Educ:* Queen Elizabeth's Grammar Sch. for Boys, Barnet; Lancaster Univ. (BA 1976; PhD 1985). CChem 1985. Lancaster University: New-Blood Lectr, 1985–91; Sen. Lectr, 1991–93; Hd, Dept of Envmtl Scis, 1996–99. Vis. Fellow and Fulbright Schol., Univ. of Colo, Boulder, 1988–89; Vis. Scientist, Nat. Center for Atmospheric Res., Boulder, Colo, 1994–95, 2010. Member: Photochemical Oxidant Rev. Gp, DoE, 1991–99; Scientific Steering Cttee, Eurotrac-2 (a Eureka project), 1996–2002. Chm., Envmtl Chemistry Gp, RSC, 1996–98. Wolfson Res. Merit Award, Royal Soc., 2010. *Publications:* Instrumental Analysis of Pollutants, 1991; Methods of Environmental Data Analysis, 1992; (with W. T. Sturges) Global Atmospheric Chemical Change, 1993; (with G. Davison) Air Pollution in the United Kingdom, 1997; Reactive Hydrocarbons in the Atmosphere, 1999; (with A. Jackson) Handbook of Atmospheric Science, 2003; (with A. Jackson) Atmospheric Science for Environmental Scientists, 2009; numerous articles in learned jls. *Recreation:* being outdoors. *Address:* Lancaster Environment Centre, Lancaster University, Lancaster LA1 4YQ. *T:* (01524) 593931.

HEWITT, Claire; *see* Hewitt, A. C.

HEWITT, Sir (Cyrus) Lenox (Simson), Kt 1971; OBE 1963; company chairman and director; *b* 7 May 1917; *s* of Cyrus Lenox Hewitt and Ella Louise Hewitt; *m* 1943, Alison Hope (*née* Tillyard) (*d* 2011); one *s* two *d* (and one *d* decd). *Educ:* Scotch Coll., Melbourne; Melbourne Univ. (BCom). FCPA, FCIS, LCA. Broken Hill Proprietary Co. Ltd, 1933–46; Asst Sec., Commonwealth Prices Br., Canberra, 1939–46; Economist, Dept of Post War Reconstruction, 1946–49; Official Sec. and Actg Dep. High Comr, London, 1950–53; Commonwealth Treasury: Asst Sec., 1953–55; 1st Asst Sec., 1955–62; Dep. Sec., 1962–66; Chm., Australian Univs Commn, 1967; Secretary to: Prime Minister's Dept, 1968–71; Dept of the Environment, Aborigines and the Arts, 1971–72; Dept of Minerals and Energy, 1972–75. Lectr, Econs and Cost Accountancy, Canberra UC, 1940–49, 1954. Acting Chairman: Pipeline Authority, 1973–75; Petroleum and Minerals Authority, 1974–75; Chairman: Qantas Airways Ltd, 1975–80 (Dir, 1973–80); Qantas Wentworth Hldgs Ltd, 1975–80; QH Tours Ltd, 1975–80 (Dir, 1974–80); Petroleum and Minerals Co. of Aust. Pty Ltd, 1975; Austmark Internat. Ltd, 1983–88; Northern Mining Corp. NL, 1984–85; State Rail Authority of NSW, 1985–88; Director: East/Aust. Pipeline Corp. Ltd, 1974–75; Mary Kathleen Uranium Ltd, 1975–80; Aust. Industry Develt Corp., 1975; Santos Ltd, 1981–82; Pontello Constructions Ltd, 1980–82; Aberfoyle Ltd, 1981–89; Endeavour Resources Ltd, 1982–86; Ansett Transport Industries Ltd, 1982–88; Short Brothers (Australia) Ltd, 1981–91; Airship Industries PLC, 1984–88; Qintex Australia Ltd, 1985–90; British Midland Airways (Australia) Pty Ltd, 1985; Universal Telecasters Securities Ltd, 1986–90; Mirage Management Ltd, 1986–91; Qintex Ltd, 1987–90; Qintex America Ltd, 1987–90; Fortis Pacific Aviation Ltd, 1987–2001; Fortis Aviation Group Ltd, 1988–2001. Dep. Chm., Aust. Atomic Energy Commn, 1972–77; Chairman: Exec. Cttee, IATA, 1976–77 (Mem., 1975–80); Orient Airlines Assoc., 1977; State Rail Authority of NSW, 1985–88; Mem., Judicial Commn of NSW, 1986–89. *Address:* (office) Level 1, 70 Pitt Street, Sydney, NSW 2000, Australia. *T:* (2) 92313233. *Clubs:* Brooks's; Melbourne (Melbourne); Union (Sydney).

See also Rt Hon. P. H. Hewitt.

HEWITT, Prof. David Sword, PhD; FRSE; Regius Professor of English Literature, University of Aberdeen, 2007–08, now Professor Emeritus; *b* 22 April 1942; *s* of Rev. George Hewitt and Elisabeth Hewitt; *m* 1967, Angela Williams; one *s* one *d*. *Educ:* Melrose Grammar Sch.; George Watson's Coll.; Univ. of Edinburgh (MA 1964); Univ. of Aberdeen (PhD 1969). University of Aberdeen: Asst Lectr, Lectr, Sen. Lectr, then Reader in English, 1964–94; Prof. of Scottish Literature, 1994–2007. Treas., Assoc. of Scottish Literary Studies, 1972–96. Elder, 1969–, Session Clerk, 2001–13, Cathedral Church of St Machar, Old Aberdeen. FRSE 1990; FEA 1996. Pres., Edinburgh Sir Walter Scott Club, 1988–89. Ed.-in-Chief, Edinburgh Edition of the Waverley Novels, 1987–2012; Man. Ed., Clarendon Dickens, 2014–. *Publications:* (ed) Scott on Himself, 1981; editions of Scott novels: The Antiquary, 1995; (jtly) Redgauntlet, 1997; (jtly) The Heart of Midlothian, 2004; Rob Roy, 2007; contrib. Oxford DNB. *Recreations:* listening to classical music and opera, visiting churches and art galleries, literature and drama. *Address:* 21 Ferryhill Place, Aberdeen AB11 7SE. *T:* (01224) 580834. *E:* david.hewitt@abdn.ac.uk.

HEWITT, Francis Anthony; Chairman, Northern Ireland Science Park, since 2008; Northern Ireland Chair, Big Lottery Fund, since 2009; *b* 1 July 1943; *s* of Joseph and Mary Hewitt; *m* 1st, 1968, Carol Burch; two *d*; 2nd, 2003, Wendy Austin. *Educ:* Queen's Univ., Belfast (BScEcon). FCIM. NI Min. of Agriculture, 1961–63; HM Customs and Excise, 1963–72; NI Min. of Commerce Rep. in W Germany, 1973–78; NI Dept of Commerce, 1978–82; HM Consulate-Gen., LA, 1982–84; Industrial Development Board for Northern Ireland: Exec. Dir, Marketing, 1984–88; Dep. Chief Exec., 1988–96; Chief Exec., NI Growth Challenge, 1996–2000; Dep. Perm. Sec., NI Dept of Culture, Arts and Leisure, 2000–02; Chief Exec., NI Chamber of Commerce, 2002–08; Mem., NI Legal Services Commn, 2003–06. Non-exec. Dir, Invest Northern Ireland, 2008–. Member Board: Ilex Urban Regeneration Co., 2010–; Strategic Investment Bd for NI, 2010–. Trustee, Grand Opera Hse, Belfast, 2007–09. Hon. Consul, Federal Republic of Germany, 2002–. Cross of Order of Merit (Germany), 2011. *Recreations:* music, walking, gun dogs, classic cars.

HEWITT, Gavin Wallace, CMG 1995; Chief Executive, Scotch Whisky Association, 2003–13; Director, Bladnoch Distillery Ltd, since 2015; Director, Scotch Malt Whisky Society, since 2015; *b* 19 Oct. 1944; *s* of George Burrill and Elisabeth Murray Hewitt; *m* 1st, 1973, Heather Mary Clayton (marr. diss. 2009); two *s* two *d*; 2nd, 2015, Amanda Harvie, *qv*. *Educ:* George Watson's Coll., Edinburgh; Edinburgh Univ. (MA). Min. of Transport, 1967–70; on secondment from MoT as Third, later Second, Sec. to UK Delegn, EEC, Brussels, 1970–72; FCO, 1972–73; First Sec., British High Commn, Canberra, 1973–78; FCO, 1978–81; First Sec. and Head of Chancery, HM Embassy, Belgrade, 1981–84; Mem., Jt FCO/BBC Review Gp, BBC External Services, 1984; Counsellor on loan to Home Civil Service, 1984–87; Counsellor, Head of Chancery and Dep. Perm. Rep., UK Mission to UN, Geneva, 1987–91; Head, SE Asia Dept, FCO, 1992–94; Ambassador: to Croatia, 1994–97; to Finland, 1997–2000; to Belgium, 2001–03. Member: Exec., Scottish Council Develt and Industry, 2004–14; Exec. Gp, Scotland Food and Drink, 2008–13; Food and Drink Leadership Forum, 2008–10; Internat. Adv. Bd, Asia Scotland Inst., 2013–. Pres., spiritsEUROPE (formerly Eur. Spirits Orgn), 2011–13. Member: Bd of Geneva English Sch., 1989–91 (Vice-Chm., 1990–91); Gen. Convocation, Heriot-Watt Univ., 2005–11; Patron, British Sch. of Brussels, 2001–03. Keeper of the Quaich, 2009. Liveryman, Distillers' Co., 2014–. *Recreations:* music, tinkering, walking.

HEWITT, Prof. Geoffrey Frederick, FRS 1989; FREng; Courtaulds Professor of Chemical Engineering, 1993–99, now Emeritus, and Senior Research Fellow, since 1999, Imperial College of Science, Technology and Medicine (Professor of Chemical Engineering, 1985–93); *b* 3 Jan. 1934; *s* of Frederick and Elaine Hewitt; *m* 1956, Shirley Foulds; two *d*. *Educ:* Boteler Grammar School, Warrington; UMIST (BScTech, PhD). CEng, FREng (FEng 1984); FIMechE, FIChemE, CChem, FRSC. Scientist, Group Leader, Div. Head, Harwell Lab., specialising in heat transfer and fluid flow in multiphase systems, 1957–90. Pres., IChemE, 1989–90. Foreign Associate, US Nat. Acad. Engrg, 1998. FCGI. Hon. DSc: Louvain, 1988; UMIST, 1998; Hon. DEng Heriot-Watt, 1995. Max Jakob Award, ASME, 1995; Nusselt-Reynolds Prize, Assembly of World Conf. on Exptl Heat Transfer, Fluid Mechs and Thermodyns, 1997; Senior Multiphase Flow Award, 2007; Global Energy Prize, 2007. *Publications:* (with N. S. Hall Taylor) Annular Two Phase Flow, 1970; (co-author) Two Phase Flow, 1973; Measurement of Two Phase Flow Parameters, 1978; (with J. G. Collier) Introduction to Nuclear Power, 1986, 2nd edn 2000; (jtly) Process Heat Transfer, 1994; (ed) International Encyclopedia of Heat and Mass Transfer, 1997; (with G. Falcone) Multiphase Flow Metering, 2009; contribs to books, numerous papers. *Recreations:* bridge, music. *Address:* Department of Chemical Engineering, Imperial College London, Prince Consort Road, SW7 2BY. *T:* (020) 7589 5111.

HEWITT, George; *see* Hewitt, B. G.

HEWITT, Guy Arlington Kenneth; High Commissioner for Barbados in the United Kingdom, since 2014; *b* London, 1967; *s* of Radcliffe and Elaine Hewitt; *m* 1995, Michelle Kirton; one *s* one *d*. *Educ:* Univ. of W Indies (BSc Hons Sociol. and Pol Sci.; MSc Develt Studies); Univ. of Kent (Postgrad. DipTh). Prog. Coordinator, Caribbean Policy Develt Centre, 1993–95; Advr, Commonwealth Secretariat, 1995–2003; Dir, Caribbean Exams Council, 2003–10; Caribbean Manager, City & Guilds Inst., 2010–14. Chm. Bd, Queen Elizabeth Hosp., 2009–11. Dep. Chm., Barbados Vocational Trng Bd, 2010–14. Ordained Minister of Religion, 2015. *Publications:* Gender Budgets Make Cents, 2001; Gender Budgets Make More Cents, 2002; Engendering Budgets, 2003. *Recreations:* gardening, scuba diving, volunteering. *Address:* Barbados High Commission, 1 Great Russell Street, WC1B 3ND. *T:* (020) 7299 7150, *Fax:* (020) 7323 6872. *E:* london@foreign.gov.bb. *Clubs:* Rotary, Kent.

HEWITT, Sir Lenox; *see* Hewitt, Sir C. L. S.

HEWITT, Martin James, QPM 2014; Assistant Commissioner, Metropolitan Police Service, since 2014; *b* London, 23 March 1966; *s* of Graham and Maureen Hewitt; *m* 2007, Louise Philpott; two *s* two *d*. *Educ:* Salesian Coll., Battersea; Royal Mil. Acad. Sandhurst; Univ. of Leicester (Postgrad. Dip. Criminal Justice Studies 2000). Commnd RA, 1987; served RA, 1987–93. Police Officer, Kent Police, 1993–2005; Metropolitan Police Service: Detective Chief Superintendent, 2005–09; Comdr, Organised Crime, 2009–12; Dep. Asst Comr, 2012–14. Associate Fellow, RUSI, 2012–. Vice Chair, Nat. Police Chiefs' Council, 2015–. Chm., Metropolitan Police Amateur Boxing Club, 2011–. *Recreations:* trying to keep ahead of four kids, two dogs and a tortoise, reading military history, keeping fit, cinema, watching and talking about Rugby and American football. *Address:* Metropolitan Police Service, New Scotland Yard, 10 Broadway, SW1H 0BG. *T:* (020) 7230 2422. *E:* martin.hewitt@met.police.uk.

HEWITT, Michael Earling; central banking and financial markets consultant; *b* 28 March 1936; *s* of late Herbert Erland Hewitt and Dorothy Amelia Hewitt; *m* 1st, 1961, Elizabeth Mary Hughes Batchelor (marr. diss. 2000); one *s* one *d*; 2nd, 2004, Galina Andreevna Utkina (marr. diss. 2008); 3rd, 2012, Olga Dolgova. *Educ:* Christ's Hospital; Merton College, Oxford

(Chancellor's Prize for Latin Prose, 1958; MA (Modern Hist.)); BSc Econ London. Bank of England, 1961–94: Economic Adviser, Govt of Bermuda, 1970–74; Financial Forecaster, 1976–78; Adviser, Financial Instns, 1981–83; Head of Financial Supervision, Gen. Div., 1984–87; Head of Finance and Industry Area, 1987–88; Senior Advr, Finance and Industry, 1988–90; Dir of Central Banking Studies, 1990–94; Project Manager (IMF), EC Technical Assistance for CIS Trng Prog. for Central Bank of Russian Fedn, 1994–99, and Nat. Bank of Ukraine, 1997–98; Resident Advr, Egyptian Capital Mkt Authy, 2000–02; Expert: Banking Sector Reform Project, Macedonia, 2003–04; Accounting Reform Project, Nat. Bank of Romania, 2006; Strengthening Financial Sector of Ukraine Project, 2008–10; Evaluation of banking sector support prog., Syria, 2011; Advr to Gov., Nat. Bank of Macedonia, 2004–05. Chm., OECD Gp of Experts on Systemic Risks in Securities Markets, 1988–90. *Recreations:* chess, wine, travel. *Address:* Villiers Lodge, 5A Villiers Road, Southsea, Hants PO5 2HG.

HEWITT, Nicholas; *see* Hewitt, C. N.

HEWITT, Sir Nicholas Charles Joseph, 3rd Bt *cr* 1921; *b* 12 Nov. 1947; *s* of Sir Joseph Hewitt, 2nd Bt and Marguerite, *yr d* of Charles Burgess; *S* father, 1973; *m* 1969, Pamela Margaret, *o d* of Geoffrey J. M. Hunt, TD; two *s* one *d*. *Heir: s* Charles Edward James Hewitt [*b* 15 Nov. 1970; *m* 2002, Alison, *d* of Peter Brown, Hobart, Tas; one *s*]. *Address:* Colswayn House, Huttons Ambo, Yorks YO60 7HJ. *T:* (01653) 696557.

HEWITT, Rt Hon. Patricia Hope; PC 2001; Chair, UK India Business Council, since 2009; *b* 2 Dec. 1948; *d* of Sir (Cyrus) Lenox (Simson) Hewitt, *qv*, and late Alison Hope Hewitt; *m* 1981, William Jack Birtles, *qv*; one *s* one *d*. *Educ:* C of E Girls' Grammar Sch., Canberra; Australian Nat. Univ.; Newnham Coll., Cambridge (MA). MA Oxon; AMusA (piano). Public Relations Officer, Age Concern (Nat. Old People's Welfare Council), 1971–73; Women's Rights Officer, Nat. Council for Civil Liberties, 1973–74, Gen. Secretary 1974–83; Press and Broadcasting Sec., 1983–88, Policy Co-ordinator, 1988–89, to Leader of Opposition; Sen. Res. Fellow, 1989, Dep. Dir, 1989–94, Inst. for Public Policy Res.; Head, then Dir, of Research, Andersen Consulting, 1994–97. Non-executive Director: BT Gp plc, 2008–14 (Sen. Ind. Dir, 2009–14); Eurotunnel, 2010–; Bupa, 2013–14; Mem., Adv. Cttee, Barclays Asia Pacific, 2009–12; Mem., Global Adv. Bd, Sutherland Global Services, 2012–; Sen. Advr, FTI Consulting, 2015–. Associate, Newnham Coll., Cambridge, 1984–97 (Hon. Associate, 2013–); Vis. Fellow, Nuffield Coll., Oxford, 1992–2001. Dep. Chair, Commn on Social Justice, 1993–95; Vice-Chairman: Healthcare 2000, 1995–96; British Council, 1997–98. Contested (Lab) Leicester E, 1983. MP (Lab) Leicester W, 1997–2010. Economic Sec., HM Treasury, 1998–99; Minister of State, DTI, 1999–2001; Sec. of State for Trade and Industry, and Minister for Women, 2001–05; Sec. of State for Health, 2005–07. Mem., Select Cttee on Social Security, 1997–98. Member: Asia Task Force, 2009–14; UK India Round Table, 2009–. Chair, Katha Children's Trust, 2011–. FRSA 1992. *Publications:* Your Rights (Age Concern), 1973; Rights for Women (NCCL), 1975; Civil Liberties, the NCCL Guide (co-ed 3rd edn), 1977; The Privacy Report (NCCL), 1977; Your Rights at Work (NCCL), 1978, 2nd edn 1981; The Abuse of Power, 1981; (jtly) Your Second Baby, 1990; About Time: the revolution in work and family life, 1993. *Recreations:* reading, theatre, music, gardening. *Address:* UK India Business Council, 12th Floor, Millbank Tower, 21–24 Millbank, SW1P 4QP. *T:* (020) 7592 3040. *E:* patricia.hewitt@ukibc.com.

HEWITT, Penelope Ann, CBE 2003; Senior District Judge (Chief Magistrate), Bow Street Magistrates' Court, 2000–03; *b* 4 May 1932; *d* of late William Mottershead, JP, MB ChB and Eileen Mottershead; *m* 1954, Peter Nisbet Hewitt; one *s* two *d*. *Educ:* Howell's Sch., Denbigh; BA Open Univ., 1975. Called to the Bar, Gray's Inn, 1978, Bencher, 2001; in practice, Liverpool, 1978–90; Mem., Northern Circuit; District Judge (Magistrates' Courts) (formerly Stipendiary Magistrate), Leeds, 1990–2000. Lay Chm., Bolton Deanery Synod, 1984–90. Member: British Acad. of Forensic Scis, 1979–2005; Magisterial Cttee, Judicial Studies Bd, 1993–98. JP Bolton, 1968–90. *Recreations:* music, reading, opera, embroidery.

HEWITT, Peter John, CBE 2008; Chief Executive, Guy's and St Thomas' Charity, since 2009; *b* 17 Nov. 1951; *m* 1st, 1977, Joan Coventry (marr. diss. 1999); three *d*; 2nd, 2013, Dr Judith Bell. *Educ:* Barnard Castle Sch.; Leeds Univ. (BA, MA). Inter-action, Kentish Town, 1976; Arts Officer, N Tyneside MBC, 1977–82; Northern Arts, 1982–97 (Chief Exec., 1992–97); Corporate Affairs Dir, Tees HA, 1997–98; Chief Exec., Arts Council of England, later Arts Council England, 1998–2008. *Recreations:* arts, walking, cycling. *Address:* Guy's and St Thomas' Charity, Francis House, King's Head Yard, SE1 1NA.

HEWITT, Sarah Louise; *see* Singleton, S. L.

HEWITT, Sheila Iffat; JP; Regional Chairman, Eastern and Southern Areas, Legal Services Commission (formerly Legal Aid Board), 1998–2004; *b* Pakistan, 6 Oct. 1952; *m* 1973, Anthony Hewitt; two *s*. *Educ:* London Sch. of Econs and Pol Sci. (BSc Econ). ACIB 1975. Member: London Rent Assessment Panel, 1985–2002; Immigration Appeals Tribunal, 1992–; Appeal Tribunal Competition Commn, 2000–10; Ind. Assessor, OCPA, 2000–. Mem., Radio Authority, 1998–2003. Non-exec. Bd Mem., Mid Surrey HA, 1992–95; Chm., Surrey Heartlands NHS Trust, 1995–98. Member: GMC, 2001–11; Fitness to Practise Panel, NMC, 2008–. JP Surrey, 1987. *Recreations:* mountain trekking, tennis. *Address:* Calderwood, Wilmerhatch Lane, Epsom, Surrey KT18 7EH. *T:* (01372) 273730. *Club:* Royal Automobile.

HEWLETT, Rev. David Jonathon Peter, PhD; Principal, Queen's Foundation for Ecumenical Theological Education, since 2003; *b* 8 Feb. 1957; *s* of Vincent and late Daphne Hewlett; *m* 1978, Penelope Skilton; three *s* one *d*. *Educ:* Durham Univ. (BA 1st cl. Hons 1979; PhD 1984). Ordained deacon, 1983, priest, 1984; Asst Curate, St James, New Barnet, 1983–86; Lectr in Systematic Theol., C of I Theol Coll., Dublin, and TCD, 1986–90; Jt Dir, SW Ministry Trng Course, and Priest i/c, Feock, Dio. of Truro, 1990–95; Principal, SW Ministry Trng Course, 1995–2003. Hon. Fellow, Dept of Theol., Exeter Univ., 1995–2003. Hon. Canon. Birmingham Cathedral, 2014–. *Recreation:* music. *Address:* Queen's Foundation for Ecumenical Theological Education, Somerset Road, Edgbaston, Birmingham B15 2QH. *T:* (0121) 454 1527, *Fax:* (0121) 454 8171. *E:* d.hewlett@queens.ac.uk.

HEWLETT, Stephen Edward; writer, broadcaster and media consultant; Managing Director: Big Pictures Ltd; Genie Pictures; *b* 8 Aug. 1958; *s* of Lawrence Edward Hewlett and Vera Mary Hewlett; partner, Karole Anne Lange; three *s*. *Educ:* Harold Malley Grammar Sch. for Boys, Solihull; Solihull Sixth Form Coll.; Univ. of Manchester (BSc Hons Liberal Studies in Sci. 1981). Researcher, Panorama, Nationwide and Watchdog, BBC, 1981–82; Producer and Dir, Diverse Reports and The Friday Alternative, Channel 4, 1982–87; BBC: Producer: Brass Tacks, 1987–88; Taking Liberties, 1988–90; Inside Story, 1990–92; Exec. Producer, Children's Hosp., The Skipper, Rough Justice, States of Terror, The Diamond Empire, 25 Bloody Years and The Dead (Best Single Documentary Award, RTS, 1994), 1992–94; Ed., Inside Story, 1992–94 (Best Single Documentary Award, BAFTA, 1994); Ed., Panorama and Exec. Ed., Special Projects, 1995–97; Hd, Factual Programmes, Channel 4, 1997–98; Dir of Progs, Carlton TV, 1998–2004; Man. Dir, Carlton Prodns, 2001–04. Non-exec. Dir, Tiger Aspect TV, 2004–07. Presenter, The Media Show, BBC Radio 4; Columnist, Guardian. Gov., Sir John Lawes Sch., Harpenden, 2003–13. FRTS 2002. Hon. MA Salford, 1999. Interview of Year and Journalist of Year Awards, RTS, 1995. *Recreations:* cricket, swimming, sailing (occasionally), Rugby Union refereeing. *E:* steve.hewlett1@btinternet.com.

HEWLETT-DAVIES, Mrs Janet Mary; journalist; public affairs consultant; *b* 13 May 1938; *d* of Frederick Charles and Margaret Ellen Hewlett; *m* 1964, Barry Davies. *Educ:* King Edward VI High School for Girls, Birmingham. Journalist, West Midlands 1956–59; BBC, 1959–65; Films Division, Central Office of Information, 1966–67; Press Officer: Prime Minister's Office, 1967–72; HM Customs and Excise, 1972–73; Principal Information Officer, Dept of Trade and Industry, 1973–74; Dep. Chief Press Secretary to Prime Minister, 1974–76; Head of Information, Dept of Transport, 1976–79; Director of Information: DoE, 1979–82; DHSS, 1982–86; Dir of Public Affairs, Pergamon, BPCC and Mirror Gp of Cos, 1986–87. Vice-Chm., WHO Working Gp on Information and Health, 1983. *Recreations:* Shakespeare's Globe, Brighton, acting. *Address:* 44 Sussex Square, Brighton BN2 1GE. *T:* (01273) 693792. *Club:* Reform.

HEWSON, (Charles) Andrew (Dale); Chairman, Johnson & Alcock Ltd, authors' agents, since 2003; *b* Tyrringham, N Bucks, 30 Dec. 1942; *s* of George Dale Hewson and Irene Hewson (*née* Richardson); *m* 1st, 1969, Margaret Cumming Watson (*d* 2002); one *d*; 2nd, 2012, Carmela Margery Bromhead; one step *s*. *Educ:* Bury Lawn Kindergarten, Newport Pagnell; St Stephen's Prep. Sch., Dundrum; Angusfield House Prep. Sch., Edinburgh; Trinity Coll., Glenalmond; Univ. of St Andrews (MA Hons). Front of House and Box Office Manager, Newcastle Playhouse, 1967–68; Agent, 1969–77, Man. Dir/Sole Proprietor, 1977–2003, John Johnson Ltd (merged with Michael Alcock Mgt, 2003). Trustee, Fenton Arts Trust, 2005–12. *Recreations:* early morning swimming, hill walking in good boots, gardening in challenging French terrain, the arts, food for free, my grandchildren. *Address:* 62 Thornhill Road, N1 1JU. *T:* (020) 7607 2108; Roquedur le Haut, Sumène, 30440 Gard, France. *T:* (4) 67825911. *E:* andrew@johnsonandalcock.co.uk. *Clubs:* Garrick, Groucho.

HEWSON, John Robert, AM 2001; PhD; investment banker and company director; *b* 28 Oct. 1946; *s* of Donald Hewson and late Eileen Isabella Hewson (*née* Tippett); *m* 1st, Margaret; two *s* one *d*; 2nd, 1988, Carolyn Judith Somerville; one *d*; 3rd, 2007, Jessica Wilson. *Educ:* Univ. of Sydney (BEc Hons); Univ. of Saskatchewan (MA 1969); Johns Hopkins Univ. (MA, PhD 1971). Economist, IMF, 1971–74; Res. Economist, Reserve Bank of Australia, 1976; Economic Advr to Fed. Treas., 1976–82; University of New South Wales: Prof. of Econs, 1978–87; Head, Sch. of Econs, 1983–86; Dir, Japanese Econs Management Studies Centre, 1984–87. Dir, Macquarie Bank, 1985–87. MP (L) Wentworth, NSW, 1987–95; Shadow Minister for Finance, 1988–89; Shadow Treas., 1989–90; Leader of the Opposition, Australian Parlt, 1990–94; Shadow Minister for Industry, Commerce, Infrastructure and Customs, 1994–95. Prof. of Mgt and Dean, Macquarie Grad. Sch. of Mgt, 2002–04. Chairman: John Hewson Gp Pty Ltd, 1995–; Gold and Resources Develt Ltd, 1996–98 (Dir, 2000–04); Australian Bus Manufacturing Co., 1999–; Universal Bus Co. Pty Ltd, 2000–; Global Renewables Ltd, 2000–04; Belle Property Pty Ltd, 2000–03; Strategic Capital Mgt Pty Ltd, 2000–04; X Capital Health, 2004–; Pisces Gp, 2008; General Security Australia Insurance Brokers Pty Ltd; Vice-Chm., Qingdao Pacific Coach Co., 2001–; Mem., Adv. Council, ABN AMRO Australia Ltd, 1998–2004 (Chm., 1996–98). Chm., RepuTex Rating Cttee, 2003–04. Chairman: Leadership Foundn Pty, 1998–2003; Investment Adv. Cttee, Australian Olympic Foundn, 2001; Foundn for New England Regl Art Mus., 2001–03; Adv. Cttee, Dunmore Lang Coll. Foundn, 2002–03; Business Leaders Forum on Sustainable Develt, 2003–09; Member, Advisory Group: Gp Training Australia, 2003–; Australia Worldwide, Solutions for a Sustainable Future, 2003–. Chairman: Osteoporosis Australia Council, 1997–; Arthritis Res. Taskforce Ltd, 2003–; KidsXpress; Director: Exec. Bd, Asia-Aust. Inst., 1999–; Positive Ageing Foundn, 1999–2003; Pres., Arthritis Foundn of Australia, 1997–2002. Chm., Freehand Gp, 2004–. Columnist, Australian Financial Review, 1998–. *Publications:* Liquidity Creation and Distribution in the Eurocurrency Market, 1975; (jtly) The Eurocurrency Markets and their Implications, 1975; Offshore Banking in Australia, 1981. *Recreations:* jazz, sport, cars, theatre, motor sports. *Clubs:* Australian; Australian Golf, Royal Sydney Golf.

HEWSON, Paul David, (Bono), Hon. KBE 2007; singer and songwriter; *b* 10 May 1960; *s* of late Robert Hewson and of Iris Hewson; *m* 1982, Alison Stewart; two *s* two *d*. *Educ:* Mount Temple Sch., Dublin. Co-founder and lead singer, U2, 1978–; nat. and internat. tours. *Albums include:* Boy, 1980; October, 1981; War, 1983; Under a Blood Red Sky, 1983; The Unforgettable Fire, 1984; Wide Awake in America, 1985; The Joshua Tree, 1987; Rattle and Hum, 1988; Achtung Baby, 1991; The Fly, 1991; Zooropa, 1993; Pop, 1997; All That You Can't Leave Behind, 2000; How to Dismantle an Atomic Bomb, 2004; No Line on the Horizon, 2009; Songs of Innocence, 2014. 22 Grammy Awards, 1987, 1988, 1992, 1993, 1994, 2000, 2001, 2004, 2005. Director: Elevation Partners, 2004–; Fender Musical Instruments Corpn, 2014–. Co-founder and Director: Debt, AIDS, Trade, Africa, 2002–; ONE Campaign to Make Poverty History (USA), 2004–; Make Poverty History (UK), 2005–. *Publications:* On the Move, 2007. *Address:* c/o Regine Moylett Publicity, 2C Woodstock Studios, Woodstock Grove, W12 8LE.

HEWSTONE, Prof. Miles Ronald Cole, DPhil, DSc; FBA 2002; Professor of Social Psychology, University of Oxford, and Fellow, New College, Oxford, since 2001; *b* 4 Aug. 1956; *s* of Ronald Keith and late Audrey Cole Hewstone; *m* 1986, Claudia Maria Hammer; one *s* one *d*. *Educ:* Univ. of Bristol (BSc 1st Cl. Hons Psychol. 1978); Trinity Coll., Oxford (DPhil 1981); Univ. of Tübingen, Germany (Habilitation); Univ. of Oxford (DSc 2007). University of Bristol: Lectr in Psychol., 1985–88; Reader in Social Psychol., 1988–91; Prof. of Social Psychol. (Personal Chair), 1991–92; Ordinarius Prof. of Social Psychol., Univ. of Mannheim, 1992–94; Prof. of Psychol., UWCC, 1994–2001. Mem., Social Integration Commn, 2014–. Invited Fellow, Center for Advanced Study in Behavioral Scis, Stanford, Calif, 1987–88 and 1999–2000. Hon. FBPsS 2003 (FBPsS 1986). Spearman Medal, 1987, Presidents' Award, 2001, BPsS; Kurt Lewin Award for Dist. Res. Achievement, Eur. Assoc. for Exptl Social Psychol., 2005; Kurt Lewin Award, Soc. for Psychol Study of Social Issues, 2012. *Publications:* Understanding Attitudes to the European Community: a social psychological study in four member states, 1986; (ed jtly) Contact and Conflict in Intergroup Encounters, 1986; Causal Attribution: from cognitive processes to collective beliefs, 1989; (ed with A. Manstead) The Blackwell Encyclopedia of Social Psychology, 1995; (ed jtly) Psychology, 2005; (ed jtly) Introduction to Social Psychology, 4th edn 2008, 5th edn 2012; (ed jtly) The Sage Handbook of Prejudice, Stereotyping and Discrimination, 2010; (ed with R. Martin) Minority Influence and Innovation: antecedents, processes and consequences, 2010; (ed with G. Hodson) Advances in Intergroup Contact, 2013. *Address:* New College, Oxford OX1 3BN. *E:* miles.hewstone@psy.ox.ac.uk.

HEXHAM AND NEWCASTLE, Bishop of, (RC), since 2009; **Rt Rev. Seamus Cunningham;** *b* Castlebar, Co. Mayo, 7 July 1942. *Educ:* St Nathy's Coll., Ballaghaderreen; St John's Coll., Waterford; Corpus Christi Coll., London. Ordained priest, 1966; Asst Priest, Our Lady and St Joseph's, Brooms, NW Durham, 1966–71; English Martyrs, Newcastle upon Tyne, 1971–72; Archdiocese of Hexham and Newcastle: Religious Educn and Catechetics Advr; Dir of Religious Educn; Spiritual Dir, Upshaw Coll., Durham, 1984–87; Administrator and Parish Priest, St Mary's Cathedral, 1987–97; Priest, Parish of St Oswin's, Tynemouth and St Mary's, Cullercoats; Vicar Gen., 2004–08. *Address:* Bishop's House, East Denton Hall, 800 West Road, Newcastle upon Tyne NE5 2BJ. *T:* (0191) 228 0003. *E:* office@rcdhn.org.uk.

HEY, Prof. Anthony John Grenville, CBE 2005; DPhil; FREng; Senior Data Science Fellow, eScience Institute, University of Washington, since 2015; *b* 17 Aug. 1946; *s* of late Colin Grenville Hey and Phyllis Gwendolen Rhodes; *m* 1969, Jessie Margaret Nancy; two *s* one *d*. *Educ:* King Edward's Sch., Birmingham; Worcester Coll., Oxford (Open Schol., 1964; BA Physics 1967); St John's Coll., Oxford; DPhil Oxon, 1970. CEng; FBCS; FIET; FREng 2001; FInstP 2005. University of Southampton: Lectr in Physics, 1974–86; Prof. of Computation, Sch. of Electronics and Computer Sci., 1986–2005; Dir, UK e-Science Core Prog., EPSRC, 2001–05 (on secondment); Microsoft Corporation: Vice-Pres. for Tech. Computing, 2005–07; Corporate Vice-Pres. for Ext. Res., 2007–11; Vice-Pres. for Res.

Connections, 2011–14. Sabbaticals at CIT, MIT and IBM Research. Member: Bd, Washington State Life Scis Discovery Fund, 2006–13; Bd, CodePlex Foundn, 2010–; Council, Res. Data Alliance, 2013–. Mem., PPARC, 2006–07. FAAAS 2010; Hon. Fellow, Cardiff Univ., 2005. Hon. DCL Newcastle, 2008; Hon. DSc: Drexel, USA, 2013; Swansea, 2014. *Publications:* (with Ian Aitchison) Gauge Theories in Particle Physics, 1982, 4th edn 2013; (with Patrick Walters) The New Quantum Universe, 1987, 2nd edn 2003; (with Patrick Walters) Einstein's Mirror, 1997; (co-ed) The Fourth Paradigm: data-intensive scientific discovery, 2009; (with Gyuri Pápay) The Computing Universe: a journey through a revolution, 2014. *Recreations:* reading, writing, hill-walking, long-term supporter of Southampton FC. *Address:* eScience Institute, Campus Box 351570, University of Washington, Seattle, WA 98195–1570, USA.

HEY, Prof. John Denis; Professor of Economics and Statistics, University of York, since 1984 (part-time, 1997–2010); *b* 26 Sept. 1944; *s* of George Brian Hey and Elizabeth Hamilton Hey (*née* Burns); *m* 1968, Margaret Robertson Bissett (marr. diss. 1998); one *s* two *d*. *Educ:* Manchester Grammar Sch.; Cambridge Univ. (MA); Edinburgh Univ. (MSc). Econometrician, Hoare & Co., 1968–69; Lectr in Economics, Univ. of Durham, 1969–73, Univ. of St Andrews, 1974–75; Lectr in Social and Economic Statistics, Univ. of York, 1975–81, Sen. Lectr, 1981–84; Professore Ordinario: Univ. of Bari, 1998–2006; Luiss Guido Carli, Italy, 2006–10. Co-Dir, Centre for Experimental Economics, Univ. of York, 1986–. Economic Consultant, Wise Speke & Co., 1972–87. Editor: Bulletin of Economic Research, 1984–87; Economic Journal, 1986–96. *Publications:* Statistics in Economics, 1974; Uncertainty in Microeconomics, 1979; Britain in Context, 1979; Economics in Disequilibrium, 1981; Data in Doubt, 1983; (ed jtly) Surveys in the Economics of Uncertainty, 1987; (ed) Current Issues in Microeconomics, 1989; (ed jtly) A Century of Economics, 1990; Experiments in Economics, 1991; (ed) The Future of Economics, 1992; (ed jtly) Recent Developments in Experimental Economics, 1993; (ed) The Economics of Uncertainty, 1997; Intermediate Microeconomics, 2003; Microeconomia, 2007; articles in academic economics jls. *Recreations:* gym, opera. *Address:* Department of Economics and Related Studies, University of York, Heslington, York YO10 5DD. *T:* (01904) 433786.

HEYES, Prof. Cecilia Mary, PhD; FBA 2010; Senior Research Fellow in Theoretical Life Sciences, All Souls College, Oxford, since 2008; Professor of Psychology, University of Oxford, since 2009; *b* Ashford, Kent, 6 March 1960; *d* of James Joseph Heyes and Helen Mary Heyes (*née* Henneker); partner, Martin Eimer. *Educ:* Highworth Grammar Sch., Ashford; University Coll. London (BSc 1981; PhD 1984). Harkness Fellow, Evolutionary Epistemology, Lehigh Univ., Univ. of Chicago and Tufts Univ., 1984–86; Res. Fellow, Psychol., Trinity Hall, Cambridge, 1986–89; Department of Psychology, University College London: Lectr, 1988–93; Sen. Lectr, 1993–96; Reader, 1996–2000; Prof., 2000–08. *Publications:* (ed jtly) Social Learning and the Roots of Culture, 1996; (ed jtly) Evolution of Cognition, 2001; (ed jtly) Selection Theory and Social Construction, 2001; contrib. papers to peer-reviewed jls of exptl psychol. and cognitive neurosci. *Recreation:* nice cup of tea and a sit down. *Address:* All Souls College, Oxford OX1 4AL. *T:* (01865) 279394. *E:* cecilia.heyes@all-souls.ox.ac.uk.

HEYES, David Alan; *b* 2 April 1946; *s* of Harold and Lilian Heyes; *m* 1968, Judith Egerton Gallagher; one *s* one *d*. *Educ:* Open Univ. (BA). Local govt manager, Manchester, 1962–86; trade union organiser, 1986–87; local govt manager, Oldham, 1987–90; self employed, computer graphics business, 1990–95; manager, CAB, Manchester, 1995–2001. MP (Lab) Ashton under Lyne, 2001–15.

HEYGATE, Sir Richard John Gage, 6th Bt *cr* 1831, of Southend, Essex; Chairman: Red Unida, since 2010; Anglo Cathay Enterprises, since 2012; Managing Partner, UK office, Oneida Associés, since 2008; *b* 30 Jan. 1940; *s* of Sir John Edward Nourse Heygate, 4th Bt and his 2nd wife, Gwyneth Eliot (*d* 1994), 2nd *d* of J. E. H. Lloyd; *S* brother, 1991; *m* 1st, 1968, Carol Rosemary (marr. diss. 1972), *d* of Comdr Richard Michell; 2nd, 1974, Jong Ja (marr. diss. 1988), *d* of In Suk, Seoul; one *d*; 3rd, 1988, Susan Fiona, *d* of late Robert Buckley; two *s*. *Educ:* Repton; Balliol Coll., Oxford. IBM (UK) Ltd, 1967–70; McKinsey & Company Inc., 1970–77; Director: Olaf Foods, 1977–85; Index Gp, 1985–87; Principal, McKinsey and Co. Inc., 1987–98; CEO, Sophron Partners Ltd, 1998–2005. Director: Isis Technology, 1999–2000; Propero Ltd, 2000–03; Web Connectivity, 2008–11; Chairman: Storks Nest Wine, 2003–04; Mouse Smart Software, 2004–06; Welford Technology Partners, 2005–10. Mem., Finance Cttee, Cancer Res., 1992–98. *Publications:* (with Michael Daunt) Endangered Species, 2008; (with Philip Carr-Gomm) The Book of English Magic, 2009. *Heir: s* Frederick Carysfort Gage Heygate, *b* 28 June 1988. *Address:* 8 Brynmaer Road, SW11 4ER.

HEYHOE, David Charles Ross, CB 1998; Director, Greenwich Hospital, 1998–2002; *b* 29 June 1938; *s* of late Cecil Ross Heyhoe and Clara Beatrice (*née* Woodard Knight); *m* 1972, Pauline Susan (*née* Morgan); one *s* one *d*. *Educ:* Beckenham and Penge Grammar Sch.; Worcester Coll., Oxford (Schol.; MA Lit.Hum.). Served HM Forces, 1957–59. Asst Principal, War Office, 1963; Asst Private Sec. to Minister (Army), 1966; Principal, MoD, 1967; Asst Sec., 1975; Res. Associate, Inst. for Strategic Studies, 1975–76; Private Sec. to Leader of H of C, 1981–84; Asst Under Sec. of State, MoD, 1986–97. Mem., Royal Patriotic Fund Corp., 1998–2002. Dir, Pollen Estate Trustee Co. Ltd, 2002–07. *Recreations:* books, sport. *Address:* 49 Westmoreland Road, Barnes, SW13 9RZ. *Clubs:* Roehampton, Rosslyn Park FC.

HEYHOE, Rosemary; Director, Human Resources Operations, Department of Trade and Industry, 2003–05; *b* 17 Sept. 1946; *d* of Herbert Arthur Mears and Mabel Mears (*née* Foster); *m* 1978, Richard John Heyhoe; two *d*. *Educ:* Wallington County Sch. for Girls. Bd of Trade, 1965–70; NEDO, 1970–73; DTI, 1973–74; Metrication Bd, 1974–75; Private Sec., Parly Under-Sec. of State, Dept of Prices and Consumer Protection, 1975–77; Personnel, DTI, 1977–82; privatisation team, Nat. Maritime Inst., 1982; internal consultancy, 1982–92; office of Principal Establishment and Finance Officer, DTI, 1992–97; Dir of Resources and Services, OFT, 1997–2001; Dir resp. for Civil Emergency Planning, DTI, 2001–03. *Recreations:* family, opera, travel. *Address:* 50 Tachbrook Street, Pimlico, SW1V 2NA.

HEYHOE FLINT, Baroness *cr* 2011 (Life Peer), of Wolverhampton in the County of West Midlands; **Rachael Heyhoe Flint,** OBE 2008 (MBE 1972); DL; public relations and sports marketing consultant; journalist, broadcaster, public speaker, sportswoman; *b* 11 June 1939; *d* of Geoffrey Heyhoe and Roma (*née* Crocker); *m* 1971, Derrick Flint, BSc; one *s*, and one step *s* two step *d*. *Educ:* Wolverhampton High Sch. for Girls; Dartford Coll. of Physical Educn (Dip. in Phys. Educn). Head of Phys. Education: Wolverhampton Municipal Grammar Sch., 1960–62; Northicote Sch., 1962–64; US Field Hockey Assoc. Coach, 1964 and 1965; Journalist, Wolverhampton Express & Star, 1965–72; Sports Editor, Wolverhampton Chronicle, 1969–71; first woman Sports Reporter, ITV, 1972; Daily Telegraph Sports Writer, 1967–90; Vice-Chm., 1981–86, and Public Relations Officer, 1982–86, Women's Cricket Assoc.; Consultant, La Manga Club, Southern Spain, 1983–; PR Exec., Wolverhampton Wanderers Football Club, 1990–2010 (Dir, 1997–2004; Vice Pres., 2003–); Mem. Bd, ECB, 2010–. England Hockey rep., 1964 (goalkeeper); Mem., England Women's Cricket team, 1960–83, Captain, 1966–77. Hit first 6 in Women's Test Cricket 1963 (England *v* Australia, Oval); scored highest test score by England player in this country, 1976 (highest in world, 1976, now fourth highest) (179 runs for England *v* Australia, Oval). Pres., Lady Taverners Charity, 2000–11. DL W Midlands, 1997. Hon. Fellow, Univ. of Wolverhampton, 2002. Hon. BSc Bradford, 2003; Hon. DSc Greenwich, 2003; Hon. Dr Sports Sci. Leeds Metropolitan, 2006. Best After Dinner Speakers Award, Guild of Professional Toastmasters, 1972. *Publications:* Just for Kicks, (Guide to hockey goalkeeping), 1966; Women's Hockey, 1975; (with Netta Rheinberg) Fair Play, The Story of Women's Cricket, 1976; (autobiog.) "Heyhoe!", 1978. *Recreations:* golf, cricket; former county squash player (Staffs). *E:* flinters@talktalk.net. *Clubs:* MCC (Hon. Life Mem., 1999; first woman Cttee Mem., 2004–11; Trustee, 2011–13), Lord's Taverners; Patshull Park Golf; South Staffs Golf; La Manga Golf Resort (Spain).

HEYLIN, Angela Christine Mary, (Mrs M. Minzly), LVO 2008; OBE 1997; *b* 17 Sept. 1943; *d* of Bernard Heylin and Ruth Victoria Heylin; *m* 1971, Maurice Minzly; one *s*. *Educ:* Apsley Grammar Sch.; Watford Coll. Charles Barker plc: Chief Exec., 1989–92; Chm., 1992–97; UK Pres., BSMG Worldwide, 1997–2000. Non-executive Director: Provident Financial, 1997–2003; Mothercare plc, 1997–2004; Austin Reed Gp plc, 2001–06. Mem. Adv. Bd, Mercer Delta Consulting, 2004–06. Prime Minister's Adv. Panel, Citizen's Charter, 1993–97. Trustee, Historic Royal Palaces, 1998–2007. Chm., Public Relations Consultants' Assoc., 1990–92. Chm., House of St Barnabas, 2001–04. *Publications:* Putting it Across, 1991. *Recreations:* theatre, gardening, music. *Address:* 46 St Augustine's Road, NW1 9RN. *T:* (020) 7485 4815, 07767 491508. *E:* angela@heylin.com.

HEYMAN, Prof. Jacques, MA, PhD; FICE; FSA; FREng; Professor of Engineering, 1971–92, and Head of Department of Engineering, 1983–92, University of Cambridge, now Emeritus Professor; Fellow of Peterhouse, 1949–51, and 1955–92, now Emeritus Fellow; *b* 8 March 1925; *m* 1958, Eva Orlans (*d* 1982); three *d*. *Educ:* Whitgift Sch.; Peterhouse, Cambridge. Senior Bursar, Peterhouse, 1962–64; University Demonstrator, Engineering Dept, Cambridge Univ., 1951, University Lectr, 1954, Reader, 1968. Vis. Professor: Brown Univ., USA, 1957–58; Harvard Univ., 1966. Consultant Engineer: Ely Cathedral, 1972–2005; St Albans Cathedral, 1978–2000; Lichfield Cathedral, 1986–91; Worcester Cathedral, 1986–90; Gloucester Cathedral, 1989–90. Member: Architectural Adv. Panel, Westminster Abbey, 1973–98; Cathedrals Fabric Commn (formerly Cathedrals Adv. Commn) for England, 1981–2001; Council, ICE, 1960–63 and 1975–78; Smeatonian Soc. of Civil Engrs, 1982– (Pres., 2004); Fabric Adv. Cttee, Ely Cathedral, 2005–. Hon. FRIBA 1998. Hon. DSc Sussex, 1975; Dr *hc* Univ. Politécnica de Madrid, 2008. James Watt Medal, 1973. Cross of St Augustine, 2005. *Publications:* The Steel Skeleton, vol. 2 (with Lord Baker, M. R. Horne), 1956; Plastic Design of Portal Frames, 1957; Beams and Framed Structures, 1964, 2nd edn 1974 (trans. Spanish 2002); Plastic Design of Frames, vol. 1, 1969 (paperback 1980), vol. 2, 1971; Coulomb's Memoir on Statics, 1972, reprinted 1997 (trans. Italian 1999); Equilibrium of Shell Structures, 1977; Elements of Stress Analysis, 1982; The Masonry Arch, 1982; Estructuras de Fábrica (collection of papers on masonry construction, trans. Spanish), 1995; The Stone Skeleton, 1995 (trans. Spanish 1999, Italian 2014); Elements of the Theory of Structures, 1996; Arches, Vaults and Buttresses, 1996; Structural Analysis, a Historical Approach, 1998 (trans. Spanish 2004); The Science of Structural Engineering, 1999 (trans. Spanish 2001); Basic Structural Theory, 2008 (trans. Spanish 2011); articles on plastic design, masonry construction and general structural theory. *Address:* 3 Banhams Close, Cambridge CB4 1HX. *T:* (01223) 357360.

HEYMANN, Amanda; *see* Rowlatt, A.

HEYN, Andrew Richard, OBE 2014; HM Diplomatic Service; Ambassador to Burma, 2009–13; *b* Prinsted, W Sussex, 14 Jan. 1962; *s* of Lt Comdr Denis Heyn and Una Heyn; *m* 1988, Jane Carmel Mulvenna; one *d*. *Educ:* Dr Challoner's Grammar Sch., Amersham; Univ. of Manchester (BA Hons Politics). DTI, 1985–88; entered FCO, 1989; Second Sec., Caracas, 1991–94; Hd, Amsterdam Intergovtl Conf. Unit, FCO, 1994–96; First Sec., Lisbon, 1996–2000; Asst Dir, HR Dept, FCO, 2000–05; Counsellor, Dep. Hd of Mission and Dir, Trade and Investment, Dublin, 2005–09. *Recreations:* tennis, football, cinema, karaoke, suffering in support of Leeds United. *Address:* c/o Foreign and Commonwealth Office, King Charles Street, SW1A 2AH. *Club:* Donnybrook Tennis (Dublin).

HEYTESBURY, 7th Baron *cr* 1828; **James William Holmes à Court;** Bt 1795; *b* 30 July 1967; *s* of 6th Baron Heytesbury and of Alison Jean (*née* Balfour); *S* father, 2004; *m* 1995, Polly Jane Kendrick (*d* 2014). *Educ:* Bryanston; Southampton Univ. (BSc Hons). *Heir: cousin* Peter Michael Hamilton Holmes à Court [*b* 1968; *m* 1995, Divonne Jarecki; two s (twins) two *d* (twins)].

HEYWOOD, Dr Ann, FRICS, FCIOB; higher education adviser, since 2013; Principal, College of Estate Management, Reading, 2007–13; *b* 9 March 1955; *d* of Philip Tassell and Mary (*née* Wicks). *Educ:* Maidstone Grammar Sch. for Girls; Bedford Coll., Univ. of London (BSc 1975); Coll. of Estate Mgt; PhD Salford Univ. 2003. FRICS 1987; FCIOB 2012. MAFF, 1975–81; Rural Planning Services, 1981–86; Founder and Man. Partner, CPM, 1986–99; owner, Principal Purpose, sustainability consultancy, 2003–08. Specialist Advr to H of C Select Cttee, 1987–88. Chair, Presidential Commn for Sustainability, RICS, 2005–07. Mem., Exec. Bd, Construction Industry Council, 2009–12. Hon. Fellow, HK Inst. of Surveyors, 2013. Green Surveyor of the Year, RICS, 1998–99. *Recreations:* sailing, walking, cinema, travel.

HEYWOOD, Barry; *see* Heywood, R. B.

HEYWOOD, Sir Jeremy (John), KCB 2012 (CB 2002); CVO 2003; Cabinet Secretary, since 2012, and Head of Civil Service, since 2014, Cabinet Office; *b* 31 Dec. 1961; *s* of late Peter Andrew Heywood and of Brenda Heywood (*née* Swinbank); *m* 1997, Dr Suzanne Elizabeth Cook (*see* S. E. Heywood); two *s* one *d* (of whom one *s* one *d* are twins). *Educ:* Bootham Sch., York; Hertford Coll., Oxford (BA Hons Modern Hist. and Econs); London Sch. of Econs (MSc Econ); Harvard Business Sch. (PMD 1994). Econ. Asst, HSE, 1983–84; HM Treasury: Econ. Asst, 1984–85; Private Sec. to Financial Sec., 1986–88; Asst to UK Dir, IMF, Washington, 1988–90 (on secondment); HM Treasury: Private Sec. to Chief Sec., 1990–91; Principal Private Sec. to Chancellor of the Exchequer, 1991–94; Head, Corporate and Mgt Change, 1994–95; Head, Securities and Markets Policy, 1995–97; Private Sec., 1997–99, Principal Private Sec., 1999–2003, to the Prime Minister; Man. Dir, Mergers and Acquisitions, subseq. Man. Dir and Co-Head, UK Investment Banking Div., Morgan Stanley, 2004–07; Hd of Domestic Policy and Strategy, Cabinet Office, 2007–08; Perm. Sec., Prime Minister's Office, 2008–11. *Recreations:* modern art, cinema, opera, ballet, Manchester United. *Address:* Cabinet Office, 70 Whitehall, SW1A 2AS.

HEYWOOD, Mark Adrian; QC 2010; a Recorder, since 2007; Senior Treasury Counsel, Central Criminal Court, since 2008; *b* 28 June 1962; *s* of Philip Gerard Heywood and Jennifer Jane Heywood; *m* 1990, Frances Jane Reid; two *s* one *d*. *Educ:* Taunton Sch.; Gonville and Caius Coll., Cambridge (BA Hons Law 1984); Inns of Court Sch. of Law. Called to the Bar, Gray's Inn, 1985, Bencher, 2014; Jun. Treasury Counsel, 2001–08. *Recreations:* sailing, motorcycling, mountains, classic tractors, agricultural machines and rural crafts. *Address:* 5 King's Bench Walk, Temple, EC4Y 7DN. *T:* (020) 7353 5638, *Fax:* (020) 7353 6166.

HEYWOOD, Matthew David, RIBA; Director, Matthew Heywood Ltd, since 2003; *b* 26 Dec. 1970; *s* of late David Main Heywood and of Patricia Ann Heywood, *qv*; *m* 2002, Sarah Elizabeth Casemore; one *s*. *Educ:* Dundee Univ. (BSc Architecture, BArch Hons). RIBA 1996. Architect: T. P. Bennett Partnership, 1994–96; Future Systems, 1996–2003 (Associate Dir, 2001–03). *Recreations:* member of Ascension Church, Balham Hill, London. *Address:* Matthew Heywood Ltd, 23 Berber Road, SW11 6RZ. *T:* (020) 7352 7583. *E:* email@matthewheywood.com.

HEYWOOD, Patricia Ann, (Mrs Michael Brown), OBE 2007; World Wide President, Mothers' Union, 2001–06; *b* 8 Feb. 1943; *d* of George and Joan Robinson; *m* 1st, 1965, David Main Heywood (*d* 1999); two *s*; 2nd, 2012, Michael Brown. *Educ:* Kendal High Sch.; Whitelands Coll., London. Teacher, 1964–68 and 1975–81. Joined, Mothers' Union, 1973; Diocesan Pres., St Andrew's, Dunkeld and Dunblane, and Mem., Central Executive, 1992–95; Provincial Pres. for Scotland and Mem., Trustee Bd, 1995–2000. *Recreations:* reading, gardening, walking, crafts. *Address:* 6 Hillside Road, Ashtead, Surrey KT21 1RX.
See also M. D. Heywood.

HEYWOOD, Sir Peter, 6th Bt *cr* 1838, of Claremont, Lancashire; company director; *b* 10 Dec. 1947; *s* of Sir Oliver Kerr Heywood, 5th Bt and of Denise Wymondham, 2nd *d* of late Jocelyn William Godefroi; *S* father, 1992; *m* 1970, Jacqueline Anne, *d* of Sir Robert Frederick Hunt, CBE; two *d*. *Educ:* Bryanston Sch.; Keble Coll., Oxford (BA Hons). *Heir:* twin *b* Michael Heywood [*b* 10 Dec. 1947; *m* 1972, Caroline Awdry Greig; one *s* one *d*].

HEYWOOD, Peter Leslie; His Honour Judge Heywood; a Circuit Judge, since 2008; *b* Bangor, N Wales, 23 Sept. 1949; *s* of Rev. Geoffrey Thomas Heywood and Irene Heywood (*née* Williams); *m* 1975, Ann Davina Morris; one *s* one *d*. *Educ:* John Bright's Grammar Sch., Llandudno; University Coll. of Wales, Aberystwyth (LLB 1977). Justices' Clerk, N Wilts, 1981–88; called to the Bar, Gray's Inn, 1988; barrister in private practice, specialising in crime, 1988–2008. Liaison Judge to Dyfed Magistrates, 2008–13, to Wales Probation Trust, 2013–. *Recreations:* flyfishing (Mem., Llandysul Angling Assoc.), Rugby, mountain biking. *Address:* Swansea Crown Court, The Law Courts, St Helens Road, Swansea SA1 4PF. *T:* (01792) 637000, *Fax:* (01792) 637049. *E:* HHJudge.Heywood@judiciary.gsi.gov.uk.

HEYWOOD, Dr (Ronald) Barry; Director, British Antarctic Survey, 1994–97; *b* 28 Sept. 1937; *s* of Ronald Heywood and Edith Henrietta Heywood (*née* Bradbury); *m* 1965, Josephine Despina Panagopoulos; two *d*. *Educ:* Ashby Grammar Sch., Leics; Birmingham Univ. (BSc 1959; MSc 1961); Queen Mary Coll., London Univ. (PhD 1970). MRSB (MIBiol 1967). British Antarctic Survey: Biologist, 1961–68; Hd, Freshwater Res., 1968–83; Chief Scientist, Offshore Biol Prog., 1978–86; Hd, Marine Life Scis Div., 1986–87; Dep. Dir, 1988–94. UK Delegate: IOC Regl Cttee for Southern Ocean, 1987–97; SCAR, 1995–97 (Mem., Wkg Gp on Human Biol and Medicine, 1995–97); Council of Managers of Nat. Antarctic Progs, 1994–97. Chairman: Eur. Bd for Polar Sci., 1995–97; Jt Exec., Eur. Bds for Marine and Polar Sci., 1995–97; Mem., British Nat. Cttee Antarctic Res., 1994–97. Pres., British Antarctic Survey Club, 2009–. Hon. Associate, RHC, 1981. Polar Medal, 1967 and Clasp, 1986. *Publications:* University Research in Antarctica, 1993; papers on freshwater and marine physics and biol. *Recreations:* walking, music, U3A Lectr on Western Classical Music. *Address:* Magdalene House, Glapthorn Road, Oundle, Peterborough PE8 4JA. *Club:* Antarctic.

HEYWOOD, Suzanne Elizabeth, (Lady Heywood); Director (Senior Partner), and Global Head, Organisation Design Service Line, McKinsey & Company, Inc., since 2013; *b* Southampton, 25 Feb. 1969; *d* of Gordon Cook and Mary Cook (*née* Brindley); *m* 1997, Sir Jeremy John Heywood, *qv*; two *s* one *d* (of whom one *s* one *d* are twins). *Educ:* on schooner Wavewalker sailing around world, recreating Capt. Cook's third voyage, 1976–86; Somerville Coll., Oxford (BA Zool. 1990); King's Coll., Cambridge (PhD 1993). HM Treasury: fast stream trainee, 1993–95; Private Sec. to Financial Sec., 1995–96; Grade 7, 1996–97; McKinsey & Company, Inc.: Consultant, 1997–2007; Partner, 2007–. Adjunct Lectr, Sch. of Econs and Mgt, Tsinghua Univ., 2014–. Trustee, Royal Opera House, 2013– (Chm., Finance and Ops Cttee, 2014–); Mem., Govg Body, RAM, 2014– (Mem., Audit Cttee, 2014–); Trustee, RA Trust, 2014–. Trustee, New Entrepreneurs Foundn, 2013–. *Publications:* articles in Wall Street Jl, McKinsey Qly and Eur. Business Rev. on range of organisational topics. *Recreations:* family, adventure travel, opera, ballet, wide range of music, art. *Address:* McKinsey & Company, Inc. United Kingdom, 1 Jermyn Street, SW1Y 4UH. *T:* (020) 7839 8040.

HEYWOOD, Prof. Vernon Hilton; Emeritus Professor, University of Reading, since 1988; *b* 24 Dec. 1927; *s* of Vernon William and Marjorie Elizabeth Heywood; *m* 1st, 1952, María de la Concepción Salcedo Manrique; four *s*; 2nd, 1980, Christine Anne Brighton. *Educ:* George Heriot's Sch., Edinburgh; Edinburgh Univ. (BSc, DSc); Pembroke Coll., Cambridge (PhD). Lecturer 1955–60, Sen. Lectr 1960–63, Reader 1963–64, Professor 1964–68, Dept of Botany, Univ. of Liverpool; University of Reading: Prof. of Botany and Hd of Dept of Botany, 1968–88; Dean, Faculty of Science, 1978–81. Dir, 1987–92, Consultant Dir, 1993, Botanic Gardens Conservation Internat.; Chief Scientist (Plant Conservation), IUCN, 1988–92; Exec. Editor, Global Biodiversity Assessment, UNEP, 1993–98. Hon. Professor: Botanical Inst., Nanjing, 1989–; Univ. Juan Agustín Maza, Mendoza, Argentina, 1997–; Hon. Fellow, Royal Botanic Garden, Edinburgh, 1995–. Storer Lectr, Univ. of California, Davis, 1990; Regents' Lectr, Univ. of Calif, Riverside, 1998. Chm., European Plants Specialist Gp, Species Survival Commn of IUCN, 1984–87; Pres. Emeritus, Internat. Council on Medicinal and Aromatic Plants, 2003– (Pres., 1994–2003); Member of Board: Genetic Resources Communications Systems Inc., 1990–94; Yves Rocher Foundn, 1991–; Conservatoire Botanique National, Porquerolles, 1991–, Bailleul, 1993–, Nancy, 1996–. Pres., Internat. Assoc. of Botanic Gdns, 2012–; Trustee: Royal Botanic Gardens, Kew, 1983–87; IUCN, UK, 1993–2005. Corresponding Mem., Botanical Soc. of Amer., 1987–. Hon. FLS 1999. Councillor of Honour, Consejo Superior de Investigaciones Científicas, Spain, 1970. Linnean Medal, Linnean Soc. of London, 1987; Hutchinson Medal, Chicago Horticl Soc., 1989; Royal Botanic Gdn Edinburgh Medal, 2012. Order of the Silver Dog, 1989, Insignia de Oro, 2003 (Gran Canaria). *Publications:* Principles of Angiosperm Taxonomy (with P. H. Davis), 1963, 2nd edn 1965; (ed jtly) Flora Europaea: vol. 1 1964 (2nd edn 1993), vol. 2 1968, vol. 3 1972, vol. 4 1976, vol. 5 1980; Plant Taxonomy, 1967, 2nd edn 1976; Flowering Plants of the World, 1978, 2nd edn 1985; (jtly) Our Green and Living World, 1984; Las Plantas con Flores, 1985; (jtly) Botanic Gardens and the World Conservation Strategy, 1987; The Botanic Gardens Conservation Strategy, 1989; (jtly) International Directory of Botanic Gardens V, 1990; (jtly) Conservation of Medicinal Plants, 1991; (jtly) Conservation Techniques in Botanic Gardens, 1991; (jtly) Tropical Botanic Gardens: their role in conservation and development, 1991; (jtly) Proceedings of the International Symposium on Botanical Gardens, 1991; (jtly) Conservation des ressources végétales, 1991; (jtly) Centres of Plant Diversity: a guide and strategy for their conservation: vol. 1 1994, vol. 2 1995, vol. 3 1996; (ed) Global Biodiversity Assessment, 1995; Les Plantes à Fleurs, 1996; (jtly) Conservation of the Wild Relatives of Cultivated Plants Native to Europe, 1997; Use and Potential of Wild Plants in Farm Households, 1998; (jtly) *In situ* Conservation: a critical review of good practices, 2006; (ed jtly) Do Conservation Targets Help?, 2006; (jtly) Flowering Plant Families of the World, 2007; (jtly) Flowering Plants: a concise pictorial guide, 2011; (with D. Hunter) Crop Wild Relatives: a manual of *in situ* conservation, 2011; (jtly) European Code of Conduct for Botanic Gardens on Invasive Alien Species, 2013; over 500 papers in sci. jls. *Recreations:* cooking, travel, music, writing. *Address:* White Mead, 22 Wiltshire Road, Wokingham RG40 1TP. *T:* (0118) 978 0185.

HEYWOOD, Victoria Mary Taylor, (Mrs C. W. Jones), CBE 2012; Chairman, Royal Society of Arts, since 2012; *b* 25 June 1956; *d* of late Kenneth Heywood Taylor and of Gillian Dorothea Taylor (*née* Black); *m* 1st, 1988, Christopher Wright (marr. diss. 1994); one *s*; 2nd, 2004, Clive William Jones, *qv*. *Educ:* Truro High Sch.; Fortismere Sch.; Central Sch. of Speech and Drama (Dip. Drama). Stage manager, 1977–84; Gen. Manager, London Bubble Th. Co., 1986–89; Exec. Dir, Contact Th., Manchester, 1989–93; Gen. Manager, London Internat. Fest. of Th., 1994; Executive Director: English Stage Co. (Royal Court Th.), 1994–2001; Royal Shakespeare Company, 2003–12. Vice-Chairman: Lyric Th., Hammersmith, 1999–2004; Young Vic Th., 2002–06. Member: Soc. of London Theatres, 1995–; Council, C&G, 2012–; Chairman: Warwick Commn into Future of Cultural Value, 2013–; 14/18 Now, 2013–. Trustee, Shakespeare Birthplace Trust, 2004–12. Lay Mem., Warwick Univ., 2008–13. Chm., Mountview Acad. of Arts, 2013–. FRSA 2005. Hon. DLitt Birmingham, 2009; Hon. DArts Ohio, 2012. *Recreations:* sleeping, eating, reading.
See also Baron Taylor of Goss Moor.

HEYWORTH, Michael Paul, MBE 2007; PhD; Director, Council for British Archaeology, since 2004; *b* 30 July 1961; *s* of Allan Keith Heyworth and Jean Barbara Heyworth (*née* Kersey); *m* 1995, Dr Catherine Jane Mortimer; one *s* one *d*. *Educ:* Univ. of Sheffield (BA Hons Prehist. and Archaeol. 1982); Univ. of Bradford (MA Scientific Methods in Archaeol. 1983; PhD 1991); OU Business Sch. (Professional Cert. in Mgt 2003). MCIfA (MIFA 1984); FSA 2001. Res. Asst, 1983–86, Postgrad. res. student, 1986–87, Univ. of Bradford; SO, 1987–89, Higher SO, 1989–90, Ancient Monuments Lab., English Heritage; Council for British Archaeology: Sen. Bibliographer, British and Irish Archaeol Bibliography, 1990–92; Inf. Officer, 1992–94; Dep. Dir and Inf. Officer, 1994–2002; Dep. Dir, 2002–04. Institute of Field Archaeologists: Mem. Council, 1985–88; Hon. Treas., 1986–88; Ed., Technical Papers, 1989–94. Co-Dir, Internet Archaeology, electronic jl, 1995–; Vice Chm., Archaeology Data Service, 1998–; Chairman: Archaeology Trng Forum, 2005–11; British Archaeol Awards, 2009–13; Adv. Bd, Nat. Heritage Protection Plan, 2011–14. Sec., All Party Parly Archaeology Gp, 2007–. Vice Pres., Eur. Forum of Heritage Assocs, 1993–98. Mem., Yorks and Humber Regl Cttee, Heritage Lottery Fund, 2009–15. Trustee: York Archaeol Trust, 1996–2007; Yorks Philosophical Soc., 2003–06; Heritage Alliance (formerly Heritage Link), 2005–11. MCMI 2003. FRSA 2014. *Publications:* (jtly) The Hamwic Glass, 1998; compiled and edited: British Archaeological Bibliography (with I. Holroyd), 1990, 1991, 1992; Archaeology in Britain, 1992; British Archaeological Yearbook 1995–96; various papers, articles and reports; over 40 Ancient Monuments Lab. tech. reports on wide variety of technol material. *Recreations:* football, current affairs, local issues. *Address:* Council for British Archaeology, Beatrice de Cardi House, 66 Bootham, York YO30 7BZ. *T:* (01904) 671417, *Fax:* (01904) 671384. *E:* mikeheyworth@archaeologyuk.org.

HIBBARD, Prof. Bryan Montague, MD, PhD; FRCOG; Professor of Obstetrics and Gynaecology, University of Wales College of Medicine (formerly Welsh National School of Medicine), 1973–91, now Emeritus Professor; *b* 24 April 1926; *s* of Montague Reginald and Muriel Irene Hibbard; *m* 1955, Elizabeth Donald Grassie. *Educ:* Queen Elizabeth's Sch., Barnet; St Bartholomew's Hosp. Med. Coll., London (MD); PhD (Liverpool). MRCS 1950; FRCOG 1965. Formerly: Sen. Lectr, Liverpool Univ.; Consultant Obstetrician and Gynaecologist, Liverpool RHB, and Univ. Hosp. of Wales. Chairman, Joint Standing Committee: Obstetric Anaesthesia, RCOG/RCAnaes, 1988–91; RCOG/RCM, 1988–91; Member: Cttee on Safety of Medicines, 1979–83; Maternity Services Adv. Cttee, 1981–85; Council, RCOG, 1982–88, 1989–92; S Glam HA, 1983–88; Medicines Commn, 1986–89. President: Welsh Obst. and Gynaecol Soc., 1985–86; History of Medicine Soc. of Wales, 1995–96. Hon. Curator of Museum, RCOG, 1986–2000 (Hon. Librarian, 1992–94). Mem. Editl Bd, Confidential Enquiries into Maternal Deaths, 1985–96 (Chm., Clinical Sub-Group, 1990–96). Pres., Contemp. Art Soc. for Wales, 2008–. Hon. FRANZCOG 1997. *Publications:* Principles of Obstetrics, 1988; The Obstetric Forceps, 1988; The Obstetrician's Armamentarium, 2000; numerous contribs to world medical literature. *Recreations:* collecting 18th century drinking glasses, fell walking, coarse gardening. *Address:* The Clock House, Cathedral Close, Llandaff, Cardiff CF5 2ED. *T:* (029) 2056 6636.

HIBBERT; *see* Holland-Hibbert, family name of Viscount Knutsford.

HIBBERT, Rev. Barrie Edward; Associate Minister, Flinders Street Baptist Church, Adelaide, 2000–03; *b* 9 June 1935; *s* of Joseph and Eva Hibbert, Gisborne, NZ; *m* 1st, 1957, Ellen Judith Eade (*d* 2010); one *s* two *d*; 2nd, 2013, Gillian Mary Arnold Collins. *Educ:* Victoria Univ. of Wellington, NZ (BA); Melbourne Coll. of Divinity, Vic, Australia (LTh); NZ Baptist Theol Coll. Minister: Baptist churches in Gore, Tawa and Dunedin, NZ, 1962–79; Flinders St Baptist Church, Adelaide, SA, 1979–87; Bloomsbury Central Baptist Church, London, 1987–99. *Address:* 53/32 Ayre Street, South Plympton, SA 5038, Australia. *T:* (8) 82978558.

HICHENS, Antony Peverell, RD 1969; Chairman, D. S. Smith (formerly David S. Smith (Holdings)) plc, 1999–2006; *b* 10 Sept. 1936; *s* of late Lt-Comdr R. P. Hichens, DSO (and Bar), DSC (and 2 Bars), RNVR, and Catherine Gilbert Enys; *m* 1963, Sczerina Neomi Hobday, DL; one *d*. *Educ:* Stowe; Magdalen Coll., Oxford (MA Law); Univ. of Pennsylvania, Wharton Sch. (MBA). Midshipman, RNVR, 1954–56. Called to Bar, Inner Temple, 1960. Rio Tinto-Zinc Corp., 1960–72; Financial Dir, Redland, 1972–81; Man. Dir and Chief Financial Officer, Consolidated Gold Fields, 1981–89; Chairman: Y. J. Lovell (Holdings), 1990–94; Caradon, 1990–98; Lasmo plc, 2000–01 (Dep. Chm., 1992–2000); Dep. Chm., Candover Investments plc, 1989–2005 (non-exec. Dir, 1989–2010). Mem. (non-exec.), British Coal Corp., 1992–97. Mem., Takeover Panel, 2001–10. Waynflete Fellow, Magdalen Coll., Oxford, 1997–. *Publications:* Gunboat Command: the life of Lieutenant Commander Robert Hichens DSO* DSC** RNVR, 2007. *Recreations:* travel, wine, shooting. *Address:* Slape Manor, Netherbury, near Bridport, Dorset DT6 5LH. *T:* (01308) 488232. *Clubs:* Brooks's, Naval.

HICKEY, Most Rev. Barry James, OAM 1982; Archbishop of Perth (Australia), (RC), 1991–2012; *b* 16 April 1936; *s* of G. Hickey. *Educ:* Christian Brothers Coll., WA; St Charles Seminary, WA; Propaganda Fide Coll., Rome; Univ. of WA. Dir, Centrecare, Perth (Catholic Family Welfare), 1972–82; Episcopal Vicar for Social Welfare, 1982–84; Parish Priest of Highgate, WA, 1983–84; Bishop of Geraldton, WA, 1984–91. Mem., Bd of Inst. of Family Studies, Melbourne, 1980–83; Chairman: Nat. Liturgical Commn, 1995–2000; Bishops' Cttee for the Media, 2000–06; Bishops' Cttee for Evangelisation and Mission, 2000–03; Bishops' Commn for Aborigines and Torres Strait Islanders, 2006–11. Mem., Australian Citizenship Council, 1998–2000. Centenary Award (Federation Medal), Australia, 2003. *Recreations:* tennis, walking. *Address:* Gibney House, 50 Vincent Street, Mt Lawley, WA 6050, Australia.

HICKEY, Christopher John, CMG 2009; Director, British Council Schools, since 2013; *b* 8 Nov. 1951; *s* of late William Joseph Hickey and Evelyn Mary Hickey; *m* 1984, Pauline Donovan; one *s* one *d*. *Educ:* Monmouth Sch.; Univ. of Sheffield (BA French and Spanish); Univ. of Leeds (PGCE); University Coll. London (MPhil French Lit.); London Business Sch. (Sen. Exec. Prog.). Dip. TEFL (RSA). English Teacher, Univ. of Rennes and Franco-American Inst., 1975–78; joined British Council, 1978: English teaching asst, 1978–80; Asst English Lang. Officer, Morocco, 1981–83; Regl Lang. Advr, London, 1983–86; First Sec. (Educn), British Embassy, Abidjan, 1986–90; English Lang. Officer, Barcelona, 1990–93; Hd, Educnl Enterprises, Madrid, 1993–95; Dep. Dir, 1996–99, Dir, 1999–2000, Educnl Enterprises, London; Director: Greece, 2000–03; Spain, 2003–09; France, 2009–13. Chm. Bd, British Council Sch., Madrid, 2003–09; Member, Board: British Hispanic Foundn, Madrid, 2003–09; Coll. Franco-Britannique, Paris, 2009–13. Chm., British Nat. Cttee for Cultural Olympiad, 2002–04. *Recreations:* literature, languages, the arts, watching football, restaurants. *Address:* British Council, 10 Spring Gardens, SW1A 2BN. *T:* (020) 7389 4143. *E:* chris.hickey@britishcouncil.org.

HICKEY, Simon Roger Greenwood; His Honour Judge Hickey; a Circuit Judge, since 2012; *b* Alton, Hants, 1 Dec. 1961; *s* of Bill and Bunty Hickey; *m* 1991, Alison Black; two *s* one *d*. *Educ:* Pocklington Sch., E Yorks; Leicester Univ. (LLB Hons). Called to the Bar, Gray's Inn, 1985 (Holt Schol., 1985; Harold Langrish Prize (Best Constitnl Essay), 1985); in practice as barrister, 1985–2009; a Recorder (Crime), 2002–12; a Recorder (Civil), 2004–12; a Dep. Dist Judge (Crime), 2006–09; a District Judge (Magistrates' Courts), 2009–12. *Recreation:* worrying about Afghanistan. *Address:* Newcastle-upon-Tyne Crown Court, The Quayside, Newcastle upon Tyne NE1 3LA. *Club:* Royal Air Force.

HICKEY, Dr Stephen Harald Frederick; Chair, Community Transport Association, since 2010; *b* 10 July 1949; *s* of late Rev. Dr James Peter Hickinbotham and Ingeborg Hickinbotham; name changed by Deed Poll to Hickey, 1976; *m* 1976, Dr Janet Elizabeth Hunter; three *s*. *Educ:* St Lawrence Coll., Ramsgate; Corpus Christi Coll., Oxford (BA, MA); St Antony's Coll., Oxford (DPhil). Joined DHSS, 1974; Asst Private Sec. to Sec. of State, 1978–79 and 1984–85; Asst Sec., DHSS, later DSS, 1985–94; seconded to Rank Xerox (UK), 1989–90; Chief Exec., Civil Service Coll., 1994–98; Prin. Finance Officer, 1998–2002, Dir, Corporate Services, 2000–02, Dir, Corporate Develt Gp, 2002–03, DSS, then DWP; Acting Chief Exec., Highways Agency, 2003; Director General: Driver, Vehicle, Operator Gp, DfT, 2003–07; Safety, Service Delivery and Logistics Gp, DfT, 2007–08. Mem., Ind. Transport Commn, 2011–. Non-exec. Dir, Wandsworth NHS PCT, 2009–13 (Vice Chair, 2011–13); Lay Mem., Wandsworth CCG, 2012– (Vice Chair, 2012–). Trustee: St George's Hosp. Charity, 2008– (Chair, 2012–); Disabled Living Foundn, 2009–14. *Publications:* Workers in Imperial Germany: the miners of the Ruhr, 1985. *Recreations:* music, tennis, walking, history.

HICKFORD, Michael Francis; Hospital Chaplain, NHS Highland, 2011–13 (Hospital and Community Healthcare Chaplain, 2004–10); Rector, St Ninian's, Invergordon, 2012–13; *b* 7 Oct. 1953; *s* of Frank Hickford and Cherryl Wendy Rosalind (*née* Mitchell). *Educ:* Gravesend Grammar Sch.; Edinburgh Theological Coll. Chaplain, St John's Cathedral, Oban, 1986–89; Rector, St Mungo, Alexandria, Dunbartonshire, 1989–95; Priest i/c, St James the Great, Dingwall with St Anne, Strathpeffer, 1995–2003; Dean of Moray, Ross and Caithness, 1998–2003; Provost and Rector, 2003–04, Hon. Canon, 2007, Chapter Canon, 2012, St Andrew's Cathedral, Inverness; Interim Priest, St Andrew's, Tain with St Ninian's, Invergordon, 2011–12. *Recreations:* music, cookery, ornithology, railways.

HICKINBOTTOM, Hon. Sir Gary (Robert), Kt 2009; FCIArb; **Hon. Mr Justice Hickinbottom;** a Judge of the High Court of Justice, Queen's Bench Division, since 2009; Judge, Supreme Court, Falkland Islands, since 2006; *b* 22 Dec. 1955; *s* of Samuel Geoffrey Hickinbottom and Jean Irene Hickinbottom (*née* Greaney); *m* 1st, 1982 (marr. diss. 2001); two *s* two *d*; 2nd, 2004, Georgina Caroline Hamilton. *Educ:* Queen Mary's Grammar Sch., Walsall; University Coll., Oxford (MA); DipICArb, 1997. FCIArb 1995. Lectr, Poly. of Central London, 1980–81; admitted Solicitor, 1981; Solicitor Advocate (all Courts), 1997; Partner, McKenna & Co., subseq. Cameron McKenna, 1986–2000; Lectr, University Coll., Oxford, 1987–89; Registered Mediator, 1991; Parking Adjudicator, Parking Appeals Service and Nat. Parking Adjudication Service, 1994–2000; Asst Recorder, 1994–98; Recorder, 1998–2000; Circuit Judge, 2000–09; Dep. High Ct Judge, 2001–09; Chief Social Security Comr and Child Support Comr, 2003–09; Chief Pensions Appeal Comr, 2005–09; Designated Civil Judge: for S and W Wales, 2005–07; for Wales, 2007–08; Dep. Sen. Pres. of Tribunals, 2008–09; Pres., Administrative Appeals Chamber, Upper Tribunal, 2008–09; Liaison Judge for Northern and N Eastern Circuits, 2012–13, for Midland, Wales and Western Circuits, 2013–, Sen. Liaison Judge for Diversity, 2012–, QBD. Asst Comr, Boundary Commn of England, 2000. Member: Gen. Council of Bar and Law Soc. Jt Wkg Party on Civil Courts, 1992–93; Law Soc. Wkg Party on Gp Actions, 1994–2000; Judicial Technol. Bd, 2004–05, 2010–13. Bencher, Middle Temple, 2009. Pres., Solicitors Assoc. of Higher Court Advocates, 2009–. Mem., Imperial Soc. of Kts Bachelor, 2009–. Freeman of the City of London, 2010; Liveryman: Arbitrators' Co., 2010– (Ct Asst, 2011–); Bakers' Co., 2012–. *Publications:* various articles on law and legal procedure. *Recreations:* choral singing, opera, ballet, sport. *Address:* Royal Courts of Justice, Strand, WC2A 2LL. *Clubs:* Reform; London Welsh.

HICKMAN, Claire Josephine; *see* Moreland, C. J.

HICKMAN, Sir (Richard) Glenn, 4th Bt *cr* 1903; *b* 12 April 1949; *o s* of Sir Alfred Howard Whitby Hickman, 3rd Bt, and of Margaret Doris (*d* 1996), *o d* of Leonard Kempson; *S* father, 1979; *m* 1981, Heather Mary Elizabeth, *er d* of late Dr James Moffett, Swindon, and late Dr Gwendoline Moffett; two *s* one *d*. *Educ:* Eton. *Heir:* *s* Charles Patrick Alfred Hickman [*b* 5 May 1983; *m* 2014, Alicia Lorraine Newson]. *Address:* Manor Farm House, Liddington, Wilts SN4 0HD. *Club:* Turf.

HICKMAN, Richard Michael, CBE 2002; Chief Inquiry Reporter, Scottish Executive (formerly Scottish Office), 1997–2002; *b* 30 April 1942; *m* 1st, 1964, Lorna Dixon (marr. diss. 1992); two *s*; 2nd, 1993, Sandie Jane Randall; one step *s* one step *d*. *Educ:* Kingswood Sch., Bath; LSE (BA Hons Geog.); Regent St Polytechnic (DipTP); Univ. of British Columbia (MA Community and Regional Planning). MRTPI 1966. Planning Depts of LCC, 1963–65, of GLC, 1965–67; Scottish Develt Dept, 1969–78; Scottish Office Inquiry Reporters' Unit, 1979–2002. *Recreations:* walking, sailing, travel.

HICKMET, Richard Saladin; barrister-at-law; *b* 1 Dec. 1947; *s* of late Ferid Hickmet and Elizabeth Hickmet; *m* 1973, Susan (*née* Ludwig); three *d*. *Educ:* Millfield Sch.; Sorbonne; Hull Univ. (BA). Called to the Bar, Inner Temple, 1974. Mem., Wandsworth Borough Council, 1978–83 (Chm., Leisure and Amenities Cttee, 1980–83; privatised street cleansing, refuse collection, parks maintenance). Contested (C): Glanford and Scunthorpe, 1987; Eastbourne, Oct. 1990. MP (C) Glanford and Scunthorpe, 1983–87. *Recreations:* squash, hunting. *Address:* The Chantry, Rhode, North Petherton, Somerset TA5 2AD. *T:* (01278) 663388, *Fax:* (01278) 663981. *E:* law@richardhickmet.co.uk.

HICKS; *see* Joynson-Hicks.

HICKS, Dr Brendan Hamilton, FRCP; Regional Postgraduate Dean Director, NHS Kent, Surrey and Sussex (formerly South East Region), 1996–2004; *b* 22 Feb. 1942; *s* of Bryan Hamilton Hicks and Winifrede (*née* O'Leary); *m* 1966, Jackie Ann Box; one *s* one *d*. *Educ:* St Brendan's Coll., Bristol; Guy's Hosp. Med. Sch., Univ. of London (BSc 1962; MB BS 1965; MD 1976). FRCP 1982. Jun. med. posts, Guy's Hosp., RPMS and Brompton Hosp., 1965–67; Governors' Res. Schol. and Lectr in Medicine, Guy's Hosp. Med. Sch., 1967–72; NIH Internat. Fellow (US Public Health Service/MRC), Univ. of Michigan, Ann Arbor, 1972–73; Sen. Lectr in Medicine, Undergrad. Tutor and Hon. Consultant Physician, Guy's Hosp. and Med. Sch., 1974–80; Sen. Lectr in Medicine, UMDS of Guy's and St Thomas' Hosps, and Consultant Physician to Guy's and St Thomas' and Lewisham Hosps, 1981–95; Postgrad. Dean and Trust Dir, Postgrad. Med. and Dental Educn, Guy's and St Thomas' Hosp., 1985–95. Hon. Prof., Univ. of Brighton, 2002–. Mem. Cttee, Friends of Greenwich Park, 2007– (Chm., 2009–11). Hon. DSc Brighton, 2005. *Publications:* contrib. chapter in: A Short Textbook of Medicine, ed jtly, biennially, 1978–92; Principles of Clinical Medicine, ed Rees and Williams, 1995; contrib. papers in Metabolism, Diabetic Medicine, Clin. Endocrinol., etc. *Recreations:* drawing, glass-blowing, stained glass. *Address:* 60 Greenwich Park Street, SE10 9LT. *T:* (020) 8858 7363. *E:* brendan.hicks@btinternet.com.

HICKS, Dr Colin Peter, CB 2007; CChem, FRSC; Director General, British National Space Centre, 1999–2006; *b* 1 May 1946; *s* of George Stephen Frederick Hicks and Irene Maud (*née* Hargrave); *m* 1967, Elizabeth Joan Payne; two *d*. *Educ:* Rutlish Grammar Sch., Merton; Univ. of Bristol (BSc, PhD). Lectr in Chemistry, Univ. of W Indies, Jamaica, 1970–73; ICI Res. Fellow, Univ. of Exeter, 1973–75; DTI, 1975–2006; NPL, 1975–80; Laboratory of Govt Chemist, 1984–87; Sec., Ind. Develt Adv. Bd, 1988–90; Hd, Res. and Technol. Policy Div., 1990–94; Hd of Envmt and Energy Technologies Div., 1994–96; Dir, Envmt, 1996–99. Mem., NERC, 2002–06. Pres., Eurisy, 2006–. Mem. Council, 2006–13, Trustee Bd, 2009–13, BUGB. *Address:* 41 Teddington Park, Teddington TW11 8DB.

HICKS, His Honour John Charles; QC 1980; a Judge of the Technology and Construction Court of the High Court (formerly the Official Referees' Courts), 1993–2000; a Circuit Judge, 1988–2000; *b* 4 March 1928; *s* of late Charles Hicks and late Marjorie Jane Hicks; *m* 1957, Elizabeth Mary, *o d* of late Rev. J. B. Jennings; one *d* (one *s* decd). *Educ:* King Edward VI Grammar Schs, Chelmsford and Totnes; London Univ. LLM 1954. Served RA (National Service), 1946–48. Admitted solicitor, 1952; called to the Bar, Middle Temple, 1966; a Recorder, 1978–88. Legal Dept, Thomas Tilling Ltd, 1953–54; Partner in Messrs Burchells, solicitors, 1955–65; Methodist Missionary Soc., Caribbean, 1965–66. Jl Sec., Methodist Conf., 1989–97. *Publications:* (contrib. precedents) George on the Sale of Flats, 1957, 4th edn 1978; (contrib. precedents) Precedents for the Conveyancer, 2004; (ed jtly) The Constitution and Discipline of the Methodist Church in the Caribbean and the Americas, 1967, with annual supplements to 1987; (ed) The Constitutional Practice and Discipline of the Methodist Church, 6th edn 1974, 7th edn 1988, with annual supplements, 1974–97; articles in Mod. Law Rev., Cambridge Law Jl, Conveyancer, and Epworth Rev. *Recreations:* singing, organ playing, theatre, opera, the Methodist Constitution. *Address:* Flat 3, 17 Montagu Square, W1H 2LE. *T:* (020) 7935 6008. *E:* john.hicks@montagusquare.net.

HICKS, Maureen Patricia; tourism consultant and freelance tour director, since 2004, now specialising in worldwide railway tours; *b* 23 Feb. 1948; *d* of Ron and Nora Cutler; *m* 1973, Keith Hicks; one *s* one *d*. *Educ:* Ashley Secondary School; Brockenhurst Grammar School; Furzedown College of Education. Teacher's Cert. Secondary Teacher, Drama and English, 1969–70; Marks & Spencer Management, 1970–74; Asst Area Educn Officer, 1974–76; Dir, Motor Museum, 1976–82; Project Dir, Stratford-upon-Avon Visitor Mgt Nat. Pilot Project, 1992–96; Dir of Fundraising and Marketing, Myton Hamlet Hospice, Warwick, 1997–2001; Stratford Upon Avon Town Centre Project Manager, 2000–04. Mem., Stratford DC, 1979–84. MP (C) Wolverhampton North East, 1987–92; contested (C) Wolverhampton NE, 1992. PPS to Minister of State and Parly Under-Sec. of State, FCO, 1991–92; Sec., H of C Tourism Cttee, 1987–92. Non-executive Director: David Clarke Associates, 1992–96; S Warwicks Combined Care (formerly Mental Health Services) NHS Trust, 1994–2002. Trustee: Kingsley Sch., Leamington Spa, 2001–; Earl Mountbatten Hospice, IoW, 2009– (Vice Chm., 2012–; Chair, Finance, Audit and Resources, 2013–). Hon. Fellow, Wolverhampton Univ., 1992. *Recreations:* MG Midget, USA, travel, theatre, golf, bridge.

HICKS, Sir Robert, Kt 1996; Chairman: Resound Health Ltd, since 2004; Marjon Tenancies Ltd, since 2012; *b* 18 Jan. 1938; *s* of W. H. Hicks; *m* 1st, 1962, Maria Elizabeth Ann Gwyther (marr. diss. 1988); two *d*; 2nd, 1991, Mrs Glenys Foote. *Educ:* Queen Elizabeth Grammar Sch., Crediton; University Coll., London; Univ. of Exeter. Taught at St Austell Grammar Sch., 1961–64; Lecturer in Regional Geography, Weston-super-Mare Technical Coll., 1964–70. MP (C): Bodmin, 1970–Feb. 1974, Oct. 1974–1983; Cornwall SE, 1983–97. An Asst Govt Whip, 1973–74; Member: Select Cttee of House of Commons, European Legislation, 1973, 1976–97; Speaker's Panel, 1992–97; Vice-Chm., Cons. Parly European Affairs Cttee, 1979–81; Chairman: Cons. Parly Agric. Cttee, 1988–90 (Vice-Chm., 1972–73 (Chm., Horticultural Sub-Cttee), and 1974–82); Westcountry Gp of Cons. MPs, 1976–77; UK Gp, Parly Assoc. for Euro-Arab Co-operation, 1982–97; Vice-Chm., Cons. Party ME Council, 1992–97 (Treasurer, 1980–92); Parly Adviser to British Hotels, Restaurants and Caterers Assoc., 1974–97, to Milk Marketing Bd, 1985–97. Chairman: Westcountry Enterprises, 1997–2003; Midas Consortium, 2003–05. Pres., Plymouth Albion RFC, 1991–96. Chm., Silvanus Trust, 1999–2010. Trustee, Peninsula Med. Sch. Foundn, 1997–2002. Chm., Bd of Govs, Plymouth Coll., 2004–09. *Recreations:* cricket, gardening, golf. *Address:* Burndoo, Luckett, Callington, Cornwall PL17 8NH. *Clubs:* Farmers, MCC.

HICKS, Robin Edgcumbe; freelance local journalist; Member, Management Board, Royal Smithfield Show, 1998–2004; *b* 6 Dec. 1942; *s* of late Ronald Eric Edgcumbe Hicks and Fredrica Hicks; *m* 1970, Sue (*née* Dalton); one *s* one *d*. *Educ:* Bancroft's Sch.; Seale Hayne Coll. (NDA; Dip. Farm Management); Univ. of Reading (DipAgric Extension). ARAgS 1995. Farm worker, 1961–63; Agricl Advr, MAFF, 1967–69; Producer/Presenter, BBC Farming Today, 1969–71; Churchill Fellow, 1973; various production posts, radio and television, 1971–77; Hd of Marketing and Develt, RASE, 1977–79; Hd of Network Radio, BBC South and West, 1979–88; Chief Exec., RASE, 1989–91; Dir, Royal Smithfield Show, 1992–98; Dir, P&O Events Ltd, 1992–98; Chief Exec., Consortium of Rural TECs, 1998–99; Dir, Expocentric.com, 1999–2001. Editor: blablablah, 2006–09; www.heraultwhatson.info, 2009–14; Reporter: French News, 2004–08; The Connexion, 2009–13; TheFrenchPaper, 2009–14. Consultant, Landscape '99; PR Consultant, Beziers Airport, 2007–14. Mem., Bristol and Weston HA, 1986–88; Vice-Chm., Radio Acad., 1986–88; Trustee: St George's Music Trust, 1981–88; Head Injury Recovery Trust, 1986–94; Rural Housing Trust, 1990–92; Avon Valley Railway, 2015–; Member: Exec. Cttee, SW Arts, 1981–85; SW Concerts Bd, 1981–88. Steward, St George's, Bristol. Hon. Life Mem., Royal Smithfield Club, 2005–. Freeman, City of London, 1977; Liveryman, Drapers' Co., 1981. Confrère, Petit Pâté de Pézenas, 2012. *Recreations:* family and friends, volunteering in Bristol, enjoying Heritage railways. *Address:* 232 The Crescent, Hannover Quay, Bristol BS1 5JR. *Clubs:* Farmers'; Midi Cricket (Pres., 2005–06; Hon. Life Pres., 2006).

HICKS, Thomas; *see* Steele, Tommy.

HICKS, William David Antony; QC 1995; *b* 11 June 1951; *s* of Maj.-Gen. William Michael Ellis Hicks, CB, OBE; *m* 1982, Jennifer Caroline Ross; one *s* two *d*. *Educ:* Eton Coll.; Magdalene Coll., Cambridge (MA Econs). Called to the Bar, Inner Temple, 1975. Freeman, Fishmongers' Co., 2012. *Recreations:* fishing, Real tennis, ski-ing, walking, bee keeping. *Address:* Landmark Chambers, 180 Fleet Street, EC4A 2HG. *Clubs:* Flyfishers', MCC.

HICKS BEACH, family name of **Earl St Aldwyn**.

HICKSON, Prof. Ian David, PhD; FRS 2010; Professor of Molecular Aging, University of Copenhagen, since 2010; *b* Blackpool, 19 Aug. 1957; *s* of Leslie Hickson and Margaret Hickson; *m* 1st, 1978, Julie Hickson (marr. diss. 2007); one *s* one *d* (and one *d* decd); 2nd, 2009, Dr Ying Liu. *Educ:* Arnold Sch., Blackpool; Univ. of Newcastle upon Tyne (BSc; PhD 1982). Lectr, Univ. of Newcastle upon Tyne, 1983–88; Sen. Scientist, 1989–95, Principal Scientist, 1995–99, ICRF; Prof. of Molecular Oncology, Univ. of Oxford, 1999–2010; Dep. Dir, CRUK Oxford Cancer Centre, 1999–2010. FMedSci 2010. *Publications:* over 200 articles in learned scientific jls. *Recreations:* swimming, cinema, food and drink, family. *Address:* Center for Healthy Aging, Department of Cellular and Molecular Medicine, Panum Institute, Building 18.1.32, University of Copenhagen, Blegdamsvej 3, Copenhagen 2200, Denmark.

HICKSON, Peter Charles Fletcher; Chairman: Communisis plc, since 2007; Chemring Group plc, since 2010; *b* Cambridge, 30 May 1945; *s* of Geoffrey and Jane Hickson; *m* 1972, Rosemary Dawson; three *s* one *d*. *Educ:* Uppingham Sch.; Fitzwilliam Coll., Cambridge (BA 1967; MA). Chief Accountant, Doulton Glass Industries Ltd, 1970–78; Finance Director: Wimpey Asphalt Ltd, 1978–80; Tarmac Buildings Products Ltd, 1980–84; Dep. Chief Exec., United Scientific Hldgs plc, 1985–89; Man. Dir, Tern plc, 1989–91; Finance Dir, MAI plc, 1991–96; Gp Finance Dir, Powergen plc, 1996–2002; Chm., Anglian Water, 2003–09. Non-executive Director: Meridian Broadcasting Ltd, 1991–96; Anglia TV plc, 1994–96; RAC plc, 1994–2002; Marconi Corp. plc, 2004–07; Scottish Power plc, 2006–07; London & Continental Railways Ltd, 2007–11; Kazakhmys plc, 2009–11; Coalfield Resources (formerly

UK Coal) plc, 2011–. Trustee, Orbis Charitable Trust, 2008– (Chm, 2015–). Chm. Govs, St John's Sch., Leatherhead, 2003–14. *Recreations:* music, golf, cricket. *Address:* Communisis plc, Longbow House, 14/20 Chiswell Street, EC1Y 4TW. *T:* (020) 7382 8850. *E:* phickson@chemring.co.uk. *Clubs:* Oxford and Cambridge, MCC, City of London; Wimbledon; Royal Wimbledon Golf, Wimbledon Park Golf; Real de Golf Las Brisas (Marbella).

HIDDEN, Hon. Sir Anthony (Brian), Kt 1989; a Judge of the High Court of Justice, Queen's Bench Division, 1989–2003; *b* 7 March 1936; *s* of late James Evelyn Harold Hidden, GM and Gladys Bessie (*née* Brooks); *m* 1982, Mary Elise Torriano Pritchard (marr. diss. 2000), *d* of R. C. Pritchard of Barton Abbotts, Tetbury, Glos; three *s* one *d*. *Educ:* Reigate Grammar Sch.; Emmanuel Coll., Cambridge (BA Hons 1957, MA 1960). 2nd Lieut, 1st Royal Tank Regt, Far East Land Forces, Hong Kong, 1958–59. Called to the Bar, Inner Temple, 1961, Bencher, 1985; Mem., Hon. Soc. of Inner Temple, 1956–, and of Lincoln's Inn (*ad eundem*), 1973–. QC 1976; a Recorder, 1977–89; Leader, SE Circuit, 1986–89. Inspector, Clapham Junction Railway Accident, 1988. *Recreations:* reading, playing bad golf.

HIDE, Prof. Raymond, CBE 1990; FRS 1971; Senior Research Investigator, Department of Mathematics, Imperial College, University of London, since 2000; Emeritus Professor of Physics, Oxford University, since 1994 (Research Professor, Departments of Physics and Earth Sciences, 1992–94); *b* 17 May 1929; *s* of late Stephen Hide and Rose Edna (*née* Cartlidge); *m* 1958, (Phyllis) Ann Licence; one *s* two *d*. *Educ:* Percy Jackson Grammar Sch., near Doncaster; Manchester Univ. (BSc 1st cl. hons Physics, 1950); Gonville and Caius Coll., Cambridge (PhD 1953, ScD 1969; Hon. Fellow, 2001). CPhys, FInstP, 1998. Res. Assoc. in Astrophysics, Univ. of Chicago, 1953–54; Sen. Res. Fellow, AERE Harwell, 1954–57; Lectr in Physics, Univ. of Durham (King's Coll., Newcastle), 1957–61; Prof. of Geophysics and Physics, MIT, 1961–67; Hd of Geophysical Fluid Dynamics Lab., Met. Office, 1967–90 (CSO 1975); Fellow, Jesus Coll., Oxford, 1983–96 (Hon. Fellow, 1997); Dir, Robert Hooke Inst. and Vis. Prof., Dept of Physics, Oxford Univ., 1990–92. Short-term vis. appts at Princeton Inst. for Advanced Study, 1954, MIT and UCLA, 1960, CIT, 1993 (Fairchild Schol.); Visiting Professor: UCL, 1967–84; Reading Univ., 1976–91; Leeds Univ., 1986–91; Gresham Prof. of Astronomy, Gresham Coll., City of London, 1985–90; Adrian Fellow, Univ. of Leicester, 1980–83. Distinguished Vis. Scientist, Jet Propulsion Lab., CIT, 1985–97; Hon. Sen. Res. Fellow, Inst. of Oceanographic Scis Deacon Lab., 1990–; Hon. Scientist, Rutherford Appleton Lab., 1992–. Member Council: RAS, 1969–72 and 1983–86 (Pres., 1983–85); Royal Meteorological Soc., 1969–72 and 1974–77 (Pres., 1974–76; Hon. Mem., 1989); NERC, 1972–75; Eur. Geophysical Soc., 1981–85 (Pres., 1982–84, Hon. Mem., 1988); Royal Soc., 1988–90. Lectures: Symons Meml, RMetS, 1970; R. A. Fisher Meml, 1977; Halley, Oxford, 1980; Jeffreys, RAS, 1981; Union, Internat. Union of Geodesy and Geophysics, Hamburg, 1983; Scott, Cambridge, 1984; Thompson, Toronto, 1984; Lindsay, NASA, 1988; Courtauld, Manchester Lit. & Phil Soc., 1996; Schuster, Manchester Univ., 1998; Starr, MIT, 2001. MAE 1988; Mem., Pontifical Acad. of Scis, 1996; Fellow: Amer. Acad. of Arts and Sciences, 1964; Amer. Geophys. Union, 1967. Hon. DSc: Leicester, 1985; UMIST, 1994; Paris, 1995. Charles Chree Medal, Inst. Physics, 1975; Holweck Medal, Soc. Franç. de Physique, 1982; Gold Medal, RAS, 1989; William Bowie Medal, Amer. Geophysical Union, 1997; Hughes Medal, Royal Soc., 1998; Richardson Medal, European Geophys. Soc., 1999; Symons Gold Medal, RMetS, 2003. *Publications:* papers in scientific jls. *Address:* Department of Mathematics, Imperial College, 180 Queen's Gate, SW7 2RH.

HIDER, David James; Director, Internal Communications Project, British Gas, 1994–95; *b* 5 Nov. 1934; *s* of Edward James Hider and Marguerite Noel Hider (*née* James); *m* 1963, Margaret Gilbert Macdonald Watson; two *s* one *d*. *Educ:* Roan Sch., Greenwich; King Edward VII Nautical Coll., Poplar. Master Mariner; DMS; CIGEM. Merchant Navy, 1952–67 (to Chief Officer); South Eastern Gas: Commercial Asst, 1967; Conversion Unit Manager, 1969; Area Service Manager, Sussex, 1973; Regl Service Manager, 1976; Dir of Marketing, 1981; British Gas: Dir of Service, 1983; Dir of Domestic Marketing, 1990; Regl Chm., British Gas S Western, 1990–94. Mem., SW IDB, 1997–99; Vice Chm., Bristol Regeneration Partnership, 2000–03; Chm., Bristol Partnership Regeneration Progs Mgt Gp (formerly Bristol Regeneration Partnership), 2003–04. Chm., Avon Youth Assoc., 1996–2015. Chm. and Man. Dir, St Peter's Hospice Enterprises, 2000–10; Trustee, CLIC, 2000–04. Gov., UWE, 1993–2004. *Publications:* contribs to Jl IGasE. *Recreations:* squash, swimming, walking, cooking, flying.

HIDER, Prof. Robert Charles, PhD; CChem, FRSC; Professor of Medicinal Chemistry, King's College, London, since 1987; *b* 14 Aug. 1943; *s* of Charles Thomas Hider and Josephine Mary (*née* Breitbach); *m* 1967, Shirley Christine Nickels; one *s* one *d*. *Educ:* King's Coll., London (BSc Chem. and Physics 1964; PhD Chem. 1967; FKC 1997). Wellcome Res. Fellow, St Thomas' Hosp., 1967–70; Lectr, then Reader, Dept of Chem., Essex Univ., 1970–87; King's College, London: Head, Sch. of Life, Basic Med. and Health Scis, then of Health & Life Scis, 1994–2000; Head, Dept of Pharmacy, 2000–03; Head, Sch. of Biomed. Scis, subseq. Sch. of Biomed. and Health Scis, 2002–07. Associated with devel of medicines for thalassaemia, anaemia, and renal failure. Visiting Professor: Dept of Biochem., Univ. of Calif, Berkeley, 1977 and 1980; Coll. of Pharmaceutical Scis, Zhejiang Univ., 2009–; Chiang Mia Univ., 2012–. Hon. MRPharmS, 1995. Hanbury Meml Medal, 2014; Thousand Talents Award, China, 2014. Member, Editorial Board: Toxicon, 1986–98; Biometals, 1990–; Biochem. Jl, 1996–2001; Jl Pharm. Sci., 2002–12; Eur. Jl Pharm. Sci., 2002–. *Publications:* contrib. articles on pharmaceutically active peptides and metal chelating agents to pharmaceutical, biochem. and chem. jls. *Recreations:* arachnology, natural history, Australian philately. *Address:* 257 Point Clear Road, St Osyth, Essex CO16 8JL. *T:* (01255) 821335.

HIELSCHER, Sir Leo (Arthur), AC 2004; Kt 1987; Foundation Chairman, Queensland Treasury Corporation, since 2010 (Chairman, 1988–2010); *b* 1 Oct. 1926; *s* of Leslie Charles Hielscher and Elizabeth Jane Petersen; *m* 1948, Mary Ellen Pelgrave; one *s* one *d* (and one *s* decd). *Educ:* Brisbane State High Sch.; Univ. of Queensland (BComm, AAUQ). FCPA; FAIM. Queensland Public Service, 1942; RAAF, 1945–47; Asst Under Sec. (Budget), Qld Treasury, 1964–69, Dep. Under Treasurer, 1969–74; Under Treas. of Qld (CS Hd of Treasury Dept of Qld Govt), 1974–88. Eisenhower Exchange Fellow, 1973. Chm., Independent Superannuation Preservation Fund Pty Ltd. *Recreations:* golf, fishing, boating, theatre. *Address:* 3301/15 Cansdale Street, Yeronga, Brisbane, Qld 4104, Australia. *T:* (home) (7) 38926296, *T:* (business) (7) 38424620, *Fax:* (7) 32100262. *Clubs:* Brisbane, Tattersalls (Brisbane).

HIGGINS, family name of **Baron Higgins**.

HIGGINS, Baron *cr* 1997 (Life Peer), of Worthing, in the co. of West Sussex; **Terence Langley Higgins,** KBE 1993; PC 1979; DL; *b* 18 Jan. 1928; *s* of late Reginald and Rose Higgins, Dulwich; *m* 1961, Dame Rosalyn Higgins, *qv*; one *s* one *d*. *Educ:* Alleyn's Sch., Dulwich; Gonville and Caius Coll., Cambridge (BA (Hons) 1958; MA 1963; Pres., Cambridge Union Soc., 1958). Brit. Olympic Team (athletics) 1948, 1952. NZ Shipping Co., 1948–55; Lectr in Economic Principles, Dept of Economics, Yale Univ., 1958–59; Economist with Unilever, 1959–64. Dir, 1980–92, Consultant, 1992–2003, Lex Service Group (Chm., Lex Pension Fund Trustees, 1994–2002); Dir, First Choice Holidays (formerly Owners Abroad) plc, 1992–97. MP (C) Worthing, 1964–97. Opposition Spokesman on Treasury and Economic Affairs, 1966–70; Minister of State, Treasury, 1970–72; Financial Sec. to Treasury, 1972–74; Opposition Spokesman: on Treasury and Econ. Affairs, 1974; for Trade, 1974–76; Principal Opposition Spokesman, H of L, on social security, 1997–2001, on work and pensions, 2001–06. Chairman: Select Cttee on Procedure, 1980–83; Select Cttee on Treasury and CS, 1983–97 (Mem., 1980–97); House of Commons Liaison Cttee, 1984–97; Sec., Cons. Parly Finance Cttee, 1965–66; Chm., Cons. Parly Cttee on Sport, 1979–81, on Transport, 1979–91; Member: Public Accounts Commn, 1984–97 (Chm., 1996–97); Exec. Cttee, 1922 Cttee, 1980–97. Member: H of L Select Cttee on Speakership of H of L, 2005, on Personal Service Companies, 2014; Jt Cttee on the Conventions of Parlt, 2006. Mem., Claims Resolution Tribunal for Dormant Accounts in Switzerland, 1998–2002. Member: Council, RIIA, 1979–85; Council, IAM, 1979–98. Governor: NIESR, 1989–; Dulwich Coll., 1980–95; Alleyn's Sch., 1995–99. Special Fellow, PSI, 1986 (Mem. Council, 1989–95); Trustee, Industry and Parlt Trust, 1985–91; Hon. Mem., Keynes College, Univ. of Kent, 1976–. DL W Sussex, 1989. *Address:* House of Lords, SW1A 0PW. *Clubs:* Reform, Yale; Hawks (Cambridge); Koninklijke Haagsche Golf.

HIGGINS, Andrew James, PhD; MRCVS; FRSB; Chairman, Retired Greyhound Trust, since 2008; Editor-in-Chief, The Veterinary Journal (formerly British Veterinary Journal), since 1991 (Deputy Editor, 1990–91); *b* 7 Dec. 1948; *s* of late Edward James Higgins and of Gabrielle Joy, *d* of late Sir John Kelland; *m* 1981, Nicola, *d* of late Peter Eliot and of Jenifer Eliot; one *s* three *d*. *Educ:* St Michael's Coll., Leeds; Royal Veterinary Coll., Univ. of London (BVetMed 1973; PhD 1985); Centre for Tropical Med., Univ. of Edinburgh (MSc 1977). FRSB (FIBiol 1993). Commnd RAVC 1973. Vet. Officer to Sultan of Oman, 1975–76; Vet. Advr, ME and N Africa, Wellcome Foundn, 1977–82; Scientific Dir and Chief Exec., Animal Health Trust, 1988–99. Cons., FAO, 1981–86. Mem., Lord Chancellor's Adv. Sub-cttee for W Suffolk, 1999–2008. Member: Conservation and Welfare Cttee, 1987–96, Ethics Cttee, 1994–2014, Welfare Cttee, 1998–2013, Zool Soc. of London; Vet. Res. Club, 1989–; Vet. Panel, BEF, 1993–2009 (Chm., 2004–09); Govt Adv. Cttee on Quarantine, 1997–98; Greyhound Board of Great Britain: Mem., UK Accreditation Service Cttee, 2009–, Disciplinary Cttee, 2009–; Chairman: Ind. Anti-doping and Medication Control Review, 2009–10; Doping and Medication Adv. Panel, 2010–12; Ind. Doping and Medication Advr, 2012–14. Trustee: Dogs Trust (formerly Nat. Canine Defence League), 1999–2009; RCVS Trust, 2001–06; Animals in War Meml Fund, 2001–08; Scientific Advr, World Horse Welfare (formerly Internat. League for the Protection of Horses), 2006–. Fédération Equestre Internationale: Hon. Scientific Advr, 1990–2010; Chm., Medication Adv. Gp, 2005–08; Mem., Vet. Cttee, 2006–10. Man. Consultant, Compton Fundraising Consultants Ltd, 2000–; Chm., Strata Technology Ltd, 2002–11. Scientific Fellow, Zool Soc. Univ. of London Laurel, 1971; Ciba-Geigy Prize for Res. in Animal Health, 1985; Equine Veterinary Jl Open Award and medal, 1986; Centenary Prize, Central Vet. Soc., 1986; George Fleming Prize, British Vet. Jl, 1987; President's Award, Vet. Mktg Assoc., 1997. *Publications:* (contrib.) An Anatomy of Veterinary Europe, 1972; (ed and contrib.) The Camel in Health and Disease, 1986; (ed) The Equine Manual, 1995, 2nd edn 2005; With the SAS and Other Animals, 2011; papers in sci. and gen. pubns and communications to learned socs. *Recreations:* ski-ing, countryside, opera. *Address:* PO Box 274, Bury St Edmunds, Suffolk IP29 5LW. *Club:* Royal Society of Medicine.

HIGGINS, Charlotte Elizabeth; Chief Culture Writer, The Guardian, since 2008; *b* Stoke-on-Trent, 6 Sept. 1972; *d* of Peter and Pamela Higgins. *Educ:* Newcastle-under-Lyme Sch.; Balliol Coll., Oxford (MA 1994). Asst Ed., Histl Collections, 1994–95; Sub-ed., Vogue, 1995–96; Chief Sub-ed., World of Interiors, 1996–97; The Guardian: Dep. Ed., Space mag., 1997–99; Classical Music Ed., 2000–04; Arts Corresp., 2004–08. Associate Fellow, Centre for Study of Greek and Roman Antiquity, Corpus Christi Coll., Oxford, 2012–. *Publications:* Latin Love Lessons, 2007; It's All Greek to Me, 2008; Under Another Sky, 2013; This New Noise, 2015. *Recreations:* chamber music, cocktail construction. *Address:* The Guardian, Kings Place, 90 York Way, N1 9GU. *E:* charlotte.higgins@theguardian.com.

HIGGINS, Christopher; *see* Higgins, J. C.

HIGGINS, Prof. Christopher Francis; DL; PhD; FRSE, FMedSci; Vice-Chancellor and Warden, 2007–14, and Pro-Chancellor, 2014–15, Durham University; *b* 24 June 1955; *s* of Prof. Philip John Higgins and Betty Ann Higgins (*née* Edmonds); *m* 1st, 1978, Elizabeth Mary Joy (marr. diss. 1994); two *d*; 2nd, 1994, Suzanne Wilson Higgins (marr. diss. 2001); three *d*. *Educ:* Univ. of Durham (BSc 1st Cl. Hons Botany 1976; PhD 1979). FRSE 1989. NATO-SERC postdoctoral Fellow, Univ. of California, Berkeley, 1979–81; University of Dundee: Lectr, 1981–87; Reader and Prof. of Molecular Genetics, 1987–89; Lister Inst. Res. Fellow, 1983–89; Oxford University: Principal Scientist, ICRF, and Dep. Dir, ICRF Labs, Inst. of Molecular Medicine, 1989–93; Fellow, Keble Coll., 1989–93; Nuffield Prof. of Clin. Biochemistry, and Fellow, Hertford Coll., 1993–97; Dir, MRC Clinical Scis Centre, and Prof. and Hd of Div. of Clinical Scis, Imperial Coll. London, 1998–2007. Howard Hughes Internat. Res. Scholar; Fellow, EMBO, 1988. Mem., BBSRC, 1997–2000; Mem., Governing Council, John Innes Centre, 1994–2000; Mem. Exec. Council, AMRC, 2003–07. Chairman: Spongiform Encephalopathy Adv. Cttee, 2004–11; Scientific Adv. Bd, Microscience; Mem., Nat. Expert Panel on New and Emerging Infections; Scientific Advr, Select Cttee on Stem Cells, H of L, 2001–02; Mem., Human Genetics Commn, 2005–08. Charity Trustee: Future Harvest, 2001–05; 2 Higher Ground, 2001–04; Kennedy Inst. for Rheumatology, 2004–07. Founding Editor and Editor-in-Chief, Molecular Microbiology, 1987–2003. Mem. Bd, One NorthEast RDA, 2008–12. Chm. Trustees, Nat. Youth Choir, 2010–. DL Co. Durham, 2008. Founder FMedSci 1998 (Mem., Council, 2000–03); FRSA. Hugh Bean Prize for Violin, 1970, Exhibr, 1970–73, RCM; Fleming Medal, Soc. for Gen. Microbiol., 1987; CIBA Medal and Prize, Biochemical Soc., 1995. *Publications:* numerous research papers in learned jls. *Recreations:* five daughters, medieval farm house, classical music and opera.

HIGGINS, Clare Frances Elizabeth; actress; *d* of James Stephen Higgins and Paula Cecilia (*née* Murphy). *Educ:* St Philomena's Convent Sch., Derbys; Ecclesbourne Sch., Derbys; LAMDA. *Theatre includes:* A View from the Bridge, Harrogate; The White Devil, Oxford Playhouse; Beethoven's Tenth, Vaudeville; Jenkin's Ear, Royal Court; Ride Down Mount Morgan, Wyndhams; A Letter of Resignation, Comedy, 1997; Heartbreak House, 2000, The Secret Rapture, 2001, Chichester; Royal Exchange, Manchester: Measure for Measure; Rollo; Blood Black and Gold; The Deep Man; Greenwich: Time and the Conways; The Rivals; A Streetcar Named Desire; Royal Shakespeare Company: A Midsummer Night's Dream, 1989; Hamlet, 1989; Antony and Cleopatra, 1992; Royal National Theatre: The Futurists, 1986; The Secret Rapture, 1988; Richard III, 1990; King Lear, 1990; Napoli Milionaria, 1991; The Absence of War, 1993 (televised, 1996); The Children's Hour, 1994 (Critics' Circle Award, 1995); Sweet Bird of Youth, 1995 (Olivier Award, Critics' Circle Award, Time Out Award, 1995); The Walls, 2001; Vincent in Brixton, 2002 (Olivier Award, Evening Standard Award, Critics' Circle Award, 2003); Major Barbara, 2008; A Slight Ache, 2008; Oedipus, 2008; All's Well That Ends Well, 2009; The Seagull, Present Laughter, W Yorks Playhouse, 1998; Who's Afraid of Virginia Woolf, Bristol Old Vic, 2002, Th. Royal, Bath, 2014; Hecuba, 2004 (Olivier Award, 2005), Phaedra, 2006, Donmar Warehouse; Death of a Salesman, The Night of the Iguana, Lyric, 2005; The Fever, Royal Court, 2009; Mrs Klein, Almeida, 2009; Other Desert Cities, Old Vic, 2014; Clarion, Arcola, 2015. *Television includes:* Pride and Prejudice; Unity; Byron; The Concubine; Mitch; The Citadel; Cover Her Face; Foreign Body; Beautiful Lies; After the War; Downtown Lagos; Circle of Deceit; Man of the Month, The Syndicate; Parade's End; Downton Abbey; Homefront. *Films include:* 1919; Hellraiser; Hellbound; The Fruit Machine; Bad Behaviour, 1993; Let it Come Down, 1995; Easter House, 1995; Small Faces, 1996; House of Mirth, 1999; The Libertine, 2004; The Golden Compass, 2007. *Address:* c/o Conway van Gelder Grant Ltd, 8–12 Broadwick Street, W1F 8HW.

HIGGINS, Daniel John P.; *see* Pearce-Higgins.

HIGGINS, His Honour David Edward Alexander; a Circuit Judge, since 2003–15; a Deputy High Court Judge, since 2007; *b* 15 Dec. 1945; *s* of Edward and Rena Higgins; *m* 1971, Roberta Jane Reading; two *d*. *Educ:* St Peter's Sch., York; Newcastle Univ. (LLB). Partner, Herbert Smith (Solicitors), 1976–2003; a Recorder of the Crown Court, 2000–03. *Recreations:* opera, equine sports, Italy. *Address:* c/o Circuit Secretariat, Rose Court, 2 Southwark Bridge, SE1 9HS.

HIGGINS, Jack; *see* Patterson, Harry.

HIGGINS, Prof. James, PhD; FBA 1999; Professor of Latin American Literature, University of Liverpool, 1988–2004, now Emeritus; *b* 28 May 1939; *s* of Peter and Annie Higgins; *m* 1962, Kirstine Anne Atwell; one *s* (and one *s* decd). *Educ:* Our Lady's High Sch., Motherwell; Univ. of Glasgow (MA); Univ. of Lyons (LèsL); PhD Liverpool 1968. Department of Hispanic Studies, Liverpool University: Asst Lectr, 1964–67; Lectr, 1967–73; Sen. Lectr, 1973–83; Reader, 1983–88; Head of Dept, 1988–97. Visiting Professor: Univ. of Pittsburgh, 1968; Univ. of Waterloo, Ont, 1974; Univ. of West Indies, Trinidad, 1979; Univ. of Wisconsin-Madison, 1990; Hon. Professor: Univ. of San Marcos, Lima, 1984; Univ. of Stirling, 2006–12. Corresp. Fellow, Peruvian Acad., 2002. Comdr, Order of Merit (Peru), 1988. *Publications:* Visión del hombre y de la vida en las últimas obras poéticas de César Vallejo, 1970; César Vallejo: an anthology of his poetry, 1970; The Poet in Peru, 1982; A History of Peruvian Literature, 1987; César Vallejo: a selection of his poetry (with trans), 1987; César Vallejo en su poesía, 1990; Cambio social y constantes humanas: la narrative corta de J. R. Ribeyro, 1991; Hitos de la poesía peruana, 1993; Myths of the Emergent: social mobility in contemporary Peruvian fiction, 1994; The Literary Representation of Peru, 2002; Lima: a cultural and literary history, 2005; Historia de la literatura peruana, 2006; John Barbour's The Bruce: a free translation in verse, 2013; numerous articles. *Recreations:* reading, gardening, walking, football, whisky, Scottish literature. *Address:* Flat 6, Carlton House, 15 Snowdon Place, Stirling FK8 2NR. *T:* (01786) 470641.

HIGGINS, Prof. Dame Joan (Margaret), DBE 2007; PhD; Professor of Health Policy, 1992–2004, now Emerita, and Director, Manchester Centre for Healthcare Management, 1998–2004, University of Manchester; *b* 15 June 1948; *d* of Kenneth and Kate Higgins; *m* 1983, John P. Martin (*d* 1997); three step *s*. *Educ:* Rutherford Coll. of Advanced Technol. (BA Hons (Sociol.), London Univ. (ext.), 1969); Univ. of York (Dip. Soc. Admin 1971); Univ. of Southampton (PhD 1979). Res. Asst, then Lectr, Portsmouth Poly., 1971–74; University of Southampton: Lectr, 1974–86, Sen. Lectr, 1986–89, in Social Policy; Prof. of Social Policy, 1989–92. Chm., Christie Hosp. NHS Trust, Manchester, 2002–07. Chairman: Manchester FHSA, 1992–96; Manchester HA, 1996–99; Patient Information Adv. Gp, 2001–08; NHS Litigation Authy, 2007–13; Regl Chm., NHS Exec. NW, 1999–2001; Interim Chm., Nat. Treatment Agency for Substance Misuse, 2001; non-executive Director: Southampton and SW Hampshire HA, 1981–90; Wessex Regl HA, 1990–92. Member: Care Record Develt Bd, 2004–07 (Chm., Ethics Adv. Gp, 2004–07); Nat. Information Governance Bd, 2007–09; Ind. Mem., H of L Appts Commn, 2008–13; Chm., Queen's Counsel Selection Panel, 2009–12 (Mem., 2005–09). Pres., European Health Mgt Assoc., 2001–03. Hon. FRCOG 2012. *Publications:* The Poverty Business: Britain and America, 1978; States of Welfare: comparative analysis in social policy, 1981; (jtly) Government and Urban Poverty, 1983; The Business of Medicine: private health care in Britain, 1988. *Recreations:* travel, gardening, walking, classical music, reading, cooking, wine, theatre, modern art. *Address:* 28 Woodbridge Street, EC1R 0HP.

HIGGINS, John Andrew; Assistant Auditor General, National Audit Office, 1989–99; *b* 19 Feb. 1940; *s* of George Henry and Mildred Maud Higgins; *m* 1965, Susan Jennifer Mathis; one *s*. *Educ:* Hendon County Sch.; Hastings Grammar Sch. ARCO. Exchequer and Audit Department: Asst Auditor, 1958; Auditor, 1968; Sen. Auditor, 1971; Chief Auditor, 1977; Dep. Dir, 1981; Office of Auditor Gen. of Canada, 1983–84; Dir, Nat. Audit Office, 1984. Treas., Crawley and Horsham Dist Organists' Assoc., 1994–2006; Trustee and Treas., Crawley Open House, 1999–. *Recreations:* classical organ playing, golf, bridge, gardening, supporting Crystal Palace and Crawley Town. *Address:* Zaria, 65 Milton Mount Avenue, Pound Hill, Crawley, Sussex RH10 3DP. *T:* (01293) 417075. *Clubs:* Ifield Golf and Country; Crawley Bridge; Horley Bridge.

HIGGINS, Prof. (John) Christopher; Director of Management Centre, University of Bradford, and Professor of Management Sciences, 1972–89, Emeritus Professor, since 1992; *b* 9 July 1932; *s* of Sidney James Higgins and Margaret Eileen Higgins (*née* Dealtrey); *m* 1960, Margaret Edna Howells; three *s*. *Educ:* Gonville and Caius Coll., Cambridge (MA); Univ. of London (BSc, MSc); PhD Bradford. Short service commission, RAF, 1953–56; 1956–70: Electronics Industry; Dept of Chief Scientist (RAF) in MoD; management consultancy; Director of Economic Planning and Research for IPC Newspapers Ltd. Member: Final Selection Bd for Civil Service Commn, 1976–91; Defence Scientific Adv. Council's Assessments Bd, 1976–83 (Chm. of its Cttee on Operational Analysis, 1980–83); UGC Sub-Cttee on Management and Business Studies, 1979–85; Yorks, Humberside and Midlands Industrial Develt Bd, 1988–91; Chm., Social Sciences Res. Council's Accountancy Steering Cttee and Member of its Management and Industrial Relns Cttee, 1976–80. Vis. Fellow, Wolfson Coll., Cambridge, 1985; Vis. Prof., Open Business School, Open Univ., 1991–97. *Publications:* Information Systems for Planning and Control: concepts and cases, 1976, new edn as Computer-Based Planning Systems, 1985; Strategic and Operational Planning Systems: Principles and Practice, 1980; numerous papers and articles on corporate planning, information systems and management educn. *Recreations:* violin/viola (ex National Youth Orchestra of Great Britain), cricket, fell-walking.

HIGGINS, John Patrick, MBE 2008; professional snooker player; *b* Motherwell, 18 May 1975; *s* of late John and Josephine Higgins; *m* 2000, Denise Whitton; two *s* one *d*. *Educ:* St Aidan's Primary Sch.; St Aidan's High Sch. Turned professional, 1992; won first tournament, 1994; wins include: Grand Prix, 1994, 1999, 2005, 2008; British Open, 1995, 1998, 2001, 2004; Internat. Open, 1995, 1996; UK Championship, 1998, 2000, 2010; Masters, 1999, 2006; World Snooker Championship, 1998, 2007, 2009, 2011; Welsh Open, 2000, 2010, 2011, 2015; Shanghai Masters, 2012; Bulgarian Open, 2013. *Address:* 76 Royal Gardens, Bothwell, Glasgow G71 8SY. *T:* (01698) 852995. *E:* john.higgins30@hotmail.co.uk.

HIGGINS, John Stuart, CBE 2005; Director General, DigitalEurope, since 2011; *b* 26 June 1954; *s* of Robert Brian Higgins and Josephine Mary Higgins; *m* 1977, Ailsa Elizabeth Ann Gibson; three *d*. *Educ:* Cardinal Langley Sch., Middleton; Univ. of East Anglia (BSc Hons Maths and Phys); CDipAF. Systems Analyst, then Project Manager, London Brick Co., 1976–81; Business Manager, Triad Computing Systems, 1982–85; Director: Wilkins Computer Systems, 1986–90; Softwright Systems, then SSA, 1991–96; CEO, Res Rocket Surfer, CA, 1997–98; Director General: Computing Services and Software Assoc., 1998–2002; Intellect, 2002–12. Chairman: GRID Computing Task Force, Information Age Partnership, 2004; IP Forum Business Opportunities Gp, 2005; CBI Trade Assoc. Council, 2009–11; Vice Chm., UK Security and Resilience Industry Suppliers' Community, 2008–11; Member, Board: Eur. Internet Forum, 2015–; Pro Europa, 2015–. Vice-Pres., Eur. Information, Communications and Consumer Electronics Technology Industry Assoc., 2006–08; Pres., Eur. Commn Strategic Policy Forum on Digital Entrepreneurship, 2014–. Mem., UK Space Leadership Council, 2012–. Lay Mem. Council, Univ. of Warwick, 2003– (Chm, Audit Cttee, 2010–15). FRSA. Editor's Award for outstanding contrib. to UK IT, Computing Awards for Excellence, 2008. *Recreations:* tennis, the outdoors, music, theatre. *Address:* DigitalEurope, 14 rue de la Science, 1040 Brussels, Belgium. *T:* (2) 6095310. *E:* john.higgins@digitaleurope.org.

HIGGINS, Dame Julia (Stretton), DBE 2001 (CBE 1996); DPhil; FRS 1995; FREng; Senior Research Investigator, Imperial College London, since 2007 (Professor of Polymer Science, 1989–2007); *b* 1 July 1942; *d* of late George Stretton Downes, CBE and Sheilah D. M. Downes (*née* Gavigan). *Educ:* Somerville Coll., Oxford (MA, DPhil 1968; Hon. Fellow, 1996). CChem 1991, FRSC 1991; CEng 1994, FREng 1999; FIM 1994; FCGI 1994; FInstP 1996; FIChemE 1997. Physics teacher, Mexborough Grammar Sch., 1966–68; Dept of Chemistry, Univ. of Manchester, 1968–72; Res. Fellow, Centre de Recherche sur les Macromolecules, Strasbourg, 1972–73; physicist, Inst Laue-Langevin, Grenoble, 1973–76; Imperial College, London: Dept of Chem. Engrg, 1976–; Dean, City and Guilds Coll., 1993–97; Dir, Graduate Sch. of Engrg and Physical Scis, 2002–06; Principal, Faculty of Engrg, 2006–07. Vis. Academic, Institut für Makromolekulare Chemie, Freiburg, 1988. Trustee, Nat. Gall., 2001–10. Chm., EPSRC, 2003–07 (Mem., 1994–2000); Science and Engineering Research Council: Member: Neutron Beam Res. Cttee, 1979–83 and 1988–91; Polymers and Composites Cttee, 1989–94 (Chm., 1991–94); Materials Commn, 1991–94; Facilities Commn, 1993–94; Member: CCLRC, 1995–2000; Sci. and Engrg Cttee, British Council, 1993–98; Council for Sci. and Technol., 1998–2004; Chm., Adv. Cttee for Maths Educn, 2008–12. Foreign Sec. and Vice Pres., Royal Soc., 2001–06; President: IChemE, 2002–03; BAAS, 2003–04; Vice-Pres. and Mem. Council, RAEng, 2008–. Foreign Associate, Nat. Acad. Engrg, USA, 1999. Hon. DSc: Nottingham, 1999; QUB, Leicester, 2002; Oxon, Sheffield, 2003; Kent, Exeter, Leeds, Sheffield Hallam, 2004; Bath, 2005; Keele, 2006; Birmingham, 2007; Manchester, Liverpool, 2008; Loughborough, 2009; Melbourne, 2011; Cardiff, 2011; UCL, 2012; Kingston, 2015; Hon. DEng Heriot-Watt, 2000. *Publications:* (with H. Benoît) Polymers and Neutron Scattering, 1994; contrib. articles on polymer science to learned jls. *Address:* Department of Chemical Engineering, Imperial College London, SW7 2AZ. *T:* (020) 7594 5565.

See also G. P. S. Downes.

HIGGINS, Rt Hon. Sir Malachy (Joseph), Kt 1993; PC 2007; a Lord Justice of Appeal, Supreme Court of Judicature, Northern Ireland, 2007–14; *b* 30 Oct. 1944; *er s* of late James and May Higgins; *m* 1980, Dorothy Ann, *d* of Dr Leslie Grech, Malta; three *d*. *Educ:* St MacNissi's Coll., Garron Tower; Queen's Univ., Belfast (LLB); Middle Temple (BL). Called to NI Bar, 1969 (Bencher, 1993), to Irish Bar, 1978; QC (NI), 1985; County Court Judge, 1988–93; Recorder of Londonderry, 1990–93; County Court Judge for Co. Armagh, 1993; Judge of the High Court of Justice, NI, 1993–2007 (Family Div., 1996–2001); Sen. Judge, QBD, 2004–07. Chairman: Criminal Justice Issues Gp, 2008–; Judicial Studies Bd for NI, 2009–. Judge in Residence, 1999–2001, Chm. Bd of Visitors, 2005–, QUB. Chm., Children Order Adv. Cttee, 1996–2001. *Recreations:* gardening, golf, sailing, walking. *Address:* Ashdene, Comber, Co. Down BT23 5SP. *Clubs:* Royal Ulster Yacht, Royal Belfast Golf.

HIGGINS, Michael D(aniel); President of Ireland, since 2011; *b* Limerick, 18 April 1941; *m* 1974, Sabina Coyne; three *s* one *d*. *Educ:* University Coll., Galway; Univ. of Manchester; Univ. of Indiana (MA Sociol.). Vis. Prof., Univ. of Southern Illinois; Lectr in Political Sci. and Sociol., UC, Galway. Mem. (Lab), Galway CC, 1974–93 (Mayor, 1982–83 and 1991–92). Member: Seanad, 1973–77 and 1983–87; Dáil (TD) (Lab) Galway W, 1981–82 and 1987–2011; Minister for Arts, Culture and Gaeltacht, 1993–97. Hon. Adjunct Prof., Irish Centre for Human Rights, NUI. Hon. LLD NUI, 2012. Seán McBride Peace Prize, Internat. Peace Bureau, Helsinki, 1991. *Publications:* (jtly) Causes for Concern: Irish politics, culture and society, 2007; Renewing the Republic, 2011; *poetry:* The Betrayal, 1990; (with M. Mulcahy) The Season of Fire, 1993; An Arid Season, 2004; New and Selected Poems, 2011. *Address:* Áras an Uachtaráin, Phoenix Park, Dublin 8, Ireland. *T:* (01) 6171000.

HIGGINS, Very Rev. Michael John, OBE 2003; Dean of Ely, 1991–2003, now Emeritus; *b* 31 Dec. 1935; *s* of Claud John and Elsie Higgins; *m* 1976, Bevyl Margaret Stringer; one *d*. *Educ:* Whitchurch Grammar Sch., Cardiff; Univ. of Birmingham (LLB 1957); Gonville and Caius Coll., Cambridge (LLB 1959, PhD 1962); Harvard Univ.; Ridley Hall, Cambridge. Lectr in English Law, Univ. of Birmingham, 1961–63. Ordained, 1965; Curate, Ormskirk Parish Church, dio. of Liverpool, 1965–68; Selection Sec., ACCM, 1968–74; Vicar, Frome and Priest-in-charge of Woodlands, dio. of Bath and Wells, 1974–80; Rector of Preston, and Leader of Preston Town Centre Team Ministry, dio. of Blackburn, 1980–91. *Publications:* The Vicar's House, 1988. *Recreations:* music, walking, travel. *Address:* Twin Cottage, Great Dunham, Norfolk PE32 2LR.

HIGGINS, Michael Selwyn L.; *see* Longuet-Higgins.

HIGGINS, Peter Raymond, RDI 2009; interior designer; Creative Director, Land Design Studio, since 1992; *b* London, 26 March 1948; *s* of late Donald Higgins and of Anneliese Higgins; *m* 2006, Shirley Walker; one *s*. *Educ:* Architectural Assoc. Sch. of Architecture (5th Yr Prize 1975). RIBA 1988. Design Dept, BBC TV, 1977–85; Associate Dir, Imagination Ltd, 1985–88; freelance designer, 1988–92; Land Design Studio, 1992–: conceptual masterplanning and exhibition design includes: River and Rowing Mus., Henley, 1998; Nat. Waterfront Mus., Swansea, 2005; UK Pavilion, Expo 2005, Japan, 2005; Golden Age of Couture, V&A, 2007; Ancient Egyptian Book of the Dead, BM, 2010. External Examiner: Leeds Metropolitan Univ., 2000–04; Kingston Univ., 2005–09; Manchester Metropolitan Univ., 2009–; Vis. Prof., Central St Martins Coll. of Art and Design, 2003–. *Publications:* (contrib.) Takeover, 2001; (contrib.) Reshaping Museum Space, 2005. *Recreation:* football. *Address:* Land Design Studio, 5 Spring Grove Road, Richmond TW10 6EH. *T:* (020) 8332 6699. *E:* peter@landdesignstudio.co.uk.

HIGGINS, Phillip John; Corporate Director (formerly Corporate Manager), Cardiff County Council, 1999–2006; *b* 9 May 1946; *s* of Eugene Oswald Higgins and Dorothy Mary Higgins; *m* 1969, Anne Elizabeth Watkin; one *s* two *d*. *Educ:* Stand Grammar Sch., Manchester; Coll. of Commerce, Manchester. IMTA 1972. Accountant, Halifax CBC, 1972–74; Sen. Accountant, West Yorks CC, 1974–76; Gp Accountant, 1976–80, Principal Asst, loans and investments, 1980–82, Principal Asst, technical, 1982–85, Gtr Manchester Council; Asst Co. Treas., S Glamorgan CC, 1985–88; Dir of Finance, Cardiff Bay Develt Corp., 1988–99. Treas., S Wales Magistrates' Courts Cttee, 1999–2006. *Recreations:* reading political history, the countryside. *Address:* Wisteria Cottage, Llantrithyd, Cowbridge, Vale of Glamorgan CF71 7UB. *T:* (01446) 781676.

HIGGINS, Dame Rosalyn, DBE 1995; JSD; FBA 1995; QC 1986; a Judge, 1995–2009, and President, 2006–09, International Court of Justice; *b* 2 June 1937; *d* of Lewis Cohen and Fay Inberg; *m* 1961, Terence Langley Higgins (*see* Baron Higgins); one *s* one *d*. *Educ:* Burlington Grammar Sch., London; Girton Coll., Cambridge (Scholar; BA 1958, 1st Cl. Law Qualifying 1, 1st Cl. Tripos Pt II; 1st Cl. LLB 1959); Yale Law Sch., (JSD 1962). UK Intern, Office of Legal Affairs, UN, 1958; Commonwealth Fund Fellow, 1959; Vis. Fellow, Brookings Instn, Washington, DC, 1960; Jun. Fellow in Internat. Studies, LSE, 1961–63; Staff Specialist in Internat. Law, RIIA, 1963–74; Vis. Fellow, LSE, 1974–78; Professor of International Law: Univ. of Kent at Canterbury, 1978–81; LSE, London Univ., 1981–95. Gen. course, Hague Acad. of Internat. Law, 1991. Visiting Professor of International Law: Stanford Univ., 1975; Yale Univ., 1977. Bencher, Inner Temple, 1989. Mem., UN Cttee on Human Rights, 1984–95. Hague Lectures on Internat. Law, 1982. Pres., British Inst. of Internat. and Comparative Law, 2011–; Vice Pres., Amer. Soc. of Internat. Law, 1972–74 (Certif. of Merit, 1971, 1995). Membre de l'Institut de Droit International, 1993 (Associé, 1987). Hon.

doctorates include: Dr *hc* Univ. of Paris XI, 1980; Hon. LLD: LSE, 1995; Cambridge, 1996; Hon. DCL Oxford, 2002. Manley Hudson Medal, 1998; Balzan Prize, Internat. Balzan Foundn, 2007. Membre de l'Ordre des Palmes Académiques (France), 1988. *Publications:* The Development of International Law through the Political Organs of the United Nations, 1963; Conflict of Interests: international law in a divided world, 1965; The Administration of the United Kingdom Foreign Policy through the United Nations, 1966; (ed with James Fawcett) Law in Movement—essays in memory of John McMahon, 1974; UN Peacekeeping: documents and commentary: Vol. I, Middle East, 1969; Vol. II, Asia, 1971; Vol. III, Africa, 1980; Vol. IV, Europe, 1981; Problems and Process, 1994; Themes and Theories: selected essays, speeches and writings in international law, 2009; articles for law jls and jls of internat. relations. *Recreations:* golf, cooking, eating.

HIGGINSON, Prof. Irene Julie, OBE 2008; PhD; FRCP, FFPHM, FMedSci; Professor of Palliative Care and Policy, since 1996 and Director, Cicely Saunders Institute, since 2010, King's College London; Scientific Director, Cicely Saunders International, since 2002; Honorary Consultant in Palliative Medicine: King's College London, since 1996; Guy's and St Thomas' Hospitals, since 2002; Lewisham Hospital, since 2004; *b* Lowton, Lancs, 25 Oct. 1958; *d* of William Leslie Higginson and Kathleen Lucille Higginson (*née* Rogers). *Educ:* Culcheth High Sch.; Univ. of Nottingham (BMedSci Hons 1980; BM BS 1982); Univ. of London (PhD 1992). MFPHM 1995, FFPHM 1997; FRCP 2005. Sen. Lectr, LSHTM, 1995–96, Dir, R&D and Consultant, Kensington, Chelsea and Westminster HA, 1995–96; Dir, Res., Educn and Quality, St Christopher's Hospice, London, 1996–2001; Dean, Grad. Studies, Guy's, King's and St Thomas' Sch. of Medicine, London, 2002–05. NIHR Sen. Investigator, 2009–. FMedSci 2013. *Publications:* (ed with J. Hanratty) Palliative Care in Terminal Illness, 1994; (ed with E. Bruera) Cachexia: anorexia in cancer patients, 1996; (ed with J. M. Addington-Hall) Palliative Care for Non-Cancer Patients, 2001; (ed jtly) Research Methods in Palliative Care, 2007; (ed jtly) Textbook of Palliative Medicine, 2009, 2nd edn 2014; over 400 papers in jls incl. Lancet, BMJ, Jl of AMA, PLOS Medicine, BMC Medicine, Palliative Medicine, Jl of Pain Symptom Mgt. *Address:* Cicely Saunders Institute, Department of Palliative Care, Policy and Rehabilitation, School of Medicine, King's College London, Bessemer Road, SE5 9PJ. *T:* (020) 7848 5516, *Fax:* (020) 7848 5517. *E:* irene.higginson@kcl.ac.uk. *Club:* Athenæum.

HIGGINSON, Lucy Amanda; equestrian writer and media consultant, since 2015; *b* 13 March 1970; *d* of late Keith Higginson and of Judith Britain; *m* 1999, Dr Alexis Warnes; one *s* one *d*. *Educ:* Manchester High Sch. for Girls; Univ. of Durham (BA Hons). Dep. Ed., The Field, 1996–2002; Dep. Ed., 2002, Ed., 2002–14, Horse & Hound. Member: Selection Panel, British Horse Soc. Hall of Fame; Adv. Panel, London Riding Club. *Recreations:* riding across country, spaniel walking, fraternising with rowers (sometimes even in a boat). *Address:* Villiers House, Common Lane, Eton College, Windsor, Berks SL4 6EG. *E:* l.higginson@etoncollege.org.uk.

HIGGS, Air Vice-Marshal Barry, CBE 1981; Assistant Chief of Defence Staff (Overseas), 1985–87; *b* 22 Aug. 1934; *s* of late Percy Harold Higgs and of Ethel Eliza Higgs; *m* 1957, Sylvia May Wilks; two *s*. *Educ:* Finchley County Secondary Grammar Sch. Served with Nos 207, 115, 138, 49 and 51 Sqdns, 1955–70; sc 1968; Forward Policy (RAF), 1971–73; ndc 1974; Comd No 39 (PR) Sqdn, 1975–77; Asst Dir Defence Policy, 1978–79; Comd RAF Finningley, 1979–81; RCDS 1982; Dep. Dir of Intelligence, 1983–85. Dir Gen., Fertiliser Manufacturers Assoc., 1987–98. ARAgS 1998. Francis New Meml Medal, Internat. Fertiliser Soc., 1999. *Recreations:* gardening, the outdoors, theatre. *Address:* 33 Parsonage Street, Cambridge CB5 8DN. *T:* (01223) 473282. *Club:* Royal Air Force.

HIGGS, Brian James; QC 1974; a Recorder of the Crown Court, 1974–98; *b* 24 Feb. 1930; *s* of James Percival Higgs and Kathleen Anne Higgs; *m* 1st, 1953, Jean Cameron DuMerton; two *s* three *d*; 2nd, 1980, Vivienne Mary Johnson; one *s*. *Educ:* Wrekin Coll.; London Univ. Served RA, 1948–50 (2nd Lieut). Called to Bar, Gray's Inn, 1955, Bencher, 1986; Mem., Hon. Soc. of Inner Temple (*ad eundem*), 1987. Contested (C) Romford, 1966. *Recreations:* wine, chess, bridge. *Address:* 5 King's Bench Walk, Temple, EC4Y 7DN. *T:* (020) 7353 5638.
See also J. A. C. Higgs.

HIGGS, Prof. Douglas Roland, DSc; FRCP, FRCPath; FRS 2005; Professor of Haematology, since 1996, Director, MRC Molecular Haematology Unit, since 2001, and Director, Weatherall Institute of Molecular Medicine, since 2012, University of Oxford; *b* 13 Jan. 1951. *Educ:* Alleyn's Sch.; King's Coll. London; King's Coll. Hosp. Med. Sch. (MB BS 1974); DSc London 1990. FRCP 1993; FRCPath 1994. SHO, 1975, Registrar in Haematol., 1976, King's Coll. Hosp., London; University of Oxford: MRC Trng Fellow, Nuffield Dept of Clinical Medicine, 1977–80; Scientific Officer (Clinical), MRC Molecular Haematol. Unit, 1980–2001; Hon. Consultant in Haematol., John Radcliffe Hosp., Oxford, 1985–. FMedSci 2001. *Address:* MRC Molecular Haematology Unit, Weatherall Institute of Molecular Medicine, John Radcliffe Hospital, Headington, Oxford OX3 9DS.

HIGGS, Elizabeth Ann; *see* Williamson, E. A.

HIGGS, Jonathan Alexander Cameron; QC 2011; *b* Chelmsford, 23 Sept. 1963; *s* of Brian James Higgs, *qv* and Jean Cameron Higgs (*née* DuMerton); *m* Caroline Sarah Darley Knight; two *s* two *d*. *Educ:* Downside; Chelmer Inst. of Higher Educn (BA Hons Law). Called to the Bar, Middle Temple, 1987. *Recreation:* watching birds. *Address:* 5 King's Bench Walk, EC4Y 7DN. *T:* (020) 7353 5638.

HIGGS, Prof. Peter Ware, CH 2013; PhD; FRS 1983; FRSE; Professor of Theoretical Physics, University of Edinburgh, 1980–96, now Emeritus; *b* 29 May 1929; *s* of Thomas Ware Higgs and Gertrude Maud (*née* Coghill); *m* 1963, Jo Ann (*d* 2008), *d* of Jo C. and Meryl Williamson, Urbana, Ill; two *s*. *Educ:* Cotham Grammar Sch., Bristol; King's Coll., Univ. of London (BSc, MSc; PhD 1954). FRSE 1974. Royal Commn for Exhibn of 1851 Sen. Student, KCL, 1953–54 and Univ. of Edinburgh, 1954–55; Sen. Res. Fellow, Univ. of Edinburgh, 1955–56; ICI Res. Fellow, UCL, 1956–57 and Imperial Coll., 1957–58; Lectr in Maths, UCL, 1958–60; Lectr in Mathematical Physics, 1960–70, and Reader in Math. Physics, 1970–80, Univ. of Edinburgh. FKC 1998. Hon. Fellow, Swansea Univ., 2008. Hon. FInstP 1998. Hon. DSc: Bristol, 1997; Edinburgh, 1998; Glasgow, 2002; KCL, 2009; UCL, 2010; Cambridge, 2012; Heriot-Watt, 2012; Durham, 2013; Manchester, 2013; St Andrews, 2014; Université libre de Bruxelles, 2014. (Jtly) Hughes Medal, Royal Soc., 1981; (jtly) Rutherford Medal, 1984, Paul Dirac Medal, 1997, Inst. of Physics; James Scott Prize, 1993, Royal Medal, 2000, RSE; High Energy Particle Physics Prize, Eur. Physical Soc., 1997; (jtly) Wolf Prize in Physics, 2004; Oskar Klein Medal, Swedish Royal Acad. of Scis, 2009; Sakurai Prize, APS, 2010; Edinburgh Award, 2011; Nonino Prize, 2013; Edinburgh Medal, 2013; (jtly) Nobel Prize in Physics, 2013; (jtly) Prince of Asturias Award, Fundación Príncipe de Asturias, 2013. *Publications:* papers on molecular vibrations and spectra, classical and quantum field theories, and on spontaneous breaking of gauge symmetries in theories of elementary particles. *Recreations:* walking, swimming, listening to music. *Address:* 2 Darnaway Street, Edinburgh EH3 6BG. *T:* (0131) 225 7060.

HIGHAM, Catherine Mary; *see* Ennis, C. M.

HIGHAM, Prof. Charles Franklin Wandesforde, PhD, ScD; FRSNZ; FRAS; FSA; FBA; Research Professor, University of Otago, New Zealand, since 2005 (Professor of Anthropology, 1968–2003; James Cook Fellow, 2003–05); *b* 19 Oct. 1939; *s* of Ernest Harry Hamilton Higham and Eileen Florence Emily Higham (*née* Woodhead); *m* 1964, Pauline Askew; two *s* two *d*. *Educ:* Raynes Park Co. Grammar Sch.; St Catharine's Coll., Cambridge (Rugby blue, 1961–62; BA, MA; PhD 1966; ScD 1991; Hon. Fellow, 2008). FSA 1984; FRAS 1986. Lectr in Prehist., Univ. of Otago, 1967–68. Vis. Prof., Univ. of London, 1978; Benians Fellow, St John's Coll., Cambridge, 1991–92; Vis. Scholar, St Catharine's Coll., Cambridge, 2003–08. Mortimer Wheeler Lectr, 1983, Reckitt Lectr, 2002, British Acad.; Golson Lectr, ANU, 2010; Keble Lectr, Oxford, 2010; McDonald Lectr, Univ. of Cambridge, 2011. FRSNZ 1992; Corresp. FBA 2000; Fellow, NZ Acad. of Humanities, 2009. Grahame Clark Medal, British Acad., 2012; Mason Durie Medal, Royal Soc. of NZ, 2014. Mem. editl bds various learned jls. *Publications:* The Archaeology of Mainland Southeast Asia, 1989; (with R. Bannanurag) The Excavation of Khok Phanom Di: Vol. I, The Excavation, Chronology and Human Burials, 1990; (ed with R. Bannanurag) The Excavation of Khok Phanom Di: Vol. II, The Biological Remains Part I, 1991; The Bronze Age of Southeast Asia, 1996; The Civilisation of Angkor, 2001; Early Cultures of Mainland Southeast Asia, 2002; The Encyclopaedia of Ancient Asian Civilizations, 2004; The Excavation of Khok Phanom Di: Vol. VII, Summary and Conclusions, 2004; (ed with A. Kijngan) The Origins of the Civilization of Angkor: Vol. II, The Excavation of Noen U-Loke and Non Muong Kao, 2007, Vol. III, The Excavation of Ban Non Wat: introduction, 2009, Vol. IV, The Neolithic Occupation, 2011, Vol. V, The Bronze Age, 2012, Vol. VI, The Iron Age: summary and conclusions, 2012; Early Thailand: from Prehistory to Sukhothai, 2012; The Origins of the Civilization of Angkor, 2013; Early Mainland Southeast Asia: from first humans to Angkor, 2014; edited with R. Thosarat: Khok Phanom Di: Vol. III: The Material Culture Part I, 1993; Khok Phanom Di: prehistoric adaptation to the world's richest habitat, 1994; The Excavation of Khok Phanom Di: Vol. IV, The Biological Remains, Part II, 1996; The Excavation of Nong Nor, a Prehistoric Site in Central Thailand, 1998; Prehistoric Thailand: from first settlement to Sukhothai, 1998; The Excavation of Khok Phanom Di: Vol. V, The People, 1999; The Excavation of Khok Phanom Di: Vol. VI, The Pottery, 2004; The Origins of the Civilization of Angkor: Vol. I, The Excavation of Ban Lum Khao, 2005. *Recreation:* classical guitar. *Address:* Department of Anthropology and Archaeology, PO Box 56, Dunedin, New Zealand. *T:* (3) 4798750; 1 Newbury Street, Company Bay, Dunedin, New Zealand. *T:* (3) 4761056. *Club:* Hawks (Cambridge).

HIGHAM, Geoffrey Arthur; Chairman, Rugby Group PLC, 1986–96 (Director, 1979–96); Director and Trustee, Building Centre Group, 1982–2001 (Chairman, 1984–88); *b* 17 April 1927; *s* of Arthur Higham and Elsie Higham (*née* Vickerman); *m* 1st, 1951, Audrey Hill (*d* 2006); one *s* one *d*; 2nd, 2007, Jenny Voice (*née* Cummins). *Educ:* King William's Coll., IOM; St Catharine's Coll., Cambridge (MA MechScis). Served RE, 1945–48. Metal Box Co., 1950–64; Montague Burton, 1964–65; Cape Industries, 1965–85: Man. Dir, 1971–80; Chm., 1980–85; Industrial Dir, Charter Consolidated, 1980–87; Director: Pirelli Gen., 1987–2006; Pirelli UK, 1997–2006; Travers Morgan, 1988–91; Try Gp, 1989–99; Vale Housing Assoc., 1998–2008; Sovereign Housing Assoc., 2007–10. Chm., BIM Foundn, 1981–83; Vice Chm., Council, BIM, 1984–88; Mem. Council, CBI, 1994–96; Mem. Council, 1978–88, Chm., 1980–82, UK S Africa Trade Assoc. Trustee, Mansfield Coll., Oxford, 1988–95. CCMI (CBIM 1975); FRSA 1989. *Recreations:* music, cricket, gardening. *Address:* 32 East St Helen Street, Abingdon, Oxfordshire OX14 5EB. *Clubs:* Army and Navy, Middlesex CC.
See also N. G. Higham.

HIGHAM, Prof. Jennifer Mary, MD; FRCOG; Consultant Gynaecologist, Imperial College Healthcare Trust, since 1997; Vice Dean, Institutional Affairs, and Director of Education (formerly Deputy Principal), Faculty of Medicine, Imperial College London, since 2010; *b* Warrington, Cheshire, 5 July 1961; *d* of late Stanley Higham and of Margaret Higham (*née* Baldwin); *m* 1992, Ed Naylor; one *s* two *d*. *Educ:* Thorpe Grammar Sch.; University Coll. London (MB BS 1985; MD 1993). MRCOG 1992, FRCOG 2005. Sen. Registrar, St Mary's Hosp., 1995–96; Hd, Undergrad. Medicine, Imperial Coll. London, 2006–09. Sen. Vice Dean, Lee Kong Chian Sch. of Medicine, Singapore, 2013–. Non-exec. Dir, W Middx Univ. Hosp. NHS Trust, 2009–. Medical Schools Council: Mem., 2010–14, Chm., 2014–, Educn Sub-cttee; Mem., Assessment Board, 2014–; Member: Bd, Health Educn NW London, 2013–; Jt Bd, Brighton and Sussex Med. Sch., 2013–; Bd, UCEA Clinical Staff Adv. Gp, 2013–; Pres., and Chm., Strategy Bd, Health Scis Acad., 2014–. Gov., Chelsea and Westminster Hosp., 2011–. Trustee: Imperial Coll. Trust, 2009–; St Mary's Develt Trust, 2014–. FHEA 2002; FFSRH (FFFP 2005). Mentor of Year, Women of Future Awards, 2011; Pres. and Rector's Award for Outstanding Contribn to Teaching Excellence, Imperial Coll. London, 2013; Imperial Coll. Medal, 2014; Nanyang Educn Gold Award, 2015. *Publications:* contrib. res. papers on abnormal uterine bleeding, gynaecol., educn, use of simulation in educn and trng. *Recreations:* art, food, ski-ing. *Address:* Faculty of Medicine, Imperial College London, S Kensington Campus, SW7 2AZ. *E:* jenny.higham@imperial.ac.uk.

HIGHAM, John Arthur; QC 1992; Partner, White & Case, since 2004; a Recorder, 2000–10; *b* 11 Aug. 1952; *s* of late Frank Greenhouse Higham and of Muriel (*née* King); *m* 1st, 1982, Francesca Mary Antonietta Ronan (decd); one *s* two *d*; 2nd, 1988, Catherine Mary Ennis, *qv*; two *s* one *d*. *Educ:* Shrewsbury Sch.; Churchill Coll., Cambridge (scholar; MA, LLM). Called to the Bar, Lincoln's Inn, 1976; an Asst Recorder, Midland and Oxford Circuit, 1998–2000; admitted solicitor and authorised as solicitor advocate, 1999; Consultant, 1999–2000, Partner, 2000–04, Stephenson Harwood, solicitors. *Publications:* (ed jtly) Loose on Liquidators, 2nd edn 1981; (ed jtly) The Law and Practice of Corporate Administration, 1994, 2nd edn as Corporate Administrations and Rescue Procedures, 2005. *Recreations:* opera, cricket, gardening. *Address:* White & Case, 5 Old Broad Street, EC2N 1DW. *T:* (020) 7532 1000, *Fax:* (020) 7532 1001. *E:* jhigham@whitecase.com.

HIGHAM, Commander Michael Bernard Shepley, CVO 1999; RN; Grand Secretary, United Grand Lodge of England, 1980–98; Secretary, Grand Charity, 1981–98; *b* 7 June 1936; *s* of late Anthony Richard Charles Higham, TD, FRCS and Mary Higham (*née* Shepley); *m* 1st, 1970, Caroline Verena Wells (marr. diss. 1996); one *s* one *d*; 2nd, 1997, Andrea Svedberg, *d* of late Elias Svedberg and Astrid Svedberg. *Educ:* Epsom Coll. Joined RN, 1954; served: HM Ships Triumph (twice), Eagle, Cavendish and Chichester; in offices of: C-in-C Portsmouth and C-in-C Plymouth; Flag Officers Plymouth, Scotland and NI; Adm. Comdg Reserves; on staff of C-in-C Fleet; retd RN, 1977. Called to the Bar, Middle Temple, 1968. Grand Secretary's Office, 1977–98, Dep. Grand Sec., 1978–80; Past Jun. Grand Warden, 1986–2005; Past Sen. Grand Warden, 2006. Mem., RNSA. Mem., Nankersey Male Choir. *Publications:* Freemasonry from Craft to tolerance, 1985. *Recreation:* sailing. *Address:* Oyster Shell, Restronguet Passage, Mylor, Falmouth, Cornwall TR11 5ST. *Club:* Royal Cornwall Yacht (Falmouth).

HIGHAM, Nicholas Geoffrey, (Nick); correspondent, BBC News, since 1988; *b* 1 June 1954; *s* of Geoffrey Arthur Higham, *qv*; *m* 1981, Deborah Starling; one *s* one *d*. *Educ:* Bradfield Coll., Berks; St Catharine's Coll., Cambridge (BA Hons English 1975). Freelance journalist, 1978–88; BBC: Media Correspondent, 1988–91; Arts and Media Correspondent, 1991–2003; analyst and roving reporter, BBC News 24, 2003–08; presenter, Meet the Author, BBC News, 2009–. Columnist, Marketing Week, 1990–2006. *Recreations:* theatre, armchair history. *Address:* c/o BBC News, BBC Broadcasting House, Portland Place, W1A 1AA. *T:* (020) 8743 8000. *E:* nick.higham@bbc.co.uk.

HIGHAM, Prof. Nicholas John, PhD; FRS 2007; Richardson Professor of Applied Mathematics, University of Manchester, since 1998; *b* Salford, 25 Dec. 1961; *s* of Kenneth Frederick Higham and Doris Higham (*née* Wilson); *m* 1998, Françoise Marie Louise Tisseur; two *s*. *Educ:* Univ. of Manchester (BSc Hons Maths 1982; MSc Numerical Analysis and Computing 1983; PhD Numerical Analysis 1985). University of Manchester: Lectr, 1985–89;

Sen. Lectr, 1989–92; Reader, 1992–96; Prof. of Applied Maths, 1996–98. Vis. Asst Prof. of Computer Sci., Cornell Univ., 1988–89; Nuffield Foundn Sci. Res. Fellow, 1991–92; Royal Soc. Leverhulme Trust Sen. Res. Fellow, 1999–2000; Royal Soc. Wolfson Res. Fellow, Royal Soc., 2003–08. Fellow, SIAM, 2009. Alston S. Householder Award VI, 1987; Leslie Fox Prize, IMA, 1988; Jun. Whitehead Prize, 1999, Fröhlich Prize, 2008, LMS. *Publications:* Handbook of Writing for the Mathematical Sciences, 1993, 2nd edn 1998; Accuracy and Stability of Numerical Algorithms, 1996, 2nd edn 2002; (with D. J. Higham) MATLAB Guide, 2000, 2nd edn 2005; Functions of Matrices: theory and computation, 2008; (ed) Princeton Companion to Applied Mathematics, 2015; contrib. numerous scientific papers. *Recreations:* photography, playing keyboards, gardening. *Address:* School of Mathematics, University of Manchester, Manchester M13 9PL. *T:* (0161) 275 5822, *Fax:* (0161) 275 5819.

HIGHFIELD, Ashley Gilroy Mark, CEng; Chief Executive, Johnston Press, since 2011; *b* 3 Oct. 1965; *s* of Roy Highfield and Sheila Highfield; one *d*. *Educ:* Elizabeth Coll., Guernsey; Royal Grammar Sch., High Wycombe; City Univ., London (BSc (Hons) Business Computing Systems). MBCS. Mgt Consultant, Coopers and Lybrand, 1988–94; Hd of IT and New Media, NBC Europe, 1994–95; Man. Dir, Flextech Interactive, Flextech Television, 1996–2000; Dir, Future (formerly New) Media and Technol., BBC, 2000–08; Chief Exec., Project Kangaroo, 2008; Man. Dir and Vice Pres., Consumer and Online, Microsoft UK, 2009–11. Non-executive Director, 1999–2000: Xrefer.com Ltd; Multimap.com Ltd; Improveline.com Ltd; WayAheadGroup (ticketing) Ltd; non-exec. Dir, WIlliam Hill plc, 2008–. Gov., BFI, 2008–. FRSA; FRTS. *Recreations:* motor racing, reading, architecture, music, film. *Clubs:* Soho House, Ivy.

HIGHFIELD, Dr Roger Ronald, FRSB; Director of External Affairs, Science Museum Group (formerly National Museum of Science and Industry), since 2011; *b* Griffithstown, Wales, July 1958; *s* of Ronald and Dorothea Highfield; *m* 1992, Julia Brookes; one *s* one *d*. *Educ:* Chase Side Primary Sch., Enfield; Christ's Hosp., Horsham; Pembroke Coll., Oxford (Domus Schol.; MA Chem. 1980); DPhil Oxon 1983. FRSB (FIBiol 2004). Clin. reporter, Pulse mag. for GPs, 1983–84; news ed., Nuclear Engrg Internat., 1984–86; Technol. Corresp., 1986, Technol. Ed., 1987–88, Sci. Ed., 1988–2008, Columnist, 2009–, Daily Telegraph; Ed., New Scientist, 2008–11. Visiting Sabbatical Fellow: Queen Elizabeth Hse, Oxford Univ., 1989; Balliol Coll., Oxford, 1994. Former contributor to Economist, Guardian, New Scientist, Sunday Times, Observer; sci. ed., Esquire, 1996–98; contrib. High Life, Spectator, Condé Nast Traveller and Science, Wired UK, Newsweek. Contrib. BBC radio, incl. Scope, Acid Test, Sci. Now, Leading Edge and Museum of Curiosity, Infinite Monkey Cage. Member: Communications and Public Engagement Cttee, RAEng; Health Protection and Society Adv. Gp, HPA; Bioscis Futures Forum; Sci. and Media Expert Gp, BIS; Adv. Cttee, Sci. Mus.; Sci. Policy Adv. Gp, Royal Soc.; Longitude Prize Cttee, 2014–. Judge: BBC Samuel Johnson Prize for Non-Fiction, 2010; British Press Awards, 2013, 2014. Hon. Fellow, BAAS. Science Writers' Award, Assoc. of British Sci. Writers, 1987, 1995, 1997, 1998; Specialist Writer of the Year, British Press Awards, 1988; Medical Journalism Award for consumer news, 1998; Tony Thistlethwaite Award, MJA, 2007; Wilkins-Bernal-Medawar Medal, Royal Soc., 2012. *Publications:* The Arrow of Time: the quest to solve time's greatest mystery, 1990; The Private Lives of Albert Einstein, 1993; Frontiers of Complexity: the search for order in a chaotic world, 1995; Can Reindeer Fly?: the science of Christmas, 1998; The Science of Harry Potter: how magic really works, 2002; After Dolly: the uses and misuses of human cloning, 2006; (ed) A Life Decoded, by Craig Venter, 2007; Supercooperators: the mathematics of evolution, altruism and human behaviour (or, why we need each other to succeed), 2011; (ed) Life at the Speed of Light, by Craig Venter, 2013. *Recreations:* Twitter (@rogerhighfield), entertainment of children, cooking. *Address:* Science Museum, Exhibition Road, SW7 2DD. *W:* www.rogerhighfield.com.

HIGHTON, David Peter; Executive Director, Corporate Development, Hamad Medical Corporation, Qatar, since 2011; Chairman, SHC Audiology, since 2011; *b* 22 May 1954; *s* of Allan Peter Highton and May Comrie Highton (*née* Doughty); *m* 2005, Wendy Ann Attree; one *d*. *Educ:* Borden Grammar Sch., Sittingbourne; Univ. of Bristol (BSc Hons Econs 1975). ACA 1978, FCA 1989. Chartered Accountant, Turquands Barton Mayhew, 1975–79; Financial Accountant, Tunnel Avebe Starches Ltd, 1979–81; Financial Controller: R. P. Martin plc, 1981–83; Grand Metropolitan Brewing, 1983–87; Regl Finance Dir, Prudential Property Services, 1987–90; Dir of Finance and Chief Exec., Ealing HA, 1990–92; Dir of Finance, Riverside Hosps, 1992–94; Chief Executive: Chelsea and Westminster Hosp., 1994–2000; Oxford Radcliffe Hosps NHS Trust, 2000–03; Managing Director: Hyperium Consulting, 2003–11; Clinicenta Ltd (formerly Patient Choice Partners), 2003–10. Non-exec. Director: Healthwork UK, 2000–05 (Chm., 2001–05); Skills for Health, 2007–11 (Chm., 2002–03); Clearview Healthcare, Delhi, 2010–14. Trustee, NHS Confedn, 2009–10. *Publications:* contribs to health mgt jls. *Recreations:* Rugby, books, films, good food. *Clubs:* Sittingbourne Rugby (Pres., 2000–09; Vice-Pres., 2009–), Imperial Medicals Rugby (Vice Pres.); Doha Rugby.

HIGNELL, Alastair James, CBE 2009; Rugby Union football player and cricketer, retired; Rugby commentator, BBC Radio Live, 1996–2008; *b* Cambridge, 4 Sept. 1955; *s* of Anthony and Patricia Hignell; *m* 1980, Jeannie Hobart; two *s*. *Educ:* Denstone Coll.; Fitzwilliam Coll., Cambridge (BA 1978; PGCE). Player: Glos CCC, 1974–83; England Rugby, 1975–79. Teacher of History: Bristol Cathedral Sch., 1978–83; Sherborne Sch., 1983–85; commentator: BBC Radio, 1985–89; ITV West, 1989–96. Patron, MS-UK, 2002–; Trustee, Leonard Cheshire Disability, 2012–. Hon. MA Bristol, 2004. Helen Rollason Award, BBC Sports Awards, 2008. *Publications:* Higgy: matches, microphones and MS, 2011. *Recreations:* family, sport, theatre, history, travel, art. *E:* alastairhignell@btconnect.com. *W:* www.alastairhignell.com. *Clubs:* Hawks; England Rugby Internationals; Gloucestershire CC, Rugby Union Writers.

HIGNETT, John Mulock, FCA; Chairman, Schroder Income Growth Fund plc, 1995–2005; *b* 9 March 1934; *s* of late Reginald and Marjorie Hignett; *m* 1961, Marijke Inge de Boer; one *s* one *d*. *Educ:* Harrow Sch.; Magdalene Coll., Cambridge (MA). Kemp Chatteris & Co., 1958–61; Deloitte & Co., 1961–63; joined Lazard Brothers & Co. Ltd, 1963; Manager, Issues Dept, 1971; Dir, 1972; Head of Corporate Finance Div., 1980; Man. Dir, 1984–88; Glaxo Holdings plc: Finance Dir, 1988–92; Man. Dir, Corporate Funds, 1992–94. Non-executive Director: TI Group plc, 1989–2000; Sedgwick Group plc, 1993–99; Alfred McAlpine plc, 1994–98; Smiths Gp plc, 2000; Camper & Nicholsons Marina Investments Ltd; World Trust Fund. Director-General: Panel on Take-Overs and Mergers, 1981–83; Council for the Securities Industry, 1983. Dep. Chm., Internat. Shakespeare Globe Centre Ltd, 1990–. *Clubs:* Royal Thames Yacht, MCC; Hawks (Cambridge).

HII, Sir Yii Ann, KBE 2012 (Hon. KBE 2007); Group Chairman and Chief Executive Officer, Investwell Group of Companies, since 1993; *b* Sarawak, Malaysia, 30 Jan. 1960; *s* of Hii Ka Kai and Sia Kiu Leng; *m* 1986, Dr Soo Hian Beh; two *s* four *d*. *Educ:* Deakin Univ., Australia (BSc Hons Civil Engrg 1983). Founder, Investwell Gp of Cos, 1993. *Address:* (office) 101 Cecil Street, #20–06, Tong Eng Building, Singapore 069533. *T:* 63241955, *Fax:* 63241966. *E:* mcompany@singnet.com.sg.

HILAIRE, Dr Ernest; High Commissioner for St Lucia in the United Kingdom, 2012–15. *Educ:* Univ. of West Indies (BSc 1st Cl. Hons Political Sci. and Sociol. (Double Major) 1993); Darwin Coll., Cambridge (MPhil Internat. Relns 1996); London Sch. of Econs and Pol Sci. (PhD Internat. Relns 2005); McKinsey Faculty (Mini MBA 2007); Univ. of Notre Dame (Exec. Cert. Negotiations and Conflict Mgt 2009). CEO, Cricket World Cup, St Lucia Inc., 2005–07; Associate, McKinsey and Co., 2007–08; Tournament Dir, ICC WT20 WI 2010, 2008–09; CEO, WI Cricket Bd, 2009–12. Chair: Sports St Lucia Inc.; Nat. Skills Develt Centre.

HILARY, John Jephson; Executive Director, War on Want, since 2008; *b* London, 11 Aug. 1964; *s* of David and Phoebe Hilary; *m* 1995, Janet Wood. *Educ:* Corpus Christi Coll., Cambridge (BA Hons Classics 1986); Sch. of Oriental and African Studies, Univ. of London (MA Chinese Politics 1992). Campaigns Officer, Amnesty Internat., 1989–91; Sub-Ed., BBC World Service, 1993–94; Ed., VSO, 1994–97; freelance trade policy consultant, 1997–2001; Trade Policy Advr, Save the Children, 2001–03; Dir of Campaigns and Policy, War on Want, 2004–08. Hon. Prof., Sch. of Politics and Internat. Relns, Univ. of Nottingham, 2013–. *Publications:* The Poverty of Capitalism, 2013; (ed) Free Trade and Transnational Labour, 2014. *Recreations:* cricket, birdwatching, classical music, modern art. *Address:* War on Want, 44–48 Shepherdess Walk, N1 7JP. *T:* (020) 7324 5040, *Fax:* (020) 7324 5041. *E:* jhilary@waronwant.org.

HILBORN, Rev. Dr David Henry Kyte; Principal, St John's College, Nottingham, since 2012; *b* 4 Jan. 1964; *s* of Edwin Henry and Constance May Hilborn; *m* 1988, Mia Alison Kyte (*see* Rev. M. A. K. Hilborn); one *s* one *d*. *Educ:* Langley Park Sch. for Boys; Nottingham Univ. (BA English; PhD Theol. and English); Mansfield Coll., Oxford (MA Theol.). Ordinand, Mansfield Coll., Oxford, 1985–89; Minister, Keyworth URC, 1989–92; research and teaching, Nottingham Univ., 1992–94; Minister: City Temple URC, 1994–99 (Jt Minister, 1997–99); Queen's Park URC, 2000–02; Theol Advr, then Head of Theology, Evangelical Alliance (UK), 1997–2006; ordained deacon and priest, C of E, 2002; Curate, St Mary's, Acton, 2002–06; Dir of Studies, 2006, Dir, N Thames Ministerial Trng Course, and Asst Dean, 2007–12, St Mellitus Coll. *Publications:* Picking Up the Pieces: can Evangelicals adapt to contemporary culture?, 1997; (ed) Faith, Hope and Homosexuality, 1998; (ed) The Nature of Hell, 2000; (jtly) One Body in Christ: the history and significance of the Evangelical Alliance, 2001; (ed) 'Toronto' in Perspective, 2001; (ed) God and the Generations, 2002; (contrib.) Evangelicalism and the Orthodox Church, 2002; (contrib.) Faith, Health and Prosperity, 2003; (ed) Movement for Change: evangelicals and social transformation, 2004; (ed) The Atonement Debate, 2008; articles in theological books and jls. *Recreations:* cricket, poetry, classic rock and pop. *Address:* St John's College, Chilwell Lane, Bramcote, Nottingham NG9 3DS. *T:* (0115) 925 1114, ext. 3210.

HILBORN, Rev. Mia Alison Kyte; Hospitaller, Head of Spiritual Health Care and Chaplaincy Team Leader, Guy's and St Thomas' Hospital NHS Foundation Trust (formerly NHS Trust), since 2001; *b* 7 March 1963; *d* of late Harry Stephen Broadbelt and Jean Margaret Broadbelt; *m* 1988, Rev. David Henry Kyte Hilborn, *qv*; one *s* one *d*. *Educ:* City Univ. (BSc (Hons) Econs and Psychol.); Mansfield Coll., Oxford (MA Theol.); Univ. of London (MA Psychol. of Religion). Ordination, URC, 1989; Minister, Friary URC, West Bridgford, Nottingham, 1989–94; City Temple URC, 1994–2000, Jt Minister, 1997–99; Free Church Chaplain, St Bart's Hosp., and Children's Chaplain, Bart's and The London NHS Trust, 1997–2001; Associate Minister, Queen's Park URC, 2000–02; ordained deacon, and priest, C of E, 2002; Hon. Asst Curate, N Lambeth Parish, 2002–09; Permission to Officiate, Stepney Area, London Dio., 2009–12; Asst Priest, St Paul's and St Mark's, Old Ford, 2009–12. Franciscan tertiary, 2010. Senior Brigade Chaplain (formerly Hd of Chaplaincy), London Fire Brigade, 2005–; Hd of Chaplaincy, London Fire and Emergency Planning Authy, 2005–; Sub-chaplain, Firefighters Meml Trust, 2013–; Chair, Chaplaincy Leadership Forum and Exec., 2013–. Governor: Evelina Hosp. Sch., 2005–14 (Chair, 2013–14); Guy's and St Thomas' NHS Foundn Trust, 2010–13. Trustee, Cecily Northcote Trust, 2015–. *Recreations:* reading, theatres. *Address:* The Chaplaincy, St Thomas' Hospital, Westminster Bridge Road, SE1 7EH.

HILBORNE, Stephanie Vera, OBE 2010; Chief Executive, The Wildlife Trusts, since 2004; *b* 3 March 1968; *d* of Derek Vance Hilborne and Mary Elizabeth Hilborne (*née* Drewett); *m* 1997, Jeremy Iain Wallace; one *s* one *d*. *Educ:* Lady Eleanor Holles Sch.; Bristol Univ. (BSc 1st Cl. Hons Biol.); University Coll. London (MSc Conservation 1993). Principal Officer, Wildlife and Countryside Link, 1994–97; Asst CEO, 1998–2000, CEO, 2000–04, Notts Wildlife Trust. FRSA 1996. *Recreations:* walking/rambling, swimming, badminton. *Address:* The Wildlife Trusts, The Kiln, Waterside, Mather Road, Newark, Notts NG24 1WT. *T:* (01636) 677711, *Fax:* (01636) 670001.

HILDEBRAND, Peter; Regional Employment Judge, London South, since 2008; *b* Lurgan, Co. Armagh, 28 June 1954; *s* of William Robert Perry Hildebrand and Olive Hildebrand; *m* 1980, Ann Purdon; one *s* two *d*. *Educ:* Campbell Coll., Belfast; Pembroke Coll., Cambridge (BA 1975). Admitted solicitor, 1978; Sacker and Partners, 1976–81, 1982–86; Stephenson Harwood, 1981–82; Burd Pearse, Exeter, 1986–97; Fee Paid Chm., Exeter, 1993–97, Salaried Chm., Leeds, 1997–2008, Employment Tribunal. *Recreations:* amateur radio, languages, running. *Address:* Regional Office of Employment Tribunals, Montague Court, 101 London Road, W Croydon CR2 0RF. *Club:* Reform.

HILDITCH, David William; Member (DemU) Antrim East, Northern Ireland Assembly, since 1998; *b* 23 July 1963; two *s*. *Educ:* Carrickfergus Grammar Sch. Carrickfergus Borough Council: Mem. (DemU), 1991–2013; Dep. Mayor, 1994–96; Mayor, 1997–98. Dist Master, Carrickfergus, Loyal Orange Instn, 1993–2000. *Address:* East Antrim Democratic Unionist Party, 31 Lancasterian Street, Carrickfergus, Co. Antrim BT38 7AB. *T:* (028) 9332 9980.

HILDRETH, (Henry) Jan (Hamilton Crossley); independent consultant; Chairman: South West London and St George's Mental Health (formerly Pathfinder) NHS Trust, 1994–2004; High Performance Sports Ltd, 1995–2011; *b* 1 Dec. 1932; *s* of Maj.-Gen. Sir (Harold) John (Crossley) Hildreth, KBE, and late Mrs Joan Elise Hallett (*née* Hamilton); *m* 1958, Wendy Moira Marjorie, *d* of late Arthur Harold Clough, CMG, OBE and Marjorie Violet Clough; two *s* one *d*. *Educ:* Wellington Coll.; The Queen's Coll., Oxford (Hon. Mods (Nat. Sci.), BA PPE 1956, MA). National Service in RA, BAOR, 1952–53; 44 Parachute Bde (TA), 1953–58. Baltic Exchange, 1956; Royal Dutch Shell Group, 1957: served Philippines (marketing) and London (finance); Kleinwort, Benson Ltd, 1963; NEDO, 1965; Member of Economic Development Cttees for the Clothing, the Hosiery and Knitwear, and the Wool Textile industries; Mem., London Transport Bd, subseq. LTE, 1968–72: main responsibilities Finance, Marketing, Corp. Plan, Data Processing, and Estates; Asst Chief Exec., John Laing & Son Ltd, 1972–74; Dir-Gen., Inst. of Directors, 1975–78. Director: Minster Trust Ltd, 1979–94; Monument Oil and Gas plc, 1984–88; non-exec. dir of several cos, 1983–96; Chairman: Carroll Securities Ltd, 1986–91; Sea Catch PLC, 1987–94; Scallop Kings PLC, 1987–97. Member: Cttee, GBA, 1978–86 and 1997–2000; Council, ISIS, 1979–82; Exec. Cttee, Industrial Soc., 1973–84 (Hon. Life Mem., 1984); Council, British Exec. Service Overseas, 1975–91; Council, SCOPE (formerly Spastic Soc.), 1980–83, 1985 (Chm. Audit Cttee, 1990–92; Hon. Treas., 1992–97); Review Body for Nursing and Midwifery Staff and Professions Allied to Medicine, 1989–95; Council, St George's Hosp. Med. Sch., 1995–2002; Dir, Contact A Family, 1980–89. Constituency Chm., 1986–89, Pres., 1989–92, Wimbledon Cons. Assoc. Governor: Wellington Coll., 1974–2003; Eagle House Sch., 1986–2003. FCILT. FRSA. *Recreations:* cross-country, mountain and road running (London Marathon, 1981–2005), photography, water mills, and others. *Address:* 50 Ridgway Place, Wimbledon, SW19 4SW. *Clubs:* Athenæum; Vincent's (Oxford); Thames Hare and Hounds.

HILDRETH, Paul Adrian; independent advisor on cities, regions and local economies, since 2005; Visiting Policy Fellow, Centre for Sustainable Urban Futures, University of Salford, since 2005; *b* London, 4 Feb. 1952; *s* of Cyril Leyland and Joan Hildreth; *m* 1987, Victoria

Anne Gauld; two *s*. *Educ:* Nobel Grammar Sch., Stevenage; Aberystwyth Univ. (BScEcon Econs 1974; MScEcon 1977); Birmingham Univ. (MSc Public Service Mgt 2006). Greater London Council: Asst Trng Officer, 1976–78; Trng Officer, 1978–79; Career Develt Officer, 1979–81; London Transport Finance, 1981; Policy Asst to Chm., Industry and Employment Cttee, 1981–83; Actg Hd, Inner City Policy, 1983–85; Chief Asst (Housing and Social Services), City of Westminster, 1985–88; London Borough of Croydon: Asst Bor. Sec., 1988–92; Hd, Econ. Prog., 1992–98; Hd, Econ. and Strategic Develt, 1998–2003; on secondment as Policy Advr, ODPM, 2003–05. Non-exec. Dir, Cambridge Econometrics, 2008–. Associate, Centre for London, 2013–. Member: Expert Panel on Cities and Regl Policy, DCLG, 2005–09; Panel for Architecture, Built Envmt and Planning, REF 2014, 2011–14; Bd, Regl Studies Assoc., 2012–15. Expert assignments, Council of Europe, 2008–13. Enabler, CABE, 2009–12. MCIPD 1981; Mem., Instn of Econ. Develt, 1999. Fellow, Regl Studies Assoc., 2014–. *Publications:* contrib. papers to peer-reviewed jls on sub-nat. econ. policy, cities and governance. *Recreations:* mountain hiking, ski-ing, tennis. *Address:* 1 Belmont Road, Reigate, Surrey RH2 7ED. *T:* (01737) 223252. *E:* pahildreth@yahoo.com, P.A.Hildreth@salford.ac.uk.

HILDYARD, Marianna Catherine Thoroton, (Lady Falconer of Thoroton); QC 2002; **Her Honour Judge Hildyard;** a Circuit Judge, since 2012; *b* 24 Nov. 1955; *d* of Sir David Hildyard, KCMG, DFC; *m* 1985, Charles Leslie Falconer (*see* Baron Falconer of Thoroton); three *s* one *d*. *Educ:* Council of Legal Educn. Called to the Bar, Inner Temple, 1977, Bencher, 2009. Asst Recorder, 1999; Recorder, 1999–2012; a Dep. High Court Judge, 2009–12. Mem. Bd, Bar Services Bd. Chm., Deborah Hutton Campaign; Ambassador, Nat. Aids Trust. *Recreations:* gardening, my children. *Address:* Luton County Court, 2nd Floor, Cresta House, Alma Street, Luton, Beds LU1 2PU.

See also Hon. Sir R. H. T. Hildyard.

HILDYARD, Hon. Sir Robert Henry Thoroton, Kt 2011; **Hon. Mr Justice Hildyard;** DL; a Judge of the High Court of Justice, Chancery Division, since 2011; *b* 10 Oct. 1952; *s* of Sir David (Henry Thoroton) Hildyard, KCMG, DFC and Millicent Hildyard, *d* of Sir Edward Baron; *m* 1980, Isabella Jane Rennie (marr. diss. 2010); two *d* (and one *d* decd); *m* 2012, Lucy Gibson; one *d*. *Educ:* Eton Coll.; Christ Church, Oxford (BA Hons Hist.). Called to the Bar, Inner Temple, 1977; Bencher, Lincoln's Inn, 2005. Jun. Counsel to Crown (Chancery), 1992–94; QC 1994; a Deputy High Court Judge, 2002–11; Attorney Gen., Duchy of Lancaster, 2006–11. Mem., Financial Reporting Review Panel, 2002–08. Mem., Adv. Council, Attingham Trust, 2011–. DL Notts, 2014. *Address:* Royal Courts of Justice, 7 Rolls Building, Fetter Lane, EC4A 1NL. *Club:* Garrick.

See also M. C. T. Hildyard.

HILHORST, Rosemary, OBE 2003; Regional Director, European Union, British Council, since 2011; *b* 10 April 1954; *d* of late Raymond Bowditch and of June Ebdon; *m* 1981, Francis Hilhorst; one *s* one *d*. *Educ:* UCL (BSc Hons (Physics) 1975); Chelsea Coll. Centre for Sci. Educn, London (PGCE (Integrated Sci.) 1976); London Business Sch. (Sen. Exec. Prog. 2003). Sci. teacher and hd of sci. depts, Sussex, Dorset, Italy and Tanzania, 1976–85; British Council, 1985–: Asst Dir, Sudan, 1986–89; mgt posts, HQ, London, 1989–91, and 1994–97; Director: Slovakia, 1991–94; Tanzania, 1997–2000; Central and E Europe, 2000–01; Connecting Futures, 2002–03; Director: Portugal, 2003–08; Russia, 2008–11. Member: Exec. Cttee, Tanzania Br., Britain-Tanzania Assoc., 1997–2000; Selection Cttee, Tanzania Bd, 1997–2000, Portuguese Bd, 2003–08, United World Colls; Governing Body, British Assoc. for Central and Eastern Europe, 2000–02. *Recreations:* gardening, running, family.

HILL; *see* Clegg-Hill, family name of Viscount Hill.

HILL; *see* Erskine-Hill.

HILL, family name of **Marquess of Downshire** and **Baron Hill of Oareford**.

HILL, 9th Viscount *cr* 1842; **Peter David Raymond Charles Clegg-Hill;** Bt 1727; Baron Hill 1814; *b* 17 Oct. 1945; *s* of Major Hon. Frederick Raymond Clegg-Hill, 2nd *s* of 6th Viscount and Alice Dorothy (*née* Chapman); *S* cousin, 2003; *m* 1973, Sharon Ruth Deane, NZ (marr. diss. 2000; she changed her name to Savanna Dawson; they re-married 2002); one *s* five *d* (and one *s* decd, Paul Andrew Raymond Clegg-Hill, *b* 1979, *d* 2003). *Heir: s* Hon. Michael Charles David Clegg-Hill [*b* 29 Feb. 1988; *m* 2010, Stephanie Riley; two *d*]. *E:* moyadrift@yahoo.co.uk.

HILL OF OAREFORD, Baron *cr* 2010 (Life Peer), of Oareford in the County of Somerset; **Jonathan Hopkin Hill,** CBE 1995; PC 2013; Member, European Commission, since 2014; *b* 24 July 1960; *s* of Rowland Louis Hill and Paddy Marguerite (*née* Henwood); *m* 1988, Alexandra Jane Nettelfield; one *s* two *d*. *Educ:* Highgate Sch.; Trinity Coll., Cambridge (MA). RIT & Northern, 1983; Hamish Hamilton, 1984–85; Conservative Research Dept, 1985–86; Special Advr to Rt Hon. Kenneth Clarke at Dept of Employment, DTI and DoH, 1986–89; Lowe Bell Communications, 1989–91; No 10 Policy Unit, 1991–92; Political Sec. to Prime Minister, 1992–94; Sen. Consultant, Bell Pottinger Consultants, 1994–98; Founding Dir, Quiller Consultants, 1998–2010; Parly Under-Sec. of State for Educn, 2010–13; Leader of the H of L and Chancellor of the Duchy of Lancaster, 2013–14. Trustee, Nat. Literacy Trust, 1995–2009; Mem. Adv. Bd, Reform, 2004–10. Governor: Highgate Sch., 1995–2010; Hanford Sch., 2004–10. *Publications:* (with Baroness Hogg) Too Close to Call, 1995. *Recreations:* reading, gardening, walking on Exmoor. *Address:* European Commission, Rue de la Loi 200, Brussels 1049, Belgium.

HILL, Prof. Adrian Vivian Sinton, DPhil, DM; FRCP; FMedSci; Director, The Jenner Institute, since 2005, and Professor of Human Genetics, since 1996, University of Oxford; Fellow, Magdalen College, Oxford, since 2004; *b* 9 Oct. 1958; *s* of late Fergus Hill and of Helen (*née* O'Donovan); *m* 1994, Sunetra Gupta, *qv*; two *d*. *Educ:* Belvedere Coll., Dublin; Trinity Coll., Dublin (Foundn Scholar; Hon. Fellow, 2008); Magdalen Coll. and Lincoln Coll., Oxford (BA 1979; BM BCh 1982; MA 1982; DPhil 1986; DM 1993). FRCP 1999. University of Oxford: Research Fellow: Exeter Coll., 1983–86, 1994–99; St John's Coll., 1988–90; Balliol Coll., 1990–93; Wellcome Trust Principal Res. Fellow, Wellcome Trust Centre for Human Genetics, 1995–2010; Chm., Centre for Clinical Vaccinology and Tropical Medicine, 2005–. Hon. Consultant Physician, Oxford Radcliffe Hosps, 1993–. FMedSci 1999. *Publications:* research papers on human genetics, vaccines and infectious diseases, esp. malaria. *Recreations:* music, travel. *Address:* The Jenner Institute, Roosevelt Drive, Oxford OX3 7DQ. *T:* (01865) 617610. *E:* adrian.hill@ndm.ox.ac.uk.

HILL, Alastair Malcolm, OBE 2000; QC 1982; *b* 12 May 1936; *s* of Prof. Sir Ian George Wilson Hill, CBE, LLD, FRCP, FRSE and Lady (Audrey) Hill; *m* 1969, Elizabeth Maria Innes; one *s* one *d*. *Educ:* Trinity Coll., Glenalmond; Keble Coll., Oxford (Stevenson-Chatterton Schol.; BA Hons Jurisp. 1959). Nat. Service, RHA, 1954–56. Called to the Bar, Gray's Inn, 1961; South Eastern Circuit; a Recorder, 1982. Former Trustee, Disability Law Service. *Recreations:* collecting prints and watercolours, opera, fly-fishing.

HILL, Allen; *see* Hill, H. A. O.

HILL, Andrea; Chief Executive, Suffolk County Council, 2008–11; *b* 12 Feb. 1964; *d* of Michael and Sheila Large; *m* 1984, Phil Hill (marr. diss. 2012); three *s*. *Educ:* N London Poly. (BA 1st Cl. Hons Modern Studies); Univ. of Birmingham (MBA Public Sector). Thurrock Borough Council: Policy Performance Rev. Officer, 1985–87; Principal Asst, 1987–90; Hd of Strategy Planning, 1990–94; Asst Chief Exec., Cambridge CC, 1994–99; Dir of Policy and Community, 1999–2000, Dep. Chief Exec., 2000–01, N Herts DC; Chief Executive: Colchester BC, 2001–04; Bedfordshire CC, 2004–08. Dir, Customer Service Direct, 2008–11. Mem. Bd, Living East, Regl Cultural Consortium for E of England, 2002–07. Non-exec. Dir, Univ. Campus Suffolk, 2008–11. Dir, DanceEast, 2010–11. Trustee, Ipswich Town Charitable (formerly Community) Trust, 2008–11. *Recreations:* marathon running, ski-ing, sailing, windsurfing.

HILL, Prof. (Anthony) Edward, OBE 2010; PhD; Executive Director, National Oceanography Centre, since 2010 (Director, 2005–10); Professor of Oceanography, University of Southampton, since 2007; *b* 30 Dec. 1959; *s* of Anthony Sidney Hill and Philomena Hill (*née* Ward); *m* 1989, Jacqueline Patricia Caukwell; two *s*. *Educ:* Bishop Wulstan RC High Sch., Rugby; Univ. of Sheffield (BSc (Applied Maths) 1st class 1981); UCNW, Bangor (MSc 1983; PhD (Physical Oceanography) 1987). Lectr in Oceanography, 1986–95, Sen. Lectr, 1995–99, UCNW, Bangor, subseq. Univ. of Wales, Bangor; Dir, Proudman Oceanographic Lab., NERC, 1999–2005. Hon. Vis. Prof., Univ. of Liverpool, 1999–2004; Hon. Prof., Univ. of Southampton, 2005–07. Interim Dir, British Antarctic Survey, 2012. Chm. Bd, Nat. Centre for Ocean Forecasting, 2005–07; Member: Exec. Bd, NERC, 2001– (Mem., Sci. and Innovation Strategy Bd, 2008–11); Steering Cttee, Global Climate Observing System, 2007–10; Council, Marine Biology Assoc., 2008–10. FIMarEST, CMarSci 2006. Hon. Fellow, Bangor Univ., 2014. Hon. DSc Sheffield, 2011. *Publications:* numerous res. contribns on oceanography of continental shelf seas to acad. jls. *Recreations:* oil painting, visiting historical monuments, walking. *Address:* National Oceanography Centre, Empress Dock, European Way, Southampton SO14 3ZH.

HILL, Antony James de Villiers; consultant; Headmaster, St Mark's School, Southborough, Mass, 1994–2006; *b* 1 Aug. 1940; *s* of James Kenneth Hill and Hon. Yvonne Aletta Hill, *d* of 2nd Baron de Villiers; *m* 1974, Gunilla Els-Charlotte Emilie (Elsa) Nilsson; one *d*. *Educ:* Sydney Grammar School; Sydney Univ. (BA Hons); Boston Univ. (MEd). Law Clerk, 1962–64; Antarctic Expedition, 1964–65; Master, Canberra Grammar Sch., 1965–66; Instructor, Himalayan Mountaineering Inst., Darjeeling, 1967–68; Master, Sydney C of E Grammar Sch., 1967–72, 1977; Mem. Faculty: Phillips Acad., Andover, Mass, 1972–74; Boston Univ., 1974–76; Senior Master, King's Sch., Parramatta, 1977–81; Headmaster: Christ Church Grammar Sch., WA, 1982–87; Melbourne C of E Grammar Sch., later Melbourne Grammar Sch., 1988–94; Dir, Wesley College Inst. for Educnl Innovation, Melbourne, 2006–07. *Recreations:* running, climbing, sailing, theatre, music, reading. *Address:* 22 Dartmouth Street, Boston, MA 02116, USA. *T:* (617) 8696935. *Clubs:* Weld (Perth, WA); Savage (Melbourne).

HILL, Sir Brian (John), Kt 1989; FRICS; FCIOB; *b* 19 Dec. 1932; *s* of Doris Winifred Hill and Gerald Aubrey Hill, OBE; *m* 1959, Janet J. Newman; two *s* one *d*. *Educ:* Stowe School; Emmanuel College, Cambridge (BA (Land Economy); MA). Managing Director, Higgs and Hill Building Ltd, 1966–78; Higgs and Hill plc: Group Managing Dir, 1972–83; Chm. and Chief Exec., 1983–89; Exec. Chm., 1989–91; non-exec. Chm., 1991–92. Director: Etonbrook Properties, 1991–93; Southern Reg. Nat. Westminster Bank, 1990–92; Chairman: Goldsborough Healthcare plc, 1993–97; Longmartin Properties Ltd, 2008–15; Member: Sackville Property Unit Trust, 1999–2002; Threadneedle Property Unit Trust, 2002–12. President: London Region, Nat. Fedn of Building Trades Employers, 1981–82; CIOB, 1987–88; Building Employers Confedn, 1992–95; Chairman: Vauxhall Coll. of Building and Further Educn, 1976–86; Nat. Contractors Group, 1983–84; Director: Building Centre, 1977–85; LDDC, 1994–98. Property Services Agency: Mem. Adv. Bd, 1981–86; Mem. Bd, 1986–88. Mem. Cttee, Lazard Property Unit Trust, 1982–98. Ext. Examr, Reading Univ., 1993–97. Chairman: Great Ormond Street Hospital, 1992–97 (Governor, then Dir, 1985–97, Special Trustee, 1990–2000); Children's Trust, Tadworth, 1998–2008; Trustee, Falkland Is Meml Trust, 1997–2007. Governor: Aberdour Sch., 1988–2007; Pangbourne Coll., 2000–04. Hon. FIStructE; Hon. FCGI; Hon. Fellow, Inst. of Child Health, 1996. Hon. DSc Westminster, 1994; Hon. LLD South Bank, 1995. *Recreations:* travelling, tennis, gardening, amateur dramatics. *Address:* Corner Oak, 5 Glen Close, Kingswood, Surrey KT20 6NT. *Club:* Royal Automobile.

HILL, Charles; *see* Hill, R. C.

HILL, Charles Edward; HM Diplomatic Service; Head of Policy and Training, Security Department, Foreign and Commonwealth Office, since 2013; *b* 31 March 1963; *s* of Anthony and Jennifer Hill; *m* 1996, Suzanne Victoria Stock; one *s* one *d*. *Educ:* Royal Holloway Coll., Univ. of London (BA Hist.). Joined HM Diplomatic Service, 1990; Third Sec. (Chancery), Doha, 1993–96; Dep. Hd of Mission, Almaty, 1997–2000; Parly Clerk, FCO, 2000–02; Hd, Central Asia and S Caucasus Section, FCO, 2002–04; Dep. Hd of Mission, Muscat, 2004–08, Oslo, 2009–13. *Recreations:* travel, tennis, backgammon, CFC. *Address:* Foreign and Commonwealth Office, King Charles Street, SW1A 2AH.

HILL, Rt Rev. Christopher John, KCVO 2014; Bishop of Guildford, 2004–13; Clerk of the Closet to the Queen, 2005–14; *b* 10 Oct. 1945; *s* of Leonard and Frances V. Hill; *m* 1976, Hilary Ann Whitehouse; three *s* one *d*. *Educ:* Sebright Sch., Worcs; King's Coll., London (BD Hons; Relton Prize for Theology, 1967; MTh 1968; AKC 1967). Deacon 1969, priest 1970. Asst Curate, Dio. of Lichfield: St Michael's, Tividale, 1969–73; St Nicholas, Codsall, 1973–74; Asst Chaplain to Archbp of Canterbury for Foreign Relations, 1974–81; Archbp's Sec. for Ecumenical Affairs, 1982–89; Hon. Canon of Canterbury Cathedral, 1982–89; Chaplain to the Queen, 1987–96; Canon Residentiary, 1989–96, Precentor, 1990–96, St Paul's Cathedral; Bishop Suffragan of Stafford, 1996–2004. Anglican Secretary: Anglican-RC Internat. Commn (I), 1974–81, Internat. Commn (II), 1983–90 (Mem., 1990–91); Anglican-Lutheran Eur. Commn, 1981–82; Consultant: C of E—German Churches Commn, 1987–90; C of E—Nordic-Baltic Churches Commn, 1989–92; Co-Chairman: C of E—French Lutheran and Reformed Conversations, 1994–98; Meissen Theol Conf., 1998–2010; Chm., C of E Council for Christian Unity, 2008–12 (Mem., 1989–96); Vice-Chm., Faith and Order Adv. Gp, 1998–2007 (Mem., 1996–2008). Member: Legal Adv. Commn, Gen. Synod of C of E, 1991–2013; House of Bishops, Gen. Synod of C of E, 1999–2013 (Chm., Women Bishops' Gp, 2005–06; Mem., Theol Gp, 2006–10; Mem., Faith and Order Commn, 2010–13); Wkg Pty on Women in the Episcopate, 2001–04 (Vice-Chm., 2003–04); Wkg Party on Bishops' Legal Costs, Fees Adv. Commn, 2003; Liturgical Commn, 2003–06; Discipline Commn, 2004–13; Anglican-RC Internat. Commn III, 2011–; Wkg Gp on Ordinariate, 2011–13. Pres., Conf. of Eur. Churches, 2013– (Vice-Pres. 2009–13). Entered H of L 2010. Mem. Council, KCL, 2009–. Guestmaster, Nikaean Club, 1982–89. Co-Chm., London Soc. of Jews and Christians, 1991–96; Vice-Chm., 1993–2002, Chm., 2002–15, Ecclesiastical Law Soc. DD Lambeth, 2014; DUniv Surrey, 2015. *Publications:* (ed jtly) Anglicans and Roman Catholics: the search for unity, 1995; (ed jtly) Documents in the Debate: papers on Anglican orders, 1997; miscellaneous ecumenical, ecclesiological and legal articles. *Recreations:* Radio 3, walking, detective stories, Italian food, GWR, unaffordable wine. *Address:* Hillview, West End, Ruardean, Glos GL17 9TP. *Clubs:* Athenæum, Sette of Odd Volumes, Nobody's Friends.

HILL, Prof. Christopher John, DPhil; FBA 2007; Sir Patrick Sheehy Professor of International Relations, University of Cambridge, since 2004; *b* 20 Nov. 1948; *s* of Peter Alan Hill and Sylvia Dawn Hill; *m* 1970, Maria McKay; one *s* one *d*. *Educ:* Merton Coll., Oxford (BA 1st Cl. Hons Modern History 1970); Nuffield Coll., Oxford (DPhil 1979). London School of Economics and Political Science: Noel Buxton Student in Internat. Relns, 1973–74; Lectr, 1974–90, Sen. Lectr, 1990–91, in Internat. Relns; Montague Burton Prof. of

Internat. Relns, 1991–2004; Convenor, Dept of Internat. Relns, 1994–97; Vice Chm., Academic Bd, 1999–2002; University of Cambridge: Dir, Centre of Internat. Studies, 2004–09; Jt Hd, 2009–10, Hd, 2012–14, Dept of Politics and Internat. Studies. Vis. Prof., Dartmouth Coll., NH, 1985; Visiting Fellow: RIIA, 1980–81; Woodrow Wilson International Centre for Scholars, Washington, 1984; European University Inst., Florence, 1992–93, 1998; UCSD, 2003; Univ. of Siena, 2003; Robert Schumann Centre of Advanced Studies, European University Inst., Fiesole, 2015; Academic Visitor, St Antony's Coll., Oxford, 2009; Vis. Researcher, Centre des Études Européennes, Paris, 2015. *Publications:* (ed) National Foreign Policies and European Political Co-operation, 1983; Cabinet Decisions in Foreign Policy, 1991; (ed jtly) Two Worlds of International Relations, 1994; (ed) The Actors in Europe's Foreign Policy, 1996; (ed jtly) European Foreign Policy: key documents, 2000; The Changing Politics of Foreign Policy, 2003; (ed jtly) International Relations and the European Union, 2005, 2nd edn 2011; (ed jtly) National and European Foreign Policies, 2011; The National Interest in Question: foreign policy in multicultural societies, 2013; (jtly) The Art of Attraction: soft power and the UK's role in the world, 2014; many articles in learned jls and contribs to books. *Recreations:* Wolverhampton Wanderers FC, the visual arts. *Address:* Department of Politics and International Studies, 7 West Road, Cambridge CB3 9DT. *T:* (01223) 767230. *E:* cjh68@cam.ac.uk.

HILL, Ven. Colin, PhD; Archdeacon of West Cumberland, 2004–08; *b* 4 Sept. 1942; *s* of William Albert Hill and Annie Hill; *m* 1965, Kathleen Chadbourne; three *d. Educ:* Leicester Univ. (BSc (Maths) 1964); Ripon Hall, Oxford; Open Univ. (PhD (Sociol. of Religion) 1988). Ordained deacon, 1966, priest, 1967; Assistant Curate: Ch of the Martyrs, Dio. Leicester, 1966–69; St Crispin's Ch, Braunstone, 1969–71; Lectr, Ecumenical Inst., Teesside, 1971–72; Vicar, St Thomas and St James, Worsbrough, 1972–78; Chs' Develt Officer for Mission and Ministry for Telford, Dios Lichfield and Hereford, 1978–96; Canon Res., and Canon Treas., Carlisle Cathedral, and Diocesan Sec., Carlisle, 1996–2004; Vice Dean, Carlisle Cathedral, 2004. Rural Dean: Telford, Dio. Lichfield, 1980–96; Telford Severn Gorge, Dio. Hereford, 1980–96; Preb., Hereford Cathedral, 1983–96. *Publications:* (contrib.) A Workbook in Popular Religion, 1986; (contrib.) A Deanery Workbook, 1988; What's Good for the Organisation: appraisal schemes, 1991; (contrib.) Religious Movements in a Neo-Weberian Perspective, 1992; Loosing the Apron Strings: devolution to deaneries, 1996; Appointing the Rural Dean, 2004; Deans and Deaneries: lessons from Norway, 2006. *Recreations:* social housing, Scandinavian travel, cultivation of bonsai. *Address:* Telford House, 1A Briery Bank, Arnside, Cumbria LA5 0HW.

HILL, Rev. Canon Colin Arnold Clifford, OBE 1996; Vicar of Croydon and Chaplain to Archbishop Whitgift Foundation, 1973–94; Chaplain to the Queen, 1990–99; *b* 13 Feb. 1929; *s* of William and May Hill; *m* 1st, 1957, Shirley (*d* 1961); one *s*; 2nd, 1971, Irene Chamberlain; one step *s. Educ:* Reading Sch.; Bristol Univ.; Ripon Hall Theol Coll., Oxford; Univ. of Wales, Bangor (MPhil 2003). Ordained deacon, Sheffield Cathedral, 1957, priest, 1958; Rotherham Parish Church; Vicar of Brightside, 1960; Rector of Easthampstead, Bracknell, 1964; Chaplain, RAF Staff Coll., Bracknell, 1968. Hon. Canon, Canterbury, 1975, Canon Emeritus, 1984; Hon. Canon, Southwark, 1984, Canon Emeritus, 1994. Proctor in Convocation and General Synod, Dio. Oxford, 1970–73, Dios of Canterbury and Southwark, 1980–84. Religious Advr, London Borough of Croydon, 1973–94; Chairman: Church Tenements Trust, 1973–94; Croydon Industrial Mission, 1975–94. Chm., Croydon Crime Prevention Initiative, 1989–94; Vice Chm., Croydon Police Consultative Cttee, 1985–94. Founder, Bracknell Samaritans, 1968; Founder Chm., Croydon Youth Counselling Agency, 1974–94. *Recreations:* walking, reading. *Address:* Silver Birches, 70 Preston Crowmarsh, Wallingford, Oxon OX10 6SL. *T:* 07837 249949.

HILL, Damon Graham Devereux, OBE 1997; motor racing driver, retired; analyst and commentator, Sky Sports F1, since 2012; *b* 17 Sept. 1960; *s* of late Graham Hill, OBE and of Bette Hill; *m* 1988, Georgie Hill; two *s* two *d. Educ:* Haberdashers' Aske's Sch. Began motorcycle racing, 1979; Formula 3, 1986; Formula 3000, 1988; Formula 1, 1992–99: Brabham team, 1992; with Williams Team, 1991–96: test driver, 1991; driver, 1993–96; Grand Prix wins: 3 in 1993, 6 in 1994, 4 in 1995, 8 in 1996 (Argentina, Australia, Brazil, Canada, France, Germany, Japan, San Marino), 1 in 1998; Drivers' World Championship, 1996; with Arrows team, 1997; with Jordan team, 1998–99. Chairman: P1 Internat. Ltd, 2001; Damon Hill BMW, Warwick, 2001. Numerous awards incl. BBC Sports Personality of the Year, 1994 and 1996. *Publications:* Grand Prix Year, 1994; Championship Year, 1996. *Club:* British Racing Drivers' (Pres., 2006–11).

HILL, David Arnold, CBE 2015; DPhil; Chairman and Owner, Environment Bank Ltd, since 2007; Owner and Director, Environmental Markets Exchange, since 2010; Deputy Chairman, Natural England, since 2011 (non-executive Director, since 2006); *b* Derby, 18 April 1958; *s* of Arnold Hill and Phyllis Joan Hill; *m* 1989, Dr Kathleen Raw; one *s* two *d. Educ:* Noel Baker Sch., Derby; Univ. of Loughborough (BSc Hons 1st Cl. 1979); Wolfson Coll., Oxford (DPhil 1982). Ecologist, Game Conservancy, 1982–86; Sen. Ecologist, RSPB, 1986–89; Dir of Develt, British Trust for Ornithology, 1989–92; Owner and Chief Exec., Ecoscope Applied Ecologists, 1992–2002, subseq. merged with RPS Gp plc, Chief Scientific Advr, 2002–06; Chief Exec., David Hill Ecology and Envmt, 2007–. Non-exec. Dir, Jt Nature Conservation Cttee, 2006–. Chm., Northern Upland Chain Local Nature Partnership, 2012–. Mem., Ecosystem Markets Taskforce, 2011–13. Vis. Prof. in Ecol., Oxford Brookes Univ., 2006–. *Publications:* The Pheasant, 1986; The Avocet, 1989; Bird Census Techniques, 1992, 2nd edn 2000; Managing Habitats for Conservation, 1996; The Handbook of Biodiversity Methods, 2005. *Recreations:* wildlife photography, bird watching, walking, mountain biking, travelling to remote places, fly fishing, my family. *E:* dhill@davidhillecology.com.

HILL, David Christopher; Executive Director, Schools, Children, Families and Adult Services, Essex County Council, since 2013 (Executive Director, Schools, Children and Families, 2010–13); *b* London, 30 March 1959; *s* of Stanley and Joyce Hill; *m* 1988, Joanne Susan Thorogood; two *d. Educ:* Brittons Sch., Rainham, Essex; Brunel Univ. (MSc; CQSW 1983). Social Worker, London Bor. of Greenwich, 1983–87; Area Dir, Family Welfare Assoc., 1987–89; Gen. Manager, City of Westminster, 1989–96; Head of Children's Services: Havering LBC, 1996–2000; Tower Hamlets LBC, 2000–05; Director of Children's Services: Merton LBC, 2005–08; Croydon LBC, 2008–10. Vice Pres., Assoc. of Dirs of Children's Services. Member: Social Work Reform Bd, 2010–; Bd, Coll. of Social Work, 2010–. Trustee, Who Cares Trust, 2010–. *Recreations:* music - choral, brass, piano, theatre performance, all sports. *Address:* Essex County Council, County Hall, Market Road, Chelmsford CM1 1QH. *T:* (01245) 431891. *E:* davechill5@sky.com.

HILL, David Graeme; Director of Strategy and Private Office, since 2013, and of Communications, since 2014, Department for Communities and Local Government (Board Member, since 2013); *b* Newcastle upon Tyne, 4 Nov. 1975; *s* of Graeme Hill and Eileen Hill; *m* 2005, Sophie Watson; two *s. Educ:* Ponteland High Sch., Northumberland; Corpus Christi Coll., Oxford (BA Hons PPE). Civil Service: fast stream, 1998–2002; Private Secretary: to Minister for Housing and Planning, 2000; to the Dep. Prime Minister, 2000–01; to Sec. of State for Transport, Local Govt and Regions, 2001–02; Propriety and Ethics Team, Cabinet Office, 2003–04; Dep. Dir, Strategy and Performance, 2005–07, Housing Supply, 2007–08, DCLG; Dep. Dir, Internat. Climate Change, DECC, 2009–11; Principal Private Sec. to Sec. of State for Communities and Local Govt, 2011–13. *Recreations:* golf, cricket, football (Newcastle United). *Address:* Department for Communities and Local Government, 2 Marsham Street, SW1P 4DF. *T:* 0303 444 0000. *E:* david.hill@communities.gsi.gov.uk.

HILL, David Neil, MA, FRCO, FRSCM; Musical Director, Bach Choir, since 1998; Chief Conductor, BBC Singers, since 2007; Principal Conductor, Yale University Schola Cantorum, since 2013; Professor of Choral Conducting, Yale University, since 2013; *b* 13 May 1957; *s* of James Brian Greatrex Hill and Jean Hill; *m* 1st, 1979, Hilary Llystyn Jones (marr. diss.); one *s* one *d*; 2nd, 1994, Alice Mary Wills; one *s* one *d. Educ:* Chetham's School of Music, Manchester; St John's College, Cambridge (organ student; toured Aust. 1977, USA and Canada, 1978, Japan, 1979; MA). FGCM 2003; FRSCM 2008. Sub-Organist, Durham Cathedral, 1980–82; Organist and Master of Music: Westminster Cathedral, 1982–88; Winchester Cathedral, 1988–2002; Organist and Dir of Music, St John's Coll., Cambridge, 2003–07. Conductor: Alexandra Choir, 1979–87; Waynflete Singers, Winchester, 1988–2002; Associate Chorus Master, 1987–98, Artistic Dir, 1992–98, Philharmonia Chorus; Principal Conductor, Southern Sinfonia, 2003–; Principal Conductor, Leeds Philharmonic, 2005–; Associate Guest Conductor, Bournemouth SO, 2009–. Dir, Southern Cathedrals' Fest., triennially 1990–2002. Mem. Council, RCO, 1984–; President: Cathedral Organists' Assoc., 2006–07; IAO, 2007–09. Recordings with choirs and orchs incl. Westminster Cathedral Choir (Gramophone award, 1985); concerts and tours abroad, including tours to Australia, USA and Philippines. Hon. RAM 2010. Hon. DMus Southampton, 2003. *Recreations:* drawing, reading, wine, cars. *Address:* c/o Catherine Strange, Rayfield Allied, Southbank House, Black Prince Road, SE1 7SJ. *Club:* Athenæum.

HILL, David Rowland; Director, Bell Pottinger Group, since 2007; *b* 1 Feb. 1948; *s* of Rowland Foster Hill and Rita Maud Hill; *m* 1974, Janet Gibson (marr. diss. 1992); one *s* one *d. Educ:* King Edward VI Sch., Birmingham; Brasenose Coll., Oxford Univ. (BA PPE). Unigate Ltd, 1970–72; Asst to Rt Hon. Roy Hattersley, MP, 1972–76; Political Advr, Dept of Prices and Consumer Protection, 1976–79; Head of Staff: Rt Hon. Roy Hattersley, 1979–83; Dep. Leader of Labour Party's Office, 1983–91; Dir of Campaigns and Communications, Lab Party, 1991–93; Chief Spokesperson for Labour Party, 1993–98; Dir, Bell Pottinger Good Relations, subseq. Good Relations, 1998–2003; Man. Dir, Keith McDowall Associates, subseq. Good Relations Political Communications, 2000–03; Dir of Communications, Prime Minister's Office, 2003–07. *Recreations:* cinema, watching sport, foreign travel. *Address:* Bell Pottinger Group, Holborn Gate, 330 High Holborn, WC1V 7QD.

HILL, Edward; *see* Hill, A. E.

HILL, Rev. Mgr Edward Peter; Parish Priest, St Andrew's Church, Tenterden, 2003–14; *b* 8 Aug. 1943; *s* of Leslie John Hill and Constance Irene Hill. *Educ:* Holy Family RC Primary Sch., Morden; John Fisher Independent Sch., Purley; St Joseph's Jun. Seminary, Mark Cross, Sussex; St John's Seminary, Wonersh. Ordained priest, 1968; Assistant Priest: St Saviour, Lewisham, 1968–72; St Thomas of Canterbury, Wandsworth, 1972–78; St Peter, Woolwich, 1978–82; served as RAF Chaplain, 1982–2000: Cranwell, Wildenrath, Brampton, Brize Norton, Rheindahlen; Asst Principal Chaplain, Support Command, Brampton, and Personnel and Trng Comd, Innsworth; Prin. RC Chaplain and Dir, Chaplaincy Services 2, RAF, 1997–2000; held rank of Gp Captain; QHC 1997–2000; Officiating Chaplain (RC), RAF Brize Norton, 2000–03. Prelate of Honour to the Pope, 1997. *Recreation:* most sports (interest in, only now, as spectator and studier). *Club:* Royal Air Force.

HILL, (Eleanor Mary) Henrietta; QC 2015; *b* Leeds, 30 July 1973; *d* of Roger Hill and Carol Hill (*née* Wright, now Lawson); *m* 2012, Richard Kenyon; two *s. Educ:* Gateway Sch., Leeds; Emmanuel Coll., Cambridge (BA Hons Law 1994; MA); Harvard Univ. (Herchel Smith Fellow 1995–96). Called to the Bar, Inner Temple, 1997; in practice as a barrister, Cloisters Chambers, 1997–2000, Doughty St Chambers, 2000–; Asst Coroner, Inner S London, 2013–. Pegasus Fellow, Center for Constitutional Rights, NY, 2002. *Publications:* Blackstone's Guide to the Race Relations (Amendment) Act 2000, 2001; (with Richard Kenyon) Promoting Equality and Diversity: a practitioner's guide, 2007; (contrib.) Halsbury's Laws, Vol. 88A, Rights and Freedoms, 2013. *Recreations:* family life, local history, travel. *Address:* Doughty Street Chambers, 54 Doughty Street, WC1N 2LS. *T:* (020) 7404 1313, *Fax:* (020) 7404 2283. *E:* h.hill@doughtystreet.co.uk.

HILL, Emma Rhian, CBE 2012; Creative Director, Mulberry, 2008–13; *b* Kingston-upon-Thames, 5 Aug. 1969; *d* of Keith Hill and Valerie Christine Hill (*née* Edwards). *Educ:* Wimbledon Sch. of Art (Art Foundn Dip. (Dist.) 1989); Ravensbourne Sch. of Design (BA Hons Fashion 1992). Designer, Accessories: Burberry, 1992–94; Liz Claiborne, 1994–97; Senior Designer, Accessories: Calvin Klein, 1998–2000; Marc Jacobs, 2000–02; Vice Pres., Accessories, Gap Inc., 2002–05; Consultant Designer: Chloe, 2006–07; Halston, 2007–08. *Club:* Soho House.

HILL, Felicity; *see* Green, F.

HILL, Air Cdre Dame Felicity (Barbara), DBE 1966 (OBE 1954); Director of the Women's Royal Air Force, 1966–69; *b* 12 Dec. 1915; *d* of late Edwin Frederick Hill and late Mrs Frances Ada Barbara Hill (*née* Cocke). *Educ:* St Margaret's Sch., Folkestone. Joined WAAF, 1939; commnd, 1940; served in: UK, 1939–46; Germany, 1946–47; Far East Air Force, 1949–51; other appts included Inspector of WRAF, 1956–59; OC, RAF Hawkinge, 1959–60; OC, RAF Spitalgate, 1960–62; Dep. Dir, 1962–65. Hon. ADC to the Queen, 1966–69. *Club:* Royal Air Force.

HILL, Sir Geoffrey (William), Kt 2012; poet and critic; University Professor, and Professor of Literature and Religion, Boston University, 1988–2006, now Emeritus; Professor of Poetry, University of Oxford, 2010–15; *b* 18 June 1932; *s* of William George Hill and Hilda Beatrice Hill; *m* 1st, 1956, Nancy Whittaker (marr. diss. 1983); three *s* one *d*; 2nd, 1987, Alice Goodman; one *d. Educ:* Fairfield Jun. Sch.; County High Sch., Bromsgrove; Keble Coll., Oxford (BA 1953, MA 1959; Hon. Fellow, 1981). Mem., academic staff, Univ. of Leeds, 1954–80 (Prof. of Eng. Lit., 1976–80); Univ. Lectr in English and Fellow of Emmanuel College, Cambridge, 1981–88; founding Co-Dir, Editorial Inst., Boston Univ., 1998–2004. Churchill Fellow, Univ. of Bristol, 1980; Associate Fellow, Centre for Res. in Philosophy and Literature, Univ. of Warwick, 2004. Lectures: Bateson Meml, Corpus Christi Coll., Oxford, 1984; Clark, Trinity Coll., Cambridge, 1986; Warton, British Acad., 1998; Tanner, Brasenose Coll., Oxford, 2000; Ward-Phillips, Univ. of Notre Dame, 2000; Empson, Univ. of Cambridge, 2005; Goldsmith, Univ. of Leeds, 2006; Lady Margaret, Christ's Coll., Cambridge, 2008; Wolfson Coll., Oxford, 2010. English version of Ibsen's Brand produced at National Theatre, London, 1978. Fellow, Amer. Acad. of Arts and Scis, 1996. Hon. Fellow, Emmanuel Coll., Cambridge, 1990. Hon. DLitt: Leeds, 1988; Warwick, 2007; Bristol, 2009; Oxford, 2010; Hon. LittD Cambridge, 2010. Whitbread Award, 1971; RSL Award (W. H. Heinemann Bequest), 1971; Loines Award, Amer. Acad. and Inst. of Arts and Letters, 1983; Ingram Merrill Foundn Award in Literature, 1985; T. S. Eliot Prize, Ingersoll Foundn, USA, 2000. *Publications: poetry:* For the Unfallen, 1959 (Gregory Award, 1961); King Log, 1968 (Hawthornden Prize, 1969; Geoffrey Faber Meml Prize, 1970); Mercian Hymns, 1971 (Alice Hunt Bartlett Award, 1971); Somewhere is Such a Kingdom: Poems 1952–1971, 1975; Tenebrae, 1978 (Duff Cooper Meml Prize, 1979); The Mystery of the Charity of Charles Péguy, 1983; Collected Poems, 1985; New and Collected Poems 1952–1992, 1994; Canaan, 1996; The Triumph of Love, 1998 (Cholmondeley Award, 1999; Heinemann Award, 2000); Speech! Speech!, 2000; The Orchards of Syon, 2002; Scenes from Comus, 2005; Without Title, 2006; Selected Poems, 2006; A Treatise of Civil Power, 2007; Oraclau/Oracles, 2010; Clavics, 2011; Odi Barbare, 2012; Broken Hierarchies: poems 1952–2012, 2013; *poetic drama:* Henrik Ibsen, Brand: a version for the English Stage, 1978, 3rd edn 1996; *criticism:* The Lords of Limit, 1984; The Enemy's Country, 1991; Style and Faith, 2003; Collected Critical Writings, 2008 (Truman Capote Prize for Literary Criticism, 2009). *Address:* The Rectory, 2 Apthorpe Street, Fulbourn, Cambs CB21 5EY.

HILL, Maj. Gen. Giles Patrick, CBE 2014; General Officer Commanding 1st (UK) Division, since 2015; *b* Leeds, 6 Jan. 1967; *s* of Donald and Patricia Hill; *m* 1995, Chantal Larocque; one *s. Educ:* Lawnswood Sch., Leeds; Cranfield Univ. (MA Mil. Sci. and Technol. 2001). Joined Army, 1989; CO, 1st Bn, Parachute Regt, 1996–98; HCSC 2011; Comdr, 16 Air Assault Bde, 2011–13; Dep. Commanding Gen., US 82nd Airborne Div., 2013–15.

HILL, Graham Chadwick, FRSC; Headmaster, Dr Challoner's Grammar School, Amersham, 1993–2001, Trustee, 2001–10; *b* 11 Jan. 1942; *s* of Harold Hill and Harriet (*née* Chadwick); *m* 1964, Elizabeth Wadsworth (*d* 2013); two *d* (and one *d* decd); *m* 2015, Katherine Anderson. *Educ:* Bacup and Rawtenstall Grammar Sch.; Trinity Coll., Cambridge (BA, MA, PGCE Dist, AdvDipEd). FRSC 1985. Asst Science Master, Marlborough Coll., 1965–70; Sen. Chemistry Master, 1970–75, Sen. Science Master, 1975–78, Bristol Grammar Sch.; Dep. Headmaster, Dr Challoner's Grammar Sch., 1978–86, 1989–93; Sen. Fellow, Univ. of York, 1986–87. Chm., 1987–89, Trustee, 1991–93 and 2001–06, ASE. FRSA 1993. Guinness Award for Sci. Teachers, 1968; Bronze Medallion, RSC, 1986. *Publications:* Chemistry in Context, 1978, 6th edn 2012; Chemistry in Context Laboratory Manual and Study Guide, 1982, 6th edn 2011; Chemistry Counts, 1986, 3rd edn 2003; Letts Revise Science, 1990; Science Scene (booklets, books and teachers' guides), 1990–92; Materials, 1992; Science for GCSE, 1998, 2nd edn 2001; Foundation Science for GCSE, 2001; Synoptic Skills in A level Chemistry, 2003; AQA GCSE Science, 2006; AQA GCSE Additional Science, 2007; co-author and editor: AQA GCSE Chemistry, 2007; AQA GCSE Physics, 2007; AQA GCSE Biology, 2007; OCR Chemistry for AS, 2008; Edexcel Chemistry for AS, 2008; OCR Chemistry for A2, 2009; Edexcel Chemistry for A2, 2009; Edexcel International GCSE Chemistry, 2013; contribs to learned jls. *Recreations:* walking, gardening, theatre, wildlife.

HILL, Graham Starforth; Resident Consultant, office in Rome 1992–94, and in Milan, 1990–94, Frere Cholmeley, later Frere Cholmeley Bischoff, solicitors; Consultant: to Monaco office, Frere Cholmeley, later Frere Cholmeley Bischoff, solicitors, 1984–94; to Rodyk and Davidson, solicitors, Singapore, 1985–96; *b* 22 June 1927; *s* of late Harold Victor John Hill and Helen Dora (*née* Starforth); *m* 1952, Margaret Elise Ambler (marr. diss.); one *s* one *d. Educ:* Dragon Sch., Oxford; Winchester Coll.; St John's Coll., Oxford (MA Hons). Called to the Bar, Grays Inn, 1951; admitted solicitor, 1961; also admitted solicitor Malaysia, Singapore and Hong Kong; Notary Public and Comr for Oaths, Singapore. Flying Officer, RAF, 1948–50. Crown Counsel, Colonial Legal Service, Singapore, 1953–56; Partner, subseq. Sen. Partner, Rodyk and Davidson, Advocates and Solicitors, Singapore, 1957–76. Chm., Guinness Mahon & Co. Ltd, 1979–83 (Dir, 1977–79); non-exec. Dir, Phelan, Lewis and Peat Ltd, 1984–86. Mem., Malayan Bd of Income Tax, 1957–60. Formerly (all Singapore): Hon. Legal Adviser to High Commn; Law Reform Comr; dir of numerous cos; Member: Univ. Faculty of Law; Constitutional Commn; Council, Law Soc. (Pres., 1970–74, Hon. Mem. 1978); Courts Martial Mil. Ct of Appeal; Council, Internat. Bar Assoc.; Discip. Cttee and Appeal Cttee, ICA, 1980–86. Trustee: Southwark Cathedral Develt Trust Fund, 1980–85; Royal Opera House Trust, 1982–85; Mem. Council, RicNic Th. Trust, 2011–. FRSA. Cavaliere dell'Ordine della Stella della Solidarietà, and Commendatore dell'Ordine al Merito, Italy. *Publications:* co-editor, The Laws of Singapore, revised edition 1970; A Lawyer's Anecdotage; report of Constitutional Commission of Singapore, 2009. *Recreations:* music, Italy. *Address:* 10 St Thomas Street, Winchester, Hants SO23 9HE. *T:* (01962) 854146. *E:* gattotrino@btinternet.com. *Club:* Garrick.

HILL, Harry Douglas; Chairman, Countrywide plc, 2007–09 (Chief Executive, 1988–2007); Co-Founder and Chairman, In-Deed Online plc, since 2010; *b* Yorks, 4 April 1948; *s* of Jack and Kathleen Hill; *m* 1986, Mandy Elizabeth Glenys; five *s. Educ:* Barnsley Grammar Sch.; Coll. of Estate Mgt. Chartered surveyor. Director: Jupiter Second Split plc, 2004–14; Milton Homes plc, 2008–09. *Recreations:* fishing, bird watching, cycling, National Hunt racing, restaurant in Portugal (owner). *Address:* Countrywide plc, Countrywide House, Perry Way, Witham, Essex CM8 3SX. *T:* (01376) 533700, *Fax:* (01376) 520465.

HILL, Henrietta; *see* Hill, E. M. H.

HILL, Prof. (Hugh) Allen (Oliver), FRS 1990; CChem, FRSC; Professor of Bioinorganic Chemistry, Oxford, 1992–2004, now Emeritus; Fellow and Praelector, 1965–2004, Hon. Fellow, 2007, The Queen's College, Oxford; *b* 23 May 1937; *s* of Hugh Rankin Stewart Hill and Elizabeth Hill (*née* Burns); *m* 1967, Boglárka Anna Pinter; two *s* one *d. Educ:* Royal Belfast Academical Institution; QUB (BSc 1959; PhD 1962); Wadham Coll., Oxford (MA 1964; DSc 1986; Hon. Fellow, 2002). Oxford University: Weir Jun. Fellow, UC, 1964–65; Deptl Demonstrator, 1965–67, Lectr, 1967–90, in Inorganic Chemistry; Reader in Bioinorganic Chemistry, 1990–92; Sen. Proctor, 1976–77. Vis. appts, Harvard, Univ. of Sydney, Univ. of California, 1970–82; Vis. Prof., Harvard Med. Sch., 1996–2002; Pacific Coast Lects, 1981; Robinson Lectr, RSC, 1994. Chm., Davy Faraday Cttee, 1996–98; Mem. Council, Royal Instn, 1995–98. Hon. DSc QUB, 1996. Interdisciplinary Award, RSC, 1987; Chemistry and Electrochemistry of Transition Metals Award, RSC, 1990; Mullard Award, Royal Soc., 1993; Breyer Medal, RACI, 1994; Royal Medal, Royal Soc., 2010. *Publications:* Physical Methods in Advanced Inorganic Chemistry (with P. Day), 1968; papers in professional jls. *Recreations:* gardening, music. *Address:* The Queen's College, Oxford OX1 4AW. *T:* (01865) 279120. *E:* allen.hill@queens.ox.ac.uk.

HILL, Sir James Frederick, 4th Bt *cr* 1917; OBE 2000; DL; Chairman, Specialist Schools and Academies Trust, 2007–09; *b* 5 Dec. 1943; *s* of Sir James Hill, 3rd Bt and Marjory, *d* of late Frank Croft; *S* father, 1976; *m* 1966, Sandra Elizabeth, *o d* of J. C. Ingram; one *s* three *d.* Dir, Yorkshire Bldg Soc., 1972–96. Chairman: British Wool Fedn, 1987–90; Sir James Hill (Wool) Ltd, 1991–. Dir, Ind. Acads Assoc., 2000–. DL West Yorks, 1994. DUniv Bradford, 1997. *Heir: s* James Laurence Ingram Hill [*b* 22 Sept. 1973; *m* 2003, Kate Elizabeth, *d* of T. Horsfield, Silkstone, Yorks; one *s* two *d*]. *Address:* Roseville, Moor Lane, Menston, Ilkley, West Yorks LS29 6AP. *T:* (01943) 874624. *Clubs:* Royal Automobile; Bradford (Yorks); St Enodoc Golf.

HILL, James Michael; QC 2006; a Recorder, since 2002; *b* 5 Oct. 1960; *s* of Michael Hill and late Doreen Hill; *m* 1986, Carolyne Dent; two *d. Educ:* Durham Johnston Sch.; Manchester Univ. (LLB Hons 1982). Called to the Bar, Inner Temple, 1984; N Eastern Circuit; in practice, specialising in criminal law and regulatory law; Hd, Fountain Chambers, 2010–. Former Gov., Red House Sch., Norton-on-Tees. Former Mem., Durham Town and Gown Soc. *Recreations:* playing golf, watching hockey. *Address:* Fountain Chambers, Cleveland Business Centre, 1 Watson Street, Middlesbrough TS1 2RQ. *T:* (01642) 804040, *Fax:* (01642) 804060. *E:* amallett@fountainchambers.co.uk; Broadway House Chambers, 9 Bank Street, Bradford BD1 1TW. *T:* (01274) 722560. *Clubs:* Durham County; Wynyard Golf; Whitley Bay and Tynemouth Hockey.

HILL, James William Thomas, (Jimmy), OBE 1995; Chairman, Jimmy Hill & Co. (formerly Jimmy Hill Ltd), 1972–2008; Presenter, Jimmy Hill's Sunday Supplement, Sky Sports, 2001–07; *m* 1st, 1950, Gloria Mary (marr. diss. 1961); two *s* one *d*; 2nd, 1962, Heather Christine (marr. diss. 1982); one *s* one *d*; 3rd, 1991, Bryony Ruth Jarvis. *Educ:* Henry Thornton School, Clapham. Player, Brentford FC, 1949–52, Fulham FC, 1952–61; Gen. Manager, Coventry City FC, 1961–67, Managing Director, 1975–83, Chm., 1980–83; Chm., Fulham Football Club (1987) Ltd, 1987–97. London Weekend Television: Head of Sport, 1967–72; Controller of Press, Promotion and Publicity, 1971–72; Deputy Controller, Programmes, 1972–73; Soccer analyst, BBC, 1973–98; Presenter, The Last Word, Sky Sports, 1998–2001. Mem., Sports Council, 1971–76. Hon. Chm., The Professional Footballers Assoc., 1957–61. *Publications:* Striking for Soccer, 1961; Improve your Soccer, 1964; Football Crazy, 1985; The Jimmy Hill Story (autobiog.), 1998. *Recreations:* keeping in touch with the world of sport in general, football in particular, but from his armchair. *Address:* Goldbridge House, Langton Lane, Hurstpierpoint, West Sussex BN6 9HA. *Club:* All England Lawn Tennis and Croquet.

HILL, Jane; presenter, BBC TV News, since 1997; *b* Eastbourne, E Sussex, 10 June 1969; *d* of David and Margaret Hill; civil partnership 2013, Sara Shepherd. *Educ:* Micklefield Sch., E Sussex; Queen Mary Coll., London Univ. (BA Hons Politics 1991). Voluntary and freelance rôles with BBC local radio, 1986–91; asst and researcher to Senate Democrats, Washington, DC, 1991; researcher, Radio 5 Live, 1994–95; trainee, BBC Regl News Trainee Scheme, 1995–96; regl TV journalist, 1995–97; presenter, BBC TV News, incl. One O'Clock, Six O'Clock and Ten O'Clock News and BBC News Channel, 1997–. *Recreations:* the arts, particularly theatre and visual art, walking our dog, food, wine, the gym, Archers addict. *Club:* Soho House.

HILL, Jeremy; *see* Hill, P. J. O.

HILL, Jimmy; *see* Hill, J. W. T.

HILL, John; *b* 28 April 1922; *s* of William Hallett Hill and Emily Hill (*née* Massey); *m* 1952, Hilda Mary Barratt (*d* 2007); (one *s* decd). *Educ:* Merchant Taylors' Sch., Crosby; Liverpool Univ. (BCom); Inst. of Public Finance and Accountancy, 1954. City Treasurer of Liverpool, 1974–82. Mem., Merseyside Residuary Body, 1985–88. Hon. Sen. Res. Fellow, Inst. of Local Govt Studies, Birmingham Univ., 1982–93. *Recreation:* music. *Address:* 325 Northway, Lydiate, Merseyside L31 0BW. *T:* (0151) 526 3699.

HILL, Sir John Alfred Rowley, 11th Bt *cr* 1779, of Brook Hall, Londonderry; *b* 29 Feb. 1940; *s* of Sir George Alfred Rowley Hill, 9th Bt and his 2nd wife, Jessie Anne (*née* Roberts; *d* 1995); *S* half-brother, 1992; *m* 1966, Diana Anne Walker (marr. diss. 1981); one adopted *s* one adopted *d. Heir: kinsman* Allan Claude Hill [*b* 10 Feb. 1936; *m* 1970, Rachel St Just (marr. diss. 1978); one *s* one *d*]. *Address:* 5 Wherry Close, March, Cambs PE15 9BX.

HILL, John Cameron, TD 1959; FRICS; Member, Lands Tribunal, 1987–99; *b* 8 April 1927; *s* of Raymond Cameron Hill and Margaret (*née* Chadwick); *m* 1954, Jane Edna Austin; one *s* one *d. Educ:* Bishop Vesey's Grammar Sch., Sutton Coldfield; Trinity Coll., Oxford; College of Estate Management, London Univ. (BSc EstMan). Hillier Parker May & Rowden, 1953–88, Partner, 1962–88. Served TA (Major), 1949–73; Metropolitan Special Constabulary (Comdt), 1973–86. Liveryman, Farriers' Co. *Publications:* (jtly) Valuations: Principles into Practice, 1980, 4th edn 1993; (jtly) Handbook of Rent Review, 1981, rev. edns to 1988. *Recreations:* shooting, DIY. *Address:* Hastoe House, Hastoe, Tring, Herts HP23 6LS. *T:* (01442) 822084. *Club:* Honourable Artillery Company.

HILL, John Lawrence; Chairman, Britannia Building Society, 1990–94; Chief Executive, Loss Prevention Council, 1986–96; *b* 21 July 1934; *s* of late Sidney Hill and Hilda Wardle Hill; *m* 1960, Elizabeth Godfrey; one *s* three *d. Educ:* Abbotsholme Sch.; Sidney Sussex Coll., Cambridge (MA). National Service, Royal Corps of Signals, 1953–55. Royal Dutch Shell Group, 1959–67; PA Consulting Group, 1967–86; Director: Britannia Building Soc., 1984–94; Britannia Life, 1989–94. Director: Loss Prevention Certification Bd, 1986–96; Nat. Approval Council for Security Systems, 1990–96. Governor, Inst. of Risk Management, 1987–93. *Recreations:* golf, bridge, music, greyhound rescue. *Address:* 23 Harvey Road, Guildford, Surrey GU1 3LU. *T:* (01483) 566413. *Clubs:* Hawks (Cambridge); Royal & Ancient Golf, Worplesdon Golf.

HILL, Rear-Adm. John Richard; naval historian and analyst; *b* 25 March 1929; *s* of Stanley Hill and May Hill (*née* Henshaw); *m* 1956, Patricia Anne Sales; one *s* two *d. Educ:* Royal Naval College, Dartmouth. China Station as midshipman, 1946–47; Sub-Lieut's Courses, 1948–49; Lieut, HM Ships: Gambia, 1950; Chevron, 1950–52; Tintagel Castle, 1952–54; Dryad (Navigation Specialist), 1954; Cardigan Bay, 1954–56; Albion, 1956–58; Roebuck, 1958–59; Lt-Comdr, Pembroke Dock, 1959–60; HMS Duchess, 1960–62; Comdr, MoD, 1963–65 and 1967–69; IDC 1965–67; HMS Dryad, 1969–71; Captain, MoD, 1973–75; Defence and Naval Attaché, The Hague, 1975–77; Cdre, MoD, 1977–80; Rear-Adm. 1981; Flag Officer, Admiralty Interview Bd, 1981–83. Editor, 1983–2002, Reviews Editor, 2002–09, The Naval Review. Under-Treas., Middle Temple, 1984–94 (Hon. Bencher, 1994); Sec., Council of Inns of Court, 1987–93. Member: Council, Greenwich Forum, 1983–; Bd of War Studies, London Univ., 1986–94; Council, Navy Records Soc., 1993–2001 (Vice Pres., 1997–2001); Council, Soc. for Nautical Res., 1993–99 (Chm., 1994–99). Trustee, Royal Naval Mus., Portsmouth, 1994–99 (Vice Pres., 2002). Defence Fellow, University of London King's College, 1972. *Publications:* The Royal Navy Today and Tomorrow, 1981; Anti-Submarine Warfare, 1984; British Sea Power in the 1980s, 1985; Maritime Strategy for Medium Powers, 1986; Air Defence at Sea, 1988; Arms Control at Sea, 1988; (Gen. Ed.) Oxford Illustrated History of the Royal Navy, 1995; The Prizes of War, 1998; War at Sea in the Ironclad Age, 2000; Lewin of Greenwich, 2000; Maritime Britain, 2005; A Light on Shore (poems and reminiscence), 2009; articles in Survival, Navy International, Brassey's Annual, NATO's 15 Nations, Naval Review, Naval Forces, DNB and Oxford DNB. *Recreations:* bridge, gardening. *Address:* Cornhill House, The Hangers, Bishop's Waltham, Southampton SO32 1EF.

HILL, Prof. Jonathan Michael, PhD; RIBA; Professor of Architecture and Visual Theory, since 2005, and Director, MPhil/PhD Architectural Design, since 2000, Bartlett School of Architecture, University College London; *b* Maidstone, 1958; *s* of George Wharton Hill and Margaret Mary Hill. *Educ:* King's Coll., Taunton; Wellington Sch.; Architectural Assoc. Sch. of Architecture (AA Dip (Hons) 1983; RIBA Pt 3 1985); Bartlett Sch. of Architecture, University Coll. London (MSc Hist. of Mod. Architecture 1990; PhD Architecture (Architectural Design) 2000). ARB (ARCUK 1985); RIBA 1994. Bartlett School of Architecture, University College London: Lectr, 1989–99, Sen. Lectr, 1999–2005, in Architecture; Head, 2004–05; Dir of Design, 2011–12. Fellow, Akademie Schloss Solitude, Stuttgart, 1998–99; Vis. Sen. Fellow, Dept of Architecture, National Univ. of Singapore, 2004. FRSA 1995. Jt Ed., Design Research in Architecture, book series, 2010–. *Publications:* The Illegal Architect, 1998; (ed) Occupying Architecture: between the architect and the user, 1998; (ed) Architecture—the Subject is Matter, 2001; Actions of Architecture: architects and creative users, 2003; Immaterial Architecture, 2006; Drawing Research, 2006; (ed jtly) Critical Architecture, 2007; Weather Architecture, 2012; A Landscape of Architecture, History and Fiction, 2015. *Recreations:* walking, gardens. *Address:* Bartlett School of Architecture, UCL Faculty of the Built Environment, 140 Hampstead Road, NW1 2BX. *T:* (020) 3108 9672. *E:* jonathan.hill@ucl.ac.uk.

HILL, Dame Judith (Eileen), DBE 2012 (CBE 2001); DL; FRCN; Chief Executive, Northern Ireland Hospice, since 2005. Sen. Nurse and Tutor, Countess Mountbatten House, Southampton; Chief Nursing Officer, Dept of Health, Social Services and Public Safety, NI, 1995–2005. Chair, NI Palliative Care Services Rev. (Report, Partnerships in Caring, 2000). Vis. Prof., Sch. of Nursing, Univ. of Ulster. Chair, Mgt Cttee, and Policy and Practice Cttee, All Ireland Inst. of Hospice and Palliative Care, 2011–. DL Belfast, 2013. FRCN 2009. Hon.

DSc Ulster, 2011. Outstanding Achievement Award, RCN, NI, 2008; Paul Harris Fellow Award, Rotary Club Belfast, 2013. *Address:* Northern Ireland Hospice, Head Office, 18 O'Neill Road, Newtownabbey, Northern Ireland BT36 6WB.

HILL, Rt Hon. Keith; *see* Hill, Rt Hon. T. K.

HILL, Leslie Francis; Chairman: HartHill Partnership Ltd, 2004–08; British Music Rights Ltd, 2005–07; ITV, 1994–2002 (Director, 1987–2002); Director, Carlton Communications PLC, 1994–2004; *b* 2 Sept. 1936; *s* of late Elizabeth May and Francis Alfred Hill; *m* 1972, Christine Susan (*née* Bush); two *s*. *Educ:* Cotham Grammar School. FCA. Qualified as Chartered Accountant; with Ware, Ward (now Ernst & Young), 1952–62, Peat, Marwick, Mitchell, 1962–65; IPC Group, 1965–70, finally Finance Director, Music for Pleasure, continuing as such with EMI Group to 1971; EMI Group: Exec. Dir, Rest of World Div., 1972–73; Man. Dir, EMI NZ, 1973–74; Asst Dir, Group Music, 1975–76; Managing Director: EMI Records (UK), 1976–78; EMI Music, Europe, 1979–80; Jt Man. Dir, HAT Group plc, 1980–86; Dir, ITN, 1987–95; Man. Dir, 1987–91, Chm. and Chief Exec., 1991–95, Central Independent Television. *Recreations:* listening to music, reading, fitness, watching cricket.

HILL, Prof. Leslie James, PhD; FBA 2003; Professor of French Studies, University of Warwick, 1998–2014, now Emeritus. *Educ:* Gonville and Caius Coll., Cambridge (BA (Mod. Langs) 1972; MA 1976; PhD (French) 1976). University of Cambridge: Res. Fellow in French, Selwyn Coll., 1974–76; Lectr in French and Dir of Studies in Mod. Langs, Clare Coll., 1976–79; University of Warwick: Lectr in French Studies, 1979–93; Sen. Lectr, 1993–96; Reader, 1996–98. *Publications:* Beckett's Fiction: in different words, 1990; Marguerite Duras: apocalyptic desires, 1993; Blanchot: extreme contemporary, 1997; Bataille, Klossowski, Blanchot: writing at the limit, 2001; The Cambridge Introduction to Jacques Derrida, 2007; Radical Indecision: Barthes, Blanchot, Derrida, and the future of criticism, 2010; Maurice Blanchot and Fragmentary Writing: a change of epoch, 2012. *Recreations:* photography, organic vegetable gardening. *Address:* Department of French Studies, School of Languages and Cultures, University of Warwick, Coventry CV4 7AL. *E:* leslie.hill@warwick.ac.uk.

HILL, Mark; *see* Hill, N. M.

HILL, Mark Roger; antiques and collectables expert, author and publisher, since 2002; *b* Guildford, 2 Feb. 1975; *s* of Roger and Angela Hill; partner, Philip Reicherstorfer. *Educ:* Royal Grammar Sch., Guildford; Reading Univ. (BA Hons Hist. of Art and Architecture). Jun. cataloguer, Bonhams, 1996–98; Specialist, Sotheby's, 1998–2000; Channel Manager, 2000, Dir, Auction Hse Services and Live Auctions, 2001–02, icollector.com; Consultant and author: Price Guide Co. (UK) Ltd and Dorling Kindersley, 2002–08; Miller's, 2008–; author and publisher, Mark Hill Publishing Ltd, 2006–. Co-presenter, BBC TV: Cracking Antiques, 2010; Antiques Uncovered, 2012; Collectaholics, 2014; specialist, Antiques Roadshow, 2007–; antiques columnist, Daily Mail, 2012–. Patron, King's Lynn Arts Centre, 2011–. Freeman: City of London, 2013; Co. of Art Scholars, Dealers and Collectors, 2009–. *Publications:* Fat Lava: West German ceramics of the 1960s and 70s, 2006, 3rd edn 2012; Michael Harris: Mdina glass and Isle of Wight studio glass, 2006; Frank Thrower and Dartington Glass, 2007; Hi Sklo Lo Sklo: post war Czech glass design from masterpiece to mass-produced, 2008; Caithness Glass: loch, heather and peat, 2011; Alla Moda: Italian ceramics of 1950s–70s, 2012; (Gen. Ed.) Beránek & Škrdlovice: legends of Czech glass, 2014; The Horrors of War by Pierre-Georges Jeanniot, 2014. *Recreations:* growing bonsai, art, reading, collecting, drinking wine. *E:* books@markhillpublishing.com. *Club:* Groucho.

HILL, Martin Henry Paul; HM Diplomatic Service, retired; property management; *b* 17 May 1961; *s* of John and Jacqueline Hill; *m* 1985, Kim Cherie Lydyard; three *d*. *Educ:* Pembroke Coll., Cambridge (BA Langs and Econs, MA). Food Standards Div., MAFF, 1983–84; Parly Clerk to Lord Privy Seal, 1985–86; Ministry of Agriculture, Fisheries and Food: Financial Mgt Team, 1986; EC Div., 1987; Sugar, Oils and Fats Div., 1988; Principal Private Sec. to Food Safety Minister, 1989–90; Trade Policy and Tropical Foods Div., 1990–92; First Sec., Agric., Fisheries and Food, Bonn, 1993–96; joined HM Diplomatic Service, 1996; SE Asian Dept, FCO, 1996–98; Dep. High Comr, Colombo, 1998–2001; Commercial Counsellor, Bangkok, 2002–05; Counsellor (Econ., Sci. and Innovation), Ottawa, 2006–09; Dep. High Comr, Ottawa, 2009–11; Dep. Hd of Mission, Bogota, 2011; Hd, Counter Proliferation Dept, FCO, 2011–12; Hd, Strategy and Network Dept, Consular Directorate, FCO, 2012–13. *Recreations:* squash, travel, reading, diving, music.

HILL, Martyn Geoffrey; tenor singer; *b* 14 Sept. 1944; *s* of Norman S. L. Hill and Gwendoline A. M. Hill (*née* Andrews); three *s* one *d*; *m* 2004, Julie Ann Moffat. *Educ:* Sir Joseph Williamson's Mathematical School, Rochester, Kent; King's College, Cambridge; Royal College of Music (ARCM); vocal studies with Audrey Langford. Prof. of Vocal Studies, Trinity Coll. of Music, 1997–2011. Concert, oratorio, recital and operatic appearances throughout the world with major orchestras, conductors and choirs; numerous radio, TV and gramophone recordings. Hon. DMus Leicester, 2009. *Address:* c/o Owen White Management, 139 Brookwood Road, SW18 5BD.

HILL, Max Benjamin Rowland; QC 2008; a Recorder, since 2004; *b* Hatfield, 10 Jan. 1964; *s* of Thomas Rowland Hill and Shirley Ann Hill; *m* 1993, Heather Faith Coombs; two *d*. *Educ:* Royal Grammar Sch., Newcastle-upon-Tyne; St Peter's Coll., Oxford (Scholar; BA Hons Juris. 1986). Called to the Bar, Middle Temple, 1987, Bencher, 2012; in practice as barrister specialising in crime; Hd of Chambers, 18 Red Lion Ct, 2011–; Leader, SE Circuit, 2014–. Chairman: Bd of Trustees, Scene and Heard, 2005–11; Criminal Bar Association, 2011–12 (Vice Chm., 2010–11); Kalisher Scholarship Trust, 2014–. Co-founder, High Stakes Persuasion, 2014–; Dir, Redmantle, 2015–. Academic Advr, Curriculum for Cohesion, 2014–. Patron, Scene and Heard, 2011–. FRSA. *Publications:* (contributing ed.) Practitioner's Guide to Terrorist Trials, 2007; (contrib.) Investigating Terrorism, 2015. *Recreations:* theatre, tennis, travel. *Address:* 18 Red Lion Court, EC4A 3EB. *T:* (020) 7520 6000, *Fax:* (020) 7520 6248. *E:* max.hill@18rlc.co.uk.

HILL, Rt Rev. Michael Arthur; *see* Bristol, Bishop of.

HILL, Michael Thomas; HM Diplomatic Service, retired; Administrator, Ascension Island, 2005–08; *b* 2 Jan. 1945; *s* of late Roland Hill and Anne Hill (*née* McIlwraith); *m* 1977, Elizabeth Louise, *d* of Derrick Charles Carden, CMG; three *s* one *d*. *Educ:* Bathgate Acad. Joined Foreign Office, 1963; served UKMIS NY, Vientiane, Kaduna, Sana'a; Dep. Hd of Mission, Ulan Bator, 1978–81; Consul, Port of Spain, 1981–85; FCO, 1985–88; Asst to Dep. Governor, Gibraltar, 1988–93; First Sec. and Hd of Aid Sect., Nairobi, 1993–96; FCO, 1996–2000; High Comr, Vanuatu, 2000–05. *Recreations:* golf, gardening, walking. *Address:* 14 Romsey Road, Winchester SO23 8TP.

HILL, Michael William; Director, Science Reference Library, British Library, 1973–86; *b* 1928; *o s* of late Geoffrey William Hill, Ross on Wye and Torquay; *m* 1st, 1957, Elma Jack Forrest (*d* 1967); one *s* one *d*; 2nd, 1969, Barbara Joy Youngman. *Educ:* King Henry VIII Sch., Coventry; Nottingham High Sch.; Lincoln Coll., Oxford (MA, MSc). MRIC 1953; CChem; FCLIP (FIInfSc 1982). Research Chemist, Laporte Chemicals Ltd, 1953–56; Morgan Crucible Group: Laboratory Head, 1956; Asst Process Control Manager, 1958; Group Technical Editor, 1963; Asst Keeper, British Museum, 1964; Dep. Librarian, Patent Office Library, 1965; Keeper, and Dir, Nat. Ref. Library of Science and Invention, BM, 1968–73; British Library: Mem., Organising Cttee, 1970–73; Associate Dir, Sci. Technology and Industry, 1986–88. Various consultancies in Europe, Asia and developing countries, 1974–92. Pres., Fédn Internat. de Documentation et Information, 1985–90. Member: Exec. Cttee, Nat. Central Library, 1971–74; EEC/CIDST Working Parties on Patent documentation, 1973–80, and on Information for Industry, 1976–80; Board, UK Chemical Inf. Service, 1974–77; Adv. Cttee for Scottish Science Reference Library, 1983–87; Chairman: Circle of State Librarians, 1977–79; Council, Aslib, 1979–81; Vice Pres., IATUL, 1976–81; Founder, Western European Round Table on Information and Documentation, subseq. European Council of Information Assocs, 1980. Series Editor (with I. McIlwaine), Guides to Information Sources. *Publications:* Patent Documentation (with Wittmann and Schiffels), 1979; Michael Hill on Science, Technology and Information (ed by P. Ward), 1988; National Information Policies and Strategies, 1994; The Impact of Information on Society, 1998, 2nd edn 2005; papers on librarianship, documentation and information science in jls and conf. proceedings. *Address:* 137 Burdon Lane, Cheam, Surrey SM2 7DB. *T:* (020) 8642 2418. *Club:* Oxford and Cambridge.

HILL, (Nicholas) Mark; QC 2009; *b* Birmingham, 7 Aug. 1965; *s* of David Hill and Stanlene Hill. *Educ:* Tudor Grange Comp. Sch., Solihull; Solihull Sixth Form Coll.; King's Coll., London (LLB Hons 1986; AKC 1986); Univ. of Wales (LLM Canon Law 1994). Called to the Bar, Middle Temple, 1987; Mem. *ad eundem*, Inner Temple, 2008, Bencher, 2011; in practice as a barrister, 3 Pump Court, 1988–2011, Francis Taylor Building, 2012–. Recorder, 2005–; Dep. Judge of Upper Tribunal (Asylum and Immigration), 2015–. Mem., Legal Aid Commn, 1995–2000, Legal Adv. Commn, 2001–, General Synod of C of E. Deputy Chancellor: dio. of Winchester, 1994–2006; dio. of York, 2007–; dio. of Blackburn, 2010–; Chancellor: dio. of Chichester, 1999–; dio. of Gibraltar in Europe, 2004–; dio. of W Yorks and the Dales, 2015–. Founder Mem., Anglican-RC Colloquium of Canon Lawyers, 1999–; Mem., Standing Cttee, Ecclesiastical Judges Assoc., 2008–; Convener, Interfaith Legal Advrs Network, 2008–; Co-Chm., Belief in Mediation and Arbitration, 2012–15. Member: Eur. Consortium for Ch and State Research, 2004– (Pres., 2012); Internat. Consortium for Law and Religion Studies, 2007–. Fellow, 1999–, Hon. Prof. of Law, 2006–, Centre for Law and Religion, Cardiff Univ.; Sen. Visitor, Emmanuel Coll., Cambridge, 2007; Ecumenical Fellow in Canon Law, Ven. English Coll., Rome, 2013–; Extraordinary Prof., Univ. of Pretoria, 2014–; Vis. Prof., Dickson Poon Sch. of Law, KCL, 2015–. Fellow, Internat. Acad. for Freedom of Religion and Belief, 2004–. Ed., Ecclesiastical Law Jl, 2002–; Member: Internat. Adv. Bd, Revista General de Derecho Canónico y Derecho Eclesiástico del Estado, 2007–; Editl Adv. Bd, Oxford Jl for Law and Religion, 2011–. *Publications:* Ecclesiastical Law, 1995, 3rd edn 2007; (ed jtly) English Canon Law, 1998; (ed) Faithful Discipleship: clergy discipline in Anglican and Roman Catholic canon law, 2001; (ed) Religious Liberty and Human Rights, 2002; (ed jtly) Jowitt's Dictionary of English Law, 2010; (ed jtly) Butterworths Costs Service, 2010; Religion and Law in the United Kingdom, 2011, 2nd edn 2014; Religion and Discrimination Law in the European Union, 2012; (ed jtly) Magna Carta, Religion and the Rule of Law, 2015; regular contrib. to legal periodicals on law and religion. *Recreations:* exotic travel, domestic theatre. *Address:* Francis Taylor Building, Temple, EC4Y 7BJ. *T:* (020) 7353 8415. *E:* mark.hill@ftb.eu.com. *Clubs:* Athenæum; Nikæan.

HILL, Rt Rev. Peter; *see* Barking, Area Bishop of.

HILL, Prof. Peter David, FRCP, FRCPsych, FRCPCH; Emeritus Professor, University of London, since 1998; Consultant Child and Adolescent Psychiatrist, in private practice, since 2003; *b* Eastbourne, 16 March 1945; *s* of Derryck and Phyllis Hill; *m* 1972, Christine Seed; two *s* one *d*. *Educ:* Leighton Park Sch., Reading; Selwyn Coll., Cambridge (BA 1966; MB BChir 1969); St Bartholomew's Hosp. Med. Sch. FRCP 1994; FRCPsych 1987; FRCPCH 1997. Hosp. posts, St Bartholomew's Hosp., London, 1969–72; Registrar and Sen. Registrar, Maudsley Hosp., 1972–79; Sen. Lectr, 1979, then Prof. of Child Mental Health, 1979–98, St George's Hosp. Med. Sch., Univ. of London; Consultant, St George's Hosp., 1979–98; Hon. Consultant, St Thomas's Hosp., 1981–89; Consultant Psychiatrist, 1998–2003, Hon. Consultant, 2003–10, Gt Ormond St Hosp. Vis. Prof., St George's, Univ. of London, 1999–. Advr, Select Cttee on Health, 1995–97. Med. Advr to British Army, 1995–2007; Consultant Advr, Huntercombe Manor Hosp., Maidenhead, 1998–2014; Specialist Advr, Health Adv. Service, 1999–2003. Chm., Faculty of Child and Adolescent Psychiatry, RCPsych, 1993–97. Pres., Union Européene de Médecins Spécialistes (Child and Adolescent Psychiatry), 2002–06. *Publications:* (jtly) Essentials of Postgraduate Psychiatry, 1979, 3rd edn 1997; (jtly) A Manual of Practical Psychiatry, 1986; Adolescent Psychiatry, 1989; (jtly) The Child Surveillance Handbook, 1990, 2nd edn 1994; (jtly) The Child with a Disability, 1996; (jtly) Child Mental Health in Primary Care, 2001; (jtly) A Perfect Start, 2007; (jtly) A Handbook for the Assessment of Children's Behaviours, 2012; contrib. papers and chapters on child and adolescent psychiatry, psychopharmacol. and child mental health services. *Recreations:* jazz trumpet, contemplation, rural wildlife. *Address:* 127 Harley Street, W1G 6AZ. *T:* (020) 7486 2332, *Fax:* (020) 7935 4612. *E:* ali@127harley.com. *Club:* Royal Society of Medicine.

HILL, (Peter) Jeremy (Oldham); HM Diplomatic Service, 1982–2007; *b* 17 April 1954; *m* 1981, Katharine Hearn; one *s* one *d*. Joined FCO as Asst Legal Advr, 1982; First Sec. (Legal Advr), Bonn, 1987–90; on loan as Legal Counsellor, Law Officers' Dept, 1991–95; Legal Counsellor, UK Rep., Brussels, 1995–98; Hd, Southern European Dept, FCO, 1999–2001; Ambassador to: Lithuania, 2001–03; Bulgaria, 2004–07.

HILL, Peter Whitehead; Editor, Daily Express, 2003–11; *b* 6 April 1945; *s* of Becket and Edith Hill; *m* 1st, 1984, Vera Marshall (marr. diss. 1998); one *d*; 2nd, 2004, Marjorie Francis; one *s*. *Educ:* Hulme Grammar Sch., Oldham; Manchester Univ. Reporter, Colne Valley Guardian, 1961–62; sub-editor: Huddersfield Examr, 1962–63; Manchester Evening News, 1963–65; leader writer, Oldham Evening Chronicle, 1965–67; sub-ed., Daily Telegraph, 1967–74; sub-ed., Daily Mirror, 1974–78; Chief Sub-Ed., Sunday People, 1970–80; Chief Sub-Ed., Night Ed., Associate Ed., and Dep. Ed., 1978–98, Ed., 1998–2003, Daily Star. Mem., Press Complaints Commn, 2003–08. *Recreations:* sailing, tennis, ski-ing, bridge, making mischief. *Address:* c/o Daily Express, 10 Lower Thames Street, EC3R 6EN. *Clubs:* Reform, Harbour.

HILL, (Robert) Charles; QC (NI) 1974; Member, Standing Advisory Commission on Human Rights under Northern Ireland Constitution Act 1973, 1991–96 (Chairman, 1992–95); *b* 22 March 1936; *s* of Benjamin Morrison Hill and Mary A. Hill (*née* Roche); *m* 1961, Kathleen Allen; three *s* one *d*. *Educ:* St Malachy's Coll., Belfast; Queen's Univ. Belfast (LLB); Trinity Coll., Dublin (MA). Called to the Bar: Inn of Court, NI, 1959, Bencher, 1988; Gray's Inn, 1971; King's Inns, Dublin, 1986; Sen. Counsel, Ireland, 1987. Official Referee under Finance Acts, 1976; Dep. County Court Judge, 1979–80. Chairman: Statutory Body, Pharmaceutical Soc. of NI, 1977–92; Poison Bd of NI, 1982–92. *Recreations:* history of art, forestry, shooting. *Address:* The Bar Library, Royal Courts of Justice, Chichester Street, Belfast BT1 3JP. *T:* (028) 9024 1523. *Club:* Kildare Street and University (Dublin).

HILL, Sir Robert (Charles Finch), KBE 1991; FREng; reliability consultant; part-time lecturer, University of Bath, since 1995; President, Institute of Marine Engineers, 1995–96; *b* 1 May 1937; *s* of late Frances Margaret Hill (*née* Lumsden) and Ronald Finch Hill; *m* 1971, Deborah Mary (*née* Windle); one *s* one *d*. *Educ:* Nautical Coll., Pangbourne; RNEC Manadon. BSc(Eng); CEng, FREng (FEng 1992). HMS Thermopylae, 1964–65; HMS Repulse, 1967–71; MoD (PE), 1971–74; RNEC Manadon, 1975–77; HMS Cleopatra, 1977–78; Nuclear Power Manager, Chatham, 1979–80; MoD (PE), 1980–84; RCDS 1985; HMS Raleigh in Comd, 1986–87; CSO (Engrg) to C-in-C Fleet, 1987–89; Chief Abovewater Systems Exec., 1989–91; Dep. Controller of the Navy (Vice-Adm.), 1989–93;

Chief Naval Engr Officer, 1989–93; Dir Gen. Submarines, 1991–93; retd. Independent Director: British Energy plc, 1999–2003; SEA (Group) Ltd, 1999–2007. Trustee, Bath Theatre Trust, 2003–. Mem. Council, Univ. of Bath, 2000–06. Hon. FIMarEST 2002. Hon. DTech Plymouth, 1995; Hon. DEng Bath, 2005. *Recreations:* rhythm guitar, theatre, sailing. *Club:* Royal Over-Seas League.

HILL, Hon. Robert Murray, AC 2012; Adjunct Professor of Sustainability, United States Studies Centre, University of Sydney, since 2009; Chairman, CRC for Low Carbon Living, since 2012; *b* 25 Sept. 1946; *s* of C. M. Hill; *m* 1969, Diana Jacka; two *s* two *d*. *Educ:* Scotch Coll., Mitcham, SA; Univ. of Adelaide (LLB 1968; BA 1982); Univ. of London (LLM 1970). In practice as barrister and solicitor, SA, 1970–. Senator (L) S Australia, 1981–2006; Fed. Shadow Minister for Foreign Affairs, 1989–93, for Defence, 1993, for Public Admin, 1993–94, for Educn, Sci. and Technol., 1994–96; Leader of the Opposition in Senate, 1993–96; Leader of the Govt in Senate, 1996–2006; Minister for the Envmt, 1996–98, for the Envmt and Heritage, 1998–2001, for Defence, 2001–06; Perm. Rep. of Australia to the UN, 2006–09. Liberal Party of Australia: Campaign Chm., 1975–77; Chm., Constitutional Cttee, 1977–81; Vice-Pres., 1977–79, Pres., 1985–87, SA Div.; Mem., Fed. Exec., 1985–87 and 1990–2006. Chm., Australian Carbon Trust, 2009. Chancellor, Univ. of Adelaide, 2010–12.

HILL, Rev. Roger Anthony John; Bishop's Missioner, Diocese of Manchester, 2007–11; Chaplain to the Queen, 2001–15; *b* 23 March 1945; *s* of Arthur and Gladys Hill; *m* 1972, Joanna Reading; three *s*. *Educ:* Univ. of Liverpool (BA 1967); Linacre Coll., Oxford (BA 1969; MA); Ripon Hall, Oxford. Ordained deacon, 1970, priest, 1971; Curate: St Peter, St Helier, Southwark, 1970–74; Dawley Parva, 1974–76; Team Vicar, 1976–81, Rector, 1981–88, Central Telford; Rector: Newark, 1988–2002; St Ann, Manchester, 2002–07. RD Newark, 1990–95; Area Dean, Hulme, 2005–07. Hon. Canon: Southwell Minster, 1998–2002; Manchester Cathedral, 2002–11, now Canon Emeritus. *Recreations:* walking, travel. *Address:* 4 Four Stalls End, Littleborough, Lancs OL15 8SB. *T:* (01706) 374719.

HILL, Roger Jonathan; Director of Community and Partnership, Sodexo Justice Services, since 2011; *b* Epsom, Surrey, 9 July 1955; *s* of John and Mary Hill; *m* 1993, Elizabeth Durrans; one *d*. *Educ:* Nork Park Sch., Banstead, Surrey; Newcastle upon Tyne Poly. (CQSW); Sunderland Univ. Business Sch. (MBA). Probation Officer, 1978–95; Asst Chief Probation Officer, Durham, 1995–2001; Chief Probation Officer: Lincs, 2001–04; London, 2004–05; Dir, Nat. Probation Service, 2005–09; Dir of Offender Mgt (SE England), Nat. Offender Mgt Service, MoJ, 2009–11. *Recreations:* contemporary music, guitar, listening and playing, photography, building renovation and DIY, walking. *Address:* Sodexo Justice Services, One Southampton Row, WC1B 5HA. *T:* (01203) 1164340, 07767 238595. *E:* roger.hill@sodexojusticeservices.com.

HILL, Shaun Donovan; consultant and writer; chef and restaurateur; *b* 11 April 1947; *s* of George Herbert Hill and Molly Hill; *m* 1966, Anja Toivonen; one *s* two *d*. *Educ:* London Oratory; St Marylebone Grammar Sch. Cook: Carrier's Restaurant, Islington, 1967–71; Gay Hussar, 1971–73; Intercontinental Hotel, London, 1973–75; Head Chef: Montcalm Hotel, London, 1976–77; Capital Hotel, London, 1978; Lygon Arms, Broadway, Worcs, 1979–81; Gidleigh Park, Chagford, 1985–94; Head Chef, Merchant House, Ludlow, 1994–2005; Head Chef and Owner, The Walnut Tree, Abergavenny, 2007–. *Publications:* Gidleigh Park Cookery Book, 1990; Shaun Hill's Cookery Book, 1994; (with John Wilkins) Archestratus: the life of luxury, 1994; Shaun Hill's Cooking at the Merchant House, 2000; How To Cook Better, 2004; (with J. Wilkins) Food in Ancient Cultures, 2005; (jtly) Cook, 2005; (jtly) The Cook's Book, 2005. *Recreations:* wine, travel. *Address:* 24 Droitwich Road, Worcester WR3 7LH. *E:* shaun@thewalnuttreeinn.com.

HILL, Stephen Guy; Executive Chairman (formerly Chairman and Chief Executive), D'Aval Ltd (formerly Harbour Group), since 2006; *b* 19 July 1960; *s* of Michael Lawrence Hill and Joan Florence Hill (*née* Luce). *Educ:* King Edward VII Sch., Lytham; St John's Coll., Cambridge (Wright Prize 1980; Whytehead Scholar; MA 1st Cl. Hons Law 1982); Harvard Business Sch. (PMD 1991). Consultant, Boston Consulting Gp, 1982–85; Exec. Asst to Chm., Guinness plc, 1985–87; Pearson plc, 1987–2002: Dir of Strategy, 1987–92; Managing Director: Watford Observer Newspapers, 1992–93; Oxford & County Newspapers Ltd, 1993–95; Chief Executive: Westminster Press Ltd, 1995–96; Financial Times Newspaper, 1996–98; Financial Times Gp Ltd, 1998–2002; Mem., Mgt Bd, 1998–2002; Chm., Interactive Data Corp. (formerly Data Broadcasting Inc.), 1998–2002; Chief Exec., Sporting Exchange Ltd (Betfair), 2003–05. Non-executive Director: Royal & Sun Alliance Gp plc, 2000–04; Psion plc, 2003–06; Channel 4, 2005–11; IG Gp plc, 2011–; Applerigg Ltd, 2013–; AZTEC Ltd, 2014–; Chm., 2Degrees.com, 2010–13. Mem. Bd, Ofcom, 2014–. Mem. Adv. Bd, Judge Business Sch., Cambridge Univ., 2007–. Mem. Council, Whitechapel Art Gall., 2000–03. Trustee, Action on Hearing Loss (formerly RNID), 2008– (Hon. Treas., 2008–12; Dep. Chm., 2012–13; Chm., 2013–). *Recreations:* triathlon, gardening, travel, classic cars. *Club:* Royal Automobile.

HILL, Prof. Stephen Roderick, PhD; Professor of Management, University of London, 2001–11, Professor Emeritus, 2012; Principal, Royal Holloway, University of London, 2002–09; *b* 15 March 1946; *s* of Alan Hill, CBE and Enid Hill (*née* Malin); *m* 1st, 1970, Jane Severn (marr. diss. 1993); one *s* one *d*; 2nd, 1996, Siobhan Rosser. *Educ:* University College Sch.; Balliol Coll., Oxford (BA Modern Hist.); London Sch. of Econs (MSc Sociol.; PhD 1973). Lectr in Sociol., Bedford Coll., London, 1968–70; London School of Economics: Lectr in Industrial Relns, 1971–74; Lectr, 1974–82, Reader, 1982–91, in Sociol.; Prof. of Sociol., 1991–2001; Pro-Dir, 1996–2001; Prof. of Mgt, 2001–02; Dir, 2001; Dep. Dir, 2001–02; Mem. Ct, 1991–2001; Mem. Council, 1996–2002; Pres., LSE Foundn Inc., 2000–02. Ed., British Jl Sociol., 1995–2002. Member: Corporate Social Responsibility Steering Gp, DTI, 2003–04; Scholarly Commns Gp, JISC, 2004–10. Mem. Bd, Surrey Bridges, 2002–08; Dir, Higher Educn SE, 2003–10; Chair, Southern Univs Mgt Services, 2003–07. Member, Court: City Univ., 2001–06; Henley Mgt Coll., 2005–08; Mem. Council, St George's, Univ. of London, 2004–09; Trustee, Univ. of London, 2008–09. Trustee, Richmond CAB (formerly Richmond CAB Service), 2010– (Vice-Chm. Trustees, 2012–). Fellow, Wellington Coll., 2009–. *Publications:* The Dockers, 1976; Competition and Control at Work, 1981; with N. Abercrombie and B. S. Turner: The Dominant Ideology Thesis, 1980; The Penguin Dictionary of Sociology, 1984, 5th edn 2006; Sovereign Individuals of Capitalism, 1986; (ed) Dominant Ideologies, 1990; (with M. White, C. Mills and D. Smeaton) Managing to Change?, 2004; (with P. McGovern, C. Mills and M. White) Market, Class, and Employment, 2007. *Recreations:* fell-walking, dinghy sailing. *E:* stephen.hill@rhul.ac.uk.

HILL, Stephen Russell, CB 2004; OBE 1982; Managing Director, Steve Hill Consultancy Ltd, since 2004; Chief Executive, Defence Aviation Repair Agency, 1999–2003; *b* 27 March 1942; *s* of late Henry Rowland Hill and Kathleen Bertha Hill; *m* 1964, Muriel Chisholm; one *s* one *d*. *Educ:* St Philip's Grammar Sch., Birmingham; Hendon CAT; BA Open Univ. 1980; Dip. Accounting and Finance 1988. CEng 1975; FIMechE 1985; FRAeS 1986. Marine Engr, BP Tanker Co., 1958–65; Civil Engrg projects, BP Refinery, Grangemouth, 1965–66; RAF, 1966–91: appts incl. Chief Engr, RAF Coningsby, 1981–84; Air Cdre, Dir of Support Mgt, 1989–91; Business Develt, BAe, 1991–95; Projects and Technical Dir, Serco Defence, 1995–96; Chief Exec., Naval Aircraft Repair Orgn, 1996–99. FCMI (FIMgt 1987). *Recreation:* hill walking.

HILL, Dr Stuart John; Vice Chair, Dudley and Walsall Mental Health Partnership NHS Trust, 2013–14 (non-executive Director, 2010–14); *b* 23 March 1950; *s* of late Maurice William Hill and of Dorothy Alice Hill (*née* Raynor); *m* 1st, 1972 (marr. diss. 1991); one *s* one *d*; 2nd, 1994, Frances Irene Susan Entwistle; one step *s*. *Educ:* Ecclesbourne GS, Duffield, Derbys; Peterhouse, Cambridge (schol.; BA Hons 1st cl. Engrg; Baker Prize; PhD Metallurgy and Materials Sci. 1977). BR Research Dept, 1975–77; GKN Technology Ltd, 1977–89; Business Develt Exec., GKN Automotive Div., 1989–90; Develt Dir, GKN Powder Metallurgy Div., 1990–91; Dir, Tech. Strategy, BRB, 1991–93; Man. Dir, BR Production Services, 1993–96; Chief Land Registrar and Chief Exec., HM Land Registry, 1996–99; Chief Exec., Housebuilders Fedn, 1999–2000; Managing Director: AEA Technology Envmt, 2000–05; AEA Technology Rail, 2005–06; Delta Rail Gp Ltd, 2006; Founding Dir, later Consultant, Kynnersley Mgt Services, 2007–11. Chair, Standards Cttee, W Midlands Police Authy, 2010–12. Lay Member: Solicitors Disciplinary Tribunal, 2009–; Professional Conduct Cttee, Nat. Register of Public Service Interpreters, 2012–; Member: Disciplinary Cttee, CIMA, 2011– (Vice Chair, 2013–); Jt Regulatory Cttee, Fixed Charge Receivership Scheme, RICS/Insolvency Practitioners Assoc., 2013–; FRC Disciplinary Tribunals, 2013–; RCVS Preliminary Investigation Cttee, 2015–. FRSA 1996. *Publications:* (trans.) F. Schmelz *et al*, Universal Joints and Driveshafts, 1992, 2nd edn 2005; ed and contrib. books and learned jls on driveline components and engrg mgt. *Recreations:* fostering cats, volunteer at Wightwick Manor (NT), family history research.

HILL, Sunetra; *see* Gupta, S.

HILL, Susan Elizabeth, (Mrs Stanley Wells), CBE 2012; novelist and playwright; *b* 5 Feb. 1942; *d* of late R. H. and Doris Hill; *m* 1975, Prof. Stanley W. Wells, *qv*; two *d* (and one *d* decd). *Educ:* grammar schs in Scarborough and Coventry; King's Coll., Univ. of London (BA Hons English 1963; Fellow, 1978). FRSL 1972. Literary critic, various jls, 1963–; numerous plays for BBC, 1970–; Presenter, Bookshelf, Radio 4, 1986–87. Founder and Publisher, Long Barn Books, 1996; Founder Publisher and Ed., Books and Company, qly mag., 1997–2000. Patron, Prince of Wales Hospice, Pontefract, 2000–. Chm., Chipping Campden Cricket Club, 1999–. *Publications:* The Enclosure, 1961; Do me a Favour, 1963; Gentleman and Ladies, 1969; A Change for the Better, 1969; I'm the King of the Castle, 1970; The Albatross, 1971; Strange Meeting, 1971; The Bird of Night, 1972; A Bit of Singing and Dancing, 1973; In the Springtime of the Year, 1974; The Cold Country and Other Plays for Radio, 1975; (ed) The Distracted Preacher and other stories by Thomas Hardy, 1979; The Magic Apple Tree, 1982; The Woman in Black: a ghost story, 1983 (adapted for stage, 1989); (ed) Ghost Stories, 1983; (ed) People, an anthology, 1983; Through the Kitchen Window, 1984; Through the Garden Gate, 1986; The Lighting of the Lamps, 1987; Lanterns Across the Snow, 1987; Shakespeare Country, 1987; The Spirit of the Cotswolds, 1988; Family (autobiog.), 1989; Air and Angels, 1991; The Mist in the Mirror: a ghost story, 1992; Mrs de Winter, 1993; (ed) Contemporary Women's Short Stories, 1995; (with Rory Stuart) Reflections from a Garden, 1995; Listening to the Orchestra (short stories), 1996; (ed) The Second Penguin Book of Women's Short Stories, 1997; The Service of Clouds, 1998; The Boy Who Taught the Bee-keeper to Read and Other Stories, 2003; The Various Haunts of Men, 2004; The Pure in Heart, 2005; The Risk of Darkness, 2006; The Man in the Picture (novella), 2007; The Vows of Silence, 2008; The Beacon, 2008; Howard's End is on the Landing: a year of reading from home, 2009; The Shadows in the Street, 2010; The Small Hand, 2010; A Kind Man, 2010; The Betrayal of Trust, 2011; Dolly, 2012; A Question of Identity, 2012; The Black Sheep, 2013; Printer's Devil Court, 2014; The Soul of Discretion, 2014; *for children:* One Night at a Time, 1984; Mother's Magic, 1986; Can it be True?, 1988; Susie's Shoes, 1989; Stories from Codling Village, 1990; I've Forgotten Edward, 1990; I Won't Go There Again, 1990; (ed) The Walker Book of Ghost Stories, 1990; Pirate Poll, 1991; The Glass Angels, 1991; Beware, Beware!, 1993; King of King's, 1993; The Battle for Gullywith, 2008; *play:* The Ramshackle Company, 1981. *Address:* Glaven Farm, Little Thornage, Holt, Norfolk NR25 7JE. *E:* mail@susan-hill.com.

HILL, Dr Susan Lesley, OBE 2005; FRSB; Chief Scientific Officer, Department of Health, since 2002; *b* Swindon, 14 April 1955; *d* of late Albert Leslie George Hill and Edna Mary Hill (*née* Bennett); civil partnership 2006, Dawn Alison Chaplin. *Educ:* Ashton Keynes Primary Sch.; Hreod Burna High Sch., Swindon; Coventry Univ. (MPhil 1986); Birmingham Univ. (PhD 1988). FRSB (FIBiol 2001). Hd, Respiratory Lab., Princess Margaret's Hosp., Swindon, 1976–80; Sen. Res. Asst, Dept of Medicine, Univ. of Birmingham, 1980–83; Chief Respiratory Physiologist, Gen. Hosp., Birmingham, 1983–88; Sen., then Prin. Clinical Scientist, S Birmingham HA, 1988–94; Res. Fellow, 1988–94, Sen. Res. Fellow, 1994–2002, Univ. of Birmingham; Consultant Clin. Scientist and Hd, Lung Resource Centre, 1994–2002, Clin. Governance Lead and Clin. Dir, Respiratory Medicine, 2000–03, University Hosp. Birmingham NHS Trust. Chm., W Midlands Regl Cttee, 1995–2002, Associate Dir, 2000–02, Healthcare Scientists. Department of Health: Nat. Dir for Audiology/Physiol Diagnostics, 2005–; SRO UK Modernising Scientific Careers prog., 2008–; Science and Society Lead, 2008–; Jt Nat. Clin. Dir for Respiratory Disease and Home Oxygen Services, 2009–. Hon. Prof. of Respiratory Medicine, Univ. of Birmingham, 2002–. Mem., Exec. Bd, Conf. of Clin. Scientists Orgns, 1995–2001. Chair: UK Healthcare Sci. Nat. Occupational Standards project, 1995–2002; Nat. Physiol Measurement Bd, 2006–; Home Oxygen Services Bd, 2009–; Co-Chair: Healthcare Sci. Prog. Bd, Med. Educn England, 2009–; Respiratory Prog. Bd, 2009–; Member: Sci. in Health Gp, Sci. Council, 2002–; Med. Technologies Adv. Cttee, NICE, 2008–; Ministerial Med. Technol. Strategic Gp, 2009–; Adv. Bd, Sci. for All, 2009–; Exec. Bd, Life Scis Industry, 2010–; Bd, Technician Council, 2010–. Mem., wkg party on Audiol Medicine, RCP, 2003–04. Vice-Pres., British Lung Foundn, 2008– (Member: Exec. Cttee, 1992–98; Breathe Easy Cttee, 1993–2000; Mem. and Chm., Midlands Cttee, 1996–2004). Member, Executive Board: British Thoracic Soc., 1992–2002; Assoc. Clin. Scientists, 2000–02; Sec., Fedn for Healthcare Sci., 2001–02. Gov., De Montfort Univ., 2009–. Co-founder and Dir, Chronic Obstructive Pulmonary Disease biannual internat. conf. series, 1997– (co-ed., conf. proc.); European Respiratory Journals: Mem., Bd of Dirs, 1998–2001; Ed., Buyers Guide, 1998–2001. Hon. MRCP 2002, Hon. FRCP 2010. Hon. DSc: Keele, 2007; De Montfort, 2008; Aston, 2009; Wolverhampton, 2009. *Publications:* Issues in Infection: the interaction between lung defences and bacteria: time for reappraisal, 1996; Practical Handbook of Respiratory Function Testing, 1999; contrib. papers and editl reviews to scientific jls on lung inflammation, infection and pathophysiol., Chronic obstructive pulmonary disease, bronchiectasis and asthma and on quality of service delivery. *Recreations:* cooking, fine dining, house renovation, reading, walking. *Address:* Department of Health, Richmond House, 79 Whitehall, SW1A 2NS. *T:* (020) 7210 5622. *E:* sue.hill@dh.gsi.gov.uk.

HILL, Rt Hon. (Trevor) Keith; PC 2003; Chair, Lambeth Living, since 2009; *b* 28 July 1943; *s* of late George Ernest Hill and Ena Ida (*née* Dakin); *m* 1972, Lesley Ann Sheppard. *Educ:* Corpus Christi Coll., Oxford (BA, MA); UCW, Aberystwyth (DipEd). Res. Asst in Politics, Univ. of Leicester, 1966–68; Belgian Govt Scholar, Brussels, 1968–69; Lectr in Politics, Univ. of Strathclyde, 1969–73; Res. Officer, Labour Party Internat. Dept, 1974–76; Political Liaison Officer, NUR, subseq. Nat. Union of Rail, Maritime and Tspt Workers, 1976–92. MP (Lab) Streatham, 1992–2010. An Asst Govt Whip, 1998–99; Parly Under-Sec. of State, DETR, 1999–2001; Treasurer of HM Household (Dep. Chief Whip), 2001–03; Minister of State (Minister for Housing and Planning), ODPM, 2003–05; PPS to Prime Minister, 2005–07. Chairman: Regulatory Panel, Assoc. of Residential Managing Agents, 2013–; London Bor. of Hammersmith and Fulham Residents' Commn on Council Housing, 2015–. *Publications:* (contrib.) European Political Parties, 1969; (contrib.) Electoral Behaviour, 1974. *Recreations:* walks, books, films, music. *Address:* 110 Wavertree Road, Streatham Hill, SW2 3ST. *T:* (020) 8674 0434.

HILL, Vernon William, II; Founder and Chairman, Metro Bank UK, since 2010; *b* San Francisco, 18 Aug. 1945; *s* of Vernon W. Hill; *m* 1973, Shirley; four *c. Educ:* Wharton Sch., Univ. of Pennsylvania. Founder and Chm., Commerce Bancorp, 1973–2007. *Publications:* Fans not Customers, 2012. *Recreation:* golf. *Address:* Metro Bank UK, One Southampton Row, WC1B 5HA. *T:* (020) 3402 8382. *E:* vernon.hill@metrobank.plc.uk.

HILL, Prof. William George, OBE 2004; FRS 1985; FRSE 1979; Professor of Animal Genetics, University of Edinburgh, 1983–2002, now Emeritus; *b* 7 Aug. 1940; *s* of late William Hill and Margaret Paterson Hill (*née* Hamilton); *m* 1971, Christine Rosemary Austin; one *s* two *d. Educ:* St Albans School; Wye Coll., Univ. of London (BSc 1961); Univ. of California, Davis (MS 1963); Iowa State Univ.; Univ. of Edinburgh (PhD 1965; DSc 1976). University of Edinburgh: Asst Lectr, 1965–67, Lectr, 1967–74, Reader, 1974–83, in Genetics; Hd, Dept of Genetics, 1989–90; Hd, Inst. of Cell, Animal and Population Biol., 1990–93; Hd, Div. of Biol Scis, 1993–98; Dean and Provost, Faculty of Sci. and Engrg, 1999–2002. Visiting Professor/Research Associate: Univ. of Minnesota, 1966; Iowa State Univ., 1967–78; N Carolina State Univ., 1979, 1985, 1992–2005. Consultant Geneticist: Cotswold Pig Develt Co., 1965–99; British Friesian Cattle Soc., 1978–88; Holstein Friesian Soc., 1988–98. Chm., Org Cttee, 4th World Congress, 1990, Pres., 5th World Congress, Genetics Applied to Livestock Prodn; Chm., Org Cttee, 4th Internat. Conf. Quantitative Genetics, 2012; Pres., British Soc. Animal Sci., 1999–2000 (Vice-Pres., 1997–99); Vice-Pres., Genetics Soc., 2004–08. Chm., Nat. Consultative Cttee, Animal Genetic Resources, 2001–02; Member: Scientific Study Group, Meat and Livestock Commn, 1969–72; Cattle Res. Consultative Cttee, 1985–86; AFRC Animals Res. Grant Bd, 1986–92; Dir's Adv. Gp, AFRC Animal Breeding Res. Orgn, 1983–86; Tech. Cttee, 1992–99 (Chm., 1995–97), Develt Cttee, 1992–98, Animal Data Centre; Inst. Animal Physiology and Genetics Res., 1986–93; Bd Govs, Roslin Inst., 1994–2002; Council, Royal Soc., 1993–94; Commonwealth Scholarship Commn, 1998–2004 (Dep.-Chm., 2002–04). Mem. 1996, Chm. 2001, RAE Biol Sci. Panel. Editor: Animal Prodn, 1971–78; Genetics, 1993–94; Livestock Prodn Sci., 1994–95; Genetics Res. (formerly Genetical Res.), 1996–2012; Proceedings of Royal Soc. B, 2005–08. Hon. DSc N Carolina State, 2003; Dr *hc* Edinburgh, 2005. *Publications:* (ed) Benchmark Papers in Quantitative Genetics, 1984; (ed) Evolution and Animal Breeding, 1989; numerous papers on quantitative and population genetics, biometrics and animal breeding, in sci. jls. *Recreations:* farming, bridge. *Address:* 4 Gordon Terrace, Edinburgh EH16 5QH. *T:* (0131) 667 3680. *Club:* Farmers.

HILL-NORTON, Vice Adm. Hon. Sir Nicholas (John), KCB 1991; Chairman, King George's Fund for Sailors, 2003–07; *b* 13 July 1939; *s* of Admiral of the Fleet Baron Hill-Norton, GCB; *m* 1966, Ann Jennifer, *d* of Vice-Adm. D. H. Mason, CB, CVO; two *s* one *d. Educ:* Marlborough Coll.; BRNC, Dartmouth; US Naval War Coll., Newport, RI. Royal Navy, 1957–95; commanded: HMS Antelope, 1974–76; Fishery Protection Sqdn, 1978–80; HMS Southampton, 1980–81; HMS Invincible, 1983–85; Flag Officer, Gibraltar, 1987–90; Flag Officer Surface Flotilla and Comdr, Anti-Submarine Warfare Striking Force Atlantic, 1990–92; Dep. Chief of Defence Staff, 1992–95. Defence Adviser: GEC-Marconi, 1995–99; BAE SYSTEMS, 1999–2000; Director: Matra Marconi Space, 1996–99; Marconi N America, 1997–2000; Lear Astronics (USA), 1996–99. Mem., UK Adv. Bd, Tenix Pty (Australia), 2003–07. Chm., British Greyhound Racing Bd, 2000–02. Vice Pres., RUSI, 1999–2003. *Recreations:* travel, cooking, country sports, golf, woodland management. *Clubs:* Royal Navy of 1765 and 1785; Goodwood Golf.

HILL-TOUT, Paul Edward; Director, Forestry Commission, 2003–10; a Forestry Commissioner, 2004–10; *b* 24 Aug. 1957; *s* of Walter Tony Hill-Tout and Evelyn Mary Hill-Tout; *m* 1982, Lin; one *s* five *d. Educ:* King's Coll. London (BA Geog.); Christ Church, Oxford (MSc Forestry and Land Mgt). Joined Forestry Commn, 1980; has held various appts across the orgn and GB. *Recreations:* owns and manages a woodland in Devon, hiking, camping, travel, all eras of history.

HILL-TREVOR, family name of **Baron Trevor**.

HILL-WOOD, Sir Samuel Thomas, 4th Bt *cr* 1921, of Moorfield, Glossop, co. Derby; business development director; *b* 24 Aug. 1971; *er s* of Sir David Basil Hill-Wood, 3rd Bt and of Jennifer Anne, *d* of Peter McKenzie-Strang; *S* father, 2002; *m* Emma Jane Dixon. *Educ:* Wellington Coll.; Kingston Univ. (BA Hons, MA). *Recreations:* golf, fishing, cricket, football, shooting. *Heir: b* Edward Charles Hill-Wood [*b* 22 April 1974; *m* 2005, Mandy Jane O'Hara; two *s* one *d*]. *Address:* Dacre Farm, Sandpit Lane, Farley Hill, Reading, Berkshire RG7 1XJ.

HILLCOAT, Polly; *see* Borland, P.

HILLEL, Mira B.; *see* Bar-Hillel.

HILLEN, John Malcolm; His Honour Judge Hillen; a Circuit Judge, since 2005; Resident Judge, Blackfriars Crown Court, since 2014; *b* 13 May 1952; *s* of late Clarence Albert and of Winifred Hillen; *m* 1985, Monica Lilian Marie Curtice; one *s* one *d. Educ:* King Edward VI Grammar Sch., Aston (Hales Scholar); Lincoln Coll., Oxford (Open Exhibn; MA Modern Hist.); Coll. of Law. Called to the Bar, Middle Temple, 1976; in practice as barrister, specialising in criminal law, 1978–2005; Asst Recorder, 1997–2000; Recorder, 2000–05. Trustee and Mem. Cttee, Barristers' Benevolent Assoc., 1996–. *Recreations:* fair-weather gardening, hibernation. *Address:* c/o Blackfriars Crown Court, 1–15 Pocock Street, SE1 0BJ. *T:* (020) 7922 5800.

HILLENBRAND, Prof. Carole, OBE 2009; PhD; FBA 2007; FRSE; FRAS; FRHistS; Professor of Islamic History, University of Edinburgh, 2000–08, now Emerita; Professor of Islamic History, University of St Andrews, since 2013; *b* Southery, Norfolk, 3 May 1943; *e d* of William Thomas Jordan and Lilian Margaret Jordan (*née* Lister); *m* 1968, Robert Hillenbrand, *qv*; two *d. Educ:* Perse Girls' Sch., Cambridge; Girton Coll., Cambridge (BA 1965); Somerville Coll., Oxford (BA 1972; Hon. Fellow 2009); Univ. of Edinburgh (PhD 1979). University of Edinburgh: Lectr in Arabic, 1979–90; Reader in Arabic, 1990–2000; Hd, Dept of Islamic and Middle Eastern Studies, 1997–2002 and 2006–08. Visiting Professor: Dartmouth Coll., 1994, 2005; Univ. of Groningen, Netherlands, 2002; Sen. Res. Fellow, Univ. of St Louis, 2011, 2013. Vice-Pres., British Soc. for Middle Eastern Studies, 2003–09. Corresp. Fellow, Medieval Acad. of America, 2012–. King Faisal Internat. Prize in Islamic Studies, 2005. FRSE 2000. *Publications:* (ed jtly) Qajar Iran: political, social and cultural change, 1800–1925, 1984; The Waning of the Umayyad Caliphate, 1989; A Muslim Principality in Crusader Times: the early Artuqid State, 1990; The Crusades, Islamic Perspectives, 1999 (trans. Russian, Indonesian, Turkish); (ed) The Sultan's Turret, 1999; Turkish Myth and Muslim Symbol: the Battle of Manzikert, 2007; Introduction to Islam: beliefs and practices in historical perspective, 2015; contribs to books and articles in jls. *Recreations:* travel, cinema. *Address:* Islamic and Middle Eastern Studies, University of Edinburgh, 19 George Square, Edinburgh EH8 9LD.

HILLENBRAND, Prof. Robert, DPhil; FBA 2008; FRSE; Honorary Professorial Fellow and Professor Emeritus, Islamic and Middle Eastern Studies, University of Edinburgh, since 2007; Professor of Islamic Art, University of St Andrews, since 2013; *b* Damgarten, Germany, 2 Aug. 1941; *s* of Fritz Hillenbrand and Margaret Hillenbrand (*née* Meinck); *m* 1968, Carole Jordan (*see* C. Hillenbrand); two *d. Educ:* Trinity Coll., Cambridge (BA 1963); Trinity Coll., Oxford (DPhil 1974). Department of Fine Art, Univ. of Edinburgh, 1971–2007, Prof. of Islamic Art, 1989–2007. Slade Prof. of Art, Univ. of Cambridge, 2008; Visiting Professor: Princeton Univ.; UCLA; Bamberg Univ.; Dartmouth Coll.; Groningen Univ.; American Univ. in Cairo. Hon. Prof., Univ. of St Andrews, 2011–12. Kevorkian Lectures, New York Univ., 1993. Dir, Centre for the Advanced Study of the Arab World, 2006–07; Vice-Pres., British Inst. of Persian Studies, 1993–2011. Alice Hitchcock Medallion, Soc. of Architectural Historians of GB, 1996; Iris Foundn Scholar's Award for Outstanding Contribn to the Decorative Arts, New York, 2008. FRSE 1991. *Publications:* (jtly) Islamic Architecture in North Africa, 1976; (ed) Proceedings of the 10th Congress of the Union Européenne des Arabisants et Islamisants, 1982; (ed) The Islamic Book, 1984; Islamic Architecture: form, function and meaning, 1994 (trans. Persian, 1998, 2000); (ed) The Art of the Saljuqs in Iran and Anatolia, 1994; The 'Amiriya in Rada': the history and restoration of a sixteenth-century Madrasa in the Yemen, 1997; (ed jtly) The Art and Archaeology of Ancient Persia: new light on the Parthian and Sasanian empires, 1998; Islamic Art and Architecture, 1999 (trans. German and Turkish, 2005; Persian and Danish, 2008); (ed jtly) Ottoman Jerusalem: the living city, 1517–1917, 2000; (ed) Persian Painting from the Mongols to the Qajars, 2001; The Architecture of Ottoman Jerusalem: an introduction, 2002; Studies in Medieval Islamic Art and Architecture, vol. 1, 2001, vol. 2, 2006; (ed) Shahnama: text and image in the Persian Book of Kings, 2004 (Book of the Year Prize, Islamic Republic of Iran, 2006); (ed) Image and Meaning in Islamic Art, 2005; (ed) Ayyubid Jerusalem: the Holy City in context, 1187–1250, 2009; The Sheikh Zayed Grand Mosque, 2010; Studies in the Islamic Arts of the Book, 2012; The Sheikh Zayed Grand Mosque: a landmark of modern Islamic architecture, 2012; (ed jtly) Ferdowsi, the Mongols and the History of Iran, 2013; 170 book chapters and articles in jls. *Recreations:* travel, cinema, hill-walking. *Address:* Islamic and Middle Eastern Studies, University of Edinburgh, 19 George Square, Edinburgh EH8 9LD.

HILLHOUSE, Prof. Edward William, PhD; FRCP; Chief of Scientific, Academic and Faculty Affairs, Hamad Medical Corporation, Dohar, Qatar, since 2013 (Senior Policy Advisor, then Chief Policy Advisor and Chief of Medical, Academic and Research Affairs, 2011–13); Professor of Medicine, Weill Cornell Medical College, New York, since 2012; Professor of Medicine, and Dean, Faculty of Medicine and Health, University of Leeds, 2002–11, now Emeritus Professor; *b* 16 March 1950; *s* of William and Joan Hillhouse; *m* 1993, Nicola Judith; three *s* three *d. Educ:* All Saints Sch., Wimbledon; Rutlish Sch., Merton; St Thomas's Hosp. Med. Sch., Univ. of London (BSc 1st Cl. Hons 1972; PhD 1975; MB BS 1981). FRCP 1995. Res. Fellow, Tufts Univ., Boston, 1986–87; Lectr in Medicine, King's Coll. Hosp., London, 1988–90; Sen. Lectr in Metabolic Medicine, Univ. of Newcastle, 1990–93; Sen. Lectr in Medicine, Univ. of Bristol, 1993–95; Prof. of Medicine, and Dir of Molecular Res. Inst., Univ. of Warwick, 1995–2002. Non-exec. Dir, Leeds Teaching Hosps NHS Trust, 2003. Dir, Internat. Assoc. of Academic Health Centers, 2010–. *Publications:* over 150 articles in learned jls. *Recreations:* yoga, tennis, watching Leeds United FC, reading, history, fine wine. *Address:* Hamad Medical Corporation, PO Box 3050, Dohar, Qatar. *E:* ehillhouse@hmc.org.qa.

HILLHOUSE, Sir (Robert) Russell, KCB 1991; FRSE; Permanent Under-Secretary of State, Scottish Office, 1988–98; *b* 23 April 1938; *s* of Robert Hillhouse and Jean Russell; *m* 1966, Alison Janet Fraser (*d* 2015); two *d. Educ:* Hutchesons' Grammar Sch., Glasgow; Glasgow Univ. (MA). FRSE 1995. Scottish Education Dept, 1962; HM Treasury, 1971; Asst Secretary, Scottish Office, 1974; Scottish Home and Health Dept, 1977; Under Sec. (Principal Finance Officer), Scottish Office, 1980; Under Sec., 1985–87, Sec., 1987–88, Scottish Educn Dept. Director: Bank of Scotland, 1998–2001; Scottish Provident Instn, 1999–2001. Chairman: Hebrides Ensemble, 1999–2003; Upper Deeside Access Trust, 1998–2003; Edinburgh Competitive Fest. Assoc., 2010–14. Gov., RSAMD, 2000–08. DUniv Glasgow, 1999; Hon. LLD Aberdeen, 1999; Hon. DLitt Napier, 1999. CCMI (CBIM 1990). FRSA 1992. *Recreations:* making music, enjoying the countryside. *Address:* 12 Russell Place, Edinburgh EH5 3HH. *T:* (0131) 476 0503. *Club:* New (Edinburgh).

HILLIARD, Lexa; *see* Hilliard, P. A.

HILLIARD, Nicholas Richard Maybury; QC 2008; **His Honour Judge Hilliard;** a Senior Circuit Judge, since 2012; Recorder of London, since 2015; *b* 1 May 1959; *s* of His Honour Judge Christopher Richard Hilliard and Anne Margaret Hilliard; *m* 2011, Jane Dorothy Garioni. *Educ:* Bradfield Coll.; Lincoln Coll., Oxford (MA). Called to the Bar, Middle Temple, 1981, Bencher, 2003; Recorder, 2001–12; Leader, SE Circuit, 2011–12. Standing Counsel to DTI, 1993–95; Jun. Treasury Counsel, 1995–2000; Sen. Treasury Counsel, Central Criminal Court, 2001–08; Resident Judge, Woolwich Crown Court, 2012–13; Common Serjeant, City of London, 2013–15. Hon. Recorder, Greenwich, 2013. Vice-Chm., 2004–05, Chm., 2005–06, Criminal Bar Assoc. Mem., Common Council, City of London, 1994–96, 2005–09. Mem., Commn of Lieutenancy, City of London, 2014–. Trustee: Ben Kinsella Trust, 2010–12; Crisis, 2011–; Finding Rhythms, 2014–. Gov., City of London Acad., Islington, 2014–. Liveryman: Wax Chandlers' Co., 1989; Feltmakers' Co. (Mem., Ct of Assts, 2005–; Third Warden, 2014–15); Hon. Liveryman: Cutlers' Co., 2014; Curriers' Co., 2015. Contrib. Ed., Archbold, Criminal Pleading, Evidence and Practice, 1994–; Ed., Criminal Appeal Reports, 1994–2000. *Address:* Central Criminal Court, Old Bailey, EC4M 7EH. *Clubs:* Garrick, Beefsteak, MCC; Surrey County Cricket; Woking Golf; Chelsea Football.

HILLIARD, Piers Alexandra, (Lexa); QC 2009; *b* London, 23 Feb. 1956; *d* of Joanne Hilliard; *m* 2003, Stephen Sands. *Educ:* London Sch. of Econs and Pol Sci. (LLB Hons); King's Coll., London (Postgrad. Dip. EC Law). Lectr in Law, Durham Univ., 1984–87; called to the Bar, Middle Temple, 1987; in practice as a barrister, 1990–. *Publications:* (contrib.) Directors: duties, liabilities and remedies, 2009. *Recreations:* walking, sailing. *Address:* 11 Stone Buildings, Lincoln's Inn, WC2A 3TG. *Club:* British Classic Yacht.

HILLIER, Andrew Charles; QC 2002; *b* 4 May 1949; *s* of late William Hillier and Rosemary (*née* Dutton); *m* 1971, Dr Geraldine Morris; one *s* one *d. Educ:* St Louis Sch.; Beaumont Coll.; Trinity Coll., Dublin (BA Hons). Called to the Bar, Gray's Inn, 1972, Bencher, 2009. Trustee: Hofesh Shechter Co., 2009–; Bar Pro Bono Unit, 2014–. *Publications:* Tolley's Employment Act, 1982. *Recreations:* gardening in France, Britain in China in the 19th century. *Address:* 11 King's Bench Walk, Temple, EC4Y 7EQ.

HILLIER, Bevis; author, art historian, journalist; *b* 28 March 1940; *s* of late Jack Ronald Hillier and Mary Louise Hillier (*née* Palmer). *Educ:* Reigate Grammar Sch.; Magdalen Coll., Oxford (demy). Gladstone Memorial Prize, 1961. Editorial staff, The Times, 1963–68 (trainee, Home News Reporter, Sale Room Correspondent); Editor, British Museum Society Bulletin, 1968–70; Guest Curator, Minneapolis Inst. of Arts, USA, 1971; Editor, The Connoisseur, 1973–76; Antiques Correspondent, 1970–84, Dep. Literary Editor, 1980–82, The Times; Editor, The Times Saturday Review, 1982; Features Editor, 1982–83, Exec. Editor, 1983–84, Telegraph Sunday Magazine; Columnist and Associate Editor, Los Angeles Times, 1984–88; Editor, Sotheby's Preview, 1990–93. Co-founder and first Chm., Thirties Soc. (now Twentieth Century Soc.), 1979; Pres., Betjeman Soc., 2006– (Vice-Pres., 1988–2006). FRSA 1967; FRSL 1997. Hon. DLitt Winchester, 2009. Commendatore, Order of Merit (Italy), 1976. *Publications:* Master Potters of the Industrial Revolution: The Turners of Lane End, 1965; Pottery and Porcelain 1700–1914, 1968; Art Deco of the 1920s and 1930s, 1968; Posters, 1969; Cartoons and Caricatures, 1970; The World of Art Deco, 1971; 100 Years of Posters, 1972; Travel Posters, 1973; Victorian Studio Photographs, 1974; (jtly) Façade, 1974; Austerity/Binge, 1975; Punorama, 1975; Dead Funny, 1975; (ed with Mary Banham) A Tonic to the Nation: The Festival of Britain 1951, 1976; The New Antiques, 1977; Fougasse, 1978; Ealing Film Posters, 1981; Bevis Hillier's Pocket Guide to Antiques, 1981; Greetings from Christmas Past, 1982; The Style of the Century 1900–1980, 1983; John

Betjeman: a life in pictures, 1984; Mickey Mouse Memorabilia, 1986; Young Betjeman, 1988; Early English Porcelain, 1992; (jtly) Art Deco Style, 1997; John Betjeman: new fame, new love, 2002; Betjeman: the bonus of laughter, 2004; The Wit and Wisdom of G. K. Chesterton, 2010; The Virgin's Baby: the battle of the Ampthill succession, 2013; Going for a Song: an anthology of poems about antiques, 2014; contributor to books, and periodicals incl. The Connoisseur, Apollo, Trans English Ceramic Circle, Proc. Wedgwood Soc., etc. *Recreations:* piano, collecting. *Address:* Flat 23, Hospital of St Cross, St Cross Road, Winchester, Hants SO23 9SD. *T:* (01962) 855294. *Club:* Garrick.

HILLIER, Malcolm Dudley; designer and author; *b* 1 Aug. 1936. *Educ:* St Paul's School; Guildhall School of Music (LGSM). Advertising career, Colman Prentis and Varley; later Dir of Television, S. H. Benson, 1958–74; started garden design co. (with Colin Hilton), and opened flower shop, specialising in dried flowers, 1974; formed design partnership, 1992; writer since 1985. *Publications:* Complete Book of Dried Flowers, 1986; Malcolm Hillier's Guide to Arranging Dried Flowers, 1987; Flowers, 1988; Container Gardening, 1991; Roses, 1991; Pot Pourri, 1991; Malcolm Hillier's Christmas, 1992; Little Scented Library, 1992; Garlands, 1994; Container Gardening throughout the Year, 1995; Good Food Fast, 1995; Malcolm Hillier's Colour Garden, 1995; Entertaining, 1997; Cat's Christmas, 1998; Flowers, 2000; Rites of Passage, 2013. *Recreations:* photography, poetry writing, pottery. *E:* malcolmhillier@yahoo.co.uk.

HILLIER, Meg; MP (Lab and Co-op) Hackney South and Shoreditch, since 2005; *b* 14 Feb. 1969; *m* 1997; one *s* two *d.* *Educ:* St Hilda's Coll., Oxford (BA Hons PPE); City Univ. (Dip. Newspaper Journalism). Reporter, S Yorks Times, 1991; Petty Officer, P & O European Ferries, 1992; PR Officer, Newlon Housing Gp, 1993; reporter, 1994–95, features editor, 1995–98, Housing Today; freelance, 1998–2000. Mem. (Lab) Islington BC, 1994–2002 (Chair, Neighbourhood Services Cttee, 1995–97); Mayor, Islington, 1998–99. Mem. (Lab) NE, London Assembly, GLA, 2000–04. Mem. Bd, Transport for London, 2004–05. PPS to Sec. of State for Communities and Local Govt, 2006–07; Parly Under-Sec. of State, Home Office, 2007–10; Shadow Sec. of State for Energy and Climate Change, 2010–11. Mem., Public Accounts Select Cttee, 2011– (Chm., 2015–). Trustee, War Memls Trust, 2001–. *Recreations:* local history, cycling. *Address:* House of Commons, SW1A 0AA.

HILLIER, Paul Douglas, OBE 2006; conductor and singer; *b* 9 Feb. 1949; *s* of Douglas and Felicity Hillier; *m* 1st, 1977, Lena-Liis Kiesel (marr. diss. 2002); two *d*; 2nd, 2004, Else Torp; two *d.* *Educ:* Guildhall School of Music and Drama, London (AGSM). Vicar-Choral, St Paul's Cathedral, 1974–76; Musical Dir, Hilliard Ensemble, 1973–90; Prof. of Music, Univ. of Calif., Davis, 1990–96; Prof. of Music and Dir, Early Music Inst., Indiana Univ., Bloomington, 1996–2003. Artistic Dir and Principal Conductor, Estonian Philharmonic Chamber Choir, 2001–07; Chief Conductor and Artistic Dir, Ars Nova, Copenhagen, 2003–; Conductor: Western Wind Chamber Choir, 1985–89; Klemetti Inst. Chamber Choir, Finland, 1989–93; Dir, Theatre of Voices, 1989–; Artistic Director: Nat. Chamber Choir of Ireland, 2008–; Coro Casa da Musica, Porto, 2009–. Hon. Prof., Univ. of Copenhagen, 2003–07. Gen. Editor, Fazer Editions of Early Music, Helsinki, 1992–99. Edison Prize (Holland), 1989; Estonian Cultural Prize, 2004; White Star of Estonia, 2007; Grammy Awards for Best Choral Perf., 2007, for Best Small Ensemble Perf., 2010. Knight, Order of Dannebrog (Denmark), 2013. *Publications:* 300 Years of English Partsongs, 1983; Romantic English Partsongs, 1986; The Catch Book, 1987; The Music of Arvo Pärt, 1997; (ed) Steve Reich, Writings on Music, 2002; On Pärt, 2005. *Recreations:* reading, walking.

HILLIER, Dr Richard John; Headmaster, Yehudi Menuhin School, since 2010; *b* Winchester, 27 April 1961; *s* of David and Shirley Hillier; *m* 1984, Elaine Hall; two *s.* *Educ:* King's Sch., Peterborough; St John's Coll., Cambridge (BA 1982; MA 1986); Univ. of Durham (PGCE 1983; PhD 1990). Classics teacher: St Leonard's Sch., St Andrews, 1986–87; Durham Sch., 1987–91; Course Tutor, Open Univ., 1989–91; Repton School: Hd of Classics, 1991–98; Housemaster and classics teacher, 1997–2006; Headmaster, Oratory Prep. Sch., 2006–10. *Publications:* Arator on the Acts of the Apostles: a Baptismal commentary, 1993; contrib. articles to Jl Theol Studies, Studia Patristica. *Recreations:* academic research (late antiquity), music and theatre, travel (Mediterranean), spending time in Northumberland and Scottish Borders, gardening, family and dog. *Address:* Yehudi Menuhin School, Stoke D'Abernon, Cobham, Surrey KT11 3QQ. *T:* (01932) 864739, *Fax:* (01932) 864633. *E:* richard.hillier@yehudimenuhinschool.co.uk.

HILLIER, Stephen Martin; Director, Althemis Ltd, since 2013; Chief Executive, Training and Development Agency for Schools, 2011–12; *b* 30 May 1957; *s* of Alfred Harley and Mabel Hillier; *m* 2004, Gillian Frances Langford; one *s* one *d* (twins). *Educ:* City of London Polytech. (BA Hons); Birkbeck Coll., Univ. of London (MSc). Exec. Officer, Schs Council, 1978–81; Department of Education and Science: Exec. Officer, Curriculum Br., 1981–82; HEO, student loans policy, 1982–85; Private Sec. to Minister of State, 1985–87; Sen. Exec. Officer, Teachers' Br., 1987–88; Teamleader, Grant-Maintained Schs, DfEE, 1988–93; Dep. Chief Exec., Teacher Trng Agency, 1994–99; Department for Education and Skills, then Department for Innovation, Universities and Skills, later Department for Business, Innovation and Skills: Divl Manager, Post-16 Educn and Trng, 1999–2001; Dep. Dir, Sch. Workforce Unit, 2001–03; Dir, Sch. Workforce Gp, 2004–06; Dir, Skills Gp, 2006–09; Regl Dir, Govt Office for E Midlands, 2010–11. Trustee: NFER, 2011–13; Mercia Learning Trust, 2013–. Chair of Govs, Valley Park Primary Sch., Sheffield, 2015–; Community Gov., King Ecgbert Acad., Sheffield, 2013–. *Recreation:* enjoying life in the Peak District and Yorkshire with our young twins Amélie and Seth. *Address:* 77 Crescent Road, Sheffield S7 1HN. *T:* 07711 847278. *E:* ginger1511@icloud.com.

HILLIER, William Edward, CEng, FIET; Visiting Industrial Fellow, Engineering Department, Cambridge University, 1996–98 and since 1999; *b* 11 April 1936; *s* of William Edward and Ivy Hillier; *m* 1958, Barbara Mary Thorpe; one *s* one *d.* *Educ:* Acton Grammar School; Open Univ. (BA). FIET (FIEE 1990). Missile Electronics Engineer, De Havilland Propellers, 1958–60; Semiconductor Test Equipment Design and Production Manager, 1960–64, Semiconductor Production Manager, 1965–70, Texas Instruments; Computer Aided Engineering Services Manager, up to Tech. Dir, CAD, Racal Redac, 1970–85 (Dep. Man. Dir, 1982–85); Dir, Application of Computers and Manufg Engrg Directorate, 1985–94, and Hd of IT, 1991–94, SERC; Corporate Industrial Marketing, EPSRC, 1994–96. Chairman: Computing and Control Div., IEE, 1993–94; Indust. Adv. Bd, Sch. of Manufg and Mech. Engrg, Birmingham Univ., 1997–2000. Dir, Heritage Rly Assoc., 2000–. FCMI. *Publications:* articles in professional papers. *Recreation:* railway preservation. *Address:* 19 Simon de Montfort Drive, Evesham, Worcs WR11 4NR. *T:* (01386) 443449.

HILLING, Julie Ann; *b* Oxford; *d* of Arthur Hilling and Penelope Hilling (*née* Whiting). *Educ:* Cedars Sch., Leighton Buzzard; Nottingham Univ. (BSc Chem.); Manchester Poly. (Dip. Youth and Community Work). Community worker: St Ann's Tenants' and Residents' Assoc., 1977–80; Sneinton Hermitage Community Assoc., 1980–81; youth worker: St Helen's BC, 1982–86; Wigan Council, 1986–2004; Learning Organiser, NASUWT, 2004–06; Sen. Regl Organiser, TSSA, 2006–10. MP (Lab) Bolton W, 2010–15; contested (Lab) same seat, 2015. PPS to Shadow Minister for Women and Equalities, 2010–12; an Opposition Whip, 2012–15. Member: Transport Select Cttee, 2010–12; Standards and Privileges Cttee, 2011–12; Chair, All Party Parly Gp on Rail of the North, 2010–15; Co-Chair, All Party Parly Gp on Youth Affairs, 2010–15.

HILLMAN, David, RDI 1997; FCSD; FRCA; Director, Studio David Hillman, since 2007; *b* 12 Feb. 1943; *s* of late Leslie Hillman and Marjorie Joan Hillman (*née* Nash); *m* 1st, 1963, Eileen Margaret Griffin (marr. diss. 1968); one *s* one *d*; 2nd, 1983, Jennie Diana Burns; two *s.* *Educ:* Aristotle Central Sch.; London Sch. of Printing and Graphic Art (NDD Graphic Design 1962). AGI 1977; FCSD 1979; Sen. FRCA 2004. Design Asst, Sunday Times mag., 1962–65; Art Editor, London Life, 1965–66; Designer/Editor, Design for Living section, Sunday Times mag., 1966–68; Art Dir and Dep. Editor, Nova, 1968–75; freelance practice, 1975–78; Dir, Pentagram Design, 1978–2007. Exhibn, Hillman in Print, The Hub, Sleaford, 2009, James Hockey & Foyer Galls, Univ. for Creative Arts, Farnham, 2010. Mem., Alliance Graphique Internat., 1977– (UK Pres., 1996–2000; Internat. Pres., 2000–03). *Publications:* (ed jtly) Ideas on Design, 1986; Puzzlegrams, 1989; Pentagames, 1992; (ed jtly) Nova, 1993; (ed jtly) The Compendium, 1993; (jtly) Puzzlegrams Too, 1994; (ed jtly) Pentagram, Book 5, 1999; (jtly) Century Makers, 1999; (jtly) Terence Donovan, The Photographs, 2000; (ed jtly) Pentagram Profile, 2004; (ed with Diana Donovan) Terence Donovan Fashion, 2012. *Recreations:* ski-ing, modern jazz. *Address:* The Barns, Wortley, Wotton-under-Edge, Glos GL12 7QP. *T:* (01453) 844266.

HILLMAN, Prof. John Richard, PhD; FRSE; FLS, FRSB, FCIHort; Scientific Adviser, Arab Academy of Sciences, since 2002; Hon. Research Fellow, James Hutton Institute, since 2011 (Director and Chief Executive, Scottish Crop Research Institute, 1986–2005); *b* 21 July 1944; *s* of late Robert Hillman and of Emily Irene (*née* Barrett); *m* 1967, Sandra Kathleen Palmer; two *s.* *Educ:* Chislehurst and Sidcup Grammar Sch. for Boys; University Coll. of Wales, Aberystwyth (BSc 1965; PhD 1968). FRSE, FRSB (FIBiol 1985); FLS 1982; FCIHort (FIHort 1997). Univ. of Nottingham: Asst Lectr in Physiology and Environmental Studies, 1968; Lectr, 1969; Univ. of Glasgow: Lectr in Botany, 1971; Sen. Lectr, 1977; Reader, 1980; Prof. of Botany, 1982. Visiting Professor: Univ. of Dundee, 1986–; Univ. of Strathclyde, 1986–; Univ. of Edinburgh, 1988–; Univ. of Glasgow, 1991–. Bawden Lectr, Brighton, 1993. Chm., Agric., Hort. and Forestry Sector Panel, UK Technology Foresight Prog., 1995–97 (Chm., Agric., Nat. Resources and Envmt Sector Panel, 1994–95); Founder and Dep. Chm., Mylnefield Research Services Ltd, 1993–2005. Pres., Agriculture & Food Sect., British Sci. Assoc. (formerly BAAS), 2000–. Member: Bd, BioIndustry Assoc., 1998–2005 (Chm., Industrial Biotechnol. Cttee, 1998–2004); Court, Univ. of Abertay Dundee, 1998–2005; Res. and Knowledge Transfer Cttee, SHEFC (later SFC), 2003–07; Commercial Farmers Gp, 2006–. Mem., Exec. Council, Scotia Agriculture Club, 2003– (Vice-Pres., 2005–07; Pres., 2007–09). Chm., Angus Cons. and Unionist Party, 2007–. FCMI (FBIM 1987); FRSA 1997; FRAgS 2004. Hon. DSc: Strathclyde, 1994; Abertay Dundee, 1996. British Potato Industry Award, 1999; Internat. Potato Industry Award, 2000; Dr Hardie Award, Virus-Tested Stem Cutting Assoc., 2001; Scottish Horticl Medal, Royal Caledonian Horticultural Soc., 2003. *Publications:* (ed) Isolation of Plant Growth Substances, 1978; (ed with A. Crozier) The Biosynthesis and Metabolism of Plant Hormones, 1984; (ed with C. T. Brett) Biochemistry of Plant Cell Walls, 1985; papers on plant physiol. and biotechnol. in learned jls. *Recreations:* horology, economics, antique woodworking and plumbing tools. *Address:* c/o James Hutton Institute, Invergowrie, Dundee DD2 5DA. *T:* (01382) 562731. *Club:* Farmers.

HILLS, Andrew Worth; Director, BBC Monitoring, 1996–2003; *b* 1 Sept. 1949; *s* of late Roland Frederick Hills and of Margaret Eunice (*née* Johnson); *m* 1st, 1974, Frances Mary Ralston (marr. diss. 1992); three *s*; 2nd, 1992, Mary Sandra Caraffi. *Educ:* Abingdon Sch.; Corpus Christi Coll., Cambridge (BA 1971; MA 1975). United Kingdom Atomic Energy Authority, 1971–96: Gen. Sec., AEE Winfrith, 1981–84; Principal Finance and Programmes Officer, 1984–86; Authority Personnel Officer, 1986–89; Exec. Dir, Finance and Personnel, 1989–91; Mem., UKAEA, 1991–94; Managing Director: Sites and Personnel, 1991–92; Corporate Services, 1992–94; Services Div., 1994–95; Dir, Special Projects, 1995–96. Trustee, Southern Sinfonia, 2003–. *Recreations:* church-crawling, music, reading. *Address:* Craven Lodge, Speen Lane, Newbury RG14 1RJ.

HILLS, Barrington William; racehorse trainer, 1969–2011 and since 2014; *b* 2 April 1937; *s* of William George Hills and Phyllis (*née* Biddle); *m* 1st, 1959, Maureen (marr. diss. 1977), *d* of late Patrick Newson; two *s* (twins) (and one *s* decd); 2nd, 1977, Penelope Elizabeth May, *d* of John Richard Woodhouse; two *s.* *Educ:* Robston Hall, Gloucester; St Mary's Convent, Newmarket; Mr Whittaker's, Worcester. National Service, King's Troop, RHA. Major race winners include: Prix de l'Arc de Triomphe, 1973 (Rheingold); 1,000 Guineas, 1978 (Enstone Spark), 2009 (Ghanaati); 2,000 Guineas, 1979 (Tap on Wood), 2004 (Haafhd); Irish Derby, 1987 (Sir Harry Lewis); Irish 1,000 Guineas, 1993 (Nicer), 1999 (Hula Angel); St Leger, 1994 (Moonax); Irish Oaks, 1994 (Bolas); Prix Royal-Oak, 1994 (Moonax). George Ennor Trophy, Horserace Writers and Photographers Assoc., 2009. *Recreations:* hunting, shooting, golf. *Address:* c/o Wetherdown House, Lambourn, Hungerford, Berks RG17 8UB. *T:* (01488) 71548. *Club:* Turf.

HILLS, Col David Henry, MBE 1986; Under Treasurer, 1997–2012, Hon. Bencher, 2012, Honourable Society of Lincoln's Inn; *b* 23 May 1946; *s* of Air Vice-Marshal (Eric) Donald Hills, CB, CBE and Pamela Mary, *d* of Col A. P. Sandeman; *m* 1970, Josephine Anne, *d* of Wing Comdr J. W. Abbott; two *s* one *d.* *Educ:* Mount St Mary's Coll.; RMA Sandhurst. Commnd 2nd Lt Royal Highland Fusiliers, 1967; regimental service, Scotland, Singapore, NI, 1967–77; Staff HQ 8 Bde, Londonderry, 1977–79; Staff Coll., Camberley, 1980; regimental service, Germany, 1981–83; MoD, 1983–85; loan service, Zimbabwe, 1985; DCOS HQ 1 Infantry Bde, 1987–88; Comd 1st Bn Royal Highland Fusiliers, 1988–90; Staff, RMA Sandhurst, 1990–93; Dep. COS Rear Support HQ ARRC, Germany and Croatia, 1993–96; DACOS G4 Ops and Plans HQ Land, 1996–97. Sec., Council of the Inns of Ct, 2007–09; Jt Rep., Council of the Inns of Ct to the Bar Standards Bd, 2008–09. *Recreations:* tennis, golf, ski-ing, bridge. *Address:* 15 Church Street, Whitchurch, Hants RG28 7AD.

HILLS, Jacqueline Sukie; *see* Binns, J. S.

HILLS, Sir John (Robert), Kt 2013; CBE 1999; FBA 2002; FAcSS; Professor of Social Policy, and Director, Centre for Analysis of Social Exclusion, London School of Economics, since 1997; *b* 29 July 1954; *s* of Derrick Walter Hills and Valerie Jean Hills (*née* Gribble); *m* 1989, Anne Elizabeth Power. *Educ:* Nottingham High Sch.; Abingdon Sch.; St John's Coll., Cambridge (BA 1976, MA); Birmingham Univ. (MSocSc 1980). Min. of Finance, Botswana, 1976–78; DoE, 1979–80; Treasury Cttee, H of C, 1980–82; Inst. for Fiscal Studies, 1982–84; Commn of Inquiry into Taxation, Zimbabwe, 1984–86; Welfare State Prog., LSE, 1986–97. Mem., Pensions Commn, 2003–06; Chair, Nat. Equality Panel, 2008–10. Ind. Review of Fuel Poverty for DECC, 2011–12 (report publd 2012). FAcSS (AcSS 2009). *Publications:* (ed) The State of Welfare: the welfare state in Britain since 1974, 1990, 2nd edn (jtly), 1998; Unravelling Housing Finance: subsidies, benefits and taxation, 1991; The Future of Welfare, 1993, 2nd edn 1997; (ed jtly) The Dynamic of Welfare, 1995; (ed) New Inequalities: the changing distribution of income and wealth in the UK, 1996; (jtly) Paying for Health, Education and Housing, 2000; (ed jtly) Understanding Social Exclusion, 2002; Inequality and the State, 2004; (ed jtly) A More Equal Society?, 2005; Ends and Means: the future roles of social housing in England, 2007; (ed jtly) Towards a More Equal Society, 2009; (jtly) An Anatomy of Economic Inequality, 2010; (jtly) Wealth in the UK: distribution, accumulation and policy, 2013; Good Times, Bad Times: the welfare myth of them and us, 2015. *Recreation:* fell walking. *Address:* Centre for Analysis of Social Exclusion, London School of Economics, Houghton Street, WC2A 2AE.

HILLS, Philip, CMG 2003; Chief Executive, Project and Export Finance, HSBC, 1990–2004; *b* 10 Feb. 1946; *s* of Frank and Lilian Elizabeth Patricia Hills; *m* 1969, Margaret Elizabeth Susan Harris; four *d*. *Educ:* Colfe's Grammar Sch., London. N. M. Rothschild & Sons Ltd, 1963–76 (Manager, Export Finance, 1969–76); Dir, Export Finance, Grindlay Brandts Ltd, 1976–81; HSBC Gp, 1981–2004. Director: Anthony Gibbs & Sons Ltd, 1981–88; Samuel Montagu & Co. Ltd, 1988–90. Chm., Export and Shipbuilding Policy Cttee, BBA, 1990–2001. *Recreations:* sport, travel, cookery. *Address:* HSBC Bank plc, 8 Canada Square, E14 5HQ.

HILLS, Prof. Richard Edwin, FRS 2014; Professor of Radio Astronomy, 1990–2012, and Deputy Head, Department of Physics, 1999–2003, University of Cambridge, Emeritus Professor of Radio Astronomy, 2012; Fellow of St Edmund's College, Cambridge, since 1993; *b* 30 Sept. 1945; *s* of Ronald Hills and Betty Dorothy Hills (*née* Davies); *m* 1973, Beverly Bevis; two *s*. *Educ:* Bedford Sch.; Queens' Coll., Cambridge (BA Physics); Univ. of California, Berkeley (PhD Astronomy). Research Scientist, Max Planck Inst. for Radio Astronomy, Bonn, 1972–74; Research Associate, 1974–84, Asst Dir of Research, 1984–90, Cavendish Lab., Cambridge; Project Scientist, James Clerk Maxwell Telescope, 1975–87. Project Scientist, Atacama Large Millimetre Array, Chile, 2007–12. FRAS. Jackson-Gwilt Medal, RAS, 1989; MacRobert Award, Fellowship of Engineers, 1990. *Publications:* contribs to professional jls. *Recreations:* travel, DIY, music. *Address:* c/o Cavendish Laboratory, J. J. Thomson Avenue, Cambridge CB3 0HE. *T:* (01223) 337369.

HILLSBOROUGH, Earl of; Edmund Robin Arthur Hill; *b* 21 May 1996; *s* and *heir* of Marquess of Downshire, *qv*.

HILLSON, Dr Rowan Mary, MBE 2006; FRCP; Consultant Physician, Diabetes and Endocrinology, General Internal Medicine, Hillingdon Hospital, 1989–2012, Hon. Consultant Physician, 2012–13; National Clinical Director for Diabetes, Department of Health, 2008–13; *b* London, 10 May 1951; *d* of Rodney and Kathleen Hillson. *Educ:* Edgbaston High Sch., Birmingham; Univ. of Birmingham (MB ChB 1974; MD 1983). MRCP 1976, FRCP 1994. Hon. Sen. Registrar, 1980–84, Sen. Registrar, 1984–89, Diabetes and Endocrinol., Gen. Internal Medicine, Radcliffe Infirmary and John Radcliffe Hosp., Oxford; diabetes and endocrinol., and gen. internal medicine roles, London Deanery, 1997–2008; Hon. Sen. Lectr, 1999–2012, and Clin. Tutor, 1998–2012, Imperial Coll. Med. Sch. Mem., Appraisal Cttee, 2005–08, Vice Chm., Vascular Topic Selection Panel, 2008–11, NICE. British Diabetic Association, later Diabetes UK: pioneered and supervised Outward Bound courses for people with diabetes, 1981–96; Member: Educn Cttee, 1989–91; Med. and Scientific Cttee, 1990–92; Chm., Sports and Exercise Wkg Party, 1991–93. Royal College of Physicians: Regl Advr, NW London, 2001–04 (CPD Advr, 2004–08); Mem. Council, 2007–10, 2013–; Trustee, 2013–. Mem. Cttee, Assoc. British Clin. Diabetologists, 2006–08. Mem., Council of Healthcare Professionals, 2013–. Trustee, Diabetes Care Trust (ABCD) Ltd, 2013–. Hon. DSc Brunel, 2011. *Publications:* Diabetes: a beyond basics guide, 1987, rev. edn 1992, 2nd edn 1996; Diabetes: a young persons guide, 1988; Diabetes Beyond Forty, 1988, 2nd edn as Late Onset Diabetes, 1996; Diabetes: a new guide, 1992, 2nd edn as Diabetes: the complete guide, 1996, 3rd edn 2002 (Spanish edn 2005); Thyroid Disorders, 1991, 3rd edn 2002; Practical Diabetes Care, 1996, 2nd edn 2002 (Polish edn 1997, Russian edn 2000); Diabetes Care: a practical manual, 2008, 2nd edn 2015; contrib. articles to learned jls on diabetes and other med. topics. *Recreations:* observing the natural world, enjoying ballet, theatre and classical music, very amateur photography.

HILSENRATH, Rebecca Jane; Chief Legal Officer, Equality and Human Rights Commission, since 2014; *b* Twickenham, 23 Feb. 1965; *d* of David Martin Loewe and Susan Flora Loewe; *m* 1992, Michael Hilsenrath; four *s*. *Educ:* Putney High Sch.; Newnham Coll., Cambridge (Exhibnr; BA Hons Law 1987); Coll. of Law. Trainee and asst solicitor, Linklaters, 1988–93; Legal Advisor: DfES, 2001–04; Attorney Gen.'s Office, 2004–08; CEO, LawWorks (Solicitors Pro Bono Gp), 2008–14. Member: Governance Expert Gp, Educn and Employers Taskforce, 2009–11; Wkg Gp on Access to Justice for Litigants in Person, Civil Justice Council, 2011–. Mem., Mgt Cttee, Bar Pro Bono Unit, 2008–. Trustee: Mary Ward Legal Centre, 2007–12; Nat. Pro Bono Centre, 2010–. Governor: Hertsmere Jewish Primary Sch., 1998–2009 (Chair of Govs, 2001–09); (and Trustee) Yavneh Coll., Borehamwood, 2000–10. *Publications:* (as Jane Diamond): A Place Called F, 2011; Visiting Sins, 2013. *Recreations:* spending time in family home in Llanegryn, mid-Wales, making myself heard above four teenage sons, writing novels, fostering. *Address:* 31 Deacons Hill Road, Elstree, Herts WD6 3HY. *T:* 07884 226444. *E:* rebecca@hilsenrath.com.

HILSON, Malcolm Geoffrey, OBE 2001; HM Diplomatic Service, retired; High Commissioner, Vanuatu, 1997–2000; *b* 28 Sept. 1942; *s* of Geoffrey Norman and Mildred Alice Hilson; *m* 1965, Marian Joan Freeman; two *s*. *Educ:* Bedford Modern School. Entered Foreign Office, 1961; served Jakarta, Singapore, Bombay, Kuala Lumpur and FCO; First Sec., Kaduna, 1982–86; FCO, 1986–90; New Delhi, 1990–93; FCO, 1993–97. *Recreations:* gardening, bowls, golf, bell ringing, photography. *Address:* Chestnuts, Long Lane, South Repps, Norfolk NR11 8NL.

HILSUM, Prof. Cyril, CBE 1990; PhD; FRS 1979; FREng; Visiting Professor of Physics, University College London, since 1988; *b* 17 May 1925; *s* of Benjamin and Ada Hilsum; *m* 1947, Betty Cooper (*d* 1987); one *d* (and one *d* decd). *Educ:* Raine's Sch., London; University Coll., London (BSc, PhD). FREng (FEng 1978); FIEEE 1984. Joined Royal Naval Scientific Service, 1945; Admiralty Res. Lab., 1947–50, and Services Electronics Res. Lab., 1950–64, working first on infra-red res., then on semiconductors; Royal Signals and Radar Estab., 1964–83, working first on compound semiconductors, later on flat panel electronic displays; CSO, 1974–83; Chief Scientist, Gen. Electric Co. Res. Labs, 1983–85; Dir of Res., GEC plc, 1985–93. Mem., SERC, 1984–88. Pres., Inst. of Physics, 1988–90; Hon. FInstP 2001 (FInstP 1960). Foreign Associate, US National Acad. of Engrg, 1983. Hon. DEng: Sheffield, 1992; Nottingham Trent, 1997. Max Born Medal and Prize, 1987, Glazebrook Medal and Prize, 1997, Inst. of Physics; Faraday Medal, IEE, 1988; Braun Prize, Soc. for Inf. Display, 1998; Royal Medal, Royal Soc., 2007. *Publications:* Semiconducting III-V Compounds, 1961; over 100 scientific and technical papers. *Recreation:* ballroom dancing. *Address:* 12 Eastglade, Pinner, Middx HA5 3AN. *T:* (020) 8866 8323.

See also L. Hilsum.

HILSUM, Lindsey; International Editor, Channel 4 News, since 2004; *b* 3 Aug. 1958; *d* of Prof. Cyril Hilsum, *qv* and late Betty Hilsum. *Educ:* City of Worcester Grammar Sch. for Girls; Exeter Univ. (BA Hons Spanish and French). Freelance journalist in Latin America, 1980–82; Information Officer, UNICEF, Nairobi, 1982–86; stringer, BBC and Guardian, Nairobi, 1986–89; producer, BBC World Service, 1989–93; freelance journalist, 1993–96; Channel 4 News: diplomatic corresp., 1996–2004; Beijing corresp., 2006–08. Specialist Journalist of the Year, 2003, Journalist of the Year, 2005, RTS; Amnesty Award, 2004; James Cameron Award, James Cameron Meml Trust, 2005; Charles Wheeler Award, British Journalism Rev., 2011; One World Journalist of Year, 2011; Special Internat. Award, Political Studies Assoc., 2011; Mungo Park Medal, RSGS, 2014. *Publications:* Sandstorm: Libya in the time of revolution, 2012; contribs to Granta, TLS, Sunday Telegraph, New Statesman, Observer, Sunday Times, etc. *Recreations:* horse riding, duck watching. *Address:* Channel 4 News, ITN, 200 Gray's Inn Road, WC1X 8XZ. *T:* (020) 7430 4606, *Fax:* (020) 7430 4608. *E:* lindsey.hilsum@itn.co.uk.

HILTON OF EGGARDON, Baroness *cr* 1991 (Life Peer), of Eggardon in the County of Dorset; **Jennifer Hilton,** QPM 1989; *b* 12 Jan. 1936; *d* of John Robert Hilton, CMG. *Educ:* Bedales Sch.; Manchester Univ. (BA Hons Psychology 1970; MA (Research) 1971); London Univ. (Dip. Criminology 1972; Dip. History of Art 1982). Joined Metropolitan Police, 1956; Univ. Scholarship, 1967; Police Staff Coll. (Directing Staff), 1973–74; Met. Police Management Services Dept, 1975–76; Supt then Chief Supt, Heathrow Airport, Battersea, Chiswick, 1977–83; New Scotland Yard (Traffic, Courts, Obscene Publications, Planning, Neighbourhood Policing), 1983–87; Comdr, 1984; Head of Training, Metropolitan Police, 1988–90. House of Lords: Opposition Whip, 1991–95; opposition spokesperson on the envmt, 1991–97; Member: EC Sub-Cttee on Envmt, 1991–95 (Chm., 1995–98); Science and Technol. Cttee, 1993–95, 2004–07, 2010–15; EC Sub-Cttee on Defence and Foreign Affairs, 2000–03; Chm., Adv. Panel on Works of Art, 1998–2003. Mem., OSCE Election Monitoring Panel, 1998–. *Publications:* The Gentle Arm of the Law, 1967, 2nd edn 1973; (with Sonya Hunt) Individual Development and Social Experience, 1975, 2nd edn 1981; articles in Police Jl, Police Review, etc. *Recreations:* gardening, history, art, travel. *Address:* House of Lords, SW1A 0PW.

HILTON, (Alan) John Howard; QC 1990; a Recorder, since 1986; *b* 21 Aug. 1942; *s* of Alan Howard Hilton and Barbara Mary Campbell Hilton; *m* 1st, 1968, Jasmina Laila Hamzavi; 2nd, 1978, Nicola Mary Bayley, *qv*; one *s*. *Educ:* Haileybury and Imperial Service Coll.; Manchester Univ. (LLB Hons). Called to the Bar, Middle Temple, 1964. *Recreations:* opera, cooking, magic, 19th century paintings of ladies, enjoying adjournments. *Address:* 1–2 Laurence Pountney Hill, EC4R 0EU. *T:* (020) 7933 8855. *Clubs:* Garrick, Les Six.

HILTON, Prof. (Andrew John) Boyd, DPhil; FBA 2007; Professor of Modern British History, University of Cambridge, since 2007; Fellow of Trinity College, Cambridge, since 1974; *b* 19 Jan. 1944; *s* of Kenneth Boyd Hilton and Irene Beryl Hilton; *m* 1971, Mary à Beckett; one *s* two *d*. *Educ:* William Hulme's Grammar Sch., Manchester; New Coll., Oxford (BA 1966; DPhil 1972). Res. Lectr, Christ Church, Oxford, 1969–74; Lectr, 1988–97, Reader, 1997–2007, Faculty of History, Univ. of Cambridge; Trinity College, Cambridge: Tutor, 1978–88, 1990–91, 1994–96; Sen. Tutor, 1985–88; Dean, 1991–93; Steward, 2000. James Ford Special Lectr, Univ. of Oxford, 1995. FRHistS 1986. *Publications:* Corn, Cash, Commerce: the economic policies of the Tory governments 1815–1830, 1969; The Age of Atonement: the influence of evangelicalism on social and economic thought, 1988; A Mad, Bad, and Dangerous People? England 1783–1846: the new Oxford history of England, 2006. *Recreations:* too few to mention. *Address:* 1 Carlyle Road, Cambridge CB4 3DN; Trinity College, Cambridge CB2 1TQ. *T:* (01223) 338425. *E:* ajbh1@cam.ac.uk.

HILTON, Anthony Victor; Financial Editor, Evening Standard, since 2002 (City Editor, 1984–89 and 1996–2002; Managing Director, 1989–95); Business and Economics columnist, Independent, Evening Standard, since 2012; *b* 26 Aug. 1946; *s* of Raymond Walwork Hilton and Miriam Eileen Norah Hilton (*née* Kydd); *m* 1st, 1969, Patricia Moore; one *s*; 2nd, 1989, Cynthia June Miles; two *s* one *d*. *Educ:* Univ. of Aberdeen (MA Hons Econs 1968). Financial columnist: Guardian, 1968; Observer, 1969; Daily Mail, 1971; Sunday Express, 1972; Editor, Accountancy Age, 1974–79; NY corresp., Sunday Times, 1979–82; City Editor, The Times, 1982–83; Dir, Associated Newspapers, 1989–95. Dir, London Forum, 1993–94; Mem. Council, London First, 1996–98 (Dir, 1993–96). Mem. Cttee, St John's Ambulance Charity Appeal, 1992–94. Vice Pres., Children's Film Unit, 1993–96. Vis. Prof., London Met. Univ., 2011–13. Hon. Dr Aberdeen, 2010. *Publications:* How to communicate financial information to employees, 1979; City within a state: a portrait of the City of London, 1987. *Recreations:* canal cruising, cycling, bonfires. *Address:* Priory Hall, Hadleigh, Suffolk IP7 5AZ. *T:* (01473) 823185. *Clubs:* Reform, Lansdowne.

HILTON, Boyd; *see* Hilton, A. J. B.

HILTON, Brian James George, CB 1992; non-executive director of public companies; Deputy Secretary, Department of Trade and Industry, 1994–99; *b* 21 April 1940; *s* of late Percival William Hilton and Gladys Hilton (*née* Haylett); *m* 1965, Mary Margaret Kirkpatrick (separated); one *s* two *d*. *Educ:* St Marylebone Grammar Sch., London. Export Credits Guarantee Dept, 1958–68; Board of Trade, 1968–71; Foreign and Commonwealth Office, 1971–74: First Secretary to UK Delegn to OECD, Paris; Asst Sec., Dept of Industry, 1976–84; RCDS 1981; Hd, Financial Services Div., DTI, 1984–87; Hd, Central Unit (Under Sec.), DTI, 1987–89; Dep. Sec., MAFF, 1989–91; Dir, Citizen's Charter Unit, Cabinet Office, 1991–94. Complaints Ombudsman, LIFFE, 2007–10. Chm., Channel Mgt Agency, Lloyd's, 2014–; non-exec. Dir, SCOR Insurance Ltd, 2009–. Foundation Governor, Hampden Gurney Primary Sch., London W1, 1976–; Gov., RAU (formerly RAC), Cirencester, 1990–91, 2005–13 (Chm., 2011–13). MRAC 2004. *Recreations:* cricket, Rugby, music, opera, gardening, fly fishing. *Address:* 1 Lake View, Shoyswell Manor, Sheepstreet Lane, Etchingham, E Sussex TN19 7AZ.

HILTON, Cara Laura; Member (Lab) Dunfermline, Scottish Parliament, since Oct. 2013; *b* Falkirk, 1975; *d* of Ian Peattie and Catherine Peattie, *qv*; *m* 2006, Simon Hilton; two *s* one *d*. *Educ:* Grangemouth High Sch.; Open Univ. (Dip. Child Develt 2008); Univ. of Strathclyde (BA Politics 1997); Univ. of Leicester (MA Eur. Law (Dist.) 2004). Asst Statistical Officer, NHS Exec., 1997–98; Educn Planning Asst, City of York Council, 1998–99; res. asst, USDAW, 1999–2007; researcher, Karen Whitefield, MSP, 2007–11; Parly Asst, Thomas Docherty, MP, 2011–13. Mem. (Lab) Fife Council, 2012–. *Recreations:* spending time with family and friends, cooking. *Address:* Unit 14, Dunfermline Business Centre, Izatt Avenue, Dunfermline KY11 3BZ. *T:* (01383) 735090. *E:* cara.hilton.msp@scottish.parliament.uk.

HILTON, John Howard; *see* Hilton, A. J. H.

HILTON, Jonathan James Robert, CEng, FIMechE; Commercial Director, Torotrak PLC, since 2014; *b* Eastbourne, 14 April 1964; *s* of John and Anne Hilton; *m* 2000, Judy Oliver; one *s* (and one *s* decd). *Educ:* Hatfield Poly. (BSc Hons Mech. Engrg 1986). CEng 1990; FIMechE 2002. Undergrad. apprentice, 1982–87, engine designer, 1987–89, Rolls Royce; Mech. engr, Graesby Dynamics Ltd, 1989–91; engine designer, 1991–94, Chief Engr, 1995–97, Cosworth; Chief Engr, TWR F1 Engines, 1998–2002; Tech. Dir, Engine Div., Renault F1 Team, 2003–06; Co-founder and Man. Dir, Flybrid Automotive Ltd, 2007–13. Trustee, IMechE, 2011– (Vice Pres., 2013–). *Publications:* named inventor on over 40 published patents. *Recreations:* family, sailing, surfing, motorsport. *Address:* Torotrak PLC, 1 Aston Way, Leyland PR26 7UX. *T:* (01772) 900900. *E:* jon.hilton@torotrak.com.

HILTON, Matthew James; Deputy Vice Chancellor (Operations) and University Secretary, Kingston University, since 2014; *b* 25 Jan. 1967; *s* of Ronald and Mary Hilton; *m* 1995, Elizabeth Sarah Jones; two *s* one *d*. *Educ:* St John Fisher High Sch., Wigan; Univ. of Sheffield (BA 1988, MA 1989); Imperial Coll., London (MBA 2000). English teacher, Prague, 1990–92; joined DTI, 1992; Private Sec. to Sec. of State and Minister for Energy and Industry, 1994–97; Dir, Business Support Rev., 2001–03; Principal Private Sec. to Sec. of State, 2003–05; Dir of Strategy and Communications, then Dir of Communications, DTI, subseq. BERR, 2005–07; Dir, Employment Relations, BERR, subseq. BIS, 2007–11; Dir of Higher Educn Student Support, 2011–12, Dir of Higher Educn, 2012–14, BIS. Trustee, Nat. Deaf Children's Soc., 2006– (Chm., 2011–). *Address:* Kingston University, River House, 53–57 High Street, Kingston upon Thames, Surrey KT1 1LQ. *Club:* Gentlemen of Lewes Cricket.

HILTON, Nicola Mary; *see* Bayley, N. M.

HILTON, Rachel; *see* Whetstone, R. M. J.

HILTON, Ronald; Chief Executive, Staffordshire County Council, 2007–10; Managing Partner, Ron Hilton Consultancy Ltd, since 2010; *b* Washington, Co. Durham, 16 Feb. 1946; *s* of James and Muriel Hilton; *m* 1968, Frances Biggs; two *s*. *Educ:* Washington Grammar Sch.; Teesside Poly. (BSc Hons). Dir, Worcester CC, 1980–85; Dep. Chief Exec., Dir of Envmt and Econ. Develt, and Dir, Stockport Direct Services, Stockport CC, 1985–2002; Corporate Dir of Develt, 2002–05, Dep. Chief Exec., 2005–07, Staffs CC. Clerk to Lord Lieutenancy of Staffs, 2007–10; Sec., Adv. Cttee, Staffs Magistrates. Chm., W Midlands Assembly Regl Adv. Gp, 2003–07. Dir, Stockport Business Link, 1998–2001. Mem., NW Business Adv. Service, 1998–2002. Econ. Develt Advr to LGA, 1997–2002. Non-exec. Dir, South Staffs and Shropshire NHS Foundn Trust, 2010– (Vice Chm. and Sen. Ind. Dir, 2012–). Mem., Regeneration and Res. Cttee, Co. Surveyors' Soc., 2003–07. Trustee, Salford Univ. Campus, 1995–2002; Gov., Staffordshire Univ., 2007–10. FRSA 2008. *Recreation:* golf. *Club:* Brocton Hall Golf.

HILTON, Prof. Sean Robert, MD; FRCGP; Professor of General Practice and Primary Care, St George's (formerly St George's Hospital Medical School), University of London, 1993–2012, now Emeritus (Director, International Relations, 2011–12); Professor of Medical Education, University of Nicosia, since 2012; *b* 31 Oct. 1949; *s* of Harold and Doris Hilton; *m* 1994, Lesley Wood; two *s* one *d*. *Educ:* Weymouth Grammar Sch.; St George's Hosp. Med. Sch., London (MB BS 1974; MD 1991). FRCGP 1990. NHS GP Principal, Kingston-upon-Thames, 1979–2009; St George's Hospital Medical School, University of London, subseq. St George's, University of London: Sen. Lectr in Gen. Practice, 1987–93; Dean of Undergrad. Medicine, 1997–2002; Vice-Principal, 2003–07; Dep. Principal, 2008–11; non-exec. Dir, St George's Healthcare Trust, 2003–11. Gov., Anglo-European Coll. of Chiropractic, 2003–12 (Chm., 2006–12); Mem. Council, Acad. of Medical Educators, 2007– (Pres., 2011–14). Trustee, Princess Alice Hospice, Esher, 2012–. FHEA 1999; FAcadMed 2009. Hon. DSc Kingston, 2012. *Publications:* (with M. Levy) Asthma in Practice, 1987, 4th edn 1999; (jtly) Asthma at Your Fingertips, 1993, 3rd edn 2006; more than 100 peer reviewed papers and book chapters on gen. practice, primary care and med. educn. *Recreations:* music (especially Schubert and songs of Jackson Browne), gardening and trees, football, cricket, WW1. *Address:* St George's, University of London, Cranmer Terrace, SW17 0RE. *T:* (020) 8286 2857. *E:* shilton.shx@gmail.com. *Clubs:* MCC; 1942.

HIMSWORTH, Emma Katherine, (Mrs N. P. Buller); QC 2012; *b* London, 17 Feb. 1968; *d* of Prof. Richard Lawrence Himsworth, *qv*; *m* 2000, Nigel Pearson Buller; two *s*, and one step *d*. *Educ:* South Hampstead High Sch.; Univ. of Edinburgh (BSc Hons Biochem.); City Univ. (DipLaw). Called to the Bar, Gray's Inn, 1993; in practice, One Essex Court, 1995–, specialising in intellectual property law and related aspects of commercial and competition law; appointed to hear trade mark appeals, 2013–. Liveryman, Goldsmiths' Co., 2000. *Address:* One Essex Court, Temple, EC4Y 9AR. *T:* (020) 7583 2000, *Fax:* (020) 7583 0118. *E:* ehimsworth@oeclaw.co.uk.

HIMSWORTH, Prof. Richard Lawrence, MD; FRCP; Professor of Health Research and Development, 1993–2002, and Director, Institute of Public Health, 1999–2002, Cambridge University; Fellow, Girton College, Cambridge, since 1995; *b* 14 June 1937; *s* of Sir Harold Himsworth, KCB, FRS; *m* 1966, Sara Margaret Tattersall; two *s* one *d*. *Educ:* Westminster Sch.; Trinity Coll., Cambridge (MB BChir 1961, MD 1971); University Coll. Hosp. Med. Sch.; University Coll. London (MA in History of Medicine 2005). FRCP 1977; FRCPE 1988; FRCPGlas 1990; FFPH (FFPHM 2002). Lectr in Medicine, UCH Med. Sch., 1967–71; MRC Travelling Fellow, New York, 1969–70; MRC Scientific Staff, Clinical Res. Centre, 1971–85: Asst Dir, 1978–82; Head, Endocrinology Res. Gp, 1979–85; Consultant Physician, Northwick Park Hosp., 1972–85; Regius Prof. of Medicine, Univ. of Aberdeen, and Hon. Consultant Physician, Aberdeen Royal Infirmary, 1985–93. Hon. Prof., UEA, 1994. Associate Dir, R&D, Anglia and Oxford RHA, 1994–98; Dir, R&D, Eastern (formerly Anglia and Oxford) Region, NHS Exec., DoH, 1998–2002. Member: NW Thames RHA, 1982–85; Scottish Nat. Med. Adv. Cttee, 1990–92; Gen. Council, King Edward's Hosp. Fund for London, 1980– (Mem. London Commns, 1990–92, 1995–97). Mem. Ct, Imperial Coll., London, 2002–09. Liveryman, 1976–, Mem. Ct of Assts, 1995–, Prime Warden, 2007–08, Goldsmiths' Co. Hon. DSc Anglia Poly., 2000. *Publications:* scientific and medical papers. *Address:* Park House, 39 High Street, Balsham, Cambridge CB21 4DJ. *T:* (01223) 893975.
See also E. K. Himsworth.

HINCE, Dr Trevor Anthony; Director and Secretary, Lister Institute for Preventive Medicine, since 2004; *b* 17 Aug. 1949; *s* of late Gerald Arthur Hince and Beryl Doris Hince (*née* Franklin); *m* 1st, 1972, Carol Jean Tarabella (marr. diss. 1996); 2nd, 1996, Sarah Elizabeth Verrall. *Educ:* Forest Grammar Sch., Winnersh; University Coll. London (BSc Hons 1971); Middlesex Hosp. Med. Sch. (PhD 1976); Brunel Univ./Henley Mgt Coll. (MSc 1988). Middlesex Hospital Medical School: Research Asst, 1971–76; Temp. Lectr in Pathology, 1976–79; Cancer Research Campaign: Asst Scientific Sec., 1980–86; Scientific Sec., 1986–89; Dep. Dir, Scientific Dept, 1989–96; Scientific Dir, 1996–2002; Dep. Dir Gen., 1998–2002; Dir, Res. Mgt and Planning, CRUK, 2002–04. Mem., Inst. of Cancer Res., 2004–. Trustee, Gibb Res. Fellowship Fund, 2004–15. *Publications:* papers in scientific jls. *Recreations:* walking, gardening, music. *Address:* (office) PO Box 1083, Bushey, Herts WD23 9AG.

HINCH, Prof. Edward John, PhD; FRS 1997; Professor of Fluid Mechanics, University of Cambridge, 1998–2014; Fellow of Trinity College, Cambridge, since 1971; *b* 4 March 1947; *s* of Joseph Edward Hinch and Mary Grace Hinch (*née* Chandler); *m* 1969, Christine Bridges; one *s* one *d*. *Educ:* Edmonton County Grammar Sch.; Trinity Coll., Cambridge (BA 1968; PhD 1973). Asst Lectr, 1972–75, Lectr, 1975–94, Reader, 1994–98, Univ. of Cambridge. Fellow, APS, 2003; MAE 2011; For. Associate, NAE, 2012. Hon Dr Inst Nat. Poly. de Toulouse, 2010. Fluid Mechanics Prize, Euro Mech, 2010; Fluid Mechanics Prize, APS, 2010. Chevalier de l'ordre national du Mérite (France), 1997. *Publications:* Perturbation Methods, 1991; papers on fluid mechanics and its applications in scientific jls. *Address:* Trinity College, Cambridge CB2 1TQ. *T:* (01223) 338427.

HINCHCLIFFE, Peter Robert Mossom, CMG 1988; CVO 1979; HM Diplomatic Service, retired; Ambassador to Jordan, 1993–97; *b* 9 April 1937; *s* of Herbert Peter and Jeannie Hinchcliffe; *m* 1965, Archbold Harriet Siddall; three *d*. *Educ:* Elm Park, Killylea, Co. Armagh, Prep. Sch.; Radley Coll.; Trinity Coll., Dublin (BA (Hons), MA). Military service, short service commission, W Yorks Regt, 1955–57; TCD, Dublin Univ., 1957–61; HMOCS: West Aden Protectorate, South Arabian Fedn, 1961–67; Admin. Asst, Birmingham Univ., 1968–69; FCO: 1st Sec., Near Eastern Dept, 1969–70; 1st Sec., UK Mission to UN, 1971–74; 1st Sec. and Head of Chancery, Kuwait, 1974–76; Asst Head of Science and Technology and Central and Southern African Depts, FCO, 1976–78; Dep. High Comr, Dar es Salaam, 1978–81; Consul-Gen., Dubai, 1981–85; Hd of Information Dept, FCO, 1985–87; Ambassador to Kuwait, 1987–90; High Comr to Zambia, 1990–93. Chm., Hutton and Paxton Community Council, 2001–05. Hon. Fellow, Edin. Univ., 1997; Hon. Adjunct Fellow, Curtin Univ., WA, 2002. *Publications:* Time to Kill Sparrows (poetry anthology), 1999; (with B. Milton-Edwards): Jordan: a Hashemite Legacy, 2001, 2nd edn 2008; Conflicts in the Middle East since 1945, 2001, 3rd edn 2007; Without Glory in Arabia: the British retreat from Aden, 2006. *Recreations:* golf, tennis, writing poetry. *Address:* The Old Bakery, Willis Wynd, Duns, Berwickshire TD11 3AD. *Clubs:* East India, Devonshire, Sports and Public Schools; Duns Golf; Royal Co. Down Golf (Newcastle, Co. Down).

HINCHCLIFFE, Dr Peter Roy; environmental consultant, since 2004; *b* 27 May 1946; *s* of Herbert Hinchcliffe and Lucy Hinchcliffe (*née* Avis); *m* 1969, Carole Musetti; one *s* one *d*. *Educ:* Liverpool Univ. (BSc; PhD 1970). FCIWEM 1991. Chemist, Lancs and Western Sea Fisheries Cttee, 1970–75; joined Department of the Environment, 1975: Chief Scientist, Marine Pollution Control Unit, 1986–91; Head: Waste Tech. Div., 1991–96; Chemicals and Biotechnol. Div., 1996–2002; Sec., Royal Commn on Envmtl Pollution, 2002–04. Gulf Medal, 1992. *Publications:* contrib. papers on marine pollution to Jl Marine Biol. Assoc. and other jls. *Recreations:* photography, computers, gardening, music. *Address:* 25 Dinorben Close, Fleet, Hants GU52 7SL. *T:* (01252) 684157. *E:* peter@hinchcliffe.me.uk.

HINCHINGBROOKE, Viscount; Luke Timothy Charles Montagu; non-executive Director, Met Film Ltd, Ealing Studios, since 2003; *b* 5 Dec. 1969; *er s* and *heir* of Earl of Sandwich, *qv*; *m* 2004, Julie, *d* of Thomas L. Fisher, Chicago; two *s*. *Educ:* Westminster Sch.; Columbia Univ., NY. Dir, Wide Multimedia, 1997–2001. *Heir:* *s* Hon. William James Hayman Montagu, *b* 2 Nov. 2004. *Address:* c/o Mapperton House, Beaminster, Dorset DT8 3NR.

HINCHLIFFE, David Martin; consultant on health and social care policy; *b* 14 Oct. 1948; *s* of late Robert Victor Hinchliffe and Muriel Hinchliffe; *m* 1982, Julia (*née* North); one *s* one *d*. *Educ:* Lawefield Lane Primary Sch., Wakefield; Cathedral C of E Secondary Modern Sch., Wakefield; Leeds Polytechnic (Cert. in Social Work); Bradford Univ. (MA Social Work and Community Work); Huddersfield Polytechnic (Cert Ed); Leeds Univ. (MA Local and Regl Hist.). Social Work with Leeds Social Services, 1968–79; Social Work Tutor, Kirklees Metropolitan Borough Council, 1980–87. MP (Lab) Wakefield, 1987–2005. An opposition front bench spokesman on personal social services and community care, 1992–95. Chairman: Health Select Cttee, 1997–2005; Select Cttee on Adoption and Children Bill, 2001 and 2002. Chm., Nat. Coal Mining Mus. for England, 2013–. Hon. Mem., Nat. Council, NSPCC. *Publications:* Rugby's Class War, 2000; (ed) A Westminster XIII: Parliamentarians and Rugby League, 2002; (jtly) Rugby's Berlin Wall, 2005; They Walked On Water: the story of Wembley, 1968, 2013. *Recreations:* Rugby League—supporter of Wakefield Trinity RLFC, genealogy, local history. *Club:* Wakefield Labour.

HINCKS, Tim; Chairman, Endemol UK, since 2012 (Chief Executive Officer, 2007–12); President, Endemol Shine Group, since 2014 (President, Endemol Group, 2012–14); *b* Windsor, 18 Aug. 1967; *s* of David Hincks and Geraldine Hincks; *m* 2000, Pippa Healy; two *s* one *d*. *Educ:* Weald Comp. Sch., Billingshurst; Bristol Univ. (BSocSc Econs and Politics). Hair gel factory, Billingshurst, 1989–90; Policy Researcher, Nat. Consumer Council, 1990; TV Researcher, Food and Drink prog., BBC Westminster and Newsnight, BBC, 1990–99; Chief Creative Officer, Endemol UK, 1999–2007. Mem., Exec. Cttee, Edinburgh Internat. Television Fest., 2006– (Exec. Chm., 2007–10). *Recreations:* my kids, Arsenal FC, member of popular rock and beat combo No Expectations. *E:* Tim.Hincks@endemoluk.com.

HIND, Andrew Fleming, CB 2011; FCA; Visiting Professor of Charity Governance and Finance, Cass Business School, City University, since 2011; Editor, Charity Finance Magazine, since 2011; *b* 29 Sept. 1955; *s* of Andrew Hind and Mary Hind; *m* 1985, Christina; three *s*. *Educ:* Portsmouth Grammar Sch.; Southampton Univ. (BSc). FCA 1979. Ernst & Young, 1976–80; Pannell Kerr Forster, Kenya, 1980–83; Divl Financial Controller, Balfour Beatty Ltd, 1983–86; Dir of Finance, 1986–89, Dep. Chief Exec., 1989–91, ActionAid; Dir of Finance and Corporate Services, Barnardo's, 1992–95; Dir of Finance and Business Develt, 1995–2002, Chief Operating Officer, 2002–04, BBC World Service; Chief Exec., Charity Commn, 2004–10. Charity Finance Directors' Group: Co-founder, 1988; Mem., Exec. Cttee, 1988–94; Chm., 1992–94. Member: Commn on Effectiveness and the Voluntary Sector, NCVO, 1990; Charity Awards Judges Panel, 2001–04, 2011– (Chm., 2003–04, 2011–); Audit Cttee, Commonwealth Secretariat, 2004–06; Commn on the Future of Volunteering, 2006–08; Professional Standards Authy for Health and Social Care (formerly Council for Healthcare Regulatory Excellence), 2009– (Chm., Audit Cttee, 2009–); Information Commn, 2010–. Chm., Public Sector Adv. Bd, ICAEW, 2007–10. Trustee: Internat. Fundraising Gp, 1992–95; VSO, 1995–98; UNICEF UK, 1995–2002 (Treas., 1996–2002); Baring Foundn, 2010–; Trustee and Treas., Diana, Princess of Wales Meml Fund, 1999–2004. *Publications:* (ed jtly) Charity Managers and Charity Trustees - Meeting the Challenges of the 1990s, 1993; (ed) The Charity Finance Handbook, 1994; The Governance and Management of Charities, 1995. *Recreations:* golf, tennis, travel, collecting old books on Africa. *Address:* 11 Byng Road, High Barnet, Herts EN5 4NW. *T:* 07703 109063. *E:* andrew@andrewhind.co.uk.

HIND, Rt Rev. Dr John William; Bishop of Chichester, 2001–12; an Honorary Assistant Bishop, Diocese of Portsmouth, since 2012; *b* 19 June 1945; *s* of late Harold Hind and Joan Mary Hind; *m* 1966, Janet Helen McLintock; three *s*. *Educ:* Watford Grammar Sch.; Leeds Univ. (BA 1966). Asst Master, Leeds Modern Sch., 1966–69; Asst Lectr, King Alfred's Coll., Winchester, 1969–70; Cuddesdon Theol Coll.; Deacon 1972, Priest 1973; Asst Curate, St John's, Catford, 1972–76; Vicar, Christ Church, Forest Hill, 1976–82 and Priest-in-Charge, St Paul's, Forest Hill, 1981–82; Principal, Chichester Theol Coll., 1982–91; Area Bishop of Horsham, 1991–93; Bishop of Gibraltar in Europe, 1993–2001. Canon Residentiary and Bursalis Preb., Chichester Cathedral, 1982–90. Mem., H of L, 2008–12. Chm., Faith and Order Commn (formerly Faith and Order Adv. Gp), C of E, 1991–2012; Mem., Faith and Order Commn, WCC, 1999–2014 (Vice-Moderator, 2006–14). DD Lambeth, 2009. *Recreations:* cooking, languages.

HIND, Kenneth Harvard, CBE 1995; barrister; *b* 15 Sept. 1949; *s* of George Edward and Brenda Hind; one *s* one *d*; *m* 2008, Sue Hall, JP; one step *d*. *Educ:* Woodhouse Grove Sch., Bradford; Leeds Univ. (LLB 1971); Inns of Court Sch. of Law. Pres., Leeds Univ. Union, 1971–72. Called to the Bar, Gray's Inn, 1973; practised North Eastern circuit, 1973–83. MP (C) West Lancashire, 1983–92; contested (C): W Lancashire, 1992; Selby, 1997. PPS to Minister of State: for Defence Procurement, 1986–87; for Employment, 1987–89; for Northern Ireland, 1989–90; PPS to Sec. of State for Northern Ireland, 1990–92. Officer, 1995–97, Chm., 1997–2002, Conservative Candidates Assoc. Member: Soc. of Conservative Lawyers, 1983–; Justice, Internat. Commn of Jurists, 1983–. Mem. (C), Ribble Valley BC, 2005–. Sen. Vice Chm., Ribble Valley Conservative Assoc., 2009– (Chm., 2006–09); Mem., Conservative Nat. Convention. Hon. Vice-Pres., Central and West Lancs Chamber of Industry and Commerce, 1983–92. *Recreations:* music, sailing Enterprise, cricket. *Address:* Newton Chambers, Newton in Bowland, Clitheroe, Lancs BB7 3DZ; 14 Water Street, Liverpool L2 8TD; 18 Ribblesdale Place, Preston PR1 3HA.

HINDE, Prof. Robert Aubrey, CBE 1988; FRS 1974; FBA; Master of St John's College, Cambridge, 1989–94 (Fellow, 1951–54, 1958–89 and since 1994); *b* 26 Oct. 1923; *s* of late Dr and Mrs E. B. Hinde, Norwich; *m* 1st, 1948, Hester Cecily (marr. diss. 1971), *d* of late C. R. V. Coutts; two *s* two *d*; 2nd, 1971, Joan Gladys, *d* of F. J. Stevenson; two *d*. *Educ:* Oundle Sch.; St John's Coll., Cambridge; Balliol Coll., Oxford (Hon. Fellow, 1986). Served Coastal Comd, RAF, Flt-Lt, 1941–45. Research Asst, Edward Grey Inst., Univ. of Oxford, 1948–50; Curator, Ornithological Field Station (now sub-Dept of Animal Behaviour), Madingley, Cambridge, 1950–65; St John's Coll., Cambridge: Steward, 1956–58; Tutor, 1958–63; Royal Soc. Res. Prof., Cambridge Univ., 1963–89. Hon. Dir, MRC Unit on Develt and Integration of Behaviour, 1970–89. Hitchcock Prof., Univ. of California, 1979; Green Vis. Scholar, Univ. of Texas, 1983. Mem. Council, Royal Soc., 1985–87. Croonian Lect., Royal Soc., 1990. Chairman: Pugwash UK, 2002–06; British Pugwash Gp, 2003–08. Mem., Academia Europaea, 1990. Hon. Member: Assoc. for the Study of Animal Behaviour, 1987; Deutsche

Ornithologische Ges., 1988; For. Hon. Mem., Amer. Acad. of Arts and Sciences, 1974; For. Associate, Nat. Acad. of Scis, USA, 1978; Hon. Fellow, Amer. Ornithologists' Union, 1977; Hon. FBPsS 1981; Hon. FRCPsych 1988; Hon. FTCD, 1990; Hon. FBA 2002. Hon. ScD: Univ. Libre, Brussels, 1974; Paris (Nanterre), 1979; Stirling, 1991; Göteborg, 1991; Edinburgh, 1992; Western Ontario, 1996; Oxford, 1998. Scientific Medal, Zoological Soc., 1961; Leonard Cammer Medal in Psychiatry, Columbia Coll., NY, 1980; Osman Hill Award, Primate Soc. of GB, 1980; Albert Einstein Award for Psychiatry, Albert Einstein Coll. of Medicine, NY, 1987; Huxley Medal, RAI, 1990; Distinguished Scientists Award, Soc. for Res. in Child Develt, 1991; Distinguished Career Award, Internat. Soc. for Study of Personal Relationships, 1992; Frink Medal, Zool Soc., 1992; G. Stanley Hall Medal, Amer. Psychol Assoc., 1993; Royal Medal, Royal Soc., 1996; Society's Medal, Assoc. for Study of Animal Behaviour, 1997; Bowlby/Ainsworth Award, Centre for Mental Health Promotion and NY Attachment Consortium, 2003. *Publications:* Animal Behaviour: a synthesis of Ethology and Comparative Psychology, 1966; (ed) Bird Vocalizations: their relations to current problems in biology and psychology, 1969; (ed jtly) Short Term Changes in Neural Activity and Behaviour, 1970; (ed) Non-Verbal Communication, 1972; (ed jtly) Constraints on Learning, 1973; Biological Bases of Human Social Behaviour, 1974; (ed jtly) Growing Points in Ethology, 1976; Towards Understanding Relationships, 1979; Ethology: its nature and relations with other sciences, 1982; (jtly) Defended to Death, 1982; (ed and contrib.) Primate Social Relationships: an integrated approach, 1983; (ed jtly) Social Relationships and Cognitive Development, 1985; Individuals, Relationships and Culture, 1987; (ed jtly) Relationships within Families, 1988; (ed jtly) Aggression and War, 1989; (ed jtly) Education for Peace, 1989; (ed and contrib.) The Institution of War, 1991; (ed jtly) Co-operation and Prosocial Behaviour, 1991; (ed jtly) War: a necessary evil? 1994; Relationships: a dialectical perspective, 1997; Why Gods Persist, 1999, 2nd edn 2010; Why Good is Good: the bases of morality, 2002; (jtly) War No More, 2003; Bending the Rules, 2007; Ending War, 2008; Changing How We Live, 2011; (ed jtly) Culture Evolves, 2011; Our Culture of Greed: when is enough enough?, 2015; sundry papers in biological and psychological journals. *Address:* St John's College, Cambridge CB2 1TP. *T:* (01223) 339356; Park Lane, Madingley, Cambridge CB23 8AL. *T:* (01954) 211816.

HINDLEY, Estella Jacqueline; QC 1992; **Her Honour Judge Hindley;** a Circuit Judge, since 1997; Designated Family Judge for Birmingham, since 2008; a Senior Circuit Judge, since 2010; *b* 11 Oct. 1948; *d* of Arthur John Hindley and Olive Maud (*née* Stanley); *m* 1980, John Gilbert Harvey; one *s*. *Educ:* Univ. of Hull (LLB Hons). Called to the Bar, Gray's Inn, 1971; a Recorder, 1989–97. Mem., Parole Bd, 1998–. Chm., Birmingham Children's Hosp. NHS Trust, 2000–04. Pres., Birmingham Medico-Legal Soc., 1999–2001; Sec., UK Assoc. of Women Judges, 2006–13. *Recreations:* book collecting, music, theatre, painting. *Address:* The Priory Courts, 33 Bull Street, Birmingham B4 6DW. *T:* (0121) 681 3000.

HINDLEY, Julia Carolyn; *see* Newton, J. C.

HINDLEY, Michael John; Director, Michael Hindley and Associates, since 1999; Member (Lab), Lancashire County Council, 2001–05; *b* 11 April 1947; *s* of John and Edna Hindley; *m* 1980, Ewa Agnieszka (*née* Leszczyc-Grabianka); one *d*. *Educ:* Clitheroe Royal Grammar School; London University (BA Hons); Lancaster University (MA); Free University of West Berlin; Univ. of Glamorgan (Postgrad. Dip. Internat. Law). Labour Councillor, Hyndburn District Council, 1979–84 (Leader, 1981–84); contested (Lab) Blackpool North, 1983. MEP (Lab) Lancashire E, 1984–94, Lancashire S, 1994–99. Mem., Exec. Bd, War on Want, 1998–2009. Special Advr, Centre for Socio-Eco-Nomic Develt, Geneva. Associate Prof., Georgetown Univ., Washington, 1993–2008. Advr on Ext. Relations, Blackburn Coll., Lancs, 2007–14; Expert Advr on Trade Issues, Eur. Econ. and Social Cttee, 2009–. *Recreations:* walking, reading, music, travel. *Address:* 27 Commercial Road, Great Harwood, Lancs BB6 7HX. *T:* (01254) 887017. *Club:* Reform.

HINDLEY, Stephen Lewis, CBE 2006; DL; FICE, FCIOB, FRICS; Executive Chairman, Midas Group Ltd, since 2002; *b* 11 March 1949; s of Arthur Stanley Hindley and Ann Hindley; *m* 1973, Moira Ann Williamson; two *d*. *Educ:* St Philip's Grammar Sch., Birmingham; Salford Univ. (BSc). FICE 1997; FCIOB 2001; FRICS 2013. Civil engr, Trafalgar House Gp, 1970–76; Project Manager, John Mowlem plc, 1976–89; Man. Dir, E. Thomas (subsid. co. of John Mowlem), 1989–98; Chief Exec., 1998–2001, Chm. and CEO, 2001–05, Midas Gp Ltd. Chairman: Construction Council, CBI; Heart of the SW Local Enterprise Partnership; Devon Community Foundn. Trustee, Children's Hospice SW. DL Devon, 2009. *Recreations:* running, hill-walking, sailing, golf, classic cars, motor sport. *Address:* Midas Group, Midas House, Pynes Hill, Exeter EX2 5WS. *T:* (01392) 356200, *Fax:* (0870) 8553814. *E:* shindley@midasgroup.co.uk. *Club:* Royal Automobile.

HINDLIP, 6th Baron *cr* 1886; **Charles Henry Allsopp;** Bt 1880; *b* 5 Aug. 1940; *e s* of 5th Baron Hindlip and Cecily Valentine Jane, *o d* of Lt-Col Malcolm Borwick, DSO; *S* father, 1993; *m* 1968, Fiona Victoria Jean Atherley (*d* 2014), *d* of late Hon. William Johnston McGowan, 2nd *s* of 1st Baron McGowan, KBE; one *s* three *d*. *Educ:* Eton. Coldstream Guards, 1959–62; joined Christie's, 1962; Gen. Manager, Christie's New York, 1965–70; Christie, Manson & Woods: Dir, 1970; Dep. Chm., 1985; Chm., 1986–96; Chm., Christie's Internat., 1996–2002; Dep. Chm., Agnew's, 2003–04. Trustee, Chatham Historic Dockyard, 1989–2000. Chevalier de la Légion d'Honneur (France), 1998. *Recreations:* painting, shooting, ski-ing. *Heir: s* Hon. Henry William Allsopp [*b* 8 June 1973; *m* 2012, Hon. Naomi Gummer, *e d* of Baron Chadlington, *qv*]. *Address:* Lydden House, King's Stag, Dorset DT10 2AU. *Clubs:* White's, Pratt's; Corviglia Ski.

HINDMARCH, Anya, MBE 2009; Founder and Executive Chairman, since 1987, and Chief Creative Officer, since 2011, Anya Hindmarch; *b* Burnham, 7 May 1968; *d* of Michael and Susan Hindmarch; *m* 1996, Hugh James Seymour; four *s* one *d*. *Educ:* New Hall Sch. Business Ambassador, UKTI, 2010–; Mem., Adv. Bd for Mayor of London, 2013–. Mem. Exec. Bd, British Fashion Council, 2010–. Trustee: RA, 2008–; Design Mus., 2009–; Mothers for Children, 2009–. Gov., Univ. of the Arts, 2010–. Hon. DArts Anglia Ruskin, 2011. Accessories Designer of Year, 2001, Designer Brand of Year, 2007, British Fashion Council; Luxury Briefing Award for Excellence, 2001, 2010; Glamour mag. Award, 2006, 2007; Elle Style Awards for Outstanding Achievement, 2008; Accessory Designer Award, British Fashion Awards, 2014. *Recreations:* art, architecture, graphic design, photography. *Address:* Anya Hindmarch Ltd, The Stable Block, Plough Brewery, 516 Wandsworth Road, SW8 3JX. *T:* (020) 7501 0177, *Fax:* (020) 7501 0170. *E:* Daisy@anyahindmarch.com.

HINDMARSH, Irene, JP, MA; Principal, St Aidan's College, University of Durham, 1970–88; Second Pro-Vice-Chancellor, University of Durham, 1982–85; *b* 22 Oct. 1923; *d* of Albert Hindmarsh and Elizabeth (*née* White). *Educ:* Heaton High Sch.; Lady Margaret Hall, Oxford (MA Hons French); King's Coll., Univ. of Durham (PGCE). Taught at St Paul's Girls' Sch., London, 1947–49, Rutherford High Sch., Newcastle upon Tyne, 1949–59; Interchange Teacher, Lycée de Jeunes Filles, Dax, Landes, France, 1954–55; Lectr in Educn and French, King's Coll., Durham, 1959–64; Headmistress, Birkenhead High Sch., GPDST, 1964–70. Vis. Prof., New York State Univ., Syracuse, Cornell, Harvard, 1962; Delegate of Internat. Fedn of Univ. Women to UNO, NY, to Commns on Human Rights and Status of Women, 1962; Vis. Professor: Fu-Dan Univ., Shanghai, 1979, and again, 1980; SW China Teachers' Univ., Beibei, Sichuan, and Fu-Dan Univ., Shanghai, 1986. Delegate/Translator to internat. confs of FIPESO, 1963–70; Chairman: Internat. Cttee of Headmistresses' Assoc., 1966–70; Internat. Panel of Joint Four, 1967–70. Mem. of Council, Chillingham Wild Cattle Assoc., 1988–98. Editor, Internat. Bull. of AHM, 1966–70. JP Birkenhead 1966, Durham 1974. FRSA 1989. *Publications:* various articles on educnl topics in AGM papers of Assoc. of Head Mistresses; contribs to prelim. papers of FIPESO meetings; seminar papers to symposia on lit. topics, Sèvres, under auspices of Council of Europe; contrib. re St Aidan's to Durham History from the Air. *Recreations:* travel, music, theatre, films, art, architecture. *Address:* 8 Dickens Wynd, Merryoaks, Elvet Moor, Durham DH1 3QR.

HINDS, Damian Patrick George; MP (C) East Hampshire, since 2010; Exchequer Secretary, HM Treasury, since 2015; *b* London, 27 Nov. 1969; *s* of Francis Hinds and Bridget Hinds; *m* 2007, Jacqui Morel; one *s* two *d*. *Educ:* St Ambrose Grammar Sch., Altrincham; Trinity Coll., Oxford (BA PPE 1992). Res. analyst, Mercer Mgt Consulting, 1992–95; Holiday Inn: Pricing Manager, 1995–96, Mktg Manager, 1996–99, Holiday Inn Europe; Vice Pres., e-Commerce, 2000–01, Vice Pres., Commercial, 2001–03, Holiday Inn and Intercontinental, EMEA; Strategy Dir, Greene King plc, 2005–07; freelance advr to hotel trade, 2003–05 and 2007–10. An Asst Govt Whip, 2014–15. *Recreation:* music. *Address:* House of Commons, SW1A 0AA. *T:* (020) 7219 7057. *E:* damian.hinds.mp@parliament.uk.

HINDS, Prof. Edward Allen, DPhil; FRS 2004; Professor of Physics, Imperial College London, since 2002; *b* 8 Sept. 1949; *s* of Laurence and Ruth Hinds; *m* 1972, Ann Carter; one *s* three *d*. *Educ:* Jesus Coll., Oxford (BA 1971; DPhil 1974). Professor of Physics: Yale Univ., 1977–95; Univ. of Sussex, 1995–2002. Alfred P. Sloan Fellow, 1981–85; Alexander von Humboldt Res. Award, 1998–2003; EPSRC Sen. Res. Fellow, 1999–2004; Royal Soc. Res. Prof., 2006–. *Publications:* articles in academic physics jls. *Recreations:* music, physics. *Address:* 213 The Blackett Laboratory, Imperial College London, Prince Consort Road, SW7 2BW. *E:* ed.hinds@imperial.ac.uk.

HINDS, Lesley Adelaide; Member (Lab) City of Edinburgh Council, since 1996 (Lord Lieutenant and Lord Provost, City of Edinburgh, 2003–07); *b* Dundee, 3 Aug. 1956; *d* of late Kenneth Nicol and of Ena Nicol; *m* 1977, Martin Hinds; one *s* two *d*. *Educ:* Kirkton High Sch., Dundee; Dundee Coll. of Educn. Primary sch. teacher, Deans Primary, W Lothian, 1977–80. Mem. (Lab), Edinburgh DC, 1984–96 (Leader, 1993–96). Chair, Health Scotland, 2001–07. Director: N Edinburgh Area Renewal; N Edinburgh Arts; Pilton Partnership. Formerly Chm., Edinburgh Internat. Conf. Centre; Chair: Edinburgh Fest. Soc., 2003–07; Edinburgh Mil. Tattoo Ltd, 2003–07. Contested (Lab) Edinburgh Western, Scottish Parlt, 2011. Convener, Transport and Envmt Cttee, Edinburgh CC, 2012–. *Recreations:* theatre, dance, swimming, travel. *Address:* City Chambers, High Street, Edinburgh EH1 1YJ. *T:* (0131) 529 3235. *E:* lesley.hinds@edinburgh.gov.uk.

HINDUJA, Gopichand Parmanand; President, Hinduja Group of Companies, since 1962; *b* 29 Feb. 1940; *s* of Parmanand Deepchand Hinduja and Jamuna Parmanand Hinduja; *m* 1963, Sunita Gurnani; two *s* one *d*. *Educ:* Jai Hind Coll., Bombay, India. Joined family business, 1958; Head, Hinduja Gp's ops in Iran, 1958–78; resident in UK, 1982–; jtly (with brother) initiated diversification and expansion of Hinduja Gp. Pres., Hinduja Foundn, 1962–. Member: Adv. Council, Hinduja Cambridge Trust, 1991–; Duke of Edinburgh's Award Fellowship, 1987–. Patron: Balaji Temple, UK; Swaminarayan Hindu Mission, London. Chm., Gurnanak Trust, Teheran. MInstD. Hon. LLD Westminster, 1996; Hon. DEc Richmond Coll., 1997. *Recreations:* Indian music, travel, sailing, yoga. *Address:* Hinduja Group of Companies, c/o Sangam Ltd, New Zealand House, 80 Haymarket, SW1Y 4TE. *T:* (020) 7839 4661. *Clubs:* Royal Automobile, Annabel's.

See also S. P. Hinduja.

HINDUJA, Srichand Parmanand; Chairman, Hinduja Group of Companies, since 1962; *b* 28 Nov. 1935; *s* of Hinduja Parmanand Deepchand and Hinduja Jamuna Parmanand Bajaj; *m* 1963, Madhu Srichand Menda; two *d*. *Educ:* National Coll., Bombay, India; Davar Coll. of Commerce, Mumbai. Joined family business; jtly (with brother) initiated diversification and expansion of Hinduja Gp. Chm., Hinduja Foundn, 1962–. Global Co-ordinator, IndusInd, 1962; Pres., IndusInd Internat. Fedn, 1996. Member, Advisory Council: Dharam Indic Res. Centres, Columbia, USA and Cambridge, UK; Hinduja Cambridge Trust, 1991–; Judge Inst. of Mgt, Cambridge, 1997. Mem., Duke of Edinburgh's Award Fellowship. Patron, Centre of India/US Educn, USA. Mem. Corp., Massachusetts Gen. Hosp. Hon. LLD Westminster, 1996; Hon. DEc Richmond Coll., 1997. *Publications:* Indic Research and Contemporary Crisis, 1995; The Essence of Vedic Marriage for Success and Happiness, 1996. *Recreations:* sports in general, but particularly tennis, volleyball and cricket, Indian classical music. *Address:* Hinduja Group of Companies, c/o Sangam Ltd, New Zealand House, 80 Haymarket, SW1Y 4TE. *T:* (020) 7839 4661. *Clubs:* Royal Over-Seas League, Les Ambassadeurs.

See also G. P. Hinduja.

HINE, Dame Deirdre (Joan), DBE 1997; FRCP, FFPH; President: Royal Medical Benevolent Fund, 2008–12; Age Cymru, since 2011; British Medical Association, 2005–06; Royal Society of Medicine, 2000–02 (Chairman, Press Board, 2004–08); *b* 16 Sept. 1937; *d* of late David Alban Curran and Noreen Mary Curran (*née* Cliffe); *m* 1963, Raymond Hine; two *s*. *Educ:* Heathfield House, Cardiff; Charlton Park, Cheltenham; Welsh Nat. Sch. of Medicine (MB BCh). DPH 1964; FFPH (FFPHM 1978); FRCP 1993. Asst MO, Glamorgan CC, 1963–74; Specialist in Community Medicine, S Glam HA, 1974–82; Sen. Lectr in Geriatric Medicine, Univ. of Wales Coll. of Medicine, 1982–84; Dep. Chief MO, Welsh Office, 1984–87; Dir, Welsh Breast Cancer Screening Service, 1987–90; CMO, Welsh Office, 1990–97. Member: Audit Commn, 1998–99; H of L Appt Commn, 2000–05; Chm., Commn for Health Improvement, 1999–2004. Non-exec. Dir, Dŵr Cymru, 2001–10. Vice President: Marie Curie Cancer Care, 1998–; British Lung Foundn, 2005–. Chairman: No Smoking Day, 1998–2001; BUPA Foundn, 2004–11. Chm., C. difficile Public Inquiry, NI, 2009–11. *Publications:* papers on health promotion, health care of elderly, breast cancer screening, epidemiol. of old age in jls and text books; Calman-Hine report on cancer services. *Recreations:* travel, theatre, reading, canal cruising.

See also P. D. Curran.

HINE, Rt Rev. John Franklin Meldon; Auxiliary Bishop in Southwark, (RC), and Titular Bishop of Beverly, 2001–13; Parish Priest, St Andrew's Church, Tenterden, since 2013; *b* 26 July 1938; *s* of Lt Comdr Jack F. W. Hine, RN and Moira E. Hine. *Educ:* Stonyhurst; Mayfield Coll.; Ven. English Coll., Rome; Pontifical Gregorian Univ., Rome (PhL 1958; STB 1961). Assistant Priest: Worcester Park, S London, 1963–70; Maidstone, 1970–73; Chatham, 1973–78; Parish Priest, Bearsted and Harrietsham, and Sec., subseq. Chm., Diocesan Schs' Commn for Kent, 1978–86; VG and Chancellor, Southwark Diocese, 1986–2001. Prelate of Honour, 1986. *Recreations:* golf, walking. *Address:* The Presbytery, 47 Ashford Road, Tenterden, Kent TN30 6LL.

HINE, Air Chief Marshal Sir Patrick (Bardon), GCB 1989 (KCB 1983); GBE 1991; Air Officer Commanding-in-Chief, RAF Strike Command and Commander-in-Chief, United Kingdom Air Forces, 1988–91; Joint Commander, British Forces, Gulf War, 1990–91; Military Adviser to British Aerospace plc, 1992–99; *b* 14 July 1932; parents decd; *m* 1956, Jill Adèle (*née* Gardner); three *s*. *Educ:* Peter Symonds Sch., Winchester. Served with Nos 1, 93 and 111 Sqns, 1952–60; Mem., Black Arrows aerobatic team, 1957–59; commanded: No 92 Sqn, 1962–64; No 17 Sqn, 1970–71; RAF Wildenrath, 1974–75; Dir, Public Relations (RAF), 1975–77; RCDS 1978; SASO, HQ RAF, Germany, 1979; ACAS (Policy), 1979–83; C-in-C RAF Germany and Comdr, Second Allied Tactical Air Force, 1983–85; VCDS, 1985–87; Air Mem. for Supply and Orgn, 1987–88. Air ADC to the Queen, 1989–91. King of Arms, Order of the British Empire, 1997–2011. CCMI; FRAeS. Winner, Carris Trophy, Hants, IoW and Channel Islands Golf Championship, and Brabazon Trophy, 1949; English Schoolboy Golf Internat., 1948–49; Inter-Services Golf, 1952–57. QCVSA 1960. *Recreations:*

golf, ski-ing, caravanning, photography. *Clubs:* Royal Air Force; Colonels (Founder Mem.); Phyllis Court (Henley-on-Thames); Royal & Ancient Golf (St Andrews) (Captain, 2010–11), Brokenhurst Manor Golf, Seniors.

HINES, James Philip; QC 2015; *b* London, 13 May 1960; *s* of late Robert Henry Hines and of Shelagh Mary Hines; *m* 1993, Siân Spier; three *s* two *d*. *Educ:* St Benedict's Sch., Ealing; Ealing Coll., London (LLB). Called to the Bar, Gray's Inn, 1982. *Recreations:* gardening, travel. *Address:* 3 Raymond Buildings, Gray's Inn, WC1R 5BH. *T:* (020) 7400 6400. *E:* james.hines@3rblaw.com.

HINES, (Melvin) Barry, FRSL; writer; *b* 30 June 1939; *s* of Richard and Annie Hines; *m* 1st (marr. diss.); one *s* one *d*; 2nd, 2004, Eleanor Mulvey. *Educ:* Ecclesfield Grammar Sch.; Loughborough Coll. of Educn (Teaching Cert.). FRSL 1977. Teacher of Physical Educn, London, 1960–62 and S Yorks, 1962–72; Yorkshire Arts Fellow in Creative Writing, Sheffield Univ., 1972–74; E Midlands Arts Fellow in Creative Writing, Matlock Coll. of Higher Educn, 1975–77; Sheffield City Polytechnic: Arts Council Fellow in Creative Writing, 1982–84; Hon. Fellow in Creative Writing, 1984; Hon. Fellow, 1985. Hon. DLitt: Loughborough, 2009; Sheffield, 2010. *Television scripts:* Billy's Last Stand, 1971; Speech Day, 1973; Two Men from Derby, 1976; The Price of Coal (2 films), 1977; The Gamekeeper, 1979; A Question of Leadership, 1981; Threads, 1984; Shooting Stars, 1990; Born Kicking, 1992; *screenplays:* Kes, 1970; Looks and Smiles, 1981. *Publications:* (fiction): The Blinder, 1966; A Kestrel for a Knave, 1968; First Signs, 1972; The Gamekeeper, 1975; The Price of Coal, 1979; Looks and Smiles, 1981; Unfinished Business, 1983; The Heart of It, 1994; Elvis over England, 1998; This Artistic Life, 2009. *Address:* c/o The Agency, 24 Pottery Lane, Holland Park, W11 4LZ. *T:* (020) 7229 9216. *Club:* Hoyland Common Workingmen's (near Barnsley).

HINES, Richard Peter Treadwell D.; *see* Davenport-Hines.

HINGLEY, Robert Charles Anthony; Partner, Ondra Partners LLP, since 2015; *b* 11 May 1960; *s* of Anthony Hingley and Ruth Hingley; *m* 1993, Arabella Ballard; one *s* one *d*. *Educ:* Rugby Sch.; Corpus Christi Coll., Cambridge (BA Hons 1981). Admitted Solicitor, 1984; Articled Clerk/Solicitor, Coward Chance, 1982–85; J. Henry Schroder & Co. Ltd, 1985–2000: Dir of Investment Banking, 1994; Hd of German Investment Banking, 1995–96; Hd of Financial Instns Gp, 1997–2000; Citigroup Investment Bank: Man. Dir and Global Co-Hd of Financial Instns Gp, 2000–03; Hd of German Investment Banking, 2001–03; Vice-Chm., Lexicon Partners, 2005–10; Chief Financial Officer, Save the Children, 2007; Dir-Gen., Panel on Takeovers and Mergers, 2007–10; Man. Dir, 2010–12, Sen. Advr, 2012–15, Lazard & Co. Ltd; Dir of Investment Affairs, ABI, 2012–14. Dir, Waterstones Hldgs, 2012–. Consultant, Strutt & Parker LLP, 2014–. Trustee: Arvon Foundn, 2006–; Save the Children, 2007–. Governor: Rugby Sch., 2007–; Chelsea Acad., 2008–. *Recreations:* golf, cricket, reading, dog-walking. *Address:* Ondra Partners LLP, 125 Old Broad Street, EC2N 1AR. *E:* roberthingley@aol.com. *Clubs:* MCC, Queen's.

HINKLEY, Prof. David Victor, PhD; Professor of Statistics, University of California at Santa Barbara, since 1995; *b* 10 Sept. 1944; *s* of Eric Samson Hinkley and Edna Gertrude (*née* Alger); *m*; one *s* one *d*. *Educ:* Birmingham Univ. (BSc 1965); Imperial Coll., London (PhD 1969). MA Oxon 1990. Asst Lectr in Maths, Imperial Coll., London, 1967–69; Asst Prof. in Stats, Stanford Univ., 1969–71; Lectr in Maths, Imperial Coll., 1971–73; Associate Prof. and Prof. in Stats, Univ. of Minnesota, 1973–80; Prof. in Maths, Univ. of Texas, 1980–91; Prof. of Statistical Sci., and Fellow of St Anne's Coll., Oxford Univ., 1989–95. Editor: Annals of Statistics, 1980–82; Biometrika, 1991–92. *Publications:* Theoretical Statistics, 1973; Problems and Solutions in Theoretical Statistics, 1977; Statistical Theory and Modelling, 1990; Bootstrap Methods and Their Application, 1997; articles in statistical and scientific jls. *Recreations:* photography, botanical observation. *Address:* Department of Statistics and Applied Probability, University of California at Santa Barbara, CA 93106–3110, USA. *T:* (805) 8932129.

HINKLEY, Sarah Ann, (Sally), CBE 1995; Director, Performance and Change Management Group, Cabinet Office, 1999–2002; *b* 28 March 1950; *d* of Eric David Booth and Mary Booth; *m* 1st, 1980, Nigel Dorling (marr. diss. 1988); one *s*; 2nd, 1998, Alan Hinkley; one step *d*. *Educ:* Kendal High Sch.; Callington Grammar Sch.; Girton Coll., Cambridge (BA 1972; MA). Joined Dept of the Environment, 1974: Private Sec. to Permanent Sec., 1980–81; Principal, 1981–86; Asst Sec., 1987; Hd, Central Policy Planning Unit, 1987–88; Dir of Finance and Resources, Historic Royal Palaces, 1989–92; Department of National Heritage, later of Culture, Media and Sport, 1992–99: Hd, Nat. Lottery Div. and Dir of Finance, 1992–94; Hd, Broadcasting Policy Div., 1994–95; Under Sec., 1995; Hd, Libraries, Galls and Museums Gp, 1995–98; Hd, Educn, Trng, Arts and Sports Gp, 1998–99; Exec. Dir, Professional Standards, ICAEW, 2003–05. FRSA 1998. *Recreations:* choral singing, writing.

HINKS, Frank Peter; QC 2000; writer and illustrator of children's stories; *b* 8 July 1950; *s* of Henry John Hinks and Patricia May Hinks (*née* Adams); *m* 1982, Susan Mary, *d* of Col J. A. Haire; three *s*. *Educ:* Bromley Grammar Sch.; St Catherine's Coll., Oxford (schol.; BA 1st Cl. Hons 1971; BCL 1st Cl. Hons 1972; MA). Called to the Bar, Lincoln's Inn, 1973, Bencher, 2008; in practice at the Bar, 1974–. Churchwarden, St Peter and St Paul, Shoreham, 1995–2005, 2010–. Liveryman, Innholders' Co. *Publications:* include: The Vicar's Chickens, 1992; The Land of Lost Hair, 1992; Creatures of the Forest, 1993; The Crystal Key, 1995; Ramion (collected stories), 2003 (trans. Korean, 2006); The Dim Daft Dwarves, 2004; The Bands of Evil, 2004; The Magic Magpie, 2004; The Cruel Count, 2004; Realm of Ramion (collected stories), 2004; The Seven Stones of Iliana, 2005; The Black Marchesa, 2005; Gary and the Frog Prince, 2005; The Embodiment of Evil, 2005; Swords of Ramion (collected stories), 2005; The Kingdom of the Deep, 2009; The Blizzard Wizard, 2010; The Body Collector, 2012; Boris and the Dumb Skulls, 2014. *Recreations:* collecting jugs, gardening. *Address:* 6 New Square, Lincoln's Inn, WC2A 3QS.

HINSLIFF, Gabrielle Seal; journalist and author; columnist and feature writer, The Guardian, since 2014; Political Editor-at-Large, Grazia, since 2012; *b* Chelmsford, 4 July 1971; *d* of Geoffrey Hinsliff and Judith Elizabeth Hinsliff; *m* 2006, James Clark; one *s*. *Educ:* Queens' Coll., Cambridge (BA Hons Eng. 1993); Centre for Journalism Studies, Univ. of Cardiff (Dip. Journalism 1994). Reporter, Grimsby Evening Telegraph, 1994–96; Daily Mail: News Reporter, then Health Reporter, 1996–97; Political Reporter, then Political Correspondent, 1997–2000; Chief Political Correspondent, 2000–04, Political Ed., 2004–09, The Observer; columnist, The Times, 2013–14. Member: Family Friendly Working Hours Taskforce, DWP, 2010–11; Resolution Foundn Commn on Living Standards, 2011–12. Trustee, 4Children, 2009–12. *Publications:* Half a Wife: the working family's guide to getting a life back, 2012. *Recreations:* my family, travel, gossip, dancing. *W:* www.twitter.com/gabyhinsliff.

HINTON, Prof. Geoffrey Everest, FRS 1998; FRSCan; PhD; Professor of Computer Science, since 2001, University Professor, since 2006, University of Toronto; *b* 6 Dec. 1947; *s* of Prof. Howard Everest Hinton, FRS and late Margaret Rose Hinton; *m* 1997, Jacqueline Ford; one *s* one *d*. *Educ:* King's Coll., Cambridge (BA Exptl Psychology 1970); Univ. of Edinburgh (PhD Artificial Intelligence 1978). Fellow: Sussex Univ., 1976–78; UCSD, 1978–80; Faculty Mem., Computer Sci. Dept, Carnegie-Mellon Univ., 1982–87; Fellow, Canadian Inst. for Advanced Res. and Prof. of Computer Science and Psychology, Univ. of Toronto, 1987–98; Dir, Gatsby Computational Neurosci. Unit, UCL, 1998–2001. Pres., Cognitive Science Soc., 1992–93. Fellow, Amer. Assoc. for Artificial Intelligence, 1991; FRSCan 1996. Hon. Fellow, Amer. Acad. of Arts and Scis, 2003; Dist. Fellow, Canadian Inst. for Advanced Res., 2014. Hon. DSc: Edinburgh, 2001; Sussex, 2011. Award for contribs to IT, IT Assoc. of Canada/NSERC, 1992; NSERC Herzberg Medal, 2010; Killam Prize in Engrg, Canada Council for Arts, 2012. *Publications:* (ed jtly) Parallel Models of Human Associative Memory, 1989; Connectionist Symbol Processing, 1992; (ed jtly) Unsupervised Learning: foundations of neural computation, 1999; numerous papers and articles in learned jls. *Address:* Department of Computer Science, University of Toronto, 6 King's College Road, Toronto, ON M5S 3G4, Canada. *T:* (416) 978 7564, *Fax:* (416) 978 1455.

HINTON, Leslie Frank; Chief Executive Officer, Dow Jones & Company, 2007–11; publisher, Wall Street Journal, 2008–11; *b* 19 Feb. 1944; *s* of late Frank Arthur Hinton and Lilian Amy Hinton (*née* Bruce); *m* 1st, 1968, Mary Christine Weadick (marr. diss. 2009); four *s* one *d*; 2nd, 2009, Katharine Margaret Raymond. *Educ:* British Army schs in Germany, Libya, Egypt, Ethiopia and Singapore. Reporter, Adelaide News, SA, 1960–65; desk editor, British United Press, London, 1965–66; reporter, The Sun, 1966–69; writer editor, Adelaide News, 1969–70; reporter, The Sun, 1971–76; US corresp., News Internat., NYC, 1976–78; news editor, 1978–80, Managing Editor, 1980–82, The Star, NYC; Associate Editor, Boston Herald, 1982–85; Editor-in-Chief, Star Mag., 1985–87; Exec. Vice Pres., 1987–90, Pres., 1990–91, Murdoch Magazines, NYC; Pres. and Chief Exec. Officer, News America Publishing Inc., NYC, 1991–93; Chm. and Chief Exec. Officer, Fox Television Stations Inc. and Fox News Inc., LA, 1993–95; Exec. Chm., News International Ltd, 1995–2007. Director: British Sky Broadcasting plc, 1999–2003; Johnston Press plc, 2005–07. Chairman: Code of Practice Cttee, Press Complaints Commn, 1998–2007; Council, CPU, 1999–2007; Director: Press Standards Bd of Finance, 2003–07; Press Assoc., 1996–2007; Associated Press, 2011. Member Board of Trustees: Amer. Sch. in London, 1999–2007; Graduate Sch. of Journalism, City Univ. of New York, 2008–11. Mem., Bd of Advrs, Dept of Ophthalmol., Columbia Univ., 2010–.

HINTZ, B. Jürgen; Group Chief Executive, Novar plc (formerly Caradon plc), 1998–2006; *b* 3 May 1942; *s* of Karl-Heinz Hintz and Elsbeth Parr; *m* 2nd, 1996, Kirsty MacMaster; one *s* one *d*, and one step *d*. *Educ:* Univ. of N Carolina State (BSc). Physicist, 1964–75; Procter & Gamble Inc.: various positions, 1976–89; Dir, 1989–91; Chief Exec., CarnaudMetalBox, 1991–95. Non-executive Director: Apple Computers Inc., 1994–97; Inchcape plc, 1994–98. Chm., Supervisory Bd, Head NV (Mem., 2003–). *Recreations:* ski-ing, tennis. *Address:* Head NV, Prins Bernhardplein 200, 1097 JB Amsterdam, Netherlands.

HINTZE, Sir Michael, Kt 2013; AM 2013; Founder, Chief Executive and Senior Investment Officer, CQS, since 1999; *b* Harbin, China, 27 July 1953; *s* of Michael Hintze and Veronica Hintze (*née* Lange, later Yakubovsky); *m* Dorothy; four *c*. *Educ:* Univ. of Sydney (BSc Physics and Pure Maths; BEng Electrical Engrg); Univ. of NSW (MSc Acoustics); Harvard Business Sch. (MBA). Electrical Design Engr, Civil and Civic Pty Ltd, Australia; served Australian Army, Royal Australian Electrical and Mech. Engrs (Captain); with Salomon Bros, NY, 1982–84; Goldman Sachs, London, 1984–96, rôles incl. Exec. Dir and Hd of UK Trading and Hd, Eur. Emerging Mkts Trading; Man. Dir and Eur. Hd of Convertibles, then Man. Dir, Leveraged Funds Gp, Credit Suisse First Boston, London, 1996–99. Estabd Hintze Family Charitable Foundn, 2005. Chm., Prince's Foundn for Building Community. Mem., Internat. Council, V&A. Trustee: IEA; Univ. of Sydney UK Trust. Trustee: Nat. Gall., 2008–; Wandsworth Mus. Patron, Arts of the Vatican Museums. Hon. DBus NSW. GCSG 2008 (KCSG 2005). (Jtly) Prince of Wales Award for Arts Philanthropy, 2009. *Address:* CQS Investment Management Ltd, 5th Floor, 33 Grosvenor Place, SW1X 7HY.

HIPKIN, John; Member (Ind), since 2008, and Leader, Independent Group, since 2013, Cambridge City Council (Member (Lib Dem), 1992–2007); Member (Ind) and Leader, Independent Group, Cambridgeshire County Council, since 2013; *b* 9 April 1935; *s* of Jack Hipkin and Elsie Hipkin; *m* 1963, Bronwyn Vaughan Dewey (marr. diss. 1985); four *s* one *d*; one *d*; *m* 2004, Marie-Louise Holland; one *d*. *Educ:* Surbiton Grammar Sch. for Boys; LSE (BScEcon). Asst Teacher, 1957–65; Research Officer: King's Coll., Cambridge, 1965–68; Univ. of East Anglia, 1968–71; Sec., Schools Council Working Party on Whole Curriculum, 1973–74; Dir, Adv. Centre for Educn, 1974–77; Hd of English, Meridian Sch., Royston, Herts, 1977–95. Mayor of Cambridge, 2005–06. Historic Envmt Champion for Cambridge, 2005–06. *Publications:* (jtly) New Wine in Old Bottles, 1967; The Massacre of Peterloo (a play), 1968, 2nd edn 1974; (ed jtly) Education for the Seventies, 1970. *Recreations:* theatre, foreign travel, history, medieval music. *Address:* 15 Oxford Road, Cambridge CB4 3PH. *T:* (01223) 564126.

HIPKINS, Michael Francis, PhD; Director, Financial Support for Learners, Department for Business, Innovation and Skills (formerly Director, Student Finance, Department for Education and Skills, then Department for Innovation, Universities and Skills), 2004–11; *b* 12 March 1951; *s* of Leonard Sidney Hipkins and Stella Frances Irving Graham; *m* 1977, Barbara Wilson; one *s* (and one *s* decd). *Educ:* Imperial Coll., London (BSc 1972; PhD 1976). MInstP 1987. EMBO Long-term Fellow, CNRS, France, 1976; Lectr, Univ. of Glasgow, 1976–86; Principal, 1988, Grade 5, 1990, DES, subseq. DFE, DFEE then DFES. Member, Council: Univ. of Bath, 2011–; Bucks New Univ., 2011– (Dep. Chair, 2014–).

HIRSCH, Andrew Mark; Chief Executive Officer, John Brown Media, since 2001; *b* London, 22 March 1959; *s* of Walter Hirsch and Doris Hirsch; *m* 1990, Jane O'Rourke; two *s*. *Educ:* Beal Grammar Sch. for Boys. Family furniture business, 1977–86; sales exec., Sydney, 1986–88; Publishing Dir, Pearl & Dean, 1988–92; John Brown Media, 1992–: set up NY office, 2000; led mgt buyout, 2004. *Recreations:* tennis, football, movies, travel, spending time with family. *Address:* John Brown Media, 136–142 Bramley Road, W10 6SR. *T:* (020) 7565 3000. *E:* andrew.hirsch@johnbrownmedia.com.

HIRSCH, Prof. Sir Peter (Bernhard), Kt 1975; MA, PhD; FRS 1963; Isaac Wolfson Professor of Metallurgy in the University of Oxford, 1966–92, Emeritus, 1992; Fellow, St Edmund Hall, Oxford, 1966–92, now Emeritus; *b* 16 Jan. 1925; *s* of Ismar Hirsch and Regina Meyerson; *m* 1959, Mabel Anne Kellar (*née* Stephens), *widow* of James Noel Kellar; one step *s* one step *d*. *Educ:* Sloane Sch., Chelsea; St Catharine's Coll., Cambridge (Hon. Fellow, 1982). BA 1946; MA 1950; PhD 1951. Reader in Physics in Univ. of Cambridge, 1964–66; Fellow, Christ's Coll., Cambridge, 1960–66, Hon. Fellow, 1978. Has been engaged on researches with electron microscope on imperfections in crystalline structure of metals and on relation between structural defects and mechanical properties. Chairman: Metallurgy and Materials Cttee (and Mem., Eng. Bd), SRC, 1970–73; UKAEA, 1982–84 (pt-time Mem., 1982–94); Technical Adv. Gp on Structl Integrity, 1993–2002; Member: Elec. Supply Res. Council, 1969–82; Council for Scientific Policy, 1970–72; Tech. Adv. Cttee, Advent, 1982–89; Tech. Adv. Bd, Monsanto Electronic Materials, 1985–88; Chm., Materials, Processes Adv. Bd, Rolls-Royce, 1996–2000. Chm., Isis Innovation Ltd, 1988–96; Director: Cogent Ltd, 1985–89; Rolls-Royce Associates, 1994–97; Oxford Med. Imaging Analysis, OMIA, 2000–01. FIC 1988. Hon. Fellow: RMS, 1977; Japan Soc. of Electron Microscopy, 1979; Japan Inst. of Metals, 1989; Inst. of Materials, 2002. Associate Mem., Royal Acad. of Sci., Letters and Fine Arts, Belgium, 1995; Hon. Member: French Electron Microscopy Soc.; Spanish Electron Microscopy Soc., 1974; Materials Res. Soc., India, 1990; Chinese Electron Microscopy Soc., 1992; For. Hon. Mem., Amer. Acad. of Arts and Scis, 2005; For. Associate, US NAE, 2001; For. Mem., Russian Acad. of Scis, 2006. Hon. DSc: Newcastle, 1979; City, 1979; Northwestern, 1982; Hon. ScD East Anglia, 1983; Hon. DEng: Liverpool, 1991; Birmingham, 1993. Rosenhain Medal, Inst. of Metals, 1961; C. V. Boys Prize, Inst. of Physics and Physical Soc., 1962; Clamer Medal, Franklin Inst., 1970; Wihuri Internat. Prize, Helsinki, 1971; Royal Soc. Hughes Medal, 1973; Metals Soc. Platinum Medal, 1976; Royal Medal, Royal Soc., 1977; A. A. Griffith Medal, Inst. of Materials, 1979; Arthur Von Hippel Award, Materials Res. Soc., 1983; (jtly) Wolf Prize in Physics, Wolf Foundn, 1983–84; Dist. Scientist Award, Electron Microscopy Soc. of America, 1986; Holweck Prize, Inst. of Physics and French Physical Soc., 1988; Gold Medal, Japan Inst. of Metals, 1989; Acta Metallurgica Gold Medal, 1997; Heyn Medal, German Soc. for Materials Sci., 2002; Lomonosov Gold Medal, Russian Acad. of Scis, 2005. *Publications:* Electron Microscopy of Thin Crystals (with others), 1965; (ed) The Physics of Metals, vol. 2, Defects, 1975; (ed jtly) Progress in Materials Science, vol. 36, 1992; (ed) Topics in Electron Diffraction and Microscopy of Materials, 1999; (ed jtly) Fracture, Plastic Flow, and Structural Integrity, 2000; Methods for the Assessment of the Structural Integrity of Components and Structures, 2003; numerous contribs to learned jls. *Recreation:* walking. *Address:* 104A Lonsdale Road, Oxford OX2 7ET.

HIRSCH, Prof. Steven Richard, FRCP; FRCPsych; expert witness in psychiatry and private practitioner, Priory Hospital, since 2002; Professor of Psychiatry, Imperial College School of Medicine (formerly Charing Cross and Westminster Medical School), 1975–2002, now Emeritus; *m* 1st, 1964, Maureen; two *d*; 2nd, 1979, Teresa (*d* 2008); one *s* one *d*; 3rd, 2011, Dr Olga Goldina. *Educ:* Amherst Coll., Mass (BA Hons); Johns Hopkins Univ. (MD); London Univ. (MPhil). Res. worker, MRC Social Psychiatry, 1971–73; Hon. Sen. Registrar, Maudsley Hosp., 1971–73; Lectr in Psychiatry, Inst. of Psychiatry, Univ. of London, 1972–73; Sen. Lectr and Hon. Cons., Depts of Psychiatry, Westminster Hosp. and Queen Mary's Hosp., 1973–75. Dir, Teaching Governance, W London Mental Health NHS Trust, 2002. *Publications:* (ed with M. Shepherd) Themes and Variations in European Psychiatry: an anthology, 1974; (with J. Leff) Abnormalities in parents of schizophrenics: review of the literature and an investigation of communication defects and deviances, (monograph) 1975; (ed with R. Farmer) The Suicide Syndrome, 1980; (ed with P. B. Bradley) The Psychopharmacology and Treatment of Schizophrenia, 1986; Psychiatric Beds and Resources: factors influencing bed use and service planning (report of a working party, RCPsych), 1988; (ed with J. Harris) Consent and the Incompetent Patient: ethics, law and medicine, 1988; (ed with D. Weinberger) Schizophrenia, 1995, 2nd edn 2003; chapters in books and abstracts; numerous contribs to scientific pubns. *Address:* Department of Psychiatry, Division of Neuroscience, Imperial College, Charing Cross Campus, St Dunstan's Road, W6 8RP. *T:* 07968 065464.

HIRST, Damien; artist; *b* Bristol, 7 June 1965; *s* of Mary Brennan; three *s* by Maia Norman. *Educ:* Goldsmiths' Coll., Univ. of London (BA Fine Art 1989). *Solo exhibitions include:* ICA, 1991; Emmanuel Perrotin, Paris, 1991; Cohen Gall., NY, 1992; Regen Projects, LA, 1993; Galerie Jablonka, Cologne, 1993; Milwaukee Art Mus., 1994; Dallas Mus., 1994; Kukje Gall., Seoul, 1995; White Cube Gall., 1995, 2003, 2007; Max Gandolph-Bibliothek, Salzburg, 1996; Gagosian Gall., NY, 1996; Bruno Bischofberger, Zurich, 1997; Astrup Fearnley, Oslo, 1997; Southampton City Art Gall., 1998; Tate Gall., 1999; Wallace Collection, 2009; retrospective exhibn, Saatchi Gall., 2003; Gagosian Gall., London, 2006; Serpentine Gall., 2006; (retrospective) Tate Modern, 2012; The Complete Spot Paintings 1986–2011, Gagosian Galls, 2012; (retrospective) New Art Gall., Walsall, 2012; Schizophrenogenesis, Paul Stolper Gall., London, 2014. Gp exhibitions in UK, Europe, USA and Australia. Co-founder and owner, Pharmacy, Notting Hill, 1998–2003 (contemp. restaurant design award, Carlton London Restaurant Awards, 1999); founder, Number 11, The Quay, Ilfracombe, 2004. Turner Prize, 1995. *Publications:* I Want to Spend the Rest of My Life Everywhere, With Everyone, One to One, Always, Forever, Now, 1997; Theories, Models, Methods, Approaches, Assumptions, Results and Findings, 2000; (illus.) Meaningless Static, by Paul Fryer, 2000; (with Gordon Burn) On the Way to Work, 2001; From the Cradle to the Grave: selected drawings, 2004. *Address:* c/o White Cube Gallery, 144–152 Bermondsey Street, SE1 3TQ.

HIRST, David Michael Geoffrey, FBA 1983; Professor of the History of Art, University of London at the Courtauld Institute, 1991–97, now Emeritus Professor of the History of Art; *b* 5 Sept. 1933; *s* of Walter Hirst; *m* 1st, 1960, Sara Vitali (marr. diss. 1970); one *s*; 2nd, 1972, Jane Martineau (marr. diss. 1984); 3rd, 1984, Diane Zervas. *Educ:* Stowe Sch.; New Coll., Oxford; Courtauld Inst. of Art (Hon. Fellow, 1998). Lectr, 1962–80, Reader, 1980–91, Courtauld Inst. Fellow at Villa I Tatti, 1969–70; Mem., Inst. for Advanced Study, Princeton, 1975. Mem., Pontifical Commn for Restoration of Sistine Ceiling, 1987–90. Mem., Florentine Accademia del Disegno; Fellow, Accademia Veneto. Arranged exhibn, Michelangelo Draftsman, Nat. Gall., Washington, 1988, Louvre, Paris, 1989; co-curated exhibn, The Young Michelangelo, Nat. Gall., 1994. Serena Medal for Italian Studies, British Acad., 2001. *Publications:* Sebastiano del Piombo, 1981; Michelangelo and his Drawings, 1988 (Italian edn 1993); Michelangelo Draftsman, Milan, 1988 (French edn 1989); (jtly) The Young Michelangelo, 1994 (Italian edn 1997); Michelangelo: the achievement of fame, 1475–1534, 2011; many contribs to British and continental books and periodicals. *Address:* 3 Queensdale Place, W11 4SQ.

HIRST, John Raymond, CBE 2014; FCA; Chief Executive, Met Office, 2007–14; *b* Nicosia, Cyprus, 9 Aug. 1952; *m* Anne; one *s* one *d*. *Educ:* Leeds Univ. (BA). FCA; ACT. ICI plc, 1979–97: CEO, ICI Autocolor, 1990–95; Gp Treas., 1995–96; CEO, ICI Perf. Chemicals, 1996–97; Gp CEO, Premier Farnell plc, 1998–2005. Chm., Asbis, 2006–; non-executive Director: Hammerson plc, 2003–14 (Chm., Audit Cttee); Marsh UK Ltd, 2014–; Ultra Electronics plc, 2015– (Chm., Audit Cttee, 2015–). Chm., Audit Cttee, WMO, 2010–. Dir, Epilepsy Research UK, 2006–. Trustee, Epilepsy Bereaved, 2008–. CCMI. Hon. DSc Exeter, 2013.

HIRST, Jonathan William; QC 1990; a Recorder, since 1997; a Deputy High Court Judge, since 2003; *b* 2 July 1953; *s* of Rt Hon. Sir David Cozens-Hardy Hirst, PC; *m* 1974, Fiona Christine Mary Hirst (*née* Tyser); one *s* (and one *s* decd). *Educ:* Eton Coll.; Trinity Coll., Cambridge (MA). Called to the Bar, Inner Temple, 1975, Bencher, 1994 (Reader, 2011; Treasurer, 2012); Jt Hd, Brick Court Chambers, 2005–. Mem., Gen. Council of the Bar, 1987–2000 (Vice Chm., 1999, Chm., 2000; Chairman: Law Reform Cttee, 1992–94; Professional Standards Cttee, 1996–98); Chm., Trinity Law Assoc., 2006–11. Mem., Baltic Exchange, 2013–. Governor: Taverham Hall Sch., Norfolk, 1991–95; Goodenough Coll., 2001– (Chm., 2008–). Church Warden, Blickling Church, Norfolk, 2015–. Chm., Cambridge Univ. Cons. Assoc., 1974. *Recreations:* shooting, gardening, other country pursuits. *Address:* Brick Court Chambers, 7–8 Essex Street, WC2R 3LD. *T:* (020) 7379 3550. *Clubs:* Boodle's, Hurlingham; Norfolk (Norwich).

HIRST, Larry, CBE 2007; Chairman, IBM Europe, Middle East and Africa, 2008–10; *b* 4 Nov. 1951; *s* of late Harold Hirst and Joan Hirst; *m* 1978, Ellen Alison; one *s* one *d*. *Educ:* Univ. of Hull (BSc Hons Maths 1973). Kodak, 1973–77; IBM Corp., 1977–2010: Dir Ops, E Europe, Russia, 1989–90; Exec. Asst to Chm., 1992–93; Vice Pres., Financial Services, EMEA, 1994–2001; Chief Exec., UK, Ireland and SA, 2001–08; Chm., IBM Netherlands, 2003–10. Non-executive Director: MITIE Gp plc, 2010–; ARM Hldgs plc, 2011–. Chm., e-skills UK Sector Skills Council for IT and Telecoms, 2001–10; Exec. Chm., Information Age Partnership, 2001–03; Chairman: Transition to Teaching Council, 2007–10; UKTI Technol. Bd, 2008–13; Mem., President's Cttee, 2001–08, Internat. Adv. Bd, 2008–10, CBI. Comr, UK Commn for Employment and Skills, 2007–10; UK Business Ambassador, 2009–12. Adjunct Prof., 2011–, Chm., Data Sci. Inst., 2014–, Imperial Coll. London (Chm., Digital Cities Exchange Bd, 2011–14); Mem. Adv. Bd, Res. Inst. in Sci. of Cyber Security, 2012–. Member: S African President's Internat. Adv. Bd, 2006–10; Bd, IMD Business Sch., Lausanne, 2008–10; Internat. Adv. Bd, BA, 2012–; Internat. Advr, Monetise Gp, 2011–; Ambassador: Everywoman, 2000–; Black British Business, 2014–. *Recreations:* golf, woodland maintenance hopefully not at the same time, reading biographies, gadgets, technology futures. *E:* larryhirst@hirst-works.com.

HIRST, Sir Michael (William), Kt 1992; LLB, CA; company director; business consultant; Founder, Michael Hirst Associates; Chairman: Pagoda Public Relations Ltd, since 2000; Millstream Associates Ltd, since 2000; *b* 2 Jan. 1946; *s* of late John Melville Hirst and Christina Binning Torrance or Hirst; *m* 1972, Naomi Ferguson Wilson; one *s* two *d*. *Educ:* Glasgow Acad., Glasgow; Univ. of Glasgow (LLB). CA 1970. Exchange Student, Univ. of Iceland, 1967; Partner, Peat, Marwick Mitchell & Co., 1978–83; Consultant, Peat Marwick UK, 1983–92. Pres., Glasgow Univ. Conservative Club, 1967; National Vice-Chm., Scottish Young Conservatives, 1971–73; Chm., Scottish Conservative Candidates Assoc., 1978–81; Vice-Chairman: Pty Organisation Cttee, 1985; Conservative Party in Scotland, 1987–89; Pres., 1989–92, Chm., 1993–97, Scottish Cons. & Unionist Party. Contested (C): Central Dunbartonshire, Feb. and Oct. 1974; E Dunbartonshire, 1979; Strathkelvin and Bearsden, 1987 and 1992. MP (C) Strathkelvin and Bearsden, 1983–87. PPS to Parly Under-Secs of State, DoE, 1985–87. Mem., Select Cttee on Scottish Affairs, 1983–87. Director: Children's Hospice Assoc., Scotland, 1993–2005; Erskine Hosp. Ltd (formerly Princess Louise Scottish Hosp.), 1980–2011 (Mem., Exec. Bd, 1997–2011). Mem., Bd of Trustees, Diabetes UK (formerly British Diabetic Assoc.), 1988–2006 (Hon. Sec., 1993–98; Vice Chm., 1998–2001; Chm., 2001–06); Pres., Internat. Diabetes Fedn, 2012– (Vice-Pres., 2006–09; Pres.-Elect, 2009–12). Chm., Park Sch. Educnl Trust, 1988–2009; Mem. Court, Glasgow Caledonian Univ., 1993–98 (Chm., Audit Cttee, 1993–98). Mem. Council, Imperial Soc. of Kts Bachelor, 2002– (Chm. Scottish Div., 2002–). Chm., Friends of Kippen Kirk Trust, 2004–. FRSA 1993; MCIPR (MIPR 2003). Hon. FRCPE 2012. Hon. DLitt Glasgow Caledonian, 2004. *Recreations:* golf, walking, ski-ing. *Address:* Glentirran, Kippen, Stirlingshire FK8 3DY. *T:* (01786) 870283. *Clubs:* Carlton; The Western (Glasgow).

HIRST, Neil Alexander Carr; Senior Policy Fellow, Grantham Institute for Climate Change, Imperial College London, since 2009; *b* 16 May 1946; *s* of Theodore James Hirst and Valerie Adamson Hirst; *m* 1984, Caroline Rokeby Collins; two *d*. *Educ:* Canford Sch.; Lincoln Coll., Oxford (BA 1st Cl. Hons PPE); Cornell Univ., USA (Telluride Schol., MBA). Jun. reporter, Eastbourne Gazette and Herald Chronicle, 1964–65; entered Civil Service, 1970: Asst Principal, Min. of Technol., 1970–73; Asst Private Sec. to Ministers for Industry and Energy and Sec. of State for Trade, 1973–75; Principal, Oil and Gas Div., then Atomic Energy Div., Dept of Energy, 1975–80; on secondment to Private Finance Dept, Goldman Sachs, NY, 1981; returned to Dept of Energy for public flotation of Britoil, 1982; Asst Sec., Atomic Energy Div., 1983–85; Counsellor (Energy), Washington DC, 1985–88; Oil and Gas Div., Dept of Energy, 1988–92; Department of Trade and Industry: coal privatisation legislation, 1992–94; Labs Unit (privatisation of Nat. Engrg Lab. and Nat. Chemical Lab.), 1995; Under Sec. and Hd, Atomic Energy Div., 1995; Dir, Nuclear Industries, 1996–98; Dep. Dir Gen., Energy, 1998–2002; Hd, Energy Mkts Unit, 2002–04; Dir, Office of Energy Technol. and R&D, 2004–08, Dir, Global Dialogue, 2008–09, Internat. Energy Agency. Mem., UKAEA, 1996–98; Chm., Nuclear Safety Wkg Gp of the G8 Summit nations, 1998. Mem., Dorset Natural Hist. and Archaeol Soc., 2000. *Recreations:* gardening, music, theatre, walking. *Address:* 3 Stockwell Park Road, SW9 0AP. *T:* (020) 7735 9615; 59 Corfe Road, Stoborough, near Wareham, Dorset BH20 5AE. *Club:* Oxford and Cambridge.

HIRST, Prof. Paul Heywood; Professor of Education, University of Cambridge, 1971–88, now Emeritus, and Fellow of Wolfson College (formerly University College), Cambridge, since 1971; *b* 10 Nov. 1927; *s* of late Herbert and Winifred Hirst, Birkby, Huddersfield. *Educ:* Huddersfield Coll.; Trinity Coll., Cambridge (BA 1948, MA 1952); Cert. Educn Cantab, 1952; DipEd London, 1955; MA Oxon (by incorporation), Christ Church, Oxford, 1955. Asst Master, William Hulme's Grammar Sch., Manchester, 1948–50; Maths Master, Eastbourne Coll., 1950–55; Lectr and Tutor, Univ. of Oxford Dept of Educn, 1955–59; Lectr in Philosophy of Educn, Univ. of London Inst. of Educn, 1959–65; Prof. of Educn, King's Coll., Univ. of London, 1965–71. Visiting Professor: Univ. of British Columbia, 1964, 1967; Univ. of Malawi, 1969; Univ. of Puerto Rico, 1984; Univ. of Sydney, 1989; Univ. of Alberta, 1989; Inst. of Educn, Univ. of London, 1991–96. De Carle Lectr, Univ. of Otago, 1976; Fink Lectr, Univ. of Melbourne, 1976. Vice-Pres., Philosophy of Educn Soc. of GB; Member: UGC Educn Sub-Cttee, 1971–80; Educn Cttee, 1972–82, Academic Policy Cttee, 1981–87, Chm., Research Cttee, 1988–92, CNAA; Swann Cttee of Inquiry into Educn of Children from Ethnic Minorities, 1981–85. Chm., Univs Council for Educn of Teachers, 1985–88. Member Court: Univ. of Derby, 1996–; Univ. of Glos, 2006–. Hon. Mem., Royal Norwegian Soc. of Scis and Letters, 1996. Hon. DEd CNAA, 1992; Hon. DPhil Cheltenham and Gloucester Coll. of Higher Educn, 2000; Hon. DLitt Huddersfield, 2002. *Publications:* (with R. S. Peters) The Logic of Education, 1970; (ed with R. F. Dearden and R. S. Peters) Education and the Development of Reason, 1971; Knowledge and the Curriculum, 1974; Moral Education in a Secular Society, 1974; (ed) Educational Theory and its Foundation Disciplines, 1984; (with V. J. Furlong) Initial Teacher Training and the Role of the School, 1988; (ed with P. A. White) Philosophy of Education: major themes in the analytic tradition, 1998; papers in: Philosophical Analysis and Education (ed R. D. Archambault), 1965; The Study of Education (ed J. W. Tibble), 1965; The Concept of Education (ed R. S. Peters), 1966; Religious Education in a Pluralistic Society (ed M. C. Felderhof), 1985; Education, Values and Mind (ed D. E. Cooper), 1986; Partnership in Initial Teacher Training (ed M. Booth *et al*), 1990; Beyond Liberal Education (ed R. Barrow and P. White), 1993; The Aims of Education (ed R. Marples), 1999; Education in Morality (ed J. M. Halstead and T. H. McLaughlin), 1999; Leaders in Philosophy of Education (ed L. J. Waks), 2008; Religious Upbringing and the Costs of Freedom (ed P. Caws and S. Jones), 2010. *Recreations:* music, especially opera. *Address:* Flat 3, 6 Royal Crescent, Brighton BN2 1AL. *T:* (01273) 684118. *Club:* Athenæum.

HISCOCK, Stephen John; HM Diplomatic Service, retired; High Commissioner to Guyana, and (non resident) Ambassador to Suriname, 2002–06; *b* 16 June 1946; *s* of Lionel Percy Hiscock and Dorothy Mabel Hiscock (*née* Wright); *m* 1st, 1967, Gillian Denise Roe; two *s*; 2nd, 1983, Dee Mary Forster; two *s* one *d*. *Educ:* Devonport High Sch. for Boys, Plymouth. With Inland Revenue, 1963–65; entered Foreign Office, 1965; FCO, 1965–68; Kuala Lumpur, 1968–72; Lusaka, 1972–76; FCO, 1976–78; Second Sec., Islamabad, 1978–82; First Secretary: Seoul, 1982–86; FCO, 1986–88; Dep. High Comr, Georgetown, 1988–93; FCO, 1993–96; Consul-Gen., Brisbane, 1997–2001; Commercial Counsellor (temp.), Bangkok, 2001–02; Dep. Hd of Mission (temp.), Kabul, March–April 2002. Mem., OAS Election Observation Mission to Guyana, 2006. Dir, Commonwealth Boxing Council Ltd, 2008. Ind. Mem., Kent Police Authy, 2008–12. Gov., Bethany Sch., Goudhurst, 2008–12. *Recreations:* Rotary, amateur dramatics, social tennis, walking. *Address:* 67 Primrose Drive, Kingsnorth, Ashford, Kent TN23 3NP. *Club:* Rotary (Ashford).

HISCOX, Robert Ralph Scrymgeour; DL; Chairman, Hiscox Ltd (formerly Hiscox plc), 1996–2013, now Honorary President; *b* 4 Jan. 1943; *s* of late Ralph Hiscox, CBE and Louisa Jeanie Hiscox; *m* 1st, 1966, Lucy Mills (marr. diss. 1978; she *d* 1996); two *s*; 2nd, 1985, Lady Julia Elizabeth Meade, 3rd *d* of Earl of Clanwilliam; three *s*. *Educ:* Rugby Sch.; Corpus Christi Coll., Cambridge (MA). ACII. Member of Lloyd's, 1967–98 (Dep. Chm., 1993–95; Dep. Chm., First Market Bd, 1993–95); Chairman: Lloyd's Underwriting Agents' Assoc., 1991; Lloyd's Corporate Capital Assoc., 1998–99; Lloyd's Market Assoc., 1999–2000. Director: Roberts & Hiscox, 1973–98; Hiscox Hldgs Ltd, 1987–99; R. K. Harrison Hldgs Ltd,

1990–99; Hiscox Syndicates Ltd, 1991–2013; Hiscox Insce Co., 1996–2013. Non-exec. Dir, Grainger (formerly Grainger Trust) plc, 2002–12. Mem., Mus. and Galls Commn, 1996–2000. Dir, Public Catalogue Foundn, 2004–12. Treasurer and Trustee: Campaign for Museums, 1998–2004; 24 Hour Mus., 2000–01; Treas., Friends of the Tate Gallery, 1990–93; Trustee: Wilts Bobby Van Trust, 1998– (Chm., 2002–); Kenneth Armitage Foundn, 2005– (Chm., 2011–); Paolozzi Foundn, 2009– (Chm., 2011–); Marlborough Brandt Gp, 2012–. Patron, Friends of Erlestoke Prison, 2012–. High Sheriff, 2011, DL, 2013, Wilts. *Recreations:* family life, country life, the arts, changing things. *Address:* Hiscox Ltd, 1 Great St Helen's, EC3A 6HX. *T:* (020) 7448 6011. *E:* robert.hiscox@hiscox.com; Rainscombe Park, Oare, Marlborough, Wilts SN8 4HZ. *T:* (01672) 563491. *Clubs:* Queen's, Shikar, White's.

HISLOP, David Seymour; QC 2010; *b* Dunedin, NZ, 17 July 1955; *s* of Alfred George Hislop and Eileen Mary Hislop; *m* 1986, Donna Joyce Bradley; one *s* one *d*. *Educ:* Whangarei Boys High Sch.; Auckland Univ. (LLB). Commercial Litigation Solicitor and Counsel, Nicholson Gribbin Solicitors, 1979–84; Litigation Partner, Thorne Dallas & Partners, 1984–88; called to the Bar, Gray's Inn, 1989; specialist defence barrister in field of serious organised crime and fraud. *Publications:* (contrib.) A Practitioner's Guide to the Law and Regulation of Financial Crime, 2011; contribs to New Law Jl, Archbold News, Butterworth's Human Rights Commentaries. *Recreations:* food, fine wine, Rugby, family. *E:* davidhislopqc@aol.com, d.hislop@doughtystreet.co.uk.

HISLOP, Ian David; Editor, Private Eye, since 1986; writer and broadcaster; *b* 13 July 1960; *s* of late David Atholl Hislop and Helen Hislop; *m* 1988, Victoria Hamson (*see* V. Hislop); one *s* one *d*. *Educ:* Ardingly College; Magdalen College, Oxford (BA Hons Eng. Lang. and Lit.; Underhill Exhibn; Violet Vaughan Morgan Scholarship). Joined Private Eye, 1981, Dep. Editor, 1985–86. Columnist, The Listener, 1985–89; Television critic, The Spectator, 1994–96; Columnist, Sunday Telegraph, 1996–2003. *Radio:* Newsquiz, 1985–90; 4th Column, 1992–96; Lent Talk, 1994; (scriptwriter, with Nick Newman) Gush, 1994; Words on Words, 1999; The Hislop Vote, 2000; A Revolution in 5 Acts, 2001; The Real Patron Saints, 2002; A Brief History of Tax, 2003; The Choir Invisible, 2003; There'll be Blue Birds over the White Cliffs of Dover, 2004; Are We Offensive Enough?, 2004; Looking for Middle England, 2006; Lord Kitchener's Image, 2007; We Three Kings, 2008; The Six Faces of Henry VIII, 2009; (with Nick Newman) Greed All About It, 2010; (with Nick Newman) What Went Wrong with the Olympics, 2010; (contrib.) A History of The World in 100 Objects, 2010; (with Nick Newman) The News at Bedtime, 2011; England Their England, 2011; *television:* scriptwriter with Nick Newman: Spitting Image, 1984–89; The Stone Age, 1989; Briefcase Encounter, 1990; The Programme, 1990–92; Harry Enfield and Chums, 1994–98; Mangez Merveillac, 1994; Dead on Time, 1995; Gobble, 1996; Sermon from St Albions, 1998; Songs and Praise from St Albions, 1999; Confessions of a Murderer, 1999; My Dad's the Prime Minister, 2003, 2004; (screenplay) A Bunch of Amateurs, 2008; The Wipers Times, 2013; performer, Have I Got News For You, 1990–; documentary presenter: Canterbury Tales, 1996; School Rules, 1997; Pennies from Bevan, 1998; Great Railway Journeys East to West, 1999; Who Do You Think You Are?, 2004; Not Forgotten, 2005; Not Forgotten: shot at dawn, 2007; Scouting for Boys, 2007; Not Forgotten: the men who wouldn't fight, 2008; Ian Hislop Goes Off the Rails, 2008; Marlow on Hogarth, 2008; Ian Hislop's Changing of the Bard, 2009; Not Forgotten: soldiers of Empire, 2009; Ian Hislop's Age of the Do-Gooders, 2010; When Bankers Were Good, 2011; Stiff Upper Lip: An Emotional History of Britain, 2012; Ian Hislop's Olden Days, 2014. Editors' Ed., 1991, Ed. of the Year, 1998, British Soc. of Mag. Editors; Award for political satire, Channel 4 Political Awards, 2004; Political Comedy Award, Channel 4, 2006; Voice of the Listener and Viewer Award for Excellence in Broadcasting, 2009; Diamond Jubilee Award for Best Political Satire, Political Studies Assoc., 2010; Liberty Human Rights Long Walk Award, 2011. *Publications:* various Private Eye collections, 1985–; contribs to newspapers and magazines on books, current affairs, arts and entertainment. *Address:* c/o Private Eye, 6 Carlisle Street, W1D 3BN. *T:* (020) 7437 4017.

HISLOP, Victoria; writer; *b* Bromley, 8 June 1959; *d* of John and Mary Hamson; *m* 1988, Ian David Hislop, *qv*; one *s* one *d*. *Educ:* Tonbridge Grammar Sch. for Girls; St Hilda's Coll., Oxford (BA Hons English). PA to Sales Dir, Sidgwick & Jackson, 1982–84; Account Dir, Good Relations, 1985–88; Account Dir, Wolff Olins, 1988–90; freelance journalist, nat. newspapers and mags incl. Daily Telegraph, Sunday Telegraph, Sunday Times, Woman & Home, Good Housekeeping, Condé Nast Traveller, 1990–. Ambassador: for tourism, Greek Tourist Orgn, 2012–; Lepra Health in Action, 2013–. *Publications:* The Island, 2005 (British Book Award for Newcomer of Year, 2007); The Return, 2008; The Thread, 2011; The Last Dance, 2012; (ed) The Story: love, loss and the lives of women, 2013; The Sunrise, 2014. *Recreations:* music, tennis, Greek language and culture. *Address:* c/o David Miller, Rogers Coleridge & White, 20 Powis Mews, W11 1JN. *T:* (020) 7221 3717. *E:* victoria@victoriahislop.com.

HITCHCOCK, Patricia Ann, (Mrs P. S. Brooke-Ball); QC 2011; *b* Epsom, Surrey, 3 Feb. 1956; *d* of Eldred Arnold Hitchcock and Muriel, (Emma), Hitchcock (*née* Bilsland); *m* 1987, Peter Stuart Brooke-Ball; one *s* one *d*. *Educ:* Westminster Sch.; Brasenose Coll., Oxford (BA Hons Eng. Lang. and Lit. 1978); City Univ., London (DipLaw 1987). Publishing trainee, Rainbird Publishing Gp, 1978–79; Asst Ed., Albany Books, 1979; Paperback Buyer, Brentano's Univ. Bookstore, LA, 1980–81; freelance proofreader, Graphic Typesetting Service, 1981–82; Prodn Ed., Sage Publications, 1982; Senior Editor: Robert Nicholson Publications, 1982–84 (Mother, NUJ Chapel); Quill Publications, 1984–85; freelance contributor and ed., 1985–86; called to the Bar, Inner Temple, 1988; joined Cloisters Chambers, Temple, from pupillage as criminal defender; in practice as a barrister, specialising in medical law. *Publications:* (contrib.) Butterworths Personal Injury Litigation Service, 2003–; (contrib.) Lewis & Buchan: Clinical Negligence, a practical guide, 7th edn 2012; contrib. articles in Solicitors Jl, AVMA Medical, Legal Jl etc. *Recreations:* friends and family, food, ballet, theatre, travel, yoga. *Address:* Cloisters, 1 Pump Court, Temple, EC4Y 7AA. *T:* (020) 7827 4000. *E:* phi@cloisters.com.

HITCHENS, Rear Adm. Gilbert Archibald Ford, CB 1988; Director General Ship Refitting, Ministry of Defence, 1985–87, retired; *b* 11 April 1932; *m* 1961, Patricia Hamilton; one *s* one *d*. BA Hons. Joined Royal Navy, 1950; Commander, 1968; Guided Weapons Staff Officer, Min. of Technology, 1968–70; Exec. Officer, RNEC, 1970–72; Senior Officer while building and Weapon Engineer Officer, HMS Sheffield, 1973–75; MoD (Navy), 1975–77; Naval Attaché, Tokyo and Seoul, 1977–79; Asst Dir, Manpower Requirements, MoD (Navy), 1979–80; Dir, Officers' Appts (Eng.), 1980–82; Captain, HMS Defiance, 1982–84; ADC to the Queen, 1984; CSO Engrg to C-in-C Fleet, 1984–85. Mem., Plymouth DHA, 1989–90. Admiralty Gov., Royal Naval Benevolent Trust, 1989–96. Competitor, Commonwealth Winter Games, 1958. Chairman: RN Ski and Mountaineering Club, 1984–86; Govs, Devonport High Sch. for Boys, 1993–97. Liveryman, Ironmongers' Co., 1994. *Recreation:* any activity in the high hills.

See also T. M. Hitchens.

HITCHENS, Peter Jonathan; journalist and author; *b* 28 Oct. 1951; *s* of late Comdr Eric Ernest Hitchens and of Yvonne Jean Hitchens (*née* Hickman); *m* 1983, Eve Ross; two *s* one *d*. *Educ:* Leys Sch., Cambridge; Oxford Coll. of Further Educn; Univ. of York (BA 1973). Journalist: Socialist Worker, 1972; Swindon Evening Advertiser, 1973–76; Coventry Evening Telegraph, 1976; Daily Express, 1977–2001: sometime industrial reporter, Labour Corresp., Dep. Pol Ed., Diplomatic Corresp., Moscow Corresp., Washington Corresp., Asst Ed.; resigned 2001; reporter and columnist, Mail on Sunday, 2001–. Orwell Prize for Journalism, 2010. *Publications:* The Abolition of Britain, 1999; (contrib.) The Rape of the Constitution, 2000; Monday Morning Blues, 2000; The Abolition of Liberty, 2004; The Broken Compass, 2009; The Rage against God, 2010; The War We Never Fought, 2012; Short Breaks in Mordor, 2014. *Recreations:* long train journeys, second-hand bookshops. *Address:* Mail on Sunday, 2 Derry Street, W8 5TS. *T:* (020) 3615 3258. *E:* peter.hitchens@mailonsunday.co.uk.

HITCHENS, Timothy Mark, CMG 2012; LVO 1997; HM Diplomatic Service; Ambassador to Japan, since 2012; *b* 7 May 1962; *s* of Rear Adm. Gilbert Archibald Ford Hitchens, *qv*; *m* 1985, Sara Kubra; one *s* one *d*. *Educ:* Dulwich Coll.; Christ's Coll., Cambridge (BA). Foreign and Commonwealth Office, 1983–; Tokyo, 1985–89; Private Sec. to Minister of State, FCO, 1991–94; Speechwriter to Foreign Sec., 1994–95; First Sec., Islamabad, 1995–97; Asst Pvte Sec. to the Queen, 1998–2002; Hd, Africa Dept (Equatorial), FCO, 2003–05; Minister, Paris, 2005–08; Dir, Eur. Pol Affairs, FCO, 2008–10; Africa Dir, FCO, 2010–12. *Recreations:* walking, gardening. *Address:* c/o Foreign and Commonwealth Office, SW1A 2AH.

HITCHIN, Prof. Nigel James, DPhil; FRS 1991; Savilian Professor of Geometry, University of Oxford, since 1997; Fellow of New College, Oxford, since 1997; *b* 2 Aug. 1946; *s* of Eric Wilfred Hitchin and Bessie (*née* Blood); *m* 1973, Nedda Vejarano Bernal; one *s* one *d*. *Educ:* Ecclesbourne Sch., Duffield; Jesus Coll., Oxford (BA 1968; Hon. Fellow, 1998); Wolfson Coll., Oxford (MA, DPhil 1972). Res. Asst, Inst. for Advanced Study, Princeton, 1971–73; Instructor, Courant Inst., New York Univ., 1973–74; SRC Res. Asst, 1974–77, SRC Advanced Res. Fellow, 1977–79, Oxford Univ.; Fellow and Tutor in Maths, St Catherine's Coll., Oxford, 1979–90 (Hon. Fellow, 2014); Prof. of Maths, Univ. of Warwick, 1990–94; Rouse Ball Prof. of Maths, Univ. of Cambridge, 1994–97; Fellow of Gonville and Caius Coll., Cambridge, 1994–97 (Hon. Fellow, 2008). Vis. Prof., SUNY, Stony Brook, 1983. Hon. DSc: Bath, 2003; Warwick, 2014. London Mathematical Society: Pres., 1994–96; Jun. Whitehead Prize, 1981; Sen. Berwick Prize, 1990; Polya Prize, LMS, 2002; Sylvester Medal, Royal Soc., 2000. *Publications:* Monopoles, Minimal Surfaces and Algebraic Curves, 1987; (with M. F. Atiyah) The Geometry and Dynamics of Magnetic Monopoles, 1988; (with G. B. Segal and R. S. Ward) Integrable Systems: twistors, loop groups and Riemann surfaces, 1999; articles in learned jls. *Address:* Hampden Manor, 81 Mill Street, Kidlington OX5 2EB.

HITCHING, His Honour Alan Norman; a Circuit Judge, 1987–2006; Resident Judge, Blackfriars Crown Court, 1998–2006; *b* 5 Jan. 1941; *s* of late Norman Henry Samuel Hitching and Grace Ellen Hitching; *m* 1st, 1967, Hilda Muriel (*née* King) (*d* 2000); one *d* two *s*; 2nd, 2003, Susan Mary (*née* Banfield), *widow* of Michael Henry Cotton. *Educ:* Forest Sch., Snaresbrook; Christ Church, Oxford (BA 1962; Radcliffe Exhibnr and Dixon Scholar, 1962; BCL 1963; MA). Harmsworth Entrance Scholar, Middle Temple, 1960; Astbury Scholar and Safford Prize, Middle Temple, 1964; called to the Bar, Middle Temple, 1964, Bencher, 2005; Standing Counsel, Inland Revenue, SE Circuit, 1974–87; Dep. Circuit Judge, 1981–85, 2006–09; a Recorder, 1985–87. Cropwood Fellow, Inst. of Criminology, Cambridge, 1990. Vice-Pres., John Grooms Assoc. for the Disabled, 1991–2007 (Chm., 1981–89; Vice-Chm., 1978–81 and 1989–91). Licensed Reader, dio. of Chelmsford, 1987–2001; ordained deacon, 2001, priest, 2002; NSM, High Ongar, Chelmsford, 2001–05; permission to officiate, Chelmsford dio., 2005–; Chaplain, Metropolitan Police, 2010–. Trustee, Tower Hamlets Mission, 2009–. *Recreations:* people, pottery, poetry, preaching. *Address:* c/o Middle Temple, Treasury Office, Middle Temple Lane, EC4Y 9AT.

HITCHINGS, (Christian Nicholas) Henry; freelance writer; Theatre Critic, London Evening Standard, since 2009; consultant editor, Oxford English Dictionary, since 2015; *b* Guildford, 11 Dec. 1974; *s* of Paul Barrington Knowles Hitchings and Mary Nichola Hitchings (*née* Adams). *Educ:* Eton Coll.; Christ Church, Oxford (BA 1996); University Coll. London (PhD 2002). *Publications:* Dr Johnson's Dictionary, 2005; The Secret Life of Words, 2008 (John Llewellyn Rhys Prize, Booktrust, 2008; Somerset Maugham Award, Soc. of Authors, 2009); Who's Afraid of Jane Austen?, 2009; The Language Wars, 2011; Sorry! The English and their Manners, 2013. *Recreations:* walking, wine. *Address:* c/o Rogers, Coleridge & White Ltd, 20 Powis Mews, W11 1JN. *Club:* Blacks.

HITCHINGS, Prof. Roger Alan, FRCS; FRCOphth; Ophthalmic Surgeon, 1978–2008, Consultant, 1981–2008 and Director, Research and Development, 2000–08, Moorfields Eye Hospital, now Honorary Consultant Ophthalmologist; Professor of Glaucoma and Allied Studies, Institute of Ophthalmology, University College London, 1999–2008, now Emeritus; *b* 30 May 1942; *s* of Alan and Mary Hitchings; *m* 1966, Virmati Talwar; two *d*. *Educ:* Steyning Grammar Sch.; Royal Free Hosp. (MB BS). FRCS 1971; FRCOphth 1988. Resident Surgical Officer, Moorfields Eye Hosp., 1969–73; Res. Fellow, Wills Eye Hosp., 1973–75; Sen. Lectr, Univ. of London, 1975–79; Consultant Ophthalmic Surgeon, KCH, 1979–81. Vis. Prof., Nat. Univ. Hosp. Singapore, 2010–13. President: Eur. Glaucoma Soc., 2000–08; World Glaucoma Assoc., 2001–03; Mem., German Ophthalmological Soc. Lectures: Duke Elder, 1997, Bowman, 2008, Royal Coll. Ophthalmologists; Shaffer, Amer. Acad. Ophthalmologists, 2000; Spaeth Commemorative, Amer. Glaucoma Soc., 2001; Ida Mann, Oxford Univ., 2002; Goldmann, Glaucoma Res. Soc., 2006; Bartisch, Univ. of Dresden, 2009. Internat. Scholar Award, American Glaucoma Soc., 2014. *Publications:* Atlas of Clinical Ophthalmology, 1984, 3rd edn 2005; The Refractory Glaucomas, 1995; Glaucoma: a practical guide, 2000; Glaucoma (2 vols), 2009, 2nd edn 2014; over 250 peer-reviewed papers on glaucoma and allied subjects. *Recreations:* Rotary, Probus, history, gardening, travel.

HITCHMOUGH, Andrew John; QC 2013; *b* Warrington, 18 Sept. 1968; *s* of Joseph Neil Hitchmough and Enid Hitchmough; *m* 2003, Sarah Baker. *Educ:* Abraham Guest High Sch., Wigan; Winstanley Coll., Wigan; Southampton Univ. (LLB 1st Cl. Hons). Called to the Bar, Inner Temple, 1991; in practice as barrister, specialising in tax, 1991–. *Recreations:* boating, diving, shooting, fly fishing, ski-ing. *Address:* Pump Court Tax Chambers, 16 Bedford Row, WC1R 4EF. *T:* (020) 7414 8080, *Fax:* (020) 7414 8099. *E:* ahitchmough@pumptax.com.

HIVES, family name of **Baron Hives**.

HIVES, 3rd Baron *cr* 1950, of Duffield, co. Derby; **Matthew Peter Hives;** engineer; Director, DWN Investments Ltd, since 2013; *b* 25 May 1971; *s* of Hon. Peter Anthony Hives (*d* 1974) and Dinah (*née* Wilson-North); *S* uncle, 1997. *Educ:* Haileybury; Newcastle Univ. (BEng); Aberdeen Univ. (MSc). MIMechE. Formerly with GEC/ALSTOM. *Heir: uncle* Hon. Michael Bruce Hives [*b* 12 March 1926; *m* 1951, Janet Rosemary (*née* Gee); two *s* one *d*]. *Address:* Gombrette House, La Rue de Gombrette, St John, Jersey JE3 4EF.

HIX, Hilary Anne; *see* Ross, H. A.

HIX, Mark; restaurateur, chef and food writer; Owner: Hix Oyster & Chop House, London, since 2008; Hix Oyster and Fish House, Dorset, since 2008; Hix Restaurant, London, since 2009; Hix Restaurant and Champagne Bar, since 2010; The Tramshed, since 2012; Hixter, since 2013; Hixter Bankside, since 2014; Director of Food, Browns Hotel, London, since 2008; *b* 10 Dec. 1962; *s* of Ernest and Gill Hix; *m* Suzie Hix (marr. diss.); three *d*. *Educ:* Colfox Sch.; Weymouth Coll. Commis Chef, Grosvenor Hse Hotel, 1981–83; Commis Chef, later Chef de Partie, Dorchester, 1983–84; Sous Chef, then Hd Chef, Mr Pontacs/Candlewick Room, 1985–90 (Michelin Red M award); Hd Chef, Le Caprice; Exec. Hd Chef, 1990–2008, Chef Dir, 1992–2008, Caprice Hldgs Ltd, overseeing Le Caprice and The Ivy (Michelin Red M award); Chef Director: J. Sheekey, Covent Gdn, 1998–2008; Daphne's, 2000–08; Bam-Bou, 2000–08; Pasha, 2000–08. Recipe column: Independent on Saturday mag. (Glenfiddich Award, Best Newspaper Cookery Writer, 2003); Country Life. Best

Cookery Writer, Guild of Food Writers, 2005; Chef of the Year, GQ Mag., 2008; Restaurateur of the Year, Tatler, 2009; Chef of the Year, Catey Awards, 2010. *Publications:* The Ivy: the restaurant and its recipes, 1997; (with A. A. Gill) Le Caprice: the book, 1999; Eat Up, 2000; British, 2003, 2nd edn 2005; Fish Etc, 2004; (with M. Gluck) The Simple Art of Food and Wine, 2005; British Regional Food: in search of the best British food today, 2006; British Seasonal Food, 2008; Hix Oyster and Chop House, 2010; Mark Hix on Baking, 2012. *Recreations:* fishing, foraging, shooting, golf, art collecting. *E:* mhix@hixfoodetc.co.uk. *Clubs:* Groucho, Soho House, Royal Automobile; Stoke Park Golf.

HOAD, Pamela Joan; *see* Gordon, P. J.

HOAR, Rev. Ronald William Cecil; Chairman, Manchester and Stockport Methodist District, 1979–95; President of the Methodist Conference, 1991–92; *b* 31 Oct. 1931; *s* of Cecil Herbert William and Lilian Augusta Hoar; *m* 1956, Peggy Jean (*née* Stubbington); three *s* two *d*. *Educ:* Shedfield Church of England Primary Sch., Hants; Price's Sch., Fareham, Hants; Richmond Coll., Univ. of London (BD). Methodist Minister: Wells, Somerset, 1955–58; Bermondsey, London, 1958–62; Westminster and Chelsea, 1962–67; Bristol Mission, 1967–76; Great Yarmouth and Gorleston, 1976–79. *Publications:* Methodism in Chelsea to 1963, 1963; A Good Ideal: a history of the Bristol Methodist Mission, 1973; Advertising the Gospel, 1991. *Recreations:* DIY, watching sport, oil painting, gardening. *Address:* 43 Green Lanes, Prestatyn, Denbighshire LL19 7BH. *T:* (01745) 886923.

HOARE, Alexander Simon; private banker; Managing Partner, C. Hoare & Co., since 2009 (Chief Executive, 2001–09); *b* 1 April 1962; *s* of Christopher E. B. Hoare and Sylvia M. Hoare; *m* 2012, Claudia, *d* of David and Suzanne Martin; one *s*. *Educ:* Winchester Coll.; Univ. of Edinburgh (BComm Hons). ACIB 1990. Consultant Analyst, PA Consulting Gp, 1985–87; joined C. Hoare & Co., 1987–. Non-exec. Dir, Jupiter Green Investment Trust Plc, 2006–09. *Address:* C. Hoare & Co., 37 Fleet Street, EC4P 4DQ. *Club:* St Mawes Billiards and Social.

HOARE, Sir Antony; *see* Hoare, Sir C. A. R.

HOARE, Rev. Brian Richard; Methodist Minister, 1971–2000; Methodist Evangelism Secretary, 1996–2000; President of the Methodist Conference, 1995–96; *b* 9 Dec. 1935; *s* of William Charles Hoare and Kathleen Nora Hoare (*née* Thwaites); *m* 1962, Joyce Eleanor Davidson; one *s* one *d*. *Educ:* Southwell Minster Grammar Sch., Notts; Westminster Coll., London (Teacher's Cert.); Richmond Coll., Univ. of London (BD 1971). Ops Clerk, RAF, 1954–56. Teacher, Col Frank Seely Secondary Sch., Calverton, Notts, 1959–62; Travelling Sec., subsequently Nat. Sec., Colls of Educn Christian Union, Inter-Varsity Fellowship, London, 1962–68. Chaplain Hunmanby Hall Sch., Filey, 1971–74; Minister, Hull Methodist Mission, 1974–77; New Testament Tutor, Cliff Coll., Sheffield, 1977–86; Superintendent Minister, Longton Central Hall, Stoke-on-Trent, 1986–88; Divl Sec. 1988–89, Dep. Gen. Sec. 1989–95, Home Mission Div. Member: World Methodist Council, Nairobi, 1986, Singapore, 1991, Rio de Janeiro, 1996, Brighton, 2001; World Methodist Exec. Cttee, Bulgaria, 1992, Estonia, 1994. Chairman: Epworth Old Rectory, 2000–08; Pratt Green Trust, 2007–15. *Publications:* (ed) Methods of Mission, 1979; Evangelism in New Testament Practice and Methodist Tradition, 1984; Hymns and Songs for Worship, 1985; Celebrate and Sing, 1991; 20 Things to do in a Decade of Evangelism, 1991; By the Way: six studies in incidental evangelism, 1995; New Creation: a full length musical presentation, 1995; Singing Faith, 1998; (ed) Leisure and Mission, 2000; (jtly) More than a Methodist, 2003; Cover to Cover: studies in Revelation, 2006; hymns and songs (words and music) published in a variety of books. *Recreations:* music, literature, travel. *Address:* 5 Flaxdale Close, Knaresborough, N Yorks HG5 0NZ.

HOARE, Sir (Charles) Antony (Richard), (Tony), Kt 2000; FRS 1982; FREng; Consultant Principal Researcher, Microsoft Research Ltd, Cambridge, since 2013 (Principal Researcher, 1999–2013); *b* 11 Jan. 1934; *s* of late Henry S. M. Hoare and Marjorie F. Hoare; *m* 1962, Jill Pym; one *s* one *d* (and one *s* decd). *Educ:* King's Sch., Canterbury; Merton Coll., Oxford (MA, Cert. Stats; Hon. Fellow, 2003); Moscow State Univ. Computer Div., Elliott Brothers, London, Ltd, 1960–68: successively Programmer, Chief Engr, Tech. Man., Chief Scientist; National Computer Centre, 1968; Prof. of Computer Science, QUB, 1968–77; Oxford University: Fellow, Wolfson Coll., 1977–99; Prof. of Computation, then James Martin Prof. of Inf. Engrg, 1977–99. Lee Kuan Yew Distinguished Visitor, Singapore, 1992; Einstein Prof., Chinese Acad. of Sci., 2006. Dist. FBCS 1978; MAE 1989; FREng 2005. For. Mem., Accademia Nazionale dei Lincei, 1988; Corresp. Mem., Bavarian Acad. of Scis, 1997; For. Associate, US NAE, 2006. Hon. Fellow: Kellogg Coll., Oxford, 1999; Darwin Coll., Cambridge, 2001. Hon. DSc: Southern California, 1979; Warwick, 1985; Pennsylvania, 1986; Belfast, 1987; York, 1989; Essex 1991; Bath, 1993; Oxford Brookes, 2000; QMC, 2005; Heriot-Watt, 2007; Athens Univ. of Econs and Business, 2007; Warsaw, 2012; Madrid, 2013; St Petersburg (Inf. Technologies, Mechanics and Optics), 2013. A. M. Turing Award, Assoc. Comp. Mach., 1980; Harry Goode Meml Award, Amer. Fedn of Inf. Processing Socs, 1981; Faraday Medal, IEE, 1985; Computer Pioneer Award, 1991, John von Neumann Medal, 2011, IEEE; Kyoto Prize, Inamori Foundn, 2000; F. L. Bauer Prize, Technical Univ. Munich, 2007; Distinguished Achievement Award, Special Interest Gp on Programming Langs, ACM, 2012. *Publications:* Structured Programming (with O.-J. Dahl and E. W. Dijkstra), 1972; Communicating Sequential Processes, 1985; (with C. B. Jones) Essays in Computing Science, 1988; (with He Jifeng) Unifying Theories of Programming, 1998; articles in Computer Jl, Commun. ACM, and Acta Informatica; *festschrift:* A Classical Mind, 1994; Reflections on the Work of C. A. R. Hoare, 2010. *Recreations:* walking, reading, listening to music. *Address:* (office) 21 Station Road, Cambridge CB1 2FB.

HOARE, Sir Charles James, 9th Bt *cr* 1784, of Annabella, Cork; International Secretary, Christian Action Research and Education, since 1998; *b* 15 March 1971; *s* of Sir Timothy Edward Charles Hoare, 8th Bt, OBE and of Felicity Anne (*née* Boddington); *S* father, 2008; *m* 2000, Hon. Eleanor Filumena Flower, *o d* of Viscount Ashbrook, *qv*; one *s* two *d*. *Educ:* Pimlico Sch.; Durham Univ. (BA); London Sch. of Econs (MSc). OStJ. *Heir:* *s* Edward Harry William Hoare, *b* 13 Feb. 2006.

HOARE, Christopher Henry St John, (Toby); Executive Chairman, since 2005, and Chief Executive Officer, Europe, since 2006, J. Walter Thomson Group; Chairman, Geometry Global, since 2013; *b* 2 Feb. 1960; *s* of J. Michael Hoare and Ann St J. Hoare; *m* 1986, Hon. Sarah Jane Dixon-Smith; two *s* one *d*. *Educ:* Harrow. Distillers Co. Ltd, 1979–80; Express Newspapers, 1980–84; Centaur Communications, 1984–85; Dorland Advertising, 1985–87; Young & Rubicam, 1987–99; Gp Chief Exec., Bates UK Ltd, 1999–2002; Chm., Bates Gp Europe, 2002–04; CEO, Team HSBC, WPP Gp, 2004–05. Governor, Harrow Sch., 2002–. Freeman, City of London, 1987; Liveryman, Co. of Distillers, 1982. *Recreations:* shooting, golf, theatre, football. *Address:* 17 Stanley Crescent, W11 2NA. *T:* (020) 7221 5159; The Old Rectory, Bradfield St George, Bury St Edmunds, Suffolk IP30 0DH. *Clubs:* Garrick; Royal Newmarket & Worlington Golf.

HOARE, Sir David (John), 9th Bt *cr* 1786, of Barn Elms, Surrey; Managing Partner, C. Hoare & Co., Bankers, since 2006 (Chairman, 2001–06); *b* 8 Oct. 1935; *s* of Sir Peter William Hoare, 7th Bt, and Laura Ray Hoare, *o d* of Sir John Esplen, 1st Bt, KBE; *S* brother, 2004; *m* 1st, 1965, Mary Vanessa Cardew (marr. diss. 1978); one *s*; 2nd, 1984, Virginia Victoria Graham Labes. *Educ:* Eton. Commnd Nat. Service, 1954–56. Joined Hoare's Bank, 1959: Man. Partner, 1964–88; Dep. Chm., 1988–2001. Dir, Mitre Court Property Holding Co., 1964. Chm., Internat. Atlantic Salmon Club, 1995–2015. Trustee, West Country Rivers Trust, 1996. *Recreations:* fishing, golf, shooting, ski-ing, forestry. *Heir:* *s* Simon Merrik Hoare [*b* 11 Oct. 1967; *m* 1st, 1999, Aurélie, *d* of Jean-François Catoire (marr. diss. 2009); two *s*; 2nd, 2011, Sandra, *d* of Alain Sortais; two *s*]. *Address:* Luscombe Castle, Dawlish, Devon EX7 0PU; C. Hoare & Co., 37 Fleet Street, EC4P 4DQ. *Clubs:* White's; Royal St George's Golf, Swinley Forest Golf.

HOARE, Henry Cadogan; Senior Partner, C. Hoare & Co., Bankers (Chairman, 1988–2001); *b* 23 Nov. 1931; *s* of late Henry Peregrine Rennie Hoare and of Lady Beatrix Fanshawe, *d* of 6th Earl Cadogan, CBE; *m* 1st, 1959, Pamela Bunbury (marr. diss. 1970); two *s* one *d*; 2nd, 1977, Caromy Maxwell Macdonald. *Educ:* Eton; Trinity Coll., Cambridge (MA). Career in banking. *Address:* c/o C. Hoare & Co., 37 Fleet Street, EC4P 4DQ.

HOARE, Michelle S., (Brie); *see* Stevens-Hoare.

HOARE, Rt Rev. Dr Rupert William Noel; Dean of Liverpool, 2000–07, now Dean Emeritus; an Assistant Bishop, Diocese of Manchester, since 2008; *b* 3 March 1940; *s* of Julian Hoare and Edith Hoare (*née* Temple); *m* 1965, Gesine (*née* Pflüger); three *s* one *d*. *Educ:* Rugby School; Trinity Coll., Oxford (BA 1961, MA 1967); Kirchliche Hochschule, Berlin; Westcott House and Fitzwilliam House, Cambridge (BA 1964); Birmingham Univ. (PhD 1973). Deacon 1964, priest 1965, Dio. Manchester; Curate of St Mary, Oldham, 1964–67; Lecturer, Queen's Theological Coll., Birmingham, 1968–72; Canon Theologian of Coventry Cathedral, 1970–75; Rector, Parish of the Resurrection, Manchester, 1972–78; Residentiary Canon, Birmingham Cathedral, 1978–81; Principal, Westcott House, Cambridge, 1981–93; Bishop Suffragan of Dudley, 1993–99. *Publications:* (trans. jtly) Bultmann's St John, 1971; (contrib.) Queen's Sermons, 1973, Queen's Essays, 1980; The Trial of Faith, 1988; articles in Theology. *Recreations:* hill walking, gardening, listening to music. *Address:* 14 Shaw Hall Bank Road, Greenfield, Saddleworth, Oldham OL3 7LD.

HOARE, Simon James; MP (C) North Dorset, since 2015; *b* Cardiff, 28 June 1969; *s* of Colin and Maria Hoare; *m* 2000, Kate, *y d* of William Lund, FRCS; three *d*. *Educ:* Bishop Hannon High Sch., Cardiff; Greyfriars, Oxford (BA Hons Modern Hist.). Business and public affairs consultant to land owners, farmers, public sector and property develt cos; family business in oil sector; Man. Dir, Community Connect Ltd, 2002–15. Member (C): W Oxfordshire DC, 2004–15 (Cabinet Mem., Resources, 2007–15); Oxfordshire CC, 2013–15. *Recreations:* gardening, collecting, horse racing, family. *Address:* House of Commons, SW1A 0AA. *T:* (020) 7219 5697. *E:* simon.hoare.mp@parliament.uk. *Clubs:* Garrick, Royal Over-Seas League; Blandford Constitutional; Newport Boat (Pembrokeshire).

HOARE, Toby; *see* Hoare, C. H. St J.

HOBAN, Mark Gerard; chartered accountant; *b* 31 March 1964; *s* of Tom Hoban and Maureen Hoban (*née* Orchard); *m* 1994, Fiona Jane Barrett. *Educ:* London Sch. of Econs (BSc Econs 1985). ACA 1989. With Coopers & Lybrand, then PricewaterhouseCoopers, 1985–2001, Sen. Manager, 1992–2001. Contested (C) South Shields, 1997. MP (C) Fareham, 2001–15. An Opposition Whip, 2002–03; Shadow Minister for Educn, 2003–05; Shadow Financial Sec., HM Treasury, 2005–10; Shadow Minister for Wearside, 2007–10; Financial Sec., HM Treasury, 2010–12; Minister of State, DWP, 2012–13. Mem., Select Cttee on Sci. and Technology, 2001–03. Chm., Flood Re, 2015–; non-exec. Dir, London Stock Exchange, 2015–; Sen. Advr, Markit Gp Ltd, 2014–. Hon. Vice-Pres., Soc. of Maritime Industries, 2003–10. Freeman, City of London, 2003; Liveryman, Fruiterers' Co., 2003. *Recreations:* cooking, entertaining, reading, travel. *Address:* 20 The Vale, Locks Heath, Southampton SO31 6NL.

HOBART (Australia), Archbishop of, (RC), since 1999; **Most Rev. Adrian Leo Doyle,** AM 2009; *b* 16 Nov. 1936; *s* of George Leo Doyle and Gertrude Mary (*née* O'Donnell). *Educ:* Urbaniana Univ., Rome (ThL, PhL); Gregorian Univ., Rome (DCL). Ordained priest, Rome, 1961; Parish Priest, Sandy Bay, Tasmania, 1974–90; VG, Archdio. of Hobart, 1997–99; apptd Coadjutor Archbishop of Hobart, 1997, ordained bishop, 1998. Judge: Regl Marriage Tribunal, Victoria and Tasmania, 1968–; Nat. Appeal Tribunal, Aust. and NZ, 1974–. *Recreations:* golf, walking, reading. *Address:* GPO Box 62, Hobart, Tas 7001, Australia. *T:* (3) 62086222. *Club:* Athenæum (Hobart).

HOBART, David Anthony, CB 2004; Chief Executive, City of London Law Society, since 2011; Gentleman Usher to the Queen, since 2007; *b* 24 Dec. 1951; *m* 1977, Mandy Wilson; one *s* one *d*. *Educ:* Magdalene Coll., Cambridge (MPhil); LLB Open Univ. rcds; jsdc; psc. Various planning and financial programming posts in MoD; promoted to Air Vice-Marshal, 2001; ACDS (Policy), 2001–04; Chief Exec., Bar Council, 2004–11. *Recreations:* golf, ski-ing. *Address:* City of London Law Society, 4 College Hill, EC4R 2RB. *Clubs:* Royal Air Force; Wildernesse (Kent), Royal Cinque Ports Golf (Deal).

HOBART, Sir John Vere, 4th Bt *cr* 1914, of Langdown, Co. Southampton; *b* 9 April 1945; *s* of Lt-Comdr Sir Robert Hampden Hobart, 3rd Bt, RN and Sylvia (*d* 1965), *d* of Harry Argo; *heir-pres.* to Earl of Buckinghamshire, *qv*; *S* father, 1988; *m* 1980, Kate, *o d* of late George Henry Iddles; two *s*. *Educ:* Royal Agricl Coll., Cirencester. Mem. (C) Isle of Wight Council, 2009–. *Heir:* *s* George Hampden Hobart, *b* 10 June 1982.

HOBART-HAMPDEN, family name of **Earl of Buckinghamshire**.

HOBBS, Prof. Angela Hunter, PhD; Professor of the Public Understanding of Philosophy, University of Sheffield, since 2012; *b* Rudgwick, Sussex, 12 June 1961; *d* of Anthony Hobbs and Rosemary Hobbs (*née* Davies); one *d*. *Educ:* Coll. of Richard Collyer, Horsham, Sussex; New Hall, Cambridge (BA Classics 1983; MA 1986; PhD Classics 1991). W. H. D. Rouse Fellow in Classics, Christ's Coll., Cambridge, 1989–92; Warwick University: Lectr in Philosophy, 1992–2001; Associate Prof. in Philosophy, 2001–09; Sen. Fellow in the Public Understanding of Philosophy, 2009–12. Chair, Arts and Ideas Trust, 2011–; Patron, Philosophy in Educn Project; Hon. Patron, Philosophy Foundn, 2011–. Associate Fellow, Crick Centre. Contributor to radio progs, incl. In Our Time, and TV progs, newspapers, audio books and websites. FRSA 2010. *Publications:* (contrib.) Concise Oxford Dictionary of Politics, 1996, 3rd edn 2008; (contrib.) Routledge Encyclopedia of Philosophy, 1998; Plato and the Hero, 2000; (contrib.) Plato's Symposium: issues in interpretation and reception, 2006; (contrib.) Maieusis: essays in ancient philosophy in honour of Myles Burnyeat, 2007; (contrib.) In Our Time, 2009; (contrib.) Oxford Encyclopedia of Ancient Greece and Rome, 2010; (contrib.) Philosophy Bites Back, 2012; (contrib.) The Philosophy Shop, 2012; (contrib.) Continuum Companion to Plato, 2012; contribs to Philosophy, Psychiatry and Psychol., Philosophical Inquiry. *Recreations:* theatre, music, reading, walking, travelling, canoeing, cricket. *Address:* Department of Philosophy, University of Sheffield, 45 Victoria Street, Sheffield S3 7QB. *T:* (0114) 222 0594, (0114) 222 0571. *E:* a.hobbs@sheffield.ac.uk. *W:* www.angiehobbs.com, www.twitter.com/drangiehobbs.

HOBBS, Christina; *see* Dodwell, C.

HOBBS, Prof. (Frederick David) Richard, FRCGP, FRCP; FMedSci; FESC; Professor and Head of Primary Care, University of Oxford, since 2011; Fellow, Harris Manchester College, Oxford, since 2011; *b* 2 Nov. 1953; *s* of Frederick Derek Hobbs and Nancy Elizabeth (*née* Wilde); *m* 1977, Jane Marilyn Porter; one *s* one *d*. *Educ:* King Edward VI Camp Hill Sch., Birmingham; Bristol Univ. (MB, ChB 1977). MRCGP 1981, FRCGP 1990; FRCP 2000. House officer posts, Bath Royal United Hosp., 1977–78; Sen. house officer posts, Selly Oak Hosp., Birmingham, 1978–80; GP trainee, Univ. Health Centre, Birmingham, 1980–81; Principal in general practice, Bellevue Med. Centre, Birmingham, 1981– (part-time, 1992–); Birmingham University: part-time Sen. Lectr in General Practice, 1985–92; Prof. and Hd,

Dept of Primary Care Clinical Scis (formerly Primary Care and Gen. Practice), 1992–2011; Asst Dean, Sch. of Medicine, 1993–96; Hd, Div. of Primary Care, Public and Occupational Health, 1998–2001; Associate Dean, Sch. of Medicine, 2002–05; Hd, Sch. of Health and Pop. Scis, 2009–11. Dir, NIHR Nat. Sch. for Primary Care Res., 2009–. FMedSci 2002; FESC 2002. *Publications:* 12 books; 30 book chapters; over 360 peer-reviewed articles. *Recreations:* gardening, travel, interests in music (passive), wine and good food. *Address:* Nuffield Department of Primary Care Health Sciences, University of Oxford, New Radcliffe House, Radcliffe Observatory Quarter, Walton Street, Oxford OX2 6GG.

HOBBS, Jennifer Lynn, MBE 1992; Principal, St Mary's College, Durham University, 1999–2007; *b* 5 March 1944; *d* of Henry Edwin Hobbs and Jean Hobbs (*née* Kennedy). *Educ:* St Paul's Girls' Sch., London; Newnham Coll., Cambridge (BA (Hons) Geog 1966; MA 1970). VSO teacher, Malacca Girls' High Sch., Malaysia, 1966–68; Geography Editor, Overseas Educ. Dept, Macmillan Education, 1968–73; British Council, 1973–94: various posts in UK; Nepal, 1979–83; Yugoslavia/Croatia, 1988–92; on secondment, Univ. of Durham, 1992–94; University of Durham, 1994–2007: Dir, Internat. Office, 1994–2004; Associate Dean for Student Support Services, 2004–05. Mem., Durham Cathedral Council, 2001–07. FRSA 2003. Governor: Durham Sch., 1998–2005; Durham High Sch. for Girls, 2007–10; Pilgrims' Sch., Winchester, 2009–. Mem., Portsmouth and Winchester Diocesan Bd of Educn, 2013 (Chm., 2010–12). *Recreations:* classical music, choral singing, sport, walking, birdwatching, gardening, environmental sustainability issues.

HOBBS, Dr Jeremy Alexander; HM Diplomatic Service; Ambassador to Paraguay, since 2013; *b* Dunfermline, 8 Feb. 1961; *s* of Brian Hobbs and Patricia Hobbs (*née* Bullman); *m* 1983, Ana Maria Erendira Granados; one *s* one *d*. *Educ:* Monterey Prep. Sch., Wynberg, SA; Arthur Mellows Village Coll., Glinton, Peterborough; Portsmouth Poly. (BA Latin American Studies); Univ. of Essex (MA Latin American Govt and Politics; PhD Govt 1991). Entered FCO, 1991; Sen. Res. Officer, FCO, 1991–95; Second Sec. (Pol/Tech. Cooperation), Bogota, 1995–99; Principal Res. Officer, FCO, 1999–2003; First Sec. (Pol), Mexico City, 2003–06; Sen. Principal Res. Officer, FCO, 2006–13; Chargé d'Affaires, Quito, 2012. *Recreations:* swimming, rowing, reading, listening to music, cooking. *Address:* 18 Groves Close, Colchester, Essex CO4 5BP. *T:* (01206) 851254. *E:* jeremy.hobbs@fco.gov.uk.

HOBBS, Prof. Kenneth Edward Frederick, ChM, FRCS; Professor of Surgery, Royal Free Hospital School of Medicine, University of London, and Consultant Surgeon, Royal Free Hampstead NHS Trust (formerly Royal Free Hospital), 1973–98, then Emeritus Professor; Chairman, Joint Board of Surgery, University College London Medical School and Royal Free Hospital School of Medicine, 1993–98; Dean, University of London Faculty of Medicine, 1994–98; *b* 28 Dec. 1936; *s* of late Thomas Edward Ernest Hobbs and Gladys May Hobbs (*née* Neave). *Educ:* West Suffolk County Grammar Sch., Bury St Edmunds; Guy's Hosp. Med. Sch., Univ. of London (MB BS 1960). ChM Bristol 1970; FRCS 1964. Lectr in Surgery, Univ. of Bristol, 1966–70; Surgical Res. Fellow, Harvard Univ., 1968–69; Sen. Lectr in Surgery, Univ. of Bristol, 1970–73; University of London: Vice-Dean, Faculty of Medicine, 1986–90; Mem. Senate, then Council, 1985–98; Chm., Acad. Adv. Bd in Medicine, 1986–90; Dep. Chm., Acad. Council Standing Sub-Cttee in Medicine, 1986–90. Mem., Systems Bd, MRC, 1982–86; Chm., Grants Cttee A, MRC, 1984–86; Member: Med. Sub-Cttee, UGC, 1986–89; Med. Cttee, UFC, 1991–92; GMC, 1996–2001 (Dep. Chm., Professional Conduct Cttee, 1999–2001; Professional Mem., Fitness to Practise Cttee, 2002–06; Mem., Fitness to Practise Panels, 2009–); Mason Med. Res. Foundn, 1988–98 (Chm., 1993–98). Vis. Prof., Univs in China, Ethiopia, S Africa, Europe, USA, West Indies. Secretary: Patey Soc., 1979–82; 1942 Club, 1985–88; Trustee and Bd Mem., Stanley Thomas Johnson Foundn, Berne, 1976–2004 (Chm., 1997–2004). Gov., Norfolk and Norwich Univ. Hosp. Foundn Trust, 2008–. Hon. Fellow, Chinese Univ. of Hong Kong, 2002. Hon. FCSSL 1995. Internat. Master Surgeon, Internat. Coll. of Surgeons, 1994. FRSocMed 1973. *Publications:* chapters on aspects of liver surgery in textbooks; contribs to professional jls. *Recreations:* gourmet cooking and dining, the countryside. *Address:* Apartment 10, Westlegate Tower, 14–18 Westlegate, Norwich NR1 3LJ. *T:* (01603) 613529. *Club:* Royal Society of Medicine.

HOBBS, Maj.-Gen. Sir Michael (Frederick), KCVO 1998; CBE 1982 (OBE 1979; MBE 1975); Governor, Military Knights of Windsor, 2000–12; *b* 28 Feb. 1937; *s* of late Brig. Godfrey Pennington Hobbs and Elizabeth Constance Mary Hobbs; *m* 1967, Tessa Mary Churchill; one *s* two *d*. *Educ:* Eton College. Served Grenadier Guards, 1956–80; Directing Staff, Staff Coll., 1974–77; MoD, 1980–82; Commander 39 Inf. Bde, 1982–84; Dir of PR (Army), 1984–85; Commander, 4th Armoured Div., 1985–87; retired. Director: Duke of Edinburgh's Award, 1988–98; Outward Bound Trust, 1995–2006.

HOBBS, Peter Thomas Goddard; HM first lay Inspector of Constabulary, 1993–98; *b* 19 March 1938; *s* of late Reginald Stanley Hobbs, BEM, Gloucester and of Phyllis Gwendoline (*née* Goddard); *m* 1964, Victoria Christabel, *d* of late Rev. Alan Matheson, Clifton Campville, Staffs; one *d*. *Educ:* Crypt Sch., Glos; Exeter Coll., Oxford (Waugh Scholar; MA). Nat. Service, 2nd Lt, RASC, 1957–59; Capt., RCT, TA, 1959–68. With ICI Ltd, 1962–79 (Jt Personnel Manager, Mond Div.); Gp Personnel Dir, Wellcome Foundn and Wellcome PLC, 1979–92. Chemical Industries Association: Dep. Chm., Pharmaceuticals and Fine Chemical Jt Industrial Council, 1979–89; Chairman: Trng Cttee, 1985–89; Employment Affairs Bd, 1989–91; Mem. Council, 1989–92; Chm., Chem. Industry Educn Centre, Univ. of York, 1992–94. Dir, Employment Conditions Abroad Ltd, 1984–91 and 1993. Confederation of British Industry: Member: Task Force on Vocational Educn and Trng, 1989–90; Educn and Trng Cttee, 1990–94; Business in the Community: Member, Target Team: for Industrial/Educn Partnerships, 1988–90; for Priority Hiring, 1988–91; Founder Chm., Employers' Forum on Disability, 1986–93; Mem., Nat. Adv. Council on Employment for People with Disabilities, 1991–93; Trustee, Learning from Experience Trust, 1988– (Chm., 1992–93 and 1998–2008). Member: Council, Contemporary Applied Arts, 1990–92; Industry Adv. Gp, Nat. Curriculum Council, 1990–92; Personnel Standards Lead Body, 1992–94; Council, EDEXCEL (formerly BTEC), 1995–98. Non-exec. Dir, Forensic Sci. Service, 1996–2006. Director: and Dep. Chm., Roffey Park Inst., 1989–93; Centre for Enterprise, London Business Sch., 1989–92; Mem. Adv. Council, Mgt Centre Europe, Brussels, 1989–97. Gov., Kent Coll., Canterbury, 2013–. Trustee, Canterbury Archaeol Trust, 2013–. CCIPD 1988 (Internat. Vice Pres., 1987–89, 1990–91); FInstD 1989 (Mem., Employment Cttee, 1989–93); FRSA 1992. Dr *hc* Internat. Mgt Centres, 2000. *Recreations:* history, archaeology, opera, turning the soil. *Address:* 105 Blenheim Crescent, W11 2EQ. *T:* (020) 7727 3054, *Fax:* (020) 7221 9542. *Club:* Oxford and Cambridge.

HOBBS, Philip John; racehorse trainer, since 1985; *b* 26 July 1955; *s* of Tony and Barbara Hobbs; *m* 1982, Sarah Louise Hill; three *d*. *Educ:* King's Coll., Taunton; Univ. of Reading (BSc). Rode 160 winners as a jockey; has trained over 2000 winners, 1985–. *Recreations:* skiing, shooting. *Address:* Sandhill Racing Stables, Bilbrook, Minehead, Somerset TA24 6HA. *T:* (01984) 640366, *Fax:* (01984) 641124. *E:* pjhobbs@pjhobbs.com. *Club:* Sportsman.

HOBBS, Richard; *see* Hobbs, F. D. R.

HOBBS, Prof. Roger Edwin, PhD, DSc; FIStructE, FICE; Director, Tension Technology International, since 1986; Professor of Engineering Structures, Imperial College of Science, Technology and Medicine, London, 1990–2003, now Emeritus; *b* 24 Feb. 1943; *s* of Edwin Daniel Hobbs and Phyllis Eileen (*née* Chapman); *m* 1st, 1965, Barbara Ann Dalton (*d* 1987); one *s* two *d*; 2nd, 1989, Dorinda Elizabeth Mitchell. *Educ:* Imperial Coll., London (PhD 1966; DSc Eng 1996). FIStructE 1990; FICE 1995; FCGI 1996. Imperial College, London: Res. Asst, 1966–70; Lectr in Civil Engrg, 1970–83; Sen. Lectr, 1983–86; Reader in Structural Engrg, 1986–90; Hd, Dept of Civil Engrg, 1994–97. *Publications:* technical papers on steel structures, wire and high strength fibre ropes, offshore pipelines. *Recreations:* walking, France, preferably in combination. *Address:* Department of Civil and Environmental Engineering, Imperial College London, SW7 2AZ.

HOBBY, Russell Keith; General Secretary, National Association of Head Teachers, since 2010; *b* Abingdon, 22 Jan. 1972. *Educ:* Corpus Christi Coll., Oxford (BA 1st Cl. Hons PPE 1993). Damascus Tech Ltd, 1993–95; Second Sight Ltd, 1995–98; joined Hay Gp, 1998, Associate Dir, 1999–2010. *Publications:* The School Recruitment Handbook, 2004. *E:* Karen.Fucella@naht.org.uk.

HOBCRAFT, Kathleen Elizabeth; *see* Kiernan, K. E.

HOBDAY, Peter James; journalist and broadcaster; *s* of Arthur John Hobday and Dorothy Ann Hobday (*née* Lewis); *m* 1st, 1959, Tamara Batcharnikoff (*d* 1984); one *s* one *d*; 2nd, 1996, Victoria Fenwick. *Educ:* St Chad's Coll., Wolverhampton; Leicester Univ. Wolverhampton Express and Star, 1960; Business magazine, 1960–61; The Director, 1961–74; joined BBC, 1970: World Service, 1970–74; Financial World Tonight, 1974–80, Moneybox, 1977–80, Radio 4; Money Programme, 1979–80, Newsnight, 1980–82, BBC TV; Today programme, Radio 4, 1982–96; Masterworks, Radio 3, 1996–2000. Hon. Dr de Montfort, 1996; Hon. DLitt Wolverhampton, 2008. *Publications:* Man the Industrialist, 1970; Saudi Arabia Today, 1974; In the Valley of the Fireflies, 1995; Managing the Message, 2000; The Girl in Rose: Haydn's last love, 2004. *Recreation:* growing olives in Italy. *Address:* 67 Highlever Road, W10 6PR. *Club:* Athenæum.

HOBHOUSE, Anna Catrina, (Kate); Chairman, Fortnum & Mason plc, since 2008; *b* Sydney, 30 July 1962; *d* of late Garfield Howard Weston and Mary Ruth Weston (*née* Kippenberger); *m* 1988, William Arthur Hobhouse; four *s* one *d*. *Educ:* Francis Holland Sch.; Univ. of Bristol (BA Ancient Mediterranean Studies). Mem., Bd of Dirs, Fortnum & Mason plc, 1998–. Trustee, Garfield Weston Foundn, 2000–. *Address:* Fortnum & Mason plc, 181 Piccadilly, W1A 1ER. *T:* (020) 7973 5610. *E:* lucy.carroll@fortnumandmason.co.uk.

See also G. G. Weston, G. H. Weston.

HOBHOUSE, Sir Charles (John Spinney), 7th Bt *cr* 1812, of Broughton-Gifford, Bradford-on-Avon and of Monkton Farleigh, Wiltshire; *b* 27 Oct. 1962; *s* of Sir Charles Chisholm Hobhouse, 6th Bt, TD and of Elspeth Jean, *yr d* of late Thomas George Spinney; *S* father, 1991; *m* 1993, Katrina (marr. diss. 1997), *d* of Maj.-Gen. Sir Denzil Macarthur-Onslow, CBE, DSO; *m* 2009, Annette Welshman; two *s*. *Recreations:* sport, travel. *Heir:* *s* Benjamin Charles Spinney Hobhouse, *b* 26 Oct. 2009. *Address:* Monkton Farleigh Manor, Bradford-on-Avon, Wilts BA15 2QE.

HOBHOUSE, Kate; *see* Hobhouse, A. C.

HOBHOUSE, Penelope, (Mrs John Malins), MBE 2014; VMH; gardener, garden writer and garden consultant, since 1976; *b* 20 Nov. 1929; *d* of late Captain J. J. L.-C. Chichester-Clark, DSO and Bar, MP and Marion Chichester-Clark (later Mrs C. E. Brackenbury); *m* 1st, 1952, Paul Hobhouse (marr. diss. 1982; he *d* 1994); two *s* one *d*; 2nd, 1983, Prof. John Malins (*d* 1992). *Educ:* Girton Coll., Cambridge (BA Hons Econs, 1951; MA). National Trust tenant of Tintinhull House garden, 1980–93. Hon. DLitt: Birmingham, 1998; Essex (Writtle Coll.), 1998. VMH 1996. *Publications:* The Country Gardener, 1976, revd edn 1989; The Smaller Garden, 1981; Gertrude Jekyll on Gardening, 1983; Colour in your Garden, 1985; The National Trust: A Book of Gardening, 1986; Private Gardens of England, 1986; Garden Style, 1988; Painted Gardens, 1988; Borders, 1989; The Gardens of Europe, 1990; Flower Gardens, 1991; Plants in Garden History, 1992; Penelope Hobhouse on Gardening, 1994; Penelope Hobhouse's Garden Designs, 1997; Penelope Hobhouse's Natural Planting, 1997; A Gardener's Journal, 1997; Gardens of Italy, 1998; The Story of Gardening, 2002; The Gardens of Persia, 2003; In Search of Paradise, 2006. *Recreations:* reading Trollope and Henry James, Italy. *Address:* Dairy Barn, Pitcombe, Bruton, Som BA10 0PF.

See also Sir R. Chichester-Clark.

HOBKIRK, Michael Dalgliesh; *b* 9 Dec. 1924; *s* of Roy and Phyllis Hobkirk; *m* 1952, Lucy Preble; two *d*. *Educ:* Marlborough Coll.; Wadham Coll., Oxford. BA (Social Studies), MA 1949. Served War of 1939–45: Army (RAC, RAEC, Captain), 1943–47. Civil Service: War Office, 1949–63; MoD, 1963–70; Directing Staff, Nat. Defence Coll., 1970–74; Brookings Instn, Washington, DC, USA, 1974–75; Lord Chancellor's Dept, 1975–80 (Principal Establishment and Finance Officer, 1977–80); Asst Under-Sec. of State, MoD, 1980–82. Sen. Fellow, Nat. Defense Univ., Washington, DC, USA, 1982–83. *Publications:* (contrib.) The Management of Defence (ed L. Martin), 1976; The Politics of Defence Budgeting, 1984; Land, Sea or Air?, 1992. *Address:* 48 Woodside Avenue, Beaconsfield, Bucks HP9 1JH. *Club:* Oxford and Cambridge.

HOBLEY, Anthony Robert; Chief Executive, Carbon Tracker Initiative, since 2014; *b* Purley, 24 Nov. 1966; *s* of Brian and Linda Hobley; *m* 2001, Geraldine Marie Ismail (marr. diss. 2010). *Educ:* St Leonards C of E Middle Sch., Chelsham; Warlingham Comprehensive Sch.; Plymouth Univ. (BSc 1st Cl. Hons Chem. with Physics 1988); Darwin Coll., Cambridge; De Montfort Univ. (CPE Law 1991); University Coll. London (LLM Envmtl Law). Trainee solicitor, Ince & Co., 1992–94; admitted as solicitor, 1994; Solicitor, Envmt Law Dept, Nabarro Nathanson, 1994–96; Sen. Solicitor, Envmt Law Team, CMS Cameron McKenna, 1996–2001; Sen. Solicitor, Global Climate Change Team, Baker & McKenzie, 2001–05; Chm., Carbon Mkts Assoc. (formerly London Climate Change Services), 2003–08; Global Hd, Climate Change and Carbon Finance, Norton Rose Gp, 2007–14; Partner, Norton Rose LLP, 2007–14. Mem., Police Liaison Cttee, Caterham Police, Surrey Constabulary, 1984–85. Sec., Climate Change Wkg Gp, UK Envmt Law Assoc., 1998–99; Chair, Legal Sub-gp, UK Emissions Trading Gp, 1999–2000. Member: Bd, Verified Carbon Standards Assoc., 2007–; Bd and Dir, Carbon Mkts & Investors Assoc., 2008–. Founder and Mem., Steering Cttee, Business for a Clean Economy (Australia), 2009–11. *Recreations:* running, ski-ing, some sailing, reading. *Address:* Carbon Tracker Initiative, The Exchange, 28 London Bridge Street, SE1 9SG. *E:* ahobley@carbontracker.org.

HOBLEY, Brian, FSA; historical and archaeological researcher and writer; Chief Urban Archaeologist, City of London, 1973–89; Director, Hobley Archaeological Consultancy Services Ltd, 1989–92; *b* 25 June 1930; *s* of William Hobley and Harriet (*née* Hobson); *m* (marr. diss. 1992); one *s* one *d*. *Educ:* Univ. of Leicester (BA Hons 1965); Univ. of Oxford (MSt 1994). FSA 1969; AMA 1970. Field Officer, Coventry Corp., 1965; Keeper, Dept Field Archaeology, Coventry Museum, 1970. Lectr, Birmingham Univ. Extra-mural Dept, 1965–74. Chm. Standing Cttee, Arch. Unit Managers, 1986–89; Jt Sec., British Archaeologists and Developers Liaison Gp, 1986–89. MCMI (MBIM 1978); MCIfA (MIFA 1982). *Publications:* (ed jtly) Waterfront Archaeology in Britain and Northern Europe, 1981; Roman Urban Defences in the West, 1983; Roman Urban Topography in Britain and the Western Empire, 1985; Roman and Saxon London: a reappraisal, 1986; British Archaeologists and Developers Code of Practice, 1986; The Rebirth of Towns in the West AD 700–1050, 1988; The Circle of God: an archaeological and historical search for the Sacred: a study in continuity, 2015; reports in learned jls incl. Proc. 7th, 8th, 9th and 12th Internat. Congresses of Roman Frontier Studies, Tel Aviv, Univ. Israel and Bucharest Univ., Rumania on excavations and reconstructions at The Lunt Roman fort, Baginton near Coventry. *Recreations:* classical music, chess. *Address:* 30 Turton Way, Kenilworth, Warwicks CV8 2RT.

HOBMAN, Anthony Hugh Burton; Member, Electoral Commission, since 2010; Senior Advisor, Lincoln International Pensions Advisory Ltd, since 2013; *b* 5 July 1955; *s* of late David Burton Hobman, CBE and of Erica Agatha Hobman (*née* Irwin); *m* 1st, 1978, Catherine Fenton (marr. diss. 1994); one *s* two *d*; 2nd, 2001, Victoria Richards (*née* Maynard); one *d* and two step *s*. *Educ:* De La Salle Coll.; Cardinal Newman Sch., Hove; N Staffs Polytech. (BA Hons (Modern Studies) 1976). Barclays Bank plc: Graduate Mgt Trainee, 1976–81; various roles in Marketing, Project, Change and Service Mgt, 1982–95; Proshare (UK) Ltd: Hd, Private Investor Services, 1996–99; Chief Exec., 1999–2000; Chief Executive: Money Channel plc, 2000–01; Occupational Pensions Regulatory Authy, 2002–05; The Pensions Regulator, 2005–10; Consumer Financial Educn Body, subseq. Money Advice Service, 2010–12. Member: Consultative Cttee, Co. Law Review, DTI, 1999–2000; Adv. Gp, Employer Task Force on Pensions, DWP, 2003–04; Man. Bd, Cttee of Eur. Insce and Occupational Pensions Supervisors, 2009–10 (Chair, Occupational Pensions Cttee, 2007–09); Simple Financial Products Steering Gp, 2012. Gov., Pensions Policy Inst., 2005–. Trustee, David Hobman Charitable Trust, 1987–96. *Recreations:* ski-ing, theatre, opera, wine, watching Time Team. *Address:* 20 Wilbury Gardens, Hove, E Sussex BN3 6HY. *T:* (01273) 727183. *E:* tonyhobman@gmail.com. *Club:* Reform.

HOBSBAWM BAMPING, Julia Nathalie, OBE 2015; Founder, Chief Executive and Director, Editorial Intelligence Ltd, since 2003; Chief Executive, Julia Hobsbawm Consulting Ltd, since 2005; *b* 15 Aug. 1964; *d* of Prof. Eric John Ernest Hobsbawm, CH, FBA and Marlene (*née* Schwarz); *m* 2004, Alaric Bamping; two *s* one *d*, and one step *s* one step *d*. *Educ:* Camden Sch. for Girls; Poly. of Central London. Asst, Martin Dunitz Med. Publrs, 1982; Publicity Officer, Penguin Books, 1983; Head of Publicity, Virago Press, 1985–87; Researcher: Books by my Bedside, Thames TV, 1987–89; Wogan, BBC, 1989–90; Forward Planning Editor, John Gau Productions, 1990–91; Fundraising Consultant, 1000 Club and High Value Donors, Labour Party, 1991–92; founded Julia Hobsbawm Associates, 1992, then, Hobsbawm Macaulay Communications, 1993 (Chair, 1993–2001); Chief Exec., HMC-Hobsbawm Media + Marketing Communications Ltd, 2001–05. Strategic Counsel to Edelman, 2009–12. Vis. Prof., London College, 2003–; Hon. Visiting Professor in Networking: Cass Business Sch., 2011–; Univ. Campus Suffolk, 2012–. Member: Commng Panel, ESRC Culture of Consumption Res. Panel, 2002–07; Public Value Adv. Panel, Arts Council, 2006–07; President's Panel, CIPR, 2007–08; Global Agenda Council on Informed Societies, World Econ. Forum, 2010–14; FCO Diplomatic Excellence Panel, 2014–. Founder, Names Not Numbers, ideas conf., 2009–. Vice Pres., Hay Fest. of Lit., 2001–. Mem., Nat. Develt Cttee, Treehouse, 2007–13. Trustee: Facial Surgery Res. Foundn, 2000–08 (Patron, 2008–); In-Kind Direct, 2003–07; Jewish Community Centre for London, 2004–05. FRSA 2003. Media Woman of the Year, First Women Awards, 2012. *Publications:* (with Robert Gray) The Cosmopolitan Guide to Working in PR and Advertising, 1996; (ed) Where the Truth Lies: trust and morality in PR and journalism, 2006, 2nd edn as Where the Truth Lies: trust and morality in the business of PR, journalism and communication, 2010; (with John Lloyd) The Power of the Commentariat: how much do commentators influence politics and public opinion?, 2008; The See-Saw: 100 ideas for work life balance, 2009; Fully Connected: working and networking in 2020, 2014. *Recreations:* conversation, reading, walking, tweeting. *W:* www.juliahobsbawm.com. *Clubs:* Groucho, Soho House.

HOBSLEY, Prof. Michael, TD 1969; PhD; FRCS; David Patey Professor of Surgery, University of London, 1986–94 (Professor of Surgery, 1984–94), now Emeritus Professor; Head, Department of Surgery, University College and Middlesex School of Medicine, University College London, 1984–93; *b* 18 Jan. 1929; *s* of Henry Hobsley and Sarah Lily Blanchfield; *m* 1953, Jane Fairlie Cambell; one *s* three *d*. *Educ:* La Martinière Coll., Calcutta; Sidney Sussex Coll., Cambridge (MA, MB, MChir); Middlesex Hosp. Med. Sch.; PhD London, 1961; DSc London, 1989. FRCS 1958. Training posts in RAMC and at Middlesex, Whittington and Chace Farm Hosps, 1951–68; Comyns Berkeley Fellow, Gonville and Caius Coll., Cambridge and Middx Hosp. Med. Sch., 1965–66; posts at Middx Hosp. and Med. Sch., 1968–: Hon. Consultant Surgeon, 1969–; Reader in Surgical Science, 1970–75; Prof. of Surg. Science, 1975–83; Dir, Dept of Surgical Studies, 1983–88. Howard C. Naffziger Surg. Res. Fellow, Univ. of Calif, 1966; Windermere Foundn Travelling Prof. of Surgery, 1984; Glaxo Visitor, Univ. of Witwatersrand, 1985; Vis. Professor: Univ. of Calif, 1980; Univ. of Khartoum, 1976; McMaster Univ., 1982; Monash Univ., 1984; Univ. of Louisville, 1995. Non-exec. Mem., Enfield HA, 1990–93. Pres., British Soc. of Gastroenterology, 1992–93; Chm., Assoc. of Profs of Surgery, 1990–94. Royal College of Surgeons: Hunterian Prof., 1962–63; Penrose May Tutor, 1973–78; Sir Gordon Gordon-Taylor Lectr, 1980; Examr, 1968–94. Examiner: Univ. of London, 1978–94; Univ. of Nigeria, 1977–94; Univ. of the WI, 1978–94; Univ. of Bristol, 1986–88; Univ. of Cambridge, 1986–94; St Mary's Hosp. Med. Sch., 1989–91; St George's Hosp. Med. Sch., 1990–93; Univ. of Birmingham, 1992–94; Univ. of Newcastle, 1992–94. Mem., Professional and Linguistics Assessment Bd and Chm., Multiple Choice Questions Panel, 1993–97; Trustee, and Chm. Academic Council, Inst. of Sports Medicine, 1995–2004. Hon. Fellow: Assoc. of Surgeons of India, 1983; Amer. Surgical Assoc., 1989. FRSocMed 1960. *Publications:* Pathways in Surgical Management, 1979, 3rd edn (ed with P. B. Boulos), 2002; Disorders of the Digestive System, 1982; Colour Atlas of Parotidectomy, 1983; Physiology in Surgical Practice, 1992; (jtly) Time to Go, 2011; articles in BMJ, Lancet, British Jl of Surgery, Gut, Klinische Wochenschrift. *Recreation:* cricket. *Address:* Fieldside, Barnet Lane, Totteridge, N20 8AS. *T:* (020) 8445 6507. *Clubs:* Athenæum, MCC.

HOBSON, John; JP; independent policy adviser; Director, Construction Industry, Department of Trade and Industry, 2001–02; *b* 30 March 1946; *s* of late John Leslie Hobson and Beatrice Edith Hobson; *m* 1970, Jeanne Gerrish (marr. diss. 1996); one *s* one *d*. *Educ:* Northampton Grammar Sch.; Manchester Grammar Sch.; King's Coll., Cambridge (MA Mathematics). Joined Min. of Transport, 1967; Asst Private Sec. to Sec. of State for the Environment, 1970–72; Private Sec. to Head of CS, 1974–78; Assistant Secretary: Dept of Transport, 1979–80; DoE, 1980–86; Under-Sec., subseq. Dir, DoE, subseq. DETR, 1986–2001 (Dir of Construction, 1997–2001). Trustee, Sustainability First, 2003–. JP Warwicks, 2002.

HOBSON, John Graham; QC 2000; a Recorder, since 2000; *s* of late John Herbert Hobson and Lilian May Hobson (*née* Mott); *m* 1976, Shirley June Palmer; one *s* one *d*. *Educ:* Monkton Combe Sch.; St John's Coll., Cambridge (LLM). Admitted Solicitor, 1968; Director: W Stepney Neighbourhood Law Centre, 1973–75; Southwark Law Project, 1975–80; called to the Bar, Inner Temple, 1980; Supplementary Panel of Counsel to Treasury, 1992–2000; Standing Counsel to Rent Assessment Panel, 1997–2000; Asst Recorder, 1999–2000. Special Advr, NI Affairs Cttee for Enquiry into Planning System in NI, H of C, 1995–96. Hon. Standing Counsel, CPRE, 2002–. *Recreations:* playing the 'cello, rowing, fishing, watching football. *Address:* Landmark Chambers, 180 Fleet Street, EC4A 2HG. *Clubs:* Travellers, London Rowing.

HOBSON, Prof. Marian Elizabeth, CBE 2002; FBA 1999; Professor of French, Queen Mary (formerly Queen Mary and Westfield College), University of London, 1992–2005, now Professorial Research Fellow; *b* 10 Nov. 1941; *d* of Baron Hobson and Doris Mary Hobson; *m* 1968, Michel Jeanneret; one *s*. *Educ:* Newnham Coll., Cambridge. Asst Lectr in French, Univ. of Warwick, 1966–71; Maître-assistante, Univ. of Geneva, 1974–76; Fellow of Trinity Coll., Cambridge (first woman Fellow), 1977–92; Univ. Lectr, Univ. of Cambridge, 1985–92. Visiting Professor: Univ. of Calif, 1990; Johns Hopkins Univ., 1995, 2005; Univ. de Paris, 1997; Harvard Univ., 2007; Eugene Freehling Vis. Prof., Univ. of Michigan, 2006; Occasional Lecturer: Ren Min Univ., Beijing, 1999, 2004; Normal Sch. of Eastern China, Shanghai, 2011; Visitor, Inst. of Advanced Study in Eur. Culture, Jiao-Tong Univ., Shanghai, 2014. Chevalier des palmes académiques (France), 1997. *Publications:* The Object of Art, 1982; Jacques Derrida: opening lines, 1998; (ed with Simon Harvey) Diderot's Lettre sur les aveugles, Lettre sur les sourds et muets, 2000; Diderot and Rousseau: networks of enlightenment, 2011; (ed) Diderot's Le Neveu de Rameau, 2013. *Address:* 21 Church Lane, Trumpington, Cambridge CB2 9LA.

HOBSON, Paul; Director, Modern Art Oxford, since 2013; *b* Wath-upon-Dearne, 18 July 1970; *s* of Alan and Carol Hobson; civil partnership, Stephen Webb. *Educ:* Brasenose Coll., Oxford (MA Modern Hist. 1991); City Univ., London (MA Arts Mgt and Policy 1995); Middlesex Univ. (MA Aesthetics and Contemp. Visual Theory 2003). Researcher, Hayward Gall., S Bank Centre, 1993–94; Develt Manager, ENO, 1994–97; Hd, Royal Acad. Trust, RA, 1997–2000; Hd, Strategy and Develt, Serpentine Gall., 2001; Dir, Private Arts Foundn, 2002–07; Interim Dir, Showroom Gall., 2007; Dir, Contemporary Art Soc., 2007–13. FRSA. *Publications:* Life is More Important than Art, 2008. *Recreations:* culture, swimming, water polo, contemporary art and dance. *Address:* Modern Art Oxford, 30 Pembroke Street, Oxford OX1 1BP. *T:* (01865) 722733.

HOCHGREB, Prof. Simone, PhD; FRAeS; Professor of Experimental Combustion, University of Cambridge, since 2002; *b* 24 July 1962; *d* of Osmar Hochgreb and Nilce F. Hochgreb; *m* 1998, Stephen Vandermark; one *d*. *Educ:* Univ. of São Paulo (BSME 1985); Princeton Univ. (PhD 1991). Asst Prof., MIT, 1991–99; Principal Investigator, Sandia Nat. Labs, Calif, 1999–2000; Man. Engr, Exponent, 2000–02. *Publications:* contrib. transactions on combustion and flame. *Address:* Department of Engineering, University of Cambridge, Trumpington Street, Cambridge CB2 1PZ. *E:* sh372@cam.ac.uk.

HOCHHAUSER, Andrew Romain; QC 1997; FCIArb; a Recorder, since 2004; a Deputy High Court Judge, since 2013; *b* 16 March 1955; *s* of late Jerome Romain, MD, FRCSE and Ruth Hochhauser. *Educ:* Highgate Sch.; Univ. of Bristol (LLB Hons); London Sch. of Econs (LLM Hons); Courtauld Inst. of Art (MA Hons). FCIArb 1995. Called to the Bar, Middle Temple, 1977 (Harmsworth Scholar), Bencher, 2000. Part-time Mem., Law Faculty, LSE, 1979–86. Hon. Counsel, Westminster Abbey, 2004–; Chm., Dance Umbrella, 2007–14; Vice-Chm., Paintings in Hosps, 2013–. Trustee: V&A Mus., 2011–; Propeller Theatre Co., 2012–; Shelter from the Storm, 2014–. Gov., Central Sch. of Ballet, 2015–. FRSA 2013. *Recreations:* collecting paintings, swimming with sharks, contemporary dance. *Address:* Essex Court Chambers, 24 Lincoln's Inn Fields, WC2A 3EG. *T:* (020) 7813 8000. *Club:* Garrick.

HOCHHAUSER, Victor, CBE 1994; impresario; *b* 27 March 1923; *m* 1949, Lilian Hochhauser (*née* Shields); three *s* one *d*. *Educ:* City of London Coll. Impresario for: Margot Fonteyn; Emil Gilels; Leonid Kogan; Natalia Makarova; Yehudi Menuhin; Rudolf Nureyev; David and Igor Oistrakh; Sviatoslav Richter; Mstislav Rostropovich; Dmitri Shostakovich; Bolshoi Ballet seasons, 1963, 1969, 1999, 2004, 2005, 2007, 2008, Bolshoi Ballet and Opera, 2001, 2006, 2007, 2010, 2013, ROH, Covent Garden; Mariinsky (formerly Kirov) Ballet and Opera, Royal Opera House, 1961, 1966, 1993, 1995, 1997, 1998, 2000, 2003, 2004, 2005, 2009, 2011, 2014; Birmingham Royal Ballet, 1994–95; Royal Ballet season, London Coliseum, 2011; Nat. Ballet of China, Royal Opera House, 2008; Guangdong Acrobatic Troupe of China, Royal Opera House, 2008, London Coliseum, 2011; concerts, Royal Albert Hall, Barbican and Royal Festival Hall; orchestras from all over the world. *Recreations:* reading, swimming, sleeping. *Address:* 4 Oak Hill Way, NW3 7LR. *T:* (020) 7794 0987.

HOCKÉ, Jean-Pierre; international consultant; United Nations High Commissioner for Refugees, 1986–89; *b* 31 March 1938; *s* of Charles and Marie Rose Hocké; *m* 1961, Michèle Marie Weber; two *s*. *Educ:* Univ. of Lausanne (grad. Econ. and Business Admin). With commercial firms in Switzerland and Nigeria, 1961–67; joined Internat. Cttee of Red Cross, 1968: Hd of Operations Dept, 1973; Mem., Directorate, 1981. Mem., Jean Monnet Foundn, Lausanne, 1984–; Chm., Bd, InterAssist, Bern, 1990–2004; Mem., Bd of Dirs, Africa Humanitarian Action, Addis Abeba, 1994–. Chm., Property Commn refugees and displaced, Bosnia, 1996–2004. Jury Mem., Prix européen de L'essai Charles Veillon, 2000–. Mem., Bd of Dirs, Lemania Gp of Schs, 2007–. Hon. Dr Lausanne, 1987. *Address:* 7 rue de l'Eglise, 1299 Crans-près-Céligny, Switzerland. *T:* (22) 7768404, 793553855. *E:* jphocke@bluewin.ch.

HOCKENHULL, Maj. Gen. James Richard, OBE 2003; Director, Cyber, Intelligence and Information Integration, since 2015; *b* Havant, Hants, 27 July 1964; *s* of William and Jean Hockenhull; *m* 1990, Karen Elizabeth Harrison; two *d*. *Educ:* Royal Hosp. Sch.; Univ. of York (BA Hons Politics); Cranfield Univ. (MA Mil. Studies). Commnd RA, 1982; Operational deployments incl. NI, Iraq and Afghanistan; CO Jt Support Gp, NI, 2001–03; Chief G5 (Planning), HQ ARRC, 2007–08; Head: Information Superiority Army HQ, 2009–11; Mil. Strategic Planning, MoD, 2011–13; Dir, Adv. Gp, Kabul, Afghanistan, MoD, 2013–14. Hon. Col Comdt, Intelligence Corps, 2014–. *Recreations:* horses, hunting, recreational ski-ing, agricultural cricket. *Address:* Royal Military Academy Sandhurst, Camberley, Surrey. *E:* jhockenhull3@gmail.com. *Club:* Philippics Cricket.

HOCKLEY, (Charles) Dair F.; *see* Farrar-Hockley.

HOCKLEY, Rear Adm. Christopher John, CBE 2014; Chief Executive Officer, MacRobert Trust, since 2014; *b* Orpington, Kent, 24 Aug. 1959; *s* of late Peter William Hockley and of Valerie Joan Hockley; *m* 2005, Kate Elizabeth Henderson; one *s* one *d*, and three step *s*. *Educ:* Dulwich Coll.; Royal Naval Engrg Coll. (BSc Hons; MSc). CMarEng 1988; CEng 1988; FIMarEST 2010. Joined RN, 1977; MEO, HMS Illustrious, HMS Invincible, 1997–99; Dep. Team Leader, Future Aircraft Carrier Proj., 1999–2002; Mil. Asst to Chief of Defence Procurement, 2002–05; Through Life Support Dir, Defence Logistics Orgn, 2005–07; Naval Base Comdr, HM Naval Base Clyde, and ADC to the Queen, 2007–11; FO Scotland, Northern England and NI, FO Regl Forces and FO Reserves, 2011–14. FCMI 2011. *Recreations:* boating, walking, watching Rugby.

HOCKMAN, Stephen Alexander; QC 1990; *b* 4 Jan. 1947; *s* of Nathaniel and Trude Hockman; *m* 1998, Elizabeth St Hill Davies. *Educ:* Eltham Coll.; Jesus Coll., Cambridge (MA). Called to the Bar, Middle Temple, 1970, Bencher, 1996 (Treas., 2015). Leader, SE Circuit, 2000–03. Mem., Apostrophe Chambers, 2011–. Chm., Bar Council, 2006 (Vice-Chm., 2005). *Recreations:* philosophy, politics, the arts. *Address:* 6 Pump Court, Temple, EC4Y 7AR. *T:* (020) 7797 8400.

HOCKNEY, Damian; Member, London Assembly, Greater London Authority, 2004–08 (UK Ind, 2004–05; Veritas, 2005; One London, 2005–08). Career in publishing. Vice-Chm., UKIP, 2001–03; Dep. Leader, Veritas, Jan.–July 2005; Leader, One London Party, 2005. Former Mem., Metropolitan Police Authy. Contested (Veritas) Broxtowe, 2005.

HOCKNEY, David, OM 2012; CH 1997; RA 1991 (ARA 1985); artist; *b* Bradford, 9 July 1937; *s* of late Kenneth and Laura Hockney. *Educ:* Bradford Grammar Sch.; Bradford Sch. of Art; Royal Coll. of Art. Lecturer: Maidstone Coll. of Art, 1962; Univ. of Iowa, 1964; Univ. of Colorado, 1965; Univ. of California, Los Angeles, 1966, Berkeley, 1967. One-man shows: Kasmin Ltd, London, 1963, 1965, 1966, 1968, 1969, 1970, 1972; Alan Gallery, New York, 1964–67; Museum of Modern Art, NY, 1964–68; Stedelijk Museum, Amsterdam, 1966; Whitworth Gallery, Manchester, 1969; Louvre, Paris, 1974; Galerie Claude Bernard, Paris, 1975 and 1985; Nicholas Wilder, LA, 1976; Galerie Neundorf, Hamburg, 1977; Warehouse Gall., 1979; Knoedler Gall., 1979, 1981, 1982, 1983, 1984, 1986 and 1988; André Emmerich Gall., 1979, 1980, annually 1982–95; Tate, 1986, 1988; Hayward Gall., 1983 and 1985; L. A.

Louver, LA, 1986, 1989, 1995, 1998, 2005, 2007, 2009; Annely Juda, 1997, 2003, 2005, 2006, 2009, 2014, 2015; Nat. Portrait Gall., 2003; Royal Acad. of Arts, 1995, 1999, 2002, 2004, 2005, 2007, 2012; Arts Club of Chicago, 2008; Kunsthalle Würth, Schwäbisch Hall, 2009; PaceWildenstein, NY, 2009; Royal W of England Acad., Bristol, 2010; touring show of drawings and prints: Munich, Madrid, Lisbon, Teheran, 1977; USA and Canada, 1978; Tate, 1980; Saltaire, Yorks, New York and LA, 1994; drawing retrospective, Hamburg, London, LA, 1996; Retrospective Exhibitions: Whitechapel Art Gall., 1970; LA County Mus. of Art, Metropolitan Mus. of Art, Tate Gall., 1988–89; Manchester City Art Galls, 1996; Centre Georges Pompidou, Paris, 1999; Bonn Mus., 1999; Mus. of Fine Arts, Boston, LA County Mus. of Art, Nat. Portrait Gall., 2006–07; Nottingham Contemporary, 2009–10; Dulwich Picture Gall., 2014; Early Drawings, Offer Waterman, London, 2015. Exhibitions of photographs: Hayward Gall., 1983; Nat. Mus. of Photography, Film and Television, 1991. 1st Prize, John Moores Exhibn, Liverpool, 1967. Designer: The Rake's Progress, Glyndebourne, 1975, La Scala, 1979; The Magic Flute, Glyndebourne, 1978; L'Enfant et les sortilèges and Nightingale, Double Bill, and Varii Capricci, Covent Garden, 1983; Tristan und Isolde, LA, 1987; Turandot, Chicago, San Francisco, 1990; Die Frau ohne Schatten, Covent Garden, 1992, LA, 1993; designing costumes and sets for Parade and Stravinsky triple bills, Metropolitan Opera House, NY, 1981. Films: A Bigger Splash, 1975; A Day on the Grand Canal with the Emperor of China or surface is illusion but so is depth, 1988; television: Secret Knowledge, 2001; Hockney on Photography, 2011. Hon. DLitt Oxford, 1995; Hon. DFA Yale, 2005. Shakespeare Prize, Hamburg Foundn, 1983; First Prize, Internat. Center of Photography, NY, 1985; Silver Progress Medal, RPS, 1988; Praemium Imperiale, Japan Art Assoc., 1989; Fifth Annual Gov's Award for Visual Arts in California, 1994. *Publications:* (ed and illustrated) 14 Poems of C. P. Cavafy, 1967; (illustrated) Six Fairy Tales of the Brothers Grimm, 1969; 72 Drawings by David Hockney, 1971; David Hockney by David Hockney (autobiog.), 1976; The Blue Guitar, 1977; David Hockney: Travels with Pen, Pencil and Ink: selected prints and drawings 1962–77, 1978; Paper Pools, 1980; (with Stephen Spender) China Diary, 1982; Hockney Paints the Stage, 1983; David Hockney: Cameraworks, 1984 (Kodak Photography Book Award); David Hockney: A Retrospective, 1988; Hockney on Photography (conversations with Paul Joyce), 1988; Hockney's Alphabet, 1991 (ed Stephen Spender); That's the Way I See It (autobiog.), 1993; Hockney on Art: photography, painting and perspective, 1999; Secret Knowledge: rediscovering the lost techniques of the old masters, 2001, 2006; Hockney's Portraits and People, 2003; Hockney's Pictures, 2004; David Hockney Portraits, 2006. *Address:* c/o 7508 Santa Monica Boulevard, Los Angeles, CA 90046, USA.

HODDER, Elizabeth; Commissioner, Equal Opportunities Commission, 1996–2002 (Deputy Chairwoman, 1996–2000); Chairman, Lifespan Healthcare NHS Trust, 2000–02 (non-executive Director, since 1993); *b* 5 Sept. 1942; *er d* of John Scruton and Beryl Haynes, High Wycombe; *m* 1st, 1962, Barry Quirke (marr. diss. 1970); two *d*; 2nd, 1971, Prof. Bramwell Hodder (*d* 2006); three step *s* two step *d*. *Educ:* High Wycombe High Sch.; Queen Mary Coll., Univ. of London. Member: Nat. Consumer Council, 1981–87; Building Societies Ombudsman Council, 1987–; Code of Banking Practice Review Cttee, 1992–2002; Comr and Chm., Consumers' Cttee, Meat and Livestock Commn, 1992–98. Founder and Hon. Pres., Nat. Stepfamily Assoc., 1985–; several positions in local and national organs. *Publications:* The Step-parents' Handbook, 1985; Stepfamilies Talking, 1989; The Book of Old Tarts, 2001. *Recreations:* Italy, cooking, painting, hill-walking. *Address:* 4 Ascham Road, Cambridge CB4 2BD. *T:* (01223) 301086.

HODDER, Prof. Ian Richard, PhD; FBA 1996; Dunlevie Family Professor, School of Humanities and Sciences, Stanford University, since 2002; *b* 23 Nov. 1948; *s* of late Prof. Bramwell William Hodder and Noreen Victoria Hodder; *m* 1st, 1975, Françoise Marguerite Hivernel; two *s*; 2nd, 1987, Christine Ann Hastorf; two *s*. *Educ:* Inst. of Archaeology, London (BA 1971); Peterhouse, Cambridge (PhD 1975). Lectr, Dept of Archaeology, University of Leeds, 1974–77; University of Cambridge: Univ. Asst, then Univ. Lectr, Dept of Archaeology, 1977–90; Reader in Prehistory, 1990–96; Dir, Cambridge Archaeol. Unit, 1990–2000; Fellow of Darwin Coll., 1990–2000; Prof. of Archaeology, 1996–2000; Prof., Dept of Cultural and Social Anthropology, 1999–2001, Co-Dir, Archaeol. Centre, 1999–2002, Stanford Univ. Adjunct Asst Prof. of Anthropology, SUNY, 1984–89; Visiting Professor: Dept of Anthropology, Univ. of Minnesota (and Adjunct Prof.), 1986–93; Van Giffen Inst. for Pre- and Proto-history, Amsterdam, 1980; Univ. of Paris I, Sorbonne, 1985; Fellow: Centre for Advanced Study in Behavioural Scis, Calif, 1987; McDonald Inst., Univ. of Cambridge, 2001–02; Guggenheim Fellow, 2005–06; Hon. Prof., Inst. of Archaeol., UCL. Hon. DSc Bristol, 2009; Hon. Dr Leiden, 2010. *Publications:* Spatial Analysis in Archaeology (with C. Orton), 1976; Symbols in Action, 1982; The Present Past, 1982; Reading the Past, 1986; The Domestication of Europe, 1990; Theory and Practice in Archaeology, 1992; The Archaeological Process, 1999; Archaeology Beyond Dialogue, 2004; The Leopard's Tale, 2006; Entangled: an archaeology of the relationships between humans and things, 2012. *Recreations:* music (playing violin and piano), tennis, golf, sailing, travel. *Address:* Department of Anthropology, Stanford University, Stanford, CA 94305, USA.

HODDINOTT, Rear-Adm. Anthony Paul, CB 1994; OBE 1979; Chairman, International Legal Assistance Consortium, 2002–11; *b* 28 Jan. 1942; *s* of late Comdr Peter Hoddinott, RN and Marjorie Hoddinott (*née* Kent); *m* 1965, Ellen Ruby, (Rue), Burton; one *s* two *d*. *Educ:* St Michael's, Otford; Bloxham; BRNC Dartmouth. Served HM Ships Chawton, Trump, Dreadnought, Repulse, Porpoise; in Comd, HMS Andrew, 1973–75; Staff of Comdr Third Fleet, USN, 1975–76; in Comd, HMS Revenge, 1976–79; Comdr, Submarine Tactics and Weapons Gp, 1979–81; in Comd, HMS Glasgow, 1981–83 (South Atlantic, 1982); Asst Dir, Naval Warfare, 1983–85; NATO Defence Coll., Rome, 1985; Dep. UK Mil. Rep. to NATO, Brussels, 1986–88; COS (Submarines), 1988–90; Naval Attaché and Comdr, British Naval Staff, Washington, 1990–94, retd. Exec. Dir, Internat. Bar Assoc., 1995–2000. Dir, Warship Preservation Trust, 1995–2006; Trustee, RN Submarine Mus., 1999–08 (Chm., Soc. of Friends, 1999–2014). Liveryman, Fan Makers' Co., 1998– (Mem., Ct of Assistants, 2007–; Master, 2016). Dir, Bentley Drivers Club, 2013–16 (Chm., Mid-West Reg., 2013–16). *Recreations:* theatre, classic Bentley cars, family, travel. *Address:* 45 Oaklands Road, Petersfield, Hants GU32 2EY.

HODDLE, Glenn; Director, Glenn Hoddle Academy, Montecastillo, Spain, since 2008; First-Team Coach, Queens Park Rangers Football Club, since 2014; *b* 27 Oct. 1957; *s* of late Derek Hoddle and of Teressa (*née* Roberts); *m* 1979, Christine Anne Stirling (marr. diss. 1999); one *s* two *d*; *m* 2000, Vanessa Shean. *Educ:* Burnt Mill Sch., Harlow. Professional football player: Tottenham Hotspur, 1976–86 (won FA Cup, 1981, 1982, UEFA Cup, 1984); AS Monaco, 1986–91 (won French Championship, 1988); Player/Manager: Swindon Town, 1991–93; Chelsea, 1993–96; Coach, England Football Team, 1996–99; Manager: Southampton, 2000–01; Tottenham Hotspur, 2001–03; Wolverhampton Wanderers, 2004–06. 53 England caps, 1980–88; represented England in World Cup, Spain, 1982, Mexico, 1986. Regular pundit, Sky TV. *Publications:* Spurred to Success (autobiog.), 1998; (with David Davies) Glenn Hoddle: the World Cup 1998 Story, 1998.

HODGE, Rt Hon. Lord; Patrick Stewart Hodge; PC 2013; a Justice of the Supreme Court of the United Kingdom, since 2013; *b* 19 May 1953; *s* of George Mackenzie Hodge and Helen Russell Hodge; *m* 1983, Penelope Jane Wigin; two *s* one *d*. *Educ:* Croftinloan Sch.; Trinity Coll., Glenalmond; Corpus Christi Coll., Cambridge (Scholar, BA; Hon. Fellow, 2014); Edinburgh Univ. (LLB). Scottish Office, 1975–78; admitted Faculty of Advocates, 1983; Standing Junior Counsel: to Dept of Energy, 1989–91; to Inland Revenue in Scotland, 1991–96; QC (Scot.) 1996; a Judge of Courts of Appeal of Jersey and Guernsey, 2000–05; Procurator to Gen. Assembly of Church of Scotland, 2000–05; a Senator of the College of Justice in Scotland, 2005–13. Comr (pt time), Scottish Law Commn, 1997–2003. Hon. Bencher, Middle Temple, 2011. Hon. Prof., Stellenbosch Univ., SA, 2014–. Trustee, David Hume Inst., 2008–13. Gov., Merchiston Castle Sch., Edinburgh, 1998–2012. Hon. LLD Glasgow, 2014. *Publications:* Scotland and the Union, 1994; various legal articles. *Recreations:* opera, ski-ing. *Address:* Supreme Court, Parliament Square, SW1P 3BD. *Club:* Bruntsfield Links Golfing Society.

HODGE, Sir Andrew (Rowland), 3rd Bt *cr* 1921, of Chipstead, Kent; *b* 4 Dec. 1968; *o s* of Sir John Rowland Hodge, 2nd Bt, MBE and of his 4th wife, Vivien Jill, *d* of A. S. Knightley; *S* father, 1995, but his name does not appear on the Official Roll of the Baronetage; *m* 2008, Dr Joyce Inma; one *s*. *Educ:* Stella Maris Coll., Malta; Benjamin Britten High Sch., Suffolk. Estate agent, 1986–91 and 1993–94. *Recreations:* tennis, ski-ing. *Heir:* *s* Aston Rowland Hodge, *b* 10 Sept. 2008.

HODGE, David Ralph; QC 1997; **His Honour Judge Hodge;** a Circuit Judge, since 2005; Specialist Chancery Judge, Northern Circuit, since 2005; *b* Prestatyn, 13 July 1956; *er s* of Ralph Noel Hodge, CBE and late Jean Margaret Hodge; *m* 2003, Jane Woosey. *Educ:* St Margaret's, Liverpool; University Coll., Oxford (BA Jurisprudence 1977; BCL 1978). Called to the Bar, Inner Temple, 1979; admitted to Lincoln's Inn, 1980 (Bencher, 2000); in practice at Chancery Bar, 1980–2005; an Asst Recorder, 1998–2000; a Recorder, 2000–05; a Dep. High Ct Judge, 2004–05; nominated Judge: of Ct of Protection (pt-time), 2007–; of Upper Tribunal (Tax and Chancery Chamber) (pt-time), 2013–; of Upper Tribunal (Lands Chamber) (pt-time). Member: Council of Circuit Judges, 2007–; Incorporated Council of Law Reporting, 2010–. Chm., Bar Representation Cttee, 1997–98, Jt Chm., Students' Activities Exec. Cttee, 2008–14, Lincoln's Inn. Tutor judge, JSB Specialist Jurisdictions Course, 2010–. *Publications:* contrib. chapter on Chancery Matters to The Law and Practice of Compromise, 4th edn, 1996 to 8th edn 2015; Rectification: the modern law and practice governing claims for rectification for mistake, 2010, 2nd edn 2015; (ed) Atkin's Court Forms titles: on Compromise & Settlements, 2013; on Declaratory Judgements, 2014; on Injunctions, 2014; on Interim Remedies, 2014. *Recreations:* wife, theatre, advocacy training. *Address:* c/o Manchester Civil Justice Centre, 1 Bridge Street West, Manchester M60 9DJ. *Clubs:* Garrick; Athenæum (Liverpool).

HODGE, Douglas; actor and director; *b* Plymouth, 25 Feb. 1960; *s* of Harry and Christine Hodge; partner, Tessa Peake-Jones; one *s* one *d*. *Educ:* Gillingham Grammar Sch.; Howard Sch., Kent; Royal Acad. of Dramatic Art; Nat. Youth Theatre. Actor: *films* include: Salome's Last Dance, 1988; Diamond Skulls, 1989; The Trial, 1993; Saigon Baby, 1995; Hollow Reed, 1996; Vanity Fair, 2004; Scenes of a Sexual Nature, 2006; The Descent 2, 2009; Robin Hood, 2010; *television* includes: Capital City, 1989–90; Anglo Saxon Attitudes, 1992; Middlemarch, 1994; The Way We Live Now, 2001; Redcap, 2003–04; Mansfield Park, 2007; One Night, 2012; Bert and Dickie, 2012; Secret State, 2012; The Town, 2012; Penny Dreadful, 2015; *theatre* includes: Moonlight, No Mans Land, 1993, Coriolanus, 1994, Almeida and Comedy; The Collection, The Lover, Donmar Warehouse, 1998; The Caretaker, Comedy, 2000; Three Sisters, Playhouse, 2003; Dumb Show, Royal Court, 2004; Guys and Dolls, Piccadilly, 2005; Titus Andronicus, Shakespeare's Globe, 2006; La Cage aux Folles, Playhouse, 2008 (Best Actor in a Musical: Olivier Awards, 2009; Tony Awards, 2010); Inadmissible Evidence, Donmar Warehouse, 2011; Torch Song Trilogy, Menier, 2012; Charlie and the Chocolate Factory, Th. Royal, 2013; National Theatre: King Lear, 1986; Pericles, Blinded by the Sun, 1994; Betrayal, 1998; A Matter of Life and Death, 2007. Director: *film*: Victoria Station, 2003; *theatre*: The Dumb Waiter, Oxford Playhouse, 2004; See How They Run, Duchess, 2006; Absurdia, Donmar, 2008; Last Easter, Birmingham Rep., 2008; Dimetos, Donmar Warehouse, 2009; Cyrano de Bergerac, NY, 2012; writer and director: Pacha Mama's Blessing, Almeida, 1989. Singer and songwriter; albums: Cowley Road Songs, 2005; Nightbus, 2009. Associate Dir, Donmar Th., 2007–09. Mem. Council, NYT, 1986–2006. *Recreations:* dive master, black belt karate. *Address:* c/o Lindy King, United Agents, 12–26 Lexington Street, W1F 0LE. *Club:* Soho House.

HODGE, Sir James (William), KCVO 1996; CMG 1996; HM Diplomatic Service, retired; Chairman, Society of Pension Consultants, since 2007; *b* 24 Dec. 1943; *s* of late William Hodge and Catherine Hodge (*née* Carden); *m* 1970, Frances Margaret, *d* of late Michael Coyne and of Teresa Coyne (*née* Walsh); three *d*. *Educ:* Holy Cross Academy, Edinburgh; Univ. of Edinburgh (MA (Hons) English Lang. and Lit.). Commonwealth Office, 1966; Third Secretary, Tokyo, 1967; Second Secretary (Information), Tokyo, 1970; FCO, 1972; First Sec. (Development, later Chancery), Lagos, 1975; FCO, 1978; First Sec. (Economic), 1981, Counsellor (Commercial), 1982, Tokyo; Counsellor: Copenhagen, 1986; FCO, 1990; RCDS, 1994; Minister, British Embassy, Peking, 1995–96; Ambassador to Thailand and (non-resident) to Lao People's Democratic Republic, 1996–2000; Consul-General, Hong Kong and (non-resident) Macao, 2000–03. MCIL 1990. FRSA 2009. Hon. DLitt Ulster, 2003; Hon. LLD Liverpool, 2004. Kt Grand Cross (1st cl.), Order of the White Elephant (Thailand), 1996. *Recreations:* books, music. *Clubs:* Oriental, MCC; Royal Scots (Edinburgh); Foreign Correspondents' (Hong Kong); Jockey (Macao).

HODGE, John Dennis; President, J. D. Hodge & Co., International Management and Aerospace Consultants, 1987–2003; *b* 10 Feb. 1929; *s* of John Charles Henry Hodge and Emily M. Corbett Hodge; *m* 1952, Audrey Cox; two *s* two *d*. *Educ:* Northampton Engineering Coll., University of London (now City Univ.). Vickers-Armstrong Ltd, Weybridge, England (Aerodynamics Dept), 1950–52; Head, Air Loads Section, Avro Aircraft Ltd, Toronto, Canada, 1952–59; Tech. Asst to Chief, Ops Div., Space Task Group, NASA, Langley Field, Va, USA, 1959; Chief, Flight Control Br., Space Task Group, NASA, 1961; Asst Chief of Flight Control, 1962, Chief, Flight Control Div., Flight Ops Directorate, NASA, MSC, 1963–68; Manager, Advanced Missions Program, NASA, Manned Spacecraft Centre, 1968–70; Dir, Transport Systems Concepts, Transport Systems Center, 1970; Vice-Pres., R&D, The Ontario Transportation Develt Corp., 1974–76; Department of Transportation, Washington, 1976–82; Chief, R&D Plans and Programs Analysis Div., 1976–77; Actg Dir, Office of Policy, Plans and Admin, 1977–79; Associate Administrator, for Policy, Plans and Program Management, Res. and Special programs Admin, 1979–82; Dir, Space Station Task Force, NASA, Washington, 1982–84; Dep. Associate Administrator for Space Station, NASA, Washington, 1984–85, Actg Associate Administrator, 1985–86. FAIAA 1991. Hon. ScD City Univ., London, Eng., 1966. NASA Medal for Exceptional Service, 1967 and 1969; Dept of Transportation Meritorious Achievement Award, 1974; Special Achievement Award, 1979; Presidential Rank Award of Meritorious Executive, NASA, 1985. *Publications:* contribs to NASA publications and various aerospace jls. *Recreations:* reading, golf. *Address:* 1951 Sagewood Lane #124, Reston, VA 20191, USA.

HODGE, Rt Hon. Dame Margaret (Eve), DBE 2015 (MBE 1978); PC 2003; MP (Lab) Barking, since June 1994; *b* 8 Sept. 1944; *d* of late Hans and Lisbeth Oppenheimer; *m* 1st, 1968, Andrew Watson (marr. diss. 1978); one *s* one *d*; 2nd, 1978, Henry Egar Garfield Hodge (later Hon. Sir Henry Hodge, OBE) (*d* 2009); two *d*. *Educ:* Bromley High Sch.; Oxford High Sch.; LSE (BSc Econ 1966). Teaching and internat. market research, 1966–73. London Borough of Islington: Councillor, 1973–94; Chair of Housing, 1975–79; Dep. Leader, 1981; Leader, 1982–92. Chair: Assoc. of London Authorities, 1984–92; London Res. Centre, 1985–92; Vice-Chair, AMA, 1991–92. Member: HO Adv. Cttee on Race Relations, 1988–92; Local Govt Commn, 1993–94; Board, Central and Inner London North TEC, 1990–92; Labour Party Local Govt Cttee, 1983–92. Parly Under-Sec. of State, DfEE,

1998–2001; Minister of State, DFES, 2001–05; Minister of State: (Minister for Employment and Welfare Reform (formerly for Work), DWP, 2005–06; DTI, 2006–07; DCMS, 2007–08 and 2009–10. Chair: Educn Select Cttee, H of C, 1997–98; Public Accounts Select Cttee, 2010–15; London Gp of Labour MPs, 1996–98; former mem., govt and local govt bodies. Sen. Consultant, Price Waterhouse, 1992–94. Director: London First, 1992; (non-exec.) UCH and Middlesex Hosp., 1992–94. Chair: Circle 33 Housing Trust, 1993–96; Fabian Soc., 1997–98. Gov., LSE, 1990–99; Mem. Council, Univ. of London, 1994–98. Hon. Fellow, Polytechnic of North London. Hon. DCL City, 1993; DUniv South Wales, 2014. Freeman, City of London, 2013. *Publications:* Quality, Equality and Democracy, 1991; Beyond the Town Hall, 1994; Elected Mayors and Democracy, 1997; contribs to numerous jls and newspapers. *Recreations:* family, opera, piano, travel, cooking. *Address:* c/o House of Commons, SW1A 0AA.

HODGE, Michael, MBE 1975; HM Diplomatic Service, retired; *b* 12 June 1944; *s* of late Howard Jack Hodge and Iris Amy Hodge (*née* Treasure); *m* 1966, Wilhelmina Marjorie Glover; one *s* one *d*. *Educ:* Cotham Grammar Sch., Bristol. With Prison Commn, 1961–62; joined HM Diplomatic Service, 1962: FO, 1962–65; Third Sec., Belgrade, 1965–67; Commercial Officer, Paris, 1968–70; Third, later Second, Sec., Bahrain Residency, 1970–72; Second Secretary: (Information), Kaduna, 1972–73; (Commercial), Kampala, 1973–74; FCO, 1974–78; First Sec. (Econ.), Copenhagen, 1978–82; FCO, 1983–87; on loan to ICI Agrochemicals, 1987–89; First Sec. (Commercial), Paris, 1989–92; Head, Services Planning and Resources Dept, FCO, 1992–96; Consul Gen., Chicago, 1996–99. Chm., Battle Meml Hall, 2001–05. Pres., Rotary Club of Battle, 2004–05, 2010–11, 2015–16. Chm., Treasure Hse Educnl Support, 2012–. Paul Harris Fellow, 2005. Kt, First Class, Order of Dannebrog (Denmark), 1978. *Recreations:* music, organising events, travel, steam railways. *Club:* Royal Over-Seas League.

HODGE, Michael John Davy V.; *see* Vere-Hodge.

HODGE, Patricia; actress; *b* 29 Sept. 1946; *d* of Eric and Marion Hodge; *m* 1976, Peter Owen; two *s*. *Educ:* Wintringham Girls' Grammar Sch., Grimsby; St Helen's Sch., Northwood, Middx; Maria Grey Coll., Twickenham; London Acad. of Music and Dramatic Art. Theatre début, No-one Was Saved, Traverse, Edinburgh, 1971; *West End theatre* includes: Popkiss, Globe, 1972; Two Gentlemen of Verona (musical), 1973; Pippin, Her Majesty's, 1973; Hair, Queen's, 1974; The Mitford Girls, Globe, 1981 (transf. from Chichester); Benefactors, Vaudeville, 1984; Noël and Gertie, Comedy, 1989–90; Shades, Albery, 1992; Separate Tables, Albery, 1993; The Prime of Miss Jean Brodie, Strand, 1994; National Theatre: A Little Night Music, 1995; Money (Best Supporting Actress, Laurence Olivier Awards, 2000); Summerfolk, 1999; Noises Off, 2000; His Dark Materials, 2003; The Country Wife, Th. Royal, 2007; Calendar Girls, Noel Coward, 2009; *other appearances* include: The Beggar's Opera, Nottingham Playhouse, 1975; Pal Joey, and Look Back In Anger, Oxford Playhouse, 1976; Then and Now, Hampstead, 1979; As You Like It, Chichester Fest., 1983; Lady in the Dark, Edinburgh Fest., 1988; Heartbreak House, Almeida, 1997; The Clean House, Crucible Th., Sheffield, 2006, and nat. tour, 2008; Calendar Girls, UK tour, 2008; The Breath of Life, Lyceum, Sheffield, 2011; Dandy Dick, nat. tour, 2012; Relative Values, Th. Royal, Bath, 2013, transf. Harold Pinter Th., 2014; *television plays and films* include: The Girls of Slender Means, 1975; The Naked Civil Servant, 1975; Hay Fever, 1984; The Death of the Heart, 1985; Hotel du Lac, 1986; Heat of the Day, 1988; The Shell Seekers, 1989; The Secret Life of Ian Fleming, 1989; The Moonstone, 1997; The Falklands Play, 2002; Marple: The Sittaford Mystery, 2006; Maxwell, 2007; *television series and serials* include: Rumpole of the Bailey, 7 series, 1978–90; Edward and Mrs Simpson, 1978; Holding the Fort, 3 series, 1979–82; The Other 'Arf, 1979–80, 1981; Nanny, 1980; Jemima Shore Investigates, 1982; The Life and Loves of a She-Devil, 1986; Rich Tea and Sympathy, 1991; The Cloning of Joanna May, 1992; The Legacy of Reginald Perrin, 1996; Sweet Medicine, 2003; Miranda, 3 series, 2009–14; *films* include: Betrayal, 1983; The Leading Man, 1996; Jilting Joe, 1997; Before You Go, 2002. Hon. DLitt: Hull, 1996; Brunel, 2001; Leicester, 2003. Female Performer of the Year, Spoken Word Awards, 2003. *Address:* c/o Paul Lyon-Maris, Independent Talent Group Ltd, 40 Whitfield Street, W1T 2RH. *T:* (020) 7636 6565.

HODGE, Patrick Stewart; *see* Hodge, Rt Hon. Lord.

HODGES, Gerald; Director of Finance, City of Bradford Metropolitan Council, 1974–85; *b* 14 June 1925; *s* of Alfred John Hodges and Gertrude Alice Hodges; *m* 1950, Betty Maire (*née* Brading); one *s* (and one *s* decd). *Educ:* King's Sch., Peterborough. CPFA. Accountancy Asst, Bexley Borough Council, 1941–48, and Eton RDC, 1948–49; Sen. Accountancy Asst, Newcastle upon Tyne, 1949–53; Chief Accountant, Hemel Hempstead, 1953–56; Dep. Treas., Crawley UDC, 1956–70; Treas., Ilkley UDC, 1970–74. Pres., Soc. of Metropolitan Treasurers, 1984–85. Gen. Comr, Inland Revenue, 1985–. Hon. Treasurer: Yorkshire Arts, 1973–86; Univ. of Bradford, 1986–97; Chm., Bradford Flower Fund Homes; Trustee, Bradford Disaster Appeal, 1985. *Publications:* occasional articles in professional jls. *Recreations:* travelling, ornithology, reading. *Address:* 23 Victoria Avenue, Ilkley, West Yorks LS29 9BW. *T:* (01943) 607346.

HODGES, Prof. John Russell, MD; FRCP, FMedSci; Principal Research Fellow and Federation Fellow, National Health and Medical Research Council, Australia, since 2007; Professor of Cognitive Neurology, UNSW Australia (formerly University of New South Wales), since 2007; *b* 7 Jan. 1952; *s* of Edward and Gwen Hodges; *m* 1952, Dr Carol Ann Gregory; two *s* one *d*. *Educ:* Kingsbridge Sch.; Royal London Hosp. Med. Sch. (MB BS Hons 1975, MD 1988). MRCP 1977, FRCP 1993. Lectr in Medicine, Southampton Univ., 1980–82; Registrar in Neurology, Radcliffe Infirmary, Oxford, 1982–85; MRC Res. Fellow, 1985–86; Lectr in Clinical Neurol., Radcliffe Infirmary, Oxford, 1986–90; MRC Travelling Fellow, UCSD, 1988–89; Lectr, Univ. of Cambridge, 1990–97; MRC Prof. of Behavioural Neurol., Univ. of Cambridge, 1997–2007. Dir, Alzheimer's Res. Trust Centre, Cambridge, 1998. Chm., British Neuropsychiatric Assoc., 1982–2001; Pres., Res. Gp on Aphasia, World Fedn of Neurol., 1998–. FMedSci 2002. *Publications:* Transient Amnesia, 1991; Cognitive Assessment for Clinicians, 1994; Memory Disorders in Psychiatric Practice, 2000; Early Onset Dementia: a multidisciplinary approach, 2001; contrib. numerous scientific papers to learned jls. *Recreations:* playing the saxophone, cinema, literature, fishing. *Address:* Neuroscience Research Australia, Hospital Road, Randwick, NSW 2031, Australia.

HODGES, John William, CMG 2003; CEng, FICE; development infrastructure consultant, since 2002; *b* 14 Nov. 1942; *s* of John Henry Hodges and Lilian Elizabeth Hodges; *m* 1962, Barbara Park; two *s* (and one *s* decd). *Educ:* Shoreditch Comprehensive Sch.; Brixton Sch. of Building; Westminster Coll. CEng 1968; FICE 1983. Exec. Engr, Govt of Zambia, 1965–68; Engr, UK Transport Res. Labs, 1969–73; Overseas Development Administration: Engrg Advr, 1974–84; Sen. Engrg Advr, 1985–86; Head: Pacific, 1987–89; Contracts, 1990–93; Chief Engrg Advr, 1994–2002. *Recreation:* restoration and rallying of classic cars.

HODGES, Lew; Chief Operating Officer, Leadership Foundation, since 2006; *b* 29 Feb. 1956. *Educ:* University Coll. London (BA (Hons) Classics); MBA London Business Sch., 1990. Chartered Accountant 1981. Subsidy Officer, then Asst Dir of Finance, Arts Council, 1981–87; Head of Finance, CNAA, 1987–89; Finance Dir, Arts Council of GB, subseq. of England, 1989–96; Dir, Corporate Services, Sports Council, 1996–97; Hd of Finance, RNT, 1997–2000; Dir of Finance and Mgt Resources, London Arts, 2000–01; Dir of Finance and Planning, Arts & Business, 2001–05. Mem., Inner London Probation Cttee, 1996–2001. Board Member: LAMDA, 2002–07; English Touring Th., 2002–11; Greenwich Fest., 2002–06; Artsadmin, 2002–13; Space, 2007–13; Nat. Youth Jazz Coll., 2009–; Wac Arts, 2014–; Protein, 2014–. *Address:* Leadership Foundation, Peer House, 8–14 Verulam Street, WC1X 8LZ.

HODGES, Nicholas Rudy; Chief Executive Officer, London International Group plc, 1993–99; *b* 26 Aug. 1939; *s* of Edward William Hodges and Gwendoline Winifred Hayward (*née* Golding); *m* 1st, 1959, Valerie Joyce Dyke (marr. diss. 1988; now Hedges); one *s* two *d*; 2nd, 1988, Christine Winifred Mary Dodd. *Educ:* Colchester Royal Grammar Sch. Salesman and Mktg, Nestlé Ltd, 1961–63; Kimberley Clark Ltd: Salesman, 1963–65; Product and Mktg Manager, 1965–67; Area Manager, 1967–69; Regl Manager, 1969–72; Regl Manager, Golden Wonder Ltd, 1972–74; Sales Dir, Johnson & Johnson Consumer, 1974–80; Man. Dir, Sangers, 1980–82; London International Group: Sales/Mktg Dir, 1982–88; World Wide Mkt Dir, Hosp. Products, 1988–90; European Man. Dir, 1990–93. Sen. non-exec. Dir and Dep. Chm., Taylor-Nelson Sofres, 1998–2002. Liveryman: Glovers' Co., 1986–2013; Co. of World Traders, 1989– (Mem. Court, 1999–2003). MCIM (MInstM 1972). *Recreations:* good food and wine, golf, fishing, horse racing. *Address:* PO Box 307, Applecross, WA 6953, Australia. *Clubs:* Royal Dornoch Golf, Burnham Beeches Golf, Busselton Golf.

HODGES, Paula; QC 2014; Partner, Herbert Smith Freehills (formerly Herbert Smith) LLP, since 1996; *b* Swansea, 20 Feb. 1965; *d* of Colin and Ann Hodges; *m* 2010, John Balsdon; three *c*. *Educ:* Olchfa Comprehensive Sch., Swansea; Girton Coll., Cambridge (BA Law 1986). Admitted solicitor, 1989; trainee solicitor, 1987–89, Asst Solicitor, 1989–96, Herbert Smith LLP. *Publications:* (contrib.) Liquefied Natural Gas: the law and business, 2006, 2nd edn 2012; (contrib.) Arbitration in England, 2013. *Recreations:* family, Chelsea Football Club, music, pilates, travel, French burgundy. *Address:* Herbert Smith Freehills LLP, Exchange House, Primrose Street, EC2A 2EG. *T:* (020) 7374 8000, *Fax:* (020) 7374 0888. *E:* paula.hodges@hsf.com.

HODGES, Prof. Richard Andrew, OBE 1995; PhD; FSA 1984; Professor of Visual Arts, and Director, Institute of World Archaeology, School of World Arts and Museology, University of East Anglia, since 1995 (on leave); President, American University of Rome, since 2012; *b* 29 Sept. 1952; *s* of Roy Clarence Hodges and Joan (*née* Hartnell); *m* 1st, 1976, Deborah Peters (marr. diss. 1998); one *s* one *d*; 2nd, 2008, Kim Bowes; one *s*. *Educ:* City of Bath Boys' Sch.; Univ. of Southampton (BA, PhD). Sheffield University: Lectr in Prehistory and Archaeology, 1976–86; Sen. Lectr, 1986–93; Prof., 1993–95. Leverhulme Res. Fellow, 1980, Dir, 1988–95 (on secondment), British Sch. at Rome; Director: Prince of Wales's Inst. of Architecture, 1996–98; Univ. of Pennsylvania Mus., Philadelphia, 2007–12. Special Advr to Minister of Culture, Albania, 1999; Mem. Bd, Packard Humanities Inst., 2003– (Advr to proj., Albania, 2000–06). Visiting Professor: in Medieval Studies, SUNY-Birmingham, 1983; in Medieval Archaeology, Siena Univ., 1984–87; in Archaeology, Copenhagen Univ., 1987–88; Sheffield Univ., 2006–09; Charles Eliot Norton Lectr, Amer. Inst. of Archaeology, 2005; Dalrymple Lectr, Univ. of Glasgow, 2009. Director: Roystone Grange landscape project, Derbyshire, 1978–88; San Vincenzo excavations, S Italy, 1980–98; co-director: Sheffield-Siena archaeological project, Montarrenti, Tuscany, 1982–87; Butrint excavations, Albania, 1994–2012; San Pietro d'Asso excavations, Tuscany, 2010. Scientific Dir, Butrint Foundn, 1995–2012. *Publications:* Walks in the Cotswolds, 1976; The Hamwih Pottery, 1981; (with G. Barker) Archaeology and Italian Society, 1981; Dark Age Economics, 1982, 2nd edn 1989; (with P. Davey) Ceramics and trade, 1983; (with D. Whitehouse) Mohammed, Charlemagne and the origins of Europe, 1983; (with John Mitchell) San Vincenzo al Volturno, 1985; Primitive and Peasant Markets, 1988; (with B. Hobley) Rebirth of the town in the West, 1988; The Anglo-Saxon Achievement, 1989; Wall to Wall History, 1991 (British Archaeological Book of the Year, 1992); (with K. Smith) Recent Developments in the Archaeology of the Peak District, 1991; (ed) San Vincenzo 1, 1993; (ed) San Vincenzo 2, 1995; (with J. Mitchell) La Basilica di Iosue a San Vincenzo al Volturno, 1995; Light in the Dark Ages, 1997; (with W. Bowden) The Sixth Century, 1998; Towns and Trade in the Age of Charlemagne, 2000; Visions of Rome: Thomas Ashby, archaeologist, 2000; (with R. Francovich) Villa to Village, 2003; (with W. Bowden and K. Lake) Byzantine Butrint, 2004; Goodbye to the Vikings?, 2006; (with L. Bejko) Eternal Butrint, 2006; New Directions in Albanian Archaeology, 2006; (with K. Bowes and K. Francis) Between Text and Territory, 2006; (with I. Hansen) Roman Butrint, 2006; The Rise and Fall of Byzantine Butrint, 2008; (with W. Bowden) Butrint 3: excavations at the Triconch Palace, 2011; (with S. Leppard and J. Mitchell) San Vincenzo Maggiore and its Workshops, 2011; Dark Age Economics: a new audit, 2012; (jtly) Butrint 4: the archaeology and histories of an Ionian town, 2012; (with S. Gelichi) From One Sea to Another, 2012. *Recreations:* hill walking, music, watching cricket. *Address:* American University of Rome, Via Pietro Roselli 4, 00153 Rome, Italy.

HODGES, Dr Wilfrid Augustine, FBA 2009; Professor of Mathematics, 1987–2006, Professorial Fellow, 2006–08, Queen Mary, University of London (formerly Queen Mary College, then Queen Mary and Westfield College); *b* Reading, 27 May 1941; *s* of Herbert Arthur Hodges and Vera Joan Hodges (*née* Willis); *m* 1965, Helen Marcia Hurst Ward; one *s* two *d*. *Educ:* King's Sch., Canterbury; New Coll., Oxford (BA 1965; DPhil 1970). Actg Asst Prof. of Philosophy, UCLA, 1967–68; University of London: Bedford College, 1968–84, Queen Mary College, then Queen Mary and Westfield College, later Queen Mary, 1984–2008: Lectr, in Philosophy and Maths, 1968–74, in Maths, 1974–81; Reader in Mathematical Logic, 1981–87. Vis. Associate Prof. of Maths, Univ. of Colo at Boulder, 1979–80. President: British Logic Colloquium, 1990–95; Eur. Assoc. for Logic, Lang. and Information, 1995–96; Internat. Union of Hist. and Philosophy of Sci., 2010–11 (Pres., Div. of Logic, Methodology and Philosophy of Sci., 2008–11). *Publications:* Logic, 1977, 2nd edn 2001; Building Models by Games, 1985; Model Theory, 1993; A Shorter Model Theory, 1997; (with I. Chiswell) Mathematical Logic, 2007; contrib. articles to mathematical and logical jls. *Recreations:* piano, Dartmoor. *Address:* Herons Brook, Sticklepath, Okehampton, Devon EX20 2PY. *T:* (01837) 840154. *E:* wilfrid.hodges@btinternet.com.

HODGETTS, Robert Bartley; Clerk to Worshipful Company of Glaziers, 1979–85; *b* 10 Nov. 1918; *s* of late Captain Bartley Hodgetts, MN and Florence Hodgetts (*née* Stagg); *m* 1st, 1945, A. K. Jeffreys; one *d*; 2nd, 1949, Frances Grace (*d* 2007), *d* of late A. J. Pepper, Worcester; two *d*. *Educ:* Merchant Taylors' Sch., Crosby; St John's Coll., Cambridge (Scholar, MA). Served RNVR (A), 1940–45. Asst Principal, Min. of Nat. Insce, 1947; Principal 1951; Asst Sec. 1964; Under-Sec., DHSS, 1973–78. *Recreation:* watching cricket and Rugby football. *Address:* 10 The Close, Winchester, Hants SO23 9LS. *T:* (01962) 890987.

HODGKIN, Sir Howard, CH 2003; Kt 1992; CBE 1977; painter; *b* 6 Aug. 1932; *m* 1955, Julia Lane; two *s*. *Educ:* Camberwell Sch. of Art; Bath Academy of Art. Taught at Charterhouse Sch., 1954–56; taught at Bath Academy of Art, 1956–66; occasional tutor, Slade Sch. of Art and Chelsea Sch. of Art. Vis. Fellow in Creative Art, Brasenose Coll. Oxford, 1976–77. A Trustee: Tate Gall., 1970–76; National Gall., 1978–85. Mem., Exec. Cttee, Nat. Art Collections Fund, 1988–90. One-man exhibitions include: Arthur Tooth & Sons, London, 1962, 1964, 1967; Kasmin Gall., 1969, 1971, 1976; Arnolfini Gall., Bristol, 1970, 1975; Dartington Hall, 1970; Galerie Müller, Cologne, 1971; Kornblee Gall., NY, 1973; Museum of Modern Art, Oxford, 1976, 1977, 2010; Serpentine Gall., London and provincial tour, Waddington Gall., 1976; André Emmerich Gall., Zürich and NY, 1977; Third Sydney Biennale, Art Gall. of NSW, 1979; Waddington Galls, 1972, 1980, 1988; Knoedler Gall. NY, 1981, 1982, 1984, 1988, 1990, 1993–94; Bernard Jacobson NY, 1980, 1981, LA, 1981, London, 1982; Tate Gall., 1982, 1985; Bath Fest., 1984; Phillips Collection, Washington DC, 1984; XLI Venice Biennale, 1984; Yale Centre for British Art, New Haven, 1985, 2007, and tour, incl. Fitzwilliam Mus., Cambridge; Kestnergesellschaft, Hanover, 1985; Whitechapel

Art Gall., 1985; Michael Werner Gall., Cologne, 1990; Nantes, Barcelona, Edinburgh and Dublin tour, 1990–91; Anthony D'Offay Gall., 1993, 1999–2000; Alan Cristea Gall., London, 1995, 2012; Metropolitan Mus. of Art, NY, 1995–96, and tour, incl. Hayward Gall., 1996–97 (retrospective); Gall. Lawrence Rubin, Zurich, 1996, 1997; Gagosian Gall., NY, 1998, 2003; Haas and Fuchs Galerie, Berlin, 1998; Gall. Lawrence Rubin, Milan, 2001; Dulwich Picture Gall., 2001; Dean Gall., Edinburgh, 2002; Gagosian Gall., LA, 2004; Galerie Lutz & Thalmann, Zürich, 2004; Irish Mus. of Modern Art, Dublin, 2006, and tour incl. London and Madrid; Gagosian Gall., London, 2008; Gagosian Gall., Paris, 2014. Group Exhibitions include: The Human Clay, Hayward Gall., 1976; British Painting 1952–1977, RA, 1977; A New Spirit in Painting, RA, 1981; Hard Won Image, Tate Gall., 1984; An International Survey of Recent Paintings and Sculpture, Mus. of Mod. Art, 1984; NY, Carnegie International, Mus. of Art, Carnegie Inst., 1985–86; British Art in 20th Century, RA, 1987; Here and Now, Serpentine Gall., 1994; and in exhibns in: Australia, Austria, Belgium, Canada, Denmark, France, Germany, GB, Holland, India, Italy, Japan, Malta, Norway, Sweden, Switzerland, USA. Designs for: Pulcinella, Ballet Rambert, 1987; Piano, Royal Ballet, 1989; mural for British Council building, New Delhi, 1992. Works in public collections: Arts Council of GB; British Council, London; Contemp. Arts Soc.; Kettering Art Gall.; Peter Stuyvesant Foundn; São Paulo Museum; Oldham Art Gall.; Tate Gall., London; V&A Museum; Swindon Central Lib.; Bristol City Art Gall.; Walker Art Center, Minneapolis; Nat. Gall. of S Aust., Adelaide; Fogg Art Museum, Cambridge, Mass; BM; Louisiana Museum, Denmark; Museum of Modern Art, Edinburgh; Southampton Art Gall.; Museum of Modern Art, and Metropolitan Mus. of Art, NY; Mus. of Art, Carnegie Inst.; Whitworth Art Gall., Manchester; City of Manchester Art Galls; Govt Picture Collection, London; Saatchi Collection, London; Nat. Gall. of Washington; Museo Nacional Centro de Arte Reina Sofia, Madrid. Hon. Fellow, Brasenose Coll., Oxford, 1988. Hon. DLitt: London, 1985; Oxford, 2000. 2nd Prize, John Moore's Exhibn, 1976 and 1980; Turner Prize, 1985. *Address:* c/o Cristina Colomar, Gagosian Gallery, 6–24 Britannia Street, WC1X 9JD.

HODGKIN, Prof. Jonathan Alan, PhD; FRS 1990; Professor of Genetics, since 2000, and Associate Head, Department of Biochemistry, since 2005, Oxford University; Fellow of Keble College, Oxford, since 2000; *b* 24 Aug. 1949; *s* of Sir Alan Hodgkin, OM, KBE, FRS and of Marion Hodgkin, *d* of late F. P. Rous; *m* 2005, Patricia Etsuko Kuwabara. *Educ:* Bryanston Sch., Dorset; Merton Coll., Oxford (BA; Hon. Fellow, 2001); Darwin Coll., Cambridge (PhD). SRC Res. Fellowship, 1974–76; Staff Scientist, MRC Lab. of Molecular Biology, 1977–2000. Vis. Prof., Univ. of Wisconsin, 1990. Mem., EMBO, 1989. *Publications:* contribs to scientific jls. *Recreations:* archaeology, cooking, cinema. *Address:* 82a Lonsdale Road, Oxford OX2 7ER. *T:* (01865) 552340.

HODGKIN, Mark William Backhouse; non-executive Director, Bury Street Capital Ltd, since 2005; *b* 26 Jan. 1949; *s* of David Kenneth and Brigit Louise Hodgkin; *m* 1978, Madeleine Alison Newton; three *d*. *Educ:* Australian National Univ. (BEc). A. Fifer Ltd, 1972–74; Laurence Prust & Co., 1974–76; Man. Dir, Rivkin & Co. (Overseas), 1976–92; Vice Pres., Bankers Trust, 1992–93; Man. Dir, West Merchant Bank (WestLB Gp), 1993–98; Chief Exec., Panmure Gordon, subseq. WestLB Panmure, Ltd, 1996–2000; CEO, Compass Capital Ltd, 2001–03; Chief Operating Officer, Cross Asset Mgt Ltd, 2003–05. Dir, Hawkesbury Capital Mgt Pte Ltd, 2005–11. *Recreations:* sailing, theatre, opera.

HODGKINS, David John, CB 1993; Director, Resources and Planning, Health and Safety Executive, 1992–94; *b* 13 March 1934; *s* of late Rev. Harold Hodgkins and Elsie Hodgkins; *m* 1963, Sheila Lacey; two *s*. *Educ:* Buxton Coll.; Peterhouse, Cambridge. BA 1956, MA 1960. Entered Min. of Labour as Asst Principal, 1956; Principal: Min. of Lab., 1961–65; Treasury, 1965–68; Manpower and Productivity Services, Dept of Employment, 1968–70; Assistant Secretary: Prices and Incomes Div., Dept of Employment, 1970–72; Industrial Relns Div., 1973–76; Under Secretary, Overseas and Manpower Divisions, Dept of Employment, 1977–84; Safety Policy Div., HSE, 1984–92. Mem., Employment Appeal Tribunal, 1996–2004. *Publications:* Sir Edward Watkin: the second railway king, 2002; The Records of the Cromford and High Peak Railway, 2009; The Diary of Edward Watkin, 2013. *Recreation:* narrow boating. *Address:* Four Winds, Batchelors Way, Amersham, Bucks HP7 9AJ. *T:* (01494) 725207.

HODGKINSON, Sir Michael Stewart, Kt 2003; Chairman, Keolis UK Ltd, since 2011; *b* 7 April 1944; *s* of Stewart Gordon Hodgkinson and Ruth Phyllis Hodgkinson; *m* 1988, Elspeth Holman; one *s* two *d*. *Educ:* Nottingham Univ. (BA Hons Industrial Econs). ACMA 1969. Finance: Ford of Europe, 1965–69; British Leyland, 1969–75; Finance and Admin. Dir, Leyland Cars Engrg, 1975–78; Man. Dir, Land Rover Ltd, 1978–83; Gp Dir, Watney Mann & Truman Brewers, 1983–85; Dep. Chief Exec., Express Dairies, 1985–89; Chief Exec., Grand Metropolitan Foods, Europe, 1989–92; Gp Airports Dir, 1992–99, Chief Exec., 1999–2003, BAA plc. Chairman: Post Office, 2003–07; First Choice plc, 2004–07; Dep. Chm., TUI Travel plc, 2007–; non-executive Director: Royal Mail, 2003–07; Dublin Airport Authy plc, 2004–11; Crossrail Ltd, 2009–12. Mem. Bd, Transport for London, 2000–12. *Recreations:* golf, theatre, travel.

HODGKINSON, Neil Robert; Editor, Hull Daily Mail, since 2011; *b* 28 May 1960; *s* of Robert Hodgkinson and Faith Hodgkinson; *m* 1st, 1984, Jacqueline Dawn Proctor; 2nd, 1993, Christine Elizabeth Talbot; 3rd, 2000, Emma Louise Schofield; one *s*. *Educ:* Baines Grammar Sch., Poulton-le-Fylde; Central Lancashire Poly. (Dip. Journalism). Trainee journalist to Dep. News Editor, W Lancs Evening Gazette, 1979–87; News Editor, then Dep. Editor, Lancs Evening Post, 1987–92; Dep. Ed., Yorkshire Evening Post, 1992–96; Editor, Lancs Evening Post, 1996–99; Editor and Dir, Yorkshire Evening Post, 1999–2006; Editl Dir, Cumbrian Newspapers Ltd, 2006–11. *Recreations:* football, Rugby Union youth coach. *Address:* Hull Daily Mail, Blundells Corner, Beverley Road, Hull HU3 1XS. *T:* (01482) 315250.

HODGKINSON, Terence, CBE 2010; DL; Principal, Terry Hodgkinson Ltd, since 2010; Chair, NCFE, since 2011; *b* 30 March 1949; *m* 1973, Anne Simpson; two *d*. *Educ:* Aston Univ. (BSc Hons). CDir 2001. Chm., Magna Hldgs Ltd, 1997–2013. Chm., Yorkshire Forward, 2003–10. Vis. Prof., Leeds Business Sch., 2010–. Non-exec. Dir, Reset Certification Scheme, 2014–. FCIOB 2001; FInstD 2008. DUniv Huddersfield, 2010. DL W Yorks, 2010. *Address:* 2 North Road Terrace, St John's North, Wakefield, W Yorks WF1 3PY. *T:* (01924) 376100. *E:* terry@terryhodgkinson.com.

HODGSON, family name of **Baroness Hodgson of Abinger** and **Baron Hodgson of Astley Abbotts**.

HODGSON OF ABINGER, Baroness *cr* 2013 (Life Peer), of Abinger in the County of Surrey; **Fiona Ferelith Hodgson,** CBE 2012; *d* of Keith Storr Allom and Jean Ferelith Maxwell Robertson; *m* 1982, Robin Granville Hodgson (*see* Baron Hodgson of Astley Abbotts); three *s* one *d* (and one twin *s* decd). *Educ:* Queen Anne's Sch., Caversham; Guildford High Sch. Res. Exec., Reader's Digest Assoc. Ltd, 1980–83; Director: Johnson Bros & Co. Ltd, 1989–; Johnson Bros Design, 1991–2006. Non-exec. Dir, Barnet DHA, 1992–94. Mem. Bd, Cons. Party, 2009–12; Pres., Nat. Cons. Convention, 2011–12 (Vice Pres., 2009–11); Hon. Vice Pres., Cons. Women's Orgn (Dep. Chm., 2002–05; Chm., 2005–08; Pres., 2008–11); Chm., Cons. Party Conf., 2011. Co-Chm., All-Party Parly Gp on Women, Peace and Security, 2014–. Member: Farm Animal Welfare Council, 1989–97; Gen. Council and Appeals Cttee, Wellbeing, 1993–2006; Adv. Cttee on Animal Foodstuffs, Food Standards Agency, 2001–04; Council of Internat. Social Services UK, 2003–04; Indep. Health Forum, 2003–04; Indep. Sector Working Gp on licensing and revalidation of private doctors, 2006–09; Indep. Sector Assessment and Adv. Cttee, Indep. Doctors Fedn, 2010–14; Women's Justice Taskforce, Prison Reform Trust, 2010–; Steering Bd, Foreign Sec.'s Initiative on Preventing Sexual Violence, 2012–. Chairman: Adv. Bd, Gender Action for Peace Security, 2009–; Governance Bd, Indep. Sector Complaints and Adjudication Service, 2012–. Member: European Union of Women, 2006–; UN Women UK, 2009–; Cons. Human Rights Commn, 2009–; Assoc. of Oxfam, 2009–. Trustee, Chalker Foundn, 2010–. Patron: Afghan Connection, 2011–; Cons. Friends of Internat. Develt, 2012–. FRGS 2011. *Recreations:* travel, riding, walking, reading, cookery. *Address:* House of Lords, SW1A 0PW. *T:* (020) 7219 3000.

HODGSON OF ASTLEY ABBOTTS, Baron *cr* 2000 (Life Peer), of Nash in the co. of Shropshire; **Robin Granville Hodgson,** CBE 1992; Chairman, Johnson Bros & Co. Ltd, Walsall, since 1989 (Director, since 1970); *b* 25 April 1942; *s* of late Henry Edward and Natalie Beatrice Hodgson; *m* 1982, Fiona Ferelith Allom (*see* Baroness Hodgson of Abinger); three *s* one *d* (and one twin *s* decd). *Educ:* Shrewsbury Sch.; Oxford Univ. (BA Hons 1964); Wharton Sch. of Finance, Univ. of Pennsylvania (MBA 1969). Investment Banker, New York and Montreal, 1964–67; Industry in Birmingham, England, 1969–72; Gp Chief Exec., 1979–95, Chm., 1995–2002, Granville plc, then Granville Baird Ltd; Chairman: Rostrum Gp Ltd, 2000–07; Nova Capital Mgt Ltd, 2002–; Carbo plc, 2002–05; RFIB Group Ltd, 2007–; Tenet Gp Ltd, 2007–12; EIS Optics Ltd (formerly Telescope Holdco), 2009–11; Cash Management Systems Ltd, 2014–; CMS Payments Intelligence Ltd, 2014–; Director: Community Hospitals plc, 1982–85 and 1995–2001; Domnick Hunter Gp, 1992–2002; Staffordshire Building Soc., 1995–2005; Marston's (formerly Wolverhampton and Dudley Breweries) plc, 2002–14. Mem., W Midlands Industrial Develt Bd, 1989–97. Contested (C) Walsall North, Feb. and Oct. 1974; MP (C) Walsall North, Nov. 1976–1979. Opposition spokesman on trade and industry, H of L, 2002–06. Official Reviewer: Charities Act, 2006, 2012; Pt 2, Transparency of Lobbying, Non Party Campaigning and Trade Union Administration Act 2014. Chm., Unshackling Good Neighbours Task Force, Cabinet Office, 2011. Chm., Birmingham Bow Gp, 1972–73; National Union of Conservative Associations: Mem. Exec. Cttee, 1988–98; Vice Pres., 1995–96; Chm., 1996–98; Chm., W Midlands Area, 1991–94. Dep. Chm., Cons. Party, 1998–2000; Chairman: Nat. Cons. Convention, 1998–2000; Trustees, Cons. Party Pension Fund, 2000–06. Member: Council for the Securities Industry, 1980–85; Securities and Investments Board, 1985–89; Dir, SFA, 1991–2001; Chm., Nat. Assoc. of Security Dealers and Investment Managers, 1979–85. Chm., Armed Forces Charities Adv. Cttee, 2009–. Pres., NCVO, 2009–12. Trustee and Hon. Fellow, St Peter's Coll., Oxford; Associate, St George's House, Windsor. Liveryman, Goldsmiths' Co., 1983. *Publications:* Britain's Home Defence Gamble, 1978. *Recreations:* squash, fishing, theatre. *Address:* House of Lords, SW1A 0PW.

HODGSON, (Adam) Robin; DL; Chief Executive, Hampshire County Council, 1985–95; *b* 20 March 1937; *s* of Thomas Edward Highton Hodgson, CB; *m* 1962, Elizabeth Maureen Linda Bovenizer; one *s* two *d*. *Educ:* William Ellis Sch., London; Worcester Coll., Oxford (MA 1969); BSc Open Univ. 1997. Admitted Solicitor, 1964. Asst Solicitor, LCC and GLC, 1964–66; Sen. Asst Solicitor, Oxfordshire CC, 1966–71; Asst Clerk, Northamptonshire CC, 1972–74; Dep. County Sec., E Sussex CC, 1974–77; Dep. Chief Exec. and Clerk, Essex CC, 1977–85. Chm., Winchester Diocesan Bd of Finance, 1996–2006. Mem. Council, Univ. of Southampton, 1996–2002; Governor, Univ. of Portsmouth, 1996–2003. Mem. Gen. Chiropractic Council, 1996–2004. DL Hampshire, 1996. *Recreations:* music, drama, geology. *Address:* Tara, Dean Lane, Winchester, Hampshire SO22 5RA. *T:* (01962) 862119.

HODGSON, Christine Mary, FCA; Executive Chairman, Capgemini UK plc, since 1997; *b* Preston, 17 Nov. 1964; *d* of Anthony Frederick and Audrey Pickles; *m* 1999, Howard Osmond Paul Hodgson, *qv*; one *s*. *Educ:* Elmslie Girls' Sch., Blackpool; Loughborough Univ. (BSc 1st Cl. Hons Accounting and Financial Mgt). ACA 1990. With Coopers & Lybrand, 1985–94; Ronson plc, 1994–97. Non-executive Director: Ladbrokes plc, 2012–; Standard Chartered Bank, 2013–. Board Member: BITC; MacIntyre Care. *Address:* Capgemini UK plc, 40 Holborn Viaduct, EC1N 2PB. *Club:* Royal Motor Yacht (Poole).

HODGSON, George Wilson; HM Diplomatic Service; Ambassador to Senegal, and concurrently to Cape Verde and Guinea Bissau, since 2015; *b* London, 17 Oct. 1980; *s* of Clive Alexander Hodgson and Dr Elizabeth Ann Hodgson; *m* 2010, Constance Maljette; two *s* one *d*. *Educ:* City of London Sch.; Pembroke Coll., Oxford (BA 1st Cl. Hons PPE); Woodrow Wilson Sch., Princeton Univ. (MPA 2008). Joined FCO, 2002; Desk Officer, EU Directorate, FCO, 2002–03; Second Secretary: Kabul, 2004; UK Representation to EU, 2005–06; First Sec., Islamabad, 2008–10; Political Counsellor, Kabul, 2010–11; Sen. Advr to Special Rep. for Afghanistan and Pakistan, State Dept, Washington (on secondment), 2011–12; Head: Parly and Communications Dept, FCO, 2012–14; Ebola Taskforce, 2014–15. *Recreations:* hiking, tennis, squash, cricket. *Address:* c/o Foreign and Commonwealth Office, King Charles Street, SW1A 0AA. *E:* george.hodgson@fco.gov.uk.

HODGSON, Guy Andrew Keith; District Judge (Magistrates' Courts) (formerly Stipendiary Magistrate), Bradford, 1993–2000; *b* 19 March 1946; *s* of Herbert and Kathleen Hodgson; *m* 1968, Kay Bampton; three *s*. *Educ:* Pocklington Sch.; Nottingham Poly. (LLB London Ext.). Articled to M. M. Rossfield, Solicitor, York; Legal Asst, Thames Valley Police, 1970–71; Asst Prosecutor, Suffolk Police, 1971–72; Asst Solicitor, Gotelee & Goldsmith, Ipswich, 1972–74; Partner, Close Thornton, Darlington, 1974–93. *Recreations:* travel, reading, painting, hobby farming, vintage tractors, family interests, canal narrow boats.

HODGSON, Howard Osmond Paul; author, scriptwriter and lyricist; Chairman and Chief Executive Officer, Memoria Ltd, since 2002; *b* 22 Feb. 1950; *s* of late Osmond Paul Charles Hodgson and of Sheila Mary (*née* Ward; now Mrs Baker); *m* 1st, 1972, Marianne Denise Yvonne (marr. diss. 1998), *d* of Samuel Katibien, Aix-en-Provence, France; two *s* one *d* (and one *s* decd); 2nd, 1999, Christine Mary Pickles (*see* C. M. Hodgson); one *s*. *Educ:* Aiglon Coll., Villars, Switzerland. DipFD 1970; MBIFD; Affiliated MRSPH (MRSH 1970). Asst Man., Hodgson & Sons Ltd, 1969–71; life assce exec., 1971–75; acquired: Hodgson & Sons Ltd, 1975 (floated USM, 1986); Ingalls from House of Fraser, 1987; launched Dignity in Destiny Ltd, 1989; merger with Pompes Funèbres Générales, France, Kenyon Securities and Hodgson Hldgs plc to form PFG Hodgson Kenyon Internat. plc, 1989; launched: Bereavement Support Service, 1990; PHKI Nat. Training Sch., 1990; retd, 1991, to pursue career in broadcasting and writing. Chief Executive: Halkin Hldgs, 1993; Hoskins Brewery plc, 1993; Ronson plc, 1995–97 (acquired Ronson plc and LGW plc, 1994, Home Shopping Marketing Ltd and associated cos, the business of DCK Marketing Ltd and Smiths Packaging Ltd, 1995; Group renamed Ronson plc, 1995; resigned, 1997); CEO, Colibri Internat., 1998–2001. Presenter, How Euro Are You, BBC2, 1991–92; panellist, Board Game, Radio 4, 1992–2001. Hon. Vice Pres., Royal Soc. of St George, 1989. USM Entrepreneur of the Year, 1987. *Publications:* How to Become Dead Rich, 1992; Six Feet Under, 2000 (film script, 2001); Exhumed Innocent?, 2002; Charles: the man who will be king, 2007 (US edn as The King and Di, 2009). *Recreations:* cricket, yachting, ski-ing, English/British Royal history, Aston Villa FC. *Address:* Mdina, Malta. *E:* hhodgson@memoria.org.uk. *Club:* Royal Motor Yacht.

HODGSON, Prof. Humphrey Julian Francis, DM; FRCP, FMedSci; Dame Sheila Sherlock Professor of Medicine, UCL Medical School (formerly Royal Free and University College Medical School), University College London, 1999–2011; Visiting Professor, University of Namibia, Windhoek, since 2011; *b* 5 April 1945; *s* of late Harold Robinson Hodgson and Celia Frances Hodgson (*née* Hodgson); *m* 1971, Shirley Victoria Penrose; one *s* one *d*. *Educ:* Westminster Sch.; Christ Church, Oxford (BA, BSc); St Thomas's Hosp. Med.

Sch. (BM BCh, DM). FRCP 1983. Trng posts at St Thomas' and Royal Free Hosps, 1970–76; Radcliffe Travelling Fellow, University Coll., Oxford, at Massachusetts Gen. Hosp., Boston, 1977; Consultant Physician, Hammersmith Hosp., 1977–99; Royal Postgraduate Medical School, London: Sen. Lectr in Medicine, 1978–89; Reader, 1989–91; Prof. of Gastroenterology, 1991–95; Vice Dean, 1986–97; Prof. of Medicine, RPMS, then ICSM, 1995–99; Jt Med. Dir, Hammersmith Hosps NHS Trust, 1994–97; Vice Dean, Royal Free Campus, Royal Free and University Coll. Med. Sch., later UCL Med. Sch., 2001–09. Chm., Scientific Co-ordinating Cttee, Arthritis Res. Campaign (formerly Arthritis and Rheumatism Council for Res.), 1996–2003. Pres., British Assoc. for Study of the Liver, 2003–05; Acad. Registrar, 1992–97, Sen. Censor and Vice-Pres., 2008–11, Ed., Clinical Medicine, 2011–, RCP. FMedSci 2002. *Publications:* Textbook of Gastroenterology, 1984; Gastroenterology: clinical science and practice, 1994; multiple articles on clinical and laboratory aspects of liver disease. *Recreations:* walking, reading, academic travel. *Address:* Department of Medicine, UCL Medical School, University College London, Rowland Hill Street, NW3 2PF. *T:* (020) 7433 2850; 40 Onslow Gardens, N10 3JU. *T:* (020) 8883 8297.

HODGSON, Ian Geoffrey; horticultural consultant and garden writer, since 2011; Editor-in-Chief, RHS Media, 2006–11 and Editor, The Garden, 1993–2011, Royal Horticultural Society; Editor at Large, Garden News and Garden Answers magazines, since 2013; *b* Mirfield, W Yorks, 2 May 1958; *s* of Geoffrey Walter Hodgson and Mary Hodgson; *m* 1993, Judith Lesley Allen; one *s*. *Educ:* Royal Botanic Gardens, Kew (Dip. Horticulture); Univ. of Sheffield (BSc Landscape Design and Plant Sci.; Dip. Landscape Arch.; MA Landscape Design). Tech. writer, Garden News, 1986–87; Tech. Ed., Practical Gardening Magazine, 1987–89; Ed., The Gardener, 1989–93. Trustee, Plant Heritage, 2011–. *Publications:* Growing Bromeliads, 1990; RHS Container Gardening, 2013; Great Garden Design, 2015. *Recreations:* music (especially classical and contemporary big band jazz), collecting old gardening books and gardening ephemera (especially history of plant hunting), garden and planting design, foreign travel (especially for natural history).

HODGSON, Keith Stephen, OBE 1997; Director, Management Support Unit, Board of Inland Revenue, 1998–2001; *b* 29 Oct. 1946; *s* of Leonard Arthur and Florence Hodgson; *m* 1969, Jean Moran. *Educ:* Wolverhampton Municipal Grammar Sch. Min. of Transport, 1965–68; Board of Inland Revenue, 1968–2001; Private Sec. to Chm. of Bd, CS Pay Res. Unit, 1978–81; Dep. Controller of Stamps, 1982–90; Dir, Stamp Office, 1990–98. FRSA 1998. *Publications:* (contrib.) Managing Change in the New Public Sector, 1994; (contrib.) Creating a Good Impression: three hundred years of the Stamp Office and Stamp Duties, 1994. *Recreations:* Freemasonry, golf, wine, Rugby, ski-ing. *Address:* Tenterden, Kent; Chandolin, Val d'Anniviers, Valais, Switzerland. *Club:* Tenterden Golf (Captain, 2011).

HODGSON, Dame Patricia (Anne), (Dame Patricia Donaldson), DBE 2004 (CBE 1995); Member of Board, since 2011, and Chair, since 2014, Ofcom (Deputy Chair, 2012–14); *b* 19 Jan. 1947; *d* of Harold Hodgson and Pat Smith; *m* 1979, George Donaldson; one *s*. *Educ:* Brentwood High Sch.; Newnham Coll., Cambridge (MA; Associate Fellow, 1994–97; Hon. Fellow, 2013); LRAM (Drama) 1968. Conservative Res. Dept, Desk Officer for public sector industries, 1968–70; freelance journalism and broadcasting in UK and USA during seventies; Chm., Bow Gp, 1975–76; Editor, Crossbow, 1976–80. BBC: joined as educn producer for Open Univ. (part of founding team pioneering distance learning techniques), 1970; most of prodn career in educn, specialising in history and philosophy, with spells in current affairs on Today and Tonight; Secretariat, 1982–83, Dep. Sec., 1983–85, The Sec., 1985–87; Hd of Policy & Planning, 1987–92; Dir of Policy & Planning, 1993–2000; Dir of Public Policy, 2000; Chief Exec., ITC, 2000–04. Principal, Newnham Coll., Cambridge, 2006–12 (Vis. Bye Fellow, 2004). Chm., Higher Educn Regulation Rev. Gp, 2004–06; Mem., HEFCE, 2005–11; Chm., School Teachers' Rev. Body, 2012–14. Non-executive Director: GCAP Media plc, 2004–06; Competition Commn, 2004–11 (Mem., Monopolies and Mergers, subseq. Competition, Commn, 1993–97); Member: Statistics Commn, 2000–05; Cttee on Standards in Public Life, 2004–08; BBC Trust, 2007–11; Commn on Freedom of Information, 2015–. Dir, BARB, 1987–98. Mem., (C) Haringey BC, 1974–77. Mem., London Arts Bd, 1991–96. Trustee, PYBT, 1992–95. Gov., Wellcome Trust, 2004–08; Mem. Adv. Bd, Judge Inst., Cambridge, 1996–2002. DU Essex, 2001; Hon. DSc City, 2002. *Television series* include: English Urban History, 1978; Conflict in Modern Europe, 1980; Rome in the Age of Augustus, 1981. *Publications:* (ed) Paying for Broadcasting, 1992; (ed) Public Purposes in Broadcasting, 1999; (ed) Culture and Communications, 2003; articles in various newspapers and jls. *Recreation:* quietness. *Address:* Ofcom, Riverside House, 2a Southwark Bridge Road, SE1 9HA. *Club:* Oxford and Cambridge.

HODGSON, Randolph Arthur, OBE 2006; owner, Neal's Yard Dairy, since 1979; *b* 29 Sept. 1956; *s* of Arthur Ralph and Monica Olive Hodgson; *m* 1982, Anita Leroy; two *s* one *d*. *Educ:* Downside Sch.; King's Coll., London (BSc Hons). Chm., Specialist Cheesemakers Assoc., 1990–94 and 2000–11. *Recreations:* cheese-making, farming.

HODGSON, Robin; *see* Hodgson, A. R.

HODGSON, Sharon; MP (Lab) Washington and Sunderland West, since 2010 (Gateshead East and Washington West, 2005–10); *b* 1 April 1966; *d* of Joan Cohen (*née* Wilson); *m* 1990, Alan Hodgson; one *s* one *d*. *Educ:* Heathfield Sen. High Sch., Gateshead; Newcastle Coll. Payroll/account clerk, Tyneside Safety Glass, 1982–88; Northern Rock Bldg Soc., Gosforth, 1988–92; Payroll administrator, Burgess Microswitch, 1992–94; Administrator, Total Learning Challenge, 1998–99; Lab. Party Orgnr, 1999–2002; Labour Link Co-ordinator, UNISON, 2002–05. PPS to Minister of State, Home Office, 2006–07, to Minister of State, MoD, 2007–08, to Minister of State, DoH, 2008–09; an Asst Govt Whip, 2009–10; Opposition Whip, 2010; Shadow Minister: for Children and Families, 2010–13; for Women and Equalities, 2013–15. Mem., Children, Schs and Families Select Cttee, 2007–09. *Address:* (office) Units 1–1a, Vermont House, Concord, Washington, Tyne and Wear NE37 2SQ; House of Commons, SW1A 0AA. *W:* www.sharonhodgson.org.

HODGSON, Ven. Thomas Richard Burnham; Archdeacon of West Cumberland, 1979–91, now Archdeacon Emeritus; *b* 17 Aug. 1926; *s* of Richard Shillito Hodgson and Marion Thomasina Bertram Marshall; *m* 1952, Margaret Esther (*d* 2007), *o d* of Evan and Caroline Margaret Makinson; one *s* one *d*. *Educ:* Heversham Grammar School; London Coll. of Divinity, Univ. of London. BD, ALCD. Deacon 1952, priest 1953, dio. Carlisle; Curate of Crosthwaite, Keswick, 1952–55; Curate of Stanwix, Carlisle, 1955–59; Vicar of St Nicholas', Whitehaven, 1959–65; Rector of Aikton, 1965–67; Vicar of Raughtonhead with Gaitsgill, 1967–73, and Domestic Chaplain to Bishop of Carlisle, 1967–73, Hon. Chaplain, 1973–79; Hon. Canon of Carlisle, 1973–91; Vicar of: Grange-over-Sands, 1973–79; Mosser, 1979–83. Mem., General Synod of C of E, 1983–90. Director of Ordination Candidates, 1970–74; RD of Windermere, 1976–79; Surrogate, 1962–91. *Publications:* Saying the Services, 1989; Speaking in Church, 2004. *Address:* 58 Greenacres, Wetheral, Carlisle CA4 8LD. *T:* (01228) 561159.

HODKINSON, Gregory Scott; Chairman, Arup Group, since 2014; *b* Newcastle, Australia, 10 June 1955; *s* of Barrie and Deirdre Hodkinson; *m* 1989, Siobhán O'Connor; two *s* three *d*. *Educ:* N Sydney Boys' High Sch.; Univ. of New South Wales; Macquarie Univ. (BA). Joined Arup, 1972: work in Australia and UK, 1972–88; Founding Principal, NY Office, 1988–2004; Chm., Americas Reg., 2004–11; Chm., Eur. Business, 2011–14. Non-exec. Dir, British American Business, 2005–. Trustee, Water Aid, 2007–14. FRSA. *Recreation:* sailing. *Address:* Arup, 13 Fitzroy Street, W1T 4BQ. *T:* (020) 7755 4300. *E:* sam.castle@arup.com. *Clubs:* Brook (New York); Shelter Island Yacht.

HODKINSON, Prof. Henry Malcolm, DM; FRCP; Barlow Professor of Geriatric Medicine, University College London, 1985–91, now Emeritus; medical expert witness, since 1990; barrister; *b* 28 April 1931; *s* of Charles and Olive Hodkinson; *m* 1st (marr. diss.); four *d*; 2nd, 1986, Judith Marie Bryant, *qv*. *Educ:* Manchester Grammar Sch.; Brasenose Coll., Oxford (MA; DM 1975); Middlesex Hospital; Westminster Univ. (Dip. in Law, 2000). FRCP 1974. Consultant Physician in Geriatrics to: Enfield and Tottenham Gps of Hosps, 1962–70; Northwick Park Hosp., 1970–78 (also Mem., Scientific Staff of Clin. Res. Centre); Sen. Lectr in Geriatric Medicine, 1978–79, Prof. of Geriatric Medicine, 1979–84, RPMS. Called to the Bar, Middle Temple, 2001; in practice as a barrister, 2001–08. Vice Pres., Research into Ageing, 1996– (Governor, 1983–96). *Publications:* An Outline of Geriatrics, 1975, 2nd edn 1981 (trans. Spanish, Dutch, German, Italian and Japanese); Common Symptoms of Disease in the Elderly, 1976, 2nd edn 1980 (trans. Turkish); Biochemical Diagnosis of the Elderly, 1977; (ed) Clinical Biochemistry of the Elderly, 1984; (with J. M. Hodkinson) Sherratt? A Natural Family of Staffordshire Figures, 1991; approx. 100 papers in learned jls, 1961–. *Recreation:* English glass and ceramics. *Address:* 8 Chiswick Square, Burlington Lane, Chiswick, W4 2QG. *T:* (020) 8747 0239.

HODKINSON, James Clifford; Chairman, Furniture Village, since 2002; non-executive Director of various companies; *b* 21 April 1944; *s* of John and Lily Hodkinson; *m* 1969, Janet Lee; one *d*. *Educ:* Salesian Coll., Farnborough. Trainee Manager, F. W. Woolworth Ltd, London, 1962–71; Manager, B & Q, Bournemouth, 1972–74; Sales Manager, B & Q (Retail) Ltd, 1974–76; Man. Dir, B & Q (Southern) Ltd, 1976–79; Dir, 1976–79, Ops Dir, 1979–84, Ops and Personnel Dir, 1984–86, B & Q (Retail) Ltd; Man. Dir, 1986–89, Chief Exec., 1989–92, B & Q plc; Internat. Develt Dir, Kingfisher plc, 1992–94; Chm. and Chief Exec., B & Q plc, 1994–98; Chief Exec., New Look Retailers Ltd, 1998–2000. *Recreation:* shooting. *Club:* Annabel's.

HODKINSON, Judith Marie, (Mrs H. M. Hodkinson); *see* Bryant, Judith M.

HODSON, Alan Charles; Chairman, Great Ormond Street Hospital Children's Charity, since 2007; *b* Bowers Gifford, 13 April 1962; *s* of John and Audrey Hodson; *m* 1986, Christiane Hyde; one *s* one *d* (and one *d* decd). *Educ:* Culford Sch.; St Peter's Coll., Oxford (MA). With Rowe & Pitman, later S. G. Warburg, then SBC, subseq. UBS, 1984–2005 (Global Hd of Equities, UBS, 2000–04). *Recreations:* golf, tennis. *Clubs:* Royal and Ancient Golf, Royal St George's Golf, Worplesdon Golf, Royal Wimbledon Golf.

HODSON, Beverley Cliffe, OBE 2003; non-executive Director, Randstad (formerly Vedior NV), since 2006; *b* 14 June 1951; *d* of Clifford Vernon Hodson and Frances Jeanne Hodson; *m* Peter John Cottingham. *Educ:* Newnham Coll., Cambridge (BA 1st cl. hons; Exhibnr). Boots, 1978–96; Sears, 1996–97; Man. Dir, UK Retail, WH Smith Gp, 1997–2004. Non-executive Director: GWR Trent FM Radio, 1990–97; M&G Gp plc, 1998–99; Legal & General, 2000–07; Robert Wiseman Dairies plc, 2005–10; Iforce Ltd, 2005–11; First Milk, 2005–11; NFU Mutual, 2007–12. Member, Council: Univ. of Gloucester (Chm., F and GP Cttee); Cheltenham Coll. Hon. Associate, Newnham Coll., Cambridge, 2012–. *Recreations:* ski-ing, tennis, reading, theatre, opera, wine, food.

HODSON, His Honour Christopher Robert; a Circuit Judge, 1993–2011; Resident Judge, Warwick and Coventry Crown Courts, 2007–11; *b* 3 Nov. 1946; *s* of James and Elizabeth Hodson; *m* 1970, Jean Patricia Anne Dayer; one *s* one *d*. *Educ:* King's Sch., Worcester. Called to the Bar, Lincoln's Inn, 1970; practised, Birmingham, 1971–93; a Recorder, 1988–93. Hon. Recorder, City of Coventry, 2007–11. *Address:* c/o Crown Court Office, Warwickshire Justice Centre, Newbold Terrace, Leamington Spa CV32 4EL.

HODSON, Clive, CBE 1992; FCCA; FCILT; Chairman, LRT Pension Fund Trustee Co. Ltd, 1998–2003; *b* 9 March 1942; *s* of late Stanley Louis Hodson and Elsie May Hodson (*née* Stratford); *m* 1976, Fiona Mary Pybus; one *s* one *d*. *Educ:* Erith Grammar Sch. FCCA 1967; FCILT (FCIT 1969); CTA (ATII 1968). LT, 1960–69; Asst Sec. and Accountant, London Country Bus Services Ltd, 1970–74; Mgt Accountant, LT, 1974–78; London Buses Ltd: Finance Dir, 1978–89; Man. Dir, 1989–95; Chm., 2000; Managing Director: LT Buses, 1994–2000; London Bus Services Ltd, 2000. Chairman: Victoria Coach Station Ltd, 1995–2000; London River Services Ltd, 1998–2000. Mem., LTB, 1995–2000. LT Project Dir, Bus Privatisation, 1993–95; Project Dir, Croydon Tramlink, 1995–2000; Dir, Capital Value Brokers Ltd, 2000–04. Freeman, City of London, 1995; Liveryman, Co. of Carmen, 1995. *Recreations:* travel, walking, reading.

HODSON, Daniel Houghton, FCT; Chairman, Berry Palmer and Lyle Holdings plc, since 2008 (Director, since 2000); *b* 11 March 1944; *s* of late Henry Vincent Hodson and Margaret Elizabeth (*née* Honey); *m* 1979, Diana Mary Ryde; two *d*. *Educ:* Eton; Merton Coll., Oxford (MA Hons PPE). FCT 1979. Chase Manhattan Bank, 1965–73; joined Edward Bates & Sons Ltd, 1973, Dir 1974–76; Unigate plc: Gp Treas., 1976–81; Gp Finance Dir, 1981–87; Pres., Unigate Inc., 1986–87; Chief Exec., 1987–88, Chm. 1988, Davidson Pearce Gp plc; Dep. Chief Exec., Nationwide Building Soc., 1989–92; Chief Exec., LIFFE, 1993–98. Director: The Post Office, 1984–95; Ransomes plc, 1993–98; Independent Insurance Gp plc, 1995–2003; London Clearing House, 1996–98; Rolfe and Nolan plc, 1999–2003; Norland Managed (formerly Reliance Environmental) Services Ltd, 1999–2006; NASDAQ OMX NLX, 2013–; Chairman: Medialink Internat., 1999–2003; Insulation and Machining Services Ltd, 2001–07; Henderson Value Trust (formerly SVM Global Fund) plc, 2004–14. Chm., European Cttee, Options and Futures Exchanges, 1996–98. Association of Corporate Treasurers: Chm., 1985–86; Pres., 1992–93. Gresham Prof. of Commerce, 1999–2002; Prof. Emeritus, Gresham Coll. Chm., Design and Artists Copyright Soc., 1999–2005. Chm., Lokahi Foundn, 2005–14; Exec. Chm., People's Pledge, 2012–13; Hon. Treas., Business for Britain, 2013–. Dep. Chm., Classical Opera Co., 1997–2005; Trustee: Hanover Band, 2012–; Chichester Cathedral Restoration and Develt Trust, 2012–. Governor: Yehudi Menuhin Sch., 1984–2005; Peter Symonds Coll., Winchester, 2000–02; St Paul's Girls' Sch., 2006–; Collyers Coll., 2011–; Chm., Bd of Govs, Univ. of Winchester (formerly King Alfred's Coll., WInchester, then University Coll., Winchester), 2001–06; Mem. Council, Gresham Coll., 2006– (Vice Chm., 2012–). Founding Editor, Corporate Finance and Treasury Management, 1984–. Master, Mercers' Co., 2008–09. Hon. DBA Winchester, 2009. *Recreations:* music, travel, photography, reading. *Address:* Chepynge House, 22 Maltravers Street, Arundel BN18 9BU. *T:* (01903) 883234. *Club:* Brooks's.

HODSON, His Honour David; *see* Hodson, His Honour T. D. T.

HODSON, Prof. Howard Peter, PhD; FREng, FRAeS; FASME; Professor of Aerothermal Technology, 2000–13, and Director, Whittle Laboratory, 2005, Department of Engineering, University of Cambridge; Fellow, Girton College, Cambridge, since 1984; *b* 18 Feb. 1957; *s* of Edward Hodson and late Kathleen Janette Hodson; *m* 1978, Dr Jane Brooks. *Educ:* Churchill Coll., Cambridge (BA Engrg 1978, MA 1982; PhD 1983). CEng 1999, FREng 2005; FRAeS 1999. Engr, Perkins Engine Co. Ltd, 1978–79; Res. Asst, Whittle Lab., Cambridge, 1982–85; Department of Engineering, University of Cambridge: Sen. Asst in Res., 1985–89; Lectr, 1989–98; Reader in Thermofluid Engrg, 1998–2000; Girton College, Cambridge: Lectr, 1985–; Dir of Studies, 1985–2000; Actg Bursar, 1994. Dir and Sec., Cambridge Turbomachinery Consultants Ltd, 1983–2005. FASME 2002. *Publications:* contrib. papers to jls of ASME, AIAA and IMechE. *Recreations:* gardening, classic vehicle restoration.

HODSON, John; Chief Executive, Singer & Friedlander Group, 1993–2004 (Director, 1987–2004; Chairman, 1999–2003); *b* 19 May 1946; *s* of Arthur and Olga Hodson; *m* 1971, Christina McLeod; one *s* two *d*. *Educ:* Worcester Coll., Oxford (PPE). Joined Singer & Friedlander, 1969: Asst Dir, 1974–83; Dir, 1983–2004; Head of Investment Dept, 1985–90. Chairman: UBC Media PLC; SEC Investment Trust; Cenkos Securities; non-executive Director: Prestbury Gp plc; Domino's Pizza UK & Ireland plc. *Recreations:* tennis, family.

HODSON, Sir Michael (Robin Adderley), 6th Bt *cr* 1789; Captain, Scots Guards, retired; *b* 5 March 1932; *s* of Major Sir Edmond Adair Hodson, 5th Bt, DSO, and Anne Elizabeth Adderley (*d* 1984), *yr d* of Lt-Col Hartopp Francis Charles Adderley Cradock, Hill House, Sherborne St John; *S* father, 1972; *m* 1st, 1963, Katrin Alexa (marr. diss. 1978), *d* of late Erwin Bernstiel, Dinas Powis, Glamorgan; three *d*; 2nd, 1978, Catherine, *d* of late John Henry Seymour, Wimpole St, W1. *Educ:* Eton. *Heir: b* Patrick Richard Hodson [*b* 27 Nov. 1934; *m* 1961, June, *o d* of H. M. Shepherd-Cross; three *s*]. *Address:* Kilgeddin House, Llanfair Kilgeddin, Monmouthshire NP7 9BB.

HODSON, Simon James; Senior Partner, DAC Beachcroft LLP (formerly Beachcroft LLP), since 2005; *b* London, 9 May 1956; *s* of Gordon Hodson and Anne Hodson; *m* 1982, Gail Lees; one *s* one *d*. *Educ:* Marlborough House Sch., Kent; Lancing Coll.; Queen Mary Coll., Univ. of London (LLB); Coll. of Law, Lancaster Gate. Admitted as solicitor, 1981; Solicitor, Clifford Turner, 1981–84; solicitor, 1984, Partner, 1985–, Beachcrofts, then Beachcroft Stanleys, later Beachcroft LLP, subseq. DAC Beachcroft LLP. Non-exec. Dir, Fresca Gp Ltd, 2009–. Gov., Marlborough Hse Sch., Kent, 2002–. *Recreations:* theatre, ski-ing, fishing, anything outdoors. *Address:* DAC Beachcroft LLP, 100 Fetter Lane, EC4A 1BN. *T:* (020) 7242 1011, *Fax:* (020) 7831 6630. *E:* shodson@dacbeachcroft.com. *Club:* City Law.

HODSON, His Honour (Thomas) David (Tattersall); an Assistant Surveillance Commissioner, 2013–15; *b* 24 Sept. 1942; *s* of late Thomas Norman Hodson and Elsie Nuttall Hodson; *m* 1969, Patricia Ann Vint; two *s* one *d*. *Educ:* Sedbergh Sch.; Manchester Univ. (LLB). Leader Writer, Yorkshire Post, 1964–65; called to the Bar, Inner Temple 1966, Bencher, 2001; in practice on Northern Circuit, 1967–87; Junior, 1969; a Recorder, 1983–87; a Circuit Judge, 1987–2010; a Sen. Circuit Judge and Hon. Recorder of Newcastle upon Tyne, 1997–2010. Mem., Parole Bd, 1996–97; pt-time judicial Mem., Parole Bd, 2010–14; Chm., Northumbria Area Criminal Justice Strategy Cttee, 2001–03. Pres., S Lancs Br., Magistrates' Assoc., 1994–96. Mem. Court, Univ. of Newcastle upon Tyne, 2000–09. Chancellor, Dio. of Newcastle, 2009–13 (Dep. Chancellor, 2003–09). Hon. Mem., N Eastern Circuit, 2007. Hon. LLD Sunderland, 2002. *Publications:* One Week in August: the Kaiser at Lowther Castle, August 1895, 1995. *Recreations:* music, family history. *Address:* c/o Ministry of Justice, North Eastern Region, 17th Floor, West Riding House, Albion Street, Leeds LS1 5AA.

HOERNER, John Lee; consultant to Tesco Stores plc, since 2008; Chief Executive, Central European Clothing, Tesco, 2005–08; *b* Lincoln, Nebraska, 23 Sept. 1939; *s* of Robert Lee Hoerner and Lulu Alice (*née* Stone); *m* 1st 1959, Susan Kay Morgan (marr. diss. 1971); one *s* one *d*; 2nd, 1973, Anna Lea Thomas. *Educ:* Lincoln High Sch.; Univ. of Nebraska (BS Business Admin 1961). Senior buying and merchandising positions, Hovland Swanson, Lincoln, Neb, 1959–68; Gen. Merchandise Manager, Ladies Div., Woolf Bros, Kansas City, Mo, 1968–72; Womenswear Merchandise Manager, Hahne & Co., NJ, Associated Dry Goods Corp., 1972–73; real est. devclt and venture capital, McLean, Va, 1973–74; Associated Dry Goods Corporation: Gen. Merchandise Manager, 1974–76; Sen. Vice Pres. and Dir of Stores, 1976–79; Sen. Vice Pres. and Gen. Merchandise Manager, 1979–81; Pres. and CEO, H. & S. Pogue Co., Cincinnati, Ohio, 1981–82; Pres. and CEO, 1982–85, Chm. and CEO, 1985–86, L. S. Ayres & Co., Indianapolis, Ind., Associated Dry Goods Corp., later May Dept Stores Co.; Burton Group, subseq. Arcadia Group, 1987–2000: Chairman: Debenhams, 1987–92; Harvey Nichols, 1988–91; Gp Chief Exec., 1992–2000; Chief Exec., Clothing, 2001–04, Clothing and Internat. Sourcing, 2004–08, Tesco. Chm., British Fashion Council, 1997–2000. Non-exec. Dir, BAA, 1998–2004. Mem., Council of Trustees, Battersea Dogs' and Cats' Home (formerly Dogs' Home, Battersea), 1991–2006 (Vice-Chm., 1995–2002; Chm., 2002–06). Lifetime Achievement Award, Univ. of Nebraska, 2008. *Publications:* Ayres Adages, 1983; The Director's Handbook, 1991; Recipes for Retailers, 2014. *Recreations:* riding, flying, dogs. *Address:* Hawling Lodge, Hawling, Cheltenham, Glos GL54 5SY. *T:* (01451) 850223. *Clubs:* Groucho, Travellers; Air Squadron.

HOEY, Catharine Letitia; MP (Lab) Vauxhall, since June 1989; *b* 21 June 1946; *d* of Thomas Henry and Letitia Jane Hoey. *Educ:* Lylehill Primary Sch.; Belfast Royal Acad.; Ulster Coll. of Physical Educn (Dip. in PE); City of London Coll. (BSc Econs). Lectr, Southwark Coll., 1972–76; Sen. Lectr, Kingsway Coll., 1976–85; Educnl Advr, London Football Clubs, 1985–89. PPS to Minister of State (Minister for Welfare Reform), DSS, 1997–98; Parliamentary Under-Secretary of State: Home Office, 1998–99; DCMS (Minister for Sport), 1999–2001. Mayor of London's Comr for Sport, 2009–. Chairman: Countryside Alliance, 2005–14; London Sport, 2014–. Hon. Pres., Clay Pigeon Shooting Assoc.; Hon. Vice Pres., British Wheelchair Basketball. *Address:* House of Commons, SW1A 0AA. *T:* (020) 7219 3000. *Club:* Surrey CC (Hon. Vice Pres.).

HOFFBRAND, Prof. (Allan) Victor, DM, DSc; FRCP, FRCPath; Professor of Haematology and Honorary Consultant, Royal Free Hospital School of Medicine, 1974–96, now Emeritus Professor of Haematology, University College London (formerly Royal Free and University College Medical School); *b* 14 Oct. 1935; *s* of late Philip Hoffbrand and Minnie (*née* Freedman); *m* 1963, Irene Jill Mellows; two *s* one *d*. *Educ:* Bradford Grammar Sch.; Queen's Coll., Oxford (BA 1956; MA 1960; BM BCh 1959; DM 1972); Royal London Hospital; DSc London 1987. FRCP 1976; FRCPath 1980. Jun. hosp. posts, Royal London Hosp., 1960–62; Res. and Registrar posts, RPMS, 1962–66; MRC Fellow, New England Med. Centre, Boston, 1967–68; Sen. Lectr, RPMS, 1968–74. Visiting Professor: Sana'a, Yemen, 1986; Armed Forces Inst. Path., Rawalpindi, 1988; Toronto Gen. Hosp., 1988; Royal Melbourne Hosp., 1991. Chairman: Standing Intercollegiate Cttee on Oncology, 1993–94; Jt Haematology Cttee, RCP, RCPath, 1994–97; Member: Systems Bd, MRC, 1986–89; Council, RCPath, 1987–90; Council, Royal Free Sch. of Med., 1991–94. Medical Advisor: Leukaemia Res. Fund; Hadassah Med. Relief; Children with Leukaemia. Fellow Commoner, Queen's Coll., Oxford, 2012–13. Member: Amer. Soc. Hematology; Brit. Soc. Haematology; Eur. Haematology Assoc. (Mem. Council, 1994–99). FMedSci 2000; Hon. FRCPE 1986. Hon. DSc QMUL, 2012. *Publications:* (ed with S. M. Lewis) Postgraduate Haematology, 1972, 7th edn 2015; (ed) Recent Advances in Haematology, 1977, 8th edn 1996; (with J. E. Pettit) Essential Haematology, 1980, 7th edn (with P. A. H. Moss) 2015; (with J. E. Pettit) Blood Diseases Illustrated, 1987, 4th edn, as Color Atlas of Clinical Hematology, 2009; (with A. B. Mehta) Haematology at a Glance, 2000, 4th edn 2014; papers on megaloblastic anaemia, iron chelation, leukaemia and related disorders. *Recreations:* music, antiques, gardening, bridge. *Address:* 12 Wedderburn Road, NW3 5QG.

HOFFMAN, Dustin Lee; actor; *b* 8 Aug. 1937; *s* of Harry Hoffman and Lillian Hoffman; *m* 1st, 1969, Anne Byrne (marr. diss. 1980); two *d*; 2nd, 1980, Lisa Gottsegen; two *s* two *d*. *Educ:* Santa Monica City Coll.; Pasadena Playhouse. Stage début in Sarah Lawrence Coll. prodn, Yes is For a Very Young Man; Broadway début, A Cook for Mr General, 1961; appeared in: Harry, and Noon and Night, Amer. Place Theatre, NY, 1964–65; Journey of the Fifth Horse, and Star Wagon, 1965; Fragments, Berkshire Theatre Festival, Stockbridge, Mass, 1966; Eh?, 1966–67; Jimmy Shine, Broadway, 1968–69; Death of a Salesman, Broadway, 1984; London début, Merchant of Venice, Phoenix, 1989. Dir, All Over Town, Broadway, 1974. Films: The Graduate, 1967; Midnight Cowboy, John and Mary, 1969; Little Big Man, Who Is Harry Kellerman and Why Is He Saying Those Terrible Things About Me?, 1971; Straw Dogs, Alfredo, Alfredo, 1972; Papillon, 1973; Lenny, 1974; All The President's Men, 1975; Marathon Man, 1976; Straight Time, 1978; Agatha, Kramer vs Kramer (Acad. Award), 1979; Tootsie, 1983; Death of a Salesman, 1985 (Emmy Award); Ishtar, 1987; Rain Man, 1989 (Academy Award; Golden Globe Award); Family Business, 1990; Billy Bathgate, 1991; Hook, 1992; Accidental Hero, 1993; Outbreak, 1995; American Buffalo, Sleepers, 1996; Mad City, Wag the Dog, 1997; Sphere, 1998; Moonlight Mile, Confidence, 2003; Runaway Jury, Finding Neverland, I Heart Huckabees, 2004; Meet the Fockers, 2005; Stranger than Fiction, Perfume, 2006; Mr Magorium's Wonder Emporium, 2007; Last Chance Harvey, 2009; Little Fockers, 2010; Barney's Version, 2011; Chef, 2014; The Choir, 2015. Director, Quartet, 2012. Record: Death of a Salesman. Obie Award as best off-Broadway actor, 1965–66, for Journey of the Fifth Horse; Drama Desk, Theatre World, and Vernon Rice Awards for Eh?, 1966; Oscar Award nominee for The Graduate, Midnight Cowboy, and Lenny; Kennedy Center Honors, 2012. *Address:* 11661 San Vicente Boulevard, Suite 222, Los Angeles, CA 90049–5110, USA.

HOFFMAN, Gary Andrew; Chief Executive, Hastings Insurance Group, since 2012; *b* 21 Oct. 1960; *m* 2003. *Educ:* Queens' Coll., Cambridge. With Barclays Bank plc, 1982–2008: Man. Dir, Telephone Banking, 1995–98; Chief Exec., UK Retail Banking, 1998; Man. Dir, Customer Service and Delivery, 1999–2001; Chief Exec., 2001–05, Chm., 2005–06, Barclaycard; Exec. Dir, 2004–08; Chm., UK Banking, 2005–06; Gp Vice Chm., 2006–08; Chief Exec., Northern Rock, 2008–09; Co-Chief Exec., Northern Rock plc and Northern Rock (Asset Mgt) plc, 2010; Chief Exec., NBNK Investments plc, 2011–12. *Recreations:* running, watching Coventry City FC.

HOFFMAN, Thomas Dieter Dirk; Chairman, Board of Governors, Guildhall School of Music and Drama, 2009–12 (Member, Board of Governors, 2002–12); *b* Cambridge, 9 Aug. 1945; *s* of late Dirk Hoffman and Marie-Luise Leyser; *m* 1971, Verena Mary Fairs; one *s*. *Educ:* St John's College Sch., Cambridge; The Leys Sch., Cambridge; Univ. of Exeter (LLB); INSEAD (Adv. Mgt Prog. for Bankers 1990). ACA 1971, FCA 1981. Spicer & Pegler, Cambridge, 1963–65, 1969–70; Arthur Andersen, London, 1970–72; Corp. Finance Dept, William & Glyn's Bank, London, 1972–76; Investment Banking Div., Hill Samuel & Co., London, 1976–78; Dir, Capital Markets Div., Lloyds Bank International, London, 1978–84; Dep. Man. Dir, Fuji International Finance, London, 1984–89; Hd, Corp. Banking in UK, ABN Bank, 1989–91; Gen. Manager, UK and Ireland, Banco Espirito Santo, 1991–2003; non-exec. Dir, Espirito Santo plc, 2003–05; Sen. Advr, Banif Financial Gp, Portugal, 2004–12. Chm., Portuguese Chamber of Commerce and Industry, 1998–2001 (Hon. Vice Pres., 2003–). City of London Corporation: Mem., Ct of Common Council, 2002–; Member: Planning and Transportation Cttee, 2002–13; Community Services Cttee, 2002–04; Mkts Cttee, 2002–; Port Health and Envmtl Services Cttee, 2004–10; Culture, Heritage and Libraries Cttee, 2005–; Livery Cttee, 2005–11; Gresham Cttee, 2005– (Chm., 2011–14); Finance Cttee, 2006–; Investment Cttee, 2006–; Financial Investment Bd, 2011–; Dep. Gov., Hon. The Irish Soc., 2009–10 (Mem. Court, 2002–11). Member, Board of Governors: City of London Sch. for Girls, 2002– (Chm., 2003–06); City of London Sch. for Boys, 2003–06; City of London Freemen's Sch., 2003–06. Member: Council, Univ. of Exeter, 2003–06 (Mem., Audit Cttee, 1998–2005; Chm., 2003–05); Bd of Govs, Birkbeck Coll., Univ. of London, 2003–11 (Fellow, 2012–); Bd of Govs, King's College Hosp., London, 2004–11; Council, Gresham Coll., 2009– (Vice Chm., 2013–14); Trustee/Almoner, Christ's Hosp. Foundn, 2006–10 (Chm., Finance Cttee, 2006–08); Mem., Council of Govs, Guy's and St Thomas' NHS Foundn Trust, 2012–. Member, Advisory Board: London Fest. Orch., 1996–2008 (Chm., 2004–08); Sixteen Choir and Orch., 2001–08 (Chm., 2004–08); Trustee: Maryport Heritage Trust, Cumbria, 1989–96; Portuguese Arts Trust, 1992–2002; Corp. of Sons and Friends of the Clergy, 1996–; City of London Fest., 2003–; Stour Fest. Co., 2008– (Chm., 2014–); Mus. of London, 2008–. Mem., Bd of Govs, Barbican Centre, 2009–. Hon. Treas., Guildhall Histl Assoc., 2008–. Trustee, Guildhall Sch. Trust, 2007–12. Fellow, Royal Commonwealth Soc., 1964. FRSA; Mem., Royal Soc. for Asian Affairs. Liveryman, Tylers' and Bricklayers' Co., 1979– (Master, 2006–07). *Publications:* articles on rowing, accounting and taxation in the EU, internat. finance, histories of guilds outside London. *Recreations:* listening to music, drinking fine wine, eating crab, collecting and reading histories of medieval guilds, collection of 1800 books on rowing from 34 countries presented to Leander Club in 2012. *Address:* Old Curteis, Biddenden, Kent TN27 8JN; 72 Gainsford Street, Tower Bridge Square, SE1 2NB. *Clubs:* City Livery; Leander.

HOFFMANN, family name of **Baron Hoffmann**.

HOFFMANN, Baron *cr* 1995 (Life Peer), of Chedworth in the County of Gloucestershire; **Leonard Hubert Hoffmann,** Kt 1985; PC 1992; a Lord of Appeal in Ordinary, 1995–2009; international commercial arbitrator, since 2009; *b* 8 May 1934; *s* of B. W. and G. Hoffmann; *m* 1957, Gillian Lorna Sterner; two *d*. *Educ:* South African College Sch., Cape Town; Univ. of Cape Town (BA); The Queen's Coll., Oxford (Rhodes Scholar; MA, BCL, Vinerian Law Scholar; Hon. Fellow, 1992). Advocate of Supreme Court of S Africa, 1958–60. Called to the Bar, Gray's Inn, 1964, Bencher, 1984; QC 1977; a Judge, Courts of Appeal of Jersey and Guernsey, 1980–85; a Judge of the High Court of Justice, Chancery Div., 1985–92; a Lord Justice of Appeal, 1992–95. Non-permanent Judge, HK Court of Final Appeal, 1998–. Stowell Civil Law Fellow, University Coll., Oxford, 1961–73 (Hon. Fellow, 1995); Vis. Prof., Faculty of Law, Oxford Univ., 2009–; Hon. Prof. of Intellectual Property Law, QMUL, 2009–. Member: Royal Commn on Gambling, 1976–78; Council of Legal Educn, 1983–92 (Chm., 1989–92); Chm., Financial Markets Law Cttee, 2009–13. Pres., British-German Jurists Assoc., 1991–2009. Dir, ENO, 1985–90, 1991–94. Chm., Arts Council Adv. Cttee on London Orchs, 1993. Pres., Heath and Hampstead Soc., 2004–. Hon. Fellow, Chartered Inst. of Taxation, 2006. Hon. DCL: City, 1992; UWE, 1995; Gloucestershire, 2003. GBS 2014. *Publications:* The South African Law of Evidence, 1963. *Address:* Brick Court Chambers, 7–8 Essex Street, WC2R 3LD.

HOFFMANN, Prof. Roald; Frank H. T. Rhodes Professor of Humane Letters, Cornell University, 1996–2009, now Emeritus; *b* 18 July 1937; *s* of Hillel Safran and Clara (*née* Rosen, who *m* 2nd, Paul Hoffmann); *m* 1960, Eva Börjesson; one *s* one *d*. *Educ:* Columbia Univ. (BA); Harvard Univ. (MA, PhD). Junior Fellow, Society of Fellows, Harvard Univ., 1962–65; Associate Professor, to Professor, 1965–74, John A. Newman Prof. of Physical Science, 1974–96, Cornell Univ. Member: Nat. Acad. of Sciences; Amer. Acad. of Arts and Sciences. Foreign Member: Royal Soc., 1984; Indian Nat. Acad. of Sciences; Royal Swedish Acad. of Sciences; USSR Acad. of Sciences; Finnish Acad. of Sciences. Hon. DTech Royal Inst. of Technology, Stockholm, 1977; Hon. DSc: Yale, 1980; Hartford, 1982; Columbia, 1982; City Univ. of NY, 1983; Puerto Rico, 1983; La Plata, 1984; Uruguay, 1984; State Univ. of NY at Binghamton, 1985; Colgate, 1985; Rennes, 1986; Ben Gurion, 1989; Lehigh Univ., 1989; Carleton Coll., 1989; Maryland, 1990; Athens 1991; Thessaloniki, 1991; Bar Ilan, 1991; St Petersburg, 1991; Barcelona, 1992; Ohio State, 1993. Nobel Prize for Chemistry, 1981. *Publications:* (with R. B. Woodward) The Conservation of Orbital Symmetry, 1970; Solids and Surfaces, 1988; (with V. Torrence) Chemistry Imagined, 1993; The Same and Not the Same, 1995; (with S. Leibowitz Schmidt) Old Wine, New Flasks, 1997; (ed jtly) Beyond the Finite, 2010; Roald Hoffmann on the Philosophy, Art and Science of Chemistry, 2011; *fiction:* The Metamict State (poetry), 1987; Gaps and Verges (poetry), 1990; Memory Effects (poetry), 1999; (with Carl Djerassi) Oxygen (drama), 2000; Soliton (poetry), 2002; Catalista (poetry),

2002; Roald Hoffmann Izbrannie Stichotvorenia (poetry), 2010 (bilingual, Russian/English edn); many scientific articles. *Address:* Department of Chemistry and Chemical Biology, Cornell University, Ithaca, NY 14853–1301, USA.

HOFFORD, Leo; QC (Scot.) 2008; *b* Singapore, 12 March 1958; *s* of Donald Hartley Hofford and Moira Macgregor (*née* Cartner); *m* 1993, Jackie Paterson; one *s* two *d*. *Educ:* Glenalmond; Edinburgh Univ. (BA, LLB, DipLP). Admitted as solicitor, 1985; called to the Scottish Bar, 1990. *Publications:* (contrib.) Parliament House Portraits. *Recreations:* writing, reading, tennis, all winter sports, piano. *Address:* 14 Chester Street, Edinburgh EH3 7RA. *T:* 07739 639086. *E:* hoffordleo@hotmail.com.

HOFMEYR, Stephen Murray; QC 2000; a Recorder, since 2005; a Deputy High Court Judge, since 2008; *b* 10 Feb. 1956; *s* of late Jan Murray Hofmeyr and of Stella Mary Hofmeyr (*née* Mills); *m* 1980, Audrey Frances Cannan; two *s* one *d*. *Educ:* Diocesan Coll., Rondebosch; Univ. of Cape Town (BCom, LLB); University Coll., Oxford (MA Juris.). Advocate, Supreme Court of S Africa; called to the Bar, Gray's Inn, 1982; Attorney and Conveyancer, Supreme Court of S Africa, 1984–85; in practice at the Bar, 1987–; Barrister, Eastern Caribbean Supreme Ct, 2005, and Supreme Ct of the Bahamas, 2012. *Recreations:* walking, ski-ing, tennis, golf. *Address:* Acre Holt, One Tree Hill Road, Guildford GU4 8PJ. *T:* (01483) 834733; 7 King's Bench Walk, Temple, EC4Y 7DS. *Clubs:* Vincent's (Oxford); Guildford Golf.

HOGAN, Prof. Brigid Linda Mary, PhD; FRS 2001; George Barth Geller Professor and Chair, Department of Cell Biology, Duke University Medical Center, since 2002; *b* 28 Aug. 1943; *d* of Edmond Hogan and Joyce Hogan (*née* Willcox). *Educ:* Wycombe High Sch. for Girls; Newnham Coll., Cambridge (MA, PhD 1968). Postdoctoral Fellowship, MIT, 1968–70; Lectr, Univ. of Sussex, 1970–74; ICRF, London, 1974–84; NIMR, London, 1985–88; Prof. of Cell Biol., Vanderbilt Univ. Med. Sch., 1988–2002; Investigator, Howard Hughes Med. Inst., 1993–2002. Fellow, Amer. Acad. of Arts and Scis, 2001. Member: Inst. of Medicine, 1996; Nat. Acad. of Sciences, USA, 2005. *Address:* Department of Cell Biology, Duke University Medical Center, Box 3709, Durham, NC 27710, USA.

HOGAN, Michael Henry; Member, Gaming Board for Great Britain, 1986–94 (Secretary, 1980–86); *b* 31 May 1927; *s* of James Joseph Hogan and Edith Mary Hogan; *m* 1st, 1953, Nina Spillane (*d* 1974); one *s* three *d*; 2nd, 1980, Mollie Burtwell. *Educ:* Ushaw Coll.; LSE. Certif. Social Sci., Certif. Mental Health. Asst Warden, St Vincent's Probation Hostel, 1949–50; London Probation Service, 1953–61; Home Office Inspectorate, 1961–80, Chief Probation Inspector, 1972–80. *Address:* Yew Tree Cottage, The Street, Capel, Surrey RH5 5LD. *T:* (01306) 711523.

HOGAN, Sir Patrick, KNZM 1999; CBE 1991; Proprietor, Cambridge Stud, since 1975; *b* 20 Oct. 1939; *s* of Thomas Hogan and Sarah Margaret Small; *m* 1961, Justine Alice Heath; two *d*. *Educ:* Goodwood Sch., Cambridge, NZ; St Peter's Convent Sch., Cambridge; Marist Brothers, Hamilton. Partner, with brother, Fencourt Thoroughbred Stud, 1965–75; estabd Cambridge Stud in partnership with wife, 1975; first to apply modern methods of promotion of progeny for sale with huge benefits to the industry as a whole. Pres., NZ Thoroughbred Breeders Assoc., 1993–96; Dir, NZ Thoroughbred Mktg Bd, 1997–99. Patron: Cambridge Chamber of Commerce, 1990–; Equine Res. Foundn, 1992. Life Mem., Cambridge Jockey Club Inc. (formerly Pres.). Hon. MSc Sport and Exercise Sci. Waikato Inst. of Technol., 2002; Hon. Dr Waikato, 2013. BMW Award for Outstanding Contribn to Racing Excellence in NZ, 1991. *Recreations:* tennis, Rugby, racing. *Address:* PO Box 108, Cambridge 3450, New Zealand. *Clubs:* Cambridge, Hautapu Rugby Football (Cambridge); Waikato Racing (Hamilton); Auckland Racing.

HOGAN-HOWE, Sir Bernard, Kt 2013; QPM 2003; Commissioner, Metropolitan Police, since 2011; *b* 25 Oct. 1957; *s* of Bernard Howe and Cecilia Hogan-Howe; *m* Marion White. *Educ:* Hinde House Comprehensive Sch.; Merton Coll., Oxford (MA Juris.; Hon. Fellow 2013); Sheffield Univ. (MBA). Joined S Yorks Police, 1979; Dist Comdr, Doncaster W Area, 1996–97; Merseyside Police: Asst Chief Constable and Hd, Community Affairs, 1997–99; Hd, Area Ops, 1999–2001; Asst Comr, Metropolitan Police, 2001–04; Chief Constable of Merseyside, 2004–09; HM Inspector of Constabulary, 2009–11. Mem., Cabinet, ACPO, 2001–04. Hon. Fellow, Liverpool John Moores Univ., 2010. Hon. LLD: Sheffield Hallam, 2012; Sheffield, 2013. *Recreations:* horse riding, playing football, supporting Sheffield Wednesday FC, opera. *Address:* Commissioner's Private Office, Metropolitan Police, 8th Floor, New Scotland Yard, The Broadway, SW1H 0BG.

HOGARTH, Adrian John; Parliamentary Counsel, since 2002; Senior Parliamentary Counsel, Law Commission, since 2011 (on secondment); *b* 7 July 1960; *s* of late Prof. Cyril Alfred Hogarth and Dr Audrey Hogarth, JP, DL; *m* 1996, Archana (*née* Singh); one *s* one *d*. *Educ:* Magdalene Coll., Cambridge (BA Archaeol. and Anthropol. Law 1981; LLM 1982; MA). Called to the Bar, Inner Temple, 1983; Coll. Supervisor, Magdalene Coll., Cambridge, 1983–85; Asst Parly Counsel, 1985–89; Sen. Asst Parly Counsel, 1989–92; Principal Asst Parly Counsel, 1992–94, seconded to Law Commn; Dep. Parly Counsel, 1994–2002. FRSA. *Recreations:* cricket, tennis, travel, reeling. *Address:* Law Commission, 52 Queen Anne's Gate, SW1H 9AG. *Clubs:* Lansdowne; Cypos? Cricket.

HOGARTH, Andrew Allan; QC 2003; *b* 21 July 1951; *s* of late William Allan Hogarth and Margaret Hogarth; *m* 1975, Elinor Mary Williams; four *s*. *Educ:* Harrow Sch.; Trinity Coll., Cambridge (MA 1973). Called to the Bar, Lincoln's Inn, 1975; in practice as barrister, specialising in employment law, 1975–. Head of Chambers, 2005–. *Address:* 12 King's Bench Walk, Temple, EC4Y 7EL. *T:* (020) 7583 0811. *E:* hogarth@12kbw.co.uk.

HOGBIN, Ann Denise, CBE 2008; multi sport operations consultant; Founder, ADH Sport Ltd, 2012; *b* Dover, 20 Dec. 1953; *d* of Gordon and Josephine Hogbin. *Educ:* Dover Grammar Sch. for Girls; Canterbury Tech. Coll. (Adv. Secretarial Course). Proj. Manager, British Olympic Assoc., 1973–94; Chief Exec., Commonwealth Games England, 1991–2011. Member: Team England HQ staff at Commonwealth Games, 1974, 1978, 1986, 1990; Fedn staff, Commonwealth Games, 1982; Team GB HQ staff at Olympics Games, Montreal, 1976, Seoul, 1988, Barcelona, 1992, and at Winter Olympics, Innsbruck, 1976, Sarajevo, 1984, Albertville, 1992; Gen. Team Manager, Commonwealth Games, Victoria, 1994; Chef de Mission: Team England, Commonwealth Games, Kuala Lumpur, 1998, Manchester, 2002, Melbourne, 2006; Team England, Commonwealth Youth Games, Edinburgh, 2000, Bendigo, 2004, Pune, 2008; Gen. Team England Manager, Commonwealth Games, Delhi, 2010; Dep. Chef de Mission, Operations, ParalympicsGB, 2012. *Recreations:* cycling, gardening, dining, cooking.

HOGBIN, Walter, CBE 1990; FREng, FICE; Consultant, Taylor Woodrow, 1997–99; Chairman, Taylor Woodrow International Ltd, 1983–96; *b* 21 Dec. 1937; *s* of Walter Clifford John Hogbin and Mary Hogbin; *m* 1968, Geraldine Anne-Marie Castley; two *s*. *Educ:* Kent Coll., Canterbury; Queens' Coll., Cambridge (MA). Joined Taylor Woodrow, 1961; Taylor Woodrow International Ltd: Divl Dir, 1975–77; Dir, 1977–79; Man. Dir, 1979–85; Dir, 1984–96, Jt Man. Dir, 1988–92, Taylor Woodrow plc; Chm., Taylor Woodrow Construction Supervisory Bd, 1991–93. Vice-Pres., Eur. Construction Industry Fedn, 1992–94; Member: Adv. Council, ECGD, 1983–88; Overseas Projects Bd, 1986–91; Export Gp for Construction Ind., 1980–97 (Chm., 1988–90); Eur. Internat. Contractors Fedn, 1988–97 (Pres., 1994–97). Col, Engr and Logistic (formerly Transport) Staff Corps, RE, 1986–2000. FREng (FEng 1994). FRSA. Telford Gold Medal, ICE, 1979. *Recreations:* golf, gardening. *Address:* Codrington Court, Wapley Road, Chipping Sodbury, S Glos BS37 6RY. *Club:* Athenæum.

HOGG, family name of **Viscount Hailsham** and of **Baroness Hogg**.

HOGG, Baroness *cr* 1995 (Life Peer), of Kettlethorpe, in the county of Lincolnshire; **Sarah Elizabeth Mary Hogg, (Viscountess Hailsham);** Chairman, Frontier Economics, 1999–2013; Lead Independent Director, HM Treasury, since 2011; *b* 14 May 1946; *d* of Baron Boyd-Carpenter, PC; *m* 1968, Rt Hon. Douglas Martin Hogg (*see* Viscount Hailsham); one *s* one *d*. *Educ:* St Mary's Convent, Ascot; Lady Margaret Hall, Oxford University (1st Cl. Hons PPE; Hon. Fellow, 1994). Staff writer, Economist, 1967, Literary Editor, 1970, Economics Editor, 1977; Economics Editor, Sunday Times, 1981; Presenter, Channel 4 News, 1982–83; Econs Editor, and Dep. Exec. Editor, Finance and Industry, The Times, 1984–86; Asst Editor, and Business and City Editor, The Independent, 1986–89; Econs Editor, Daily Telegraph and Sunday Telegraph, 1989–90; Hd, Prime Minister's Policy Unit, 1990–95; Dir, 1995–97, Chm., 1997–99, London Economics. Director: London Broadcasting Co., 1982–90; Royal Nat. Theatre, 1988–91. A Gov., BBC, 2000–04. Non-executive Director: Foreign and Colonial Smaller Cos Investment Trust, 1995–2002 (Chm., 1997–2002); Nat. Provident Instn, 1996–99; GKN, 1996–2006 (Dep. Chm., 2003–06); The Energy Group, 1996–98; 3i Group plc, 1997–2010 (Dep. Chm., 2000–02; Chm., 2002–10); Scottish Eastern Investment Trust, 1998–99; Martin Currie Portfolio Investment Trust, 1999–2002; P&O, 1999–2000; P&O Princess, 2000–03; Carnival Corp., 2003–08; Carnival plc, 2003–08; BG Group, 2005–15; Cadbury plc, 2008–10; John Lewis Partnership, 2011–; Nat. Dir, Times Newspapers Ltd, 2015–. Member: Internat. Adv. Bd, Nat. Westminster Bank, 1995–98; Adv. Bd, Bankinter, 1995–98. Chairman: Financial Reporting Council, 2010–14 (Mem., 2004–14; Dep. Chm., 2007–10); Hogg Tendering Adv. Cttee for LIBOR, 2012–14. Mem., Takeover Panel, 2011–. Member: House of Lords Select Cttee on Sci. and Technol., 1996–99; H of L Monetary Policy and Econs Cttee, 2000–03. Member: REconS, 1996–2000; Council, IFS, 1998–2005; Cemmap, 2002–04. Governor: Centre for Economic Policy Research, 1985–92; IDS, 1987; Univ. of Lincoln, 2002–05; London Business Sch., 2004–10; Fellow, Eton Coll., 1996–2008. Trustee: St Mary's Sch., Ascot, 1994–; Trusthouse Foundn, 2003–; Cicely Saunders Internat., 2009–11; Queen Elizabeth Diamond Jubilee Trust, 2012–; Historic Lincoln Trust, 2013–; NIESR, 2014–. Hon. MA Open Univ., 1987; Hon. DLitt Loughborough, 1992; Hon. LLD Lincoln, 2001; Hon. DPhil: City, 2002; Cranfield, 2006. Wincott Foundation Financial Journalist of the Year, 1985. *Publications:* (with Jonathan Hill) Too Close to Call, 1995. *Address:* House of Lords, SW1A 0PW.

See also Hon. Sir T. P. J. Boyd-Carpenter, Hon. C. M. Hogg.

HOGG, Hon. Charlotte Mary; Chief Operating Officer, Bank of England, since 2013; *b* London, 26 Aug. 1970; *d* of Viscount Hailsham, *qv*, and Baroness Hogg, *qv*; *m* 1999, Stephen Kenneth Sacks; two *c*. *Educ:* St Mary's Sch., Ascot; Hertford Coll., Oxford (BA); Harvard Univ. (Kennedy Schol.). Principal, McKinsey & Co., 1994–2001; Man. Dir, Morgan Stanley, 2001–07; Discover Financial Services, 2007–08; Man. Dir, UK and Ireland, Experian, 2008–11; Hd, Retail and Intermediaries, Santander UK, 2011–13. Non-exec. Dir, BBC Worldwide, 2010–. Mem., Finance Cttee, OUP, 2006–. Gov., Nottingham Trent Univ., 2010–. Trustee, First Story, 2008– (Chm., 2008–12). *Recreation:* eventing. *Address:* The Cottage, Kettlethorpe Hall, Kettlethorpe, Lincs LN1 2LD.

HOGG, Sir Christopher (Anthony), Kt 1985; Chairman: Financial Reporting Council, 2006–10; Reuters Group (formerly Reuters Holdings) PLC, 1985–2004 (Director, 1984–2004); GlaxoSmithKline, 2002–04 (Director, SmithKline Beecham, subseq. GlaxoSmithKline, 1993–2004); *b* 2 Aug. 1936; *s* of late Anthony Wentworth Hogg and Monica Mary (*née* Gladwell); *m* 1st, 1961, Anne Patricia (*née* Cathie) (marr. diss. 1997); two *d*; 2nd, 1997, Miriam Stoppard, *qv*. *Educ:* Marlborough Coll.; Trinity Coll., Oxford (MA; Hon. Fellow 1982); Harvard Univ. (MBA). National Service, Parachute Regt, 1955–57. Harkness Fellow, 1960–62; IMEDE, Lausanne, 1962–63; Hill, Samuel Ltd, 1963–66; IRC, 1966–68; Courtaulds plc, 1968–96: Chief Exec., 1979–91; Chm., 1980–96; Chm., Courtaulds Textiles, 1990–95; Dep. Chm., 1995–96, Chm., 1996–2002, Allied Domecq. Dir, Air Liquide SA, 2000–05. Advr, Corporate Governance Cttee, Financial Reporting Council/Stock Exchange (Cadbury Cttee), 1992. Member: Indust. Develt Adv. Bd, 1976–81; Cttee of Award for Harkness Fellowships, 1980–86; Internat. Council, J. P. Morgan, 1988–2003; Court, Bank of England, 1992–96. Chm. Bd, RNT, 1995–2004. Trustee, Ford Foundn, 1987–99. For. Hon. Mem., Amer. Acad. of Arts and Scis, 1991. Hon. FCSD 1987; Hon. Fellow, London Business Sch., 1992; Hon. FCGI 1992; Hon. FCA 2013. Hon. DSc: Cranfield Inst. of Technol., 1986; Aston, 1988. BIM Gold Medal, 1986; Centenary Medal, Soc. of Chemical Industry, 1989; Hambro Businessman of the Year, 1993. *Publications:* Masers and Lasers, 1963. *Recreations:* grandchildren, friends, golf.

See also Hon. H. Legge.

HOGG, David Alan, CB 1997; Director-General and General Counsel and Solicitor, HM Revenue and Customs, 2005–09; *b* 8 Oct. 1946; *s* of Donald Kenneth Hogg and Alwyn Lilian Hogg (*née* Chinchen); *m* 1st, 1969, Geraldine Patricia Smith (marr. diss. 1979); one *s* one *d*; 2nd, 1981, Pauline Pamela Papworth; two *s*. *Educ:* Brighton Coll.; Coll. of Law. Admitted solicitor, 1969; in private practice, 1969–78; Treasury Solicitor's Department: Sen. Legal Asst, 1978–85; Asst Treasury Solicitor, 1985–89; Dept of Energy, 1989–90; Treasury Solicitor's Department: Principal Asst Solicitor and Hd, Litigation Div., 1990–93; Dep. Treasury Solicitor, 1993–97; Solicitor and Legal Adviser: DETR, 1997–2001; DTLR, 2001–02; ODPM and Dept for Transport, 2002–03; ODPM, 2003–04; Actg Solicitor, HM Customs and Excise, 2004–05. Vice Pres., Valuation Tribunal for England, 2009–10. *Recreations:* inland waterways, theatre, reading, watching sport. *E:* hogg.david@hotmail.co.uk.

HOGG, Prof. Dorothy, MBE 2001; Professor, 2004–07, and Head, Jewellery and Silversmithing Department, 1985–2007, Edinburgh College of Art, now Professor Emeritus; craft artist in residence, Victoria and Albert Museum, 2008; *b* 19 May 1945; *d* of William Hogg and Alice Hogg (*née* Murdoch); *m* 1973, Lachlan MacColl; one *s*. *Educ:* Glasgow Sch. of Art (Dip of Art); Royal Coll. of Art (Master of Design, Silver Medal for work of special distn); Moray House Coll. of Educn, Edinburgh (CertEd). Freelance designer, 1970–; Lecturer: Glasgow Sch. of Art, 1972–73; Duncan of Jordanstone Coll. of Art, 1974–85; Lectr, 1985–98, Reader, 1998–2004, Edinburgh Coll. of Art. External examr, UK instns. Chm. Contemp. Cttee, and Trustee, Scottish Goldsmiths Trust, 2000–05; Purchase Advr, 1997–2001, and Selected Index Advr, 2000–03, Crafts Council, London; Specialist Advr, Scottish Arts Council, 2003–05. Trustee, Crafts Council, 2008–. Solo retrospective exhibn, Scottish Gall., Edinburgh, 1994; many group exhibns, UK, Germany, Italy, Japan and USA, 1967–. Work in public and private collections incl. Royal Mus. of Scotland, Crafts Council, Goldsmiths' Co., Aberdeen Art Gall. and Mus., Koch Ring Collection, V&A, and Mus. of Arts and Design, NY; awarded first craft residency, V&A, 2008. Freeman, City of London, 1998; Mem., Incorporation of Goldsmiths, City of Edinburgh, 1992; Freeman, Co. of Goldsmiths, London, 1997. FRSA 2007. Hon. FRCA 2006. Lifetime Achievement Medal, Goldsmiths' Craft and Design Council, 2010. *Recreations:* drawing, gardening, golf. *Address:* c/o The Scottish Gallery, 16 Dundas Street, Edinburgh EH3 6HZ. *T:* (0131) 558 1200, *Fax:* (0131) 558 3900. *E:* dorothy_hogg@hotmail.com.

HOGG, Gilbert Charles; author, since 2000; *b* 11 Feb. 1933; *s* of Charles and Ivy Ellen Hogg; *m* 1st, Jeanne Whiteside; one *s* one *d*; 2nd, 1979, Angela Christina Wallace. *Educ:* Victoria University Coll., Wellington, NZ (LLB 1956). Called to the New Zealand Bar and admitted

Solicitor, 1957; admitted Solicitor, GB, 1971. Served RNZAC (TF), 1955–62 (Lieut). Partner, Phillips, Shayle-George and Co., Solicitors, Wellington, 1960–66; Sen. Crown Counsel, Hong Kong, 1966–70; Editor, Business Law Summary, 1970–73; Divl Legal Adviser, BSC, 1974–79; British Gas Corporation, subseq. British Gas: Dir of Legal Services, 1979–84; Sec., 1984–90; Dir, Regulatory Ops, 1990–95; solicitor and regulatory consultant, 1995–2000. Mem., Competition Commn (formerly Monopolies and Mergers Commn), 1998–2003. Mem., Professional Ethics Cttee, 1994–97, and Council, Energy Section, 1993–98, Internat. Bar Assoc. Chairman: Phoenix House, 1996–2004; Charterhouse-in-Southwark, 1999–2004; Trustee, IBA Educn Trust, 1995–98. *Publications:* Teaching Yourself Tranquillity, 2005; The Happy Humanist, 2011; *novels:* A Smell of Fraud, 1974; The Predators, 2002; Caring for Cathy, 2008; Blue Lantern, 2009; Present Tense, 2010; The Cruel Peak, 2012; Codename Wolf, 2013; Don't Cry for the Brave, 2014; The Unforgiving Shore, 2015. *Address:* 73 Ellerby Street, SW6 6EU. *T:* (020) 7736 8903. *W:* www.gilhogg.co.uk.

HOGG, Hon. Dame Mary (Claire), (Hon. Dame Mary Koops), DBE 1995; **Hon. Mrs Justice Hogg;** a Judge of the High Court of Justice, Family Division, since 1995; *b* 15 Jan. 1947; *d* of Rt Hon. Baron Hailsham of St Marylebone, PC, KG, CH, FRS; *m* 1987, Eric Koops (LVO 1997); one *s* one *d. Educ:* St Paul's Girls' Sch. Called to the Bar, Lincoln's Inn, 1968 (Bencher, 1995), NI, 1993; QC 1989; Asst Recorder, 1986–90; Recorder, 1990–95. Mem. Council, Children's Soc., 1990–95; Trustee, Harrison Homes, 1983–2009. Gov., Univ. of Westminster, 1992– (Poly. of Central London, 1983–92). FRSA 1991. Freeman, City of London, 1981. Hon. LLD Westminster, 1995. *Address:* Royal Courts of Justice, Strand, WC2A 2LL.

See also Viscount Hailsham.

HOGG, Sir Michael Edward L.; *see* Lindsay-Hogg.

HOGG, Sir Piers Michael James, 9th Bt *cr* 1846, of Upper Grosvenor Street, Middlesex; *b* 25 April 1957; *e s* of Sir Michael Hogg, 8th Bt and of Elizabeth Anne Thérèse, *e d* of Sir Terence Falkiner, 8th Bt; *S* father, 2001; *m* 1982, Vivien (marr. diss. 1996), *y d* of Dr Philip Holman; one *s* one *d. Educ:* St Paul's Sch. *Heir: s* James Edward Hogg, *b* 11 Sept. 1985.

HOGG, Rear-Adm. Robin Ivor Trower, CB 1988; FNI; Managing Director: Raidfleet Ltd, since 1988; Shinbond Ltd, since 1998; Robstar Productions Ltd, since 1998; *b* 25 Sept. 1932; *s* of Dudley and Nancy Hogg; *m* 1st, 1958, Susan Bridget Beryl Grantham; two *s* two *d*; 2nd, 1970, Angela Sarah Patricia Kirwan. *Educ:* The New Beacon, Sevenoaks; Bedford School. Directorate of Naval Plans, 1974–76; RCDS 1977; Captain RN Presentation Team, 1978–79; Captain First Frigate Sqdn, 1980–82; Director Naval Operational Requirements, 1982–84; Flag Officer, First Flotilla, 1984–86; COS to C-in-C Fleet, 1986–87, retd. CEO, Colebrand Ltd, 1988–97. Chm., 2011–13, Pres., 2013–, CPRE for Devon (Chm., Plymouth and South Hams, 2007–). FCMI; FRSA. *Recreation:* private life. *Address:* c/o Barclays Bank, Blenheim Gate, 22/24 Upper Marlborough Road, St Albans AL1 3AL. *T:* (01752) 872366.

HOGGARD, Robin Richard; Director of Government Relations, London School of Economics and Political Science, since 2014 (Director of External Relations, 2007–14); *b* 26 Nov. 1956; *s* of George Lawrence Hoggard and Frances Mary Christine Hoggard (*née* Stephenson); *m* 1988, Tonoko Komuro; one *s. Educ:* Cheadle Hulme Sch.; Univ. of Newcastle upon Tyne (BA Hons Politics 1979); SOAS, Univ. of London (MSc 1982). HM Diplomatic Service, 1982–2007: FCO, 1982; Tokyo, 1984–89; FCO, 1989–91; DTI, 1991–93; UK Deleg. to NATO, 1994–98; Counsellor (Mgt) and Consul Gen., Tokyo, 1998–2003; Counsellor, FCO, 2003–04; Hd of Res. Analysts, FCO, 2004–07. *Address:* London School of Economics and Political Science, Houghton Street, WC2A 2AE.

HOGGER, Henry George, CMG 2004; HM Diplomatic Service, retired; Senior Consultant, MEC International Ltd, since 2005; *b* 9 Nov. 1948; *s* of late Rear-Adm. Henry Charles Hogger, CB, DSC and Ethel Mary Hogger; *m* 1972, Fiona Jane McNabb; two *s* two *d. Educ:* Winchester Coll.; Trinity Hall, Cambridge (MA Hons). Joined FCO 1969; MECAS, Lebanon, 1971–72; served Aden, Caracas, Kuwait; FCO, 1978–82; Head of Chancery, Abu Dhabi, 1982–86; FCO, 1986–89; Counsellor and Dep. Head of Mission, Amman, 1989–92; High Comr, Namibia, 1992–96; Head, Latin America, later Latin America and Caribbean Dept, FCO, 1996–2000; Ambassador to Syria, 2000–03; Governorate Co-ordinator for Basra, Coalition Provisional Authy, Iraq, 2003–04 (on secondment). Chm., Council for British Research in the Levant, 2008–13. Co-Chair, Damask Rose Trust, 2008–. Member: Inst. of Advanced Motorists; RGS. *Recreations:* golf, sailing, music, travel. *Address:* Shop Farm House, Briantspuddle, Dorchester, Dorset DT2 7HY.

HOGGETT, Anthony John Christopher, PhD; QC 1986; a Recorder, 1988–2006; *b* 20 Aug. 1940; *s* of late Christopher Hoggett and Annie Marie Hoggett; *m* 1968, Brenda Marjorie Hale (*see* Baroness Hale of Richmond) (marr. diss. 1992); one *d. Educ:* Leeds Grammar Sch.; Hymers Coll., Hull; Clare Coll., Cambridge (MA, LLB); PhD Manchester. Asst Juridique, Inst. of Comparative Law, Paris, 1962–63; Lectr in Law, Univ. of Manchester, 1963–69; called to Bar, Gray's Inn, 1969, Head of Chambers, 1985–96; Asst Recorder, 1982. Res. Fellow, Univ. of Michigan, 1965–66. Mem., Civil Service Final Selection Bd for Planning Inspectors, 1987–91. Dir, Eur. Youth Parlt Internat., 1993–2003. Mem. Adv. Council, Rural Bldgs Preservation Trust, 1994–2002 (Trustee, 2000–02). Mem. Editl Bd, Envmtl Law Reports, 1992–2006. *Publications:* articles in Criminal Law Rev., Mod. Law Rev. and others. *Recreations:* swimming, music. *Address:* Kings Chambers, 36 Young Street, Manchester M3 3FT.

HØJ, Prof. Peter Bordier, PhD; Vice Chancellor and President, University of Queensland, since 2012; *b* Hundested, Denmark, 29 April 1957; *s* of John and Bodil Høj; *m* 1983, Dr Robyn Van Heeswijk (*d* 2003); one *s* one *d*; partner, Prof. Mandy Thomas. *Educ:* Univ. of Copenhagen (MSc; PhD 1987). FTSE 2004. Foundn Prof. of Viticultural Sci., Univ. of Adelaide, 1995–97; Man. Dir, Wine Res. Inst., 1997–2004; CEO, Australian Res. Council, 2004–07; Vice Chancellor and Pres., Univ. of S Australia, 2007–12. Director: Provisor Pty Ltd, 2002–04; CRC Viticulture, 2002–04. Co-Dep. Chair, Strengthened Export Controls Steering Gp, 2012–. Member: Cttee, Nat. Res. Infrastructure, 2009–11; Australian Qualifications Framework Council, 2011–13; Australian Res. Cttee, 2012–; Adv. Bd, edX Univ., 2014–. Member, Board: Educn Australia, 2008–10; Open Univs Australia, 2008–09; Univs Australia, 2009–13 (Dep. Chair and Lead Vice Chancellor of Res., 2011–13); CSIRO, 2011–. Mem. Council, Australian Inst. Marine Scientists, 2005–07. DUniv Copenhagen, 2008. *Publications:* contrib. scientific pubns. *Recreations:* soccer, biking, classical music, bush walking, wine show judging. *Address:* c/o University of Queensland, Brisbane, Qld 4072, Australia.

HOLBOROW, Jonathan; Editor, Mail on Sunday, 1992–98; Member, Editorial Integrity Board, Express Newspapers, 2000–02; *b* 12 Oct. 1943; *s* of late Prof. Eric John Holborow and of Cicely Mary (*née* Foister); *m* 1st, 1965, Susan Ridings (*d* 1993); one *s* one *d*; 2nd, 1994, Vivien Ferguson. *Educ:* Charterhouse. Reporter, Maidenhead Advertiser, 1961–65; Lincs Echo, 1965–66; Lincoln Chronicle, 1966–67; Daily Mail, Manchester, 1967–69; Scottish News Editor, Daily Mail, Glasgow, 1969–70; Daily Mail, Manchester: Northern Picture Editor, 1970–72; Northern News Editor, 1972–74; Daily Mail, London: Dep. News Editor, 1974–75; News Editor, 1975–80; Editor, Cambrian News, Aberystwyth, 1980–82; Asst Editor, then Associate Editor, Mail on Sunday, 1982–86; Dep. Editor, Today, 1986–87; Daily Mail: Asst Editor, then Associate Editor, 1987–88; Dep. Editor, 1988–92; Dir, Associated Newspapers Ltd, 1992–98. Chm., Folkestone and Hythe Cons. Assoc., 2004–09; Mem., Area Mgt Exec., Kent Conservatives, 2009–12 (Dep. Chm., 2010–12). *Recreation:* golf.

HOLBOROW, Prof. Leslie Charles, MA; QSO 2009; Vice-Chancellor, Victoria University of Wellington, 1985–98, now Emeritus Professor; *b* 28 Jan. 1941; *s* of George and Ivah Vivienne Holborow; *m* 1965, Patricia Lynette Walsh (*d* 2012); one *s* two *d. Educ:* Henderson High Sch.; Auckland Grammar Sch.; Univ. of Auckland (MA 1st Cl. Hons Philosophy); Oxford Univ. (BPhil). Jun. Lectr, Auckland Univ., 1963; Commonwealth schol. at Merton Coll., Oxford, 1963–65; Lectr, then Sen. Lectr, Univ. of Dundee (until 1967 Queen's Coll., Univ. of St Andrews), 1965–74, Mem. Court, 1972–74; University of Queensland, Brisbane: Prof. of Philosophy, 1974–85; Pres., Academic Bd, 1980–81; Pro-Vice-Chancellor (Humanities), 1983–85. Sen. Fellow, Centre for Strategic Studies, Victoria Univ. of Wellington, 2003–14. Pres., Qld Br., Aust. Inst. of Internat. Affairs, 1984–85; Nat. Pres., 1987–90, Hon. Vice Pres., 1991–, Mem., Standing Cttee, 2002–, NZ Inst. of Internat. Affairs; Member: NZ Cttee for Pacific Economic Co-operation, 1986–97; Bd, Inst. of Policy Studies, 1986–98; Bd, NZ Inst. of Econ. Res., 1986–91; Bd, Victoria Univ. Foundn, 1990–98; NZ Cttee for Security Co-operation in Asia Pacific, 1994–. Chair: NZ Vice-Chancellors' Cttee, 1990, 1996; Cttee on Univ. Academic Progs, 1993–95; Bd, NZ Univs Acad. Audit Unit, 2003–08; Member: Council, ACU, 1990–91, 1996; Educn Sub-Commn, UNESCO Commn for NZ, 1997–2000. Member: Musica Viva Nat. Bd, 1984–85; Bd of Management, Music Fedn of NZ, 1987–90; Bd, NZ Sch. of Dance, 2010–. Trustee: NZ String Quartet, 1988–2011; Lilburn Residence Trust, 2005–; Chm., NZ String Quartet Foundn, 1999–. Hon. LLD Victoria Univ. of Wellington, 1998. *Publications:* articles on NZ foreign policy, opera reviews, contrib. philosophical and legal jls. *Recreations:* tramping, golf, listening to music. *Address:* 16 Ames Street, Paekakariki, Wellington 5034, New Zealand. *Clubs:* Wellington, Victoria University Staff (Wellington).

HOLBOROW, Lady Mary (Christina), DCVO 2010; JP; Lord-Lieutenant of Cornwall, 1994–2011; *b* 19 Sept. 1936; *d* of 8th Earl of Courtown, OBE, TD, DL, and Christina Margaret Tremlett (*née* Cameron); *m* 1959, Geoffrey Jermyn Holborow, OBE; one *s* one *d. Educ:* Tudor Hall Sch., Banbury. Mem., Regional Board, TSB, 1981–89; Director: SW Water, 1989–95; Devon and Cornwall TEC, 1990–96; TSW Broadcasting, 1990–91. Vice-Chm., Cornwall and Isles of Scilly HA, 1990–2000; SW Regl Chm., FEFC, 1993–94; Chm., Cornwall Rural Develt Cttee, 1987–99. Patron or Pres., numerous charitable orgns in Cornwall. Hon. LLD Exeter, 1997; Hon. DBus Plymouth, 2010. JP Cornwall 1970. DStJ 1987 (Comr, Cornwall St John Ambulance, 1982–87). *Address:* The Coach House, Ladock, Truro, Cornwall TR2 4PL. *T:* (01726) 882274.

HOLBROOK, Rt Rev. John Edward; *see* Brixworth, Bishop Suffragan of.

HOLBROOK, Peter, CBE 2015; Chief Executive, Social Enterprise UK, since 2010; *b* Tooting, London, 12 March 1971; *s* of Keith Holbrook and Pamela Holbrook (now O'Brien). *Educ:* Tamworth Manor High Sch.; Univ. of Central Lancashire (BSc Hons Envmtl Mgt). Res. and Media Officer, Greenpeace UK, 1993–94; London Shops Manager, Oxfam GB, 1994–98; Retail and Mktg Manager, Focus on Blindness, 1998–2001; Founding Chief Exec., Sunlight Develt Trust, 2001–10. Chair, Social Enterprise World Forum, 2012–. Member: Mutuals Taskforce, Cabinet Office, 2010–; Employee Engagement Taskforce, BIS, 2010–; EU Social Business Expert Gp, 2012–. Trustee, Big Society Trust, 2010–. Mem., House of St Barnabas, 2013–. *Recreations:* theatre, film, festivals, literature, social entrepreneurship. *Address:* Social Enterprise UK, Third Floor, Fire Station, 139 Tooley Street, SE1 2HZ. *T:* (020) 3589 4950, *Fax:* (020) 7403 7184.

HOLCROFT, Sir Charles (Anthony Culcheth), 4th Bt *cr* 1921, of Eaton Mascott, Berrington, co. Salop; *b* Ludlow, Shropshire, 22 Oct. 1959; *e s* of Sir Peter George Culcheth Holcroft, 3rd Bt and of Rosemary Rachel (*née* Deas, now Firbank); *S* father, 2009; *m* 1986, Mrs Elizabeth Carter, *y d* of late John Raper, Powys; one *s* one *d*, and one step *s. Educ:* Royal Agricultural Coll., Cirencester; Univ. of Manchester Inst. of Sci. and Technol. (BSc Hons Computing Sci. 1999). *Recreations:* the countryside, tennis, cricket, computer technology, fencing. *Heir: s* Toby David Culcheth Holcroft, *b* 5 Feb. 1990. *Address:* Poligono 5, Parcela 320, Cami de na Bubota, 07210 Algaida, Mallorca, Spain. *T:* (971) 665836. *E:* cholcroft@gmail.com.

HOLCROFT, Christopher Mark, FRGS; Business and Client Services Consultant, Informed Solutions Ltd, since 2015; *b* Burnley, Lancs, 8 March 1966; *s* of Raymond and Anne Holcroft; *m* 1998, Jane Arwen Senton; one *s* two *d. Educ:* Burnley Grammar Sch.; London Sch. of Econs and Pol Sci. (BSc Hons Geog.). CGeog (GIS) 2011. Cartographer, LSE, 1988–90; freelance cartographer, The Independent, 1989–90; Geographic Information Systems Specialist, Informatix (Japan), 1990–95; Corporate Sales, Autodesk, 1996–98; Corporate Mktg Manager, Cadcorp, 1998–2004; Sen. Product Manager, Ordnance Survey, 2004–05; Business Develt Manager (Asia Pacific), Cadcorp, 2005–07; Chief Executive: AGI, 2007–12; RMetS, 2012–13; Dir of Strategic Business Develt, Ordnance Survey Internat., 2013–15. Member: UK Geographic Inf. Panel, DCLG, 2007–08; UK Location Council, DEFRA, 2009–12; Ordnance Survey Derived Data Adv. Gp, 2011–13; Geographic Inf. Customer Gp, BIS, 2012–; Readers Panel for the Queen's Anniv. Prizes for Higher and Further Educn, Royal Anniversary Trust, 2012–. FRGS 1993. Past Chair's Award, AGI, 2011, 2012. *Recreations:* bass guitar, classical piano, weather observations, running, walking, family history books. *Address:* Informed Solutions, 11 Old Queen Street, Westminster, SW1H 9JA. *T:* (020) 3042 2000. *E:* chris.holcroft@informed.com.

HOLCROFT, Lt Col Patrick Roy, LVO 2013; OBE 1986; Lord-Lieutenant of Worcestershire, since 2012; *b* Birmingham, 17 March 1948; *e s* of Oliver Roy Holcroft and Gabrielle Mary Holcroft (*née* Perry); *m* 1982, Annie Kathleen Roberts; three *s. Educ:* Downside Sch.; RMA Sandhurst; Nottingham Univ. (BA Hons 1972). Commnd 2nd Bn, Grenadier Guards, 1969; Adjt, 1973–75; Instructor, RMA Sandhurst, 1975–77; i/c 2nd Bn Inkerman Co., 1977–78; psc 1980; The Captain, 1st Bn, Queen's Co., 1981–82; SO2 (MO1), MoD (A), 1982–84; MA to Adjt Gen. (Lt Col), MoD (A), 1984–87. Robert Fleming & Co.: investment analyst, 1988–90; Dir, Fleming Investment mgt, 1990–92; CEO, Robert Fleming Insce Brokers, 1992–2001; led mgt buy-out, 2001, co. renamed RFIB Gp; CEO, RFIB Gp, 2001–09; non-exec. Dir, 2009–13. Non-executive Director: Griffin Insce Assoc., 2002–13; Thomas Miller Hldgs, 2010–. Trustee: Grenadier Guards, 1992–; Hedley Foundn, 1995–; Lloyds Patriotic Fund, 2004–13; Nuffield Trust for Forces of the Crown, 2011–. *Recreations:* field sports, cricket, golf, reading, theatre, cooking. *Address:* c/o Lieutenancy Office, County Hall, Spetchley Road, Worcester, Worcs WR5 2NP. *Clubs:* Cavalry and Guards, Pratt's.

HOLDAWAY, Prof. Richard, CBE 2013; PhD; FREng; Director, Space Science and Technology, Science and Technology Facilities Council (formerly Council for the Central Laboratory of the Research Councils), since 1998; *b* 22 Feb. 1949; *s* of Maurice Holdaway and Margaret Holdaway; two *s. Educ:* Univ. of Southampton (BSc Aeronautics/Astronautics Engrg 1970; PhD Astrodynamics 1974). Design Engr, Harrier, Hawker Siddeley Aviation, 1970; Proj. Engr, Appleton Lab., 1974–80; Project Engr, then Div. Head (Space), Rutherford Appleton Lab., 1980–98. Visiting Professor: Univ. of Southampton, 1995–; Univ. of Kent, 1996–; Beijing Univ. of Aeronautics and Astronautics, 2006–. FAIAA 1996; FREng 2001. *Publications:* 80 jtly edited books and articles on space technology. *Recreations:* sport (squash, soccer, hockey), season ticket holder and fanatical supporter of Portsmouth Football Club. *Address:* Rutherford Appleton Laboratory, Chilton, Didcot, Oxon OX11 0QX. *T:* (01235) 445527, *Fax:* (01235) 446640. *E:* r.holdaway@rl.ac.uk.

HOLDEN, Amanda Juliet; musician, writer; *b* 19 Jan. 1948; *d* of Sir Brian Warren and Dame Josephine Barnes, DBE; *m* 1971, Anthony Holden, *qv* (marr. diss. 1988); three *s. Educ:* Benenden Sch.; Lady Margaret Hall, Oxford (MA); Guildhall Sch. of Music and Drama (Piano

Accompanying Schol.; LGSM); American Univ., Washington (Hall of Nations Schol.; MA); ARCM; LRAM. Music staff: St Michael's Comprehensive, Watford, 1970–72; Watford Sch. of Music, 1971–75; Guildhall Sch., 1973–87; Founder, Music Therapy Dept, Charing Cross Hosp., London, 1973–75. Mem., Opera Adv. Bd, Royal Opera House, 1998; Advr, Opera Genesis Prog., ROH2, 2006–09. Has translated *c* 60 opera libretti, 1985–, including: The Coronation of Poppea (Monteverdi), Les Boréades, Castor and Pollux (Rameau), Armide (Gluck), Agrippina, Alcina, Ariodante, Partenope, Rodelinda (Handel), La finta giardiniera, Il re pastore, Idomeneo, Die Entführung, The Marriage of Figaro, Don Giovanni, The Magic Flute, La clemenza di Tito, The Barber of Seville, La Cenerentola, L'elisir d'amore, Maria Stuarda, Lucia di Lammermoor, Beatrice and Benedict, The Bartered Bride, Lohengrin, Rigoletto, A Masked Ball, Aida, Falstaff, Faust, The Pearl Fishers, The Fair Maid of Perth, Carmen, Werther, La bohème, Tosca, Madam Butterfly, Il Trittico, Pagliacci (Leoncavallo), Francesca da Rimini (Rachmaninov), Volo di notte (Dallapiccola), Experimentum Mundi (Battistelli), Caligula (Glanert); *cartoon film script:* Rhinegold, 1995; *play translation,* Amphitryon (Kleist); *adaptations for concert hall:* The Epic of Gilgamesh (Martinů); Der Freischütz; *libretti:* The Selfish Giant (after Wilde); The Silver Tassie (after O'Casey) (Outstanding Achievement in Opera (jtly), Laurence Olivier Awards, 2001); Family Matters (after Beaumarchais), The Piano Tuner (after Daniel Mason); Bliss (after Peter Carey). *Publications:* The Magic Flute (arr. for children), 1990; (contrib.) The Mozart Compendium, 1990; (trans.) Lohengrin, 1993; (ed) The Viking Opera Guide, 1993; (ed) The Penguin Opera Guide, 1995, 2nd edn 1997; (ed) The New Penguin Opera Guide, 2001; (ed) The Penguin Concise Guide to Opera, 2005. *Recreations:* birdwatching, gardening, swimming. *W:* www.amandaholden.org.uk.

HOLDEN, Anthony Ivan; writer; *b* 22 May 1947; *s* of late John Holden and Margaret Lois Holden (*née* Sharpe); *m* 1st, 1971, Amanda Juliet Warren (*see* A. J. Holden) (marr. diss. 1988); three *s*; 2nd, 1990, Cynthia Blake, *d* of Mrs George Blake, Brookline, Mass. *Educ:* Tre-Arddur House Sch., Anglesey; Oundle Sch.; Merton Coll., Oxford (MA Hons Eng. Lang. and Lit.; Editor, Isis). Trainee reporter, Thomson Regional Newspapers, Evening Echo, Hemel Hempstead, 1970–73; home and foreign corresp., Sunday Times, 1973–77; columnist (Atticus), Sunday Times, 1977–79; Washington corresp. and US Editor, Observer, 1979–81; Features Editor and Asst Editor, The Times, 1981–82; freelance journalist and author, 1982–85 and 1986–; Exec. Editor, Today, 1985–86; music critic, The Observer, 2002–08. Fellow, Center for Scholars and Writers, NY Public Liby, 1999–2000. Broadcaster, radio and TV; TV documentaries include: The Man Who Would Be King, 1982; Charles at Forty, 1988; Anthony Holden on Poker, 1992; Who Killed Tchaikovsky, 1993. Member, Board of Governors: South Bank Centre, 2002–08; Northern Shakespeare Trust, 2006–. Pres., Internat. Fedn of Poker, 2009–13. Young Journalist of 1972; commended for work in NI, News Reporter of the Year, British Press Awards, 1976; Columnist of the Year, British Press Awards, 1977. Opera translations: Don Giovanni, 1986; La Bohème, 1986; The Barber of Seville, 1987. *Publications:* (trans. and ed) Aeschylus' Agamemnon, 1969; (contrib.) The Greek Anthology, 1973; (trans. and ed) Greek Pastoral Poetry, 1974; The St Albans Poisoner, 1974, 2nd edn 1996; Charles, Prince of Wales, 1979; Their Royal Highnesses, 1981; Of Presidents, Prime Ministers and Princes, 1984; The Queen Mother, 1985, 3rd edn 1995; (trans.) Mozart's Don Giovanni, 1987; Olivier, 1988; Charles, 1988; Big Deal, 1990, 3rd edn 2002; (ed) The Last Paragraph, 1990; A Princely Marriage, 1991; The Oscars, 1993; The Tarnished Crown, 1993; (contrib.) Power and the Throne, 1994; Tchaikovsky, 1995; Diana: her life and legacy, 1997; Charles: a biography, 1998; William Shakespeare: his life and work, 1999; (ed jtly) The Mind Has Mountains, 1999; (ed jtly) There are Kermodians, 1999; The Drama of Love, Life and Death in Shakespeare, 2000; Shakespeare: an illustrated biography, 2002; The Wit in the Dungeon: the life of Leigh Hunt, 2005; All In, 2005; The Man Who Wrote Mozart, 2006; Bigger Deal, 2007; Holden on Hold'em, 2008; (ed jtly) Poems that Make Grown Men Cry, 2014. *Recreations:* poker, Arsenal FC, Lancashire CC. *Address:* c/o Rogers Coleridge White, 20 Powis Mews, W11 1JN. *T:* (020) 7221 3717.

HOLDEN, Prof. David William, PhD; FRS 2004; FMedSci; Professor of Molecular Microbiology, since 1997, and Director, MRC Centre for Molecular Bacteriology and Infection, since 2012, Imperial College London; *b* 3 Nov. 1955; *s* of John and Bronwen Holden; *m* 2000, Belinda Sinclair. *Educ:* George Watson's Coll., Edinburgh; Univ. of Durham (BSc Hons (Botany) 1977); UCL (PhD 1982). Research Fellow: Agriculture Canada, 1982–84; Univ. of Wisconsin, 1985–88; NIMR, London, 1988–90; Royal Postgraduate Medical School, London: Lectr, 1990–93; Sen. Lectr, 1993–95; Prof., 1995–97. Scientific Founder and Consultant, Microscience Ltd, 1997–2005. FMedSci 2002. *Publications:* numerous articles in learned jls; several patents. *Recreations:* climbing, reading, cycling. *Address:* Section of Microbiology, MRC Centre for Molecular Bacteriology and Infection, Imperial College London, Armstrong Road, SW7 2AZ. *T:* (020) 7594 3073, *Fax:* (020) 7594 3095. *E:* d.holden@imperial.ac.uk.

HOLDEN, His Honour Derek; a Circuit Judge, 1984–2000; a Chairman, Asylum and Immigration Tribunal (formerly Immigration Appeal Tribunal), 2000–11; *b* 7 July 1935; *s* of Frederic Holden and Audrey Holden (*née* Hayes); *m* 1961, Dorien Elizabeth Holden (*née* Bell); two *s*. *Educ:* Cromwell House; Staines Grammar Sch. Served Army; Lieut East Surrey Regt, 1953–56. Qualified as Solicitor, 1966; Derek Holden & Co., Staines, Egham, Camberley, Feltham, Basingstoke and Ashford, 1966–84; Consultant, Batt Holden & Co., 1966–84; Principal, Dorien Property Co., 1974–84; Partner, Black Lake Securities, 1978–84. A Recorder, 1980–84; President: Social Security Appeal Tribunals and Medical Appeal Tribunals, Vaccine Damage Tribunals, and Disability Appeals Tribunal, 1990–92; Child Support Tribunal, 1993; Chm., Tribunals Cttee, Judicial Studies Bd, 1991–93; Mem., Criminal Injuries Compensation Appeal Panel, 2000–08; Chm., Ind. Appeals Body, ICSTIS, 2001–11. Mem., Royal Yachting Assoc., 1975– (Dept of Trade Offshore Yachtmaster Instr with Ocean Cert.; Advanced Open Water Diving Cert., 2000); Principal, Chandor Sch. of Sailing, Lymington, 1978–85. *Recreations:* sailing, snow-boarding, photography, music, scuba-diving. *Address:* Beech House, Treveor Gardens, Modbury, Devon PL21 0TE. *Clubs:* Western (Glasgow); Leander, Remenham (Henley); Burway Rowing (Laleham); Eton Excelsior Rowing (Windsor); Staines Boat; Port Solent Yacht.

HOLDEN, Sir John David, 4th Bt *cr* 1919; *b* 16 Dec. 1967; *s* of David George Holden (*d* 1971) (*e s* of 3rd Bt), and of Nancy, *d* of H. W. D. Marwood, Foulrice, Whenby, Brandsby, Yorks; *S* grandfather, 1976; *m* 1987, Suzanne Cummings; three *d*. *Heir: uncle* Brian Peter John Holden [*b* 12 April 1944; *m* 1984, Bernadette Anne Lopez, *d* of George Gerard O'Malley].

HOLDEN, John Stewart; Lay Member and Vice Chair, Bath and North East Somerset Clinical Commissioning Group, since 2013; *b* 23 July 1945; *s* of William Stewart Holden and Jenny Holden (*née* Brelsford); *m* 1st, 1970, Pamela (marr. diss. 1984); 2nd, 1984, Margaret Newport. *Educ:* Merchant Taylors'; Emmanuel Coll., Cambridge (BA Hons Natural Scis/Law 1967; MA). British Petroleum and subsidiaries, 1964–93: Manager, Gas (Western Hemisphere), 1981–84; Area Oil Co-ordinator and Dir, BP (Schweiz) AG, 1984–87; Dir, Alexander Duckham & Co., 1991–93; Manager, European Lubricants & Bitumen, 1991–93; Develt Dir, Electricity Pool, 1994–96; Chief Exec., Companies House and Registrar of Cos for England and Wales, 1996–2002; Registrar of Political Parties, 1998–2000; Board Member: UK Passport Service, 2002–07; Criminal Records Bureau, 2002–06. Mem., Home Office Review of Criminal Records Bureau, 2002. Mem., Audit Cttee, Ind. Police Complaints Commn, 2005–09. Board Member and Audit Chair: Wiltshire PCT, 2006–13; NHS Bath and NE Somerset, 2012–13. Vice Chm., Nat. Council, Light Aircraft Assoc., 2013–. *Publications:* The Watlington Branch, 1974; The Manchester and Milford Railway, 1979, 2nd edn 2007. *Recreations:* flying, Italian opera, history, industrial archaeology.

HOLDEN, Patrick Brian, MA, FCIS; Chairman: Ainsfield PLC, since 1991; Holden Homes (Southern) Ltd, since 1984; *b* 16 June 1937; *s* of Reginald John and Winifred Isabel Holden; *m* 1972, Jennifer Ruth (*née* Meddings), MB, BS (marr. diss. 2001). *Educ:* Allhallows Sch. (Major Schol.); St Catharine's Coll., Cambridge (BA Hons Law 1960, MA 1963). FCIS 1965. Served Royal Hampshire Regt, 1955–57 (regular commn), seconded 1 Ghana Regt, RWAFF. Fine Fare Group: Sec., 1960–69; Legal and Property Dir, 1965–69; Pye of Cambridge Gp, 1969–74; Dir, Pye Telecom. Ltd, 1972–74; Sec., then Dir, Oriel Foods Gp, 1975–81; Gp Sec., Fisons plc, 1981–83; Dir, Legal Affairs, Nabisco, 1983–85. Non-exec. Dir, Mortimer Growth II plc, 1997–2007. Sec., New Town Assoc., 1974–75. Lloyd's Name, 1984–. Trustee, Cartoon Mus., 2012–; Dir, Cartoon Art Trust, 2012–. *Publications:* Map of Tewin and its Rights of Way, 1991; A–Z of Dog Training and Behaviour, 1999; The Old School House: a Dickensian school, 2000; Agility: a step by step guide, 2001. *Recreations:* dogs, bridge, walking, cartoons, limericks. *Address:* The Old School House, Lower Green, Tewin, Herts AL6 0LD. *T:* (01438) 717573. *Club:* Naval and Military.

HOLDEN, Patrick Hyla, CBE 2005; Director, Sustainable Food Trust, since 2010; International Ambassador, Soil Association, since 2010 (Director, 1995–2010); *b* 9 Sept. 1950; *s* of Dr Hyla Montgomery Holden and Joan Elizabeth Holden; *m* 1st, 1977, Louise Richards (marr. diss.); two *s* two *d*; 2nd, 2002, Rebecca Mary Hiscock; four *s*. *Educ:* Dulwich Hamlet Primary Sch.; Alleyn's Sch., Dulwich; Mount Grace Comp. Sch., Potters Bar; Emerson Coll., Sussex (biodynamic agric. course). Farmer, 240-acre mixed organic dairy farm, W Wales, 1973– (pt-time, 1988–); Dir, British Organic Farmers, 1988–92. Mem., UK Register of Organic Food Standards Bd, 1987–97. Patron: Soil Assoc. Land Trust, 2010–; Bio-Dynamic Agricl Assoc., 2011–; Living Earth Land Trust, 2011–. *Recreations:* Hebridean Islands, all year swimming, tennis, hill walking, Bach. *Address:* 38 Richmond Street, Totterdown, Bristol BS3 4TQ. *T:* (0117) 987 1467. *E:* patrickholden@me.com. *Club:* Farmers.

HOLDEN, Sir Paul, 7th Bt *cr* 1893, of Oakworth House, Keighley, Yorkshire; *b* 3 March 1923; *s* of Sir Isaac Holden Holden, 5th Bt and Alice Edna Holden (*née* Byrom); *S* brother, 2003; *m* 1950, Vivien Mary Oldham; one *s* two *d*. *Educ:* Leys Sch., Cambridge; Oriel Coll., Oxford. Fellow, Inst. of Amateur Cinematographers, 2011. *Recreations:* film making (Pres., Surrey Border Movie Makers), swimming, diving. *Heir: s* Michael Peter Holden [*b* 19 June 1956; *m* 1990, Irene Yvonne Salmon; three *d*]. *Address:* 122 Clare Park Private Retirement Residences, Crondall, Farnham, Surrey GU10 5DT. *Club:* Lions (Farnham).

HOLDEN, Robert David, CBE 2009; independent consultant for long-term complex projects, since 2011; Chairman, High Speed 1 Ltd, since 2011; *b* Manchester, 6 April 1956; *s* of Robert Holden and Gladys Holden; *m* 1993, Jill Benson; one *s* one *d*. *Educ:* Lancaster Univ. (BA Financial Control and Econs 1977). ACA 1980. With Arthur Young; joined Vickers Shipbuilding and Engineering Ltd, 1983, Finance Dir, 1994; Finance Dir, GEC Marine, 1995; London & Continental Railways Ltd: Finance Dir, 1996–99; CEO, 1999–2009; CEO, Crossrail Ltd, 2009–11. Dir, Cammell Laird Shipbuilders, 1990–96. Chm., Eurostar (UK) Ltd, 1998–2010; non-executive Director: Eurostar Gp Ltd, 1999–2010; Viridor Ltd, 2012–; Nuclear Decommissioning Authy, 2015–. Mem., Exec. Cttee, Railway Industry Pension Scheme, 2008–14. Mem. Council, UCL, 2005–12. Hon. FICE 2010. *Address:* High Speed 1 Ltd, 1 Euston Square, Melton Street, NW1 2FD.

HOLDEN, Susan Anne; Chief Executive, Earthwatch Institute (Europe), since 2014; *b* Morden, 13 May 1966; *d* of John Holden and Sheila Holden. *Educ:* Newnham Coll., Cambridge (BA Geog. 1987; MA); Henley Sch. of Mgt (Dip. Mgt). Various roles, Shell Internat. and Shell UK, 1988–93; National Trust: Property Manager, 1996–99; Area Manager, 1999–2002; Business Admin Dir, 2002–05; Chief Exec., Woodland Trust, 2005–14. FRSA. *Recreations:* hill-walking, gardening, piano, tree planting. *Address:* Earthwatch Institute (Europe), Mayfield House, 256 Banbury Road, Oxford OX2 7DE. *E:* sholden@earthwatch.org.uk.

HOLDEN-BROWN, Sir Derrick, Kt 1979; Chairman, Allied-Lyons PLC, 1982–91 (Chief Executive, 1982–88); Director, Allied Breweries, 1967–91 (Chairman, 1982–86); *b* 14 Feb. 1923; *s* of Harold Walter and Beatrice Florence (*née* Walker); *m* 1st, 1950, Patricia Mary Ross Mackenzie (*d* 2001); one *d* (one *s* decd); 2nd, 2005, Farideh Pelham. *Educ:* Westcliff. Mem., Inst. of Chartered Accountants of Scotland. Served War, Royal Navy, 1941–46, Lt RNVR, Coastal Forces. Chartered Accountant, 1948; Hiram Walker & Sons, Distillers, 1949; Managing Director: Cairnes Ltd, Brewers, Eire, 1954; Grants of St James's Ltd, 1960; Dir, Ind Coope Ltd, 1962; Chm., Victoria Wine Co., 1964; Finance Dir, 1972, Vice-Chm., 1975–82, Allied Breweries; Director: Sun Alliance & London Insurance plc, 1977– (Vice Chm., 1983, Dep. Chm., 1985–92); Midland Bank, 1984–88. Chm., FDIC, 1984–85 (Dep. Chm. 1974–76). President: Food and Drink Fedn, 1985–86; Food Manufacturers' Fedn Inc., 1985. Chairman: Brewers' Soc., 1978–80 (Master, Brewers' Co., 1987–88); White Ensign Assoc., 1987–90; Portsmouth Naval Heritage Trust, 1989–. *Recreations:* sailing, offshore cruising. *Address:* 6 Ashburn Gardens, SW7 4DG. *T:* (020) 7370 1597. *Clubs:* Boodle's; Royal Yacht Squadron; Royal Lymington Yacht.

HOLDER, Eric H., Jr; Attorney General of the United States of America, 2009–15; Partner, Covington & Burling, Washington, DC, 2001–09 and since 2015; *b* New York City, 21 Jan. 1951; *s* of Eric Holder and Miriam R. Holder; *m* Sharon Malone; three *c*. *Educ:* Stuyvesant High Sch., NYC; Columbia Univ. (BA American Hist. 1973); Columbia Law Sch. (JD 1976). Called to the Bar, NY, 1977; Public Integrity Section, Dept of Justice, 1976–88; Associate Judge, Superior Court, DC, 1988–93; US Attorney, DC, Dept of Justice, 1993–97; Dep. Attorney Gen., 1997–2001; Actg Attorney Gen., 2001. Mem., Ad Hoc Adv. Gp, US Sentencing Commn. Member Board: Columbia Univ.; Nat. Center for Victims of Crime; Meyer Foundn; Save the Children Foundn. Hon. Bencher, Middle Temple, 2012.

HOLDER, Sir (John) Henry, 4th Bt *cr* 1898, of Pitmaston, Moseley, Worcs; Production Director and Head Brewer, Elgood & Sons Ltd, North Brink Brewery, Wisbech, 1975–93, retired; *b* 12 March 1928; *s* of Sir John Eric Duncan Holder, 3rd Bt and Evelyn Josephine (*d* 1994), *er d* of late William Blain; *S* father, 1986; *m* 1st, 1960, Catharine Harrison (*d* 1994), *yr d* of late Leonard Baker; twin *s* one *d*; 2nd, 1996, Josephine Mary (*d* 2013), *d* of late A. Elliott and *widow* of G. Rivett. *Educ:* Eton Coll.; Birmingham Univ. (Dip. Malting and Brewing); Dip. in Safety Management, British Safety Council. Mem., Inst. of Brewing and Distilling (Diploma Mem., Inst. of Brewing). National Service, RAC; commnd 5th Royal Tank Regt, 1947. Shift Brewer, Mitchells & Butlers Ltd, 1951–53; Brewer, Reffels Bexley Brewery Ltd, 1953–56; Asst Manager, Unique Slide Rule Co., 1956–62; Brewer, Rhymney Brewery Co. Ltd, 1962–75. *Recreations:* sailing, computing. *Heir: er* twin *s* Nigel John Charles Holder, *b* 6 May 1962. *Address:* Westering, Holt Road, Cley-next-the-Sea, Holt, Norfolk NR25 7UA. *Club:* Brancaster Staithe Sailing (King's Lynn).

HOLDER, Most Rev. Dr John Walder Dunlop; *see* West Indies, Archbishop of the.

HOLDERNESS, Sir Martin (William), 4th Bt *cr* 1920, of Tadworth, Surrey; Financial Planner, Succession Group, independent financial advisers; *b* 24 May 1957; *s* of Sir Richard William Holderness, 3rd Bt and of Pamela Mary Dawsett (*née* Chapman); *S* father, 1998; *m* 1st (marr. diss. 2013); one *s* one *d*; 2nd, 2014, Amanda Jane Robinson (*née* Hayes). *Educ:* Bradfield Coll., Berkshire; Portsmouth Poly. (BA Accountancy 1979). CA 1983; MSFA 1995. Articled KMG Thomson McLintock, 1978–83; financial adviser, 1984–; Man. Dir, MH Financial Mgt Ltd, 2002–14. *Recreations:* theatre, films, football, family life. *Heir: s* Matthew William Thornton Holderness, *b* 23 May 1990. *Address:* 109 Sandpit Lane, St Albans, Herts AL4 0BP. *Club:* Two Brydges.

HOLDERNESS-RODDAM, Jane Mary Elizabeth, CBE 2004; LVO 1999; Chairman, Riding for the Disabled Association, 2000–10, now Hon. Life Vice-President; *b* 7 Jan. 1948; *d* of Jack and Anne Bullen; *m* 1974, Timothy David Holderness-Roddam, *qv. Educ:* Westwing Sch., Thornbury, Glos. SRN, Middlesex Hosp., London, 1970. Owner, W Kington Stud Farm. Olympic Team Gold Medallist, Equestrian 3 day Event, 1968. President: Fortune Centre of Riding Therapy, 1969–; British Equestrian Trade Assoc., 2004–; British Eventing, 2004– (Chm., 1999–2004). Chairman: Nat. Riding Fest., 1999–2010; Council, British Equestrian Fedn, 2010–; Pres., Caspian Horse Soc., 2007–; Trustee: World Horse Welfare, 2007–13; Brooke, 2013–; Patron, Side Saddle Assoc., 2008–. Dir, Nat. Equine Database, 2009–13. Hon. Freeman, Co. of Loriners, 2001; Yeoman, Co. of Saddlers, 2005. Hon. Dr UWE, 2004. Queen's Award for Equestrianism, British Horse Soc., 2009. *Publications:* equestrian books include: Competitive Riding, 1988; Complete Book of Eventing, 1988; Showing, 1989; Show Jumping, 1990; Fitness for Horse and Rider, 1993; Practical Cross Country, 1994; The Life of Horses, 1999; Horse Riding in a Weekend, 2004; contrib. to equestrian magazines. *Recreations:* travel, antique collecting. *Address:* Church Farm, West Kington, Chippenham, Wilts SN14 7JE. *T:* (01249) 782050, *Fax:* (01249) 782940. *E:* jhroddam@aol.com.

HOLDERNESS-RODDAM, Timothy David; Director, Abercrombie & Kent Ltd, since 2003; *b* 23 Nov. 1942; *s* of David and Susan Holderness-Roddam; *m* 1974, Jane Mary Elizabeth Bullen (*see* J. M. E. Holderness-Roddam). *Educ:* Radley Coll. Partner, West Kington Farms, 1988–. Man. Dir, UM Gp, 1993–2000; Dep. Chm., Countrywide Farmers plc, 2004–13. Chairman: Horse Trials Support Gp, 1974–2010; British Equestrian Fedn Fund, 2008–. Dir, British Eventing Ltd, 2010–. Trustee, Friends of Conservation, 1976–. *Recreations:* travel, shooting, country pursuits. *Address:* Church Farm, West Kington, Chippenham, Wilts SN14 7JE. *T:* (01249) 782050, *Fax:* (01249) 782940. *E:* jhroddam@aol.com. *Club:* Cavalry and Guards.

HOLDGATE, Sir Martin (Wyatt), Kt 1994; CB 1979; PhD; FRSB; President: Zoological Society of London, 1994–2004; Freshwater Biological Association, 2002–10; *b* 14 Jan. 1931; *s* of late Francis Wyatt Holdgate, MA, JP, and Lois Marjorie (*née* Bebbington); *m* 1963, Elizabeth Mary (*née* Dickason), *widow* of Dr H. H. Weil; two *s. Educ:* Arnold Sch., Blackpool; Queens' Coll., Cambridge (BA 1952; MA 1956; PhD 1955). FRSB (FIBiol 1967). Jt Leader and Senior Scientist, Gough Is Scientific Survey, 1955–56; Lecturer in Zoology: Manchester Univ., 1956–57; Durham Colleges, 1957–60; Leader, Royal Society Expedition to Southern Chile, 1958–59; Asst Director of Research, Scott Polar Research Institute, Cambridge, 1960–63; Senior Biologist, British Antarctic Survey, 1963–66; Dep. Dir (Research), The Nature Conservancy, 1966–70; Director: Central Unit on Environmental Pollution, DoE, 1970–74; Inst. of Terrestrial Ecology, NERC, 1974–76; Dep. Sec., 1976, Dir-Gen. of Res., 1976–79, Chief Scientist, 1979–85, Depts of the Environment and of Transport; Dep. Sec., Environment Protection and Chief Envmt Scientist, DoE, and Chief Scientific Advr, Dept of Transport, 1985–88; Dir Gen., IUCN, 1988–94. Hon. Professorial Fellow, UC Cardiff, 1976–83. Member: NERC, 1976–87; SERC (formerly SRC), 1976–87; ABRC, 1976–88; Bd, World Resources Inst., Washington, 1985–94; China Council for Internat. Co-operation on Envmt and Develt, Beijing, 1992–94; Chairman: Review of Scientific Civil Service, 1980; Renewable Energy Adv. Gp, 1992; Energy Adv. Panel, 1993–96; Internat. Inst. for Envmt and Develt, 1994–99; Co-Chm., Intergovtl Panel on Forests, UN Commn on Sustainable Develt, 1995–97; Mem., Royal Commn on Envmtl Pollution, 1994–2002; Trustee: Nat. Heritage Meml Fund and Heritage Lottery Fund, 1995–98; Cumbria Wildlife Trust, 2004–15. Chm., British Schools Exploring Society, 1967–78; Vice-Pres., Young Explorer's Trust, 1981–90 (Chm., 1972, 1979–81). President: Governing Council, UN Environment Prog., 1983–84; Global 500 Forum, 1992–97; Chm., Commonwealth Expert Gp on Climate Change, 1988–89. Chm., Governing Council, Arnold Sch., 1997–2004. Pres., Friends of the Lake District, 2014–. Hon. Mem., IUCN, 2000. Hon. FZS 2005. Hon. Fellow: RHBNC, 1997; Univ. of Cumbria, 2015. Hon. DSc: Durham, 1991; Sussex, 1993; Lancaster, 1995; QMUL, 2006. Bruce Medal, RSE, 1964; UNEP Silver Medal, 1983; UNEP Global 500, 1988; Patron's Medal, RGS, 1992; Livingstone Medal, RSGS, 1993. Comdr, Order of The Golden Ark (Netherlands), 1991. *Publications:* A History of Appleby, 1956, rewritten as The Story of Appleby in Westmorland, 2006; Mountains in the Sea, The Story of the Gough Island Expedition, 1958; (ed jtly) Antarctic Biology, 1964; (ed) Antarctic Ecology, 1970; (with N. M. Wace) Man and Nature in the Tristan da Cunha Islands, 1976; A Perspective of Environmental Pollution, 1979; (ed jtly) The World Environment 1972–82, 1982; (ed jtly) The World Environment 1972–92, 1992; From Care to Action: making a sustainable world, 1996; The Green Web: a union for world conservation, 1999; Penguins and Mandarins: memories of natural and un-natural history, 2003; Arnold: the story of a Blackpool school, 2009; numerous papers and articles on Antarctica, environment and conservation. *Address:* Fell Beck, Hartley, Kirkby Stephen, Cumbria CA17 4JH. *Club:* Athenæum.

HOLDHAM, Susan Pauline, (Mrs Charles Llewellyn); a District Judge (Magistrates' Courts), since 2014; *b* Stoke-on-Trent, 11 Oct. 1960; *d* of late James Stanley Holdham and of Betty Holdham; *m* 1992, Charles Llewellyn; one *s. Educ:* Blythe Bridge High Sch.; Univ. of Bristol (LLB Hons 1982); Inns of Court Sch. of Law. Called to the Bar, Gray's Inn, 1983, Middle Temple *ad eundem*; in practice as barrister: SE Circuit, 1983–99; Criminal Appeal Office, 1999–2014; a Dep. Dist Judge (Magistrates' Courts), 2006–14. *Publications:* (with A. Beldam) The Court of Appeal Criminal Division: a practitioner's guide, 2012. *Recreations:* medieval history, greyhounds, theatre, cocktails, opera. *Address:* c/o Westminster Magistrates' Court, 181 Marylebone Road, NW1 5BR.

HOLDING, John Francis; HM Diplomatic Service, retired; business adviser and director, and active Rotarian in New Zealand, since 1996; *b* 12 Aug. 1936; *s* of late Francis George Holding, CA, Inland Revenue, and Gwendoline Elizabeth Holding (*née* Jenkins); *m* 1st, 1970, Pamela Margaret Straker-Nesbit (marr. diss. 1984); two *d*; 2nd, 1993, Susan Ann Clark (marr. diss. 1999). *Educ:* Colwyn Bay Grammar Sch.; LSE (externally). Mil. service, 1955–57; Min. of Housing and Local Govt, 1957; CRO (later FCO), 1964; served Karachi, Islamabad and Kinshasa; First Sec., 1973; Canberra, 1973–78; The Gambia, 1978–80; Grenada and Barbados, 1984–87; Dep. High Comr, Dhaka, 1987–90; Consul-General, Auckland, and Dir UK Trade Promotion in NZ, 1990–96. *Recreations:* tennis, walking, photography, pianoforte. *Address:* 36 Bell Road, Remuera, Auckland 1050, New Zealand.

HOLDING, Malcolm Alexander; HM Diplomatic Service, retired; Consul-General, Naples, 1986–90; *b* 11 May 1932; *s* of Adam Anderson Holding and Mary Lillian (*née* Golding); *m* 1955, Pamela Eve Hampshire; two *d. Educ:* King Henry VIII Sch., Coventry. Foreign Office, 1949–51; HM Forces, 1951–53; FO, 1953–55; Middle East Centre for Arab Studies, 1956–57; Third Secretary (Commercial), Tunis, 1957–60; Second Sec. (Commercial), Khartoum, 1960–64; Second, later First Sec. (Commercial), Cairo, 1964–68; Consul, Bari, 1969; FCO, 1970–73; First Sec., British Dep. High Commission, Madras, 1973–75; FCO, 1976–78; Canadian National Defence Coll., Kingston, Ontario, 1978–79; Counsellor (Commercial), Rome, 1979–81; Consul-Gen., Edmonton, 1981–85. Commendatore, Order of Merit of the Republic of Italy, 1980. *Address:* 18 Strand Court, The Strand, Topsham, Exeter EX3 0AZ.

HOLDING, Dr Peter; Headmaster, Sir William Borlase's Grammar School, Marlow, since 1997; *b* Leigh-on-Sea, 5 April 1954; *s* of John and Joan Holding; *m* 2007, Sarah Woodman. *Educ:* Brockway High Sch., USA; Univ. of Pennsylvania (BA); Open Univ. (MA Ed.); Shakespeare Inst. (MA); Univ. of Michigan (PhD 1988); Westminster Coll., Oxford (PGCE). Asst Lectr in English and Film Studies, Univ. of Michigan, 1978–82; Head: of Drama, Forest Sch., London, 1982–87; of English, Rugby Sch., 1988–94; Dep. Hd, Lawrence Sheriff Sch., Rugby, 1994–97. Chairman: Bucks Assoc. of Secondary Heads, 2003–12; Bucks Learning Trust, 2013–; Mem. Bd, Bucks Acad. for Sch. Leadership, 2004–10; Nat. Leader of Educ., 2012–; Trustee, La Retraite Sch., 2012–. *Publications:* Romeo and Juliet: text and performance, 1989. *Recreations:* theatre, opera, travel, cooking. *Address:* Sir William Borlase's Grammar School, West Street, Marlow SL7 2BR. *E:* pholding@swbgs.com.

HOLDRIDGE, Ven. Bernard Lee; Archdeacon of Doncaster, 1994–2001; *b* 24 July 1935; *s* of Geoffrey and Lucy Medlow Holdridge. *Educ:* Grammar Sch., Thorne; Lichfield Theol Coll. Ordained deacon, 1967, priest, 1968; Curate, Swinton, S Yorks, 1967–71; Vicar, St Jude, Hexthorpe, Doncaster, 1971–81; Rector, St Mary, Rawmarsh with Parkgate, 1981–88; RD of Rotherham, 1986–88; Vicar, Priory Church of St Mary and St Cuthbert, Worksop, with St Giles, Carburton and St Mary the Virgin, Clumber Park, dio. of Southwell, 1988–94; permission to officiate, dio. of Guildford, 2006–. Dignitary in Convocation, 1999–2001. Chairman: DAC for Care of Churches and Churchyards, Southwell, 1990–94; ACS, 1998–2003. Guardian, Shrine of Our Lady of Walsingham, 1996–. *Recreations:* foreign travel, reading, theatre, a glass of wine with friends. *Address:* Flat 35, Denehyrst Court, York Road, Guildford, Surrey GU1 4EA. *T:* (01483) 570791.

HOLDSWORTH, Ven. Dr John Ivor; Executive Archdeacon for the Diocese of Cyprus and the Gulf, since 2010; Chaplain, St Helena's Church, Larnaca, since 2010; *b* 10 Feb. 1949; *s* of Harold Holdsworth and Edith Mary Holdsworth; *m* 1971, Susan Annette Thomas; one *s* one *d. Educ:* Leeds Grammar Sch.; University Coll. of Wales, Aberystwyth (BA); University Coll., Cardiff (BD, MTh); St David's University Coll., Lampeter (PhD 1992). Ordained deacon 1973, priest 1974; Curate, St Paul's, Newport, 1973–77; Vicar: Abercrave and Callwen, 1977–86; Gorseinon, 1986–97; Principal and Warden, St Michael's Theol Coll., Llandaff, 1997–2003; Archdeacon of St Davids, Vicar of Steynton, and Canon of St Davids Cathedral, 2003–10. Presenter, HTV Wales Religious Affairs, 1988–98. Vis. Prof., Glyndwr Univ., 2012–. *Publications:* Communication and the Gospel, 2003; Dwelling in a Strange Land, 2003; SCM Study Guide to the Old Testament, 2005; Getting Started with the Bible, 2007; Lies, Sex and Politicians: communicating the Old Testament in contemporary culture, 2010; Conversations with the New Testament, 2014. *Recreations:* walking, armchair supporter of Leeds United and Yorkshire County Cricket Club, broadcasting. *Address:* (office) PO Box 22075, Nicosia 1517, Cyprus.

HOLDSWORTH, Very Rev. Kelvin; Provost, St Mary's Episcopal Cathedral, Glasgow, since 2006; *b* 22 Oct. 1966; *s* of John Stuart Holdsworth and Joyce Holdsworth (*née* Kew). *Educ:* Manchester Poly. (BSc Hons Computing Sci. and Maths 1989); Univ. of St Andrews (BD Hons Practical Theol. and Christian Ethics 1992); Univ. of Edinburgh (MTh Ministry 1996). Lay Worker, St Benet's Ecumenical Chaplaincy, QMW, 1992–95; ordained deacon, 1997, priest, 1998; Precentor, St Ninian's Cathedral, Perth, 1997–2000; Rector, St Saviour's Ch, Bridge of Allan, 2000–06. Contested (Lib Dem) Stirling, 2005. Dir, Newscan Pubns, 2006–09; Mem. Editl Bd, 2005–09, Ed., 2010–14, Inspires (mag. of Scottish Episcopal Ch). *Recreations:* politics, blogging, opera critic (Scotland) for Opera Britannia, sinking other people's yachts. *Address:* St Mary's Episcopal Cathedral, 300 Great Western Road, Glasgow G4 9JB. *T:* (0141) 339 6691. *E:* provost@thecathedral.org.uk. *Club:* Arlington Baths (Glasgow).

HOLDSWORTH HUNT, Christopher; Founder Director and Managing Director, KBC Peel, Hunt Ltd (formerly Peel, Hunt plc), 1989–2004; Chairman, Melchior Japan Investment Trust plc, 2006–10; *b* 2 Aug. 1942; *s* of late Peter Holdsworth Hunt and Monica (*née* Neville); *m* 1st, 1969, Charlotte Folin (marr. diss. 1974); 2nd, 1976, Joanne Lesley Starr Minoprio (*née* Reynolds); two *s. Educ:* Summer Fields, St Leonards; Eton Coll.; Tours Univ. Commnd Coldstream Guards, 1961–64. Joined Murton & Adams, Stockjobbers, 1964; firm acquired by Pinchin Denny, 1969; Partner, Pinchin Denny, 1971; firm acquired by Morgan Grenfell, 1986; Dir, Morgan Grenfell Securities, 1987–88. Non-exec. Dir, Octopus IHT AIM VCT plc, 2008–10. *Recreations:* opera, ballet, theatre, golf, tennis, walking. *Address:* 1 Hillsleigh Road, W8 7LE. *T:* (020) 7229 9903. *Clubs:* White's, City of London, Pratt's; Sunningdale Golf; Swinley Forest Golf.

HOLE, Christopher Charles Maximilian, (Max), CBE 2015; Chairman and Chief Executive Officer, Universal Music Group International, since 2013; *b* London, 26 May 1951; *s* of Frederick and Barbara Mary Hole; *m* 1999, Jan Ravens; three *s*, and two step *s. Educ:* Haileybury; Univ. of Kent. Founder: Gemini Artists, 1972–74; Criminal Records, 1976–81; Dir, A&R, 1982–87, Man. Dir, UK, 1987–90, WEA; Man. Dir, East West Records, 1990–98; Universal Music Group International: Sen. Vice Pres., Mktg and A&R, 1998–2005; Pres., Asia Pacific, 2005–10; Chief Operating Officer, 2010–13. Mem. Bd, ENO, 2012–. Trustee, EMI Music Sound Foundn, 2013–. *Recreations:* cricket, music, spending time at his houses in Cornwall and Corfu. *Address:* Universal Music Group International, 364–366 Kensington High Street, W14 8NS. *T:* (020) 7471 5603, *Fax:* (020) 7471 5605. *E:* max.hole@umusic.com. *Clubs:* MCC, Groucho.

HOLE, Very Rev. Derek Norman; Provost of Leicester, 1992–99, now Emeritus; *b* Plymouth, 5 Dec. 1933; *s* of Frank Edwin Hole and Ella Evelyn Hole (*née* Thomas). *Educ:* Public Central Sch., Plymouth; Lincoln Theological College. Nat. service, RAF, 1952–54. Asst Librarian, Codrington Liby, Oxford, 1954–56. Ordained deacon, 1960, priest, 1961; Asst Curate, St Mary Magdalen, Knighton, Leicester, 1960–62; Domestic Chaplain to Archbishop of Cape Town, 1962–64; Asst Curate, St Nicholas, Kenilworth, 1964–67; Rector, St Mary the Virgin, Burton Latimer, 1967–73; Vicar, St James the Greater, Leicester, 1973–92; Chaplain to the Queen, 1985–92. Hon. Canon, Leicester Cathedral, 1983–92. Rural Dean, Christianity South, Leicester, 1983–92; Chm., House of Clergy, 1986–94; Vice-Pres., Diocesan Synod, 1986–94; Member: Bishop's Council, 1986–99; Assoc. of English Cathedrals, 1992–99; Cathedral Music Wkg Party, 1993–99. Chaplain to: Lord Mayor of Leicester, 1976–77, 1994–95, 1996–97; High Sheriffs of Leics, 1980–85, 1987–88, 1995–96, 1999–2000, 2001–02, 2007–08, 2013–14; Leicester High Sch., 1983–93; Haymarket Theatre, Leicester, 1980–83, 1993–95; Leicester Br., RAFA, 1978–92; Master of Merchant Taylors' Co., 1995–96; Leicester Guild of Freemen, 1996–99; Royal Soc. of St George, 2000–06; Mayor of Oadby and Wigston BC, 2005–06; Leics br., Royal Soc. of St George, 2006–10; Leics br., British Korean Veterans Assoc., 2006–. Commissary to Bishop of Wellington, NZ, 1998–2012. Priest Associate, Actors' Church Union, 1995– (Mem., 1980–95); Vice-Pres., English Clergy Assoc., 1993–. Chm. Leicester Diocesan Redundant Churches Uses Cttee, 1985–99. Dir and Trustee, Leicester Charity Orgn Soc., 2001–05 (Mem., 1983–2001); Trustee: Leicester Church Charities, 1983–; Leics Historic Churches Preservation Trust, 1989–2014; Bernard Fawcett Meml Trust, 1993–99; North Meml Homes, 1999–2012; President: Leicester Rotary Club, 1987–88; Friends, Ch of St Mary the Virgin, Burton Latimer, 2000–; Leics Probus Club, 2010–11; Leics Book Soc., 2011–12; Vice-President: Leics County Scout Council, 1992–99; Leics Guild of the Disabled, 1992–99; Leicester Cathedral Old Choristers' Assoc., 1999–; Chm., Friends, Ch of St James the Greater, Leicester, 2012–. Patron, Victoria County History of Leics Trust, 2008–; Mem., Victorian Soc., 1986–2011; Hon. Life Mem., Leics Br., BRCS, 1995; Mem., Bd of Mgt, Britain-Australia Soc., 2001–05 (Chm., Leics Br., 2000–08; Treas., 2008–11). Governor: Alderman Newton's Sch., Leicester, 1976–82; Leicester High Sch., 1992–2004; Alderman Newton Foundn, 1992–2007; Leicester GS, 1992–99 (Trustee, 1999–2006; Patron, 2006–); St John's C of E Sch., Leicester, 1997–2000. Mem. (Ind.), Burton Latimer UDC, 1971–73. Sen. Fellow, De Montfort Univ., 1998–; Mem. of Ct, Univ. of Leicester, 2011–. Freeman, City of London, 2003; Liveryman, Framework Knitters' Co., 2003– (Chaplain to Master, 2004–).

Hon. DLitt De Montfort, 1999; Hon. LLD Leicester, 2005. Paul Harris Award, Rotary Club, 2012; High Sheriff of Leics's Award, 2014. *Publications:* (contrib.) Century to Millennium: St James the Greater, Leicester 1899–1999, compiled by Dr A. McWhirr, 1999. *Recreations:* bridge, music, walking, reading biographies and Victorian history. *Address:* 25 Southernhay Close, Leicester LE2 3TW. *T:* and *Fax:* (0116) 270 9988, (mobile) 07799 892615. *E:* dnhole@btinternet.com.

HOLE, Max; *see* Hole, C. C. M.

HOLES, Prof. Clive Douglas, FBA 2002; Khalid Bin Abdullah Al-Saud Professor for the Study of the Contemporary Arab World, University of Oxford, 1997–2014; Fellow, Magdalen College, Oxford, 1997–2014, now Emeritus; *b* 29 Sept. 1948; *s* of Douglas John Holes and Kathryn Mary (*née* Grafton); *m* 1st, 1980, Gillian Diane Pountain (marr. diss.); two *s*; 2nd, 2004, Deidre Margaret Thorn. *Educ:* High Arcal Grammar Sch., Dudley, Worcs; Trinity Hall, Cambridge (BA Hons 1969; MA 1973); Univ. of Birmingham (MA 1972); Wolfson Coll., Cambridge (PhD 1981). UNA volunteer teacher, Bahrain, 1969–71; British Council Officer, Kuwait, Algeria, Iraq, Thailand and London, 1971–76 and 1979–83; Lectr in Arabic and Applied Linguistics, Univ. of Salford, 1983–85; Dir, Lang. Centre, Sultan Qaboos Univ., Oman, 1985–87; University of Cambridge: Lectr in Islamic Studies, 1987–96; Reader in Arabic, 1996; Fellow, Trinity Hall, 1989–96. Fellow: British Soc. for Middle Eastern Studies, 1989; Anglo-Oman Soc., 1990; Bahrain-British Soc., 1991. Mem., Philological Soc., 1984–. *Publications:* Colloquial Arabic of the Gulf and Saudi Arabia, 1984, 2nd edn 2010; Language Variation and Change in a Modernising Arab State, 1987; Gulf Arabic, 1990; Breakthrough Arabic, 1992; (ed) Perspectives on Arabic Linguistics, Vol. 5, 1993; Modern Arabic: structures, functions and varieties, 1995, 2nd edn 2004; Dialect, Culture and Society in Eastern Arabia, Vol. I, 2001, Vol. II, 2005, Vol. III, 2014; Poetry and Politics in Contemporary Bedouin Society, 2009; The Nabati Poetry of the United Arab Emirates, 2011; articles in professional jls concerned with Arabic language, culture, society and literature. *Recreations:* keeping fit, watching Wolverhampton Wanderers FC, visiting the Middle East. *Address:* The Nook, Church Lane, Harwell, Didcot, Oxon OX11 0EZ.

HOLFORD-STREVENS, Bonnie Jean; *see* Blackburn, B. J.

HOLGATE, Andrew James Headley; Literary Editor, Sunday Times, since 2008 (Deputy Literary Editor, 1999–2008); *b* Reigate, 31 Dec. 1958; *s* of Headley Holgate and Evelyn Holgate (*née* Owen); *m* 1986, Gün Akyuz; one *s* one *d*. *Educ:* Christ's Hosp.; Durham Univ. (BA Hons Hist. 1981). Bookseller, then Mktg Manager, Hatchard's, 1983–88; Mktg Officer, Chatto & Windus, 1988–89; Mktg Manager, Hatchard's, 1989–90; Ed., W Mag., WH Smith, 1990–99. *Publications:* (ed jtly) The Cost of Letters, 1998; (ed jtly) The Test of Time, 1999. *Recreations:* reading, art, theatre, walking, gardening, sport. *Address:* c/o News UK, 1 London Bridge Street, SE1 9GF.

HOLGATE, Hon. Sir David (John), Kt 2014; **Hon. Mr Justice Holgate;** a Judge of the High Court, Queen's Bench Division, since 2014; *b* 3 Aug. 1956; *s* of late John Charles Holgate and of Catherine Philbin Holgate (*née* Rooney); civil partnership 2006, Alexander Nicholas Constantine. *Educ:* Davenant Foundation Grammar Sch., Loughton; Exeter Coll., Oxford (BA Hons 1977). Called to the Bar, Middle Temple, 1978, Bencher, 2004; admitted to Hong Kong Bar, 2001; QC 1997; Recorder, 2002–14; Dep. High Court Judge, 2008–14. Mem., Supplementary Panel, Jun. Counsel to the Crown (Common Law), 1986–97; Standing Jun. Counsel to the Inland Revenue in rating and valuation matters, 1990–97. *Recreations:* music, particularly opera, travel, reading. *Address:* Royal Courts of Justice, Strand, WC2A 2LL. *Club:* Travellers.

HOLGATE, Nicholas Ian; Town Clerk, Royal Borough of Kensington and Chelsea, since 2011; *b* 26 March 1962; *s* of late John Holgate and of Josephine Holgate (*née* Neve); *m* 2005, Natalie Cronin. *Educ:* Hall Grove Sch., Bagshot; Charterhouse; Trinity Coll., Cambridge (BA 1984). ACMA. HM Treasury, 1984–2004: Private Secretary: to Chief Sec. to the Treasury, 1991–92; to Sec. of State for Nat. Heritage, 1992–93; Govt Res. Fellow, 1993–94; Team Leader: Strategy, Finance and Purchasing, 1995–98; Educn and Trng, 1998–2001; Dir, Welfare Reform, Budget and Public Finances Directorate, 2001–04; Chief Operating Officer, then Dir Gen., Corporate Strategy and Services, DCMS, 2004–08; Exec. Dir, Finance, Inf. Systems and Property, Royal Bor. of Kensington and Chelsea, 2008–11. *Recreations:* food, film, games. *Address:* Royal Borough of Kensington and Chelsea, Town Hall, Hornton Street, W8 7NX.

HOLGATE, Prof. Stephen Townley, CBE 2011; MD, DSc; FRCP, FRCPE, FRCPath, FMedSci, FIBMS, FRSB; Medical Research Council Clinical Professor of Immunopharmacology, University of Southampton, and Hon. Consultant Physician, School of Medicine, Southampton University Hospital Trust (formerly Southampton General Hospital), since 1987; *b* 2 May 1947; *s* of William Townley Holgate and Margaret Helen (*née* Lancaster); *m* 1972, Elizabeth Karen Malkinson; three *s* one *d*. *Educ:* London Univ. (BSc 1968; MB BS 1971; MD 1979); DSc Soton 1991. FRCP 1984; FRCPE 1995; FRCPath 1999; CBiol, FRSB (FIBiol 1999); FIBMS 2009. House Physician and Surgeon, Charing Cross Hosp., 1971–72; Sen. Hse Physician, Nat. Hosp. for Nervous Diseases and Brompton Hosp., 1972–74; Registrar in Medicine, Salisbury and Southampton Gen. Hosps, 1974–76; Lectr in Medicine, 1976–80, Sen. Lectr, 1980–86, Reader and Prof. (personal Chair), 1986–87, Univ. of Southampton. MRC/Wellcome Trust Res. Fellow, Harvard Univ., 1978–80. Mem., Royal Commn on Envmtl Pollution, 2002–08; Chairman: Population and Systems Medicine Bd, MRC, 2007–12; MRC Translation Res. Gp, 2014–; REF 2014 Main Panel A. Member: Med. Scis Cttee, Sci. Europe, 2012–; Horizon 2020 Scientific Panel for Health, EC, 2014–. MAE. Founder FMedSci, 1998. FRSA 1997. Hon. CSci 2009. Hon. MD: Ferrara, Italy, 1997; Jagiellonian, Poland, 1999; Naples Federico II, 2012; Hon. DSc Exeter, 2015. Rhône Poulenc Rorer World Health Award, 1995; (jtly) King Faisal Internat. Prize in Medicine, 1999; Paul Ehrlich Award, Eur. Acad. of Allergy, Asthma and Clin. Immunol., 2008; Sci. Achievement Award, Amer. Thoracic Soc., 2012; William Frankland Award, BSACI, 2012. *Publications:* (ed jtly) Asthma and Rhinitis: implications for diagnosis and treatment, 1995, 2nd edn 2000; (jtly) Health Effects of Air Pollutants, 1999; (ed jtly) Allergy, 1999, 4th edn 2012; Difficult Asthma, 1999; (ed jtly) Middleton's Allergy: principles and practice, 2 vols, 6th edn 2004 to 8th edn 2014; 1010 peer-reviewed articles. *Recreations:* gardening, walking, theatre. *Address:* Clinical and Experimental Sciences, Level F South Pathology and Laboratory Block, Southampton General Hospital, Southampton SO16 6YD.

HOLLAMBY, David James; HM Diplomatic Service, retired; Governor and Commander-in-Chief, St Helena and Dependencies, 1999–2004; *b* 19 May 1945; *s* of Reginald William Hollamby and Eva May Hollamby (*née* Ponman); *m* 1971, Maria Helena Guzmán; two step *s*. *Educ:* Albury Manor Sch., Surrey. Joined Foreign Office, 1964: Beirut, 1967–69; Latin American Floater, 1970–72; Third Sec. and Vice Consul, Asunción, 1972–75; Second Sec., FCO, 1975–78; Vice Consul (Commercial), NY, 1978–82; Consul (Commercial), Dallas, 1982–86; First Secretary: FCO, 1986–90; Rome, 1990–94; Asst Hd, Western Eur. Dept, FCO, 1994–96; Dep. Hd, W Indian and Atlantic Dept, FCO, 1996–98; Dep. Hd, Overseas Territories Dept, FCO, 1998–99. Volunteer Co-ordinator, Volunteer Centre, Westminster, 2006–09. *Recreations:* travel, reading, music, golf, ski-ing. *Address:* 42 Oakbark House, High Street, Brentford Lock TW8 8LF.

HOLLAND, Hon. Sir Alan (Douglas), Kt 1995; Judge, High Court (formerly Supreme Court) of New Zealand, 1978–94, retired; *b* 20 June 1929; *s* of Clarence Cyril Holland and Marjorie Evelyn Holland; *m* 1961, Felicity Ann Ower; one *s*. *Educ:* Waitaki Boys' High Sch.; Canterbury Coll., Univ. of New Zealand (LLB). Part-time Lectr in Law and Commerce Faculties of Canterbury Univ., 1953–63; Partner, Wynn Williams & Co., Solicitors, Christchurch, 1956–78. Pres., Canterbury Dist Law Soc., 1973 (Mem. Council, 1963–73); Mem. Council and associated cttees, NZ Law Soc., 1970–74. *Recreations:* general. *Address:* Villa 18, 60 Browns Road, Merivale, Christchurch 8014, New Zealand. *T:* (3) 3557102. *Club:* Christchurch.

HOLLAND, Rt Rev. Alfred Charles; Bishop of Newcastle, NSW, 1978–92; *b* 23 Feb. 1927; *s* of Alfred Charles Holland and Maud Allison; *m* 1954, Joyce Marion Embling; three *s* one *d*. *Educ:* Raine's Sch., London; Univ. of Durham (BA 1950; DipTh 1952). RNVR, 1945–47; Univ. of Durham, 1948–52; Assistant Priest, West Hackney, London, 1952–54; Rector of Scarborough, WA, 1955–70; Asst Bishop, Dio. Perth, WA, 1970–77. Chaplain, St George's Coll., Jerusalem, 1993. Life Member: Stirling Rugby Football Club, 1969; Durham Univ. Society, 1984. *Publications:* Luke Through Lent, 1980; (ed) The Diocese Together, 1987; Eyes' Delight, 2001. *Recreations:* reading, painting. *Address:* 52 Windsor Gardens, 244–264 Mowbray Road, Chatswood, NSW 2067, Australia. *Club:* Australian (Sydney).

See also Rt Rev. J. C. Holland.

HOLLAND, Sir Anthony; *see* Holland, Sir J. A.

HOLLAND, Hon. Sir Christopher (John), Kt 1992; a Judge of the High Court of Justice, Queen's Bench Division, 1992–2007; a Judge of the Employment Appeal Tribunal, 1994–2007; *b* 1 June 1937; *er s* of late Frank and Winifred Mary Holland; *m* 1967, Jill Iona Holland; one *s* one *d*. *Educ:* Leeds Grammar Sch.; Emmanuel Coll., Cambridge (MA, LLB). National Service (acting Lance-Corp.), 3rd Royal Tank Regt, 1956–58. Called to the Bar, Inner Temple, 1963, Bencher, 1985; commenced practice on North Eastern Circuit (Presiding Judge, 1993–97); QC 1978; a Recorder, 1992. Mem., Criminal Injuries Compensation Bd, 1992. Mem., Oxford Univ. Appeal Court, 2009–. Vice Chm., Cttee of Inquiry into Outbreak of Legionnaires' Disease at Stafford, 1985; Chm., Azelle Rodney Inquiry, 2010–13. Chm., Lower Washburn Parish Council, 1975–91. *Address:* c/o Royal Courts of Justice, Strand, WC2A 2LL.

HOLLAND, David Moore; QC 2011; *b* Belfast, 22 Nov. 1961; *s* of John Holland and Olive Holland; two *s* one *d*; *m* 2013, Sarah Morley. *Educ:* Campbell Coll., Belfast; Pembroke Coll., Cambridge (BA Hons Law 1984; MA); Univ. of Toronto (LLM; Commonwealth Scholar). Called to the Bar, Inner Temple, 1986; in practice as a barrister, specialising in property law and costs, 1988–; Dep. Adjudicator to HM Land Registry, 2009–13; Judge of First-tier Tribunal (Property Chamber) (pt-time), 2013–. *Recreations:* watching cricket and football, food and wine, ferrying children around. *Address:* Landmark Chambers, 180 Fleet Street, EC4A 2HG. *E:* clerks@landmarkchambers.co.uk. *Clubs:* MCC, Century; Lancashire County Cricket, Surrey County Cricket, Arsenal Football, Spirochaetes Hockey.

HOLLAND, Rt Rev. Edward; an Hon. Assistant Bishop, Diocese of London, and Hon. Assistant Bishop, Diocese in Europe, since 2002; *b* 28 June 1936; *s* of Reginald Dick Holland and Olive Holland (*née* Yeoman). *Educ:* New College School; Dauntsey's School; King's College London (AKC). National Service, Worcestershire Regt, 1955–57; worked for Importers, 1957–61; KCL, 1961–65. Deacon 1965, priest 1966, Rochester; Curate, Holy Trinity, Dartford, 1965–69; Curate, John Keble, Mill Hill, 1969–72; Precentor, Gibraltar Cathedral, and Missioner for Seamen, 1972–74; Chaplain at Naples, Italy, 1974–79; Vicar of S Mark's, Bromley, 1979–86; Suffragan Bishop of Gibraltar in Europe, 1986–95; Area Bishop of Colchester, 1995–2001. Mem., Churches Conservation Trust, 1998–2001; Chm., Friends of Anglican Centre in Rome, 2002–15. *Recreations:* travel, being entertained and entertaining. *Address:* 37 Parfrey Street, Hammersmith, W6 9EW. *T:* (020) 8746 3636.

HOLLAND, Frank Robert Dacre; Chairman, C. E. Heath PLC, 1973–84, non-executive Director, 1984–86; *b* 24 March 1924; *s* of Ernest Albert Holland and Kathleen Annie (*née* Page); *m* 1st, 1948, Margaret Lindsay Aird (*d* 2004); one *d*; 2nd, 2005, Charmian Julie Marchal Watford. *Educ:* Whitgift Sch., Croydon. Joined C. E. Heath & Co. Ltd, 1941; entered Army, 1942; Sandhurst, 1943; commissioned 4th Queen's Own Hussars, 1944; served, Italy, 1944–45, Austria and Germany, 1945–47; returned to C. E. Heath & Co. Ltd, 1947; Joint Managing Director, North American Operation, 1965; Director, C. E. Heath & Co. Ltd, 1965, Dep. Chm., 1969. Director: British Aviation Insce Co., 1974–84; Trade Indemnity plc, 1974–86; Greyhound Corp., USA, 1974–87. Liveryman, Insurers' Co., 1980– (Master, 1985–86). *Recreations:* travel, gardening. *Address:* 2001/184 Forbes Street, Darlinghurst, NSW 2010, Australia. *Club:* Cavalry and Guards.

HOLLAND, Sir Geoffrey, KCB 1989 (CB 1984); President, Marine Biological Association of the United Kingdom, 2008–14; *b* 9 May 1938; *s* of late Frank Holland, CBE and of Elsie Freda Holland; *m* 1964, Carol Ann Challen. *Educ:* Merchant Taylors' Sch., Northwood; St John's Coll., Oxford (BA 1st cl. Hons; MA; Hon. Fellow, 1991). 2nd Lieut, RTR, 1956–58. Entered Min. of Labour, 1961, Asst Private Sec., 1964–65; Principal Private Sec. to Sec. of State for Employment, 1971–72; Manpower Services Commission: Asst Sec., Hd of Planning, 1973; Dir of Special Progs, 1977; Dep. Sec., 1981; Dir, 1981; Second Perm. Sec., 1986; Perm. Sec., Dept of Employment, subseq. Employment Dept Gp, 1988–93; Perm. Sec., DFE, 1993–94; Vice-Chancellor, Exeter Univ., 1994–2002. Director: Shell UK, 1994–98; Exeter Investment Gp plc, subseq. iimia plc, 2002–06. Mem., Nat. Cttee of Inquiry into Higher Educn, 1996–97. Chairman: Govt's Sustainable Develt Educn Panel, 1998–2003; Learning and Skills Develt Agency, 2003–06; Quality Improvement Agency for Lifelong Learning, 2006–08. Mem. Bd, MLA, 2004–09 (Chm., SW MLA, 2002–08). Liveryman, Merchant Taylors' Co., 1967– (Master, 2000–01). CCMI (CBIM 1987). Fellow, Eton Coll., 1994–2009; Hon. Fellow, Polytechnic of Wales, 1986. Hon. FIPD (Hon. FITD 1986; Pres., IPD, 1998–2000); Hon. FCGI 1994. Hon. LLD: Sheffield, 1994; Exeter, 2003. *Publications:* Young People and Work, 1977; many articles on manpower, educn, training, management etc in professional jls. *Recreations:* journeying, opera, exercising the dog. *Club:* East India, Devonshire, Sports and Public Schools.

HOLLAND, James; historian, writer and broadcaster; *b* Salisbury, 27 June 1970; *s* of Martin and Jans Holland; *m* 1995, Rachel Thwaites; one *s* one *d*. *Educ:* Chafyn Grove Prep. Sch., Salisbury; King's Sch., Bruton, Som; Univ. of Durham (BA Hons Hist. 1992). Publicity Manager, Penguin Books UK, 1997–2001. Contributions to television programmes: Victory in Europe, 2005; Battle of Britain: the real story, 2010; Dambusters: the race to smash the German dams, 2012; The Battle for Malta, 2013; Cold War, Hot Jets, 2013; Normandy '44: the battle beyond D-Day, 2014. Co-Chair, Co-Founder and Prog. Dir, Chalke Valley Hist. Fest., 2011–. Trustee, Barnes Wallis Meml Trust, 2012–. *Publications: non-fiction:* Fortress Malta: an island under siege, 2003; Together We Stand: North Africa - turning the tide in the West 1942–43, 2005; Heroes: the greatest generation and the Second World War, 2007; Italy's Sorrow: a year of war 1944–45, 2008; The Battle of Britain, 2010; Dam Busters: race to smash the dams 1943, 2012; The Authors' XI: a season of English cricket from Hackney to Hambledon, 2013; (ed) An Englishman at War: the wartime diaries of Stanley Christopherson, 2014; *fiction:* The Burning Blue, 2004; A Pair of Silver Wings, 2006; The Odin Mission, 2008; Darkest Hour, 2009; Blood of Honour, 2010; Hellfire, 2011; Duty Calls: Dunkirk, 2011; Duty Calls: Battle of Britain, 2012; Devil's Pact, 2013. *Recreations:* cricket, walking. *Address:* Maud's Cottage, Broad Chalke, Salisbury, Wilts SP5 5QH. *T:* (01722) 781111. *E:* james@jholland.co.uk. *Club:* Royal Air Force.

See also T. Holland.

HOLLAND, Sir (John) Anthony, Kt 2003; Chairman: Northern Ireland Parades Commission, 2000–05; Standards Board for England, 2001–08; Joint Insolvency Monitoring Unit, 2001–05; Complaints Commissioner, Financial Services Authority, 2004–14; *b* 9 Nov. 1938; *s* of John and Dorothy Rita Holland; *m* 1963, Kathleen Margaret Anderson; three *s*. *Educ:* Ratcliffe Coll., Leics; Nottingham Univ. (LLB 1959); Financial Planning Cert., Chartered Insce Inst., 1997; MPhil UWE 1998. Admitted Solicitor of Supreme Court, 1962; notary public. Joined Foot & Bowden, 1964, Partner, 1964–90, Sen. Partner, 1990–97; Principal Ombudsman, PIA, 1997–2000. Chairman: Social Security Appeals Tribunal, 1974–97; South Western Regl Adv. Council, BBC, 1984–87; a Chm., SFA, 1993–2001; Access Dispute (formerly Access Dispute Resolution) Cttee, 2002–10; Dep. Chm., Regulatory Decisions Cttee, 2002–04; Mem., Investigatory Powers Tribunal, 2009–14; Member: Council, Law Soc., 1976–95 (Vice-Pres., 1989–90; Pres., 1990–91; Chm., Young Solicitors Gp, 1972); Marre Cttee on future of the Legal Profession, 1986–88; Council, Justice, 1991–2003 (Chm., Exec. Bd, 1996–99); Mem. Council, Howard League for Penal Reform, 1992–2002; Hon. Mem., SPTL, 1992. Mem. Bd, Pension Protection Fund, 2007–13; Lay Mem., Speaker's Cttee for Ind. Parly Standards Authy, 2011–14. President: Plymouth Law Soc., 1986–87; Cornwall Law Soc., 1988–89. Mem., Plymouth Diocesan Finance Cttee, 1986–94. Chm., Plymouth Chamber of Commerce and Industry, 1994–96. Governor: Plymouth Coll., 1976–93; Coll. of Law, 1991–97. Hon. Mem., Canadian Bar Assoc., 1990. Liveryman, Tallow Chandlers' Co. Hon. LLD Plymouth. *Publications:* (jtly) Principles of Registered Land Conveyancing, 1966; (jtly) Landlord and Tenant, 1968; (Jt Adv. Ed.) Mines and Quarries Section, Butterworth's Encyclopædia of Forms and Precedents, 1989; (Gen. Ed.) Cordery on Solicitors, 9th edn, 1995–2004. *Recreations:* opera, literature, the cinema. *Address:* 262 Lauderdale Tower, Barbican, EC2Y 8BY. *T:* (020) 7638 5044. *Clubs:* Athenæum; Royal Western Yacht (Plymouth).

HOLLAND, John Lewis; Managing Director, Herts & Essex Newspapers, 1990–2000; *b* 23 May 1937; *s* of George James Holland and Esther Holland; *m* 1958, Maureen Ann Adams; one *s* one *d*. *Educ:* Nottingham Technical Grammar Sch. Trainee Reporter, Nottingham Evening News, subseq. Jun. Reporter, Mansfield Br. Office, 1953–55; Sports Reporter, Mansfield Reporter Co., 1955–56; Sports Reporter, subseq. Sports Editor, Aldershot News Group, 1956–59; News Editor, West Bridgford & Clifton Standard, Nottingham, 1959–61; Chief Sports Sub Editor, Bristol Evening Post, and Editor, Sports Green 'Un (sports edn), 1961–64; Editor, West Bridgford & Clifton Standard, Nottingham, and Partner, Botting & Turner Sports Agency, Nottingham, 1964–66; Birmingham Evening Mail: Dep. Sports Editor, 1966–71; Editor, Special Projects Unit (Colour Prodn Dept), 1971–75; Editor, 1975–79, and Gen. Man., 1979–81, Sandwell Evening Mail; Marketing/Promotions Gen. Man., Birmingham Post & Mail, 1981–82; Editor, The Birmingham Post, 1982–86. Director: Birmingham Post & Mail Circulation and Promotions, 1986–88; Birmingham Post & Mail Publications and Promotions, 1988–90; Birmingham Convention and Visitor Bureau, 1982–90. President: Chartered Inst. of Marketing, 1989–90; Chiltern Newspaper Proprietors Assoc., 1995–99 (Vice-Pres., 1994–95). Member: Hertford Business Club, 1994–2000; Soc. of Cambs Area Golf Captains, 1999–2007. *Recreations:* journalism, golf, keeping horses, gardening, keep fit. *Address:* Carob Lodge, Marathounda, PO Box 60151, Paphos 8101, Cyprus. *Clubs:* Press (Birmingham); Heydon Grange Golf (Captain, 1998–99) (Royston); Tsada Golf (Captain, 2003–04), Secret Valley Golf, Elea Golf (Cyprus).

HOLLAND, Rt Rev. Dr Jonathan Charles; an Assistant Bishop, Diocese of Brisbane, Queensland, since 2006; *b* Perth, 26 Sept. 1956; *s* of Rt Rev. Alfred Charles Holland, *qv*; *m* 1980, Kerry Anne Minchin; two *s* one *d*. *Educ:* Univ. of Western Australia (BA Hons 1978); Queen's Coll., Oxford (BA Hons 1982); Univ. of Queensland (MA 1999; PhD 2007). Ordained deacon, 1982, priest, 1983; Rector: Church of the Ascension, Midland, 1989–93; Christ Church, St Lucia, Qld, 1993–2006. Archbishop's Examining Chaplain, 1995–2006; Canon, St John's Cathedral, 2004–06. *Publications:* Eyes Delight: six paintings and their theological meaning, 1999; Jesus Unbound: the story of Jesus of Nazareth, 2008; Anglicans, Trams and Paw Paws: the story of the Diocese of Brisbane 1945–1980, 2013. *Recreations:* reading, poetry, gardening. *Address:* 63 Cavendish Street, Nundah, Qld 4012, Australia. *T:* (7) 38352213, *Fax:* (7) 32569436. *E:* jholland@anglicanchurchsq.org.au. *Club:* Australian (Sydney).

HOLLAND, Julian Miles, (Jools), OBE 2003; DL; pianist and broadcaster; *b* 24 Jan. 1958; *s* of Derek Holland and June Rose Holland (*née* Lane); one *s* one *d* by Mary Leahy; *m* 2005, Christabel Durham; one *d*. *Educ:* Invicta Sherington Sch.; Shooters Hill Sch. Keyboard player with Squeeze, 1974–80; band leader, Rhythm & Blues Orch., 1993–; regular tours in UK. Architect: Helicon Mountain, Greenwich; gatehouse, Witton Castle. *Television:* presenter: The Tube, 1981–86; Juke Box Jury, 1989; Sunday Night, 1990; The Happening, 1990; Later with Jools Holland, 1993–; presenter and writer, Jools' History of the Piano, 2002; actor and writer, The Groovy Fellers, 1988; writer and producer: Walking to New Orleans, 1985; Mr Roadrunner, 1991; Beat Route, 1998; Jools Meets the Saint, 1999; *radio:* presenter, The Jools Holland Show; *films:* musical director, Spiceworld the Movie, 1997; writer of film score, Milk, 1999. *Solo albums:* A World Of His Own, 1990; Full Complement, 1991; The A-Z Geographer's Guide To The Piano, 1993; Solo Piano, 1995; Sex & Jazz & Rock & Roll, 1996; Lift The Lid, 1997; Sunset Over London, 1999; Hop The Wag, 2000; Small World Big Band, 2001; More Friends, 2002; Friends 3, 2003; Swinging The Blues, Dancing The Ska, 2005; Moving Out To The Country, 2006; The Informer, 2008; Rockinghorse, 2010; The Golden Age of Song, 2012; jt album, Tom Jones and Jools Holland, 2004. DL Kent, 2006. *Publications:* Beat Route, 1998; (with Dora Loewenstein) Rolling Stones: a life on the road, 1998; Barefaced Lies & Boogie-Woogie Boasts: the autobiography, 2007. *Address:* One Fifteen, 1 Globe House, Middle Lane Mews, N8 8PN.

HOLLAND, Katharine Jane; QC 2010. *Educ:* Hertford Coll., Oxford (BCL; MA). FCIA 2010; DipICArb 2010. Called to the Bar, Middle Temple, 1989. *Address:* Landmark Chambers, 180 Fleet Street, EC4A 2HG. *T:* (020) 7430 1221, *Fax:* (020) 7421 6060.

HOLLAND, Kevin John William C.; *see* Crossley-Holland.

HOLLAND, Norman James Abbott; Group Standards Manager, Philips UK, 1983–90; President, British National Electrotechnical Committee, 1993–99; *b* 16 Dec. 1927; *s* of James George Holland and May Stuart Holland; *m* 1951, Barbara Florence Byatt; one *s* one *d*. *Educ:* Sir Walter St John's Grammar Sch.; Regent Street Polytechnic. UK Delegate: IEC Council, 1987–92 (Delegn Leader, 1993–99; Mem. Bd, 1998–99); CENELEC Gen. Assembly, 1987–92 (Delegn Leader, 1993–99); Chm., Electrotechnical Sector Bd, 1993–99, Mem., Standards Bd, 1993–99, BSI. Member: IEC Finance Cttee, 1985–91; Engrg Council, 1985–91; Bd, Electronic Engrg Assoc., 1985–92 (Chm., Standards Policy Gp); NACCB, 1987–92. *Recreation:* golf. *Address:* 12 Pine Road, Chandler's Ford, Hants SO53 1LP.

HOLLAND, Prof. Peter William Harold, PhD, DSc; FRS 2003; Linacre Professor of Zoology, since 2002, and Head, Department of Zoology, since 2011, University of Oxford; Fellow, Merton College, Oxford, since 2002; *b* 17 Aug. 1963; *s* of late William Harold Bolton and of Christine (*née* Bartrop) and step *s* of Franklin Holland; *m* 1996, Amanda Susan Horsfall; two *s*. *Educ:* Marple Hall Sch.; Queen's Coll., Oxford (MA); NIMR, London (PhD 1987); DSc Reading 2002. University of Oxford: Demonstrator, Dept of Zool., 1987–91; Browne Res. Fellow, Queen's Coll., 1988–91; Royal Soc. Univ. Res. Fellow, 1991–94; Prof. of Zool., Univ. of Reading, 1994–2002. Member: Cttee, British Soc. Develtl Biol., 1990–95; Genes Develtl Biol. Cttee, BBSRC, 1997–99; Council, Marine Biol. Assoc., 1998–2001, 2003– (Gov., 2003–); Funding Panel, NSF, 2002–03; Comparative Genomics Wkg Gp, NIH, 2004–06; Individual Merit Promotion Panel, BBSRC, 2004–10. Hon. Res. Fellow, Natural History Mus., 2005–. FLS 2002; FMBA 2014. Scientific Medal, Zool Soc. of London, 1996; De Snoo van 't Hoogerhuijs Medal, 1999; Genetics Soc. Medal, 2004; Blaise Pascal Medal, European Acad. of Scis, 2005; Kowalevsky Medal, St Petersburg Soc. of Naturalists, 2006; Linnean Medal for Zoology, Linnean Soc., 2012. *Publications:* (ed with C. Stern) Essential Developmental Biology, 1993; (ed jtly) The Evolution of Developmental Mechanisms, 1994; Swifter than the Arrow: Wilfred Bartrop, football and war, 2009; The Animal Kingdom, 2011; res. papers in scientific jls. *Recreations:* the natural world, Lepidoptera, table tennis, sporting history, fishing. *Address:* Merton College, Oxford OX1 4JD.

HOLLAND, Richard; District Judge (Magistrates' Courts) (formerly Stipendiary Magistrate), Leicestershire, 1999–2011; *b* 23 Jan. 1951; *s* of late Clifford Holland and Mary Holland (*née* Gledhill, later Smithies); *m* 2001, Ann, *d* of Charles and Mavis Mortimer, Wakefield. *Educ:* Colne Valley High Sch., W Yorks; Queen Mary Coll., Univ. of London (BA Hons 1971). Admitted Solicitor 1974. Articled Clerk, Magistrates' Courts Service, WR of Yorks, 1972–74; Sen. Court Clerk, 1974–75, Dep. Justices' Clerk, 1975–79, Oldham; Justices' Clerk, Rochdale, 1979–89; Justices' Clerk, and Clerk to the Magistrates' Courts Cttee, Wakefield Metropolitan Dist, 1990–97; Justices' Clerk and Chief Exec., Leeds City, 1997–99. *Recreations:* birdwatching, canal boating, the sport of Kings, feigning indolence.

HOLLAND, Stuart (Kingsley); political economist; Chief Executive, Alter-Europe, 1998–2003; Director, Associate Research in Economy and Society Ltd, 1993–98; *b* 25 March 1940; *y s* of late Frederick Holland and May Holland, London; *m* 1976, Jenny Lennard; two *c*. *Educ:* state primary schs; Christ's Hosp.; Univ. of Missouri (Exchange Scholar); Balliol Coll., Oxford (Domus Scholar; 1st Cl. Hons Mod. History); St Antony's Coll., Oxford (Sen. Scholar; DPhil Econs). Econ. Asst, Cabinet Office, 1966–67; Personal Asst to Prime Minister, 1967–68; Res. Fellow, Centre for Contemp. European Studies, Univ. of Sussex, 1968–71, Assoc. Fellow and Lectr, 1971–79. Vis. Scholar, Brookings Instn, Washington, DC, 1970. Adviser to Commons Expenditure Cttee, 1971–72; Special Adviser to Minister of Overseas Develt, 1974–75. MP (Lab) Vauxhall, 1979–89; Opposition frontbench spokesman on overseas develt and co-operation, 1983–87, on treasury and economic affairs, 1987–89; Prof. of Econs, Eur. Univ. Inst., Florence, 1989–93. Res. Specialist, RIIA, 1972–74; Associate, Inst. of Develt Studies, 1974–89 (Gov., 1983–91). Consultant: Econ. and Social Affairs Cttee, Council of Europe, 1973; Open Univ., 1973. Rapporteur, Trades Union Adv. Cttee, OECD, 1977. Chm., Public Enterprise Gp, 1973–75. European Community Commission: Mem., Expert Cttee on Inflation, 1975–76; Consultant to Directorate Gen. XVI, 1989; Dir, Proj. on Econ. and Social Cohesion, 1991–93; Adviser: to Merger Task Force, DG IV, 1991–93; to Region of Tuscany, 1992–96. Member: Council, Inst. for Workers' Control, 1974–; UN Univ. Working Party on Socio-Cultural Factors in Develt, Tokyo, 1977. Vis. Prof., Faculty of Econs, Univ. of Coimbra, 2003–; Sen. Scholar, Inst. for Social and Eur. Studies, Kőszeg, Hungary, 2014–. Lubbock Lectr, Oxford Univ., 1975; Tom Mann Meml Lectr, Australia, 1977. Mem., Labour Party, 1962–; Mem. sub-cttees (inc. Finance and Econ. Policy, Indust. Policy, EEC, Economic Planning, Defence, Development Cooperation, Public Sector), Nat. Exec. Cttee, Labour Party, 1972–89; Executive Member: Labour Coordinating Cttee, 1978–81; European Nuclear Disarmament Campaign, 1980–83; Mem., Economic Cttee, Socialist International, 1984–. Hon. MRTPI 1980. Dr *hc* Roskilde Univ., Denmark, 1992. *Publications:* (jtly) Sovereignty and Multinational Corporations, 1971; (ed) The State as Entrepreneur, 1972; Strategy for Socialism, 1975; The Socialist Challenge, 1975; The Regional Problem, 1976; Capital versus the Regions, 1976; (ed) Beyond Capitalist Planning, 1978; Uncommon Market, 1980; (ed) Out of Crisis, 1983; (with Donald Anderson) Kissinger's Kingdom, 1984; (with James Firebrace) Never Kneel Down, 1984; The Market Economy, 1987; The Global Economy, 1987; The European Imperative: economic and social cohesion in the 1990s, 1993; Towards a New Bretton Woods: alternatives for the global economy, 1994; (with Ken Coates) Full Employment for Europe, 1995; Europe in Question: constitution, cohesion and enlargement, 2004; Europe in Question: and what to do about it, 2014; contrib. symposia; articles in specialist jls and national and internat. press. *Recreation:* singing in the bath. *E:* sholland@fe.uc.pt.

HOLLAND, Thomas; historian, translator and novelist; *b* Oxford, 5 Jan. 1968; *s* of Martin and Jans Holland; *m* 1993, Sadie Lowry; two *d*. *Educ:* Chafyn Grove Prep. Sch.; Canford Sch.; Queens' Coll., Cambridge (BA 1989). FEA 2008. Chm., Soc. of Authors, 2009–11. Presenter: Making History, BBC Radio 4, 2011–; Islam: the Untold Story, Channel 4, 2012. *Publications:* The Vampyre, 1995; Supping with Panthers, 1996; Deliver us from Evil, 1997; The Sleeper in the Sands, 1998; The Bonehunter, 2001; Rubicon, 2003; Persian Fire, 2005; Millennium, 2008; In the Shadow of the Sword, 2012; (trans.) Herodotus, The Histories, 2013; Dynasty: the rise and fall of the House of Caesar, 2015. *Recreations:* cricket (hitter of a six and bowler of the Prince of Udaipur), walking ancient roads, dinosaurs, wombats. *Address:* c/o Conville and Walsh, 2 Ganton Street, W1F 7QL.

See also J. Holland.

HOLLAND, Prof. Walter Werner, CBE 1992; MD; FRCP, FRCPE, FRCGP, FRCPath, FFPH; Professor of Public Health Medicine, 1991–94, now Emeritus, and Hon. Director, 1968–94, Social Medicine and Health Service Research Unit, United Medical and Dental Schools of Guy's and St Thomas' Hospitals (formerly St Thomas's Hospital Medical School); *b* 5 March 1929; *s* of Henry Holland and Hertha Zentner; *m* 1964, Fiona Margaret Auchinleck Love; three *s*. *Educ:* St Thomas's Hosp. Med. Sch., London (BSc Hons 1951; MB, BS Hons 1954; MD 1964). FFCM 1972; FRCP 1973; FRCGP 1982; FRCPE 1990; FRCPath 1992. House Officer, St Thomas' Hosp., 1954–56; MRC Clin. Res. Fellow, London Sch. of Hygiene, 1959–61; Lectr, Johns Hopkins Univ., Md, USA, 1961–62; St Thomas's Hospital Medical School, later United Medical and Dental Schools of Guy's and St Thomas' Hospitals: Sen. Lectr, Dept of Medicine, 1962–64; Reader and Chm., Dept of Clin. Epidemiol. and Social Medicine, 1965–68; Prof. of Clin. Epidemiol., 1968–91. Fogarty Scholar-in-Residence, NIH, Bethesda, Md, 1984–85; Sawyer Scholar-in-Residence, Case Western Reserve Med. Sch., Cleveland, Ohio, 1985. Vis. Prof., LSE, 1998–. Queen Elizabeth, Queen Mother Lectr, FPHM, 1995; Harben Lectr, 1995; Rock Carling Lectr, Nuffield Trust, 1997. President: Internat. Epidemiol Assoc., 1987–90; Faculty of Public Health (formerly Community) Medicine, RCP, 1989–92. Non-exec. Mem., Glos HA, 1992–96. FKC 1999. Life Mem., Soc. of Scholars, Johns Hopkins Univ., 1970; Hon. Mem., Amer. Epidemiol Soc., 1985. Hon. FFPHMI 1993; Hon. Fellow, UMDS, 1996. Dr *hc*: Univ. of Bordeaux, 1981; Free Univ. of Berlin, 1990. *Publications:* Data Handling in Epidemiology, 1970; Air Pollution and Respiratory Disease, 1972; Epidemiology and Health, 1977; Health Care and Epidemiology, 1978; Measurement of Levels of Health, 1979; Evaluation of Health Care, 1983; Chronic Obstructive Bronchopathies, 1983; Oxford Textbook of Public Health, 1984, 2nd edn 1991; (with Susie Stewart) Screening in Health Care, 1990; (ed jtly) Public Health Policies in the European Union, 1999; Foundations for Health Improvement, 2002; (with S. Stewart) Screening for Health Improvement: a good use of resources, 2005; Improving Health Services, 2013; pubns on health services res., epidemiol methods and on respiratory disease. *Recreations:* reading, walking. *Club:* Athenæum.

HOLLAND-HIBBERT, family name of **Viscount Knutsford**.

HOLLAND-KAYE, (William) John, FRICS; Chief Executive, Heathrow Airport Holdings Ltd, since 2014. *Educ:* Peterhouse, Cambridge (BA 1986; MA 1991); INSEAD, France (MBA). Man. Dir, Nat. Sales Div., Bass Brewers, 1999–2002; appts with Taylor Woodrow, incl. Ops Dir, Taylor Woodrow Develts and Commercial Dir, Taylor Woodrow Inc.,

2002–07; Divl Chm., Taylor Wimpey plc, 2007–09; Commercial Dir, BAA, 2009–12; Develt Dir, Heathrow, 2012–14. *Recreations:* cooking, books, swimming, hill walking. *Address:* Heathrow Airport Ltd, The Compass Centre, Nelson Road, Hounslow, Middx TW6 2GW.

HOLLAND-MARTIN, Robert George, (Robin); Director, Henderson (formerly Henderson Administration Group) plc, 1983–98; *b* 6 July 1939; *y s* of late Cyril Holland-Martin and Rosa, *d* of Sir Gerald Chadwyck-Healey, 2nd Bt, CBE; *m* 1976, Dominique, 2nd *d* of Maurice Fromaget; two *d. Educ:* Eton. Cazenove & Co., 1960–74 (partner, 1968–74); Finance Director, Paterson Products Ltd, 1976–86; Consultant: Newmarket Venture Capital plc (formerly Newmarket Co.), 1982–94; Investindustrial Gp of Cos, 1997–2013. Non-executive Director: Dorling Kindersley Hldgs plc, 1992–2000; Fine Art Soc. plc, 1995–; Service Point Solutions (formerly Grupo Picking Pack) SA (Spain), 1998–2006; Grapes Direct Ltd, 2000–06. Hon. Dep. Treasurer, Cons. and Unionist Party, 1979–82. Mem., Trustee Bd (formerly Council), Metropolitan Hospital-Sunday Fund, 1964–2002 (Chm., 1977–2002); Mem. Council, Homoeopathic Trust, 1970–90 (Vice Chm., 1975–90). Victoria & Albert Museum: Mem. Adv. Council, 1972–83; Mem. Cttee, Associates of V&A, 1976–85 (Chm., 1981–85); Dep. Chm., Trustees, 1983–85. Mem., Visiting Cttee for Royal Coll. of Art, 1982–93 (Chm., 1984–93). Trustee: Blackie Foundn Trust, 1971–96 (Chm., 1987–96; Pres., 1998–); King's Med. Res. Trust, 2000–; C&G of London Art Sch., 2001– (Chm., 2002–). Mem., Court of Assts, Fishmongers' Co., 1999– (Prime Warden, 2010–11). *Address:* 94 Old Church Street, SW3 6EP. *T:* (020) 7352 7871. *Clubs:* White's, Royal Automobile.

HOLLANDE, François Gérard Georges; President of France, since 2012; Leader, Socialist Party, since 2011; *b* Rouen, 12 Aug. 1954; *s* of Georges Hollande and Nicole Hollande (*née* Tribert); two *s* two *d* by Marie-Ségolène Royal; former partner, Valérie Trierweiler. *Educ:* Lycée Pasteur, Neuilly; Faculté de Droit, Paris (Licencié en Droit); Ecole des hautes études commerciales, Paris (Dip.); Inst. d'études politiques, Paris; Ecole Nat. d'Admin. Auditor, 1980–84, Clerk, 1984, Court of Auditors; Lectr, 1982–88, Prof. of Econs, 1988–91, Inst. d'études politiques. Special Advr to Pres. of France, 1981; Chief of Staff to Sec. of State, 1983–84. Member: Ussel CC, 1983–89; Limousin Regl Council, 1992 and 1998–2001 (Vice-Pres., 1998–2001); Tulle CC, 1995–2001 (Mayor, 2001–08); Mem. (Soc.) Corrèze, Nat. Assembly, 1988–93 and 1997–2012; MEP, 1999; Pres., Gen. Council of Corrèze, 2008–12. Joined Socialist Party, 1979, Nat. Sec., 1994–97, First Sec., 1997–2008; Vice Pres., Socialist Internat., 1999. *Publications:* (jtly) l'Heure des choix, 1991; Devoirs de vérité, 2006; Changer de destin, 2012. *Address:* Palais de l'Elysée, 75008 Paris, France.

HOLLANDER, Prof. Anthony Peter, PhD; Professor of Stem Cell Biology, and Head, Institute of Integrative Biology, University of Liverpool, since 2014; *b* London, 4 Feb. 1964; *s* of Otto Hollander and Miriam Hollander; *m* 1990, Catriona Lamont (marr. diss. 2013); two *s* one *d*; *m* 2015, Dr Anna Salerno. *Educ:* Christ's Coll. Finchley; Univ. of Bath (BSc 1987; 1st Cl. Hons Pharmacol.); Univ. of Bristol (PhD Pathol. 1990). Postdoctoral Scientist, McGill Univ., Montreal, 1990–93; Lectr, 1993–99, Reader, 1999–2000, Univ. of Sheffield; Prof. of Rheumatol. and Tissue Engrg, 2000–14, Hd, Sch. of Cellular and Molecular Medicine, 2009–14, Univ. of Bristol. CSO, Azellon Cell Therapeutics, 2009– (Dir, 2009–). Pres., Internat. Cartilage Repair Soc., 2012–13. *Publications:* over 100 articles in learned jls. *Recreations:* cooking, opera, theatre, reading, walking, ski-ing. *Address:* Institute of Integrative Biology, University of Liverpool, First Floor, Biosciences Building, Crown Street, Liverpool L69 7ZB. *T:* (0151) 795 4413. *E:* A.Hollander@liv.ac.uk.

HOLLANDER, Charles Simon; QC 1999; a Recorder, since 2000; a Deputy High Court Judge; *b* 1 Dec. 1955; *s* of Paul and Eileen Hollander; *m* 1986, Heather Pilley; two *s* two *d. Educ:* University College Sch.; King's Coll., Cambridge (BA 1977; MA 1981). Called to the Bar, Gray's Inn, 1978, Bencher, 2008; in practice at the Bar, 1978–. Mem., Bar Standards Bd, 2006– (Chm., Standards Cttee, 2006–). CEDR accredited mediator. *Publications:* Documentary Evidence, 1985, 10th edn 2009; Conflicts of Interest and Chinese Walls, 2000, 3rd edn 2008; (ed jtly) Phipson on Evidence, 15th edn 2000, 16th edn 2005. *Recreations:* tennis, food, wine. *Address:* Brick Court Chambers, 7/8 Essex Street, WC2R 3LD. *T:* (020) 7379 3550.

HOLLANDS, Maj.-Gen. Graham Spencer; *b* 14 Feb. 1942; *s* of Ernest Darrell Hollands and Gwendoline Isobel Hollands (*née* Matheson); *m* 1968, Lesley Clair Billam; one *s* one *d. Educ:* King Edward VI Sch., Bath; RMA Sandhurst; RMCS; Staff Coll., Camberley. Commissioned RA, 1963; served BAOR and UK; MoD, 1980–81; CO 25 Field Regt RA, 1981–84; CO 3rd Regt RHA, 1984–85; COS Artillery Div., HQ 1 (BR) Corps, 1985–86; Comdr, British Trng Teams, Nigeria, 1986–87; CRA 2nd Inf. Div., 1987–89; DCOS, HQ BAOR, 1989–92; Comdr Artillery, 1st British Corps, 1992–94. Chief Exec., W Kent Coll., 1994. *Recreations:* golf, ski-ing, country pursuits.

HOLLENDEN, 4th Baron *cr* 1912, of Leigh, Kent; **Ian Hampden Hope-Morley;** part-owner and Trustee, The Hampden Estate; *b* 23 Oct. 1946; *e s* of 3rd Baron Hollenden and Sonja (*née* Sundt); *S* father, 1999; *m* 1st, 1972, Beatrice (*née* d'Anchald) (marr. diss. 1985); one *s* one *d*; 2nd, 1988, Caroline (*née* Ash); two *s. Educ:* Maidwell Hall; Eton Coll. Shipbroker: Asmarine SA, Paris, 1969–72; Eggar Forrester, London, 1972–77; Mktg Mgr, British Shipbuilders, 1977–79; Shipbroker, Galbraith Wrightson, 1979–86; Proprietor, The Hampden Wine Company, Thame, 1988–98. *Recreations:* shooting, ski-ing. *Heir: s* Hon. Edward Hope-Morley, *b* 9 April 1981. *Address:* The Estate Office, Great Hampden, Great Missenden, Bucks HP16 9RE. *Club:* Brooks's.

HOLLENWEGER, Prof. Walter Jacob; Professor of Mission, University of Birmingham, 1971–89, now Emeritus; *b* 1 June 1927; *s* of Walter Otto and Anna Hollenweger-Spörri; *m* 1951, Erica Busslinger. *Educ:* Univs of Zürich and Basel. Dr theol Zürich 1966 (and degrees leading up to it). Stock Exchange, Zürich, and several banking appts, until 1948. Pastor, 1949–57; ordained, Swiss Reformed Church, 1961. Study Dir, Ev. Acad., Zürich, 1964–65; Research Asst, Univ. of Zürich, 1961–64; Exec. Sec., World Council of Churches, Geneva, 1965–71; regular guest prof. in Switzerland, Germany and USA. Hon. Fellow, Selly Oak Colls, Birmingham, 1996. Prize for Theol., Sexau, Germany, 1995; Lifetime Achievement Award, Soc. for Pentecostal Studies, USA, 1999. *Publications:* Handbuch der Pfingstbewegung, 10 vols, 1965/66; (ed) The Church for Others, 1967 (also German, Spanish and Portuguese edns); (ed) Die Pfingstkirchen, 1971; Kirche, Benzin und Bohnensuppe, 1971; The Pentecostals, 1972, 1988 (also German and Spanish edns); Pentecost between Black and White, 1975 (also German and Dutch edns); Glaube, Geist und Geister, 1975; (ed) Studies in the Intercultural History of Christianity, 150 vols, 1975–2010; Evangelism Today, 1976 (also German edn); (with Th. Ahrens) Volkschristentum und Volksreligion in Pazifik, 1977; Interkulturelle Theologie, vol. I, 1979, vol. II, 1982, vol. III, 1988 (abridged French edn); Erfahrungen in Ephesus, 1979; Wie Grenzen zu Brücken werden, 1980; Besuch bei Lukas, 1981; Conflict in Corinth—Memoirs of an Old Man, 1982 (also German, Italian, Indonesian and French edns; musical and drama edn, 1999); Jüngermesse/Gomer: Das Gesicht des Unsichtbaren, 1983 (music edns 1994 and 1995); Zwingli zwischen Krieg und Frieden, 1983, 1988; Das Fest der Verlorenen, 1984; Der Handelsreisende Gottes, 1985 (music edn 1994); Das Wagnis des Glaubens, 1986 (music edn 1993); Weihnachtsoratorium, 1986; Mirjam, Mutter, and Michal: Die Frauen meines Mannes (zwei Monodramen), 1987 (music edn 1994); Bonhoeffer Requiem, 1990 (music edn 1992); Ostertanz der Frauen/Veni Creator Spiritus, 1990; Kommet her zu mir/Die zehn Aussätzigen, 1990; Fontana (musical), 1991; Jona (musical), 1992; Hiob im Kreuzfeuer der Religionen, 1993; Jürg Rathgeb (oratorio), 1993; Der Kommissar auf biblischer Spurensuche, 1993; Ruth, die Ausländerin, 1993; Kamele und Kapitalisten, 1994; Johannestexte, 1995; Scherben, 1996; Pentecostalism, 1997 (also German edn); Maria von Wedemeyer, 1997; Nympha und Onesimus, 1999; Neuer Himmel—neue Erde, 1999; Der Klapperstorch und die Theologie, 2000; Das Kirchenjahr inszenieren, 2002; Petrus, der Pontifex, 2002; Der Freund der Frauen, 2008; Albert Schweitzer, 2008; *relevant publication:* Theology Out of Place: a theological biography of Walter J. Hollenweger, by Lynne Price, 2002. *Address:* Alte Gasse 58, 3704 Krattigen, Switzerland. *T:* (33) 6544302.

HOLLERN, Catherine Molloy; MP (Lab) Blackburn, since 2015; *b* Dumbarton, 12 April 1955; two *d*; partner, John. Work study manager, Newman's Footwear; Contracts Manager, Blackburn Coll. Mem. (Lab), Blackburn with Darwen Council, until 2015 (Leader Lab Gp, 2004–15; Leader of Council, 2004–07 and 2010–15). *Address:* House of Commons, SW1A 0AA.

HOLLICK, family name of **Baron Hollick**.

HOLLICK, Baron *cr* 1991 (Life Peer), of Notting Hill in the Royal Borough of Kensington and Chelsea; **Clive Richard Hollick;** Partner, G. P. Bullhound, since 2010; Director, Honeywell Inc., since 2003; *b* 20 May 1945; *s* of late Leslie George Hollick and Olive Mary (*née* Scruton); *m* 1977, Susan Mary Woodford (*see* Lady Hollick); three *d. Educ:* Taunton's Sch., Southampton; Univ. of Nottingham (BA Hons). Joined Hambros Bank Ltd, 1968, Dir, 1973–96; Chairman: Shepperton Studios Ltd, 1976–84; Garban Ltd (USA), 1983–97; Founder and Chm., Meridian Broadcasting Ltd, 1992–96; Chief Executive: Mills & Allen Internat., subseq. MAI PLC, 1974–96; United News & Media, subseq. United Business Media plc, 1996–2005; Man. Dir, 2005–06, Partner, 2006–09, Sen. Advr, 2009–10, Kohlberg Kravis Roberts; Director: Logica plc, 1987–91; Avenir Havas Media SA, 1989–92; Satellite Information Systems Ltd, 1990–94; British Aerospace, 1992–97; Anglia Television, 1994–97; TRW Inc., 2000–02; Diageo plc, 2001–11 (Sen. Dir, 2004–11); Nielsen Inc., 2007–09; Pro Sieben Sat1 (formerly Pro Sieben Media) AG, 2007–14; BMG Music Rights Mgt, 2009–14; Chm., WePredict Ltd, 2013–15; Member, Advisory Board: Jefferies Inc., 2011–; Ambassador Th. Gp, 2011–; Market Share Inc., 2013–. Special Advr to Pres. of BoT and Sec. of State for Trade and Industry, 1997–98; Prime Minister's Trade and Investment Envoy to Kenya and Tanzania, 2014–. Chm., South Bank Centre, 2002–08. Member: Nat. Bus Co. Ltd, 1984–91; Adv. Cttee, Dept of Applied Econs, Univ. of Cambridge, 1989–97; Financial Law Panel, 1993–97; Commn on Public Policy and British Business, 1995–97; H of L Select Cttee on Econ. Affairs, 2010– (Chm., 2014–); Adv. Bd, Royal Soc., 2010–. Chm., Galleon Trust, 1992–97. Founding Trustee, IPPR, 1988–. Gov., LSE, 1997–2003. Hon. LLD Nottingham, 1993. *Recreations:* reading, theatre, music, cinema, golf, countryside.

HOLLICK, Lady; Susan Mary Woodford-Hollick, OBE 2011; Founder and Director, Bringing Up Baby Ltd, since 1989; *b* 16 May 1945; *d* of late Ulric Cross, DSO, DFC, ORTT and Joan Woodford; *m* 1977, Clive Richard Hollick (*see* Baron Hollick); three *d. Educ:* La Retraite Convent High Sch., London; Univ. of Sussex (BA Hons). Producer/Dir, World in Action, Granada TV, 1969–81; Founding Commissioning Ed. for multicultural progs, Channel 4 TV, 1980–84. Chm., Index on Censorship, 1993–2000. Member: Arts Council England (formerly Arts Council of England), 2002–09 (Chair, London Regl Council (formerly London Arts Bd), 2000–09); Adv. Bd, Tate Modern, 2000–09; Chair: Tate Members' Council, 1999–2005; AMREF UK, 2007–11 (Dir, AMREF Internat. Bd, 2008–); Leaders Quest Foundn, 2011–14; Stuart Hall Foundn, 2015–; Director: Free Word, 2009–; Theatre de Complicite, 2009–. Trustee, Reprieve, 2014–. FRSA. *Publications:* The Good Nursery Guide, 1992. *Recreations:* the arts, television, cinema, tennis, golf, horse riding. *Club:* Queenwood Golf (Ottershaw, Surrey).

HOLLIDAY, Sir Frederick (George Thomas), Kt 1990; CBE 1975; FRSE; Chairman, Northumbrian Water Group, 1993–2006 (Director, 1991); *b* 22 Sept. 1935; *s* of late Alfred C. and Margaret Holliday; *m* 1957, Philippa Mary Davidson; one *s* one *d. Educ:* Bromsgrove County High Sch.; Sheffield Univ. BSc 1st cl. hons Zool. 1956; FRSB (FIBiol 1970), FRSE 1971. Fisheries Research Trng Grant (Develt Commn) at Marine Lab., Aberdeen, 1956–58; Sci. Officer, Marine Lab., Aberdeen, 1958–61; Lectr in Zoology, Univ. of Aberdeen, 1961–66; Prof. of Biology, 1967–75, Dep. Principal, 1972, Acting Principal, 1973–75, Univ. of Stirling; Prof. of Zoology, Univ. of Aberdeen, 1975–79; Vice-Chancellor and Warden, Univ. of Durham, 1980–90. Member: Scottish Cttee, Nature Conservancy, 1969; Council, Scottish Field Studies Assoc., 1970–78 (Pres., 1981–90); Council, Scottish Marine Biol Assoc., 1967–85 (Pres., 1979–85); Scottish Wildlife Trust (Vice-Pres.); Council, Freshwater Biol Assoc., 1969–72, and 1993–2000 (Pres., 1995–2001); NERC Oceanography and Fisheries Research Grants Cttee, 1971; Council, NERC, 1973–79; Nature Conservancy Council, 1975–80 (Dep. Chm., 1976–77, Chm., 1977–80); Scottish Economic Council, 1975–80; Council, Marine Biol Assoc. UK, 1975–78 (Vice-Pres., 1994–); Oil Develt Council for Scotland, 1976–78; Standing Commn on Energy and the Environment, 1978–82; Adv. Cttee, Leverhulme Trust Res. Awards, 1978–95 (Chm., 1989–95); PCFC, 1989–93; Awards Council, Royal Anniv. Trust, 1993–95; Council, Water Aid, 1994–98; Envmtl Cttee, CBI, 1994–2006; Chm., Independent Review of Disposal of Radioactive Waste at Sea, 1984; Ind. Chm., Jt Nature Conservation Cttee, 1991. Dir, Shell UK, 1980–99; Mem., Shell UK Audit Cttee, 1993–94; Chairman: Investors' Cttee, Northern Venture Partnership Fund, 1990–2001; Northern Venture Capital Fund, 1996–2009; Go-Ahead Gp, 1998–2002 (Dir, 1997–2002); Dep. Chm., Northern Regional Bd, Lloyd's Bank, 1989–91 (Mem., 1985–91; Chm., 1986–89); Director: Northern Investors Ltd, 1984–90; BRB, 1990–94 (Chm., BR (Eastern), 1986–90); Union Railways, 1993–97; Lyonnaise des Eaux SA, 1996–97; Lyonnaise Europe plc, 1996–2000; Suez Lyonnaise des Eaux, 1997–2001; Wisespeke Plc, 1997–98; Brewin Dolphin Gp, 1998–2005 (Chm., 2003–05); Northern 2 Venture Capital Fund, 1999–2011. Pres., NE Reg. Assoc. for Sci. Educn, 2004–06. Trustee, Nat. Heritage Meml Fund, 1980–91; Vice-Pres., Civic Trust for NE; Mem., Scottish Civic Trust, 1984–87; Pres., British Trust for Ornithology, 1996–2001. Member, Board of Governors: Rowett Res. Inst., 1976–84; Lathallan Sch., 2005–08. DUniv Stirling, 1984; Hon. DSc: Sheffield, 1987; Cranfield, 1991; Hon. DCL Durham, 2002. DL Durham, 1985–90. *Publications:* (ed and contrib.) Wildlife of Scotland, 1979; numerous on fish biology and wildlife conservation in Adv. Mar. Biol., Fish Physiology, Oceanography and Marine Biology, etc. *Recreations:* ornithology, microscopy, walking, gardening. *Address:* East Rosehill, Northwaterbridge, Laurencekirk AB30 1QD. *T:* (01674) 840544.

HOLLIDAY, Rev. Canon Peter Leslie, QHC 2015; Group Chief Executive, St Giles Hospice, 2000–15; Canon Custos, Lichfield Cathedral, since 2013; *b* Sutton Coldfield, 3 July 1948; *s* of John Kenneth Holliday and Marjorie Doris Holliday; *m* 1969, Ruth Mary Page; one *s* two *d. Educ:* Bishop Vesey's Grammar Sch.; Birmingham Univ. (BCom 1970; MA 1992); Queen's Theol Coll., Birmingham. FCA 1979. Articled clerk, Peat, Marwick, Mitchell & Co., 1970–73; Dir, Chart Tutors Ltd, 1974–81; ordained deacon, 1983, priest, 1984; Curate, Burton on Trent, 1983–87; Priest-in-charge, Longdon, and Subchanter, Lichfield Cathedral, 1987–93; Vicar, Stratford upon Avon, 1993–2000; Chancellor's Vicar, Lichfield Cathedral, 2002–13. Chm., Chart Foulks Lynch plc, 1981–88; Dir, Cowan De Groot plc, 1985–87. Deputy Chair: Hospice UK, 2007–15 (Chair, Adv. Council, 2007–15); Lichfield Cathedral Sch., 2008–. Dir, Stratford Music Festival, 1997–. Contested (C) Warley E, Oct. 1974. *Recreations:* classical music, family and friends, gardening. *Address:* St Giles Hospice, Fisherwick Road, Whittington, Lichfield WS14 9LH. *Club:* Burton (Burton on Trent; Chaplain, 2006–).

HOLLIDAY, Steven John, FREng; Chief Executive, National Grid, since 2007; *b* Exeter, 26 Oct. 1956; *s* of Michael and Jean Holliday; *m* 1996, Kate Patterson; three *d*. *Educ:* Univ. of Nottingham (BSc Mining Engrg 1978). Esso/Exxon, 1978–97: Ops Manager, Fawley Refinery, Esso UK, 1988–92; Supply and Transportation Divl Dir, Esso UK, 1992–94; Regl Vice-Pres. Gas, Exxon Co. Internat., 1994–97; Bd Dir, British Borneo Oil and Gas, 1997–2000; National Grid: Bd Dir responsible for Transmission, 2001–03; Gp Dir responsible for UK Gas Distribution and Business Services, 2003–07. Non-exec. Dir, Marks & Spencer, 2004–14. Chm., Talent and Skills Leadership Team, 2009–, Vice Chm., 2014–, BITC; Vice Chm., Enterprise for Educn Ltd, 2015–. Chm., Crisis, 2012–. FREng 2010. *Recreations:* sports, Rugby, ski-ing, arts. *Address:* National Grid, 1–3 Strand, WC2N 5EH. *T:* (020) 7004 3021, *Fax:* (020) 7004 3022. *E:* steven.holliday@nationalgrid.com.

HOLLIGER, Heinz; oboist, composer and conductor; *b* Langenthal, Switzerland, 21 May 1939; *m* Ursula Holliger, harpist. *Educ:* Berne Conservatoire; Paris; Basle; studied with Cassagnaud, Lefébure, Veress, Pierlot and Boulez. Played with Basle Orch., 1959–63; Prof. of oboe, Freiburg Music Acad., 1965–2003. Has appeared as soloist and conductor at all major European music festivals, and with Chamber Orch. of Europe, English Chamber Orch., etc; has directed all major Swiss orchs, Cleveland Orch., Philharmonia, Vienna Philharmonic, Vienna SO, CBSO, Berlin Philharmonic, Concertgebouw, etc. Has inspired compositions by Berio, Penderecki, Stockhausen, Henze, Martin and others. *Compositions include:* Der magische Tänzer, Trio, Dona nobis pacem, Pneuma, Psalm, Cardiophonie, Kreis, Siebengesang, H for wind quintet, string quartet Atembogen, Scardanelli-Cycle, Gesänge der Frühe, (S)irato for orch., Violin Concerto, Partita, Puneigä. Has won many international prizes, including: Geneva Competition first prize, 1959; Munich Competition first prize, 1961; Sonning Prize; Frankfurt Music Prize; Ernst von Siemens Prize. *Address:* Konzertgesellschaft, Peter Merian-Strasse 28/Postfach, 4002 Basel, Switzerland.

HOLLINGBERY, George; MP (C) Meon Valley, since 2010; a Lord Commissioner of HM Treasury (Government Whip), since 2015; *b* 12 Oct. 1963; *m* 1991, Janette Marie White; one *s* two *d*. *Educ:* Radley Coll.; Lady Margaret Hall, Oxford (BA Human Scis 1985); Wharton Sch., Univ. of Pennsylvania (MBA 1991). Stockbroker, Robert Fleming Securities, 1985–89; non-exec. Dir and shareholder, Lister Bestcare Ltd, 1991–95; Dir and Founder, Pet Depot Ltd, 1994–99; Chm. and Founder, Companion Care Vet. Gp, 1998–2001; property investment business, 2005–. Mem. (C) Winchester CC, 1999–2010. Contested (C) Winchester, 2005. PPS to Secretary of State for Home Dept, 2012–15. Mem., Communities and Local Govt Select Cttee, 2010–15. Mem. Exec., 1922 Cttee, 2012–. *Address:* House of Commons, SW1A 0AA.

HOLLINGHURST, Alan James, FRSL; writer; *b* 26 May 1954; *s* of James Kenneth Hollinghurst and Elizabeth Lilian Hollinghurst (*née* Keevil). *Educ:* Canford Sch.; Magdalen Coll., Oxford (BA 1975; MLitt 1979; Hon. Fellow 2013). On staff, TLS, 1982–95. Vis. Prof., Univ. of Houston, 1998; Old Dominion Fellow, Princeton Univ., 2004. FRSL 1995. Hon. DLit UCL, 2012. *Publications:* The Swimming-Pool Library, 1988 (Somerset Maugham Award, E. M. Forster Award, AAAL); The Folding Star, 1994 (James Tait Black Meml Prize); The Spell, 1998; The Line of Beauty (Man Booker Prize), 2004; The Stranger's Child, 2011; *translations:* Racine, Bajazet, 1991; Racine, Berenice and Bajazet, 2012. *Recreations:* looking at buildings, listening to music. *Address:* 15 Tanza Road, NW3 2UA. *Club:* Cranium.

HOLLINGHURST, Rt Rev. Anne Elizabeth; *see* Aston, Bishop Suffragan of.

HOLLINGHURST, Edmund, FREng, FICE, FIStructE; FCIHT; Director and Partner, 1986, then Senior Partner, Gifford & Partners; *b* 27 June 1944; *s* of Rev. Dr George Frederick Hollinghurst and Rachel Hollinghurst (*née* Cooper); *m* 1986, Glenys Helen Davis; three *d*. *Educ:* Dragon Sch., Oxford; Kingswood Sch., Bath; Sidney Sussex Coll., Cambridge (MA). CEng 1971; FCIHT (FIHT 1985); FICE 1995; FIStructE 1995; FREng (FEng 1997). Trainee, Ove Arup & Partners, 1962–63; Engineer: Ninham Shand, Cape Town, SA, 1965–66; Ove Arup & Partners, London, Africa and Middle East, 1967–70; Kier Ltd, UK and overseas, 1970–73; Gifford & Partners, 1973–86, seconded as staff consultant, Asian Develt Bank, 1978. Mem., Royal Fine Art Commn, 1996–99. Vis. Prof., Univ. of Southampton. Major designs include: Bray Viaduct, Devon; Kwai Chung, Hong Kong; Dee Crossing, Wales; Second Severn Crossing; Camel Estuary Bridge, Cornwall; Kingston Bridge, Glasgow; River Tyne Millennium Bridge. Fédération Internationale de la Précontrainte Design Award, for Bray Viaduct, 1994. *Publications:* contrib. to ICE and IStructE texts. *Recreation:* sailing.

HOLLINGSWORTH, Michael Charles; Chairman, Venture Television Ltd (trading as Venture Artists, Venture Broadcasting, and Venture Correspondents), 2007 (Chief Executive, 1993–2007); *b* 22 Feb. 1946; *s* of Albert George Hollingsworth and Gwendoline Marjorie Hollingsworth; *m* 1st, 1968, Patricia Margaret Jefferson Winn (marr. diss. 1987); one *d*; 2nd, 1989, Anne Margaret Diamond (marr. diss. 1999); four *s* (and one *s* decd). *Educ:* Carlisle Grammar Sch.; Ruskin Coll., Oxford. Programme Editor, Anglia Television, 1964–67; Producer, BBC Local Radio, 1967–74; Northern Editor, Today, Radio Four, 1974–75; Editor, News and Current Affairs: Southern Television Ltd, 1975–79; ATV Network/Central, 1979–82; Sen. Producer, Current Affairs, BBC TV, 1982–84; Dir of Programmes, TV-am Ltd, 1984–86; Man. Dir, Music Box Ltd, 1986–89. Agent and consultant to television and radio cos, and to charities. FRSA. *Recreation:* DIY (house renovation).

HOLLINGSWORTH, Timothy Philip; Chief Executive Officer, British Paralympic Association, since 2011; *b* Farnborough, Kent, 10 April 1967; *s* of Michael and Marjorie Hollingsworth; *m* 2000, Emma Houston; two *s*. *Educ:* Lancing Coll., Sussex; Sevenoaks Sch., Kent; Univ. of Exeter (BA Hons English and Drama; MA Drama 1990). Press Officer, 1993–95, Hd of Communications, 1995–2000, CBI; Hd, Corporate and Internal Communications, Granada plc, 2000–01; Dir, HBL Media, 2001–04; Dir, Policy and Communications, 2004–10, Chief Operating Officer, 2010–11, UK Sport. Mem. Bd, Youth Sport Trust, 2011–. Hon. LLD: Exeter, 2014; Bath, 2014. *Recreations:* theatre, current affairs, guitar, family, sport, Fulham FC. *Address:* British Paralympic Association, 60 Charlotte Street, W1T 2NU. *T:* (020) 7842 5789, *Fax:* (020) 7842 5777. *E:* tim.hollingsworth@paralympics.org.uk.

HOLLINGTON, Robin Frank; QC 1999; a Recorder, since 2004; a Deputy High Court Judge, Chancery Division, since 2013; *b* 30 June 1955; *s* of late Reginald Barrie Hollington and Eleanor Gwendoline Hollington (*née* Paxton); *m* 1988, Jane Elizabeth Cadogan Gritten; one *s*. *Educ:* Haileybury; University Coll., Oxford (MA); Univ. of Pennsylvania (LLM). Called to the Bar, Lincoln's Inn, 1979, Bencher, 2007. *Publications:* Minority Shareholders' Rights, 1990, 7th edn as Shareholders' Rights, 2013. *Recreations:* lawn tennis, golf. *Address:* New Square Chambers, 12 New Square, Lincoln's Inn, WC2A 3SW. *T:* (020) 7419 8000. *Clubs:* Royal Automobile, MCC; Walton Heath Golf.

HOLLINGWORTH, Clare, OBE 1984; Correspondent in Hong Kong for Sunday Telegraph, since 1981; Research Associate (formerly Visiting Scholar), Centre of Asian Studies, University of Hong Kong, since 1981; *b* 10 Oct. 1911; *d* of John Albert Hollingworth and Daisy Gertrude Hollingworth; *m* 1st, 1936, Vyvyan Derring Vandeleur Robinson (marr. diss. 1951); 2nd, 1952, Geoffrey Spencer Hoare (*d* 1965). *Educ:* Girls' Collegiate Sch., Leicester; Grammar Sch., Ashby de la Zouch, Leics; Sch. of Slavonic Studies, Univ. of London. On staff, League of Nations Union, 1935–38; worked in Poland for Lord Mayor's Fund for Refugees from Czechoslovakia, 1939; Correspondent in Poland for Daily Telegraph: first to report outbreak of war from Katawice; remained in Balkans as Germans took over; moved to Turkey and then Cairo, 1941–50, covering Desert Campaigns, troubles in Persia and Iraq, Civil War in Greece and events in Palestine; covered trouble spots from Paris for Manchester Guardian, 1950–63, incl. Algerian War, Egypt, Aden and Vietnam (Journalist of the Year Award and Hannan Swaffer Award, 1963); Guardian Defence Correspondent, 1963–67; Daily Telegraph: foreign trouble shooter, 1967–73, covering war in Vietnam; Correspondent in China, 1973–76; Defence Correspondent, 1976–81. Hon. DLitt Leicester, 1993. James Cameron Award for Journalism, 1994. *Publications:* Poland's Three Weeks War, 1940; There's a German Just Behind Me, 1942; The Arabs and the West, 1951; Mao and the Men Against Him, 1984; Front Line, 1990. *Recreations:* visiting second-hand furniture and bookshops, collecting modern pictures and Chinese porcelain, music. *Club:* Foreign Correspondents' (Hong Kong).

HOLLINGWORTH, John Harold; *b* 11 July 1930; *s* of Harold Hollingworth, Birmingham; *m* 1969, Susan Barbara (marr. diss. 1985), *d* of late J. H. Walters, Ramsey, IoM. *Educ:* Chigwell House Sch.; King Edward's Sch., Edgbaston. MP (C) All Saints Division of Birmingham, 1959–64; contested (C) Birmingham, All Saints, 1966 and 1970. Chairman: Birmingham Young Conservatives, 1958–62; Edgbaston Div. Conservative Assoc., 1967–72; Vice-Chm., Birmingham Conservative Assoc., 1958–61, 1972–78 (Vice-Pres. 1960–66). Chm., Forward Housing Assocs, 1962–80. Dir and Gen. Manager, Cambridge Symphony Orch. Trust, 1979–82 (Gov., 1982–92); Dir, Thaxted Fest. Foundn, 1987–93. Chm., Elmdon Trust Ltd, 1984–91; dir of other cos; mem. of various charitable activities. Trustee, 1991–98, Hon. Chief Exec., 1992–93, Hon. Treas., 1993–98, British Performing Arts Medicine Trust. Member: Viola d'Amore Soc. of GB; ESU. *Publications:* contributions to political journals. *Recreations:* exercising Rough Collie dogs, planning third British Empire. *Address:* 10 Hamel Way, Widdington, Saffron Walden CB11 3SJ. *T:* (01799) 542445. *Club:* Lansdowne.

HOLLINGWORTH, Rt Rev. Hon. Dr Peter John, AC 2001 (AO 1988); OBE 1976; Governor General of the Commonwealth of Australia, 2001–03; *b* 10 April 1935; *m* 1960, Kathleen Ann Turner; three *d*. *Educ:* Murrumbeena and Lloyd Street State Schools; Scotch Coll., Melbourne; Trinity Coll., Univ. of Melbourne (BA 1958; MA 1980); Australian Coll. of Theol. (ThL 1959); Univ. of Melbourne (Dip. Social Studies, 1970). Commercial Cadet, Broken Hill Pty, 1952–53. Ordained, 1960; Priest in charge, St Mary's, N Melbourne, 1960–64; Brotherhood of St Laurence: Chaplain and Dir of Youth Work, 1964–70; Assoc. Dir, 1970–79; Exec. Dir, 1980–90; Canon, St Paul's Cathedral, Melbourne, 1980; Bishop in the Inner City, dio. of Melbourne, 1985–90; Archbishop of Brisbane and Metropolitan, Province of Queensland, 1990–2001. Chairman: Social Responsibilities Commn, Gen. Synod, Anglican Church of Aust., 1990–98; Nat. Council for the Centenary of Fedn, 2000. Mem., Australian Assoc. of Social Workers, 1970–78. Paul Harris Fellow, Rotary Internat., 1989; FAIM 1997; Hon. Fellow: Trinity Coll., Melbourne, 1998; St John's Coll., Brisbane, 2006. Hon. LLD: Monash, 1986; Melbourne, 1990; DUniv: Griffith, 1993; Qld Univ. of Technol., 1994; Univ. of Central Qld, 1995; DLitt Univ. of Southern Qld, 1999; DLitt Lambeth 2001. KStJ 2001; Nat. ChLJ 1998–2001; GCLJ 1998. Australian of the Year, 1991. *Publications:* Australians in Poverty, 1978; The Powerless Poor, 1972; The Poor: victims of affluence, 1975; Kingdom Come!, 1991; Public Thoughts of an Archbishop, 1996. *Recreations:* writing, reading, swimming, music, the arts, philanthropy, welfare. *Address:* PO Box 18081, Collins Street East, Melbourne, Vic 8003, Australia.

HOLLINRAKE, Kevin Paul; MP (C) Thirsk and Malton, since 2015; *b* Easingwold, 28 Sept. 1963; *m* Nikky; four *c*. *Educ:* Easingwold Sch.; Sheffield Poly. Prudential Property Services: Branch Manager, Haxby, then Burnley, Lancs, 1985–87; Area Manager, 1987–91; Jt Founder and Man. Dir, Hunters Property Gp, 1992–; Co-owner, Vizzihome, 2008–13; Chm., Shoptility.com, 2013–. *Address:* House of Commons, SW1A 0AA.

HOLLINS, family name of **Baroness Hollins**.

HOLLINS, Baroness *cr* 2010 (Life Peer), of Wimbledon in the London Borough of Merton and of Grenoside in the County of South Yorkshire; **Sheila Clare Hollins,** FRCPsych; FRCPCH; Professor of Psychiatry of Disability, St George's, University of London (formerly St George's Hospital Medical School), 1990–2011, now Emeritus; *b* 22 June 1946; *d* of late Captain Adrian Morgan Kelly, Bristol, and of Monica Dallas Kelly (*née* Edwards); *m* 1969, Martin Prior Hollins, *s* of late Harry Pryor Hollins; one *s* three *d*. *Educ:* Notre Dame High Sch., Sheffield; St Thomas' Hosp. Med. Sch., London (MB BS). MRCPsych 1978, FRCPsych 1988; FRCPCH. Sen. Registrar in Child Psychiatry, Earls Court Child Guidance Unit and Westminster Children's Hosp., 1979–81; Sen. Lectr in Psychiatry of Learning Disability, 1981–90, Hd, Div. of Mental Health, 2003–05, St George's Hosp. Med. Sch.; Winston Churchill Fellow, 1993; Hon. Consultant: Wandsworth Community Health Trust and Richmond, Twickenham and Roehampton Healthcare Trust, 1981–99; SW London Community Trust, 1999–2002; SW London and St George's Mental Health Trust, 2002–11. On secondment to Policy Div., DoH, as pt-time Policy Advr on learning disability, 1993–94 and 2001–03; Member: Minister's Adv. Gp on Learning Disability, 1999–2001; Learning Disability Task Force, 2001–04; Expert Panel, Ind. Enquiry into Access to Healthcare for People with Learning Disabilities, 2007–08; Prime Minister's Standing Commn on Carers, 2007–09; Chairman: NHS Wkg Party on Breast and Cervical Screening in Learning Disability, 1999–2000; External Adv. Gp, Nat. Confidential Inquiry into Suicides and Homicides, 2007–11; Dep. Chm., Nat. Specialist Commissioning Adv. Gp, 2006–08. Hon. Prof., Dept of Theol. and Religion, Univ. of Durham, 2012–. Royal College of Psychiatrists: Vice-Pres., 2003–04; Pres., 2005–08; Chm., Exec. Cttee, Psychiatry of Learning Disability Faculty, 1994–98; Mem., Ct of Electors, 1999–2005; Mem., Bd of Internat. Affairs, 2001–05. Pres., 2012–13, Chm., Bd of Sci., 2013–, BMA. Mem., Acad. of Med. Royal Colls, 2005–08. Mem., Community Care and Disability Sub-cttee, Joseph Rowntree Foundn, 1989–93. Exec. Chm., Books Beyond Words Community Interest Co., 2010–. Mem., Pontifical Commn for the Protection of Minors, 2014–. FRSocMed. Hon. FRCP 2007. Mem., Lay Community of St Benedict. Hon. DD London, 2013; Hon. MD Sheffield, 2014; Hon. LLD Bath, 2014; Hon. DS Worcester, 2014. *Publications:* (ed with M. Craft) Mental Handicap: a multi-disciplinary approach, 1985; (with M. Grimes) Going Somewhere: pastoral care for people with mental handicap, 1988; (with J. Curran) Understanding Depression in People with Learning Disabilities, 1996; (with L. Sireling) Understanding Grief, 1999; editor and joint author 44 titles in Books Beyond Words series, including: Hug Me, Touch Me, 1994 (Best Author, Read Easy Awards Book Trust and Joseph Rowntree Foundn); (with J. Bernal) Getting on with Epilepsy, 1999; Looking After My Breasts, 2000; (jtly) George Gets Smart, 2001; with L. Sireling: When Dad Died, 1990, 3rd edn 2004; When Mum Died, 1990, 3rd edn 2004; with V. Sinason: Jenny Speaks Out, 1992; Bob Tells All, 1992; Mugged, 2002; Supporting Victims, 2007; (jtly) You're in Prison, 2013; (with Hugh Grant and Nigel Hollins) The Drama Group, 2015; contrib. numerous peer-reviewed papers on mental health and learning disability. *Recreations:* family, walking, music. *Address:* House of Lords, SW1A 0PW. *T:* (020) 7219 0520. *E:* hollinss@parliament.uk.

See also J. M. Kelly.

HOLLINS, Peter Thomas; Chief Executive (formerly Director General), British Heart Foundation, 2003–13; *b* 22 Oct. 1947; *m* 1973, Linda Pitchford; two *d*. *Educ:* Hertford Coll., Oxford (2nd Cl. Hons Chem.). British Oxygen, 1970–73; ICI UK, 1973–89; ICI Holland, 1989–92; EVC Brussels, 1992–98; Chief Exec., British Energy, 1998–2001. Holds various non-exec. directorships. Chm., CLIC Sargent, 2014–. *Recreations:* fluent in Dutch, German and French, classical music, travelling, Rugby, hill-walking. *Address:* c/o CLIC Sargent, Horatio House, 77–85 Fulham Palace Road, W6 8JA.

HOLLIS, family name of **Baroness Hollis of Heigham**.

HOLLIS OF HEIGHAM, Baroness *cr* 1990 (Life Peer), of Heigham in the City of Norwich; **Patricia Lesley Hollis;** PC 1999; DL; DPhil; FRHistS; *b* 24 May 1941; *d* of (Harry) Lesley (George) Wells and Queenie Rosalyn Wells; *m* 1965, (James) Martin Hollis, FBA (*d* 1998); two *s*. *Educ:* Plympton Grammar Sch.; Cambridge Univ. (MA); Univ. of California; Columbia Univ., NY; Nuffield Coll., Oxford (DPhil). Harkness Fellow, 1962–64; Nuffield Scholar, 1964–67. University of East Anglia: Lectr, 1967, then Reader, and Sen. Fellow in Modern Hist.; Dean, School of English and American Studies, 1988–90. Councillor: Norwich City Council, 1968–91 (Leader, 1983–88); Norfolk CC, 1981–85. Member: Regional Econ. Planning Council, 1975–79; Govt Commn on Housing, 1975–77; RHA, 1979–83; BBC Regional Adv. Cttee, 1979–83; Bd, Pensions Adv. Service, 2006–. Vice-President: ADC, 1990–97; AMA, 1990–97; Assoc. of Envmtl Health Officers, 1992–97; NFHA, 1993–97. Dir, Radio Broadland, 1983–97. Chm., Broadland Housing Assoc., 2009–. Nat. Comr, English Heritage, 1988–91; Mem. Press Council, 1989–90. Contested (Lab) Gt Yarmouth, Feb. and Oct. 1974, 1979. An opposition whip, 1990–97; opposition frontbench spokesperson on social security, disability, local govt and housing, 1992–97; Parly Under-Sec. of State, DSS, 1997–2001, DWP, 2001–05. Trustee: Hist. of Parlt Trust, 2005–; Policy Studies Inst., 2006–; Pensions Adv. Service, 2006–. Hon. Pres., Women's Local Govt Soc., 2007–. FRHistS. DL Norfolk, 1994. Hon. DLitt: Anglia Poly. Univ., 1995; London Guildhall, 2001; DUniv Open, 2000. Campaigning Politician of the Year Award, Channel 4, 2009; Peer of the Year, Dods and Scottish Widows Awards, 2009. *Publications:* The Pauper Press, 1970; Class and Conflict, 1815–50, 1973; Pressure from Without, 1974; Women in Public 1850–1900, 1979; (with Dr B. H. Harrison) Robert Lowery, Radical and Chartist, 1979; Ladies Elect: women in English local government 1865–1914, 1987; Jennie Lee: a life, 1997 (Orwell Prize; Wolfson Hist. Prize, 1998); A New State Pension, 2010. *Recreations:* boating, singing, domesticity. *Address:* House of Lords, SW1A 0PW. *T:* (020) 7219 3000.

HOLLIS, Rt Rev. Crispian; *see* Hollis, Rt Rev. R. F. C.

HOLLIS, Daniel Ayrton; QC 1968; a Recorder of the Crown Court, 1972–96; *b* 30 April 1925; *m* 1st, 1950, Gillian Mary Turner (marr. diss. 1961); one *d* (one *s* decd); 2nd, 1963, Stella Hydleman; one *s*. *Educ:* Geelong Grammar Sch., Australia; Brasenose Coll., Oxford. Served N Atlantic and Mediterranean, 1943–46. Lt-Commander, RNVR. Called to Bar, Middle Temple, 1949; Bencher, 1975; Treas., 1994; Head of Chambers, 1968–95. A Comr, CCC, 1971; a Dep. High Ct Judge, 1982–93. Mem., Criminal Injuries Compensation Bd, 1995–2000. Mem., Home Sec.'s Adv. Bd on Restricted Patients, 1986–92. *Address:* 22 St James's Square, SW1Y 4JH; 8 place Fontaine Vieille, La Garde Freinet 83680, France. *Club:* Travellers.

HOLLIS, Geoffrey Alan; Director, Drew Associates, 1997–2009; *b* 25 Nov. 1943; *s* of late William John Hollis and of Elsie Jean Hollis (*née* Baker); *m* 1967, Ann Josephine Prentice; two *s*. *Educ:* Hastings Grammar Sch.; Hertford Coll., Oxford (MA); Polytechnic of Central London (Dip. Management Studies). International Computers, 1966; International Publishing Corp., 1967; Gulf Oil, 1969; MAFF, 1974–96; seconded to FCO, First Sec., 1977–80, UK Perm. Rep., EC, Brussels; Under Sec. and Hd of Meat, later Livestock Gp, 1991–96. Non-executive Director: Lucas Ingredients (Dalgety plc), 1991–95; E and N Herts HA, 1998–2001; Mem., Welwyn Hatfield PCT, 2001–06. Chm., Welwyn & Hatfield CAB, 2006–12. Admitted to Co. of Clockmakers, 1997. Clocks Advr, St Albans Dio. *Recreations:* chess, golf, horology. *Address:* 12 Lodge Drive, Hatfield, Herts AL9 5HN.

HOLLIS, His Honour Keith Martin John; a Circuit Judge, 2000–13; a Deputy Circuit Judge, since 2013; mediator and legal consultant, since 2013; *b* 9 June 1951; *s* of Eric and Joan Hollis; *m* 1979, Mariana Roberts; one *s* one *d*. *Educ:* Whitgift Sch., Croydon. Admitted Solicitor, 1975; Partner, Davies Brown & Co., Solicitors, 1976–82; Sole Principal, then Sen. Partner, Hollis Wood & Co., Solicitors, 1982–92; Dist Judge, 1992–2000; Associate Mem., 1 Crown Office Row Chambers, 2014–. Accredited Mediator 2013. Dir of Studies, Commonwealth Magistrates' and Judges' Assoc., 1999–2010; Mem., Working Pty on Latimer House Guidelines on Parly Supremacy and Judicial Independence in the Commonwealth, 2000. Chm., New Sussex Opera, 2011–13; Trustee: Sussex Community Foundn, 2014–; Ouse and Adur Rivers Trust, 2015–. *Recreations:* music, hill-walking, gardening. *Address:* Crown Office Row, 119 Church Street, Brighton BN1 1UD.

HOLLIS, Kim; QC 2002; *b* 19 Sept. 1957; *d* of Gurbaksh Singh Salariya and Jean Taylor; *m* 1987, Andrew Charles Hollis; two *s*. *Educ:* Cheltenham Ladies' Coll.; QMC, Univ. of London (LLB Hons). Called to the Bar, Gray's Inn, 1979, Bencher, 2008. Vice Chm., 2005–11, Chm., 2011–14, Race and Religion Cttee, then Diversity Cttee, later Equality and Diversity Cttee, Bar Council; Hd, Equality and Diversity Cttee, Criminal Bar Assoc., 2004–. Chair: Minority Lawyers Conf., 2009; Bar Conf., 2010 (Vice Chair, 2009); N London Bar Mess, 2011–14. Mem., FCO Diplomatic Excellence Panel, 2013–; Diversity Advr to FCO, 2014–. Chair, Assoc. of Women Barristers, 2009–10; Vice Pres., British Assoc. of Counselling and Psychotherapy, 2014–. (Jtly) Most Successful Lawyers' Award, Soc. of Asian Lawyers, 2005. *Recreations:* opera, theatre, ski-ing. *Address:* 25 Bedford Row, WC1R 4HD. *T:* (020) 7067 1500, *Fax:* (020) 7067 1507. *E:* Kimhollis2@msn.com. *Clubs:* National Liberal, Royal Over-Seas League.

HOLLIS, Posy; *see* Simmonds, P.

HOLLIS, Richard Graham; designer, writer and publisher; *b* 4 Dec. 1934; *s* of late George Harry Hollis and Mary Dorothy Hollis (*née* Doughty); *m* 1974, Posy Simmonds, *qv*; one *s* (and one *s* decd) from a previous marr. *Educ:* Aldenham Sch.; Chelsea Sch. of Art; Wimbledon Coll. of Art; Central Sch. of Arts and Crafts. RDI 2005. Nat. Service, 2nd Lieut, RASC. Lecturer: London Sch. of Printing and Graphic Arts, 1959–61; Chelsea Sch. of Art, 1961–63; staff designer, Galeries Lafayette, Paris, 1963–64; Hd, Dept of Graphic Design, W of England Coll. of Art, Bristol, 1964–66; Art Ed., New Society weekly, 1966–68; Sen. Lectr, Central Sch. of Art and Design, 1967–69 and 1976–78. Consultant Designer: Sadler's Wells Th., 1959–61; Finmar Ltd, 1962–64; Modern Poetry in Translation, 1964–2003; Whitechapel Art Gall., 1969–72 and 1976–85; Art Ed. and designer, Pluto Press, 1972–76. Solo travelling exhibn, Libby Sellers Gall., 2012, Centre Pompidou, Paris, Univ. of Art and Design, Lausanne, Artists' Space, NY, 2013. *Publications:* Graphic Design: a concise history, 1994, rev. and expanded edn 2001; (with Lutz Becker) Avant-Garde Graphics 1918–1934, 2005; Swiss Graphic Design: the origins and growth of an international style 1920–1965, 2006; About Graphic Design, 2012. *Address:* c/o Laurence King Publishing Ltd, 361–363 City Road, EC1V 1LR.

HOLLIS, Rt Rev. (Roger Francis) Crispian; Bishop of Portsmouth, (RC), 1988–2012, now Emeritus; *b* 17 Nov. 1936; *s* of Christopher and Madeleine Hollis. *Educ:* Stonyhurst College; Balliol Coll., Oxford (MA); Venerable English College, Rome (STL). National Service as 2nd Lt, Somerset Light Infantry, 1954–56. Ordained priest, 1965; Assistant in Amesbury, 1966–67; RC Chaplain, Oxford Univ., 1967–77; RC Assistant to Head of Religious Broadcasting, BBC, 1977–81; Administrator, Clifton Cathedral, Bristol, 1981–87; Auxiliary Bishop of Birmingham (Bishop in Oxfordshire), 1987–88. Chm., Dept of Mission and Unity, 2001–05, Chm., Dept for Internat. Affairs, 2005–09, Catholic Bishops' Conf. of England and Wales. *Recreations:* occasional golf, walking, cricket watching. *Address:* Stable House, Fairview, Mells, Somerset BA11 3PP.

HOLLOBONE, Philip Thomas; MP (C) Kettering, since 2005; *b* 7 Nov. 1964. *Educ:* Dulwich Coll.; Lady Margaret Hall, Oxford (MA 1987). Industry res. analyst, 1987–2003. Served TA, 1984–93. Member (C): Bromley BC, 1990–94; Kettering BC, 2003–. Contested (C): Lewisham E, 1997; Kettering, 2001. *Address:* House of Commons, SW1A 0AA.

HOLLOWAY, Adam James Harold; MP (C) Gravesham, since 2005; *b* 1965; *s* of Rev. Roger Holloway, OBE and Anne (*née* Alsop). *Educ:* Cranleigh Sch.; Magdalene Coll., Cambridge (BA Social and Pol Sci. 1987); RMA Sandhurst; Imperial Coll. of Sci. and Technol. (MBA). Travelled with the Afghan Resistance, 1982; classroom asst, Pace Coll., Soweto, S Africa, 1985. Grenadier Guards, 1987–92 (Captain); service in Gulf War, 1991. Presenter, 1992–94: World in Action (undercover, living homeless in London for 3 months, as homeless psychiatric patient for 2 months, as Muslim refugee in Serb territory, Bosnia, living homeless in NYC for 2 weeks); Disguises (reports from UK and Balkans); Sen. Reporter, ITN, 1994–97: Bosnia reporter, Sarajevo, 1994; News at Ten Special Reports; Reporter, Tonight with Trevor MacDonald (undercover as asylum seeker), 2001; Iraq War (Northern front) reports for ITN and Sky News, 2003. PPS to Minister of State, FCO, 2011–12. Member: Defence Select Cttee, 2006–10 and 2012–14; Public Admin Select Cttee, 2014–15; Foreign Affairs Select Cttee, 2015–. Dep. Chm., Cons. Middle East Council, 2010–. Chm., Council for Arab-British Understanding, 2009–14. Trustee: Christian Aid, 1997–2001; MapAction, 2004–10. *Publications:* In Blood Stepp'd in Too Far?: towards a realistic policy for Afghanistan, 2009. *Recreation:* being with my family and godchildren. *Address:* House of Commons, SW1A 0AA. *T:* (020) 7219 3000; c/o 440 Strand, WC2R 0QS. *E:* hollowaya@parliament.uk, ajhholloway@gmail.com. *Clubs:* Pratt's; Gravesend Conservative, Northfleet Conservative.

HOLLOWAY, His Honour Frederick Reginald Bryn; a Circuit Judge, 1992–2012; *b* 9 Jan. 1947; *s* of William Herbert Holloway and Audrey (*née* Hull-Brown); *m* 1974, Barbara Bradley; two *s*. *Educ:* Mill Mead, Shrewsbury; Wrekin Coll., Wellington, Salop; Coll. of Law. Entered chambers in Liverpool, 1972; Asst Recorder, 1984–89; Recorder, 1989–92. *Recreations:* gardening, Shrewsbury Town FC, cricket, tennis.

HOLLOWAY, James Essex, CBE 2012; Director (formerly Keeper), Scottish National Portrait Gallery, 1997–2012; *b* 24 Nov. 1948; *s* of Roland David Holloway and Nancy Briant Holloway (*née* Evans). *Educ:* Marlborough Coll.; Courtauld Inst. of Art, London Univ. (BA Hons). Res. Asst, Nat. Gall. of Scotland, 1972–80; Asst Keeper, Nat. Mus. of Wales, 1980–83; Dep. Keeper, Scottish Nat. Portrait Gall., 1983–97. *Publications:* The Discovery of Scotland, 1978; James Tassie, 1986; Jacob More, 1987; William Aikman, 1988; Patrons and Painters: art in Scotland 1650–1760, 1989; The Norie Family, 1994. *Recreations:* motorbikes, India, French horn. *Address:* 20 India Street, Edinburgh EH3 6HB. *Clubs:* New, Puffin's (Edinburgh).

HOLLOWAY, Michael John, OBE 2009; HM Diplomatic Service, retired; Director, MJ Holloway Consultancy Services Ltd, since 2014; Board Member, King's Group, since 2013; *b* Minster-in-Kent, 14 Jan. 1957; *s* of Robert Lawrence Holloway and Jean Olive Dormedy. *Educ:* St Edmund's Sch., Canterbury. Joined FCO, 1976; Finance Dept, FCO, 1976–77; Vice Consul, Dubai, 1978; Asst Mgt Officer/Accountant, Bucharest, 1979–81; African/Middle East Floater, 1981–82; Asst Reviewer, Mgt Officer/Accountant, FCO, 1984–87; Vice Consul, Barcelona, 1988–90; Parly Desk Officer, Europe Dept, FCO, 1990–92; Know How Fund Manager, Czech and Slovak Republics, 1992–93, FCO/ODA; Second Sec. (Pol and Press), Mexico City, 1994–97; Dep. Consul-Gen., Rio de Janeiro, 1998–2002; Dir, Immigration, Dhaka, 2002–03; Dep. Hd, Resource Mgt Unit, Europe Directorate, FCO, 2003–05; Consul Gen., Spain, 2005–10; Ambassador to Panama, 2011–13. Member (C): Dover DC, 2015–; Sandwich Town Council, 2015–. *Recreations:* dogs, painting, gardening, walking.

HOLLOWAY, Neil John; Corporate Vice President, Sales and Operations, Microsoft Business Solutions, since 2012; *b* 14 May 1960; *s* of Jenny Holley; *m*; one *s* one *d*. *Educ:* Univ. of Bath (BSc 1982); Jesus Coll., Cambridge (MPhil 1984). Man. Dir, Migent UK, 1988–90; Microsoft UK, 1990–2003: Dir, 1994–96; Dep. Gen. Manager, 1996–98; Man. Dir, 1998–2003; Vice-Pres., 2000–05 and Vice-Pres., Sales, Marketing and Services, 2003–05, Pres., 2005–07, Microsoft Europe, ME and Africa; Vice Pres., Business Strategy, Microsoft Internat., 2007–12. *Recreations:* golf, swimming.

HOLLOWAY, Reginald Eric, CMG 1984; HM Diplomatic Service, retired; *b* 22 June 1932; *s* of late Ernest and Beatrice Holloway; *m* 1958, Anne Penelope, *d* of late Walter Robert and Doris Lilian Pawley; one *d*. *Educ:* St Luke's, Brighton. Apprentice reporter, 1947–53; served RAF, 1953–55; journalist in Britain and E Africa, 1955–61; Press Officer, Tanganyika Govt, 1961–63; Dir, British Inf. Service, Guyana, 1964–67; Inf. Dept, FCO, 1967–69 (Anguilla, 1969); 2nd, later 1st Sec., Chancery in Malta, 1970–72; E African Dept, FCO, 1972–74; Consul and Head of Chancery, Kathmandu, 1974–77 (Chargé d'Affaires *ai*, 1975 and 1976); Asst Head, S Asian Dept, FCO, 1977–79; Counsellor, 1979; Inspector, 1979–81; Consul-Gen., Toronto, 1981–85; Sen. British Trade Comr, Hong Kong, 1985–89, and Consul-Gen. (non-resident), Macao, 1986–89; Consul-Gen., Los Angeles, 1989–92. Business consultant, 1992–97; tree farmer, 1998–2001. Chm., Canadian Urban Inst., 1993–98. *Publications:* The Evolution and Demise of the Larger Format Press Camera, 2008. *Recreations:* gardening, old press cameras. *Address:* 6811 Carmella Place, Niagara Falls, ON L2J 4J4, Canada.

HOLLOWAY, Richard Arthur; Managing Director, Thames, since 2011; *b* Watford, 16 March 1949; *s* of Gordon Roy Holloway and Iris Harriet Holloway; *m* (marr. diss.). *Educ:* Watford Grammar Sch. Producer, 1982, Controller of Entertainment, 1992–98, Central Television; Hd of Entertainment, 1998–2010, Dir of Entertainment, 2010–11, Pearson Television, then Thames Television, later talkbackThames; executive producer: Pop Idol, 2001–03; X Factor, 2004–; Britain's Got Talent, 2007–. FRTS 2009. Lifetime Achievement Award, RTS, 2009. *Recreations:* golf, gardening, all things Italian. *Address:* Thames, 1 Stephen Street, W1T 1AL. *T:* (020) 7691 6000. *E:* richard.holloway@thames.tv. *Clubs:* Ivy, Soho House.

HOLLOWAY, Rt Rev. Richard Frederick; Bishop of Edinburgh, 1986–2000 and Primus of the Episcopal Church in Scotland, 1992–2000; Chairman: Scottish Arts Council, 2005–10; Joint Board, Scottish Arts Council and Scottish Screen, 2007–10; *b* 26 Nov. 1933; *s* of Arthur and Mary Holloway; *m* 1963, Jean Elizabeth Kennedy, New York; one *s* two *d*. *Educ:* Kelham Theol Coll.; Edinburgh Theol Coll.; Union Theol Seminary, New York (STM); BD (London). FRSE 1995. Curate, St Ninian's, Glasgow, 1959–63; Priest-in-charge, St Margaret and St Mungo's, Glasgow, 1963–68; Rector, Old St Paul's, Edinburgh, 1968–80; Rector, Church of the Advent, Boston, Mass, USA, 1980–84; Vicar, St Mary Magdalen's, Oxford, 1984–86. Gresham Prof. of Divinity, 1997–2001. Member: Human Fertilisation and Embryo Authority, 1991–97; Broadcasting Standards Commn, 2001–03; Chm., Edinburgh Voluntary Orgns Council, 1991–95. FRSE 1995. DUniv: Strathclyde, 1994; Open, 2005; Hon. DLitt Napier, 2000; Hon. DD: Aberdeen, 1995; Glasgow, 2001; Hon. LLD Dundee, 2009; DUniv Stirling, 2010; Hon. Dr Drama Royal Conservatoire of Scotland, 2012. *Publications:* Let God Arise, 1972; New Vision of Glory, 1974; A New Heaven, 1978; Beyond Belief, 1982; Signs of Glory, 1983; The Killing, 1984, 2nd edn as Behold Your King, 1995; (ed) The Anglican Tradition, 1984; Paradoxes of Christian Faith and Life, 1984; The Sidelong Glance, 1985; The Way of the Cross, 1986; Seven to Flee, Seven to Follow, 1987; Crossfire: faith and doubt in an age of certainty, 1988; Another Country, Another King, 1991; Who Needs Feminism?, 1991; Anger, Sex, Doubt and Death, 1992; The Stranger in the Wings, 1994; (jtly) Churches and How to Survive Them, 1994; Limping Towards the Sunrise, 1995; Dancing on the Edge, 1997; Godless Morality, 1999; Doubts and Loves: what is left of Christianity, 2001; On

Forgiveness, 2002; Looking in the Distance, 2004; How to Read the Bible, 2006; Between the Monster and the Saint: reflections on the human condition, 2008; Leaving Alexandria: a memoir of faith and doubt, 2012. *Recreations:* long-distance walking, reading, cinema, music. *Address:* 6 Blantyre Terrace, Edinburgh EH10 5AE.

HOLLOWAY, Prof. Robin Greville, PhD, MusD; composer; Fellow of Gonville and Caius College, Cambridge, since 1969, and Professor of Musical Composition, University of Cambridge, 2001–11, now Emeritus; *b* 19 Oct. 1943; *s* of Robert Charles Holloway and Pamela Mary Jacob. *Educ:* St Paul's Cathedral Choir Sch.; King's Coll. Sch., Wimbledon; King's Coll., Cambridge (MA 1968; PhD 1972; MusD 1976); New Coll., Oxford. Lectr in Music, 1975–99, Reader in Music, 1999–2001, Cambridge Univ. *Compositions* include: Garden Music, 1962; First Concerto for Orchestra, 1966–69; Scenes from Schumann, 1969–70; Evening with Angels, 1972; Domination of Black, 1973–74; Sea Surface full of Clouds, 1974–75; Clarissa, 1976 (premièred ENO, 1990); Romanza, 1976; The Rivers of Hell, 1977; Second Concerto for Orchestra, 1978–79; Serenade in C, 1979; Aria, 1980; Peer Gynt, 1980–97; Brand, 1981; Women in War, 1982; Second Idyll, 1983; Seascape and Harvest, 1984; Viola Concerto, 1984; Serenade in E flat, 1984; Ballad for harp and orch., 1985; Inquietus, 1986; Double Concerto for clarinet and saxophone, 1988; The Spacious Firmament, 1989; Violin Concerto, 1990; Boys and Girls Come Out to Play, 1992; Gilded Goldbergs, 1992–98; Missa Caiensis, 1993–2001; Third Concerto for Orchestra, 1994; Canterbury Concerto for clarinet and orch., 1997; Scenes from Antwerp, 1998; Double Bass Concerto, 1998; Symphony, 1999; Spring Music, 2002; String Quartet no 1, 2003; String Quartet no 2, 2004; Fourth Concerto for Orchestra, 2006; Five Temperaments, 2008; Fifth Concerto for Orchestra, 2009; Reliquary, 2010; String Quartet no 4, trio for oboe, violin and piano, 2011; C'est l'extase, after Debussy, for soprano and orchestra, 2012; Europa and the Bull, for tuba and orchestra, 2014. *Publications:* Wagner and Debussy, 1978; On Music: essays and diversions 1963–2003, 2003; Essays and Diversions II, 2008; numerous articles and reviews. *Recreation:* playing on two pianos. *Address:* Gonville and Caius College, Cambridge CB2 1TA. *T:* (01223) 335424.

HOLLOWELL, Rt Rev. Barry Craig Bates, PhD; Bishop of Calgary, 2000–05; Registered Psychologist, since 2013; *b* Boston, Mass, 14 April 1948; *m* 1976, Linda Barry (*d* 2008); two *s* one *d*. *Educ:* Valparaiso Univ., Indiana (BA 1970); Westcott House and Fitzwilliam Coll., Cambridge (BA 1972, MA 1976); Episcopal Divinity Sch., Cambridge, Mass (MDiv 1973); St Paul Univ., Ottawa (MPastStudies 1979); Univ. of NB (MA Psychol. 1986); Univ. of Calgary (PhD Counselling Psychol. 2012). Ordained deacon, 1973, priest, 1974; Deacon, All Saints', Chelmsford, Mass, 1973–74; Asst Curate, Christ Church Cath., Fredericton, NB, 1974–75; pastoral and liturgical work, Christ Church Cath., and Anglican Chaplain, Univ. of NB, 1975–86; pastoral work, St Barnabas, Ottawa, 1978–79; interim Priest-in-charge, St Margaret's Chapel-of-Ease, 1983; Rector, St George's Anglican Ch, St Catharines, Niagara, 1986–2000; Archdeacon, Lincoln, Niagara, 1991–2000. Mem., Gen. Synod, 1989–2005 (Chm., Faith, Worship and Ministry Cttee, 1995–2001). Rep. Anglican Ch of Canada at signing of Porvoo Agreement, Westminster Abbey, 1996. *Recreations:* photography, music, cooking, stained and fused glass. *Address:* (home) 26 Shannon Square SW, Calgary, AB T2Y 4K1, Canada. *T:* (587) 2154939. *W:* www.bcbhcounselling.com.

HOLLOWS, Dame Sharon, DBE 2001; Principal, Charter Academy, Portsmouth, since 2009; consultant on management and leadership, since 2004; *b* 14 Dec. 1958; *d* of Jack and Margaret Hollows; one *s* one *d*. *Educ:* Haslingden Grammar Sch.; W London Inst. of Higher Educn; Greenwich Univ. (MA Ed). Teacher, 1979–93: Furness Jun. Sch. and Manor Special Sch., Brent; St James' Jun. Sch. and Manor Primary Sch., Newham; Head Teacher, Calverton Primary Sch., Newham, 1994–2002; Adv. Head Teacher, Plumcroft Primary Sch., Greenwich, 2002–04; Dir, Sharon Hollows Consultancy Ltd, 2004–12. Mem., Standards Task Force, 2000–02. *Recreations:* horse riding, motor cycling, eating. *Address:* The Oast House, Hartfield Road, Edenbridge, Kent TN8 5NH.

HOLM, Sir Ian, Kt 1998; CBE 1989; actor, since 1954; *b* 12 Sept. 1931; *s* of Dr James Harvey Cuthbert and Jean Wilson Cuthbert; *m* 1st, 1955, Lynn Mary Shaw (marr. diss. 1965); two *d*; and one *s* one *d*; 2nd, 1982, Sophie Baker (marr. diss. 1986); one *s*; 3rd, 1991, Penelope Wilton, *qv* (marr. diss. 2002); one step *d*; 4th, 2003, Sophie de Stempel. *Educ:* Chigwell Grammar Sch., Essex. Trained RADA, 1950–53 (interrupted by Nat. Service); joined Shakespeare Memorial Theatre, 1954, left after 1955; Worthing Rep., 1956; tour, Olivier's Titus Andronicus, 1957; re-joined Stratford, 1958: roles include: Puck; Ariel; Gremio; Lorenzo; Prince Hal; Henry V; Duke of Gloucester; Richard III; The Fool in Lear; Lennie in The Homecoming (also on Broadway, 1966) (Evening Standard Actor of the Year, 1965); left RSC, 1967; Moonlight, Almeida, 1993 (Evening Standard Actor of the Year, Critics Circle Award); King Lear, RNT, 1997 (Olivier award for Best Actor, 1998); The Homecoming, Comedy, 2001. Major film appearances include: Young Winston, The Fixer, Oh! What a Lovely War, The Bofors Gun, Alien, All Quiet on the Western Front, Chariots of Fire (Best Supporting Actor: Cannes, 1981; BAFTA, 1982); Return of the Soldier; Greystoke; Brazil; Laughterhouse; Dance With a Stranger; Wetherby; Dreamchild; Another Woman; Hamlet; Kafka; Naked Lunch; Blue Ice; Mary Shelley's Frankenstein, 1994; The Madness of King George, Big Night, Night Falls on Manhattan, 1995; Lochness, 1996; A Life Less Ordinary, The Sweet Hereafter, The Fifth Element, 1997; Simon Magus, eXistenZ, The Match, Joe Gould's Secret, 1998; Esther Kahn, Beautiful Joe, 1999; Bless the Child, Fellowship of the Ring, 2001; From Hell, 2002; Return of the King, 2003; The Emperor's New Clothes, Garden State, Strangers with Candy, 2004; Chromophobia, Beyond Friendship, The Treatment, Lord of War, 2005; The Hobbit: An Unexpected Journey, 2012; The Hobbit: The Battle of the Five Armies, 2014. TV series include: J. M. Barrie in trilogy The Lost Boys (RTS Best Actor Award, 1979); We, the Accused, 1980; The Bell, 1981; Game, Set and Match, 1988; other TV appearances include: Lech Walesa in Strike, 1981; Goebbels in Inside the Third Reich, 1982; Mr and Mrs Edgehill, 1985; The Browning Version, 1986; Uncle Vanya, 1990; The Last Romantics, 1991; The Borrowers, 1992; The Deep Blue Sea, 1994; Landscape, 1995; King Lear, 1997; Alice Through the Looking Glass, 1998. *Publications:* (with Steven Jacobi) Acting My Life (autobiog.), 2004. *Recreations:* tennis, walking, general outdoor activities. *Address:* c/o Markham, Froggatt & Irwin, 4 Windmill Street, W1T 2HZ.

HOLM, Niels; Official Secretary to Governor-General of New Zealand, 2010–14; *b* Rotherham, NZ, 12 Jan. 1955; *s* of Helge Holm and Janet Holm; *m* 1975, Suzette Parks. *Educ:* Canterbury Univ., Christchurch (MA Hons 1975; Dip. Teaching 1976). Teacher, Dannevirke High Sch., 1977–78; joined Dept of Trade and Industry, NZ, 1979; Private Sec. to Minister of For. Affairs and Overseas Trade, 1982–84, to Minister for Overseas Trade, 1984–85; Japanese lang. trng, 1985–87; Trade Comr, Tokyo, 1987; joined Min. of For. Affairs and Trade, 1988; First Sec., 1988–90; N Asia Div., 1990–92; Dep. Hd of Mission, Manila, 1992–95; Econ. First Sec., Tokyo, 1995–99; Internat. Security and Arms Control Div., 1999; Dep. Dir, Asia-Pacific Econ. Cooperation Div., 1999–2001; Ambassador to Iran and High Comr to Pakistan, 2001–04, and concurrently first Ambassador to Afghanistan, 2003–04; Regl Dep. Dir, Pacific Div., 2005–07; High Comr to PNG, 2007–10. *Recreations:* reading, ski-ing, travel.

HOLMAN, Hon. Sir (Edward) James, Kt 1995; **Hon. Mr Justice Holman;** a Judge of the High Court of Justice, Family Division, since 1995; *b* 21 Aug. 1947; *o s* of late Dr Edward Theodore Holman and Mary Megan Holman, MBE (*née* Morris), formerly of Ringwood, Hants, and Manaccan, Cornwall; *m* 1979, Fiona Elisabeth, *er d* of late Dr Ronald Cathcart Roxburgh, FRCP; two *s* one *d*. *Educ:* Dauntsey's; Exeter College, Oxford (BA Jurisp., MA). Called to the Bar, Middle Temple, 1971, Bencher, 1995; QC 1991; Western Circuit; in practice, 1971–95; Standing Counsel to HM Treasury (Queen's Proctor), 1980–91; a Recorder, 1993–95; Family Div. Liaison Judge, Western Circuit, 1995–2002. A Legal Assessor, UK Central Council for Nursing, Midwifery and Health Visiting, 1983–95. Member: Family Proceedings Rules Cttee, 1991–95; Supreme Court Procedure Cttee, 1992–95; ex-officio Mem., Bar Council, 1992–95. Chm., Family Law Bar Assoc., 1992–95 (Sec., 1988–92). Mem., Council, RYA, 1980–83, 1984–87, 1988–91. *Recreations:* sailing, ski-ing, music. *Address:* Royal Courts of Justice, Strand, WC2A 2LL. *Clubs:* Royal Ocean Racing (Mem. Cttee, 1984–87); Royal Yacht Squadron, Ocean Cruising.

HOLMAN, Sir John (Stranger), Kt 2010; Salters Professor of Chemical Education, University of York, 2000–04, Emeritus Professor of Chemistry, 2010; Senior Adviser for Education: Wellcome Trust, since 2011; Gatsby Foundation, since 2011; *b* Bath, 16 Sept. 1946; *s* of Leslie Holman and Elizabeth Holman; *m* 1969, Wendy North; two *s* one *d*. *Educ:* Royal Grammar Sch., Guildford; Gonville and Caius Coll., Cambridge (BA Hons 1967). CChem 1985; FRSC 1985. Chemistry teacher: Radley Coll., 1967–71; Bristol Grammar Sch., 1972–76; Hd of Sci., Watford Grammar Sch., 1976–84; educnl consultant, author and pt-time teacher, 1984–94; Headmaster, Watford Grammar Sch. for Boys, 1994–2000. Dir, Nat. Sci. Learning Centre, 2004–10; Nat. Dir, Sci., Technol., Engrg and Maths prog., 2006–10. Chm., Teacher Develt Trust, 2014–; Trustee: Natural History Mus., 2011–; RSC, 2013–. Lord Lewis Award, RSC, 2014; Kavli Educn Medal, Royal Soc., 2014. *Publications:* (with G. Hill) Chemistry in Context, 1978, 6th edn 2011; (jtly) Chemistry^3, 2009, 2nd edn 2013; author/ed. of 15 other text books; contrib. articles to numerous educnl jls. *Recreations:* spending time with my large family, growing, cooking and eating food, walking, cycling, reading novels, biography and poetry. *Address:* Chemistry Department, University of York, York YO10 5DD. *E:* jsh4@york.ac.uk.

HOLMAN, Rev. Michael Mark, SJ; Principal, Heythrop College, University of London, since 2012; *b* 4 Nov. 1954; *s* of Michael and Sonja Holman. *Educ:* Wimbledon Coll.; Heythrop Coll., Univ. of London (BA); Weston Jesuit Sch. of Theol. (MDiv); Fordham Univ., NY (MSc). Entered Society of Jesus, 1974; ordained priest, 1988; Dep. Headmaster, Mt St Mary's Coll., 1992–94; Headmaster, Wimbledon Coll., 1995–2004; Provincial Superior (British Province), 2005–11. FRSA. *Recreations:* classical music, hill walking, Ignatian spirituality. *Address:* Heythrop College, University of London, Kensington Square, W8 5HN.

HOLMAN, His Honour Richard Christopher; a Senior Circuit Judge, 2002–11 (a Circuit Judge, 1994–2011); Designated Civil Judge, 1998–2011; *b* 16 June 1946; *s* of Frank Harold Holman and Joan (*née* Attrill); *m* 1st, 1969, Susan Whittaker, MBE, DL (*d* 2007); two *s*; 2nd, 2009, Kathleen Hendry. *Educ:* Watford Grammar Sch. for Boys; Eton Coll.; Gonville and Caius Coll., Cambridge (MA 1968). Admitted as solicitor, 1971; Partner, Foysters, later Davies Wallis Foyster, 1973–94, Man. Partner, 1988–89; Dep. Dist Registrar of High Court and Dep. Registrar of County Court, 1982–88; Asst Recorder, 1988–92; a Recorder, 1992–94. Member: NW Legal Aid Area Cttee, 1980–94; Civil Procedure Rule Cttee, 1997–2002. Mem. Council, Manchester Law Soc., 1983–90. Gov., Pownall Hall Sch., Wilmslow, 1990–98 (Chm., 1993–98). Trustee, Crossroads Care Cheshire East, 2008–11. *Recreations:* golf, gardening, theatre, music. *Club:* Wilmslow Golf (Captain, 1999).

HOLMBERG, Eric Robert Reginald; Deputy Chief Scientist (Army), Ministry of Defence, 1972–77; *b* 24 Aug. 1917; *s* of Robert and May Holmberg; *m* 1940, Wanda Erna Reich (*d* 2003); one *s* one *d*. *Educ:* Sandown (Isle of Wight) Grammar Sch.; St John's Coll., Cambridge (MA); Imperial Coll., London (PhD). Joined Mine Design Department, Admiralty, 1940; Admiralty Gunnery Establishment, 1945; Operational Research Department, Admiralty, 1950; appointed Chief Supt Army Operational Research Group, 1956; Dir, Army Operational Science and Res., subseq. Asst Chief Scientist (Army), MoD, 1961–72. *Publications:* The Trouble with Relativity, 1986; papers in Proc. Royal Astronomical Society, and Proc. of Physical Interpretations of Relativity Theory.

HOLMES OF RICHMOND, Baron *cr* 2013 (Life Peer), of Richmond in the London Borough of Richmond upon Thames; **Christopher Holmes,** MBE 1993; Director of Paralympic Integration, London Organising Committee of the 2012 Olympic Games and Paralympic Games, 2009–13; *b* Peterborough, 15 Oct. 1971; *s* of Michael John Holmes and Margaret Mary Holmes. *Educ:* Harry Cheshire High Sch., Kidderminster; King's Coll., Cambridge (BA 1994; MA 1998). Paralympic swimmer; winner of Paralympic Gold Medals: 6 at Barcelona Games, 1992; 3 at Atlanta Games, 1996. Public speaker, 1992–. Admitted Solicitor, 2004; with Ashurst, 2002–07. Non-executive Director: Disability Rights Commn, 2002–07; UK Sport, 2005–; Equality and Human Rights Commn, 2013–; Mem., Pensions Client Bd, 2009–10. Mem., Digital Skills Cttee, H of L, 2014–15. Patron: Youth Sport Trust, 1995–; British Paralympic Assoc., 2004–; Help for Heroes, 2008–. Ambassador, Queen Elizabeth Diamond Jubilee Trust, 2013–. Hon. LLD: Bath, 2012; BPP Law Sch., 2014. *Publications:* contrib. articles to Daily Telegraph, Observer, Spectator and European. *Recreations:* ski-ing, reading, wine. *Address:* Kew, Surrey. *T:* 07961 358136. *E:* cholmes128@btinternet.com. *Club:* Hawke's (Cambridge).

HOLMES, Prof. Andrew Bruce, AM 2004; FRS 2000; FAA; FTSE; CSIRO Fellow, CSIRO Materials Science and Engineering, 2008–14, now Emeritus; University Laureate Professor, University of Melbourne, 2009–14, now Emeritus; Emeritus Professor and Distinguished Research Fellow, Imperial College London, since 2009; President, Australian Academy of Science, since 2014 (Member, Council, since 2007); *b* 5 Sept. 1943; *s* of late Bruce Morell Holmes and Frances Henty Graham Holmes; *m* 1971, Jennifer Lesley; three *s*. *Educ:* Scotch Coll., Melbourne; Univ. of Melbourne (BSc, MSc); University Coll. London (PhD 1971; Hon. Fellow, 2012); ScD Cantab 1997; DSc Oxon 2011. Royal Soc. European Postdoctoral Fellow, ETH Zürich, 1971–72; University of Cambridge: Demonstrator, 1972–77; Lectr, 1977–94; Dir, Melville Lab. for Polymer Synthesis, 1994–2004; Reader in Organic and Polymer Chemistry, 1995–98; Prof. of Organic and Polymer Chemistry, 1998–2004; Fellow, Clare Coll., Cambridge, 1973–; Dir, Cambridge Quantum Fund, 1995–2004; Mem., CUP Syndicate, 2000–04; ARC Fedn and VESKI Fellow, and Prof. of Chem., Univ. of Melbourne/CSIRO Molecular and Health Technologies, 2004–09; Prof. of Chem., Imperial Coll., London, 2004–09. Member: Internat. Sci. Adv. Bd, A*Star Inst. of Materials Sci. and Engrg, Singapore, 2008–11; External Rev. Panel, Internat. Council for Sci., 2013–14. Principal Ed., Jl Materials Res., 1994–99; Chm., Editl Bd, Chemical Communications, 2000–03; Member: Bd of Editors, Organic Syntheses, Inc., 1996–2001; Publishing Bd, RSC, 2003–06; Publishing Adv. Cttee, CSIRO, 2006–14; Editl Bd, New Jl of Chemistry, 2000–03; International Advisory Board: Macromolecular Chem. and Physics, 1999–2006; Jl Mater. Chem., 1996–2006; Chemical Communications, 2004–12; Chem. World, 2004–; Aust. Jl of Chem., 2004–; Bulletin, Chemical Soc. of Japan, 2004–; Beilstein Jl Organic Chem., 2005–; Angewandte Chemie, 2006–13; Associate Ed., Organic Letters, 2006–. Vis. Fellow, La Trobe Univ., 1977; Visiting Professor: Univ. of Calif, Berkeley, 1984; Univ. of Calif, Irvine, 1991; Royal Soc. Leverhulme Sen. Res. Fellow, 1993–94; Wilsmore Fellow, Univ. of Melbourne, 2002–03; Hans Kupczyk Foundn Guest Prof., Univ. of Ulm, Germany, 2009; Newton Abraham Vis. Prof. and Fellow, Lincoln Coll., Univ. of Oxford, 2011–12; Fellow, Materials Res. Soc., 2013; Hon. Fellow, Chemical Res. Soc. of India, 2013. Lectures: W. G. Dauben, Univ. of Calif, Berkeley, 1999–2000; Aggarwal, Cornell Univ., 2002; Tilden, RSC, 2003; Merck-Karl Pfister, MIT, 2005; W. Heinlen Hall, Bowling Green State Univ., Ohio, 2006; Merck Res., RSC, 2008; Merck, Univ. of Cambridge, 2009; Robert Robinson, Oxford, 2010; Ta-shue Chou, Academia Sinica Taiwan, 2010; H. Dudley Wright Colloquium, Univ. of Geneva, 2012; Chemical Record, Chemical Soc., Japan, 2013; Nozoe, Internat. Symposium on Novel Aromatic Compounds, Taipei, 2013; C. N. R. Rao,

Chem. Res. Soc. India, 2014; McRae, Queens Univ., Ont, 2014. FAA 2006; FTSE 2006; FRACI 2014. Hon. FRSC, 2013. Dr *hc* Hasselt, 2010. Alfred Bader Award, 1994, Materials Chem. Award, 1995, John B. Goodenough Award, 2011, RSC; Descartes Prize, EU, 2003; Macro Gp Medal UK for Outstanding Achievement, 2003; Royal Medal, Royal Soc., 2011; Glenn Award, Energy and Fuels Div., American Chem. Soc., 2015. *Publications:* contribs to various learned chem., physics and materials sci. jls on subject of synthesis and properties of polymeric and organic semiconductor materials and of natural products. *Recreations:* musical appreciation, walking. *Address:* Bio21 Institute, University of Melbourne, 30 Flemington Road, Vic 3010, Australia. *T:* (3) 83442344, *Fax:* (3) 83442384. *E:* aholmes@unimelb.edu.au.

HOLMES, Andrew Mayhew; Chairman, Highland Perthshire Ltd, since 2010; *b* Haltwhistle, Northumberland, 20 June 1947; *s* of Walter Holmes and Nancy Holmes; *m* 1970, Catherine Roth; three *s* one *d*. *Educ:* Millom Sch.; Harrogate Grammar Sch.; Leeds Univ. (BSc Civil Engrg); Newcastle Univ. (MSc Civil Engrg). MICE 1973. Various engrg posts, 1968–94; Dep. Dir, Transportation, Lothian Region, 1994–96; Dep. Dir, Develt, Edinburgh, 1996–98; Dir, City Develt, Edinburgh CC, 1998–2008. Mem., Mobility and Access Cttee for Scotland, 2008–. Trustee: Nat. Mus of Scotland, 2009–; Historic Envmt Scotland, 2015–. *Publications:* articles in engrg and transport jls. *Recreations:* mountaineering, gardening, travelling in Italy. *Address:* Strathtummel, Lower Oakfield, Pitlochry PH16 5DS. *E:* a.m.holmes@btinternet.com. *Club:* Italian Alpine.

HOLMES, David, CB 1985; Director, Corporate Resources, British Airways plc, 1996–99; Chairman, British Airways Regional, 1998–99; *b* 6 March 1935; *s* of late George A. Holmes and Annie Holmes; *m* 1963, Ann Chillingworth; one *s* two *d*. *Educ:* Doncaster Grammar Sch.; Christ Church, Oxford (MA); Birkbeck Coll., Univ. of London (BA). Asst Principal, Min. of Transport and Civil Aviation, 1957; Private Sec. to Jt Parly Sec., 1961–63; HM Treasury, 1965–68; Principal Private Sec. to Minister of Transport, 1968–70; Asst Sec., 1970, Under Sec., 1976, Dep. Sec., 1982–91, Dept of Transport; Dir, Govt and Industry Affairs, British Airways, 1991–95. Trustee: Motorway Archive Trust, 2002–; RAC Foundn, 2003–11 (Chm., 2003–09). *Recreations:* history, archaeology, music. *Address:* Dormer Lodge, 31 Little Park Gardens, Enfield, Middx EN2 6PQ. *Club:* Royal Automobile.

HOLMES, David Charles, CBE 2014; Chief Executive, Family Action, since 2013; *b* Wallasey, 29 Dec. 1967; *s* of Denis and Rene Holmes; *m* 1992, Tracey Angela Chippendale; one *s*. *Educ:* London Sch. of Econs and Pol Sci. (LLB Hons 1989); Univ. of Bristol (LLM 1990). Admitted as solicitor, 1993; Solicitor: Clifford Chance, 1991–94; Mayer Brown, 1994–95; Department of Health: Dep. Hd, Emergency Care, 1995–96; Head: Legal Services, Medicines Control Agency (on secondment), 1996–97; Hosp. Policy, 1997–99; Children's Safeguarding Unit, 1999–2002; Dep. Dir, Adoption and Children's Trusts, 2002–03; Deputy Director: Looked After Children and Adoption, DFES, 2003–05; Children's Services, London Bor. of Haringey, 2005–06; Chief Exec., British Assoc. for Adoption and Fostering, 2006–13. Chair: End Child Poverty Coalition, 2013–; Connaught Gp, 2013–15. Trustee, Children England, 2011– (Vice Chair, 2012–14; Chair, 2014–); Chair, Naomi Hse, 2013–. *Recreations:* enjoying family time, music, Spanish language, literature and culture, sport. *Address:* Family Action, 24 Angel Gate, City Road, EC1V 2PT. *T:* (020) 7241 7601. *E:* david.holmes@family-action.org.uk.

HOLMES, David Robert; Registrar, University of Oxford, and Professorial Fellow, St John's College, Oxford, 1998–2006; *b* 2 May 1948; *s* of late Leslie Howard Holmes and Joyce Mary Holmes (*née* Stone); *m* 1st, 1974, Lesley Ann Crone (marr diss. 1989); one *s* one *d*; 2nd, 1989, Susan, *d* of William John and Edna Bayley. *Educ:* Preston GS; Merton Coll., Oxford (MA; Hon. Fellow, 2000; Chancellor's Prize for Latin Prose, Oxford Univ., 1968). University of Warwick: Admin. Asst, 1970–74; Asst Registrar, 1974–78; seconded as Asst Registrar, Univ. of Sheffield, 1975–76; Sen. Asst Registrar, 1978–82; University of Liverpool: Acad. Sec., 1982–86; Dep. Registrar and Acad. Sec., 1987–88; Registrar and Sec., Univ. of Birmingham, 1988–98. Member: Council, Univ. of Warwick, 2006–09; Academic Council, BPP Univ. (formerly Coll. of Professional Studies), 2007– (Chm., 2014–). Trustee: Ind. Schs Governing Body, Foundn for Schs of King Edward VI in Birmingham, 2006–14 (Chm., 2008–14); James Martin 21st Century Foundn, 2006–09; Arthur Thomson Trust, 2008–. Mem., Birmingham Speculative Club 1870, 2014–. Hon. DCL Oxon, 2006. *Publications:* (contrib.) Beyond the Limelight, 1986; Perspectives, Policy and Practice in Higher Education, 1998; The State of UK Higher Education, 2001. *Recreations:* reading the classics, squash, cricket, golf, tennis, music, gardening. *Address:* 20 Goodby Road, Moseley, Birmingham B13 8NJ. *T:* (0121) 249 9714. *Club:* Edgbaston Golf (Chm., 2009–14).

See also Sir J. E. Holmes.

HOLMES, David Vivian; journalist and broadcaster; Member, Broadcasting Complaints Commission, 1987–92; *b* 12 Oct. 1926; *s* of Vivian and Kathleen St Clair Holmes; *m* 1st, 1957, Rhoda Ann, *d* of late Col N. J. Gai; two *d*; 2nd, 1979, Linda Ruth Alexander (*née* Kirk). *Educ:* Ipswich Sch.; Allhallows Sch. Served KRRC, 1944–47. Evening Standard, 1951–56; Reporter, BBC News, 1956–61; BBC political reporter, 1961–72; Asst Head, BBC Radio Talks and Documentary Programmes; launched Kaleidoscope arts programme, 1973; Political Editor, BBC, 1975–80; Chief Asst to Dir-Gen., BBC, 1980–83; Sec. of the BBC, 1983–85. Chm., Parly Lobby Journalists, 1976–77. Member: Council, Hansard Soc., 1981–83; MoD Censorship Study Gp, 1983; Exec. Cttee, Suffolk Historic Churches Trust, 1989–90. Founder and Organiser, Blyth Valley Chamber Music concerts, 1988–2000. *Publications:* An Inglorious Affair, 2002. *Recreations:* history of 17th century Dissent, gardening. *Address:* 5 Salters Lane, Walpole, Halesworth, Suffolk IP19 9BA. *T:* (01986) 784412.

HOLMES, Eamonn; broadcast journalist; Anchor, Sunrise, Sky News, since 2005; presenter, This Morning, ITV, since 2006; *b* 3 Dec. 1959; *s* of Leonard Holmes and Josephine Holmes; three *s* one *d*. *Educ:* St Malachy's Coll., Belfast. Reporter, Ulster TV, 1980–86; presenter of TV programmes including: Good Evening Ulster, Ulster TV, 1982–86; Open Air, 1986–91, Holiday, 1989–92, Jet Set, 2001–07, BBC; GMTV, 1993–2005; presenter, Eamonn Holmes Show, BBC Radio Five Live, 2004–09. Mem. Adv. Panel, DCMS Free-to-Air Events Listing Rev., 2009. Mem. Bd, Manchester United Charitable Foundn, 2007–. DUniv: Staffs, 2004; QUB, 2006. *Publications:* Eamonn Holmes: this is my life (autobiog.), 2006. *Recreation:* watching Manchester United. *E:* info@eamonn.tv.

HOLMES, George Dennis, CB 1979; FRSE; Director-General and Deputy Chairman, Forestry Commission, 1977–86, retired; *b* 9 Nov. 1926; *s* of James Henry Holmes and Florence Holmes (*née* Jones); *m* 1953, Sheila Rosemary Woodger; three *d*. *Educ:* John Bright's Sch., Llandudno; Univ. of Wales (BSc (Hons)); FRSE 1982; FICFor. Post-grad. Research, Univ. of Wales, 1947; appointed Forestry Commission, 1948; Asst Silviculturist, Research Div., 1948; Asst Conservator, N Wales, 1962; Dir of Research, 1968; Comr for Harvesting and Marketing, 1973. Mem., Scottish Legal Aid Bd, 1989–94. Hon. Prof., Univ. of Aberdeen, 1984–2000. Pres., Capability Scotland, 2003–13. Hon. DSc Wales, 1985. *Publications:* contribs to Forestry Commission pubns and to Brit. and Internat. forestry jls. *Recreations:* golf, fishing. *Address:* 7 Cammo Road, Barnton, Edinburgh EH4 8EF. *T:* (0131) 339 7474.

HOLMES, Janice Elizabeth; *see* Ward, J. E.

HOLMES, Sir John (Eaton), GCVO 2004 (CVO 1998); KBE 1999; CMG 1997; Director, Ditchley Foundation, since 2010; *b* 29 April 1951; *s* of late Leslie Howard Holmes and Joyce Mary (*née* Stone); *m* 1976, Margaret Penelope Morris; three *d*. *Educ:* Preston Grammar Sch.; Balliol Coll., Oxford (BA 1st Cl. Hons Lit. Hum., MA). HM Diplomatic Service, 1973–2007: FCO, 1973–76; 3rd Sec., then 2nd Sec., Moscow, 1976–78; Near East and N Africa Dept, FCO, 1978–82; Asst Private Sec. to Foreign Sec., 1982–84; 1st Sec. (Economic), Paris, 1984–87; Asst Hd of Soviet Dept, FCO, 1987–89; seconded to Thomas de la Rue & Co., 1989–91; Counsellor, Econ. and Commercial, New Delhi, 1991–95; Head of European Union Dept (External), FCO, 1995; on secondment as Private Sec. (Foreign Affairs), 1996–99 and Principal Private Sec., 1997–99, to the Prime Minister; Ambassador to Portugal, 1999–2001; Ambassador to France, 2001–07; Under-Sec. Gen. for Humanitarian Affairs, UN, 2007–10. Chm. Bd, Internat. Rescue Cttee UK, 2012–. Member: Council, Radley Coll., 2010–; Exec. Cttee, Pilgrims, 2011–. *Publications:* The Politics of Humanity, 2013. *Recreations:* sport (tennis, cricket, golf), music, reading. *Address:* c/o Ditchley Foundation, Ditchley Park, Enstone, Chipping Norton, Oxon OX7 4ER.

See also D. R. Holmes.

HOLMES, Dr John Ernest Raymond; Director, Quality and Performance, United Kingdom Atomic Energy Authority, 1989–90; *b* Birmingham, 13 Aug. 1925; *s* of late Dr John K. Holmes and of Ellen R. Holmes; *m* 1949, Patricia Clitheroe; one *s* one *d*. *Educ:* King Edward's School, Birmingham; University of Birmingham (BSc, PhD). Asst Lectr in Physics, Manchester Univ., 1949–52; Research Scientist, AERE Harwell, 1952–59; Atomic Energy Establishment, Winfrith: Research Scientist, 1959–66; Chief Physicist, 1966–73; Dep. Dir, 1973–86; Dir, 1986–89. *Publications:* technical papers on nuclear power. *Address:* Flat 1, St Antony's School House, Westbury, Sherborne, Dorset DT9 3QF. *T:* (01935) 817335.

HOLMES, Jonathan Roy; Managing Director, Jon Holmes Media Ltd, since 2006; *b* 26 June 1950; *s* of Roy Coulson Holmes and Margery Eleanor Heathcote Holmes (*née* Adams); *m* 1981, Margaret Helen Shipman; one *s* two *d*. *Educ:* Oundle Sch., Northants; Leeds Univ. (BA Hons (Political Studies) 1971). Reporter, Leicester Mercury, 1971–72; Dir, Pointon York Gp, 1972–80; Founder and Man. Dir, Park Associates Ltd, 1981–98; Partner, Benson McGarvey & Co., 1983–2001; Chm. and CEO, SFX Sports Gp, 1998–2006. Non-executive Director: Sportech plc, 2007–10; Brand meets Brand Ltd, 2011–. Chairman: Leicester City FC, 2003; Cultivate East Midlands, 2006–11. Co-Founder, Mick Fitzgerald Racing Club, 2012. Hon. MBA De Montfort, 2005. *Recreations:* theatre, sport, esp. football, cricket and National Hunt racing, causing trouble. *Address:* Norwood Farmhouse, Cobham, Surrey KT11 1BS. *T:* 07802 461706. *E:* jon@jonholmesmedia.com. *Clubs:* Garrick, Groucho, MCC.

HOLMES, Dame Kelly, DBE 2005 (MBE 1998); National Schools Sports Champion, 2006–08; Director, Double Gold Enterprises, since 1996; *b* 19 April 1970; *d* of Michael Norris and Pamela Thomson. *Educ:* Hugh Christie Sch., Tonbridge. Nursing Asst for mentally handicapped, 1987; served Army, 1988–97. International athlete, 1993–2005: winner: Commonwealth Games: Gold, 1994 and 2002, Silver, 1998, 1500m; European Championships: Silver, 1500m, 1994; Bronze, 800m, 2002; World Championships: Silver, 1500m, Bronze, 800m, 1995; Silver, 800m, 2003; Olympic Games: Bronze, 800m, 2000; Gold, 1500m and 800m, 2004; Silver, World Indoor Championships, 2003; 1500m, 1st World Athletics Final, 2004. Founder and Chair, Dame Kelly Holmes Legacy Trust, 2008–. Pres., Commonwealth Games England. Performance of Year Award, IAAF, 2004; BBC Sports Personality of Year, 2004; European Athlete of Year, 2004; World Female Athlete of Year, 2004. *Publications:* (with R. Lewis) My Olympic Ten Days, 2004; (with F. Blake) Black, White and Gold: my autobiography, 2005; (with G. Walden) Katy and the Shooting Star, 2008.

HOLMES, Prof. Kenneth Charles, PhD; FRS 1981; Director of the Department of Biophysics, Max-Planck-Institute for Medical Research, Heidelberg, 1968–2003; Professor of Biophysics, Heidelberg University, 1972–99, now Emeritus; *b* 19 Nov. 1934; *m* 1957, Mary Scruby; one *s* three *d*. *Educ:* St John's Coll., Cambridge (MA 1959); London Univ. (PhD 1959). Res. Associate, Children's Hosp., Boston, USA, 1960–61; Mem., Scientific Staff, MRC Lab. of Molecular Biology, Cambridge, 1962–68. Mem., EMBO; Scientific mem., Max Planck Gesellschaft, 1972–; Mem., Heidelberg Acad. of Scis, 1991. Corresp. Mem., Soc. Royale des Scis, Liège. *Publications:* (with D. Blow) The Use of X-ray Diffraction in the Study of Protein and Nucleic Acid Structure, 1965; papers on virus structure, molecular mechanism of muscular contraction and the structure of actin. *Recreations:* rowing, singing. *Address:* Emeritus Group Biophysics, Max-Planck-Institute for Medical Research, Jahnstrasse 29, 69120 Heidelberg, Germany. *T:* (6221) 486270.

HOLMES, Maurice Colston, OBE 1985; Director, Safety, British Railways Board, 1989–92; *b* 15 Feb. 1935; *s* of Charles Edward Holmes and Ellen Catherine Mary Holmes (*née* Colston); *m* 1985, Margaret Joan Wiscombe. *Educ:* Presentation Coll., Reading. British Rail: Divl Man., Liverpool Street, 1976–79; Chief Operating Man., 1979–80, Dep. Gen. Man., 1980–82, Southern Region; Dir of Operations, BRB, 1982–88. Dir and Trustee, Railway Pension Trustee Co. Ltd, 1994–96. Pres., British Transport Pension Fedn, 1993–. Col, RE, Engrg and Logistic Staff Corps (TA), 1990–2001. *Recreations:* travel, transport, gardens. *Address:* 9 High Tree Drive, Earley, Reading, Berks RG6 1EU. *T:* (0118) 966 8887.

HOLMES, Michael Harry; Chairman, fountains plc, 2007–09; *b* 10 March 1945; *s* of Harry Albert Holmes and Doris Rachel (*née* Linihan); *m* 1968, Ellen van Caspel; three *s*. *Educ:* Alleyn's Sch., Dulwich; Gonville and Caius Coll., Cambridge (MA). Costain Civil Engineering Ltd, 1966–70; Ready Mixed Concrete Ltd, 1970–73; Pioneer Concrete Ltd, 1973–77; Rentokil Group plc, 1977–95: Regl Man. Dir, UK Property Services, 1988–91; Regl Man. Dir, N America, Caribbean and E Africa, 1992–95; self-employed, 1995–97; Chief Executive: Chesterton Internat. plc, 1997–2001; Orbis plc, 2002–08. *Recreations:* fishing, sailing, old cars, motorcycles, theatre. *Address:* Beechcroft, Hophurst Hill, Crawley Down, W Sussex RH10 4LW. *T:* (01342) 716101. *Club:* Oriental.

HOLMES, Michael John; Member (Ind) South West Region, England, European Parliament, 1999–2002 (UK Ind, 1999–2000, subseq. non-aligned); retired; *b* 6 June 1938; adopted *s* of Albert and Elsie Holmes; *m* 1974, Carolyn Allen Jee; two *s* one *d*. *Educ:* Sevenoaks Sch. SSC, Royal Warwicks Regt, 1958–60. Sales and Mkting Exec., Sunday Times, Evening Standard, and Observer, 1962–69; Owner Publisher, Independent Gp of Free Newspapers, 1970–87; voluntary and charity work, 1987–99. European Parliament: Voting Member: Fisheries Cttee; Budgetary Control Cttee. Leader, UK Independence Party, 1998–2000. *Recreations:* travel, reading, politics. *Address:* Highfield House, North Street, Charminster, Dorchester, Dorset DT2 9QS. *T:* (01305) 268599.

HOLMES, Prof. Patrick, PhD; Professor of Hydraulics, Imperial College of Science, Technology and Medicine, 1983–2003; Dean, City and Guilds College, 1988–91; *b* 23 Feb. 1939; *s* of Norman Holmes and Irene (*née* Shelbourne); *m* 1963, Olive (*née* Towning); one *s* one *d*. *Educ:* University Coll. of Swansea, Univ. of Wales (BSc 1960, PhD 1963). CEng, MICE. Res. Engr, Harbour and Deep Ocean Engrg, US Navy Civil Engrg Lab., Port Hueneme, Calif, 1963–65; Lectr, Dept of Civil Engrg, Univ. of Liverpool, 1966–72, Sen. Lectr, 1972–74, Prof. of Maritime Civil Engrg, 1974–83. Vis. Prof., Univ. of the WI, Trinidad, 2001. Chm., Environment Cttee, SERC, 1981–85. Pres., Conf. of European Schs of Advanced Engrg Educn and Res., 1993–95. Hon. Mem., C&G, 1992 (FCGI 1999). *Publications:* (ed) Handbook of Hydraulic Engineering (English edn), by Lencastre, 1987; articles on ocean and coastal engineering, wave motion, wave loading, coastal erosion and accretion, and harbour and breakwater design, in Proc. ICE and Proc. Amer. Soc. of Civil Engrs. *Recreations:* golf, yachting, walking, choral music. *Address:* Cliff Hanger, 2A Claybush Road, Ashwell, Baldock, Herts SG7 5RA. *T:* (01462) 742979.

HOLMES, Paul Robert; *b* 16 Jan. 1957; *s* of Frank and Dorothy Holmes; *m* 1978, Raelene Palmer; three *c*. *Educ:* York Univ. (BA Hons Hist); Sheffield Univ. (PGCE). Teacher, Chesterfield Boys' High Sch., 1979–84; Hd of History, Buxton Coll., 1984–90; Hd of Sixth Form, Buxton Community Sch., 1990–2001. Mem., Chesterfield BC, 1987–95, 1999–2002. MP (Lib Dem) Chesterfield, 2001–10; contested (Lib Dem) same seat, 2010. Lib Dem spokesman on disability, 2001–05, and on work and pensions, 2002–05, on housing, 2007, on home affairs and justice, 2008–10; Shadow Minister for Arts and Heritage, 2006–07. Member: Educn and Skills Select Cttee, 2001–07; Children, Schs and Families Cttee, 2008–10. Chm., Lib Dem Parly Party, 2005–07. *Recreations:* reading, walking, history.

HOLMES, Prof. Peter Henry, OBE 2007; PhD; FRCVS; FRSE; Professor of Veterinary Physiology, 1982–2008, now Emeritus, and Honorary Senior Adviser, since 2008, University of Glasgow; *b* Cottingham, E Yorks, 6 June 1942; *s* of Frank Holmes and Edna Holmes (*née* Wiles); *m* 1965, Ruth Helen Mack; two *d*. *Educ:* Beverley Grammar Sch.; Univ. of Glasgow (BVMS 1966; PhD 1969). MRCVS 1966. University of Glasgow: Asst Lectr, 1966–69, Lectr, 1969–76, Sen. Lectr, 1976–80, Reader, 1980–82, in Vet. Physiol.; Hd, Dept of Vet. Physiol., 1978–97; Vice-Principal for Res., 1997–2004; Territorial Vice-Principal for Faculties of Vet. Medicine, Medicine and Biomed. and Life Scis, 1997–2005; Mem., Sen. Mgt Cttee, 1997–2005; Chm., Univ. Res. Planning and Strategy Cttee, 1997–2004. Jt Chm., Univs of Glasgow and Strathclyde Synergy Partnership, 1997–2004. Chairman: Livestock Res. Strategy Cttee, Natural Resources Dept, ODA, 1992–97; (Founding) Internat. Steering Cttee, Prog. against African Trypanosomiasis, UN, 1997–2002; Strategic Sci. Adv. Panel, Scottish Exec. Envmt and Rural Affairs Dept, 2005–08; Strategic and Tech. Adv. Gp for Neglected Tropical Diseases, WHO, 2013–15; Member: SFC (formerly SHEFC), 2003–10 (Chm., Res. Policy Adv. Cttee, 2003–05; Chm., Res. and Knowledge Transfer Cttee, 2005–10); DTI Res. Council Econ. Impact Wkg Gp (Warry Cttee), 2006. Mem. Council, Treas. and Pres., Assoc. of Vet. Teachers and Res. Workers, 1985–92; Mem., Vet. Policy Gp, BVA, 1993–97; Mem. Council, Treas. and Chm., UFAW, 1991–98. Chm., Res. Awards Cttee, 2005–08, Fellowship Sec., 2008–, RSE. FRSE 1999. Hon. FRCVS 2007. Hon. DUniv Strathclyde, 2004; Hon. DSc Hull, 2013. Comdr, Ordre des Palmes Académiques (France), 2009. *Publications:* (ed jtly) The Trypanosomiases, 2003; numerous research papers on pathophysiology and control of parasite infections in domestic animals. *Recreations:* cycling, hill-walking, golf, painting. *Address:* 2 Barclay Drive, Helensburgh G84 9RD. *T:* (01436) 674165. *E:* peter.holmes@glasgow.ac.uk.

HOLMES, Peter Rodney; HM Diplomatic Service, retired; *b* 29 July 1938; *m* Anne Cecilia Tarrant; one *s* three *d*. Diplomatic Service: served Strasbourg, Belgrade, Paris, Cento, Ankara; Stockholm, 1974; Consul, Douala, 1978; Dep. Head of Mission, Bahrain, 1983; Commercial Counsellor, Santiago, 1987; Ambassador to Honduras, 1995–98. *Address:* 15 Cavalier Way, Alton, Hampshire GU34 1QX.

HOLMES, Peter Sloan; development consultant, since 2010; Chief Executive: Sheridan Group, 2004–10 (Director, 2000–10); Sheridan Millennium Ltd, 2000–07; *b* 8 Dec. 1942; *s* of George H. G. and Anne S. Holmes; *m* 1966, Patricia McMahon; two *s*. *Educ:* Rossall Sch.; Magdalen Coll., Oxford (BA English Lang. and Lit.). Teacher, Eastbourne Coll., 1965–68; Head of English, Grosvenor High Sch., Belfast, 1968–71; Lectr, then Sen. Lectr, Stranmillis Coll. of Educn, Belfast, 1971–75; Department of Education for Northern Ireland: Inspector, 1975–83 (Sen. Inspector, 1980; Staff Inspector, 1982); Asst Sec., 1983–87; Under Sec., 1987; Dep. Sec., 1996–2000. Chairman: Arts & Business NI, 2000–06; Bytes Project, 2009–13. *Recreations:* singing, cycling, gliding. *Address:* 15a Ochlochy Park, Dunblane, Perthshire FK15 0DU. *T:* (01786) 824525, 07801 989938.

HOLMES, Richard Gordon Heath, OBE 1992; FBA 1997; FRSL; writer, biographer and lecturer; Professor of Biographical Studies, School of English and American Studies, University of East Anglia, 2001–07; *b* 5 Nov. 1945; *s* of late Dennis Patrick Holmes and Pamela Mavis Holmes (*née* Gordon); partner, Rose Tremain, *qv*. *Educ:* Downside Sch.; Churchill Coll., Cambridge (BA; Hon. Fellow, 2011). FRSL 1975. Reviewer and historical features writer for The Times, 1967–92. Mem. Cttee, Royal Literary Fund, 1990–. Vis. Fellow, Trinity Coll., Cambridge, 2000, 2002. Lectures: Ernest Jones Meml, British Inst. of Psycho-Analysis, 1990; John Keats Meml, RCS, 1995; Johan Huizinga Meml, Univ. of Leiden, 1997; Seymour Biography, ANU, 2008; Wordsworth, Univ. of London, 2011; Dibner, Smithsonian Inst., Washington, 2012; Gesellschaft für englische Romantik, Ludwig Maximilian Univ., Munich, 2013; Byron, Univ. of Nottingham, 2014; Leon Levy Biography, NY, 2014. Hon. DLitt: UEA, 2000; E London, 2001; Kingston, 2008. *Publications:* Thomas Chatterton: the case re-opened, 1970; One for Sorrow (poems), 1970; Shelley: the pursuit, 1974 (Somerset Maugham Award, 1977); Gautier: my fantoms (trans.), 1976, enlarged edn 2008; Inside the Tower (radio drama documentary), 1977; (ed) Shelley on Love, 1980; Coleridge, 1982; (with Peter Jay) Nerval: the chimeras, 1985; Footsteps: adventures of a romantic biographer, 1985; (ed) Mary Wollstonecraft and William Godwin, 1987; (ed with Robert Hampson) Kipling: something of myself, 1987; De Feministe en de Filosoof, 1988; Coleridge: vol. 1, Early Visions (Whitbread Book of the Year Prize), 1989, vol. 2, Darker Reflections (Duff Cooper Memorial Prize), 1998; To the Tempest Given (radio drama documentary), 1992; Dr Johnson & Mr Savage, 1993 (James Tait Black Meml Prize, 1994); The Nightwalking (radio drama documentary), 1995 (Sony Award); (ed) Coleridge: selected poems, 1996; Insights: the Romantic poets and their circle, 1997, enlarged edn 2005; Clouded Hills (radio documentary), 1999; Runaway Lives (radio documentary), 2000; Sidetracks: explorations of a romantic biographer, 2000; Romantics and Revolutionaries: Regency portraits, 2002; The Frankenstein Project (radio documentary), 2002; (ed) Classic Biographies (series), 2004; A Cloud in a Paper Bag (radio documentary), 2007; The Age of Wonder, 2008 (Royal Soc. Sci. Book Prize 2009; US Nat. Book Critics Circle Award for Non Fiction, 2010; US NAS Communication Award, 2010); Anaesthesia (radio drama), 2009; Thomas Lawrence Portraits, 2010; Falling Upwards: how we took to the air, 2013. *Recreations:* sailing, downhill-walking, French gardening, hot-air ballooning, stargazing. *Address:* c/o HarperCollins, 77 Fulham Palace Road, W6 8JB.

HOLMES, Robin Edmond Kendall; Head of Judicial Appointments, Lord Chancellor's Department, 1992–98; *b* 14 July 1938; *s* of Roy Frederick George and Kaye Holmes; *m* 1964, Karin Kutter; two *s*. *Educ:* Wolverhampton Grammar Sch.; Clare Coll., Cambridge (BA); Birmingham Univ. (LLM). Articles, Wolverhampton CBC, 1961–64; admitted solicitor, 1964; Min. of Housing and Local Govt, subseq. DoE, 1965–73 and 1976–82; Colonial Secretariat, Hong Kong, 1973–75; Lord Chancellor's Dept, 1982–98; Grade 3, 1983–98; Circuit Administrator, Midland and Oxford Circuit, 1986–92. *Recreation:* travelling.

HOLMES, Roger; Managing Director, Change Capital Partners, since 2005; *b* 21 Jan. 1960. Strategy Consultant, then Principal, McKinsey & Co.; Kingfisher: Finance Dir, B & Q, 1994–97; Man. Dir, Woolworths, 1997–99; Chief Exec., electrical retailing div., 1999–2000; Marks and Spencer plc: Head, UK retailing business, 2001–02; Exec. Dir, 2001–04; Chief Exec., 2002–04. *E:* rholmes@changecapitalpartners.com.

HOLMES, Roger de Lacy, CB 2002; Chief Executive, St John Ambulance, 2002–07; *b* 15 Jan. 1948; *s* of Stephen and Muriel Holmes; *m* 1st, 1970, Jennifer Anne Heal (marr. diss. 2005); one *s* one *d*; 2nd, 2005, Rosalind Joy Halstead. *Educ:* Huddersfield New Coll.; Balliol Coll., Oxford (BA). DTI, 1969–74; Dept of Prices and Consumer Protection, 1974–77; Dept of Industry, 1977–79; Asst to Chm., British Leyland, 1980–82; Company Sec., Mercury Communications, 1982–83; Jt Sec and Dir, Corporate Affairs, ICL, 1984; Exec. Dir, Dunlop Holdings, 1984–85; Euroroute, 1985–86; Chloride Group: Man. Dir, Power Electronics, 1986–88; Corporate Affairs Dir, 1989–92; Dep. Master and Comptroller, Royal Mint, 1993–2001. Non-executive Director: Cygnet Health Care, 1993–2000; Yorks Ambulance Service NHS Trust, 2006–12. Mem. Council, Univ. of London, 2003–08. CStJ 2007 (OStJ 2004). *Recreations:* golf, bridge. *Address:* 6 Lakeside Gardens, Strensall, York YO32 5WB.

HOLMES, Timothy Charles; Executive Director, UK-Korea Forum for the Future, 2010–14; *b* 26 April 1951; *s* of late Ronald William Holmes and Barbara Jean (*née* Mickleburgh); *m* 1973, Anna-Carin Magnusson; one *s* one *d*. *Educ:* Bec Sch.; Selwyn Coll., Cambridge (MA); Univ. of Aix-Marseille. Joined FCO, 1974; Second, later First, Sec., Tokyo, 1976–80; seconded to Invest in Britain Bureau, Dept of Industry, 1981–83; FCO, 1983–86; First Sec., Islamabad, 1986–90; FCO, 1990–94; Dep. Head of Mission and Commercial and Econ. Counsellor, Seoul, 1994–97; Dep. Hd of Mission, 1997–2002, Consul-Gen., 2000–02, The Hague; Dir, Asia Pacific, Internat. Gp, Trade Partners UK, then UK Trade & Investment, 2002–04; Consul Gen., Sydney and Dir Gen., Trade and Investment, 2004–08; Dep. CEO and Dir, Corporate Prog., Asia House, 2009–11. Gen. Sec., Workability Internat., 2011–12. Exec. Dir, Pakistan-Britain Trade and Investment Forum, 2009–12. FLS 2012. *Publications:* The Wild Flowers of Islamabad, 1990. *Recreations:* botany, ornithology, reading.

HOLMES, Prof. William Neil; Professor of Physiology, University of California, since 1964; *b* 2 June 1927; *s* of William Holmes and Minnie Holmes (*née* Lloyd); *m* 1955, Betty M. Brown, Boston, Mass; two *s* two *d*. *Educ:* Adams Grammar Sch., Newport, Salop; Liverpool Univ. (BSc, MSc, PhD, DSc); Harvard Univ., Cambridge, Mass. National Service, 2nd Bn RWF, 1946–48. Visiting Scholar in Biology, Harvard Univ., 1953–55; Post-grad. Research Schol., Liverpool Univ., 1955–56; ICI Fellow, Glasgow Univ., 1956–57; Asst Prof. of Zoology, 1957–63, Associate Prof. of Zoology, 1963–64, Univ. of British Columbia, Canada; John Simon Guggenheim Foundn Fellow, 1961–62; Visiting Professor of Zoology: Univ. of Hull, 1970; Univ. of Hong Kong, 1973, 1982–83 and 1987. Scientific Fellow, Zoological Soc. of London, 1967; External examiner: for undergraduate degrees, Univ. of Hong Kong, 1976–79, 1985–88; for higher degrees, Univs of Hong Kong and Hull, 1976–; Consultant to: Amer. Petroleum Inst., Washington, DC (environmental conservation), 1972–74; US Nat. Sci. Foundn (Regulatory Biology Prog.), 1980–83; US Bureau of Land Management (petroleum toxicity in seabirds), 1982–. Mem. Editorial Bd, American Journal of Physiology, 1967–70. Member: Endocrine Soc., US, 1957–; Soc. for Endocrinology, UK, 1955–; Amer. Physiological Soc., 1960–; Zoological Soc. of London, 1964–. *Publications:* numerous articles and reviews in Endocrinology, Jl of Endocrinology, Gen. and Comp. Endocrinology, Cell and Tissue Res., Archives of Environmental Contamination and Toxicology, Environmental Res., Jl of Experimental Biology. *Recreations:* travel, old maps and prints, carpentry and building. *Address:* 117 East Junipero Street, Santa Barbara, CA 93105, USA. *T:* (805) 6827256. *Club:* Tennis (Santa Barbara).

HOLMES à COURT, family name of **Baron Heytesbury**.

HOLMES à COURT, Janet Lee, AC 2007 (AO 1995); Chairman: Heytesbury Pty Ltd, Australia, 1991–2009; John Holland Group, 1991–2012 (Chairman, Advisory Board, 2013–14); *b* 29 Nov. 1943; *m* 1966, (Michael) Robert (Hamilton) Holmes à Court (*d* 1990); three *s* one *d*. *Educ:* Perth Modern Sch.; Univ. of Western Australia (BSc Chemistry; DipEd). Former Chemistry Teacher, Perth. Member Board: Reserve Bank of Australia, 1992–97; Rio Tinto Community Investment (formerly WA Future) Fund, 2006–. Bd Mem., Aust. Res. Council, 2003–05; Bd Dir, Vision 2020 Aust., 2004–13. Comr, Tourism WA, 2002–07. Chairman: Australian Children's TV Foundn, 1986–; Black Swan Theatre Co., Perth, 1991–2005; WA Symphony Orch., 1998–; Member: Bd, Australian Urban Design Res. Centre, WA, 2005– (Chm., 2005–14); Bd, Australian Nat. Acad. of Music, 2009–; Bd, Australian Major Performing Arts Gp, 2010–; Chamber of Arts and Culture WA, 2010–; Internat. Adv. Bd, NY Philharmonic, 2015–; Bd of Advrs, Centenary Trust for Women, 2015–. Gov., Sony Foundn Australia, 1999–2009. Hon. FAIB 1998; Hon. FAHA 2011. DUniv: Qld, 1994; Murdoch, 1997; Hon. DLitt WA, 1997; Hon. DBus: Ballarat, 2007; Charles Sturt, 2008; Hon. DArts Edith Cowan, 2011. Veuve Clicquot Business Woman of the Year, 1996; John Shaw Medal, Roads Australia, 2014. *Address:* PO Box 7255, Cloisters Square, WA 6850, Australia.

HolmPATRICK, 4th Baron *cr* 1897; **Hans James David Hamilton;** *b* 15 March 1955; *s* of 3rd Baron Holmpatrick and Anne Loys Roche (*d* 1998), *o d* of Commander J. E. P. Brass, RN (retd); *S* father, 1991; *m* 1984, Mrs Gill du Feu, *e d* of K. J. Harding; one *s* and one step *s*. *Heir:* *b* Hon. Ion Henry James Hamilton, *b* 12 June 1956.

HOLROYD, Andrew; *see* Holroyd, W. A. M.

HOLROYD, Dame Margaret; *see* Drabble, Dame M.

HOLROYD, Sir Michael (de Courcy Fraser), Kt 2007; CBE 1989; CLit 2004; author; *b* London, 27 Aug. 1935; *s* of Basil Holroyd and Ulla (*née* Hall); *m* 1982, Margaret Drabble (*see* Dame Margaret Drabble). *Educ:* Eton Coll.; Maidenhead Public Library. Vis. Fellow, Pennsylvania State Univ., 1979. Chm., Soc. of Authors, 1973–74; Chm., Nat. Book League, 1976–78; Pres., English PEN, 1985–88. Chm., Strachey Trust, 1990–95. Member: BBC Archives Adv. Cttee, 1976–79; Arts Council of England (formerly of GB), 1992–95 (Vice-Chm., 1982–83, Chm., 1992–95, Literature Panel); Chm., Public Lending Right Adv. Cttee, 1997–2000. Vice-Pres., Royal Literary Fund, 1997–. Pres., Stephen Spender Trust, 1998–. Nat. Gov., Shaw Fest. Theatre, Ontario, 1993–2014. FRSL 1968 (Mem. Council, 1977–87; Chm. Council, 1998–2001; Vice Pres., 2001–03; Pres., 2003–10; Pres. Emeritus, 2010); FRSA. Saxton Meml Fellowship, 1964; Bollingen Fellowship, 1966; Winston Churchill Fellowship, 1971. Hon. DLitt: Ulster, 1992; Sheffield, 1993; Warwick, 1993; East Anglia, 1994; LSE, 1998; Sussex, 2009. Heywood Hill Prize, 2001; David Cohen British Lit. Prize, 2005; Golden Award, PEN, 2006. *Publications:* Hugh Kingsmill: a critical biography, 1964; Lytton Strachey, 2 vols, 1967, 1968 (Yorkshire Post Prize, 1968), rev. edn 1994 (Prix du Meilleur Livre Etranger, 1995); A Dog's Life: a novel, 1969, rev. edn 2014; (ed) The Best of Hugh Kingsmill, 1970; (ed) Lytton Strachey By Himself, 1971; Unreceived Opinions, 1973; Augustus John, 2 vols, 1974, 1975, rev. edn 1996; (with M. Easton) The Art of Augustus John, 1974; (ed) The Genius of Shaw, 1979; (ed with Paul Levy) The Shorter Strachey, 1980; (ed with Robert Skidelsky) William Gerhardie's God's Fifth Column, 1981; (ed) Essays by Divers Hands, vol. XLII, 1982; Bernard Shaw: Vol. I, The Search for Love 1856–1898, 1988 (Irish Life Arts Award, 1988); Vol. II, The Pursuit of Power 1898–1918, 1989; Vol. III, The Lure of Fantasy 1918–1950, 1991; Vol. IV, The Last Laugh 1950–1991, 1992; Vol. V, The Shaw Companion, 1992; abridged edn, 1997; Basil Street Blues, 1999; Works on Paper: the craft of biography and autobiography, 2002; Mosaic: portraits in fragments, 2004; A Strange Eventful History, 2008 (James Tait Black Meml Prize, Sheridan Morley Prize, 2009); A Book of Secrets, 2010; On Wheels, 2012; various radio and television scripts. *Recreations:* listening to stories, watching people dance, avoiding tame animals, being polite, music, siestas. *Address:* c/o AP Watt at United Agents, 12–26 Lexington Street, W1F 0LE.

HOLROYD, Robert Anthony; Headmaster, Repton School, 2003–14; *b* 9 Dec. 1962; *s* of Anthony Holroyd and Jean Elizabeth Holroyd; *m* 1988, Penelope Claire Riddell; two *d*. *Educ:* Birkenhead Sch.; Christ Church, Oxford (Schol. 1981; BA 1st cl. Hons (Mod. Langs) 1985; MA 1988; PGCE 1989). Asst Master, Oakham Sch., 1985–86; Colegio Anglo Colombiano, Bogota, 1986–88; Hd of Dept and Housemaster, Radley Coll., 1989–2003. *Recreations:* the hills and the classics.

HOLROYD, (William) Andrew (Myers), CBE 2009 (OBE 2003); Chief Executive Officer, Jackson Canter Ltd, since 2014; President, Law Society, 2007–08; *b* 13 April 1948; *s* of Bill Holroyd and Joan Holroyd; *m* 1975, Caroline Skerry; two *d*. *Educ:* Univ. of Nottingham (BA Law 1969). Admitted solicitor, 1974; Partner, Jackson & Canter, Liverpool, 1977–2014. Lay Canon, Liverpool Cathedral, 2009–. Gov., Liverpool John Moores Univ., 2009– (Hon. Fellow, 2008). Trustee, Liverpool Community Spirit, 2011. Hon. DLaws Nottingham, 2009. *Recreations:* music, golf. *Address:* c/o Jackson Canter Ltd, 3rd Floor, Walker House, Exchange Flags, Liverpool L2 3YL. *Club:* Woolton Golf (Liverpool).

HOLROYD, William Arthur Hepworth, FHSM; Chief Executive, North Durham Health Authority, 1992–93; *b* 15 Sept. 1938; *s* of late Rev. Harry Holroyd and Annie Dodgshun Holroyd; *m* 1967, Hilary Gower; three *s*. *Educ:* Kingswood Sch., Bath; Trinity Hall, Cambridge (MA History); Manchester Univ. (DSA). Hospital Secretary: Crewe Memorial Hosp., 1963–65; Wycombe General Hosp., 1965–67; secondment to Dept of Health, 1967–69; Dep. Gp Sec., Blackpool and Fylde HMC, 1969–72; Regional Manpower Officer, Leeds RHB, 1972–74; District Administrator, York Health Dist, 1974–82; Regional Administrator, Yorkshire RHA, 1982–85; Dist Gen. Man., Durham HA, 1985–92. Non-exec. Dir, York Waterworks, plc, 1996–99. Member: National Staff Cttee for Admin. and Clerical Staff in NHS, 1973–82; General Nursing Council for England and Wales, 1978–83; English Nat. Board for Nursing, Midwifery and Health Visiting, 1980–87; NHS Trng Authority, 1988–91. Director, Methodist Chapel Aid Ltd, 1978–2011 (Chm., 2000–11). Mem. Ind. Monitoring Bd (formerly Bd of Visitors), HM Prison Full Sutton, 1995–2008. *Publications:* (ed) Hospital Traffic and Supply Problems, 1968. *Recreations:* walking, music, visiting the Shetland Isles, research into Handel's Messiah libretto.

HOLROYDE, Geoffrey Vernon; Director, Coventry (formerly Coventry Lanchester) Polytechnic, 1975–87; *b* 18 Sept. 1928; *s* of late Harold Vincent Holroyde and Kathleen Olive (*née* Glover); *m* 1960, Elizabeth Mary, *d* of Rev. E. O. Connell; two *s* two *d*. *Educ:* Wrekin Coll.; Birmingham Univ. (BSc); Birmingham Conservatoire (BMus 1995); ARCO. Royal Navy, 1949–54 and 1956–61; School-master, Welbeck Coll., 1954–56; English Electric, becoming Principal of Staff Coll., Dunchurch, 1961–70; British Leyland, Head Office Training Staff, 1970–71; Head, Sidney Stringer Sch. and Community Coll., Coventry, 1971–75; Higher Educn Adviser to Training Commn, 1987–88; Dir, GEC Management Coll., Dunchurch, 1989–92. Chairman: Industrial Links Adv. Gp to Cttee of Dirs of Polytechnics, 1980–87; National Forum for the Performing Arts in Higher Educn, 1987–91; Develt Training Steering Gp, 1983–88; Mem., W Midlands RHA, 1985–89 (Chm., Non Clinical Res. Cttee; Vice-Chm., AIDS Task Force); Mem., RSA Educn Industry Forum, 1986–90. Dir of Music, St Mary's Church, Warwick, 1962–72; Dir, Coventry Cathedral Chapter House Choir, 1982–95; Asst Dir, Warwickshire County Youth Chorale, 1999–2006. Mem., Exec. Cttee, British Fedn of Young Choirs, 1993–95. Member: Council, Upper Avon Navigation Trust, 1994–2001; Steering Cttee, Assoc. of Inland Navigation Authorities, 1997–2003. Governor, 1978–91, Trustee, 1979–91, Chm., Governing Body, 1984–89, Brathay Hall Trust; Chm. Trustees, St Mary's Hall, Warwick, 1984–90; Governor: Mid Warwicks Coll. of Further Educn, 1976–87; Kings School, Worcester, 1983–88; Coten End Co. Jun. Sch., 2006–. Hon. Dir of Music, 2006–14, Organist Emeritus, 2015, Holy Trinity, Gosport. Hon. Life Mem., RSCM, 1970; Hon. Life Fellow, Birmingham Conservatoire, UCE, 2002. *Publications:* Managing People, 1968; Delegations, 1968; Communications, 1969; Organs of St Mary's Church, Warwick, 1969; 900 years of Music in St Mary's Warwick, 2010. *Recreations:* music (organ and choir), canals, sailing, outdoor pursuits. *Address:* 38 Coten End, Warwick CV34 4NP. *T:* (01926) 492329.

HOLROYDE, Hon. Sir Timothy Victor, (Sir Tim), Kt 2009; **Hon. Mr Justice Holroyde;** a Judge of the High Court of Justice, Queen's Bench Division, since 2009; a Presiding Judge of the Northern Circuit, 2012–15; *b* 18 Aug. 1955; *s* of Frank Holroyde and Doreen Holroyde; *m* 1980, Miranda Elisabeth Stone; two *d*. *Educ:* Bristol Grammar Sch.; Wadham Coll., Oxford (BA Hons Juris.). Called to the Bar, Middle Temple, 1977, Bencher, 2005; in practice on Northern Circuit, 1978–2008; QC 1996; Recorder, 1997–2008. Mem., Sentencing Council, 2015–. *Recreation:* tennis. *Address:* Royal Courts of Justice, Strand, WC2A 2LL.

HOLST, Dame Alison (Margaret), DNZM 2011; CBE 1987; QSM 1983; food writer, 1966–2014; *b* Dunedin, NZ, 1 Feb. 1938; *d* of Arthur Hollier Payne and Margaret Ardagh Ursula Payne (*née* Dickie); *m* 1961, Dr Peter Eugene Holst; one *s* one *d*. *Educ:* Opoho Prim. Sch., Dunedin; Dunedin North Intermediate Sch.; Otago Girls High Sch., Dunedin; Univ. of Otago (BHSc 1960). Lectr, Sch. of Home Sci., Univ. of Otago, 1961–65. Television and radio presenter. Hon. DSc Otago, 1997. *Publications:* Here's How, 1966; Meals with the family, 1967; Food Without Fuss, 1972; (ed) The New Zealand Radio and Television Cookbook, 1974; More Food Without Fuss, 1974; Simply Delicious, 1975; Lamb for all Seasons, 1976; What's Cooking?, 1978; Kitchen Diary, 1–12, 1978–89; Alison Holst's Food Processor Book, 1980; Alison Holst's Microwave Book, 1982; Let's Cook, 1982; Alison Holst Cooks, 1984; Dollars and Sense, 1984; Let's Cook Some More, 1984; Cooking Class 1, 1986, 2, 1987, 3, 1988; Family Cookbook, 1987; Lambtastic, 1987; New Zealand Recipe Notes, 1987; Microwave Menus 1, 1988, 2, 1989; Complete Cooking Class, 1989; Meals Without Meat, 1990; Recipes to Remember, 1990; Barbecue Cooking, 1991; Best of Alison Holst, 1991; Best of Home Cooking, 1991; Cooking the New Zealand Way, 1991; Food for Healthy Appetites, 1991; Kitchen Diary Collection, 1991; New Kitchen Diary, 1–3, 1991–93; New Microwave Cookbook, 1991; Mini Money Meals, 1992; Family Favourites, 1993; Everyday Cookery, 1993; Breakfasts and Brunches, 1994; Marvellous Muffins, 1994; Alison's Kitchen, 1995; Cooking for Christmas, 1995; Food for Young Families, 1995; Best Potato Recipes, 1995; Good Food, 1995; Chocolate Temptations, 1996; Sausage Book, 1996; Soup Book, 1997; Ultimate Collection, 2000; Alison's Pantry, 2003; Cool Food for Warmer Days, 2006; Fast and Fun Family Food, 2009; (with Barbara Larson) Home-Grown Cook, 2011; with Simon Holst: Bread Book, 1997; More Marvellous Muffins, 1997; Best Baking, 1998; Best Mince Recipes, 1998; Very Easy Vegetarian, 1998; School Lunches and After School Snacks, 1999; Sensational Salads, 1999; Really Easy Chicken Recipes, 2000; Baby Food and Beyond, 2000; Healthy and Delicious Muffins, 2000; More for Less Cookbook, 2001; Quick and Easy Twenty Minute Meals, 2001; 100 Favourite Muffins and Slices, 2003; 100 Favourite Cakes and Biscuits, 2004; 100 Favourite Twenty Minute Dishes, 2004; 100 Great Ways to use Slow Cookers, 2006; Food to Go, 2006; New Zealand Diabetes Cookbook, 2006; Year-Round Ways to use Slow Cookers, 2007; Popular Potatoes, 2008; Kiwi Favourites, 2008; Marvellous Mince and Sensational Sausages, 2009; New Zealand Barbecue Book, 2009; New Zealand Bread Book, 2010; My Own Kiwi Favourites, 2010; Delicious Slow Cooker Recipes, 2011. *Recreations:* walking, reading, cooking, gardening. *Address:* PO Box 482, Orewa 0946, New Zealand.

HOLT, Alexis Fayrer B.; *see* Brett-Holt.

HOLT, Dr Andrew Anthony, CBE 2004; Head, Information Services Division, Department of Health, 1990–2005; *b* 4 Jan. 1944; *s* of Josef Holzmann and Livia Holzmann; *m* 1969, Janet Margery; three *s*. *Educ:* Latymer Upper Sch.; University Coll. London (BSc Maths 1965; PhD 1969). ICI Paints Div., 1968–70; entered Civil Service, 1970: Principal, Treasury, 1974–78; Head, Operational Research: Inland Revenue, 1978–87; DHSS, 1987–90. Tutor, Open Univ., 1972–; Nat. Subject Advr for Maths and Stats, Univ. of the Third Age, 2012–. *Publications:* History of Teddington, 2005; contrib. to jls and OR Society papers.

HOLT, Catherine; *see* Johnstone, C.

HOLT, Prof. Christine Elizabeth, (Mrs W. A. Harris), PhD; FRS 2009; FMedSci; FRSB; Professor of Developmental Neuroscience, University of Cambridge, since 2003; Fellow, Gonville and Caius College, Cambridge, since 1997; *b* 28 Aug. 1954; *d* of (Robert) Clifford Holt and Elizabeth, (Betty), Gertrude Ann Holt (*née* Buist); *m* 1983, Prof. William Anthony Harris, *qv*; one *s* one *d*. *Educ:* St Elizabeth's Sch., Stocksfield; Harrogate Coll.; St Clare's, Oxford; Sussex Univ. (BSc Hons Biol Scis); King's Coll., London (PhD Zool. 1982). FRSB (FSB 2011). Postdoctoral Fellow, UCSD, 1982 and 1984–89 (Alexander von Humboldt Fellow, 1986–87; McKnight Scholar, 1986–89); Jun. Res. Fellow, Worcester Coll., Oxford, 1983–84; Asst Prof.-in-Residence, 1989–92, Asst Prof. 1992–96, Associate Prof., 1996–97, UCSD (Pew Scholar in Biomed. Scis, 1991–96); Lectr, 1997–99, Reader in Develtl Neurobiol., 1999–2003, Cambridge Univ. Mem., EMBO, 2005–. FMedSci 2007. *Publications:* contrib. papers to sci. jls. *Recreations:* music, fell walking, art, wildlife. *Address:* Department of Physiology, Development and Neuroscience, Anatomy Building, University of Cambridge, Downing Street, Cambridge CB2 3DY. *T:* (01223) 333750. *E:* ceh33@cam.ac.uk.

See also R. C. S. Holt.

HOLT, Prof. David, (Tim), CB 2000; PhD; FSS; President, Royal Statistical Society, 2005–07 (Vice-President, 2003–04); Chair, UK Data Forum, since 2012; *b* 29 Oct. 1943; *s* of late Ernest Frederick Holt and Catherine Rose (*née* Finn); *m* 1966, Jill Blake; one *s* one *d*. *Educ:* Coopers' Company's Sch.; Exeter Univ. (BSc Maths 1966; PhD Mathematical Stats 1969). FSS 1973. Res. Fellow, Univ. of Exeter, 1969–70; Survey Statistician, Statistics Canada, 1970–73 (Consultant, 1974–75); University of Southampton: Lectr in Social Stats, 1973–80; Leverhulme Prof. of Social Stats, 1980–2005; Dean, Social Sci. Faculty, 1981–83; Dep. Vice Chancellor, 1990–95; Dir, CSO, 1995–96; Hd, Govt Statistical Service, 1995–2000; Dir, ONS, and Registrar Gen. for England and Wales, 1996–2000. Consultant: NZ Dept of Stats, 1981; OPCS, 1983, 1987, 1991; ESRC, 1990; Australian Bureau of Stats, 1990; EU, 2001–02; UN, 2001–02; IMF, 2002; Scientific Advr to Chief Scientist, DHSS, 1983–88. Vis. Fellow, Nuffield Coll., Oxford, 1995–2003. Associate Editor: Jl Royal Statistical Soc. B, 1983–88; Survey Methodology, 1988–2002; Editor: Jl Royal Statistical Soc. A: Stats and Society, 1991–94; Jl Official Stats, 2001–. Vice-President: Internat. Assoc. of Survey Statisticians, 1989–91 (Scientific Sec., 1985–87); UN Statistical Commn, 1997–99; Mem., Internat. Statistical Inst., 1985 (Vice-Pres., 1999–2001); Fellow, Amer. Statistical Assoc., 1990; Founding Academician, Acad. of Social Scis, 1999. Trustee, Newitt Trust, 1990–. Hon. DSc (SocSci) Southampton, 1999. *Publications:* (jtly) Analysis of Complex Surveys, 1989; papers in academic jls. *Recreations:* golf, travelling.

HOLT, Dame Denise Mary, DCMG 2009 (CMG 2002); HM Diplomatic Service, retired; Ambassador to Spain, 2007–09; *b* 1 Oct. 1949; *d* of William Dennis and Mary Joanna Mills; *m* 1987, David Holt; one *s*. *Educ:* New Hall Sch., Chelmsford; Bristol Univ. Res. Analyst, FCO, 1970–84; First Sec., Dublin, 1984–87; Head of Section, FCO, 1988–90; First Sec., Brasilia, 1991–93; Dep. Hd, Eastern Dept, FCO, 1993–94; Asst Dir, Personnel, 1996–98; Dep. Hd of Mission, Dublin, 1998–99; Dir, Personnel, FCO, 1999–2002; Ambassador to Mexico, 2002–05; Dir for Migration and Overseas Territories, FCO, 2005–07. Non-executive Director: HSBC Bank plc, 2011–; Scottish Power Renewable Energy Ltd, 2011–12; Scottish Power Energy Network Hldgs, 2012–14; M&S Bank, 2013– (Chm., 2013–); Iberdrola SA, 2014–; non-exec. Dir and Gov., Nuffield Health, 2013–. Member: Bd, Ofqual, 2010–13; NHS Pay Review Bd, 2010–14; Ind. Chm., Nominations Cttee, Alzheimer's Soc. Member: Mgt Council, Canada Blanch Centre for Contemp. Spanish Studies, LSE, 2010–; Internat. Adv. Panel, Univ. of Birmingham, 2012–13; Chm., Inst. of Latin American Studies (formerly for Study of the Americas), Sch. of Advanced Studies, Univ. of London, 2012–. Member: Adv. Council, Wilton Park, 2012–; Council, Bristol Univ., 2014–. Trustee, FCO Liby, 2012–. Chm. Trustees, Anglo-Spanish Soc., 2010–13. Hon. DLaws Bristol, 2012. *Recreations:* theatre, reading, needlework. *E:* ddpholt@aol.com.

HOLT, Prof. Douglas Brewster, PhD; Founder and President, Cultural Strategy Group, since 2010. *Educ:* Stanford Univ. (AB); Univ. of Chicago (MBA); Northwestern Univ. (PhD). Brand manager: Clorox Co.; Dole Packaged Foods; Assistant Professor: Penn State Univ., 1992–97; Univ. of Illinois, 1997–2000; Associate Prof., Harvard Business Sch., 2000–04; L'Oréal Prof. of Marketing, Univ. of Oxford, 2004–10; Fellow, Worcester Coll., Oxford, 2004–10. Founding Partner, Amalgamated, advertising agency, 2004–09. *Publications:* (ed jtly) The Consumer Society Reader, 2000; How Brands Become Icons: the principles of cultural branding, 2004; Cultural Strategy: using innovative ideologies to build breakthrough brands, 2010; articles in learned jls. *Address:* Cultural Strategy Group, 2945 Juilliard Street, Boulder, CO 80305, USA.

HOLT, Elaine Karen, FCILT; Founder and Director, Cat Street Consulting, since 2013; Executive Vice President Operations, Carnival Cruises UK, since 2014; *b* Oxford, 5 June 1966; *d* of Michael and June Brown; *m* 1995, Stephen Holt. *Educ:* Stroud Girls' High Sch. British Airways: Reservations Agent, 1985–87; Sales Agent, 1987–89; Project Exec., 1989–90; Support Exec., 1990–92; British Airways (Galileo): Nat. Acct Manager, 1992–96; Manager, Nat. Accts, 1996–97; Hd of Sales, 1997–98; Managing Director: FirstInfo, 2000; TotalJourney, 2001; Commercial Services Dir, First Great Western, 2001–03; Regl Dir, First South & Wales, 2003–04; Dir, First Rail, 2004–06; Man. Dir, First Capital Connect, 2006–09; Chm. and Chief Exec., Directly Operated Railways, 2009–11; Chm., East Coast, 2009–11; Bd Dir, Rail Franchise Procurement Team, National Express, 2012; Rail Franchise Director, RATP Dev UK, 2013–14. Non-exec. Dir, Highways Agency, 2014–. Mem. Bd, Rail Delivery Gp, Assoc. of Train Operating Cos, 2011–12. FCILT 2010. *Recreations:* running (half marathons), keep fit, yoga, dancing. *Address:* 1 Hockley Mill, Church Lane, Twyford, Winchester SO21 1NT. *E:* ekholt@icloud.com.

HOLT, His Honour John Frederick; a Circuit Judge, 1998–2015; *b* 7 Oct. 1947; *s* of Edward Basil Holt and Monica Holt; *m* 1970, Stephanie Ann Watson; three *s*. *Educ:* Ampleforth; Bristol Univ. (LLB). Called to the Bar, Lincoln's Inn, 1970; barrister, E Anglian Chambers, 1970–98 (Head of Chambers, 1993–98); Asst Recorder, 1989–92; a Recorder, 1992–98. ECB cricket coach. *Recreations:* village cricket, classic motor cars. *Clubs:* Strangers (Norwich); MG Car, Octagon Car, Jaguar Drivers; Twinstead Cricket.

HOLT, John Michael, MD, FRCP; Consultant Physician, John Radcliffe Hospital (formerly Radcliffe Infirmary), Oxford, 1974–2000, now Emeritus; Fellow, 1968–2000, now Emeritus, and Vice Principal, 1999–2000, Linacre College, Oxford; *b* 8 March 1935; *s* of late Frank Holt, BSc and of Constance Holt; *m* 1959, Sheila Margaret Morton; one *s* three *d*. *Educ:* St Peter's Sch., York; Univ. of St Andrews. MA Oxon; MD St Andrews; MSc Queen's Univ. Ont. Registrar and Lectr, Nuffield Dept of Medicine, Radcliffe Infirmary, Oxford, 1964–66, Cons. Physician 1968; Chm., Medical Staff, Oxford Hosps, 1982–84. University of Oxford: Med. Tutor, 1967–73; Dir of Clinical Studies, 1971–76; Mem., Gen. Bd of Faculties, 1987–91; Chm., Clinical Medicine Bd, 1992–94. Civilian Advr in Medicine, RAF, 1994–2000. Formerly Examiner in Medicine: Univ. of Oxford; Hong Kong; London; Glasgow; Dublin; RCP. Censor, RCP, 1995–97. Member: Assoc. of Physicians; Soc. of Apothecaries; Cttee on Safety of Medicines, 1979–86; Oxford RHA, 1984–88. Pres., Oxford Medical Alumni, 2003–07. Editor, Qly Jl of Medicine, 1975–92. *Publications:* papers on disorders of blood and various med. topics in BMJ, Lancet, etc. *Recreation:* sailing. *Address:* Old Whitehill, Tackley, Oxon OX5 3AB. *T:* (01869) 331241. *Club:* Oxford and Cambridge.

HOLT, Karen Jane, (Mrs Paul Smith); Her Honour Judge Karen Holt; a Circuit Judge, since 2014; *b* Woking, 13 May 1964; *d* of Michael Holt and Christine Holt; *m* 1993, Paul Smith; one *s* one *d* (and one *s* decd). *Educ:* Univ. of Leeds (LLB). Called to the Bar, Lincoln's Inn, 1987; barrister, 1987–2014; a Recorder, 2009–14. *Recreations:* travel, family, school governor (secondary). *Address:* Aylesbury Crown Court, County Hall, Market Square, Aylesbury, Bucks HP20 1XD. *T:* (01296) 434401. *E:* HHJudgeKaren.Holt@judiciary.gsi.gov.uk.

HOLT, Her Honour Mary; a Circuit Judge, 1977–95; *d* of Henry James Holt, solicitor, and of Sarah Holt (*née* Chapman); unmarried. *Educ:* Park Sch., Preston; Girton Coll., Cambridge (MA, LLB, 1st cl. Hons). Called to the Bar, Gray's Inn, 1949 (Atkin Scholar). Practised on Northern circuit. Former Vice-Chm., Preston North Conservative Assoc.; Member: Nat. Exec. Council, 1969–72; Woman's Nat. Advisory Cttee, 1969–70; representative, Central Council, 1969–71. MP (C) Preston N, 1970–Feb. 1974. Contested (C) Preston N, Feb. and Oct. 1974. Dep. Pres., Lancs Br., BRCS, 1976–95. Freedom of Cities of Dallas and Denton, Texas, 1987. Badge of Honour, BRCS, 1989. *Publications:* 2nd edn, Benas and Essenhigh's Precedents of Pleadings, 1956. *Recreation:* walking. *Club:* Royal Over-Seas League.

HOLT, Oliver Charles Thomas; Chief Sports Writer, Mail on Sunday, since 2015; *b* 22 May 1966; *s* of Thomas and Eileen Holt; *m* 1995, Sarah Llewellyn-Jones; one *s* two *d*. *Educ:* Christ Church, Oxford (BA Hons Modern Hist.). Reporter, Daily Post & Echo, Liverpool, 1990–93; The Times: Motor Racing Corresp., 1993–97; Football Corresp., 1997–2000; Chief Sports Corresp., 2000–02; Chief Sports Writer, The Mirror, 2002–15. Sports Writer of the Year, British Press Gazette, 2005, 2006; Sports Columnist of the Year, Sports Journalists' Assoc., 2012. *Publications:* The Bridge, 1998; If You're Second, You're Nothing: Ferguson and Shankly, 2006; End of the Rainbow: England's quest for glory in South Africa, 2010; Miracle at Medinah, 2012. *Recreations:* Marlon Brando, Bob Dylan, Stockport County. *Address:* c/o Mail on Sunday, Northcliffe House, 2 Derry Street, W8 5TS.

HOLT, (Robert Charles) Stephen; His Honour Judge Stephen Holt; a Circuit Judge, since 2009; *b* Wylam, Northumberland, 30 July 1952; *s* of (Robert) Clifford Holt and Elizabeth Gertrude Ann Holt (*née* Buist); civil partnership 2005, Jonathon Charles Hill. *Educ:* Gordonstoun Sch.; Newcastle Univ. (BSc Hons). Called to the Bar, Gray's Inn, 1978; a Recorder, 2005–09. Mem., Parole Bd, 2010–. Hon. Recorder of Norwich, 2013–. *Recreations:* walking, sailing, gardening, reading. *E:* sholt100@gmail.com. *Clubs:* Royal Automobile; Norfolk.

See also C. E. Holt.

HOLT, Stuart; Headmaster, Clitheroe Royal Grammar School, 1991–2004; *b* 12 Sept. 1943; *s* of Alan and Irene Holt; *m* 1968, Valerie Hollows; one *s* one *d*. *Educ:* Leeds Univ. (BSc 2nd Cl. Hons Zool., MPhil); Univ. of Lancaster (MA Educn). Biol. Master, Adwick Sch., Doncaster, 1968–71; Hd of Biol., King's Sch., Pontefract, 1971–73; Hd of Sci., Whitley High Sch., Wigan, 1973–78; Dep. Hd Curriculum, Wright Robinson High Sch., Manchester, 1978–84; Headmaster, Failsworth Sch., Oldham, 1984–91. Mem., Rotary Internat. *Recreations:* Rossendale Male Voice Choir, theatre, photography, Italy, fell-walking, cabinet making. *Address:* c/o Clitheroe Royal Grammar School, York Street, Clitheroe, Lancs BB7 2DJ.

HOLT, Thelma Mary Bernadette, CBE 1994; Managing Director, Thelma Holt Ltd, since 1990; Associate Producer, Royal Shakespeare Company, since 2004; *b* 4 Jan. 1932; *d* of David Holt and Ellen Finagh (*née* Doyle); *m* 1st, 1956, Patrick Graucob (marr. diss. 1968; remarried 2011); 2nd, 1969, David Pressman (marr. diss. 1970). *Educ:* St Ann's Sch., Lytham; RADA. Actress, 1953; Founder, Open Space Theatre (with Charles Marowitz), 1968; Dir, Round House Theatre, 1977; Exec. Producer, Theatre of Comedy, 1983; Head of Touring and Commercial Exploitation, Royal Nat. Theatre, 1985 (Laurence Olivier/Observer Award for Outstanding Achievement, 1987); Exec. Producer, Peter Hall Co., 1989; formed Thelma Holt Ltd, 1990, productions include: The Three Sisters, 1990; Tango at the End of Winter, 1991; Electra, Hamlet, Les Atrides, La Baruffe Chiozotte, Six Characters in Search of an Author, The Tempest, 1992; Much Ado About Nothing, 1993; Peer Gynt, The Clandestine Marriage, 1994; The Seagull, A Midsummer Night's Dream, Antony and Cleopatra, The Glass Menagerie, 1995; Observe the Sons of Ulster Marching Towards the Somme, A Doll's House, 1996; The Maids, Les Fausses Confidences, Oh Les Beaux Jours, Shintoku-Maru, 1997; The Relapse, 1998; Macbeth, King Lear, 1999; Miss Julie, 2000; Semi-Monde, 2001; Via Dolorosa, The Tempest, 2002; Pericles, Ghosts, Hamlet, The Taming of the Shrew, 2003; We Happy Few, Hamlet, 2004; Man and Boy, Primo (NT, NY), Twelfth Night, 2005; The Crucible, Hay Fever, Breakfast with Mugabe, Titus Andronicus, The Canterbury Tales, 2006; Coriolanus, Kean, The Giant, 2007; Measure for Measure, Twelfth Night, The English Samurai, 2009; Ghosts, Bedroom Farce, Musashi, 2010; Ruby Wax Losing It, 2011; Cymbeline, Volcano, All That Fall, 2012; Anjin, 2013; Forbidden Broadway, 2014; for Royal Shakespeare Company: The Jacobeans, 2003; The Taming of the Shrew/The Tamer Tamed, All's Well that Ends Well, Othello, 2004; A Midsummer Night's Dream, 2005; Written on the Heart, 2012; Anjin - The Shogun and the English Samurai, 2013. Member: Arts Council, 1993–98 (Chm., Drama Adv. Panel, 1994–98); Council, RADA, 1985–2011. Director: Stage One (formerly Theatre Investment Fund) Ltd, 1982–; Citizens Theatre, Glasgow, 1989– (Vice-Pres., 1997–); Almeida Th., 2001–09; Chm., Yvonne Arnaud Th., 2002–05; Trustee, Rose Th., 2009–. Cameron Mackintosh Vis. Prof. of Contemporary Theatre, Oxford Univ., 1998; Fellow, St Catherine's Coll., Oxford, 1998–2003, then Emeritus. Patron, OUDS, 2001. Companion, Liverpool Inst. for Performing Arts, 2002; Dist. Friend of Oxford Univ., 2006. DUniv Middlesex, 1994; Hon. MA Open, 1988; Hon. DLitt UEA, 2003; Hon DA Plymouth, 2010. Special Award for Individual Achievement, TMA Awards, 2006. Order of the Rising Sun, Gold Rays with Rosette (Japan), 2004. *Recreation:* bargain hunting at antique fairs. *Address:* Noël Coward Theatre, 85 St Martin's Lane, WC2N 4AU. *T:* (020) 7812 7455, *Fax:* (020) 7812 7550. *E:* thelma@dircon.co.uk.

HOLT, Tim; *see* Holt, David.

HOLTAM, Rt Rev. Nicholas Roderick; *see* Salisbury, Bishop of.

HOLTBY, Christopher Bruce, OBE 2000; HM Diplomatic Service; Ambassador to Estonia, since 2012; *m* Polly Jane; one *s* two *d*. Entered CS, 1992; Desk Officer, NATO and Eur. Policy Dept, 1992–93, Navy Resources and Progs Dept, 1993–94, MoD; Second Sec., UK Delegn to NATO and WEU, Brussels, 1994–98; Hd, Policy and Ops Section, Balkans Dept, 1998–99, Hd, Kosovo Rev. Team, 1999–2000, MoD; Hd, Kosovo Section, FCO, 2000–02; UK Liaison Officer and Policy Advr on Asia and Pacific to EU High Rep., EU Council Secretariat, Brussels, 2002–07; Dep. Hd, Security Policy Dept, FCO, 2007–11. *Address:* c/o Foreign and Commonwealth Office, King Charles Street, SW1A 2AH.

HOLTEN, Kasper; Director of Opera, Royal Opera House, Covent Garden, since 2011; *b* Copenhagen, 29 March 1973; *s* of Henning Holten and Bodil Nyboe Andersen; partner, Signe Fabricius; one *d*. *Educ:* Univ. of Copenhagen. Asst dir to leading stage dirs, 1992–; début as stage dir, Musikteatret Undergrunden Odense, 1993; Dramaturg, Aalborg Teater, 1996–2000; Artistic Dir, Aarhus Sommeropera, 1996–99; Dir of Opera, Royal Danish Th., 2000–11. Stage productions include: Ring, Copenhagen, 2003–06; Le Nozze di Figaro, Theater an der Wien, 2007; Die Frau Ohne Schatten, Copenhagen, 2011; Lohengrin, Deutsche Oper Berlin, 2012; Eugene Onegin, ROH, 2013; Don Giovanni, ROH, L'Ormindo, Sam Wanamaker Playhouse, Idomeneo, Wiener Staatsoper, 2014; Król Roger, ROH, 2015. Dir of prodns of opera, drama, musical and operetta in Denmark, Sweden, Norway, Finland, Iceland, Latvia, Russia, France, Germany, Italy, Austria, UK, USA, Japan and Australia; dir, film, Juan, 2010. Mem., Arts Council Denmark (Music), 1995–99. Knight, Order of the Dannebrog (Denmark), 2003; Ingenio et Arti Medal (Denmark), 2011. *Address:* Royal Opera House, Bow Street, Covent Garden, WC2E 9DD. *T:* 07572 603935. *E:* kasper@holten.com.

HOLTHAM, Gerald Hubert, FLSW; Managing Partner, Cadwyn Capital LLP, since 2005; Adviser to Finance Minister, Welsh Assembly Government, 2012–14; *b* Aberdare, 28 June 1944; *s* of late Denis Arthur Holtham and Dilys Maud Holtham (*née* Bull); *m* 1st, 1969, Patricia Mary Blythin (marr. diss. 1976); one *d*; 2nd, 1979, Edith Hodgkinson; one *s* one *d*. *Educ:* King Edward's Sch., Birmingham; Jesus Coll., Oxford (BA 1st Cl. PPE); Nuffield Coll., Oxford (MPhil Econ). ODI, 1973–75; Economist, OECD, Paris, 1975–82; Head, Gen. Econ. Div., Dept of Econs, OECD, 1982–85; Vis. Fellow, Brookings Inst., Washington, 1985–87; Chief Internat. Economist, Shearson Lehman, 1988–91; Econs Fellow, Magdalen Coll., Oxford, 1991–92; Chief Economist, Lehman Brothers, Europe, 1992–94; Dir, IPPR, 1994–98; Dir, Global Strategy, Norwich Union Investment Mgt, 1998–2000; Chief Investment Officer, Morley Fund Mgt, 2000–04. Chm., Ind. Commn on Financing, Welsh Assembly Govt, 2008–10. Visiting Professor: Univ. of Strathclyde, 1990–93; Cardiff Univ. Business Sch., 2004–; Affiliated Prof., London Business Sch., 1992–99. FLSW 2015. Hon. Fellow, Swansea Univ., 2011. *Publications:* (with Roger Busby) Main Line Kill (novel), 1967; (with Arthur Hazlewood) Aid and Inequality in Kenya, 1975; (jtly) Empirical Macroeconomics for Interdependent Economies, 1988; (with Ralph Bryant and Peter Hooper) External Deficits and the Dollar, 1988; articles on economics in learned jls. *Recreations:* gardening, windsurfing, listening to jazz. *Address:* 13 Lansdowne Gardens, SW8 2EQ. *T:* (020) 7622 8673.

HOLWELL, Peter, FCA; Principal, University of London, 1985–97; *b* 28 March 1936; *s* of Frank Holwell and Helen (*née* Howe); *m* 1959, Jean Patricia Ashman; one *s* one *d*. *Educ:* Palmers Endowed Sch., Grays, Essex; Hendon Grammar Sch.; London Sch. of Econs and Pol Science (BSc Econ). FCA 1972; MBCS 1974; FRSocMed 1991. Articled Clerk, 1958–61, Management Consultant, 1961–64, Arthur Andersen and Co.; University of London: Head of Computing, Sch. Exams Bd, 1964–67; Head of University Computing and O & M Unit, 1967–77; Sec. for Accounting and Admin. Computing, 1977–82; Clerk of the Court, 1982–85; Dir, School Exams Council, 1988–94; Mem., Univ. of London Exams and Assessments Council, 1991–96. Chm., UCCA Computing Gp, 1977–82. Chm., City and E London FHSA, 1994–96; Mem., Quality Cttee, NHS Canterbury and Coastal CCG, 2013–. Director: Zoo Operations Ltd, 1988–92; London E Anglian Gp Ltd, 1990–93; non-exec. Mem., NE Thames RHA, 1990–94. Consultant: POW Sch. of Architecture and the Bldg Arts, 1998–99; Chatham Historic Dockyard Trust, 1999–2001. FZS, 1988–2001 (Treas., 1991–92). Chm., St Mark's Res. Foundn and Educnl Trust, 1995–2000; Trustee: Samuel Courtauld (formerly Home House) Trust, 1985–97; Leeds Castle Foundn, 2001–03. Mem. Council, Sch. of Pharmacy, Univ. of London, 1996–2001; Vice-Chm., Wye Coll., 1996–2000. *Recreations:* military history, music, travel. *Address:* Hookers Green, Bishopsbourne, Canterbury, Kent CT4 5JB.

HOM, Ken, Hon. OBE 2009; BBC TV presenter; author; *b* 3 May 1949; *s* of late Thomas Hom and Ying Fong Hom. *Educ:* Univ. of Calif, Berkeley. Public television producer, 1974–75; cookery teacher, 1975–78; Cookery prof., Calif. Culinary Acad., San Francisco, 1978–82; Presenter: BBC TV series: Ken Hom's Chinese Cookery, 1984; Hot Chefs, 1991; Ken Hom's Hot Wok, 1996; Ken Hom Travels with a Hot Wok, 1998; Foolproof Chinese Cookery, 2000; The Noodle Road (series), Korean Broadcasting Service, 2009; Exploring China: A Culinary Adventure, 2012. Consultant Chef, Maison Chin, Bandara Hotel, Bangkok, 2008–13; Exec. Consultant Chef, MEE restaurant, Copacabana Palace Hotel, Rio de Janeiro, 2014–. Hon. Chm., Inst. for Advancement of Sci. and Art of Chinese Cuisine, NY, 1993–. Founding Patron, Oxford Gastronomica, 2007. Ambassador, Action Against Hunger, 2008–. Hon. Dr Oxford Brookes, 2007. *Publications:* Ken Hom's Encyclopaedia of Chinese Cookery Techniques, 1984 (US edn as Chinese Technique, 1981); Ken Hom's Chinese Cookery, 1984, anniversary edn, 2009; Ken Hom's Vegetable and Pasta Book, 1987; Ken Hom's East Meets West Cuisine, 1987; Fragrant Harbour Taste, 1988; Asian Vegetarian Feast, 1988; Ken Hom's Quick and Easy Chinese Cookery, 1988; The Taste of China, 1989; The Cooking of China, 1992; Ken Hom's Chinese Kitchen, 1993; Ken Hom's Hot Wok, 1996; Ken Hom's Asian Ingredients and Posters, 1997; Ken Hom Travels with a Hot Wok, 1997; Easy Family Dishes: a memoir with recipes, 1998 (Andre Simon Award, 1999; US edn as Easy Family Recipes from a Chinese-American Childhood, 1998); Ken Hom Cooks Thai, 1999; Foolproof Chinese Cookery, 2000; Quick Wok, 2001; Foolproof Thai Cookery, 2002; Foolproof Asian Cookery, 2003; 100 Top Stir Fries, 2004; Simple Chinese Cookery, 2005; Simple Thai Cookery, 2006; Simple Asian Cookery, 2007; (with Wynnie Chan) The Ken Hom Nutri Wok Kit Recipe Book, 2008; Complete Chinese Cookbook, 2011; Classic Chinese Recipes, 2011; My Kitchen Table: 100 quick stir-fry recipes, 2011; My Kitchen Table: easy Chinese suppers, 2012; Asian, 2012; (with Ching-He Huang) Exploring China: a culinary adventure: 100 recipes from our journey, 2012; (with Pierre-Jean Pébeyre) Truffle, 2014. *Recreations:* Bordeaux vintage wine, bicycling, reading, swimming.

HOMA, Peter Michael, CBE 2000; Chief Executive, Nottingham University Hospitals NHS Trust, since 2006; *b* 3 Jan. 1957; *s* of late Karol Anthony Homa and Anne Kathleen Homa (*née* Dixon); *m* 2006, Deborah Hallas; one *s* one *d* from previous marriage. *Educ:* Ernest Bevin Sch., London; Univ. of Sussex (BA Hons Econs 1979); Univ. of Hull (MBA 1993); Henley Management Coll. and Brunel Univ. (DBA 1998). Comp IHM 2003 (MHSM 1985, FHSM 1999). Self-employed, 1979–81; nat. admin. trainee, SW Thames RHA, 1981–82; Operational Services Adminr, St George's Hosp., London, 1983–84; Dep. Unit Adminr, Bristol Children's and Maternity Hosps, 1984–86; Dep. Unit Gen. Manager, Acute Services, Bromsgrove and Redditch HA, 1986–89; Leicester Royal Infirmary: Associate Gen. Manager, 1989–90; Unit. Gen. Manager, 1990–93; Chief Exec., Leicester Royal Infirmary NHS Trust, 1993–98; Hd, Nat. Patients' Access Team, NHS Exec., 1998–99; Chief Executive: Commn for Health Improvement, 1999–2003; St George's Healthcare NHS Trust, 2003–06. Visiting Professor: LSE, 2000–03; Univ. of Lincoln, 2006; Univ. of Surrey, 2006–09; Univ. of Nottingham, 2008. Pres., IHSM, 1998–99 (Vice-Chm., 1996–97; Chm., 1997–98). *Recreations:* running, cycling, reading, writing, picture framing. *Address:* Nottingham University Hospitals NHS Trust, Queen's Medical Centre Campus, Nottingham NG7 2UH.

HOMAN, Maj.-Gen. John Vincent, CB 1980; CEng, FIMechE; Facilities Manager, Matra Marconi Space (formerly Marconi Space Systems), Portsmouth, 1982–92; *b* 30 June 1927; *s* of Charles Frederic William Burton Homan and Dorothy Maud Homan; *m* 1953, Ann Bartlett; one *s* two *d*. *Educ:* Haileybury; RMA Sandhurst; RMCS Shrivenham. BSc (Eng). Commnd, REME, 1948; Lt-Col 1967; Comdr REME 2nd Div., 1968–70; Col 1970; MoD 1970–72; CO 27 Comd Workshop REME, 1972–74; Brig. 1974; Dep. Dir, Electrical and Mechanical Engineering, 1st British Corps, 1974–76; Dir of Equipment Management, MoD, 1976–77; Dir Gen., Electrical and Mechanical Engrg, MoD, 1978–79; Maj.-Gen. 1978; Sen. Army Mem., RCDS, 1980–82. Col Comdt, REME, 1982–88. *Address:* Roedean, 25 The Avenue, Andover, Hants SP10 3EW. *T:* (01264) 351196.

HOMDEN, Dr Carol Ann, CBE 2013; Chief Executive, Thomas Coram Foundation for Children (Coram) (formerly Coram Family), since 2007; *b* 9 April 1960; *d* of Dick Homden and Beryl Homden (*née* Kinnersley, now Rabbage); *m* Steve Caplin; two *s*. *Educ:* Shrewsbury High Sch.; Univ. of East Anglia (BA Hons English Lit.; PhD 1986). Publicity Asst, Poly. of N London, 1985–86; Polytechnic of Central London, subsequently University of Westminster: PR Officer, 1986–87; Dir, Corporate Communications, 1987–97; Dir, Mktg and Develt, 1997–99; Dir, Mktg and Public Affairs, BM, 1999–2003; Commercial Dir, Prince's Trust, 2003–07. Chair: Avenues Trust, 2005–11; Nat. Autistic Soc., 2012–. *Publications:* The Plays of David Hare, 1986. *Recreations:* cottage in Suffolk, visiting museums. *Address:* Coram, 49 Mecklenburgh Square, WC1N 2QA. *T:* (020) 7520 0304. *E:* carol@coram.org.uk.

HOME; *see* Douglas Home, and Douglas-Home, family name of Baroness Dacre and Earl of Home.

HOME, 15th Earl of, *cr* 1605; **David Alexander Cospatrick Douglas-Home,** KT 2013; CVO 1997; CBE 1991; Baron Home 1473; Baron Dunglass 1605; Baron Douglas (UK) 1875; Chairman: Coutts & Co., 1999–2013; Coutts & Co. Ltd (formerly Coutts Bank von Ernst, then RBS Coutts Bank Ltd), 2004–15 (Director, 1999, Chairman, 2000, Coutts (Switzerland); Chairman, Bank von Ernst (Switzerland), 2003); *b* 20 Nov. 1943; *o s* of Baron Home of the Hirsel (Life Peer), KT, PC (who disclaimed his hereditary peerages for life, 1963) and Elizabeth Hester (*d* 1990), *d* of Very Rev. C. A. Alington, DD; *S* father, 1995; *m* 1972, Jane Margaret, *yr d* of late Col J. Williams-Wynne, CBE, DSO; one *s* two *d*. *Educ:* Eton College; Christ Church, Oxford (BA 1966). Director: Morgan Grenfell & Co. Ltd, 1974–99; Morgan Grenfell Egyptian Finance Co. Ltd, 1975–77; Morgan Grenfell (Scotland), then Deutsche Morgan Grenfell (Scotland) Ltd, 1978–99 (Chm., 1986–99); Morgan Grenfell (Asia) Ltd, 1978–82 (Dep. Chm., 1979–82); Arab Bank Investment Co., 1979–87; Agricultural Mortgage Corp., 1979–93; Arab-British Chamber of Commerce, 1975–84; Tandem Group (formerly EFG plc), 1981–96 (Chm., 1993–96); Credit for Exports, 1984–94; Deutsche Morgan Grenfell (Hong Kong), 1989–99; Deutsche Morgan Grenfell Asia Pacific Holdings Pte Ltd, 1989–99; Morgan Grenfell Thai Co., 1990–96; K & N Kenanga Bhd, 1995–99; Kenanga DMG Futures Sdn Bhd, 1995–99; Deutsche Morgan Grenfell Group plc, 1996–99 (Chm., Jan.–March, 1999); Wheatsheaf Investments Ltd (formerly Deva Gp), 1999–2010; Deva Gp Ltd (formerly Deva Hldgs), 1999–2010; Dubai Financial Services Authy, 2005–11; Chairman: Morgan Grenfell Export Services, 1984–99; Morgan Grenfell Internat. Ltd, 1987–99; Cegelec Controls Ltd, 1991–94; K & N Kenanga Holdings Bhd, 1993–99; Grosvenor Estate Hldgs, 1993–99; Grosvenor Gp Ltd, 2007–10 (Dep. Chm., 2005–07); MAN Ltd, 2000–09; Trustee, Grosvenor Estate, 1993–2010. Chm., Committee for Middle East Trade, 1986–92 (Mem., 1973–75). Governor: Ditchley Foundn, 1977–2011; Commonwealth Inst., 1988–98. Trustee, RASE, 1999–2004 (Hon. Trustee, 2004–). Pres., Old Etonian Assoc., 2002–03. Elected Mem., H of L, 1999. *Recreation:* outdoor sports. *Heir:* *s* Lord Dunglass, *qv*. *Address:* 43 Chelsea Towers, Chelsea Manor Street, SW3 5PN. *T:* (020) 3730 1690; The Hirsel, Coldstream, Berwickshire TD12 4LP. *T:* (01890) 882345. *Club:* Turf.
See also Viscount Lifford.

HOME, Anna Margaret, OBE 1993; Chair, Children's Media Foundation, since 2012; *b* 13 Jan. 1938; *d* of James Douglas Home and Janet Mary (*née* Wheeler). *Educ:* Convent of Our Lady, St Leonard's-on-Sea, Sussex; St Anne's Coll., Oxford (MA (Hons) Mod. Hist.). BBC Radio Studio Man., 1960–64; Res. Asst, Dir, Producer, Children's TV, 1966–70; Exec. Producer, BBC Children's Drama Unit, 1970–81: responsible for series such as Lizzie Dripping, Bagthorpe Saga, Moon Stallion; started Grange Hill, 1977; Controller of Programmes SE, later Dep. Dir of Programmes, TVS (one of the original franchise gp), 1981–86; Hd of Children's Programmes, BBC TV, 1986–98; Chief Exec., Children's Film and Television Foundn, 1998–2012. Chair: Cinemagic, 1999–2005; Eurokidnet, 2002–06; Children's Television Trust Internat., 2005–11; Kidnet, 2006–12; Save Kids TV, 2006–12; Board Member: Screen South, 2002–; Unicorn Th. for Children, 2004–11; Mem. Adv. Bd, Ability Media, 2009–13. Chm., 2nd World Summit on TV for Children, London, 1998. Chairman: Showcommotion Children's Media Fest., 2005–09; Children's Media Conf., 2010–. Trustee, Prince of Wales Arts and Kids Foundn, 2005–14. FRTS 1987. Pye Award for distinguished services to children's television, 1984; Eleanor Farjeon Award for services to children's literature, 1989; Judges Award, RTS, 1993; Lifetime Achievement Award, Women in Film and TV, 1996; BAFTA Special Award for Lifetime Achievement in Children's Programmes, 1997. *Publications:* Into the Box of Delights: a history of children's television, 1993. *Recreations:* theatre, literature, travel, gardening. *Address:* 3 Liberia Road, N5 1JP.

HOME, Sir William (Dundas), 14th Bt *cr* 1671 (NS), of Blackadder, Co. Berwick; consultant tree surgeon and horticulturalist; *b* 19 Feb. 1968; *s* of late John Home, *er s* of 13th Bt, and of Nancy Helen, *d* of H. G. Elliott, Perth, WA (she *m* 1993, Rt Hon. Sir John Grey Gorton, GCMG, AC, CH); *S* grandfather, 1992; *m* 1995, Dominique Meryl, *d* of Sydney Fischer, OBE; one *s* one *d*. *Educ:* Cranbrook Sch., Sydney, NSW. Member: Bd, Internat. Soc. of Arboriculture, 1991 (Founding Mem., Australian Chapter, 1997); Aust. Inst. of Horticulture, 1992; Nat. Arborists' Assoc. of Aust., 1999. *Recreations:* golf, scuba diving, fishing, tennis. *Heir:* *s* Thomas John Home, *b* 24 Nov. 1996. *Address:* 53 York Road, Queen's Park, NSW 2022, Australia. *Club:* Royal Sydney Golf (Sydney).

HOME ROBERTSON, John David; Member (Lab) East Lothian, Scottish Parliament, 1999–2007; *b* 5 Dec. 1948; *s* of late Lt-Col J. W. Home Robertson and Mrs H. M. Home Robertson; *m* 1977, Catherine Jean Brewster; two *s*. *Educ:* Ampleforth Coll.; West of Scotland Coll. of Agriculture. Farmer. Mem., Berwicks DC, 1975–78; Mem., Borders Health Bd, 1976–78. Chm., Eastern Borders CAB, 1977. MP (Lab) Berwick and E Lothian, Oct. 1978–83, E Lothian, 1983–2001. Opposition Scottish Whip, 1983–84; opposition spokesman on agric., 1984–87, 1988–90, on Scotland, 1987–88; PPS to Minister of Agriculture, Fisheries and Food, 1997–98; PPS to Minister for Cabinet Office, 1998–99; Member: Select Cttee on Scottish affairs, 1980–83; Select Cttee on Defence, 1990–97; British-Irish Parly Body, 1993–99. Chm., Scottish Gp of Lab MPs, 1983. Dep. Minister for Rural Affairs, Scottish Exec., 1999–2000. Convener, Holyrood Progress Gp, 2000–05. Mem., Press Complaints Commn, 2008–11. Founder, Paxton Trust, 1989 (Man. Trustee, 2009–11); Mem., Mgt Cttee, Edinburgh Direct Aid, 2005–09. Pres., Berwickshire Naturalists Club, 2015.

HOMER, Linda Margaret, CB 2008; a Commissioner, Chief Executive Officer and Permanent Secretary for Tax, HM Revenue and Customs, since 2012; *b* 4 March 1957; *d* of John and Jean Risebrow; *m* 1979, Ian James Homer; three *d*. *Educ:* University Coll. London (LLB). Admitted solicitor, 1980; Lawyer, Reading BC, 1979–82; Solicitor, then Asst Chief Exec., 1982–94, Dir, Corporate Services, 1994–97, Herts CC; Chief Executive: Suffolk CC, 1998–2002; Birmingham CC, 2002–05; Dir Gen., Immigration and Nationality, then Chief Exec., Border and Immigration Agency, later UK Border Agency, Home Office, 2005–11; Permanent Sec., DfT, 2011–12. DUniv Birmingham, 2010. *Recreations:* ski-ing, alpine walking, gardening. *Address:* HM Revenue and Customs, 100 Parliament Street, SW1A 2BQ.

HOMMEN, Johannes Henricus Maria, (Jan); Chief Executive Officer, ING Group, 2009–13 (Member, 2005–09, Chairman, 2008–09, Supervisory Board); *b* 29 April 1943; *s* of Joseph Hommen and Johanna van Herpen; *m* 1969, Gertrudis, (Tucke), van Enschot; two *s* two *d*. *Educ:* St Jans Lyceum, Gymnasium B, Den Bosch; Univ. of Tilburg (Business 1970). Controller, Lips Aluminium, 1970–74; Financial Dir, Alcoa Nederland, 1974–78; Alcoa, USA: Asst Treas., 1978–86, Vice Pres. Treas., 1986–91; Exec. Vice Pres. and Chief Financial Officer, 1991–97; Philips Electronics: Exec. Vice Pres. and Chief Financial Officer, Netherlands, 1997–2002; Vice Chm. and Chief Financial Officer, 2002–05; Chm., Reed Elsevier, 2005–09. Chairman, Supervisory Board: Academic Hosp., Maastricht, 2001–; TNT, 2005–09; Tias Nimbas Business Sch., Univ. of Tilberg; Member, Supervisory Board: Ahold, 2003–07, 2013–; Campina, until 2009. Commander, Orde van Oranje Nassau (Netherlands), 2013. *Recreations:* golf, tennis, swimming, reading, music, chess. *Address:* c/o ING Group, ING House, Amstelveenseweg 500, 1081 KL Amsterdam, Netherlands.

HONDERICH, Prof. Edgar Dawn Ross, (Ted), PhD; Grote Professor of the Philosophy of Mind and Logic, University College London, 1988–98, now Emeritus; Chairman, Royal Institute of Philosophy, 2006–11; *b* 30 Jan. 1933; *s* of John William Honderich and Rae Laura Armstrong, Baden, Canada; *m* 1st, 1964, Pauline Ann Marina Goodwin (marr. diss. 1972), *d* of Paul Fawcett Goodwin and Lena Payne, Kildare; one *s* one *d*; 2nd, 1989, Jane Elizabeth O'Grady (marr. diss. 1998), *d* of Major Robert O'Grady and Hon. Joan Ramsbotham, Bath; 3rd, 2003, Ingrid Coggin Purkiss, *d* of Maurice Edward Henry Coggin and Eleonora Illeris, Cambridge. *Educ:* Kitchener Sch., Kitchener, Canada; Lawrence Park Sch., Toronto; University Coll., Univ. of Toronto (BA 1959); University Coll. London (PhD 1968). Literary Editor, Toronto Star, 1957–59; Lectr in Phil., Univ. of Sussex, 1962–64; Lectr in Phil., 1964–73, Reader in Phil., 1973–83, Prof. of Phil., 1983–88, and Head of Dept of Philosophy, 1988–93, UCL; Chm., Bd of Phil Studies, Univ. of London, 1986–89. Vis. Prof., Yale Univ., and CUNY, 1970. Editor: Internat. Library of Philosophy and Scientific Method, 1966–98; Penguin philosophy books, 1967–98; The Arguments of the Philosophers, 1968–98; The Problems of Philosophy: their past and present, 1984–98; radio, television, journalism. *Publications:* Punishment: the supposed justifications, 1969, 5th edn as Punishment: the supposed justifications reconsidered, 2005; (ed) Essays on Freedom of Action, 1973; (ed) Social Ends and Political Means, 1976; (ed with Myles Burnyeat) Philosophy As It Is, 1979; Violence for Equality: inquiries in political philosophy (incorporating Three Essays on Political Violence, 1976), 1980, 3rd edn as Terrorism for Humanity: inquiries in political philosophy, 2003; (ed) Philosophy Through Its Past, 1984; (ed) Morality and Objectivity, 1985; A Theory of Determinism: the mind, neuroscience, and life-hopes, 1988, 2nd edn, as The Consequences of Determinism, 1990; Mind and Brain, 1990; Conservatism, 1990, revd edn as Conservatism: Burke, Nozick, Bush, Blair?, 2005; How Free Are You? The Determinism Problem, 1993, 2nd edn 2002 (trans. German, Japanese, Chinese, Swedish, Italian, Polish, Romanian, French, Spanish); (ed) The Oxford Companion to Philosophy, 1995, new edn 2005; Philosopher: a kind of life, 2000; After the Terror, 2002, 2nd edn 2003; Political Means and Social Ends: collected papers, 2003; On Consciousness: collected papers, 2004; On Determinism and Freedom: collected papers, 2005; Humanity, Terrorism, Terrorist War (USA edn as Right and Wrong, and Palestine, 9/11, Iraq, 7/7...), 2006; Radical Externalism: Honderich's Theory of Consciousness discussed, ed Anthony Freeman, 2006; Actual Consciousness, 2014; (ed) Philosophers of Our Times: Royal Institute of Philosophy annual lectures, 2014; phil articles in Amer. Phil Qly, Analysis, Inquiry, Jl of Theoretical Biol., Mind, Phil., Pol Studies, Proc. Aristotelian Soc., Jl of Consciousness Studies, Jl of Ethics, Rechtsphilosophische Hefte, etc. *Recreations:* wine, Queen's Wood, Highgate Wood, inexpensive restaurants. *Address:* 66 Muswell Hill Road, N10 3JR. *T:* (020) 8350 4936. *E:* t.honderich@ucl.ac.uk. *Club:* Garrick.

HONDROS, Ernest Demetrios, CMG 1996; DSc; FRS 1984; Director: Petten Establishment, Commission of European Communities' Joint Research Centre, 1985–95; Institute of Advanced Materials, Petten (Netherlands) and Ispra (Italy), 1988–95; *b* 18 Feb. 1930; *s* of Demetrios Hondros and Athanasia Paleologos; *m* 1968, Sissel Kristine Garder-Olsen; two *s*. *Educ:* Univ. of Melbourne (DSc MSc); Univ. of Paris (Dr d'Univ.). CEng, FIMMM. Research Officer, CSIRO Tribophysics Laboratory, Melbourne, 1955–59; Research Fellow, Univ. of Paris, Lab. de Chimie Minérale, 1959–62; National Physical Laboratory: Sen. Research Officer, Metallurgy Div., 1962–65; Principal Res. Fellow, 1965–68; Sen. Principal Res. Officer (Special Merit), 1974; Supt, Materials Applications Div., 1979–85. Vis. Prof., Dept of Materials, ICSTM, 1988–2004. Membre d'Honneur, Société Française de Métallurgie, 1986; Mem., Academia Europaea, 1988. Hon. DSc London, 1997. Rosenhain Medallist, Metals Soc., 1976; Howe Medal, Amer. Soc. for Metals, 1978; A. A. Griffiths Medal and Prize, Inst. of Metals, 1987. *Publications:* numerous research papers and reviews in learned jls. *Recreations:* music, literature, walking.

HONE, David; landscape and portrait painter; President, Royal Hibernian Academy of Arts, 1978–83; *b* 14 Dec. 1928; *s* of Joseph Hone and Vera Hone (*née* Brewster); *m* 1962, Rosemary D'Arcy; two *s* one *d*. *Educ:* Baymount School; St Columba's College; University College, Dublin. Studied art at National College of Art, Dublin, and later in Italy. Hon. RA, HRSA (ex-officio). *Recreations:* walking dogs, photography. *Address:* 4 Ailesbury Gardens, Sydney Parade, Dublin 4, Ireland. *T:* (1) 2692809.

HONE, Michael Stuart, OBE 1993 (MBE 1978); JP; HM Diplomatic Service, retired; Ambassador and Consul-General, Iceland, 1993–96; *b* 19 May 1936; *s* of William John Hone and Marguerite (*née* Howe); *m* 1st, 1957; three *s*; 2nd, 1983, Dr Elizabeth Ann Balmer; one *s* one *d*. *Educ:* Westham Secondary Sch. Entered RN 1951; joined CRO, 1961; served Kingston, Nairobi, Lisbon, Bridgetown; FCO 1972; served Beirut, Baghdad, Canberra; Resident British Rep., St Vincent and Grenadines; Chief Secretary, St Helena, 1990. JP Hasting and Rother, 2001. *Recreations:* family, walking. *Address:* Hillcroft, Station Approach, Crowhurst, Sussex TN33 9DB. *T:* (01424) 830444.

HONE, Richard Michael; QC 1997; **His Honour Judge Hone;** a Circuit Judge at the Central Criminal Court, since 2005; *b* 15 Feb. 1947; *s* of Maj. Gen. Sir Ralph Hone, KCMG, KBE, MC, TD, QC and Sybil Mary Hone (*née* Collins); *m* 1st, Sarah Nicholl-Carne (marr. diss.); two *s*; 2nd, Diana Pavel; two *s*. *Educ:* St Paul's Sch. (Schol.); University Coll., Oxford (MA). Called to the Bar, Middle Temple, 1970 (Bencher, 1994; Cocks' Referee, 1988–94); an Asst Recorder, 1987–91; a Recorder, 1991–2004. Mem., Bar Professional Conduct Cttee, 1993–97; Chm., Jt Regulations Cttee, Inns of Court and Bar, 1995–2000; Legal Mem., Mental Health Review Tribunals, 2000–. Freeman, City of London, 2004; Liveryman, Ironmongers' Co., 2008–. Pres., Freemasons' Grand Charity, 2012–. KStJ 2000 (Asst Dir of Ceremonies, 1996). *Recreations:* wine, travel, fine art. *Address:* Central Criminal Court, Old Bailey, EC4M 7EH. *T:* (020) 7248 3277. *Clubs:* Boodle's, Pratt's, Beefsteak.

HONEY, Elizabeth; *see* Filkin, E. J.

HONEY, Michael John; Chief Executive, London Ambulance Service, 1996–2000; *b* 28 Nov. 1941; *s* of Denis Honey and Mary Honey (*née* Henderson); four *d*; *m* 1996, Elizabeth Filkin, *qv*. *Educ:* Clifton College; Regent Street Polytechnic (DipArch); Columbia Univ. MArch (Urban Design); MSc (City Planning). City Planner, Boston Redevelopment Authority, 1968–70; Corporate Planning Manager, Bor. of Greenwich, 1970–74; Head, Exec. Office, Bor. of Croydon, 1974–80; Chief Executive: Bor. of Richmond upon Thames, 1980–88; LDDC, 1988–90; Gloucestershire CC, 1990–96. *Recreation:* sailing.

HONEY, Air Vice-Marshal Robert John, CB 1991; CBE 1987; Air Secretary, 1989–94; *b* 3 Dec. 1936; *s* of F. G. Honey; *m* 1956, Diana Chalmers; one *s* one *d*. *Educ:* Ashford Grammar Sch. Joined RAF as pilot, 1954; served: Germany, 1956–59; Singapore, 1961–64; Canada, 1968–69; India, 1982; UK intervening years; Dep. Commander RAF Germany, 1987–89. Dir, RAF Sports Bd, 1994–2001. Mountaineering expedns to Mulkila, India, 1979, Masherbrum, Pakistan, 1981, Greenland, 1998. *Recreations:* climbing, mountaineering, ski-ing, watercolour painting.

HONEYBALL, Mary; Member (Lab) London Region, European Parliament, since Jan. 2000; *b* 12 Nov. 1952; *d* of Stanley James Honeyball and Betty Gath Honeyball (*née* Tandy). *Educ:* Pate's Grammar Sch. for Girls, Cheltenham; Somerville Coll., Oxford (MA). Admin. Officer, GLC, 1975–77; Negotiations Officer, Soc. of Civil and Public Servants, 1977–83; Political Organiser, RACS, 1983–85; Gen. Sec., Newham Voluntary Agencies Council, 1986–90; Chief Exec., Gingerbread Lone Parents' Charity, 1992–94; Gen. Sec., Assoc. of Chief Officers of Probation, 1994–98; Chief Exec., Nat. Childbirth Trust, 1999–2000. Mem. (Lab) Barnet LBC, 1978–86. Mem., RSA. Governor: Grahame Park Comprehensive Sch., London NW,

1978–84; Sir Francis Drake Primary Sch., SE8, 1986–90; Deptford Green Comprehensive Sch., SE8, 1986–90. Liveryman, City of London, 2011–. *Recreations:* modern fiction, art. *Address:* 4G Shirland Mews, W9 3DY. *T:* (020) 8964 9815, *Fax:* (020) 8960 0150. *E:* mary@maryhoneyball.net.

HONEYCOMBE, (Ronald) Gordon; author, playwright, television presenter, actor and narrator; *b* Karachi, British India, 27 Sept. 1936; *s* of Gordon Samuel Honeycombe and Dorothy Louise Reid Fraser. *Educ:* Edinburgh Acad.; University Coll., Oxford (MA English). National Service, RA, mainly in Hong Kong, 1955–57. Announcer: Radio Hong Kong, 1956–57; BBC Scottish Home Service, 1958; actor: with Tomorrow's Audience, 1961–62; with RSC, Stratford-on-Avon and London, 1962–63; Newscaster with ITN, 1965–77; Newscaster, TV-am, 1984–89. Acted in TV plays, series and shows including: That Was the Week that Was, 1964; The Brack Report, 1982; CQ, 1984; Numbats, 1994; appearances as TV presenter include: (also writer) A Family Tree and Brass Rubbing (documentaries), 1973; The Late Late Show (series), and Something Special (series), 1978; (also ed and jt writer) Family History (series), 1979; appearances as TV narrator include: Arthur C. Clarke's Mysterious World (series), 1980; A Shred of Evidence, 1984; stage appearances include: Playback 625, Royal Court, 1970; Paradise Lost, York and Old Vic, 1975; Suspects, Swansea, 1989; Aladdin, Wimbledon, 1989–90, Bournemouth, 1990–91; Run For Your Wife!, tour, 1990; The Taming of the Shrew, Perth, WA, 1998; film appearances include: The Medusa Touch; The Fourth Protocol; Let's Get Skase; The Sculptor; Short Film Maker. Author of stage productions: The Miracles, Oxford, 1960 and (perf. by RSC), Southwark Cath., 1963 and Consett, 1970; The Princess and the Goblins (musical), Great Ayton, 1976; Paradise Lost, York, Old Vic and Edinburgh Fest., 1975–77; Waltz of my Heart, Bournemouth, 1980; Lancelot and Guinevere, Old Vic, 1980; author of TV plays: The Golden Vision, 1968; Time and Again, 1974 (Silver Medal, Film and TV Fest., NY, 1975); The Thirteenth Day of Christmas, 1986; radio dramatisations (all Radio 4): Paradise Lost, 1975; Lancelot and Guinevere, 1976; A King shall have a Kingdom, 1977; devised Royal Gala performances: God save the Queen!, Chichester, 1977; A King shall have a Kingdom, York, 1977. Directed and prod, The Redemption, Fest. of Perth, 1990. *Publications: non-fiction:* Nagasaki 1945, 1981; Royal Wedding, 1981; The Murders of the Black Museum, 1982; The Year of the Princess, 1982; Selfridges, 1984; TV-am's Official Celebration of the Royal Wedding, 1986; More Murders of the Black Museum, 1993; The Complete Murders of the Black Museum, 1995; Australia For Me, 1996; Murders of the Black Museum, 2009; *documentary novels:* Adam's Tale, 1974; Red Watch, 1976; Siren Song, 1992; *fiction:* The Redemption (play), 1964; Neither the Sea nor the Sand, 1969; Dragon under the Hill, 1972; The Edge of Heaven, 1981; Beach, 2005; contrib. national newspapers and magazines. *Recreations:* bridge, crosswords, genealogy. *Address:* c/o RGM WA, 649 Beaufort Street, Mt Lawley, Perth, WA 6050, Australia. *T:* (8) 93285788.

HONORÉ, Prof. Antony Maurice; QC 1987; DCL Oxon; FBA 1972; Regius Professor of Civil Law, University of Oxford, 1971–88; Fellow, 1971–89, Acting Warden, 1987–89, All Souls College, Oxford; *b* 30 March 1921; *o s* of Frédéric Maurice Honoré and Marjorie Erskine (*née* Gilbert); *m* 1st, Martine Marie-Odette Genouville; one *s* one *d*; 2nd, Deborah Mary Cowen (*née* Duncan). *Educ:* Diocesan Coll., Rondebosch; Univ. of Cape Town; New Coll., Oxford (Rhodes Scholar, 1940; Hon. Fellow 2008); DCL Oxon 1969. Union Defence Forces, 1940–45; Lieut, Rand Light Infantry, 1942. BCL 1948. Vinerian Scholar, 1948. Advocate, South Africa, 1951; called to Bar, Lincoln's Inn, 1952, Hon. Bencher, 1971. Lectr, Nottingham Univ., 1948; Rhodes Reader in Roman-Dutch Law, 1957–70, Fellow of Queen's Coll., Oxford, 1949–64, of New Coll., 1964–70. Visiting Professor: McGill, 1961; Berkeley, 1968. Lectures: Hamlyn, Nottingham, 1982; J. H. Gray, Cambridge, 1985; Blackstone, Oxford, 1988; H. L. A. Hart, University Coll., Oxford, 1992; Maccabean, British Acad., 1998. Member: Internat. Acad. of Comparative Law, 1994; Accademia Costantiniana, 1994. Corresp. Member: Bavarian Acad. of Scis, 1992; Serbian Phil. Soc., 1988; Hon. Fellow: Harris Manchester Coll., Oxford, 2000; All Souls Coll., Oxford, 2008; Queen's Coll., Oxford, 2010. Hon. LLD: Edinburgh, 1977; South Africa, 1984; Stellenbosch, 1988; Cape Town, 1990; Witwatersrand, 2002. Hon. Citizen, San Ginesio, Italy, 2004. *Publications:* (with H. L. A. Hart) Causation in the Law, 1959, 2nd edn 1985 (trans. Japanese 1991, Chinese 2004); Gaius, 1962; The South African Law of Trusts, 1965, 5th edn 2002; Tribonian, 1978; Sex Law, 1978; (with J. Menner) Concordance to the Digest Jurists, 1980; Emperors and Lawyers, 1981, 2nd edn 1994; The Quest for Security, 1982; Ulpian, 1982, 2nd edn 2002; Making Law Bind, 1987; About Law, 1996 (trans. Arabic and Ukrainian 1999); Law in the Crisis of Empire, 1998; Responsibility and Fault, 1999; Justinian's Digest: character and compilation, 2010; *festschriften:* The Legal Mind (ed N. MacCormick and P. Birks), 1986; (also contrib.) Relating to Responsibility (ed P. Cane and J. Gardner), 2001. *Address:* 94C Banbury Road, Oxford OX2 6JT. *T:* (01865) 559684.

HONOUR, (Patrick) Hugh, FBA; FRSL; writer; *b* 26 Sept. 1927; *s* of late Herbert Percy Honour and Dorothy Margaret Withers. *Educ:* King's Sch., Canterbury; St Catharine's Coll., Cambridge (BA). Asst to Dir, Leeds City Art Gall. and Temple Newsam House, 1953–54. Guest Curator for exhibn, The European Vision of America, National Gall. of Art, Washington, Cleveland Museum of Art, and, as L'Amérique vue par l'Europe, Grand Palais, Paris, 1976. FRSL 1972. Corresp. FBA 1986 (Serena Medal, 1995). *Publications:* Chinoiserie, 1961, 2nd edn 1973; Companion Guide to Venice, 1965, rev. edn 1997; (with Sir Nikolaus Pevsner and John Fleming) The Penguin Dictionary of Architecture, 1966, 5th rev. edn as Penguin Dictionary of Architecture and Landscape Architecture, 1998; Neo-classicism, 1968, 4th edn 1977; The New Golden Land, 1976; (with John Fleming) The Penguin Dictionary of Decorative Arts, 1977, rev. edn 1989; Romanticism, 1979; (with John Fleming) A World History of Art, 1982 (Mitchell Prize, 1982) (USA as The Visual Arts: a history, 7th edn 2005); The Image of the Black in Western Art IV, from the American Revolution to World War I, 1989 (Anisfield-Wolf Book Award in Race Relations, 1990); (with John Fleming) The Venetian Hours of Henry James, Whistler and Sargent, 1991; (ed) Edizione Nazionale delle Opere di Antonio Canova, vol. I, Scritti, 1994, 2nd edn 2007, (with Paolo Mariuz), vol. XVIII, 1, 2002 and 2, Epistolario, 2003; Carnets Khmers, 1998; I gessi di Canova per l'ambasciatore Zulian, 2007. *Recreation:* gardening.

HONYWOOD, Sir Filmer (Courtenay William), 11th Bt *cr* 1660; FRICS; Regional Surveyor and Valuer, South Eastern Region, Central Electricity Generating Board, 1978–88; *b* 20 May 1930; *s* of Col Sir William Wynne Honywood, 10th Bt, MC, and Maud Naylor (*d* 1953), *d* of William Hodgson Wilson, Hexgreave Park, Southwell, Notts; *S* father, 1982; *m* 1956, Elizabeth Margaret Mary Cynthia (*d* 1996), *d* of Sir Alastair George Lionel Joseph Miller of Glenlee, 6th Bt; two *s* two *d*. *Educ:* Downside; RMA Sandhurst; Royal Agricultural College, Cirencester (MRAC Diploma). Served 3rd Carabiniers (Prince of Wales' Dragoon Guards). Farmed, 1954–64 (Suffolk Co. Dairy Herd Prodn Awards, 1955 and 1956); joined Agricl Land Service, MAFF, Maidstone, 1964; Asst Land Comr, 1966; Surveyor, Cockermouth, Cumbria, 1973–74; Senior Lands Officer, South Eastern Region, CEGB, 1974–78; pt time Sen. Valuer, Inland Revenue Valuation Service, Folkestone, 1989–90. Consultant on agricultural compensation/restoration, UK Nirex Ltd, 1988–90; Land Agency consultant, Nuclear Electric plc, 1993–94. Examiner in Agriculture: Incorporated Soc. of Estates & Wayleaves Officers, 1989–95; Soc. of Surveying Technicians, 1996–97. *Heir: s* Rupert Anthony Honywood, *b* 2 March 1957. *Address:* Greenway Forstal Farmhouse, Hollingbourne, Maidstone, Kent ME17 1QA. *T:* (01622) 880418.

HOOD, family name of **Viscounts Bridport** and **Hood**.

HOOD, 8th Viscount *cr* 1796, of Whitley, co. Warwick; **Henry Lyttelton Alexander Hood;** Bt 1778; Baron (Ire.) 1782, GB 1795; Partner, Hunters, Solicitors, since 1991; a Lord in Waiting to the Queen, since 2008; *b* 16 March 1958; *e s* of 7th Viscount Hood and Diana Maud Hood, CVO (*née* Lyttelton); *S* father, 1999; *m* 1991, Flora, *yr d* of Comdr M. B. Casement, OBE, RN; three *s* two *d* (of whom one *s* one *d* are twins). *Educ:* Edinburgh Univ. (MA 1981). Qualified as solicitor, 1987. *Heir: s* Hon. Archibald, (Archie), Lyttelton Samuel Hood, *b* 16 May 1993.

HOOD, Prof. Christopher Cropper, CBE 2011; DLitt; FBA 1996; FAcSS; Gladstone Professor of Government, Oxford University, 2001–14, now Emeritus; Fellow of All Souls College, Oxford, 2001–14, now Emeritus; *b* 5 March 1947; *s* of David White Hood and Margaret Cropper; *m* 1979, Gillian Thackwray White; two *d*. *Educ:* Univ. of York (BA 1968; DLitt 1987); Univ. of Glasgow (BLitt 1971). Lectr in Politics, Glasgow Univ., 1972–77 and 1979–86; Res. Fellow, Univ. of York, 1977–79; Prof. of Govt and Public Administration, Univ. of Sydney, 1986–89; Prof. of Public Admin and Public Policy, LSE, 1989–2000. Chair, Politics and Internat. Relations Section, British Acad., 2002–05. Chm., Wkg Party on Personalised Medicine, Nuffield Council on Bioethics, 2008–10. Vis. Res. Fellow, Zentrum für interdisziplinäre Forschung, Univ. of Bielefeld, 1982 and 1989; Sen. Teaching Fellow, Nat. Univ. of Singapore, 1984–85; Fellow, US Nat. Acad. of Public Administration, 2010–; Professorial Fellow, ESRC, 2011–14. FAcSS (AcSS 2001). FRSA 2007. *Publications:* Limits of Administration, 1976; (ed jtly) Big Government in Hard Times, 1981; (with A. Dunsire) Bureaumetrics, 1981; The Tools of Government, 1983; Administrative Analysis, 1986; (ed jtly) Delivering Public Services in Western Europe, 1988; (with A. Dunsire) Cutback Management in Public Bureaucracies, 1989; (with M. W. Jackson) Administrative Argument, 1991; Explaining Economic Policy Reversals, 1994; (ed jtly) Rewards at the Top, 1994; The Art of the State, 1998; (with C. Scott *et al*) Regulation inside Government, 1999; (jtly) Telecommunications Regulation, 1999; (with Henry Rothstein and Robert Baldwin) The Government of Risk: understanding risk regulation regimes, 2001; (ed jtly) Rewards at the Top: Asian and Pacific Rim states, 2003; (ed jtly) Controlling Modern Government, 2004; (with Martin Lodge) Politics of Public Service Bargains, 2006; (ed with David Heald) Transparency: the key to better governance?, 2006; (with H. Margetts) The Tools of Government in the Digital Age, 2007; The Blame Game, 2011; (ed jtly) Forging a Discipline, 2014; (ed jtly) When the Party's Over; the politics of fiscal squeeze in perspective, 2014; (with R. Dixon) A Government that Worked Better and Cost Less?, 2015. *Address:* All Souls College, Oxford OX1 4AL. *T:* (01865) 279379. *W:* www.christopherhood.net.

HOOD, Very Rev. (Elizabeth) Lorna; Minister, Renfrew North, since 1979; Chaplain to the Queen in Scotland, since 2008; Moderator of the General Assembly of the Church of Scotland, 2013–14; *b* Irvine, 21 April 1953; *d* of James Mitchell and Elizabeth Mitchell (*née* Sharpe); *m* 1979, Peter Hood; one *s* one *d*. *Educ:* Glasgow University (MA 1974; BD Hons 1977). Ordained Minister, C of S, 1978; Moderator, Paisley Presbytery, 1995–96; Nominations Convenor, Church of Scotland, Renfrew North, 1996–99; Vice-Convenor: Bd of Ministry, 2005–06; Assembly Arrangements Cttee, 2010–. Mem., Bd of Studies, Inst. of Counselling, Glasgow, 2000–. Gen. Trustee, C of S, 2001–. Hon. DD Glasgow, 2014. *Recreations:* golf, reading, travel. *Address:* Church of Scotland, 121 George Street, Edinburgh EH2 4YN.

HOOD, James; *b* 16 May 1948; *m* 1967, Marion McCleary; one *s* one *d*. *Educ:* Lesmahagow High Sch.; Motherwell Tech. Coll.; Nottingham Univ.; WEA. Miner, Nottingham, 1968–87; NUM official, 1973–87 (Mem., NEC, 1990–92); Leader, Nottingham striking miners, 1984–85. Member: Ollerton Parish Council, 1973–87; Newark and Sherwood Dist Council, 1979–87. MP (Lab) Clydesdale, 1987–2005, Lanark and Hamilton E, 2005–15; contested (Lab) same seat, 2015. Member: Select Cttee on European Legislation, 1987–97 (Chm., 1992–98); Speaker's Panel of Chairmen, 1997–2015; Chair, European Scrutiny Cttee, 1998–2006; founder Chm., All Party Gp on ME (Myalgic Encephalomyelitis), 1987–92; Chm., Miners' Parly Gp, 1991–92; Convenor: Home Affairs Cttee, 1992–97; Scottish Lab. Gp of MPs, 1995–96; sponsor of four Private Members' Bills: on under-age drinking, on ME, on road transport safety and on shops. UK Member: NATO Parly Assembly, 2005–10; Parly Assembly for Council of Europe, 2005–15; Eur. Security and Defence Assembly, WEU, 2005–11. *Recreations:* reading, gardening. *Club:* Lesmahagow Miners Welfare Social (Hon. Mem.).

HOOD, Sir John (Antony), KNZM 2014; PhD; President and Chief Executive, Robertson Foundation, since 2010; Chair, Rhodes Trust, since 2011. *Educ:* Westlake Boys' High Sch., Auckland; Univ. of Auckland (BE; PhD 1976); Worcester Coll., Oxford (Rhodes Schol. 1976; MPhil 1978). With Fletcher Hldgs, subseq. Fletcher Challenge, Ltd, 1979–97: Head, Fletcher Challenge Paper, Fletcher Challenge Building, then Fletcher Construction Co.; Vice-Chancellor: Univ. of Auckland, 1999–2004; Univ. of Oxford, 2004–09. Formerly: Chm., Tonkin and Taylor Ltd; Director: ASB Bank Ltd; Fonterra Co-operative Gp Ltd; BG Gp plc, 2007–; Study Gp Pty Ltd, 2011–; Matakina Ltd; WPP plc, 2014–; Chm., Urenco, 2012–. Gov., NZ Sports Foundn. Hon. Dr Beida, 2005; Hon. LLD: Auckland, 2004; UBC, 2006; Hon. PhD (Business Admin) Korea, 2008. Sir Peter Blake Medal, 2009.

HOOD, Sir John Joseph Harold, 3rd Bt *cr* 1922, of Wimbledon, Co. Surrey; *b* 27 Aug. 1952; *e s* of Sir Harold Joseph Hood, 2nd Bt and Hon. Ferelith Rosemary Florence Kenworthy, *o d* of 10th Baron Strabolgi; *S* father 2005, but his name does not appear on the Official Roll of the Baronetage.

HOOD, Very Rev. Lorna; *see* Hood, Very Rev. E. L.

HOOD, (Martin) Sinclair (Frankland), FSA; FBA 1983; archaeologist; *b* 31 Jan. 1917; *s* of late Lt-Comdr Martin Hood, RN, and late Mrs Martin Hood, New York; *m* 1957, Rachel Simmons; one *s* two *d*. *Educ:* Harrow; Magdalen Coll., Oxford. FSA 1953. British Sch. at Athens: student, 1947–48 and 1951–53; Asst Dir, 1949–51; Dir, 1954–62; Vice-Pres., 1996–. Student, British Inst. Archaeology, Ankara, 1948–49. Geddes-Harrower Vis. Prof. of Greek Art and Archaeology, Univ. of Aberdeen, 1968. Took part in excavations at: Dorchester, Oxon, 1937; Compton, Berks, 1946–47; Southwark, 1946; Smyrna, 1948–49; Atchana, 1949–50; Sakca-Gozu, 1950; Mycenae, 1950–52; Knossos, 1950–51, 1953–55, 1957–61, 1973 and 1987; Jericho, 1952; Chios, 1952–55. Hon. Dr, Univ. of Athens, 2000. *Publications:* The Home of the Heroes: The Aegean before the Greeks, 1967; The Minoans, 1971; The Arts in Prehistoric Greece, 1978; various excavation reports and articles. *Address:* The Old Vicarage, Great Milton, Oxford OX44 7PB. *T:* (01844) 279202. *Club:* Athenæum.

HOOD, Nicholas; *see* Hood, W. N.

HOOD, Peter Charles Freeman G.; *see* Gregory-Hood.

HOOD, Prof. Roger Grahame, CBE 1995; DCL; FBA 1992; Professor of Criminology, 1996–2003, and Director of the Centre for Criminological Research, 1973–2003, University of Oxford; Fellow of All Souls College, Oxford, 1973–2003, now Emeritus; *b* 12 June 1936; 2nd *s* of Ronald and Phyllis Hood; *m* 1963, Barbara Blaine Young (marr. diss. 1985); one *d*; *m* 1985, Nancy Stebbing (*née* Lynah). *Educ:* King Edward's Sch., Five Ways, Birmingham; LSE (BSc Sociology); Downing Coll., Cambridge (PhD); DCL Oxon 1999. Research Officer, LSE, 1961–63; Lectr in Social Admin, Univ. of Durham, 1963–67; Asst Dir of Research, Inst. of Criminology, Univ. of Cambridge, 1967–73; Fellow of Clare Hall, Cambridge, 1969–73; Reader in Criminology, Oxford Univ., 1973–96; Sub-Warden, All Souls Coll., Oxford, 1994–96. Vis. Prof., Univ. of Virginia Sch. of Law, 1980–90, and

2005–11; Dist. Vis. Prof., Univ. of Hong Kong, 2003–04; Adjunct Prof., City Univ., Hong Kong, 2008–11. Expert Consultant, UN, on death penalty, 1988, 1995–96, 2000 and 2005. Member: Parole Bd, 1972–73; SSRC Cttee on Social Sciences and the Law, 1975–79; Judicial Studies Bd, 1979–85; Parole System Review, 1987–88; Foreign Secretary's Death Penalty Expert Gp (formerly Panel), 1998–. Pres., British Soc. of Criminology, 1986–89. Hon. QC 2000. Hon. LLD: Birmingham, 2008; Edinburgh Napier, 2011. Sellin-Glueck Award, Amer. Soc. of Criminology, 1986; Cesare Beccaria Medal, Internat. Soc. of Social Defence and for a Humane Criminal Policy, 2011; Eur. Criminology Award, Eur. Soc. of Criminology, 2012. *Publications:* Sentencing in Magistrates' Courts, 1962; Borstal Re-assessed, 1965; (with Richard Sparks) Key Issues in Criminology, 1970; Sentencing the Motoring Offender, 1972; (ed) Crime, Criminology and Public Policy: Essays in Honour of Sir Leon Radzinowicz, 1974; (with Sir Leon Radzinowicz) Criminology and the Administration of Criminal Justice: a bibliography, 1976; (with Sir Leon Radzinowicz) A History of English Criminal Law, vol. 5, The Emergence of Penal Policy, 1986; The Death Penalty: a world-wide perspective, 1989, 5th edn (with Carolyn Hoyle) 2015; Race and Sentencing, 1992; (with Stephen Shute) The Parole System at Work, 2000; (with Martina Fielzer) Differences or Discrimination?, 2004; (with Stephen Shute and Florence Seemungal) A Fair Hearing?: ethnic minorities in the Criminal Court, 2005; (with Florence Seemungal) A Rare and Arbitrary Fate, 2006; (jtly) A Penalty without Legitimacy, 2009; (jtly) Public Opinion on the Mandatory Death Penalty in Trinidad, 2011; Enhancing EU Action on the Death Penalty in Asia, 2012; The Death Penalty in Malaysia, 2013; (ed with Surya Deva) Confronting Capital Punishment in Asia: human rights, politics and public opinion, 2013. *Address:* 36 The Stream Edge, Fisher Row, Oxford OX1 1HT. *T:* (01865) 243140. *E:* roger.hood@all-souls.ox.ac.uk.

HOOD, Sinclair; *see* Hood, M. S. F.

HOOD, (William) Nicholas, CVO 2012; CBE 1991; Chairman: Wessex Water Authority, 1987–89; Wessex Water plc, 1989–99; *b* 3 Dec. 1935; *s* of Sir Tom Hood, KBE, CB, TD and of Joan, *d* of Richmond P. Hellyar; *m* 1st, 1963, Angela Robinson (marr. diss. 1990); one *s* one *d*; 2nd, 1994, Ann E. H. Reynolds (marr. diss. 2003); 3rd, 2007, Patricia Lang. *Educ:* Clifton Coll. FIWEM 1992. Served DCLI, 1955–57. NEM General Insce Assoc. Ltd and Credit Insce Assoc. Ltd, 1958–64; G. B. Britton UK Ltd, eventually Sales and Marketing Dir, 1964–70; UBM Gp Plc, eventually Dir of Central Reg., 1970–84; Man. Dir, UBM Overseas Ltd, 1972–82; Dir, HAT Gp Ltd, 1984–86. Director: Bremhill Industries Plc, 1987–93; Winterthur Life UK (formerly Provident Life Assoc.) Ltd, 1988–2007 (Chm., 2002–07); Western Adv. Bd, Nat. Westminster Bank, 1990–92; CU Environmental Trust Plc, 1992–98; APV plc, 1994–97; QHIT plc, 1998–2003; Brewin Dolphin plc, 2000–12 (Dep. Chm., 2005–12); Dep. Chm., Azurix, 1998–99; Chairman: MHIT plc, 1998–2003; Frogmat Ltd, 2001–09; Mem., Strategic Adv. Bd, First Gp, 2005–. Dep. Chm., BITC, 1993–2007. Mem., DTI/DoE Adv. Cttee on Business and the Envmt, 1991–93. Chm., Water Aid Council, 1990–95; Chm., Water Services Assoc., 1995; Pres., IWSA, 1997–99 (Vice-Pres., 1993–97); Life Vice-Pres., Internat. Water Assoc., 2001; Hon. Life Vice-Pres., Amer. Waterworks Assoc., 1996; Member: Water Trng Council, 1987–99; Foundn for Water Res., 1989–99; Sustainability South West, 2000–02. Director: Harbourside Centre, 1996–99; Harbourside Foundn, 1998–2001; Clifton College Services Ltd, 2000–; Royal United Hosp., Bath, 2012–. Chairman: Bristol 2000, 1995–98; At-Bristol, 1998–2001 (Life Pres., 2002). Mem., Prince of Wales Council for Duchy of Cornwall, 1993–2011. Chm. Trustees, Penny Brohn Cancer Centre (formerly Bristol Cancer Help Centre), 2000–07; Trustee, West Country Rivers, 2000–; Chm., Walk the Walk, 2006–13. Dir, West of England Philharmonic Orch., 2003–07. Gov., Merchants' Acad., 2010–. Master, Soc. of Merchant Venturers, 2007–08. CCMI (CBIM 1990). Hon. MBA UWE, 2002. *Recreations:* fishing, painting. *Address:* One Queen's Parade, Bath BA1 2NJ. *T:* (01225) 334423. *Clubs:* Army and Navy, Boodle's, MCC.

HOODLESS, Donald Bentley, OBE 2005; Chairman, Northern Ireland Housing Executive, since 2012; *b* 14 Oct. 1942; *s* of Ernest William Hoodless and Rosina Mary Hoodless; *m* 1965, Elisabeth Marian Anne Frost Plummer (*see* Dame E. M. A. F. Hoodless); two *s*. *Educ:* Univ. of Durham (BA Hons Econs 1964); Central London Poly. (Dip. Public Admin London Univ. 1968). FCIH 1997. Dir, Circle 33 Housing Trust, 1975–86; Chief Executive: Notting Hill Housing Trust, 1986–93; Circle 33 Housing Trust, 1993–2005. Chm., Skills for Care, 2005–08; Member Board: Housing Corp., 2005–08; Tenant Services Authy, 2008–12. Chm., Royal Nat. Orthopaedic Hosp., 2002–10. Mem. (Lab), Islington LBC, 1968–82 (Leader, 1982). *Recreations:* golf, Arsenal Football Club, reading. *Address:* 10 Eclipse Building, 26 Laycock Street, N1 1AH. *T:* and *Fax:* (020) 7359 0231. *E:* donald@hoodless.org. *Club:* Highgate Golf.

HOODLESS, Dame Elisabeth (Marian Anne Frost), DBE 2004 (CBE 1992); Executive Director, Community Service Volunteers, 1986–2011; *b* 11 Feb. 1941; *d* of late Raymond Evelyn Plummer, TD and Maureen Grace Plummer (*née* Frost); *m* 1965, Donald Bentley Hoodless, *qv*; two *s*. *Educ:* Redland High Sch., Bristol; Univ. of Durham (BA (Social Studies) 1962); LSE (DASS, CQSW 1963). Asst Dir, 1963–75, Dep. Dir, 1975–86, CSV. Churchill Fellow, consultant to US Govt VISTA (Volunteers in Service to America) prog., 1966; Commonwealth Youth Fellow, consultant to Govt of Jamaica, Nat. Youth Service prog., 1974. Mem. (Lab) London Borough of Islington, 1964–68. Dep. Chm., Speaker's Commn on Citizenship, 1987–90; Member: Personal Social Services Council, 1973–80; DoH Wkg Gp on Volunteering in the NHS, 1994–96; Sec. of State's Adv. Gp on Citizenship Educn, 1997–98. Member: IBM Community Adv. Bd, 1988–91; Bd, Innovations in Civic Participation, USA, 2001–11 (Vice-Chm., 2006–11); Bd, Attend (formerly Nat. Assoc. of Hosp. and Community Friends), 2002–06 (Vice Pres., 2006–). Pres., Volonteurope (European Network of Volunteer Agencies), 1988–2011; Chairman: Nat. Network of Volunteer Involving Agencies, 2004–11; Internat. Assoc. for Nat. Youth Service, 2007–11. Trustee, UK Disasters Emergency Appeal, 2010–12. Freeman, City of London, 1992. JP Inner London Youth Courts, 1969–2011 (Chm.). Chm. Govs, Barnsbury Sch. for Girls, 1971–89; Governor: Reeves Foundn, 1981–2003; Redland High Sch., 2011–. DUniv Sheffield Hallam, 2004. *Publications:* Getting Money from Central Government, 1981; Managing Innovation, 1997; (contrib.) Any Volunteers for a Good Society, 2002; Citoyenneté active: intégrer la théorie à la pratique par le volontariat, 2002; Senior Volunteers: solutions waiting to happen, 2003. *Recreations:* grandchildren, growing orchids, ballet, shopping. *Address:* 10 The Eclipse Building, 26 Laycock Street, N1 1AH. *T:* (020) 7359 0231. *E:* donald@hoodless.org.

HOOK, Prof. Andrew Dunnet, PhD; FBA 2002; FRSE; Bradley Professor of English Literature, University of Glasgow, 1979–98, now Professor Emeritus; *b* 21 Dec. 1932; *s* of Wilfred Thomas Hook and Jessie Hook (*née* Dunnet); *m* 1966, Judith Ann Hibberd (*d* 1984); one *s* (and one *s* one *d* decd). *Educ:* Univ. of Edinburgh (MA 1st Cl. Hons 1954); Princeton Univ. (PhD 1960). Asst Lectr in English Lit., 1961–63, Lectr in American Lit., 1963–71, Univ. of Edinburgh; Sen. Lectr in English, Univ. of Aberdeen, 1971–79. Vis. Fellow, Dept of English, Princeton Univ., 1999–2000; Gillespie Vis. Prof., Coll. of Wooster, Ohio, 2001–02; Visiting Professor: Dartmouth Coll., 2003, 2006, 2007; Univ. of St Thomas, St Paul, Minnesota, 2005. FRSE 2000. *Publications:* (ed) Scott: Waverley, 1972; (ed with J. Hook) Charlotte Bronte: Shirley, 1974; (ed) John Dos Passos: Twentieth Century Views, 1974; Scotland and America: a study of cultural relations 1750–1835, 1975, 2nd edn 2008; American Literature in Context 1865–1900, 1983; (ed) History of Scottish Literature 1660–1800, 1987; Scott Fitzgerald, 1992; (ed with R. Sher) The Glasgow Enlightenment, 1995; From Goosecreek to Gandercleugh: studies in Scottish-American literary and cultural history, 1999; (ed with D. Mackenzie) Scott: The Fair Maid of Perth, 1999; F. Scott Fitzgerald: a literary life, 2002; (ed with C. Elliott) Francis Jeffrey's American Journal: New York to Washington 1813, 2011; (ed) Eliza Oddy: A Mississippi Diary: from St Paul, Minnesota to Alton, Illinois, October 1894 to May 1895, 2013. *Recreations:* golf, watching sport on TV. *Address:* 5 Rosslyn Terrace, Glasgow G12 9NB. *T:* (0141) 334 0113. *E:* nassau@palio2.vianw.co.uk.

HOOK, David Morgan Alfred, FREng; Partner, 1963–93, Managing Director, 1984–88, Deputy Chairman, 1989–90, G. Maunsell & Partners; *b* 16 April 1931; *m* 1957, Winifred (*née* Brown); two *s* one *d*. *Educ:* Bancroft's School; Queens' College, Cambridge (MA). FICE, FIStructE; FREng (FEng 1985). Holland & Hannen and Cubitts, 1954–58; Nuclear Civil Constructors, 1958–62; G. Maunsell & Partners (Consulting Engineers), 1962–93. Liveryman, Engineers' Co., 1985. *Publications:* papers in Jl of IStructE. *Recreations:* golf, bowls, bridge. *Club:* Oxford and Cambridge.

HOOK, Neil Kenneth, MVO 1983; HM Diplomatic Service, retired; Consul-General, Osaka, 2001–05; UK Commissioner-General, Expo 2005; *b* 24 April 1945; *s* of George Edward Hook and Winifred Lucy Hook (*née* Werrell); *m* 1973, Pauline Ann Hamilton; one *s* one *d*. *Educ:* Varndean Grammar Sch., Brighton; Sheffield Univ. (Dip. Management Studies). Joined Diplomatic Service, 1968; served FCO, Moscow, Tokyo; Dhaka, 1980–83; S Africa Dept, FCO, 1984; S Asia Dept, FCO, 1985–86; Tokyo, 1987–92; N America Dept, FCO, 1993–95; Ambassador to Turkmenistan, 1995–98; FCO, 1998–99; High Comr, Swaziland, 1999–2001. *Recreations:* ballads, bridge, Hash House Harriers, photography, walking.

HOOKEM, Michael; Member (UK Ind) Yorkshire and the Humber Region, European Parliament, since 2014; *b* Hull, 9 Oct. 1953. Served RAF, 1970–74; Commando Engr, RE; Property Manager, Residential Property Gp Ltd, 2011–13. Chm., Yorks and N Lincs Regl Cttee, UKIP, 2012–15. Contested (UK Ind): Kingston upon Hull E, 2010; Wentworth and Dearne, 2015. *Address:* European Parliament, 60 Rue Wiertz, 1047 Brussels, Belgium.

HOOKER, Prof. Morna Dorothy, DD; Lady Margaret's Professor of Divinity, University of Cambridge, 1976–98; Fellow of Robinson College, Cambridge, since 1976; *b* 19 May 1931; *d* of Percy Francis Hooker, FIA, and Lily (*née* Riley); *m* 1978, Rev. Dr W. David Stacey, MA (*d* 1993); one step *s* two step *d*. *Educ:* Univ. of Bristol (research schol.; MA 1956); Univ. of Manchester (research studentship; PhD 1966); MA Oxford 1970 and Cambridge 1976; DD Cambridge 1993. Research Fellow, Univ. of Durham, 1959–61; Lectr in New Testament Studies, King's Coll., London, 1961–70; Lectr in Theology, Oxford, and Fellow, Linacre Coll., 1970–76 (Hon. Fellow, 1980); Lectr in Theology, Keble Coll., 1972–76. Visiting Fellow, Clare Hall, Cambridge, 1974; Visiting Professor: McGill Univ., 1968; Duke Univ., 1987 and 1989; York St John Univ., 2008–. FKC 1979. Lectures: T. W. Manson meml, 1977; A. S. Peake meml, 1978; Henton Davies, 1979; Ethel M. Wood, 1984; James A. Gray, Duke Univ., 1984; W. A. Sanderson, Melbourne, 1986; Didsbury, Manchester, 1988; Brennan, Louisville, 1989; St Paul's, 1989; Perkins, Texas, 1990; Shaffer, Yale, 1995; John Albert Hall, Victoria, BC, 1996; Smyth, Columbia Decatur, 1996; Chuen King, Hong Kong, 2001; Lund, Chicago, 2003; Newell, Anderson Univ., 2006; C. K. Barrett, Durham, 2010; Hugh Price Hughes, Hinde Street Methodist Church, London, 2010; Fernley-Hartley, 2011. Pres., SNTS, 1988–89. Jt Editor, Jl of Theological Studies, 1985–2005. Hon. Fellow, Westminster Coll., Oxford, 1996. Hon. DLitt Bristol, 1994; Hon. DD Edinburgh, 1997. Burkitt Medal for Biblical Studies, British Acad., 2004. *Publications:* Jesus and the Servant, 1959; The Son of Man in Mark, 1967; (ed jtly) What about the New Testament?, 1975; Pauline Pieces, 1979; Studying the New Testament, 1979; (ed jtly) Paul and Paulinism, 1982; The Message of Mark, 1983; Continuity and Discontinuity, 1986; From Adam to Christ, 1990; A Commentary on the Gospel according to St Mark, 1991; Not Ashamed of the Gospel, 1994; The Signs of a Prophet, 1997; Beginnings, 1997; Paul: a short introduction, 2003; Endings, 2003; (ed) Not in Word Alone, 2003; Paul: a beginner's guide, 2008; The Drama of Mark, 2010; (with Frances Young) Holiness and Mission, 2010; contribs to New Testament Studies, Jl of Theological Studies, Theology, Epworth Review, etc. *Recreations:* Molinology, walking, music. *Address:* Robinson College, Grange Road, Cambridge CB3 9AN.

HOOKS, Air Vice-Marshal Robert Keith, CBE 1979; CEng, FRAeS; RAF retired; *b* 7 Aug. 1929; *s* of late Robert George Hooks and Phyllis Hooks; *m* 1954, Kathleen (*née* Cooper); one *s* one *d*. *Educ:* Acklam Hall Sch.; Constantine Coll., Middlesbrough; BSc(Eng) London. Commnd RAF, 1951; served at RAF stations West Malling, Fassberg, Sylt, 1952–55; RAF Technical Coll., Henlow, 1956; Fairey Aviation Co., 1957–58; Air Ministry, 1958–60; Skybolt Trials Unit, Eglin, Florida, 1961–63; Bomber Command Armament Sch., Wittering, 1963–65; OC Engrg Wing, RAF Coll., Cranwell, 1967–69; HQ Far East Air Force, 1969–71; Supt of Armament A&AEE, 1971–74; Director Ground Training, 1974–76; Director Air Armament, 1976–80; Vice-Pres. (Air), Ordnance Board, 1980; Dir Gen. Aircraft 2, MoD (Procurement Exec.), 1981–84; Divl Dir (European Business), Westland Helicopters, 1984–85; Projects Dir, Helicopter Div., Westland plc, 1985–87. Dep. Man. Dir, E H Industries Ltd, 1987–94. *Address:* 34 Thames Crescent, Maidenhead, Berks SL6 8EY. *Club:* Royal Air Force.

HOOLE, John George Aldick; independent curator and researcher; Arts and Culture Worker, Oxford Brookes University, 2003–08; *b* 3 Feb. 1951; *s* of John Aldick Hoole and Pamela Betty Coleman; *m* 1975, Lindsey G. Rushworth; one *s* one *d*. *Educ:* Univ. of East Anglia (BA Hons History of Art). Asst Keeper of Art, Southampton Art Gall., 1974–78; Asst Dir, Museum of Modern Art, Oxford, 1978–82; Curator, Barbican Art Gall., 1982–98; Dir, Barbican Art Galls, 1998–2001. Chair, Chiltern Sculpture Trust, 2003–08. *Publications:* (with Margaret Simons) James Dickson Innes, 1887–1914, 2013. *Recreation:* horticulture. *Address:* 54 Western Road, Oxford OX1 4LG. *T:* (01865) 245268.

HOOLEY, Prof. Christopher, FRS 1983; Visiting Heilbronn Professor, University of Bristol, since 2008; *b* 7 Aug. 1928; *s* of Leonard Joseph Hooley, MA, BSc, and Barbara Hooley; *m* 1954, Birgitta Kniep (*d* 2013); two *s*. *Educ:* Wilmslow Preparatory Sch.; Abbotsholme Sch.; Corpus Christi Coll., Cambridge (MA, PhD, ScD). Captain, RAEC, 1948–49 (SO III, British Troops in Egypt). Fellow, Corpus Christi Coll., Cambridge, 1955–58; Lectr in Mathematics, Univ. of Bristol, 1958–65; Prof. of Pure Mathematics, Univ. of Durham, 1965–67; University College, Cardiff, subseq. University of Wales, Cardiff: Prof. of Pure Maths, 1967–95; Hd of Dept of Pure Maths, 1967–88; Dean of Faculty of Science, 1973–76; Dep. Principal, 1979–81; Hd of Sch. of Maths, 1988–95; Dep. Principal, 1991–94; Distinguished Res. Prof., Sch. of Maths, 1995–2008. Visiting Member: Inst. for Advanced Study, Princeton, 1970–71, and Fall Terms, 1976, 1977, 1982, 1983; Institut des Hautes Etudes Scientifiques, Paris, 1984. Founding FLSW 2010. Adams Prize, Cambridge, 1973; Sen. Berwick Prize, London Mathematical Soc., 1980. *Publications:* Applications of Sieve Methods to the Theory of Numbers, 1976; (ed with H. Halberstam) Recent Progress in Analytic Number Theory, 1981; memoirs in diverse mathematical jls. *Recreations:* classic cars; antiquities. *Address:* Rushmoor Grange, Backwell, Bristol BS48 3BN. *T:* (01275) 462363.

HOOLEY, John Rouse; DL; Chief Executive, West Sussex County Council, 1975–90; Clerk to the Lieutenancy of West Sussex, 1976–90; *b* 25 June 1927; *s* of Harry and Elsie Hooley; *m* 1953, Gloria Patricia Swanston; three *s* one *d*. *Educ:* William Hulme's Sch., Manchester; Lincoln Coll., Oxford; Manchester Univ. LLB London. Admitted Solicitor (Hons), 1952. Served Lancashire Fusiliers, 1946–48. Asst Solicitor, Chester, Carlisle and Shropshire, 1952–65; Asst Clerk, Cornwall, 1965–67; Dep. Clerk and Dep. Clerk of the Peace, W Sussex, 1967–74; County Sec., W Sussex, 1974–75. Member: Chichester HA, 1990–95 (Chm.,

1993–95); W Sussex HA, 1995–96. Chm., Downland Housing Gp, 1990–2003. DL W Sussex, 1991. *Recreations:* gardening, music. *Address:* Bosvigo, Lavant Road, Chichester PO19 5RQ.

HOON, Rt Hon. Geoffrey (William); PC 1999; Managing Director, International Business, AgustaWestland, since 2011; *b* 6 Dec. 1953; *s* of Ernest and June Hoon; *m* 1981, Elaine Ann Dumelow; one *s* two *d*. *Educ:* Nottingham High Sch.; Jesus College, Cambridge (MA). Called to the Bar, Gray's Inn, 1978. Labourer at furniture factory, 1972–73; Lectr in Law, Leeds Univ., 1976–82. Vis. Prof. of Law, Univ. of Louisville, 1979–80. In practice at Nottingham, 1982–84. MP (Lab) Ashfield, 1992–2010. An Opposition Whip, 1994–95; opposition spokesman on IT, 1995–97; Parly Sec., 1997–98, Minister of State, 1998–99, Lord Chancellor's Dept; Minister of State, FCO, 1999; Sec. of State for Defence, 1999–2005; Lord Privy Seal and Leader of H of C, 2005–06; Minister of State for Europe, FCO, 2006–07; Parly Sec. to HM Treasury (Govt Chief Whip), 2007–08; Sec. of State for Transport, 2008–09. European Parliament: Mem. (Lab) Derbyshire, 1984–94; Mem., Legal Affairs Cttee, 1984–94; President: Standing Delegn to China, 1987–89; Standing Delegn to US, 1989–92. Chm., Friends of Music, 1992–94; Vice-Chm. and Gov., Westminster Foundn, 1994–97. *Recreations:* football, running, cinema, music, cycling.

HOOPER, family name of **Baroness Hooper**.

HOOPER, Baroness *cr* 1985 (Life Peer), of Liverpool and of St James's in the City of Westminster; **Gloria Dorothy Hooper,** CMG 2002; *b* 25 May 1939; *d* of late Frances and Frederick Hooper. *Educ:* University of Southampton (BA Hons Law); Universidad Central, Quito, Ecuador (Lic. de Derecho Internacional). Admitted to Law Society, Solicitor, 1973; Partner, Taylor and Humbert, subseq. Taylor Garrett, 1974–84. MEP (C) Liverpool, 1979–84; contested (C) Merseyside West, European Parly elecn, 1984. Baroness in Waiting, 1985–87; Parly Under Sec. of State, DES, 1987–88, Dept of Energy, 1988–89, DoH, 1989–92; Dep. Speaker, H of L, 1993–. Member: Parly Delegns to Council of Europe and WEU, 1992–97, 2002–08; EU Select Cttee, Sub Cttee B, Internal Market (formerly Sub Cttee on Finance, Econs and Internat. Trade, later Econ. and Financial Affairs), 2009–; Chm., All-Party Parly Gp for Latin America, 2009–. Chm., Adv. Cttee, UCL Inst. of Americas, 2012–. Pres., Canning House, 1997–2002. Chm., Dance Teachers' Benevolent Fund, 2009–. FRGS 1982; Fellow, Industry and Parlt Trust, 1983; FRSA 1986. Hon. DLaws Southampton, 2009. Order of Francisco de Miranda (Venezuela); Order of Boyaca Gran Cruz (Colombia); Order of Merit (Ecuador); Order of Bernardo O'Higgens (Chile); Dame, Order of St Gregory the Great (Holy See). *Publications:* Cases on Company Law, 1967; Law of International Trade, 1968. *Recreations:* theatre, walking. *Address:* House of Lords, Westminster, SW1A 0PW. *T:* (020) 7219 3000.

HOOPER, Rt Hon. Sir Anthony, Kt 1995; PC 2004; a Lord Justice of Appeal, 2004–12; *b* 16 Sept. 1937; *s* of late Edwin Morris Hooper and Greta Lillian Chissim; *m* 1st, Margrethe Frances (*née* Hansen) (marr. diss. 1986); one *s* one *d*; 2nd, Heather Christine (*née* Randall) (*d* 2005); 3rd, Fiona Mary (*née* Baigrie). *Educ:* Sherborne; Trinity Hall, Cambridge (Scholar; MA, LLB; Hon. Fellow, 2009). 2nd Lieut, 7th RTR, 1956–57. Called to the Bar, Inner Temple, 1965, Bencher, 1993; admitted to Law Society of British Columbia, 1969; QC 1987; a Recorder, 1986–95; a Judge of the High Ct of Justice, QBD, 1995–2004; Presiding Judge, NE Circuit, 1997–2000. Associate Mem., Matrix Chambers, 2013–. Asst Lectr and Lectr, Univ. of Newcastle upon Tyne, 1962–65; Asst and Associate Prof., Faculty of Law, Univ. of British Columbia, 1965–68; Prof. Associé, Univ. de Laval, 1969–70; Prof., Osgoode Hall Law Sch., York Univ., 1971–73. Visiting Professor: Univ. de Montréal, 1972, 1973; Osgoode Hall, 1984; Judicial Fellow and Hon. Prof., UCL, 2012–. Mem., Criminal Procedure Rules Cttee, 2004–12. Chm., Public Concern at Work Whistleblowing Commn, 2013. Pres., British Acad. of Forensic Scis, 2001–03. Chm. Govs, Inns of Court Sch. of Law, 1996–99; Chm., Expert Witness Inst., 2013–. Gen. Ed., Blackstone's Criminal Practice, 2008–14. *Publications:* (ed) Harris's Criminal Law, 21st edn 1968; articles in legal jls. *Club:* Athenæum.

See also R. Hooper.

HOOPER, David John; QC 2010; *b* London, 14 Oct. 1946; *s* of John and Rachel Hooper; *m* 1976, Nicole; one *s*. *Educ:* Highfield Coll., Chertsey; Univ. of Kent; Jesus Coll., Cambridge. Called to the Bar, Middle Temple, 1971; in practice at the Bar, specialising in internat. criminal law. *Recreations:* beer sampling, walking, reading. *Address:* (chambers) 25 Bedford Row, WC1R 4HD. *T:* (020) 7067 1500. *E:* davidhooper@btopenworld.com.

HOOPER, Dr John David, CDir; Chief Executive, Chartered Association of Building Engineers (formerly Association of Building Engineers), since 2011; *b* 22 March 1947; *s* of Wilfred John Hooper and Vera Hooper; *m* 1991, Veronica Jane Bligh; one *s* four *d* by previous marriages. *Educ:* Bath Univ. (BSc 1972); Salford Univ. (MSc 1982); Columbia Pacific Univ. (PhD 1985). CEng 1980; CDir 2001. Apprentice engr, UKAEA, 1964–69; Project Engr, United Glass Ltd, 1969–74; Sen. Project Engr, Cadbury Schweppes Ltd, 1974–78; Dep. Gp Chief Engr, Gp Energy Manager and Sales Manager, Glaxo Pharmaceuticals PLC, 1978–85; Chief Exec., Chartered Inst. Building, 1985–87; Dir, Pan European Ops, Carlson Mktg Gp, Inc., 1987–90; Business Strategy Manager, Scottish Hydro Electric PLC, 1990–94; Chief Executive: British Sports Fedn, 1994–97; RoSPA, 1997–2004; Inst. of Clinical Res., 2004–09; British Polio Fellowship, 2009–11. Patron, Lifeskills Learning for Living, 1997–. Advr, Business in the Arts, 1993–. Dir, Thera Trust, 2012–. FCMI (FBIM 1985); FInstD 1985; FRSA 1999; FRSPH (FRIPH 2002). *Publications:* Heat Energy Recovery in the Pharmaceutical Industry, 1982; Energy Management and Marketing in the Pharmaceutical Industry, 1985; monthly contribs to jls. *Recreations:* flying light aircraft, DIY.

HOOPER, Rt Rev. Michael Wrenford; Bishop Suffragan of Ludlow and Archdeacon of Ludlow, 2002–09; Honorary Assistant Bishop, Diocese of Worcester, since 2010; *b* 2 May 1941; *m* 1968, Rosemary Anne Edwards; two *s* two *d*. *Educ:* Crypt Sch., Gloucester; St David's Coll., Lampeter; St Stephen's House, Oxford. Ordained deacon, 1965, priest, 1966; Asst Curate, St Mary Magdalene, Bridgnorth, Shropshire, dio. of Hereford, 1965–70; Vicar of Minsterley and Rector of Habberley, 1970–81; Rural Dean of Pontesbury, 1976–81; Rector and Rural Dean of Leominster, 1981–97; Archdeacon of Hereford, 1997–2002; Prebendary of Hereford Cathedral, 1981–2002. *Recreations:* walking, cycling, dogs, reading, music. *Address:* 6 Avon Drive, Eckington, Pershore WR10 3BU. *T:* (01386) 751589. *E:* bishopmichael@btinternet.com.

HOOPER, Ven. Paul Denis Gregory; Archdeacon of Leeds, since 2012; *b* Winchester, 24 April 1952; *s* of Robert and Mary Hooper; *m* 1983, Judith Innes Rollison; three *s*. *Educ:* Eastbourne Coll.; Manchester Univ. (BA Town and Country Planning 1975); Wycliffe Hall, Oxford (BA Theology 1980; MA 1985). Sen. Planning Officer, Plymouth City Council, 1975–78; ordained deacon, 1981, priest, 1982; Curate, St George's, Leeds, 1981–84; Youth Officer, 1984–87, Communications Officer, 1987–96, Dio. of Ripon; Chaplain to Bishop of Ripon, 1987–95; Vicar, St Mark's, Harrogate, 1995–2009; Dir of Clergy Develt, Dio. of Ripon and Leeds, 2009–12. Gov., St Aidan's C of E High Sch., Harrogate, 1997–2012. *Publications:* Being Young in an Old Church, 1986. *Recreations:* sailing, hill-walking, music, motor caravanning, civic design, modern literature. *Address:* 2 Wike Ridge Avenue, Leeds LS17 9NL. *T:* (0113) 269 0594. *E:* paul.hooper@westyorkshiredales.anglican.org.

HOOPER, Richard, CBE 2005; Managing Partner, Hooper Communications, since 1988; *b* 19 Sept. 1939; *s* of late Edwin Morris Hooper and Greta Lillian (*née* Goode); *m* 1964, Meredith Jean Rooney; two *s* one *d*. *Educ:* Sherborne Sch.; Worcester Coll., Oxford (BA German and Russian, 1963; MA). National Service, 2nd Lieut 7th RTR, BAOR, 1958–59. Gen. trainee, BBC, 1963; Radio Producer, BBC Further Educn, 1964–66; Harkness Fellow, USA, 1967–68; Sen. Radio and TV Producer, BBC Open Univ. Prodns, 1969–72; Dir, National Develt Prog. in Computer Assisted Learning, 1973–77; Man. Dir, Mills & Allen Communications, 1978–79; Dir, Prestel, Post Office Telecommunications, 1980–81; Chief Exec., Value Added Systems and Services, BT, 1982–86; Man. Dir, Super Channel, 1986–88. Chm., Radio Authy, 2000–03; Dep. Chm., OFCOM, 2002–05; Chairman: Ind. Review of Postal Services Sector, 2008– (report updated 2010); Broadband Stakeholder Gp, 2010–; Digital Copyright Exchange Feasibility Study, 2011–. Non-exec. Chm., IMS Gp plc, 1997–2002; Chairman: Informa (formerly T & F Informa) plc, 2005–07 (Sen. non-exec. Dir, 1999–2005); Copyright Hub Ltd, 2013–; non-executive Director: MAI, 1993–96; United News & Media, 1996–97; LLP Gp plc, 1997–98; Informed Sources Internat., 1997–99; Superscape plc, 2000–02; UK eUniversities Worldwide, 2002–04; hibu (formerly Yell Gp) plc, 2006–14 (Sen. Ind. Dir, 2009–); Sen. Ind. Dir, VocaLink Hldgs Ltd, 2008–; Principal Mentor, Bird & Co. Boardroom and Exec. Mentoring, 2009–. Special Staff Consultant to President Lyndon Johnson's Commn on Instructional Technology, 1968. *Publications:* (ed) Colour in Britain, 1965; (ed) The Curriculum, Context, Design and Development, 1971; Unnatural Monopolies, 1991; contrib. to books and jls. *Recreations:* the family, theatre, golf. *Clubs:* Garrick; Vincent's (Oxford).

See also Rt Hon. Sir A. Hooper, T. G. Hooper.

HOOPER, Susannah Jemima; *see* Storey, S. J.

HOOPER, Thomas George; film director; *b* London, 5 Oct. 1972; *s* of Richard Hooper, *qv*. *Educ:* Highgate Sch.; Westminster Sch.; University Coll., Oxford (BA Hons English Lit.). Director: *films:* Painted Faces (short film), 1992; Red Dust, 2004; The Damned United, 2009; The King's Speech, 2010 (Acad. Award for Best Dir, BAFTA Award (jtly) for Outstanding British Film, Directors Guild of America Award for Outstanding Directing, 2011); Les Misérables, 2012; *television:* Quayside, 1996; Byker Grove, 1997; Eastenders, 1997–98; Cold Feet, 1999; Love in a Cold Climate, 2001; Daniel Deronda, 2002; Prime Suspect 6: The Last Witness, 2003; Elizabeth I, 2005 (Emmy Award for Best Dir of a Miniseries, 2006); Longford, 2006; John Adams, 2008. Member: Bd, Directors UK, 2006–07; London Coordinating Cttee, Directors Guild of America, 2010–. Gov., BFI, 2011–. *Address:* c/o Independent Talent Group, 40 Whitfield Street, W1T 2RH.

HOOPER, Toby Julien Anderson; QC 2000; **His Honour Judge Hooper;** a Circuit Judge, since 2007; *b* 14 Dec. 1950; *o s* of Lt Col Denys Anderson Hooper and late Paula Hooper (*née* Glascoe); *m* 1981, Anna, *d* of late Dr Brian Locke, FRCR and of Rachel Locke; one *s* two *d*. *Educ:* Downside Sch.; Durham Univ. (BA Hons 1972). Called to the Bar, Inner Temple, 1973, Bencher, 2000; in practice at the Bar, 1974–2007; Asst Recorder, 1998–2000; a Recorder, 2000–07. Hon. Recorder, City of Hereford, 2009–. Mem., Parole Bd, 2010–13. Bar Council: Additional Mem., Remuneration Cttee, 1998–2003 (Vice-Chm. (Civil), 2000–03); Mem. (as SE Circuit Rep.), 2000–03; Chm., Pupillage Bd, 2001–03; Mem., General Management Cttee, 2003–05; Mem. (co-opted), Costs Sub-Cttee, Civil Justice Council, 2002–04; Mem., Incorporated Council of Law Reporting, 2004–07. Hon. Sec., Incorp. Inns of Court Mission (Gainsford Youth Club, Covent Garden), 1979–90. *Publications:* (ed) Inner Temple Advocacy Handbook, 1998, 7th edn 2004; (Gen. Ed.) Bar Council Taxation and Retirement Benefits Handbook, 3rd edn 2000, 4th edn 2002. *Recreations:* choral singing, walking. *Address:* Worcester Combined Court Centre, The Shirehall, Worcester WR1 1EQ.

HOOTON, His Honour Patrick Jonathan; a Circuit Judge, 1994–2010; *b* 30 June 1941; *s* of late John Charles Hooton, CMG, MBE, QC (Bermuda) and of Patricia Jessica Hooton (*née* Manning); *m* 1st, 1970, Anne Josephine Wells; one *s*; 2nd, 1980, Jocelyn Margaret East; one *s* one *d*. *Educ:* Downside Sch., Somerset; Trinity Coll., Cambridge. Commonwealth Develt Corp., 1964–68; Van Moppes & Co., 1969–71; called to the Bar, Gray's Inn, 1973; practised on Western Circuit, 1973–94. Mem., Club Taurino, 1994–. *Recreations:* field sports, sailing, ski-ing, Southampton FC and Hampshire CC. *Clubs:* Lawyers' Fishing; Hampshire CC.

HOPCROFT, George William; HM Diplomatic Service, retired; consultant on international relations; *b* London, 30 Sept. 1927; *s* of late Frederick Hopcroft and Dorothy Gertrude (*née* Bourne); *m* 1951, Audrey Joan Rodd; three *s* one *d*. *Educ:* Chiswick County Sch. for Boys (sch. 'MP' July 1945); London Univ. (BCom); Brasenose Coll., Oxford; INSEAD, Fontainebleau; Univ. of Miami. Auditor with Wm R. Warner, 1946; entered Export Credits Guarantee Dept, 1946; Asst Trade Comr, Madras, 1953–57; Sen. Credit Underwriter, ECGD, 1957–64; on secondment to HM Treasury, 1964; joined FO, 1965; First Sec. (Commercial), Amman, 1965–69; First Sec. (Econ.), Bonn, 1969–71; First Sec. (Comm.), Kuala Lumpur, 1971–75; FCO, 1975–78; Counsellor (Comm. and Econ.), Bangkok, 1978–81; FCO 1981; Lloyds of London antibiosis underwriter, 1982–92. Founder Mem., Export and Overseas Trade Adv. Panel (EOTAP), 1982–; operational expert in for. affairs, attached to Govt of Belize, 1982–83. Mem., FCO Assoc. *Recreations:* leisure and circumnavigation (Pilot's A Licence, 1956), German and French literature, song, film, sport (Civil Service ½ mile champion, 1947; Venables Bowl for coxless pairs, Amateur Rowing Assoc. of E, Colombo, 1957; double-marathon in 6 hours, 1959 & 1960; Kow Yai sen. marathon, 1979; British Masters Athletic Fedn M80 400m and 800m champion, 2008 and 2009, M85 400m and 800m champion, 2013), serendipity. *Clubs:* Civil Service, Royal Over-Seas League; British (Bangkok).

HOPE, family name of **Marquess of Linlithgow**, and of **Barons Glendevon, Hope of Craighead** and **Rankeillour**.

HOPE OF CRAIGHEAD, Baron *cr* 1995 (Life Peer), of Bamff in the District of Perth and Kinross; **James Arthur David Hope,** KT 2009; PC 1989; FRSE; Deputy President of the Supreme Court of the United Kingdom, 2009–13; HM Lord High Commissioner to the General Assembly of the Church of Scotland, 2015; *b* 27 June 1938; *s* of late Arthur Henry Cecil Hope, OBE, WS, Edinburgh and Muriel Ann Neilson Hope (*née* Collie); *m* 1966, Katharine Mary Kerr, *d* of W. Mark Kerr, WS, Edinburgh; twin *s* one *d*. *Educ:* Edinburgh Acad.; Rugby Sch.; St John's Coll., Cambridge (Open Schol. 1956, BA 1962, MA 1978; Hon. Fellow, 1995); Edinburgh Univ. (LLB 1965). FRSE 2003. National Service, Seaforth Highlanders, 1957–59 (Lieutenant 1959). Admitted Faculty of Advocates, 1965; Standing Junior Counsel in Scotland to Board of Inland Revenue, 1974–78; Advocate-Depute, 1978–82; QC (Scotland) 1978; Dean, Faculty of Advocates, 1986–89; Lord Justice-Gen. of Scotland and Lord Pres. of Court of Session, 1989–96; a Lord of Appeal in Ordinary, 1996–2009; Second Sen. Law Lord, 2009. Chm., Med. Appeal Tribunal, 1985–86; Legal Chm., Pensions Appeal Tribunal, 1985–86. Mem., Scottish Cttee on Law of Arbitration, 1986–89. Mem. Bd of Trustees, Nat. Liby of Scotland, 1989–96. Chm. Bd, Inst. of Advanced Legal Studies, 2000–13. President: Stair Soc., 1993–2013; Internat. Criminal Law Assoc., 2000–13; Commonwealth Magistrates' and Judges' Assoc., 2003–06 (Hon. Life Vice-Pres., 2009). Chm., Sub-Cttee E (Law and Instns), H of L Select Cttee on EU, 1998–2001. Convenor of Crossbench Peers, 2015–. Hon. Professor of Law: Aberdeen, 1994–; Strathclyde, 2013– (Chancellor, 1998–2013; Fellow, 2000). Chm., Botanic Cottage Trust, 2009–12. Fellow, Soc. of Writers to the Signet, 2011. Hon. Member: Canadian Bar Assoc., 1987; Soc. of Legal Scholars (formerly SPTL), 1991; Hon. Fellow, Amer. Coll. of Trial Lawyers, 2000. Hon. Bencher: Gray's Inn, 1989; Inn of Court of NI, 1995. Hon. LLD: Aberdeen, 1991; Strathclyde, 1993; Edinburgh, 1995; Glasgow, 2013; BPP, 2014; Abertay, 2014; DUniv Strathclyde, 2013. David Kelbie Award, Inst. Contemporary Scotland, 2007. *Publications:* (ed jtly) Gloag & Henderson's Introduction to the Law of Scotland, 7th edn 1968, asst editor, 8th edn 1980 and 9th edn 1987, (contrib.) 11th edn 2001; (ed jtly) Armour on Valuation for Rating, 4th edn 1971, 5th edn 1985; (with A. G. M. Duncan) The Rent (Scotland) Act 1984, 1986; (contrib.) Stair Memorial Encyclopaedia of Scots Law; (contrib.) Court of Session Practice. *Recreations:* walking, ornithology, music. *Address:* 34 India Street, Edinburgh EH3 6HB. *T:* (0131) 225 8245; House of Lords, SW1A 0PW. *Club:* New (Edinburgh).

HOPE OF THORNES, Baron *cr* 2005 (Life Peer), of Thornes in the County of West Yorkshire; **Rt Rev. and Rt Hon. David Michael Hope,** KCVO 1995; PC 1991; DPhil; Vicar, St Margaret's, Ilkley, 2005–06; Archbishop of York, 1995–2005; *b* 14 April 1940. *Educ:* Nottingham Univ. (BA Hons Theol); Linacre Coll., Oxford (DPhil; Hon. Fellow, 1993). Curate of St John, Tuebrook, Liverpool, 1965–70; Chaplain, Church of Resurrection, Bucharest, 1967–68; Vicar, St Andrew, Warrington, 1970–74; Principal, St Stephen's House, Oxford, 1974–82; Warden, Community of St Mary the Virgin, Wantage, 1980–87; Vicar of All Saints', Margaret Street, 1982–85; Bishop of Wakefield, 1985–91; Bishop of London, 1991–95. Mem., H of L, 2005–15. Prelate, Order of British Empire, 1991–95; Dean of the Chapels Royal, 1991–95. Hon. DD: Nottingham, 1999; Hull, 2005. *Publications:* The Leonine Sacramentary, 1971; Living the Gospel, 1993; Signs of Hope, 2001; (with Hugh Little) Better to Travel Hopefully, 2007. *Address:* 35 Hammerton Drive, Hellifield, Skipton, N Yorks BD23 4LZ.

HOPE, Sir Alexander (Archibald Douglas), 19th Bt *cr* 1628 (NS), of Craighall; OBE 2011; Managing Director, Double Negative VFX Ltd, since 1998; *b* London, 16 March 1969; *s* of Sir John Carl Alexander Hope, 18th Bt and of Merle Pringle, *d* of late Robert Douglas; *S* father, 2007; *m* 2002, Emmeline Grace, *d* of Simon H. Barrow; two *s*. *Educ:* Eton; Univ. of Bristol (BSocSc). *Heir: s* William John Hope, *b* 7 March 2004. *E:* alex@dneg.com. *Club:* Soho House.

HOPE, His Honour Antony Derwin; a Circuit Judge, 2002–14; *b* 22 Aug. 1944; *s* of John and Lorna Hope; *m* 1979, Heidi Saure; one *s* one *d*. *Educ:* Leighton Park Sch., Reading; Coll. of Estate Mgt (BSc Estate Mgt); Coll. of Law. Called to the Bar, Middle Temple, 1970; in practice as barrister, London and Winchester, 1971–2002; Judge: Bolton Crown Court, 2002–04; Portsmouth Crown Court, 2004–06; Resident Judge, Southampton Crown Court, 2006–14. UK Delegate to Internat. Assoc. of Judges, 2006–11. Hon. Recorder of Southampton, 2008–. *Publications:* The 1990–91 Planning Acts, 1993; Charles Dickens: from Portsmouth to Pickwick, 2012. *Recreations:* cricket, walking, studying history, foreign travel, classic cars, membership of Dickens Fellowship.

HOPE, Prof. Charles Archibald, DPhil; Director, and Professor of the History of the Classical Tradition, Warburg Institute, University of London, 2002–10, now Emeritus Professor; *b* 11 April 1945; 2nd *s* of Sir Archibald Philip Hope, 17th Bt, OBE, DFC, AE and of Ruth, *y d* of Carl Davis; *m* 1st, 1977, Jennifer Katharine Hadley (marr. diss.); one *s*; 2nd, 2003, Donatella Sparti; one *d*. *Educ:* Eton; Balliol Coll., Oxford (BA 1967; DPhil 1975); Courtauld Inst., London (MA 1968); MA Cantab 1972. Res. Lectr, Christ Church, Oxford, 1968–72; Jun. Res. Fellow, King's Coll., Cambridge, 1972–76; Warburg Institute: Lectr in Renaissance Studies, 1976–92; Sen. Lectr, 1972–2002; Dep. Dir, 1999–2002. Slade Prof. of Fine Art, Oxford Univ., 1985–86. *Publications:* Masterpieces of Renaissance Painting, 1979; Titian, 1980; (ed) Autobiography of Benvenuto Cellini, 1984; contrib. learned jls. *Address:* Warburg Institute, Woburn Square, WC1H 0AB.

HOPE, Christopher David Tully, FRSL; writer; *b* 26 Feb. 1944; *s* of Dennis Tully and Kathleen Mary Hope (*née* McKenna); *m* 1967, Eleanor Klein (marr. diss. 1994); two *s*. *Educ:* Christian Brothers College, Pretoria; Univ. of Natal (BA Hons 1970); Univ. of Witwatersrand (MA 1973). FRSL 1990. Founder and Dir, Franschhoek Literary Fest., S Africa, 2007–10. A Distant Drum (play for music), Carnegie Hall, 2014. Pringle Prize, English Acad. of Southern Africa, 1972; Cholmondeley Award, Soc. of Authors, 1974; Arts Council Bursary, 1982; Travelex, Travel Writers' Award, 1997. *Publications:* Cape Drives, 1974; A Separate Development, 1981 (David Higham Prize for Fiction); In the Country of the Black Pig, 1981; Private Parts and Other Tales, 1982 (rev. edn as Learning to Fly and Other Tales, 1990) (Internat. PEN Silver Pen Award); Kruger's Alp, 1984 (Whitbread Prize for Fiction); Englishmen, 1985; The Hottentot Room, 1986; Black Swan, 1987; White Boy Running, 1988 (CNA Award, S Africa); My Chocolate Redeemer, 1989; Moscow! Moscow!, 1990; Serenity House, 1992; The Love Songs of Nathan J. Swirsky, 1993; Darkest England, 1996; (ed jtly) New Writing, 1996; Me, the Moon and Elvis Presley, 1997; Signs of the Heart: love and death in Languedoc, 1999; Heaven Forbid, 2002; Brothers Under the Skin: travels in tyranny, 2003; My Mother's Lovers, 2006; The Garden of Bad Dreams, 2008; Shooting Angels, 2011; Jimfish, 2015; contribs to BBC, newspapers, jls. *Recreation:* getting lost. *Address:* c/o Rogers, Coleridge & White, 20 Powis Mews, W11 1JN.

HOPE, Derwin; *see* Hope, A. D.

HOPE, Marcus Laurence Hulbert, OBE 1998; HM Diplomatic Service, retired; Consul-General, Montreal, 1998–2002; *b* 2 Feb. 1942; *s* of late Laurence Frank Hope, OBE; *m* 1980, Uta Maria Luise Müller-Unverfehrt; one *s*. *Educ:* City of London Sch.; Sydney C of E Grammar Sch.; Univ. of Sydney (BA); Univ. of London (BA Hons); Open Univ. (Dip. Physical Sci. 2006). Joined HM Diplomatic Service, 1965; Third Sec., CRO, 1965; MECAS, 1966; Second Sec., Tripoli, 1968; FCO, 1970; First Sec., 1972; Head of Chancery, Dubai, 1974; First Sec. (Commercial), Bonn, 1976; FCO, 1980; NATO Defence Coll., Rome, 1984; Counsellor, Beirut, 1984–85; Counsellor and Head of Chancery, Berne, 1985–89; Dep. Head of Mission and Counsellor (Commercial and Aid), Jakarta, 1989–92; Hd, Western Europe Dept, FCO, 1992–95; Ambassador to Zaire, also (non-resident) to the Congo, 1996–98. Trustee, Congo Church Assoc., 2002–. FRAS 2004. JP Wandsworth, 2003–12. *Recreations:* classical guitar, astronomy, scuba diving. *Address:* 29 Narbonne Avenue, SW4 9JR.

HOPE, Philip Ian; Director, Improving Care Ltd, since 2010; *b* 19 April 1955; *s* of A. G. Hope and Grace Hope; *m* 1980, Allison, *d* of John and Margaret Butt; one *s* one *d*. *Educ:* Wandsworth Comp. Sch.; St Luke's Coll., Exeter Univ. (BEd). Teacher, Kettering Sch. for Boys; Youth Policy Advr, NCVO; Hd, Young Volunteer Resources Unit, Nat. Youth Bureau; Mgt and Community Work Consultant, Framework, 1985–96; Dir, Framework in Print publishing co-operative. Member (Lab and Co-op): Kettering BC, 1983–87; Northants CC, 1993–97. Contested (Lab and Co-op) Kettering, 1992. MP (Lab and Co-op) Corby, 1997–2010; contested (Lab and Co-op) same seat, 2010. PPS to Minister of State for Housing and Planning, 1999–2001, to Dep. Prime Minister, 2001–03; Parliamentary Under-Secretary of State: ODPM, 2003–05; DfES, then Dept for Children, Schools and Families, 2005–07; a Parly Sec. and Minister for the Third Sector, Cabinet Office, 2007–08; Minister for the E Midlands, 2008–10; Minister of State, DoH, 2008–10. Member: Public Accounts Select Cttee, 1997–98; NI Grand Cttee, 1997–2005; Cttee of Selection, 1999–2005; Chairman: All-Party Parly Gp for charities and voluntary orgns, 1997–2001; All-Party Lighting Gp, 2001–05. Vice Chm., PLP Social Security Deptl Cttee, 1997–2001; Mem., Leadership Campaign Team with responsibility for educn, 1997–99. Adjunct Prof. for Ageing and Health, Global Health Inst., Imperial Coll. London, 2010–. *Publications:* Making Best Use of Consultants, 1993; (jtly) Performance Appraisal, 1995; various curriculum and training packs for schs and youthworkers and information booklets for young people. *Recreations:* tennis, juggling, computing, gardening.

HOPE, Prof. Ronald Anthony, (Tony), PhD; FRCP, FRCPsych; Professor of Medical Ethics, University of Oxford, 2000–12; Fellow, St Cross College, Oxford, 1990–2012, now Emeritus; *b* 16 March 1951; *s* of Ronald Sidney Hope and Marion Nuttall Hope (*née* Whittaker); *m* 1981, Sally Louise Hirsh; two *d*. *Educ:* Dulwich Coll.; New Coll., Oxford (Bosanquet Open Schol. in Medicine; MA, PhD 1978; BM BCh 1980). FRCPsych 1997; FRCP 2011. W. H. Rhodes Travel Schol., 1969; doctoral res. in neurobiol. at NIMR, 1973–76; preclinical trng, Middx Hosp., 1976–77; clinical trng, Univ. of Oxford, 1977–80; House surgeon, Royal United Hosp., Bath, 1980–81; House physician, John Radcliffe Hosp., Oxford, 1981; SHO-Registrar rotation in Psychiatry, Oxford, 1981–85; Wellcome Trust Trng Fellow in Psychiatry, Oxford hosps, 1985–87; University of Oxford: Clin. Lectr in Psychiatry, 1987–90; Leader, Oxford Practice Skills Project, 1990–95; Lectr in Practice Skills, 1995–2000; Reader in Medicine, 1996–2000; Dir, Ethox (Oxford Centre for Ethics and Communication in Health Care Practice), 1999–2005; Hon. Consultant Psychiatrist, Warneford Hosp. Oxford, 1990–2012. Chairman: Wellcome Trust Strategy Cttee on Med. Humanities, 2005–08; Wkg Party on Ethics and Dementia, Nuffield Council on Bioethics, 2007–09. Res. Prize and Medal, RCPsych, 1989. *Publications:* Oxford Handbook of Clinical Medicine, 1985 (trans. 9 langs), 4th edn 1998; Essential Practice in Patient-Centred Care, 1995; Manage Your Mind, 1995 (trans. 5 langs), 2nd edn 2007; Medical Ethics and Law: the core curriculum, 2003, 2nd edn 2008; Medical Ethics: a very short introduction, 2004; Empirical Ethics in Psychiatry, 2008; contrib. numerous papers and chapters, mainly in fields of Alzheimer's Disease and med. ethics. *Recreations:* family, literature, wine, walking. *Address:* St Cross College, Oxford OX1 3LZ.

HOPE-DUNBAR, Sir David, 8th Bt *cr* 1664; *b* 13 July 1941; *o s* of Sir Basil Douglas Hope-Dunbar, 7th Bt, and of his 2nd wife, Edith Maude Maclaren (*d* 1989), *d* of late Malcolm Cross; *S* father, 1961; *m* 1971, Kathleen, *yr d* of late J. T. Kenrick; one *s* two *d*. *Educ:* Eton; Royal Agricultural College, Cirencester. MRICS (ARICS 1966). Founder, Dunbar & Co., now Allied Dunbar PLC. *Recreations:* fishing, shooting. *Heir: s* Charles Hope-Dunbar, *b* 11 March 1975. *Address:* Banks Farm, Kirkcudbright DG6 4XF. *T:* (01557) 330424.

HOPE HAILEY, Prof. Veronica, PhD; Professor of Management Studies (formerly of Strategy and Human Resources), since 2012, and Dean, School of Management, since 2013, University of Bath; *b* Nottingham, 30 Nov. 1956; *d* of Morrison Gilbert Hope and Pauline Hope; *m* 1st, 1979, Charles Philip Edwards (marr. diss. 1994); three *d*; 2nd, 1995, John Martin Hailey, *qv*; two *d*. *Educ:* Univ. of York (BA Hons 1978); Aston Univ. (MSc 1986); Univ. of Manchester (PhD 1993). Res. Fellow, Judge Inst., Univ. of Cambridge, 1993–96; Professor: of Human Resource Mgt, Cranfield Sch. of Mgt, Cranfield Univ., 1996–2004; of Strategy, Univ. of Bath, 2004–06; Associate Dean and Prof. of Human Resource Mgt, Cass Business Sch., City Univ., 2006–12. MCIPD 1986. *Publications:* (with J. Balogun) Exploring Strategic Change, 1999, 4th edn 2015; Strategic Human Resource Management, 1999; contribs to internat. jls. *Recreations:* family, dog walking, cooking, pilates. *Address:* University of Bath, Claverton Down, Bath BA2 7AY. *T:* (01225) 388388. *E:* vhh20@management.bath.ac.uk.

HOPE JOHNSTONE, family name of **Earl of Annandale and Hartfell**.

HOPE-MORLEY, family name of **Baron Hollenden**.

HOPES, Rt Rev. Alan Stephen; *see* East Anglia, Bishop of, (RC).

HOPETOUN, Earl of; Andrew Victor Arthur Charles Hope; *b* 22 May 1969; *s* and *heir* of Marquess of Linlithgow, *qv*; *m* 1993, Skye, *e d* of Major Bristow Bovill; twin *s* two *d*. *Educ:* Eton; Exeter Coll., Oxford. A Page of Honour to the Queen Mother, 1985–87. Mem., Royal Co. of Archers, 2002–. *Heir: s* Viscount Aithrie, *qv*. *Address:* Hopetoun House, South Queensferry, West Lothian EH30 9SL.

HOPEWELL, Peter David F.; *see* Fraser-Hopewell.

HOPGOOD, Richard Simon; Director, Henry Smith Charity, 2002–12; *b* 7 Oct. 1952; *s* of Ronald and Daphne Hopgood; *m* 1988, Elizabeth Wakefield; one *d*. *Educ:* Christ's Hosp.; Wadham Coll., Oxford (BA). On staff of Church Comrs, 1977–98 (Dep. Sec., Policy and Planning, 1994–98); Dir of Policy and Dep. Sec.-Gen., Archbishops' Council, 1999–2002. Trustee: Escaping Victimhood, 2013–; Inst. for Voluntary Action Res., 2013–; Thames Valley Partnership; Church and Community Fund. *Recreations:* reading, photography, cycling.

HOPKIN, Sir Deian (Rhys), Kt 2009; PhD; FRHistS; Vice-Chancellor and Chief Executive, London South Bank University (formerly South Bank University), 2001–09, now Professor Emeritus; President, National Library of Wales, since 2011; *b* 1 March 1944; *s* of late Islwyn Hopkin and Charlotte Hopkin (nee Rees); *m* 1st, 1966, Orian Jones (marr. diss. 1989); two *d*; 2nd, 1989, Lynne Hurley; two *s*. *Educ:* Llandovery Coll.; University Coll. of Wales, Aberystwyth (BA 1965; PhD 1981). FRHistS 1984. Lectr, 1967–84, Sen. Lectr, 1984–91, Hd of Dept, 1989–91, Dept of History, UCW Aberystwyth; Staff Tutor, Open Univ., 1974–76; Dean, Human Scis, 1992–96, Vice-Provost, 1996–2001, City of London Poly., then London Guildhall Univ. Chm., Cityside Regeneration Ltd, 1997–2002. Member: Council, Nat. Liby of Wales, 1975–88; Gen. Adv. Council, BBC, 1988–95; Exec., UK Arts and Humanities Service, 1996–2002; Skills for Health UK, 2004–08; Bd, Foundn Degree Forward, 2007–11; Learning and Skills Council, 2007–09; Council for Industry and Higher Educn, 2007–09; Public Interest Gen. Council, 2007–; Educn Honours Cttee, 2010–; Higher Educn Commn, 2012–. Chairman: Univs UK Skills Task Gp, 2006–09; Local Economy Policy Unit, 2010–. Member: London Eur. Progs Cttee, 2000–05; Bd, Central London Partnership, 2001–06; One London Ltd, 2002–05; South Bank Employers Gp, 2005–07; Vice Chm., London Higher, 2006–08. Member: Hackney Community Coll. Corp., 2000–02; Lambeth Coll. Corp., 2002–05; Council, City and Guilds Inst. of London, 2009–; Council, Essex Univ., 2011–15. Chm., CEL Transact Ltd, 2011–. Freeman: City of London, 2003; Co. (formerly Guild) of Educators, 2004 (Liveryman). FCGI 2010 (Hon. Mem., 2008). Chm., UNIAID Foundn, 2004–09; Vice-Chm., Council for Assisting Refugee Academics, 2005–; Patron: Bishopsgate Inst., 2008–11; Hillcroft Coll., 2009–; Southwark Theatres and Educn Partnership, 2008–12; Futureversity (formerly Summer Univ.), 2008–13; Cerebra, 2009–; Trustee: Bishopsgate Foundn, 1999–2003; Aldgate and Allhallows Foundn, 2004–06; Campaign for Learning, 2009–; Inst. of Historical Res. Trust, 2009–14; North-West Univ., S Africa, 2009–; Improving Dispute Resolution Adv. Service for Further and Higher Educn, 2011–. Chm. Emeritus, Univ. Centre, Jersey, 2011–; Prof. Emeritus, Univ. of E London, 2010; Hon. Prof., Univ. of Essex, 2015–. Hon. FCIBSE 2008. Hon. Fellow: Univ. of Wales, Aberystwyth, 2003; Univ. of Wales, Trinity St Davids, 2012. Hon. DLitt Glamorgan, 2008; Hon. LLD McGill, 2010; DUniv Open, 2012. *Publications:* (ed jtly) History and Computing, 1987; (ed jtly) Class, Community and the Labour Movement: Wales and Canada 1850–1930, 1989; (ed jtly) The Labour Party in Wales 1900–2000, 2000; Universities in the Modern Economy, 2002; contrib. articles to Internat. Rev. Social Hist., Llafur, etc. *Recreations:* music (especially jazz), writing, broadcasting. *Address:* 4 Eversleigh Place, Beckenham, Kent BR3 1DF. *T:* (020) 8658 0903. *Club:* Athenæum.

HOPKIN, Prof. Julian Meurglyn, CBE 2011; MD; FRCP, FRCPE, FMedSci; FLSW; Professor of Experimental Medicine, since 2012 (Professor of Experimental Medicine, then Professor of Medicine, 1999–2010; Professor Emeritus, 2010), and Chairman, Advisory Board, College of Medicine, since 2012, Swansea University (formerly University of Wales, Swansea) (Head, School of Medicine, 2001–08; Rector, 2008–10); Honorary Consultant Physician, Abertawe Bro Morgannwg University Health Board (formerly Swansea Hospitals), 1999–2010 and since 2012; *b* 30 Aug. 1948; *s* of Meurglyn Hopkin and Mair Hopkin (*née* Watkins); *m* 1st, 1973, Janina Macczak (*d* 2009); two *s* one *d*; 2nd, 2011, Amanda Louise Moorhouse. *Educ:* Maesydderwen Sch., Ystradgynlais; Univ. of Wales (MB BCh; MD 1981); Univ. of Edinburgh (MSc 1978); MA Oxon 1992. FRCP 1988; FRCPE 2000. Med. House

Officer and Registrar, Univ. Hosps of Wales, Oxford and Edinburgh, 1972–77; MRC Advanced Student and Clinical Scientist, MRC, Edinburgh, 1977–79; Lectr in Medicine, Univ. of Birmingham, 1979–84; Clinical Sen. Lectr and Consultant Physician, Oxford, 1984–98; Fellow, Brasenose Coll., Oxford, 1992–98. Visiting Professor: Univ. of Osaka, 1994; Tor Vergata Univ., Rome, 2001; Univ. of Kyoto, 2002. Dir, Allerna Therapeutics, 2007–11; non-exec. Dir, Abertawe Bro Morgannwg Univ. NHS Trust, 2008–. Chm., Trustees, St David's Med. Foundn, 2008–. FMedSci 2005; FLSW 2011. Hon. Fellow, Swansea Univ., 2011. (Jtly) Daiwa-Adrian Prize in Medicine, Daiwa Anglo-Japanese Foundn, 2001. Hon. Druid, Bardic Circle of Isle of Britain, 2008. *Publications:* Pneumocystis Carinii, 1991; (contrib.) Oxford Textbook of Medicine, 2nd edn 1987 to 5th edn 2010; contribs on clinical medicine, human genetic variation, allergy and infection to Lancet, BMJ, Nature and Science. *Recreation:* the outdoors. *Address:* Hafod, Llanrhidian, Gwyr SA3 1EH. *T:* (01792) 390033. *E:* j.m.hopkin@swan.ac.uk.

HOPKIN, Sir Royston (Oliver), KCMG 2005 (CMG 1995); Chairman and Managing Director, Spice Island Beach Resort (formerly Spice Island Inn), since 1987; Owner, Blue Horizons Cottage Hotel, since 1978; *b* 10 Jan. 1945; *s* of late Curtis Hopkin and Audrey Hopkin; *m* 1st, 1975, Floreen Hope (decd); one *s* one *d*; 2nd, 1983, Betty Grell-Hull; one *d*. *Educ:* Grenada Boys' Secondary Sch. British Amer. Insce Co., 1963–65; joined family business, Ross Point Inn, 1965, Manager, 1969–78. Member: Grenada Tourist Bd, 1965–83; Grenada Bd of Tourism, 1998–2001; Pres., Grenada Hotel Assoc., 1969–89; Caribbean Hotel Association: Dir, 1970–; Pres., 1994–96; Chm., 1996–98; Chm., Memship Policy Cttee, 2000–06; Caribbean Tourism Organization: Dir, 1990–98; Exec. Cttee, 1994–98. Chm., Caribbean Alliance (formerly Action) for Sustainable Tourism, 2002– (Vice-Chm., 1996–2002). Mem. Bd of Trustees, Queen Elizabeth Home, Grenada, 1996– (Dep. Chm., 2006–); Trustee, Duke of Edinburgh's Award of Grenada, 2004–10. Ambassador at Large for Tourism, 2013–. Numerous awards incl. Caribbean Hotelier of the Year, 1991; Special Service Award, Grenada Bd of Tourism, 2006; Lifetime Achievement Award: Caribbean Hotel and Tourism Assoc., 2011; Caribbean Tourism Orgn, 2012; 40th Anniv. Independence Award, Most Outstanding Hotelier, 2014. *Recreations:* reading, tennis, travelling. *Address:* Mace Point Villa, True Blue, Box 6, St George's, Grenada, West Indies. *T:* (home) 4444584, (business) 4444258. *E:* roystonhopkin@spicebeachresort.com.

HOPKINS, Adrian Mark; QC 2003; *b* 16 May 1961; *s* of Thomas and Brenda Hopkins; *m* 2010, Tanno Udema. *Educ:* Warwick Sch.; St Peter's Coll., Oxford (Exhibnr; BA Hons Juris. 1983). Called to the Bar, Lincoln's Inn, 1984; in practice, specialising in healthcare law, clinical negligence and professional disciplinary hearings. Member: Supplementary Panel, Counsel to Treasury (Common Law), 1995–99; Attorney Gen.'s London B Panel for Crown's Civil Litigation, 1999–2002; Mem., Bar's and Council of the Inns of Court's Disciplinary Tribunals, 2005–12. Contributing Ed., Medical Law Reports, 1999–. *Address:* Serjeants' Inn Chambers, 85 Fleet Street, EC4Y 1AE. *T:* (020) 7427 5000, *Fax:* (020) 7353 0425.

HOPKINS, Sir Anthony; *see* Hopkins, Sir P. A.

HOPKINS, Anthony Strother, CBE 1996; BSc(Econ); FCA; Civil Service Commissioner for Northern Ireland, 2009–12; *b* 17 July 1940; *s* of Strother Smith Hopkins, OBE, and Alice Roberta Hopkins; *m* 1965, Dorothy Moira (*née* McDonough); one *s* two *d*. *Educ:* Campbell Coll., Belfast; Queen's University of Belfast (BScEcon). Manager, Thomson McLintock & Co., Chartered Accountants, London, 1966–70; Principal, Dept of Commerce, N Ireland, 1970–74; Northern Ireland Development Agency, 1975–82, Chief Executive, 1979–82; Under Secretary, 1982–88, Second Perm. Sec., 1988–92, Dept of Economic Development for N Ireland; Dep. Chief Exec., 1982–88, Chief Exec., 1988–92, Industrial Develt Bd for NI; Sen. Partner, Deloitte & Touche (formerly Touche Ross & Co.), NI, Chartered Accountants, 1992–2001; Dep. Chm., 1995–96, Chm., 1997–2007, Laganside Corp. Chairman: MMB for NI, 1995–2003; NI Higher Educn Council, 2002–09. Dep. Chm., Probation Bd for NI, 1997–98. Member: NI Tourist Bd, 1992–98; Council, NI Chamber of Commerce and Industry, 1992–95; NI Skills Task Force, 1999–2003. Mem., Bd of Advrs, Crescent Capital (formerly Hambro NI Ventures), 1995–2007 (Mem., Investment Cttee, 2003–); Dir, QUBIS Ltd, 2002–05; Chm., Kestrel Superyachts Ltd, 2007–14. Vis. Prof., Univ. of Ulster, 1992–. Mem. Adv. Bd, Ulster Business Sch., 1992–99. Member, Appeal Committee: Relate, 1994–97; Mencap (NI), 1997–2005; Mem., Management Cttee, Ulster Garden Village Ltd Charitable Trust, 2003– (Chm., 2006–). Hon. Treas., Prince's Trust NI Appeal, 1995–97. CCMI (CBIM 1990; Chm. NI Regl Bd, 1992–97). DUniv Ulster, 2010. *Recreations:* golf, sailing. *Clubs:* Royal Belfast Golf, Royal Ulster Yacht (Co. Down).

HOPKINS, Prof. Antony Gerald, PhD; FBA 1996; Smuts Professor of Commonwealth History, University of Cambridge, 1994–2002, now Emeritus; Emeritus Fellow, Pembroke College, Cambridge, 2002; Walter Prescott Webb Professor of History, University of Texas at Austin, 2002–13; *b* 21 Feb. 1938; *s* of George Henry Hopkins and Queenie Ethel (*née* Knight); *m* 1964, Wendy Beech; two *s*. *Educ:* St Paul's Sch.; QMC, Univ. of London (BA); SOAS (PhD). Asst Lectr, Lectr, then Reader, 1964–77, Prof. of Economic History, 1977–88, Univ. of Birmingham; Prof. of Internat. History, Grad. Inst. of Internat. Studies, Univ. of Geneva, 1988–94. DUniv Stirling, 1996; Hon. DLitt Birmingham, 2013. Forkosch Prize, Amer. Historical Assoc., 1995. *Publications:* An Economic History of West Africa, 1973, revd 1988; (with P. J. Cain) British Imperialism: innovation and expansion 1688–1914, 1993, (with P. J. Cain) British Imperialism: crisis and deconstruction 1914–90, 1993, joint 2nd edn as British Imperialism 1688–2000, 2001; (ed) Globalization in World History, 2002; (ed) Global History: interactions between the universal and the local, 2006; articles in learned jls. *Recreation:* worrying. *Address:* Pembroke College, Cambridge CB2 1RF.

HOPKINS, Prof. Colin Russell, PhD; Professor of Molecular Cell Biology, 2000–06, Senior Research Investigator, 2006–10, Imperial College of Science, Technology and Medicine; *b* 4 June 1939; *s* of Bleddyn Hopkins and Vivienne Russell (*née* Jenkins); *m* 1964, Hilary Floyd; one *s* one *d*. *Educ:* UC, Swansea, Univ. of Wales (BSc; PhD 1964). University of Liverpool: Asst Lectr, Dept of Physiol., Med. Sch., 1964–66; Lectr, Dept of Histology, 1966–70; Sen. Lectr, Dept of Histology and Cell Biol. (Medical), 1971–75; Fulbright Fellow, Dept of Cell Biol., 1970, Fulbright Travelling Schol. and Vis. Associate Prof., 1971–72, Rockefeller Univ., NY; Prof. and Head, Dept of Medical Cell Biol., Univ. of Liverpool, 1975–86; Rank Prof. of Physiological Biochem., ICSTM, 1986–91; Dir, MRC Lab. for Molecular Cell Biol., UCL, 1991–2000. *Publications:* Cell Structure and Function, 1964; numerous scientific papers. *Recreations:* natural history, music.

HOPKINS, David Rex Eugène; Director of Quality Assurance/Administration, Ministry of Defence, 1983–90; *b* 29 June 1930; *s* of late Frank Hopkins and Vera (*née* Wimhurst); *m* 1st, 1955, Brenda Joyce Phillips (*d* 2005); two *s* one *d* (and one *d* decd); 2nd, 2006, Gwyneth Vick (*née* Rees). *Educ:* Worthing High Sch.; Christ Church, Oxford (MA 1950; Dip. in Econs and Pol Science, 1951). National Service Commn, RA, 1952; service in Korea. Asst Principal, WO, 1953; Principal, WO, 1957, MoD 1964; Asst Sec., 1967; Home Office, 1969–70; RCDS, 1971; Defence Equipment Secretariat, 1972; Dir, Headquarters Security, 1975; Financial Counsellor, UK Delegn to NATO, 1981–83. *Recreations:* church life, travel, fell-walking, military history. *Address:* 6 Hitherwood Court, SE19 1UX. *T:* (020) 8670 7504.

HOPKINS, Prof. David William, PhD; Professor of Soil Science and Dean of Agriculture, Food and Environment, Royal Agricultural University, since 2014; *b* London, 12 March 1963; *s* of Robert David Hopkins and Frances Margaret Hopkins; two *s* one *d*. *Educ:* Manchester Poly. (HND Biol. 1983; BSc Biol. 1985); Univ. of Newcastle (PhD Soil Sci. 1988). Postdoctoral Res. Scientist, Univ. of Newcastle, 1988–90; Lectr, then Sen. Lectr, Biol Scis, Univ. of Dundee, 1990–99; Prof. of Envmtl Sci. and Hd of Sch., Univ. of Stirling, 1999–2006; Dir of Sci., Scottish Crop Res. Inst., Dundee, 2006–11; Prof. of Envmtl Biol. and Hd, Sch. of Life Scis, Heriot-Watt Univ., 2011–14. Adjunct Prof. of Antarctic Studies, Univ. of Canterbury, Christchurch, 2006–. Res. Fellow, RSE, 2002. *Publications:* over 100 res. articles. *Address:* School of Agriculture, Food and Environment, Royal Agricultural University, Cirencester, Glos GL7 6JS.

HOPKINS, Prof. David William Richard, PhD; HSBC Professor of International Leadership, Institute of Education, University of London, 2005–09, now Emeritus; Director of Education, Bright Tribe Trust, since 2012; *b* 30 Jan. 1949; *s* of David Clifford Hopkins and Thelma Hopkins; *m* 1985, Marloes de Groot (marr. diss. 2013); two *s* one *d*; partner, 2014, Trish Franey. *Educ:* Univ. of Reading (BA Hons Politics 1970); UCNW, Bangor (PGCE 1971); Univ. of Sheffield (MEd 1976); Simon Fraser Univ., BC (PhD 1980). Outward Bound instructor, 1969–72; teacher, Minsthorpe High Sch. and Community Coll., 1973–75; mountain guide and grad. student, 1976–80; Lectr, Simon Fraser Univ., BC, 1980–82; Sen. Lectr, W Glam Inst. for Higher Educn, 1983–85; Tutor, Inst. of Educn, Univ. of Cambridge, 1985–96; Prof., Hd of Sch. and Dean of Educn, Univ. of Nottingham, 1996–2002; now Emeritus; Dir, Standards and Effectiveness Unit, DfES, 2002–05. Hon. Prof., Univ. of Hull, 2002; Professorial Fellow, Univ. of Melbourne, 2005; Visiting Professor: Univ. of Edinburgh, 2007–; Catholic Univ. of Santiago, 2007–; Chinese Univ. of HK, 2007–; Univ. of Wales, 2008–; Univ. of Cumbria, 2013–. Chm., Leicester City Partnership Bd, 1999–2002. Chm., Professional Standards Cttee, British Mountain Guides, 1997–2002. Mem., All Souls Gp, 2003. Trustee: Outward Bound, 2008–12; Adventure Learning Schs Charity, 2013– (Exec. Dir, 2010–13). Freeman, Guild of Educators, 2005. IFMGA 1978; FRSA 2002. Hon. DEd Nottingham Trent, 2014. *Publications:* over 40 books including: A Teacher's Guide to Classroom Research, 1985, 5th edn 2014; Evaluation for School Development, 1989; (jtly) The Empowered School, 1991; (jtly) Personal Growth through Adventure, 1993; (jtly) School Improvement in an Era of Change, 1994; Improving the Quality of Education for All, 1996, 2nd edn 2002; (jtly) Models of Learning, 1997, 2nd edn 2002; (ed jtly) The International Handbook of Educational Change, 4 vols, 1998, 2nd edn 2010; (jtly) Improving Schools: performance and potential, 1999; School Improvement for Real, 2001; Every School a Great School, 2007; (jtly) System Leadership in Practice, 2009; (ed jtly) Powerful Learning, 2011; Exploding the Myths of School Reform, 2013; contrib. numerous articles on educn. *Recreations:* mountaineering, ski-ing, modern literature, current affairs, friends and family. *Address:* 6 Calver Mill, Calver, Hope Valley, Derbys S32 3YU; L'Aiguillette, 35 Chemin des Grands Bois, 74400 Argentière-Mt Blanc, France. *Clubs:* Alpine, Frontline; Climbers'.

HOPKINS, John Humphrey David; Golf Correspondent, The Times, 1993–2010; *b* 26 March 1945; *s* of late Leslie Charles Hopkins and Mary Eileen Hopkins (*née* Ellis); *m* 1970, Suzanne Ernestine Kommenda (marr. diss. 1998); one *s* one *d*; *m* 2006, Ysobel Jane Jones. *Educ:* Llandaff Cathedral Sch., Cardiff (Choral Schol.); Wrekin Coll., Telford, Salop. Sunday Times: Rugby Corresp., 1976–80; Golf Corresp., 1980–91; golf and Rugby writer, Financial Times, 1991–93. *Publications:* Life with the Lions, 1977; The British Lions, 1980; Nick Faldo in Perspective, 1985; Golf: the four Majors, 1988; Golfer's Companion, 1990; Golf in Wales: the Centenary 1895–1995, 1995; Fore! The Best of John Hopkins on Golf, 2013. *Recreations:* squash, golf, Rugby, theatre, reading. *Address:* 12 Village Farm, Bonvilston, Vale of Glamorgan CF5 6TY. *T:* (01446) 781576. *Clubs:* Royal Automobile, MCC; Jesters; Cardiff and County (Cardiff); Royal and Ancient (St Andrews), Royal Porthcawl Golf.

HOPKINS, Julian; *see* Hopkins, R. J.

HOPKINS, Kelvin Peter; MP (Lab) Luton North, since 1997; *b* 22 Aug. 1941; *s* of late Prof. Harold Horace Hopkins, FRS and Joan Avery Frost; *m* 1965, Patricia Mabel Langley; one *s* one *d*. *Educ:* Nottingham Univ. (BA Hons Politics, Economics, Maths with Stats). Economic Dept, TUC, 1969–70 and 1973–77; Lectr, St Albans Coll. of Further Educn, 1971–73; Policy and Res. Officer, NALGO, then UNISON, 1977–94. Member: Public Administration Select Cttee, 2002–10 and 2011–; Transport Select Cttee, 2010–11; Eur. Scrutiny Cttee, 2007–; Chm., All Party Parly Gp on Alcohol Misuse, 1998–2001, for Social Sci. and Policy, 2010–; Co-Chm., All Party Parly Gp for Further Educn and Lifelong Learning, 2005–; Secretary: All Party Parly Gp for Jazz Appreciation, 1997–2001; All Party Parly Gp on Conflict Issues, 2007–10. Founder Mem., Old Testament Prophets, 1997–. Columnist, Socialist Campaign Gp News, 1998–2008. Gov., Luton Sixth Form Coll., 1993–. Hon. Fellow: Univ. of Luton, 1993; Univ. of Bedfordshire, 2010. *Publications:* NALGO papers. *Recreations:* music, wine, collecting antique glassware. *Address:* House of Commons, Westminster, SW1A 0AA. *T:* (020) 7219 6670; (home) (01582) 722913; 3 Union Street, Luton LU1 3AN. *T:* (01582) 488208.

HOPKINS, Kristan Frederick; MP (C) Keighley, since 2010; Vice Chamberlain of HM Household (Government Whip), since 2015; *b* 8 June 1963; one *d*. *Educ:* Leeds Univ. (BA). Served Army, Duke of Wellington's Regt. Lectr (pt-time) in media theory, communications and digital media. Chairman: Bradford Vision; Yorks and Humber Regl Housing Bd. Mem. (C) Bradford MDC, 1998–2010 (Leader, 2006–10). Parly Under-Sec. of State, DCLG, 2013–15. Contested (C): Leeds W, 2001; Halifax, 2005. *Address:* House of Commons, SW1A 0AA.

HOPKINS, Matthew John; Chief Executive, Barking, Havering and Redbridge University Hospitals NHS Trust, since 2014; *b* Brawdy, Wales, 31 July 1966; *s* of John Hopkins and Valerie Meeks; *m* 2000, Pauline Fahy; one *s* one *d*. *Educ:* Cambridge Sch. of Nursing (RGN 1988); Kingston Univ. (MBA with Dist.). Staff Nurse: Haematol. Unit, Addenbrooke's Hosp., Cambridge, 1988–91; Teenage Cancer Unit, Middx Hosp., 1991–93; Macmillan Cancer Support Nurse, Queen Mary's Univ. Hosps NHS Trust, 1993–98; Dep. Dir of Nursing, Trinity Hospice, London, 1998–2001; Dep. Gen. Manager, Guy's and St Thomas's NHS Foundn Trust, 2001–03; Gen. Manager, St Mary's NHS Trust, 2003–05; Dir of Ops, Imperial Coll. Healthcare NHS Trust, 2005–07; Chief Operating Officer, Barts and the London NHS Trust, 2007–08; Dep. Dir, NHS London, 2008–10; Chief Exec., Epsom and St Helier Univ. Hosps NHS Trust, 2011–14. *Recreations:* cycling, surfing, ski-ing, coaching youth Rugby, sailing, theatre. *Address:* Barking, Havering and Redbridge University Hospitals NHS Trust, Rom Valley Way, Romford, Essex RM7 0AG. *T:* (01708) 435444. *E:* sue.williams@bhrhospitals.nhs.uk. *Club:* Old Emanuel Rugby Football.

HOPKINS, Sir Michael (John), Kt 1995; CBE 1989; RA 1992; RIBA; RWA; Founding Partner, Hopkins Architects (formerly Michael Hopkins & Partners), since 1976; *b* 7 May 1935; *s* of late Gerald and Barbara Hopkins; *m* 1962, Patricia Ann Wainwright (*see* P. A. Hopkins); one *s* two *d*. *Educ:* Sherborne Sch.; Architectural Assoc. (AA Dip. 1964). RIBA 1966; RWA 1989. Worked in offices of Sir Basil Spence, Leonard Manasseh and Tom Hancock; partnership with Norman Foster, 1969–75 and with Patricia Hopkins, 1976–; *projects include*: own house and studio, Hampstead, 1976 (RIBA Award, 1977; Civic Trust Award, 1979); brewery bldg for Greene King, 1979 (RIBA Award, 1980); Patera Bldg System, 1984; Res. Centre for Schlumberger, Cambridge, 1984 (RIBA and Civic Trust Awards, 1988); infants sch., Hampshire, 1986 (RIBA and Civic Trust Awards, 1988); Mound (formerly Bicentenary) Stand, Lord's Cricket Ground, 1987 (RIBA, Civic Trust Awards, 1988); R&D Centre, Solid State Logic, 1988 (RIBA Award, 1989; Civic Trust Award, 1990); London office and country workshop for David Mellor, 1989 and 1991 (RIBA Award, 1989; Civic Trust Award, 1990; RIBA Award, 1993); redevelt of Bracken House, St Paul's, for Ohbayashi Corp., 1992 (RIBA Award, 1992; Civic Trust Award, 1994); offices at New Square, Bedfont Lakes, 1992; Glyndebourne Opera House, 1994 (RIBA Award, 1994; Civic

Trust Award, 1995); Inland Revenue Centre, Nottingham, 1995 (Civic Trust Award, 1997); Queen's Bldg, Emmanuel Coll., Cambridge, 1995 (RIBA Award, 1996); Lady Sarah Cohen House, 1996; Saga Gp HQ, 1999; Jubilee Campus, Nottingham Univ., 1999 (RIBA and BCI Awards); Dynamic Earth, Edinburgh, 1999 (Civic Trust and RIBA Awards); Westminster Underground Station, 1999 (BCI Award, 2000, Civic Trust Award 2002); Portcullis House, Westminster, 2000 (Civic Trust and RIBA Awards); Wildscreen @ Bristol, 2000 (Civic Trust Award); Pilkington Labs, Sherborne Sch., 2000; Housing, Charterhouse, 2000; Parade Ground, Goodwood Racecourse, 2001 (Civic Trust Award 2003); The Forum, Norwich, 2001; Manchester Art Gall., 2002; Haberdashers' Hall, 2002; Nat. Coll. of Sch. Leadership, Nottingham Univ. (RIBA Award), 2002; GEK HQ, Athens, 2003 (RIBA Award, 2004); Norwich Cathedral Refectory, 2004 (RIBA and Civic Trust Award, 2005) and Hostry, 2009 (RIBA Award, 2010); Inn The Park, London, 2004 (Civic Trust Award, 2006); Wellcome Trust HQ, London, 2004 (RIBA Award, 2005); Evelina Children's Hosp., London, 2005 (RIBA and Civic Trust Award, 2006); Utopia, Broughton Hall Pavilion, Yorkshire, 2005 (RIBA Award, 2006, Civic Trust Award, 2007); Alnwick Garden Pavilion, Northumberland, 2006; Shin-Marunouchi Towers, Japan, 2007; LTA's Nat. Tennis Centre, Roehampton, 2007; Dubai Gate Village, 2007; Northern Arizona Univ., 2007 (RIBA Award, 2009); Bryanston Sch. Sci. Bldg, 2007; Faculty of Envmtl Studies, Yale Univ., 2008 (RIBA Award, 2010); North and South Colls, Rice Univ., 2010; Velodrome, Olympic Park, 2011; Chepauk Stadium, Chennai, 2011; Long House, Cockthorpe, Norfolk, 2011; MCA Pune Internat. Cricket Centre, 2012; Macmillan Cancer Centre, UCH, London, 2012. Pres., Architectural Assoc., 1997–99 (Vice Pres., 1987–93); Trustee, British Mus., 1993–2004. Hon. FAIA 1996; Hon. FRIAS 1996. Hon. Mem., Bund Architekten, 1996. Dr *hc* RCA 1994; Hon. DLitt Nottingham, 1995; Hon. DTech London Guildhall, 1996. RIBA Royal Gold Medal (with Patricia Hopkins), 1994. *Recreations:* Blackheath, sailing, Catureglio. *Address:* 49A Downshire Hill, NW3 1NX. *T:* (020) 7435 1109; (office) 27 Broadley Terrace, NW1 6LG. *T:* (020) 7724 1751.

HOPKINS, Patricia Ann, (Lady Hopkins); Partner, Hopkins Architects (formerly Michael Hopkins & Partners), since 1976; *b* 7 April 1942; *d* of Denys Wainwright, MB, Dsc, FRCS and Dr Shelagh Wainwright, MB, ChB; *m* 1962, Michael John Hopkins (*see* Sir Michael Hopkins); one *s* two *d*. *Educ:* Wycombe Abbey Sch.; Architectural Assoc. (AA Dip. 1968). Own practice, 1968–76; in partnership with Michael Hopkins, 1976–. Buildings include: own house and studio, Hampstead, 1976 (RIBA Award, 1977; Civic Trust Award, 1979); Hopkins office, Marylebone, London, 1985; Fleet Velmead Infants Sch., Hants, 1986 (RIBA Award, Civic Trust Award, 1988); Masterplan, 1988, Raphael Cartoon Gall., 1993, V&A Mus.; Glyndebourne Opera House, 1994 (RIBA Award, Royal Fine Art Commn Award, 1994; Civic Trust Award, FT Award, 1995); Queen's Bldg, Emmanuel Coll., Cambridge, 1995 (RIBA Award, Royal Fine Art Commn Award, 1996); Jewish Care residential home for the elderly, 1996; Preachers Court, Charterhouse, 2000; Wildscreen @ Bristol, 2000 (Civic Trust, DTLR Urban Design Awards); Haberdashers' Hall, 2002 (Wood Award, 2003); Manchester Art Gall., 2002 (RIBA Award, Civic Trust Award, 2003); Villas at Emirates Hills, Dubai, 2003; West Wing, Ickworth House, 2006; Alnwick Garden Pavilion, 2006; Long House, Cockthorpe, Norfolk, 2011. Member: Nat. Lottery Bd, Arts Council England (formerly Arts Council of England), 1994–2000; Foundn Campaign Bd, AA, 1994–2000. Trustee, Nat. Gall., 1998–2005. Gov., Queen's Coll., Harley St, 1997–. Hon. FRIAS 1996; Hon. FAIA 1997. Hon. DTech London Guildhall, 1996. *Recreations:* family, friends, Blackheath, Catureglio. *Address:* 49A Downshire Hill, NW3 1NX. *T:* (020) 7435 1109; (office) 27 Broadley Terrace, NW1 6LG. *T:* (020) 7724 1751.

HOPKINS, Paul Andrew; QC 2009; a Recorder, since 2006; *b* Maesteg, Wales, 1 Feb. 1966; *s* of late Clifford Hopkins and Marjorie Hopkins (*née* Forrester); *m* 1994, Lisa Danielle Richards; one *s*. *Educ:* Maesteg Comprehensive Sch.; Univ. of Birmingham (LLB Hons 1987; NFU Mutual Assce Prize for Commercial Law); Inns of Court Sch. of Law. Called to the Bar, Gray's Inn, 1989 (Pres., Gray's Inn Student Barristers, 1988–89), Bencher, 2013; Mem. Wales and Chester Circuit; in practice as barrister specialising in family law, 1989–; Hd, Family Law Dept, 2001–12, Dep. Hd, 2011–12, Hd, 2012–, of Chambers, 9 Park Place, Cardiff. Door Tenant, 4 Paper Bldgs, Temple, 2011–. Approved Counsel, Panel of Advocates to Welsh Assembly Govt, later Welsh Govt, 2009–12. Dir, Family Contact, Cardiff, 1999–2014. Ext. Examr, Bar Professional Trng Course, Cardiff Law Sch., 2010–13. Member: Family Law Bar Assoc., 1993–; Assoc. of London Welsh Lawyers, 2012–. Mem., Children in Wales, 2012–. *Recreations:* travel, gardening, sport, choral music (Member: Nat. Eisteddfod of Wales Choir, 2012; Cor Tabernacl (Tabernacle Chapel) Cardiff Choral Soc. Choir, 2013–; Cor Meibion Taf Cardiff (Taf Male Voice Choir), 2013–). *Address:* (chambers) 9 Park Place, Cardiff CF10 3DP. *T:* (029) 2038 2731, *Fax:* (029) 2022 2542. *E:* clerks@9parkplace.co.uk. *Clubs:* Cardiff and County, Cameo (Cardiff).

HOPKINS, Sir (Philip) Anthony, Kt 1993; CBE 1987; actor since 1961; *b* Port Talbot, S Wales, 31 Dec. 1937; *s* of late Richard and of Muriel Hopkins; *m* 1st, 1968, Petronella (marr. diss. 1972); one *d*; 2nd, 1973, Jennifer (marr. diss. 2002), *d* of Ronald Lynton; 3rd, 2003, Stella Arroyave. *Educ:* Cowbridge, S Wales; RADA; Cardiff Coll. of Drama. London début as Metellus Cimber in Julius Caesar, Royal Court, 1964; National Theatre: Juno and the Paycock, A Flea in Her Ear, 1966; The Dance of Death, The Three Sisters, As You Like It (all male cast), 1967; The Architect and the Emperor of Assyria, A Woman Killed with Kindness, Coriolanus, 1971; Macbeth, 1972; Pravda, 1985 (Laurence Olivier/Observer Award for outstanding achievements, 1985; (jtly) Best Actor, British Theatre Assoc. and Drama Magazine Awards, 1985; Royal Variety Club Stage Actor Award, 1985); King Lear, 1986; Antony and Cleopatra, 1987. Other stage appearances include: The Taming of the Shrew, Chichester, 1972; Equus, USA, 1974–75, 1977 (Best Actor Award, NY Drama Desk, Amer. Authors and Celebrities Forum Award, Outer Critics Circle Award, 1975; LA Drama Critics' Award, 1977); The Tempest, LA, 1979; Old Times, New York, 1984; The Lonely Road, Old Vic, 1985; M. Butterfly, Shaftesbury, 1989; Director: Dylan Thomas: return journey, Lyric, Hammersmith, 1992; August, Theatr Clwyd, 1994. *Films:* The Lion in Winter, 1968; The Looking Glass War, 1969; Hamlet, 1969; When Eight Bells Toll, 1971; Young Winston, 1972; A Doll's House, 1973; The Girl from Petrovka, 1974; All Creatures Great and Small, 1974; Juggernaut, 1974; Audrey Rose, 1977; A Bridge Too Far, 1977; International Velvet, 1978; Magic, 1978; The Elephant Man, A Change of Seasons, 1980; The Bounty (Variety Club Film Actor Award), 1984; The Good Father, 1986; 84 Charing Cross Road (Best Actor Award, Moscow Film Fest.), 1986; The Dawning, 1988; A Chorus of Disapproval, 1989; Desperate Hours, 1991; The Silence of the Lambs, 1991 (Acad., BAFTA and NY Film Critics Circle, Awards for Best Actor, 1992); Freejack, Howard's End, Chaplin, 1992; Bram Stoker's Dracula, The Trial, The Innocent, The Remains of the Day, 1993 (BAFTA Best Actor Award); Shadowlands, 1994; The Road to Wellville, Legends of the Fall, 1995; Nixon, 1996; August (also dir), 1996; Surviving Picasso, 1996; Amistad, 1998; The Edge, 1998; The Mask of Zorro, 1998; Meet Joe Black, 1999; Instinct, 1999; Titus, 2000; Hannibal, 2001; Hearts in Atlantis, 2002; Bad Company, 2002; Red Dragon, 2002; The Human Stain, 2004; Alexander, 2005; Proof, 2006; The World's Fastest Indian, 2006; Bobby, 2006; All the King's Men, 2006; Fracture, 2007; Beowulf, 2007; The Wolfman, 2010; You Will Meet a Tall Dark Stranger, 2011; Thor, 2011; 360, 2012; Hitchcock, 2013; Thor: The Dark World, 2013; Noah, 2014; Kidnapping Freddy Heineken, 2015. *American television films:* QB VII, 1973; Dark Victory, 1975; Bruno Hauptmann in The Lindbergh Kidnapping Case (Emmy Award), 1976; The Voyage of the Mayflower, 1979; The Bunker (Emmy Award, 1981), The Acts of Peter and Paul, 1980; The Hunchback of Notre Dame, 1981; The Arch of Triumph, 1984; Hollywood Wives, 1984; Guilty Conscience, 1984; The Tenth Man, 1988; To Be the Best, 1991; *BBC television:* Pierre Bezukhov in serial, War and Peace (SFTA Best TV Actor award), 1972; Kean, 1978; Othello, 1981; Little Eyolf, 1982; Guy Burgess in Blunt (film), 1987; Donald Campbell in Across the Lake, 1988; Heartland, 1989; Gwyn Thomas: A Few Selected Exits, 1993; Ind. TV performances incl. A Married Man (series), 1983. Fellow, BAFTA, 2008. Hon. Fellow, St David's Coll., Lampeter, 1992. Hon. DLitt Wales, 1988. Commandeur, Ordre des Arts et des Lettres (France), 1996. *Recreations:* reading, walking, piano.

HOPKINS, (Richard) Julian; Development Director, 2006–10, and part-time Development Adviser, 2010–11, St Albans Cathedral; *b* 12 Oct. 1940; *s* of late Richard Robert Hopkins, CBE and Grace Hilda (*née* Hatfield); *m*; two *s* one *d*; *m* 3rd, 2005, Stella Louise (*née* Marino). *Educ:* Bedford School. Asst Manager, London Palladium, 1963; Central Services Manager, BBC, 1965; joined RSPCA as Accounts Manager, 1972, appointed Admin. and Finance Officer, 1976; Exec. Dir, 1978–82; Gen. Manager, Charity Christmas Card Council, 1982–83; Admin. and Develt Dir, War on Want, 1984–88; Dir, CARE Britain, 1988–94; Dir, ORBIS USA, ORBIS Internat., NY, 1994–95; Exec. Vice Pres., American SPCA, NY, 1995–2000; Develt Dir, IUCN, Washington, DC, 2000–05. Dir, and Mem. Exec. Cttee, World Soc. for Protection of Animals, 1980–82; Mem., Farm Animal Welfare Council, 1980–83. FCMI. *Publications: novels:* Conducting Terror, 2007; In The Thick Of It, 2010. *Recreations:* genealogy, opera, orchestral music, writing, 6 grandchildren. *E:* julianhop2010@gmail.com.

HOPKINS, Robert John, PhD; author and environmentalist; Catalyst and Outreach Manager, Transition Network, since 2007; *b* Chiswick, London, 24 June 1968; *s* of late John Murray Hopkins and of Heather Mary Elmhirst (*née* King); *m* 2007, Emma Louise Schofield; four *s*. *Educ:* Univ. of West of England (BSc 1st Cl. Hons Envmtl Quality and Resource Mgt 1996); Univ. of Plymouth (MSc Soc. Res. 2007; PhD 2010). Teacher and course co-ordinator, Practical Sustainability course, Kinsale Further Educn Coll., Co. Cork, Ire., 2000–05. Vis. Fellow, Univ. of Plymouth, 2012–. Ashoka Fellow, 2008. Hon. DSc UWE, 2013. *Publications:* The Transition Handbook: from oil dependency to local resilience, 2007; The Transition Companion: making your community more resilient in uncertain times, 2011; The Power of Just Doing Stuff: how local action can change the world, 2013. *Recreations:* gardening, swimming, time with my children. *Address:* Transition Network, 43 Fore Street, Totnes, Devon TQ9 5HN. *T:* (01803) 865669. *E:* robhopkins@transitionnetwork.org.

HOPKINS, Russell, OBE 1989; FDSRCS; Consultant Oral and Maxillo-Facial Surgeon, Cardiff Royal Infirmary, 1968–95; Director of Medical Audit, South Glamorgan Health Authority, 1991–95; *b* 30 April 1932; *s* of Charles Albert Hopkins and Frances Doris Hopkins; *m* 1970, Jill Margaret Pexton; two *s* one *d*. *Educ:* Barnard Castle Sch.; King's Coll., Durham Univ. (BDS 1956); Royal Free Hosp., London Univ. LRCP, MRCS 1964; FDSRCS 1961. Gen. dental practice, 1956–58; SHO, Oral Surgery, Nottingham Gen. Hosp., 1958–59; Registrar, Oral Surgery, St Peter's Hosp., Chertsey, 1959–61; Sen. Registrar, Royal Victoria Infirmary, Newcastle upon Tyne, 1965–68; Consultant, 1968–95, Gen. Manager, 1985–91, Univ. Hosp. of Wales, Cardiff. Member: Central Cttee, Hosp. Med. Services, 1975–88; Jt Consultant Cttee, London, 1980–93 (Chm., Welsh Sub-Cttee, 1986–93); Chairman: Med. Bd, S Glamorgan, 1980–82; Welsh Council, BMA, 1991–94 (Chm., Welsh Consultant and Specialist Cttee, 1989–93); BMA Gen. Managers' Gp, 1988–90; Glan-Y-Môr NHS Trust, 1995–99; Brô Morgannwg NHS Trust, 1999–2005 (Lead Chair, 2002–04). Pres., BAOMS, 1992–93; Mem., Eur. Assoc. of Max.-Fac. Surgery, 1980–95; Fellow, BMA, 1998. Ext. Examr, Univ. of Hong Kong, 1990–93. *Publications:* Pre-Prosthetic Oral Surgery, 1986; A Journey Through a Life, 2014; chapters in numerous medical works. *Recreations:* grass cutting, photography, reading, having joints replaced! *Address:* 179 Cyncoed Road, Cardiff CF23 6AH. *T:* (home) (029) 2075 2319.

HOPKINS, Sidney Arthur; Managing Director, Guardian Royal Exchange plc, 1990–94; *b* 15 April 1932; *m* 1955, Joan Marion Smith; one *d*. *Educ:* Battersea Grammar Sch. ACII. Joined Royal Exchange Assce, 1948, Man., Organisation and Methods, 1966; Guardian Royal Exchange Assurance Ltd: Chief Claims Man. (UK), 1974; Man., Home Motor, 1976; Asst Gen. Man. (Life), 1979; Guardian Royal Exchange Assurance plc: Asst Gen. Man. (Field Operations), 1983; Gen. Man. (UK), 1985; Guardian Royal Exchange (UK) Ltd: Man. Dir, 1987; Guardian Royal Exchange plc: Dir, 1986; Dep. Chief Exec., 1989. Dir, Residuary MMB, 1994–2002. Freeman, City of London; Liveryman, Company of Insurers. *Recreations:* sports, films. *Address:* Woodlands, 8 Littleworth Lane, Esher, Surrey KT10 9PF. *Club:* Royal Automobile.

HOPKINSON, family name of **Baron Colyton**.

HOPKINSON, Ven. Barnabas John; Archdeacon of Wilts, 1998–2004; *b* 11 May 1939; *s* of late Prebendary Stephan Hopkinson and Mrs Anne Hopkinson; *m* 1968, Esmé Faith (*née* Gibbons); three *d*. *Educ:* Emanuel School; Trinity Coll., Cambridge (MA); Lincoln Theological Coll. Curate: All Saints and Martyrs, Langley, Manchester, 1965–67; Great St Mary's, Cambridge, 1967–70; Chaplain, Charterhouse School, 1970–75; Team Vicar of Preshute, Wilts, 1975–81; RD of Marlborough, 1977–81; Rector of Wimborne Minster, Dorset, 1981–86; RD of Wimborne, 1985–86; Archdeacon of Sarum, 1986–98; Priest-in-charge, Stratford-sub-Castle, 1987–98. Canon of Salisbury Cathedral, 1983–2004, now Emeritus. *Recreations:* gardening, amateur dramatics. *Address:* Tanners Cottage, Frog Street, Bampton, Devon EX16 9NT.

HOPKINSON, Prof. Brian Ridley, FRCS; Professor of Vascular Surgery, University of Nottingham, 1996–2003, now Emeritus; Consultant General Surgeon, Queen's Medical Centre, Nottingham, 1973–2003; *b* 26 Feb. 1938; *s* of Edward Alban Ernest Hopkinson and May Olive Hopkinson (*née* Redding); *m* 1962, Margaret Ruth Bull; three *s* one *d*. *Educ:* Birmingham Univ. (MB ChB 1961; ChM 1972). FRCS 1964. Hse Surgeon, 1961–62, Resident Surgical Officer, 1964–65, Hallam Hosp., W Bromwich; Registrar, Cardiac Surgery, Queen Elizabeth Hosp., Birmingham, 1965–66; Buswell Res. Fellow, Buffalo, NY, 1966–67; Sen. Surgical Registrar, Birmingham Gen. Hosp. and Wolverhampton Royal Infirmary, 1967–69; Lectr in Surgery, Univ. of Birmingham, 1969–73; Consultant Gen. Surgeon specialising in vascular surgery, Queen's Med. Centre, Nottingham, 1973–96. Hon. Prof., Chinese Med. Univ., Shenyang, China, 1999. Various BMA posts including: Sec. and Chm., Nottingham Div., 1975–83; Chm., Trent Regl Council, 1992–95; Chm., Regl Consultant and Specialist Cttee, 1987–92; Chm., Annual Reps' Meeting, 1998–2001. Licensed Lay Reader, C of E, St Jude's, Mapperley. *Publications:* Endovascular Surgery for Aortic Aneurysms, 1997; Operative Atlas of Endovascular Aneurysm Surgery, 1999; contrib. Lancet. *Recreations:* swimming, motor caravanning, coal fired steamboats. *Address:* Lincolnsfield, 18 Victoria Crescent, Private Road, Sherwood, Nottingham NG5 4DA. *T:* (0115) 960 4167.

HOPKINSON, Bryan; Strategy Co-ordinator, United Nations Mission in Kosovo, 2006–08; Political Consultant, Skorgg International, 2000–14; *b* 24 Nov. 1956; *s* of Brian Hopkinson and Florance Hopkinson (*née* Richardson), Huddersfield; *m* 1987, Stephanie Burd (*née* Perkins). *Educ:* King James's Grammar Sch., Huddersfield; King's Coll., Cambridge (BA, MA). Joined FCO, 1980; Kampala, 1981–84; songwriter and musician, 1985–87; rejoined FCO, 1987; Lisbon, 1989–93; FCO, 1993–95; Ambassador to Bosnia-Herzegovina, 1995–96; Hon. Dir, British Council, Sarajevo, 1995–96; International Crisis Group: Director: Bosnia Proj., Sarajevo, Jan.–July 1999; Kosovo Proj., Pristina, July–Dec. 1999; Montenegro Proj., Podgorica, Jan.–June 2000; Political Dir, OSCE Mission in Kosovo, 2002–04. *Publications:*

numerous Balkans reports. *Recreations:* walking, music, board and computer games. *Address:* Apt 206, 1535 The Melting Point, Commercial Street, Huddersfield, W Yorks HD1 3DN. *T:* (01484) 469804.

HOPKINSON, Prof. David Albert, MD; Professor of Human Biochemical Genetics, University College London, 1993–2000, now Emeritus; Director, Medical Research Council Human Biochemical Genetics Unit, 1976–2000; *b* 26 June 1935; *s* of George Albert and Lily Hopkinson; *m* 1st, 1959, Josephine Manze; two *s* one *d*; 2nd, 1980, Yvonne Edwards. *Educ:* Chesterfield Grammar Sch.; St Catharine's Coll., Cambridge; Royal London Hosp. Med. Coll. (MA, MD); Open Univ. (BSc Hons 1st Cl. Geol. 2008). FGS 2009. Royal London Hospital: House Surgeon and House Physician, 1959–60; Jun. Lectr, Biochem., 1960; Resident Pathologist, 1961; Scientific Staff, MRC Human Biochemical Genetics Unit, 1962–2000. Volunteer Advr and Social Policy Coordinator, Chiltern CAB, 2002–. Hon. Life Mem., Internat. Forensic Haemogenetics Soc., 1992. *Publications:* Handbook of Enzyme Electrophoresis in Human Genetics, 1976. *Recreations:* vegetable gardening, hill and mountain walking, furniture restoration, watching Rugby. *Address:* Swan Cottage, 42 Church Street, Great Missenden, Bucks HP16 0AZ.

HOPKINSON, David Hugh; editorial consultant, The Times, 1995–2005; *b* 9 June 1930; *er s* of late C. G. Hopkinson; *m* Patricia Ann Eaton (decd); one *s* one *d*; and three *s* one *d* by previous marriage. *Educ:* Sowerby Bridge Grammar Sch. Entered journalism on Huddersfield Examiner, 1950; Yorkshire Observer, 1954; Yorkshire Evening News, 1954; Evening Chronicle, Manchester, 1956; Chief Sub-Editor, Sunday Graphic, London, 1957; Asst Editor, Evening Chronicle, Newcastle upon Tyne, 1959; Chief Asst Editor, Sunday Graphic, 1960; Dep. Editor, Sheffield Telegraph, 1961, Editor, 1962–64; Editor, The Birmingham Post, 1964–73; Dir, Birmingham Post & Mail Ltd, 1967–80; Editor, Birmingham Evening Mail, 1974–79; Editor-in-Chief, Evening Mail series, 1975–79, Birmingham Post and Evening Mail, 1979–80; The Times: Asst to Editor, 1981; Chief Night Ed., 1982–89; Dep. Man. Ed., 1990–95. Mem., Lord Justice Phillimore's Cttee inquiring into law of contempt. National Press Award, Journalist of the Year, 1963. *Address:* c/o The Times, 1 London Bridge Street, SE1 9GF.

HOPKINSON, David Hugh Laing, CBE 1986; RD 1965; DL; Deputy Chairman and Chief Executive, M&G Group PLC, 1979–87; Chairman, Harrisons and Crosfield, 1988–91 (Deputy Chairman, 1987–88, Director, 1986–91); Deputy Chairman, ECC Group (formerly English China Clays), 1986–91 (Director, since 1975); *b* 14 Aug. 1926; *s* of late Cecil Hopkinson and Leila Hopkinson; *m* 1951, Prudence Margaret Holmes, OBE, JP, DL; two *s* two *d*. *Educ:* Wellington Coll.; Merton Coll., Oxford (BA 1949). RNVR and RNR, 1944–65. A Clerk of the House of Commons, 1948–59; Robert Fleming, 1959–62; M&G Investment Management, 1963–87 (Chm., 1975–87); Director: Lloyds Bank Southern Regional Board, 1977–88; BR (Southern) Bd, 1978–87 (Chm., 1983–87); Wolverhampton and Dudley Breweries, 1987–96; Mem., Adv. Gp of Governor of Bank of England, 1984. Mem., Housing Corp., 1986–88. Director: English Chamber Orchestra and Music Soc., 1970–89; Charities Investment Managers, 1970–2014; Merchants Trust, 1976–99; RTZ Pension Trustees, 1993–99; SE Arts Board, 1994–97. Member: General Synod of C of E, 1970–90; Central Bd of Finance, 1970–90; a Church Comr, 1973–82, 1984–94; Mem., Chichester Dio. Bd of Finance, 1970–2001 (Chm., 1977–88); Chm., Chichester Cathedral Finance Cttee, 2000–05. Chm., Church Army Bd, 1987–89. Trustee: Nat. Assoc. of Almshouses; Chichester Cathedral Development Trust; Pallant House Gall., Chichester, 1992–2002 (Chm. of Trustees); Royal Pavilion, Brighton; RAM Foundn; Edward James Foundn, 1990–2002 (Chm.). Governor: Sherborne Sch., 1970–96 (Vice-Chm., Bd, 1987–96); Wellington Coll., 1978–96. DL 1986, High Sheriff, 1987–88, W Sussex. Hon. Fellow: St Anne's Coll., Oxford, 1984–; Chichester Univ., 2007–. Dist. Friend, Univ. of Oxford, 2007. *Recreations:* travelling, walking, opera. *Address:* St John's Priory, Poling, Arundel, W Sussex BN18 9PS. *T:* (01903) 882393. *Club:* Brooks's.

HOPKINSON, George William; Deputy Director and Director of Studies, Royal Institute of International Affairs, 1999–2000; retired writer and speaker on international relations; *b* 13 Sept. 1943; *s* of William Hartley Hopkinson and Mary (*née* Ashmore); *m* 1st, 1973, Mary Agnes Coverdale (marr. diss. 1997); one *s*; 2nd, 2010, Virginia Frances Dewhurst. *Educ:* Tupton Hall Grammar Sch.; Pembroke Coll., Cambridge (BA 1965; MA 1969). Inland Revenue, 1965–73; CSD, 1973–81; HM Treasury, 1981–86; Ministry of Defence, 1986–97: Hd, Defence Arms Control Unit, 1988–91; Vis. Fellow, Global Security Programme, Cambridge Univ., 1991–92 (on secondment); Hd, Defence Lands Service, 1992–93; Asst Under-Sec. of State (Policy) 1993–97; Royal Institute of International Affairs: Hd of Internat. Security Prog., 1997–99. Associate Fellow: RUSI, 1997–2008; RIIA, 2000–03; Sen. Vis. Fellow, WEU Inst., Paris, 2001. *Publications:* The Making of British Defence Policy, 2000; The Atlantic Crises, Britain, Europe and Parting from the United States, 2005; contribs to books on security policy, international affairs and arms control; occasional papers. *Recreations:* reading, walking. *Address:* Gloucester House, The Southend, Ledbury, Herefordshire HR8 2HD. *Club:* Oxford and Cambridge.

HOPKINSON, Giles, CB 1990; Under-Secretary, Departments of the Environment and Transport, 1976–90, retired; *b* 20 Nov. 1931; *s* of late Arthur John Hopkinson, CIE, ICS, and Eleanor (*née* Richardson); *m* 1956, Eleanor Jean Riddell; three *d*. *Educ:* Marlborough Coll.; Leeds Univ. (BSc). E. & J. Richardson Ltd, 1956–57; Forestal Land, Timber and Rly Co. Ltd, 1957–58; DSIR: Scientific Officer, 1958–61; Sen. Scientific Officer, 1961–64; Private Sec. to Perm. Sec., 1963–64; Principal, MoT, 1964–71; Asst Sec., DoE, 1971; Under-Secretary: DoE (Personnel Mgt and Trng), 1976; Dept of Transport (Ports and Freight Directorate), 1979; Dir, London Region, PSA, DoE, 1983–90. *Recreations:* music, painting, restoration of antique furniture, church bellringing. *Address:* 12 Barn Hill, Stamford, Lincs PE9 2AE.

HOPKINSON, Maj.-Gen. John Charles Oswald Rooke, CB 1984; Director, British Field Sports Society, 1984–93; *b* 31 July 1931; *s* of Lt-Col John Oliver Hopkinson and Aileen Disney Hopkinson (*née* Rooke); *m* 1956, Sarah Elizabeth, *d* of Maj.-Gen. M. H. P. Sayers, OBE; three *s* one *d*. *Educ:* Stonyhurst Coll.; RMA, Sandhurst. sc 1963, jssc 1968, rcds 1979. Commanding Officer, 1st Bn Queen's Own Highlanders, 1972–74 (despatches); Dep. Comdr 2nd Armoured Division, and Comdr Osnabrück Garrison, 1977–78; Director Operational Requirements 3 (Army), 1980–82; Chief-of-Staff, HQ Allied Forces Northern Europe, 1982–84. Colonel, Queen's Own Highlanders, 1983–94. Chm., Wye Salmon Fishery Owners Assoc., 1993–2002; Vice-Chm., Atlantic Salmon Trust, 1995–2004. Dir, Green Bottom Property Co. Ltd, 1995–2007. Trustee, Wye Foundn, 1996–2005. *Recreations:* shooting, fishing, sailing. *Address:* Bigsweir, Gloucestershire. *Club:* Army and Navy.

HOPKINSON, Simon Charles; restaurateur, chef, writer; *b* 5 June 1954; *s* of Bruce and late Dorothie Hopkinson. *Educ:* St John's Coll. Sch., Cambridge (chorister); Trent Coll., Derbyshire. Normandie Hotel, Birtle, 1972; Hat and Feather Restaurant, Knutsford, 1973; St Non's Hotel, St David's, 1973–74; Druidstone Hotel, Broadhaven, 1974–75; chef and proprietor: Shed Restaurant, Dinas, 1975–77; Hoppy's Restaurant, 1977–78; Egon Ronay Inspector, 1978–80; private chef, London, 1980–83; Hilaire Restaurant, Kensington, 1983–87; co-proprietor, Bibendum, 1987– (head chef, 1987–95). Presenter, TV series, The Good Cook, 2011. Cookery writer for The Independent and Food Illustrated. Awards: Glenfiddich, 1995, 1997, 1998, 2000; André Simon Meml, 1995. *Publications:* (with Lindsey Bareham) Roast Chicken and Other Stories, 1994; (contrib.) The Conran Cook Book, 1997; (with Lindsey Bareham) The Prawn Cocktail Years, 1997; Gammon & Spinach, 1998; Roast Chicken and Other Stories: Second Helpings, 2001; Week In Week Out, 2007; The Vegetarian Option, 2009; The Good Cook, 2011. *Recreations:* poker, wine. *Address:* c/o David Higham Associates, 7th Floor, Waverley House, 7–12 Noel Street, W1F 8GQ.

HOPKIRK, Jennifer; DL; Vice Lord-Lieutenant for Buckinghamshire, 2006–11; *b* 4 Dec. 1941; *d* of Bertie and Lilian Manser; *m* 1967, Paddy Hopkirk; two *s* one *d*. *Educ:* Clifton High Sch., Bristol; St Godric's, Hampstead. Commercial TV film prodn, 1960–69. Various posts with Central London Cttee, RNLI, 1977–2004; Mem., Bucks Br., NSPCC, 1985– (Chm., 2006–09; Pres., 2009–); Co-Vice Chm., London Cttee, British Paraplegic Sports Soc., 1986–94. Patron, Chilterns MS Centre, 2006–12. High Sheriff Bucks, 2005–06, DL Bucks, 2006. *Recreations:* reading, gardening, tennis, bridge, Lucas Terriers, 6 grandchildren. *Address:* Penn, Buckinghamshire. *Club:* Queen's.

HOPKIRK, Joyce, (Mrs W. J. Lear); writer; *b* 2 March; *d* of Walter Nicholson and Veronica (*née* Keelan); *m* 1st, 1962, Peter Hopkirk (marr. diss. 1966; he *d* 2014); one *d*; 2nd, 1974, William James Lear; one *s*. *Educ:* Middle Street Secondary Sch., Newcastle upon Tyne. Reporter, Gateshead Post, 1955; Founder Editor, Majorcan News, 1959; Reporter, Daily Sketch, 1960; Royal Reporter, Daily Express, 1961; Ed., Fashion Magazine, 1967; Women's Ed., Sun, 1967; Launch Ed., Cosmopolitan, 1971–72 (launched 1972); Asst Ed., Daily Mirror, 1973–78; Women's Ed., Sunday Times, 1982; Editl Dir, Elle, 1984; Asst Ed., Sunday Mirror, 1985; Ed.-in-Chief, She Magazine, 1986–89; Dir, Editors' Unlimited, 1990–92; Founder Ed., Chic Magazine 1994. Mem., Competition Commn, 1999–2004. Co-Chm., PPA Awards, 1998. Editor of the Year, 1972; Women's Magazines Editor of the Year, 1988. FRSA 1990. *Publications:* Successful Slimming, 1976; Successful Slimming Cookbook, 1978; (jtly) Splash!, 1995; (jtly) Best of Enemies, 1996; (jtly) Double Trouble, 1997; Unfinished Business, 1998; Relative Strangers, 1999; The Affair, 2000. *Recreations:* conversation, sleeping, gardening, boating.

HOPMEIER, Michael Andrew Philip; His Honour Judge Hopmeier; a Circuit Judge, since 2009; *b* Oldham, 25 Oct. 1950; *s* of Lucian Hopmeier and Yolanda Hopmeier. *Educ:* Dulwich Coll.; Wadham Coll., Oxford (MA); University Coll. London (LLM). Called to the Bar, Middle Temple, 1974, Bencher, 2014; Asst Recorder, 1990–94; Recorder, 1994–2009. Hon. Vis. Prof., City Univ., London, 2014–. *Publications:* (ed) Millington and Sutherland Williams on the Proceeds of Crime, 4th edn, 2013. *Recreations:* sailing, ski-ing, travel, music. *Address:* Kingston Crown Court, 6–8 Penrhyn Road, Kingston-upon-Thames, Surrey KT1 2BB. *T:* (020) 8240 2500. *Clubs:* Bar Yacht; Weirwood Sailing, Emsworth Sailing.

HOPPEN, Prof. (Karl) Theodore, PhD; FBA 2001; FRHistS; Professor of History, University of Hull, 1996–2003; *b* 27 Nov. 1941; *s* of Paul Ernst Theodore Hoppen and Edith Margaretha Hoppen (*née* Van Brussel); *m* 1st, 1970, Alison Mary Buchan (*d* 2002); one *s* two *d*; 2nd, 2007, Anne Patricia Drakeford. *Educ:* Glenstal Abbey Sch., Co. Limerick; University Coll., Dublin (BA 1961; MA 1964); Trinity Coll., Cambridge (PhD 1967). University of Hull: Asst Lectr, 1966–68; Lectr, 1968–74; Sen. Lectr, 1974–86; Reader, 1986–96. Benjamin Duke Fellow, Nat. Humanities Center, NC, 1985–86; Vis. Fellow, Sidney Sussex Coll., Cambridge, 1988; Res. Reader in Humanities, British Acad., 1994–96. FRHistS 1978. Hon. MRIA 2010. Mem. Editl Bd, Dictionary of Irish Biography, 2003–13 (9 vols publd 2009). *Publications:* The Common Scientist in the Seventeenth Century, 1970, 2nd edn 2008; (ed) Papers of the Dublin Philosophical Society 1683–1709, 1982, 2nd edn 2008; Elections, Politics and Society in Ireland 1832–1885, 1984; Ireland since 1800: conflict and conformity, 1989, 2nd edn 1999; The Mid-Victorian Generation 1846–1886, vol. in New Oxford History of England, 1998; (ed with Mary E. Daly) Gladstone: Ireland and beyond, 2011; contrib. numerous articles to learned jls. *Recreations:* idleness, bel canto operas. *Address:* 1 Greyfriars Crescent, Beverley HU17 8LR. *T:* (01482) 861343. *E:* K.T.Hoppen@hull.ac.uk. *Club:* Oxford and Cambridge.

HOPPER, Prof. Andrew, CBE 2007; PhD; FRS 2006; FREng, FIET; Professor of Computer Technology and Head of Department, Computer Laboratory, University of Cambridge, since 2004; *b* Warsaw, Poland, 9 May 1953; *s* of William John Hopper and Maria Barbara Wyrzykowska; *m* 1988, Prof. Alison Gail Smith; one *s* one *d*. *Educ:* Quintin Kynaston Sch., London; University Coll. of Swansea (BSc); Trinity Hall, Cambridge (PhD 1978; Hon. Fellow, 2011). FREng (FEng 1996); FIET (FIEE 1993). University of Cambridge: Res. Asst, 1977–79; Asst Lectr, 1979–83; Lectr, 1983–92; Reader in Computer Technol., 1992–97; Prof. of Communications, Dept of Engrg, 1997–2004; Fellow, 1981–2011, Dir of Studies in Computer Sci., 1981–93, Corpus Christi Coll., Cambridge. Res. Dir, Acorn Computers Ltd, Cambridge, 1979–84; Man. Dir, Olivetti Oracle Res. Lab., Cambridge, subseq. AT&T Labs Cambridge, 1986–2002; Director: Qudos Ltd, Cambridge, 1985–89; Virata Corp. (formerly Advanced Telecommunications Modules Ltd), 1993–2001; Acorn Computer Gp plc, Cambridge, 1996–98; Adaptive Broadband Ltd, 1998–2001; Telemedia Systems Ltd, Cambridge, 2000–03 (Chm., 1995–2003); Real VNC Ltd, 2002– (Chm., 2002–); Solarflare Inc. (formerly Level 5 Networks Ltd), 2002–08; Ubisense (formerly Ubiquitous Systems) Ltd, 2003– (Chm., 2006–); Chairman: Cambridge Broadband Ltd, 2000–05; Adventiq Ltd, Cambridge, 2005–09; Vice-Pres., Res., Ing. C. Olivetti & C., SpA, Italy, 1993–98. Pres., IET, 2012–13 (Dep. Pres., 2010–12). Clifford Paterson Lecture, Royal Soc., 1999. Hon. Fellow: Univ. of Wales, Swansea, 2005; Corpus Christi Coll., Cambridge, 2013. Hon. DSc (Eng) QUB, 2010. Silver Medal, Royal Acad. of Engrg, 2003; Sigmobile, outstanding contribn award, ACM (USA), 2004; Mountbatten Medal, IEE, 2004; MacRobert Award, RAEng, 2013. *Publications:* (jtly) Local Area Network Design, 1986. *Recreations:* ski-ing (Univ. of Cambridge half-blue), flying, farming. *Address:* Computer Laboratory, William Gates Building, J. J. Thomson Avenue, Cambridge CB3 0FD.

HOPPER, Andrew Christopher Graham; QC 2001; *b* 1 Oct. 1948; *s* of late Hugh Christopher Hopper and Doreen Adele Hopper (*née* Harper); *m* 1980, Rosamund Heather Towers. *Educ:* Monkton Combe Sch., Bath. Admitted solicitor, 1972; Higher Courts (Civil) Qualification 1994; Partner, Adams & Black, Cardiff, 1972–88 (Sen. Partner, 1982–88); HM Dep. Coroner for S Glamorgan, 1977–83; estabd own practice, 1988; Consultant: Cartwrights Adams & Black, Cardiff, 1988–2003; Jay Benning & Peltz, 1997–2000; Geoffrey Williams and Christopher Green, Cardiff, 1998–2013; Radcliffes Le Brasseur (formerly Radcliffes), 2001–; MLM Cartwright (formerly Cartwrights Adams & Black, then Cartwright Black), Cardiff, 2003–12. Law Society: Mem., Disciplinary Prosecuting Panel, 1979–2002; Mem., Regulatory Affairs Bd, 2009–; Chm., Regulatory Processes Cttee, 2009–. Jt Gen. Ed., Cordery on Solicitors, subseq. Cordery on Legal Services, 2011–. *Publications:* (ed) Cordery on Solicitors, 9th edn, 1995, 10th edn, 1999; (contrib.) Legal Problems in Emergency Medicine, 1996; (ed) Guide to Professional Conduct of Solicitors, 8th edn, 1999; (with Gregory Treverton-Jones) The Solicitor's Handbook, 2008, 6th edn 2015; (ed) Halsbury's Laws of England, 5th edn, 2008; (contrib.) Butterworths Guide to the Legal Services Act 2007, 2009; (with Gregory Treverton-Jones) Outcomes Focused Regulation: a practical guide, 2011; (ed) Atkin's Court Forms, Legal Professions, 2013. *Recreation:* mostly Burgundy. *Address:* PO Box 7, Pontyclun, Mid Glamorgan CF72 9XN.

HOPPER, Shami; *see* Chakrabarti, S.

HOPPER, Prof. Stephen Donald, AC 2012; PhD; FLS, FTSE; Winthrop Professor of Biodiversity, University of Western Australia, since 2012; *b* 18 June 1951; *s* of Donald Arthur Hopper and Patricia Love Hopper; *m* 1975, Christine Rigden; two *s* one *d*. *Educ:* Univ. of Western Australia (BSc 1st Cl. Hons 1973; PhD 1978). Pt-time music teacher (guitar and mandolin), Zenith Music, Claremont, WA, 1970–75; botany lab. demonstrator, Univ. of WA, 1973–77; contractual botanist, Western Australian Herbarium, Dept of Agriculture,

1977; Res. Officer (flora conservation), Dept of Fisheries and Wildlife, 1977–85; Sen. Res. Scientist, flora conservation, 1985–88, Sen. Principal Res. Scientist and Officer i/c, 1988–92, Dept of Conservation and Land Mgt, Western Australian Wildlife Res. Centre; Dir, Kings Park and Botanic Garden, Perth, WA, 1992–99; CEO, Botanic Gdns and Park Authy (which manages Kings Park and Botanic Gdn and Bold Park), 1999–2004; Foundn Prof. of Plant Conservation Biol., Univ. of WA, 2004–06; Dir, Royal Botanic Gardens, Kew, 2006–12. Co-presenter, TV prog., The West, 2003. Corresp. Mem., Botanical Soc. of America, 2007. FLS 2007; FTSE 2011. Hon. DSc: Western Australia, 2010; Sussex, 2012. *Publications:* (jtly) Western Australia's Endangered Flora, 1990; (jtly) Leaf and Branch, 1990; (jtly) The Banksia Atlas, 1991; Kangaroo Paws and Catspaws, 1993; (ed jtly) Gondwanan Heritage, 1996; (with P. Nikulinsky) Life on the Rocks, 1999, 2nd edn 2008; (with P. Nikulinsky) Soul of the Desert, 2005; (jtly) Orchids of Western Australia, 2008; jl articles and scientific papers. *Recreations:* music, walking, photography, travelling. *Address:* Centre of Excellence in Natural Resource Management, University of Western Australia, Proudlove Parade, Albany, WA 6330, Australia.

HOPPER, William Joseph; author; merchant banker, retired; *b* 9 Aug. 1929; *s* of I. Vance Hopper and Jennie Josephine Hopper; one *d* by a former marriage. *Educ:* Langside Elementary Sch., Glasgow; Queen's Park Secondary Sch., Glasgow; Glasgow Univ. (MA 1st Cl. Hons (Mod. Langs) 1953). Educn Officer, RAF, 1953–55. Financial Analyst, W. R. Grace & Co., NY, 1956–59; London Office Manager, H. Hentz & Co., Members, NY Stock Exchange, 1960–66; Gen. Manager, S. G. Warburg & Co. Ltd, 1966–69; Director: Hill Samuel & Co. Ltd, 1969–74; Morgan Grenfell & Co. Ltd, 1974–79 (Adviser, 1979–86) (bond issue for EIB selected as Deal of the Year by Institutional Investor, 1976); Wharf Resources Ltd, Calgary, 1984–87; Manchester Ship Canal Co., 1985–87; Chairman: Robust Mouldings, 1986–90; GCP (Australia) Ltd, 2010–12; Exec. Chm., Shire Trust, 1986–91; Advr, Yamaichi Internat. (Europe), 1986–88. Exec. Chm., WJ Hopper & Co. Ltd, investment bankers and placement agents, 1996–2009. MEP (C), Greater Manchester West, 1979–84. Co-founder (1969) and first Chm. (now Mem., Exec. Cttee), Inst. for Fiscal Studies, London; Treasurer, Action Resource Centre, 1985–94; Trustee: Nat. Hosp. for Nervous Diseases Develt Fund, 1986–90; Hampstead, Wells and Campden Trust, 1989–2000; London Rep., Cambodian Arts and Scholarship Foundn, 2004–. Chm. Cttee of Management, Rosslyn Hill Unitarian Chapel, 1995–98 and 2004–10. Mem., London Dist and SE Provincial Assembly of Unitarian and Free Christian Churches, 2000–04. Governor, Colville Primary Sch., Notting Hill Gate, 1978–80. Vis. Fellow and Exec. in Residence, Manchester Business Sch., 2009–12. Author in Residence, Edinburgh Bookfest, 2009; Writer in Residence, Drucker Inst., Claremont, 2009–. *Publications:* A Turntable for Capital, 1969; The Puritan Gift: triumph, collapse and revival of an American dream, 2007 (trans. Mandarin, 2013). *Recreations:* singing in church choir, watching old films, chatting to friends. *Address:* 9a Flask Walk, NW3 1HJ. *T:* (020) 7435 6414, 07545 025692. *E:* will@puritangift.com. *Club:* Garrick.

HOPPIT, Prof. Julian, PhD; FBA 2012; FRHistS; Astor Professor of British History, University College London, since 2006; *b* Knutsford, Cheshire, 14 Aug. 1957; *s* of Geoffrey and May Hoppit; *m* 1984, Karin Horowitz. *Educ:* Watford Boys Grammar Sch.; Selwyn Coll., Cambridge (BA 1979; PhD 1984). FRHistS 1988. Res. Fellow, Pembroke Coll., Cambridge, 1982–83; Coll. Fellow, Magdalene Coll., Cambridge, 1983–86; Lectr, then Reader, 1987–2001, Prof., 2001–06, Dept of Hist., UCL. Ed., Histl Jl, 2009–12. Treas., RHistS, 2001–05. *Publications:* Risk and Failure in English Business, 1700–1800, 1987; Failed Legislation, 1600–1800, 1997; A Land of Liberty?: England, 1689–1727, 2000; contrib. articles to Past and Present, Econ. Hist. Rev., Histl Jl. *Recreations:* golf, gardening, cooking. *Address:* Department of History, University College London, Gower Street, WC1E 6BT. *T:* (020) 7679 3603. *E:* j.hoppit@ucl.ac.uk.

HOPSON, Christopher Ian; Chief Executive, NHS Providers (formerly Foundation Trust Network), since 2012; *b* 9 April 1963; *s* of David Joseph Hopson and Susan Hopson (*née* Buckingham); *m* 1994, Charlotte Gascoigne; two *s*. *Educ:* Marlborough Coll.; St Andrew's Sch., Del, USA (ESU Scholarship); Univ. of Sussex (BA Hons Pols 1985); Cranfield Sch. of Mgt (MBA 1992). Social Democratic Party: constituency agent, 1985–87; Researcher to Rosie Barnes, MP, 1987–88; Dir, Elections and Campaigns, 1988–89; Chief Exec. (Nat. Sec.), 1989; consultant, corporate communications strategy, 1989–91; Pol Advr to Sec. of State, Dept of Nat. Heritage, 1992; Granada Media Group: Corp. Affairs Dir, 1993–99; Bd Dir, 1996–99; Man. Dir, Result e-learning business, 1999–2002; Consultant, DfES, 2002–04; HM Revenue and Customs: Dir, Communications and Mktg, 2005–07; Dir, Change and Capability, 2007; Bd Dir, 2006–08; Dir, Customer Contact, 2008–12. Mem. Council, RTS, 1993–97. Trustee, Foyer Fedn, 1999–2010 (Chm. of Trustees, 2004–10). *Recreations:* family, reading, theatre, cinema, football (West Ham), good food and wine (not necessarily in that order). *Address:* NHS Providers, One Birdcage Walk, SW1H 9JJ. *T:* (020) 7304 6805. *E:* chris.hopson@nhsproviders.org.

HOPTON, Nicholas Dunster; HM Diplomatic Service; Ambassador to Qatar, since 2013; *b* Manchester, 8 Oct. 1965; *s* of David Samuel Hopton, MD, FRCS and Janet Sealy Hopton (*née* Dunster), MBE, DL; *m* 1993, Alejandra Echenique; three *s* two *d*. *Educ:* St Peter's Sch., York; Magdalene Coll., Cambridge (BA 1989); La Sapienza Univ., Rome. Entered FCO, 1989; European Communities Dept, FCO, 1990–91; Second Sec. (Pol/Inf.), Rabat (and Nouakchott), 1991–95; News Dept, FCO, 1995–97; EU Dept (Ext.), FCO, 1997–98; Private Sec. to Minister for Europe, FCO, 1998–2000; First Sec., Rome, 2000–03; Counsellor (EU/Econ.), Paris, 2003–07; Nat. Security Strategy Team, Cabinet Office, 2007–08; No 10 Policy Unit, 2008; Hd, Internat. Orgns Dept, FCO, 2008–11; Ambassador to Yemen, 2012–13. Vis. Academic, St Antony's Coll., Oxford, 2013–14. *Publications:* In Pieces, 1999. *Recreations:* squash, sailing, hill walking, music. *Address:* c/o Foreign and Commonwealth Office, King Charles Street, SW1A 2AH. *E:* Nicholas.Hopton@fco.gov.uk. *Clubs:* Royal Automobile; Hawks (Cambridge).

HOPWOOD, Sir David (Alan), Kt 1994; FRS 1979; John Innes Professor of Genetics, University of East Anglia, Norwich, 1968–98, now Emeritus Professor of Genetics; Head of the Genetics Department, John Innes Centre, 1968–98, now Emeritus Fellow; *b* 19 Aug. 1933; *s* of Herbert Hopwood and Dora Hopwood (*née* Grant); *m* 1962, Joyce Lilian Bloom; two *s* one *d*. *Educ:* Purbrook Park County High Sch., Hants; Lymm Grammar Sch., Cheshire; St John's Coll., Cambridge (MA, PhD; Hon. Fellow, 2007). DSc (Glasgow). Whytehead Major Scholar, St John's Coll., Cambridge, 1951–54; John Stothert Bye-Fellow, Magdalene Coll., Cambridge, 1956–58 (Hon. Fellow, 1991); Res. Fellow, St John's Coll., 1958–61; Univ. Demonstrator, Univ. of Cambridge, 1957–61; Lectr in Genetics, Univ. of Glasgow, 1961–68. Pres., Genetical Soc. of GB, 1985–87. Foreign Fellow, Indian Nat. Science Acad., 1987. Hon. Professor: Chinese Acad. of Med. Scis, 1987; Insts of Microbiology and Plant Physiology, Chinese Acad. of Scis, 1987; Huazhong Agricl Univ., Wuhan, China, 1989; Jiao Tong Univ., Shanghai, 2004; Guangxi Univ., Nanning, China, 2004. Hon. FIBiol 2001. Hon. Fellow: UMIST, 1990; Magdalene Coll., Cambridge, 1992. Hon. Member: Spanish Microbiol. Soc., 1985; Hungarian Acad. of Scis, 1990; Soc. for Gen. Microbiol., 1990 (Pres., 2000–03); Kitasato Inst., Tokyo, 1997. Hon. DSc: Eidgenössische Technische Hochschule, Zürich, 1989; UEA, 1998; Athens, 2012. Mendel Medal, Czech Acad. of Scis, 1995; Stuart Mudd Prize, Internat. Union of Microbiol Socs, 2002; Ernst Chain Prize, Imperial Coll. London, 2003; André Lwoff Prize, Fedn of Eur. Microbiol Socs, 2003; Prize Medal, Soc. for Gen. Microbiol., 2011. *Publications:* Streptomyces in Nature and Medicine, 2007; numerous articles and chapters in scientific jls and books. *Recreations:* cooking, gardening, natural history. *Address:* John Innes Centre, Colney Lane, Norwich NR4 7UH. *T:* (01603) 450000, *Fax:* (01603) 450778.

HORAM, Baron *cr* 2013 (Life Peer), of Grimsargh in the County of Lancashire; **John Rhodes Horam;** Member, Electoral Commission, since 2012; *b* 7 March 1939; *s* of Sydney Horam, Preston; *m* 1987, Judith Jackson. *Educ:* Silcoates Sch., Wakefield; St Catharine's Coll., Cambridge (BA 1960; Fellow Commoner, 2010). Marketing Executive, Rowntree & Co., 1960–62; leader and feature writer: Financial Times, 1962–65; The Economist, 1965–68; Man. Dir, Commodities Research Unit Ltd, 1968–70 and 1983–92; Dep. Chm., 1992–95, non-exec. Dir, 1997–, CRU Internat. Ltd. MP Gateshead West, 1970–83 (Lab, 1970–81, SDP, 1981–83); MP (C) Orpington, 1992–2010. Parly Under-Sec. of State, Dept of Transport, 1976–79; Labour spokesman on econ. affairs, 1979–81; Parly spokesman on econ. affairs, SDP, 1981–83; Parly Sec., OPSS, 1995; Parly Under-Sec. of State, DoH, 1995–97. Chm., Envmtl Audit Select Cttee, 1997–2003; Mem., Foreign Affairs Select Cttee, 2005–10. Mem. Exec., 1922 Cttee, 2004–07. Chm., St Catharine's Soc., Cambridge, 2005–13 (Pres., 2014–15). *Address:* 6 Bovingdon Road, SW6 2AP.

HORBURY, Rev. Prof. William, PhD, DD; FBA 1997; Professor of Jewish and Early Christian Studies, University of Cambridge, 1998–2009; Fellow of Corpus Christi College, Cambridge, since 1978; *b* 6 June 1942; *m* 1966, Katharine Mary, *d* of late Rt Rev. D. R. Feaver; two *d*. *Educ:* Charterhouse; Oriel Coll., Oxford (MA 1967); Clare Coll., Cambridge (MA 1968; PhD 1971); Westcott House, Cambridge; DD Cantab 2000. Res. Fellow, Clare Coll., Cambridge, 1968–72; ordained deacon, 1969, priest, 1970; Vicar, Great Gransden, and Rector, Little Gransden, 1972–78; Cambridge University: Dean of Chapel, Corpus Christi Coll., 1978–85; Univ. Lectr in Divinity, 1984–96; Reader, 1996–98; Dir, Jewish Inscriptions Project, Divinity Faculty, 1989–95. Leverhulme Emeritus Fellow, 2010–11. T. W. Manson Meml Lect., 2009. NSM, St Botolph, Cambridge, 1990–. Pres., British Assoc. for Jewish Studies, 1996. Hon. DD Aberdeen, 2009; Hon. DTheol Münster, 2014. *Publications:* (ed jtly) Suffering and Martyrdom in the New Testament, 1981; (ed jtly) Essays in Honour of Ernst Bammel, 1983; (ed) *Templum Amicitiae*: essays on the Second Temple, 1991; (jtly) Jewish Inscriptions of Graeco-Roman Egypt, 1992; (jtly) The Jewish-Christian Controversy, 1996; Jews and Christians in Contact and Controversy, 1998; Jewish Messianism and the Cult of Christ, 1998; (ed) Hebrew Study from Ezra to Ben-Yehuda, 1999; (ed jtly) The Cambridge History of Judaism, vol. iii, The Early Roman Period, 1999; Christianity in Ancient Jewish Tradition, 1999; Messianism among Jews and Christians: twelve Biblical and historical studies, 2003; Herodian Judaism and New Testament Study, 2006; Jewish War under Trajan and Hadrian, 2014; articles in Vetus Testamentum, Jl of Theol Studies, New Testament Studies, Palestine Exploration Qly, Jewish Studies Qly, and other jls. *Recreations:* railways, cats. *Address:* Corpus Christi College, Cambridge CB2 1RH; 5 Grange Road, Cambridge CB3 9AS. *T:* (01223) 363529.

See also W. A. Feaver.

HORDEN, Richard, RIBA; Chairman: Horden Cherry Lee Architects Ltd, since 1999; micro compact home ltd, since 2005; Managing Director, Richard Horden Associates, since 1985; *b* Leominster, 26 Dec. 1944; *s* of Peter Horden and Irene Horden (*née* Kelly); *m* 1972, Kathleen Gibson Valentine (*d* 1998); one *s* one *d*. *Educ:* Perrott Hill Sch.; Bryanston Sch.; Architectural Assoc. (AA Dip.). RIBA 1974. Work with Sir Norman Foster, 1974–84: Design Assistant for the Sainsbury Centre for Visual Arts, UEA; Stansted Airport; estabd Richard Horden Associates, 1985. Prof. of Architecture and Product Design, Technical Univ., Munich, 1996–2011. Projects include: Poole Mus.; Study Gall., Poole; Kingsgate House, Kings Road, London. Mem., German Inst. of Architects. RIBA Commendation for Courtyard House, Poole, 1974; FT Award and RIBA Nat. Award for Architecture for Queen's Stand, Epsom, 1993; Building of the Year Award, Royal Fine Arts Commn, for House on Evening Hill, Poole, 2003. *Publications:* Light Tech: towards a light architecture, 1995; Richard Horden: architecture and teaching, 1999; Peak Lab, 2003; Sixty Projects, 2004; Micro Architecture: lightweight, mobile and ecological buildings for the future, 2008. *Recreations:* yachting, ski-ing, running, rowing. *Address:* Horden Cherry Lee Architects Ltd, 36-38 Berkeley Square, W1J 5AE. *T:* (020) 7495 4119. *Clubs:* Royal Motor Yacht (Poole); Erlenbach Rowing (Lake Zurich).

HORDER, Prof. Jeremy Christian Nicholas, DPhil; FBA 2014; Professor of Criminal Law, London School of Economics and Political Science, since 2013; *b* 25 Feb. 1962; *s* of John and Sylvia Horder; one *d*. *Educ:* Felsted Sch.; Univ. of Hull (LLB Law 1984); Keble Coll., Oxford (BCL, MA; DPhil 1990). Oxford University: Jun. Res. Fellow, Jesus Coll., 1987–89; Tutorial Fellow, Worcester Coll., 1989–2005; Reader in Criminal Law, 2001–06; Prof. of Criminal Law, 2006–10; Edmund Davies Prof. of Criminal Law, KCL, 2010–13. A Law Comr for England and Wales, 2005–10. Hon. Bencher, Middle Temple, 2012. Hon. LLD Hull, 2012. *Publications:* Provocation and Responsibility, 1992; Excusing Crime, 2004; Homicide and the Politics of Law Reform, 2012. *Recreations:* supporting Arsenal Football Club, reading crime fiction, swimming, running. *Address:* Department of Law, London School of Economics and Political Science, Houghton Street, WC2A 2AE. *T:* (020) 7955 7246. *E:* j.horder@lse.ac.uk.

HORDERN, His Honour (Alfred) Christopher (Willoughby); QC 1979; a Circuit Judge, 1983–2003; *m*; one *s* two *d*. *Educ:* Oxford Univ. (MA). Called to the Bar, Middle Temple, 1961; a Recorder of the Crown Court, 1974–83. *Recreations:* ski-ing, sailing, gardening of course. *Address:* Broom House, High House Farm Road, Sudbourne, Woodbridge, Suffolk IP12 2BL.

HORDERN, Rt Hon. Sir Peter (Maudslay), Kt 1985; PC 1993; DL; Chairman, Fina (formerly Petrofina (UK)), 1987–98 (Director, 1973–98); *b* 18 April 1929; British; *s* of C. H. Hordern, MBE; *m* 1964, Susan Chataway; one *s* one *d* (and one *s* decd). *Educ:* Geelong Grammar Sch., Australia; Christ Church, Oxford, 1949–52 (MA). Mem. of Stock Exchange, London, 1957–74. Chm., Foreign & Colonial Smaller Cos (formerly Foreign & Colonial Alliance Investment), 1986–97 (Dir, 1976–99); Dir, TR Technology, 1975–98. MP (C) Horsham, 1964–74 and 1983–97, Horsham and Crawley, 1974–83. Chm., Cons. Parly Finance Cttee, 1970–72; Member: Exec., 1922 Cttee, 1968–97 (Jt Sec., 1988–97); Public Accts Cttee, 1970–97; Public Accounts Commn, 1984–97 (Chm., 1988–97). Mem. Bd, British Liby, 1996–99. DL West Sussex, 1988. *Recreations:* golf, reading and travel.

HORE, Julia Mary; *see* Yeomans, J. M.

HORE-RUTHVEN, family name of **Earl of Gowrie**.

HORE RUTHVEN, Hon. Malise Walter Maitland Knox; *see* Ruthven, Hon. M. W. M. K. H.

HORLEY, Sandra, CBE 2011 (OBE 1999); Chief Executive, Refuge, since 1983; *b* Sarnia, Canada, 11 Jan. 1952; *m* 1983, Julian Nieman; one *d*. *Educ:* McGill Univ. (BA Dist. Sociol. 1977). Homelessness Officer, Shrewsbury and Atcham BC, 1978–79; Dir, Haven Project (for homeless and abused women), 1979–82; Housing Advr, London Bor. of Lambeth, 1982–83. Mem. Bd, Stonham Housing Assoc., 1996–99. Hon. Fellow, London Southbank Univ., 2006. Voluntary Sector Achiever of Year and Outstanding Achiever of Year, Dods and Scottish Widows Women in Public Life Awards, 2008. *Publications:* Love and Pain, 1990; The Charm

Syndrome, 1991, new edn as Power and Control, 2003. *Address:* Refuge, 4th Floor, International House, 1 St Katharine's Way, E1W 1UN. *T:* (020) 7395 7711, *Fax:* (020) 7395 7790. *E:* pauline_persaud@refuge.org.uk.

HORLICK, Vice-Adm. Sir Edwin John, (Sir Ted), KBE 1981; FREng, FIMechE, MIMarEST; part-time consultant; *b* 28 Sept. 1925; *m* Jean Margaret (*née* Covington) (*d* 1991); four *s*. *Educ:* Bedford Modern Sch. Joined RN, 1943; Sqdn Eng. Officer, 2nd Frigate Sqdn, 1960–63; Ship Dept, MoD, 1963–66; First Asst to Chief Engineer, HM Dockyard, Singapore, 1966–68; Asst Dir Submarines, 1969–72; SOWC 1973; Fleet Marine Engineering Officer, Staff of C-in-C Fleet, 1973–75; RCDS 1976; Dir Project Team Submarine/Polaris, 1977–79; Dir Gen. Ships, 1979–83; Chief Naval Engineer Officer, 1981–83. FREng (FEng 1983). *Recreations:* golf, Rugby administration, DIY.

HORLICK, Sir James Cunliffe William, 6th Bt *cr* 1914, of Cowley Manor, Gloucester; *b* 19 Nov. 1956; *o s* of Sir John James Macdonald Horlick, 5th Bt and June, *d* of Douglas Cory-Wright, CBE; *S* father, 1995; *m* 1st, 1985, Fiona Rosalie (marr. diss. 1998), *e d* of Andrew McLaren; three *s*; 2nd, 1999, Mrs Gina Hudson. *Educ:* Eton. *Heir: s* Alexander Horlick, *b* 8 April 1987.

HORLICK, Nicola Karina Christina, (Mrs M. F. D. Baker); Chairman, Rockpool Investments LLP, since 2011; Chief Executive Officer, Bramdean Asset Management, since 2004; Co-founder and Chief Executive Officer, Money&Co., since 2013; *b* Nottingham, 28 Dec. 1960; *d* of Michael Robert Dudley Gayford and Suzanna Christina Victoria Gayford (*née* Czyzewska); *m* 1st, 1984, Timothy Piers Horlick (marr. diss. 2005); two *s* three *d* (and one *d* decd); 2nd, 2006, Martin Francis Damian Baker. *Educ:* Cheltenham Ladies' Coll.; Birkenhead High Sch., GDST; Phillips Exeter Acad., USA (ESU Schol.); Balliol Coll., Oxford (BA Juris.). S. G. Warburg, 1983–91, Dir, 1989–91; Managing Director: Morgan Grenfell Investment Mgt, 1991–97; SG Asset Mgt (UK), 1997–2003. Founder and Chm., Glentham Capital, 2013–. *Publications:* Can You Have It All?, 1997, 3rd edn 1999. *Recreations:* theatre, listening to music, ski-ing. *Address:* Money&Co., 42 Bruton Place, W1J 6PA. *T:* (020) 7052 9272. *E:* chani@moneyandco.com.

HORLICK, Sir Ted; *see* Horlick, Sir Edwin John.

HORLOCK, Timothy John; QC 1997; a Recorder, since 2000; *b* 4 Jan. 1958; *s* of Sir John Harold Horlock, FRS; *m*; four *s*. *Educ:* Manchester Grammar Sch.; St John's Coll., Cambridge (MA). Called to the Bar, Middle Temple, 1981 (Bencher, 2007); Asst Recorder, 1997–2000. *Recreations:* football, tennis, cricket. *Address:* Deans Court Chambers, 24 St John Street, Manchester M3 4DF.

HORN, Bernard Philip; Chairman: Social Finance Ltd, since 2008; Econiq (Ireland), since 2007; *b* 22 April 1946; *s* of late Robert Horn and Margaret Mary Horn; *m* 1988, Clare Margaret Gilbert; one *s* two *d*, and two *s* one *d* by previous marriage. *Educ:* Catholic Coll., Preston; John Dalton Faculty of Technol., Manchester (DMS); Harvard Business Sch. With National Westminster Bank, 1965–2000: Sen. Internat. Exec., Corp. Financial Services, 1986–88; Chief of Staff, 1989–90; Gen. Manager, Gp Strategy and Communications, 1990–91; Chief Exec., Internat. Businesses, 1991–96; Dir, 1995–2000; Exec. Dir, Gp Ops, 1996–2000. Chairman: Netik Hldgs Ltd, 2002–10; Eontec Ltd, 2003–04; E-Box, 2004–15; non-exec. Dir, InvestCloud Inc., 2013–. Mem., Commn on Unclaimed Assets, 2005–07. Chm., Magic Bus (UK) (Indian charity), 2007–; Vice Pres., Enham Trust (Trustee, 2007–14). Freeman, City of London, 2001; Mem., Co. of Information Technologists, 2001–14. *Recreations:* music, theatre. *E:* bph@bernardhorn.com. *Clubs:* Royal Automobile, Hurlingham.

HORN, Helen Margaret, MBE 1994; Chief Executive Officer, Womankind Worldwide, 2013–15; freelance consultant, since 2015; *b* 27 April 1961; *d* of Kenneth and Mary Horn. *Educ:* Dover Grammar Sch. for Girls; Thanet Tech. Coll.; Heidelberg Univ. HM Diplomatic Service, 1981–2007: former diplomatic postings: Warsaw; Zurich; Dhaka; Dubai; Kinshasa; Vienna; Johannesburg; Ambassador to Guinea, 2003–04; Consul-Gen., Brisbane, 2004–05; Pretoria, 2006–07; Hd, SE Asia Maritime Team, FCO, 2007; Dir, Qld Br., ESU, 2007–09; Humanitarian Programme Manager Africa, Christian Aid, 2009–11; Dir, Humanitarian Partnership Agreement, Australia, 2011–13. Trustee: People in Aid, 2014–; Ethiopiaid, 2015–. *Recreations:* African wildlife, outdoor pursuits, swimming, ballet, theatre, opera.

HORN-SMITH, Sir Julian (Michael), Kt 2004; Senior Adviser: UBS, since 2007; CVC, since 2009; non-executive Director, Lloyds Banking Group (formerly Lloyds TSB Group) plc, 2006–12; *b* 14 Dec. 1948. *Educ:* London Univ. (BSc Econ); Bath Univ. (MSc). Vodafone, then Vodafone AirTouch, subseq. reverted to Vodafone Gp plc, 1984–2006: Dir, 1996–2006; Chief Exec., Internat., 1999; Chief Operating Officer, 2001–04; Dep. Chief Exec., 2005–06. Dep. Chm. and Sen. Ind. Dir, Asia Resource Minerals plc (formerly Bumi plc), 2011–14; non-executive Director: Smiths Gp plc, 2006; Digicel Gp (Caribbean and Pacific), 2006–13; De La Rue plc, 2009–13; Acer Gp, 2011–; Chm., Sage Gp, 2006–07. Chm., Altimo Adv. Bd (Alfa Telecoms), 2006–11; Co-Chair, Turkish British Tatlidil. Pro Chancellor, Bath Univ., 2010–. Pres., Egyptian Exploration Soc., 2006–. DLaws Bath, 2007. *Address:* c/o Lloyds Banking Group plc, 25 Gresham Street, EC2V 7HN. *Clubs:* Army and Navy; Royal Ascot Racing.

HORNBLOWER, Prof. Simon, DPhil; FBA 2004; Senior Research Fellow, All Souls College, Oxford, since 2010; *b* 29 May 1949; *s* of George Alexander Hornblower and Edith Faith Hornblower; *m* 1st, 1975, Jane Custance (marr. diss. 1989); 2nd, 2010, Esther Eidinow. *Educ:* Eton Coll. (Schol.); Jesus Coll., Cambridge (Schol.; 1st cl. (Classical Tripos Pt I) 1969); Balliol Coll., Oxford (BA 1st cl. (Lit.Hum.) 1971); DPhil Oxon 1978. Prize Fellow, All Souls Coll., Oxford, 1971–77; Lectr in Ancient Hist., Univ. of Oxford, and Tutorial Fellow, Oriel Coll., Oxford, 1978–97; University College London: Sen. Lectr, Dept of Greek and Latin and of Hist., 1997–98; Prof. of Classics and Ancient Hist., 1998–2010; Grote Prof. of Ancient Hist., 2006–10. Mem., Inst. for Advanced Study, Sch. of Historical Studies, Princeton, NJ, 1994–95. *Publications:* Mausolus, 1982; The Greek World 479–323 BC, 1983, 4th edn 2011; Thucydides, 1987; Commentary on Thucydides, 3 vols, 1991, 1996 and 2008; (ed) Greek Historiography, 1994; (ed jtly) Cambridge Ancient History, vol. 6, 1994; (ed jtly) Ritual, Finance, Politics, 1994; (ed jtly) Oxford Classical Dictionary, 3rd edn 1996, 4th edn 2012; (ed jtly) Greek Personal Names: their value as evidence, 2000; Thucydides and Pindar, 2004; (ed jtly) Pindar's Poetry, Patrons and Festivals, 2007; Thucydidean Themes, 2011; (ed) Herodotus, Histories Book V, 2013; Lykophron, Alexandra, Text, Translation and Commentary, 2015. *Address:* All Souls College, Oxford OX1 4AL.

HORNBY, Andrew Hedley; Chief Executive, Coral, since 2011; *b* 21 Jan. 1967; *s* of James and Clare Hornby; *m* Catherine. *Educ:* Univ. of Oxford; Harvard Business Sch. (MBA). Boston Consulting Gp; Blue Circle; ASDA, 1996–99: Dir of Corp. Develt; Retail Man. Dir; Man. Dir, George; Halifax, subseq. HBOS plc: Chief Exec., Halifax Retail, 1999–2001; Chief Exec., Retail Div., 2001–05; Chief Operating Officer, 2005–06; Chief Exec., HBOS plc, 2006–09; Gp Chief Exec., Alliance Boots, 2009–11. *Address:* Gala Coral Group, New Castle House, Castle Boulevard, Nottingham NG7 1FT.

HORNBY, Derrick Richard; *b* 11 Jan. 1926; *s* of late Richard W. Hornby and Dora M. Hornby; *m* 1948, June Steele; two *s* one *d*. *Educ:* University Coll., Southampton (DipEcon). Early career in accountancy; Marketing Dir, Tetley Tea Co. Ltd, 1964–69; Man. Dir, Eden Vale, 1969–74; Chm., Spillers Foods Ltd, 1974–77; Divisional Managing Director: Spillers Internat., 1977–80; Spillers Grocery Products Div., 1979–80; Chm., Carrington Viyella Ltd, 1979. Pres., Food Manufrs Fedn Incorp., 1977–79; Mem., Food and Drinks EDC. Member Council: CBI, to 1979; Food and Drinks Industry Council, to 1979. Chairman: Appeal Fund, Nat. Grocers Benefit Fund, 1973–74; London Animal Trust, 1978–80. FCMI; FIGD, ACommA. *Recreations:* golf, fly-fishing. *Address:* Northside, Romsey Road, Whiteparish, Wilts SP5 2SD.

HORNBY, Jonathan Peter; Founding Partner, CHI & Partners (formerly Clemmow Hornby Inge Ltd), advertising agency, 2001; Chief Executive, The&Partnership, since 2013; *b* Leamington Spa, 29 March 1967; *s* of Sir Derek Peter Hornby and Sonia Margaret Hornby (*née* Beesley); two *s* one *d*; *m* 2003, Clare Griffiths; two *d*. *Educ:* Marlborough Coll.; Univ. of Edinburgh (MA Hons). Joined Ogilvy & Mather, 1990, Account Dir, 1993–94; Brand Account Dir, 1995–96, Client Services Dir, 1996–98, Collett Dickenson Pearce & Partners; Jt Man. Dir, TBWA GGT Simons Palmer, 1998–2001. Non-exec. Dir, Mobile Money Network, 2011–. Trustee, English Heritage Foundn, 2011–. Gov., Marlborough Coll., 2007–. *Recreations:* sailing, eventing. *Address:* CHI & Partners, 7 Rathbone Street, W1T 1LY. *Clubs:* Soho House, George, Thirty, Marketing Group of Great Britain, 5 Hertford Street; Itchenor Sailing.

HORNBY, His Honour Keith Anthony Delgado; a Circuit Judge, 1995–2015; *b* 18 Feb. 1947; *s* of late James Lawrence Hornby and Naomi Ruth Hornby (*née* Delgado); *m* 1970, Judith Constance Fairbairn (*d* 2010); two *s* one *d*. *Educ:* Oratory Sch.; Trinity Coll., Dublin (BA Hons Legal Sci.). Lectr in Commercial Law, PCL, 1969–70; called to the Bar, Gray's Inn, 1970; practised on SE Circuit, 1970–95; Asst Recorder, 1988–92; Recorder, 1992–95; a Circuit Judge: Bow County Court, 1995–2012 (Lead Judge, 2007–12); Central London County Court, 2013–14; Mayors and City of London Court, 2014–15. Mem., Equal Treatment Adv. Cttee, Judicial Studies Bd, 2006–10. Gov., Oratory Sch., 2007–. *Recreations:* art, theatre, cricket, squash, golf. *Clubs:* Hurlingham; Refreshers Cricket (Pres., 2011–), Old Oratorian Cricket (Pres., 2011–).

HORNBY, Richard; Chief Finance Officer, Coastal West Sussex Clinical Commissioning Group, since 2014; *b* Bradford, 10 Dec. 1969; *s* of Michael Hornby and Caroline Hornby; *m* 2004, Zoë Phillips; two *s*. *Educ:* Univ. of Kent (BA Theol.). CIPFA 1997. Hd, Financial Services, Liberata plc, 2000–03; Hd of Finance, City of Westminster, 2003; Divl Dir, Housing, Regeneration and Envmt, Lambeth Council, 2003–09; Treas., Sussex Police Authy, 2009–12; County Treas., W Sussex CC, 2009–14. Chm., W Sussex Finance Officers Assoc., 2010. Former Hon. Sec., Soc. of County Treasurers (Hon. Auditor, 2010). Gov., Univ. of Chichester, 2010–12. *Recreations:* classical music, collecting art. *Address:* NHS Coastal West Sussex Clinical Commissioning Group, 1 The Causeway, Goring-by-Sea, W Sussex BN12 6BT. *T:* 07554 553924. *E:* richard.hornby@nhs.net.

HORNE, Sir (Alan) Gray (Antony), 3rd Bt *cr* 1929; *b* 11 July 1948; *s* of Antony Edgar Alan Horne (*d* 1954) (*o s* of 2nd Bt), and of Valentine Antonia, *d* of Valentine Dudensing; *S* grandfather, 1984; *m* 1980, Cecile Rose, *d* of Jacques Desplanche. *Heir:* none. *Address:* Château du Basty, 24210 Thenon, Dordogne, France.

HORNE, Alexander James; advisor to sports and leisure clients, since 2015; UK Chairman, FanZone Ltd, since 2015; *b* Cambridge, 13 July 1972; *s* of Martin and Phyll Horne; *m* 2005, Lisa Quail; two *d*. *Educ:* Manchester Univ. (BSc Maths 1993). ACA 1997. Trainee, Coopers & Lybrand, Manchester, 1993–96; Business Recovery Services Manager, Manchester, 1996–98; Financial Restructuring Sen. Manager, Bangkok, 1999–2000; Business Restructuring/Turnaround Sen. Manager, London, 2000–03; Finance Dir, FA, 2003–06; Man. Dir, Wembley Stadium, 2006–08; Chief Operating Officer, FA, 2008–10; Gen. Sec., Football Assoc., 2010–15. Chm., NSPCC Sports Bd, 2013–.

HORNE, Sir Alistair Allan, Kt 2003; CBE 1992; LittD; author, journalist, lecturer; *b* 9 Nov. 1925; *s* of late Sir (James) Allan Horne and Lady (Auriol) Horne (*née* Hay), *widow* of Capt. Noel Barran; *m* 1st, 1953, Renira Margaret (marr. diss. 1982), *d* of Adm. Sir Geoffrey Hawkins, KBE, CB, MVO, DSC; three *d*; 2nd, 1987, Hon. Mrs Sheelin Eccles. *Educ:* Le Rosey, Switzerland; Millbrook, USA; Jesus Coll., Cambridge (MA); LittD Cantab 1993. Served War of 1939–45: RAF, 1943–44; Coldstream Gds, 1944–47; Captain, attached Intelligence Service (ME). Foreign Correspondent, Daily Telegraph, 1952–55. Founded Alistair Horne Res. Fellowship in Mod. History, St Antony's Coll., Oxford, 1969, Hon. Fellow, 1988. Fellow, Woodrow Wilson Center, Washington, DC, USA, 1980–81 and 2005; Vis. Scholar, Library of Congress, USA, 2005. Lectures: Lees Knowles, Cambridge, 1982; Goodman, Univ. of West Ontario, 1983. Member: Management Cttee, Royal Literary Fund, 1969–89; Franco-British Council, 1979–93; Cttee of Management, Soc. of Authors, 1979–82; Trustee, Imperial War Museum, 1975–82. FRSL. Chevalier, Légion d'Honneur (France), 1993. *Publications:* Back into Power, 1955; The Land is Bright, 1958; Canada and the Canadians, 1961; The Price of Glory: Verdun 1916, 1962 (Hawthornden Prize, 1963); The Fall of Paris: The Siege and The Commune 1870–71, 1965, rev. 2nd edn 1990; To Lose a Battle: France 1940, 1969, rev. 2nd edn 1990; Death of a Generation, 1970; The Terrible Year: The Paris Commune, 1971; Small Earthquake in Chile, 1972, rev. 2nd edn 1990; A Savage War of Peace: Algeria 1954–62, 1977 (Yorkshire Post Book of Year Prize, 1978; Wolfson Literary Award, 1978), 3rd edn 1996; Napoleon, Master of Europe 1805–1807, 1979; The French Army and Politics 1870–1970, 1984 (Enid Macleod Prize, 1985); Macmillan: the official biography, Vol. I, 1894–1956, 1988, Vol. 2, 1957–1986, 1989, 2nd edn 2008; A Bundle from Britain (memoirs), 1993; (with David Montgomery) The Lonely Leader: Monty 1944–45, 1994; How Far from Austerlitz?: Napoleon 1805–1815, 1996; (ed) Telling Lives, 2000; Seven Ages of Paris: portrait of a city, 2002; Friend or Foe, 2004; Age of Napoleon, 2004; La Belle France, 2004; The French Revolution, 2009; Kissinger: 1973, the crucial year, 2009; But What Do You Actually Do?: a literary vagabondage (memoirs), 2011; *contribs to books:* Combat: World War I, ed Don Congdon, 1964; Impressions of America, ed R. A. Brown, 1966; Marshal V. I. Chuikov, The End of the Third Reich, 1967; Sports and Games in Canadian Life, ed N. and M. L. Howell, 1969; Decisive Battles of the Twentieth Century, ed N. Frankland and C. Dowling, 1976; The War Lords: Military Commanders of the Twentieth Century, ed Field Marshal Sir M. Carver, 1976; Regular Armies and Insurgency, ed R. Haycock, 1979; Macmillan: a life in pictures, 1983; The Art of War, ed A. Roberts, 2009; Hubris: tragedy of war in the 20th century, 2015. *Recreations:* curiosity, staying afloat. *Address:* The Old Vicarage, Turville, near Henley-on-Thames, Oxon RG9 6QU. *Club:* Garrick.

HORNE, David Oliver, FCA; Chairman and Chief Executive, Lloyds Merchant Bank, 1987–92; *b* 7 March 1932; *s* of Herbert Oliver Horne, MBE and Edith Marion Horne (*née* Sellers); *m* 1959, Joyce Heather (*née* Kynoch); two *s* two *d*. *Educ:* Fettes College, Edinburgh. Director: S. G. Warburg & Co., 1966–70; Williams & Glyn's Bank, 1970–78; Lloyds Bank International, 1978–85; Managing Dir, Lloyds Merchant Bank, 1985–87. Dep. Chm., Serif, 1993–97; Director: Waterman Partnership Hldgs, 1992–2003; Black Arrow Gp, 1993–. *Recreation:* golf. *Address:* Four Winds, 5 The Gardens, Esher, Surrey KT10 8QF. *T:* (01372) 463510.

HORNE, Sir Gray; *see* Horne, Sir A. G. A.

HORNE, Marilyn (Bernice); mezzo-soprano; Director, Voice Program, Music Academy of the West, Santa Barbara; *b* 16 Jan. 1934; *m* 1960, Henry Lewis (marr. diss.); one *d*. *Educ:* Univ. of Southern California. US opera début, 1954; sings at Covent Garden, La Scala, Metropolitan Opera and other major venues; rôles include Adalgisa, Amneris, Carmen, Eboli, Isabella, Mignon, Orlando, Rosina, Tancredi, concerts and recitals. *Publications:* (with J. Scovell):

Marilyn Horne - My Life (autobiog.), 1983; Marilyn Horne: the song continues, 2004. *Address:* c/o Colombia Artists Management, 1790 Broadway, 6th Floor, New York, NY 10019, USA.

HORNE, Robert Drake; Senior Researcher, Finance for Technical Education, Papua New Guinea, 2012–14; *b* 23 April 1945; *s* of late Harold Metcalfe Horne and Dorothy Katharine Horne; *m* 1972, Jennifer Mary (*née* Gill); three *d*. *Educ:* Mill Hill Sch.; Oriel Coll., Oxford (MA Classics). Asst Master, Eton Coll., Windsor, 1967–68; DES, later DFE, then DFEE, 1968–97; seconded to Cabinet Office, 1979–80; Under Sec., 1988–97; Dir of Finance and Planning, Employment Service, 1995–97; First Asst Sec., Dept of Educn (formerly Employment and Educn), Trng and Youth Affairs, Canberra, 1998–2001. Budget Planning Advr, Dept of Educn, PNG, 2004–06; Financial Advr, Targeted Budget Support Prog., Vietnam, 2007–08; Economic Advr, Higher Educn Sector Develt Prog., Vietnam, 2009–11. *Recreations:* cycling, sun-soaking. *Address:* 53 Gulfview Road, Blackwood, SA 5051, Australia.

HORNER, Christian, OBE 2013; Team Principal, Infiniti Red Bull (formerly Red Bull) Racing, Formula One, since 2005; *b* Leamington Spa, 16 Nov. 1973; *m* 2015, Geri Halliwell. *Educ:* Warwick Sch. for Boys. Won Formula Renault scholarship, 1991; racing driver: with Manor Motorsport, race winner and highest placed rookie, British Formula Renault, 1992; F3000, 1996; Internat. F3000, 1997, driver and entrant in own racing team, Arden Internat.; retired from competitive driving to run Arden Internat., 1998; entered Arden Internat. in F3000 and Euro F3000 Championships. *Recreations:* tennis, ski-ing, water ski-ing. *Address:* Infiniti Red Bull Racing, Bradbourne Drive, Tilbrook, Milton Keynes MK7 8BJ. *T:* (01908) 279702, *Fax:* (01908) 279703.

HORNER, Frederick, DSc; CEng, FIET; Director, Appleton Laboratory, Science Research Council, 1977–79; *b* 28 Aug. 1918; *s* of late Frederick and Mary Horner; *m* 1946, Elizabeth Bonsey; one *s* one *d*. *Educ:* Bolton Sch.; Univ. of Manchester (Ashbury Scholar, 1937; Fairbairn Engrg Prize, 1939; BSc 1st Cl. Hons 1939; MSc 1941; DSc 1968). CEng, FIET (FIEE 1959). On staff of DSIR, NPL, 1941–52; UK Scientific Mission, Washington DC, 1947; Radio Research Station, later Appleton Lab. of SRC, 1952–79, Dep. Dir, 1969–77; Admin. Staff Coll., Henley, 1959. Delegate: Internat. Union of Radio Science, 1950–90 (Chm., Commn VIII, 1966–69); Internat. Radio Consultative Cttee, 1953–90 (Internat. Chm., Study Group 2, 1980–90). Member: Inter-Union Commn on Frequency Allocations for Radio Astronomy and Space Science, 1965–92 (Sec., 1975–82); Electronics Divl Bd, IEE, 1970–76. Mem. Council: RHC, 1979–85 (Vice-Chm., 1982–85); RHBNC, 1985–89; Hon. Associate, Physics, RHC, 1975–85. Diplôme d'Honneur, Internat. Radio Cons. Cttee, 1989. *Publications:* more than 50 scientific papers. *Recreations:* genealogy, gardening, wildlife studies. *Address:* Gordano Lodge, Clevedon Road, Weston-in-Gordano, Bristol BS20 8PZ.

HORNER, Dr Susan Margaret, MBE 2013; education and arts consultant, since 2010; *b* Kingston-upon-Thames, 15 July 1948; *d* of William and Marjorie Galyer; *m* 1974, Peter Horner. *Educ:* Birmingham Univ. (BA Hons); Hughes Hall, Cambridge (PGCE); Leeds Univ. (PhD 1990). Teacher of English, Sheffield: Rowlinson Sch., 1971–73; Abbeydale Grange Sch., 1974–79; High Green Sch., 1980–84; Educn Advr, Sheffield, 1984–92; English Officer, Nat. Curriculum Council, 1992–94, SCAA, 1994–98; Sen. Manager, 1998–2008, Dir of Curriculum, 2009–10, QCA. Advr to Govts of Oman and Rwanda on curriculum and assessment, 2012–. Adviser: Clore Duffield Foundn, 2011–; RSC, 2012–. Chair, RSA Acads Trust, 2012–; Trustee: First Story, 2011–; Min. of Stories, 2013–; CapeUK, 2013–. Author, Magic Dust that Lasts, report on writers in schs, Arts Council England, 2010. *Publications:* contrib. nat. curriculum and assessment advice and specifications. *Recreations:* literature, theatre, travel, birdwatching. *Address:* 14 Whirlow Park Road, Sheffield S11 9NP. *T:* (0114) 236 3465. *E:* sue@suehorner.com. *W:* www.suehorner.com; RSA Academies Trust, 8 John Adam Street, WC2N 6EZ.

HORNER, Hon. Sir (Thomas) Mark, Kt 2013; **Hon. Mr Justice Horner;** a Judge of the High Court of Justice, Northern Ireland, since 2012; *b* Belfast, 3 July 1956; *s* of Dr Thomas Horner and Mabel Horner; *m* 1981, Karin van der Ree; two *s* one *d*. *Educ:* Campbell Coll., Belfast; St Catharine's Coll., Cambridge (BA 1978); Inst. of Professional Legal Studies, Queen's Univ. Belfast (Professional Cert.). Called to the Bar, NI, 1979; QC (NI), 1996. *Recreations:* reading, golf, watching Rugby. *Address:* Royal Courts of Justice, Chichester Street, Belfast BT1 3JF.

HORNSBY, Timothy Richard, CBE 2008; MA; Chair, International Tree Foundation; *b* 22 Sept. 1940; *s* of late Harker William Hornsby and Agnes Nora French; *m* 1971, Dr Charmian Rosemary Newton; one *s* one *d*. *Educ:* Bradfield Coll.; Christ Church, Oxford Univ. (MA 1st C1. Hons Modern History). Harkness Fellow, USA, at Harvard, Columbia, Henry E. Huntington Research Inst., 1961–63; Asst Prof., Birmingham Southern Coll., Alabama, 1963–64; Research Lectr, Christ Church, Oxford, 1964–65; Asst Principal, Min. of Public Building and Works, 1965–67; Private Sec. to Controller General, 1968–69; HM Treasury, 1971–73; Prin., then Asst Sec., DoE, 1975; Dir, Ancient Monuments and Historic Buildings, 1983–88, and Dir of Rural Affairs, 1984–88, DoE; Dir Gen., Nature Conservancy Council, 1988–91; Dir, Construction Policy Directorate, DoE, 1991; Chief Executive: Royal Bor. of Kingston upon Thames, 1991–95; Nat. Lottery Charities Bd, 1995–2001. A Comr, Nat. Lottery Commn, 2001–08 (Chm., 2004–05); Ind. Mem., Consumer Council for Water, 2005–14; Mem. Bd, Audience Agency, 2014–. Chair, Harkness Fellows Assoc., 2002–. Chm. Trustees, Horniman Mus. and Gardens, 2004–14; Trustee: Charles Darwin Trust, 2002–10; Internat. Inst. for Envmt and Develt, 2005–11; Royal Botanical Gardens, Kew, 2007–14; Castle Howard Arboretum, 2008–; Field Lane, 2014–; British Architectural Trust Bd, 2014–. Gov., Legacy Trust, 2007–; Comr, Marshall Aid Commemoration Commn, 2011–. FRSA. *Recreations:* conservation, ski-ing, talking. *Address:* c/o Marshall Aid Commemoration Commission, Association of Commonwealth Universities, Woburn House, WC1H 9HF. *E:* thornsby@timothyhornsby.freeserve.co.uk. *Club:* Athenæum.

HOROWITZ, Anthony, OBE 2014; children's writer; *b* 5 April 1955; *s* of late Mark and Celia Joyce Horowitz; *m* 1988, Jill Green; two *s*. *Educ:* Rugby Sch.; Univ. of York (BA). Screenwriter: *film:* Stormbreaker, 2006; *television* includes: Robin of Sherwood; Poirot; Midsomer Murders; Murder in Mind; Crime Traveller; (with J. Green) Foyle's War (series), 2002–15 (Lew Grade People's Award, 2003); Collision (series), 2009; Injustice (series), 2011; writer of play, Dinner with Saddam, 2015. *Publications:* Devil's Doorbell, 1983; Night of the Scorpion, 1985; Groosham Grange, 1989; Myths and Legends, 1991; Granny, 1995; Falcon's Malteser, 1995; The Switch, 1997; Public Enemy No 2, 1997; The Devil and His Boy, 1999; Horowitz Horror, 1999; Unholy Grail, 1999; More Horowitz Horror, 2000; Mindgame (play), 2000; Stormbreaker, 2000; Point Blanc, 2001; Skeleton Key, 2002 (Red House Children's Book Award, 2003); Eagle Strike, 2003; Scorpia, 2004; The Killing Joke (adult novel), 2004; Ark Angel, 2005; Raven's Gate, 2005; Evil Star, 2006; Nightrise, 2007; Snakehead, 2007; Crocodile Tears, 2009; More Bloody Horowitz, 2010; Scorpia Rising, 2011; The House of Silk, 2011; Oblivion, 2012; Russian Roulette, 2013; Moriarty, 2014; Trigger Mortis, 2015. *Recreations:* scuba-diving, cinema, walking in Suffolk. *Address:* c/o United Agents, 12–26 Lexington Street, W1F 0LE. *T:* (020) 3214 0800.

HOROWITZ, His Honour Michael; QC 1990; a Circuit Judge, 2004–13; *b* 18 Oct. 1943; *s* of late David and Irene Horowitz; *m*; one *d* (one *s* decd). *Educ:* St Marylebone Grammar School; Pembroke College, Cambridge (BA 1966; LLB 1967). Pres., Cambridge Union Soc., 1967; English-Speaking Union Debating Tour of USA, 1967. Called to the Bar, Lincoln's Inn, 1968, Bencher, 1997; Asst Recorder, 1987; a Recorder, 1991–2004. Senate of Inns of Court and Bar, 1982–85; Mem., Professional Conduct Cttee, Bar Council, 1997–2000. Dir, Bar Mutual Indemnity Fund, 1999–2004. *Publications:* (contrib.) Rayden on Divorce, 17th edn 1997, 18th edn 2005; Essential Family Practice, 2002. *Recreations:* reading history, listening.

HOROWITZ, Prof. Myer, OC 1990; EdD; Adjunct Professor of Education, University of Victoria, since 1998 (Interim Director, Centre for Early Childhood Research and Policy, 2012–14); Professor Emeritus of Education, since 1990, President Emeritus, since 1999, University of Alberta; *b* 27 Dec. 1932; *s* of Philip Horowitz and Fanny Cotler; *m* 1956, Barbara, *d* of Samuel Rosen and Grace Midvidy, Montreal; two *d*. *Educ:* High Sch., Montreal; Sch. for Teachers, Macdonald Coll.; Sir George Williams Univ. (BA); Univ. of Alberta (MEd); Stanford Univ. (EdD). Teacher, Schs in Montreal, Sch. Bd, Greater Montreal, 1952–60. McGill University: Lectr in Educn, 1960–63; Asst Prof., 1963–65; Associate Prof., 1965–67; Asst to Dir, 1964–65; Prof. of Educn, 1967–69 and Asst Dean, 1965–69; University of Alberta: Prof. and Chm., Dept Elem. Educn, 1969–72; Dean, Faculty of Educn, 1972–75; Vice-Pres. (Academic), 1975–79; Pres., 1979–89. Hon. Dr: McGill, 1979; Concordia, 1982; Athabasca, 1989; British Columbia, 1990; Alberta, 1990; Victoria, 2000; Brock, 2000; Calgary, 2005; Royal Roads, 2012. Diamond Jubilee Medal, 2012. *Address:* A459 MacLaurin Building, University of Victoria, PO Box 3010 STN CSC, Victoria, BC V8W 3N4, Canada.

HORRELL, Roger William, CMG 1988; OBE 1974; HM Diplomatic Service, retired; *b* 9 July 1935; *s* of William John Horrell and Dorice Enid (*née* Young); *m* 1970, Patricia Mildred Eileen Smith (*née* Binns) (marr. diss. 1975); one *s* one *d*. *Educ:* Shebbear College; Exeter College, Oxford. MA. Served in Devonshire Regt, 1953–55; HM Colonial Service, Kenya, 1959–64; joined Foreign Office, 1964; Economic Officer, Dubai, 1965–67; FCO, 1967–70; First Sec., Kampala, 1970–73; FCO, 1973–76; First Sec., Lusaka, 1976–80; Counsellor, FCO, 1980–93. *Recreations:* watching cricket and Rugby Union - now mostly on TV, playing bridge. *Address:* 51 Oatlands Drive, Weybridge, Surrey KT13 9LU. *Club:* Reform.

HORRIDGE, Prof. (George) Adrian, FRS 1969; FAA 1971; Professor, Australian National University, 1969–92, Emeritus Professor, since 1993; *b* Sheffield, England, 12 Dec. 1927; *s* of George William Horridge and Olive Stray; *m* 1954, Audrey Anne Lightburne; one *s* four *d*. *Educ:* King Edward VII Sch., Sheffield. Fellow, St John's Coll., Cambridge, 1953–56; on staff, St Andrews Univ., 1956–69; Dir, Gatty Marine Laboratory, St Andrews, 1960–69. Vis. Fellow, Churchill Coll., Cambridge, 1993–94. *Publications:* Structure and Function of the Nervous Systems of Invertebrates (with T. H. Bullock), 1965; Interneurons, 1968; (ed) The Compound Eye and Vision of Insects, 1975; Monographs of the Maritime Museum at Greenwich nos 38, 39, 40, 54, 1979–82; The Prahu: traditional sailing boat of Indonesia, 1982 (Oxford in Asia); Sailing Craft of Indonesia, 1985 (Oxford in Asia); Outrigger Canoes of Bali & Madura, Indonesia, 1986; (contrib.) The Austronesians, 1995; What Does the Honeybee See?, 2009; contribs 240 scientific papers to jls, etc, on behaviour and nervous systems of lower animals, and vision of the honeybee. *Recreations:* optics, mathematics, cultivating *Vanessa itea*, marine biology; sailing, language, arts, boat construction in Indonesia. *Address:* 76 Mueller Street, Yarralumla, ACT 2600, Australia.

HORROBIN, James, FWCB; artist blacksmith, since 1966; *b* 22 March 1946; *s* of Harry Horrobin and Betty Mary Horrobin; *m* 1st, 1966, Shirley Fitzgerald (marr. diss. 1983); one *s* one *d*; 2nd, 2007, Gabrielle Ridler. *Educ:* apprenticeship with his father on Exmoor, 1961–66; Hereford Tech. Coll. Set up own workshop, W Somerset, 1969; Lectr, Haystack Sch. of Craft, Maine, and Nat. Ornamental Metal Mus., Memphis, 1984–85. Chm., British Artist Blacksmith Assoc., 1983. Featured artist, Crafts Council exhibn, 1990. Commissions include: gates for Metalwork Gall., V&A Mus., 1981; portcullis and railings, Richmond Terrace, Whitehall, 1986; staircase, Chelsea residence of Charles Saatchi, 1989; screens, gate, address plates and emblem, 66 Cheapside, London, 1991; screens, railings and figure of Koko, Savoy Th., London, 1993; dossal rail, plaques and choir stalls, Church of Heavenly Rest, NY, 1997; lanterns, portico of St Paul's Chapel, Broadway, NY, 1998; gates, summer garden, Antony House, Cornwall, 1999; cloister railings, St John of Lattingtown, NY, 2003; Churchill Meml Screen, St Paul's Cathedral, London, 2003–04; screen, Torre Abbey, Devon, 2008; restoration of garden gates and new entrance gates, Bradfield Hall, Devon, 2010–11. FWCB 1996 (Silver Medal, 1996, Tonypandy Award, 2006, Co. of Blacksmiths). *Recreations:* painting, art history, architecture, reading, swimming, surfing, travel. *Address:* Furze View, Timberscombe, Minehead, Somerset TA24 7TY. *T:* (01643) 841402. *E:* jh@doverhay.co.uk. *W:* www.doverhay.co.uk.

HORROCKS, Prof. Geoffrey Charles, PhD; Fellow, St John's College, Cambridge, since 1983; Professor of Comparative Philology, University of Cambridge, since 1997; *b* 3 Feb. 1951; *s* of Roland Horrocks and Marjorie Horrocks (*née* Atkinson); *m* 1973, Gillian Elizabeth Tasker; two *d*. *Educ:* Manchester Grammar Sch.; Downing Coll., Cambridge (BA 1972; PhD 1978). Employee Relns Manager, Mobil North Sea Ltd, 1972–73; Res. Fellow, Downing Coll., Cambridge, 1976–77; Lectr in Linguistics, SOAS, 1977–83; Lectr in Classics, Univ. of Cambridge, 1983–97. Hon. Dr Athens, 2012. *Publications:* Space and Time in Homer, 1981; Generative Grammar, 1987; Greek: a history of the language and its speakers, 1997, 2nd edn 2010; (with J. Clackson) The Blackwell History of Latin Language, 2007; contrib. numerous articles in jls of general, theoretical and historical linguistics, and Classics. *Recreations:* travel, guitar, football, gardening, gossip, talking to the members of my family (in no particular order). *Address:* St John's College, Cambridge CB2 1TP. *T:* (01223) 338600.

HORROCKS, Prof. Ian Robert, PhD; FRS 2011; Professor of Computer Science, University of Oxford, since 2007; Fellow of Oriel College, Oxford, since 2007; *b* Liverpool, 11 March 1958; *s* of William Joseph Horrocks and Barbara Francis Horrocks; *m* 1981, Maureen Mary Healy. *Educ:* Univ. of Manchester (BSc Hons Computer Sci. 1981; MSc 1995; PhD 1997). Res. Associate, Dept of Computer Sci., Univ. of Manchester, 1981–83; Tech. Dir, Scientex Ltd, 1983–94; Department of Computer Science, University of Manchester: Res. Associate, 1998–99; Lectr, 1999–2002; Sen. Lectr, then Reader, 2002–03; Prof., 2003–07. Vis. Scientist, Istituto per la Ricerca Scientifica e Tecnologica, Trento, 1997–98. Chief Scientist, Cerebra Inc., Carlsbad, Calif, 2001–06. *Publications:* contrib. numerous articles to computer sci. jls and confs. *Recreations:* mountain biking, ski-ing, reading, cinema, music. *Address:* Department of Computer Science, Wolfson Building, Parks Road, Oxford OX1 3QD. *T:* (01865) 273939, *Fax:* (01865) 521093. *E:* ian.horrocks@cs.ox.ac.uk.

HORROCKS, Jane; actress; *b* 18 Jan. 1964; *d* of John and Barbara Horrocks; partner, Nick Vivian; one *s* one *d*. *Educ:* Fearns Co. Secondary Sch., Rossendale, Lancs; RADA (Dip.). *Films:* The Dressmaker, 1989; The Witches, 1990; Life is Sweet, 1991 (Best Supporting Actress, LA Critics Award, 1992); Little Voice, 1998; Chicken Run, 2000; The Corpse Bride, 2006; Sunshine on Leith, 2013; *plays:* Road, Royal Court, 1987; The Rise and Fall of Little Voice, RNT and Aldwych, 1992–93; Cabaret, Donmar Warehouse, 1993–94; Sweet Panic, Duke of York's, 2003; Absurd Person Singular, Garrick, 2007; The Good Soul of Szechuan, Young Vic, 2008; Aunt Dan and Lemon, Royal Court, 2009; (musical) Annie Get Your Gun, Young Vic, 2009; East is East, Trafalgar Studios, 2014; *television:* Road, 1987; Storyteller, 1988; Bad Girl, 1992; Suffer the Little Children, 1994 (Best Actress Award, RTS, 1995); Absolutely Fabulous, 1992–94, 2001–04, 2011; Mirrorball, 2000; The Street, 2006, 2007; The Amazing Mrs Pritchard, 2006; Gracie, 2009; The Road to Coronation Street, 2010; This is Jinsy, 2011; Trollied, 2011–13; True Love, 2011; The Cruise, 2014; Inside No. 9, 2015. *Address:* c/o United Agents, 12 Lexington Street, W1F 0LE.

HORROCKS, Paul John; DL; Director, Essential Communications, since 2010; Partner, Gordon Burns Partnership, since 2011; Editor, Manchester Evening News, 1997–2009; *b* 19 Dec. 1953; *s* of Joe and Eunice Horrocks; *m* 1976, Linda Jean Walton; two *s* one *d*, and one step *d.* *Educ:* Bolton Sch. Reporter, Daily Mail, 1974; Manchester Evening News: gen. reporter, 1975–80; crime corresp., 1980–87; news editor, 1987–91; Asst Editor, 1991–95; Dep. Editor, 1995–97. Dir, Soc. of Editors, 2001–10 (Pres., 2007); Member: PCC, 2002–06; Defence Press and Broadcasting Adv. Cttee, 2007–09; Appts Panel, IPSO, 2014–. Chm., Bury NHS PCT, 2010–13; non. exec. Dir, NHS Greater Manchester, 2010–13; Mem., Appeals Bd, Royal Manchester Children's Hosp., 2007–; Ethics Panel, Gtr Manchester Police Crime Comr, 2014. Communications Advr, NHS Gtr Manchester Service Transformation, 2011. Vice-Pres., Community Foundn for Greater Manchester, 2000–08; Mem., Organising Council, Commonwealth Games, Manchester 2002, 1998–2002. Mem., Bd of Govs, Univ. of Bolton, 2010–. Trustee, Tatton Park Trust, 2008–. Patron, Francis House Children's Hospice, 1999–. DL Greater Manchester, 2011. *Recreations:* sailing, golf, Rugby Union.

HORROCKS, Peter John Gibson, CBE 2015; Vice-Chancellor, Open University, since 2015; *b* 8 Oct. 1959; *s* of James Nigel Gibson Horrocks and Ellen Elizabeth Gibson Horrocks; *m* 1987, Katharine Rosemary Rogers; two *s* one *d.* *Educ:* King's Coll. Sch., Wimbledon; Christ's Coll., Cambridge (BA). BBC: Dep. Ed., Panorama, 1988–90; Editor: Election '92; Public Eye, 1992–94; Here and Now, 1994; Newsnight, 1994–97; Election '97; Panorama, 1997–2000; Hd of Current Affairs, 2000–05; Hd of TV News, 2005–07; Hd of Multimedia Newsroom, 2007–09; Director: BBC World Service, 2009–15; BBC Global News, 2010–15. *Address:* Vice Chancellor's Office, Open University, Walton Hall, Milton Keynes MK7 6AA.

HORSBRUGH-PORTER, Sir (Andrew) Alexander (Marshall), 5th Bt *cr* 1902, of Merrion Square, City and Co. of Dublin; Senior Associate, Mourant Ozannes, Guernsey, since 2011; *b* 19 Jan. 1971; *s* of Sir John Horsbrugh-Porter, 4th Bt and of Lavinia Rose (*née* Turton); *S* father, 2013; *m* 2005, Jennie, *d* of Keith Downing; one *s* one *d.* *Educ:* Winchester Coll.; Univ. of Birmingham (BSc Politics and Econ. Hist.). Qualified Solicitor, 1998, Insolvency Practitioner, 2007. Solicitor: Davies Arnold Cooper, 1996–2000; Ince & Co., 2000–03; Attorney, Ritch & Conolly, Cayman Islands, 2004–11; Advocate, Royal Court of Guernsey, 2014. *Publications:* (contrib.) Personal Insolvency: a practical guide, 2013; contribs INSOL Jl. *Recreations:* cricket, tennis, golf, history, reading. *Heir:* *s* William John Ernest Horsbrugh-Porter, *b* 25 Sept. 2006. *Address:* Chatwall Barn, Rue de Heche, St Peters, Guernsey GY7 9AD. *T:* (01481) 263006. *E:* alex.horsbrugh-porter@mourantozannes.com. *Club:* MCC.

HORSBURGH, John Millar Stewart; QC (Scot.) 1980; Sheriff of Lothian and Borders at Edinburgh, 1990–2011; *b* 15 May 1938; *s* of late Alexander Horsburgh and Helen Margaret Watson Millar or Horsburgh; *m* 1966, Johann Catriona Gardner, MB, ChB, DObst RCOG; one *s* one *d.* *Educ:* Hutchesons' Boys' Grammar Sch., Glasgow; Univ. of Glasgow (MA Hons, LLB). Admitted to Scots Bar, 1965; Advocate-Depute, 1987–89. Part-time Mem., Lands Tribunal for Scotland, 1985–87. *Address:* 8 Laverockbank Road, Edinburgh EH5 3DG. *T:* (0131) 552 5328.

HORSEY, Gordon; a District Judge, 1991–94; *b* 20 July 1926; *s* of late E. W. Horsey, MBE, and of H. V. Horsey; *m* 1951, Jean Mary (*née* Favill); one *d.* *Educ:* Magnus Grammar Sch., Newark, Notts; St Catharine's Coll., Cambridge. BA, LLB. Served RN, 1944–45, RE, 1945–48 (Captain). Admitted solicitor, 1953; private practice in Nottingham, 1953–71; Registrar: Coventry County Court, 1971; Leicester County Court, 1973; a Recorder, 1978–84. JP Leics, 1975. *Recreation:* fly-fishing. *Address:* The Old Woodyard, 55 Swithland Lane, Rothley, Leics LE7 7SG. *T:* (0116) 230 2545.

HORSFALL, Sir Edward (John Wright), 4th Bt *cr* 1909, of Hayfield, Glusburn, co. York; *b* 17 Dec. 1940; *s* of Sir John Horsfall, 3rd Bt, MC, TD and Cassandra Nora Bernadine Horsfall (*née* Wright); *S* father, 2005; *m* 1965, Rosemary King; three *s.* *Educ:* Uppingham. Dir, Hayfield Textiles Ltd, 1961–78. Mem. (C) Cotswold DC, 2003–15 (Cabinet Mem., 2004–10). *Recreations:* theatre, travel, the arts, music. *Heir:* *e s* David Edward Horsfall [*b* 3 Sept. 1966; *m* 1996, Maria Gloria Sandoval; one *d*]. *Address:* York House, 4 The Mead, Cirencester, Glos GL7 2BB. *T:* (01285) 652012.

HORSHAM, Area Bishop of, since 2009; **Rt Rev. Mark Crispin Rake Sowerby;** *b* Ripon, 28 Oct. 1963; *s* of Rev. Geoffrey Sowerby and Hilary Sowerby (*née* Evans); *m* 1989, Ruth Mary Jones; three *d.* *Educ:* Barnard Castle Sch.; St Aidan and St John Fisher's Sixth Form, Harrogate; King's Coll., London (BD 1985; AKC 1985); Univ. of Lancaster (MA 1994); Coll. of the Resurrection, Mirfield. Ordained deacon, 1987, priest, 1988; Curate: Knaresborough, 1987–90; Darwen St Cuthbert with Tockholes, 1990–92; Vicar, St Mary Magdalen, Accrington, 1992–97; Selection Sec./Vocations Officer, Ministry Div. of Archbishop's Council, 1997–2001; Vicar, St Wilfrid's, Harrogate, 2001–09 (Team Rector, 2004–09). Assistant Director of Ordinands: Dio. of Blackburn, 1993–96; Dio. of Ripon and Leeds, 2005–09. Chaplain: St Christopher's C of E Sch., Accrington, 1992–97; Victoria Hosp., Accrington, 1992–97. *Recreations:* cooking, sea fishing, opera. *Address:* Bishop's House, 21 Guildford Road, Horsham, W Sussex RH12 1LU. *T:* (01403) 211139, *Fax:* (01403) 217349. *E:* bishop.horsham@chichester.anglican.org.

HORSHAM, Archdeacon of; *see* Windsor, Ven. J. F.

HORSLEY, Very Rev. Canon Dr Alan Avery Allen; Provost of St Andrew's Cathedral, Inverness, 1988–91; Canon Emeritus, Peterborough Cathedral, since 1986; *b* 13 May 1936; *s* of Reginald James and Edith Irene Horsley; *m* 1966, Mary Joy Marshall, MA; two *d.* *Educ:* St Chad's Coll., Durham (BA 1958); Birmingham Univ.; Pacific Western Univ., Calif (MA 1984; PhD 1985); Queen's Coll., Birmingham. Ordained deacon 1960, priest 1961, Peterborough; Assistant Curate: Daventry, 1960–63; St Giles, Reading, 1963–64; St Paul's, Wokingham, 1964–66; Vicar of Yeadon, dio. Bradford, 1966–71; Rector of Heyford and Stowe Nine Churches, dio. Peterborough, 1971–78; RD of Daventry, 1976–78; Vicar of Oakham with Hambleton and Egleton (and Braunston and Brooke from 1980), 1978–86; Non-Residentiary Canon of Peterborough Cathedral, 1979–86; Chaplain: Catmose Vale Hosp., 1978–86; Rutland Memorial Hosp., 1978–86; Vicar of Lanteglos-by-Fowey, dio. Truro, 1986–88; Daventry ATC, 2005; Northants Burma Star Assoc., 2008–; Priest in Charge: St Mary in the Fields, Culloden, 1988–91; St Paul, Strathnairn, 1988–91; Vicar, Mill End and Heronsgate with West Hyde, 1991–2001; acting RD, Rickmansworth, 1998–2000, RD, 2000–01. Permission to officiate: dio. Truro, 1998–2005; dio. Peterborough, 2003–. Hon. Assistant Priest: All Saints', Northampton, 2003–10 (Choirs' Chaplain, 2005–10); Holy Sepulchre, Northampton, 2010–14. *Publications:* (with Mary J. Horsley) A Lent Course, 1967, 3rd edn 2007; Lent with St Luke, 1978, 3rd edn 1997; Action at Lanteglos and Polruan, 1987; The Parish Church at Mill End, Rickmansworth, Hertfordshire: Pt I, 1999, 2nd edn 2000; Pt II, 2000; Forty-One Men: a biblical course for Lent, 2008; (with Lee Dunleavy) Kalendar for All Saints Church with St Katherine and St Peter in Northampton, 2008, 2nd edn 2009; Kalendar for St Crispin's Group, Northampton, 2011; contribs to Rutland Record Soc. Jl. *Recreations:* music, piano and organ, cultivation of flowers, historical research. *Address:* 22 Vyner Close, Thorpe Astley, Leicester LE3 3EJ. *T:* (0116) 289 2695, 07503 321553. *E:* canonalanahorsley@gmail.com.

HORSLEY, (Christine) Ruth; *see* Mercer, C. R.

HORSLEY, Nicola Jane; *see* Spence, N. J.

HORSLEY, Stephen Daril; Director of Operations, Clinicard Ltd, since 2014; *b* 23 June 1947; *s* of Donald Vincent Horsley and Marie Margaret Horsley; *m* 1974, Vivienne Marjorie Lee; one *s* two *d.* *Educ:* Guy's Hosp.; Manchester Business Sch. (MBSc 1985); Manchester Univ. (MA Health Ethics and Law 2004). FRCP 1988 (MRCP 1976); FFPH. Gen. Hosp. Medicine, Truro, 1971–75; Community Medicine, Yorks RHA, 1975–79; District Community Physician, E Cumbria HA, 1979–82; District MO, S Cumbria HA, 1982–85; Specialist in Community Medicine, Oxford RHA, 1985–86; Regl MO, N Western RHA, 1986–94; Consultant in Public Health, Morecambe Bay HA, 1994–2000; Locum Consultant in Public Health: St Helens and Knowsley DHA, 2000–02; St Helens PCT, April 2002; Director of Public Health: Northants Heartlands PCT, 2002–06; Northants Teaching PCT, 2007–13 (Acting Dir, 2006–07); Interim Dir of Public Health, Plymouth CC, 2013–14. Vis. Prof. of Public Health, Leicester Univ., 1997–. *Publications:* contribs to BMJ, Community Medicine. *Recreations:* wind surfing, walking.

HORSMAN, Malcolm; *b* 28 June 1933. *Educ:* Open Univ. (BSc 2006); King's Coll. London (MA 2007); Birkbeck, Univ. of London (MRes 2008). Commnd Sherwood Foresters, Nat. Service, 1952. Director, Slater Walker Securities Ltd, 1967–70; Chm., Ralli International Ltd, 1969–73; Director: The Bowater Corporation Ltd, 1972–77; Tozer Kemsley & Millbourn (Holdings) Ltd, 1975–82. Member: Study Group on Local Authority Management Structures, 1971–72; South East Economic Planning Council, 1972–74; Royal Commission on the Press, 1974–77; Institute of Contemporary Arts Ltd, 1975–78; Council, Templeton Coll. (formerly Oxford Centre for Management Studies), 1973–84; Chm., British Centre, Internat. Theatre Inst., 1982–84 (Mem. Exec. Council, 1980–87). Visiting Fellow, Cranfield Univ. (formerly Cranfield Institute of Technology)/The School of Management, 1977–97. Vis. Lectr, Univ. of Transkei, 1977. Chm., Nat. Youth Theatre, 1982–90 (Dep. Chm. 1971–82); Director: Hackney New Variety Ltd (Hackney Empire Trust), 1995–97; Gate Theatre, 1997–2000; Member: Court, RCA, 1977–80; Editorial Bd, DRAMA, 1978–81; Royal Court Develt Cttee, 1995–98; Council, Birthright, 1974–85; Council, Anti-Slavery Internat., 1998–2000. Chairman: Alice Hoffman Homes, later Hoffman De Visme Foundn, 1992–98; Open School Trust, 1998–2000. *Club:* Harlequins Rugby Football.

HORSMAN, Michael John; Special Professor, Nottingham University Business School, 2003–06; Independent Member, House of Commons Senior Pay Panel, since 2003; *b* 3 March 1949; *s* of late Graham Joseph Vivian Horsman and Ruth (*née* Guest); *m* 1977, Dr Anne Margaret Marley; three *s.* *Educ:* Dollar Acad.; Glasgow Univ. (MA Hist. and Politics, 1st cl. Hons, 1971); Balliol Coll., Oxford (Snell Exhibnr, Brackenbury Scholar). Entered Civil Service, 1974; Private Sec. to Chm., MSC, 1978–79; Dept of Employment, 1979–84, on secondment to Unilever, 1981–82; Dir, PER, 1984–85; Hd, Finance Policy, and Resource Controller, MSC, 1985–87; Hd, Ops Br., Employment Service, 1987–89; Regl Dir, London and SE, Employment Service, 1989–92; Dir, Office of Manpower Economics, 1992–2003. *Recreations:* historical research, literature, cycling.

HORT, Sir Andrew (Edwin Fenton), 9th Bt *cr* 1767, of Castle Strange, Middlesex; *b* 15 Nov. 1954; *e s* of Sir James Fenton Hort, 8th Bt and Joan, *d* of Edward Peat; *S* father, 1995; *m* 1986, Mary, *d* of Jack Whibley; one *s* one *d.* *Heir:* *s* James John Fenton Hort, *b* 26 Nov. 1989. *Address:* Welle House, East Prawle, Kingsbridge, Devon TQ7 2BU.

HORTA-OSÓRIO, António Mota de Sousa; Group Chief Executive, Lloyds Banking Group, since 2011; *b* Lisbon, 28 Jan. 1964. *Educ:* Colégio de São João de Brito, Lisbon; Universidade Católica Portuguesa (Licenciatura Mgt and Business Admin doctoral degree 1987); INSEAD (MBA 1991; Henry Ford II Prize); Harvard Business Sch. (AMP 2003). Asst Prof. in Finance and Econometrics, Universidade Católica Portuguesa, 1985–90 (Guest Prof., MBA Prog. in Financial Strategic Planning, 1992–96); Vice Pres. and Hd, Capital Mkts, Citibank Portugal, 1987–90; Corporate Finance, Goldman Sachs Internat., NY and London, 1991–93; Banco Santander SA, 1993–2010: CEO, Banco Santander de Negócios Portugal, 1993–2000; CEO, Banco Santander Brasil, 1997–2000; CEO, 2000–06, Chm., 2006–10, Banco Santander Totta; Exec. Vice Pres., and Mem., Mgt Cttee, 2000–10; CEO, Santander UK plc, 2006–10. Non-executive Director: Abbey National plc, 2004–06; Bank of England, 2009–11; Champalimaud Foundn, 2011–; Sociedade Francisco Manuel dos Santos BV, 2011; Exor, 2015–. Guest Prof., Portuguese Banking Trng Inst., 1985–90. Member, Governing Body: Universidade Católica Portuguesa, 2007–10; London Business Sch., 2010–; Member, Advisory Council: Saïd Business Sch., Univ. of Oxford, 2008–12; Judge Business Sch., Univ. of Cambridge, 2009–11; CityUK, 2010–12. Chm., Wallace Collection, 2015–. Hon. Dr: Edinburgh, 2011; Bath, 2012. Order of Merit Grã-Cruz (Portugal), 2014; Comdr, Order of Civil Merit (Spain), 1998; Order of Southern Cross (Brazil), 1998; Encomienda de Numero, Orden de Isabel la Católica (Spain), 2009. *Recreations:* tennis, scuba diving, ski-ing. *Address:* Lloyds Banking Group plc, 25 Gresham Street, EC2V 7HN. *Clubs:* Queen's; Clube VII (Lisbon).

HORTON, Claire Ellen; Chief Executive, Battersea Dogs & Cats Home, since 2010; *b* Skipton, Yorks, 20 May 1962; *d* of Michael and Mildred Weir; *m* 1985, Paul Horton; one *s.* *Educ:* Dudley Girls High Sch.; Univ. of Warwick Business Sch. (MBA 2007). Special Constable, W Midlands Police Constabulary, 1980–87; Area Manager, NSPCC, 1988–93; Regl Dir, Cats Protection League, 1994–99; Dir, Brewed Infusion Ltd, 1999–2002; Chief Exec., Univ. of Warwick Students' Union, 2002–08; Chief Operating Officer, Variety Club of GB, 2008–10. Non-executive Director: Membership Solutions Ltd, 2006–; Animal Health and Welfare Bd for England, DEFRA, 2014–; Chm., Assoc. of Dogs and Cats Homes, 2015–. Ind. Chair and Panel Mem., Appeals Service, Worcester CC, 2004–08. FRSA 2012; FInstD 2012. Hon. LLD Roehampton, 2015. *Publications:* (jtly) Universities and their Unions, 2006. *Recreations:* enjoying poverty through horse ownership, writing, reading, eating, but *not* cooking. *Address:* Battersea Dogs & Cats Home, 4 Battersea Park Road, SW8 4AA. *T:* (020) 7627 9207. *E:* c.horton@battersea.org.uk.

HORTON, Geoffrey Robert; Economic Consultant, Horton 4 Consulting, since 1998; *b* 23 July 1951; *s* of late Leonard Horton and Joan Horton; *m* 1991, Dianne Alexandra Craker; two *d.* *Educ:* Bristol Grammar Sch.; Exeter Coll., Oxford (MA); University Coll. London (MSc Econ). Economic asst, HM Treasury, 1974–76; Lectr in Econs, University Coll. of Swansea, 1976–78; Economic Advr, HM Treasury, 1978–85; Chief Economist, DRI (Europe) Ltd, 1985–88; Sen. Economic Advr, Dept of Energy, 1988–90; Sen. Consultant, Nat. Economic Research Associates, 1990–92; Dir, Regulation and Business Affairs, Office of Electricity Regulation, 1990–95; Dir Gen., Electricity Supply for NI, 1992–95; Dir of Consumer Affairs, OFT, 1995–98. Member: Panel of Experts for Reform of the Water Service in NI, 2003–06; Energy and Climate Security Panel, BERR, later DECC, 2007–10. Award for Gallantry, Royal Humane Soc., 2005. *Publications:* articles and research papers on economics. *Recreations:* reading, cooking, sailing. *Address:* 43 Grove Park, Camberwell, SE5 8LG. *T:* (020) 7733 6587. *E:* Geoff@Horton4.co.uk.

HORTON, Mark Anthony; His Honour Judge Horton; a Circuit Judge, since 2008; *b* Crediton, Devon, 30 Sept. 1953; *s* of Robert Anthony Horton, DFC and Helene Renee Horton; *m* 1986, Madeleine Curry; two *s.* *Educ:* Blundell's Sch., Tiverton; Birmingham Univ. (LLB Hons). Called to the Bar, Middle Temple, 1976; in practice as barrister specialising in crime and personal injury; Hd, Criminal Dept, St John's Chambers, Bristol, 1995–2008; Recorder, 2000–08. *Recreations:* tennis, football, Rugby, languages, French, German, Spanish, Russian. *Address:* Bristol Crown Court, The Law Courts, Small Street, Bristol BS1 1DA.

HORTON, Matthew Bethell; QC 1989; *b* 23 Sept. 1946; *s* of Albert Leslie Horton, BSc, FRICS and Gladys Rose Ellen Harding; *m* 1972, Liliane Boleslawski (marr. diss. 1984); one *s* one *d.* *Educ:* Sevenoaks School; Trinity Hall, Cambridge (Open Exhibn, Hist.; Squire Law Scholar; 1st Cl. Hons Law 1967; MA 1967; LLM 1968); Astbury Scholar, Middle Temple, 1968. Called to the Bar, Middle Temple, 1969. Western Circuit; Mem., Parly Bar Mess, 1977.

Member: Cttee, Jt Planning Law Conf., 1983–97; European Environmental Law Cttee, Internat. Bar Assoc.; Admin. Law Cttee of Justice. *Recreations:* ski-ing, windsurfing, tennis. *Address:* 39 Essex Street, WC2R 3AT. *Club:* Tramp.

HORTON, Prof. Peter, DPhil, DSc; FRS 2010; Professor of Biochemistry, University of Sheffield, 1990–2010, now Emeritus. *Educ:* Univ. of York (BA 1st Cl. Hons Biol.; DPhil; DSc); Dip. Teaching and Learning in Higher Educn. FHEA. Postdoctoral trng, Purdue Univ.; University of Sheffield: Lectr, then Reader, Dept of Molecular Biol. and Biotechnol., 1978–90; Chm., Robert Hill Inst., 1989–2003; Res. Advr, Project Sunshine, 2011–. Ext. Advr to Internat. Rice Res. Inst. *Publications:* contribs to jls incl. Nature, Jl Exptl Botany, Jl Biol Chem. *Address:* Department of Molecular Biology and Biotechnology, University of Sheffield, Firth Court, Western Bank, Sheffield S10 2TN.

HORTON, Dr Richard Charles, FRCP; Editor, since 1995, and Publishing and Editorial Director, since 2001, The Lancet; *b* 29 Dec. 1961; *s* of Ole Bjarne Kverneland and Barbara Gwendoline Beddow, and adopted *s* of Charles Kenneth Horton and Clarice Audrey Ward; *m* 1998, Ingrid Johanna Wolfe; one *d. Educ:* Bristol GS; Univ. of Birmingham (BSc 1st, MB ChB Hons). FRCP 1997. Sen. House Officer, Queen Elizabeth Hosp., Birmingham, 1987–88; Clin. Res. Fellow, Royal Free Hosp., London, 1988–90; Asst Editor, 1990–93, N American Editor (New York), 1993–95, The Lancet. Med. Columnist, The Observer, 1996–98. Visiting Professor: Cleveland Clinic, USA, 1997, 2007; Duke Univ., USA, 2000; Yale Univ., 2000; Arthur Thomson Vis. Prof., Univ. of Birmingham, 2000; Arnold Johnson Vis. Prof., McMaster Univ., Canada, 2000; Mayo Clinic, USA, 2002; Potiker Prof., Cleveland Clinic, USA, 2002; Hon. Professor: LSHTM, 2000–; UCL, 2005–; Univ. of Oslo, 2013–. Writer and Presenter, The Citadel (TV), 1998. Member: Exec. Cttee, UK Medical Journalists Assoc., 1991–93, 1995–97; Internat. Cttee of Medical Jl Editors, 1995–; Evaluation Gp, Acheson Ind. Inquiry into Inequalities in Health, 1998; RCP Wkg Party on Defining and Maintaining Professional Values in Medicine, 2004–05; Co-Chair, WHO Scientific Adv. Gp on Internat. Clinical Trials Registration, 2006–; Chair, RCP Wkg Party on Physicians and the Pharmaceutical Industry, 2007–08. Sen. Associate, Nuffield Trust, 2008–; Member: Council, Acad. of Med. Scis, 2010–13; Council, Univ. of Birmingham, 2010–14; Ind. Adv. Gp, WHO AFRO, 2015–. President: World Assoc. of Med. Editors, 1995–96; US Council of Science Editors, 2005–06; Foundn Council, Global Forum for Health Res., 2003–06. Patron, Medsin, 2006–; Chair, Health Metrics Network, 2010–12; Co-Chair, Ind. Expert Advr Gp on women's and children's health, 2012–15 (annual reports, 2012, 2013, 2014). Fellow, Amer. Acad. for Advancement of Sci., 1997; Founder FMedSci 1998. Hon. FRCPCH, 2013. Foreign Associate, US Inst. of Medicine, 2012. Hon. MD: Umeå, 2007; Birmingham, 2008; Gothenburg, 2014. Med. Pubn of the Year, Med. Journalists' Assoc., 2004; Edinburgh Medal, 2007; Dean's Medal, John's Hopkins Sch. of Med., 2009. *Publications:* Second Opinion: doctors, diseases and decisions in modern medicine, 2003; Doctors in Society, 2005; Innovating for Health, 2009; books and articles on cardiovascular pharmacol., gastroenterol., global health and journalology; reviews and essays in New York Review of Books, London Review of Books, TLS. *Recreation:* horizontal reflection. *Address:* The Lancet, 125 London Wall, EC2Y 5AS. *T:* (020) 7424 4929.

HORTON, Roger Graham; Chief Executive Officer, Taylor & Francis Group, since 2003; *b* 11 June 1957; *s* of late Bertram Horton and of Joan Horton; *m* 1986, Deborah; two *d.* Sales and mktg roles with Internat. Thomson, 1977–87; Editl Dir, McGraw-Hill, Europe, 1987–94; Man. Dir, Taylor & Francis, 1994–2003. *Publications:* business and industry related articles. *Recreations:* Reading FC home games fanatic, rock 'n' roll bass player, occasional barn dance caller, golf. *Address:* c/o Taylor & Francis, 2 Park Square, Abingdon, Oxon OX14 4RN. *T:* (020) 7017 6000.

HORTON, Dame Rosemary Anne, (Dame Rosie), DNZM 2011; QSO 2004; QSM 1993; *b* Christchurch, NZ; *d* of Ellis George Moon and Olga Reama Moon (*née* Raphael); *m* 1st, Donald Ronald Keith Smith (marr. diss.); one *d*; 2nd, Henry Michael Horton. Patron: Starship Foundn (Vice-Chm., 1991); NZ Breast Cancer Foundn (Founder Trustee and Chm., 1995–2005; Chm., Bequest Cttee); Rautakauri Music Therapy Trust; Star Jam; World Child Cancer; Ambassador for: Macular Degeneration; Centre for Brain Res., Univ. of Auckland; former Chair: Friends of Starship, NZ Breast Cancer Foundn; Aotea Women's Cttee; Aotea Performing Arts Trust; former Vice Chair, Laura Fergusson Trust (former Chm., Laura Fergusson Women's Cttee); Edge Bd of Mgt. Former Trustee: Arts Regl Service Trust; Parks and Wilderness Trust; SPCA; Dame Malvina Major Trust; Women's Refuge Foundn; Bethany Adv. Bd; Salvation Army; Prince of Wales Trust; Santa Parade Trust; NZ/UK Link Foundn. Distinguished Citizen Award, Auckland City, 2010. Commemoration Medal, 1990. *Recreations:* bridge, collecting Aboriginal art, travel, ballet, opera, theatre. *Address:* 179 Victoria Avenue, Remuera, Auckland, New Zealand. *T:* 274986586. *E:* rosiehorton@ihug.co.nz.

HORTON, Sharon Margaret; *see* Bowles, S. M.

HORVITZ, Prof. (Howard) Robert, PhD; Professor of Biology, Massachusetts Institute of Technology, since 1986; *b* 8 May 1947; *s* of late Oscar Horvitz and of Mary Horvitz; *m* 1993, Martha Constantine Paton; one *d. Educ:* Massachusetts Inst. of Technol. (BS 1968); Harvard Univ. (MA 1972; PhD 1974). Asst Prof. of Biol., 1978–81, Associate Prof. of Biol., 1981–86, MIT; Investigator, Howard Hughes Med. Inst., 1988–. Foreign Mem., Royal Soc., 2009. (Jtly) Nobel Prize in Physiol. or Medicine, 2002. *Address:* Department of Biology, Massachusetts Institute of Technology, 77 Massachusetts Avenue, Cambridge, MA 02139, USA.

HORWELL, Richard Eric; QC 2006; a Recorder, since 2004; *b* 14 Nov. 1953; *s* of John and Edna Horwell; *m* 2002, Lindsay; one *s. Educ:* Ewell Castle Sch.; Council of Legal Educn. Called to the Bar, Gray's Inn, 1976, Bencher, 2009; Jun. Treasury Counsel, 1991–96; Sen. Treasury Counsel, 1996–2002; First Sen. Treasury Counsel, 2002–06. *Recreations:* motor sport, travel, photography, film, dogs. *Address:* 3 Raymond Buildings, Gray's Inn, WC1R 5BH.

HORWICH, Prof. Alan, PhD; FRCR, FMedSci; Professor of Radiotherapy, since 1986, and Dean, 1992–97 and 2005–13, Institute of Cancer Research and Royal Marsden Hospital; *b* 1 June 1948; *s* of William and Audrey Horwich; *m* 1981, Pauline Amanda Barnes; two *s* one *d. Educ:* William Hulme's Grammar Sch., Manchester; University College Hosp. Med. Sch. (MB BS 1971; PhD 1981). MRCP 1974, FRCP 1994; FRCR 1981. Postgrad. medicine, London, 1971–74; Fellowship in Oncology, Harvard, 1975; res. on ribonucleic acid tumour viruses, ICRF, 1976–79; radiation oncology, Royal Marsden Hosp. and Inst. of Cancer Res., 1979–; Dir, Clinical R&D, Royal Marsden Hosp., 1994–2005; Hd, Clinical Labs, Inst. of Cancer Res., 1995–2011. Chm., MRC Testicular Tumour Working Party, 1988–94. Civilian Consultant to RN, 1989–2013. Warden, RCR, 1998–2002. FMedSci 2003. *Publications:* Testicular Cancer: investigation and management, 1991, 2nd edn 1996; Combined Radiotherapy and Chemotherapy in Clinical Oncology, 1992; Oncology: a multidisciplinary text book, 1995; Systemic Treatment of Prostate Cancer, 2010; numerous articles in med. jls on urological cancers and lymphomas. *Address:* Royal Marsden Hospital, Downs Road, Sutton, Surrey SM2 5PT. *T:* (020) 8661 3274.

See also P. G. Horwich.

HORWICH, Prof. Paul Gordon, PhD; Professor of Philosophy, New York University, since 2005; *b* 7 Feb. 1947; *s* of William Horwich and Audrey (*née* Rigby). *Educ:* Brasenose Coll., Oxford (BA Physics); Yale Univ. (MA Physics & Phil.); Cornell Univ. (MA, PhD Phil. 1975). Massachusetts Institute of Technology: Asst Prof. in Philosophy, 1973–80; Associate Prof., 1980–87; Prof. of Philosophy, 1987–95; Prof. of Philosophy, UCL, 1994–2000; Kornblith Prof. of Philosophy, Grad. Center, CUNY, 2000–05. *Publications:* Probability and Evidence, 1982; Asymmetries in Time, 1987; Truth, 1992, 2nd edn 1998; Meaning, 1998; From a Deflationary Point of View, 2004; Reflections on Meaning, 2005; Truth - Meaning - Reality, 2010; Wittgenstein's Metaphilosophy, 2012. *Recreations:* opera, ski-ing, summers in Tuscany. *Address:* Department of Philosophy, New York University, 5 Washington Place, New York, NY 10003, USA. *Club:* Black's.

See also A. Horwich.

HORWITZ, Prof. Frank Martin, PhD; Professor of International Human Resource Management, Cranfield School of Management, Cranfield University, since 2009 (Director, 2009–13); *b* Bloemfontein, S Africa; *m* 1976, Dianne; one *s* two *d. Educ:* Grey Coll.; Univ. of Witwatersrand (BA (SocSci); PhD 1985). Higher Dip. Personnel Mgt; Masters in Personnel Mgt. Sen. Lectr, Wits Business Sch., Univ. of Witwatersrand, 1982–83; Graduate School of Business, University of Cape Town, 1981–2009: Dir, MBA Course, 1986–91; Dir of Res., 1993–2001; Acad. Dir, 2002–03; Dir, 2004–09. Visiting Professor: Haskayne Sch. of Business, Univ. of Calgary, 1992–93; Nanyang Business Sch., Singapore, 2001–02; Rotterdam Sch. of Mgt, Erasmus Univ., 2003–05. Mem. Bd of cos; Consultant in organisational change and human capital strategies for cos in Canada, Namibia, SA and UK. *Publications:* (jtly) Managing Resourceful People, 1991; (jtly) On the Edge: how South African companies cope with change, 1992; (jtly) Employment Equity and Affirmative Action: an international comparison, 2003; (jtly) Managing Human Resources in Africa, 2004; contrib. articles to learned jls incl. Human Resources Mgt Jl, Internat. Jl Cross-Cultural Mgt, Jl Internat. Compensation and Benefits, Business in the Contemporary World, Internat. Jl Human Resource Mgt, Internat. Jl Manpower. *Recreations:* cycling, good wine, playing guitar. *Address:* Cranfield School of Management, Cranfield University, Cranfield, Bedford MK43 0AL.

HORWOOD, Dr Joseph William, FSS, CStat; FIMA; CMath, CSci; Chief Scientist, 1994–2010, non-executive Director, 2010–12, Centre for Environment, Fisheries and Aquaculture Science; Chief Fisheries Science Adviser, Department for Environment, Food and Rural Affairs, 1994–2010; *b* Birmingham, 1948; *s* of Jennifer Horwood. *Educ:* King Edward VI Sch., Stratford upon Avon; Univ. of London (BSc ext.); Univ. of E Anglia (ScD 1992). FSS 1970; CStat 1993; FIMA 1992; CMath 1992; CSci 2005. Marine and Fisheries Scientist, CEFAS, 1970–2010, now Emeritus Fellow. Member: Scientific Cttee, Internat. Whaling Commn, 1976–89; Scientific, Tech. and Econ. Cttee on Fisheries, EU, 1990–92; UK Marine Sci. Co-ordination Cttee, 2008–10; Marine Protected Areas Sub-Cttee, JNCC, 2009–. Chm., Sci. Adv. Cttee, CEFAS, 2006–12. International Council for Exploration of the Sea: Mem., Adv. Cttee on Fisheries Mgt, 1990–93; Vice Pres., 2000–03; Pres., 2006–09. Mem. Bd, Marine Biol Assoc., 1998–2001. Natural England: non-exec. Dir, 2009–; Mem., Audit and Risk Cttee, 2010–11; Mem., Sci. Adv. Cttee, 2010–; Mem., Jt Nature Conservancy Council, 2014–; Dir, JNCC Support Co., 2014–. *Publications:* The Sei Whale: population biology, ecology and management, 1987; Population Biology and Exploitation of the Minke Whale, 1989; contrib. scientific pubns. *Recreation:* being outside. *Address:* CEFAS Laboratory, Pakefield Road, Lowestoft NR33 0HT. *T:* (01502) 524563, *Fax:* (01502) 513865. *E:* Joe.horwood@cefas.co.uk. *Clubs:* Southwold Golf; Rookery Park Golf.

HORWOOD, Martin Charles; *b* 12 Oct. 1962; *s* of Don Horwood, ISO and Nina Horwood; *m* 1995, Dr Shona Arora; one *s* one *d. Educ:* Queen's Coll., Oxford (BA 1984). Account Exec., Ted Bates Advertising, 1985–86; Dir of Develt, British Humanist Assoc., 1986–88; Creative Co-ordinator, Help the Aged, 1988–90; Donor Marketing Manager, Oxfam, 1990–95; Dir of Communications and Fundraising, Oxfam (India), 1995–96; Dir of Fundraising, Alzheimer's Soc., 1996–2001; Sen. Consultant, 2001–03, Hd of Consultancy, 2003–05, Target Direct Marketing. MP (Lib Dem) Cheltenham, 2005–15; contested (Lib Dem) same seat, 2015. Lib Dem spokesman on envmt, 2006–10. Member: Select Cttee on Communities and Local Govt (formerly ODPM), 2005–07; Envmtl Audit Select Cttee, 2007–10; Sec., All-Party Gp for corporate responsibility, 2005; Chm., All-Party Gp for tribal peoples, 2007–15; Chairman: Lib Dem Transport Cttee, 2010–11; Lib Dem Internat. Affairs Cttee, 2011–15. *Recreations:* cycling, drawing, astronomy.

HORWOOD-SMART, Rosamund, (Mrs R. O. Bernays); QC 1996; a Recorder, since 1995; *b* 21 Sept. 1951; *d* of late John Horwood-Smart and Sylvia Horwood-Smart; *m* 1st, 1983, Richard Blackford (marr. diss. 1994); one *s* one *d*; 2nd, 1996, Richard O. Bernays. *Educ:* Felixstowe Coll.; Cambridgeshire High Sch. for Girls; Inns of Court Sch. of Law. Called to the Bar, Inner Temple, 1974, Bencher, 1998. Trustee: Nat. Music Day, 1992–98; Prisoners of Conscience Appeal Fund, 1990–2001 (Chm., then Patron); Toyota Trevelyan-shi Trust, 1990–2007; Temple Music Foundn, 2006–; Handel House, 2008–; Longborough Fest. Opera, 2014–. Patron, New English Ballet Theatre, 2011–. Vice Pres., Internat. Students House, 2007– (Gov., 1978–2007; Chm., 2001–07). *Recreations:* music, gardening, theatre.

HOSE, John Horsley, CBE 1987; Forest Craftsman, Forestry Commission, 1975–88 (Forest Worker, 1949, Skilled Forest Worker, 1950); President, National Union of Agricultural and Allied Workers, 1978–82; *b* 21 March 1928; *s* of Harry and Margaret Eleanor Hose; *m* 1st, 1967, Margaret Winifred Gaskin (marr. diss. 1987); 2nd, 1987, Linda Sharon Morris. *Educ:* Sneinton Boulevard Council Sch.; Nottingham Bluecoat Sch. Architects' Junior Asst, 1943–46. National Service, with Royal Engineers, 1946–48. Chm., Nat. Trade Gp, Agricultural and Allied Workers/TGWU, 1982–86 (Mem., 1982–89); Mem., Gen. Exec. Council, TGWU, 1986–88. *Recreations:* reading, drinking real ale. *Address:* St Martin's Rectory, St Agnes Close, Wigman Road, Bilborough, Nottingham NG8 4BJ. *T:* (0115) 929 1534.

HOSIE, Stewart; MP (SNP) Dundee East, since 2005; *b* 3 Jan. 1963; *m* 1997, Shona Robison, *qv*; one *d. Educ:* Carnoustie High Sch.; Dundee Coll. of Technol. Gp Inf. Systems Manager, MIH, 1988–93; systems analyst, 1993–96; Year 2000/EMU Project Manager, Stakis/Hilton, 1996–2000. Nat. Sec., 1999–2003, Dep. Leader, 2014–, SNP. Contested (SNP): Kirkcaldy, 1992, 1997; Kirkcaldy, Scottish Parlt, 1999. *Address:* (office) 8 Old Glamis Road, Dundee DD3 8HP; House of Commons, SW1A 0AA.

HOSKER, Edmund Nigel Ronald; Director, International Energy, EU and Energy Resilience (formerly Energy Security), Department of Energy and Climate Change, since 2011; *b* 25 April 1958; *s* of Ronald Reece Hosker and Hilda Gertrude Hosker (*née* Harrington); *m* 1983, Elizabeth Miranda Thornely; three *d. Educ:* Slough Grammar Sch.; St Catharine's Coll., Cambridge (BA Hons English 1979). Joined Department of Trade and Industry, 1979: Private Sec. to Minister for Industry and subseq. to Sec. of State for Trade and Industry, 1983–84; Principal, 1984; on secondment to British Embassy, Washington, 1990–94; Asst Sec., 1994; transf. to Cabinet Office, 1995–97; Dir of Finance, DTI, 1997–2000; Dir, Finance and Resource Mgt, DTI, 2000–02; on secondment to Scottish Power, 2003; Dir, Europe and World Trade, DTI, subseq. BERR, 2003–08; Dir, Energy Markets Unit, BERR, 2008; acting Dir Gen. for Corporate Services, then Corporate Support and Shared Services, later Corporate and Professional Services, subseq. Acting Chief Operating Officer, DECC, 2008–11. Chair, Governing Bd, Internat. Energy Agency, 2013–. *Address:* Department of Energy and Climate Change, 3 Whitehall Place, SW1A 2AW.

HOSKER, Sir Gerald (Albery), KCB 1995 (CB 1987); HM Procurator General, Treasury Solicitor and Queen's Proctor, 1992–95; *b* 28 July 1933; *s* of Leslie Reece Hosker and Constance Alice Rose Hosker (*née* Hubbard); *m* 1956, Rachel Victoria Beatrice Middleton; one *s* one *d. Educ:* Berkhamsted Sch., Berkhamsted, Herts; Law Soc. Coll. of Law. Admitted Solicitor, 1956; Corporate Secretary 1964; Associate of the Faculty of Secretaries and

Administrators 1964. Articled to Derrick Bridges & Co., 1951–56; with Clifford-Turner & Co., 1957–59; entered Treasury Solicitor's Dept as Legal Asst, 1960; Sen. Legal Asst, 1966; Asst Solicitor, 1973; Under Sec. (Legal), 1982; Dep. Treasury Solicitor, 1984–87; Solicitor to the DTI, 1987–92. Conducted enquiry into: Customs and Excise aspects of Simon de Danser case, 1999; C. W. Cheney Pension Fund for DSS, 2001; Public Inquiry Comr, Falkland Is, 1999–2000. Dir, RAFM Investments Ltd, 2003–09. Mem. Bd, Inst. of Advanced Legal Studies, Univ. of London, 1992–95; Governor, Lyonsdown Sch., New Barnet, 1996–2006 and 2009–12. Trustee, RAF Mus., 1998–2009; Mem., Governing Bodies Forum, Mus Assoc., 2005–09. FRSA 1964. Hon. QC 1991. *Recreations:* the study of biblical prophecy, walking. *Address:* (office) c/o Treasury Solicitor, One Kemble Street, WC2B 4TS. *Club:* Royal Over-Seas League.

HOSKING, Barbara Nancy, CBE 1999 (OBE 1985); Deputy Chairman, Westcountry Television, 1997–99 (non-executive Director, 1992–99); *b* 4 Nov. 1926; *d* of late William Henry Hosking and Ada Kathleen Hosking (*née* Murrish). *Educ:* West Cornwall School for Girls, Penzance; Hillcroft College, Surbiton; and by my friends. Secretary to Town Clerk, Council of Isles of Scilly, and local corresp. for BBC and Western Morning News, 1945–47; Editl Asst, The Circle, Odeon and Gaumont cinemas, 1947–50; Asst to Inf. Officer, Labour Party, 1952–55; Asst to Gen. Manager, Uruwira Minerals Ltd, Tanzania, 1955–57; Res. Officer, Broadcasting Section, Labour Party, 1958–65; Press and Inf. Officer posts, Civil Service, 1965–77; Controller of Inf. Services, IBA, 1977–86; Political Consultant, Yorkshire TV, 1987–92. Mem. (Lab), Islington BC, 1962–64. Non-exec. Dir, Camden and Islington Community Health Services NHS Trust, 1992–93. Pres., Media Soc., 1987–88; Jt Vice-Chm., NCVO, 1987–92. Mem. Council, Family Policy Studies Centre, 1994–97. Trustee: Charities Aid Foundn, 1987–92; 300 Gp, 1988–91; Nat. Literacy Trust, 1993–99. Associate, Women's Advertising Club of London, 1994–. Patron, Clean-Break Theatre Co., 1992–. Hon. Vice Pres., London Cornish Assoc., 1992; Bard, Gorsedd Kernow. Occasional radio broadcaster. FRTS 1988; FRSA (Mem. Council, 1992–96). DUniv Ulster, 1996. Special citation, Internat. Women's Forum, NY, 1983, Boston, 1996. *Publications:* contribs to Punch, New Scientist, Spectator. *Recreations:* opera, lieder, watching politics. *Address:* 15 Regency Court, 4 Regency Street, SW1P 4BZ. *T:* (020) 7821 1207. *Club:* Reform.

HOSKING, Prof. Geoffrey Alan, OBE 2015; FBA 1993; FRHistS; Professor of Russian History, 1984–2007, now Emeritus, and Leverhulme Personal Research Professor, 1999–2004, University College London; *b* 28 April 1942; *s* of Stuart William Steggall Hosking and Jean Ross Hosking; *m* 1970, Anne Lloyd Hirst; two *d. Educ:* Maidstone Grammar Sch.; King's Coll., Cambridge (MA, PhD); St Antony's Coll., Oxford. FRHistS 1998. Asst Lectr in Government, 1966–68, Lectr in Government, 1968–71, Univ. of Essex; Vis. Lectr in Political Science, Univ. of Wisconsin, Madison, 1971–72; Lectr in History, Univ. of Essex, 1972–76; Sen. Research Fellow, Russian Inst., Columbia Univ., New York, 1976; Sen. Lectr and Reader in Russian History, Univ. of Essex, 1976–84; Dep. Dir, SSEES, London Univ., 1996–98. Vis. Prof., Slavisches Inst., Univ. of Cologne, 1980–81; Mem., IAS, Princeton, 2006–07. BBC Reith Lectr, 1988 (The Rediscovery of Politics: authority, culture and community in the USSR). Member: Council, Writers and Scholars Educnl Trust, 1985–2007; Overseas Policy Cttee, British Acad., 1994–2000; Council, RHistS, 2002–06; Jury, Booker Prize for Russian Fiction, 1993. Member: Internat. Academic Council, Mus. of Contemporary History (formerly Mus. of the Revolution), Moscow, 1994–; Admin. Bd, Moscow Sch. of Pol Studies, 1992–2000; Exec. Cttee, Britain-Russia Centre, 1994–2000. Trustee, J. S. Mill Inst., 1992–96; Governor, Camden Sch. for Girls, 1989–94. Member: Editl Bd, Jl of Contemporary History, 1988–99; Editl Cttee, Nations and Nationalism, 1994–2012; Editl Bd, Nationalities Papers, 1997–2005; Editl Bd, Reviews in History, 1999–2004; Editl Bd, Ab Imperio, 2002–; Editl Bd, Otechestvennaia Istoriia, 2007–12. Hon. Dr Russian Acad. Scis, 2000. *Publications:* The Russian Constitutional Experiment: Government and Duma 1907–14, 1973; Beyond Socialist Realism: Soviet fiction since Ivan Denisovich, 1980; A History of the Soviet Union, 1985, 3rd edn 1992 (Los Angeles Times Hist. Book Prize, 1986); The Awakening of the Soviet Union, 1990, 2nd edn 1991; (with J. Aves and P. J. S. Duncan) The Road to Post-Communism: independent political movements in the Soviet Union 1985–91, 1992; Russia: people and Empire 1552–1917, 1997; (ed with George Schöpflin) Myths and Nationhood, 1997; (ed with Robert Service) Russian Nationalism Past and Present, 1998; (ed with Robert Service) Reinterpreting Russia, 1999; Russia and the Russians: a history, 2001 (history prize, Ind. Publisher Book Awards, USA, 2002), 2nd edn 2012; Rulers and Victims: the Russians in the Soviet Union, 2006 (Alec Nove Book Prize, 2008); Trust: money, markets and society, 2010; Russian History: a very short introduction, 2012; Trust: a history, 2014. *Recreations:* music, chess, walking. *Address:* School of Slavonic and East European Studies, University College London, Gower Street, WC1E 6BT. *T:* (020) 7267 5543; Flat 15, Julian Court, 150 Camden Road, NW1 9HU. *E:* geoffreyhosking@mac.com.

HOSKING, John Everard, CBE 1990; JP; DL; Chairman, Agra Europe (London) Ltd, 1989–94 (Director and Chief Executive, 1974–89); Vice-President, Magistrates' Association, since 1990 (Chairman of Council, 1987–90); *b* 23 Oct. 1929; *s* of J. Everard Hosking, OBE and E. Margaret (*née* Shaxson); *m* 1953, Joan Cecily Whitaker, BSc; two *s. Educ:* Marlborough Coll.; Wye Coll., London Univ. (BScA 1953). NDA 1954. Farming and forestry in Kent, 1953–69; Man. Dir, Eastes and Loud Ltd, 1965–69; Director: Newgrain-Kent, 1969–74; Ashford Corn Exchange Co., 1965–69; Agroup Ltd, 1987–94; Bureau Européen de Recherches SA, 1987–90; European Intelligence Ltd, 1987–94. Tax Comr, 1980–2004. Chairman: Centre for European Agricultural Studies Assoc., 1977–83; European Agricultural Outlook Conference, 1981–95; Kent Magistrates' Courts Cttee, 1984–88; Member: Kent Police Authority, 1970–74; Lord Chancellor's Adv. Cttee on the Appointment of Magistrates, 1977–89; Central Council, Magistrates' Courts Cttees, 1980–83; Bar Council Professional Conduct Cttee, 1983–86; Senate of Inns of Court and the Bar Disciplinary Tribunal, 1983–86; Council, Commonwealth Magistrates' and Judges' Assoc., 1989–92; Lord Chief Justice's Working Party on Mode of Trial, 1989; Lord Chancellor's Adv. Cttee on Legal Educn and Conduct, 1991–94. Pres., Kent Magistrates' Assoc., 2001–12, now Life Vice-Pres. (Chm., 1973–78). Pres., Wye Coll. Agricola Club, 1995–2004. Vice-Patron, Ashford Community Arts Trust, 2001–11. Governor: Ashford Sch., 1976–2006 (Chm., 1994–2001); Wye Coll., Univ. of London, 1995–2000; Mem. Governing Council, Church Schs Co., 1999–2001. Ed., Common Agricl Policy Monitor, 1994–2011. JP Kent, 1962 (Chm., Ashford Bench, 1975–85); DL Kent, 1992. British Univs Ploughing Champion, 1952. *Publications:* (ed) Rural Response to the Resource Crisis in Europe, 1981; The Agricultural Industry of West Germany, 1990. *Recreations:* the arts, the countryside. *Address:* Pett House, Charing, Kent. *Club:* Farmers.

HOSKINS, Sir Brian (John), Kt 2007; CBE 1998; PhD; FRS 1988; Chair (formerly Director), Grantham Institute for Climate Change, Imperial College London, since 2008; Professor of Meteorology, University of Reading, since 1981; *b* 17 May 1945; *s* of George Frederick Hoskins and Kathleen Matilda Louise Hoskins; *m* 1968, Jacqueline Holmes; two *d. Educ:* Bristol Grammar Sch.; Trinity Hall, Cambridge (BA 1966; MA, PhD 1970; Hon. Fellow 2011). FRMetS 1970 (Hon. FRMets 2001); Fellow, Amer. Meteorol Soc., 1985 (Hon. Mem., 2014); FAAAS 2012; FEI 2012. Post-doctoral Fellow, Nat. Center for Atmospheric Res., Boulder, Colo, 1970–71; Vis. Scientist, GFD Program, Univ. of Princeton, 1972–73; Univ. of Reading: Post-doctoral Fellow, 1971–72, Gp Leader, 1973–, Atmospheric Modelling Gp; Reader in Atmospheric Modelling, 1976–81; Head, Dept of Meteorol., 1990–96. Royal Soc. Res. Prof., 2001–10. Special Advr to Sec. of State for Transport, 1990. Meteorological Office: Chm., SAC, 1995–2013; non-exec. Dir, 2000–13. Member: NERC, 1988–94; Jt Scientific Cttee, World Climate Res. Prog., 1995–2004 (Vice Chm., 2000–04); Royal Commn on Envmtl Pollution, 1998–2005; Intergovtl Panel on Climate Change, 2005–07; UK Govt Climate Change Cttee, 2008–; Mem. Council, 2000–01, Chair, Global Envmtl Res. Cttee, 1999–2006, Royal Soc. Pres., IAMAS, 1991–95. Mem., Academia Europaea, 1989; Corresp. Academician, Real Acad. de Ciencias y Artes de Barcelona, 1994; Foreign Associate, US NAS, 2002; Foreign Mem., Chinese Acad. of Scis, 2002; FAAAS 2012. Lectures: Starr Meml, MIT, 1989; Bernard Haurwitz Meml, Amer. Meteorol Soc., 1995; Welsh, Univ. of Toronto, 2006; 12th IMO Lectr, 2011; Bjerknes, Amer. Geophysical Union, 2014. Hon. Mem., Amer. Meteorol Soc., 2014. Hon. FCGI 2011. Hon. DSc: Bristol, 2008; UEA, 2009. Royal Meteorological Society: Pres., 1998–2000; Symons Meml Lecture, 1982; L. F. Richardson Prize, 1972; Buchan Prize, 1976; Symons Medal, 2006; Charles Chree Silver Medal, Inst. of Physics, 1987; Carl-Gustaf Rossby Res. Medal, Amer. Meteorol Soc., 1988; Vilhelm Bjerknes Prize, Eur. Geophys. Soc., 1997; Buys Ballot Medal, 2014; Gold Medal, Internat. Union of Geodesy and Geophysics, 2015. *Publications:* (ed with R. P. Pearce) Large-scale Dynamical Processes in the Atmosphere, 1983; (with Dr I. N. James) Dynamics of the Midlatitude Atmosphere, 2014; 180 papers in meteorol jls. *Recreations:* music, sport, gardening. *Address:* Anchor House, Green Lane, Pangbourne, Berks RG8 7BG. *T:* (0118) 984 1308.

HOSKINS, Paul Trevor; Music Director, Rambert (formerly Rambert Dance Company), since 1996; *b* Benghazi, Libya, 15 Oct. 1966; *s* of Trevor Hoskins and Jenny Hoskins (*née* Lloyd); *m* 1992, Clare Holmes; one *s* two *d. Educ:* Christ's Hosp. Sch., Horsham; Gonville and Caius Coll., Cambridge (BA Hons 1989); Royal Coll. of Music. Conductor, Cambridge New Music Players, 1992; as freelance conductor, débuts with: English Nat. Ballet, 1993; Opera Factory, 1994; BBC Nat. Orch. of Wales, 1998; Royal Ballet, 2001; New York City Ballet, 2001; San Francisco Ballet, 2001; Royal Swedish Ballet, 2008; Swedish Radio Symphony Orch., 2010. Gov., Childs Hill Sch., 2006–. *Recreations:* family, home, sport, crosswords, cinema. *Address:* 99 Upper Ground, SE1 9PP. *E:* paul.hoskins@rambert.org.uk.

HOSKYNS, Sir Robin Chevallier, 18th Bt *cr* 1676, of Harewood, Herefordshire; *b* 5 July 1989; *o s* of Sir (Edwyn) Wren Hoskyns, 17th Bt, FRCPCH and of Jane Hoskyns (*née* Sellers); *S* father, 2015. *Heir: uncle* John Chandos Hoskyns [*b* 4 April 1961; two *d* by Jennifer Biondi].

HOSSAIN, Ajmalul; QC 1998; *b* 18 Oct. 1950; *s* of late Asrarul Hossain, barrister and Senior Advocate, Supreme Court of Bangladesh, and Rabia Hossain; *m* 1970, Nasreen Ahmed; two *s. Educ:* King's Coll., London (LLB Hons 1976; LLM 1977). FCIArb 1994. Called to the Bar, Lincoln's Inn, 1976 (Buchanan Prize), Bencher, 2012; SE Circuit; in practice at the Bar, Bangladesh, 1977–, England, 1978–; Supreme Court of Bangladesh: enrolled in High Court Div., 1977, Appellate Div., 1986; Senior Advocate, 1998. Pt-time Chm., Southampton Reg., Employment (formerly Industrial) Tribunals, 1995–2005. Member: Internat. Court of Arbitration, 2006–09, Commn on Arbitration, 2009–, Internat. Chamber of Commerce, Paris; Code of Conduct Commn, Internat. Cricket Council, 2006–; Ethics Cttee, Fédération Internationale de l'Automobile, Paris, 2013–. Member: Supreme Court Bar Assoc., Bangladesh, 1986; Chancery Bar Assoc., 2002. Fellow, Soc. for Advanced Legal Studies, 2000. *Recreations:* travelling, bridge. *Address:* Selborne Chambers, 10 Essex Street, WC2R 3AA. *T:* (020) 7420 9500, *Fax:* (020) 7420 9555. *E:* ajmalul.hossain@selbornechambers.co.uk; A. Hossain & Associates, 3B Outer Circular Road, Maghbazar, Dhaka 1217, Bangladesh. *T:* (2) 8311492, *Fax:* (2) 9344356.

HOSSAIN, (Syed Mohammad) Sa'ad (Ansarul); QC 2013; *b* Belfast, 11 Aug. 1971; *s* of Quamer and Mary Hossain; *m* 2000, Anna Thomas; two *s* one *d. Educ:* Methodist Coll., Belfast; Gonville and Caius Coll., Cambridge (BSc Hons Natural Scis 1992). Called to the Bar, Gray's Inn, 1995; in practice as barrister, specialising in commercial law, 1996–. *Recreations:* running, surfing, tennis, trekking. *Address:* One Essex Court, Temple, EC4Y 9AR. *T:* (020) 7583 2000, *Fax:* (020) 7583 0118. *E:* shossain@oeclaw.co.uk.

HOTHAM, family name of **Baron Hotham**.

HOTHAM, 8th Baron *cr* 1797; **Henry Durand Hotham;** DL; Bt 1621; *b* 3 May 1940; *s* of 7th Baron Hotham, CBE, and Lady Letitia Sibell Winifred Cecil (*d* 1992), *er d* of 5th Marquess of Exeter, KG; *S* father, 1967; *m* 1972, Alexandra Stirling Home, *d* of late Maj. Andrew S. H. Drummond Moray; two *s* one *d. Educ:* Eton; Cirencester Agricultural Coll. Late Lieut, Grenadier Guards; ADC to Governor of Tasmania, 1963–66. DL Humberside, 1981. *Heir: s* Hon. William Beaumont Hotham [*b* 13 Oct. 1972; *m* 2005, Katrina Heyward; one *s* two *d*]. *Address:* The Dower House, Mere Lane, South Dalton, Beverley, E Yorks HU17 7PL; Scorborough Hall, Driffield, Yorks YO25 9AZ.

HOTHFIELD, 6th Baron *cr* 1881; **Anthony Charles Sackville Tufton;** DL; Bt 1851; *b* 21 Oct. 1939; *s* of 5th Baron Hothfield, TD and Evelyn Margarette (*d* 1989), *e d* of late Eustace Charles Mordaunt; *S* father, 1991; *m* 1975, Lucinda Marjorie, *d* of Captain Timothy John Gurney; one *s* one *d. Educ:* Eton; Magdalene Coll., Cambridge (MA). MICE. DL Cumbria, 2004. *Recreations:* Real tennis, lawn tennis, bridge, shooting. *Heir: s* Hon. William Sackville Tufton, MD [*b* 14 Nov. 1977; *m* 2006, Elizabeth, *o d* of Robin Burgess; two *s* one *d*]. *Address:* Drybeck Hall, Appleby, Cumbria CA16 6TF. *Clubs:* Hawks (Cambridge); Jesters; almost every Real tennis club.

HOTSPUR; *see* McGrath, J. A.

HOTTEN, Christopher Peter; QC 1994; a Recorder, since 1990; *b* 7 July 1949; *s* of Alan John Hotten and Ida Lydia Hotten; *m* 1973, Lone Elisabeth Nielsen; one *s* two *d. Educ:* Hornchurch Grammar Sch.; Leicester Univ. (LLB). Called to the Bar, Inner Temple, 1972. *Recreations:* golf, going to the gym. *Address:* No5 Chambers, Fountain Court, Steelhouse Lane, Birmingham B4 6DR. *Club:* Stetchford (Birmingham).

HOTUNG, Sir Joseph (Edward), Kt 1993; Chairman, Ho Hung Hing Estates Ltd, 1962–2011; *b* 25 May 1930; *s* of Edward Sai-kim Hotung and Maud Alice (*née* Newman); *m* 1957, Mary Catherine McGinley (marr. diss. 1969); two *s* two *d. Educ:* St Francis Xavier Coll., Shanghai; St Louis Coll., Tientsin; Catholic Univ. of America (BA); Univ. of London (LLB ext.). With Marine Midland Bank, 1957–60. Director: HSBC Hldgs plc, 1991–98; Hongkong & Shanghai Banking Corp. Ltd, 1991–96; Hongkong Electric Hldgs Ltd, 1984–97; China & Eastern Investment Co. Ltd, 1989–98. Member: Judicial Services Commn, Hong Kong, 1990–97; Inland Revenue Bd of Review, Hong Kong, 1989–95. University of Hong Kong: Mem. Council, 1984–96; Chm. and Trustee, Staff Terminal Benefits Scheme, 1987–96; Mem. Council, Business Sch., 1990–96; Chm., Arts Develt Council, Hong Kong, 1994–96; Dir, E Asian Hist. of Sci. Foundn, 1991–2001; Member: Governing Body, SOAS, 1997–2005; St George's Hosp. Med. Sch., London Univ., 2001–07. Trustee: British Mus., 1994–2004, now Trustee Emeritus; Asia Soc., NY, 1991–97; MMA, NY, 2000–05, now Trustee Emeritus. Hon. Mem., Freer Gall. of Art and Sackler Gall., Washington, 1990. Honorary Fellow: Hong Kong Univ., 1995; SOAS, 2009. Hon. DLitt Hong Kong, 1997; Hon. DSc Econs London, 2003. NACF Award, 1993. *Recreation:* Oriental art. *Address:* 1203 Prince's Building, 10 Chater Road, Central, Hong Kong. *T:* 25229929. *Clubs:* Reform, Beefsteak; Hong Kong (Hong Kong); Century Assoc. (New York).

HOUGH, Prof. James, OBE 2013; PhD; FRS 2003; FRSE; CPhys, FInstP; FRAS; Kelvin Professor of Natural Philosophy, 2009–11, now Emeritus (Professor of Experimental Physics, 1986–2009), Associate Director, Institute for Gravitational Research, since 2009 (Director, 2000–09), and Research Professor in Natural Philosophy, since 2010, University of Glasgow; *b* 6 Aug. 1945; *s* of Frederick and Lillias Hough; *m* 1972, Anne Park McNab (*d* 2000); one *s* one *d*. *Educ:* Univ. of Glasgow (BSc 1st Cl. Hons Natural Philosophy 1967; PhD 1971). FInstP 1993; CPhys 2002. University of Glasgow: Res. Fellow, 1970–72; Lectr in Natural Philosophy, 1972–83; Sen. Lectr, 1983–86. Chief Exec., Scottish Univs Physics Alliance, 2011–15. Vis. Fellow, JILA, Univ. of Colorado, 1983; PPARC Sen. Fellow, 1997–2000. RSE GV Prize Lectr, 2008. Member: PPARC, 2005–07; Scottish Science Advrs Council, 2010–15; Council, Inst. of Physics, 2011–15. FRAS 1983; FRSE 1991; FAPS 2001; FRSA 2012. Max Planck Res. Prize, 1991; Duddell Medal and Prize, Inst. of Physics, 2004. *Publications:* contribs to learned jls and to books and conf. reports. *Recreations:* sports cars, photography. *Address:* Institute for Gravitational Research, Department of Physics and Astronomy, University of Glasgow, Glasgow G12 8QQ. *T:* (0141) 330 4706, *Fax:* (0141) 330 6833. *E:* j.hough@physics.gla.ac.uk.

HOUGH, Prof. James Harley, PhD; CPhys, FInstP; FRAS; Professor of Astrophysics, University of Hertfordshire (formerly Hatfield Polytechnic), since 1989 (Director of Astronomy Research, 2003–10); *b* 2 July 1943; *s* of John Harley Hough and Sarah Ann (*née* Lomax); *m* 1966, Monica Jane Dent; one *s* one *d*. *Educ:* Prince Henry's GS, Otley, Yorks; Univ. of Leeds (BSc 1st Cl. Hons; PhD 1967). FRAS 1997; FInstP 1998. Res. Fellow, Univ. of Calgary, 1967–71; SERC Res. Fellow, Univ. of Durham, 1971–72; Hatfield Polytechnic, subseq. Univ. of Hertfordshire: Lectr, 1972–83; Reader in Astronomy, 1983–89; Hd of Physical Scis, 1987–98; Dean of Natural Scis, 1998–2003. Particle Physics and Astronomy Research Council: Mem. Council 1997–2000; Chm., Educn and Trng Panel, 1998–2001; Mem. or Chm., numerous SERC/PPARC Cttees and Bds, 1980–. Herschel Medal, RAS, 2010. *Publications:* PPARC reports on future of UK Ground-Based Astronomy; numerous scientific papers in learned jls, mostly on active galaxies, star formation, interstellar dust, astronomical polarimetry. *Address:* Centre for Astrophysics Research, Science & Technology Research Institute, University of Hertfordshire, Hatfield AL10 9AB. *T:* (01707) 284500.

HOUGH, Jonathan Anthony; QC 2014; *b* Colchester, 3 June 1973; *s* of Kenneth and Ellen Josephine Hough; *m* 2005, Caroline Elizabeth Brennan; one *d*. *Educ:* Bradford Grammar Sch.; St Hugh's Coll., Oxford (BA 1st Cl; MA); City Univ. (DipLaw). Called to the Bar, Middle Temple, 1997; in practice as barrister, specialising in commercial, public and administrative law, 1997–. *Publications:* (ed) Jackson & Powell on Professional Liability, 7th edn 2012. *Recreations:* theatre, ski-ing, riding. *Address:* 4 New Square, Lincoln's Inn, WC2A 3RJ. *T:* (020) 7822 2000, *Fax:* (020) 7822 2001. *E:* j.hough@4newsquare.com. *Club:* Garrick.

HOUGH, Julia Marie, (Judy); *see* Taylor, Judy.

HOUGH, Robert Eric, CBE 2015; DL; Chairman, Northwest Regional Development Agency, 2009–12 (Board Member, 2007–12); *b* 18 July 1945; *s* of Gordon Hough and Joyce Hough (*née* Davies); *m* 1975, Pauline Elizabeth Arch; two *s*. *Educ:* William Hulme's Grammar Sch., Manchester; Univ. of Bristol (LLB 1967). Admitted solicitor, 1970; NP, 1982–92; Partner, Slater Heelis, solicitors, Manchester, 1974–89; Peel Holdings: Dir, 1986–; Exec. Dep. Chm., 1989–2002; non-exec. Dep. Chm., 2002–09; Manchester Ship Canal Company: non-exec. Chm., 1987–89; Exec. Chm., 1989–2002; Chairman: Liverpool Airport Ltd, 1997–2009, 2014–; Doncaster Sheffield Airport, 1999–2009, 2012–; Durham Tees Valley Airport, 2002–09, 2012–. Non-executive Chairman: New East Manchester Ltd, 2002–10; Cheshire Building Soc., 2006–08 (non-exec. Dir, 2002–08); Turley Associates Ltd, 2008–14 (non-exec. Dir, 2003–14); non-executive Director: Brammer plc, 1993–2003 (non-exec. Dep. Chm., 1998–2003); PJ Kennedy Investments Ltd, 1997–2011; Alfred McAlpine plc, 2003–08; Styles & Wood Gp plc, 2006–; Provident Financial plc, 2007–13. Mem., 2000–04, Mem. Exec. Bd, 2006–07, NW Regl Assembly; Mem., NW Regl Leaders Bd, 2013–. Pres., Manchester Chamber of Commerce, 1994–95; Chm., Organising Cttee, 1995–99, Vice-Pres., 1999–2002, Manchester Commonwealth Games 2002; Chairman: NW Business Leadership Team, 2000–03; Liverpool City Reg. Local Enterprise Partnership, 2012–. Member: Learning and Skills Council, 2009–10; Adv. Council, Tate Liverpool, 2013–. Gov., Univ. of Manchester, 2005– (Dep. Chm. Govs, 2012–). Mem., Law Soc. DL 1997, High Sheriff 2004, Gtr Manchester. Hon. DBA Manchester Metropolitan, 1996; Hon. DLitt Salford, 1996. *Recreations:* golf, gardening, walking. *Address:* Peel Holdings, Peel Dome, The Trafford Centre, Manchester M17 8PL. *T:* (0161) 629 8202, *Fax:* (0161) 629 8333. *E:* rhough@peel.co.uk. *Club:* Hale Golf.

HOUGH, Stephen, CBE 2014; concert pianist; composer; *b* 22 Nov. 1961. *Educ:* Chetham's Sch. Music, Manchester; Royal Northern Coll. of Music (Fellow, 1993); Juilliard Sch. Numerous recitals and concerto appearances with LSO, LPO, RPO, Philharmonia, Chicago SO, Philadelphia Orchestra, Cleveland Orchestra, NY Philharmonic, LA Philharmonic, San Francisco SO, Boston SO, Pittsburgh SO, Orchestre Nat. de France, Deutsches Symphonie Orchester, Berlin Philharmonic, Russian Nat. Orchestra; festival performances incl.: Ravinia, Mostly Mozart, Waldbühne, Hollywood Bowl, Blossom, Proms, Le Grange de Meslay, La Roque d'Antheron, Edinburgh, Sapporo, Salzburg, Tanglewood. *Recordings:* Hummel Piano Concertos and Sonatas; 3 Liszt Recitals; 3 Piano Albums; Schumann Recital; Brahms Piano Concertos Nos 1 and 2; Complete Britten Piano Music; Schubert Sonatas; Mendelssohn Piano Concertos; (with Robert Mann) Complete Beethoven and Brahms Violin Sonatas; Chopin Ballades and Scherzos; Scharwenka Piano Concerto No 4, and Sauer Piano Concerto No 1 (Gramophone Record of the Year, 1996); (with Steven Isserlis) Cello Sonatas of Grieg, Rachmaninoff, Franck and Rubinstein; Piano Concertos of Lowell Liebermann; Brahms Sonata; (with Michael Collins and Steven Isserlis) Clarinet Trios; Complete Piano and Orchestra Music of Saint-Saëns (Gramophone CD of the Year, 2003; Gold Disc Award, Gramophone Mag., 2008); Complete Rachmaninoff Piano Concertos; English Piano Album; piano music of York Bowen, Franck and Mompou; Mozart Album; Beethoven and Mozart Piano and Wind Quartets; Spanish Album; Stephen Hough in recital; music of Corigliano Tsontakis, Copland and Weber; Complete music for piano and orchestra by Tchaikovsky; Chopin: Late Masterpieces; Chopin Complete Waltzes (Diapason d'Or de l'Année, 2011); Broken Branches (compositions by Stephen Hough); Liszt and Grieg Piano Concertos; French Album; Brahms Piano Concertos (with Salzburg Mozarteum Orch.); In The Night (recital disc). Internat. Chair of Piano Studies, RNCM, 2003– (Dayas Gold Medal, 1981); Vis. Prof. of Piano, RAM, 2002– (Hon. RAM 2002). MacArthur Fellowship, MacArthur Foundn, 2001–. Writer of cultural blog for Daily Telegraph website, 2008–. Hon. DMus Liverpool, 2011. Internat. Terence Judd Award, 1982; Naumburg Internat. Piano Competition, 1983; Jean Gimbel Lane Prize in Piano Perf., Northwestern Univ., 2009; Royal Philharmonic Soc. Instrumentalist Award, 2010. *Compositions:* Suite R-B and other enigmas, 2003; Three Marian Hymns for children's choir and organ, 2005; On Falla, 2005; Advent Calendar, 2005; 3 Songs From War, 2006; Mass of Innocence and Experience, 2006; The Loneliest Wilderness: elegy for cello and orch., 2006; Missa Mirabilis, 2007 (orchestral version, 2011); Londinium Magnificat and Nunc Dimittis, 2007; Three Grave Songs, 2007; Herbstlieder, 2008; Un Piccolo Sonatina, 2008; Was mit den Tränen geschieht: trio for piccolo, contrabassoon and piano, 2008; Requiem Æternum: after Victoria, 2009; Other Love Songs for SATB and piano duet, 2010; Sonata for piano (broken branches), 2010; Piano Sonata no 2 (notturno luminoso), 2012; December: a choral album, 2012; Sonata for cello and piano (les adieux), 2013; Dappled Things: a cycle of six songs for baritone and piano, 2014; Piano Sonata III (Trinitas), 2015. *Publications:* (contrib.) The Way We Are Now, 2006; The Bible as Prayer, 2007; (contrib.) Elgar: an anniversary portrait, 2007; (contrib.) Britten's Century: celebrating 100 years of Britten, 2013; vols of transcriptions incl. Rodgers and Hammerstein, 1999, Franck, Choral No 3, 2000, Tributes, 2015, Sonata for Viola and Piano, 2015. *Recreations:* reading, painting. *Address:* HarrisonParrott Ltd, 5–6 Albion Court, Albion Place, W6 0QT. *W:* www.stephenhough.com.

HOUGHAM, John William, CBE 1996; Commissioner and Deputy Chairman, Disability Rights Commission, 2000–07; *b* 18 Jan. 1937; *s* of late William George Hougham and Emily Jane (*née* Smith); *m* 1961, Peggy Edith Grove (*d* 2006); one *s* one *d*. *Educ:* Sir Roger Manwood's Sch., Sandwich; Leeds Univ. (BA Hons). National Service: commnd 2nd Lieut RA, 1955–57. British Home Stores, 1960–63; Ford Motor Company Ltd, 1963–93: Director: Industrial Relns, Ford España SA, 1976–80; Industrial Relns, Mfg, Ford of Europe Inc., 1982–86; Personnel, and Exec. Bd Mem., Ford UK, 1986–93. Mem. Bd, Personnel Mgt Services Ltd, 1989–93. Chm., ACAS, 1993–2000; Member: Review Body on Doctors' and Dentists' Remuneration, 1992–93; Adv. Bd of CS Occupational Health Service, 1992–96; Employment Appeal Tribunal, 1992–93 and 2000–07; Bluewater Chaplaincy Team, 2013–. Member: Engrg ITB, 1987–90; IPM Nat. Cttee for Equal Opportunities, 1987–92; CBI Employment Policy Cttee, 1987–93; Council, CRAC, 1988–2000; Bd, Trng and Employment Agency for NI, 1990–93; Council, Engrg Trng Authy, 1990–93; Chairman: Employment Occupational Standards Council, 1994–97; Employment NTO, 1997–2002, subseq. ENTO, 2002–04; Adv. Cttee, ESRC Future of Work Prog., 1998–2005. Vis. Prof., Univ. (formerly Poly.) of E London, 1991–2000; Vis. Fellow, City Univ., 1991–2000. Pres., Manpower Soc., 1997–2001; Mem. Adv. Council, Involvement & Participation Assoc., 1997–2000 (Vice-Pres., 1994–97, Hon. Vice-Pres., 1997–); Chm. Disciplinary Cttee, British Health Trades Assoc., 2000–. Governor: St George's C of E Sch., Gravesend, 1990–2008; Gravesend GS for Boys, 1990–2003. Trustee: Ellenor Lions Hospices (formerly Ellenor Foundn), 2004–13; Kent Workplace Mission, 2014–. St John Ambulance: Comdr, Kent, 2007–12; Mem., County Priory Gp, 2013–; Pres., Northfleet, 2014–. Reader, dio. of Rochester, 1998–. CCIPD (CIPM 1986); CCMI (CIMgt 1986); FRSA 1998. Freeman, City of London, 1995. Liveryman, Wheelwrights' Co., 2009. Member, Editorial Advisory Board: Human Resource Mgt Jl, 1991–2000; People Mgt Mag., 1993–2003. Hon. LLD Leeds, 1997; Hon. DBA De Montfort, 1997. SBStJ 2009. *Publications:* (contrib.) Legal Intervention in Industrial Relations (ed William McCarthy), 1992. *Recreations:* collecting books on Kent, watching cricket and Rugby football, family history. *Address:* 12 Old Road East, Gravesend, Kent DA12 1NQ. *T:* (01474) 352138. *Club:* Harlequin Football.

HOUGHTON, Brian Thomas, CB 1991; Director, International Division (formerly International Tax Policy Division), Inland Revenue, 1987–91; *b* 22 Aug. 1931; *s* of Bernard Charles Houghton and Sadie Houghton; *m* 1953, Joyce Beryl (*née* Williams); three *s* one *d*. *Educ:* City Boys' Sch., Leicester; Christ's Coll., Cambridge (Scholar; BA 1st cl. (Mod. Langs); MA 1957). Inland Revenue, 1957; Private Sec. to Chief Sec., HM Treasury, 1966–68; Assistant Secretary: Inland Revenue, 1968–75; HM Treasury, 1975–77; Under Sec., 1977, Principal Finance Officer and Dir of Manpower, Inland Revenue, 1977–83; Policy Div. Dir, Inland Revenue, 1983–87. Consultant, OECD, 1991–93. Vis. Professorial Fellow, QMW, 1992–97. *Recreation:* sailing. *Address:* 19 Rookes Lane, Lymington, Hants SO41 8FP. *T:* (01590) 670375.

HOUGHTON, Dr John; Director, Teesside Polytechnic, 1971–79, retired (Principal, Constantine College of Technology, 1961–70); *b* 12 June 1922; *s* of George Stanley Houghton and Hilda (*née* Simpson); *m* 1951, Kathleen Lamb; one *s* one *d*. *Educ:* King Henry VIII Sch., Coventry; Hanley High Sch.; Coventry Tech. Coll.; King's Coll., Cambridge; Queen Mary Coll., London Univ. BSc (Hons) Engrg 1949; PhD 1952. CEng, MIMechE, FRAeS. Aircraft Apprentice, Sir W. G. Armstrong-Whitworth Aircraft Ltd, 1938–43; design and stress engr, 1943–46; student at univ. (Clayton Fellow), 1946–51; Lectr, Queen Mary Coll., London Univ., 1950–52; Sen. Lectr and Head of Aero-Engrg, Coventry Techn. Coll., 1952–57; Head of Dept of Mech. Engrg, Brunel Coll. Advanced Technology, 1957–61. Freeman, City of Coventry, 1943. JP Middlesbrough, 1962–92. *Publications:* (with D. R. L. Smith) Mechanics of Fluids by Worked Examples, 1959; various research reports, reviews and articles in professional and learned jls. *Recreations:* keen sportsman (triple Blue), do-it-yourself activities, gardening.

HOUGHTON, Gen. Sir (John) Nicholas (Reynolds), GCB 2011 (KCB 2008); CBE 2000 (OBE 1992); Chief of the Defence Staff, since 2013; Aide-de-Camp General to the Queen, since 2009; *b* 18 Oct. 1954; *s* of Frank and Margaret Houghton; *m* 1982, Margaret Glover; one *s* one *d*. *Educ:* Woodhouse Grove Sch., Bradford; RMA, Sandhurst; St Peter's Coll., Oxford (MA). Commissioned, Green Howards, 1974; psct 1985–86; CO, 1 Green Howards, 1991–94; hcsc 1997; Comdr, 39th Inf. Bde (NI), 1997–99; DMO, MoD, 1999–2002; COS HQ ARRC, 2002–04; ACDS (Ops), MoD, 2004–05; Dep. Comdg Gen., Multinational Force, Iraq, 2005–06; Chief of Jt Ops, MoD, 2006–09; Vice Chief of Defence Staff, 2009–13. Col, Yorks Regt, 2006–11; Col Comdt, Intelligence Corps, 2008–14. Officer, Legion of Merit (USA), 2006. *Recreations:* golf, shooting, history, family, watching sport, travel. *Address:* RHQ The Yorkshire Regiment, Trinity Church Square, Richmond, N Yorks DL10 4QN. *T:* (01748) 822133.

HOUGHTON, Sir John (Theodore), Kt 1991; CBE 1983; FRS 1972; Chief Executive (formerly Director General) of the Meteorological Office, 1983–91; Chairman, Royal Commission on Environmental Pollution, 1992–98 (Member, 1991–98); *b* 30 Dec. 1931; *s* of Sidney M. Houghton, schoolmaster, and Miriam Houghton; *m* 1st, 1962, Margaret Edith Houghton (*née* Broughton) (*d* 1986), MB, BS, DPH; one *s* one *d*; 2nd, 1988, Sheila Houghton (*née* Thompson). *Educ:* Rhyl Grammar Sch.; Jesus Coll., Oxford (Scholar). BA hons Physics 1951, MA, DPhil 1955. Research Fellow, RAE Farnborough, 1954–57; Lectr in Atmospheric Physics, Oxford Univ., 1958–62; Reader, 1962–76; Professor, 1976–83; Fellow, Jesus Coll., Oxford, 1960–83, Hon. Fellow 1983; on secondment as Dir (Appleton), 1979–83, and Dep. Dir, 1981–83, Rutherford Appleton Laboratory, SERC, Hon. Scientist, 1992–. Member: Astronomy, Space and Radio Bd, SERC (formerly SRC), 1970–73 and 1976–81; Exec. Cttee, WMO, 1983–91 (Vice-Pres., 1987–91); Astronomy and Planetary Sci. Bd, SERC, 1987–93; Meteorological Cttee, 1975–80; Jt Organising Cttee, Global Atmospheric Res. Programme, 1976–79; Exec. Management Bd, British Nat. Space Centre, 1986–91; UK Govt Panel on Sustainable Develt, 1994–2000; Chairman: Jt Scientific Cttee, World Climate Research Programme, 1981–84; Earth Observation Adv. Cttee, ESA, 1982–93; Scientific Assessment, Intergovtl Panel for Climate Change, 1988–2002; Jt Scientific and Tech. Cttee, Global Climate Observing System, 1992–95; John Ray Initiative, 1997–2006 (Pres., 2006–). Pres., RMetS, 1976–78 (Hon. Mem.). Trustee, Shell Foundn, 2000–10. MAE 1988; Fellow, Optical Soc. of America; FInstP. Lectures: Cherwell-Simon Meml, 1983–84, Halley, 1992, Templeton, 1992, Oxford Univ.; Bakerian, Royal Soc., 1991. Hon. Mem., Amer. Met. Soc.; Hon. FRIBA 2001. Hon. Fellow: Univ. of Wales, Lampeter, 1994; Univ. of Wales, Bangor, 2003; Univ. of Wales, Aberystwyth, 2006. Hon. DSc: Wales, 1991; UEA, 1993; Leeds, 1995; Heriot-Watt, 1996; Greenwich, 1997; Glamorgan, 1998; Reading, 1999; Birmingham, 2000; Gloucestershire, 2001; Hull, 2002; Oxford, 2006; DUniv Stirling, 1992; Hon. DLaws Dalhousie, 2010. Buchan Prize, RMetS, 1966; Charles Chree medal and prize, Inst. of Physics, 1979; (with F. W. Taylor, C. D. Rodgers and G. D. Peskett) Rank Prize for opto-electronics, 1989; Symons Meml Medal, RMetS, 1991; Glazebrook Medal and Prize, Inst. of Phys, 1990; Global 500 Award, UN Envmt Programme, 1994; Gold Medal, RAS, 1995; Internat. Meteorological Orgn Prize, 1998; Japan Prize, Foundn of Sci. and Technol., Japan, 2006; Champion for Wales, Welsh Assembly, 2008; Albert Einstein Sci. Award, World Cultural Council, 2009. *Publications:* (with S. D. Smith) Infra-Red Physics, 1966; The Physics of Atmospheres, 1977, 3rd edn 2002; (with F. W. Taylor and C. D. Rodgers) Remote Sounding of Atmospheres, 1984; Does God play dice?, 1988; Global Warming: the complete briefing, 1994, 4th edn 2009; The Search for God: can science help?, 1995; In The Eye of the

Storm, 2013 (autobiog.); papers in learned jls on atmospheric radiation, spectroscopy, remote sounding from satellites and climate change. *Recreations:* walking, sailing. *Address:* c/o Hadley Centre, Meteorological Office, Fitzroy Road, Exeter EX1 3PB.

HOUGHTON, Gen. Sir Nicholas; *see* Houghton, Gen. Sir J. N. R.

HOUGHTON, Peter; Director of Innovation, South East Coast Strategic Health Authority, 2009–11; *b* 7 Dec. 1957; *s* of late Peter Houghton and of Verde Cicely Houghton. *Educ:* Barnsley Grammar Sch.; Keble Coll., Oxford (BA Classics); Aberdeen Univ. (Cert Health Econs 1988). NHS nat. admin trainee, 1981–83; Dep. Administrator, Royal Nat. Orthopaedic Hosp., London, 1983–85; Gen. Manager, Mental Health and Learning Disability Services, Cambridge, 1985–91; Chief Exec., Hinchingbrooke Healthcare NHS Trust, Huntingdon, 1991–93; Actg Dir of Planning, E Anglian RHA, 1993–94; Director: Strategic Develt, Anglia and Oxford Reg., NHS Exec., 1994–99; Eastern Reg., NHS Exec., DoH, 1999–2002; Chief Exec., Norfolk, Suffolk and Cambs Strategic HA, 2002–05; Dir, NHS Nat. Leadership Network, DoH, 2005–06; Chief Exec., SW London and St George's Mental Health NHS Trust, 2006–09. Mem., Inst. Health Mgt, 1984. *Recreations:* classical music and opera, travel, gardening, cycling.

HOUGHTON, Sir Stephen (Geoffrey), Kt 2013; CBE 2004; Leader, Barnsley Metropolitan Borough Council, since 1996 (Member (Lab), since 1988); *b* Barnsley, 27 April 1958; *s* of William and Ivy Houghton; *m* 1985, Karen Eastwood; one *s* one *d.* *Educ:* Barnsley Coll. (NHC Electrical and Electronic Engrg); Univ. of Birmingham (MSc Local Governance). British Coal: apprentice electrician, 1974–78; electrician, 1978–85; Electrical Inspector, 1985–93; Manager, Bargaining for Skills Prog., Barnsley & Doncaster TEC, 1993–96. Mem., Audit Commn, 2005–11. Mem. Bd, 1999–2005, Dep. Chm., 2003–05, Yorkshire Forward RDA. Houghton Rev. into rôle of local authorities in tackling worklessness, 2008 (report published, 2009). Mem., Doncaster and Wirral Councils Improvement Bd, 2010–. Non-exec. Dir, Barnsley Hosp. Foundn Trust, 2012–. Chm., Special Interest Gp of Municipal Authorities, 1998–; Local Govt Improvement Peer, 2008–. *Publications:* contribs to jls and discussion documents and pamphlets of Local Govt Information Unit, Solace Foundn, LGA, Centre for Econ. and Social Inclusion and Progress. *Recreations:* cricket, football, walking, running. *Address:* 7 Paddock Grove, Cudworth, Barnsley S72 8GF. *T:* (01226) 717348, 07968 130102. *E:* cllrstephenhoughton@barnsley.gov.uk.

HOULDEN, Rev. Prof. (James) Leslie; Professor of Theology, King's College, London, 1987–94, now Emeritus; *b* 1 March 1929; *s* of late James and Lily Alice Houlden. *Educ:* Altrincham Grammar Sch.; Queen's Coll., Oxford. Asst Curate, St Mary's, Hunslet, Leeds, 1955–58; Chaplain, Chichester Theological Coll., 1958–60; Chaplain Fellow, Trinity Coll., Oxford, 1960–70; Principal, Cuddesdon Theol Coll., later Ripon Coll., Cuddesdon, 1970–77; King's College, London: Lectr, 1977; Sen. Lectr in New Testament Studies, 1985; Dean, Faculty of Theology and Religious Studies, 1986–88; Head, Dept of Biblical Studies, 1988–89; Actg Dean, 1993–94; FKC 1994. Hon. Canon of Christ Church Oxford, 1976–77. Member: Liturgical Commn, 1969–76; Doctrine Commn of C of E, 1969–76; Gen. Synod of C of E, 1980–90. Editor, Theology, 1983–91. DD Lambeth, 2005. *Publications:* Paul's Letters from Prison, 1970; (ed) A Celebration of Faith, 1970; Ethics and the New Testament, 1973; The Johannine Epistles, 1974; The Pastoral Epistles, 1976; Patterns of Faith, 1977; Explorations in Theology 3, 1978; What Did the First Christians Believe?, 1982; Connections, 1986; Backward into Light, 1987; (ed jtly) The World's Religions, 1988; History, Story and Belief, 1988; (ed jtly) Dictionary of Biblical Interpretation, 1990; Truth Untold, 1991; (ed) Austin Farrer: the essential sermons, 1991; Bible and Belief, 1991; Jesus: a question of identity, 1992; (ed jtly) Austin Farrer, Words for Life, 1993; (ed) The Interpretation of the Bible in the Church, 1995; (ed jtly) Companion Encyclopedia of Theology, 1995; The Public Face of the Gospel, 1997; (ed jtly) The Common Worship Lectionary: a scripture commentary, Year A, 2001, Year B, 2002, Year C, 2003; The Strange Story of the Gospels, 2002; (ed) Jesus in History, Thought and Culture: an encyclopedia, 2003, reissued as Jesus: the complete guide, 2005; (jtly) Services for Weekdays, 2006; (with J. Woodward) Praying the Lectionary, 2007; (ed jtly) Decoding Early Christianity, 2007; *contributed to:* The Myth of God Incarnate, 1977; Incarnation and Myth, 1979; Alternative Approaches to New Testament Study, 1985; The Reality of God, 1986; A New Dictionary of Christian Ethics, 1986; The Trial of Faith, 1988; God's Truth, 1988; Embracing the Chaos, 1990; Tradition and Unity, 1991; Using the Bible Today, 1991; Fundamentalism and Tolerance, 1991; Anchor Bible Dictionary, 1992; The Resurrection of Jesus Christ, 1993; Crossing the Boundaries, 1994; Divine Revelation, 1997; New Soundings, 1997; Theological Liberalism, 2000; The Oxford Bible Commentary, 2001; reviews and articles in learned jls. *Address:* 5 The Court, Temple Balsall, Knowle, Solihull B93 0AN. *Club:* Athenæum.

HOULDER, Bruce Fiddes, CB 2014; QC 1994; DL; independent consultant on rule of law, nation building and criminal and military justice issues, since 2014; Director of Service Prosecutions (Armed Forces), 2008–13; a Recorder, since 1991; *b* 27 Sept. 1947; *s* of late Charles Alexander Houlder and Jessie Houlder (*née* Fiddes); *m* 1974, Stella Catherine Mattinson; two *d.* *Educ:* Felsted Sch., Dunmow. Called to the Bar, Gray's Inn, 1969, Bencher, 2001. Bar Council: Mem., 1995–97, 1998–2000, 2003–05; Vice Chm., Professional Standards Cttee, 1996–98; Chairman: Public Affairs Cttee, 1999–2000 (Vice Chm., 1996–98); Equal Opportunities Cttee, 2003; Bar Quality Adv. Panel, 2007–08; Vice-Chm., Bar IT Panel, 2004–08; Judicial Studies Board: Mem., Criminal Cttee, 2003–06; Mem., Working Pty on Criminal Justice Reforms; Chm., Criminal Bar Assoc. of England and Wales, 2001–02 (Vice Chm., 2000–01); Member: Criminal Law Adv. Cttee, Law Commn, 2007–; Service Justice Bd, 2009–13; Sheffield Hallam Univ. Law and Criminology Adv. Cttee, 2012–. Tutor, Judicial Coll., 2010–. Dir, Barco Ltd, 2003–08. DL Greater London, 2009; Rep. Lieut for London Bor. of Hillingdon, 2014–. *Recreations:* watercolour painting, opera, cycling, theatre, music. *E:* bhqc@aol.com. *Club:* Garrick.

HOULDING, Rev. Preb. David Nigel Christopher; Vicar, St Stephen's with All Hallows, Hampstead, since 1985; *b* Fawkham, Kent, 25 July 1953; *s* of Reginald Houlding and Vera Houlding (*née* Bellini). *Educ:* King's Sch., Canterbury; King's Coll., London (AKC 1976); St Augustine's Coll., Canterbury. Lay Chaplain, Christian Medical Coll., Vellore, S India, 1976–77; ordained deacon, 1977, priest, 1978; Curate, All Saints, Hillingdon, 1977–81; Asst Priest, St Alban the Martyr, Holborn, 1981–85; Area Dean, N Camden, 2001–03; Preb., Consumpta per Mare, St Paul's Cathedral, 2004–. Chair: House of Clergy, Dio. of London, 2000–; C of E Appts Cttee, 2004; Mem., Archbishop's Council, 2003–. Pres., Church Union, 2012–. Trustee, Additional Curates Soc., 1996–; Master Gen., Soc. of the Holy Cross, 1997–. Gov., St Stephen's House, Oxford, 2001–. Hon. DD Nashotah House, Wisconsin, 2005. *Publications:* Consecrated Women? Reception and Communion, 2004; In this sign, Conquer, 2006; Who is this Man: Christ in the renewal of the Church, 2006. *Recreations:* capital cities of Europe, France, house restoration, dining. *Address:* All Hallows House, 52 Courthorpe Road, Hampstead, NW3 2LD. *T:* (020) 7267 7833, 07710 403294. *E:* fr.houlding@lineone.net. *Club:* National Liberal.

HOULDSWORTH, Sir Richard (Thomas Reginald), 5th Bt *cr* 1887, of Reddish and Coodham; Farm Manager, since 1988; *b* 2 Aug. 1947; *s* of Sir Reginald Douglas Henry Houldsworth, 4th Bt, OBE, TD and Margaret May (*d* 1995), *d* of late Cecil Emilius Laurie; *S* father, 1989; *m* 1st, 1970, Jane Elizabeth (marr. diss. 1982), *o d* of Alistair Orr; two *s*; 2nd, 1992, Ann Catherine Tremayne; one *s.* *Educ:* Bredon School, Tewkesbury, Glos; Blanerne School, Denholm, Roxburghshire. *Recreations:* shooting, fishing, tennis, squash, horse racing. *Heir:* *s* Simon Richard Henry Houldsworth [*b* 6 Oct. 1971; *m* 2003, Rosamond Louise Frayling-Kelly]. *Address:* April Cottage, Naunton, Cheltenham, Glos GL54 3AA.

HOULIHAN, Michael Patrick; Chief Executive, Museum of New Zealand Te Papa Tongarewa, 2010–14; Special Adviser on Military Heritage, Ministry of Culture and Heritage, New Zealand, 2014; *b* 27 Sept. 1948; *s* of Michael Houlihan and Kathleen (*née* Small); *m* 1969, Jane Hibbert; one *s* one *d.* *Educ:* St Francis Xavier's Coll., Liverpool; Univ. of Bristol (BA Hons Hist.). Imperial War Museum: Research Asst, 1971–75, Dep. Keeper, 1975–76, Dept of Exhibits; Keeper, Dept of Permanent Exhibns, 1976–84; Dep. Dir, 1984–94, Dir, 1994–98, Horniman Mus. and Gardens; Dir, subseq. Chief Exec., Nat. Museums and Galls of NI, 1998–2003; Dir Gen., Amgueddfa Cymru—Nat. Museum Wales (formerly Nat. Museums and Galls of Wales), 2003–10. Chairman: Collections Trust (formerly MDA), 2003–09; ICOM UK, 2008–10; Dep. Chm., ICOM NZ, 2012. Member: British Commn for Military Hist., 1982–; NI Cttee, British Council, 1998; Bd, NI Mus Council, 1998. Vis. Prof., Ulster Univ., 1999. Trustee: Nat. Self-Portrait Collection of Ireland, 1998–2003; Nat. Coal Mining Mus., 2004–10. Mem. Council, Goldsmiths Coll., Univ. of London, 1997–98. *Publications:* Trench Warfare 1914–18, 1974; (with B. Yale) No Man's Land, 1984. *Recreations:* military history, cycling, Romanesque architecture, battlefields.

HOULSBY, Prof. Guy Tinmouth, DSc; FREng; Professor of Civil Engineering, University of Oxford, since 1991 (Head, Department of Engineering Science, 2009–14); Fellow of Brasenose College, Oxford, since 1991; *b* 28 March 1954; *s* of late Lt Col Thomas Tinmouth Houlsby, TD and of Vivienne May Houlsby (*née* Ford); *m* 1985, Jenny Lucy Damaris Nedderman; two *s.* *Educ:* Trinity College, Glenalmond; St John's College, Cambridge (MA, PhD); DSc Oxon 2003. CEng 1983, FREng 1999; FICE 1997. Engineer, Binnie and Partners, 1975–76, Babtie Shaw and Morton, 1976–77; Research Student, Cambridge, 1977–80; Oxford University: Jun. Res. Fellow, Balliol Coll., 1980–83; Lectr in Engineering, 1983–91; Fellow, Keble College, 1983–91. Rankine Lect., British Geotech. Soc., 2014. *Publications:* (with A. M. Puzrin) Principles of Hyperplasticity, 2006; contribs to learned jls on soil mechanics. *Recreations:* ornithology, woodwork, Northumbrian small pipes, rowing. *Address:* 25 Purcell Road, Marston, Oxford OX3 0HB. *T:* (01865) 722128.

HOULT, Frederick Wilson; JP; Vice Lord-Lieutenant of Tyne and Wear, 2007–13; *b* 18 June 1938; *s* of late Frederick Hoult and Beatrice Hoult (*née* Wilson); *m* 1962, Peta Ann Wood; one *s* two *d.* *Educ:* Beadnell Village Sch.; St Mary's Sch., Melrose; Sedbergh Sch., Yorks; Rutherford Coll., Newcastle upon Tyne. Apprentice engr, CA Parsons, Newcastle upon Tyne, 1955–60; joined Hoults Ltd, family removals co., 1960, sold 1983; Chm., Hoults Hldgs Ltd, 1983–. A Tax Comr, 1981–2007. Vice Chm., NHS Supplies Authy, 1991–98. Mem., Newcastle HA, 1986–90; Chm., Freeman Hosp. NHS Trust, 1990–94. Pres., British Assoc. of Removers, 1976–77. Chairman: Tyneside Carr-Gomm, 1988–91; Mowden Hall Sch., 1998–2002. JP 1970, High Sheriff, 1986–87, Tyne and Wear. *Recreations:* family, sailing, ski-ing, tennis, countryside. *Address:* Stavros, 43 The Grove, Gosforth, Newcastle upon Tyne NE3 1NH. *T:* (0191) 285 3456. *Club:* Northern Counties (Newcastle upon Tyne).

HOULT, Helen Isabel; *see* Cleland, H. I.

HOURIGAN, Rhian Sara; *see* Harris, R. S.

HOURSTON, Sir Gordon (Minto), Kt 1997; FRPharmS; Chairman, United Biscuits plc, 1999–2000 (non-executive Director, 1995–99); *b* 24 July 1934; *s* of William A. M. Hourston and Vera W. (*née* Minto); *m* 1962, Sheila Morris; two *s.* *Educ:* Daniel Stewart's Coll., Edinburgh; Heriot-Watt Univ. FRPharmS 1982 (MRPharmS 1957). Joined Boots The Chemists, 1958: Dir, 1978; Dep. Man. Dir, 1984–88; Chm. and Man. Dir, 1988–95; Dir, Boots Co. plc, 1981–95. Chm., Homestyle plc (formerly Roseleys plc), 1996–2004. Chm., Company Chemists' Assoc., 1988–95. Chm., Armed Forces Pay Rev. Body, 1993–99 (Mem., 1989–99); Mem., Sen. Salaries Rev. Body, 1993–99. Trustee, Pharmacy Practice Res. Trust, 1999–2003. Hon. DSc Robert Gordon, 2004. *Recreations:* golf, walking, modern history, reading. *Address:* Tullich Lodge, Ballater, Aberdeenshire AB35 5SB.

HOUSDEN, Sir Peter (James), KCB 2010; Permanent Secretary, Scottish Government, 2010–15; *b* 7 Dec. 1950. Teacher, Madeley Court Sch., Telford, 1975–79; Professional Asst, Humberside LEA, 1979–82; Asst Dir of Educn, Notts LEA, 1982–86; Sen. Educn Officer, Lancs LEA, 1986–88; Dep. Chief Educn Officer, Notts LEA, 1988–91; Dir of Educn, 1991–94, Chief Exec., 1994–2001, Notts CC; Dir Gen., Schs, DfES, 2001–05; Permanent Sec., ODPM, then DCLG, 2005–10. Mem., Chartermark Panel, 1997–2001. Advr, LGA, 1997–2001. Chm., Nottingham Drug Action Team, 1994–2000; Mem., Adv. Council on Misuse of Drugs, 1998–2003. Associate Fellow, Warwick Univ. Business Sch., 1996–2002. Trustee: Work Foundn, 2007–11; RNLI, 2014–. Mem. Ct, Univ. of Greenwich, 2008–10. DUniv Nottingham Trent, 2014.

HOUSE, James Michael; QC 2015; *b* Oxford, 3 May 1970; *s* of Peter House and Judith House; *m* 1997, Kirsten Esther; one *s* one *d.* *Educ:* Chew Valley Comp. Sch.; Lancaster Univ. (BA Hons Politics and Internat. Relns); Univ. of Central England (CPE). Called to the Bar, 1995. *Recreations:* my family, cycling, sailing, golf. *Address:* 7 Bedford Row, WC1R 4BS. *T:* (020) 7242 3555. *E:* jhouse@7br.co.uk.

HOUSE, Roger Keith; a District Judge (Magistrates' Courts) (formerly Metropolitan Stipendiary Magistrate), 1995–2013; Chairman, Youth Court, 1995–2013; *b* 24 Jan. 1944; *s* of Donald Stuart House and Kathleen Mary House; *m* 1971, Elizabeth Anne Hall; two *s.* *Educ:* Wychwood Prep. Sch.; Sherborne. Admitted Solicitor, 1972; Asst Solicitor with various firms, 1972–76; sole practitioner, 1976–95. *Recreations:* singing, reading, walking the countryside, shooting, surfing.

HOUSE, Sir (William) Stephen, Kt 2013; QPM 2004; Chief Constable, Police Scotland, 2012–15; *b* 19 Oct. 1957; *s* of William Cullingford House and Alice Reid House; *m* 1987, Caroline Jose; one *s* two *d.* *Educ:* Kelvinside Acad., Glasgow; University College Sch., Hampstead; Aberdeen Univ. (MA Hons Hist./Eng. Lit.); Brunel Univ. (MBA). Joined Sussex Police, 1981; Supt, W Yorks Police, 1994–98; Asst Chief Constable, Staffs Police, 1998–2001; Dep. Asst Comr, 2001–05, Asst Comr, 2005–07, Metropolitan Police; Chief Constable, Strathclyde Police, 2007–12. *Recreations:* reading (science fiction and history), running, hill walking.

HOUSLAY, Prof. Miles Douglas, PhD; FRSE; FMedSci; Professor of Pharmacological Innovation (part-time), King's College London, since 2011; Professor of Pharmacology (part-time), University of Strathclyde, since 2011; Chief Executive, BioGryffe Consulting Ltd, since 2011; *b* 25 June 1950; *s* of Edwin Douglas Houslay and Georgina Marie Houslay; *m* 1972, Rhian Mair Gee; two *s* one *d.* *Educ:* UC Cardiff (BSc Hons Biochem. 1971); King's Coll., Cambridge (PhD Biochem. 1974). FRSE 1986. ICI Res. Fellow, Dept Pharmacol., Univ. of Cambridge, 1974; Res. Fellow, Queens' Coll., Cambridge, 1975; Lectr in Biochem., 1976–82, Reader, 1982–84, UMIST; University of Glasgow: Gardiner Prof. of Biochemistry, 1984–2011, now Emeritus; Chair, Neurosci. and Molecular Pharmacol., 2008–11; Co-Dir, Inst. of Neurosci. and Psychol., 2010–11. Ed.-in-Chief, Cellular Signalling, 1987–2014. Chairman: Cell Bd Grant Panel, MRC, 1990–93; Project Grant Panel, Wellcome Trust, 1996–2000, BHF, 1997–99; former Member: Grant Panels for MRC, AFRC, SHHD, Brit. Diabetic Assoc. and Health Res. Bd (Eire); RAE panels, HEFC, 1992, 1996. Selby Fellow, Aust. Acad. Scis, 1984. Minshull Meml Lectr, Univ. of Edinburgh, 1990. Trustee, BHF, 1997. Consultant and mem. scientific adv. bds at various pharmaceutical cos in UK, Europe and

USA, including: Celgene Corp., 2002–05; Fission Pharmaceuticals, 2007–; Chm., Scientific Adv. Bd, BioTheryX Corp., 2011–14; Dir and CSO, Mironid Ltd, 2014–. FMedSci, 1998. Colworth Medal, Biochem. Soc., 1984; Most Cited Scientist in Scotland, Edinburgh Sci. Fest. Award, 1992; Joshua Lederburg Soc. Award, Celgene Corp., 2012. *Publications:* Dynamics of Biological Membranes, 1982; over 460 contribs on cell signalling systems to learned jls. *Recreations:* walking (hill, coastal and desert), reading, driving, cooking, music, eating out, photography. *E:* miles.houslay@kcl.ac.uk.

HOUSSEMAYNE du BOULAY, Sir Roger (William), KCVO 1982 (CVO 1972); CMG 1975; HM Diplomatic Service, retired; Vice Marshal of the Diplomatic Corps, 1975–82; *b* 30 March 1922; *s* of Charles John Houssemayne du Boulay, Captain, RN, and Mary Alice Veronica, *née* Morgan; *m* 1957, Elizabeth (*d* 2014), *d* of late Brig. Home, late RM, and Molly, Lady Pile; one *d*, and two step *s*. *Educ:* Winchester; Oxford. Served RAFVR, 1941–46 (Pilot). HM Colonial Service, Nigeria, 1949–58; HM Foreign, later Diplomatic, Service, 1959; FO, 1959; Washington, 1960–64; FCO 1964–67; Manila, 1967–71; Alternate Director, Asian Development Bank, Manila, 1967–69, and Director, 1969–71; Counsellor and Head of Chancery, Paris, 1971–73; Resident Comr, New Hebrides, 1973–75. Adviser: Solomon Is Govt, 1986; Swaziland Govt, 1992. *Recreation:* painting. *Address:* Anstey Cottage, Swallowfield Park, Reading, Berks RG7 1TG.

HOUSTON, Anne Catherine, OBE 2015; Independent Chair, North Ayrshire Child Protection Committee, since 2014; *b* 28 Aug. 1954; *d* of Robert and Marta Houston. *Educ:* Glasgow Coll. of Technol. (HNC Applied Physics and Electronics 1975); Jordanhill Coll. of Further Educn (CQSW, Dip SW, 1980); OU Business Sch. (mgt of non-profit enterprises 1992); Social Enterprise Acad., Edinburgh (ILM Cert. in Leadership and Mgt 2009). Various sen. mgt posts in soc. work related fields; Counselling Manager, 1990–94, Dir, 1994–2006, ChildLine Scotland; Dep. Chief Exec., ChildLine UK, 2003–06, Dir, ChildLine UK within NSPCC, 2006; Chief Exec., CHILDREN 1ST, 2004–14. Mem., Partnership Drugs Initiative, Lloyds TSB Foundn for Scotland, 2001–12; Vice Chair, Nat. Strategic Gp, Scotland, Stop It Now!, 2007–14. Trustee, Cattanach Trust, 2007– (Vice Chm., 2011–); Chm., Postcode Culture Trust, 2012–14. Mem. Counselling Team, consultant on Human Relns and Counselling Course, and student tutor, Scottish Inst. of Human Relns, 1989–94; Member: Adv. Cttee on Prison Mgt, Scottish Prison Service, 1994–2000; Cross Party Parly Gp for Children, 2003–06; Bd, Coalition of Care and Support Providers Scotland (formerly Community Care Providers Scotland), 2009–14; Scottish Govt Early Years Task Force, 2011–14; Bd, Care Inspectorate, 2014–; Putting the Baby in the Bathwater Coalition, 2014–; Vice Chairman: Scottish Alliance on Children's Rights, 1999–2005 (Founder Mem.); Scottish Pre-school Play Assoc., 2000–06; Anti-bullying Network Adv. Cttee, 2001–06; Chm., Justice for Children Alliance, 2007–14. Treas., Assoc. of Chief Officers of Scottish Voluntary Orgns, 2000–04. Mem., Annie Dow Heroism Award panel, 2014–. FRSA. *Publications:* Beyond the Limit: children living with parental alcohol misuse, 1998; Young People Helping Young People: international telephone helpline guidelines, 2000. *Recreations:* reading, music, gardening, food and wine. *E:* anne@achouston.plus.com.

HOUSTON, Robert Graham; Chairman, Scottish Qualifications Authority, since 2009; *b* Glasgow, 7 Oct. 1948; *s* of David Houston and Catherine Houston; *m* 1976, Jenifer Hastie; one *s* one *d*. *Educ:* Penilee Secondary Sch., Glasgow. Regl Dir, Ellerman Travel and Leisure Ltd, 1976–86; Dir, Scotland, Industrial Soc., 1986–2003; exec. business coach, 1990–. Mem. Bd, UK Skills, 1996–2010; Vice Chm., BBC Scotland Broadcasting Council, 2002–07. Mem. (SNP), Stirling Council (Leader, 2008–12). Mem. Bd, Scottish Police Authy, 2012–. Contested (SNP) Glasgow Craigton, Feb. and Oct. 1974. *Recreations:* golf, tai chi, reading, gardening. *Address:* Scottish Qualifications Authority, Optima Building, 58 Robertson Street, Glasgow G2 8DQ; Stirling Council, Old View Forth, Stirling FK8 2ET.

HOUSTON, Stewart, CBE 2007; FRAgS; Managing Director, Microware Pig Systems, since 1989; Chair, British Pig Executive, since 2004; *b* Hebburn, Co. Durham, 24 Oct. 1946; *s* of Alfred and Jean Houston; *m* 1970, Janet Margaret Pugh; two *s*. *Educ:* Jarrow Grammar Sch. Full-time farmer until 1989. Non-executive Director: Agric. and Horticulture Develt Bd, 2008–; Animal Health Welfare Bd, DEFRA, 2011–; Scottish Agricl Colls, 2012–. Chm., Nat. Pig Assoc., 2003–13. FRAgS 2010. Liveryman: Farmers' Co., 2007–; Butchers' Co., 2012–. *Recreations:* fly fishing, Sunderland Football Club. *Address:* Wayside, Thornborough, Bedale, N Yorks DL8 2RQ. *T:* (01677) 470656. *E:* stewart@mpsagri.co.uk. *Clubs:* Farmers (Chm., 2013); Tanfield Fishing.

HOUSTOUN-BOSWALL, Sir (Thomas) Alford, 8th Bt *cr* 1836; founder and Chairman, The Harrodian School, since 1993; international economics and business consultant; *b* 23 May 1947; *s* of Sir Thomas Houstoun-Boswall, 7th Bt, and Margaret Jean, *d* of George Bullen-Smith; *S* father, 1982; *m* 1st, 1971, Eliana Michele (marr. diss. 1996), *d* of Dr John Pearse, New York; one *s* one *d*; 2nd, 2007, Malgosia, *d* of Grzegorz Stepnik. *Educ:* Lindisfarne College. Partner, Rosedale-Engel, Houstoun-Boswall Partnership, Bermuda; Director, Stair & Co., New York (specialising in fine 18th century English furniture and works of art); Pres., Houstoun-Boswall Inc. (Fine Arts), New York. Lecturer, New York Univ. and Metropolitan Museum of Art, New York. *Heir: s* Alexander Alford Houstoun-Boswall, *b* 16 Sept. 1972. *Address:* The Harrodian School, Lonsdale Road, SW13 9QN; 18 rue Basse, 06410 Biot, France; 11 East 73rd Street, New York, NY 10021, USA.

HOVELL-THURLOW-CUMMING-BRUCE, family name of **Baron Thurlow**.

HOVEN, Helmert Frans van den; Knight, Order of Netherlands Lion, 1978; Commander, Order of Orange Nassau, 1984; Hon. KBE 1980. Chairman, Unilever NV, 1975–84; Vice-Chairman, Unilever Ltd, 1975–84; *b* 25 April 1923; *m* 1st, 1950, Dorothy Ida Bevan (marr. diss. 1981); one *s*; 2nd, 1981, Cornelia Maria van As. *Educ:* Grammar and Trade schs in The Netherlands. Joined Unilever NV, Rotterdam, 1938; transf. to Unilever Ltd, London, 1948, then to Turkey, 1951, becoming Chm. of Unilever's business there, 1958; Chm., Unilever's Dutch margarine business, Van den Bergh en Jurgens BV, 1962; sen. marketing post, product gp, Margarine, Edible Fats and Oils, 1966; Mem. Bds of Unilever, and responsible for product gp, Sundry Foods and Drinks, 1970; Dir, Fidelity Investments, 1984–2012; non-exec. Dir, Hunter Douglas NV, 1984–; formerly: Mem. Supervisory Bd of Shell; Chm. Supervisory Bds of ABN/Amro Bank and various other cos; Mem., Eur. Adv. Bd, AT & T and Rockwell. Pres., ICC, Paris, 1984–86. Mem. Council, North Western (Kellogg) Business Sch., 1984–2006. *Recreations:* rowing, walking.

HOW, Timothy Francis; Chairman: Enotria Wine Group Ltd, since 2012; Roys (Wroxham) Ltd, since 2014; *b* 29 Dec. 1950; *s* of Mervyn Henry How and Margaret Helen How; *m* 1975, Elizabeth Mary Howard; four *d*. *Educ:* Churchill Coll., Cambridge (MA); London Business Sch. (MSc Business Studies). Gen. Manager, Polaroid (UK) Ltd, 1979–83; Man. Dir, Bejam Gp PLC, 1983–89; Chief Exec., Majestic Wine PLC, 1989–2008. Non-executive Director: Henderson Gp plc, 2008–; Rayner & Keeler Ltd, 2008–13 (Chm., 2009–13); Dixons Carphone (formerly DSG Internat., later Dixons Retail) plc, 2010–; Chairman: Framlington AIM VCT plc, later Downing Income 4 VCT plc, 2004–13; Woburn Enterprises Ltd, 2011–. Chm., Wine and Spirit Trade Assoc., 2009–11. Dir, Norfolk and Norwich Univ. Hosps Foundn Trust, 2013–. Gov., Peabody Trust, 2008–14. *Recreations:* sailing, golf. *Address:* Norvista, Main Road, Brancaster Staithe, Norfolk PE31 8BY. *Clubs:* Sloane; Oxford and Cambridge Sailing, Brancaster Staithe Sailing.

HOWAR, Valentine Ruth; *see* Henshall, V. R.

HOWARD; *see* Fitzalan-Howard.

HOWARD, family name of **Earls of Carlisle, Effingham,** and **Suffolk,** and of **Barons Howard of Lympne, Howard of Penrith, Howard of Rising** and **Strathcona**.

HOWARD DE WALDEN, Baroness (10th in line), *cr* 1597; **Mary Hazel Caridwen Czernin;** *b* 12 Aug. 1935; *e d* of 9th Baron Howard de Walden and 5th Baron Seaford (*d* 1999) and Countess Irene Harrach; *S* to Howard de Walden Barony of father, called out of abeyance in her favour, 2004; *m* 1957, Count Joseph Czernin (*d* 2015); one *s* five *d*. *Heir: s* Hon. Peter John Joseph Czernin, *qv*.

HOWARD OF EFFINGHAM, Lord; Edward Mowbray Nicholas Howard; Mizuho Bank Ltd, since 2013; *b* 11 May 1971; *s* and *heir* of Earl of Effingham, *qv*, and *s* of Anne M. Howard (who *m* 1978, Prof. P. G. Stein, *qv*); *m* 2002, Tatiana Tafur; one *s* one *d* (twins). *Educ:* Oundle; Bristol Univ. ANZ Investment Bank, 1998–2003; Barclays Capital, 2004–13. *Recreation:* ski-ing. *Heir: s* Hon. Frederick Henry Charles Howard, *b* 19 March 2007. *Address:* Vermont 10, Domaine de la Résidence, Villars, Switzerland.

HOWARD OF LYMPNE, Baron *cr* 2010 (Life Peer), of Lympne in the County of Kent; **Michael Howard,** CH 2011; PC 1990; QC 1982; *b* 7 July 1941; *s* of late Bernard and Hilda Howard; *m* 1975, Sandra Clare, *d* of Wing-Comdr Saville Paul; one *s* one *d*, and one step *s*. *Educ:* Llanelli Grammar School; Peterhouse, Cambridge. MA, LLB; President of the Union, 1962. Major Scholar, Inner Temple, 1962; called to the Bar, Inner Temple, 1964, Bencher, 1992. Junior Counsel to the Crown (Common Law), 1980–82; a Recorder, 1986. Contested (C) Liverpool, Edge Hill, 1966 and 1970; Chm., Bow Group, 1970–71. MP (C) Folkestone and Hythe, 1983–2010. PPS to Solicitor-General, 1984–85; Parly Under-Sec. of State, DTI, 1985–87; Minister of State, DoE, 1987–90; Secretary of State for: Employment, 1990–92; the Environment, 1992–93; the Home Dept, 1993–97; Shadow Foreign Sec., 1997–99; Shadow Chancellor, 2001–03; Leader of the Conservative Party and Leader of the Opposition, 2003–05. Member: H of L Appts Commn, 2010–; Commn on Freedom of Information, 2015–. Jt Sec., Cons. Legal Cttee, 1983–84; Jt Vice-Chm., Cons. Employment Cttee, 1983–84; Vice-Chm., Soc. of Cons. Lawyers, 1985. Pres., Atlantic Partnership; Chairman: Entrée Gold Inc., 2013– (Dir, 2007–); Soma Oil and Gas Ltd, 2013–; Sen. Ind. Dir, Quindell, 2015–. Sen. Advr, Canaccord Genuity, 2013–. Chm., Help the Hospices, 2010–. *Recreations:* watching football (Swansea, Liverpool) and baseball (New York Mets). *Address:* House of Lords, SW1A 0PW. *Clubs:* Carlton, Pratt's, Coningsby (Chm., 1972–73).

HOWARD OF PENRITH, 3rd Baron *cr* 1930, of Gowbarrow, co. Cumberland; **Philip Esme Howard;** Chief Investment Officer, Beazley Group, since 2012; *b* 1 May 1945; *e s* of 2nd Baron Howard of Penrith and Anne (*née* Hotham, *widow* of Anthony Bazley); *S* father, 1999; *m* 1969, Sarah Sophia Walker; two *s* two *d*. *Educ:* Ampleforth Coll.; Christ Church, Oxford. Journalist, Scotsman, then Daily Mail, 1967–71; Dir, Deltec Trading Co. Ltd, 1972–77; Partner, Phillips and Drew, 1977–84; Man. Dir, Lehman Brothers, 1984–97; Chm., Tarchon (formerly Esperia) Capital Mgt Ltd, 1999–2013. Non-exec. Dir, Schroders plc, 2008–. *Heir: s* Hon. Thomas Philip Howard, *b* 8 June 1974. *Address:* 45 Erpingham Road, SW15 1BQ. *T:* (020) 8789 7604. *Clubs:* Turf, Portland.

HOWARD OF RISING, Baron *cr* 2004 (Life Peer), of Castle Rising in the County of Norfolk; **Greville Patrick Charles Howard;** Chairman, Wicksteed Leisure Ltd, 1984–2003; *b* 22 April 1941; *s* of Col Henry and Patience Howard; *m* 1981, Mary Cortlandt (*née* Culverwell); two *s* one *d*. *Educ:* Eton. Private Sec. to Rt Hon. Enoch Powell, MBE, PC, 1968–70. Chm., Fortress Holdings plc, 1995–2004. Dir, Keep Trust, 1980–89. Chm., Nat. Playing Fields Assoc., 2004–13. Mem. (C) King's Lynn and W Norfolk DC, 2003–. *Address:* Castle Rising, Norfolk. *Club:* White's.

HOWARD, Charles Anthony Frederick; QC 1999; *b* 7 March 1951; *s* of late Hon. John Algernon Frederick Charles Howard and Naida Howard (later Mrs Geoffrey Royal); *m* 1st, 1978, Geraldine Dorman (marr. diss.); one *s* one *d*; 2nd, 1999, Rosie Boycott, *qv*; one step *d*. *Educ:* Sherborne Sch.; St John's Coll., Cambridge (Open Hist. Schol.; BA 1972; MA 1976; McMahon Student). Called to the Bar, Inner Temple, 1975. Mem., Family Law Bar Assoc. *Recreations:* cricket, tennis, gardening, walking, films. *Address:* 1 King's Bench Walk, Temple, EC4Y 7DB. *T:* (020) 7736 1500. *Clubs:* Groucho; Somerset CC.
See also Earl of Effingham.

HOWARD, Rear-Adm. Christopher John, (Jack); Chief of Staff, C-in-C Naval Home Command, 1987–89, retired; *b* 13 Sept. 1932; *s* of late Claude Albert Howard and Hilda Mabel Howard (*née* Norton); *m* 1st, 1960, Jean Webster (marr. diss. 1987); two *d*; 2nd, 1987, Hilary Troy; one *s* one *d*. *Educ:* Newton Abbot Grammar School; King's College London; Imperial College, London. MSc, DIC. MIET. Entered RN 1954; served in HM Ships Ocean, Pukaki, Roebuck, Urchin, Tenby; Officer i/c RN Polaris School, 1978–80; Dean, RN Engineering College, 1980–82; Dir, Naval Officer Appts (Instructor), 1982–84; Commodore, HMS Nelson, 1985–87. NDC Latimer, 1975; Chief Naval Instructor Officer, 1987. Consultant, PA Consulting Group, 1989–91; Dir of Ops, Devon and Cornwall TEC, 1992–97. Gov. Maynard Sch., Exeter, 2002–06. *Recreation:* family.

HOWARD, Sir David (Howarth Seymour), 3rd Bt *cr* 1955, of Great Rissington, co. Gloucester; Chairman, Charles Stanley & Co., Stockbrokers, since 1999 (Managing Director/Chief Executive Officer, 1971–2014); Lord Mayor of London, 2000–01; *b* 29 Dec. 1945; *s* of Sir Edward Howard, 2nd Bt, GBE; *S* father, 2001; *m* 1968, Valerie Picton Crosse, *o d* of Derek W. Crosse; two *s* two *d*. *Educ:* Radley Coll.; Worcester Coll., Oxford (MA Hons). Director: Wealth Mgt Assoc. (formerly Assoc. of Pvte Client Investment Managers and Stockbrokers), 2001–; CISI (formerly Securities Inst., then Securities and Investment Inst., 2002–14 (Chm., Exam. Bd, 2003–14; Hon. FCSI); Financial Services Skills Council, 2004–07. Mem., Sutton BC, 1974–78; Common Councilman, City of London, 1972–86, Alderman, 1986–, Sheriff, 1997–98. Master, Gardeners' Co., 1990–91. Chm., London Gardens Soc., 1996–. Pres., Chartered Mgt Inst., 2008–10 (Pres., City Br., 2002–12). Pro-Chancellor and Chm. Council, City Univ., 2003–08. KStJ 2000. Grand Cordon (1st class), Order of Independence (Jordan), 2001. *Recreation:* gardening. *Heir: s* Robert Picton Seymour Howard, *b* 28 Jan. 1971. *Clubs:* City Livery, United Wards, Lime Street Ward.

HOWARD, Prof. Deborah Janet, PhD; FSA, FSAScot; FRSE; FBA 2010; Professor of Architectural History, 2001–13, now Emerita, and Director of Research, since 2014, University of Cambridge (Head, Department of History of Art, 2002–06 and 2007–09); Fellow of St John's College, Cambridge, since 1992; *b* 26 Feb. 1946; *d* of Thomas Were Howard, OBE and Isobel Howard (*née* Brewer); *m* 1975, Prof. Malcolm Sim Longair, *qv*; one *s* one *d*. *Educ:* Loughton High Sch. for Girls; Newnham Coll., Cambridge (BA 1st Cl. Hons Architecture and Fine Arts 1968; MA 1972); Courtauld Inst. of Art, Univ. of London (MA 1969; PhD 1973). FSA 1984; FSAScot 1991; FRSE 2004. Leverhulme Fellow in History of Art, Clare Hall, Cambridge, 1972–73; Lectr in History of Art, UCL, 1973–76; pt-time Lectr, 1982–90, Sen. Lectr, 1990–91, Reader, 1991, Dept of Architecture, Univ. of Edinburgh; pt-time Lectr, Courtauld Inst. of Art, Univ. of London, 1991–92; Cambridge University: Librarian, Faculty of Architecture and History of Art, 1992–96; Reader in Architectl History, 1996–2001. Kennedy Prof. of Renaissance Studies, Smith Coll., Mass, 2006; Vis. Prof., Harvard (Villa i Tatti), 2007; Robert Johnson-La Palme Vis. Prof., Princeton Univ., 2009; McGeorge Fellow, Univ. of Melbourne, 2012; Daphne Mayo Vis. Scholar, Univ. of Qld, 2012. Member: Royal Fine Art Commn for Scotland, 1987–95; Royal Commn on Ancient and Historical Monuments of Scotland, 1990–99; Scientific Cttee, Centro di Studi di

Architettura Andrea Palladio, Vicenza, Italy, 2011–; Scientific Adv. Bd, Max Planck Insts—Bibliotheca Hertziana, Rome, and Kunsthistorisches Institut, Florence, 2008–14; Comitato Scientifico, Centro di Studi di Architettura 'Andrea Palladio', Vicenza, 2011–; Chm., Soc. of Architectl Historians of GB, 1997–2000. Trustee: British Archtl Liby Trust, 2001–10; British Archtl Trust Bd (formerly RIBA Trust), 2010–; Venice in Peril, 2015–. Hon. FRIAS 1995. LittD UCD, 2014. *Publications:* (jtly) The Art of Claude Lorrain, 1969; Jacopo Sansovino: architecture and patronage in Renaissance Venice, 1975, 2nd edn 1987; The Architectural History of Venice, 1980, 2nd edn 1987, rev. and enlarged edn 2002; (ed and jtly) The Architecture of the Scottish Renaissance, 1990; (ed) William Adam, 1990; (ed) Scottish Architects Abroad, 1991; Scottish Architecture from the Reformation to the Restoration 1560–1660, 1995; (ed) Architecture in Italy 1500–1600 by Wolfgang Lotz, 2nd edn, 1995; (jtly) La Scuola Grande della Misericordia di Venezia, 1999; Venice & the East: the impact of the Islamic world on Venetian architecture, 2000; (ed with L. Moretti) Architettura e musica nella Venezia del Rinascimento, 2006; (with L. Moretti) Sound and Space in Renaissance Venice: architecture, music, acoustics, 2009; Venice Disputed: Marc'Antonio Barbaro and Venetian architecture 1550–1600, 2011; (ed with L. Moretti) The Music Room in Early Modern France and Italy: sound, space and object, 2012; (ed jtly) Architecture and Pilgrimage: Southern Europe and beyond, 1000–1500, 2013; (ed with H. McBurney) The Image of Venice: Fialetti's View and Sir Henry Wotton, 2014; numerous articles and book reviews in learned jls. *Recreations:* mountain walking (completed Scottish Munros, 2011), music, photography, gardening. *Address:* St John's College, Cambridge CB2 1TP. *T:* (01223) 339360; Faculty of Architecture and History of Art, University of Cambridge, 1 Scroope Terrace, Cambridge CB2 1PX. *T:* (01223) 332975.

HOWARD, Air Vice Marshal Graham John, CB 2014; FCILT; Assistant Chief of Defence Staff (Logistic Operations), 2011–14; *b* Spalding, Lincs, 29 Aug. 1960; *s* of Albert John Howard and Josephine Ann Howard (*née* Mason); *m* 1st, 1985, Penelope Ann Tiffany Richmond (marr. diss. 2004); two *d*; 2nd, 2006, Jacqueline Samantha (*née* Wilson); one step *d*. *Educ:* Gleed Boys' Sch.; Spalding Grammar Sch.; King's Coll., London (MA Defence Studies 1998). FCILT 2008. Commnd RAF, 1979; jun. logistics roles, 1980–95; acsc 1996; SO 1 Logistic Ops HQ Strike Comd, 1997–98; OC, Tactical Supply Wing, 1998–2000; PJHQ, 2000–04; CO, RAF Stafford, 2004–06; HCSC 2006; Strategic Delivery Unit, British Embassy, Kabul, 2006; Comdr, Jt Force Logistics HQ, PJHQ, 2007–08; Hd, Defence Logistics Policy, 2008–10; Hd, Defence Support Chain Ops and Movements, 2010–11. President: Movement Control Assoc., 2008–; Tactical Supply Wing and Servicing Commando Assoc., 2012–. *Recreations:* family, keeping fit, travel.

HOWARD, Prof. Ian George, RSA 1998; Principal, Edinburgh College of Art, 2001–11; Emeritus Professor, University of Edinburgh, since 2011; *b* 7 Nov. 1952; *s* of Harold Geoffrey Howard and Violet Howard (*née* Kelly); *m* 1977, Ruth D'Arcy; two *d*. *Educ:* Aberdeen Grammar Sch.; Univ. of Edinburgh; Edinburgh Coll. of Art. MA Hons Fine Art 1975; Postgrad. Dip. 1976. Lectr in Painting, Gray's Sch. of Art, Aberdeen, 1977–86; Head of Painting, Duncan of Jordanstone Coll. of Art, Dundee, 1986–95; Prof. of Fine Art (personal chair), Dundee Univ., 1995–2001; Mem., Faculty of Fine Art, British Sch. at Rome, 1996–2002; Dean, Duncan of Jordanstone Coll. of Art and Design, 1999–2001; Prof., Heriot-Watt Univ., 2001–11. Dir, Dundee Contemporary Arts Ltd, 1997–2004. Treas., Royal Scottish Acad., 2008–13. Numerous exhibns internationally; work in collections, including: Scottish Arts Council; Arts Council England; Contemporary Art Soc.; Edinburgh City Art Centre; Hunterian Art Gall., Glasgow; Fleming Collection, London; Royal Scottish Acad., V&A Mus. Trustee, Nat. Galls of Scotland, 2010–. Hon. Vice-Principal, Univ. of Edinburgh, 2009–11. Dr *hc* Edinburgh, 2007. *Publications:* Heretical Diagrams, 1995; Emblemata, 1998; Uncertain Histories, 2000. *Recreations:* travel, cooking, wild mushrooms. *Address:* Royal Scottish Academy, The Mound, Edinburgh EH2 2EL. *W:* http://ianhoward-art.net.

HOWARD, Rear-Adm. Jack; *see* Howard, Rear-Adm. C. J.

HOWARD, Prof. (James) Kenneth, OBE 2010; RA 1991 (ARA 1983); painter; Professor of Perspective, Royal Academy of Arts, 2001–11; *b* 26 Dec. 1932; *s* of Frank and Elizabeth Howard; *m* 1st, Ann Howard (*née* Popham), dress designer (marr. diss. 1974); 2nd, 1990, Christa Gaa (*née* Köhler), RWS (*d* 1992); 3rd, 2000, Dora Bertolutti. *Educ:* Kilburn Grammar School; Hornsey School of Art; Royal College of Art (ARCA). NEAC 1962 (Pres., 1998–2003); ROI 1966 (Hon. ROI 1988; Hon. Fellow 2007); RWA 1981; RWS 1983. British Council scholarship to Florence, 1958–59; taught various London Art Schools, 1959–73; Official Artist for Imperial War Museum in N Ireland, 1973, 1978; painted for the British Army in N Ireland, Germany, Cyprus, Hong Kong, Brunei, Nepal, Belize, Norway, Lebanon, Canada, Oman, 1973–; one man exhibitions: Plymouth Art Centre, 1955; John Whibley Gallery, 1966, 1968; New Grafton Gallery, 1971–2000; Jersey, 1978, 1980, 1983; Hong Kong, 1979; Nicosia, 1982; Delhi, 1983; Lowndes Lodge Gall., 1987, 1989, 1990, 1991; Sinfield Gall., 1991, 1993, 1995; Bankside Gall., 1996; Everard Reid Gall., Johannesburg, 1998; Richard Green Gall., 2002, 2003, 2004, 2005, 2006, 2009, 2011, 2013, 2015, 2016; RA Friends Room, 2009. Works purchased by Plymouth Art Gall., Imperial War Mus., Guildhall Art Gall., Ulster Mus., Nat. Army Mus., Hove Mus., Sheffield Art Gall., Southend Mus.; commissions for UN, BAOR, Drapers' Co., Stock Exchange, States of Jersey, Banque Paribas, Royal Hosp. Chelsea. Freeman: City of London, 2007; Painter-Stainers' Co., 2007 (Liveryman, 2007–). Hon. RBA 1989; RBSA 1991; Hon. SGA 2008. First Prize: Hunting Group Award, 1982; Sparkasse Karlsruhe, 1985. Gen. Editor, Art Class series, 1988. *Publications:* contribs to: The War Artists, 1983; 60th Vol. of The Old Water-Colour Societies' Club, 1985; Painting Interiors, 1989; Art of Landscape and Seascape, 1989; Visions of Venice, 1990; Venice: the artist's vision, 1990; 20th Century Painters and Sculptors, 1991; Oils Masterclass, 1996; (jtly) Ken Howard: a personal view—Inspired by Light, 1998; Dictionary of Artists in Britain since 1945, 1998; Britain's Paintings, 2003; St Ives 1975–2005: art colony in transition, 2007; Light and Dark, 2011; In the Footsteps of Turner, 2013; *relevant publication:* The Paintings of Ken Howard, by Michael Spender, 1992. *Recreations:* cinema, opera. *Address:* 8 South Bolton Gardens, SW5 0DH. *T:* (020) 7373 2912; (studio) St Clements Studio, Mousehole, Cornwall TR19 6TR. *T:* (01736) 731596; (studio) Ramo e Corte del Paludo, 6262 Cannaregio, Venice, Italy. *T:* 0415202277. *Clubs:* Arts, Chelsea Arts.

HOWARD, Hon. John (Winston), OM 2012; AC 2008; Prime Minister of Australia, 1996–2007; *b* 26 July 1939; *s* of Lyall F. Howard and Mona Howard; *m* 1971, Alison Janette Parker; two *s* one *d*. *Educ:* Canterbury Boys' High Sch.; Sydney Univ. Solicitor of NSW Supreme Court, 1962. MP (L) for Bennelong, NSW, 1974–2007. Minister for Business and Consumer Affairs, Australia, 1975; Minister assisting Prime Minister, May 1977; Minister for Special Trade Negotiations, July 1977; Federal Treasurer, 1977–83; Dep. Leader of the Opposition, 1983–85; Leader, Parly Liberal Party, 1985–89 and 1995–2007; Leader of the Opposition, Australia, 1985–89, 1995–96. Chm., Manpower and Labour Market Reform Gp, 1990–93. Chm., Internat. Dem. Union, 2002–. Hon. LLD Notre Dame. Centenary Medal, Australia, 2003; Gold Olympic Order, IOC, 2003; US Presidential Medal of Freedom, 2009. *Publications:* Lazarus Rising, 2010; The Menzies Era, 2014. *Recreations:* cricket, films, reading, golf. *Address:* GPO Box 36, Sydney, NSW 2001, Australia. *Club:* Australian (Sydney).

HOWARD, Prof. Jonathan Charles, DPhil; FRS 1995; Professor of Genetics, Institute for Genetics, University of Cologne, 1994–2011, now Emeritus; Director, Instituto Gulbenkian de Ciência, Oeiras, Portugal, since 2012; Max-Planck Fellow, Max-Planck Institute of Plant Breeding, Cologne, since 2013; *b* 24 June 1943; *s* of John Eldred Howard and Marghanita (*née* Laski); *m* 1990, Maria Leptin; two *s*. *Educ:* Westminster Sch.; Magdalen Coll., Oxford (BA Zool. 1964; DPhil Medicine 1969). Mem., Scientific Staff, MRC, at Cellular Immunology Res. Unit, Sir William Dunn Sch. of Pathology, Univ. of Oxford, 1968–73; Weir Jun. Res. Fellow, University Coll., Oxford, 1970–73; Babraham Institute, Cambridge: Mem. Staff, Dept of Immunology, 1974–94; Head of Dept, 1985–94; Res. Fellow, Clare Hall, Cambridge, 1975–78; sabbaticals at: Depts of Pathology and Cell Biol., Stanford Univ., 1983, 1987; Div. of Biol., CIT, 1983; EMBL, 1992. Mem., EMBO, 1993; MAE 2008. *Publications:* Darwin, 1982; papers in learned jls on immunology and evolution. *Recreations:* fishing, piano. *Address:* Institut für Genetik, Universität zu Köln, Zülpicher Strasse 47, 50674 Köln, Germany. *T:* (221) 4704864; Heinestrasse 19, 50931 Köln, Germany. *T:* (221) 4200320.

HOWARD, Prof. Judith Ann Kathleen, CBE 1996; FRS 2002; Professor of Chemistry, University of Durham, since 1991; *b* 21 Oct. 1945; *d* of James and Kathleen Duckworth. *Educ:* Univ. of Bristol (BSc Hons 1966; DSc 1986); Somerville Coll., Oxford (DPhil 1971). CChem, FRSC 1991; EurChem 1996; CPhys, FInstP 1996. Sen. Res. Fellow, 1987–91, Reader, 1991, Univ. of Bristol; Sen. Fellow, Royal Soc. Leverhulme Trust, 1996–97; Sir Derman Christopherson Fellow, Univ. of Durham, 1997–98; EPSRC Sen. Res. Fellow, 1998–2003. DUniv Open, 1998; Hon. DSc: Bristol, 2004; Bath, 2005. *Publications:* (contrib.) Encyclopedia of Inorganic Chemistry, 1994; Crystallographic Instrumentation, 1998; Implications of Molecular and Materials Structure for New Technologies, 1999; over 1100 jl articles. *Recreations:* music, reading, hiking, art, swimming. *Address:* Department of Chemistry, University of Durham, Durham DH1 3LE. *T:* (0191) 334 2047, *Fax:* (0191) 334 2051. *E:* j.a.k.howard@durham.ac.uk.

HOWARD, Kenneth; *see* Howard, J. K.

HOWARD, Laurence, OBE 2004; PhD; Lord-Lieutenant of Rutland, since 2003; *b* 29 March 1943; *s* of Henry Lovering Howard and Beryl Cicely Howard; *m* 1966, Christine Mary Kinver; one *s* one *d*. *Educ:* Strode's Sch.; Nottingham Univ. (BSc 1967); Leicester Univ. (PhD Neurophysiol. 1971). Wolfson Fellow, 1970–73; Leicester University: Lectr, 1974, Sen. Lectr, 1988–90, in Physiology; Sub-Dean, Med. Sch., 1990–2003; Associate Lectr in Physiology, 2003–06. Chairman: Bd of Visitors, HM Prison Stocken, 1988–91; Leicester Magistrates' Courts Cttee, 1997–2002; Central Council, Magistrates' Courts Cttees, 2002–03; Pres., Leics and Rutland Magistrates' Assoc., 2004–; Mem., Unified Courts Admin Bd, 2002–04. President: Leics and Rutland Headway, 2005–; Leics and Rutland Community Foundn, 2010–; Rutland Sinfonia, 2012–. Patron, Leicester Charity Link, 2010–. Freeman, City of London, 1966. JP Rutland, 1979 (Chm. Bench, 1988–94). Hon. Fellow, UC Northampton, 2001. Hon. Air Cdre, 504 (Notts) Sqdn, 2008–. Hon. LLD Leicester, 2013. *Publications:* articles on physiology in scientific jls. *Recreations:* travel, horse riding, music. *Address:* Daventry House, Main Street, Whissendine, Rutland LE15 7ET. *T:* (01664) 474662. *E:* laurence@whiss64.plus.com.

HOWARD, Margaret; freelance broadcaster and concert presenter, since 1969; presenter, with Classic FM, 1992–99; *b* 29 March 1938; *d* of John Bernard Howard and Ellen Corwena Roberts. *Educ:* St Mary's Convent, Rhyl, N Wales; St Teresa's Convent, Sunbury; Guildhall Sch. of Music and Drama; Indiana Univ., Bloomington, USA; Open Univ. (BA Hons Hum. 2013). LGSM; LRAM 1960. Joined BBC, 1955; British govt tech. asst, Nigerian Broadcasting Corp., 1965–66 (on secondment); BBC World Service Announcer, 1967–69; Teaching Asst, Dept of Radio and TV, Indiana Univ., 1969–70; Reporter: The World This Weekend, BBC Radio 4, 1970–74; Edition, BBC TV, 1971; Tomorrow's World, BBC TV, 1972; Editor and Presenter: Pick of the Week, BBC Radio 4, 1974–91; Classic Reports, Classic FM, 1992–94; Howard's Week, Classic FM, 1994–97; Presenter: It's Your World, BBC World Service, 1981–86; Masterclass, 1994–99, Music and the Mind, concert series with Medici Quartet, 1995, Classic FM; concerts: Haydn's Seven Last Words from the Cross, Medici Quartet, 2001, 2002; Viva Verdi, Opera Nazionale Italiana, UK tour, 2001; Interviewer/Presenter, Strictly Instrumental, occasional BBC series, 1980–85; consultant and recording artist, Classical Communications Ltd, 2003–. Radio critic, The Tablet; columnist, The Universe; record columnist, Chic magazine. Female UK Radio Personality of the Year, Sony Awards, 1984; Sony Radio Awards Roll of Honour, 1988; Voice of the Listener Award for excellence, 1991; Radio Personality of the Year, TRIC Awards, 1996; inducted into Radio Acad. Hall of Fame, 2013. *Publications:* Margaret Howard's Pick of the Week, 1984; Court Jesting, 1986. *Recreations:* swimming, tasting wine, dog walking, Nordic walking. *Address:* 215 Cavendish Road, SW12 0BP. *T:* (020) 8673 7336. *Club:* South London Swimming (Tooting).

HOWARD, Martin Lloyd, CB 2007; Chief of Assessments Staff, Cabinet Office, since 2014; *b* 1 Oct. 1954; *s* of late Leonard Lloyd Howard and of Joan Mary Howard; *m* 1993, Caroline Jane Delves. *Educ:* Gravesend Grammar Sch. Joined MoD, 1975; apptd Sen. CS, 1993; Dir, Central and Eastern Europe, MoD, 1993–94; Private Sec. to Sec. of State for NI (on loan), 1994–96; Dep. Chief, Assessments Staff, Cabinet Office (on loan), 1996–98; Ministry of Defence: Hd, Overseas Secretariat, 1998–99; Dir of News, 1999–2001; Dir Gen., Corporate Communications, 2001–03; Dep. Chief of Defence Intelligence, 2003–04; Dir Gen., Operational Policy, 2004–07; Asst Sec. Gen. (Ops), NATO, 2007–11; Dir, Cyber Policy Support, later Cyber Policy and Internat. Relns, GCHQ, 2011–14. *Recreations:* classical and contemporary guitar, sailing, reading, music. *Address:* Cabinet Office, 70 Whitehall, SW1A 2AS. *T:* (020) 7276 0292.

HOWARD, Prof. Maurice, PhD; Professor of Art History, University of Sussex, since 2001; *b* Isleworth, London, 16 June 1948; *s* of Henry George Howard and Elsie May Howard (*née* Minter). *Educ:* Walpole and Langley Grammar Schs; Christ's Coll., Cambridge (BA Hons 1970); Courtauld Inst. of Art (MA 1972); Univ. of London (PhD 1985). Lecturer in Art History: Pennsylvania State Univ., 1972–73; Univ. of St Andrews, 1974–76; University of Sussex: Lectr in Art Hist., 1976–96; Reader, 1996–2001. Hon. Res. Fellow, V&A Mus., 2001–06, 2008–11. Chm., 1991–94, Pres., 2013–, Soc. of Architectural Historians of GB; Pres., Soc. of Antiquaries of London, 2010–14 (Dir, 2007–10). *Publications:* The Early Tudor Country House: architecture and politics 1490–1550, 1987; The Tudor Image, 1995; (jtly) Ornament: a social history since 1450, 1996; (jtly) The Vyne: a Tudor house revealed, 2003; The Building of Elizabethan and Jacobean England, 2007. *Recreations:* opera, tennis. *Address:* Arts Building, University of Sussex, Falmer, Brighton BN1 9QN. *T:* (01273) 606755. *E:* M.Howard@sussex.ac.uk.

HOWARD, Sir Michael (Eliot), OM 2005; CH 2002; Kt 1986; CBE 1977; MC 1943; DLitt; FBA 1970; FRHistS; Emeritus Professor of Modern History, University of Oxford, since 1989; *b* 29 Nov. 1922; *y s* of late Geoffrey Eliot Howard, Ashmore, near Salisbury, and of Edith Julia Emma, *o d* of Otto Edinger; civil partnership 2006, Mark Anthony James. *Educ:* Wellington; Christ Church, Oxford (BA 1946, MA 1948; Hon. Student, 1990). Served War, Coldstream Guards, 1942–45. Asst Lecturer in History, University of London, King's Coll., 1947; Lecturer, 1950; Lecturer, then Reader, in War Studies, 1953–63; Prof. of War Studies, 1963–68; University of Oxford: Fellow of All Souls Coll., 1968–80 (Hon. Fellow, 2014); Chichele Prof. of History of War, 1977–80; Regius Prof. of Modern History and Fellow of Oriel Coll., 1980–89 (Hon. Fellow, 1990); Robert A. Lovett Prof. of Military and Naval Hist., Yale Univ., 1989–93. Vis. Prof. of European History, Stanford Univ., 1967; Kluge Vis. Prof., Library of Congress, 2003. Ford's Lectr in English History, Oxford, 1971; Radcliffe Lectr, Univ. of Warwick, 1975; Trevelyan Lectr, Cambridge, 1977; Leverhulme Lectr, 1996; Lee Kuan Yew Distinguished Visitor, Nat. Univ. of Singapore, 1996. FKC. Pres. and co-Founder, Internat. Institute for Strategic Studies; Vice-Pres., Council on Christian Approaches to Defence and Disarmament; Pres., Army Records Soc. Hon. Gov., Ditchley Foundn, 2011–. Gov., Wellington Coll., 1979–90. For. Hon. Mem., Amer. Acad. of Arts and Scis, 1983. Hon. LittD Leeds, 1979; Hon. DLit London, 1988; Hon. DHumLit Lehigh Univ.,

Pa, USA, 1990. Chesney Meml Gold Medal, RUSI, 1973; NATO Atlantic Award, 1989. *Publications:* The Coldstream Guards, 1920–46 (with John Sparrow), 1951; Disengagement in Europe, 1958; Wellingtonian Studies, 1959; The Franco-Prussian War, 1961 (Duff Cooper Memorial Prize, 1962); The Theory and Practice of War, 1965; The Mediterranean Strategy in the Second World War, 1967; Studies in War and Peace, 1970; Grand Strategy, vol IV (in UK History of 2nd World War, Military series), 1971 (Wolfson Foundn History Award, 1972); The Continental Commitment, 1972; War in European History, 1976; (with P. Paret) Clausewitz On War, 1977; War and the Liberal Conscience, 1978; (ed) Restraints on War, 1979; The Causes of Wars, 1983; Clausewitz, 1983; Strategic Deception in World War II, 1990; The Lessons of History, 1991; (ed with W. R. Louis) The Oxford History of the Twentieth Century, 1998; The Invention of Peace, 2000 (Pol Book Prize, Friedrich Ebert Stiftung); The First World War, 2002; Captain Professor: a life in war and peace (autobiog.), 2006; Liberation or Catastrophe?: reflections on the history of the 20th century, 2007. *Address:* The Old Farm, Eastbury, Hungerford, Berks RG17 7JN. *Clubs:* Athenæum, Garrick, Pratt's.

HOWARD, Michael Newman; QC 1986; a Recorder of the Crown Court, since 1993; *b* 10 June 1947; *s* of late Henry Ian Howard and of Tilly Celia Howard. *Educ:* Clifton College; Magdalen College, Oxford (MA, BCL). Lecturer in Law, LSE, 1970–74; called to the Bar, Gray's Inn, 1971, Bencher, 1995; in practice at Bar, 1971–; Asst Recorder, 1989–93; Leader of Admiralty Bar, 1999–. Visiting Professor: Law, Univ. of Essex, 1987–92; Maritime Law, UCL, 1996–99; Maritime Law, Tulane Univ., 2011–. Mem. of Panel, Lloyd's Salvage Arbitrators, 1987–2009. *Publications:* Phipson on Evidence, ed jtly, 12th edn 1976 to 14th edn 1990, Gen. Ed., 15th edn 2000; *contributions to:* Frustration and Force Majeure, 1991, 2nd edn 1995; *Consensus ad Idem:* essays for Guenter Treitel, 1996; Halsbury's Laws of England, 4th edn (Damages); Butterworth's Commercial Court and Arbitration Pleadings, 2005; Palmer on Bailment, 3rd edn, 2009; articles and reviews in legal periodicals. *Recreations:* books, music, sport. *Address:* Quadrant Chambers, Quadrant House, 10 Fleet Street, EC4Y 1AU. *T:* (020) 7583 4444, *Fax:* (020) 7583 4455. *E:* michael.howard@quadrantchambers.com. *Clubs:* Royal Automobile, Oxford and Cambridge, Garrick.

HOWARD, Philip Ewen; Head Chef and Co-owner, The Square, W1, since 1991; *b* Johannesburg, SA, 5 June 1966; *s* of Francis and Lynne Howard; *m* 1990, Jennifer Collier; one *s* one *d*. *Educ:* Bradfield Coll.; Univ. of Kent at Canterbury (BSc Microbiol. 1987). Commis Chef, Roux Restaurants, 1987–88; Chef de Partie: Harveys, 1988–89; Bibendum, 1989–90; Co-owner: The Ledbury, 2005–; Kitchen W8, 2009–; Sonny's Kitchen, 2012–. 2 Michelin Stars, 1994, 1998; 4 AA Rosettes, 2012. Catey Award for Restaurateur of Year, 2011; Restaurateurs Chefs Chef of Year, AA, 2013. *Publications:* The Square: The Cook Book, vol. 1: savoury, 2012; The Square: The Cook Book, vol. 2: sweet, 2013. *Recreations:* ski-ing, running, travelling. *Address:* The Square, 6–10 Bruton Street, W1J 6PU. *T:* (020) 7495 7100. *E:* phil@squarerestaurant.com.

HOWARD, Rebecca Mary; *see* Sabben-Clare, R. M.

HOWARD, Robert, (Bob); Northern Regional Secretary, Trades Union Congress, 1980–2000; *b* 4 April 1939; *s* of Robert and Lily Howard; *m* 1984, Valerie Stewart; two *s* one *d*. *Educ:* Gregson Lane County Primary Sch.; Deepdale Secondary Modern Sch.; Queen Elizabeth's Grammar Sch., Blackburn, Lancs; Cliff Training Coll., Calver via Sheffield, Derbyshire. British Leyland, Lancs, 1961–68: Member, Clerical and Admin. Workers' Union Br. Exec.; Councillor, Walton le Dale UDC, 1962–65; GPO, Preston, Lancs, 1969–80: Telephone Area UPW Telecomms Representative Member: Jt Consultative Council, Jt Productivity Council, Council of PO Unions Area Cttee, Delegate to Preston Trades Council; Secretary, Lancashire Assoc. of Trades Councils, 1977–79; created 14 specialist cttees for LATC; appointment as N Reg. Sec., TUC, 1980, by Gen. Sec., TUC, first full-time secretary to a TUC region. Member: Industrial Tribunals, 1979–80; Northumbria Regional Cttee, Nat. Trust, 1989–; Council, Northern Exams Assoc., 1986–; Board: Durham Univ. Business Sch., 1987–; Tyneside TEC, 1989–99; Northern Develt Co., 1991–99; Nat. Resource for Innovative Trng Res. and Employment Ltd, later Northern Informatics, 1995–99. Northern Region Coordinator, Jobs March, 1983; Exec. Organiser, Great North Family Gala Day, 1986–90. JP Duchy of Lancaster, 1969–74. *Publications:* North-East Lancashire Structure Plan—The Trades Councils' View (with Peter Stock), 1979; Organisation and Functions of TUC Northern Regional Council, 1980. *Recreations:* fell walking, opera, ballet, classical music, camping, cricket, football, spectating outdoor sports, reading, chess. *Address:* 8 Caxton Way, North Lodge, Chester le Street, County Durham DH3 4BW. *Club:* Durham CC.

HOWARD, Stephen Lee, LVO 2015; Chief Executive, Business in the Community, since 2008 (Managing Director, 2005–08); *b* 25 March 1953; *s* of Richard and Marilyn Howard; *m* 1976, Holly Grothe; three *s*. *Educ:* Michigan State Univ. (BA 1975); Univ. of Michigan Law Sch. (JD *cum laude* 1978). In practice as lawyer, Providence, RI, 1978–85; Cookson America Inc.: General Counsel, 1985–86; Vice-Pres., Corporate Develt and General Counsel, 1986–91; Cookson Group plc: Chief Exec., Gp Develt, 1991–92; Dir and Chief Exec., Engineered Prods Div. and Gp Corporate Develt, 1992–94; Chief Exec., Ceramic and Engineered Prods Div. and Gp Corporate Develt, 1994–97; Gp Jt Man. Dir, 1995–97; Gp Chief Exec., 1997–2004; Chief Exec., Novar plc, 2004–05. Non-executive Director: SEGRO plc (formerly Slough Estates plc), 2001–10; Balfour Beatty plc; In Kind Direct, 2008–. Mem., Adv. Bd, Veolia. Dep. Chm., Habitat, Humanity GB. Gov., St George's Coll. *Recreations:* tennis, basketball. *Address:* Business in the Community, 137 Shepherdess Walk, N1 7RQ. *Club:* Royal Automobile.

HOWARD, Victoria; *see* Barnsley, V.

HOWARD-JOHNSTON, Angela Maureen; *see* Huth, A. M.

HOWARD-LAWSON, Sir John (Philip), 6th Bt *cr* 1841, of Brough Hall, Yorkshire; *b* 6 June 1934; *s* of Sir William Howard Lawson, 5th Bt and Joan Eleanor (*d* 1989), *d* of late Arthur Cowie Stamer, CBE; assumed by Royal Licence surname and arms of Howard, 1962, of Howard-Lawson, 1992; *S* father, 1990; *m* 1960, Jean Veronica (*née* Marsh) (*d* 2001); two *s* one *d*. *Educ:* Ampleforth. *Heir: s* Philip William Howard [*b* 28 June 1961; *m* 1st, 1988, Cara Margaret Browne (marr. diss. 1992); 2nd, 1993, Isabel Anne Oldridge de la Hey; one *d*]. *Address:* Wood House, Otters Holt, Culgaith, Penrith, Cumbria CA10 1SG. *T:* (01768) 88315.

HOWARTH, family name of **Baron Howarth of Newport**.

HOWARTH OF BRECKLAND, Baroness *cr* 2001 (Life Peer), of Parson Cross in the County of South Yorkshire; **Valerie Georgina Howarth,** OBE 1999; founding Chief Executive, ChildLine, 1987–2001; *b* 5 Sept. 1940. *Educ:* Abbeydale Girls' Grammar Sch.; Univ. of Leicester. MBASW; Associate Mem., ADASS. Caseworker, Family Welfare Assoc., 1963–68; London Borough of Lambeth: Sen. Child CareWorker and Trng Officer, 1968–70; Area Co-ordinator, 1970–72; Chief Co-ordinator of Social Work, 1972–76; Asst Dir of Personal Services, 1976–82; Dir of Social Services, London Borough of Brent, 1982–86. Board Member: Food Standards Agency, 2000–07; Nat. Care Standards Commn, 2001–04; Children and Family Courts Adv. and Support Services, 2004–12 (Chm., 2008–12). Founder Member: King's Cross Homelessness Project (first Chm.), 1986–87; London Homelessness Forum, 1986–87; Home Office Steering Gp on Child Witnesses, 1991–97; Telephone Helplines Assoc. (first Chm.); NCH Commn considering Children as Abusers, 1991–92. Dir and Mem. Cttee, ICSTIS, 1988–2000; Mem., NSPCC Professional Adv. Panel, 1993–94; UK Rep., Euro Forum for Child Welfare, 1994–97. Member: Sub cttee G on EU, H of L, 2005–10 (Chm., 2007–10); EU Select Cttee, H of L, 2007–10; Sub cttee D on Agric. and Fisheries, H of L, 2010–. Trustee, Livability (formerly John Grooms Assoc. for Disabled People, later Grooms-Shaftesbury), 1987– (Chair, 2007–10; Pres., 2005–14; Sen. Vice-Pres., 2014–); Trustee: Lucy Faithfull Foundn, 1992– (Vice Chm.); NCVCCO, 1990–95 (Vice Chm.); Stop It Now, 1992–2009 (Chm.); Nat. Children's Bureau, 1993–94; Michael Sieff Foundn, 1994–2004; Little Hearts Matter, 2002– (Patron, 2002–); Children's Internat. Helplines Assoc., 2003–07 (Chm. Trustees, 2003–07; Pres., 2007–); Patron, TRACKS, 2011–. DUniv Open, 2007. *Recreations:* gardening, reading, walking, people, church activities. *Address:* House of Lords, SW1A 0PW. *E:* howarthv@parliament.uk.

HOWARTH OF NEWPORT, Baron *cr* 2005 (Life Peer), of Newport in the county of Gwent; **Alan Thomas Howarth,** CBE 1982; PC 2000; *b* 11 June 1944; *e s* of late T. E. B. Howarth, MC, TD and Margaret Howarth; *m* 1967, Gillian Martha (marr. diss. 1996), *d* of Mr and Mrs Arthur Chance, Dublin; two *s* two *d*. *Educ:* Rugby Sch. (scholar); King's Coll., Cambridge (major scholar in History; BA 1965). Sen. Res. Asst to Field-Marshal Montgomery on A History of Warfare, 1965–67; Asst Master, Westminster Sch., 1968–74; Private Sec. to Chm. of Conservative Party, 1975–79; Dir, Cons. Res. Dept, 1979–81; Vice-Chm., Conservative Party, 1980–81. MP: Stratford on Avon, 1983–97, (C) 1983–95, (Lab) 1995–97; (Lab) Newport E, 1997–2005. PPS to Dr Rhodes Boyson, MP, 1985–87; an Asst Govt Whip, 1987–88; Lord Comr of HM Treasury, 1988–89; Parliamentary Under-Secretary of State: DES, 1989–92 (Schools Minister, 1989–90; Minister for Higher Educn and Sci., 1990–92); DFEE, 1997–98 (Employment Minister and Minister for Disabled People); DCMS, 1998–2001 (Minister for the Arts). Secretary: Cons. Arts and Heritage Cttee, 1984–85; PLP Social Security Cttee, 1996–97; Member: Nat. Heritage Select Cttee, 1992–94; Social Security Select Cttee, 1995–97; Intelligence and Security Cttee, 2001–05; Ad Hoc Cttee on Internat. Orgns, 2008–09; Chm., All Party Parly Gp on Charities and Vol. Sector, 1992–97; Treas., 1993–97, Vice-Pres., 2002–, All Party Arts and Heritage Gp; Co-Chairman: All Party Parly Gp on Architecture and Planning, 2005–11; All Party Parly Gp on Arts, Health and Wellbeing, 2014–; Hon. Treas. and Vice-Chm., All Party Parly Gp for Drug Policy Reform, 2013–. Chm., Friends, Huntington's Disease Assoc., 1988–97; Mem. Adv. Council, Nat. Listening Library, 1992–97; Vice-Pres., British Dyslexia Assoc., 1994–97; Chm., UK Literary Heritage Wkg Gp, 2006–12; Mem. Bd, Norwich Heritage and Econ. Regeneration Trust, 2006–. Mem. Bd, Poetry Archive, 2006–13. Mem. Court: Univ. of Warwick, 1987–97; Univ. of Birmingham, 1992–97. Mem. Bd, Inst. of Historical Res., 1992–97. Gov., Royal Shakespeare Theatre, 1984–97; Chm., Trustees and Govs, Royal Pavilion Museums Foundn (formerly Friends of Royal Pavilion Art Gall. and Mus), Brighton and Hove, 2006–11. FSA 2007. *Publications:* (jtly) Monty at Close Quarters, 1985; jt author of various CPC pamphlets. *Recreations:* books, the arts, walking. *Address:* House of Lords, SW1A 0PW.

HOWARTH, David Ross; Reader in Private Law, since 2005 and Director, MPhil in Public Policy, since 2012, University of Cambridge; *b* 10 Nov. 1958; *s* of George Albert Howarth and Jean Howarth (*née* Rowbotham); *m* 1985, Edna Helen Murphy; two *s*. *Educ:* Queen Mary's Grammar Sch., Walsall; Clare Coll., Cambridge (BA 1981); Yale Univ. (MA 1982; LLM 1983; MPhil 1985). University of Cambridge: William Sen. Res. Fellow in Comparative Law, 1985–87, Lectr, 1987, Clare Coll.; Univ. Asst Lectr, 1987–92, Univ. Lectr, 1992–2005, Dir, Graduate Prog., 2011–12, Dept of Land Economy; Associate Fellow, Cambridge Centre for Sci. and Policy, 2010–. Mem. (Lib Dem), Cambridge CC, 1987–2004 (Leader, 2000–03; Hon. Councillor, 2010). MP (Lib Dem) Cambridge, 2005–10. Lib Dem Shadow to Energy Minister, 2005–07, Solicitor-Gen., 2007, Sec. State for Justice, 2008–10. Member: Envmtl Audit Select Cttee, 2005–07; Constit. Affairs, later Justice, Select Cttee, 2005–08. Member: Electoral Commn, 2010–; Council of Advrs, Rand Europe, 2012–; Founding Mem., Cambridge Cttee for Public Policy, 2012–; Co-Chair, Univ. of Cambridge Strategic Res. Initiative in Public Policy, 2013–. *Publications:* Textbook on Tort, 1995; (jtly) Tort: cases and materials, 2000, 6th edn 2008; (jtly) The Law of Tort, 2001; (jtly) Reinventing the State, 2007; Law as Engineering: thinking about what lawyers do, 2013; numerous articles in learned jls and edited books. *Address:* Clare College, Cambridge CB2 1TL. *T:* (01223) 333200.

HOWARTH, Elgar; freelance musician; *b* 4 Nov. 1935; *s* of Oliver and Emma Howarth; *m* 1958, Mary Bridget Neary; one *s* two *d*. *Educ:* Manchester Univ. (MusB); Royal Manchester Coll. of Music (ARMCM 1956; FRMCM 1970). Royal Opera House, Covent Garden (Orchestra), 1958–63; Royal Philharmonic Orchestra, 1963–69; Mem., London Sinfonietta, 1968–71; Mem., Philip Jones Brass Ensemble, 1965–76; freelance conductor, 1970–; Principal Guest Conductor, Opera North, 1985–88; Musical Advisor, Grimethorpe Colliery Brass Band, 1972–2007. Hon. RAM 1989; FRNCM 1994; FRWCMD (FWCMD 1997); FRCM 1999. Hon. Fellow, UC Salford, 1992. DUniv: Birmingham, 1993; York, 1999; Hon. DMus Keele, 1995; DLitt: Salford, 2003; Huddersfield, 2009. Olivier Award for Outstanding Achievement in Opera (for Die Soldaten, and The Prince of Hamburg, ENO), 1997. *Publications:* various compositions mostly for brass instruments.

HOWARTH, Rt Hon. George (Edward); PC 2005; MP (Lab) Knowsley, since 2010 (Knowsley North, Nov. 1986–1997; Knowsley North and Sefton East, 1997–2010); *b* 29 June 1949; *m* 1977, Julie Rodgers; two *s* (one *d* decd). *Educ:* Liverpool Polytechnic. Formerly: engineer; teacher; Chief Exec., Wales TUC's Co-operative Centre, 1984–86. Former Mem., Huyton UDC; Mem., Knowsley BC, 1975–86 (Dep. Leader, 1982). Parliamentary Under-Secretary of State: Home Office, 1997–99; NI Office, 1999–2001. Mem., Intelligence and Security Cttee, 2015–. *Address:* House of Commons, SW1A 0AA.

HOWARTH, Sir (James) Gerald (Douglas), Kt 2012; MP (C) Aldershot, since 1997; *b* 12 Sept. 1947; *s* of late James Howarth and Mary Howarth, Hurley, Berks; *m* 1973, Elizabeth Jane, *d* of late Michael and Muriel Squibb, Crowborough, Sussex; two *s* one *d*. *Educ:* Haileybury and ISC Jun. Sch.; Bloxham Sch.; Southampton Univ. (BA Hons). Commnd RAFVR, 1968. Gen. Sec., Soc. for Individual Freedom, 1969–71; entered internat. banking, 1971; Bank of America Internat., 1971–77; European Arab Bank, 1977–81 (Manager, 1979–81); Syndication Manager, Standard Chartered Bank, 1981–83; Dir, Richard Unwin Internat., 1983–87; Jt Man. Dir, Taskforce Communications, 1993–96. Dir, Freedom Under Law, 1973–77; estabd Dicey Trust, 1976. Mem., Hounslow BC, 1982–83. MP (C) Cannock and Burntwood, 1983–92. Parliamentary Private Secretary: to Parly Under-Sec. of State for Energy, 1987–90; to Minister for Housing and Planning, 1990–91; to Rt Hon. Margaret Thatcher, MP, 1991–92; Shadow Defence Minister, 2002–10; Parly Under-Sec. of State, MoD, 2010–12. Member: Select Cttee on Sound Broadcasting, 1987–92; Home Affairs Select Cttee, 1997–2001; Defence Select Cttee, 2001–03. Chairman: Lords and Commons Family and Child Protection Gp, 1999–2005; All Party RAF Gp, 2005; Vice-Chairman: Parly Aerospace Gp, 1997; All-Party Photography Gp, 2004–; Jt Sec., Cons. Parly Aviation Cttee, 1983–87; Vice-Chm., Cons. Parly Envmt, Transport and the Regions Cttee, 1997–99; Jt Vice-Chm., Cons. Parly Home Affairs Cttee, 2000–02. Mem. Exec., 1922 Cttee, 1999–2002; Chm., 92 Gp, 2001–07, 2013–. Chm., Conservative Way Forward, 2013–. Pres., British Air Display Assoc. (formerly Air Display Assoc. Europe), 2002–; Mem. Council, Air League. Trustee: Vulcan to the Sky Trust, 2006–; British Forces Foundn, 2008–. Jt Patron, Aerobility (formerly British Disabled Flying Assoc.), 2009–. CRAeS 2004. Liveryman, Hon. Co. of Air Pilots (formerly GAPAN), 2011. Britannia Airways Parly Pilot of the Year, 1988. Contributor to No Turning Back Gp pubns. *Recreations:* flying (private pilot's licence, 1965), photography, walking up hills, normal family pursuits. *Address:* House of Commons, SW1A 0AA. *T:* (020) 7219 5650.

HOWARTH, Judith; soprano; *b* 11 Sept. 1962; *m* 1986, Gordon Wilson. *Educ:* Royal Scottish Acad. of Music and Drama. Rôles include: *Royal Opera:* 1985–86: Oscar, in Un Ballo in Maschera (also in Florida); Elvira, in L'Italiana in Algeri; Iris, in Semele; 1989–: Adele, in Die Fledermaus; Ännchen, in Der Freischutz; Gilda, in Rigoletto; Liu, in Turandot; Marguerite de Valois, in Les Huguenots; Marzelline, in Fidelio; Morgana, in Alcina; Musetta, in La Bohème; Norina, in Don Pasquale; *Opera North:* 1992–: Cressida, in Troilus and Cressida; Norina; Susanna, in Le Nozze di Figaro; *English National Opera:* Madame Mao, in Nixon in China; Fiorilla, in Il Turko in Italia; Leila, in Les Pêcheurs des Perles; Butterfly, in Madame Butterfly; other rôles and productions include: Violetta, in La Traviata, Glyndebourne Touring Opera; Anne Trulove, in The Rake's Progress, Brussels; Marie, in La Fille du Régiment, Geneva; Hasse's Solimano and Cavilli's La Didone, Berlin; Countess Olga Sukarev, in Fedora, Washington; Soprano Heroines, in Les Contes d'Hoffmann, Nedda, in I Pagliacci, Florida; Aithra, in Die Ägyptische Helena, Santa Fe; Ellen Orford, in Peter Grimes, Toulouse; Pamina, in Die Zauberflöte, Strasbourg; title rôle in Maria Stuarda, WNO. Many concerts and festival appearances, incl. Salzburg, Aix-en-Provence, Edinburgh.

HOWARTH, His Honour Nigel John Graham; commercial and civil arbitrator, since 2011; accredited mediator, since 2012; a Circuit Judge, 1992–2006; a Deputy Circuit Judge, 2006–11; *b* 12 Dec. 1936; *s* of Vernon and Irene Howarth; *m* 1962, Janice Mary Hooper; two *s* one *d*. *Educ:* Manchester Grammar Sch.; Manchester Univ. (LLB, LLM). Called to the Bar, Gray's Inn, 1960; private practice at Chancery Bar, Manchester, 1961–92; Actg Deemster, IOM, 1985, 1989; a Recorder, 1989–92. ACIArb 2012. Chm., Northern Chancery Bar Assoc., 1990–92. Pres., Manchester Incorp. Law Library Soc., 1985–87. Vice Pres., Disabled Living, 1993–2008. *Recreations:* music, theatre, fell walking, Assoc. football (Altrincham FC). *Address:* Exchange Chambers, 7 Ralli Courts, W Riverside, Manchester M3 5FT.

HOWARTH, Paul John Arton; Managing Director, National Nuclear Laboratory, since 2009; *b* Manchester, 6 Aug. 1970; *s* of Dr Graham Arton and Edith May Howarth; *m* 1995, Victoria Dawn Cooper; three *s*. *Educ:* Knutsford High Sch.; Univ. of Birmingham (BSc Hons Phys and Astrophys; PhD Nuclear Phys 1995); Univ. of Salford (MSc Business Admin). British Nuclear Fuels plc, 1995–2006: Consultant Physicist, BNFL Instruments, 1995–96; Royal Soc. Fellowship, Kyushu Technol. Transfer Centre, then Japan Atomic Energy Res. Inst., 1997–98; Res. and Technol. Commercial Manager, 1998–2000; Special Asst to Dir of Technol. and Ops, 2000–01; Hd of Technol. for Nuclear Generation, Berkeley Labs, 2001–02; Prog. Dir for Advanced Reactor Res., then Hd, Gp Science and Skills Strategy, 2002–06; Executive Director: Dalton Nuclear Inst., Univ. of Manchester, 2007–09; Battelle Energy UK, 2011–. Vis. Prof., Univ. of Manchester, 2009–. Non-exec. Dir, NPL, 2015–; Chm., Centre of Nuclear Excellence, 2015–. Mem. Bd, Assoc. of Independent Res. and Technol. Orgns, 2014–. FREng 2014. *Recreations:* cycling, hockey, fell walking, squash. *Address:* Whirlwind, 1 Hermitage Lane, Goostrey, Cheshire CW4 8HB. *E:* paul.ja.howarth@nnl.co.uk.

HOWARTH, Peter Andreas; Managing Director, Show Media Ltd, since 2002; *b* 12 Sept. 1964; three *s*; partner, Emma Tucker. *Educ:* Gonville and Caius Coll., Cambridge (BA English 1986). Projects Manager, Paul Smith Ltd, 1986–88; Head of Menswear, Nicole Farhi, 1988–91; Style Ed., 1991–93, Style Dir, 1993–95, GQ; Editor: Arena, 1995–96; Esquire, 1996–2002. *Publications:* (ed) Fatherhood, 1997.

HOWARTH, Robert Lever; Member (Lab), Bolton County Borough, then Metropolitan Borough, Council, 1972–2004 (Leader, Labour Group, 1975–2004; Leader of the Council, 1980–2004); *b* 31 July 1927; *s* of James Howarth and Bessie (*née* Pearson); *m* 1952, Josephine Mary Doyle; one *s* one *d*. *Educ:* Bolton County Grammar Sch.; Bolton Technical Coll. Draughtsman with Hawker Siddeley Dynamics. MP (Lab) Bolton East, 1964–70. Lectr in Liberal Studies, Leigh Technical Coll., 1970–76; Senior Lectr in General Studies, Wigan Coll. of Technology, 1977–87. Dep. Chm., 1986–87, Chm., 1987–88 and 2002–03, Manchester Airport. Mem. (Lab), Bolton BC, 1958–60, 1963–66; Freeman, 2001, Hon. Alderman, 2004, Bolton MBC. *Recreations:* gardening, reading, walking, films. *Address:* 93 Markland Hill, Bolton, Lancs BL1 5EQ. *T:* (01204) 844121.

HOWARTH, Stephen Frederick; HM Diplomatic Service, retired; UK Permanent Representative to Council of Europe, Strasbourg (with personal rank of Ambassador), 2003–07; *b* 25 Feb. 1947; *s* of Alan Howarth and Alice Howarth (*née* Wilkinson); *m* 1966, Jennifer Mary Chrissop; one *s* two *d*. *Educ:* Switzerland; Rossall Sch.; Norwich Sch. Joined HM Diplomatic Service, 1966; FCO, 1966–71; Vice Consul, Rabat, 1971–74; Second Sec., Washington, 1975–80; Second, later First, Sec., Near East and N Africa Dept, FCO, 1980–82; seconded to Ecole Nationale d'Admin, Paris, 1982–83; Asst Head, Trade Relations and Export Dept, FCO, 1983–84; Dep. Head of Mission, Dakar, 1984–88; Asst Head of Cultural Relations Dept, FCO, 1989–90; Counsellor and Dep. Head, Perm. Under Sec.'s Dept, FCO, 1990–92; Head of Consular Dept, later Div., 1993–97; Minister, Paris, 1997–2002. *Publications:* contribs to jl of Institut Internat. de l'Admin Public, ENA Mensuel, Paris. *Recreations:* books, buildings, landscape, gardens. *Address:* Le Matha, Caplong, Ste Foy-la-Grande, 33220, France.

HOWARTH, Rt Rev. Toby Matthew; *see* Bradford, Area Bishop of.

HOWATCH, Susan; writer; *b* 14 July 1940; *d* of George Stanford Sturt and Ann Sturt; *m* 1964, Joseph Howatch (separated 1975); one *d*. *Educ:* Sutton High Sch. GPDST; King's Coll. London (LLB 1961; FKC 1999). Established Starbridge Lectureship in Theology and Natural Science, Cambridge University, 1992. Hon. LittD Hope Coll., Mich, 2012. *Publications:* The Dark Shore, 1965; The Waiting Sands, 1966; Call in the Night, 1967; The Shrouded Walls, 1968; April's Grave, 1969; The Devil on Lammas Night, 1970; Penmarric, 1971; Cashelmara, 1974; The Rich are Different, 1977; Sins of the Fathers, 1980; The Wheel of Fortune, 1984; *Starbridge novels:* Glittering Images, 1987; Glamorous Powers, 1988; Ultimate Prizes, 1989; Scandalous Risks, 1991; Mystical Paths, 1992; Absolute Truths, 1994; *St Benet's trilogy:* A Question of Integrity, 1997, renamed as The Wonder Worker; The High Flyer, 1999; The Heartbreaker, 2003. *Recreation:* reading theology. *Address:* c/o Aitken Alexander Associates Ltd, 291 Gray's Inn Road, WC1X 8EB. *T:* (020) 7373 8672.

HOWATSON, William, FRAgS; freelance rural affairs journalist; Member (Lib Dem), Aberdeenshire Council, since 1999; Provost of Aberdeenshire, 2007–12; *b* 22 Jan. 1953; *s* of William Smith Howatson and Bessie Howatson; *m* 1985, Hazel Symington Paton; two *d*. *Educ:* Lockerbie Acad.; Univ. of Edinburgh (MA Hons 1975). Reporter: Scottish Farmer newspaper, 1979–83; Dumfries and Galloway Standard, 1983–84; Agricl Ed. and Leader Writer, 1984–96, columnist, 1996–2005, The Press and Journal, Aberdeen; columnist, The Courier, Dundee, 2012–. Chm., Guild of Agricl Journalists, 1995. Member: Scottish Water and Sewerage Customers Council, 1995–99; Health Educn Bd for Scotland, 1996–2003, subseq. NHS Health Scotland, 2003–05 (Vice Chm., 2003–05); E Areas Bd, Scottish Natural Heritage, 1997–2003 (Vice Chm., 1999–2003); Bd, SEPA, 1999–2005 (Chm. E Regl Bd, 2003–05); Rail Passenger Cttee for Scotland, 2001–03; Scottish Agricl Wages Bd, 2013–. Non-exec. Dir, Angus NHS Trust, 1998–99; Chairman: Aberdeen City Community Health Partnership, 2008–12; NHS Grampian, 2011–14 (non-exec. Mem., 2007–11). Mem. Bd of Mgt, Angus Coll., 1996–2009; Gov., Macaulay Land Use Res. Inst., 1998–2003. Assessor to Court, Univ. of Aberdeen, 2010–12. FRAgS 2003. JP S Aberdeenshire, 1999–2007. Netherthorpe Award, Guild of Agricl Journalists, 2008. *Publications:* (contrib.) Farm Servants and Labour in Lowland Scotland 1770–1914, 1984. *Recreations:* gardening, hill-walking, cooking, reading Scottish history. *Address:* Stone of Morphie, Hillside, Montrose, Angus DD10 0AA. *T:* (01674) 830746, *Fax:* (01674) 830114. *E:* billhowatson@btinternet.com.

HOWDEN, Alan Percival; Director, Picturedrome Media Ltd, since 2001; non-executive Director, UK Film and Television Production Co. Ltd, since 2001; *b* 28 Aug. 1936; *s* of C. P. Howden and Marian Grindell; *m* 1981, Judith South; one *d*. *Educ:* Sale Grammar Sch.; UMIST (BSc Tech Mech. Engrg). Joined BBC, 1964: Programme Exec., 1964–70; Sen. Programme Exec., 1970–77; Hd of Purchased Programmes, 1977–83; Gen. Manager, Programme Acquisition, 1983–91; Controller, Prog. Acquisition, 1991–99; Advr, Prog. Acquisition, BBC TV, 1999–2000. Mem. Bd, BBC Enterprises, 1989–94. British Film Institute: Gov., 1994–2001; Chm., Film Educn Rev. Cttee for DCMS, 1998–99; British Federation of Film Societies: Vice-Chm., 1965–80; Chm., 1980–82; Vice Pres., 1982–. MInstD 1994. *Recreations:* theatre, early music, English countryside. *E:* alanhowden@btconnect.com.

HOWDEN, Robert Ellis; President and Chairman, British Cycling Federation, since 2013 (Director, 1998–2000 and since 2001); *b* Barnsley, 11 June 1955; *s* of Leonard and Elizabeth Howden; *m* 1975, Ceri; one *d*. *Educ:* Wombwell High Sch.; Thornes House Sch., Wakefield; Wakefield Coll. Managing Director: Grass Concrete Ltd, 1981–; Chantry Contractors Ltd, 1981–. FRSA 2007. *Recreations:* cycling, painting, history. *Address:* c/o Duncan House, 142 Thornes Lane, Thornes, Wakefield, W Yorks WF2 7RE. *T:* (01924) 379443, *Fax:* (01924) 290289. *E:* bobhowden@grasscrete.com. *Club:* Wakefield Cycling.

HOWDEN, Timothy Simon; Director, Hay Hill Management Ltd, since 2006; *b* 2 April 1937; *s* of Phillip Alexander and Rene Howden; *m* 1st, 1958, Penelope Mary Wilmott (marr. diss. 1984); two *s* one *d*; 2nd, 1999, Lois Robin Chesney. *Educ:* Tonbridge Sch. Served RA, 1955–57, 2nd Lieut. Floor Treatments Ltd, 1957–59; joined Reckitt & Colman, 1962; France, 1962–64; Germany, 1964–70; Dir, Reckitt & Colman Europe, 1970–73; Ranks Hovis McDougall, 1973–92: Dir, RHM Flour Mills, 1973–75; Man. Dir, RHM Foods, 1975–81; Chm. and Man. Dir, British Bakeries, 1981–85; Planning, then Dep. Man. Dir, 1985–89; Man. Dir, 1989–92; Gp Chief Exec. for Europe, The Albert Fisher Group, 1992–96; CEO, Albert Fisher Inc., N America, 1996–97. Director: Finning Internat. Inc., 1998–2007; Hyperion Insce Gp, 2000–; SSL Internat. plc, 1999–2005. *Recreations:* ski-ing, tennis, golf, sailing. *Club:* Annabel's.

HOWDLE, Prof. Peter David, MD; FRCP; Professor of Clinical Medicine, University of Leeds, 2006–09, now Emeritus; Consultant Physician, St James's University Hospital, Leeds, 1987–2009; *b* 16 June 1948; *s* of George Henry Howdle and Mary Jane Howdle (*née* Baugh); *m* 1972, Susan Ruth Lowery. *Educ:* King's Sch., Pontefract; Univ. of Leeds Med. Sch. (BSc 1969; MB ChB 1972; MD 1985). FRCP 1992. Jun. med. appts, St James's Univ. Hosp., Leeds, 1972–82; University of Leeds: Lectr in Medicine, 1982–87, Sen. Lectr, 1987–96; Prof. of Clinical Educn, 1996–2006; Hd, Acad. Unit of Gen. Surgery, Medicine and Anaesthesia, Univ. of Leeds Med. Sch., 1999–2005; Hd, Section of Medicine, Surgery and Anaesthesia, Leeds Inst. of Molecular Medicine, 2005–09. Vis. Lectr (Fulbright Schol.), Harvard Univ., 1984–85. Coeliac UK: Med. Advr, 1995–2011; Gov. and Trustee, 2006–11; Chm., Health Adv. Council, 2006–11; Chm., Guidelines Develt Gps, NICE, 2008–12; Med. Vice-Chair, Adv. Cttee on Clinical Excellence Awards Yorks and Humber Sub-cttee, 2009–. Vice-Pres., Methodist Conf., 2002–03; Co-Chm., Jt Implementation Commn for the Anglican-Methodist Covenant, 2003–14; Chairman: Wesley Study Centre Cttee, St John's Coll., Durham Univ., 2009–14; Strategy and Resources Cttee, Methodist Council, 2012–. *Publications:* Comprehensive Clinical Hepatology, 2000; Your Guide to Coeliac Disease, 2007; contrib. over 100 articles mainly on coeliac disease and mucosal immunity. *Recreations:* classical music, modern literature, Methodist history and liturgy. *E:* p.d.howdle@leeds.ac.uk.

HOWE, family name of **Baron Howe of Aberavon** and **Baroness Howe of Idlicote**.

HOWE, 7th Earl *cr* 1821; **Frederick Richard Penn Curzon;** PC 2013; Baron Howe, 1788; Baron Curzon, 1794; Viscount Curzon, 1802; farmer; Parliamentary Under-Secretary of State, Ministry of Defence, since 2015; Deputy Leader, House of Lords, since 2015; Chairman, London and Provincial Antique Dealers' Association, 1999–2010, Honorary President, since 2010; *b* 29 Jan. 1951; *s* of Chambré George William Penn Curzon (*d* 1976) (*g s* of 3rd Earl) and Enid Jane Victoria Curzon (*née* Fergusson) (*d* 1997); *S* cousin, 1984; *m* 1983, Elizabeth Helen Stuart, DL; one *s* three *d*. *Educ:* Rugby School; Christ Church, Oxford (MA Hons Lit. Hum.; Chancellor's Prize for Latin Verse, 1973). AIB. Entered Barclays Bank Ltd, 1973; Manager, 1982; Sen. Manager, 1984–87. Director: Adam & Co., 1987–90; Provident Life Assoc. Ltd, 1988–91. A Lord in Waiting (Govt Whip), 1991–92; front bench spokesman, H of L, on employment and transport, 1991, on environment and defence, 1992; Parly Sec., MAFF, 1992–95; Parly Under-Sec. of State, MoD, 1995–97; opposition front bench spokesman on health, H of L, 1997–2010; Parly Under-Sec. of State, DoH, 2010–15; elected Mem., H of L, 1999. Governor: King William IV Naval Foundation, 1984–; Trident Trust, 1985–2008; Trustee, Milton's Cottage, 1985–2012 (Chm., 2006–11); Member: Council, RNLI, 1997–2014 (Pres., Chilterns Br., 1985–); Council of Mgt, Restoration of Appearance and Function Trust, 2000–10 (Chm., 2008–10); President: S Bucks Assoc. for the Disabled, 1984–; Nat. Soc. for Epilepsy, 1986–2010 (Vice-Pres., 1984–86); Penn Country Br., CPRE, 1986–92; Abbeyfield Beaconsfield Soc., 1991–2013. Patron: Demand, 2000–10; Chiltern Soc., 2001–. Hon. FRCP 2008. *Recreations:* spending time with family, music. *Heir:* *s* Viscount Curzon, *qv*. *Address:* c/o House of Lords, SW1A 0PW.

HOWE OF ABERAVON, Baron *cr* 1992 (Life Peer), of Tandridge, in the County of Surrey; **Richard Edward Geoffrey Howe,** CH 1996; Kt 1970; PC 1972; QC 1965; *b* 20 Dec. 1926; *er s* of late B. E. Howe and Mrs E. F. Howe, JP (*née* Thomson), Port Talbot, Glamorgan; *m* 1953, Elspeth Rosamund Morton Shand (*see* Baroness Howe of Idlicote); one *s* two *d*. *Educ:* Winchester Coll. (Exhibitioner); Trinity Hall, Cambridge (Scholar, MA, LLB; Hon. Fellow, 1992); Pres., Trinity Hall Assoc., 1977–78. Lieut Royal Signals 1945–48. Chm. Cambridge Univ. Conservative Assoc., 1951; Chm. Bow Group, 1955; Managing Dir, Crossbow, 1957–60, Editor 1960–62. Called to the Bar, Middle Temple, 1952, Bencher, 1969, Reader, 1993; Mem. General Council of the Bar, 1957–61; Mem. Council of Justice, 1963–70. Dep. Chm., Glamorgan QS, 1966–70. Contested (C) Aberavon, 1955, 1959; MP (C): Bebington, 1964–66; Reigate, 1970–74; Surrey East, 1974–92. Sec. Conservative Parliamentary Health and Social Security Cttee, 1964–65; an Opposition Front Bench spokesman on labour and social services, 1965–66; Solicitor-General, 1970–72; Minister for Trade and Consumer Affairs, DTI, 1972–74; opposition front bench spokesman on social services, 1974–75, on Treasury and economic affairs, 1975–79; Chancellor of the Exchequer, 1979–83; Sec. of State for Foreign and Commonwealth Affairs, 1983–89; Lord Pres. of the Council, Leader of H of C, and Dep. Prime Minister, 1989–90. Mem., H of L, 1992–2015. Chm., Interim Cttee, IMF, 1982–83. Chm., Framlington Russian Investment Fund, 1994–2003; Director: Sun Alliance & London Insce Co. Ltd, 1974–79; AGB Research Ltd, 1974–79; EMI Ltd, 1976–79; BICC plc, 1991–97; Glaxo Hldgs, 1991–95; Glaxo Wellcome plc, 1995–96. Special Advr, Internat. Affairs, Jones, Day, Reavis and Pogue, 1991–2000; Member: J. P. Morgan Internat. Adv. Council, 1992–2001; Adv. Council, Bertelsmann Foundn, 1992–97; Fuji Wolfensohn Internat. European Adv. Bd, 1996–98; Carlyle Gp Eur. Adv. Bd, 1997–2001; Fuji Bank Internat. Adv. Council, 1999–2002. Member: (Latey) Interdeptl Cttee on Age of Majority, 1965–67; (Street) Cttee on Racial Discrimination, 1967; (Cripps) Cons. Cttee on Discrimination against Women, 1968–69; Chm. Ely Hospital, Cardiff, Inquiry, 1969. Chm. Steering Cttee, Tax Law Rewrite Project, Inland Revenue, 1996–2005. Visitor, SOAS, Univ. of London, 1991–2001; Vis. Fellow, John F. Kennedy Sch. of Govt, Harvard Univ., 1991–92; Herman Phleger Vis. Prof., Stanford Law Sch., Calif, 1993. Member, International Advisory Council: Inst. of Internat. Studies, Stanford Univ., Calif, 1990–2005; Centre for Eur. Policy Studies, 1992–2005; Chm., Adv. Bd, English Centre for Legal Studies, Warsaw Univ.,

1992–99; Pres., Acad. of Experts, 1996–2005; Vice-President: RUSI, 1991–; English Coll. Foundn in Prague, 1992–. President: Cons. Political Centre Nat. Adv. Cttee, 1977–79; Nat. Union of Cons. and Unionist Assocs, 1983–84; GB China Centre, 1992–; Russian/European Trust, 1997–; Jt Pres., Wealth of Nations Foundn, 1991–2004; Chm., Thomson Foundn, 2004–07 (Trustee, 1995–2007); Trustee: Cambridge Commonwealth Trust, 1993–2010; Cambridge Overseas Trust, 1993–2010. Mem., Adv. Council, Presidium of Supreme Rada of Ukraine, 1991–97. Mem. Council of Management, Private Patients' Plan, 1969–70; Mem., Steering Cttee, Project Liberty, 1991–97; Patron: Enterprise Europe, 1990–2004; UK Metric Assoc., 2003– (Pres., 2005–); McKechnie Foundn, 2005–. Pres., Which? (formerly Assoc. for Consumer Res.), 1992–2010 (an Hon. Vice-Pres., 1974–92). Freeman, City of London, 2004; Hon. Freeman, Co. of Tax Advisors, 2004. Hon. Fellow: UCW, Swansea, 1996; UCW, Cardiff, 1999; Amer. Bar Foundn, 2000; Chartered Inst. of Taxation, 2000; SOAS, 2003. Hon. Freeman, Port Talbot, 1992. Hon. LLD: Wales, 1988; LSE, 2004; Glamorgan, 2004; Hon. DCL City, 1993. Joseph Bech Prize, FVS Stiftung, Hamburg, 1993; Paul Harris Fellow, Rotary Internat., 1995. Grand Cross, Order of Merit (Portugal), 1987; Grand Cross, Order of Merit (Germany), 1992; Order of Public Service (Ukraine), 2001. *Publications:* Principles in Practice, 1960; Conservative Opportunity, 1965; Conflict of Loyalty (memoirs), 1994; *contributed:* The Chancellors' Tales: managing the British economy, 2006; British Diplomacy: foreign secretaries reflect, 2007; World Crisis: the way forward after Iraq, 2008; various political pamphlets for Bow Group and Conservative Political Centre. *Clubs:* Athenæum, Garrick.

HOWE OF IDLICOTE, Baroness *cr* 2001 (Life Peer), of Shipston-on-Stour in the County of Warwickshire; **Elspeth Rosamund Morton Howe,** CBE 1999; JP; Chairman: Broadcasting Standards Commission, 1997–99 (Chairman, Broadcasting Standards Council, 1993–97); BOC Foundation for the Environment and Community, 1990–2003; *b* 8 Feb. 1932; *d* of late Philip Morton Shand and Sybil Mary (*née* Sissons); *m* 1953, Baron Howe of Aberavon, *qv*; one *s* two *d*. *Educ:* Bath High Sch.; Wycombe Abbey; London Sch. of Econs and Pol Science (BSc 1985; Hon. Fellow, 2001). Vice-Chm., Conservative London Area Women's Adv. Cttee, 1966–67, also Pres. of the Cttee's Contact Gp, 1973–77; Mem., Conservative Women's Nat. Adv. Cttee, 1966–71. Member: Lord Chancellor's Adv. Cttee on appointment of Magistrates for Inner London Area, 1965–75; Lord Chancellor's Adv. Cttee on Legal Aid, 1971–75; Parole Board, 1972–75. Dep. Chm., Equal Opportunities Commn, 1975–79. Co-opted Mem., ILEA, 1967–70; Member: Briggs Cttee on Nursing Profession, 1970–72; Justice Cttee on English Judiciary, 1992. Chairman: Hansard Soc. Commn on Women at the Top, 1990–91; The Quality of Care, Local Govt Management Bd Inquiry and Report, 1991–92; Archbishop's Commn on Cathedrals, 1992–94. Director: Kingfisher (formerly Woolworth Holdings) PLC, 1986–2000; United Biscuits (Holdings) PLC, 1988–94; Legal & General Group, 1989–97; Chm., Opportunity 2000 Target Team, Business in the Community, 1990–99. President: Peckham Settlement, 1976–; Women's Gas Fedn, 1979–93; Fedn of Personnel Services, subseq. of Recruitment and Employment Services, 1980–94; UNICEF UK, 1993–2002; Member Council: NACRO, 1974–93; PSI, 1983–92; St George's House, Windsor, 1989–93; Vice-Pres., Pre-Sch. Playgroups Assoc., 1979–83. Trustee, Westminster Foundn for Democracy, 1992–96. Has served as chm. or mem. of several sch. governing bodies in Tower Hamlets; Governor: Cumberlow Lodge Remand Home, 1967–70; Wycombe Abbey, 1968–90; Froebel Educn Inst., 1968–75; LSE, 1985–2006; Mem. Bd of Governors, James Allen's Girls' Sch., 1988–93; Mem. Council, Open Univ., 1996–2003 (Vice-Chm. Council, 2001–03). JP Inner London Juvenile Court Panel, 1964–92 (Chm. of Court, 1970–90). Hon. LLD: London, 1990; Aberdeen, 1993; Liverpool, 1994; DUniv: Open, 1993; South Bank, 1996; Hon. DLitt: Bradford, 1990; Sunderland, 1995. *Publications:* Under Five (a report on pre-school education), 1966. *Address:* House of Lords, SW1A 0PW.

HOWE, Sir Bernard H.; *see* Hogan-Howe.

HOWE, Hon. Brian Leslie, AO 2008 (AM 2001); *b* 28 Jan. 1936; *s* of John P. Howe and Lillian M. Howe; *m* 1962, Renate Morris; one *s* two *d*. *Educ:* Melbourne High Sch.; Melbourne Univ. (BA, DipCrim); McCormick Theol Seminary, Chicago (MA). Ordained Minister of Methodist Church, 1963; parishes at Eltham, Morwell and Fitzroy, 1960–69; Dir, Centre for Urban Research and Action, Fitzroy, and Lectr in Sociology, Swinburne Inst. of Technology, 1970–77. Professorial Associate, Centre for Public Policy, Univ. of Melbourne, 1996–; Woodrow Wilson School of Public and International Affairs, Princeton University: Res. Fellow, Centre of Domestic and Comparative Policy Studies, 1997; Frederick H. Schultz Class of 1951 Prof., 1998. MP (ALP) Batman, Vic, 1977–96; Minister: for Defence Support, 1983–84; for Social Security, 1984–89; for Community Services and Health, 1990–91; for Health, Housing and Community Services, 1991–93; for Housing, Local Govt and Community (then Human) Services, 1993–94; for Housing and Regional Develt, 1994–96; Minister assisting the Prime Minister for Social Justice, 1988–93, for Commonwealth-State Relations, 1991–93; Dep. Prime Minister of Australia, 1991–95. Life Mem., ALP, 2005. Bd Mem., 2003–08, Fellow, 2011, Australia & NZ Sch. of Govt. Life Mem., Victorian Council of Social Service, 2007. Patron, Royal Melbourne Philharmonic Orch., 1998–. Charter Mem. and Mem. Bd, Brotherhood of St Laurence, 1998– (Life Mem., 2005). Hon. Fellow, Queen's Coll., Univ. of Melbourne, 2000. Hon. FPIA (Hon. FRAPI 1995). STD *hc* Melbourne Coll. of Divinity, 2009; Hon. DLitt Melbourne, 2014. *Publications:* Weighing up Australian Values, 2007; numerous papers, contribs to books, jls and conf. procs. *Recreations:* golf, reading, films, Australian Rules football. *Address:* PO Box 459, North Carlton, Vic 3054, Australia.

HOWE, Prof. Christine Joyce, PhD; Professor of Education, University of Cambridge, since 2006; *b* Birmingham, 21 Nov. 1948; *d* of Walter Virgil Howe and Joyce Winifred Howe (*née* Barmby); *m* 1979, William John Robertson; one *s* one *d*. *Educ:* Univ. of Sussex (BA 1st Cl. Hons); Univ. of Cambridge (PhD 1975). Lectr, Sussex Univ., 1974–76; Strathclyde University: Lectr, 1976–90; Sen. Lectr, 1990–95; Reader, 1995–98; Prof. of Psychol., 1998–2006. Mem., ESRC, 2004–08. Chm., Develtl Section, BPsS, 2006–08. FAcSS (AcSS 2008). *Publications:* Learning Language in a Conversational Context, 1983; Language Learning: a special case for developmental psychology, 1993; Group and Interactive Learning, 1994; Gender and Classroom Interaction, 1997; Conceptual Structure in Childhood and Adolescence: the case of everyday physics, 1998; Peer Groups and Children's Development, 2010; Educational Dialogues: understanding and promoting productive interactions, 2010. *Recreations:* bridge, tennis, hill-walking, music, theatre.

HOWE, Prof. Christopher Barry, MBE 1997; PhD; FBA 2001; Professor, Chinese Business Management, School of Oriental and African Studies, University of London, 2001–03, now Emeritus (Research Professor, 2003–06); Research Professor, School of East Asian Studies, University of Sheffield, 2006–08 (Hon. Professor, since 2009); *b* 3 Nov. 1937; *s* of Charles Roderick Howe and Patricia (*née* Creeden); *m* 1967, Patricia Anne Giles; one *s* one *d*. *Educ:* William Ellis Sch., London; St Catharine's Coll., Cambridge (MA); PhD London. Economic Secretariat, FBI, 1961–63; Sch. of Oriental and African Studies, London Univ., 1963–2006: Head, Contemp. China Inst., 1972–78; Prof. of Economics with ref. to Asia, 1979–2001. Member: Hong Kong Univ. and Polytechnic Grants Cttee, 1974–93; UGC, 1979–84; ESRC Res. Develt Gp, 1987–88; Hong Kong Res. Grants Council, 1991–99; HEFCE Wkg Party on Chinese Studies, 1998; China Panel, British Acad., 2002–. Foreign Advr to Haut Conseil de l'évaluation de la recherche et de l'ensignment supérieur, Paris, 2010–. Fellow, 48 Gp Club, 2003. *Publications:* Employment and Economic Growth in Urban China 1949–57, 1971; Industrial Relations and Rapid Industrialisation, 1972; Wage Patterns and Wage Policy in Modern China 1919–1972, 1973; China's Economy: a basic guide, 1978; (ed) Studying China, 1979; (ed) Shanghai: revolution and development, 1980; (ed) The Readjustment in the Chinese Economy, 1984; (with Kenneth R. Walker) The Foundations of the Chinese Planned Economy, 1989; (ed) China and Japan: history, trends and prospects, 1990; The Origins of Japanese Trade Supremacy, 1996; (ed with C. H. Feinstein) Chinese Technology Transfer in the 1990s, 1997; (with R. A. Ash and Y. Y. Kueh) China's Economic Reform, 2003; (with T. Kambara) China and the Global Energy Crisis, 2007; The Long March to Science and Innovation in China and Hong Kong: progress and the contemporary challenges, 2016. *Recreations:* music, walking, cycling, swimming. *Address:* 12 Highgate Avenue, N6 5RX. *T:* (020) 8340 8104.

HOWE, Prof. Daniel Walker, FRHistS; Rhodes Professor of American History, 1992–2002; Fellow of St Catherine's College, Oxford, 1992–2002, now Fellow Emeritus; *b* 10 Jan. 1937; *s* of Maurice Langdon Howe and Lucie Walker Howe; *m* 1961, Sandra Shumway; two *s* one *d*. *Educ:* Harvard (BA); Magdalen Coll., Oxford (MA); Univ. of California at Berkeley (PhD). Lieut, US Army, 1959–60. Yale University: Instructor, 1966–68; Asst Prof., 1968–73; University of California at Los Angeles: Associate Prof., 1973–77; Prof., 1977–92; Chm., History Dept, 1983–87. Harmsworth Vis. Prof., Oxford, 1989–90. Fellow: Charles Warren Center, Harvard, 1970–71; Nat. Endowment for Humanities, 1975–76; Guggenheim Foundn, 1984–85; Res. Fellow, Huntington Library, 1991–92, 2002–03. FRHistS 2002. Hon. DHum Weber State Univ., 2014. Amer. Historian Laureate, 2008; Pulitzer Prize in History, 2008. *Publications:* The Unitarian Conscience, 1970, 2nd edn 1988; Victorian America, 1976; The Political Culture of the American Whigs, 1980; Making the American Self, 1997; What Hath God Wrought, 2007; articles in learned jls. *Recreations:* music, grandchildren. *Address:* St Catherine's College, Oxford OX1 3UJ. *T:* (01865) 271700; 3814 Cody Road, Sherman Oaks, CA 91403, USA.

HOWE, Darren Francis; QC 2015; a Deputy District Judge, since 2010; a Recorder, since 2012; *b* Cuckfield, Sussex, 3 April 1969; *s* of Peter John Howe and Carmel Howe; *m* 2006, Antonio Delgado. *Educ:* Chailey Comprehensive Sch.; Haywards Heath Sixth Form Coll., Univ. of Hull (LLB Hons); Inns of Court Sch. of Law. Called to the Bar, Gray's Inn, 1992; in practice as barrister, Brighton, 1993–2006, London, 2006–. *Publications:* (contrib.) DIY Divorce and Separation: the expert guide to representing yourself, 2014. *Recreations:* running, off-road cycling, travel, cinema, music. *Address:* 1 Garden Court Family Law Chambers, 1 Garden Court, Temple, EC4Y 9BJ. *T:* (020) 7797 7900. *E:* clerks@1gc.com. *Club:* Hospital.

HOWE, Prof. Denis; Professor of Aircraft Design, 1973–92, College of Aeronautics, Cranfield Institute of Technology, now Professor Emeritus, Cranfield University; *b* 3 Sept. 1927; *s* of Alfred and Alice Howe; *m* 1st, 1954, Audrey Marion Wilkinson; two *s* three *d*; 2nd, 1981, Catherine Bolton. *Educ:* Watford Grammar Sch.; MIT (SM); College of Aeronautics (PhD). CEng, FIMechE, FRAeS. Project Engineer, Fairey Aviation Co., 1945–54; College of Aeronautics, Cranfield Institute of Technology: Lectr, Sen. Lectr and Reader, 1954–73; Head of College, 1986–90; Dean of Engineering, 1988–91. *Publications:* Aircraft Conceptual Design Synthesis, 2000; Aircraft Loading and Structural Layout, 2004; contribs to learned jls. *Recreations:* gardening, church administration. *Address:* 78 Albert Road, Gourock PA19 1NL. *T:* (01475) 633468.

HOWE, Derek Andrew, CBE 1991; former public affairs and political consultant and company director; *b* 31 Aug. 1934; *o s* of late Harold and Elsie Howe; *m* 1st, 1958, Barbara (*née* Estill); two *d*; 2nd, 1975, Sheila (*née* Digger), MBE (*d* 1990); one *s*; 3rd, 1996, Penny (*née* James) (*d* 2012). *Educ:* City of Leeds Sch.; Cockburn High Sch., Leeds. Journalist, Yorkshire Evening News, 1951–61; Conservative Central Office, 1962–70; Parliamentary Liaison Officer, 1970–73; Special Adviser, 1973–75; Press Officer, Leader of HM Opposition, 1975–79; special adviser to: Paymaster Gen., 1979–81; Chancellor of Duchy of Lancaster, 1981; Political Secretary, 10 Downing Street, 1981–83 and Special Adviser to Leader of the House of Commons, 1982–83. Chm., Churchill Clinic, 1996–99 (Dep. Chm., 1995–96). Trustee, London Youth Trust, 1985–2005 (Chm. Trustees, 1988–2004). Freeman of the City of London. *Recreations:* gardening, reading, antiques, philately, Freemasonry. *Address:* The Vines, Kimpton, near Andover, Hampshire SP11 8NU; 47 Old Market Street, Usk NP15 1AL.

HOWE, Eric James, CBE 1990; Data Protection Registrar, 1984–94; *b* 4 Oct. 1931; *s* of Albert Henry Howe and Florence Beatrice (*née* Hale); *m* 1967, Patricia Enid (*née* Schollick); two *d*. *Educ:* Stretford Grammar Sch.; Univ. of Liverpool (BA Econs 1954). FIDPM 1990; FBCS 1972. NCB, 1954–59; British Cotton Industry Res. Assoc., 1959–61; English Electric Computer Co., 1961–66; National Computing Centre, 1966–84: Dep. Dir, 1975–84; Mem. Bd of Dirs, 1976–84. Chairman: National Computer Users Forum, 1977–84; Focus Cttee for Private Sector Users, DoI, 1982–84; Member: User Panel, NEDO, 1983–84; Council, British Computer Soc., 1971–74 and 1980–83; NW Regional Council, CBI, 1977–83. Chm. Bd, N Wales Housing Assoc., 2003–05 (Bd Mem., 1997–2006). Rep. UK, Confedn of Eur. Computer Users Assocs, 1980–83. *Recreations:* gardening, golf.

HOWE, Geoffrey Michael Thomas; Chairman: Jardine Lloyd Thompson Group plc, since 2006 (Director, 2002–04, Joint Deputy Chairman, 2004–06); Nationwide Building Society, 2007–15 (Director, 2005–15); *b* 3 Sept. 1949; *s* of Michael Edward Howe and Susan Dorothy Howe (*née* Allan); *m* 1995, Karen Mary Webber (*née* Ford); two *d*. *Educ:* Manchester Grammar Sch.; St John's Coll., Cambridge (MA). Solicitor. Stephenson Harwood, 1971–75; joined Clifford Chance, 1975; Partner, Corporate Dept, 1980; Man. Partner, 1989–97; Gen. Counsel and Dir, Robert Fleming Hldgs Ltd, 1998–2000; Chm., Railtrack Gp plc, 2002. Director: Gateway Electronic Components Ltd, 2000–; Investec plc, 2003–10; Close Brothers Gp, 2011–. *Recreations:* opera, wine, antiques, paintings.

HOWE, Ven. George Alexander; Chief of Staff and Chaplain to Bishop of Carlisle, and Diocesan Director of Ordinands, Diocese of Carlisle, 2011–15; Archdeacon of Westmorland and Furness, 2000–11, now Archdeacon Emeritus; *b* 22 Jan. 1952; *s* of late Eugene Howe and Olivia Lydia Caroline Howe (*née* Denroche); *m* 1980, Jane Corbould; one *s* one *d*. *Educ:* Liverpool Inst. High Sch.; Univ. of Durham (BA 1973); Westcott House, Cambridge. Ordained deacon, 1975, priest, 1976; Curate: St Cuthbert, Peterlee, 1975–79; St Mary, Norton, Stockton-on-Tees, 1979–81; Vicar, Utd Benefice of Hart with Elwick Hall, 1981–85; Rector, St Edmund, Sedgefield, 1985–91; Rural Dean of Sedgefield, 1988–91; Vicar, Holy Trinity, Kendal, 1991–2000; Rural Dean of Kendal, 1994–99. Hon. Canon, Carlisle Cathedral, 1994–. Diocesan Ecumenical Officer (formerly Bishop's Advr for Ecumenical Affairs), dio. of Carlisle, 2001–11. Chm., Church and Community Fund, 2007–13. *Recreations:* listening to The Archers, walking the dog, good food and wine, cartology. *Address:* 1 St John's Gate, Threlkeld, Keswick, Cumbria CA12 4TZ. *T:* (01768) 779168. *E:* george.howe@carlislediocese.org.uk.

HOWE, Jeremy Peter; Commissioning Editor, Drama, BBC Radio 4, since 2006; *b* London, 16 Nov. 1956; *s* of Robert and Marjorie Howe; *m* 1st, 1981, Elizabeth Milicevic (*d* 1992); two *d*; 2nd, 1998, Jennifer Howarth. *Educ:* Dulwich Coll.; St Edmund Hall, Oxford (BA Hons English). Associate Dir, York Th. Royal, Colchester Mercury, then freelance dir, Royal Court, Lyric Belfast, Nottingham Playhouse, 1981–86; Drama Producer, BBC NI, 1986–89; Asst Commng Ed., Film 4/Channel 4, 1989–91; Ed., Drama, BBC Radio 3, 1991–94; Exec. Producer, Television, Bristol, BBC, 1994–2006. *Publications:* Mummydaddy, 2012. *Recreations:* my family, writing, travelling Europe, being in the desert. *Address:* c/o BBC Broadcasting House, W1A 1AA. *E:* jeremy.howe@bbc.co.uk. *Club:* Groucho.

HOWE, John Francis, CB 1996; OBE 1974; Chairman, Citylink Telecommunications Ltd, since 2004; *b* 29 Jan. 1944; *s* of late Frank and Marjorie Howe; *m* 1981, Angela Ephrosini (*née* Nicolaides); one *d* one step *d. Educ:* Shrewsbury Sch.; Balliol Coll., Oxford (Scholar; MA). Pirelli General Cable Works, 1964; joined MoD as Asst Principal, 1967; Principal, 1972; Civil Adviser to GOC NI, 1972–73; Private Sec. to Perm. Under-Sec. of State, 1975–78; Asst Sec., 1979; seconded to FCO as Defence Counsellor, UK Delegn to NATO, 1981–84; Head, Arms Control Unit, MoD, 1985–86; Private Sec. to Sec. of State for Defence, 1986–87; Asst Under-Sec. of State (Personnel and Logistics), 1988–91; Dep. Under-Sec. of State (Civilian Management), 1992–96; Dep. Chief of Defence Procurement (Support), 1996–2000; on secondment to Thomson CSF Racal, subseq. Thales, plc, 2000–02, Sen. Defence Advr, 2001–02. Vice Chm., 2002–09, non-exec. Mem., Adv. Bd, 2009–, Thales UK plc. Chm., Security and Resilience Industry Suppliers' Community, 2009–11; Pres., EuroDefense UK, 2010–. Chm., Frederick Bonnart-Braunthal Scholarship Trust, 2014– (Trustee, 2002–); Trustee: MapAction, 2010–; RUSI, 2011–. *Recreations:* travel, garden labour, paintings, charity work. *Club:* Athenæum.

HOWE, Air Vice-Marshal John Frederick George, CB 1985; CBE 1980; AFC 1961; Commandant-General, RAF Regiment and Director General of Security (RAF), 1983–85, retired; *b* 26 March 1930; *m* 1961, Annabelle Gowing; three *d. Educ:* St Andrew's Coll., Grahamstown, SA. SAAF, 1950–54 (served in Korea, 2nd Sqdn SAAF and 19 Inf. Regt, US Army, 1951); 222 Sqdn, Fighter Comd, 1956; 40 Commando RM, Suez Campaign, 1956; Fighter Command: Flt Comdr, 222 Sqdn, 1957; Flt Comdr, 43 Sqdn, 1957–59; Sqdn Comdr, 74 Sqdn, 1960–61; Air Staff, HQ Fighter Command, 1961–63; RAF Staff Coll., 1964; USAF Exchange Tour at Air Defence Comd HQ, Colorado Springs, 1965–67; 229 Operational Conversion Unit, RAF Chivenor, 1967–68; OC 228 OCU, Coningsby, 1968–69; Central Tactics and Trials Org., HQ Air Support Comd, 1969–70; MoD, 1970–72; Station Comdr, RAF Gutersloh, 1973–74; RCDS, 1975; Gp Capt. Ops, HQ No 11 Gp, 1975–77; Comdt, ROC, 1977–80; Comdr, Southern Maritime Air Region, 1980–83. Hon. Colonel: Field Sqns (Airfield Damage Repair) (Vol.) (South), 1988–93; 77 Engr Regt (Vol.), 1993. American DFC 1951; Air Medal 1951. *Recreations:* country pursuits, ski-ing, sailing. *Club:* Royal Air Force.

HOWE, Martin, CB 1995; PhD; self-employed consultant on competition policy, since 1998; Director, Competition Policy Division, Office of Fair Trading, 1984–96; *b* 9 Dec. 1936; *s* of late Leslie Wistow Howe and Dorothy Vernon Howe (*née* Taylor Farrell); *m* 1959, Anne Cicely Lawrenson; three *s. Educ:* Leeds Univ. (BCom (Accountancy)); Sheffield Univ. (PhD). Asst Lectr, Lectr, Sen. Lectr, in Economics, Univ. of Sheffield, 1959–73; Senior Economic Adviser: Monopolies Commn, 1973–77; Office of Fair Trading, 1977–80; Asst Secretary, OFT and DTI, 1980–84. Special Prof., Univ. of Nottingham Business Sch., 1994–2003. Associate, Europe Economics, 1998–2006. *Publications:* Equity Issues and the London Capital Market (with A. J. Merrett and G. D. Newbould), 1967; Rockley Wilson: remarkable cricketer, singular man, 2008; Frank Sugg: a man for all seasons, 2011; articles on variety of topics in learned and professional jls; articles in cricket jls. *Recreations:* theatre (including amateur dramatics), cricket, gardening, bowls. *Address:* 6 Mansdale Road, Redbourn, Herts AL3 7DN. *T:* (01582) 792074. *E:* martinhowe1@sky.com.

HOWE, Martin John; Founding Partner and Senior Partner, Howe & Co. Solicitors, since 1991; *b* London, 12 Dec. 1958; *s* of Michael Howe and Margaret Howe (*née* O'Brien); *m* 1992, Guldil Dilmec; one *s* one *d. Educ:* Sheffield Univ. (BA Hons Law 1980). Admitted solicitor, 1983; in practice as solicitor, Sheffield, until 1986, London, 1986–91; estab. Howe & Co., specialising in human rights and personal injury cases. Founding Mem., HUSH, 1997; co-founder, Gurkha Justice Campaign, 2008. *Recreations:* travel (especially road trips), reading, playing the guitar, sport. *Address:* Howe & Co. Solicitors, 1010 Great West Road, Brentford TW8 9BA. *T:* (020) 8840 4688. *E:* law@howe.co.uk.

HOWE, Martin Russell Thomson; QC 1996; *b* 26 June 1955; *s* of late Colin Howe, FRCS and Dr Angela Howe, *d* of Baron Brock, surgeon; *m* 1989, Lynda Barnett; one *s* three *d. Educ:* Trinity Hall, Cambridge (BA, Pt I Engrg, Pt II Law; Baker Prize for Engrg, 1974; MA). Called to the Bar, Middle Temple, 1978 (Harmsworth Exhibnr), Bencher, 2013; in practice, specialising in intellectual property and European law, 1980–; Appointed Person for design appeals under Intellectual Property Act 2014, 2015–. Councillor (C), London Borough of Hammersmith and Fulham, 1982–86 (Chm., Planning Cttee, 1985–86). Contested (C) Neath (S Wales), 1987. Member: Coalition Govt Commn on a Bill of Rights for the UK, 2011–13; Cons. Party Commn on Human Rights and Eur. Convention, 2013–. *Publications:* Europe and the Constitution after Maastricht, 1992; (ed) Russell-Clarke on Industrial Designs, 6th edn, 1998, 8th edn, as Russell-Clarke & Howe on Industrial Designs, 2010; contrib. Halsbury's Laws of England, 1986, 1995, 2000; Tackling Terrorism: the European Human Rights Convention and the enemy within, 2001, 2nd edn 2003; A Constitution for Europe: a legal assessment of the Treaty, 2003, 2nd edn 2005; numerous articles in legal jls and pamphlets on European constitutional issues and intellectual property law. *Address:* 8 New Square, Lincoln's Inn, WC2A 3QP.

See also R. P. T. Howe.

HOWE, Robert Paul Thomson; QC 2008; *b* England, 12 May 1964; *s* of late Colin Howe and Hon. Angela Howe; *m* 1998, Rosella Albano; two *d. Educ:* Trinity Hall, Cambridge (BA 1986); St Edmund Hall, Oxford (BCL). Called to the Bar, Middle Temple, 1988. *Address:* Blackstone Chambers, Blackstone House, Temple, EC4Y 9BW.

See also M. R. T. Howe.

HOWE, His Honour Ronald William; Director of Appeals, General Dental Council, 1999–2004; a Circuit Judge, 1991–97 (Deputy Circuit Judge, 1997–2000); *b* 19 June 1932; *s* of William Arthur and Lilian Mary Howe; *m* 1956, Jean Emily Goodman; three *s* one *d. Educ:* Morpeth Sch.; Coll. of Law, London. Admitted Solicitor, 1966; partner with Ronald Brooke & Co., Ilford, then Brooke, Garland & Howe, 1966–75; Registrar of County Court, subseq. Dist Judge, 1975–91. Mem., Judicial Studies Bd, 1990–91 (Mem., Civil and Family Cttee, 1988–91; Tutor, 1987–91); Advocacy Trng Advr, Law Soc., 1998–2000. *Recreations:* gardening, an increasing use of my computer, golf (not as often as I would like), masonry.

HOWE, Stephen Douglas; Editor, Farmers Weekly, 1991–2005; Associate Publisher, Farmers Weekly Group, 2000–05; *b* 28 Feb. 1948; *m* 1971, Susan Jane Apps; one *s* one *d. Educ:* Brymore Sch., Somerset; Seale-Hayne Coll. (DipAgr); NDA, Dip Farm Management. Lectr in Crop Husbandry and Farm Manager, Lackham Coll. of Agric., Wilts, 1969–72; Power Farming magazine: Management Specialist, 1972–82; Managing Editor, 1982–85; Agricultural Machinery Jl, 1985–87; Editor, Crops, 1987–91. Dir, British Crop Protection Enterprises Ltd, 2005–08; Business Develt Advr, UBM/Farmers Guardian, 2007–12. Governor: Inst. of Grassland and Environmental Res., 1996–2000; Nat. Fedn of Young Farmers, 1999–2000. Pres., Eurofarm, 1999–2006. Member: Council, RASE, 2005– (Trustee, 2009–); Exec., BCPC, 2008– (Trustee, 2014–); Trustee, Guild of Agricultural Journalists' Charitable Trust, 2005– (Chm., 2008–). Fellow, Guild of Agricultural Journalists, 1991; FRAgS 2008 (ARAgS 2003). Hon. Life Mem., Royal Smithfield Club, 2004. Hon. DArts Plymouth, 2000. *Recreations:* gardening, sailing, farming. *Address:* Springfield Cottage, Byers Lane, South Godstone, Surrey RH9 8JH. *T:* (01342) 893018. *Club:* Farmers.

HOWE, Timothy Jean-Paul; QC 2008; *b* London, 12 June 1963; *s* of late Prof. Alan Howe and of Mireille Howe; *m* 1990, Katharine Jane Zisman; one *s* two *d. Educ:* St Paul's Sch., London (First Foundn Schol.); Magdalen Coll., Oxford (Anne Shaw Open Schol.; BA 1st Cl. Hons Lit.Hum. 1985; Editor, Isis, 1983–84); City Univ. (Dip. Law with Dist. 1986). Called to the Bar, Middle Temple, 1987 (Queen Mother's Fund, Astbury and Harmsworth Scholarships); in practice as barrister, specialising in commercial law, 1988–. Sec. and Mem., Exec. Cttee, Commercial Bar Assoc., 1997–; Chm., Member Services Bd, Bar Council, 2008–10. CEDR Accredited Mediator, 2004. Gov., Godolphin and Latymer Sch., 2011–. *Publications:* (ed jtly) Commercial Court Procedure, 2001; (contrib.) Law of Bank Payments, 2004. *Recreations:* collecting modern British art, wine, travel, ballet and opera. *Address:* Fountain Court Chambers, Temple, EC4Y 9DH. *T:* (020) 7583 3335, *Fax:* (020) 7353 0329. *E:* th@fountaincourt.co.uk. *Club:* Hurlingham.

HOWELL, family name of **Baron Howell of Guildford**.

HOWELL OF GUILDFORD, Baron *cr* 1997 (Life Peer), of Penton Mewsey in the co. of Hampshire; **David Arthur Russell Howell;** PC 1979; journalist and economist; *b* 18 Jan. 1936; *s* of late Colonel A. H. E. Howell, DSO, TD, DL and Beryl Howell, 5 Headfort Place, SW1; *m* 1967, Davina Wallace; one *s* two *d. Educ:* Eton; King's Coll., Cambridge (BA 1st class hons 1959). Lieut Coldstream Guards, 1954–56. Joined Economic Section of Treasury, 1959; resigned, 1960. Leader-Writer and Special Correspondent, The Daily Telegraph, 1960–64; Chm. of Bow Gp, 1961–62; Editor of Crossbow, 1962–64; contested (C) Dudley, 1964. MP (C) Guildford, 1966–97. A Lord Comr of Treasury, 1970–71; Parly Sec., CSD, 1970–72; Parly Under-Sec.: Dept of Employment, 1971–72; NI Office, March–Nov. 1972; Minister of State: NI Office, 1972–74; Dept of Energy, 1974; Secretary of State: for Energy, 1979–81; for Transport, 1981–83. Chairman: Select Cttee on Foreign Affairs, 1987–97; H of L Sub-Cttee on EC Foreign and Security Policy, 1999–2000. H of L Opposition spokesman on foreign affairs, 2000–10; Dep. Leader of the Opposition, H of L, 2005–10; Minister of State, FCO, 2010–12. Chairman: Cons. One Nation Gp, 1987–97; UK-Japan 21st Century (formerly 2000) Group, 1990–2001. Sen. Vis. Fellow, PSI, 1983–85; Vis. Fellow, Nuffield Coll., Oxford, 1993–2001. Dir of Conservative Political Centre, 1964–66. Director: Jardine Insurance Brokers, 1991–97; Monks Investment Trust, 1993–2004; John Laing Plc, 1999–2002; Adv. Dir, UBS (formerly SBC Warburg), 1997–2000; Advisor: Japan Central Railway Co., 2001–10, 2013–; Mitsubishi Electric, Europe, BV, 2003–10, 2013–; Kuwait Investment Office, 2003–10, 2013–; Hermitage Global Fund, 2007–10. Mem., Internat. Adv. Council, Swiss Bank Corp., 1988–97. President: BIEE, 2006–13; Energy Industries Council, 2013–. Governor, Sadler's Wells Trust, 1995–98; Trustee: Shakespeare Globe Theatre, 2000–10; Duke of Edinburgh's Commonwealth Conferences, 2008–10; Chm. Council, Commonwealth Socs, 2013–; Pres., Royal Commonwealth Soc., 2013–. *Publications:* (co-author) Principles in Practice, 1960; The Conservative Opportunity, 1965; Freedom and Capital, 1981; Blind Victory: a study in income, wealth and power, 1986; The Edge of Now, 2000; Out of the Energy Labyrinth, 2007; Old Links and New Ties: power and persuasion in an age of networks, 2013; various pamphlets and articles. *Recreations:* writing, history, gardening. *Address:* House of Lords, SW1A 0PW. *Club:* Beefsteak.

See also Rt Hon. G. G. O. Osborne.

HOWELL, Anthony; Chief Education Officer, 2002–11, Strategic Director, Children, Young People and Families (formerly Learning and Culture), 2003–11, Birmingham City Council; *b* 7 Jan. 1951; *s* of late Bernard Howell and Katherine Howell; *m* 1975, Hilary Helen Ellis; one *s* one *d. Educ:* Xaverian Coll., Manchester; Univ. of Liverpool (BSc Zool.); Univ. of Bristol. Teacher, 1975; Chief Advr, Derbys LEA, 1995–2002; Dep. Chief Educn Officer, Birmingham CC, 2002. Bd Mem., Birmingham and Solihull Connexions, 2002; Bd Mem. and Trustee, Acad. of Youth/Univ. of the First Age, 2002; BECTA Educn Cttee, 2002–11. Pres., Soc. of Chief Inspectors and Advrs, 1999.

HOWELL, Gareth, CBE 1993; PhD; CChem; Director, British Council, Malaysia, 1990–95; *b* 22 April 1935; *s* of Amwel John and Sarah Blodwen Howell; *m* 1957, Margaret Patricia Ashelford; one *s* two *d. Educ:* Ferndale Grammar Sch., Rhondda; University College London; Inst. of Education, Univ. of London. BSc, PhD; PGCE London. MRSC. Asst Master, Canford Sch., Wimborne, Dorset, 1957–61; Lectr, Norwich City Coll., 1961–65; British Council: Science Educn Officer, London, 1965–66; Science Educn Officer, Nigeria, 1966–70; Head, Science Educn Section, 1970–74; Director, Science and Technology Dept, 1974; Representative, Malawi, 1974–76; on secondment to Min. of Overseas Development as Educn Adviser, 1976–79; Counsellor and Dep. Educn Adviser, British Council Div., British High Commn, India, 1979–83; Controller: Sci., Technol. and Educn Div., 1983–87; Americas, Pacific and E Asia Div., 1987–90. *Recreations:* photography, philately, gardening, tennis, walking, travel. *Address:* 9 Alderway, West Cross, Swansea SA3 5PD.

HOWELL, Gwynne Richard, CBE 1998; Principal Bass, Royal Opera House, 1971; *b* Gorseinon, S Wales, 13 June 1938; *s* of Gilbert and Ellaline Howell; *m* 1968, Mary Edwina Morris; two *s. Educ:* Pontardawe Grammar Sch.; Univ. of Wales, Swansea (BSc; Hon. Fellow 1986); Manchester Univ. (DipTP); MRTPI 1966. Studied singing with Redvers Llewellyn while at UCW; pt-time student, Manchester RCM, with Gwilym Jones, during DipTP trng at Manchester Univ.; studied with Otakar Kraus, 1968–72. Planning Asst, Kent CC, 1961–63; Sen. Planning Officer, Manchester Corp., 1965–68, meanwhile continuing to study music pt-time and giving public operatic performances which incl. the rôle of Pogner, in Die Meistersinger; as a result of this rôle, apptd Principal Bass at Sadler's Wells, 1968; also reached final of BBC Opera Singers competition for N of Eng., 1967. In first season at Sadler's Wells, sang 8 rôles, incl. Monterone and the Commendatore; appearances with Hallé Orch., 1968 and 1969; Arkel in Pelleas and Melisande, Glyndebourne and Covent Garden, 1969; Goffredo, in Il Pirato, 1969. *Royal Opera House, Covent Garden:* début as First Nazarene, Salome, 1969–70 season; the King, in Aida; Timur, in Turandot; Mephisto, in Damnation of Faust; Prince Gremin, in Eugene Onegin; High Priest, in Nabucco; Reinmar, in Tannhauser, 1973–74 (later rôle, Landgraf); Colline, in La Bohème; Pimen, in Boris Godunov; Ribbing, Un ballo in maschera; Padre Guardiano, in La forza del destino; Hobson, in Peter Grimes, 1975; Sparafucile, in Rigoletto, 1975–76 season; Ramfis in Aida, 1977; Tristan und Isolde, 1978, 1982; Luisa Miller, 1978; Samson et Delilah, 1981; Fiesco in Simon Boccanegra, 1981; Pogner in Die Meistersinger, 1982; Arkel in Pelléas et Mélisande, 1982; Dossifei in Khovanshchina, 1982; Semele, 1982; Die Zauberflöte, 1983; Raimondo, in Lucia di Lammermoor, 1985; Rocco in Fidelio, 1986; Marcel in Les Huguenots, 1991; Daland in Der Fliegende Holländer, 1992; Katya Kabanova, 1994; Stiffelio, 1995; Mathis der Maler, 1995; The Bartered Bride, 1998; Greek Passion, 2000; The Tempest (world première), 2004; *English National Opera:* Don Carlos, Die Meistersinger, 1974–75; The Magic Flute, Don Carlos, 1975–76; Duke Bluebeard's Castle, 1978, 1991; The Barber of Seville, 1980; Tristan and Isolde, 1981; Hans Sachs in Die Meistersinger, 1984; Parsifal, 1986; Don Carlos, 1992; Banquo in Macbeth, 1993; Fidelio, 1996; Mary Stuart, 1998; Silver Tassie (world première), 2000; War and Peace, 2001; Lulu, 2002; Dansker in Billy Budd, 2005, 2012; Aida, 2007; *Metropolitan Opera House, New York:* début as Lódovico in Otello, and Pogner in Die Meistersinger, 1985; *Bastille, Paris:* début in Parsifal, 1997; *sacred music:* Verdi and Mozart Requiems, Missa Solemnis, St Matthew and St John Passions; sings in Europe and USA; records for BBC and for major recording companies. *Recreations:* tennis, golf, Rugby enthusiast, gardening. *Address:* 197 Fox Lane, N13 4BB. *T:* and *Fax:* (020) 8886 1981.

HOWELL, John Frederick; Senior Research Associate, Overseas Development Institute, since 1997 (Director, 1987–97); *b* 16 July 1941; *s* of late Frederick Howell and Glenys Griffiths; *m* 1993, Paula Wade; two *s*, and one step *s. Educ:* Univ. of Wales (BA Hons 1963); Univ. of Manchester (MA Econ. Dist. 1965); Univ. of Reading, (external; PhD). Lectr, Univ. of Khartoum, 1966–73; correspondent, Africa Confidential, 1971–75; Sen. Lectr, Univ. of Zambia, 1973–77; Overseas Development Institute, 1977–; seconded as Advr, Min. of Agric. and Land Affairs, S Africa, 1997–2001. Vis Lectr, Mananga Agric. Management Centre,

Swaziland, 1978–80; Vis. Prof. in Agricl Develt, Wye Coll., Univ. of London, 1988–96. Consultant on aid and agricl devel: World Bank; EC; FAO; Commonwealth Secretariat; DFID in S Africa, India, Nepal, Nigeria, Brazil, Tanzania, Malaŵi, Sudan; Adviser: All-Party Parly Gp on Overseas Develt, 1985–86; Princess Royal's Africa Review Gp, 1987–89; Economic Advr, Chagos Refugees Gp, 2008–10. Mem. Council, VSO, 1991–97. Pres., UK Chapter, Soc. of Internat. Develt, 1991–93. *Publications:* Local Government and Politics in the Sudan, 1974; (ed) Borrowers and Lenders: rural financial markets and institutions in developing countries, 1980; Administering Agricultural Development for Small Farmers, 1981; (ed) Recurrent Costs and Agricultural Development, 1985; (ed) Agricultural Extension in Practice, 1988; (with Alex Duncan) Structural Adjustment and the African Farmer, 1992; Returning Home: a proposal for the resettlement of the Chagos Islands, 2008. *Address:* 3 Elers Road, Ealing, W13 9QA.

HOWELL, John Michael, OBE 2000; DPhil; MP (C) Henley, since June 2008; *b* London, 27 July 1955; *s* of Alexander J. Howell and Gladys S. Howell; *m* 1987, Alison Parker; one *s* two *d. Educ:* Battersea Grammar Sch.; Univ. of Edinburgh (MA 1978); St John's Coll., Oxford (DPhil 1981). Ernst & Young, 1987–96; Business Presenter, BBC World Service TV, 1996–97; Director: Fifth World Prodns Ltd, 1996–2003; Media Presentation Consultants Ltd, 2005–08. Mem. (C), Oxfordshire CC, 2004–09 (Cabinet Mem. for Change Mgt, 2005–08). PPS to Leader, H of C, 2010–14, to Minister of State, DCLG, 2010–12. Member: Justice Select Cttee, 2014–; Executive, 1922 Cttee, 2014–. *Publications:* Neolithic Northern France, 1983; Understanding Eastern Europe: the context of change, 1994. *Recreations:* music, theatre. *Address:* House of Commons, SW1A 0AA. *T:* (020) 7219 4828, 7219 6676, *Fax:* (020) 7219 2606. *E:* howellJm@parliament.uk; PO Box 84, Watlington, Oxon OX49 5XD. *T:* (01491) 613072. *Club:* Leander (Henley).

HOWELL, Leslie, CBE 1996; Chairman, St Helens and Knowsley Teaching Hospital NHS Trust, 2008–13; *b* Liverpool, 11 Oct. 1943; *s* of Philip Leslie Howell and Gladys Howell; *m* 1969, Joan; one *s* one *d. Educ:* Liverpool Collegiate Sch.; Open Univ. (BA 1973); INSEAD (MBA Gen. Mgt Prog. 1986). FCII. Trainee, Liverpool and London Globe Insce Co., 1962; Royal Insurance, later Royal Sun Alliance: Claims Hd, 1965–68; Sen. Tutor, Trng Sch., 1968–70; Mktg Admin. Manager, 1970–72; Mgt Trng Officer, 1972–75; Mgt Trng Manager, 1975–78; HR Dir, British Engine Insce, 1978–81; on secondment to Govt Task Force, Liverpool, 1981–82; Trng and Develt Manager, 1982–83; BCG Consultants, 1984–85 (on secondment); Regl Manager, NW England, 1985–86; Dir and Gen. Manager, 1986–95; Gen. Manager, Gp Strategy, 1996–98; Sec. Gen., Comité Européen des Assurances, 1999–2002. Chairman: British Engine Insce, 1990–95; CIG Hldgs Ltd, 2002–06. Dir, Insce Ombudsman Bd, 1992–98; Chairman: Motor Insurers Bureau, 1994–98; Eur. Motor Cttee, Comité Européen des Assurances, 1994–98; Mem., British Insurers Internat. Cttee, 1993–98. Member: Nat. Council, TEC, 1996–98 (Chm., Merseyside TEC, 1995–98); Bd, NACETT, 1997–98. Member: Govt Task Force in Liverpool, 1981–82; Bd, Liverpool City Challenge, 1995–98. Vis. Prof., Business Sch., 1998–2008, Dir, 2002–, Liverpool John Moores Univ.; Director: Liverpool Univ., 1995–98; Liverpool Sch. of Tropical Medicine, 1996–98. Trustee, Lung Cancer Fund, 2001–04. *Recreations:* walking, music, family, cricket. *E:* les.howell1@btinternet.com. *Club:* Artists'.

HOWELL, Margaret, CBE 2007; RDI 2007; Designer and Creative Director, Margaret Howell Ltd, since 1986; *b* Tadworth, Surrey, 5 Sept. 1946; *d* of Edwin Harris Howell and Gladys Ivy Howell; *m* 1972, Paul Andrew Renshaw (marr. diss. 1987); one *d* (one *s* decd). *Educ:* Goldsmith's Coll., Univ. of London (DipAD). Self-employed clothes designer, 1970–86; founded Margaret Howell Ltd, 1986. Hon. Dr Univ. of Arts, London, 2010. *Recreations:* walking, swimming, photography, art exhibitions. *Address:* 6 Welbeck Way, W1G 9RZ. *T:* (020) 7009 9000, *Fax:* (020) 7009 9001. *E:* admin@margarethowell.co.uk.

HOWELL, Michael Edward, CMG 1989; OBE 1980; HM Diplomatic Service; High Commissioner, Mauritius, 1989–93; *b* 2 May 1933; *s* of Edward and Fanny Howell; *m* 1958, Joan Little; one *s* one *d. Educ:* Newport High Sch. Served RAF, 1951–53. Colonial Office, 1953; CRO, 1958; Karachi, 1959; 2nd Secretary: Bombay, 1962; UK Delegn to Disarmament Cttee, Geneva, 1966; 1st Sec. (Parly Clerk), FCO, 1969; Consul (Comm.), New York, 1973; ndc 1975; FCO, 1976; Hd of Chancery, later Chargé d'Affaires, Kabul, 1978; Consul-General: Berlin, 1981; Frankfurt, 1983; High Comr to Papua New Guinea, 1986. *Recreation:* golf. *Address:* c/o Foreign and Commonwealth Office, SW1A 2AH.

HOWELL, Michael William Davis; Deputy Chairman, Future Brilliance Ltd, since 2013 (Chairman, 2012–13); *b* 11 June 1947; *s* of late Air Vice-Marshal Evelyn Michael Thomas Howell, CBE, and Helen Joan Hayes; *m* 1975, Susan Wanda Adie; two *s* one *d. Educ:* Charterhouse Sch., Godalming; Trinity Coll., Cambridge (BA 1968, MA 1969); INSEAD, Fontainebleau (MBA 1975); Harvard Business Sch. (MBA 1976). British Leyland Truck and Bus Division: Graduate Trainee, 1969–71; Personnel Manager, Leyland Nat., 1971–74; Cummins Engine Co. Inc.: Asst to Vice-Pres. Internat. (USA), 1976–77; Dir, European Mktg, Brussels, 1977–80; Vice-President: Europe (based in London), 1981–84; Corporate Strategy, 1984–88; Vice-Pres., GE Canada Inc., 1988–89; Gen. Manager, GE Transportation, 1989–91; Dir, Arlington Capital Partners (formerly Mgt) Ltd, 1991–96 (non-exec. Dir, 1996–2010); Commercial Dir, Railtrack Gp plc, 1996–97; Chm., FPT Gp Ltd, 1998–2002; Chief Exec., Transport Initiatives Edinburgh, subseq. tie ltd, 2002–06. Chm., Evo Electric Ltd, 2007–12; Director: Westinghouse Air Brake Technol. Corp. (USA), 2003–; Hutchison China Meditech Ltd, 2006–. City and Guilds of London Institute: Treas., 2003–06; Chm., 2006–12. Gov., Clothworkers' Foundn, 1999– (Master, 2014–15). *Recreations:* hill-walking, sailing. *Address:* London, E1 8JA. *E:* mwdhowell@aol.com. *Club:* Oxford and Cambridge.

HOWELL, Patrick Leonard; QC 1990; *b* 4 Dec. 1942; *s* of Leonard Howell, MC, and Mary Isobel (*née* Adam); *m* 1966, Sandra Marie McColl; two *s* one *d. Educ:* Radley; Christ Church, Oxford (MA); London Sch. of Econs and Pol Science (LLM). Called to the Bar: Inner Temple, 1966; Lincoln's Inn, 1968. Teaching Fellow, Osgoode Hall Law Sch., Toronto, 1965–66. An Upper Tribunal Judge (Administrative Appeals, Tax and Chancery Chambers) (formerly Social Security Comr and Child Support Comr), 1994–2012; a Judge, Employment Appeal Tribunal, 1999–2012.

HOWELL, Peter Adrian; Senior Lecturer, Department of Classics, Royal Holloway and Bedford New College, University of London, 1994–99 (Lecturer, 1985–94), now Hon. Research Fellow; *b* 29 July 1941; *s* of Lt-Col Harry Alfred Adrian Howell, MBE and Madge Maud Mary, *d* of Major-Gen. R. L. B. Thompson, CB, CMG, DSO. *Educ:* Downside School; Balliol College, Oxford (BA 1963; MA; MPhil 1966). Asst Lectr and Lectr, Dept of Latin, Bedford Coll., Univ. of London, 1964–85. Dep. Chm., Jt Cttee, Nat. Amenity Socs, 1991–93; Member: Cttee, Victorian Soc., 1968–2005 (Chm., 1987–93); Westminster Cathedral Art Cttee, 1974–91, 1993–; Dept of Art and Architecture, Liturgy Commn, RC Bishops' Conf., 1977–84; Churches Cttee, English Heritage, 1984–88; RC Historic Churches Cttee for Wales and Herefordshire, 1995–; Westminster Diocesan Historic Churches Cttee, 1995–99. *Publications:* Victorian Churches, 1968; (with Elisabeth Beazley) Companion Guide to North Wales, 1975; (with Elisabeth Beazley) Companion Guide to South Wales, 1977; A Commentary on Book I of the Epigrams of Martial, 1980; (ed with Ian Sutton) The Faber Guide to Victorian Churches, 1989; (ed and trans.) Martial: the Epigrams Book V, 1995; Martial, 2009; articles in Architectural History, Country Life. *Recreations:* art, architecture, music. *Address:* 127 Banbury Road, Oxford OX2 6JX. *T:* (01865) 515050.

HOWELL, Robert; theatre designer; *b* Liverpool, 14 Nov. 1966; *s* of Stuart and Doreen Howell; *m* 1996, Gail Lonsdale; two *s. Educ:* John Hamden Grammar Sch.; Bucks Coll. of Higher Educn; Birmingham Poly. (BA 1st Cl. Hons). Resident Design Asst, RSC, 1989–91; freelance theatre designer, 1991–; *productions:* Relative Values, Chichester Fest. Th., 1993, then tour, transf. Savoy Th.; Eurovision, Sydmonton Fest. and Vaudeville Th., 1993; Oliver, Crucible Th., Sheffield, 1993; Private Lives, Dalateatern, Sweden, 1994; Julius Caesar, Royal Exchange, 1994; The Shakespeare Revue, RSC, 1994; True West, Donmar, 1994; Simpatico, Royal Ct, 1995; The Painter of Dishonour, RSC, 1995; The Glass Menagerie, Donmar, 1995; Tartuffe, Almeida, 1996; The Loves of Cass Maguire, Druid Th. Co., 1996; Habeas Corpus, Donmar, 1996; Peter Pan, W Yorks Playhouse, 1996; Little Eyolf, RSC, 1996; Tom and Clem, Aldwych, 1997; Chips with Everything, RNT, 1997; Entertaining Mr Sloane, Th. Clywd, 1997; The Government Inspector, Almeida, 1997; The Fix, Donmar, 1997; Eddie Izzard: Glorious Tour, 1997, 2000; How I Learned to Drive, Donmar, 1998; Richard III, RSC, 1998; Real Classy Affair, Royal Ct, 1998; Vassa, Almeida, 1999; Troilus and Cressida, Money, RNT, 1999; The Family Reunion, RSC, 1999; Betrayal, Th. d'Atelier, Paris, 1999; Battle Royal, RNT, 1999; Little Malcolm and his Struggle Against the Eunuchs, Hampstead and West End, 1999; Eddie Izzard, UK Tour, 1999–2000; Hard Fruit, Royal Ct, 2000; Turn of the Screw, WNO, 2000; Conversations After a Burial, Almeida, 2000; The Caretaker, Guildford and Comedy Th., 2000; Lulu, Almeida, transf. Kennedy Th., Washington, 2001; Howard Katz, RNT, 2001; Sunset Boulevard, UK tour, 2001; Faith Healer, Almeida, 2001; Proof, Donmar, 2002; Our House, West End, 2002; Sophie's Choice, ROH, 2002; The Graduate, Gielgud and Broadway, 2002 (UK tour, 2004); Simply Heavenly, Young Vic, 2003, transf. West End, 2004; The Lady from the Sea, Almeida, 2003; Tell Me on a Sunday, West End and UK tour, 2003; Endgame, West End, 2004; Buried Child, RNT, 2004; Hedda Gabler, Almeida, 2005 (Best Set Design, Olivier Awards, 2006); Lord of the Rings, Toronto, 2006, transf. Th. Royal Drury Lane, 2007 (Best Designer, What's On Stage Awards, Outstanding Costume Design, Dora Mavor Awards, 2006); Bash, Trafalgar Studios, 2007; The Reporter, RNT, 2007; Boeing Boeing, Comedy Th., 2007, transf. Broadway and UK tour, 2008; Speed-the-Plow, Old Vic, 2008; Our House, Birmingham Repertory and UK tour, 2008; Her Naked Skin, RNT, 2008; The Norman Conquests, Old Vic, 2008, transf. NY, 2009; Complicit, Old Vic, 2009; The Last Cigarette, Chichester and West End, 2009; The Observer, RNT, 2009; Inherit the Wind, Old Vic, 2009; Carmen, Metropolitan Opera, NY, 2009; Private Lives, The Prisoner of Second Avenue, Vaudeville, 2010; Deathtrap, Noel Coward, 2010; Matilda (The Musical), RSC, 2010 (Best Set Design, Olivier Awards, 2012); Ghost (The Musical), Manchester and London, 2011 (Outstanding Set Design, Drama Desk Awards, 2012); Stephen Ward, Aldwych, 2013; Fathers and Sons, Donmar Warehouse, 2014. Best Set Designer for Troilus and Cressida, Vassa and Richard III, Olivier Awards, 2000; Best Designer, for Matilda (The Musical) and Ghost (The Musical), What's On Stage Awards, 2012. *Address:* c/o Judy Daish Associates, 2 St Charles Place, W10 6EG. *T:* (020) 8964 8811. *E:* judy@judydaish.com.

HOWELL, Rupert Cortlandt Spencer, FIPA; Group Development Director (formerly Group Transformation Director), Trinity Mirror plc, since 2013; *b* 6 Feb. 1957; *s* of late Lt Col F. R. Howell, MBE, RE, and of S. D. L. Howell (*née* McCallum); *m* 1987, Claire Jane Ashworth; one *s* one *d. Educ:* Wellington Coll.; Univ. of Warwick (BSc Mgt Scis). FIPA 1995; Fellow, Marketing Soc., 2008. Mkting trainee, Lucas Service Overseas, 1978; Account Exec., Mathers Advertising, 1979–81; Account Supervisor, Grey Advertising, 1981–83; Young & Rubicam: Account Dir, 1983–84; New Business Dir, 1985–86; Hd, Client Services, 1987; Howell Henry Chaldecott Lury Ltd, subseq. HHCL & Partners: Founder, 1987; Man. Partner, 1987–97; Jt Chief Exec., 1997–98; Chm., 1999–2002; Jt Chief Exec., Chime Communications plc, 1997–2002; Chm., UK & Ireland, and Pres., Europe, Middle E and Africa, Interpublic Gp, subseq. McCann Worldgroup, 2003–07; Man. Dir, ITV Brand and Commercial, 2007–10; CEO, Phoenix Newspaper Publishing, 2011–13. Non-exec. Chm., Hey Human (formerly Billington Cartmell) Gp, 2012–; non-exec. Dep. Chm., Matomy Media Ltd, 2014–. President: Inst. of Practitioners in Advertising, 1999–2001; Eur. Assoc. of Communication Agencies, 2006–07; Vice-Chm., Advertising Assoc., 2008–12. Trustee, Media Trust, 2008–. *Recreations:* golf, shooting, cricket, Rugby Union, soccer. *Clubs:* MCC, Lord's Taverners, Thirty, Solus.

HOWELL, Prof. Simon Laurence, PhD, DSc; Professor of Physiology, since 1985, Director of Research and Development, since 2007, Guy's Campus Dean, since 2005, and Dean of Faculty of Life Sciences and Medicine, since 2014, King's College London; *b* 29 June 1943; *s* of Laurence James Howell and Joan Kathleen Rosemary (*née* Wheelwright); *m* 1969, Linda Margaret Chapman (marr. diss. 2012); one *d. Educ:* St John's Sch., Leatherhead; Chelsea Coll., London (BSc Hons 1964); KCL (PhD 1967); DSc London 1983. Res. Fellow, Univ. of Sussex, 1968–78; Lectr, Charing Cross Hosp. Med. Sch., London, 1978–80; Reader, Queen Elizabeth Coll., London, 1980–85; Hd, Biomed. Scis Div., 1988–98, Hd, GKT Sch. of Biomed. Scis, 1998–2003, KCL. Chm., Diabetes UK, 2006–09 (Vice Chm., 2002–06). Chm., Lord Brock Meml Trust, 2011–. Minkowski Prize, Eur. Assoc. Study of Diabetes, 1983. *Publications:* (jtly) Biochemistry of the Polypeptide Hormones, 1985; (jtly) Diabetes and its Management, 5th edn 1996, 6th edn 2003; The Biology of the Pancreatic B Cell, 1999. *Recreations:* gardening, opera. *Address:* King's College London Faculty of Life Sciences and Medicine, Guy's Campus, SE1 1UL.

HOWELL WILLIAMS, Craig; QC 2009; *b* Liverpool; *s* of Peter and Fiona Elizabeth Howell Williams; *m* 1994, Elizabeth Jill Ainger; one *s* one *d. Educ:* Univ. of Leeds (BA Hons); Council of Legal Educn. Called to the Bar, Gray's Inn, 1983; Accredited Mediator, CEDR, 2005. Jun. Counsel to Crown B Panel, 1993–99. Chm., London Luton Airport Consultative Cttee, 1999–2002; Lead Asst Comr, Boundary Commn for England, 2011–13; Member: RICS Mediation Panel, 2010–; Planning Mediation Panel, DCLG, 2013–. MCIArb 2012. Trustee, Planning Aid for London, 2007–11. *Recreations:* music, theatre.

HOWELLS, family name of **Baroness Howells of St Davids**.

HOWELLS OF ST DAVIDS, Baroness *cr* 1999 (Life Peer), of Charlton in the London Borough of Greenwich; **Rosalind Patricia-Anne Howells,** OBE 1994; Chancellor, University of Bedfordshire, 2009–14; Vice Chair, London Voluntary Services Council, 1978–83; *b* Grenada, WI, 10 Jan. 1931; *m* 1955, John Charles Howells (decd); two *d. Educ:* St Joseph's Convent, Grenada; South West London Coll. (Cert. Welfare and Counselling); City Univ., Washington. Formerly Dep. High Comr for Grenada in London; Equal Opportunities Dir, Greenwich Council for Racial Equality, 1980–87; Chair, Lewisham Racial Equality Council, 1994–97; Mem., Commn on Future of Multi-Ethnic Britain, 1998–2000. Governor, Avery Hill Coll., later Thames Poly., then Univ. of Greenwich, 1985–97. Trustee: West Indian Standing Conf.; City Parochial Foundn; Museum of Ethnic Arts; Women of the Year Cttee; Stephen Lawrence Charitable Trust; Pres., Windward Is Res. and Educn Foundn Trust, Univ. of St George's, Grenada, 2014–. Patron: Greenwich and Bexley Hospice, 2014–; Jason Roberts Foundn, 2012–. DUniv Greenwich, 1998. *Recreations:* travelling, adventurous food, all types of music. *Address:* c/o House of Lords, SW1A 0PW.

HOWELLS, Anne Elizabeth; opera, concert and recital singer; Professor, Royal Academy of Music, since 1997; *b* 12 Jan. 1941; *d* of Trevor William Howells and Mona Hewart; *m* 1st, 1966, Ryland Davies, *qv* (marr. diss. 1981); 2nd, 1981, Stafford Dean (marr. diss. 1996); one *s* one *d*; 3rd, 1999. *Educ:* Sale County Grammar Sch.; Royal Manchester (subseq. Royal Northern) Coll. of Music (ARMCM; Hon. FRMCM); studied under Frederick Cox and Vera Rosza. Three seasons (Chorus), with Glyndebourne, 1964–66; at short notice given star rôle there in Cavalli's L'Ormindo, 1967; rôles there also include: Dorabella in Così fan Tutte;

Cathleen in (world première of) Nicholas Maw's Rising of the Moon, 1970; the Composer in Ariadne; Diana in Calisto; under contract, 1969–71, subseq. Guest Artist, Royal Opera, Covent Garden; sings with Scottish Opera, ENO and major orchs in UK; recitals in Brussels and Vienna; operatic guest performances incl. La Scala (Milan), Chicago, Metropolitan (NY), San Francisco, Geneva, Brussels, Salzburg, Amsterdam, Hamburg (W German début), W Berlin, Paris. Rôles include: Lena in (world première of) Richard Rodney Bennett's Victory; Rosina in Barber of Seville; Cherubino in Marriage of Figaro; Zerlina in Don Giovanni; Giulietta in The Tales of Hoffmann; Orsini in Lucrezia Borgia; Ascanius in Benvenuto Cellini; Helen in King Priam; Judit in Bluebeard's Castle; Octavian in Der Rosenkavalier (video recording), 1985; Annius in La Clemenza di Tito (film of Salzburg prodn); Lady Hautdesert in (world première of) Gawain, 1994. Hon. RAM. *Recreations:* theatre, cinema, reading, writing (articles published in The Oldie Mag.). *Address:* c/o Royal Academy of Music, Marylebone Road, NW1 5HT.

HOWELLS, Sir Eric (Waldo Benjamin), Kt 1993; CBE 1986; farmer and landowner, since 1966; *b* 9 Aug. 1933; *s* of Vincent Vaughan Howells and Amy (*née* Jones); *m* 1960, Margaret Maisie Edwards; one *s* twin *d.* Sec. and Gen. Manager of a limited co., 1959–66; Director: Carmarthen and Pumsaint Farmers Ltd, 1997–2001; Welsh Milk Ltd, 2000–06. Chm., Whitland and Dist Abattoir Cttee, 2001–05; New Enterprise Timber Recycling Plant, 2007–. Former Chm., Pembrokeshire NFU. Mem., Llanddewi Velfrey Parish Community Council, 1967–2008 (Chm., 1967, 1974, 1981, 1988, 1995, 2001); Chm., 1978–87, Pres., 1987–90, Pembrokeshire Cons. and Unionist Assoc.; Wales Area Conservative Party: Treas., 1984–88; Dep. Chm., 1988–90; Chm., 1990–95; Pres., 1996–99; Life Vice-Pres. Chm., Wales Area Cons. European Co-ordinating Cttee, 1992–95; Mem. of numerous other local and nat. Cons. and other bodies; regular broadcaster on radio and television in English and Welsh. Deacon and Treas., Bethel Congregational Chapel, Llanddewi Velfrey, 1974–. *Recreations:* music, bee keeping, DIY, reading, writing. *Address:* Meadow View, Llanddewi Velfrey, Narberth, Pembrokeshire SA67 7EJ. *T:* (01994) 240205.

HOWELLS, Gwyn; Marketing and Communications Consultant, Gwyn Howells Marketing, since 2002; *b* 21 May 1949; *s* of late Emrys Howells and Edith Frances (*née* Taylor); *m* 1st, 1976, Margaret Anne Farrall (*d* 1995); one *s* one *d*; 2nd, 2003, Virginia Ann McCarthy. *Educ:* Lewis Sch. for Boys, Pengam; City of London Poly. (BSc Econs 1970). Sen. Brand Manager, Gallaher Ltd, 1971–82; Dir, Brand and Trade Mktg, Courage Ltd, 1982–89; Marketing Dir, Reebok UK Ltd, 1989–92; Marketing Dir, 1992–99, Dir Gen., 1999–2002, Meat and Livestock Commn. Liveryman, Butchers' Co., 2001 (Court Asst, 2013–). *Recreations:* Rugby football, tennis, theatre. *Address:* 30 Bewdley Street, N1 1HB. *Clubs:* Hampstead Rugby Football, Rhymney Rugby Football.

HOWELLS, James Richard; QC 2014; *b* Kent, 10 July 1971; *s* of Russell Mervyn Howells and Margaret Anne Howells; *m* 2001, Zoë Yasmin Khan; three *s. Educ:* Magdalene Coll., Cambridge (BA 1992; MA); Brasenose Coll., Oxford (BCL 1994). Called to the Bar, Middle Temple, 1995. *Recreations:* family, cinema, art and antiques, gym, obstacle course racing. *Address:* Boothby Graffoe; 1 Atkin Building, Gray's Inn, WC1R 5AT.

HOWELLS, Rt Hon. Kim (Scott), PC 2009; PhD; writer, painter and television presenter, since 2010; *b* 27 Nov. 1946; *s* of Glanville James and Joan Glenys Howells; *m* 1983, Eirlys Howells (*née* Davies); two *s* one *d. Educ:* Mountain Ash Grammar Sch.; Hornsey College of Art; Cambridge College of Advanced Technology (BA (Jt Hons)); Warwick Univ. (PhD). Steel-worker, 1969–70; Coal-miner, 1970–71; Lectr, 1975–79; Research Officer: Swansea Univ., 1979–82; NUM, S Wales Area, 1982–89. MP (Lab) Pontypridd, Feb. 1989–2010. Opposition Front bench spokesman on aid and develt, 1993–94, on foreign affairs, 1994, on home affairs, 1994–95, on trade and industry, 1995–97; Parliamentary Under-Secretary of State: DFEE, 1997–98; DTI, 1998–2001; DCMS, 2001–03; Minister of State: DfT, 2003–04; DfES, 2004–05; (Minister for the Middle East), FCO, 2005–08; Chm., Intelligence and Security Cttee, 2008–10. Mem., British Mountaineering Council, 1993–. *Recreations:* climbing, painting, jazz, cinema, literature, art, growing vegetables.

HOWELLS, Michael Dennis; production designer, since 1989; *b* Droxford, Hants, 13 Jan. 1957; *s* of Victor Dennis Howells and Mollie Howells (*née* Thomas); partner, David, Frieherr Pretorius von Richthofen (*d* 1993). *Educ:* Marling Sch., Glos; Cheltenham Coll. of Art (Foundn); Camberwell Sch. of Art (BA). Production designer, films: Second Best, 1994; Princess Caraboo, 1994; Emma, 1996; Fairy Tale: A True Story, 1998; Ever After, 1998; An Ideal Husband, 1999; Miss Julie, 2000; Ohio Impromptu, 2000; About Time 2 (segment of Ten Minutes Older: The Cello, 2002; Shackleton, 2002; Bright Young Things, 2003; Nanny McPhee, 2005; Sixty Six, 2006; Death at a Funeral, 2007; Blackwood, 2012; The Game, 2013; designer, fashion sets including: Christian Lacroix couture shows; Christian Dior, 1998–2003, 2006–11; Associate Designer, Rambert Dance Co., 2007–: ballets include: Constant Speed, 2007; Lady into Fox, 2007; Eternal Light, 2008; Cardoon Club, 2010; Seven for a Secret, 2011; What Wild Ecstasy, 2012. Artistic Dir, Port Eliot Fest. (Associate Designer, 2011). Dance/ballet: prodn designer/costumes, Fier!, Dansgroep, Amsterdam, 2009; prodn designer/set, Dark Arteries, Rambert, 2015; theatre: costume designer, Chariots of Fire, Hampstead, transf. Gielgud, 2012; prodn designer/sets/costumes, Not a Cloud in the Sky, Staats Th., Saarbruecken, 2014. Isabella Blow Award for Fashion Creator of the Year, British Fashion Council, 2007. *Address:* (film, ballet, theatre) c/o Casarotto Marsh, Waverley House, 7–12 Noel Street, W1F 8GQ. *T:* (020) 7287 4450; (fashion, photography) c/o Camilla Lowther Management, 19 All Saints Road, W11 1HE. *T:* (020) 7313 8314.

HOWES, Maj. Gen. Buster; *see* Howes, Maj. Gen. F. H. R.

HOWES, Sir Christopher (Kingston), KCVO 1999 (CVO 1997); CB 1993; Second Commissioner and Chief Executive of the Crown Estate, 1989–2001; Senior Advisor, Barclays Wealth and Investment Management, since 2013; Member: HRH Prince of Wales's Council, 1990–2011; Council, Duchy of Lancaster, 1993–2005; *b* 30 Jan. 1942; *yr s* of late Leonard Howes, OBE and Marion Howes (*née* Bussey); *m* 1967, Clare, *o d* of Gordon and Lilian Cunliffe; one *s* one *d* (and one *s* one *d* decd). *Educ:* Gresham's Sch.; Coll. of Estate Management, Univ. of London (BSc 1965); Univ. of Reading (MPhil 1976). ARICS 1967, FRICS 1977. Valuation and Planning Depts, GLC, 1965–67; Partner and Sen. Partner, Chartered Surveyors, Norwich, 1967–79; Department of the Environment: Dep. Dir, Land Economy, 1979–81; Chief Estates Officer, 1981–85; Dir, Land and Property Div., 1985–89. Sen. Vis. Fellow, Sch. of Envmtl Scis, UEA, 1975; Visiting Lecturer: Dept of Land Economy, Univ. of Cambridge, 1976–81; Univ. of Reading, 1974–80; Aberdeen 1982; UCLA and UCS Los Angeles, 1983; Harvard, 1985; Univ. N Carolina, Chapel Hill, 1985; Miami, 1985; Vis. Prof., Bartlett Sch. of Architecture and Planning, UCL, 1984–. Member: Sec. of State for the Envmt's Thames Adv. Cttee, 1995–98; CNAA Surveying Bd, 1978–82; OECD Urban Policy Gp, 1985–88; Planning and Develt Divl Council, RICS, 1983–92; Policy Review Cttee, RICS, 1984–90; RIBA Awards Gp, 1997–2002; Council: Norfolk Archaeol Trust, 1979–; British Property Fedn, 1992–2001. Jt Chm., World Land Policy Congress, London, 1986. Vis. Speaker, Commonwealth Assoc. of Surveying and Land Economy Conf., Trinidad, 1982 and Cyprus, 1984, 2009. Hon. Mem., Cambridge Univ. Land Soc., 1989–. Founder Mem., Norwich Third World Centre, 1970; dir of various housing assocs, 1970–80; Dep. Chm., Howard de Walden Estate, 2012– (non-exec. Dir, 2002–12); non-executive Director: Norwich & Peterborough Building Soc., 1998–2005; Compco Hldg Ltd, 2004–; Dir, Colville Estates Ltd, 2003–12; non-exec. Chm., Barclays Real Estate (formerly Property Finance) Team, 2005–10; Member, Advisory Board: Barclays Private Banking, 2001–; Three Delta LLP, 2006–11; Advr, Operational Efficiency Prog., HM Treasury, 2008–09; Mem., Barclays Private Bank Adv. Cttee, 2008–13. Member: Bd, Norwich Theatre Royal Trust, 1969–79; Adv. Bd, Aldeburgh Music, 1998–2010. Steward and Hon. Surveyor to Dean and Chapter, Norwich Cathedral, 1973–79; Trustee: HRH The Prince of Wales's Inst. of Architecture, 1992–99; British Architectural Library Trust, 1997–2010; Suffolk Historic Churches Trust, 2009–14; Ore and Alde Estuary Trust, 2013–; Mem., British Archtl Trust Bd (formerly RIBA Trust), 2010–. Member: Court of Advisers, 1980–99, Investment Adv. Cttee, 1999–2011, St Paul's Cathedral; Court, UEA, 1992–. Patron, Heatherley Sch. of Fine Art Chelsea, 2008–. Norwich CC, 1969–73; JP Norfolk 1973–80. Hon. FRIBA 1995. Hon. LittD E Anglia, 2000. Mem. of various editorial bds. *Publications:* (jtly) Acquiring Office Space, 1975; Value Maps: aspects of land and property values, 1979; Economic Regeneration (monograph), 1988; Urban Revitalization (monograph), 1988; papers on land and planning policy in learned jls. *Recreations:* music, art, architecture, sailing. *Address:* 8 Millennium House, 132 Grosvenor Road, SW1V 3JY. *T:* (020) 7828 9920; Westerly House, Aldeburgh, Suffolk IP15 5EL. *Clubs:* Athenæum, Garrick; Norfolk (Norwich); Aldeburgh Yacht; Aldeburgh Golf.

HOWES, Maj. Gen. Francis Hedley Roberton, (Buster), CB 2013; OBE 2003; Defence Attaché and Head of British Defence Staff, Washington, 2012–15; *b* Newcastle upon Tyne, 22 March 1960; *s* of Martin and Lolita Howes; *m* 2011, Jennifer Catherine Quinton; three *d. Educ:* York Univ. (BA Chem.); City Univ. London (MA Strategic Studies). Joined RM, 1982; rcds 2002; CO, 42 Commando RM, 2003–05; Divl Dir, JCSC, 2005–06; HCSC, 2006; Dir, Naval Staff, MoD, 2007; Comdr, 3 Commando Bde, RM, 2008; Hd, Overseas Ops, MoD, 2008–09; Comdt Gen., RM and Comdr, UK Amphibious Forces, 2010–11. *Recreations:* art, bodging, growing vegetables, admiring trees, laughing.

HOWES, Rupert Spencer; Chief Executive Officer, Marine Stewardship Council, since 2004; *b* London, 1 April 1963; *s* of Peter John Howes and Elizabeth Jane Howes; *m* 1995, Louise Ann Hulton; three *s* one *d. Educ:* Haverstock Comprehensive Sch., N London; Sussex Univ. (BA (Econ) Hons 1985); Imperial Coll. London (MSc Envmtl Technol. 1992). ACA 1991. Trainee accountant, KPMG, 1987–91; Res. Officer, Internat. Inst. for Envmt and Develt, 1991–94; Sen. Res. Fellow, Sci. Policy Res. Unit, Sussex Univ., 1994–97; Dir, Sustainable Econ. Prog., Forum for the Future, 1997–2004. Social Entrepreneur Award, SKOLL Foundn, 2007; Leaders for a Living Planet Award, WWF, 2009; Schwab Foundn Social Entrepreneur of the Year, 2014. *Publications:* (jtly) Clean and Competitive?: motivating environmental performance in industry, 1997; (contrib.) The Triple Bottom Line: does it all add up?, 2004. *Recreations:* treasure hunting, fishing, occasional diver, country walks and time with family and dog. *Address:* Marine Stewardship Council, Marine House, 1 Snow Hill, EC1A 2DH. *T:* (020) 7246 8903. *E:* rupert.howes@msc.org.

HOWES, Dr Sally, OBE 2004; Executive Leader, National Audit Office, since 2013; *b* Peterborough, 17 Jan. 1961; *d* of Stanley and Dorothy Howes; *m* 2003, Paul Becksmith. *Educ:* Fitzwilliam Coll., Cambridge (BA Geog. 1982; MA); Bristol Univ. (PhD 1985). Software engr, Logica Space & Defence Systems, 1985–90; Commercial Dir, 1990–99, Man. Dir, 1999–2002, Esys plc; Dir Gen., Soc. of British Aerospace Cos, 2003–07; Commercial Dir, MoD, 2008–10; Dir, Nat. Audit Office, 2010–13. Vis. Prof., Surrey Univ., 2014–. Chair, Policy Panel, IET, 2014–. *Recreations:* gardening, reading, ski-ing, interior design. *E:* showes@ntlworld.com.

HOWES, Sally Ann; actress (stage, film and television); *b* 20 July; *d* of late Bobby Howes; *m* 1958, Richard Adler (marr. diss.); *m* 1969, Andrew Maree (marr. diss.). *Educ:* Glendower, London; Queenswood, Herts; privately. *Films include:* Thursday's Child, 1943; Halfway House, 1943; Dead of Night, 1945; Nicholas Nickleby, 1947; Anna Karenina, 1948; My Sister and I; Fools Rush In; History of Mr Polly, 1949; Stop Press Girl; Honeymoon Deferred; The Admirable Crichton, 1957; Chitty, Chitty Bang Bang, 1968. First appeared West End stage in (revue) Fancy Free, at Prince of Wales's, and at Royal Variety Performance, 1950. *Stage Shows include:* Caprice (musical debut); Paint Your Wagon; Babes in the Wood; Romance by Candlelight; Summer Song; Hatful of Rain; My Fair Lady; Kwamina, NY; What Makes Sammy Run?, NY; Brigadoon (revival), NY City Center, 1962; Sound of Music, Los Angeles and San Francisco, 1972; Lover, St Martin's; The King and I, Adelphi, 1973, Los Angeles and San Francisco, 1974; Hans Andersen, Palladium, 1977; Hamlet (tour), 1983; The Dead, NY, 2000. Has appeared on television: in England from 1949 (Short and Sweet Series, Sally Ann Howes Show, etc); in USA from 1958 (Dean Martin Show, Ed Sullivan Show, Mission Impossible, Marcus Welby MD); Play of the Week; Panel Shows: Hollywood Squares; Password; Bell Telephone Hour; US Steel Hour, etc. *Recreations:* reading, riding, theatre.

HOWES, Sally Margaret; QC 2003; *b* 10 Sept. 1959; *d* of Patrick George Howes and Janet Howes. *Educ:* Polam Hall Sch., Co. Durham; Univ. of Newcastle upon Tyne (BA Hons (Classics); Dip. Law). Called to the Bar, Middle Temple, 1983; Judge Advocate (pt-time), 1993–. Specializes in criminal law. *Recreations:* polo, racing, walking the South Downs with my labrador Shamba. *Address:* Atkinson Bevan Chambers, 2 Harcourt Buildings, EC4Y 9DB. *T:* (020) 7353 2112, *Fax:* (020) 7353 8339. *Clubs:* National Liberal; Cowdray Park Polo.

HOWESON, Captain Charles Arthur, RNR; Chairman: Harvey Nash plc (SW), since 2010; SPS (Pathology and Microbiology), since 2012; Bristol Water plc, since 2015; *b* 27 Nov. 1949; *s* of Arthur C. Howeson and Sheila B. Howeson; *m* 1978, Emma Jane Stevenson; one *s* two *d. Educ:* Uppingham Sch.; Royal Naval Coll. Dartmouth; Royal Naval Staff Coll. RN 1968–90, Chief of Allied Staffs and Dep. COS (Ops) to Comdr British Forces Gibraltar, 1990; retired in rank of Comdr, 1991; Hon. Captain, RNR, 2010. Exec. Dir, Plymouth Area Groundwork Trust, 1991–93. Member: Nat. Consumer Council for Water, 2006–15 (Chm., Western Reg., 2006–15; Chm., Adv. Bd, 2009–14); Nat. Consumer Council for Postal Services (Chm., Western Reg.), 2000–07. Chairman: Horizon Roofing Ltd, 2004–10; UK Seafish Industry Authy, 2007–10; Coutts & Co. Private Bankers (SW), 2009; non-executive Chairman: Rowe Gp, 2003–10; St Piran Homes Ltd, 2004–10; Clearwood Joinery Ltd, 2004–10; First Great Western Trains, 2007–09 (Chm., Adv. Bd, 2009–); Crownhill Estates Ltd; Eko-Tek Gp of Cos; Buckland Corporate Finance Ltd; NHS Property Services Ltd, 2011–13; non-exec. Dir, Duchy of Somerset Estates Ltd. Chm., SW Strategic HA, 2009–11; NHS Lead for Veterans, 2009; Vice Chm., NHS South of England, 2011–12. Pres., Millfields Community Econ. Devel Trust; Vice-Pres., Plymouth Chamber of Commerce and Industry, 2006–10; Chairman: Plymouth Area Business Council (formerly Plymouth Econ. Develt Gp), 1999–; Seaton Area Residents' Assoc., 2000–14; Plymouth Policing Adv. Bd, 2007–08; Plymouth Employment Action Zone Bd and Working Links Partnership Bd; Plymouth's Econ. Task Force; Vice-Chm. and Dir, City of Plymouth's Local Strategic Partnership; Vice Chm., Plymouth Sub-Regl Econ. Partnership of Local Authorities, 2000–09; Director: Millfields Estate Mgt Co. Ltd, 2000–; London and West Country Estates Ltd; Frog Construction Ltd; Sailport plc and Solemeasure Ltd; Radio Plymouth Ltd, 2008–12; RNH (West End) Ltd, 2000–; Plymouth Naval Base Visitors' Centre and Mus. Ltd, 2000–12. Gp Chm. Bd, Mount Batten Sailing and Water Sports Centre, 2000–07; Chm., Plymouth Branch, STA, later Tall Ships Youth Trust. Patron, St Austell Br., Royal Naval Assoc., 1995–2010; Vice-Patron, Tomorrow's People; Pres., G-Scale Soc., SW; Chm. Trustees and Govs, Plymouth Drake Foundn, 2006–12, now Life Vice Pres.; Governor and Trustee: Plymouth Coll. Sch., 1997–2009; St Dunstan's Abbey Sch.; Gov., Plymouth Coll. of Further Educn; Trustee: Estates of 19th Duke of Somerset, 1995–; Bermuda Inst. for Oceanographic Sci., 2008–; Hon. Sec. and Treas., 1999–2009, and Dep. Vice Patron, Britannia Assoc., 2009–. Mem., RNSA, 1968–. MRIN; FInstD; FCMI; FRSA; FFB; FNI. Freeman, City of London; Liveryman, Shipwrights' Co.; Mem., Guild of Freemen; Younger Brother, Trinity House. Hon. DPhil (Mgt) Plymouth, 2009. SLJ (Brunei) 1983. *Recreations:* competent international cruising yachtsman, tennis, adequate but still improving jazz pianist, designing and operating substantial garden railway called Third Great Western, wine tasting in heavy seas on board friends' yachts. *Address:* The Water Tower, 91 Craigie Drive, The Millfields, Plymouth PL1 3JB. *E:* charles@smallack.com. *Clubs:* Army and Navy, Naval and Military, 1910 (Goring Hotel); Royal Yacht Squadron.

HOWICK OF GLENDALE, 2nd Baron *cr* 1960; **Charles Evelyn Baring;** a Director, Northern Rock plc (formerly Northern Rock Building Society), 1987–2001; a Managing Director, Baring Brothers & Co. Ltd, 1969–82; *b* 30 Dec. 1937; *s* of 1st Baron Howick of Glendale, KG, GCMG, KCVO, and Lady Mary Cecil Grey, *er d* of 5th Earl Grey; *S* father, 1973; *m* 1964, Clare Nicolette, *y d* of Col Cyril Darby; one *s* three *d*. *Educ:* Eton; New Coll., Oxford. Director: The London Life Association Ltd, 1972–82; Swan Hunter Group Ltd, 1972–79. Member: Exec. Cttee, Nat. Art Collections Fund, 1973–86; Council, Friends of Tate Gall., 1973–78; Adv. Cttee, Westonbirt Arboretum, 1995–2001; Adv. Cttee, Nat. Arboreta, 2001–. Trustee: Chelsea Physic Garden, 1994–2012; Royal Botanic Gdns, Edinburgh, 2001–09; Pres., NE Div., Plant Heritage, 2009–. Chm., Botanics Foundn, 2010–13; Mem. Council, Baring Foundn, 1982–99; Trustee, Northern Rock Foundn, 1997–2007. *Heir: s* Hon. David Evelyn Charles Baring [*b* 26 March 1975; *m* 2003, Victoria Jane, *d* of Owen and Margaret Sutherland]. *Address:* Howick, Alnwick, Northumberland NE66 3LB. *T:* (01665) 577624.

See also Sir E. H. T. Wakefield.

HOWIE, family name of **Baron Howie of Troon**.

HOWIE OF TROON, Baron *cr* 1978 (Life Peer), of Troon in the District of Kyle and Carrick; **William Howie;** civil engineer, publisher, journalist; Consultant, George S. Hall Ltd, since 2001; Chairman, Parliamentary Perceptions, since 2011; *b* Troon, Ayrshire, 2 March 1924; *er s* of late Peter and Annie Howie, Troon; *m* 1951, Mairi Margaret (*d* 2005), *o d* of late Martha and John Sanderson, Troon; two *d* two *s*. *Educ:* Marr Coll., Troon; Royal Technical Coll., Glasgow (BSc, Diploma). Civil engineer in practice, 1944–63, 1970–73; MP (Lab) Luton, Nov. 1963–70; Asst Whip, 1964–66; Lord Comr of the Treasury, 1966–67; Comptroller, HM Household, 1967–68. A Vice-Chm., Parly Labour Party, 1968–70. Gen. Man., 1976–87, Dir (Internal Relns), 1987–96, Thomas Telford Ltd; Dir, SETO, 1996–2000; Dir, 1996–2001, Consultant, 2001–11, PMS Publications Ltd. MICE 1951, FICE 1984; Member: Council, Instn of Civil Engineers, 1964–67; Cttee of Inquiry into the Engineering Profession, 1977–80; President: Assoc. of Supervisory and Exec. Engrs, 1980–85; Assoc. for Educnl and Trng Technol., 1982–93; Ind. Publishers Guild, 1987–93; Vice-President: PPA, 1990–; Combustion Engrg Assoc., 1999–2009. Member: Governing Body, Imperial Coll. of Science and Technology, 1965–67; Pro-Chancellor, City Univ., 1984–91 (Mem. Council 1968–91). MSocIS (France), 1978. Hon. FIStructE 1995; Hon. FABE 2000. Hon. DSc City Univ., 1992; Hon. LLD Strathclyde, 1994. *Publications:* (jtly) Public Sector Purchasing, 1968; Trade Unions and the Professional Engineer, 1977; Trade Unions in Construction, 1981; (ed jtly) Thames Tunnel to Channel Tunnel, 1987. *Recreation:* opera. *Address:* 34 Temple Fortune Lane, NW11 7UL. *T:* (020) 8455 0492. *Clubs:* Luton Labour, Lighthouse, Architecture.

HOWIE, Prof. Archibald, CBE 1998; PhD; FRS 1978; Professor of Physics, Cavendish Laboratory, University of Cambridge, 1986–2001, now Emeritus; Fellow of Churchill College, Cambridge, since 1960; *b* 8 March 1934; *s* of Robert Howie and Margaret Marshall McDonald; *m* 1964, Melva Jean Scott; one *d* (one *s* decd). *Educ:* Kirkcaldy High Sch.; Univ. of Edinburgh (BSc); California Inst. of Technology (MS); Univ. of Cambridge (PhD). English Speaking Union, King George VI Memorial Fellow (at Calif. Inst. of Technology), 1956–57; Cambridge University: Research Scholar, Trinity Coll., 1957–60; Research Fellow, Churchill Coll., 1960–61; Cavendish Laboratory: ICI Research Fellow, 1960–61; Demonstrator in Physics, 1961–65; Lecturer, 1965–79; Reader, 1979–86; Hd of Dept of Physics, 1989–97. Visiting Scientist, Nat. Research Council, Canada, 1966–67; Vis. Prof. of Physics, Univ. of Aarhus, Denmark, 1974. Dir, NPL Management Ltd, 1995–2001. Pres., Internat. Fedn of Socs for Electron Microscopy, 1999–2002. Hon. Prof., Univ. of York, 2008–. Hon. Member: Chinese Electron Microscopy Soc., 2000; Japanese Soc. of Microscopy, 2003. Hon. FRMS 1978 (Pres., 1984–86); Hon. FRSE 1995. Hon. Dr (Physics): Bologna, 1989; Thessaloniki, 1995; DUniv York, 2011. Distinguished Scientist Award, Electron Microscopy Soc. of America, 1991; Guthrie Medal, Inst. of Physics, 1992; Royal Medal, Royal Soc., 1999; (jtly with M. J. Whelan): C. V. Boys Prize, Inst. of Physics, 1965; Hughes Medal, Royal Soc., 1988; Gjønnes Medal, Internat. Union of Crystallography, 2012. *Publications:* (co-author) Electron Microscopy of Thin Crystals, 1965, 2nd edn 1977; papers on electron microscopy and diffraction in scientific jls. *Recreations:* gardening, wine-making. *Address:* 194 Huntingdon Road, Cambridge CB3 0LB. *T:* (01223) 570977.

HOWIE, Prof. John Garvie Robertson, CBE 1996; MD, PhD; FRCGP, FRCPE, FMedSci; Professor of General Practice, University of Edinburgh, 1980–2000; *b* 23 Jan. 1937; *s* of Sir James Howie and Isabella Winifred Mitchell, BSc; *m* 1962, Elizabeth Margaret Donald; two *s* one *d*. *Educ:* High School of Glasgow; Univ. of Glasgow (MD); PhD Aberdeen. House officer, 1961–62; Laboratory medicine, 1962–66; General practitioner, Glasgow, 1966–70; Lectr/Sen. Lectr in General Practice, Univ. of Aberdeen, 1970–80. Founder FMedSci 1998. Hon. DSc Aberdeen, 2002. *Publications:* Research in General Practice, 1979, 2nd edn 1989; A Day in the Life of Academic General Practice, 1999; Academic General Practice in the UK Medical Schools 1948–2000, 2011; articles on appendicitis, prescribing and general medical practice and education, in various jls. *Recreations:* golf, gardening, music. *Address:* 4 Ravelrig Park, Balerno, Midlothian EH14 7DL. *T:* (0131) 449 6305. *E:* john.howie23@btinternet.com.

HOWIE, Robert Bruce McNeill; QC (Scot.) 2000; *b* 24 Aug. 1960; *s* of Dr William Bruce McNeill Howie, OBE, and Dr Theresa Grant or Howie; *m* 1996, Deirdre Elizabeth Hughes Clark or Haigh; one *s*. *Educ:* Aberdeen Grammar Sch.; Aberdeen Univ. (LLB, DLP). Admitted Advocate, 1986. *Address:* 41a Fountainhall Road, Edinburgh EH9 2LN.

HOWITT, Richard Stuart; Member (Lab) Eastern Region, England, European Parliament, since 1999 (Essex South, 1994–99); *b* 5 April 1961. *Educ:* Lady Margaret Hall, Oxford (BA); Univ. of Hertfordshire (DMS). Community worker, 1982–94. Mem. (Lab), Harlow DC, 1984–94 (Leader, 1991–94). Contested (Lab) Billericay, 1987. Hon. Pres., SE Econ. Develt Strategy Assoc., 1994– (Chm., 1986–94); Hon. Vice-President: ADC, 1994–97; LGA, 1997–; Trustee, Centre for Local Econ. Strategies, 1994–. Mem., Labour Party Nat. Policy Forum and NEC Local Govt sub-cttee, 1994–. European Parliament: First Vice-Pres., Regl Affairs Cttee, 1997–99 (Mem., 1994–96); Pres., All-Party Disability Gp, 1999–; Rapporteur: Europe and UN Social Summit, 1995; European Funding for Local and Regl Authorities, 1995; European Refugee Policy, 1996; Guidelines for Effective European Projects, 1998; European Code of Conduct for Enterprises, 1999; Corporate Social Responsibility, 2002–03, 2007; Budget, 2002; Participation of Non-state Actors in EC Develt Policy, 2003; Human Right Report, 2006. *Address:* Labour European Office, Unit 3, Frohock House, 222 Mill Road, Cambridge CB1 3NF. *T:* (01223) 240202, *Fax:* (01223) 241900. *E:* richard.howitt@geo2.poptel.org.uk.

HOWKER, David Thomas; QC 2002; *b* 29 Oct. 1959; *s* of late Kenneth Howker and Miriam Howker; *m* 1994, Shani Estelle Barnes, *qv*; two *s* three *d*. *Educ:* Blackpool Grammar Sch.; Birmingham Univ. (LLB); Inns of Court Sch. of Law. Called to the Bar, Inner Temple, 1982; in practice, specialising in criminal law; Standing Counsel to HM Customs and Excise, 1998–2002; a Recorder, 1999. *Address:* No5 Chambers, Greenwood House, 4–7 Salisbury Court, EC4Y 8AA.

HOWKER, Shani Estelle; *see* Barnes, S. E.

HOWKINS, John Anthony; consultant and writer; *b* 3 Aug. 1945; *s* of Col Ashby Howkins and Lesley (*née* Stops); *m* 1st, 1971, Jill Liddington; 2nd, 1977, Annabel Whittet. *Educ:* Rugby Sch.; Keele Univ.; Architectural Association Sch. of Architecture (Dip.). Marketing Manager, Lever Bros, 1968–70; founder, TV4 Gp, 1971; TV/Radio Editor, Books Editor, Time Out, 1971–74; Sec., Standing Conf. on Broadcasting, 1975–76; Editor, InterMedia, Journal of Internat. Inst. of Communications, 1975–84; Exec. Dir, Internat. Inst. of Communications, 1984–89. Gov., London Film Sch. (formerly London Internat. Film Sch.), 1976–2014 (Chm., 1979–84); Member: Interim Action Cttee on the Film Industry, DTI, 1980–84; British Screen Adv. Council, DTI, 1985– (Dep. Chm., 1991–2013); Vice-Chm. (New Media), Assoc. of Independent Producers, 1984–85. Exec. Editor, National Electronics Review, 1981–99; TV Columnist, Illustrated London News, 1981–83. Chairman: Tornado Productions, 2000–03; BOP Consulting, 2007–11; Director: Television Investments, 1993–; Equator Gp plc, 1999–2006; HandMade plc, 2006–10; Hotbed Media Ltd, 2006–; Screen East, 2006–10; Project Dir, World Learning Network, 1996–2005; Bd Dir, Norfolk and Norwich Festival, 2010–. Dir, Adelphi (formerly Intellectual Property) Charter, RSA, 2004–06. Mem., AHRC, 2008–13. Specialist Advr, Select Cttee on European Communities, House of Lords, 1985–87; Adviser: Broadcasting Reform Commn, Poland, 1989–90; Polish-Radio-and-Television, 1991–94; Minister of Film, Poland, 1991–92; Chm., Adv. Bd, Createc, 1996–2000; Co-ordinator, Eur. Audiovisual Conf., 1997–98. Associate, Coopers Lybrand Deloitte, 1990–91. Special European Consultant, HBO Inc. (and other Time Warner Inc. cos), 1981–85 and 1989–95. Visiting Professor: Lincoln Univ., 2003–13; City Univ., London, 2009–; Vis. Prof. and Internat. Vice-Pres., Sch. of Creativity, Shanghai, 2006–; Executive-in-Residence, Drucker Sch. of Mgt, LA, 2014–. Chm., John Howkins Res. Centre on the Creative Economy, Shanghai, 2006–. UK Rep., Transatlantic Dialogue on Broadcasting and Information Soc., 1998–2008. *Publications:* Understanding Television, 1977; The China Media Industry, 1980; Mass Communications in China, 1982; New Technologies, New Policies, 1982; Satellites International, 1987; (with Michael Foster) Television in '1992': a guide to Europe's new TV, film and video business, 1989; Four Global Scenarios on Information and Communication, 1997; The Creative Economy, 2001, 2nd edn 2013; CODE, 2002; Creative Ecologies, 2009; Dutty's Dare, 2009. *Address:* E6 Albany, Piccadilly, W1J 0AR. *T:* (020) 7434 1400. *E:* john@johnhowkins.com.

HOWLETT, Ben; MP (C) Bath, since 2015; *b* Colchester, 21 Aug. 1986; *s* of Clive Howlett and Beverley Howlett; partner, Josh Jones. *Educ:* Manningtree High Sch.; Colchester Sixth Form Coll.; Durham Univ. (BA Hons Hist. and Politics 2007); Univ. of Cambridge (MA Econ. Hist. 2008). Recruitment Consultant, Venn Gp, 2008–10; Managing Consultant, Finegreen Associates, 2010–15. *Recreations:* running (Bath half), Bath Rugby fan, charity work (healthcare and mental health), cooking, socialising, school governor. *Address:* House of Commons, SW1A 0AA. *T:* (020) 7219 8755. *E:* ben.howlett.mp@parliament.uk.

HOWLETT, Elizabeth, (Elizabeth Robson); Professor of Singing, Royal College of Music, since 1989; *b* 17 Jan. 1938; *d* of Walter James Robson and Lizzie Mason Robson (*née* Houston); *m* 1962, Neil Baillie Howlett (marr. diss. 1987); two *d*. *Educ:* Royal Scottish Acad. of Music (Sir James Caird Jun. and Sen. Scholarships; DRSAMD). Leading Lyric Soprano, Sadler's Wells Opera Co., 1961–65; Leading Soprano, Royal Opera House, Covent Gdn, 1965–70; Soprano, Staatsoper, Hamburg, 1970–74; guest engagements in Europe, S Africa, Japan, Korea, Canada, USA, Scottish Opera, WNO, Opera North, ENO, 1974–. Nat. and Internat. Examr, 1997–; Adjudicator, Festivales Musicales, Buenos Aires, 1995–2004. Mem. (C) Wandsworth BC, 1986– (Chairman: Social Services Cttee, 1989–92; Educn Cttee, 1992–98; Chief Whip, 1999–2000); Mayor of Wandsworth, 1998. Mem. (C) Merton and Wandsworth, London Assembly, GLA, 2000–08. Mem., Inner London Probation Bd, 1995–2001. Non-exec. Dir and Chm., Nat. Hosp. for Neurol. and Neurosurgery, 1990–96. Founder and Trustee, Margaret Dick Award for young Scottish singers, 1982–; Trustee, Foundn for Young Musicians, 1996–2007. Hon. Vice Patron, Ystradgynlais Male Voice Choir, 1985–. JP Wimbledon, 1985–2006. Freeman, City of London, 1999. Eschanson of Roi René Award, Aix-en-Provence, 1970. *Recreations:* walking, theatre, music. *E:* elizabethhowlett@btconnect.com.

HOWLETT, Gen. Sir Geoffrey (Hugh Whitby), KBE 1984 (OBE 1972); MC 1952; Chairman: Leonard Cheshire Foundation, 1990–95; Services Sound & Vision Corporation, 1991–99 (Vice-Chairman, 1989–91); *b* 5 Feb. 1930; *s* of Brig. B. Howlett, DSO, and Mrs Joan Howlett (later Latham); *m* 1955, Elizabeth Anne Aspinal (*d* 2006); one *s* two *d*. *Educ:* Wellington Coll.; RMA, Sandhurst. Commnd Queen's Own Royal W Kent Regt, 1950; served, 1951–69: Malaya, Berlin, Cyprus and Suez; 3 and 2 Para, 16 Parachute Bde and 15 Para (TA); RAF Staff Coll. and Jt Services Staff Coll.; Mil. Asst to CINCNORTH, Oslo, 1969–71; CO 2 Para, 1971–73; RCDS, 1973–75; Comd 16 Parachute Bde, 1975–77; Dir, Army Recruiting, 1977–79; GOC 1st Armoured Div., 1979–82; Comdt, RMA, Sandhurst, 1982–83; GOC SE District, 1983–85; C-in-C Allied Forces Northern Europe, 1986–89, retd. Colonel Commandant: ACC, 1981–89; Parachute Regt, 1983–90. Comr, Royal Hosp., Chelsea, 1989–95. President: CCF, 1989–2000; Army Benevolent Fund for Dorset, 1992–2000; Regular Forces Employment Assoc., 1993–97 (Vice-Chm., 1989–90; Chm., 1990–93); Army Cricket Assoc., 1984–85; Combined Services Cricket Assoc., 1985; Stragglers of Asia Cricket Club, 1989–94. Visitor, Milton Abbey Sch., 2001–05 (Chm. of Govs, 1994–2000). Liveryman, Cooks' Co., 1991–2013. Cross of Merit, 1st cl. (Lower Saxony), 1982. *Recreations:* cricket, racing. *Address:* 58 Hascombe Court, Somerleigh Road, Dorchester DT1 1AG. *Club:* MCC.

HOWLETT, Air Vice-Marshal Neville Stanley, CB 1982; RAF retired, 1982; Member: Lord Chancellor's Panel of Independent Inquiry Inspectors, 1982–95; Pensions Appeal Tribunal, 1988–2000; *b* 17 April 1927; *s* of Stanley Herbert Howlett and Ethel Shirley Howlett (*née* Pritchard); *m* 1952, Sylvia (*d* 2005), *d* of J. F. Foster; one *s* one *d*. *Educ:* Liverpool Inst. High Sch.; Peterhouse, Cambridge. RAF pilot training, 1945–47; 32 and 64 (Fighter) Squadrons, 1948–56; RAF Staff Coll. Course, 1957; Comdr, 234 Sqn at 229 (Fighter) OCU, RAF Chivenor, 1958–59; flew Hunter in London-Paris Air Race, 1959; OC Flying Wing, RAF Coltishall, 1961–63; Directing Staff, RAF Staff Coll., 1967–69; Station Comdr, RAF Leuchars, 1970–72; RCDS, 1972; Dir of Operations (Air Defence and Overseas), 1973–74; Air Attaché, Washington DC, 1975–77; Dir, Management Support of Intelligence, MoD, 1978–80; Dir Gen. of Personal Services (RAF), MoD, 1980–82. Consultant, Defence Intelligence Staff, 1982–93. Vice-Pres., RAFA, 1984–2003 (Chairman: Exec. Cttee, 1990–97; Central Council, 1999–2001). *Recreations:* golf, fishing. *Address:* Milverton, Bolney Trevor Drive, Lower Shiplake, Oxon RG9 3PG. *Clubs:* Royal Air Force; Leander, Phyllis Court (Henley); Huntercombe Golf.

HOWLETT, Ronald William, OBE 1986; Managing Director, Cwmbran Development Corporation, 1978–88, retired; *b* 18 Aug. 1928; *s* of Percy Edward Howlett and Lucy Caroline Howlett; *m* 1st, 1954, Margaret Megan Searl (marr. diss. 1990); two *s*; 2nd, 1996, Judith Lloyd Wade-Jones, *d* of Lt-Col N. L. Wade, OBE, TD. *Educ:* East Ham Grammar Sch. for Boys; University Coll. London (BSc Eng (Hons)). CEng; FICE. Nat. Service, Royal Signals, BAOR, 1947–49. Crawley Develt Corp., 1953–56; Exec. Engr, Roads and Water Supply, Northern Nigeria, 1956–61 (Resident Engr, Kaduna River Bridge; Water Engr, Kano); Bor. of Colchester, 1961–64; Cwmbran Develt Corp., 1964–65; Bor. of Slough, 1965–69; Dep. Chief Engr, 1969–74, Chief Admin. Officer, 1974–77, Cwmbran Develt Corp. Major undertakings: design/construction main drainage and waste treatment works; new town residential, commercial, industrial develt. *Recreations:* fishing, music, furniture restoration.

HOWLETT, Stephen William; Chief Executive, Peabody Trust, since 2004 (Board Member, since 2011); *b* 18 Nov. 1951; *s* of late Ivan William and Marjorie Elsie Howlett; *m* 1989, Jane Elizabeth Everton; two *s* one *d*. *Educ:* King Edward VI Sch., Bury St Edmunds; West Suffolk Coll. of Further Educn; Thames Polytech. (BA Hons). Admin. Officer, Housing Corp., 1975–76; Housing Officer, Warden Housing Assoc., 1976–78; London Regl Officer, NFHA, 1978–82; Director: Croydon Churches Housing Assoc., 1982–88; Notting Hill Housing Trust, 1988–92; Chief Executive: Swale Housing Assoc., 1992–99; Amicus, 1999–2004. Member: Bd, Asset Skills, 2004–13; Residential Cttee, British Property Fedn, 2005–; Chm., G15 London Housing Assocs, 2009–11. A London Leader, London Sustainable Develt Commn, 2007–. Academician, Inst. of Urbanism 2009–. Mem. Bd, 1995–2004, Vice-Chm., 1999–2004, Canterbury Coll.; Mem. Court, 2008– (Vice-Chm., 2010–13; Chm., 2013–), Pro Chancellor, 2013–, Univ. of Greenwich. Trustee, Open City, 2012–. FRSA 2008. *Recreations:* family, cinema, opera, sport. *Address:* Peabody Trust, 45 Westminster Bridge Road, SE1 7JB. *T:* (020) 7021 4230, *Fax:* (020) 7021 4070. *E:* stephenh@peabody.org.uk. *Club:* MCC.

HOWLING, Rex Andrew; QC 2011; *b* Bromley, Kent, 15 June 1961; *s* of Richard John Howling and Shirley Maureen Howling; *m* 1985, Carol Melanie Dell; two *s* two *d*. *Educ:* Charterhouse Sch.; Univ. of Sussex (BSc Biochem. 1982); Britannia Royal Naval Coll.; Poly. of Central London (DipLaw). Officer, Submarine Services, RN, 1980–89. Called to the Bar, Middle Temple, 1991; in practice as a barrister specialising in child care and matrimonial finance, Field Court Chambers, 1992–2007, 4 Paper Buildings, 2007–. Member: Family Law Bar Assoc., 1991–; Resolution, 2010–; Assoc. of Lawyers for Children, 2010–. Member: RYA; RNSA. *Publications:* contrib. to Family Law. *Recreations:* sailing, hockey, reading, skiing, family. *Address:* Old Hill, Sampford Road, Radwinter, near Saffron Walden, Essex CB10 2TL. *T:* (01799) 599674, 07973 623876. *E:* rexhowling@btinternet.com. *Clubs:* Bar Yacht; Helford River Sailing; Old Carthusian Yacht.

HOWSON, Peter John, OBE 2009; painter, since 1981; *b* 27 March 1958; *s* of Tom and Janet Howson; *m* 1983, Frances Nevay (marr. diss.); *m* 1989, Terry Cullen; one *d*. *Educ:* Glasgow Sch. of Art (BA Hons 1981). Official British War Artist in Bosnia, 1993–95; The Times War Artist, Kosovo, 1999. DUniv Strathclyde, 1996.

HOY, Sir Christopher (Andrew), Kt 2009; MBE 2005; Member, Great Britain Cycling Team, 1996–2013; Founder, Hoybikes, 2013; *b* 23 March 1976; *s* of David Hoy and Carol Jane Hoy (*née* Reid) (MBE 2009); *m* 2010, Sarra Kemp; one *s*. *Educ:* George Watson's Coll., Edinburgh; Univ. of Edinburgh (BSc Hons Sport Sci.). Olympic Games: Silver Medal, team sprint, 2000; Gold Medal, 1 km time trial cycling, 2004; Gold Medals, team sprint, keirin, and sprint, 2008; Gold Medals, team sprint and keirin, 2012; world champion: 1 km time trial and team sprint, 2002; team sprint, 2005; 1 km time trial, 2004, 2006, keirin and 1 km time trial, 2007; keirin and sprint, 2008; keirin, 2010, 2012; Commonwealth champion, 2002, 2006; world record holder, 500 m; Olympic record holder: 1000 m, 2004; 200 m time trial, 2008; team sprint, 2012. Dr *hc*: Edinburgh, 2005; St Andrews, 2009; Hon. Dr Heriot-Watt, 2005. BBC Sports Personality of the Year, 2008; Lifetime Achievement Award, BBC Sports Awards, 2014. *Publications:* Heroes, Villains and Velodromes, 2008; Chris Hoy: the autobiography, 2009. *W:* www.chrishoy.com.

HOY, John Francis Dudley, FRICS; Chief Executive, Blenheim Palace, since 2003; *b* Cambridge, 19 Jan. 1957; *s* of Dudley and Joan Hoy; *m* 1998, Tracy Lorraine Rogers; two *d*. *Educ:* Leys Sch., Cambridge; Royal Agricl Coll., Cirencester (Dip. Rural Estate Mgt 1979). FRICS 1990. Asst Resident Land Agent, Goodwood Estate, 1979–84; Resident Agent and Gen. Manager, Knebworth Estate, 1985–97; Hd of Ops, Warwick Castle, 1997–2000; Gen. Manager, Madame Tussaud's, London, 2000–02; Commercial Project Manager, NMSI Trading Ltd, 2002–03. Mem. Bd, VisitEngland, 2011–. *Recreations:* theatre, historic houses, golf, tennis, cinema, family, travel and tourism. *Address:* Upper Campsfield Farm, Upper Campsfield Road, Woodstock, Oxon OX20 1QG. *T:* (home) (01993) 810440, (office) (01993) 810501. *E:* (home) JohnFDHoy@aol.com, (office) johnhoy@blenheimpalace.com.

HOYER, Dr Werner; President, European Investment Bank, since 2012; *b* Wuppertal, 17 Nov. 1951; *m* Katja; one *s* one *d*. *Educ:* High Sch., Hannover; Univ. of Cologne (Dip. Econs 1974; PhD Econs 1977). University of Cologne: Sen. Res. Asst in Econs, 1974–84; Associate Lectr for Foreign Trade, 1978–93; Dir, Econs and Information Dept, Carl-Duisberg Soc., 1985–87. Mem., Bundestag, 1987–2011; Dep. Foreign Minister, 1994–98 and 2009–11. *Publications:* Vermögenseffekte des Geldes: theoretische Ansätze zur Rolle des geldes als Vermögensobjekt im Wirtschaftsprozeß, 1978; (with W. Eibner) Mikroökonomische Theorie, 1984, 4th edn 2011; (contrib.) Maastricht II: entwicklungschancen und Risiken der EU: erweiterung, vertiefung oder stagnation?, 1996; (ed jtly) Der Vertrag von Amsterdam, 1997; (ed with G. F. Kaldrak) Europäische Sicherheits und Verteidigungspolitik (ESVP): der weg zu integrierten europäischen streitkräften?, 2002. *Address:* European Investment Bank, Office of the President, 98–100 Boulevard Konrad Adenauer, 2950 Luxemburg. *T:* 43791, *Fax:* 437704.

HOYLAND, Jeremy Quentin; Managing Partner, Simmons & Simmons, since 2011; *b* Sheffield, 25 April 1967; *s* of James Irwin Hoyland and Janet Elizabeth Hoyland (*née* Green); *m* 1997, Oonagh Anne MacNamara; two *s* one *d*. *Educ:* High Storrs Sch., Sheffield; St Aidan's Coll., Durham Univ. (BA Hons Law); Trent Poly. Admitted as solicitor, England and Wales, 1991, Hong Kong, 1998; joined Simmons & Simmons, 1989: Partner, Banking and Capital Mkts Dept, 1997; Head: of Finance, Hong Kong, 1998–2001; of Capital Mkts, London, 2002–05; of Financial Mkts, 2005–10. *Recreations:* family, walking, gardening, sport. *Address:* Simmons & Simmons, CityPoint, One Ropemaker Street, EC2Y 9SS. *T:* (020) 7628 2020. *E:* jeremy.hoyland@simmons-simmons.com.

HOYLE, family name of **Baron Hoyle**.

HOYLE, Baron *cr* 1997 (Life Peer), of Warrington in the co. of Cheshire; **Eric Douglas Harvey Hoyle;** consultant; *b* 17 Feb. 1930; *s* of late William Hoyle and Leah Ellen Hoyle; *m* 1953, Pauline Spencer (*d* 1991); one *s*. *Educ:* Adlington C of E Sch.; Horwich and Bolton Techn. Colls (HNC Mech. Engrg). Engrg apprentice, British Rail, Horwich, 1946–51; Sales Engr, AEI, Manchester, 1951–53; Sales Engr and Marketing Executive, Charles Weston Ltd, Salford, 1951–74. Mem., Manchester Regional Hosp. Bd, 1968–74; Mem., NW Regional Health Authority, 1974–75. Contested (Lab): Clitheroe, 1964; Nelson and Colne, 1970 and Feb. 1974; MP (Lab): Nelson and Colne, Oct. 1974–1979; Warrington, July 1981–1983; Warrington N, 1983–97. Chm., PLP, 1992–97 (Mem., Trade and Industry Cttee, 1987–92); Mem., Select Cttee on Trade and Industry, 1984–92. Mem. Nat. Exec., Labour Party, 1978–82, 1983–85. A Lord in Waiting (Govt Whip), 1997–99. Pres., ASTMS, 1977–81, 1985–88 (Vice-Pres., 1981–85), MSF, 1988–91 (Jt Pres., 1988–90; Pres., 1990–91); Chm., ASTMS Parly Cttee, 1975–76. Pres., Adlington Cricket Club, 1974–; Chm., 1999–2010, Pres., 2010–, Warrington Rugby League Club. JP Chorley, 1958. Freeman: Gibraltar, 2004; Warrington, 2005. *Recreations:* sport, cricket, theatre-going, reading. *Address:* House of Lords, SW1A 0PW.

See also Rt Hon. L. H. Hoyle.

HOYLE, Very Rev. Dr David Michael; Dean of Bristol, since 2010; *b* Edgeside, Waterfoot, Lancs, 1957; *s* of Michael and Yvonne Hoyle; *m* 1981, Janet Susan; one *s* one *d*. *Educ:* Watford Boys' Grammar Sch.; Corpus Christi Coll., Cambridge (BA 1980; MA 1983; PhD 1991); Ripon Coll., Cuddesdon (Cert. Theol.). Ordained deacon, 1986, priest, 1987; Curate, Good Shepherd, Chesterton, 1986–88; Chaplain, 1988–91, Fellow, 1988–95, Dean, 1991–95, Magdalene Coll., Cambridge; Vicar, Christ Church, Southgate, 1995–2002; Dir, Post-ordination Trng, Edmonton Area, 2000–02; Diocesan Dir of Ministry and Residentiary Canon, Gloucester Cathedral, 2002–10. Sec., Theol Gp, House of Bishops, 2002–06. *Publications:* (jtly) A History of Magdalene College Cambridge, 1994; Reformation and Religious Identity in Cambridge, 2007. *Recreations:* hill-walking, company and conversation. *Address:* Bristol Cathedral, College Green, Bristol BS1 5TJ. *T:* (0117) 926 4879, *Fax:* (0117) 925 3678. *E:* dean@bristol-cathedral.co.uk.

HOYLE, Prof. Eric; Professor of Education, 1971–96, now Professor Emeritus, and Senior Research Fellow, since 1996, Graduate School of Education, University of Bristol; *b* 22 May 1931; *s* of Percy and Bertha Hoyle; *m* 1954, Dorothy Mary Morley; one *s* two *d*. *Educ:* Preston Grammar Sch.; Univ. of London (BSc Sociology, MA). Taught, Harehills Secondary Sch., Leeds, 1953–58 (Head of English Dept, 1956–58); Head, English Dept, Batley High Sch., 1958–60; Lectr and Sen. Lectr in Educn, James Graham Coll., Leeds, 1961–64; Lectr and Sen. Lectr in Educn, Univ. of Manchester, 1965–71; Bristol University: Hd, Sch. of Educn, 1971–91; Dean, Faculty of Educn, 1974–77, 1983–86. Vis. Prof., Sch. of Management, Univ. of Lincs and Humberside, 1995–2000. Member: Avon Educn Cttee, 1977–80; Educnl Res. Bd, SSRC, 1973–78 (Vice-Chm., 1976–78); Bd of Management, NFER, 1976–94; Council, Exec. Council for Educn of Teachers, 1971 (Mem. Exec., 1978–81, 1987–90); Adviser to Public Schools Commn, 1968–70; consultant and advr on educnl mgt and professional develt of teachers to UNESCO, World Bank etc, SE Asia and Africa, 1972–. Editor, World Yearbook of Educn, 1980–86; founding Co-Editor, Research in Educn, 1969. *Publications:* The Role of the Teacher, 1969; (with J. Wilks) Gifted Children and their Education, 1974; The Politics of School Management, 1986; (with Peter John) Professional Knowledge and Professional Practice, 1995; (with Mike Wallace) Educational Leadership: ambiguity, professionals and managerialism, 2005; *festschrift:* Teaching: professionalization, development and leadership, ed D. Johnson and R. Maclean, 2008; contribs to professional jls. *Recreations:* music, reading, collecting first editions, cooking. *Address:* 42 Oakwood Road, Henleaze, Bristol BS9 4NT. *T:* (0117) 962 0614; Graduate School of Education, University of Bristol, 35 Berkeley Square, Bristol BS8 1JA. *T:* (0117) 928 3000.

HOYLE, Rt Hon. Lindsay (Harvey); PC 2013; MP (Lab) Chorley, since 1997; Chairman of Ways and Means and a Deputy Speaker, House of Commons, since 2010; *b* 10 June 1957; *s* of Baron Hoyle, *qv*; *m* 1st, Lynda Anne Fowler (marr. diss. 1982); 2nd, Catherine Swindley; two *d*. *Educ:* Adlington County Sch.; Lord's Coll., Bolton. Owner of building co.; Man. Dir, textile printing co. Mem. (Lab) Chorley BC, 1980–98 (Dep. Leader, 1995–97; Chair, Economic Develt and Tourist Cttee); Mayor, 1997–98. Member: Trade and Industry Select Cttee, 1998–2010; H of C Catering Cttee, 1997–2005; European Scrutiny Cttee, 2005–10; Finance Select Cttee, 2010–; All Pty Rugby League Gp, 1997– (Vice Chm., 1997–); All Pty Cricket Gp, 1997– (Treas., 1998–); All Pty Parly Gp on Financial Educn for Young People; Unite Parly Gp; Vice Chm., All Pty Tourism Gp, 1999–; Chm., All Pty BVI Gp, 2007–10; Pres., All Pty Gp on Gibraltar, 2001–. Member: Royal Lancs Agricl Show Soc.; Unite the Union. Hon. Colonel: C (64) Med. Sqdn (Vols); 5 Gen. Support Med. Regt. *Recreations:* Rugby League (former Chm., Chorley Lynx), cricket, football. *Address:* House of Commons, SW1A 0AA. *T:* (020) 7219 3000. *Clubs:* Adlington Cricket, Chorley Cricket.

HOYLE, Martin Trevor William Mordaunt; Television, Radio, Arts and Media Writer, Financial Times, since 1994; *s* of Capt. T. W. Hoyle and Dora Marie (*née* Muller). *Educ:* Egypt and Canada; Clifton Coll.; Wadham Coll., Oxford (BA); Bristol Old Vic Sch.; Poly. of Central London Business Sch. Music Critic, Bristol Evening Post, 1963–67; freelance researcher, BBC TV 1965–; Sub-editor, John Calder Publishers, 1979–82; Theatre Critic, Financial Times, 1983–90; Classical Music and Opera Editor, Time Out, 1988–2008; freelance writer on theatre, music, TV, film, books for Financial Times, Time Out, The Times, Mail on Sunday, Herald, The House, Independent on Sunday; reviews for Meridian (BBC World Service). *Publications:* The World of Opera: Mozart, 1996. *Recreation:* shouting at cyclists. *Address:* 22 Scotland Street, Edinburgh EH3 6PX. *T:* (0131) 556 6093.

HOYLE, Prof. Richard William, DPhil; FAcSS; Professor of Regional and Local History, and Director and General Editor, Victoria County History, Institute of Historical Research, University of London, since 2014; *b* 4 Dec. 1958; *s* of C. and H. M. Hoyle; *m* 1981, Gillian M. Bishop (marr. diss. 2012); two *s*; *m* 2014, Catherine Glover. *Educ:* Univ. of Birmingham (BA 1981); Corpus Christi Coll., Oxford (DPhil 1987). Res. Fellow, Magdalen Coll., Oxford, 1985–87; Lectr, Univ. of Bristol, 1987–89; British Acad. Res. Fellow, Magdalen Coll., Oxford, 1989–92; University of Central Lancashire: Lectr, then Sen. Lectr, 1993–96; Reader, 1997; Prof. of Hist., 1998–2000; Prof. of Rural History, 2000–14, Dir, Rural Hist. Centre, 2000–03, Univ. of Reading. British Acad. Res. Reader, 2004–06. Vis. Fellow, Folger Shakespeare Liby, Washington DC, 2014. Mem., Res. Grants Bd, ESRC, 1997–2001. Sec., British Agricl Hist. Soc., 1996–98. Ed., Agricl Hist. Review, 1998–. FAcSS (AcSS 2006). *Publications:* books include: (ed) The Estates of the English Crown 1558–1640, 1992; The Pilgrimage of Grace and the Politics of the 1530s, 2001; (ed) People, Landscape and Alternative Agriculture, 2004; (with H. French) The Character of English Rural Society: Earls Colne 1550–1750, 2007; (ed) Our Hunting Fathers: field sports in England since 1850, 2007; (ed) Custom, Improvement and Landscape in Early Modern Britain, 2011; (ed) The Farmer in England, 2013; contrib. articles to Past and Present, English Histl Review, Histl Jl, Econ. Hist. Review, Northern Hist., Yorks Archaeol Jl. *Recreations:* gardening, twentieth-century music, walking. *Address:* Institute of Historical Research, University of London, Senate House, Malet Street, WC1E 7HU. *E:* richard.hoyle@sas.ac.uk.

HOYLE, Susan Linda, OBE 2011; Director, Clore Leadership Programme, since 2008 (Deputy Director, 2003–08); *b* 7 April 1953; *d* of Roland and Joan Hoyle; *m* 2005, Graham Thomas Devlin, *qv*. *Educ:* Univ. of Bristol (BA Drama and French). Education Officer, London Festival Ballet, 1980–83; Administrator, Extemporary Dance Th., 1983–86; Dance and Mime Officer, 1986–89, Dir of Dance, 1989–94, Arts Council of GB; Dep. Sec.-Gen., Arts Council of England, 1994–97; Head of Arts, British Council, France, 1997–98; Gen. Manager, then Exec. Dir, The Place, 1998–2003. Director: Shobana Jeyasingh Dance Co., 1998–2002; Ricochet Dance Co., 2001–03; DV8 Physical Th., 2003–09; LPO, 2003–05; Create KX, 2007–11. Trustee, British Council, 2008–14. Hon. Fellow, Falmouth Univ., 2014. Chevalier, Ordre des Palmes Académiques, 2010. *Address:* Clore Leadership Programme, South Building, Somerset House, Strand, WC2R 1LA.

HOYLES, Dame Celia (Mary), (Dame Celia Noss), DBE 2014 (OBE 2004); PhD; Professor of Mathematics Education, Institute of Education, University College London (formerly Institute of Education, University of London), since 1984; *b* London, 18 May 1946; *d* of Harold French and Elsie French (*née* Last); *m* 1st, Martin Hoyles (marr. diss.); 2nd, 1996, Prof. Richard Noss; one step *s* one step *d*. *Educ:* Univ. of Manchester (BSc 1st Cl. Hons Maths 1967); Chelsea Coll., Univ. of London (PGCE 1971; MEd 1973; PhD 1980). Teacher in London schs, 1967–72; Sen. Lectr, then Principal Lectr, Poly. of N London, 1972–84; Dean of Res. and Consultancy, Inst. of Educn, Univ. of London, 2002–04. Govt Chief Advr for Maths, 2004–07; Dir, 2007–13, Exec. Chair, 2013–14, Nat. Centre for Excellence in Teaching of Mathematics. Pres., Inst. of Mathematics and its Application, 2013–15. DUniv Open, 2006; Hon. DSc Loughborough, 2008. Hans Freudenthal Medal for res. in maths educn, Internat. Commn on Mathematical Instruction, 2004; Kavli Educn Medal, Royal Soc., 2011. *Publications:* (with R. Sutherland) Logo Mathematics in the Classroom, 1992; (ed with R. Noss) Learning Mathematics and Logo, 1992; (ed jtly) Computers for Exploratory Learning, 1995; (with R. Noss) Windows on Mathematical Meanings: learning cultures and computers, 1996; (ed jtly) Mathematics Education and Technology, 2009; (jtly) Improving

Mathematics at Work: the need for techno-mathematical literacies, 2010; contrib. res. jls. *Recreations:* tennis, swimming, walking, reading. *Address:* UCL Institute of Education, 20 Bedford Way, WC1H 0AL. *T:* (020) 7612 6659. *E:* c.hoyles@ioe.ac.uk.

HOYT, Hon. William Lloyd, OC 2007; Chief Justice of New Brunswick, 1993–98; *b* 13 Sept. 1930; *m* 1954, Joan Millier; three *d. Educ:* Woodstock High Sch.; Acadia Univ. (BA, MA); Emmanuel Coll., Cambridge (BA, MA; Hon. Fellow, 2001). Called to New Brunswick Bar, 1957; QC (NB) 1972; Associate, Limerick & Limerick, 1957–59; Partner, Limerick, Limerick & Hoyt and successor firm, Hoyt, Mockler, Allen & Dixon, 1959–81; Judge, 1981–84, Court of Appeal, 1984–98, New Brunswick. Mem., Bloody Sunday Tribunal of Inquiry (UK), 1998–2010. Member: Fredericton Barristers' Soc., 1957–81 (Pres., 1970–71); New Brunswick Barristers' Soc., 1957–81 (Council, 1970–72, 1975–79); Cttee on Canadian Constitution, Canadian Bar Assoc., 1977–78; Director: Canadian Inst. for Admin of Justice, 1979–83; Canadian Judges' Conf., 1985–89; Canadian Inst. of Advanced Legal Studies, 1994–2008; Chm., New Brunswick Judicial Council, 1993–98 (Vice-Chm., 1988–93). Hon. LLD: St Thomas Univ., Fredericton, 1997; Univ. of New Brunswick, 1998; Hon. DCL Acadia Univ., 2001. *Publications:* Married Women's Property, 1961; Professional Negligence, 1973.

HRUSKA, Dr Jan; Managing Director, LogicIQ Ltd, since 2006; *b* 22 April 1957; *s* of Ivan Hruska and Bozena Bozicek-Ferrari; *m* 2000, Regula Voellm. *Educ:* 1st Gymnasium, Zagreb; King's Sch., Canterbury; Downing Coll., Cambridge (BA 1978); Magdalen Coll., Oxford (DPhil 1984). Co-founder, and Technical Dir, 1985–2000, Jt Chief Exec. Officer, 2000–05, non-exec. Dir, 2006–, Sophos Ltd. *Publications:* The PC Security Guide, 1988; Computer Security Solutions, 1990; Computer Viruses and Anti-Virus Warfare, 1990, 2nd edn 1992; Computer Security Reference Book, 1992. *Recreations:* sub-aqua diving, running, piano-playing, lock-picking, ex-flying (Private Pilots Licence, Instrument Meteorological Conditions, Night), ex-ski-ing. *Address:* c/o Sophos Ltd, The Pentagon, Abingdon, Oxon OX14 3YP. *T:* (01235) 559933, *Fax:* (01235) 559935. *E:* jh@sophos.com.

HTUT, U Kyaw Myo; Ambassador of Myanmar to the United States of America, since 2013; *b* Meiktila, 9 Dec. 1957; *s* of U Tin Tut and Daw Yi Yi San; *m* 1984, Daw Khin Myint Kyi; one *s* two *d. Educ:* Basic Educn High Sch. I; Rangoon Univ. (Botany); Defence Service Acad. (BSc 1981); Nat. Defence Coll. (MA Defence Studies 2006). Served Defence Services to rank of Col, Myanmar, 1981–2008 (Mil. Meritorious Services Medal, 2nd and 3rd Cl.). Minister Counsellor, Min. of Foreign Affairs, 2008; Minister Counsellor, 2008–10, Ambassador, 2010–11, Perm. Mission of Myanmar to UN, Geneva; Ambassador to the Court of St James's, 2011–13; non-resident Ambassador to Sweden, 2012–13, and to Norway, 2013. *Recreations:* golf, football. *Address:* c/o Embassy of Myanmar, 2300 S Street NW, Washington, DC 20008, USA.

HU JINTAO; General Secretary, Communist Party of China, 2002–13; President, People's Republic of China, 2003–13 (Vice-President, 1998–2003); Chairman, Central Military Commission, 2004–13 (Vice-Chairman, 1999–2004); *b* 21 Dec. 1942; *m* Liu Yongqing; one *s* one *d. Educ:* Tsinghua Univ., Beijing. Engineer; joined Min. of Water Conservancy, 1968, Technician, 1969–74; Gansu Provincial Construction Committee: Sec., 1974–75; Dep. Dir of Design Mgt, 1975–80; Vice-Chm., 1980–82. Communist Youth League of China: Sec., Gansu Provincial Cttee, 1982; Sec., 1982–84; First Sec., 1984–85; Communist Party of China: Mem., Central Cttee, 1985–; Sec., Guizhou, 1985–88, Tibet, 1988–92; Mem., Standing Cttee, Political Bureau, 1992–2013. *Address:* c/o Office of the President, Zhong Nan Hai, Beijing, People's Republic of China.

HUANG, Prof. Christopher Li-Hur; Professor of Cell Physiology, Cambridge University, since 2002; Fellow, Murray Edwards College (formerly New Hall), Cambridge, since 1979; *b* 28 Dec. 1951; *s* of late Rayson Lisung Huang, CBE. *Educ:* Methodist Boys' Sch., Kuala Lumpur; Nat. Jun. Coll., Singapore; Queen's Coll., Oxford (Singapore President's Scholar; Florence Heale Scholar; Benefactors Prize; BA, BM, BCh, MA; DM 1985; DSc 1995); Gonville and Caius Coll., Cambridge (MA; PhD 1980; MD 1986; ScD 1995). House Physician, Nuffield Dept of Medicine, Oxford Univ., 1977–78; Cambridge University: MRC Schol., Physiological Lab., 1978–79; Asst Lectr, 1979–84; Lectr in Physiol., 1984–96; Reader in Cellular Physiol., 1996–2002; Hon. Sen. Res. Fellow in Biochemistry, 2006–; New Hall, Cambridge: Fellow and Lectr in Physiol., 1979–2002; Dir of Studies in Med. Sci., 1981–; Professorial Fellow, 2002–. Hon. Res. Fellow, RCS, 1985–88; Hon. Sen. Res. Fellow, St George's Hosp. Med. Sch., London Univ., 1991–. Procultura Foundn Vis. Prof., Debrecen Univ., Hungary, 1996; Vis. Prof., 2001–04, Ext. Assessor, 2007, Mount Sinai Med. Sch., NY; Vis. Prof., 2005, Ext. Assessor, 2005–06 and 2008, Univ. of HK; Ext. Assessor, Univ. of Leeds, 2008; Adjunct Prof., First Affiliated Hosp., Med. Coll., Xi'an Jiaotong Univ. Med. Centre, China, 2008–11. Consulting Ed., John Wiley, 1986–2008; Mem. Editl Bd, 1990–96, Distributing Ed., 1991–94, Jl Physiol.; Chm., Editl Bd, Monographs of Physiol Soc., 1994–99; Member Editorial Board: BioMed Central Physiology, 2005–; Europace, 2008–; Biological Revs, 2009– (Chm., 2000–08). Mem. Ct of Examrs, RCSE, 1999–2004. Cambridge Philosophical Society: Council Mem., 1994–; Biol Sec., 2000–08; Adjudicator and convenor, 2008, Adjudicator, 2010, Wm Bate Hardy Prize; Vice-Pres., 2010–13; Pres., 2014–15. Manager, Prince Philip Scholarship Fund, 1986–. Dir, Aw Boon Haw Foundn, 2004–09; ind. non-exec. Dir, Hutchison China Meditech Ltd, 2006–; Dir, Cambridge Cardiac Systems, 2009–14. Fellowships Cttee, British Heart Foundn UK, 2014–. FRSB (FSB 2011). Brian Johnson Prize in Pathology, Univ. of Oxford, 1976; Lepra Award, Brit. Leprosy Relief Assoc., 1977; Rolleston Meml Prize for Physiological Res., Oxford Univ., 1980; Gedge Prize in Physiol., Cambridge Univ., 1981 (Adjudicator, 2007–). *Publications:* Companion to Neonatal Medicine, 1982; Companion to Obstetrics, 1982; Companion to Gynaecology, 1985; Research in Medicine: a guide to writing a thesis in the medical sciences, 1990, 3rd edn as Research in Medicine: planning a project - writing a thesis, 2010; Intramembrane Charge Movements in Striated Muscle, 1993; (ed jtly) Applied Physiology for Surgery and Critical Care, 1995; (ed jtly) Molecular and Cellular Biology of Bone, 1998; (ed jtly) Translational Models for Cardiac Arrhythmogenesis, 2008; Nerve and Muscle, 2011; (ed jtly) Sudden Arrhythmic Death: from basic science to clinical practice, 2013; Basic Physiology for Anaesthetists, 2015; over 300 original scientific papers and reviews on striated muscle activation and homeostasis, peripheral nerve growth and repair, physiol magnetic resonance imaging, cellular triggering processes in osteoclasts and cardiac arrhythmogenesis. *Recreations:* music, playing the violin (Cambridge String Players, 2001–08; City of Cambridge SO, 2008–), reading Shakespeare plays, Impressionist and Post-Impressionist art history. *Address:* Murray Edwards College, Huntingdon Road, Cambridge CB3 0DF.

HUBBARD, family name of **Baron Addington**.

HUBBARD, David; *see* Hubbard, R. D. C.

HUBBARD, Ven. Julian Richard Hawes; Director, Ministry Division, Archbishops' Council, since 2011; *b* 15 Feb. 1955; *m* 1984, Rachel (*née* Ashton); three *s* one *d. Educ:* Emmanuel Coll., Cambridge (BA 1976, MA 1981); Wycliffe Hall, Oxford (BA 1980, MA 1985). Ordained deacon, 1981, priest, 1982; Curate, St Dionis, Parson's Green, 1981–84; Tutor, Wycliffe Hall, Oxford, and Chaplain, Jesus Coll., Oxford, 1984–89; Selection Sec., ACCM, 1989–91, Sen. Selection Sec., ABM, 1991–93; Vicar, Bourne, 1993–99; RD, Farnham, 1996–99; Priest-in-charge, Tilford, 1997–99; Canon Residentiary, Guildford Cathedral, and Dir, Ministerial Trng, Dio. Guildford, 1999–2005; Archdeacon of Oxford and Residentiary Canon, Christ Church, Oxford, 2005–11. *Address:* Ministry Division, Church House, Great Smith Street, SW1P 3NZ.

HUBBARD, (Richard) David (Cairns), OBE 1995; Chairman: London and Manchester Group, 1993–98 (Director, 1989–98); Exco plc, 1996–98 (Deputy Chairman, 1995); *b* 14 May 1936; *s* of late John Cairns Hubbard and Gertrude Emilie Hubbard; *m* 1964, Hannah Neale (*née* Dennison); three *d. Educ:* Tonbridge. FCA. Commissioned, Royal Artillery, 1955–57; Peat Marwick Mitchell & Co., 1957–65; Cape Asbestos Co., 1965–74; Bache & Co., 1974–76; Finance Dir, 1976–86, Chm., 1986–96, Powell Duffryn; Chm., Andrew Sykes Group, 1991–94; non-executive Director: Blue Circle Industries, 1986–96; City of London Investment Trust (formerly TR City of London Trust), 1989–2002; Slough Estates, 1994–2001; Medical Defence Union Ltd, 1998–2000; Mem., Southern Adv. Bd, Nat. Westminster Bank, 1988–91. Mem., Bd of Crown Agents for Oversea Govts and Admins, 1986–88. Mem. Council, Inst. of Dirs, 1991–97. Chm., CRC Council, 1996–98 (Council Mem., 1982–98). Liveryman, Skinners' Co.; Freeman, City of London. *Recreation:* golf. *Address:* Meadowcroft, Windlesham, Surrey GU20 6BJ. *T:* (01276) 472198. *Clubs:* Royal & Ancient Golf (St Andrews); Berkshire Golf (Pres., 1999–2004), Lucifer Golfing Society, Elders Golfing Society (Capt., 2002–04; Pres., 2007–10).

HUBBLE, Benedict John Wakelin; QC 2009; *b* Taplow; *s* of late John Clifford Hubble and Gillian Mary Hubble; *m* 1995, Zara Jane Sinclair; two *d. Educ:* University Coll., Oxford (BA Hons; Dip. Law). Called to the Bar, Middle Temple, 1992; in practice as barrister specialising in professional liability and commercial law. *Recreations:* family, ski-ing, hiking. *Address:* 4 New Square, Lincoln's Inn, WC2A 3RJ. *T:* (020) 7822 2000, *Fax:* (020) 7822 2001. *E:* b.hubble@4newsquare.com.

HUBER, Prof. Robert; Director, Max-Planck-Institut für Biochemie, and Scientific Member, Max-Planck Society, 1972–2005, now Director Emeritus; *b* 20 Feb. 1937; *s* of Sebastian and Helene Huber; *m* 1960, Christa Essig; two *s* two *d. Educ:* Grammar Sch. and Humanistisches Gymnasium, München; Technische Univ., München (Dr rer. nat. 1963). Lecturer, 1968, Associate Prof., 1976–, Technische Univ., München. Scientific Mem., Max-Planck Soc. Editor, then Adv. Ed., Jl of Molecular Biology, 1976–. Visiting Professor: Univ. Autónoma de Barcelona, 2001; Nat. Univ. of Singapore, 2005; Univ. Duisburg-Essen, 2005; Cardiff Univ., 2007. Member: EMBO (also Mem. Council); Deutsche Chem. Ges.; Ges. für Biologische Chem.; Bavarian Acad. of Scis, 1988; Deutsche Akademie der Naturforscher Leopoldina; Accademia Nazionale dei Lincei, Rome; Orden pour le mérite für Wissenschaft und Künste; Corresp. Mem., Croatian Acad. of Scis and Arts; Fellow, Amer. Acad. of Microbiology, 1996; Associate Fellow, Third World Acad. of Scis, 1995; Foreign Associate, Nat. Acad. of Scis, USA, 1995; Foreign Mem., Royal Soc., 1999. Hon. Member: Amer. Soc. of Biolog. Chemists; Swedish Soc. for Biophysics; Japanese Biochem. Soc.; Sociedad Española de Bioquímica y Biología Molecular. Hon. Professor: Ocean Univ., Qingdao, 2002; Peking Univ., 2003; Sichuan Univ., Chengdu, 2003; Shanghai Second Med. Univ., 2004; Shanghai Jiao Tong Univ., 2005; Univ. de Sevilla, 2006; Lotte Dist. Prof., Seoul Nat. Univ., 2005. Dr *hc:* Catholic Univ. of Louvain, 1987; Univ. of Ljubljana, Jugoslavia, 1989; Univ. Tor Vergata, Rome, 1991; Univ. of Lisbon, 2000; Univ. of Barcelona, 2000; Tsinghua Univ., Peking, 2003. E. K. Frey Medal, Ges. für Chirurgie, 1972; Otto-Warburg Medal, Ges. für Biolog. Chem., 1977; Emil von Behring Medal, Univ. of Marburg, 1982; Keilin Medal, Biochem. Soc., 1987; Richard Kuhn Medal, Ges. Deutscher Chem., 1987; (jtly) Nobel Prize for Chemistry, 1988; E. K. Frey-E. Werle Gedächtnismedaille, 1989; Kone Award, Assoc. of Clin. Biochemists, 1990; Sir Hans Krebs Medal, FEBS, 1992; Linus Pauling Medal, 1993–94; Distinguished Service Award, Miami Winter Symposia, 1995; Max Tishler Prize, Harvard Univ., 1997; Max Bergmann Medal, 1997. Bayerischer Maximiliansorden für Wissenschaft und Kunst, 1993; Das Grosse Verdienstkreuz mit Stern und Schulterband (Germany), 1997; Röntgenplakette der Stadt Remscheid-Lennep, 2004; Premio Città di Firenze sulle Scienze Molecolari, 2004. *Publications:* numerous papers in learned jls on crystallography, immunology and structure of proteins. *Recreations:* cycling, hiking, ski-ing. *Address:* Max-Planck Institut für Biochemie, Am Klopferspitz 18a, 82152 Martinsried, Germany. *T:* (089) 85782677/8.

HÜBNER, Danuta Maria, PhD; Member (Christian Democrats), European Parliament, since 2009; *b* 8 April 1948; two *d. Educ:* Central Higher Sch. of Planning and Statistics, Warsaw (MSc (Econs) 1971; PhD 1974). Researcher, 1971–92, Prof. of Econs, 1992–, Central Higher Sch. of Planning and Statistics, Warsaw, subseq. Warsaw Sch. of Econs; Dep. Dir, Inst. of Develt and Strategic Studies, Warsaw, 1991–94; Under-Sec. of State, Min. of Industry and Trade, 1994–96; Sec. of State for European Integration, 1996–97; Hd, Chancellery of Pres. of Poland, 1997–98; Dep. Exec. Sec., 1998–2000, Exec. Sec., 2000–01, UN Econ. Commn for Europe, Geneva; Sec. of State, Min. of Foreign Affairs, 2001–03; Minister for European Affairs, 2003–04. Mem., Eur. Commn, 2004–09. *Publications:* books and scientific articles. *Address:* European Parliament, 60 rue Wiertz, 1047 Brussels, Belgium.

HÜBSCHER, Prof. Stefan Georg, FRCPath; Professor of Hepatic Pathology, since 2005, and Leith Professor, since 2011, University of Birmingham; Hon. Consultant Histopathologist, University Hospitals Birmingham NHS Foundation Trust, since 1989; *b* Birmingham, 6 Oct. 1956; *s* of Georg and Agnes Hübscher; *m* 1981, Dawn Emeny; three *s. Educ:* King Edward's Sch., Birmingham; Nottingham High Sch.; Univ. of Birmingham (MB ChB 1979). MRCPath 1985, FRCPath 1995. Hse Surgeon, Selly Oak Hosp., Birmingham, 1979–80; Hse Physician, Dudley Rd Hosp., Birmingham, 1980; Senior House Officer: in Histopathol., Queen Elizabeth Hosp., Birmingham, 1980–81; in Microbiol., Children's Hosp., Birmingham, 1981; University of Birmingham: Lectr in Pathol., 1981–89; Sen. Lectr in Pathol., 1989–2000; Reader in Hepatic Pathol., 2000–05. *Publications:* contrib. papers to peer-reviewed jls, review articles and book chapters. *Recreations:* swimming, gardening, cookery, season ticket holder and shareholder at West Bromwich Albion FC. *Address:* Department of Cellular Pathology, Level -1, Queen Elizabeth Hospital, Birmingham B15 2WB. *T:* (0121) 371 3345, *Fax:* (0121) 371 3333. *E:* s.g.hubscher@bham.ac.uk.

HUCK, Prof. Steffen, PhD; Director, Economics of Change, Wissenschaftszentrum Berlin für Sozialforschung, since 2012; Professor of Economics, University College London, since 2003; *b* Seligenstadt, 2 Oct. 1968; *s* of Jochen and Waltraud Huck; *m* 2010, Heike Harmgart. *Educ:* Goethe Univ., Frankfurt (Dip. Econs); Humboldt Univ. (PhD). Res. Fellow, Humboldt Univ., Berlin, 1995–97; Res. Scholar, German Sci. Foundn, 1998–99; Sen. Lectr in Econs, Royal Holloway, Univ. of London, 2000–01; Reader in Econs, 2002–03, Hd, Dept of Econs, 2008–11, UCL. *Publications:* (trans. and ed) Wilfred Owen, Gedichte aus dem Krieg; (ed) Das Narrenschiff, vol. 1 1993, vol. 2 1994; (ed as Julian Weiss) Pop, 1999; (ed) Advances in Understanding Strategic Behaviour, 2004; contribs to learned jls on econs, biol., physics, political sci. and opera. *Recreations:* opera and more opera, TV series binge watching. *Address:* c/o Department of Economics, University College London, Gower Street, WC1E 6BT. *T:* (Germany) (30) 25491421. *E:* s.huck@ucl.ac.uk.

HUCKER, Rev. Michael Frederick, MBE 1970; Principal Chaplain, Church of Scotland and Free Churches, Royal Air Force, 1987–90; Secretary, Forces Board, Methodist Church, 1990–96; *b* 1 May 1933; *s* of William John and Lucy Sophia Hucker; *m* 1961, Katherine Rosemary Parsons; one *s* one *d. Educ:* City of Bath Boys' Sch.; Bristol Univ. (MA); London Univ. (BD). Ordained Methodist minister, 1960; commnd as RAF chaplain, 1962. QHC 1987–90. Mem. Bd, Orbit Housing Assoc., 1996–2004, Orbit Housing Gp Ltd, 2004–05. *Recreations:* gardening, music. *Address:* Jeffries Mill, Spring Gardens, Frome, Somerset BA11 2NZ.

HUCKFIELD, Leslie (John); Director, Leslie Huckfield Research (services for higher education and research for non profit organisations), since 1997; *b* 7 April 1942; *s* of Ernest Leslie and Suvla Huckfield. *Educ:* Prince Henry's Grammar Sch., Evesham; Keble Coll.,

Oxford; Univ. of Birmingham; Heriot Watt Univ.; Glasgow Caledonian Univ. Lectr in Economics, City of Birmingham Coll. of Commerce, 1963–67. Advertising Manager, Tribune, 1983; Co-ordinator, CAPITAL (transport campaign against London Transport Bill), 1983–84. Prin. Officer, External Resources, St Helen's Coll., Merseyside, 1989–93; European Officer, Merseyside Colls, 1994–95; Eur. Funding Manager, Wirral Metropolitan Coll., 1995–97. Contested (Lab) Warwick and Leamington, 1966; MP (Lab) Nuneaton, March 1967–1983. PPS to Minister of Public Building and Works, 1969–70; Parly Under-Secretary of State, Dept of Industry, 1976–79. MEP (Lab) Merseyside E, 1984–89. Member: Nat. Exec. Cttee, Labour Party, 1978–82; W Midlands Reg. Exec. Cttee, Labour Party, 1978–82; Political Sec., Nat. Union Lab. and Socialist Clubs, 1979–81. Chairman: Lab. Party Transport Gp, 1974–76; Independent Adv. Commn on Transport, 1975–76; Pres., Worcs Fedn of Young Socialists, 1962–64; Member: Birmingham Regional Hosp. Bd, 1970–72; Political Cttee, Co-op. Retail Soc. (London Regional), 1981–93; British Consultants and Construction Bd, 2003–04; Bd, Senscot (Scottish Social Entrepreneurs' Network), 2007–; Associate, W Midlands Office in Europe, 2004–07; community develt, HE and FE projects in W Midlands and Scotland, 2006–. Chartered Mem., RTPI, 2010–13 (Associate Mem., 2007–10). Vis. Fellow, Yunus Centre for Social Business and Health, Glasgow Caledonian Univ., 2012–. *Publications:* various newspaper and periodical articles. *Recreation:* running marathons. *Address:* Leslie Huckfield Research, PO Box 6000, Auchterarder PH3 1YX. *T:* (01764) 660080, 07796 266002, *Fax:* 0871 717 1957. *E:* les@huckfield.com. *W:* www.huckfield.com.

HUCKLE, Alan Edden; HM Diplomatic Service, retired; re-employed as Research Analyst, Overseas Territories Directorate, Foreign and Commonwealth Office, 2012–14; Chairman, Falkland Islands Association, since 2011; *b* 15 June 1948; *m* 1973, Helen Gibson; one *s* one *d*. *Educ:* Univ. of Warwick (BA 1st Cl. Hons Hist. 1969; MA Renaissance Studies 1970). Leverhulme Trust Schol., 1971; British Sch. at Rome Schol., 1971; Personnel Mgt Div., CSD, 1971–74; Asst Private Sec. to Sec. of State for NI, Belfast, 1974–75; Machinery of Govt Div., CSD, 1975–78; Pol Affairs Div., NI Office, Belfast, 1978–80; FCO, 1980–83; Exec. Dir, British Inf. Services, NY, 1983–87; Hd of Chancery, Manila, 1987–90; Dep. Hd, Arms Control and Disarmament Dept, FCO, 1990–92; Counsellor and Dep. Hd of Delegn to CSCE, Vienna, 1992–96; Head: Dependent Territories Regl Secretariat, Bridgetown, 1996–98; OSCE/Council of Europe Dept, FCO, 1998–2001; Overseas Territories Dept, FCO, and Comr (non-resident), British Antarctic Territory and British Indian Ocean Territory, 2001–04; Gov. of Anguilla, 2004–06; Gov., Falkland Is and Comr for S Georgia and S Sandwich Is, 2006–10. Chm., Chagos Conservation Trust, 2011–14; Trustee, Falkland Is Maritime Heritage Trust, 2015–.

HUCKLE, Theodore David; QC 2011; Counsel General for Wales, since 2011; *b* Blaenavon, Mon, 27 May 1962; *s* of Sylvia Huckle (*née* Lewis); *m* 1994, Alison Claire Bird; four *d*. *Educ:* Jones's West Mon Grammar Sch., Pontypool; Jesus Coll., Cambridge (Titular Exhibnr; BA 1983; LLM 1985; MA 1987). Called to the Bar, Lincoln's Inn, 1985 (Hardwicke & Megarry Schol.), Bencher, 2012. Formerly Member: Treasury Panel of Counsel; Panel of Counsel, Nat. Assembly for Wales; Panel of Counsel, Serious Fraud Office. Ed., Div. I, Butterworth's Personal Injury Litigation Service, 2013–. *Publications:* (contrib.) Occupational Illness Litigation, 2005–; Future Loss in Practice: periodical payments and lump sums, 2007; (contrib.) Munkman on Employer's Liability, 15th edn 2009 to 16th edn 2013; contribs to New Law Jl, Jl Personal Injury Law, Personal Injury Law Jl, Personal Injury Focus. *Recreations:* sculling, karaoke, walking, drumming, opera, ski-ing. *Address:* Civitas Law Chambers, Global Reach, Celtic Gateway, Cardiff Bay, Cardiff CF11 0SN. *T:* (0845) 0713007. *E:* theohuckleqc@civitaslaw.com; Office of the Counsel General, Crown Buildings, Cathays Park, Cardiff CF10 3NQ. *E:* PSCounselGeneral@wales.gsi.gov.uk. *Club:* Llandaff Rowing.

HUDD, Roy, OBE 2004; actor; *b* 16 May 1936; *s* of Harold Hudd and Evalina Barham; *m* 1st, 1963, Ann Lambert (marr. diss. 1983); one *s*; 2nd, 1988, Deborah Flitcroft. *Educ:* Croydon Secondary Technical School. Entered show business, 1957, as half of double act Hudd & Kay; Butlin Redcoats; started as a solo comedian, 1959; first pantomime, Empire Theatre, Leeds, 1959; 4 years' concert party Out of the Blue, 1960–63; first radio broadcast Workers Playtime, 1960; *stage includes:* The Merchant of Venice, 1960; The Give Away, 1969; At the Palace, 1970; Young Vic Co. seasons, 1973, 1976, 1977; Oliver!, 1977; Underneath the Arches, 1982 (SWET Actor of the Year); Run For Your Wife, 1986, 1989; The Birth of Merlin, Theatre Clwyd, 1989; The Fantasticks, 1990; Midsummer Night's Dream, 1991; Friends Like This, 1998; A Funny Thing Happened on the Way to the Forum, 1999; Hard Times, Haymarket, 2000; Theft, 2001; Roy Hudd's Exceedingly Entertaining Evening, 2005–08; The Solid Gold Cadillac, Garrick, 2006; The Merry Widow, Coliseum, 2008; The Wizard of Oz, RFH, 2008; When We Are Married, Garrick, 2010–11; An Evening/Afternoon with Roy and Debbie Hudd, 2012–14; *films include:* Blood Beast Terror, 1967; Up Pompeii; The Seven Magnificent Deadly Sins; Up the Chastity Belt; The Garnet Saga; An Acre of Seats in a Garden of Dreams, 1973; The Sweet Life, 1998; Kind of Hush, 1998; Purely Belter, 2000; Our Robot Overlords, 2012; *television series include:* Not So Much a Programme, More a Way of Life, 1964; Illustrated Weekly Hudd, 1966–68; Roy Hudd Show, 1971; Comedy Tonight, 1970–71; Up Sunday, 1973; Pebble Mill, 1974–75; Hold the Front Page, 1974–75; The 60 70 80 show, 1974–77; Movie Memories, 1981–85; Halls of Fame, 1985; The Puppet Man, 1985; Cinderella, 1986; Hometown, 1987, 1988–89; What's My Line?, 1990; Lipstick On Your Collar, 1993; Common as Muck, 1994–96; What's My Line, 1994–96; Karaoke, 1996; The Quest, 2002; Coronation Street, 2002–04, 2006–09; The Quest 2, 2004; The Final Quest, 2005; In the City, 2006; *radio series:* The News Huddlines, 1975–2003; Like They've Never Been Gone, 2001–04; Tickling Tunes, 2006; *author of stage shows:* Victorian Christmas, 1978; Just a Verse and Chorus, 1979; Roy Hudd's Very Own Music Hall, 1980; Beautiful Dreamer, 1980; Underneath the Arches, 1982; While London Sleeps, 1983; They Called Me Al, 1987; numerous pantomimes, 1980–. Columnist, Yours magazine, 1991–. Chm., Entertainment Artistes Benevolent Fund, 1980–90. President: British Music Hall Soc., 1992–; TRIC, 2000–01. Trustee, British Actors Equity, 2007–. King Rat, Grand Order of Water Rats, 1989, 2000. Hon. DCL E Anglia, 2007; Hon. DLitt Westminster, 2010. Variety Club BBC Radio Personality, 1976, 1993; Gold Badge of Merit, BASCA, 1981; Sony Gold Award, 1990; British Comedy Lifetime Achievement, LWT, 1990; EMAP Columnist of the Year, 1995; Crystal Award for services to entertainment, Inst. of Entertainment & Arts Mgt, 1995; Roy Castle Award for outstanding services to variety, 2003; The Oldie Diamond Geezer of the Year, 2012. *Publications:* Music Hall, 1976; Roy Hudd's Book of Music Hall, Variety and Show Biz Anecdotes, 1993; Roy Hudd's Who's Who in Variety 1945–60, 1997; Twice Nightly, 2007; A Fart In a Colander (autobiog.), 2009. *Recreations:* collecting old songs, sleeping. *Address:* PO Box 604, Ipswich IP6 9WZ. *Club:* Garrick.

HUDDERSFIELD, Area Bishop of, since 2014; Rt Rev. Dr Jonathan Robert Gibbs; *b* Manchester, 6 May 1961; *s* of Phillip and Jean Gibbs; *m* 1986, Toni Millsted; two *s* one *d*. *Educ:* King's Sch., Chester; Jesus Coll., Oxford (MA 1989); Jesus Coll., Cambridge (PhD Theol. 1990); Ridley Hall, Cambridge. Ordained deacon, 1989, priest, 1990; Asst Curate, Stalybridge, 1989–92; Chaplain, Basle with Freiburg-im-Breisgau, 1992–98; Rector, Heswall, 1998–2014. *Recreations:* reading and collecting books, wines and the culture of France, hill-walking. *Address:* Stone Royd, 9 Valley Head, Huddersfield, W Yorks HD2 2DH. *T:* (01484) 900656. *E:* bishop.jonathan@westyorkshiredales.anglican.org.

HUDDLESTON, Nigel Paul; MP (C) Worcestershire Mid, since 2015; *b* Lincs, 13 Oct. 1970; *m* 1999, Melissa Peters; one *s* one *d*. *Educ:* Robert Pattinson Comprehensive Sch., N Hykeham; Christ Church, Oxford (BA Hons PPE 1992); Anderson Sch. of Mgt, Univ. of Calif, Los Angeles (MBA 1998). Sen. Manager, Arthur Andersen Business Consulting, 1993–2002; Dir, Strategy Practice, Deloitte Consulting, 2002–10; Industry Hd of Travel, Google, 2011–15. Mem. (C) St Albans DC, 2011–15. Contested (C) Luton S, 2010. *Address:* House of Commons, SW1A 0AA.

HUDGELL, Susan Alison; *see* Pember, S. A.

HUDGHTON, Ian Stewart; Member (SNP) Scotland, European Parliament, since 1999 (Scotland North East, Nov. 1998–1999); *b* 19 Sept. 1951; *m* 1981, Lily M. Ingram; one *s* one *d* (and one *s* decd). *Educ:* Forfar Acad.; Kingsway Technical Coll., Dundee. Partner and Jt Proprietor, then Proprietor, F. Hudghton & Son, Painters and Decorators, 1971–95. Mem., Cttee of Regions, 1998. Member (SNP): Angus DC, 1986–96 (Housing Convener, 1988–96); Angus Council, 1995–99 (Leader, 1995–99); Tayside Regl Council, 1994–96 (Depute Leader, 1994–96). Pres., SNP, 2005–. *Recreations:* family, theatre, music, horse riding. *Address:* (office) 8 Old Glamis Road, Dundee DD3 8HP. *T:* (01382) 623200.

HUDSON, Andrew Peter, CB 2012; Senior Adviser, Big Lottery Fund, 2012–15; Chair, Circle 33 Housing Trust, since 2012; *b* 22 March 1958; *s* of late John Thomas David Hudson and of Margaret Hudson; *m* 2002, Judith Simpson. *Educ:* King Edward's Sch., Birmingham; New Coll., Oxford (BA Hons). Inland Revenue, 1980–82, 1984–86; HM Treasury: 1982–84; Chancellor of the Exchequer's Office, 1986–89; Local Govt Finance Div., 1989–91; seconded to Interconnection Systems Ltd, 1991–92; Press Sec. to Chancellor of the Exchequer and Hd of Communications, 1992–96; Hd, Health Team, 1996–99; Essex County Council: Asst Chief Exec., 1999–2002; Dep. Chief Exec. (Finance and Performance), 2002–04; Chief Exec., Valuation Office Agency, 2004–09; Dir Gen., Public Services (formerly Man. Dir, Public Services and Growth), HM Treasury, 2009–11. Chair, The Old Church, arts centre, 2012–. Trustee, Hackney Doorways, 2012– (Chair, 2014–). *Recreations:* running, walking, watching sport. *E:* ap.hudson@btinternet.com.

HUDSON, Prof. Anne Mary, DPhil; FRHistS; FBA 1988; Professor of Medieval English, Oxford, 1989–2003; Fellow of Lady Margaret Hall, Oxford, 1963–2003, now Hon. Fellow; *b* 28 Aug. 1938; *d* of late R. L. and K. M. Hudson. *Educ:* Dartford Grammar Sch. for Girls; St Hugh's Coll., Oxford (BA English cl. I; MA; DPhil 1964). FRHistS 1976. Lectr in Medieval English, 1961–63, Tutor, 1963–91, LMH, Oxford; Oxford University: CUF Lectr, 1963–81; Special Lectr, 1981–83; British Acad. Reader in the Humanities, 1983–86; Lectr in Medieval English, 1986–89. Early English Text Society: Exec. Sec., 1969–82; Mem. Council, 1982–; Dir, 2006–13. Sir Israel Gollancz Prize, British Acad., 1985, 1991. Dr Hist. *hc* Charles Univ. of Prague, 2010. *Publications:* (ed) Selections from English Wycliffite Writings, 1978; (ed) English Wycliffite Sermons, i, 1983, iii, 1990, iv and v (with P. Gradon), 1996; Lollards and their Books, 1985; (ed jtly) From Ockham to Wyclif, 1987; The Premature Reformation, 1988; (ed) Two Wycliffite Texts, 1993; (ed jtly) Heresy and Literacy 1000–1500, 1994; (ed) The Works of a Lollard Preacher, 2001; Studies in the Transmission of Wyclif's Writings, 2008; (ed) Two Revisions of Rolle's English Psalter Commentary and the Related Canticles, vol. 1, 2012, vol. 2, 2013, vol. 3, 2014; Doctors in English: a study of the Wycliffite Gospel commentaries, 2015. *Address:* Lady Margaret Hall, Oxford OX2 6QA.

HUDSON, Anthony Sean; QC 2015; *b* Gateshead, 23 Sept. 1969; *s* of Tony and Eva Hudson; *m* 2000, Shereener Browne; two *s* one *d*. *Educ:* Bedale Secondary Sch.; Univ. of Exeter (LLB Hons). Called to the Bar, Middle Temple, 1996; in practice as barrister, 1996–. *Recreations:* swimming, cycling, running, jazz. *Address:* Matrix Chambers, Griffin Buildings, Gray's Inn, WC1R 5LN. *T:* (020) 7404 3447. *E:* anthonyhudson@matrixlaw.co.uk.

HUDSON, Barrie; *see* Hudson, N. B.

HUDSON, Dr Ian Robert Burton, FRCP, FFPM; Chief Executive, Medicines and Healthcare Products Regulatory Agency, since 2013; *b* Middlesbrough, 18 Sept. 1958; *s* of Eric Hudson and Matilda Hudson; *m* 1987, Denise; one *c*. *Educ:* Kingswood Sch., Bath; London Hosp. Med. Coll., Univ. of London (BSc 1979; MB BS 1982; DCH 1985; Dip. Pharm. Med. 1991; MD 1992). FFPM 2001; FRCP 2006. Mainly paediatrics, NHS, 1982–87; Res. Fellow, Univ. of Glasgow, 1987–89; various posts in R&D, SmithKline Beecham, 1989–2001; Dir, Licensing Div., Medicines and Healthcare Products Regulatory Agency, 2001–13. *Publications:* contrib. book chapters in pharmaceutical lit.; articles in jls on paediatrics, anti-infectives, oncology and pharmaceutical regulation. *Recreations:* hiking, kayaking, photography, theatre, opera, restaurants. *Address:* Medicines and Healthcare Products Regulatory Agency, 151 Buckingham Palace Road, SW1W 9SZ. *E:* ian.hudson@mhra.gsi.gov.uk. *Club:* Athenæum.

HUDSON, Isabel Frances; Chairman, National House Building Council, since 2011 (Deputy Chairman, 2011); *b* Leicester, 8 Dec. 1959; *d* of Prof. Ronald Philip Draper, *qv*; *m* 1982, Adrian Hudson; two *d*. *Educ:* Collegiate Grammar Sch., Leicester; St Margaret's Sch., Aberdeen; Harlaw Acad., Aberdeen; Lady Margaret Hall, Oxford (MA 1st Cl. Modern Langs 1981). Corporate develt, Royal Internat. and Royal Global, with secondments to Germany and Italy, Royal Insce Gp, 1981–93; Hd, Eur. Develt and Ops, Lloyd's of London, 1993–95; Develt Dir, GE Insce, 1996–99; Chief Financial Officer, Eureko BV, 1999–2002; Exec. Dir, Prudential UK, 2002–06; CEO, Synesis Life, 2006–08. Non-executive Director: Fineos, Ireland, 2002–06; QBE Insce, Australia, 2005–14; Pensions Regulator, 2009–14; Phoenix Gp Hldgs, 2010–; MGM Advantage, 2010–13; Standard Life, 2014–; BT plc, 2014–. Chm., Business Develt Bd, 2008–11, Ambassador, 2013–, Scope. Mem., Adv. Council, Lady Margaret Hall, Oxford, 2011–. FCII 1985. Rutter Gold Medal, Chartered Insce Inst., 1985. *Recreations:* travel, restaurants, financing daughters' shopping, French DIY.

HUDSON, Kathryn Margaret; Parliamentary Commissioner for Standards, since 2013; *b* 28 March 1949; *d* of William and Annie Stead; *m* 1971, Michael Hudson; two *s*. *Educ:* Univ. of Southampton (BSc Sociol./Law); Univ. of S Bank (MSc Public Sector Mgt 1994); letter of accreditation as Probation Officer, Home Office, 1971. Probation Officer, 1971–75; Youth Worker, ILEA, 1979–83; Social Worker, Bromley, 1983–86; Sen. Social Worker, Greenwich, 1986–90; Team Ldr, Adoption and Fostering, 1990–92, Principal Officer, 1992–94, Bexley; Assistant Director of Social Services: Bexley, 1994–98; Lewisham, 1998–2000 (Actg Dir, 2000); Dir, Social Services, Newham, 2001–04; Nat. Dir for Social Care, DoH, 2004–08; Dep. Parly and Health Service Ombudsman, 2008–12. *Address:* Office of the Parliamentary Commissioner for Standards, House of Commons, SW1A 0AA. *T:* (020) 7219 0320. *E:* hudsonk@parliament.uk.

HUDSON, Keith William, FRICS; Technical Secretary, Cost Commission, Comité Européen des Economistes de la Construction, 1989–94; *b* 2 June 1928; *s* of William Walter Hudson and Jessie Sarah Hudson; *m* 1952, Ailsa White; two *s* two *d*. *Educ:* Sir Charles Elliott Sch.; Coll. of Estate Management. FRICS 1945. Served Army, 1948–50 (Lieut). Private practice, 1945–48 and 1950–57; Min. of Works, Basic Grade, 1957–64; Min. of Health (later DHSS), 1964–86: Main Grade, 1964–66; Sen. Grade, 1966–74; Superintending, 1974–76; Dir B, 1976–79; Under Sec., 1979; Dir of Construction and Cost Intelligence, and Chief Surveyor, DHSS, 1979–86, retd. *Publications:* articles in Chartered Surveyor and in Building. *Recreations:* painting, walking.

HUDSON, Kirsty; *see* McLeod, K.

HUDSON, Lucian John; Director of Communications, Open University, since 2011 (Acting Director of Marketing Communications, since 2014); *b* 5 July 1960; *s* of late John and Vanda Hudson; *m* 1982, Margaret Prythergch. *Educ:* Ecole Montalembert, Paris; Lycée Français de

Londres; St Catherine's Coll., Oxford (MA (Hons) PPE); London Business Sch.; exec. educn courses at Judge Business Sch., Cambridge Univ. and Saïd Business Sch., Oxford Univ. Strategic communications specialist, with expertise in advocacy, negotiation, collaboration and mediation; BBC: producer and sen. producer, Nine O'Clock News, 1988–93; night editor, Breakfast News, news editor, party confs, 1993–94; strand editor, BBC World, 70 live events and breaking news specials inc. first 6 hrs of death of Diana, Princess of Wales, 1994–97; Hd of Programming and Chief Editl Advr, BBC Worldwide, 1997–99; Dir of e-Communications Gp, Cabinet Office, 2000–01; seconded to MAFF to run media ops during foot and mouth disease, 2001; Dir of Commns, DEFRA, 2001–04; Dir of Commns, DCA, 2004–06; Dir of Communication and Press Sec., FCO, 2006–08; special assignment: on collaborative partnerships, FCO, 2008; MoJ, 2008–09; on secondment from MoJ as Interim Man. Dir, Cornerstone Global Associates and Sen. Advr to Chief Exec., Marie Curie Cancer Care, 2009–10; Partner and Man. Dir, Cornerstone Global Associates, 2010–11. Ind. Reviewer, No 10 and Cabinet Office communications review, 2013. Mem., Nat. Criminal Justice Bd, 2004–06. Expert Panel Mem., CEDR Panel on Inquiry into Public Inquiries, 2011–, on Collaborative Working, 2011–. Mem. Adv. Bd, Global Thinkers Forum, 2014–. Founding editorial dir, Justpeople.com, 1999–2000. Chm., Liberal Judaism, 2009–15; Mem., 2009–, Chm., Strategic Communications Task Force, 2010–11, Jewish Leadership Council, 2009–. Chm., Citizens MK Leadership Team, 2015–. Chm., Rory Peck Trust, 1998–2000. Chm., Council, Tavistock Inst., 2003–07. Gov. and Trustee, Leo Baeck Coll., 2009–12. CEDR Accredited Mediator, 2010. MCIPR 2005. FInstD 2015. *Publications:* (contrib.) Corporate Responsibility: a research handbook, 2012; (contrib.) Social Partnerships and Responsible Business: a research handbook, 2013; (contrib. jtly) Sustainability, Accounting, Mgt and Policy Jl. *Recreations:* writing, reading, swimming, listening to music. *E:* lucian.hudson@open.ac.uk. *Club:* Royal Automobile.

HUDSON, Mark Henry; Chairman, NWF Group plc, since 2006 (Director, since 1985); *b* 27 Jan. 1947; *s* of Tom Hudson and Peggy Hudson (*née* Field); *m* 1970, Susan Gordon Russell; two *s*. *Educ:* Sedbergh Sch.; St Catharine's Coll., Cambridge (BA 1969, MA 1974); Wye Coll., Univ. of London (Dip. Farm Business Admin 1970). Principal, Mark Hudson Associates, 1991–; Chm., Game Conservancy Trust Ltd, later Game and Wildlife Conservation Trust, 2006–10. Panel Mem., Agricultural Land Tribunal, 1981–99, 2013–. Pres., CLA, 2003–05. Mem. Council, Duchy of Lancaster, 2006– (Chm., 2015–). Chm., Oxford Farming Conf., 1990–91. Author of report, Food, Flora and Fauna: can land managers deliver?, RICS/RAC, 2009. ARAgS 2007. *Recreations:* family, fishing, golf. *Address:* c/o NWF Group plc, Wardle, Nantwich, Cheshire CW5 6BP. *Clubs:* Farmers (Chm., 1990), MCC.

HUDSON, Michael William; Director of Finance, Wiltshire Council, since 2010; *b* Liverpool, 21 Jan. 1970; *s* of William Hudson and Norma Hudson; *m* 2010, Catriona Hughes; one *s* three *d*. *Educ:* Woodhey High Sch.; Holy Cross Coll.; Huddersfield Univ. (LLB Hons 1991); Univ. of Manchester (LLM 1992); Liverpool John Moores Univ. (CIPFA 1996). Sen. Auditor, Audit Commn, 1992–98; Dir, KPMG, 1998–2004; Hd of Finance, Oldham Council, 2004–06; Dir of Resources and Treas. to Humber Bridge, Hull CC, 2006–10. Ind. Mem., Audit Cttee, NE Lincs Council, 2000–02. Chm. Govs, North Thoresby Sch., 2000–02. *Recreations:* sports including football, walking, climbing. *Address:* Wiltshire Council, County Hall, Bythesea Road, Trowbridge, Wilts BA14 8JN.

HUDSON, Rt Rev. Nicholas; an Auxiliary Bishop of Westminster, (RC), since 2014; Titular Bishop of St Germans, since 2014; *b* 14 Feb. 1959; *s* of Richard Hudson and Marie-Charlotte Hudson (*née* Valdelièvre). *Educ:* Wimbledon Coll. Prep. Sch.; Jesus Coll., Cambridge (BA 1981); Venerable English Coll., Rome (LTh); Catholic Univ. of Leuven (studies in RE and catechesis). Ordained priest, 1986; Asst Priest, St Thomas of Canterbury, Canterbury, 1987–91; Dir, Southwark Christian Educn Centre, 1992–2000; Vice-Rector, 2000–04, Rector, 2004–13, Venerable English Coll., Rome; Parish Priest, Sacred Heart, Wimbledon, 2014. *Address:* c/o Diocese of Westminster, Vaughan House, 46 Francis Street, SW1P 1QN.

HUDSON, (Norman) Barrie, CB 1996; Director, International Development Affairs (formerly Under Secretary, International Division), Overseas Development Administration, 1993–97, retired; *b* 21 June 1937; *s* of William and Mary Hudson; *m* 1963, Hazel (*née* Cotterill); two *s* one *d*. *Educ:* King Henry VIII Sch., Coventry; Univ. of Sheffield (BA Hons 1958); University Coll., London (MScEcon 1960). Economist, Tube Investments Ltd, 1960; Economist, Economist Intell. Unit, 1962; National Accounts Statistician (UK Technical Assistance to Govt of Jordan), 1963; Statistician, ODM, 1966; Econ. Adviser, ME Develt Div., Beirut, 1967; Overseas Development Administration: Econ. Adviser, 1972, Sen. Econ. Adviser, 1973; Head, SE Asia Develt Div., Bangkok, 1974; Asst Sec., 1977; Under Sec. (Principal Establishments Officer), 1981; Under Sec. for Africa, 1986. Trustee, SCF, 1998–2005. *Recreations:* theatre, reading, music, watching football and cricket. *Address:* 2 Pine Rise, Meopham, Kent DA13 0JA. *T:* (01474) 814419.

HUDSON, Pamela May; *see* Hudson-Bendersky, P. M.

HUDSON, Vice Adm. Peter Derek, CB 2015; CBE 2005; Commander Maritime Command, NATO Headquarters Northwood, 2013–15; *b* Manchester, 25 June 1961; *s* of Brian and Elizabeth Hudson; *m* 1997, Linda Williams; three *s*. *Educ:* Netherthorpe Grammar Sch., Staveley, Derbys; Britannia Royal Naval Coll.; Open Univ. (BSc Maths/Econs). Joined Royal Navy, 1980; in command: HMS Cottesmore, 1994–96; HMS Norfolk, 1996–98; Fleet Ops Officer, 1998–2000, Team Leader, Fleet Change Prog., 2000–02, Fleet HQ; in command, HMS Albion, 2002–04; Hd of Personnel, C-in-C Fleet, 2005; Dir, Naval Resources and Programming, MoD, 2005–07; Comdr, UK Amphibious Forces, 2008–09; Comdr, UK Maritime Forces, 2009–11; COS (Capability) to C-in-C Fleet, 2011–13. ADC to the Queen, 2008–09. Younger Brother, Trinity Hse, 2005. Freeman, City of London, 2003. *Recreations:* cricket, fly fishing, hill walking, entertaining my children. *Address:* Marchbank, Fordwater Road, Chichester, W Sussex PO19 6PS. *E:* Peter@bethwines.org.uk.

HUDSON, Prof. Peter John, DPhil; FRS 2008; Willaman Professor of Biology and Director, Huck Institutes of the Life Sciences, Pennsylvania State University, since 2002. *Educ:* Univ. of Leeds (BSc Zool.); Magdalen Coll., Oxford (DPhil). Hd, Upland Res. Gp, Game Conservancy Trust; Prof., Univ. of Stirling, 1995–2002. Corresp. FRSE 2010. Laurent Perrier Award, 1985; Carlton Herman Award, 2005. *Publications:* The Red Grouse: the biology and management of a wild gamebird, 1986; (with M. W. R. Rands) Ecology and Management of Gamebirds, 1988; Grouse in Space and Time, 1992; (with D. Newborn) A Handbook of Grouse and Moorland Management, 1995; (jtly) Ecology of Wildlife Diseases, 2001; contribs to jls incl. Nature, Science, Ecol., Amer. Naturalist, Internat. Jl Parasitol., Parasitol., Proc. Royal Soc., Jl Helminthol., Oikos, Jl Applied Ecol. *Address:* Huck Institutes of the Life Sciences, Pennsylvania State University, University Park, PA 16802, USA.

HUDSON, Rachel Sophia Margaret; Her Honour Judge Hudson; a Circuit Judge, since 2009; a Deputy High Court Judge, since 2008; Designated Family Judge for Northumbria and North Durham, since 2014; *b* Cranleigh, Surrey, 29 Jan. 1963; *d* of late Stuart Hudson and Olive Hudson; *m* 2013, Gary Stacey; one *s* by a previous marriage. *Educ:* Newcastle Church High Sch.; Queen Elizabeth Grammar Sch., Hexham; London Sch. of Econs (LLB). Called to the Bar, Middle Temple, 1985; in practice as a barrister, Trinity Chambers, Newcastle upon Tyne, 1985–2009; a Recorder, 2005–09. *Recreation:* family life. *Address:* Newcastle upon Tyne Combined Court Centre, Quayside, Newcastle upon Tyne NE1 3LA. *T:* (0191) 201 2000.

HUDSON, Prof. Raymond, PhD, DLitt, DSc; FBA 2006; Professor of Geography, since 1990, and Deputy Vice-Chancellor, 2012–14 and since 2015, University of Durham (Acting Vice-Chancellor, 2014–15); *b* 7 March 1948; *s* of John and Jean Hudson; *m* 1975, Geraldine Holder Jones; one *s* one *d*. *Educ:* Bristol Univ. (BA 1st Cl. Hons 1969; PhD 1974; DSc 1996); DLitt Durham 2013. University of Durham: Lectr in Geog., 1972–83; Sen. Lectr, 1983–87; Reader, 1987–90; Head of Geog. Dept, 1992–97; Dir, Centre for European Studies, 1990–99; Chair, Internat. Centre for Regl Regeneration and Develt Studies, 1999–2005; Dir, Wolfson Res. Inst., 2003–07; Pro Vice-Chancellor, Partnerships and Engagement, 2007–12. Chairman: Conf. of Heads of Geog. Depts in HE Instns in UK, 1995–99; Human Geog. Subject Area Panel, ESRC, 1999–2001; Member: Trng and Develt Bd, ESRC, 2002–06; Higher Educn Acad., 2007–; HEFCE Strategic Adv. Cttee for Enterprise and Skills, 2010–13, for Res. and Knowledge Exchange, 2013–14; Bd, Health and Educn Innovation Cluster North East, 2012–14. Vice-Pres., RGS with IBG, 1999–2004; Pres., Geog. Sect., BAAS, 2001–02. FAcSS (AcSS 2001); MAE 2007; FRSA 2009; Fellow, Regl Studies Assoc., 2010. Editor, European Urban and Regional Studies, 1994–2007. Hon. DSc Roskilde, 1987. Edward Heath Award, 1989, Victoria Medal, 2005, RGS; Sir Peter Hall Award, Regl Studies Assoc., 2014. *Publications:* (with D. Pocock) Images of the Urban Environment, 1978; (contrib. and ed, jtly) Regions in Crisis, 1980; (with D. W. Rhind) Land Use, 1980; (contrib. and ed, jtly) Regional Planning in Europe, 1982; (contrib. and ed, jtly) Redundant Spaces in Cities and Regions, 1983; (jtly) An Atlas of EEC Affairs, 1984; (contrib. and ed, jtly) Uneven Development in Southern Europe, 1985; (with A. Williams) The United Kingdom, 1986; Wrecking a Region, 1989; (with D. Sadler) The International Steel Industry, 1989; (with A. Williams) Divided Britain, 1989; (jtly) A Tale of Two Industries, 1991; (jtly) A Place called Teesside, 1994; (ed and contrib., jtly) Towards a New Map of Automobile Manufacturing in Europe?, 1995; (with M. Dunford) Successful European regions, 1996; (contrib. and ed jtly) Divided Europe, 1998; (jtly) Digging up Trouble: environment, protest and opencast coal mining, 2000; Production, Place and Environment: changing perspectives in economic geography, 2000; (jtly) Coalfields Regeneration: dealing with the consequences of industrial decline, 2000; Producing Places, 2001; (jtly) Placing the Social Economy, 2002; Economic Geographies: circuits, flows and spaces, 2005; numerous articles in scientific and scholarly jls. *Recreations:* reading, music, watching sport, travel. *Address:* 7 Oliver Place, Merryoaks, Durham DH1 3QS. *T:* (home) (0191) 386 2963, (office) (0190) 334 6045, (mobile) 07793 903351.

HUDSON, Prof. Richard Anthony, FBA 1992; Professor of Linguistics, University College London, 1989–2004, now Emeritus; *b* 18 Sept. 1939; *s* of late Prof. John Pilkington Hudson, CBE, GM and Mary Gretta Hudson (*née* Heath); *m* 1970, Gaynor Evans; two *d*. *Educ:* Loughborough Grammar Sch.; Corpus Christi Coll., Cambridge (BA); Sch. of Oriental and African Studies, London (PhD). University College London: Research Asst, Linguistics, 1964–70; Lectr 1970, Reader 1980, Dept of Phonetics and Linguistics. *Publications:* English Complex Sentences: an introduction to systemic grammar, 1971; Arguments for a Non-Transformational Grammar, 1976; Sociolinguistics, 1980; Word Grammar, 1984; An Invitation to Linguistics, 1984; English Word Grammar, 1990; Teaching Grammar: a guide for the national curriculum, 1992; Word Meaning, 1995; English Grammar, 1998; Language Networks: the new word grammar, 2007; An Introduction to Word Grammar, 2010; articles in jls. *Recreations:* walking, cycling, music. *Address:* Research Department of Linguistics, University College London, Chandler House, 2 Wakefield Street, WC1N 1PF. *T:* (020) 7679 2000.

HUDSON, Richard Bayliss, RDI 1999; stage designer; *b* 9 June 1954; *s* of Peter Obank Hudson and Ella Joyce Bayliss. *Educ:* Peterhouse Sch., Rhodesia; Wimbledon Sch. of Art (BA Hons 1976). Designer of sets and costumes, 1986–, for major theatre companies in Britain, and for Royal Opera, ENO, Glyndebourne, Chicago Lyric Opera, La Fenice, Vienna State Opera, Bayerische Staatsoper; designs include: King Lear and Candide, Old Vic (Olivier award for season), 1988; A Night at the Chinese Opera, Kent Opera, 1990; The Queen of Spades, 1992, Eugene Onegin, 1994, Manon Lescaut, 1997, Le Nozze di Figaro and Don Giovanni, 2000, Glyndebourne; Die Meistersinger, Royal Opera, 1993; The Cherry Orchard, RSC, 1995; The Lion King, Broadway, 1997 (Tony Award, 1998), also London, Tokyo, Osaka, Toronto, Los Angeles, Hamburg; Samson et Dalila, Met. Opera, New York, 1998; Guillaume Tell and Ernani, Vienna State Opera, 1998; Peter Grimes, Amsterdam, 2000; Pique Dame, Chicago Lyric Opera, 2000; Tamerlano, Maggio Musicale Fiorentino, 2001; The Cunning Little Vixen, Opera North, 2001; Khovanshchina, Opéra de Paris, 2001; Doctor Faustus, Young Vic, 2002; Benvenuto Cellini, Zurich, 2002; Les Vêpres Siciliennes, Opéra de Paris, 2003; Ring Cycle, ENO, 2004–05; Emperor Jones, Gate, 2005; Women Beware Women, 2006, Coriolanus, 2007, RSC; L'après-midi d'un Faune, Jeux, Fall of the House of Usher, Bregenz Fest., 2006; The Makropulos Case, Royal Danish Opera, 2006; Death in Venice (costumes), Aldeburgh Fest., La Bohème, Greek Nat. Opera, 2007; La Forza del Destino, Vienna State Opera, Rushes, Royal Ballet, 2008; Divorzio all'Italiana, 2008, Kafka's Monkey, 2009, Young Vic; Goldberg Variations, ROH2, 2009; Rigoletto, Vienna Volksoper, 2009; Armida, Metropolitan Opera, NY, Tamerlano, Royal Opera, The Nutcracker, Amer. Ballet Th., 2010; Eidolon, Royal Danish Ballet, Invitus Invitam, Royal Ballet, 2010; Die Entführung aus dem Serail, Rome Opera, Romeo and Juliet, Nat. Ballet of Canada, 2011; La Nuit de Gutenberg, Opéra du Rhin (costumes), Terre et Cendres, Opéra de Lyon (costumes), Pêcheurs des Perles, Opéra Comique, Paris (costumes), La Bayadère and Le Coq d'Or, Royal Danish Ballet, 2012. British Scenographic Comr, Orgn Internat. des Scénographes, Techniciens et Architectes de Théâtre, 1996–2011. Pres., Soc. of British Stage Designers, 2008–. Companion, Liverpool Inst. for Perf. Arts, 2009. FRWCMD 2010. DUniv Surrey, 2005. Gold Medal for set design, Prague Quadrennial, 2003. *Address:* c/o Judy Daish Associates, 2 St Charles Place, W10 6EG.

HUDSON-BENDERSKY, Pamela May, CBE 1988; JP; Regional Nursing Director, North West Thames Regional Health Authority, 1985–88, retired; *b* 1 June 1931; *d* of late Leonard Joshua Hudson and of Mabel Ellen Hudson (now Baker); *m* 1987, David Bendersky (*d* 2012), NY State and Kansas City. *Educ:* South West Essex High School. SRN. Nursing Officer, Charing Cross Hosp., 1966–67; Matron, Fulham Hosp., 1967–70; Principal Regl Nursing Officer, SE Thames RHB, 1970–73; Area Nursing Officer, Lambeth, Southwark and Lewisham AHA(T), 1973–82; Regional Nursing Officer, NW Thames RHA, 1982–85. Member, Alcohol Education and Research Council, 1982–87. JP: Inner London SE Div., 1983–88; N Glos (formerly Cheltenham) Petty Sessional Div., 1989–2001 (Chm., 1998–2001). *Publications:* contribs to nursing profession jls. *Recreations:* embroidery, theatre, gardening. *Address:* 15 Horsefair, Campden Road, Shipston on Stour CV36 4PD. *T:* (01608) 661158.

HUDSON DAVIES, (Gwilym) Ednyfed; *see* Davies, Ednyfed H.

HUDSON-SMITH, Dr Andrew Paul; Director and Deputy Chair, Bartlett Centre for Advanced Spatial Analysis, since 2010, and Reader in Digital Urban Systems, since 2012, University College London; *b* Wokingham, Berks, 15 Oct. 1970; *s* of John and Barbara Smith. *Educ:* Plymouth Univ. (BSc Geog. 1992); Univ. of Wales Coll., Cardiff (MSc Town Planning 1996); University Coll. London (PhD Digital Planning 2003). Bartlett Centre for Advanced Spatial Analysis, University College London: res. asst, 1996–99; Res. Fellow, 2004–05; Sen. Res. Fellow, 2005–08; Lectr and Res. Manager, 2008–10. Ed.-in-Chief, Future Internet Jl, 2010–. Mem., All Party Parly Gp, Smart Cities, 2014–. Mem., Smart London Bd, GLA,

2013–. FRSA 2011. *Recreations:* theatre, meteorology, horology. *Address:* Bartlett Centre for Advanced Spatial Analysis, UCL Faculty of the Built Environment, 1st Floor, 90 Tottenham Court Road, W1T 4TJ. *T:* (020) 3108 3877. *E:* a.hudson-smith@ucl.ac.uk.

HUDSON-WILKIN, Rev. Rose Josephine; Chaplain to the Queen, since 2008; Chaplain to the Speaker of the House of Commons, and Priest Vicar, Westminster Abbey, since 2010; Prebendary, St Paul's Cathedral, since 2013; Priest-in-charge, St Mary at Hill with St Andrew Hubbard, St George Botolph Lane, and St Botolph by Billingsgate, since 2014; *b* 19 Jan. 1961; *m* 1983, Rev. Kenneth Wilkin; one *s* two *d. Educ:* Montego Bay High Sch.; Church Army Coll.; Queen's Theol Coll. (W Midlands Ministerial Trng Course); Birmingham Univ. (BPhil Ed 2000). Lay Trng Officer, Anglican Dio. Jamaica, 1982; ordained deacon, 1991, priest, 1994; Curate, St Matthew, Wolverhampton, 1991–94; Priest, Good Shepherd, W Bromwich, 1995–98; Officer for Black Anglican Concerns, Lichfield Dio., 1995–98; Vicar, Holy Trinity, Dalston and All Saints, Haggerston, 1998–2014. Mem., Broadcasting Standards Commn, 1998–2004. Member: Gen. Synod of C of E, 1995–98, 2005–10 (Chm., Cttee for Minority Ethnic Anglican Concerns, 1999–2009); Theol Bd, WCC, 1996–98; Chm., Worldwide Cttee, SPCK, 1998–2004. Trustee, Trusthouse Charitable Foundation, 2009–; Patron, City YMCA, 2011–. *Recreations:* reading, travelling, entertaining, tennis, scrabble. *Address:* St Mary at Hill, Lovat Lane, EC3R 8EE.

HUEBNER, Michael Denis, CB 1994; Director General, Judicial Group, and Secretary of Commissions, Lord Chancellor's Department, 1998–2000; Deputy Clerk of the Crown in Chancery, 1993–2000; *b* 3 Sept. 1941; *s* of late Dr Denis William Huebner and Rene Huebner (*née* Jackson); *m* 1965, Wendy Ann, *d* of Brig. Peter Crosthwaite; one *s* one *d. Educ:* Rugby Sch.; St John's Coll., Oxford (BA Modern History). Called to the Bar, Gray's Inn, 1965, Bencher, 1994; Master of the House, 2001–03. Lord Chancellor's Department, 1966–68; Law Officers' Dept, 1968–70; rejoined Lord Chancellor's Dept, 1970: Asst Solicitor, 1978; Under Sec., Circuit Administrator, NE Circuit, 1985–88; Prin. Estabt and Finance Officer, 1988–89; Dep. Sec., Judicial Appts, 1989; Sec. of Commns, 1989–91; Hd of Law and Policy Gps, 1991–93; Head, 1993–95, Chief Exec., 1995–98, Court Service. Pres., Electricity Arbitration Assoc., 2002–08. Trustee, St Luke's Community Trust, 2000–07. Liveryman, Clockmakers' Co., 2003–. *Publications:* brief guide to Ormesby Hall (Nat. Trust); contrib. (jtly) Courts, Halsbury's Laws of England, 4th edn 1975; legal articles in New Law Jl. *Recreations:* looking at pictures, architecture, theatre going. *Club:* Athenæum.

HUEY EVANS, Gay Jeanette; Deputy Chair, Financial Reporting Council, since 2014 (Member since 2012); *b* New York, 17 July 1954; *d* of late Clarence Calvin Huey and of Frances Huey; *m* (marr. diss.); one *d. Educ:* Bucknell Univ. (BA Econs). Sen. Man. Dir, Bankers Trust, NY and London, 1984–98; Dir, Mkts Div., FSA, 1998–2005; Pres., Tribeca Global Mgt and Hd of Governance, Citigroup Alternatives, 2005–08; Vice-Chm., Investment Banking and Investment Mgt, Barclays, 2008–10. Chm., 1994–98, Vice-Chm., 2011–12, non-exec. Chm. (Europe), 2011–12, Internat. Swaps and Derivatives Assoc., Inc. Non-executive Director: London Stock Exchange Gp, 2010–13; Itau BBA International, 2012–; Standard Chartered plc, 2015–; Ind. non-exec. Dir, Aviva plc, 2011–. Mem., Lord Mayor's Appeal Cttee, 2009–10. Mem., Council of Foreign Relns, 2009–. Mem., Forum UK, 2010–. Trustee: Wigmore Hall, 2005–13; Bucknell Univ., 2009–11; Wellbeing of Women, 2011–. FRSA. *Recreations:* tennis, music, cooking, trekking.

HUFFINGTON, Arianna Stassinopoulos; Co-founder, Huffington Post, 2005; President and Editor-in-Chief, Huffington Post Media Group, since 2011; *b* Athens, 15 July 1950; *d* of Kostantinos and Elli Stassinopoulos; *m* 1986, Michael Huffington (marr. diss. 1997); two *d. Educ:* Girton Coll., Cambridge (BA Econs 1972; MA). Pres., Cambridge Union. Co-founder, Detroit Project, 2003. Board Member: El País; Cttee to Protect Journalists. Hon. Dr Brown, 2011. Awards include: Best Political Blog, Webby Awards, 2008; President's Award, LA Press Club, 2009; Oceana Partners Award, 2009; Fred Dressler Lifetime Achievement Award, 2009; Emery Award, Hetrick-Martin Inst., 2010; Media/Entertainment Design Award, Global Green Sustainable Design Awards, 2010; Online Commentary/Blogging Award, Online Journalism Awards, 2011; Forces for Nature Award, Natural Resources Defense Council, 2011; Aenne Burda Award, 2012. *Publications:* The Female Woman, 1974; After Reason, 1978; Maria Callas: the woman behind the legend, 1981, 2002; The Gods of Greece, 1983, 2000; Picasso: creator and destroyer, 1988, 1996; The Fourth Instinct: the call of the soul, 1994, 2003; Greetings from the Lincoln Bedroom, 1998, 1999; How to Overthrow the Government, 2000, 2001; Pigs at the Trough: how corporate greed and political corruption are undermining America, 2003, 2004; Fanatics and Fools: the game plan for winning back America, 2004; On Becoming Fearless … in Love, Work and Life, 2006, 2007; Right is Wrong: how the lunatic fringe hijacked America, shredded the Constitution and made us all less safe, 2008; Third World America: how our politicians are abandoning the middle class and betraying the American dream, 2010, 2011; Thrive: the third metric to redefining success and creating a life of well-being, wisdom and wonder, 2014. *Address:* Huffington Post, 770 Broadway, Fifth Floor, New York, NY 10003, USA. *Fax:* (212) 6526332. *E:* arianna@huffingtonpost.com.

HUFFINLEY, Beryl; Vice-President and Vice-Chair, Labour Action for Peace, since 2005 (Chair, 1987–2005); formerly: President, National Assembly of Women; Vice President, British Peace Assembly; *b* 22 Aug. 1926; *d* of Wilfred and Ivey Sharpe; *m* 1948, Ronald Brown Huffinley. Secretary: Leeds Trades Council, 1966; Yorkshire and Humberside TUC Regional Council, 1974. Chairman: Leeds and York Dist Cttee, T&GWU, 1974; Regional Cttee, T&GWU No 9 Region, 1972. Member: Regional Econ. Planning Council (Yorkshire and Humberside), 1975–79; Leeds AHA, 1977; Press Council, 1978–84; Leeds CC Peace-Link Gp. Trustee, Yeadon Trade Council Club. *Address:* Cornerways, 29 South View, Menston, Ilkley, West Yorks LS29 6JX. *T:* (01943) 875115. *Club:* Trades Council (Leeds).

HUFTON, Dame Olwen, DBE 2004; PhD; FBA 1993; Professor of History, University of Oxford, 1997–2003 (Leverhulme Personal Research Professor, 1997–2002); Senior Research Fellow, Merton College, Oxford, 1997–2003, now Fellow Emeritus; *d* of Joseph Hufton and Caroline Hufton; *m* 1965, Brian Taunton Murphy; two *d. Educ:* Hulme Grammar Sch., Oldham; Royal Holloway Coll., Univ. of London (BA 1959; Hon. Fellow, 2000); UCL (PhD 1962; Hon. Fellow, 1999). Lectr, Univ. of Leicester, 1963–66; Reading University: Lectr, then Reader, 1966–75; Prof. of Modern Hist., 1975–88; Vis. Fellow, All Souls Coll., Oxford, 1986–87; Prof. of Modern Hist. and Women's Studies, Harvard Univ., 1987–91; Prof. of History, Eur. Univ. Inst., Florence, 1991–97. Hon. DLitt: Reading, 1999; Southampton, 2006. *Publications:* Bayeux in the Late Eighteenth Century, 1967; The Poor of Eighteenth Century France, 1974; Europe, Privilege and Protest 1730–1789, 1980, 2nd edn 2001; Women and the Limits of Citizenship in the French Revolution, 1992; The Prospect before Her: a history of women in Western Europe, vol. 1, 1500–1800, 1995; articles in Past and Present, Eur. Studies Rev., and French Hist. Studies. *Address:* 40 Shinfield Road, Reading, Berks RG2 7BW. *T:* (0118) 987 1514.

HUGGINS, family name of **Viscount Malvern**.

HUGGINS, Rt Rev. Philip James; an Assistant Bishop, Diocese of Melbourne (Bishop of the North & West Region (formerly Bishop of the Northern Region)), since 2004; *b* 16 Oct. 1948; *s* of Alf Huggins and Mary Nutt; *m* 1976, Elizabeth Cuming; three *s. Educ:* Monash Univ. (BEcon, Grad. Dip. Welfare Admin, MA). Teaching Fellow, Univ. of New England, 1971–74; ordained priest, 1977; worked in parishes, Dio. of Bendigo, 1977–80; Industrial Chaplain, dio. Melbourne, 1980–83; Univ. Chaplain, Monash Univ., 1983–89; Exec. Officer, Archbishop of Melbourne's Internat. Devclt Fund, 1990–91; Rector of Williamstown, 1991–95; Archdeacon of Essendon, 1994–95; Regl Bishop, Dio. of Perth, 1995–98; Bishop of Grafton, NSW, 1998–2003; Parish Priest, St Stephen's Anglican Church, Richmond, Vic, 2003–04. ChLJ 1997. *Recreations:* varied sports, poetry, the arts. *Address:* The Anglican Centre, 209 Flinders Lane, Melbourne, Vic 3000, Australia.

HUGH-JONES, George; QC 2010; *b* London, 7 March 1958; *s* of late Kenneth Hugh-Jones and Denise Hugh-Jones; *m* 1993, Shelley North; one *s* one *d. Educ:* Downside Sch.; Downing Coll., Cambridge (BA Mod. Langs (French and Russian) 1979; MA); City Univ. (DipLaw 1982). Called to the Bar, Middle Temple, 1983; in practice as barrister, 1983–, specialising in clinical negligence and healthcare disciplinary work. *Recreations:* tennis, swimming. *Address:* Serjeants' Inn Chambers, 85 Fleet Street, EC4Y 1AE. *E:* ghugh-jones@serjeantsinn.com.

HUGH-JONES, Sir Wynn Normington, (Sir Hugh Jones), Kt 1984; LVO 1961; Joint Hon. Treasurer, Liberal Party, 1984–87; *b* 1 Nov. 1923; *s* of Huw Hugh-Jones and May Normington; *m* 1st, 1958, Ann (*née* Purkiss) (marr. diss. 1987); one *s* two *d*; 2nd, 1987, Oswynne (*née* Buchanan). *Educ:* Ludlow; Selwyn Coll., Cambridge (Scholar; MA). Served in RAF, 1943–46. Entered Foreign Service (now Diplomatic Service), 1947; Foreign Office, 1947–49; Jedda, 1949–52; Paris, 1952–56; FO, 1956–59; Chargé d'Affaires, Conakry, 1959–60; Head of Chancery, Rome, 1960–64; FO, 1964–66, Counsellor, 1964; Consul, Elizabethville (later Lubumbashi), 1966–68; Counsellor and Head of Chancery, Ottawa, 1968–70; FCO, 1971, attached Lord President's Office; Cabinet Office, 1972–73; Director-Gen., ESU, 1973–77; Sec.-Gen., Liberal Party, 1977–83. A Vice-Chm., European-Atlantic Gp, 1985–92; Vice-Pres., Lib. Internat. British Gp, 1995–98 (Patron, 1998–). Chm., Avebury in Danger, 1988–89. Gov., Queen Elizabeth Foundn for Disabled People, 1985–2001; Trustee, Wilts Community Foundn, 1991–93. FCMI. *Publications:* Diplomacy to Politics by Way of the Jungle, 2002; Campaigning Face to Face, 2007; American Prospects under Obama, 2008. *Recreations:* golf, gardening. *Address:* 45 Queens Road, Devizes, Wilts SN10 5HP. *Clubs:* English-Speaking Union; N Wilts Golf.

HUGH SMITH, Col Henry Owen, LVO 1976; Defence Adviser to British High Commissioner, Nairobi, 1987–90; *b* 19 June 1937; *s* of Lt-Comdr Colin Hugh Smith and late Hon. Mrs C. Hugh Smith. *Educ:* Ampleforth; Magdalene Coll., Cambridge. BA Hons 1961. Commnd Royal Horse Guards, 1957; Blues and Royals, 1969; psc 1969; served Cyprus and Northern Ireland (wounded); Equerry in Waiting to The Duke of Edinburgh, 1974–76; CO The Blues and Royals, 1978–80; GSO1, MoD, 1980–87. Chm., BLESMA, 1996–2010. *Recreation:* sailing. *Clubs:* Boodle's, Pratt's; Royal Yacht Squadron.

HUGHES, family name of **Baroness Hughes of Stretford** and **Baron Hughes of Woodside**.

HUGHES OF STRETFORD, Baroness *cr* 2010 (Life Peer), of Ellesmere Port in the County of Cheshire; **Beverley June Hughes;** PC 2004; *b* 30 March 1950; *d* of Norman Hughes and Doris Hughes (*née* Gillard); *m* 1973, Thomas K. McDonald; one *s* two *d. Educ:* Manchester Univ. (BSc Hons, MSc); Liverpool Univ. (DSA, DASS). Merseyside Probation Service, 1973; Manchester University: Res. Fellow, 1976; Lectr, Sen. Lectr and Head of Dept of Social Policy and Social Work, 1981–97. Mem. (Lab), Trafford MBC, 1986–97 (Leader, 1995–97). MP (Lab) Stretford and Urmston, 1997–2010. Parly Under-Sec. of State, DETR, 1999–2001, Home Office, 2001–02; Minister of State: Home Office, 2002–04; DFES, later DCSF, 2005–09; Minister for the NW, 2007–09. *Publications:* Community Care and Older People, 1995. *Recreations:* jazz, walking, family. *Address:* House of Lords, SW1A 0PW.

HUGHES OF WOODSIDE, Baron *cr* 1997 (Life Peer), of Woodside in the City of Aberdeen; **Robert Hughes;** *b* Pittenweem, Fife, 3 Jan. 1932; *m* 1957, Ina Margaret Miller; two *s* three *d. Educ:* Robert Gordon's Coll., Aberdeen; Benoni High Sch., Transvaal; Pietermaritzburg Tech. Coll., Natal. Emigrated S Africa, 1947, returned UK, 1954. Engrg apprentice, S African Rubber Co., Natal; Chief Draughtsman, C. F. Wilson & Co. (1932) Ltd, Aberdeen, until 1970. Mem., Aberdeen Town Council, 1962–70; Convener: Health and Welfare Cttee, 1963–68; Social Work Cttee, 1969–70. Mem., AMICUS (formerly AEU, then AEEU), 1952–. Contested (Lab) North Angus and Mearns, 1959; MP (Lab) Aberdeen North, 1970–97. Member: Standing Cttee on Immigration Bill, 1971; Select Cttee, Scottish Affairs, 1971 and 1992–97; introd Divorce (Scotland) Bill 1971 (failed owing to lack of time); Parly Under-Sec. of State, Scottish Office, 1974–75; sponsored (as Private Member's Bill) Rating (Disabled Persons) Act 1978; Principal Opposition Spokesman: on agriculture, 1983–84; on transport, 1985–88 (Jun. Opp. Spokesman, 1981–83); Mem., PLP Shadow Cabinet, 1985–88. Chm., Aberdeen City Labour Party, 1961–69. Vice-Chm., Tribune Gp, 1984–85. Founder Mem. and Aberdeen Chm., Campaign for Nuclear Disarmament; Vice-Chm., 1975–76, Chm., 1976–94, Anti-Apartheid Movement; Member: GMC, 1976–79; Movement for Colonial Freedom, 1955 (Chm. Southern Africa Cttee); Scottish Poverty Action Group; Aberdeen Trades Council and Exec. Cttee, 1957–69; Labour Party League of Youth, 1954–57; Chm., 1994–99, Hon. Pres., 1999–, Action for Southern Africa; Hon. Pres., Mozambique Angola Cttee, 2001–; Trustee, Canon Collins Educn Trust for Southern Africa, 1997–2007. Grand Companion, Order of Oliver Tambo (SA), 2004. *Recreation:* fishing. *Address:* House of Lords, SW1A 0PW.

HUGHES, Rt Hon. Lord; Anthony Philip Gilson Hughes, Kt 1997; PC 2006; a Justice of the Supreme Court of the United Kingdom, since 2013; *b* 11 Aug. 1948; *s* of late Patrick and Patricia Hughes; *m* 1972, Susan Elizabeth March; one *s* one *d. Educ:* Tettenhall Coll., Staffs; Van Mildert Coll., Durham (BA 1969). Sometime Lectr, Durham Univ. and QMC. Called to the Bar, Inner Temple, 1970, Bencher, 1997; in practice at the Bar, 1971–97; a Recorder, 1988–97; QC 1990; a Judge of the High Court of Justice, Family Div., 1997–2003, QBD, 2004–06; a Lord Justice of Appeal, 2006–13; Vice-Pres., Court of Appeal (Criminal Div.), 2009–13. Presiding Judge, Midland (formerly Midland and Oxford) Circuit, 2000–03. Hon. LLD Birmingham, 2009. *Recreations:* garden labouring and mechanics, bellringing. *Address:* Supreme Court of the United Kingdom, Parliament Square, SW1P 3BD. *Clubs:* Athenæum; Worcester Rowing.

HUGHES, Alan; Managing Director, Whitechapel Bell Foundry Ltd (established 1570), since 1982; *b* 25 Aug. 1948; *s* of William A. Hughes and Florence I. Hughes; *m* 1985, Kathryn Smith; two *d. Educ:* Christ's Hosp. Church bell founder, 1966–. Freeman, City of London, 1984; Liveryman, Founders' Co., 2000. *Address:* Whitechapel Bell Foundry Ltd, 32 & 34 Whitechapel Road, E1 1DY.

HUGHES, Prof. Alan; Professor of Innovation, Imperial College Business School, Imperial College London, since 2014; Margaret Thatcher Professor of Enterprise Studies, Judge Business School (formerly Judge Institute of Management Studies), 1999–2013, now Emeritus, and Director, Centre for Business Research, 1994–2013, now Director Emeritus, University of Cambridge; Life Fellow, Sidney Sussex College, Cambridge, since 2013 (Fellow, 1973–2013); Senior Research Fellow, National Centre for Universities and Business, since 2013; *b* 1 Aug. 1946; *s* of Benjamin Redshaw Hughes and Lilias Hughes; *m* 1968, Jean Braddock; two *s* one *d. Educ:* King's Coll., Cambridge (BA Econs 1968). Sen. Economic Asst, NEDO, 1971–73; University of Cambridge: Univ. Asst Lectr, then Univ. Lectr in Econs, 1973–94; Chm., Faculty Bd of Econs and Pols, 1983–88; Dir, ESRC Small Business Res. Centre, Dept of Applied Econs, 1989–93; Dir of Res., Judge Inst. of Mgt Studies, 2001–04; Dir, Nat. Competitiveness Network Prog., Cambridge-MIT Inst., 2000–03; Dir, ESRC Impact Acceleration A/c Prog. Dist. Vis. Prof., Doshisha Univ., Kyoto, 2005–; Hon. Prof., Univ. of Queensland Business Sch., 2012–. Member: Commn on Public Policy and British Business, 1995–96; DfES Expert Panel on Educn, Learning and Lifelong Skills, 2000–05;

Prime Minister's Council for Sci. and Technol., 2004–13; Expert Panel, Australian Nat. Innovation Rev., 2008–09; Adv. Panel, Excellence Initiative, Wissenschaftsrat, Germany, 2011–12; EPSRC Strategic Adv. Network, 2011–13; Lead Expert Gp, Foresight Future of Manufg Proj., 2012–14; Patents Expert Adv. Gp, IP Office, 2012. *Publications:* (ed with D. J. Storey) Finance and the Small Firm, 1994; (ed with S. Deakin) Enterprise and Community: new directions in corporate governance, 1997; edited with A. D. Cosh: The Changing State of British Enterprise: growth, innovation and competitive advantage in SMEs 1986–1995, 1996; Enterprise Britain: growth innovation and public policy in the small and medium sized enterprise sector 1994–1997, 1998; British Enterprise in Transition: growth innovation and public policy in the small and medium sized enterprise sector 1994–1999, 2000; Enterprise Challenge: policy and performance in the British SME Sector 1999–2002, 2003; British Enterprise: thriving or surviving, 2007; (jtly) Knowledge Exchange Between Academics and the Business, Public and Third Sectors, 2009; (jtly) Growing Value: business-university collaboration for the 21st century, 2012; (with M. Kitson) Connecting with the Ivory Tower: business perspectives on knowledge exchange in the UK, 2013; (jtly) Cultural Connections: the role of the arts and humanities in competitiveness and local development, 2014; (ed) The Future of UK Manufacturing: scenario analysis, capital markets and industrial policy, 2014; (jtly) The Economic Significance of the UK Science Base, 2014; over 200 articles in jls etc. *Recreations:* photography, walking, golf, gardening, watching football and Rugby. *Address:* Centre for Business Research, Top Floor, Judge Business School Building, Trumpington Street, Cambridge CB2 1AG. *T:* (01223) 765335, *Fax:* (01223) 765338. *E:* a.hughes@cbr.cam.ac.uk.

HUGHES, Ven. Dr Alexander James; Archdeacon of Cambridge, since 2014; *b* Honiara, Solomon Islands, 3 Oct. 1975; *s* of John and Jill Hughes; *m* 1998, Sarah Newman; two *s*. *Educ:* Priory Sch., Lewes; Eton Coll.; Greyfriars, Oxford (BA 1997; MA 2004); St Edmund's Coll., Cambridge (MPhil 1999; PhD 2011). Ordained deacon, 2000, priest, 2001; Asst Curate, Headington Quarry, Oxford, 2000–03; Bishop's Domestic Chaplain, Portsmouth, 2003–08; Vicar, St Luke and St Peter, Southsea, 2008–14. Hon. Canon, Ely Cathedral, 2014–. *Publications:* Public Worship with Communion by Extension: some pastoral and theological issues, 2002; (contrib.) The Anglican Religious Communities Yearbook, 2005; (contrib.) Fear and Friendship: Anglicans engaging with Islam, 2012; contrib. to jls incl. Third Millennium, Theology, Anaphora, Modern Believing. *Recreations:* running, music, reading, writing. *Address:* 1A Summerfield, Cambridge CB3 9HE. *T:* (01223) 355013. *E:* alexanderjameshughes@gmail.com. *Club:* Newnham Riverbank.

HUGHES, Aneurin Rhys; Ambassador and Head of Delegation of European Commission to Australia and New Zealand, 1995–2002; *b* 11 Feb. 1937; *s* of William and Hilda Hughes; *m*; two *s*; *m* 2001, Lisbeth Lindbaeck. *Educ:* University College of Wales, Aberystwyth (BA; Fellow, 2002). President, National Union of Students, 1962–64. Research in S America, 1964–66; HM Diplomatic Service, 1967–73: served, Singapore and Rome; Commission of the European Communities, 1973–2002: Head of Division for Internal Coordination in Secretariat-General, 1973–77; Adviser to Dir Gen. for Information, 1977–80; Chef de Cabinet to Mr Ivor Richard, Comr responsible for Employment, Social Affairs and Educn, 1981–85; Adviser to Dir Gen. for Information, and Chm., Selection Bd for Candidates from Spain and Portugal, 1985–87; Amb. and Head of Delegn in Norway, 1987–95. *Publications:* Billy Hughes - Founding Father of the Australian Labour Party, 2005. *Recreations:* golf, music.

HUGHES, Anthony Philip Gilson; *see* Hughes, Rt Hon. Lord.

HUGHES, Antony; *see* Hughes, M. A.

HUGHES, Dr Antony Elwyn; consultant, 1996–2003; Director, Engineering and Science, and Deputy Chief Executive, Engineering and Physical Sciences Research Council, 1994–96; *b* 9 Sept. 1941; *s* of Ifor Elwyn Hughes and Anna Betty Hughes (*née* Ambler); *m* 1963, Margaret Mary Lewis; one *s* two *d* (and one *s* decd). *Educ:* Newport High Sch., Gwent; Jesus Coll., Oxford (MA; DPhil). CPhys; FInstP. Harkness Fellow, Cornell Univ., 1967–69. United Kingdom Atomic Energy Authority, Atomic Energy Research Establishment (Harwell): Scientific Officer, 1963–67; Sen. Scientific Officer, 1969–72; Principal Scientific Officer, 1972–75; Leader: Defects in Solids Gp, 1973; Solid State Sciences Gp, 1978; Individual Merit Appointment, 1975–81; Sen. Personal Appointment, 1981–83; Head, Materials Physics Div., 1983–86; Dir, Underlying Res. and Non-Nuclear Energy Res., 1986–87; Authority Chief Scientist and Dir, Nuclear Res., 1987–88. Science and Engineering Research Council: Dir, Labs, 1988–91; Dir, Progs, and Dep. Chm., 1991–93; acting Chief Exec., 1993–94. Mem., NI Higher Educn Council, 1993–2001. Member Council: Royal Instn of GB, 1995–98; Careers Res. and Adv. Centre, 1994–2007. *Publications:* Real Solids and Radiation, 1975; (ed) Defects and their Structure in Non-Metallic Solids, 1976; review articles in Contemporary Physics, Advances in Physics, Jl of Materials Science, Jl of Nuclear Materials, Reports on Progress in Physics. *Recreations:* walking, watching Rugby and cricket, playing the trumpet, gardening. *Address:* Kingswood, King's Lane, Harwell, Didcot, Oxfordshire OX11 0EJ. *T:* (01235) 835301.

HUGHES, Belinda Carol, (Bee); Headmistress, Maynard School, Exeter, since 2009; *b* Liverpool, 12 Dec. 1962; *d* of Derek Visick Hughes and Gillian Hughes. *Educ:* Helsby Grammar Sch.; Liverpool Sir John Moores Univ. (BEd Hons); Univ. of Leicester (MBA); Nat. Coll. of Sch. Leaders (NPQH). Hd of House, Island Sch., Hong Kong, 1987–97; Hd, Lower Sch., West Island Sch., Hong Kong, 1997–2001; Dep. Headteacher, Hitchin Girls' Sch., 2001–08. Chair, GSA SW and Wales Reg.; Ind. Sch. Rep., ASCL Nat. Council. Mem., CBI. *Recreations:* photography, tennis, theatre, international cinema, Renaissance Italy. *Address:* Maynard School, Denmark Road, Exeter EX1 1SJ. *T:* (01392) 273417, *Fax:* (01392) 355999. *E:* beehughes@maynard.co.uk.

HUGHES, Hon. Claudia Madeleine; *see* Ackner, Hon. C. M.

HUGHES, His Honour Dafydd Lloyd; a Circuit Judge, 2004–14; Deputy Designated Family Judge, Caernarfon and Rhyl, 2007–14; *b* 3 June 1947; *s* of Rev. Elwyn Morris Hughes and Gwen Mai Hughes (*née* Evans); *m* 1971, Ann Tegwen Davies; one *s* two *d*. *Educ:* Grove Park Grammar Sch. for Boys, Wrexham; University Coll. London (LLB Hons). Admitted solicitor, 1971; Asst Solicitor and Partner, Edmund Pickles & Upton, Solicitors, Wrexham, 1971–90; Co. Court Registrar, later Dist Judge, 1990–2004; Asst Recorder, 1994–98; Recorder, 1998–2004; Liaison Judge, N Wales Magistrates, 2007–14; Nominated Judge to hear Court of Protection cases for N Wales, 2012–. Mem., Ministerial Steering Gp on Childcare Proceedings Rev., Welsh Assembly Govt, later Welsh Govt, 2006–. Mem., Adv. Cttee, CAFCASS Cymru, 2006–14. Hon. Recorder of Caernarfon, 2012–15. *Recreations:* theatre, museums and galleries, travel, cookery, developing and refining grandparenting skills.

HUGHES, (David Evan) Peter, MA; Head of Science, Westminster School, 1984–89; *b* 27 April 1932; *s* of late Evan Gwilliam Forrest-Hughes, OBE; *m* 1956, Iris (*née* Jenkins); one *s* one *d* (and one *d* decd). *Educ:* St Paul's Sch.; St John's Coll., Oxford (Gibbs Schol. in Chemistry; MA). National Service, 5 RHA, 1954. Assistant Master, Shrewsbury School, 1956; Head of Chemistry, 1958, Science, 1965; Nuffield Foundation, 1967–68; Second Master, Shrewsbury Sch., 1972; Headmaster, St Peter's Sch., York, 1980–84; part-time teacher, Westminster Sch., 1994–2011; Dir, Understanding Science Project, and Leverhulme Res. Fellow, Imperial Coll. and Westminster Sch., 1989–94. Chief Examr, Univ. of Cambridge Local Exam. Syndicate, 1968–2006. Chm., Friends' Cttee, Imperial Coll., 1992–94. *Publications:* Advanced Theoretical Chemistry (with M. J. Maloney), 1964; Chemical Energetics, 1967; (ed) Awareness of Science, 4 vols, 1993–94; (with P. F. Cann) Chemistry, 2015; contrib. Oxford DNB; articles in professional jls. *Recreations:* music, bridge, hill-walking. *Address:* 5 Woodbank Drive, Porthill, Shrewsbury SY3 8RW.

HUGHES, David Glyn; National Agent, 1979–88, Senior National Officer, 1986–88, the Labour Party; *b* 1 March 1928; *s* of Richard and Miriam Hughes; *m* 1958, Mary Atkinson (*d* 2002); one *d*. *Educ:* Darwin St Secondary Modern Sch. Apprentice, later fitter and turner, 1944–52; Labour Party Agent: Northwich, Bolton, Tonbridge, Portsmouth, 1952–69; Asst Regional Organiser, 1969–75, Regional Organiser, 1975–79, Northern Region. *Recreations:* computing, reading. *Address:* 65 Bourne Way, Hayes, Bromley, Kent BR2 7HA. *T:* (020) 8462 8921.

HUGHES, Prof. David John, CEng, FREng, FIMechE, CDir; Managing Director, Business Innovation Group LLP, since 2006; Professor of Engineering Management, City University, since 2006; *b* 5 May 1947; *m* 1970, Dawn Anne Newman; two *d*. *Educ:* Royal Grammar Sch., High Wycombe; Aston Univ. (MSc 1970). CEng 1975, FREng 2001; FIMechE 1996; MIEEE 2000; CDir 2007. Hd, Electrical/Electronic Systems, Ford Motor Co., 1970–91; Director: Advanced Vehicle Systems, Lucas plc, 1991–97; Technol. Planning, GEC plc, 1997–99; Exec. Vice Pres., Marconi plc, 1999–2001; Dir, Special Projects, BAE Systems, 2002; Dir Gen., Innovation Gp, and Chief Scientific Advr, DTI, 2002–06. Member: Technol. and Innovation Cttee, CBI, 1999–2003; EPSRC, 2003–06; Innovation and Engagement Bd, Cardiff Univ., 2005–11; Innovation Adv. Bd, Surrey Univ., 2006–11; Chairman: Industrial Partnership Panel, City Univ., 2009–12; Mgt Bd, Additive Manufacturing Centre, Loughborough Univ., then at Nottingham Univ., 2011–14. Vis. Prof., Engrg Mgt, City Univ., 2006–. Hon. DTech Loughborough, 2008. *Publications:* articles for various jls and mgt confs. *Recreations:* walking, 20th century British art, antique metalware, African tribal art. *Address:* School of Engineering and Mathematical Sciences, City University, Northampton Square, EC1V 0HB.

HUGHES, His Honour David Morgan; a Circuit Judge, 1972–98; *b* 20 Jan. 1926; *s* of late Rev. John Edward Hughes and Mrs Margaret Ellen Hughes; *m* 1956, Elizabeth Jane Roberts; one *s* two *d*. *Educ:* Beaumaris Grammar Sch.; LSE (LLB). Army, 1944–48: Captain, Royal Welch Fusiliers; attached 2nd Bn The Welch Regt; Burma, 1945–47. London Univ., 1948–51; Rockefeller Foundn Fellowship in Internat. Air Law, McGill Univ., 1951–52; called to Bar, Middle Temple, 1953; practised Wales and Chester Circuit; Dep. Chm., Caernarvonshire QS, 1970–71; a Recorder, Jan.–Nov. 1972; Dep. Chm., Agricultural Lands Tribunal, 1972; Mem., Mental Health Review Tribunal, 1989–98. Pres., Council, HM Circuit Judges for England and Wales, 1995. *Recreations:* tennis, cricket, gardening. *Address:* Bryn, Quarry Lane, Kelsall, Cheshire CW6 0PA. *T:* (01829) 751349.

HUGHES, David Richard; journalist; Chief Leader Writer, Daily Telegraph, 2006–13; *b* 3 April 1951; *s* of John Arfon Hughes and Lilian Elvira Hughes (*née* Jones); *m* 1973, Christine O'Brien; two *s*. *Educ:* Cowbridge Grammar Sch.; Univ. of Leicester (BA Hons Hist.). Reporter, Merthyr Express, 1973–76; Leader Writer, 1976–79, Political Corresp., 1979–84, Western Mail; Political Reporter, Daily Mail, 1984–86; Political Corresp., 1986–89, Chief Political Corresp., 1989–92, Sunday Times; Editor, Western Mail, 1992–94; Political Ed., 1994–2005, Leader Writer, 2005–06, Daily Mail. *Recreations:* Rugby, walking in Wales. *Address:* 7 Southfield Gardens, Strawberry Hill, Twickenham TW1 4SZ. *T:* (020) 8892 5726.

HUGHES, Dr David Treharne Dillon, FRCP; Consultant Physician, Royal London (formerly London) Hospital, 1970–96; Director, Respiratory Medicine, Royal Hospitals NHS Trust, 1994–96; Head, Department of Clinical Investigation, Wellcome Research Laboratories, 1978–93; *b* 31 Oct. 1931; *s* of Maj.-Gen. W. D. Hughes, CB, CBE; *m* 1959, Gloria Anna Bailey; one *s* two *d*. *Educ:* Cheltenham Coll.; Trinity Coll., Oxford (BSc, MA); London Hosp. Medical Coll. (BM BCh); RPMS. MRCP 1959, FRCP 1972. Jun. hosp. posts, London Hosp., 1957–59; Capt. RAMC, 1959–61 (jun. med. specialist, BMH Hong Kong); Res. Fellow, Univ. of Calif, 1963–64; jun. hosp. appts, London Hosp., 1964–70. Mem., GMC, 1993–96. Clinical Dir, Atos Origin Coalminers Medical Assessment Process for DTI, 1999–2010. Past President: Internat. Soc. Internal Medicine; Hunterian Soc. Chm., Bd of Govs, Moving Theatre Trust, 1994–2000; Hon. Vice-Pres., Royal Theatrical Fund, 2010–. Master, Soc. of Apothecaries, 1992–93. *Publications:* Tropical Health Science, 1967; Human Biology and Hygiene, 1969; Lung Function for the Clinician, 1981; numerous scientific papers on respiratory function and chest disease. *Recreations:* cricket, rowing, horse racing, theatre. *Address:* 94 Overbury Avenue, Beckenham, Kent BR3 6PY. *T:* (020) 8650 3983; Littleport Farm, Sedgeford, Norfolk PE36 5LR. *T:* (01485) 570955. *Clubs:* Savage, Garrick; Leander (Henley-on-Thames).

HUGHES, Dr (Edgar) John; HM Diplomatic Service, retired; Chairman, Canning House, since 2012 (Trustee, since 2010); *b* 27 July 1947; *s* of William Thomas Hughes and Martha Hughes (*née* Riggs); *m* 1982, Lynne Evans; two *s*. *Educ:* Lewis Sch., Pengam, Wales; LSE (BSc Econ 1969); Lehigh Univ., USA (MA 1970); Pembroke Coll., Cambridge (Univ. of Cambridge Sara Norton Res. Prize in Amer. Hist., 1972; PhD 1973). FCO, 1973–79; on secondment to Cabinet Office, 1979–81; First Sec., UK Delegn to CSCE, Madrid, 1981–82; FCO, 1982–83; First Sec. and Head of Chancery, Santiago, 1983–85, First Sec. (Inf.), Washington, 1985–89; Counsellor and Hd of Aviation and Maritime Dept, FCO, 1990–93; Dep. Hd of Mission, Norway, 1993–97; Change Manager, FCO, 1997–99; on secondment to BAE Systems, 1999–2000; Ambassador to Venezuela, 2000–03; on secondment to Shell, 2003–04; Ambassador to Argentina, 2004–08; non-resident Ambassador to Paraguay, 2005–08. Robin Humphreys Fellow, Inst. for Study of the Americas, Univ. of London, 2008–10. Chm., Marshall Scholarships Commn, 2011– (Comr, 2009–). Chm., LatAmConsult Ltd, 2009–. Sen. Vis. Fellow, LSE, 2011–12. Trustee, Atlantic Coll., Wales, 2010–. FRSA 2010. *Publications:* The Historian as Diplomat (with P. A. Reynolds), 1976; articles in internat. affairs jls. *Recreations:* running, ski-ing, tennis, watching Rugby, reading. *Club:* Rhymney Rugby Football.

HUGHES, Frances Mary Theresa; Senior Partner, Hughes Fowler Carruthers, since 2001; *b* Richmond, Surrey, 15 June 1954; *d* of Noel and Joanna Hughes; *m* 2003, Jonathan Buckeridge; two *s* one *d*. *Educ:* Ursuline Convent, Wimbledon; St Anne's Coll., Oxford (BA 1976; MA 1981). Admitted solicitor, 1981; Solicitor: Theodore Goddard, 1981–83; Bates Wells & Braithwaite, 1983–2001. Vice Pres., Eur. Br., 2003–09, Gov. at Large, Internat. Br., 2005–11, Internat. Acad. of Matrimonial Lawyers. Mediator, 1990–. Gov., Hanover Primary Sch., 1993–98. Co-Founder, Poet in the City, 1999 (Mem., Steering Cttee, 1999–2002); Mem. Bd, Poetry Soc., 2001–05; Trustee: Shelter from the Storm, 2009–11; Arts Patrons Trust, 2010–; Complicité Th., 2014–. FRSA. *Recreations:* viola player, both orchestral and in string quartets, opera, theatre, poetry, Hampstead Ladies Pond. *Address:* Hughes Fowler Carruthers, Academy Court, 94 Chancery Lane, WC2A 1DT. *T:* (020) 7421 8383, *Fax:* (020) 7421 8384. *E:* f.hughes@hfclaw.com. *Club:* Union.

HUGHES, Francine Elizabeth; *see* Stock, F. E.

HUGHES, Very Rev. Geraint Morgan Hugh; Dean of Brecon, 1998–2000; *b* 21 Nov. 1934; *s* of late Ven. Hubert Hughes, Archdeacon of Gower, and late Blodwen Hughes; *m* 1959, Rosemary Criddle; one *s* one *d*. *Educ:* Brecon Grammar Sch.; Keble Coll., Oxford (BA 1958; MA 1963); St Michael's Coll., Llandaff. Nat. Service, RAF, 1953–55. Ordained deacon, 1959, priest, 1960; Curate: Gorseinon, 1959–63; Oystermouth, 1963–68; Rector: Llanbadarn Fawr Group, 1968–76; Llandrindod with Cefnllys, 1976–98; Canon of Brecon Cathedral, 1989–98; RD of Maelienydd, 1995–98. Chaplain, Mid and West Wales Fire Bde, 1996–2009

(Supervisory Chaplain, 2002–09); Mid Wales Regl Chaplain, SJAB, 2003–. Pres., Llandrindod Hosp. Friends, 2002–. Paul Harris Fellow, Rotary Club, 1991. OStJ 2004. *Recreations:* gardening, computing, sheep husbandry, wood turning. *Address:* Hafod, Cefnllys Lane, Penybont, Llandrindod Wells, Powys LD1 5SW. *T:* (01597) 851830.

HUGHES, Rev. Dr Gerard Joseph, SJ; Tutor in Philosophy, since 1998, Master, 1998–2006, Campion Hall, University of Oxford; *b* 6 June 1934; *s* of Henry B. Hughes and Margaret (*née* Barry). *Educ:* Campion Hall, Oxford (MA Greats 1962); Heythrop Coll. (STL 1967); Univ. of Michigan (PhD 1970). Entered Society of Jesus, 1951; ordained priest, 1967; Heythrop College, University of London: Lectr in Philosophy, 1970–98; Head, Dept of Philosophy, 1974–96; Vice-Principal, 1984–98. Hon. DLit London, 2009. *Publications:* Authority in Morals, 1978; (ed) The Philosophical Assessment of Theology, 1987; The Nature of God, 1995; Aristotle on Ethics, 2001; Is God to Blame?, 2007; Fidelity without Fundamentalism, 2010. *Recreations:* classical music, gardening. *Address:* Campion Hall, Oxford OX1 1QS. *T:* (01865) 286111.

HUGHES, Glyn Tegai, MA, PhD; Warden of Gregynog, University of Wales, 1964–89; *b* 18 Jan. 1923; *s* of Rev. John Hughes and Keturah Hughes; *m* 1957, Margaret Vera Herbert (*d* 1996), Brisbane, Qld; two *s.* *Educ:* Newtown and Towyn County Sch.; Liverpool Institute; Manchester Grammar Sch.; Corpus Christi Coll., Cambridge (Schol., MA, PhD). Served War, Royal Welch Fusiliers, 1942–46 (Major). Lector in English, Univ. of Basel, 1951–53; Lectr in Comparative Literary Studies, Univ. of Manchester, 1953–64, and Tutor to Faculty of Arts, 1961–64. Contested (L) Denbigh Div., elections 1950, 1955 and 1959. Mem., Welsh Arts Council, 1967–76; Nat. Governor for Wales, BBC, and Chm., Broadcasting Council for Wales, 1971–79; Member: Bd, Channel Four Television Co., 1980–87; Welsh Fourth TV Channel Authy, 1981–87. Chm., Welsh Broadcasting Trust, 1988–96; Vice-Pres., N Wales Arts Assoc., 1977–94; Chm., Undeb Cymru Fydd, 1968–70. Fellow, Univ. of Wales Aberystwyth, 2000; Hon. Fellow, Univ. of Wales Bangor, 2004. Methodist local preacher, 1942–2012. *Publications:* Eichendorffs Taugenichts, 1961; Romantic German Literature, 1979; (ed) Life of Thomas Olivers, 1979; Williams Pantycelyn, 1983; (with David Esslemont) Gwasg Gregynog: a descriptive catalogue, 1990; Islwyn, 2003; (ed) The Romantics in Wales, 2009; articles in learned journals and Welsh language periodicals. *Recreation:* book-collecting. *Address:* Rhyd-y-gro, Tregynon, Newtown, Powys SY16 3PR. *T:* (01686) 650609.

HUGHES, Prof. Graham Robert Vivian, MD; FRCP; Professor of Medicine, King's College London, since 2005; Head, London Lupus Centre, London Bridge Hospital, since 2005; *b* 26 Nov. 1940; *s* of G. Arthur Hughes and Elizabeth Emily Hughes; *m* 1966, Monica Ann Austin; one *s* one *d.* *Educ:* Cardiff High Sch. for Boys; London Hosp. Med. Coll. (MB BS 1967; MD 1973). Trng posts, London Hosp., 1967–69; Vis. Fellow, Columbia Univ., NY, 1969–70; Sen. Registrar, Hammersmith Hosp., 1970–73; Consultant, Univ. Hosp. of WI, Kingston, Jamaica, 1974; Consultant, and Reader in Medicine, Hammersmith Hosp., 1975–85; Consultant, and Hd, Lupus Arthritis Res. Unit, subseq. Lupus Unit, St Thomas' Hosp., 1985–2005. Ed., Lupus, 1991–; mem., editl bds of numerous jls. Consultant, RAF, 1985–. Life Pres., Lupus UK, 1985; Chm., Hughes Syndrome Foundn, 2001–; Patron, Arthritis Research UK, 2011–. Dr *hc:* Marseilles, 2001; Barcelona, 2004. Rheumatology World Prize, Internat. League against Rheumatism, 1993; Lifetime Achievement Award: Internat. Soc. for Immunology, 2006; European Lupus Soc., 2011; Master, Amer. Coll. of Rheumatol., 2006. *Publications:* Connective Tissue Diseases, 1977, 4th edn 1994; Modern Topics in Rheumatology, 1977; Clinics in Rheumatic Diseases: Systemic Lupus Erythematosus, 1982; Lupus: a guide for patients, 1985; Lecture Notes in Rheumatology, 1986; Problems in the Rheumatic Diseases: lessons from patients, 1988; Phospholipid Binding Antibodies, 1991; Autoimmune Connective Tissue Diseases, 1993; Antibodies to Endothelial Cells and Vascular Damage, 1993; Hughes Syndrome, 1998; Lupus: the facts, 2000; Hughes Syndrome: a patients' guide, 2001; Understanding Hughes Syndrome, 2009; The London Lupus Centre, Book of Lupus: a patients' guide, 2009; Tales of a Flying Doctor, 2011; Hughes Syndrome: highways and byways, 2013; Sjogren's Syndrome in Clinical Practice, 2014; contrib. numerous papers on lupus and related diseases. *Recreations:* tennis, golf, sailing, piano (classical and jazz). *Address:* London Lupus Centre, London Bridge Hospital, 27–29 Tooley Street, SE1 2PR. *T:* (020) 7234 2155. *E:* graham.hughes@hcaconsultant.co.uk.

HUGHES, (Harold) Paul; Director of Finance, BBC, 1971–84; Director, Lazard Select Investment Trust Ltd, 1988–2001; *b* 16 Oct. 1926; *o s* of Edmund and Mabel Hughes; *m* 1955, Beryl Winifred Runacres; one *s* one *d.* *Educ:* Stand Grammar Sch., Whitefield, near Manchester. Certified Accountant. Westminster Bank Ltd, 1942–45; Royal Marines and Royal Navy, 1945–49; Arthur Guinness Son & Co. Ltd, 1950–58; British Broadcasting Corporation: Sen. Accountant, 1958–61; Asst Chief Accountant, Finance, 1961–69; Chief Accountant, Television, 1969–71; Pension Fund Consultant, 1984–89; Chm., BBC Enterprises Ltd, 1979–82; Chm., Visnews Ltd, 1984–85; Chief Exec., BBC Pension Trust Ltd, 1987–89. Chm., Pan European Property Unit Trust, 1987–96; Director: Kleinwort Benson Farmland Trust (Managers) Ltd, 1976–89; Keystone Investment Co. PLC, later Mercury Keystone Investment Trust PLC, 1988–96. *Recreations:* opera, gardening. *Address:* 26 Downside Road, Guildford, Surrey GU4 8PH. *T:* (01483) 569166.

HUGHES, (Harold) Victor, CBE 1989; FRAgS; Principal, Royal Agricultural College, Cirencester, 1978–90, Principal Emeritus 1990; *b* 2 Feb. 1926; *s* of Thomas Brindley Hughes and Hilda Hughes (*née* Williams). *Educ:* Tenby County Grammar Sch.; UCW, Aberystwyth (BSc). FRAgS 1980. Lectr, Glamorgan Training Centre, Pencoed, 1947–49; Crop Husbandry Adv. Officer, W Midland Province, Nat. Agricultural Adv. Service, 1950; Lectr in Agric., RAC, 1950–54; Vice Principal, Brooksby Agricultural Coll., Leics, 1954–60; Royal Agricultural College: Farms Dir and Principal Lectr in Farm Management, 1960–76; Vice Principal and Farms Dir, 1976–78. Hon. MRICS (Hon. ARICS 1984). FIAgrM 1992. *Publications:* articles in learned jls and agric. press. *Recreation:* shooting. *Address:* No 17 Quakers Row, Coates, Cirencester, Glos GL7 6JX.

HUGHES, Henry Andrew Carne M.; *see* Meyric Hughes.

HUGHES, Iain; QC 1996; **His Honour Judge Iain Hughes;** a Circuit Judge, since 2002; Designated Civil Judge for Hampshire, Isle of Wight, Dorset and Wiltshire, since 2003; a Senior Circuit Judge, since 2010; *b* 7 Dec. 1950; *s* of late John Sidney Mather and of Jessica Hamilton-Douglas; *m* 1978, Hon. Claudia Madeleine Ackner, *qv*; one *s* one *d* (and one *s* decd). *Educ:* Moseley Hall Grammar Sch., Cheadle; Univ. of Bristol (LLB); King's Coll. London (MA Dist. War Studies 2011). Called to the Bar, Inner Temple, 1974; Bencher, 2001. Recorder, 2000–02. Chm., Professional Negligence Bar Assoc., 2000–01. *Publications:* (ed) Jackson and Powell on Professional Negligence, 3rd edn 1992, 4th edn 1997. *Recreations:* military history, opera, theatre. *Address:* c/o The Law Courts, Winchester SO23 9EL.

HUGHES, Prof. Ian Edward, PhD; Professor of Pharmacology, University of Leeds, 1999–2006, now Emeritus, and Visiting Professor, Institute of Membrane and Systems Biology, since 2010; *b* Southport, 9 Aug. 1941; *s* of Lawrence Edward Hughes and late Elizabeth Winifred Hughes (*née* Aspinwall); *m* 1966, Patricia Anne Frettsome (*d* 2003); two *s.* *Educ:* Worksop Coll.; Univ. of Leeds (BSc Pharmacy 1962; BSc Pharmacol. 1963; PhD Pharmacol. 1965). FBPhS (FBPharmacolS 2000). Asst Lectr in Pharmacol., Univ. of Leeds, 1966; Sen. Tutor in Pharmacol., Univ. of WA, 1966–68; University of Leeds: Lectr in Pharmacol., 1968–79; Sen. Lectr, 1979–99; Actg Hd of Dept, 1984–90. Dir, UK Centre for Biosci., Higher Educn Acad., 2000–07. Chair, 1998–2010, Mental Health Act Manager, 2010–, Leeds Partnerships NHS Foundn Trust. Panel Chair, Judicial Appts Commn, 2007–. Chair, Speciality Sch. Bds (Medicine, Pathol., Oncol., Radiol.), London Deanery, 2010–14. Member: Fitness to Practise panels, Gen. Social Care Council, 2007–12; Nat. Coll. for Teaching and Leadership (formerly Teaching Agency), 2012–; Health and Care Professions Council, 2012–. Member: Gen. Osteopathic Council, 2003–13; GMC, 2004–08. Vice-Chm., Qualifications Cttee, Bar Council, 2006–11. Mem. and Vice-Chm., Wellcome Trust/MRC UK Biobank Ethics and Governance Council, 2004–11. UK Nat. Teaching Fellowship holder, 2001. Mem., Bd of Mgt, Richmond Fellowship, 2005–14. FHEA 2001. *Publications:* MCQ in Dental Pharmacology and Therapeutics, 1984; Learning Pharmacology through MCQ, 1985, 2nd edn 1990 (Japanese edn 1990); contribs to jls incl. British Jl Pharmacol., Eur. Jl Pharmacol., Jl Pharmacy and Pharmacol., Trends in Pharmacol Scis. *Recreations:* gardening, walking, wood turning. *Address:* Faculty of Biological Sciences, University of Leeds, Leeds LS2 9JT.

HUGHES, Ian Noel, CMG 2014; HM Diplomatic Service, retired; Ambassador to the Republic of South Sudan, 2013–15; *b* 5 Dec. 1951; *s* of Robert John Hughes and Sylvia Betty Hughes (*née* Lewis); *m* 1978, Tereasa June Tinguely; two *s* one *d.* *Educ:* Khormaksar, Aden; St John's, Singapore. FCO, 1971–74; Latin America Floater, 1974–76; Vice-Consul: Kabul, 1976–80; Warsaw, 1980–82; S Pacific Dept, FCO, 1982–85; Second Sec. and Vice-Consul, Tegucigalpa, 1985–88; First Sec. (Political), Berne, 1988–90; News Dept, FCO, 1991–93; First Sec. (Press/Information), New Delhi, 1993–97; Dep. Hd, Near East and N Africa Dept, FCO, 1997–2000; Dep. Hd of Mission and Consul-Gen., Mexico City, 2000–03; Dep. High Comr, Mumbai, 2003–05; Ambassador to Guatemala, El Salvador and Honduras, 2006–09; High Comr to Sierra Leone, and Ambassador (non-resident) to Liberia, 2009–13. *Recreations:* reading, history, travel, playing golf badly.

HUGHES, Prof. Ieuan Arwel, MD; FRCP, FRCPCH, FMedSci; FLSW; Professor and Head of Department of Paediatrics, 1989–2011, Foundation Professor, 2011, Emeritus Professor, 2012, University of Cambridge; Member, Fitzwilliam College, Cambridge, since 2012 (Bye Fellow, 2007–12); Visiting Fellow, PHG Foundation (Foundation for Genomics and Population Health), since 2012; *b* 9 Nov. 1944; *s* of Arwel Hughes and Enid Phillips (*née* Thomas); *m* 1969, Margaret Maureen Davies; two *s* one *d.* *Educ:* Univ. of Wales Coll. of Medicine, Cardiff (MB, BCh, MD); MA Cantab, 1991. MRCP 1971, FRCP 1984; FRCPC 1974; FRCPCH 1997; MRSocMed. Medical Registrar, UCH, 1970–72; Senior Paediatric Resident, Dalhousie Univ., Canada, 1972–74; Endocrine Research Fellow, Manitoba Univ., Canada, 1974–76; MRC Fellow, Tenovus Inst., Cardiff, 1976–78; Consultant Paediatrician, Bristol, 1978–79; Senior Lectr in Child Health, 1979–85, Reader in Child Health, 1985–89, Univ. of Wales Coll. of Medicine, Cardiff; Fellow, Clare Hall, Cambridge, 1994–2007, now Life Mem. Chm., DoH Cttee on Toxicity of Chemicals in Food, Consumer Products and the Envmt (Phytoestrogen Working Gp), 2002–08. President: European Soc. for Paediatric Endocrinology, 1993– (Sec., 1987–92); Assoc. of Clinical Profs of Paediatrics, 1995–99; Section of Endocrinology, RSocMed, 2005–07; Chm., Clinical Cttee, British Soc. for Paediatric Endocrinology and Diabetes, 2009–12; Coordinator, Eur. Soc. of Paediatric Endocrinology-supported Paediatric Endocrine Trng Centres in Africa (Nairobi, Lagos), 2013–; Member: Council, Soc. for Endocrinology; Expert Gp on Androgens and Women in Sport, IAAF, 2010–; Cambridge Univ. Adv. Gp on Africa, 2014–. Trustee, Newlife Foundn, 2012–. Sen. (formerly Perspectives) Ed., Archives of Disease in Childhood, 2003–. Member: Ralph Vaughan Williams Soc., 2000–; Wagner Soc., 2009–. Founder FMedSci 1998; FLSW 2011. Andrea Prader Prize, European Soc. for Paediatric Endocrinology, 2006; James Spence Medal, RCPCH, 2014. *Publications:* Handbook of Endocrine Tests in Children, 1986; 300 articles on paediatric endocrine disorders, steroid biochemistry and mechanism of steroid hormone action; 74 chapters in standard endocrine textbooks. *Recreations:* music (choral singing, bassoon, piano, concert-going), travel, hill walking, cycling, ski-ing. *Address:* 4 Latham Road, Cambridge CB2 7EQ.

HUGHES, Ignatius Loyola; QC 2009; a Recorder, since 2005; *b* Liverpool, 1962; *s* of late Peter Hughes and of Rose Mary Hughes; *m* 1994, Dagmar Steffens; one *s* one *d.* *Educ:* St Anselm's Coll., Birkenhead; Univ. of Newcastle upon Tyne (LLB Hons). Called to the Bar, Middle Temple, 1986; in practice as barrister specialising in criminal law. *Recreations:* ski-ing, surfing, real ale, football. *Address:* Albion Chambers, Broad Street, Bristol BS1 1DR. *T:* (0117) 927 2144, *Fax:* (0117) 926 2569. *E:* Ignatius.hughesqc@albionchambers.co.uk. *Club:* Liverpool Football.

HUGHES, James Ernest, PhD; FREng; Director, 1973–85 and Managing Director and Chief Executive, 1983–84, Johnson Matthey PLC; *b* 3 Nov. 1927; *s* of Herbert Thomas Hughes and Bessie Beatrice Hughes; *m* 1950, Hazel Aveline (*née* Louguet-Layton); three *d.* *Educ:* Spring Grove Sch.; Imperial Coll., London Univ., (BSc, ARSM (Bessemer Medalist); DIC); PhD London 1952. FIMMM; FREng (FEng 1981). Associated Electrical Industries, 1952–63; Johnson Matthey PLC, 1963–85. Vis. Professor, Univ. of Surrey, 1974–78. President: Inst. of Metals, 1972–73; Metals Soc., 1981–82; Instn of Metallurgists, 1982–83. *Publications:* scientific papers in learned jls. *Recreations:* antiques, music, gardening. *Address:* Fieldfayres, 44 Chitterne Road, Codford, Warminster, Wilts BA12 0PG.

HUGHES, Janis; Member (Lab) Glasgow Rutherglen, Scottish Parliament, 1999–2007; *b* 1 May 1958; *d* of Thomas Nish and Janet (*née* Cumming); *m* (marr. diss.). *Educ:* Queen's Park Sch., Glasgow; Western Coll. of Nursing, Glasgow. Nursing: Royal Hosp. for Sick Children, Glasgow, 1980–82; Victoria Infirmary, Glasgow, 1982–86; Belvidere Hosp., Glasgow, 1986–88; Health Service Adminr, Renal Unit, Glasgow Royal Infirmary, 1988–99. Steward, 1980–83, Sec., Glasgow Royal Infirmary Br., 1993–99, NUPE, then UNISON. *Recreations:* reading, cooking.

HUGHES, Jeremy Michael, CBE 2015; Chief Executive, Alzheimer's Society, since 2010; *b* 15 Aug. 1957; *s* of Rev. Martyn L. Hughes and Mary D. Hughes; *m* 1989, Caroline Anne Chappell; two *s.* *Educ:* Harrow Sch.; St Edmund Hall, Univ. of Oxford (BA 1st cl., MA). Man. Dir, LMS Public Relns Ltd, 1983–89; Asst Dir, Nat. Children's Home, 1989–92; Director: Muscular Dystrophy Gp, 1992–93; Leonard Cheshire, 1994–99; BRCS, 1999–2003; Hd, External Relns, Internat. Fedn of Red Cross and Red Crescent Socs, 2003–04; Chief Exec., Breakthrough Breast Cancer, 2005–10. Bd Mem., NCRI, 2007–10. Trustee: Ockenden Internat., 2002–06; Sightsavers Internat., 2006–14; AMRC, 2006–09; Chairman: Nat. Voices, 2009–14 (Jt Chm., 2008–09); Global Alzheimer's and Dementia Action Alliance, 2014–; Co-Chm., Prime Minister's Champion Gp on Dementia Friendly Communities, 2012–. Mem. Adv. Bd, Foundn for Excellence in Business Practice, Geneva, 2003–05. *Publications:* (contrib.) Sweet Charity: the role and workings of voluntary organisations, 1996. *Recreations:* hill-walking, house renovation. *Address:* Alzheimer's Society, Devon House, 58 St Katharine's Way, E1W 1LB. *T:* (020) 7423 3507, *Fax:* (020) 7423 3501. *E:* jeremy.hughes@alzheimers.org.uk.

HUGHES, John; *see* Hughes, Edgar J. and Hughes, Robert J.

HUGHES, Prof. John, PhD; FRS 1993; FBPhS; Director, Parke-Davis Neuroscience Research Centre (formerly Parke-Davis Research Unit), Cambridge, 1983–2000; Chairman and Joint Founder, Cambridge Biotechnology Ltd, 2000–03; Senior Research Fellow, 1983–2009, Emeritus Fellow, 2010, Wolfson College, University of Cambridge; *b* London, 6 Jan. 1942; *s* of Joseph and Edith Hughes; *m* 1967, Madelaine Carol Jennings (marr. diss. 1981); one *d*; three *s* one *d*; *m* 1997, Ann Rosemary Elizabeth, *d* of Joseph and Norma Mutty; one step *s* one step *d.* *Educ:* Mitcham County Grammar Sch. for Boys; Chelsea Coll., London (BSc); Inst. of Basic Med. Sciences, London (PhD). MA Cantab, 1988. Res. Fellow, Yale Univ. Med. Sch., 1967–69; University of Aberdeen: Lectr in Pharmacology, 1969–77; Dep.-Dir, Drug Res. Unit, 1973–77; Imperial College, London University: Reader in Pharmacol

Biochemistry, 1977–79; Prof. of Pharmacol Biochemistry, 1979–82; Vis. Prof., 1983–. Hon. Professor: of Pharmacol., Univ. of Cambridge, 1989–2000 (Vis. Res. Fellow, Dept Pharmacol., 2000–); of Pharmacol., Aberdeen Univ., 1998–. Vice-Pres., Drug Discovery Europe, Warner-Lambert Co., 1987; Vice-Pres. of Res., Warner-Lambert/Parke-Davis Co., 1988–2000; Chm., Scientific Adv. Bd, Synaptica Ltd, 2002–. Member: Substance Abuse Cttee, Mental Health Foundn, 1986–; Scientific Cttee, Assoc. of British Pharmaceutical Industry, 1990–95; Bd, Nat. Inst. for Biol Standards and Control, 1999–; Chm., Res. Cttee, Chronic Fatigue Syndrome (formerly Persistent Virus Disease) Res. Foundn, 1992– (Trustee of the Foundn, 1997–). Mem. Council, Internat. Sch. Neuroscience, 1988–. Editor: Brit. Jl Pharmacol., 1977–83; Brain Res., 1976–; Mem. Editl Bd, Neuropeptides, 2010– (Jt Chief Exec. Ed., 1980–2010). J. Y. Dent Meml Lectr, Soc. for Study of Drug Addiction, 1976; Oliver-Sharpey Lectr, RCP, 1980; Gaddum Lectr and Medal, British Pharmacol Soc., 1982. Mem., Royal Acad. of Medicine, Belgium, 1983. Fellow, Internat. Neuropeptide Soc., 2002; FBPhS (FBPharmacolS, 2008). DMed *hc* Univ. of Liège, 1978; Hon. DSc Aberdeen, 2010. Sandoz Prize, British Pharmacol Soc., 1975; Pacesetter Award, US Nat. Inst. on Drug Abuse, 1977; Lasker Prize, Albert and Mary Lasker Foundn, NY, 1978; Scientific Medal, Soc. for Endocrinology, 1980; W. Feldberg Foundn Award, 1981; Lucien Dautrebande Prize, Fondation de Pathophysiologie, Belgium, 1983; Lilly Award, European Coll. of Neuropsychopharmacology, 1992. *Publications:* Centrally Acting Peptides, 1978; Opioids Past, Present and Future, 1984; (ed jtly) The Neuropeptide Cholecystokinin (CCK), 1989; articles in Nature, Science, Brit. Jl Pharmacol., and Brain Res. *Recreations:* family, friends, gardening, golf. *Address:* Wolfson College, Barton Road, Cambridge CB3 9BB. *E:* john@sbulbeck.com.

HUGHES, John Dennis; Principal, Ruskin College, Oxford, 1979–89 (Tutor in Economics and Industrial Relations, 1957–70, and Vice Principal, 1970–79); *b* 28 Jan. 1927; *m* 1949, Violet (*née* Henderson); four *d. Educ:* Westminster City Sch.; Lincoln Coll., Oxford (MA). Lieut, RAEC, 1949–50. Extramural Tutor, Univs of Hull and Sheffield, 1950–57. Founded, Trade Union Res. Unit, 1970; Dep. Chm., Price Commn, 1977–79. Non-exec. Dir, BRB, 1997–99. Member: Industrial Develt Adv. Bd, 1975–79; Nat. Consumer Council, 1982–94; Ind. Mem., Rail Passengers Council, 2001–05. Governor, London Business Sch., 1979–92. Mem. Council, St George's House, 1978–83; Trustee Dir, Merchant Navy and Airline Officers Assoc., later NUMAST, then Nautilus UK), 1981–2009. *Publications:* Trade Union Structure and Government, 1968; (with R. Moore) A Special Case? Social Justice and the Miners, 1972; (with H. Pollins) Trade Unions in Great Britain, 1973; Industrial Restructuring: some manpower aspects, 1976; Britain in Crisis, 1981; The Social Charter and the European Single Market, 1991; contrib. Eur. Labour Forum jl. *Recreation:* cycling. *Address:* Rookery Cottage, Stoke Place, Old Headington, Oxford OX3 9BX. *T:* (01865) 763076.

HUGHES, John Gerard, PhD; FBCS; FLSW; Vice-Chancellor, Bangor University, since 2010; *b* Belfast, 28 Aug. 1953; *s* of John Hughes and Mary Hughes; *m* 1975, Maura Smyth; two *s*; *m* 2007, Xinyu Wu; one *s*. *Educ:* Queen's Univ., Belfast (BSc 1st Cl. Maths 1975; PhD Theoretical Physics 1978). Lectr, QUB, 1980–84; Scientist, IAEA, 1984–86; Prof. of Information Systems Engrg, 1991–2004, Pro Vice-Chancellor, 2000–04, Univ. of Ulster; Pres., NUI, Maynooth, 2004–10. Chair, Higher Educn Wales, 2011–13; Vice-Chair, Universities UK, 2011–13. FBCS 1996; FLSW 2013. *Publications:* Database Technology, 1985; Object-Oriented Databases, 1991. *Recreations:* football, walking, gardening, history, music. *Address:* Bangor University, College Road, Bangor, Gwynedd LL57 2DG. *T:* (01248) 382001. *E:* john.hughes@bangor.ac.uk.

HUGHES, Jonathan; Chief Executive, Scottish Wildlife Trust, since 2014 (Deputy Chief Executive, 2008–14); *b* Wrexham; *s* of Gwynfor and Meryl Hughes; partner, Emmi Hartikainen; two *s* one *d*. *Educ:* Univ. of Wales, Bangor; Univ. degli Studi di Firenze, Italy (MSc Ecol. 1991). Policy Advr, Forestry Commn England, 2004–06; Hd of Policy, Scottish Wildlife Trust, 2006–08. Mem. Bd, Architecture and Design Scotland, 2010–. Sci. Advr, European Outdoor Conservation Assoc., 2012–; Councillor for IUCN, 2012–. Chm., Postcode Heroes Trust, 2013–. Contributor: Guardian; Scotsman; Huffington Post. *Publications:* contrib. papers to scientific jls. *Recreations:* tennis, theatre, architecture, Italian cinema, comics, opera, table-football. *Address:* (office) Harbourside House, 110 Commercial Street, Leith, Edinburgh EH6 6NF. *T:* (0131) 312 7765. *E:* jhughes@swt.org.uk.

HUGHES, Judith Caroline Anne, (Mrs Inigo Bing); QC 1994; **Her Honour Judge Judith Hughes;** a Circuit Judge, since 2001; a Deputy High Court Judge, since 1997; *b* 13 Oct. 1950; 3rd *d* of Frank and Eva Hughes; *m* 1st, 1977, Mark G. Warwick (marr. diss. 1998); two *d*; 2nd, 2004, Inigo Geoffrey Bing, *qv*. *Educ:* Univ. of Leeds (LLB 1973). Called to the Bar, Inner Temple, 1974 (Bencher, 1994); Asst Recorder, 1991–95; a Recorder, 1995–2001; a Judicial Mem., Parole Bd, 2002–09. Vice Chm., Legal Services Cttee, Bar Council, 1999. Trustee: Gilbert Place Centre, 1995–98; Children's Soc., 1996–2003; Help African Schs to Educate, 2000– (Chm., 2001–); Mem. Cttee, Bottoms Up, 2001–. Hon. Mem., Harrow Rotary Club, 2004. *Publications:* (jtly) Butterworths Guide to Family Law, 1996. *Recreations:* theatre, reading, handicrafts, travel, gardening, philately, opera. *Address:* Principal Registry of the Family Division, First Avenue House, High Holborn, WC1V 6NP. *Club:* Reform.

HUGHES, Staff Sgt Kim Spencer, GC 2009; High Threat Counter Improvised Explosive Device Specialist, since 2010; *b* Münster, 12 Sept. 1979; *s* of Barry Melvin Hughes and Francis Mary Elizabeth Hughes (*née* Trask); one *s*. *Educ:* William Reynolds Jun. Sch.; Thomas Telford Sch.; Cranfield Univ. (Ammunition Technician course Cl. 2). Basic trng, Army Trng Regt Pirbright, 1997; driver, 8 Transport Regt RLC, 1997–2000; Ammunition Technician Cl. 2, 2000–01; Troop Corp., Fallingbostel, Germany, 2001–03; Troop Sgt, Bielefeld, Germany, 2003–07; Instructor: B Team (Jt Service), 2007–09; A Team (High Threat), 2009–10; High Threat IED Disposal Operator, 19 Light Bde, Helmand Province, Afghanistan, 2009; High Threat Counter Terrorist Bomb Disposal Instructor, 2009–10. Captain Webb Medal, Shropshire Soc. in London, 2011. *Recreations:* deer stalking, target shooting, practical shot gun, practical mini rifle, motorcycle.

HUGHES, Lewis Harry, CB 1996; consultant in public sector audit, 2004–10; Deputy Auditor General for Wales, 2000–04; *b* 6 March 1945; *s* of Reginald Harry Hughes, retired MoD official, and Gladys Lilian Hughes; *m* 1975, Irene June Nash, violinist and teacher; one *s*. *Educ:* Devonport High Sch. for Boys; City of London Coll. CIPFA. Exchequer and Audit Dept, 1963–83 (Associate Dir, 1982–83); National Audit Office, 1983–2000: Dir of Health Audit and of Defence Audit to 1990; Asst Auditor Gen., 1991–2000. *Recreations:* golf, music, family life. *Address:* 1 Wood End Road, Harpenden, Herts AL5 3EB. *T:* (01582) 764992. *Club:* Redbourn Golf.

HUGHES, Louis Ralph; Chief Executive Officer, InZero Systems (formerly GBS Laboratories LLC), since 2004; *b* Cleveland, Ohio, 10 Feb. 1949. *Educ:* General Motors Inst., Flint (BMechEng 1971); Harvard Univ. (MBA 1973). General Motors Corp., 1973–2000: financial staff, 1973; Asst Treasurer, 1982; Vice-Pres., of Finance, Gen. Motors of Canada, 1985; Vice-Pres. of Finance, General Motors Europe, Zürich, 1987; Chm. and Man. Dir, Adam Opel AG, Rüsselsheim, 1989; Pres., General Motors Europe, 1992; Exec. Vice Pres., 1992–2000; Pres., Internat. Ops, 1994–98; Pres. and Chief Operating Officer, Lockheed Martin Corp., 2000. C of S, Afghanistan Reconstruction Gp, US Embassy, Kabul, 2004–05. Non-exec. Chm., OutPerformance (formerly Maxager Technology Inc.), 2001–08; non-exec. Dir, ABB Ltd, 2003–. *Recreations:* ski-ing, climbing, cuisine, antiques. *Address:* InZero Systems, 13755 Sunrise Valley Drive, #750, Herndon, VA 20171–4608, USA.

HUGHES, Prof. Medwin, DPhil; DL; FLSW; Vice Chancellor: University of Wales Trinity St David, since 2010; University of Wales, since 2011; *s* of Mildred Emily Hughes, MBE; *m* 1986, Fiona Campbell Gray; three *s*. *Educ:* Llangefni Secondary Sch.; Univ. of Wales, Aberystwyth (BA Hons 1st cl. 1983); Jesus Coll., Oxford (Meyrick Grad. Scholar; Sir John Rhys Scholar; DPhil 1987; Welsh Supernumerary Fellow, 2012–13). DPS. Researcher and lectr, NE Wales Inst. of Higher Educn, 1987–89; Sen. Lectr, Trinity Coll., Carmarthen, 1989–91; Lectr, Univ. of Wales, Cardiff, 1991–94; Trinity College, Carmarthen: Dean, 1994–97; Asst Principal, 1997–98; Dep. Principal, 1998–2000; Principal and Vice Chancellor, 2000–09; Vice Chancellor: Trinity UC, 2009–10; Univ. of Wales, Lampeter, 2009–10; Swansea Metropolitan Univ., 2013. Chairman: Citizenship 2000 Project, 1992–95; Kaleidoscope UK, 2006–12; Vice Chm., Higher Educn Wales, 2012–13. Welsh Language Board: Vice Chm., 1999–2003; Chm., Adv. Cttee, 2003; Chm., Jt Adv. Cttee, Welsh Language Bd and Nat. Assembly of Wales, 1999–2000; Mem., Statutory Welsh Language Bd, 1993–2003; Council of Europe: Mem., UK Intergovtl Educn Delegn, 1989; Project Dir, Minorities and Teacher Educn, 1990–95; Educnl Advr, Citizenship and Educn, 1996–; Rapporteur, Language Learning for Eur. Citizenship, 1997. Member: Wales Digital Coll., 2000–03; Governing Body, Ch in Wales, 2000–05; Nat. Soc. for Educn, C of E, 2000–; Wales Cttee, Duke of Edinburgh Award, 2000–04; Ct, Aberystwyth Univ., 2000–; Ct, Cardiff Univ., 2003–; Graham Commn, Nat. Assembly of Wales, 2005–07; Educn Commn, Ch in Wales, 2007–08; Founding Mem., Welsh American Acad., 2001–. Chm., Llandovery Coll., 2015–. Trustee, Heritage Regeneration Trust, 2012–13. Mem., Swansea Bay City Reg. Bd, 2015–. High Sheriff, Dyfed, April 2016–. Hon. DPA Univ. Rio Grande Ohio, 2001. FRSA 2001; FLSW 2013. DL Dyfed, 2011. *Recreations:* music, reading, walking. *Address:* University of Wales Trinity St David, College Road, Carmarthen Campus, Carmarthen SA31 3EP. *Club:* Oxford and Cambridge.

HUGHES, Merfyn; *see* Hughes, T. M.

HUGHES, Michael, CBE 1998; Chief Investment Officer, Baring Asset Management Ltd, 2000–07 (Director, 1998–2000); *b* 26 Feb. 1951; *s* of late Leonard and Gwyneth Mair Hughes; *m* 1978, Jane Ann Gosham; two *d*. *Educ:* Univ. of Manchester (BA Econs); London School of Economics and Political Science (MSc Econs). Economist, BP Pension Fund, 1973–75; Partner and Chief Economist, de Zoete and Bevan, Stockbrokers, 1976–86; Dir, BZW Securities, 1986–89; Man. Dir, BZW Strategy, 1989–98; Chm., Barclays Capital Pension Fund, 1995–2000. Chm., Financial Panel, Foresight Prog., DTI, 1994–97; Mem., ESRC, 1995–98. Sen. Ind. Dir, JPMorgan Mid-Cap Investment Trust, 2008–; non-exec. Dir, T Bailey Ltd, 2009–. Investment Consultant, Guide Dogs for the Blind, 1995–; Consultant: Seven Investment Mgt, 2008–14; Fiducia Wealth Mgt, 2008–; Sen. Advr, BT Pension Scheme, 2010–12. Mem. Council, Univ. of Essex, 1997–2006. Trustee: Littlegarth Sch., 2006–13; Duntons Charity, 2011–14. FRSA 2005. *Recreations:* horses, gardening. *Club:* National Liberal.

HUGHES, (Michael) Antony; His Honour Judge Antony Hughes; a Circuit Judge, South Eastern Circuit, since 2006; Designated Family Judge, Milton Keynes and Oxford, 2007, and Northampton, since 2014; Deputy High Court Judge, since 2007; *b* 26 May 1953; *s* of late Joseph Frederick Hughes, MA Oxon, BSc, and Doris Anne Hughes, MBE; *m* 1977, Ann Holdsworth; three *d*. *Educ:* King's Sch., Canterbury; Coll. of Law. Articled with Cole & Cole, Oxford, 1973–77; admitted as solicitor, 1977; Partner with Linnell & Murphy, then Linnells, subseq. Borneo Linnells, Solicitors, Oxford, 1979–2006; NP, 1985–2006; Dep. Metropolitan Stipendiary Magistrate, 1993–2000; a Recorder, 2000–06. Hon. Recorder of Milton Keynes, 2012. *Recreations:* walking, growing vegetables, fly fishing. *Address:* Milton Keynes County Court, 351 Silbury Boulevard, Milton Keynes MK9 2DT. *T:* (01908) 302810. *Club:* Lansdowne.

HUGHES, Miranda, PhD; CPsychol; Regional Commissioner, Northern and Yorkshire, Appointments (formerly NHS Appointments) Commission, 2004–12; *b* 18 Oct. 1952; *d* of John and Diana Hughes; *m* 1987, Paul Rayner; two *s* one *d*. *Educ:* Univ. of Keele (BA 1976; PhD 1981); Univ. of Stirling (MSc 1978). CPsychol 1988. Lectr in Psychol., Leeds Univ., 1979–84; Mgt Consultant, KPMG, 1984–87; consultancy and non-exec. appts in private and public sectors, 1987–2001. Chair, W Yorks Probation Bd, 2001–05.

HUGHES, Nigel Howard, FREng; Director of Technology, Smiths Industries Aerospace and Defence Systems Ltd, 1992–97; *b* 11 Aug. 1937; *s* of late William Howard Hughes and of Florence Hughes (*née* Crawshaw); *m* 1962, Margaret Ann Fairmaner; three *d*. *Educ:* St Paul's Sch.; Queen's Coll., Oxford (MA). CEng, FIMechE; FRAeS 1993; FREng (FEng 1995). Pilot Officer, RAF, 1956–58. RAE, Bedford, 1961–73; Head of Radio and Navigation Div., 1973–77, Head of Flight Systems Dept, 1977–80, RAE, Farnborough; MoD Central Staffs, 1980–82; Asst Chief Scientific Advr (Projects), MoD, 1982–84; Dep. Chief Scientific Advr, MoD, 1985–86; Dir, RSRE, 1986–89; Chief Exec., Defence Res. Agency, 1989–91. Mem., 1992–98, Chm., 1998–2003, Airworthiness Requirements Bd, CAA. *Recreations:* pre-1940 Rolls-Royce cars, model engineering, amateur radio, vintage radio and TV, music.

HUGHES, Owain Arwel, CBE 2009 (OBE 2004); orchestral conductor, since 1970; Principal Conductor, Aalborg Symphony Orchestra, Denmark, 1995–99; Principal Associate Conductor, Royal Philharmonic Orchestra, 2003–10; Professor of Music, University of Wales Trinity St David, since 2014; *b* 21 March 1942; *s* of Arwel Hughes and Enid Hughes (*née* Thomas); *m* 1966, Jean Lewis; one *s* one *d*. *Educ:* Howardian High Sch., Cardiff; University Coll., Cardiff (BA Hons); Royal Coll. of Music. Has conducted all major UK orchs and their choirs and also orchs throughout Europe; Associate Conductor: BBC Welsh Symphony Orch., 1980–86; Philharmonia Orch., London, 1985–90; Musical Dir, Huddersfield Choral Soc., 1980–86; Founder and Artistic Dir, Annual Welsh Proms, 1986–; Music Dir, NYO of Wales, 2003–10; Founder and Music Dir, Camerata, Wales, 2005–; Principal Guest Conductor, Cape Town Philharmonic Orch., S Africa, 2007–. Television: Blodeugerdd (series), BBC Wales, 1974–76; Development of English Choral Tradition, 1975; Walton Belshazzar's Feast, 1975; Music in Camera, 1976–86; Much Loved Music Show, 1977–83; Verdi Requiem, 1986; Requiem series, 1987; Easter series, 1988; Mahler Symphony No 8, 1990; Pantycelyn, 1995, Dewi Sant, 2002 (S4C oratorios); Divas, 2002, 2004; Codi Canu (3 series, 2006, 2008, 2010); documentaries: Remembering Wales, 2002; Maestro, 2005; Centenary documentary on Arwel Hughes, 2009. Has made numerous recordings for a range of companies. Vice-Pres., NCH Action for Children, 1988–. Founding Fellow, George Thomas Soc., 1989. FRWCMD (FWCMD 1995). Hon. Fellow: Univ. of S Wales (formerly Poly. of Wales, then Univ. of Glamorgan), 1986; UC, Cardiff, 1991; Trinity Coll., Carmarthen, 2004; UC, Lampeter, 2007; UC, Bangor, 2007. Hon. DMus: CNAA, 1986; Wales, 1991. Gold Medal, Welsh Tourist Bd, 1988; Jubilee Award, Guild of Welsh Music, 2006; Sir Geraint Evans Meml Award, Welsh Music Guild, 2011. *Publications:* My Life in Music (autobiog.), 2012. *Recreations:* Rugby, cricket, golf. *E:* patrick@patrickgarvey.com. *Clubs:* Lord's Taverners; London Welsh Rugby.

HUGHES, Paul; *see* Hughes, H. P.

HUGHES, Paul Michael; General Manager: BBC Symphony Orchestra, and BBC Symphony Chorus, since 1999; BBC Singers, since 2012; *b* Malvern, 16 June 1956; *s* of Charles Bernard Hughes and June Patricia Hughes. *Educ:* King's Sch., Worcester; Trinity Coll. of Music, London (LTCL; GTCL; FTCL; Hon. Fellow, Trinity Laban Conservatoire, 2012). Gen. Manager, Acad. of Ancient Music, 1985–89; Events Manager and Artist Manager, IMG Artists, 1989–93; Chief Exec., Royal Scottish Nat. Orch., 1993–96; Gen. Manager, Monteverdi Choir and Orch., 1997–98. Governor, Board: RSAMD, 1994–96; GSMD,

2007–. Hon. RCM 2012; Hon. FGS 2014. *Recreations:* cooking, hiking, attending the theatre. *Address:* 31 Sabine Road, SW11 5LN. *T:* 07799 625180, *Fax:* (020) 7286 3251. *E:* paulmh@me.com, paul.hughes-bbcso@bbc.co.uk. *Club:* Two Brydges.

HUGHES, Ven. Paul Vernon; Archdeacon of Bedford, since 2003; *b* 4 Aug. 1953; *s* of Reginald Harry Hughes and Eileen Mary Hughes; *m* 1984, Elizabeth Jane Hawkes, (Rev. Canon Liz Hughes, Lead Chaplain, London Luton Airport); one *s* one *d*. *Educ:* Ghyll Royd Prep. Sch., Ilkley; Pocklington Sch.; Central London Poly. (Dip. Urban Estate Mgt); Ripon Coll., Cuddesdon. Residential Property Surveyor, Chestertons, 1974–79. Ordained deacon, 1982, priest, 1983; Curate, Chipping Barnet with Arkley, 1982–86; Team Vicar, Dunstable, 1986–93; Vicar, Boxmoor, 1993–2003. RD Hemel Hempstead, 1996–2003. *Recreations:* music, amateur operatics, walking (country and coast), reading. *Address:* 17 Lansdowne Road, Luton, Beds LU3 1EE. *T:* (01582) 730722, *Fax:* (01582) 877354. *E:* archdbedf@stalbans.anglican.org. *Club:* Lansdowne (Luton).

HUGHES, Peter; *see* Hughes, D. E. P.

HUGHES, Peter John, OBE 2012; HM Diplomatic Service; High Commissioner to Belize, since 2013; *b* 14 Sept. 1953. Entered FCO, 1976; Caribbean Dept, FCO, 1976–78; Islamabad, 1978–80; Vice-Consul, Rome, 1980–83; Warsaw, 1983–85; Desk Officer, Defence Dept, FCO, 1985–87; Dep. Hd of Area, Personnel Ops Dept, FCO, 1987–89; Vice-Consul (Commercial), Sydney, 1989–94; Hd, Korea Section, Far East and Pacific Dept, FCO, 1994–98; Resident Comr, Castries, 1998–2001; Dep. High Comr, Colombo, 2001–05; First Sec. (Pol/Mil.), Kabul, 2005–08; Ambassador to the Democratic People's Republic of Korea, 2008–11; FCO, 2011–13. *Address:* c/o Foreign and Commonwealth Office, King Charles Street, SW1A 2AH.

HUGHES, Peter Thomas; QC 1993; **His Honour Judge Peter Hughes;** a Circuit Judge, since 2007; Judge of the Court of Protection, since 2010; *b* 16 June 1949; *s* of late Peter Hughes, JP, and Jane Blakemore Hughes (*née* Woodward); *m* 1974, Christine Stuart Taylor; one *s* one *d*. *Educ:* Bolton Sch.; Bristol Univ. (LLB Hons). Called to the Bar, Gray's Inn, 1971, Bencher, 2001; Mem., Wales and Chester Circuit, 1971–2007 (Junior, 1991; Treas., 1999–2000), Northern Circuit, 2007–; Asst Recorder, 1988–92; Recorder, 1992–2007; Dep. High Ct Judge, 2001–07; Liaison Judge: Cumbria Magistrates, 2012–; between English and Scottish Judiciary, 2014–. Tutor Judge, Judicial Studies Bd, 2008–12. Chairman: Medical Appeal Tribunals, 1988–93; Registered Homes Tribunals, 1993–2002 (Lead Chm., 2000–02); Mental Health Review Tribunals, 1999–. Member: Gen. Council of the Bar, 1993–98; Council of Circuit Judges, 2011–. Freeman, 2005, Liveryman, 2015, Clockmakers' Co.; Freeman, City of London, 2014. *Recreations:* trying to keep on top of the garden, and travelling to far away places when the garden allows. *Address:* Carlisle Combined Court Centre, Earl Street, Carlisle CA1 1DJ. *T:* (01228) 882120.

HUGHES, Philip; *see* Hughes, R. P.

HUGHES, Philip Arthur Booley, CBE 1982; artist; Director, Thames and Hudson Ltd, since 1991; *b* 30 Jan. 1936; *s* of Leslie Booley Hughes and Elizabeth Alice Hughes (*née* Whyte); *m* 1964, Psiche Maria Anna Claudia Bertini; two *d*, and two step *d*. *Educ:* Bedford Sch.; Clare Coll., Cambridge (BA). Engineer, Shell Internat. Petroleum Co., 1957–61; Computer Consultant, SCICON Ltd (formerly CEIR), 1961–69; Co-Founder, Logica, 1969: Man. Dir, 1969–72; Chm., 1972–90; Dir, 1990–95. Vis. Prof., UCL, 1981–90. Member: SERC, 1981–85; Nat. Electronics Council, 1981–88. Governor, Technical Change Centre, 1980–88. Mem. Council, RCA, 1988–92. Trustee: Design Museum, 1990–96; Inst. for Public Policy Res., 1988–99; Nat. Gall., 1996–2002 (Chm., Bd of Trustees, 1996–99). Official Vis. Artist to Antarctica, British Antarctic Survey, 2001–02. Exhibn of paintings with Beryl Bainbridge, Monks Gall., Sussex, 1972; exhibited: Contemp. British Painting, Madrid, 1983; Contemp. Painters, Ridgeway Exhibn Museum and Art Gall., Swindon, 1986; exhibitions with: Philip Wolfhagen, Sherman Gall., Sydney, 2002; Keith Grant, Churchill Coll., Cambridge, 2003; with Antoine Poncet, Château la Nerthe, Châteauneuf-du-Pape, 2004; one-man exhibitions: Parkway Focus Gall., London, 1976; Angela Flowers Gall., London, 1977; Gal. Cance Manguin, Vaucluse, France, 1979, 1985, 2000; Francis Kyle Gall., London, 1979, 1982, 1984, 1987, 1989, 1992, 1994, 1997, 2000, 2003, 2007, 2010, 2012; Gal. La Tour des Cardinaux, Vaucluse, France, 1993; Mus. of Contemp. Art, Monterrey, Mexico, 1997; Mus. Rufino Tamayo, Mexico City, 1998; Tate St Ives, 2000; V&A Mus., 2001; Musée du Châtillonais, Châtillon-sur-Seine, 2002; Star Gall., Lewes, 2004; Watermill Gall., Aberfeldy, 2005, 2012; Rex Irwin Gall., Sydney, 2005, 2008; Galerie Pascal Lainé, Ménerbes, Vaucluse, France, 2007, 2010, 2014; Charleston, E Sussex, 2008; Pier Arts Centre, Stromness, Orkney, 2008; Galerie Gimpel et Müller, Paris, 2011; Brighton Mus. and Art Gall., 2012; Cromarty Arts Trust, 2012; Univ. of Stirling, 2012; Salisbury and S Wilts Mus., 2012; Jerwood Gall., Hastings, 2014; Kent Univ., 2015; retrospectives: Inverness Mus. and Art Gall., 1990; Ambassade d'Australie, Paris, 1995; Drill Hall Gall., Canberra, 1998, 2002, 2008; Volvo Gall., Sydney, George Adams Gall., Melbourne, 1999; Maison de la Truffe et du Vin, Ménerbes, 2007. CompOR 1985. Hon. Fellow, QMC, 1987. DUniv Stirling, 1985; Hon. DSc: Kent, 1988; London, 2000. *Publications:* Patterns in the Landscape, 1998; Tracks: walking the ancient landscapes of Britain, 2012; articles in nat. press and learned jls on management scis and computing. *E:* studio@philiphughesart.com.

HUGHES, Prof. Richard Anthony Cranmer, MD; FRCP; FMedSci; Professor of Neurology, King's College London (formerly Guy's, King's and St Thomas's School of Medicine, King's College London), 1999–2007, now Emeritus; *b* 11 Nov. 1942; *s* of late Dr Anthony Chester Cranmer Hughes and Lilian Mildred Hughes; *m* 1968, Coral Stephanie Whittaker; one *s* two *d*. *Educ:* Marlborough Coll.; Clare Coll., Cambridge (BA Double First); Guy's Hosp. Med. Sch. (MB BChir (Dist. in Pathol.), MD). MRCP 1970, FRCP 1980. Sen. Lectr, Guy's Hosp. Med. Sch., 1975–87; Prof. of Neurol., UMDS, 1987–98, Hd, Div. of Clin. Neuroscis, GKT, 1999–2001. Vis. Prof. of Neurol., UCL, 2008–. Hon. Consultant Neurologist: Guy's Hosp., 1975–2007; KCH, 1995–2007; Nat. Hosp. for Neurol. and Neurosurgery, 1996–. Ed., Jl Neurol., Neurosurgery and Psychiatry, 1989–96; Founding Co-ordinating Ed., Cochrane Neuromuscular Disease Gp, 1998–2010. Pres., Clinical Neuroscis Section, RSocMed, 2002–03. Mem. Council, Assoc. British Neurologists, 2001–03. Pres., Eur. Fedn of Neurol Socs, 2009–14 (Vice-Pres., 2001–05). Trustee, Muscular Dystrophy UK (formerly Muscular Dystrophy Campaign), 2010–. FMedSci 2000. Gov., Highgate Sch., 1991–95. Hughlings Jackson Lect., RSocMed, 2009. Medal, Assoc. of British Neurologists, 2006. *Publications:* Guillain-Barré Syndrome, 1990; Neurological Emergencies, 1994, 4th edn 2003; European Handbook of Neurological Management, 2006; contrib. numerous articles to New England Jl of Medicine, Lancet, Annals of Neurol., Brain and other jls on neuroimmunol., multiple sclerosis and peripheral neuropathy. *Recreations:* botany, theatre, tennis. *Address:* PO Box 114, National Hospital, Queen Square, WC1N 3BG. *Clubs:* Athenæum, Royal Society of Medicine.

HUGHES, Richard John C.; *see* Carey-Hughes.

HUGHES, Robert Gurth; Chief Executive, Sight for Surrey (formerly Surrey Association for Visual Impairment), since 2013; *b* 14 July 1951; *s* of late Gurth Martin Hughes and Rosemary Dorothy Hughes (*née* Brown), JP; *m* 1986, Sandra Kathleen (*née* Vaughan); four *d*. *Educ:* Spring Grove Grammar Sch.; Harrow Coll. of Technology and Art. Trainee, then Film Producer, BAC Film Unit, 1968–73; News Picture Editor, BBC Television News, 1973–87. Greater London Council: Mem., 1980–86; Opposition Dep. Chief Whip, 1982–86; Opposition spokesman on arts and recreation, 1984–86. MP (C) Harrow West, 1987–97; contested (C) same seat, 1997. PPS to Rt Hon. Edward Heath, 1988–90, to Minister of State, DSS, 1990–92; an Asst Govt Whip, 1992–94; Parly Sec., OPSS, Cabinet Office, 1994–95; Gen. Sec. (subseq. Exec. Dir), Fedn of Ophthalmic and Dispensing Opticians, 1997–2005; Chief Exec., Assoc. of Optometrists, 2005–11. National Chm., Young Conservatives, 1979–80. A Governor, BFI, 1990–92. Hon. DSc Anglia Poly. Univ., 1998. *Recreations:* watching cricket, listening to music.

HUGHES, (Robert) John; journalist; Syndicated Columnist, The Christian Science Monitor, since 1985; Director, International Media Studies Program, 1991–97 (on leave of absence, 1997–2006), Professor of Communications, since 2007, Brigham Young University, Utah; *b* Neath, S Wales, 28 April 1930; *s* of Evan John Hughes and Dellis May Hughes (*née* Williams); *m* 1st, 1955, Vera Elizabeth Pockman (marr diss. 1987); one *s* one *d*; 2nd, 1988, Peggy Janeane Chu; one *s*. *Educ:* Stationers' Company's Sch., London. Reporter, sub-editor, corresp. for miscellaneous London and S African newspapers and news agencies (Natal Mercury, Durban; Daily Mirror, Daily Express, Reuter, London News Agency), 1946–54; joined The Christian Science Monitor, Boston, USA, 1954: Africa Corresp., 1955–61; Asst Foreign Editor, 1962–64; Far East Corresp., 1964–70; Man. Editor, 1970; Editor, 1970–76; Editor and Manager, 1976–79; Pres. and Publisher, Hughes Newspapers Inc., USA, 1979–81, 1984–85; Associate Dir, US Information Agency, 1981–82; Dir, Voice of America, 1982; Asst Sec. of State for Public Affairs, USA, 1982–84; Pres., Concord Communications Inc., 1989–91; Asst Sec.-Gen., UN, 1995 (on leave of absence); special advr on communications to Sec.-Gen., UN, 1996–; Ed., 1997–2006, and Chief Operating Officer, 1999–2006, Deseret Morning News, Salt Lake City. Chairman: Presidential Commn on US Govt Internat. Broadcasting, 1991; Congressional Commn on Broadcasting to China, 1992. Nieman Fellow, Harvard Univ., 1961–62. Pres., Amer. Soc. of Newspaper Editors, 1978–79. Pulitzer Prize for Internat. Reporting, 1967; Overseas Press Club of America award for best daily newspaper or wire service reporting from abroad, 1970; Sigma Delta Chi's Yankee Quill Award, 1977. Hon. LLD Colby Coll., 1978; Hon. DH Southern Utah, 1995. *Publications:* The New Face of Africa, 1961; Indonesian Upheaval (UK as The End of Sukarno), 1967; Islamic Extremism and the War of Ideas: lessons from Indonesia, 2010; Paper Boy to Pulitzer, 2014; articles in magazines and encyclopaedias. *Recreations:* reading, walking. *Address:* Department of Communications, Brigham Young University, Provo, UT 84602, USA. *Clubs:* Foreign Correspondents' (Hong Kong); Overseas Press (New York).

HUGHES, His Honour (Robert) Philip; a Circuit Judge, 1998–2015; Community Relations Judge (North Wales), 2007–15; *b* 4 June 1947; *s* of late Peredur and Myra Hughes; *m* 1973, Kathleen, (Katie), Dolan; two *s*. *Educ:* Valley Sch., Anglesey; Wrekin Coll., Shropshire. Called to the Bar, Gray's Inn, 1971; in practice at the Bar, 1971–98, Hd of Chambers, 1994–98; Asst Recorder, 1990–93, a Recorder, 1993–98, Wales and Chester Circuit; Designated Family Judge at Warrington, 2000–07; Liaison Judge, Powys Magistrates, 2007–13. Asst Boundary Comr, 1996–98. Mem. Cttee, Council of HM Circuit Judges, 2007–15. Mem., Bd of Govs, Glyndŵr Univ. (formerly NE Wales Inst. of Higher Educn), 2008–11 (Hon. Fellow, 2012). *Recreations:* sailing, vegetable gardening, coarse cooking, theatre. *Club:* Holyhead Sailing.

HUGHES, Robert Valentine, CBE 1999; Chairman, Horserace Betting Levy Board, 1998–2009; *b* 13 Feb. 1943; *s* of Robert Canning Hughes and Betty Bertha Hughes; *m* 1968, Eryl Lumley. *Educ:* Univ. of Birmingham (DMS 1976; MSocSc 1979). Review Leader (Performance Rev.), W Midlands Co. Transport and Engrg Dept, 1977–81; Birmingham District Council: Principal Asst to Chief Exec., 1981–83; Develt and Promotion Officer, 1983–84; Town Clerk and Chief Exec., Great Grimsby BC, 1984–88; Chief Exec., Kirklees Metropolitan Council, 1988–98. Pres., SOLACE, 1997–98. DUniv UCE, 1999. *Recreations:* playing the piano, accordion and melodian, cooking, watching Birmingham City FC. *Address:* Highbury, Parish Lane, King's Thorn, Herefordshire HR2 8AT.

HUGHES, Rodger Grant, FCA; Senior Independent Director, Chime Communications plc, since 2007; *b* 24 Aug. 1948; *s* of Eric and Doreen Hughes; *m* 1973, Joan Clare Barker; two *s*. *Educ:* Rhyl Grammar Sch.; Queens' Coll., Cambridge (BA 1970; MA). FCA 1973. PricewaterhouseCoopers (formerly Price Waterhouse): joined 1970; Partner, 1982–2007: i/c Ind. Business Gp, 1988–91; i/c NW Reg., 1991–95; Mem., Supervisory Bd, 1991–95; Hd, Audit and Business Adv. Services, 1995–2002; Mem., Mgt Bd, 1995–2007; Managing Partner, Clients and Mkts, 2002–06. Auditor to Duchy of Cornwall, 1998–2007. Mem., Steering Bd and Chm., Audit Cttee, Companies House, 2008–10; non-exec. Mem. Bd and Chm., Audit Cttee, Simmons & Simmons, 2008–; non-executive Director: Friends Provident plc, 2009; Bell Pottinger Communications USA LLC, 2010–12; Nat. Counties Building Soc., 2013– (Chm., 2015–; Chm., Audit Cttee, 2013–15); Mem., UK Adv. Council, Raab Karcher AG, 1995–97. Mem., Educn Leadership Team, BITC, 2005–08.

HUGHES, Rosemary Ann, (Rosemary, Lady Hughes); DL; President, Special Educational Needs and Disability Tribunal, 2003–08; *b* 30 June 1939; *d* of Rev. John Pain and Barbara Pain; *m* 1964, Sir David Collingwood Hughes, 14th Bt (*d* 2003); three *s* (and one *s* decd). *Educ:* Girton Coll., Cambridge (BA 1960; LLB 1962). Dep. Metropolitan Stipendiary Magistrate, 1990–95. Chm. (pt-time), Special Educnl Needs and Disability Tribunal, 1995–2003. Lay Canon, Ely Cathedral, 2000–13, now Lay Canon Emerita. DL Cambs, 1997. *Recreations:* playing double bass, ski-ing, horse racing, bridge. *Address:* The Coach House, High Street, Wilburton, Ely, Cambs CB6 3RA.

See also Sir T. C. Hughes, Bt.

HUGHES, Prof. Sean Patrick Francis, MS; FRCS, FRCSEd, FRCSI, FRCSEd (Orth); Professor of Orthopaedic Surgery, Imperial College London (formerly at Royal Postgraduate Medical School), University of London, 1991–2006, now Emeritus; Medical Director, Ravenscourt Park Hospital, 2002–04; Hon. Consultant Orthopaedic Surgeon: Imperial College Healthcare NHS Trust (formerly Hammersmith Hospitals), since 1991; Medway Maritime Hospital NHS Trust, since 2007; *b* 2 Dec. 1941; *s* of late Patrick Joseph Hughes and Kathleen Ethel Hughes (*née* Bigg); *m* 1972, Felicity Mary (*née* Anderson); one *s* two *d*. *Educ:* Downside Sch.; St Mary's Hospital, Univ. of London (MB BS, MS). DHMSA. Senior Registrar in Orthopaedics, Middlesex and Royal National Orthopaedic Hosp., 1974–76; Research Fellow in Orthopaedics, Mayo Clinic, USA, 1975; Sen. Lectr, and Dir Orthopaedic Unit, RPMS, Hammersmith Hosp., 1977–79; George Harrison Law Prof. of Orthopaedic Surgery, Univ. of Edinburgh, 1979–91; Chief of Orthopaedic Service, 1995–98, Clin. Dir, Surgery and Anaesthesia, 1998–2002, Hammersmith Hosps NHS Trust; Hd of Surgery, Anaesthesia and Intensive Care, Imperial Coll. Faculty of Medicine, 1997–2004; Dir, Inst. of Musculoskeletal Surgery, Imperial Coll. London, 2004–06. Hon. Civilian Consultant, RN, 1985–2012; Hon. Consultant, Nat. Hosp. for Nervous Diseases, Queen Sq., 1994–2010. Non-exec. Dir, W Middlesex Univ. Hosp. NHS Trust, 1998–2006. Vice President: RCSE, 1994–97 (Mem. Council, 1984–97); Assoc. Res. Circulation Bone, 1994–97; Mem. Council, British Orthopaedic Assoc., 1989–92. Fellow: Brit. Orthopaedic Assoc.; Royal Soc. Med.; Member: Orthopaedic Research Soc.; British Orth. Res. Soc. (Pres., 1995–97); Soc. Internat. de Chirurgie Orth. et de Traumatologie; World Orth. Concern; Internat. Soc. for Study of the Lumbar Spine. Primary Ed., Bone and Joint Jl, 2012–. *Publications:* Astons Short Text Book of Orthopaedics, 2nd edn 1976 to 5th edn (jtly) 1997; Basis and Practice of Orthopaedics, 1981; Basis and Practice of Traumatology, 1983; Musculoskeletal Infections, 1986; (ed jtly) Orthopaedics: the principles and practice of musculoskeletal surgery, 1987; (ed jtly) Orthopaedic Radiology, 1987; papers on blood flow and mineral exchange, fracture healing, bone scanning, antibiotics and infection in bone, external fixation of fractures, surgery of the lumbar and cervical spine. *Recreations:* walking, music. *Address:* 5 Meadow Place, Edensor Road, W4 2SY. *T:* (020) 8995 7708. *Club:* Athenæum.

HUGHES, Shirley, (Mrs J. S. P. Vulliamy), OBE 1999; FRSL; free-lance author/illustrator; *b* 16 July 1927; *d* of Thomas James Hughes and Kathleen Dowling; *m* 1952, John Sebastian Papendiek Vulliamy (*d* 2007); two *s* one *d*. *Educ:* West Kirby High Sch. for Girls; Liverpool Art Sch.; Ruskin Sch. of Art, Oxford. Illustrator/author; overseas edns or distribn in France, Spain, W Germany, Denmark, Holland, Sweden, Aust., NZ, Japan, USA, China and Canada. Lectures to Teacher Trng Colls, Colls of Further Educn, confs on children's lit. and to children in schs and libraries; overseas lectures incl. tours to Aust. and USA. Mem., Cttee of Management, 1983–86, Chm., Children's Writers and Illustrators Gp, 1994–96, Soc. of Authors; Member: Public Lending Right Registrar's Adv. Cttee, 1984–88; Library and Information Services Council, 1989–92. FRSL 2000. Hon. FCLIP (Hon. FLA 1997); Hon. Fellow, Liverpool John Moores Univ., 2004. Hon. LittD: UEA, 2004; Liverpool, 2004. Eleanor Farjeon Award for services to children's lit., 1984. *Publications:* illustrated about 200 books for children of all ages; written and illustrated: Lucy and Tom's Day, 1960, 2nd edn 1979; The Trouble with Jack, 1970, 2nd edn 1981; Sally's Secret, 1973, 3rd edn 1976; Lucy and Tom go to School, 1973, 4th edn 1983; Helpers, 1975 (Children's Rights Other Award, 1976), 2nd edn 1978; Lucy and Tom at the Seaside, 1976, 3rd edn 1982; Dogger, 1977 (Kate Greenaway Medal, 1978; Silver Pencil Award, Holland, 1980; Greenaway Picture Book of All Time, 2007), 4th edn 1980; It's Too Frightening for Me, 1977, 4th edn 1982; Moving Molly, 1978, 3rd edn 1981; Up and Up, 1979, 3rd edn 1983; Here Comes Charlie Moon, 1980, 3rd edn 1984; Lucy and Tom's Christmas, 1981; Alfie Gets in First, 1981, 2nd edn 1982; Charlie Moon and the Big Bonanza Bust-up, 1982, 2nd edn 1983; Alfie's Feet, 1982, 2nd edn 1984; Alfie Gives a Hand, 1983; An Evening at Alfie's, 1984; Lucy and Tom's abc, 1984; A Nursery Collection, 6 vols, 1985–86; Chips and Jessie, 1985; Another Helping of Chips, 1986; Lucy and Tom's 123, 1987; Out and About, 1988; The Big Alfie and Annie Rose Story Book, 1988; Angel Mae, 1989; The Big Concrete Lorry, 1989; The Snowlady, 1990; Wheels, 1991; The Big Alfie Out-of-Doors Story Book, 1992; Bouncing, 1993; Giving, 1993; Stories by Firelight, 1993; Chatting, 1994; Hiding, 1994; Rhymes for Annie Rose, 1995; Enchantment in the Garden, 1996; Alfie and the Birthday Surprise, 1997; The Lion and the Unicorn, 1998; Abel's Moon, 1999; Alfie's Numbers, 1999; The Shirley Hughes Collection, 2000; Alfie Weather, 2001; A Life Drawing: recollections of an illustrator (memoirs), 2002; Annie Rose is My Little Sister, 2002; Olly and Me, 2003; Ella's Big Chance, 2003 (Kate Greenaway Medal, 2004); Alfie Wins a Prize, 2004; A Brush with the Past, 2005; Alfie's World, 2006; Alfie and the Big Boys, 2007; Jonadab and Rita, 2008; Olly and Me 1, 2, 3, 2009; Bye Bye Birdie, 2009; Don't Want to Go!, 2010; The Christmas Eve Ghost, 2010; All About Alfie, 2011; (ed) Mother and Child Treasury, 1998; Hero on a Bicycle, 2012; Bobbo Goes to School, 2012; Alfie's Christmas, 2013; Dixie O'Day in the Fast Lane!, 2012; Dixie O'Day and the Great Diamond Robbery, 2014; Alfie Outdoors, 2015. *Recreations:* looking at paintings, dressmaking, writing books for children. *Address:* c/o Random House Children's Books, 61–63 Uxbridge Road, W5 5SA.

See also E. S. Vulliamy.

HUGHES, Rt Hon. Sir Simon (Henry Ward), Kt 2015; PC 2010; barrister; *b* 17 May 1951; *s* of late James Henry Annesley Hughes and of Sylvia (Paddy) Hughes (*née* Ward). *Educ:* Llandaff Cathedral Sch., Cardiff; Christ Coll., Brecon; Selwyn Coll., Cambridge (BA 1973, MA 1978); Inns of Court Sch. of Law; Coll. of Europe, Bruges (Cert. in Higher European Studies, 1975). Trainee, EEC, Brussels, 1975–76; Trainee and Mem. Secretariat, Directorate and Commn on Human Rights, Council of Europe, Strasbourg, 1976–77. Called to the Bar, Inner Temple, 1974; in practice, 1978–. MP: Southwark and Bermondsey, Feb. 1983–1997 (L, 1983–88, Lib Dem, 1988–97); (Lib Dem) Southwark N and Bermondsey, 1997–2010; (Lib Dem) Bermondsey and Old Southwark, 2010–15; contested (Lib Dem) same seat, 2015. Spokesman: (L), on the environment, 1983–Jan. 1987 and June 1987–March 1988; (Alliance), on health, Jan.–June 1987; (Lib Dem), on education and science, 1988–90, on envmt, 1988–94, on natural resources, 1992–94, on community and urban affairs and young people, 1994–95, on social welfare, 1995–97, on health, 1995–99, on home affairs, 1999–2003, on London, 2003–05, on ODPM affairs, 2005; Lib Dem shadow to Attorney-Gen., 2005–07, to Leader of H of C, 2007–09; Lib Dem spokesman on energy and climate change, 2009–10; Dep. Leader, Lib Dems, 2010–14; Minister of State, MoJ, 2013–15. Mem., Accommodation and Works Select Cttee, 1992–97; Co-Chair, All Party Gp on Youth Affairs. Advocate for Access to Education, 2011–15. Jun. Counsel, Lib. Party application to European Commn on Human Rights, 1978–79; Chm., Lib. Party Adv. Panel on Home Affairs, 1981–83; Vice-Chm., Bermondsey Lib. Assoc., 1981–83. Jt Pres., British Youth Council, 1983–84. President: Young Liberals, 1986–88 (Vice-Pres., 1983–86, Mem. 1973–78); Democrats Against Apartheid, 1988; Lib Dem Party, 2004–08. Pres., Southwark Chamber of Commerce, 1984–87, 2004–07, 2013– (Mem., 1987–); Vice-President: Union of Liberal Students, 1983–88 (Mem., 1970–73); Student Democrats, 1988. Member: the Christian Church; Gen. Synod of Church of England, 1984–85; Southwark Area Youth Cttee; Council of Management, Cambridge Univ. Mission, Bermondsey; Anti-Apartheid Movement. Trustee: Salmon Youth Centre, Bermondsey; Rose Theatre Trust; Gov., St James C of E Sch., Bermondsey. Hon. Fellow, South Bank Univ., 1992. Member to Watch Award, 1985. *Publications:* pamphlets on human rights in Western Europe, the prosecutorial process in England and Wales, Liberal values for defence and disarmament. *Recreations:* music, theatre, listening to the radio, sport (Millwall and Hereford FC, Glamorgan CCC, Wales RFU), travel, the open air. *Address:* 6 Lynton Road, Bermondsey, SE1 5QR.

HUGHES, Stephen Edward; local government consultant, since 2014; *b* 18 Feb. 1954; *s* of Lawrence Edward Hughes and Dorothy Hughes (*née* Merricks); *m* 1991, Marian Nicholls (marr. diss. 2007); one step *s* one step *d*. *Educ:* Lincoln Grammar Sch.; Tettenhall Coll., Wolverhampton; Peterhouse, Cambridge (BA Hons Econs). CPFA 1997. Res. Officer, Internat. Wool Secretariat, 1976–79; Economist, Coventry CC, 1979–81; Principal Officer (Finance), AMA, 1981–84; Dep. Sec., ALA, 1984–90; seconded to Policy Unit, Islington LBC, 1990–92; Principal Asst Dir of Finance, 1992–97, Head of Finance and Property Services, 1997–98, Islington LBC; Divl Manager, Local Govt Taxation, DETR, 1998–99; Dir of Finance, London Bor. of Brent, 1999–2004; Birmingham City Council: Strategic Dir of Resources, 2004–05; Acting Chief Exec., 2005–06; Chief Exec., 2006–14; interim Exec. Dir, LGA, 2015. Strategic Advr on local govt, CIPFA, 2014–; Assoc. Consultant, Bevan Brittan, 2014–. Non-executive Director: Business Link W Midlands, 2008–09; Big Bang Ltd, 2013–; Housing and Care 21, 2014–. Dir, Walterton and Elgin Community Homes Ltd, 2001–04. Mem. (Lab), Didcot Town Council, 1987–95 (Chair, Finance Cttee, 1991–93; Dep. Leader, 1991–95). *Publications:* contribs to various local govt jls. *Recreations:* golf, ski-ing, sailing, chess, Go, surfing the net.

HUGHES, Stephen Skipsey; Member (Lab) North East Region, England, European Parliament, 1999–2014 (Durham, 1984–99); *b* 19 Aug. 1952; *m* 1988, Cynthia Beaver; one *s* one *d*, and one *s* twin *d* by previous marriage. *Educ:* St Bede's School, Lanchester; Newcastle Polytechnic (DMA). European Parliament: Dep. Ldr, Lab. Pty, 1991–93; Substitute Member: Legal Affairs Cttee, 1989–94; Citizens Rights Cttee, 1989–94; Mem., Environment Cttee, 1984–94; former Member: Rules Cttee; Security and Defence Cttee; Mem., Intergroup on Nuclear Disarmament, 1988–2014 (Chm., 1988–90); Chm., 1994–99, Socialist Co-ordinator, 1999–2014, Social Affairs and Employment Cttee; Vice-Pres., Progressive Alliance of Socialists and Democrats Gp, 2009–14. Vice-President: Fedn of Industrial Develt Authorities, 1990–; Assoc. of District Councils, 1990–. *Address:* 19 Oakdene Avenue, Darlington, Co. Durham DL3 7HR.

HUGHES, Sir Thomas (Collingwood), 15th Bt *cr* 1773, of East Bergholt, Suffolk; FRCEM; consultant in emergency medicine informatics and medical educator; Consultant in Emergency Medicine, John Radcliffe Hospital, Oxford, since 2005; Hon. Senior Clinical Lecturer in Emergency Medicine, University of Oxford, since 2008; Partner, Circle Healthcare, since 2011; Medical Director, L2S2 Ltd, since 2014; *b* 16 Feb. 1966; *s* of Sir David Collingwood Hughes, 14th Bt and of Rosemary Ann Hughes, *qv*; *S* father, 2003; *m* 1996, Marina Louise Barbour, MB BS, DPhil, MRCP, FRACP, consultant in paediatric cardiology, Gt Ormond St Hosp., *d* of Richard Barbour, Albany, WA; one *s* two *d*. *Educ:* Oundle; Soham Village Coll.; Hills Road Sixth Form Coll.; Univ. of Sheffield (MB ChB); Univ. of Wales Coll. of Medicine (MSc); Open Univ. (MBA). MRCP. PhD student, Univ. of Melbourne. Consultant in Emergency Medicine, Ballarat, 1999–2004; Dir of Acute Care, Hinchingbrooke Hosp., 2012–13. FRCEM (FCEM 2008). Major Educator Award, Univ. of Oxford, 2009. *Publications:* Adult Emergency Medicine at a Glance, 2011. *Heir:* *s* Alfred Collingwood Hughes, *b* 24 May 2001. *E:* mail@berristead.com.

HUGHES, Thomas George; Sheriff of Tayside, Central and Fife at Dundee, since 2004; *b* 2 Jan. 1955; *s* of Thomas and Patricia Hughes; *m* 1995, Janice Owens; one *s* one *d*. *Educ:* Strathclyde Univ. (LLB). Admitted solicitor, 1979; in practice as solicitor, 1979–2003; pt-time Sheriff, 2003–04. *Recreations:* sport, reading. *Address:* Sheriff Court House, 6 West Bell Street, Dundee DD1 9AD. *T:* (01382) 229961. *E:* sheriffthughes@scotcourts.gov.uk.

HUGHES, Thomas Lowe; Trustee, since 1971, and President Emeritus, since 1991, Carnegie Endowment for International Peace, Washington (President, 1971–91); *b* 11 Dec. 1925; *s* of Evan Raymond Hughes and Alice (*née* Lowe); *m* 1st, 1955, Jean Hurlburt Reiman (*d* 1993); two *s*; 2nd, 1995, Jane Dudley Casey Kuczynski. *Educ:* Carleton Coll., Minn (BA); Balliol Coll., Oxford (Rhodes Schol., BPhil); Yale Law Sch. (LLB, JD). USAF, 1952–54 (Major). Member of Bar: Supreme Court of Minnesota; US District Court of DC; Supreme Court of US. Professional Staff Mem., US Senate Sub-cttee on Labour-Management Relations, 1951; part-time Prof. of Pol Sci. and Internat. Relations, Univ. of Southern California, Los Angeles, 1953–54, and George Washington Univ., DC, 1957–58; Exec. Sec. to Governor of Connecticut, 1954–55; Legislative Counsel to Senator Hubert H. Humphrey, 1955–58; Admin. Asst to US Rep. Chester Bowles, 1959–60; Staff Dir of Platform Cttee, Democratic Nat. Convention, 1960; Special Asst to Under-Sec. of State, Dept of State, 1961; Dep. Dir of Intelligence and Research, Dept of State, 1961–63; Dir of Intell. and Res. (Asst Sec. of State), 1963–69; Minister and Dep. Chief of Mission, Amer. Embassy, London, 1969–70; Mem., Planning and Coordination Staff, Dept of State, 1970–71. Vis. Sen. Res. Fellow, German Histl Inst., Washington, 1997–. Chm., Nuclear Proliferation and Safeguards Adv. Panel, Office of Technology Assessment, US Congress; Chm., Bd of Editors, Foreign Policy Magazine; Sec., Bd of Dirs, German Marshall Fund of US; Dir, Arms Control Assoc. Chairman: Oxford-Cambridge Assoc. of Washington; US-UK Bicentennial Fellowships Cttee on the Arts. Member Bds of Visitors: Harvard Univ. (Center for Internat. Studies); Princeton Univ. (Woodrow Wilson Sch. of Public and Internat. Affairs); Georgetown Univ. (Sch. of Foreign Service); Bryn Mawr Coll. (Internat. Adv. Bd.); Univ. of Denver (Soc. Sci. Foundn); Atlantic Council of US (Exec. Cttee). Member Bds of Advisers: Center for Internat. Journalism, Univ. of S Calif; Coll. of Public and Internat. Affairs, Amer. Univ., Washington, DC; Washington Strategy Seminar; Cosmos Club Jl (Chm.). Member Bds of Trustees: Civilian Military Inst.; Amer. Acad. of Political and Social Sci.; Amer. Cttee, IISS; Hubert H. Humphrey Inst. of Public Affairs; Amer. Inst. of Contemp. German Studies, Washington, DC; Arthur F. Burns Fellowship Program. Mem. Adv. Bd, Fundación Luis Munoz Marin, Puerto Rico. Member: Internat. Inst. of Strategic Studies; Amer. Assoc. of Rhodes Scholars; Amer. Political Sci. Assoc.; Amer. Bar Assoc.; Amer. Assoc. of Internat. Law; Amer. For. Service Assoc.; Amer. Acad. of Diplomacy; Internat. Studies Assoc.; Washington Inst. of Foreign Affairs (Pres.); Trilateral Commn; Assoc. for Restoration of Old San Juan, Puerto Rico; Soc. Mayflower Descendants. Arthur S. Flemming Award, 1965. Hon. LLD: Washington Coll., 1973; Denison Univ., 1979; Florida Internat. Univ., 1986; Hon. HLD: Carleton Coll., 1974; Washington and Jefferson Coll., 1979. KStJ 1984. *Publications:* Perilous Encounters: the Cold War collisions of domestic and world politics: oral history interviews with Thomas L. Hughes, 2011; Oxford After Dinner, 2011; Speaking Up and Speaking Out, 2013; Anecdotage: some authentic retrievals, 2014; occasional contribs to professional jls, etc. *Recreations:* swimming, tennis, music, 18th century engravings. *Address:* 5636 Western Avenue, Chevy Chase, MD 20815, USA. *T:* (301) 6561420. *Clubs:* Yale, Century Association, Council on Foreign Relations (New York); Cosmos, Chevy Chase (Washington).

HUGHES, His Honour (Thomas) Merfyn; QC 1994; a Circuit Judge, 2001–14; Resident Judge, North Wales Crown Courts, 2010–14; a Deputy Circuit Judge, since 2014; *b* 8 April 1949; *s* of John Medwyn Hughes and Blodwen Jane Hughes (*née* Roberts); *m* 1977, Patricia Joan (DL; High Sheriff, Gwynedd, 2002–03), *d* of John Talbot, surgeon, Brentwood; two *s* one *d*. *Educ:* Rydal Sch., Colwyn Bay; Liverpool Univ. (LLB Hons 1970); Council of Legal Educn. Called to the Bar, Inner Temple, 1971; in practice at the Bar, Chester, 1971–94, Temple, 1994–2001; Asst Recorder, 1987–91; a Recorder, 1991–2001; Leading Counsel to Local Authorities, Waterhouse Tribunal on Child Abuse, 1996–98; Pres., Mental Health Review Tribunal, 1999–2011; Member: Parole Bd for England and Wales, 2004–11; Courts Bd for N Wales, 2005–14; N Wales Probation Bd, 2005–10. Chm., Chester Bar Cttee, 1999–2001; Mem., Wales and Chester Circuit Mgt Bd, 1999–2001. Contested (Lab) Caernarfon, 1979. *Recreations:* sailing, watching Rugby, golf. *Clubs:* Royal Anglesey Yacht; Bangor Rugby Union Football (Pres., 2012–).

HUGHES, Sir Trevor (Poulton), KCB 1982 (CB 1974); FICE; Permanent Secretary, Welsh Office, 1980–85; *b* 28 Sept. 1925; *y s* of late Rev. John Evan and Mary Grace Hughes; *m* 1st, 1950, Mary Ruth Walwyn (marr. diss.); two *s*; 2nd, 1978, Barbara June Davison. *Educ:* Ruthin Sch. RE, 1945–48, Captain 13 Field Survey Co. Municipal engineering, 1948–61; Min. of Transport, 1961–62; Min. of Housing and Local Govt: Engineering Inspectorate, 1962–70; Dep. Chief Engineer, 1970–71; Dir, 1971–72 and Dir-Gen., 1972–74, Water Engineering, DoE; Dep. Sec., DoE, 1974–77; Dep. Sec., Dept of Transport, 1977–80. Mem., British Waterways Bd, 1985–88. Chairman: Building and Civil Engrg Holidays Scheme Mgt Ltd, 1987–99; Building and Civil Engrg Benefits Scheme Trustee Ltd, 1987–99. Vice-Chm., Public Works Congress Council, 1975–89, Chm., 1989–91. Chief British Deleg., Perm. Internat. Assoc. of Navigation Congresses, 1985–91; Mem., Water Panel, Monopolies and Mergers Commn, 1991–97. A Vice-Pres., ICE, 1984–86. Hon. Fellow, Univ. of Glamorgan (formerly Poly. of Wales), 1986. Hon. FCIWEM. *Recreations:* music, gardening, reading. *Address:* Clearwell, 13 Brambleton Avenue, Farnham, Surrey GU9 8RA. *T:* (01252) 714246.

HUGHES, Victor; *see* Hughes, H. V.

HUGHES, William Frederick, CBE 2009; QPM 2001; Chief Executive Officer, Probimus Ltd, since 2013; Director General, Serious Organised Crime Agency, 2006–10 (Director General designate, 2004–06); *b* Aug. 1950. *Educ:* Univ. of Aston in Birmingham (BSc Hons Mech. Engrg 1973). PC to Supt, Thames Valley Police, 1975–91; Asst Chief Constable, W Yorks Police, 1991–97; Dep. Chief Constable, Herts Constabulary, 1997–2000; Dir Gen., Nat. Crime Squad, 2000–06; seconded to SOCA, 2004. Internat. Dir, Bluelight Global Solutions Ltd, 2010–12. *Recreations:* aviation, personal computers, music.

HUGHES, William Lloyd; QC 2013; *b* 26 Nov. 1964; *s* of Dr Gwilym Hughes and Maureen Anne Hughes (*née* Day); *m* 1994, (Katharine) Louise D'Arcy, QC (*d* 2010); two *d*. *Educ:* Merchant Taylors' Sch., Northwood; Leicester Poly. (BSc Hons Law with Chem.); Inns of Court Sch. of Law. Called to the Bar, Gray's Inn, 1989; in practice as barrister, 1989–. Freeman, City of London, 2013. *Recreations:* being a father to Daisy and Emily and their wonderful company, most sport, particularly Rugby Union, football, cricket, kayaking, swimming, music of Bruce Springsteen, the Clash, the Ramones, attending concerts (eclectic), theatre, cinema. *Address:* 9–12 Bell Yard, WC2A 2JR. *T:* (020) 7400 1800, *Fax:* (020) 7404 1405. *E:* w.hughes@9-12bellyard.com; 9 Park Place, Cardiff CF10 3DP. *T:* (029) 2038 2731. *Clubs:* Watford Football, London Welsh Rugby Football, Surrey County Cricket; United Services Mess (Cardiff).

HUGHES, William Young, CBE 1987; Chairman, Aberforth Smaller Companies Trust plc, 1990–2005; Chief Executive, 1976–98, and Chairman, 1985–98, Grampian Holdings plc; non-executive Chairman, Palm Tree Technology plc, since 2007; *b* 12 April 1940; *s* of Hugh Prentice Hughes and Mary Henderson Hughes; *m* 1964, Anne Macdonald Richardson; two *s* one *d*. *Educ:* Firth Park Grammar Sch., Sheffield; Univ. of Glasgow (BSc Hons Pharmacy, 1963). MPS 1964. Research, MRC project, Dept of Pharmacy, Univ. of Strathclyde, 1963–64; Lectr, Dept of Pharmacy, Heriot-Watt Univ., 1964–66; Partner, R. Gordon Drummond (group of retail chemists), 1966–70; Man. Dir, MSJ Securities Ltd (subsid. of Guinness Gp), 1970–76; Grampian Holdings, Glasgow, 1977–98 (holding co. in transport, tourism and retail). Non-exec. Chm., Fairfax I.S. plc, 2005–12; non-executive Director: Cashbox plc, 2007–10; Frenkel Topping plc, 2007–10. Dir, Royal Scottish Nat. Hosp. and Community NHS Trust, subseq. Central Scotland Healthcare NHS Trust, 1992–97; Mem. Council, Strathcarron Hospice, 2000–. Chairman: CBI Scotland, 1987–89; Prince's Scottish Youth Business Trust, 2000–07; Prince's Trust—Scotland, 2003–07; Trustee, Prince's Trust (UK), 2003–07. Hon. Chm., European Summer Special Olympic Games (1990), Strathclyde, 1988–91. Pres., Right Track (formerly Work Wise), 1994–. Treas., Scottish Conservative Party, 1993–98 (Dep. Chm., 1989–92).

HUGHES HALLETT, Prof. Andrew, DPhil; FRSE; Professor of Economics and Public Policy, George Mason University, since 2006; Professor of Economics, University of St Andrews, since 2007; *b* London, 1 Nov. 1947; *s* of Vice-Adm. Sir (Cecil) Charles Hughes Hallett and Joyce Hughes Hallett; *m* 1982, Claudia Becker; two *s* one *d*. *Educ:* Radley Coll., Abingdon; Univ. of Warwick (BA Hons 1st Cl. 1969); London Sch. of Econs and Pol Sci. (MSc Econ. 1971); Nuffield Coll., Oxford (DPhil 1976). Associate Prof., Erasmus Univ., Rotterdam, 1977–85; David Dale Prof. of Econs, Univ. of Newcastle, 1985–89; Jean Monnet Prof. of Econs, Strathclyde Univ., Glasgow, 1989–2001; Prof. of Econs, Vanderbilt Univ., 2001–06. Vis. Prof. of Econs and Fulbright Scholar, Princeton Univ., 1992–94; Visiting Professor: Univ. of Rome Sapienza, 1986–87, 2006, 2010; Univ. of Paris X, 2002; Univ. of Frankfurt, 2006; Bundesbank Prof., Free Univ. of Berlin, 2005; Faculty Associate, Kennedy Sch., Harvard Univ., 2012–13. Consultant: World Bank; IMF; UNDP; EC; Eur. Central Bank. Mem., Council of Econ. Advrs to Scottish Govt, 2007–; Comr, Scottish Fiscal Commn, 2014–; Advr, Econs and Monetary Cttee, Eur. Parlt, 2015–; consultant to various national central banks and govts. FRSE 2000. *Publications:* Quantitative Economic Policies and Interactive Planning, 1983; Stabilising Speculative Commodity Markets, 1987; Optimal Control, Expectations and Uncertainty, 1989; The Theory of Economic Policy in a Strategic Context, 2012; 210 articles in learned jls on policy design, coordination, monetary union, fiscal policies, monetary policy and debt. *Recreations:* history, beer graduating to malt whisky, blues music. *Address:* School of Public Policy, George Mason University, 3351 N Fairfax, Arlington, VA 22201, USA. *T:* (703) 9932280. *E:* ahughesh@gmu.edu; School of Economics, St Andrews University, Fife KY16 9AJ. *T:* (01334) 462420.

HUGHES-HALLETT, David John, FRICS; chartered surveyor; consultant, since 1999; *b* 19 June 1947; *s* of Peter Hughes-Hallett and Pamela (*née* Marshall); *m* 1976, Anne Mary Wright; two *s* one *d*. *Educ:* Fettes Coll., Edinburgh; Coll. of Estate Mgt, Reading. FRICS 1982. Director: Scottish Landowners' Federation, 1982–89; Scottish Wildlife Trust, 1989–98; main Bd Mem., SEPA, 1995–2002; Bd Mem., 2002–10, Depute Convener, 2006–09, Loch Lomond and Trossachs Nat. Park Authy; Mem., East Areas Bd, 2005–07, Local Advr, 2007–12, SNH; Panel Mem., Waterwatch Scotland, 2006–09; Member: Bd, Office of Scottish Charity Regulator, 2008–; Registration and Conduct Cttee, Scottish Social Services Council, 2010–; adjudication panels, Gen. Teaching Council for Scotland, 2012–; Home Owners Housing Panel and Private Rented Housing Panel, Scottish Govt, 2012–; Ind. Mem. Bd, Public Prosecution Service NI, 2011–. Chm., RICS in Scotland, 1987–88; Chm., Balerno High Sch. Bd, 1994–96. *Recreations:* sailing, cycling, choral singing, Scottish countryside and its wildlife. *Address:* The Old School, Back Latch, Ceres, Fife KY15 5NT. *T:* (01334) 829333. *E:* david@hugheshallett.co.uk.

HUGHES-HALLETT, James Wyndham John, CMG 2012; FCA; Director: John Swire & Sons Ltd, since 2005 (Chairman, 2005–14); Chairman, Clarkson plc, since 2015; *b* 10 Sept. 1949; *s* of late Michael Wyndham Norton Hughes-Hallett and Penelope Ann Hughes-Hallett (*née* Fairbairn); *m* 1991, Lizabeth Louise Hall (marr. diss. 2009); two *d*. *Educ:* Eton Coll.; Merton Coll., Oxford (MA; Hon. Fellow 2007). FCA 1973. Articled Clerk, Dixon, Wilson, Tubbs and Gillett, 1970–73; chartered accountant, 1974–76; various posts in Japan, Taiwan, Hong Kong and Australia, Swire Gp, 1976–2000; Chairman: John Swire & Sons (HK) Ltd, 1999–2004; Cathay Pacific Ltd, 1999–2004; Swire Pacific Ltd, 1999–2004 (Dir, 1995–2014); Director: Cathay Pacific Airways Ltd, 1999–2014; HSBC Hldgs plc, 2005–14. Trustee: Esmée Fairbairn Foundn, 2005– (Chm., 2013–); Dulwich Picture Gall., 2005–12; China Now, 2006–09; Dep. Chm., Attingham Trust, 2013–. Governor: SOAS, Univ. of London, 2005–10; Courtauld Inst., 2008– (Chm., 2012–). Hon. Fellow, Univ. of Hong Kong, 2004. Silver Bauhinia Star (Hong Kong), 2003. *Address:* c/o John Swire and Sons Ltd, Swire House, 59 Buckingham Gate, SW1E 6AJ. *T:* (020) 7834 7717. *Clubs:* Brooks's, Beefsteak; Hong Kong.

See also L. Hughes-Hallett, Sir T. Hughes-Hallett.

HUGHES-HALLETT, Lucy, FRSL; author; *b* London, 7 Dec. 1951; *d* of late Michael Wyndham Norton Hughes-Hallett and Penelope Ann Hughes-Hallett (*née* Fairbairn); *m* 1984, Dan Franklin; two *d*. FRSL 2011. *Publications:* Cleopatra, 1990; Heroes, 2004; The Pike: Gabriele d'Annunzio, 2013 (Samuel Johnson Non-Fiction Prize, 2013; Costa Biography Award, 2013; Duff Cooper Prize, 2013). *Address:* c/o Lutyens & Rubinstein, 21 Kensington Park Road, W11 2EU. *T:* (020) 7792 4855. *E:* felicity@lutyensrubinstein.co.uk.

See also J. W. J. Hughes-Hallett, Sir T. Hughes-Hallett.

HUGHES-HALLETT, Sir Thomas, Kt 2012; DL; Chief Executive, Marie Curie Cancer Care, 2000–12; *b* 28 Aug. 1954; *s* of late Michael Wyndham Norton Hughes-Hallett and Penelope Ann Hughes-Hallet (*née* Fairbairn); *m* 1979, Juliet, *o d* of Col Anthony Rugge-Price; two *s* one *d*. *Educ:* Eton Coll.; Oriel Coll., Oxford (MA Modern Hist. 1974); Coll. of Law. Called to the Bar, Inner Temple, 1975. J. Henry Schroder Wagg & Co. Ltd, 1978–82; Enskilda Securities, 1982–93 (Chief Exec., Enskilda Corp., London, 1991–93); Robert Fleming & Co. Ltd, 1993–2000: Chm., Robert Fleming Securities, 1993–99; Chm., Fleming Private Asset Mgt, 1999–2000. Chairman: End of Life Care Implementation Adv. Bd, DoH, 2009–; End of Life Palliative Care Funding Review, 2010–11; Chelsea and Westminster Hosp. NHS Foundn Trust, 2014–. Mem., Gen. Adv. Council, King's Fund, 2010–. Chairman: English Churches Housing Gp, 2000–04; Michael Palin Centre for Stammering Children, 2002–09. Special Trustee, Great Ormond St Hosp. Children's Charity, 2004–08. DL Suffolk, 2013. *Recreations:* music, tennis, cooking, walking.

See also J. W. J. Hughes-Hallett.

HUGHES JONES, Dr Nevin Campbell, FRS 1985; on scientific staff, Medical Research Council, 1954–88; Fellow of Hughes Hall, Cambridge, 1987–90, now Emeritus; *b* 10 Feb. 1923; *s* of William and Millicent Hughes Jones; *m* 1952, Elizabeth Helen Dufty; two *s* one *d*. *Educ:* Berkhamsted Sch., Herts; Oriel Coll., Univ. of Oxford; St Mary's Hosp. Med. School. MA, DM, PhD; FRCP. Medical posts held at St Mary's Hosp., Paddington, Radcliffe Infirmary, Oxford, and Postgrad. Med. Sch., Hammersmith, 1947–52; Member: MRC's Blood Transfusion Unit, Hammersmith, 1952–79 (Unit transferred to St Mary's Hosp. Med. Sch., Paddington, as MRC's Experimental Haematology Unit, 1960); MRC's Mechanisms in Immunopathology (formerly in Tumour Immunity) Unit, Cambridge, 1979–88. *Publications:* Lecture Notes on Haematology, 1970, 8th edn 2009. *Recreations:* making chairs, walking the Horseshoe Path on Snowdon. *Address:* 65 Orchard Road, Melbourn, Royston, Herts SG8 6BB. *T:* (01763) 260471.

HUGHES-MORGAN, Sir (Ian) Parry (David), 4th Bt *cr* 1925, of Penally, co. Pembroke; *b* 22 Feb. 1960; *e s* of His Honour Maj.-Gen. Sir David John Hughes-Morgan, 3rd Bt, CB, CBE and Isabel Jean Hughes-Morgan (*née* Lindsay); *S* father, 2006; *m* 1992, Julia Katrin, *er d* of R. J. S. Ward; three *d*. *Heir:* *b* Jonathan Michael Vernon Hughes-Morgan [*b* 19 Feb. 1962; *m* 1996, Gail Christine Melling; one *s* one *d*].

HUGHES-PENNEY, Robert Charles; Investment Director, Rathbone Brothers plc, since 1999; *b* Rio de Janeiro, 2 March 1968; *s* of Roger Hughes-Penney and Angela Hughes-Penney; *m* 1998, Elspeth Hoare; two *s* one *d*. *Educ:* Haberdashers' Aske's Sch., Elstree; Manchester Poly. (BSc Hons); RMA Sandhurst. Chartered Fellow CISI 2010. Joined Army, 1990; Lieut 13th/18th Royal Hussars, QMO, 1990–92; Capt., Light Dragoons, 1993; Laurence Keen Ltd, 1993–95; Dir, Rathbone Investment Mgt Ltd, 2003–06. Mem. Council, C&G, 2006–11 (Hon. Mem., 2010–). Trustee: Mercy Ships UK, 1999–2004; City Parochial Foundn, 2004–10 (Vice-Chm., Investment Cttee, 2008–10). Mem., Court of Common Council, 2004–12 (Member: Finance Cttee, 2006–12; Policy and Resources Cttee, 2007–12; Property Investment Bd, 2011–12; Chairman: Investment Cttee, 2011–12; Financial Investment Bd, 2011–12). Mem. Court, Haberdashers' Co., 2008– (Third Warden, 2014–). Gov., Haberdashers' Aske's Sch., Elstree, 2009–. *Recreation:* family. *Address:* Rathbone Investment Management Ltd, 1 Curzon Street, W1J 5FB. *T:* (020) 7399 0000. *E:* Robert.Hughes-Penney@Rathbones.com. *Club:* Cavalry and Guards.

HUGHES-YOUNG, family name of **Baron St Helens**.

HUGHESDON, John Stephen, FCA; Partner, 1977–2004, Consultant, 2004–06, Mazars (formerly Neville Russell); *b* 9 Jan. 1944; *s* of Eric Hughesdon and Olive Mona (*née* Quirk); *m* 1970, Mavis June Eburne; one *s* one *d*. *Educ:* Eltham Coll. ACA 1967, FCA 1977. Articled Clerk, then Manager, Peat Marwick Mitchell, 1962–73; Manager, Neville Russell, 1973–76. Common Councilman, 1991–96, Alderman, 1997–2008, Sheriff, 2004–05, City of London. Liveryman: Co. of Coopers, 1992– (Master, 2006–07); Co. of Chartered Accountants, 2003–12; Freeman: Co. of Parish Clerks, 2001–; Co. of Watermen and Lightermen, 2005–. Trustee: Christ's Hosp. Foundn, 1993–2007 (Trustee, Pension Scheme, 2007–10); British and Foreign Bible Soc., 1997–2012 (Chm., 2010–12; Trustee, Pension Scheme, 2000–); Culham Inst., 2012–. Chm., Southwark Dio. Welcare, 2005–07; Lay Chm., Newbury Deanery Synod, 2010–; Pres., Boys' Bde London Dist, 2005–08; Hon. Treasurer: Girls' Bde Nat. Council for England and Wales, 1979–91; Tear Fund, 1992–96. *Recreations:* family, church, golf. *Address:* 44 Speen Lane, Speen, Newbury, Berks RG14 1RN. *T:* (01635) 43120. *E:* john.hughesdon@hotmail.com. *Club:* City Livery.

HUGHFF, Victor William, FIA; Chief General Manager, Norwich Union Insurance Group, 1984–89; *b* 30 May 1931; *s* of William Scott Hughff and Alice Doris (*née* Kerry); *m* 1955, Grace Margaret (*née* Lambert) one *s* one *d*. *Educ:* City of Norwich School. Served in RAF, 1951–53; commnd in Secretarial Br., National Service List. Joined Norwich Union Life Insce Soc., 1949; Assistant Actuary, 1966; General Manager and Actuary, 1975; Main Board Director, 1981–89. Director: Stalwart Assurance Group, 1989–93; Congregational & General Insurance, 1989–2001; United Reformed Church Ministers' Pension Trust Ltd, 1993–2005; Norwich Centre Projects Ltd, 1994–2006. CCMI. Liveryman, Actuaries' Co., 1990–. Elder of United Reformed Church, 1972–. *Recreation:* bowls. *Address:* 18 Hilly Plantation, Thorpe St Andrew, Norwich NR7 0JN. *T:* (01603) 434517.

HUHNE, Christopher Murray Paul; Chairman, Europe, Zilkha Biomass Energy, since 2013; Strategic Adviser: Anaerobic Digestion and Bioresources (formerly Biogas) Association, since 2013; British Photovoltaic Association; *b* 2 July 1954; *s* of Peter Ivor Paul Huhne and Ann Gladstone Murray; *m* 1984, Vicky Pryce, *qv* (marr. diss. 2011); two *s* one *d*, and two step *d*. *Educ:* Université de Paris-Sorbonne (Certificat 1972); Magdalen Coll., Oxford (BA 1st Cl. Hons PPE 1975). Freelance journalist, India, 1975–76; Liverpool Daily Post and Echo, 1976–77; Brussels Corresp., Economist, 1977–80; Economics Leader Writer, 1980–84, Economics Editor, 1984–90, Columnist, Guardian, 2013–; Business Editor and Asst Editor, Independent on Sunday, 1990–91; Economic Columnist and Business and City Editor, Independent and Independent on Sunday, 1991–94; Founder and Man. Dir, sovereign ratings div., Ibca Ltd, 1994–97; Gp Man. Dir, Fitch Ibca Ltd, 1997–99. Mem. Council, REconS, 1993–98. Contested (SDP/Lib Dem Alliance): Reading E, 1983; Oxford W and Abingdon, 1987. Liberal Democrats: Chair, Press and Broadcasting Policy Panel, 1994–95; Econ. Advr, General Election, 1997; Mem., Econ. Policy Commn, 1998; Mem. Adv. Bd, Centre Forum (formerly Centre for Reform), 1998–; Jt Chair, Policy Panel on Global Stability, Security and Sustainability, 1999–2000; Chairman: Expert Commn on Britain's adoption of Euro, 1999–2000; Commn on public services, 2001–02. MEP (Lib Dem) SE Reg., England, 1999–2005. European Parliament: spokesman: European Lib Dem and Reformist Gp, Econ. and Monetary Affairs Cttee, 1999–2004; Alliance of Liberals and Democrats for Europe, 2004–05; Substitute Mem., Budget Cttee, 1999–2005. MP (Lib Dem) Eastleigh, 2005–Feb. 2013; PC 2010–13. Lib Dem dep. Treasury spokesman, 2005–06, spokesman on the envmt, 2006–07, on home affairs, 2007–10; Sec. of State for Energy and Climate Change, 2010–12. Mem., Standing Cttee, Finance Act, 2005. Mem. Council, Britain in Europe, 1999–2005. Mem. Council, Consumers' Assoc., 2002–04. Vis. Fellow, Nuffield Coll., Oxford, 2009–12. Young Financial Journalist of the Year, 1981, Financial Journalist of the Year, 1990, Wincott Awards. *Publications:* (jtly) Debt and Danger: the world financial crisis, 1984, 2nd edn 1987; Real World Economics, 1990; (jtly) The Ecu Report, 1991; Both Sides of the Coin: the case for the Euro, 1999, 2nd edn 2001. *E:* chris@chrishuhne.org.uk. *W:* www.chrishuhne.org.uk.

HUHNE, Vicky; *see* Pryce, V.

HUISMANS, Sipko; non-executive Director, Imperial Tobacco, 1996–2006; *b* 28 Dec. 1940; *s* of Jouko and Roelofina Huismans; *m* 1969, Janet; two *s* one *d*. *Educ:* primary sch., Holland; secondary sch., Standerton, S Africa; Stellenbosch Univ., S Africa (BA Com). Shift chemist, Usutu Pulp Co. Ltd, 1961–68; Gen. Man., Springwood Cellulose Co., 1968–74; Man. Dir, Courtaulds Central Trading, 1974–80; Dir, 1980–96, Man. Dir, 1982–84, Courtaulds Fibres; Dir, 1984–96, Man. Dir, 1990–91, Chief Exec., 1991–96, Courtaulds PLC; Chairman: Internat. Paints Ltd, 1987–90; Courtaulds Chemical and Industrial Exec., 1988–96; Special Advr to Chm., Texmaco, Indonesia, 1996–2000. Non-exec. Dir, Vickers, 1996; Mem., Supervisory Bd, Reemtsma, 2002–. *Recreations:* motor racing, sailing, competition. *Clubs:* Royal Lymington Yacht, Royal Southampton Yacht.

HULANÌCKI, Barbara, OBE 2012; RDI 2009; Designer, Hu Design Inc., since 2004; *b* Warsaw, Poland, 8 Dec. 1936; *d* of late Witold Hulanicki and Victoria Hulanìcki; *m* 1963, Stephen Charles Fitz-Simon (*d* 1997); one *s*. *Educ:* Brighton Sch. of Art (Fashion). Freelance fashion illustrator, incl. for Women's Wear Daily, Vogue, The Times, Sunday Times, Observer; Founder (with Stephen Fitz-Simon), Biba, London, 1964–76, Biba Cosmetics, 1964–76; opened shop, Barbara Hulanicki, Brazil, 1978; fashion designer for: Cacharel, 1977–80; Fiorucci, 1977–80; Minirock, Japan, 1980–92; Barbara Hulanicki, London, 1980–84; Barbara Hulanicki Cosmetics, worldwide, 1985–87; Fitz & Fitz, NY, 1996; IslandLife Ministore, Miami Beach, 2002; B with G, Miami Beach, 2003; Coccinelle, Italy, 2007–; Top Shop, UK and USA, 2008–10; George, Asda, UK, 2010–; interior designer, 1987–, projects include: Woody's on the Beach, Miami Beach, 1986; Who's in the Grove, Miami, 1988; Sempers, Miami Beach, 1988; Match Club, Bolera Restaurant, Miami Beach, 1989; Marlin Hotel, South Beach, 1990–92 (Miami Design Preservation League Award), 1996 and 1998; Gloria and Emilio Estefan Recording Studio, 1992–93 and Star Island, 1996–97, Miami; Cavalier Hotel, Leslie Hotel, South Beach, 1993; Compass Point Beach Club, Bahamas, 1994–95; The Netherlands, South Beach, 1995 (AIA award, Florida Architects Assoc. award, 1993); Pink Sands Hotel, Bahamas, 1998, 2004–06, 2010–; Coral Sands Hotel, Bahamas, 2004–05, 2006; Goldeneye Develt, Jamaica, 2004; product designer for: Habitat (textiles and wallpapers), 2005–; Graham & Brown (wallpaper and paint collection), 2007–; V&A Mus. (jewellery, scarves and cards), 2007–; Virago Press (book cover), 2008. Hon. Dr Design: Wolverhampton, 2008; Heriot-Watt, 2009; Brighton, 2010. Dress of the Yr Award, Bath Mus. of Costume, 1972; Cosmetic Achievement Lifetime Award, Cosmetic Exec. Women, 2005. *Publications:* From A to Biba (autobiog.), 1983; Disgrace, 1990. *Address:* Hu Design Inc., 1300 Collins Avenue #200, Miami Beach, FL 33139, USA. *T:* (305) 6959966, *Fax:* (305) 6959228. *E:* info@barbarahulanickidesign.com.

HULDT, Prof. Bo Kristofer Andreas; Professor of Strategic Studies, Department of Security and Strategy, Swedish National Defence College, 2002–08, now Emeritus; *b* 24 April 1941; *s* of Bo and Marta Huldt; *m* Ingrid Mariana Neering (*d* 2009); two *d*. *Educ:* Lund Univ., Sweden (PhD Hist.); Augustana Coll., USA (BA); graduate work, Princeton. Asst and Associate Prof. of History, Lund and Växjö Univs, 1974–79; Res. Associate, Secretariat for Future Studies, Swedish Cabinet Office, 1975–78; Swedish Institute of International Affairs: Res. Associate, 1979; Asst Dir, 1983; Dep. Dir and Dir of Studies, 1985; Dir, 1988–97 (on leave of absence, 1992–95); Dir, IISS, 1992–93; Dir, Dept of Security Policy, Strategy and Mil. Hist., Royal Swedish Mil. Staff and War Coll., Stockholm, 1994–95; Prof. of Strategic Studies, 1996, Dir, Dept of Strategic Studies, 1997–2001, Swedish Nat. Defence Coll. Hd, Res. Council, Folke Bernadotte Acad., 2006–. Special Consultant to Swedish Dept of Defence, 1981–82. Pres., Swedish Nat. Defence Assoc., 1997–2000. Member: Swedish Royal Acad. of War Sciences, 1984 (Pres., 2006–10); Swedish Royal Naval Acad., 1991. Editor: Yearbook of Swedish Inst. of Internat. Affairs, 1983–92; Swedish Nat. Defence Coll. Strategic Yearbook, 2002–. *Publications:* Sweden, the United Nations and Decolonization, 1974; (jtly) Sweden in World Society, 1978; World History 1945–65, Norwegian edn, 1982, Swedish and Finnish edns, 1983, Icelandic edn, 1985, French edn, 1995; contribs to learned jls on history, internat. politics and security. *Recreations:* shooting, literature. *Address:* Swedish National Defence College, Box 27805, 11593 Stockholm, Sweden.

HULINE-DICKENS, Frank William, (Frank Dickens); cartoonist, since 1959; writer; *b* 9 Dec. 1931; *s* of William James Charles Huline-Dickens and Lucy Sarah White; one *d* by Maria del Sagrario. *Educ:* Stationers' Co.'s Sch., London. Creator of cartoons 'Bristow', 1960–2002, 'Patto', 2002–04, Evening Standard. Plays: Fantasyland; No to be in England; three series of Bristow, BBC Radio, 1999–2000. *Publications:* 42 books including: Bristow collections, 1980–98; A Curl Up and Die Day (novel), 1980; Three Cheers for the Good Guys (novel), 1984; The Big Big Big Bristow Book, 2001; A Calmer Sutra, 2002; *for children:* Fly Away Peter (with Ralph Steadman), 1961; The Great Boffo, 1969; Boffo and the Great Motor Cycle Race; Boffo and the Great Air Race; Boffo and the Great Balloon Race; Boffo and the Great Cross Country Race; Teddy Pig; Albert Herbert Hawkins, the Naughtiest Boy in the World, 1971, and the Queen's Birthday, and the Space Rocket, 1978, and the Olympics, 1980; (with Raoul Dufy) Il Violino D'Oro. *Recreations:* cycling, painting. *Club:* Unity Cycling (Pres., 2006–08).

HULL, Bishop Suffragan of, since 2015; **Rt Rev. Alison Mary White;** *b* 1956; *d* of Dr Keith Rodney Dumbell, *qv*; *m* 1982, Rt Rev. Francis, (Frank), White, *qv*. *Educ:* St Aidan's Coll., Durham (BA English 1978); Cranmer Hall, Durham; Leeds Univ. (MA Theol. 1994). Ordained deaconess, 1986, deacon, 1987, priest, 1994; non-stip. Minister, St Mary and St Cuthbert, Chester le Street, 1986–89; Hon. Parish Deacon, St John the Evangelist, Birtley, 1989–93; Diocesan Missioner, Dio. of Durham, 1989–93; Dir, Past Studies, Cranmer Hall, Durham, 1993–98; Dir of Ordinands, Durham, 1998–2000; Springboard Missioner, 2000–04; Adult Educn Officer, Dio. of Peterborough, 2005–10; Canon, Peterborough Cathedral, 2009–10; Hon. Canon Theologian, Sheffield Cathedral, 2010–15; Priest-in-charge, St James, Riding Mill, 2011–15; Advr for Spirituality and Spiritual Direction, Dio. of Newcastle, 2011–15. *Address:* Hullen House, Woodfield Lane, Hessle, E Yorks HU13 0ES.

HULL, Prof. Christopher Michael, FRS 2012; Professor of Theoretical Physics, Imperial College London, since 2003 (Head, Theoretical Physics Group, 2007–11); *b* London, 20 April 1957; *s* of Charles Hull and Margaret Hull (*née* Gordon); one *s* one *d*. *Educ:* Haberdashers' Aske's Sch., Elstree; King's Coll., Cambridge (BA 1st Cl. Maths 1979; PhD Maths 1983). Res. Fellow, MIT, 1983–85; Res. Fellow, King's Coll., Cambridge, 1985–87; SERC Advanced Res. Fellow, Imperial Coll. London, 1987–88; Queen Mary College, then Queen Mary and Westfield College, later Queen Mary, University of London: SERC Advanced Res. Fellow, 1988–92; Lectr in Physics, 1992–93; Reader in Theoretical Physics, 1993–95; Prof. of Theoretical Physics, 1995–2003. FInstP. Dirac Medal, Inst. of Physics, 2003. *Publications:* articles on theoretical physics in scientific jls. *Recreations:* music, theatre, cinema, art, hiking, cycling, guitar. *Address:* Blackett Laboratory, Imperial College London, Prince Consort Road, SW7 2AZ. *T:* (020) 7594 7867. *E:* c.hull@imperial.ac.uk.

HULL, Prof. Sir David, Kt 1993; FRCP, FRCPCH; Foundation Professor of Child Health, University of Nottingham, 1972–96; *b* 4 Aug. 1932; *s* of late William and Nellie Hull; *m* 1960, Caroline Elena Lloyd; two *s* one *d*. *Educ:* Univ. of Liverpool (BSc Hons, MB ChB). DCH, DObstRCOG; FRCP 1974; FRCPCH 1996. Lectr in Paediatrics, Oxford, 1963–66; Consultant Paediatrician, Hosp. for Sick Children, London, 1966–72; Sen. Lectr, Inst. of Child Health, Univ. of London, 1966–72. President: Neonatal Soc., 1987–91; British Paediatric Assoc., 1991–94. Hon. FFPH 2000. *Publications:* (with D. I. Johnston) Essential Paediatrics, 1981, 4th edn 1999; (with A. D. Milner) Hospital Paediatrics, 1984, 3rd edn 1997; (with E. F. St J. Adamson) Nursing Sick Children, 1984; (with L. Polnay) Community Paediatrics, 1984, 2nd edn 1993. *Recreations:* gardening, drawing.
See also Derek Hull.

HULL, Air Vice-Marshal David Hugill, FRCP; Dean of Air Force Medicine and Clinical Director, RAF, 1994–96, retired; *b* 21 Aug. 1931; *s* of late T. E. O. and M. E. Hull (*née* Dinsley); *m* 1957, Ann Thornton-Symington; two *d*. *Educ:* Rugby; Trinity Hall, Cambridge; St Thomas' Hosp. MA, MB BChir. Royal Waterloo and Kingston upon Thames Hosps, 1956–57; RAF 1957; Consultant in Medicine, PMRAF Hosp., Akrotiri, 1966–67; RAF Hosp., Cosford, 1967–74; Exchange Consultant, Aeromedical Consultation Service, USAF Sch. of Aerospace Medicine, 1974–77; PARAF Hosp., Wroughton, 1977–82; Consultant Advr in Medicine, RAF, 1983–93; Reader, Clinical Aviation Medicine, RAF IAM, 1981–93. QHS, 1991–96. Lady Cade Medal, RCS, 1973. Hon. Texas Citizen, 1977. OStJ 1997. *Publications:* chapters in books on aviation and aerospace medicine; papers in professional jls. *Recreations:* sailing, gardening, cross-country ski-ing. *Club:* Royal Air Force.

HULL, Prof. Derek, FRS 1989; FREng, FIMMM; Senior Fellow, University of Liverpool, since 1991; Goldsmiths' Professor of Metallurgy, University of Cambridge, 1984–91, now Professor Emeritus; Fellow, Magdalene College, Cambridge, 1984–91; *b* 8 Aug. 1931; *s* of late William and Nellie Hull (*née* Hayes); *m* 1953, Pauline Scott; one *s* four *d*. *Educ:* Baines Grammar School, Poulton-le-Fylde; Univ. of Wales (PhD, DSc). AERE, Harwell and Clarendon Lab., Oxford, 1956–60; University of Liverpool: Senior Lectr, 1960–64; Henry Bell Wortley Prof. of Materials Engineering, 1964–84; Dean of Engineering, 1971–74; Pro-Vice-Chancellor, 1983–84. Dist. Vis. Prof. and Senior Vis. NSF Fellow, Univ. of Delaware, 1968–69; Monash Vis. Prof., Univ. of Monash, 1981; Andrew Laing Lecture, NECInst, 1989. FREng (FEng 1986). Hon. Fellow, University Coll. Cardiff, 1985. Hon. DTech Tampere Univ. of Technology, Finland, 1987. Rosenhain Medal, 1973, A. A. Griffith Silver Medal, 1985, Inst. of Metals; Medal of Excellence in Composite Materials, Univ. of Delaware, 1990. *Publications:* Introduction to Dislocations, 1966, 5th edn 2011; An Introduction to Composite Materials, 1981, 2nd edn 1996; Fractography: observing, measuring and interpreting fracture surface topography, 1999; Celtic and Anglo-Saxon Art: geometric aspects, 2003; numerous contribs to Proc. Royal Soc., Acta Met., Phil. Mag., Jl Mat. Sci., MetalScience, Composites. *Recreations:* golf, music, fell-walking, early Medieval art. *Address:* School of Engineering, University of Liverpool, Liverpool L69 3GH. *Club:* Heswall Golf.
See also Sir David Hull.

HULL, John Folliott Charles, CBE 1993; Chairman, 1997–98, Deputy Chairman, 1976–97 and 1998–99, Land Securities plc; *b* 21 Oct. 1925; *er s* of Sir Hubert Hull, CBE, and Judith, *e d* of P. F. S. Stokes; *m* 1951, Rosemarie Waring; one *s* three *d*. *Educ:* Downside; Aberdeen Univ.; Jesus Coll., Cambridge (Titular Schol.; 1st cl. hons Law; Keller Prize; MA). RA, 1944–48 (attached Royal Indian Artillery, 1945–48). Called to Bar, Inner Temple, 1952, *ad eund* Lincoln's Inn, 1954. J. Henry Schroder Wagg & Co. Ltd, 1957–72, 1974–85: a Man. Dir, 1961–72; Dep. Chm., 1974–77; Chm., 1977–83; Dir, 1984–85; Schroders plc: Dir, 1969–72, 1974–85; Dep. Chm., 1977–85. Director: Lucas Industries plc, 1975–90; Legal and General Assurance Soc., 1976–79; Legal & General Group plc, 1979–90; Goodwood Racecourse Ltd, 1987–93. Dir-Gen., City Panel on Take-overs and Mergers, 1972–74 (Dep. Chm., 1987–99); Chm., City Company Law Cttee, 1976–79. Lay Mem., Stock Exchange, 1983–84. Mem., Council, Manchester Business Sch., 1973–86. *Recreation:* reading 19th century novelists. *Address:* 33 Edwardes Square, W8 6HH. *T:* (020) 7603 0715. *Club:* MCC.
See also Duke of Somerset.

HULL, His Honour John Grove; QC 1983; a Circuit Judge, 1991–2003; *b* 21 Aug. 1931; *s* of Tom Edward Orridge Hull and Marjory Ethel Hull; *m* 1961, Gillian Ann, *d* of Leslie Fawcett Stemp; two *d*. *Educ:* Rugby School; King's College, Cambridge. BA (1st cl. in Mech. Scis Tripos) 1953, MA 1957; LLB 1954. National Service, commissioned RE, 1954–56; called to the Bar, Middle Temple, 1958 (Cert. of Honour, Bar Final), Bencher, 1989; in practice, common law Bar, 1958–91; a Recorder, 1984–91. *Recreations:* gardening, English literature.

HULL, Leslie David; His Honour Judge Leslie Hull; a Circuit Judge, since 2001; *b* 7 Jan. 1950; *s* of Leslie and Irene Hull; *m* Susanna; two *s* one *d*. *Educ:* Cowley Sch., St Helens; Brasenose Coll., Oxford (MA Juris.). Called to the Bar, Middle Temple, 1972 (Harmsworth Schol.); a Recorder, 1988–2001. *Recreations:* sport, music, wine.

HULL, Robert; Director, Consultative Work, European Economic and Social Committee, 2002–06; *b* 23 Jan. 1947; *s* of John Whitfield Hull and Marguerite (*née* Stace); *m* 1972, Christine Elizabeth Biffin; one *s* two *d*. *Educ:* Dame Allan's Sch., Newcastle upon Tyne; Univ. of Leicester (BA Hist. 1968); Manchester Business Sch. (MBA 1973); King's Coll. London/RADA (MA Text and Performance Studies 2007). UKAEA, 1968–69; PO Telecommunications, 1969–71; North of England Develt Council, 1973–74; EC Commission, 1974–79: Customs Service, 1974–76; Ext. Relns, SE Asia, 1976–79; Civil Servant, Scottish Office, 1979–82; European Commission, 1982–98: Ext. Relns, ME, 1982–86; Asst to Dir Gen., Financial Instns and Co. Law, 1986–90; Head, Policy Co-ordination Unit for Envmt and Sustainable Develt, 1990–98; Dir, Common Services Orgn, subseq. Jt Services, Eur. Econ. and Social Cttee and Eur. Cttee of Regs, 1998–2002. Contested (C) Durham, EP elecn, 1989. Chm., Hexham Community Partnership, 2010–; non-executive Director: Queens Hall Arts, 2007–; Théâtre Sans Frontières, 2009–; Five-Quarter Energy, 2010–. Mem. Council, Newcastle Univ., 2006–15. FRSA. *Publications:* various articles on EU ext. relns, financial services, envmt and sustainable develt, lobbying the EU. *Recreations:* sailing, ski-ing, music, theatre, local history. *Address:* Maiden Cross, Allendale Road, Hexham, Northumberland NE46 2DH. *T:* (01434) 606192. *Club:* Travellers.

HULL, Robert David, (Rob), PhD; *b* 17 Dec. 1950; *s* of David Archibald Hull and late Rosalie Joy Hull (*née* Cave); *m* 1973, Sarah, (Sally), Ann, *d* of late Frank Bernard Cockett, FRCS; one *s* one *d*. *Educ:* Royal Grammar Sch., Guildford; Jesus Coll., Cambridge (BA 1st cl. Hons Mathematics; MA; PhD Linguistics 1975). Civil Service Dept, 1974–81; HM Treasury, 1981–82; Dept of Educn and Science, later Dept for Educn, 1982–94; Sec., HEFCE, 1994–98 (on secondment); Dir for Qualifications and Occupational Standards, subseq. for Qualifications and Young People, DFEE, subseq. DFES, 1998–2004. Mem., NIHEC, 1994–98. Chm., E London Advanced Technol. Trng, 2005–13. Chm., On Golden Lane, 2007–10; Mem. Bd, Islington Giving, 2012–. Trustee, Education Action, 2008–10. Governor: Holloway Sch., 1999– (Chm., 2010–); Richard Cloudesley Sch., 2007–10; Prior Weston Sch., 2007–10; Cripplegate Foundn, 2008– (Chair, 2014–15); London Metropolitan Univ., 2010– (Dep. Chm., 2013–). FRSA 2007. *Recreations:* chess, photography, theatre, cinema, walking. *Address:* 27 Myddelton Square, EC1R 1YE. *T:* (020) 7713 5343. *Clubs:* Surrey County Cricket; Cavendish Chess.

HULLAH, Rt Rev. Peter Fearnley; Director, Together for Sudan (Women's Education Partnership), since 2012; *b* 7 May 1949; *s* of late Ralph and Mary Hullah; *m* 1st, 1971, Hilary Sargent Long (marr. diss. 2008); one *s* one *d*; 2nd, 2008, Penelope Ann Bristow. *Educ:* Bradford Grammar Sch.; King's Coll., London (BD, AKC); Makerere Univ., Kampala; Cuddesdon Coll., Oxford. Curate, St Michael and All Angels, Summertown, Oxford, 1974–77; Asst Chaplain, St Edward's Sch., Oxford, 1974–77; Chaplain, 1977–82, Housemaster, 1982–87, Internat. Centre, Sevenoaks Sch.; Sen. Chaplain, King's Sch., Canterbury, 1987–92; Headmaster, Chetham's Sch. of Music, 1992–99; Area Bishop of Ramsbury, 1999–2005; Principal, Northampton Acad., 2005–11. Regl Exec. Dir, United Learning Trust, 2009–11; Gp Exec. Dir Ethos and Values, Nat. Executive, United Learning Trust and United Church Schs Trust, 2011–13. Chm., Chaplains' Conf., 1987–92. Canon, Manchester Cathedral, 1995–99. Archbishops' Advr for Secondary Sch. Chaplaincy, 2001–06; Licensed to officiate, St Martin in the Fields, Dio. of London, 2010. Chm. Trustees, Bloxham Project, 2000–06 (Mem., 1979–99, Chm., 1996–99, Steering Cttee). Feoffee, Chetham's Hosp., 2005–10. Mem. Council, RSCM, 2002–05; Gov., Marlborough Coll., 2000–08; Trustee, Uppingham Sch., 2008–12. FRSA 1993. *Recreations:* nurturing hopeful schools, pilgrimage, music. *Address:* 62 St Margaret's Road, Twickenham TW1 2LP. *Club:* Athenæum.

HULME, Prof. Charles, DPhil; CPsychol, FBPsS; Professor of Psychology, University College London, since 2011; *b* 12 Oct. 1953; *s* of Norman and Edith Hulme; *m* 1995, Margaret Jean Snowling, *qv*; three *d*, and one step *s*. *Educ:* Oriel Coll., Oxford (MA; DPhil 1979). CPsychol 1989; FBPsS 1990. University of York: Lectr in Psychol., 1978–88; Reader,

1988–92; Prof., 1992–2011. *Publications:* Reading Retardation and Multi-sensory Teaching, 1981; (with S. Mackenzie) Working Memory and Severe Learning Difficulties, 1992; (with M. Snowling) The Science of Reading, 2005; (with M. Snowling) Developmental Disorders of Language and Cognition, 2009. *Recreations:* walking, music, wine. *Address:* Division of Psychology and Language Sciences, University College London, Room 210, Chandler House, 2 Wakefield Street, WC1N 1PF.

HULME, Geoffrey Gordon, CB 1984; Chairman, Knowledge Aid for Sierra Leone, 2001–13; *b* 8 March 1931; *s* of Alfred and Jessie Hulme; *m* 1956, Shirley Leigh Cumberlidge (*d* 2003); one *s* one *d*. *Educ:* King's Sch., Macclesfield; Corpus Christi Coll., Oxford (MA, 1st Cl Hons Mod. Langs). Nat. Service, Intelligence Corps, 1949–50; Oxford, 1950–53; Ministry of Health, subseq. Department of Health and Social Security, latterly Department of Health: Asst Principal, 1953–59; Principal, 1959–64; Principal Regional Officer, W Midlands, 1964–67; Asst Sec., 1967–74; Under-Sec., 1974–81; Principal Finance Officer, 1981–86; Dep. Sec., 1981–91; seconded to Public Finance Foundn as Dir, Public Expenditure Policy Unit, 1986–91; consultant, Office of Health Econs, CIPFA, 1991–2001. Trustee: Council for Educn in the Commonwealth, 2001–13; Disabled Living Foundn, 2001–06 (Chm., 2001–06). *Recreations:* most of the usual things, collecting edible fungi. *Address:* 314 Metro Central Heights, SE1 6DB. *E:* g.hulme@ntlworld.com. *Club:* Royal Automobile.

HULME, Margaret Jean; *see* Snowling, M. J.

HULME, Prof. Michael, PhD; Professor of Climate and Culture, King's College London, since 2013; *b* 23 July 1960; *s* of Ralph Hulme and Shelagh Mary Hulme (*née* Close); *m* 1987, Gillian Margaret Walker; one *d*. *Educ:* Madras Coll., St Andrews; Univ. of Durham (BSc); UC, Swansea (PhD 1985). Lectr in Geog., Univ. of Salford, 1984–88; Sen. Res. Associate, 1988–97, Reader, 1998–2002, Prof. of Climate Change (formerly Envmtl Sci.), 2002–13, UEA; Dir, Tyndall Centre for Climate Change Res., 2000–07. Manager, Intergovtl Panel on Climate Change Data Distribution Centre, 1997–2002; Convening Lead Author, Lead Author and Review Ed., UN Intergovtl Panel on Climate Change, 3rd Assessment Report, 2001. Editor-in-Chief, Wiley Interdisciplinary Reviews: Climate Change, 2008–. *Publications:* (ed) Climates of the British Isles, 1997; Climate Change Scenarios for the United Kingdom, 1998, 2nd edn 2002; Imagined Memories and the Seductive Quest for a Family History, 2008; Why we Disagree about Climate Change, 2009; (ed) Making Climate Change Work For Us, 2010; Exploring Climate Change Through Science and In Society, 2013; Can Science Fix Climate Change: a case against climate engineering, 2014; (ed) Climates and Cultures, 6 vols, 2015; contrib. numerous climate-related articles to acad., professional and popular jls. *Recreations:* cricket, modern history, genealogy. *Address:* Department of Geography, King's College London, Strand, WC2R 2LS. *E:* mike.hulme@kcl.ac.uk. *W:* www.mikehulme.org.

HULME, Rev. Paul; Minister, Guildford Circuit, since 2012; *b* 14 May 1942; *s* of Harry Hulme and Elizabeth Hulme; *m* 1976, Hilary Frances Martin; three *s*. *Educ:* Hatfield House, Yorks; Didsbury Theological Coll., Bristol (BA). Minister: Bungay, Suffolk, 1968–70; Brighton, (also Chaplain, Sussex Univ.), 1970–75; Newquay, Cornwall, 1975–79; Taunton, 1979–86; Enfield, 1986–88; Supt Minister, Wesley's Chapel, London, 1988–96; Minister: New River Circuit, N London, 1997–2003; Orpington and Chislehurst Circuit, 2003–12. Duty Chaplain, Westminster Abbey, 1996–. Mem., BBC Churches Religious Adv. Council, 1992–95. Trustee, Joseph Rank Trust, 1991. Freeman, City of London, 1990. *Recreations:* walking, music. *Address:* Epworth, Charterhouse Road, Godalming, Surrey GU7 2AL. *T:* (01483) 414709. *Club:* National Liberal.

HULME, Tom; Design Director, IDEO, since 2008; Founder and Managing Director, openideo.com and oiengine.com, since 2010; *b* London, 27 June 1976; *s* of Phil and Jan Hulme; *m* 2010, Anna; one *s* one *d*. *Educ:* Univ. of Bristol (BSc 1st Cl. Hons Physics); Harvard Business Sch. (MBA; Baker Schol. Award). Man. Dir, Marcos Sportscars, 1998–99; Founder and Man. Dir, Fluid Conditioning Systems, 2000. Gen. Partner, Google Ventures, 2014–. Young Global Leader, World Econ. Foundn, 2012. *Address:* IDEO, White Bear Yard, 144a Clerkenwell Road, EC1R 5DF. *T:* 07932 033553. *E:* thulme@mba2007.hbs.edu.

HULME CROSS, Peter; Member, London Assembly, Greater London Authority, 2004–08 (UK Ind, 2004–05; One London, 2005–08). Computer engr, then trainer. Former Mem., London Fire and Emergency Planning Authy.

HULSE, Christopher, CMG 1992; OBE 1982; HM Diplomatic Service, retired; Ambassador to the Swiss Confederation, and concurrently (non-resident) to the Principality of Liechtenstein, 1997–2001; *b* 31 July 1942; *s* of late Eric Cecil Hulse and Joan Mary Hulse (*née* Tizard); *m* 1966, Dimitra (*d* 2010), *d* of Brig. and Mrs D. Karayannakos, Karayanneïka-Trypi, Sparta, Greece; one *d*. *Educ:* Woking Grammar Sch.; Trinity Coll., Cambridge (BA 1964). Entered Foreign Office, 1964; UN Dept, FO, 1964–67; Third Sec., later Second Sec., Prague, 1967–70; Eastern European and Soviet Dept, FCO, 1970–72; First Sec., Bangkok, 1973; Western European Dept, FCO, 1973–77; UK Delegn to NATO, Brussels, 1977–80; UK Delegn to CSCE Conf., Madrid, 1980–81; Asst Hd, Defence Dept, FCO, 1981–82; Counsellor, NATO Defence Coll., Rome, 1983; Political Counsellor and Consul-Gen., Athens, 1983–88; Hd of Eastern European, subseq. Central European Dept, FCO, 1988–92; Permt Rep., UN, Vienna, 1992–97. *Recreations:* books, music, walking, gardening, carpentry. *Address:* Karayanneïka-Trypi, near Sparta, 23100, Greece.

HULSE, Sir Edward (Jeremy Westrow), 10th Bt *cr* 1739, of Lincoln's Inn Fields; DL; *b* 22 Nov. 1932; *er s* of Sir Westrow Hulse, 9th Bt and his 1st wife Philippa Mabel Hulse (decd) (*née* Taylor, later Lamb); *S* father, 1996; *m* 1957, Verity Ann Pilkington; one *s* one *d*. *Educ:* Eton; Sandhurst. Late Captain, Scots Guards. High Sheriff, Hampshire, 1978; DL Hampshire, 1989. *Recreations:* tennis, shooting. *Heir: s* Edward Michael Westrow Hulse [*b* 10 Sept. 1959; *m* 1986, Doone Brotherton; three *s* three *d*]. *Address:* Topps Farm House, Breamore, Fordingbridge, Hampshire SP6 2BU. *T:* (01725) 512233. *Club:* White's.

HULSE, Dr Russell Alan; Regental Professor and Associate Vice President for Strategic Initiatives, since 2007, and Founding Director, Science and Engineering Education Center, since 2009, University of Texas at Dallas; *b* 28 Nov. 1950; *s* of Alan Earle Hulse and Betty Joan Hulse (*née* Wedemeyer); *m* 2010, Jeanne V. Kuhlman. *Educ:* The Cooper Union, NY (BS Physics 1970); Univ. of Massachusetts, Amherst (MS Physics 1972; PhD Physics 1975; DSc 1994). National Radio Astronomy Observatory, 1975–77; Plasma Physics Lab., Princeton Univ., 1977–2007, Principal Res. Physicist, 1992–2007, Dist. Res. Fellow, 1994. Vis. Prof. of Physics and Sci. Educn, Univ. of Texas at Dallas, 2004–07. Mem. Bd, Battelle Meml Inst., 2006–12. Fellow, Amer. Physical Soc., 1993. (Jtly) Nobel Prize in Physics, 1993. *Publications:* papers in professional jls and conf. procs in fields of pulsar astronomy, controlled fusion plasma physics and computer modeling. *Recreations:* nature photography, bird watching, clay target shooting, hunting, other outdoor activities. *Address:* University of Texas at Dallas, 800 West Campbell Rd, AD 15, Richardson, TX 75080–3021, USA.

HULYER, Douglas, CBiol, FRSB; independent adviser on environment and heritage and on environmental communications and learning; artist and writer; Director, Naturalhistories (consultancy), since 2006; *b* 13 April 1952; *s* of Charles and Florence Hulyer; *m* 1975, Beth Woodward (*d* 2012); two *d*. *Educ:* Colfe's Sch.; Avery Hill Coll. of Educn (Cert Ed Dist.; BEd 1st Cl. Hons London). CBiol, MIBiol, FRSB (FIBiol 2008). Educn Officer, Surrey Wildlife Trust, 1977–84; Wildfowl and Wetlands Trust: Educn Officer, 1984–88; Dir, Educn and Public Affairs, 1988–97; Dir, Conservation Progs, 1997–2005. Member: Council for Envmtl Educn, 1998–2002; Council, English Nature, 2002–06; Bd, Natural England, 2006–14. Member: Commn on Educn and Communication, IUCN, 1996–; Learning Panel, NT, 2008–. Trustee: Nat. Heritage Meml Fund, 2006–13; Heritage Lottery Fund, 2006–12; Earth Trust, 2012– (Chm., 2014–); Woodchester Mansion Trust, 2012–. Vice-Pres., Surrey Wildlife Trust, 2003–. MInstD. *Recreations:* art, gardening, design, music. *Address:* Thornton, Thrupp Lane, Thrupp, Stroud, Glos GL5 2EF. *E:* doug.hulyer@btinternet.com.

HUM, Sir Christopher (Owen), KCMG 2003 (CMG 1996); HM Diplomatic Service, retired; Master of Gonville and Caius College, Cambridge, 2006–12, now Life Fellow; *b* 27 Jan. 1946; *s* of late Norman Charles Hum and Muriel Kathleen (*née* Hines); *m* 1970, Julia Mary, second *d* of Hon. Sir Hugh Park; one *s* one *d*. *Educ:* Berkhamsted Sch.; Pembroke Coll., Cambridge (Foundn Scholar; 1st Cl. Hons; MA; Hon. Fellow 2004); Univ. of Hong Kong; Sch. of Oriental and African Studies, Univ. of London. Joined FCO, 1967; served in: Hong Kong, 1968–70; Peking, 1971–73; Office of the UK Perm. Rep. to the EEC, Brussels, 1973–75; FCO, 1975–79; Peking, 1979–81; Paris, 1981–83; Asst Head, Hong Kong Dept, FCO, 1983–85; Counsellor, 1985; Dep. Head, Falkland Is Dept, FCO, 1985–86; Head, Hong Kong Dept, FCO, 1986–89; Counsellor (Political) and Hd of Chancery, UK Mission to UN, New York, 1989–92; Asst Under-Sec. of State (Northern Asia), 1992–94, (Northern Asia and Pacific), 1994–95; Ambassador to Poland, 1996–98; Dep. Under-Sec. of State and Chief Clerk, FCO, 1998–2001; Ambassador to the People's Republic of China, 2002–05. Dir, Laird, plc, 2006–15. Adv. Cttee, China Policy Inst., Univ. of Nottingham, 2006–; Exec. Cttee, GB-China Centre, 2006– (Vice-Chm., 2013–). Gov., SOAS, 1998–2001; Mem. Council, Cambridge Univ., 2009–12; Syndic, Fitzwilliam Mus., 2008–14; Chm., Cambridge Assessment, 2010–12; Trustee, Young Classical Artists Trust, 2006–14. Hon. Pres., China Assoc. Hon. LLD Nottingham, 2006; Hon. PhD London Metropolitan, 2006. *Recreations:* all the arts, walking, Asia. *Address:* Gonville and Caius College, Cambridge CB2 1TA. *E:* ch407@cam.ac.uk. *Club:* Athenæum.

HUMBLE, James Kenneth, OBE 1996; fair trading consultant, since 1998; *b* 8 May 1936; *s* of Joseph Humble and Alice (*née* Rhodes); *m* 1962, Freda (*née* Holden); three *d*. Served RN, 1954–56. Weights and Measures, Oldham, 1952–62; Fed. Min. of Commerce and Industry, Nigeria, 1962–66; Chief Trading Standards Officer, Croydon, 1966–74; Asst Dir of Consumer Affairs, Office of Fair Trading, 1974–79; Dir of Metrication Bd, 1979–80; Dir, Nat. Metrological Co-ordinating Unit, 1980–87; Chief Exec., Local Authorities Co-ordinating Body on Food and Trading Standards, 1982–98. Non-exec. Dir, NCC, 1997–2002. Sec., Trade Descriptions Cttee, Inst. of Trading Standards, 1968–73; Examr, Dip. in Trading Standards, 1978–94; Vice Chm., Council of Europe Cttee of Experts on Consumer Protection, 1976–79. Member: Council for Vehicle Servicing and Repair, 1972–75; Methven Cttee, 1974–76; OECD Cttee, Air Package Tours, 1978–79; BSI Divl Council, 1976–79; Eden Cttee on Metrology, 1984; Food Codes Cttee, DoH, 1998–; Group Chairman: World Conf. on Safety, Sweden, 1989; Yugoslavian Conf. on Fair Trading, 1992; Member: European Consumer Product Safety Assoc., 1987–97; W European Legal Metrology Co-operation, 1989–98; European Forum Food Law Enforcement Practitioners, 1990–98; Consumer Congress, 1998–2002. Non-executive Director: Wine Standards Bd, 1999–2003; Dignity in Dying, 2007– (Chm., Orgnl Develt Cttee, 2007–). Organiser, First European Metrology Symposium, 1988. Conf. papers to USA Western States Conf. on Weights and Measures, 1989. FITSA 1974– (Vice Pres., 1997–; Orator, 1998–); FRSA 1996. Trustee, Golden Leaves, 2002–. Rugby, Devonport Services, 1954–56; Captain, Oldham Rugby Union, 1957–59; Professional Rugby, Leigh RFC, 1959–65. *Publications:* (contrib.) Marketing and the Consumer Movement, 1978; European Inspection, Protection and Control, 1990; A Grandad's Life, 2008; (jtly) A History of the Trading Standards Institute, 2014; contrib. to various jls. *Recreations:* bridge, golf, opera. *Address:* 153 Upper Selsdon Road, Croydon, Surrey CR2 0DU. *T:* (020) 8657 6170.

HUMBLE, (Jovanka) Joan; JP; *b* 3 March 1951; *d* of John and Dora Piplica; *m* 1972, Paul Nugent Humble; two *d*. *Educ:* Lancaster Univ. (BA Hons). DHSS, 1972–73; Inland Revenue, 1973–77. Mem. (Lab), Lancs CC, 1985–97. MP (Lab) Blackpool N and Fleetwood, 1997–2010. Chair, Blackpool FC Rangers Junior Football Club, 2011–; Mem., Adv. Bd, Blackpool Salvation Army Bridge project, 2012–; Chm., Blackpool Civic Trust, 2013– (Treas., 2012–13). JP Preston, 1993. *Recreations:* gardening, cooking, reading.

HUME, Gary, RA 2001; artist; *b* 9 May 1962; *m* Georgie Hopton. *Educ:* Goldsmiths' Coll., Univ. of London (BA 1988). Prof. of Drawing, RA, 2004. *Solo exhibitions* include: Karsten Schubert Ltd, 1989, 1991; Galerie Tanja Grünert, Cologne, 1991, 1993; Matthew Marks Gall., NY, 1992, 1994, 1997, 1998, 2001, 2005, 2009; White Cube, ICA, Kunsthalle Bern, 1995; Galleria il Ponte, Rome, 1996; Hayward Gall., Sadler's Wells Th., 1998; Whitechapel Art Gall., Dean Gall., Edinburgh, 1999; La Caixa, Barcelona, 2000; White Cube, 2002; MOMA, Dublin, 2003; MOMA, Oxford, 2008; New Art Centre, Salisbury, 2010; White Cube, Leeds Art Gall., 2012; *group exhibitions* include: Karsten Schubert Ltd, 1990, 1992, 1993, 1995; British Art Show, McLellan Galls, Glasgow, Leeds City Art Gall. and Hayward Gall., 1990; Matthew Marks Inc., NY, 1991; Musée Nat. d'Histoire, Luxembourg, Times Sq., NY, 1993; Stedelijk Mus., Amsterdam, 1995; Venice Biennale, 1995, 1999; Saatchi Gall., 1997, 2000; White Cube², NPG, 2000; Tate Modern, 2001; Tate Liverpool, 2002; Tate Britain, 2004, 2013; *work in public collections* including Arts Council, British Council, Saatchi Collection, Tate Gall., Paine Webber Art Collection, NY, DESTE Foundn for Contemp. Art, Athens, and Art Inst. of Chicago. Jerwood Painting Prize, 1997. *Address:* c/o Royal Academy of Arts, Burlington House, Piccadilly, W1J 0BD.

HUME, James Bell; Under-Secretary, Scottish Office, 1973–83; *b* 16 June 1923; *s* of late Francis John Hume and Jean McLellan Hume; *m* 1950, Elizabeth Margaret Nicolson (*d* 2008). *Educ:* George Heriot's Sch., Edinburgh; Edinburgh Univ. (MA Hons History, 1st Cl.). RAF, 1942–45. Entered Scottish Office, 1947; Jt Sec., Royal Commn on Doctors' and Dentists' Remuneration, 1958–59; Nuffield Trav. Fellowship, 1963–64; Head of Edinburgh Centre, Civil Service Coll., 1969–73. *Publications:* Mandarin Grade 3, 1993. *Recreations:* dance music, walking, enjoying silence. *Address:* 2/9 Succoth Court, Succoth Park, Edinburgh EH12 6BZ.

HUME, James Robert, (Jim); Member (Lib Dem) Scotland South, Scottish Parliament, since 2007; *b* 4 Nov. 1962; *s* of Walter and Joyce Hume; *m* 1986, Lynne White; two *s* one *d*. *Educ:* Selkirk High Sch.; East of Scotland Coll. of Agric. (Dip. Agric. 1982); Univ. of Edinburgh (MBA 1997). Farmer; Partner, John Hume & Son, 1988–. Dir, NFU Scotland, 2004–06 and 2007. Mem. (Lib Dem), Scottish Borders Council, 2007–. Chm., Borders Foundn for Rural Sustainability, 2002–07; Mem. Bd, Scottish Enterprise Borders, 2002–07. Trustee, Borders Forest Trust, 2000–06. *Publications:* (contrib.) Shepherds, by Walter Elliot, 2000. *Recreations:* amateur radio, gardening, motorcycling, conservation work. *Address:* Sundhopeburn, Yarrow, Selkirk TD7 5NF; Scottish Parliament, Holyrood Road, Edinburgh EH99 1SP. *T:* (0131) 348 6703, *Fax:* (0131) 348 6705. *E:* jim.hume.msp@scottish.parliament.uk. *Club:* Cockenzie and Port Seton Amateur Radio.

HUME, Prof. John; Tip O'Neill Professor of Peace Studies, Faculty of Social Sciences, University of Ulster, 2002–10, now Hon. Professor; *b* 18 Jan. 1937; *s* of Samuel Hume; *m* 1960, Patricia Hone; two *s* three *d*. *Educ:* St Columb's Coll., Derry; St Patrick's Coll., Maynooth, NUI (MA). Res. Fellow in European Studies, TCD; Associate Fellow, Centre for Internat. Affairs, Harvard, 1976. Pres., Credit Union League of Ireland, 1964–68; MP for Foyle, NI Parlt, 1969–73; Member (SDLP): Londonderry: NI Assembly, 1973–75; NI Constitutional Convention, 1975–76; NI Assembly, 1982–86; Foyle, NI Assembly, 1998–2000; Minister of Commerce, NI, 1974. Mem. (SDLP) NI, European Parlt, 1979–2004. Leader, SDLP, 1979–2001. Mem. (SDLP) New Ireland Forum, 1983–84.

Contested (SDLP) Londonderry, UK elections, Oct. 1974. Member: Cttee on Regl Policy and Regl Planning, European Parlt, 1979–2004; ACP-EEC Jt Cttee, 1979–2004; Bureau of European Socialist Gp, 1979–2004. MP (SDLP) Foyle, 1983–2005. Mem., Irish T&GWU (now Services, Industrial, Professional & Technical Union). Hon. DLitt: Massachusetts, 1985; Catholic Univ. of America, 1986; St Joseph's Univ., Philadelphia, 1986; Tusculum Coll., Tennessee, 1988. St Thomas More Award, Univ. of San Francisco, 1991; (jtly) Nobel Peace Prize, 1998; Freedom of Londonderry, 2000. KCSG 2012. *Address:* c/o Faculty of Social Sciences, University of Ulster, Magee Campus, Londonderry BT48 7JL.

HUME, Dr Robert, FRCPE, FRCPGlas, FRCPI, FRCPath, FRCSE; Consultant Physician, Southern General Hospital, Glasgow, 1965–93; *b* 6 Jan. 1928; *m* 1958, Kathleen Ann Ogilvie; two *s* one *d. Educ:* Univ. of Glasgow (MB, ChB, MD, DSc). FRCPGlas 1968; FRCPE 1969; FRCPath 1992; FRCSE 1992; FRCPI 1993. Nat. Service in India and Germany, 1946–48, commnd into Gordon Highlanders. Glasgow University: Hutcheson Res. Scholar, 1955–56; Hall Fellow, 1956–58; Hon. Clinical Sub-Dean, 1985–93. Dir, HCI Internat. Med. Centre, 1996–2002. Pres., RCPSGlas, 1990–92. Chm., Jt Cttee on Higher Med. Trng for UK Colls, 1990–93. Member: Acad. of Medicine, Malaysia, 1991; Royal Philosophical Soc. of Glasgow; Glasgow Antiques and Fine Arts Soc.; NT for Scotland. Hon. FACP; Hon. FRACP; Hon. FCSSA; Hon. FRCP&S (Canada). *Publications:* on haematological and vascular diseases. *Recreations:* hill-walking, swimming, reading, art appreciation, gardening, talking, golf. *Address:* 6 Rubislaw Drive, Bearsden, Glasgow G61 1PR. *T:* (0141) 586 5249. *Club:* Buchanan Castle Golf.

HUMFREY, Charles Thomas William, CMG 1999; HM Diplomatic Service, retired; *b* 1 Dec. 1947; *s* of Brian and Marjorie Humfrey; *m* 1971, Enid Thomas; two *s* one *d. Educ:* The Lodge Sch., Barbados (Barbados Scholar, 1966); St Edmund Hall, Oxford (Webb Medley Jun. Prize, 1968). FCO 1969; Tokyo, 1971–76; SE Asian Dept, FCO, 1976–79; Private Sec. to Minister of State, 1979–81; UK Mission, NY, 1981–85; Southern African Dept, FCO, 1985–87; Counsellor, Ankara, 1988–90; Counsellor (Econ.), Tokyo, 1990–94; Head of African Dept (Southern), FCO, 1994–95; Minister, Tokyo, 1995–99; Ambassador: Republic of Korea, 2000–03; Republic of Indonesia, 2004–08. Exec. Dir, UK-Japan 21st Century Gp, 2008–11. Chm., Anglo-Indonesian Soc., 2010–; Mem. Council, RSAA, 2011–. Chm., Welford Place Ltd, 2009–. *Address:* 31 Welford Place, Wimbledon, SW19 5AJ.

HUMM, Robert Peter, CBE 2011; Head of Regulatory Development, General Pharmaceutical Council; *b* 8 June 1949; *s* of Joseph Robert Humm and Winifred Maud Humm (*née* Fox). Chartered Sec. Formerly Solicitor to HSC and HSE; Dir, Legal Services, DEFRA, 2004–09; Dir, Tax Litigation, then Legal Dir, HMRC, 2009. *Recreations:* opera, travel. *Address:* General Pharmaceutical Council, 25 Canada Square, Canary Wharf, E14 5LQ. *T:* (020) 3713 7842. *E:* Robert.Humm@pharmacyregulation.org.

HUMM, Roger Frederick; Director: Andrew Macdonald (London) Ltd, since 2002; St James and Country Estates Ltd, since 2004; Mount Securities Ltd, since 2006; *b* 7 March 1937; *s* of Leonard Edward Humm, MBE, and Gladys Humm; *m* 1966, Marion Frances (*née* Czechman) (marr. diss.). *Educ:* Hampton Sch., Hampton, Middx; Univ. of Sheffield (BA Hons Econ). Graduate trainee, Ford Motor Co. Ltd (UK), 1960, Sales Manager, 1973; Marketing Dir, 1977, Internat. Gp Dir, N Europe, 1978, Ford of Europe Inc.; Exec. Dir of Sales, 1980, Man. Dir, 1986–90, Ford Motor Co. Ltd; Director: Henry Ford & Son Ltd (Cork), 1978–90; Ford Motor Credit Co. Ltd, 1980–90; Vice-Chm. and Chief Exec., 1992–2000, non-exec. Dir, 2000–02, Alexanders Holdings plc. FRSA 1987; FInstD; FIMI. Liveryman, Worshipful Co. of Carmen, 1986; Freeman, City of London, 1986. *Recreations:* golf, scuba diving, writing. *Address:* The Clock House, Kelvedon, Essex CO5 9DG. *Clubs:* Royal Automobile, Lord's Taverners, Variety Club of Great Britain; Wentworth.

HUMPHERSON, Edward Allen; Head of Assessment, UK Statistics Authority, since 2014; *b* Salisbury, 2 June 1970; *s* of late William Allen Humpherson and Rosemary Elizabeth Humpherson (*née* Arbuthnot); *m* 2004, Fiona Kathryn James; one *s* two *d. Educ:* Univ. of Edinburgh (MA 1st Cl. Hons Politics and Econ. Hist.). Chartered Accountant 1996. Nat. Audit Office, 1993–2007; Asst Auditor Gen., Nat. Audit Office, 2007–13. *Publications:* National Audit Office reports. *Recreations:* cricket, contemporary art. *Address:* UK Statistics Authority, 1 Drummond Gate, SW1V 2QQ. *T:* (020) 7592 8675.

HUMPHERY-SMITH, Cecil Raymond Julian, OBE 2004; FSA; Principal, 1983–2010, now Emeritus, and Trustee, since 1964, Institute of Heraldic and Genealogical Studies, Canterbury; *b* 29 Oct. 1928; *s* of Frederick Humphery-Smith, MBE and Agnes Violet (*née* Boxall); *m* 1951, Alice Elizabeth Gwendoline Cogle; one *s* five *d. Educ:* Hurstpierpoint Coll.; London Sch. of Hygiene and Tropical Medicine, Univ. of London (BSc 1950); Parma-Piacenza Dept of Agronomy; Univ. of Kent at Canterbury. Consumer Services Manager, H. J. Heinz Corp., 1955–60; UK Rep. and Internat. Consultant, DeRica SpA, 1961–74; Man. Dir, Achievements Ltd, 1961–91; script ed. and writer, Media Internat., 2001–04. Founder and Director: Sch. of Family History, 1957; Inst. of Heraldic and Genealogical Studies, 1961. Pt-time Extra Mural Lectr, Univs of Oxford, London and Kent, 1951–2000. Ed., Family History, 1962–. Vis. Prof., Univ. of Minho, 1975. Co-Founder, Fedn of Family Hist. Socs, 1974; formerly Mem. Cttees, Soc. of Genealogists (FSG 1970); Heraldry Society: Mem. Council, 1953–2003; Fellow, 1960; Vice-Pres., 1993; Vice-Pres., Cambridge Univ. Heraldry Soc., 1954; Hon. Vice Pres., Cambridge Univ. Heraldic and Genealogical Soc., 1994. Pres. Emeritus, Confedn Internat. des Sciences Généalogique et Héraldique (Pres., 1986–90); Mem., Bureau Perm. des Congrès internationaux, 1976–; Academician, 1976, Mem. Council, 1994–, Acad. Internat. d'Héraldique; Pres., Internat. Fedn of Schs of Family Hist. Studies, Bologna, 2001. Mem., Governing Council, Rutherford Coll., Univ. of Kent at Canterbury, 1992–2001. FSA 1982. Hon. Fellow, Canterbury Christ Ch Univ., 2008. Freeman, City of London, 1967; Liveryman: Co. of Broderers, 1973–; Co. of Scriveners, 1979– (Hon. Historian, 1983; Mem. Court, 1999). DLit Minho, 1975. Kt of Obedience, SMO Malta, 1977; Founding Co-ordinator, Order of Malta Volunteers, 1974. *Publications:* (jtly) The Colour of Heraldry, 1958; General Armory Two, 1973; Sonnets of Life, 1973; Anglo-Norman Armory, vol. 1, 1973, vol. 2, 1993; Atlas and Index of Parish Registers, 1974, as Phillimore's Atlas and Index of Parish Registers, 1995, 3rd edition 2003; A Genealogist's Bibliography, 1985; Hugh Revel, Master of the Hospital 1257–1277, 1994; Armigerous Ancestors, 1997; (jtly) A History of the Worshipful Company of Scriveners of London, 2001; A Tudor Armorial, 2004; several pamphlets and studies in the heraldry of Canterbury Cathedral; contrib. articles to proc. of internat. congresses and colloquia in genealogy and heraldry; contrib. encyclopedias, DNB, The Coat of Arms, Genealogists Mag., Family History, etc. *Recreations:* music, writing sonnets, enjoying four generations of family, trundling on my electric disability scooter to look at the sea and the junction of the estuaries of the waters of Thames, Medway and Swale. *Address:* Institute of Heraldic and Genealogical Studies, Northgate, Canterbury, Kent CT1 1BA; Saint Michael's, Allan Road, Seasalter, Whitstable, Kent CT5 4AH. *T:* (01227) 275791. *E:* scatterbr@sky.com.

HUMPHREY, Dame Caroline, (Lady Rees of Ludlow), DBE 2011; PhD; FBA 1998; Fellow, King's College, Cambridge, since 1978; Sigrid Rausing Professor of Collaborative Anthropology, University of Cambridge, 2006–10, now Emeritus; *b* 1 Sept. 1943; *d* of Prof. C. H. Waddington, CBE, FRS and M. J. Waddington; *m* 1st, 1967, Nicholas Humphrey (marr. diss. 1977); 2nd, 1986, Prof. Martin Rees (*see* Baron Rees of Ludlow). *Educ:* St George's High Sch., Edinburgh; Girton Coll., Cambridge (BA 1965; PhD 1973); Leeds Univ. (MA Mongolian Studies 1971). University of Cambridge: Research Fellow, Girton Coll., 1971–74; Sen. Asst in Res., Scott Polar Res. Inst., 1973–78; Asst Lectr, 1978–83; Lectr, 1983–95; Reader, 1995–98; Prof. of Asian Anthropology, 1998–2006. British Acad. Research Reader, 1990–92; Vis. Fellow, Inst. for Humanities, Univ. of Michigan, 1992. MAE 2007. Internat. Mem. (formerly Foreign Mem.), Amer. Philosophical Soc., 2004. Staley Prize in Anthropology, Sch. of Amer. Res., USA, 1990. Chevalier, Ordre des Palmes Académiques (France), 2004. *Publications:* Karl Marx Collective: economy, society and religion in a Siberian collective farm, 1983, rev. edn 1998; (with J. Laidlaw) The Archetypal Actions of Ritual, 1994; Shamans and Elders: experience, knowledge and power among the Daur Mongols, 1996; (with D. Sneath) The End of Nomadism?: pastoralism and the state in Inner Asia, 1998; The Unmaking of Soviet Life, 2002. *Recreation:* classical music. *Address:* River Farm House, Latham Road, Cambridge CB2 7EJ. *T:* (01223) 369043.

HUMPHREY, John Eugene; Acting Chief Executive and Interim Accounting Officer, UK Hydrographic Office, since 2015; *b* Norwich, 12 Oct. 1962; *s* of John Edwin and Anne Theresa Humphrey; *m* 1991, Kathryn Anne; two *s. Educ:* Thornleigh Salesian Coll., Bolton; Univ. of Bradford (BA Hons Interdisciplinary Human Studies); Grad. DipM. Articled Clerk, Arthur Young, 1986–87; Grad. trainee, then Sales Exec., Unisys, 1987–90; Sales Exec., then Divl Mktg Manager, ICL plc, 1990–95; Sales and Mktg Dir, Seaward Electronic Ltd, 1995–96; Gen. Manager and Sales Dir, AlliedSignal Laminate Systems Ltd, 1996–98; Gp Man. Dir, Dedicated Micros Gp Ltd, 1999–2001; Man. Dir, Braddahead Ltd, 2001–04; Vice Pres., Infrastructure Solutions, Verint, Canada, 2004–07; Hd, Sales and Mktg, UK Hydrographic Office, 2007–08; Geschäftsführer, Admiralty Deutschland GmbH, 2008–12; UK Hydrographic Office: Interim Commercial Dir, 2012–14; Chief Commercial Officer and Dep. Chief Exec., 2014–15. *Recreations:* classic cars, private flying, ski-ing, theatre, walking. *Address:* UK Hydrographic Office, Admiralty Way, Taunton, Som TA1 2DN. *T:* (01823) 337900. *E:* John.Humphrey@ukho.gov.uk. *Club:* Civil Service.

HUMPHREYS, Baroness *cr* 2013 (Life Peer), of Llanrwst in the County of Conwy; **Christine Mary Humphreys;** President, Welsh Liberal Democrats, since 2007. Former teacher. Mem. (Lib Dem) Wales N, Nat. Assembly for Wales, 1999–2003.

HUMPHREYS, Sir Colin (John), Kt 2010; CBE 2003; FRS 2011; FREng, FIMMM, FInstP; Director of Research, Department of Materials Science and Metallurgy, University of Cambridge, since 2008 (Goldsmiths' Professor of Materials Science, 1992–2008); Professor of Experimental Physics, Royal Institution of Great Britain, since 1999; Director, Rolls-Royce University Technology Centre, since 1994; Fellow of Selwyn College, Cambridge, since 1990; *b* 24 May 1941; *s* of Arthur William Humphreys and Olive Annie (*née* Harton); *m* 1966, Sarah Jane Matthews; two *d. Educ:* Luton Grammar Sch.; Imperial Coll., London (BSc); Churchill Coll., Cambridge (PhD); Jesus Coll., Oxford (MA). Sen. Res. Officer 1971–80, Lectr 1980–85, in Metallurgy and Science of Materials, Univ. of Oxford; Sen. Res. Fellow, Jesus Coll., Oxford, 1974–85; Henry Bell Wortley Prof. of Materials Engrg and Hd of Dept of Materials Sci. and Engrg, Liverpool Univ., 1985–89; Prof. of Materials Sci., 1990–92, Hd, Dept of Materials Sci. and Metallurgy, 1991–95, Univ. of Cambridge. Visiting Professor: Univ. of Illinois, 1982–86; Arizona State Univ., 1979. Lectures: D. K. C. MacDonald Meml, Toronto, 1993; Hume-Rothery Meml, Oxford, 1997; Gladstone, London, 1999; Hatfield Meml, Sheffield, 2000; Royal Acad. of Engrg Sterling, Singapore and Malaysia, 2001; John Matthews Meml, Durban, 2002; Robert Warner, Founders' Co., London, 2002; Sigma Xi, McGill Univ., 2004; Golden Jubilee Oration, Defence Res. Develt Orgn, Delhi, 2008; IEEE Dist. Lect., IIT, Bombay, 2008; Sir D. Owen Evans Meml, Univ. of Wales, Aberystwyth, 2010; John Cowley Dist. Lect., Arizona State Univ., 2011; Winegard Lect., Guelph and Toronto, 2012; Finniston, IMMM, London, 2012; Armourers' and Brasiers' Kelly Lect., Cambridge, 2013. Chm., Commn on Electron Diffraction, and Mem. Commn on Internat. Tables, Internat. Union of Crystallography, 1984–87. Member: SERC, 1988–92 (Chm., Materials Sci. and Engrg Commn, 1988–92; Mem., Science Bd, 1990–92); Adv. Cttee, Davy-Faraday Labs, Royal Instn, 1989–92; Scientific Adv. Cttee on Advanced Materials for EC Internat. Scientific Co-opn Prog., 1990–2000; Metallurgy and Materials Panel, RAE 2001, HEFCE; BERR (formerly DTI) Nat. Adv. Cttee on Electronic Materials and Devices, 1999–2006; Internat. Adv. Panel, Etisalat, UAE, 2003–04; Adv. Panel, Leverhulme Trust, 2005–; Internat. Review Panel, Japan World Premier Res. Centre Initiative, 2008–; Res. Appt Panel, Royal Soc., 2010–12 (Co-Chm., 2013; Chm., 2014–Dec. 2016); External Adv. Bd, Energy Frontier Res. Center for Solid-State Lighting Sci., Sandia National Labs, 2010–14; Tribology Trust Awards Cttee, 2011–; Internat. Scientific Adv. Bd, Photon Sci. Inst., Manchester, 2012–15; Internat. Scientific Adv. Panel, Monash Centre for Electron Microscopy, Australia, 2013–16; Chairman: Internat. Adv. Bd, Nat. Inst. for Materials Sci., Tsukuba, Japan, 2003–; Internat. Review Panel, Dept of Materials, Technion, Israel, 2004. Member Council: RMS, 1988–89; Inst. of Metals, 1989–91; President: Physics sect., BAAS, 1998–99; Inst. of Materials, 2002 (Mem. Council, 1992–2002; Sen. Vice-Pres., 2000–01); Inst. of Materials, Minerals and Mining, 2002–03 (Chm., Managing Bd, 2004–05); Awards Cttee, Royal Acad. of Engrg, 2003–06. Director: Camgan Ltd, 2011–; Intellec Ltd, 2011–; Plessey Lighting Ltd, 2012–. Fellow in Public Understanding of Physics, Inst. of Phys, 1997–98; Selby Fellow, Aust. Acad. of Scis, 1997; Fellow, Sch. of Engrg, Univ. of Tokyo, 2007; FCGI 2011. Hon. Pres., Canadian Coll. for Chinese Studies, 1996–2007; Member Court: Univ. of Bradford, 1990–92; Univ. of Cranfield, 1992–. Trustee, Link House Trust, Cambridge, 1994–. Freeman, City of London, 1994; Liveryman: Goldsmiths' Co., 1997– (Freeman, 1992; Mem., Technology and Promotions Cttee, 2002–); Armourers' and Brasiers' Co., 2001– (Freeman, 1998; Mem., Ct of Assts, 2004–; Master, 2010–11). FREng (FEng 1996); MAE 1991. Hon. Fellow Royal Microscopical Soc., 2014. Hon. DSc Leicester, 2001. RSA Medal, 1963; Reginald Mitchell Meml Lecture and Medal, 1989; Rosenhain Medal and Prize, Inst. of Metals, 1989; Templeton Award, 1994; Elegant Work Prize, Inst. of Materials, 1996; Kelvin Medal and Prize, Inst. of Physics, 1999; Gold Medal, Fedn of Eur. Materials Socs, 2001; Robert Franklin Mehl Gold Medal, Minerals, Metals and Materials Soc., USA, 2003; Platinum Medal, IMMM, 2013. Editor, Reports on Progress in Physics, 2001–06. *Publications:* (ed) High Voltage Electron Microscopy, 1974; (ed) Electron Diffraction 1927–77, 1978; Creation and Evolution, 1985 (trans. Chinese 1988); (ed) Understanding Materials, 2002; The Miracles of Exodus, 2003 (trans. German 2007); The Mystery of the Last Supper: reconstructing the final days of Jesus, 2011 (trans. German, Japanese, Portuguese, Russian, 2012, Greek, 2013); patents and numerous sci. and tech. pubns mainly on electron microscopy, semiconductors, superconductors and nanometre scale electron beam lithography. *Recreations:* chronology of ancient historical events, contemplating gardening. *Address:* Department of Materials Science and Metallurgy, 27 Charles Babbage Road, Cambridge CB3 0FS. *T:* (01223) 334457.

HUMPHREYS, Emyr Owen, FRSL; author; *b* 15 April 1919; *s* of William and Sarah Rosina Humphreys, Prestatyn, Flints; *m* 1946, Elinor Myfanwy, *d* of Rev. Griffith Jones, Bontnewydd, Caerns; three *s* one *d. Educ:* University Coll., Aberystwyth; University Coll., Bangor (Hon. Fellow, Univ. of Wales, 1987). Gregynog Arts Fellow, 1974–75; Hon. Prof., English Dept, Univ. Coll. of N Wales, Bangor, 1988. FRSL 1993. Hon. DLitt Wales, 1990. Cymmrodorion Medal, 2003. *Publications:* The Little Kingdom, 1946; The Voice of a Stranger, 1949; A Change of Heart, 1951; Hear and Forgive, 1952 (Somerset Maugham Award, 1953); A Man's Estate, 1955; The Italian Wife, 1957; Y Tri Llais, 1958; A Toy Epic, 1958 (Hawthornden Prize, 1959); The Gift, 1963; Outside the House of Baal, 1965; Natives, 1968; Ancestor Worship, 1970; National Winner, 1971 (Welsh Arts Council Prize, 1972); Flesh and Blood, 1974; Landscapes, 1976; The Best of Friends, 1978; Penguin Modern Poets No 27, 1978 (Soc. of Authors Travelling Award, 1979); The Kingdom of Brân, 1979; The Anchor Tree, 1980; Pwyll a Riannon, 1980; Miscellany Two, 1981; The Taliesin Tradition, 1983 (Welsh Arts Council Non-Fiction Prize, 1984); Jones: a novel, 1984; Salt of the Earth,

1985; An Absolute Hero, 1986; Darn o Dir, 1986; Open Secrets, 1988; The Triple Net, 1988; The Crucible of Myth, 1990; Bonds of Attachment, 1991 (Book of the Year, Welsh Arts Council, 1992); Outside Time, 1991; Brodyr a Chwiorydd, 1994; Unconditional Surrender, 1996; The Gift of a Daughter, 1998 (Book of the Year, Welsh Arts Council, 1999); Collected Poems, 1999; Dal Pen Rheswm, 1999; Ghosts and Strangers, 2001; Conversations and Reflections, 2002; Old People Are a Problem, 2003; The Shop, 2005; Welsh Time, 2009; The Woman at the Window, 2009. *Recreation:* walking. *Address:* Llinon, Penyberth, Llanfairpwll, Ynys Môn, Gwynedd LL61 5YT.

HUMPHREYS, Prof. Glyn William, PhD; FRSocMed; FBA 2009; Watts Professor of Psychology, University of Oxford, since 2011; Fellow of Wolfson College, Oxford, since 2011; *b* Ormskirk, Lancs, 28 Dec. 1954; *s* of Glyn and Dorothy Humphreys; *m* 1984, M. Jane Riddoch; two *s* one *d. Educ:* Univ. of Bristol (BSc 1st Cl. Hons Psychol. 1976; PhD 1980). Birkbeck College, University of London: Lectr in Psychol., 1979–87; Sen. Lectr, 1987–88; Prof., 1988–89; Prof. of Cognitive Psychol., Univ. of Birmingham, 1989–2011. Leibniz Prof. and Humboldt Fellow, Leipzig Univ., 1998. FRSocMed 2008. *Publications:* (with V. Bruce) Visual Cognition: computational, experimental and neuropsychological perspectives, 1989; (ed with D. Besner) Basic Processes in Reading: visual word recognition, 1991; (ed) Understanding Vision: an inter-disciplinary approach, 1992; (ed with M. Davies) Approaches to Consciousness and Intention, 1993; (ed jtly) Prospects for Artificial Intelligence, 1993; (ed with V. Bruce) Object and Face Processing, 1994; (with R. Ellis) Connectionist Psychology, 1999; (jtly) Connectionist Models in Cognitive Neuroscience, 1999; (ed) Case Studies in the Neuropsychology of Vision, 1999; (jtly) Attention, Space and Action: studies in cognitive neuroscience, 1999; (ed with E. M. E. Forde) Category Specificity in Mind and Brain, 2002; (ed jtly) Attention and Performance in Computational Vision, 2005; *with M. J. Riddoch:* (ed) Visual Object Processing: a cognitive neuropsychological approach, 1987; To See But Not to See: a case study of visual agnosia, 1987; The Birmingham Object Recognition Battery, 1993; (ed) Cognitive Neuropsychology and Cognitive Rehabilitation, 1994; (ed) Attention in Action: The Behavioural Brain Sciences/EPS Symposium, 2004. *Recreations:* swimming, all forms of music, gardening, hill walking, guitar. *Address:* Department of Experimental Psychology, University of Oxford, South Parks Road OX1 3UD.

HUMPHREYS, Janet, (Mrs V. W. Humphreys); *see* Anderson, Janet.

HUMPHREYS, Kate; *see* Priestley, K.

HUMPHREYS, Dr Keith Wood, CBE 1992; Chairman, The Technology Partnership plc, 1998–2008; *b* 5 Jan. 1934; *s* of William and Alice Humphreys; *m* 1964, Tessa Karen Shepherd; three *d. Educ:* Manchester Grammar School; Trinity Hall, Cambridge (MA, PhD). FRSC. Managing Dir, Plastics Div., Ciba-Geigy (UK), 1972–78; Jt Managing Dir, Ciba-Geigy (UK), 1979–82; Managing Dir, 1982–84, Chm. and Man. Dir, 1984–95, May & Baker, later Rhône-Poulenc Ltd. Director: Hickson Internat. plc, 1995–2000; BIP Ltd, 1996–2001. Mem., BBSRC, 1994–98. CCMI. *Recreations:* music, bridge.

HUMPHREYS, Richard William; QC 2006; barrister; *b* 22 Feb. 1963; *s* of Ian Richardson Humphreys and Valerie Thursby Trewin; *m* 1988, Rosalind Julia Birley; one *s* two *d. Educ:* Aldwickbury Sch., Wheathampstead; Stowe Sch.; Nottingham Univ. (LLB); Gonville and Caius Coll., Cambridge (LLM 1985). Called to the Bar, Inner Temple, 1986. *Recreations:* history, tennis, ski-ing.

HUMPHRIES, Barry; *see* Humphries, J. B.

HUMPHRIES, Chris, CBE 1998; Chief Executive Officer, UK Commission for Employment and Skills, 2008–10; Pro Chancellor, since 2012, and Chairman, Board of Governors, since 2010, University of West London; *b* 31 Aug. 1948; *s* of John Joseph Humphries and Neradah Merle Humphries; *m* 1996, Hazel Maxwell Cross; one *s* two *d. Educ:* Univ. of NSW (BA 1972). Media Resources Officer, ILEA, 1975–79; Producer, Promedia, 1979–82; IT Prog. Manager, 1982–84, Asst Dir, 1984–87, CET; Production Manager, ICL Interactive Learning Services, 1987–88; Educn Business Unit Manager, Acorn Computers Ltd, 1988–91; Chief Exec., Hertfordshire TEC, 1991–94; Dir, then Chief Exec., TEC Nat. Council, 1994–98; Director General: British Chambers of Commerce, 1998–2001; City & Guilds of London Inst., 2001–07. Chairman: Nat. Skills Task Force, 1998–2000; UK Skills, 2000–13; WorldSkills London 2011, 2008–12; Nat. Numeracy, 2012–14 (Trustee, 2014–); Member: Nat. Learning and Skills Council, 2000–02; Nat. Adult Learning Cttee, 2000–07; Council for Excellence in Leadership and Mgt, 2001–02; BBC Educn Adv. Gp, 2002–07; Skills Strategy Steering Gp, 2002–04. Mem. Council, Gresham Coll., 2003–07. Bd Mem., NHSU Trust, 2003–05.

HUMPHRIES, David Ernest; defence science consultant; Director, Materials Research Laboratory, Defence Science and Technology Organisation, Melbourne, Australia, 1992–94; *b* 3 Feb. 1937; *er s* of late Ernest Augustus Humphries and Kathleen Humphries; *m* 1959, Wendy Rosemary Cook; one *s* one *d. Educ:* Brighton Coll.; Corpus Christi Coll., Oxford (Scholar; MA). RAE Farnborough: Materials Dept, 1961; Avionics Dept, 1966; Head of Inertial Navigation Div., 1974; Head of Bombing and Navigation Div., 1975; Head of Systems Assessment Dept, 1978; Dir Gen. Future Projects, MoD PE, 1981–83; Chief Scientist (RAF) and Dir Gen. of Res. (C), MoD, 1983–84; Dir Gen. Res. Technol., MoD (PE), 1984–86; Asst Chief Scientific Advr (Projects and Research), MoD, 1986–90; Dir, Australian Aeronautical Res. Lab., 1990–92. *Recreations:* music, theatre. *Address:* Lynmouth Cottage, 28 Howard Road, Dorking, Surrey RH4 3HP.

HUMPHRIES, His Honour Gerard William; a Circuit Judge, 1980–2003; *b* 13 Dec. 1928; *s* of late John Alfred Humphries and Marie Frances Humphries (*née* Whitwell), Barrow-in-Furness; *m* 1st, 1957, Margaret Valerie (*d* 1999), *o d* of late W. W. Gelderd and Margaret Gelderd (*née* Bell), Ulverston; four *s* one *d*; 2nd, 2007, Elizabeth Anne Swinburne. *Educ:* St Bede's Coll., Manchester; Manchester Univ. (LLB Hons). Served RAF, 1951–53, Flying Officer. Called to Bar, Middle Temple, 1952; admitted to Northern Circuit, 1954; Asst Recorder of Salford, 1969–71; a Recorder of the Crown Court, 1974–80. Chairman: Medical Appeals Tribunal, 1976–80; Vaccine Damage Tribunals, 1979–80. Charter Mem., Serra Club, N Cheshire, 1963– (Pres. 1968, 1973, 1995–96, 2003–04). Trustee: SBC Educnl Trust, 1979– (Chm., 1979–90); Serra Foundn, 1998–. Foundn Governor, St Bede's Coll., Manchester, 1978–2008. KCHS 1996, with star 2003 (KHS 1986). *Publications:* The Stations of the Cross: stations for vocation, 1995. *Recreations:* travel, music, caravanning, gardening, lecturing on New Testament trials and other subjects.

HUMPHRIES, Prof. Jane; *see* Humphries, K. J.

HUMPHRIES, John Anthony Charles, OBE 1980; Senior Partner, Travers Smith Braithwaite, 1980–95; *b* 15 June 1925; *s* of Charles Humphries; *m* 1951, Olga June, *d* of Dr Geoffrey Duckworth, MRCP; four *d. Educ:* Fettes; Peterhouse, Cambridge (1st Law). Served War, RNVR, 1943–46. Solicitor (Hons), 1951. Chairman: Water Space Amenity Commn, 1973–83; Southern Council for Sport and Recreation, 1987–92; Vice-Pres., Inland Waterways Assoc., 1973– (Chm., 1970–73); Mem. Inland Waterways Amenity Adv. Council, 1971–89; Adviser to HM Govt on amenity use of water space, 1972; Member: Nat. Water Council, 1973–83; Thames Water Authy, 1983–87. Mem., Sports Council, 1987–88. Chm., Evans of Leeds plc, 1982–97; Mem., London Bd, Halifax Building Soc., 1985–92; Dep. Chm., Environment Council, 1985–94. Chm., Lothbury Property Trust, 1996–99. Vice Chm., Council, Surrey Univ., 1995–99. Governor, Sports Aid Foundn, 1990–96. Trustee, Thames Salmon Trust, 1987–2001. *Publications:* A Lifetime of Verse, 2006. *Recreations:* inland waters, gardening. *Address:* 21 Parkside, Wimbledon, SW19 5NA. *T:* (020) 8946 3764. *Club:* Naval.

HUMPHRIES, (John) Barry, AO 1982; CBE 2007; music-hall artiste and author; *b* 17 Feb. 1934; *s* of J. A. E. Humphries and L. A. Brown; *m* 1959, Rosalind Tong; two *d*; *m* 1979, Diane Millstead; two *s*; *m* 1990, Lizzie, *d* of Sir Stephen (Harold) Spender, CBE, CLit. *Educ:* Melbourne Grammar Sch.; Univ. of Melbourne. Repertory seasons, Union Theatre, Melbourne, 1953–54; Phillip Street Revue Theatre, Sydney, 1956; Demon Barber, Lyric, Hammersmith, 1959; Oliver!, New, 1960, Piccadilly, 1968, London Palladium, 1997; Treasure Island, Mermaid, 1968; Dick Whittington, New Wimbledon Th., 2011. One-man shows (author and performer): A Nice Night's Entertainment, 1962; Excuse I, 1965; Just a Show, Australia, 1968, Fortune Theatre, 1969; A Load of Olde Stuffe, 1971; At Least You Can Say That You've Seen It, 1974; Housewife Superstar, 1976; Isn't It Pathetic at His Age, 1979; A Night with Dame Edna, 1979; An Evening's Intercourse with Barry Humphries, 1981–82; Tears Before Bedtime, 1986; Back with a Vengeance, 1987; Look At Me When I'm Talking To You!, 1994; Rampant in Whitehall, Les Patterson Has a Stand Up, 1996; New Edna, the Spectacle, 1998; Edna's Royal Tour, 1998, NY, 2000 (Special Tony Award); Remember You're Out, 1999; Nat. American Tour, 2001; Back to My Roots and Other Suckers, Australia, 2003; Dame Edna Back With a Vengeance, NY, 2004 and US nat. tour, 2005; Back With a Vengeance, a New Effort, Australia, 2006; Last Night of the Poms, UK tour, 2009; All About Me, Broadway, 2010; Eat Pray Laugh!, farewell Australian tour, 2012–13, UK tour, 2013. TV series: The Dame Edna Experience, 1987; Ally McBeal, 2002; The Dame Edna Treatment, 2007. Numerous plays, films, broadcasts and recordings. Exhibition: Wish You Were Here!: travels with a brush, Savill Galls, Melbourne, 2007. Patron of Honour, Internat. League of Antiquarian Booksellers, 2012–. Pres., Frans de Boever Soc. (Belgium). DUniv Griffith Univ., Qld, 1994. Lifetime Achievement Award, Sydney Theatre Awards, 2012. *Publications:* Bizarre, 1964; Innocent Austral Verse, 1968; (with Nicholas Garland) The Wonderful World of Barry McKenzie, 1970; (with Nicholas Garland) Bazza Holds His Own, 1972; Dame Edna's Coffee Table Book, 1976; Les Patterson's Australia, 1979; Treasury of Australian Kitsch, 1980; A Nice Night's Entertainment, 1981; Dame Edna's Bedside Companion, 1982; The Traveller's Tool, 1985; (with Nicholas Garland) The Complete Barry McKenzie, 1988; My Gorgeous Life: the autobiography of Dame Edna Everage, 1989; The Life and Death of Sandy Stone, 1991; More Please (autobiog.), 1992; Women in the Background (novel), 1995; My Life As Me (autobiog.), 2002; Handling Edna: the unauthorised biography, 2010. *Recreations:* kissing, inventing Australia, painting beautifully. *Clubs:* Garrick, Beefsteak, Pratt's, Roxburgh; Savage (Melbourne).

HUMPHRIES, John Charles Freeman; Founder and Trustee, since 1987, and Director, 1993–2002, British Bone Marrow Donor Appeal; Chief Executive, Cymru Annibynnol Independent Wales Party, 2000–03; *b* 2 Jan. 1937; *s* of Charles Montague Humphries and Lilian Clara Humphries; *m* 1959, Eliana Paola Julia Mifsud; two *s* one *d. Educ:* St Julian's High Sch., Newport, Gwent. Western Mail: News Editor, 1966–73; Dep. Editor, 1973–80; Thomson Regional Newspapers: European Bureau Chief, 1980–86; London/City Editor, 1986–87; Editor, Western Mail, 1988–92; Launch Editor, Wales on Sunday, 1989. Mem., Wales Cttee, Consumer Council for Water, 2005–09. *Publications:* The Man From the Alamo: why the Welsh Chartist uprising 1839 ended in a massacre, 2004; Gringo Revolutionary: the amazing adventures of Caryl ap Rhys Pryce, 2005; Freedom Fighters: Wales' forgotten 'war' 1963–1993, 2008; Spying for Hitler: the Welsh doublecross, 2012; Welsh Explorer of the Nile: the ruined reputation of John Petherick, nineteenth-century adventurer, 2013. *Recreations:* walking, opera, reading, Rugby, gardening. *Address:* Cwr y Coed, Usk Road, Tredunnoc, Gwent NP15 1PE. *Club:* Cardiff and County.

HUMPHRIES, Prof. (Katherine) Jane, PhD; FBA 2012; Professor of Economic History, University of Oxford, since 2004; Fellow of All Souls College, Oxford, since 1998; *b* Rotherham, Yorks, 9 Nov. 1948; *d* of John Humphries and Doris Humphries; *m* 1975, Michael Hepburn Best; one *s* one *d*, and four step *d. Educ:* Mexborough Grammar Sch.; Mexborough Sixth Form Coll.; Newnham Coll., Cambridge (BA 1st Cl. Econs 1970); Cornell Univ. (PhD Econs 1973). Asst Prof., Econs, 1973–79, Associate Prof., Econs, 1979–80, Univ. of Massachusetts; University of Cambridge: Lectr in Econs, 1980–95; Reader in Econs and Econ. Hist., 1995–98; Fellow, Newnham Coll., Cambridge, 1980–98; Reader in Econ. Hist., Univ. of Oxford, 1998–2004. Pres., Econ. Hist. Soc., 2010–13. Editor, Econ. Hist. Review, 2004–09. *Publications:* Childhood and Child Labour in the British Industrial Revolution, 2010; papers in learned jls and edited collections. *Recreations:* family, tennis, walking, fiction, cinema. *Address:* All Souls College, Oxford OX1 4AL. *T:* (01865) 279346. *E:* jane.humpries@all-souls.ox.ac.uk.

HUMPHRIES, Prof. Martin James, PhD; FMedSci; FRSB; Professor of Biochemistry, since 1995, Vice-President and Dean, Faculty of Life Sciences, since 2008, University of Manchester; *b* 26 Nov. 1958; *s* of Terence and Kathleen Lesley Humphries; *m* 1982, Sandra Ceinwen Jones; two *d. Educ:* Nottingham High Sch.; Univ. of Manchester (BSc 1980; PhD 1983). Guest Researcher, Nat. Cancer Inst., NIH, Bethesda, Md, 1983–88; Postdoctoral Res. Associate, 1983–87, Associate Dir for Res., 1987–88, Howard Univ. Cancer Center, Washington; Wellcome Trust Sen. Res. Fellow, 1988–95, Principal Res. Fellow, 1995–2008, Univ. of Manchester; Dir, Wellcome Trust Centre for Cell-Matrix Research, 2000–10. Vice-Chm., 2005–07, Chm., 2008–10, Biochemical Soc.; Vice-Pres., Acad. of Med. Scis, 2012–. FMedSci 2000; FRSB (FSB 2010). MAE 2006. *Publications:* The Extracellular Matrix Factsbook, 1993, 2nd edn 1998; contrib. numerous articles to learned jls. *Recreations:* golf, red wine. *Address:* Faculty of Life Sciences, University of Manchester, Michael Smith Building, Oxford Road, Manchester M13 9PT. *E:* martin.humphries@manchester.ac.uk.

HUMPHRIES, Michael John; QC 2003; *b* 15 June 1959; *s* of Derek James Humphries and Joan Irene Humphries; *m* 1989, Juliet Claire Hampton; one *s* two *d. Educ:* Univ. of Leicester (BL). Called to the Bar, Inner Temple, 1982, Bencher, 2009. Sen. Editor, Tottel's (formerly Butterworths) Compulsory Purchase and Compensation Service, 1999–. *Recreations:* house in France, music, literature. *Address:* Francis Taylor Building, Inner Temple, EC4Y 7BY. *T:* (020) 7353 8415. *E:* mhumphries@ftb.eu.com. *Club:* Reform.

HUMPHRYES, Jane Carole; QC 2003; a Recorder, since 1999; *d* of Alan John Humphryes and Avril Pamela Gloria Humphryes; *m* Timothy Stephen Robert Wakefield; one *s* four *d*, and one step *s* one step *d. Educ:* Univ. of Kent at Canterbury; Council of Legal Educn. Called to the Bar, Middle Temple, 1983. *Recreations:* walking, watercolours, travel, cuisine, theatre, ski-ing. *Address:* 3 Raymond Buildings, Gray's Inn, WC1R 5BH. *T:* (020) 7400 6400.

HUMPHRYS, John; Presenter: Today Programme, Radio 4, since 1987; On the Ropes, Radio 4, since 1994; Mastermind, BBC TV, since 2003; *b* 17 Aug. 1943; *s* of George and Winifred Humphrys; *m* 1965, Edna Wilding (marr. diss. 1991; she *d* 1997); one *s* one *d*; one *s* with Valerie Sanderson. *Educ:* Cardiff High School. BBC TV: Washington Correspondent, 1971–77; Southern Africa Correspondent, 1977–80; Diplomatic Correspondent, 1980–81; Presenter: 9 O'Clock News, 1981–86; On the Record, 1993–2002. Hon. Fellow, Cardiff Univ., 1998. Hon. DLitt Abertay Dundee, 1996; Hon. MA Wales, 1998; Hon. LLD St Andrews, 1999. *Publications:* Devil's Advocate, 1999; The Great Food Gamble, 2001; Lost for Words: the mangling and manipulation of the English language, 2004; Beyond Words: how language reveals the way we live now, 2006; In God We Doubt: confessions of a failed atheist, 2007; (with Dr Sarah Jarvis) The Welcome Visitor: living well, dying well, 2009; (with C.

Humphrys) Blue Skies and Black Olives, 2009. *Recreations:* music, attempting to play the 'cello, hill walking. *Address:* c/o BBC News Centre, New Broadcasting House 03B, Portland Place, W1A 1AA.

HUNJAN, Satinder Pal Singh; QC 2002; a Recorder, since 2003; a Deputy High Court Judge, since 2008; *b* 5 Nov. 1960; *s* of Nasib Singh Hunjan and Rajinder Kaur Hunjan; one *s* one *d*. *Educ:* Univ. of Birmingham (LLB Hons). Called to the Bar, Gray's Inn, 1984; specialises in clinical negligence, personal injuries and general commercial law. *Recreations:* travelling, tennis, ski-ing, football, theatre. *Address:* 5 Fountain Court, Steelhouse Lane, Birmingham B4 6DR. *T:* (0121) 606 0500, *Fax:* (0121) 606 1501. *E:* sh@no5.com.

HUNKIN, Timothy Mark Trelawney; artist, cartoonist, engineer; *s* of late Oliver John Hunkin and of Frances Elizabeth Hunkin; *m* 2005, Meg; one step *d*. *Educ:* St Paul's Sch., Hammersmith; Caius Coll., Cambridge (BA Engrg 1972). Launched Phlegethon Fireworks, staging public displays and building fireworks, 1971; cartoonist, Rudiments of Wisdom (cartoon strip), Observer, 1973–87; worked for Oxfam, Africa, 1980; Osher Fellow, Exploratorium Sci. Centre, San Francisco, 1993; British Council lect. tour, How to Cheat at Art, Australia and USA, 1997; Fellowship, Xerox Parc, 1998; Co-founder Mongrel Media, designing and building exhibns, 1999; Nesta Dreamtime Fellowship, 2004. Projects include: inflatable pigs and sheep shot from mortar shells, developed for Pink Floyd's Animal tour, 1977; designed and built 50-ft high water clock, Neal's Yd, Covent Gdn, 1982; designed How Television Works (gallery), Nat. Museum of Photography, Bradford, 1986; designed Ride of Life (ride), 1989; created The Secret Life of the Home (gallery), Sci. Mus., London, 1994–95; created, with Mongrel Media, visitor centre, Eden Project, 2000, Science in the Dock (sci. ethics automata show), Glasgow Sci. Centre, 2001; opened Under the Pier Show (amusement arcade of homemade slot machines), Southwold Pier, 2002; public clocks, Hawkins Bazaar and London Zoo, 2008; clock for The Exploratorium, San Francisco, 2013; opened Novelty Automation (amusement arcade), London, 2015. Exhibitions include: The Disgusting Spectacle (mechanical sculptures), ICA, London, 1981; The Art Gallery (mechanical art gall. spectators), tour of 20 provincial galls, 1983. Researcher, writer and presenter, Channel 4: Secret Life of Machines, series 1, 1988, series 2, 1990; Secret Life of the Office (series), 1992. *Publications:* Mrs Gronkwonk and the Post Office Tower (for children), 1973; Almost Everything There is to Know: the Rudiments of Wisdom cartoons, 1988; Hunkin's Experiments, 2003. *E:* hunkin@timhunkin.com.

HUNNINGS, Mary Rosa Alleyne; *see* Berry, M. R. A.

HUNSDON OF HUNSDON, Baron; *see* Aldenham, Baron.

HUNT, family name of **Barons Hunt of Chesterton, Hunt of Kings Heath** and **Hunt of Wirral**.

HUNT OF CHESTERTON, Baron *cr* 2000 (Life Peer), of Chesterton in the co. of Cambridgeshire; **Julian Charles Roland Hunt,** CB 1998; PhD; FRS 1989; Professor in Climate Modelling, University College London, 1999–2008, now Emeritus; Visiting Fellow, Malaysian Commonwealth Studies Centre, University of Cambridge, since 2008; *b* 5 Sept. 1941; *s* of Roland Charles Colin Hunt, CMG; *m* 1965, Marylla Ellen Shephard; one *s* two *d*. *Educ:* Westminster Sch.; Trinity Coll., Cambridge (BA 1963; PhD 1967); Univ. of Warwick. Post-doctoral res., Cornell Univ., USA, 1967; Res. Officer, Central Electricity Res. Labs, 1968–70; University of Cambridge: Fellow, 1966–, Sen. Res. Fellow, 1998–99, Trinity Coll.; Lectr in Applied Maths and in Engrg, 1970–78; Reader in Fluid Mechanics, 1978–90; Prof., 1990–92, Hon. Prof., 1992–, in Fluid Mechanics; Chief Exec., Meteorol Office, 1992–97. Hon. Dir, Lighthill Inst. for Math. Scis, 2003–06, Acad. Dir, Lighthill Risk Network, 2006–, UCL. Vis. Scientist, 1997, 1998, Pierre Fermat Vis. Prof., 2007, 2008, Cerfacs and Inst de Mécanique des Fluides de Toulouse; Visiting Professor: Colorado State Univ., 1975; NC State Univ., and Envmtl Protection Agency, 1977; Univ. of Colorado, 1980; Nat. Center for Atmospheric Res., Boulder, Colo, 1983; Arizona State Univ., 1997–98, 2007–; Stanford Univ., 1998; Univ. of Notre Dame, Indiana, 2011–; Hong Kong Univ., 2011–; J. M. Burgers Prof., Tech. Univ., Delft, 1998–; Mary B. Upson Vis. Prof., Cornell Univ., 2003–06. Founder Dir, 1986–91, Dir and Chm., 1997–, Cambridge Envmtl Res. Consultants Ltd. President: IMA, 1993–95 (Hon. Sec., 1984–89; Vice-Pres., 1989–93; Hon. Fellow, 2003); Adv. Cttee on Protection of the Sea, 2003– (Chm., 2001–03); Nat. Soc. for Clean Air, 2006–07; Vice Pres., Globe Internat., 2006–14. Member: Mgt Bd, European Res. Community for Flow Turbulence and Combustion, 1988–95; Exec. Council, WMO, 1992–97; NERC, 1994–96; Stakeholder Adv. Panel, EDF Energy, 2006–09; Chair, Adv. Cttee, Tokamak Solutions Ltd, 2010–; Co-Chair, Asian Network on Climate Science and Technol., 2013–. Hon. Chm., Just Ghana Ltd. Councillor, Cambridge CC, 1971–74 (Leader, Labour Gp, 1972). Branch Sec., Electrical Power Engrs Assoc., 1970. Fellow, APS, 2003; Hon. FICE 2003. Hon. DSc: Salford, 1995; Bath, 1996; UEA, 1997; Grenoble, Uppsala, Warwick, 2000; Dundee, 2005; Western Univ., Ont, 2014. L. F. Richardson Medal, Eur. Geophysical Soc., 2001. *Publications:* (contrib.) New Applications of Mathematics, ed C. Bondi, 1991; (ed) London's Environment, 2005; scientific pubns in Jl of Fluid Mechanics, Atmospheric Envmt, Qly Jl of Royal Meteorol Soc., Proc. Royal Soc., Jl of the Atmospheric Scis, Jl Flow Turb Combustion. *Address:* Department of Earth Sciences, University College London, Gower Street, WC1E 6BT.

See also Hon. T. J. W. Hunt.

HUNT OF KINGS HEATH, Baron *cr* 1997 (Life Peer), of Birmingham in the co. of West Midlands; **Philip Alexander Hunt,** OBE 1993; PC 2009; *b* 19 May 1949; *s* of Rev. Philip Lacey Winter Hunt and Muriel Hunt; *m* 1st, 1974 (marr. diss.); one *d*; 2nd, 1988, Selina Ruth Helen Stewart; three *s* one *d*. *Educ:* City of Oxford High Sch.; Oxford Sch.; Leeds Univ. (BA). Oxford RHB, 1972–74; Nuffield Orthopaedic Centre, 1974–75; Mem., Oxfordshire AHA, 1975–77; Sec. Edgware/Hendon Community Health Council, 1975–78; Asst Sec., 1978–79, Asst Dir, 1979–84, NAHA; Dir, NAHA, then NAHAT, 1984–97; Chief Exec., NHS Confedn, 1997. Chair, Nat. Patient Safety Agency, 2004–05. Sen. Policy Advr, Sainsbury Centre for Mental Health, 1997; Sen. Policy Associate, King's Fund, 1998. Member: Oxford City Council, 1973–79; Birmingham City Council, 1980–82. A Lord in Waiting (Govt Whip), 1998–99; Parly Under-Sec. of State, DoH, 1999–2003, DWP, 2005–06; Minister of State, DoH, 2006–07; Parly Under-Sec. of State, MoJ, 2007–08; Minister of State, DEFRA, 2008–09, DECC, 2008–10; Dep. Leader, 2009–10, Dep. Leader of Opposition, 2010–, H of L. Chm., H of L Select Cttee on Merits of Statutory Instruments, 2004; Co-Chm., All-Party Gp on Public Health and Primary Care, 1997–98. Chm., Heart of England NHS Foundn Trust, 2011–14; Member: Council, Internat. Hosp. Fedn, 1986–91; King's Fund Inst. Adv. Cttee, 1991–93; Council, Assoc. for Public Health, 1992 (Co-Chm., 1994). Pres., FPA, 1998. *Publications:* The Health Authority Member (discussion paper) (with W. E. Hall), 1978; articles in Health Service publications. *Recreations:* music, cycling, swimming, football. *Address:* House of Lords, SW1A 0PW.

HUNT OF WIRRAL, Baron *cr* 1997 (Life Peer), of Wirral in the co. of Merseyside; **David James Fletcher Hunt,** MBE 1973; PC 1990; Chairman, Financial Services and Partner, DAC Beachcroft (formerly Beachcroft) LLP, solicitors; Chairman, Press Complaints Commission, 2011–14; *b* 21 May 1942; *s* of late Alan Nathaniel Hunt, OBE and Jessie Edna Ellis Northrop Hunt; *m* 1973, Patricia, (Paddy), Margery (*née* Orchard); two *s* two *d*. *Educ:* Liverpool Coll.; Montpellier Univ.; Bristol Univ. (LLB); Guildford Coll. of Law. Solicitor of Supreme Court of Judicature, admitted 1968; Partner: Stanleys & Simpson North, 1977–88; Beachcroft Stanleys, 1988–99; Beachcroft Wansbroughs, 1999–2006; Beachcroft LLP, 2006–; Partner, then Consultant, Stanley Wansbrough & Co., 1965–85; Director: BET Omnibus Services Ltd, 1980–81; Solicitors Indemnity Mutual Insce Assoc. Ltd, 2001–05. Chartered Insurance Institute: Chm., Professional Standards Bd, 2004–06; Dep. Pres., 2006–07; Pres., 2007–08; Chm., Assoc. of Ind. Financial Advisers, 1999–2002. Contested (C) Bristol South, 1970, Kingswood, 1974; MP (C) Wirral, March 1976–1983, Wirral West, 1983–97; contested (C) Wirral West, 1997. PPS to Sec. of State for Trade, 1979–81, to Sec. of State for Defence, 1981; an Asst Govt Whip, 1981–83; a Lord Comr of HM Treasury, 1983–84; Parly Under-Sec. of State, Dept of Energy, 1984–87; Treasurer of HM Household and Dep. Chief Whip, 1987–89; Minister for Local Govt and Inner Cities, DoE, 1989–90; Secretary of State: for Wales, 1990–93; for Employment, 1993–94; Chancellor, Duchy of Lancaster and Minister for Public Service and Sci., 1994–95. Chm., Cons. Shipping and Shipbuilding Cttee, 1977–79; Vice-Chairman: Parly Youth Lobby, 1978–80; Parly War Crimes Gp, 2000–; Vice-Pres., Cons. Group for Europe, 1984–87 (Vice-Chm., 1978–81; Chm., 1981–82); Pres., All Party Parly Gp on Occupational Safety and Health, 1999–. Chm., Inter-Parly Council against Anti-Semitism, 1996–. Chm., Bristol Univ. Conservatives, 1964–65; winner of Observer Mace for British Universities Debating Competition, 1965–66; Nat. Vice-Chm., FUCUA, 1965–66; Chm., Bristol City CPC, 1965–68; Nat. Vice-Chm., YCNAC, 1967–69; Chm., Bristol Fedn of YCs, 1970–71; Chm., British Youth Council, 1971–74 (Pres., 1978–80); Vice-Pres., Nat. YCs, 1986–88 (Chm., 1972–73); Vice-Chairman: Nat. Union of Cons. and Unionist Assocs, 1974–76; Cons. Party, 1983–85. Pres., Tory Reform Gp, 1991–97. Vice-Pres., Nat. Playbus Assoc., 1981–. Member: South Western Economic Planning Council, 1972–76; CBI Council, 1999–2006; Chairman: McDonald's Educn Co. Ltd, 2009–; Lending Standards Bd, 2011–. Mem. Adv. Cttee on Pop Festivals, 1972–75. Trustee, Holocaust Educnl Trust, 1998–; Chm., ESU, 2005–11 (Gov., 1999–2011; Dep. Chm., 2000–05). Bencher, Inner Temple, 2015. Mem., Rotary Club, London, 2000– (Dep. Pres., 2011–). Churchwarden, Parish of Chewton Mendip with Emborough, Somerset, 2007–. Fellow, Internat. Inst. of Risk and Safety Mgt, 2002. Hon. FIA 2003; Hon. FCII 2004. *Publications:* pamphlets on political subjects. *Recreations:* cricket, walking. *Address:* DAC Beachcroft LLP, 100 Fetter Lane, EC4A 1BN. *T:* (020) 7894 6066, *Fax:* (020) 7894 6158. *E:* lordhunt@dacbeachcroft.com. *Club:* Hurlingham.

HUNT, Alan Charles, CMG 1990; HM Diplomatic Service, retired; trainer and consultant in diplomatic practice, since 2010; *b* 5 March 1941; *s* of John Henry Hunt and Nelly Elizabeth Hunt (*née* Hunter); *m* 1978, Meredith Margaret Claydon; two *d*. *Educ:* Latymer Upper School, Hammersmith; Univ. of East Anglia. First Cl. Hons BA in European Studies. Clerical Officer, Min. of Power, 1958–59; FO, 1959–62; Vice-Consul, Tehran, 1962–64; Third Sec., Jedda, 1964–65; floating duties, Latin America, 1965–67; University, 1967–70; Second, later First Sec., FCO, 1970–73; First Sec., Panama, 1973–76; FCO 1976–77; First Sec. (Commercial), Madrid, 1977–81; FCO, 1981–83; Counsellor (Econ. and Commercial), Oslo, 1983–87; Head of British Interests Section, subseq. Chargé d'Affaires, Buenos Aires, 1987–90; Counsellor, FCO, 1990–91; Consul-Gen., Düsseldorf, and Dir-Gen. of Trade and Investment Promotion in Germany, 1991–95; Sen. Directing Staff (Civilian), RCDS, 1995–96; Dir of Trade and Investment Promotion, FCO, and Dep. Dir-Gen. for Export Promotion, DTI, 1996–97; High Comr, Singapore, 1997–2001. Dir, Oxford Univ. Foreign Service Prog., 2003–10. Vis. Prof., Coll. of Europe, 2012–. *Publications:* No Immunity, 2014. *Recreations:* golf, bridge, travel, reading, music.

HUNT, Anthony Blair, DLitt; FBA 1999; Senior Research Fellow, St Peter's College, Oxford, 2009–11, now Emeritus Fellow (Fellow and Tutor in French, 1990–2009; Vice Master, 2007–09); Lecturer in Mediaeval French Literature, Oxford University, 1990–2009; *b* 21 March 1944; *s* of Norman Blair Hunt and Dorothy Gaskell Hunt (*née* Mottershead). *Educ:* Birkenhead Sch.; Worcester Coll., Oxford (BLitt, MA 1971); St Andrews Univ. (DLitt 1991). University of St Andrews: Asst Lectr, 1968–72; Lectr, 1972–79; Reader, 1979–90; British Acad. Res. Reader, 1986–88. Vis. Prof. of Mediaeval Studies, Westfield Coll., London Univ., 1986–88. Jt Pres., Anglo-Norman Text Soc., 2011–. FSA 1986–2009. Foreign Mem., Norwegian Acad. of Sci. and Letters, 1999; Officier, Ordre des Palmes Académiques, 2008. *Publications:* Rauf de Linham, Kalender, 1983; Chrétien de Troyes, Yvain, 1986; Les giupartiz des eschez, 1986; Plant Names of Medieval England, 1989; Popular Medicine in Thirteenth-Century England, 1990; Teaching and Learning Latin in Thirteenth-Century England, 1991; The Medieval Surgery, 1992; Anglo-Norman Medicine, vol. 1, 1994, vol. 2, 1997; Le Livre de Catun, 1994; Villon's Last Will, 1996; Sermons on Joshua, 1998; Three Receptaria from Medieval England, 2001; Le Chant des Chanz, 2004; Les Paraboles maistre Alain en Françoys, 2005; Les Cantiques Salomon, 2006; Les Proverbez d'Alain, 2006; Miraculous Rhymes: the writing of Gautier de Coinci, 2007; Ovide, Du remede d'amours, 2008; An Old French Herbal, 2009; Three Anglo-Norman Treatises on Falconry, 2009; Old French Medical Texts, 2011; Cher Alme: texts of Anglo-Norman piety, 2010; Les Paroles Salomon, 2012; Writing the Future: prognostic texts of Anglo-Norman England, 2013; An Anglo-Norman Medical Compendium, 2014; articles in learned jls, contribs to collective vols, etc. *Recreations:* fell-walking, playing the double bass, opera. *Address:* 140 Main Road, Long Hanborough, Witney OX29 8JY.

HUNT, Anthony James, CEng, FIStructE; Chairman: Anthony Hunt Associates, 1988–2002; YRM plc, 1993–94; *b* 1932; *s* of late James Edward Hunt and of Joan Margaret (*née* Cassidy); *m* 1st, 1957, Patricia Daniels (marr. diss. 1972; remarried 1975; marr. diss. 1982); one *s* one *d*; 3rd, 1985, Diana Joyce Collett (marr. diss. 2007); 4th, 2013, Hélène Moore (*née* Etchats). *Educ:* Salesian Coll., Farnborough; Westminster Tech. Coll. CEng 1961; FIStructE 1973. Articled via Founders' Co. to J. L. Wheeler Consulting Engr, 1948–51; F. J. Samuely and Partners, Consulting Engrs, 1951–59; Morton Lupton, Architects, 1960–62; founded Anthony Hunt Associates, Consulting Engrs, 1962; acquired by YRM plc, Bldg Design Consultants, 1988; became separate limited co., 1997. Major buildings: Sainsbury Centre for the Visual Arts, Norwich, 1978, 1993; Willis Faber Dumas HQ, Ipswich, 1975; Inmos Micro Electronics Factory, Gwent, 1982; Schlumberger Cambridge Research, 1985; Waterloo Internat. Terminal, 1993; Law Faculty, Cambridge, 1995; Nat. Botanic Gdn, Wales, 1998; New Mus. of Scotland, Edinburgh, 1998; Lloyd's Register of Shipping, London, 1998–99; Eden Project, Cornwall, 1998–99. Willis Vis. Prof. of Architecture, Sheffield Univ., 1994–; Graham Vis. Prof. of Architecture, Univ. of Penn, 2002; Velux Vis. Prof., KAA Sch. of Art and Architecture, Copenhagen, 2009–; Visiting Professor: Chinese Univ. of Hong Kong, 2004; Univ. du Québec, Montreal, 2004–; Inst. Superior Técnico, Lisbon, 2005–. FRSA 1989. Hon. FRIBA 1989. Hon. DLitt Sheffield, 1999; Hon. DEng Leeds, 2003; Hon. Dr RCA, 2012. Gold Medallist, IStructE, 1995. *Publications:* Tony Hunt's Structures Notebook, 1997, 2nd edn 2003; Tony Hunt's Sketchbook, 1999, vol. 2, 2003; *relevant publications:* The Engineer's Contribution to Contemporary Architecture—Anthony Hunt, by Angus Macdonald, 2000; Connexions: the unseen hand of Tony Hunt, by N. Dale, 2012. *Recreations:* furniture restoration, music, sailing, ski-ing, painting. *Address:* Dolphin House, Vicarage Street, Painswick, Stroud, Glos GL6 6XR. *Clubs:* Chelsea Arts, Oriental.

HUNT, Barbara L.; *see* Leigh-Hunt.

HUNT, Christopher H.; *see* Holdsworth Hunt.

HUNT, Christopher John, FSA; Acting Director of Library Services, University of London, 2003–04; Director and University Librarian, John Rylands University Library of Manchester, 1991–2002, now University Librarian Emeritus; *b* 28 Jan. 1937; *s* of Richard John Hunt and Dorothy (*née* Pendleton); *m* 1963, Kathleen Mary Wyatt. *Educ:* Rutlish Sch., Merton; Univ. of Exeter (BA); King's Coll., Univ. of Durham (MLitt). FSA 1995. Asst Librarian, Univ. of Newcastle upon Tyne, 1960–67; Sub Librarian, Univ. of Manchester, 1967–74; University Librarian: James Cook Univ. of N Queensland, 1974–81; La Trobe Univ., 1981–85;

Librarian, British Library of Political and Economic Science, LSE, 1985–91. Chairman: Internat. Cttee for Social Sci. Inf. and Documentation, 1989–92; Library Panel, Wellcome Trust, 1993–99 (Mem., 1988–99). Curator of Libraries, Univ. of Oxford, 2000–02; Acting Dir of Library Servs, London Univ., 2003. Academic Gov., LSE, 1989–91; Mem. Council, Univ. of Manchester, 2000–02; Feoffee of Chetham's Hosp. and Library, Manchester, 1993–2005. *Publications:* The Leadminers of the Northern Pennines, 1970; The Book Trade in Northumberland and Durham to 1860, 1975; papers in professional and learned jls. *Recreations:* book collecting, wine. *Address:* 35 South End, Longhoughton, Alnwick, Northumberland NE66 3AW.

HUNT, David John; HM Diplomatic Service; Ambassador to Lithuania, 2011–15; *m* Sarah; one *s* one *d*. *Educ:* Hull Univ. Entered FCO, 2001; Hd, US Section, N America Dept, 2001–03, Hd, Sanctions Unit, UN Dept, 2003–04, FCO; Deputy Head: of Mission and Consul Gen., Zagreb, 2005–08; Conflict Dept, FCO, 2008–11. *Address:* c/o Foreign and Commonwealth Office, King Charles Street, SW1A 2AH.

HUNT, (David) Peter; His Honour Judge Peter Hunt; a Circuit Judge, since 1997; Designated Family Judge for West Yorkshire, Leeds County Court (formerly Care Centre), since 2000; a Senior Circuit Judge, since 2010; *b* 25 April 1951; *s* of late Rev. Charles Christopher Hunt and of Edna Hunt; *m* 1984, Cherryl Janet Nicholson; two *s*. *Educ:* Grangefield Grammar Sch., Stockton-on-Tees; Keble Coll., Oxford (MA). Called to the Bar, Gray's Inn, 1974; in practice at the Bar, 1974–97; Junior, North Eastern Circuit, 1981–82; a Recorder, 1993–97. Mem., Gen. Council of the Bar, 1981–84. Chm., Inquiry into multiple abuse of nursery sch. children, Newcastle, 1993–94. Dep. Chancellor, Diocese of Ripon and Leeds, 2011–. *Publications:* (with M. L. Rakusen) Distribution of Assets on Divorce, 1979, 3rd edn 1990. *Address:* Leeds Combined Court, The Courthouse, 1 Oxford Row, Leeds LS1 3BG. *T:* (0113) 306 2800.

HUNT, David Roderic Notley; QC 1987; a Recorder, since 1991; Commissioner of the Royal Court of Jersey, since 2012; *b* 22 June 1947; *s* of Dr Geoffrey Notley Hunt and Deborah Katharine Rosamund Hunt; *m* 1974, Alison Connell Jelf; two *s*. *Educ:* Charterhouse School; Trinity College, Cambridge (MA Hons). Called to the Bar, Gray's Inn, 1969, Bencher, 1996 (Vice-Treas., 2015; Treas., 2016). *Recreations:* sailing, ski-ing, golf. *Address:* Blackstone Chambers, Blackstone House, Temple, EC4Y 9BW. *T:* (020) 7583 1770.

HUNT, Donald Frederick, OBE 1993; FRCO; Principal, 1997–2007, Music Adviser, 2007–10, Elgar School of Music; Master of the Choristers and Organist, Worcester Cathedral, 1975–96; *b* 26 July 1930; *m* 1954, Josephine Benbow; two *s* two *d*. *Educ:* King's School, Gloucester. ARCM; ARCO 1951; FRCO(CHM) 1954. Asst Organist, Gloucester Cathedral, 1947–54; Director of Music: St John's Church, Torquay, 1954–57; Leeds Parish Church, 1957–75; Leeds City Organist, 1973–75. Chorus Dir, Leeds Festival, 1962–75; Conductor: Halifax Choral Soc., 1957–88; Leeds Philharmonic Soc., 1962–75; Worcester Festival Choral Soc., 1975–97; Worcester Three Choirs Festival, 1975–96; Elgar Chorale, 1980–2014; Elgar Camerata, 1999–2014; Guest Conductor, Cape Town Philharmonia, 1997–2008; Artistic Advisor: Bromsgrove Festival, 1981–91, 2008–13; N Staffs Triennial Fest., 1999; Artistic Dir and Conductor, Elgar 150th Anniv., Worcester, 2007. Vice President: Elgar Soc., 2002–; Elgar Foundn, 2007–. FRSCM 2011. Hon. DMus Leeds 1975; Hon. MA Worcester, 2010. *Publications:* S. S. Wesley: cathedral musician, 1990; Festival Memories, 1996; Elgar and the Three Choirs Festival, 1999; (ed) Elgar Complete Edition, vol. 13; *compositions:* Magnificat and Nunc Dimittis, 1972; Missa Brevis, 1973; Versicles and Responses, 1973; God be gracious, 1984; Worcester Service, 1984; Missa Nova, 1985; Mass for Three Voices, 1986; A Song of Celebration, 1995; Hymnus Paschalis, 1999; The Joys of Christmas, 2010; On Christmas Night (cantata), 2012; Five Pastoral Partsongs (for unaccompanied SATB), 2013; anthems, carols and songs. *Recreations:* cricket, poetry, gardening, Leeds United. *Address:* 13 Bilford Avenue, Worcester WR3 8PJ. *T:* (01905) 756329. *E:* dandjhunt54@yahoo.co.uk.

HUNT, (Henry) Holman, CBE 1988; Deputy Chairman, 1985–91, Member, 1980–91, Monopolies and Mergers Commission; *b* 13 May 1924; *s* of Henry Hunt and Jessie Brenda Beale; *m* 1954, Sonja Blom; one *s* two *d*. *Educ:* Queen's Park Sch., Glasgow; Glasgow Univ. (MA). FCMA, FIMC, FBCS, FInstAM. Caledonian Insce Co., 1940–43; RAF, 1943–46; Glasgow Univ., 1946–50; Cadbury Bros, 1950–51; PA Management Consultants: Consultant, 1952–57; Manager, Office Organisation, 1958–63; Dir, Computer Div., 1964–69; Bd Dir, 1970–83; Man. Dir, PA Computers and Telecommunications, 1976–83. Pres., Inst. of Management Consultants, 1974–75. *Recreations:* music, reading, walking, travel, photography. *Address:* 28 The Ridings, Epsom, Surrey KT18 5JJ. *T:* (01372) 720974. *Club:* Caledonian.

HUNT, Jacqueline Leigh, (Jay); Chief Creative Officer, Channel 4, since 2011; *b* Sydney, Australia, 20 Jan. 1967; *d* of John Hunt and Wendy Hunt (*née* Smith); *m* 2005, Ian Blandford; one *s* one *d*. *Educ:* St John's Coll., Cambridge (BA English). Joined BBC, 1989; Assistant Editor: Breakfast News, 1990–95; Newsnight, 1995–98; Panorama, 1999; Editor: One O'Clock News, 2000–03; Six O'Clock News, 2003–05; Controller, Daytime, 2005–07; Hd of Progs, Five, 2007–08; Controller, BBC One, 2008–10. *Recreations:* travel, running, cycling. *Address:* Channel 4, 124 Horseferry Road, SW1P 2TX. *E:* jhunt@channel4.co.uk.

HUNT, Rt Hon. Jeremy; PC 2010; MP (C) South West Surrey, since 2005; Secretary of State for Health, since 2012; *b* 1 Nov. 1966; *s* of Adm. Sir Nicholas John Streynsham Hunt, GCB, LVO; *m* 2009, Lucia Guo; one *s* one *d*. *Educ:* Charterhouse; Magdalen Coll., Oxford (BA 1st Cl. Hons PPE 1988). Co-Founder and Man. Dir, Hotcourses, 1991–2005; Co-Founder, Hotcourses Foundn, 2004. Shadow Sec. of State for Culture, Media and Sport, 2007–10; Sec. of State for Culture, Olympics, Media and Sport, 2010–12. *Recreation:* Latin music and dancing. *Address:* 23 Red Lion Lane, Farnham, Surrey GU9 7QN. *T:* (01252) 712536, *Fax:* (01428) 607498. *E:* huntj@parliament.uk.

HUNT, Sir John (Leonard), Kt 1989; *b* 27 Oct. 1929; *s* of late William John Hunt and Dora Maud Hunt, Keston, Kent; unmarried. *Educ:* Dulwich Coll. Councillor, Bromley Borough Council, 1953–65; Alderman, Bromley Borough Council, 1961–65; Mayor of Bromley, 1963–64. Contested (C) S Lewisham, 1959. MP (C): Bromley, 1964–74; Ravensbourne, 1974–97. Member: Select Cttee on Home Affairs (and Mem., Sub-Cttee on Race Relations and Immigration), 1979–87; Speaker's Panel of Chairmen, 1980–97. Chm., Indo-British Parly Gp, 1979–91; UK Rep. at Council of Europe and WEU, 1973–77 and 1988–97. Mem., BBC Gen. Adv. Council, 1975–87. Pres., Inst. of Administrative Accountants, subseq. of Financial Accountants, 1970–88. Mem. of London Stock Exchange, 1958–70. Freeman, City of London, 1986; Freeman, Haberdashers' Co., 1986. *Recreations:* good food, reading autobiographies. *Address:* 164 Sutherland Avenue, W9 1HR.

HUNT, John Michael Graham, OBE 2000; Chief Executive and Secretary, British Dental Association, 1993–2001; Director, Smile-on Ltd, 2001–11; *b* 5 Feb. 1942; *s* of Robert Graham Hunt and Patricia Mary Hunt; *m* 1966, Jill Mason Williams; one *s* two *d*. *Educ:* Guy's Hosp. Dental Sch., Univ. of London (BDS 1965). LDS RCS 1965. Resident House Officer, Guy's Hosp., 1965; Fulbright Travelling Schol., Clinical Dental Fellow, Eastman Dental Centre, NY, 1966–67; London Hospital Dental Institute: Registrar, Conservative Dentistry, 1967–70; Lectr in Oral Surgery, 1968–70; General Dental Practice, Torquay, 1970–80; Clinical Dental Surgeon, Prince Philip Dental Hosp., Univ. of Hong Kong, 1980–84; Dental Officer, 1984–89, Sen. Dental Officer, 1989–93, DoH. Hon. Lectr, London Hosp. Med. Coll., 1989–93; Speaker, FDI, World Dental Fedn, 1999–2005. FRSA. Hon. FFGDP(UK) 2001. *Recreations:* walking, ski-ing, tennis, sailing. *Address:* Ryden, Paternoster Lane, Ipplepen, Totnes, Devon TQ12 5RY.

HUNT, Rt Hon. Jonathan (Lucas), ONZ 2005; PC 1987; High Commissioner for New Zealand in the United Kingdom, and Ambassador to Eire, 2005–08; *b* 2 Dec. 1938; *s* of Henry Lucas Hunt and Alison Zora Hunt. *Educ:* Auckland Grammar Sch.; Univ. of Auckland (MA Hons). Teacher, Kelston Boys' High Sch., 1961–66; MP NZ, 1966–2005 (MP (Lab) New Lynn, Auckland, 1966–96). New Zealand Parliament: Dep. Speaker, 1974–75; Sen. Opposition Whip, 1980–84; Minister of Broadcasting and Communications, 1984–90; Leader of the House, 1987–90; Speaker, 1999–2005. *Recreations:* music, cricket, wine appreciation, reading. *Club:* Wellington (New Zealand).

HUNT, Judith Anne, OBE 1999; consultant and executive coach, since 1999; Board Member, Transport for London, 2006–12; *b* 13 Sept. 1945; *d* of late Philip E. Riley and Amy Riley; *m* 1st, 1967, Alan J. Hunt (marr. diss. 1979); two *d*; 2nd, 1988, Daniel W. Silverstone, *qv*. *Educ:* Cheadle Hulme Sch.; Leeds Univ. (BA Hons). Lectr, Stockport Coll. and Salford Coll. of Technology, and teacher, Salford, 1967–74; Nat. Organiser, 1974–80 and Asst Gen. Sec., 1980–82, AUEW (TASS); Equal Opportunities Advr and Dep. Head, Personnel Services, GLC, 1982–84; Dir of Personnel (Staffing), GLC, 1984–86; Acting Dir of Personnel, ILEA, 1986–87; Chief Executive: London Borough of Ealing, 1987–93; Local Govt Mgt Bd, 1993–99. Special Advr, LGA, 1999–2000. CS Comr, 1995–98; Mem. Adv. Council, CS Coll., 1995–99. Non-exec. Dir, CPS, 2002–05. Chairman: Camden and Islington HA, 2000–02; London Health Observatory, 2002–06; Lay Mem., Camden CCG, 2013–. Parent Governor, ILEA; Member: Governing Body, Ruskin Coll.; Exec. Council, Solace; Women's Nat. Commn, 1976–82; ESRC Res. Priorities Bd, 1995–99; W London TEC; W London Leadership, 1989–93; London First, 1992–95; Camden CCG, 2013–. Trustee, Common Purpose, 1994–2004. FRSA 1990. *Publications:* Organising Women Workers, 1985; (ed) Jackie West: work, women and the labour market; contribs to jls. *Recreations:* books, gardening, opera, painting.

HUNT, Rev. Canon Dr Judith Mary; Rector, St Alkmund's Parish Church, Whitchurch, since 2012; Priest-in-charge, Edstaston, Fauls, Prees, Tilstock and Whixall, since 2013; *b* Darwen, Lancs, 16 April 1957. *Educ:* Bristol Univ. (BVSc 1980); London Univ. (PhD 1985); Ridley Hall, Cambridge; Fitzwilliam Coll., Cambridge (BA 1990). MRCVS 1980. House Surgeon, 1980–82, Res. Scholar, 1982–85, Royal Vet. Coll., London; Lectr in Equine Vet. Sci., Univ. of Liverpool, 1985–88; ordained deacon, 1991, priest, 1994; Parish Deacon, 1991–94, Asst Curate, 1994–95, St Peter's and Church of the Good Shepherd, Heswall; Priest-in-charge, St Mary's, Tilston and Shocklach, 1995–2003; Diocese of Chester: Bishop's Advr for Women in Ministry, 1995–2000; Dir of Mission and Ministry, 2003–09; Archdeacon of Suffolk, 2009–12. Canon Res., 2003–09, Canon Emeritus, 2012–, Chester Cathedral.

HUNT, Maj.-Gen. Malcolm Peter John, OBE 1984; Royal Marines retired, 1992; General Secretary, Association of British Dispensing Opticians, 1995–99; *b* 19 Nov. 1938; *s* of Peter Gordon Hunt and Rachel Margaret Hunt (*née* Owston); *m* 1st, 1962, Margaret Peat (*d* 1996); two *s*; 2nd, 2004, Angela Jean Payne (*née* Oats), *widow* of Capt. R. N. E. Payne, RN. *Educ:* St John's Sch., Leatherhead; Staff Coll., Camberley. Joined Royal Marines, 1957; service in Malta, Aden and NI; OC RM Detachment, HMS Nubian, 1966–68; Instructor, Army Staff Coll., 1979–81; CO, 40 Commando RM, 1981–83 (Falklands, NI); Internat. Mil. Staff, HQ NATO, 1984–87; Dir, NATO Defence Commitments Staff, MoD, 1987–90; Comdr, British Forces Falkland Islands, 1990–91. Exec. Dir, Nat. Back Pain Assoc., 1993–94. Member: Metropolitan Police Cttee, 1995–2000; Gen. Optical Council, 1999–2001. Pres., S Atlantic Medal Assoc. 1982, 2002–11. Gov., St John's Sch., Leatherhead, 1993–2007 (Vice-Chm., 1997–2006). FRSA 1993. Freeman, City of London, 1999; Liveryman, Co. of Spectacle Makers, 2000. *Recreations:* golf, politics, reading, theatre. *Address:* Gillons Lawn, Woolston, N Cadbury, Somerset BA22 7BP. *T:* (01963) 440929.

HUNT, Margaret Corinna; *see* Phillips, M. C.

HUNT, Group Captain Mark, OBE 2015; CEng, FIMechE, FRAeS; Commandant, Defence School of Aeronautical Engineering and Station Commander, Royal Air Force Cosford, since 2015; President, Institution of Mechanical Engineers, 2014–15 (Deputy President, 2012–14); *b* Shoreham-by-Sea, 9 Sept. 1971; *s* of Robert Henry Hunt and Angela Gillian Hunt; *m* 1996, Lisa Rogers; three *s*. *Educ:* Cardinal Newman Sch., Hove; Univ. of Brighton (BEng Mech. Engrg 1993); RAF Coll., Cranwell; Cranfield Univ. (MBA (Def) 2004); UK Defence Acad. (Staff Coll.); King's Coll. London (MA Defence Studies 2009); Open Univ. (Foundn French 2009); Windsor Leadership Prog., 2012; Exeter Univ. (RAF Strategic Leadership Develt Prog. 2015). CEng 1999; FIMechE 2004; FRAeS 2015. Jun. Engr Officer, 20 Sqdn, RAF Wittering, 1997–99; Sen. Engr Officer, IV (AC) Sqdn, RAF Cottesmore, 2005–07; Chief Air Engr, RAF Brize Norton, 2010–12; Sentinel and Sentry Type Airworthiness Authy, ISTAR Force, RAF Waddington, 2012–15. RAEng Arkwright Schol. Mentor, 2009–. Registered with Internat. Project Mgt Assoc., 2014. Trustee, IMechE, 2007–15. Freeman, City of London, 2005; Liveryman, Engineers' Co., 2005 (Mem., Ct of Assts, 2015). FCMI 2006. *Publications:* (contrib.) RAF Engineer Yearbook, 2005, 2007; contrib. articles to IMechE Jl. *Recreations:* practising heartily to become a Master of Wines, investing in sons' early adoption of mobile technology, rescuing chocolate labradors, fusion cooking, watching cricket and Rugby, marathons (personal best 3 hours 29 minutes) and sprint triathlons (1 hour 10 minutes). *Club:* Royal Air Force.

HUNT, Martin Robert, RDI 1981; Partner, Queensberry Hunt (formerly Queensberry Hunt Levien), design consultancy, since 1966; *b* 4 Sept. 1942; *s* of Frederick and Frances Hunt; *m* 1st, 1963, Pauline Hunt; one *s* one *d*; 2nd, 1980, Glenys Barton; one *s*. *Educ:* Monmouth. DesRCA, FCSD. Graduated RCA 1966 (Hon. Fellow 1987); formed Queensberry Hunt Partnership, 1966. Part time Tutor, 1968, Head of Glass Sch., 1974–86, Vis. Prof., 1997–2000, Royal Coll. of Art; Vis. Prof., De Montfort Univ., 1997–. Master, Faculty of RDI, 2001–03. *Recreation:* sailing. *Address:* Queensberry Hunt, 19 Fermoy Road, W9 3NH. *T:* (020) 8206 7690.

HUNT, Maurice William; Deputy Director-General, 1989–97, and Secretary, 1986–97, Confederation of British Industry; *b* 30 Aug. 1936; *s* of Maurice Hunt and Helen Hunt (*née* Andrews); *m* 1960, Jean Mary Ellis; one *s* one *d*. *Educ:* Selhurst Grammar School, Croydon; LSE (BSc Econ). ACIB. Nat. Service, RAF, 1955–57. ANZ Bank, 1953–66; Joint Iron Council, 1966–67; Board of Trade, 1967; Asst Sec., DTI, 1974; RCDS 1982; Dir, Membership, CBI, 1984; Exec. Dir (Ops), CBI, 1987. Dir, Pool Reinsurance Co. Ltd, 1994–2002. *Recreations:* walking, gardening, sailing. *Address:* Archway House, Old Place, Lindfield, Haywards Heath, W Sussex RH16 2HU. *T:* (01444) 482687.

HUNT, Neil Philip; Chief Executive, Royal College of General Practitioners, since 2011; *b* 2 May 1954; *s* of Keith Hunt and Doreen Hunt; *m* Tracey Ellen Hassell; two *s* (twins). *Educ:* Univ. of Sussex (BA Hons); Goldsmiths Coll., London (PGCE); Croydon Coll. (DipASS; CQSW). Social worker, 1977–84; Team/Area Manager, London Borough of Lewisham, 1984–89; Divl Manager, Kent CC, 1989–91; NSPCC: Regl Dir, 1991–97; Dir of Child Protection, 1997–2003; on secondment to Home Office, then to DfES, 2002–03; Chief Exec., Alzheimer's Soc., 2003–10. *Recreation:* striving to survive the increasingly effective assaults launched by my soon-to-be-teenage sons!

HUNT, Prof. Nigel Peter, PhD; FDSRCS, FDSRCPSGlas, FDSRCSE, FGDP(UK); Clinical Professor of Orthodontics and Head, Division of Craniofacial Development, UCL Eastman Dental Institute (formerly Eastman Dental Institute), University College London, since 1998; Honorary Consultant in Orthodontics, Eastman Dental Hospital, University College London Hospital, since 1984; *b* Horbury, Yorks, 21 May 1952; *s* of Ralph Hunt and Vera Hunt (*née* Phelps); *m* 1st, 1980, Gillian von Klemperer (marr. diss. 2001); one *s* one *d*; 2nd, 2002, Susan Cochrane; one *s* one *d*. *Educ:* Queen Elizabeth Grammar Sch., Wakefield; Guy's Hosp. Dental Sch., Univ. of London (BDS 1974; MSc 1980; PhD 1992). FDSRCPSGlas 1978; DOrthRCS 1980, MOrthRCS 1988; FDSRCSE 1994; FDSRCS 2001; FGDP(UK) 2014. Hse Surgeon, SHO and Registrar, Guy's Hosp., 1975–78; Clinical Asst, Eastman Dental Hosp., 1978–80; Sen. Registrar, Guy's Hosp. and Orpington Hosp., 1980–84; Sen. Lectr and Hon. Consultant, Inst. of Dental Surgery, London, 1984–90; Consultant Orthodontist, Eastman Dental Hosp., London and Regl Plastic Surgery Unit, Queen Victoria Hosp., E Grinstead, 1990–92; Consultant, Sen. Lectr and Dir, Orthodontic Res., Eastman Dental Inst. and Hosp., 1992–96; Hd, Orthodontics Unit, Eastman Dental Inst. and Consultant in Orthodontics, UCL Hosps Trust, 1996–98. Royal College of Surgeons: Trustee, 2012–; Mem. Council, 2012–; Dean, Faculty of Dental Surgery, 2014– (Hon. Vice-Dean, 2010–12). Pres., British Orthodontic Soc., 2015– (Chm., 2011–14; Hon. Life Mem., 2014); Hon. Life Mem., World Fedn of Orthodontists, 2015. FHEA 2002. Mem., Council Club, RCS. *Publications:* (with M. Harris) Fundamentals of Orthodontic Surgery, 2008; contrib. scientific articles to peer-reviewed jls. *Recreations:* ski-ing, walking, cricket. *Address:* Department of Orthodontics, UCL Eastman Dental Institute, 256 Grays Inn Road, WC1X 8LD. *T:* (020) 3456 1239, *Fax:* (020) 3456 1238. *E:* n.hunt@ucl.ac.uk. *Clubs:* MCC; Surrey County Cricket.

HUNT, Peter; *see* Hunt, D. P.

HUNT, Peter Lawrence, CMG 2001; HM Diplomatic Service, retired; Managing Director, London, British-American Business Council, 2005–12; *b* 10 June 1945; *s* of late Lawrence Hunt and Catherine Hunt (*née* Bree); *m* 1972, Anne Langhorne Carson; two *s* two *d*. *Educ:* St Anselm's Coll.; Birkbeck Coll., Univ. of London (BA Hons). Joined HM Diplomatic Service, 1962: African floater duties, 1967–69; Managua, 1970–73; FCO, 1973–78; Second Sec., (Commercial), Caracas, 1978–82; First Secretary: FCO, 1982–87; Dep. Head of Mission and Consul, Montevideo, 1987–90; Dep. Head, S Atlantic and Antarctic Dept and Dep. Comr, British Antarctic Territory, 1990–93; Minister-Counsellor, Dep. Head of Mission, and Consul-Gen., Santiago, 1993–96; Consul-General: Istanbul, 1997–2001; Los Angeles, 2001–05. *Recreations:* chess, golf, tennis, hill-walking.

HUNT, Richard Bruce; Chairman, R. B. Hunt and Partners Ltd, 1966–95; Deputy Chairman, Howe Robinson and Co. Ltd, 1990–97; *b* 1927; *s* of Percy Thompson Hunt and Thelma Constance Hunt; *m* 1972, Ulrike Dorothea Schmidt; two *d*. *Educ:* Christ's Hospital. FICS. Served Royal Signals, 1946–48; joined Merchant Bankers Ralli Brothers, 1949–66; formed own company, R. B. Hunt and Partners, 1966. Chm., Baltic Exchange Ltd, 1985–87 (Dir, 1977–80, re-elected, 1981–87). Liveryman, Shipwrights' Co. *Recreations:* golf, ski-ing. *Clubs:* Hurlingham, Royal Wimbledon Golf; Royal Lymington Yacht.

HUNT, Sir Richard Timothy; *see* Hunt, Sir Tim.

HUNT, Sally Colette; General Secretary, University and College Union, since 2007 (Joint General Secretary, 2006–07); *b* 14 July 1964; *d* of Barry Hunt and Catherine Hunt (*née* Cox); one *d*. *Educ:* Univ. of Sussex (BA Hons Internat. Relns 1987). Researcher, Ind. Union of Halifax Staff, 1990–91; Asst Gen. Sec., Nationwide Gp Staff Union, 1991–95; Association of University Teachers: London Regl Official, 1995–97; Asst Gen. Sec., 1997–2002; Gen. Sec., 2002–06. Mem., Gen. Council, 2002–, Exec. Cttee, 2008–, TUC; Member: Gen. Council, ITUC (formerly Exec. Bd, ICFTU), 2004–; Exec., European TUC, 2005–; Council, ACAS, 2015–. *Address:* University and College Union, Carlow Street, NW1 7LH. *T:* (020) 7756 2559.

HUNT, Terence, CBE 1996; Chief Executive (formerly National Director), NHS Supplies, 1991–2000; *b* 8 Aug. 1943; *s* of Thomas John Hunt and Marie Louise Hunt (*née* Potter); *m* 1967, Wendy Graeme George; one *s* one *d*. *Educ:* Huish's Grammar Sch., Taunton. Associate Mem. Inst. of Health Service Management. Tone Vale Group HMC, 1963–65; NE Somerset HMC, 1965–67; Winchester Gp HMC, 1967–69; Lincoln No 1 HMC, 1969–70; Hosp. Sec., Wycombe General Hosp., 1970–73; Dep. Gp Sec., Hillingdon Hosp., 1973–74; Area General Administrator, Kensington and Chelsea and Westminster AHA(T), 1974–77; District Administrator: NW Dist of KCW AHA(T), 1977–82; Paddington and N Kensington, 1982–84; Regl Gen. Manager, NE Thames RHA, 1984–91. Member: Steering Gp on Undergrad. Med. and Dental Educn and Res., 1987–91; NHS Central R&D Cttee, 1991–94; Hosp. Cttee, EEC, 1991–93; Med. Cttee, UFC, 1989–91. Member: Twyford & Dist Round Table, 1975–84 (Chm., 1980–81; Pres., 1988–89); Cttee, Reading Town Regatta, 1984–95 (Treas., 1984–86; Chm., 1989–93); Rotary Club of Reading Maiden Erlegh, 2004–11. Church Warden, St Andrew's Ch, Sonning, Berks, 2010–. Member: Council of Govs, London Hosp. Med. Coll., 1985–91; Council, UCL, 1985–91. CCMI. Freeman, 1991, Liveryman, 1998, Barbers' Co. Knight's Cross, Order of Falcon (Iceland), 2001. *Recreations:* motor cycling, cycling, clockmaking. *Address:* 36 Old Bath Road, Charvil, Reading, Berks RG10 9QR. *T:* (0118) 934 1062. *Club:* Royal Society of Medicine.

HUNT, Sir Tim, Kt 2006; PhD; FRS 1991; Principal Scientist, Cancer Research UK (formerly Senior Scientist, Imperial Cancer Research Fund), 1990–2010; *b* 19 Feb. 1943; *s* of Richard William Hunt and Katherine Eva Rowland; christened Richard Timothy, name changed by Deed Poll to Tim, 2004; *m* 1st, 1971, Missy Cusick (marr. diss. 1974); 2nd, 1995, Prof. Mary Katharine Levinge Collins; two *d*. *Educ:* Dragon Sch.; Magdalen Coll. Sch., Oxford; Clare Coll., Cambridge (BA Nat. Sci. 1964; PhD 1968; Hon. Fellow, 2002). University of Cambridge: Fellow, Clare Coll., 1968–2002; Univ. Lectr in Biochem., 1981–90; Junior Proctor, 1982–83. Mem., Scientific Council, European Res. Council, 2011–15. Mem., EMBO; MAE 1998. Founder FMedSci 1998. Foreign Hon. Mem., Amer. Acad. of Arts and Scis, 1997; Foreign Associate, US Nat. Acad. of Scis, 1999. (Jtly) Nobel Prize for Physiology or Medicine, 2001. Officier, Légion d'Honneur (France), 2002. *Publications:* Molecular Biology of the Cell: the problems book (with John Wilson), 1989, 6th edn 2014; The Cell Cycle: an introduction (with Andrew Murray), 1993; articles in cell and molecular biology jls. *Recreations:* cooking, eating, photography. *Address:* Rose Cottage, Ridge, Herts EN6 3LH. *E:* rtimhunt@gmail.com.

HUNT, Hon. Tristram Julian William, PhD; FRHistS; MP (Lab) Stoke-on-Trent Central, since 2010; Senior Lecturer in Modern British History, Queen Mary University of London, since 2010 (Lecturer, 2003–10); *b* 31 May 1974; *s* of Baron Hunt of Chesterton, *qv*; *m* 2004, Juliet Thornback; one *s* two *d*. *Educ:* University Coll. Sch.; Trinity Coll., Cambridge (BA 1995; PhD 2000); Univ. of Chicago (Exchange Fellow). FRHistS 2005. Sen. researcher, Labour Party election campaign, 1997; Special Advr to Parly Under-Sec. of State, DTI, 1998–2001; Res. Fellow, IPPR, 2001; Associate Fellow, Centre for Hist. and Econs, King's Coll., Cambridge, 2001–02. Vis. Prof., Arizona State Univ., 2004–05. Author and presenter, television: Civil War (series), 2002; Isaac Newton: Great Briton, 2002; British Middle Class, 2005; The Protestant Revolution (series), 2007. Trustee: Heritage Lottery Fund, 2005–10; Nat. Heritage Meml Fund, 2005–10; History of Parliament Trust, 2011–. Shadow Sec. of State for Educn, 2013–15. *Publications:* The English Civil War, 2002, 3rd edn 2006; Building Jerusalem: the rise and fall of the Victorian city, 2004, 2nd edn 2005; Friedrich Engels: the frock-coated communist, 2009 (Elizabeth Longford Histl Biog. Prize, 2010); Ten Cities that made an Empire, 2014; contribs to History Today, Jl Social Hist. *Recreations:* Victorian urban architecture, fresh-water swimming, ceramics, book-browsing. *Address:* c/o Georgina Capel Associates Ltd, 29 Wardour Street, W1D 6PS. *T:* (020) 7734 2414, *Fax:* (020) 7734 8101; House of Commons, SW1A 0AA. *E:* tristram.hunt.mp@parliament.uk.

HUNT, William George, TD 1988 (and Clasp 1994); Windsor Herald of Arms, since 1999; Registrar, College of Arms, 2007–14; Genealogist, Order of St John, since 2010; HM Lieutenant, City of London, since 2012; *b* 8 Dec. 1946; *s* of late Frank Williams Hunt, TD, MA, and Mary Elizabeth Leyland Hunt (*née* Orton), JP; *m* 1998, Michaela Wedel; two *s*. *Educ:* Liverpool Coll.; Univ. of Southampton (BA); Univ. of Constance; Univ. of Lausanne; Univ. of Caen (Dip.). FCA 1979. Mentor, Salem Sch., 1967–69; Audit Manager, Arthur Young McClelland Moores, 1970–83; Financial Controller and Partnership Sec., Frere Cholmeley, 1983–92; Finance Dir, Hopkins & Wood, 1993–95; Portcullis Pursuivant of Arms, 1992–99. Clerk, HM Commn of Lieutenancy for City of London, 1990–2013; Mem., Ct of Common Council, City of London, 2004–13. Dir, Heraldry Soc., 1997–2006. Treas., HAC Biographical Dictionary (1537–1914) Trust, 1993–. Gov., City of London Sch., 2009–13. Mem., RFCA, 1990– (Exec. Mem., City of London Assoc., 2007–). Freeman, City of London; Founder Mem., Treas., 1976–78, Chm., 1978–79, Soc. of Young Freemen of City of London; Maj. and Mem., Ct of Assts, 1988–2000, HAC; Mem., Ct of Assts, 1996–, Master, 2000–01, Co. of Makers of Playing Cards. CStJ 2011 (SBStJ 1999). *Publications:* Guide to the Honourable Artillery Company, 1987; (ed jtly) Dictionary of British Arms, Vol. 1, 1992. *Recreation:* orders and decorations. *Address:* College of Arms, 130 Queen Victoria Street, EC4V 4BT. *T:* (020) 7329 8755.

HUNT-DAVIS, Brig. Sir Miles (Garth), GCVO 2010 (KCVO 2003; CVO 1998); CBE 1990 (MBE 1977); Private Secretary, 1993–2010, and Treasurer, 2000–10, to HRH The Duke of Edinburgh (Assistant Private Secretary, 1991–92); *b* Johannesburg, SA, 7 Nov. 1938; *s* of late Lt-Col Eric Hunt-Davis, OBE, ED and Mary Eleanor Turnbull (*née* Boyce); *m* 1965, Anita (Gay) Ridsdale, *d* of Francis James Ridsdale; two *s* one *d*. *Educ:* St Andrew's Coll., Grahamstown, SA. Commnd 6th QEO Gurkha Rifles, 1962; active service in Borneo and Malaya, 1964–66; student, Canadian Land Forces Comd and Staff Coll., 1969–70; Bde Maj., 48 Gurkha Inf. Bde, 1974–76; Comdt, 7th Duke of Edinburgh's Own Gurkha Rifles, 1976–79; School of Infantry: Chief Instructor, Tactics Wing, 1979–80; GSO 1 Tactics, 1980–82; Instr, Staff Coll., Camberley, 1982–83; Commander: British Gurkhas, Nepal, 1985–87; Bde of Gurkhas, 1987–90; retd, 1991. Col, 7th Duke of Edinburgh's Own Gurkha Rifles, 1991–94. Chm., Gurkha Bde Assoc., 1991–2003. Trustee, Gurkha Welfare Trust (UK), 1987–2002; Gov., Sutton's Hosp. in Charterhouse, 2009–. Freeman, City of London, 2002. Yr Brother, Trinity House, 2004. Hon. MA Cambridge, 2009; Hon. Dr Edinburgh, 2010. *Publications:* (with Col E. D. Powell-Jones) Abridged History of the 6th Queen Elizabeth's Own Gurkha Rifles, 1974. *Recreations:* golf, elephant polo.

HUNTER, Air Vice-Marshal Alexander Freeland Cairns, CBE 1982 (OBE 1981); AFC 1978; Deputy Chairman, Annington Holdings plc, 1996–2013; *b* 8 March 1939; *s* of late H. A. C. and L. E. M. Hunter; *m* 1964, Wilma Elizabeth Bruce Wilson. *Educ:* Aberdeen Grammar Sch.; Aberdeen Univ. (MA 1960, LLB 1962). Commissioned RAFVR 1959; RAF 1962; flying training 1962; Pilot, 81 (PR) Sqn, FEAF, 1964–67; Central Flying Sch., 1967–68; Instructor, Northumbrian Univ. Air Sqn, 1968–69; Asst Air Attaché, Moscow, 1971–73; RAF Staff Coll., 1974; Flight Comdr, 230 Sqn, 1975–77; OC 18 Sqn, RAF Germany, 1978–80; Air Warfare Course, 1981; MoD (Air), 1981; OC RAF Odiham, 1981–83; Gp Captain Plans, HQ Strike Comd, 1983–85; RCDS 1986; Dir of Public Relations (RAF), 1987–88; Comdt, RAF Staff Coll., 1989–90; Comdr British Forces Cyprus and Adminr of Sovereign Base Areas, 1990–93. Chm., Home Housing Assoc., 1995–98; Member, Board: North Housing Assoc. Ltd, 1993–95 (Vice Chm. (NE), 1994); Warden Housing Assoc., 1996–98. Chairman: Home in Scotland Ltd, 1998–2000; Home Gp, 1998–2003; Paramount Homes Ltd, 1998–2003; Kenton Bar Bunker Co. Ltd, 1999–2004; UK Haptics Ltd, 2006–07; Chm., Annington Trust, 2008– (Dep. Chm., 1996–2008); Dep. Chm., Urban Housing Trust Ltd, 2001–03; Director: Clyde Helicopters Ltd, 1993–95; Newcastle Bldg Soc., 1993–2004; Newcastle Bank (Gibraltar), 1995–99; Great NE Air Ambulance Trading Co. Ltd, 2000–01. Vice-Pres., HMS Trincomalee Trust, 2007–. Chm., N of England, RFCA, 2003–06 (Vice Chm. (Air), 1996–2003); Vice Chm. (Air), Council of RFCAs (formerly TAVRAs), 1999–2004. Hon. Col, Tyne-Tees Regt, 1999–2006; Hon. Air Cdre, No 609 (W Riding) Sqdn, RAuxAF, 2001–06. Gentleman of the Four and Twenty, Rothbury, 2002–. DL Northumberland, 1994. OStJ 1994 (Chm. Council, Northumbria, 1998–2000). *Recreations:* shooting, fishing, hill-walking, military history, living in Germany. *Address:* c/o Clydesdale Bank, Business Banking Centre, Wakefield Road, Carlisle CA3 0HE. *Clubs:* Royal Air Force; Northern Counties (Newcastle upon Tyne).

HUNTER, Sir Alistair (John), KCMG 1994 (CMG 1985); DL; HM Diplomatic Service, retired; *b* 9 Aug. 1936; *s* of Kenneth Clarke Hunter and Joan Tunks; *m* 1st, 1963, Gillian Bradbury; one *s* two *d*; 2nd, 1978, Helge Milton (*née* Kahle); two step *s*. *Educ:* Felsted; Magdalen Coll., Oxford. Royal Air Force, 1955–57; CRO, 1961–65; Private Sec. to Permanent Under-Sec., 1961–63; 2nd Sec., Kuala Lumpur, 1963–65; 1st Sec. (Commercial), Peking, 1965–68; seconded to Cabinet Office, 1969–70; FCO, 1970–73; 1st Sec., Rome, 1973–75; FCO, 1975–80; Hd of Chancery, Bonn, 1980–85; seconded to DTI as Under Sec., Overseas Trade, 1985–88; Consul-Gen., Düsseldorf, and Dir-Gen. of British Trade and Investment Promotion in FRG, 1988–91; Consul-Gen., NY, and Dir-Gen. of Trade and Investment, USA, 1991–96. Exec. Chm., British-Amer. Chamber of Commerce, London, 1996–98. Chairman: British Music Rights, 1998–2005; E Kent Forum, 1998–2001; Manston Airport Consultative Cttee, 1999–2006; Margate Th. Royal Trust, 2000–07. Dir, PRS, 1996–2002; Dep. Chm., Locate in Kent, 1996–2005. Trustee, Horniman Mus. and Gdns, 1996–99. DL Kent, 2001. *Address:* Bay View House, 2A Bay View Road, Broadstairs CT10 2EA.

HUNTER, Andrew Reid; Headmaster, Merchiston Castle School, since 1998; *b* Nairobi, 28 Sept. 1958; *s* of John Horatio Hunter and Irene Hunter (*née* Fish); *m* 1981, Barbara Gandy Bradford; two *s* one *d*. *Educ:* Univ. of Manchester (BA Hons). Teacher of English, 1983–91, Housemaster, 1991, Worksop Coll.; Housemaster and Teacher of English and Religious Studies, Bradfield Coll., 1991–98. *Recreations:* previously county tennis, hockey and squash player; theatre, literature. *Address:* Merchiston Castle School, Colinton Road, Edinburgh EH13 0PU. *T:* (0131) 312 2203, *Fax:* (0131) 441 6060. *E:* headmaster@merchiston.co.uk. *Clubs:* New (Edinburgh), Western (Glasgow).

HUNTER, Andrew Robert Frederick Ebenezer; *b* 8 Jan. 1943; *s* of late Sqdn Leader Roger Edward Hunter, MBE, DFC and Winifred Mary Hunter (*née* Nelson); *m* 1972, Janet (*d* 2002), *d* of late Samuel Bourne of Gloucester; one *s* one *d*. *Educ:* St George's Sch., Harpenden; Durham Univ.; Jesus Coll., Cambridge; Westcott House, Cambridge. In industry, 1969; Asst Master, St Martin's Sch., Northwood, 1970–71; Asst Master, Harrow Sch., 1971–83. Contested: (C) Southampton, Itchen, 1979; (DemU) Lagan Valley, NI Assembly, 2003. MP (C, 1983–2002, Ind C, 2002–04, DemU, 2004–05) Basingstoke. PPS to Minister of State, DoE, 1985–86. Member: NI Select Cttee, 1994–2001; NI Grand Cttee, H of C, 1996–2005; Chm., Cons. NI Cttee, 1992–97. Chm., Monday Club, 2006–15. Mem., NFU, 1984–2005. Vice-Pres., Nat. Prayer Book Soc., 1987–97. Mem. Ct, Univ. of Southampton, 1983–2005. Commnd TAVR (resigned commn as Major, 1984). Hon. Mem., Soc. of the Sealed Knot, 1987–. *Recreations:* watching cricket and Rugby football, collecting model soldiers, reading. *Address:* 21 Manor Court, Meeting Street, Moira, Co. Down BT67 0TL. *Club:* Carlton.

HUNTER, Angela Margaret Jane, (Anji); Senior Adviser, Edelman, since 2013; *b* 29 July 1955; *d* of Arthur John, (Mac), Hunter and Joy Lorraine Hunter; *m* 1st, 1980, Nick Cornwall (marr. diss. 2004); one *s* one *d*; 2nd, 2006, (Thomas) Adam (Babington) Boulton, *qv*. *Educ:* St Leonard's Sch., St Andrews, Fife; St Clare's Hall, Oxford; Brighton Poly. (BA 1987). Teacher of English as a Foreign Language, Academia Británica, Córdoba, Spain, 1976–78; Legal Asst, Hodge Jones & Allen, then Offenbach & Co., 1978–80; Res. Asst to Tony Blair, MP, 1986–90, Head of Office, 1990–97; Special Asst to Prime Minister, 1997–2001; Dir of Govt Relations, Prime Minister's Office, 2001–02; Dir of Communications, BP plc, 2002–07; Gp Hd of Govt Relations and Social Affairs, Anglo American plc, 2009–11; Dir, Queen Elizabeth Prize for Engrg, RAEng, 2011–13. UK Adv. Bd, All Nippon Airways. Trustee: Snowdon Awards Scheme; Three Faiths Forum; Turner Contemporary. Mem., Bd of Govs, Birmingham Business Sch., 2005–. DUniv: Birmingham, 2013; Brighton, 2014. *Recreations:* diving, ski-ing, horse-riding.

HUNTER, Prof. (Ann) Jacqueline, CBE 2010; PhD; FBPhS; FMedSci; Chief Executive, Biotechnology and Biological Sciences Research Council, since 2013 (Member, since 2004); Professor of Life Science Innovation, St George's Hospital Medical School, since 2013; *m*; one *d* and two step *d*. *Educ:* Selwyn Sch.; Kings Secondary Sch.; Bedford Coll., Univ. of London (BSc Jt Hons Physiol. and Psychol. 1977; PhD 1980). Wellcome Trust Post-doctoral Res. Fellow, St George's Hosp. Med. Sch., 1982–83; Sen. Pharmacologist, Dept of Neuropharmacol., Glaxo Gp Res., 1983–86; Hd of Behavioural Pharmacol., Astra Neurosci. Res., 1986–88; Asst Dir, Pharmacol., SmithKline and French, 1989–90; Prog. Manager, SmithKline Beecham Pharmaceuticals, 1990–92; Dir, Neurol. Res., 1992–97, Gp Dir, Neurobehavioural Res., 1997–2000, SmithKline Beecham; GlaxoSmithKline: Vice Pres., Biol., 2000–02; Sen. Vice Pres. and Hd, Neurol. and G1 Centre of Excellence for Drug Discovery, 2002–08; Sen. Vice Pres. and Hd, Sci. Envmt Develt, 2008–10; Founder and CEO, OI Pharma Partners Ltd, 2010–; CEO, NeuroSymptomatix Ltd, 2010–13; non-executive Director: Proximagen Neuroscience Gp plc, 2010–12; Stratified Medical, 2015–. Trustee, Age Care, 2010–13. Member, Council: RHUL, 2011–13; Univ. of Herts, 2013–. FBPhS (FBPharmacolS 2012); FMedSci 2014. *Publications:* (ed jtly) Memory: neurochemical and abnormal perspectives, 1991; (ed jtly) Neurodegeneration, 1992; (ed jtly) Inflammatory Cells and Mediators in CNS Diseases, 1999; (ed jtly) Antisense Technology in the Central Nervous System, 1999; contribs to scientific jls. *Address:* BBSRC, Polaris House, North Star Avenue, Swindon, Wilts SN2 1UH. *E:* jackie.hunter@bbsrc.ac.uk.

HUNTER, Anthony John, OBE 2010; Chief Executive, Social Care Institute for Excellence, since 2014; *b* 9 March 1954; *s* of Robert and Elizabeth Hunter; *m* 1986, Tatyana Fomina; one *s* one *d*. *Educ:* Doncaster Grammar Sch.; Queen's Coll., Oxford (MA PPE 1976); Nottingham Univ. (MA Applied Social Studies, CQSW, 1980); Sheffield Poly. (DMS 1984). Social Worker and Social Services Manager, Doncaster MBC, 1976–84; Day and Home Services Manager, Barnsley MBC, 1985–86; Res. and Develt Manager, Barnardo's, 1986–89; Health and Social Care Consultant, Price Waterhouse, 1989–95; Dir of Social Services, Housing and Public Protection, ER of Yorks Council, 1995–2003; Exec. Dir, Community Services, Liverpool CC, 2004–08; Chief Exec., NE Lincs Council, 2008–13. Pres., Assoc. of Dirs of Social Services, 2004–05. *Publications:* articles on social care, local govt develt and change mgt issues. *Recreations:* football, rock'n'roll singing, comedy. *E:* tony.hunter@scie.org.uk.

HUNTER, Anthony Rex; *see* Hunter, Tony.

HUNTER, Archibald Sinclair; DL; CA; Chairman, Macfarlane Group PLC, 2004–12 (Director, since 1998); *b* 20 Aug. 1943; *s* of late John Lockhart Hunter and Elizabeth Hastings (*née* Sinclair); *m* 1969, Patricia Ann Robertson; two *s* one *d*. *Educ:* Queen's Park Sch., Glasgow. CA 1966. With Mackie & Clark, Glasgow, 1966; joined Thomson McLintock, 1966: Partner, 1974–87; Glasgow Office Managing Partner, 1983–87; Glasgow Office Managing Partner, KPMG Peat Marwick, 1987–92; Sen. Partner, Scotland, 1992–99, Consultant, 1999–2001, KPMG. Pres., ICAS, 1997–98. Non-executive Director: Clydeport plc, 1999–2002; N American Income Trust (formerly Edinburgh US Tracker Trust), 2003–; Royal Bank of Scotland, 2004–10; Chm., Le Chardon d'Or Ltd, 2001–. Dir, Beatson Inst., 1999–2010; Treas., Scottish Cancer Foundn, 2003–. Mem. Court, Univ. of Strathclyde, 1999–2007 (Chm., 2002–07). DL Renfrewshire, 1995. DUniv Strathclyde, 2006. *Recreations:* golf, swimming, hill-walking. *Address:* Macfarlane Group, Clansman House, 21 Newton Place, Glasgow G3 7PY. *T:* (0141) 314 3979. *Clubs:* Williamwood Golf (formerly Capt.) (Glasgow); Western Gailes Golf (Ayrshire).

HUNTER, Rt Rev. Barry Russell, AM 1992; Bishop of Riverina, 1971–92; permission to officiate, diocese of Newcastle, NSW, 1996–2001, diocese of Armidale, NSW, since 2001; *b* Brisbane, Queensland, 15 Aug. 1927; *s* of late John Hunter; *m* 1961, Dorothy Nancy, *d* of B. P. Sanders, Brisbane; three *d*. *Educ:* Toowoomba Grammar Sch.; St Francis' Theological Coll., Brisbane; Univ. of Queensland (BA, ThL). Assistant Curate, St Matthew's, Sherwood, 1953–56; Member, Bush Brotherhood of St Paul, Cunnamulla, Queensland, 1956–61; Rector, St Cecilia's, Chinchilla, 1961–66; Rector, St Gabriel's, Biloela, 1966–71; Archdeacon of the East, Diocese of Rockhampton, 1969–71; Locum Tenens in parish of Cudal, NSW, 1992–96. DLitt (*hc*) Charles Sturt Univ., 1994. *Recreation:* music. *Address:* 90 Calala Lane, Tamworth, NSW 2340, Australia.

HUNTER, Prof. Christopher Alexander, FRS 2008; Herchel Smith Professor of Organic Chemistry, University of Cambridge, since 2014; *b* Dunedin, NZ, 19 Feb. 1965; *s* of John Alexander Hunter and Alice Mary Hunter; *m* 2008, Rosaleen Theresa McHugh; two *s* one *d*. *Educ:* Churchill Coll., Cambridge (BA 1986; PhD 1989). Lectr, Dept of Chem., Univ. of Otago, NZ, 1989–91; Lectr, 1991–94, Reader, 1994–97, Prof. of Chemistry, 1997–2014, Dept of Chem., Univ. of Sheffield; Lister Inst. Res. Fellow, 1994–99. EPSRC Sen. Res. Fellow, 2005–10. Hon. DSc Ulster, 2013. Meldola Medal, 1992, Corday Morgan Medal, 1999, Tilden Prize, 2009, Physical Organic Chem. Award and Ingold Lectr, 2011, RSC. *Publications:* contrib. papers to scientific jls. *Address:* Department of Chemistry, University of Cambridge, Lensfield Road, Cambridge CB2 1EW. *T:* (01223) 336710. *E:* ch664@cam.ac.uk.

HUNTER, Craig; *see* Hunter, J. C.

HUNTER, David Peter; Director, Department for Environment, Food and Rural Affairs, 1996–2007; *b* 31 Dec. 1948; *o s* of Mr and Mrs D. Hunter, Southampton; *m* 1973, Judith, *d* of Mr and Mrs G. A. Baker, Worcester; two *s* two *d*. *Educ:* Regent's Park Sch.; Shirley Sch.; King Edward VI Sch., Southampton; Magdalen Coll., Oxford (MA). MAFF, 1972–82; Cabinet Office, 1982–83; rejoined MAFF, 1983; Head: Beef Div., 1984–87; Trade Policy and Tropical Products Div., 1987–93; Agencies and Citizen's Charter Div., 1993–96; EU and Livestock Gp, 1996–98; Agricl Gp, MAFF, subseq. DEFRA, 1998–2001; Dir, EU and Internat. Policy Directorate, 2001–06, Review of Rural Payments Agency, 2006–07, DEFRA. *Recreations:* theatre, vegetables, Soton FC, country walks.

HUNTER, Rear-Adm. Ian Alexander, CB 1993; Chief of Naval Staff, New Zealand, 1991–94; *b* 23 Oct. 1939; *s* of late A. A. Hunter and O. R. Hunter; *m* 1965, Hilary R. Sturrock; two *s*. *Educ:* Christchurch Boys' High Sch.; BRNC Dartmouth. Joined RNZN 1957; served HMNZS Otago, HMS Tabard, USS Arneb, HMNZS Rotoiti (Antarctic), N Ireland Anti-Submarine Sch., HM Ships Torquay and Eastbourne, HMNZ Ships Taranaki, Blackpool, Canterbury, Waikato (Command), Southland (Command); posts with Chief of Naval Staff; RCDS 1985; ACDS (Develt Plans), 1987–88; Commodore Auckland, 1988–91 (concerned with Govt financial reforms for RNZN, restructuring Dockyard, orgn of Whitbread Round the World Yacht Race). Pres., Sea Cadet Assoc. of NZ, 1998–. Trustee, United Services Medal Collection Trust 2006–; Patron, Wellington Returned Services Assoc., 2001–13. *Address:* 108B Messines Road, Karori, Wellington, New Zealand.

HUNTER, Prof. Ian Charles, PhD; FREng, FIET, FIEEE; Radio Design/Royal Academy of Engineering Professor of Microwave Signal Processing, since 2012, and Deputy Head, School of Electronic and Electrical Engineering, since 2013, University of Leeds; *b* Fleetwood, Lancs, 1 Sept. 1957; one *s* two *d*. *Educ:* Univ. of Leeds (BSc 1st Cl. Hons 1978; PhD 1981). FIET 2000; FIEEE 2007; FREng 2013. With Aercom Industries, Inc., Sunnyvale, Calif; KW Engrg, San Diego; Principal Engr, Filtronic Components Ltd, UK; Fellow Engr, Filtronic Comtek, 1995–2001; Mem., academic staff, Univ. of Bradford, 1991–97 (Sen. Lectr, 1995–97); Sen. Res. Fellow (pt-time), 1999–2001, Reader, 2001–03, Prof., 2003–12, Univ. of Leeds. Ed-in-Chief, Internat. Jl Electronics, 2006–. *Publications:* (jtly) Practical Microstrip Circuit Design, 1991; Theory and Design of Microwave Filters, 2001; The Story of Filtronic, 2003; contrib. papers to IEEE and IEE jls. *Recreations:* walking, sailing. *Address:* School of Electronic and Electrical Engineering, University of Leeds, Woodhouse Lane, Leeds LS2 9JT. *E:* i.c.hunter@leeds.ac.uk.

HUNTER, Ian Gerald Adamson; QC 1980; SC (NSW) 1994; a Recorder, 1986–2000; *b* 3 Oct. 1944; *s* of late Gerald Oliver Hunter and Jessie Hunter; *m* 1975, Maggie (*née* Reed) (marr. diss. 1999); two *s*; *m* 2000, Jill (*née* Nichols). *Educ:* Reading Sch.; Pembroke Coll., Cambridge (Open Scholar, Squire Univ. Law Scholar, Trevelyan Scholar, BA (double first in Law), MA, LLB); Harvard Law Sch. (Kennedy Memorial Scholar, LLM). Called to the Bar, Inner Temple, 1967 (Duke of Edinburgh Entrance Scholar, Major Scholar), Bencher, 1986; Mem. Bar, NSW, 1993; Avocat à la cour de Paris, 1995–2010. CEDR Accredited Mediator, 1998–. Chm., Consolidated Regulations and Transfer Cttee, Senate of Inns of Court, 1986–87 (Mem., 1982–85); Member: International Relations Cttee, Bar Council, 1982–90; Exec. Cttee, Bar Council, 1985–86. Mem. and Rapporteur, Internat. Law Assoc. Anti-Trust Cttee, 1968–72; Pres., Union Internat. des Avocats, 1989 (UK Vice-Pres., 1982–86; first Vice Pres., 1986–; Dir of Studies, 1990–91); Vice Pres., Franco-British Lawyers Soc., 1996–99; Pres., Anglo-Australasian Lawyers Soc., 1998–; Treas., Bar Pro Bono Unit, 1997–99; Hon. Mem., Canadian Bar Assoc., 1990. FCIArb. *Publications:* articles on public international law. *Recreations:* bebop, other good music, French cooking. *Address:* Essex Court Chambers, 24 Lincoln's Inn Fields, WC2A 3EG. *T:* (020) 7813 8000.

HUNTER, Jacqueline; *see* Hunter, A. J.

HUNTER, James, CBE 2001; PhD; FRSE; Director, Centre for History, UHI Millennium Institute, Dornoch, 2005–10, now Emeritus Professor of History, University of the Highlands and Islands; *b* 22 May 1948; *s* of Donald and Jean Hunter; *m* 1972, Evelyn Ronaldson; one *s* one *d*. *Educ:* Oban High Sch.; Aberdeen Univ. (MA Hons 1971); Edinburgh Univ. (PhD 1974). Res. Fellow, Aberdeen Univ., 1974–76; journalist: Press and Jl, 1976–81; Sunday Standard, 1981–82; freelance journalist and broadcaster, 1982–85; Founding Dir, Scottish Crofters' Union, 1985–90. Chairman: Skye and Lochalsh Enterprise, 1995–98; Highlands and Is Enterprise, 1998–2004 (Bd Mem., 1991–95); Isle of Eigg Heritage Trust, 2004–07; Member: Scottish Tourist Bd, 1995–98; Council, NT for Scotland, 1995–98; Convention of the Highlands and Is, 1996–2004; Bd, Scottish Natural Heritage, 2004–10 (Mem., N Areas Bd, 1992–98); Vice-Chair, Land Reform Rev. Gp, Scottish Govt, 2012–13. Mem., BBC's Broadcasting Council for Scotland, 1999–2002. FRSE 2007. *Publications:* The Making of the Crofting Community, 1976; For the People's Cause, 1986; Skye: the island, 1986; The Claim of Crofting, 1991; Scottish Highlanders: a people and their place, 1992; A Dance Called America: the Scottish Highlands, the United States and Canada, 1994; On the Other Side of Sorrow: nature and people in the Scottish Highlands, 1995; Glencoe and the Indians, 1996 (US edn as Scottish Highlanders, Indian Peoples); Last of the Free: a millennial history of the Highlands and Islands of Scotland, 1999; Culloden and the Last Clansman, 2001; Scottish Exodus: travels among a worldwide clan, 2005; From the Low Tide of the Sea to the Highest Mountain Tops: community ownership of land in the Scottish Highlands and Islands, 2012. *Recreations:* walking, helping on occasion with grandchildren. *Address:* 19 Mansefield Park, Kirkhill, Inverness IV5 7ND. *T:* (01463) 831228. *E:* jameshunter22548@btinternet.com.

HUNTER, Prof. John Angus Alexander, OBE 1997; MD; Grant Professor of Dermatology, University of Edinburgh, 1981–99, now Emeritus; *b* 16 June 1939; *s* of Dr John Craig Alexander Hunter and Alison Hay Shand Alexander; *m* 1968, Ruth Mary Farrow; one *s* two *d*. *Educ:* Loretto Sch., Musselburgh; Pembroke Coll., Cambridge (BA 1960); Univ. of Edinburgh (MB ChB 1963; MD 1977 (Gold Medal)). FRCPE 1978. Gen. med. posts, Edinburgh, 1963–66; Research Fellow in Dermatology: Inst. of Dermatology, London, 1967; Univ. of Minnesota, 1968–69; Lectr, Dept of Dermatology, Univ. of Edinburgh, 1970–74; Consultant Dermatologist, Lothian Health Bd, 1974–80. Chm., Specialist Adv. Cttee (Dermatol.), JCHMT, 1986–90. President: Section of Dermatol., RSocMed, 1993–94; Scottish Dermatol Soc., 1994–97; Hon. Member: British Assoc. of Dermatologists, 1999 (Pres., 1998–99); Dermatological Socs of N America, Greece, Germany, Poland, Austria and USA. *Publications:* (jtly) Common Diseases of the Skin, 1983; (jtly) Clinical Dermatology, 1989, 4th edn 2008; (jtly) Skin Signs in Clinical Medicine, 1997; (ed jtly) Davidson's Principles and Practice of Medicine, 18th edn 1999 to 20th edn 2006; (ed jtly) Davidson's Clinical Cases in Medicine, 2008, 2nd edn as Davidson's 100 Clinical Cases, 2012; numerous articles in dermatol jls. *Recreations:* family archives, golf, gardening, music. *Address:* Sandy Lodge, Nisbet Road, Gullane, E Lothian EH31 2BQ. *E:* jaa.hunter@virgin.net. *Clubs:* Hawks (Cambridge); Hon. Company of Edinburgh Golfers.

HUNTER, (John) Craig; Founder Director and Managing Director, VERSEC Ltd, since 1998; *b* Hitchin, Herts, 16 Jan. 1961; *s* of Ronald Hunter and Hazel Hunter; civil partnership 2010, Nick Hazell. *Educ:* Hitchin Boys' Grammar Sch.; Sheffield City Poly. (BA Hons Business Studies with Law 1983). Fellow, ICSA, 1998; Chartered Sec. in Public Practice 1998. Dep. Company Sec., NFC plc, 1991–98. Specialist Dir (non-exec.), British Swimming, 2007–; Member: Technical Swimming Cttee, Ligue Européenne de Natation, 2008–; Mission Control Panel, UK Sport, 2011–; Ind. Dir, English Inst. of Sport (Ind. Mem., Audit Cttee, 2014–); Ind. Mem., Audit Cttee, UK Sport Gp, 2014–. Founding Dir, Onboard Associated Ltd, 2014–. Chef de Mission, Commonwealth Games England: Commonwealth Games, 2010, Commonwealth Youth Games, 2011; Chef de Mission, Eur. Youth Olympic Fest., British Olympic Assoc., 2011; Chef de Mission, ParalympicsGB, London 2012, 2011–12. Ext. Examr, MSc Finance and Corporate Governance, Univ. of Hertfordshire, 2007–11. President: Herts Amateur Swimming Assoc., 1991–92; Hatfield Swimming Club, 2008–. Outstanding Achievement Award, ICSA 2013. *Recreations:* ski-ing, yoga, theatre, French conversation. *Address:* 39 Alma Road, St Albans, Herts AL1 3AT. *T:* (01727) 855512, 07771 814929. *E:* craig.hunter@btinternet.com.

HUNTER, John Garvin, CB 2004; Permanent Secretary, Department of Finance and Personnel, Northern Ireland Civil Service, 2003–07; *b* 9 Aug. 1947; *s* of Garvin and Martha Hunter; *m* 1976, Rosemary Alison Haire; one *s* two *d*. *Educ:* Merchant Taylors' Sch., Liverpool; Queen's Univ., Belfast (BA); Cornell Univ., NY (MBA). Asst Principal, NICS, 1970; Department of Health and Social Services: Dep. Principal, 1973; Harkness Fellow, 1977–79; Principal Officer, 1979; Asst Sec., 1982; Dir Gen., Internat. Fund for Ireland, 1986; Under Sec., 1988; Chief Exec., Mgt Exec., Health and Personal Social Services, NI, 1990–96; Dir of Personnel, NICS, 1997–99; Perm. Sec., Dept for Social Develt, NICS, 1999–2003. Chm., Chief Executives' Forum, 2008–; Member: Council, Univ. of Ulster, 2008–; Bd of Finance and Personnel, Presbyterian Church in Ireland, 2009–; Chm. Council, Corrymeela

Community, 2011–. Trustee, Age NI, 2009–13. *Publications:* contribs to conf. papers on the conflict in NI and on health service planning. *Recreations:* Corrymeela Community, Abbey Singers, Ulster Historical Foundation, U3A.

HUNTER, Prof. John Rotheram, OBE 2011; PhD; FSA, FSAScot, FCSFS; Professor of Ancient History and Archaeology, University of Birmingham, 1996–2010, now Emeritus; *b* 4 Jan. 1949; *s* of William Rotherham Hunter and Stella Maud Hunter (*née* Atthill); *m* 1971, Margaret Suddes; three *s* one *d*. *Educ:* Merchant Taylors' Sch., Crosby; Univ. of Durham (BA 1970; DipArch 1971; PhD 1977); Univ. of Lund. FSAScot 1980; MCIfA (MIFA 1985); FSA 1986. Lectr, 1974–83, Sen. Lectr, 1983–95, Reader, 1995–96, in Archaeology, Univ. of Bradford. Vis. Prof. of Archaeol., Univ. of Oxford, 2010–. Cathedral Archaeologist, Bradford Cathedral, 1990–99. Registered Forensic Practitioner, 2003–; Dir, Centre for Internat. Forensic Assistance, 2003–05. Mem., Royal Commn on Ancient and Histl Monuments of Scotland, 2004–. FCSFS (FFSSoc 2007). *Publications:* Rescue Excavations on the Brough of Birsay, Orkney, 1986; (with I. B. M. Ralston) Archaeological Resource Management in the UK, 1993; (with C. Roberts and A. Martin) Studies in Crime: an introduction to forensic archaeology, 1996; Fair Isle: the archaeology of an island community, 1996; (with I. B. M. Ralston) The Archaeology of Britain: an introduction, 1998, 2nd edn 2010; (with M. Cox) Advances in Forensic Archaeology, 2005; Investigations in Sanday, Orkney: vol. 1, Excavations at Pool, Sanday, 2007; (with A. Woodward) An Examination of Prehistoric Stone Bracers from Britain, 2011; (with B. Simpson and C. Sturdy Colls) Forensic Approaches to Buried Remains, 2013. *Recreations:* rowing, watching football, walking the dog. *Address:* School of History and Culture, Arts Building, University of Birmingham, Birmingham B15 2TT. *T:* (0121) 414 5497.

HUNTER, Keith Robert, OBE 1981; British Council Director, Italy, 1990–96; *b* 29 May 1936; *s* of Robert Ernest Williamson and Winifred Mary Hunter; *m* 1st, 1959, Ann Patricia Fuller (marr. diss. 1989); one *s* two *d*; 2nd, 1991, Victoria Solomonidis. *Educ:* Hymers Coll., Hull; Magdalen Coll., Oxford (MA); Sch. of African and Oriental Studies, Univ. of London; Chinese Univ. of Hong Kong; Inst. of Educn, Univ. of London. Joined British Council, 1962; Lectr, Royal Sch. of Admin, Phnom Penh, 1960–64; Schs Recruitment Dept, 1964–66; SOAS, 1966–67; Asst Rep., Hong Kong, 1967–69; Dir, Penang, 1970–72; Dep. Rep., Kuala Lumpur, 1972–74; London Univ. Inst. of Educn, 1974–75; Rep., Algeria, 1975–78; First Sec. (Cultural), subseq. Cultural Counsellor (British Council Rep.), China, 1979–82; Sec. of Bd, and Hd of Dir-Gen.'s Dept, 1982–85; Controller, Arts Div., 1985–90. Trustee, British Sch. at Rome, 1997–2001. Chm., Parkhouse Award Trust, 1999–. *Recreations:* music, printmaking, restoration. *Address:* 15 Queensdale Road, W11 4SB.

HUNTER, Sir Laurence (Colvin), Kt 1995; CBE 1987; FRSE 1986; Professor of Applied Economics, University of Glasgow, 1970–2003, now Professor Emeritus and Hon. Senior Research Fellow; *b* 8 Aug. 1934; *s* of Laurence O. and Jessie P. Hunter; *m* 1958, Evelyn Margaret (*née* Green); three *s* one *d*. *Educ:* Hillhead High Sch., Glasgow; Univ. of Glasgow (MA); University Coll., Oxford (DPhil). Asst, Manchester Univ., 1958–59; National Service, 1959–61; Post-Doctoral Fellow, Univ. of Chicago, 1961–62; University of Glasgow: Lectr, 1962; Sen. Lectr, 1967; Titular Prof., 1969; Vice-Principal, 1982–86; Dir of External Relations, 1987–90; Dir, Business Sch., 1996–99. Member: Ct of Inquiry into miners' strike, 1972; Council, Advisory, Conciliation and Arbitration Service, 1974–86; Royal Commn on Legal Services in Scotland, 1976–80; Council, ESRC, 1989–92; Chairman: Post Office Arbitration Tribunal, 1974–92; Police Negotiating Bd, 1987–99 (Dep. Chm., 1980–86). Pres., Scottish Econ. Soc., 1993–96; Treas., RSE, 1999–2004. DUniv Paisley, 1999. *Publications:* (with G. L. Reid) Urban Worker Mobility, 1968; (with D. J. Robertson) Economics of Wages and Labour, 1969, 2nd edn (with C. Mulvey), 1981; (with G. L. Reid and D. Boddy) Labour Problems of Technological Change, 1970; (with A. W. J. Thomson) The Nationalised Transport Industries, 1973; (with R. B. McKersie) Pay, Productivity and Collective Bargaining, 1973; (with L. Baddon *et al.*) People's Capitalism, 1989; other pubns in economics and industrial relations. *Recreations:* golf, painting, curling. *Address:* 7 Boclair Crescent, Bearsden, Glasgow G61 2AG. *T:* (0141) 563 7135.

HUNTER, Mack Robert; a District Judge (Magistrates' Courts), since 2004; *b* 21 Oct. 1954; *s* of Mack and Joan Hunter; *m* 1996, Margaret (*née* Campbell); one *s* one *d*. *Educ:* Sevenoaks Sch.; Worcester Coll., Oxford (MA). Called to the Bar, Gray's Inn, 1979; in practice as barrister, 1979–2004; Actg Stipendiary Magistrate, then Dep. Dist Judge, 1998–2004. *Recreations:* swimming, tennis, history, spending time with family. *Address:* c/o Chief Magistrates' Office, Westminster Magistrates' Court, 181 Marylebone Road, NW1 5BR.

HUNTER, Mark James; *b* 25 July 1957; *s* of Arthur Brian Hunter and Betty Elizabeth Mary Hunter; *m* 1997, Lesley Graham (*d* 2013); one *s* one *d*. *Educ:* Audenshaw Grammar Sch. Employed in newspaper advertising industry, latterly as business develt manager, local newspaper div., Guardian Media Gp. Member (Lib Dem): Tameside MBC, 1980–89; Stockport MBC, 1996–2005 (Chm., Educn Cttee; Dep. Leader, 2001–02; Leader, 2002–05). Contested: (Liberal SDP Alliance) Ashton under Lyne, 1987; (Lib Dem) Stockport, 2001. MP (Lib Dem) Cheadle, July 2005–2015; contested (Lib Dem) same seat, 2015. Lib Dem spokesman on foreign affairs, 2007, dep. spokesperson on transport and PPS to Lib Dem Leader, 2007–10; Lib Dem Dep. Chief Whip, 2010–15; an Asst Govt Whip, 2010–14. Hon. Pres., Stockport Br., Parkinson's UK, 2009–. Member: Nat. Trust; Amnesty Internat.; CAMRA.

HUNTER, Prof. Michael Cyril William, FSA; FRHistS; FBA 2007; Professor of History, Birkbeck College, University of London, 1992–2011, now Emeritus; *b* 22 April 1949; *s* of Francis Hunter and Olive Hunter (*née* Williams). *Educ:* Christ's Hospital; Jesus Coll., Cambridge (BA 1971, MA 1975); Worcester Coll., Oxford (DPhil 1975). Research Fellow: Worcester Coll., Oxford, 1972–75; Univ. of Reading, 1975–76; Birkbeck College, University of London: Lectr in History, 1976–84; Reader in History, 1984–92. Longstanding activist on issues concerning historic preservation; also involved in projects for making digital resources available online. *Publications:* John Aubrey and the Realm of Learning, 1975; Science and Society in Restoration England, 1981; The Victorian Villas of Hackney, 1981; (with Annabel Gregory) An Astrological Diary of the Seventeenth Century, 1988; Establishing the New Science, 1989; (jtly) Avebury Reconsidered, 1991; The Royal Society and its Fellows 1660–1700, 1982, rev. edn 1994; Robert Boyle by Himself and his Friends, 1994; Science and the Shape of Orthodoxy, 1995; (ed) Preserving the Past, 1996; (ed) Archives of the Scientific Revolution, 1998; (ed with Edward B. Davis) The Works of Robert Boyle, vols 1–7, 1999, vols 8–14, 2000; Robert Boyle: scrupulosity and science, 2000; (ed jtly) The Correspondence of Robert Boyle, 6 vols, 2001; The Occult Laboratory, 2001; (jtly) London's Leonardo, 2003; The Boyle Papers, 2007; Editing Early Modern Texts, 2007; Boyle: between God and science, 2009 (Samuel Pepys Award, 2011; Roy G. Neville Prize, 2011); (ed) Printed Images in Early Modern Britain, 2010; Boyle Studies: aspects of the life and thought of Robert Boyle, 2015. *Recreations:* book-collecting, motorcycling, historic buildings. *Address:* Exmouth House, Exmouth Place, Hastings, East Sussex TN34 3JA. *T:* (01424) 430727.

HUNTER, Paul Anthony, FRCS, FRCP, FRCOphth; Consultant Ophthalmic Surgeon, King's College Hospital, 1982–2013, Honorary Consultant, 2013–14; President, Royal College of Ophthalmologists, 2000–03; *b* 22 Nov. 1944; *s* of Gordon Nicholson Hunter and Kathleen Margaret (*née* Tyldesley); *m* 1971, Elizabeth Alex Pearse; one *s* one *d*. *Educ:* Leys Sch., Cambridge; Queens' Coll., Cambridge (BA Hons 1966; MB BChir 1969); Middlesex Hosp. Med. Sch. DO RCP&RCS 1974. FRCS 1977; FRCOphth 1993; FRCP 2002. Resident Surgical Officer, Moorfields Eye Hosp., 1976–79; Sen. Registrar, Middx Hosp., 1980–81; Hon. Lectr, King's Coll. Med. Sch., London Univ., 1982–2013. *Publications:* (ed jtly) Atlas of Clinical Ophthalmology, 1988, 3rd edn 2005; contribs on cornea and external eye disease to professional jls. *Recreations:* travel, ski-ing, gardening, grandchildren.

HUNTER, Prof. Peter John, DPhil; FRS 2006; FRSNZ; Professor of Engineering Science, since 1997 and Director, Bioengineering Institute, since 2001, University of Auckland; *b* Auckland, NZ, 30 July 1948. *Educ:* Univ. of Auckland (BE 1971; ME 1972); Univ. of Oxford (DPhil 1975). Res. Fellow, Rutherford Lab., 1975–77; Fellow, St Catherine's Coll., Oxford, 1975–77; Lectr in Engrg Sci., Univ. of Auckland, 1978–97. Dir of Computational Physiol., Univ. of Oxford. Co-Chm., Physiome Cttee, IUPS. FRSNZ 1994. Rutherford Medal, Royal Soc. of NZ, 2009. *Publications:* articles in learned jls. *Address:* Bioengineering Institute, Faculty of Engineering, University of Auckland, Private Bag 92019, Auckland Mail Centre, Auckland 1142, New Zealand.

HUNTER, Sir Philip (John), Kt 2008; CBE 1999; PhD; Chief Schools Adjudicator, 2002–09; Chair, North Staffordshire Combined Healthcare Trust, 2009–12; *b* 23 Nov. 1939; *m* Ruth Bailey; two *s* one *d*. *Educ:* Univ. of Durham (BSc 1962); Univ. of Newcastle upon Tyne (PhD 1965). Lectr, Univ. of Khartoum, 1965–67; Senior Scientific Officer: ARC, Cambridge, 1967–69; DES, 1969–71; Course Dir, CS Staff Coll., 1971–73; posts at DES, including science, schools, finance and Private Office, 1973–79; Dep. Chief Educn Officer, ILEA, 1979–85; Chief Educn Officer, then Dir of Educn, Staffs, 1985–2000. Dir, Staffs TEC, 1990–2001; Member of Council: Keele Univ., 1987–99; BTEC, 1990–95; Member: Nat. Council for Educnl Technol., 1986–91; Nat. Curriculum Wkg Gp on Design and Technol., 1988–89; Design Council Educn Cttee, 1990–94; Qualifications and Curriculum Authy, 1997–2001. Chm., West Midlands Chief Educn Officers, 1995–97; Pres., Soc. of Educn Officers, 1998–99 (Vice-Pres., 1997). Vis. Prof. of Educn, Keele Univ., 1998–2005. Trustee, Staffs Wildlife Trust, 2012–. Hon. DTech Staffs, 1999. *Publications:* (jtly) Terrestrial Slugs, 1970; (jtly) Pulmonates, 1978; (ed) Developing Education: fifteen years on, 1999; papers on ecology of invertebrates; contrib. educnl jls on educn policy matters. *Recreation:* gardening. *Address:* Park Farm, Vicarage Lane, Little Eaton, Derbyshire DE21 5EA.

HUNTER, Prof. Richard Lawrence, PhD; FBA 2013; Regius Professor of Greek, Cambridge University, since 2001; Fellow, Trinity College, Cambridge, since 2001; *b* 30 Oct. 1953; *s* of John Lawrence Hunter and Ruth Munro Hunter; *m* 1978, Iris Temperli; one *s* one *d*. *Educ:* Cranbrook Sch., Sydney; Univ. of Sydney (BA Hons 1974); Pembroke Coll., Cambridge (PhD 1979). University of Cambridge: Fellow, 1977–2001, Dir of Studies in Classics, 1979–99, Asst Tutor, 1985–87, Tutor for Admissions, 1987–93, Pembroke Coll.; Univ. Lectr in Classics, 1987–97; Reader in Greek and Latin Lit., 1997–2001; Chm., Sch. of Arts and Humanities, 2007–08. Visiting Professor: Princeton Univ., 1991–92, 2012–13; Univ. of Virginia, 1979, 1984. Pres., Council, Aristotle Univ. of Thessaloniki, 2013–. MAE 2013. Fellow, Alexander S. Onassis Public Benefit Foundn, 2006. Ed., Jl of Hellenic Studies, 1995–2000. Corresp. Fellow, 2001, Foreign Fellow, 2014, Acad. of Athens; Hon. Fellow, Aust. Acad. of Humanities, 2005. Hon. Dr Phil. Thessaloniki, 2004. Premio Anassilaos, Reggio Calabria, 2006. *Publications:* Eubulus: the fragments, 1983; A Study of Daphnis and Chloe, 1983; The New Comedy of Greece and Rome, 1985; Apollonius of Rhodes, Argonautica III, 1989; The Argonautica of Apollonius, Literary Studies, 1993; trans., Jason and the Golden Fleece (The Argonautica), 1993; Theocritus and the Archaeology of Greek Poetry, 1996; (ed) Studies in Heliodorus, 1998; Theocritus: a selection, 1999; Theocritus, Encomium of Ptolemy, 2003; Plato's Symposium, 2004; (with M. Fantuzzi) Tradition and Innovation in Hellenistic Poetry, 2004 (Italian edn 2002); (ed) The Hesiodic Catalogue of Women: constructions and reconstructions, 2005; The Shadow of Callimachus, 2006; On Coming After (collected papers), 2008; (ed with I. Rutherford) Wandering Poets in Ancient Greek Culture, 2009; Critical Moments in Classical Literature, 2009; (ed with K. Carvounis) Signs of Life?: studies in later Greek poetry, 2009; (with D. Russell) Plutarch: how to study poetry (De audiendis poetis), 2011; Plato and the Traditions of Ancient Literature, 2012; Hesiodic Voices, 2014; Apollonius of Rhodes, Argonautica IV, 2015; articles and reviews in learned jls. *Recreation:* travel. *Address:* Faculty of Classics, Sidgwick Avenue, Cambridge CB3 9DA. *T:* (01223) 335960, 335152.

HUNTER, Robert Walter, Lord-Lieutenant for Shetland, since 2011; *b* 1949; *m* 1971, Mabel Joan Hawick; three *c*. *Educ:* Strathclyde Univ. Work in shipbuilding and marine electrical equipment supply, then fish processing industry; Manager: Shetland Oil Industries Gp, 1990–2002; Grimista Property Ltd, 2003–04; Electrical Manager, Camvo 86 Ltd, 2004–06. Dir, Shetland Livestock Mktg Gp. DL Shetland, 2002. *Address:* Millburn, Bridge End, Shetland ZE2 9LD.

HUNTER, Sir Thomas (Blane), Kt 2005; Chairman: West Coast Capital, since 1998; Hunter Foundation, since 1998; *b* 6 May 1961; *m* 1990, Marion McKillop; two *s* one *d*. *Educ:* Strathclyde Univ. (BA Mktg and Econs). Founder: Sports Div., 1984, sold 1998; Hunter Foundn, 1998; West Coast Capital, 2001. Founder and Mem. Bd, Clinton-Hunter Develt Initiative, 2005–. Beacon Prize, 2004. *Recreations:* ski-ing, water sports, music. *Address:* Marathon House, Olympic Business Park, Drybridge Road, Dundonald KA2 9AE. *T:* (01563) 852226, *Fax:* (01563) 850091.

HUNTER, Dr Tony, (Anthony Rex Hunter), FRS 1987; Professor, since 1982, and Renato Dulbecco Professor, since 2011, Molecular and Cell Biology Laboratory, Salk Institute, San Diego, California; concurrently Adjunct Professor of Biology, University of California, San Diego; Director, Salk Institute Cancer Centre, since 2008; *b* 23 Aug. 1943; *s* of Ranulph Rex Hunter and Nellie Ruby Elsie Hunter (*née* Hitchcock); *m* 1969, Philippa Charlotte Marrack (marr. diss. 1974); *m* 1992, Jennifer Ann Maureen Price; two *s*. *Educ:* Felsted Sch., Essex; Gonville and Caius Coll., Cambridge (BA, MA, PhD). Research Fellow, Christ's Coll., Cambridge, 1968–71 and 1973–74; Salk Inst., San Diego: Res. Associate, 1971–73; Asst Prof., 1975–78; Associate Prof., 1978–82. American Cancer Soc. Res. Prof., 1992–2008. Einstein Prof., Chinese Acad. of Scis, 2013. Assoc. Mem., EMBO, 1992. FRSA 1989; Fellow: Amer. Acad. of Arts and Scis, 1992; Amer. Assoc. for Cancer Res. Acad., 2013; For. Associate, US Nat. Acad. of Scis, 1998; Member: Inst. of Medicine, US Nat. Acads, 2004; Amer. Philos. Soc., 2006. Katharine Berkan Judd Award, Meml Sloan-Kettering Cancer Center, 1992; Gairdner Foundn Internat. Award, 1994; Hopkins Meml Medal, Biochemical Soc., 1994; Mott Prize, Gen. Motors Cancer Res. Foundn, 1994; Feodor Lynen Medal, Univ. of Miami, 1999; J. Allyn Taylor Internat. Prize in Medicine, John P. Robarts Res. Inst. and C. H. Stiller Meml Foundn, 2000; Keio Med. Sci. Prize, Keio Univ. Med. Sci. Fund, Tokyo, 2001; Sergio Lombroso Award in Cancer Res., Weizman Inst. Sci., 2003; Amer. Cancer Soc. Medal of Honor, 2004; Kirk A. Landon Amer. Assoc. for Cancer Res. Prize, 2004; Prince of Asturias Award, 2004; Louis Gross Horowitz Prize, 2004; Wolf Prize in Medicine, 2005; Daniel Nathans Meml Award, Van Andel Inst., 2005; Pasarow Award in Cancer, Robert J. and Claire Pasarow Foundn, 2007; Herbert Tabor Award, Amer. Soc. of Biochem. and Molecular Biol., 2007; Clifford Prize for Cancer Res., Inst. of Med. and Veterinary Sci., Adelaide, 2007; Signal Transduction Soc. Hon. Medal, 2011; Royal Medal, Royal Soc., 2014; BBVA Foundn Frontiers of Knowledge Award in Biomedicine, 2014. *Publications:* numerous, in leading scientific jls. *Recreations:* white water rafting, exploring the Baja peninsula. *Address:* Molecular and Cell Biology Laboratory, The Salk Institute, 10010 North Torrey Pines Road, La Jolla, CA 92037, USA. *T:* (858) 4534100, ext. 1385, *Fax:* (858) 4574765. *E:* hunter@salk.edu.

HUNTER, William John, MB, BS; FRCP, FRCPE, FFOM; Director, Public Health, European Commission, 1999–2000; *b* 5 April 1937; *m*; two *s* one *d*. *Educ:* Westminster Medical Sch. (MB, BS). LRCP 1961, FRCP 1995; FRCPE 1999; MRCS 1961; FFOM 1978. Commission of the European Communities: Principal Administrator, 1974–82; Hd of Div., Industrial Medicine and Hygiene, 1982–88; Dir, Public Health and Safety at Work, 1988–99. Hon. DG, EC, 2000–. Permt Mem., Caducée Gp, Commissariat Gén. du Plan advising Prime Minister of France, 2004–. Internat. Advr, 1998–2007, Mem., European Wkg Gp, 2001–07, RCP. Member: Admin. Bd, Assoc. Internat. des Anciens des Communautés Européennes, 2001–12; Adv. Bd, Inst des Scis de la Santé, 2004–06; Admin. Bd, Ribérac Hosp., 2006–. Member, Administrative Board: Cercle d'Histoire et de Généalogie du Perigord, 1998–2005; Ensemble Vocal Arnaut de Mareuil, 2004–05. Hon. FFPH (Hon. FFPHM 1997). OStJ 1993. Ed., Internat. Jl of Integrated Care, 1999–2002. *Publications:* many on public health and safety at work. *Recreations:* swimming, diving, music.

HUNTER, Winston Ronald O'Sullivan; QC 2000; a Recorder, since 2000; *b* 7 Sept. 1960; *m* 1988, Louise Mary Blackwell; three *s*. *Educ:* Leeds Univ. (LLB 1st Cl. Hons). Called to the Bar, Lincoln's Inn, 1985, Bencher, 2011. *Recreations:* cricket, shooting, antiques. *Address:* 12 Byrom Street, Manchester M3 4PP. *T:* (0161) 829 2100.

HUNTER BLAIR, Sir Patrick (David), 9th Bt *cr* 1786, of Dunskey; owner, Milton of Blairquhan, Ayrshire; *b* 12 May 1958; *s* of Francis John Hunter Blair and of Joyce Adeline Mary (*née* Graham); *S* cousin, 2006; *m* 1984, Marguerite Catherine O'Neill; three *s* (incl. twins) two *d*. *Educ:* Edinburgh Acad.; Univ. of Aberdeen (BSc Forestry). FICFor. Dir of Policy Standards, NI Forest Service, 1998–2005. Non-exec. Dir, Scottish Natural Heritage, 2007–13. Chm., S Scotland Regl Forestry Forum, 2010–. *Recreations:* family, friends, forestry and fishing. *Heir:* *s* Ronan Patrick Hunter Blair, *b* 10 Feb. 1995. *Address:* Milton of Blairquhan, Maybole, Ayrshire KA19 7LY.

HUNTING, Richard Hugh, CBE 2010; Chairman, Hunting plc, since 1991 (Deputy Chairman, 1989–91); *b* 30 July 1946; *s* of late Charles Patrick Maule Hunting, CBE, TD and Diana, *d* of Brig. A. B. P. Pereira, DSO; *m* 1970, Penelope, *d* of Col L. L. Fleming, MBE, MC; one *s* two *d*. *Educ:* Rugby Sch.; Sheffield Univ. (BEng); Manchester Business Sch. (MBA). Joined Hunting Gp, 1972; worked at Hunting Surveys and Consultants, Field Aviation, E. A. Gibson Shipbrokers, Hunting Oilfield Services, Hunting Engineering; Director: Hunting Associated Industries, 1986–89 (Chm., 1989); Hunting Petroleum Services, 1989; Hunting plc, 1989–. Dir, Yule Catto & Co. plc, 2000–09. Non-exec. Dir, Royal Brompton and Harefield NHS Foundn Trust (formerly NHS Trust), 2007–15. Mem. Council, CBI, 1992–97. Comr, Royal Hosp., Chelsea, 2002–08; Mem., Adv. Bd, Greenwich Hosp., 2011–. Trustee: Geffrye Mus., 1995–2009 (Chm., 2000–09); Battle of Britain Meml Trust, 1998– (Chm., 2000–); Chm., Royal Brompton and Harefield Hosps Charity, 2012–. Mem. Court, Ironmongers' Co., 1986– (Master, 1996). *Recreations:* arts, ski-ing, family history. *Address:* (office) 5 Hanover Square, W1S 1HQ. *T:* (020) 7321 0123. *Clubs:* Boodle's, Chelsea Arts, Hurlingham.

HUNTINGDON, 17th Earl of, *cr* 1529 (by some reckonings 16th Earl of); **William Edward Robin Hood Hastings Bass,** LVO 1999; farmer and consultant; *b* 30 Jan. 1948; *s* of Capt. Peter Robin Hood Hastings Bass (who assumed additional surname of Bass by deed poll, 1954) (*d* 1964); *g s* of 13th Earl and Priscilla Victoria, *d* of Capt. Sir Malcolm Bullock, 1st Bt, MBE; *S* kinsman, 1990; *m* 1989, Sue Warner (marr. diss. 2001). *Educ:* Winchester; Trinity Coll., Cambridge. Began as racehorse trainer, 1976; Trainer, West Ilsley Stables, Berks, 1989–98. *Heir:* *b* Hon. Simon Aubrey Robin Hood Hastings Bass, *b* 2 May 1950. *Address:* Wells Head House, Kingsclere, near Newbury, Berks RG20 5PX.

HUNTINGDON, Bishop Suffragan of, since 2008; **Rt Rev. David Thomson,** DPhil; FSA, FRHistS; *b* 2 Feb. 1952; *s* of Canon Ronald and Coral Thomson; *m* 1974, Jean Elliot Douglas-Jones; two *s* two *d*. *Educ:* Keble Coll., Oxford (MA, DPhil 1978); Selwyn Coll., Cambridge (BA 1980, MA 1984); Westcott House, Cambridge. FSA 2008; FRHistS 2008. Lectr, Wentworth Castle Coll. of Educn, 1976–78. Ordained deacon, 1981, priest, 1982; Curate, Maltby Team Ministry, 1981–84; Team Vicar, Banbury, 1984–94; Team Rector, Cockermouth, 1994–2002; Archdeacon of Carlisle, and Canon Residentiary, 2002–08; Interim Bishop of St Edmundsbury and Ipswich, 2013–15. Mem., Gen. Synod, 2013–. Vice-Chair, Nat. Soc. and Bd of Educn, 2013–15; Chair, Schs Develt Gp, Nat. Soc., 2015–. Sen. Mem., St Edmund's Coll., Cambridge, 2012–. Hon. Canon, Ely Cathedral, 2008–. Gov., Trinity Sch., Carlisle, 2002–08 (Chair, 2003–05). Sec., Parish and People, 1984–93. Chair, Little Gidding Council of Reference, 2012–. FRSA. *Publications:* A Descriptive Catalogue of Middle English Grammatical Texts, 1979; An Edition of the Middle English Grammatical Texts, 1984; A Journey with John, 2004; Lent with Luke, 2005; Christmas by Candlelight, 2006; Ways to Pray, 2007; contribs to collaborative works; articles in learned jls on medieval and theol subjects. *Recreations:* medieval studies, detective fiction, fine art. *Address:* 14 Lynn Road, Ely, Cambs CB6 1DA. *T:* (01353) 662137, *Fax:* (01353) 669357. *E:* bishop.huntingdon@ely.anglican.org.

HUNTINGDON AND WISBECH, Archdeacon of; *see* McCurdy, Ven. H. K.

HUNTINGFIELD, 7th Baron *cr* 1796 (Ire.); **Joshua Charles Vanneck;** Bt 1751; Lecturer, Cambridge Enterprise Agency, since 1999; Development Manager, Young Enterprise Cambridgeshire, 2001–08; *b* 10 Aug. 1954; *o s* of 6th Baron Huntingfield and Janetta Lois, *er d* of Captain R. H. Errington, RN; *S* father, 1994; *m* 1982, Arabella Mary (*d* 2011), *d* of A. H. J. Fraser, MC; four *s* one *d* (incl. twin *s*). *Educ:* West Downs, Winchester; Eton; Magdalene Coll., Cambridge (MA). ACA. With Gerald Eve & Co., London, 1976, Chestertons, London, 1977–82; Highland Wineries, Inverness, 1982–87; accountant: Deloitte Haskin & Sells, later Coopers & Lybrand, Cambridge, 1987–91; NFU Mutual, Cambridge, 1993–96; Stafford & Co., Cambridge, 1996–2001. *Recreations:* family, history, writing. *Heir:* *s* Hon. Gerard Charles Alastair Vanneck, *b* 12 March 1985. *Address:* 69 Barrons Way, Comberton, Cambridge CB23 7EQ. *Club:* Pratt's.

HUNTINGFORD, Richard Norman Legh; Chairman: Prince's Trust Trading Ltd, since 2010; Creston plc, since 2011; UTV Media plc, since 2012; *b* Winchester, 14 May 1956; *s* of Jonathan and Joanna Huntingford; *m* 1996, Nicky; one *s* two *d* and one step *s*. *Educ:* Radley Coll. FCA 1979. With Peat Marwick, subseq. KPMG, 1975–87; Dir, 1987–2000, Chief Exec., 2000–07, Chrysalis plc; Chairman: Virgin Radio, 2007–08; Boomerang Plus plc, 2008–12. *Recreations:* tennis, Rugby, cricket, restaurants. *Address:* Creston plc, 10 Great Pulteney Street, W1F 9NB. *Clubs:* MCC, Queen's.

HUNTINGTON-WHITELEY, Lt Comdr Sir (John) Miles, 4th Bt *cr* 1918, of Grimley, Worcester; VRD (and 2 clasps); RNR (retired); *b* Fareham, Hants, 18 July 1929; *y s* of Captain Sir Maurice Huntington-Whiteley, 2nd Bt, RN and Lady Margaret Huntington-Whiteley, *d* of 1st Earl Baldwin of Bewdley, KG, PC, FRS; *S* brother, 2014; *m* 1960, HIllH Countess Victoria zu Castell-Rüdenhausen; one *s* two *d*. *Educ:* Eton Coll.; Trinity Coll., Cambridge. RN 1947–49; RNR, 1949–90. *Recreations:* applied and fine arts, music, the paranormal. *Heir:* *s* Leopold Maurice Huntington-Whiteley, *b* 15 July 1965. *Address:* Flat 4, 39 Courtfield Gardens, SW5 0PJ. *T:* (020) 7341 0833. *Club:* Naval.

HUNTINGTOWER, Lord; James Patrick Grant of Rothiemurchus; *b* 14 Sept. 1977; *s* and *heir* of Earl of Dysart, *qv*; *m* 2009, Daisy Sandy Ziani, *d* of Mark de Ferranti; one *s*. *Educ:* Eton; Edinburgh Univ. (BSc 2003). ACA 2004. *Heir:* *s* Hon. John Peter Grant, yr of Rothiemurchus, Master of Huntingtower, *b* 13 July 2011.

HUNTLEY, Andrew John Mack, FRICS; Chairman, Insignia Richard Ellis (formerly Richard Ellis, Chartered Surveyors), 1993–2001; *b* 24 Jan. 1939; *s* of William Mack Huntley and Muriel Huntley (*née* Akehurst); *m* 1963, Juliet Vivien Collum; three *d*. *Educ:* Monkton Combe Sch., Bath. FRICS 1963. Davis & Son, Bristol, 1956–58; D. Ward & Son, Plymouth, 1958–61; Davige & Partners, London, 1961–65; with Richard Ellis, subseq. Insignia Richard Ellis, 1965–2001. Director: Pillar Property, 2002–05; Miller Gp, 2002–; Charities Official Investment Fund, 2002–08. Chairman: Panceltica Hldgs Ltd, 2007–09; Metric Property Investments plc, 2010–13; Dir, Capital & Counties plc, 2010–; Sen. Ind. Dir, Intu Properties plc (formerly Capital Shopping Centres), 2010–. *Recreations:* shooting, tennis. *Address:* Ashurst, Fernhurst, Haslemere, Surrey GU27 3JB. *Club:* Boodle's.

HUNTLEY, Gillian Lesley; *see* Slater, G. L.

HUNTLEY, Maj. Gen. Michael, CB 2005; Director General Logistics (formerly Equipment Support) (Land), 2002–06; Defence Analyst, Louisburg Keane Ltd, since 2006; *b* 24 Dec. 1950. *Educ:* BSc. Commnd REME, 1972; rcds; psc; hcsc; Dep. COS 1st (UK) Armoured Div.; Dir Equipment Support (Army); Comdr Equipment Support, HQ Land Comd; Dir Support Ops, Equipment Support (Land), until 2002. Col Comdt, REME, 2004–10. *Address:* c/o Army Personnel Centre, Kentigern House, 65 Brown Street, Glasgow G2 8EX.

HUNTLY, 13th Marquess of, *cr* 1599 (Scot.); **Granville Charles Gomer Gordon;** Earl of Huntly, 1450; Earl of Aboyne, Baron Gordon of Strathavon and Glenlivet, 1660; Baron Meldrum (UK), 1815; Premier Marquess of Scotland; Chief of House of Gordon; *b* 4 Feb. 1944; *s* of 12th Marquess of Huntly and Hon. Mary Pamela Berry (*d* 1998), *d* of 1st Viscount Kemsley; *S* father, 1987; *m* 1st, 1972, Jane Elizabeth Angela (marr. diss. 1990), *d* of late Col Alistair Gibb and Lady McCorquodale of Newton; one *s* two *d*; 2nd, 1991, Mrs Catheryn Millbourn; one *d*. *Educ:* Gordonstoun. Chm., Cock o' the North Liqueur Co. Ltd, 1998–; Dir, Hintlesham Hldgs Ltd, 1987–. *Heir:* *s* Earl of Aboyne, *qv*. *Address:* Aboyne Castle, Aberdeenshire AB34 5JP. *T:* (01339) 887778.

See also Baron Cranworth.

HUNTON, Christopher John; Global Managing Partner, WPP, since 2007; *b* 12 Aug. 1961; *s* of Thomas and Elsie Hunton; *m* 1992, Dr Sara Hunton; one *s* one *d*. *Educ:* Bedford Coll., London (BA Hons); Hughes Hall, Cambridge (PGCE 1983). Teacher, Knox Sch., NY, 1984–85; Asst Housemaster, Wellingborough Sch., Northants, 1985–86; Account Manager, Foote, Cone & Belding, 1986–88; Account Dir, Ayer Barker, 1988–90; Bd Account Dir, Young & Rubicam, 1990–94; Gp Account Dir, Lowe Howard-Spink, 1994–98; CEO, McCann-Erickson, 1998–2004; Man. Dir, Lowe London, 2005–07. *Recreations:* family, sport, musical theatre, fishing.

HUNTSMAN, Peter William, FRICS; FAAV; Principal, College of Estate Management, University of Reading, 1981–92, Hon. Fellow, 1993; *b* 11 Aug. 1935; *s* of late William and Lydia Irene Huntsman (*née* Clegg); *m* 1st, 1961, Janet Mary Bell (marr. diss.); one *s* one *d*; 2nd, 1984, Cicely Eleanor (*née* Tamblin) (*d* 2013). *Educ:* Hymers Coll., Hull; Coll. of Estate Management, Univ. of London (BSc Estate Man.). Agricultural Land Service, Dorset and Northumberland, 1961–69; Kellogg Foundn Fellowship, Cornell Univ., USA, 1969–70; Principal Surveyor, London, ADAS, 1971–76; Divl Surveyor, Surrey, Middx and Sussex, 1976–81. Liveryman, Chartered Surveyors' Co., 1985; Freeman, City of London, 1985. Hon. FSVA 1993. *Publications:* (contrib.) Walmsley's Rural Estate Management, 6th edn 1978; contribs to professional jls. *Recreations:* sport, Dorset countryside, reading. *Address:* 28 Mowlem Court, Rempstone Road, Swanage, Dorset BH19 1DR. *T:* (01929) 761659.

HUOT, Prof. Sylvia, PhD; FBA 2011; Professor of Medieval French Literature, University of Cambridge, since 2007; Fellow, Pembroke College, Cambridge, since 1996. *Educ:* Univ. of Calif., Santa Cruz (BA 1976); Princeton Univ. (PhD 1982). William Rainey Harper Post-doctoral Teaching Fellow, Univ. of Chicago, 1982–84; Asst Prof. of French, later Assoc. Prof., then Presidential Res. Prof., Dept of Foreign Langs and Lits, Northern Illinois Univ., 1986–95; Lectr, 1996–99, Reader in Medieval French Lit., 1999–2007, French Dept, Univ. of Cambridge. *Publications:* From Song to Book, 1987; (ed jtly) Rethinking the Romance of the Rose, 1992; The Romance of the Rose and its Medieval Readers, 1993; Allegorical Play in the Old French Motet, 1997; Madness in Medieval French Literature, 2003; Postcolonial Fictions in the Roman de Perceforest, 2007; Dreams of Lovers and Lies of Poets: poetry, knowledge and desire in the Roman de la Rose, 2010.

HUPPERT, Prof. Herbert Eric, ScD; FRS 1987; Professor of Theoretical Geophysics and Foundation Director, Institute of Theoretical Geophysics, Cambridge University, 1989–2011, now Professor Emeritus; Leverhulme Emeritus Research Fellow, 2013–15; Fellow of King's College, Cambridge, since 1970; Dean of Science Professor, University of Bristol, since 2012; Professor, School of Mathematics and Statistics, University of New South Wales, since 2012 (Visiting Professor, 1991–96); *b* 26 Nov. 1943; *er s* of Leo Huppert and Alice Huppert (*née* Neuman); *m* 1966, Felicia Adina Huppert (*née* Ferster), PhD; two *s*. *Educ:* Sydney Boys' High Sch.; Sydney Univ. (BSc 1963); ANU (MSc 1964); Univ. of California at San Diego (MS 1966, PhD 1968); Univ. of Cambridge (MA 1971, ScD 1985). ICI Research Fellow, 1968–70; University of Cambridge: Asst Dir of Research, 1970–81; Lectr in Applied Maths, 1981–88; BP Venture Unit Sen. Res. Fellow, 1983–89; Reader in Geophysical Dynamics, 1988–89. Visiting research scientist: ANU; Univ. of California, San Diego; Canterbury Univ.; Caltech; MIT; Univ. of NSW; Univ. of WA; Univ. of Sydney; Tata Inst., Mumbai; Weizmann Inst. of Sci., Rehovot; Woods Hole Oceanographic Inst. Member: NERC, 1993–98; Council, Royal Soc., 2001–03. MAE 2011. Fellow: Amer. Geophysical Union, 2002; APS, 2004. Lectures: Evnin, Princeton, 1995; Midwest Mechanics, 1996–97; Henry Charnock Dist., Southampton Oceanography Centre, 1999; Smiths Industries, Oxford Univ., 1999; Arthur L. Day (also Prize), Nat. Acad. of Sci., USA, 2005; Dist. Israel Pollak, Technion, 2005; Bakerian (also Prize), Royal Soc., 2011. Associate Editor, Jl Fluid Mechanics, 1971–90; Editor, Jl of Soviet Jewry, 1985–; Member, Editorial Board: Philosophical Trans of Royal Soc. (series A), 1994–99; Reports on Progress in Physics, 1997–2003. William Hopkins Prize, Cambridge Philos. Soc., 2005; Wolfson Merit Award, Royal Soc., 2006; Murchison Medal, London Geol Soc., 2007. *Publications:* approximately 240 papers on applied mathematics, crystal growth, fluid mechanics, geology, geophysics, oceanography and meteorology. *Recreations:* my children, squash, tennis, mountaineering, cycling. *Address:* Institute of Theoretical Geophysics, Department of Applied Mathematics and Theoretical Physics, Centre for Mathematical Sciences, Wilberforce Road, Cambridge CB3 0WA. *T:* (office) (01223) 337853, *Fax:* (01223) 765900; 46 De Freville Avenue, Cambridge CB4 1HT. *T:* (01223) 356071. *E:* heh1@esc.cam.ac.uk.

See also J. L. Huppert.

HUPPERT, Julian Leon, PhD; *b* 21 July 1978; *s* of Prof. Herbert Eric Huppert, *qv*; partner, Dr Caroline Wright. *Educ:* Trinity Coll., Cambridge (MSci 2000; PhD 2005). Business Analyst, Monis Software Ltd, 2000–01; CEO, Cambridge Laboratory Innovations Ltd, 2003–05. Fellow: Trinity Coll., Cambridge, 2004–08; Clare Coll., Cambridge, 2009–; RCUK Fellow, Cavendish Lab., 2009–12, Lectr, 2012–, Univ. of Cambridge. Mem. (Lib Dem) Cambridgeshire CC, 2001–09 (Leader, Lib Dem Gp, 2004–07). Contested (Lib Dem) Huntingdon, 2005. MP (Lib Dem) Cambridge, 2010–15; contested (Lib Dem) same seat, 2015. Mem. Council, Liberty, 2009–10. *Publications:* various scientific papers and political articles. *Recreations:* cycling, hiking, cooking.

HUQ, Dr Rupa Asha; MP (Lab) Ealing Central and Acton, since 2015; *b* Ealing, 2 April 1972; *d* of late Muhammad Huq and of Roshan Huq. *Educ:* Montpelier Primary Sch.; Notting Hill and Ealing High Sch.; Newnham Coll., Cambridge (BA Hons Social and Pol Scis with Law 1993); Univ. of E London (PhD Cultural Studies 1999). Asst to Carole Tongue, MEP, Strasbourg, 1996; Lectr, Manchester Univ., 1998–2004 (Leverhulme Trust Fellow); Sen. Lectr in Sociol. and Criminol., Kingston Univ., 2004–15. Dep. Mayoress of Ealing, 2010–11. Contested (Lab): North West, EP, 2004; Chesham and Amersham, 2005. *Publications:* Beyond Subculture, 2006; On the Edge: the contested cultures of English suburbia, 2013; Making Sense of Suburbia Through Popular Culture, 2013; contrib. articles to Guardian, Tribune, THES. *Address:* House of Commons, SW1A 0AA.

HURD, family name of **Baron Hurd of Westwell**.

HURD OF WESTWELL, Baron *cr* 1997 (Life Peer), of Westwell in the co. of Oxfordshire; **Douglas Richard Hurd,** CH 1996; CBE 1974; PC 1982; Deputy Chairman, Coutts & Co., 1998–2009; *b* 8 March 1930; *e s* of Baron Hurd (*d* 1966) and Stephanie Corner (*d* 1985); *m* 1st, 1960, Tatiana Elizabeth Michelle (marr. diss. 1982), *d* of A. C. Benedict Eyre, Westburton House, Bury, Sussex; three *s*; 2nd, 1982, Judy (*d* 2008), *d* of Sidney and Pamela Smart; one *s* one *d*. *Educ:* Eton (King's Scholar and Newcastle Scholar; Fellow, 1981–96); Trinity Coll., Cambridge (Major Scholar). Pres., Cambridge Union, 1952. HM Diplomatic Service, 1952–66; served in: Peking, 1954–56; UK Mission to UN, 1956–60; Private Sec. to Perm. Under-Sec. of State, FO, 1960–63; Rome, 1963–66. Joined Conservative Research Dept, 1966; Head of Foreign Affairs Section, 1968; Private Sec. to Leader of the Opposition, 1968–70; Political Sec. to Prime Minister, 1970–74. MP (C): Mid-Oxon, Feb. 1974–1983; Witney, 1983–97. Opposition Spokesman on European Affairs, 1976–79; Minister of State, FCO, 1979–83; Minister of State, Home Office, 1983–84; Sec. of State for NI, 1984–85, for Home Dept, 1985–89; Sec. of State for Foreign and Commonwealth Affairs, 1989–95. Dir, NatWest Gp, 1995–99; Dep. Chm., NatWest Markets, 1995–98; Chm., British Invisibles, 1997–2000; Sen. Advr, Hawkpoint, 2000–11. Member: Royal Commn on H of L reform, 1999; H of L Appointments Commn, 2000–10. Chairman: Prison Reform Trust, 1997–2001 (Hon. Pres., 2001–); CEDR, 2001–04; Canterbury Review Gp, 2000–01. Co-Pres., RIIA, 2001–07. Chm., German British Forum, 2000–05. Vis. Fellow, Nuffield Coll., Oxford, 1978–86. Chm. Booker Prize Judges, 1998. High Steward, Westminster Abbey, 2000–11. *Publications:* The Arrow War, 1967; An End to Promises, 1979; The Search for Peace (televised), 1997; Ten Minutes to Turn the Devil (short stories), 1999; Memoirs, 2003; Robert Peel, 2007; Choose Your Weapons, 2010; (with Edward Young) Disraeli: the two lives, 2013; Elizabeth II: the steadfast, 2015; *novels:* Truth Game, 1972; Vote to Kill, 1975; The Shape of Ice, 1998; Image in the Water, 2001; with Andrew Osmond: Send Him Victorious, 1968; The Smile on the Face of the Tiger, 1969, repr. 1982; Scotch on the Rocks, 1971; War Without Frontiers, 1982; (with Stephen Lamport) Palace of Enchantments, 1985. *Recreation:* writing. *Address:* c/o House of Lords, SW1A 0PW. *Clubs:* Pratt's, Travellers, Beefsteak.

See also N. R. Hurd.

HURD, Nicholas Richard; MP (C) Ruislip, Northwood and Pinner, since 2010 (Ruislip Northwood, 2005–10); *b* 13 May 1962; *s* of Baron Hurd of Westwell, *qv* and Tatiana Elizabeth Michelle Hurd; *m* 1st, 1988, Kim Richards (marr. diss.); two *s* two *d*; 2nd, 2010, Lady Clare Kerr, *er d* of Marquess of Lothian, *qv*; one *s* one *d*. *Educ:* Eton Coll.; Exeter Coll., Oxford (BA Classics 1985). Investment Manager, Morgan Grenfell, 1985–90; Corporate Finance Exec., Crown Communications, 1990–92; Managing Director: Passport Magazine Directories, 1992–94; Robert Fleming Do Brasil, 1994–2000; Business Develt Dir, Band-X Ltd, 2000–04; COS to Tim Yeo, MP, 2004–05. Shadow Minister for Charities, Social Enterprise and Volunteering, 2008–10; Parly Sec., Cabinet Office, 2010–14. Trustee, Greenhouse Sports Charity, 2004–. *Recreations:* sport, music. *Address:* House of Commons, SW1A 0AA. *T:* and *Fax:* (020) 7219 1053. *E:* nick.hurd.mp@parliament.uk.

HURFORD, Prof. James Raymond, PhD; FBA 2015; Professor of General Linguistics, University of Edinburgh, 1979–2008, now Emeritus; *b* Reading, 16 July 1941; *s* of James H. Hurford and Muriel K. L. W. Crocker; *m* 1964, Sue Ann Davis; one *d* (and one *d* decd). *Educ:* Exeter Sch.; St John's Coll., Cambridge (BA 1963); University Coll. London (PhD 1967). Post Doctoral Fellow, Systems Develt Corp., 1967–68; Asst Prof., Univ. of Calif at Davis, 1968–71; Lectr, 1972–76, Sen. Lectr, 1976–79, Univ. of Lancaster. *Publications:* The Linguistic Theory of Numerals, 1975; (with B. Heasley) Semantics: a coursebook, 1983; Language and Number, 1987; Grammar: a student's guide, 1994; The Origins of Meaning, 2007; The Origins of Grammar, 2011; The Origins of Language, 2014. *Recreations:* gardening, squash, hiking. *Address:* Linguistics and English Language, University of Edinburgh, Dugald Stewart Building, 3 Charles Street, Edinburgh EH8 9AD. *T:* (0131) 650 3959. *E:* jim@ling.ed.ac.uk.

HURFORD, Peter (John), OBE 1984; organist; *b* 22 Nov. 1930; *e c* of H. J. Hurford, Minehead and Gladys Winifred Hurford (*née* James); *m* 1955, Patricia Mary Matthews, *e d* of late Prof. Sir Bryan Matthews, CBE, FRS; two *s* one *d*. *Educ:* Blundell's Sch.; Royal Coll. of Music; Jesus Coll., Cambridge (MA, MusB; Hon. Fellow, 2006). FRCO. Commnd, Royal Signals, 1954–56. Director of Music, Bablake Sch., Coventry and Conductor, Leamington Spa Bach Choir, 1956–57; Master of the Music, Cathedral and Abbey Church of St Alban, 1958–78; Conductor, St Albans Bach Choir, 1958–78; Founder, Internat. Organ Festival, St Albans, 1963. Artist-in-Residence: Univ. of Cincinnati, 1967–68; Sydney Opera Ho., 1980, 1981, 1982; Acting Organist, St John's Coll., Cambridge, 1979–80; recital and lecture tours throughout Europe, USA, Canada, Japan, Philippines, Taiwan, Australia and NZ, 1960–98; perf. the organ works of J. S. Bach, in 34 progs for BBC, 1980–82, and at 50th Edinburgh Fest., 1997. Vis. Prof. of Organ, Univ. of Western Ontario, 1976–77; Prof., RAM, 1982–88; Betts Fellow, Oxford Univ., 1992–93; Hon. Fellow in Organ Studies, Bristol Univ., 1997–98. Mem. Council, 1963–2003, Pres., 1980–82, RCO; Pres., IAO, 1995–97; Mem., Hon. Council of Management, Royal Philharmonic Soc., 1983–87. Has made numerous LP records and CDs, incl. complete organ works of J. S. Bach (Gramophone Award, 1979; Silver Disc, 1983), F. Couperin, G. F. Handel, P. Hindemith. Hon. FRSCM 1977; Hon. Mem., RAM, 1981; Hon. FRCM 1987. Hon. Dr, Baldwin-Wallace Coll., Ohio, 1981; Hon. DMus Bristol, 1992; Hon. DArts Hertfordshire, 2007. RCO Medal, 2013. *Publications:* Making Music on the Organ, 1988; Suite: Laudate Dominum; sundry other works for organ; Masses for Series III, and Rite II of Amer. Episcopal Church; sundry church anthems. *Recreations:* walking, wine, silence. *Address:* Broom House, St Bernard's Road, St Albans, Herts AL3 5RA.

HURLSTON, Malcolm, CBE 2013; social entrepreneur; Founding Chairman: Malcolm Hurlston Corporate Consultancy, since 1980; Registry Trust, since 1985; Employee Share Ownership Centre, since 1986; *b* Southport, Lancs, 7 July 1938; *s* of Robert Hurlston and Alice Mary Hurlston (*née* Taylor); three *s* two *d*; *m* 2002, Linda Wilbert. *Educ:* Sunnymede, Southport; Magdalene Coll., Cambridge (Open Maj. Schol.; BA 1961; MA). Nat. Service, Jt Services Sch. for Linguists (Flying Officer). Reporter, City Press; Dir, London Press Exchange; DJ, BBC Serbo Croat Service; Chairman: Open Shop; Euroshop; Student Loans Co.; Irish Judgements; Financial Inclusion Centre; Founding Chairman: Foundn for Credit Counselling, 1992–2010 (Pres., 2010–); StepChange (formerly CCCS); Proof of Age Standards Scheme; devised Unity Trust Bank (co-operative and trade union bank); Founder: Retail Credit Gp; Standing Cttee on Reciprocity; Credit Card Res. Gp; Office of Travel Charter. Campaigner: *for*: opening shops on Sundays; Co-operative Bank into clearing; liberalisation of pharmacies; tax simplification of share schemes; Company Share Option Plan; *against*: insce nationalisation; takeover of Cooperative Wholesale Soc. by City interests. Mentor, Univ. of Westminster. Remy Schlumberger Award, Internat. Assoc. for Financial Participation, 2012. *Publications:* Samovar (poems); *translations:* L'art de la drague, by Alain Krief; Leda, by Miroslav Krleža; monographs. *Recreations:* Eton fives (Cambridge 2nd VI), tennis, dining, reading, humming, this transitory life. *Address:* Maida Vale, London and La Napoule, France. *E:* mhurlston@hurlstons.com. *Clubs:* Royal Air Force; Omnisport de Tanneron.

HURN, Sir (Francis) Roger, Kt 1996; Chairman, Prudential plc, 2000–02; Deputy Chairman, Cazenove Group plc, 2003–09 (Director, 2001–09); *b* 9 June 1938; *s* of Francis James Hurn and Joyce Elsa Hurn (*née* Bennett); *m* 1980, Rosalind Jackson; one *d*. *Educ:* Marlborough Coll. Engrg apprentice, Rolls Royce Motors, 1956; joined Smiths Industries, 1958. National Service, 1959–61. Smiths Industries: Export Dir, Motor Accessory Div., 1969; Man. Dir, Internat. Operations, 1974; Exec. Dir, 1976; Man. Dir, 1978; Chief Exec., 1981–96; Chm., 1991–98; Chm., GEC, subseq. Marconi, 1998–2001; Dep. Chm., Glaxo Wellcome, 1997–2000, GlaxoSmithKline, 2000–03. Non-executive Director: Ocean Transport & Trading, 1982–88; Pilkington, 1984–94; S. G. Warburg Gp, 1987–95; ICI, 1993–2001. Gov., Henley Mgt Coll., 1986–2004 (Chm. Govs, 1996–2004). Liveryman, Coachmakers and Coach Harness Makers' Co., 1979–. *Recreations:* outdoor pursuits, travel. *Address:* Stonesdale, Bulstrode Way, Gerrards Cross, Bucks SL9 7QT.

HURRELL, Prof. Andrew James, DPhil; FBA 2011; Montague Burton Professor of International Relations, University of Oxford, since 2008; Fellow, Balliol College, Oxford, since 2008; *b* 2 Feb. 1955; *s* of late William Palmer Hurrell and Brenda Joan Hurrell (*née* Batch); *m* 1977, Yasmin Ahmed; one *s* one *d*. *Educ:* Gresham's Sch.; St John's Coll., Cambridge (BA 1977); St Antony's Coll., Oxford (MPhil 1982; DPhil 1986). Lloyds Bank Internat., London and Brazil, 1978–80; Res. Fellow, Christ Church, Oxford, 1983–86; Asst Prof. of Internat. Relns, Bologna Center, Sch. of Advanced Internat. Studies, Johns Hopkins Univ., 1986–89; Lectr in Internat. Relns, Oxford Univ., 1989–2008; Fellow, Nuffield Coll., Oxford, 1989–2008, now Emeritus. Visiting Professor: Univ. of São Paulo, 1994, 1997; Univ. of Brasilia, 2005; Fundação Getúlio Vargas, Rio de Janeiro, 2009; Inaugural Fellow, Straus Inst. for Advanced Study of Law and Justice, NYU Law Sch., 2009–10. Delegate, OUP, 2010– (Mem., Finance Cttee). Mem., Soc. of Scholars, Johns Hopkins Univ., 2010. Susan Strange Award, Internat. Studies Assoc., 2015. *Publications:* (ed with L. Fawcett) Regionalism in World Politics, 1995; (ed with N. Woods) Inequality, Globalisation and World Politics, 1999; (with K. Alderson) Hedley Bull on International Society, 2000; (ed jtly) Order and Justice in International Relations, 2003; On Global Order: power, values and the constitution of international society, 2007; contribs to jls incl. Internat. Affairs, Rev. Internat. Studies, Metaphilosophy. *Recreations:* theatre, cooking, travel, books. *Address:* Balliol College, Oxford OX1 3BJ. *E:* andrew.hurrell@politics.ox.ac.uk.

HURST, Alan Arthur; Partner, Law Hurst & Taylor, since 1980; *b* 2 Sept. 1945; *s* of George Arthur Hurst and Eva Grace Hurst; *m* 1976, Hilary Caroline Burch; two *s* one *d*. *Educ:* Westcliff High Sch.; Univ. of Liverpool (BA Hons). Admitted Solicitor, 1975. Member (Lab): Southend BC, 1980–96; Essex CC, 1993–98. MP (Lab) Braintree, 1997–2005; contested (Lab) same seat, 2005. Pres., Southend-on-Sea Law Soc., 1992–93. *Recreations:* bird watching, local history, canvassing. *Address:* 28 Whitefriars Crescent, Westcliff-on-Sea, Essex SS0 8EU. *T:* (01702) 337864.

HURST, Sir Geoffrey Charles, Kt 1998; MBE 1977; Director, Aon Warranty Group (formerly London General Insurance), 1995–96; Director of Football, McDonald's, UK, since 2002; professional football player, 1957–76; *b* 8 Dec. 1941; *s* of Charles and Evelyn Hurst; *m* 1964, Judith Helen Harries; three *d*. Professional Football Player: West Ham United, 1957–72; Stoke City, 1972–75; West Bromwich Albion, 1975–76; Player-Manager, Telford United, 1976–79; Manager, Chelsea, 1979–81; English Football International, 1966–72. Joined London General Insurance, 1981. *Publications:* The World Game, 1970; (with Michael Hart) 1966 and All That, 2001; World Champions, 2006. *Recreations:* sport in general, family.

HURST, (Jonathan) Martin (Stuart), PhD; Commercial Director, Department for Environment, Food and Rural Affairs, since 2011; *b* 7 Sept. 1960; *s* of John Stuart Hurst and Jeanette Rose Hurst; *m* 2007, Stephanie (*née* Cottrill); one *d*, and one step *d*. *Educ:* Queens' Coll., Cambridge (BA 1982); Univ. of Southampton (MSc 1983; PhD 1989). Economist, HM Treasury, 1985–95; Divl Manager, DETR, 1995–2002; Sen. Policy Advr (envmt, farming, housing, planning), 10 Downing Street, 2002–05; Transformation Dir, Natural England, 2005; Dir, Regulation, 2006–07, Water, 2007–10, Arms Length Bodies and Estates, 2010–11, DEFRA. Vice Chm., Wandle Housing Assoc., 2008–. Trustee, Groundwork SE London, 2005–11. *Recreations:* hill walking, cricket, choral singing, bird watching. *Address:* Department for Environment, Food and Rural Affairs, Nobel House, Smith Square, SW1P 3JR. *T:* (020) 7238 5247. *E:* martin.hurst@defra.gsi.gov.uk.

HURST, Prof. Laurence Daniel, DPhil; FMedSci; FRS 2015; Professor of Evolutionary Genetics, since 1997, Director, Genetics and Evolution Teaching Project, since 2012 and Director, Milner Centre for Evolution, since 2015, University of Bath; *b* Ilkley, Yorks, 6 Jan. 1965; *s* of John Stuart Hurst and Jeanette Rose Hurst; *m* 1999, Clair Florence Ann Brunton; two *d*. *Educ:* Truro Sch.; Churchill Coll., Cambridge (BA Nat. Scis (Zool.) 1987); University Coll., Oxford (DPhil 1991). Henry Fellowship, Harvard Univ., 1987–88; Browne Res. Fellow, Queen's Coll., Oxford, 1991–93; University of Cambridge: Res. Fellow, Dept of Genetics, 1994–97; Sen. Res. Fellow, Churchill Coll., 1995–97. Horace le Marquand and Dudley Bigg Res. Fellow, Royal Soc., 1993–2001. Professorial Res. Fellow, Inst. for Advanced Study, Collegium Budapest, 1995; External Faculty, John Innes Centre, Norwich, 2010–14. Mem., EMBO, 2004; FMedSci 2015. Charles Darwin Award, BAAS, 1999; Scientific Medal, Zool Soc., 2003; Medal, Genetics Soc., 2010. *Publications:* papers on evolution, genetics and genomics in Nature, Nature Genetics, Public Liby of Sci. Biol. *Recreations:* music (listening and performing, playing the trumpet), collecting antique maps. *Address:* Department of Biology and Biochemistry, University of Bath, Bath BA2 7AY. *T:* (01225) 386424, *Fax:* (01225) 386779. *E:* l.d.hurst@bath.ac.uk.

HURST, Peter Thomas; Arbitrator and Mediator, 39 Essex Chambers, since 2015; Senior Costs Judge of England and Wales (formerly Chief Master of the Supreme Court Taxing Office), 1992–2014 (Master, 1981–92); a Recorder, since 2000; *b* Troutbeck, Westmorland, 27 Oct. 1942; *s* of Thomas Lyon Hurst and Nora Mary Hurst; *m* 1968, Diane Irvine; one *s* two *d*. *Educ:* Stonyhurst College; LLB 1973, MPhil 2000, London. Admitted as Solicitor of the Supreme Court, 1967; Partner: Hurst and Walker, Solicitors, Liverpool, 1967–77; Gair Roberts Hurst and Walker, Solicitors, Liverpool, 1977–81; Judicial Taxing Officer: H of L, 2002–09; Privy Council, 2002–14; Supreme Court of UK, 2009–14. Greffier Substitute, Royal Court of Jersey, 2005–. Assessor to Lord Justice Jackson's Rev. of Civil Costs, 2009. Chair, Ind. Rev. Panel, NHS Continuing Healthcare, 2014–; Mem., CIArb, 2014–15; Accredited Mediator, 2014. Hon. Bencher, Gray's Inn, 2007. Mem. Sen. Editl Bd, Civil Procedure (The White Book) (formerly The Supreme Court Practice), 2000–15 (contrib., 1986–; Advisory Ed., 2015–). *Publications:* (ed jtly) Butterworth's Costs Service, 1986–; (contrib.) Cordery on Solicitors, 8th edn 1988; (ed jtly) Legal Aid, 1994, Solicitors, 1995, Halsbury's Laws of England, 4th edn; Civil Costs, 1995, 5th edn 2013; (ed jtly) Legal Aid Practice 1996–97, 1996; (ed jtly) The New Civil Costs Regime, 1999; Criminal Costs, 2007; (contrib.) Civil Procedure Rules Ten Years On, 2009; (contrib.) Civil Justice Qly; (contrib.) European Business Law Rev. (Special Edn), 2014; Costs and Funding Following the Civil Justice Reforms, 2015. *Recreation:* music. *Address:* 39 Essex Chambers, 81 Chancery Lane, WC2A 1BQ. *Club:* Athenæum.

HURT, Sir John (Vincent), Kt 2015; CBE 2004; actor, stage, films and television; *b* 22 Jan. 1940; *s* of Rev. Arnould Herbert Hurt and Phyllis Massey; *m* 1984, Donna Peacock (marr. diss. 1990); *m* 1990, Jo Dalton (marr. diss. 1995); two *s*; *m* 2005, Anwen Rees-Myers. *Educ:* The Lincoln Sch., Lincoln; RADA. Started as a painter. *Stage:* début, Arts Theatre, London, 1962; Chips With Everything, Vaudeville, 1962; The Dwarfs, Arts, 1963; Hamp (title role), Edin. Fest., 1964; Inadmissible Evidence, Wyndham's, 1965; Little Malcolm and his Struggle Against the Eunuchs, Garrick, 1966; Belcher's Luck, Aldwych (RSC), 1966; Man and Superman, Gaiety, Dublin, 1969; The Caretaker, Mermaid, 1972; The Only Street, Dublin Fest. and Islington, 1973; Travesties, Aldwych (RSC), 1974; The Arrest, Bristol Old Vic, 1974; The Shadow of a Gunman, Nottingham Playhouse, 1978; The Seagull, Lyric, Hammersmith, 1985; A Month in the Country, Albery, 1994; Krapp's Last Tape, New Ambassadors, 2000, Barbican, 2006, Shakespeare Th., Washington, Brooklyn Acad. of Music, Kirk Douglas Th., LA, 2011–12; Heroes, Wyndham's, 2005. *Films include:* With The Wild and the Willing, 1962; A Man for All Seasons, 1966; Sinful Davey, 1967; Before Winter Comes, 1969; In Search of Gregory, 1970; Mr Forbush and the Penguins, (Evans in) 10 Rillington Place, 1971; The Ghoul, Little Malcolm, 1974; East of Elephant Rock, 1977; The Disappearance, The Shout, Spectre, Alien, Midnight Express (BAFTA award, 1978), 1978; Heaven's Gate, 1979; The Elephant Man, 1980 (BAFTA award, 1981); History of the World Part 1, 1981; Partners, 1982; Champions, Nineteen Eighty-Four, The Osterman Weekend, The Hit, 1984; Jake Speed, Rocinate, 1986; Aria, 1987; White Mischief, 1988; Scandal, 1989; Frankenstein Unbound, The Field, 1990; King Ralph, Lapse of Memory, 1991; Dark at Noon, 1992; Second Best, 1994; Even Cowgirls Get the Blues, Rob Roy, 1995; Dead Man, Wild Bill, 1996; Contact, 1997; Love and Death on Long Island, 1998; All the Little Animals, You're Dead, 1999; Night Train, 2000; Lost Souls, Captain Corelli's Mandolin, 2001; Miranda, 2002; Dogville, 2003; Hellboy, 2004; The Skeleton Key, 2005; The Proposition, V for Vendetta, Shooting Dogs, Manderlay, Perfume, 2006; Oxford Murders, Indiana Jones and the Kingdom of the Crystal Skull, Lecture 21, 2008; Outlander, The Limits of Control, 2009; 44 Inch Chest, Harry Potter and the Deathly Hallows, Pt 1, 2010, Pt 2, 2011; Brighton Rock, Tinker, Tailor, Soldier, Spy, 2011; Only Lovers Left Alive, 2014; Hercules 3D, 2014. *Television:* The Waste Places, 1968; The Naked Civil Servant, 1975 (Emmy Award, 1976); Caligula, in I Claudius (series), 1976; Treats, 1977; Crime and Punishment (series), 1979; Deadline, 1988; Poison Candy, 1988; Who Bombed Birmingham, 1990; Red Fox, 1991; Six Characters in Search of an Author, 1992; The Alan Clark Diaries, 2004; An Englishman in New York, 2009; Whistle and I'll Come to You, 2010; Henry V, 2012; Dr Who: the day of the Doctor, 2013. War and Peace, BBC Radio 4, 2015. Dir, United British Artists, 1982. Outstanding Contribution to Cinema Award, BAFTA, 2012; Cultural Honour Award, Liberatum, 2013. *Address:* c/o Independent Talent Group Ltd, 40 Whitfield Street, W1T 2RH.

HURWITZ, Michael; Director, Greener Transport and International, Department for Transport, since 2013; *b* Leeds, 25 April 1971; *s* of His Honour Vivian Ronald Hurwitz and of Dr Ruth Hurwitz; *m* 1999, Anna Turner; one *s* two *d*. *Educ:* Leeds Grammar Sch.; Univ. of Manchester (BA 1st Cl. Psychol.; MSc Psychol.). Andersen Business Consulting, 1998–2000; Deloitte MCS Ltd, 2000–04; Hd, Planning and Performance, 2004–06, Envmt Policy, 2006–09, DfT; Dir, Office for Low Emission Vehicles, BIS, 2009–11; Dir, Analysis and Strategy, DfT, 2012–13. *Address:* Department for Transport, 33 Horseferry Road, SW1P 4DR. *E:* michael.hurwitz@dft.gsi.gov.uk.

HUSAIN, Saleem, (Sam); non-executive Director, W & G Foyle Ltd (Chief Executive Officer, 2007–15); *b* New Delhi, 27 April 1947; *s* of late Dr Mumtaz Husain and Mary Husain; *m* 1977, Lesley Mary Todd (marr. diss. 2005). *Educ:* St Mary's Acad., Pakistan; Open Univ. (MBA 1993). ACA 1972, FCA 1979. Articled clerk, David J. Jones & Co., Manchester, 1965–70; Audit Senior: Mann Judd & Co., Manchester, 1970–73; Tansley Witt & Co., 1973–74; Hudson Group Ltd: Mgt Accountant, 1974; Gp Mgt Accountant, 1975; Gp Chief Accountant, 1976–78; Finance Dir, 1978–82; Dep. Chm., 1982–87; Man. Dir, HEP Hldgs Ltd, 1987– (consultancy appts, 2004–07); Ascent Media Group (formerly Liberty Livewire): UK Gp Chief Finance Officer and Dir, Corporate Affairs, 2001; UK Gp Man. Dir, Corporate and Finance, 2002–04. Mem. Council, 2009–15, Vice Pres., 2012–15, Bookseller Assoc. FInstD 1986. Pres.'s Award, 1995, Roland Chase Award, 1997, BKSTS. *Recreations:* golf, motor boating, bridge. *Address:* 60 Raleigh Drive, N20 0UU. *T:* (020) 8368 1005. *E:* shusain@btclick.com. *Club:* Hadley Wood Golf (Captain, 2011).

HUSBAND, Dame Janet (Elizabeth Siarey), DBE 2007 (OBE 2002); FRCP, FRCR, FMedSci; Professor of Diagnostic Imaging, Institute of Cancer Research, University of London, 1996–2007, now Emeritus; Chairman, National Cancer Research Institute, 2011–13; *b* 1 April 1940; *d* of late Ronald Howard Siarey and Clarissa Marian Siarey; *m* 1963, Peter Husband; three *s*. *Educ:* Headington Sch., Oxford; Guy's Hosp. Med. Sch., Univ. of London (MB BS 1964). MRCS, LRCP 1964; DCH 1966; DObstRCOG 1967; DMRD 1974; FRCR 1976; FRCP 1987. Registrar in Diagnostic Radiol., Guy's Hosp. and KCH (pt-time), 1971–76; Clinical Scientist, MRC Div. of Radiol., Northwick Park Hosp., 1976; Royal Marsden Hospital, later Royal Marsden NHS Foundation Trust: Radiol. Res. Fellow, 1977–80; Consultant Radiologist, 1980–2007; Hd, Academic Dept of Radiol., 1985–2007; Med. Dir, 2003–06; non-exec. Dir, 2014–. Co-dir, CRUK (formerly CRC) Clinical Magnetic Resonance Res. Gp, Inst. Cancer Res., London Univ., 1986–2005. Special Comr, Royal Hosp. Chelsea, 2007–13. Non-executive Director: Nuada Medical Gp, 2009–; Spire Healthcare plc, 2014–. Member: Cooperation and Competition Panel, Monitor, 2009–14; Health Honours Cttee, 2009–. Co-founder and Trustee, Internat. Cancer Imaging Soc., 2000; President: BIR, 2003–04; RCR, 2004–07. Hon. Mem., 5 internat. med. socs. FMedSci 2001. Hon. DSc Inst. of Cancer Res., London 2013. Gold Medal: RCR; ECR; ICIS. *Publications:* (ed) Computed Tomography Review, 1989; (ed jtly) Imaging in Oncology, 2 vols, 1998, 3rd edn 2009; (jtly) Guide to the Practical Use of MRI in Oncology, 1999; articles in learned jls. *Recreations:* walking, opera. *Address:* The Old Bakehouse, High Street, Longborough, Glos GL56 0QE. *Club:* Sloane.

HUSBAND, Prof. Thomas Mutrie, PhD; FREng, FIMechE; Chairman: UKERNA, 1997–2000; East and North Herts NHS Trust, 2000–01; Vice-Chancellor, University of Salford, 1990–97; *b* 7 July 1936; *s* of Thomas Mutrie Husband and Janet Clark; *m* 1st, 1962, Pat Caldwell (*d* 2001); two *s*; 2nd, 2003, Gwen Fox. *Educ:* Shawlands Acad., Glasgow; Univ. of Strathclyde (BSc(Eng), MA, PhD). Weir Ltd, Glasgow: Apprentice Fitter, 1953–58; Engr/Jun. Manager, 1958–62; sandwich degree student (mech. engrg), 1958–61; various engrg and management positions with ASEA Ltd in Denmark, UK and S Africa, 1962–65; postgrad. student, Strathclyde Univ., 1965–66; Teaching Fellow, Univ. of Chicago, 1966–67; Lectr, Univ. of Strathclyde, 1967–70; Sen. Lectr, Univ. of Glasgow, 1970–73; Prof. of Manufacturing Organisation, Loughborough Univ., 1973–81; Prof. of Engrg Manufacture, 1981–90, Dir of Centre for Robotics, 1982–90, Hd of Dept of Mech. Engrg, 1983–90, Imperial Coll., London Univ. Member: Standing Cttee for Educn, Training and Competence to Practise, Royal Acad. of Engrg (formerly Fellowship of Engrg), 1989–93; Engrg Technol. Adv. Cttee, DTI, 1990–93; Council, Engrg Council, 1992–95; Manufacturing Div. Bd, IEE, 1992–95; McRobert Award Cttee, Royal Acad. of Engrg, 2000–05. Mem., Univ. Bd, Bournemouth Univ., 2003–09. Non-executive Director: Royal Exchange Theatre, Manchester, 1993–97; Univs and Colls Employers Assoc., 1994–97. FREng (FEng 1988). Hon. DSc: Manchester, 1997; Salford, 1998. *Publications:* Work Analysis and Pay Structure, 1976; Maintenance and Terotechnology, 1977; Education and Training in Robotics, 1986; articles in Terotechnica, Industrial Relations Jl, Microelectronics and Reliability, etc. *Recreations:* watching Arsenal FC, music, theatre. *Address:* 12 Roscrea Drive, Wick Village, Bournemouth BH6 4LU.

HUSBAND, William Anthony, (Tony); freelance cartoonist and writer; *b* 28 Aug. 1950; *s* of Henry Ronald and Vera Husband; *m* 1976, Carole Garner; one *s*. *Educ:* Holy Trinity Primary Sch., Hyde; Greenfield Secondary Sch., Hyde. Full-time cartoonist, 1984–; works for Private Eye, The Spectator, The Oldie, Playboy, Punch, Golf International, Nursing Standard, The Idler, TES, The Dalesman, The Cumbrian, Down Your Way, Practical Caravan and many more; campaign work with Envmtl Investigation Agency; co-devised and co-wrote: Oink (comic), 1985–88; Round the Bend (children's TV prog.), 1988–90; co-wrote: (with David Wood) Save The Human (play), UK tour, 1991; Hanger 17 (children's TV series), 1993; episode of Chucklevision, 1994; series of greetings cards, Camden, Carlton, Hallmark Cards and Paperhouse; (with Ian McMillan, poet) performs cartoon/poetry event in front of live audiences. Several solo exhibns, incl. Ruby Lounge, Temple, Richard Goodhall Gall. and Jackalope, Manchester; exhibn accompanying Lowry's paintings, The Lowry, Salford, 2001; Cartoonist in Residence, The Lowry, 2006–. Edited and helped create first prison comic 'The Bird'. Awards: Cartoonist Club of GB: Gag Cartoonist, 1985, 1986, 1988; Strip Cartoonist, 1987; Cartoon Arts Trust: Sports Cartoonist, 1995, 2001; Gag Cartoonist, 2000, 2002; Strip Cartoonist, 2000; Pont Award, 2005. *Publications:* Use Your Head, 1985; Bye Bye Cruel World, 1986; Animal Husbandry, 1987; 102 Uses for a Black Lace Album, 1988; The Greatest Story Never Told, 1988; Yobs 1, 1989; Another Pair of Underpants, 1990; Yobs 2, 1993; (with David Day) True Tales of Environmental Madness, 1993; (with David Wood) Save The Human, 1993; (with David Day) The Complete Rhino, 1994; Football Food Guide, 1995; Reduced History of Football, 2004; Reduced History of Cricket, 2005; Reduced History of Golf, 2005; Reduced History of Rugby, 2006; Reduced History of Britain, 2006; The World's Worst Jokes, 2006; Reduced History of Tennis, 2006; (illus.) Private Eye's Coleman Balls, 2006; Reduced History of Sex, 2007; Reduced History of Cats, 2007; Reduced History of Dogs, 2007; The Calmer Sutra, 2008; (with Deborah Hudson) Sing Your Heart Out, 2010; I Nearly Died Laughing, 2012; It's Only a Game, 2012; (with Dan Cockrill) Sellotaping Rain to my Cheek, 2013; (ed) Propaganda Cartoons of World War II, 2013; Take Care, Son: the story of my dad and his dementia, 2014; with Ian McMillan: Yorkshire Humour, 2009; Daft Yorkshire Customs, 2010; Yorkshire T'Olympics, 2011; 100 Uses for a Yorkshire Pudding, 2011; The Tale of Walter the Pencil Man, 2013; 101 Uses for a Flat Cap, 2013; 10 books pubd in Germany. *Recreations:* golf (10 handicap), music, photography (Mem., Hyde Photographic Soc.), Manchester United, playing the drums, wine and good food. *Address:* Hicroft, 132 Joel Lane, Gee Cross, Hyde, Cheshire SK14 5LN. *T:* (0161) 366 0262, *Fax:* (0161) 368 8479. *E:* toonyhusband@hotmail.com. *W:* www.tonyhusband.co.uk. *Clubs:* Groucho; Werneth Low Golf (Hyde).

HUSBANDS, Prof. Christopher Roy, PhD; Director, Institute of Education, University College London (formerly University of London), since 2011; Vice Provost (Academic Development), University College London; *b* Nuneaton, Warwickshire, 29 May 1959; *s* of Humphrey Roy and Pearl Husbands; *m* 1983, Nicola Owen-Jones; four *d*. *Educ:* King Edward VI Sch., Nuneaton; Nuneaton Sixth Form Coll.; Emmanuel Coll., Cambridge (BA 1980; PhD 1985); Inst. of Educn, Univ. of London (PGCE 1984). Teacher: Heartsease Sch., 1984–88; Fearnhill Sch., 1988–90; Lectr, 1991–93, Sen. Lectr, 1993–95, in Educn, UEA; University of Warwick: Reader, 1995–98; Prof., 1998–2003; Dir, Inst. of Educn, 2001–03; Dean of Educn and Lifelong Learning, UEA, 2003–07; Prof. of Educn and Dean of Faculty, Inst. of Educn, Univ. of London, 2007–10. Hon. Prof., E China Normal Univ., Shanghai, 2013. Member: Bd, TDA, 2006–12; RSA/Pearson Academies Commn, 2012–13. Non-exec. Dir, Edexcel, 2000–04. Trustee, AQA, 2005–08. Mem., Learning Panel, Nat. Trust, 2007–. *Publications:* What is History Teaching?, 1995; Professional Learning, 1998; The Performing School, 2001; Understanding History Teaching, 2003; (jtly) Transforming Education for All, 2013; *Recreations:* reading, writing, cycling, walking, playing the piano badly. *Address:* UCL Institute of Education, 20 Bedford Way, WC1H 0AL. *T:* (020) 7911 5409.

HUSBANDS, Sir Clifford (Straughn), GCMG 1996; KA 1995; CHB 1989; GCM 1986; Governor-General of Barbados, 1996–2011; President, Privy Council for Barbados, 1996–2011; *b* 5 Aug. 1926; *s* of Adam Straughn Husbands and Ada Augusta (*née* Griffith); *m* 1959, Ruby C. D. Parris; one *s* two *d*. *Educ:* Parry Sch., Barbados; Harrison Coll., Barbados; Middle Temple, Inns of Court, London. Called to the Bar, Middle Temple, 1952, Bencher, 2007; in private practice, Barbados, 1952–54; Actg Dep. Registrar, Barbados, 1954; Legal Asst to Attorney Gen., Grenada, 1954–56; Magistrate: Grenada, 1956–57; Antigua, 1957–58; Crown Attorney, Magistrate and Registrar, Montserrat, 1958–60; Actg Crown Attorney, 1959, Actg Attorney Gen., 1960, St Kitts-Nevis-Anguilla; Asst to Attorney Gen., Barbados, 1960–67 (Legal Draughtsman, 1960–63); DPP, Barbados, 1967–76; QC Barbados 1968; Judge, Supreme Court, Barbados, 1976–91; Justice of Appeal, 1991–96. Chairman: Community Legal Services, 1985–96; Penal Reform Cttee, Barbados, 1995–96; Mem., Judicial and Legal Service Commn, Barbados, 1987–96. Mem. Council, Barbados FPA, 1960–96. Vice-Pres., Barbados LTA, 1970s. Pres., Old Harrisonian Soc., 1983–87. Chief Scout, Barbados Boy Scouts Assoc., 2006–11, Hon. Chief Scout, 2012. Hon. Mem., Royal Commonwealth Soc., 2012. Paul Harris Fellowship Award, 2001. KStJ 2004. Silver Jubilee Medal, 1977. *Recreations:* music, swimming, photography, cricket. *Address:* Seamoon, Mount Standfast, St James, Barbados. *Clubs:* Rally, Spartan (Barbados).

HUSH, Prof. Noel Sydney, AO 1993; DSc; FRS 1988; FAA; Foundation Professor and Head of Department of Theoretical Chemistry, University of Sydney, 1971–92, now Professor Emeritus, and Hon. Associate, Chemistry School and School of Molecular and Microbial Biosciences, since 1990; *b* 15 Dec. 1924; *s* of Sidney Edgar Hush and Adrienne (*née* Cooper); *m* 1949, Thea L. Warman (decd), London; one *s* one *d*. *Educ:* Univ. of Sydney (BSc 1946; MSc 1948); Univ. of Manchester (DSc 1959). FAA 1977. Res. Fellow in Chemistry, Univ. of Sydney, 1946–49; Lectr in Phys. Chem., Univ. of Manchester, 1950–54; Lectr, subseq. Reader in Chem., Univ. of Bristol, 1955–71. Visiting Professor: ANU, 1960; Florida State Univ., 1965; Case Western Reserve Univ., 1968; Cambridge Univ., 1981; Stanford Univ., 1987; Vis. Fellow, Cavendish Lab., 1971; Vis. Sen. Scientist, Brookhaven Nat. Lab., USA, 1959–. Mem., Aust. Res. Grants Cttee, 1984–90 (Chm., Chem. Cttee, 1987–90). Director: Molecular Electronics Res. Ltd, 1997–; Quadrant Ltd, 2009–. Adv. Editor, Chemical Physics, 1973–; Mem. Bd of Mgt, Quadrant Magazine, 2002–08. Foreign Member: Amer. Acad. of Arts and Scis, 1999; US NAS, 2011. Fellow, Royal Soc. of NSW, 2011. Hon. DSc Sydney, 2009. Centenary Medal, RSC, 1990; Flinders Medal, 1994, Inaugural Award, David Craig Medal, 2000, Australian Acad. of Science; Centenary Medal, Australia, 2004; Physical Chem. Medal, RACI, 2006; Robert A. Welch Award in Chem., Welch Foundn, USA, 2007. *Publications:* (ed) Reactions of Molecules at Electrodes, 1971; *c* 350 papers in Jl of Chemical Physics, Chemical Physics, Jl of Amer. Chemical Soc., etc. *Recreations:* literature, music, travel. *Address:* 170 Windsor Street, Paddington, Sydney, NSW 2021, Australia. *T:* (2) 93281685; School of Molecular Bioscience, University of Sydney, Sydney, NSW 2006, Australia. *T:* (2) 96923330. *Clubs:* Athenæum; Union, University and Schools (Sydney).

HUSKINSON, (George) Nicholas (Nevil); His Honour Judge Nicholas Huskinson; a Circuit Judge, since 2003; a Member, Upper Tribunal (Lands Chamber) (formerly Lands Tribunal), since 2006; *b* 7 Dec. 1948; *s* of Leonard and Margaret Huskinson; *m* 1972, Pennant Elfrida Lascelles Iremonger; two *s*. *Educ:* Eton (King's Schol.); King's Coll., Cambridge (MA). Called to the Bar, Gray's Inn, 1971 (Arden Schol.); Asst Recorder, 1995–99; a Recorder, 1999–2003; a Vice Pres., Immigration Appeal Tribunal, subseq. a Sen. Immigration Judge and

Mem., Asylum and Immigration Tribunal, 2003–05. Asst Ed., Woodfall's Law of Landlord and Tenant, 28th edn, 1978–89. *Recreations:* bridge, gardening, walking, cooking. *Address:* Snaresbrook Crown Court, 75 Hollybush Hill, Snaresbrook, E11 1QW. *T:* (020) 8530 0000. *Clubs:* MCC, Garrick.

HUSKISSON, Edward Cameron, MD; FRCP; Consultant Rheumatologist, King Edward VII's Hospital Sister Agnes (formerly King Edward VII Hospital for Officers), since 1982; *b* 7 April 1939; *s* of Edward William Huskisson, Northwood, Middx and late Elinor Margot Huskisson (*née* Gibson); *m* 1990, Janice Elizabeth Louden; three *s* one *d. Educ:* Eastbourne Coll.; King's Coll., London (BSc); Westminster Hosp. Med. Sch. (MB BS 1964); MD London 1974. MRCS 1964; LRCP 1964, MRCP 1967, FRCP 1980. Consultant Physician and Head of Rheumatology, St Bartholomew's Hosp., 1976–93. *Publications:* (jtly) Joint Disease: all the arthropathies, 1973, 4th edn 1988; Repetitive Strain Injury, 1992. *Address:* 14A Milford House, 7 Queen Anne Street, W1G 9HN. *T:* (020) 7636 4278, *Fax:* (020) 7323 6829. *E:* edwardhuskisson@aol.com.

HUSSAIN, Baron *cr* 2011 (Life Peer), of Luton in the County of Bedfordshire; **Qurban Hussain;** *b* Kashmir, 27 March 1956; *m*; six *c. Educ:* Rochdale Coll.; Bedford Coll., Univ. of London; Luton Univ. Came to live in UK, 1971. Partner, BMQ Properties. Sec., Luton TUC, 1994–96. Member: Labour Party, 1996–2003; Lib Dem Party, 2003–. Mem. (Lib Dem), Luton BC, 2003–10 (Dep. Leader, 2005–07; Dep. Leader, Lib Dem Gp). Contested (Lib Dem) Luton S, 2005, 2010. *Address:* House of Lords, SW1A 0PW.

HUSSAIN, Altaf; Member (C) South Wales West, National Assembly for Wales, since May 2015; *b* Srinagar, 31 July 1944; *s* of Mohamed Saiyed and Amira Saiyed; *m* 1973, Khalida Sultan; one *s* one *d. Educ:* Med. Coll. Srinagar, Kahmir, India (MS BS 1966); Kashmir Univ. (MS 1973); Liverpool Univ. (MChOrth 1982). FICS. Resident, 1967–70, Registrar of Orthopaedics, 1970–74, Lectr in Orthopaedics, 1974–81, SMHS Hosp. and Med. Coll., Srinagar; Resident, then Registrar, Royal Liverpool Hosp., 1979–83; Consultant Orthopaedic Surgeon: Al Zulfi Hosp., Riyadh, 1983–86; Prince Salman Hosp., Riyadh, 1986–92; various NHS hospitals, 1992–2000; Prince Charles Hosp., Merthyr Tydfil, 2000–10. Tutor, RCS, 2004–. Consultant Ed., Internat. J&K Practitioner. Invented Notch Trial in total knee replacement and Thumb Index Reference in total hip replacement. Shadow Minister for Social Services, Nat. Assembly for Wales, 2015–. Dep. Chm., Bridgend Cons. Assoc., 2009–11; Chm., S Wales W, Cons. Party, 2011–15. Mem., New Castle Higher Community Council, 2012–. Gov., St Robert's Catholic Sch., Aberkenfig, 2013–. Life Member: Indian Orthopaedic Soc., UK; Indian Orthopaedic Assoc.; Member: British Orthopaedic Assoc.; Western Orthopaedic Assoc.; Amnesty Internat. UK. Best Practice Team Award, 2007; Glory of India Award, India Internat. Friendship Soc., 2008; Bharat Gaurav Award, 2009; Lifetime Achievement Award, 2009. *Publications:* contrib. articles to internat. professional jls. *Recreations:* golf, swimming, keep fit, South East politics. *Address:* National Assembly for Wales, Cardiff Bay, Cardiff CF99 1NA. *T:* 0300 200 7259, 07725 497846. *E:* altaf.hussain@assembly.wales; (office) 11 St James Gardens, Swansea SA1 6DY; (home) 20 Plas Ty Mawr, Penyfai, Bridgend CF31 4NH. *T:* (01656) 660483, 07817 506004. *E:* draltafhussain1@gmail.com.

HUSSAIN, Rear Adm. Amjad Mazhar, CB 2011; CEng; Executive Director, Jacobs (UK), 2012; Chairman, SQR Systems Ltd, 2013; *b* Rawalpindi, Pakistan, 15 May 1958; *s* of Mazhar Hussain and Tahira Hussain (*née* Begum); *m* 1983, Wendy Downer; one *s* two *d. Educ:* Downer Grammar Sch.; Harrow Weald 6th Form Coll.; Univ. of Durham (BSc Engrg Sci. and Mgt 1979); Cranfield Univ. (MSc 1987); London Business Sch. (MSc 2002). MIET. Joined RN, 1976; served: HMS Dido, 1982–83; HMS Cornwall, 1989–91; HMS Invincible, 1995–97; Integrated Project Team Leader, 1997–99; Asst Dir, Capability Strategy, 1999–2002; Naval Base Comdr, Portsmouth, 2002–05; Director General: Logistics (Fleet), 2006–07; Weapons, 2007–09; Dir, Precision Attack, 2009–12; Controller of the Navy, 2009–12. Trustee, Imperial War Mus., 2015–. FCGI 2013. Freeman, City of London, 2006; Liveryman, Lightmongers' Co., 2006. Hon. DCL Durham, 2011. *Recreations:* family life, all sports. *Address:* 1180 Eskdale Road, Winnersh, Wokingham RG41 5TU. *Club:* Army and Navy.

HUSSAIN, Imran; MP (Lab) Bradford East, since 2015; *b* 7 June 1978. *Educ:* Univ. of Huddersfield (LLB). Called to the Bar, Lincoln's Inn. Mem. (Lab), City of Bradford MDC, 2002– (Dep. Leader, 2010–15). *Address:* House of Commons, SW1A 0AA. *T:* (020) 7219 8636. *E:* imran.hussain.mp@parliament.uk.

HUSSAIN, Mamnoon; President of Pakistan, since 2013; *b* Agra, India, 23 Dec. 1940; *s* of Haji Azhar Hussain and Siraj Begum; *m* 1970, Mehmooda Kamil; three *s. Educ:* Karachi Secondary Educn Bd; Karachi Univ. (BCom Hons 1963); Inst. of Business Admin, Karachi (MBA 1965). Advr to Chief Minister of Sindh, 1997–98; Gov. of Sindh, 1999. Pres., Chamber of Commerce and Industry, Karachi, 1999. Hon. PhD Inst. of Business Admin, Karachi, 2014; Hon. Dr Bako Siaje, 2015. *Recreations:* games, cricket, reading. *Address:* President's Secretariat, Aiwan-e-Sadr, Islamabad, Pakistan. *Club:* Karachi Gymkhana.

HUSSAIN, Mukhtar; QC 1992; a Recorder of the Crown Court, since 1989; *b* 22 March 1950; *s* of late Karam Dad and Rehmi Bi; *m* 1972, Shamim Akhtar Ali; three *d. Educ:* William Temple Secondary School. Came to UK, 1964. Called to the Bar, Middle Temple, 1971, Bencher, 2000; Asst Recorder, 1986–89; Head of Chambers, 1992–2012. Chm., Police Discipline Appeals Tribunal, 1997–; Member: Mental Health Review Tribunal, 2000–; CICB, 2000–; Bar Council, 2001. Presenter, Granada TV, 1982–87. *Recreations:* cricket, squash, bridge, golf, reading. *Address:* Lincoln House, 1 Brazennose Street, Manchester M2 5EL.

HUSSAIN, Nasser, OBE 2002; columnist, Daily Mail, since 2003; cricket commentator, Sky Sports, since 2004; *b* Madras, India, 28 March 1968; *s* of Joe Hussain and Shireen Hussain (*née* Price); *m* Karen Birch; two *s* one *d. Educ:* Univ. of Durham (BSc). Essex County Cricket Club: first-class début, 1987; county cap, 1989; Vice-Captain, 1995–99; Captain, 1999–2004, retired; England: début, 1990; Vice-Captain, 1998–99; Captain, 1999–2003; toured India, W Indies, Zimbabwe, NZ, Aust., S Africa, Pakistan, Sri Lanka; highest test score 207 *vs* Aust., Edgbaston, 1997. Player of the Series, England *vs* India, 1996. *Publications:* (with Steve Waugh) An Ashes Summer, 1997; Playing with Fire (autobiog.), 2004. *Address:* The Old Rectory, Colam Lane, Little Baddow, Chelmsford, Essex CM3 4SY.

HUSSEIN-ECE, Baroness *cr* 2010 (Life Peer), of Highbury in the London Borough of Islington; **Meral Hussein Ece,** OBE 2009; Member, Equality and Human Rights Commission, 2009–12; *b* Islington, 10 Oct. 1953; one *s* two *d. Educ:* BA (Hons). Mem. (Lab) 1994–96, (Lib Dem) 1997–2002, Hackney LBC (Dep. Leader, 1995–96); Mem. (Lib Dem) Islington LBC, 2002–10 (Cabinet Mem. for Health and Social Care, 2002–06). Chm., Islington Health Partnership Bd, 2004–06; Mem. Bd, Islington PCT, 2002–06. Non-exec. Dir, Camden and Islington Mental Health and Social Care Trust, 2004–06. Chair, Ethnic Minority Liberal Democrats, 2006–10; Special Advr to Nick Clegg, MP, on community cohesion and black and minority ethnic communities, 2008–. Mem., Black, Asian and Minority Ethnic Women Councillors' Govt Taskforce, 2008–09. Mem., Lib Dem Federal Exec., 2005–10. Hon. DLitt Coventry, 2012. *Address:* House of Lords, SW1A 0PW.

HUSSEY, Ann Elizabeth, (Mrs Alastair Sharp); QC 2009; *b* London, 5 March 1959; *d* of Arnold Hussey and Jean Hussey; *m* 1984, Alastair Sharp; one *s* three *d. Educ:* St Albans Girls Sch.; Univ. of Kent (BA Hons Law). Called to the Bar, Middle Temple, 1981 (Blackstone Law Scholar), Bencher, 2012; in practice as barrister specialising in matrimonial finance. *Recreations:* riding, showing native ponies, ski-ing. *Address:* 1 Hare Court, Temple, EC4Y 7BE. *E:* hussey@1hc.com.

HUSSEY, Derek Robert; Member (UU) Tyrone West, Northern Ireland Assembly, 1998–2007; *b* 12 Sept. 1948; *s* of Sydney Robert Hussey and Rachel Hussey (*née* Maguire); *m* 1st (marr. diss.); one *s*; 2nd, Karen (*née* Vaughan); one *s* one *d. Educ:* Model Sch., Omagh; Omagh Acad.; Stranmillis Coll., Belfast (Cert Ed). Head of Business Studies, Castlederg High Sch., 1972–98, retired. Mem. (Ind. U 1989–97, UU 1997–), Strabane DC. Mem., N Ireland Forum, 1996–98. Dep. Whip, UUP, NI Assembly, 1998–99; former UU spokesman on victims' issues. Contested (UU) Tyrone West, NI Assembly, 2007. *Recreations:* country and western music, soccer, Rugby, ski-ing, Ulster-Scots history and culture. *E:* drhussey@hotmail.com.

HUSSEY, Hon. James Arthur; Advisor to Chairman, Oberthur Fiduciaire, since 2011; *b* 15 Aug. 1961; *s* of Baron Hussey of North Bradley and of Lady Susan Katharine Hussey, *qv*; *m* 1994, Emma Betty Shelley; one *s* two *d. Educ:* Harrow Sch.; Trinity Coll., Oxford (BA Hons Modern Hist.). De La Rue PLC, 1983–2010: Commercial Dir, Thomas De La Rue, 1990–95; Managing Director: Portals Ltd, 1995–98; Currency Div., 1998–2006; Security and Paper Div., 2006–08; Chief Exec., 2009–10. Dir, Camelot, 2006–09. Bd Advr, Currency Res., 2013–. Trustee, Ruffer CP, 2011–; Trustee and Vice Chm., Friends of the Elderly, 2012–. *Recreations:* shooting, football, Rugby, cricket. *Address:* Old Rectory, Wylye, Warminster BA12 0RN. *T:* (01985) 248280. *Clubs:* Brooks's; MCC.

HUSSEY, Ross Michael; Member (UU) West Tyrone, Northern Ireland Assembly, since 2011; *b* Omagh, 25 Feb. 1959; *s* of Sydney Robert Hussey and Rachel Hussey. *Educ:* Omagh Co. Primary Sch.; Omagh Acad.; Omagh Technical Coll.; Open Univ. (BA Hons); Nat. Univ. of Ireland, Galway (Dip. Community Develt); Queen's Univ. Belfast (Cert. Effective Mgt of Volunteers). Pearl Assurance plc, 1976–2002. Reserve Constable (pt-time), RUC GC, 1977–2001; Police Service, NI, 2001–02. Mem., Omagh DC, 2005–12 (Vice Chm., 2011–12). Mem., Finance and Personnel Cttee, 2011–12, Public Accounts Cttee, 2011–, NI Assembly. Contested (UU) W Tyrone, 2015. Mem., NI Policing Bd, 2011–; Chm., Part-time Officers Welfare Gp, RUC GC Assoc., 2002–. *Recreations:* historical research, First World War. *Address:* (office) 64 Market Street, Omagh, Co. Tyrone BT78 1EN. *T:* (028) 8224 5568. *E:* ross.hussey@mla.niassembly.gov.uk.
See also D. R. Hussey.

HUSSEY, Lady Susan Katharine, GCVO 2013 (DCVO 1984; CVO 1971); Lady-in-Waiting to the Queen, since 1960; *b* 1 May 1939; 5th *d* of 12th Earl Waldegrave, KG, GCVO; *m* 1959, Marmaduke Hussey (later Baron Hussey of North Bradley) (*d* 2006); one *s* one *d. Address:* 18 Lochmore House, Cundy Street, SW1W 9JX.
See also Sir Francis Brooke, Bt, Hon. J. A. Hussey.

HUSTLER, Dr Margaret Joan; Headmistress, Harrogate Ladies' College, 1996–2007; Director, International School of Choueifat-Amman, Jordan, since 2007; *b* 1 Nov. 1949; *d* of Harry Hustler and Dorothy (*née* Kaye); *m* 1976, David Thomas Wraight; three *s* five *d. Educ:* Marist Convent, London; Westfield Coll., London Univ. (BSc Hons); Royal Holloway Coll., London Univ. (PhD Biochem). Teacher, Lady Eleanor Holles Sch., Hampton, 1977–85; Dep. Headmistress, Atherley Sch., Southampton, 1985–89; Headmistress, St Michael's Sch., Limpsfield, 1989–96. *Recreations:* walking, sewing, knitting, reading.

HUSTON, Felicity Victoria; public affairs and recruitment consultant, since 2011; Partner, Huston & Co., Tax Consultants, since 1994; *b* May 1963; *d* of Jim McCormick and Joy McCormick (*née* Day); *m* 1992, Adrian Robert Arthur Huston, JP; two *s. Educ:* Strathearn Sch., Belfast; Campbell Coll., Belfast; Nottingham Univ. (BA Hons 1985). HM Inspector of Taxes, 1988–94. Commissioner: H of L Appts Commn, 2000–08; Public Appts for NI, 2005–11. Director: Cassandra Consulting (NI) Ltd, 2003–07; Moyle Interconnector (Financing) plc, 2003–10; Moyle Interconnector plc; NI Energy Hldgs Ltd and gp cos, 2005–10. Gen. Comr of Income Tax, 2002–09 (Chm., NI Reg., Assoc. of Gen. Comrs of Income Tax, 2005–07). Mem., Industrial Tribunals Panel, 1999–2000. Member: Consumer Panel, PIA, 1996–98; PO Users' Council, NI, 1996–2000; Gen. Consumer Council, 1996–2000 (Dep. Chm., 1999–2000); Chm., NI Consumer Cttee for Electricity, 2000–03. Chm., Selection Panel, Ind. Parly Standards Authy, 2009; Ind. Mem., QC Selection Panel, England and Wales, 2011–13, NI, 2011–. Member Board: NI Charities Adv. Cttee, 1998–2000; Clifton House (Belfast Charitable Soc.), 1995–2007 (Hon. Treas., 2000–05). Dir, Team NI Ltd, 2004–06. Chm., Point Fields Th. Co., 1996. Trustee, Assisi Animal Sanctuary, 2006–11. *Recreations:* cookery, family, pets. *Address:* c/o Huston & Co., 13 Cabin Hill Gardens, Belfast BT5 7AP. *T:* (028) 9080 6080. *E:* felicity@huston.co.uk.

HUTCHEON, Joy Louise; Director General, Country Programmes (formerly Africa, South and East Asia and Western Hemisphere), Department for International Development, since 2011; *b* 26 Feb. 1965; *d* of Keith Hutcheon and Margaret (*née* Swindells); partner, Christopher Peter Nuttall, *qv. Educ:* University Coll. London (BA English). Home Office: Private Sec. to Minister of State, 1991–92; Hd, Sentencing Policy, 1992–95; Private Sec. to Perm. Sec., 1995–97; Franchising Exec., Office of Passenger Rail Franchising, 1997–99; Team Leader, Performance and Innovation Unit, Cabinet Office, 1999–2000; Consultant, Caribbean, 2000–03; Department for International Development: Hd, Western Asia Dept, 2003–05; Dir, Communication and Knowledge Sharing, 2005–07; Hd, Zambia, 2007–09; Dir, E and Central Africa, 2009–11. *Publications:* Winning the Generation Game, 2000; Prime Minister's Review of Adoption, 2000; Sentencing for Drug and Drug Related Cases in OECS Magistrates' Courts, 2005. *Recreations:* weekends in Suffolk, playing the saxophone, California. *Address:* Department for International Development, 22 Whitehall, SW1A 2EG.

HUTCHEON, William Robbie; Editor, The Courier and Advertiser, 2002–11 (Deputy Editor, 2001); *b* 19 Jan. 1952; *s* of Alexander Hutcheon and Williamina Hutcheon (*née* Robbie); *m* 1974, Margo Martin; one *s* two *d. Educ:* Aberdeen Acad. D. C. Thomson & Co. Ltd: joined as reporter, Aberdeen, 1969; Sports Sub-ed., Dundee, 1970; various posts, The Courier and Advertiser, inc. Sports Ed., Chief Sub-ed., Night News Ed., to 2001. Mem., Editors' Cttee, Scottish Daily Newspapers Soc., 2002–11 (Chm., 2007–08). *Recreations:* sport, music, travel, computing. *Address:* 42 Ferndale Drive, Broughty Ferry, Dundee DD5 3DF. *T:* (01382) 774552. *E:* hutcheon642@btinternet.com.

HUTCHESON, Linda Dolores; *see* Cardozo, L. D.

HUTCHINGS, Prof. Graham John, PhD, DSc; FRS 2009; FRSC, FIChemE; FInstP; FLSW; Professor of Physical Chemistry, since 1997, and Director, Cardiff Catalysis Institute, since 2008, Cardiff University (Pro-Vice-Chancellor Research, 2010–12); *b* Weymouth, 3 Feb. 1951; *s* of Duncan Herbert and Celia Doris Hutchings; *m* 1973, Sally Joanna Dalton; one *s* three *d. Educ:* Weymouth Grammar Sch.; University Coll. London (BSc 1st Cl. Hons; PhD Chem. 1975; DSc 2002). FRSC 1987; FIChemE 2006; FInstP 2009. SO, 1975–79, Res. and Prodn Manager, 1979–81, ICI Petrochem. Div.; CSO, AECI, S Africa, 1981–84; Lectr, Sen. Lectr, then Prof., Dept of Chem., Univ. of Witwatersrand, Johannesburg, 1984–87; Asst Dir, 1987–94, Prof. and Dep. Dir, 1994–97, Leverhulme Centre for Innovative Catalysis, Univ. of Liverpool. MAE 2010. Founding FLSW 2010. Ed., Jl Catalysis, 1999–. Treas., Internat. Catalysis Socs, 2000–08. Davy Medal, Royal Soc., 2013. *Publications:* contrib. papers to scientific jls, incl. Nature and Science, on subject of heterogeneous catalysis; more than 30 patents on subject of catalysis. *Recreations:* walking, sketching landscapes. *Address:* Cardiff Catalysis Institute, School of Chemistry, Cardiff University, Park Place, Cardiff CF10 3AT. *T:* (029) 2087 4059, *Fax:* (029) 2087 4030. *E:* hutch@cf.ac.uk.

HUTCHINGS, Gregory Frederick; Chairman, GCH Capital Ltd, since 2010. *Educ:* Uppingham Sch.; University of Aston (BSc); MBA Aston Mgt Centre. Dir, 1983–2000, Chief Exec., 1984–95, Chm., 1995–2000, Tomkins plc; Exec. Chm., Lupus Capital plc, 2004–09. Bd Mem., RNT, 1996–2002; Gov., Mus. of London, 1999–2008. England veterans hockey teams, 1998–. Hon. DBA Sunderland, 2000.

HUTCHINGS, Prof. Ian Michael, PhD; FInstP, FIMMM; FREng; GKN Professor of Manufacturing Engineering, University of Cambridge, since 2001; Fellow, St John's College, Cambridge, since 1975; *b* Barnet, Herts, 6 May 1950; *s* of Douglas and Sheila Hutchings; *m* 1973, Jennifer Farrant; three *s* one *d*. *Educ:* Rugby Sch.; Trinity Coll., Cambridge (BA 1971; MA; PhD 1975). FIMMM 1993; FInstP 1994; FREng 2002. Department of Materials Science, University of Cambridge: demonstrator, 1977–82; Lectr, 1982–97; Reader in Tribology, 1997–2000; St John's College, Cambridge: Lectr, 1978–2001; Dir of Studies in Materials Sci. and Metallurgy, 1990–2000. Hon. Prof., China Univ. of Mining and Technol., Beijing, 1999; Vis. Prof., Xi'an Univ. of Architecture and Technol., China, 2004; Adjunct Prof., Xi'an Jiaotong Univ., China, 2004. Chm., St John's Innovation Centre Ltd, Cambridge, 1996–. Ed.-in-Chief, Wear, 1998–2012. Tribology Silver Medal, 1994, Donald Julius Groen Prize, 2000, IMechE; NPL Award for Materials Metrol., Inst. of Materials, 2000; Staudinger-Durrer Prize and Medal, ETH Zürich, 2007. *Publications:* Tribology: friction and wear of engineering materials, 1992; contrib. papers to scientific and engrg jls on tribology, materials engrg and manufg engrg incl. engrg aspects of ink-jet printing. *Recreation:* not gardening. *Address:* University of Cambridge, Institute for Manufacturing, 17 Charles Babbage Road, Cambridge CB3 0FS. *E:* imh2@cam.ac.uk.

HUTCHINGS, Martin Anthony; QC 2011; *b* Farnborough, Kent, 14 July 1959; *s* of Donald Hutchings and Mary Hutchings; *m* 1990, Claudia Dalton; one *s* one *d*. *Educ:* Ravensbourne Sch.; St Catherine's Coll., Oxford (BA). Called to the Bar, Middle Temple, 1986; in practice as barrister, specialising in property litigation; Mem., Wilberforce Chambers, 2006–. *Recreations:* walking, cinema, swimming. *Address:* Wilberforce Chambers, 8 New Square, Lincoln's Inn, WC2A 3QP. *T:* (020) 7306 0102. *E:* mhutchings@wilberforce.co.uk.

HUTCHINS, Bonnie; *see* Greer, B.

HUTCHINS, (Hazel) Patricia, (Pat); freelance writer and illustrator of children's books, since 1964; *b* 18 June 1942; *d* of Edward and Lily Victoria Goundry; *m* 1966, Laurence Edward Hutchins (*d* 2008); two *s*. *Educ:* Darlington Art Sch.; Leeds Coll. of Art (NDD). Asst Art Dir, J. Walter Thompson Advertising Agency, 1962–64. Dir and writer, Hutchins Film Co., 1997–; wrote and co-produced 39 ten-minute animated children's films, based on Titch books, for television. Hon. DCL UEA, 2006. Kate Greenaway Medal, 1974. *Publications:* Rosie's Walk, 1968; Tom and Sam, 1968; The Surprise Party, 1968; Clocks and More Clocks, 1970; Changes, Changes, 1971; Titch, 1971; Goodnight Owl, 1972; The Wind Blew, 1974; The Silver Christmas Tree, 1974; The House That Sailed Away, 1975; Don't Forget the Bacon, 1976; Happy Birthday Sam, 1979; Follow That Bus!, 1978; One-Eyed Jake, 1978; The Best Train Set Ever, 1978; The Mona Lisa Mystery, 1981; One Hunter, 1982; King Henry's Palace, 1983; You'll soon Grow into them, Titch, 1983; The Curse of the Egyptian Mummy, 1983; The Very Worst Monster, 1985; The Tale of Thomas Mead, 1986; The Doorbell Rang, 1986; Where's the Baby?, 1987; Which Witch is Which?, 1989; Rats!, 1989; What Game Shall We Play?, 1990; Tidy Titch, 1991; Silly Billy, 1992; My Best Friend, 1992; Little Pink Pig, 1993; Three Star Billy, 1994; Titch and Daisy, 1996; Shrinking Mouse, 1997; It's My Birthday, 1999; Ten Red Apples, 2001; We're Going on a Picnic, 2002; There's only one of me, 2003; Don't Get Lost!, 2004; Bumpety Bump, 2006; Barn Dance, 2007; Where, Oh Where, is Rosie's Chick?, 2015. *Recreations:* music, reading, gardening, cooking. *Address:* Random House Children's Books, 61–63 Uxbridge Road, W5 5SA. *Club:* Chelsea Arts.

HUTCHINSON; *see* Hely-Hutchinson.

HUTCHINSON, family name of **Baron Hutchinson of Lullington**.

HUTCHINSON OF LULLINGTON, Baron *cr* 1978 (Life Peer), of Lullington in the County of E Sussex; **Jeremy Nicolas Hutchinson;** QC 1961; *b* 28 March 1915; *o s* of late St John Hutchinson, KC; *m* 1st, 1940, Dame Peggy Ashcroft (marr. diss. 1966; she *d* 1991); one *s* one *d*; 2nd, 1966, June Osborn (*d* 2006). *Educ:* Stowe Sch.; Magdalen Coll., Oxford. Called to Bar, Middle Temple, 1939, Bencher 1963. RNVR, 1939–46. Practised on Western Circuit, N London Sessions and Central Criminal Court. Recorder of Bath, 1962–72; a Recorder of the Crown Court, 1972–76. Mem., H of L, 1978–2011. Member: Cttee on Immigration Appeals, 1966–68; Cttee on Identification Procedures, 1974–76. Prof. of Law, RA, 1987–2005. Mem., Arts Council of GB, 1974–79 (Vice-Chm., 1977–79); Trustee: Tate Gallery, 1977–84 (Chm., 1980–84); Chantrey Bequest, 1977–99. *Address:* 10 Blenheim Road, NW8 0LU.

HUTCHINSON, Alison Elizabeth; Chief Executive, Pennies Foundation, since 2009; *b* Dumbarton, Scotland, 5 Feb. 1967; *d* of Charles and Elizabeth McCrea; *m* 1995, David John Hutchinson; one *s* two *d*. *Educ:* Strathclyde Univ. (BSc Technol. and Business Studies). IBM Corporation: Systems Engr, 1986–89; Software Sales Manager, 1989–91; Sales Exec., 1991–93; Eur. Customer Progs Manager, 1993–95; Global Manager, Smart Cards, 1995–97; Chief Exec., E-Net, 1997–99; Dir, Global Financial Solutions, 1999–2000; CEO, Barclays B2B, 2000–01, Mktg Dir, Barclaycard, 2002–03, Barclays Bank plc; Man. Dir, Kensington Mortgages, 2003–07, Gp CEO, 2007–08, Kensington Gp plc. Independent non-executive Director: LMAX Ltd, 2010–15; Aviva Life Hldgs Ltd, 2014–; Yorkshire Building Soc. Gp, 2015. Trustee, CAF, 2010–. *Recreations:* variety of sports, including cross country running and fitness training, sampling wine of many different varieties. *Address:* Beacon Underwood, Wood Road, Hindhead, Surrey GU26 6PX. *T:* 07917 064176. *E:* alison.hutchinson3@btinternet.com.

HUTCHINSON, Anne-Marie, OBE 2002; Partner, Dawson Cornwell, since 1998; *b* Donegal, 1 Aug. 1957; *d* of Samuel Gerald Hutchinson and Catherine Hutchinson; one *s* one *d*. *Educ:* St Peter's Sch., Huntingdon; Univ. of Leeds (BA Internat. Hist. and Politics). Admitted solicitor, 1985; Partner, Beckman and Beckman, 1988–98. Mem., Nat. Commn on Forced Marriage, H of L, 2013–. Chair, Family Law Cttee, 2007–10, Chair, Women Lawyers' Interest Gp, 2011–13, Internat. Bar Assoc.; Gov. at Large, Internat. Acad. of Matrimonial Lawyers, 2011–. Trustee, Reunite, 1990–; Ambassador, Sharan Proj., 2014–. *Publications:* (jtly) International Parental Child Abduction, 2003. *Recreations:* travel, reading, charity work. *Address:* Dawson Cornwell, 15 Red Lion Square, WC1R 4QT. *T:* (020) 7242 2556, *Fax:* (020) 7539 4841. *E:* amh@dawsoncornwell.com.

HUTCHINSON, Elisabeth Helen; *see* Wicksteed, E. H.

HUTCHINSON, (George) Malcolm, CB 1989; CEng, FIET; Director, Malcolm Hutchinson Ltd, since 1992; *b* 24 Aug. 1935; *s* of Cecil George Hutchinson and Annie Hutchinson; *m* 1958, Irene Mary Mook; four *d*. *Educ:* Pocklington Sch.; Queens' Coll., Cambridge (MA). Develt Engr, Metropolitan Vickers, 1957; short service commn, 1958, regular commn, 1961, REME; RMCS, 1967; sc Camberley, 1968; CO 12 Armd Workshop, REME, 1968–70; Staff appts, 1970–74; British Liaison Officer, USA Army Materiel Comd, 1974–76; Comdr REME 1 British Corps troops, 1977–79; REME staff, 1979–82; Project Man., Software Systems, 1982–85; Dep. to DGEME, 1985–86; Dir Procurement Strategy MoD(PE), 1986–88; Vice Master-Gen. of the Ordnance, 1988–90. Mem., Defence Prospect Team, 1990. Procurement and logistic consultant, 1991–92. Managing Director: DLR, 1992–97; Docklands Rly Mgt Ltd, 1997–99; Chm., Atomic Weapon Estabt Mgt Ltd, 1999–2003; Exec. Chm., Atomic Weapon Estabt plc, 2002–05. Chm., Serco Docklands Ltd, 2006–10. Mem., Engrg Council, 1993–99. Pres., IEEIE, 1990–94. Col Comdt, REME, 1991–96. *Recreations:* Rugby, cricket, sailing. *Address:* Rectory Cottage, Little Ann Road, Little Ann, Andover, Hants SP11 7SN.

HUTCHINSON, Prof. Gregory Owen, DPhil; Regius Professor of Greek, University of Oxford, since 2015; Student of Christ Church, Oxford, since 2015; *b* London, 5 Dec. 1957; *s* of Jeremy Hutchinson and Daphne Hutchinson; *m* 1979, Yvonne Downing; one *d*. *Educ:* City of London Sch.; Balliol Coll., Oxford (BA 1979); Christ Church, Oxford (DPhil 1983). University of Oxford: Res. Lectr, Christ Church, 1981–84; Fellow and Tutor in Classics, Exeter Coll., 1984–2015; Reader in Classical Lit., 1996–98; Prof. of Greek and Latin Langs and Lit., 1998–2015. *Publications:* Aeschylus, Septem contra Thebas, 1985; Hellenistic Poetry, 1988; Latin Literature from Seneca to Juvenal: a critical study, 1993; Cicero's Correspondence: a literary study, 1998; Greek Lyric Poetry: a commentary on selected larger pieces, 2001; Propertius: Elegies Book IV, 2006; Talking Books: readings in Hellenistic and Roman books of poetry, 2008; Greek to Latin: frameworks and contexts for intertextuality, 2013. *Recreations:* playing the piano, reading literature in various languages, washing up to music. *Address:* Christ Church, Oxford OX1 1DP. *E:* gregory.hutchinson@classics.ox.ac.uk.

HUTCHINSON, Henry; *see* Hutchinson, M. H. R.

HUTCHINSON, (John) Maxwell, PPRIBA; architect, writer, broadcaster; *b* 3 Dec. 1948; *s* of late Frank Maxwell Hutchinson and Elizabeth Ross Muir (*née* Wright); marr. diss. *Educ:* Wellingborough Prep. Sch.; Oundle; Scott Sutherland Sch. of Arch., Aberdeen; Architectural Assoc. Sch. of Arch. (AA Dip. 1972); RIBA 1972. Founder, Hutchinson and Partners, Chartered Architects, 1972, Chm., 1987–93; Dir, The Hutchinson Studio Architects, 1993–. Chairman: Permarock Products Ltd, Loughborough, 1985–95; Holland, Hannen and Cubitts, 2010–; non-exec. Dir, Archial Gp plc, 2005–10. Royal Institute of British Architects: Mem. Council, 1978–93, Sen. Vice Pres., 1988–89, Pres., 1989–91; Chairman: East Midlands Arts Bd Ltd, 1991–95; Industrial Bldg Bureau, 1987–89; Vice-Chm., Construction Industry Council, 1990–92. Vis. Prof., Architecture, QUB, 1989–93; Special Prof. of Architecture, Nottingham Univ., 1993–96; Vis. Prof., Westminster Univ., 1998–2000. Founder and Chm., Article 25 (Architects for Aid), 2005–. Chm., British Architectural Library Trust, 1991–99; Mem. Council, RSCM, 1997–2000. Associate Mem., PRS, 1988. Trustee: Univ. of London; Univ. of London Inst. in Paris. Fellow, Chartered Inst. of Building, 2011. Hon. Fellow: Greenwich Univ., 1990; Royal Soc. of Ulster Architects, 1991; UCL, 2008. Hon. DDes, Robert Gordon, 2007. Church Warden Emeritus, Our Most Holy Redeemer, Clerkenwell; ordained deacon, 2014; Asst Curate, St John on Bethnal Green, 2014–. *Compositions:* The Kibbo Kift, Edinburgh Fest., 1976; The Ascent of Wilberforce III, Lyric Hammersmith, 1982; Requiem in a Village Church (choral), 1986; St John's Cantata, 1987. *Publications:* The Prince of Wales: right or wrong?, 1989; Number 57: the storey of a house, 2003. *Recreation:* jazz piano. *Address:* 17 Chart Street, N1 6DD.

HUTCHINSON, Malcolm; *see* Hutchinson, G. M.

HUTCHINSON, Prof. (Marcus) Henry (Ritchie), PhD; Director, Central Laser Facility, CCLRC Rutherford Appleton Laboratory, 1997–2005; *b* 2 Dec. 1945; *s* of Marcus Henry McCracken Hutchinson and Maud Hutchinson; *m* 1973, Gillian Ruth Harris; one *s* two *d*. *Educ:* Coleraine Academical Instn; Queen's Univ. of Belfast (BSc 1st cl. Hons Physics 1968; PhD Physics 1971). FInstP 1998. Imperial College, London: Lectr in Physics, 1973–83; Sen. Lectr, 1983–86; Reader in Optics, 1986–89; Prof. of Laser Physics, 1989–2002; Dir, Blackett Lab. Laser Consortium, 1986–97; Associate Dir, Centre for Photomolecular Scis, 1992–97. Chief Scientist, CCLRC, 2004–07. Chief Scientific Advr, PETAL (Petawatt Aquitaine Laser) Prog., 2009–. Vis. Res. Prof., Univ. of Illinois at Chicago, 1986; Vis. Prof., Univ. of Oxford, 2003–; Invited Prof., Univ. of Bordeaux 1, 2009–11. Member: SERC Physics Cttee, 1990–92; Wissenschaftliche Rat, Gesellschaft für Schwerionenforschung mbH, Darmstadt, 2001–05 (Chm., Plasma Physics Adv. Cttee, 2004–10); UK Mem., European Strategy Forum for Res. Infrastructures, 2005–07. FRSA 2007. *Publications:* contrib. numerous scientific papers and articles in physics. *Recreations:* walking, gardening. *Address:* 16 Chiltern Hills Road, Beaconsfield, Bucks HP9 1PL.

HUTCHINSON, Maxwell; *see* Hutchinson, J. M.

HUTCHINSON, Prof. Peter John Ashton, PhD; FRCS; Professor of Neurosurgery, University of Cambridge, since 2014; Director of Clinical Studies and Fellow, Robinson College, Cambridge, since 2008; Hon. Consultant Neurosurgeon, Cambridge University Hospitals NHS Foundation Trust, since 2003; *b* Plymouth, 16 Dec. 1965; *s* of David and Rosalind Hutchinson; *m* 1998, Elizabeth Barr; two *s*. *Educ:* Judd Sch., Tonbridge; St Bartholomew's Hosp. Med. Sch., Univ. of London (BSc Hons; MB BS); Robinson Coll., Cambridge (PhD 2001). FRCS 1994 (FRCS (Surg. Neurol. 2002)). Hse Officer, St Bartholomew's and Homerton Hosps, 1990–91; SHO, St Bartholomew's and Oxford rotation, 1991–94; Registrar: St Bartholomew's, 1994; Addenbrooke's Hosp., Cambridge, 1994–2002; Acad. of Med. Scis/Health Foundn Sen. Fellow, 2003–13; Reader in Neurosurgery, Univ. of Cambridge, 2008–13. Mem., Sec. of State for Transport's Hon. Med. Adv. Panel on Driving and Disorders of the Nervous System, 2008–. Speciality Lead for Neurosurgery, RCS Academic and Res. Bd, 2013–. Chair, Trauma Gp, Soc. of British Neurol Surgeons, 2010–. Vice Pres., Eur. Assoc. of Neurosurgeons, 2010–; Treas., Internat. Neurotrauma Soc., 2013–. *Publications:* (jtly) Intracranial Pressure and Brain Biochemical Monitoring XI, 2002; (jtly) Intracranial Pressure and Brain Biochemical Monitoring XII, 2005; (ed jtly) Head Injury: a multidisciplinary approach, 2009; contribs to learned jls, incl. Lancet. *Recreation:* Chief Medical Officer of Formula One British Grand Prix. *Address:* Box 167, Academic Division of Neurosurgery, University of Cambridge, Addenbrooke's Hospital, Cambridge CB2 0QQ. *T:* (01223) 336946, *Fax:* (01223) 216926. *E:* pjah2@cam.ac.uk.

HUTCHINSON, Prof. Philip; DL; FREng; CPhys; Principal, Royal Military College of Science, Cranfield University, 1996–2006, now Emeritus Professor; Chairman, Letcombe Technology Ltd, 2006–13; *b* 26 July 1938; *s* of George and Edna Hutchinson; *m* 1960, Joyce Harrison; one *s* one *d*. *Educ:* King James 1st Grammar Sch., Bishop Auckland, Co. Durham; King's Coll., Univ. of Durham (BSc); Univ. of Newcastle upon Tyne (PhD). MInstP. SO and SSO, Theoretical Phys. Div., AERE, Harwell, 1962–69; Vis. Fellow, Chem. Engrg Dept, Univ. of Houston, Texas, 1969–70; AERE, Harwell: SSO and PSO, Theoretical Phys Div., 1970–75; Hd of Thermodynamics and Fluid Mechanics Gp, Engrg Scis Div., 1975–80; Hd of Engrg Phys Br., Engrg Scis Div., 1980–85; Hd of Engrg Scis Div., 1985–87; Hd, Harwell Combustion Centre, 1980–87; Cranfield Institute of Technology, then Cranfield University: Head, Sch. of Engrg, 1987–2002; Pro Vice-Chancellor, 1996–99; Dep. Vice Chancellor, 1996–2003. Visiting Professor: Imperial Coll., London, 1980–85; Univ. of Leeds, 1985–. Chairman: Exec. Cttee on Fundamental Res. in Combustion, 1977–81, Exec. Cttee on Energy Efficiency and Emissions Reduction in Combustion, 1997–98, Internat. Energy Agency; Combustion Phys Gp of InstP, 1985–89; MRI 1989; Mem., Combustion Inst., 1977–2003; Past Mem., Watt Cttee on Energy, representing InstP and Combustion Inst. respectively; Founding Bd Mem., Eur. Research Community on Flow Turbulence and Combustion, 1988 (Chm., 1994–2000; Treas., 2000–02). 27th Leonardo da Vinci Lectr for

IMechE, 1983. Liveryman, Engineers' Co., 2004–. DL Oxon, 2003. FREng (FEng 1997). Hon. DTech Lund, 1999. *Publications:* papers in learned jls on statistical mechanics, fluid mechanics, combustion and laser light scattering. *Recreations:* music, reading, Go, gadgets.

HUTCHINSON, His Honour Richard Hampson; a Circuit Judge, 1974–2000; *b* 31 Aug. 1927; *s* of late John Riley Hutchinson and May Hutchinson; *m* 1954, Nancy Mary (*née* Jones); two *s* three *d.* *Educ:* St Bede's Grammar Sch., Bradford; UC Hull (LLB 1st Cl. Hons London). National Service, RAF, 1949–51. Called to Bar, Gray's Inn, 1949; practised on NE Circuit, 1951–74. Recorder: Rotherham, 1971–72; Crown Court, 1972–74; Hon. Recorder of Lincoln, 1991–2000; Resident Judge, Lincoln Crown Court, 1985–2000. Mem., County Court Rules Cttee, 1990–94; Technical Rep., Central Council of Probation Cttees, 1989–2000. *Recreations:* reading, conversation, history. *Address:* c/o Lincoln Combined Court Centre, 360 High Street, Lincoln LN5 7RL.

HUTCHISON, family name of **Baroness Kennedy of the Shaws**.

HUTCHISON, Most Rev. Andrew Sandford; Primate of the Anglican Church of Canada, 2004–07; *b* 19 Sept. 1938; *s* of Ralph Burton Hutchison and Kathleen Marian (*née* Van Nostrand); *m* 1960, Lois Arlene Knight; one *s.* *Educ:* Lakefield Coll. Sch.; Upper Canada Coll.; Trinity Coll. Toronto (LTh). Ordained deacon, 1969, priest, 1970; served fifteen years in the dio. of Toronto; Dean of Montreal, 1984–90; Bp of Montreal, 1990–2004, Archbishop, 2002–04; Metropolitan, Ecclesiastical Province of Canada, 2002–04. Pres., Montreal Diocesan Theol Coll., 1990–2004; Visitor, Bishops Univ., Lennoxville, 1990–2004; Chaplain: Canadian Grenadier Guards, 1986–90 (Hon. Chaplain, 1990–2004); 6087 and 22 CAR, 1986–2004; Order of St John of Jerusalem, Quebec, 1987–2004; Bishop Ordinary, Canadian Forces, 1997–2004. Pres., Fulford Residence, Montreal, 1990–2004. Trustee, Lakefield Coll. Sch., 1997–2000. Hon. DD: Montreal Diocesan Theol Coll., 1993; Trinity Coll., Toronto, 1994; Huron Univ. Coll., London, Ont, 2007; Hon. DCL Bishop's Univ., Lennoxville, 2003. OStJ 1991. Ecclesiastical Grand Cross, Order of St Lazarus, 1992.

HUTCHISON, Geordie Oliphant; Managing Director, Calders & Grandidge, timber importers and manufacturers, 1974–96; *b* 11 June 1934; *s* of late Col Ronald Gordon Oliphant Hutchison and of Ruth Gordon Hutchison-Bradburne; *m* 1964, Virginia Barbezat; two *s* one *d.* *Educ:* Eton Coll. Served RN, 1952–54: commnd as aircraft pilot, 1953. Calders Ltd, 1954–59; Calders & Grandidge Ltd, 1959–96: Dir, 1969. Comr, Forestry Commn, 1981–89. High Sheriff, Lincs, 1998. *Recreations:* golf, shooting. *Address:* Collairnie House, Cupar, Fife KY15 7RX. *T:* (01337) 810309. *Club:* Royal and Ancient Golf (St Andrews).

HUTCHISON, Prof. James Douglas, PhD; FRCSE, FRCS, FRCSGlas; Regius Professor of Surgery, since 2000 and Sir Harry Platt Professor of Orthopaedics, since 1995, University of Aberdeen; Hon. Consultant Orthopaedic Surgeon, Aberdeen Royal Infirmary, since 1991; *b* 8 Oct. 1955; *s* of James Hutchison, FRCS and Grace J. J. Holloway, MA; *m* 1985, Catherine, (Kate), MacLeod Douglas; two *s* one *d.* *Educ:* High Sch. of Dundee; Univ. of Dundee (MB ChB 1979); Univ. of Aberdeen (PhD 1988). FRCSE 1984; FRCS 2000; FRCSGlas 2002. Orthopaedic Registrar and Sen. Registrar, Royal Infirmary, Edinburgh, and Princess Margaret Rose Orthopaedic Hosp., 1986–90; Sen. Lectr in Orthopaedics, Univ. of Aberdeen, 1991–95. Speciality Advr in Orthopaedics and Trauma to CMO (Scotland), 1998–2007. Chairman: Scottish Cttee for Orthopaedics and Trauma, 2000–04; Scottish Hip Fracture Audit, 2004–06; Hip Fracture Delivery Team for Scottish Exec. Health Dept, 2005–09; Orthopaedics Task and Finish Gp for 18 weeks Referral to Treatment Team, 2008–, Spinal Collaboration Clinical Reference Gp, 2010–, Scottish Govt; Scottish Surgical Mortality Audit, 2011–14. Chairman: Intercollegiate Specialty Bd in Trauma and Orthopaedic Surgery, 2005–08; Specialty Exams Quality Assce Cttee, FRCS, 2009–11; Royal College of Surgeons of Edinburgh: Trustee (Mem. Council), 2008–12; Vice-Pres., 2012–15; Mem., Specialty Adv. Bd in Orthopaedics, 1997– (Chm., 2007–11); Chm., Heritage Cttee, 2009–. Member: Harveian Soc., 1997 (Pres., 2008); Moynihan Chirurgical Club, 2005; President: Aberdeen Medico-Chirurgical Soc., 2005–06; Assoc. of Profs of Orthopaedic Surgery, 2010–; ex officio Mem. Council, British Orthopaedic Assoc., 2010–. Chm., Bd of Govs, Surgeons Hall Trust, 2007–09; Pres., Dundee High Sch. Old Boys' Club, 2007–08; Mem., Bd of Govs, Robert Gordon's Coll., Aberdeen, 2011– (Chm., 2013–). *Publications:* contribs to scientific and clinical jls incl. Lancet, BMJ, Jl Bone and Joint Surgery. *Recreations:* family, dogs, golf, shooting, art, curling. *Address:* Cowiehillock Cottage, Echt, Skene, Aberdeenshire AB32 6XD. *T:* (01330) 860716. *E:* j.d.hutchison@abdn.ac.uk. *Clubs:* Royal Northern and University (Aberdeen); Aesculapian (Edinburgh).

HUTCHISON, Rt Hon. Sir Michael, Kt 1983; PC 1995; a Lord Justice of Appeal, 1995–99; *b* 13 Oct. 1933; *s* of Ernest and Frances Hutchison; *m* 1957, Mary Spettigue; two *s* three *d.* *Educ:* Lancing; Clare College, Cambridge (MA). Called to Bar, Gray's Inn, 1958, Bencher, 1983; a Recorder, 1975–83; QC 1976; a Judge of the High Court, QBD, 1983–95; Judge, Employment Appeal Tribunal, 1984–87; Presiding Judge, Western Circuit, 1989–92. Surveillance Comr, 1998–2006. Member: Judicial Studies Bd, 1985–87; Parole Bd, 1987–89.

HUTCHISON, Sir Peter Craft, 2nd Bt *cr* 1956; CBE 1992; FRSE; Chairman: Hutchison & Craft Ltd, Insurance Brokers, Glasgow, 1979–96; Forestry Commission, 1994–2001; *b* 5 June 1935; *s* of Sir James Riley Holt Hutchison, 1st Bt, DSO, TD, and Winefryde Eleanor Mary (*d* 1988), *d* of late Rev. R. H. Craft; *S* father, 1979; *m* 1966, Virginia, *er d* of late John Millar Colville, Gribloch, Kippen, Stirlingshire; one *s.* *Educ:* Eton; Magdalene Coll., Cambridge. Mem., Scottish Tourist Bd, 1981–87; Mem., 1987–98, Vice-Chm., 1989–98, British Waterways Bd; Chm., Loch Lomond and Trossachs Wkg Party, 1991–92. Dep. Convenor, Loch Lomond and the Trossachs Nat. Park Authy, 2002–. Chm. of Trustees, Royal Botanic Gdn, Edinburgh, 1985–94; Mem. Bd, Scottish Natural Heritage, 1994. Hon. Pres., Royal Caledonian Horticultural Soc., 1994–2010. Deacon, Incorporation of Hammermen, 1984–85. FRSE 1997. *Publications:* (with P. Cox) Seeds of Adventure, 2008. *Heir: s* James Colville Hutchison [*b* 7 Oct. 1967; *m* 1996, Jane, *d* of Peter Laidlaw]. *Address:* Broich, Kippen, Stirlingshire FK8 3EN.

HUTCHISON, Sir Robert, 3rd Bt *cr* 1939, of Thurle, Streatley, co. Berks; independent financial adviser, since 1978; *b* 25 May 1954; *er s* of Sir Peter Hutchison, 2nd Bt and Mary-Grace (*née* Seymour); *S* father, 1998; *m* 1987, Anne Margaret, *e d* of Sir (Godfrey) Michael (David) Thomas, 11th Bt; two *s.* *Educ:* Orwell Park Sch., Ipswich; Marlborough Coll. With J. & A Scrimgeour Ltd, 1973–78. *Recreations:* golf, tennis, watching Association Football, family life. *Heir: s* Hugo Thomas Alexander Hutchison, *b* 16 April 1988. *Address:* Hawthorn Cottage, Lower Road, Grundisburgh, Woodbridge, Suffolk IP13 6UQ. *Clubs:* Ipswich & Suffolk (Ipswich), Woodbridge Golf.

HUTH, Angela Maureen, (Mrs J. D. Howard-Johnston); writer; *b* 29 Aug. 1938; *d* of late Harold Edward Strachan Huth and Bridget Huth (*née* Nickols); *m* 1961, Quentin Hugh Crewe (marr. diss. 1970; he *d* 1998); one *d* (one *s* decd); *m* 1978, James Douglas Howard-Johnston; one *d* (one *s* decd). *Educ:* Lawnside, Gt Malvern, Worcs; Beaux Arts, Paris; Annigoni Sch. of Painting, Florence; Byam Shaw Art Sch., London. Harpers Bazaar, 1957–58; Art dept, J. Walter-Thompson, 1958–59; Queen mag., 1959–61; reporter, Man Alive, BBC, 1965–67; BBC TV presenter, How It Is, 1969–70; Kaleidoscope, Radio 4, 1970; freelance, 1968–. Radio and TV: plays: The Drip (radio); I didn't take my mother (radio); Past Forgetting (radio), 2001; Special Co-respondent; The Emperor's New Hat; The Summer House; Virginia Fly is Drowning; Sun Child; documentaries: The English Woman's Wardrobe, 1987; Land Girls, 1995; stage plays: The Understanding, 1982; The Trouble with Old Lovers, 1995. FRSL 1975. *Publications:* Nowhere Girl, 1970; Virginia Fly is Drowning, 1972; Sun Child, 1975; South of the Lights, 1977; Monday Lunch in Fairyland and Other Stories, 1978; The Understanding (play), 1982; Wanting, 1984; The English Woman's Wardrobe (non-fiction), 1986; Eugenie in Cloud Cuckoo Land (for children), 1986; Such Visitors and Other Stories, 1989; Invitation to the Married Life, 1991; Land Girls, 1994; The Trouble with Old Lovers (play), 1995; Another Kind of Cinderella, 1996; Wives of the Fishermen, 1998; Easy Silence, 1999; Of Love and Slaughter, 2002; The Collected Stories of Angela Huth, 2003; (ed) Well Remembered Friends: eulogies on celebrated lives, 2004; Once a Land Girl, 2010. *Recreations:* collecting antique paste jewellery, re-visiting favourite places in Britain, tap dancing. *Address:* c/o Caroline Michel, PFD, Drury House, 34–43 Russell Street, WC2B 5HA.

HUTH, Johannes Peter; Managing Director, Kohlberg Kravis Roberts & Co. Partners LLP (formerly Ltd), since 1999; *b* Heidelberg, Germany, 27 May 1960; *s* of Prof. Karl Otto Huth and Dr Brigitte Marielouise Soergel; *m* 1st, 1991, Leili (marr. diss. 2008); two *s* three *d*; 2nd, 2011, Helene. *Educ:* London Sch. of Econs and Pol Sci. (BSc Econ. 1984); Univ. of Chicago (MBA 1986). Vice Pres., Mergers and Acquisitions Dept, NY, Salomon Brothers, 1986–91; Mem., Mgt Cttee, Investcorp, 1991–99. Chm. Trustees, Private Equity Foundn, then Impetus - Private Equity Foundn, 2011–; Trustee: Design Mus., 2011– (Vice Chm.); Staedel Mus.; Educnl Endowment Foundn. Gov., LSE, 2002–. Vis. Fellow, Oxford Univ. FRSA. *Recreations:* cycling, ski-ing. *Address:* Kohlberg Kravis Roberts & Co. Partners LLP, Stirling Square, 7 Carlton Gardens, SW1Y 5AD. *E:* huthj@kkr.com.

HUTSON, Prof. Jeremy Mark, DPhil; FRS 2010; CChem, FRSC; FInstP; Professor of Chemistry and Physics (formerly Chemistry), University of Durham, since 1996; *b* 7 May 1957; *s* of James Murray Hutson and Margaret Joyce Hutson (*née* Pearson). *Educ:* Brentwood Sch.; Wadham Coll., Oxford (MA); Hertford Coll., Oxford (DPhil 1981). CPhys, MInstP 1994; FInstP 2004; MRSC, CChem 1988; FRSC 1999. NATO/SERC Res. Fellow, Univ. of Waterloo, Canada, 1981–83; Drapers' Co. Res. Fellow, 1983–84, Stokes Res. Fellow, 1984–86, Pembroke Coll., Cambridge; Lectr, 1987–93, Reader, 1993–96, Hd, Dept of Chem., 1998–2001, Univ. of Durham. JILA Vis. Fellow, Univ. of Colo, Boulder, 2001–02. Chairman: EPSRC Collaborative Computational Project on Molecular Quantum Dynamics, 2000–05; ESF Sci. Cttee, EuroQUAM, 2007–10. Member: EPSRC Peer Review College, 1994–; Bd, Atomic Molecular and Optical Physics Div., European Physical Soc., 2004–07. Ed., Internat. Rev. in Physical Chem., 2000–. Corday-Morgan Medal, 1991, Tilden Prize, 2011, RSC; Kołos Medal, Univ. of Warsaw and Polish Chemical Soc., 2007; Computational Chem. Award, RSC, 2007; Humboldt Prize, Alexander von Humboldt Foundn, 2010. *Publications:* numerous contribs to jls incl. Jl Chem. Physics, Jl Physical Chem., Physical Rev. *Recreations:* hiking, diving, paddling, local history. *Address:* Department of Chemistry, University of Durham, South Road, Durham DH1 3LE. *E:* J.M.Hutson@durham.ac.uk.

HUTSON, John Whiteford, OBE 1966; HM Diplomatic Service, retired; Consul-General, Casablanca, 1984–87; *b* 21 Oct. 1927; *s* of John Hutson and Jean Greenlees Laird; *m* 1954, Doris Kemp (*d* 2014); one *s* two *d.* *Educ:* Hamilton Academy; Glasgow Univ. (MA (Hons)). MCIL (MIL 1987). HM Forces, 1949–51; Foreign Office, 1951; Third Secretary, Prague, 1953; FO, 1955; Second Sec., Berlin, 1956; Saigon, 1959; First Sec., 1961; Consul (Commercial) San Francisco, 1963–67; First Sec. and Head of Chancery, Sofia, 1967–69; FCO, 1969; Counsellor, 1970; Baghdad, 1971–72; Inspector, FCO, 1972–74; Head, Communications Operations Dept, FCO, 1974–76; Counsellor (Commercial), Moscow, 1976–79; Consul-Gen., Frankfurt, 1979–83. *Recreations:* British diplomatic oral history project, church yesterday and today, elementary bridge.

See also L. M. Hutson.

HUTSON, Prof. Lorna Margaret, DPhil; Berry Professor of English Literature, University of St Andrews, 2004–Sept. 2016 (Head of School, 2008–11); Merton Professor of English Literature, University of Oxford, from Sept. 2016; Fellow of Merton College, Oxford, from Sept. 2016; *b* Berlin, 27 Nov. 1958; *d* of John Whiteford Hutson, *qv*; civil partnership 2005, Catherine M. Sprent (*d* 2011); partner, 2013, Linda R. Hardy; one adopted *d.* *Educ:* St Hilary's Sch., Edinburgh; Tormead Sch., Guildford; Somerville Coll., Oxford (MA Hons 1st Cl.; DPhil 1983). Lectr, 1985–95, Reader in English Lit., 1995–98, QMC; Prof. of English Lit., Univ. of Hull, 1998–2000; Prof., Univ. of California at Berkeley, 2000–04. John Simon Guggenheim Meml Fellowship, 2004; Leverhulme Trust Major Res. Fellowship, 2014–. *Publications:* Thomas Nashe in Context, 1989; The Usurer's Daughter, 1994; (with V. Kahn) Rhetoric and Law in Early Modern Europe, 2000; The Invention of Suspicion, 2007; Circumstantial Shakespeare, 2015; articles in Representations, English Lit. Hist., Texas Studies in Lit. and Lang., Huntington Library Qly. *Recreations:* walking, swimming, cooking, art galleries. *Address:* (from Sept. 2016) Merton College, Oxford OX1 4JD. *E:* (until Sept. 2016) lmh10@st-andrews.ac.uk.

HUTSON, Robin Charles; Chairman and Chief Executive Officer: Lime Wood Group Ltd, since 2009; Home Grown Hotels Ltd, since 2011; *b* Beckenham, Kent, 9 Jan. 1957; *s* of Derek and Eileen Hutson; *m* 1983, Judith Alison Hill; two *s.* *Educ:* Godalming Grammar Sch.; Brooklands Tech. Coll. Mgt trainee, Savoy Hotel Gp, 1975–78; Trainee, Le Crillon, Paris, 1978–79; Front Office Manager, Berkeley Hotel, 1979–84; Ops Manager, Elbow Beach, Bermuda, 1984–86; Gen. Manager, then Man. Dir, Chewton Glen Hotel, 1986–94; Co-Founder, Chm. and CEO, Hotel du Vin Gp Ltd, 1994–2004; Chm., Soho Hse Gp, 2004–08. Outstanding Contribution Award, Hotel Cateys, 2014. *Recreations:* fly-fishing, motorcycling, food, wine, travel. *Address:* Lime Wood Group Ltd, Clayhill, Beechen Lane, Lyndhurst, Hants SO43 7DD. *E:* robin@robinhutson.com. *Clubs:* Soho House, Groucho; Mottisfont Fly Fishing.

HUTT, Ven. David Handley; Canon, 1995–2005, now Emeritus, and Archdeacon, 1999–2005, of Westminster; Steward, 1995–2005, and Sub-Dean, 1999–2005, Westminster Abbey; *b* 24 Aug. 1938; *s* of late Frank and of Evelyn Hutt. *Educ:* Brentwood; RMA Sandhurst; King's College London (Hanson Prize for Christian Ethics; Barry Prize for Theology; AKC). Regular Army, 1957–64. KCL, 1964–68. Deacon 1969, priest 1970; Curate: Bedford Park, W4, 1969–70; St Matthew, Westminster, 1970–73; Priest Vicar and Succentor, Southwark Cathedral, 1973–78; Sen. Chaplain, King's Coll., Taunton, 1978–82; Vicar: St Alban and St Patrick, Birmingham, 1982–86; All Saints, Margaret St, 1986–95. Mem. Court, Sion Coll., 2005–07 (Pres., 1996–97; Fellow, 2007–). Nat. Co-ordinator, Affirming Catholicism, 1990–98. Mem. Council, ALVA, 2000–05. Trustee, Utd Westminster Schs' Foundn, 2006–14; Gov., Sutton Valence Sch., 2007–13. Patron, London Parks and Gardens Trust, 2003–. MA Lambeth, 2005. *Publications:* miscellaneous theol articles and reviews. *Recreations:* reading, travel, the enjoyment of fine wine. *Address:* 14 Up The Quadrangle, Morden College, Blackheath, SE3 0PW.

HUTT, Sir Dexter (Walter), Kt 2004; education consultant, since 2011; Chief Executive (formerly Executive Head), Ninestiles Federation of Schools, Birmingham, 2004–11; Executive Leader, Hastings Schools Federation, 2008–11; *b* Georgetown, Guyana, 25 July 1948; *s* of Walter and Binks Hutt; *m* 1976, Rosemary Lyn Jones; two *s* one *d.* *Educ:* Birmingham Univ. (BScSoc). Hd, Middle Sch., Holte Sch., Birmingham, 1978–82; Dep. Hd and Actg Hd, Sidney Stringer Sch., Coventry, 1982–88; Headteacher, Ninestiles Sch., Birmingham, 1988–2004. Chief Exec., Ninestiles Plus, 2003–11. Member: DFE Reference Gp, 1998–2011; Bd, Young People's Learning Agency, 2010–12; Bd, CBSO, 2014–. Comr, Commn for Racial Equality, 2004–07. Trustee: Villiers Park, 2005–11; Ninestiles Acad.

Trust, 2013–. FRSA. *Recreations:* current affairs, reading novels and biographies, horse-racing, golf. *Address:* Orchard House, 7 Hole Farm Road, Birmingham B31 2BS. *T:* (0121) 477 4385. *E:* dexterhutt@gmail.com.

HUTT, Jane Elizabeth; Member (Lab) Vale of Glamorgan, National Assembly for Wales, since 1999; Minister for Finance and Government Business, since 2014; *b* 15 Dec. 1949; *d* of late Prof. Michael Stewart Rees Hutt and of Elizabeth Mai Hutt; *m* 1984, Michael John Hillary Trickey; two *d. Educ:* Highlands Sch., Eldoret, Kenya; Rosemead Sch., Littlehampton; Univ. of Kent (BA Hons 1970); London Sch. of Econs (CQSW 1972); Bristol Univ. (MSc Mgt Develt and Social Responsibility 1995). Community worker: IMPACT (Town Planners & Architects), Wales, 1972–74; Polypill (Community Projects Foundn), Wales, 1975–77; Co-ordinator, Welsh Women's Aid, 1978–88; Director: Tenant Participation Adv. Service, (Wales), 1988–92; Chwarae Teg (Wales), 1992–99. National Assembly for Wales: Sec., then Minister, for Health and Social Services, 1999–2005; Business Minister and Minister for Children, 2005–07; Minister for Children, Educn, Lifelong Learning and Skills, 2007–09; Minister for Business and Budget, 2009–11; Minister for Finance and Leader of the House, 2011–14. Hon. Fellow, UWIC, 1996. *Publications:* Opening the Town Hall: an introduction to local government, 1989; Making Opportunities: a guide for women and employers, 1992. *Recreations:* music, reading. *Address:* National Assembly for Wales, Cardiff Bay, Cardiff CF99 1NA. *T:* 0300 200 7110.

HUTTER, Prof. Otto Fred, PhD; Regius Professor of Physiology, University of Glasgow, 1971–90, now Emeritus; *b* 29 Feb. 1924; *s* of Isak and Elisabeth Hutter; *m* 1948, Yvonne T. Brown; two *s* two *d. Educ:* Chajes Real Gymnasium, Vienna; Bishop's Stortford Coll., Herts; University Coll., London (BSc, PhD). Univ. of London Postgrad. Student in Physiology, 1948; Sharpey Scholar, UCL, 1949–52; Rockefeller Travelling Fellow and Fellow in Residence, Johns Hopkins Hosp., Baltimore, 1953–55; Lectr, Dept of Physiology, UCL, 1953–61; Hon. Lectr, 1961–70. Visiting Prof., Tel-Aviv Univ., 1968, 1970; Scientific Staff, Nat. Inst. for Medical Research, Mill Hill, London, 1961–70. Hon. Mem., Physiological Soc., 1992. Hon. DSc Glasgow Caledonian, 1994. *Publications:* papers on neuromuscular and synaptic transmission, cardiac and skeletal muscle, in physiological jls. *Address:* 60 Browning Avenue, Bournemouth BH5 1NW.

HUTTON, family name of **Barons Hutton** and **Hutton of Furness**.

HUTTON, Baron *cr* 1997 (Life Peer), of Bresagh in the county of Down; **James Brian Edward Hutton,** Kt 1988; PC 1988; a Lord of Appeal in Ordinary, 1997–2004; *b* 29 June 1931; *s* of late James and Mabel Hutton, Belfast; *m* 1st, 1975, Mary Gillian Murland (*d* 2000); two *d*; 2nd, 2001, Lindy, *widow* of Christopher H. Nickols; two step *s* one step *d. Educ:* Shrewsbury Sch.; Balliol Coll., Oxford (1st Cl. final sch. of Jurisprudence; Hon. Fellow, 1988); Queen's Univ. of Belfast. Called to the Northern Ireland Bar, 1954; QC (NI) 1970; Bencher, Inn of Court of Northern Ireland, 1974; called to English Bar, 1972. Junior Counsel to Attorney-General for NI, 1969; Legal Adviser to Min. of Home Affairs, NI, 1973; Sen. Crown Counsel in NI, 1973–79; Judge of the High Court of Justice (NI), 1979–88; Lord Chief Justice of NI, 1988–97. Hon. Bencher: Inner Temple, 1988; King's Inns, Dublin, 1988. Mem., Jt Law Enforcement Commn, 1974; Dep. Chm., Boundary Commn for NI, 1985–88. Chm., Inquiry into death of Dr David Kelly, 2003–04. Visitor, Univ. of Ulster, 1999–2004. Hon. LLD: QUB, 1992; Ulster, 2004. *Address:* House of Lords, SW1A 0PW.

HUTTON OF FURNESS, Baron *cr* 2010 (Life Peer), of Aldingham in the County of Cumbria; **John Matthew Patrick Hutton;** PC 2001; Chairman: Independent Public Service Pensions Commission, since 2010; MyCSP Ltd, since 2012; *b* 6 May 1955; *m* (marr. diss.); three *s* one *d* (and one *s* decd); *m* 2004, Heather Rogers, OBE. *Educ:* Magdalen Coll., Oxford (BA, BCL). Research Associate, Templeton Coll., Oxford, 1980–81; Sen. Lectr, Newcastle Poly., 1981–92. Contested (Lab): Penrith and Borders, 1987; Cumbria and Lancs N, European Parlt, 1989. MP (Lab) Barrow and Furness, 1992–2010. Parly Under-Sec. of State, 1998–99, Minister of State, 1999–2005, DoH; Chancellor, Duchy of Lancaster, 2005; Secretary of State: for Work and Pensions, 2005–07; for Business, Enterprise and Regulatory Reform, 2007–08; for Defence, 2008–09. Chm., RUSI, 2010–15. *Publications:* Kitchener's Men, 2008; August 1914: surrender at St Quentin, 2010; (with Sir Leigh Lewis) How to be a Minister: a 21st-century guide, 2014; The Gunners of August 1914, 2014; articles on labour law in Industrial Law Jl. *Recreations:* football, cricket, cinema, music, First World War history. *Address:* House of Lords, SW1A 0PW.

HUTTON, Alasdair Henry, OBE 1990 (MBE 1986); TD 1977; writer and narrator of public events, UK and overseas; Member (C), Scottish Borders Council, 2002–12 (Convener, 2003–12); *b* 19 May 1940; *s* of Alexander Hutton and Margaret Elizabeth (*née* Henderson); *m* 1975, Deirdre Mary Cassels (*see* Dame D. M. Hutton); two *s. Educ:* Dollar Academy; Brisbane State High Sch., Australia. Radio Station 4BH, Brisbane, 1956; John Clemenger Advertising, Melbourne, 1957–59; Journalist: The Age, Melb., 1959–61; Press and Journal, Aberdeen, Scotland, 1962–64; Broadcaster, BBC: Scotland, N Ireland, London, Shetland, 1964–79. MEP (C) S Scotland, 1979–89; European Democratic Gp spokesman on regional policy, 1983–87, on budgetary control, 1987–89; contested (C) S Scotland, EP elecn, 1989 and 1994. Contested (C) Roxburgh and Berwickshire, Scottish Parly elecn, 1999. Sen. Consultant, Coutts Career Consultants, Scotland, 1994–97; Sen. Advr, Career Associates, 1998–2003. European Adviser: Royal Bank of Scotland, 1989–94; IOM Parlt, 1989–94; Scottish Police Coll., 1989–94. Board Mem., Scottish Agricl Coll., 1992–95. Chm., Crime Concern, Scotland, 1990–95. Member: Internat. Relns Cttee, Law Soc. of Scotland, 1991–99; Church and Nation Cttee, Church of Scotland, 1992–96; Social Security Adv. Cttee, 1996–99. Presenter, The Business Programme, BBC Radio Scotland, 1989–90; Narrator, Edinburgh Mil. Tattoo, later Royal Edinburgh Mil. Tattoo, 1992–. Mem., Queen's Body Guard for Scotland, Royal Co. of Archers. Hon. Col, Lothian and Borders Bn, ACF, 2006–09. Former Vice Pres., John Buchan Soc.; Chm. and Life Mem., Edinburgh Sir Walter Scott Club. Scottish Chm. and Trustee, Community Service Volunteers, 1985–2010. President: RBL Scotland, Kelso, 2000–, Border Area, 2014–; Kelso Farmers' Mkt, 2006–12. Patron: Overseas Projects, ROKPA UK, 1997–; Borders Ind. Advocacy Service, 2001–; Borders Talking Newspaper, 2008–. Chm., SE Scotland Br., Order of St John, 2012–. Elder, Kelso N, Church of Scotland. MStJ 2013. *Publications:* 15 Para 1947–1993, 1997; The Tattoo Fox, 2013; The Tattoo Fox Makes New Friends, 2014. *Address:* 4 Broomlands Court, Kelso, Roxburghshire TD5 7SR. *T:* (01573) 224369, 07753 625734. *E:* AlasdairHutton@yahoo.co.uk. *W:* www.alasdairhutton.co.uk. *Clubs:* New, Royal Scots (Edinburgh).

HUTTON, Anthony Charles, CB 1995; Executive Director, OECD, Paris, 2001–07; *b* 4 April 1941; *s* of Charles James Hutton and Athene Mary (*née* Hastie); *m* 1963, Sara Flemming; two *s* one *d. Educ:* Brentwood School; Trinity College, Oxford (MA). HM Inspector of Taxes, 1962; joined Board of Trade, 1964; Private Sec. to 2nd Perm. Sec., 1967–68; Principal Private Sec. to Sec. of State for Trade, 1974–77; Asst Sec., DoT, 1977, DTI, 1983; Under Sec., 1984–91; Dep. Sec., 1991–96; Principal Estabt and Finance Officer, 1991–97; Dir Gen., Resources and Services, 1996–97; Dir Gen., Trade Policy, DTI, 1997–2000; Dir, Public Mgt Service, OECD, 2000–01. *Recreations:* music, reading, 20th century history.

HUTTON, Brian Gerald, PhD; Secretary, 1976–88, Deputy Librarian, 1983–88, National Library of Scotland (Assistant Keeper, 1974–76); *b* Barrow-in-Furness, 1 Nov. 1933; *s* of James and Nora Hutton; *m* 1958, Serena Quartermaine May; one *s* one *d. Educ:* Barrow Grammar Sch.; Nottingham Univ. (BA Hons Hist. 1955); University Coll. London (Dip. Archive Admin and Churchill Jenkinson prizeman, 1959); Oxford Brookes Univ. (LLB 1st Cl. 1996); PhD Brunel 2002. National Service as Russian Linguist, RN, 1955–57. Asst Archivist, Herts County Record Office, 1959–60; Asst Keeper and Dep. Dir, Public Record Office, N Ireland, also Administrator, Ulster Hist. Foundn and Lectr in Archive Admin, Queen's Univ., Belfast, 1960–74; Stagiaire, Archives Nationales, Paris, 1970. County Sec., Bucks CPRE, 1990–93. Chm., Friends of Oxfordshire Museums, 1991–96; Member: Exec. Cttee, Bucks Record Soc., 1999–; Cttee, Bucks Br., Histl Assoc., 2010– (Chm., 2005–10). Lectr in local history studies and on legal topics. Commissioned, Kentucky Colonel, 1982. *Publications:* contribs to library, archive and legal hist. jls. *Recreations:* visiting art galleries, listening to music, enjoying the company of grandsons. *Address:* Robin Cottage, The Green, Kingston Blount, Oxon OX39 4SE. *T:* (01844) 354173.

HUTTON, Dame Deirdre (Mary), DBE 2004 (CBE 1998); Chairman, Civil Aviation Authority, since 2009; *b* 15 March 1949; *d* of Kenneth Alexander Home Cassels and Barbara Kathleen Cassels; *m* 1975, Alasdair Henry Hutton, *qv* (marr. diss. 2010); two *s. Educ:* Sherborne Sch. for Girls; Hartwell House Coll. Researcher, Glasgow Chamber of Commerce, 1975–80; freelance researcher, 1980–86; Scottish Consumer Council: Mem. Council, 1987–89; Vice Chm., 1990–91; Chm., 1991–99; Vice-Chm., 1997–2000, Chm., 2001–05, Nat. Consumer Council. Dep. Chm., Financial Services Authy, 2004–07 (non-exec. Dir, 1998–2007); Chm., Food Standards Agency, 2005–09. Vice Chm., Borders Local Health Council, 1991–94; Chairman: Enterprise Music Scotland Ltd, 1992–95 (also Founder); Rural Forum (Scotland) Ltd, 1992–99; Council, PIA Ombudsman, 1997–2000 (Dep. Chm., 1995–97); DTI Foresight Panel on Food Chains and Crops for Industry, 1999–2000; Steering Gp, Food Chain Centre, 2002–05; Vice-Chm., Scottish Envmt Protection Agency, 1999–2002; Dep. Chm., European Food Safety Authy, 2003–08; Member: Music Cttee, Scottish Arts Council, 1985–91; Scottish Consultative Council on the Curriculum, 1987–91; Parole Bd for Scotland, 1993–97; Minister's Energy Adv. Panel, DTI, 1997–99; Sec. of State for Scotland's Constitutional Steering Gp on Scottish Parliament, 1998; Sec. of State's Competitiveness Council, DTI, 1999–2000; Better Regulation Task Force, 1999–2005; Sustainable Develt Commn, 2000–01; Curry Commn on Future of Agriculture and Food, 2001; non-exec. Mem. Bd, HM Treasury, 2008–13. Board Member: Picker Inst. Europe, 2003–06; Castle Trust, 2011–. Non-executive Director: Edinburgh Festival Theatres Ltd, 1997–99; Borders Health Bd, 1997–2002; Thames Water Utilities Ltd, 2010–. Honorary Vice-President: Inst. of Food Sci. and Technol., 2007; Trading Standards Inst., 2007. FCGI 2010. Pro-Chancellor, Cranfield Univ., 2012–. DUniv Stirling, 2000; Hon. DSc: Loughborough, 2005; Cranfield, 2007. *Recreations:* reading, eating, talking, music. *Address:* Civil Aviation Authority, CAA House, 45–59 Kingsway, WC2B 6TE.

HUTTON, His Honour Gabriel Bruce; a Circuit Judge, 1978–2003; *b* 27 Aug. 1932; *y s* of late Robert Crompton Hutton, and Elfreda Bruce; *m* 1st, 1963, Frances Henrietta Cooke (*d* 1963); 2nd, 1965, Deborah Leigh Windus; one *s* two *d. Educ:* Marlborough; Trinity Coll., Cambridge (BA). Called to Bar, Inner Temple, 1956; Dep. Chm., Glos QS, 1971. A Recorder of the Crown Court, 1972–77. Liaison Judge for Glos, 1987–2003, and Resident Judge for Gloucester Crown Court, 1990–2003. Chairman: Glos and Wilts Area Criminal Justice Liaison Cttee, 1992–2000; Glos Criminal Justice Strategy Cttee, 2001–03. Chm., Glos Br., CPRE, 1993–2005. *Recreations:* hunting (Chm., Berkeley Hunt, 1973–2005), shooting, fishing. *Address:* Chestal House, Chestal, Dursley, Glos GL11 5AA. *T:* (01453) 543285.

HUTTON, Janet; nursing/management adviser, self-employed consultant, 1988–99; *b* 15 Feb. 1938; *d* of Ronald James and Marion Hutton. *Educ:* Gen. Infirmary at Leeds Sch. of Nursing. SRN 1959. Ward Sister, Leeds Gen. Infirmary, 1962–64, 1966–68; Nursing Sister, Australia, 1964–66; Commng Nurse, Lister Hosp., Stevenage, 1968–71; Planning and Develts Nurse, N London, 1971–73; Divl Nursing Officer, Colchester, 1973–79; Dist Nursing officer, E Dorset, 1979–83; Regl Nursing Officer, 1983–88, Quality Assurance Manager, 1986–88, Yorks RHA. Trustee, Sue Ryder Care (formerly Sue Ryder Foundn), 1998–2007 (Vice Chm., 2004–07). *Recreations:* music, needlework, walking, gardening, tennis (spectator). *Club:* Soroptimist International of Harrogate and District (Harrogate).

HUTTON, Prof. John Philip, MA; Emeritus Professor of Economics, since 2013, Professor of Economics and Econometrics, 1982–2004, and Head of Department of Economics and Related Studies, 2001–04, University of York; *b* 26 May 1940; *s* of Philip Ernest Michelson Hutton and Hester Mary Black Hutton; *m* 1964, Sandra Smith Reid (*d* 2009); one *s* one *d. Educ:* Daniel Stewart's Coll., Edinburgh; Edinburgh Univ. (MA 1st Cl.). York University: Junior Research Fellow, 1962; Lecturer, 1963; Sen. Lectr, 1973; Reader, 1976. Economic Adviser, HM Treasury, 1970, 1971; Advr to Malaysian Treasury, 1977, Mem., Technical Assistance Mission, Kenya, 1990, IMF; Consultant to: NEDO, 1963; Home Office, 1966; Royal Commission on Local Govt in England and Wales, 1967; NIESR, 1980. Chairman, HM Treasury Academic Panel, 1980, 1981; Mem. Council, Royal Economic Soc., 1981–86. Jt Managing Editor, Economic Journal, 1980–86; Jt Editor, Bulletin of Economic Research, 1986–91 (Chm., Bd of Trustees, 2000–); Associate Editor, Applied Economics, 1986–2004. *Publications:* contribs to learned jls, incl. Economic Jl, Rev. of Economic Studies, Oxford Economic Papers. *Recreations:* golf, modern fiction, cinema, music, especially cello playing. *Address:* 1 The Old Orchard, Fulford, York YO10 4LT. *T:* (01904) 638363.

HUTTON, Kenneth; Chairman, Peterborough Development Agency, 1987–92; *b* 11 May 1931; *s* of Wilks and Gertrude Hutton; *m* 1981, Georgia (*née* Hutchinson); one *s*, and two step *s* one step *d. Educ:* Bradford Belle Vue Grammar School; Liverpool University (Thomas Bartlett Scholar; BEng). FICE; FCIHT. Graduate Asst, Halifax CBC, 1952–54; Royal Engineers, 1954–56; Sen Engineer, Halifax CBC, 1956–59; Sen. Asst Engineer, Huddersfield CBC, 1959–63; Asst Chief Engineer, Skelmersdale Develt Corp., 1963–66; Dep. Chief Engineer, Telford Develt Corp., 1966–68; Chief Engineer, 1968–84, Gen. Manager, 1984–88, Peterborough Develt Corp. Gov., Peterborough Enterprise Programme, 1988–92. *Recreations:* crosswords, reconnecting with the past. *Address:* 2 Barkston Drive, Peterborough PE1 4LA.

HUTTON, Prof. Peter, PhD; FRCP, FRCA; CEng, FIMechE; Professor of Anaesthesia, 1986–2009, and Head, Department of Anaesthesia and Intensive Care, 1986–2001, University of Birmingham; Hon. Consultant Anaesthetist, University Hospital Birmingham NHS Trust, since 1986; President, Royal College of Anaesthetists, 2000–03; *b* 9 Nov. 1947; *s* of Peter Hutton and Lily Hutton (*née* Draper); *m* 1973, Barbara Meriel Johnson; two *s* two *d. Educ:* Morecambe GS; Birmingham Univ. (BSc 1st Cl. Hons Mech. Engrg 1969, PhD 1973; MB ChB 1978). FRCA 1982; FRCP 2001; CEng, FIMechE 2003; FRCS 2004. SERC Res. Fellow, Birmingham Univ., 1969–72; jun. doctor trng posts in anaesthesia and medicine, Birmingham and Bristol, 1978–82; Clinical Lectr in Anaesthesia, Univ. of Bristol and Hon. Sen. Registrar, Avon AHA, 1982–86. Mem., Jt Cttee for Higher Trng in Anaesthesia, 1988–92; Chm., Nat. Clinical Adv. Bd, 2003–04. Pres., Anaesthetic and Recovery Nurses Assoc., 1989–90; Council Member: Assoc. Anaesthetists of GB and Ireland, 1989–92; RCAnaes, 1993– (Sen. Vice Pres., 1999–2000); Chm., Acad. of Med. Royal Colls, 2002–04 (Vice-Chm., 2001–02). Founder FMedSci 1998; FRCPGlas (*ad eundem*) 2003; Hon. FRCEM (Hon. FFAEM 2003); Hon. FCA(SA) 2003; Hon. Fellow, Coll. of Anaesthetists, RCSI, 2003. *Publications:* (with G. M. Cooper) Guidelines in Clinical Anaesthesia, 1985; (ed. with C. Prys-Roberts) Monitoring in Anaesthesia and Intensive Care, 1994; (ed) jtly) Fundamental Principles and Practice of Anaesthesia, 2001; contrib. numerous scientific and rev. papers. *Recreations:* family, woodwork, fell-walking. *Address:* University Department of Anaesthesia, North 5, Queen Elizabeth Hospital, University Hospital Birmingham NHS Trust, Edgbaston, Birmingham B15 2TH. *T:* (0121) 627 2060, *Fax:* (0121) 627 2062. *Club:* Athenæum.

HUTTON, Dr Roger Martin Stanley; Director, PricewaterhouseCoopers (on secondment), since 2015; *b* Broxbourne, Herts, 24 Oct. 1960; *s* of Stanley and Pamela Hutton; *m* 1990, Karen Applegate; two *d. Educ:* Kingsbridge Sch., Devon; Sussex Univ. (BSc Hons Physics with Eur. Studies 1983; MSc Sci., Technol. and Industrialisation 1984); Lancaster Univ. (MA Sci. and Technol. in Internat. Affairs 1985); European University Inst., Florence (PhD Political and Social Sci. 1989). Joined MoD as admin fast streamer, 1988; Asst Dir, Defence Policy, 1992–93; househusband, 1993–96; Asst Dir, Resources and Progs (Navy), 1996–99; Hd, Arts Funding and Orgn Br., DCMS (on secondment), 1999–2000; Dep. Dir, NATO and Eur. Policy Gp, MoD, 2000–03; on secondment: Dir, Corporate Affairs, Bromley PCT, 2003; Project Manager, Efficiency Study into Criminal Injuries Compensation Authy and Appeals Panel, Home Office, 2003; Dir, Jt Commitments Policy, MoD, 2003–06; Head: of Defence Resources and Plans, 2006–09; of Strategy Develt, 2009–11; Hd, Defence Transformation Unit, then Dir, Defence Transformation, 2011–13; Dir Defence Strategy, then Dir Corporate Strategy, 2013–15. *Recreations:* family, ski-ing, classical music, guitar, Charlton Athletic FC. *Address:* PricewaterhouseCoopers LLP, 7 More London Riverside, SE1 2RT.

HUTTON, Prof. Ronald Edmund, DPhil; FBA 2013; FRHistS, FSA, FLSW; Professor of History, University of Bristol, since 1996; *b* 19 Dec. 1953; *s* of Geoffrey Edmund Hutton and late Elsa Edwina (*née* Hansen); *m* 1988, Lisa Radulovic (marr. diss. 2003); one *d. Educ:* Pembroke Coll., Cambridge (BA 1976; MA 1980); St John's Coll., Oxford (DPhil 1980). FRHistS 1981; FSA 1993; FLSW 2011. Prize Fellow, Magdalen Coll., Oxford, 1979–81; University of Bristol: Lectr, 1981–89; Reader, 1989–96. Comr, English Heritage, 2009–14. *Publications:* The Royalist War Effort 1642–1646, 1981, 2nd edn 1999; The Restoration, 1985; Charles II, 1989; The British Republic, 1990, 2nd edn 2000; The Pagan Religions of the Ancient British Isles, 1991; The Rise and Fall of Merry England, 1994; The Stations of the Sun, 1996; The Triumph of the Moon, 1999; Shamans, 2001; Witches, Druids and King Arthur, 2003; Debates in Stuart History, 2004; The Druids, 2007; Blood and Mistletoe, 2009; A Short History of Britain 1485–1660, 2011; Pagan Britain, 2013. *Recreation:* conviviality. *Address:* Department of Historical Studies, University of Bristol, 13 Woodland Road, Bristol BS8 1TB. *T:* (0117) 928 7595, *Fax:* (0117) 928 8276. *E:* r.hutton@bristol.ac.uk.

HUTTON, Tracy Jane; *see* Ayling, T. J.

HUTTON, William Nicholas; Principal, Hertford College, Oxford, since 2011; *b* 21 May 1950; *s* of late William Thomas Hutton and Dorothy Anne (*née* Haynes); *m* 1978, Jane Anne Elizabeth Atkinson; one *s* two *d. Educ:* Chislehurst and Sidcup GS; Bristol Univ. (BSocSc); INSEAD (MBA). With Phillips & Drew, Stockbrokers, 1971–77; Sen. Producer, Current Affairs, BBC Radio 4, 1978–81; Dir and Producer, Money Programme, BBC 2, 1981–83; econs corresp., Newsnight, BBC 2, 1983–88; Ed., European Business Channel, 1988–90; The Guardian: Econs Ed., 1990–95; Asst Ed., 1995–96; The Observer: Ed., 1996–98; Ed.-in-Chief, 1998–99; Contributing Ed. and columnist, 2000–; Chief Exec., 2000–08, Vice-Chm., 2008–11, Industrial Soc., later The Work Foundn; Chm., Big Innovation Centre, 2011–. Rapporteur, Kok Gp, 2004; Chairman: Review into Fair Pay in Public Sector, 2011; Ind. Univ. Tuition Fees Commn, 2012–. Vis. Fellow, Nuffield Coll., Oxford, 1995; Visiting Professor: Manchester Business Sch., 1996–99; Bristol Univ., 1996–; Univ. of the Arts, 2006. Fellow, Sunningdale Inst., 2006. Chm., Employment Policy Inst., 1995–2002. Hon. Fellow, Mansfield Coll., Oxford. Hon. DLitt: Kingston, 1995; De Montfort, 1996; Strathclyde, London Guildhall, UCE, 1997; Bristol, Glasgow, 2003; Greenwich, 2013; York St John, 2014; DUniv Open, 2001. Political Journalist of Year, What The Papers Say, 1993. *Publications:* The Revolution That Never Was: an assessment of Keynesian economics, 1986; The State We're In, 1995; The State To Come, 1997; The Stakeholding Society, 1998; (with Anthony Giddens) On the Edge: living with global capitalism, 2000; The World We're In, 2002; The Writing on the Wall, 2007; Staying Ahead: the economic performance of the UK's creative industries, 2007; Them and Us: changing Britain - why we need a fair society, 2010; How Good We Can Be: ending the mercenary society and building a great country, 2015. *Recreations:* family, reading, eating, tennis, cinema, writing. *Address:* Hertford College, Cattle Street, Oxford OX1 3BW. *T:* (01865) 279407.

HUXLEY, Air Vice-Marshal Brian, CB 1986; CBE 1981; Deputy Controller, National Air Traffic Services, 1985–86; retired 1987; *b* 14 Sept. 1931; *s* of Ernest and Winifred Huxley; *m* 1955, Frances (*née* Franklin) (*d* 2007); two *s. Educ:* St Paul's Sch.; RAF College, Cranwell. Commissioned 1952; No 28 Sqdn, Hong Kong, 1953–55; qual. Flying Instructor, 1956; Cranwell, Central Flying Sch. and No 213 Sqdn, 1956–65; MoD, 1966–68; Chief Flying Instr, Cranwell, 1969–71; Commanding RAF Valley, 1971–73; RAF Staff Coll., 1973–74; RCDS 1975; Defence Intelligence Staff, 1976–77; AOC Mil. Air Traffic Ops, 1978–80; Dir of Control (Airspace Policy), and Chm., Nat. Air Traffic Management Adv. Cttee, 1981–84. Mem., CAA Ops Adv. Cttee, 1987–99. Chm., Review of Helicopter Offshore Safety and Survival, 1993–94. *Publications:* contribs to Children's Encyclopaedia Britannica, 1970–72, and to Railway Modeller, 1974–83. *Recreations:* flying, model-making. *Club:* Royal Air Force.

HUXLEY, Prof. George Leonard, FSA; MRIA; Hon. Professor, Trinity College Dublin, since 1989 (Research Associate, 1983–89); Professor Emeritus, Queen's University, Belfast, since 1988; Adjunct Professor in Mathematics and Ancient Classics, National University of Ireland, Maynooth, since 2007; *b* Leicester, 23 Sept. 1932; *s* of late Sir Leonard Huxley, KBE and Ella M. C., *d* of F. G. and E. Copeland; *m* 1957, Davina Best; three *d. Educ:* Blundell's Sch.; Magdalen Coll., Oxford (Demy; 2nd Mods, 1st Greats, Derby Scholar 1955). Commnd in RE, 1951, Actg Op. Supt, Longmoor Mil. Rly. Fellow of All Souls Coll., Oxford, 1955–61; Asst Dir, British School at Athens, 1956–58; Prof. of Greek, QUB, 1962–83; Dir, Gennadius Library, Amer. Sch. of Classical Studies, Athens, 1986–89. Harvard University: Vis. Lectr, 1958 and 1961; Loeb Lectr, 1986; Leverhulme Fellow, European Sci. Foundn, 1980–81; Vis. Lectr, St Patrick's Coll., Maynooth, 1984–85 and 1993; Faber Lectr, Princeton Univ., 1987; Vis. Prof., UCSD, 1990. Examiner for Newcastle Award, Eton, 1960. Mem. of Exec., NI Civil Rights Assoc., 1971–72. Member: Irish Nat. Cttee, Greek and Latin Studies, 1972–86, 1991–99 (Chm., 1976–79); Irish Adv. Cttee, Liverpool Univ. Inst. of Irish Studies, 1996–2004; Exec., Nat. Library of Ireland Soc., 1997–2000; Member, Managing Committee: British Sch. at Athens, 1967–79; Amer. Sch. of Classical Studies, Athens, 1991–; Irish Mem., Standing Cttee on Humanities, European Science Foundn, Strasbourg, 1978–86. Royal Irish Academy: Sec., Polite Literature and Antiquities Cttee, 1979–86; Sen. Vice-Pres., 1984–85 and 1999–2000; Vice-Pres., 1997–98; Hon. Librarian, 1990–94; Special Envoy, 1994–97; Hon. Pres., Classical Assoc. of Ireland, 1999; Mem., Bureau, Fédn Internat. d'Etudes Classiques, 1981–89 (Senior Vice-Pres. 1984–89); Mem., Internat. Commn, Thesaurus Linguae Latinae, Munich, 1999–2001; MAE 1990. Patron, Irish Inst. of Hellenic Studies, Athens, 1998–. Hon. Freeman of Kythera, 2012. Hon. LittD TCD, 1984; Hon. DLit: QUB, 1996; NUI Maynooth, 2013. Cromer Greek Prize, British Acad., 1963. *Publications:* Achaeans and Hittites, 1960; Early Sparta, 1962; The Early Ionians, 1966; Greek Epic Poetry from Eumelos to Panyassis, 1969; (ed with J. N. Coldstream) Kythera, 1972; Pindar's Vision of the Past, 1975; On Aristotle and Greek Society, 1979; Homer and the Travellers, 1988; articles on Hellenic, Byzantine, mathematical and railway subjects. *Recreation:* siderodromophilia. *Address:* Department of Classics, Trinity College, Dublin 2, Ireland; Forge Cottage, Church Enstone, Oxfordshire OX7 4NN. *Club:* Athenæum.

HUXLEY, Paul, RA 1991 (ARA 1987); artist; Professor of Painting, Royal College of Art, 1986–98, now Emeritus; Treasurer, Royal Academy, 2000–14; *b* 12 May 1938; *m* 1st, 1957, Margaret Doria Perryman (marr. diss. 1972); two *s*; 2nd, 1990, Susan Jennifer Metcalfe. *Educ:* Harrow Coll. of Art; Royal Acad. Schs (Cert.). Harkness Fellow, 1965–67; Vis. Prof., Cooper Union, New York, 1974; Vis. Tutor, RCA, 1974–85. Member: Serpentine Gallery Cttee, 1971–74; Art Panel and Exhibns Sub-Cttee, Arts Council of GB, 1972–76; Trustee, Tate Gall., 1975–82. Mem. Council, British Sch. at Rome, 2000–05. Commnd by London Transport to design 22 ceramic murals for King's Cross Underground Stn, 1984; commnd by Rambert Dance Co. to design sets and costumes for Cat's Eye, 1992. *One-man exhibitions:* Rowan Gall., London, 1963, 1965, 1968, 1969, 1971, 1974, 1978, 1980; Juda Rowan Gall., London, 1982; Kornblee Gall., New York, 1967, 1970; Galeria da Emenda, Lisbon, 1974; Forum Kunst, Rottweil, W Germany, 1975; Mayor Rowan Gall., 1989; Galerie zur alten deutschen Schule, Switzerland, 1992; Gillian Jason Gall., 1993; Gardner Art Centre, Sussex Univ., 1994; Jason & Rhodes Gall., London, 1998; Rhodes & Mann Gall., London, 2001; Watergate Gall., Seoul and Chang Art Gall., Beijing, 2009; Gall. Reis, Singapore, 2011; *group exhibitions:* Whitechapel Art Gall., London, and Albright-Knox Gall., Buffalo, NY, 1964; Paris Biennale, and Marlborough-Gerson Gall., New York, 1965; Galerie Milano, Milan, 1966; Carnegie Inst., Pittsburgh, 1967; UCLA, Calif (also USA tour), and touring show of Mus. of Modern Art, New York, 1968; Mus. am Ostwall, Dortmund (also Eur. tour), and Tate Gall., 1969; Walker Art Gall., Liverpool, 1973; Hayward Gall., 1974; São Paulo Bienal, and Forum Gall., Leverkusen, 1975; Palazzo Reale, Milan, 1976; Royal Acad., 1977; Nat. Theatre, 1979; Arts Council tour, Sheffield, Newcastle upon Tyne and Bristol, 1980; Museo Municipal, Madrid, and Eastern Arts 4th Nat. Exhibn and British tour, 1983; Juda Rowan Gall., 1985; Künstlerhaus, Vienna, 1986; Mappin Art Gall., Sheffield, 1988; British Council tour, Eastern Europe, 1990–93; South Bank Centre, and Arts Council tour, 1992–93; Barbican Gall., London, 1993; British Council tour, Africa, 1994–96; Gallery 7, HK, 1996; Gulbenkian Foundn Center for Modern Art, Lisbon, 1997; Pallant House Gall., Chichester, 1998; Kettle's Yard, Cambridge, 1999; Rhodes+Mann, London, 2000; Kunstmus., Wolfsburg, 2002; Mus. of Contemp. Art, Andros, Greece and China Nat. Mus. of Fine Arts, Beijing, 2005; Falmouth and Hayward Gall., London, 2006; Centre Culturel Calouste Gulbenkian, Paris, 2010; *works in public collections:* Tate Gall., V&A Mus., Arts Council of GB, British Council, Royal Acad., RCA, Contemp. Arts Soc., Camden Council, Govt Art Collection, Nuffield Foundn, London; Whitworth Art Gall., Manchester; Graves Art Gall., Sheffield; Walker Art Gall., Liverpool; City Art Gall., Leeds; Creasey Collection of Modern Art, Salisbury; Leics Educn Authority; Fitzwilliam Mus., Cambridge; Ulster Mus., Belfast; Art Gall. of NSW, and Mus. of Contemp. Art, Sydney; Art Gall. of SA, Adelaide; Albright-Knox Gall., Buffalo, Neuberger Mus., Purchase, and MOMA, NY; Centro Cultural Arte Contemporáneo, Mexico City; Art Gall. of Ontario, Toronto; Moroccan Govt Collection, Asilah; Szépmüvészeti Mus., Budapest; Technisches Mus., Vienna; Seoul Mus. of Art, and Bukchon Mus., Seoul. *Publications:* (ed) Exhibition Road: painters at the Royal College of Art, 1988. *Address:* 2 Dalling Road, W6 0JB.

HUXLEY, Dr Peter Arthur, PhD; CBiol; FRSB; agroforestry education consultant, 1992–2002; *b* 26 Sept. 1926; *s* of Ernest Henry Huxley and Florence Agnes (*née* King); *m* 1st, 1954, Betty Grace Anne Foot (marr. diss. 1980); three *s* one *d*; 2nd, 1980, Jennifer Margaret Bell (*née* Pollard); one *s* one *d. Educ:* Alleyn's Sch.; Edinburgh Univ.; Reading Univ. (BSc, PhD). FRSB (FIBiol 1970). RNVR, 1944–46. Asst Lectr to Sen. Lectr, Makerere University Coll., Uganda, 1954–64; Dir of Res., Coffee Res. Foundn, Kenya, 1965–69; Prof. of Horticulture, Univ. of Reading, 1969–74; Prof. of Crop Science, Univ. of Dar es Salaam/FAO, 1974–76; Agric. Res. Adviser/FAO, Agric. Res. Centre, Tripoli, 1977–78; International Council for Research in Agroforestry, Nairobi, 1979–92: Dir, Res. Develt Div., 1987–90; Principal Res. Advr, 1991–92. *Publications:* (ed jtly) Soils Research in Agroforestry, 1980; (ed jtly) Plant Research and Agroforestry, 1983; (ed) Manual of Research Methodology for the Exploration and Assessment of Multipurpose Trees, 1983; (ed jtly) Multipurpose trees: selection and testing for agroforestry, 1989; (ed jtly) Tree-crop Interactions: a physiological approach, 1996; (ed jtly) Agroforestry for Sustainable Development in Sri Lanka, 1996; (ed jtly) Glossary for Agroforestry, 1997; (compiled and ed jtly) Tropical Agroforestry, 1999; approx. 135 pubns in agric., horticult., agroforestry, meteorol and agricl botany jls. *Recreations:* music, philosophy. *Address:* Flat 4, 9 Linton Road, Oxford OX2 6UH.

HUXTABLE, Gen. Sir Charles Richard, KCB 1984 (CB 1982); CBE 1976 (OBE 1972; MBE 1961); DL; Commander-in-Chief, United Kingdom Land Forces, 1988–90; Aide-de-Camp General to the Queen, 1988–90; *b* 22 July 1931; *m* 1959, (Margaret) Mary (OBE 2002), *d* of late Brig. J. H. C. Lawlor; three *d. Educ:* Wellington Coll.; RMA Sandhurst; Staff College, Camberley; psc, jssc. Commissioned, Duke of Wellington's Regt, 1952; Captain, 1958, Major, 1965; GSO2 (Ops), BAOR, 1964–65; GSO1 Staff College, 1968–70; CO 1 DWR, 1970–72; Col, 1973; MoD, 1974; Brig., Comd Dhofar Bde, 1976–78; Maj.-Gen., 1980; Comdr, Land Forces, NI, 1980–82; Dir, Army Staff Duties, 1982–83; Comdr, Training and Arms Dirs (formerly Training Estabts), 1983–86; QMG, 1986–88. Colonel: DWR, 1982–90; Col, Royal Irish Regt, 1992–96; Colonel Commandant: The King's Div., 1983–88; UDR, 1991–92. Pres., Ex-Services Mental Welfare Soc., 1990–2001. DL N Yorks, 1994. *Address:* Long Bank House, Leyburn, North Yorks DL8 5HD.

HYAMS, Edward Barnard; Owner, Lexdenergy Ltd, since 2012; *b* London, 1951; *s* of Leonard Hyams and Jean Hyams; *m* 1974, Janet; two *s* one *d. Educ:* Ipswich Sch., Ipswich; Imperial Coll., London (BSc Eng Electrical Engrg); CDipAF 1979. CEng 1981. Dir, Engrg, Southern Electric plc, 1992–96; Man. Dir, Eastern Gp plc, 1996–2000; CEO, BizzEnergy Ltd, 2000–02; Chm., Ergo Services, Beaufort, 2003–08; Investment Partner, Englefield Capital LLP, 2005–12; Founding Partner, Rockfield Energy Partners, 2012–14. Chm., Energy Saving Trust, 2005–12; Dir, Carbon Trust, 2005–11. Member: Adv. Bd, Estover Ltd, 2012–; Bd, CPREL Ltd, 2012–. Trustee, Ipswich Sch. Foundn, 2011–14; Gov., Ipswich Sch., 2014. *Recreations:* gardening, ski-ing, classical music, occasional attempts at golf.

HYDE, Lord; Edward George James Villiers; *b* 17 April 2008; *s* and *heir* of Earl of Clarendon, *qv*.

HYDE, Charles Gordon; QC 2006; a Recorder, since 2004; a Deputy High Court Judge, since 2011; *b* 27 Feb. 1963; *s* of Gordon and Ann Hyde; *m* 2001, Liz Cunningham; two *s* one *d. Educ:* Rugby Sch.; Manchester Univ. (LLB Hons). Called to the Bar, Middle Temple, 1988. Mem., Family Procedure Rule Cttee, 2004–. *Recreations:* fly fishing, walking, watching sport, natural history. *Address:* Queen Elizabeth Building, Temple, EC4Y 9BS.

HYDE, Daniel Stephen, FRCO; Informator Choristarum, Tutorial Fellow and Organist, Magdalen College, Oxford, since 2009; *b* Matlock, 24 April 1980; *s* of Nigel and Susan Hyde; *m* 2005, Salima Virji. *Educ:* Durham Cathedral Choir Sch.; Oakham Sch.; King's Coll., Cambridge (MA). Dir, Chapel Music, Jesus Coll., Cambridge, 2004–09. *Recreations:* opera, reading, food and wine. *Address:* Magdalen College, Oxford OX1 4AU. *T:* (01865) 276000. *E:* daniel.hyde@magd.ox.ac.uk.

HYDE, Dame Helen (Yvonne), DBE 2013; MA; Headmistress, Watford Grammar School for Girls, since 1987; *b* 11 May 1947; *d* of Henry and Tilly Seligman; *m* 1968, Dr John Hyde; two *d. Educ:* Parktown Girls' High Sch., Johannesburg; Witwatersrand Univ. (BA 1967; BA Hons 1969); King's Coll., London (MA 1974). Teacher of French, 1970, Head of Modern Languages, 1978, Acland Burghley; Dep. Headmistress, Highgate Wood, 1983. Student of Yad Vashem in Holocaust Studies, 2007–10; Fellow of Imperial War Mus. in Holocaust Studies, 2008; Mem., Holocaust Commn, 2014. Pres., Freedom and Autonomy - Nat. Schs Assoc. (formerly Assoc. of Heads of Grant Maintained Schs, later Assoc. of Heads of Foundn and Aided Schs, subseq. Foundn and Aided Schs Nat. Assoc., then Freedom and Autonomy for Schs - Nat. Assoc.), 2006– (Treas., 1995–2006). Accredited Trainer: Edward de Bono

Thinking Skills, 2003; Mind Mapping (Buzan), 2004. *Recreations:* tapestry, exercise, cycling, theology. *Address:* Watford Grammar School for Girls, Lady's Close, Watford, Herts WD18 0AE.

HYDE, Margaret Sheila, OBE 2006; Director, Esmée Fairbairn Foundation (formerly Esmée Fairbairn Charitable Trust), 1994–2005; *b* 11 Sept. 1945; *er d* of late Gerry Tomlins and Sheila (*née* Thorpe); *m* 1966, Derek Hyde (marr. diss. 1976). *Educ:* Watford Grammar Sch. for Girls; London Sch. of Econs and Political Science (DSA 1969; BSc Hons Social Admin 1971; Mostyn Lloyd Meml Prize, 1969; Janet Beveridge Award, 1971). Blackfriars Settlement, 1965–67; Home Office, 1972–77: served in Probation, Prison and Gen. Depts, 1972–76; Private Sec. to Perm. Under Sec. of State, 1976–77; Head of Information, NCVO, 1977–85; Chief Exec., Action Resource Centre, 1985–91 (Trustee, 1992–94); Dep. Sec. Gen., Arts Council of GB, 1991–92; Prog. Consultant, Internat. Save the Children Alliance and Save the Children UK, 1992–94. Mem., Exec. Cttee, 300 Gp, 1984–87 (Treas., 1985–87). Member: Exec. Cttee, Assoc. of Charitable Foundns, 1995–99 (Vice Chm., 1997–99); Venturesome Investment Cttee, 2005–10; Futurebuilders Adv. Panel, 2005–07; England Cttee, Big Lottery Fund, 2007–11; Charity Tribunal, 2008–; Trustee: Peter Bedford Trust, 1983–92 (Chm., 1985–87); Charities Effectiveness Review Trust, 1986–91; New Econs Foundn, 2005–14; Hammersmith United Charities, 2012–14; Allen Lane Foundn, 2013–. Mem. Ct of Govs, LSE, 1987–2014, now Emeritus Gov. FRSA 1991 (Mem. Council, 1994–99). *Recreation:* hill walking.

HYDE, Matthew Thomas; Chief Executive, Scout Association, since 2013; *b* Peterborough, 22 Feb. 1975; *s* of Richard and Diana Hyde; *m* 2005, Laura Bates; one *s*. *Educ:* Queen Mary and Westfield Coll., Univ. of London (BA 1st Cl. Hons English); Univ. of Westminster (MBA Dist.). President: Students' Union, QMW, 1996–98; Univ. of London Union, 1998–99; Dep. Gen. Manager, Students' Union, KCL, 1999–2001; Gen. Manager, Students' Union, Goldsmiths' Coll., 2001–06; Chief Exec., NUS, 2006–13. Trustee: NCVO, 2011–; Step up to Serve, 2014–. Hon. Fellow, QMUL, 2012. *Recreations:* family, football (supporting Peterborough United), cricket, art, food, travel. *Address:* Scout Association, Gilwell Park, Chingford, E4 7QW. *T:* (020) 8433 7105. *E:* matt.hyde@scouts.org.uk.

HYDE-CHAMBERS, Fredrick Rignold, OBE 2003; Executive Chairman, Enterprise and Parliamentary Dialogue International (formerly International Association of Business and Parliament), since 2012 (Secretary-General, 1997–2012); *b* 12 May 1944; *s* of late Derek Christie Hyde-Chambers and Margaret M. Rignold; *m* 1976, Audrey Christine Martin (*née* Smith) (separated 2008); two *s*; partner, 2009, Fuad Janmohamed. *Educ:* Buckingham Coll., Harrow; Arts Educnl Sch. Child actor, TV and stage, 1958–64; The Tibet Relief Fund, UK, 1965–68; Gen. Sec., Buddhist Soc., 1968–72; Private Sec. to MPs, 1974–80; Industry and Parliament Trust, 1980–, Dir, 1987–2003. Co-Founder and Hon. Advr, All-Party Parly Tibet Gp. Member: Adv. Bd, State Legis. Leaders' Foundn, USA; Council, Buddhist Soc.; Bd, Crystal Fund, Georgia, 2014; Chairman: Tibet Soc. of UK, 2004–; Tibet Relief Fund, 2007–; Buddhist Chaplaincy Support Gp, 2009–; Hon. Advr, Nepalese Buddhist Community Centre, 2012–. Co-Founder, Tanzanian Fine Art Project, 2014. Script writer and consultant, BBC TV and Channel 4 documentaries. First Novel Award, Authors' Club, 1988; Airey Neave Trust Human Rights Scholarship, 1989. *Publications:* The Mouse King, 1976; (with Audrey Hyde-Chambers) Tibetan Folktales, 1979, repr. 2002 (Japan, 1997); Tibet and China, 1988; Lama, 1988 (also USA, Germany, Sweden, Argentina and France). *Recreation:* carriage driving. *Address:* Enterprise and Parliamentary Dialogue International, 14 Great College Street, SW1P 3RX. *T:* (020) 7878 1036, 07812 691071. *E:* frhc@epdi.eu; 12 Gloucester Court, Swan Street, SE1 1DQ.

HYDE-PARKER, Sir Richard William; *see* Parker.

HYDON, Kenneth John; non-executive Director: Reckitt Benckiser plc, since 2003; Pearson plc, since 2006; Merlin Entertainments plc, since 2013; *b* Leicester, 1944; *s* of John Thomas and Vera Hydon; *m* 1966, Sylvia Sheila Johnson; one *s* one *d*. FCMA 1970; FCCA 1983; FCT 1997. Financial Director: Racal Electronics subsids, 1979–85; Vodafone Gp plc, 1985–2005. Non-executive Director: Cellco Partnership (dba Verizon Wireless USA), 2000–05; Tesco plc, 2004–13; Mem., Supervisory Bd, Vodafone Deutschland (formerly Mannesman), 2000–03. Non-exec. Dir, Royal Berks NHS Foundn Trust, 2005–12. Patron, Dixie GS, 2000–. FRSA. *Recreations:* dinghy sailing, golf, track days, gym, cycling, watching Rugby and horse-racing. *Address:* Oxon. *Clubs:* Royal Automobile; Leander (Henley-on-Thames).

HYETT, Paul David Etheridge, PPRIBA; Principal, HKS Inc. (Architects), since 2008; *b* 18 March 1952; *s* of Derek James and Josephine Mable Hyett (*née* Sparks); *m* 1976, Susan Margaret Beavan; three *s*. *Educ:* Architectural Assoc. (AA Dip.); Bartlett Sch. of Planning (MPhil Planning). Career Assistant: Cedric Price Architects, 1974–78; Alan Baxter Associates, 1978–80; Partner: Arno Jobst & Paul Hyett Architects, 1981–82; Nicholas Lacey, Jobst and Hyett Architects, 1982–87; Paul Hyett Architects, 1987–97; Hyett Salisbury Whiteley, 1997–2001; Chm., Ryder, later Ryder HKS, then Principal, HKS Architects Ltd, 2001–. Dir, Building Centre, 2004–08. Tutor: Dusseldorf Fachhochschule (Architecture), 1987–90; Bartlett Sch. of Planning, 1996–98. Chm., Carbon Trust Res. Prog., 2004–08. Royal Institute of British Architects: Vice Pres., Educn, 1998–2001; Pres., 2001–03; Vice Pres., Internat. Affairs, 2003–05. Mem., Architectl Assoc., 1972–. Columnist: Architects Jl; RIBA Jl. Trustee: British Architectural Liby Trust, 2004–06; Civic Trust, 2004–07. Hon. FAIA 2005; Hon. Fellow, Royal Soc. of Architects of Wales, 2006. Hon. DArt Lincoln, 2004. *Publications:* In Practice, 2000; (with B. Edwards) Rough Guide to Sustainability, 2001; (contrib.) Sustaining Architecture in the Anti-Machine Age, 2001; (with John Jenner) Tomorrow's Hospitals, 2004; Changing Hospital Architecture, 2008; contribs to Building Design, Architects' Jl, RIBA Jl, Moscow DOM. *Recreations:* trekking, political biographies, history, writing. *Address:* HKS Inc. (Architects), 82 Dean Street, W1D 3SP. *T:* (020) 7292 9494, *Fax:* (020) 7292 9495. *E:* phyett@hksinc.com.

HYLAND, Susan Margaret; HM Diplomatic Service; Political Counsellor, Islamabad, since 2011; *b* 30 Oct. 1964; *d* of Alan and Joan Frances Hyland (*née* Beddow). *Educ:* Somerville Coll., Oxford (MA; BPhil; Nuffield Exhibn Grad. Scholarship); Yale Univ. (Henry Fellowship); Ecole Nationale d'Admin, France (diplôme). Joined HM Diplomatic Service, 1990; Second Sec., Oslo, then UK Mission to the UN, NY, 1992; Second Sec., UK Delegn to the OECD, 1993; Ecole Nationale d'Admin, 1994–95; First Secretary: FCO, 1996; Moscow, 2000; Private Sec. to Perm. Under-Sec., FCO, 2001; seconded to Westminster Foundn for Democracy, 2004; First Sec., Paris, 2005; Head, Human Rights, Democracy and Governance Gp, subseq. Human Rights and Democracy Dept, FCO, 2006–11. *Recreations:* theatre, travel, reading. *Address:* Foreign and Commonwealth Office, King Charles Street, SW1A 2AH.

HYLTON, 5th Baron *cr* 1866; **Raymond Hervey Jolliffe,** MA; *b* 13 June 1932; *er s* of 4th Baron Hylton and Perdita Rose Mary (*d* 1996), *d* of late Raymond Asquith and *sister* of 2nd Earl of Oxford and Asquith, KCMG; *S* father, 1967; *m* 1966, Joanna Ida Elizabeth, *d* of late Andrew de Bertodano; four *s* one *d*. *Educ:* Eton (King's Scholar); Trinity Coll., Oxford (MA). ARICS. Lieut R of O, Coldstream Guards. Asst Private Sec. to Governor-General of Canada, 1960–62; Trustee, Shelter Housing Aid Centre, 1970–76; Chairman: Catholic Housing Aid Soc., 1972–73; Nat. Fedn of Housing Assocs, 1973–76; Housing Assoc. Charitable Trust; Help the Aged Housing Trust, 1976–82; Hugh of Witham Foundn, 1978–; Vice-Pres., Age Concern (Nat. Old People's Welfare Council), 1971–77; President: SW Reg. Nat. Soc. for Mentally Handicapped Children, 1976–79; NI Assoc. for Care and Resettlement of Offenders, 1989–2010. An indep. mem. of H of L; Member, All Party Parliamentary Group: on Penal Affairs; on Human Rights; British-Russian; British-Armenian; British-Albanian; British-Palestine; elected Mem., H of L, 1999. Founder and Mem., Mendip and Wansdyke Local Enterprise Gp, 1979–85. Hon. Treas., Study on Human Rights and Responsibilities in Britain and N Ireland, 1985–88. Mem., Nat. Steering Gp, Charter '87, 1987–99; Signatory of Charter '88 and of Charter '99. Trustee: Christian Internat. Peace Service, 1977–82; Acorn Christian Healing Trust, 1983–98; Action around Bethlehem among Children with Disabilities, 1993–2000; Forward Thinking, 2004–; Chairman: Moldovan Initiatives Cttee of Mgt, 1993–; Adv. Council, Foundn for Reconciliation and Relief in Middle East, 2006–; Member: Council for Advancement of Arab-British Understanding; RIIA; Patron, Soul of Europe Trust, 2009–. Gov., Ammerdown Centre, Bath, 1972–. Mem., Frome RDC, 1968–72. DL Somerset, 1975–90. Hon DSc (SocSci) Southampton, 1994. *Heir: s* Hon. William Henry Martin Jolliffe [*b* April 1967; *m* 2015, Dr Pia M. Vogler]. *Address:* c/o House of Lords, SW1A 0PW.

HYMAN, Prof. Anthony Arie, PhD; FRS 2007; Research Group Leader and Director, Max Planck Institute of Molecular Cell Biology and Genetics, since 1999 (Managing Director, 2011–13); *b* Haifa, Israel, 27 May 1962. *Educ:* University Coll. London (BSc 1984); King's Coll., Cambridge (PhD 1988). Res. Asst, Dept of Zool., UCL, 1981; Gp Leader, 1993–97, Vis. Sen. Scientist, 1998–99, Eur. Molecular Biol. Lab., Heidelberg. Prof. of Molecular Cell Biol., Dresden Univ. of Technol., 2002. Lucille P. Markey Vis. Fellow, 1988–90, Sen. Fellow, 1991–94; Amer. Cancer Soc. Fellow, 1990. Mem., EMBO, 2000– (Gold Medal, 2003). *Publications:* contribs to jls incl. Cell Biol., Current Biol., Methods in Cell Biol., Nature, Science, Natural Cell Biol., Cell, EMBO, Development. *Address:* Max Planck Institute of Molecular Cell Biology and Genetics, Pfotenhauerstrasse 108, 01307 Dresden, Germany.

HYMAN, Howard Jonathan; Chairman: Hyman Associates, since 1997; VinoVeritas Asia Ltd, since 2012; *b* 23 Oct. 1949; *s* of late Joe Hyman and Corrine Irene (*née* Abrahams); *m* 1972, Anne Moira Sowden; two *s* one *d*. *Educ:* Bedales Sch., Hants; Manchester Univ. (BA Hons Econs 1972); Sch. of Oriental and African Studies, Univ. of London; Beijing Normal Univ. ACA 1975, FCA 1982. Price Waterhouse: articled clerk, 1972–75; Partner, 1984; seconded to HM Treasury as specialist privatisation adviser, 1984–87; Founder and Partner i/c of Privatisation Services Dept, 1987–90; Head of Corporate Finance, Europe, 1990; Member: E European Jt Venture Bd, 1990–94; European Mgt Bd, 1991–94; China Bd, 1993–94; World Gen. Council, 1992–94; World Head, Corporate Finance, 1994; Dep. Chm., Charterhouse Bank Ltd, 1994–96; Man. Dir, Charterhouse plc, 1994–96. Dir, Kingstream Steel plc, Perth, Australia, 2000–02. Mem., Chartered Accountants' Co. *Publications:* Privatisation: the facts, 1988; The Implications of Privatisation for Nationalised Industries, 1988; chapters in: Privatisation and Competition, 1988; Privatisation in the UK, 1988; articles in Electrical Rev., Equities Internat., Public Finance and Accountancy, Business and Govt, Administrator. *Recreations:* Chinese culture and language, walking, golf, watching cricket, reading, gardening, classical music. *Address:* 1 Cato Street, W1H 5HG. *T:* (020) 7258 0404. *Clubs:* Reform, MCC; Minchinhampton Golf.

HYMAN, Peter Jonathan; Founder and Headteacher, School 21, since 2012; *b* London, 23 Nov. 1968; *s* of Robin Philip Hyman, *qv*; *m* 1999, Corinna Little; one *s* two *d*. *Educ:* University Coll. Sch.; Bristol Univ. (BA 1st Cl. Hons Hist. 1991); City Univ. (Dip. Journalism 1992). QTS 2006; NPQH 2010. Researcher, Behind the Headlines prog., BBC, 1992–93; Advisor: Shadow Chancellor, 1993; Shadow Social Security Sec., 1993–94; Advr and speechwriter to Leader of the Opposition, later Prime Minister, 1994–2001; Hd, Prime Minister's Strategic Communication Unit, 2001–03; teaching asst, 2004–05, trainee hist. teacher, 2005–06, Islington Green Sch.; hist. teacher, Seven Kings High Sch., 2006–07; Dep. Headteacher and on Future Leaders Headship Prog., Greenford High Sch., 2007–11. *Publications:* 1 Out of 10: from Downing Street vision to classroom reality, 2005. *Recreations:* family, cooking, reading, politics, writing, Arsenal FC. *Address:* School 21, Pitchford Street, E15 4RZ. *T:* (020) 8262 2121. *E:* phyman@school21.org.uk.

HYMAN, Richard Allan; Founder, 2012, and Retail Advisor, since 2012, RAH Advisory Ltd; Founder, richardtalksretail.com, 2014; *b* Ilford, Essex, 6 Aug. 1951; *s* of David and Rose Hyman; *m* 1st, 1976, Sandra Levy (marr. diss. 1993); two *d*; 2nd, 1998, Debbie Grant (*d* 2008); one *d*. *Educ:* Shoreditch Sch. Researcher, Financial Times, 1972–78; Editl and Mktg Dir, Mintel, 1979–84; Verdict Research: Founder and Chm., 1984–2005; Man. Dir, 2005–08; Strategic Adviser: Deloitte, 2008–12. Pres., PatelMiller, 2012–13. *Recreations:* jazz, football, tennis, current affairs, business, visiting shops. *Address:* RAH Advisory Ltd, 10 Northaw Place, Coopers Lane, Northaw, Potters Bar, Herts EN6 4NQ. *E:* richard.hyman@btconnect.com. *Clubs:* Home House, Ronnie Scott's.

HYMAN, Robin Philip; publisher; Chairman, Laurence King Publishing Ltd (formerly Calmann & King Ltd), 1991–2004; *b* 9 Sept. 1931; *s* of late Leonard Hyman and Helen Hyman (*née* Mautner); *m* 1966, Inge Neufeld; two *s* one *d*. *Educ:* Henley Grammar Sch.; Christ's Coll., Finchley; Univ. of Birmingham (BA (Hons) 1955). National Service, RAF, 1949–51. Editor, Mermaid, 1953–54; Bookselling and Publishing: joined Evans Brothers Ltd, Publishers, 1955: Dir, 1964; Dep. Man. Dir, 1967; Man. Dir, 1972–77; Chm., Bell & Hyman Ltd, 1977–86, which merged with Allen & Unwin Ltd, 1986, to form Unwin Hyman Ltd, Man. Dir, 1986–88, Chm. and Chief Exec., 1989–90. Mem. Editorial Bd, World Year Book of Education, 1969–73. Publishers' Association: Mem. Council, 1975–92; Treasurer, 1982–84; Vice-Pres., 1988–89, 1991–92; Pres., 1989–91; Member: Exec. Cttee, Educnl Publishers' Council, 1971–76 (Treas., 1972–75); Publishers' Adv. Cttee, British Council, 1989–92; BBC Gen. Adv. Council, 1992–97. Dir, Spiro Inst., 1991–98. Trustee: ADAPT, 1997–2006; Samuel Pepys Award Trust, 2001– (Chm., 2007–14). Mem., First British Publishers' Delegn to China, 1978. FRSA. *Publications:* A Dictionary of Famous Quotations, 1962; (with John Trevaskis) Boys' and Girls' First Dictionary, 1967; Bell & Hyman First Colour Dictionary, 1985; Universal Primary Dictionary (for Africa), 1976; (with Inge Hyman) 11 children's books, incl. Barnabas Ball at the Circus, 1967; Runaway James and the Night Owl, 1968; The Hippo who Wanted to Fly, 1973; The Magical Fish, 1974; Peter's Magic Hide-and-Seek, 1982. *Recreations:* theatre, reading, travel, enjoying grandchildren. *Address:* 101 Hampstead Way, NW11 7LR. *T:* (020) 8455 7055. *Clubs:* Garrick, MCC.
See also P. J. Hyman.

HYMAN, Timothy James, RA 2011; painter and writer; *b* Hove, 17 April 1946; *s* of Alan Hyman and Noreen Hyman; *m* 1982, Judith Ravenscroft. *Educ:* Hall Sch., Hampstead; Charterhouse; Slade Sch. of Fine Art, London (Dip. 1967). Curator, Narrative Paintings, ICA and tour, 1979–80; *solo exhibitions* include: Blond Fine Art, London, 1981, 1983, 1985; Usher Gall., Lincoln, Ferens Art Gall., Hull and tour, 1984; Westfield Coll., London, 1985; Contemporary Art Gall., Ahmedabad, 1988; Austin/Desmond Fine Art, London, 1990; Castlefield Gall., Manchester, 1993; Gall. M, London, 1994; Gall. Chemould, Bombay, 1994; Mid River: Paintings and Drawings of a Decade, 2000, London Mappings and Panoramas, 2006, Austin/Desmond Fine Art, London; The Man Inscribed with London, Gall. of the Artists' Studios, Tel Aviv, 2006, Austin/Desmond Fine Art, London, 2009; A Year with Maggie's, RA, 2015; *works in public collections* include: Arts Council; British Mus.; British Council; Contemporary Art Soc.; Deutsche Bank; Mus. of London; LA County Mus.; lead curator, Stanley Spencer, Tate Britain, 2001; co-curator, British Vision, Ghent, 2007–08. Artist-in-Residence: Lincoln Cath., 1983–84; Westfield Coll., 1984–85; Sandown Racecourse, 1992; Maggie Cancer Caring Centres, 2011–12. Mem., Powys Soc., 1970– (Chm., 2010–). *Publications:* Bonnard, 1998; Bhupen Khakhar, 1998; Carnivalesque, 2000;

Sienese Painting, 2003; Timothy Hyman: fifty drawings, 2010; Refiguring: painting and experience in the twentieth century, 2016; contrib. TLS, London Mag., Artscribe, etc. *Recreations:* novels of John Cowper Powys, cinema, walking, travel, looking at paintings. *Address:* 62 Myddelton Square, EC1R 1XX. *T:* (020) 7837 1933.

HYND, Annette, (Mrs Ronald Hynd); *see* Page, Annette.

HYND, Ronald; choreographer; Ballet Director, National Theater, Munich, 1970–73 and 1984–86; *b* 22 April 1931; *s* of William John and Alice Louisa Hens; *m* 1957, Annette Page, *qv*; one *d*. *Educ:* erratically throughout England due to multiple wartime evacuation. Joined Rambert School, 1946; Ballet Rambert, 1949; Royal Ballet (then Sadler's Wells Ballet), 1952, rising from Corps de Ballet to Principal Dancer, 1959; danced Siegfried (Swan Lake), Florimund (Sleeping Beauty), Albrecht (Giselle), Poet (Sylphides), Tsarevitch (Firebird), Prince of Pagodas, Moondog (Lady and Fool), Tybalt (Romeo), etc; produced first choreography for Royal Ballet Choreographic Group followed by works for London Festival Ballet, Royal Ballet, Dutch National Ballet, Munich Ballet, Houston Ballet, Australian Ballet, Tokyo Ballet, Nat. Ballet of Canada, Grands Ballets Canadiens, Santiago Ballet, Cincinnati Ballet, Pact Ballet, Malmö Ballet, Ljubljana Ballet, Northern Ballet, Ballet of La Scala, Milan, Bonn Ballet, Vienna State Ballet, Amer. Ballet Theatre, New London Ballet, Deutsche Oper Berlin, Hungarian Na. Ballet, Royal Danish Ballet, Chicago Joffrey Ballet, Tulsa Ballet Theater, Texas Ballet Theater. *Ballets include:* Le Baiser de la Fée, 1968, new production 1974; Pasiphaë, 1969; Dvorak Variations, 1970; Wendekreise, 1972; In a Summer Garden, 1972; Das Telefon, 1972; Mozartiana, 1973; Charlotte Brontë, 1974; Mozart Adagio, 1974; Galileo (film), 1974; Orient/Occident, 1975; La Valse, 1975; Valses Nobles et Sentimentales, 1975; The Merry Widow, 1975, 17 subseq. prodns incl. Amer. Ballet Th. at Met. Opera, NY, 1997 and Royal Danish Ballet, 1998; L'Eventail, 1976; The Nutcracker (new version for Festival Ballet), 1976, new prodns for Ballet de Nice, 1997, La Scala, 2000; ice ballets for John Curry, 1977; Rosalinda, 1978, eleven subseq. prodns incl. Berlin, 1998; La Chatte, 1978; Papillon, 1979; The Seasons, 1980; Alceste, 1981; Scherzo Capriccioso, 1982; Le Diable a Quatre, 1984; Fanfare für Tänzer, 1985; Coppelia (new prodn for Festival Ballet), 1985, new prodns for Santiago and Berlin, 2000, Hong Kong Ballet, 2008, Estonian Nat. Ballet, 2010; Ludwig-Fragmente Eines Rätsels, 1986; The Hunchback of Notre Dame, 1988; Ballade, 1988; Liaisons Amoureuses, 1989; Sleeping Beauty (new prodn for English Nat. Ballet), 1993 and Pacific Northwest Ballet, 2001; *musicals:* Sound of Music, 1981; Camelot, 1982; *TV productions:* The Nutcracker, The Sanguine Fan (Fest. Ballet); The Merry Widow (Nat. Ballet of Canada and Aust. Ballet); operas, La Traviata and Amahl and the Night Visitors. *Recreations:* the gramophone, garden, travel.

HYNES, Dame Ann Patricia; *see* Dowling, Dame A. P.

HYNES, Paul Richard; QC 2010; *b* London, 17 Dec. 1963; *s* of Patrick Hynes and Joan Hynes (*née* Pritchard); *m* 1992, Michelle Simpson; two *d*. *Educ:* Forest Sch.; North East London Poly. (BA Hons Law). Called to the Bar, Lincoln's Inn, 1987; in practice as a barrister, 1987–, specialising in criminal defence. Hon. LLD UEL, 2011. *Publications:* (contrib.) Abuse of Process: a practical approach, 2006, 2nd edn 2011; (jtly) International Money Laundering and Terrorist Financing: a UK perspective, 2009. *Recreation:* being grumpy. *Address:* 25 Bedford Row, WC1R 4HD. *T:* (020) 7067 1500, *Fax:* (020) 7067 1507. *E:* phynes@25bedfordrow.com.

HYNES, Prof. Richard Olding, FRS 1989; Daniel K. Ludwig Professor for Cancer Research, Massachusetts Institute of Technology, since 1999; Investigator, Howard Hughes Medical Institute, since 1988; *b* 29 Nov. 1944; *s* of late Hugh Bernard Noel Hynes and Mary Elizabeth Hynes; *m* 1966, Fleur Marshall; two *s*. *Educ:* Trinity Coll., Cambridge (BA 1966; MA 1970); MIT (PhD Biology 1971). Res. Fellow, Imperial Cancer Res. Fund, 1971–74; Massachusetts Institute of Technology: Asst Prof., 1975–78, Associate Prof., 1978–83, Prof., 1983–, Dept of Biology and Center for Cancer Res.; Associate Hd, 1985–89, Head, 1989–91, of Biology Dept; Dir, Center for Cancer Res., 1991–2001. Gov., Wellcome Trust, 2007–. Hon. Res. Fellow, Dept of Zoology, UCL, 1982–83. Guggenheim Fellow, 1982. Mem., Inst. of Medicine, US NAS, 1995; Mem., US NAS, 1996. FAAAS, 1987; Fellow, Amer. Acad. of Arts and Scis, 1994. Gairdner Internat. Award, Gairdner Foundn, Toronto, 1997; Pasarow Med. Res. Award, Robert J. and Claire Pasarow Foundn, 2008. *Publications:* (ed) Surfaces of Normal and Malignant Cells, 1979; (ed) Tumor Cell Surfaces and Malignancy, 1980; Fibronectins, 1990; (ed with K. Yamada) Extracellular Matrix Biology, 2012; over 350 articles in professional jls. *Recreations:* reading, music, gardening, ski-ing. *Address:* 76–361D, Koch Institute for Integrative Cancer Research, Massachusetts Institute of Technology, Cambridge, MA 02139–4307, USA. *T:* (617) 2536422, *Fax:* (617) 2538357.

HYNES, Prof. Samuel, DFC 1945; PhD; Woodrow Wilson Emeritus Professor of Literature, Princeton University, since 1990; *b* 29 Aug. 1924; *s* of Samuel Hynes and Margaret Turner Hynes; *m* 1944, Elizabeth Igleheart (*d* 2008); two *d*. *Educ:* Univ. of Minnesota (AB 1947); Columbia Univ. (PhD 1956). Pilot, US Marine Corps: 2nd Lieut, 1943–46; Capt., then Major, 1952–53. Instructor to Prof. of English, Swarthmore Coll., 1949–52 and 1954–68; Professor: Northwestern Univ., 1968–76; Princeton Univ., 1976–90. Woodrow Wilson Prof. of Literature, 1977–90. FRSL 1978. Air Medal, 1945. *Publications:* (ed) Further Speculations by T. E. Hulme, 1955; The Pattern of Hardy's Poetry, 1961; The Edwardian Turn of Mind, 1962; William Golding, 1964; (ed) The Author's Craft and Other Critical Writings of Arnold Bennett, 1968; (ed) Romance and Realism, 1970; Edwardian Occasions, 1972; The Auden Generation, 1976; (ed) Complete Poetical Works of Thomas Hardy, Vol. I 1982, Vol. II 1984, Vol. III 1985, Vols IV and V 1995; (ed) Thomas Hardy, 1984; Flights of Passage: reflections of a World War II aviator, 1988; A War Imagined, 1990; (ed) Joseph Conrad: complete short fiction, 4 vols, 1992–93; The Soldiers' Tale: bearing witness to modern war, 1997; The Growing Seasons, 2003; The Unsubstantial Air: American fliers in the First World War, 2014. *Address:* 130 Moore Street, Princeton, NJ 08540, USA. *T:* (609) 9211930.

HYSLOP, Fiona Jane; Member (SNP) Linlithgow, Scottish Parliament, since 2011 (Lothians, 1999–2011); Cabinet Secretary for Culture, Europe and External Affairs, since 2014; *b* 1 Aug. 1964; *d* of Thomas Hyslop and Margaret Birrell; *m* 1994; two *s* one *d*. *Educ:* Ayr Acad.; Glasgow Univ. (MA Hons 1985); Scottish Coll. of Textiles (Post Grad. Dip. 1986). Mkting Manager, Standard Life, 1986–99. Scottish Parliament: Cabinet Sec. for Educn and Lifelong Learning, 2007–09; Minister for Culture and External Affairs, 2009–11; Cabinet Sec. for Culture and External Affairs, 2011–14. Mem., SNP, 1986– (Mem., Nat. Exec., 1990–). Contested (SNP): Edinburgh Leith, 1992; Edinburgh Central, 1997. *Address:* Scottish Parliament, Edinburgh EH99 1SP. *T:* (0131) 348 5920.

HYSLOP, Peter Henry St G.; *see* St George-Hyslop.

HYTNER, Benet Alan; QC 1970; a Recorder of the Crown Court, 1972–97; a Deputy High Court Judge, 1974–97; Judge of Appeal, Isle of Man, 1980–97; Expert to Asbestos Trust, 2006–12; *b* 29 Dec. 1927; *s* of late Maurice and Sarah Hytner, Manchester; *m* 1954, Joyce Myers (OBE 2004); three *s* one *d*. *Educ:* Manchester Grammar Sch.; Trinity Hall, Cambridge (Exhibr; MA). National Service, RASC, 1949–51 (commnd). Called to Bar, Middle Temple, 1952, Bencher, 1977, Reader, 1995; in practice as barrister, 1952–2010; Leader, Northern Circuit, 1984–88. Member: Gen. Council of Bar, 1969–73, 1986–88; Senate of Inns of Court and Bar, 1977–81, 1984–86. *Recreations:* walking, music, theatre, reading. *Address:* 42 Bedford Row, WC1R 4LL.

See also J. E. Hytner, Sir N. R. Hytner.

HYTNER, James Edward; Chief Executive Officer, G14 and President, Global Clients, IPG Mediabrands, since 2013; *b* Manchester, 22 July 1964; *s* of Benet Alan Hytner, *qv*; *m* 2008, Joanna; two *s* two *d*. *Educ:* Oxford Poly.; Wharton Business Sch. Marketing Director: Coca-Cola, 1991–95; Sky TV, 1995–2001; ITV, 2001–05; Barclays, 2005–09; Universal McCann: Chief Executive Officer: EMEA, 2009–11; G14, 2011–12; Worldwide CEO, Initiative, 2012–13. Trustee, Comic Relief, 2006–; Mem., Commercial Bd, BAFTA, 2012. *Recreations:* Manchester United, ski-ing, wine, theatre. *Address:* IPG Mediabrands, 42 St John's Square, EC1M 4EA. *T:* (020) 7073 7333. *E:* jim.hytner@mbww.com. *Club:* Thirty.

See also Sir N. R. Hytner.

HYTNER, Sir Nicholas (Robert), Kt 2010; theatre and film director; Director, National Theatre, 2003–15; *b* 7 May 1956; *s* of Benet Alan Hytner, *qv*. *Educ:* Manchester Grammar School; Trinity Hall, Cambridge (MA; Hon. Fellow, 2003). Associate Director: Royal Exchange Theatre, Manchester, 1985–89; NT, 1989–97. Vis. Prof. of Contemporary Theatre, Oxford Univ., 2000–01; Emeritus Fellow, St Catherine's Coll., Oxford, 2003. Trustee, ROH, 2008–; non-exec. Dir, BBC, 2014–. Director of many theatre and opera productions including: *theatre:* As You Like It, 1985, Edward II, 1986, The Country Wife, 1986, Don Carlos, 1987, Royal Exchange; Measure for Measure, 1987, The Tempest, 1988, RSC; Ghetto, National Theatre, 1989; Miss Saigon, Drury Lane, 1989, Broadway, 1991; Volpone, Almeida, 1990; King Lear, RSC, 1990; The Wind in the Willows, NT, 1990; The Madness of George III, NT, 1991; The Recruiting Officer, NT, 1992; Carousel, NT, 1992, Shaftesbury, 1993, NY, 1994; The Importance of Being Earnest, Aldwych, 1993; The Cripple of Inishmaan, NT, 1997; Twelfth Night, NY, 1998; Lady in the Van, Queen's 1999; Cressida, Albery, 2000; Orpheus Descending, Donmar Warehouse, 2000; The Winter's Tale, Mother Clapp's Molly House, NT, 2001; Sweet Smell of Success, NY, 2002; National Theatre: Henry V, His Dark Materials, 2003; The History Boys, 2004, NY, 2006; Stuff Happens, 2004; Henry IV, Pts 1 and 2, 2005; Southwark Fair, The Alchemist, 2006; The Man of Mode, The Rose Tattoo, Rafta, Rafta, Much Ado About Nothing, 2007; Major Barbara, 2008; England People Very Nice, Phèdre, The Habit of Art, 2009; London Assurance, Hamlet, 2010; One Man, Two Guvnors (transf. Adelphi), Collaborators, 2011; Travelling Light, Timon of Athens, People, Cocktail Sticks, 2012; Great Britain, 2014; The Hard Problem, 2015; *opera:* English National Opera: Rienzi, 1983; Xerxes, 1985 (Laurence Olivier and Evening Standard Awards); The Magic Flute, 1988; The Force of Destiny, 1992; King Priam, Kent Opera, 1983; Giulio Cesare, Paris Opera, Houston Grand Opera, 1987; Le Nozze di Figaro, Geneva Opera, 1989; La Clemenza di Tito, Glyndebourne, 1991; Don Giovanni, Bavarian State Opera, 1994; The Cunning Little Vixen, Paris, 1995; Così fan tutte, Glyndebourne, 2006; Don Carlo, Covent Garden, 2008, 2013, Metropolitan Opera, NY, 2010; *films:* The Madness of King George, 1994 (Evening Standard and BAFTA Awards for Best British Film); The Crucible, 1997; The Object of My Affection, 1998; The History Boys, 2006; The Lady in the Van, 2015. Awards for Best Director: Evening Standard, 1989, 2012; Critics Circle, 1989; Olivier, 1993, 2005; Tony, 1994, 2006; Lebedev Special Award, London Evening Standard Theatre Award, 2012. Hon. FKC 2012. Hon. DLit London, 2009; Hon. DFA Juilliard Sch., NY, 2015. Freeman, City of London, 2015. Chevalier, Ordre des Arts et des Lettres (France), 2009.

See also J. E. Hytner.

I

IACOBESCU, Sir George, Kt 2012; CBE 2003; Chief Executive Officer, since 1997, and Chairman, since 2011, Canary Wharf Group plc; *b* 9 Nov. 1945; *m* 1976, Gabriela; one *d*. *Educ:* Lyceum D. Cantemir (BSc 1963); Univ. of Civil & Industrial Engrg, Bucharest (Masters degree in professional engrg 1968). Construction Dir, Homeco Invst, Montreal and Toronto, 1975–78; Project Dir, Olympia Center and Neiman Marcus Bldgs, Chicago, 1981–84; Vice-Pres., Develt and Construction, World Financial Center, 1984–87; Vice-Pres., Construction, 1987–92; Dir, CWL, 1993–95; Dep. CEO, Canary Wharf Gp plc, 1995–97. Co-Chm., Teach First; Director: London First; Gateway to London; Wood Wharf (Gen. Partners) Ltd. Member: Adv. Bd, UK Acad. of Finance; Defence Reform Unit, MoD, 2010–. Trustee, British Mus., 2007–. CCMI. Hon. DBA East London, 2007. *Recreations:* jazz, opera, antiques, football, tennis. *Address:* Canary Wharf Group plc, 1 Canada Square, E14 5AB. *T:* (020) 7418 2209.

IAN, David; *see* Lane, D. I.

IANNUCCI, Armando Giovanni, OBE 2012; freelance writer, director and comedy producer; *b* 28 Nov. 1963; *s* of Armando and Gina Iannucci; *m* 1990, Rachael Jones; two *s* one *d*. *Educ:* St Peter's Primary Sch., Glasgow; St Aloysius Coll., Glasgow; Glasgow Univ.; University Coll., Oxford (MA English Lang. and Lit. 1986). Writer for television: and performer, The Friday Night Armistice, 1995, 1997, 1998; and producer, The Day Today, 1995; and dir, The Armando Iannucci Shows, 2001; and producer, I'm Alan Partridge, 1997 and 2001; deviser and dir, The Thick of It, 2005–07, 2009 and 2012; dir, In the Loop (film), 2009; creator, Veep, 2012. Libretto, Skin Deep, Opera North, 2009. Columnist: Daily Telegraph, 1998–2005; Sunday Observer, 2006–; Gramophone mag., 2006–. Writers' Guild of Britain Award, British Comedy Awards, 2011. *Publications:* Facts and Fancies, 2000; Alan Partridge: every ruddy word, 2005; The Audacity of Hype: bewilderment, sleaze and other tales of the 21st century, 2009. *Recreations:* prevaricating, bad piano, astronomy, fearing, re-assuring, theology. *Address:* c/o PBJ Management, 22 Rathbone Street, W1T 1LG. *T:* (020) 7287 1112. *E:* general@pbjmanagement.co.uk; c/o CAA, 2000 Avenue of the Stars, Los Angeles, CA 90067, USA. *T:* 4242882000.

IBBETSON, Prof. David John, PhD, DPhil; FBA 2003; Regius Professor of Civil Law, University of Cambridge, since 2000; President, Clare Hall, Cambridge, since 2013. *Educ:* Corpus Christi Coll., Cambridge (BA 1976; PhD 1980); DPhil Oxon. Formerly Lectr in Law, Univ. of Oxford, and Fellow of Magdalen Coll., Oxford; Fellow of Corpus Christi Coll., Cambridge, 2000–13. Hon. Bencher, Gray's Inn, 2008. *Publications:* (ed with A. D. E. Lewis) Roman Law Tradition, 1994; Historical Introduction to the Law of Obligations, 1999. *Address:* Clare Hall, Herschel Road, Cambridge CB3 9AL.

IBBOTSON, Peter Stamford; broadcasting and media consultant; *b* 13 Dec. 1943; *s* of Arthur Ibbotson and Ivy Elizabeth (*née* Acton); *m* 1975, Susan Mary Crewdson; two *s* (one *d* decd). *Educ:* Manchester Grammar Sch.; St Catherine's Coll., Oxford (BA Modern History). BBC: Editor, Newsweek, 1978–82; Editor, Panorama, 1983–85; Asst Head, Television Current Affairs, 1985–86; Chief Asst to Dir of Programmes, Television, 1986–87; Dep. Dir of Progs, TV, 1987–88; Dir of Corporate Affairs, Carlton Television Ltd, 1991–94. Director: UK Radio Develts Ltd, 1990–94; Film and Television Completions PLC, 1990–98. Corporate Consultant, Channel 4, 1988–91 and 1994–2004; Consultant: to BBC Govs, 2004–06; to Chm., ITV plc, 2007–09. Dir, BARB, 1987–88. Gov., ESU, 2000–05. FRTS 1994. *Publications:* (jtly) The Third Age of Broadcasting, 1978. *Recreations:* silviculture, reading, photography. *Address:* Newnham Farm, Wallingford, Oxon OX10 8BW. *T:* (01491) 833111.

IBBOTSON, Vice Adm. Sir Richard (Jeffery), KBE 2011; CB 2008; DSC 1992; DL; Deputy Commander-in-Chief Fleet and Chief Naval Warfare Officer, 2009–11; *b* 27 June 1954; *s* of Jeffrey Ibbotson and Joan Ibbotson; *m* 1975, Marie; two *d*. *Educ:* Univ. of Durham (BSc); RNEC Manadon (MSc). CGIA. Capt., First Frigate Sqdn and HMS Boxer, 1998–99; Asst Dir, MoD, 1999–2001; Comdr, British Forces Falkland Is, 2001–02; Comdr, Standing Naval Forces Atlantic, 2003–04; CO, Britannia RNC, 2004–05; Naval Sec. and Dir Gen. Human Resources Navy, 2005–07; Flag Officer Sea Training, 2007–09. Mem., Armed Forces Pay Rev. Body, 2011–. Chm., S Devon Healthcare NHS Foundn Trust, 2014–. DL Devon, 2011. Hon. DTech Plymouth, 2008. *Recreations:* water sports, classic cars.

IBBOTSON, His Honour Roger; a Circuit Judge, 2001–13; *b* 2 Jan. 1943; *s* of Harry and Lily Ibbotson; *m* 1967, Susan Elizabeth Dalton; three *d*. *Educ:* Cockburn High Sch., Leeds; Univ. of Manchester (LLB). Articled clerk, Burton and Burton, Leeds, 1963–66; admitted solicitor, 1966; Asst Solicitor, 1966–70, Partner, 1970–2001, Booth & Co., later Addleshaw Booth & Co.; Asst Recorder, 1994–98; Recorder, 1998–2001. Pres., Leeds Law Soc., 1996–97; Council Mem., Law Soc., 1997–2001. *Recreations:* walking, reading, the language and modern history of France.

IBBOTT, Alec, CBE 1988; HM Diplomatic Service, retired; *b* 14 Oct. 1930; *s* of Francis Joseph Ibbott and Madge Winifred Ibbott (*née* Graham); *m* 1964, Margaret Elizabeth Brown; one *s* one *d*. Joined Foreign (subseq. Diplomatic) Service, 1949; served in HM Forces, 1949–51; FCO, 1951–54; ME Centre for Arab Studies, 1955–56; Second Secretary and Vice Consul, Rabat, 1956–60; Second Secretary, FO, 1960–61; Second Sec. (Information), Tripoli, 1961; Second Sec., Benghazi, 1961–65; First Sec. (Information), Khartoum, 1965–67; First Sec., FO (later FCO), 1967–71; Asst Political Agent, Dubai, 1971; First Secretary, Head of Chancery and Consul: Dubai, 1971–72; Abu Dhabi, 1972–73; First Secretary and Head of Chancery: Nicosia, 1973–74; FCO, 1975–77; Carácas, 1977–79; Counsellor, Khartoum, 1979–82; seconded to IMS Ltd, 1982–85; Ambassador to Liberia, 1985–87; High Comr to the Republic of The Gambia, 1988–90. Chief Exec., Southern Africa Assoc., 1992–95; Gen. Manager, UK Southern Africa Business Assoc., 1994–95. Mem. Council, Anglo-Arab Assoc., 1992–2003. Trustee, Charlton Community Develt Trust, 1995–2003.

IBELL, Prof. Timothy James, PhD; FREng, FIStructE, FICE; Professor of Civil Engineering, since 2003, and Associate Dean, Faculty of Engineering and Design, since 2008, University of Bath; *b* Cape Town, 25 Feb. 1967; *s* of Anthony James Ibell and Elizabeth Diane Ibell (*née* Hall); partner, Jacqueline Ann Hatton; one *s*. *Educ:* Western Province Prep. Sch., Cape Town; Diocesan Coll. (Bishops), Cape Town; Univ. of Cape Town (BScEng 1st Cl. Hons 1988); Univ. of Cambridge (PhD 1992). FREng 2013; FIStructE 2007; FICE 2013. Sen. Civil Engr, Sasol Technol., 1993–94; Sen. Res. Associate, Univ. of Cambridge, 1994–97; Department of Architecture and Civil Engineering, University of Bath: Lectr, 1997–2000; Sen. Lectr, 2000–03; Hd of Dept, 2005–08 and 2010–13. Pres., IStructE, 2015. FHEA 1998. *Publications:* contribs to peer-reviewed jls. *Recreations:* cricket, killer sudoku, swimming. *Address:* Department of Architecture and Civil Engineering, University of Bath, Bath BA2 7AY. *T:* (01225) 386365, *Fax:* (01225) 386691. *E:* t.j.ibell@bath.ac.uk.

ICHIOKA, Sarah Mineko; Principal, New Intentional Communities Project, since 2014; *b* Berkeley, Calif, 9 Feb. 1979; *d* of Victor Masaru Ichioka and Marilyn Jane Ichioka; *m* 2012, Jack Stiller; one *d*. *Educ:* Berkeley High Sch.; Univ. of Paris; Yale Univ. (BA Hist. 2001); London Sch. of Econs and Pol Sci. (MSc City Design and Social Sci. 2003). Housing and Community Develt Fellow, NY City Dept of Housing Preservation and Develt, 2001–02; Associate, Enterprise LSE Cities Ltd, 2003–05; Exhibn Content Coordinator and Catalogue Ed., 10th Venice Architecture Biennale, 2005–06; Founding Res. Associate, Urban Age Project, 2004–07; Consultant Curator, Tate Modern, 2006–07; Dep. Dir, 2007–08, Co-Dir, 2009–, London Fest. of Architecture; Dir, Architecture Foundn, 2008–14. Dir, London Sch. of Architecture, 2013–14. Mem., Curatorial Cttee, Design Mus., 2013–14. Hon. FRIBA 2013. Cultural Leadership Internat. Grant Recipient, British Council, 2009. *Publications:* (ed jtly) Cities: people, society, architecture: 10th International Architecture Exhibition - Venice Biennale, 2006; (contrib.) The Endless City, 2008; (contrib.) In Favour of Public Space: ten years of the European Prize for Urban Public Space, 2010; (contrib.) The Union Street Urban Orchard, 2011; (ed jtly) South Kilburn Studios: notes on an experiment, 2012; (contrib.) Constructing Worlds: photography and architecture in the modern age, 2014. *Recreations:* travel, reading, cycling, gardening, walking, art, cooking, sewing, Yale Alumni Schools Committee member. *Address:* Brendon Cottage, Henshaw Lane, Siddington near Macclesfield, Cheshire SK11 9JW. *T:* 07791 732478. *E:* mail@sarahichioka.com.

ICKE, Robert William; freelance writer and director; Associate Director, Almeida Theatre, since 2013; *b* Stockton-on-Tees, 29 Nov. 1986; *s* of Stephen W. Icke and Morag Mackenzie. *Educ:* Ian Ramsey C of E Comp. Sch., Stockton-on-Tees; King's Coll., Cambridge (BA; Scholar). Artistic Dir, Arden Theatre Co., 2003–07; Associate Dir, Headlong, 2010–13. *Publications:* adaptations for theatre: 1984, by George Orwell (with Duncan Macmillan), 2013; Oresteia, by Aeschylus, 2015. *E:* roberticke@gmail.com.

IDDESLEIGH, 5th Earl of, *cr* 1885; **John Stafford Northcote;** Bt 1641; Viscount St Cyres, 1885; *b* 15 Feb. 1957; *s* of 4th Earl of Iddesleigh, and of Maria Luisa Alvarez-Builla y Urquijo (Condesa del Real Agrado in Spain), OBE, DL; S father, 2004; *m* 1983, Fiona Caroline Elizabeth (marr. diss. 1999; she *d* 2006), *d* of P. Wakefield, Barcelona, and Mrs M. Hattrell, Burnham, Bucks; one *s* one *d*; *m* 2000, Maria Ann Akaylar. *Educ:* Downside Sch.; RAC Cirencester. *Heir:* *s* Viscount St Cyres, *qv*.

IDDON, Dr Brian, CChem, FRSC; *b* 5 July 1940; *s* of John Iddon and Violet (*née* Stazicker); *m* 1st, 1965, Merrilyn Ann Muncaster (marr. diss. 1989); two *d*; 2nd, 1995, Eileen Harrison; two step *s*. *Educ:* Univ. of Hull (BSc Chem. 1961; PhD Organic Chem. 1964; DSc 1981). FRSC (FCS 1959), Hon. FRSC 2010; CChem 1980. Temp. Lectr in Organic Chem., 1964–65, Sen. Demonstrator, 1965–66, Univ. of Durham; University of Salford: Lectr in Organic Chem., 1966–78; Sen. Lectr, 1978–86; Reader, 1986–97. Vis. Prof., Dept of Chemistry, Liverpool Univ., 2002–07. Has lectured worldwide, incl. lect. The Magic of Chemistry presented to schs and univs in UK and Europe, 1968–98. Chm., Bolton Technical Innovation Centre Ltd, 2003–08. Has made TV and radio broadcasts. Mem. (Lab) Bolton MDC, 1977–98, Hon. Alderman, 1998 (Vice-Chm., 1980–82, Chm., 1986–96, Housing Cttee). MP (Lab) Bolton SE, 1997–2010. Mem., Ext. Adv. Bd, Sch. of Chemistry, Univ. of Manchester, 2006–. Chm., Govt Affairs Cttee, RSC, 2012–. Chm., Care Not Killing Alliance Ltd, 2006–10 and 2012–. Trustee, SCI, 2011– (Hon. Mem., 2003). Hon. Fellow, Univ. of Bolton, 2005. Hon. FIChemE 2010. Hon. Dr Bolton, 2010. President's Award, RSC, 2006; Citizens Advice Parliamentarian of the Year Award, 2010. *Publications:* (jtly) Radiation Sterilization of Pharmaceutical and Biomedical Products, 1974; The Magic of Chemistry, 1985; James Lawrence Isherwood (1917–1989), 2013; Science and Politics: an unlikely mixture (autobiog.), vol. 1, 2014; contrib. chapters in books; numerous papers and reviews and articles in learned jls incl. Jl Chem. Soc., Perkin Trans, Tetrahedron, Chem. Comm., Sch. Sci. Rev., Heterocycles. *Recreations:* gardening, philately, cricket (spectator). *Address:* 3 Avoncliff Close, Bolton BL1 8BD. *T:* (01204) 491785. *E:* iddonb@hotmail.co.uk.

IDIENS, Dale; Depute Director, National Museums of Scotland, 2000–01 and Acting Director, 2001–02; Vice-Chair, Scottish Arts Council, 2002–05 (Member, 1998–2005; Acting Chair, 2004–05); *b* 13 May 1942; *d* of Richard Idiens and Ruth Christine Idiens (*née* Hattersley). *Educ:* High Wycombe High Sch.; Univ. of Leicester. BA (Hons); DipEd. Department of Art and Archaeology, Royal Scottish Museum, later National Museums of Scotland: Asst Keeper in charge of Ethnography, 1964; Dep. Keeper, 1979; Keeper, Dept of Hist. and Applied Art, 1983; Depute Dir (Collections), 1992. Mem. Council, Architectural Heritage Soc. of Scotland, 2003–06; Ind. Mem., Conservation Cttee, NT for Scotland, 2007–11. *Publications:* Traditional African Sculpture, 1969; Ancient American Art, 1971; (ed with K. G. Ponting) African Textiles, 1980; The Hausa of Northern Nigeria, 1981; Pacific Art, 1982; (contrib.) Indians and Europe, an Interdisciplinary Collection of Essays, 1987; Cook Islands Art, 1990; (contrib.) No Ordinary Journey: John Rae, Arctic explorer 1813–1893, 1993; articles and papers in Jl of the Polynesian Soc., African Arts, Textile History, Jl History of Collections; reviews and lectures. *Recreations:* travel, film, wine. *Address:* 97/10 East London Street, Edinburgh EH7 4BF. *T:* (0131) 557 8481. *Club:* Naval and Military.

IDLE, Eric; actor and writer; *b* 29 March 1943; *m* 1st, Lynn Ashley (marr. diss.); one *s*; 2nd, Tania Kosevich; one *d*. *Educ:* Royal Sch., Wolverhampton; Pembroke Coll., Cambridge (BA 1965; Pres., Cambridge Footlights, 1964–65). Pres., Prominent Features. *Stage* includes: I'm Just Wild About Harry, Edinburgh Fest., 1963; Monty Python Live at Drury Lane,

1974; Monty Python Live at the Hollywood Bowl, 1980; The Mikado, ENO, 1987, Houston Opera House, 1989; writer: Spamalot (musical), Chicago, 2004, NY, 2005, Palace Th., 2007; (with J. Du Prez) Not the Messiah, (He's a Very Naughty Boy) (comic oratorio), Toronto, 2007, toured Australia, NZ and USA, 2008, Royal Albert Hall, 2009; What About Dick?, LA, 2008; Rutlemania! The Tribute Concert, 2008; Monty Python Live (Mostly), 02 Arena, 2014; concert tours: Eric Idle Exploits Monty Python, USA, 2000; The Greedy Bastard Tour, USA, 2003; *television* includes: joint writer: The Frost Report, 1967; Marty Feldman, 1968–69; joint writer and actor: Monty Python's Flying Circus, 4 series, 1969–74; Rutland Weekend Television, 1978; actor: Do Not Adjust Your Set, 1968–69; Around the World in 80 Days, 1989; Nearly Departed, 1989; *films* include: joint writer and actor: And Now for Something Completely Different, 1970; Monty Python and the Holy Grail, 1974; Life of Brian, 1978; The Rutles, 1978; The Meaning of Life, 1982; Splitting Heirs, 1993; actor: The Adventures of Baron Munchausen, 1988; Nuns on the Run, 1990; Casper, 1995; Wind in the Willows, 1996. *Publications:* The Greedy Bastard Diary, 2005; *novels:* Hello Sailor, 1975; The Road to Mars, 1999; The Pythons Autobiography by the Pythons, 2003.

IDLE, Prof. Jeffrey Robert, PhD; CSci; CChem, FRSC, EurChem; CBiol, FRSB, EurProBiol; FBPhS; Visiting Professor and Research Fellow, Hepatology Research Group, Department of Clinical Research, University of Bern, since 2003; Scientific Contractor and Consultant, Laboratory of Metabolism, Center for Cancer Research, National Cancer Institute, National Institutes of Health, USA, since 2002; *b* 17 Sept. 1950; *s* of Robert William Idle and Margaret Joyce Idle (*née* Golightly). *Educ:* Hatfield Polytechnic (BSc 1972, BSc Hons 1973); St Mary's Hosp. Med. Sch. (PhD 1976). CChem 1987; FRSC 1987; CBiol 1999; FRSB (FIBiol 1999); EurChem 2000; EurProBiol 2000; CSci 2004; FBPhS (FBPharmacolS 2005). St Mary's Hospital Medical School, London: Lectr in Biochem., 1976; Lectr in Biochemical Pharmacol., 1976–83; Wellcome Trust Sen. Lectr, 1983–88; Reader in Pharmacogenetics, 1985–88; University of Newcastle upon Tyne: Prof. of Pharmacogenetics, 1988–95; Hd, Sch. of Clinical Med. Scis, 1992–95; Hd, Dept of Pharmacol. Scis, 1992–95; Consultant in Med. Genetics, Regl Hosp., Trondheim, 1996–99; Prof. in Medicine and Molecular Biol., Norwegian Univ. of Sci. and Technol., 1996–2004; Prof. of Pharmacology, Charles Univ., Prague, 2004–10. Founding Editor and Editor-in-Chief, Pharmacogenetics, 1991–98. Chief Executive: Genotype Ltd, 1993–95; VitOmega Internat., 1995–98; Pres., Radka LLC, 2009–10. Dir, Nivy Blacksmith Music sro, 1999–2010; Exec. Producer, Sixth Ave Records LLC, 2009–10. *Publications:* over 300 peer reviewed articles, reviews and chapters in internat. scientific and med. jls and books in the fields of pharmacogenetics, drug metabolism and metabolomics. *Recreation:* music and film.

IDRIS, Kamil E., PhD; Director General, World Intellectual Property Organization, 1997–2008 (Deputy Director General, 1994–97); Secretary General, International Union for the Protection of New Varieties of Plants, 1997–2008; *b* 26 Aug. 1954. *Educ:* Univ. of Cairo (BA); Univ. of Geneva (PhD Internat. Law); Univ. of Ohio (Master Internat. Affairs); Inst. of Public Admin, Khartoum (DPA); Univ. of Khartoum (LLB). Part-time Journalist, El-Ayam and El-Sahafa (newspapers), Sudan, 1971–79; Lecturer: in Philosophy and Jurisp., Univ. of Cairo, 1976–77; in Jurisp., Ohio Univ., 1978; Asst Dir, Res. Dept, subseq. Dep. Dir, Legal Dept, Min. of Foreign Affairs, Sudan, 1978; Vice-Consul in Switzerland, and Legal Advr, Sudan Perm. Mission to UN Office, Geneva, 1979–82; Sen. Prog. Officer, Develt Co-operation and External Relns Bureau for Africa, 1982–85, Dir, Develt Co-operation and External Relns Bureau for Arab and Central and European Countries, 1985–94, WIPO. Prof. of Public Internat. Law, Univ. of Khartoum. Advocate and Comr of Oaths, Republic of Sudan. Member: UN Internat. Law Commn, 1992–96, 2000–01; Sudan Bar Assoc.; African Jurists Assoc. Comdr, Ordre Nat. du Lion (Senegal), 1998. *Publications:* articles on law, econs, jurisp. and aesthetics in jls.

IDRIS JONES, Denise; *see* Jones, Denise I.

IEMMA, Hon. Morris; MP (ALP) Lakemba, New South Wales, 1999–2008; Premier of New South Wales, 2005–08; *b* July 1961; *s* of George and Maria Iemma; *m* 1997, Santina Raiti; three *s* one *d*. *Educ:* Narwee Boys' High Sch.; Univ. of Technology, Sydney (LLB); Univ. of Sydney (BEc). Industrial Officer, Commonwealth Bank Officers Assoc., 1984–86; Advr to Senator Graham Richardson, Minister for Envmt, Arts, Sport, Tourism and Territories, Australian Nat. Parlt, 1986–91. Government of New South Wales: MP (ALP) Hurstville, 1991–99; Member: Parly Constitutional Fixed Terms Cttee, 1991–92; Parly Regulation Rev. Cttee, 1991–95; Parly Sec. to the Premier, 1995–99; Minister: for Public Works and Services, 1999–2003; Assisting the Premier on Citizenship, 1999–2003; for Sport and Recreation, 2001–03; for Health, 2003–05; for Citizenship, 2005–08; for State and Regl Develt, 2006–07; Treasurer, 2005–06. Mem., ALP, 1977–. *Recreations:* all sports, particularly Australian Rules, league and soccer, blues music, cinema.

IFE, Prof. Barry William, CBE 2000; PhD; Principal, Guildhall School of Music & Drama, since 2004; *b* 19 June 1947; *s* of Bernard Edward Ife and Joan Mary (*née* Thacker); *m* 1st, 1968, Anne Elizabeth Vernon (marr. diss. 1985); 2nd, 1986, Christine Mary Whiffen (marr. diss. 1998); two *s*; 3rd, 2012, Dr Trudi Laura Darby. *Educ:* King's Coll., London (BA Hons 1968; FKC 1992); Birkbeck Coll., London (PhD 1984). ALCM 1965. Asst Lectr in Spanish, 1969–71, Lectr, 1971–72, Univ. of Nottingham; Lectr in Spanish, Birkbeck Coll., London, 1972–88; King's College, London: Cervantes Prof of Spanish, 1988–2004; Hd, Sch. of Humanities, 1989–96; Vice-Principal, 1997–2003; Actg Principal, 2003–04. Leverhulme Res. Fellow, 1983–85. Trustee: Boise Foundn, 2004–12; Mendelssohn Scholarship Foundn, 2004–12; Chm., Mendelssohn Boise Foundn, 2013–; City Arts Trust, 2004–; Mem. Bd, Universities UK, 2010–13. Gov., RAM, 1998–2004. President: British Harpsichord Soc., 2009–; Incorporated Soc. of Musicians, 2014–15. Fellow, Birkbeck, Univ. of London, 2007. FRCM 2013. Hon. FRAM 2001. *Publications:* Dos Versiones de Piramo y Tisbe, 1974; Francisco de Quevedo: La Vida del Buscón, 1977; Anthology of Early Keyboard Methods, 1981; Domenico Scarlatti, 1985; Reading and Fiction in Golden-Age Spain, 1985; Early Spanish Keyboard Music, 1986; Antonio Soler: Twelve Sonatas, 1989; Christopher Columbus: Journal of the First Voyage, 1990; Lectura y Ficción, 1992; Letters from America, 1992; Miguel de Cervantes: Exemplary Novels, 1993; Corpus of Contemporary Spanish, 1995; Don Quixote's Diet, 2000; contrib. articles and reviews to Bull. Hispanic Studies, MLR, Jl Inst. Romance Studies, TLS, Music and Letters, Eighteenth Century Music and others. *Recreations:* music, literature, sorting things out. *Address:* Guildhall School of Music & Drama, Barbican, EC2Y 8DT. *E:* barry.ife@gsmd.ac.uk; Hasketon Grange, Grundisburgh Road, Hasketon, Woodbridge, Suffolk IP13 6HN.

IGGULDEN, Conn Francis Harry Nicholls; author, since 2002; *b* Hillingdon, London, 24 Feb. 1971; *s* of Henry and late Kathy Iggulden; *m* 1997, Ella D'Urso; two *s* two *d*. *Educ:* Merchant Taylors' Sch., Middx; Queen Mary and Westfield Coll., London Univ. (BA Hons); Univ. of Greenwich (PGCE). Hd of English, St Gregory's RC High Sch., Kenton, Middx, 1999–2001. *Publications:* The Gates of Rome, 2003; The Death of Kings, 2004; The Field of Swords, 2005; The Gods of War, 2006; The Dangerous Book for Boys, 2006; Blackwater, 2006; The Dangerous Book for Boys Yearbook, 2007; Wolf of the Plains, 2007; Lords of the Bow, 2008; Bones of the Hills, 2008; The Dangerous Book of Heroes, 2009; Tollins, 2009; Empire of Silver, 2010; Conqueror, 2011; Quantum of Tweed, 2012; Emperor: the blood of gods, 2013; Wars of the Roses: Stormbird, 2013; Wars of the Roses: Trinity, 2014. *Recreations:* carpentry, reading, copying out poems by hand, Tae Kwon Do (Mem., Tae Kwon Do Assoc. of GB). *Address:* c/o A. M. Heath, 6 Warwick Court, WC1R 5DJ. *W:* www.conniggulden.com, www.twitter.com/Conn_Iggulden.

IGNARRO, Prof. Louis J., PhD; Professor, Department of Molecular and Medical Pharmacology, University of California, Los Angeles, since 1985; *b* 31 May 1941; *m* 1st (marr. diss.); one *d*; 2nd, 1997, Sharon Elizabeth Williams. *Educ:* Long Beach High Sch.; Columbia Univ. (BA 1962); Univ. of Minnesota (PhD 1966). Post-doctoral Fellow, NIH, 1966–68; Hd, Biochem. and Anti-inflammatory Prog., Geigy Pharmaceuticals, 1968–73; Asst Prof., 1973–79, Prof., 1979–85, Dept of Pharmacol., Sch. of Medicine, Tulane Univ. Mem., US Nat. Acad. of Scis. Nobel Prize for Medicine (jtly), 1998. *Publications:* articles in scientific jls. *Address:* Department of Molecular and Medical Pharmacology, University of California, 10833 Le Conte Avenue, Los Angeles, CA 90095, USA.

IGNATIEFF, Prof. Hon. Michael; PC (Can.) 2010; PhD; writer; Edward R. Murrow Professor of Press, Politics and Public Policy, Kennedy School of Government, Harvard University, since 2014 (Edward R. Murrow Professor of Practice, 2012–14); *b* 12 May 1947; *s* of George Ignatieff and Alison (*née* Grant); *m* 1st, 1977, Susan Barrowclough (marr. diss. 1998); one *s* one *d*; 2nd, 1999, Suzanna Zsohar. *Educ:* Upper Canada Coll., Toronto; Univ. of Toronto (BA 1969); Cambridge Univ. (MA 1978); Harvard Univ. (PhD 1976). Asst Prof. of History, Univ. of BC, 1976–78; Sen. Res. Fellow, King's Coll., Cambridge, 1978–84; Vis. Fellow, Ecole des Hautes Etudes, Paris, 1985; Alistair Horne Fellow, St Antony's Coll., Oxford, 1993–95; Visiting Professor: Univ. of Calif, Berkeley, 1997; LSE, 1998–2000; Carr Prof. of Human Rights Policy, Kennedy Sch. of Govt, Harvard Univ., 2000–06; Sen. Resident, Massey Coll., Toronto, 2011–12; Prof., Munk Sch. of Global Affairs, Univ. of Toronto, 2011–14. MP (L) Etobicoke-Lakeshore, Canada, 2006–11; contested (L) same seat, 2011. Leader, Liberal Party of Canada and of the Opposition, 2009–11. Presenter: Voices, Channel 4, 1986; Thinking Aloud, BBC TV Series, 1987–88; The Late Show, BBC TV, 1989–95; Blood and Belonging, BBC, 1993; Trial of Freedom, C4, 1999; The Future of War, BBC, 2000. Editorial Columnist, The Observer, 1990–93. Hon. DPhil Stirling, 1996; Hon. Dr: Bishop's, 1995; Trinity Coll., Toronto, 1999; New Brunswick, 2001; Queen's, 2001; Western Ontario, 2001; McGill, 2002; Regina, 2003; Whitman Coll., 2004; Niagara, 2008; Tilborg, 2009. *Publications:* A Just Measure of Pain, 1978; The Needs of Strangers, 1984; The Russian Album, 1987 (Canadian Governor General's Award, 1988; Heinemann Prize, RSL, 1988); Asya, 1991; Scar Tissue, 1993; Blood and Belonging, 1993; The Warrior's Honour: ethnic war and the modern conscience, 1998; Isaiah Berlin: a life, 1998; Virtual War: Kosovo and beyond, 2000; The Rights Revolution, 2000; Human Rights as Politics and Idolatry, 2001; Empire Lite, 2003; Charlie Johnson in the Flames, 2003; The Lesser Evil: political ethics in an age of terror, 2004; True Patriot Love, 2009; Fire and Ashes: success and failure in politics, 2013. *Recreations:* walking, talking, wine, theatre, music. *Address:* c/o United Agents LLP, 12–26 Lexington Street, W1F 0LE.

IKRAM, Tanweer; a District Judge (Magistrates' Courts), since 2009; Diversity and Community Relations Judge, since 2011 (Deputy Lead Diversity and Community Relations Judge, since 2013); *b* Taplow, Bucks, 1965; *s* of Mohammed Ikram and Azmat Sultana; *m* 2007, Nusrat Baig. *Educ:* Univ. of Wolverhampton (LLB 1988); Nottingham Trent Univ. (Postgrad. Dip. Mgt of Legal Practice 2003). Called to the Bar, Inner Temple, 1990; Partner, IBB Solicitors, 1993–2007; Consultant, ABV Solicitors, 2007–09. Lectr, BPP Law Sch., 2002–04. Vis. Fellow, London South Bank Univ., 2010–; Hon. Vis. Prof., Pakistan Law Coll., Lahore, 2010–. Hon. Pres., London Criminal Courts Solicitors' Assoc., 2007–08. Fellow, Soc. of Advanced Legal Studies, 2009. Hon. LLD West London, 2012. *Publications:* (Contributing Ed.) Archbold Magistrates' Court Criminal Practice, 2013, 2014, 2015, 2016. *Recreations:* classic cars, travel. *Address:* Westminster Magistrates' Court, 181 Marylebone Road, NW1 5BR. *T:* (020) 3126 3050. *E:* tan@ikram.eu.

ILCHESTER, 10th Earl of, *cr* 1756; **Robin Maurice Fox-Strangways;** Baron Ilchester of Ilchester, Somerset, and Baron Strangways of Woodsford, Dorset, 1741; Baron Ilchester and Stavordale of Redlynch, Somerset, 1747; *b* 2 Sept. 1942; *s* of Hon. Raymond Fox-Strangways, 2nd *s* of 8th Earl of Ilchester and Margaret Vera (*née* Force); *S* uncle, 2006; *m* 1969, Margaret Elizabeth, *d* of late Geoffrey Miles; one *s* one *d*. *Educ:* Loughborough Coll. *Heir:* *s* Lord Stavordale, *qv*.

ILES, Isobel Christine, (Chrissie); Anne and Joel Ehrenkranz Curator, Whitney Museum of American Art, New York, since 1997; *b* Beirut, Lebanon, 30 Nov. 1957; *d* of Albert Ronald Iles and Isobel Campbell Iles. *Educ:* Univ. of Bristol (BA Jt Hons Hist. of Art and Political Hist. 1979); City Univ., London (Post-grad. Dip. Arts Admin 1980). Curator, Waterloo Gall., London, 1980–82; Curatorial Asst, B2 Gall., London, 1982–84; freelance curator, London, 1984–86; Curatorial Asst, Matt's Gall., London, 1986–88; Hd of Exhibns, MOMA, Oxford, 1988–97. *Publications:* monographs and exhibn catalogues; contribs to jls incl. Frieze Mag., Artforum, Parkett, Coil Mag. of the Moving Image, Performance Mag. *Recreations:* contemporary art, medieval, renaissance and eighteenth century art and architecture. *Address:* Whitney Museum of American Art, 99 Gansevoort Street, New York, NY 10014, USA. *T:* (212) 5703600. *E:* chrissie_iles@whitney.org.

ILEY, Jason; Chairman and Chief Executive Officer, Sony Music, since 2014; *b* Farnborough, 15 Jan. 1969; *s* of Michael and Zandra Iley; *m* 1997, Nadia Adorni; two *s*. *Educ:* Trent Poly. (BA Hons Modern Eur. Studies). Product Manager: Epic, 1995–97; Polydor, 1997–2000; Gen. Manager, Island Records, 2000–05; Man. Dir, 2005–06, Pres., 2006–13, Mercury Records; Pres., ROC Nation Records, 2013–14. *Recreations:* cycling, running. *Address:* Sony Music Entertainment, 9 Derry Street, W8 5HY. *T:* (020) 7361 8000.

ILIC, Fiona Jane; *see* Alexander, F. J.

ILIESCU, Ion; Member of Senate, Romania, 1996–2000 and 2004–08; President of Romania, 1990–96 and 2000–04; *b* 3 March 1930; *s* of Alexandru and Maria Iliescu; *m* 1951, Elena Şerbănescu. *Educ:* Bucharest Poly. Inst.; Moscow Energy Inst. Design Engr and Researcher, Energy Engrg Inst., Bucharest, 1955–56; Chm., Nat. Water Resources Council, 1979–84; Dir, Tech. Publishing House, 1984–89. President: Council, Nat. Salvation Front, 1989–90; Provisional Council for Nat. Unity, 1990; Pres. of Romania, 1990–92, then, on first constitutional mandate, 1992–96; Pres., Social Democratic Party (formerly Party of Social Democracy) of Romania, 1996–2000, now Hon. Pres. *Publications:* Global Issues: Creativity, 1992; Revolution and Reform, 1993; Romania in Europe and in the World, 1994; The Revolution as I lived it, 1995; Diplomatic Autumn, 1995; Moments of History, vol. I 1995, vols II and III 1996; Romanian-American Dialogues, 1998; Political Life Between Dialogue and Violence, 1998; Where to? - Romanian Society, 1999; Hope Reborn, 2001; Romanian Revolution, 2001; Integration and Globalisation, 2003; The Great Shock at the End of a Short Century, 2004; Romanian Culture and European Identity, 2005; For Sustainable Development, 2005; Romania and the World at the Crossroad of XX and XXI Centuries, 2009; After 20 Years, 2010; Fragments of Life and Lived History, 2011. *Recreations:* reading, theatre, opera, classical music concerts. *Address:* Str. Molière 3, Bucharest, Romania.

ILIFFE, family name of **Baron Iliffe**.

ILIFFE, 3rd Baron *cr* 1933, of Yattendon; **Robert Peter Richard Iliffe;** DL; Chairman, Yattendon Group (formerly Investment Trust) PLC, since 1984; *b* Oxford, 22 Nov. 1944; *s* of late Hon. W. H. R. Iliffe and Mrs Iliffe; *S* uncle, 1996; *m* 1966, Rosemary Anne Skipwith; three *s* one *d* (of whom one *s* one *d* are twins). *Educ:* Eton; Christ Church, Oxford. Subsidiary cos of Yattendon Group (formerly Investment Trust): Marina Developments Ltd; Iliffe News & Media Ltd; Yattendon Estates Ltd; Dir, Scottish Provincial Press. Former Chairman: Birmingham Post and Mail Ltd; West Midlands Press Ltd; Dillons Newsagents; Coventry Newspapers Ltd; Cambridge Newspapers Ltd; Herts & Essex Newspapers Ltd; Staffs

Newspapers Ltd. Member of Council, RASE, 1972– (Chm., 1994–98). Pres., Rare Breeds Survival Trust, 1999–2003. Mem., Governing Body, Bradfield Coll., 1996–2008 (Warden, 2001–06). High Sheriff of Warwicks, 1983–84; DL Berks, 2007. *Recreations:* yachting, shooting, fishing, old cars. *Heir: s* Hon. Edward Richard Iliffe, *b* 13 Sept. 1968. *Address:* Barn Close, Yattendon, Thatcham, Berks RG18 0UX. *Clubs:* Boodle's; Royal Yacht Squadron (Cdre, 2005–09).

ILIFFE, Prof. John; Professor of African History, University of Cambridge, 1990–2006, now Emeritus; Fellow of St John's College, Cambridge, since 1971; *b* 1 May 1939; 2nd *s* of late Arthur Ross Iliffe and Violet Evelyn Iliffe. *Educ:* Framlingham Coll.; Peterhouse, Cambridge (BA 1961; MA; PhD 1965; LittD 1990). Lectr, then Reader, in History, Univ. of Dar-es-Salaam, 1965–71; University of Cambridge: Asst Dir of Res. in Hist., 1971–80; Reader in African Hist., 1980–90. FBA 1989–2006. *Publications:* Tanganyika under German Rule, 1969; A Modern History of Tanganyika, 1979; The Emergence of African Capitalism, 1983; The African Poor: a history, 1987; Famine in Zimbabwe, 1989; Africans: the history of a continent, 1995, 2nd edn 2007; East African Doctors: a history of the modern profession, 1998; Honour in African History, 2005; The African Aids Epidemic: a history, 2006; Obasanjo, Nigeria and the World, 2011. *Recreation:* cricket. *Address:* St John's College, Cambridge CB2 1TP. *T:* (01223) 338714. *Club:* MCC.

ILLINGWORTH, David Jeremy, FCA; Partner, 1975–2001, Senior Adviser, 2001–04, KPMG (formerly KMG Thomson McLintock); President, Institute of Chartered Accountants in England and Wales, 2003–04; *b* Stockport, Cheshire, 28 April 1947; *s* of late Prof. Charles Raymond Illingworth and Joan Ellen Mary Illingworth; *m* 1968, Annie Vincenza Bailey; two *d. Educ:* Stockport Sch.; Emmanuel Coll., Cambridge (BA 1968). ACA 1971, FCA 1972. Trainee, KMG Thomson McLintock, 1968–71. Non-exec. Dir, Nuclear Decommng Authy, 2004–11 (Chm., Audit Cttee). Independent Chairman: Trinity Retirement Benefit Scheme, 2006–; Places for People Retirement Benefit Scheme, 2011–; Wolseley plc Pension Scheme, 2011–. Mem., Cttee, Manchester Soc. of Chartered Accountants, 1983–2004 (Pres., 1992–93); Institute of Chartered Accountants in England and Wales: Mem. Council, 1997–2006; Vice-Pres., 2001–02; Dep. Pres., 2002–03; Chairman: NW Regl Bd, 2004–07; Staff Pension Fund, 2007–14; Foundn charity, 2007–13; Ind. Chm., Combined Nuclear Pension Plan, 2014–. NW Regl Council Mem., CBI, 1993–2003. Mem. Cttee, Duke of Westminster Awards for Business and Industry in the NW, 1995–2001. Mem. Council, 2006–, Trustee and Mem. Exec. Cttee, 2007–, Chm., Audit Cttee, 2009–, C&G. Governor: Oldham Hulme Grammar Sch. (formerly Hulme Grammar Sch., Oldham), 1992– (Chm., 2008–); Withington Girls Sch., 2006– (Treas., 2007–). FRSA. Liveryman, Co. of Chartered Accountants, 2002– (Mem. Court, 2007–; Master, 2014–15). *Recreations:* travel, golf, music, theatre, opera, walking. *Address:* Alphin, 7 Park Lane, Greenfield, Oldham OL3 7DX. *T:* (01457) 875971. *Clubs:* St James' (Manchester); Saddleworth Golf (Oldham).

ILLINGWORTH, Raymond, CBE 1973; cricketer; Manager, Yorkshire County Cricket Club, 1979–84; Chairman of Selectors, Test and County Cricket Board, 1994–96; and Manager, England Cricket Team, 1995–96; *b* 8 June 1932; *s* of late Frederick Spencer Illingworth and Ida Illingworth; *m* 1958, Shirley Milnes; two *d. Educ:* Wesley Street Sch., Farsley, Pudsey. Yorkshire County cricketer; capped, 1955. Captain: MCC, 1969; Leics CCC, 1969–78; Yorks CCC, 1982–83. Toured: West Indies, 1959–60; Australia twice (once as Captain), 1962–63 and 1970–71. Played in 66 Test Matches (36 as Captain). Pres., Yorks CCC, 2010–12. Hon. MA Hull, 1983; Hon. Dr Leeds Metropolitan, 1997. *Publications:* Spinners Wicket, 1969; The Young Cricketer, 1972; Spin Bowling, 1979; Captaincy, 1980; Yorkshire and Back, 1980; (with Kenneth Gregory) The Ashes, 1982; The Tempestuous Years 1977–83, 1987; One Man Committee, 1996. *Recreations:* golf, bridge. *Address:* The Mistle, 4 Calverley Lane, Farsley, Pudsey, West Yorkshire LS28 5LB.

ILLSLEY, Anthony Kim; non-executive Chairman, Plastic Logic Ltd, since 2006; *b* 8 July 1956. *Educ:* Loughborough Grammar Sch.; Bath Univ. (BSc Business Admin). Mktg and Sales Trainee, subseq. Gp Brand Manager, Colgate Palmolive, 1979–84; joined Pepsico, 1984: European Mktg Manager, subseq. Ops Dir, Pepsicola International; resp. for business in France, Belgium and Scandinavia, Pepsi-Cola; President: Pepsicola Japan; Asia Pacific Div., Hong Kong; Walkers Snack Foods UK Ltd, 1995–98; CEO, Telewest Communications, 1998–2000. Non-executive Chairman: Power Paper Ltd, 2005–06; Velocix Ltd, 2007–09; non-executive Director: EasyJet, 2000–05; GCap Media plc (formerly Capital Radio), 2000–08; Northern Foods plc, 2006–11; Sepura plc, 2007–13; KCOM Gp plc, 2009–; Datalase Ltd, 2009–13; Camelot UK Lotteries Ltd, 2011–; Quindell, 2015–.

ILLSLEY, Eric Evlyn; *b* 9 April 1955; *s* of John and Maude Illsley; *m* 1978, Dawn Webb; two *d. Educ:* Barnsley Holgate Grammar Sch.; Leeds Univ. (LLB Hons 1977). NUM, Yorkshire Area: Compensation Officer, 1978–81; Asst Head of General Dept, 1981–84; Head of Gen. Dept and Chief Admin. Officer, 1984–87. MP Barnsley Central, 1987–Feb. 2011 (Lab, 1987–2010, Ind, 2010–11). An Opposition Whip, 1991–94; Opposition spokesperson: on health, 1994–95; on local govt, April–Oct. 1995; on NI, 1995–97. Member, Select Committee: on televising proceedings of H of C, 1988–91; on Energy, 1987–91; on Procedure, 1991–2010; on Foreign Affairs, 1997–2010; Mem., Speaker's Panel of Chairmen, 1999–2010; Chm., All Party Parly Packaging Manufg Industry Gp, 2005–10; Jt Chm., All Party Parly Glass Gp, 1992–2002; Vice Chm., All Party Parly Gp on Occupnl Pensions, 1997–2011 (Treas., 1993–97); Mem., Parly and Scientific Cttee, 1987–2011 (Jt Hon. Sec., 1994–95; Jt Dep. Chm., 1995–98; Vice-Pres., 1998–2001). Sec., Barnsley Constit. Lab. Pty, 1980–83 (Treas., 1979–80); Sec. and Election Agent, Yorks S Eur. Constit. Lab. Pty, 1983–87; Treas., Yorks Gp of Lab. MPs, 1988–2010. Member Executive Committee: CPA, 1997–2010; IPU, 1997–2010. *Recreation:* golf.

ILLSTON, Prof. John Michael, CEng, FICE; Director of the Hatfield Polytechnic, 1982–87, Professor and Professor Emeritus, 1987, Fellow, 1991; *b* 17 June 1928; *s* of Alfred Charles Illston and Ethel Marian Illston; *m* 1951, Olga Elizabeth Poulter; one *s* two *d. Educ:* Wallington County Grammar Sch.; King's Coll., Univ. of London (BScEng, PhD, DScEng; FKC 1985). CEng, FICE 1975. Water engr, then schoolmaster, 1949–59; Lectr, Sen. Lectr and Reader in Civil Engrg, King's Coll., London, 1959–77; Dir of Studies in Civil Engrg, Dean of Engrg, and Dep. Dir, Hatfield Polytechnic, 1977–82. Member: Commonwealth Scholarships Commn, 1983–92; Engrg Bd, SERC, 1983–86; Engrg Council, 1984–90; Council, BTEC, 1986–89; Chm., CNAA Cttee for Engrg, 1987–91; Visitor, Building Res. Stn, 1989–95. Chairman: Govs, Bishop Wordsworth Sch., 1994–98; Salisbury Br., CRUSE Bereavement Care, 1998–2001; Salisbury and Dist, Univ. of Third Age, 2002–05. *Publications:* (with J. M. Dinwoodie and A. A. Smith) Concrete, Timber and Metals, 1979; (ed) Construction Materials, 2nd edn 1994, 3rd edn 2001; contrib. Cement and Concrete Res. and Magazine of Concrete Res. *Address:* 10 Merrifield Road, Ford, Salisbury, Wilts SP4 6DF.

ILVES, Toomas Hendrik, Hon. GCB 2006; President of Republic of Estonia, 2006–Oct. 2016; *b* Stockholm, 26 Dec. 1953; *m* Evelin Int-Lambert; one *d*, and one *s* one *d* by a previous marriage. *Educ:* Columbia Univ., USA (BA Psychol. 1976); Pennsylvania Univ. (MA Psychol. 1978). Res. Asst, Dept of Psychol., Columbia Univ., 1974–79; Asst Dir and English teacher, Open Educn Center, Englewood, NJ, 1979–81; Dir, Literary Storefront Soc., Vancouver, 1981–83; Lectr in Estonian Lit. and Linguistics, Dept of Interdisciplinary Studies, Simon Fraser Univ., Vancouver, 1983–84; analyst and researcher, res. unit, 1984–88, Hd, Estonian desk, 1988–93, Radio Free Europe, Munich; Ambassador of Estonia to USA, Canada and Mexico, 1993–96; Minister of Foreign Affairs, 1996–98; Chm., N Atlantic Inst., 1998; Minister of Foreign Affairs, 1999–2002; MP (Moderate People's Party) Estonia, 2002–04; MEP (Socialist Gp), 2004–06. Co-Dir, World Develt Report Steering Gp on Internet and Develt, World Bank, 2014. Chairman: EU Task Force on e-Health, 2011–12; Steering Bd, Eur. Cloud Computing, 2012–14; High-Level Panel on Global Internet Cooperation and Governance Mechanisms, Internat. Corp. for Assigned Names and Numbers, 2013; Global Agenda Council on Cyber Security, WEF, 2014. Democracy Award, Nat. Democratic Inst., 2013; Freedom Award, Atlantic Council Expert Assignments, 2014. Knight First Cl., Royal Norwegian Order of Merit, 1999; Grand Cross, Order of Honour (Greece), 1999; Grand Comdr, Légion d'Honneur (France), 2001; Third Cl. Order of the Seal (Estonia), 2004; Three Star Order of Republic (Latvia), 2004; Collar: Order of Cross of Terra Mariana (Estonia), 2006; Order of Nat. Coat of Arms (Estonia), 2008; Order of White Rose (Finland), 2007; Golden Fleece Order (Georgia), 2007; Collar, Order of Isabel la Católica (Spain), 2007; Order of Vytautas the Gt with the Golden Chain (Lithuania), 2008; Grand Cross, Order of Netherlands Lion, 2008; Grand Cordon, Leopold of Belgium, 2008; Chain, Three Star Order of Republic (Latvia), 2009; Grand Cross, Order of Merit of Republic (Hungary), 2009; Order of St George (Georgia), 2011; Collar, Nat. Order Star (Romania), 2011; Dostyk, Star of Award 1 (Kazakhstan), 2012; Grand Collar, Nat. Order of Merit of Republic (Malta), 2012; Cross of Recognition 1 Cl. (Lativa), 2012; Grand Cross, Special Cl. Order of Merit (Germany), 2013; Order of White Eagle (Poland), 2013; Grand Cross, Order of St Olav (Norway). *Publications:* Eesti jõudmine: compilation of speeches and writings from 1986–2006, 2006; A nagy európai fal?, 2007; Atvērtā pasaule un nacionālās vērtības: runas, raksti, viedokļi, 2010; Omalla äänellä, 2011; Suurem Eesti: a selection of the President's speeches and essays from 2006–2011, 2011; In Our Own Voice, 2012; The Head of State Speaking, 2014. *Address:* Office of the President, A. Weizenbergi 39, 15050 Tallinn, Estonia. *T:* 6316202, *Fax:* 6316250.

IMBERT, family name of **Baron Imbert**.

IMBERT, Baron *cr* 1999 (Life Peer), of New Romney, in the county of Kent; **Peter Michael Imbert,** Kt 1988; CVO 2008; QPM 1980; Lord-Lieutenant of Greater London, 1998–2008; Commissioner, Metropolitan Police, 1987–93 (Deputy Commissioner, 1985–87); *b* 27 April 1933; *s* of late William Henry Imbert and of Frances May (*née* Hodge); *m* 1956, Iris Rosina (*née* Dove); one *s* two *d. Educ:* Harvey Grammar Sch., Folkestone, Kent. Joined Metropolitan Police, 1953; Asst Chief Constable, Surrey Constabulary, 1976, Dep. Chief Constable, 1977; Chief Constable, Thames Valley Police, 1979–85. Metropolitan Police Anti-Terrorist Squad, 1973–75; Police negotiator at Balcome Street siege, Dec. 1975; visited Holland following Moluccan sieges, and Vienna following siege of OPEC building by terrorists, Dec. 1975. Lectures in UK and Europe to police and military on terrorism and siege situations; lecture tours to Australia, 1977, 1980 and 1986, to advise on terrorism and sieges, and to Canada, 1981 re practical effects on police forces of recommendations of Royal Commn on Criminal Procedure; Vis. Internat. Fellow, Australian Police Staff College, 1994 and 1997. Leader, Internat. Criminal Justice Delegn to Russia, 1993. Sec., Nat. Crime Cttee-ACPO Council, 1980–83 (Chm., 1983–85). Non-executive Director: Securicor Gp, 1993–2001; Camelot Gp, 1994–2001; Retainagroup, 1995–2004; non-executive Chairman: Capital Eye Security, 1997–2014; iRisk, 2013–15. Member: Gen. Advisory Council, BBC, 1980–87; Criminal Justice Consultative Cttee, 1992–93; Mental Health Foundn, Cttee of Inquiry into Care in the Community for the Severely Mentally Ill, 1994; Academic Consultative Cttee, King George VI and Queen Elizabeth Foundn of St Catharine's, Cumberland Lodge, Windsor, 1983–2001; Ministerial Adv. Gp, Royal Parks, 1993–2001; Public Policy Cttee, RAC, 1993–2003. Trustee, Queen Elizabeth Foundn of St Catharine's, 1988–2001. Chm., Surrey CCC Youth Trust, 1993–96; Hon. Life Vice Pres., Surrey CCC, 2004–; President: Richmond Horse Show, 1993–99; Littlestone Golf Club, 2013–. Gov., Harvey Grammar Sch., 1994–2002. CCMI (CBIM 1982). DL Greater London, 1994. Hon. DLitt Reading, 1987; Hon. DBA IMCB, 1989. *Publications:* occasional articles and book reviews. *Recreations:* bad bridge, coarse golf, talking about my grandchildren. *Address:* House of Lords, SW1A 0PW.

IMBERT-TERRY, Sir Michael Edward Stanley, 5th Bt *cr* 1917, of Strete Ralegh, Whimple, Co. Devon; *b* 18 April 1950; *s* of Major Sir Edward Henry Bouhier Imbert-Terry, 3rd Bt, MC, and Jean (who *m* 1983, 6th Baron Sackville), *d* of late Arthur Stanley Garton; *S* brother, 1985; *m* 1975, Frances Dorothy, *d* of late Peter Scott, Ealing; two *s* two *d. Educ:* Cranleigh. *Heir: s* Brychan Edward Imbert-Terry, *b* 1975.

IMBODEN, Dr Christoph Niklaus; consultant ecologist; *b* 28 April 1946; *s* of Max Imboden and Elisabeth Imboden-Stahel; one *s* one *d*; *m* 2009, Maria Reich-Rohrwig. *Educ:* Univ. of Basel (PhD). New Zealand Wildlife Service: Sen. Scientist, 1977; Asst Dir (Research), 1978; Dir-Gen., ICBP, later BirdLife Internat., 1980–96; Interim CEO, WWF Switzerland, 2002–03. Former Mem., Bd of Dirs, Plantlife International. Premio Gaia, Sicily, 1993; RSPB Conservation Medal, 1993. Officer, Order of the Golden Ark (Netherlands), 1996. *Publications:* papers on ornithology, ecology, conservation. *Recreations:* classical music, birdwatching, hill-walking, travelling.

IMISON, Dame Tamsyn, DBE 1998; education strategist; Headteacher, Hampstead School, 1984–2000; *b* 1 May 1937; *m* 1958, Michael Imison; two *d* (one *s* decd). *Educ:* Hitchin Girls' GS; Milham Ford Sch., Oxford; Somerville Coll., Oxford (Hon. Fellow, 1999); Queen Mary Coll., London (BSc Hons Zoology 1964; Hon. Fellow, 2004); Ruskin Sch. of Drawing and Fine Art, Oxford; Inst. of Education, London Univ. (PGCE 1972; Hon. Fellow, 2001); Open Univ. (Cert. of Prof. Develt in Educn 1994; MA Educn 1996). Freelance scientific, exhibn and illustration work for Oxford Mus., British Mus. (Natural History), and Publisher's Editor, Elsevier, 1960–70; Teacher: Brentford Sch. for Girls, 1972–76; Pimlico Sch., 1976–79; Abbey Wood Sch., 1979–84. Member: Secondary Exam. Council, 1986–88 (Chair, A Level and GCSE Biology and Music Cttees); Secondary Heads Council, 1993–98; SHA Exec., 1994–98; various DES Steering Gps; Adv. Gp on Raising Achievement of Ethnic-minority Children; Dir, CRAC Council, 1996–2002; Mem., Nat. Adv. Cttee on Creativity and Cultural Educn, 1997–99; Founder, Nat. Schs Playwright Commng Gp, 1995–2004; Heads' Appraiser, GDST, 1998–2004; Director: Lifelong Learning Foundn, 1999–; 5x5x5=creativity, 2007–; Vice-Pres., Soc. for Promoting the Trng of Women, 2002–12; Trustee: Menerva (formerly 300 Gp) Educnl Trust, 1990–99 (Patron, 2001–); Soc. for Furtherance of Critical Philosophy (also Chair), 1994–; I Can (Special Needs charity), 1997–2001; Eastfeast, 2005–. Mem. Council, UCS, 1995–2002. Patron: Explore (formerly Students Exploring Marriage), 2001–10; Campaign for Learning, 2003–. Scientific Fellow, Zoological Soc. of London, 1966–2012; FRSA 1995. *Publications:* (contrib.) Education 14–19: critical perspectives, 1997; (contrib.) New Teachers in an Urban Comprehensive School, 1997; Managing ICT in the Secondary School, 2001; (contrib.) Enquiring Minds, 2004; (contrib.) Creativity in Education, 2001; scientific illustrations in textbooks; *editor:* Comprehensive Achievements: all our geese are swans, 2013. *Recreations:* fun, theatre, painting, gardening, walking, swimming, sailing, singing. *Address:* Magnolia House, Station Road, Halesworth, Suffolk IP19 8BZ. *T:* (01986) 873354. *E:* tamsyn_imison@mac.com.

IMPEY, Dr Edward Alexander, FSA, FRHistS; Director-General and Master of the Royal Armouries, since 2013; *b* 28 May 1962; *s* of late Oliver Richard Impey and Jane Impey (*née* Mellanby); *m* 2008, Karen Lundgren; two *d. Educ:* Dragon Sch., Oxford; Bedales Sch. (Schol.); Oriel Coll., Oxford (BA; MA; MPhil; DPhil 1991). FRHistS 2011. British Acad. Post-doctoral Res. Fellow, Oriel Coll., Oxford, 1992–95; Asst Curator, Historic Bldgs, 1995–97, Curator, 1997–2002, Historic Royal Palaces; English Heritage: Dir of Res. and Standards, 2002–09; Dir, Conservation and Protection, 2009–10; Dir, Heritage Protection and Planning, 2010–13. Chercheur Associé, Univ. of Caen, 1992–; Vis. Res. Fellow, Univ.

of Reading, 2011–. Trustee, Ancient Monuments Soc., 1994–. FSA 1996; MCIfA (MIFA 2003). *Publications:* (jtly) The Tower of London, 2000, rev. edn 2009; Kensington Palace, 2003, rev. edn 2012; (ed and contrib.) The White Tower, 2008; contrib. articles and guidebooks on architecture and hist. *Recreations:* shooting, antiquarianism. *Address:* Royal Armouries, Armouries Drive, Leeds LS10 1LT. *T:* (0113) 220 1898. *E:* edward.impey@armouries.org.uk. *Club:* Athenæum.

IMRAN KHAN, (Imran Ahmad Khan Niazi); *see* Khan.

IMRAY, Sir Colin (Henry), KBE 1992; CMG 1983; HM Diplomatic Service, retired; *b* 21 Sept. 1933; *s* of late Henry Gibbon Imray and Frances Olive Imray; *m* 1957, Shirley Margaret Matthews; one *s* three *d*. *Educ:* Highgate Sch.; Hotchkiss Sch., Conn; Balliol Coll., Oxford (2nd cl. Hons PPE, MA). Served in Seaforth Highlanders and RWAFF, Sierra Leone, 1952–54. CRO, 1957; Canberra, 1958–61; CRO, 1961–63; Nairobi, 1963–66; FCO, 1966–70; British Trade Comr, Montreal, 1970–73; Counsellor, Head of Chancery and Consul-Gen., Islamabad, 1973–77; RCDS, 1977; Commercial Counsellor, Tel Aviv, 1977–80; Rayner Project Officer, 1980; Dep. High Comr, Bombay, 1980–84; Asst Under-Sec. of State (Dep. Chief Clerk and Chief Inspector), FCO, 1984–85; High Commissioner: Tanzania, 1986–89; Bangladesh, 1989–93. Order of St John: Sec. Gen., 1993–97; Dir, Overseas Relns, 1997–98. Vice Pres., Royal Over-Seas League, 2005– (Mem., Central Council, 1998–2005; Mem., Exec. Council, 1999–2005; Chm., 1999–2005); Trustee, Jt Commonwealth Societies Trust, 2000–05; Patron, Wallingford Chameleon Arts, 2010– (Chm., 2008–10). Freeman, City of London, 1994. High Steward, Wallingford, 2002–15. KStJ 1993. *Publications:* Remember and Be Glad, 2009. *Address:* 1A St John's Road, Wallingford, Oxon OX10 9AD. *Club:* Royal Over-Seas League.
See also F. King.

IMRIE, Celia Diana Savile; actress; *b* 15 July 1952; *d* of David and Diana Imrie; one *s*. *Educ:* Guildford High Sch. Advanced Greek Dancing Cert. *Theatre* includes: The Sea, National Th., 1992 (Best Supporting Actress Award); Acorn Antiques, Theatre Royal, Haymarket, 2005 (Olivier Award for Best Musical Supporting Actress); Unsuspecting Susan, East 59th Street Th., New York, 2005; Plague Over England, Duchess, 2009; Mixed Up North, Wilton's Music Hall, 2009; Noises Off, Old Vic, 2011, Novello, 2012; *films* include: Highlander, 1986; In the Bleak Midwinter, 1995; The Borrowers, 1997; Hilary and Jackie, 1998; Star Wars: Episode 1, 1999; Bridget Jones's Diary, 2001; Lucky Break, 2001; Calendar Girls, 2003; Wimbledon, 2004; Bridget Jones: The Edge of Reason, 2004; Nanny McPhee, 2005; The Best Exotic Marigold Hotel, 2012; Love Punch, What We Did on Our Holiday, Nativity 3: Dude, Where's my Donkey?!, 2014; The Second Best Exotic Marigold Hotel, 2015; *television* includes: Bergerac, 1981; Victoria Wood: As Seen on TV, 1985; Acorn Antiques, 1986; Oranges are not the Only Fruit, 1990; The Riff Raff Element, 1993; Blackhearts in Battersea, 1996; The History of Tom Jones, 1997; dinnerladies, 1998; Gormenghast, 2000; Love in a Cold Climate, 2001; Doctor Zhivago, 2002; Daniel Deronda, 2002; After You've Gone, 2007; Cranford, 2009; Titanic, 2012; Dr Who, 2013; Love and Marriage, 2013; The Blandings, 2013; Vicious, 2015. *Publications:* Not Quite Nice, 2015. *Recreations:* biking by the sea, going to Nice. *Address:* c/o Clare Eden, 194 Amyand Park Road, Twickenham TW1 3HY.

INCH, Thomas David, OBE 2000; CChem, FRSC; Secretary-General, Royal Society of Chemistry, 1993–2000; *b* 25 Sept. 1938; *s* of Thomas Alexander Inch and Sarah Lang Graves Inch; *m* 1964, Jacqueline Vivienne Pudner; one *d*. *Educ:* St Austell Grammar Sch.; Univ. of Birmingham (BSc 1st Cl. Hons Chem. 1960; PhD 1963; DSc 1971). Salters Fellow, Univ. of Birmingham, 1963–64; Vis. Fellow, NIH, USA, 1964–65; Chemical Defence Estabt, MoD, 1965–87 (RCDS 1985); Gen. Manager, Research Business Development, BP Research, 1987–90; Vice-Pres., R&D, BP America, 1990–93. Director: BP Ventures, 1987–89; Edison Polymer Innovation Corp., 1990–92; Ohio Science and Technology Commn, 1992. Chm., Nat. Adv. Cttee, Chemical Weapons Convention, 1997–2005. *Publications:* papers and reviews on chemistry and related topics. *Recreation:* golf. *Address:* 16 Ashlands, Ford, Salisbury SP4 6DY. *Club:* High Post Golf.

INCHCAPE, 4th Earl of, *cr* 1929; **Kenneth Peter Lyle Mackay,** AIB; Viscount Glenapp 1929; Viscount Inchcape 1924; Baron Inchcape 1911; Director: Glenapp Estate Co. Ltd, since 1980 (Chairman, since 2002); Inchcape Family Estates (formerly Investments) Ltd, since 1980 (Chairman, since 2002); Gray Dawes Travel Ltd, since 1996 (Chairman, since 2002); Duncan MacNeill & Co. Ltd, since 1986; Assam Oil and Gas, since 2006; farmer in Wiltshire; *b* 23 Jan. 1943; *er s* of 3rd Earl of Inchcape, and of his 1st wife, Mrs Aline Thorn Hannay, *d* of Sir Richard Pease, 2nd Bt; *S* father, 1994; *m* 1966, Georgina, *d* of late S. C. Nisbet and Mrs G. R. Sutton; one *s* two *d*. *Educ:* Eton. Late Lieut 9/12th Royal Lancers. Inchcape PLC, 1970–91. Master, Grocers' Co., 1993–94; Prime Warden, Shipwrights' Co., 1998–99. *Recreations:* shooting, fishing, golf, travel, ski-ing. *Heir: s* Viscount Glenapp, *qv*. *Address:* Manor Farm, Clyffe Pypard, Swindon SN4 7PY. *Clubs:* White's, Oriental, Pratt's; New (Edinburgh); Prestwick (Ayrshire); Royal Sydney (Sydney, NSW).
See also Baron Camoys.

INCHIQUIN, 18th Baron of, *cr* 1543; **Conor Myles John O'Brien;** (The O'Brien); Bt 1686; Prince of Thomond; Chief of the Name; *b* 17 July 1943; *s* of Hon. Fionn Myles Maryons O'Brien (*d* 1977) (*y s* of 15th Baron) and Josephine Reine (*d* 2011), *d* of late Joseph Eugene Bembaron; *S* uncle, 1982; *m* 1988, Helen, *d* of Gerald Fitzgerald O'Farrell; two *d*. *Educ:* Eton. Served as Captain, 14th/20th King's Hussars. *Heir: cousin* Conor John Anthony O'Brien, *b* 24 Sept. 1952. *Address:* Thomond House, Dromoland, Newmarket on Fergus, Co. Clare, Ireland.

INCHYRA, 3rd Baron *cr* 1962, of St Madoes, Co. Perth; **Christian James Charles Hoyer Millar;** *b* 12 Aug. 1962; *o s* of 2nd Baron Inchyra and of Fiona Mary (*née* Sheffield); *S* father, 2011; *m* 1992, Caroline Jane, *d* of late Robin Swan; one *s* two *d*. *Educ:* Eton; Edinburgh Univ. *Heir: s* Hon. Jake Christian Robert Hoyer Millar, *b* 10 July 1996.

IND, Hugh Timothy; Director, Compliance and Returns, Immigration Enforcement, Home Office (formerly Crime and Enforcement, UK Border Agency), since 2012; *b* Pembury, Kent, 13 July 1969; *s* of Jack Kenneth Ind, *qv*; *m* 2003, Jo Grinter; one *s* one *d*. *Educ:* Tonbridge Sch., Kent; St John's Coll., Oxford (BA PPE 1991). Various roles, Home Office, 1991–99; Bill Manager, Regulation of Investigatory Powers Act, 1999–2000; Principal Private Sec., DCMS, 2001–04; Dir of Ops, Nat. Asylum Support Service, 2005–06; Strategic Dir Asylum, 2007–10, Regl Dir, 2010–12, UK Border Agency. *Recreations:* reading, cricket, walking. *Address:* Immigration Enforcement, Home Office, 2 Marsham Street, SW1P 4DF. *T:* (020) 7035 1205. *E:* hugh.ind@homeoffice.gsi.gov.uk.

IND, Jack Kenneth; Headmaster, Dover College, 1981–91; *b* 20 Jan. 1935; *s* of late Rev. William Price Ind and Mrs Doris Maud Ind (*née* Cavell); *m* 1964, Elizabeth Olive Toombs; two *s* two *d*. *Educ:* Marlborough Coll.; St John's Coll., Oxford (BA Hons Mods, 2nd Cl. Class. Lit. and Lit. Hum.). Teacher: Wellingborough Sch., 1960–63; Tonbridge Sch., 1963–81 (Housemaster, 1970–81) and 1991–92; Eastbourne Coll., 1992–93; Gymnásium, Nové Zámky, Slovakia, 1994; Talbot Heath Sch., Bournemouth, 1996–97; Eastbourne Coll., 1997–98; Prior Park Coll., Bath, 1999–2001; Eastbourne Coll., 2001–02; (part time) Brighton Coll., 2002–04; Guildford High Sch., 2004–05 and 2009–10; St Catherine's Sch., Bramley, 2006–07 and 2008–09. Trustee, HMC projects in Central and Eastern Europe, 1997–2003. Reader in Ch of England, 1963–. *Recreations:* tennis, Rugby football, music, reading. *Address:* 68 Whitelake Road, Tonbridge, Kent TN10 3TJ. *T:* (01732) 300367.
See also H. T. Ind.

IND, Rt Rev. William; Bishop of Truro, 1997–2008; Assistant Bishop, Diocese of Salisbury, since 2009; *b* 26 March 1942; *s* of William Robert and Florence Emily Ind; *m* 1967, Frances Isobel Bramald; three *s*. *Educ:* Univ. of Leeds (BA); College of the Resurrection, Mirfield. Asst Curate, St Dunstan's, Feltham, 1966–71; Priest in charge, St Joseph the Worker, Northolt, 1971–74; Team Vicar, Basingstoke, 1974–87; Director of Ordinands, dio. of Winchester, 1982–87; Hon. Canon of Winchester, 1985–87; Bishop Suffragan of Grantham, 1987–97; Dean of Stamford, 1988–97. Hon. DD Exeter, 2009. *Recreations:* bird watching, cricket watching, orchid finding. *Address:* 15 Dean Close, Melksham, Wilts SN12 7EZ. *T:* (01225) 340979.

INDIAN OCEAN, Archbishop of the, since 2006; **Most Rev. (Gerald James) Ian Ernest,** GOSK 2006; *b* 30 Aug. 1954; *s* of Gerald and Jessie Ernest; *m* 1983, Kamla Ramloll; one *s*. *Educ:* Madras Univ., India (BCom 1979); St Paul's Theol Coll., Mauritius; Westhill Coll., Univ. of Birmingham, UK (CPS 1986); Procter Schol., Episcopal Div. Sch., Cambridge, Mass and Boston Inst. of Theol., 2005. Ordained priest, 1985; Bishop of Mauritius, 2001–. Mem., 1989–93, Chm., 2001–, Bd of Comrs, Dio. Mauritius; Member: Provincial Standing Cttee and Provincial Electoral Coll., Ch of Province of Indian Ocean, 1992–2001; Council of Religious and Spiritual Leaders of Mauritius, 1996–. Chm., Council of Provinces in Africa, 2007–12. Convener, Target Gp for Bps Trng, Task Force of Theol Educn for Anglican Communion, 2003–; Mem., Eight Mems Design Gp Cttee, apptd by Archbp of Canterbury to prepare for Lambeth Conf. and Anglican Gathering 2008, 2003–. Pres., Prison Fellowship Internat., Mauritius. Main translator of New Testament into Creole, 1987–91; Ed., Anglican Diocesan Mag., 1990–95. *Publications:* (jtly) Autonomy for Rodrigues Island; articles on peace, justice and family issues. *Recreations:* reading, music, swimming. *Address:* Bishop's House, Nalletamby Avenue, Phoenix, Republic of Mauritius. *T:* (home) (230) 6960767, (office) (230) 6865158, *Fax:* (230) 6971096. *E:* dioang@intnet.mu.

INGE, family name of **Baron Inge**.

INGE, Baron *cr* 1997 (Life Peer), of Richmond in the co. of North Yorkshire; **Field Marshal Peter Anthony Inge,** KG 2001; GCB 1992 (KCB 1988); PC 2004; DL; Chief of the Defence Staff, 1994–97; Constable, HM Tower of London, 1996–2001; *b* 5 Aug. 1935; *s* of late Raymond Albert Inge and Grace Maud Caroline Inge (*née* Du Rose); *m* 1960, Letitia Marion Beryl, *yr d* of late Trevor and Sylvia Thornton-Berry; two *d*. *Educ:* Summer Fields; Wrekin College; RMA Sandhurst. Commissioned Green Howards, 1956; served Hong Kong, Malaya, Germany, Libya and UK; ADC to GOC 4 Div., 1960–61; Adjutant, 1 Green Howards, 1963–64; student, Staff Coll., 1966; MoD, 1967–69; Coy Comdr, 1 Green Howards, 1969–70; student, JSSC, 1971; BM 11 Armd Bde, 1972; Instructor, Staff Coll., 1973–74; CO 1 Green Howards, 1974–76; Comdt, Junior Div., Staff Coll., 1977–79; Comdr Task Force C/4 Armd Bde, 1980–81; Chief of Staff, HQ 1 (BR) Corps, 1982–83; GOC NE District and Comdr 2nd Inf. Div., 1984–86; Dir Gen. Logistic Policy (Army), MoD, 1986–87; Comdr 1st (Br.) Corps, 1987–89; Comdr Northern Army Gp, and C-in-C, BAOR, 1989–92; CGS 1992–94. ADC Gen. to the Queen, 1991–94. Colonel, The Green Howards, 1982–94. Col Comdt: RMP, 1987–92; APTC, 1988–97. Non-exec. Dir, Racal Electronics plc, 1997–2000. Comr, Royal Hosp. Chelsea, 1998–2004; Trustee, Historic Royal Palaces, 1999–2007. President: Army Benevolent Fund, 1998–2002; The Pilgrims, 2002–; Member Council: St George's House, Windsor Castle; Marlborough Coll., 1998–2006, 2010–. Mem., Hakluyt Foundn, 1999–2004; Chm., King Edward VII's Hosp. Sister Agnes, 2004–12. DL N Yorks, 1994. Hon. DCL Newcastle, 1995. *Recreations:* cricket, walking, music and reading, especially military history. *Address:* c/o House of Lords, SW1A 0PW. *Clubs:* Boodle's, Beefsteak, Army and Navy, Travellers, MCC.

INGE, George Patrick Francis, FRICS; Chairman: Savills plc, 1987–95; FPD Savills (formerly Savills Land & Property) Ltd, 1992–2000; *b* 31 Aug. 1941; *s* of late John William Wolstenholme Inge and Alison Lilias Inge; *m* 1977, Joyce (*née* Leinster); one *s* one *d*. *Educ:* Old Malthouse Prep. Sch., Dorset; Sherborne Sch. Joined Alfred Savill & Sons, 1960; Partner, 1968; Man. Partner, Savills, 1985; Chief Exec., Savills plc, 1987–91. Non-exec. Chm., Severn Trent Property Ltd, 1995–2006; non-exec. Dir, Westbury plc, 1995–2003. Governor: Old Malthouse Sch., Dorset, 1977–98 (Chm., 1986–98); Cothill House Sch., 1989–2013; Nottingham Trent Univ., 1994–96; Downe House Sch., 1996–2004 (Chm., 1999–2004). *Recreations:* shooting, fishing, golf. *Address:* The Old Vicarage, Little Milton, Oxford OX44 7QB. *T:* (01844) 279538. *Club:* Flyfishers'.

INGE, Rt Rev. John Geoffrey; *see* Worcester, Bishop of.

INGESTRE, Viscount; James Richard Charles John Chetwynd-Talbot; *b* 11 Jan. 1978; *s* and *heir* of 22nd Earl of Shrewsbury and Waterford, *qv*; *m* 2006, Polly Elizabeth, *d* of Henry Blackie; one *s* three *d*. *Educ:* Shrewsbury Sch.; Royal Agricl Coll. MRICS 2002. *Heir: s* Hon. George Henry Charles John Alton Chetwynd-Talbot, *b* 3 May 2013.

INGHAM, Sir Bernard, Kt 1990; Secretary, Supporters of Nuclear Energy, 1998–2008 and 2010–14; *b* 21 June 1932; *s* of Garnet and Alice Ingham; *m* 1956, Nancy Hilda Hoyle; one *s*. *Educ:* Hebden Bridge Grammar Sch., Yorks. Reporter: Hebden Bridge Times, 1948–52; Yorkshire Post and Yorkshire Evening Post, Halifax, 1952–59; Yorkshire Post, Leeds, 1959–61; Northern Industrial Correspondent, Yorkshire Post, 1961; Reporter, The Guardian, 1962–65; Labour Staff, The Guardian, London, 1965–67; Press and Public Relns Adviser, NBPI, 1967–68; Chief Inf. Officer, DEP, 1968–73; Dir of Information: Dept of Employment, 1973; Dept of Energy, 1974–77; Under Sec., Energy Conservation Div., Dept of Energy, 1978–79; Chief Press Sec. to Prime Minister, 1979–90; Head, Govt Inf. Service, 1989–90. Chm., Bernard Ingham Communications, 1990–2011. Columnist: The Express (formerly Daily Express), 1991–98; PR Week, 1994–2001; Yorkshire Post, 2003–. Non-executive Director: McDonald's Restaurants Ltd, 1991–2005 (Mem. Adv. Bd, 2005–10); Hill and Knowlton (UK) Ltd, public relations counsel, 1991–2002. Mem. Exec. Cttee, Meml to Women of WWII, 2004–05. Vis. Fellow, Univ. of Newcastle, 1989–2004; Vis. Prof., Middlesex Univ. Business Sch., 1998–. Pres., British Franchise Assoc., 1993–2012. Mem. Council Univ. of Huddersfield, 1994–2000. Hon. DLitt: Buckingham, 1997; Bradford, 2004; DUniv Middlesex, 1999. *Publications:* Kill The Messenger, 1991; Yorkshire Millennium, 1999; Yorkshire Castles, 2001; Yorkshire Villages, 2001; The Wages of Spin, 2003; Yorkshire Greats, 2005. *Recreations:* walking, gardening, reading. *Address:* 9 Monahan Avenue, Purley, Surrey CR8 3BB. *T:* (020) 8660 8970, 07860 535962. *E:* bernardinghamcom@aol.com. *Clubs:* Reform; Midgehole Working Men's, Pennine (Hebden Bridge).

INGHAM, Christopher John, CMG 2002; HM Diplomatic Service, retired; Ambassador to Republic of Uzbekistan and (non-resident) to Republic of Tajikistan, 1999–2002; *b* 4 June 1944; *s* of Dr Roland Ingham and Dorothy Ingham; *m* 1968, Jacqueline Anne Clarke; one *s* two *d*. *Educ:* St John's Coll., Cambridge (MA). Mgt trainee, Cadbury Bros Ltd, 1966–68; joined HM Diplomatic Service, 1968; Moscow, 1972–74; Calcutta, 1974; Kuwait, 1974–76; FCO, 1976–80; Dep. Perm. Rep. to IAEA/UNIDO, Vienna, 1980–85; FCO, 1985–87; Hd, Commercial Section, Mexico City, 1987–89; FCO, 1989–91; Counsellor and Dep. Hd of Mission, Bucharest, 1991–95; Counsellor, EU and Economic, Madrid, 1995–99. *Recreations:* hill-walking, choral singing.

INGHAM, Rt Rev. Michael; Bishop of New Westminster, 1994–2013; *b* 25 Aug. 1949; *s* of Herbert and Dorothy Ingham. *Educ:* Univ. of Edinburgh (MA 1970; BD 1973 (First Class Hons)). Ordained deacon and priest, 1974; Asst Curate, St John the Evangelist, Ottawa, Ontario, 1974–76; Rector: Christ the King, Burnaby, BC, 1976–80; St Francis-in-the-Wood, W Vancouver, 1980–89; Principal Sec. to the Primate, Toronto, 1989–92; Dean of Christ Church Cathedral, Vancouver, 1992–94. Hon. DD: Vancouver Sch. of Theol., 1998; Episcopal Divinity Sch., Cambridge, MA, 2009; Hon. LLD Simon Fraser, 2013. *Publications:* Rites for a New Age, 1985, 2nd edn 1990; Mansions of the Spirit, 1997; More Than I can Say: Michael Peers: a memoir, 2014. *Recreations:* sailing, golf.

INGHAM, Prof. Philip William, DPhil; FMedSci; FRS 2002; FRSB; Research Director (formerly Deputy Director), Institute of Molecular and Cell Biology, Singapore, since 2006; Professor of Developmental Biology, Lee Kong Chian School of Medicine, Nanyang Technological University, since 2013; Professor of Developmental Biology, Imperial College London, since 2013; *b* 19 March 1955; *s* of late George Philip Ingham and Dorothy Ingham; *m* 1993, Anita Maria Taylor; one *s* two *d*. *Educ:* Queens' Coll., Cambridge (BA, MA); Univ. of Sussex (DPhil 1981). Res. Scientist, MRC, 1986; Imperial Cancer Research Fund: Res. Scientist, 1986–91; Sen. Scientist, 1991–94; Principal Scientist, 1994–96; Prof. of Develtl Genetics and Dir, MRC Centre for Develtl and Biomed. Genetics (formerly Centre for Develtl Genetics), Univ. of Sheffield, 1996–2009. Chm., British Soc. for Develtl Biol., 1999–2004. Mem., EMBO, 1995. FRSB (FIBiol 2000); FMedSci 2001. Hon. FRCP 2007. Genetics Soc. Medal, 2005. *Publications:* contrib. scientific papers to Cell, Nature, Science, Genes and Develt, Develt, Develtl Biol. *Recreations:* music, playing tennis, walking, ski-ing, travelling, reading. *Address:* Institute of Molecular and Cell Biology, 61 Biopolis Drive, Proteos, Singapore 138673. *E:* pingham@imcb.a-star.edu.sg.

INGHAM, Stuart Edward; Chief Executive, United Leeds Teaching Hospitals NHS Trust, 1991–98; *b* 9 Oct. 1942; *s* of Edward Ingham and Dorothy Mary (*née* Pollard); *m* 1969, Jane Stella Wilkinson; one *s* one *d*. *Educ:* Canon Slade Grammar Sch., Bolton. AHSM 1970. Bolton and District HMC: Trainee in Hosp. Admin, 1965–66; HCO, 1966–67; Dep. Gen. Supt, Ancoats Hosp., 1967–69; Sen. Admin. Asst, Royal Bucks and Associated HMC, 1969–70; Hospital Secretary: Harefield Hosp., 1970–73; St James's Univ. Hosp., Leeds, 1973–74; Leeds Area Health Authority (Eastern): General Administrator, 1974–77; Dist Administrator, 1977–82; York Health Authority: Dist Administrator, 1982–84; Dist Gen. Manager, 1985–88; Dist Gen. Manager, Leeds Western HA, 1988–90. *Recreations:* equestrian sports, bad golf. *Address:* The Turnings, Woodacre Crescent, Bardsey, Leeds LS17 9DQ.

INGILBY, Sir Thomas (Colvin William), 6th Bt *cr* 1866; FAAV; managing own estate; *b* 17 July 1955; *s* of Sir Joslan William Vivian Ingilby, 5th Bt, DL, JP, and Diana, *d* of late Sir George Colvin, CB, CMG, DSO; *S* father, 1974; *m* 1984, Emma Clare Roebuck, *d* of Major R. R. Thompson, Whinfield, Strensall, York; four *s* one *d*. *Educ:* Aysgarth Sch., Bedale; Eton Coll.; Royal Agricultural Coll., Cirencester. MRAC; ARICS, MRICS; FBII. Joined Army, May 1974, but discharged on death of father; Assistant: Stephenson & Son, York, 1978–80; Strutt & Parker, Harrogate, 1981–83. Chairman: Harrogate Mgt Centre Ltd, 1991–99; Action Harrogate Ltd, 1992–98. Dir, Yorks Tourist Bd, 1997–2009 (Dep. Chm., 2005–09); Dir, Welcome to Yorkshire, 2014–. Founder and Nat. Co-ordinator, Stately Homes Hotline, 1988–; Pres., Council for Prevention of Art Theft, 1991–2001; Chairman: Yorkshire's Great Houses, Castles and Gardens, 1995–; Great Inns of Britain, 1996–2013; Fest. Dir, Air NZ Golden Oldies Internat. Cricket Fest., 2010. Chm., Bd of Govs, Cundall Manor Sch., Helperby, 2007–. President: Nidderdale Amateur Cricket League, 1979–; Harrogate Gilbert and Sullivan Soc., 1988–. Internat. Hon. Citizen, New Orleans, 1979; Lifetime Achievement Award, Harrogate Business Awards, 2011. *Publications:* Yorkshire's Great Houses: behind the scenes, 2005. *Recreations:* cricket, tennis, reading, writing, lecturing, historical research, walking. *Heir:* *s* James William Francis Ingilby [*b* 15 June 1985; *m* 2014, Sara Nicholson]. *Address:* Ripley Castle, Ripley, near Harrogate, North Yorkshire HG3 3AY. *T:* (01423) 770152. *E:* enquiries@ripleycastle.co.uk.

INGLE, Alan Richmond, CMG 2000; HM Diplomatic Service, retired; *b* 16 Oct. 1939; *s* of late Henry Ingle and of Helen Ingle (*née* Keating); *m* 1963, Gillian Hall; one *s* one *d*. *Educ:* Stand Grammar Sch. and Prince Rupert Sch., Wilhelmshaven. Entered BoT, 1957; Accra (Trade Commn Service), 1961–65; FO, 1965–66; Kingston, 1966–70; Third Sec., Christchurch, 1970–74; Second Secretary: FCO, 1974–77; (Commercial), Singapore, 1977–81; First Sec., FCO, 1981–83; Consul and Dir, British Inf. Services, NY, 1983–88; First Sec., FCO 1988–93; Counsellor (Mgt), Lagos and Abuja, 1993–96; Hd of Delegn, Jt Mgt Office, Brussels, 1996–99; Counsellor: FCO, 2000; UK Mission to UN, NY, 2001. *Address:* Chaseley, Higher Broad Oak Road, West Hill, Ottery St Mary, Devon EX11 1XJ. *Club:* Royal Over-Seas League.

INGLEDOW, Anthony Brian, OBE 1969; HM Diplomatic Service, retired; Counsellor, Foreign and Commonwealth Office, 1983–93; *b* 25 July 1928; *s* of Cedric Francis Ingledow and Doris Evelyn Ingledow (*née* Worrall); *m* 1956, Margaret Monica, *d* of Sir Reginald Watson-Jones, FRCS; one *s* one *d*. *Educ:* St Bees School; London Univ. Served HM Forces, 1947–49. Joined Colonial Administrative Service, Nigeria, 1950; District Officer: Auchi, 1954; Oyo, 1956; Secretariat, Ibadan, 1958, retired 1960; joined HM Diplomatic Service, 1961; 2nd Secretary, Khartoum, 1962; FO, 1964; 1st Secretary, Aden, 1966; Lagos, 1967; FCO, 1970; Dakar, 1972; FCO, 1975. *Recreations:* reading, travel. *Address:* c/o Lloyds Bank, 8–10 Waterloo Place, SW1Y 4BE. *Club:* Athenæum.

INGLESE, Anthony Michael Christopher, CB 2008; General Counsel and Solicitor, HM Revenue and Customs, 2008–14; *b* 19 Dec. 1951; *s* of Angelo Inglese and Dora Inglese (*née* Di Paola); *m* 1974, Jane Elizabeth Kerry Bailes; one *s* one *d*. *Educ:* Salvatorian Coll., Harrow Weald; Fitzwilliam Coll., Cambridge (MA, LLB). Called to the Bar, Gray's Inn, 1976, Bencher, 2002; Legal Advr's Br., Home Office, 1975–86; Legal Secretariat to Law Officers, 1986–88; Legal Advr's Br., Home Office, 1988–91; Legal Dir, OFT, 1991–95; Legal Advr, MoD (Treasury Solicitor's Dept), 1995–97; Dep. Treasury Solicitor, 1997–2001; Solicitor and Dir Gen., Legal Services, DTI, later BERR, 2002–08. *E:* anthony.inglese@btinternet.com.

INGLEWOOD, 2nd Baron *cr* 1964; **(William) Richard Fletcher-Vane;** farmer, landowner and businessman; Vice Lord-Lieutenant of Cumbria, since 2012; *b* 31 July 1951; *e s* of 1st Baron Inglewood, TD and Mary (*d* 1982), *e d* of Major Sir Richard George Proby, 1st Bt, MC; *S* father, 1989; *m* 1986, Cressida, *y d* of late Desmond Pemberton-Pigott, CMG; one *s* two *d*. *Educ:* Eton; Trinity Coll., Cambridge (MA); Cumbria Coll. of Agriculture and Forestry. MRICS. Called to the Bar, Lincoln's Inn, 1975. Member: Lake Dist Special Planning Bd, 1984–90 (Chm., Develt Control Cttee, 1984–89); NW Water Authority, 1987–89. Pres., Cumbria Tourist Bd, 2004–. Non-executive Director: CN Group, 1997– (Chm., 2002–); Carr's Milling Industries, 2004–13 (Chm., 2005–13). Chm., Reviewing Cttee on Export of Works of Art, 2002–14; Pres., British Art Market Fedn, 2014–. Contested (C) Houghton and Washington, 1983; Durham, EP elecns, 1984; MEP (C) Cumbria and Lancashire N, 1989–94; contested (C) same reg., 1994; MEP (C) NW Reg., England, 1999–2004. Cons. spokesman on legal affairs, EP, 1989–94 and 1999–2004, on constitutional affairs, 2001–04; Dep. Whip, EDG, 1992–94, Chief Whip, 1994. A Lord in Waiting (Govt Whip), 1994–95; Captain of HM Yeomen of the Guard (Dep. Govt Chief Whip), 1995; Parly Under-Sec. of State, DNH, 1995–97; elected Mem., H of L, 1999. Chm., H of L Select Cttee on Communications, 2011–13, on Extradition, 2013–14. Mem., Delegn to Parly Assembly, Council of Europe, 2010–11. FSA 2002. DL Cumbria, 1993. *Heir:* *s* Hon. Henry William Frederick Fletcher-Vane, *b* 24 Dec. 1990. *Address:* Hutton-in-the-Forest, Penrith, Cumbria CA11 9TH. *T:* (01768) 484500, *Fax:* (01768) 484571. *Clubs:* Pratt's, Travellers.

INGLIS, George Bruton; Senior Partner, Slaughter and May, 1986–92; *b* 19 April 1933; *s* of late Cecil George Inglis and Ethel Mabel Inglis; *m* 1968, Patricia Mary Forbes; three *s*. *Educ:* Winchester College; Pembroke College, Oxford (MA). Solicitor. Partner, Slaughter and May, 1966–92. *Recreation:* gardening.

INGLIS, Heather Hughson; *see* Swindells, H. H.

INGLIS, Ian Grahame, CB 1983; Chairman, State Grants Commission, Tasmania, 1990–2001; *b* 2 April 1929; *s* of late William and Ellen Jean Inglis; *m* 1952, Elaine Arlene Connors; three *s* one *d*. *Educ:* Hutchins Sch., Hobart; Univ. of Tasmania (BCom). Agricl Economist, Tasmanian Dept of Agric., 1951–58; Economist, State Treasury, 1958–69; Chairman: Rivers and Water Supply Commn, and Metropolitan Water Bd, 1969–77; NW Regl Water Authority, 1977; State Under Treasurer, Tas, 1977–89. Dir, TGIO Ltd (formerly Tasmanian Govt Insce Bd), 1989–96. Chm., Retirement Benefits Fund Investment Trust, 1989–95. Member: Ambulance Commn of Tasmania, 1959–65; Tasmanian Grain Elevators Bd, 1962–65; Clarence Municipal Commn, 1965–69; Motor Accidents Insurance Bd, 1991–95. Dir, Comalco Aluminium (Bell Bay) Ltd, 1980–95. *Recreations:* yacht-racing, gardening, bridge. *Address:* 5 Sayer Crescent, Sandy Bay, Hobart, Tas 7005, Australia. *T:* (3) 62231928. *Clubs:* Tasmanian, Royal Yacht of Tasmania (Hobart).

INGLIS, Prof. Kenneth Stanley, AO 2003; DPhil; Professor of History, Australian National University, 1977–94, retired; *b* 7 Oct. 1929; *s* of S. W. Inglis; *m* 1st, 1952, Judy Betheras (*d* 1962); one *s* two *d*; 2nd, 1965, Amirah Gust. *Educ:* Univ. of Melbourne (MA); Univ. of Oxford (DPhil). Sen. Lectr in History, Univ. of Adelaide, 1956–60; Reader in History, 1960–62; Associate Prof. of History, Australian National Univ., 1962–65; Prof., 1965–66; Prof. of History, Univ. of Papua New Guinea, 1966–72, Vice-Chancellor, 1972–75; Professorial Fellow in Hist., ANU, 1975–77. Vis. Prof. of Australian Studies, Harvard, 1982; Vis. Prof., Univ. of Hawaii, 1985; Vis. Fellow, St John's Coll., Cambridge, 1990–91; Hon. Prof., Monash Univ., 2009–. Hon. DLitt Melbourne, 1996. Jt Gen. Editor, Australians: a historical library, 1987–88. *Publications:* Hospital and Community, 1958; The Stuart Case, 1961, 2nd edn 2002; Churches and the Working Classes in Victorian England, 1963; The Australian Colonists, 1974; This is the ABC: the Australian Broadcasting Commission, 1932–1983, 1983; The Rehearsal: Australians at War in the Sudan 1885, 1985; (ed and introduced) Nation: the life of an independent journal 1958–1972, 1989; Sacred Places: war memorials in the Australian landscape, 1998, rev. edn 2008; Anzac Remembered: selected writings, 1998; Observing Australia, 1959–1999, 1999; Whose ABC?: the Australian Broadcasting Corporation 1983–2006, 2006. *Address:* Rathdowne Place, 497 Rathdowne Street, Carlton, Vic 3053, Australia.

INGLIS, His Honour Richard Anthony Girvan; a Circuit Judge, 1996–2014; *b* 28 Dec. 1947; *s* of Angus Inglis and Kathleen Flora Inglis; *m* 1976, Heather Hughson Swindells, *qv*; one *s*. *Educ:* Marlborough Coll.; Selwyn Coll., Cambridge (BA 1969). Called to the Bar, Middle Temple, 1971; Jun., Midland and Oxford Circuit, 1984; Recorder, 1993–96; Hon. Recorder of Newark, 2002–14. *Recreations:* garden, music, church bell ringing.

INGLIS of Glencorse, Sir Roderick (John), 10th Bt *cr* 1703 (then Mackenzie of Gairloch); MB, ChB; *b* 25 Jan. 1936; *s* of Sir Maxwell Ian Hector Inglis of Glencorse, 9th Bt and Dorothy Evelyn (*d* 1970), MD, JP, *d* of Dr John Stewart, Tasmania; *S* father, 1974; *m* 1960, Rachel (marr. diss. 1975), *d* of Lt-Col N. M. Morris, Dowdstown, Ardee, Co. Louth; twin *s* one *d* (and *e s* decd); *m* 1975 (marr. diss. 1977); one *d*. *Educ:* Winchester; Edinburgh Univ. (MB, ChB 1960). *Heir:* *s* Ian Richard Inglis [*b* 9 Aug. 1965; *m* 1st, 1990, Lesley Margaret Moss (marr. diss. 1994); one *s*; 2nd, 2000, Yvonne Rossina Hird; one *s* one *d*]. *Address:* Clarendon House, 93 Villiers Drive, Clarendon, 3201Pietermaritzburg, KZN, S Africa.

INGLIS, Dr Stephen Charles; Director, National Institute for Biological Standards and Control, 2002–April 2016 (a Health Protection Agency centre, 2009–13; a Medicines and Healthcare products Regulatory Agency centre, since 2013); *b* 1 Sept. 1952; *s* of John Reid Inglis and Joan Inglis (*née* Devear); *m* 1975, Moira Margaret Hunter; two *s* one *d*. *Educ:* Aberdeen Grammar Sch.; Aberdeen Univ. (BSc Hons Biochem. 1974); Churchill Coll., Cambridge (PhD 1978). University of Cambridge: Res. Fellow, Churchill Coll., 1978–80; Demonstrator, 1979–84, Lectr, 1984–90, Dept of Pathol.; Fellow, Darwin Coll., 1984–90; Hd, Molecular Scis, 1990–95, Res. Dir, 1995–2001, Cantab Pharmaceuticals, subseq. Xenova PLC. Chm., Phogen, 1997–2001. Member, Corporate Executive Team: HPA, 2005–09; MHRA, 2012–. Member: Scientific Pandemic Influenza Adv. Cttee, 2005–, Expert Scientific Gp on Phase One Clin. Trials, 2006–, DoH; Bd, Nat. Measurement Systems, DIUS, then BIS, 2007–. Chm., MRC/HFEA Wkg Party on evaluation of clin. procedures for assisted reprodn, 2003–; Member: Molecular and Cellular Medicine Bd, MRC, 1996–2000; Scientific Adv. Cttee, CRC Ventures, 2000–01; Scientific Adv. Cttee, Edward Jenner Inst. Vaccine Res., 2000–12; Jt Professional Adv. Cttee on Blood Safety, 2002–; Biologicals Subcttee, Cttee for Safety of Medicines, 2002–05; Jt Cttee on Vaccines and Immunisation, 2002–09 (Chm., sub-gp on varicella-zoster); Nat. Biol Standards Bd, 2002–09; Biologicals and Vaccines Expert Adv. Gp, Commn for Human Medicines, 2006–13; Steering Cttee, Nat. Genetics Ref. Lab., 2007–09; Steering Bd, Health Tech. and Medicines Knowledge Transfer Network, 2010–13. Mem., Governing Body, Lister Inst. of Preventative Medicine, 2003–10. MInstD 1997. *Publications:* contrib. scientific papers to professional jls in fields of virology, molecular biol., vaccine develt. *Recreations:* music: jazz piano, saxophone and bagpipes (occasionally), sport: tennis, ski-ing, diving. *Address:* (until April 2016) National Institute for Biological Standards and Control, Medicines and Healthcare products Regulatory Agency, Blanche Lane, South Mimms, Potters Bar, Herts EN6 3QG. *T:* (01707) 641400.

INGLIS-JONES, Nigel John; QC 1982; Barrister-at-Law; *b* 7 May 1935; 2nd *s* of Major John Alfred Inglis-Jones and Hermione Inglis-Jones; *m* 1st, 1965, Lenette Bromley-Davenport (*d* 1986); two *s* two *d*; 2nd, 1987, Ursula Culverwell; one *s*. *Educ:* Eton; Trinity Coll., Oxford (BA). Nat. Service with Grenadier Guards (ensign). Called to the Bar, Inner Temple, 1959, Bencher, 1981. A Recorder, 1976–93. Dep. Social Security Comr, 1993–2002; Gen. Comr of Income Tax, 1992–2005. *Publications:* The Law of Occupational Pension Schemes, 1989. *Recreations:* gardening, fishing, collecting English drinking glass. *Address:* Woolston Manor Farm House, Woolston, North Cadbury, Yeovil BA22 7BL. *T:* (01963) 441031.

INGMAN, David Charles, CBE 1993; Chairman, British Waterways Board, 1987–93; *b* 22 March 1928; *s* of Charles and Muriel Ingman; *m* 1951, Joan Elizabeth Walker; two *d*. *Educ:* Grangefield Grammar Sch., Stockton-on-Tees; Durham Univ. (BSc, MSc). Imperial Chemical Industries, 1949–85: Dir, then Dep. Chm., Plastics Div., 1975–81; Gp Dir, Plastics and Petrochemicals Div., 1981–85; Chm. and Chief Exec., Bestobell, 1985–86. Dir, Engineering Services Ltd, 1975–78; Alternative Dir, AECI Ltd, SA, 1978–82; non-exec. Dir, Negretti-Zambra, 1979–81. Mem., Nationalised Industries Chairmen's Gp, 1987–93. *Recreations:* golf, walking, travel.

INGOLD, Dr Keith Usherwood, OC 1994; FRS 1979; FRSC 1969; Distinguished Research Scientist, National Research Council, Canada, since 1991; *b* Leeds, 31 May 1929; *s* of Christopher Kelk Ingold and Edith Hilda (*née* Usherwood); *m* 1956, Carmen Cairine Hodgkin; one *s* one *d* (and one *s* decd). *Educ:* University Coll. London (BSc Hons Chem., 1949; Fellow, 1987); Univ. of Oxford (DPhil 1951). Emigrated to Canada, 1951; Post-doctorate Fellow (under Dr F. P. Lossing), Div. of Pure Chem., Nat. Res. Council of Canada, 1951–53; Def. Res. Bd Post-doctorate Fellow (under Prof. W. A. Bryce), Chem. Dept, Univ. of BC, 1953–55; National Research Council of Canada: joined Div. of Appl. Chem., 1955; Head, Hydrocarbon Chem. Section of Div. of Chem., 1965; Associate Dir, Div. of Chemistry, 1977–90. Adjunct Professor: Brunel Univ., 1983–94; Univ. of Guelph, 1985–87; Carleton Univ., 1991–; Van Arkel Vis. Prof., Leiden Univ., Holland, 1992; Vis. Lectr, Japan Soc. for Promotion of Science, 1982. Hon. Treas., RSC, 1979–81; Canadian Society for Chemistry: Vice-Pres., 1985–87, Pres., 1987–88. Hon. Mem., Argentinian Soc. for Res. in Organic Chem., 1997. Lectures: Frontiers in Chem., Case Western Res. Univ., and Frank Burnett Dains Meml, Univ. of Kansas, 1969; J. A. McRae Meml, Queen's Univ., Ont, 1980; Canadian Industries Ltd, Acadia Univ., NS, Imperial Oil, Univ. of Western Ont, and Douglas Hill Meml, Duke Univ., NC, 1987; Rayson Huang, Univ. of Hong Kong, 1988; 3M University, Univ. of Western Ont, Peter de la Mare Meml, Univ. of Auckland, and Gilman, Iowa State Univ., 1993; Marjorie Young Bell, Mount Allison Univ., NB, and Bergman, Yale Univ., 1994; Weissberger-Williams, Kodak Res. Center, Rochester, NY, and Stanley J. Cristol, Univ. of Colorado, 1995; (first) Cheves Walling, Gordon Res. Conf., 1997; Max T. Rogers, Michigan State Univ., 2000. Hon. FRSE 2001. Hon. DSc: Univ. of Guelph, 1985; St Andrews, 1989; Carleton, 1992; McMaster, 1995; Hon. LLD: Mount Allison, New Brunswick, 1987; Dalhousie, 1996; Dr *hc* Ancona, 1999. Awards: American Chemical Society: Award in Petroleum Chem., 1968; Pauling Award, 1988; Arthur C. Cope Scholar Award, 1992; James Flack Norris Award in Physical Organic Chem., 1993; Award in Kinetics and Mechanism, Chem. Soc., 1978; Chemical Institute of Canada: Medal, 1981; Syntex Award for Physical Organic Chem., 1983; Royal Society of Canada: Centennial Medal, 1982; Henry Marshall Tory Medal, 1985; Humboldt Res. Award, Alexander von Humboldt Foundn, W Germany, 1989; Alfred Bader Award in Organic Chem., Canadian Soc. for Chem., 1989; Sir Christopher Ingold Lectureship Award, Royal Soc. of Chem., 1989; VERIS Award, Vitamin E Res. Inf. Services, 1989; Lansdowne Visitor Award, Univ. of Victoria, Canada, 1990; Mangini Prize in Chem., Univ. of Bologna, 1990; Royal Society: Davy Medal, 1990; Royal Medal A, 2000; Izaak Walton Killam Meml Prize, Canada Council, 1992; Angelo Mangini Medal, Italian Chem. Soc., 1997; Canada Gold Medal for Sci. and Engrg, Natural Scis and Engrg Res. Council of Canada, 1998. Silver Jubilee Medal, 1977; Golden Jubilee Medal, 2002; Gold Medal, Professional Inst. of Public Service, Canada, 2009; Diamond Jubilee Medal, 2012. *Publications:* over 500 scientific papers in field of physical organic chemistry, partic. free-radical chemistry. *Recreation:* ski-ing. *Address:* 72 Ryeburn Drive, Ottawa ON K1V 1H5, Canada. *T:* (613) 8221123, (office) (613) 9900938.

INGOLD, Prof. Timothy, PhD; FBA 1997; FRSE; Professor of Social Anthropology, University of Aberdeen, since 1999 (Head, School of Social Science, 2008–11); *b* 1 Nov. 1948; *s* of late Cecil Terence Ingold, CMG and Leonora Mary Ingold (*née* Kemp); *m* 1972, Anna Kaarina Väli-Kivistö; three *s* one *d*. *Educ:* Churchill Coll., Cambridge (BA 1st cl. Hons 1970; PhD Social Anthropol. 1976). Department of Social Anthropology, University of Manchester: Lectr, 1974–85; Sen. Lectr, 1985–90; Prof., 1990–99 (Max Gluckman Prof. of Social Anthropology, 1995–99); Hd of Dept, 1993–97. British Academy Res. Readership, 1997–99; ESRC Professorial Fellowship, 2005–08; Adjunct Prof., Univ. of Tromsø, Norway, 1997–2000. Corresp. Mem., Finnish Literary Soc., 1993. FRSE 2000. Rivers Meml Medal, RAI, 1989; Jean-Marie Delwart Foundn Award, Royal Belgian Acad. of Scis, 1994; Anders Retzius Gold Medal, Swedish Soc. for Anthropol. and Geog., 2004; Huxley Meml Medal, RAI, 2014. Kt, 1st Class, Order of White Rose (Finland), 2014. *Publications:* The Skolt Lapps today, 1976; Hunters, pastoralists and ranchers, 1980; Evolution and social life, 1986; The appropriation of nature, 1986; (ed) What is an animal?, 1988; (ed jtly) Hunters and gatherers, 2 vols, 1988; (ed jtly) Tools, language and cognition in human evolution, 1993; (ed) Companion encyclopedia of anthropology, 1994; (ed) Key debates in anthropology, 1996; The Perception of the Environment, 2000; (ed jtly) Creativity and Cultural Improvisation, 2007; Lines, 2007; (ed jtly) Ways of Walking, 2008; Being Alive, 2011; Redrawing Anthropology, 2011; (ed jtly) Imagining Landscapes, 2012; (ed jtly) Biosocial Becomings, 2013; Making, 2013; (ed jtly) Making and Growing, 2014; The Life of Lines, 2015; articles in academic books and learned jls. *Recreation:* music ('cello and piano). *Address:* Department of Anthropology, University of Aberdeen, Aberdeen AB24 3QY. *T:* (01224) 274350.
See also P. Healey.

INGRAHAM, Rt Hon. Hubert Alexander; PC 1993; Prime Minister, Commonwealth of the Bahamas, 1992–2002 and 2007–12; Member, National Assembly, 1977–2012 (PLP, 1977–86, Ind, 1987–90, FNM, 1990–2012); *b* 4 Aug. 1947; *m* Delores Velma Miller; five *c*. *Educ:* Cooper's Town Public Sch.; Southern Senior Sch.; Govt High Sch. Evening Inst., Nassau. Called to Bahamas Bar, 1972; Sen. Partner, Christie, Ingraham & Co. Formerly: Mem., Air Transport Licensing Authy; Chm., Real Property Tax Tribunal. Chm., Bahamas Mortgage Corp., 1982. Mem., Progressive Liberal Party, 1975–86; Minister of Housing, Nat. Insurance and Social Services, 1982–84; Leader, Free National Movement, 1990–2012; Leader of Opposition, 1990–92, 2005–07. *Address:* c/o Free National Movement, PO Box N–10713, Nassau, Bahamas.

INGRAM, Adam Hamilton; Member (SNP) Carrick, Cumnock and Doon Valley, Scottish Parliament, since 2011 (South of Scotland, 1999–2011); *b* 1 May 1951; *m* 1977, Gerry; three *s* one *d*. *Educ:* Kilmarnock Acad.; Paisley Coll. (BA Hons Business Economics, 1980). Family bakery business, 1971–76; Sen. Economic Asst, Manpower Services Commn, 1985–86; Researcher and Lectr, Paisley Coll., 1987–88; Hd of Res., Development Options Ltd; Economic Develt consultant, 1990–99. Minister for Children and Early Years, Scottish Parlt, 2007–11. Joined SNP, 1983 (Mem., Nat. Exec. Cttee, 1994–99). *Address:* Scottish Parliament, Edinburgh EH99 1SP.

INGRAM, Rt Hon. Adam (Paterson); PC 1999; *b* 1 Feb. 1947; *s* of Bert Ingram and Louisa Paterson; *m* 1970, Maureen Georgina McMahon. *Educ:* Cranhill Secondary School. Commercial apprentice, 1965, computer programmer, 1966–69, J. & P. Coats, Glasgow; programmer/analyst, Associated British Foods, 1969–70; programmer/systems analyst, SSEB, 1970–77; Trade Union Official, NALGO, 1977–87. Chair, East Kilbride Constituency Labour Party, 1981–85; Councillor, E Kilbride DC, 1980–87, Leader, 1984–87. MP (Lab) E Kilbride, 1987–2005, E Kilbride, Strathaven and Lesmahagow, 2005–10. An Opposition Whip, Feb.–Nov. 1988 (responsible for Scottish business and Treasury matters); PPS to Leader of the Opposition, 1988–92; front bench spokesman on social security, 1993–95, on sci. and technol., 1995–97; Minister of State: NI Office, 1997–2001; MoD, 2001–07. Mem., Select Cttee on Trade and Industry, 1992–93; Vice-Chm., British-Japanese All-Party Parly Gp, 1992–97; Sec., British-Singapore All-Party Parly Gp, 1992–97; Vice-Chm., All-Party Parly Gp on Nuclear Energy, 2007–10; Sec., All-Party Parly Gp on Iraq, 2008–10. Head, Study Team on Defence role in counter-terrorism and resilience, 2007–09. JP E Kilbride, 1980–2008. Hon. Col, 154 Scottish Regt, RLC, 2013–. *Recreations:* fishing, cooking, reading, golf. *E:* adam_ingram@compuserve.com.

INGRAM, Christopher John; Partner, Ingram Enterprise LLP, since 2008; *b* 9 June 1943; *s* of Thomas Frank Ingram and Gladys Agnes Ingram; *m* 1964, Janet Elizabeth Rye; one *s* one *d*. *Educ:* Woking Grammar Sch. KMP, 1970–72; Man. Dir, TMD Advertising, 1972–76; Founder Chris Ingram Associates (CIA), later Tempus Group plc, 1976, Chm., 1976–2002; Partner, Genesis Investments, 2002–08; Founder, The Ingram Partnership Ltd, 2003–07. Owner, Woking FC, 2002–12. Chm., Vitesse Media, 2014–. Dep. Chm., Foundn for Entrepreneurial Mgt, 2003–07, Chm., Centre for Creative Business, 2005–08, London Business Sch. Exec. Chm., Sports Revolution, 2009–13. Mem., Vice-Chancellor's Adv. Council, Univ. of Arts London, 2012–. Vice Pres., Shelter, 2001–08. Trustee, Ingram Trust, 1992–. Hon. Fellow, London Business Sch., 2007–. *Recreations:* theatre, football, modern British art, eating out, travel in cold climates. *Address:* (office) 85 Tottenham Court Road, W1T 4TQ.

INGRAM, Prof. David Stanley, OBE 1999; botanist and plant pathologist; Hon. Professor: University of Edinburgh, since 1992; University of Lancaster, since 2009; Master, St Catharine's College, Cambridge, 2000–06; *b* 10 Oct. 1941; *s* of Stanley Arthur Ingram, toolmaker and Vera May Ingram (*née* Mansfield); *m* 1965, Alison Winifred Graham; two *s*. *Educ:* Yardley Grammar School, Birmingham; Univ. of Hull (BSc, PhD); MA, ScD Cantab. CBiol, FRSB (FIBiol 1986); FLS 1991; FRSE 1993; FCIHort (FIHort 1997); FRCPE 1998. Research Fellow, Univ. of Glasgow Dept of Botany, 1966–68; ARC Unit of Develt Botany, Cambridge, 1969–74; University of Cambridge: Research Fellow, Botany Sch., 1968–69; Univ. Lectr, 1974–88; Reader in Plant Pathology, 1988–90; Mem. Gen. Board, 1984–88; Fellow, Downing Coll., Cambridge, 1974–90 (Dean, 1976–82; Tutor for Graduate Students, 1982–88; Dir of Studies in Biology, 1976–89; Hon. Fellow, 2000); Regius Keeper, Royal Botanic Garden, Edinburgh, 1990–98 (Hon. Fellow, 1998); Advr to Univ. of Edinburgh on public engagement with science, 1998– (Mem. Adv. Cttee, Div. of Biol Scis, 1991–98); Cambridge University: Chairman: Cttee for Interdisciplinary Envmtl Studies, 2001–03; Colls Cttee, 2003–05; Mem., Council, 2003–05. Visiting Professor: Univ. of Glasgow, 1991–2005 (Hon. Prof., 2005–10); of Envmtl Sci. and Horticulture, Napier Univ., 1998–2005; Glyndwr Univ., 2012–; Prof. of Horticulture, RHS, 1995–2000; Vis. Sen. Res. Fellow, ESRC Genomics Forum, Edinburgh, 2006–09 (Mem. Adv. Cttee, 2005–); Hon. Professorial Fellow, Sci., Technol. and Innovation Studies, 2012–, Hon. Associate, Innogen, 2015–, Univ. of Edinburgh; Fellow, Ruskin Foundn, 2014–. Chairman: Scientific Council, Sainsbury Lab. for Plant Pathology, 1990–92; Science and Plants for Schools Trust, 1991–98; Science and Plants for Schs, Scotland, 1998–2000; Scientific and Horticultural Advice Cttee, RHS, 1995–2000 (Mem., Scientific Cttee, 1992–95); Adv. Cttee, Darwin Initiative for Survival of the Species, 1999–2005; Prog. Convener and Chair, Sci. and Soc. Steering Gp, RSE, 2005–09; Member: Adv. Cttee, St Andrews Botanic Garden, 1990–95; Exec. Cttee, Scotland's Nat. Gardens Scheme, 1990–96; Adv. Cttee on SSSI in Scotland, 1992–98; Council, Linnean Soc., 1992–95 (Vice Pres., 1993–94); Council, Internat. Assoc. of Botanic Gardens; Main Bd and Scientific Adv. Cttee, Scottish Natural Heritage, 1999–2000; Jt Nature Conservation Cttee, 1999–2000 and 2002– (Dep. Chm., 2006–); Forestry Commn Adv. Panel, 2004–06. Member: Editl Cttee, Flora of China, 1992–98; Editorial Board: Biol Revs, 1984–98, 2001–05; Annals of Botany, 1992–2001; Advances in Plant Path., 1992–95; Food Security, 2009– (Mem., Adv. Bd, 2006–). Hon. Mem., Inst. of Analytical Plant Illustration, 2016–. Trustee: Grimsthorpe and Drummond Castle Trust, 1990–98; John Fife Meml Trust, 1990–98; Younger Botanic Garden Trust, 1990–2000; Royal Botanic Garden (Sibbald) Trust, 1990–98; Botanic Gardens Conservation International, 1991–98; Scottish Sci. Trust, 1998–99 (Mem. Scientific Adv. Cttee, 1999–2002); Dynamic Earth Proj., 1998–2000; World Conservation Monitoring Centre 2000, 2001–04. President: 7th Internat. Congress of Plant Pathology, 1994–98; British Soc. for Plant Pathology, 1998 (Hon. Mem., 2008); Hon. Vice-Pres., Royal Caledonian Horticultural Soc., 1990. Hon. Fellow: Myerscough Coll., 2001; Worcester Coll., Oxford, 2003; St Catharine's Coll., Cambridge, 2006. Hon. FRSGS 1998. DUniv Open, 2000. VMH 2004. *Publications:* (with D. N. Butcher) Plant Tissue Culture, 1974; (with J. P. Helgeson) Tissue Culture Methods for Plant Pathologists, 1980; (with A. Friday) Cambridge Encyclopedia of Life Sciences, 1985; (with P. H. Williams) Advances in Plant Pathology, vol. 1, 1982 to vol. 9, 1993; (with A. Hudson) Shape and Form in Plants and Fungi, 1994; (with A. Karp and P. G. Isaac) Molecular Tools for Screening Biodiversity, 1998; (with N. F. Robertson) Plant Disease, 1999; (with D. Vince-Prue and P. J. Gregory) Science and the Garden, 2002, 3rd edn 2015; The Gardens at Brantwood: evolution of John Ruskin's Lakeland paradise, 2014; contrib. papers dealing with research in plant pathology, plant tissue culture, botany, horticultural science, garden history and history of art to learned jls; contrib. articles to magazines and newspapers dealing with horticulture and sci. *Recreations:* listening to classical music and jazz, theatre, ceramics and other decorative arts, gardening, reading, strolling around cities. *Address:* c/o Royal Society of Edinburgh, 22–26 George Street, Edinburgh EH2 2PQ. *Club:* New (Edinburgh).

INGRAM, Edward John W.; *see* Winnington-Ingram.

INGRAM, Sir James (Herbert Charles), 4th Bt *cr* 1893; *b* 6 May 1966; *s* of (Herbert) Robin Ingram (*d* 1979) and of Shiela, *d* of late Charles Peczenik; *S* grandfather, 1980; *m* 1998, Aracea Elizabeth (marr. diss. 2014), *d* of Graham Pearce; one *s*. *Educ:* Eton; Cardiff Univ. *Heir:* *s* Herbert Rufus Ingram, *b* 12 Aug. 2010.

INGRAM, Paul; Head of Agricultural Services, Barclays Bank plc, 1988–94; *b* 20 Sept. 1934; *s* of John Granville Ingram and Sybil Ingram (*née* Johnson); *m* 1st, 1957, Jennifer Gillian (*née* Morgan) (*d* 1988); one *s* one *d*; 2nd, 2013, Janet Elizabeth Farmer. *Educ:* Manchester Central High School; University of Nottingham (BSc 1956). Dept of Conservation and Extension, Fedn of Rhodesia and Nyasaland, 1956–63; Nat. Agricl Adv. Service, later ADAS, MAFF, 1965–88; County Livestock Officer, Lancs, 1969–70; Policy Planning Unit, MAFF, 1970–72; Farm Management Adviser, Devon, 1972–76; Regional Farm Management Adviser, Wales, 1976–77; Dep. Sen. Livestock Advr, 1977–79, Sen. Agricl Officer, 1979–85, Chief Agricl Officer, 1985–87, Dir of Farm and Countryside Service, 1987–88, ADAS. *Address:* 36 Ceylon Road, W14 0PY.

INGRAM, Robert Alexander; General Partner, Hatteras Venture Partners, since 2007; Chairman, Elan Corporation plc, 2011–13 (Director, 2010–13); *b* 6 Dec. 1942; *s* of Myra L. Ingram; *m* 1962, Carolyn Jean Hutson; three *s*. *Educ:* Eastern Illinois Univ. (BSc Business Admin); Lumpkin Coll. of Business. Sales rep., 1965; Merrell Dow Pharmaceuticals: various sales mgt, then govt and public affairs posts; Vice Pres., Public Affairs, until 1985; Vice Pres., Govt Affairs, Merck & Co. Inc., 1985–88; Pres., Merck Frosst Canada Inc., 1988–90; joined Glaxo Inc., 1990: Exec. Vice Pres., Admin and Regulatory Affairs, 1990–93; Exec. Vice Pres., then Pres. and Chief Operating Officer, 1993–94; Pres. and CEO, 1994–99; Chm., Glaxo Wellcome Inc., and Chief Exec., Glaxo Wellcome plc, 1997–2000; Chm., Glaxo Inc., 1999–2000; GlaxoSmithKline: Chief Operating Officer and Pres., Pharmaceutical Ops, 2000–02; Vice Chm., Pharmaceuticals, 2003–09; Strategic Advr to CEO, 2010–. Director: Wachovia Corp., 1997; TheraCom, 1998; Northern Telecom Ltd (NORTEL), 1999–2006; Valeant Pharmaceuticals Internat., 2003–. Hon. LLD: Eastern Illinois, 1988; Univ. of Scis, Philadelphia, 1999. *Recreations:* Formula One motor racing, Porsche restoration. *Address:* Hatteras Venture Partners, 280 S Mangum Street, Suite 350, Durham, NC 27701, USA. *Club:* Royal Automobile.

INGRAM, Stanley Edward; solicitor; *b* 5 Dec. 1922; *o s* of late Ernest Alfred Stanley Ingram and Ethel Ann Ingram; *m* 1948, Vera (*née* Brown); one *s* one *d*. *Educ:* Charlton Central School. Articled clerk with Wright & Bull, Solicitors; admitted Solicitor, 1950. Served RAF, 1942–46; maintained machines used to break Enigma code at Bletchley Park, 1943–45. Legal Asst, Min. of Nat. Insurance, 1953; Sen. Legal Asst, Min. of Pensions and Nat. Insurance, 1958; Asst Solicitor, 1971, Under Sec. (Legal), 1978–83, DHSS. Member Council: Civil Service Legal Soc. and of Legal Section of First Division Assoc., 1971–82; Mem., Salaried Solicitors' Cttee of Law Society, 1978–81. Secretary: Romsey Gp, CS Retirement Fellowship, 1989–97; Test Valley Croquet Club, 1995–2002 (Treas., 1994–95); Winchester Croquet Club, 1998–2006; Romsey Abbey Probus Club, 2000–12 (Vice-Pres., 1996; Pres.,

1997). Freedom of Bletchley Park, 2001. Bletchley Park Commemorative Badge, 2009. *Publications:* The Enigma Mission (novel), 2010. *Recreation:* gardening. *Address:* 2 Little Woodley Farm, Winchester Hill, Romsey, Hants SO51 7NU. *Club:* Law Society.

INGRAM, Tamara, OBE 2011; President and Chief Executive Officer, Team P&G, WPP, since 2007; *b* 1 Oct. 1960; *d* of John Ingram and Sonia (*née* Bolson); *m* 1989, Andrew Millington; one *s* one *d.* *Educ:* Queen's Coll., Harley St; Univ. of E Anglia (BA Hons Eng.). Joined Saatchi & Saatchi, 1985: Account Exec., 1985–87; Bd Account Dir, 1989–90; Gp Account Dir, 1990–93; Exec. Bd Dir, 1993–95; Saatchi & Saatchi Advertising Ltd: Jt CEO, 1995–99; Chief Exec., 1999–2001; Chm., 2001; Chm. and Chief Exec., McCann-Erickson London, 2002; Global CEO, Added Value, Henley Centre, and Fusion5, Kantar Div., WPP, 2003–05; CEO, Grey Gp UK, WPP, 2005–07. Non-exec. Dir, Serco, 2014–. Chm., Visit London, 2002–09; Mem. Bd, London Develt Agency, 2000–06. Chm., Develt Bd, Royal Court Th., 2004–08. Board Member: Sage Gp, 2005–13; Almeida Th., 2008–13. Member Council: IPA, 1995–; Mktg Soc., 1995–. *Recreations:* theatre, football, tennis, family.

INGRAM, Timothy Charles William; Chairman: Wealth Management Association, since 2012; Greencoat UK Wind plc, since 2012; *b* 18 June 1947; *s* of Stanley Ingram and Sheila Ingram; *m* 1975, Christine Cooper; three *s.* *Educ:* Harrow Sch.; Churchill Coll., Cambridge (MA Econs); INSEAD Business Sch. (MBA). Gen. Manager, ANZ Bank, 1985–91; First National Finance Corporation: Finance Dir, 1992–94; Chief Exec., 1994–2002; Man. Dir, Abbey National plc, 1996–2002; Chief Exec., Caledonia Investments plc, 2002–10; Chairman: Collins Stewart plc, 2010–12; RSM Tenon plc, 2012–13. Non-executive Director: Hogg Robinson plc, 1999–2000; Sage Group plc, 2002–11; Savills plc, 2002–12; ANZ Bank (Europe) Ltd, 2004–10; Alliance Trust plc, 2010–12. *Recreations:* ski-ing, opera, travel. *Clubs:* Reform, Hurlingham.

INGRAMS, family name of **Baron Darcy de Knayth**.

INGRAMS, Richard Reid; journalist; Editor: Private Eye, 1963–86; The Oldie, 1992–2014; *b* 19 Aug. 1937; *s* of late Leonard St Clair Ingrams and Victoria (*née* Reid); *m* 1st, 1962, Mary Morgan (marr. diss. 1993; she *d* 2007); one *s* (and one *s* one *d* decd); 2nd, 2011, Sara Soudain. *Educ:* Shrewsbury; University Coll., Oxford. Joined Private Eye, 1962; columnist: Observer, 1988–90, 1992–2005; The Independent, 2005–11. *Publications:* (with Christopher Booker and William Rushton) Private Eye on London, 1962; Private Eye's Romantic England, 1963; (with John Wells) Mrs Wilson's Diary, 1965; Mrs Wilson's 2nd Diary, 1966; The Tale of Driver Grope, 1968; (with Barry Fantoni) The Bible for Motorists, 1970; (ed) The Life and Times of Private Eye, 1971; (as Philip Reid, with Andrew Osmond) Harris in Wonderland, 1973; (ed) Cobbett's Country Book, 1974; (ed) Beachcomber: the works of J. B. Morton, 1974; The Best of Private Eye, 1974; God's Apology, 1977; Goldenballs, 1979; (with Fay Godwin) Romney Marsh and the Royal Military Canal, 1980; (with John Wells) Dear Bill: the collected letters of Denis Thatcher, 1980; (with John Wells) The Other Half: further letters of Denis Thatcher, 1981; (with John Wells) One for the Road, 1982; (with John Piper) Piper's Places, 1983; (ed) The Penguin Book of Private Eye Cartoons, 1983; (with John Wells) My Round!, 1983; (ed) Dr Johnson by Mrs Thrale, 1984; (with John Wells) Down the Hatch, 1985; (with John Wells) Just the One, 1986; John Stewart Collis: a memoir, 1986; (with John Wells) The Best of Dear Bill, 1986; (with John Wells) Mud in Your Eye, 1987; The Ridgeway, 1988; You Might As Well Be Dead, 1988; England (anthology), 1989; (with John Wells) Number 10, 1989; On and On…, 1990; (ed) The Oldie Annual, 1993; (ed) The Oldie Annual 2, 1994; Malcolm Muggeridge: the authorized biography, 1995; (ed) I Once Met, 1996; (ed) The Oldie Annual 3, 1997; (ed) Jesus: authors take sides (anthology), 1999; (ed) The Oldie Annual 4, 1999; The Life and Adventures of William Cobbett, 2005; My Friend Footy: a memoir of Paul Foot, 2005; Quips & Quotes: a journalist's commonplace book, 2012. *Recreation:* piano. *Address:* Forge House, Downs Road, Reading, Berks RG8 9TU.

INJIA, Hon. Sir Salamo, Kt 2005; Chief Justice of Papua New Guinea, since 2008 (Deputy Chief Justice, 2003–08); *b* 12 Sept. 1958; *s* of Kapo Injia and Anna Injia; *m* 1994, Peam; three *s* two *d.* *Educ:* Univ. of Papua New Guinea (LLB); Harvard Law Sch. (LLM). Dep. Public Solicitor, 1989–90; private legal practice, 1991–93; a Judge of the Nat. and Supreme Courts, PNG, 1993–2003. *Publications:* (jtly) Criminal Law and Practice in Papua New Guinea, 3rd edn, 2001. *Recreation:* social golf. *Address:* PO Box 1300, Waigani, Papua New Guinea. *T:* 3245715, *Fax:* 3257732. *E:* SInjiaKt@pngjudiciary.gov.pg.

INKSTER, Nigel Norman, CMG 2003; Counsellor, Foreign and Commonwealth Office, 1998. Entered FCO, 1975; Third Secretary: FCO, 1975; Kuala Lumpur, 1976; Third, later Second Sec., FCO, 1976–79; Second, later First Sec., Bangkok, 1979–82; First Secretary: FCO, 1982–83; Peking, 1983–85; Buenos Aires, 1985–89; FCO, 1989–92; Counsellor: Athens, 1992–94; Hong Kong, 1994–98.

INMAN, His Honour Derek Arthur; a Circuit Judge, 1993–2008; *b* 1 Aug. 1937; *s* of Arthur and Marjorie Inman; *m* 1st, 1963, Sarah Juliet Cahn (marr. diss. 1982); one *s* two *d*; 2nd, 1983, Elizabeth (*née* Dickinson), *widow* of Lt-Col C. Thomson. *Educ:* Roundhay Sch., Leeds; RNC, Dartmouth. RN; served in HM Ships Sheffield, Belfast and Bulwark; Staff of C-in-C Home Fleet; Sec. to Comdr Naval Forces Gulf and HMS Hermione; retired as Lieut Comdr, 1974. Called to the Bar, Middle Temple, 1968; in Chambers at 2 Harcourt Bldgs, 1974–93. *Recreations:* watching cricket and Rugby, compulsory gardening. *Address:* c/o Lloyds Bank, High Street, Godalming, Surrey GU7 1AT.

INMAN, Edward Oliver, OBE 1998; FRAeS; Chief Executive, South Bank Employers' Group, since 2004; *b* 12 Aug. 1948; *s* of late John Inman and of Peggy Inman (*née* Beard); *m* 1st, 1971, Elizabeth (*née* Douglas) (marr. diss. 1982); one *s* one *d*; 2nd, 1984, Sherida (*née* Sturton) (marr. diss. 2005); one *d*; 3rd, 2009, Julia Heasman. *Educ:* King's College Sch., Wimbledon; Gonville and Caius Coll., Cambridge (MA); School of Slavonic and East European Studies, London (MA). FRAeS 1999. Joined Imperial War Museum as Res. Asst, 1972; Asst Keeper 1974; Keeper of Exhibits (Duxford) 1976; Dir, Imperial War Mus., Duxford, 1978–2004. Trustee, American Air Mus. in Britain, 2004–. Chm., Jubilee Gardens Trust, 2010–; Bd Mem., Waterloo Quarter Business Improvement District, 2006–. *Address:* South Bank Employers' Group, 91 Waterloo Road, SE1 8RT. *T:* (020) 7202 6900, *Fax:* (020) 7202 6904. *E:* email@southbanklondon.com.

INMAN, Melbourne Donald; QC 1998; **His Honour Judge Melbourne Inman;** a Circuit Judge, since 2007; a Senior Circuit Judge, since 2014; Recorder of Birmingham; *b* 1 April 1957; *s* of Melbourne and Norah Inman. *Educ:* Bishop Vesey's Grammar Sch.; Regent's Park Coll., Oxford (MA). Called to the Bar, Inner Temple, 1979, Bencher, 2002. Asst Recorder, 1996–99; Recorder, 1999–2007. Hd of Advocacy Trng and Continuing Professional Develt, Midland Circuit, 1998–2007. *Recreations:* ski-ing, listening to the piano. *Address:* Queen Elizabeth II Law Courts, 1 Newton Street, Birmingham B4 7NA.

INNES of Coxton, Sir Alastair (Charles Deverell), 13th Bt *cr* 1686 (NS), of Coxton, co. Moray; *b* 17 Sept. 1970; *o s* of Sir David Innes of Coxton, 12th Bt and of Marjorie Alison (*née* Parker); *S* father, 2010; *m* 2008, Sarah Louise, *d* of Robin and Carolyn Jones, Chester; two *d.* *Educ:* Haileybury; Southampton Univ. Admitted Solicitor, 1999; Solicitor, 2010–, Legal Dir, Amey plc, 2013–. *Recreations:* golf, tennis, running and walking.

INNES, Alistair Campbell M.; *see* Mitchell-Innes.

INNES of Edingight, Sir Malcolm (Rognvald), KCVO 1990 (CVO 1981); Orkney Herald of Arms Extraordinary, since 2001; *b* 25 May 1938; 3rd *s* of late Sir Thomas Innes of Learney, GCVO, LLD, and Lady Lucy Buchan, 3rd *d* of 18th Earl of Caithness; *m* 1963, Joan (*d* 2013), *o d* of Thomas D. Hay, CA, Edinburgh; three *s.* *Educ:* Edinburgh Acad.; Univ. of Edinburgh (MA, LLB). WS 1964. Falkland Pursuivant Extraordinary, 1957–58; Carrick Pursuivant, 1958–71; Lyon Clerk and Keeper of the Records, 1966–81; Marchmont Herald, 1971–81; Lord Lyon King of Arms, 1981–2001; Sec., Order of the Thistle, 1981–2001. Mem., Queen's Body Guard for Scotland (Royal Company of Archers), 1971. Fellow, Heraldry Socs of NZ, 1978, Canada, 1982, and Scotland, 2001. Grand Officer of Merit, SMO Malta. *Recreation:* visiting places of historic interest. *Clubs:* New, Puffin's (Edinburgh).

INNES, Sir Peter (Alexander Berowald), 17th Bt *cr* 1628, of Balvenie; *b* 6 Jan. 1937; *s* of Lt-Col Sir (Ronald Gordon) Berowald Innes, 16th Bt, OBE and Elizabeth Haughton (*d* 1958), *e d* of late Alfred Fayle; *S* father, 1988; *m* 1959, Julia Mary, *d* of A. S. Levesley; two *s* one *d.* *Educ:* Prince of Wales School, Nairobi, Kenya; Bristol Univ. (BSc). Scott Wilson Kirkpatrick and Partners, then Scott Wilson Kirkpatrick & Co. Ltd, Consulting Engineers, 1964–2000: Associate, 1982–87; Partner, 1987–95; Dir, 1995–2000; responsible for several airport projects in UK, Africa and Middle East, including major military airbases. Lt-Col Engr and Logistic (formerly Transport) Staff Corps, RE (TA). Voluntary guide, Winchester Cathedral, 2001–. *Heir:* *s* Alexander Guy Berowald Innes, *b* 4 May 1960. *Club:* S Winchester Golf.

INNES, Peter Maxwell; HM Diplomatic Service, retired; Consul-General, Melbourne, 1998–2001; *b* 9 Aug. 1941; *s* of James Innes and Agnes Margaret Innes (*née* Dea); *m* 1965, Robina Baillie Walker; one *s* one *d.* *Educ:* Morrison's Acad., Crieff; Open Univ. (BA Hons Hum 2011). Min. of Aviation, 1960–72; Department of Trade and Industry, 1972–77; Asst Airport Manager, Aberdeen Airport, 1972–73; on secondment to British Embassy, Washington, 1973–76; joined FCO, 1977; Seoul, 1979–83; FCO, 1983–85; First Sec. (Agric.), Dublin, 1985–89; FCO, 1989–92 (EC Monitoring Mission in Bosnia, 1991); Dir, British Information Services, NY, 1992–97; FCO, 1997–98. *Recreations:* reading, walking, travel, watching most sports. *Address:* Alberton, South Crieff Road, Comrie, Perthshire PH6 2HF. *Clubs:* Royal Over-Seas League; Probus (Comrie); 30 (Crieff); Comrie Golf.

INNES, Rt Rev. Dr Robert Neil; *see* Gibraltar in Europe, Bishop of.

INNES, Sheila Miriam; consultant (education and media); *b* 25 Jan. 1931; *d* of late Dr James Innes, MB, ChB, MA and of Nora Innes. *Educ:* Talbot Heath School, Bournemouth; Lady Margaret Hall, Oxford (Exhibnr; BA Hons Mod. Langs; MA). BBC Radio Producer, World Service, 1955–61; BBC TV producer: family programmes, 1961–65; further education, 1965–73; exec. producer, further education, 1973–77; Head, BBC Continuing Educn, TV, 1977–84; Controller, BBC Educnl Broadcasting, 1984–87; Dir, BBC Enterprises Ltd, 1986–87; Chief Exec., 1987–89, Dep. Chm., 1989–92, Open Coll. Non-exec. Dir, Brighton Health Care NHS Trust, 1993–96. Chairman: Cross-Sector Cttee for Development and Review, BTEC, 1986–87; Cross-Sector Cttee for Product Develt, BTEC, 1989–92; British Gas Training Awards, 1988–92. Member: Gen. Board, Alcoholics Anonymous, 1980–; Board of Governors, Centre for Information on Language Teaching and Research, 1981–84; Council, Open Univ., 1984–87; Council for Educational Technology, 1984–87; EBU Educational Working Party, 1984–87; Educn Cttee, 1990–95, Women's Adv. Gp, 1992–95, RSA; Standing Conf. on Schools' Science and Technol., 1990–93 (Mem. Council, 1993–98); Age Concern Training Validation (later Quality) Cttee, 1992–94; IMgt Management Develt Proj., 1992–95. Vice-Pres., Educn Sect., British Sci. Assoc. (formerly BAAS), 1990–. Mem., Clothing and Allied Products ITB Management 2000 Cttee of Enquiry, 1989. Patron, One World Broadcasting Trust, 1988–98. Gov., Talbot Heath Sch., Bournemouth, 1989–95. Vice-Pres., Abbeyfield Eastbourne Soc., 2005–. Mem., RTS, 1984; FRSA 1986; FITD 1987; CCMI (CIMgt 1987). Hon. DLitt South Bank, 1992. *Publications:* BBC publications; articles for language jls and EBU Review. *Recreations:* music (classical and jazz), country pursuits, sketching, photography, travel, languages. *Address:* Wychwood, Barcombe, East Sussex BN8 5TP. *T:* (01273) 400268. *Clubs:* Reform; Oxford Society.

INNES-KER, family name of **Duke of Roxburghe**.

INSALL, Sir Donald (William), Kt 2010; CBE 1995 (OBE 1981); FSA, RWA, FRIBA; architect and planning consultant; Founder, Donald Insall Associates Ltd (formerly Donald W. Insall & Associates), 1958 (Principal, 1958–81; Chairman, 1981–98); *b* 7 Feb. 1926; *o s* of late William R. Insall and Phyllis Insall, Henleaze, Bristol; *m* 1964, Amy Elizabeth, MA, *er d* of Malcolm H. Moss, Nanpantan, Leics; two *s* one *d.* *Educ:* Bristol Univ.; RA Sch. of Architecture; Sch. of Planning, London (Dip. (Hons)); SPAB Lethaby Schol. 1951. FRIBA 1968, FRTPI 1973. Coldstream Guards, 1944–47. Architectural and Town-Planning Consultancy has included town-centre studies, civic and univ., church, domestic and other buildings, notably in conservation of historic towns and buildings (incl. restoration of ceiling, House of Lords, and Windsor Castle after fire, 1992); Medal (Min. of Housing and Local Govt), Good Design in Housing, 1962. Visiting Lecturer: RCA, 1964–69; Coll. d'Europe, Bruges, 1976–81; Catholic Univ. of Leuven, 1982–2003; Adjunct Prof., Univ. of Syracuse, 1971–81. Mem., Council of Europe Working Party, 1969–70; Nat. Pilot Study, Chester: A Study in Conservation, 1968; Consultant, Chester Conservation Programme, 1970–87 (EAHY Exemplar; European Prize for Preservation of Historic Monuments, 1981; Europa Nostra Medals of Honour, 1983 and 1989). Member: Historic Buildings Council for England, 1971–84; Grants Panel, EAHY, 1974; Council, RSA, 1976–80 (FRSA, 1948); Council, SPAB, 1979–2007; Ancient Monuments Bd for England, 1980–84; UK Council, ICOMOS, 1998–2014; Royal Parks Adv. Bd, 2000–02; Comr, Historic Bldgs and Monuments Commn, 1984–89; Member: Standing Adv. Cttee, Getty Grant Program, 1988–92; EC Expert Cttee on Architectl Heritage, 1990, 1993–; DNH Inquiry into Fire Protection at Royal Palaces, 1993; Architectl Adv. Cttee, World Monuments Fund in Britain, 1996–; Vice-Chm., Conf. on Trng in Architectural Conservation, 1990–2000 (Hon. Sec., 1959–89); Vice-President: Bldg Crafts and Conservation Trust, 1994–2010; City of Winchester Trust, 2002–. Member: Architectl Adv. Cttee, Westminster Abbey, 1993–98; Fabric Adv. Cttee, Southwark Cathedral, 1992–, Canterbury Cathedral, 1997–. Patron: Kew Soc., 2001–; Envmtl Trust for Richmond-on-Thames, 2001–; Bedford Park Soc., 2001–. RIBA: Banister Fletcher Medallist, 1949; Neale Bursar, 1955; Examr, 1957; Competition Assessor, 1971. Conferences: White House (Natural Beauty), 1965; Historic Architectural Interiors, USA, 1988, 1993; Singapore, 1994. Lecture tours: USA, 1964, 1972 (US Internat. Reg. Conf. on Conservation), 2003; Mexico, 1972; Yugoslavia, 1973; Canada, 1974, 1999; Argentina, 1976; India, 1979; Portugal, 1982. Hon. Freeman, City of Chester, 2000. Hon. LLD Bristol, 2004; Hon. DArch Chester, 2012. European Architectural Heritage Year Medal (for Restoration of Chevening), 1973; Harley J. McKee Award, Assoc. for Preservation Technol. Internat., 1999; People in Conservation Award, RICS, 1999; Europa Nostra Medal of Honour, 2000; Plowden Medal, Royal Warrant Holders' Assoc., 2001. Silver Jubilee Medal, 1977. *Publications:* (jtly) Railway Station Architecture, 1966; (jtly) Conservation Areas 1967; The Care of Old Buildings Today, 1973; Historic Buildings: action to maintain the expertise for their care and repair, 1974; Conservation in Action, 1982; Conservation in Chester, 1988; Living Buildings, Architectural Conservation: philosophy, principles and practice, 2008; contrib. to Encyclopædia Britannica, professional, environmental and internat. jls. *Recreations:* visiting, sketching, photographing and enjoying places; appreciating craftsmanship; Post-Vintage Thoroughbred Cars (Mem., Rolls Royce Enthusiasts' Club). *Address:* 73 Kew Green, Richmond, Surrey TW9 3AH; (office) 12 Devonshire Street, W1G 7AB. *T:* (020) 7245 9888. *Club:* Athenæum.

INSCH, Elspeth Virginia, OBE 1998; Headmistress, King Edward VI Handsworth School, Birmingham, 1989–2012; *b* 21 Aug. 1949; *d* of John Douglas Insch and Isabella Elizabeth Campbell (*née* Brodie). *Educ:* Newarke Girls' Sch., Leicester; Birkbeck Coll., Univ. of London (BSc); Univ. of Edinburgh (MPhil, DipEd, PGCE). CGeog 2002. Demonstrator, Univ. of Edinburgh, 1970–73; Teacher: Abington High Sch., Leics, 1974–77; Nottingham High Sch. for Girls (GPDST), 1977–84; Dep. Head, Kesteven and Sleaford High Sch. for Girls, 1984–89. Consultant, Springbank Sand and Gravel Co. Ltd, 1970–79. Pres., Assoc. of Maintained Girls' Schools, 1999–2000; Mem. Cttee, Nat. Grammar Schools Assoc., 1990–2006. FRGS 1968 (Mem., 1994–, Chm., 2003–06, Educn Cttee; Vice Pres., 2003–06). Fellow, Winston Churchill Meml Trust, 1980; Trustee, Grantham Yorke Trust, 1990–2005. DL W Midlands, 2008–12. Hon. DSc Aston, 2006. *Address:* Cramond, Rowgate, Kirkby Stephen, Cumbria CA17 4SP.

INSHAW, Maj. Gen. Timothy Gordon, CB 2011; Head, Strategy and Policy, London Operations, L-3 Communications, since 2014; *b* Hong Kong, 14 Aug. 1957; *s* of Gordon Henry William Inshaw and Rita Inshaw; *m* 1982, Sally Patricia Roe; three *s*. *Educ:* Wilsthorpe Comp. Sch.; Welbeck Coll.; RMA Sandhurst; RMCS (BSc 1981). CE; MIET 2000, FIET 2009; CITP 2008; FBCS 2009. SO3 Comms HQN1, 1985–86; Instructor, Sch. of Signals, 1987; Army Staff Coll., 1988–89; OC 212 (12 Armoured Bde) Signal Sqn, 1990–92; Instructor, Jun. Div. of Staff Course, 1992–93; SO2 Operational Requirements, 1994; SO1 Mgt Plans, Directorate Gen. CIS, 1995; CO 9th Signal Regt (Radio), 1995–98; Dep. Dir Defence Resources and Plans, 1998–2000; rcds 2001; Comdr 1st Signal Bde, 2002–04; Dir Capability Integration (Army), 2004–07; Dir Gen. Trng and Educn, 2007–10; Dir, Inf. Systems and Services, Defence Equipment and Support, 2010–13. Controller, Royal Signals Trustees Ltd, 2014–. *Recreations:* cricket, gardening, walking, DIY.

INSKIP, family name of **Viscount Caldecote**.

INSOLE, Douglas John, CBE 1979; Marketing Director, Trollope & Colls Ltd, 1975–91; *b* 18 April 1926; *s* of John Herbert Insole and Margaret Rose Insole; *m* 1948, Barbara Hazel Ridgway (*d* 1982); two *d* (and one *d* decd). *Educ:* Sir George Monoux Grammar Sch.; St Catharine's Coll., Cambridge (MA). Cricket: Cambridge Univ., 1947–49 (Captain, 1949); Essex CCC, 1947–63 (Captain, 1950–60); played 9 times for England; Vice-Captain, MCC tour of S Africa, 1956–57. Chairman: Test Selectors, 1965–68; TCCB, later ECB, 1975–78 (Chm., Cricket Cttee, 1968–87; Chm., Internat. Cttee, 1988–2000); Mem., MCC Cttee, 1955–94; Manager, England cricket team, Australian tours, 1978–79 and 1982–83. Soccer: Cambridge Univ., 1946–48; Pegasus, and Corinthian Casuals; Amateur Cup Final medal, 1956. Member: Sports Council, 1971–74; FA Council, 1979– (Life Vice-Pres., 1999). Pres., Essex CCC, 1994–. JP Chingford, 1962–74. *Publications:* Cricket from the Middle, 1960. *Recreations:* cricket, soccer, theatre, jazz. *Address:* 8 Hadleigh Court, Crescent Road, Chingford, E4 6AX. *T:* (020) 8529 6546. *Club:* MCC (Trustee, 1988–94; Hon. Life Vice Pres., 1995; Pres., 2006–07).

INSTANCE, Caroline Mary; Chief Executive, Actuarial Profession, 2002–11; *b* 4 May 1957; *d* of William Henry and late Hilary Willatt; *m* 1st (marr. diss. 1995); one *s* one *d*; 2nd, 1998, John Instance; two step *d*. *Educ:* Henley Grammar Sch.; Sheffield Univ. (BSc Hons Psychol. 1978). MIPD. With Rank Orgn, 1978–82; United Friendly, 1982–96 (Human Resources Dir, 1993–96); Chief Exec., OPRA, 1996–2002. Non-exec. Dir, Omnilife, 2015–. Trustee, ShareAction, 2011–. Mem., Thakeham Parish Council. *Recreations:* theatre, opera, enjoying countryside, voluntary work with Age UK (Horsham Dist) and Pallant Gallery.

INSTONE, Daniel Richard; independent environmental advisor, since 2013; *b* London, 17 Dec. 1947; *s* of Ralph and Sybil Instone; *m* 1986, Anne Scrope; two *d*. *Educ:* Westminster Sch.; Christ Church, Oxford (MA Hons Classics). Ministry of Technology, later Department of Trade and Industry: Asst Principal, 1970–73; Asst Pte Sec. to Minister of Industrial Develt, 1973; Pte Sec. to Minister of State for Industry, 1974; Grade 7, 1975–83 (seconded to Econ. Secretariat, Cabinet Office, 1978–80); Department of Transport: Dep. Dir, 1983–91 (seconded to HM Treasury, 1985–88); Hd, Transport Policy Unit, 1991–98; Team Leader, Prime Minister's Strategy Unit, 1998–2001; Department for Environment, Food and Rural Affairs: Hd, Water Quality Div., 2001–05; Waste Strategy Div., 2005–08; Sen. Responsible Owner, Waste Prog., 2008–09; Prog. Dir, Atmosphere and Local Envmt Prog., 2009–13. *Recreations:* walking, music, literature, interesting ideas.

INVERDALE, John Ballantyne; sports presenter, BBC; *b* 27 Sept. 1957; *s* of Capt. John Ballantyne Inverdale, CBE, RN and Stella Norah Mary Westlake (*née* Richards); *m* Jacqueline Elizabeth Knight; two *d*. *Educ:* Clifton Coll.; Univ. of Southampton (BA Hons). Journalist, Lincolnshire Echo, 1979–82; BBC Radio Lincs, 1982–85; BBC Radio 2, 1985–88; presenter: Sport on 5 (formerly Sport on 2), BBC Radio, 1988–94; Drivetime, BBC Radio 5 Live, 1994–97, and Rugby Special, BBC TV, 1994–; Onside, 1997–2001, Grandstand, 1999–2004, BBC TV. Pres., British Univs and Colls Sport, 2005–; Chm., Esher Rugby FC, 1998–. Hon. Fellow, UWIC, 2009. Hon. DLitt Soton, 2001; Hon. DArts Lincoln, 2006. *Address:* c/o BBC News Centre, Broadcasting House, Portland Place, W1A 1AA.

INVERFORTH, 4th Baron *cr* 1919, of Southgate; **Andrew Peter Weir;** *b* 16 Nov. 1966; *s* of 3rd Baron Inverforth and of Jill Elizabeth, *o d* of late John W. Thornycroft, CBE; *S* father, 1982; *m* 1992, Rachel Sian Shapland Davies. *Educ:* Marlborough College; Trinity Coll., Cambridge; London Hosp. Med. Coll. MB BS 1994.

INVERNE, James Allan Marshall; journalist, author and artist manager; Co-Managing Director, Inverne Price Music Consultancy, since 2013; Founder and Editor-in-Chief, www.thepianoforum.org, 2014; *b* Bournemouth, 5 May 1975; *s* of Richard Inverne and late Susan Inverne; *m* 2004, Kareen Cartier; one *s*. *Educ:* Bournemouth Grammar Sch.; Queen Mary and Westfield Coll., Univ. of London (BA Hons). Arts Ed., Performance TV, 1996–2001; Classical CD reviewer, Mail on Sunday, 1996–98; Eur. Performing Arts corresp., Time mag., 1999–2005; London Th. corresp., Playbill Online, 2003–05; Ed., Gramophone mag., 2005–11; Founder Ed., Inside Sundance Institute mag., 2009–; Contributing Editl Dir, programmes, Delfont Mackintosh Theatres, 2013–; contrib. Wall St Jl, Sunday Telegraph, The Times and Jerusalem Report. Dir and Co-Founder, Interact: Interfaith Action, 2007–. *Publications:* Jack Tinker: a life in review, 1997; The Impresarios, 2000; Wrestling with Elephants: the authorised biography of Don Black, 2003; Inverne's Stage and Screen Trivia, 2004; The Faber Pocket Guide to Musicals, 2009. *Recreations:* theatre, concert and cinema-going, reading (especially biographies), museums. *T:* 07870 203181. *E:* james.inverne@gmail.com.

INVERNESS (St Andrew's Cathedral), Provost of; *no new appointment at time of going to press*.

INVERURIE, Lord; Tristan Michael Keith; *b* 28 May 2010; *s* and *heir* of Earl of Kintore, *qv*.

INWOOD, Rt Rev. Richard Neil; Bishop Suffragan of Bedford, 2003–12; an Honorary Assistant Bishop: Diocese of Derby, since 2012; Diocese of Southwell and Nottingham, since 2012; *b* 4 March 1946; *s* of Cyril and Sylvia Inwood; *m* 1969, Elizabeth Joan Abram; three *d*. *Educ:* University Coll., Oxford (MA, BSc Chem.); Univ. of Nottingham (BA Theol.). Teacher, Uganda, 1969; Works R & D chemist, Dyestuffs Div., ICI, 1970–71; ministerial trng, St John's Coll., Nottingham, 1971–74; ordained deacon, 1974, priest, 1975; Curate: Christ Church, Fulwood, Sheffield, 1974–78; All Souls, Langham Place, W1, 1978–81; Vicar, St Luke's, Bath, 1981–89; Hon. Chaplain, Dorothy House Foundn, Bath, 1984–89; Rector, Yeovil with Kingston Pitney, 1989–95; Prebendary of Wells, 1990–95; Archdeacon of Halifax, 1995–2003; Central Chaplain, Mothers' Union, 2004–09. Acting Bishop of Southwell and Nottingham, 2014. *Publications:* Biblical Perspectives on Counselling, 1980; (jtly) The Church, 1987; (with Mike Smith) Moved by Steam, 2009; (with Mike Smith) Steam Tracked Back, 2011. *Recreations:* fell walking, gardening, music, family, railway nostalgia. *Address:* 43 Whitecotes Park, Chesterfield S40 3RT.

ION, Dame Susan (Elizabeth), DBE 2010 (OBE 2002); PhD; FREng, FIMMM, FNucI; consultant; Vice-President, Royal Academy of Engineering, 2002–08; *b* 3 Feb. 1955; *d* of Lawrence James Burrows and Doris Burrows (*née* Cherry); *m* 1980, John Albert Ion. *Educ:* Penwortham Girls' Grammar Sch., Preston, Lancs; Imperial Coll., London (BSc 1st Cl. Hons, DIC; PhD Materials Sci./Metallurgy 1979). FREng (FEng 1996). British Nuclear Fuels Ltd: Hd, R & D, Fuel Div., 1990–92; Dir, Technol. Develt, 1992–96; Dir of Technol., 1996–2006; Mem., Company Executive, 1996–2006. Member: PPARC, 1994–2000; Council for Sci. and Technol., 2004–11; EPSRC, 2005–10. Chairman: UK Fusion Adv. Bd, 2006–12; Nuclear Innovation and Res. Adv. Bd, 2014–. Non-exec. Dir, Health and Safety Lab., HSE, 2005–. Visiting Professor: Imperial Coll. London, 2006–; London Southbank Univ., 2011–; Hon. Prof., Univ. of Central Lancs, 2007–. Pres., British Nuclear Soc., 2004–06. Gov., Univ. of Manchester, 2004–. Hinton Medal for Outstanding Contribn to Nuclear Engrg, INucE, 1993; President's Medal, RAEng, 2014. *Recreations:* ski-ing, fell walking, playing the violin.

IPGRAVE, Rt Rev. Michael Geoffrey; *see* Woolwich, Area Bishop of.

IPSWICH, Bishop of; *see* St Edmundsbury and Ipswich.

IPSWICH, Archdeacon of; *no new appointment at time of going to press*.

IQBAL, Abdul Shaffaq; QC 2014; a Recorder, since 2008; *b* Wolverhampton, 3 Aug. 1969; *s* of Mohammed Iqbal and Zubaida Bibi; *m* 1996, Rifat Parveen; one *s* one *d*. *Educ:* Moor End High Sch., Huddersfield; Univ. of Bradford (BPharm Hons 1991); Univ. of Northumbria (DipLaw 1993); Inns of Court Sch. of Law. Pharmacist, 1991–92; called to the Bar, Gray's Inn, 1994; in practice as criminal barrister, 1994–. *Recreations:* football, cricket, motorsport, travel, family. *Address:* 6 Park Square, Leeds LS1 2LW. *T:* (0113) 245 9763, *Fax:* (0113) 242 4395. *E:* iqbalqc@psqb.co.uk. *Clubs:* Huddersfield Town Football, Wolverhampton Wanderers Football.

IRBY, family name of **Baron Boston**.

IREDALE, Prof. John Peter, DM; FRCP, FRCPE; FRSE; FMedSci; Dean of Clinical Medicine, since 2010, Regius Professor of Medical Science, since 2013, and Vice Principal, Health Services, since 2014, University of Edinburgh; Consultant Hepatologist, Royal Infirmary of Edinburgh, since 2006; *b* Oxford, 9 Nov. 1960; *s* of Peter Iredale, *qv*; *m* 1990, Dr Catriona Jean Gunn; two *s* one *d*. *Educ:* City of Oxford Sch. for Boys; Univ. of Southampton (BM Hons 1985; DM 1995). MRCP 1988, FRCP 1999; FRCPE 2007. Vis. Clin. Scientist, UCL, 1994–98; University of Southampton: MRC Clinician Scientist, 1994–98; MRC Sen. Clin. Fellow, 1998–2004; Prof. of Hepatol., 2000–04, of Medicine, 2004–06; University of Edinburgh: Prof. of Medicine, 2006–13; Dir, MRC Centre for Inflammation Res., 2009–15. FMedSci 2003; FRSE 2011. *Publications:* contribs to learned jls on tissue scarring and regeneration, incl. Jl Clin. Investigation, Procs NAS, Nature Medicine. *Recreations:* family, cycling, watercolour painting, fishing. *Address:* MRC Centre for Inflammation Research, Queen's Medical Research Institute, 47 Little France Crescent, Edinburgh EH16 4TJ. *T:* (0131) 242 6687, *Fax:* (0131) 242 6682. *E:* carolynn.walthew@ed.ac.uk.

IREDALE, Peter, PhD; FInstP, FIET; Chairman: Oxfordshire Health Authority, 1996–2001; Four Counties Public Health Resources Unit, 1997–2000; *b* Brownhills, Staffs, 15 March 1932; *s* of late Henry and Annie Iredale; *m* 1957, Judith Margaret (*née* Marshall); one *s* three *d*. *Educ:* King Edward VI Grammar Sch., Lichfield; Univ. of Bristol (BSc, PhD). AERE Harwell (subseq. Harwell Laboratory), 1955–92: research: on Nuclear Instrumentation, 1955–69; on Non Destructive Testing, 1969–70; Computer Storage, 1970–73; Commercial Officer, 1973–75; Gp Leader, Nuclear Instrumentation, 1975–77; Dep. Hd, Marketing and Sales Dept, 1977–79; Hd of Marine Technology Support Unit, 1979–81; Chm., UK Wave-Energy Steering Cttee, 1979–84; Dir, Engrg, 1981–84; Dir, Engrg and Non Nuclear Energy, 1984–86; Dep. Dir, 1986–87, Dir, 1987–90, Harwell Lab.; Dir, Culham/Harwell Sites, UKAEA, 1990–92. Chairman: Oxfordshire DHA, 1992–96; Develt Bd, Oxford Inst. of Health Scis, 1993–2001; Elliot-Smith Clinic, 2002–. Supernumerary Fellow, 1991–99, Mem. of Common Room, Wolfson Coll., Oxford, 1999–. Hon. DSc Oxford Brookes, 1993. *Publications:* papers on high energy physics, nuclear instrumentation. *Recreations:* family, music, working with wood, gardening. *Address:* 25 Kirk Close, Oxford OX2 8JL.

See also J. P. Iredale.

IREDALE, Prof. Roger Oliver, PhD; Professor of International Education, 1993–96, now Professor Emeritus, and Director (formerly Dean), Faculty of Education, 1994–96, University of Manchester; *b* 13 Aug. 1934; *s* of Fred Iredale and Elsie Florence (*née* Hills); *m* 1968, Mavis Potter; one *s* one *d*. *Educ:* Harrow County Grammar Sch.; Univ. of Reading (BA 1956, MA 1959, PhD 1971; Hurry Medal for Poetry; Early English Text Soc.'s Prize; Seymour-Sharman Prize for Literature; Graham Robertson Travel Award); Peterhouse Coll., Univ. of Cambridge (Cert. Ed. 1957). Teacher, Hele's Sch., Exeter, 1959–61; Lectr and Senior Lectr, Bishop Otter Coll., Chichester, 1962–70; British Council Officer and Maître de Conférences, Univ. of Algiers, 1970–72; Lectr, Chichester Coll. of Further Educn, 1972–73; British Council Officer, Madras, 1973–75; Dir of Studies, Educnl Admin, Univ. of Leeds, 1975–79; Educn Adviser, 1979–83, Chief Educn Advr, 1983–93, ODA. Sen. Consultant, Iredale Develt Internat., 1996–2003. Member: Commonwealth Scholarship Commn, 1984–93; Unesco-Unicef Jt Cttee, 1991–96; VSO Educn Adv. Cttee, 2002–04; Comr, Sino-British Friendship Scholarship Scheme Commn, 1986–96. Hon. Leader Writer, Western Daily Press, 2011–13. Governor: Sch. of Oriental and African Studies, 1983–95; Queen Elizabeth House, Oxford, 1986–87; Commonwealth of Learning, 1988–93; Sidcot Sch., 2001–03. Trustee, 1993–98, non-exec. Dir, 1998–2007, CfBT Educn Services, subseq. CfBT Educn Trust; Chm., CfBT LLC, Abu Dhabi, 2006–08. Trustee: War on Want, 1998–2000; BookPower, 1999–2006. Hon. FCP 1995. Poetry Society's Greenwood Prize, 1974; First Prize for Poetry, Sherborne Literary Fest., 2013. *Publications:* Turning Bronzes (poems), 1974; Out Towards the Dark (poems), 1978; An Inventory of Time (poems), 2010; articles in The Times, Guardian, Western Daily Press, Comparative Education and other jls; poems for BBC Radio 3 and in anthologies and jls. *Recreations:* poetry writing, championing the oppressed, journalism. *Address:* Northsyde House, 17 High Street, West Coker, Yeovil BA22 9AP. *T:* (01935) 864422.

IRELAND, Mary Elizabeth; Head, Bancroft's School, since 2008; *b* Dumbarton, 5 April 1956; *d* of Denis Ferguson and Elizabeth Ferguson (*née* Gilchrist); *m* 1979, Simon Ireland; one *s*. *Educ:* Notre Dame High Sch.; Univ. of St Andrews (BSc Biochem.); Univ. of Dundee (DipEd). CBiol 1994; MBS 1994. Manufacturing Exec., Procter and Gamble, 1977–79; Hd, Sci. and Technol., King's Hall Sch., Taunton, 1985–89; Housemistress, Ardingly Coll., 1991–2000; Dep. Hd, Christ's Hospital, 2000–07. FRSA 2012. Trustee, Sue Thompson Foundn, 2013–. Freeman, City of London, 2011. *Recreations:* dogs, music (particularly early music and opera), Italy, theatre, cricket, science fiction. *Address:* Bancroft's School, 611–627 High Road, Woodford Green IG8 0RF. *T:* (020) 8506 6760. *E:* head@bancrofts.org. *Clubs:* Lansdowne, East India.

IRELAND, Patrick Gault de C.; *see* de Courcy-Ireland.

IRELAND, Prof. Peter Thomas, DPhil; CEng, FIMechE; Donald Schultz Professor of Turbomachinery, Head, Osney Thermo-Fluids Laboratory, and Director, Rolls-Royce University Technology Centre, University of Oxford, since 2011; Fellow of St Catherine's College, Oxford, since 2011; *b* Coventry, 23 April 1962; *s* of John Ireland and Edna Merry; *m* 2004, Melanie Rigby; one *d. Educ:* St John's Coll., Oxford (BA Engrg Sci.; DPhil Turbine Cooling 1987). CEng 1995; FIMechE 2004. Tutorial Fellow in Engrg Sci., St Anne's Coll., Oxford, 1989–2007; UK Corporate Specialist in Heat Transfer, Rolls-Royce Aerospace, Derby, 2007–11. Dir, Fire Precautions Ltd, 2006–. *Publications:* over 120 papers in heat transfer, turbine cooling and heat transfer measurement method. *Address:* Department of Engineering Science, University of Oxford, Thermo-Fluids Laboratory, Southwell Building, Osney Mead Industrial Estate, Oxford OX2 0ES. *T:* (01865) 288723. *E:* peter.ireland@eng.ox.ac.uk.

IRELAND, Ronald David; QC (Scot.) 1964; Sheriff Principal of Grampian, Highland and Islands, 1988–93; *b* 13 March 1925; *o s* of William Alexander Ireland and Agnes Victoria Brown. *Educ:* George Watson's Coll., Edinburgh; Balliol Coll., Oxford (Scholar; BA 1950, MA 1958); Edinburgh Univ. (LLB 1952). Served Royal Signals, 1943–46. Passed Advocate, 1952; Clerk of the Faculty of Advocates, 1957–58; Aberdeen University: Prof. of Scots Law, 1958–71; Dean of Faculty of Law, 1964–67; Hon. Prof., Faculty of Law, 1988–; Sheriff of Lothian and Borders (formerly Lothians and Peebles) at Edinburgh, 1972–88. Governor, Aberdeen Coll. of Education, 1959–64 (Vice-Chm., 1962–64). Comr, under NI (Emergency Provisions) Act, 1974–75. Member: Bd of Management, Aberdeen Gen. Hosps, 1961–71 (Chm., 1964–71); Departmental Cttee on Children and Young Persons, 1961–64; Cttee on the Working of the Abortion Act, 1971–74; Hon. Sheriff for Aberdeenshire, 1963–88. Member: North Eastern Regional Hosp. Bd, 1964–71 (Vice-Chm. 1966–71); After Care Council, 1962–65; Nat. Staff Advisory Cttee for the Scottish Hosp. Service, 1964–65; Chm., Scottish Hosps Administrative Staffs Cttee, 1965–72. Dir, Scottish Courts Admin, 1975–78. Hon. LLD Aberdeen, 1994. *Address:* 6A Greenhill Gardens, Edinburgh EH10 4BW. *Clubs:* New (Edinburgh); Royal Northern and University (Aberdeen); Highland (Inverness).

IRELAND, Seith; *see* Ireland, W. S. S.

IRELAND, Susan Jean; Director of Open Spaces, City of London Corporation, since 2008; *b* Hertford, 9 May 1956; *d* of late Prof. Geoffrey Dowrick and of Pamela Dowrick; *m* 1980, Clive Ireland (marr. diss. 1991). *Educ:* Ashford Grammar Sch.; Newton Abbot Grammar Sch.; University Coll. Wales (BSc Hons Geog. 1977); Wye Coll., Univ. of London (MSc Landscape Ecol., Design and Maintenance 1978). Tech. Officer, Ashford BC, 1978–82; Chelmsford Borough Council: Sen. Tech. Officer, 1982–86; Inf. and Support Services Manager, 1986–88; Asst Dir, Leisure Services, 1988–2002; Hd of Parks, 2002–04; Dir, Parks and Heritage Services, 2005–08. *Recreations:* reading, travel, caring for a walled garden with luscious fruit, preparing for climate change. *Address:* City of London Corporation, Open Spaces Department, PO Box 270, Guildhall, EC2P 2EJ. *T:* (020) 7332 3033. *Clubs:* Guildhall, Gardeners' Livery.

IRELAND, (William) Seith (Stanners); Sheriff of North Strathclyde at Paisley, since 2014; *b* 5 April 1956; *s* of Samuel Ireland and Isobel Ireland (*née* Stanners); *m* 2006, Elizabeth Crombie. *Educ:* High Sch. of Glasgow; Univ. of Glasgow (LLB Hons 1979). Pres., Students' Rep. Council, Univ. of Glasgow, 1977–78. Admitted as solicitor, 1982; asst solicitor, 1982–85; founded own practice, Ireland & Co., 1986–2003. Temp. Sheriff, 1999; Sheriff (pt-time), 2000–03; Floating Sheriff, 2003–04; Sheriff of N Strathclyde at Kilmarnock, 2004–14. Pres., Glasgow Bar Assoc., 1993–94; Member, Council: Law Soc. of Scotland, 1995–98; Sheriffs' Assoc., 2009–13 (Hon. Sec. and Treas., 2010–12); Scottish Assoc. for the Study of Offending, 2013–. Mem. Business Cttee, Gen. Council, Univ. of Glasgow, 2005–09. Mem., Scottish Bd, Phoenix Futures, 2013–. *Recreations:* golf, cinema, cooking. *Address:* Sheriff's Chambers, Sheriff Court House, Paisley, Renfrewshire PA3 2HW. *T:* (0141) 887 5291, *Fax:* (0141) 887 6702. *E:* sheriffwsireland@scotcourts.gov.uk.

IRENS, Nicholas James, FCA; Director, Sporting Index Ltd, since 2006; *b* 6 Oct. 1946; *s* of late Gp Capt. Henry James Irens and of Helen Margaret Irens; *m* 1972, Fiona Mary Walker; three *s* one *d. Educ:* Blundell's Sch., Tiverton. FCA 1970. Partner, Turner Easdale & Co., Chartered Accountants, 1970–78; Finance Director: Juliana's Hldgs plc, 1979–87; First Leisure Corp. plc, 1988–92; Chm., Cannons Gp plc, 1992–2001. Chm., Esporta Gp Ltd, 2002–06. *Recreations:* bridge, cricket, racing. *Address:* Saxby's Mead, Cowden, Kent TN8 7DR. *T:* (01342) 850520. *E:* nirens@btopenworld.com. *Clubs:* Portland, MCC.

IRETON, Barrie Rowland, CB 2000; Director, Copperbelt Development Foundation, 2002; *b* 15 Jan. 1944; *s* of Philip Thomas Ireton, CBE, and Marjorie Rosalind Ireton; *m* 1965, June Collins; one *s* one *d* (and one *s* decd). *Educ:* Alleyne's Grammar Sch., Stevenage; Trinity Coll., Cambridge (MA); London School of Economics (MSc 1970). Economic Statistician, Govt of Zambia, 1965–68; Economist, Industrial Develt Corp., Zambia, 1968–69; Development Sec., The Gambia, 1970–73; Overseas Development Administration: Economic Advr, 1973–76; Sen. Economic Advr, 1976–84; Asst Sec., 1984–88; Under Sec., 1988–96; Principal Finance Officer, 1988–93; Dir, Africa Div., 1993–96; Dir-Gen., Progs, subseq. Internat. and Resources, ODA, FCO, then DFID, 1996–2003. Sen. Fellow, Inst. of Commonwealth Studies, 2005. Director: Zambia Copper Investments, 2002–05; European Investment Bank, 2002–05; Dir, 2002–05, Business Advr, 2006, Konkola Copper Mines. *Publications:* Britain's International Development Policies: a history of DFID and overseas aid, 2013. *Recreations:* tennis, gardening, walking.

IRONS, Jeremy; actor; *b* 19 Sept. 1948; *s* of late Paul Dugan Irons and of Barbara Anne Brereton (*née* Sharpe); *m* 1st (marr. diss.); 2nd, 1978, Sinead Cusack; two *s. Educ:* Sherborne; Bristol Old Vic Theatre Sch. *Theatre* appearances include: Bristol Old Vic Theatre Co., 1968–71; Godspell, Round House, transf. Wyndham's, 1971; The Taming of the Shrew, New Shakespeare Co., Round House, 1975; Wild Oats, RSC, 1976–77; The Rear Column, Globe, 1978; The Real Thing, Broadway, 1984 (Tony Award for Best Actor); The Rover, Mermaid, 1986; A Winter's Tale, RSC, 1986; Richard II, RSC, 1986; A Little Night Music, NY, 2003; Camelot, Hollywood Bowl, 2004; Embers, Duke of York, 2006; Never So Good, Lyttelton, 2008; The Gods Weep, Hampstead, 2010; *television* appearances include: The Pallisers; Love for Lydia; Brideshead Revisited, 1981; The Captain's Doll, 1983; Longitude, 2000; Elizabeth I, 2005 (Best Supporting Actor, Emmy Awards, 2006, Golden Globe Awards, 2007); The Borgias, 2011, 2012, 2013; Henry IV, 2012; *films* include: The French Lieutenant's Woman, 1981; Moonlighting, 1982; Betrayal, 1982; Swann in Love, 1983; The Wild Duck, 1983; The Mission, 1986; A Chorus of Disapproval, 1988; Dead Ringers, 1988 (Best Actor, New York Film Critics Circle Awards, 1988, Genie Awards, 1989); Danny Champion of the World, 1988; Reversal of Fortune, 1990 (Academy Award for Best Actor, 1991); Australia, 1991; Kafka, 1992; Waterland, 1992; Damage, 1993; M. Butterfly, 1994; The House of the Spirits, 1994; Die Hard: with a vengeance, 1995; Stealing Beauty, 1996; Lolita, 1997; The Man in the Iron Mask, 1998; Chinese Box, 1998; Dungeons and Dragons, And Now Ladies and Gentlemen, Callas Forever, Last Call, 2001; The Time Machine, 2002; Being Julia, 2004; Merchant of Venice, 2004; Kingdom of Heaven, 2005; Casanova, Eragon, Inland Empire, 2006; Appaloosa, 2008; The Pink Panther 2, 2009; Beautiful Creatures, 2013; Night Train to Lisbon, 2014; The Man Who Knew Infinity, 2015. Member: Gaia Foundn; European Film Acad.; Patron: Prison Phoenix Trust; Archway Foundn. *Address:* c/o Hutton Management, 4 Old Manor Close, Askett, Bucks HP27 9NA.

IRONS, Norman MacFarlane, CBE 1995; DL; CEng; Lord Provost and Lord Lieutenant of Edinburgh, 1992–96; Partner, IFP Consulting Engineers, 1983–2006; *b* 4 Jan. 1941; *s* of Dugald Paterson Irons and Anne Galbraith Irons (*née* Rankin); *m* 1966, Anne Wyness Buckley; one *s* one *d. Educ:* George Heriot's Sch.; Borough Road Coll.; Napier Tech. Coll. CEng; MCIBSE 1968; MIMechE 1973. Building Services Engr, 1962–. Mem. (SNP) City of Edinburgh Council, 1976–96. JP 1983–2008, DL 1988, Edinburgh. Pres., Lismore RFC, 1989–94. Hon. Consul: for Denmark, 1999–2011; for Hungary, 2013–. Dean of Consular Corps, Edinburgh and Leith, 2010–11. Paul Harris Fellow, Rotary Internat., 1996; Hon. Mem. Rotary Club of Edinburgh, 2007. Hon. FRCSE 1994. Hon. DLitt Napier, 1993; DUniv Heriot-Watt, 1997. Royal Order of Merit (Norway), 1994; Kt, Order of Dannebrog (Denmark), 2008. *Recreations:* enjoying life with his wife, Rugby. *Address:* 141 Saughtonhall Drive, Edinburgh EH12 5TS. *T:* (0131) 337 6154. *Club:* New (Edinburgh).

IRONSIDE, family name of **Baron Ironside**.

IRONSIDE, 2nd Baron *cr* 1941, of Archangel and of Ironside; **Edmund Oslac Ironside;** Defence Consultant, Rolls-Royce Industrial Power Group, 1989–95; *b* 21 Sept. 1924; *o s* of 1st Baron Ironside, Field Marshal, GCB, CMG, DSO, and Mariot Ysabel Cheyne (*d* 1984); *S* father, 1959; *m* 1950, Audrey Marigold, *y d* of late Lt-Col Hon. Thomas Morgan-Grenville, DSO, OBE, MC; one *s* one *d. Educ:* Tonbridge Sch. Joined Royal Navy, 1943; retd as Lt, 1952. Marconi Co., 1952–59; English Electric Leo Computers, 1959–64; Cryosystems Ltd, 1964–68; International Research and Development Co., 1968–84; Market Co-ordinator (Defence), NEI plc, 1984–89. Mem., EC Select Cttee, H of L, 1974–90; Vice-Pres., Parly and Scientific Cttee, 1977–80 and 1983–86 (Dep. Chm., 1974–77); Treas., All Party Energy Studies Gp, 1979–92; Chm., All Party Defence Study Gp, 1994–99 (Hon. Sec., 1992–94). Mem., Organising Cttee, British Library, 1972–74. President: Electric Vehicle Assoc., 1975–83; European Electric Road Vehicle Assoc., 1980–82; Vice-Pres., Inst. of Patentees and Inventors, 1976–90; Chm., Adv. Cttee, Science Reference Lib., 1975–85. Member: Court, 1975–94, Council, 1986–88, City Univ.; Court, 1982–, Council, 1984–87, Essex Univ. Pres., Sea Cadet Corps, Chelmsford, 1959–88. Mem. Ct Assts, Skinners' Co. (Master, 1981–82). Hon. FCGI (CGIA 1986). *Publications:* (ed) High Road to Command: the diaries of Major-General Sir Edmund Ironside, 1920–22, 1972. *Heir: s* Hon. Charles Edmund Grenville Ironside [*b* 1 July 1956; *m* 1st, 1985, Hon. Elizabeth Law (marr. diss. 2000), *e d* of Lord Coleraine, *qv*; one *s* two *d*; 2nd, 2001, Katherine Rowley; one *d*]. *Address:* Priory House, Old House Lane, Boxted, Colchester, Essex CO4 5RB.

IRONSIDE, Gordon Douglas; Headmaster, Sutton Grammar School, since 1990; *b* 11 Aug. 1955; *s* of Douglas William Ironside and Doreen Grant Ironside; *m* 1979, Rachael Elizabeth Ann Golder; two *s* one *d. Educ:* Pembroke Coll., Cambridge (BA 1977; Scholar); Durham Univ. (PGCE). CMath; FIMA. Hd of Maths, 1983–89, Dep. Headmaster, 1987–90, Sutton Grammar Sch. *Recreations:* tennis, golf, Rotary, mathematics. *Address:* Sutton Grammar School, Manor Lane, Sutton SM1 4AS. *T:* (020) 8642 3821. *E:* gironside@aol.com. *Clubs:* Sutton Rotary (Pres., 1998–2000); Cuddington Golf; Surrey Racquets.

IRONSIDE, Prof. James Wilson, CBE 2006; FRCPath, FRCPE; FMedSci; FRSE; Professor of Clinical Neuropathology, National CJD Research and Surveillance Unit, University of Edinburgh, since 2000; *b* 18 Nov. 1954; *s* of James F. Ironside and Jessie C. Ironside (*née* Moir); *m* 1979, Janet A. D. Cruickshank (marr. diss. 1992); one *s* one *d. Educ:* Univ. of Dundee (BMSc, MB ChB). FRCPath 1997; FRCPE 1999. Lectr in Pathology, Univ. of Leeds, 1986–90; Consultant Neuropathologist, Western Gen. Hosp., Edinburgh, 1990–; Sen. Lectr in Pathology, 1994–98, Reader, 1998–2000, Univ. of Edinburgh. Hon. Consultant Neuropathologist, Lothian Univ. Hosps NHS Trust, 1994–. FMedSci 2002; FRSE 2011. *Publications:* (jtly) Neuropathology: a color atlas and text, 1994; (jtly) Intraoperative Diagnosis of CNS Tumours, 1997; (jtly) Diagnostic Pathology of Nervous System Tumours, 2002; (ed jtly) Greenfield's Neuropathology, 9th edn, 2015; numerous contribs to scientific jls. *Recreations:* opera, early music, piano, Renaissance Art, wine. *Address:* National CJD Research and Surveillance Unit, Western General Hospital, Crewe Road, Edinburgh EH4 2XU. *T:* (0131) 537 3109, *Fax:* (0131) 343 1404. *E:* james.ironside@ed.ac.uk.

IRONSIDE, Leonard, CBE 2003; JP; Scottish Manager for Information and Support (formerly Information and Support Manager for Scotland), Parkinson's Disease Society, since 2007; *b* Aberdeen; *b* 16 Feb.; *s* of Alexander and Olive Ironside; *m* 1992, Wendy Anita Cook (marr. diss. 2011); two *d. Educ:* Hilton Acad., Aberdeen. Professional Lightweight Wrestler, 1973–91 (Commonwealth Middleweight Champion, 1979–81, 1981–91; European Lightweight title, 1985–89). Department of Social Security, Aberdeen: Welfare Benefits Manager, 1976–79; Manager, Pensions Section, 1980–85; Adjudication Officer, 1985–87; Nat. Insce Inspector, 1987–99; Nat. Minimum Wage Officer, 1999–2000. Area Develt Officer, N of Scotland, Parkinson's Disease Soc., 2003–07. Convention of Scottish Local Authorities: social works spokesman, 1997–99; Chm., Urban Affairs, 1999–2001. Freelance feature writer, Aberdeen Independent Newspapers and Evening Express, 2000–. Mem., Grampian Regl Council, 1982–96. Mem. (Lab) Aberdeen CC, 1995– (Convener: Social Work Cttee, 1995–97; Social Care and Well Being Cttee, 2012–; Leader, 1999–2003). Chm., Grampian Initiative, 1990–94 (Founder Mem., 1988). Mem. Bd, NHS Grampian, 2001–03. Member: Bd, Aberdeen Exhibn and Conf. Centre, 1986–96; Aberdeen Voluntary Service, 1995–99; Bd of Govs, Robert Gordon Univ., 1999–2008. Chm., Aberdeen Internat. Youth Fest., 1995–2003. Patron, Grampian Special Olympics, 1988–; Athletics Coach, Bon Accord (Special Needs), 1987–. Chm., Horizon Rehabilitation Centre, 1997–2004; Dir, Albyn Hse, Alcohol Support Orgn, Aberdeen. Director: Scottish Sub-Sea Technol. Gp, 1988–92; Grampian Food Resource Centre Ltd, 1990–96; Grampian Enterprise Ltd, 1990–94; Mem., Grampian Racial Equality Commn, 1986–90; Mem. Bd, Aberdeen Sports Council, 1986–94. FRSA 2003. JP Aberdeen, 1995. Rose Bowl Award for services to disabled sport, Scottish Sports Council, 1990; Veteran of Year in Sport Award, Aberdeen Sports Council, 2014. *Publications:* When You're Ready Boys… Take Hold, 2008; articles in local govt mags, local press, etc. *Recreations:* Granite City Chorus (barbershop harmony), yoga teacher, plays tennis, squash, badminton, cycling, after-dinner speaking. *Address:* (home) 42 Hillside Terrace, Portlethen, Aberdeen AB12 4QG. *T:* (01224) 780929, 07802 332656; (office) 239 North Anderson Drive, Aberdeen AB16 7GR. *E:* Lironside@aberdeencity.gov.uk.

IRRANCA-DAVIES, (Ifor) Huw; MP (Lab) Ogmore, since Feb. 2002; *b* 22 Jan. 1963; *s* of Gethin Davies and Anne Teresa Davies; *m* 1991, Joanna Teresa Irranca; three *s. Educ:* Crewe and Alsager Coll. (BA Hons Combined Studies); Swansea Inst. of Higher Educn (MSc Eur. Leisure Resource Mgt (Univ. of Wales Award)). Recreation Asst, then Duty Manager, Lliw Valley BC, 1986–89; Manager, CLM Ltd and Serco Ltd, 1989–92; Facilities Manager, Swansea Coll., 1994–96; Sen. Lectr, Swansea Inst. of Higher Educn, 1996–2002. An Asst Govt Whip, 2006–07; Parly Under-Sec. of State, Wales Office, 2007–08, DEFRA, 2008–10; Shadow Minister for Energy, 2010–11, for Food and Farming, 2011–15. Chm., Envmtl Audit Select Cttee, 2015–. All-Party Parliamentary Groups: Chm., Recognition of Munitions Workers; Co-Chm., Patient and Public Involvement in Health and Social Care; Vice Chairman: Energy Intensive Industries; British Council; University. *Recreations:* family activities, hill-walking, cycling, reading biographies and historical fiction, Rugby. *Address:* House of Commons, SW1A 0AA. *T:* (020) 7219 2952.

IRVINE, family name of **Baron Irvine of Lairg**.

IRVINE OF LAIRG, Baron *cr* 1987 (Life Peer), of Lairg in the District of Sutherland; **Alexander Andrew Mackay Irvine;** PC 1997; Lord High Chancellor of England and Wales, 1997–2003; *b* 23 June 1940; *s* of Alexander Irvine and Margaret Christina Irvine; *m* 1974, Alison Mary, *y d* of Dr James Shaw McNair, MD, and Agnes McNair, MA; two *s*. *Educ:* Inverness Acad.; Hutchesons' Boys' Grammar Sch., Glasgow; Glasgow Univ. (MA, LLB); Christ's Coll., Cambridge (Scholar; BA 1st Cl. Hons with distinction; LLB 1st Cl. Hons; George Long Prize in Jurisprudence; Hon. Fellow, 1996). Called to the Bar, Inner Temple, 1967, Bencher, 1985; QC 1978; a Recorder, 1985–88; Dep. High Court Judge, 1987–97. Univ. Lectr, LSE, 1965–69. Contested (Lab) Hendon North, 1970. Opposition spokesman on legal and home affairs, 1987–92; Shadow Lord Chancellor, H of L, 1992–97. Joint President: Industry and Parlt Trust, 1997; British-Amer. Parly Gp, 1997; IPU, 1997; CPA, 1997; Pres., Magistrates' Assoc., 1997–2003. Church Comr, 1997–2003. Trustee, John Smith Meml Trust, 1992–97; Foundn Trustee, Whitechapel Art Gall., 1990–97; Trustee, Hunterian Collection, 1997–. Mem. Cttee, Friends of the Slade, 1990–. Vice-Patron, World Fedn of Mental Health, 1998–. Hon. Bencher, Inn of Court of NI, 1998. Fellow, US Coll. of Trial Lawyers, 1998; Hon. Fellow: Soc. for Advanced Legal Studies, 1997; LSE, 2000. Hon. Mem., Polish Bar, 2000. Hon. LLD: Glasgow, 1997; Siena, 2000. *Recreations:* cinema, theatre, collecting paintings, reading, travel. *Address:* House of Lords, SW1A 0PW. *Club:* Garrick.

IRVINE, Alan Montgomery, RDI 1964; DesRCA, ARIBA; architect in private practice; *b* 14 Sept. 1926; *s* of Douglas Irvine and Ellen Marler; *m* 1st, 1955; (one *s* decd); 2nd, 1966, Katherine Mary Buzas; two *s*. *Educ:* Regent Street Polytechnic, Secondary Sch. and Sch. of Architecture; Royal College of Art. RAF (Aircrew), 1944–47. Worked in Milan with BBPR Gp, 1954–55. In private practice since 1956, specialising in design of interiors, museums and exhibitions; partnership Buzas and Irvine, 1965–85. Work has included interior design for Schroder Wagg & Co., Lazards, Bovis, S Australian Govt, Nat. Enterprise Bd; Mem. of design team for QE2, 1966. Various exhibns for V&A Museum, Tate Gallery, Royal Academy, Imperial War Museum, RIBA, British Council, British Museum, Wellcome Inst., Olivetti, Fiat etc including: Treasures of Cambridge, 1959; Book of Kells, 1961; Internat. Exhibn of Modern Jewellery, 1961; Architecture of Power, 1963; Mellon Collection, 1969; Art and the E India Trade, 1970; Age of Charles I, 1972; Internat. Ceramics, 1972; Pompeii AD79, 1976; Gold of El Dorado, 1978; The Medal: Mirror of History, 1979; Horses of San Marco (London, NY, Milan, Berlin), 1979–82; Great Japan Exhibition, 1981; Art and Industry, 1982; Cimabue Crucifix (London, Madrid, Munich), 1982–83; Treasures of Ancient Nigeria, 1983; The Genius of Venice, 1983; Leonardo da Vinci: studies for the Last Supper (Milan, Sydney, Toronto, Barcelona, Tokyo), 1984; Art of the Architect, 1984; Re dei Confessori (Milan, Venice), 1985; C. S. Jagger: War and Peace Sculpture, 1985; Queen Elizabeth II: portraits of 60 years, 1986; Eye for Industry, 1986; Glass of the Caesars (London, Cologne, Rome), 1988; Michelangelo Drawings, Louvre, 1989; Conservation Today, 1989; Paul de Lamerie, 1990; Lion of Venice (London, Amsterdam), 1991; David Smith Medals, 1991; Leonardo and Venezia, Venice, 1992. Museum work includes: Old Master Drawings Gallery, Windsor Castle, 1965; New Galleries for Royal Scottish Museum, 1968; Crown Jewels display, Tower of London, 1968; Heinz Gallery for Architectural Drawings, RIBA, London, 1972; War Meml, Winchester Coll., 1973; Museum and Art Gallery for Harrow School, 1975; Heralds' Museum, London, 1980; Housesteads Roman Fort Mus., 1982; Al Shaheed Museum, Baghdad, 1983; Cabinet War Rooms, London, 1984; West Wing Galls, Nat. Maritime Mus., Greenwich, 1986; Beatrix Potter Museum, Cumbria, 1988; George III Gall., Science Mus., 1993; English Sculpture Gall., V&A Mus., 1999; Fleming Collection Gall., London, 2001; Project, Monumental Tower, Bologna Airport, 2003; Treasuries at: Winchester Cathedral, 1968; Christ Church, Oxford, 1975; Winchester Coll., 1982; Lichfield Cath., 1993. Retrospective personal exhibitions: RIBA Heinz Gall., 1989; Portraits from Detroit: US cars 1940s–60s, photographs by Alan Irvine, RCA, 1996. Accredited corresp. to NASA, Apollo 13 Mission, 1970. Consultant designer to Olivetti, Italy, 1979–89; Consultant architect to British Museum, 1981–84. Mem., Crafts Council, 1984–86. Liveryman, Worshipful Co. of Goldsmiths. Hon. Fellow, RCA. *Recreations:* travel, photography. *Address:* 1 Aubrey Place, St John's Wood, NW8 9BH.

IRVINE, Rev. Canon Christopher Paul; Canon Librarian, Canterbury Cathedral, since 2007; *b* 17 Dec. 1951; *s* of Joseph Ernest Irvine and Phyllis Irvine; *m* 1978, Rosemary Hardwicke; two *d*. *Educ:* Univ. of Nottingham (BTh); Univ. of Lancaster (MA); Kelham Theol Coll.; St Martin's Coll., Lancaster (PGCE). Ordained deacon and priest, 1976; Asst Curate, St Mary, Stoke Newington, 1977–80; Anglican Chaplain, Sheffield Univ., 1980–85; Chaplain, St Edmund Hall, Oxford, 1985–90; Tutor, 1985–90, Vice-Principal, 1991–94, St Stephen's House, Oxford; Vicar, Cowley St John, Oxford, 1994–98; Principal, Coll. of the Resurrection, Mirfield, 1998–2007. Hon. Sen. Res. Fellow, Sch. of History, Univ. of Kent, 2009–. Chm., Soc. of Liturgical Study, 1998–2002; Member: C of E Liturgical Commn, 2011– (Consultant, 2006–10); Cathedrals Fabric Commn for England, 2011–. Trustee, Art and Christian Enquiry, 2008–. *Publications:* Worship, Church and Society, 1993; (ed) Celebrating the Easter Mystery, 1996; (ed) They shaped our Worship, 1998; (with Anne Dawtry) Art and Worship, 2002; The Art of God: the making of Christians and the meaning of worship, 2005; (ed) The Use of Symbols in Worship, 2007; (ed) Anglican Liturgical Identity, 2008; (contrib.) Anglican Words for Worship, 2012; (contrib.) The Study of Liturgy and Worship, 2013; The Cross and Creation in Christian Liturgy and Art, 2013; (contrib.) The Edinburgh Companion to the Bible and the Arts, 2014. *Recreations:* art galleries and exhibitions, poetry, gardening, film. *Address:* 19 The Precincts, Canterbury, Kent CT1 2EP. *T:* (01227) 865226. *E:* Christopher.Irvine@canterbury-cathedral.org.

IRVINE, Sir Donald (Hamilton), Kt 1994; CBE 1987 (OBE 1979); MD; FRCGP; FMedSci; Principal in General Practice, Ashington, 1960–95; Regional Adviser in General Practice, University of Newcastle, 1973–95; President, General Medical Council, 1995–2002; *b* 2 June 1935; *s* of late Dr Andrew Bell Hamilton Irvine and Dorothy Mary Irvine; *m* 1st, 1960, Margaret McGuckin (marr. diss. 1983); two *s* one *d*; 2nd, 1986, Sally Fountain (marr. diss. 2004); 3rd, 2007, Cynthia Rickitt, MBE. *Educ:* King Edward Sixth Grammar Sch., Morpeth; Medical Sch., King's Coll., Univ. of Durham (MB BS); DObstRCOG 1960; MD Newcastle 1964; FRCGP 1972 (MRCGP 1965). House Phys. to Dr C. N. Armstrong and Dr Henry Miller, 1958–59. Initiated and led develt of new code of practice for UK med. profession, Good Med. Practice, 1990–95; led reform of GMC through overhaul of constitution of Council and its governance processes, 1995–2002. Chm. Council, RCGP, 1982–85 (Vice-Chm., 1981–82); Hon. Sec. of the College, 1972–78; Jt Hon. Sec., Jt Cttee on Postgrad. Trng for Gen. Practice, 1976–82; Fellow, BMA, 1976; Member: GMC, 1979– (Chm., Cttee on Standards and Medical Ethics, 1985–95); UKCC, 1983–93; Chairman: Picker Inst. Europe, 2002–13; Dr Foster Ethics Cttee, 2008– (Vice Chm., 2002–08); Gov., MSD Foundn, 1982–89 (Chm., Bd of Govs, 1983–89). Vice-Pres., Medical Defence Union, 1974–78. Vis. Prof. in Family Practice, Univ. of Iowa, USA, 1973; (first) Vis. Prof. to RACGP, 1977; Hon. Prof., Sch. of Health, Durham Univ., 2002–. Vis. Cons. on Postgrad. Educn for Family Medicine to Virginia Commonwealth Univ., 1971, Univ. of Wisconsin-Madison, 1973, Med. Univ. of S Carolina, 1974. 30th Sir William Osler Lectr, McGill Univ., 2006; 29th John P. McGovern Award Lectr, Amer. Osler Soc. Mem., Audit Commn, 1990–96. Mem., Internat. Adv. Council, Pfizer Inc., 2004–. Chm., Adv. Bd for Medicine, Univ. of Warwick, 2003–09. Pres., Age UK, Northumbria, 2009–; Vice Pres., Patients Assoc., 2010–. Founder FMedSci 1998. Hon. FRCP 1997; Hon. FRCPE 1997; Hon. FPHM 1998; Hon. FRCS 2000; Hon. FAcadMed, 2010. Hon. DSc: Exeter, 1997; Leicester, 1998; Durham, 2002; Warwick, 2009; Hon. DCL: Newcastle, 2002; Northumbria at Newcastle, 2002; DUniv York, 1997. *Publications:* The Future General Practitioner: learning and teaching, (jtly), 1972 (RCGP); Managing for Quality in General Practice, 1990; (ed jtly) Making Sense of Audit, 1991, 2nd edn 1997; (with Sally Irvine) The Practice of Quality, 1996; The Doctors' Tale: professionalism and public trust, 2003; (contrib.) Maintaining Patients' Trust: modern medical professionalism, 2011; chapters to several books on gen. practice; papers on clinical and educnl studies in medicine, in jls incl. BMJ, Lancet, Jl of RCGP, Med. Jl Australia. *Recreations:* bird watching, gardening, walking, watching television. *Address:* Mole End, Fairmoor, Morpeth NE61 3JL.

IRVINE, Hazel Jane; broadcast journalist and television presenter, BBC Sport, since 1990; *b* 26 May 1965; *d* of William and Norma Irvine; *m*; one *d*. *Educ:* St Andrews Univ. (MA Hons Art Hist.). Prodn asst, Radio Clyde, 1986–87; sports broadcaster and journalist: Scottish Television, 1987–90; BBC Scotland, 1990–99; based in London, 1999–. Best Regl Presenter/Reporter, 1999, Sports Presenter of the Year, 2006, RTS. *Recreations:* golf, hill-walking, travelling, playing piano. *Address:* c/o Jane Morgan Management, Argentum, 2 Queen Caroline Street, W6 9DX. *T:* (020) 3178 8071.

IRVINE, Very Rev. John Dudley; Associate Vicar, Holy Trinity, Cambridge, since 2012; *b* 2 Jan. 1949; 3rd *s* of Rt Hon. Sir Arthur Irvine, QC, MP and Eleanor Irvine; *m* 1972, Andrea Mary Carr; three *s* one *d*. *Educ:* Haileybury Coll. (Hd of Sch.); Sussex Univ. (BA (Hons) Law, 1970); Wycliffe Hall, Oxford (BA (Hons) Theol., 1980; MA 1985). Called to the Bar, Middle Temple, 1973; in practice, Inner Temple, 1973–78. Ordained deacon, 1981, priest, 1982; Curate, Holy Trinity, Brompton with St Paul's, Onslow Sq., 1981–85; Priest i/c, 1985–95, Vicar, 1995–2001, St Barnabas, Kensington; Dean of Coventry, 2001–12; Priest-in-charge, St Francis's, North Radford, 2006–12. *Recreations:* travel, film, theatre, walking. *Address:* Holy Trinity Church, Market Street, Cambridge CB2 3NZ.

See also M. F. Irvine.

IRVINE, John Jeremy; Senior International Correspondent, ITN, since 2014; *b* 2 June 1963; *s* of Dr Kenneth Irvine and Jacqueline Irvine; *m* 1992, Libby McCann; one *s* one *d*. *Educ:* Brackenber House Prep. Sch., Belfast; Campbell Coll., Belfast. Reporter: Tyrone Constitution, Omagh, 1983–87; Ulster TV, Belfast, 1987–94; ITN: Ireland Corresp., 1994–2000; Middle East Corresp., 2000–03; Asia Corresp., 2003–06; Washington Corresp., 2006–10; Internat. Corresp., 2010–14. *Recreation:* golf. *Address:* c/o ITN, 200 Gray's Inn Road, WC1X 8XZ. *Clubs:* Malone Golf (Belfast); Royal County Down Golf (Newcastle).

IRVINE, Air Vice-Marshal Lindsay John, CB 2014; FRAeS; Director of Legal Services, Royal Air Force, since 2009; *b* Aberdeen, 5 Nov. 1959; *s* of late Jack Irvine and of Christine Irvine; *m* 1981, Claire Negus; one *s* one *d*. *Educ:* Robert Gordon's Coll., Aberdeen; University Coll., Oxford (MA Classics); City Univ., London (Dip. Law); King's Coll. London (MA Internat. Relns). Called to the Bar, Middle Temple, 1983; in practice as barrister, 1983–86; commnd Legal Br., RAF, 1986; MoD, 1986–89; HQ British Forces, Cyprus, 1989–93; HQ PTC, 1994–96; PJHQ, 1996–99; HQ STC, 1999–2000; MoD, 2000–02; Dep. Dir, Legal Services (RAF), 2003–09; rcds 2006. FRAeS 2009. *Recreations:* running, ski-ing, old cars, flying old de Havilland aeroplanes, playing clarinet and saxophone. *Address:* HQ Air Command, RAF High Wycombe, Bucks HP14 4UE. *E:* lindsay.irvine425@mod.uk. *Club:* Royal Air Force.

IRVINE, Michael Fraser; *b* 21 Oct. 1939; *s* of Rt Hon. Sir Arthur Irvine, PC, QC, MP, and Eleanor Irvine. *Educ:* Rugby; Oriel College, Oxford (BA). Called to the Bar, Inner Temple, 1964; in practice as barrister, 1964–2004. Sen. Legal Assessor, NMC, 2004–06. Contested (C): Bishop Auckland, 1979; Ipswich, 1992; MP (C) Ipswich, 1987–92. PPS to Attorney-Gen., 1990–92. Pres., Ipswich Cons. Assoc., 1998–2011. *Recreation:* hill walking in Scotland. *Address:* 13 East Sheen Avenue, SW14 8AR. *T:* (020) 8392 9337.

See also Very Rev. J. D. Irvine.

IRVINE, Oliver Henry U.; *see* Urquhart Irvine.

IRVINE, Prof. Robin Francis, FRS 1993; Royal Society Research Professor, Department of Pharmacology, University of Cambridge, since 1996; *b* 10 Feb. 1950; *s* of Charles Donald Irvine and June (*née* Ievers); *m* 1973, Sandra Jane Elder; two *s*. *Educ:* Stroud Sch., Romsey; Sherborne Sch., Dorset; St Catherine's Coll., Oxford (MA Biochem. 1972); Corpus Christi Coll., Cambridge (PhD Botany 1976). SRC Res. Student, ARC Unit of Developmental Botany, Cambridge, 1972–75; Beit Meml Fellow, ARC Inst. of Animal Physiol., Babraham, 1975–78; Mem. of Scientific Staff, 1978–95, UG5, 1993–95, AFRC Inst. of Animal Physiol. and Genetics Res., subseq. AFRC Babraham Inst., Cambridge. Mem., Wellcome Trust Cell and Molecular Panel, 1989–92. Mem. Council, Royal Soc., 1999–2001. Morton Lectr, Biochem. Soc., 1994. FRSB (FIBiol 1998); Founder FMedSci 1998. Member Editorial Board: Biochemical Jl, 1988–96; Cell, 1994–2008; Current Biology, 1994–2014; Molecular Pharmacology, 2000–09. J. R. Vane Medal, British Pharmacol Soc., 2010; Van Deenan Medal, Utrecht Univ., 2013. *Publications:* (ed) Methods in Inositide Research, 1990; contribs to Nature, Biochem. Jl and other scientific jls. *Recreations:* playing the lute and guitar, music (especially pre-1650), ornithology, reading. *Address:* Department of Pharmacology, Tennis Court Road, Cambridge CB2 1PD. *T:* (01223) 334000.

IRVINE, Sarah Frances; *see* Beamish, S. F.

IRVING, Gillian; QC 2006; *b* 1 Nov. 1958; *d* of Roger Irving and Mary Holliday Irving; *m* 1988, Peter Cadwallader. *Educ:* Caldew Comprehensive Sch., Dalston; Trent Poly., Nottingham (BA Hons Law); Inns of Court Sch. of Law. Called to the Bar, Inner Temple, 1984; in practice specialising in family law, Court of Protection, and community and mental health law. Part-time Judge of First-tier Tribunal (Health, Educn and Social Care Chambers). *Recreations:* gardening, racing (flat and National Hunt), country pursuits. *Address:* 15 Winckley Square, Preston PR1 3JJ; Linenhall Chambers, 1 Stanley Place, Chester CH1 2LU; 1 Hare Court, EC4Y 7BE; Dere Street Barristers, 33 Broad Chare, Newcastle upon Tyne NE1 3DQ; Broadway House Chambers, 1 The Square, Leeds LS1 2ES.

IRVING, Prof. John Alan, PhD; Professor of Music, Trinity Laban Conservatoire of Music and Dance, since 2013; *b* Rotherham, S Yorks, 20 May 1959; *s* of Alan Arthur Irving and Iris June Irving (*née* Cartright); *m* 2006, Jane Booth. *Educ:* Old Hall Comp. Sch.; Thomas Rotherham Coll.; Univ. of Sheffield (BMus Hons 1980; PhD 1985). LRAM 1978; ARCM Hons 1981. Ida Carroll Res. Fellow, RNCM, 1984–86; Temp. Lectr in Music, Univ. of Birmingham, 1986–87; Stipendiary Music Lectr, New Coll., Oxford, 1987–88; University of Bristol: Lectr, 1988–99; Sen. Lectr, 1999–2003; Reader, 2003–07; Prof. of Music Hist. and Performance Practice, 2007–11; Dir, Inst. of Musical Res., Sch. of Advanced Study, Univ. of London, 2009–11 (on secondment), Associate Fellow, 2011–; Prof. of Music Hist. and Performance Practice, Canterbury Christ Ch Univ., 2011–12. Trustee: Royal Musical Assoc., 2009–14 (Vice Pres., 2009–); Horniman Mus., 2010–14. FRSA 2011; FRHistS 2011; Sen. FHEA 2014. *Publications:* Mozart's Piano Sonatas: contexts, sources, style, 1997; Mozart: the 'Haydn' Quartets, 1998; Mozart's Piano Concertos, 2003; The Treasures of Mozart, 2009; Understanding Mozart's Piano Sonatas, 2010; The Mozart Project, 2014. *Recreations:* concert-going, reading. *E:* johnirvingimr@googlemail.com. *Club:* Athenæum.

IRVING, John Winslow; novelist; *b* Exeter, New Hampshire, 2 March 1942; *s* of Colin Franklin Newell Irving and Frances Winslow Irving; *m* 1st, 1964, Shyla Leary (marr. diss. 1981); two *s*; 2nd, 1987, Janet Turnbull; one *s*. *Educ:* Phillips Exeter Acad., USA; Univ. of New Hampshire (BA 1965); Univ. of Iowa (MFA 1967). Professor of English: Windham Coll., 1967–72; Univ. of Iowa, 1972–75; Mount Holyoke Coll., 1975–78; Brandeis Univ.,

1978–79. Wrestling Coach: Northfield Mt Hermon Sch., 1981–83; Fessenden Sch., 1983–86; Vermont Acad., 1987–89. Rockefeller Foundn grantee, 1971–72; Nat. Endowment for the Arts Fellow, 1974–75; Guggenheim Fellow, 1976–77. Mem., AAAL, 2001. *Publications:* Setting Free the Bears, 1968; The Water-Method Man, 1972; The 158-Pound Marriage, 1974; The World According to Garp, 1978 (Nat. Book Award, USA, 1979); The Hotel New Hampshire, 1981; The Cider House Rules, 1985 (screenplay, 1999; Best Screenplay Award, Nat. Bd of Review, 1999; Academy Award for best adapted screenplay, 2000); A Prayer for Owen Meany, 1989; A Son of the Circus, 1994; Trying to Save Piggy Sneed, 1996; A Widow for One Year, 1998; My Movie Business: a memoir, 1999; The Fourth Hand, 2001; Until I Find You, 2005; Last Night in Twisted River, 2009; In One Person, 2012. *Address:* c/o The Turnbull Agency, POB 757, Dorset, VT 05251, USA.

IRVING, Prof. Malcolm, PhD; FRS 2003; Professor of Biophysics, since 1998, and Director, Randall Division of Cell and Molecular Biophysics, since 2003, King's College London; *b* 23 July 1953. *Educ:* Emmanuel Coll., Cambridge (BA 1974); University Coll. London (MSc 1976; PhD 1979). Research Fellow: UCLA, 1979–80; Yale Univ., 1980–81; King's College London: Res. Asst, 1982–83; Royal Soc. Univ. Res. Fellow, 1983–91; Lectr in Biophysics, 1991–94; Reader in Biophysics, 1994–98. FMedSci 2006. *Address:* Randall Division of Cell and Molecular Biophysics, King's College London, New Hunt's House, Guy's Campus, SE1 1UL.

IRVING, Sir Miles (Horsfall), Kt 1995; MD; FRCS; FMedSci; Professor of Surgery, University of Manchester, 1974–99, now Emeritus; Chairman: Newcastle upon Tyne NHS Hospitals Trust, 1998–2006; Northeast Health Innovation and Education Cluster, 2010–13; *b* 29 June 1935; *s* of Frederick William Irving and Mabel Irving; *m* 1965, Patricia Margaret Blaiklock; two *s* two *d*. *Educ:* King George V Sch., Southport; Liverpool Univ. (MB, ChB 1959; MD 1962; ChM 1968); Sydney Univ., Australia; MSc Manchester Univ., 1977. FRCS 1964; FRCSE 1964. Robert Gee Fellow, Liverpool Univ., 1962; Phyllis Anderson Fellow, Sydney Univ., 1967; St Bartholomew's Hospital, London: Chief Asst in Surgery, 1969–71; Reader in Surgery, Asst Dir of Professorial Surgical Unit, and Hon. Consultant Surgeon, 1972–74. Hon. Consultant Surgeon: Hope Hosp., Salford, 1974–99; Manchester Royal Infirmary, 1993–2005; to the Army, 1989–2002. Hunterian Prof., 1967, Hunterian Orator, 1993, RCS; Sir Gordon Bell Meml Orator, NZ, 1982. Regl Dir of R&D, N Western RHA, 1992–94; Chm., Standing Gp on Health Technol., DoH, 1993–99; Nat. Dir, NHS Health Technol. Prog., 1994–99; Chm., NHS Innovations (N), 2004–10. Member: Expert Adv. Gp on AIDS, DoH, 1991–96; MRC Health Services and Public Health Res. Bd, 1993–96. Member: Council, RCS, 1984–95; GMC, 1989–92; President: Ileostomy Assoc. of GB and Ireland, 1982–92; Assoc. of Surgeons of GB and Ireland, 1995–96; Internat. Surgical Gp, 1995–96; Section of Coloproctology, RSM, 1997–98; Assoc. of Coloproctology of GB and Ireland, 1998–99; Manchester Med. Soc., 1999–2000. Mem. Bd, Imperial War Mus., 2006–14; Dir, Imperial War Mus. Trading Co., 2012–. Mem. Council, Newcastle Univ., 2001–11. Chm. Council, Northumbria, Order of St John, 2007–. Founder FMedSci 1998. Hon. Fellow: Amer. Assoc. for Surgery of Trauma, 1985; Amer. Surgical Assoc., 2000; Barbers' Co., 2014; Hon. FRCEM (Hon. FFAEM 1995); Hon. FRCSCan; FRCSGlas *ad eund*; Hon. FACS 2000. Hon. Member: Assoc. Française de Chirurgie, 1996; Romanian Soc. of Surgeons. Hon. DSc Salford, 1996; DSc (*hc*) Sibiu Univ., Romania, 1997; Hon. DCL Northumbria, 2007; Dr *hc* Univ. of Medicine and Pharmacy, Iasi, Romania, 2014. Moynihan Medal, Assoc. of Surgeons of GB and Ire., 1968; Pybus Medal, N of England Surgical Soc., 1986; John Loewenthal Medal, Sydney Univ., 1993; Canet Medal, Inst. of Mech. Incorp. Engrs, 1995; Bryan Brooke Medal, Ileostomy Assoc. of GB and Ire., 1996; Presidents Medal, British Soc. of Gastroenterology, 1999; Guthrie Medal, RAMC, 2005. Hon. Col 201 (Northern) Fd Hosp. Vol., 1999–2006. SBStJ 2009. *Publications:* Gastroenterological Surgery, 1983; Intestinal Fistulas, 1985; ABC of Colorectal Diseases, 1993; Introduction to Minimal Access Surgery, 1995; 100 Years of the RVI, 2006. *Recreations:* thinking about and occasionally actually climbing mountains, reading, opera. *Address:* 12 Ashford Close, Woodstock, Oxon OX20 1FF. *T:* (01993) 811761.

IRWIN, Lord; James Charles Wood; Managing Director, The Handy Squad, 2005; *b* 24 Aug. 1977; *s* and *heir* of 3rd Earl of Halifax, *qv*; *m* 2006, Georgia Emily, *d* of Patrick Robert James Clarkson; one *s* one *d*. *Educ:* Eton; Keble Coll., Oxford. *Heir:* *s* Hon. Rex Patrick Wood, *b* 12 Aug. 2010. *Address:* Garrowby, York YO41 1QD.

IRWIN, Alan; *see* Irwin, G. A.

IRWIN, Lt Gen. Sir Alistair (Stuart Hastings), KCB 2002; CBE 1994 (OBE 1987); Adjutant General, 2003–05; Director, Balhousie Publications Ltd, since 2008; *b* 27 Aug. 1948; *s* of late Brig. Angus Digby Hastings Irwin, CBE, DSO, MC and of Elizabeth Bryson Irwin (*née* Cumming); *m* 1972, Nicola Valentine Blomfield Williams; one *s* two *d*. *Educ:* Wellington Coll.; St Andrews Univ. (MA); Univ. of Baluchistan (BSc Hons 1980). Commnd The Black Watch (RHR), 1970; Staff Coll., Quetta, Pakistan, 1980; CO 1st Bn, The Black Watch, 1985–88 (despatches, 1987); Instructor, Staff Coll., Camberley, 1988–92; Comd, 39 Inf. Bde, 1992–94; Dir Land Warfare, MoD, 1994–95; Prog. Dir, PE, MoD, 1996; Comdt, RMCS, 1996–99; Military Sec., 1999–2000; GOC NI, 2000–03. Member: Commonwealth War Graves Commn, 2006–13 (Vice-Chm., 2011–13); Scottish Govt Great War Commemoration Panel, 2013–. Mem., Adv. Bd, Inst. of Continuing Professional Develt, 2004–. Strategic Advr, Eruma plc, 2008–14. President: Quetta Assoc., 2004–; RBL Scotland, 2006–; Earl Haig Fund for Scotland, 2006–; Officers' Assoc. Scotland, 2006–; (Army) Officers' Assoc., 2006–; Veterans Scotland, 2006–11; Chairman: Christina Mary Hendrie Trust, 2006–11; Black Watch Heritage Appeal, 2007–. Trustee, Queen Mother Meml Fund for Scotland, 2003–08. Col, The Black Watch, 2003–06; Chm., Black Watch Castle and Museum Trust, 2013–. Col Comdt, Scottish Div., 2000–04; Hon. Col Tayforth Univs OTC, 1998–2009. Officer, Royal Co. of Archers (Queen's Bodyguard for Scotland), 2007– (Mem., 1989–2007). Pres., Army Angling Fedn, 1997–2005; Mem., Atlantic Salmon Trust, 2008–. Life Mem., Highland Soc. of London, 2003–. Vice-Pres., Royal Caledonian Educn Trust (formerly Royal Caledonian Schs Trust), 2007–; Patron, Annan Juvenile Pipe Band, 2007–; Hon. Pres., Dundee Ex-Servicemen's Assoc., 2010–. FCMI 2005. Hon. Keeper of the Quaich, 2007–. Hon. Mem., Dundee Weavers, 2012–. *Recreations:* shooting, fishing, photography, small scale farming, writing. *Address:* c/o Adam & Co. plc, 25 St Andrews Square, Edinburgh EH2 1AF. *Clubs:* Boodle's; Highland and Lowland Brigade, Royal Scots.

IRWIN, David; Partner, Irwin Grayson Associates (consultants in enterprise and economic development), since 2002; *b* 5 Sept. 1955; *s* of Hew Irwin and Ann (*née* Tattersfield); *m* 1st, 1983, Jane Christine Kinghorn (marr. diss. 2008); one *s* one *d*; 2nd, 2013, Penny Hawley; two *s*. *Educ:* Worksop Coll.; Durham Univ. (BSc (Hons) Engrg Sci and Mgt 1977); Cambridge Univ. (Adv. Course Prodn Methods and Mgt 1978); Newcastle Univ. (MBA 1986). Develt Engr, Hydraulic Hose Div., Dunlop, 1978–80; Co-founder and Dir, Project North East, 1980–2000; Chief Exec., Small Business Service, 2000–02; Chm., Cobweb Information Ltd, 2002–. Chm., Internat. Assoc. for Enterprise Promotion, 2009–15. Trustee, Speakers' Corner Trust, 2010–. FRSA 1993. Queen's Award for Enterprise Promotion, 2009. *Publications:* Financial Control, 1991; Planning to Succeed in Business, 1995; Financial Control for Non Financial Managers, 1995; Make Your Business Grow, 1998; On Target, 1999; Advocacy for Business Associations, 2012. *Recreations:* squash, photography. *Club:* Northern Rugby Football (Newcastle upon Tyne).

IRWIN, Prof. (George) Alan, PhD; Professor, Department of Organization, Copenhagen Business School, since 2015 (Dean of Research, 2007–14); *b* Sunderland, 16 July 1955; *s* of late George William Irwin and of Doreen Irwin (*née* Payne, now Bittlestone); *m* 2008, Maja Horst; one *s* two *d*. *Educ:* St Aidan's Grammar Sch., Sunderland; Univ. of Salford (BSc); Univ. of Manchester (MSc; PhD 1980). Lectr in Sci. and Technol. Policy and Sociol., Univ. of Manchester, 1981–91; Brunel University: Sen. Lectr, 1991–94, Reader, 1994–98, Prof., 1998–2004, Hd of Dept, 1998–2001, Dept of Human Scis; Dean of Arts and Social Scis, 2001–04; Pro-Vice-Chancellor for Res. and Enterprise, 2004; Dean, Social and Envmtl Studies, Univ. of Liverpool, 2004–07; Acting Pres., Copenhagen Business Sch., 2011. Vis. Prof., Dept of Mgt, Univ. of Glasgow, 2010–15; Carl and Thecla Lamberg Guest Prof., Faculty of Social Sci., Univ. of Gothenburg, 2015. Mem., 2005–07, Chair, 2008–10, Biosci. for Society Strategy Panel, BBSRC. Member: Public Engagement Strategy Adv. Gp, Wellcome Trust, 2002–04; R&D Steering Cttee, Eur. Foundn for Mgt Develt, 2011–; Strategy Adv. Bd for Global Food Security Prog., 2011–. Foreign Mem., Royal Danish Acad. of Scis and Letters, 2013. FAcSS (AcSS 2014). Hon. Fellow, British Assoc. for Advancement of Sci., 2008. Knight, Order of Dannebrog (Denmark), 2014. *Publications:* Risk and Control of Technology, 1985; Citizen Science, 1995; (ed with B. Wynne) Misunderstanding Science?, 1996; Sociology and the Environment, 2001; (with M. Michael) Science, Social Theory and Public Knowledge, 2003; (ed with J. Molin) The Distinctiveness of Diversity, 2009. *Recreations:* music, literature, running, Sunderland FC, good company, fresh air. *Address:* Department of Organization, Copenhagen Business School, Kilevej 14a, Frederiksberg 2000, Denmark. *T:* 38153815. *E:* ai.ioa@cbs.dk.

IRWIN, Dr Gregor, CMG 2014; Chief Economist, Global Counsel, since 2014; *b* Glasgow, 26 Jan. 1971; *s* of Robert and Anne Irwin; *m* 2002, Dr Kersti Berge; one *s*. *Educ:* Thomas Muir High Sch., Bishopbriggs, Glasgow; Glasgow Univ. (BAcc Econs and Accountancy 1991); Balliol Coll., Oxford (MPhil Econs 1994; DPhil Econs 1996). Strategy Consultant, Marakon Associates, 1996–97; Fellow in Economics: Lady Margaret Hall, Oxford, 1997–2000; University Coll., Oxford, 2000–02; Econ. Advr, Internat. Debt and Capital Mkts, HM Treasury, 2002–04; Hd of Res., 2004–06, Hd of Policy, 2006–08, Internat. Finance Div., Bank of England; Chief Economist, 2008–14, Dir for Economics, 2011–14, FCO. *Publications:* contrib. papers to jls incl. Internat. Jl Finance and Econs, Econs Jl, Oxford Econ. Papers, Rev. Internat. Econs, Develt Policy Rev. *Address:* 92 Croftdown Road, NW5 1HA. *T:* 07729 420518. *E:* gregor.irwin@icloud.com.

IRWIN, Helen Elizabeth; Clerk of Committees, House of Commons, 2005–08; *b* 21 April 1948; *d* of late Walter William Taylor and Kathleen Taylor (*née* Moffoot); *m* 1972, Robert Graham Irwin; one *d*. *Educ:* Whalley Range Grammar Sch., Manchester; King's Coll., London (BA Hons Hist. 1969); SSEES, Univ. of London (MA Soviet Studies 1970). Asst Clerk, H of C, 1970–72; Admin. Asst, Univ. of St Andrews, 1972–75; a Clerk, House of Commons, 1977–2008: Cttee of Public Accounts, 1977–81; served in Table Office, 1981–85; Social Services Cttee, 1985–89; Health Cttee, 1989–91; Foreign Affairs Cttee, 1991–94; Principal Clerk, Committee Office, 1994–99; Clerk of Bills, 1999–2001; Principal Clerk, Table Office, 2001–05. Mem. Council, Hansard Soc., 1990–99. Life Mem., Study of Parlt Gp. Fellow, Industry and Parlt Trust. Hon. Res. Fellow, UCL, 2009–11. *Publications:* occasional contribs to books on parliamentary practice and procedure. *Recreations:* family, friends, travel, Vauxhall. *E:* helenirwin@aol.com.

IRWIN, Ian Sutherland, CBE 1982; Executive Chairman (formerly also Chief Executive), Scottish Transport Group, 1987–2002; *b* Glasgow, 20 Feb. 1933; *s* of Andrew Campbell Irwin and Elizabeth Ritchie Arnott; *m* 1959, Margaret Miller Maureen Irvine; two *s*. *Educ:* Whitehill Sen. Secondary Sch., Glasgow; Glasgow Univ. (BL). CA, IPFA, FCILT. Commercial Man., Scottish Omnibuses Ltd, 1960–64; Gp Accountant, Scottish Bus Gp, 1964–69; Gp Sec., 1969–75, Dep. Chm. and Man. Dir, 1975–87, Scottish Transport Gp; Chairman: Scottish Bus Gp Ltd, 1975–2002; Caledonian MacBrayne Ltd, 1975–90; STG Properties Ltd (formerly Scottish Transport Investments Ltd), 1975–2002; STG Pension Funds, 1975–2002. Dir, Scottish Mortgage & Trust plc, 1986–99. Pres., Bus and Coach Council, 1979–80; Hon. Vice-Pres., Internat. Union of Public Transport; Member Council: CIT, 1978–87 (Vice Pres., 1984–87); CBI, 1987–93; Mem., Nationalised Industries Chairmen's Gp, 1987–91. Hon. Col, 154 Regt RCT (V), 1986–93. FInstD; CCMI. *Publications:* various papers. *Recreations:* golf, foreign travel, walking, reading. *Address:* 10 Moray Place, Edinburgh EH3 6DT. *T:* (0131) 225 6454. *Club:* Bruntsfield Links Golfing Soc.

IRWIN, Dr Michael Henry Knox; Chairman, Voluntary Euthanasia Society, 1996–99 and 2001–03 (Vice-Chairman, 1995 and 1999–2001); *b* 5 June 1931; *s* of late William Knox Irwin, FRCS and of Edith Isabel Mary Irwin; *m* 1st, 1958, Elizabeth Naumann (marr. diss. 1982); three *d*; 2nd, 1983, Frederica Harlow (marr. diss. 1991); 3rd, 1994, Patricia Walters (marr. diss. 2000); partner, Angela Farmer. *Educ:* St Bartholomew's Hosp. Med. Coll., London (MB, BS 1955); Columbia Univ., New York (MPH 1960). House Phys. and House Surg., Prince of Wales' Hosp., London, 1955–56; MO, UN, 1957–61; Dep. Resident Rep., UN Technical Assistance Bd, Pakistan, 1961–63; MO, 1963–66, SMO, 1966–69, and Med. Dir, 1969–73, United Nations; Dir, Div. of Personnel, UNDP, 1973–76; UNICEF Rep., Bangladesh, 1977–80; Sen. Advr (Childhood Disabilities), UNICEF, 1980–82; Sen. Consultant, UN Internat. Year of Disabled Persons, 1981; Med. Dir, UN, UNICEF and UNDP, 1982–89; Director: Health Services Dept, IBRD, 1989–90; Westside Action, 1991–93. Founder, Doctors for Assisted Dying, 1998. Pres., Assistance for Blind Children Internat., 1978–84. Consultant, Amer. Assoc. of Blood Banks, 1984–90; Advr, ActionAid, 1990–91; Vice Pres., UNA, 1999– (Vice-Chm., 1995–96; Chm., 1996–98); Chm., UK Cttee, UNHCR, 1997–2002; Vice Pres., Nat. Peace Council, 1996–2000. Director: World Fedn of Right-to-Die Socs, 2004–06 (Vice-Pres., 2000–02; Pres., 2002–04; Treas., 2008–12); Right-to-Die Europe, 2011–13. Co-ordinator, Secular Med. Forum, 2006–08; Founder and Co-ordinator, Soc. for Old Age Rational Suicide, 2009–. Hon. Associate, Nat. Secular Soc., 2011; Hon. Med. Advr, Friends at the End, 2004–. Patron, British Humanist Assoc., 2015. Contested (Living Will Campaign) Kensington and Chelsea, Nov. 1999. Mem. Editl Adv. Panel, Medicine and War, 1985–95. Officer Cross, Internat. Fedn of Blood Donor Organizations, 1984; Tenrei Ohta Award, World Fedn of Right-to-Die Socs, 2014. *Publications:* Check-ups: safeguarding your health, 1961; Overweight: a problem for millions, 1964; Travelling without Tears, 1964; Viruses, Colds and Flu, 1966; Blood: new uses for saving lives, 1967; The Truth About Cancer, 1969; What Do We Know about Allergies?, 1972; A Child's Horizon, 1982; Aspirin: current knowledge about an old medication, 1983; Can We Survive Nuclear War?, 1984; Nuclear Energy: good or bad?, 1985; Peace Museums, 1991; Pro-Choice Living Will, 2003; Psyche-Anima, 2004; What Survives?, 2005; Tilting at Windmills, 2007; Irish Living Will, 2008; Old Age Rational Suicide, 2009; Approaching Old-Old, 2014; I'll See Myself Out, Thank You, 2015; *novel:* Talpa, 1990. *Recreations:* politics, metaphysics. *Address:* 9 Waverleigh Road, Cranleigh, Surrey GU6 8BZ.

IRWIN, Rear-Adm. Richard Oran, CB 1995; Member, Tribunal (Criminal Injuries Compensation) (formerly Criminal Injuries Compensation Appeals Panel), 2000–12; *b* 3 Sept. 1942; *s* of Lt Col Richard Arthur Irwin, TD and Catherine Millicent (*née* Palmer); *m* 1st, 1965, Coreen Jill Blackham (marr. diss. 2005), *d* of Rear-Adm. J. L. Blackham, CB; one *s* one *d*; 2nd, 2006, Rosemary Sylvia Helen Groves, PhD, *widow* of Richard Groves, and *d* of R. E. Storrar. *Educ:* Sherborne; Dartmouth; RN Engrg Coll., Manadon (BSc Engrg). FIEE 1986. Served in 7th, 3rd and 10th Submarine Sqdns, 1968–78; on Naval Staff, 1978–81; on staff of Flag Officer, Submarines, 1981–83; on staff, Strategic Systems Exec., 1983–86; RCDS, 1987; Dir, Nuclear Systems, 1988–91; Captain, HMS Raleigh, 1991–92; Chief, Strategic Systems

Exec., MoD, 1992–95; RN retd, 1996. Mem., DFEE Panel of Ind. Assessors, 1996–2008; Panel of Ind. Assessors, DCMS, 2004–08. Ind. Investigator, Financial Services Compensation Scheme, 2002–08. Chm., W Sussex HA, 1996–2000. Non-exec. Dir, Halmatic Ltd, 1996–98. Chm., Queen Alexandra Hosp. Home, 1998–2011. Trustee, 2003–08, Vice Pres., 2008–, Royal Naval Mus. (Chm., Friends of RN Mus. and HMS Victory, 1999–2010). Member: RNSA; Assoc. of Retired Naval Officers. Chairman: Selborne Assoc., 2010–; Selborne PCC, 2010–; Friends of Gilbert White's House and Garden and Oates Collections, 2014–. Gov., Kingsham Primary Sch., 1996–2004; Pres., Old Shirburnian Soc., 1999–2000. Officer, Legion of Merit (US), 1996. *Recreations:* sailing, squash, tennis, ski-ing, bridge. *Address:* Deep Thatch, Gracious Street, Selborne, Hants GU34 3JB. *Club:* Lansdowne.

IRWIN, Hon. Sir Stephen (John), Kt 2006; **Hon. Mr Justice Irwin;** a Judge of the High Court of Justice, Queen's Bench Division, since 2006; Presiding Judge, Northern Circuit, 2008–12; *b* 5 Feb. 1953; *s* of late John McCaughey Irwin and of Norma Gordon Irwin; *m* 1978, Deborah Rose Ann Spring; one *s* two *d. Educ:* Methodist Coll., Belfast; Jesus Coll., Cambridge (BA Hons 1975). Called to the Bar: Gray's Inn, 1976 (Bencher, 2002); Northern Ireland, 1997; QC 1997; a Recorder, 2000–06. Chairman: Bar Council, 2004; Special Immigration Appeals Commn, 2013– (Mem., 2012–). Chm., Trustees, Poetry Soc., 2011–14. *Publications:* Medical Negligence: a practitioner's guide, 1995; legal articles in learned jls. *Recreations:* walking, Irish history, music, verse. *Address:* Royal Courts of Justice, Strand, WC2A 2LL.

IRWIN, Prof. Terence Henry, PhD; FBA 2010; Professor of Ancient Philosophy, University of Oxford, since 2007; Fellow, Keble College, Oxford, since 2007; *b* Enniskillen, NI, 21 April 1947. *Educ:* Univ. of Oxford (BA 1969); Princeton Univ. (PhD 1973). Loeb Fellow in Classical Phil., 1971–72, Asst Prof. of Phil. and Classics, 1972–75, Santayana Fellowship, 1975, Harvard Univ.; Cornell University: Associate Prof. of Phil., 1975–82; Prof. of Phil., 1982–94; Prof. of Classics, 1994–95; Susan Linn Sage Prof. of Phil. and Humane Letters, 1995–2008, now Emeritus. Mem., Amer. Acad. of Arts and Scis, 1995. *Publications:* Plato's Moral Theory, 1977; Plato's Gorgias, 1979; Aristotle's Nicomachean Ethics, 1985, 2nd edn, 1999; Aristotle's First Principles, 1988 (trans. Italian); Classical Thought, 1988 (trans. Chinese, Japanese, Greek); Plato's Ethics, 1995 (trans. Spanish); (jtly) Aristotle: selections, 1995; Oxford Reader in Classical Philosophy, 1999; The Development of Ethics, vol. 1, Socrates to the Reformation, 2007, vol. 2, Suarez to Rousseau, 2008, vol. 3, Kant to Rawls, 2009; (ed) Classical Philosophy, 8 vols, 1995. *Address:* Keble College, Oxford OX1 3PG.

ISAAC, Anthony Eric; Chief Executive, The BOC Group, 2000–06; *b* 24 Nov. 1941; *m* Janice Donovan; one *s* one *d.* Finance Director: GEC Plessey Telecommunications, 1988–90; Arjo Wiggins Appleton plc, 1990–94; BOC Gp, 1994–2000. Non-executive Director: GDF SUEZ Energy Internat. (formerly Internat. Power plc), 2000–13; Schlumberger plc, 2003– (Chm., 2012–); Hogg Robinson Gp plc, 2006–15.

ISAAC, Anthony John Gower, CB 1985; fiscal consultant; a Deputy Chairman, Board of Inland Revenue, 1982–91 (a Commissioner of Inland Revenue, 1973–77 and 1979–91); *b* 21 Dec. 1931; *s* of Ronald and Kathleen Mary Gower Isaac; *m* 1963, Olga Elizabeth Sibley; one *s* two *d* (and two *d* decd). *Educ:* Malvern Coll.; King's Coll., Cambridge (BA). HM Treasury, 1953–70: Private Sec. to Chief Sec. to Treasury, 1964–66; Inland Revenue, 1971; on secondment to HM Treasury, 1976–78. Mem., Tax Law Rev. Cttee, 1994–2006. *Publications:* A Local Income Tax, 1992; A Comment on the Viability of the Allowance for Corporate Equity, 1997. *Recreations:* gardening, fishing, grandchildren.

ISAAC, David, CBE 2011; Partner, since 2000, and Head, Advanced Manufacturing and Technology Sector, since 2012, Pinsent Masons LLP; *b* Johannesburg, SA, 31 March 1958; *s* of Glen Isaac and Jill Isaac (*née* Edge); civil partnership 2005, Paul John Thornton Keene. *Educ:* King Henry VIII Sch., Abergavenny; Trinity Hall, Cambridge (BA 1979); Wolfson Coll., Oxford. Admitted as solicitor, 1985; Solicitor: Morgan Cole, 1984–2000; Pinsent Masons, 2000–. Mem. Bd, Big Lottery Fund, 2014–. Chairman: Modern Art Oxford, 2001–; Stonewall, 2003–12; Trustee: Diana, Princess of Wales Meml Fund, 2007–13; British Future, 2011–14. *Recreations:* visual arts, walking, bee keeping. *Address:* Pinsent Masons LLP, 30 Crown Place, EC2A 4ES. *T:* (020) 7490 6375. *E:* david.isaac@pinsentmasons.com.

ISAAC, James Keith, CBE 1985; FCILT; Chairman, West Midlands Travel Ltd, 1986–94 (Managing Director, 1986–90; Chief Executive, 1986–92); *b* 28 Jan. 1932; *s* of late Arthur Burton Isaac and Doreen (*née* Davies); *m* 1957, Elizabeth Mary Roskell; two *d. Educ:* Leeds Grammar Sch. Mem., Inst. of Traffic Admin; FCILT (FCIT 1978). National Service, RE 2nd Lieut, 1952–54. Asst to Traffic Manager, Aldershot and Dist Traction Co. Ltd, 1958–59; Asst Traffic Man., Jamaica Omnibus Services Ltd, Kingston, Jamaica, 1959–64; Dep. Traffic Man., Midland Red (Birmingham and Midland Motor Omnibus Co. Ltd), Birmingham, 1965–67; Traffic Manager: North Western Road Car Co. Ltd, Stockport, Cheshire, 1967–69; Midland Red, Birmingham, 1969–73; Dir of Ops, 1973–77, Dir Gen., 1977–86, W Midlands Passenger Transp. Exec., Birmingham. Dir, London Transport Buses Ltd, 1994–99. Chm., Bus and Coach Services Ltd, 1986–90. Chm., Internat. Commn on Transport Economics, 1981–88. International Union of Public Transport: Vice-Pres., 1989–93; Pres., 1993–97; Hon. Pres., 1997–. President: Omnibus Soc., 1982; Bus and Coach Council, 1985–86; Mem. Council, CIT, 1982–85. *Recreations:* reading, travel, grandchildren. *Address:* 2 St Elphin's House, St Elphin's Park, Darley Dale, Derbys DE4 2RL. *T:* (01629) 736762. *E:* james.isaac@outlook.com. *Club:* Army and Navy.

ISAACS, family name of **Marquess of Reading**.

ISAACS, Dr Anthony John; Consultant Endocrinologist, London Medical (formerly London Diabetes and Lipid Centre, then London Medical London Diabetes), 2002–13; *b* 22 Oct. 1942; *s* of late Benjamin H. Isaacs, BSc and Lily Isaacs (*née* Rogol); *m* 1st, 1971, Jill Kathleen Elek; three *s*; 2nd, 1986, Dr Edie Friedman; one *d. Educ:* Wanstead County High Sch.; Hertford Coll., Oxford (Open Exhibnr; Domus Scholar; BA Animal Physiology, 1st Cl. Hons 1965; MA 1968; BM, BCh 1968); Westminster Med. Sch. (Barron Schol.); MSc (Public Health Medicine), London, 1992. MRCP 1971, FRCP 1997. House posts, Westminster, Whittington and Hammersmith Hosps, 1968–70; Med. Registrar, Westminster Hosp., 1971–73; Research Fellow (Endocrinology), Royal Free Hosp., 1973–75; Sen. Med. Registrar, Westminster Hosp., 1975–84; SMO, Medicines Div., 1984–85, PMO, and Med. Assessor, Cttee on Safety of Medicines, 1985–86, SPMO/Under Sec., and Hd, Med. Manpower and Educn Div., 1986–91, DHSS, subseq. DoH; Regl Consultant (Service Policy and Clinical Audit), NE Thames, later N Thames RHA, 1993–95; Consultant Endocrinologist: Charing Cross Hosp., 1993–95; Chelsea & Westminster Hosp., 1993–2003, Emeritus, 2003–. Sen. Med. Assessor, Medicines and Healthcare products Regulatory (formerly Medicines Control) Agency, 2002–08. Consultant in Clinical Audit, Educn and Trng, Barnet HA, 1995–2001; Hon. Consultant Physician, Barnet, Enfield and Haringey HA, 2001–02. Hon. Consultant Phys. (Endocrinology), UC and Middx Hosps, 1986–96. Vice-Chm., Jt Planning Adv. Cttee, 1986–91; Member: Steering Gp for Implementation of Achieving a Balance (and Co-Chm., Technical sub-gp), 1986–91; 2nd Adv. Cttee on Med. Manpower Planning, 1986–89; Steering Gp on Undergrad. Med. and Dental Educn and Res., 1987–91 (Chm., Implementation Task Gp, 1989–90 and Working Gp, 1990–91); Ministerial Gp on Junior Doctors' Hours, 1990–91; GMC Associate, Fitness to Practise Panels, GMC, 2006–12; Med. Panellist, MPTS, 2012– (Mem., Interim Orders Panels, 2013–); Partner and Lay Panel Mem., Health and Care Professionals Council, 2014–. Chairman: Barnet Health Promoting Schs, later Barnet Healthy Schs Scheme, Steering Gp, 1995–2002; Barnet Cardiovascular Strategy Steering Gp (formerly Barnet Coronary Heart Disease, Stroke and Smoking Focus Gp), 1995–2001; Barnet Adv. Gp on Palliative Care Services, 1996–2000. Gov., Royal Free Hampstead NHS Trust, 2012–. Hon. Vis. Fellow, LSHTM, 1992–93; Associate Prof., Sch. of Health, Biol and Envmtl Scis, subseq. of Health and Social Scis, Middlesex Univ., 2002–05 (Hon. Vis. Prof., 2001–02, 2006–07). Chm., New End Sch. PTA, 1983–85; Parent Governor, 1987–92, Partnership (formerly First) Gov., 1992–2010, Chm. Governing Body, 2002–10, Hendon Sch. Mem., Soc. for Endocrinology, 1998–. Chm., Friends of Belsize Community Library, 2012–. DFPHM 1999. FRSocMed 1971 (Hon. Treas., 2001–03, Hon. Sec., 2003–05, Vice-Pres., 2005–07, Section of Endocrinol. and Diabetes). *Publications:* Anorexia Nervosa (with P. Dally and J. Gomez), 1979; papers in med. jls on rheumatol and endocrinol topics. *Recreations:* music, cinema, table tennis, chess, travel.

ISAACS, Barry Russell; QC 2011; *b* London, 27 Oct. 1964; *s* of Sam Isaacs and Rita Isaacs; *m* 1995, Deborah De Groen; one *s* two *d. Educ:* Ilford Co. High Sch. for Boys; Oriel Coll., Oxford (BA 1987); Harvard Univ. (AM 1989). ASA 1989. Mgt Consultant, Bain & Co., 1987–90; Investment Manager, Venture Capital, Touche Remnant, 1990–91; called to the Bar, Inner Temple, 1994; in practice as a barrister, specialising in insolvency, banking and commercial law, South Square, 1994–. *Recreation:* tennis. *Address:* 3–4 South Square, Gray's Inn, WC1R 5HP. *T:* (020) 7696 9900. *E:* practicemanagers@southsquare.com. *Club:* Chandos Lawn Tennis.

ISAACS, Elizabeth; QC 2013; a Recorder, since 2009; *b* London, 8 March 1963; *d* of Eliot and Gloria Isaacs; one *d. Educ:* Sponne Sch., Towcester; Univ. of Durham (BA Hons Psychol. 1984); Univ. of Leicester (MA Social Work 1989); Univ. of Coventry (LLB Hons 1997); Inns of Court Sch. of Law. Social worker, Warks CC, 1990–97; called to the Bar, Lincoln's Inn, 1998; in practice as family barrister, 1998–; fee-paid Judge and Chair, Mental Health Tribunal, 2014–. Mem., Family Justice Council, 2015–. *Publications:* (with C. Shepherd) Social Work Decision Making: a guide for childcare lawyers, 2008, 2nd edn 2012; (jtly) Challenging and Defending Local Authority Childcare Decisions, 2013; (contrib.) Family Court Practice, 2014; (contrib. Ed.) Clarke, Hall & Morrison on Children, 2014. *Recreations:* theatre, cinema, walking, art, reading Hello magazine. *Address:* St Ives Chambers, Whittall Street, Birmingham B4 6DH. *T:* (0121) 236 0853. *E:* elizabeth.isaacs@stiveschambers.co.uk.

ISAACS, Jane; *see* King, Jane.

ISAACS, Sir Jeremy (Israel), Kt 1996; General Director, Royal Opera House, Covent Garden, 1988–97 (Member, Board of Directors, 1985–97); Chief Executive, Jeremy Isaacs Productions, 1998–2008; *b* 28 Sept. 1932; *s* of Isidore Isaacs and Sara Jacobs; *m* 1st, 1958, Tamara (*née* Weinreich) (*d* 1986), Cape Town; one *s* one *d*; 2nd, 1988, Gillian Mary Widdicombe. *Educ:* Glasgow Acad.; Merton Coll., Oxford (MA; Hon. Fellow 2006). Pres. of the Union, Hilary, 1955. Television Producer, Granada TV (What the Papers Say, All Our Yesterdays), 1958; Associated-Rediffusion (This Week), 1963; BBC TV (Panorama), 1965; Controller of Features, Associated Rediffusion, 1967; with Thames Television, 1968–78: Controller of Features, 1971–74; Producer, The World at War, 1974; Director of Programmes, 1974–78; Chief Exec., Channel Four TV Co., 1981–87; TV programmes: A Sense of Freedom, STV; Ireland, a Television History, BBC; Cold War, CNN; Millennium, CNN; Millennium Minds, Channel 4; Artists At Work, Artsworld, 2001; interviewer, Face to Face, BBC. Chm., Artsworld Channels Ltd, 2000–03. Dir, Glasgow 1999, 1996–99. Chairman: DCMS Adv. Panel, European Capital of Culture UK Nomination for 2008, 2002–03; EU Selection Panel, European Capitals of Culture 2010, 2006, and Eur. Capitals of Culture 2016, 2011–13. Chm., Salzburg Festival Trust, 1997–2001; Trustee, IPPR, 1989–99. Member: Somerset House Trust, 1997–2003; Council, UEA, 1997–2000; Trustee: European Opera Centre, 1996–2008; Children's Music Workshop, 1997–2007; 2011 Trust, 2009–. Dir, Open College, 1987–92. Governor, BFI, 1979–84 (Chm., BFI Production Bd, 1979–81). President: RTS, 1997–2000; Merton Soc., 2005–07; Merton Founder's Soc., 2009–. Organised A Statue for Oscar Wilde, Adelaide Street, 1998. James MacTaggart Meml Lectr, Edinburgh TV Fest., 1979; Jonathan Dennis Meml Lectr, Giornate del Cinema Muto, Pordenone, 2010. FRSA 1983; Fellow: BAFTA, 1985; BFI, 1986; FRSAMD 1989; FGS (FGSM 1989). Hon. FRIBA 2004. Hon. DLitt: Strathclyde, 1984; CNAA, 1987; Bristol, 1988; Hope, Liverpool, 2009; Hon. LLD Manchester, 1999. Desmond Davis Award for outstanding creative contrib. to television, 1972; George Polk Meml Award, 1973; Cyril Bennett Award for outstanding contrib. to television programming, RTS, 1982; Lord Willis Award for Distinguished Service to Television, 1985; Bidlake Meml Prize for services to cycling, 1986; Directorate Award, Internat. Council of Nat. Acad. of TV Arts and Scis, NY, 1987; Lifetime Achievement Award, Banff, 1988; BAFTA Scotland Award, 2009. Commandeur de l'Ordre des Arts et des Lettres (France), 1988; Mem., Ordre pour le Mérite (France), 1993. *Publications:* Storm over Four: a personal account, 1989; (jtly) Cold War, 1998, 2nd edn 2008; Never Mind the Moon: my time at the Royal Opera House, 1999; Look Me in the Eye: a life in television, 2006. *Recreations:* reading, walking, cooking, drinking, watching TV sport. *Club:* Garrick.

ISAACS, Stuart Lindsay; QC 1991; a Recorder, since 1997; a Deputy High Court Judge, since 2004; *b* 8 April 1952; *s* of late Stanley Leslie Isaacs and of Marquette Isaacs; *m* 2000, Melodie, *e d* of Mannie and Judy Schuster; two *s* one *d. Educ:* Haberdashers' Aske's Sch., Elstree; Downing Coll., Cambridge (Law, Double 1st cl. Hons); Univ. Libre de Bruxelles (Licence spéciale en droit européen, grande distinction). Called to the Bar, Lincoln's Inn, 1975, Bencher, 1999; admitted NY Bar, 1985. An Asst Recorder, 1992–97. Member: Internat. Panel of Arbitrators, Singapore Internat. Arbitration Centre, 1998–; Restricted Patients Panel, Mental Health Review Tribunal, 2000–04; Internat. Panel of Mediators, Singapore Mediation Centre, 2007–. Mem. Law Adv. Cttee, British Council, 1996–99. Formerly Consultant Ed., Butterworth's EC Case Citator; Consultant Ed., Banking Law Reports, 1996–98. *Publications:* EC Banking Law, 1985, 2nd edn 1994; Banking and the Competition Law of the EEC, 1978; (ed jtly) The EC Regulation on Insolvency Proceedings, 2003, 2nd edn 2009. *Recreations:* family, travel, languages. *Address:* King & Spalding, 125 Old Broad Street, EC2N 1AR. *E:* sisaacsqc@kslaw.com, stuart@stuartisaacsqc.com.

ISAACS, Tamara Margaret; *see* Finkelstein, T. M.

ISAACSON, Laurence Ivor, CBE 1998; Chairman, World Cancer Research Fund (UK), since 2012 (Director and Trustee, since 2003); *b* 1 July 1943; *s* of Henry Isaacson and Dorothy (*née* Levitt). *Educ:* London Sch. of Econs (BSc Econ). FIH (FHCIMA 1996). Mgt trainee, Unilever, London and Rotterdam, 1964–67; Doyle Dane Bernbach Advertising, 1967–70; Foote Cone & Belding Advertising, 1970–72; Jt Founder and Man. Dir, Creative Business Ltd, 1972–83; Dir, Kennedy Brookes Plc, 1983–86; Jt Founder and Dep. Chm., Groupe Chez Gérard PLC, 1986–2002; Partner and Dir, Paris Commune LLC (USA), 2005–10. Chm., MAP Travel-Canada, 2001–04. Mem. Adv. Bd, UK in NY, 2001. Chairman: Contemp. Dance Trust, 1988–94; BOC Covent Gdn Fest. of Opera and Music Theatre, 1993–2001; London Restaurant Week, 1999; L'Escargot Restaurant, 2014–; Dir and Mem. Council, Arts & Business (formerly ABSA), 1987–2002; Mem. Council, RADA, 2014–. Royal Shakespeare Co.: Director: RSC Foundn, 1998–2000; Main Bd, 2003–11; RSC America Inc., 2004–; Gov., 2000–; Chm., Actors' Circle, 2001–; non-exec. Dir, Ambassador Theatre Gp, 2000–. Dir, London Tourist Bd, 1994–2002; Mem., London First Visitors Council, 1994–98; Creative Dir, Ampersand Travel, 2013–. Dir, Crusaid, 1994–2008; Director: World Cancer Res. Fund (Hong Kong), 2010–; World Cancer Res. Fund (Holland), 2013–. Patron: Cardiff Internat. Fest. of Music Theatre, 2001–; PKD Kidney Charity, 2011–. FRSA 1997. *Address:* 5 Chalcot Crescent, NW1 8YE. *T:* (020) 7586 3793. *E:* laurencei@aol.com. *Clubs:* Garrick, Groucho, Home House (Founding Partner, and Dir, 1999–2005); Norwood (NYC).

ISAACSON, Prof. Peter Gersohn, DM, DSc; FRCPath; FRS 2009; Professor of Morbid Anatomy, University College London, 1982–2002, now Emeritus; Consultant Histopathologist, University College London Hospitals NHS Foundation Trust, since 2002; *b* 24 Nov. 1936; *s* of Robert and Freda Isaacson; *m* 1959, Maria de Lourdes Abranches Pinto; one *s* three *d*. *Educ:* Prince Edward Sch., Salisbury, Rhodesia; Univ. of Cape Town (MB ChB); DM Southampton, 1980; DSc London, 1992. FRCPath 1972. Sen. Lectr, then Reader, Southampton Univ. Med. Sch., 1974–82. Founder FMedSci 1998. Hon. MD: Free Univ. of Berlin, 1998; Universidade Nova de Lisboa, 2005. San-Salvatore Prize, Lugano, 1999. *Publications:* Biopsy Pathology of the Lymphoreticular System, 1983; Oxford Textbook of Pathology, 1993; Extranodal Lymphoma, 1994; numerous contribs to med. jls. *Address:* Cellular Pathology - 2nd Floor, Royal Free Hospital, Pond Street, NW3 2QG. *T:* (secretary) (020) 7830 2227, (direct) (020) 7794 0500 ext. 33844, *Fax:* (020) 7435 3289.

ISAAMAN, Gerald Michael, OBE 1994; journalist and consultant; Editorial Consultant, Home Counties Newspapers plc, 1994–99; Editor, 1968–94, and General Manager, 1990–94, Hampstead and Highgate Express; *b* 22 Dec. 1933; *s* of Asher Isaaman and Lily Finklestein; *m* 1962, Delphine Walker, *e d* of Cecile and Arnold Walker; one *s*. *Educ:* Dame Alice Owen's Grammar School. Reporter, North London Observer Series, 1950, Hampstead and Highgate Express, 1955. Director: Pipistrel Retail Solutions, 1994–; Pipistrel Education Systems, 1994–; Health Independent Ltd, 2002–; non-exec. Dir, Whittington Hosp. NHS Trust, 1994–98. Founder Trustee, Arkwright Arts Trust, 1971; Chairman: Camden Arts Trust Management Board, 1970–82; Exhibns Cttee, Camden Arts Centre, 1971–82; Russell Housing Soc., 1976–82; Trustees, King's Cross Disaster Fund, 1987–89; Dep. Chm., Assoc. of British Editors, 1996–2000 (Mem. Council, 1985–93); Member: Press Complaints Commn, 1993–95; Bd, Camden Trng Centre, 1997–2001; Camden Festival Trust, 1982–; Cheltenham Literary Fest. Cttee, 1998–2011; Patron and Trustee, Hamden Trust, 1995–; Patron, Ledbury Poetry Fest., 1997–. Jt Founder, Marlboroughnewsonline.co.uk, 2011. FRSA 1992–2005. Special presentation, for distinguished services to journalism, British Press Awards, 1994. *Recreations:* work, listening to jazz, talking to my grandson Max. *Address:* 13 George Lane, Marlborough, Wilts SN8 4BX. *T:* (01672) 519375. *E:* gerald@isaaman.com. *Club:* Garrick.

ISCHINGER, Wolfgang Friedrich; Chairman, Munich Security Conference, since 2008; *b* 6 April 1946; *s* of Karl and Margarete Ischinger; *m* 2002, Jutta Falke; one *s* two *d* (and one *s* decd). *Educ:* German Law Sch.; Fletcher Sch. of Law and Diplomacy, Medford, Mass. (MA 1973). Joined German Foreign Service, 1975; Policy Planing Staff, Foreign Ministry, Bonn, 1977–79; Washington, 1979–82; Pvte Sec. to Foreign Minister, 1982–90; Minister, Paris, 1990–93; Dir, Policy Planning Staff, 1993–95, Political Dir, 1995–98, State Sec., 1998–2001, Foreign Ministry; Ambassador to USA, 2001–06; Ambassador to UK, 2006–08. Holds numerous foreign decorations incl. Comdr, Légion d'Honneur (France), 1999. *Publications:* numerous contribs on foreign and security policy issues. *Recreations:* mountaineering, ski-ing. *Address:* Munich Security Conference, Prinzregentenstrasse 7, 80538 Munich, Germany. *E:* office@securityconference.de.

ISENBERG, Prof. David Alan, MD; FRCP, FMedSci; Arthritis Research UK (formerly Arthritis Research Campaign) Diamond Jubilee Professor of Rheumatology and Academic Director of Rheumatology, University College London, since 1996; *b* 20 Oct. 1949; *s* of late Dr Harry and of Sheila Isenberg; *m* 1975, Lucy Fischel; one *s* one *d*. *Educ:* St Bartholomew's Hosp. Med. Coll. (MB BS 1973); MD London 1984. MRCS 1973; LRCP 1973, MRCP 1976, FRCP 1990. Various trng posts in internal medicine, N London hosps, 1976–79; Sir Jules Thorn Res. Fellow, UCL, 1979–81; Sir Stanley Thomas Johnson Res. Fellow, Tufts-New England Med. Center, Boston, 1982–83; University College London: Consultant Rheumatologist, Middlesex Hosp., 1984–; Sen. Lectr, Middlesex Hosp., 1984–92; Prof. of Rheumatology, 1992–95. Non-exec. Dir, Royal Nat. Orthopaedic Hosp., Stanmore, 2011–. Pres., British Soc. of Rheumatology, 2004–06. FMedSci 2006. Evelyn Hess Award, Lupus Foundn of America, 2010; Roger Demers Award, 2012. *Publications:* (jtly) Autoimmune Rheumatic Disease, 1987, 2nd edn 1999; (ed jtly) Oxford Textbook of Rheumatology, 1993, 3rd edn 2004; (jtly) Friendly Fire: explaining autoimmune disease, 1995; (ed jtly) Controversies in Rheumatology, 1997; (ed jtly) Adolescent Rheumatology, 1998; (ed jtly) Imaging in Rheumatology, 2002; Lupus: the facts, 2008; 500 res. papers; 225 reviews and chapters. *Recreations:* playing tennis and guitar, writing short stories, watching football, going to the theatre and classical music concerts. *Address:* Room 424, The Rayne Building, University College London, 5 University Street, WC1E 6JF. *T:* (020) 3108 2150, 2148. *E:* d.isenberg@ucl.ac.uk.

ISH-HOROWICZ, Prof. David, FRS 2002; PhD; Professor of Cell and Developmental Biology, University College London, since 2013; *b* 2 Aug. 1948; *s* of Moshe Ish-Horowicz and Hava Ish-Horowicz (*née* Berman); *m* 1988, Rosamund Diamond. *Educ:* Manchester Grammar Sch.; Pembroke Coll., Cambridge (BA 1969); Darwin Coll., Cambridge/MRC Lab. of Molecular Biol. (PhD 1973). Post-doctoral Res. Fellow, Basel Univ., Switzerland, 1973–76; Imperial Cancer Research Fund, later Cancer Research UK: Res. Scientist, 1977–81; Sen. Res. Scientist, 1981–87; Principal Scientist, 1987–2013. Hon. Prof., UCL, 1997–2013. Mem., EMBO, 1985. *Publications:* contrib. papers to research jls. *Recreations:* music, swimming, ski-ing, eating.

ISHAM, Sir Norman (Murray Crawford), 14th Bt *cr* 1627, of Lamport, Northamptonshire; OBE 1988; Chartered Architect, now retired; *b* 28 Jan. 1930; *yr s* of Lt-Col Vere Arthur Richard Isham, MC (*d* 1968) and Edith Irene (*d* 1973), *d* of Harry Brown; *S* brother, 2009; *m* 1956, Joan, *d* of late Chief Inspector Leonard James Genet, BEM, BSAP; two *s* one *d*. *Educ:* Stowe; Univ. of Cape Town (BArch Dist.). ARIBA 1958. Study Bursary, Italian Govt, 1958–59. Projects include Browning Barracks, Parachute Regiment Depot, Aldershot, 1968 (Civic Trust Award, 1968; Concrete Soc. Award, 1969). Mem. Cttee, Alton Soc.; Pres., Orton Trust, Northants; establd Anglo-American Isham Ancestry Assoc., 2012. *Heir: s* Richard Leonard Vere Isham [*b* 30 Dec. 1958; *m* 1990, Julia Claire Mary, *d* of David Frost Pilkington, CBE; two *s*].

ISHERWOOD, John David Gould, CMG 2001; Chairman, Hampshire Archives Trust, 2001–11; consultant solicitor, 1991–2002; *b* 8 Feb. 1936; *s* of Frank Hilton Isherwood and Beatrice Marion Isherwood (*née* Gould); *m* 1967, Anne Isobel Inglis; one *s* one *d*. *Educ:* Cheltenham Coll.; Merton Coll., Oxford (MA 1963; MSt 1997); Stanford Univ., California. Lieut, RA, 1954–56. Admitted Solicitor, 1964; VSO, 1964–68; Solicitor, 1969, Sen. Partner, 1985–91, Barker, Son & Isherwood, Andover. Mem., Law Soc. Trustee: Oxfam, 1968–98 (Chm., Exec. Cttee, 1979–85); Wateraid, 1981–2001 (Chm., 1995–2001); NCVO, 1996–2003. Trustee, SE Museums, Libraries and Archives Council, 2003–08. Hon. Sec., Hants New Victoria Co. Hist. Project, 2008–. *Recreations:* local history, theatre, travel. *Address:* Chalcot, Penton Mewsey, Andover, Hants SP11 0RQ.

ISHERWOOD, Mark; Member (C) Wales North, National Assembly for Wales, since 2003; *b* 21 Jan. 1959; *s* of Rodney Isherwood and Patricia McLean; *m* 1985, Hilary Fleming; two *s* four *d*. *Educ:* Univ. of Newcastle-upon-Tyne (BA Hons Politics). Trainee Manager, subseq. Br. Manager, Cheshire Building Soc., 1981–89; Commercial Business Develt Manager, NWS Bank, 1989–90; Wirral Area Manager, 1990–94, N Wales Area Manager, 1994–2003, Cheshire Building Soc. Mem., Treuddyn Community Council, 1999–2004 (Vice-Chm., 2002–03). Bd Mem., Venture Housing Assoc., 1992–2003. Gov., Ysgol Parc-y-Llon, 1996–2004. Contested (C): Alyn and Deeside, 2001; Delyn, 2015. Mem., Mold Round Table, 1984–2009. ACIB. *Recreations:* sailing, spending time with family. *Address:* National Assembly for Wales, Cardiff Bay, Cardiff CF99 1NA. *T:* 0300 200 7219. *E:* mark.isherwood@assembly.wales; (constituency office) 5 Halkyn Street, Holywell, Flintshire CH8 7TX.

ISHIGURO, Kazuo, OBE 1995; FRSL; author; *b* 8 Nov. 1954; *s* of Shizuo and Shizuko Ishiguro; *m* 1986, Lorna Anne MacDougall; one *d*. *Educ:* Univ. of Kent (BA English/Philosophy); Univ. of East Anglia (MA Creative Writing). Began publishing short stories, articles, in magazines, 1980; writer of TV plays, 1984–; filmscripts: (jtly) The Saddest Music in the World, 2004; The White Countess, 2006. Mem. Jury, Cannes Film Festival, 1994. FRSL 1989. Hon. DLitt: Kent, 1990; UEA, 1995; St Andrews, 2003. Premio Scanno for Literature, Italy, 1995; Premio Mantova, Italy, 1998. Chevalier de l'Ordre des Arts et des Lettres (France), 1998; Peggy V. Helmerich Distinguished Author Award, 2013; Sunday Times Award for Literary Excellence, 2014; Lion Medal, NY Public Liby, 2014. *Publications:* A Pale View of Hills, 1982 (Winifred Holtby Prize, RSL); An Artist of the Floating World, 1986 (Whitbread Book of the Year, Whitbread Fiction Prize); The Remains of the Day, 1989 (Booker Prize; filmed 1993); The Unconsoled, 1995 (Cheltenham Prize, 1995); When We Were Orphans, 2000; Never Let Me Go, 2005 (Premio Serono, Italy, Corine Internat. Book Prize, Germany, Casino de Santiago Eur. Novel Award, Spain, 2006; filmed 2010); Nocturnes: five stories of music and nightfall, 2009 (Giuseppe Tomasi di Lampedusa Internat. Literary Prize); The Buried Giant, 2015. *Recreations:* music; playing piano and guitar. *Address:* c/o Faber & Faber, Bloomsbury House, 74–77 Great Russell Street, WC1B 3DA.

ISLE OF MAN, Archdeacon of; *see* Brown, Ven. A.

ISLE OF WIGHT, Archdeacon of; *see* Sutton, Ven. P. A.

ISLINGTON, Bishop Suffragan of, since 2015; **Rt Rev. Richard Charles Thorpe;** *b* 1965. *Educ:* Birmingham Univ. (BSc 1987); Wycliffe Hall, Oxford. Ordained deacon, 1996, priest, 1997; Curate, Holy Trinity, Brompton, with St Paul's, Onslow Square, 1996–2005; Priest-in-charge, 2005–10, Rector, 2010–15, St Paul's, Shadwell, with Ratcliffe St James; Priest-in-charge, All Hallows, Bromley-by-Bow, 2010–14.

ISON, Very Rev. David John, PhD; Dean of St Paul's, since 2012; *b* 15 Sept. 1954; *s* of Richard Lea Ison and Maureen Jean Ison; *m* 1977, Hilary Margaret Powell; two *s* two *d*. *Educ:* Univ. of Leicester (BA 1976); Univ. of Nottingham (BA 1978); St John's Coll., Nottingham (DPS 1979); King's Coll. London (PhD 1985). Ordained deacon, 1979, priest, 1980; Asst Curate, St Nicholas and St Luke, Deptford, 1979–85; Tutor, Church Army Trng Coll., 1985–88; Vicar, Potters Green, Coventry, 1988–93; Officer for Contg Ministerial Educn, Dio. Exeter, 1993–2005; Dean of Bradford, 2005–12. *Publications:* (ed) Pilgrim Guide to Exeter Cathedral, 1999; (ed) The Vicar's Guide, 2005. *Recreations:* building a car, bodgery. *Address:* The Chapter House, St Paul's Churchyard, EC4M 8AD. *T:* (020) 7236 2827. *E:* deanspa@stpaulscathedral.org.uk.

ISRAEL, Prof. Jonathan Irvine, DPhil; FBA 1992; Professor of Modern History, Institute for Advanced Study, Princeton, since 2000; *b* 22 Jan. 1946; *s* of David and Miriam Israel; *m* 2009, Annette Munt; one *s* one *d* by a previous marriage. *Educ:* Kilburn Grammar Sch.; Queens' Coll., Cambridge; St Antony's Coll., Oxford (DPhil 1972). Lectr, Hull Univ., 1972–74; Lectr, 1974–81, Reader, 1981–84, Prof. of Dutch History and Instns, 1985–2000, UCL. *Publications:* Race, Class and Politics in Colonial Mexico, 1975; The Dutch Republic and the Hispanic World, 1982; European Jewry in the Age of Mercantilism 1550–1750, 1985; Dutch Primacy in World Trade 1585–1740, 1989; Empires and Entrepots: the Dutch, the Spanish monarchy and the Jews 1585–1713, 1990; (ed) The Anglo-Dutch Movement: essays on the Glorious Revolution and its world impact, 1991; The Dutch Republic, 1995; Conflicts of Empires: Spain, the Low Countries and the struggle for world supremacy 1585–1713, 1997; Radical Enlightenment: philosophy and the making of modernity 1650–1750, 2001; Enlightenment Contested, 2006; A Revolution of the Mind: radical enlightenment and the intellectual origins of modern democracy, 2010; Democratic Enlightenment: philosophy, revolution, and human rights, 1750–1790, 2011; Revolutionary Ideas: an intellectual history of the French Revolution from The Rights of Man to Robespierre, 2014. *Address:* School of Historical Studies, Institute for Advanced Study, Einstein Drive, Princeton, NJ 08540, USA.

ISRAEL, Prof. Werner, OC 1994; FRS 1986; Adjunct Professor of Physics, University of Victoria, since 1997; *b* 4 Oct. 1931; *s* of Arthur Israel and Marie Kappauf; *m* 1958, Inge Margulies; one *s* one *d*. *Educ:* Cape Town High Sch.; Univ. of Cape Town (BSc 1951, MSc 1954); Dublin Inst. for Advanced Studies; Trinity Coll., Dublin (PhD 1960). Lectr in Applied Maths, Univ. of Cape Town, 1954–56; University of Alberta: Asst Prof., 1958; Associate Prof., 1964; Prof. of Maths, 1968–71; Prof. of Physics, 1972–96; Univ. Prof., 1985–96. Sherman Fairchild Dist. Schol., CIT, 1974–75; Vis. Prof., Dublin Inst. for Advanced Studies, 1966–68; Sen. Visitor, Dept of Applied Maths and Theoretical Physics, Univ. of Cambridge, 1975–76; Maître de Recherche Associé, Inst. Henri Poincaré, Paris, 1976–77; Visiting Professor: Berne, 1980; Kyoto, 1986, 1998; Vis. Fellow, Gonville and Caius Coll., Cambridge, 1985. Fellow, Canadian Inst. for Advanced Research, 1986–. Pres., Internat. Soc. of Gen. Relativity and Gravitation, 1998–2001. Hon. DSc: Queen's, Kingston, Ont, 1987; Victoria, BC, 1999; Dr *hc* Tours, 1994. *Publications:* (ed) Relativity, Astrophysics and Cosmology, 1973; (ed with S. W. Hawking) General Relativity: an Einstein centenary survey, 1979; (ed with S. W. Hawking) 300 Years of Gravitation, 1987; numerous papers on black hole physics, general relativity, relativistic statistical mechanics. *Recreation:* music. *Address:* Department of Physics and Astronomy, University of Victoria, Victoria, BC V8W 2Y2, Canada.

ISRAELACHVILI, Prof. Jacob Nissim, FRS 1988; FAA; Professor of Chemical Engineering and Materials Science, Department of Chemical Engineering and Materials Department, University of California, Santa Barbara, since 1986; *b* 19 Aug. 1944; *s* of Haim and Hela Israelachvili; *m* 1st, 1971, Carina (marr. diss. 2010); two *d*; 2nd, 2012, Trudi Carey. *Educ:* Univ. of Cambridge (MA; PhD 1972). FAA 1982. Post-doctoral res. into surface forces, Cavendish Lab., Cambridge, 1971–72; EMBO Res. Fellow, Biophysics Inst., Univ. of Stockholm, 1972–74; Res. Fellow, subseq. Professorial Fellow, Res. Sch. of Physical Scis, Inst. of Advanced Studies, ANU, Canberra, 1974–86. Council Mem., 1983–87, Vice-Pres., 1986–87, Internat. Assoc. of Colloid and Interface Scientists. Foreign Associate, US NAE, 1996; Fellow, APS, 2004; FAAAS 2012; MNAS 2004. Dr sc *hc* ETH Zürich, 2007; Hon. DEng S Florida, 2008. Pawsey Medal, 1977, Matthew Flinders Lectr medallist, 1986, Aust. Acad. of Sci.; (jtly) David Syme Res. Prize, 1983; (jtly) Medal, US Materials Res. Soc., 2004; Nat. Award in Colloid and Surface Chem., ACS, 2009; H. Walker Award for excellence in chem. engrg lit., AIChE, 2012; Tribology Gold Medal Laureate, IMechE, 2013. *Publications:* Intermolecular and Surface Forces: with applications to colloidal and biological systems, 1985, 3rd edn 2011; about 400 pubns in learned jls, incl. Nature, Science, Procs Royal Soc. *Recreation:* history of science. *Address:* 713 Via Airosa, Santa Barbara, CA 93110, USA. *T:* (mobile) (805) 2525568, (office) (805) 8938407.

ISSA, Caroline; Chief Executive Officer: Tank Publications Ltd, since 2002; Tank Form Ltd, since 2004; *b* Montreal, 18 April 1977; *d* of Farah Issa and Lee Chin Lim. *Educ:* Royal West Acad., Montreal; Marianopolis Coll., Westmount, Quebec; Wharton Sch., Univ. of Pennsylvania (BScEcon). Analyst, Marakon Associates, San Francisco, 1999–2002. *Address:* Tank, 91–93 Great Portland Street, W1W 7NX. *T:* (020) 7637 0303. *E:* caroline@tankmagazine.com.

ISSERLIS, Steven John, CBE 1998; 'cellist; *b* 19 Dec. 1958; *s* of late George and Cynthia Isserlis; partner, Pauline Mara (*d* 2010); one *s*. *Educ:* City of London School; International 'Cello Centre; Oberlin College. London recital début, Wigmore Hall, 1977; concerts in Europe, Asia, N America, Australia, 1978–; tours in USSR, later Russia, 1984–; débuts, 1990–, in New York, Paris, Berlin, Vienna, Tokyo, Sydney, Seoul, Taipei, etc; numerous recordings. Awards for recordings include: Gramophone Award (Contemporary Music), for John Tavener's The Protecting Veil, 1992; Deutsche Schallplattenpreis, for Schumann Cello Concerto, 1998; Classic CD Award, for Haydn Concertos, 1999; Gramophone Award (Instrumental Recording), Critics' Award, Classical Brits and CD of the Year, BBC R3 CD Review, for Bach Cello Suites, 2007. Piatigorsky Artist Award, USA, 1993; Instrumentalist Award, Royal Philharmonic Soc., 1993; Schumann Prize, City of Zwickau, 2000; Red F Award, Classic FM, 2002; Classical Artist of the Year, Time Out, 2002; Gramophone Hall of Fame, 2013. *Publications:* Cello World, 1999; Beethoven: mandolin variations (arr. violin or cello and piano), 1990; (with Sabina Teller Ratner) Saint-Saens Complete Shorter Works for cello and piano, 1998; Unbeaten Tracks (short pieces for cello by various contemporary composers), 2000; for children: Why Beethoven Threw the Stew, 2001; Why Handel Waggled His Wig, 2006; (with A. Dudley) Little Red Violin (musical story), 2008; (with A. Dudley) Goldiepegs and the 3 Cellos, 2010; (with A. Dudley) Cindercella, 2012. *Recreations:* talking on the telephone, e-mailing everybody I know (usually for no good reason), eating too much, regretting it, watching videos, reading, panicking about upcoming concerts, sleeping, jet-lag, telling people how tired I am, wondering if I should have any more worthwhile recreations. *Address:* c/o IMG Artists, The Light Box, 111 Power Road, W4 5PY. *T:* (020) 7957 5800.

ISSING, Dr Otmar; President, Center for Financial Studies, Goethe University, Frankfurt, since 2006; Member, Executive Board, European Central Bank, 1998–2006; *b* 27 March 1936. *Educ:* Univ. of Würzburg (BA Econs; PhD 1961). Res. Asst, Inst. of Econs and Social Scis, 1960–66, Lectr, 1965–66, Univ. of Würzburg; Temp. Prof., Univ. of Marburg, 1965–66; Professor: Faculty of Econs and Social Scis, and Dir, Inst. for Internat. Econ. Relns, Univ. of Erlangen-Nuremberg, 1967–73 (Temp. Prof., 1966–67); of Econs, Monetary Affairs and Internat. Econ. Relns, Univ. of Würzburg, 1973–90 (Hon. Prof., 1991–); Mem. Directorate, Deutsche Bundesbank, 1990–98. Co-founder and Jt Ed., WiSt (scientific jl), 1972–90. Hon. doctorates from: Bayreuth, 1996; Constance, 1998; Frankfurt am Main, 1999; Laurea *hc* in Internat. Econ. Integration, Univ. of Pavia, 2010. Internat. Prize, Friedrich August von Hayek Stiftung, 2004; Bernhard Harms Medal, Inst. for World Econs, Kiel, 2004; Hans Möller Medal, Univ. of Munich, 2005; Ludwig Erhard Prize (for econ. writing), 2006. Grand Cross, Order of Merit (Germany), 2006; Grand Officer, Order of Merit (Luxemburg), 2006; Silver Insignia, Würzburg, 2007. *Publications* include: Leitwährung und internationale Währungsordnung, 1965; Indexklauseln und Inflation, 1973; Einführung in die Geldtheorie, 1974, 15th edn 2011 (trans. Chinese and Bulgarian); Investitionslenkung in der Marktwirtschaft?, 1975; (jtly) Kleineres Eigentum: Grundlage unserer Staats- und Wirtschaftsordnung, 1976; Einführung in die Geldpolitik, 1981, 6th edn 1996; Internationale Währungsordnung, 1991; Von der D-Mark zum Euro, 1998; (jtly) Monetary Policy in the Euro Area, 2001; Der Euro: Geburt, Erfolg, Zukunft, 2008 (The Birth of the Euro, 2008; trans. Chinese, 2011); contrib. learned jls. *Address:* Georg Sittig Strasse 8, 97074 Würzburg, Germany.

IVANYI, Prof. Juraj, MD; PhD; Director, Tuberculosis and Related Infections Unit, MRC Clinical Sciences Centre, Hammersmith Hospital, 1984–97; Hon. Professor of Immunology of Infectious Diseases, Guy's Campus of King's College London (formerly Guy's, King's and St Thomas's Hospital Medical and Dental School), since 1998; *b* 20 June 1934; *s* of Dr Arnold Ivanyi and Maria (*née* Keszner); *m* 1st, 1960, Dr Ludmila Svobodova (*d* 2002); 2nd, 2009, Katharine Mary Honey. *Educ:* Charles Univ., Prague (MD); Acad. of Scis, Prague (PhD 1963). Czechoslovak Acad. of Scis, Prague, 1961–68 (Hd, Dept of Immunochem., Inst. of Experimental Biol. and Genetics, 1966–68); Head, Dept of Immunobiol., Wellcome Res. Labs, Beckenham, 1970–84; Prof. of Mycobacteriological Immunol., RPMS, Univ. of London, 1990–97. Hon. Mem., Slovak Soc. for Immunology, 1995. Garnet Immunoglobulin Award, Czech Immunology Soc., 2006. *Publications:* over 300 in field of immunology. *Address:* 3 Grotes Place, Blackheath, SE3 0QH. *T:* (020) 8318 1088.

IVE, Sir Jonathan (Paul), KBE 2012 (CBE 2006); RDI 2003; Senior Vice President and Head of Design, since 1996, Head of Human Interface, since 2012, and Chief Design Officer, since 2015, Apple; *b* London, 1967; *m*; twin *s*. *Educ:* Newcastle upon Tyne Poly. (BA 1st Cl. Hons Industrial Design 1989). Partner, Tangerine, design consultancy, London, 1989–92; joined Apple, 1992. *Designs* include: ceramic-ware, electrical appliances; consumer electronics, computers (incl. iMac, PowerBook, iBook, iPod, iPhone, iPad). Hon. Dr: Newcastle Poly.; Univ. of the Arts, London; RCA. Inaugural medal, RSA, 1999; Designer of Year, Design Mus., 2003; Benjamin Franklin Medal, RSA, 2004; President's Award, D&AD, 2005, and Royal Acad. of Engrs, 2005. *Address:* c/o Apple, 1 Infinite Loop, Cupertino, CA 95014, USA. *T:* (408) 9740419.

IVEAGH, 4th Earl of, *cr* 1919; **Arthur Edward Rory Guinness;** DL; Chairman, Elveden Farms; Bt 1885; Baron Iveagh 1891; Viscount Iveagh 1905; Viscount Elveden 1919; *b* 10 Aug. 1969; *s* of 3rd Earl of Iveagh and Miranda Daphne Jane, *d* of Maj. Michael Smiley; *S* father, 1992; *m* 2001, Clare Hazell; two *s*. Dir, Burhill Estates; Chm., Iveagh Ltd. Mem. Bd, Iveagh Trust; Chm., Chadacre Agricl Trust; Trustee: Robert Black Meml Fund; East Anglian Air Ambulance. DL Suffolk, 2008. FIAgrM 2008. *Heir: s* Viscount Elveden, *qv*. *Address:* The Estate Office, Elveden, Thetford, Norfolk IP24 3TQ.

IVENS, Anne; *see* McElvoy, A.

IVENS, Martin Paul; Editor, Sunday Times, since 2013 (Deputy Editor, 1996–2013); *b* London, 29 Aug. 1958; *s* of Michael William and Rosalie Joy Evans; *m* 1994, Anne McElvoy, *qv*; two *s* one *d*. *Educ:* Finchley Catholic High Sch.; St Peter's Coll., Oxford (BA 1st Cl. Modern Hist.). Foreign Ed., Sunday Telegraph, 1986–88; The Times: Foreign News Ed., 1988–90; Foreign Ed., 1990–94; Exec. Ed. (News and Comment), 1994–96. Directory Trustee, Social Mkt Foundn. *Recreations:* mediaeval and modern history, running, classical music. *Address:* The Sunday Times, 1 London Bridge Street, SE1 9GF. *Club:* Travellers.

IVERSEN, Prof. Leslie Lars, CBE 2013; PhD; FRS 1980; Professor of Pharmacology and Director, Wolfson Centre for Age-Related Diseases, King's College London, 1999–2004; Visiting Professor of Pharmacology, University of Oxford, since 2007; *b* 31 Oct. 1937; *s* of Svend Iversen and Anna Caia Iversen; *m* 1961, Susan Diana (*née* Kibble) (*see* S. D. Iversen); one *s* one *d* (and one *d* decd). *Educ:* Trinity Coll., Cambridge (BA Biochem., PhD Pharmacol). Harkness Fellow, United States: with Dr J. Axelrod, Nat. Inst. of Mental Health, and Dr E. Kravitz, Dept of Neurobiology, Harvard Med. Sch., 1964–66; Fellow, Trinity Coll., Cambridge, 1964–84; Locke Research Fellow of Royal Society, Dept of Pharmacology, Univ. of Cambridge, 1967–71; Dir, MRC Neurochemical Pharmacology Unit, Cambridge, 1971–82; Dir, Merck, Sharp & Dohme Neurosci. Res. Centre, Harlow, 1982–95; Sen. Vis. Scientist, Dept of Pharmacology, 1995–96, Vis. Prof. of Pharmacol., 1996–2007, Oxford Univ. Chm., Adv. Council on Misuse of Drugs, 2011– (interim Chm., 2010). Foreign Associate, Nat. Acad. of Scis (USA), 1986. *Publications:* The Uptake and Storage of Noradrenaline in Sympathetic Nerves, 1967; (with S. D. Iversen) Behavioural Pharmacology, 1975, 2nd edn 1981; The Science of Marijuana, 2000; Speed, Ecstasy, Ritalin: the science of amphetamines, 2007; (jtly) Introduction to Neuropsychopharmacology, 2009. *Recreations:* reading, gardening. *Address:* Department of Pharmacology, University of Oxford, Mansfield Road, Oxford OX1 3QT.

IVERSEN, Prof. Susan Diana, CBE 2005; PhD, ScD; FMedSci; Professor of Psychology, 1993–2005, now Emeritus, and Pro-Vice-Chancellor, (Planning and Resource Allocation), 2000–05, (Special Projects), 2005–12, Oxford University; Fellow of Magdalen College, Oxford, 1993–2005, now Emeritus; *b* 28 Feb. 1940; *d* of Jack Bertram Kibble and Edith Margaret Kibble; *m* 1961, Leslie Lars Iversen, *qv*; one *s* one *d* (and one *d* decd). *Educ:* Girton Coll., Cambridge (BA Zoology, PhD Exp. Psych, ScD). NATO Science Fellow, Nat. Inst. Mental Health and Dept of Pharmacology, Harvard Med. Sch., 1964–66; Fellow: Girton Coll., Cambridge, 1964–75; Jesus Coll., Cambridge, 1981–93; Dept of Exp. Psychology, Cambridge, 1966–83; Merck Sharp & Dohme, Neuroscience Research Centre, Harlow, 1983–93; Oxford University: Prof. and Head of Dept of Experimental Psychol., 1993–2000; Pro-Vice-Chancellor (Res.), 1998–2000. Oxford University Press: Psychology Delegate, 1994–2005; Chm., Finance Cttee, 2001–05. Member: Council, SERC, 1991–94; BBSRC, 1994–97. Member: Animal Procedures Cttee, Home Office, 1989–98; Mental Health and Neurosci. Grant Cttee, Wellcome Trust, 1990–98 (Chm. Panel, 1995–98); Health and Life Scis Panel, 1993–98, Brain Sci., Addiction and Drug Project Panel, 2004, Foresight. President: British Assoc. of Psychopharmacol., 1984–86; Experimental Psychol. Soc., 1988–90; Med. Sect., 1989, Psychol. Sect., 1997, BAAS; Chm., Brain Res. Assoc., 1994–96. Mem. Council, Bioscis Fedn, 2004–08; Trustee, Inst. for Animal Health, 2004–09; Trustee and Mem. Council, GDST, 2005–14 (Chm., Acad. Trust Bd, 2007–14); Mem. Council, 2004–07, Treas., 2010–14, Acad. of Med. Scis. Chm., Internat. Adv. and Scientific Bd, Inst. of Neurosci., TCD; Mem. Adv. Bd, Brain, Mind and Behavior Prog., J. S. McDonnell Foundn, St Louis, USA, 1999–2008. A. Vibert Douglas Fellow, Internat. Fedn of Univ. Women, 1964–65. FMedSci 1999. Hon. Fellow, Cardiff Univ., 1999. Hon. DSc St Andrews, 2005. K. M. Stott Prize, Newnham Coll., Cambridge, 1972; Spearman Medal, BPsS, 1974; Lifetime Achievement Award, British Assoc. for Psychopharmacol., 2003. Receiving Ed., Science, 1994–99; Chief Ed., Neuropsychologia, 1997–2000. *Publications:* (with L. L. Iversen) Behavioural Pharmacology, 1975, 2nd edn 1981; (ed with L. L. Iversen and S. H. Snyder) Handbook of Psychopharmacology, 20 vols; (jtly) Introduction to Neuropsychopharmacology, 2008. *Recreations:* history, wildlife, modern art, theatre. *Address:* Magdalen College, Oxford OX1 4AU.

IVES, Charles John Grayston, (Bill); Informator Choristarum, Organist, and Tutor in Music, Magdalen College, Oxford, 1991–2009; Fellow of Magdalen College, 1991–2009, now Emeritus; *b* 15 Feb. 1948; *s* of Harold James Ives and Catherine Lilla Ives; *m* 1st, 1972, Bethan Eleri Jones (marr. diss. 1986); one *s* one *d*; 2nd, 1988, Janette Ann (*née* Buqué). *Educ:* King's Sch., Ely; Selwyn Coll., Cambridge. Asst Dir of Music, Reed's Sch., Cobham, 1971–76; Lectr in Music, Coll. of Further Educn, Chichester, 1976–78; tenor, The King's Singers, 1978–85; freelance composer, 1985–91. Examr, Associated Bd of Royal Schs of Music, 1988–2006. Hon. FRSCM 2008. DMus Lambeth 2008. *Publications:* (as Grayston Ives) musical compositions of sacred choral music, including Canterbury Te Deum (commnd for Enthronement of Archbishop George Carey, Canterbury Cathedral, 1991), The Gift of Grace (commnd for Nat. Commemoration Service, Westminster Abbey, 2007) and Requiem (commnd for 550th anniv. of Magdalen Coll., Oxford, 2008). *Recreations:* books, wine, travel. *Address:* Potmans Heath Cottage, Wittersham, Tenterden, Kent TN30 7PU. *T:* (01797) 270525.

IVISON, David Malcolm; Director, British Metallurgical Plant Constructors' Association, 1994–2002; *b* 22 March 1936; *s* of John and Ruth Ellen Ivison; *m* 1961, Lieselotte Verse; one *s* one *d*. *Educ:* King Edward VI School, Lichfield; RMA Sandhurst; Staff College, Camberley. Army, Gurkha Transport Regt, 1955–83 (Lt-Col). Tate & Lyle, 1984–85; Chief Exec., Inst. of Road Transport Engrs, 1985–89. Mem. (C) Surrey CC, 2005–. *Recreations:* learning languages, tennis, reading. *Address:* 1 Dundaff Close, Camberley, Surrey GU15 1AF. *T:* (01276) 27778.

IVORY, Sir Brian (Gammell), Kt 2006; CBE 1999; CA; FRSE; Chairman, Marathon Asset Management LLP, since 2011; *b* 10 April 1949; *s* of late Eric James Ivory and Alice Margaret Joan, *d* of Sir Sydney James Gammell; *m* 1981, Oona Mairi Macphie Bell-MacDonald (*see* O. M. M. Ivory); one *s* one *d*. *Educ:* Eton College; Magdalene College, Cambridge (MA). The Highland Distilleries Co., subseq. Highland Distillers plc: Dir, 1978–99; Man. Dir, 1988–94; Gp Chief Exec., 1994–97; Exec. Chm., 1997–99. Executive Chairman: Macallan Glenlivet plc, 1996–99; Scottish American Investment Co. plc, 2001–; Retec Digital plc, 2006–13; Arcus Eur. Infrastructure Fund, 2010–; Dep. Chm., Shawbrook Bank Ltd, 2011–15; Director: Rémy Cointreau SA, 1991–2014; Bank of Scotland, 1998–2007; HBOS plc, 2001–07; Orpar SA, 2003–13; Insight Investment Mgt Ltd, 2003–; Synesis Life Ltd, 2007–08. Vice-Chm., Scottish Arts Council, 1988–92; Mem., Arts Council of GB, 1988–92; Mem., Scottish Economic Council, 1996–98; Chm. of Trustees, Nat. Galleries of Scotland, 2001–09; Chm. of Trustees, Gt Steward of Scotland's Dumfries House Trust, 2011–. Chair, Governance and Nominations Cttee, St Andrews Univ., 2007–. Founder and Chm., Nat. Piping Centre, 1996–. Mem., Royal Co. of Archers (Queen's Body Guard for Scotland), 1996–. FRSA 1993; FRSE 2001. Freeman, City of London, 1996. Paolozzi Gold Medal, Nat. Galls of Scotland, 2009. *Recreations:* the arts, farming, hill walking. *Address:* 12 Ann Street, Edinburgh EH4 1PJ. *Club:* New (Edinburgh).

IVORY, James Francis; film director; Partner in Merchant Ivory Productions, since 1961; *b* 7 June 1928; *s* of Edward Patrick Ivory and Hallie Millicent De Loney. *Educ:* Univ. of Oregon (BA Fine Arts); Univ. of Southern California (MFA Cinema). Guggenheim Fellow, 1974. Collaborator with Ruth Prawer Jhabvala and Ismail Merchant on the following films: The Householder, 1963; Shakespeare Wallah, 1965; The Guru, 1969; Bombay Talkie, 1970; Autobiography of a Princess, 1975; Roseland, 1977; Hullabaloo over Georgie and Bonnie's Pictures, 1978; The Europeans, 1979; Jane Austen in Manhattan, 1980; Quartet, 1981; Heat and Dust, 1983; The Bostonians, 1984; A Room With a View, 1986; Mr and Mrs Bridge, 1990; Howards End, 1992; The Remains of the Day, 1993; Jefferson in Paris, 1995; Surviving Picasso, 1996; A Soldier's Daughter Never Cries, 1998; The Golden Bowl, 2000; Le Divorce, 2003; The City of Your Final Destination, 2008; collaborator with Ismail Merchant (producer) on: (with Nirad Chaudhuri) Adventures of a Brown Man in Search of Civilization, 1971; (with George W. S. Trow and Michael O'Donoghue) Savages, 1972; (with Walter Marks) The Wild Party, 1975; (with Kit Hesketh-Harvey) Maurice, 1987; (with Tama Janowitz) Slaves of New York, 1989; (with Kazuo Ishiguro) The White Countess, 2006; other films: (with Terrence McNally) The Five Forty Eight, 1979; documentaries: Venice, Theme and Variations, 1957; The Sword and the Flute, 1959; The Delhi Way, 1964. D. W. Griffith Award, Directors Guild of America, 1995. Commandeur, Ordre des Arts et des Lettres (France), 1996. *Publications:* Autobiography of a Princess (Also Being the Adventures of an American Film Director in the Land of the Maharajas), 1975. *Recreations:* looking at pictures, Ancient Egypt and Rome. *Address:* PO Box 93, Claverack, NY 12513, USA. *T:* (office) (212) 5828049.

IVORY, Oona Mairi Macphie, (Lady Ivory); DL; Founder and Director, since 1996 and Deputy Chairman, since 1999, National Piping Centre; *b* 21 July 1954; *d* of late Archibald Ian Bell-Macdonald and Mary Rae (*née* Macphie); *m* 1981, Brian Gammell Ivory (*see* Sir B. G. Ivory); one *s* one *d*. *Educ:* Royal Scottish Acad. of Music and Drama; King's Coll., Cambridge (MA); Royal Acad. of Music. ARCM. Dir, 1988–97, Chm., 1995–97, Scottish Ballet; Dir,

RSAMD, 1989–2002. Dir, Glasgow Internat. Piping Fest., 2004–. Trustee, Sri Lanka Reconciliation Music Trust, 2010–. FRSA 1993. DL Edinburgh, 1998. *Recreations:* the arts, sailing, wild places. *Address:* 12 Ann Street, Edinburgh EH4 1PJ.

IWAN, Dafydd; President, Plaid Cymru, 2003–10 (Vice-President, 2001–03); *b* 24 Aug. 1943; *s* of Rev. Gerallt Jones and Elizabeth Jane Jones; *m* 1988, Bethan; two *s*; two *s* one *d* from previous marriage. *Educ:* Welsh Sch. of Architecture, Cardiff (BArch 1968). Chair, Cymdeithas yr Iaith Gymraeg, 1968–71; Dir, 1969–, Man. Dir, 1982–2004, Sain Recording Co. Organiser, Tai Gwynedd Housing Assoc., 1974–82. Mem., Gwynedd Council, 1996–2008 (Leader, Develt Portfolio, 2004–08). Hon. Fellow: Univ. of Wales, Bangor; Univ. of Wales, Aberystwyth. Hon. Mem., Gorsedd of Bards. Hon. LLD Wales, 2004. *Publications:* First Autobiography, 1983; Holl Ganeuon (song collection), 1992; Cân Dros Gymru (autobiog.), 2002; Pictorial Biography, 2005. *Recreations:* writing poetry, composing, art, Rugby. *Address:* Carrog, Caeathro, Caernarfon, Gwynedd LL55 2TF. *T:* (01286) 676004. *E:* dafyddiwan2@gmail.com.

IYER, Kumar Sabapathy; HM Diplomatic Service; Deputy High Commissioner, Mumbai and Director General, UK Trade and Investment, India, since 2013; *b* London; *s* of Sabapathy Iyer and Mahalakshmi Iyer; *m* 2004, Kathryn Ann Worth; one *s* one *d*. *Educ:* Blurton High Sch.; Stoke-on-Trent Sixth Form Coll.; University Coll., Durham Univ. (BA Hons 1st Cl. Econs); Corpus Christi Coll., Cambridge (MPhil Econs; Bank of England Schol.); Harvard Univ. (Kennedy Schol.). Teaching Fellow, Harvard Univ.; Boston Consulting Gp, until 2008; Dep. Dir, Prime Minister's Strategy Unit, No 10 Downing St, 2008–10; Dep. Dir, Strategy, Planning and Budget, 2010–12, Hd, Financial Sector Interventions, 2012–13, HM Treasury. *Publications:* (contrib.) The Internet Revolution: a global perspective, 2003. *Recreations:* cricket, chess. *Address:* c/o Foreign and Commonwealth Office, King Charles Street, SW1A 2AH.

IZZA, Michael Donald McCartney, FCA; Chief Executive, Institute of Chartered Accountants in England and Wales, since 2006; *b* 13 Dec. 1960; *s* of late Salvatore Izza and of Jean Izza (*née* McCartney); *m* 1991, Gillian Johnston; one *s* one *d*. *Educ:* Thornleigh Salesian Coll., Bolton; Durham Univ. (BA Hons Law). ACA 1987, FCA 2007. Coopers & Lybrand, 1983–89; John Labatt Ltd, 1989–96 (Man. Dir, John Labatt Retail, 1992–96); Spring Group plc, 1996–2000: Man. Dir, Spring Skills, 1996–97; Divl Man. Dir, 1997–98; Actg Gp Finance Dir, 1999–2000; Divl Dir, Professional Services and Exec. Dir, Support Services, Carlisle Support Services, 2001; Institute of Chartered Accountants in England and Wales, 2002–: Exec. Dir, Finance and Ops, 2002–03; Chief Operating Officer, 2004–06. Chm., HM Treasury cttees to appoint ind. valuers for financial instns; mem., Govt cttees and gps. *Recreations:* running, hill walking, gardening, Bolton Wanderers FC, history, philately. *Address:* Institute of Chartered Accountants in England and Wales, Chartered Accountants' Hall, PO Box 433, Moorgate Place, EC2P 2BJ. *T:* (020) 7920 8419. *E:* michael.izza@icaew.com.

J

JABALÉ, Rt Rev. (John) Mark, OSB; Bishop of Menevia, (RC), 2001–08; Parish Priest, Holy Trinity Catholic Church, Chipping Norton, 2008–14; *b* 16 Oct. 1933; *s* of John and Arlette Jabalé. *Educ:* Belmont Abbey Sch.; Fribourg Univ. (LèsL); St Mary's Coll., London (DipEd). Belmont Abbey School: Games Master and House Master, 1963–69; Headmaster, 1969–83; built Monastery of the Incarnation, in Tambogrande, Perú; Prior, 1986–93, Abbot, 1993–2000, Belmont Abbey; Bp Coadjutor of Menevia, 2000–01. Steward, Henley Royal Regatta, 1985–. *Recreations:* computers, rowing. *Address:* 14 Egerton Gardens, NW4 4BA. *Club:* Leander (Henley-on-Thames).

JACK, David M.; *see* Morton Jack.

JACK, Ian Grant; writer and editor; columnist, Guardian, since 2001; *b* 7 Feb. 1945; *s* of Henry Jack and Isabella Jack (*née* Gillespie); *m* 1st, 1979, Aparna Bagchi (marr. diss. 1992); 2nd, 1998, Rosalind Sharpe; one *s* one *d*. *Educ:* Dunfermline High School, Fife. Trainee journalist, Glasgow Herald, 1965; reporter, Cambuslang Advertiser and East Kilbride News, 1966; journalist, Scottish Daily Express, 1966–70; Sunday Times, 1970–86; Observer and Vanity Fair (NY), 1986–88; Dep. Editor, 1989–91, Exec. Editor, 1991–92, Editor, 1992–95, Independent on Sunday; Editor, Granta, 1995–2007. FRSL 2009. Journalist of the Year, Granada TV What The Papers Say award, 1985; Colour Magazine Writer of the Year, 1985, Reporter of the Year, 1988, British Press Awards; Nat. Newspaper Editor of the Year, Newspaper Focus Awards, 1992. *Publications:* Before the Oil Ran Out, 1987; The Crash That Stopped Britain, 2001; The Country Formerly Known as Great Britain, 2009; Mofussil Junction, 2013. *Address:* c/o Rogers, Coleridge and White, 20 Powis Mews, W11 1JN. *Clubs:* Groucho; India International Centre (New Delhi).

JACK, Prof. (James) Julian (Bennett), PhD; FRS 1997; Professor of Physiology, 1996–2003, and Fellow of University College, since 1966, University of Oxford; *b* Invercargill, NZ, 25 March 1936. *Educ:* Univ. of Otago (MMedSci, PhD); Magdalen Coll., Oxford (BM 1963; MA). Rhodes Scholarship, 1960–63; House Officer, Radcliffe Infirmary, Oxford, 1963–64; Foulerton Gift Res. Fellow, Royal Soc., 1964–68; University of Oxford: Weir Jun. Res. Fellow in Natural Sci., UC, 1966; Lectr in Physiology, 1970–94; Reader in Cellular Neurosci., 1994–96. Visiting Professor: UCL, 2003–10; KCL, 2012–. Chm., Sci. Adv. Bd, Syntaxin plc, 2005–14; Member, Scientific Advisory Board: Rose Kennedy Center, NY, 2002–; OXION, Oxford, 2006–13; Coco Therapeutics, 2013–14. Mem. Council, Action Res., 1988–91; Chm. Res. Panel, Multiple Sclerosis Soc., 2001–10; Gov., Wellcome Trust, 1987–2004 (Dep. Chm. of Govs, 1994–99); Trustee, Brain Res. Trust, 2006–13. Founder FMedSci 1998; FRCP 1999. Hon. FRSNZ 1999. Hon. DSc Otago. *Address:* 24 Claylands Road, SW8 1NZ. *T:* (020) 7582 3085.

JACK, Rt Hon. (John) Michael, CBE 2015; PC 1997; Chairman, Topps Tiles plc, 2011–15 (non-executive Director, 2000–15); *b* 17 Sept. 1946; *m* 1976, Alison Jane Musgrave; two *s*. *Educ:* Bradford Grammar Sch.; Bradford Tech. Coll.; Leicester Univ. BA(Econs); MPhil. Shipping, subseq. Advertising, Depts, Procter & Gamble, 1970–75; PA to Sir Derek Rayner, Marks & Spencer, 1975–80; Sales Dir, L. O. Jeffs Ltd, 1980–87. Mem., Mersey RHA, 1984–87. Contested (C) Newcastle upon Tyne Central, Feb. 1974. MP (C) Fylde, 1987–2010. PPS to Minister of State, DOE, 1988–89, to Minister of Agric., Fisheries and Food, 1989–90; Parly Under Sec. of State, DSS, 1990–92; Minister of State: Home Office, 1992–93; MAFF, 1993–95; Financial Sec. to HM Treasury, 1995–97; Opposition front bench spokesman on health, 1997, on agric., fisheries and food, 1998. Member: Agriculture Select Cttee, 2000–01; Envmt, Food and Rural Affairs Select Cttee, 2001–07 (Chm., 2003–10); Tax Law Rewrite Steering Cttee, 1999–2010; Exec., 1922 Cttee, 2000–03. Sec., Cons. Back-bench Transport Cttee, 1987–88; Chm., Cons. Back-bench sub-cttee on Horticulture and Markets, 1987–88; Sec., Cons. NW Members Gp, 1988–90. Nat. Chm., Young Conservatives, 1976–77. Chm., Office of Tax Simplification, 2010–11. Agric. and Food Advr, HSBC Bank, 2010–. Lay Canon, Blackburn Cathedral, 2008–. Trustee: MedAlert, 1990–; Lytham Community Sports Assoc., 1997. Vice-Pres., Think Green, 1989–90; Pres., Nat. Fruit Show, 2009–; Judge, BBC Food and Farming Awards, 2010–11. *Recreations:* cycling, mountain biking, olive tree cultivation, vegetable growing, motor sport, boules. *E:* michaeljack17@gmail.com.

JACK, Julian; *see* Jack, J. J. B.

JACK, Lorna Burn, CA; Chief Executive, Law Society of Scotland, since 2009; *b* Fraserburgh, 20 Aug. 1962; *d* of George Buchan Jack and Mary Strachan Jack; *m* Lucas Hooijenga. *Educ:* Univ. of Aberdeen (MA Accountancy and Econs); Harvard Business Sch.; Exec. Develt Prog., Inst. of Chartered Accountants. CA 1984. Audit Senior, Arthur Andersen & Co., 1982–85; Finance Dir, Aberdeen Cable Services Ltd, 1985–89; Scottish Enterprise: Hd of Food Sector Team, 1989–97; Hd of Global Companies Research, 1997–98; Dir of Ops and Dep. Chief Exec., 1998–2000, Chief Exec., 2000–02, Scottish Enterprise Forth Valley; Pres. Americas, Scottish Develt Internat., 2002–08. Non-exec. Dir, Highlands and Islands Airport Ltd, 2014–. Trustee and Treas., McConnell Internat. Foundn, 2013–. *Recreations:* ski-ing, reading, music. *Address:* Law Society of Scotland, 26 Drumsheugh Gardens, Edinburgh EH3 7YR. *T:* (0131) 226 7411, *Fax:* (0131) 225 2934.

JACK, Sir Malcolm (Roy), KCB 2011; PhD; FSA; author, historian and lecturer; Clerk and Chief Executive of the House of Commons, 2006–11; *b* 17 Dec. 1946; *s* of late Iain Ross Jack and Alicia Maria Eça da Silva, Hong Kong. *Educ:* school in Hong Kong; Univ. of Liverpool (Hong Kong Govt Scholar; BA Hons 1st Class); LSE, Univ. of London (PhD). A Clerk, House of Commons, 1967–; Private Sec. to Chm. of Ways and Means, 1977–80; Clerk to Agriculture Select Cttee, 1980–88; Clerk of Supply, 1989–91; Clerk of Standing Cttees, 1991–95; Sec. to H of C Commn, 1995–2001; Clerk of the Journals, 2001–03; Clerk to Jt Cttee on H of L Reform, 2002–03; Clerk of Legislation, 2003–06. Presidential Advr, OSCE Parly Assembly, 1992–96. Vis. Prof., Nanyang Univ., Singapore, 2015. Pres., Beckford Soc., 2015– (Chm., 1996–2015); Sec., Johnson Club, 1998–; Mem., Adv. Bd, Constitution Soc., 2013–. FSA 2012. *Publications:* The Social and Political Thought of Bernard Mandeville, 1987; Corruption and Progress: the eighteenth-century debate, 1989; (ed with Anita Desai) The Turkish Embassy Letters of Lady Mary Wortley Montagu, 1993; (ed) Vathek and Other Stories: a William Beckford Reader, 1993; (ed) The Episodes of Vathek of William Beckford, 1994; William Beckford: an English Fidalgo, 1996; Sintra: a glorious Eden, 2002; Lisbon: city of the sea, 2007; (ed) Erskine May's Parliamentary Practice, 24th edn, 2011; articles and essays in books, learned and literary jls; reviews in TLS, APN Lisbon, QB S Africa. *Recreations:* thinking for oneself (Enlightenment), empires adrift, Johnsoniana, oriental ceramics, Africana, escaping southwards. *E:* Malcolm.Jack@btinternet.com. *Club:* East India.

JACK, Rt Hon. Michael; *see* Jack, Rt Hon. J. M.

JACK, Sir Raymond (Evan), Kt 2001; a Judge of the High Court, Queen's Bench Division, 2001–11; *b* 13 Nov. 1942; *s* of Evan and Charlotte Jack; *m* 1976, Elizabeth Alison, *d* of Rev. Canon James Seymour Denis Mansel, KCVO; one *s* two *d*. *Educ:* Rugby; Trinity Coll., Cambridge (MA). Called to Bar, Inner Temple, 1966, Bencher, 2000; QC 1982; a Recorder, 1989–91; a Circuit Judge, 1991–2001; Judge of the Bristol Mercantile Court, 1994–2001. Gov., Salisbury NHS Foundn Trust, 2012–. *Publications:* Documentary Credits, 1991, 4th edn 2009. *Recreations:* words and wood. *Address:* Serle Court, 6 New Square, Lincoln's Inn, WC2A 3QS.

JACK, Simon Michael; His Honour Judge Jack; a Circuit Judge, North Eastern Circuit, since 2004; *b* 29 Oct. 1951; *s* of Donald Fingland Jack and Hilary Jack (*née* Gresham); *m* 1st, 1973, Christine Anne King (separated 2004; marr. diss. 2010); one *s* two *d*; 2nd, 2013, Sarah Louise Fearon. *Educ:* Richard Hale Sch., Hertford; Winchester Coll.; Trinity Coll., Cambridge (BA (Langs and Law) 1973). Called to the Bar, Middle Temple, 1974; in practice as barrister, N Eastern Circuit, 1975–2003 (specialized in criminal and family law, and civil actions involving police). *Recreations:* triathlon, sailing, ski-ing, cinema. *Address:* Kingston upon Hull Combined Court Centre, Lowgate, Hull HU1 2EZ. *Clubs:* Barracuda Triathlon; Hull Thursday Road.

JACK, Stuart Duncan Macdonald, CVO 1994; HM Diplomatic Service, retired; Governor, Cayman Islands, 2005–09; *b* 8 June 1949; *s* of William Harris Jack and Edith Florence Jack (*née* Coker); *m* 1977, Mariko Nobechi; one *s* two *d*. *Educ:* Westcliff High Sch. for Boys; Merton Coll., Oxford (BA 1971). VSO, Laos, 1971; joined HM Diplomatic Service, 1972: Eastern European and Soviet Dept, FO, 1972–73; Tokyo, 1974–79; Far Eastern Dept, FCO, 1979–81; Moscow, 1981–84; on secondment with Bank of England, 1984–85; Tokyo, 1985–89; Overseas Inspector, 1989–92; Consul Gen., St Petersburg, 1992–95; Hd of Research and Analysis, FCO, 1996–99; Minister, Tokyo, 1999–2003; FCO, 2003–05. *Recreations:* reading, photography, music.

JACK, Dr William Hugh, CB 1988; management consultant, 1994–2005; Comptroller and Auditor General, Northern Ireland Audit Office, 1989–94; *b* 18 Feb. 1929; *s* of John Charles Jack and Martha Ann Jack; *m* 1953, Beatrice Jane Thompson; three *s* one *d*. *Educ:* Ballymena Acad.; Univ. of Edinburgh (BSc(For); PhD); Queen's Univ., Belfast (BScEcon). MICFor 1959. Min. of Agriculture for NI, 1948–49; Colonial Forest Service, Gold Coast/Ghana, 1949–59 (Conservator of Forests, 1957); Dept of Agriculture for NI, 1959–89 (Permanent Sec., 1983). CCMI. *Publications:* various articles in forestry research and economic jls. *Recreations:* walking, reading. *Address:* 22 Viewfort Park, Belfast BT17 9JY.

JACKAMAN, Michael Clifford John; Chairman of Grand Appeal, Royal Hospital for Sick Children, Bristol, 1995–2001; Chairman, Allied Domecq (formerly Allied-Lyons) plc, 1991–96 (Vice-Chairman, 1988–91); *b* 7 Nov. 1935; *s* of Air Cdre Clifford Thomas Jackaman, OBE and Lily Margaret Jackaman (*née* Turner); *m* 1960, Valerie Jane Pankhurst; one *s* one *d*. *Educ:* Felsted Sch., Essex; Jesus Coll., Cambridge (MA Hons). Lieut RA, 1955–56. Dep. Man. Dir, Harveys of Bristol, 1976–78; Marketing Dir, Allied Breweries, 1978–83; Dir, Allied Domecq (formerly Allied Lyons) plc, 1978–96; Chairman: Showerings Vine Products and Whiteways, 1983–86; Hiram Walker Allied Vintners, 1986–91; John Harvey & Sons Ltd, 1983–93; Mem., Council of Admin, Château Latour, 1983–93; Director: Fintex of London Ltd, 1986–92; Rank Orgn, 1992–97; Kleinwort Benson Gp, 1994–98. Governor, Bristol Polytechnic, 1988–91. Dir, Th. Royal, Bath, 1999–2005. Founder Mem., Wine Guild of UK. Vice Pres., Internat. Wine and Spirits Comp. Liveryman, Distillers' Co.; Grand Master, Keepers of the Quaich (Scotland), 1996; Commanderie des Bontemps du Médoc et des Graves (France); Confraria do Vinho do Porto (Portugal). Hon. DBA UWE, 1993. *Publications:* contribs to periodicals, incl. Arts Review. *Recreations:* Budleigh Salterton Literary Festival, Iford Arts, thrown and handmade pottery, opera, walking. *Club:* Army and Navy.

JACKLIN, Anthony, CBE 1990 (OBE 1970); professional golfer, 1962–85 and 1988–99; Director of Golf, San Roque Club, 1988–90; golf course designer, since 2002; *b* 7 July 1944; *s* of Arthur David Jacklin; *m* 1st, 1966, Vivien (*d* 1988); two *s* one *d*; 2nd, 1988, Astrid May Waagen; one *s*, one step *s* one step *d*. Successes include: British Assistant Pro Championship, 1965; Pringle Tournament, 1967; Dunlop Masters, 1967; Greater Jacksonville Open, USA, 1968; British Open Championship, 1969; US Open Championship, 1970; Benson & Hedges, 1971; British Professional Golfers Assoc., 1972, 1982; Gtr Jacksonville Open, 1972; Bogota Open, 1973 and 1974; Italian Open, 1973; Dunlop Masters, 1973; Scandinavian Open, 1975; Kerrygold International, 1976; English National PGA Championship, 1977; German Open, 1979; Jersey Open, 1981; PGA Champion, 1982; Ryder Cup player, 1967–80, Team Captain, Europe, 1983–89; Champion Tour wins: First of America Classic, 1994; Franklin Quest, 1995. Life Mem., PGA (Hon. Life Mem., European Tournament Players Div.). Inducted, World Golf Hall of Fame, 2002. *Publications:* Golf with Tony Jacklin, 1969; The Price of Success, 1979; (with Peter Dobereiner) Jacklin's Golfing Secrets, 1983; Tony Jacklin: the first forty years, 1985; (with Bill Robertson) Your Game and Mine, 1990; Tony Jacklin: my autobiography, 2006. *Recreations:* shooting, marquetry. *Address:* Jacklin Design Group LLC, 1175 51st Street West, Bradenton, FL 34209, USA. *Clubs:* Royal & Ancient Golf (Hon. Mem., 2002); Potters Bar Golf; Hon. Mem. of others.

JACKLIN, Susan Elizabeth; QC 2006; a Recorder, since 1998; *b* 4 Aug. 1958; *d* of Joseph and Alice Jacklin. *Educ:* Winckley Sq. Convent Sch., Preston; Univ. of Durham (BA Hons Law); Inns of Court Sch. of Law. Called to the Bar, Inner Temple, 1980, Bencher, 2011; in practice at the Bar, 1982–. Advocacy Trainer: Western Circuit, 1996–; Hon. Soc. of Inner Temple, 2003–. Ext. Examr, Bar Vocational Course, UWE, 2002–06. Chm., Access to the Bar Cttee, 2011–13, Mem., 2012, Bar Council; Vice-Chm., 2012–13, Chm., 2014–15,

Family Law Bar Assoc. *Recreations:* international travel, walking, cooking and entertaining. *Address:* 1 Garden Court, Family Law Chambers, Temple, EC47 9BJ. *T:* (020) 7797 7900. *E:* jacklin@1gc.com. *Club:* Athenæum.

JACKLIN, William, (Bill), RA 1991 (ARA 1989); *b* 1 Jan. 1943; *s* of Harold and Alice Jacklin; *m* 1st, 1979, Lesley Sarina Berman (marr. diss. 1993); 2nd, 1993, Janet Ann Russo. *Educ:* Walthamstow Sch. of Art; Royal College of Art (NDD, MARCA). Part-time Lectr at various art colleges, 1967–75; Arts Council Bursary, 1975; lives and works in New York and Newport, RI, 1985–; Artist in Residence, British Council, Hong Kong, 1993–94. One man exhibns, London galleries, 1970– (incl. Marlborough Fine Art, 1980, 1983, 1988, 1992, 1994, 1995, 1997, 2000, 2004, 2005, 2007, 2008, 2013, 2016), USA, 1985– (incl. Marlborough Gall., NY, 1985, 1987, 1990, 1997, 1999, 2002, 2003, 2007, 2012), Hong Kong, 1995, Marlborough Gall., Monaco, 2009; retrospective exhibn, Mus. of Modern Art, Oxford, 1992; graphic retrospective, RA, 2016; frequent shows in internat. exhibns; works in major collections including Arts Council, British Mus., Metropolitan Mus. NY, Mus. of Modern Art NY, Tate Gall., V&A. *Publications:* catalogues to one man exhibns, London and New York; Bill Jacklin New York: New York paintings 1985 to 2015 (monograph), 2016; *relevant publication:* Bill Jacklin (monograph), by John Russell-Taylor, 1997; Bill Jacklin: Graphics (monograph), by Nancy Campbell, 2016. *Recreation:* planting trees. *Address:* c/o Marlborough Fine Art, 6 Albemarle Street, W1S 4BY. *T:* (020) 7629 5161. *Clubs:* Arts, Chelsea Arts.

JACKLING, Sir Roger Tustin, KCB 2001 (CB 1995); CBE 1982; Director, Defence Academy of the UK, 2002–05; *b* 23 Nov. 1943; *s* of Sir Roger Jackling, GCMG and late Joan (*née* Tustin) (Lady Jackling); *m* 1976, Jane Allen Pritchard; two *s*. *Educ:* Wellington Coll.; New York Univ. (BA); Jesus Coll., Oxford. Asst Principal, MoD, 1969, Principal, 1972; London Executive Prog., London Business Sch., 1974; Sec. of State's Office, MoD, 1976–79; Asst Sec. and Hd of DS11, 1979–82; Prime Minister's Office, 1983; Head of DS7/Resources and Programmes (Army), MoD, 1983–85; Fellow, Center for Internat. Affairs, Harvard Univ., 1985–86; Principal, CS Coll., 1986–89; Asst Under-Sec. of State (Progs), MoD, 1989–91; Dep. Under-Sec. of State (Resources, Progs and Finance), MoD, 1991–96; Second Perm. Under Sec. of State, MoD, 1996–2002. Visiting Professor: War Studies Dept, KCL, 2002–; Durham Business Sch., 2003–; Cranfield Univ. at Shrivenham, 2003–. Trustee: Imperial War Mus., 1997–2003; RAF Mus., 2002–. Member Council: RIPA, 1987–92; RUSI, 1993–2005; Chairman: Toc H, 2004–06; Internat. Military Services, 2005–; Council of Voluntary Welfare Work, 2005–; non-exec. Dir, Moorfield Eye Hosp., 2008–. Member, Advisory Board: Durham Business Sch., 1999–; Kent Business Sch., 2005– (Chm., 2008–). Chm. Govs, Purcell Sch., 2012–. Liveryman, Tallow Chandlers' Co., 2011. *Recreations:* books, theatre, opera, playing golf, watching cricket. *Clubs:* Garrick; Highgate Golf, Faversham Golf, Tandridge Golf.

JACKSON, Adam Edward; Head, Public Affairs, Grant Thornton UK LLP, since 2014; *b* 5 March 1969; *s* of Michael and Patricia Jackson; *m* 2011, Holly Hodges. *Educ:* University Coll. London (BA Modern Hist.; MA Legal and Pol Theory). Industry and Consumer Affairs Attaché, UK Perm. Repn to EU, Brussels, 1994–96; Number Portability Manager, Oftel, 1996–97; Department of Trade and Industry: Asst Dir, Regl Policy, 1997–99; Hd, Strategic Communications and Speechwriting, 2000–02; Dep. Dir, Sen. Staff Mgt, 2002–03; Dir, Business Planning, 2003–05; Dir of Finance, 2005–06; Tesco: Dir of Public Policy, 2006–08; Dir, Climate Change Prog., 2008; Dir, Enterprise, BERR, then BIS, 2008–13; led review of DfT Rail Gp, 2013; Dir, Change and Capability, Rail Exec., DfT, 2013–14. Mem. Bd, London Retail Consortium, 2007–08. Trustee: Akosia, 2013–; Watermans Arts Centre, 2014–. MCIPR. *Recreations:* cooking and eating, real ale, gardening, walking Dolly and Spud the dogs. *Address:* Grant Thornton UK LLP, Grant Thornton House, Melton Street, Euston Square, NW1 2EP. *T:* (020) 7728 2385. *E:* adam.e.jackson@uk.gt.com. *Club:* Bournemouth Exiles (Bournemouth FC Supporters).

JACKSON, Alan Robert, AO 1991; Chairman: Australian Trade Commission, 1996–2001; Austrim Nylex (formerly Austrim) Ltd, 1990–2001 (Chief Executive, 1990–2001); *b* 30 March 1936; *m* 1962, Esme Adelia Giles; four *d*. FCA, FASA, FAIM, FCPA. Accountant to Man. Dir, Mather & Platt, 1952–77; Man. Dir, 1977–90, Chm., 1990–97, BTR Nylex Ltd; Man. Dir and Chief Exec. Officer, BTR plc, 1991–95. Director: Australia Reserve Bank, 1990–2001; Seven Network Ltd, 1995–2001; Titan Petrochemicals and Polymers Berhad (Malaysia), 1997–2001. Dir, St Frances Xavier Cabrini Hosp., 1995–2001. *Recreations:* tennis, golf.

JACKSON, Alison Mary; artist, photographer, film-maker; *b* 15 May 1960; *d* of George Hulbert Mowbray Jackson and Catherine Mary Jackson (*née* Harvey Kelly). *Educ:* Chelsea Coll. of Art (BA Hons Fine Art Sculpture); Royal Coll. of Art (MA Fine Art Photography). *Solo art exhibitions* include: Richard Salmon Gall., London, 1999, 2000, 2003; Jerwood Space, London, 2001; Musée de la Photographie à Charleroi, Brussels, 2002; Le Mois de la Photo, Montreal, Photo London, Pro-gram Gall., 2004; Julie Saul Gall., NY, 2005; M&B Gall., Los Angeles, 2007; Hamiltons Gall., London, 2008; Mitchell Liby, Glasgow, 2009; Ben Brown Fine Arts, 2011; *group art exhibitions* include: Edinburgh Fest., Art 2000, London, 2000; Paris Photo, Louvre, Photographers' Gall./Julie Saul Gall., NY, 2002–05; Internat. Center of Photography (ICP), NY, Musée de l'Elysée, Lausanne, 2003; Photo London, Hayward Gall., London, 2004; KunstForum, Vienna, 2005–06; Liverpool Biennial, Tate, 2008; New Art Gall. Walsall, 2008; Tate Britain, 2010; MOMA, San Francisco, 2010; Tate Modern, 2010. *Television*: creator, writer, dir, Doubletake, 2001–03 (BAFTA Award for Innovation, 2002); producer/dir, Saturday Night Live, USA, 2004–05; writer and director: Royal Wedding Special, 2005; The Secret Election, 2005; Sven: the coach, the cash and his lovers, 2006; Blaired Vision, 2007; The South Bank Show: Alison Jackson on Andy Warhol, 2009; dir, Tony Blair Rock Star, 2006; The Alison Jackson Review, 2011; Private Lies, 2012. Schweppes advertising campaign, 2001–03 (Best of the Best Award for Photography, IPA, 2002, 2003; Creative Circle Award, 2002) and 2007. Ambassador, Spinal Injuries Assoc. Photographers' Gall. Award, London, 1999; Infinity Award for Photography, ICP, NY, 2004. *Publications:* Private, 2003; Confidential, 2007; Up the Aisle, 2011; Exposed! 2011, 2011. *Recreation:* tennis. *Address:* c/o Kevin Cooper, CAA, 2000 Avenue of the Stars, Los Angeles, CA 90212, USA. *T:* (424) 2884545.

JACKSON, Alison Muriel; Team Leader, Public Issues, Methodist Church, 2005–08; Director, Wales Office, 1999–2005; *b* 24 Sept. 1947; *d* of John McIntyre and Muriel McIntyre (*née* Brookes); *m* 1970, Alan D. Jackson; one *s*. *Educ:* Sydenham High Sch., GPDST; St Anne's Coll., Oxford (BA (Lit. Hum.) 1970, MA 1976); Bristol Univ. (Dip. Adult Educn (ext.) 1982). Land Registry, Gloucester, 1983–86; Welsh Office: Local Govt Finance, 1986–88; Private Sec. to Perm. Sec., 1988–90; Urban Affairs Div., 1990–93; Agric. Div., 1993–98. Panel Chair, Judicial Appts Commn, 2005–. Chm., Church Action on Poverty, 2015–. Methodist Local Preacher, 1976–. *Recreations:* walking, cooking.

JACKSON, (Ann) Merenid; *see* Edwards, A. M.

JACKSON, Sir Barry (Trevor), Kt 2001; MS, FRCS; Serjeant Surgeon to the Queen, 1991–2001; Consultant Surgeon: St Thomas' Hospital, 1973–2001; Queen Victoria Hospital, East Grinstead, 1977–98; King Edward VII Hospital for Officers, 1983–2002; President, Royal Society of Medicine, 2002–04; *b* 7 July 1936; *er s* of Arthur Stanley Jackson and Violet May (*née* Fry); *m* 1962, Sheila May Wood; two *s* one *d*. *Educ:* Sir George Monoux Grammar Sch.; King's College London (FKC 2012); Westminster Med. Sch. (Entrance Scholar). MB, BS 1963; MRCS, LRCP 1963; MS 1972; FRCS 1967; FRCP 1999; FRCSGlas 1999. Down Bros Ltd, 1952–54; RAF 1954–56; junior surgical appts, Gordon Hosp., St James' Hosp., Balham, St Peter's Hosp., Chertsey, St Helier Hosp., Carshalton, St Thomas' Hosp. Surgeon to the Royal Household, 1983–91; Hon. Consultant in Surgery to the Army, 1990–2006. Royal College of Surgeons: Arris & Gale Lectr, 1973; Vicary Lectr, 1994; Bradshaw Lectr, 1998; Examr Primary FRCS, 1977–83; Mem. Court of Examrs, 1983–89; Mem. Council, 1991–2001; Pres., 1998–2001; Mem., Court of Patrons, 2008–; Asst Editor 1984–91, Editor, 1992–97, Annals RCS; Pres., Assoc. of Surgeons of GB and Ireland, 1994–95 (Mem. Council, 1982–85; Hon. Sec., 1986–91; Vice Pres., 1993–94); Mem. Council, RSocMed, 1987–92 (Pres., Sect. of Coloproctology, 1991–92; Steven's Lect. for the Laity, 2001; Stuart Lectr, 2005); Mem., GMC, 1999–2003. Pres., British Acad. Forensic Scis, 2005–07. External examr in surgery: Khartoum, 1981, 1997; Ibadan, 1982; Colombo, 1984, 1988; Abu Dhabi, 1989. Mem., W Lambeth HA, 1982–83; Special Trustee: St Thomas' Hosp., 1982–84, 1994–99; Guy's Hosp., 1996–99; Trustee: Smith & Nephew Foundn, 1995–2002; Hunterian Collection, 2004– (Chm., 2008–14); Refresh, 2005– (Chm., 2006–); Surgical Foundn, 2009–13; Bowel and Cancer Res., 2012– (Chm., 2012–15). Chm., SE Thames Regional Med. Adv. Cttee, 1983–87. Mem. Council of Govs, UMDS of Guy's and St Thomas' Hosps, 1989–94. Mem. Council, Imperial Soc. of Kts Bachelor, 2012–. President: Royal Med. Benevolent Fund, 2002–08; Med. Artists Assoc. of GB, 2005–; Patron, Bowel Disease Res. Foundn, 2010–. Liveryman, Barbers' Co. (Master, 2003–04; Charles Bernard Lectr, 2007). Hon. FRCSI, 1999; Hon. FRCSEd, 1999; Hon. FDSRCS, 1999; Hon. FACS, 2000; Hon. FRACS, 2000; Hon. FRCSCan, 2003; Hon. FRSocMed 2005. Hon. DSc Hull, 2001. *Publications:* contribs to surgical jls and textbooks (surgery of gastro-intestinal tract). *Recreations:* book collecting, reading, medical history, music, especially opera, cryptic crosswords. *T:* (020) 8399 3157. *E:* barryjck7@aol.com. *Club:* Garrick.

JACKSON, Betty, CBE 2007 (MBE 1987); RDI 1988; Designer Director, Betty Jackson Ltd, since 1981; *b* 24 June 1949; *d* of Arthur and Phyllis Gertrude Jackson; *m* 1985, David Cohen; one *s* one *d*. *Educ:* Bacup and Rawtenstall Grammar Sch.; Birmingham Coll. of Art (DipAD fashion and textiles). Freelance fashion illustrator, 1971–73; design asst, 1973–75; chief designer, Quorum, 1975–81. Part-time Tutor, 1982–90, Vis. Prof., 1998–, RCA. Fellow: Birmingham Polytechnic, 1989; Univ. of Central Lancs, 1992. Hon. Fellow, RCA, 1989. Trustee, V&A Mus., 2005–12. Mem. Bd, Creative Skillset, 2010. DUniv Huddersfield, 2012. Awards include: British Designer of the Year, Harvey Nichols and British Fashion Council, 1985; Viyella, 1987; Fil d'Or, Internat. Linen, 1989; Contemporary Designer of the Year, British Fashion Awards, 1999. *Address:* Betty Jackson Ltd, 4b Ledbury Mews North, W11 2AF. *T:* (020) 7243 4727. *E:* info@bettyjackson.com. *Clubs:* Groucho, Chelsea Arts, Soho House, Ivy.

JACKSON, Very Rev. Brandon Donald; Dean of Lincoln, 1989–97, now Emeritus; *b* 11 Aug. 1934; *s* of Herbert and Millicent Jackson; *m* 1958, Mary Lindsay, 2nd *d* of John and Helen Philip; two *s* one *d*. *Educ:* Stockport School; Liverpool Univ.; St Catherine's Coll. and Wycliffe Hall, Oxford (LLB, DipTh). Curate: Christ Church, New Malden, Surrey, 1958–61; St George, Leeds, 1961–65; Vicar, St Peter, Shipley, Yorks, 1965–77; Provost of Bradford Cathedral, 1977–89. Mem., Gen. Synod, 1970–77, 1980–89. Religious Adviser to Yorkshire Television, 1969–79; Church Commissioner, 1971–73; Mem., Marriage Commn, 1975–78; Examining Chaplain to Bishop of Bradford, 1974–80. Chm., Wensleydale CPRE, 1998–2005. Mem., Ind. Monitoring Bd, HM Prison Gartree, 2008–13. Member Council: Wycliffe Hall, Oxford, 1971–85; St John's Coll., Nottingham, 1987–89; Governor: Harrogate College, 1974–86; Bradford Girls' GS, 1977–81; Bradford Grammar Sch., 1977–89; Bishop Grosseteste Coll., Lincoln, 1989–97; Lincoln Christ's Hosp. Sch., 1989–97. Hon. DLitt Bradford, 1990. *Recreations:* sport (mainly watching), Sale RFC (former playing member), long suffering supporter of Man. City, cycling, fell-walking, fishing, enjoying grandchildren, reading, playing the cornet in brass bands (Mem., 60s Club Band). *Address:* 1 Kingston Way, Market Harborough, Leics LE16 7XB. *T:* (01858) 462425. *E:* brandon.j@talktalk.net.

JACKSON, Caroline Frances; environmental consultant and speaker, since 2009; Member (C) South West Region, England, European Parliament, 1999–2009 (Wiltshire, 1984–94; Wiltshire North and Bath, 1994–99)); *b* 5 Nov. 1946; *d* of G. H. Harvey; *m* 1975, Robert Victor Jackson, *qv*; one *s* decd. *Educ:* School of St Clare, Penzance; St Hugh's and Nuffield Colleges, Oxford. MA, DPhil. Elizabeth Wordsworth Research Fellow, St Hugh's College, Oxford, 1972. Oxford City Councillor, 1970–73; contested (C) Birmingham, Erdington, 1974. European Parliament: Secretariat of Cons. Group, 1974–84; Chm., Envmt, Consumer Protection and Public Health Cttee, 1999–2004. Chm., Inst. for European Envmt Policy, 2006–10; Pres., Envmtl Protection UK, 2010–12; Mem., Foresight Adv. Council, GDF Suez Envmt (formerly SITA), 2009–13. Dir, Peugeot Talbot (UK) Ltd, 1987–99. Mem., Nat. Consumer Council, 1982–84. *Publications:* A Student's Guide to Europe, 1988; Europe's Environment, 1989; The End of the Throwaway Society, 1998; Playing by the Green Rules, 2000; Britain's Waste: the lessons we can learn from Europe, 2006. *Recreations:* walking, painting, golf. *Address:* New House, Hanney Road, Southmoor, Abingdon, Oxon OX13 5HR. *T:* (01865) 821243. *E:* contactcfjackson@gmail.com. *W:* www.drcarolinejackson.com.

JACKSON, Christopher Murray; Partner, Christopher Jackson Associates, since 1994; Chairman: CJA Consultants Ltd, 1995–2002 (Director, since 1995); Member of Council, Bethany School Ltd, Goudhurst, since 2011 (Chairman, 1999–2009; Director, 1999–2011); *b* 24 May 1935; *s* of Rev. Howard Murray Jackson and Doris Bessie Jackson (*née* Grainger); *m* 1971, Carlie Elizabeth Keeling; one *s* one *d*. *Educ:* Kingswood Sch., Bath; Magdalen Coll., Oxford (Open Exhibnr, BA Hons (Physics) 1959, MA 1964); Goethe Univ., Frankfurt; London Sch. of Economics. National Service, commnd RAF, Pilot, 1954–56. Unilever, 1959–69, Sen. Man., 1967; Save and Prosper Gp, 1969–71; D. MacPherson Gp, 1971–74; Dir of Corporate Development, Spillers Ltd, 1974–80; Chairman: Wellmeade Ltd, 1998–2010; Natural Resources Internat. Ltd, 1997–2003; European Broadcasting Network plc, 1997–99. Contested (C): East Ham South, 1970; Northampton North, Feb. 1974. MEP (C) Kent E, 1979–94; contested (C) Kent E, EP elecns, 1994; Hon. MEP, 1994–; European Parliament: spokesman, on develt and co-op., 1981–87, on foreign affairs, 1991–92, on econ. affairs, 1992–94; Cons. spokesman on agric., 1987–89; Chm., Intergroup on Frontier Controls, 1987–94; Co-Pres., Working Gp on Population and Develt, 1990–94; Mem., Bureau of EDG, 1984–91; Dep. Ldr, Cons. MEPs, 1989–91; Rapporteur-General, ACP-EEC Jt Assembly, 1985–86. Nat. Chm., Cons. Countryside (formerly Nat. Agricl and Countryside) Forum, 1995–98. Mem., Cons. Nat. Union Exec. Cttee, 1995–98. Dir, Politics International Ltd, 1995–98. Vice President: Assoc. of Dist Councils, 1980–95; Assoc. of Local Councils, 1984–95; Assoc. of Port Health Authorities, 1989–99. Member: Chatham Hse (RIIA); Inst. of Dirs, 1998–2008. Treas., St Martin-in-the-Fields, 1975–77. Pres., Kent Hotels and Restaurants Assoc., 1988–94. *Publications:* Towards 2000—People Centred Development, 1986 (major report); (ed) Your European Watchdogs, 1990; Shaking the Foundations: Britain and the New Europe, 1991; The Maastricht Summit, 1992; Whose Job is it Anyway?—decentralisation (or subsidiarity) and the EC, 1992; Working for the European Community, 1990, 2nd edn 1992; (ed) Industrial Property Rights, 1997 (official EC pubn); (with B. Patterson) Both Sides of the Coin: arguments for and against UK membership of the EU, 2014; pamphlets on Britain and Europe. *Recreations:* music, tennis, walking, travel. *Address:* Flackley Ash Farmhouse, Peasmarsh, Rye, E Sussex TN31 6TB. *T:* (01797) 230660. *E:* flackley.ash2@btinternet.com. *Clubs:* Athenæum; Rye Lawn Tennis.

JACKSON, Colin Ray, CBE 2003 (OBE 2000; MBE 1990); former athlete; broadcaster and television presenter; *b* Cardiff, 18 Feb. 1967. *Educ:* Llanederyn High Sch., Cardiff. Gold Medals won in 110m hurdles: European Cup, 1989, 1993, 1998; Commonwealth Games, 1990, 1994; European Championships, 1990, 1994, 1998, 2002; World Cup, 1992; World

Championships, 1993, 1999; also Silver Medal, Olympic Games, 1988; Gold Medals won in 60m hurdles: European Indoor Championships, 1989, 1994, 2002; World Indoor Championships, 1999; set world record for 110m hurdles (12.91 secs), 1993, and 60m indoor hurdles (7.30 secs), 1994. Silver Medal for 4 x 100m relay, World Championships, 1993. *Publications:* Colin Jackson: the autobiography, 2003; Life's New Hurdles, 2008. *Address:* c/o MTC (UK) Ltd, 71 Gloucester Place, W1U 8JW.

JACKSON, Daphne Diana; Assistant Personnel Officer, City Engineer's Department, City of Birmingham, 1986–93; *b* 8 Oct. 1933; *d* of Major Thomas Casey, MC, South Lancs Regt, and Agnes Nora Casey (*née* Gradden); *m* 1953, John Hudleston Jackson (*d* 2014). *Educ:* Folkestone County Grammar School for Girls; South West London College. ACIS. Westminster Bank, 1951–53; Kent Educn Cttee, 1953–57; Pfizer Ltd, Sandwich, 1957–67; Southern Transformer Products, 1967–68; Borough of Hounslow, 1968–86, Personnel and Central Services Officer, Borough Engr and Surveyor's Dept, 1978–86. Mem., NACRO Employment Adv. Cttee, 1984–86; Chm., Gen. Adv. Council to IBA, 1985–89 (Mem., 1980). Mem., Soroptimists International (Pres., Stratford-upon-Avon, 1995–96). Mem., Cleeve Prior PCC, 1991–; Gov., Cleeve Prior C of E Controlled First Sch., 1989–2005; Chm. Mgt Cttee, Cleeve Prior Meml Village Hall, 1994–97. Freeman, City of London, 1980; Liveryman, Chartered Secretaries and Administrators Co., 1980. *Recreations:* bereavement counselling, learning about antiques, reading. *Address:* 3 Manor Court, Bidford Road, Cleeve Prior, Evesham, Worcs WR11 8HZ. *T:* (01789) 772817.

JACKSON, Prof. David Cooper; Chairman, Immigration Appeal Tribunal, 1996–2003 (Vice-President, 1984–96); Professor of Law (part time), 1984–98, now Emeritus, and Director, Institute of Maritime Law, 1987–90, University of Southampton; *b* 3 Dec. 1931; *s* of late Rev. James Jackson and Mary Emma Jackson; *m* Roma Lilian (*née* Pendergast). *Educ:* Ashville Coll., Harrogate; Brasenose Coll., Oxford. MA, BCL; Senior Hulme Scholar, 1954; LLD Southampton, 1997. Called to the Bar, Inner Temple, 1957, and Victoria, Australia, 1967. Bigelow Fellow, Univ. of Chicago, 1955; Fellow, Assoc. of Bar of City of New York, 1956; National Service, 1957–59; Senior Lectr, Univ. of Singapore, 1963–64; Sir John Latham Prof. of Law, Monash Univ., 1965–70 (Carnegie Travelling Fellow, 1969); Prof. of Law, Southampton Univ., 1970–83 (Dean of Law, 1972–75, 1978–81; Dep. Vice-Chancellor, 1982–83); Consultant, UNCTAD, 1980, 1983. Visiting Professor: Queen Mary Coll., London, 1969; Arizona State Univ., 1976; Melbourne Univ., 1976. JP Hants 1980–84. Editor, World Shipping Laws, 1979–89 (and contrib.). *Publications:* Principles of Property Law, 1967; The Conflicts Process, 1975; Enforcement of Maritime Claims, 1985, 4th edn 2005; Civil Jurisdiction and Judgments: maritime claims, 1987; Immigration Law and Practice, 1996, 4th edn (jtly) 2008; articles in legal jls, Australia, UK, USA. *Recreations:* walking, travel, theatre.

JACKSON, David Richard Holmes, CBE 2004; JP; Chief Executive, Bradford Teaching Hospitals NHS Foundation Trust (formerly Bradford Hospitals NHS Trust), 1992–2005; *b* 24 Sept. 1948; *s* of Samuel Horace Jackson and Pauline Jackson (*née* Blockey); *m* 1973, Frances Bush; two *s* two *d*. *Educ:* Kingswood Sch., Bath; Univ. of Leeds (LLB). DipHSM 1978. Trainee and Dep. Hosp. Sec., Leeds (St James) Univ. HMC, 1970–73; Sen. Adminr, Hull A Gp HMC, 1973–74; Dep. Dist Adminr, Gen. Infirmary, Leeds, 1974–78; Dist Adminr, Beverley Health Dist, 1978–82; Grimsby Health Authority: Dist Adminr, 1982–85; Dist Gen. Manager, 1985–92. JP Bradford, 1998. *Recreations:* walking, travelling, good living. *Address:* 10 Southway, Ilkley LS29 8QG. *T:* (01943) 609521. *E:* davidrhjackson@hotmail.com. *Club:* Ilkley Bowling.

JACKSON, Donald, MVO 1985; artist calligrapher; Scribe, since 1964, and Senior Illuminator, since 1985, to Crown Office; *b* 14 Jan. 1938; *s* of Wilfred Jackson and Helena Ruth Jackson (*née* Tolley); *m* 1962, Mabel Elizabeth Morgan; one *s* one *d*. *Educ:* Bolton Sch. of Art; City & Guilds, London; Central Sch. of Art; Goldsmiths' Coll. FSSI 1960 (Chm., 1973). Preparer of Letters Patent and Royal Charters under Great Seal, incl. 1974 redesignated Royal Cities, towns and boroughs in England and Wales; Dir, Calligraphy Centre, 1984–97; Artistic Director: The St John's Bible (handwritten and illuminated Bible in seven vols to mark Millennium, for St John's Univ. and Benedictine Abbey, Minn), 1997–2011; Heritage Series of Fine Art Facsimile Reproductions, 2007–12. Vis. Lectr, Camberwell Sch. of Art, 1958–75; Distinguished Vis. Prof. of Art, California State Univ., 1976–77; lectr in USA and Australia. 30-year personal retrospective exhibn, Painting with Words, in USA, Puerto Rico, Hong Kong, Europe, 1988–91; exhibition series, Illuminating the Word: the St John's Bible, incl. Minneapolis Inst. of Arts, 2005, Joslyn Mus., Omaha, V&A, Mus. of Biblical Image and Art, NY, Liby of Congress, Washington, and Tyler Art Mus., Texas, 2006, Naples Art Mus., Fla, and Phoenix Art Mus., Arizona, 2007, Winnipeg Art Gall., Canada, Tacoma Art Mus., Washington, and Mobile Mus. of Art, Alabama, 2008, Walters Art Mus., Baltimore, 2009; Sci. Mus. of Minnesota (with Dead Sea Scrolls exhibn), St Paul, Minneapolis, 2010; Minneapolis Inst. of Arts, 2011; New Mexico History Mus., Sante Fe, 2011–12; work in internat. public and private collections, incl. perm. display at St Martin-in-the-Fields, London. Founding Trustee, Irene Wellington Educnl Trust, 1987. Presenter, and producer with Jeremy Bennett: Alphabet (film series), 1979; The Illuminator (documentary), BBC Wales, 2005. Liveryman, Scriveners' Co., 1973 (Master, 1997–98). *Publications:* The Story of Writing, 1980, 3rd edn 1994; (jtly) The Calligraphers' Handbook, 1985; (jtly) More than Fine Writing, 1986; Gospel and Acts (facsimile edn), 2005; Psalms (facsimile edn), 2006; Pentateuch (facsimile edn), 2006; Prophets (facsimile edn), 2007; Wisdom (facsimile edn), 2007; (jtly) The Lion Companion to Christian Art, 2008; Historical (facsimile edn), 2010; Letters and Revelation (facsimile edn), 2012. *Recreations:* friends, family, other people's art, country sports. *Address:* The Scriptorium, The Hendre, Monmouth NP25 5HG. *T:* (01600) 714222.

JACKSON, Prof. Emily Meg; Professor of Law, since 2007, and Head of Law Department, since 2012, London School of Economics and Political Science; *b* London, 28 Dec. 1966; *d* of Douglas Jackson and Lesley Jackson. *Educ:* Bushey Meads Sch.; Brasenose Coll., Oxford (BA Juris. 1989). Fellow and Lectr in Law, St Catharine's Coll., Cambridge, 1991–93; Lectr in Law, Birkbeck Coll., Univ. of London, 1993–97; Sen. Lectr in Law, LSE, 1998–2004; Prof. of Medical Law, QMUL, 2004–07. Dep. Chm., Human Fertilisation and Embryology Authy, 2008–12 (Mem., 2003–12). Mem., Judicial Appointments Commn, 2014–. *Publications:* Regulating Reproduction, 2001; Medical Law, 2006, 3rd edn 2013; Debating Euthanasia, 2011; Law and the Regulation of Medicines, 2012. *Recreations:* art, architecture, walking, food and wine. *Address:* Law Department, London School of Economics and Political Science, Houghton Street, WC2A 2AE. *T:* (020) 7955 6368. *E:* e.jackson@lse.ac.uk.

JACKSON, Ven. Frances Anne, (Peggy); Archdeacon of Llandaff, since 2009; Priest-in-charge, St Fagans and Michaelston-super-Ely, since 2014; *b* Loughborough, 1 Aug. 1951; *d* of Wilfrid Ernest, (Bill), Pegg and Eileen Florence Pegg; *m* 1972, Tony Jackson (marr. diss. 1981); one *d*. *Educ:* Somerville Coll., Oxford (BA Modern History 1972; MA 1976); Ripon Coll., Cuddesdon. FCA 1981 (ACA 1976). Chartered Accountant: Robson Rhodes, 1973–76; Deloitte, Haskins & Sells, 1976–85; ordained deacon, 1987, priest, 1994; Asst Curate, St Mary the Virgin, Ilkeston, Derbyshire, 1987–90; Team Vicar, St Paul's, Highfield, Hemel Hempstead, 1990–98; Team Rector, Mortlake with E Sheen, 1998–2009; Area Dean, Richmond and Barnes, 2000–05; Dean, Women's Ministry, Dio. of Southwark, 2004–09; Priest-in-charge, Penmark with Llancarfan with Llantrithyd, 2009–14. Member: WATCH, 1994–; Gp for Rescinding the Act of Synod, 2000–14; elected Mem., Governing Body, Church in Wales, 2012– (co-opted Mem., 2010–12). Member: Amnesty Internat., 1987–; Fawcett Soc., 2005–; Friends of Llandaff Cath., 2009–. *Recreations:* flying (private pilot's licence, 2008–), circle dancing, bell-ringing, singing. *Address:* The Rectory, Greenwood Lane, St Fagans, Cardiff CF5 6EL. *T:* (029) 2056 7393. *E:* archdeacon.llandaff@churchinwales.org.uk. *Clubs:* Oxford Union; Soroptimist Internat. (Cardiff).

JACKSON, Francis Alan, CBE 2007 (OBE 1978); Organist and Master of the Music, York Minster, 1946–82, Organist Emeritus, since 1988; *b* 2 Oct. 1917; *s* of W. A. Jackson; *m* 1950, Priscilla, *d* of Tyndale Procter; two *s* one *d*. *Educ:* York Minster Choir Sch.; Sir Edward Bairstow. Chorister, York Minster, 1929–33; ARCO, 1936; BMus Dunelm 1937; FRCO (Limpus Prize), 1937; DMus Dunelm 1957. Organist Malton Parish Church, 1933–40. Served War of 1939–45, with 9th Lancers in Egypt, N Africa and Italy, 1940–46. Asst Organist, York Minster, 1946; Conductor York Musical Soc., 1947–82; Conductor York Symphony Orchestra, 1947–80. Pres. Incorp. Assoc. of Organists, 1960–62; Pres., RCO, 1972–74. Hon. FRSCM 1963; Hon. Fellow, Westminster Choir Coll., Princeton, NJ, 1970; Hon. FRNCM, 1982; Hon. FGCM 2005; Hon. FGMS; Hon. FNMSM 2015. DUniv York, 1983; DMus Lambeth, 2012. Medal, RCO, 2012. Order of St William of York, 1983. *Publications:* Blessed City: the life and works of Sir Edward C. Bairstow 1874–1946, 1996; Piano Trio, 2001; Fantasy for Two Organs, 2014; Music for a Long While (autobiog.), 2014; organ music, including 6 sonatas and 40 organ pieces, 3 duets, symphony, organ concerto, church music, including 80 anthems, songs, monodramas. *Recreation:* gardening. *Address:* Nether Garth, East Acklam, Malton, N Yorks YO17 9RG. *T:* (01653) 658395.

JACKSON, Prof. Frank Cameron, AO 2006; Distinguished Professor, 2003–15, and Fractional Professor of Philosophy, 2011–15, Australian National University, now Professor Emeritus (Professor of Philosophy, 1986–90 and 1992–2007); *b* 31 Aug. 1943; *s* of Allan Cameron Jackson and Ann Elizabeth Jackson; *m* 1966, Morag Elizabeth Fraser; two *d*. *Educ:* Melbourne Univ. (BA, BSc, 1966); La Trobe Univ. (PhD 1975). Temp. Lectr, Adelaide Univ., 1967; Lectr, Sen. Lectr, then Reader, La Trobe Univ., 1968–77; Prof., Monash Univ., 1978–86 and 1991; Australian National University: Dir, Inst. of Advanced Studies, 1998–2001; Dir, Res. Sch. of Soc. Scis, 2004–07; Fractional Prof. of Philosophy, La Trobe Univ., 2008–10. Vis. Prof., Princeton Univ., 2007–14. Corresp. FBA 2000. *Publications:* Perception, 1977; Conditionals, 1987; (with D. Braddon-Mitchell) Philosophy of Mind and Cognition, 1996; From Metaphysics to Ethics, 1998; Mind, Method, and Conditionals, 1998; Language, Names, and Information, 2010. *Recreation:* reading. *Address:* 33 David Street, O'Connor, ACT 2602, Australia.

JACKSON, Glenda May, CBE 1978; *b* Birkenhead, 9 May 1936; *d* of Harry and Joan Jackson; *m* 1958, Roy Hodges (marr. diss. 1976); one *s*. *Educ:* West Kirby Co. Grammar Sch. for Girls; RADA. Actress, 1957–92; with various repertory cos, 1957–63, stage manager, Crewe Rep.; joined Royal Shakespeare Co., 1963. Dir, United British Artists, 1983. Parly Under-Sec. of State, DETR, 1997–99. Pres., Play Matters (formerly Toy Libraries Assoc.), 1976–. *Plays:* All Kinds of Men, Arts, 1957; The Idiot, Lyric, 1962; Alfie, Mermaid and Duchess, 1963; Royal Shakespeare Co.: Theatre of Cruelty Season, LAMDA, 1964; The Jew of Malta, 1964; Marat/Sade, 1965, NY and Paris, 1965; Love's Labour's Lost, Squire Puntila and his Servant Matti, The Investigation, Hamlet, 1965; US, Aldwych, 1966; Three Sisters, Royal Ct, 1967; Fanghorn, Fortune, 1967; Collaborators, Duchess, 1973; The Maids, Greenwich, 1974; Hedda Gabler, Australia, USA, London, 1975; The White Devil, Old Vic, 1976; Stevie, Vaudeville, 1977; Antony and Cleopatra, Stratford, 1978; Rose, Duke of York's, 1980; Summit Conference, Lyric, 1982; Great and Small, Vaudeville, 1983; Strange Interlude, Duke of York's, 1984; Phedra, Old Vic, 1984, Aldwych, 1985; Across from the Garden of Allah, Comedy, 1986; The House of Bernarda Alba, Globe, 1986; Macbeth, NY, 1988; Scenes from an Execution, Almeida, 1990; Mother Courage, Mermaid, 1990; *films:* This Sporting Life, 1963; Marat/Sade, 1967; Negatives, 1968; Women in Love (Oscar Award, 1971), 1970; The Music Lovers, 1971; Sunday, Bloody Sunday, 1971; The Boyfriend, 1972; Mary, Queen of Scots, 1972; Triple Echo, 1972; Il Sorviso de Grande Tentatore (The Tempter), 1973; Bequest to the Nation, 1973; A Touch of Class (Oscar Award, 1974), 1973; The Maids, 1974; The Romantic Englishwoman, 1974; Hedda Gabler, 1975; The Incredible Sarah, 1976; House Calls, 1978; Stevie, 1978; The Class of Miss MacMichael, 1978; Lost and Found, 1979; Hopscotch, 1980; Return of the Soldier, 1982; Health, 1982; Giro City, 1982; Sacharov, 1983; Turtle Diary, 1985; Business as Usual, 1987; Beyond Therapy, 1987; Salome's Last Dance, 1988; The Rainbow, 1989; The Secret Life of Sir Arnold Bax, 1992; *TV:* Elizabeth in Elizabeth R, 1971; The Patricia Neal Story (Amer.). Best film actress awards: Variety Club of GB, 1971, 1975, 1978; NY Film Critics, 1971; Nat. Soc. of Film Critics, US, 1971. MP (Lab) Hampstead and Highgate, 1992–2010, Hampstead and Kilburn, 2010–15. *Recreations:* cooking, gardening, reading Jane Austen.

JACKSON, Gordon; *see* Jackson, W. G.

JACKSON, Helen Margaret, CBE 2010; Member, Women's Income (formerly Women and Pensions) Network, Equality and Human Rights Commission, since 2006 (voluntary outreach worker on women and pensions, Equal Opportunities Commission, 2005–06); *b* 19 May 1939; *d* of Stanley Price and Katherine (*née* Thornton); *m* 1960, Keith Jackson (marr. diss. 1998); two *s* one *d*. *Educ:* St Hilda's Coll., Oxford (BA Hons Mod. Hist., MA); C. F. Mott Coll. of Educn, Prescot (Cert Ed 1972). Asst Librarian, 1961; mother, housewife and voluntary worker, 1961–72; teacher, 1972–80; City Cllr, Sheffield, 1980–91 (Chm., Public Works and Econ. Develt Cttees). Founder Mem. and Chair, Centre for Local Economic Strategies, 1986–91. MP (Lab) Sheffield, Hillsborough, 1992–2005. PPS to Sec. of State for NI, 1997–2001. Member: Envmt Select Cttee, 1992–97; Modernisation of H of C Select Cttee, 1997–2001; Transport, Local Govt and the Regions Select Cttee, 2001–03; Chair: All-Party Parly Water Gp, 1993–97; Party Envmt Gp, 1997–2005; All-Party Parly Gp on S Africa, 1997–2005; Founder and Chair, All-Party Parly Steel Gp, 2002–05; Co-Chair, PLP Women's Gp, 1992–97; Sec., PLP Gp on Envmtl Protection, 1995–97; Vice-Chair, PLP, 2001–02 (Mem., Parly Cttee, Labour Party, 2001–05); Mem., NEC, Labour Pty, 1999–2005. UK Parly Rep., Assoc. of Eur. Parliamentarians for Africa, 1997–2005. Vice Chair, Fawcett Soc., 2007–10; Comr, Women's Nat. Commn, 2008–10. Pres., Sheffield Homestart, 2005–; Trustee: S Yorks Women's Develt Trust, 2005–10; Age Concern, Sheffield, 2005; Grandparents Plus, 2011– (Co-Chm., 2015). *Publications:* The Active Citizen, 2007. *Recreations:* walking, music, grandchildren. *Address:* 2 Topside, Grenoside, Sheffield S35 8RD.

JACKSON, Prof. James Anthony, CBE 2015; PhD; FRS 2002; Professor of Active Tectonics, since 2002, and Head, Department of Earth Sciences, since 2008, Cambridge University; Fellow, Queens' College, Cambridge, since 1979; *b* 12 Dec. 1954; *s* of Richard Owen Jackson and Honor (*née* Thomason); *m* 1984, Susan Elliott; one *s* one *d*. *Educ:* Cranleigh Sch.; Queens' Coll., Cambridge (BA 1976, PhD 1980). Res. Fellow, NERC, 1979–82; Asst Lectr, 1984–88, Lectr, 1988–96, Reader, 1996–2002, Dept of Earth Scis, Cambridge Univ. Allan Cox Vis. Prof., Stanford Univ., 1990–91; Visiting Professor: CIT, 2006; CNRS Grenoble, 2006. Royal Instn Christmas Lects, Planet Earth: an Explorer's Guide, 1995. Fellow, Amer. Geophys. Union, 2003. Pres.'s Award, 1985, Bigsby Medal, 1997, Wollaston Medal, 2015, Geol. Soc. London. *Publications:* contribs to professional jls in earth scis. *Recreations:* swimming, tandeming. *Address:* Bullard Laboratories, Madingley Road, Cambridge CB3 0EZ. *T:* (01223) 333478, *Fax:* (01223) 360779.

JACKSON, Jane Thérèse, (Tessa), OBE 2011; Director, Institute of International Visual Arts, since 2010; *b* 5 Nov. 1955; *d* of John Nevill Jackson and Viva Christian Thérèse Jackson (*née* Blomfield). *Educ:* Univ. of East Anglia (BA Hons Fine Art); Univ. of Manchester (Dip. Museum Studies); Univ. of Bristol (MA Film and TV Prodn 1998). Art Editor, OUP, 1979–80; Exhibns Organiser, SPAB, 1981–82; Curator: Eyemouth Museum, 1982; Collins

Gallery, Univ. of Strathclyde, 1982–88; Visual Arts Officer, Glasgow 1990—European City of Culture, 1988–91; Director: Arnolfini, Bristol, 1991–99; Scottish Arts Council, 1999–2001; Owner, Internat. Cultural Develt, 2002–10; Chief Exec. and Artistic Dir, Artes Mundi Prize, 2002–10. Consultant, Arts Council England Rev. of Presentation of Contemporary Visual Arts, 2005. FRSA 2000. *Publications:* (with John R. Hume) George Washington Wilson and Victorian Glasgow, 1983; (jtly) Signs of the Times: art and industry in Scotland 1750–1985, 1985; (ed jtly) A Platform for Partnership (Glasgow City Council), 1991; contrib. exhibn catalogues. *Recreations:* travel, walking, architecture. *E:* tessajackson@aol.com.

JACKSON, John Bernard Haysom; Chairman: Xenova Group plc, 1990–2005; Oxford Technology Venture Capital Trusts plc, since 1997; *b* 26 May 1929; *m* 1st, 1955, Ann Nichols (marr. diss. 1984); one *s* two *d*; 2nd, 1984, Rowena Thomas. *Educ:* King's School, Canterbury; Queens' Coll., Cambridge (BA, LLB). Called to the Bar, Inner Temple, 1954. Philips Electronics, 1952–80 (Dir, 1966–94); Dir, 1980–2001, Vice-Chm., 1991–94, Chm., 1994–2001, Hilton Gp. Non-solicitor Chm., Mishcon de Reya, 1992–; Chairman: Celltech Gp, 1982–2003; Wyndeham Press Gp plc, 1990–2003; Dep. Chm., BHP Billiton plc, 2001–02; Director: WPP Group plc, 1993–2004 (Founding Mem., Adv. Bd, 2004–); Instore (formerly Brown & Jackson) plc, 1994–2013; Billiton plc, 1997–2001; Opendemocracy Ltd, 2000–. Chairman: Countryside Alliance, 1999–2005; Rural Regeneration Unit, 2003–06; Trustee, One World Action, 1998–2005. Chm. and co-owner, History Today magazine, 1981–. *Publications:* A Bucket of Nuts and a Herring Net, 1979, 3rd edn as A Little Piece of England: a tale of self-sufficiency, 2011; (contrib.) Even Paranoids have Enemies, 1998. *Recreations:* growing rare plants, breeding butterflies, fishing, painting, writing.

JACKSON, John Henry; Clerk to the Governors, Dulwich College, 1998–2007; Company Secretary, BG plc (formerly British Gas), 1990–97; *b* 7 Aug. 1948; *s* of late John and of May Jackson; *m* 1975, Patricia Mary Robinson; one *s* one *d*. *Educ:* Trinity School, Croydon; St Catherine's College, Oxford (MA). FCIS. Joined SE Gas Board, 1970; Asst Sec., 1977, Sen. Asst Sec., 1983, British Gas Corp., later British Gas plc. Mem., Solicitors Disciplinary Tribunal, 2002–12. Assessor, Nat. Clinical Assessment Service (formerly Authy), 2003–07. Mem., Ind. Monitoring Bd, HMP High Down, 2004–05; Independent Member: Parole Bd, 2005–14; CIPFA Disciplinary Cttee, 2007–10. Mem. UK and Internat. Councils, ICSA, 1996–2002 (a Chief Examr, 1997–2000). Non-exec. Dir, Queen Victoria Hosp. NHS Trust, E Grinstead, 1996–98. Chm., Horsham and Crawley Samaritans, 2008–10. Clerk to Govs, Alleyn's Sch., 1998–2004.

JACKSON, (John) Patrick; Director, Portugal, British Council, 1993–96; *b* 18 Sept. 1940; *s* of Godfrey Jackson and Mary Jackson (*née* Worthington); *m* 1st, 1963, Marieliese de Vos van Steenwyk (marr. diss.); three *d* (and one *d* decd); 2nd, 1978, Hélène Mellotte; two *d*. *Educ:* Worksop Coll.; Midhurst Grammar Sch.; New Coll., Oxford (MA); Moscow Univ. (postgrad. studies); London Univ. Inst. of Educn (postgrad. Cert Ed). British Council, 1963–96: English Language Teaching Inst., London, 1964–66; Asst Dir, Bahrain, 1966–69; Asst Cultural Attaché, Moscow, 1969–71; Dep. Dir, Higher Educn Dept, 1971–73; Regl Dir, Calcutta, 1973–75; Dir, N Europe Dept, 1975–79; Rep., Senegal, 1979–83; Regl Dir, São Paulo, 1983–88; Dep. Controller, Home Div., 1988–91; Dir, Exchanges and Training Div., 1991–93; early retirement, 1996; kidney transplant, 1997; Baggage Agent, Gatwick Handling Ltd, 1997–2000; Homesearch consultant, 2000–04; retd, 2004. *Recreations:* birdwatching, languages, IT, crosswords. *Address:* The Two Houses, Hollow Lane, East Grinstead, W Sussex RH19 3PS.

JACKSON, Judith Mary; QC 1994; *b* 18 Sept. 1950; *d* of Thomas Worthington Jackson and Betty Jackson (*née* Kinsey); one *d*. *Educ:* Queen Mary College, London (LLB, LLM); Birkbeck, Univ. of London (MRes (Dist.) Spanish and Latin American Cultural Studies 2012). Called to the Bar, Inner Temple, 1975; Bencher, Lincoln's Inn, 2001. Dir, Bar Mutual Insce Fund Ltd, 1999–2009. Chm., Young Barristers' Cttee, 1984–85. *Recreations:* music, cycling, trekking in the Andes and Andean culture. *Address:* Maitland Chambers, 7 Stone Buildings, Lincoln's Inn, WC2A 3SZ. *T:* (020) 7406 1200.

JACKSON, Prof. Julian Timothy, PhD; FBA 2003; FRHistS; Professor of Modern French History, Queen Mary, University of London, since 2003; *b* 10 April 1954; *s* of Edward Francis Jackson and Marion Marianne Marris (*née* Ellinger). *Educ:* Peterhouse, Cambridge (BA 1976; PhD 1982). Res. Asst to Robert Rhodes James, MP, for biog. of Eden, 1983; University College of Swansea, subseq. University of Wales, Swansea: Lectr, 1983–90, Sen. Lectr, 1990–95, Reader, 1995–2000, in Hist.; Prof. of Hist., 2000–03. FRHistS 1985. Commandeur, Ordre des Palmes Académiques (France), 2010. *Publications:* The Politics of Depression in France, 1985 (trans. Japanese 2001); The Popular Front in France: defending democracy, 1988 (trans. Japanese 1992); De Gaulle, 1990, rev. edn 2003 (trans. French 2004, Portuguese 2010); France: the dark years 1940–44, 2001 (trans. French 2004, Czech 2006); (ed) Europe 1900–1945, 2002 (trans. Spanish 2003); The Fall of France, 2003 (trans. Czech 2006); Living in Arcadia: homosexuality, politics and morality in France from the Liberation to Aids, 2010 (trans. French 2010); Jean Renoir, 2010. *Recreations:* cinema, theatre, travel, food. *Address:* Department of History, Queen Mary, University of London, Mile End Road, E1 4NS. *T:* (020) 7727 9930, *Fax:* (020) 8980 8400. *E:* j.t.jackson@qmul.ac.uk.

JACKSON, Sir Kenneth Joseph, (Sir Ken), Kt 1999; Chairman, Nirex Ltd, 2001–05. *Educ:* St Joseph's Sch., Wigan. Electrical technician, RAF, 1956–61; joined ETU, 1966: Br. Sec., Wigan; area officer, Preston; officer, Merseyside and NW; Exec. Councillor, EETPU, 1987; Pres., EETPU section, 1992–96, Gen. Sec., 1996–2003, AEEU.

JACKSON, (Kenneth) Robin, CBE 2014; PhD; Chief Executive and Secretary, British Academy, 2006–15; *b* 7 Oct. 1949; *s* of Kenneth and Lily Jackson; *m* 1985, Joanna Motion; one *s*. *Educ:* RGS Newcastle upon Tyne; Pembroke Coll., Oxford (MA Lit.Hum. 1973); Princeton Univ. (PhD Classical Philos. 1982). Classics Fellow, Marlboro Coll., Vermont, 1973–75; Seymour Reader in Greek Philos., Ormond Coll., and Lectr, then Sen. Lectr, in Classics, Univ. of Melbourne, 1977–94; Associate Dir, QAA, 1995–98; Res. Policy Advr, UUK, 1998–2002; Regl Consultant, London, 2002–06, Actg Dir, Corporate Resources, 2006, HEFCE. *Publications:* Olympiodorus: commentary on Plato's Gorgias, 1998; articles on Greek philosophy; policy papers on higher educn funding and res. policy. *Recreations:* listening to music, reading, walking in London. *Address:* The Secret Garden, Back Street, Reepham, Norfolk NR10 4SJ. *T:* 07500 010430. *E:* krobinj2015@yahoo.co.uk. *Clubs:* Athenæum; Newcastle United Football.

JACKSON, (Kevin) Paul; freelance consultant, since 2014; Creative Director, Houghton Street Media, Beijing, 2012–14; *b* 2 Oct. 1947; *s* of late T. Leslie Jackson and of Jo (*née* Spoonley); *m* 1981, Judith Elizabeth Cain; two *d*. *Educ:* Gunnersbury Grammar Sch.; Univ. of Exeter (BA 1970); Stanford Univ. (Exec. Program 1993). Stage manager: Marlowe Theatre, Canterbury, 1970; Thorndike Theatre, Leatherhead, 1971. BBC Television: Production Assistant, 1971–79; Producer, 1979–82: programmes include: The Two Ronnies, Three of a Kind (BAFTA Award 1982), Carrot's Lib, The Young Ones (BAFTA Award 1984), Happy Families; freelance producer and director, 1982–84: programmes include: Cannon & Ball, Girls On Top; Producer and Chm., Paul Jackson Prodns Ltd, 1984–86: programmes include: Red Dwarf, Don't Miss Wax, Saturday Live; Man. Dir, Noel Gay TV, 1987–91: progs include The Appointments of Dennis Jennings (Oscar for Best Live Action Short, 1989); Dir of Progs, 1991–93, Man. Dir, 1993–94, Carlton TV; Man. Dir, Carlton UK Productions, 1994–96; Head, then Controller, BBC Entertainment, 1997–2000; Man. Dir, Granada Media Australia and Chief Exec., Red Heart Prodns, 2000–02; Dir, Internat. Prodn and Entertainment, Granada, London, 2002; CEO, Granada America, 2002–06; Chm., Granada Productions (Australia), 2002–06 (CEO, 2000–02); Dir, Entertainment and Comedy, ITV plc, 2006–09; CEO, 2009–12, Consultant, 2012, Eyeworks UK; progs with Houghton Street Media, Beijing incl. Mama Mia, Chinese Gadget Show. Chairman: RTS, 1994–96; Comic Relief, 1985–98; Charity Projects, 1992–98; Trustee, Pilotlight, 1996–2003 (Chm., 1996–2000); Chm. Trustees, 1999–2012, Patron, 2000–12, Timebank. Academic Visitor, 1996–2004, Vis. Prof., 2004–, Exeter Univ. FInstD 1992; FRTS 1993. Hon. LLD Exeter, 2004. *Recreations:* my family, theatre, Rugby, travel, food and wine. *Address:* c/o Anita Land Ltd, 10 Wyndham Place, W1H 2PU. *Clubs:* Groucho, Ivy.

JACKSON, Prof. Mark Andrew, PhD; Professor of the History of Medicine, University of Exeter, since 2003; *b* Horley, 10 Sept. 1959; *s* of Richard and Valerie Jackson; *m* 1993, Siobhan Deehan; two *s* one *d*. *Educ:* Reigate Grammar Sch.; St Thomas' Hosp., Univ. of London (BSc 1983; MB BS 1985); Univ. of Leeds (PhD 1992). Res. Fellow, Univ. of Manchester, 1992–98; University of Exeter: Sen. Lectr, 1998–2000; Reader, 2000–03. Wellcome Trust: Chair: Hist. of Medicine Panel, 2003–08; Res. Resources in Med. Hist. Panel, 2008–13; Sen. Acad. Advr (Med. Humanities), 2013–. Mem., Hist. Sub-Panel, REF 2014, 2011–14. Dir, Medical Humanities Consultancy Ltd, 2013–. Gov., Colyton GS, 2011–14. *Publications:* (with G. Feinberg) The Chain of Immunology, 1983 (trans. Italian, Spanish and Japanese, 1985); New-Born Child Murder: women, illegitimacy and the Courts in Eighteenth-Century England, 1996; (ed jtly) Forgotten Lives: exploring the history of learning disability, 1997; The Borderland of Imbecility: medicine, society and the fabrication of the feeble mind in late Victorian and Edwardian England, 2000; (ed jtly) Crossing Boundaries: change and continuity in the history of learning disability, 2000; (ed) Infanticide: historical perspectives on child murder and concealment, 1520–2000, 2002; Allergy: the history of a modern malady, 2006 (trans. German, Japanese, Korean, 2007); (ed) Health and the Modern Home, 2007; Asthma: the biography, 2009; (ed) Oxford Handbook of the History of Medicine, 2011; The Age of Stress: science and the search for stability, 2013; History of Medicine: a beginner's guide, 2014; contribs to jls incl. Social Hist. of Medicine, British Jl for Hist. of Sci., Studies in Hist. and Philosophy of Biol and Biomed. Scis, Hist. of the Human Scis, Lancet. *Recreations:* family, Queens Park Rangers FC, classical music. *Address:* Centre for Medical History, University of Exeter, Amory Building, Rennes Drive, Exeter EX4 4RJ. *T:* (01392) 723003. *E:* m.a.jackson@exeter.ac.uk.

JACKSON, Michael; Founder, and Chairman, Shaping Tomorrow Ltd, since 2003; *b* 12 March 1948; *s* of Stanley Jackson and Maisie Joan Jackson. *Educ:* Salford Univ. (BSc Electronics). Hawker Siddeley, 1970–73; Vice Pres., Citibank NA, 1973–86; Sen. Vice Pres., Bank of America, 1986–90; Chief Exec., Birmingham Midshires Bldg Soc., 1990–98; Chm., Results Plus Ltd, 1998–2004. Non-exec. Dir, GallifordTry plc, 1997–2004. Hon. DBA Wolverhampton, 1997. *Recreations:* genealogy, music, sport. *Address:* The Habit, Blackladies, Kiddemore Green Road, Brewood, Staffs ST19 9BQ.

JACKSON, Gen. Sir Michael David, (Sir Mike), GCB 2005 (KCB 1998; CB 1996); CBE 1992 (MBE 1979); DSO 1999; DL; *b* 21 March 1944; *s* of George Jackson and Ivy (*née* Bower); *m* 1985, Sarah Coombe; two *s* one *d*. *Educ:* Stamford Sch.; RMA Sandhurst; Birmingham Univ. (BSocSc 1967). Commnd Intelligence Corps, 1963; transf. to Parachute Regt, 1970; Staff Coll., 1976; Bde Major, Berlin, 1977–78; ndc 1981; Directing Staff, Staff Coll., 1981–83; Comd 1st Bn Parachute Regt, 1984–86; Sen. DS, Jt Service Defence Coll., 1986–88; Services Fellow, Wolfson Coll., Cambridge, 1989; Comdr, 39 Inf. Bde, 1990–92; Dir Gen. Personal Services (Army), MoD, 1992–94; GOC 3 (UK) Div., 1994–95; Comdr, Implementation Force Multinat. Div. SW, Bosnia Herzegovina, 1995–96; Dir Gen., Develt and Doctrine, MoD, 1996–97; Comdr, ACE Rapid Reaction Corps, 1997–2000; Comdr, Kosovo Force, March–Oct. 1999; C-in-C, Land Comd, 2000–03; ADC Gen. to the Queen, 2001–06; CGS, 2003–06. Non-exec. Dir, ForceSelect, 2010–; Sen. Advr, PA Consulting Gp, 2007–; Mem. Internat. Adv. Bd, Rolls-Royce, 2007–. Col Comdt, Parachute Regt, 1998–2004; Hon. Col, Rifle Vols, TA, 1999–2007. DL Wilts, 2007. Hon. LLD: Birmingham, 2000; Sheffield, 2005. Freeman, City of London, 1988. *Publications:* Soldier: the autobiography, 2007. *Recreations:* travel, music, ski-ing, tennis. *Address:* Regimental Headquarters, Parachute Regiment, Merville Barracks, Colchester, Essex CO2 7UT. *Clubs:* Army and Navy, Buck's, Garrick; St Moritz Tobogganing.

JACKSON, Most Rev. Michael Geoffrey St Aubyn; *see* Dublin, Archbishop of, and Primate of Ireland.

JACKSON, Michael Richard; television executive and producer; President of Programming, IAC, 2006–09; *b* 11 Feb. 1958; *s* of Ernest Jackson and Margaret (*née* Kearsley). *Educ:* King's Sch., Macclesfield; Poly. of Central London (BA (Hons) Media Studies). Organiser, Channel Four Gp, 1979; Producer, The Sixties, 1982; Independent Producer, Beat Productions Ltd, 1983–87, produced Whose Town is it Anyway?, Open the Box, The Media Show; joined BBC Television; Editor: The Late Show (BFI Television Award), 1988–90; Late Show Productions, 1990–91, progs incl. The Nelson Mandela Tribute, Tales from Prague (Grierson Documentary Award), Moving Pictures, The American Late Show (PBS), Naked Hollywood (BAFTA Award, Best Factual Series); Head of Music and Arts, BBC Television, 1991–93; Controller, BBC 2, 1993–96; Controller, BBC 1 and BBC Dir of Television, 1996–97; Dir of Progs, 1997–98, Chief Exec., 1997–2001, C4; Chm., Film Four Ltd, 1997–2001; Pres. and Chief Exec., USA Entertainment, 2001–02; Chm., Universal Television Gp, 2002–04; Sen. Advr, Lepe Partners, 2012–14. Executive Producer: The Genius of Photography (series), BBC, 2007; America: the Story of Us (series), 2010. Co-Founder, veryshortlist.com, 2007–. Non-executive Director: EMI Gp, 1999–2002; Scottish TV, 2009–; Nutopia, 2011–; Peters, Fraser and Dunlop, 2015–; Dir, DIC Entertainment, 2006–09. Chm., Photographers' Gall., 2001–02. FRTS 1997. Hon. DLitt Westminster, 1995. *Recreations:* reading, films, collecting photography, walking.

JACKSON, Air Vice-Marshal Michael Richard, CB 1998; independent consultant, since 2004; Director General, Intelligence Staff, Ministry of Defence, 1996–98; *b* 28 Dec. 1941; *s* of Felix Ralph Jackson and Margaret Jackson (*née* Marshall); *m* 1967, Kay Johnson; two *s*. *Educ:* Cardinal Vaughan Sch.; RAF Coll., Cranwell. Joined RAF, 1965: sqdn flying duties, 1965–69; navigation instructor, 1969–70; Exchange Officer, USA, 1971–74; RAF Staff Coll., 1974; Sqdn Comdr, 1975–77; Mem., Directing Staff, Army Staff Coll., Camberley, 1977–80; Ops Wing Comdr, 1981–84; Defence and Air Attaché, Warsaw, 1985–87; Unit Comdr, 1987–89; Defence Fellow, Rand Corp. and Cambridge Univ., 1989–90; Dir, MoD Central Staffs, 1991–95. Exec. Dir, Oracle Corp., 1998–2004; Dir, Market Develt, Silicon Graphics, 2002–04; Dep. Chm., Alpha Intelligence Mgt Ltd, 2007–09. Fellow, Centre for Security and Intelligence Studies, Buckingham Univ., 2009–. Trustee and Project Dir, Bury St Edmunds Heritage Trust, 2011–. *Recreations:* music, walking, gardening. *Address:* c/o RAF Record Office, High Wycombe, Bucks HP14 4UE. *Club:* Royal Air Force.

JACKSON, (Michael) Rodney; Consultant, Sandersons, Solicitors, 2001–05; a Recorder, 1985–2001; *b* 16 April 1935; *s* of John William Jackson and Nora Jackson (*née* Phipps); *m* 1968, Anne Margaret, *d* of late Prof. Eric William Hawkins, CBE; two *s*. *Educ:* King Edward VII Sch., Sheffield; Queen Elizabeth Grammar Sch., Wakefield; Queens' Coll., Cambridge (MA, LLM). Admitted Solicitor of the Supreme Court, 1962; Notary Public, 1967; Solicitor Advocate, 1996–2005. Partner, 1964–94, Sen. Partner, 1992–94, Consultant, 1994–2001, Andrew M. Jackson & Co., Solicitors. *Recreations:* reading, rail travel. *Address:* 11 The Paddock, Swanland, North Ferriby, E Yorks HU14 3QW. *T:* (01482) 633278.

JACKSON, Sir Michael (Roland), 5th Bt *cr* 1902; MA; CEng, MIET; *b* 20 April 1919; *s* of Sir W. D. Russell Jackson, 4th Bt, and Kathleen (*d* 1975), *d* of Summers Hunter, CBE, Tynemouth; *S* father 1956; *m* 1st, 1942, Hilda Margaret (marr. diss. 1969), *d* of late Cecil George Herbert Richardson, CBE, Newark; one *s* one *d*; 2nd, 1969, Hazel Mary, *d* of late Ernest Harold Edwards. *Educ:* Stowe; Clare Coll., Cambridge. Served War of 1939–45; Flt-Lieut, Royal Air Force Volunteer Reserve. *Heir: s* Thomas St Felix Jackson [*b* 27 Sept. 1946; *m* 1st, 1980, Victoria, *d* of late George Scatliff, Wineham, Sussex (marr. diss. 2009); two *d*; 2nd, 2013, Annie von Brockdorff, *d* of late Frank Gleave]. *Address:* Pennys Cottage, Rockbourne, Fordingbridge, Hants SP6 3NL.

JACKSON, Mike; *see* Jackson, R. M.

JACKSON, Sir Neil Keith, 9th Bt *cr* 1815, of Arlsey, Bedfordshire; *b* 12 May 1952; *s* of Sir Keith Arnold Jackson, 8th Bt and of Pauline Mona (*née* Climo); *S* father, 2000, but his name does not appear on the Official Roll of the Baronetage; *m* 1973, Sandra Whitehead (marr. diss.); two *s*. *Heir: s* Stephen Keith Jackson, *b* 27 Sept. 1973.

JACKSON, Sir Nicholas (Fane St George), 3rd Bt *cr* 1913; organist, harpsichordist and composer; Director, Concertante of London, since 1987; *b* 4 Sept. 1934; *s* of Sir Hugh Jackson, 2nd Bt, and Violet Marguerite Loftus (*d* 2001), *y d* of Loftus St George; *S* father, 1979; *m* 1972, Nadia Françoise Genevieve (*née* Michard); one *s*. *Educ:* Radley Coll.; Wadham Coll., Oxford; Royal Acad. of Music. LRAM; ARCM. Organist: St Anne's, Soho, 1963–68; St James's, Piccadilly, 1971–74; St Lawrence, Jewry, 1974–77; Organist and Master of the Choristers, St David's Cathedral, 1977–84. Musical Dir, St David's Cathedral Bach Fest., 1979; Dir, Bach Festival, Santes Creus, Spain, 1987–89. Organ recitals and broadcasts: Berlin, 1967; Paris, 1972, 1975; USA (tour), 1975, 1978, 1980 and 1989; Minorca, 1977; Spain, 1979; Madrid Bach Festival, 1980; RFH, 1984; Croatia (tour), annually, 2002–08; France, 2009–12; concert tours of Spain and Germany, annually 1980–. Début as harpsichordist, Wigmore Hall, 1963; directed Soho Concertante, Queen Elizabeth Hall, 1964–72. Mem. Music Cttee, Welsh Arts Council, 1981–84. Examiner, Trinity Coll. of Music, 1985–99. Lectr on work of Sir Thomas Graham Jackson incl. Venice, 2008. Recordings: Mass for a Saint's Day, 1971; organ and harpsichord music, incl. works by Arnell, Bach, Couperin, Langlais, Mozart, Vierne and Walther; Spanish organ music; own organ music, recorded at Chartres Cath., 2000; Requiem and other choral music, 2006; own instrumental works, 2012. Hon. Patron, Hertford Coll. Music Soc., 1996–. Master, Drapers' Co., 1994–95; Liveryman, Musicians' Co., 1985. Hon. Fellow, Hertford Coll., Oxford, 1995. *Publications:* (ed) Sir Thomas Graham Jackson, Recollections: the life and travels of a Victorian architect, 2003; Requiem, 2007; *compositions:* Mass for a Saint's Day, 1966; 20th Century Merbecke, 1967; 4 Images (for organ), 1971; Divertissement (organ), 1983; Organ Mass, 1984; 2 Organ Sonatas, 1985; Suite, for brass quintet and organ, 1986; The Reluctant Highwayman (opera), 1992 (world première, 1995); (completed) Bach's Fugue, BWV 906, 1996; Missa Cum Jubilo, 1998; Venetian Serenade, 2008; The Four Temperaments, 2009; Six Elizabethan Songs, 2010; Piano Trio, 2011. *Recreations:* sketching, writing. *Heir: s* Thomas Graham St George Jackson, *b* 5 Oct. 1980.

JACKSON, Patrick; *see* Jackson, J. P.

JACKSON, Paul; *see* Jackson, K. P.

JACKSON, Paul Edward; Managing Director (International) (Amex), Ogilvy Group, 2006–07; *b* 8 July 1953; *s* of George Edward Jackson and Joan (*née* Barry); *m* 2000, Elaine Claire Adams; two *s*. *Educ:* Taunton Sch.; Watford Sch. of Art; Canterbury Coll. of Art (BA Hons Graphic Design); Bradford Univ. Mgt Centre. MIPA 1987. Account Executive: Saatchi & Saatchi, 1978–80; Mathers, 1980–81; Account Supervisor, Fletcher Shelton Delaney, 1981–83; Account Manager, Publicis, 1983–85; Bd Dir, BSB Dorland, 1985–92; Man. Dir, Kevin Morley Mktg, 1992–95; Exec. Man. Partner and Vice Chm., Ammirati Purlis Lintas, 1995–97; Client Service Dir, Dewe Rogerson, 1997–99; Ogilvy & Mather: Exec. Mgt Dir, 1999–2002; CEO, 2002–06. Non-exec. Dir, Aga Rangemaster Gp (formerly AGA Foodservice) plc, 2005–. MInstD 1992. FRSA 1993. *Recreations:* sailing, fly fishing.

JACKSON, Ven. Peggy; *see* Jackson, Ven. F. A.

JACKSON, Prof. Peter, PhD; FBA 2012; Professor of Medieval History, Keele University, 2002–11, now Emeritus; *b* Rochdale, Lancs, 27 Jan. 1948; *s* of Frank Jackson and Dorothy Jackson; *m* 1990, Rebecca Oswald. *Educ:* Northern Grammar Sch., Portsmouth; St John's Coll., Cambridge (BA 1st Cl. Hist. 1971; PhD 1977). Jun. Res. Fellow, Churchill Coll., Cambridge, 1975–79; Keele University: Lectr in Hist., 1979–91; Sen. Lectr in Hist., 1991–2000; Reader in Hist., 2000–02. Vis. Fellow, Inst. for Advanced Studies, Hebrew Univ. of Jerusalem, 2000. *Publications:* (ed) The Cambridge History of Iran, vol. 6, 1986; (trans. and ed jtly) The Mission of Friar William of Rubruck, 1990; The Delhi Sultanate, 1999; The Mongols and the West 1221–1410, 2005; The Seventh Crusade, 1244–1254: sources and documents, 2007; Studies on the Mongol Empire and Early Muslim India, 2009.

JACKSON, Hon. Sir Peter (Arthur Brian), Kt 2010; **Hon. Mr Justice Peter Jackson;** a Judge of the High Court of Justice, Family Division, since 2010; *b* 9 Dec. 1955; *s* of late Guy Jackson and of Amanda Jackson (now Park); *m* 1983, Deborah Sanderson; two *d*. *Educ:* Marlborough Coll.; Brasenose Coll., Oxford (BA Hons). Called to the Bar, Inner Temple, 1978, Bencher, 2010; barrister specialising in family law, 1978–2010; QC 2000; Recorder, 2000–10; Family Div. Liaison Judge, Northern Circuit, 2011–. Gov., 2000–13, Trustee, 2013–, Camden Sch. for Girls. *Address:* Royal Courts of Justice, Strand, WC2A 2LL.

JACKSON, Peter John; Chairman, Kingfisher plc, 2006–09; *b* 16 Jan. 1947; *s* of Jack and Joan Jackson; *m* 1974, Anne Campbell; two *s* one *d*. *Educ:* Leeds Univ. (BA Econs). Industrial Relations Officer, BSC, 1968–71; Res. Officer, Commn on Industrial Relns, 1971–73; Personnel Manager, Guthrie Industries Europe, 1973–76; Perkins Engines: Indust. Relns Manager, 1976–80; Personnel Dir, 1980–83; Man. Dir, Rolls Royce Diesels, 1983–84; Dir and Gen. Manager, Gp Parts and Distribn, 1985–87; joined Associated British Foods, 1987; British Sugar plc: Exec. Dir, 1987–88; Dep. Man. Dir, 1988–89; Chief Exec., 1989–99; Chief Exec., Associated British Foods, 1999–2005. Non-exec. Dir, Smiths Group plc, 2003–09. Chm. Trustees, Disabilities Trust, 2007–. *Recreations:* garden, golf, Sheffield United.

JACKSON, Peter (Michael); Senior Lecturer in Industrial Studies, Institute of Extra-mural Studies, National University of Lesotho, 1980; *b* 14 Oct. 1928; *s* of Leonard Patterson Jackson; *m* 1961, Christine Thomas. *Educ:* Durham Univ.; University Coll., Leicester. Lecturer, Dept of Sociology, University of Hull, 1964–66; Fellow, Univ. of Hull, 1970–72; Tutor, Open Univ., 1972–74; Senior Planning Officer, S Yorks CC, 1974–77. MP (Lab) High Peak, 1966–70; contested (Lab) Birmingham North, European Parly elecns, 1979. Member: Peak Park Jt Planning Bd, 1973–77, 1979–82; Derby CC, 1973–77. *Recreations:* numismatics, book collecting, ski-ing. *Address:* 82 Vandon Court, 64 Petty France, SW1H 9HG. *Club:* Maseru (Lesotho).

JACKSON, Sir Peter (Robert), ONZ 2012; KNZM 2010 (CNZM 2002); film producer, director, writer and actor; *b* Pukerua Bay, NZ, 31 Oct. 1961; *s* of late Bill and Joan Jackson; *m* 1987, Frances Walsh; one *s* one *d*. Formerly photographer, Evening Post, Wellington, NZ; Founder and Partner: WingNut Films Ltd (acquired Nat. Film Unit, NZ, 2000); Weta Ltd; Three Foot Six Ltd, 1999–. *Films:* producer, director, co-writer and actor: Bad Taste, 1987; Braindead, 1992; Heavenly Creatures, 1994; Forgotten Silver, 1995; The Frighteners, 1997; The Lord of the Rings trilogy: The Fellowship of the Ring, 2001 (BAFTA Awards for Best Film and Best Dir, 2002); The Two Towers, 2002; The Return of the King, 2003 (Acad. Awards for Best Dir, Best Picture and Best Adapted Screenplay, 2004); prod., dir and co-writer: Meet the Feebles, 1989; King Kong, 2005; The Lovely Bones, 2010; The Adventures of Tintin, 2011; The Hobbit Trilogy: An Unexpected Journey, 2012; The Desolation of Smaug, 2013; The Battle of the Five Armies, 2014; prod. and co-writer, Jack Brown Genius, 1994; prod. and actor, The Long and Short of it, 2003; producer: Valley of the Stereos, 1992; District 9, 2009.

JACKSON, Philip Henry Christopher, CVO 2009; DL; FRBS; sculptor; *b* 18 April 1944; *s* of Humphrey Hoskins Jackson and Margaret Jackson (*née* Edwards); *m* 1979, Jean Barbara Welch; two *s* one *d*, and one step *s* one step *d*. *Educ:* Farnham Sch. of Art. Vice Pres., RBS, 1991–93; Pres., W Sussex Art Soc., 2001–; Member: Art Workers Guild, 1988–; Fabric Adv. Cttee, Chichester Cath., 2006–; Lambert Barnard Paintings Steering Gp, 2009–. *Major commissions* include: Manchester Peace Gp, St Peters Sq., Manchester, 1988; Falklands War Monument, Portsmouth, 1992; The Young Mozart, Orange Sq., London, 1994; Liberation Sculpture Jersey, St Helier, 1995; Sir Matt Busby, Manchester United FC, Manchester, 1996; Wallenberg Monument, Great Cumberland Place, London, 1997; Minerva Sculpture, Chichester Fest. Th., 1997; Gurkha Monument, Horse Guards Ave., London, 1997; Constantine the Great, York Minster, 1998; Christ in Judgement, 1998, St Richard, 2000, Chichester Cath.; Empress Elizabeth of Austria, Geneva, 1998; Wallenberg Monument, Buenos Aires, 1998; The In Pensioner, Royal Hosp. Chelsea, London, 2000; King George VI, RNC, Dartmouth, 2002; Champions, the World Cup Sculpture, West Ham, London, 2003; equestrian sculpture of HM the Queen, Windsor Great Park, 2003; Terence Cuneo, Waterloo Station, London, 2003; Bobby Moore Sculpture, new Wembley Stadium; Queen Mother Meml, The Mall, London, 2008; United Trinity sculpture, Manchester United FC, 2008; Sir Alf Ramsey sculpture, New Wembley Stadium, 2008; British Diplomats commemorative sculpture, FCO, London, 2008; Lord Glenconner sculpture, Mustique, 2009; Archangel Gabriel sculpture, S Harting Church, W Sussex, 2009; St John the Evangelist, Portsmouth RC Cathedral, 2010; Peter Osgood sculpture, Chelsea FC, 2010; Bomber Command Meml, Green Park, 2012; Sir Alex Ferguson, Manchester United FC, 2012; HRH Prince Philip, Windsor Great Park, 2013; Joan Littlewood, Stratford East, 2013; Korean War Meml, Victoria Embankment, London, 2014; Mahatma Gandhi sculpture, Parliament Sq., London, 2015. DL W Sussex, 2008. Hon. MA UC Chichester. Silver Medal, 1990, Sir Otto Beit Medal for Sculpture, 1991, 1992 and 1993, RBS. *Publications:* Philip Jackson: sculptures since 1987, 2002. *Recreations:* messing about in boats, Real tennis. *Address:* The Sculpture Studio, Mill Lane, Cocking, West Sussex GU29 0HJ. *T:* (01730) 816872, *Fax:* (01730) 812618. *E:* philipjackson@sculpturestudiolimited.co.uk. *Clubs:* Athenæum, Sloane.

JACKSON, Ralph S.; *see* Seymour-Jackson.

JACKSON, Rt Rev. Richard Charles; *see* Lewes, Bishop Suffragan of.

JACKSON, Prof. Richard James, PhD; FRS 2006; Professor of RNA Biochemistry, University of Cambridge, 2000–07, now Emeritus; Fellow of Pembroke College, Cambridge, 1967–2007, now Emeritus; *b* 1 July 1940; *s* of James Rufus Jackson and Edith Winifred Jackson (*née* Clark); *m* 1967, Wiltrud Elfriede Klippel; two *d*. *Educ:* Bryanston Sch., Blandford Forum; Pembroke Coll., Cambridge (BA Natural Scis (Biochem.) 1962; PhD 1966). Res. Fellow, Dept of Molecular Biol., Univ. of Geneva, 1966–67; University of Cambridge: Res. Fellow, Pembroke Coll., 1967–70; Univ. Demonstrator, 1970–73; Lectr, 1973–94; Reader in the Biochem. of Nucleic Acids, 1994–2000. Roche Res. Fellow, Dept of Molecular Biol., Univ. of Geneva, 1977 (on sabbatical). Mem. EMBO, 1990. Jubilee Lect. and Harden Medal, Biochem. Soc., 2005. *Publications:* articles, esp. on the mechanism and regulation of mammalian protein biosynthesis, in scientific jls. *Recreations:* walking, bird watching, travel, music, reading. *Address:* Department of Biochemistry, University of Cambridge, Tennis Court Road, Cambridge CB2 1QW. *T:* (01223) 333682, *Fax:* (01223) 333345. *E:* rjj1000@cam.ac.uk.

JACKSON, Richard Michael, (Mike), CVO 1983; HM Diplomatic Service, retired; Ambassador to Costa Rica, 1995–97; *b* 12 July 1940; *s* of Richard William Jackson and Charlotte (*née* Wrightson); *m* 1961, Mary Elizabeth Kitchin; one *s* one *d*. *Educ:* Queen Elizabeth Grammar Sch., Darlington; Paisley Grammar Sch.; Glasgow Univ. (MA Hons 1961). Joined Home Civil Service, 1961; Scottish Office, 1961–70; seconded to MAFF, 1971–72; seconded to FCO and served in The Hague, 1973–74; trans. to HM Diplomatic Service, 1974; European Integration Dept (External), FCO, 1975–76; Panama City, 1976–79; Arms Control and Disarmament Dept, FCO, 1979–81; Buenos Aires, 1981–82; Falkland Islands Dept, FCO, 1982; Stockholm, 1982–87; Dep. Head of Mission, Seoul, 1987–91; Ambassador to Bolivia, 1991–95. *Recreations:* conservation, birdwatching, real ale. *E:* mollieandmike@yahoo.com.

JACKSON, Robert Victor; *b* 24 Sept. 1946; *m* 1975, Caroline Frances Harvey (*see* C. F. Jackson); one *s* decd. *Educ:* Falcon Coll., S Rhodesia; St Edmund Hall, Oxford (H. W. C. Davis Prize, 1966; 1st Cl. Hons Mod. Hist. 1968); President Oxford Union, 1967. Prize Fellowship, All Souls Coll., 1968 (Fellow, 1968–86). Councillor, Oxford CC, 1969–71; Political Adviser to Sec. of State for Employment, 1973–74; Member, Cabinet of Sir Christopher Soames, EEC Commn, Brussels, 1974–76; Chef de Cabinet, President of EEC Economic and Social Cttee, Brussels, 1976–78; Mem. (C) Upper Thames, European Parlt, 1979–84; Special Adviser to Governor of Rhodesia (Lord Soames), 1979–80; European Parlt's Rapporteur-Gen. on 1983 European Community Budget. MP Wantage, 1983–2005 (C, 1983–2005, Lab, 2005). Parly Under Sec. of State, DES, 1987–90, Dept of Employment, 1990–92, Office of Public Service and Sci., 1992–93. Mem., Select Cttee on Sci. and Technol., 1999–2001. Mem., Adv. Cttee on Works of Art, H of C; Treas., Cons. Mainstream Parly Gp. Mem., UK Delegn, Council of Europe and WEU, 2000–01. Contested (C) Manchester Central Div., Oct. 1974. Co-Chm., CAABU, 2001. Trustee: Hattori Foundn; Hattori Trust Co. Ltd. Editor: The Round Table: Commonwealth Jl of Internat. Relations, 1970–74; International Affairs (Chatham House), 1979–80. *Publications:* South Asian Crisis: India, Pakistan, Bangladesh 1972, 1975; The Powers of the European Parliament, 1977; The European Parliament: Penguin Guide to Direct Elections, 1979; Reforming the European Budget, 1981; Tradition and Reality: Conservative philosophy and European integration 1982; From Boom to Bust?—British farming and CAP reform, 1983; Political Ideas in Western Europe Today, 1984. *Recreations:* reading, music, walking. *Address:* New House, Hanney Road, Southmoor, Abingdon OX13 5HR.

JACKSON, Ven. Robert William; Archdeacon of Walsall, 2004–09; freelance church growth consultant, since 2009; *b* 21 June 1949; *s* of Joseph William and Mary Edith Jackson; *m* 1973, Anne Christine Day; one *s* one *d* (and one *s* decd). *Educ:* King's Coll., Cambridge (MA 1973); Univ. of Manchester (MA 1973); Univ. of Nottingham (DipTh). Govt Economic Advr, 1972–78. Ordained deacon, 1981, priest, 1982; Curate, Christ Church, Fulwood, 1981–84; Vicar: St Mark's, Grenoside, 1984–92; St Mary, Scarborough, 1992–2001; Springboard Res. Missioner, 2001–04. *Publications:* Matthew, 1987, 2nd edn 1993; Godspeed, 1994; Till the Fat Lady Sings, 1996; Higher than the Hills, 1999; Hope for the Church, 2002; The Road to Growth: towards a thriving church, 2005; Going for Growth, 2006; (jtly) Everybody Welcome: the course where everybody helps grow their church, 2009; Growing Through a Vacancy, 2013; (jtly) LyCiG Local Course, 2013. *Recreations:* tennis, cricket, walking, trains. *Address:* 4 Glebe Park, Eyam, Hope Valley S32 5RH. *E:* venerablebob@gmail.com.

JACKSON, Robin; *see* Jackson, K. R.

JACKSON, Rodney; *see* Jackson, Michael R.

JACKSON, Sir Roland; *see* Jackson, Sir W. R. C.

JACKSON, Rosemary Elizabeth; QC 2006; a Recorder, since 2002; mediator, adjudicator and arbitrator, since 2014; *b* 16 April 1958; *d* of Douglas and Pauline Jackson; *m* (marr. diss. 2010); one *s* one *d*. *Educ:* King's Coll. London (LLB Hons 1980; AKC 1980). Called to the Bar, Middle Temple, 1981; Accredited Mediator, 2001. *Address:* Keating Chambers, 15 Essex Street, WC2R 3AA. *T:* (020) 7544 2600, *Fax:* (020) 7544 2700.

JACKSON, Prof. Roy, DSc; FRS 2000; Class of 1950 Professor of Engineering and Applied Science, Princeton University, 1983–98, now Professor Emeritus; *b* 6 Oct. 1931; *s* of Harold and Ellen Jackson; *m* 1957, Susan Margaret Birch (*d* 1991); one *s* one *d*. *Educ:* Trinity Coll., Cambridge (BA 1954, MA 1959); Univ. of Edinburgh (DSc 1968). ICI Ltd, 1955–61; Reader in Chemical Engrg, Univ. of Edinburgh, 1961–68; A. J. Hartsook Prof. of Chemical Engrg, Rice Univ., 1968–77; Prof. of Chemical Engrg, Univ. of Houston, 1977–82; Sherman Fairchild Dist. Schol., CIT, 1982–83. Alpha Chi Sigma Award, 1980, Thomas Baron Award, 1993, AIChE. *Publications:* Transport in Porous Catalysts, 1977; The Dynamics of Fluidized Particles, 2000. *Recreations:* sailing, water colour painting. *Address:* 311 Johnson Street, New Bern, NC 28560, USA. *T:* (252) 5142493.

JACKSON, Rt Hon. Sir Rupert (Matthew), Kt 1999; PC 2008; **Rt Hon. Lord Justice Jackson;** a Lord Justice of Appeal, since 2008; *b* 7 March 1948; *s* of late George Henry Jackson and Nancy Barbara Jackson (*née* May); *m* 1975, Claire Corinne Potter; three *d*. *Educ:* Christ's Hospital; Jesus College, Cambridge (MA, LLB; Hon. Fellow, 2009). Pres., Cambridge Union, 1971. Called to the Bar, Middle Temple, 1972, Bencher, 1995; QC 1987; a Recorder, 1990–98; a Dep. High Court Judge, 1993–98; a Judge of the High Court of Justice, QBD, 1999–2008; Judge in charge of Technol. and Construction Ct, 2004–07. Chm., Professional Negligence Bar Assoc., 1993–95. Ed., 1982–99, consultant ed., 2000–, Jackson and Powell on Professional Liability; Ed., 2000–10, Ed.-in-Chief, 2011–, Civil Procedure (The White Book). *Recreations:* bridge, chess, gardening, walking. *Address:* Royal Courts of Justice, Strand, WC2A 2LL. *Club:* Reform.

JACKSON, Prof. Stephen Philip, PhD; FRS 2008; Frederick James Quick and Cancer Research UK Professor of Biology, Department of Biochemistry, Cambridge University, since 2009 (Frederick James Quick Professor of Biology, Department of Zoology, 1995–2009); Senior Scientist, since 1996, Head, Cancer Research UK Laboratories, since 2004, Wellcome Trust/Cancer Research UK Gurdon Institute (formerly Wellcome/CRC Institute of Cancer and Developmental Biology), Cambridge University; Fellow of St John's College, Cambridge, since 1995; *b* 17 July 1962; *s* of Philip George Jackson and Marian Margaret (*née* Smith); *m* 1991, Teresa Margaret Clarke; two *s*. *Educ:* Univ. of Leeds (BSc 1st Cl. Hons Biochem. 1983); Univ. of Edinburgh (PhD Molecular Biol. 1987). Postgraduate research: Imperial Coll., London, 1983–85; Univ. of Edinburgh, 1985–87; Postdoctoral Fellow, Univ. of Calif, Berkeley, 1987–91; Research Gp Leader, 1991–95, Dep. Dir, then Dep. Chm., 2001–04, Wellcome/CRC Inst., subseq. Wellcome Trust/CRUK Gurdon Inst., Univ. of Cambridge. Founder, and Chief Scientific Officer: KuDOS Pharmaceuticals Ltd, 1997–2008; Mission Therapeutics Ltd, 2011–. Tenovus Medal Lecture, Tenovus-Scotland, 1997. FMedSci 2001; Mem. EMBO, 1997–. Eppendorf European Investigator Award, 1995; Colworth Medal, 1997, GlaxoSmithKline Award, 2008, Biochemical Soc.; Anthony Dipple Carcinogenesis Young Investigator Award, 2002; Innovator of Year Award, BBSRC, 2009; Buchanan Medal, Royal Soc., 2011. *Publications:* over 200 research papers and review articles in leading scientific jls, particularly in areas of DNA repair. *Recreations:* my children, gardening, travel. *Address:* Wellcome Trust/Cancer Research UK Gurdon Institute, University of Cambridge, Tennis Court Road, Cambridge CB2 1QN. *T:* (office) (01223) 334102.

JACKSON, Stewart James; MP (C) Peterborough, since 2005; *b* 31 Jan. 1965; *s* of Raymond Thomas Jackson and Sylvia Alice Theresa Jackson; *m* 1999, Sarah O'Grady; one *d*. *Educ:* Royal Holloway Coll., Univ. of London (BA Hons (Econs and Public Admin) 1988); Thames Valley Univ. (MA Human Resource Mgt). MCIPD 2001. Pres., Univ. of London, 1988–89. Retail Banker, Lloyds TSB, 1993–98; Business Services Manager, AZTEC (Trng and Enterprise Council for SW London), 1998–2000; Business Advr, Human Resources, Business Link for London, 2000–05. Mem. (C) Ealing BC, 1990–98. Contested (C) Brent S, 1997, Peterborough, 2001. *Recreations:* family, cinema, travel, biographies, local history. *Address:* House of Commons, SW1A 0AA. *T:* (020) 7219 8286. *E:* jacksonsj@parliament.uk. *Club:* Peterborough Conservative.

JACKSON, Dr Sylvia; Member (Lab) Stirling, Scottish Parliament, 1999–2007; *b* 3 Dec. 1946; *d* of Herbert Edward Woodforth and Lucy Franklin; *m* 1970, Michael Peart Jackson (*d* 2001); one *s* one *d*. *Educ:* Brigg Girls' High Sch.; Univ. of Hull (BSc Hons Chemistry; PGCE; BPhil Educn); Univ. of Stirling (PhD Educn). Teacher of chemistry and physics, schools in Hull, Alva, Stirling, Cumbernauld and Kirkintilloch; Asst Sci. Advr, Edinburgh CC and Lothian Regl Council; Res. Fellow, Univ. of Stirling; Lectr, Moray House Inst. of Educn, Univ. of Edinburgh. Scottish Parliament: Dep. Convenor, Local Govt Cttee, 2000; Convenor, Subordinate Legislation Cttee, 2003–07; Mem., Local Govt and Transport Cttee, 2003–07; Cross Party Groups: Convenor, Animal Welfare; Co-Convenor, Affordable Housing; Vice Convenor, Drugs and Alcohol, 2004–07. Exec. Mem., CPA, 2003–07. *Publications:* Introducing Science (series of 12 pupil books and 6 teacher guides); contribs to jls, mainly dealing with professional develt of teachers. *Recreations:* walking, photography.

JACKSON, Dame Temuranga B.; *see* Batley-Jackson, Dame T.

JACKSON, Tessa; *see* Jackson, J. T.

JACKSON, (William) Gordon; QC (Scot) 1990; Member (Lab) Glasgow Govan, Scottish Parliament, 1999–2007; *b* 5 Aug. 1948; *s* of Alexander Jackson and Margaret Shillinglaw or Jackson; *m* 1972, Anne Stevely; one *s* two *d*. *Educ:* Ardrossan Academy; St Andrews Univ. (LLB). Advocate, 1979; called to the Bar, Lincoln's Inn, 1989; Advocate Depute, Scotland, 1987–90.

JACKSON, Sir (William) Roland (Cedric), 9th Bt *cr* 1869, of The Manor House, Birkenhead; DPhil; Executive Chair, Sciencewise, since 2012; *b* 9 Jan. 1954; *s* of Sir (William) Thomas Jackson, 8th Bt and Gillian Malise (*née* Stobart); *S* father, 2004; *m* 1977, Nicola Mary, MA, DPhil, *yr d* of Prof. Peter Reginald Davis, PhD, FRCS; three *s*. *Educ:* Wycliffe Coll.; St Peter's Coll., Oxford (MA); Exeter Coll., Oxford (DPhil). Hd of Science, Backwell Sch., 1986–89; Educn Advr, ICI, 1989–93; Science Museum: Hd of Learning, 1993–2002; Hd of Mus., 2001–02; Chief Exec., BAAS (British Sci. Assoc.), 2002–13. Res. Associate, UCL, 2014–. Dir, Big Bang Educn CIC, 2010–13. Chair, Biosci. for Society Strategy Panel, BBSRC, 2011–14; Member: Nuffield Council on Bioethics, 2013–; Mgt Bd, Industrial Biotechnol. Catalyst, 2014–. Vis. Fellow, Royal Instn, 2013–. Trustee: Mather-Jackson Library, 2007–; Lowther Castle and Gardens Trust, 2014–. Sec., Alpine Club Library, 2011–. Hon. DSc Aston, 2011; DHC Aberdeen, 2012. *Recreation:* collecting and reading mountaineering and rock-climbing literature and occasionally repeating some of the feats described therein. *Heir:* *s* Adam William Roland Jackson, *b* 19 May 1982. *Clubs:* Athenæum, Alpine.

JACKSON-NELSON, Marjorie, AC 2001; CVO 2002; MBE 1953; Governor, South Australia, 2001–07; *b* 13 Sept. 1931; *d* of William Alfred Jackson and Mary Jackson; *m* 1953, Peter Nelson (*d* 1977); one *s* two *d*. *Educ:* Lithgow High Sch., NSW. Athlete (the Lithgow Flash): holder, Australian 100 yards, 100 metres, 220 yards and 200 metres sprint titles, 1950–54; broke world sprint records on ten occasions; Olympic Gold Medals for 100m and 200m, Helsinki, 1952; 7 Commonwealth Games Gold Medals. Australian Commonwealth Games teams: Women's Section Manager, Auckland, 1982, Edinburgh, 1986, Auckland, 1990; Gen. Team Manager, Victoria, Canada, 1994; Athletes' Liaison Officer, Malaysia, 1998. Member Board: S Australian Govt's Sports Inst., 1985–90; Sydney Organising Cttee for 2000 Olympic Games, 1998–2000. Launched Peter Nelson Leukaemia Res. Fellowship, 1977; has raised over Aust. 6 million to sponsor research into fighting leukaemia; funds raised have sponsored a leukaemia lab. in Adelaide. Freedom of City of London, 2006. Hon. Dr, Charles Sturt, NSW, 2001. Australian Sports Medal, 2000; Olympic Order, IOC, 2008.

JACKSON-STOPS, Timothy William Ashworth, FRICS; Chairman, 1978–98, Consultant, since 1998, Jackson-Stops & Staff; *b* 1942; *s* of late Anthony and Jean Jackson-Stops; *m* 1987, Jenny MacArthur; two *s*. *Educ:* Eton; Agricultural Coll., Cirencester. Jackson-Stops & Staff, 1967–: Dir, 1974. *Recreations:* ski-ing, sailing, shooting. *Address:* Wood Burcote Court, Towcester, Northants NN12 6JP. *T:* (01327) 350443.

JACOB, Rt Hon. Sir Robert Raphael Hayim, (Sir Robin), Kt 1993; PC 2003; a Lord Justice of Appeal, 2003–11; Sir Hugh Laddie Professor in Intellectual Property and Director, Institute of Brand and Innovation Law, University College London, since 2011; *b* 26 April 1941; *s* of Sir Isaac Hai, (Sir Jack) Jacob, QC; *m* 1967, Wendy Jones; three *s*. *Educ:* King Alfred Sch., Hampstead; Mountgrace Secondary Comprehensive Sch., Potters Bar; St Paul's Sch.; Trinity Coll., Cambridge (BA, MA); LSE (LLB; Hon. Fellow, 2005). Called to the Bar, Gray's Inn, 1965 (Atkin Scholar; Bencher, 1989; Vice-Treas., 2006; Treas., 2007); teacher of law, 1965–66; pupillage with Nigel Bridge (later Lord Bridge of Harwich), 1966–67, with A. M. Walton, 1967; entered chambers of Thomas Blanco White, 1967; Junior Counsel to Treasury in Patent Matters, 1976–81; QC 1981; a Judge of the High Court of Justice, Chancery Div., 1993–2003. Dep. Chm., Copyright Tribunal, 1989–93; apptd to hear appeals to Sec. of State under the Trade Marks Acts, 1988–93. Member: Adv. Bd, Centre for European Law, KCL, 2002–; Adv. Council on Intellectual Property Law, Osgoode Hall Law Sch., 2009–; Econ. and Scientific Adv. Bd, Eur. Patent Office, 2012–. Governor: LSE, 1994–; Expert Witness Inst., 1996–2006, 2011–. Hon. Vis. Prof. of Law, Univ. of Birmingham, 1999–; Dist. Judicial Visitor, UCL, 2002–11. Pres., Intellectual Property Judges' Assoc., 2013–; Hon. President: Assoc. of Law Teachers, 2002–; Licensing Exec. Soc., 2003–. Hon. Fellow, St Peter's Coll., Oxford, 1998. Hon. LLD Wolverhampton, 2009. Jt Editor, Encyclopedia of UK and European Patent Law, 1977–. *Publications:* Kerly's Law of Trade Marks (ed jtly), 1972, 1983 and 1986 edns; Patents, Trade Marks, Copyright and Designs (ed jtly), 1970, 1978, 1986; Editor, Court Forms Sections on Copyright (1978), Designs and Trade Marks (1975–86); section on Trade Marks (ed jtly), 4th edn, Halsbury's Laws of England, 1985, 1995; Guidebook of Intellectual Property, 1993, 6th edn 2013; IP and Other Things, 2015; articles and lectures. *Recreations:* Arsenal FC, photography, country garden. *Address:* Faculty of Laws, University College London, Bentham House, Endsleigh Gardens, WC1H 0EG. *E:* rjacob@ucl.ac.uk.

JACOB, Ven. William Mungo, PhD; FRHistS; Archdeacon of Charing Cross, 1996–2015, now Archdeacon Emeritus; Rector, St Giles-in-the-Fields, 2000–15; Priest-in-charge: St Anne's, Soho with St Thomas and St Peter, 2011–13; St John's, East Dulwich, since 2015; *b* 15 Nov. 1944; *s* of John William Carey Jacob and Mary Marsters Dewar. *Educ:* King Edward VII School, King's Lynn; Hull Univ. (LLB); Linacre Coll., Oxford (MA); Exeter Univ. (PhD). FRHistS 2013. Deacon 1970, priest 1971; Curate of Wymondham, Norfolk, 1970–73; Asst Chaplain, Exeter Univ., 1973–75; Lecturer, Salisbury and Wells Theological Coll., 1975–80, Vice-Principal, 1977–80; Sec. to Cttee for Theological Education, ACCM, 1980–86; Warden, Lincoln Theol Coll., 1986–96; Canon of Lincoln Cathedral, 1986–96. D. J. James Prof. of Pastoral Theol., Univ. of Wales, Lampeter, 2006–09. Vis. Res. Fellow, KCL, 2011–. Ed., Theology, 1998–2008. *Publications:* (ed with P. Baelz) Ministers of the Kingdom, 1985; (contrib.) Religious Dissent in East Anglia, 1991; (contrib.) The Weight of Glory, 1991; (ed with N. Yates) Crown and Mitre, 1993; Lay People and Religion in the Early Eighteenth Century, 1996; The Making of the Anglican Church Worldwide, 1997; (contrib.) The National Church in Local Perspective, 2003; (contrib.) Studies in Church History, vols 16, 28, 31, 38, 40, 42, 50; (contrib.) Anglicanism and the Western Christian Tradition, 2003; (contrib.) The Pastor Bonus, 2004; (contrib.) St Paul's: the Cathedral Church of London 604–2004, 2004; (contrib.) Cambridge History of Libraries in Britain and Ireland, vol. 2, 2006; The Clerical Profession in the Long Eighteenth Century, 1680–1840, 2007; (contrib.) Treasures of the English Church, 2008; (contrib.) Lambeth Palace Library: treasures from the collections of the Archbishops of Canterbury, 2010; (contrib.) Comfortable Words: polity, piety and the Book of Common Prayer, 2012; contribs to Jl Anglican Studies, Liby and Information Studies. *Address:* 4 St Mary's Walk, SE11 4UA. *T:* (020) 7582 2025.

JACOBI, Sir Derek (George), Kt 1994; CBE 1985; actor; *b* 22 Oct. 1938; *s* of Alfred George Jacobi and Daisy Gertrude Masters. *Educ:* Leyton County High Sch.; St John's Coll., Cambridge (MA Hons; Hon. Fellow, 1987). Artistic Associate, Old Vic Co. (formerly Prospect Theatre Co.), 1976–81; associate actor, RSC; Artistic Dir, Chichester Fest. Th., 1995–96. Vice-Pres., Nat. Youth Theatre, 1982–. *Stage:* Birmingham Repertory Theatre, 1960–63 (first appearance in One Way Pendulum, 1961); National Theatre, 1963–71; Prospect Theatre Co., 1972, 1974, 1976, 1977, 1978; Hamlet (for reformation of Old Vic Co., and at Elsinore), 1979; Benedick in Much Ado About Nothing (Tony Award, 1985), title rôle in Peer Gynt, Prospero in The Tempest, 1982, title rôle in Cyrano de Bergerac, 1983 (SWET Award; Plays and Players Award), RSC; Breaking the Code, Haymarket, 1986, Washington and NY 1987; Dir, Hamlet, Phoenix, 1988; title rôle in Kean, Old Vic, 1990; title rôle in Becket, Haymarket, 1991; Byron, in Mad, Bad and Dangerous to Know, Ambassadors, 1992; Macbeth, RSC, 1993; title rôle in Hadrian VII, Playing the Wife, Chichester, 1995; Uncle Vanya, Chichester, 1996, NY, 2000; God Only Knows, Vaudeville, 2001; The Tempest, Old Vic, 2003; Don Carlos, Gielgud, 2005; A Voyage Round My Father, Wyndham's, 2006; Malvolio in Twelfth Night, Wyndham's, 2008 (Olivier Award, Best Actor); title rôle in King Lear, Donmar Warehouse, 2010; Heartbreak House, Chichester, 2012; *appearances include: TV:* She Stoops to Conquer, Man of Straw, The Pallisers, I Claudius, Philby, Burgess and Maclean, Richard II, Hamlet, Inside the Third Reich, Mr Pye, Cadfael; The Gathering Storm, 2002; The Jury, 2002; The Long Firm, 2004; The Old Curiosity Shop, 2007; Last Tango in Halifax, 2012–15; Vicious, 2013, 2015; *films:* 1971–: Odessa File; Day of the Jackal; The Medusa Touch; Othello; Three Sisters; Interlude; The Human Factor; Charlotte; The Man Who Went Up in Smoke; Enigma; Little Dorrit (Best Actor Award, Evening Standard); Henry V; The Fool; Dead Again; Hamlet; Love is the Devil (Best Actor Award, Evening Standard); Gladiator; The Body; Gosford Park; A Revenger's Tragedy; Nanny McPhee; The Golden Compass; A Bunch of Amateurs; The King's Speech; Anonymous; Grace of Monaco; Cinderella. *Awards:* BAFTA Best Actor, 1976–77; Variety Club TV Personality, 1976; Standard Best Actor, 1983. *Publications:* As Luck Would Have It, 2013. *Address:* c/o Independent Talent Group Ltd, 40 Whitfield Street, W1T 2RH.

JACOBS, Edward John; an Upper Tribunal Judge (Administrative Appeals Chamber) (formerly Social Security and Child Support Commissioner), since 1998; *b* 20 Nov. 1952; *m* Jill, *d* of W. J. Langford. *Educ:* Paston Sch.; Univ. of Southampton. Called to the Bar, Inner Temple, 1976. *Publications:* Effective Exclusion Clauses, 1990; (with M. Jones) Company Meetings: law and procedure, 1991; Child Support: the legislation, 1993, 12th edn 2015; Tribunal Practice and Procedure, 2009, 3rd edn 2014; (ed and contrib.) Jowitt's Dictionary of

English Law, 3rd edn 2010; contrib. articles to legal jls. *Recreations:* ancient and medieval murder, cross-country ski-ing. *Address:* Upper Tribunal, Administrative Appeals Chamber, 5th Floor, Rolls Building, 7 Rolls Buildings, Fetter Lane, EC4A 1NL.

JACOBS, Rt Hon. Sir Francis (Geoffrey), KCMG 2006; PC 2005; Professor of Law, since 2006, and President, Centre of European Law, since 2007, King's College London; an Advocate General, Court of Justice of the European Communities, 1988–2006; *b* 8 June 1939; *s* of late Cecil Sigismund Jacobs and Louise Jacobs (*née* Fischhof); *m* 1st, 1964, Ruth (*née* Freeman); one *s*; 2nd, 1975, Susan Felicity Gordon (*née* Cox); one *s* three *d*. *Educ:* City of London Sch.; Christ Church, Oxford; Nuffield Coll., Oxford. MA, DPhil. Called to the Bar, Middle Temple, 1964, Bencher, 1990, Reader, 2009; in part-time practice, 1974–88, 2006–; QC 1984; Lectr in Jurisprudence, Univ. of Glasgow, 1963–65; Lectr in Law, LSE, 1965–69; Secretariat, European Commn of Human Rights, and Legal Directorate, Council of Europe, Strasbourg, 1969–72; Legal Sec., Court of Justice of European Communities, Luxembourg, 1972–74; Prof. of European Law, Univ. of London, 1974–88; Dir, Centre of Eur. Law, 1981–88, Vis. Prof., 1989–2006, KCL. Pres., UK Assoc. for European Law, 2009–13 (Hon. Sec., 1974–81; a Vice-Pres., 1988–2009); Trustee, British Inst. of Internat. and Comparative Law, 2006–09, 2010–. Chm., Eur. Maritime Law Orgn, 2005–12; Pres., Admin. Tribunal, Internat. Inst. for Unification of Private Law, 2009–; Pres., 2011–13, Mem. Senate, 2013–, European Law Inst. Cooley Lectr, 1983, Bishop Lectr, 1989, LeRoy Fellow, 1993, 2002, Jean Monnet Fellow, 2006, Univ. of Mich.; Hamlyn Lectr, 2006; British Acad. Law Lect., 2008. Marcel Storme Prof., Univ. of Ghent, 2005–06; Jean Monnet Prof., KCL, 2006–; Prof., Coll. of Europe, Bruges, 2006–09. Governor: British Inst. of Human Rights, 1985–; Inns of Court Sch. of Law, 1996–2001. Patron, UK Envmtl Law Assoc., 2007–; Pres., 2007–13, Patron, 2013–, Missing Children Europe. FKC, 1990. Hon. Fellow, Soc. for Advanced Legal Studies, 1998; Hon. Mem., Soc. of Legal Scholars, 2003; Foreign Mem., Royal Flemish Acad. of Belgium for Sci. and Arts, 2005. Hon. LLD: Birmingham, 1996; Glasgow, 2006; Kingston, 2012; Hon. DCL City, 1997; Hon. Dr Ghent, 2007; Hon. DLaws, Groningen, 2014. Hon. Texan, 2000. Commandeur de l'Ordre de Mérite, Luxembourg, 1983. Founding Editor, Yearbook of European Law, 1981–88; Mem. Editl Bd, Yearbook of European Law and many law reviews. Gen. Ed., Oxford EC Law Library (formerly Oxford European Community Law series), 1986–2010. *Publications:* Criminal Responsibility, 1971; The European Convention on Human Rights, 1975, 2nd edn (with Robin C. A. White), 1996; (jtly) References to the European Court, 1975; (ed) European Law and the Individual, 1976; (jtly) The Court of Justice of the European Communities, 1977; (jtly) The European Union Treaty, 1986; (joint editor): The European Community and GATT, 1986; The Effect of Treaties in Domestic Law, 1987; Liber Amicorum Pierre Pescatore, 1987; European Community Law in English Courts, 1998; (contrib.) de Smith, Woolf and Jowell, Judicial Review of Administrative Action, 1995; The Sovereignty of Law: the European way, 2007; *relevant publications:* Continuity and Change in EU Law: essays in honour of Sir Francis Jacobs, 2008; Making Community Law: the legacy of Advocate General Jacobs at the European Court of Justice, 2008. *Recreations:* family life, books, music, nature, travel. *Address:* Wayside, 15 St Alban's Gardens, Teddington, Middx TW11 8AE. *T:* (020) 8943 0503. *E:* francis.jacobs@kcl.ac.uk; Fountain Court, Temple, EC4Y 9DH.

JACOBS, Prof. Ian Jeffrey, MD; FRCOG; President and Vice-Chancellor, UNSW Australia, since 2015; *b* 6 Oct. 1957; *s* of Sidney and Shirley Jacobs; *m* 1988, Chris Steele; two *s* one *d*. *Educ:* Trinity Coll., Cambridge (BA 1980, MA 1983); London Univ. (MB BS 1983; MD 1991). FRCOG (MRCOG 1990). Consultant Gynaecological Oncologist, Bart's and the London NHS Trust, 1996–2004; Prof. of Gynaecological Oncology, 1999–2004, and Dir, Cancer Inst., 2002–04, Bart's and the London, Queen Mary's Sch. of Medicine; Hd of Res., Dept. of Gynaecological Cancer, UCL, 2004–11; Gynaecol Oncologist, UCLH, 2004–11; Director: Inst. for Women's Health, UCL, 2004–09; UCLH/UCL Comprehensive Biomed. Res. Centre, 2007–10; Dean of Biomed. Scis, UCL, 2009–10; Res. Dir, UCL Partners Academic Health Sci. Centre, 2009–10; Prof. of Women's Health and Cancer, UCL, 2004–11; Sen. Investigator, NIHR, 2009–14; Vice Pres. and Dean, Faculty of Med. and Health Scis, Manchester Univ., 2010–15; Hd, Manchester Academic Health Sci. Centre, 2011–15. Hon. Consultant: Royal Marsden Hosp., 1996–2010; Central Manchester NHS Trust, Manchester, 2011–14. Non-exec. Dir, Abcodia Ltd, 2012–. Founder and Mem. Bd, Uganda Women's Health Initiative, 2005– (Chm., 2005–15). *Publications:* over 200 articles on Ovarian Cancer; numerous contribs to med. and scientific jls, incl. Lancet, BMJ and Cancer Res. *Recreations:* Arsenal football fan, dogs, family life, running, charitable work. *Address:* Office of the President and Vice-Chancellor, UNSW Australia, Sydney, NSW 2052, Australia.

JACOBS, Rabbi Irving, PhD; Principal, Jews' College, London, 1990–93; *b* 2 Aug. 1938; *s* of Solomon Jacobs and Bertha (*née* Bluestone); *m* 1963, Ann Klein; one *s* three *d*. *Educ:* Jews' Coll., London; Univ. of London (BA, PhD); Rabbinical Dip. Jews' College, London: Res. Fellow, 1966–69; Lectr, 1969–75; Sen. Lectr, 1975–84; Dean, 1984–90. *Publications:* The Midrashic Process, 1995; The Impact of Midrash, 2006; articles on Midrash Apocryphal lit. and Jewish liturgy in scholarly jls. *Address:* 28 Elmstead Avenue, Wembley, Middx HA9 8NX. *T:* (020) 8248 5777.

JACOBS, Jeffrey, CB 2002; Head of Paid Service and Director of Communities and Intelligence, since 2011, and Greater London Returning Officer, since 2014, Greater London Authority; *b* 20 July 1949; *s* of late Sydney and Jane Jacobs; *m* 1974, Mary Jane Whitelegg; one *s* one *d*. *Educ:* Enfield Grammar Sch. Joined Ministry of Housing and Local Government, later Department of the Environment, 1965: Asst Private Sec. to Sec. of State for Envmt, 1979–82; Head: Housing Policies Studies Div., 1987–90; Envmt Agency Project Team, 1990–92; Manchester Olympic Unit, 1992–94; Regeneration Div., 1994–97; Principal Private Sec. to Dep. Prime Minister, 1997–98; Dir, Planning Directorate, DETR, 1998–2001; Exec. Dir, Policy and Partnerships, GLA, 2001–04; Dir Gen., Children and Young People and Communities, 2004–06, Chief Exec., Govt Olympic Exec., 2006–07, DCMS; Sen. Advr to Mayor of London, 2007–08; Exec. Dir and Dep. Chief Exec., GLA, 2008–11. Fellow, Hubert H. Humphrey Inst., Minneapolis, 1986–87. *Recreations:* sport, walking. *E:* jacobs116@sky.com.

JACOBS, John Robert Maurice, OBE 1997; golf entrepreneur; *b* 14 March 1925; *s* of Robert and Gertrude Vivian Jacobs; *m* 1949, Rita Wragg; one *s* one *d*. *Educ:* Maltby Grammar School. Asst Professional Golfer, Hallamshire Golf Club, 1947–49; Golf Professional: Gezira Sporting Club, Cairo, 1949–52; Sandy Lodge Golf Club, 1952–64; Man. Dir, Athlon Golf, 1967–75; Professional Golfers' Association: Tournament Dir-Gen., 1971–76, Advr to Tournament Div., 1977; European Ryder Cup Captain, 1979–81 (player, 1955); Golf Instructor: Golf Digest Magazine Schs, 1971–76; Golf Magazine Schs, US, 1977. Adviser to: Walker Cup Team; Spanish and French nat. teams; Past Adviser to: Curtis Cup Team; English Golf Union team; Scottish Union team; German, Swedish and Italian teams. Golf Commentator, ITV, 1967–87. Currently associated with John Jacobs' Practical Golf Schools, based in USA. Golf adviser to Golf World Magazine, 1962–86. President: PGA of Europe, 1999–2000; Orgn of Golf Range Owners, 2002–; Founder Mem., Professional Golfers' Architects Assoc., 2002–; Vice-Pres., Assoc. of Golf Writers, 1996– (Michael Williams Award, 2003). Legends in Golf Award, Irish Legends Golf Soc., 1994; Medal of Merit, Spanish Royal Golf Fedn, 1995; 5-Star Professional Award, PGA of Europe, 1996; Lifetime Achievement Award, 1996; Geoffrey Dyson Trophy, Sportscoach UK, 2002; Lindberg Bowl for services to European golf, PGA, 2005; PGA Master Professional, 2006; Lifetime Achievement Award, Sportscoach UK, 2008. Inducted World Golf Hall of Fame, 2000, World Golf Teaching Hall of Fame, 2001. *Publications:* Golf, 1961; Play Better Golf, 1969; Practical Golf, 1973; John Jacobs Analyses the Superstars, 1974; Golf Doctor, 1979; The Golf Swing Simplified, 1993; Golf in a Nutshell, 1995; 50 Greatest Golf Lessons of the Century, 1999; 50 Years of Golfing Wisdom, 2005. *Recreations:* shooting, fishing. *Address:* Stable Cottage, Chapel Lane, Lyndhurst, Hants SO43 7FG. *T:* (023) 8028 2743. *Clubs:* Royal and Ancient Golf (St Andrews), Sandy Lodge Golf, New Forest Golf, Brokenhurst Manor Golf, Bramshaw Golf, Burley Golf, Hamptworth Golf and Country, Wellow Golf (Vice Pres., 2002–), Walton Heath Golf; Lake Nona Golf and Country (Florida).

JACOBS, Laurence Warren; Partner, Milbank Tweed, since 2004; *b* London, 21 March 1960; *s* of Sidney and Shirley Jacobs; *m* 1984, Ann Gainsford; one *s* three *d*. *Educ:* Haberdashers' Aske's Sch., Elstree; Queens' Coll., Cambridge (BA Hist. 1982); King's Coll., Cambridge. Admitted Solicitor, 1990; Articled Clerk, 1988–90, Associate, 1990–92, Clifford Chance; Associate, 1992–98, Partner, 1998–2004, Allen & Overy. *Recreations:* reading, hiking, family, living in Jerusalem. *Address:* Milbank Tweed, 10 Gresham Street, EC2V 7JD. *T:* (020) 7615 3000, *Fax:* (020) 7615 3100. *E:* ljacobs@milbank.com.

JACOBS, Michael Upton; Senior Adviser, Global Commission on the Economy and Climate, since 2013; *b* London, 3 Dec. 1960; *s* of Arthur Jacobs and Betty Upton Hughes; *m* 1997, Catherine McKenzie; one *s* two *d*. *Educ:* Woodhouse Sch.; Wadham Coll., Oxford (BA Hons PPE); Middlesex Poly. (Postgrad. Dip. Employment and Planning). Dir, then Man. Dir, CAG Consultants, 1990–94; ESRC Res. Fellow, Centre for Study of Envmtl Change and Dept of Geog., LSE, 1994–97; Gen. Sec., Fabian Soc., 1997–2003; Mem., Council of Econ. Advrs, HM Treasury, 2004–07; Special Advr to Prime Minister, 10 Downing St, 2007–10; Sen. Advr, Inst. du Développement Durable et des Relations Internationales, 2013–14. Visiting Professor: Grantham Res. Inst. on Climate Change and Envmt, LSE, 2010–; Dept of Political Sci., UCL, 2011–; Associate Fellow, IPPR, 2011–. Mem., Editl Bd, 2002–, Co-Ed., 2012–14, Political Qly. Member: Climate Change Adv. Bd, Children's Investment Fund Foundn, 2010–; Supervisory Bd, Eur. Climate Foundn, 2011–13. Trustee: Action Aid, 2004–07. *Publications:* The Green Economy: environment, sustainable development and the politics of the future, 1991; The Politics of the Real World, 1996; (ed) Greening the Millennium: the new politics of the environment, 1997; Paying for Progress: a new politics of tax for public spending, 2000. *Recreations:* art, theatre, cycling, 5-a-side football, sailing, school governor. *Address:* c/o New Climate Economy, Overseas Development Institute, 203 Blackfriars Road, SE1 8NJ.

JACOBS, Nigel Robert; QC 2006; barrister and arbitrator; *b* 31 May 1960; *m* 1993, Suzanne Tanchan; two *d*. *Educ:* Highgate Sch.; Pembroke Coll., Cambridge (BA 1982); Trinity Coll., Cambridge (LLM 1984). Called to the Bar, Middle Temple, 1983. *Recreations:* tennis, theatre, cinema. *Address:* Quadrant Chambers, 10 Fleet Street, EC4Y 1UA. *T:* (020) 7583 4444, *Fax:* (020) 7583 4455.

JACOBS, Prof. Patricia Ann, OBE 1999; FRS 1993; Co-Director of Research, Wessex Regional Genetics Laboratory, 2001–15 (Director, 1988–2001); *b* 8 Oct. 1934; *d* of Cyril Jacobs and Sadie Jacobs (*née* Jones); *m* 1972, Newton Ennis Morton; three step *s* two step *d*. *Educ:* St Andrews Univ. (BSc 1st Cl. Hons 1956; D'Arcy Thomson Medal 1956; DSc 1966; Sykes Medal 1966). FRSE 1977; FRCPath 1987; FRCPE 1998; FRCOG 1999. Res. Asst, Mount Holyoke Coll., USA, 1956–57; Scientist, MRC, 1957–72; Prof., Dept of Anatomy and Reproductive Biology, Univ. of Hawaii Sch. of Medicine, 1972–85; Prof. and Chief of Div. of Human Genetics, Dept of Pediatrics, Cornell Univ. Med. Coll., 1985–87. Hon. Prof. of Human Genetics, Univ. of Southampton Med. Sch., 1993. Mem., MRC, 1996–98. Founder FMedSci 1998; FRSA 1993. Foreign Associate, NAS, 2009. Hon. DSc St Andrews, 2002. Allan Award, Amer. Soc. of Human Genetics, 1981; Regents Medal, Univ. of Hawaii, 1983; Premio Phoenix Anni-Verdi, 1998; Mauro Baschirotto Award, European Soc. of Human Genetics, 1999; March of Dimes Prize in Develtl Biol., 2011. *Publications:* numerous articles in learned jls. *Recreations:* walking, botany, gardening.

See also Peter A. Jacobs.

JACOBS, Peter Alan; non-executive Chairman: L. A. Fitness (formerly L. A. Leisure), 1999–2005; W. T. Foods, 2002–05; *b* 22 Feb. 1943; *s* of Cyril and Sadie Jacobs; *m* 1966, Eileen Dorothy Naftalin; twin *s* one *d*. *Educ:* Glasgow Univ. (BSc Hons MechEng); Aston Univ. (Dip. Management Studies). Tube Investments: grad. trainee, 1965–67; Production Controller, Toy Div., 1968–70; Pedigree Petfoods: Production Shift Manager, 1970–72; Purchasing Dept, 1972–81; Production Manager, 1981–83; Sales Dir, Mars Confectionery, 1983–86; Berisford International: Man. Dir, British Sugar, 1986–89; Chief Exec., Berisford and Chm., British Sugar, 1989–91; Chief Exec., BUPA, 1991–98; non-executive Chairman: Healthcall Ltd, 1998–2001; Hillsdown Holdings plc, 1999–2000; abc Media, 2005–10; non-executive Director: Allied Domecq, 1998–2004; Bank Leumi (UK), 1999–2003; Virtual Communities Inc., 1999–2000; RAF Air Command (formerly RAF Strike Command), 2002–09. *Recreations:* tennis, theatre, music. *Address:* Garden Flat, 29 Daleham Gardens, NW3 5BY. *Club:* Royal Automobile.

See also Patricia A. Jacobs.

JACOBS, His Honour Peter John; a Circuit Judge, 1997–2013; *b* 16 April 1943; *s* of Herbert Walter Jacobs and Emma Doris Jacobs; *m* 1975, Dr Ruth Edwards; two *s*. *Educ:* King Edward VII Sch., King's Lynn; University Coll., Cardiff (BA Hons 1964). Schoolmaster: Barry Boys' Grammar Sch., 1965–68; Cathays High Sch., 1968–72; called to the Bar, Gray's Inn, 1973; practice, 1973–97; Standing Counsel to Inland Revenue, 1995–97; Resident Judge, Norwich Crown Court, 2004–13. Mem. (L), Barry Borough Council, 1966–69. Pres., Old Lennensians Assoc., 2006–. Hon. Recorder of Norwich, 2008–13. *Recreations:* watching Norwich City Football Club, fine art, Norfolk railways and churches. *Address:* White Lodge, 133 Lower Street, Horning, Norwich, Norfolk NR12 8PF. *Clubs:* Norfolk (Norwich); Norwich City Football.

JACOBS, Richard David; QC 1998; a Recorder, since 2002; *b* 21 Dec. 1956; *s* of late Elliott Jacobs, chartered accountant, and of Ruth Jacobs (*née* Ellenbogen); *m* 1990, Pamela Fine; one *s* two *d*. *Educ:* Highgate Sch.; Pembroke Coll., Cambridge. Called to the Bar, Middle Temple, 1979, Bencher, 2011. Vis. Fellow, LSE, 2003. *Publications:* (jtly) Liability Insurance in International Arbitration: the Bermuda form, 2004, 2nd edn 2011. *Recreations:* tennis, Arsenal FC, theatre, piano. *Address:* Essex Court Chambers, 24 Lincoln's Inn Fields, WC2A 3EG. *T:* (020) 7813 8000. *Clubs:* MCC, Royal Automobile.

JACOBSON, Howard Eric, FRSL; novelist; critic; *b* 25 Aug. 1942; *s* of Max Jacobson and Anita (*née* Black); *m* 1st, 1964, Barbara Starr (marr. diss.); one *s*; 2nd, 1978, Rosalin Sadler (marr. diss.); 3rd, 2005, Jenny De Yong. *Educ:* Stand Grammar Sch., Whitefield; Downing Coll., Cambridge (BA, MA; Hon. Fellow). Lectr in English Lit., Univ. of Sydney, Australia, 1965–67; Tutor in English, Selwyn Coll., Cambridge, 1968–72; Sen. Lectr, Wolverhampton Poly., 1974–80. Vis. Prof., New Coll. of Humanities, 2012–. Writer and presenter, TV documentaries: Into the Land of Oz, 1991; Yo, Mrs Askew, 1991; Roots Schmoots, 1993; Sorry, Judas, 1993; Seriously Funny, 1997; Howard Jacobson Takes on the Turner, 2000; Why the Novel Matters: a South Bank Show Special, 2002; Jesus the Jew, 2009; Creation, 2010; Flesh, 2010; Rebels of Oz, 2014; contrib. to Late Show, 1989–, Late Rev., 1995–. TV critic, The Correspondent, 1989–90; columnist, The Independent, 1998–. Mem., Editl Bd, Modern Painters, 1990–2005. FRSL 2012. *Publications:* (with W. Sanders) Shakespeare's Magnanimity, 1978; In the Land of Oz, 1987; Roots Schmoots, 1993; Seeing with the Ear (Peter Fuller Meml Lecture), 1993; Seriously Funny, 1997; Whatever It Is, I Don't Like It, 2011; *novels:* Coming from Behind, 1983; Peeping Tom, 1984; Redback, 1986; The Very

Model of a Man, 1992; No More Mister Nice Guy, 1998; The Mighty Walzer, 1999 (Everyman Bollinger Wodehouse Prize for Comic Writing, Jewish Qly Wingate Prize, 2000); Who's Sorry Now?, 2002; The Making of Henry, 2004; Kalooki Nights, 2006 (Jewish Qly Wingate Prize, 2007); The Act of Love, 2008; The Finkler Question, 2010 (Man Booker Prize, 2010); Zoo Time, 2012 (Everyman Bollinger Wodehouse Prize for Comic Writing, 2013); J, 2014. *Address:* c/o Curtis Brown, Haymarket House, 28–29 Haymarket, SW1Y 4SP. *T:* (020) 7393 4400. *Clubs:* Chelsea Arts, Groucho.

JACOBUS, Prof. Mary Longstaff, CBE 2012; DPhil; FBA 2009; Professor of English (Grace 2), 2000–11, now Emerita, and Director, Centre for Research in the Arts, Social Sciences and Humanities, 2006–11, University of Cambridge; Fellow of Churchill College, Cambridge, since 2000; *b* 4 May 1944; *d* of Marcus Jacobus and Diana (*née* Longstaff); *m* 1981, A. Reeve Parker; one *s* one *d*. *Educ:* Oxford High Sch. for Girls, GPDST; Lady Margaret Hall, Oxford (BA 1st Cl. Hons English 1965, MA; DPhil 1970; Hon. Fellow, 2000). Oxford University: Randall McIver Jun. Res. Fellow, 1968–70, Fellow and Tutor in English, 1971–80, Lady Margaret Hall; CUF Lectr, English Faculty, 1972–80; Lectr, Manchester Univ., 1970–71; Cornell University: Associate Prof. of English, 1980–82; Prof. of English, 1982–89, now Emerita; John Wendell Anderson Prof. of English and Women's Studies, 1989–2000. Hon. Res. Fellow, LMH, Oxford, 1980–2000. Guggenheim Fellow, 1988–89. M. H. Abrams Distinguished Vis. Prof., Cornell Univ., 2011–12. *Publications:* Tradition and Experiment in Wordsworth's Lyrical Ballads (1798), 1976; (ed) Women Writing and Women Writing About Women, 1979; Reading Woman: essays in feminist criticism, 1986; (ed jtly) Body/Politics: women and the discourse of science, 1989; Romanticism, Writing and Sexual Difference: essays on The Prelude, 1989; First Things: the maternal imaginary in literature, art and psychoanalysis, 1996; Psychoanalysis and the Scene of Reading, 1999; The Poetics of Psychoanalysis: in the wake of Klein, 2005; Romantic Things: a tree, a rock, a cloud, 2012; Cy Twombly: poet in paint, 2015. *Address:* Faculty of English, University of Cambridge, 9 West Road, Cambridge CB3 9DP. *T:* (01223) 335070.

JACOBY, Stefan; Executive Vice President, Consolidated International Operations, General Motors Co., since 2013; *b* Hannover, Germany, 10 April 1958; *s* of Hans Albin Jacoby and Anne Marie Jacoby; *m* 2006, Roberta Bantel; two *s* one *d*. *Educ:* Univ. of Cologne (Dip. KFM; MBA). Analyst, Industrial Sales and Controlling Dept, Volkswagen AG, 1985–88; Pricing Manager, Product and Mktg Depts, Volkswagen of America, 1988–90; Manager, Pricing Dept, Commercial Vehicle Div., Volkswagen AG, 1989–90; Gen. Manager of Controlling, Volkswagen Audi Nippon KK, Japan, 1990–92; Volkswagen AG: Gen. Manager, Export Sales Planning Dept, 1992–95; Hd, Gen. Office of Chm., Bd of Mgt, 1995–97; Vice Pres., Asia-Pacific, Volkswagen Asia-Pacific Ltd, 1997–2001; Pres. and CEO Europe, Mitsubishi Motors Europe BV (Amsterdam), 2001–04; Exec. Vice Pres. and Gen. Rep., Mktg and Sales, Volkswagen AG, 2004–07; Pres. and CEO, Volkswagen Gp of America Inc., 2007–10; Pres. and CEO, Volvo Car Corp., 2010–12.

JACOMB, Sir Martin (Wakefield), Kt 1985; Advisor: Share plc, since 2013 (Chairman, 2001–13); Pension Insurance Corporation Ltd, since 2013 (Chairman, 2006–12); Special Advisor, Canary Wharf Group PLC, since 2011 (Chairman, 2003–11; Director, 2009–11); *b* 11 Nov. 1929; *s* of Hilary W. Jacomb and Félise Jacomb; *m* 1960, Evelyn Heathcoat Amory (MBE 2007); two *s* one *d*. *Educ:* Eton Coll.; Worcester Coll., Oxford (MA Law 1953; Hon. Fellow, 1994). 2nd Lieut, RA, 1948–49. Called to the Bar, Inner Temple, 1955 (Hon. Bencher, 1987); practised at the Bar, 1955–68. Kleinwort Benson Ltd, 1968–85; Dep. Chm., Barclays Bank PLC, 1985–93; Chairman: Barclays de Zoete Wedd, 1986–91; Postel Investment Management, 1991–95; Delta plc, 1993–2003; Prudential Corp., 1995–2000 (Dir, 1994–2000); Director: The Telegraph plc (formerly Daily Telegraph), 1986–2000; Rio Tinto plc (formerly RTZ Corp.), 1988–2000; Marks and Spencer, 1991–2000; formerly Director: John Mowlem and Co. Ltd; Merchants Trust plc; Mercantile Credit Co. Ltd; British Gas; Christian Salvesen; Hudson's Bay Co.; Australian and NZ Bank. A Dir, Bank of England, 1986–95. Chm., British Council, 1992–98. Chm., Internat. Adv. Bd, First Avenue Partners, 2006–. External Mem., Finance Cttee, OUP, 1971–95. Mem., Nolan Cttee on Standards in Public Life, 1994–97. Director, Oxford Playhouse Trust, 1999–2006. Trustee, Nat. Heritage Meml Fund, 1982–97. Chancellor, Univ. of Buckingham, 1998–2010. Hon. FKC 2007. Hon. Dr: Humberside, 1993; Buckingham, 1997; Hon. DCL Oxford, 1997. *Recreations:* theatre, family bridge, visual arts, the outdoors.

JACOVIDES, Mario; Global Head of Structured and Asset Finance, Allen & Overy LLP, since 2009 (Partner, since 1999); *b* London, 1964; *s* of Christakis and Yiannoulla Jacovides; *m* 1995, Maria Pieretti; two *s*. *Educ:* Chace Sch.; Univ. of E Anglia (LLB Hons). Admitted solicitor, 1989. Wilde Sapte: trainee, 1987, then solicitor; Partner, 1995–99. *Recreations:* ornithology, fishing, golf, tennis. *Address:* Allen & Overy LLP, One Bishops Square, E1 6AB. *T:* (020) 3088 2659. *E:* mario.jacovides@allenovery.com.

JACQUES, Dr David Lawson; garden historian; owner, Sugnall Estate, since 2003; *b* 29 Sept. 1948; *s* of late Greville Lawson Jacques and Anne Grace Jacques; *m* 1st, 1973, Rosalind Catherine Denny (marr. diss. 1993); two *d*; 2nd, 2004, Karen Sims-Neighbour. *Educ:* Univ. of Leeds (MSc Transportation Engrg 1972); Poly. of N London (DipTP 1977); Courtauld Inst., Univ. of London (PhD 1999). MCIHT (MIHT 1977); MRTPI 1981. Land Use Consultants, 1973–76; Jacques Miller Partnership, 1977–78; Associate, Travers Morgan Planning, 1978–87; Inspector of Historic Parks and Gardens, English Heritage, 1987–93; Consultant on historic landscapes, parks and gardens, 1993– (e.g. Privy Garden, Hampton Court; Tudor Garden, Kenilworth Castle); Lectr (pt-time) Landscapes and Gardens, Dept of Archaeol., Univ. of York, 1994–98; Prog. Dir, MA in Landscape Conservation and Change, Architectural Assoc., 2000–06. Vis. Prof., De Montfort Univ., 1999–2003. Mem. Council, 1975–2001, Chm., 1998–2000, Garden Hist. Soc.; International Council on Monuments and Sites: Co-ordinator, Landscapes Wkg Gp, 1991–95; Corresp. Mem., Internat. Cttee for Gdns and Sites, 1991–; Chm., UK Historic Gdns and Landscapes Cttee, 1993–98. Trustee and Chm., Gdns Cttee, Castle Bromwich Hall Gdns Trust, 1985–87; Chm., Bishop's Park Co-ordinating Gp, 1985–87; Trustee: Landscape Design Trust, 1994–; Chiswick House & Garden Trust, 2005–. Chairman: Staffs Gdns and Parks Trust, 1994–97; Friends of the William Salt Liby, 2004–. Chm., Hammersmith and Fulham Liberal Democrats, 1987–93. *Publications:* Georgian Gardens: the reign of nature, 1983, repr. 1990; (with A. J. Van der Horst) The Gardens of William and Mary, 1988; Strategic Guidance for Heritage Land in London, 1988; Essential to the pracktick part of phisick: the London apothecaries 1540–1617, 1994; Landscape Modernism Renounced: the career of Christopher Tunnard, 2009; Gardens of Court and Country: English design, 1630s to 1730s, 2015; contrib. chapters in books and articles to jls incl. Jl Gdn Hist. Soc., Landscape Design, Country Life, Jl Envmtl Mgt, Jl RTPI, Monuments Historiques, English Heritage Conservation Bull., Die Gartenkunst, Arte dei Giardini, Internat. Jl Heritage Studies, Jl Architectural Conservation, Schriftenreihe des Deutschen Rates für Landespflege, Tuinjournaal and Architectural Hist. *Recreations:* local history, croquet, visiting historic gardens. *Address:* Sugnall Hall, Sugnall, Stafford ST21 6NF. *T:* (01785) 851711. *Club:* Farmers.

JACQUES, Peter Roy Albert, CBE 1990; Secretary, TUC Social Insurance and Industrial Welfare Department, 1971–2000; *b* 12 Aug. 1939; *s* of George Henry Jacques and Ivy Mary Jacques (*née* Farr); *m* 1965, Jacqueline Anne Sears; one *s* one *d*. *Educ:* Archbishop Temple's Secondary Sch.; Newcastle upon Tyne Polytechnic (BSc Sociology); Univ. of Leicester. Building labourer, 1955–58; market porter, 1958–62; Asst, TUC Social Insce and Industrial Welfare Dept, 1968–71. Member: Industrial Injuries Adv. Council, 1972; Nat. Insce Adv. Cttee, 1972–78; Health and Safety Commn, 1974–95; Royal Commn on the Nat. Health Service, 1976–79; EEC Cttee on Health-Safety, 1976; NHS London Adv. Cttee, 1979; Social Security Adv. Cttee, 1980–95; Health Educn Council, 1984–87; Civil Justice Review Adv. Cttee, 1985–; Royal Commn on Envmtl Pollution, 1989–95; Employment Appeal Tribunal, 1996–2009. Jt Sec., BMA/TUC Cttee, 1972; Secretary: TUC Social Health and Envmt Protection Cttee (formerly Social Insurance and Industrial Welfare Cttee), 1972–93; TUC Health Services Cttee, 1979–2000; TUC Special Advr, 1992–95. Vice-Chm., Redbridge and Waltham Forest HA, 1996–99. Mem. Exec. Cttee, Royal Assoc. for Disability and Rehabilitation, 1975. *Publications:* responsible for TUC pubns Health-Safety Handbook; Occupational Pension Schemes. *Recreations:* reading, yoga, walking, camping, vegetable growing. *Address:* 8 Osborne Road, Buckhurst Hill, Essex IG9 5RR. *T:* (020) 8257 7757.

JAFFÉ, David Andrew, FSA; Senior Curator, National Gallery, 1998–2012; art consultant, since 2012; *b* 7 July 1953; *s* of Peter John Jaffé and Patricia Willis Jaffé (*née* Andrew); *m* 1988, Elizabeth Kate Stephen; two *s*. *Educ:* Geelong Grammar Sch.; Melbourne Univ. (BSc); Courtauld Inst. of Art, Univ. of London (MA). Lectr, Univ. of Qld, 1979–81; Curator, Australian Nat. Gall., 1982–90; engaged in research, 1990–94; Curator of Paintings, J. Paul Getty Mus., 1994–98. FSA 1989. Hon. Life Mem., Art Exhibns Australia, 2005. Commendatore, Stella della Solidarietà (Italy), 2004. *Publications:* Rubens: self portrait in focus, 1988; Rubens and the Italian Renaissance, 1992; Titian, 2003; Rubens: the making of a master, 2005; Rubens: Massacre of the Innocents, 2009; contrib. articles to jls incl. Apollo, Burlington mag., Jl Warburg and Courtauld Insts. *Recreations:* tennis, gymnastics. *Address:* 97 Knatchbull Road, SE5 9QU. *E:* davidjaffe7@gmail.com. *Club:* Melbourne (Melbourne).

JAFFERJEE, Aftab Asger; QC 2008; Senior Treasury Counsel, Central Criminal Court, 2001–11; *b* 25 June 1956; *s* of Asger Jafferjee and Tara Kajiji; *m* 2001, Nazli Javeri; two *d*. *Educ:* St Paul's Sch., Darjeeling; Rugby Sch.; Durham Univ. (BA Hons). Called to the Bar, Inner Temple, 1980, Bencher, 2011; Jun. Treasury Counsel, 1997–2001. Member: Professional Conduct Cttee of Bar (of England and Wales), 1994–96; Cttee, Criminal Bar Assoc., 1995–97. Criminal Lawyer of Year Award, Soc. of Asian Lawyers, 2012. *Recreations:* cuisine, travel, theatre (Founder, Castle Th. Co., Durham, 1977). *Address:* 2 Harcourt Buildings, Temple, EC4Y 9DB. *T:* (020) 7353 2112. *E:* ajafferjee@2hb.co.uk.

JAFFRAY, Alistair Robert Morton, CB 1978; Deputy Under-Secretary of State, Ministry of Defence, 1975–84; *b* 28 Oct. 1925; *s* of late Alexander George and Janet Jaffray; *m* 1st, 1953, Margaret Betty Newman (decd); two *s* one *d*; 2nd, 1980, Edna Mary (decd), *e d* of late S. J. Tasker, Brasted Chart. *Educ:* Clifton Coll.; Corpus Christi Coll., Cambridge. BA First Cl. Hons, Mod. Langs. Served War, RNVR, 1943–46. Apptd Home Civil Service (Admty), 1948; Private Sec. to First Lord of Admty, 1960–62; Private Sec. to successive Secretaries of State for Defence, 1968–70; Asst Under-Sec. of State, MoD, 1971, Dep. Sec. 1975; Sec. to Admty Bd, 1981–84. Governor, Clifton Coll., 1980–; Chm. Management Cttee, Royal Hospital Sch., Holbrook, 1985–91. *Address:* Okeford, 10 Lynch Road, Farnham, Surrey GU9 8BZ.

JAFFRAY, Sir William Otho, 5th Bt *cr* 1892; *b* 1 Nov. 1951; *s* of Sir William Edmund Jaffray, 4th Bt, TD, JP, DL and of Anne, *d* of Captain J. Otho Paget, MC, Thorpe Satchville, Leics; *S* father, 1953; *m* 1981, Cynthia Ross Corrington (marr. diss. 1997); three *s* one *d*; *m* 2009, Constance Haynes. *Heir:* *s* Nicholas Gordon Alexander Jaffray, *b* 18 Oct. 1982. *Address:* c/o 79 Carter Lane, EC4V 5EP.

JAFFREY, Saeed, OBE 1995; actor and writer; *b* 8 Jan. 1929; *s* of late Dr Hamid Hussain Joffrey and Hadia Begum Joffrey; *m* 1st, 1958, Madhur Bahadur (marr. diss. 1966); three *d*; 2nd, 1980, Jennifer Irene Sorrell. *Educ:* Allahabad Univ. (MA Medieval Hist. 1950); Catholic Univ., Washington DC (MFA Drama 1958). First Indian actor to tour USA in Shakespeare, 1958, and to appear on Broadway, in A Passage to India, 1962; *films* include: The Wilby Conspiracy, 1974; The Man Who Would Be King, 1975; The Chess Players, 1977 (Best Actor Awards, Filmfare, and Filmworld, 1978); Touch Wood, 1981; Masoom, 1982; Gandhi, 1982; My Beautiful Laundrette, 1985 (BAFTA award, 1986); A Passage to India, 1985; Ram Teri Ganga Maili, 1985; Henna, 1989; Masala (Canadian Acad. Award), 1992; *television* includes: Gangsters, 1975–77; Jewel in the Crown, Staying On, 1980–82; Far Pavilions, 1985; Partition, Tandoori Nights, 1985–87; Love Match, 1986; Killing on the Exchange, 1986; Rumpole, 1990; Little Napoleons, 1994–95; Common as Muck, 1996–97; Ravi Desai in Coronation Street, 1998–99; *theatre* includes: Captain Brassbound's Conversion, 1972; Midsummer Night's Dream, 1989; White Chameleon, 1991; My Fair Lady, 1997; The King & I, 2001; *radio* includes: wrote and presented first programme on India in America, Reflections of India, 1961–63; numerous plays incl. Art of Love (Kama Sutra), The Pump, Shakuntala, Savitri, A Suitable Boy, and The Silver Castle. *Publications:* Saeed: an actor's journey, 1998. *Recreations:* snooker, cartooning and caricatures, watching cricket and tennis.

JAGDEO, Bharrat; High Level Envoy for Sustainable Development in Forest Countries and Patron of Nature, International Union for the Conservation of Nature, since 2012; President and Commander-in-Chief of the Armed Forces, Republic of Guyana, 1999–2011; *b* 23 Jan. 1964; *m* 1998, Varshnie Jagdeo. *Educ:* Gibson Primary Sch.; Mahaica Multilateral Sch.; Univ. of Moscow (MSc Econs 1990). Economist, Macro-economic Planning Div., State Planning Secretariat, 1990–92; Special Advr to Minister of Finance, 1992–93; Jun. Minister of Finance, 1993–95; Minister of Finance, 1995–2001. Director: Guyana Water Authy; Nat. Bank of Industry and Commerce; Governor: IMF; World Bank; Caribbean Develt Bank (Dir); Inter American Develt Bank (Chm., Caribbean Gp of Govs). Nat. Authorising Officer, EU.

JAGGER, Bianca; Founder, President and Chief Executive, Bianca Jagger Human Rights Foundation, since 2005; *b* Managua, Nicaragua, 2 May 1950; *d* of Carlos Pérez-Mora and Dora Macias; *m* 1971, Michael Philip Jagger (*see* Sir M. P. Jagger) (marr. diss. 1979); one *d*. *Educ:* La Immaculada, Managua; Univ. Sciences Po, Paris. Actress: *films*: The Rutles: All You Need is Cash, 1978; Flesh Colour, 1978; The American Success Company, 1980; Cannonball Run, 1981; C.H.U.D II, 1989; *television*: Street Hawk, 1985; Miami Vice, 1986; Hotel, 1986; The Colbys, 1987. Writer of blog for Huffington Post, USA. Chair, World Future Council, 2007–09. Member: Coalition for Internat. Criminal Court; Exec. Dir's Leadership Council, Amnesty Internat., USA; Adv. Cttee, Human Rights Watch America; Adv. Bd, Creative Coalition; Women and Girls' Lead Initiative, Ind. Television Service, 2013–. Former Member: Adv. Bd, Coalition for Internat. Justice; Bd, People for the American Way; Twentieth Century Task Force to Apprehend War Criminals. Council of Europe Goodwill Ambassador, 2003–; Bonn Challenge Ambassador, IUCN, 2012–. Patron: Circle of Conscience, Amnesty Internat.; Global Network for Study of Human Rights and the Envmt, 2014–. Hon. DHum Stonehill Coll., Mass, 1983; Hon. Dr Human Rights Simmons Coll., Boston, 2008; Hon. LLD E London, 2010. Earth Day Internat. Award, UN, 1994; USA Media Spotlight Award for Leadership, Amnesty Internat., 1997; Green Globe Award, Rainbow Alliance, 1997; American Civil Liberties Union Award, 1998; Right Livelihood Award, 2004; World Achievement Award, Mikhail Gorbachev's World Awards, 2004; World Citizenship Award, Nuclear Age Peace Foundn, 2006; Latin American UK Award for Lifetime Achievement, Latin-UK Awards, 2014. *Publications:* contribs to newspapers incl. Observer, Guardian, Independent, Mail on Sunday, Sunday Express, New Statesman, European, NY Times, Washington Post, Dallas Morning News, Columbus Dispatcher, Libération, Le Journal du Dimanche, Le Juriste Internat., Panorama, Der Spiegel, Süddeutsche Zeitung. *Recreations:* family, nature, walking in the rainforest, photography, music, opera, art, cinema, theatre, yoga, horseback riding. *Address:* Unit 246, 272 Kensington High Street, W8 6ND. *E:* biancajagger1@gmail.com. *W:* www.biancajagger.com, www.twitter.com/BiancaJagger.

JAGGER, Ven. Ian; Archdeacon of Durham and Canon Residentiary of Durham Cathedral, since 2006; *b* 17 April 1955; *m* 1993, Ruth Green; one *s. Educ:* Huddersfield New Coll.; King's Coll., Cambridge (BA 1977, MA 1981); St John's Coll., Durham (BA 1980, MA 1987). Ordained deacon, 1982, priest, 1983; Curate, St Mary, Twickenham, 1982–85; Team Vicar, Willen, Milton Keynes, 1985–94; Team Rector, Fareham, 1994–98; RD Fareham, 1996–98; Canon Residentiary, Portsmouth Cathedral, 1998–2001; Archdeacon of Auckland, Dio. Durham, 2001–06. *Address:* 15 The College, Durham DH1 3EQ.

JAGGER, Jonathan David, LVO 2012; FRCS, FRCOphth; Surgeon-Oculist to the Queen, since 2002; Consultant Ophthalmologist: Royal Free Hospital, since 1986; King Edward VII's Hospital for Officers, since 1995; St Luke's Hospital for the Clergy, since 2000; *b* 12 April 1951; *s* of Lt-Col Derek Bourne Jagger and Pamela (*née* Jarratt); *m* 1977 Sarah Elisabeth Lee; one *s* one *d. Educ:* Uppingham; St Thomas' Hosp., London (MB, BS 1974); DO 1979. FRCS 1981; FRCOphth 1989. Registrar, Westminster Hosp., 1979–80; Resident Surgical Officer, 1980–83, Sen. Resident, 1983, Moorfields Eye Hosp.; Sen. Registrar, Western Ophthalmic Hosp. and Moorfields Eye Hosp., 1983–86; Cons. Ophthalmic Surgeon, UCH and Middx Hosp., 1986–89; Surgeon-Oculist to HM Household, 1999–2002. Cons. Ophthalmologist, Assoc. of Royal Naval Officers, 1998–. Mem. Council, RCOphth, 1990–94; Mem., Ophthalmic Qualifications Cttee, 1993–. FRSocMed. *Publications:* articles on cataract surgery, lasers, retinal disorders. *Recreations:* travel, ski-ing, DIY. *Address:* 119 Harley Street, W1G 6AU.

JAGGER, Sir Michael Philip, (Sir Mick), Kt 2002; singer, songwriter and film producer; *b* Dartford, Kent, 26 July 1943; *s* of late Basil Fanshawe, (Joe), Jagger and Eva Jagger; *m* 1st, 1971, Bianca Rose Pérez Morena de Macías (*see* Bianca Jagger) (marr. diss. 1979); one *d*; 2nd, 1990, Jerry Hall (marr. diss. 1999); two *s* two *d*; one *d* by Marsha Hunt; one *s* by Luciana Gimenez Morad. *Educ:* Dartford Grammar Sch.; LSE. Lead singer, Rolling Stones, 1962–; tours worldwide, 1964–. *Records include: albums:* The Rolling Stones, 1964; The Rolling Stones No 2, 1965; Out of Our Heads, 1965; Aftermath, 1966; Between the Buttons, 1967; Their Satanic Majesties Request, 1967; Beggars' Banquet, 1968; Let It Bleed, 1969; Get Yer Ya-Ya's Out!, 1970; Sticky Fingers, 1971; Exile on Main Street, 1972; Goat's Head Soup, 1973; It's Only Rock 'n' Roll, 1974; Black and Blue, 1976; Some Girls, 1978; Emotional Rescue, 1980; Tattoo You, 1981; Still Life, 1982; Undercover, 1983; Dirty Work, 1986; Steel Wheels (also prod.), 1989; Flashpoint, 1991; Voodoo Lounge, 1994; Bridges to Babylon, 1997; Bent, 1997; No Security, 1998; Forty Licks, 2002; A Bigger Bang, 2005; GRRR!, 2012; *solo albums:* She's the Boss, 1985; Primitive Cool, 1987; Wandering Spirit, 1993; Goddess in the Doorway, 2001; album with SuperHeavy, SuperHeavy, 2011. *Films include:* Performance, 1970; Ned Kelly, 1970; Freejack, 1992; Shine a Light, 2008; producer: Enigma, 2001; Get On Up, 2014. Founded film prodn co., Jagged Films.

JAGLAND, Thorbjørn; Secretary General, Council of Europe, since 2009; *b* 5 Nov. 1950; *m* 1975, Hanne Grotjord; two *s. Educ:* Univ. of Oslo. Leader, Labour Youth League, 1977–81; Labour Party of Norway: Res. and Analysis Sec., 1981–86; Party Sec., 1986–92; Leader, 1992–2002. MP (Lab) Buskerud County, Norway, 1993–2009. Prime Minister of Norway, 1996–97; Minister of Foreign Affairs, 2000–01; Pres. of Storting, 2005–09. Chm., Standing Cttee on Foreign Affairs, 2001–05. Chm., Norwegian Nobel Cttee, 2009–15. Chm., Bd of Dirs, Oslo Centre for Peace and Human Rights, 2006–09. *Publications:* My European Dream, 1990; New Solidarity, 1993; Letters, 1995; Our Vulnerable World, 2001; Ten Theses on the EU and Norway, 2003. *Recreations:* ski-ing, outdoor activities, literature. *Address:* Council of Europe, Avenue de l'Europe, 67075 Strasbourg Cedex, France.

JAGO, David Edgar John; Communar of Chichester Cathedral, 1987–92; *b* 2 Dec. 1937; *s* of late Edgar George Jago and of Violet Jago; *m* 1st, 1963, Judith Lissenden, DPhil (*d* 1995); one *s* one *d*; 2nd, 1997, Gertraud Marianne, (Gerty), Apfelbeck. *Educ:* King Edward's Sch., Bath; Pembroke Coll., Oxford (MA). National Service, RA, 1956–58. Asst Principal, Admiralty, 1961; Private Sec. to Permanent Under Sec. of State (RN), 1964–65; Principal 1965; Directing Staff, IDC, 1968–70; Private Sec. to Parly Under Sec. of State for Defence (RN), 1971–73; Ministry of Defence: Asst Sec., 1973; Asst Under Sec. of State: Aircraft, 1979–82; Naval Staff, 1982–84; Under Sec., Cabinet Office, 1984–86. Gov., Bedgebury Sch., 1996–2000. *Recreations:* theatre, opera, military history, supporting Arsenal FC. *Club:* Oxford and Cambridge.

JAGPAL, Jagdip; Manager, International Programmes, Tate, since 2014; *b* London, 22 Nov. 1964; *d* of late Darshan Singh and of Jaswant Kaur. *Educ:* London Sch. of Econs and Pol Sci. (LLB Hons); Coll. of Law; London Business Sch. Man. Ed., Butterworths Ltd, 1986–91; Solicitor, Rubinstein Callingham Polden & Gale, 1992–95; BBC Radio: lawyer, 1995–96; Chief Asst to Controller, Radio 4, 1996–99; Man. Dir, Network Television Prodn, SMG plc, 1999–2002; Associate, 2002–04, non-exec. Dir, 2004–11, Franklin Rae Communications, 2002–04; Chief Exec., Cloisters, 2004–07; exec. search consultant, 2007–09; Man. Dir, Anareva, 2009–14. Non-executive Director: Noel Gay Artists Ltd, 2004–08; Bend It Networks Gp, 2015–. Mem Bd, Almeida Theatre, 2009–14. Trustee, Wallace Collection, 2007–. Mem., Ct of Govs, LSE, 2011–. *Recreations:* art, theatre, travel, London, watching television. *Address:* c/o Anareva, Gridiron Building, One Pancras Square, N1C 4AG. *E:* jagdip@mac.com.

JAGUARIBE, Roberto; Ambassador of Brazil to the Court of St James's, 2010–15; *b* Rio de Janeiro, 27 Dec. 1952; *s* of Hélio Jaguaribe and Maria Lúcia Jaguaribe; *m* Cinara Lima; two *d* and two step *s. Educ:* Pontifical Catholic Univ. of Rio de Janeiro (BE Systems Engrg). Public Entry Exam Diplomat, Brazil, 1978; Mission to UN, NY, 1983–87; Montevideo, 1987–90; Head: Div. for Intellectual Property and Sensitive Technologies, 1990–93; Intellectual Property Sect. and Disarmament Sect., Internat. Orgns, Mission in Geneva, 1993–95; Sec. for Internat. Affairs, Min. of Planning and Budget, 1995–98; Dir-Gen. for Trade Promotion, Min. of Ext. Relns, 1998–2000; Dep. Hd of Mission, Washington, 2000–03; Sec. for Industrial Technol., Min. of Develt, Industry and Foreign Trade, 2003–05; Pres., Nat. Inst. of Industrial Property of Brazil, 2005–06; Under Sec.-Gen. for Political Affairs, Min. of Ext. Relns, 2007–10. *Recreations:* music, reading, outdoors, golf. *Address:* c/o Embassy of Brazil, 14–16 Cockspur Street, SW1Y 5BL.

JAHODA, Prof. Gustav, FBA 1988; FRSE; Professor of Psychology, University of Strathclyde, 1964–85, now Emeritus Professor; *b* 11 Oct. 1920; *s* of late Olga and Leopold Jahoda; *m* 1950, Jean Catherine (*née* Buchanan) (*d* 1991); three *s* one *d. Educ:* Vienna, Paris, Univ. of London. MScEcon, PhD. FRSE 1993. Tutor, Oxford Extra-Mural Delegacy, 1946–68; Lectr, Univ. of Manchester, 1948–51; Univ. of Ghana, 1952–56; Sen. Lectr, Univ. of Glasgow, 1956–63. Visiting Professor, Universities of: Ghana, 1968; Tilburg, 1984; Kansai, Osaka, 1985; Ecole des Hautes Etudes, Paris, 1986; Saarbrücken, 1987; New York, 1987; Geneva, 1990. Fellow, Netherlands Inst. of Advanced Studies, 1980–81; Hon. Fellow, Internat. Assoc. for Cross-Cultural Psychology (Pres., 1972–74); Membre d'Honneur, Assoc. pour la Recherche Inter-culturelle, 1986. *Publications:* White Man, 1961, 2nd edn 1983; The Psychology of Superstition, 1969, 8th edn 1979; Psychology and Anthropology, 1982 (French edn 1989; Japanese edn 1992); (with I. M. Lewis) Acquiring Culture, 1988; Crossroads between Culture and Mind, 1992; Images of Savages, 1999; A History of Social Psychology, 2007; contribs to learned jls. *Recreations:* photography, reading. *Address:* c/o Department of Psychology, University of Strathclyde, Glasgow G1 1QE. *Club:* University of Strathclyde Staff.

JAINE, Tom William Mahony; freelance writer; Proprietor, Prospect Books, 1993–2014; *b* 4 June 1943; *s* of William Edwin Jaine and Aileen (*née* Mahony); *m* 1st, 1965, Susanna F. Fisher; 2nd, 1973, Patience Mary Welsh (decd); two *d*; 3rd, 1983, Sally Caroline Agnew; two *d. Educ:* Kingswood Sch., Bath; Balliol Coll., Oxford (BA Hons). Asst Registrar, Royal Commn on Historical Manuscripts, 1967–73; Partner, Carved Angel Restaurant, Dartmouth, 1974–84; publisher, The Three Course Newsletter (and predecessors), 1980–89; Editor: Good Food Guide, 1989–94; Petits Propos Culinaires. Wine and Food Writer of the Year, Glenfiddich Awards, 2000; Derek Cooper Lifetime Achievement Award, BBC Food and Farming Awards, 2014. *Publications:* Cooking in the Country, 1986; Cosmic Cuisine, 1988; Making Bread at Home, 1995; Building a Wood-Fired Oven, 1996; (ed) Oxford Companion to Food, 2nd edn 2006, 3rd edn 2014; contribs Guardian, etc. *Recreations:* baking, buildings. *Address:* Allaleigh House, Blackawton, Totnes, Devon TQ9 7DL.

JAITLEY, Arun; Member, Rajya Sabha for Gujarat, since 2000; Minister of Finance, India, since 2014; *b* New Delhi, 28 Dec. 1952; *s* of Maharaj Krishan Jaitley and Ratan Praba Jaitley; *m* 1982, Sangeeta Dogra; one *s* one *d. Educ:* Shri Ram Coll., Delhi (BCom Hons); Delhi Univ. (LLB 1977). Started practising law, 1977; Sen. Advocate, 1990–2009; Additional Solicitor Gen. of India, 1989–90. Minister of State: Information and Broadcasting, 1999–2000; Dept of Disinvestment, 1999–2000; Law, Justice and Co. Affairs, 2000; Minister: of Law, Justice and Co. Affairs, 2000–02; of Shipping, 2001; of Commerce and Industry and of Law and Justice, 2003–04; Leader of Opposition, 2009–14; Minister of Defence, 2014. Bharatiya Janata Party: Mem., 1980–; Mem., Nat. Exec., 1991–; spokesperson, 1999; Gen. Sec., 2002–03 and 2004–09. *Recreation:* cricket. *Address:* Ministry of Finance, Room No 134, North Block, New Delhi 110 001, India. *T:* 23092510, 23092810, 23092830. *E:* fmo@nic.in.

JAKEMAN, Prof. Eric, FRS 1990; Professor of Applied Statistical Optics, University of Nottingham, 1996–2004, now Professor Emeritus; *b* 3 June 1939; *s* of Frederick Leonard Jakeman and Hilda Mary Hays; *m* 1968, Glenys Joan Cooper; two *d. Educ:* Brunts Grammar Sch., Mansfield; Univ. of Birmingham (BSc, PhD). FInstP 1979. Asst Res. Physicist, UCLA, 1963–64. DRA (formerly RRE, subseq. RSRE), 1964–95 (DCSO, 1985–95). Hon. Sec., Inst. of Physics, 1994–2003 (Vice-Pres. for Publications, 1989–93); Mem. Exec. Cttee, European Physical Soc., 1990–94. Fellow, Optical Soc. of America, 1988. Maxwell Medal and Prize, Inst. of Physics, 1977; (jtly) MacRobert Award, 1977; (jtly) Instrument Makers' Co. Award. *Publications:* numerous contribs to learned jls. *Recreations:* gardening, music, beekeeping. *Address:* University of Nottingham, University Park, Nottingham NG7 2RD.

JAKENS, Claire; Her Honour Judge Jakens; a Circuit Judge, since 2010; *b* Brighton, 23 May 1952; *d* of Arthur George Jakens and Frances Bell Jakens; *m* 1984, Prof. Nicholas Hamlyn; one *s. Educ:* Reading Univ. (BA Hons Italian); Warburg Inst., London Univ. (MPhil Combined Histl Studies; Dip. Law 1987). Various posts in UK and Italy; Lectr (pt-time) in Italian, Reading Univ., 1975–77; teacher of Italian, St Paul's Girls' Sch., 1977–87; called to the Bar, Middle Temple, 1988; in practice as barrister, 1988–2010. FRSA. *Recreations:* walking, travel, opera and theatre, friends and family.

JAKUB, Claire; *see* Curtis-Thomas, C.

JAMES; *see* Streatfeild-James.

JAMES, family name of **Baron Northbourne**.

JAMES OF BLACKHEATH, Baron *cr* 2006 (Life Peer), of Wildbrooks in the County of West Sussex; **David Noel James,** CBE 1992; Chairman, Litigation Control Group Ltd, 2002–06; *b* 7 Dec. 1937; *m* 2004, Caroline Webster. Lloyds Bank, 1959–64; Chairman: Eagle Trust plc, 1989–97; Davies & Newman, 1990–92; New Millennium Experience Co., 2000–01; Racecourse Holdings Trust, 2003–05. *Address:* House of Lords, SW1A 0PW.

JAMES, Alex; *see* James, S. A.

JAMES, Christopher John; Deputy Chairman, R. Griggs Group Ltd, 1994–2000 (Director, 1993–2000); *b* 20 March 1932; *s* of John Thomas Walters James, MC and Cicely Hilda James; *m* 1958, Elizabeth Marion Cicely Thomson; one *s* one *d. Educ:* Clifton Coll., Bristol; Magdalene Coll., Cambridge (MA). Served RA, 2nd Lieut, 1951–52; TA, 1952–60. Admitted Solicitor, 1958; Partner, Johnson & Co., Birmingham, 1960–87 (Sen. Partner, 1985–87); Dep. Sen. Partner, Martineau Johnson, 1987–89, Sen. Partner, 1989–94. Director: Birmingham Building Soc., then Birmingham Midshires Building Soc., 1980–96 (Dep. Chm., 1988–90; Chm., 1990–96); Police Mutual Assurance Soc., 1996–2001. Gen. Comr for Income Tax, 1974–82. Pres., Birmingham Law Soc., 1983–84. Chm., Kalamazoo Trust, 1997–2001. Mem. Council, Edgbaston High Sch. for Girls, 1980–90 (Chm., 1987–90); Gov., Clifton Coll., 1980–99. *Recreations:* photography, railways, trying to get the better of my computer, water colour painting.

JAMES, His Honour Christopher Philip; a Circuit Judge, 1980–97; *b* 27 May 1934; *yr s* of late Herbert Edgar James, CBE, and Elizabeth Margaret James. *Educ:* Felsted School; Magdalene Coll., Cambridge (MA). Commnd RASC, 1953. Called to the Bar, Gray's Inn, 1959; a Recorder of the Crown Court, 1979; Judge of Woolwich County Court, 1982–92, of Lambeth County Court, 1992–97. *Address:* Flat 8, 93 Elm Park Gardens, SW10 9QW. *Club:* Oxford and Cambridge.

JAMES, Clive Vivian Leopold, CBE 2012; AO 2013 (AM 1992); writer and broadcaster; Director, clivejames.com, since 2005; *b* 7 Oct. 1939; *s* of Albert Arthur James and Minora May (*née* Darke). *Educ:* Sydney Technical High Sch.; Sydney Univ. (BA Hons); Pembroke Coll., Cambridge (MA; Hon. Fellow). President of Footlights when at Cambridge. Dir, Watchmaker Prodns, 1994–99. Record albums as lyricist for Pete Atkin: Beware of the Beautiful Stranger; Driving through Mythical America; A King at Nightfall; The Road of Silk; Secret Drinker; Live Libel; The Master of the Revels; Touch has a Memory, 1991; Midnight Voices, the Clive James-Pete Atkin Songbook Vol. 1, 2008. Song-book with Pete Atkin: A First Folio. *Television series:* Cinema, Up Sunday, So It Goes, A Question of Sex, Saturday Night People, Clive James on Television; Postcard series, 1989–: Rio, Chicago, Paris, Miami, Rome, Shanghai, Sydney, London, Cairo, New York, Bombay, Berlin, Buenos Aires, Nashville, Hong Kong, Mexico City, Las Vegas, Havana. Hon. Mem., Australian Acad. of the Humanities, 2006. Hon. DLitt: Sydney, 1999; UEA, 2006. Philip Hodgins Meml Medal, 2003; George Orwell Special Prize, 2008; NSW Premier's Award, 2012; British Academy President's Medal, 2014; Special Award, BAFTA, 2015. *Publications: non-fiction:* The Metropolitan Critic, 1974, 2nd edn 1994; The Fate of Felicity Fark in the Land of the Media, 1975; Peregrine Prykke's Pilgrimage through the London Literary World, 1976; Britannia Bright's Bewilderment in the Wilderness of Westminster, 1976; Visions Before Midnight, 1977; At the Pillars of Hercules, 1979; First Reactions, 1980; The Crystal Bucket, 1981; Charles Charming's Challenges on the Pathway to the Throne, 1981; From the Land of Shadows, 1982; Glued to the Box, 1982; Flying Visits, 1984; Snakecharmers in Texas, 1988; On Television, 1991; The Dreaming Swimmer, 1992; Fame, 1993; Reliable Essays, 2001; Even As We Speak, 2001; The Meaning of Recognition: new essays 2001–2005, 2005; Cultural Amnesia, 2007; The Revolt of the Pendulum, 2009; A Point of View, 2011; Poetry Notebook: 2006–2014, 2014; Latest Readings, 2015; *fiction:* Brilliant Creatures, 1983; The Remake, 1987; Brrm! Brrm!, 1991; The Silver Castle, 1996; *verse:* Fan-Mail, 1977; Poem of the Year, 1983; Other Passports: poems 1958–85, 1986; The Book of my Enemy: collected verse 1958–2003, 2003; Opal Sunset: selected poems 1958–2008, 2008; Angels Over Elsinore: collected poems 2003–2008, 2008; Nefertiti in the Flak Tower, 2012; (trans.) Dante, The Divine Comedy, 2013; Sentenced to Life, 2015; *autobiography:* Unreliable Memoirs, 1980;

Falling Towards England: Unreliable Memoirs II, 1985; May Week Was in June: Unreliable Memoirs III, 1990; Always Unreliable, 2001; North Face of Soho: Unreliable Memoirs IV, 2006; The Blaze of Obscurity, 2009.

JAMES, Colin John Irwin, FCIPD; Chief Executive, Roads Service, Northern Ireland, 1999–2002; *b* 17 Sept. 1942; *s* of William and Evelyn James; *m* 1968, Monica Jean Patston; one *s* one *d*. *Educ:* Royal Belfast Academical Instn; Queen's Univ., Belfast (BSc Hons 1965); University Coll. London (MPhil 1967). FCIPD (FIPD 1988); MCIH 1992; MCIHT (MIHT 1999). GLC, 1967–71; DoE (NI), 1971–73; NI Housing Exec., 1973–94; joined Defence Housing Exec., 1994, Chief Exec., 1995–99. Dir, Waldovision Ltd, 2012–14. *Recreations:* local history, photography, walking, home cinema. *Address:* 10 Fort Road, Helens Bay, Co. Down BT19 1LA.

JAMES, Darius; Artistic Director, Ballet Cymru, since 1986; *b* Newport, 18 Feb. 1966; *s* of Bernard Williams and Yvonne Williams (*née* Greenleaf); *né* Darius James Williams; *m* 2012, Amy Doughty. *Educ:* Royal Ballet Sch. Dancer: Northern Ballet Th., 1984–86; Alexander Roy London Ballet Th., 1987–92. Dir, Community Dance Wales, 2008–10. Creative Wales Major Award, Arts Council of Wales, 2008. *Recreations:* theatre, ballet, dance, surfing. *Address:* Ballet Cymru, 30 Glasllwch Crescent, Newport, S Wales NP20 3SE. *T:* (01633) 253985. *E:* dariusjames@welshballet.co.uk.

JAMES, Rt Rev. David Charles, PhD; Bishop of Bradford, 2002–10; Honorary Assistant Bishop, Diocese of York, since 2010; *b* 6 March 1945; *s* of Charles George Frederick James and Cecilia Lily James; *m* 1971, Gillian Patricia Harrop; four *d*. *Educ:* Nottingham High Sch.; Exeter Univ. (BSc 1966; PhD 1971); Nottingham Univ. (BA 1973); St John's Theol Coll., Nottingham. Asst Lectr in Chemistry, Southampton Univ., 1969–70. Ordained deacon, 1973, priest, 1974; Curate: Highfield Church, Southampton, 1973–76; Goring by Sea, Worthing, 1976–78; Anglican Chaplain, UEA, 1978–82; Vicar of Ecclesfield, Sheffield, 1982–90; RD, Ecclesfield, 1987–90; Vicar of Highfield, Southampton, 1990–98; Bp Suffragan of Pontefract, 1998–2002. Hon. Canon of Winchester, 1998. Took seat in H of L, 2009. Gov., King Alfred's UC, Winchester, 1992–97. *Address:* 7 Long Lane, Beverley, E Yorks HU17 0NH.

JAMES, Prof. David Edward; Professor (formerly Director) of Adult Education, 1969–2002, University Professor, and Special Adviser to the Vice-Chancellor on Regional Academic Affairs, 2002–05, University of Surrey; *b* 31 July 1937; *s* of Charles Edward James and Dorothy Hilda (*née* Reeves); *m* 1963, Penelope Jane Murray; two *s* one *d*. *Educ:* Universities of Reading, Oxford, Durham, London (Bsc Hons Gen., BSc Hons Special, MEd, DipEd, DipFE); FRSPH; FITD 1992; FRSB. Lectr in Biology, City of Bath Tech. Coll. 1961–63; Lectr in Sci. and Educn, St Mary's Coll. of Educn, Newcastle upon Tyne, 1963–64; University of Surrey: Lectr in Educnl Psych., 1964–69; Hd, Dept of Educnl Studies, 1982–93; Dean of Associated Instns, 1996–2002. FRSA. *Publications:* A Student's Guide to Efficient Study, 1966, Amer. edn 1967; Introduction to Psychology, 1968, Italian edn 1972. *Recreation:* farming. *Address:* 30 Glendale Drive, Burpham, Guildford, Surrey GU4 7HZ.

JAMES, (David) Keith (Marlais), OBE 2005; Chairman: Julian Hodge Bank Ltd, since 2012; Hodge Life Assurance Co. Ltd, since 2012; *b* Carmarthen, 16 Aug. 1944; *s* of James Lewis James and Margaret Evelyn James; *m* 1973, Kathleen Linda Marrs; one *s* two *d*. *Educ:* Cardiff High Sch.; W Monmouth Sch.; Queens' Coll., Cambridge (MA). Admitted as solicitor, 1969; Partner, Phillips and Buck Solicitors, 1969–95; Chairman: Eversheds LLP, 1995–2004; Admiral Insce Co. Ltd, 2003–; Internat. Greetings plc, 2006–11. Non-executive Director: Bank of Wales plc, 1988–2001; Axa Insce Co. Ltd, 1992–99; HTV Gp Ltd, 1997–98 and 1999–2006. Dep. Chm., Inst. of Welsh Affairs, 1987–2007 (Hon. Fellow, 2009). Trustee, Nat. Trust, 2011–14. *Recreations:* hill walking, theatre, golf. *Address:* Trehedyn Cottage, Peterston-super-Ely, Vale of Glamorgan CF5 6LG. *T:* (029) 2078 7674. *Clubs:* Oxford and Cambridge; Cardiff and County; Royal Porthcawl Golf.

JAMES, Derek Claude, OBE 1989; Director of Social Services, Leeds, 1978–89; *b* 9 March 1929; *s* of Cecil Claude James and Violet (*née* Rudge); *m* 1954, Evelyn (*née* Thomas); one *s* one *d*. *Educ:* King Edward's Grammar Sch., Camp Hill, Birmingham; Open Univ. (BA). Dip. in Municipal Admin. Local Government: Birmingham, 1946–60; Coventry, 1960–63; Bradford, 1963–69; Leeds, 1969–89. Mem., Yorks and Humberside RHA, 1976–82; Chm., Leeds Area Review Cttee (Child Abuse), 1978–89; Mem., Nat. Adv. Council on Employment of Disabled People, 1984–89; Pres., Nat. Assoc. of Nursery and Family Care, 1988–92; Chairman: Nightstop Homeless Persons Project, 1989–92; Nightstop Trust, Leeds, 1993–2000; Disabled Living Centre, Leeds, 1994–2002 (Mem. Exec. Cttee, 2002–11); Vice-Chm., Nat. Family Service Units, 1992–96 (Mem. Nat. Cttee, 1992–96); Expert Panel Mem., Registered Homes Tribunal, 1990–96; Adviser: AMA Social Services Cttee, 1983–89; Physical Disablement Res. Liaison Gp, 1986–89. Sanctuary Housing Association: Chm., North and West Yorks Area Cttee, 1992–2001; Member: North Divl Cttee, 1992–97; North Regl Cttee, 2004–09; Central Council, 1993–97, 2001–03; Scrutiny Cttee, 2004–09; Chm., Care Cttee, 1998–2003; Chairman and non-executive Director: Sanctuary Care Co., 2002–09; Sanctuary Home Care Co., 2003–09. Non-exec. Dir, Neuroscis and Maxillo-Facial Surgery Subsid. Governing Body, United Leeds Teaching Hosps Trust, 1997–98. *Recreations:* watching sport, garden pottering, acceding to my grandchildren's wishes, gentle holidays. *Address:* 10 Emmandjay Court, Valley Drive, Ilkley, W Yorks LS29 8PF. *T:* (01943) 603659.

JAMES, Diane Martine; Member (UK Ind) South East Region, European Parliament, since 2014; *b* 20 Nov. 1959; *d* of Edwin James and Margaret (*née* Wrape); *m* 1st, John Stuart Smith; 2nd, John Richard Forrest. *Educ:* Thames Valley Univ. Mem. (UK Ind) Waverley BC, 2006–. *Recreations:* travel, fitness, antiques, animal rescue. *Address:* European Parliament, Rue Wiertz, Brussels 1047, Belgium.

JAMES, Hon. Edison Chenfil; MP (UWP) Marigot, Dominica; Leader, United Workers' Party, since 2012; *b* 18 Oct. 1943; *s* of David and Patricia James; *m* 1970, Wilma; one *s* two *d*. *Educ:* North East London Poly. (BSc Hons); Univ. of Reading (MSc); Imperial Coll., London (Dip. Pest Management). Teacher, St Mary's Acad., 1973; Agronomist, Min. of Agriculture, Dominica, 1974–76; Farm Improvement Officer, Caribbean Develt Bank and Agric. and Indust. Develt Bank, 1976–80; Project Co-ordinator, Coconut Rehabilitation; Gen. Manager, Dominica Banana Marketing Corp., 1980–87; Man. Dir, Agric. Managing Corp., 1987–95. Prime Minister, Dominica, 1995–2000; Leader of the Opposition, 2000–07. *Recreations:* cricket, football, table tennis, politics, international affairs. *Address:* Parliament of Dominica, Roseau, Dominica, West Indies. *T:* 4482401. *Club:* Rotary Club of Dominica.

JAMES, Erwin; *see* Monahan, E. J.

JAMES, Prof. Frank Arthur John Lord, PhD; FRAS; Professor of the History of Science, since 2004, and Head, Collections and Heritage, since 1998, Royal Institution; Professor of History of Science, University College London, since 2013; *b* 7 March 1955; *s* of Arthur Montague James and Mary Patricia James (*née* Lord); *m* 1986, Joasia Hermaszewska; two *s* one *d*. *Educ:* Chelsea Coll. (BSc); Imperial Coll., London (MSc, DIC; PhD 1981). FRAS 1981. Associate, Univ. of London Inst. of Educn, 1981–82; Royal Institution: Res. Fellow, 1982–86; seconded to Marine Soc. serving in S Atlantic, 1984; Lectr, 1986–97; Reader in Hist. of Sci., 1997–2004. Vis. Res. Fellow, Sci. Studies Centre, Univ. of Bath, 1998–; Visiting Professor: UCL, 2007–13; Centro Simão Mathias, São Paulo, 2008. Earnshaw Lectr, QUB, 2004. Mem., Exec. Cttee, COPUS, 1989–97. British Society for History of Science: Officer and Council Mem., 1989–2005; Vice-Pres., 2005–06, 2008–09; Pres., 2006–08; Newcomen Society for History of Engineering and Technology: Mem. Council, 1991–94, 1996–99, 2005–07, 2010–; Vice Pres., 1999–2003; Pres., 2003–05; Treas., 2011–; British Association for Advancement of Science, later British Science Association: Recorder of Hist. of Sci. Section, 1992–97; Mem. Council, 1995–2000; Pres., 2009–10; Member, Council: Div. of Hist. of Sci. Technol., Internat. Union for the Hist. and Philosophy of Sci., 2009–; Soc. for Hist. of Alchemy and Chem., 2010–. MAE 2012. Chm., Nat. Organising Cttee, 24th Internat. Congress for Hist. of Sci. and Technol., 2009–13. Jt Ed., History of Technol., 1989–96. Liveryman, Scientific Instrument Makers' Co., 2010–. Corresp. Mem., 2011, Membre Effectif, 2014, Acad. internat. d'histoire des scis. *Publications:* (ed jtly) Faraday Rediscovered: essays on the life and work of Michael Faraday, 1791–1867, 1985; Chemistry and Theology in mid-Victorian London: The Diary of Herbert McLeod 1860–1870, 1987; (ed) The Place of Experiment: essays on the development of laboratories in industrial civilisation, 1989; (jtly) Faraday, 1991; (ed) The Correspondence of Michael Faraday, vol. 1 1991, vol. 2 1993, vol. 3 1996, vol. 4 1999, vol. 5 2008, vol. 6 2012; (ed jtly) Renaissance and Revolution: humanists, scholars, craftsmen and natural philosophers in early modern Europe, 1993; (jtly) Science in Art: works in the National Gallery that illustrate the history of science and technology, 1997; (ed) Semaphores to Short Waves, 1998; Guide to the Microfilm edition of the Manuscripts of Michael Faraday (1791–1867) from the Collections of the Royal Institution, Institution of Electrical Engineers and Guildhall Library, 2000–01; (ed) The Common Purposes of Life: science and society at the Royal Institution of Great Britain, 2002; Guide to the Microfilm edition of the Letters of John Tyndall (1820–1893) from the Collections of the Royal Institution, 2003; Christmas at the Royal Institution: an anthology of lectures, 2007; Michael Faraday: a very short introduction, 2010; (ed) Faraday's Chemical History of a Candle, 2011; contrib. many articles on nineteenth century science in its social, religious, military and cultural contexts. *Recreations:* walking in the country, visiting historic buildings, browsing in second hand bookshops. *Address:* Royal Institution, 21 Albemarle Street, W1S 4BS. *T:* (020) 7670 2924. *E:* fjames@ri.ac.uk.

JAMES, Geraldine, OBE 2003; actress; *b* 6 July 1950; *d* of Gerald Trevor Thomas and Annabella Doogan Thomas; adopted stage name, Geraldine James, 1972; *m* 1986, Joseph Sebastian Blatchley; one *d*. *Educ:* Downe House, Newbury; Drama Centre London Ltd. *Stage:* repertory, Chester, 1972–74, Exeter, 1974–75, Coventry, 1975; Passion of Dracula, Queen's, 1978; The White Devil, Oxford, 1981; Turning Over, Bush, 1984; When I was a Girl I used to Scream and Shout, Whitehall, 1987; Cymbeline, National, 1988; Merchant of Venice, Phoenix, 1989, NY (Drama Desk Best Actress Award), 1990; Death and the Maiden, Duke of York's, 1992; Lysistrata, Old Vic and Wyndham's, 1993; Hedda Gabler, Royal Exchange, Manchester, 1993; Give Me Your Answer Do!, Hampstead, 1998; Faith Healer, Almeida, 2001; The Cherry Orchard, 2003, Home, 2004, Oxford Stage Co.; UN Inspector, RNT, 2005; The Exonerated, Riverside Studios, 2006; Victory, Arcola, 2009; Hamlet, Donmar on Broadway, 2009; The Seagull, Arcola, 2011; 13, NT, 2011; *TV series include:* The History Man, 1980; Jewel in the Crown, 1984; Blott on the Landscape, 1985; Echoes, 1988; Band of Gold, 1994, 1995; Kavanagh QC, 1994, 1995, 1997, 1998; Drovers' Gold, 1996; Seesaw, 1998; The Sins, 2000; White Teeth, State of Play, 2002; Jane Hall, 2004; The Amazing Mrs Pritchard, 2006; Time of Your Life, 2007; The Last Enemy, City of Vice, 2008; Utopia, 2012, 2013; Black Work, 2015; *TV films include:* Dummy (Best Actress, BPG), 1977; A Doll's House, 1992; Doggin' Around, 1994; Crime and Punishment, 2001; Hound of the Baskervilles, 2002; Hex, 2004; Poirot, 2005; A Harlot's Progress, 2006; The Heist, Rapunzel, Caught in a Trap, 2008; The Other Woman, 2012; *films include:* Sweet William, Night Cruiser, 1978; Gandhi, 1981; The Storm, 1985; Wolves of Willoughby Chase, 1988; The Tall Guy, She's Been Away, (Best actress, Venice Film Festival, 1989), 1989; If Looks Could Kill, The Bridge, 1990; Prince of Shadows, 1991; No Worries Australia, 1993; Words on the Window Pane, 1994; Moll Flanders, 1995; The Man Who Knew Too Little, 1998; All Forgotten, The Testimony of Taliesin Jones, The Luzhin Defence, 2000; An Angel for May, 2001; Calendar Girls, 2002; The Fever, 2003; Sherlock Holmes, 2009; Alice in Wonderland, Made in Dagenham, 2010; Arthur, Sherlock Holmes 2, The Girl with the Dragon Tattoo, 2011; Diana, 2013; Robot Overlords, 45 Years, 2015; *radio includes:* The Raj Quartet, 2006; The Waves, 2007; Dombey and Son, 2007; Sacred Hearts, 2009; The Carhullan Army, 2010. *Recreation:* music. *Address:* c/o Julian Belfrage Associates, 3rd Floor, 9 Argyll Street, W1F 7TG.

JAMES, Rt Rev. Graham Richard; *see* Norwich, Bishop of.

JAMES, Hamilton E.; President, Blackstone Group, since 2002; *b* 3 Feb. 1951; *s* of Hamilton R. James and Waleska Bacon Evans; *m* 1973, Amabel G. Boyce; one *s* two *d*. *Educ:* Harvard Coll. (AB *magna cum laude* 1973); Harvard Business Sch. (MBA with High Dist., Baker Schol. 1975). Chairman: Banking Gp, Donaldson, Lufkin & Jenrette, 1975–2000; Global Investment Banking and Private Equity, Credit Suisse First Boston, 2000–02. Dir, Costco Corp., 1988–; has served on other corporate bds. Mem., various cttees, Harvard Univ., 1990–; former Mem., Subcttee on Technology and Competitiveness, US President's Export Council. Vice Chm., Coldwater Conservation Fund, Trout Unlimited. Trustee: (and Chm. Emeritus) American Ballet Th., 1992–2000; (and Mem., Exec. Cttee) Second Stage Th., 1995–; MMA; Woods Hole Oceanographic; Wildlife Conservation Soc. Trustee: Brearley Sch., 1996–2001. Mem., Adv. Bd, Montana Land Reliance; Mem., Bd of Trustees, Center for American Progress. *Recreations:* fly-fishing, hunting, soccer, cycling, ski-ing, racquet sports. *Address:* Blackstone Group, 345 Park Avenue, New York, NY 10154, USA. *T:* (212) 5835455, *Fax:* (212) 5835460. *E:* James@Blackstone.com. *Clubs:* River, Links (New York); Wee Burn Country (Darien, Conn.); Little Harbor (Harbor Springs, MI).

JAMES, Howell Malcolm Plowden, CBE 1997; Chief Executive, Quiller Consultants, since 2014; *b* 13 March 1954; *s* of late T. J. and Virginia James. *Educ:* Mill Hill Sch., London. Head of Promotions, Capital Radio, 1978–82; Organiser, Help a London Child Charity, 1979–82; Head of Press and Publicity, TV-am, 1982–85; Special Adviser: Cabinet Office, 1985; Dept of Employment, 1985–87; DTI, 1987; Dir of Corporate Affairs, BBC, 1987–92; Dir of Corporate and Govt Affairs, Cable and Wireless, 1992–94; Pol Sec. to Prime Minister, 1994–97; Dir, Brown Lloyd James, 1997–2004; Permanent Sec., Govt Communications, 2004–08; Barclays Bank plc: Gp Corporate Affairs Dir, 2008–11; Vice Chm., Corporate Affairs, 2011–12; Global Hd, Corporate Communications, Christie's, 2012–14. Mem., Review of Govt Communication, 2003. Dir, Broadcast Audience Res. Bd, 1987–92. Dir, Equilibrium Hotels (Riad El Fenn), 2003–. Director: English Nat. Ballet Sch., 1990–96; Chichester Fest. Th., 2005–; Trustee, British Council, 2010–. Gov., George Eliot Sch., 1989–92; Mem., Ct of Govs, Mill Hill Sch., 1996–2003. Trustee, Queen Elizabeth's Foundn for Disabled People Develt Trust, 1992–96; Trustee and non-exec. Dir, Employers' Forum on Disability, 2012–. *Recreations:* theatre, movies, food. *Address:* Quiller Consultants, 5th Floor, 22 Arlington Street, SW1A 1RD. *T:* (020) 7233 9444. *E:* james@quillerconsultants.com. *Clubs:* Garrick, Soho House.

JAMES, Prof. Ioan Mackenzie, FRS 1968; MA, DPhil; Savilian Professor of Geometry, Oxford University, 1970–95, Professor Emeritus, since 1995; Fellow of New College, Oxford, 1970–95, Emeritus Fellow, 1995, Leverhulme Emeritus Fellow, 1996–98, Hon. Fellow, 1999; *b* 23 May 1928; *o s* of Reginald Douglas and Jessie Agnes James; *m* 1961, Rosemary Gordon Stewart, *qv*; no *c*. *Educ:* St Paul's Sch. (Foundn Schol.); Queen's Coll., Oxford (Open Schol.). Commonwealth Fund Fellow, Princeton, Berkeley and Inst. for Advanced Study, 1954–55; Tapp Res. Fellow, Gonville and Caius Coll., Cambridge, 1956; Reader in Pure Mathematics, Oxford, 1957–69, and Senior Research Fellow, St John's Coll., 1959–69, Hon. Fellow, 1988. Hon. Prof., Univ. of Wales, 1989; Vis. Prof., Univ. of Paris, 1995–97. Ed., Topology, 1962–90. London Mathematical Society: Treasurer, 1969–79; Pres.,

1985–87; Whitehead Prize and Lectr, 1978. Mem. Council, Royal Soc., 1982–83. Gov., St Paul's Schs, 1970–99. Hon. DSc Aberdeen, 1993. *Publications:* The Mathematical Works of J. H. C. Whitehead, 1963; The Topology of Stiefel Manifolds, 1976; Topological Topics, 1983; General Topology and Homotopy Theory, 1984; Aspects of Topology, 1984; Topological and Uniform Spaces, 1987; Fibrewise Topology, 1988; Introduction to Uniform Spaces, 1990; Handbook of Algebraic Topology, 1995; Fibrewise Homotopy Theory, 1998; Topologies and Uniformities, 1999; History of Topology, 1999; Remarkable Mathematicians, 2002; Remarkable Physicists, 2003; Asperger's Syndrome and High Achievement, 2006; The Mind of the Mathematician, 2007; Remarkable Biologists, 2009; Driven to Innovate, 2009; Remarkable Engineers, 2010; papers in mathematical, medical and historical jls. *Address:* Mathematical Institute, Radcliffe Observatory Quarter, Woodstock Road, Oxford OX2 6GG.

JAMES, Irene; Member (Lab) Islwyn, National Assembly for Wales, 2003–11; *b* 1952. Formerly special needs teacher, Risca Primary Sch. Agent to Don Touhig, MP, gen. election, 2001.

JAMES, Isabella Garden; *see* McColl, I. G.

JAMES, Jason Charles; Director General, Daiwa Anglo-Japanese Foundation, since 2011; *b* Edinburgh, 15 Feb. 1965; *s* of Donald William James and Lorna Constance James (*née* Dunford); *m* 1992, Kyoko Igarashi; two *s* one *d*. *Educ:* King's Coll., Cambridge (BA 1987; MA 1990). Gaimuin, Tokyo Stock Exchange; Associate, Soc. of Investment Analysts. Sec. to Principal, Ueno Gakuen Coll., Tokyo, 1983; analyst, Nat. Securities, Tokyo, 1985–86; Japanese Equity Fund Manager, Robert Fleming Asset Mgt, 1987–89; HSBC, Tokyo: Japanese Equity Strategist, 1989–96; Head: Japanese Equity Strategy, 1990–96; Japanese Equity Res., 1996–98; HSBC, London: Global Strategist, 1998–99; Head: Eur. Equity Strategy, 1999–2002; Global Equity Strategy, 2002–04; Dir, Japan, British Council, 2007–11. *Publications:* (jtly) The Political Economy of Japanese Financial Markets: myths versus reality, 1999; (contrib.) Britain and Japan: biographical portraits, vol. VIII, 2013; academic papers in DBJ Discussion Paper Series and Trans of Asiatic Soc. of Japan. *Recreations:* singing, piano, cryptic crosswords. *Address:* Daiwa Anglo-Japanese Foundation, Daiwa Foundation Japan House, 13/14 Cornwall Terrace (Outer Circle), NW1 4QP. *Clubs:* Reform; Tokyo (Tokyo).

JAMES, Jeffrey Daniel Dominic; Chief Executive, Keeper of Public Records and Historical Manuscripts Commissioner, since 2014; *b* Solihull, 11 March 1968; *né* Walker; adopted *s* of late Edwin and Edith James; *m* 2010, Joanne Knight; three *s* (incl. twin *s*). *Educ:* Open Univ. (BSc Hons 2001); Univ. of Hertfordshire (MA Hist. 2010). Electronic technician, 1984–92, Chief Petty Officer, 1992–98, RN. Network Gp Manager, Univ. of Leeds, 1998–2003; Ops Manager, Swift Res. Ltd, 2003–04; Hd of Ops, BL, 2004–07; Dir of Ops and Services, Nat. Archives, 2007–13; Dep. Chief Exec., Chartered Inst. of Housing, 2013–14. *Address:* National Archives, Kew, Richmond, Surrey TW9 4DU. *T:* (020) 8392 5220. *E:* jeff.james@nationalarchives.gsi.gov.uk.

JAMES, Sir Jeffrey (Russell), KBE 2001; CMG 1994; HM Diplomatic Service, retired; UK Special Representative for Nepal, 2003–05; *b* 13 Aug. 1944; *s* of Lewis Charles James and Ruth James; *m* 1965, Mary Longden; two *d*. *Educ:* Whitgift Sch.; Keele Univ. (BA Hons Internat. Relations). FCO 1967; served Tehran and Kabul; Dep. Political Advr, BMG Berlin, 1978; FCO 1982; Counsellor on loan to Cabinet Office, 1984; Counsellor and Head of Chancery, Pretoria/Cape Town, 1986; Counsellor (Economic and Commercial), New Delhi, 1988; Head, Edinburgh European Council Unit, FCO, 1992; Chargé d'Affaires, Tehran, 1993; High Comr, Nairobi, 1997–2001. Lay Mem., Asylum and Immigration Tribunal, 2005–14. Dir, Eastern Africa Assoc., 2006–. Mem., Chatham House (RIIA), 2002– (Assoc. Fellow, 2006–11). Mem. Governing Council, Keele Univ., 2006–14. *Recreations:* birding, golf, hill walking. *Address:* 7 Rockfield Close, Oxted, Surrey RH8 0DN. *Club:* Tandridge Golf.

JAMES, John Christopher Urmston, OBE 2003; Honorary Life President, European Tennis Federation, since 2008 (President, 2002–08); Life Vice-President, Lawn Tennis Association, since 2007 (Vice-President, 2003–07); Chairman, British Olympic Foundation, since 1989; *b* 22 June 1937; *s* of John Urmston James and Ellen Irene James; *m* 1st, 1959, Gillian Mary Davies (marr. diss. 1982); two *s*; 2nd, 1982, Patricia Mary, *d* of late Arthur Leslie Walter White. *Educ:* St Michael's, Llanelli; Hereford Cathedral Sch. Harrods, 1954; Jaeger, 1961; Pringle, 1972; Asst Sec., 1973–81, Sec., 1981–2002, LTA. Pres., Middx Tennis Assoc., 2003–. Mem., Internat. Council, Tennis Hall of Fame, 2003–. Vice Chm., BOA, 2001–04. Mem., Olympic Cttee, ITF, 1991–2009. Trustee: Torch Trophy Trust, 2003–; Tennis Foundn (formerly British Tennis Foundn), 2003–10; Dan Maskell Trust, 2003–. Member: NT; Ealing NT; Friends of Osterley Park (Chm., 2012–); Wildfowl & Wetlands Trust, Barnes. Lay Vice Chm., St Mary's, Osterley PCC; Lay Mem., Hounslow Deanery Synod, 2004–; Mem. House of Laity, London Diocesan Synod, 2010–. Mem., Lib Dem Party (Pres., Hounslow Lib Dems, 2005–). *Recreations:* tennis, Rugby football, walking, architecture, the countryside, gardening, theatre. *Address:* Parkfield Cottage, Osterley Road, Isleworth, Middx TW7 4PF. *T:* (020) 8232 8683. *Clubs:* All England Lawn Tennis and Croquet, Queen's, International of GB; Cambridge University Tennis (Hon. Vice Pres.); Llanelli Lawn Tennis and Squash; Isleworth Probus (Vice Chm., 2013–).

JAMES, John Douglas, OBE 1996; conservationist and environmental arts consultant; *b* 28 July 1949; *s* of late William Antony James, ERD, MA and Agnes Winifred James (*née* Mitchell); *m* 1971, Margaret Patricia Manton. *Educ:* Spalding Grammar School; Dip. in Co. Direction, Inst. of Dirs, 1994; MBA Nottingham Univ. 1999. Articled pupil, William H. Brown & Son, 1967–68; Marketing Dept, Geest Industries, 1969–71; Marketing Dept, John Player & Sons, 1971–77; Woodland Trust: Nat. Develt Officer, 1977; (first) Director, 1980; Exec. Dir, 1985; Chief Exec., 1992–97. Forestry Comr, 1998–2004 (Mem. Nat. Cttee for England, 2003–04). Co-owner: Focus Gall., Nottingham, 1995–2004; Church Street Gall., Cromer, 2004–12; Cromerart, 2012–. Nottingham Roosevelt Scholar, 1975 (Trustee, Nottingham Roosevelt Scholarship, 1997–2004); Churchill Fellow, 1980. Founder Mem., S Lincs Nature Reserves Ltd, 1968. FRSA 1995. *Recreations:* woodland walks, writing about natural history. *Address:* c/o Cromerart, Merchants' Place, Cromer NR27 9ES.

JAMES, John Henry; Chief Executive, Kensington & Chelsea and Westminster Health Authority (formerly Commissioning Agency), 1992–2002; *b* 19 July 1944; step *s* of late George Arthur James and *s* of late Doris May James; *m* 3rd, 1987, Anita Mary Stockton, *d* of Brian Scarth, QPM and of late Irene Scarth. *Educ:* Ludlow Grammar Sch.; Keble Coll., Oxford (BA Mod. Hist. 1965; postgrad. dip. in Econ. and Pol Sci. 1966). AHSM 1991 (LHSM 1989). Entered Home Civil Service 1966; Asst Principal, Min. of Pensions and Nat. Insurance; Private Sec. to First Perm. Sec., 1969–71, Principal, 1971–74, DHSS; seconded to HM Treasury, 1974–76; Principal, 1976–78, Asst Sec., 1978–86, Under Sec., 1986–91, DHSS, later Dept of Health; Dir of Health Authority Finance, NHS Management Bd, 1986–89; General Manager: Harrow DHA, 1990–92; Parkside DHA, 1991–93. Chm. of reviews and dir of projects, DoH, 2002–05. Co-ordinator, London Cardiac Specialty Rev., 1993. Non-exec. Dir, Laing Homes Ltd, 1987–89. Member: Adv. Council, King's Fund Inst., 1990–93; NHS Res. Task Force, 1993; NHS Central R&D Council, 1994–99; MRC Health Services and Public Health Res. Bd, 1995–99; NHS Adv. Cttee on Resource Allocation, 1997–99; Accessible Transport Commn for London, 1998–2002; Nat. Strategic Gp tackling Racial Harassment in NHS, 1999–2001. Mem. Editl Bd, Milbank Foundn, NY, 2000–12. Mem. Bd, Enfield Healthwatch, 2013–. FRSA 1994. *Publications:* Transforming the NHS, 1994; contributed: Oxford Textbook of Public Health, 1985, 2nd edn 1991; Health Care UK, 1993; Rationing of Health and Social Care, 1993; Information Management in Health Services, 1994; articles in jls. *Recreations:* chess, cricket, travel, food and wine, collecting edible fungi. *E:* anj.james@btinternet.com. *Club:* Athenæum.

JAMES, Sir John (Nigel Courtenay), KCVO 1997; CBE 1990; FRICS; Secretary and Keeper of the Records, Duchy of Cornwall, 1993–97; Trustee of the Grosvenor Estate, 1971–2000; a Crown Estate Commissioner, 1984–99; *b* 31 March 1935; *s* of Frank Courtenay James and Beryl May Wilford Burden; *m* 1961, Elizabeth Jane St Clair-Ford; one *s* one *d*. *Educ:* Sherborne Sch., Dorset. Chief Agent and Estate Surveyor, Grosvenor Estate, 1968–71. Director: Sun Alliance & London Insurance Gp, 1972–93 (a Vice-Chm., 1988–93); Woolwich Equitable Building Soc., 1982–89; Williams & Glyn's Bank plc, 1983–85; Royal Bank of Scotland, 1985–93. Member: Commn for the New Towns, 1978–86; Cttee of Management, RNLI, 1980–2005 (Dep. Chm., 1999–2005); Council, Architectural Heritage Fund, 1983–2001 (Chm., 1999–2001); Prince of Wales' Council, 1984–97. Pres., RICS, 1980–81. Trustee, Henry Smith's Charity, 1991–2005. Gov., Sherborne Sch., 1990–2002. *Recreation:* sailing. *Club:* Brooks's.

JAMES, Jonathan Elwyn Rayner; QC 1988; a Recorder, 1998–2002; *b* 26 July 1950; *s* of late Basil James and of Moira James; *m* 1981, Anne Henshaw (*née* McRae); one *s*. *Educ:* King's College Sch., Wimbledon; Christ's Coll., Cambridge (MA, LLM); Brussels Univ. (Lic. Spécial en Droit Européen 1973). Called to Bar, Lincoln's Inn (Hardwicke Schol.), 1971, Bencher, 1994. Asst Recorder, 1994–98. Mem. Editl Bd, Entertainment Law Rev., 1990. *Publications:* (co-ed) EEC Anti-Trust Law, 1975; (co-ed) Copinger and Skone James on Copyright, 12th edn 1980–14th edn 1998; (jt consulting editor) Encyclopaedia of Forms and Precedents, Vol. 15 (Entertainment), 1989. *Recreations:* DIY, opera, 007, squash, France. *Address:* Hogarth Chambers, 5 New Square, Lincoln's Inn, WC2A 3RJ. *T:* (020) 7404 0404.

JAMES, Julie; Member (Lab) Swansea West, National Assembly for Wales, since 2011; *b* Swansea, 25 Feb. 1958; *d* of Derek James and Lorna James; *m* 1988, David Flatt; two *s* one *d*. *Educ:* Penzance Girls' Grammar Sch.; Univ. of Sussex (BA Hons 1980); Poly. of Central London (DipLaw 1982); Inns of Court Sch. of Law. Called to the Bar, 1983. Policy Lawyer, London Bor. of Camden, 1986–93; Asst County Sec., West Glamorgan CC, 1993–96; Asst Chief Exec. (Governance), City and Co. of Swansea, 1996–2005; Consultant, Clarkslegal LLP, 2005–11. Dep. Minister for Skills and Technol., Welsh Govt, 2014–. *Recreations:* swimming, ski-ing, gardening, family. *Address:* (office) 4th Floor, Sun Alliance House, 166–167 St Helen's Road, Swansea SA1 4DQ. *T:* (01792) 460836. *E:* julie.james@assembly.wales.

JAMES, Rt Rev. Kay; *see* Gippsland, Bishop of.

JAMES, Keith; *see* James, D. K. M.

JAMES, Lawrence Edwin; historian and journalist, since 1985; *b* 26 May 1943; *s* of Arthur and Laura James; *m* 1967, Mary Charlotte Williams; two *s*. *Educ:* Weston-super-Mare GS; York Univ. (BA 1966); Merton Coll., Oxford (MLitt 1979). Schoolmaster: Merchant Taylors' Sch., Northwood, 1969–76; Sedbergh Sch., Cumbria, 1976–85. *Publications:* Crimea: the war with Russia in contemporary photographs, 1981; The Savage Wars: the British conquest of Africa 1870–1920, 1985; Mutiny, 1987; Imperial Rearguard: wars of empire 1919–1985, 1988; The Golden Warrior: the life and legend of Lawrence of Arabia, 1990, 3rd edn 2005; The Iron Duke: a military biography of the Duke of Wellington, 1992, 2nd edn 2001; Imperial Warrior: the life and times of Field-Marshal Viscount Allenby, 1993; The Rise and Fall of the British Empire, 1994, 2nd edn 1997; Raj: the making and unmaking of British India, 1997; Warrior Race: the British experience of war, 2001; The Middle Class: a history, 2006; Aristocrats, 2009; Churchill and Empire: portrait of an Imperialist, 2013. *Recreations:* bird watching, pipe smoking, maintenance of a Springer spaniel and two Border Terriers, brass rubbing. *Address:* 4 Lechlade Road, Langford, Glos GL7 3LE. *Club:* Travellers.

JAMES, Linda Elizabeth Blake; *see* Sullivan, L. E.

JAMES, Margot; MP (C) Stourbridge, since 2010; an Assistant Government Whip, since 2015; *b* Coventry, 1958; *d* of Maurice James; partner, Jay. *Educ:* Millfield Sch., Som; London Sch. of Econs and Pol Sci. (BSc Econs and Govt). Work in sales and mktg for Maurice James Industries; consulting firm; Co-founder, Shire Health, 1986–98; Hd, Eur. Healthcare, 1998, Regl Pres., Pharmaceutical Div., 2005, Ogilvy & Mather. Non-exec. Dir, Parkside NHS Trust, 1998–2003. Mem. (C) Kensington and Chelsea LBC, 2006–08. Contested (C) Holborn and St Pancras, 2005. Mem., Business, Innovation and Skills Select Cttee, 2010–12; PPS to Minister for Trade and Investment, BIS and FCO, 2012, to Leader of H of C, 2014–15. *Address:* House of Commons, SW1A 0AA.

JAMES, Prof. Mary Elizabeth, PhD; FAcSS; Professor, Faculty of Education, University of Cambridge, 2008–13; *b* Dorking, 21 March 1946; *d* of Robert Henry James and Florence Edna James; *m* 2013, David Peter Ebbutt; one *s*. *Educ:* Brighton Coll. of Educn (Teachers' Cert. 1967); Univ. of Sussex (BEd 1968); Inst. of Educn, Univ. of London (MA 1979); Open Univ. (PhD 1990); MA Cantab 1992. Teacher of RE, Park Barn Secondary Sch., Guildford, 1968–70; Hd of Yr and English Teacher, Portsmouth Southern Grammar Sch. for Girls, 1970–74; Hd of Social Studies and Sociol., Hatch End High Sch., Harrow, 1974–79; Res. Asst in Curriculum, Faculty of Educnl Studies, Open Univ., 1979–82; Sen. Res. Associate, Dept of Educn, Univ. of Cambridge, 1982–85; Res. Fellow, Sch. of Educn, Open Univ., 1985–89; Tutor in Educn, Cambridge Inst. of Educn, 1989–92; University of Cambridge: Lectr in Educn, 1992–2000; Sen. Lectr, 2000–02; Reader in Educn, 2002–04; Associate Dir of Res., Faculty of Educn, 2008–13; Fellow, Lucy Cavendish Coll., Cambridge, 1996–2004, Fellow Commoner, 2004–; Chair in Educn, Inst. of Educn, London Univ., 2005–07, 2008; Chair, Scientific Adv. Panel for NordForsk Prog., 2012–. Non-exec. Dir, Bell Educnl Services Ltd, 2013–15. Mem., Expert Panel for Nat. Curriculum Rev., 2010–11. Overseas Mem., Curriculum Develt Council, Educn Bureau, Govt of Hong Kong, 2004–07. Pres., British Educnl Res. Assoc., 2011–13 (Vice Pres., 2010–11, 2013–14). FAcSS (AcSS 2006). *Publications:* (ed jtly) Calling Education to Account, 1982; (with R. McCormick) Curriculum Evaluation in Schools, 1983, 2nd edn 1988 (trans. Spanish, 1996); Using Assessment for School Improvement, 1998; (jtly) Learning How to Learn: tools for schools, 2006; (jtly) Improving Learning How to Learn, in classrooms, schools and networks, 2007; (contrib. ed.) International Encyclopedia of Education, 3rd edn 2010; (with A. Pollard) Principles for Effective Pedagogy, 2012; Educational Assessment, Evaluation and Research: the selected works of Mary E. James, 2013; contribs to jls. *Recreations:* riding my beautiful mare around the local RSPB nature reserve, book club, visiting gardens, houses, galleries, theatre, cinema, making things with textiles, travel (especially on horse-back). *T:* 07714 652809. *E:* mej1002@cam.ac.uk. *Club:* Farmers.

JAMES, Michael; *see* James, R. M. and Jayston, M.

JAMES, Michael Francis; a District Judge (Magistrates' Courts) (formerly Stipendiary Magistrate), West Midlands, 1991–2002; *b* 30 Oct. 1933; *s* of Francis and Eveline James; *m* 1958, Lois Joy Elcock. *Educ:* King Charles I Grammar Sch., Kidderminster. Admitted solicitor, 1956. National Service: commnd RAF, 1957; qualified as air navigator, 1958. Partner, Ivens Morton & Greville-Smith (later Morton Fisher), 1959–86; Sen. Partner, 1986–91. Part-time ind. prison adjudicator, 2002–08. Vis. Fellow, UWE, 1996–99. *Recreations:* books, wine, walking, music.

JAMES, Michael Leonard, (Michael Hartland), MBE 2012; writer and broadcaster, since 1983; *b* 7 Feb. 1941; *m* 1975, Jill Tarján (marr. diss. 1992); two *d*. *Educ:* Latymer Upper Sch.; Christ's Coll., Cambridge. Entered British govt service, 1963; Private Sec. to Rt Hon. Jennie Lee, MP, Minister for the Arts, 1966–68; DES, 1968–71; Planning Unit of Rt Hon. Margaret Thatcher, MP, Sec. of State for Educn and Science, 1971–73; Asst Sec., 1973; DCSO 1974; served London, Milan, Paris, Tokyo, 1973–78; Director, IAEA, Vienna, 1978–83; Advr on Internat. Relations, CEC, Brussels, 1983–85. Member: CSSB, 1983–93; Immigration Appeal Tribunal, 1987–2005; Asylum and Immigration Tribunal, 2005–13; a Chm., Fitness to Practise Cttee, GMC, 2000–06. Governor: Colyton Grammar Sch., 1985–90; Sidmouth Community Coll., 1988–2004 (Chm., 1998–2001). Chm., 2001–11, Pres., 2011–, Kennaway House Trust. Feature writer and book reviewer for The Times (thriller critic, 1989–90; travel correspondent, 1993–), Daily Telegraph (thriller critic, 1993–), Sunday Times and Guardian, 1986–2014. Television and radio include: Sonja's Report (ITV), 1990; Masterspy, interviews with Oleg Gordievsky (BBC Radio 4), 1991. FRSA 1982. Hon. Fellow, Univ. of Exeter, 1985. *Publications: as M. L. James:* (jtly) Internationalization to Prevent the Spread of Nuclear Weapons, 1980; *as Michael Hartland:* Down Among the Dead Men, 1983; Seven Steps to Treason, 1985 (SW Arts Lit. Award; dramatized for BBC Radio 4, 1990); The Third Betrayal, 1986; Frontier of Fear, 1989; The Year of the Scorpion, 1991; The Verdict of Us All (short stories), 2006; Masters of Crime: Lionel Davidson and Dick Francis, 2006; *as Ruth Carrington:* Dead Fish, 1998. *Address:* Kennaway House Trust, Sidmouth, Devon EX10 8NG. *Clubs:* Athenæum, PEN, Detection.

JAMES, Prof. Michael Norman George, DPhil, FRS 1989; FRS(Can) 1985; Professor of Biochemistry, 1978, and Distinguished University Professor of Biochemistry, 1993, University of Alberta, now Emeritus Distinguished Professor; *b* 16 May 1940; *s* of Claud Stewart Murray James and Mimosa Ruth Harriet James; *m* 1961, Patricia McCarthy; one *s* one *d*; *m* 1977, Anita Sielecki; *m* 1996, Deborah Brown; one *d*. *Educ:* Univ. of Manitoba (BSc, MSc); Linacre Coll., Oxford (DPhil). University of Alberta: Asst Prof., then Associate Prof., 1968–78; Canada Res. Chair in Protein Structure and Function, 2001–08. Mem., MRC of Canada Group in Protein Structure and Function, 1974. Hon. DSc Manitoba, 2010. *Publications:* over 300 contribs to learned jls. *Address:* Department of Biochemistry, University of Alberta, Edmonton, AB T6G 2H7, Canada. *T:* (780) 4924550, (780) 6412978.

JAMES, Dame Naomi (Christine), DBE 1979; PhD; author and philosopher; former yachtswoman; *b* 2 March 1949; *d* of Charles Robert Power and Joan Power; *m* 1st, 1976, Robert Alan James (*d* 1983); one *d*; 2nd, 1990, Eric G. Haythorne (marr. diss.), *o s* of G. V. Haythorne, Ottawa, Canada. *Educ:* Rotorua Girls' High Sch., NZ; UC, Cork (BA Philosophy and Eng. Lit. 1997; MA Philosophy 1999); Milltown Inst. of Theology and Philosophy (PhD Philosophy 2005). Hair stylist, 1966–71; language teacher, 1972–74; yacht charter crew, 1975–77. Sailed single handed round the world via the three great Capes, incl. first woman solo round Cape Horn, on 53 ft yacht, Express Crusader, Sept. 1977–June 1978; sailed in 1980 Observer Transatlantic Race, winning Ladies Prize and achieving women's record for single-handed Atlantic crossing, on 53 ft yacht Kriter Lady; won 1982 Round Britain Race with Rob James, on multihull Colt Cars GB. Trustee, Nat. Maritime Museum, 1985–92; Council Mem., Winston Churchill Meml Trust, 1986–93. Royal Yacht Sqdn Chichester Trophy, 1978; NZ Yachtsman of the Year, 1978. *Publications:* Woman Alone, 1978; At One with the Sea, 1979; At Sea on Land, 1981; Courage at Sea, 1987. *Recreations:* literature, philosophy, walking. *Address:* Shore Cottage, Currabinny, Carrigaline, Co. Cork, Ireland. *Clubs:* Royal Dart Yacht (Dartmouth); Royal Lymington Yacht (Lymington); Royal Western Yacht (Plymouth).

JAMES, Prof. Oliver Francis Wintour, FRCP, FMedSci; Medical Director, North East and North Cumbria Academic Health Science Network; President, British Liver Trust; *b* 23 Sept. 1943; *s* of Baron James of Rusholme and Cordelia Mary (*née* Wintour); *m* 1965, Rosanna Foster; one *s* one *d*. *Educ:* Winchester; Balliol Coll., Oxford (MA 1964; BM BCh 1967); Middlesex Hosp. Med. Sch. Registrar and Fellow, Royal Free Hosp., 1971–74; University of Newcastle upon Tyne: First Asst in Medicine, 1974–75; Reader in Medicine (Geriatrics), 1975–85; Prof. of Geriatric Medicine, 1985–2008; Hd, Sch. of Clin. Med. Scis, 1994–2004; Pro Vice Chancellor, 2004–08. Consultant Physician, Freeman Hosp., Newcastle, 1977. Vis. Prof., Univs of Hong Kong, Indianapolis and St Louis. Chairman: Liver Section, EC Concerted Action on Cellular Aging, 1982–86; Jt Cttee for Higher Med. Trng, SAC in Geriatrics, 1992–95. Pres., Brit. Assoc. for Study of Liver, 1992–94. Royal College of Physicians: Censor, 1994–96; Sen. Vice Pres., 1997–2001. Non-exec. Bd Mem., North of England Strategic HA (formerly NE Strategic HA), 2009–13. Chair, Sir James Knott Charitable Trust, 2006–. Trustee, Help the Aged, 2001–. Medical Assessor, Penrose Inquiry, 2015. Founder FMedSci 1998. *Publications:* numerous papers and chapters on aspects of liver disease, geriatric medicine and training of physicians. *Recreations:* vegetable growing, wine, golf, long distance cycling. *Address:* Aumery Park, Fadmoor, York YO62 7JG.

JAMES, Peter John, CBE 2011; Principal, London Academy of Music and Dramatic Art, 1994–2010, now Emeritus; *b* 27 July 1940; *s* of Arthur Leonard James and Gladys (*née* King); *m* 1st, 1964, Anthea Olive (marr. diss. 1972); one *d*; one *s* by Bernadette McKenna; 2nd, 1999, Alexandra Paisley. *Educ:* Birmingham Univ. (BA Hons English, Philosophy); Bristol Univ. (Postgrad. Cert. Drama). Founder Dir, Liverpool Everyman Theatre, 1964–71; Associate Dir, NT at Young Vic, 1971–73; Director: Crucible Theatre, Sheffield, 1974–81; Lyric Theatre, Hammersmith, 1981–94 (numerous first productions; Theatre Awards, 1986, 1992). Dir of plays, UK and overseas, incl. Russia. Former cttee memberships incl. Arts Council, European Theatre Convention, Internat. Theatre Inst. (Award for Excellence, 1990). *Recreations:* cooking, watching boxing and football matches. *Address:* 68a Springfield Road, Tottenham, N15 4AZ. *T:* 07784 245563.

JAMES, Peter John; author; *b* Hove, 22 Aug. 1948; *s* of John James and Cornelia James (*née* Katz). *Educ:* Charterhouse; Ravensbourne Film Sch. Director: Quadrant Prodn Ltd, Toronto, 1971–76; Yellowbill Prodn Ltd, 1976–85; Cornelia James Ltd, 1977–95; Ministry of Vision, 1990–; CEO, Movision Ltd, 2001–05. Film productions: The Corpse Grinders, 1971; Blood Orgy of the She-Devils, Under Milk Wood, 1972; Blue Blood, Children Shouldn't Play with Dead Things, The Blockhouse, 1973; Deranged, Dead of Night, Sunday in the Country, 1974; It Seemed Like a Good Idea at the Time, Shivers, 1975; Spanish Fly, Find the Lady, 1976; Biggles, 1986; Jericho Mansions, 2003; A Different Loyalty, The Merchant of Venice, Head in the Clouds, The Bridge of San Luis Rey, 2004; The Last Sign, Bailey's Billions, Guy X, Beowulf & Grendel, The River King, 2005; Perfect Creature, 2006. Stage adaptation: The Perfect Murder, UK tour, 2014; Dead Simple, UK tour, 2015. Hon. Chair, CWA, 2011, 2012. Chair, Brighton Drugs Commn, 2012–. Patron, Sussex Crimestoppers, 2009–. Hon. DLitt Brighton, 2009. *Publications:* Dead Letter Drop, 1981; Atom Bomb Angel, 1982; Billionaire, 1983; Possession, 1988; Dreamer, 1989; Twilight, 1991; Sweet Heart, 1991; Prophecy, 1993; Host, 1994; Alchemist, 1996; The Truth, 1997; Denial, 2000; Faith, 2000; Dead Simple, 2005; Looking Good Dead, 2006; Not Dead Enough, 2007; Dead Man's Footsteps, 2008; Dead Tomorrow, 2009; The Perfect Murder, 2010; Dead Like You, 2010; Dead Man's Grip, 2011; Perfect People, 2011; Not Dead Yet, 2012; Dead Man's Time, 2013; Want You Dead, 2014; A Twist of the Knife, 2014; You Are Dead, 2015; The House on Cold Hill, 2015. *Recreations:* motor racing, ski-ing, tennis, running, fine wine. *Address:* c/o Carole Blake, Blake Friedmann Literary, TV and Film Agency, First Floor, Selous House, 5–12 Mandela Street, NW1 0DU. *T:* (020) 7387 0842. *E:* carole@blakefriedmann.co.uk. *Clubs:* Ivy, Groucho, Annabel's, British Automobile Racing.

JAMES, Philip; *see* James, W. P. T.

JAMES, (Robert) Michael; UK Trade Adviser, International Tropical Timber Organisation, 1998–2000; *b* 2 Oct. 1934; *s* of late Rev. B. V. James and Mrs D. M. James; *m* 1959, Sarah Helen (*née* Bell); two *s* one *d*. *Educ:* St John's, Leatherhead; Trinity Coll., Cambridge (BA Hons History). Schoolmaster: Harrow Sch., 1958–60; Cranleigh Sch., 1960–62; joined CRO, 1962; 3rd Sec., Wellington, NZ, 1963–65; 1st Sec., Colombo, Sri Lanka, 1966–69; FCO, 1969–71; Dep. High Comr and Head of Chancery, Georgetown, Guyana, 1971–73; Econ. Sec., Ankara, Turkey, 1974–76; FCO, 1976–80; Commercial Counsellor and Deputy High Commissioner: Accra, 1980–83; Singapore, 1984–87; Dep. High Comr, Bridgetown, Barbados, 1987–90. Exec., Timber Trade Fedn, 1990–98; Dir, Forests Forever Campaign, 1990–98. *Recreations:* sport (cricket Blue, 1956–58), drawing, travel. *Address:* 17 North Grove, Highgate, N6 4SH. *T:* (020) 8245 3763. *Clubs:* MCC; Hawks (Cambridge); Hunstanton Golf, Highgate Golf.

JAMES, Rosemary Gordon; *see* Stewart, R. G.

JAMES, Roy Lewis, CBE 1998; independent educational consultant, since 1997; HM Chief Inspector of Schools in Wales, 1992–97; *b* 9 Feb. 1937; *s* of David John and Eleanor James; *m* 1962, Mary Williams; one *d*. *Educ:* Llandysul Grammar School; University College of Wales, Aberystwyth (BSc Hons, DipEd). Asst Master, Strode's Grammar Sch., Egham, 1959–60; Head of Maths Dept, Lampeter Comp. Sch., 1960–62; Head of Maths Dept, Cyfarthfa Castle Sch., Merthyr Tydfil, 1962–70; HM Inspector of Schs, 1970–84, seconded as Sec., Schs Council Cttee for Wales, 1975–77; Staff Inspector, 1984–90; Chief Inspector of Schs (Wales), 1990–97. External Prof., Univ. of Glamorgan, 1997–2002. Chairman: Techniquest (Wales) Educn Adv. Gp, 1997–2002; Awards Panel Wales (Teaching Awards), 2000–06; Chair: Denbighshire Educn Recovery Bd, 2007–11; Welsh for Adults Mid-Wales Centre Strategic Bd, 2013–. Trustee, Welsh Dyslexia Proj., 2004–11. Admitted to Gorsedd of Bards, Nat. Eisteddfod of Wales, 1997. *Publications:* numerous res. reports and articles on educn policy, curriculum and assessment, and initial trng and continuous professional develt of teachers. *Recreations:* travel, walking, reading, wine, chess, snooker, eating out. *Address:* Bryn Cemais, Llanfarian, Aberystwyth SY23 4BX.

JAMES, Hon. Sebastian Richard Edward Cuthbert; Group Chief Executive Officer, Dixons Carphone, since 2014; *b* London, 11 March 1966; *s* of Baron Northbourne, *qv*; *m* 1998, Anna Katherine Gregory; three *s* one *d*. *Educ:* Eton Coll.; Magdalen Coll., Oxford (BA Hons Law 1987); INSEAD (MBA 1991). Associate, Bain & Co., 1987–90; Case Leader, Boston Consulting Gp, 1991–94; Man. Dir, Longwall Hldgs Ltd, 1995–2001; Partner, iFormation Gp, 2001–02; Strategy Dir, Mothercare plc, 2002–03; Founder and Chief Exec., Silverscreen Ltd, 2004–06; CEO, Synergy Insce Services, 2006–08; Dixons Retail plc: Transformation Dir, 2008–12; Gp Services Dir, 2008–12; Gp Ops Dir, 2008–12; Gp CEO, 2012–14. Chm., Ink Publishing, 2001–12; Ind. Dir, Direct Line, 2014–. Advr DFE, 2010–11. Co-Founder, Tablets for Schools, 2012–. Trustee, Save the Children, 2014–. *Recreations:* ski-ing, scuba diving, playing guitar. *Address:* Dixons Carphone, 1 Portal Way, North Acton Business Park, W3 6RS. *E:* sebastian@james.net. *Club:* Soho House.

JAMES, Shani R.; *see* Rhys-James.

JAMES, Siân Catherine; *b* 24 June 1959; *d* of Melbourne Griffiths and Martha Griffiths (*née* Morgan); *m* 1976, Martin R. James; one *s* one *d*. *Educ:* University Coll. of Wales, Swansea (BA Hons Welsh). Field Officer, Wales, Nat. Fedn of Young Farmers Clubs, 1990–91; Fundraiser, Wales, SCF, 1991–95; Dep. Public Affairs Manager, Wales, NT, 1995–98; Communications Manager, Securicor, HMP Parc, 1998–99; Assembly Liaison Manager, ATOL, 1999–2003; Dir, Welsh Women's Aid, 2003–05. MP (Lab) Swansea E, 2005–15. *Recreations:* dolls houses, model railways, antiques, spending quality time with family.

JAMES, Simon John; His Honour Judge Simon James; a Circuit Judge, since 2010; *b* Plymouth, 24 Jan. 1966; *s* of Comdr David John Dicks James, RN and Anne James; *m* 1991, Dawn Hilditch; one *s* one *d*. *Educ:* Brookfield Comprehensive Sch.; Leeds Univ. (LLB Hons); Inns of Court Sch. of Law. Called to the Bar, Lincoln's Inn, 1988; in practice at the Bar on Northern Circuit, specialising in crime, 1988–2010; Recorder, 2005–10. *Recreations:* family, friends, food and wine, watching sport. *Address:* The Law Courts, Chaucer Road, Canterbury, Kent CT1 1ZA.

JAMES, Stanley Francis; Head of Statistics Division 1, Department of Trade and Industry, 1981–84; *b* 12 Feb. 1927; *s* of H. F. James; unmarried. *Educ:* Sutton County Sch.; Trinity Coll., Cambridge. Maths Tripos Pt II; Dip. Math. Statistics. Research Lectr, Econs Dept, Nottingham Univ., 1951; Statistician, Bd of Inland Revenue, 1956; Chief Statistician: Bd of Inland Revenue, 1966; Central Statistical Office, 1968; Asst Dir, Central Statistical Office, 1970–72; Dir, Stats Div., Bd of Inland Revenue, 1972–77; Head, Econs and Stats Div. 6, Depts of Industry and Trade, 1977–81. Hon. Treasurer, Royal Statistical Soc., 1978–83. *Recreations:* travel, theatre, gardening. *Club:* Royal Automobile.

JAMES, Stephen Howard George Thompson B.; *see* Bellamy-James.

JAMES, Stephen Lawrence; Consultant, Simmons & Simmons, Solicitors, 1992–2002 (Partner, 1961; Senior Partner, 1980–92); *b* 19 Oct. 1930; *s* of Walter Amyas James and Cecile Juliet (*née* Hillman); *m* 1st, 1955, Patricia Eleanor Favell James (marr. diss. 1986); two *s* two *d*; 2nd, 1998, Monique Whittome (Dame, Order of Royal Crown of Crete), *d* of Count Dom Joseph Borda of Kalkara, Malta. *Educ:* Clifton Coll.; St Catharine's Coll., Cambridge (BA History and Law). Mem., Gray's Inn, 1953, Bar finals, 1956; admitted Solicitor: England and Wales, 1959; Hong Kong, 1980. Director: Horace Clarkson PLC (formerly H. Clarkson (Holdings) PLC), 1975–2002; Shipping Industrial Holdings Ltd, 1972–82; Tradinvest Bank & Trust Co. of Nassau Ltd, 1975–85; Nodiv Ltd, 1975–78; Silver Line Ltd, 1978–82; Thompson Moore Associates Ltd, 1984–88; Greycoat PLC, 1994–99; Kiln Capital PLC, 1994–99. Mem., Law Soc., 1961–. *Recreations:* yachting, gardening. *Address:* 6 Elystan Place, SW3 3LF; Widden, Shirley Holms, Lymington, Hants SO41 8NL. *Clubs:* Royal Yacht Squadron; Royal Thames Yacht.

JAMES, Steven Alexander, (Alex); musician, journalist, cheesemaker; *b* Bournemouth, 21 Nov. 1968; *s* of Jason Bernard James and Kelly Joyce James; *m* 2003, Claire Louise Neate; three *s* two *d*. *Educ:* Bournemouth Sch.; Goldsmiths Coll., Univ. of London (Hon. Fellow, 2008). Bass guitarist in Blur, 1989–; other musical projects incl. Me, Me, Me (with Stephen Duffy) and band, Fat Les; writer and producer with Marianne Faithfull, Sophie Ellis-Bextor, Florence and the Machine, Bernard Sumner and Kevin Rowland (Dexys); weekly columnist: Alex James on Food, The Sun, 2010–14; Mucking In…, The Sunday Telegraph, 2011–; weekly radio show, Date Night, Classic FM, 2008–; producer of award-winning artisan cheeses; host, annual food and music festival, The Big Feastival, 2011–. Hon. DArts: Bournemouth, 2010; Gloucestershire, 2013. *Publications:* Bit of a Blur (autobiog.), 2007; All Cheeses Great and Small (autobiog.), 2012. *Recreations:* building, napping. *E:* ellie@neatejames.tv. *Clubs:* Groucho, 5 Hertford Street.

JAMES, Steven Wynne Lloyd; Circuit Administrator, North-Eastern Circuit, Lord Chancellor's Department, 1988–94; *b* 9 June 1934; *s* of Trevor Lloyd James and Olwen James; *m* 1962, Carolyn Ann Rowlands (*d* 1995), *d* of James Morgan Rowlands and Mercia Rowlands; three *s*. *Educ:* Queen Elizabeth Grammar Sch., Carmarthen; LSE. LLB 1956. Admitted solicitor, 1959. Asst Solicitor in private practice, 1959–61; Legal Asst, HM Land Registry, 1961; Asst Solicitor, Glamorgan CC, 1962–70; Asst Clerk of the Peace, 1970–71; Lord Chancellor's Dept, 1971–94: Wales and Chester Circuit: Courts Administrator,

(Chester/Mold), 1971–76; Asst Sec., 1976; Dep. Circuit Administrator, 1976–82; Under Sec., 1982; Circuit Administrator, 1982–88. *Address:* Westlake, 2 Heol-y-Bryn, The Knap, Barry, Vale of Glamorgan CF62 6SY. *T:* (01446) 420677. *Club:* Civil Service.

JAMES, Prof. Vivian Hector Thomas; Professor and Head of Department of Chemical Pathology, St Mary's Hospital Medical School, London University, 1973–90, now Professor Emeritus; Hon. Chemical Pathologist, St Mary's NHS Trust (formerly Paddington and North Kensington Health Authority), since 1973; *b* 29 Dec. 1924; *s* of William and Alice James; *m* 1958, Betty Irene Pike. *Educ:* Latymer Sch.; London Univ. BSc, PhD, DSc; FRCPath 1977. Flying duties, RAFVR, 1942–46. Scientific Staff, Nat. Inst. for Med. Res., 1952–56; St Mary's Hospital Medical School, London: Lectr, Dept of Chemical Pathol., 1956; Reader, 1962; Prof. of Chem. Endocrinol., 1967; Chm., Div. of Pathology, St Mary's Hosp., 1981–85. Emeritus Fellow, Leverhulme Trust, 1991. Mem., Herts AHA, 1974–77. Secretary: Clin. Endocrinol. Cttee, MRC, 1967–72; Cttee for Human Pituitary Collection, MRC, 1972–76 (Chm., 1976–82); Endocrine Sect., RSocMed, 1972–76 (Pres., 1976–78); Gen. Sec., Soc. for Endocrinology, 1979–85 (Treas., 1986–91; Hon. Mem., 2003); Sec.-Gen., European Fedn of Endocrine Socs, 1986–; Chairman: UKSport Expert Cttee, 1999–; UK Anti-Doping Scientific Expert Gp, 2010–; Member, Review Bd: Internat. Tennis Fedn, 2007–; ICC, 2009–; Mem., 2012 Olympics Anti-Doping Gp, 2008–; Standing Scientific Consultant, Irish Sports Council, 2008–. Clinical Endocrinology Medal Lectr, Clin. Endocrinol. Trust, 1990; Jubilee Medal, Soc. for Endocrinology, 1992. Hon. MRCP 1989. Hon. Mem., Italian Endocrine Soc., 1980. Freeman, Haverfordwest, 1946. Fiorino d'oro, City of Florence, 1977. Editor, Clinical Endocrinology, 1972–74. Editor-in-Chief, 1993–2000, Founder Editor, 2000–, Endocrine-Related Cancer; Editl Advr, European Jl of Endocrinology, 1994–2002. *Publications:* (ed jtly) Current Topics in Experimental Endocrinology, 1971, 5th edn 1983; (ed) The Adrenal Gland, 1979, 2nd edn 1992; (ed jtly) Hormones in Blood, 1961, 3rd edn 1983; contribs to various endocrine and other jls. *Club:* Royal Society of Medicine.

JAMES, Prof. Wendy Rosalind, (Mrs D. H. Johnson), CBE 2011; DPhil; FBA 1999; Professor of Social Anthropology, University of Oxford, 1996–2007, now Emeritus; Fellow, St Cross College, Oxford, 1972–2007, now Emeritus; President, Royal Anthropological Institute, 2001–04; *b* 4 Feb. 1940; *d* of William Stanley James and Isabel James (*née* Lunt); *m* 1977, Douglas Hamilton Johnson; one *s* one *d*. *Educ:* Kelsick Grammar Sch., Ambleside; St Hugh's Coll., Oxford (BA 1962; BLitt 1964; DPhil 1970). Lectr in Social Anthropol., Univ. of Khartoum, 1964–69; Leverhulme Res. Fellow, St Hugh's Coll., Oxford, 1969–71; Lectr in Social Anthropol., Univ. of Oxford, 1972–96. Vis. Lectr, Univ. of Bergen, 1971–72. Vice-Pres., British Inst. in Eastern Africa, 2001–11. Hon. Dr Scientiarum Anthropologicarum Copenhagen, 2005. Rivers Meml Medal for anthropological res., RAI, 2009. *Publications:* 'Kwanim Pa: the making of the Uduk people, 1979; (ed with D. L. Donham) The Southern Marches of Imperial Ethiopia, 1986; The Listening Ebony: moral knowledge, religion and power among the Uduk of Sudan, 1988; (ed with D. H. Johnson) Vernacular Christianity, 1988; (ed) The Pursuit of Certainty: religious and cultural formulations, 1995; (ed jtly) Juan Maria Schuver's Travels in North East Africa 1880–1883, 1996; (ed with N. J. Allen) Marcel Mauss: a centenary tribute, 1998; (ed jtly) Anthropologists in a Wider World: essays on field research, 2000; (ed jtly) Remapping Ethiopia: socialism and after, 2002; The Ceremonial Animal: a new portrait of anthropology, 2003; (ed with D. Mills) The Qualities of Time: anthropological approaches, 2005; (ed jtly) R. G. Collingwood, The Philosophy of Enchantment: studies in folktale, cultural criticism and anthropology, 2005; War and Survival in Sudan's Frontierlands: voices from the Blue Nile, 2007; (ed jtly) Early Human Kinship: from sex to social reproduction, 2008; (contrib.) An Autobiography and Other Writings: with essays on Collingwood's life and work, 2013; contrib. Jl of Classical Sociol. *Recreations:* travel, vegetarian cookery, gardening. *Address:* c/o Institute of Social and Cultural Anthropology, 51 Banbury Road, Oxford OX2 6PE. *T:* (01865) 559041.

JAMES, Prof. (William) Philip (Trehearne), CBE 1993; MD, DSc; FRCP, FMedSci; FRSE; FRSB; President, World Obesity Federation (formerly International Association for the Study of Obesity), 2009–14 (Senior Vice-President, 2004–06; President Elect, 2006–09; Past President, 2014–16); *b* 27 June 1938; *s* of Jenkin William James and Lilian Mary James; *m* 1961, Jean Hamilton (*née* Moorhouse); one *s* one *d*. *Educ:* Ackworth Sch., Pontefract, Yorks; University Coll. London (BSc Hons 1959; DSc 1983); University Coll. Hosp. (MB, BS 1962; MD 1968). FRCP 1978; FRCPE 1983; FRSE 1986; FRSB (FIBiol 1988). Sen. House Physician, Whittington Hosp., London, 1963–65; Clin. Res. Scientist, MRC Tropical Metabolism Res. Unit, Kingston, Jamaica, 1965–68; Harvard Res. Fellow, Mass Gen. Hosp., 1968–69; Wellcome Trust Res. Fellow, MRC Gastroenterology Unit, London, 1969–70; Sen. Lectr, Dept of Human Nutrition, London Sch. of Hygiene and Trop. Medicine, and Hon. Consultant Physician, UCH, 1970–74; Asst Dir, MRC Dunn Nutrition Unit, and Hon. Consultant Physician, Addenbrooke's Hosp., Cambridge, 1974–82; Dir, Rowett Res. Inst., Aberdeen, 1982–99. Res. Prof., Aberdeen Univ., 1983–; Hon. Prof. of Nutrition, LSHTM, 2004–. Dir, Public Health Policy Gp, 1999–2010. Chairman: FAO Consultation on internat. food needs, 1987; Nat. Food Alliance, 1988–90 (Pres., 1990–98); Coronary Prevention Gp, 1988–95 (Pres., 1999–); WHO Consultation on world food and health policies, 1989; DoH Panel on Novel Foods, 1992–98; DoH Task Force on Obesity, 1994; RCPE Wkg Pty on Mgt of Obesity in NHS, 1994–97; Eur. Panel, Eur. Heart Foundn's Analysis of Cardiovascular Risk, 1994; Planning Gp, Eur. Young Nutrition Leadership Courses, 1994–2001; Internat. Obesity Task Force, 1995–2009; UN Commn on Food and Health, later Nutrition Needs in new Millennium, 1997–99; Assoc. of Profs of Human Nutrition, 1994–97; Member: MAFF Adv. Cttee on Novel Foods and Processes, 1986–88; EC Scientific Cttee for Food, 1992–95; DoH (formerly MAFF) Nutrition Task Force, 1992–95; DoH Cttee on Med. Aspects of Food Policy, 1990–99; Internat. Panel on Diet and Cancer, World Cancer Res. Fund, 1994–97, 2004–09; WHO Non-communicable Diseases Internat. Adv. Council, 2010–14; Independent Member: Scientific Steering Cttee, DGXXIV, Brussels, 1997–2000; BSE Cttee, 2001–02. Advr, Eur. Dirs of Agricl Res. on Diet and Health, 1995–2000; Chief Advr on non-communicable diseases, WHO Eastern Mediterranean Region Office, 2012–. Author, proposals on Food Standards Agency for Prime Minister, 1997 and EU, 1999. Vice-Pres., Internat. Union of Nutritional Scis, 2001–05. Founder FMedSci 1998. Hon. MFPHM 1994. FRSA 1988. Hon. MA Cantab, 1977; Hon. DSc: City, 2004; Buckingham, 2012; Aberdeen, 2013. *Publications:* The Analysis of Dietary Fibre in Food, 1981; The Body Weight Regulatory System: normal and disturbed mechanisms, 1981; Assessing Human Energy Requirements, 1990; (ed) Human Nutrition and Dietetics, 1992, 2nd edn 1999; documents on European national nutrition policy and energy needs for Scottish Office, DoH, FAO, NACNE and WHO; scientific pubns on energy metabolism, salt handling, obesity and heart disease in Lancet, Nature, Clin. Science, New England Jl of Medicine; policy commentaries in World Nutrition for the World Public Health Nutrition Assoc. *Recreations:* talking, writing reports; eating, preferably in France. *Address:* 1 Gatti's Wharf, 5 New Wharf Road, N1 9RS. *E:* jeanhjames@aol.com. *Club:* Athenæum.

JAMESON, Prof. (Guy) Antony, PhD; FRS 1995; FREng; Thomas V. Jones Professor of Engineering, Stanford University, since 1997; *b* 20 Nov. 1934; *s* of Brig. Guy Oscar Jameson and late Olive Maud Helen Jameson (*née* Turney); *m* 1st, 1964, Catharina Selander (marr. diss.); one *s* one *d*; 2nd, 1985, Charlotte Ansted. *Educ:* Trinity Hall, Cambridge (MA; PhD 1963). FREng 2005. Nat. Service, 2nd Lieut, RE, 1953–55. Research Fellow, Trinity Hall, Cambridge, 1960–63; Economist, TUC, 1964–65; Chief Mathematician, Hawker Siddeley Dynamics, Coventry, 1965–66; Aerodynamics Engineer, Grumman Aerospace, Bethpage, NY, 1966–72; Courant Institute of Mathematical Sciences, New York University: Research Scientist, 1972–74; Prof. of Computer Sci., 1974–80; Prof. of Aerospace Engrg, 1980–82, James S. McDonnell Dist. Univ. Prof. of Aerospace Engrg, 1982–96, Princeton Univ. *Publications:* numerous articles in jls and conference proceedings. *Recreations:* squash, tennis, ski-ing. *Address:* Department of Aeronautics and Astronautics, Stanford University, Durand Building, Stanford, CA 94305, USA.

JAMESON, Brig. Melville Stewart, CBE 1994; Lord-Lieutenant for Perth and Kinross, since 2006; *b* 17 July 1944; *s* of Melville Stewart Jameson and Mary Bowring Jameson; *m* 1973, Sarah Amy Walker-Munro; two *s*. *Educ:* Glenalmond; RMA Sandhurst. Commnd Royal Scots Greys, 1965; CO, Royal Scots Dragoon Guards, 1986–88; Comdr, 51 Highland Bde, 1993–96; Col, Royal Scots Dragoon Guards, 2003–09. Chief Exec. and Producer, 1995–2007, Sen. Advr, 2012–, Royal Edinburgh Mil. Tattoo; consultant to: Windsor Castle Royal Tattoo, 2007–, Basel Tattoo, 2007–. Chm., Royal Scots Dragoon Guards Mus. Trust, 2012–; President: Perth Coll. UHI Develt Trust, 2008–; Perth and Kinross, SSAFA, 2010–; Perth and Kinross, Order of St John, 2010–. Patron: Perth and Kinross Assoc. of Voluntary Services, 2007–; Pitlochry Fest. Th., 2010–. Officer, Royal Co. of Archers, Queen's Body Guard for Scotland, 1983–. Mem., Royal Caledonian Hunt. CStJ 2010. *Recreations:* shooting, music, Highland bagpipes, gardening, trees. *Address:* Easter Logie, Blairgowrie, Perthshire PH10 6SL. *T:* (01250) 884258, *Fax:* (01250) 884351. *E:* production@melvillejameson.co.uk. *Club:* Cavalry and Guards.

JAMESON, Michael Peter; Strategic Director, Bradford City Council, since 2014; *b* Blackburn, Lancs, 26 June 1961; *s* of Peter and Patricia Jameson; *m* 1994, Deborah Harrison; one *s* two *d*. *Educ:* St Mary's Coll., Blackburn; Hull Univ. (BA Hons Hist. 1983); Manchester Univ. (MA Econ. and Social Studies 1988; CQSW 1988). Social work and mgt posts, Lancs CC, 1984–86, Bolton MBC, 1988–96; Resource Manager, Wigan MBC, 1996–98; Gp Manager, Blackburn with Darwen BC, 1998–2002; Service Dir, Stockport MBC, 2002–09; Exec. Dir and Dir of Children's Services, Oldham MBC, 2009–14. *Recreations:* golf, football, Rugby, walking, family, fine wines. *Address:* 21 Knowsley Road West, Clayton-Le-Dale, Blackburn, Lancs BB1 9PW. *T:* (01254) 245592. *E:* michael_jameson@btinternet.com. *Club:* Wilpshire Golf (Blackburn).

JAMESON, Rodney Mellor Maples; QC 2003; **His Honour Judge Jameson;** a Circuit Judge, since 2012; *b* 22 Aug. 1953; *s* of late Denys and of Rosemary Jameson; *m* 1977, Clare Fiona Mary Agius; two *s*. *Educ:* Charterhouse; Univ. of York (BA Hons). Called to the Bar, Middle Temple, 1976; a Recorder, 2001–12; Hd of Chambers, No 6 Park Square, Leeds, 2009–12. *Recreations:* opera, wine, ski-ing, golf, tennis. *Address:* Leeds Combined Court Centre, The Courthouse, 1 Oxford Row, Leeds LS1 3BG.

JAMIESON, Brian George, PhD; FRSB; research management consultant, since 1997; *b* 7 Feb. 1943; *s* of late George and Amy Jamieson; *m* 1966, Helen Carol Scott. *Educ:* Boroughmuir Sch.; Edinburgh Univ. (BSc, PhD). FRSB (FSB 2010). Research Assistant: Brigham Young Univ., Utah, 1967–68; Edinburgh Univ., 1968–70; Natural Environment Res. Council, 1970–73 and 1975–77; Principal, ARC, 1973–75; Cabinet Office, 1977–78; Agricultural and Food Research Council: Asst Sec., 1978–87; Dir, Central Office, 1987–91; Acting Sec., Oct.–Dec. 1990; Dir of Admin, 1991–94; Dep. Chief Exec., BBSRC, 1994–97. Mem., Univ. of Bristol Agriculture Cttee, 1997–2001. Mem., Remuneration Cttee, Royal Soc., 1995–2000. Chm., Silbury Housing Ltd, 2012–; Member: Bd, Sarsen Housing Assoc., 1997–2012 (Vice-Chm., 2004–08; Chm., 2008–12); Bd, Mendip Housing Ltd, 2005–06; Bd, Aster Communities, 2012–14. Mem. Court, Univ. of Salford, 1996–98. Associate Mem., Inst. of Wines and Spirits, 2015. *Publications:* papers on igneous petrology and research management. *Recreations:* running, keeping fit, ski-ing, travelling, family history, studying and tasting wine. *Address:* 8 Orwell Close, Caversham, Reading, Berks RG4 7PU. *T:* (0118) 954 6652. *E:* brianjamieson@compuserve.com.

JAMIESON, Cathy; *b* 3 Nov. 1956; *d* of Robert and Mary Jamieson; *m* 1976, Ian Sharpe; one *s*. *Educ:* James Hamilton Acad., Kilmarnock; Glasgow Art Sch. (BA Hons Fine Art); Goldsmiths' Coll. (Higher Dip. Art); Glasgow Univ. (CQSW); Glasgow Caledonian Univ. (Cert. Management). Social Worker, Strathclyde Regl Council, 1980–92; Principal Officer, Who Cares? Scotland, 1992–99. MSP (Lab and Co-op) Carrick, Cumnock and Doon Valley, 1999–2011. Scottish Executive: Minister: for Educn and Young People, 2001–03; for Justice, 2003–07. MP (Lab and Co-op) Kilmarnock and Loudoun, 2010–15; contested (Lab and Co-op) same seat, 2015. Mem., Scottish Exec. Cttee, 1996–2008, NEC, 1998–99, Lab Party.

JAMIESON, David Charles; Police and Crime Commissioner (Lab) for West Midlands, since Aug. 2014; *b* 18 May 1947; *s* of Frank and Eileen Jamieson; *m* 1971, Patricia Hofton; one *s* one *d* (and one *s* decd). *Educ:* Tudor Grange Sch., Solihull; St Peter's, Birmingham; Open Univ. (BA). Teacher, Riland Bedford Sch., 1970–76; Head, Maths Dept, Crown Hills Sch., Leicester, 1976–81; Vice-Principal, John Kitto Community Coll., Plymouth, 1981–92. MP (Lab) Plymouth Devonport, 1992–2005. An Asst Govt Whip, 1997–98; a Lord Comr of HM Treasury (Govt Whip), 1998–2001; Parly Under-Sec. of State, DTLR, subseq. DfT, 2001–05. Mem., Select Cttee on Educn, 1992–97. Sponsored Private Mem.'s Bill for Activity Centres (Young Persons' Safety) Act, 1995. Mem. (Lab), Solihull BC, 1970–74; Mem. (Lab), Solihull MBC, 2010–14. Member: Bd, Roadsafe, 2007–; IAM, 2007–11 (Vice Chm., 2010–11). Fellow, Inst. of Couriers, 2007. *Recreations:* music, classic cars, gardening. *E:* davidcj@hotmail.co.uk.

JAMIESON, George; Sheriff of South Strathclyde, Dumfries and Galloway at Dumfries, since 2009; *b* Paisley, 21 Aug. 1961; *s* of George Jamieson and Isabella Jamieson. *Educ:* Paisley Grammar Sch.; Univ. of Strathclyde (LLB Hons, DipLP). Trainee Solicitor, Hart, Abercrombie Caldwell & Co., 1984–86; admitted Solicitor, Scotland, 1985, England and Wales, 2002; Asst Solicitor, 1986–90, Partner, 1990–2001, Walker Laird; Consultant, Pattison & Sim, Solicitors, 2001–08; Immigration Adjudicator, then Immigration Judge, 2002–09; pt-time Sheriff, 2006–09. *Publications:* Parental Responsibilities and Rights, 1995; Summary Applications and Suspensions, 2000; Family Law Agreements, 2005. *Recreations:* swimming, walking, history, travel, Dutch language, culture and history. *Address:* Sheriff Court House, Buccleuch Street, Dumfries DG1 2AN. *T:* (01387) 262334. *E:* sheriffgjamieson@scotcourts.gov.uk.

JAMIESON, Rt Rev. Hamish Thomas Umphelby; Bishop of Bunbury, 1984–2000; *b* 15 Feb. 1932; *s* of Robert Marshall Jamieson and Constance Marzetti Jamieson (*née* Umphelby); *m* 1962, Ellice Anne McPherson (*d* 2013); one *s* two *d*. *Educ:* Sydney C of E Grammar Sch.; St Michael's House, Crafers (ThL); Univ. of New England (BA). Deacon 1955; Priest 1956. Mem. Bush Brotherhood of Good Shepherd, 1955–62. Parish of Gilgandra, 1957; Priest-in-Charge, Katherine, NT, 1957–62; Rector, Darwin, 1962–67; Canon of All Souls Cathedral, Thursday Island, 1963–67; Royal Australian Navy Chaplain, 1967–74; HMAS Sydney, 1967–68; HMAS Albatross, 1969–71; Small Ships Chaplain, 1972; HMAS Cerberus, 1972–74; Bishop of Carpentaria, 1974–84. Liaison Bp to the West and Chm. Australian Council, Mission to Seafarers (formerly to Seamen), 1992–2000. Chm. Nat. Exec., Anglican Renewal Ministries of Australia, 1984–2000; Exec. Mem., Internat. Charismatic Consultation on World Evangelisation, 1994–2002; Member: Anglican Bd of Mission, 1977–98; Bd of Reference, Christian Solidarity Australasia, 1990–99; Internat. Bd, Sharing of Ministries Abroad, 1998–2008; Bd, People Alive Prayer Ministry, 2001–08; Advr, Fremantle Aglow, 2000–; Nat. Advr, Aglow Australia, 2005–07. Mem. Bd, Australian Coll. of Theology, ACT, 1993–97. *Recreations:* reading, music, cricket. *Address:* Villa 339 Springfields, 17 Hefron Street, Rockingham, WA 6168, Australia.

JAMIESON, Margaret; *see* Wallace, M.

JAMIESON, Rt Rev. Penelope Ann Bansall, DCNZM 2004; PhD; Bishop of Dunedin, 1990–2004; *b* Chalfont St Peter, Bucks, 21 June 1942; *m* 1964, Ian William Andrew Jamieson; three *d*. *Educ:* St Mary's Sch., Gerrards Cross; High Sch., High Wycombe; Edinburgh Univ. (MA 1964); Victoria Univ., Wellington (PhD 1977); Otago Univ. (BD 1983). Ordained deacon 1982; priest 1983; Asst Curate, St James', Lower Hutt, 1982–85; Vicar, Karori West with Makara, dio. Wellington, 1985–90. *Publications:* Living at the Edge, 1997. *Address:* c/o Diocesan Office, PO Box 13–170, Green Island, 9052, Dunedin, New Zealand.

JAMIESON, Peter Nicholas; Executive Chairman, British Phonographic Industry, 2002–07; *b* 4 April 1945; *s* of William Herbert Jamieson and Mary Elaine Jamieson; *m* 1989, Jane Elinor Dalzell; one *s* two *d*. *Educ:* St George's Coll., Buenos Aires; Eastbourne Coll. Managing Director: EMI-AL Greece, 1972–75; EMI NZ, 1977–79; EMI Australia, 1979–83; EMI Records UK, 1983–86; Chm., RCA BMG UK, 1986–89; Vice-Pres., BMG Asia Pacific, 1989–95; Pres., MTV Asia, 1995–98; CEO, Linguaphone Gp, 1998–2002. Director: Combe House Hotel, Devon, 1998–; pjams Ltd, 2009–; Bat out of Hell Hldgs, 2009–; The Dots UK, 2014–. *Recreations:* tennis, golf. *Address:* Newlands, South Road, St George's Hill, Surrey KT13 0NA. *T:* (01932) 855822. *E:* pj@jamiesonslive.com. *Clubs:* Hurlingham, Royal Automobile; St George's Hill Tennis (Chm., 2011–); St George's Hill Golf.

JAMIESON, William Bryce; commentator and policy analyst; Executive Editor, The Scotsman, 2000–12; Director, The Policy Institute, 2000–08; *b* 9 June 1945; *s* of John Bryce Jamieson and Anne Jamieson (*née* Leckie); *m* 1971, Elaine Margaret Muller; one *s*. *Educ:* Sedbergh Sch., Yorks; Manchester Univ. (BA Econs). Sub-Editor, Gwent Gazette, 1969–70; Chief Sub-Editor, Celtic Press, 1970–71; Sub-Editor, Western Mail, 1971–73; Thomson Regional Newspapers: City Reporter, 1973–75; Economics Correspondent, 1975–76; City Reporter, Daily Express, 1976–78; City Editor, 1978–86; Dep. City Editor, Today, 1986; Dep. City Editor, 1986–95, Econs Editor, 1995–2000, Sunday Telegraph. Business Journalist of the Year, Overall Journalist of the Year, 2009, Lifetime Achievement Award, 2012, Scottish Press Awards. *Publications:* Goldstrike: Oppenheimer empire in crisis, 1989; Britain Beyond Europe, 1994; UBS Guide to Emerging Markets, 1997; EU Enlargement: a coming home or poisoned chalice?, 1998; Britain: free to choose, 1998; Illustrated Guide to the British Economy, 1998; Illustrated Guide to the Scottish Economy, 1999; A Constitution to Destroy Europe, 2003; Scotland's Ten Tomorrows, 2005. *Recreations:* reading, opera, gardening. *Address:* Inverogle, Lochearnhead, Stirlingshire FK19 8PR. *T:* 07771 800587. *E:* wbjamieson@supanet.com.

JAMISON, Fr Christopher; *see* Jamison, Fr P. C.

JAMISON, James Kenneth, OBE 1978; Director, Arts Council of Northern Ireland, 1969–91; *b* 9 May 1931; *s* of William Jamison and Alicia Rea Jamison; *m* 1964, Joan Young Boyd; one *s* one *d*. *Educ:* Belfast College of Art (DA). Secondary school teacher, 1953–61; Art Critic, Belfast Telegraph, 1956–61; Art Organiser, Arts Council of Northern Ireland, 1962–64, Dep. Director, 1964–69. Hon. DLitt Ulster, 1989. *Publications:* miscellaneous on the arts in the North of Ireland. *Recreation:* the arts.

JAMISON, Fr (Peter) Christopher, OSB; Director, National Office for Vocation of the Catholic Church in England and Wales, since 2010; *b* 26 Dec. 1951; *s* of John Warren Jamison and Mary Beverley (*née* Allen). *Educ:* Downside Sch.; Oriel Coll., Oxford (MA Mod. Langs 1973); Heythrop Coll., Univ. of London (BA Theol. and Philos. 1977). Entered Worth Abbey, 1973; ordained priest, 1978; Worth School: Head of RE and Housemaster, 1979–93; Headmaster, 1994–2002; Abbot of Worth, 2002–10. Pres., Internat. Commn on Benedictine Educn, 2002–13. Hon. Fellow, Rank Foundn, 2012. *Publications:* (with D. Lundy and L. Poole) To Live is to Change: a way of reading Vatican II, 1994; (with R. Steare) Integrity in Practice, 2003; Finding Sanctuary, 2006; Finding Happiness, 2008; (ed) The Disciples' Call, 2013; articles in The Tablet. *Address:* Catholic Bishops' Conference, 39 Eccleston Square, SW1V 1BX. *T:* (020) 7901 4867. *E:* christopher.jamison@ukvocation.org.

JAMMEH, Alhaji Yahya Abdulaziz Jemus Junkung; President, Republic of the Gambia, since 1996; *b* 25 May 1965; *m* 1998, Zineb Yahya Souma. *Educ:* Gambia High Sch. Joined Gambia Nat. Gendarmerie, 1984; commnd 1989; served: Special Intervention Unit, 1984–86; Mobile Gendarmerie Special Guards Unit, 1986–87; Gendarmerie Trng Sch., 1987–89; 2nd Lieut, 1989; OC, Mobile Gendarmerie, Jan.–June 1991; OC, Mil. Police Unit, June–Aug. 1991; Gambia Nat. Army, 1991–93; Lieut, 1992; Mil. Police Officers' Basic Course, Alabama, 1993–94; Capt., 1994; Chm., Armed Forces Provisional Ruling Council and Hd of State, 1994–96; Col, 1996; retd from Army, 1996. Chm., CILLS (Inter-states cttee for control of drought in Sahel), 1997–2000; Vice-Chm., Orgn of Islamic Conf., 2000–. Hon. DCL St Mary's, Halifax, Canada, 1999. Has received numerous awards and decorations from USA, Libya, China, Liberia and Senegal. *Recreations:* tennis, soccer, hunting, reading, correspondence, driving, riding motorcycles, music, movies, world events, animal rearing. *Address:* Office of the President, State House, Banjul, The Gambia.

JANDRELL, Steven Richard; Principal, Queen Ethelburga's Collegiate Foundation, since 2006; *b* Llanidloes, Powys, 25 Nov. 1957; *s* of Donald and Patricia Jandrell; *m* 1991, Margaret Healey; one *s*. *Educ:* Univ. of Sussex (BA Hons Music 1979); University Coll. of N Wales, Bangor (PGCE Music and Drama 1980). ARCM (Organ) 1987; ARCO 1987. Organist and Choirmaster, Parish of Holyhead, freelance musician, actor and teacher, 1980–83; Organist and Choirmaster, Cath. of St Mary the Crowned, Gibraltar, and music teacher, 1983–85; music teacher, Sandwell, 1985–86; Organist and Choirmaster, Parish of Holyhead and Choirmaster, UC of N Wales Choir, 1986–90; Dir of Music, Penrhos Coll., 1990–95; Dir of Music, 1995–99, Vice Principal, 1999–2001, Dep. Hd and Hd of Sen. Sch., 2001–06, Area Co-ord. for N and Exec. Council, 2014–, Queen Ethelburga's Coll. Mem., Ind. Schs Assoc., 2014–. *Recreations:* music of all genres, early church music, theatre, travelling, swimming, walking, chocolate tasting, avoiding management speak. *Address:* Queen Ethelburga's Collegiate Foundation, Thorpe Underwood Estate, Ouseburn, York YO26 9SS. *T:* (01423) 333300. *E:* sj@qe.org.

JANIS SMITH, Niove Rachel, (Nia Janis); Director, Playful Productions, since 2010; *b* London, 18 Feb. 1977; *d* of Nikolas Janis and Roberta Aarons; *m* 2010, Richard Smith; one *d*. *Educ:* Godolphin and Latymer Sch.; Univ. of Bristol (BA Hons). Prodn Asst, Upstairs at the Gatehouse, 1998–99; Asst Producer, The Connection Ltd, 1999–2000; Prodn Asst, RSC, 2000–01; Administrator, Royal Court, 2001–05; Gen. Manager, Act Productions, 2005–10. Mem. Bd, Paines Plough, 2012–. Mem., Soc. of London Th., 2011–. *Recreations:* reading, pilates, running. *Address:* Playful Productions, 4th Floor, 41–44 Great Queen Street, WC2B 5AD. *T:* (020) 7811 4600. *E:* annie@playfuluk.com.

JANKE, family name of **Baroness Janke**.

JANKE, Baroness *cr* 2014 (Life Peer), of Clifton in the City and County of Bristol; **Barbara Lilian Janke;** *b* Liverpool, 5 June 1947; *m* John Janke; one *s* one *d*. Former teacher. Mem. (Lib Dem) Bristol CC, 1995– (Leader, 2003–07 and 2009–12). Contested (Lib Dem) Surbiton, 1992.

JANKOVIĆ, Dr Vladeta; Ambassador of Serbia to the Holy See, 2007–12; *b* 1 Sept. 1940; *s* of Dr Dragoslav and Bosiljka Janković; *m* 1970, Slavka Srdić; one *s* one *d*. *Educ:* Univ. of Belgrade (BA 1964; MA 1967; PhD Lit. 1975). University of Belgrade, Faculty of Philology: Asst Lectr, 1970–78; Lectr, 1978–83; Prof. of Classical Lit. and Comparative Hist. of Eur. Drama, 1983–2000; Hd, Dept of Comparative Lit. and Theory of Lit., 1992–2000. Lectr, Univ. of Ann Arbor, and Univ. of Columbia (Fulbright Schol.), 1987–88. Co-founder (with Vojislav Kostunica), Democratic Party of Serbia, 1992 (Pres., Political Council, 2012–). MP Serbia, 1992–93 and Jan.–June 2007; Mem., Fed. Parlt of Yugoslavia, 1996–2000; Chm., Foreign Affairs Cttee, Upper Chamber of Parlt, 2000–01. Ambassador of Federal Republic of Yugoslavia, then Serbia and Montenegro, to UK, 2001–04; Diplomatic Advr to Prime Minister of Serbia, 2004–07. *Publications:* Menander's Characters and the European Drama, 1978; Terence, Comedies, 1978; The Laughing Animal: on classical comedy, 1987; Comedies of Hroswitha, 1988; Who's Who in Classical Antiquity, 1991, 2nd edn 1996; Myths and Legends, 1995, 5th edn 2006; The Link (essays), 2011. *Recreation:* tennis. *Address:* 16 Vlajkovićeva, 11000 Belgrade, Serbia.

JANMAN, Timothy Simon; Senior Consultant, Hoggett Bowers, since 2003; *b* 9 Sept. 1956; *s* of Jack and Irene Janman; *m* 1990, Shirley Buckingham (marr. diss. 2000). *Educ:* Sir William Borlase Grammar Sch., Marlow, Bucks; Nottingham Univ. (BSc Hons Chemistry). Ford Motor Co., 1979–83; IBM UK Ltd, 1983–87; Manpower PLC: Nat. Account, subseq. Public Sector Business, Manager, 1993–95; Sen. Nat. Account Manager, 1995–97; Dir, Boyden Internat. Ltd, 1997–2003. Nat. Sen. Vice-Chm., FCS, 1980–81; Vice-President: Selsdon Gp, 1988– (Chm., 1983–87); Jordan is Palestine Cttee, 1988–. Mem., Southampton City Council, May–July 1987. MP (C) Thurrock, 1987–92; contested (C) Thurrock, 1992. Mem., Select Cttee on Employment, 1989–92. Vice-Chm., Cons. Backbench Employment Cttee, 1988–92 (Sec., 1987–88); Sec., Cons. Backbench Home Affairs Cttee, 1989–92. Pres., Thurrock Cons. Assoc., 2002–. *Publications:* contribs to booklets and pamphlets. *Recreations:* restaurants, theatre. *Address:* 35c Weltje Road, Hammersmith, W6 9LS.

JANNER, family name of **Baron Janner of Braunstone**.

JANNER OF BRAUNSTONE, Baron *cr* 1997 (Life Peer), of Leicester in the co. of Leicestershire; **Greville Ewan Janner;** QC 1971; barrister, author, lecturer, journalist and broadcaster; *b* 11 July 1928; *s* of Baron Janner and Lady Janner; *m* 1955, Myra Louise Sheink (*d* 1996), Melbourne; one *s* two *d*. *Educ:* Bishop's Coll. Sch., Canada; St Paul's Sch. (Foundn Schol.); Trinity Hall, Cambridge (Exhibnr; MA); Harvard Post Graduate Law School (Fulbright and Smith-Mundt Schol.); Harmsworth Scholar, Middle Temple, 1955. Nat. Service: Sgt RA, BAOR, War Crimes Investigator. Pres., Cambridge Union, 1952; Chm., Cambridge Univ. Labour Club, 1952; Internat. Sec., Nat. Assoc. of Labour Students, 1952; Pres., Trinity Hall Athletic Club, 1952. Contested (Lab) Wimbledon, 1955. MP (Lab) Leicester NW, 1970–74, Leicester W, 1974–97. Mem., Select Cttee on Employment, 1982–96 (Chm., 1992–96); Co-Chm., All Party Employment Gp, 1996–97; Chairman: All-Party Industrial Safety Gp, 1975–97; All-Party Magic Group, 1991–97; Founder, 1973, and former Chm., All-Party Cttee for Homeless and Rootless People; Founder, 1990, and Vice-Chm., 1990–92, All Party Race and Community Gp; Vice-Chairman: All-Party Parly Cttee for Jews in the Former Soviet Union (formerly Cttee for Release of Soviet Jewry), 1971–97; (Jt), British-Israel Parly Gp, 1983–2008 (Chm., 2008–); British-India Parly Gp, 1991–97 (Jt Vice-Chm., 1987–91); British-Spanish Parly Gp, 1987–97 (Sec., 1986); All-Party British-Romanian Gp, 1990–92; All-Party Parly Cttee for E Eur. Jewry, 1990–97; Sec., All-Party War Crimes Gp, 1987–97, 2000–; Founder and Pres. of World Exec., Inter-Parly Council Against Anti-Semitism, 1990–97. President: National Council for Soviet Jewry, 1979–85; Bd of Deputies of British Jews, 1979–85; Commonwealth Jewish Council, 1983–2012 (Founder Pres., 2012–); Assoc. of Jewish Ex-Servicemen and Women, 2009–12; Vice-President: Assoc. for Jewish Youth, 1970–; IVS, 1983–; World Jewish Congress: European Vice-Pres., 1984–86; Mem. World Exec., 1986–; Vice-Pres., 1990–2009; Hon. Vice-Pres., 2009–; Jt Pres., Coexistence Trust (formerly Political Council for Co-existence), 2005–12; Mem., Adv. Bd, Community Security Trust, 2006–. Partner, JSB Associates, 1984–88; Chm., JSB Gp Ltd, 1988–97 (Hon. Pres., 1997); non-exec. Dir, Ladbroke Plc, 1986–95. Member: Nat. Union of Journalists (Life Mem.); Soc. of Labour Lawyers; Magic Circle; Internat. Brotherhood of Magicians; Pres., REACH, 1982–; Pres., Jewish Museum, 1985–2001; Mem. Bd of Dirs, Jt Israel Appeal, 1985–; Vice-Pres., Guideposts Trust, 1983–; Founder and Pres., Maimonides Foundn, 1992–2002; Chairman: Holocaust Educnl Trust, 1987–2012 (Founding Patron, 2012–); Lord Forte Charitable Foundn, 1995–. Formerly Dir, Jewish Chronicle Newspaper Ltd; Trustee, Jewish Chronicle Trust. Hon. Mem., Leics NUM, 1986–. FIPD (FIPM 1976). Hon. PhD Haifa Univ., 1984; Hon. LLD: De Montfort, 1998; Leicester, 2008. Comdr, Order of Grand Duke Gediminas (Lithuania), 2002; Freedom of City of Gibraltar, and Gibraltar Medallion of Honour, 2012. *Publications:* 66 books, mainly on employment and industrial relations law, presentational skills, and on public speaking, including: Complete Speechmaker; Janner on Presentation; One Hand Alone Cannot Clap; To Life! (memoirs). *Recreations:* family, magic, languages—speaks nine.

See also Hon. D. J. M. Janner.

JANNER, Hon. Daniel (Joseph Mitchell); QC 2002; *b* 27 April 1957; *s* of Lord Janner of Braunstone, *qv* and late Myra Janner, JP; *m* 1983, Caroline Gee; three *d*. *Educ:* University College Sch.; Trinity Hall, Cambridge (MA; Pres., Cambridge Union Soc., 1978; Dr Cooper's Law Scholarship, 1979). Called to the Bar, Middle Temple (Jules Thorn Scholar), 1980, Bencher, 2009. Accredited Mediator, CIArb, 2004. Dir of Res., Soc. of Conservative Lawyers, 1996–99. Mem., Cttee, Criminal Bar Assoc., 1999–2005. Member: Bd of Deputies of British Jews, 2000–05; Cttee, Dermatrust, 2000–05. Contested (Lab) Bosworth, 1983. Trustee, Cambridge Union Soc., 2010–. Gov., The Hall Sch., Hampstead, 2005–10; Chm. Govs, Immanuel Coll., Herts, 2007–09. Editor: Litigation Law Jl, 1986–90; Criminal Appeal Reports, 1994–. *Recreations:* walking in the Cotswolds, swimming, ski-ing, Arsenal Football Club. *Address:* 23 Essex Street, WC2R 3AA.

JANŠA, Janez; MP (Soc Dem), Slovenia, 2008–12; Prime Minister of Slovenia, 2004–08 and 2012–13; *b* 17 Sept. 1958; one *s* one *d*; *m* 2009, Urška Bačkovnik; one *s*. *Educ:* Univ. of Ljubljana (Defence Studies). Trainee, Republican Secretariat for Defence, 1982; Pres., Cttee for Basic People's Defence and Social Self-Protection, 1983–89; Ed.-in-Chief, Democracy, 1989–90. Minister of Defence and MP (SDZ), Slovenia, 1990–94; MP (Soc. Dem.), 1994–2004; Leader of the Opposition, 1994–2000; Minister of Defence, 2000. Vice Pres., later Pres. Council, Slovene Democratic Alliance (SDZ), 1989–91; Mem., 1992–, Pres., 1993–2012, Social Democratic Party. *Publications:* On My Own Side, 1988; Movements, 1992; The Barricades, 1994; (jtly) Seven Years Later, 1995.

JANSEN, Elly, (Mrs Elly Whitehouse-Jansen), OBE 1980; Founder and Chief Executive Officer: The Richmond Fellowship for Community Mental Health, 1959–91; The Richmond Fellowship International, 1981–2000; Fellowship Charitable Foundation, 1983–93; Richmond Psychosocial Foundation International (formerly Richmond Fellowship Foundation International), 2006–10 (Consultant, since 2010); *b* 5 Oct. 1929; *d* of Jacobus Gerrit Jansen and Petronella Suzanna Vellekoop; *m* 1969, Alan Brian Stewart Whitehouse (known as George); three *d*. *Educ:* Paedologisch Inst. of Free Univ., Amsterdam; Boerhave Kliniek (SRN); London Univ. Founded: Richmond Fellowship of America, 1968, of Australia, 1973, of New Zealand, 1978, of Austria, 1979, of Canada, 1981, of Hong Kong, of India, of Israel, 1984, and of the Caribbean, 1987; Richmond Fellowship Internat., 1981; Richmond Fellowship branches in France, Malta, Peru, Bolivia, Uruguay, Costa Rica, Mexico, Ghana, Nigeria, Zimbabwe, Pakistan, Philippines, Nepal and Bangladesh, 1981–93; Richmond Companions Internat., 2015. Organised internat. confs on therapeutic communities, 1973, 1975, 1976, 1979, 1984, 1988 and 1999; acted as consultant to many govts on issues of community care. Fellowship, German Marshall Meml Fund, 1977–78. Templeton Award, 1985. *Publications:* (ed) The Therapeutic Community Outside the

Hospital, 1980; (contrib.) Mental Health and the Community, 1983; (contrib.) Towards a Whole Society: collected papers on aspects of mental health, 1985; (contrib.) R. D. Laing: creative destroyer, 1997; contribs to Amer. Jl of Psychiatry, L'Information Psychiatrique, and other jls. *Recreations:* literature, music, interior design. *Address:* 21 Thames Eyot, Cross Deep, Twickenham TW1 4QL. *T:* (020) 8891 3643.

JANSON-SMITH, (Peter) Patrick; Chairman, Kingsford Campbell Literary and Marketing Agency, since 2014; *b* 28 July 1949; *s* of (John) Peter Janson-Smith and (Diana) Mary Janson-Smith (*née* Whittaker); *m* 1st, 1972, Lavinia Jane Priestley (marr. diss.); one *s* one *d*; 2nd, 1987, Pamela Jean Gossage (marr. diss.); two *s*; 3rd, 2006, Anne-Louise Fisher. *Educ:* Cathedral Sch., Salisbury; Cokethorpe Park Sch., Witney. Asst to Export Publicity Manager, Univ. of London Press Ltd, 1967–69; Granada Publishing: asst to Publicity Manager, Panther Books Ltd, 1969–70; ed., 1970–71, 1973–74, press officer, 1971–72, Mayflower Books; Publicity Manager, Octopus Books, 1972; Transworld Publishers: ed., 1974–78, Associate Editl Dir, 1978–79, Corgi Books; Editl Dir, Nationwide Book Service, 1979–81; Publisher: Corgi and Black Swan Books, 1981–95; Adult Trade Div., 1995–2005; Literary Agent, Christopher Little Literary Agency, 2005–07; Publisher, Blue Door, HarperCollins, 2008–14. Member: Bd, Edinburgh Book Fest., 1994–97; Soc. of Bookmen, 1998–; Cttee, Imaginative Book Illustration Soc., 2010–. *Recreations:* book collecting, late 19th and early 20th century illustrations, wine, food. *Clubs:* Beefsteak, Century.

JANSONS, Mariss; conductor; Music Director, Bavarian Radio Symphony Orchestra, Munich, since 2003; *b* Riga, Latvia, 14 Jan. 1943; *s* of late Arvid Jansons; *m* 1998, Irina; one *d* from previous marr. *Educ:* Leningrad Conservatory; studied in Vienna with Prof. Hans Swarowsky and in Salzburg with Herbert von Karajan. Leningrad Philharmonic (later renamed St Petersburg Philharmonic): Associate Conductor, 1973–85; Associate Principal Conductor, 1985–; Music Director: Oslo Philharmonic Orch., 1979–2002; Pittsburgh SO, 1997–2004; Principal Guest Conductor, LPO, 1992–; Principal Conductor, Royal Concertgebouw Orch., Amsterdam, 2004–15. Has conducted leading orchestras of Europe and America incl. Boston and Chicago Symphony Orchestras, Berlin and Vienna Philharmonic, Royal Concertgebouw, etc; conductor, Vienna New Year's concert, Vienna Philharmonic Orch., 2006, 2012. Has toured extensively in Europe, America and Japan. Prof. of Conducting, St Petersburg Conservatoire, 1992–2000. Numerous recordings. Hon. RAM 1999; Hon. Mem., Ges. der Musikfreunde, Vienna, 2001. Hon. Dr: Oslo, 2006; Riga, 2006. Eddison Award for recording of Shostakovich's 7th Symphony, Holland, 1989; Dutch Luister Award for recording of Berlioz Symphonie fantastique with Royal Concertgebouw Orch., 1982; Norwegian Culture Prize of Anders Jahre, 1991; Artist of the Year, EMI Classics, 1996, MIDEM, 2006; Grammy Award for Shostakovich's 13th Symphony, 2006; Conductor of Yr, Opernwelt, 2011; Ernst von Siemens Music Prize, 2013. Comdr with Star, Royal Norwegian Order of Merit, 1995; Three Stars Medal (Latvia), 2006; Medal of Merit of St Petersburg, 2013; German Federal Cross of Merit with Star, 2013; Knight of Lion (Netherlands), 2013. *Address:* c/o Bavarian Radio Symphony Orchestra, Rundfunkplatz 1, 80335 Munich, Germany. *T:* (89) 590034120.

JANUARY, Peter, PhD; HM Diplomatic Service, retired; *b* 13 Jan. 1952; *s* of late Eric Frank January and Hetty Amelia January (*née* Green); *m* 2000, Catherine Helen Courtier Jones, MBE. *Educ:* Sexey's Sch., Bruton; Univ. of Reading (BA 1st Cl. Hons History and Italian 1974); University Coll. London (PhD Italian History 1983). Asst Master, Chatham Grammar Sch. for Girls, 1975–80; joined FCO, 1983; First Sec. (Commercial), Hungary, 1985–88; FCO, 1988–91; Dep. Head of Mission, Mozambique, 1991–93; FCO, 1993–99; Ambassador to Albania, 1999–2001; Hd, OSCE and Council of Europe Dept, FCO, 2001–04; Hd of Private Military/Security Co. policy rev. team, Internat. Security Directorate, FCO, 2004–08. *Recreations:* spending time with my wife and golden retriever, watching and reading about cricket, Shakespeare, Elizabethan and Jacobean tragedy, European and Levantine history (articles on military history of the Venetian Republic incl. in Ateneo Veneto), medieval English churches, travel in Italy and elsewhere in the Mediterranean, Roman and Byzantine mosaics and frescoes, poetry, English detective novels, British coins, Falkland Island and other Commonwealth stamps, Times crossword, English countryside, daydreaming. *Address:* 8 New Road, Trull, Taunton TA3 7NJ. *Club:* Somerset County Cricket (Chm., Taunton Area Cttee, 2009–).

JANVRIN, family name of **Baron Janvrin**.

JANVRIN, Baron *cr* 2007 (Life Peer), of Chalford Hill in the County of Gloucestershire; **Robin Berry Janvrin,** GCB 2007 (KCB 2003; CB 1997); GCVO 2007 (KCVO 1998; CVO 1994; LVO 1983); QSO 2007; PC 1998; Deputy Chairman, HSBC Private Bank (UK) Ltd, since 2008; *b* 20 Sept. 1946; *s* of Vice Adm. Sir Richard Janvrin, KCB, DSC; *m* 1977, Isabelle de Boissonneaux de Chevigny; two *s* two *d*. *Educ:* Marlborough Coll.; Brasenose Coll., Oxford (BA 1970; Hon. Fellow, 1999). Royal Navy, 1964–75; joined Diplomatic Service, 1975; First Secretary: UK Delegn to NATO, 1976–78; New Delhi, 1981–84; Counsellor, 1985; Press Sec. to the Queen, 1987–90; Asst Private Sec. to the Queen, 1990–95; Dep. Private Sec. to the Queen, 1996–99; Private Sec. to the Queen and Keeper of the Queen's Archives, 1999–2007. Trustee: Entente-Cordiale Scholarship Scheme, 2008–; Nat. Portrait Gall., 2008–; Gurkha Welfare Trust, 2009–; Charitable Foundn of the Duke and Duchess of Cambridge and Prince Harry, 2009–. *Recreations:* family, painting, gardening. *Address:* House of Lords, SW1A 0PW.

JANZON, Mrs Bengt; *see* Dobbs, M.

JAPAN, Emperor of; *see* Akihito.

JARAY, Tess, RA 2010; artist; *b* Vienna, 31 Dec. 1937; *d* of Francis Ferdinand Jaray and Pauline Jaray; two *d* by Marc Vaux. *Educ:* Alice Ottley Sch., Worcester; St Martin's Sch. of Art, London; Slade Sch. of Fine Art, University Coll. London (Slade Dip.). Teacher: Hornsey Sch. of Art, 1964–68; Slade Sch. of Fine Art, UCL, 1968–99; Emeritus Reader in Fine Art, UCL, 2000–. First solo exhibn, Grabowski Gall., London, 1963; *solo exhibitions* include: Whitechapel Gall., 1973; Ashmolean Mus., Oxford, Whitworth Art Gall., Manchester, 1984; Serpentine Gall., London, 1988; Djanogly Gall., Nottingham, 2013; *work in public collections* including: British Mus., Arts Council, V&A Mus., Tate Gall.; *public commissions* include: Centenary Sq., Birmingham, 1992; Wakefield Cathedral Precinct, 1992; forecourt of new British Embassy, Moscow, 2000; paving for St Mary's Church, Nottingham, 2012. Hon. FRIBA 2000. *Publications:* For Years Now: poems by W. G. Sebald, images by Tess Jaray, 2001; Painting: mysteries and confessions, 2010; (with Richard Davey) Thresholds, 2012; The Art of Tess Jaray, 2014; The Blue Cupboard: inspirations and recollections, 2014. *Address:* Lion East Apartment, 24 North Road, N7 9EA. *T:* (020) 7607 1263. *E:* email@tessjaray.com.

JARDINE, Sir Andrew (Colin Douglas), 5th Bt *cr* 1916; charity and property consultant, since 2015; Estates Bursar and Fellow, Worcester College, Oxford, 2010–14; *b* 30 Nov. 1955; *s* of Brigadier Sir Ian Liddell Jardine, 4th Bt, OBE, MC, and Priscilla Daphne, *d* of Douglas Middleton Parnham Scott-Phillips; *S* father, 1982; *m* 1997, Dr Claire Vyvien Griffith, *d* of Dr William and Dr Vyvien Griffith; one *s* two *d*. *Educ:* Charterhouse; Royal Agricultural Coll., Cirencester; Reading Univ. (BSc Hons 1996). MRICS (ARICS 1998). Commissioned Royal Green Jackets, 1975–78. With C. T. Bowring & Co. Ltd, 1979–81; with Henderson Administration Gp, 1981–92; Dir, Gartmore Investment Trust Management Ltd, 1992–93; with Strutt & Parker, 1996–99; resident land agent, 2000–10. MCSI (MSI 1993). Mem., Queen's Body Guard for Scotland, Royal Company of Archers, 1990–2007. *Heir: s* Guy Andrew Jardine, *b* 15 March 2004. *Address:* Caudle Farm, Caudle Green, near Cheltenham, Glos GL53 9PR.

See also Sir J. A. G. Baird, Bt.

JARDINE, Edgar Frederick, CB 2012; independent consultant; Interim Chief Executive, Northern Ireland Policing Board, 2011–12; *b* Dungannon, Co. Tyrone, 19 March 1951; *s* of late James and Rachael Jardine; *m* 1972, Sandra Givans; one *s* one *d*. *Educ:* Royal Sch., Dungannon; Queen's Univ., Belfast (BSc, MSc). Statistician/Researcher, Policy, Planning and Res. Unit, Dept of Finance and Personnel, NI, 1979–96; Chief Exec., NI Stats and Res. Agency, 1996–2002; Dep. Sec., Office of First Minister and Dep. First Minister, NI, 2002–04; Dep. Sec., Dept of Culture, Arts and Leisure, NI, 2004–11. Non-exec. Mem. Bd, Probation Bd for NI; Mem. Bd, NI Educn Authy, 2015–. Dir, N Down YMCA, 1988–. Gov., Stranmillis Univ. Coll. *Recreation:* Ulster Rugby.

JARDINE, Dr Ian William; Chief Executive, Scottish Natural Heritage, since 2002; National Expert, European Commission (on secondment); *b* 22 May 1959; *s* of William Laing Jardine and Isabel Dakers Jardine (*née* Ferguson); *m* 1986, Anne Scott Daniel; three *s*. *Educ:* Royal High Sch., Edinburgh; Univ. of Durham (BSc Biol. (Ecol.) 1980); Univ. of Leeds (PhD Zool. 1984). Various posts, mainly in urban renewal, housing and industry, Scottish Office, 1984–91; Dir, NE Scotland, Nature Conservancy Council for Scotland, 1991–92; Scottish Natural Heritage, 1992–: Director: NE Scotland, 1992–97; Strategy and Ops, 1997–2002. Pres., Eurosite, 2007–10. Mem. Council, RZSScot, 2005–08. *Recreations:* natural history, walking, reading (fiction, science, history), theatre. *Address:* Scottish Natural Heritage, Great Glen House, Leachkin Road, Inverness IV3 8NW. *T:* (01463) 725001, *Fax:* (01463) 725044. *E:* ian.jardine@snh.gov.uk.

JARDINE, James Christopher Macnaughton; Sheriff of Glasgow and Strathkelvin, 1979–95; *b* 18 Jan. 1930; *s* of James Jardine; *m* 1955, Vena Gordon Kight; one *d*. *Educ:* Glasgow Academy; Gresham House, Ayrshire; Glasgow Univ. (BL). National Service (Lieut RASC), 1950–52; TA, 1952–54. Admitted as solicitor, in Scotland, 1953. Practice as principal (from 1955) of Nelson & Mackay, and as partner of McClure, Naismith, Brodie & Co., Solicitors, Glasgow, 1956–69; Sheriff of Stirling, Dunbarton and Clackmannan, later N Strathclyde, at Dumbarton, 1969–79. A Vice-Pres., Sheriffs' Assoc., 1976–79. Sec., Glasgow Univ. Graduates Assoc., 1956–66; Mem., Business Cttee of Glasgow Univ. Gen. Council, 1964–67. Member: Consultative Cttee on Social Work in the Criminal Justice System (formerly Probation) for Strathclyde Region, 1980–94; Professional Advisory Cttee, Scottish Council on Alcoholism, 1982–85. *Recreation:* enjoyment of music and theatre.

JARDINE, Sir John Christopher Rupert B.; *see* Buchanan-Jardine.

JARDINE, Prof. Lisa Anne, CBE 2005; FRS 2015; PhD; Director, Centre for Editing Lives and Letters, since 2002; Professor of Renaissance Studies, and Director, UCL Centre for Humanities Interdisciplinary Research Projects, University College London, since 2012; *b* 12 April 1944; *d* of Jacob Bronowski and Rita (*née* Coblenz); *m* 1st, 1969, Nicholas Jardine, *qv* (marr. diss. 1979); one *s* one *d*; 2nd, 1982, John Robert Hare; one *s*. *Educ:* Cheltenham Ladies' Coll.; Newnham Coll., Cambridge (BA Maths and English 1966; MA 1968; PhD 1973); Univ. of Essex (MA 1967). Res. Fellow, Warburg Inst., Univ. of London, 1971–74; Lectr in Renaissance Literature, Univ. of Essex, 1974; Res. Fellow, Cornell Univ., 1974–75; University of Cambridge: Res. Fellow, Girton Coll., 1974–75; Fellow: King's Coll., 1975–76 (Hon. Fellow, 1995); Jesus Coll., 1976–89 (Hon. Fellow, 2006); Lectr in English, 1976–89; Reader in Renaissance English, 1989; Associate, Newnham Coll., 1992–2002; Prof. of Renaissance Studies, 1989–2005, Centenary Prof. of Renaissance Studies, 2005–12, QMW, later QMUL. Davis Center Fellow, Princeton Univ., 1987–88; Francis Bacon Vis. Prof. of Hist., Calif Inst. of Technol., 2014. Chm., AHRB Wkg Party on public understanding of the arts and humanities, 2002; Mem., AHRC (formerly AHRB), 2003–07 (Chm., Mus and Collections Cttee, 2004–07). Trustee: V & A Mus., 2003–11 (Chm., Collections Cttee, 2004–11; Chm., Bethnal Green Mus. Cttee, 2007–09); Artangel, 2006–08; Sir Joseph Banks Archive Proj., 2007; Chelsea Physic Garden 2011–; Mem. Council, Royal Instn, 2004–09; Patron: Nat. Council on Archives, 2007–09; Archives and Records Assoc., 2009–; non-exec. Dir, National Archives, 2011–. Chair, Human Fertilisation and Embryology Authy, 2008–14. Presenter: Night Waves, BBC Radio 3, 1992–96; author and presenter: A Point of View, 2006–; Seven Ages of Science, BBC Radio 4, 2013. Chair of Govs, Westminster City Sch., 1999–2006; London Dio. Bd for Schs Foundn Gov., St Marylebone Secondary Sch., 2006–11. Tanner Lectures, Yale Univ., 2012. Chair of Judges: Baileys Women's Prize for Fiction (formerly Orange Prize for Fiction), 1997 (Patron, 2010–); Booker Prize for Fiction, 2002; Mem., Michael Faraday Prize Cttee, Royal Soc., 2003–06. Mem., Apeldoorn British Dutch Conf. Steering Bd, 2009–12. President: British Sci. Assoc., 2013–14 (Hon. Fellow, 2012); Antiquarian Horology Assoc., 2014–. MAE 2013. FRHistS 1992; FRSA 1992. Hon. Bencher, Middle Temple, 2012. Hon. Dr: Sheffield Hallam, 2004; York, 2015; Hon. DLitt: St Andrews, 2005; Keele, 2014; DUniv Open, 2006; Hon. DSc Aberdeen, 2011. President's Medal, British Acad., 2012; Bacon Medal for History of Sci., CIT, 2012. *Publications:* Francis Bacon: discovery and the art of discourse, 1974; Still Harping on Daughters: women and drama in the age of Shakespeare, 1983; (jtly) From Humanism to the Humanities: education and the liberal arts in fifteenth- and sixteenth-century Europe, 1986; (jtly) What's Left? Women In Culture and the Labour Movement, 1989; Erasmus, Man of Letters, 1993; Reading Shakespeare Historically, 1996; Wordly Goods: a new history of the Renaissance, 1996; Erasmus, the Education of a Christian Prince, 1997; (jtly) Hostage to Fortune: the troubled life of Francis Bacon, 1998; Ingenious Pursuits: building the scientific revolution, 1999; Francis Bacon, A New Organon and Other Writings, 1999; (jtly) Global Interests: Renaissance art between East and West, 2000; On a Grander Scale: the outstanding career of Sir Christopher Wren, 2002; The Curious Life of Robert Hooke: the man who measured London, 2003; (jtly) London's Leonardo, 2003; The Awful End of Prince William the Silent, 2005; Going Dutch: how England plundered Holland's glory, 2008 (Cundill Internat. History Prize, 2009); A Point of View, 2008; Another Point of View, 2009; Temptation in the Archives: essays in Golden Age Dutch culture, 2015; contribs to newspapers, numerous articles in learned jls. *Recreations:* conversation, cookery, contemporary art. *Address:* 51 Bedford Court Mansions, Bedford Avenue, WC1B 3AA.

JARDINE, Prof. Nicholas, PhD; FBA 2004; Professor of History and Philosophy of the Sciences, University of Cambridge, 1991–2010, now Emeritus; Fellow, Darwin College, Cambridge, since 1975; *b* 4 Sept. 1943; *s* of Michael James Jardine and Jean Caroline (*née* Crook); *m* 1992, Marina Frasca-Spada; two *s* two *d* from previous marriages. *Educ:* Monkton Combe; King's Coll., Cambridge (BA 1965; PhD 1969). Jun. Res. Fellow, 1967–71, Sen. Res. Fellow, 1971–75, King's Coll., Cambridge; Royal Soc. Res. Fellow, 1968–73; University of Cambridge: Lectr, 1975–86; Reader, 1986–91. Dir, Cambridge Scientific Heritage Project, 2010–13. Mem., Internat. Acad. of Hist. of Sci., 1991–. Editor: Studies in Hist. and Philosophy of Sci., 1982–2012; Studies in Hist. and Philosophy of Biol and Biomedic. Scis, 1998–2012. *Publications:* (with R. Sibson) Mathematical Taxonomy, 1971; The Birth of History and Philosophy of Science, 1984, rev. edn 1988; The Fortunes of Inquiry, 1986; (ed jtly) Romanticism and the Sciences, 1990; The Scenes of Inquiry, 1991, 2nd edn 2000; (ed jtly) Cultures of Natural History, 1996; (ed jtly) Books and Sciences in History, 2000; (with A. Segonds) La guerre des astronomes, 2 vols, 2008; (with M. Granada and A. Mosley) Christoph Rothmann's Discourse on the Comet of 1585, 2014; (ed jtly) Observing the World through Images, 2014. *Recreation:* plant hunting. *Address:* 83 Alpha Road, Cambridge CB4 3DQ. *T:* (01223) 313734.

JARDINE of Applegirth, Sir William Murray, 13th Bt *cr* 1672 (NS); 24th Chief of the Clan Jardine; *b* 4 July 1984; *s* of Sir Alec Jardine of Applegirth, 12th Bt and of Mary Beatrice, posthumous *d* of Hon. John Cross, 3rd *s* of 2nd Viscount Cross; *S* father, 2008; *m* 2011, Gemma, *d* of Maurice Clish; two *s*. *Educ:* Strathallan Sch., Perthshire. Outdoor sports educator. *Recreations:* windsurfing, sailing. *Heir: s* Alexander Jardine, *b* 5 May 2012. *Address:* Ash House, Millom, Cumbria LA18 5HY. *E:* jardinesglobal@aol.com.

JARDINE-YOUNG, Eve; Principal, Cheltenham Ladies' College, since 2011; *b* Malawi, 1972; *d* of Ian and Anne Jardine-Young; *m* 2008, James Postle. *Educ:* St Andrew's Sch., Malawi; Cheltenham Ladies' Coll.; Pembroke Coll., Cambridge (BA Engrg Sci. 1994). Teacher of Econs, Radley Coll., 1994–95; Founding Housemistress, Raven House, and Hd of Sixth Form, Epsom Coll., 1995–2005; Dir of Studies, Blundell's Sch., 2005–11. *Recreations:* music, drama, literature, conservation and sustainability initiatives, architecture and design. *Address:* Cheltenham Ladies' College, Bayshill Road, Cheltenham, Glos GL50 3EP. *T:* (01242) 520691, *Fax:* (01242) 227882. *E:* principal@cheltladiescollege.org.

JARMAN, Andrew Miles, MA; Teacher of Mathematics, Ripley St Thomas Church of England Academy, since 2012; *b* 16 May 1957; *s* of Basil Jarman and Josephine Mary Jarman (*née* Lockyer); *m* 1980, Kerstin Maria Bailey; one *s* two *d*. *Educ:* Hertford Coll., Oxford (PGCE 1979; MA 1992); NPQH 2000. Mathematics teacher: Aylesbury GS, 1979–80; Portsmouth GS, 1980–84; Haberdashers' Aske's Sch., Elstree, 1984–88; Cheltenham College, 1988–2001: Hd of Maths, 1988–92; Dir of Studies, 1992–2001; Headmaster, Lancaster Royal GS, 2001–12. OMLJ 2008. *Recreations:* golf, family. *Address:* Westwood, Westbourne Drive, Lancaster LA1 5EE. *T:* (01524) 35524. *E:* jarman67@yahoo.com.

JARMAN, Sir Brian, Kt 1998; OBE 1988; PhD; FRCP, FRCGP, FFPH, FMedSci; Professor of Primary Health Care, Imperial College School of Medicine (formerly St Mary's Hospital Medical School), 1984–98, now Emeritus; President, British Medical Association, 2003–04; *b* 9 July 1933; *m* 1963, Marina Juez Uriel; three *s*. *Educ:* Barking Abbey Sch.; St Catharine's Coll., Cambridge (Open Exhibn; BA Nat. Sci. 1954; MA 1957); Imperial Coll., London (DIC 1957, PhD 1960, Geophysics); St Mary's Hosp. Med. Sch., London Univ. (MB BS 1st Cl. Hons 1969). MRCP 1972, FRCP 1988; MRCGP (Hons) 1978, FRCGP 1984; MFPHM 1994, FFPH (FFPHM 1999). National Service, 2nd Lt, 19 Field Regt, RA, 1954–55, Army Opnl Res. Gp, 1955–56. Geophysicist: Royal Dutch Shell Oil Co., 1960–63; Geophysical Services Inc., 1963–64; House appts: St Mary's Hosp., London, 1969; St Bernard's Hosp., Gibraltar, 1970; Beth Israel Hosp., Harvard Med. Sch., 1970; Clin. Fellow, Harvard Univ., 1970; GP, London, 1971–98; St Mary's Hospital Medical School, later Imperial College School of Medicine: pt-time Sen. Lectr, Dept of Gen. Practice, 1973–83; Hd of Community Health Scis Div., 1995–97; Hd, Div. of Primary Care and Population Health Scis, 1997–98; Dir, Dr Foster Unit, 2001–. Med. Advr and Cons., Barnet FHSA, 1991–95. Member: Sci. Consultative Gp, BBC, 1983–89; Health Services Res. Cttee, MRC, 1987–89; Requirements Bd, Advanced Informatics in Medicine, EC, 1989–90; Kensington, Chelsea & Westminster FHSA, 1990–96; Standing Med. Adv. Cttee, 1998–2005. Mem. Council, RCP, 1995–98. Med. Mem., Bristol Royal Infirmary Inquiry, 1999–2001. Sen. Fellow, Inst. for Healthcare Improvement, Boston, USA, 2001–. Trustee, Wytham Hall Unit for the Homeless, 1979–; Chm., Trustees, Anna Freud Centre, 1995–2003. Founder FMedSci 1998. *Publications:* (ed and contrib.) Primary Care, 1988; contribs to books, papers, reviews, articles in med. jls, conf. proceedings. *Recreations:* music, reading, family, travel, squash, friends. *Address:* 62 Aberdare Gardens, NW6 3QD. *T:* (020) 7624 5502.

JARMAN, (John) Milwyn; QC 2001; **His Honour Judge Jarman;** a Specialist Chancery Circuit Judge, since 2007; *b* 30 April 1957; *s* of Thomas Jarman and Mary Elizabeth Jarman; *m* 1983, Caroline Anne Joyce Newman (marr. diss.); two *s* one *d*. *Educ:* UCW, Aberystwyth (LLB 1st Cl. Hons); Sidney Sussex Coll., Cambridge (LLM). Called to the Bar, Gray's Inn, 1980, Bencher, 2006; in practice, Cardiff, 1981–2007, specialising in chancery, planning and local government, and personal injuries law; Recorder, 2002–07; Principal Technol. and Construction Ct Judge for Wales, 2008–12; Additional Judge, Upper Tribunal (Lands, Immigration and Asylum, and Property Chambers) (formerly Lands Tribunal), 2009–; Diversity and Community Relations Judge for Swansea and West/Mid Wales, 2009–; authorised to sit in Administrative Ct, 2009–, Planning Ct, 2014–. Treasurer: Wales and Chester Circuit, 2006–07; Assoc. of Judges of Wales. An Asst Boundary Comr. Hon. Counsel, Welsh Books Council, 2002–07. Chm., Legal Wales Foundn Bd, 2011–. *Recreations:* ski-ing, snooker, Welsh affairs and sport. *Address:* Civil Justice Centre, 2 Park Street, Cardiff CF10 1ET.

JARMAN, Pauline; Member (Plaid Cymru), Rhondda Cynon Taff County Borough Council, since 1995 (Leader, 1999–2004); *b* 15 Dec. 1945; *m* Colin Jarman; two *s*. *Educ:* Mountain Ash Grammar Sch. Export Officer, AB Metals, 1962–65; Export/Import Officer, Fram Filters, 1965–68; self-employed retailer, 1976–88. Member: Cynon Valley BC, 1976–96 (Leader, Plaid Cymru Gp; Mayor, 1987–88); Mid-Glamorgan CC, 1981–96 (Leader, Plaid Cymru Gp; Leader of Council); (Plaid Cymru) S Wales Central, Nat. Assembly for Wales, 1999–2003. *Address:* 3 Middle Row, Mountain Ash, Aberdare CF45 4DN.

JARMAN, Richard Neville; arts consultant; General Director, Britten-Pears Foundation, 2002–15; *b* 24 April 1949; *s* of late Dr Gwyn Jarman and Pauline (*née* Lane). *Educ:* King's Sch., Canterbury; Trinity Coll., Oxford (MA English). Sadler's Wells Opera and ENO, 1971–76; Touring Officer, Dance, Arts Council, 1976–77; Edinburgh International Festival: Artistic Asst, 1978–82; Fest. Adminr, 1982–84; Gen. Adminr, London Fest. and English Nat. Ballet, 1984–90; Gen. Dir, Scottish Opera, 1991–97; Interim Gen. Manager, Arts Theatre, Cambridge, 1997–98; Artistic Dir, Royal Opera House, 1998–2000; Interim Gen. Dir, Scottish Opera, 2005–06; Interim Chief Exec., Nat. Dance Co. Wales, 2014–15. Chm., Dance Umbrella, 1997–2007; Dir, Canterbury Fest., 2001–05. Artistic Assessor, Arts Council, 2010–12. Gov., Central Sch. of Speech and Drama, 2000–05. Trustee: British Performing Arts Medicine Trust, 1999–2004; Music Preserved, 2014–. *Publications:* History of Sadler's Wells Opera, 1974; History of London Coliseum Theatre, 1979. *Recreations:* listening to music, going to the theatre, gardening, food and drink, travel, reading. *Address:* 19 Belsize Avenue, Palmers Green, N13 4TL. *T:* (020) 8350 3603, 07710 313147.

JARMAN, Roger Whitney; Under Secretary, Local Government Finance, Housing and Social Services Group, Welsh Office, 1994–95; *b* 16 Feb. 1935; *s* of Reginald Cecil Jarman and Marjorie Dix Jarman; *m* 1959, Patricia Dorothy Odwell; one *s*. *Educ:* Cathays High Sch., Cardiff; Univ. of Birmingham (BSocSc Hons; Cert. in Educn). Recruitment and Selection Officer, Vauxhall Motors Ltd, 1960–64; Asst Sec., Univ. of Bristol Appts Bd, 1964–68; Asst Dir of Recruitment, CSD, 1968–72; Welsh Office: Principal, European Div., 1972–74; Asst Sec., Devolution Div., 1974–78; Asst Sec., Perm. Sec.'s Div., 1978–80; Under Secretary: Land Use Planning Gp, 1980–83; Transport, Highways and Planning Gp, 1983–88; Transport, Planning, Water and Environment Gp, 1988; Housing, Health and Social Services Policy Gp, 1988–94. Standing Orders Comr, Nat. Assembly for Wales, 1998. Mem. Panel of Chairmen, RAS, 1995–2002; Lay Chm., NHS Complaints Procedure, 1996–2007; Bd Mem., Linc-Cymru (formerly Glamorgan and Gwent) Housing Assoc., 1996–2009. Mem., Nat. Trust Cttee for Wales, 2000–06. *Recreations:* walking, reading, wine and food. *Club:* Civil Service.

JAROSZEK, Jeremy; Chief Executive, Erewash Borough Council, since 2006; *b* 5 Dec. 1951; *s* of Walenty Jaroszek and Sylvia Jaroszek (*née* Stanley); *m* 1989, Rosemary Moon; one *s* one *d*. *Educ:* Vyners Sch.; Selwyn Coll., Cambridge (MA); Imperial Coll., London (MSc 1974). CPFA 1982. Greater London Council, 1974–85; Camden LBC, 1985–86; Dep. Dir of Finance, London Borough of Hillingdon, 1986–89; Dir of Finance, 1990–99, Strategic Dir of Resources, 1999–2002, London Borough of Barnet; Dir, J. J. Global Ltd, financial consultancy and mgt for local govt, 2002–06. Treas., Middlesex Probation Service, 1990–2001. *Recreations:* ski-ing, stargazing, family pursuits.

JARRATT, Sir Alexander Anthony, (Sir Alex), Kt 1979; CB 1968; DL; Chancellor, University of Birmingham, 1983–2002; Chairman, Centre for Dispute Resolution, 1990–2000, Life President, since 2000; *b* 19 Jan. 1924; *o s* of Alexander and Mary Jarratt; *m* 1946, Mary Philomena Keogh; one *s* two *d*. *Educ:* Royal Liberty Gram. Sch., Essex; University of Birmingham. War Service, Fleet Air Arm, 1942–46. University of Birmingham, BCom, 1946–49. Asst Principal, Min. of Power, 1949, Principal, 1953, and seconded to Treas., 1954–55; Min. of Power: Prin. Priv. Sec. to Minister, 1955–59; Asst Sec., Oil Div., 1959–63; Under-Sec., Gas Div., 1963–64; seconded to Cabinet Office, 1964–65; Secretary to the National Board for Prices and Incomes, 1965–68; Dep. Sec., 1967; Dep. Under Sec. of State, Dept of Employment and Productivity, 1968–70; Dep. Sec., Min. of Agriculture, 1970. Man. Dir, IPC, 1970–73; Chm. and Chief Executive, IPC and IPC Newspapers, 1974; Chm. and Chief Exec., Reed Internat., 1974–85 (Dir, 1970–85); Chm., Smiths Industries, 1985–91 (Dir, 1984–96); a Dep. Chm., Midland Bank, 1980–91; Jt Dep. Chm., Prudential Corp. plc, 1987–91, 1992–94 (Dir, 1985–94); Director: ICI, 1975–91; Thyssen-Bornemisza Group, 1972–89; Mem., Ford European Adv. Council, 1983–88. Confederation of British Industry: Mem., Council, 1972–92; Mem., President's Cttee, 1983–86; Chairman: Economic Policy Cttee, 1972–74; Employment Policy Cttee, 1983–86; Mem., NEDC, 1976–80. President: Advertising Assoc., 1979–83; PPA 1983–85. Chairman: Industrial Soc., 1975–79; Henley: The Management Coll., 1977–89; Gov., Ashridge Management Coll., 1975–91. Vice-Pres., Inst. of Marketing, 1982–92. Pres., Age Concern, Essex, 2000–. FRSA. DL Essex, 1995. Hon. CGIA 1990. Hon. DSc Cranfield, 1973; DUniv: Brunel, 1979; Essex, 1997; Hon. LLD Birmingham, 1982. *Recreations:* walking, the countryside, reading, music. *Address:* Barn Mead, Fryerning, Essex CM4 0NP.

JARRATT, Prof. Peter, CEng; FBCS; FSS; FIMA; CITP; Professor of Computing, University of Birmingham, 1975–2000, now Emeritus; *b* 2 Jan. 1935; *s* of Edward Jarratt and Edna Mary Jarratt; *m* 1972, Jeanette Debeir; one *s* two *d*. *Educ:* Univ. of Manchester (BSc, PhD). Programmer, Nuclear Power Plant Co. Ltd, 1957; Chief Programmer, Nuclear Power Gp, 1960; Lectr in Mathematics, Bradford Inst. of Technology, 1962; Asst Dir, Computing Lab., Univ. of Bradford, 1966; Dir, Computing Lab., Univ. of Salford, 1972; University of Birmingham: Dir, Computer Centre, 1975–91; Dep. Dean, Faculty of Science and Engrg, 1984; first Dean of Faculty of Science, 1985–88; Develt Advr to Vice-Chancellor, 1988–93. Director: Birmingham Res. and Develt Ltd, 1986–88; BISS Ltd, 1993–96; Carma Ltd, 1993–2008; Wang-Inet Ltd, 1996–97; Wang Global Ltd, 1997–99. Chm., Birmingham Inst. for Conductive Educn, 1987–90. Member: Birmingham Lunar Soc., 1991–93; Anglo-Belgian Soc., 2009–. Gov., Royal Nat. Coll. for the Blind, 1986–95; Patron, Henshaw's Soc. for the Blind, 1993–. *Publications:* numerous res. papers on mathematics, computer sci. and risk mgt. *Recreations:* classical music, mountain walking, gardening, chess. *Address:* c/o The University of Birmingham, Edgbaston, Birmingham B15 2TT. *Club:* Athenæum.

JARRAUD, Michel; Secretary-General, World Meteorological Organization, since 2004; *b* 31 Jan. 1952; *s* of René Jarraud and Simone Blanchet; *m* 1975, Martine Camus; one *s* one *d*. *Educ:* Ecole Polytechnique, Paris; Ecole de la Météorologie Nationale, Paris (Ingénieur de la Météorologie 1976). Researcher in Numerical Weather Prediction: Météo France, Paris, 1976–78; Eur. Centre for Medium-range Weather Forecast, Reading, 1978–85; Dir, French Nat. Forecasting, Météo France, Paris, 1986–89; Hd, Ops Dept, 1990–94, Dep. Dir, 1991–94, ECMWF, Reading; Dep. Sec.-Gen., WMO, 1995–2003. *Address:* World Meteorological Organization, 7bis avenue de la Paix, Case Postale No 2300, 1211 Geneva 2, Switzerland. *T:* (22) 7308200. *E:* sgomm@wmo.int.

JARRETT, Keith; pianist and composer; *b* Allentown, Penn, 8 May 1945; *s* of Daniel and Irma Jarrett; *m* Margot (marr. diss.); two *s*. *Educ:* Berklee Sch. of Music. Pianist with jazz gps led by Art Blakey, 1965, Charles Lloyd, 1966–69, Miles Davis, 1970–71; tours of Europe and numerous recordings; soloist and leader of own gps, 1969–. Concert soloist with various US orchs; numerous recordings of classical music. *Albums include:* Life Between the Exit Signs, 1968; Restoration Ruin, 1968; Birth, 1971; Expectations, 1971; Facing You, 1972; In the Light, 1973; Belonging, 1974; Treasure Island, 1974; Death and the Flower, 1974; Personal Mountains, 1979; Nude Arts, 1979; Invocations, 1981; Standards, 1983; The Cure, 1990; Bye Bye Black Bird, 1991; At the Deer Head Inn, 1992; Bridge of Light, 1993; At the Blue Note, 1994; La Scala, 1995; Tokyo '96, 1998; Expectations, 1999; Melody at Night with You, 1999; Whisper Not, 2000; Inside Out, 2001; Always Let Me Go, 2002; Yesterdays, 2009; Hamburg '72, 2014. *Compositions include:* Celestial Hawk, 1980; Sonata for Violin and Piano, 1985; Elegy for Violin and String Orchestra, 1985; Sacred Ground, 1985.

JARRETT, Rt Rev. Martyn William; Bishop Suffragan of Beverley, 2000–12; Episcopal Visitor for the Northern Province, 2000–12; *b* 25 Oct. 1944; *s* of Frederick and Ivy Jarrett, Bristol; *m* 1968, Betty, *d* of Frank and Mabel Wallis, Bristol; two *d*. *Educ:* Cotham GS, Bristol; King's Coll., London (BD 1967; AKC 1967); Hull Univ. (MPhil 1991); St Boniface, Warminster. Ordained deacon, 1968, priest, 1969; Curate: St George, Bristol, 1968–70; Swindon New Town, 1970–74; St Mary, Northolt, 1974–76; Vicar: St Joseph the Worker, Northolt West End, 1976–81; St Andrew, Hillingdon, 1981–83; Priest-in-charge, Uxbridge Moor, 1982–83; Vicar, St Andrew with St John, Uxbridge, 1983–85; Selection Sec., 1985–88, Sen. Selection Sec., 1989–91, ACCM; Vicar, Our Lady and All Saints, Chesterfield, 1991–94; Suffragan Bp of Burnley, 1994–2000; Hon. Assistant Bishop: Ripon and Leeds, 2000–12; Durham, 2000–12; Sheffield, 2000–12; Manchester and Wakefield, 2001–12; Southwell and Nottingham (formerly Southwell), 2001–; Bradford, 2002–12; Liverpool, 2003–12; Newcastle, 2010–12. Member: Bishops' Urban Panel, 1998–2010; Gen. Synod, 2000–12; Churches Commn for Inter-Faith Relations, 2000–06; Council for Christian Unity, 2001–10; C of E and C of S Jt Study Gp, 2006–10; Church Union Council, 2011–. Chm., Worksop Priory and Gatehouse Trust, 2012–. Vice Chm., Internat. Bps' Conf. on Faith and Order, 1998–2013. Vice-Pres., Soc. for the Maintenance of the Faith, 2011–. Patron, Coll. of Readers, 2003–12 (Co-Patron, 2012–). *Recreations:* psephology, reading, bird watching. *Address:* 91 Beaumont, Worksop, Notts S80 1YG. *T:* (01909) 477847. *E:* martyn.jarrett@yahoo.co.uk. *Club:* Farmers.

JARROLD, Kenneth Wesley, CBE 1997; Partner, Dearden Partnership LLP, since 2012 (Senior Consultant, 2006–07, Director, 2007–09, Chair, 2009–11, Dearden Consulting); *b* 19 May 1948; *s* of William Stanley Jarrold and Martha Hamilton Jarrold (*née* Cowan); *m* 1973, Patricia Hadaway (marr. diss. 2010); two *s*. *Educ:* St Lawrence Coll., Ramsgate; Sidney Sussex Coll., Cambridge (Whittaker Schol.; BA Hons Hist. 1st cl.; Pres., Cambridge Union Soc.) Dip. IHSM (Hons Standard). E Anglian RHB, 1969–70; Briggs Cttee on Nursing, 1970–71; Dep. Supt, Royal Hosp., Sheffield, 1971–74; Hosp. Sec., Derbyshire Royal Infirmary, 1974–75; Sector Administrator, Nottingham Gen. and Univ. Hosps, 1975–79; Asst Dist Administrator (Planning), S Tees HA, 1979–82; Dist Administrator, 1982–84, Dist Gen. Manager, 1984–89, Gloucester HA; Regl Gen. Manager, Wessex RHA, 1990–94; Dir of Human Resources and Dep. Chief Exec., NHS Exec., 1994–97; Chief Executive: Co. Durham HA, 1997–2002; Co. Durham and Tees Valley Strategic HA, 2002–05. Non-exec. Dir, Serious Organised Crime Agency, 2005–09. Chm., Co. Durham Econ. Partnership, 2006–12. Member: NHS Training Authy (and Chm., Training Cttee), 1984–87; Nat. Adv. Gp, NHS Leadership Centre, 2002–04; Nat. Mental Health Taskforce, 2003–05; Govt Programme Bd on Health Inequalities, 2004–05; Chairman: Management Educn System by

Open Learning Project Group, 1986–89, and 1991–93; Durham and Teesside Workforce Develt Confedn, 2001–02; DoH Wkg Party on Code of Conduct of NHS Managers, 2002; NHS Reference Gp on Health Inequalities, 2003–05; DoH Task Gp on maximising NHS contrib. to Public Health, 2004; Pharmacy Regulation and Leadership Oversight Gp, 2007–09; Partnership Cttee, Child Exploitation and Online Protection Centre, 2009–12; N Staffordshire Combined Healthcare NHS Trust, 2011–; Prog. Bd for Govts work on rebalancing of medicines legislation and pharmacy regulation, 2013–; Patron: NHS Retirement Fellowship, 2009–; Cavell Nurses Trust, 2013–. Pres., IHSM, 1985–86 (Mem., Nat. Council, 1977–89). Hon. Visiting Professor: York Univ., 1998–2006; Salford Univ., 1998–2004; Durham Univ., 2005–07. Hon. Fellow, John Snow Coll., Durham Univ., 2006. DUniv Open, 1999. *Publications:* Challenges for Health Services in the 1990s, 1990; (contrib.) Health Care Systems in Canada and the UK, 1994; Minding Our Own Business: healing division in the NHS, 1995; Servants and Leaders, 1998; articles in professional jls. *Address:* 75 Beechwood Road, Eaglescliffe, Stockton-on-Tees TS16 0AE. *Club:* Athenæum.

JARROLD, Nicholas Robert; HM Diplomatic Service, retired; Director, British Association for Central and Eastern Europe, 2004–09; *b* 2 March 1946; *s* of late Albert and Dawn Jarrold; *m* 1972, Anne Catherine Whitworth; two *s*. *Educ:* Shrewsbury Sch.; Western Reserve Acad., Ohio (ESU Scholar); St Edmund Hall, Oxford (Exhibnr, MA). Entered Diplomatic Service, 1968: FCO, 1968–69; The Hague, 1969–72; Dakar, 1972–75; FCO, 1975–79; 1st Sec. and Hd of Chancery, Nairobi, 1979–83; FCO, 1983–89; Counsellor and Dep. Head of Mission, Havana, 1989–91; Vis. Fellow, St Antony's Coll., Oxford, 1991–92; Counsellor (Economic and Commercial), Brussels and Luxembourg, 1992–96; Ambassador to: Latvia, 1996–99; Croatia, 2000–04. Chairman: British-Latvian Assoc., 2009–14; British-Croatian Soc., 2014–. *Recreations:* reading history, cricket, the theatre. *Address:* 9 Park Drive, SW14 8RB. *Club:* Athenæum.

JARROW, Bishop Suffragan of, since 2007; **Rt Rev. Mark Watts Bryant;** *b* 8 Oct. 1949; *s* of Douglas William and Kathleen Joyce Bryant; *m* 1976, Elisabeth Eastaugh; two *s* one *d*. *Educ:* St John's Sch., Leatherhead; St John's Coll., Univ. of Durham (BA); Cuddesdon Theol Coll. Ordained deacon, 1975, priest, 1976; Curate, Addlestone, 1975–79; Asst Priest, 1979–83; Vicar, 1983–88, St John Studley, Trowbridge; Chaplain, Trowbridge FE Coll., 1979–83; Dir of Ordinands and Hd, Vocations and Trng Dept, Dio. Coventry, 1988–96; Team Rector, Caludon, Coventry, 1996–2001; Archdeacon of Coventry, 2001–07; Residentiary Canon, Coventry Cathedral, 2006–07. *Recreations:* music, walking, popular television. *Address:* Bishop's House, Ivy Lane, Low Fell, Gateshead NE9 6QD.

JÄRVI, Neeme; Chief Conductor, Residentie Orkest, The Hague, since 2005; Conductor Laureate and Artistic Advisor, New Jersey Symphony Orchestra (Principal Conductor and Music Director, 2005–09); Music Director, Estonian National Symphony Orchestra, since 2010; *b* Tallinn, Estonia, 7 June 1937; *s* of August and Elss Järvi; *m* 1961, Liilia Järvi; two *s* one *d*. *Educ:* Estonia-Tallinn Conservatory of Music; Leningrad State Conservatory. Chief Conductor: Estonian Radio Symphony Orch., 1963–77 (Conductor, 1960–63); Estonia opera house, Tallinn, 1963–77; toured USA with Leningrad Phil. Orch., 1973 and 1977; Chief Conductor, Estonian State Symph. Orch., 1976–80; since emigration to USA in 1980 has appeared as Guest Conductor with New York Phil. Orch., Philadelphia Orch., Boston Symph., Chicago Symph., Los Angeles Phil., Met. Opera (New York) and in San Francisco, Cincinnati, Indianapolis, Minneapolis and Detroit; has also given concerts in Vienna, London, Canada, Sweden, Finland, Norway, Denmark, Holland, Switzerland and W Germany; Principal Guest Conductor, CBSO, 1981–84; Chief Conductor, Gothenburg SO, Sweden, 1982–2004, now Principal Conductor Emeritus; Musical Dir and Principal Conductor, Royal Scottish Nat. Orch., 1984–88, Conductor Laureate, 1989; Music Dir, Detroit SO, 1990–2005, now Music Dir Emeritus; First Principal Guest Conductor, Japan Philharmonic SO. 1st Prize, Internat. Conductors Competition, Accademia Santa Cecilia, Rome, 1971. Over 310 CDs including: works by Bartok, Dvorak, Medtner, Barber, Prokofiev (symphonic cycle), Shostakovich; complete works of Sibelius and all symphonies of Nielsen and Mahler (Toblach Prize for best recording, 1993, for No 3); Saul and David, opera by Nielsen; Don Giovanni; Schmidt symphonies. *Recreation:* traveller. *Address:* c/o HarrisonParrott International Artists Management Ltd, 5–6 Albion Court, Albion Place, W6 0QT.

JARVIE, Elizabeth (Marie-Lesley); QC (Scot.) 1995; Sheriff of Lothian and Borders at Edinburgh, 1997–2013; *b* 22 Jan. 1952; *d* of Dr James Leslie Rennie and Marie-Thérèse (*née* Loyseau de Mauléon); *m* 1976, John Jarvie; one *s* four *d*. *Educ:* Larbert High Sch., Stirlingshire; Univ. of Edinburgh (MA Hons, LLB). Apprentice, Biggert Baillie & Gifford WS, 1978–79; admitted to Scots Bar, 1981; Advocate-Depute, 1991–94. Part-time Chm., Social Security Appeal Tribunal, 1986–89. *Recreations:* ski-ing, music, lunching, news. *Address:* Rowallan, Barnton Avenue, Edinburgh EH4 6JJ. *T:* (0131) 336 2117.

JARVIS, Alison; freelance management consultant, since 1998; *b* Barnstaple, N Devon, 11 March 1966; *d* of late Adrian John Wilson Jarvis and of Stella Christine Jarvis (now Philp); civil partnership 2006, Madeline Jane Smith. *Educ:* Univ. of Bristol (BA Modern Langs 1988). Graduate Trainee, Lyons Tetley, 1988–90; Mktg Manager, Ind Coope Retail, 1990–94; Dir of Change, Allied Domecq, 1994–99; Dir, Stonewall Scotland, 2000–04; Dir of Countries, Regions and Communities and Dir of Scotland, CRE, 2005–07. Assessor, Office of Comr for Public Appts Scotland, 2008–. Member: SFC, 2008–; NHS Health Scotland, 2011–. *Address:* Scottish Funding Council, Donaldson House, 97 Haymarket Terrace, Edinburgh EH12 5HD.

JARVIS, Anne Elizabeth; University Librarian, University of Cambridge, since 2009; Fellow, Wolfson College, Cambridge, since 2000; *b* Dublin, 31 July 1962; *d* of late P. J. Murray and Maeve Keelan; *m* 2007, David Jarvis. *Educ:* Our Lady's Sch., Terenure, Dublin; Univ. of Dublin (BA 1984); Dublin City Univ. (MA 1997); Univ. of Cambridge (MA 2003). Asst Librarian, Coopers & Lybrand, London, 1989–92; Asst Librarian, 1992–97, Sub-Librarian, 1997–98, Dublin City Univ.; Sub-Librarian, TCD, 1998–2000; Dep. Librarian, Cambridge Univ. Liby, 2000–09. Member: Legal Deposit Adv. Panel, DCMS, 2009–10; Bd, Res. Libraries UK, 2010–. Vice-Pres., Wolfson Coll., Cambridge, 2005–07. *Recreations:* cinema, theatre, tennis. *Address:* Cambridge University Library, West Road, Cambridge CB3 9DR. *T:* (01223) 333045.

JARVIS, Anthony, MA; Headmaster, St Olave's and St Saviour's Grammar School, 1994–2010; Chairman, Council of Governors, Hurstpierpoint College, since 2013; *b* Oxford, 30 March 1945; *s* of Donald Anthony Jarvis and Ida Jarvis (*née* Allmond); *m* Brigit Mary, *d* of Baillie Andrew Convery and Elizabeth Convery; one *s* one *d*. *Educ:* City of Oxford High Sch.; Brighton Coll. of Educn (Cert Ed); Univ. of Sussex (BEd Hons; MA). Haywards Heath County School: Asst Master, 1968–71; Librarian, 1971–72; Hd, Social Studies, 1972–73; Housemaster, Beckworth Boarding Hse, Lindfield, 1969–72; Oathall School: Hd of Year, 1973–74; Hd, Social Studies and Curriculum Co-ordinator, 1974–79; Hd of English, 1979–84; Dep. Principal and Headmaster of Secondary Sch., St George's English Sch., Rome, 1984–90 (Acting Principal, 1987–88); Headmaster, Sir Thomas Rich's Sch., Gloucester, 1990–94. PGCE teacher and tutor, Univ. of Sussex, 1975–79. Educn consultancies in UK and Europe, 2004–. Addnl Mem., HMC, 1996–2010. Mem., Nationally Recognised Outstanding Leaders in Educn, 2008–; Chartered London Teacher, 2008–; Leadership Pathways Coach, Nat. Coll. of Sch. Leadership, 2009–. Headteacher Mem., Army Scholarship Bd, 1997–2001. Woodard Corporation: Fellow, 2002–; Dir, 2006–12; Chm., Educn Cttee, 2006–12. Governor: Hurstpierpoint Coll., 2001–; Christ's Hosp., Horsham, 2007–12. FRSA 1993. Hon. Mem., East India and Public Schs Club, 1996–2010. *Recreations:* travel and restaurants, books and newspapers, Rugby Union, Italy. *Address:* The Severals, Bury Road, Newmarket, Suffolk CB17 8EN. *Club:* Sir Thomas Rich's Bowling.

JARVIS, Catriona, (Mrs P. St J. Bolton); a Judge of the Upper Tribunal (Immigration and Asylum Chamber) (formerly a Vice-President, Immigration Appeal Tribunal, later a Senior Immigration Judge, Asylum and Immigration Tribunal), 2004–13; writer; *b* 16 April 1950; *d* of late Stanley and Isabella Jarvis; *m* 1996, Philip St John Bolton; one *s*. *Educ:* Manresa House Coll. of Educn (Cert Ed 1972); Univ. of Paris, Sorbonne (Cert. de Langue Française Degré Supérieur 1975); Univ. of E London (LLM Dist. 2000); Univ. of London (MA Merit 2009). Admitted solicitor, 1985; solicitor in private practice and local govt, 1985–92; Immigration Adjudicator (pt-time), 1992–96; Immigration Adjudicator, Immigration Appellate Authy, 1996–2004. Founder Mem., 1997, Dep. Pres., 1997–98, Council of Immigration Judges. Mem., Internat. Assoc. of Refugee Law Judges, 1999– (Mem. Council, 2005–11; Rapporteur, Vulnerable Persons Working Party, 2007–14). Member, Board of Trustees: Inderpal Rahal Meml Trust, 1998–; English PEN, 2012–13; Prisoners of Conscience, 2013–. Fellow, Centre for Social Policy, Dartington Social Res. Unit, 2015–. *Publications:* (contrib.) Security of Residence and Expulsion: protection of aliens in Europe, 2001; contrib. papers and articles on internat. refugee, immigration and human rights law. *Recreations:* literary debate, creative writing, theatre and cinema, yoga, swimming, walking, tennis. *Club:* Highbury Group.

JARVIS, Daniel Owen Woolgar, MBE 2011; MP (Lab) Barnsley Central, since March 2011; *b* Nottingham, 30 Nov. 1972; *m* 2001, Caroline (*d* 2010); one *s* one *d*; *m* 2013, Rachel Jarvis; one *d*. *Educ:* Aberystwyth Univ.; RMA Sandhurst. Served Parachute Regt; deployed to Kosovo, Sierra Leone, NI, Iraq and Afghanistan; ADC to Gen. Sir Mike Jackson; Adjutant, 3 Para; Staff Planner, Perm. Jt HQ Northwood and Army HQ, Salisbury; Co. Comdr, Special Forces Support Gp. Shadow Culture Minister, 2011–13, Shadow Justice Minister, 2013. Mem., Business, Innovation and Skills Select Cttee, 2011–12. *Address:* House of Commons, SW1A 0AA.

JARVIS, Frederick Frank, (Fred), CBE 2015; General Secretary, National Union of Teachers, 1975–89; Member of General Council, 1974–89, President, 1987, Trades Union Congress (Chairman, 1986–87); *b* 8 Sept. 1924; *s* of Alfred and Emily Ann Jarvis; *m* 1954, Elizabeth Anne Colegrove, Stanton Harcourt, Oxfordshire; one *s* one *d*. *Educ:* Plaistow Secondary Sch., West Ham; Oldershaw Grammar Sch., Wallasey; Liverpool Univ. (Dip. in Social Science with dist.); St Catherine's Society, Oxford (BA Hons PPE; MA). Contested (Lab) Wallasey, Gen. Elecn, 1951; Chm., Nat. Assoc. of Labour Student Organisations, 1951; Pres., Nat. Union of Students, 1952–54 (Dep. Pres., 1951–52); Asst Sec., Nat. Union of Teachers, 1955–59; Head of Publicity and Public Relations, 1959–70; Dep. Gen. Sec., NUT, 1970–74 (apptd Gen. Sec. Designate, March 1974). Pres., Eur. Trade Union Cttee for Educn, 1983–84, 1985–86 (Vice-Pres., 1981–83); Chairman, TUC Cttees: Local Govt, 1983–88; Educn Training, 1985–88; Chm., TUC Nuclear Energy Review Body, 1986–88. Member: Central Arbitration Cttee, 1985–94; Franco-British Council, 1986–98. Mem. Council, Nat. Youth Theatre; Trustee, Trident Trust; Mem. Bd, Univ. of First Age, Birmingham. *Photographic exhibitions:* Days of Rallies and Roses, London, Manchester, Norwich and Grantham, 1997; Politicians, Poppies and other Flowers, London, 1998; Monet's Garden and the lesser known Provence, London, Birmingham, 2000, Poole, Edinburgh, Alton, Provence, Oxford, 2001; Homage to the Hammers, London, 2001; Market Day, Provence, 2002; Forty Years On: a year in the life of St Catherine's College, Oxford, 2002; London's Future: the spirit of its schools, London, 2004; Photo Opportunities, London, 2004; Pictures for a Hospice, London, 2010. FRSA. Hon. FEIS 1980; Hon. FCP 1982. DUniv UCE, 2004. *Publications:* The Educational Implications of UK Membership of the EEC, 1972; Education and Mr Major, 1993; (autobiog.) You Never Know Your Luck: reflections of a Cockney campaigner for education, 2014; Ed, various jls including: 'Youth Review', NUT Guide to Careers; NUT Univ. and Coll. Entrance Guide. *Recreations:* swimming, cycling, gardening, cinema, theatre, photography. *Address:* 92 Hadley Road, New Barnet, Herts EN5 5QR.

JARVIS, His Honour (James) Roger; a Circuit Judge, 2000–14; *b* 7 Sept. 1944; *s* of late Flt Lieut Douglas Bernard Jarvis, DFC, RAF (retd), and Elsie Vanessa Jarvis; *m* 1972, Kerstin Marianne Hall; one *s* two *d*. *Educ:* Latymer Upper Sch.; Brockenhurst County Grammar Sch.; Peter Symonds. Articled Clerk, Bernard Chill & Axtell; admitted Solicitor, 1969; joined Andrews McQueen, later McQueen Yeoman, 1972; Asst Solicitor, 1972–73; Partner, 1973–2000. *Recreations:* jogging, walking, reading.

JARVIS, John Francis, CVO 2001; CBE 1993; Chairman, Jarvis Hotels Ltd, 1990–2011 (Chief Executive, 1990–2002); *b* 15 Feb. 1943; *s* of Thomas Jarvis and Mary Jarvis; *m* 1984, Sally Ann Garrod; one *s* two *d*. *Educ:* Scarborough Grammar Sch.; S Devon Hotel Coll. FIH (FHCIMA 1975). With Rank Orgn, 1965–75; Ladbroke Gp plc, 1975–90: Chairman: Ladbroke Hotels, Holidays and Entertainment, 1975–87; Texas Homecare, 1985–87; Hilton Internat., 1987–90; Prince's Trust-Action, 1993–98; Prince's Trust Trading, 1998–2000; Prince's Foundn, 2001–03. Director: Shepperton Hldgs Ltd, 1995–2001; Apollo Leisure Gp, 1998–99; non-exec. Dir, Ladbrokes plc, 2006–14; non-executive Chairman: On Board Services Ltd, later Eur. Rail Catering (Hldgs) Ltd, 1995–97; Sandown Park, 2003–12. Member: English Tourist Bd, 1983–96; BTA, 1995–2000; Chm., British Hospitality Assoc. Council, 2000–01. Mem., Exec. Bd, Variety Club of GB, 1986–98. Mem., Jockey Club, 2005–. *Recreation:* tennis.

JARVIS, Dr John Herbert; Senior Vice President Advisor, John Wiley & Sons Inc., 2007–09 (Senior Vice President, John Wiley and Sons - Europe, 1997–2007); *b* 16 May 1947; *s* of Herbert Henry Wood Jarvis and Mabel (*née* Griffiths); *m* 1970, Jean Elizabeth Levy; one *s* one *d*. *Educ:* UC of Swansea (BSc; PhD 1972). Research Fellow: Welsh Nat. Sch. of Medicine, 1972–75; Univ. of Bristol, 1975–77; Ed., Elsevier Sci. Pubns, 1977–79; John Wiley Publishers, 1979–2009: Publishing Dir, 1987–93; Man. Dir, 1993–97. Director: STM Publishing Gp, 1999–2005; Royal Pharmaceutical Soc. Publishing; Maney Publishing. Mem. Council, Publishers' Assoc., 1998–2005. Mem. Bd, Chichester Fest. Th., 2001–10. Gov., Chichester Coll., 2005–11. Trustee Dir, Weald and Downland Open Air Mus., 2010–. *Publications:* contrib. articles to various med. and biomed. jls on aspects of cancer. *Recreations:* boating, walking, guitar, reading, theatre, hypochondria. *Address:* Chilgrove Barn, Chilgrove, Chichester, West Sussex PO18 9HX. *T:* (01243) 535323, *Fax:* (01243) 770122. *E:* johnhjarvis@btinternet.com. *Clubs:* Groucho; Goodwood (Sussex).

JARVIS, John Manners; QC 1989; a Recorder, since 1992; a Deputy High Court Judge, since 1998; *b* 20 Nov. 1947; *s* of late Donald Edward Manners Jarvis and Theodora Brixie Jarvis; *m* 1972, Janet Rona Kitson; two *s*. *Educ:* King's Coll. Sch., Wimbledon; Emmanuel Coll., Cambridge (MA (Law)). Called to Bar, Lincoln's Inn, 1970, Bencher, 1998; practising barrister specialising in Commercial Law, particularly banking; Jt Hd of Chambers, 1999–2009. An Asst Recorder, 1987–92. CEDR Mediator, 2000–. Chm., Commercial Bar Assoc., 1995–97 (Treas., 1993–95); Mem., Bar Council, 1995–97. Gov., King's Coll. Sch., Wimbledon, 1987– (Chm., 2008–13). Overseas Editor, Jl of Banking and Finance—Law and Practice, 1990–; Consultant Editor, Jl of Internat. Banking and Finance, 2006–. *Publications:* (jtly) Lender Liability, 1993; (contrib.) Banks, Liability and Risk, 2nd edn 1995. *Recreations:* tennis, horse-riding, sailing, ski-ing, cycling, music. *Address:* 3 Verulam Buildings, Gray's Inn, WC1R 5NT. *T:* (020) 7831 8441, *Fax:* (020) 7831 8479. *E:* jjarvis@3vb.com. *Club:* Hurlingham.

JARVIS, Surg. Rear Adm. Lionel John, CBE 2012; FRCR; Chief Executive, Qatar Heart Hospital, Hamad Medical Corporation, Doha, 2012–15; *b* Windsor, 13 May 1955; *s* of Steve and Eileen Jarvis; *m* 1998, Dr Penelope Gordon; one *s* one *d*. *Educ:* Wellington Coll., Berks; Guy's Hosp., London (MB BS 1977). MRCS, LRCP 1977; FRCR 1988; MIET 2003. Defence consultant advr in radiol., 1995–2000; Cons. Radiologist and CO, Royal Hosp., Haslar, 2001–03; rcds 2004; Dir, Med. Policy, MoD, 2005–08; ACDS (Health), 2008–11; Chief Naval Med. Officer and Med. Dir Gen. (Naval), 2009–12. QHS, 2006–12. Pres., Royal Navy Cresta, 2010–12. Vice Patron, Poppy Factory, 2012–. Gov., Royal Star and Garter Homes, 2009–12. Diagnostic Imaging Dr of Year, 1999; Crookshank Medal, RCR, 2007. Gulf War Medal (with clasp), 1991; Queen's Jubilee Medal, 2002, 2012; Iraq War Medal (with clasp), 2003. OStJ 2012. *Publications:* contribs to med. jls, incl. Lancet, American Jl Radiol., Clinical Radiol., BMJ. *Recreations:* sailing, ski-ing, cresta, riding. *Address:* Midlington Farmhouse, Droxford, Hants SO32 3PU. *Clubs:* Army and Navy, Royal Society of Medicine; Royal Naval Sailing Association.

JARVIS, Martin, OBE 2000; actor, director and producer; *b* 4 Aug. 1941; *s* of late Denys Jarvis and of Margot Jarvis; *m*; two *s*; *m* 1974, Rosalind Ayres. *Educ:* Whitgift School; RADA (Hons Dip., 1962, Silver Medal, 1962, Vanbrugh Award, 1962; RADA Associate, 1980). Nat. Youth Theatre, 1960–62; played Henry V, Sadler's Wells, 1962; Manchester Library Theatre, 1962–63; *stage:* Life of Galileo, Mermaid, 1963; Cockade, Arts, 1963; Poor Bitos, Duke of York's, 1963; Man and Superman, Vaudeville, 1966; The Bandwagon, Mermaid, 1970; The Rivals, USA, 1973; Hamlet (title rôle), Fest. of British Th., 1973; The Circle, Haymarket, 1976; She Stoops to Conquer, Canada, and Hong Kong Arts Festival, 1977; Caught in the Act, Garrick, 1981; Importance of Being Earnest, NT, 1982; Victoria Station, NT, 1983; The Trojan War Will Not Take Place, NT, 1983; Woman in Mind, Vaudeville, 1986; The Perfect Party, Greenwich, 1987; Henceforward, Vaudeville, 1989; Exchange, Vaudeville, 1990, Los Angeles, 1992; You Say Potato, Los Angeles, 1990; Twelfth Night, Playhouse, 1991; Leo in Love, Southampton, 1992; Just Between Ourselves, Greenwich, 1992; Make and Break, 1993, Man of the Moment, 1994, Los Angeles; On Approval, Playhouse, 1994; Table Manners, LA, 1995; The Doctor's Dilemma, Almeida, 1998; Skylight, LA, 1999; Passion Play, Donmar, 2000; By Jeeves, NY, 2001; recitals of Paradise Lost, Old Vic, Chichester and QEH, 1975–77; The Queen's Birthday Concert, Royal Festival Hall, 1996; narrator, Peter and the Wolf, Barbican, 1997; An Audience with Martin Jarvis, RNT, 2003; Gielgud Centenary Gala, Gielgud, 2004; Twelfth Night, Regent's Pk, 2005; Honour, Wyndham's, 2006; Dir, The Life of Galileo, LA, 2008; recitals of Beloved Clara and Odyssey of Love, Chichester, Wigmore Hall, Kings Place, St John Smith's Square and Los Angeles, 2007–15; The Importance of Being Earnest, Harold Pinter Th., 2014; Racing Demon, LA, 2014; The Guilty Mother, LA, 2015; *films:* The Last Escape, Ike, The Bunker, Taste the Blood of Dracula, Buster; The Fool of the World and the Flying Ship, 1991 (Emmy Award); Emily's Ghost, 1992; Calliope; Absence of War, 1995; Titanic, 1997; The X-Ray Kid, Sex 'n' Death, 1999; Mrs Caldicot's Cabbage War, By Jeeves, 2002; Much Ado About Nothing, 2005; Framed, 2006; The Legend of Spyro, 2007; Return of the Neanderthal Man, 2009; Neander Jin, 2010; Cars 2, The Girl with the Dragon Tattoo, 2011; Wreck-It Ralph, 2013; Phil Spector (USA), 2013; United Passions, 2014; *television series:* The Forsyte Saga, 1967; Nicholas Nickleby, 1968; Little Women, 1969; The Moonstone, 1971; The Pallisers, 1974; David Copperfield, 1975; Killers, 1976; Rings on Their Fingers, 1978–80; Breakaway, 1980; The Black Tower, 1985; Chelworth, 1988; Countdown, 1990–; Murder Most Horrid, 1991; The Good Guys, 1992; Woof!, 1992; Library of Romance, 1992; Girl from Ipanema (British Comedy Award); Scarlet and Black, 1993; Brillat Saverin, 1994; Lovejoy, 1994; Murder She Wrote, 1995; Supply and Demand, 1998; Space Island One, 1998; Lorna Doone, 2000; Micawber, 2001; Bootleg, 2002; Psi-Kix (USA), 2003; Doctors, 2004, 2009; Numb3rs (USA), 2007; The Bill, 2008; Stargate Atlantis (USA), 2008; Taking the Flak, 2009; Eastenders, 2010; Marple: The Mirror Crack'd From Side to Side, 2010; Just William, 2011; Funny or Die (USA), 2011; Endeavour; By Any Means, 2013; Poirot: Dead Man's Folly, 2013; Law and Order UK, 2014; Cosmos, 2014; American Dad, 2015; *radio:* numerous performances, incl. one-man series, Jarvis's Frayn; as Charles Dickens in series, The Best of Times; Gush, 1994; (and prod.) Speak After the Beep, 2 series, 1997; Spies, 2002; Ring for Jeeves, 2014; productions of plays; script writing and adaptations; prod. and dir dramas, 2002–, incl. Dr No, 2008; Jeeves Live, BBC and Cheltenham Fest., 2008; Dir, A Small Family Business, 2009; Man of the Moment, 2009; Dir, Goldfinger, 2010 (Earphones Award, 2010); Dir, Widowers' Houses, The Browning Version, England, Their England, 2011; Henceforward…, From Russia With Love, 2012; Dir, Skios, You Never Can Tell, Air Force One, 2013, On Her Majesty's Secret Service, 2014; Dir, for LATW-NPR (USA), The Rivals, Macbeth, Hamlet, Romeo and Juliet, Copenhagen, 2011–12, An Enemy of the People, 2014; Dir, A Midsummer Night's Dream, The Liar (Corneille), 2013; Dir, Diamonds Are Forever, Michael Frayn's Matchbox Th., 2015; commentaries for TV and film documentaries and for arts programmes; has adapted and read over 100 of Richmal Crompton's Just William stories for radio, TV and CD; Just William Live!, Best of British Fest., Th. Royal Winchester and radio, 2012; Jeeves Live and Just William Live, BBC Radio and Cheltenham Fest.; recorded one-man performance of David Copperfield for cassette, 1991; one-man perf., Oscar Wilde, 1996; co-produced cassette 2nd World War Poetry, 1993; produced and directed cassettes, Lord of the Flies; Tales from Shakespeare; P. G. Wodehouse recordings, 2007–; Voice of God, OT CD recordings (USA), 2009. Writer/presenter, Concorde Playhouse, 1994–97. Dir, Children's Film Unit, 1993–2000. Co-founder (with Rosalind Ayres), Jarvis & Ayres Productions, 2000–. Mem., Artist Adv. Council, LA Theatre Works, 2000–. Vice-Pres., Salamander Oasis Trust, 1990–2007. Mem., BAFTA. Sony Silver Award, 1991; NY Internat. Award, for contribn to broadcasting, 1994; British Talkies award, 1995, 1997, 1998; US Audie Award, 1999; Theatre World Award for Outstanding Broadway Debut, 2002; US Earphones Award, 2003, 2005, 2007, 2009; Radio Independents Gp Award, for outstanding contribn to broadcasting, 2007. *Publications:* Bright Boy, 1977; William Stories: a personal selection, 1992; Meet Just William, 1999; Acting Strangely (autobiog.), 1999; Broadway, Jeeves?, 2003; short stories for radio; contribs to many anthologies; articles in The Listener, Punch, Tatler, The Times, Daily Express, Daily Telegraph and Daily Mail. *Recreations:* Beethoven, Mozart, Schumann, growing lemons. *Address:* c/o Amanda Howard Associates, 74 Clerkenwell Road, EC1M 5QA. *Club:* Ivy.

JARVIS, Prof. Martin John, OBE 2002; DSc; Principal Scientist, Cancer Research UK (formerly Imperial Cancer Research Fund), 1991–94; Professor of Health Psychology, University College London, 1999–2004, now Emeritus; *b* 30 June 1939; s of Richard William Jarvis and Mary May Jarvis (*née* Utting); *m* 1969, Muriel Richardson; one *s* one *d*. *Educ:* Watford Grammar Sch.; Corpus Christi Coll., Cambridge (MA); Birkbeck Coll., London (BA Psychol.); Inst. of Psychiatry (MPhil Clin. Psychol); UCL (DSc Medicine 1997). Res. worker, 1978–89, Sen. Lectr, 1986–89, Addiction Res. Unit, Inst. Psychiatry; Sen. Scientist, Health Behaviour Unit, ICRF, 1989–91; Reader in Health Psychol., UCL, 1996–99. Mem., CMO's Scientific Cttee on Tobacco and Health, 1994–. Dir, ASH, 1996–. Mem., Scientific Cttee on Tobacco Product Regulation, WHO, 2000–. *Publications:* numerous res. papers on tobacco smoking and nicotine addiction. *Recreations:* growing vegetables, bee-keeping, walking, gym. *Address:* Department of Epidemiology and Public Health, University College London, 1–19 Torrington Place, WC1E 6BT; 118 Woodwarde Road, SE22 8UT. *T:* (020) 8693 3508. *E:* martin.jarvis@ucl.ac.uk.

JARVIS, Richard James; Consultant in Communicable Disease Control, Public Health England (formerly Health Protection Agency), since 2003; Head of School, North West School of Public Health, since 2013; *b* Stoke-on-Trent, 28 March 1966; *s* of Victor and Dorotheamaria Jarvis; *m* 1996, Kathryn Simpson; one *s* one *d*. *Educ:* Cotton Coll., N Staffs; King's Coll. London (BSc Immunol. and Basic Med. Scis 1988; MB BS Medicine and Surgery 1991); Univ. of Birmingham (MPH 1998); Univ. of Salford (Postgrad. Envmtl Protection 2006). MFPH 2001, FFPH 2005. Jun. med. posts, N Staffs Hosp., 1991–93, Trent Postgrad. Hosp., 1993–95; GP registrar, Bath Rd Surgery, Buxton, 1995–96; specialist registrar, W Midlands Public Health Trng Scheme, 1996–2001; Consultant in communicable disease control, Liverpool HA, 2001–03. Hon. Clin. Lectr, Liverpool Univ., 2011–. Chm., Public Health Medicine Cttee, BMA, 2008–12. *Recreations:* photography, astronomy, amateur meteorology, walking, cinema. *Address:* Cheshire and Merseyside Health Protection Unit, Floor 5, Rail House, Lord Nelson Street, Liverpool L1 1JF. *T:* 0344 225 1295. *E:* richard.jarvis@phe.gov.uk.

JARVIS, Roger; *see* Jarvis, J. R.

JARVIS, Sian Elizabeth, CB 2010; strategic communications consultant, Asda, since 2013 (Director, Corporate Relations, 2012–13); *b* Bromsgrove, 11 April 1963; *d* of Anthony and Marjorie Jarvis; twin *s* and *d*. *Educ:* Loughborough Univ. (BA Hons). With BBC, 1986–92: Current Affairs, Radio 4, 1986–88; news trainee, 1988–89; reporter/presenter, Look East, 1989–92; Political Corresp., GMTV, 1992–99; Hd of News, 1999–2001, Dir-Gen. Communications, 2001–11, DoH. Partner, African Horseback Safaris, 2007–. *Recreations:* opera and theatre, horseback riding, ski-ing.

JARY, Michael Keith, FRAS; Founder Member, 1987, and Senior Partner, OC&C Strategy Consultants (Partner, since 1993); *b* Cambridge, 15 June 1963; *s* of Keith Jary and late Jacqueline Ann Jary (*née* Pogue); *m* 2015, Jonathan Jimenez Ferrer. *Educ:* Berkhamsted Sch. (Schol.); Merton Coll., Oxford (Postmaster 1982; BA Hons Physics 1985; MA 1989); INSEAD (Louis Franck Schol.; Kitchener Schol.; MBA Dist. 1989); Sch. of Oriental and African Studies, Univ. of London (Postgrad. Cert. Asian Art (Dist.) 2008). Associate, Booz Allen & Hamilton, 1985–87; OC&C Strategy Consultants: Man. Partner, London and Hd, Worldwide Retail Practice, 2000–05; Worldwide Man. Partner and Chm., Internat. Exec. Cttee, 2005–11. Mem., Investment Cttee, Web-Angel plc, 1999–2001; non-executive Chairman: Duchy Originals Ltd, 2008–; The Prince's Social Enterprises, 2010–; non-executive Director: Wax Lyrical Ltd, 1995–96; Nationwide Building Soc., 2009–. Member: Adv. Bd, World Retail Congress, 2009–12; Exec. Sub-cttee, The Prince's Charities, 2010–13. Chair, Bd of Trustees, Fairtrade Foundn, 2013–. Ambassador, Retail Trust, 2014–. FRAS 2011. *Publications:* (jtly) Retail Power Plays, 1997; (jtly) Markenpower, 1998; (jtly) Brands: the new wealth creators, 1998; (contrib.) Market Leader, 2009; In the Footsteps of a Himalayan Pilgrimage, 2013. *Recreations:* collecting Indian and South East Asian art and cultural artefacts, organic farming (pigs, sheep, poultry, bees and vegetables), opera-going, playing croquet, classic cars, cooking, Himalayan trekking. *Address:* c/o OC&C Strategy Consultants, 6 New Street Square, EC4A 3AT. *T:* (020) 7010 8024, *Fax:* (020) 7010 8100. *Club:* Royal Automobile.

JASON, Sir David, Kt 2005; OBE 1993; actor; *b* 2 Feb. 1940; *s* of Arthur and Olwyn White; adopted stage name, David Jason, 1965; *m* 2005, Gill Hinchcliffe; one *d*. Stage career began with a season in repertory, Bromley Rep.; *theatre includes:* Under Milk Wood, Mayfair, 1971; The Rivals, Sadler's Wells, 1972; No Sex Please … We're British!, Strand, 1972; Darling Mr London, tour, 1975; Charley's Aunt, tour, 1975; The Norman Conquests, Oxford Playhouse, 1976; The Relapse, Cambridge Theatre Co., 1978; Cinderella, 1979; The Unvarnished Truth, Mid/Far East tour, 1983; Look No Hans!, tour and West End, 1985; *films:* Under Milk Wood, 1970; Royal Flash, 1974; The Odd Job, 1978; Only Fools and Horses; Wind in the Willows, 1983; *television includes:* Do Not Adjust Your Set, 1967; The Top Secret Life of Edgar Briggs, 1973–74; Mr Stabbs, 1974; Ronnie Barker Shows, 1975; Open All Hours, 1975; Porridge, 1975; Lucky Feller, 1975; A Sharp Intake of Breath, 1978; Del Trotter in Only Fools and Horses, 1981–91 (Best Light Entertainment Perf., BAFTA, 1990); Porterhouse Blue, 1986; Jackanory, 1988; A Bit of A Do, 1988–89; Single Voices: The Chemist, 1989; Amongst Barbarians, 1989; Pa Larkin in The Darling Buds of May, 1990–93; A Touch of Frost, 1992–2010; The Bullion Boys, 1993; All the King's Men, 1999; Micawber, 2001; The Quest (also dir), 2002; The Hogfather, 2006; The Colour of Magic, 2008; The Royal Bodyguard, 2011; Still Open All Hours, 2015; *voice work:* Dangermouse, Count Duckula, The Wind in the Willows. Awards include Best Actor Award, BAFTA, 1988; Special Recognition Award for Lifetime Achievement in Television, Nat. Television Awards, 1996; Best Comedy Perf. Award, BAFTA, 1997; BAFTA Fellowship, 2003. *Publications:* David Jason: my life, 2013. *Recreations:* diving, flying, motorcycles. *Address:* c/o Richard Stone Partnership, Suite 3, De Walden Court, 85 New Cavendish Street, W1W 6XD.

JASPAN, Andrew; Founder, Executive Director and Editor, The Conversation website, Melbourne, since 2010; Editor-in-Chief and Trustee, The Conversation website, UK, since 2012; Editor-in-Chief and Board Member, The Conversation website, USA; Asia-Pacific Director, Innovation Media Consulting, since 2009; *b* 20 April 1952; *s* of Mervyn and Helen Jaspan; *m* 1991, Karen Jane Grant; two *s*. *Educ:* Beverley GS; Manchester Univ. (BA Hons Politics). Co-Founder, New Manchester Review, 1976–79; Daily Telegraph features, 1979; Fellowship, Journalists in Europe, Paris, 1980–81; freelance journalist, Daily Mirror and Daily Telegraph, 1982; News Sub-Ed., The Times, 1983–85; Asst News Ed., Sunday Times, 1985–88; Editor: Sunday Times Scotland, 1988–89; Scotland on Sunday, 1989–94; The Scotsman, 1994–95; The Observer, 1995–96; Publr and Man. Dir, The Big Issue, 1996–98; Ed., Sunday Herald, 1999–2004; Ed.-in-Chief, The Age, 2004–08. Consultant, 2008–10, Sen. Res. Fellow, Faculty of Engrg and Infrastructure, 2011–, Univ. of Melbourne; Bd Mem. and Adjunct Prof., Global Studies Inst., 2008–11, Adjunct Prof., Sch. of Media and Communications, 2011–, Royal Melbourne Inst. of Technol. *Publications:* Exams and Assessment, 1975; Preparing for Higher Education, 1975. *Recreations:* sailing, tennis, travelling. *Address:* The Conversation, 33 Lincoln Square South, Melbourne, Vic 3010, Australia.

JASUDASEN, Thambynathan; High Commissioner for Singapore in the United Kingdom, 2011–14; *b* Malaysia, 20 June 1952; *m* 1980, Patricia Ibbotson; one *s* twin *d*. *Educ:* Raffles Instn; Nat. Jun. Coll., Singapore; Nat. Univ. of Singapore (LLB Hons 1977); Ecole Nat. d'Admin, Paris. Nat. Service as Armour Officer, Singapore Armed Forces, 1971–73. Joined Min. of Foreign Affairs, Singapore, 1977; served: Singapore Perm. Mission to UN, NY, 1979–81: Manila, 1988–90; Kuala Lumpur, 1991–94; Dir, ASEAN Directorate and Dir, Policy, Planning and Analysis Directorate IV, Min. of Foreign Affairs; Ambassador: to France, 1997–2004; to Myanmar, 2004–06; High Comr in Malaysia, 2006–11. Freeman, City of London, 2013. Public Admin Medal, Silver, 1990, Gold, 2011 (Singapore); Comdr, Palmes Académiques (France), 2002; Officer, Légion d'Honneur (France), 2004; Darjah Sultan Ahmad Shah of Pahang (Malaysia), 2010. *Address:* c/o Singapore High Commission, 9 Wilton Crescent, Belgravia, SW1X 8SP. *Clubs:* Travellers, Royal Over-Seas League, Mosimann, Caledonian; Wentworth; Brocket Hall.

JAUNZENS, Serena Michelle; *see* Best, S. M.

JAVACHEFF, Christo; *see* Christo and Jeanne-Claude.

JAVID, Rt Hon. Sajid; PC 2014; MP (C) Bromsgrove, since 2010; Secretary of State for Business, Innovation and Skills and President, Board of Trade, since 2015; *b* Rochdale, 5 Dec. 1969; *m* 1997, Laura; one *s* three *d*. *Educ:* Univ. of Exeter (BA Hons Econs and Politics 1991). Analyst and Associate, 1991–94, Vice Pres., 1994–2000, Chase Manhattan Bank, N. A.; Dir, 2000–04, Man. Dir, 2004–09, Deutsche Bank AG; Mem. Bd, Deutsche Bank Internat. Ltd,

2007–09. Economic Sec., 2012–13, Financial Sec., 2013–14, HM Treasury; Minister for Equalities, 2014; Sec. of State for Culture, Media and Sport, 2014–15. *Address:* House of Commons, SW1A 0AA. *T:* (020) 7219 7027. *E:* sajid.javid.mp@parliament.uk.

JAWARA, Alhaji Sir Dawda Kairaba, Kt 1966; Hon. GCMG 1974; Grand Master, Order of the Republic of The Gambia, 1972; President of the Republic of The Gambia, 1970–94; Vice-President of the Senegambian Confederation, 1982; *b* Barajally, MacCarthy Island Div, 16 May 1924. *Educ:* Muslim Primary Sch. and Methodist Boys' Grammar Sch., Bathurst; Achimota Coll.; Glasgow Univ. FRCVS 1988 (MRCVS 1953); Dip. in Trop. Vet. Med., Edinburgh, 1957. Veterinary Officer for The Gambia Govt, 1954–57, Principal Vet. Officer, 1957–60. Leader of People's Progressive Party (formerly Protectorate People's Party), The Gambia, 1960; MP 1960; Minister of Education, 1960–61; Premier, 1962–63; Prime Minister, 1963–70. Chairman: Permanent Inter State Cttee for Drought in the Sahel, 1977–79; Organisation pour la Mise en Valeur du Fleuve Gambie Conf., Heads of State and Govt, 1987–88; Authy of Heads of State and Govt, Economic Community of W African States, 1988–89. Patron, Commonwealth Vet. Assoc., 1967–. Hon. LLD Ife, 1978; Hon. DSc Colorado State Univ., USA, 1986. Peutinger Gold Medal, Peutinger-Collegium, Munich, 1979; Agricola Medal, FAO, Rome, 1980. Grand Cross: Order of Cedar of Lebanon, 1966; Nat. Order of Republic of Senegal, 1967; Order of Propitious Clouds of China (Taiwan), 1968; Nat. Order of Republic of Guinea, 1973; Grand Cordon of Most Venerable Order of Knighthood, Pioneers of Republic of Liberia, 1968; Grand Comdr, Nat. Order of Federal Republic of Nigeria, 1970; Comdr of Golden Ark (Netherlands), 1979; Grand Gwanghwa Medal of Order of Diplomatic Service (Republic of Korea), 1984; Nishan-i-Pakistan (Pakistan), 1984; Grand Officer of Nat. Merit, Islamic Republic of Mauritania, 1992; Grand Comdr, Nat. Order of Republic of Portugal, 1993. *Publications:* Kaibara (autobiog.), 2009. *Recreations:* golf, gardening, sailing. *Address:* 40 Atlantic Blvd, Fajara, The Gambia.

JAY, family name of **Baroness Jay of Paddington**.

JAY OF EWELME, Baron *cr* 2006 (Life Peer), of Ewelme, in the County of Oxfordshire; **Michael Hastings Jay,** GCMG 2006 (KCMG 1997; CMG 1992); HM Diplomatic Service, retired; Chairman, House of Lords Appointments Commission, 2008–13; *b* 19 June 1946; *s* of late Alan David Hastings Jay, DSO, DSC, RN and Vera Frances Effa Vickery, MBE; *m* 1975, Sylvia Mylroie (*see* Lady Jay of Ewelme). *Educ:* Winchester Coll.; Magdalen Coll., Oxford (MA; Hon. Fellow, 2004); School of Oriental and African Studies, London Univ. (MSc 1969). ODM, 1969–73; UK Delegn, IMF-IBRD, Washington, 1973–75; ODM, 1976–78; First Sec., New Delhi, 1978–81; FCO, 1981–85; Counsellor: Cabinet Office, 1985–87; (Financial and Commercial), Paris, 1987–90; Asst Under-Sec. of State for EC Affairs, FCO, 1990–93; Dep. Under-Sec. of State (Dir for EC and Economic Affairs), FCO, 1994–96; Ambassador to France, 1996–2001; Prime Minister's Personal Rep. for G8 Summits, 2005–06; Perm. Under-Sec. of State, FCO and Head of the Diplomatic Service, 2002–06. Non-executive Director: Associated British Foods, 2006–15; Credit Agricole SA, 2007–11; Valeo SA, 2007–15; Candover Investments plc, 2008–; EDF SA, 2009–. Chairman: Merlin, 2007–13; Culham Langs and Scis, 2009–11. Vice Chm., Business for New Europe, 2006–; Assoc. Mem., BUPA, 2006–11. Mem., Adv. Council, 2011–, Chm., 2014–, BL. Sen. Associate Mem., St Antony's Coll., Oxford, 1996. *Address:* House of Lords, SW1A 0PW.

JAY OF EWELME, Lady; Sylvia Jay, CBE 2005; Chairman, L'Oréal UK and Ireland, 2011–13 (Vice-Chairman, L'Oréal (UK) Ltd, 2005–11); *b* 1 Nov. 1946; *d* of William Edwin Mylroie and Edie Mylroie (*née* Chew); *m* 1975, Michael Hastings Jay (*see* Baron Jay of Ewelme). *Educ:* Nottingham Univ. (BA (Hons) Soc. Sci.); London Sch. of Econs. Home Civil Service: Admin. grade, ODA, 1971–87; secondments to French Ministère de la Coopération, 1988–89, to French Trésor, Paris, 1990, to EBRD, London, 1990–93; Clerk to European Union Sub-cttee A, H of L, 1994–96; accomp. husband, Ambassador to France, Paris, 1996–2001; Dir Gen., Food and Drink Fedn, 2001–05. Non-executive Director: Saint-Gobain, 2001–; Carrefour, 2003–05; Lazard Ltd, 2006–; Alcatel-Lucent, 2006–14; Casino Supermarket Gp, 2012–. Chm., Food from Britain, 2006–09 (Mem., 2003–). Chm., Pilgrim Trust, 2005–14; Trustee: Entente Cordiale Scholarships Scheme, 2001–14; Prison Reform Trust, 2006–14; Body Shop Foundn, 2006–11. Hon. DLaws Nottingham, 2009. Chevalier, Légion d'Honneur (France), 2008. *Address:* 38 Markham Street, SW3 3NR.

JAY OF PADDINGTON, Baroness *cr* 1992 (Life Peer), of Paddington in the City of Westminster; **Margaret Ann Jay;** PC 1998; Leader of the House of Lords, 1998–2001; Minister for Women, 1998–2001; *b* 18 Nov. 1939; *er d* of Baron Callaghan of Cardiff, KG, PC and late Audrey Elizabeth (*née* Moulton); *m* 1961, Peter Jay, *qv* (marr. diss. 1986); one *s* two *d*; *m* 1994, Prof. M. W. Adler, *qv*. Principal Opposition Spokesman on Health, H of L, 1995–97; Minister of State, DoH, 1997–98. Chm., H of L Select Cttee on Constitution, 2010–. Dir, Nat. Aids Trust, 1988–92. Non-executive Director: Carlton Television, 1996–97; Scottish Power, 1996–97; Independent Media Gp, 2001–; BT Gp, 2002–08. Mem., Kensington, Chelsea & Westminster HA, 1992–97; Chm., Nat. Assoc. of Leagues of Hosp. Friends, 1994. Chm., ODI, 2002–08 (Mem. Council, 2008–); Jt Pres., Foreign Policy Centre, 2009–. Mem. Bd, Hansard Soc., 2013–. *Address:* c/o House of Lords, SW1A 0PW.

JAY, Sir Antony (Rupert), Kt 1988; CVO 1993; freelance writer and producer, since 1964; Chairman, Video Arts Ltd, 1972–89; *b* 20 April 1930; *s* of Ernest Jay and Catherine Hay; *m* 1957, Rosemary Jill Watkins; two *s* two *d*. *Educ:* St Paul's Sch. (scholar); Magdalene Coll., Cambridge (major scholar; BA (1st cl. Hons) Classics and Comparative Philology, 1952; MA 1955; Hon. Fellow, 2001). 2nd Lieut Royal Signals, 1952–54. BBC, 1955–64: Editor, Tonight, 1962–63; Head of Talks Features, TV, 1963–64; (with Jonathan Lynn) writer of BBC TV series, Yes, Minister and Yes, Prime Minister, 1980–88 (BAFTA Writers' Award 1987), 2013, (stage version) Yes, Prime Minister, 2010. Mem., Cttee on Future of Broadcasting, 1974–77. FRSA 1992; CCMI (CIMgt 1992). Hon. MA Sheffield, 1987; Hon. DBA IMCB, 1988. *Publications:* Management and Machiavelli, 1967, 2nd edn 1987; (with David Frost) To England with Love, 1967; Effective Presentation, 1970; Corporation Man, 1972; The Householder's Guide to Community Defence against Bureaucratic Aggression, 1972; (with Jonathan Lynn): Yes, Minister, Vol. 1 1981, Vol. 2 1982, Vol. 3 1983; The Complete Yes, Minister, 1984; Yes, Prime Minister, Vol. 1 1986, Vol. 2 1987; The Complete Yes, Prime Minister, 1989; Elizabeth R, 1992; (ed) Oxford Dictionary of Political Quotations, 1996, 4th edn 2010; How to Beat Sir Humphrey, 1997; Not In Our Back Yard, 2005; Yes, Prime Minister (play), 2010. *Address:* c/o Alan Brodie Representation Ltd, Paddock Suite, 55 Charterhouse Street, EC1M 6HA. *T:* (020) 7253 6226.

JAY, John Philip Bromberg; Business Development Partner, Brompton Asset Management, since 2009; *b* 1 April 1957; *s* of late Alec Jay and June (*née* Bromberg); *m* 1st, 1987, Susy Streeter (marr. diss. 1992); 2nd, 1992, Judi Bevan (*née* Leader); one *d*. *Educ:* University Coll. Sch.; Magdalen Coll., Oxford (BA Hons Mod. Hist.). Journalist, Western Mail, 1979–81; financial journalist: Thomson Regl Newspapers, 1981–84; Sunday Telegraph, 1984–86; City Editor, Sunday Times, 1986–89; City and Business Editor, Sunday Telegraph, 1989–95; Man. Ed., Business News, Sunday Times, 1995–2001; Dir, New Star Asset Mgt, 2001–09. *Publications:* (with Judi Bevan) The New Tycoons, 1989. *Recreations:* ski-ing, cinema, theatre, walking. *Address:* Brompton Asset Management, 1 Knightsbridge Green, SW1X 7QA. *T:* (020) 7045 0600.

JAY, Hon. Martin, CBE 2000; DL; Chairman: VT Group (formerly Vosper Thornycroft Holdings) plc, 2002–05 (Chief Executive, 1989–2002); Invensys plc, 2003–09; Oxensis Ltd, since 2009; *b* 18 July 1939; *s* of Baron Jay, PC and Margaret Christian Jay; *m* 1969, Sandra Mary Ruth Williams; one *s* two *d*. *Educ:* Winchester Coll.; New Coll., Oxford (MA). With BP, 1962–69; GEC plc, 1969–85 (Man. Dir, GEC Inf. Services, and Mem., Mgt Bd, 1980–85); Man. Dir, Lewmar plc, 1985–87; Man. Dir, Electronics Components Div., GEC plc, 1987–89. Chm., EADS UK Ltd, 2005–06. Advr to HM Treasury, to lead collaborative procurement strand of operational efficiency prog., 2008–; Dir, Office of Govt Commerce, 2009–. Mem., Nat. Defence Industries Council, 1997–2005; Pres., British Maritime Equipment Council, subseq. Soc. for Maritime Industries, 1997–2003. DL Hants, 2001. Chairman: Rose Rd Children's Appeal, 1997–2003; Tall Ships Youth Trust, 2005–10; Vice Pres., RNLI, 2010–. Hon. DBA Southampton Inst., 2001; Hon. LLD Portsmouth, 2004. *Recreations:* sailing, gardening, tennis. *Address:* Bishops Court, Bishops Sutton, Alresford, Hants SO24 0AN. *T:* (01962) 732193. *Club:* Garrick.

See also C. I. Arney, P. Jay.

JAY, Peter; writer and broadcaster; *b* 7 Feb. 1937; *s* of Baron Jay, PC and Margaret (Peggy) Christian Jay; *m* 1st, 1961, Margaret Ann (*see* Baroness Jay of Paddington) (marr. diss. 1986), *d* of Baron Callaghan of Cardiff, KG, PC; one *s* two *d*; one *s*; 2nd, 1986, Emma, *d* of late P. K. Thornton, CBE; three *s*. *Educ:* Winchester Coll.; Christ Church, Oxford (MA 1st cl. hons PPE, 1960). President of the Union, 1960. Nuffield Coll., 1960. Midshipman and Sub-Lt RNVR, 1956–57. Asst Principal 1961–64, Private Sec. to Jt Perm. Sec. 1964, Principal 1964–67, HM Treasury; Economics Editor, The Times, 1967–77, and Associate Editor, Times Business News, 1969–77; Presenter, Weekend World (ITV Sunday morning series), 1972–77; The Jay Interview (ITV series), 1975–76; Ambassador to US, 1977–79; Dir Economist Intelligence Unit, 1979–83. Consultant, Economist Gp, 1979–81; Chm. and Chief Exec., TV-am Ltd, 1980–83 and TV-am News, 1982–83, Pres., TV-am, 1983; Presenter, A Week in Politics, Channel 4, 1983–86; COS to Robert Maxwell (Chm., Mirror Gp Newspapers Ltd), 1986–89; Supervising Editor, Banking World, 1986–89 (Editor, 1984–86); Economics and Business Editor, BBC, 1990–2001. Non-exec. Dir, Bank of England, 2003–09. Presenter, The Road to Riches, BBC TV series, 2000. Chairman: NACRO Working Party on Children and Young Persons in Custody, 1976–77; NCVO, 1981–86 (Vice-Pres., 1986–92); Trustee, Charities Aid Foundn, 1981–86; Chm., Charities Effectiveness Review Trust, 1986–87. Vis. Scholar, Brookings Instn, Washington, 1979–80; Wincott Meml Lectr, 1975; Copland Meml Lectr, Australia, 1980; MacTaggart Meml Lectr, 1981; Shell Lectr, Glasgow, 1985. Hon. Prof., Univ. of Wales, Aberystwyth, 2001–; Exec. Prof. of Political Economy, Henley Business Sch. (formerly Henley Mgt Coll.), 2006–10. Governor, Ditchley Foundn, 1982–; Mem. Council, St George's House, Windsor, 1982–85. Mem., Woodstock Town Council, 2004– (Dep. Mayor, 2004–06; Mayor, 2008–10). Dir, New Nat. Theater, Washington, DC, 1979–81. Political Broadcaster of Year, 1973; Harold Wincott Financial and Economic Journalist of Year, 1973; RTS Male Personality of Year (Pye Award), 1974; SFTA Shell Internat. TV Award, 1974; RTS Home News Award, 1992. FRGS 1977. Hon. DH Ohio State Univ., 1978; Hon. DLitt Wake Forest Univ., 1979; Berkeley Citation, Univ. of Calif, 1979. *Publications:* The Budget, 1972; (contrib.) America and the World 1979, 1980; The Crisis for Western Political Economy and other Essays, 1984; (with Michael Stewart) Apocalypse 2000, 1987; Road to Riches, or The Wealth of Man, 2000; contrib. Foreign Affairs jl. *Recreations:* sailing, bridge. *Address:* The Retreat, Woodstock, Oxon OX20 1LJ. *T:* (01993) 811222, 07860 355557, *Fax:* (01993) 812861. *E:* thepeterjay@btinternet.com. *Clubs:* Garrick; Royal Naval Sailing Association, Royal Cork Yacht.

See also Hon. M. Jay.

JAY, Hon. Sir Robert Maurice, Kt 2013; **Hon. Mr Justice Jay;** a Judge of the High Court of Justice, Queen's Bench Division, since 2013; *b* 20 Sept. 1959; *s* of late Prof. Barrie Samuel Jay and of Marcelle Ruby Jay; *m* 1997, Deborah Jacinta Trenner; one *d*. *Educ:* King's Coll. Sch. (Open Schol.); New Coll., Oxford (Open Schol.; BA 1st cl. Hons Jurisp. 1980). Called to the Bar, Middle Temple, 1981, Bencher, 2007; in practice at the Bar, 1981–2013; QC 1998; a Recorder, 2000–13; a Dep. High Ct Judge, 2008–13. Jun. Counsel to the Crown (Common Law), 1989–98. Gov., King's Coll. Sch., 2012–. *Recreations:* golf, opera, bridge, politics, history, cooking. *Address:* Royal Courts of Justice, Strand, WC2A 2LL. *T:* (020) 7947 6387.

JAY-O'BOYLE, Fionnuala Mary, CBE 2008 (MBE 2000); Principal, Jay Associates Public and Government Affairs, since 1991; Lord-Lieutenant, County Borough of Belfast, since 2014; *b* Londonderry, 22 March 1960; *d* of Thomas Boyle and Elizabeth Boyle (*née* McGrory); *m* 1989, Richard Jay. *Educ:* Thornhill Coll., Londonderry; Queen's Univ., Belfast (BA Hons Pol Sci. and Ancient Hist. 1982). Communications and PR Manager, Bryson House, 1986–90; Dir, PR and Mktg, Andras House Ltd, 1990–91. Founder and Working Dir, Belfast Buildings Preservation Trust, later Belfast Buildings Trust, 1995–. Chm., Belfast Civic Trust. Mem. Council, Architectural Heritage Fund. Founder, NI Schs Debating Competition. Vice Chair, NI Opera. Trustee: Prince's Regeneration Trust; Teachers of Singers in Ireland. Hon. RSUA 2008. DL Belfast 2009. *Recreations:* opera, theatre, food and wine, travel, history. *Address:* Elderslie House, 18 Ashley Avenue, Belfast, Northern Ireland BT9 7BT. *T:* (028) 9066 5630. *E:* jay.associates@btconnect.com.

JAYARATNE, Dissanayake Mudiyanselage; Prime Minister of Sri Lanka, 2010–15; Minister of Buddhist and Religious Affairs, 2010–15; *b* Gampola, Ceylon, 4 June 1931; *s* of Dissanayake Mudiyanselage Punchirala and Dissanayake Mudiyanselage Bandaramenika; *m* 1981, Dona Anula Yapa; one *s* two *d*. *Educ:* Gampola Zahira Vidyalaya; Gampola Gandhi Vidyalaya. Postmaster. Mem., Doluwa Village Council, Gampola, 1959; Chm., Pahala Korale Village Council, 1961. MP (Sri Lanka Freedom Party) Gampola, 1970–77 and 1989–2015; Minister: of Lands, Agric. and Envmt, 1994–2000; of Agric., Food and Co-operatives, 2000–01; of Post, Telecommunication and Rural Devlt, 2004–07; of Plantation Industries, 2008–10. Exec. Mem., Telecommunication Commn. Founder Mem., Sri Lanka Freedom Party, 1951 (Vice Pres.); Gen. Sec., United People's Alliance. President: Fedn of Village Councils of Kandy Dist, 1965; Fedn of All Village Councils, 1965. Pres., Internat. Youth Conf. *Address:* c/o Parliament of Sri Lanka, Sri Jayewardenepura Kotte, Colombo, Sri Lanka.

JAYASINGHE, Nihal; Justice Jayasinghe; Judge, Supreme Court of Extraordinary Chamber of Courts of Cambodia, United Nations, since 2006; *m* 1977, Indira Wickremasinghe; one *s* one *d*. *Educ:* Univ. of Colombo (LLB 1969). State Counsel, Attorney Gen's Dept, Sri Lanka, 1975–83; Sen. State Counsel, 1983–94; Dep. Solicitor Gen., 1994–97; Judge, 1997–2002, Pres., 2002, Court of Appeal; Judge, 2002–06, Sen. Presiding Judge, 2006–08, Supreme Court of Sri Lanka; High Comr for Sri Lanka in the UK, and concurrently Ambassador to Ireland, 2008–10. Vis. Schol., Univ. of Illinois at Chicago, 1989–90. *Recreations:* music, cricket. *Address:* No 12 De Soyza Mawatha, Templars Road, Mount Lavinia, Sri Lanka. *T:* 112726880.

JAYAWARDENA, Ranil Malcolm; MP (C) North East Hampshire, since 2015; *b* London, 3 Sept. 1986; *s* of Nalin Mahinda Jayawardena and Indira Maureen Jayawardena; *m* 2011, Alison Lyn Roberts; one *d*. *Educ:* Robert May's Sch., Odiham; Alton Coll., Alton; London Sch. of Econs and Political Sci. (BSc Hons). Various roles, from commercial banking to gp exec. functions, Lloyds Banking Gp, 2008–15. Mem., Basingstoke and Deane BC, 2008–15 (Dep. Leader, 2012–15). Mem., Home Affairs Select Cttee, 2015–. *Recreations:* cricket, golf, tennis, shooting, walking, local history, film, theatre. *Address:* House of Commons, SW1A 0AA. *T:* (020) 7219 3637. *E:* ranil.jayawardena.mp@parliament.uk.

JAYNE, Dr David Roland Walker, FRCP, FRCPE, FMedSci; Reader in Vasculitis, Department of Medicine, University of Cambridge, since 2013; *b* Sutton, Surrey, 19 Jan. 1957; *s* of Freeman Oliver Jayne and Ruth Margaret Jayne; *m* 1982, Lucinda Higson Smith; two *s* one *d*. *Educ:* King's Sch., Canterbury; Corpus Christi Coll., Cambridge (BA 1978;

BChir 1981; MB 1981; MD 1993). MRCP 1985, FRCP 1999; FRCPE 2009. Hse Surgeon, Royal Northern Hosp., 1981–82; Hse Physician, St Peter's Hosp., Chertsey, 1982; Senior House Officer: UCH, 1982–83; St Thomas' Hosp., 1983–84; Nat. Heart Hosp., 1984–85; Registrar, St Mary's Hosp., 1985–87; Clinical Research Fellow: Addenbrooke's Hosp., Cambridge, 1987–90; Gonville and Caius Coll., Cambridge, 1990–95; Sen. Lectr, St George's Hosp., London, 1996–2001; Consultant in Nephrology and Vasculitis, Addenbrooke's Hosp., Cambridge, Cambridge Univ. Hosps NHS Foundn Trust, 2001–13. Pres., Eur. Vasculitis Soc., 2011–. FMedSci 2013. *Recreation:* horse riding. *Address:* Department of Medicine, Addenbrooke's Hospital, Cambridge CB2 2SP. *T:* (01223) 586796. *E:* dj106@cam.ac.uk.

JAYSON, Prof. Malcolm Irving Vivian, MD; FRCP; Professor of Rheumatology and Director, University Centre for the Study of Chronic Rheumatism, University of Manchester, 1977–96, now Emeritus Professor; *b* 9 Dec. 1937; *s* of Joseph and Sybil Jayson; *m* 1962, Judith Tauber; two *s*. *Educ:* Middlesex Hosp. Med. Sch., Univ. of London (MB, BS 1961); MD Bristol, 1969; MSc Manchester, 1977. FRCP 1976. House Physician, 1961, House Surgeon, 1962, Middlesex Hosp.; House Physician: Central Middlesex Hosp., 1962; Brompton Hosp., 1963; Sen. House Officer, Middlesex Hosp., 1963; Registrar: Westminster Hosp., 1964; Royal Free Hosp., 1965; Lectr, Univ. of Bristol, Royal Nat. Hosp. for Rheumatic Diseases, Bath, and Bristol Royal Infirmary, 1967; Sen. Lectr, Univ. of Bristol, and Consultant, Royal Nat. Hosp. for Rheumatic Diseases, Bath, and Bristol Royal Infirmary, 1979. Visiting Professor: Univ. of Iowa, 1984; Univ. of Queensland, 1985; Univ. of Cairo, 1992. Gen. Sec., Internat. Back Pain Soc., 1986–; President: Soc. of Chiropodists, 1984; Arachnoiditis Self-Help Gp, 1989–; Pres., Internat. Soc. for Study of the Lumbar Spine, 1995–96. *Publications:* (with A. St J. Dixon) Rheumatism and Arthritis, 1974, 8th edn 1991; The Lumbar Spine and Back Pain, 1976, 4th edn 1992; Back Pain: the facts, 1981, 3rd edn 1992; (with C. Black) Systemic Sclerosis: Scleroderma, 1988; Understanding Back Pain, 2001, 8th edn 2009; contribs to Lancet, BMJ and other med. jls. *Recreations:* antiques (especially sundials), trout fishing. *Address:* The Gate House, 8 Lancaster Road, Didsbury, Manchester M20 2TY. *T:* (0161) 445 1729.

JAYSTON, Michael, (Michael James); actor; *b* 29 Oct. 1935; *s* of Aubrey Vincent James and Edna Myfanwy Llewelyn; *m* 1st, 1965, Lynn Farleigh (marr. diss. 1970); 2nd, 1970, Heather Mary Sneddon (marr. diss. 1977); 3rd, 1978, Elizabeth Ann Smithson; three *s* one *d*. *Educ:* Becket Grammar School, Nottingham; Guildhall Sch. of Music and Drama (FGS). *Stage:* Salisbury Playhouse, 1962–63 (parts incl. Henry II, in Becket); Bristol Old Vic, 1963–65; RSC, 1965–69 (incl. Ghosts, All's Well That Ends Well, Hamlet, The Homecoming (NY), The Relapse); Equus, NT, 1973, Albery, 1977; Private Lives, Duchess, 1980; The Sound of Music, Apollo, 1981; The Way of the World, Chichester, 1984, Haymarket, 1985; Woman in Mind, Vaudeville, 1987; Dancing at Lughnasa, Garrick, 1992; The Wind in the Willows, NT, 1994; Easy Virtue, Chichester, 1999; Wild Orchids, Chichester, 2001; The Rivals, Moment of Weakness, tour, 2002; The Marquise, tour, 2004; Heroes, tour, 2006; Last Confession, Haymarket, 2007; Quartet, Yvonne Arnaud Th., 2010; *films include:* Midsummer Night's Dream, 1968; The Power Game, 1968; Cromwell, 1969; Nicholas and Alexandra, 1970; *television includes:* Beethoven, 1969; Mad Jack, 1970; Wilfred Owen, 1971; Tinker, Tailor, Soldier, Spy, 1979; Dr Who, 1986; A Bit of a Do, 1988, 1989; Haggard, 1990; Darling Buds of May, 1992; Outside Edge, 1995, 1996; Only Fools and Horses, 1996; Eastenders, 2001; The Bill, 2005; Emmerdale, 2008–09. Life Mem., Battersea Dogs and Cats Home. *Recreations:* cricket, darts, chess. *Address:* c/o Diamond Management, 31 Percy Street, W1T 2DD. *Clubs:* MCC, Lord's Taverners, Cricketers'; Sussex CC, Gedling Colliery CC (Vice-Pres.); Rottingdean CC (Pres.).

JEAN, Rt Hon. Michaëlle, CC 2005; CMM 2005; CD 2005; PC (Can.) 2012; UNESCO Special Envoy to Haiti, since 2010; Governor General of Canada, 2005–10; *b* Port au Prince; *m* Jean-Daniel Lafond (CC 2005); one *d*, and two step *d*. *Educ:* Univ. of Montreal (BA Italian and Hispanic Langs and Lit; MA Comparative Lit); Univ. of Perouse; Univ. of Florence; Catholic Univ. of Milan. Worked with Québec shelters for battered women, 1979–86; taught at Faculty of Italian Studies, Univ. of Montreal, 1984–86; Employment and Immigration Canada; Conseil des Communautés culturelles du Québec; joined Radio-Canada, 1988; reporter and host on news and public affairs progs incl. Actuel, Montréal ce soir, Virages and Le Point; presenter of several Réseau de l'Information à Radio-Canada progs, 1995; presenter: The Passionate Eye and Rough Cuts, CBC Newsworld, 1999; weekend edns of Le Téléjournal, 2001, daily edn of Le Téléjournal, Le Midi, 2003, Radio-Canada; own show, Michaëlle, 2004. Co-Founder and Co-Chm., Michaëlle Jean Foundn, 2009–. Chancellor, Univ. of Ottawa, 2012–. *Address:* Michaëlle Jean Foundation, 143 Séraphin-Marion Street, Ottawa, ON K1N 6N5, Canada.

JEANES, Ronald Eric; Deputy Director, Building Research Establishment, 1981–86; *b* 23 Sept. 1926; *s* of Edwin and Eunice Jeanes; *m* 1951, Helen Field (*née* Entwistle); one *s* one *d*. *Educ:* University Coll., Exeter (BSc 1951). Served HM Forces, 1945–48. Royal Naval Scientific Service, 1951–62; BRE, 1962–86. *Publications:* DoE and BRE reports. *Recreation:* amateur theatre. *Address:* 10 Whybrow Gardens, Berkhamsted, Herts HP4 2GU. *T:* (01442) 870242.

JEANNERET, Marian Elizabeth; *see* Hobson, M. E.

JEANNIOT, Pierre Jean, OC 1988; CQ 2002; Director General and Chief Executive Officer, International Air Transport Association, 1993–2002, now Director General Emeritus; President and Chief Executive Officer, Jinmag Inc., since 1990; *b* Montpellier, France, 9 April 1933; *s* of Gaston and Renée Jeanniot; *m* 1979, Marcia David; two *s* one *d*. *Educ:* Sir George Williams Univ. (BSc); McGill Univ. (Management Prog.). Sperry Gyroscope, 1952–55; Air Canada, 1955–68; Vice-Pres., Computers and Communications, Québec Univ., 1969; Air Canada: Vice-Pres., Computer and Systems Services, 1970–76; subseq. Exec., sales, marketing, planning subsid. cos; Exec. Vice-Pres. and Chief Operating Officer, 1980; Pres. and CEO, 1984–90. Dir of many cos. Pres., Canadian OR Soc., 1966; Chm., Air Transport Assoc. of Canada, 1984; Mem., Exec. Cttee and Chm., Strategic Planning Sub-Cttee, IATA, 1988–90. Chairman: Thales Canada Inc., 2003–09; Laurentian Aerospace Inc., 2006–; Luxell Inc., 2009–11; Adv. Bd, Star Navigation Inc., 2006–. Internat. Aviation Consultant, Gerson Lehrman Gp, 2010–. Chm., Council for Canadian Unity, 1991–94. University of Québec: Chm. Bd, 1972–78; Pres., Foundn, 1978–92; Chancellor, 1995–2008. Chm. and participant, numerous charitable bodies. FRAeS, 2007. Hon. Dr Quebec, 1988; Hon. LLD Concordia, 1997; Hon. DSc McGill, 2006. Airline Business Strategy Award, Airline Business Magazine, 2002; Canadian Aviation Hall of Fame, 2012. Chevalier, Légion d'Honneur (France), 1991; Independence Medal (First Order) (Kingdom of Jordan), 1995. *Address:* 1010 de la Gauchetière West # 960, Montreal, QC H3B 2N2, Canada. *W:* www.pierrejeanniot.com.

JEANS, Ven. Alan Paul; Archdeacon of Sarum, since 2003; *b* 18 May 1958; *s* of Brian Edward and Jacqueline Rosemary Jeans; *m* 1981, Anita Gail (*née* Hobbs); two *d*. *Educ:* Bournemouth Sch.; Bournemouth and Poole Coll. (MIAS, MIBC 1983); Southampton Univ. (BTh 1989); Salisbury and Wells Theol Coll.; Univ. of Wales, Lampeter (MA 2002). Building Surveyor, 1976–86. Ordained deacon, 1989, priest, 1990; Curate, Parkstone with Branksea, 1989–93; Priest i/c, Bishop's Cannings, All Cannings and Etchilhampton, 1993–98; Advr for Parish Develt, 1998–2005, Diocesan Dir of Ordinands, 2007–12, Dio. of Salisbury; Rural Dean, Alderbury, 2005–07. Canon, Salisbury Cathedral, 2002–. Asst Chaplain, Dauntsey's Sch., 1995–2007; Chaplain to the Forces (Reserves), 2002–. Mem., Gen. Synod of C of E, 2000–05 and 2010–. *Recreations:* food, architectural history, classic motors cars. *Address:* Ramsbury Office, Church House, Crane Street, Salisbury SP1 2QB. *T:* (01722) 438662. *E:* adsarum@salisbury.anglican.org.

JEANS, Christopher James Marwood; QC 1997; a Recorder, since 2009; *b* 24 Jan. 1956; *s* of late David Marwood Jeans and Rosalie Jean Jeans; *m* 1998, Judith Mary Laws; one *d*. *Educ:* Minchenden Sch.; King's Coll. London (LLB 1977); St John's Coll., Oxford (BCL 1979). Called to the Bar, Gray's Inn, 1980, Bencher, 2007; Lectr, City of London Poly., 1981–83; in practice at the Bar, 1983–. Part-time Employment Judge (formerly part-time Chm.), Employment Tribunals, 1998–2008. Mem., Law Panel, The Times, 2007–08. Pres. (pt-time), Commonwealth Secretariat Arbitral Tribunal, 2011– (Mem., 2008–11). FICPD 1998. *Recreations:* football (Spurs), cricket, walking, swimming, cinema, theatre, arctic and world travel. *Address:* 11 King's Bench Walk, Temple, EC4Y 7EQ.

JEAPES, Maj.-Gen. Anthony Showan, CB 1987; OBE 1977; MC 1960; retired; Consultant Inspector, Lord Chancellor's Panel of Independent Inspectors, 2003–05 (Member, 1991–2003); *b* 6 March 1935; *s* of Stanley Arthur Jeapes; *m* 1959, Jennifer Clare White; one *s* one *d*. *Educ:* Raynes Park Grammar Sch.; RMA Sandhurst. Commissioned Dorset, later Devonshire and Dorset, Regt, 1955; joined 22 SAS Regt, 1958; attached US Special Forces, 1961; Staff College, 1966; Brigade Major, 39 Inf. Bde, NI, 1967; Sqn Comdr, 22 SAS Regt, 1968; Nat. Defence Coll., 1971; Directing Staff, Staff Coll., Camberley, 1972; CO 22 SAS Regt, 1974; Mem., British Mil. Adv. Team, Bangladesh, 1977; Dep. Comdr, Sch. of Infantry, 1979; Comdr, 5 Airborne Brigade, 1982; Comdr, Land Forces NI, 1985–87; GOC, SW Dist, 1987–90. Vice-Chairman: Romanian Orphanage Trust, 1991–99; European Children's Trust, 1995–99. Vice-Patron, Poppy Factory, 2015–. *Publications:* SAS Operation Oman, 1980; SAS Secret War, 1996. *Recreations:* offshore sailing, country pursuits. *Address:* c/o National Westminster Bank, Warminster, Wilts BA12 9AW.

JEARY, Anthony John P.; *see* Pye-Jeary, A. J.

JEAVONS, (Robert) Clyde (Scott); Curator, National Film and Television Archive, British Film Institute, 1990–97; *b* 30 June 1939; *s* of Frank Rechab Scott-Jeavons and Olive Edith (*née* Robins); *m* 1st, 1963, Hilary Coopey (marr. diss.); one *d*; 2nd, 1977, Orly Yadin (marr. diss.); 3rd, 2007, Shirley Ann Tait. *Educ:* St Lawrence Coll.; Royal Russell Sch.; University Coll. London (BA Hons Scandinavian Studies). Asst Stage Manager, Det Norske Riksteatret, Norway, 1963; financial journalist, Investors' Rev., 1964; Chief Sub, Features Ed. and book reviewer and film critic, SHE mag., 1964–69; Dep. Curator and Hd, Film and TV Acquisitions, Nat. Film Archive, BFI, 1969–85; freelance author and film programmer, 1986–90. Archive Consultant, London Film Fest. Member: Satyajit Ray Foundn (Vice-Chair, 2010–14); BAFTA; Critics' Circle; British Cinema and TV Veterans. Hon. Mem., BFI. Mem., Islington Choral Soc. FRSA 1992–2002. Hon. FBKS 1994. *Publications:* (with Michael Parkinson) A Pictorial History of Westerns, 1974; A Pictorial History of War Films, 1975; (with Jeremy Pascall) A Pictorial History of Sex in the Movies, 1976; British Film-Makers of the Eighties, 1990; contrib. Sight & Sound, Monthly Film Bull., Guardian, Sunday Times, Jl of Film Preservation, etc. *Recreations:* cricket, golf, travel, cooking and dining, music, film, choral singing, reading the New Yorker. *Address:* Garden Flat, 110A Highbury New Park, N5 2DR. *T:* (020) 7226 6778. *Clubs:* Union; Middlesex CC, Brondesbury Cricket, Barnes Cricket (Hon. Mem.), Bertie Joel Net XI, Bushmen Cricket and Dining; Surrey Seniors; Kent Golf Union.

JEBB, family name of **Baron Gladwyn**.

JEEVES, Prof. Malcolm Alexander, CBE 1992; FMedSci, FBPsS; PPRSE; Professor of Psychology, University of St Andrews, 1969–93, Hon. Research Professor, since 1993; *b* 16 Nov. 1926; *s* of Alderman Alexander Frederic Thomas Jeeves and Helena May Jeeves (*née* Hammond); *m* 1955, Ruth Elisabeth Hartridge; two *d*. *Educ:* Stamford Sch.; St John's Coll., Cambridge (MA, PhD). Commissioned Royal Lincs Regt, served 1st Bn Sherwood Foresters, BAOR, 1945–48. Cambridge University: Exhibnr, St John's Coll., 1948, Res. Exhibnr, 1952; Burney Student, 1952; Gregg Bury Prizeman, 1954; Kenneth Craik Res. Award, St John's Coll., 1955. Rotary Foundn Fellow, Harvard, 1953; Lectr, Leeds Univ., 1956; Prof. of Psychology, Adelaide Univ., 1959–69, and Dean, Faculty of Arts, 1962–64; Vice-Principal, St Andrews Univ., 1981–85; Dir, MRC Cognitive Neuroscience Res. Gp, St Andrews, 1984–89. Lectures: Abbie Meml, Adelaide Univ., 1981; Cairns Meml, Aust., 1986; New Coll., Univ. of NSW, 1987; Boyle, St Mary le Bow, Cheapside, 2008. Member: SSRC Psych. Cttee, 1972–76; Biol. Cttee, 1980–84, Science Bd, 1985–89, Council, 1985–89, SERC; MRC Neuroscience and Mental Health Bd, 1985–89; Council, 1984–88, Exec., 1985–87, Vice-Pres., 1990–93, Pres., 1996–99, RSE; ABRC Manpower Sub-Cttee, 1991–93; Pres., Section J, BAAS, 1988. Founder FMedSci 1998. Hon. Sheriff, Fife, 1986–. Hon. DSc: Edinburgh, 1993; St Andrews, 2000; DUniv Stirling, 1999. Editor-in-Chief, Neuropsychologia, 1990–93. *Publications:* (with Z. P. Dienes) Thinking in Structures, 1965 (trans. French, German, Spanish, Italian, Japanese); (with Z. P. Dienes) The Effects of Structural Relations upon Transfer, 1968; The Scientific Enterprise and Christian Faith, 1969; Experimental Psychology: an introduction for Biologists, 1974; Psychology and Christianity: the view both ways, 1976 (trans. Chinese); (with G. B. Greer) Analysis of Structural Learning, 1983; (with R. J. Berry and D. Atkinson) Free to be Different, 1984; Behavioural Sciences: a Christian perspective, 1984; (with D. G. Myers) Psychology—through the eyes of faith, 1987, 2nd edn 2002; Mind Fields, 1994; Human Nature at the Millennium, 1997; (with R. J. Berry) Science, Life and Christian Belief, 1998; (ed and contrib.) From Cells to Souls, 2004; (ed and contrib.) Human Nature, 2005; (with W. S. Brown) Neuroscience, Psychology and Religion, 2009 (trans. Spanish, Greek and Chinese); (ed and contrib.) Rethinking Human Nature, 2011; Minds, Brains, Souls and Gods, 2013; The Emergence of Personhood - a quantum leap?, 2015; papers in sci. jls, mainly on neuropsychology and cognition. *Recreations:* music, fly fishing, walking. *Address:* Psychology Laboratory, The University, St Andrews KY16 9JU. *T:* (01334) 462057.

See also E. R. Dobbs.

JEEWOOLALL, Sir Ramesh, GCSK 2007; Kt 1979; Speaker, Mauritius Parliament, 1979–82 and 1996–2000; *b* 20 Dec. 1940; *s* of Shivprasad Jeewoolall; *m* 1971, Usweenee (*née* Reetoo); two *s*. *Educ:* in Mauritius; Inns of Court Sch. of Law. Called to the Bar, Middle Temple, 1968; practising at the Bar, 1969–71; Magistrate, 1971–72; practising at the Bar and Chm., Mauritius Tea Develt Authority, 1972–76. Mem., Mauritius Parlt, 1976–82 and 1987–91; Minister of Housing, Lands, Town and Country Planning and the Envmt, 1987–90; Dep. Speaker, 1977–79. Pres., CPA, 1996–97 (Vice-Pres., 1995–96). Chancellor, Univ. of Mauritius, 2006–. *Publications:* Who Owns Your Agenda?, 2013. *Recreations:* reading, conversation, chess. *Address:* 92 Belle Rose Avenue, Quatre Bornes, Mauritius. *T:* 4645371.

JEFFCOTT, Prof. Leo Broof, PhD, DVSc; FRCVS; Professor of Veterinary Science, University of Sydney, 2004–12, now Emeritus (Dean, Faculty of Veterinary Science, 2004–09); *b* 19 June 1942; *s* of late Edward Ian Broof Jeffcott and Pamela Mary (*née* Hull); *m* 1969, Tisza Jacqueline (*née* Hubbard); two *d*. *Educ:* Univ. of London (BVetMed 1967, PhD 1972); Univ. of Melbourne (DVSc 1989); MA Cantab 1994. FRCVS 1978. Animal Health Trust, Newmarket: Asst Pathologist, 1967–71; Clinician, 1972–77; Head, Clinical Dept, 1977–81; Professor: of Clinical Radiology, Swedish Univ. of Agricl Scis, Uppsala, 1981–82; of Veterinary Clinical Sciences, Univ. of Melbourne, 1982–91; Prof. of Vet. Clin. Studies and Dean of Vet. Sch., 1991–2004, Fellow of Pembroke Coll., 1993–2004, Cambridge Univ. Mem. Council, RCVS, 1992–2004. Chm., Internat. Cttee for 5th Internat. Conf. on Equine Exercise Physiology, 1994–98; Mem. Bureau, FEI, 1998–2006 (Hon. Mem., 2006; Chm.,

Vet. Cttee, 1998–2006). Lectures: Sir Frederick Hobday Meml, BEVA, 1977; Peter Hernqvist, Swedish Univ. of Agricl Scis, Skara, 1991; Share-Jones, RCVS, 1993; J. D. Stewart Address, Univ. of Sydney, 2004; R. R. Pascoe Peroration, Australian Equine Vet. Assoc., 2005; John Hickman Meml, 50th BEVA Congress, 2011. FEI Official Veterinarian: Seoul Olympics, 1988; World Equestrian Games, Stockholm, 1990, The Hague, 1994, Rome, 1998; Jerez, Spain, 2002; Barcelona Olympics, 1992; Atlanta Olympics, 1996; Sydney Olympics, 2000; Athens Olympics, 2004; Beijing Olympics, 2008; Beijing Paralympics, 2008. Hon. FRVC 1997. VetMedDr *hc* Swedish Univ. of Agricl Scis, 2000. Norman Hall Medal for Research, RCVS, 1978; Internat. Prize of Tierklinik Hochmoor, Germany, 1981; Equine Veterinary Jl Open Award, BEVA, 1982; John Hickman Orthopaedic Prize, BEVA, 1991; Internat. Hall of Fame Award for Equine Res., Univ. of Kentucky, 1991; UK Equestrian Award for Scientific Achievement, 1994; Sefton Award for Services to Equestrian Safety, 1997; Dalrymple-Champneys Cup and Medal, 2001. Hon. Order of Kentucky Cols, Gov. of Kentucky, 2011. *Publications:* (with R. K. Archer) Comparative Clinical Haematology, 1977; (ed jtly) Equine Exercise Physiology 3, 1991; (with G. Dalin) Osteochondrosis in the 90s, 1993; (with A. F. Clarke) On to Atlanta '96, 1994; (with A. F. Clarke) Progress towards Atlanta '96: thermoregulatory responses during competitive exercise with performance horse, Vol. I 1995, Vol. II 1996; Equine Exercise Physiology 5, 1999; (ed jtly) Osteochondrosis and Musculoskeletal Development in the Foal Under the Influence of Exercise, 1999; (ed with P. D. Rossdale) A Tribute to Colonel John Hickman, 2001; 350 articles in equine veterinary sci. jls. *Recreations:* swimming, photography, equestrian sports. *Address:* Faculty of Veterinary Science, University Veterinary Teaching Hospital, University of Sydney, 410 Werombi Road, Camden, NSW 2570, Australia.

JEFFERIES, Andrew; QC 2009; *b* 18 April 1968; *s* of Alan Jefferies and Ann Jefferies (*née* Shearden); one *s* one *d*. *Educ:* Priestley Sixth Form Coll.; Univ. of E Anglia (LLB Hons); Inns of Court Sch. of Law. Called to the Bar, Middle Temple, 1990; in practice as barrister specialising in criminal defence. *Recreations:* reading, motorbikes, languages, scuba diving, music. *Address:* Mansfield Chambers, 5 Chancery Lane, WC2A 1LG.

JEFFERIES, David George, CBE 1990; FREng; Chairman: National Grid Group plc, 1990–99; Viridian Group (formerly Northern Ireland Electricity) plc, 1994–98; *b* 26 Dec. 1933; *s* of Rose and George Jefferies; *m* 1959, Jeanette Ann Hanson. *Educ:* SE Coll. of Technology. FREng (FEng 1989); FIET, FInstE. Southern Electricity Board: Area Manager, Portsmouth, 1967–72; Staff Coll., Henley, 1970; Chief Engr, 1972–74; Dir, NW Region, CEGB, 1974–77; Dir Personnel, CEGB, 1977–81; Chm., London Electricity Bd, 1981–86; Dep. Chm., Electricity Council, 1986–89. Non-exec. Dir, Strategic Rail Authy, 1999–2001; Chairman: 24/Seven Utilities Service Co., 1999–2002; Smartlogik, 2000–02; Costain, 2001–07; Geotrupes, 2004–07. Chm., Electricity Pension Scheme, 1986–97. Chm., Power Sector Working Gp, 1993–2002; Co-Chm., Indo-British Partnership, 1999–2003. President: Energy Industries Club, 1991–93; Inst. of Energy, 1994–96; Electricity Assoc., 1996–97; IEE, 1997–98; Electrical and Electronic Industries Benevolent Assoc., 1998–99; Henley Mgt Coll. UK Alumni, 2009–. Mem. Bd, Royal Instn, 2000–05. Liveryman, Wax Chandlers' Co., 1984– (Master, 2005–06). CCMI. Hon. DTech Brunel, 1992; Hon. LLD Manchester, 1993. *Recreations:* golf, gardening, music. *Address:* Espada, 30 Abbots Drive, Virginia Water, Surrey GU25 4SE. *Clubs:* Athenæum, Royal Automobile; Wentworth.

JEFFERIES, Roger David; Independent Housing Ombudsman, 1997–2001; *b* 13 Oct. 1939; *s* of George Edward Jefferies and Freda Rose Jefferies (*née* Marshall); *m* 1st, 1962, Jennifer Anne Southgate (marr. diss.); one *s* two *d*; 2nd, 1974, Margaret Sealy (marr. diss.); 3rd, 1984, Pamela Mary Elsey (*née* Holden); one *s*. *Educ:* Whitgift School; Balliol College, Oxford. BA, BCL; solicitor. Member: Law Society, 1965–; British and Irish Ombudsman Assoc., 1997–. Asst Solicitor, Coventry Corporation, 1965–68; Asst Town Clerk, Southend-on-Sea County Borough Council, 1968–70; Director of Operations, London Borough of Hammersmith, 1970–75; Chief Exec., London Borough of Hounslow, 1975–90; Under Secretary, DoE, 1983–85 (on secondment); Chief Exec., London Bor. of Croydon, 1990–93; Housing Assoc. Tenants' Ombudsman, 1993–97. Chm., Discipline Cttees, Lambeth, Southwark and Lewisham HA, 1998–2004. Non-executive Director: Nat. Clinical Assessment Authy, 2001–05; Financial Ombudsman Service, 2002–08; Telecommunications Ombudsman Service, 2002–07. Ind. Adjudicator for Lewisham LBC, 2006–07; Ind. Assessor for Telecommunications and Energy Ombudsman, 2007–11. Member: Regl Planning Bd, Arts Council of GB, 1986–88; Adv. Bd, Lewisham Theatre, 1994–99; Council, RIPA, 1982–88; Bd, Public Finance Foundn, 1987–93; Pres., SOLACE, 1990–91. Clerk: Mortlake Crematorium Bd, 1973–90; W London Waste Authy, 1986–90. Director: Extemporary Dance Co., 1989–91; Croydon Business Venture, 1991–93; Solotec, 1992–93. Hon. Sec., Commn for Local Democracy, 1993–96. Trustee: S African Advanced Educn Project, 1989–96; Barnes Workhouse Fund, 2002–10. *Publications:* Tackling the Town Hall, 1982; Ursula's Secrets (novel), 2014. *Recreations:* the novel, genealogy, the Languedoc.

JEFFERIES, Stephen; freelance teacher and choreographer, since 2008; international ballet competition judge, 2014–15; *b* 24 June 1951; *s* of George and Barbara Jefferies; *m* 1972, Rashna Homji; one *s* one *d*. *Educ:* Turves Green Sch., Birmingham; Royal Ballet Sch. ARAD (Advanced Hons). Joined Sadler's Wells Royal Ballet, 1969; created 10 leading roles whilst with Sadler's Wells; Principal Dancer, 1973–76 and 1977–79, Sen. Principal Dancer, 1979–95, Character Principal, 1994–95, Royal Ballet; joined National Ballet of Canada as Principal Dancer, 1976; created role of Morris, in Washington Square, 1977; returned to Royal Ballet at Covent Garden, 1977; Rehearsal Dir, Rambert Dance Co., Jan.–July 1995 (on leave of absence); Artistic Dir, Hong Kong Ballet, 1996–2006; Artistic Dir and Choreographer, Suzhou Kewen Promotion Co., 2007–08; co-choreographer (with Wayne Eagling), Beauty and the Beast, Kremlin Ballet, 2013. *Major roles include:* Prince in Sleeping Beauty, Swan Lake and Giselle, Prince Rudolf in Mayerling, Petruchio in Taming of the Shrew, Romeo and Mercutio in Romeo and Juliet, Lescaut in Manon; lead, in Song and Dance, 1982; *roles created:* Yukinojo (mime role), in world première of Minoru Miki's opera An Actor's Revenge, 1979; male lead in Bolero, Japan (chor. by Yashiro Okamoto), 1980; Antonio in The Duenna, S Africa (chor. by Ashley Killar), 1980; lead, in Dances of Albion (chor. by Glen Tetley), 1980; Esenin in Kenneth Macmillan's ballet, Isadora, Covent Garden, 1981; lead, in L'Invitation au Voyage, Covent Garden (chor. by Michael Corder), 1982; Consort Lessons, and Sons of Horos, 1986, Still Life at the Penguin Café, and The Trial of Prometheus, 1988 (chor. by David Bintley); title role in Cyrano (chor. by David Bintley), 1991. Choreographed ballets: Bits and Pieces, in Canada, 1977; Mes Souvenirs, in London, 1978; Magic Toyshop, 1987; *for Hong Kong Ballet:* Swan Lake, 1996; Giselle, Nutcracker, 1997; Tango Ballet Tango, 2000; Sleeping Beauty, 2002; (and designed) The Legend of the Great Archer, 2004; Suzie Wong, 2006. *Film:* Anna, 1988. *Recreations:* golf, football, gardening, swimming and various other sports. *Address:* Flat 37, Regatta Point, 38 Kew Bridge Road TW8 0EB.

JEFFERISS, Dr Paul Howard; Head of Policy, BP, since 2010 (Director of Environmental Policy, 2006–09; Head of Energy, Climate and Environmental Policy, 2009–10); *b* 29 Oct. 1955; *s* of Leonard James Jefferiss and Elsie Jefferiss (*née* Shenton). *Educ:* Peterhouse, Cambridge (BA Hons Anglo-Saxon, Norse and Celtic 1977, MA 1990); Harvard Univ. (MA Celtic Langs and Lit. 1980; PhD 1991); Tufts Univ. (Cert. Envmtl Mgt 1992; MA Envmtl (and Urban) Policy 1994). Publicity Asst, OUP, 1978–79; Harvard University: Hd Teaching Fellow, 1982–91; Lectr, 1988–91; Asst Sen. Tutor, 1988–91, Tutor, 1991–93, Dunster House; Lectr in Envmtl Mgt, UNEP at Tufts Univ., 1995–97; Dir of Energy, Union of Concerned Scientists, 1994–98; Hd, Envmtl Policy, RSPB, 1998–2000 and 2001–06; Dir, Green Alliance, 2000–01. Member: Renewables Wkg Gp, US President's Initiative on Climate Change Technol. Strategy, 1997; Energy Adv. Panel, 1999–2003, Renewables Adv. Bd, 2006–10, DECC (formerly DTI); Envmtl Adv. Gp, Ofgem, 2002–10; Envmtl Innovations Adv. Gp, BERR (formerly DTI)–DEFRA, 2003–08; Sustainable Develt Task Force, DEFRA, 2003–05; Bd, Renewable Fuels Agency, 2007–10; World Business Council on Sustainable Develt, 2015–. Non-executive Director: Renewable Energy Policy Project, 1997–98; Carbon Trust, 2001–; Carbon Trust Investments Ltd, 2003–12; SITA Trust, 2005–08; Mem., Adv. Bd, SITA UK, 2009–11. Member: Adv. Bd and Annual Assessment Panel, Tyndall Centre for Climate Change Res., 2000–06; Steering Bd, (Univ. of) Sussex Energy Gp, 2005–10. Member: Green Globe Network, 2000; Bd, Eur. Envmtl Bureau, 2000–01 (Chm., EEB-UK, 2000–01); Bd, Low-Carbon Vehicle Partnership, 2003–08. Trustee, Nat. Energy Foundn, 2005–08. *Publications:* (ed with W. J. Mahon) Proceedings of the Harvard Celtic Colloquium, Vol IV 1984, Vol V 1985; reports, briefing papers and articles on sustainable develt, envmt, energy and transport policy, incl. contribs to Science jl. *Recreations:* reading, running, travelling, maintaining a listed building. *Address:* The Mill House, 61 Mill Street, Gamlingay, Cambs SG19 3JS. *T:* 07770 342123. *E:* paul.jefferiss@bp.com.

JEFFERSON, Prof. Ann Margaret, FBA 2004; Fellow and Tutor in French, New College, Oxford, since 1987; Professor of French, University of Oxford, since 2006; *b* 3 Nov. 1949; *d* of Antony and Eirlys Jefferson; *m* 1st, 1971, Anthony Glees (marr. diss. 1992); two *s* one *d*; 2nd, 2011, Michael Holland. *Educ:* St Anne's Coll., Oxford (BA Hons 1971; MA); Wolfson Coll., Oxford (DPhil 1976). University of Oxford: Jun. Res. Fellow, 1978–82, Lectr in French, 1982–87, St John's Coll.; CUF Lectr in French, Fac. of Mod. Langs, 1987–2006. Visiting Professor: Columbia Univ., 2006; (Chaire Dupront), Sorbonne, Univ. Paris IV, 2008. Commandeur, Ordre des Palmes Académiques (France), 2012 (Officière, 2001). *Publications:* The Nouveau Roman and the Poetics of Fiction, 1980; (with D. Robey) Modern Literary Theory: a comparative introduction, 1982, rev. edn 1986; Reading Realism in Stendhal, 1988; Nathalie Sarraute, Fiction and Theory: questions of difference, 2000; Stendhal: La Chartreuse de Parme, 2003; Biography and the Question of Literature in France, 2007; (trans.) Le Défi biographique, 2012; Genius in France: an idea and its uses, 2014. *Address:* New College, Oxford OX1 3BN. *T:* and *Fax:* (01865) 279521. *E:* ann.jefferson@new.ox.ac.uk.

JEFFERSON, Joan Ena; *see* Appleyard, J. E.

JEFFERSON, Sir John Alexander D.; *see* Dunnington-Jefferson.

JEFFERSON, William Hayton, OBE 1985; Director, Portugal, British Council, and Cultural Counsellor, Lisbon, 1996–98; *b* 29 July 1940; *s* of late Stanley Jefferson and Josephine (*née* Hayton); *m* 1st, 1963, Marie-Jeanne Mazenq (marr. diss. 1986); three *s*; 2nd, 1986, Fadia Georges Tarraf; one *s*. *Educ:* Nelson-Thomlinson Grammar Sch., Wigton, Cumbria; Wadham Coll., Oxford (MA 1966). Russian teacher, 1963–66; with British Council, 1967–98: Tripoli, 1967–70; Kuwait, 1970–72; Algeria, 1972–75; Director: Qatar, 1975–79; Overseas Co-operation, London, 1979–82; United Arab Emirates, 1982–85; Algeria, 1985–90; Dir, Czechoslovakia, and Cultural Counsellor, Prague, 1990–96. Mem. (Ind), Allerdale Borough Council, Cumbria, 1999–; Chairman: N Allerdale Regeneration Gp, 2001–06; Jt Adv. Cttee, Solway Coast Area of Outstanding Natural Beauty, Cumbria, 2002–; Lake Dist Nat. Park Authy, 2008– (Mem., 2007–). Pres., Cumbria Co. Bowling Assoc., 2005–07. Gold Medal: Czech Scientific Univ., 1995; Palacky Univ., Olomouc, 1996; Silver Medal: Charles Univ., Prague, 1996; Masaryk Univ., Brno, 1996. *Recreations:* Cumbrian local history and dialect, wine, bowls. *Address:* 3 Marine Terrace, Silloth, Cumbria CA7 4BZ. *T:* (01697) 332526. *Club:* Silloth-on-Solway Bowls.

JEFFERSON SMITH, Peter, CB 1992; Trustee, South East London Community Foundation, 1995–2005 (Chair of Trustees, 1995–2000); *b* 14 July 1939; *m* 1964, Anna Willett; two *d*. *Educ:* Trinity College, Cambridge. HM Customs and Excise, 1960; Commissioner, 1980; Dep. Chm., 1988–94. *Address:* 22 Iveley Road, SW4 0EW. *T:* (020) 7622 8285.

JEFFERTS SCHORI, Most Rev. Katharine, PhD; Presiding Bishop, Episcopal Church in the United States of America, 2006–15; *b* 26 March 1954; *m* 1979, Richard Miles Schori; one *d*. *Educ:* Stanford Univ. (BS 1974); Oregon State Univ. (MS Oceanography 1977; PhD 1983); Church Divinity Sch. of the Pacific (MDiv 1994). Ordained deacon and priest, 1994; Pastoral Associate, then Asst Rector, Episcopal Ch of the Good Samaritan, Corvallis, Oregon, and Priest-in-charge, El Buen Samaritano, Corvallis, 1994–2001; Bishop of Nevada, 2001–06. *Publications:* A Wing and a Prayer: a message of faith and hope, 2007; The Gospel in the Global Village: seeking God's dream of Shalom, 2009; Gathering at God's Table: the five marks of mission in the feast of faith, 2012. *Address:* c/o Episcopal Church Center, 815 Second Avenue, New York, NY 10017, USA.

JEFFERY, Prof. Charles Adrian, PhD; Professor of Politics, since 2004, and a Vice Principal, since 2011, University of Edinburgh; *b* 27 July 1964; *yr s* of late Frank Jeffery and of June Jeffery (now Addington); *m* 1998, Elke Lieve Versmessen; one *s* two *d*. *Educ:* Univ. of Loughborough (BA 1985; PhD 1990). Lecturer: in Eur. Hist., N Staffs Poly., 1988–89; in W Eur. Politics, Leicester Univ., 1989–94; Institute for German Studies, University of Birmingham: Sen. Res. Fellow, 1994–96; Reader, 1996–99; Prof. of German Politics and Dep. Dir, 1999–2004. Joint Editor: Regl and Fed. Studies, 1995–2012; German Politics, 2001–05. Member: Res. Adv. Bd, Cttee on Standards in Public Life, 2001–06; Commn on Consequences of Devolution for H of C, 2012–13. Specialist Advr, Select Cttee on ODPM, 2004–05. Dir, ESRC Res. Prog. on Devolution and Const. Change, 2000–06. Mem., ESRC, 2005–11. Chairman: Assoc. for Study of German Politics, 1999–2000 and 2005–08; Political Studies Assoc., 2011–. FAcSS (AcSS 2004). FRSE 2007. *Publications:* (jtly) German Federalism Today, 1991; Social Democracy in the Australian Provinces 1918–1934, 1995; The Regional Dimension of the European Union, 1997; Recasting German Federalism, 1998; (jtly) Germany's European Diplomacy, 2000; Verfassungspolitik und Verfassungswandel: Deutschland und Grossbritannien im Vergleich, 2001; (jtly) Devolution and Electoral Politics, 2006; (jtly) The Scottish Parliament, The First Decade, 2009; (jtly) Rethinking Germany and Europe, 2010. *Recreations:* food and cooking, rock music. *Address:* School of Social and Political Science, Chrystal Macmillan Building, 15A George Square, Edinburgh EH8 9LD. *T:* (0131) 650 3941. *E:* charlie.jeffery@ed.ac.uk.

JEFFERY, David John, CBE 2000; Chief Executive, British Marine Equipment Council, 2000–01; *b* 18 Feb. 1936; *s* of late Stanley John Friend Jeffery and Sylvia May (*née* Mashford); *m* 1959, Margaret (*née* Yates); one *s* two *d*. *Educ:* Sutton High Sch., Plymouth; Croydon Coll. of Technology. Nat. Service, RAOC, 1954–56; Admiralty Dir of Stores Dept, 1956–66; RN Staff Coll., 1967; MoD, 1968–70; on secondment, 1970–76: Treasury Centre for Admin. Studies, 1970–72; Management Science Training Adviser, Malaysian Govt, Kuala Lumpur, 1972–74; Civil Service Dept, 1974–76; MoD, 1976–83; RCDS, 1983; Dir, Armaments and Management Services, RN Supply and Transport Service 1984–86; Chief Exec. and Bd Mem., PLA, 1986–99. Chm., Estuary Services Ltd, 1988–99. Director: UK Major Ports Ltd, 1993–99; British Ports Industry Trng Ltd, 1993–99 (Chm., 1998–99); Trustee Dir, Pilots' Nat. Pension Fund, 1987–95; Vice-Pres. of Conf., Internat. Assoc. of Ports and Harbors, 1995–97; Chairman: European Sea Ports Orgn, 1997–99; DTI Ports Sector Gp, 1998–2002; Mem., European Maritime Industries High Level Panel, 1994–95, Marine Foresight Panel, 1997–99. Orgnl Develt Advr, VSO, Kathmandu, 2004–06. Chm., Frome CAB, 2001–04. Governor: Selwood Middle Sch., Frome, 2001–04; Trinity Sch., Frome, 2014–. Freeman,

City of London, 1987; Mem., Co. of Watermen and Lightermen of River Thames, 1987. *Recreations:* theatre, music, travel, trekking. *Address:* The Old Coach House, High Street, Nunney, Frome, Somerset BA11 4LZ.

JEFFERY, Prof. Nicholas David, PhD; FRCVS; Professor of Neurology and Neurosurgery, Lloyd Veterinary Medical Center, Iowa State University, since 2010; *b* 1 May 1958; *s* of John and Jill Jeffery; *m* 2005, Kat (marr. diss. 2010); three *s*; *m* 2011, Unity Locke. *Educ:* Bristol Univ. (BVSc); Wolfson Coll., Cambridge (PhD). FRCVS; Dip. ECVN; Dip. ECVS; Dip. SAS. Veterinary Officer, PDSA, 1981–83; Veterinary Surgeon: Citivet, E1, 1983–90; Animal Health Trust, 1990–93; Wellcome Trust Scholarship, Cambridge Univ., 1993–97; Wellcome Trust Fellowship, UCL, 1997–2000; Lectr in Veterinary Neurol., 2000–06, Prof. of Veterinary Clinical Studies, 2006–10, Univ. of Cambridge. *Publications:* Handbook of Small Animal Spinal Surgery, 1995; contrib. veterinary and neurosci. jls. *Recreations:* dog walking, TV, crosswords, reading the newspaper. *Address:* Lloyd Veterinary Medical Center, Iowa State University, 1600 S 16th Street, Ames, IA 50011–1250, USA.

JEFFERY, Maj.-Gen. the Hon. (Philip) Michael, AC 1996 (AO (mil.) 1988); CVO 2000; MC 1971; Governor-General of Australia, 2003–08; *b* 12 Dec. 1937; *s* of Philip Frederick Jeffery and Edna Mary Jeffery (*née* Johnson); *m* 1967, Marlena Joy Kerr; three *s* one *d*. *Educ:* Kent Street High Sch., WA; Royal Mil. Coll., Duntroon. Served Infantry, 1958–93: jun. regtl appts, 17 Nat. Service Trng Co. and SAS Regt, 1959–62; Operational Service, Malaya, Borneo and Vietnam, 1962–72; psc 1972; Commanding Officer: 2nd Bn Pacific Islands Regt, PNG, 1974–75; SAS Regt, Perth, 1976–77; jssc 1978; Dir, Special Forces, 1979–81; Comd, 1 Bde, Sydney, 1983–84; rcds 1985; comd, 1 Div., Brisbane, 1986–88; DCGS, Canberra, 1990–91; ACGS Materiel, 1991–93. Gov., WA, 1993–2000. Founding Chm. and Patron, Future Directions Internat. Ltd, 2001–03 and 2008–. Chairman: Outcomes Australia, 2008–; Royal Flying Doctor Service of Australia, 2009–12; Global Foundn, 2009–12; Diamond Jubilee Trust of Australia, 2012; Nat. Advocate for Soil Health, 2012–. Mem., United Services Inst., Canberra, 1978–. Hon. DTech Curtin, 2000. Citizen of WA, 2000. KStJ 1995. Grand Companion, Order of Logohu (PNG), 2005. *Recreations:* golf, fishing, music. *Address:* 18 Hampton Circuit, Yarralumla, ACT 2600, Australia. *Clubs:* Commonwealth (Canberra); Royal Canberra Golf.

JEFFERY, Very Rev. Robert Martin Colquhoun; Canon and Sub-Dean of Christ Church, Oxford, 1996–2002; *b* 30 April 1935; *s* of Norman Clare Jeffery and Gwenyth Isabel Jeffery; *m* 1968, Ruth Margaret Tinling (*d* 1995); three *s* one *d*. *Educ:* St Paul's School; King's Coll., London (BD, AKC). Assistant Curate: St Aidan, Grangetown, 1959–61; St Mary, Barnes, 1961–63; Asst Sec., Missionary and Ecumenical Council of Church Assembly, 1964–68; Sec., Dept of Mission and Unity, BCC, 1968–71; Vicar: St Andrew, Headington, Oxford, 1971–78; St Bartholomew, Tong, 1978–87; RD of Cowley, 1973–78; Lichfield Diocesan Missioner, 1978–79; Archdeacon of Salop, 1980–87; Dean of Worcester, 1987–96, now Dean Emeritus. Mem., Gen. Synod of C of E, 1982–87 and 1988–96 (Member: Standing Cttee, 1990–96; Business Cttee, 1990–96); Mem., Crown Appointments Commn, 1996. Chm. Trustees, Emmaus Oxford, 2003–05. Select Preacher, Univ. of Oxford, 1990, 1997, 1999, 2002. Chm., Churches Together in Oxfordshire, 1997–2000. Gov., Ripon Coll., 1976–2007 (Hon. Fellow, 2007). FRSA 1992. Hon. DD Birmingham, 1999. *Publications:* (with D. M. Paton) Christian Unity and the Anglican Communion, 1965, 3rd edn 1968; (with T. S. Garret) Unity in Nigeria, 1964; (ed) Lambeth Conference 1968 Preparatory Information; Areas of Ecumenical Experiment, 1968; Ecumenical Experiments: A Handbook, 1971; Case Studies in Unity, 1972; (contrib.) Benson of Cowley, 1980; (ed) By What Authority?, 1987; Anima Christi, 1994; (contrib.) Coventry's First Cathedral, 1994; (contrib.) A Scandalous Prophet, 2002; (contrib.) Ambassadors for Christ, 2004; (contrib.) In Search of Humanity and Deity, 2006; Imitating Christ, 2006; Discovering Tong, 2007; (trans.) Imitation of Christ, by Thomas A. Kempis, 2013. *Recreations:* local history, cooking, writing obituaries and book reviews. *Address:* 47 The Manor House, Bennett Crescent, Cowley, Oxford OX4 2UG. *T:* (01865) 749706. *E:* rmcj@btopenworld.com.

JEFFERY, Sir Thomas (Baird), Kt 2015; CB 2006; Director General, Children Services and Departmental Strategy (formerly Children, Young People and Families), Department for Education (formerly Director General, Children, Young People and Families, Department for Education and Skills, then Director General, Children and Families, Department for Children, Schools and Families), 2003–14; *b* 11 Feb. 1953; *s* of Herbert George, (Jeff), Jeffery and Margaret (*née* Thornton); *m* 1987, Alison Nisbet; one *s* one *d*. *Educ:* King's Sch., Canterbury; Jesus Coll., Cambridge (MA Eng. Lit.); Centre for Contemporary Cultural Studies, Univ. of Birmingham. Joined DES, 1981; Private Sec. to Perm. Sec., 1984–85; Principal Private Sec. to Sec. of State, 1987–89; Dir, Student Loans Co., 1989–92; Head: Special Educnl Needs Div., 1992–95; Personnel and Related Roles, 1995–98; on secondment to DoH as Hd, Children's Services, 1998–2001; Dir, Children and Families Group, DfES, 2001–03. *Publications:* (contrib.) Impacts and Influences, 1987; (contrib.) Metropolis London, 1989; (contrib.) Splintered Classes, 1990; Mass-Observation: a short history, 1999. *Recreations:* family, walking, cricket, modern history and literature. *Club:* MCC.

JEFFERYS, Dr David Barrington, FFPM, FRCP, FRCPE; Senior Vice President, Global Regulatory Affairs, Government Relations and Patient Safety, Eisai Europe Ltd, since 2011; *b* 1 Aug. 1952; *s* of Godfrey B. Jefferys and Joyce E. Jefferys; *m* 1985, Ann-Marie Smith; one *s* one *d*. *Educ:* St Dunstan's Coll.; Guy's Hosp. Med. Sch., Univ. of London (BSc Hons; MB BS 1976; MD 1983). FFPM 1990; FRCPE 1990; FRCP 1992. Medical posts at Guy's and St Thomas' Hosps, 1976–83; locum consultant physician, Tunbridge Wells, 1983–84; SMO, DoH, 1984–86; PMO and Principal Assessor to Cttee on Safety of Medicines, 1986; Medicines Control Agency: Business Manager, Eur. and New Drug Licensing, 1986–94; Dir, Licensing Div., 1994–2000; Chief Exec. and Dir, Medical Devices Agency, 2000–03; Actg Hd, Med. Devices Sector, Medicines and Healthcare products Regulatory Agency, 2003. Sen. Strategic Regulatory Advr, Eisai Europe, 2005–06; Vice Pres., 2006–08, Sen. Vice Pres., Global Regulatory Affairs, 2008–11, Eisai Research and Develt Co. Ltd, subseq. Eisai Europe Ltd. Vis. Prof. in Medicine, Univ. of Newcastle upon Tyne, 1994. UK Deleg. to Cttee on Proprietary Medicinal Products, 1995–2000. Chm., Mutual Recognition Facilitation Gp, EU, 1997–98. Member: EU Med. Device Expert Gp; Global Harmonisation Task Force Steering Cttee. Pres., Regulatory Affairs Professional Soc., 2008–10 (Chm. Bd, 2009–10); Pres. and Chm., Orgn for Professionals in Regulatory Affairs, 2011–12; Co-Chm., Regulatory Policy and Tech. Standards Cttee, Internat. Fedn of Pharmaceutical Manufrs and Assocs, 2013–. Vice Chm., Health and Wellbeing Bd, 2013–; Mem., President's Cttee, Young Epilepsy, 2012–. Mem. (C), Bromley LBC, 2011–. Pres., Old Dunstonian Assoc., 2013–14. Church Warden, St Mary's Shortlands, 2009–. FRSocMed 2004. Freeman, City of London, 2002–; Liveryman, Soc. of Apothecaries, 2008–. *Publications:* chapters in books and articles on medicines regulation, regulatory policy and quality assurance. *Recreations:* sport, ski-ing, theatre, music, art. *Club:* Surrey County Cricket.

JEFFERYS, Judith Patricia; *see* Armitage, J. P.

JEFFORD, Andrew Christopher; author, journalist and broadcaster, since 1988; *b* Berkeley, 14 March 1956; *s* of Peter and Celia Jefford; *m* 1st, 1980, Bogumila Magdalena Kaczanowska (marr. diss. 2006); 2nd, 2008, Paula Tracy Grech; two *s*. *Educ:* Gresham's Sch., Norfolk; Reading Univ. (BA 1st Cl. Hons English Lit.); Univ. of E Anglia (MA with dist. 19th and 20th Century Novel 1980). Ed., Octopus Books, 1983–88; Wine Corresp., Evening Standard, 1992–2002; columnist: Decanter mag., 1998–; Waitrose Food Illustrated mag., 2000–10; World of Fine Wine mag., 2003–; travel and drink writer, FT, 2004–; Wine Writer-in-Residence, Wine 2030 Res. Network, 2009–10. Occasional presenter, Food Prog., BBC Radio 4, 1995–2008. Sen. Res. Fellow, Univ. of Adelaide, 2009–10. *Publications:* Port: an essential guide to the classic drink, 1988; Which? Wine Guide, 1991; The Wines of Germany, 1994; The Evening Standard Wine Guide, 1996, 1997; Smokes, 1997; One Hundred and One Things You Need to Know About Wine, 1998; Wine Tastes, Wine Styles, 2000; The New France, 2002; After-Dinner Drinks, 2003; Choosing Wine, 2003; Peat Smoke and Spirit: a portrait of Islay and its whiskies, 2004; Andrew Jefford's Wine Course, 2008; contributor: Robert Louis Stevenson, 1983; (with P. Draper) Questions of Taste: the philosophy of wine, 2007; Whiskey and Philosophy: a small batch of spirited ideas, 2009. *Recreations:* family life, classical music, travel, swimming, walking, writing haiku (published via Twitter @andrewcjefford). *Address:* c/o Watson Little, Suite 315, Screenworks, 22 Highbury Grove, N5 2ER. *E:* andrewjefford@gmail.com. *W:* www.andrewjefford.com.

JEFFORD, Barbara Mary, OBE 1965; actress; *b* Plymstock, Devon, 26 July 1930; *d* of late Percival Francis Jefford and Elizabeth Mary Ellen (*née* Laity); *m* 1953, Terence Longdon (marr. diss. 1961); *m* 1967, John Arnold Turner. *Educ:* Weirfield Sch., Taunton, Som. Studied for stage, Bristol and Royal Academy of Dramatic Art (Bancroft Gold Medal). *Royal Shakespeare Co.:* Stratford-on-Avon, 1950–54: Isabella in Measure for Measure; Anne Bullen in Henry VIII; Hero in Much Ado About Nothing; Lady Percy in Henry IV parts I and II; Desdemona in Othello; Rosalind in As You Like It; Helena in A Midsummer Night's Dream; Katharina in The Taming of the Shrew; Patsy Newquist in Little Murders, Aldwych, 1967; Volumnia in Coriolanus, 1989 and 1990; Tatyana in Barbarians, 1990; Countess in All's Well That Ends Well, Mistress Quickly in The Merry Wives of Windsor, 1992; Katia in Misha's Party, 1993; Countess Terzky in Wallenstein, 1993–94; *Old Vic Company:* (1956–62) Imogen in Cymbeline; Beatrice in Much Ado About Nothing; Portia in The Merchant of Venice; Julia in Two Gentlemen of Verona; Tamora in Titus Andronicus; Lady Anne in Richard III; Queen Margaret in Henry VI parts I, II and III; Isabella in Measure for Measure; Regan in King Lear; Viola in Twelfth Night; Ophelia in Hamlet; Rosalind in As You Like It; St Joan; Lady Macbeth; Gwendoline in The Importance of Being Earnest; Beatrice Cenci; Lavinia in Mourning Becomes Electra; *for Prospect, at Old Vic:* (1977–79) Gertrude in Hamlet; Cleopatra in All for Love; Cleopatra in Antony and Cleopatra; Nurse in Romeo and Juliet; Anna in The Government Inspector; RSC Nat. Tour, 1980, Mistress Quickly in Henry IV pts 1 and 2; *National Theatre:* Gertrude in Hamlet, Zabina in Tamburlaine the Great, 1976; Mother in Six Characters in Search of an Author, Arina Bazarov in Fathers and Sons, Salathiel in Ting Tang Mine (Clarence Derwent Award, 1988), 1987; Sanctuary, 2002; Anne of Austria in Power, 2003. *Other London stage appearances include:* Andromache in Tiger at the Gates, Apollo, 1955, NY, 1956; Lina in Misalliance, Royal Court and Criterion, 1963; step-daughter in Six Characters in Search of an Author, Mayfair, 1963; Nan in Ride a Cock Horse, Piccadilly, 1965; Mother Vauzou in Mistress of Novices, Piccadilly, 1973; Filumena, Lyric, 1979; Duchess of York in Richard II, and Queen Margaret in Richard III, Phoenix, 1988–89; Oenone in Phèdre, Albina in Britannicus, Albery, 1998, NY, 1999; Duchess of York in Richard II, and Volumnia in Coriolanus, Almeida at Gainsborough Studios, NY and Tokyo, 2000; Mary in The Old Masters, Comedy, 2004; Hanna in Mary Stuart, Donmar, 2005; *other stage appearances include:* Hedda Gabler, Medea; Phaedra, Oxford Playhouse, 1966; Lady Sneerwell in The School for Scandal, toured UK, 1995; Our Betters, Chichester, 1997; Queen Margaret in Richard III, Crucible Th., Sheffield, 2002; Mrs Higgins in Pygmalion, Th. Royal Bath and tour, 2007, transf. Old Vic, 2008; has toured extensively in UK, Europe, USA, Near East, Far East, Africa, Australia, Russia, Poland and Yugoslavia. *Films:* Ulysses, 1967; A Midsummer Night's Dream, 1967; The Shoes of the Fisherman, 1968; To Love a Vampire, 1970; Hitler: the last ten days, 1973; And the Ship Sails On, 1983; Why the Whales Came, 1988; Reunion, 1988; Where Angels Fear to Tread, 1991; The Ninth Gate, 1999; The Deep Blue Sea, 2011; Philomena, 2012. Has appeared in numerous television and radio plays. Hon. DLitt Exeter, 2004. Pragnell Shakespeare Award, 1994. Silver Jubilee Medal, 1977. *Recreations:* music, swimming, gardening. *Address:* c/o United Agents Ltd, 12–26 Lexington Street, W1F 0LE.

JEFFORD, Nerys Angharad; QC 2008; a Recorder, since 2007; *b* Swansea, 25 Dec. 1962; *d* of John Keith Jefford and late Eirlys Rona Jefford. *Educ:* Olchfa Comprehensive Sch.; Lady Margaret Hall, Oxford (Schol.; BA 1984); Univ. of Virginia (Fulbright Schol.; LLM 1985). MCIArb 2006. Called to the Bar, Gray's Inn, 1986 (Lord Justice Holker Schol.; Karmel Schol.), Bencher, 2007; in practice at the Bar, 1988–. Mem., Educn and Trng Cttee, Bar Standards Bd, 2007– (Vice Chm., 2013–). Mem. Council, Soc. of Construction Law, 2002–09 (Chm., 2007–08). Mem., Adv. Council, Lady Margaret Hall, Oxford, 2006–. Trustee, Tech 4 All, 2013–. Sec., London Welsh Chorale, 2011–14. *Publications:* Keating on Construction Contracts, 8th edn 2006 to 9th edn 2012; (contrib.) Keating on Building Contracts, 5th edn 1991 to 8th edn 2006; (ed) Bullen, Leake and Jacob's Precedents of Pleadings, HK edn, 2013. *Recreation:* choral singing (London Welsh Chorale; Gray's Inn Chapel Choir; The Harry Ensemble). *Address:* Keating Chambers, 15 Essex Street, WC2R 3AA. *T:* (020) 7544 2600, *Fax:* (020) 7544 2700. *E:* njefford@keatingchambers.com.

JEFFREY, Dianne Michele, CBE 2011; DL; Chairman, Age UK, since 2009; *b* Sheffield, 23 Nov. 1944; *d* of Cyril and Eve Cantor; *m* 1965, Nicholas Jeffrey; two *s* two *d*. *Educ:* Sheffield High Sch.; Badminton Sch., Bristol; Sheffield Univ. (BA). Chm., Digital Outreach Ltd, 2007–. Chm., Community Healthcare (N Derbys) NHS Trust, 1994–2002. Chm., NHS Confedn, 2000–03. Mem., Regl Cttee, HLF, 2007–. Vice Chm., Derwent Valley Mills World Heritage Site, 2011–; Chair, Strategic Adv. Gp, Peak Nat. Park, 2012–. Chm., Anchor Trust, 2003–08. Chm., Governing Council, Univ. of Derby, 2002–11. Hon. Col, Derbys Army Cadet Force, 2004–. High Sheriff, 2002–03, DL 2004, Derbys. DUniv Derby, 2012. *Recreations:* music, ski-ing, opera, gardening, walking. *Address:* Age UK, Tavis House, 1–6 Tavistock Square, WC1H 9NA. *E:* diannejeffrey@gmail.com. *Clubs:* Royal Automobile, Royal Society of Medicine.

JEFFREY, Joan; *see* MacNaughton, J.

JEFFREY, Dr Robin Campbell, FREng, FIChemE, FIMechE; Chairman and Chief Executive, British Energy, 2001–02; Chairman, Bruce Power, 1999–2002; *b* 19 Feb. 1939; *s* of Robert Stewart Martin Jeffrey and Catherine Campbell McSporran; *m* 1962, Barbara Helen Robinson; two *s* one *d*. *Educ:* Kelvinside Acad.; Royal Technical Coll. (Glasgow Univ.) (BSc); Pembroke Coll., Cambridge (PhD). With Babcock & Wilcox, 1956–79; South of Scotland Electricity Board, later Scottish Power: Engrg Resources Manager, 1964–79; Technical Services Manager, 1979–80; Torness Project Manager, 1980–88; Chief Engr, 1988–89; Man. Dir, Engrg Resources Business, 1989–92; Chief Exec., 1992–95, Chm., 1995–98, Scottish Nuclear Ltd; Dep. Chm., 1996–2001, Exec. Dir, N America, 1998–2001, British Energy. Board Member: London Transport, 1996–98; London Underground Ltd, 1996–98. Former Member: Scottish Council, CBI; Exec., Scottish Council for Develt and Industry. Vis. Prof., Univ. of Strathclyde, 1994–2004. FREng (FEng 1992). *Publications:* (jtly) Open Cycle MHD Power Generation, 1969; pubns on energy related issues. *Recreations:* squash, tennis, ski-ing, playing musical instruments. *Address:* Brambles, Spring Copse, Oxford OX1 5BJ. *Clubs:* Cambridge University Royal Tennis; Hinksey Heights Golf.

JEFFREY, Sir William Alexander, KCB 2008 (CB 2001); Permanent Secretary, Ministry of Defence, 2005–10; *b* 28 Feb. 1948; *s* of Alexander and Joyce Jeffrey; *m* 1979, Joan MacNaughton, *qv*. *Educ:* Allan Glen's, Glasgow; Univ. of Glasgow (BSc Hons). Home Office, 1971–94: Private Sec. to Permanent Under Sec. of State, 1975–76; Principal, 1976–84; Assistant Secretary: Criminal Policy Dept, 1984–88; HM Prison Service, 1988–91; Asst Under Sec. of State, Immigration and Nationality Dept, 1991–94; Under Sec., Economic and

Domestic Affairs Secretariat, Cabinet Office, 1994–98; Dep. Sec., NI Office, 1998–2002; Dir Gen., Immigration and Nationality, Home Office, 2002–05; Security and Intelligence Co-ordinator and Permanent Sec., Cabinet Office, 2005. Chm. of Trustees, Police Foundn, 2011–; Chm., Civil Service Healthcare, 2011–; Chair, Implementation Bd for successor to ACPO. Reviewer, Rev. of Ind. Advocacy in Criminal Courts, 2013–14. *Recreations:* reading, hill-walking, watching football.

JEFFREYS, family name of **Baron Jeffreys**.

JEFFREYS, 3rd Baron *cr* 1952, of Burkham; **Christopher Henry Mark Jeffreys;** stockbroker, since 1992; *b* 22 May 1957; *s* of 2nd Baron Jeffreys and of Sarah Annabelle Mary, *d* of late Major Henry Garnett; *S* father, 1986; *m* 1985, Anne Elisabeth Johnson; one *s* one *d*. *Educ:* Eton. With: GNI Ltd, 1985–90; Raphael Zorn Hemsley, 1992–2000; Savoy Investment Mgt, 2000–12; Ashcourt Rowan Asset Mgt, 2012–. *Recreation:* country sports. *Heir: s* Hon. Arthur Mark Henry Jeffreys, *b* 18 Feb. 1989. *Address:* Bank House, 3 Main Street, Sproxton, Leics LE14 4QS. *T:* (01476) 861008.

JEFFREYS, Alan Howard; QC 1996; a Recorder, 1993–2004; *b* 27 Sept. 1947; *s* of late Hugh and Rachel Jeffreys; *m* 1975, Jane Olivia Sadler; one *s* one *d*. *Educ:* Ellesmere Coll.; King's College, London (LLB Hons). Called to the Bar, Gray's Inn, 1970; South Eastern Circuit; Asst Recorder, 1989–93. Mem., Criminal Injuries Compensation Appeals Panel (formerly Criminal Injuries Compensation Bd), 1999–2002. Mem., Exec. Cttee, Personal Injuries Bar Assoc., 2006–09. *Recreations:* fishing, chess, music. *Address:* Farrar's Building, Temple, EC4Y 7BD. *T:* (020) 7583 9241. *Club:* Hurlingham.

JEFFREYS, Sir Alec John, Kt 1994; FRS 1986; Wolfson Research Professor of the Royal Society, University of Leicester, since 1991 (Professor of Genetics, since 1987); *b* 9 Jan. 1950; *s* of Sidney Victor Jeffreys and Joan (*née* Knight); *m* 1971, Susan Miles; two *d*. *Educ:* Luton Grammar School; Luton VIth Form College; Merton College, Oxford (Postmaster; Christopher Welch Schol.; BA, MA, DPhil 1975; Hon. Fellow, 1990). EMBO Research Fellow, Univ. of Amsterdam, 1975–77; Leicester University: Lectr, Dept of Genetics, 1977–84; Reader, 1984–87; Lister Inst. Res. Fellow, 1982–91. Member: EMBO, 1983; Human Genome Orgn, 1989. Editor, Jl of Molecular Evolution, 1985. FRCPath 1991; FLS 1994; Founder FMedSci 1998. Hon. FRCP 1993; Hon. FIBiol 1998; Hon. FRSocMed 2001. Fellow, Forensic Sci. Soc. of India, 1989; Hon. Mem., Amer. Acad. of Forensic Scis, 1998. Hon. Fellow, Univ. of Luton, 1995. DUniv Open, 1991; Hon. DSc: St Andrews, 1996; Strathclyde, 1998; Hull, 2004; Oxford, 2004. Colworth Medal for Biochemistry, Biochem. Soc., 1985; Carter Medal, Clinical Genetics Soc., 1987, 2003; Davy Medal, Royal Soc., 1987; Linnean Soc. Bicentenary Medal, 1987; Analytika Prize, German Soc. for Clin. Chem., 1988; Press, Radio and TV Award, Midlander of the Year, 1989; Linnean Medal, 1994; Sir Frederick Gowland Hopkins Meml Medal, Biochem. Soc., 1996; Albert Einstein World of Science Award, World Cultural Council, 1996; Baly Medal, RCP, 1997; SCI Medal, 1997; Sir George Stokes Medal, RSC, 2000; Gold Medal, RCS, 2004; Copley Medal, Royal Soc., 2014. Hon. Freeman, City of Leicester, 1993. UK Patents on genetic fingerprints. *Publications:* research articles on molecular genetics and evolution in Nature, Cell, etc. *Recreations:* walking, swimming, postal history, reading unimproving novels.

JEFFREYS, Annabel Kate; *see* Arden, A. K.

JEFFREYS, David Alfred; QC 1981; a Recorder of the Crown Court, 1979–99; *b* 1 July 1934; *s* of late Coleman and Ruby Jeffreys; *m* 1964, Mary Ann Elizabeth Long; one *s* one *d*. *Educ:* Harrow; Trinity Coll., Cambridge (BA Hons). Served, Royal Signals, 1952–54; City, 1958. Called to the Bar, Gray's Inn, 1958, Bencher, 1989; Junior Prosecuting Counsel to the Crown, Central Criminal Court, 1975; Sen. Prosecuting Counsel to the Crown, CCC, 1979–81; Jt Head, Hollis Whiteman Chambers, 1995–99, retd. Mem., Bar Council, 1977–80. *Address:* c/o 1–2 Laurence Pountney Hill, EC4R 0EU.

JEFFREYS, Prof. Elizabeth Mary; Bywater and Sotheby Professor of Byzantine and Modern Greek Language and Literature, University of Oxford, 1996–2006; Fellow of Exeter College, Oxford, since 1996; *b* 22 July 1941; *d* of Lawrence R. Brown and Veronica Thompson; *m* 1965, Michael J. Jeffreys; one *d*. *Educ:* Blackheath High Sch. for Girls (GPDST); Girton Coll., Cambridge (MA (Class. Tripos)); St Anne's Coll., Oxford (BLitt; Hon. Fellow, 1997). Classics Mistress, Mary Datchelor Girls' Sch., 1965–69; Sen. Res. Fellow, Warburg Inst., London Univ., 1969–72; Vis. Fellow, Dumbarton Oaks Centre for Byzantine Studies, 1972–74, 1984; Res. Fellow, Ioannina Univ., Greece, 1974–76; part-time Lectr, univs in Sydney, Australia, 1976–86; Vis. Fellow, Humanities Centre, Canberra, 1978; Res. Fellow, Melbourne Univ., 1987–89; Res. Fellow, 1990–92, Australian Sen. Res. Fellow, 1993–95, Sydney Univ. Fellow, Australian Acad. of Humanities, 1993. *Publications:* Byzantine Papers, 1981; Popular Literature in Late Byzantium, 1983; The Chronicle of John Malalas: a translation, 1986; Studies in John Malalas, 1990; The War of Troy, 1996; Digenis Akritis, 1998; Through the Looking Glass, 2000; Rhetoric in Byzantium, 2003; The Age of the Dromon, 2006; Oxford Handbook of Byzantine Studies, 2008; Iacobi Monachi Epistulae, 2009; Four Byzantine Novels, 2012. *Recreation:* walking. *Address:* Exeter College, Oxford OX1 3DP.

JEFFREYS, Louise; Director of Arts (formerly Director of Programming), Barbican Centre, since 2010; *b* Whitstable, Kent; *d* of Peter Jeffreys and Sylvia Taylor. *Educ:* City of London Freemen's Sch.; Univ. of Manchester (BA Hons Drama 1978). Tech. Dir, ENO, 1990–94; Hd of Prodn, Bavarian State Opera, Munich, 1994–96; Admin. Dir, Nottingham Playhouse, 1996–98; Hd of Theatre, Barbican, London, 1999–2010. Chm., Assoc. of British Theatre Technicians. Mem. Bd, Told by an Idiot, 2011–. *Recreations:* reading, walking, gardening. *Address:* Barbican Centre, Silk Street, EC2Y 8DS. *T:* (020) 7382 7381. *E:* louise.jeffreys@barbican.org.uk.

JEFFREYS, Prof. Paul William, PhD; CPhys; Professor of Computing, since 2002, Director, IT Risk Management, since 2012, and Fellow, e-Research Centre, since 2006, University of Oxford; Fellow, Keble College, Oxford, since 2001; *b* 4 July 1954; *s* of George Lewis Jeffreys and Naomi Emily Jeffreys; *m* 1985, Linda Christine Pay; two *s* one *d*. *Educ:* Drayton Manor Grammar Sch., Hanwell; Univ. of Manchester (BSc Hons); Univ. of Bristol (PhD 1980); MA Oxon. CPhys 1982; MInstP 1982. CERN Fellow, Geneva, 1979–82; Rutherford Appleton Laboratory: physicist, 1982–95; Hd, Computing and Resource Mgt Div., Particle Physics Dept, 1995–2001; Leader, CCLRC e-Science Centre, 2000–01; University of Oxford: Dir, Oxford Univ. Computing Services, 2001–05; Dir, e-Science Centre, 2001–06; Dir, e-Horizons Inst., 2005–10; Acting Dir, 2005–07, Dir, 2007–12, Inf. and Communications Technol.; Vice-Pres., Sen. Common Room, Keble Coll., 2013–. Dir, Digitalspires, 2006–08. Mem., FCO Academic Expert Network for internat. cyber security policy, 2014–. Trustee, Jisc, 2012–14. Mem., Editl Bd, British Jl of Interdisciplinary Studies, 2014–. *Recreations:* family life, ski-ing, squash, running, Real tennis. *Address:* Keble College, Oxford OX1 3PG. *T:* (01865) 273229, *Fax:* (01865) 283346. *E:* paul.jeffreys@it.ox.ac.uk.

JEFFRIES, Hon. Sir John (Francis), Kt 1993; Chairman, New Zealand Press Council, 1997–2005; *b* 28 March 1929; *s* of Frank Leon Jeffries and Mary Jeffries; *m* 1951, Joan Patricia Christensen (*d* 2001); one *s* one *d*. *Educ:* St Patrick's Coll., Wellington; Victoria Univ. of Wellington (BA, LLB). Clerical, 1946–50; school teaching, 1950–55; Law, 1956–76; Judge of the High Court of New Zealand, 1976–92; NZ Police Complaints Authority, 1992–97. Chm., Air New Zealand, 1975. Wellington City Council, 1962–74; Dep. Mayor, Wellington, 1971–74. Chm., Nat. Housing Commn, 1973–75. Vice-Pres., NZ Law Soc., 1973–76; Member: Trust for Intellectually Handicapped, 1980–88; NZ Inst. of Mental Retardation, 1984–88. Comr of Security Warrants, 1999–2013. Hon. Life Mem., Amer. Bar Assoc., 1974. *Recreations:* reading, music, sports generally. *Address:* 4/310 Oriental Parade, Oriental Bay, Wellington, New Zealand. *T:* (4) 3859995. *Clubs:* Wellington; Royal Wellington Golf.

JEFFRIES, Michael Makepeace Eugene, RIBA; FICE; Chairman: Civica Group Ltd, since 2010; Mouchel Group plc, since 2013; *b* 17 Sept. 1944; *s* of William Eugene Jeffries and Margaret Jeffries (*née* Makepeace); *m* 1966, Pamela Mary Booth; two *s* two *d*. *Educ:* Poly. of North London (DipArch Hons). RIBA 1973; FICE 2003. Architectural Assistant: John Laing & Sons Ltd, 1963–67; Surrey CC, 1967–68; Gillespie & Steele, Trinidad, 1968–69; Deeks Bousell Partnership, London, 1969–73; Senior Architect: Bradshaw Gass & Hope, Lancs, 1973–75; W. S. Atkins Ltd, 1975–78; Man. Dir, ASFA Ltd, 1978; Dir, W. S. Atkins Gp Consultants Ltd, 1979–92; Mkting and Business Develt Dir, W. S. Atkins Ltd, 1992–95; W. S. Atkins plc: Chief Exec., 1995–2001; Chm., 2001–04. Non-executive Director: De La Rue, 2000–07; Worksmart Ltd, 2013–. Chairman: Wembley Nat. Stadium Ltd, 2002–08; Parking Internat. Hldgs Ltd (NCP), 2005–07; NCP Services Ltd, 2008–10; VT Group plc, 2005–10; Priory Group, 2011–14. Governor: RNLI, 2007–14; Canford Sch., 2014–. *Publications:* various technical papers in jls. *Recreations:* sailing, golf, water colour painting, antiquarian horology. *Address:* 1 The Whitehouse, 326 Sandbanks Road, Poole, Dorset BH14 8HY. *T:* (01202) 706051. *Club:* Royal Motor Yacht (Poole).

JEFFS, Julian; QC 1975; author; *b* 5 April 1931; *s* of Alfred Wright Jeffs, Wolverhampton, and Janet Honor Irene (*née* Davies); *m* 1966, Deborah, *d* of Peter James Stuart Bevan; three *s*. *Educ:* Wrekin Coll.; Downing Coll., Cambridge (MA; Associate Fellow, 1986; Emeritus Associate Fellow 1915). Nat. Service, Naval rating, 1949–50. Sherry Shipper's Asst, Spain, 1956. Barrister, Gray's Inn, 1958 (Bencher 1981), Inner Temple, 1971; Midland and Oxford Circuit; Hong Kong Bar; retired from practice, 1991; a Recorder, 1975–96; a Dep. High Court Judge, Chancery Div., 1981–96. Chm., Patent Bar Assoc., 1980–89; Member: Senate of Inns of Court and Bar, 1984–85; Bar Council, 1988–89. Gen. Comr of Income Tax, 1983–91. Editor, Wine and Food, 1965–67; Mem., Cttee of Management, International Wine & Food Soc., 1965–67, 1971–82; Chm., 1970–72, Vice-Pres., 1975–91, Pres., 1992–96, Life Trustee, 2014, Circle of Wine Writers. Gen. Editor, Faber's Wine Series, 1985–2002. Dep. Gauger, City of London, 1979. Freeman, City of London. Lauréat de l'Office International de la Vigne et du Vin, 1962 and 2001; Glenfiddich wine writer awards, 1974 and 1978. Mem., Gran Orden de Caballeros del Vino. Encomienda, Orden de Isabel la Católica (Spain), 2004. *Publications:* Sherry, 1961, 6th edn 2014; (an editor) Clerk and Lindsell on Torts, 13th edn 1969 to 16th edn 1989; The Wines of Europe, 1971; Little Dictionary of Drink, 1973; (jtly) Encyclopedia of United Kingdom and European Patent Law, 1977; The Wines of Spain, 1999, 2nd edn 2006; A Short History of the Lodge of Antiquity No 2, 2007; (ed with Jocelyn Hillgarth) Maurice Baring: letters, 2007. *Recreations:* freemasonry, wine, rambling, old cars, musical boxes, follies, Iberian things. *Address:* Church Farm House, East Ilsley, Newbury, Berks RG20 7LP. *T:* (01635) 281216. *E:* julian.jeffs@btopenworld.com. *Clubs:* Beefsteak, Garrick, Reform, Saintsbury.

JEFFS, Kenneth Peter, CMG 1983; FRAeS; consultant; *b* 30 Jan. 1931; *s* of Albert Jeffs and Theresa Eleanor Jeffs; *m* Iris Woolsey; one *s* two *d*. *Educ:* Richmond and East Sheen County Sch. jssc. National Service, RAF, 1949–51. Entered CS as Clerical Officer, Bd of Control, 1947; Air Min., 1952; Principal, 1964; JSSC, 1966–67; Private Secretary: to Under-Sec. of State (RN), MoD, 1969–71; to Minister of Defence, 1971–72; Asst Sec., Dir Defence Sales, MoD, 1972–75; Counsellor, Defence Supply, Washington, DC, 1976–79; Dir Gen. (Marketing), MoD, 1979–83; Exec. Vice-Pres., (Mil. Affairs), 1984–87, Dir, 1985–87, British Aerospace Inc.; Pres., MLRS Internat. Corp., 1987–92; Dir, Studley Associates, 1994–99. FRAeS 1985. *Recreations:* granddaughters, golf, horse racing. *Address:* Old Studley, Howell Hill Grove, Ewell, near Epsom, Surrey KT17 3ET. *Clubs:* Royal Automobile; Bude and North Cornwall Golf.

JEHANGIR, Sir Cowasji, 4th Bt *cr* 1908, of Bombay; *b* 23 Nov. 1953; *er s* of Sir Hirji Jehangir, 3rd Bt and of Jinoo, *d* of K. H. Cama; *S* father, 2000; *m* 1988, Jasmine, *d* of Beji Billimoria; one *s* one *d*. *Educ:* Cathedral and John Connon Sch., Bombay; Elphinstone Coll., Bombay (BA Econ). National Radio and Electronics Co. Ltd, Bombay, 1976–80. Chairman: Jehangir Hosp., Pune, 1989–; Jehangir Clinical Develt Centre Ltd, Pune, 2006–. Hon. Dir, Centre for Photography as an Art Form, Bombay, 1986–. Mem. Senate, Univ. of Pune, 1992–95. Trustee: Sir Cowasji Jehangir Sch., Bombay, 1976–; Jehangir Art Gall., Bombay, 2000–. *Recreations:* wildlife, photography, jazz, squash. *Heir: s* Cowasji Jehangir, *b* 28 March 1990. *Clubs:* Willingdon Sports, Bombay Gymkhana (Bombay); Royal Western India Turf (Bombay and Pune); Poona (Pune).

JEJEEBHOY, Sir Jamsetjee, 8th Bt *cr* 1857, of Bombay; *b* 16 Nov. 1957; *o s* of Sir Jamsetjee Jejeebhoy, 7th Bt and Shirin J. H. Cama; *S* father, 2006, and assumed name of Jamsetjee Jejeebhoy in lieu of Rustom Jejeebhoy; *m* 1984, Delara Jal Bhaisa; one *s*. *Educ:* Bombay Univ. (BCom 1979; LLM 1984). Dep. Man., Legal, Tata Exports Ltd, 1983–98; Vice Pres., India, Quantum Technologies Inc., 1998–2004. Dir, Beaulieu Investment Pvt. Ltd, 1975. Chairman: Parsi Dhandha Rojgar Fund, 2004; Bombay Panjrapole, 2006; Sett Rustomjee Jamsetjee Jejeebhoy Gujarati Sch. Fund, 2006; Sir Jamsetjee Jejeebhoy Parsee Benevolent Institution, 2006; Sir Jamsetjee Jejeebhoy Charity Fund, 2006; Parsi Surat Charity Fund, 2013. Trustee: Destitute Eranis Charity Fund, 1990; Zoroastrian Building Fund, 2004; K. N. Bahadurji Meml Sanatorium for Parsis. Hon. Freeman and Liveryman, Clockmakers' Co., 2008. *Recreation:* collecting antiques. *Heir: s* Jehangir Jejeebhoy [*b* 20 Jan. 1986; *m* 2012, Naira Sam Variava]. *Address:* (residence) Beaulieu, 95 Worli Seaface, Mumbai 400030, India. *T:* 24938517; (office) Sir J J Charity Fund, Kalpataru Heritage Building, 5th Floor, 127 Mahatma Gandhi Road, Mumbai 400001, India. *T:* 22673843. *E:* jj@sjjcf.org. *Clubs:* Willingdon Sports, Royal Western India Turf, Ripon (Mumbai).

JELINEK, Elfriede; writer; *b* Mürzzuschlag, Austria, 20 Oct. 1946; *m* 1974, Gottfried Hüngsberg. *Educ:* Vienna Conservatory; Albertsgymnasium, Vienna; Univ. of Vienna. Writer of plays for radio, and for theatre incl. Raststätte, Das Werk; screenplays: Die Ausgesperrten (TV), 1982; Malina (film), 1991; Das Werk (TV), 2004; opera libretto, Lost Highway, 2003. Nobel Prize for Literature, 2004. *Publications:* Lisas Schatten (poems), 1967; ende: Gedichte von 1966–1968, 1980; Die endlose Unschuldigkeit (essays), 1980; Was geschah, nachdem Nora ihren Mann verlassen hatte oder Stützen der Gesellschaften, 1980; Theaterstücke, 1984; Oh Wildnis, oh Schutz vor ihr, 1985; Krankheit oder moderne Frauen, 1987; Isabelle Huppert in Malina, 1991; Sturm und Zwang, 1995; Stecken, Stab und Stangl, 1997; er nicht als er, 1998; Macht nichts: eine kleine Trilogie des Todes, 1999; Der Tod und das Mädchen I–V: Prinzessinnendramen, 2003; Rein Gold, 2013; *novels:* wir sind lockvögel baby!, 1970; Michael: ein Jugendbuch für die Infantilgesellschaft, 1972; Die Liebhaberinnen, 1975 (Women as Lovers, 1994); bukolit, 1979; Die Ausgesperrten, 1980 (Wonderful, Wonderful Times, 1990); Die Klavierspielerin, 1983 (The Piano Teacher, 1988) (filmed, 2001); Lust, 1989 (Lust, 1992); Die Kinder der Toten, 1995; Gier: ein Unterhaltungsroman, 2000 (Greed, 2006); *plays:* Wolken. Heim, 1990; Totenauberg: ein Stück, 1991; Ein Sportstück, 1998; Das Lebewohl, 2000; In den Alpen, 2002; Bambiland, Babel, 2004; Ulrike Maria Stuart, 2007; also translations of other writers' works. *Address:* c/o Serpent's Tail, 3A Exmouth House, Pine Street, EC1R 0JH.

JELLICOE, family name of **Earl Jellicoe**.

JELLICOE, 3rd Earl *cr* 1925; **Patrick John Bernard Jellicoe;** Viscount Jellicoe of Scapa, 1918; Viscount Brocas of Southampton, 1925; *b* 29 Aug. 1950; *s* of 2nd Earl Jellicoe, KBE, DSO, MC, PC, FRS and his 1st wife, Patricia Christine (*née* O'Kane) (*d* 2012); *S* father, 2007; *m* 1971, separated 1971, marr. diss. 1981; two *s* (*b* 1970, 1977). *Educ:* Eton. Profession, engineer. *Heir: b* Hon. Nicholas Charles Joseph John Jellicoe [*b* 23 March 1953; *m* 1982, Patricia, *d* of late Count Arturo Ruiz de Castilla; two *d*].

JELLICOE, (Patricia) Ann, (Mrs Roger Mayne), OBE 1984; playwright and director; *b* 15 July 1927; *d* of John Andrea Jellicoe and Frances Jackson Henderson; *m* 1st, 1950, C. E. Knight-Clarke (marr. diss. 1961); 2nd, 1962, Roger Mayne (*d* 2014); one *s* one *d*. *Educ:* Polam Hall, Darlington; Queen Margaret's, York; Central Sch. of Speech and Drama (Elsie Fogarty Prize, 1947). Actress, stage manager and dir, London and provinces, 1947–51; privately commnd to study relationship between theatre architecture and theatre practice, 1949; founded and ran Cockpit Theatre Club to experiment with open stage, 1952–54; taught acting and directed plays, Central Sch., 1954–56; Literary Manager, Royal Court Theatre, 1973–75; Founder, 1979, Director, 1979–85 and Pres., 1986, Colway Theatre Trust to produce community plays; Life Pres., Dorchester Community Plays Assoc., 1999. *Plays:* The Sport of My Mad Mother (also dir with George Devine), Royal Court, 1958; (also dir) For Children, 1959; The Knack, Arts (Cambridge), 1961 (also dir with Keith Johnstone), Royal Court, 1962, New York, 1964, Paris, 1967 (filmed, 1965; Palme d'Or, Cannes, 1965); Shelley or The Idealist (also dir), Royal Court, 1965; The Rising Generation, Royal Court, 1967; The Giveaway, Garrick, 1969; Flora and the Bandits (also dir), Dartington Coll. of Arts, 1976; The Bargain (also dir), SW Music Theatre, 1979; *community plays:* (also directed): The Reckoning, Lyme Regis, 1978; The Tide, Seaton, 1980; (with Fay Weldon and John Fowles) The Western Women, Lyme Regis, 1984; Mark og Mønt (Money and Land), Holbæk, Denmark, 1988; Under the God, Dorchester, 1989; Changing Places, Woking, 1992; *plays for children:* (also directed): You'll Never Guess!, Arts, 1973; Clever Elsie, Smiling John, Silent Peter, Royal Court, 1974; A Good Thing or a Bad Thing, Royal Court, 1974; *translations:* Rosmersholm, Royal Court, 1960; The Lady from the Sea, Queen's, 1961; (with Ariadne Nicolaeff) The Seagull, Queen's, 1963; Der Freischütz, Sadlers Wells, 1964; *directed:* Skyvers, 1963; A Worthy Guest, 1974; (community plays): The Poor Man's Friend, Bridport, 1981; The Garden, Sherborne, 1982; Entertaining Strangers, Dorchester, 1985. *Publications:* Some Unconscious Influences in the Theatre, 1967; (with Roger Mayne) Shell Guide to Devon, 1975; Community Plays: how to put them on, 1987; *plays:* The Sport of My Mad Mother, 1958 (USA 1964); The Knack, 1962 (USA 1964; trans. various langs); Shelley or The Idealist, 1966; The Rising Generation, 1969; The Giveaway, 1970; 3 Jelliplays, 1975. *Address:* Harbour House, George Street, West Bay, Bridport, Dorset DT6 4EY.

JENCKS, Charles Alexander, PhD; landscape architect, designer and writer; *b* 21 June 1939; *s* of Gardner Platt Jencks and Ruth Pearl Jencks; *m* 1st, 1960, Pamela Balding (marr. diss. 1973); two *s*; 2nd, 1978, Margaret Keswick (*d* 1995); one *s* one *d*; 3rd, 2006, Louisa Lane Fox. *Educ:* Harvard University (BA Eng. Lit. 1961; BA, MA Arch. 1965); London University (PhD Arch. Hist., 1970). Joined Architectural Association, 1968: Lectr in Architecture, 1970–91; Lectr in Arch., 1974–85, Vis. Prof. of Arch., 1985–94, Univ. of Calif at LA Sch. of Arch. Writer on Post-Modern architecture, 1975–, Late-Modern architecture, 1978–; designer of furniture, gardens, and sculpture, incl. DNA sculpture for James Watson, Kew Gardens, and Landform for Scottish Nat. Gall. of Modern Art (Gulbenkian Prize 2004); Parco Portello, Milan, 2002–11; various landforms, 2005–, incl. Doublewalk, Midpark Hosp., Dumfries, 2010–12, Holding the Eco-Line, Suncheon, S Korea, 2011–13, Crawick Multiverse, 2015; numerous Univ. lectures, incl. Peking, Warsaw, Tokyo, USA, Paris; house designs incl. The Garagia Rotunda, 1976–77, The Elemental House, 1983, The Thematic House, 1984. Fulbright Schol., Univ. of London, 1965–67; Melbourne Oration, Australia, 1974; Bossom Lectr, RSA, 1980; Mem., Cttee for selection of architects, Venice Biennale, 1980; Curator, Post-Modern London, exhibn, 1991. Editor at Academy Editions, 1979–; Editl Consultant, Architectural Design, 1979–. Co-Founder, Maggie Centres, 1995. Member: Architectural Assoc.; RSA. Gold Medal for Architecture, Nara, Japan, 1992; Gardener of the Year, Country Life, 1998. *TV films:* (wrote) Le Corbusier, BBC, 1974; (wrote and presented) Kings of Infinite Space (Frank Lloyd Wright and Michael Graves), 1983. *Publications:* Meaning in Architecture, 1969; Architecture 2000, 1971; Adhocism, 1972; Modern Movements in Architecture, 1973, 2nd edn 1985; Le Corbusier and the Tragic View of Architecture, 1974, 2nd edn 1987; The Language of Post-Modern Architecture, 1977, 6th edn 1991; Late-Modern Architecture, 1980; Post-Modern Classicism, 1980; Free-Style Classicism, 1982; Architecture Today (Current Architecture), 1982, 2nd edn 1988; Abstract Representation, 1983; Kings of Infinite Space, 1983; Towards a Symbolic Architecture, 1985; What is Post-Modernism? 1986, 3rd edn 1989; Post-Modernism—the new classicism in art and architecture, 1987; The Architecture of Democracy, 1987; The Prince, The Architects and New Wave Monarchy, 1988; The New Moderns, 1990; (ed) The Post Modern Reader, 1992; Heteropolis, Los Angeles, the Riots and the Strange Beauty of Heteroarchitecture, 1993; The Architecture of the Jumping Universe, 1995, 2nd edn 1997; Frank O. Gehry: cultural conservation and individual imagination, 1995; (ed jtly) Theories and Manifestos of Contemporary Architecture, 1997; Ecstatic Architecture, 1999; Le Corbusier and the Continual Revolution in Architecture, 2000; Architecture 2000 and Beyond, 2001; The New Paradigm in Architecture, 2002; The Garden of Cosmic Speculation, 2003; Scottish Parliament, 2005; The Iconic Building, 2005; Critical Modernism, 2007; (with E. Heathcote) The Architecture of Hope, Maggie Cancer Caring Centres, 2010; The Universe in the Landscape, 2011; The Story of Post-Modernism: five decades of ironic, iconic and critical architecture, 2011; articles in professional jls incl. Architecture Forum, Architecture Rev., Domus, A&U, Architectural Design; occasional contrib. Sunday Times Mag., Encounter, TLS, The Observer, The Independent, Prometheus. *Recreations:* travel, collecting Chinese (bullet-hole) rocks. *Address:* 19 Lansdowne Walk, W11 3AH.

JENKIN, family name of **Baroness Jenkin of Kennington** and **Baron Jenkin of Roding**.

JENKIN OF KENNINGTON, Baroness *cr* 2011 (Life Peer), of Hatfield Peverel in the County of Essex; **Anne Caroline Jenkin;** *b* 8 Dec. 1955; *d* of late Hon. Charles Richard Strutt and of Hon. Jean Elizabeth, *d* of 1st Viscount Davidson, GCVO, CH, CB, PC; *m* 1988, Hon. Bernard Christison Jenkin, *qv*; two *s*. Vice Chairman: All Party Women in Parlt Gp, 2011–; All Party Agroecology Gp, 2012–; Co-chair: Cons. Friends of Internat. Develt, 2011–; Associate Parly Sustainable Resource Gp, 2012–. Pres., Harwich and North Essex Cons. Women's Gp, 1992–. Co-Founder, 2005, Co-Chair, 2011–, Women2Win. Mem., Adv. Bd, Global Property Project, 2011–. Patron: Soham for Kids, 2011–; Restless Development, 2011–; Trustee, UNICEF (UK), 2013–. *Address:* House of Lords, SW1A 0PW.
See also Baron Rayleigh.

JENKIN OF RODING, Baron *cr* 1987 (Life Peer), of Wanstead and Woodford in Greater London; **Charles Patrick Fleeming Jenkin;** PC 1973; MA; President, Foundation for Science and Technology, since 2006 (Vice-President, 1996–97; Chairman, 1997–2006); *b* 7 Sept. 1926; *s* of late Mr and Mrs C. O. F. Jenkin; *m* 1952, Alison Monica Graham; two *s* two *d*. *Educ:* Dragon Sch., Oxford; Clifton Coll.; Jesus Coll., Cambridge (MA 1951). Served with QO Cameron Highlanders, 1945–48. Harmsworth Scholar, Middle Temple, 1951; called to the Bar, 1952. Distillers Co. Ltd, 1957–70. Member: Hornsey Borough Council, 1960–63; London Council of Social Service, 1963–67. MP (C) Wanstead and Woodford, 1964–87. An Opposition front bench spokesman on Treasury, Trade and Economics, 1965–70; Jt Vice-Chm., Cons. Parly Trade and Power Cttee, 1966–67; Founder Chm., All Party Parly Group on Chemical Industry, 1968–70; Financial Sec. to the Treasury, 1970–72; Chief Sec. to Treasury, 1972–74; Minister for Energy, 1974; Opposition front bench spokesman: on Energy, 1974–76; on Soc. Services, 1976–79; Secretary of State: for Social Services, 1979–81; for Industry, 1981–83; for the Environment, 1983–85. Mem., H of L, 1987–2015; Mem., Select Cttee on Sci. and Technol., H of L, 1996–2001 (Chm., Sub-Cttee II on Sci. and Soc., 1999–2000); Pres., Parly and Scientific Cttee, 2009–14. Mem., Exec. Cttee, Assoc. of Cons. Peers, 1996–2000. President: National CPC Cttee, 1983–86; Greater London Area, Nat. Union of Cons. Assocs, 1989–93 (Vice-Pres., 1987–89). Chm., Friends' Provident Life Office, 1988–98 (Dep. Chm., Friends' Provident Life Office (Dir, 1986–88) and UK Provident Institution (Dir, 1987–88), 1987–88, when merged). Chm., Forest Healthcare NHS Trust, 1991–97. Director: Tilbury Contracting Gp Ltd, 1974–79; Royal Worcester Ltd, 1975–79; Continental and Industrial Trust Ltd, 1975–79; Chairman: Crystalate Hldgs PLC, 1988–90 (Dir, 1987–90); Lamco Paper Sales Ltd, 1987–93; Consultant, Thames Estuary Airport Co. Ltd, 1994–; Mem. Internat. Adv. Bd, Marsh and McLennan, 1993–98. UK Co-Chm., UK-Japan 2000 Gp, 1986–90 (Bd Mem., 1990–99); Vice-Pres., 1991 Japan Festival Cttee, 1987–91. Adviser: Andersen Consulting, Management Consultants, 1985–96; Sumitomo Trust and Banking Co. Ltd, 1989–2010; Member: UK Adv. Bd, Nat. Economic Res. Associates Inc., 1985–98; Supervisory Bd, Achmea Hldg NV, Netherlands, 1992–98. Member, Council: UK CEED, 1987–2003; Guide Dogs for the Blind Assoc., 1987–97; ICRF, 1991–97 (Dep. Chm., 1994–97); Royal Instn, 2002–05; Chm., Visual Handicap Gp, 1990–98; Pres., Friends of Wanstead Hosp., 1987–91. Pres., British Urban Regeneration Assoc., 1990–96; Sen. Vice Pres., World Congress on Urban Growth and Develt, 1992–95; Vice President: Nat. Housing Fedn, 1992–2000; LGA, 1997–; Jt Pres., London Councils (formerly Assoc. of London Govt), 1995–. Pres., ASE, 2002–03. Chm. Trustees, Westfield Coll. Trust, 1988–2000 (Gov., Westfield Coll., 1964–70; Fellow, QMW, 1991); Gov., Clifton Coll., 1969– (Mem. Council, 1972–79; Pres. of School, 1994–99; Pres., Old Cliftonian Soc., 1987–89); Mem. Internat. Adv. Bd, Nijenrode Univ., Netherlands, 1994–98. Trustee, Monteverdi Choir, 1992–2001. Patron, St Clare West Essex Hospice Trust, 1991–; Patron and Hon. Fellow, Nuclear Inst., 2011–. Freeman: City of London, 1985; London Bor. of Redbridge, 1988. FRSA 1985. Hon. FRSE 2001; Hon. FCOptom 2003; Hon. Fellow, British Sci. Assoc. (Hon. Fellow, BAAS, 2007). Hon. LLD South Bank, 1997; Hon. DSc Ulster, 2001. *Recreations:* music, gardening, sailing, bricklaying, reading.
See also Hon. B. C. Jenkin, Rear Adm. D. C. Jenkin.

JENKIN, Hon. Bernard Christison; MP (C) Harwich and North Essex, since 2010 (Colchester North, 1992–97; North Essex, 1997–2010); *b* 9 April 1959; *s* of Lord Jenkin of Roding, *qv*; *m* 1988, Anne Caroline Strutt (*see* Baroness Jenkin of Kennington); two *s*. *Educ:* Highgate Sch.; William Ellis Sch.; Corpus Christi Coll., Cambridge (BA Hons Eng. Lit., MA). Ford Motor Co., 1983–86; 3i, 1986–88; Hill Samuel Bank, 1988–89; Legal & General Ventures, 1989–92. Contested (C) Glasgow Central, 1987. PPS to Sec. of State for Scotland, 1995–97; Opposition spokesman on constitutional affairs, 1997–98, on transport, 1998–99; Opposition front bench spokesman on transport, and for London, 1999–2001; Shadow Defence Sec., 2001–03; Shadow Sec. of State for the Regions, 2003–04; Shadow Minister for Energy, 2005; Dep. Chm., Conservative Party (Candidates), 2005–06. Chm., Select Cttee on Public Admin, 2010–; Member: Select Cttee on Social Security, 1992–97; Select Cttee on Defence, 2006–10; Sec., Cons. Backbench Small Business Cttee, 1992–97; Jt Sec., Cons. Backbench Foreign Affairs Cttee, 1994–95; Mem. Exec., 1922 Cttee, 2010–. Vice Pres., Combat Stress, 2009–. Mem., St Paul's Cathedral Council, 2005–. Pres., Cambridge Union Soc., 1982. *Publications:* (jtly) Defence Acquisition for the Twenty-First Century, 2015. *Recreations:* family, music (esp. opera), fishing, shooting, sailing, ski-ing, DIY, arguing the Conservative cause. *Address:* House of Commons, SW1A 0AA. *T:* (020) 7219 3000. *Clubs:* Pratt's; Colchester Conservative.
See also Baron Rayleigh.

JENKIN, Rear Adm. (David) Conrad, CB 1983; Commandant, Joint Service Defence College (formerly National Defence College), 1981–84, retired; *b* 25 Oct. 1928; *s* of Mr and Mrs C. O. F. Jenkin; *m* 1958, Jennifer Margaret Nowell; three *s* one *d*. *Educ:* Dragon Sch., Oxford; RNC, Dartmouth. Entered RN at age of 13½, 1942; qual. in Gunnery, 1953; commanded: HMS Palliser, 1961–63; HMS Cambrian, 1964–66; HMS Galatea, 1974–75; HMS Hermes (aircraft carrier), 1978–79; Flag Officer, First Flotilla, 1980–81. President: Hong Kong Flotilla Assoc., 1999–2012; HMS Cambrian Assoc., 2005–13. *Recreations:* sailing, scale model-making. *Address:* Knapsyard House, West Meon, Hants GU32 1LF. *T:* (01730) 829227.
See also Baron Jenkin of Roding.

JENKIN, Guy Arthur Allen; writer, director and producer for television and film; *b* Carmarthen, 27 April 1955; *s* of Allen and Hazel Jenkin; *m* 2010, Bernadette Davis; two *s* one *d*. *Educ:* King Edward's Sch., Bath; Trinity Coll., Cambridge (BA English Lit. 1978). Television: contributor: Weekending, 1978–82; Not the Nine O'Clock News, 1979; Spitting Image, 1984; Who Dares Wins, 1982–86; writer: Shelley, 1983–89; Rebecca's Daughters (film), 1992; The Private Life of Samuel Pepys, 2004; co-writer and producer, Drop the Dead Donkey, 1990–98; writer and director: A Very Open Prison, 1995; Lord of Misrule, 1996; Crossing the Floor, 1997; Sex 'n' Death, 2001; The Sleeping Dictionary (film), 2002; Jeffrey Archer: the truth, 2003; Hacks, 2012; co-writer, director and producer, Outnumbered, 2007–11; co-writer and dir, Just Around the Corner, 2012; co-writer and co-director: What We Did on Our Holiday (film), 2014; Ballot Monkeys, 2015; writer, Fighting for the Dunghill (theatre), 1992; writer and dir, Bugsplat!, 2015.

JENKIN, Simon William Geoffrey, OBE 2006; education consultant, retired; Chief Education Officer, Devon County Council, 1989–98; *b* 25 July 1943; *s* of Dudley Cyril Robert Jenkin and Muriel Grace (*née* Mather); *m* 1973, Elizabeth Tapsell; two *d*. *Educ:* Univ. of London (BSc Econs); Jesus Coll., Oxford (DipEd). Lectr, 1967–72, Sen. Lectr, 1972–75, Bournemouth Coll. of Technology; Educn Officer, Essex CC, 1975–80; Area Educn Officer, NE Essex, 1980–83; Principal Educn Officer, Derbys CC, 1983–87; Dep. Chief Educn Officer, Devon CC, 1988–89. Mem., SW Regl Cttee, FEFCE, 1993–98. Director: Cornwall and Devon Careers Co. Ltd, 1995–98; Cambridge Education, 2001–09. Advr, LGA, 1991–98. Gov., United World Coll. of the Atlantic, 1991–98. Trustee, Bath Technology Centre, 2006–09. FRSA 1992. *Recreation:* my wife. *Address:* Grainge House, 10 Matford Avenue, Exeter EX2 4PW. *T:* (01392) 499798.

JENKINS, family name of **Baroness Morgan of Ely**.

JENKINS OF HILLHEAD, Lady; *see* Jenkins, Dame M. J.

JENKINS, Adrian Richard; Director, Bowes Museum, Barnard Castle, since 2001; *b* 23 Jan. 1965; *s* of George and Mary Jenkins; *m* 2006, Lucy Whetstone; one *s* one *d*. *Educ:* Tasker Milward Comp. Sch.; Univ. of Leicester (BA Hons Ancient Hist. 1986); Barber Inst. of Fine Arts, Univ. of Birmingham (MPhil Art Hist. 1990); Bolton Business Sch. (MBA 2001). Curatorial Asst, English Heritage, 1990–92; Asst Keeper of Art, Laing Art Gall., Newcastle upon Tyne, 1992–96; Sen. Keeper of Fine and Applied Art, Bolton Mus. and Art Gall., 1996–2001. Hon. Fellow, Inst. of Advanced Study, Univ. of Durham, 2013–16. *Publications: catalogues:* (with Lucy Whetstone) Expressionism in Germany 1905–1925, 1999; Painters and Peasants: Henry La Thangue and British Rural Naturalism 1880–1905, 2000; (ed) The Road to Impressionism: Josephine Bowes and painting in nineteenth century France, 2002; (jtly) Creative Tension: British art 1900–1950, 2005; Goya's Prison: the year of despair, 2009; various contribs to jls. *Recreations:* looking at paintings, drainage issues, enjoying

Upper Teesdale, celebrating the flair of Welsh Rugby. *Address:* c/o The Bowes Museum, Barnard Castle, Co. Durham DL12 8NP. *T:* (01833) 690606, *Fax:* (01833) 637163. *E:* adrian.jenkins@thebowesmuseum.org.uk.

JENKINS, Alan Dominique; Chairman, Eversheds, solicitors, 2004–11; *b* 27 May 1952; *s* of Ian Samuel and Jeannette Juliette Jenkins; *m* 1979, Caroline (*née* Treverton Jones); one *s* three *d*. *Educ:* Clifton Coll., Bristol; New Coll., Oxford (MA Jurisprudence). Admitted solicitor, 1977; Partner, 1983–98, Man. Partner, 1996–98, Frere Cholmeley Bischoff; Eversheds: Partner, 1998–2011; Hd of Internat., 2002–09. Non-executive Member, Board: UK Trade and Investment, 2009–; CPS, 2011–; non-executive Director: Financial Ombudsman Service, 2011–; Northcourt Ltd, 2011–; Sydney and London Properties Ltd, 2011–; Pension Protection Fund, 2013–. Trustee: Foundn for Internat. Envmtl Law and Develt, 1998–2011 (Chm., 2003–05); Internat. Inst. for Envmt and Develt, 2005–13 (Vice-Chm., 2005–13); London Middle East Inst., 2011–; Trustee and Chm., Mencap Trust Co. Ltd, 2009–. FInstD (Mem., Council, 2007–). FRSA. *Publications:* (contrib.) International Commercial Fraud, 2002. *Recreations:* ski-ing, tennis, watching sport in general (especially cricket and Rugby), theatre, music. *Clubs:* MCC, Roehampton.

JENKINS, Alun; *see* Jenkins, T. A.

JENKINS, Antony Peter; Chairman, Business in the Community, since 2015 (Director, since 2014); *b* Blackburn, Lancs, 11 July 1961; *s* of Peter Jenkins and Patricia Jenkins (*née* Salter); *m* 1984, Amanda Mary Benson; one *s* one *d*. *Educ:* Malbank Sch., Nantwich; University Coll., Oxford (BA PPE 1982); Cranfield Inst. of Technol. (MBA 1988). Barclays plc, 1983–89; Citigroup, 1989–2005: Hd of Product Develt, 1989–91, Regl Product Manager, 1991–93, Eur. Securities Services; Dir of Strategic Implementation, Worldwide Securities Services/Global Transaction Services, 1993–95; Exec. Dir, N America Cash Mgt, 1995–98; Head, College Strategic Business Unit, 1998–99, Internet Initiatives, 1999–2000, Citi Cards; Chief Executive: c2it, 2000–02; eConsumer, 2002; Executive Vice President: US Hispanic, Global and Strategic Delivery Strategic Business Unit, 2002–04; Citibrands, 2004–05; Chief Executive Officer: Barclaycard, 2006–09; Global Retail Banking, Barclays Bank plc, 2009–12; Group Chief Exec., Barclays Bank plc, 2012–15. ACIB 1986; ACIM 1987. *Recreations:* family, running and fitness, ski-ing. *Club:* New York Road Runners.

JENKINS, (Archibald) Ian; *b* 18 March 1941; *s* of Archibald Jenkins and Margaret (*née* Duncan); *m* 1967, Margery MacKay. *Educ:* Rothesay Acad., Isle of Bute; Glasgow Univ. (MA 1963; DipEd 1964). Teacher of English, Clydebank High Sch., 1964–70; Principal Teacher of English, Peebles High Sch., 1970–99. Mem. (Lib Dem) Tweeddale, Ettrick and Lauderdale, Scottish Parlt, 1999–2003; Lib Dem spokesman on educn, culture and sport, 2000–03. *Recreations:* jazz, reading. *Address:* 1 South Park Drive, Peebles EH45 9DR. *T:* (01721) 720528.

JENKINS, Prof. Aubrey Dennis; Professor of Polymer Science, University of Sussex, 1971–92, now Emeritus; *b* 6 Sept. 1927; *s* of Arthur William Jenkins and Mabel Emily (*née* Street); *m* 1st, 1950, Audrey Doreen Middleton (marr. diss. 1987); two *s* one *d*; 2nd, 1987, Jitka Horská, *er d* of late Josef Horský and Anna Horská, Hradec Králové, Czechoslovakia. *Educ:* Dartford Grammar Sch.; Sir John Cass Technical Inst.; King's Coll., Univ. of London. BSc 1948, PhD 1951; DSc 1961. FRIC 1957. Research Chemist, Courtaulds Ltd, Fundamental Research Laboratory, Maidenhead, 1950–60; Head of Chemistry Research, Gillette Industries Ltd, Reading, 1960–64 (Harris Research Labs, Washington, DC, 1963–64); University of Sussex, 1964–92: Sen. Lectr in Chemistry, 1964–68; Reader, 1968–71; Dean, Sch. of Molecular Scis, 1973–78. Visiting Professor: Inst. of Macromolecular Chemistry, Prague, 1978 and 1986; Univ. of Massachusetts, Amherst, 1979; ETH Zürich, 2002. Mem. Council, RSC, 2003–05. Member: Internat. Union of Pure and Applied Chemistry, Commn on Macromolecular Nomenclature, 1974– (Chm., 1977–85; Sec., Macromolecular Div., 1985–93); British Assoc. for Central and Eastern Europe (formerly GB/E Europe Centre), 1975–2005; British, Czech and Slovak Assoc., 1990–. Mem., Brighton HA, 1983–90. Examining chaplain to Bishop of Chichester, 1980–90. Hon. Fellow, Soc. of Organic Chemistry of Argentina, 1993. Geza Zemplen Medal, Budapest, 1984; Heyrovský Gold Medal for Chemistry, Czechoslovak Acad. of Scis, 1990. *Publications:* Kinetics of Vinyl Polymerization by Radical Mechanisms (with C. H. Bamford, W. G. Barb and P. F. Onyon), 1958; Polymer Science, 1972; (with A. Ledwith) Reactivity, Mechanism and Structure in Polymer Chemistry, 1974; (with J. F. Kennedy) Macromolecular Chemistry, Vol. I 1980, Vol. II 1982, Vol. III 1984; Progress in Polymer Science (12 vols), 1967–85; (with J. N. Murrell) Properties of Liquids and Solutions, 1994; papers in learned jls. *Recreations:* music, travel, photography. *Address:* Vixen's, 22A North Court, Hassocks, West Sussex BN6 8JS. *T:* (01273) 845410. *E:* polygon@vixens.eclipse.co.uk.

JENKINS, Bethan Maeve; Member (Plaid Cymru) South Wales West, National Assembly for Wales, since 2007; *b* 9 Dec. 1981; *d* of Mike Jenkins and Marie Jenkins. *Educ:* Ysgol Gyfun Rhydfelen, Pontypridd; Univ. of Wales, Aberystwyth (BScEcon Internat. Pol. and Internat. Hist.). Equal Opportunities Officer, 2003–04, Pres., 2004–05, Aberystwyth Guild of Students; Youth Organiser, Plaid Cymru, 2005–07. Plaid Cymru spokesperson on Welsh language, heritage and sport; Mem., Communities, Equality and Local Govt Cttee. *Recreations:* blogging, playing viola, swimming. *Address:* 75 Briton Ferry Road, Neath SA11 1AR. *T:* (01639) 643549. *E:* bethan.jenkins@assembly.wales. *W:* www.bethanjenkins.org.uk.

JENKINS, Brian David; *b* 19 Sept. 1942; *s* of Hiram Jenkins and Gladys (*née* Morgan); *m* 1963, Joan Dix; one *s* one *d*. *Educ:* Aston Coll.; Coventry Coll.; Coleg Harlech; London Sch. of Econs (BSc Econ); Wolverhampton Poly. (PGCE). With CEGB, 1963–68; Jaguar Cars, 1968–73; Percy Lane, 1973–75; Lecturer: Isle of Man Coll., 1981–83; Tamworth Coll., 1983–96. Mem., USDAW. Tamworth Borough Council: Mem. (Lab), 1985–96; Dep. Mayor, 1992–93; Mayor, 1993–94; Leader, 1995–96. Contested (Lab) SE Staffs, 1992. MP (Lab) SE Staffs, April 1996–1997, Tamworth, 1997–2010; contested (Lab) same seat, 2010. Mem., Tamworth Br., RBL. *Recreations:* music, reading, watching sport.

JENKINS, Sir Brian (Garton), GBE 1991; FCA; Deputy Chairman, Barclays Bank plc, 2000–04; Prior, England and the Islands, Order of St John of Jerusalem, 2004–10; Lord Mayor of London, 1991–92; *b* 3 Dec. 1935; *s* of late Owen Garton Jenkins and Doris Enid (*née* Webber); *m* 1967, (Elizabeth) Ann Prentice; one *s* one *d*. *Educ:* Tonbridge; Trinity Coll., Oxford (State Scholar; MA; Hon. Fellow, 1992). FCA 1974. Served RA, Gibraltar, 1955–57 (2nd Lieut). With Cooper Brothers & Co., later Coopers & Lybrand, 1960–95; Chm., Woolwich Bldg Soc., later Woolwich plc, 1995–2000. Pres., ICAEW, 1985–86. Pres., London Chamber of Commerce, 1996–98. Chm., 1998–2003, Pres., 2003–08, Charities Aid Foundn. Alderman, City of London (Ward of Cordwainer), 1980–2004 (Sheriff, 1987–88); Liveryman: Chartered Accountants' Co., 1980– (Master, 1990–91); Merchant Taylors' Co., 1984– (Master, 1999–2000); Information Technologists' Co., 1985– (Master, 1994–95). Dep. Pres., 1996–97, Pres., 1997–98, BCS. Hon. Bencher, Inner Temple, 1992; Hon. Mem., Baltic Exchange, 1993. Hon. DSc City Univ., 1991; Hon. DLitt London Guildhall Univ., 1991; Companion, De Montfort Univ., 1993; Hon. Fellow, Goldsmiths Coll., London, 1998. FBCS. CCMI. FRSA. Centenary Award, Chartered Accountants Founding Socs, 1993. KStJ 1991. *Publications:* An Audit Approach to Computers, 1978, 4th edn 1992. *Recreations:* walking, reading, ephemera. *Address:* 4 Park Gate, SE3 9XE. *Clubs:* Brooks's, City of London, City Livery.

JENKINS, Lt-Col Charles Peter de Brisay, MBE 1960; MC 1945; Clerk, Worshipful Company of Goldsmiths, 1975–88, retired; *b* 19 Aug. 1923; *s* of late Brig. A. de B. Jenkins and of Mrs Elizabeth Susan Jenkins; *m* 1949, Joan Mary, *e d* of late Col and Mrs C. N. Littleboy, Thirsk; one *s*. *Educ:* Cheltenham Coll.; Selwyn Coll., Cambridge. Commnd RE, 1943; served in Italy, 1943–45; subseq. Hong Kong, Kenya and Germany; jssc 1960; Instructor, Staff Coll., Camberley, 1961–63; Comdr, RE 1st Div., 1965–67; retd 1967. Asst Clerk, Goldsmiths' Co., 1968. Mem., Hallmarking Council, 1977–88; Vice-Chm., Goldsmiths' Coll. (Univ. of London) Council, 1983–91. Trustee Nat. Centre for Orchestral Studies, 1980–89. *Publications:* Unravelling the Mystery - the Story of the Goldsmiths' Company in the Twentieth Century, 2000. *Recreations:* swimming, gardening, Wagner. *Address:* Oak Hill, South Brent, Devon TQ10 9JL.

JENKINS, Sir Christopher; *see* Jenkins, Sir J. C.

JENKINS, Rt Rev. David Edward; Bishop of Durham, 1984–94; an Assistant Bishop, Diocese of Ripon and Leeds, 1994–2014; *b* 26 Jan. 1925; *er s* of Lionel C. Jenkins and Dora (*née* Page); *m* 1949, Stella Mary Peet (*d* 2008); two *s* two *d*. *Educ:* St Dunstan's Coll., Catford; Queen's Coll., Oxford (MA; Hon. Fellow, 1991). EC, RA, 1945–47 (Captain). Priest, 1954. Succentor, Birmingham Cath. and Lectr, Queen's Coll., 1953–54; Fellow, Chaplain and Praelector in Theology, Queen's Coll., Oxford, 1954–69; Dir, Humanum Studies, World Council of Churches, Geneva, 1969–73 (Consultant, 1973–75); Dir, William Temple Foundn, Manchester, 1973–78 (Jt Dir, 1979–84); Prof. of Theology, Univ. of Leeds, 1979–84, Emeritus Prof., 1985; Hon. Prof. of Divinity, Univ. of Durham, 1994–. Exam. Chaplain to Bps of Lichfield, 1956–69, Newcastle, 1957–69, Bristol, 1958–84, Wakefield, 1978–84, and Bradford, 1979–84; Canon Theologian, Leicester, 1966–82, Canon Emeritus, 1982–. Lectures: Bampton, 1966; Hale, Seabury-Western, USA, 1970; Moorehouse, Melbourne, 1972; Cadbury, Birmingham Univ., 1974; Lindsay Meml, Keele Univ., 1976; Heslington, York Univ., 1980; Drummond, Stirling Univ., 1981; Hibbert, Hibbert Trust, 1985; Hensley Henson, Oxford, 1987; Gore, Westminster Abbey, 1990; Samuel Ferguson, Manchester Univ., 1997. Chm., SCM Press, 1987–92; Trustee, SCM Press Trust, 1992–97. Hon. Fellow: St Chad's Coll., Durham, 1986; Univ. of Sunderland (formerly Sunderland Poly.), 1986. Hon. DD: Durham, 1987; Trinity Coll., Toronto, 1989; Aberdeen, 1990; Birmingham, 1996; Leeds, 1996; Hon. DLitt Teesside, 1994; Hon. DCL Northumbria, 1994. DUniv Open 1996. Jt Editor, Theology, 1976–82. *Publications:* Guide to the Debate about God, 1966; The Glory of Man, 1967; Living with Questions, 1969; What is Man?, 1970; The Contradiction of Christianity, 1976; God, Miracle and the Church of England, 1987; God, Politics and the Future, 1988; God, Jesus and Life in the Spirit, 1988; Still Living with Questions, 1990; (with Rebecca Jenkins) Free to Believe, 1991; Market Whys and Human Wherefores, 2000; The Calling of a Cuckoo (memoirs), 2003; contrib. Man, Fallen and Free, 1969, etc. *Recreations:* music, reading, walking, birdwatching. *Address:* c/o PO Box 35, Barnard Castle DL12 8WZ.

See also D. M. Jenkins.

JENKINS, David Edward Stewart; Managing Consultant, Lateral Research Consultants, since 2003 (Senior Partner, 1994–2003); *b* 9 May 1949; *s* of late William Stephen Jenkins and of Jean Nicol Downie; *m* 1972, Maggie Steele, *d* of Dr C. H. and Mrs J. D. Lack; two *s* one *d*. *Educ:* Univ. of London Goldsmiths' College (BA(Soc) 1977); LSE. Warden, Ellison Hse Adult Probation Hostel, SE17, 1973–74; Lecturer: (part-time) in Sociology, Brunel Univ., 1980–81; (part-time) in Social Administration, LSE and Goldsmiths' Coll., 1980–81; in Criminology, Univ. of Edinburgh, 1981; Dir, Howard League, 1982–86; Res. Fellow, PSI, 1986–87; Res. Consultant to HM Chief Inspector of Prisons, 1987–95. Morris Ginsburg Fellow in Sociology, LSE, 1986–87. *Recreations:* music, swimming, cycling.

JENKINS, Ven. David Harold, PhD; Archdeacon of Sudbury, since 2010; *b* Belfast, 19 Oct. 1961; *s* of Joseph Jenkins and Janet Jenkins; *m* 1997, Sarah Gillian Benjamin; two *s* one *d*. *Educ:* Belfast Royal Acad.; Sidney Sussex Coll., Cambridge (BA 1984; MA 1987); Ripon Coll., Cuddesdon (BA 1989, MA 1994, Oxon); Univ. of Wales, Lampeter (MA 2001; PhD 2008). Ordained deacon, 1989, priest, 1990; Vicar: St Michael and All Angels, Blackpool, 1994–99; St John the Baptist, Broughton, 1999–2004; Rural Dean, Preston, 2004; Diocesan Dir of Educn, Dio. of Carlisle, 2004–10. Canon, Carlisle Cathedral, 2004–10; Hon. Canon, St Edmundsbury Cathedral, 2010–. FRHistS 2011. *Publications:* Holy, Holier, Holiest: the sacred topography of the early medieval church, 2010; (contrib.) English Cathedrals and Monasteries through the Ages, 2013. *Recreations:* reading, music, jogging, my family! *Address:* Sudbury Lodge, Stanningfield Road, Great Whelnetham, Bury St Edmunds IP30 0TL. *T:* (01284) 386942. *E:* archdeacon.david@cofesuffolk.org.

JENKINS, David Hugh; DL; Chief Executive, Dorset County Council, 1999–2012; Deputy Chairman, NHS Dorset Clinical Commissioning Group, since 2013; *b* 28 April 1952; *s* of David Lyndhurst Jenkins and Charlotte Elizabeth Jenkins; *m* 1980, Ethna Geraldine Trafford; one *d*. *Educ:* Barry Boys' Comprehensive Sch.; Jesus Coll., Oxford (MA); Coll. of Law, Chester. Asst Master, Fairfield GS, Bristol, 1973–74; admitted solicitor (Hons), 1977; Articled Clerk then Asst Solicitor, Oxon CC, 1975–79; Solicitor, Commn for Local Admin in Wales, 1979–84; Asst Co. Sec., Hants CC, 1984–89; Dorset County Council: Dep. Co. Solicitor, 1989–91; Asst Chief Exec., 1991–93; Co. Solicitor, 1993–96; Dir, Corporate Services, 1996–99. Pres., Dorset Law Soc., 1993–94. Clerk to: Dorset Fire Authy, 1999–2008; Dorset Lieutenancy, 1999–2012; Secretary: Dorset Probation Cttee, 1999–2009; Dorset Strategic Partnership, 2002–12. Chairman: Wessex Regl Flood and Coastal Cttee, 2015–; Inquiry into Infant Cremations in Shropshire, 2014–15. Dep. Chair, Nat. Efficiency Taskforce, 2008–10. Board Member: Dorset TEC, 1999–2001; Dorset Business Link, 1999–2001; Bournemouth SO, 2000–13 (Trustee, 2013–, Chm., 2014–, Bournemouth SO Endowment Trust); Dorset Connexions Partnership, 2001–06 (Chair, 2005–06). Pres., Dorset Assoc. of Parish and Town Councils, 2013–. Ind. Chair, Glos CC Waste Working Gp, 2013–14. Chair: SW Centre for Excellence Bd, 2004–07; Bd, SW Regl Improvement and Efficiency Partnership, 2007–12. Chm., Dorset Working Gp for 2012 Games, 2003–12; Mem., SW Bd for 2012 Games, 2011–12. Chm., ACCE, 2006–07; Mem. Council, SOLACE, 2005–07. Trustee: Burton Bradstock Fest., 2012–; Richard Ely Trust, 2012–. Patron, Bridport Arts Centre, 2009–. FRSA 2009. DL Dorset, 2012. *Recreations:* music, theatre, travel, family. *Address:* Bucklers Bid, Shipton Lane, Burton Bradstock, Bridport DT6 4NQ.

JENKINS, David John, OBE 2004 (MBE 1993); Chairman, Aneurin Bevan Local Health Board, since 2009; *b* 21 Sept. 1948; *s* of William and Dorothy Jenkins; *m* 1976, Felicity Anne (*née* Wood); two *s* one *d*. *Educ:* Canton High Sch., Cardiff; Liverpool Univ. (BA Hons); Garnett Coll., London (CertEd). Industrial Sales Organiser, ITT (Distributors), 1970–74; steel worker, GKN, 1974; Lectr, Peterborough Tech. Coll., 1975–78; Wales Trades Union Congress: Research and Admin. Officer, 1978–83; Gen. Sec., 1983–2004. Chairman: Health Professions Wales, 2004–06; Nat. Leadership and Innovation Agency for Healthcare in Wales, 2007–09. Chm., Wales Co-op. Devclt Centre, 1994–. Pt-time Mem., Competition (formerly Monopolies and Mergers) Commission, 1993–2002; Member: Employment Appeal Tribunal, 1994–; Fitness to Practise Panel, GMC, 2006–14. *Recreations:* walking, fishing, family. *Address:* Ty Brith Cottage, Twyn Square, Usk, Monmouthshire NP15 1BH. *T:* (01291) 673570.

JENKINS, Maj.-Gen. David John Malcolm, CB 2000; CBE 1994; Under-Treasurer, Honourable Society of Gray's Inn, 2000–08; *b* 2 Jan. 1945; *m* 1969, Ann Patricia Sharp; one *s* two *d*. *Educ:* Sherborne Sch.; Reading Univ. (BA Hons); Magdalene Coll., Cambridge (MPhil). Commissioned The Queen's Own Hussars, 1964; regimental service, 1964–75; RMCS and Staff Coll., 1976–77; Allied Staff, Berlin, 1983–85; CO, The Queen's Own

Hussars, 1985–87; COS, 3 Armd Div., 1988–90; Comdr Armd 1 (Br) Corps, 1990–91; Dir, Military Ops, 1991–93; Commandant, RMCS, 1994–96; DG Land Systems, MoD, 1996–2000; Master Gen. of the Ordnance, 1998–2000. Col Comdt, REME, 1997–2002; Col, Queens Royal Hussars, 1999–2004; Hon. Col, Inns of Court and City Yeomanry, 2003–10. *Recreations:* ski-ing, country sports, music, military history. *Clubs:* Beefsteak, Garrick.

JENKINS, Deborah Mary, (Mrs Ivor Stolliday), MBE 1995; Director and owner, Kindling Ltd, since 1997; Chairman, South Tees Hospitals NHS Foundation Trust, since 2008; *b* Oxford, 14 July 1959; *d* of Rt Rev. David Edward Jenkins, *qv*; *m* 1997, Ivor Stolliday. *Educ:* LTCL, piano, 1976; Brasenose Coll., Oxford (BA 1981); Durham Univ. Business Sch. (MBA 1995). Tutor, Tübingen Univ., and British Council Student, Budapest, 1981–83; Manager, Caravanserai, Bishop Auckland, 1983–85; Owner, The Silver Swan, 1985–88; Personnel Dir, Impasse, 1986–87; Project Dir, Inner Cities Unit, Industrial Soc., 1987–89; Regl Dir, Common Purpose, 1989–95; Chair and CEO, The Derwent Initiative, 1993–. Vice Chair, Mental Health Act Commn, 2001–08. Vice Chair, Newcastle City Health NHS Trust, 1995–97. Non-executive Director: Northern Arts, 1992–95; NE SHA, 2006–08. Chair: Barnard Castle Vision, 2006–; Northern Neonatal Network, 2009–. Gov., Newcastle Coll., 1993–95. *Recreations:* domesticity, lustreware, pretending to be Niçoise. *Address:* 28 The Bank, Barnard Castle, Co. Durham DL12 8PQ. *E:* kindlingltd@msn.com.

JENKINS, Prof. Edgar William, CChem, FRSC; FRSB; JP; Professor of Science Education Policy, University of Leeds, 1993–2000, now Emeritus; *b* 7 Jan. 1939; *s* of Lewis Morgan Jenkins and Eira Gwyn (*née* Thomas); *m* 1961, Isobel Harrison; two *d*. *Educ:* Univ. of Leeds (BSc, MEd). CChem, FRSC 1974; FRSB (FSB 2010). Teacher: Keighley Grammar Sch., 1961–62; Leeds Grammar Sch., 1962–67; University of Leeds: Lectr and Sen. Lectr, 1967–76; Reader in Science Education, 1980–92; Head, Sch. of Education, 1980–84, 1991–95; Dir, Centre for Studies in Science Educn, 1997–2000. Chm., Bd, Grad. Teacher Trng Registry, 1995–2001. JP W Yorks, 1977. FRSA. Editor: Studies in Science Education, 1986–98; Internat. Jl of Technology and Design Education, 1994–2000. *Publications:* A Safety Handbook for Science Teachers, 1973, 4th edn 1991; From Armstrong to Nuffield, 1979; Inarticulate Science?, 1983; Technological Revolution?, 1985; A Magnificent Pile, 1985; Policy, Practice and Professional Judgement, 1993; Investigations by Order, 1996; Junior School Science Education since 1900, 1998; Learning from Others, 2000; Policy, Professionalism and Change, 2001; Innovations in Science and Technology Education, 2003; Guidelines for Policy-making in Secondary School Science and Technology Education, 2003; 75 Years and more: the ASE in Yorkshire, 2009; Advancing Science Education: the first fifty years of the Association for Science Education, 2013; books for schools. *Recreations:* choral music, walking, lay administration of justice.

JENKINS, Edward Nicholas; QC 2000; a Recorder, since 2000; *b* 27 July 1954; *m* 1979; one *s* one *d*. *Educ:* Trinity Hall, Cambridge (BA Hons). Called to the Bar, Middle Temple, 1977; Asst Recorder, 1999–2000. *Address:* 5 Paper Buildings, Temple, EC4Y 7HB. *T:* (020) 7583 6117.

JENKINS, Sir Elgar (Spencer), Kt 1996; OBE 1988; Member (C), Bath and North East Somerset Council, and Executive Member for Transport, 2003–07; *b* 16 June 1935; *s* of late Spencer and Mabel Jenkins. *Educ:* Monmouth Sch.; St Edmund Hall, Oxford (Pres., Oxford Univ., Cons. Assoc., 1955); St Luke's Coll., Exeter; Open Univ. (BA, Teaching Cert.). Commission, RAF, 1956–59. Asst Master, Bath and Bristol, 1962–73; Dep. Headmaster, Cardinal Newman Sch., then St Gregory's Catholic Comp. Sch., Bath, 1973–88. Chairman: Bath and Dist HA, 1989–93; Bath Mental Health Care NHS Trust, 1993–97. Member: Local Govt Mgt Bd, 1990–96; Nat. Adv. Cttee on Libraries, 1995–96. Bath City Council: Mem. (C), 1966–72, 1973–96; Mayor, Leader of Council, Chm. of Cttees. Association of District Councils: Mem., 1985–96; Leader, Cons. Gp, 1991–96; Dep. Chm., 1991–93; Vice-Chm., 1993–96. Mem., Nat. Exec., Cons. Party, 1994–96. Contested (C) Ebbw Vale, 1970. Mem. Council, 1968–96, Mem. Court, 1968–, Bath Univ. Chm. of Trustees, Bath Postal Mus., 1986–2002; Trustee, Holburne Mus. of Art, 2003–07. Mem., Bath Archaeol Trust, 1994–2005. FRSA. *Recreations:* history, reading, theatre. *Address:* 55 Uphill Drive, Bath BA1 6PB.

JENKINS, Emyr; *see* Jenkins, J. E.

JENKINS, Ffion Llywelyn; *see* Hague, F. L.

JENKINS, Prof. George Charles, MB, BS, PhD; FRCPE, FRCPath; Consultant Haematologist, The Royal London (formerly London) Hospital, 1965–92, now Hon. Consulting; Hon. Consultant, St Peter's Hospitals, 1972–86; Professor of Haematology in the University of London, 1974–92, now Emeritus; Consultant to the Royal Navy, now Emeritus; *b* 2 Aug. 1927; *s* of late John R. Jenkins and Mabel Rebecca (*née* Smith); *m* 1956, Elizabeth (*d* 2014), *d* of late Cecil J. Welch, London; one *s* two *d*. *Educ:* Wyggeston, Leicester; St Bartholomew's Hosp. Med. Coll. MB, BS, PhD; MRCS 1951; LRCP 1951; FRCPath 1975 (MRCPath 1964); FRCPE; FRSocMed. House Phys. and Ho. Surg., St Bart's Hosp., 1951–52. Sqdn Ldr, RAF Med. Br., 1952–54. Registrar in Pathology, St Bart's Hosp., 1954–57; MRC Research Fellow, Royal Postgraduate Med. Sch., 1957–60; Sen. Registrar, Haematology, London Hosp., 1960–63; Cons. Haematologist, N Middlesex Hosp., 1963–65. Examiner: Univ. of London, 1971–95; Univ. of Cambridge, 1984–95; Sen. Examiner, RCPath, 1971–92, Mem. Council, 1979–84, Vice-Pres., 1981–84. Member, sub-cttee on biologicals, 1976–86, cttee on dental and surgical materials, 1988–92, Cttee on Safety of Medicines. Pres., British Acad. of Forensic Scis, 1990–91 (Mem., 1977–; Chm. Exec. Council, 1985–89); Member: British Soc. for Haematology, 1962– (formerly Hon. Sec.; Pres., 1988–89); Internat. Soc. of Haematology, 1975–95; Assoc. of Clinical Pathologists, 1958–92. Gov. and Mem. Council, Home Farm Trust, 1993–2002. *Publications:* (jtly) Advanced Haematology, 1974; (jtly) Infection and Haematology, 1994; papers and contribs to med. and sci. books and jls. *Recreations:* theatre, music, art, talking to people, attempting to paint pictures. *Address:* 3 Lambert Jones Mews, Barbican, EC2Y 8DP.

JENKINS, Prof. Geraint Huw, PhD, DLitt; FBA 2002; FLSW; Director, University of Wales Centre for Advanced Welsh and Celtic Studies, 1993–2008, Hon. Senior Fellow, 2009; Professor Emeritus, University of Wales, 2009; *b* 24 Jan. 1946; *s* of David Hugh Jenkins and Lilian Jenkins (*née* Phillips); *m* 1972, Ann Ffrancon; three *d*. *Educ:* Ardwyn Grammar Sch., Aberystwyth; UCW, Swansea (BA 1st Cl. Hons 1967; Hon. Fellow, Univ. of Wales Swansea, 2004); UCW, Aberystwyth (PhD 1974); DLitt Wales 1994. University of Wales, Aberystwyth: Lectr in Welsh Hist., 1968–81; Sen. Lectr, 1981–88; Reader, 1988–90; Prof. of Welsh Hist., 1990–93; Head of Welsh History, 1991–93. Vis. Prof., UCLA, 2003. Member: Univ. of Wales Bd of Celtic Studies, 1985– (Chm., 1993–2007); Council and Court, Univ. of Wales, Aberystwyth, 1991–2006; Cardiganshire Historical (formerly Antiquarian) Soc. (Chm., 1998–); Council, British Acad., 2007–09; Univ. of Wales Press Bd, 2009–12. Founding FLSW 2010. Hon. Fellow: Swansea Univ., 2004; Swansea Metropolitan Univ., 2010. Editor: Ceredigion, 1985–95; Cof Cenedl, 1986–2009. *Publications:* Cewri'r Bêl-droed yng Nghymru, 1977; Literature, Religion and Society in Wales 1660–1730, 1978; Thomas Jones yr Almanaciwr, 1980; Hanes Cymru yn Cyfnod Modern Cynnar, 1983, rev. edn 1988 (Welsh Arts Council Prize, 1989); The Foundations of Modern Wales, 1987, rev. edn 1993; (ed jtly) Politics and Society in Wales 1840–1922, 1988; Llunio Cymru Fodern, 1989; The Making of Modern Wales, 1989; Cymru Ddoe a Heddiw, 1990; Wales Yesterday and Today, 1990; Cadw Tŷ mewn Cwmwl Tystion, 1990 (Welsh Arts Council Prize, 1991); Protestant Dissenters in Wales 1639–1689, 1992; The Illustrated History of the University of Wales, 1993; (ed jtly) Merêd: Casgliad o'i Ysgrifau, 1995; (ed) Y Gymraeg yn ei Disgleirdeb, 1997; (ed) The Welsh Language before the Industrial Revolution, 1997; (ed jtly) Cardiganshire in Modern Times, 1998; (ed) Iaith Carreg fy Aelwyd, 1998; (ed) Language and Community in the Nineteenth Century, 1998; (ed) Gwnewch Bopeth yn Gymraeg, 1999; Doc Tom: Thomas Richards, 1999; (ed) Welsh and its Social Domains 1801–1911, 2000; (ed jtly) Eu Hiaith a Gadwant?, 2000; (ed jtly) Let's Do Our Best for the Ancient Tongue, 2000; (ed) Cymru a'r Cymry 2000, 2001; (ed jtly) From Medieval to Modern Wales, 2004; A Rattleskull Genius: the many faces of Iolo Morganwg, 2005; A Concise History of Wales, 2007; (ed jtly) The Correspondence of Iolo Morganwg, 2007; (ed jtly) Degrees of Influence, 2008; Iolo Morganwg y Gweriniaethwr, 2010; The Swans Go Up, 2011; Yr Elyrch: Dathlu'r Cant, 2012; Bard of Liberty: the political radicalism of Iolo Morganwg, 2012; Proud to be a Swan: the centenary history of Swansea City FC, 2012. *Recreations:* music, sport, gardening. *Address:* Llain Wen, Blaenplwyf, Aberystwyth, Ceredigion SY23 4QJ. *T:* (01970) 612024.

JENKINS, Hugh Royston, CBE 1996; FRICS, FPMI; Chairman and Chief Executive, Prudential Portfolio Managers, and Director, Prudential Corporation, 1989–95; Chairman: Falcon Property Trust, 1995–2003; Development Securities plc, 1999–2003; *b* 9 Nov. 1933; *m* 1988, Mrs Beryl Kirk. *Educ:* Llanelli Grammar Sch. National Service, Royal Artillery, 1954–56. Valuer, London County Council, 1956–62; Assistant Controller, 1962–68, Managing Director, 1968–72, Coal Industry (Nominees) Ltd; Dir Gen. of Investments, NCB, 1972–85. Vice Chm., National Assoc. of Pension Funds, 1979–80; Chief Exec. Officer, Heron Financial Corp., 1985–86; Gp Investment Dir, Allied Dunbar Assce, 1986–89; Dep. Chm. and Chief Exec., Allied Dunbar Unit Trusts, 1986–89; Chm., Dunbar Bank, 1988–89; Chm. and Chief Exec., Allied Dunbar Asset Management, 1987–89. Dep. Chm., 1996–97, Chm., 1997–98, Thorn plc; Director: Unilever Pensions Ltd, 1985–89; IBM Pensions Trust PLC, 1985–89; Heron International, 1985–89; EMI, 1995–2003; Rank Gp plc, 1995–2001; Johnson Matthey, 1996–2003. Chm., Property Adv. Gp, DoE, 1990–96; Member: The City Capital Markets Cttee, 1982; Private Finance Panel, 1994–95; Lay Mem. of the Stock Exchange, 1984–85. *Address:* Flat 3, 36 Sloane Court West, SW3 4TB.

JENKINS, Ian; *see* Jenkins, A. I.

JENKINS, Sir (James) Christopher, KCB 1999 (CB 1987); First Parliamentary Counsel, 1994–99; *b* 20 May 1939; *s* of Percival Si Phillips Jenkins and Dela (*née* Griffiths); *m* 1962, Margaret Elaine Edwards, *yr d* of Rt Hon. L. John Edwards and Dorothy (*née* Watson); two *s* one *d*. *Educ:* Lewes County Grammar Sch.; Magdalen Coll., Oxford (Mackinnon Schol.; BA 1st class Hons Jurisprudence 1961; MA 1968). With Slaughter and May, 1962–67, solicitor, 1965. Joined Office of Parly Counsel, 1967; at Law Commn, 1970–72 and 1983–86; Parly Counsel, 1978–91; Second Parly Counsel, 1991–94. Adv. Council, Citizenship Foundn, 1989–2010; Adv. Law Cttee, British Council, 1998–2001; Adv. Council, Constitution Unit, UCL, 1999–2010; Council, Statute Law Soc., 2000–02. Hon. QC 1994.

JENKINS, Dame Jennifer; *see* Jenkins, Dame M. J.

JENKINS, Sir John, KCMG 2011 (CMG 2003); LVO 1989; HM Diplomatic Service, retired; Executive Director, Middle East, International Institute for Strategic Studies, since 2015; *b* 26 Jan. 1955; *s* of John Malsbury Jenkins and Mabel Lilleen Norah Jenkins (*née* Gardiner); *m* 1982, Nancy Caroline Pomfret. *Educ:* St Philip's Grammar Sch., Birmingham; Becket Sch., Nottingham; Jesus Coll., Cambridge (BA 1977; PhD 1980). Joined FCO, 1980; full-time lang. trng, SOAS, Univ. of London and London Centre for Arabic Studies, 1981–83 and 1998–99; Second, later First, Sec., Abu Dhabi, 1983–86; First Sec., FCO, 1986–89; Head of Chancery, Kuala Lumpur, 1989–92; First Sec., FCO, 1992–95; Counsellor and Dep. Head of Mission, Kuwait, 1995–98; lang. trng, SOAS, Univ. of London, 1998–99; Ambassador to Burma (Union of Myanmar), 1999–2002; Consul-Gen., Jerusalem, 2003–06; Ambassador to Syria, 2006–07; Dir, Middle East and N Africa, FCO, 2007–09; Ambassador to Iraq, 2009–11; UK Special Rep. to Nat. Transitional Council, Benghazi, 2011; Ambassador to Libya, 2011; Ambassador to Saudi Arabia, 2012–15. *Recreations:* Nottingham Forest FC, walking, theatre, films and books, the ancient world, drumming, the Middle East. *Address:* International Institute for Strategic Studies Middle East, 14th Floor, GPCorp Tower, Bahrain Financial Harbour, Manama, POB 11095, Kingdom of Bahrain. *Club:* Oxford and Cambridge.

JENKINS, John David; QC 1990; a Recorder, since 1990; *b* 7 Dec. 1947; *s* of late Vivian Evan Jenkins, MBE and of Megan Myfanwy Evans; *m* 1972, Susan Elizabeth Wilkinson; two *s*. *Educ:* Ashville Coll., Harrogate; King's Coll. London (LLB Hons). Called to the Bar, Gray's Inn, 1970; in practice at the Bar, Wales and Chester Circuit, 1970–2008. *Recreations:* football, cricket, psephology. *Address:* (office) 30 Park Place, Cardiff CF10 3BS. *T:* (029) 2039 8421. *Club:* Pentyrch Cricket.

JENKINS, (John) Emyr; Chief Executive, Arts Council of Wales, 1994–98; *b* 3 May 1938; *s* of Llewellyn Jenkins and Mary Olwen Jenkins; *m* 1964, Myra Bonner Samuel; two *d*. *Educ:* Machynlleth County Sch.; UCW, Aberystwyth (BSc Physics). BBC Studio Manager, 1961–63; BBC Announcer and Newsreader, 1963–71; Anchorman, Heddiw (Daily TV Mag.), 1968–69; BBC Wales Programme Organiser, 1971–77; First Dir, Royal Nat. Eisteddfod of Wales, 1978–93; Dir, Welsh Arts Council, 1993–94. Mem., IBA Welsh Adv. Cttee, 1986–90. Foundn Chm., Mudiad Ysgolion Meithrin (Assoc. of Welsh Playgroups), 1971–73; Member: Welsh Lang. Educn Develt Cttee, 1987–88; Council, UCW Aberystwyth, 1982–86; Steering Cttee/Council, Voluntary Arts Network, 1988–94; Voluntary Arts Wales Cttee, 1999–2001; Bd, Univ. of Wales Press, 1999– (Chm., 2003–06). Chm., Welsh Music Inf. Centre, 2000–05; Foundn Chm., Sherman Cymru Th., 2006–12. Gov., RWCMD, 1998– (Dep. Chm., 2000–06). FRSA 1992. Hon. FRWCMD (Hon. FWCMD 1997). Hon. MA Wales, 1993. Hon. Mem., Gorsedd of Bards, 1982. Elder, Crwys Presbyterian Church of Wales, 1984 (Treas., 2009–); Trustee, Presbyterian Church of Wales, 2014–. *Recreations:* music, theatre, walking, sport.

See also F. L. Hague, M. B. Antoniazzi.

JENKINS, Sir Karl (William Pamp), Kt 2015; CBE 2010 (OBE 2005); DMus; FRAM; composer; *b* 17 Feb. 1944; *s* of late David and Lily Jenkins; *m* 1973, Carol Barratt, composer; one *s*. *Educ:* Gowerton Grammar Sch.; University Coll. of Wales, Cardiff (BMus); DMus Wales 2006; Royal Acad. of Music (LRAM 1966; ARAM 2001; FRAM 2003). Played saxophone, keyboards and oboe with Ronnie Scott's jazz band, Nucleus (co-founder) and Soft Machine (1972–80); composer of advertising music for Levi's, British Airways, Pepsi, etc (D&AD award for best music, 1985, 1989; Creative Circle Gold Award, 1986). *Compositions:* Adiemus: Songs of Sanctuary, 1995; Cantata Mundi, 1997; Dances of Time, 1998; The Journey, 1999; The Eternal Knot, 2000; Vocalise, 2003; Diamond Music/Palladio, 1996; Imagined Oceans, 1998; Eloise (opera), 1999; The Armed Man: A Mass for Peace (for soloists, chorus and orch.) (commnd by Royal Armouries), 2000; Dewi Sant, 2000; Over the Stone (harp concerto), 2002; In These Stones Horizons Sing, 2004; Requiem, 2005; Quirk (concertante), 2005; Tlep, 2006; Stabat Mater, 2008; Joy to the World, Stella Natalis, 2009; Gloria, 2010; film score: River Queen, 2005. FRWCMD (FWCMD 2003); Fellow: Cardiff Univ., 2004; Trinity Coll., Carmarthen, 2005; Swansea Inst., 2005. *Publications:* Still with the Music: my autobiography, 2015. *Recreations:* travel, food, sport. *Address:* c/o Karl Jenkins Music Ltd, 46 Poland Street, W1F 7NA. *T:* (020) 7434 2225. *E:* info@karljenkins.com.

JENKINS, Katharine Mary; Visiting Professor, Department of Government, London School of Economics and Political Science, since 2002; *b* 14 Feb. 1945; *d* of late Rev. Dr Daniel Thomas Jenkins and Nell Jenkins; *m* 1967, Euan Sutherland, *qv* (marr. diss. 1995); one *s* one *d*. *Educ:* South Hampstead High Sch.; St Anne's Coll., Oxford (BA Hons); London School of

Economics (MScEcon). Called to Bar, Inner Temple, 1971. Asst Principal, 1968, Principal, 1973, Dept of Employment; Central Policy Review Staff, Cabinet Office, 1976; Asst Sec., Dept of Employment, 1979; Dep. Head of Efficiency Unit, 1984; Dir, Prime Minister's Efficiency Unit, and Under Sec., Cabinet Office, 1986–89; Dir, Personnel, Royal Mail, 1989–91; Chm., Kate Jenkins Associates, 1991–2008. Dir, Carrenza Ltd, 2003–; Chm., Carrenza Consulting Ltd, 2007–14. Member: NHS Policy Bd, 1992–95; Audit Commn, 1993–99; Council, Hansard Soc., 2003–10 (Vice Chm., 2005–10). Dir, London and Manchester Gp, 1989–97. Special Trustee, St Thomas' Hosp., 1992–95. Member: Barbican Centre Cttee, 2000–06; Council, Spitalfields Fest., 2003–06; St Bartholomew's Hosp. Trust Med. Coll., 2003–12 (Vice Chm., 2006–12). London School of Economics and Political Science: Mem., Ct of Govs, 1990– (Vice Chm., 2009–14); Mem. Council, 2000–03, 2008– (Vice Chm., 2009–14). *Publications:* (with W. Plowden) Governance and Nationbuilding: the failure of international intervention, 2006; Politicians and Public Services: a clash of cultures, 2008; reports: Making Things Happen: the implementation of government scrutinies, 1985; Improving Management in Government: the next steps, 1988; (with W. Plowden) Keeping Control: the management of public sector reform programmes, 1995. *Address:* 513 Gilbert House, Barbican, EC2Y 8BD.

See also Sir S. D. Jenkins, B. J. Mack.

JENKINS, Dame (Mary) Jennifer, (Lady Jenkins of Hillhead), DBE 1985; Member of Council, National Trust, 1985–90 (Chairman, 1986–90); *b* 18 Jan. 1921; *d* of late Sir Parker Morris; *m* 1945, Baron Jenkins of Hillhead, OM, FBA (*d* 2003); two *s* one *d*. *Educ:* St Mary's Sch., Calne; Girton Coll., Cambridge (scholar). Chm., Cambridge Univ. Labour Club. With Hoover Ltd, 1942–43; Min. of Labour, 1943–46; Political and Economic Planning (PEP), 1946–48; part-time extra-mural lectr, 1949–61; part-time teacher, Kingsway Day Coll., 1961–67. Chairman: Consumers' Assoc., 1965–76; Historic Buildings Council for England, 1975–84; Member: Exec. Bd, British Standards Instn, 1970–73; Design Council, 1971–74; Cttee of Management, Courtauld Inst., 1981–84; Ancient Monuments Bd, 1982–84; Historic Buildings and Monuments Commn, 1984–85 (Chm., Historic Buildings Adv. Cttee, 1984–85); Pres., Ancient Monuments Soc., 1985– (Sec., 1972–75). Chairman: N Kensington Amenity Trust, 1974–77; Royal Parks Review Gp, 1991–96; Architectural Heritage Fund, 1994–97; Adv. Panel, Heritage Lottery Fund, 1995–99; Civic Trust, 2003–04. Trustee, Wallace Collection, 1977–83. Director: J. Sainsbury Ltd, 1981–86; Abbey National plc (formerly Abbey National Building Soc.), 1984–91. Liveryman, Goldsmiths' Co., 1980. Freeman, City of London, 1982. JP London Juvenile Courts, 1964–74. Hon. FRICS 1981; Hon. FRIBA 1982; Hon. MRTPI 1988; Hon. FLI 1995. Hon. LLD: London, 1988; Bristol, 1990; DUniv: York, 1990; Strathclyde, 1993; Hon. DCL: Newcastle, 1992; Oxford, 2003; Hon. DArch Oxford Brookes, 1993; Hon. DLitt Greenwich, 1998; Hon. DSc St Andrews, 2006. *Publications:* (with Patrick James) From Acorn to Oak Tree, 1994; (ed) Remaking the Landscape: the changing face of Britain, 2002. *Address:* St Amand's House, East Hendred, Oxon OX12 8LA.

JENKINS, Sir Michael (Nicholas Howard), Kt 1997; OBE 1991; *b* 13 Oct. 1932; *s* of C. N. and M. E. S. Jenkins; *m* 1957, Jacqueline Frances Jones; three *s*. *Educ:* Tonbridge School; Merton College, Oxford (MA Jurisp.). Shell-Mex & BP, 1956–61; IBM UK, 1961–67; Partner, Robson, Morrow, Management Consultants, 1967–71; Technical Dir, Stock Exchange, 1971–77; Man. Dir, European Options Exchange, Amsterdam, 1977–79; Chief Executive, LIFFE, 1981–92; Chairman: London Commodity Exchange, 1992–96; Futures and Options Assoc., 1993–99; Dir, 1991–2003, Chm., 1996–2003, London Clearing House Ltd. Chm., E-Crossnet Ltd, 1999–2005; Director: Tradepoint Financial Networks plc, 1995–99; British Invisibles, 1998–2001; EasyScreen plc, 1999–2005. Trustee: Brain and Spine Foundn, 1993–2010; Success in Shortage Subjects, 2007–. Pres., Merton Soc., 2007–10. Gov., Sevenoaks Sch., 1993–2007. Liveryman: Information Technologists' Co., 2004–; World Traders' Co., 2009–. *Recreations:* golf, music, wood turning. *Club:* Wildernesse (Sevenoaks).

JENKINS, Neil Martin James; opera singer; tenor; music editor; *b* 9 April 1945; *s* of Harry James Jenkins and Mary Morrison Jenkins (*née* Terry); *m* 1st, 1969, Sandra Wilkes; one *s*; 2nd, 1982, Penny (*née* Underwood); one *s*, and two step *s* one step *d*. *Educ:* Westminster Abbey Choir School; Dean Close School (music Scholar); King's College Cambridge (Choral Scholar; MA). Recital début, Kirkman Concert Series, Purcell Room, 1967; operatic début, Menotti's The Consul, Israel Festival, 1968; major rôles with English Music Theatre, Glyndebourne Fest. Opera, Kent Opera, New Sussex Opera, Scottish Opera, WNO; ENO; numerous recordings, film sound tracks and videos. Prof. of Singing, RCM, 1975–76; teacher, summer schools, incl. Canford, AIMS (formerly Ardingly) and Dartington, 1989–. Cummins Harvey Vis. Fellow, Girton Coll., Cambridge, 2003. President: Grange Choral Soc., Hants; Haywards Heath Music Soc., 2000–; Shoreham Oratorio Choir, 2003–; Basildon Choral Soc., 2008–; Kent Chorus, 2011–; Vice-President: Hunts Philharmonic; Brighton Competitive Music Festival. Geoffrey Tankard Lieder Prize, 1967; NFMS Award, 1972; Sir Charles Santley Award, Musicians' Co., 2004. *Publications: choral music* (edited and arranged): The Carol Singer's Handbook, 1993; O Praise God, 1994; O Holy Night, 1994; Sing Solo Sacred, 1997; works by J. S. Bach: St Matthew Passion, 1997; St John Passion, 1998; Christmas Oratorio, 1999; Magnificat, 2000; B Minor Mass, 2002; Easter Oratorio, 2003; Haydn The Seasons, 2003; Ascension Oratorio, 2004; The Creation, 2005; Handel The Passion of Christ, 2014; Haydn The Seven Last Words, 2015; Schutz: The Christmas Story, 2000; The Seven Last Words, 2015; The Resurrection Story, 2015; articles in: Haydn Soc. of Great Britain Jl, 2005; Göttinger Händel-Beiträge XII, 2008; (contrib.) Handel, 2011; John Beard, Handel and Garrick's Favourite Tenor, 2012. *Recreations:* visiting ancient monuments, 18th century music research. *Address:* c/o Music International, 13 Ardilaun Road, N5 2QR. *T:* (020) 7359 5813.

JENKINS, Paul, OBE 2001; Chief Executive, Tavistock and Portman NHS Foundation Trust, since 2014; *b* 11 Feb. 1963; *s* of Ifor and Sheila Jenkins; *m* 1989, Catherine Bannister; two *s*. *Educ:* Solihull Sch.; Balliol Coll., Oxford (MA Ancient and Modern Hist.); Manchester Business Sch. (MBA). Admin. trainee, DoH, 1985; Project Manager, DoH, 1998–2004: Next Steps Proj. Team, Cabinet Office, 1988–91; Policy Lead for NHS Community and Continuing Care, 1991–96; Dir, Service Develt, NHS Direct, 2004–07; Chief Exec., Rethink, later Rethink Mental Illness, 2007–14. Mem., Standing Commn for Carers, 2009–. *Recreations:* Welsh language and culture, Rugby, cricket, history, archaeology, hill-walking. *Address:* Tavistock and Portman NHS Foundation Trust, Tavistock Centre, 120 Belsize Lane, NW3 5BA. *E:* PJenkins@tavi-port.nhs.uk.

JENKINS, Sir Paul (Christopher), KCB 2012; HM Procurator General, Treasury Solicitor and Head of Government Legal Service, 2006–14; *b* 22 Sept. 1954; *s* of late Reginald Turberville Jenkins and Elsie Jenkins (*née* Williams); civil partnership 2009, René Finne Hansen. *Educ:* Harrow County Sch. for Boys; Univ. of Manchester (LLB Hons 1976). Called to the Bar, Middle Temple, 1977, Bencher, 2002; Treasury Solicitor's Dept, 1979–90; Monopolies and Mergers Commn, 1990–92; Legal Adviser: DNH, subseq. DCMS, 1992–98; LCD, 1998–2002; Dir Gen., Legal and Internat. Gp, LCD, subseq. DCA, 2002–04; Solicitor to DWP and to DoH, and Dir Gen., Law, Governance and Special Policy, DWP, 2004–06. Gov., Europäische Rechtsakad., Trier, 2002–05, 2007–14; Trustee: Inns of Court and Bar Educnl Trust, 2005–12; British Inst. of Internat. and Comparative Law, 2012–. Hon. QC 2009. Dir, Hampstead Theatre, 2006–12. *Recreations:* opera, London, gardening. *Address:* c/o Treasury Solicitor's Department, 1 Kemble Street, WC2B 4TS.

JENKINS, Peter Redmond, CMG 2005; HM Diplomatic Service, retired; Partner, Ambassador Partnership (formerly ADRg Ambassadors), since 2010; *b* 2 March 1950; *s* of late Denys Arthur Reali Jenkins and Monique Marie-Louise Jenkins; *m* 1990, Angelina Chee-Hung Yang; one *s* one *d*. *Educ:* Downside Sch.; Corpus Christi Coll., Cambridge (BA Hons, MA); Harvard Univ. Graduate Sch. of Arts and Scis (Harkness Fellow). Joined HM Diplomatic Service, 1973: FCO, 1973–75; UK Mission to Internat. Orgns, Vienna, 1975–78; FCO, 1978–82; Private Sec. to HM Ambassador, Washington, 1982–84; FCO, 1984–87; Paris, 1987–91; Minister-Counsellor and Consul Gen., Brasilia, 1992–95; Dep. Perm. Rep., 1996–2001, and Minister, 1998–2001, UK Mission to UN, Geneva; Perm. Rep. to UN and other Internat. Orgns, Vienna, 2001–06; Special Rep. for the Renewable Energy and Energy Efficiency Partnership, 2006–08. Special Advr to Dir, Internat. Inst. for Applied Systems Analysis, 2006–08. Associate Fellow, Geneva Centre for Security Policy, 2010–12. Non-executive Director: Ecoenergen, 2009–; Oceana, 2015–. Chm., IAEA Conference on Illicit Trafficking of Nuclear Materials, 2007. Vis. Lectr, Univ. of Bath, 2009–. Gov., Downside Sch., 2012–. Member: Cttee, Harkness Fellows Assoc., 2012–; Exec. Cttee, British Pugwash Gp, 2014–. *Publications:* many articles on nuclear issues, esp. the problem posed by Iran's nuclear prog. *Recreations:* ski-ing, hill/mountain walking, reading, travelling. *Address:* 14 Great Bedford Street, Bath BA1 2TZ. *E:* prjs@post.harvard.edu. *Clubs:* Brooks's, Beefsteak.

JENKINS, Peter White, MBE 2007; County Treasurer, Merseyside County Council, 1973–84; *b* 12 Oct. 1937; *s* of John White Jenkins, OBE, and Dorothy Jenkins; *m* 1961, Joyce Christine Muter; one *s* one *d*. *Educ:* Queen Mary's Grammar Sch., Walsall; King Edward VI Grammar Sch., Nuneaton. CIPFA. Local govt service in Finance Depts at Coventry, Preston, Chester, Wolverhampton; Dep. Treasurer, Birkenhead, 1969–73; Dir of Finance, Welsh Water Authority, 1984–87. Hon. Treas., 1994–98, Chapter Clerk, 2006–, Brecon Cathedral. *Recreations:* walking, gardening, local history, reading. *Address:* 9 Camden Crescent, Brecon, Powys LD3 7BY.

JENKINS, His Honour Richard Peter Vellacott; a Circuit Judge, 1989–2015; *b* 10 May 1943; *s* of late Gwynne Jenkins and Irene Lilian Jenkins; *m* 1st, 1975, Agnes Anna Margaret Mullan (*d* 2003); one *s* one *d*; 2nd, 2010, Jennifer Christine Kershaw, (Her Honour Judge Kershaw, QC) (*d* 2012). *Educ:* Edge Grove School, Aldenham; Radley College; Trinity Hall, Cambridge (MA). Called to the Bar, Inner Temple, 1966; Midland Circuit, 1966–72; Midland and Oxford Circuit, 1972–89 (Remembrancer and Asst Treasurer, 1984–89); a Recorder, 1988–89; Designated Family Judge, Lincoln, 1997–2007. Mem., Humberside Probation Cttee Policy Sub-Cttee, 1996–2000; Mem., Lincs Probation Bd, 2001–03. Chairman: Lincolnshire Family Mediation Service, 1997–2002 (Hon. Pres., 2005–10); Lincs Area Criminal Justice Strategy Cttee, 2000–02. Council of Circuit Judges: Mem. Cttee, 2000–09; Chm., Family Sub-Cttee, 2003–08; Jun. Vice Pres., 2007; Sen. Vice Pres., 2008; Pres., 2009; Mem., Judges' Council, 2009. Mem. Court, Univ. of Lincoln, 2011– (Chm., Adv. Bd, Law Sch., 2006–10). Liveryman, Co. of Barbers, 1967–. Hon. LLD Lincoln, 2004. *Clubs:* MCC, Lansdowne.

JENKINS, Richard Thomas, OBE 1986; HM Diplomatic Service, retired; Ambassador to Georgia, 1998–2001; *b* 19 Aug. 1943; *s* of Vincent Arthur Wood Jenkins and Edna Jenkins (*née* Frith); *m* 1976, Maurizia Marantonio; two *s*. *Educ:* Plaistow Co. GS; Nottingham Univ. (BA Hons 1964); Warsaw Univ.; Glasgow Univ. Entered HM Diplomatic Service, 1967; FCO, 1967–70; Warsaw, 1970; FCO, 1970–76; Second, subseq. First Sec., E Berlin, 1976–79; Res. Dept, FCO, 1979–83; First Sec. (Commercial), Warsaw, 1983–85; Head, Central European Sect., 1985–89, Dep. Head, Jt Assistance Unit (Know How Fund), 1989–94, FCO Res. Dept; Dep. Head of Mission and Consul-Gen., Kiev, 1994–97. Election monitoring for OSCE Office for Democratic Instns and Human Rights: Albania, 2003; Georgia, Macedonia, 2004; Belarus, Tajikistan, Kazakhstan, 2005; Kosovo (Council of Europe), 2006. Mem., Fabian Soc. Freeman, City of London, 1998. Hon. Fellow, Univ. of E London, 1995.

JENKINS, (Sir) Simon David, Kt 2004; columnist, The Guardian, since 2005; Chairman, National Trust, 2008–14; *b* 10 June 1943; *s* of late Rev. Dr Daniel Thomas Jenkins and Nell Jenkins; *m* 1978, Gayle Hunnicutt (marr. diss. 2008); one *s*, and one step *s*; *m* 2014, Hannah Kaye. *Educ:* Mill Hill Sch.; St John's Coll., Oxford (BA Hons; Hon. Fellow 2004). Country Life magazine, 1965; Univ. of London Inst. of Educn, 1966; Times Educational Supplement, 1966–68; Evening Standard, 1968–74; Insight Editor, Sunday Times, 1974–75; Dep. Editor, Evening Standard, 1976, Editor, 1976–78; Political Editor, The Economist, 1979–86; The Sunday Times: columnist, 1986–90; editor, Books Section, 1988–89; The Times: Editor, 1990–92; columnist, 1992–2005. Member: British Railways Bd, 1979–90; LRT Bd, 1984–86; South Bank Bd, 1985–90; Calcutt Cttee on Privacy, 1989–90; Grade Cttee on Fear of Crime, 1989; Runciman Cttee on Misuse of Drugs Act 1971, 1998–2000; HFEA, 2001–06. Chm., Commn for Local Democracy, 1994–95. Director: Municipal Journal Ltd, 1980–90; Faber & Faber, 1980–90. Chm., Booker Prize, 2000. Mem. Council, Bow Group, and Editor of Crossbow, 1968–70; Member: Cttee, Save Britain's Heritage, 1976–; Historic Buildings and Monuments Commn, 1985–90 (Dep. Chm., 1988–90); Millennium Commn, 1994–2000; Mem. Council, Old Vic Co., 1979–81; Chm., Pevsner Books Trust, 1994–2011; Dep. Chm., Thirties Soc., 1979–85; Founder and Dir, Railway Heritage Trust, 1985–90; Trustee: World Monuments Fund, 1995–98; Somerset House Trust, 2003–09. Gov., Mus. of London, 1985–87. FSA 2004; FRSL 2004; Hon. RIBA, 1997. Hon. Dr UCE, 1998; Hon. DLitt: London, 2000; City, 2001; Univ. of Wales, Lampeter, 2001; Exeter, 2003; Univ. of London Inst. of Educn, 2005. What The Papers Say Journalist of the Year, 1988; Columnist of the Year, British Press Awards, 1993; Edgar Wallace Trophy for Outstanding Reporting, London Press Club, 1997; David Watt Meml Prize, Rio Tinto, 1998; Commentariat of the Year, Comment Awards, 2010. *Publications:* A City at Risk, 1971; Landlords to London, 1974; (ed) Insight on Portugal, 1975; Newspapers: the power and the money, 1979; The Companion Guide to Outer London, 1981; (with Max Hastings) The Battle for the Falklands, 1983; Images of Hampstead, 1983; (with Anne Sloman) With Respect Ambassador, 1985; The Market for Glory, 1986; The Times Guide to English Style and Usage, 1992; The Selling of Mary Davies, 1993; Against the Grain, 1994; Accountable to None: the Tory nationalization of Britain, 1995; England's Thousand Best Churches, 1999; England's Thousand Best Houses, 2003; Big Bang Localism, 2005; Thatcher and Sons, 2006 (Political Book of the Year, Channel 4, 2007); Wales: churches, houses, castles, 2009; A Short History of England, 2011; England's Hundred Best Views, 2013; Mission Accomplished, 2015. *Recreations:* London, the English countryside. *Address:* c/o The Guardian, King's Place, 90 York Way, N1 9GU. *Club:* Garrick.

See also K. M. Jenkins.

JENKINS, Stanley Kenneth; HM Diplomatic Service, retired; *b* 25 Nov. 1920; *s* of Benjamin and Ethel Jane Jenkins; *m* 1957, Barbara Mary Marshall Webb (*d* 2004); four *d*. *Educ:* Brecon; Cardiff Tech. Coll. President, Nat. Union of Students, 1949–51. LIOB 1950. Served War, Royal Artillery and Royal Engineers, 1942–46, retiring as Major. Joined Foreign (later Diplomatic) Service, 1951; Singapore, 1953; Kuala Lumpur, 1955; FO, 1957; Singapore, 1959; Rangoon, 1961; FO, 1964; Nicosia, 1967; FO, 1970–78, Counsellor. Chancellor's Medal, Univ. of Glamorgan, 2012. *Publications:* So Much to Do, So Little Time (autobiog.), 2000. *Recreations:* gardening, tennis. *Address:* Willow Cottage, 1 Beehive Lane, Ferring, Worthing, W Sussex BN12 5NL. *T:* (01903) 247356.

JENKINS, Stephen Lewis; public relations consultant, since 2013; Head of Media Relations, Archbishops' Council of the Church of England, 1999–2013 (Acting Head of Communications, 2002–04; Acting Director of Communications, 2011–12); *b* 1 Dec. 1955;

s of Charles Lewis Jenkins and Marjorie Jenkins (*née* Negus); *m* 1979, Susan Jane Varley; two *s*. *Educ:* Reading Sch.; UCNW, Bangor (BSc Hons (Agric. with Agricl Econs)). Technical and news reporter, Big Farm Weekly, 1977–80; Dep. Ed., Big Farm Management, subseq. Farm Business, 1980–84; freelance, 1984–85; tech. journalist, Farm Contractor Mag., 1985–87; Press Officer: Children's Soc., 1987–90; Gen. Synod of C of E, 1991–99. Develt Officer, Mothers' Union, Dio. of Oxford, 2015–. *Recreation:* family life and the search for time. *Address:* 34 Dickens Close, Caversham, Reading RG4 5LZ. *T:* 07768 764783.

JENKINS, Prof. Stephen Pryse, DPhil; Professor of Economic and Social Policy, London School of Economics and Political Science, since 2011; *b* 11 June 1956; *s* of David W. P. Jenkins and Katherine E. Jenkins (*née* Gillingham). *Educ:* Univ. of Otago, Dunedin (BA 1977); Univ. of York (DPhil 1983). Jun. Lectr, Massey Univ., 1978; Res. Fellow, Univ. of York, 1979–80, 1981–83; Lectr, Univ. of Bath, 1983–91; Prof. of Applied Econs, Univ. of Wales, Swansea, 1991–94; Prof. of Econs, 1994–2011, Dir, 2006–09, Inst. for Social and Economic Res., Univ. of Essex. *Publications:* (ed jtly) The Distribution of Household Welfare and Household Production, 1998; (ed jtly) The Dynamics of Child Poverty in Industrialized Countries, 2001; Changing Fortunes: income mobility and poverty dynamics in Britain, 2011 (ed jtly) The Great Recession and the Distribution of Household Income, 2013; numerous articles in learned jls. *Recreations:* music, running, cycling. *Address:* Department of Social Policy, London School of Economics and Political Science, Houghton Street, WC2A 2AE. *T:* (020) 7955 6527. *E:* s.jenkins@lse.ac.uk.

JENKINS, (Thomas) Alun; QC 1996; Advocate, Public Defender Service, since 2014; *b* 19 Aug. 1948; *s* of Seward Thomas Jenkins and Iris, *d* of Alderman W. G. H. Bull, miner and sometime Chm. of Monmouthshire CC; *m* 1971, Glenys Maureen Constant; one *s* two *d*. *Educ:* Ebbw Vale Tech. Sch.; Bristol Univ. (LLB Hons 1971). Called to the Bar, Lincoln's Inn, 1972, Bencher, 2008; in private practice, Bristol, 1972–2014, and London, 1996–2014, specialising in law of serious crime, esp. large diversion frauds, large scale drug importations, organised crime, and conspiracies; Head of Chambers, Queen Square, Bristol, 1995–2014. Asst Recorder, 1992–2000; Recorder, 2000–14. *Recreations:* cultural: opera, Shakespeare and literature generally; sport: horse riding, Rugby, motor cars, point to point.

JENKINS, Thomas Lawrence; Sports Photographer: The Guardian, since 1990; Observer, since 1993; *b* 1 Jan. 1968; *s* of Richard and Mary Jenkins; *m* 2003, Rosamund Harris; one *s* one *d*. *Educ:* Sevenoaks Sch.; Gwent Coll. of Higher Educn (BTEC HND Documentary Photography 1989). Freelance sports photographer: Allsport, 1989; Sunday Telegraph, 1989; Sunday Express, 1990. Young Photographer of the Year, 1990, Sports Photographer of the Year, 2004, 2006, 2007, British Press Awards; Sports Photographer of the Year, 2000, Photograph of the Year, 2004, What the Papers Say; Sports Photographer of the Year, Nikon, 2002, Sports Journalists Assoc., 2003, 2004; Barclays Football Photographer of the Year, 2008–09; 4 awards, Press Photographer's Year, 2009; Sports Portfolio of the Year, Sports Journalists Assoc., 2011. *Publications:* In the Moment: the sports photography of Tom Jenkins, 2012. *Recreation:* spending time with my family. *E:* tom.jenkins@guardian.co.uk.

JENKINS, Victor, CEng; Director ISTAR, Defence Equipment and Support, Ministry of Defence, 2007–11; *b* Cardiff, 17 April 1950; *s* of Roy and Hazel Jenkins; *m* 1995, Sheila Lonsdale (*née* Richardson); one step *d*. *Educ:* Paston Sch., Norfolk; Univ. of Kent at Canterbury (BSc Hons Electronics). CEng 1991; Certificated Project Manager, 1994. Systems Engr, Cossor Electronics Ltd, 1972–76; Manager, res. and projects, 1976–90, Dir, Procurement Policy for Project Mgt, 1990–92, PE, MoD; rcds 1993; Dir of Projects, Al Yamamah Prog., MoD, 1994–98; Dir of Ops and Dep. Chief Exec., UK Hydrographic Office, 1998–2004; Dir of Ops and Actg Chief Exec., HM Govt Communications Centre, 2004–07. *Recreations:* cycling, walking, dining.

JENKINSON, Eric, CVO 2009; OBE 2003; HM Diplomatic Service; Information Management Department, Foreign and Commonwealth Office, 2011; *b* 13 March 1950; *s* of Horace and Bertha Jenkinson; *m*; two *s*; *m* 2004, Máire Donnelly. Joined FCO, 1967; Protocol Div., FCO, 1967–70; Brussels, 1971–73; Islamabad, 1973–76; full-time language training, 1976–77; temp. duty, then Third Sec., Commercial, Jedda, 1978–80; Second Sec., Commercial, Riyadh, 1980–82; Sci., Energy and Nuclear Dept, FCO, 1982–84; Asst Private Sec., FCO, 1984–86; First Sec., Econ., Bonn, 1986–90; Dep. Consul General, Frankfurt, 1990–91; full-time language training, 1991–92; Dep. Head of Mission, Bahrain, 1992–95; Head, Parly Relns Dept, FCO, 1995–98; First Sec., Commercial/Econ., then Dep. Head of Mission, Tehran, 1999–2002; High Commissioner: The Gambia, 2002–06; Trinidad and Tobago, 2007–11. *Recreations:* cooking, photography, Rugby, cricket, reading.

JENKINSON, Jeffrey Charles, MVO 1977; Chief Executive, Harwich Haven Authority, 1992–97; *b* 22 Aug. 1939; *s* of late John Jenkinson and Olive May Jenkinson; *m* 1962, Janet Ann (*née* Jarrett); one *s* two *d*. *Educ:* Royal Liberty Sch., Romford; City of London Coll. National Service, RN, 1957–59. Port of London Authority: Port operations and gen. management, 1959–71; British Transport Staff Coll., 1972; PLA Sec., 1972–81; Dir of Admin, 1982–86; Bd Mem., 1982–92; Chief Exec., Property, 1987–92; Dir, Placon Ltd and other PLA gp subsid. cos, 1978–92. Dir, E London Small Business Centre Ltd, 1977–92; Mem. Bd, Globe Centre Ltd, 1992–96. Envmt Agency Chm., Essex Area Envmt Gp, 1996–2002; Mem., Anglian (Eastern) Regl Flood Defence Cttee, 2003–11 (Vice Chm., 2005–11). Member: Bd, and Council, London Chamber of Commerce and Industry, 1989–92; Council, British Ports Assoc., 1993–96; Chm., Thames Riparian Housing Assoc., 1986–92; Member: Newham CHC, 1974–80; Committee of Management: Seamen's Gp of Hosps, 1972–74; Seamen's Hosp. Soc., 1974– (Hon. Treas., 1998–2002). Mem. Bd, Colne Housing Soc., 2009–14. Freeman, City of London, 1975; Mem. Ct, Co. of Watermen and Lightermen of River Thames, 1990– (Master, 1997–98). *Recreations:* sailing, walking, music.

JENKINSON, Sir John (Banks), 14th Bt *cr* 1661; *b* 16 Feb. 1945; *o s* of Sir Anthony Banks Jenkinson, 13th Bt and Frances (*d* 1996), *d* of Harry Stremmel; *S* father, 1989; *m* 1979, Josephine Mary Marshall-Andrew; one *s* one *d*. *Educ:* Eton; Univ. of Miami. *Heir: s* George Samuel Anthony Banks Jenkinson, *b* 8 Nov. 1980.

JENKINSON, Kenneth Leslie; Headmaster, Colchester Royal Grammar School, 2000–15 (Deputy Headmaster, 1994–2000); *b* 4 Oct. 1955; *s* of Reginald and Margaret Jenkinson; *m* 1979, Jacqueline Anne Loose; two *d*. *Educ:* Danum Grammar Sch., Doncaster; Univ. of Leeds (BA, PGCE); Univ. of Sheffield (MA); NPQH. Teacher, Modern Languages, Hayfield Sch., Doncaster, 1979–88; Head, Modern Languages, Blundell's Sch., Tiverton, 1988–94. *Recreations:* family, travel, sport.

JENKINSON, Nigel Harrison; Adviser, Financial Stability Board, Bank for International Settlements, since 2009; *b* 18 June 1955; *s* of Alan and Jean Jenkinson; two *s*. *Educ:* Birmingham Univ. (BSocSc 1st cl. Hons Mathematics, Econs and Statistics); London Sch. of Economics (MSc Econometrics and Mathematical Econs (Dist)). Bank of England: Economist, 1977–90; Mem., Economic Unit, Secretariat of Cttee of Govs, European Union Central Banks, 1990–93 (on secondment); Dep. Head, Reserves Mgt, 1993–94; Head, Structural Economic Analysis Div., 1994–98; Dep. Dir, Monetary Analysis and Statistics, 1999–2003; Exec. Dir, Financial Stability, 2003–09; Advr to Gov., 2009. Mem., REconS. *Recreations:* football, cricket, reading. *Address:* Financial Stability Board, Bank for International Settlements, Centralbahnplatz 2, 4002, Basel, Switzerland. *Club:* Colchester United Supporters Association.

JENKINSON, Philip; DL; Chairman, Active Devon Sports Partnership, since 2005; *b* 2 June 1948; *s* of Harold Jenkinson and Edith Florence Jenkinson (*née* Phillipson); *m* 1970, Sandra Elizabeth Cornish; four *s*. *Educ:* Manchester Grammar Sch.; Univ. of Exeter (LLB 1st Cl. Hons); Liverpool Poly. Trainee solicitor, Gillingham BC, Kent, 1970–72; admitted solicitor, 1972; Asst Solicitor, Bath CC, 1972–74; Devon County Council: Solicitor, 1974–95; Chief Exec., and Clerk to the Lieutenancy, 1995–2006. Director: Prosper (formerly Devon and Cornwall TEC), 1995–2002; Cornwall and Devon Connexions, 2001–12. Governor: Exeter Coll., 2005–13 (Chm., 2008–10); Southbrook Special Sch., 2010–; Exeter Mathematics Sch., 2014–. DL Devon, 2006. FRSA. *Recreations:* walking designated footpaths, music.

JENKINSON, Prof. Timothy John, DPhil; Professor of Finance, Saïd Business School, University of Oxford, since 2006; Fellow, Keble College, Oxford, since 1987; *b* Hockley, Essex, 12 April 1961; *s* of John and Jean Jenkinson; *m* 1986, Rebecca Priestman; two *s*. *Educ:* Greensward Sch.; Churchill Coll., Cambridge (BA Econs 1982); Univ. of Pennsylvania (MA Econs 1983); Christ Church, Oxford (DPhil Econs 1986). Lectr in Econs, 1987–2000, Reader in Business Econs, 2000–05, Oxford Univ.; Dir, Oxford Private Equity Inst., 2009–. Chm., Oxera Ltd, 2008–. *Publications:* Going Public, 1996, 2nd edn 2001; Readings in Microeconomics, 1996, 2nd edn 2000; Readings in Macroeconomics, 1996, 2nd edn 2000; Competition in Regulated Industries, 1998; contrib. articles to internat. academic jls. *Recreations:* travel, cycling, family, theatre, watching football and Rugby. *Address:* Saïd Business School, University of Oxford, Park End Street, Oxford OX1 1HP. *T:* (01865) 288916. *E:* tim.jenkinson@sbs.ox.ac.uk.

JENKS, Prof. Christopher, FAcSS; sociologist; Vice-Chancellor and Principal, Brunel University, 2006–12, now Emeritus Professor; *b* 12 June 1947; *y s* of late Arthur Jenks and Alice Elizabeth Jenks; *m* Barbara Read; two *d*. *Educ:* Westminster City Sch.; Univ. of Surrey (BSc 1969); Univ. of London; PGCE 1970, MSc Econ 1971, London Univ. Goldsmiths' College, London University: Lectr, 1971–76, Sen. Lectr, then Reader, 1976–94, in Sociology; Prof. of Sociology, 1995–2004; Pro-Warden, 1995–2000; Prof. of Sociology and Pro-Vice-Chancellor, Brunel Univ., 2004–06. Ed., Childhood jl, 1995–. FAcSS (AcSS 2000). FRSA 2006; FRSocMed 2008; FCGI 2011; FGCL 2012. Hon. Freeman, Water Conservators' Co., 2011. Hon. PhD Univ. of Sci. and Technol., Trondheim, 2005. *Publications:* Rationality, Education and the Social Organization of Knowledge, 1976; (ed jtly) Worlds Apart, 1977; (jtly) Toward a Sociology of Education, 1977; (ed) The Sociology of Childhood, 1982; Culture, 1993, 2nd edn 2005; Cultural Reproduction, 1993; Visual Culture, 1995; Childhood, 1996, 2nd edn 2005; (jtly) Theorizing Childhood, 1998; (ed) Core Sociological Dichotomies, 1998; (jtly) Images of Community: Durkheim, social systems and the sociology of art, 2000; Aspects of Urban Culture, 2001; Culture, 4 vols, 2002; Transgression, 2003; Urban Culture, 4 vols, 2004; Subculture: the fragmentation of the social, 2004; Childhood, 3 vols, 2005; (jtly) Qualitative Complexity, 2006; Transgression, 4 vols, 2006; articles in British Jl of Sociology, Theory, Culture and Society, Cultural Values and others. *Recreations:* cricket, art and literature, previously rock climbing and mountaineering. *Address:* c/o Brunel University, Uxbridge, Middx UB8 3PH. *Clubs:* Athenæum, Chelsea Arts, MCC.

JENKS, Sir (Richard) Peter, 4th Bt *cr* 1932, of Cheape in the City of London; FCA; *b* 28 June 1936; *yr s* of Sir Richard Atherley Jenks, 2nd Bt and of Marjorie Suzanne Arlette Jenks (*née* du Cros); *S* brother, 2004; *m* 1963, Juniper Li-Yung Foo; one *s* two *d*. *Educ:* Charterhouse; Grenoble Univ. FCA 1959. Lieut, Royal Inniskilling Dragoon Guards, 1959–61. Articled chartered accountancy clerk, 1954–59; stockbroking, 1962–88: Partner, Govett Sons & Co.; Partner and Finance Dir, Hoare Govett; Dir, Security Pacific Bank Ltd. *Recreations:* ski-ing, mountaineering, olive farming, butterflies, wine, travel, astronomy, charity work. *Heir: s* Richard Albert Benedict Jenks, *b* 27 Feb. 1965. *Address:* 81 Onslow Square, SW7 3LT. *T:* (020) 7589 6295, *Fax:* (020) 7584 9952. *E:* peter.jenks@virgin.net; Sornanino, Loc. Casafrassi, 53011 Castellina in Chianti, Siena, Italy.

JENKYNS, Andrea Marie; MP (C) Morley and Outwood, since 2015; *b* Beverley, 16 June 1974; *d* of late Clifford Jenkyns. *Educ:* Marton Primary Sch., Holderness; Open Univ. (Dip. Econs); Univ. of Lincoln (BA Internat. Relns and Politics 2014). Soprano singer and songwriter; music tutor in secondary schs, Lincs CC; musical theatre dir, two children's performing arts academies. Mem. (C), Lincs CC, 2009–13. Trustee, MRSA Action UK. *Address:* House of Commons, SW1A 0AA.

JENNER, Ann Maureen; freelance ballet teacher; Ballet Teacher, Australian Ballet School, 1999–2008; Guest Ballet Teacher: Royal Ballet School; Australian Ballet; Queensland Ballet, and many other schools in Sydney and Melbourne; also guest choreographer; *b* 8 March 1944; *d* of Kenneth George Jenner and Margaret Rosetta (*née* Wilson); *m* 1980, Dale Robert Baker; one *s*. *Educ:* Royal Ballet Junior and Senior Schools. Royal Ballet Co., 1961–78: Soloist 1964; Principal Dancer 1970. Australian Ballet, 1978–80. Associate Dir, 1987, Dir, 1988–94, Nat. Theater Ballet Sch., Melbourne. Roles include: Lise, Fille Mal Gardée, 1966; Swanhilda, Coppelia, 1968; Cinderella, 1969; Princess Aurora, Sleeping Beauty, 1972; Giselle, 1973; Gypsy, Deux Pigeons, 1974; White Girl, Deux Pigeons, 1976; Juliet, Romeo and Juliet, 1977; Countess Larisch, Mayerling, 1978; Flavia, Spartacus, 1979; Kitri, Don Quixote, 1979; Anna, Anna Karenina, 1980; Poll, Pineapple Poll, 1980; one-act roles include: Symphonic Variations, 1967; Firebird, 1972; Triad, 1973; Les Sylphides; Serenade; Les Patineurs; Elite Syncopations, Concert, Flower Festival Pas de Deux, etc. Guest Teacher, San Francisco Ballet Co. and San Francisco Ballet Sch., 1985.

JENNER, Prof. Peter George, PhD, DSc; FRPharmS; Professor of Pharmacology, King's College London School of Biomedical Sciences (formerly Guy's, King's, and St Thomas' School of Biomedical Sciences), King's College London, 1989–2008, now Emeritus Professor; *b* 6 July 1946; *s* of late George Edwin Jenner and Edith (*née* Hallett); *m* (marr. diss. 2003); one *s*; *m* 2014, Melanie Gardner. *Educ:* Chelsea Coll., London Univ. (BPharm Hons 1967; PhD 1970; DSc 1987). FRPharmS 1994; FBPhS (FBPharmacolS 2005). Post-doctoral Fellow, Dept of Pharmacy, Chelsea Coll., London, 1970–72; Lectr in Biochem., 1972–78, Sen. Lectr, 1978–85, Dept of Neurol., Inst. of Psychiatry, Univ. of London, 1972–78; King's College, London University: Reader in Neurochem. Pharmacol., Inst. of Psychiatry and KCH Med. Sch., 1985–89; Hon. Sen. Lectr, Inst. of Neurol., 1988–2000; Prof. of Pharmacology and Head, Dept of Pharmacology, 1989–98, Head, Div. of Pharmacology and Therapeutics, GKT Sch. of Biomed. Scis, 1998–2004; FKC 2006. Director: Exptl Res. Labs, Parkinson's Disease Soc., 1988–99; Neurodegenerative Diseases Res. Centre, 1993–. Dir, Primagen Ltd, 1999–; Dir and CSO, Proximagen Ltd, 2005–10; CSO, Chrnos Therapeutics, 2015–. Adjunct Prof. of Neurology, Univ. of Miami, USA, 1997–99. Parkinson's Disease Society: Mem. Council, 1993–99 (Hon. Sec. to Council, 1996–99); Mem., Med. Adv. Panel, 1993–99. Mem., Molecular and Cellular Pharmacol. Gp Cttee, Biochem. Soc., 1993–2000. Mem., Bd of Mgt, Inst. of Epileptology, KCL, 1994–2003. Vice-Pres., Eur. Soc. for Clin. Pharmacol., 2001–08. Mem., Med. Adv. Bd, Bachman-Strauss Foundn, 2000–05. FRSocMed 2011. European Ed., Synapse, 1990–2015; Series Editor: Neurosci. Perspectives, 1991–96; (jtly) Internat. Review of Neurobiol., 1996–; Handling Editor: Jl of Neurochemistry, 1998–2008; Neuropharmacology, 2002–; Jl of Neural Transmission; Member, Editorial Board: Jl of Pharmacy and Pharmacology; Polish Jl of Pharmacology, 2002–. *Publications:* (with B. Testa) Drug Metabolism: chemical and biochemical aspects, 1976; (ed with B. Testa) Concepts in Drug Metabolism, Part A 1980, Part B 1981; (ed jtly) Approaches to the Use of Bromocriptine in Parkinson's Disease, 1985; (ed jtly) Neurological Disorders, 1987; (ed) Neurotoxins and their Pharmacological Implications, 1987; (ed jtly) Disorders of Movement, 1989; (ed jtly) Neuroprotection in Parkinson's Disease, vol. 3:

beyond the decade of the brain, 1998; (ed jtly) Biomedical and Health Research, vol. 19: dopamine receptor subtypes, 1998; contrib. Lancet, Jl Neurochem., Annals Neurol., Biochem. Pharmacol., Brain Res., Psychopharmacol., Neurosci.; Exptl Neurol.; Jl Pharmacol Exptl Therapeutics; Pharmacol. & Therapeutics; Eur. Jl of Pharmacol.; Clinical Neuropharmacol.; Jl of Neurochem. *Recreations:* gardening, driving. *Address:* Neurodegenerative Diseases Research Centre, Hodgkin Building, King's College London School of Biomedical Sciences, Guy's Campus, London Bridge, SE1 1UL. *T:* (020) 7848 6010. *Club:* Athenæum.

JENNER, Air Marshal Sir Timothy (Ivo), KCB 2000 (CB 1996); FRAeS; Chairman, Board of Trustees, Thames Valley and Chiltern Air Ambulance, since 2011; *b* 31 Dec. 1945; *s* of Harold Ivo Jenner and Josephine Dorothy Jenner; *m* 1968, Susan Lesley Stokes; two *d. Educ:* Maidstone Grammar Sch.; RAF Coll., Cranwell. Wessex Sqdn Pilot and Instructor, UK, ME and Germany, 1968–75; Puma Pilot and Instructor, 1976–78; MoD Desk Officer, Helicopter, 1979–80; Army Staff Coll., Camberley, 1981; OC 33 Sqdn, 1982–84; Military Assistant to: ACDS (Commitments), 1985; DCDS (Programmes & Personnel), 1986; OC, RAF Shawbury, 1987–88; RCDS 1989; Dep. Dir, Air Force Plans, 1990–91; Dir, Defence Progs, 1992–93; AO Plans, HQ Strike Command, 1993; Asst Chief of Defence Staff (Costs Review), 1993–95; ACAS, 1995–98; COS and Dep. C-in-C, Strike Comd, 1998–2000; Comdr, NATO Combined Air Ops Centre 9, 2000; Dir, European Air Gp, 2000; Strategic Advr, Serco Gp, 2001–03; Chm., Serco Defence, then Serco Defence and Aerospace, 2003–05; Sen. Advr, Serco Defence, Sci. and Nuclear (formerly Sen. Military Advr, Serco Defence and Aerospace, then Sen. Advr, Serco Defence, Sci. and Technol.), 2005–11. Advr, Atmaana Ltd, 2006–10. Non-exec. Dir, NATS, 1996–98. FRAeS 1997 (Mem. Council, 2001–03; Pres., Coventry Br., 2002–). *Recreations:* old cars, photography, mountain walking. *Address:* c/o Lloyds, PO Box 1190, 7 Pall Mall, SW1Y 5NA. *Club:* Royal Air Force.

JENNINGS, Alex Michael; actor; *b* 10 May 1957; *s* of Michael Thomas Jennings and Peggy Patricia Jennings (*née* Mahoney); partner, Lesley Moors; one *s* one *d. Educ:* Abbs Cross Tech. High Sch., Hornchurch; Univ. of Warwick (BA); Bristol Old Vic Theatre Sch. *Theatre:* début, Orchard Theatre Co., 1980; The Country Wife, Royal Exchange, Manchester, 1986; seasons at York, Cambridge Th. Co., Bristol Old Vic; Associate Actor with RSC, Stratford and London: Measure for Measure, Taming of the Shrew, Hyde Park, 1987–88; Richard II, 1991–92; Peer Gynt (Olivier Award for Best Actor, 1996), Measure for Measure, A Midsummer Night's Dream, 1994–96; Hamlet (also in NY and Washington) (Helen Hayes Award for Best Actor, 1999), Much Ado About Nothing, 1996–98; Associate Actor with Royal National Theatre: Ghetto, 1989; The Recruiting Officer, 1992; The Winter's Tale, The Relapse (Evening Standard Award for Best Actor), 2001; Albert Speer, 2000; His Girl Friday, 2003; Stuff Happens, 2004; The Alchemist, 2006; Present Laughter, 2007; The Habit of Art, 2009; Collaborators, 2011; Hymn, 2012; Cocktail Sticks, 2012; other London appearances include: Too Clever By Half, 1986 (Olivier Award for Best Comedy Performance, London Theatre Critics' Award for Best Actor, 1987), The Liar, 1987, Old Vic; The Wild Duck, Peter Hall Co., 1990; The Importance of Being Earnest, Aldwych, 1993; My Fair Lady, Th. Royal, Drury Lane (Olivier Award for Best Actor in a Musical), 2002; Candide, ENO, 2008, Japan, 2010; My Fair Lady, Théâtre du Châtelet, 2010, 2013; Charlie and the Chocolate Factory, Th. Royal, Drury Lane, 2014; *films:* War Requiem, 1988; A Midsummer Night's Dream, 1995; Wings of the Dove, 1996; The Four Feathers, 2002; Five Children and It, 2004; Bridget Jones: The Edge of Reason, 2004; The Queen, 2006; Babel, 2007; Trap for Cinderella, 2013; Belle, 2014; *television*: Ashenden, 1992; Bad Blood, 1999; Riot at the Rite, 2005; A Very Social Secretary, 2005; State Within, 2006; Cranford, 2007; 10 Days to War, 2008; Hancock and Joan, 2008; Whitechapel, 2009, 2010; Return to Cranford, 2009; On Expenses, 2010; Silk, 2011–14; We'll Take Manhattan, 2012; The Lady Vanishes, 2013; Castles in the Sky, 2014; Foyle's War, 2015; *concert work:* Peer Gynt (with Gothenberg SO), 1993; with London Mozart Players: The Soldier's Tale, 2001; The Crocodiamond, 2004; Tamos, King of Egypt, 2006; with Medici Quartet, Hymn, 2011; extensive radio work. Hon. DLitt Warwick, 1999. *Recreations:* books, painting, shopping. *Address:* c/o Independent Talent Group Ltd, 40 Whitfield Street, W1T 2RH. *T:* (020) 7636 6565.

JENNINGS, Audrey Mary; Metropolitan Stipendiary Magistrate, 1972–99; *b* 22 June 1928; *d* of Hugh and Olive Jennings, Ashbrook Range, Sunderland; *m* 1961, Roger Harry Kilbourne Frisby, QC (marr. diss. 1980; he *d* 2001); two *s* one *d. Educ:* Durham High Sch.; Durham Univ. (BA); Oxford Univ. (DPA). Children's Officer, City and County of Cambridge, 1952–56. Called to Bar, Middle Temple, 1956 (Harmsworth Schol.); practised at Criminal Bar, London, 1956–61 and 1967–72. Occasional opera critic, Musical Opinion. *Recreations:* theatre, music, gardening, writing short stories.

JENNINGS, Colin Brian; Special Professor of Diplomacy, University of Nottingham, since 2006; *b* 27 Nov. 1952; *s* of Brian Jennings and Jean (*née* Thomas); *m* 1978, Jane Barfield. *Educ:* Hereford Cathedral Sch.; Univ. of Leicester (BA 1975; MA 1976). Joined MoD, 1976; Procurement Executive, 1976–78; Defence Secretariat, 1979; Second Sec., UK Delegn to NATO, 1980–81 (on secondment); Principal Defence Secretariat, 1982–83; HM Diplomatic Service, 1983–2006; Policy Planning Staff, FCO, 1983–86; First Sec. (Economic), Lagos, 1986–89; Asst, Central and Southern Africa Dept, FCO, 1990–92; Dep. High Comr, Nicosia, 1992–96; Chief Exec., Wilton Park Exec. Agency, FCO, 1996–2006. Vice Chair, Diplomatic Service Appeal Bd, 2007–11. Vis. Lectr, Inst. of Policy Studies, Rennes and Univ. of Rennes, 2007–10. Internat. Advr, Electoral Reform Internat. Services, 2009–11. West Cornwall Rep., Cornwall Homeseekers Ltd, 2011–13; Partner, Sherlock Homes, 2013–. *Recreations:* supporting the Cornish Pirates Rugby team, walking the fox terrier. *Address:* The Print Works, Market Place, Marazion, Cornwall TR17 0AR.

JENNINGS, Rt Rev. David Willfred Michael; Bishop Suffragan of Warrington, 2000–09; an Honorary Assistant Bishop: Diocese of Gloucester, since 2010; Diocese of Oxford, since 2013; *b* 13 July 1944; *s* of late Rev. Willfred Jennings and Nona Jennings (*née* de Winton); *m* 1969, Sarah Catherine Fynn, *d* of late Dr Robert Fynn of Harare, Zimbabwe; three *s. Educ:* Summer Fields, Oxford; Radley Coll.; King's Coll., London (AKC 1966). Ordained deacon, 1967, priest, 1968; Assistant Curate: St Mary, Walton on the Hill, Liverpool, 1967–69; Christchurch Priory, Christchurch, Hants, 1969–73; Vicar: Hythe, Southampton, 1973–80; St Edward, Romford, 1980–92; Rural Dean of Havering, 1985–92; Archdeacon of Southend, 1992–2000. Commissary for Bishop of Bahamas, 1986–; Commissary (Acting Bishop), Dio. of Sodor and Man, 2007–08; non-residentiary Canon, Chelmsford Cathedral, 1987–92. Chair, Retired Clergy Assoc., 2012–. Mem., Governing Council, Liverpool Hope Univ. (formerly UC), 2000–09 (Vice Chm., 2007–09); Gov., Summer Fields, Oxford, 2010–. *Recreations:* exploring the buildings of the British Isles, walking, reading, listening to music. *Address:* Laurel Cottage, East End, Northleach, near Cheltenham, Glos GL54 3ET. *T:* (01451) 860743.

JENNINGS, Sir John (Southwood), Kt 1997; CBE 1985; PhD; FRSE; Director, Shell Transport and Trading Company plc, 1987–2001 (Chairman, 1993–97); Vice Chairman, Committee of Managing Directors, Royal Dutch/Shell Group of Companies, 1993–97; Managing Director, Royal Dutch/Shell Group of Companies, 1987–97; *b* 30 March 1937; *s* of George Southwood Jennings and Irene Beatrice Jennings; *m* 1961, Gloria Ann Griffiths (marr. diss. 1996); one *s* one *d*; *m* Linda Elizabeth Baston. *Educ:* Oldbury Grammar Sch.; Univ. of Birmingham (BSc Hons Geology, 1958); Univ. of Edinburgh (PhD Geology, 1961); London Business Sch. (Sloan Fellow, 1970–71). Various posts, Royal Dutch/Shell Group, 1962–2001, including: Gen. Man. and Chief Rep., Shell cos in Turkey, 1976–78; Man. Dir, Shell UK Exploration and Prodn, 1979–84; Exploration and Prodn Co-ordinator, Shell Internationale Petroleum Mij., The Hague, 1985–90. Non-executive Director: Robert Fleming Holdings, 1997–2000; Det Norske Veritas, 1997–2001; MITIE Gp, 1997–2007 (Dep. Chm., 1997–2007); Bechtel Gp Internat., 2002–08; Mem., Internat. Adv. Bd, Toyota, 1997–2005; Chairman: Spectron Gp, 2000–05; Intelligent Energy, 2001–05. Vice Chm., Governing Body, London Business Sch., 1993–97 (Mem., 1992–); Vice Pres., Liverpool Sch. of Tropical Medicine, 1991–97; Member Council: RIIA, 1994–97; Exeter Univ., 1997–99. Chancellor, Loughborough Univ., 2003–10. FRSE 1992. Hon. FGS 1992. Hon. DSc: Edinburgh, 1991; Birmingham, 1997. Commandeur de l'Ordre National du Mérite (Gabon), 1989. *Recreations:* fly fishing, travel. *Clubs:* Brooks's, Flyfishers'.

JENNINGS, Rev. Jonathan Peter; Priest-in-charge, St Augustine's, Gillingham, since 2008; *b* 6 March 1961; *s* of John Harold Jennings and Margaret Jennings (*née* Amps); *m* 1998, Helen Jarvis; two *s* one *d. Educ:* Grangefield Grammar Sch., Stockton-on-Tees; Stockton 6th Form Coll.; KCL (BD); Westcott House, Cambridge. Ordained deacon, 1986, priest, 1987; Curate: St Cuthbert Peterlee, 1986–89; St Cuthbert Darlington, 1989–92; Press and Communications Officer, Dio. Manchester, 1992–95; Broadcasting Officer, Gen. Synod of C of E, 1995–98; Hd of Broadcasting, Archbps' Council, 1998–2001; Press Sec. to Archbp of Canterbury, 2001–08. Rural Dean of Gillingham, 2010–11. Producer, religious progs, and news and sports journalist, 1987–2000. Chaplain to HM Forces (V), 1993–. *Recreations:* early music, Middlesbrough FC, cricket, sea fishing, steam railways. *Address:* St Augustine's Vicarage, Rock Avenue, Gillingham, Kent ME7 5PW.

JENNINGS, Rev. Peter; educational and interfaith consultant; *b* 9 Oct. 1937; *s* of Robert William Jennings and Margaret Irene Jennings; *m* 1963, Cynthia Margaret Leicester; two *s. Educ:* Manchester Grammar Sch.; Keble Coll., Oxford (MA); Hartley Victoria Methodist Theological Coll.; Manchester Univ. (MA). Ordained 1965. Minister: Swansea Methodist Circuit, 1963–67; London Mission (East) Circuit, 1967–78, and Tutor Warden, Social Studies Centre, 1967–74; Gen. Sec., Council of Christians and Jews, 1974–81; Associate Minister, Wesley's Chapel, 1978–81; Asst Minister, Walthamstow and Chingford Methodist Circuit, 1981–82; Superintendent Minister: Whitechapel Mission, 1982–91; Barking and Ilford Methodist Circuit, 1991–93; Dir, N E London Religious Educn Centre, 1993–98; Associate Minister: Cambridge Methodist Circuit, 1998–2003; Welshpool and Bro Hafren Methodist Circuit, 2003–06; retired to Wales Circuit, Synod Cymru, 2006. Pastoral Tutor, Centre for Jewish-Christian Relns, Wesley House, Cambridge Univ., 1999–2003. *Publications:* papers and articles on aspects of Christian-Jewish relations. *Recreations:* photography, being educated by Tim and Nick and now by their respective children, Dan, Leah, Dillon and Rosie. *Address:* 5 Cuffnell Close, Liddell Park, Llandudno LL30 1UX. *T:* (01492) 860449.

JENNINGS, Sir Peter (Nevile Wake), Kt 2000; CVO 1999; Serjeant at Arms, House of Commons, 1995–99; *b* 19 Aug. 1934; *s* of late Comdr A. E. de B. Jennings, RN and Mrs V. Jennings, MBE; *m* 1958, Shirley Anne (*d* 2012), *d* of late Captain B. J. Fisher, DSO, RN and Mrs C. C. Fisher; one *s* two *d. Educ:* Marlborough College; psc (m)†, osc (US). Commissioned 2/Lt, RM, 1952; retired, 1976. Appointed to staff of House of Commons, 1976. Chairman: Central London Br., SSAFA Forces Help, 2001–12; St Martin-in-the-Fields Almshouse Charity, 2004–10; Bowles (formerly Bowles Outdoor Centre), 2004–10; Dep. Chm., 2011–14, Chm., 2014–15, ESU. *Address:* Cross Farm, Chilmark, Salisbury SP3 5AR.

JENNINGS, Robert Samuel, MBE 2003; DPhil; Principal, Slemish College, Ballymena, 1996–2010; *b* 29 Aug. 1949; *s* of James and Elizabeth Jennings; *m* 1978, Jennifer Titterington; one *s* one *d. Educ:* Stranmillis Coll., Belfast (Cert Ed); London Bible Coll. (BA Hons Theol.); Queen's Univ., Belfast (MTh); Univ. of Ulster (DPhil); Open Univ. (MA). Head of physical educn, 1971–73, and of RE, 1973–75, Antrim High Sch.; Asst Teacher of RE, Wallace High Sch., Lisburn, 1978–80; Head of RE, Rainey Endowed Sch., Magherafelt, 1980–94; Asst Adv. Officer for RE, Western Educn and Library Bd, 1994–96. Pt-time Lectr, Post Grad. Cert. in Expert Teaching, Univ. of Ulster, 1999–. *Publications:* (contrib.) New International Version Thematic Study Bible, 1996. *Recreations:* golf, walking.

JENNINGS, Saira Kabir; *see* Sheikh, S. K.

JENNINGS, Thomas James, CBE 2004; CEng, FIMechE; Chairman, Ducales Capital Ltd, since 2013; *b* 1 March 1954; *s* of Gerald and Dorithia Jennings; *m* 1978, Jane Speers; two *s* one *d. Educ:* Queen's Univ. of Belfast (BSc). CEng, FIMechE. Grad. engr, 1975; subseq. held mgt posts; Chm. and Man. Dir, Rotary Gp Ltd, 1997–2009; Chm., Ballyrogan Hldgs Ltd, 2008. FRSA 2004. *Recreation:* country sports. *T:* (028) 9181 1361.

JENNY, Prof. Frédéric, PhD; Professor of Economics, Business School, since 1972, and Co-director, European Centre for Law and Economics, since 2010, École Supérieure des Sciences Économiques et Commerciales, Paris; *b* Geneva, 29 Sept. 1943; *s* of Frederic Marc Jenny and Madeleine Jenny (*née* Permezel); *m* 1984, Sarah Harrison Beers. *Educ:* Business Sch., École Supérieure des Scis Écon. et Commerciales, Paris (MBA 1966); Harvard Univ. (PhD Econs 1975); Univ. of Paris (Dr Econs 1977). Judge, French Supreme Court, 2004–12. Visiting Professor: Keio Univ., Tokyo, 1984; UCL, 2005–; Faculty of Law, Haifa Univ., Israel, 2012; Vis. Lectr, Cape Town Business Sch., SA, 1991. French Competition Authority: Rapporteur, 1978–84, Rapporteur Gen., 1984–93; Vice-Chm., 1993–2004. Mem. Bd, OFT, 2007–14. Chm., Competition Cttee, OECD, 1994–; Pres., Wkg Gp on Trade and Competition, WTO, 1994–2003; Mem., Adv. Bd, Interdisciplinary Centre for Competition Law and Initiative, Middle East Initiative, 2010–. Chm., Scientific Bd, Consumer Unity Trust of India (CUTS), 2009–. Member, Editorial Board: Concurrences, 2008–; World Competition, 2009–; Jl Competition Law and Econs, 2012–. Officier de la Légion d'honneur (France), 2003 (Chevalier, 1992); Officier de l'Ordre du Mérite (France), 1999 (Chevalier, 1988). *Publications:* book chapters; contribs to jls incl. Actualité Juridique, Droit Administratif, Antitrust Bull., Competition Policy, Concurrences, Economia Industrial, Eur. Business Orgn Law Rev., Eur. Econ. Rev., Eur. Merger Control Reporter, Fordham Internat. Law Jl, Internat. Antitrust Law and Policy, Internat. Business Lawyer, Jl Econ. Literature, OECD Jl Competition Law and Policy, Oxera, Rev. d'Economie Industrielle, Rev. française de gestion, Semaine Juridique, Rev. des Affaires Européennes, Rev. de la Concurrence et de la Consommation, Rev. de jurisprudence commerciales, Rev. Lamy de la Concurrence, World Competition Law and Econs Rev. *Recreations:* hiking, sailing. *Address:* 19 rue de l'Estrapade, 75005 Paris, France. *T:* 674654437. *E:* frederic.jenny@gmail.com.

JENRICK, Robert; MP (C) Newark, since June 2014; *b* Wolverhampton, 1982; *m* 2009, Michal Berkner; three *d. Educ:* Wolverhampton Grammar Sch.; St John's Coll., Cambridge (BA 1st Cl. Hist. 2003); Univ. of Pennsylvania (Thouron Fellow 2004); Coll. of Law (Grad. Dip. Law 2005); BPP Law Sch. (Legal Practice Course 2006). Trainee solicitor, Skadden Arps, Slate, Meagher & Flom LLP, 2006–08; admitted as solicitor, 2008; Solicitor, Sullivan & Cromwell LLP, 2008–10; Sen. Exec. and Internat. Man. Dir, Decorative Arts Div., Christie's, 2010–14. PPS to Parly Under-Sec. for Energy and Climate Change, 2014–15, to Employment Minister, 2015. Mem., Health Select Cttee, 2014–15. Contested (C) Newcastle-under-Lyme, 2010. *Address:* House of Commons, SW1A 0AA; Belvedere, 29a London Road, Newark-on-Trent NG24 1TN.

JENSEN, Elisabeth, (Liz), FRSL; writer; *b* Oxon, 26 Nov. 1959; *d* of Niels Rosenvinge Jensen and Valerie Jensen (*née* Corcos); *m* 2010, Carsten Jensen; two *s. Educ:* Oxford High Sch.; Somerville Coll., Oxford (BA Hons Eng. Lang. and Lit.). Journalist, South China Morning Post, Hong Kong, 1979–80; radio journalist, ICRT, Taiwan, 1982–83; news reporter and documentary producer, BBC, 1983–87; freelance radio producer and journalist,

1987–95; novelist, critic and creative writing teacher, 1995–. Writer in Residence, Kingston Univ., 2006. FRSL 2005. *Publications:* Egg Dancing, 1995; Ark Baby, 1998; The Paper Eater, 2000; War Crimes for the Home, 2002; The Ninth Life of Louis Drax, 2004; My Dirty Little Book of Stolen Time, 2006; The Rapture, 2009; The Uninvited, 2012. *Address:* c/o Aitken Alexander Associates, 291 Gray's Inn Road, WC1X 8EB. *E:* liz.jensen@rocketmail.com.

JENSEN, Rt Rev. Peter; Archbishop of Sydney, and Metropolitan of the Province of New South Wales, 2001–13; *b* 11 July 1943; *s* of Arthur Henry Jensen and Dorothy Lake Jensen (*née* Wilins); *m* 1968, Christine Willis Jensen (*née* O'Donell); three *s* two *d*. *Educ:* Univ. of London (BD 1970); Sydney Univ. (MA 1976); Magdalen Coll., Oxford (DPhil 1980). Ordained deacon, 1969, priest, 1970, Anglican Ch of Australia; Curate, Broadway, 1969–76; Asst Minister, St Andrew, N Oxford, 1976–79; Moore College: Lectr, 1973–76 and 1980–84; Principal, 1985–2001. *Publications:* The Quest for Power, 1973; At the Heart of the Universe, 1991; The Revelation of God, 2002; The Future of Jesus, 2005; Power and Promise, 2014. *Recreations:* golf, reading. *Address:* 102/7 Karrabee Avenue, Huntleys Cove, NSW 2111, Australia.

JENSEN, Tom Risdahl; Ambassador of Denmark to Russia, 2010–15; *b* 28 Sept. 1947; *s* of Laust and Eva Jensen; *m* 2001, Helle Bundgaard. *Educ:* Univ. of Aarhus, Denmark (BA Scand. Lit. and Langs; MSc Political Sci.). Entered Ministry of Foreign Affairs, Copenhagen, 1977; First Sec., Danish Perm. EU Repn, 1981–84; Hd of Section, 1984–88; Econ. Counsellor, Bonn, 1988–92; Hd of Dept, 1992–97; Under-Sec., 1997–2001; Ambassador: to UK, 2001–06; to Sweden, 2006–10.

JEPHCOTT, Sir David Welbourn, 4th Bt *cr* 1962, of East Portlemouth, Devon; *b* 9 Aug. 1952; *er s* of Sir Neil Welbourn Jephcott, 3rd Bt and Mary Denise (*née* Muddiman); *S* father, 2012; *m* 1977, Madeleine Ann, *d* of Maurice Arthur Burridge; one *d*. *Heir:* *b* Mark Lanwer Jephcott [*b* 23 Feb. 1957; *m* 1st, 1983, Lysa Ann Rigden; one *s* one *d*; 2nd, 2010, Dr Sarah Brigitte Vardy].

JEPSON, Martin Clive; President and Chief Operating Officer, Brookfield Office Properties, Europe, since 2013; *b* Leeds, 6 April 1962; *s* of Donald Jepson and Mildred Jepson; *m* 1988, Anne Cleaver; one *s* one *d*. *Educ:* Garforth Comp. Sch.; Bristol Poly. (BSc Hons Valuation and Estate Mgt 1983). ARICS 1986, FRICS 1999. Director: Sinclair Goldsmith, 1987–93; Conrad Ritblat, 1993–95; Milner Estates, 1995–98; Delancey, 1998–2000; London Regl Dir, Taylor Woodrow Property Co., 2000–03; Chief Exec., Southside Capital, 2003–05; UK Man. Dir, Howard Hldgs, 2005–08; Man. Dir, London Gp, Hammerson plc, 2008–11; Sen. Vice Pres., Brookfield Office Properties, 2011–13. Trustee and Dir, Sparks, 2012–. *Recreations:* golf, Rugby, cricket, football, walking, cinema, family, reading. *Address:* Brookfield Office Properties, Europe, 99 Bishopsgate, EC2M 3XD. *T:* (020) 7408 8277. *E:* martin.jepson@brookfield.com. *Clubs:* Arts; Walton Heath Golf.

JEREMIAH, Melvyn Gwynne, CB 1994; Chairman, Wages and Salary Commission, Republic of Namibia, 1995–97; *b* 10 March 1939; *s* of Bryn Jeremiah and Evelyn (*née* Rogers); *m* 1960, Lilian Clare (*née* Bailey) (marr. diss. 1966). *Educ:* Abertillery County Sch. Apptd to Home Office, 1958; HM Customs and Excise, 1963–75; Cabinet Office, 1975–76; Treasury, 1976–79; Principal Finance Officer (Under Sec.), Welsh Office, 1979–87; Under Sec., DHSS, later DoH, 1987–95; Chief Exec., Disablement Services Authy, 1987–91, on secondment from DoH. Special Advr to Govt of Repub. of Namibia, 1995–97. Sec., Assoc. of First Div. Civil Servants, 1967–70. Pres., Internat. Assoc. of Amateur Heralds, 2006–10 (Sec., 2002–04); Hon. Secretary: Heraldry Soc., 2002–09 (Vice-Pres., 2013; Hon. Fellow, 2014); Friends of City Churches, 2006–11; Chm., White Lion Soc., 2008–. Churchwarden, 2009–15, Parish Clerk, 2011–, St Stephen Walbrook. Gov., Chelsea and Westminster Hosp. Foundn Trust, 2010–. Life FRSA 2005. Freeman, City of London, 2002; Liveryman: Co. of Scriveners, 2002; Parish Clerks' Co., 2012. JP Inner London, 2002–09. *Recreations:* heraldry, genealogy, ecclesiology. *Club:* Reform.

JEREMY, David Hugh Thomas; QC 2006; a Recorder, since 1999; *b* 3 March 1955; *s* of Tom and Sarah Jeremy; *m* 1991, Caroline Jacobs; three *s* one *d*. *Educ:* Cheltenham Coll.; Exeter Univ. (LLB). Called to the Bar, Middle Temple, 1977; in practice at the Bar specialising in criminal law. *Recreations:* reading newspapers, studying maps, watching my children play sport, camping, researching cheap red wines. *Address:* Hollis Whiteman Chambers, 1–2 Laurence Pountney Hill, EC4R 0EU. *T:* (020) 7933 8855, *Fax:* (020) 7929 3732. *E:* david.jeremy@holliswhiteman.co.uk.

JERMEY, Dominic James Robert, CVO 2010; OBE 2001; HM Diplomatic Service; International Counter-Extremism Coordinator, Foreign and Commonwealth Office, since 2015; *b* 26 April 1967; *s* of Kevin Jermey and Maureen Jermey; *m* 2003, Clare Judith Roberts; one *s* one *d*. *Educ:* Tonbridge Sch.; Clare Coll., Cambridge (BA Hons 1989). Corp. Finance Dept, J. H. Schroder Wagg & Co. Ltd, 1990–93; Foreign and Commonwealth Office, 1993–: Second Sec. (Pol), then First Sec. (Afghanistan), Islamabad, 1995–99; First Sec., Skopje, 1999; British Rep., East Timor, 2000; peacekeeping and crisis related roles, London and Kabul, 2000–03; Hd, British Embassy Office (Tsunami Crisis), Phuket, Jan.–Feb. 2005; Dir of Trade and Investment, 2004–06, and Dep. Hd of Mission, 2006–07, Madrid; Man. Dir, Sectors Gp, UK Trade & Investment, 2007–10 (Actg Chief Exec., 2009); Ambassador to the UAE, 2010–14; Chief Exec., UKTI, 2014–15. Trustee and Mem. Bd, CAFOD, 2008–. Freeman, 2002, Liveryman, 2009–, Cutlers' Co. *Recreations:* slow triathlete, adventure travel, diving, Hospitalité Notre Dame de Lourdes. *Address:* c/o Foreign and Commonwealth Office, King Charles Street, SW1A 2AH.

JERMEY, Michael Francis; Director of News and Current Affairs, ITV, since 2009 (Director of Sport, 2009–12); *b* London, 24 March 1964; *s* of late Clifford George Gray Jermey and Patience Jermey (*née* Hughes); *m* 2003, Caroline, *d* of Baron Taverne, *qv*; one *s*. *Educ:* City of London Sch.; Brasenose Coll., Oxford (BA PPE 1985). Current affairs journalist, Central Television, 1985–86; ITN: trainee, 1986–87; prodn journalist, News, 1987–90; Prog. Ed., News at Ten, 1990–91; Hd, Foreign News, 1991–93; Associate Ed., 1993–95, Dep. Ed., 1995–99, News; Dir of Develt, 1999–2004; Launch Man. Dir, News Channel, 2000–01; Man. Dir, ITN Internat., 2002–04; ITV plc: Ed., Regl News, 2004–07; Dir, Regions and Network News Ops, 2007–09. Commissioning Editor: First Election Debate, ITV, 2010; The Royal Wedding, ITV, 2011; ITV series: Tonight, 2009; Exposure, 2011; The Agenda, 2012; On Assignment, 2014. Non-exec. Dir, Parliamentary Broadcasting Unit Ltd, 2007–11. Chm., Creative Diversity Network's News Wkg Gp, 2013–; Mem., Defence Press and Broadcasting Adv. Cttee, 2007–. Mem., TV Cttee, BAFTA, 2009–12. Trustee, Rory Peck Trust, 2002–14 (Chm., 2011–14). Ext. Examr, Cardiff Sch. of Journalism, Cardiff Univ., 2013–. *Recreations:* family, reading, supporting Arsenal FC. *Address:* ITV plc, London Television Centre, Upper Ground, SE1 9LT. *T:* (020) 7157 6425. *E:* Michael.Jermey@itv.com.

JERRAM, (Jeremy) James, CBE 1995; Director, Railways Pension Scheme, 2007–10 (Chairman, 1996–2007); *b* 7 Aug. 1939; *s* of Lionel Jerram and Kathleen (*née* Cochrane); *m* 1965, Ruth Middleton; four *d*. *Educ:* Selwyn Coll., Cambridge (MA). FCA 1966. Arthur Andersen & Co., 1963–71; Standard Telephones & Cables, 1971–87; finance dir, computer software cos, 1987–90; Bd Mem. for Finance, then Vice-Chm., BRB, 1991–2000.

JERSEY, 10th Earl of, *cr* 1697; **George Francis William Child Villiers;** Viscount Grandison of Limerick (Ire.), 1620; Viscount Villiers of Dartford and Baron Villiers of Hoo, 1691; actor; *b* 5 Feb. 1976; *s* of George Henry Child Villiers, Viscount Villiers (*d* 1998), and of his 2nd wife, Sacha Jane Hooper Valpy (now Mrs Raymond Hubbard); *S* grandfather, 1998; *m* 2003, Marianne Simonne, *d* of Peter and Jeannette De Guelle; one *s* three *d*. *Educ:* Canford Sch.; Birmingham Sch. of Speech and Drama. Patron: Jersey RFC; Macmillan Cancer Support, Jersey; Relate, Jersey. *Recreations:* Rugby, squash, tennis, cricket, sailing, shooting. *Heir:* *s* Viscount Villiers, *qv*. *Club:* Royal Automobile.

JERSEY, Dean of; *see* Key, Very Rev. R. F.

JERVIS, family name of **Viscount St Vincent**.

JERVIS, Roger P.; *see* Parker-Jervis.

JERVIS, Simon Swynfen, FSA; Director of Historic Buildings (formerly Historic Buildings Secretary), National Trust, 1995–2002; *b* 9 Jan. 1943; *s* of late John Swynfen Jervis and Diana (*née* Marriott); *m* 1969, Fionnuala MacMahon; one *s* one *d*. *Educ:* Downside Sch.; Corpus Christi Coll., Cambridge (schol.). Student Asst, Asst Keeper of Art, Leicester Mus. and Art Gall., 1964–66; Department of Furniture, Victoria and Albert Museum: Asst Keeper, 1966–75; Dep. Keeper, 1975–89; Actg Keeper, 1989; Curator, 1989–90; Dir, Fitzwilliam Mus., Cambridge, 1990–95. Guest Schol., J. Paul Getty Mus., 1988–89, 2003; Ailsa Mellon Bruce Sen. Fellow, Center for Advanced Study in Visual Arts, Nat. Gall. of Art, Washington, 2006–07. Mem., Reviewing Cttee on Export of Works of Art, 2007–15. Chairman: Nat. Trust Arts Panel, 1987–95; Furniture Hist. Soc., 1998–2013 (Ed. Furniture Hist., 1987–92); Walpole Soc., 2003–13. Dir, Burlington Magazine, 1993– (Trustee, 1996–). Trustee: Royal Collection Trust, 1993–2001; Leche Trust, 1995–2013 (Chm., 2007–13); Sir John Soane's Mus., 1999–2002 (Life Trustee, 2002–13; Chm., 2008–13); Emery Walker Trust, 2003–12; Mem., Adv. Council, NACF, 2002–. FSA 1983 (Pres., 1995–2001). Iris Foundn award, Bard Center, NY, 2003. *Publications:* Victorian Furniture, 1968; Printed Furniture Designs Before 1650, 1974; High Victorian Design, 1983; Penguin Dictionary of Design and Designers, 1984; British and Irish Inventories, 2010; (with Dudley Dodd) Roman Splendour, English Arcadia, 2015; many articles in learned jls. *Address:* 45 Bedford Gardens, W8 7EF. *T:* (020) 7727 8739.

JESKY, John Sydney; Chair, Pennine Acute Hospitals NHS Trust, since 2006; *b* London, 12 Dec. 1945; *s* of Isaac and Elizabeth Joan Jesky; *m* 1st, 1972, Lynne Behrens (marr. diss.); twin *s*; 2nd, 2008, Christine Knight. *Educ:* William Ellis Grammar Sch.; London Univ. (BSc (Econ) Hons). Econ. and Mkt Res. Exec., Food Manufacturers' Fedn, 1969–72; Strategic Planning Exec., 1973–76, Business Develt Manager, 1976–77, Mktg and Business Develt Dir, 1977–83, Rank Hovis Ltd; Dep. Man. Dir, Campbell's Foods Ltd, 1984–88; Man. Dir, Crossley Carpets & Yarns Ltd, 1988–90; Gp Man. Dir, Waterford Foods (UK) Ltd, 1992–96; Chief Exec., Lyndale Foods Ltd, 1996–2001; Exec. Chm., FHSC Ltd, 2002–06. Chm., Organisation Development Services Ltd, 2010–11. Non-exec. Dir, Gtr Manchester Strategic HA, 2002–06. Trustee: Princess Royal Trust for Carers, 1999–2009; Music in Hospitals, 2009–13 (Chm., NW Cttee, 2009–13). Mem. Bd, Buxton Fest., 2015–. Gov., RNCM, 2000–09. Freeman, City of London, 2003. *Recreations:* opera, cricket, collecting cricket prints and forgetting their names, collecting clocks and watches. *Address:* Pennine Acute Hospitals NHS Trust, Trust Headquarters, North Manchester General Hospital, Delaunays Road, Manchester M8 5RB. *T:* (0161) 604 5451, *Fax:* (0161) 604 5470. *E:* john.jesky@pat.nhs.uk. *Club:* MCC.

JESSEL, Sir Charles (John), 3rd Bt *cr* 1883; farmer; nutrition consultant, since 1987; *b* 29 Dec. 1924; *s* of Sir George Jessel, 2nd Bt, MC, and Muriel (*d* 1948), *d* of Col J. W. Chaplin, VC; *S* father, 1977; *m* 1st, 1956, Shirley Cornelia (*d* 1977), *o d* of John Waters, Northampton; two *s* one *d*; 2nd, 1979, Gwendolyn Mary (marr. diss. 1983), *d* of late Laurance Devereux, OBE, and *widow* of Charles Langer, MA. *Educ:* Eton; Balliol College, Oxford; Northants Inst. of Agric., Moulton, 1952 (Dip with distinction); Dip., Inst. for Optimum Nutrition, 1987. Served War of 1939–45, Lieut 15/19th Hussars (despatches). Chm., Ashford Br., NFU, 1963–64; Mem., Exec. Cttee, Kent Br., NFU, 1960–73; Pres., Kent Br., Men of the Trees, 1979–85, and 1995–. Life Vice Pres., British Soc. of Dowsers, 1994 (Pres., 1987–93). Gov., Inst. for Optimum Nutrition, 1994–98 (Chm., 1997–98). Life Mem., British Inst. for Allergy and Envmtl Therapy; Mem., British Assoc. of Nutritional Therapists, 1997–2008 (Fellow, 2008). Patron, Nutritional Cancer Therapy Trust, 1998–2005. Hon. Fellow, Psionic Med. Soc., 1977 (Pres., 1995–2002; Vice Pres., 2003–); Hon. Mem., Inst. of Psionic Med., 2008. JP Kent 1960–78. *Publications:* (ed) An Anthology of Inner Silence, 1990; Memories by Request, 2011. *Recreations:* gardening, planting trees, opera, choral works. *Heir:* *s* George Elphinstone Jessel [*b* 15 Dec. 1957; *m* 1st, 1988, Rose (marr. diss. 1993), *yr d* of James Coutts-Smith; 2nd, 1998, Victoria, *y d* of Captain A. J. B. Naish, CBE, RN]. *Address:* South Hill Farm, Hastingleigh, near Ashford, Kent TN25 5HL. *T:* (01233) 750325. *Club:* Cavalry and Guards.

JESSEL, Oliver Richard; Chairman of numerous companies in the Jessel Group, 1954–89; *b* 24 Aug. 1929; *s* of late Comdr R. F. Jessel, DSO, OBE, DSC, RN; *m* 1950, Gloria Rosalie Teresa (*née* Holden); one *s* five *d*. *Educ:* Rugby. Lieut RNVR, 1953. Founded group of companies, incl. Jessel Securities Ltd, 1954; opened office in City of London, 1960; Chm., London, Australian and General Exploration Co. Ltd, 1960–75; formed: New Issue Unit Trust, Gold & General Unit Trust and other trusts, 1962–68; Castle Communications, 1983; Standard Financial Holdings, 1987; responsible for numerous mergers, incl. Johnson & Firth Brown Ltd, and Maple Macowards Ltd; Chm., Charles Clifford Industries Ltd, 1978–81; reorganised Belvoir Petroleum Corp., 1987–89; Chm., Thomas Seager PLC, 1993–2000. Mem. Cttee, Unit Trust Assoc., 1964–68. *Address:* Tilts House, Boughton Monchelsea, Maidstone, Kent ME17 4JE.

JESSEL, Toby Francis Henry; *b* 11 July 1934; *y s* of late Comdr R. F. Jessel, DSO, OBE, DSC, RN; *m* 1st, 1967 (marr. diss. 1973); one *d* decd; 2nd, 1980, Eira Gwen, *y d* of late Horace and Marigwen Heath. *Educ:* Royal Naval Coll., Dartmouth; Balliol Coll., Oxford (MA). Sub-Lt, RNVR, 1954. (Co-opted) LCC Housing Cttee, 1961–65; Councillor, London Borough of Southwark, 1964–66; Mem. for Richmond-upon-Thames, GLC, 1967–73 (Chm., S Area Bd, Planning and Transportation Cttee, 1968–70). Contested (C): Peckham, 1964; Hull North, 1966. MP (C) Twickenham, 1970–97; contested (C) same seat, 1997. Mem., Nat. Heritage Select Cttee, 1992–97. Chairman: Cons. Parly Arts and Heritage Cttee, 1983–97 (Vice-Chm., 1979); Anglo-Belgian Parly Gp, 1983–97; Indo-British Parly Gp, 1991–97 (Hon. Sec., 1972–87; Vice-Chm., 1987); Treas., Anglo-Chilean Parly Gp, 1991–93. Parliamentary delegate: to India and Pakistan, 1971; to India, 1982, 1992, 1994; to Belgium, 1994; Member: Council of Europe, 1976–92; WEU, 1976–92. Hon. Sec., Assoc. of Adopted Cons. Candidates, 1961–66. Hon. Sec., Katyn Meml Fund, 1972–75. Mem. Metropolitan Water Bd, 1967–70; Mem., London Airport Consultative Cttee, 1967–70. Mem. Council, Fluoridation Soc., 1976–83. Dir, Warship Preservation Trust, 1994–2006. Member: Exec. Cttee and Organizing Cttee, European Music Year, 1985; Council, Assoc. of British Orchestras, 1991–94. Liveryman, Worshipful Co. of Musicians. Chevalier, Ordre de la Couronne (Belgium), 1980; Order of Polonia Restituta (Polish Govt in Exile); Commander's Cross with Star, Order of Merit (Liechtenstein), 1979. *Recreations:* music (has performed Mozart, Beethoven and Schumann piano concertos; raised £30,000 for NSPCC, Nov. perf., 1993, and £40,000 Dec. perf., 1995), gardening, croquet (Longworth Cup, 1961, Younger Cup, 2002, 2004, 2008, Fox Cup, 2004, Lomas A. Cup, 2009, Hurlingham), skiing. *Address:* Alureds, Staplecross Road, Northiam, E Sussex TN31 6JJ. *Clubs:* Garrick, Hurlingham.

See also O. R. Jessel.

JESSELL, Prof. Thomas Michael, PhD; FRS 1996; FMedSci; Professor, Departments of Neuroscience and of Biochemistry and Molecular Biophysics, Columbia University, New York, since 1989; Investigator, Howard Hughes Medical Institute, since 1985; *b* 2 Aug. 1951;

s of Andre Hubert Jessell and Bettina Maria Anna Jessell (*née* Arndt); *m* 1973, Jennet Ann Priestland (marr. diss. 1981); partner, Jane Dodd; three *d. Educ:* Chelsea Coll., Univ. of London (BPharm); Trinity Coll., Cambridge Univ. (PhD 1977; Hon. Fellow, 2014). Harkness Fellow, Harvard Univ., 1978–80; Res. Fellow, Trinity Coll., Cambridge, 1979; Royal Soc. Locke Res. Fellow, St George's Hosp., London, 1980–81; Asst Prof., Dept of Neurobiol., Harvard Med. Sch., 1981–85; Associate Prof., Dept of Biochem. and Molecular Biophysics, Columbia Univ., 1985–89. FMedSci 2006. Fellow, Amer. Acad. of Arts and Scis, 1992; Mem., Inst. of Med., 2001; Foreign Assoc., NAS, 2002. Hon. DPhil Umeå, Sweden, 1998; Hon. DSc London, 2004. March of Dimes Prize, 2001; Kavli Prize in Neurosci., Norwegian Acad. of Scis and Letters, 2008; Canada Gairdner Internat. Award, 2012; Scolnick Prize, 2013; Vilcek Foundn Prize, 2014. *Publications:* edited with E. Kandel and J. Schwartz: Principles of Neural Science, 3rd edn 1991, 5th edn 2011; Essentials of Neural Science, 1995; contrib. to scientific jls. *Recreation:* art. *Address:* Columbia University Medical Center, 701 West 168th Street, New York, NY 10032, USA. *T:* (212) 3051531.

JESSOP, Alexander Smethurst; Sheriff of Grampian, Highland and Islands at Aberdeen, 1990–2008; *b* 17 May 1943; *s* of Thomas Alexander Jessop and Ethel Marion Jessop; *m* 1967, Joyce Isobel Duncan; two *s* one *d. Educ:* Montrose Acad.; Fettes Coll.; Aberdeen Univ. (MA, LLB). Solicitor in private practice, Montrose, 1966–76; Depute Procurator Fiscal, Perth, 1976–78; Asst Solicitor, Crown Office, 1978–80; Sen. Asst Procurator Fiscal, Glasgow, 1980–84; Regional Procurator Fiscal: Aberdeen, 1984–87; Glasgow, 1987–90. Member: Scottish Legal Aid Bd, 1996–2004; Bd, Montrose Port Authy, 2008–. External Examr, Aberdeen Univ., 1998–2004. Gov., Rossie Secure Unit, 2008–. *Recreation:* sport. *Address:* 1 Hillhead of Hedderwick, Hillside, Montrose DD10 9JS. *Club:* Royal Montrose Golf (Captain).

JEVANS, Deborah Ann, CBE 2013; Chief Executive Officer, England Rugby 2015, 2012–15; *b* London, 20 May 1960; *d* of Reginald Thomas George Jevans and Leslie Isobel Jevans. *Educ:* Loughton County High Sch. Professional tennis player, 1977–83; International Tennis Federation: Dir, Women's Tennis, 1987–91; Gen. Sec., 1991–2001; owner, sports consultancy co., 2001–03; Dir, Sport and Venues, 2012 Olympic Bid, 2003–05; Dir, Sport, LOCOG, 2006–12. Member: Bd, WTA Tour, 1990–2000; Women in Sport Commn, IOC, 2000–03; Bd, Sport England, 2013–. Director: All England Lawn Tennis and Croquet Club Ltd, 2008–14; All England Lawn Tennis Championships Ltd, 2008–14; non-exec. Dir, Football League, 2014–. *Recreations:* playing and watching sport, history and art, particular interest in sports participation. *Club:* All England Lawn Tennis.

JEVON, Louise Mary; *see* Richardson, L. M.

JEWELL, Prof. Derek Parry, DPhil; FRCP, FMedSci; Professor of Gastroenterology, University of Oxford, 1999–2008, now Emeritus; Fellow, Green Templeton College (formerly Green College), Oxford, since 1995; Consultant Physician, John Radcliffe Hospital, Oxford, since 1980; *b* 14 June 1941; *s* of Ralph Parry Jewell and Eileen Rose Jewell; *m* 1974, Barbara Margaret Lockwood; one *s* one *d. Educ:* Bristol Grammar Sch.; Pembroke Coll., Oxford (MA, DPhil 1972). FRCP 1979. Radcliffe Travelling Fellow, 1973; Associate Prof. in Medicine, Stanford Univ., USA, 1973–74; Sen. Lectr in Medicine, Royal Free Sch. of Medicine, 1974–80; Sen. Lectr, 1980–97, Reader, 1997–99, Univ. of Oxford. Pres., British Soc. of Gastroenterology, 2001–02. Pres., Oxford Medical Alumni, 2007–10. FMedSci 1999. *Publications:* (with H. C. Thomas) Clinical Gastrointestinal Immunology, 1979; Challenges in Inflammatory Bowel Disease, 2001; (contrib.) Topics in Gastroenterol., 1972, 1980–90; over 400 original papers. *Recreations:* music, reading, gardening. *Address:* Nuffield Department of Medicine, John Radcliffe Hospital, Oxford OX3 9DU.

JEWELL, John Anthony, (Tony), FRCGP, FFPH; Chief Medical Officer for Wales, 2006–12; *b* 6 May 1950; *s* of late John Jewell and of Madelon Jewell; *m* 1978, Jane Rickell; two *s. Educ:* Christ's Coll., Cambridge (BA 1972; MB BChir 1976); London Hosp. Med. Coll. DRCOG 1977, DCH 1979; FFPH 1998; FRCGP 2001. Principal in gen. practice, 1989; Consultant, 1994; Director of Public Health: Peterborough, 1996–98; NW Anglia, 1996–98; Cambridgeshire, 1998–2002; Clin. Dir and Dir, Public Health, Norfolk, Suffolk and Cambs SHA, 2002–06. Mem., Tower Hamlets HA, 1982–88. Pres., UK Assoc. of Dirs of Public Health, 2001–06. Hon. DSc Glamorgan, 2011. Alwyn Smith Prize, 2011; President's Award, Chartered Inst. of Envmtl Health, 2012. *Publications:* (with S. Hillier) Healthcare and Traditional Medicine in China 1800–1982, 1984, 2nd edn 2005; (contrib.) Oxford Handbook of Public Health; (contrib.) Perspectives in Public Health; contribs to jls on road traffic injuries, primary care, counselling and politics of the NHS. *Recreation:* travelling with DK guidebooks. *Address:* 34 Marlow House, Kingsley Walk, Cambridge CB5 8NY.

JEWERS, William George, CBE 1982 (OBE 1976); Managing Director, Finance, and Member, British Gas plc (formerly British Gas Corporation), 1976–87; *b* 18 Oct. 1921; *s* of late William Jewers and Hilda Jewers (*née* Ellison); *m* 1955, Helena Florence Rimmer; one *s* one *d. Educ:* Liverpool Inst. High Sch. for Boys. Liverpool Gas Co., 1938–41. Served War: RAFVR Observer (Flying Officer), 1941–46: Indian Ocean, 265 Sqdn (Catalinas), 1943–44; Burma 194 Sqdn (Dakotas), 1945. Liverpool Gas Co./NW Gas Bd, Sen. Accountancy Asst, 1946–52; W Midlands Gas Bd: Cost Acct, Birmingham and Dist Div., 1953–62; Cost Acct, Area HQ, 1962–65; Asst Chief Acct, 1965–66; Chief Acct, 1967; Dir of Finance, 1968; Gas Council, Dir of Finance, 1969–73; British Gas Corp., Dir of Finance, 1973–76. FCMA, FCCA, JDipMA, CompIGasE. *Publications:* papers and articles to gas industry jls. *Recreations:* music, reading. *Address:* 17 South Park View, Gerrards Cross, Bucks SL9 8HN. *T:* (01753) 886169.

JEWITT, (Anselm) Crispin; historian of cartography; specialist in 19th and 20th century British military cartography, since 2007; Director, National Sound Archive, British Library, 1992–2007; *b* 30 July 1949; *s* of Vivian Henry Anselm Jewitt and Helen Phyllis Jewitt (*née* Charles); *m* 1970, Mary Lee Lai-ling; two *s* one *d. Educ:* Skinners' Sch., Tunbridge Wells; Polytech. of N London. ALA 1974. Curator, Map Liby, 1980–83, Nat. Conspectus Officer, 1984–88, BL; Asst Dir, Nat. Sound Archive, 1988–92. Pres., Internat. Assoc. of Sound and Audiovisual Archives, 1999–2002; Convenor, Co-ordinating Council of Audiovisual Archives Assocs, 2003–07. Advisor: Arkivet för Ljud och bild, 1998; ScreenSound Australia, 2001. Trustee: Nat. Life Stories Collection, 1992–2007; Wildlife Sound Trust, 1992–; Saga Trust, 1999–2007; Bridges, 2008–11. *Publications:* Maps for Empire, 1992; Intelligence Revealed, 2011; book reviews and articles in professional jls. *Recreations:* dogs, trees, whisky. *Address:* Edenbridge, Kent. *E:* crispinjewitt@hotmail.com.

JEWKES, Sir Gordon (Wesley), KCMG 1990 (CMG 1980); HM Diplomatic Service, retired; Director, Slough Estates plc, 1992–2002; *b* 18 Nov. 1931; *er s* of late Jesse Jewkes; *m* 1954, Joyce Lyons (*d* 2005); two *s*; *m* 2008, Estelle Heime (*née* Houghton). *Educ:* Barrow Grammar Sch.; Magnus Grammar Sch., Newark-on-Trent, and elsewhere. Colonial Office, 1948; commnd HM Forces, Army, 1950–52; Gen. Register Office, 1950–63; CS Pay Res. Unit, 1963–65; Gen. Register Office, 1965–68; transf. to HM Diplomatic Service, 1968; CO, later FCO, 1968–69; Consul (Commercial), Chicago, 1969–72; Dep. High Comr, Port of Spain, 1972–75; Head of Finance Dept, FCO, and Finance Officer of Diplomatic Service, 1975–79; Consul-General: Cleveland, 1979–82; Chicago, 1982–85; Gov., Falkland Is and High Comr, British Antarctic Territory, 1985–88; Dir-Gen. of Trade and Investment, USA, and Consul-Gen., NY, 1989–91. Dir, Hogg Group, 1992–94; Exec. Dir, Walpole Cttee, 1992–96. Member: Council, Univ. of Buckingham, 1996–2001; Marshall Aid Commemoration Commn, 1996–99; London Metropolitan Adv. Bd, Salvation Army, 1996–2002. DUniv Buckingham, 2007. *Recreations:* music, travel, walking. *Address:* 53 Woodside Avenue, Beaconsfield, Bucks HP9 1JH. *T:* (01494) 678564.

JEWSON, Richard Wilson; Lord-Lieutenant of Norfolk, since 2004; Chairman, Archant (formerly Eastern Counties Newspapers Group Ltd), 1997–2014 (Director, 1982–2014); *b* 5 Aug. 1944; *s* of Charles Boardman and Joyce Marjorie Jewson; *m* 1965, Sarah Rosemary Spencer; one *s* three *d. Educ:* Rugby; Pembroke Coll., Cambridge (MA). Joined Jewson & Sons, 1965, Man. Dir, 1974–86; Meyer International: Dir, 1983–93; Group Man. Dir, 1986–91; Dep. Chm., 1990–91; Chm., 1991–93; Chairman: Danogue (formerly Ideal Hardware, then Inter X) plc, 1994–2002; Anglian Housing Gp Ltd, 1996–2001; Octagon Healthcare (Holdings) Ltd, 1998–2006; Hy-phen.com Ltd, 2000–01; East Port Great Yarmouth Ltd, 2000–07; PFI Infrastructure plc, 2004–07; Raven Russia Ltd, 2007–; Tritax Big Box REIT plc, 2013–; Dep. Chm., Anglian Water, 1994–2002 (Dir, 1991–2002); non-executive Director: Pro Share (UK), 1992–95; Building Centre Gp Ltd, 1992–95; Delian Lloyds Investment Trust, 1993–95; Savills plc, 1994–2004 (Chm., 1995–2004); Queens Moat Houses, 1994–2003 (Chm., 2001–03); Grafton Gp plc, 1995–2013; Miller Insurance Group Ltd, 1995–96; Angerstein Underwriting Trust, 1995–96; Taverham Hall Educnl Trust Ltd, 1998–2004; Temple Bar Investment Trust plc, 2001–; Anglian Water Services Ltd, 2002–04; Jarrold and Sons Ltd, 2003–13; Watts, Blake, Bearne & Co. plc, 2004–07; Clean Energy Brazil plc, 2007–09. Mem., CBI London Region Cttee, 1986–93. CCMI. DL Norfolk, 2000. *Recreations:* golf, sailing, Real tennis, horse trials, gardening, opera, visual arts. *Address:* Dades Farm, Barnham Broom, Norfolk NR9 4BT. *T:* (01603) 757909, *Fax:* (01603) 757909. *Clubs:* Boodle's; Royal West Norfolk Golf; Brancaster Staithe Sailing.

JEZZARD, Prof. Peter Hamish, PhD; FInstP; Herbert Dunhill Professor of Neuroimaging, University of Oxford, since 2003; Fellow, University College, Oxford, since 2003; *b* Middlesbrough, 6 Nov. 1965; *s* of Frank Ernest Jezzard and Kathleen May Jezzard; *m* 2000, Helen Rachel Simms; two *s* one *d. Educ:* Univ. of Manchester (BSc Physics 1987); Darwin Coll., Cambridge (PhD MRI Physics 1991). FInstP 2007. National Institutes of Health, USA: Vis. Fellow, 1991–95; Unit Chief, Unit on MRI Physics, 1995–97; MRC Ext. Scientific Staff, Univ. of Oxford, 1998–2003; Res. Fellow, Wolfson Coll., Oxford, 2000–03. Pres., Internat. Soc. for Magnetic Resonance in Medicine, 2013–14 (Fellow, 2008). *Publications:* (jtly) Functional MRI: an introduction to methods, 2001; (contrib.) Quantitative Magnetic Resonance in the Brain: monitoring disease progression and treatment response, 2003; (contrib.) MR Imaging in White Matter Diseases of the Brain and Spinal Cord, 2005; (contrib.) Handbook of Medical Image Processing, 2nd edn 2008; (contrib.) Clinical MR Neuroimaging, 2nd edn 2010; (contrib.) Clinical Perfusion MRI, 2013; (contrib.) Brain Mapping: an encyclopedic reference, 2014; contribs to scientific jls incl. Radiol., Proc. NAS, Neuroimage, Neurol., Magnetic Resonance in Medicine. *Recreations:* walking, pottering in my woodshop, making furniture. *Address:* Oxford Centre for Functional Magnetic Resonance Imaging of the Brain, John Radcliffe Hospital, Oxford OX3 9DU. *T:* (01865) 222727. *E:* peter.jezzard@univ.ox.ac.uk.

JI Chaozhu; Under-Secretary General of the United Nations, 1991–96; *b* Shanxi Province, 30 July 1929; *s* of Dr Chi Kung-Chuan, Commissioner of Education, and Chang Tao-Jan; *m* 1957, Wang Xiangtong; two *s. Educ:* Primary and secondary schools in Manhattan; Harvard Univ. (reading Chemistry); Tsinghua Univ. (graduated 1952). English stenographer at Panmunjom, Korea, for Chinese People's Volunteers, 1952–54; English interpreter for Chinese leaders, incl. Chairman Mao, Premier Chou En-Lai, 1954–73; Dep. Dir, Translation Dept, Foreign Ministry, 1970–73; Counsellor, Liaison Office, Washington DC, 1973–75; Dep. Dir, Dept of Internat. Organisations and Confs, Foreign Min., 1975–79; Dep. Dir, Dept of American and Oceanic Affairs, Foreign Min., 1979–82; Minister-Counsellor, US Embassy, 1982–85; Ambassador to Fiji, Kiribati and Vanuatu, 1985–87; Ambassador to UK, 1987–91. Vice Pres., All China Fedn of Returned Overseas Chinese, 1996–2005. *Publications:* The Man on Mao's Right: from Harvard Yard to Tiananmen Square, my life inside China's foreign ministry (autobiog.), 2008. *Recreations:* swimming, music.

JIANG ENZHU; Chairman, Foreign Affairs Committee, National People's Congress, China, 2003–08; *b* 14 Dec. 1938; *s* of Jiang Guohua and Yu Wen Guizhen; *m* 1967, Zhu Manli; one *s. Educ:* Beijing Foreign Languages Inst. Teacher, Beijing Foreign Languages Inst., 1964; London Embassy, People's Republic of China, 1964–77; Ministry of Foreign Affairs: Dep. Dir, 1978, Dir, 1983, Dep. Dir-Gen. and Dir-Gen., 1984–90, Dept of W European Affairs; Asst Minister, 1990–91; Vice Foreign Minister, 1991–95; Chinese Ambassador to UK, 1995–97; Dir, Xinhua News Agency (Hong Kong Br.), 1997–2000; Minister, Liaison Office of Central People's Govt, HKSAR, 2000–02. Chief Negotiator for People's Republic of China in Sino-British talks over future of Hong Kong, 1993; a Dep. Hd, Prelim. Wkg Cttee of Preparatory Cttee, HKSAR, 1993–95. Res. Fellow, Center for Internat. Affairs, Harvard Univ., and Sen. Vis. Scholar, Brookings Inst., USA, 1981–82. *Address:* Foreign Affairs Committee, National People's Congress, 23 XI Jiao Min Xiang, Beijing 100805, People's Republic of China.

JIANG ZEMIN; President, People's Republic of China, 1993–2003; Chairman, Central Military Commission, 1990–2004; *b* Yangzhou City, Aug. 1926. *Educ:* Jiaotong Univ., Shanghai. Participated in student movement led by underground Party orgns, 1943; joined Communist Party of China, 1946. Associate engr, section chief and power workshop dir, factory Party sec., then First Dep. Dir, Shanghai Yimin No 1 Foodstuffs Factory; First Dep. Dir, Shanghai Soap Factory; Section Chief of electrical machinery, Shanghai No 2 Designing Sub-bureau, First Min. of Machine-building Industry; trainee, Stalin Automobile Plant, Moscow, 1955; Dep. Chief, Power Div., Dep. Chief Power Engr, and Dir, Power Plant, Changchun No 1 Auto Works, 1956–62; Dep. Dir, Shanghai Electric Equipt Res. Inst., 1962; Dir and actg Party sec., Wuhan Thermo-Tech. Machinery Res. Inst.; Dep. Dir, and Dir, Foreign Affairs Bureau, First Min. of Machine-building Industry; Vice-Chm. and Sec.-Gen., State Commns on Admin of Imports and Exports and on Admin of Foreign Investment, 1980–82; Vice Minister and Dep. Sec., Party Gp, later Minister and Sec., Party Gp, Min. of Electronics Industry, 1982–85. Mayor of Shanghai and Dep. Sec., later Sec., Shanghai Municipal Party Cttee, 1985. Communist Party of China Central Committee: Mem., 1982; Mem., Political Bureau, 1987 (Mem., Standing Cttee, 1989, Gen. Sec.); Chm., Military Cttee, 1989. *Address:* 25 Huangsi Dajie, Beijing 100011, People's Republic of China.

JILANI, Asaf; journalist and broadcaster; a pioneer of Urdu journalism in the UK; Senior Producer, South Asia Region (formerly Eastern) Service, BBC World Service, 1983–2010; *b* 24 Sept. 1934; *s* of Abdul Wahid Sindhi and Noor Fatima Jilani; *m* 1961, Mohsina Jilani; two *s* one *d. Educ:* Jamia Millia, Delhi; Sindh Madrasa, Karachi; Karachi Univ. (MA, Economics). Sub-Editor, Daily Imroze, Karachi (Progressive Papers Ltd), 1952; Political Corresp., Daily Imroze, 1954; Special Corresp., Daily Jang, Karachi (posted in India), 1959–65; first Urdu journalist to be posted as a foreign correspondent; held prisoner in Delhi during India/Pakistan War, 1965; London Editor: Daily Jang (Karachi, Rawalpindi, Quetta); Daily News, Karachi, and Akhbar-Jehan, Karachi, 1965–73; Editor, Daily Jang, London (first Urdu Daily in UK), 1973–82; writer: London Letter for Akhbar-e-jahan, Karachi, 2009–; columns for Daily Jehan Pakistan, Karachi, Lahore and Islamabad, 2013–14; columns for Daily Jasarat, Karachi and Lahore, 2014–; columns for Daily Aag, Luckhnow, 2013–. Iqbal Medal (Pakistan), for journalistic contribution to exposition of Islamic poetic philosopher Dr Mohammed Iqbal, during his centenary celebrations, 1979. *Publications:* Wast Asia, Nai Azadi Nay Challenge (Central Asian Journey, in Urdu; based on 21 prog. series for BBC World Service), 1994; Gaon Gaon Badalti Dunia (Changing Villages, in Urdu; based on 36 prog. series for BBC

Urdu Service), 1998; Saghar Shishay Lalo Gohar: a collection of articles, 2009; Shehar e Bekaran (Problems and Challenges Faced by the Large Cities of the India/Pakistan Subcontinent, in Urdu; based on 30 prog. series for BBC Urdu Service), 2009; Durope Ke Asiai (Asians in Europe), 2012. *Recreations:* walking, swimming, painting. *Address:* 17 Leys Gardens, Cockfosters, Herts EN4 9NA.

JILES, Prof. David Collingwood, PhD, DSc; CEng, FREng, FInstP, FIEEE, FIET, FIMA, FIMMM; Anson Marston Distinguished Professor of Engineering, 2003–05 and since 2010, Palmer Endowed Chair in Electrical and Computer Engineering, and Chairman, Department of Electrical and Computer Engineering, since 2010, Iowa State University, Ames; *b* London, 28 Sept. 1953; *s* of Kenneth Gordon Jiles and Vera Ellen (Johnson) Jiles; *m* 1979, Helen Elizabeth Graham; two *s* two *d. Educ:* Univ. of Exeter (BSc 1975); Univ. of Birmingham (MSc 1976; DSc 1990); Univ. of Hull (PhD 1979). CEng; FInstP 1988; FIEEE 1994; FIET (FIEE 1995); FIMA 1999; FIMMM 2007; FREng 2014; Registered Professional Engr, USA. Postdoctoral Fellow, Phys Dept, Victoria Univ., NZ, 1979–81; Res. Associate, Phys Dept, Queen's Univ., Kingston, Canada, 1981–84; Ames Laboratory, US Dept of Energy: Res. Fellow, 1984–86; Associate Physicist, then Physicist, 1986–90; Sen. Scientist, 1990–2005; Iowa State University: Asst Prof., then Associate Prof., 1986–90; Prof. of Materials Sci. and Engrg, 1990–2005; Prof. of Electrical and Computer Engrg, 1992–2005; Prof., Dir and Royal Soc. Res. Fellow, Wolfson Centre for Magnetics, Cardiff Univ., 2005–10 (Hon. Prof., 2010–). Visiting Professor: Dept of Applied Phys, Univ. of Hull, 1991, 1994; Fraunhofer Inst., Univ. of the Saarland, 1992, 1997; Vienna Univ. of Technol., 2000, 2003, 2007; Wolfson Centre for Magnetics, Cardiff Univ., 2004; Univ. of Sheffield, 2010; Vis. Scientist, Inst. of Phys, Czech Acad. of Scis, 1999. Fellow: Magnetics Soc., 1994; APS 1997; Japanese Soc. for the Promotion of Sci., 2006. Hon. Fellow, Indian Soc. for Nondestructive Testing, 2011. Member: Eta Kappa Nu, IEEE, 2011–; Tau Beta Pi, 2011–. Editor-in-Chief, IEEE Trans. on Magnetics, 2005–11. *Publications:* Introduction to Magnetism and Magnetic Materials, 1991, 3rd edn 2015; Introduction to the Electronic Properties of Materials, 1994, 2nd edn 2001; Introduction to the Principles of Materials Evaluation, 2007; over 600 scientific papers in learned jls and confs; 18 patents. *Recreations:* classical music, opera, chess, running, soccer, squash. *Address:* Department of Electrical and Computer Engineering, Iowa State University, Ames, IA 50011, USA. *T:* (515) 2941097, *Fax:* (515) 2943637.

JILLINGS, Godfrey Frank; Deputy Chairman, Gladedale Holdings plc, 2000–09; *b* 24 May 1940; *s* of late Gerald Frank Jillings and Dorothy Marjorie Jillings; *m* 1967, Moira Elizabeth McCoy (*d* 1986); one *s. Educ:* Tiffin Sch., Kingston; Inst. of Personnel Management. DMS; FCIB. S. G. Warburg & Co. Ltd, 1956–58; National Westminster Bank Ltd, 1958–90: Head of Industrial Section, 1983; Sen. Project Manager, 1985–86; Director: County Unit Trust Managers Ltd, 1986–87; Natwest Stockbrokers Ltd, 1986–89; Chief Exec., Natwest Personal Financial Management Ltd, 1987–89; Senior Exec., Group Chief Exec.'s Office, 1989–90; Chief Exec., FIMBRA, 1990–94; Dir, Financial Services Initiative, later Dir, London Office, WDA, 1994–97. A Dep. Chief Exec., PIA, 1992–94. Chm., John Gater Holdings Ltd, 1994–95; Director: DBS Mgt plc, 1994–2001 (Dep. Chm., 1996–2001); Baronsmead VCT plc, 1995–2014; DBS Financial Management plc, 1997–2001; Baronsmead VCT 2 plc, 1998–2010; Spring Studios Ltd, 2004–14 (Chm., 2006–13); Chm., Ma Potter's plc, 2002–07. *Recreations:* travel, chess, golf. *Address:* 1 Fairacres, Roehampton Lane, SW15 5LX. *Club:* Royal Automobile.

JINGA, Ion, PhD; Ambassador and Permanent Representative of Romania to the UN, New York, since 2015; *b* Daneasa, Romania, 1 Sept. 1961; *s* of Ion Jinga and Viorica Jinga; *m* 1987, Daniela Doina; one *d. Educ:* Dinicu Golescu High Sch., Câmpulung-Muscel; Univ. of Bucharest (BSc Physics 1986; BA Law 1992); National Sch. for Pol and Admin. Studies, Bucharest (MA Public Admin 1992); College of Europe, Bruges (MA Eur. Admin 1992); Inst. for Internat. Studies, Univ. of Leeds, 1993; Al. I. Cuza Acad., Bucharest (PhD Law 1999). Teacher: Economic High Sch. no. 4, Bucharest, 1984–85; Secondary Sch. no. 127, Bucharest, 1985–86; Physicist Engr, Nuclear Energy Reactors Inst., Pitesti, 1986–91; Hd of Protocol, Mass Media and External Relns Office, Arges Co. Govt, Pitesti, 1991–92; Third Sec., Directorate for EU Affairs, 1992–94, Second Sec., Minister's Office, 1994–95, Min. of Foreign Affairs, Bucharest; First Sec., 1995–98, Dep. Hd of Mission, 1998–99, Mission of Romania to the EU, Brussels; Counsellor, Directorate for EU Affairs, Min. of Foreign Affairs, 1999–2000; Dep. Hd of Mission, then Chargé d'Affaires ai, Mission of Romania to the EU, Brussels, 2000–01; Mem., Romanian Delegn, and Coordinator of Nat. Secretariat, Convention on the Future of Europe, 2002; Dir Gen. for EU Affairs, Min. of Foreign Affairs, Bucharest, 2002–03; Ambassador of Romania to Belgium, 2003–08, to the UK, 2008–15. NATO Res. Fellow, 1997–99. Member: Scientific Council, Romanian Magazine for Community Law, 2003–; Eur. Gp for Evaluation and Prospective, 2005–; Founder Mem., Romanian Soc. for Eur. Law, 2009–. Co-Patron, Scottish Romanian Univs Exchange, 2010–; Member: Bd, Mid-Atlantic Club, London, 2010–; Manchester Debating Union, Manchester Univ., 2011–; Atlantic Council of UK, 2011–. Patriarchal Cross, Romanian Orthodox Church, 2005; Hon. Citizen, Câmpulung-Muscel, 2007; Dip. of Excellence and Son of the Arges County, 2007; Medal of Excellence, Nat. Sch. for Pol and Admin. Studies, Bucharest, 2012; Hon. Award of Achievement, Romanian Nat. Union of Students UK, 2014. Officer, Nat. Order for Merit (Romania), 2000; Cross, Romanian Royal House, 2008; Officier, l'Ordre national du mérite (France), 2003; Grand Cross, Order of the Crown (Belgium), 2008; Silver Medal (State of Jersey), 2014. *Publications:* over 100 articles and interviews published in British media, mainly on Romanians living in UK, free movement of people, Romania's economy and British-Romanian relations. *Recreations:* literature, history, travelling, tennis, ski-ing, swimming. *Clubs:* Athenæum, Royal Automobile; Cercle Gaulois (Brussels).

JINKINSON, Alan Raymond; General Secretary, UNISON, 1993–96; *b* 27 Feb. 1935; *s* of Raymond and Maggie Jinkinson; *m* 1968, Madeleine Gillian Douglas (*d* 1995). *Educ:* King Edward VII Sch., Sheffield; Keble Coll., Oxford (BA Hons). National and Local Government Officers' Association: Education Dept, 1960; District Officer, 1967; District Orgn Officer, 1973; National Officer (Local Govt), 1976; Asst Gen. Sec., 1981; Dep. Gen. Sec., 1983; Gen. Sec., 1990. *Recreations:* cinema, opera, theatre, walking, watching cricket. *Address:* 10 Princethorpe Road, SE26 4PF. *T:* (020) 8778 1098.

JIRIČNA, Eva Magdalena, CBE 1994; RA 1997; RDI 1991; architect; Principal of own practice, since 1984; President, Architectural Association, 2003–05; *b* 3 March 1939; *d* of Josef Jiričny and Eva (*née* Svata); *m* 1963, Martin Holub (marr. diss. 1973). *Educ:* Coll. of Architecture and Town Planners, Univ. of Prague (Engr Architect 1962); Acad. of Fine Arts, Prague (Acad. Architect 1967). Professional practice and management examination, RIBA, 1973. Main projects include: AMEC plc, London HQ; Boodle & Dunthorne (later Boodles), Jewellers, Dublin, London, Chester, Manchester and Liverpool; Prague HQ, Andersen Consulting; Canada Water Bus Stn, Jubilee Line Extension; Orangery, Prague Castle; Hotel Josef, Prague; RA shop, London; V&A Museum: masterplan; Modernism Exhibn; Jewellery Gall.; Canary Wharf penthouses; Selfridges shopfronts, London; Faith Zone, Millennium Dome. Hon. Prof. of Architecture and Design, Univ. of Applied Arts, Prague, 2002. Hon. AIA 2006. *Address:* 3rd Floor, 38 Warren Street, W1T 6AE. *T:* (020) 7554 2400, *Fax:* (020) 7388 8022. *E:* mail@ejal.com.

JOACHIM, Rev. Dr Margaret Jane; Operations Manager, Fujitsu Services Ltd, 2011–14; Minister in Secular Employment, Diocese of London, since 1997; *b* 25 June 1949; *d* of late Reginald Carpenter and Joyce Margaret Carpenter; *m* 1970, Paul Joseph Joachim (*d* 2011); one *d. Educ:* Brighton and Hove High School; St Hugh's College, Oxford (MA Geology); Univ. of Birmingham (PhD Geology); Southern Dioceses Ministerial Trng Scheme. FRES 1983; FGS 1991. Grammar school teacher, 1971–76; post-doctoral research Fellow, Univ. of Birmingham, 1976–79; computer consultant, 1979–84; Futures Database Manager, Rudolf Wolff & Co., 1984–87; EDS (Electronic Data Systems) Ltd: Manager, UK Insurance Services, 1988–91; Leadership and Professional Develt Instr, 1991–93; Sen. Relationship Manager (Insce), 1994–96; Manager, EMEA Year 2000 Services, 1997–2000; Client Delivery Manager, 2000–02; Global Support Manager, 2002–03; UK Applications Prog. Manager, ABN Amro Account, 2003; Prog. Dir, 2003–04, EMEA Applications Delivery Manager (Insce), 2004–05, Applications Develt Manager, EMEA Financial Services Applications Industry Unit, 2005–06, EDS Credit Services Ltd; Prog. Manager, 2006–10, Hd, Progs, Information and Technol. Gp, 2010–11, Fujitsu Services Ltd. Asst Dir, Taskforce 2000, 1997 (on secondment). Training Officer, Liberal Parly Assoc., 1979–84; Mem., Exec. Cttee, Women's Liberal Fedn, 1984–85; Chair, Fawcett Soc., 1984–87 (Vice-Chair, 1993–95; Mem. Exec. Cttee, 1990–95); Trustee, Fawcett Trust, 1995–2005; Chair, internat. working gp to set up EEC Women's Lobby, 1988–90; Chair, 1989–90, Vice-Chair, 1990–92, WLD (formerly SLD Women's Orgn). Co-ordinator, Women into Public Life Campaign, 1987–88; Vice-Chair, 1989, Mem. Exec. Cttee, 1989–91, 300 Gp. Contested: (L) West Gloucestershire, 1979; (L/Alliance) Finchley, 1983; (L/Alliance) Epsom and Ewell, 1987. Chair: Lib Dem London Region Candidates' Cttee, 2007–10; Lib Dem English Candidates' Cttee, 2011–13; Regl Parties Cttee, 2015–; Vice-Chair, Lib Dem English Pty, 2015–. Ordained deacon, 1994, priest, 1995; Asst Curate (non-stipendiary), St Barnabas, Ealing, 1994–97, St Peter's, Mount Park, Ealing, 1998–. Moderator, 1999–2002, 2007–09, Sec., 2009–, CHRISM (Christians in Secular Ministry). Trustee: Christians in Secular Employment Trust, 2003–; Royal Assoc. for Deaf People, 2007–13. Mem., Exec. Cttee, Nat. Traction Engine Club, 1976–79; Founder, Steam Apprentice Club, 1978; Founder, Oxford Univ. Gilbert and Sullivan Soc., 1968. *Publications:* papers in: Studies in the Late-Glacial of North-West Europe, 1980; Holocene Palaeoecology and Palaeohydrology, 1986. *Recreations:* walking, reading, going to traction engine rallies, making jam, research into book history. *Address:* 8 Newburgh Road, W3 6DQ. *T:* (020) 8723 4514. *E:* margaret.joachim@london.anglican.org. *Club:* Reform.

JOB, Rev. Canon (Evan) Roger (Gould); Canon Residentiary, Precentor and Sacrist, 1979–94, Vice Dean, 1991–94, Canon Emeritus, since 2003, Winchester Cathedral; *b* 15 May 1936; 2nd *s* of late Thomas Brian and Elsie Maud Job, Ipswich; *m* 1964, Rose Constance Mary, *o d* of late Stanley E. and Audrey H. Gordon, Hooton, Wirral; two *s. Educ:* Cathedral Choir School and King's Sch., Canterbury; Magdalen Coll., Oxford; Cuddesdon Theol Coll. BA 1960, MA 1964; ARCM 1955. RN, 1955–57. Deacon 1962, priest 1963. Asst Curate, Liverpool Parish Church, 1962–65; Vicar of St John, New Springs, Wigan, 1965–70; Precentor of Manchester Cath., 1970–74; Precentor and Sacrist of Westminster Abbey, 1974–79; Chaplain of The Dorchester, 1976–79. Chaplain: to first High Sheriff of Gtr Manchester, 1973–74; to High Sheriff of Hampshire, 2004–05, 2016–. Occasional officiant, Royal Chapel, Windsor Great Park, 2007–. Select Preacher, Univ. of Oxford, 1974, 1991. *Recreations:* gardening, piano. *Address:* Kitwood Farm-house, Ropley, Alresford, Hants SO24 0DB.

JOB, Sir Peter James Denton, Kt 2001; Chief Executive, Reuters Group PLC, 1991–2001; *b* 13 July 1941; *s* of late Frederick Job and of Marion Job (*née* Tanner); *m* 1966, Christine Cobley, *d* of Frederick Cobley; one *s* one *d. Educ:* Clifton College; Exeter College, Oxford (BA). Trainee Reuter journalist, 1963; reporter then manager in Paris, New Delhi, Kuala Lumpur, Jakarta and Buenos Aires, 1963–78; Man. Dir, Reuters Asia, based in Hong Kong, 1978–90; Dir, Reuters Gp, 1989–2001; Chm., Visnews Ltd, 1991–92. Non-executive Director: Grand Metropolitan, 1994–97; Glaxo Wellcome, 1997–99; Diageo, 1997–99; Schroders, 1999–2010 (Sen. Ind. Dir, 2004–10); GlaxoSmithKline, 2000–04; Instinet, 2000–05; TIBCO Software Inc., 2000–14 (Presiding Dir, 2007–14); Royal Dutch Shell (formerly Shell Transport & Trading), 2001–10. Member Supervisory Board: Deutsche Bank AG, 2001–11; Bertelsmann AG, 2002–05. Chm., Internat. Adv. Council, NASDAQ, 1999; Member: DTI Multimedia Adv. Gp, 1994–97; DTI Japan Trade Gp, 1994–98; HM Treasury Adv. Panel, 1995; High Level Adv. Gp on Information Society, EU, 1996; FCO Business Panel, 1998; INSEAD UK Nat. Council, 1993–2001. Trustee, Action on Hearing Loss (formerly RNID), 2010–14. Mem., Madrigal Soc., 2011–. Hon. Fellow, Green Coll., Oxford, 1995. Hon. DLitt Kent, 1998; Hon. DLaws Exeter, 2008. Comdr, Order of the Lion (Finland), 2001. *Recreations:* boating, golf, tennis, early choral music, gardening, theatre, country sports. *Address:* 701 Rowan House, 9 Greycoat Street, SW1P 2QD. *Clubs:* Garrick, Oriental; Hong Kong (Hong Kong); Tadmarton Golf.

JOBBINS, Robert, OBE 2001; PhD; media consultant, since 2001; Director of News, BBC World Service, 1996–2001; *b* 2 Nov. 1941; *s* of Henry Robert Jobbins and Miriam Jeffrey Jobbins; *m* 1st, 1962, Jenifer Ann Rowbotham (marr. diss. 1991); two *s*; 2nd, 1992, Jacqueline Duff. *Educ:* Rickmansworth Grammar Sch.; Univ. of Essex (MA Art History, 2005; PhD 2015). BBC Foreign Correspondent: Cairo, 1977–83; Singapore, 1983–86; Head of BBC Arabic Service, 1986–89; Editor, BBC World Service News and Current Affairs, 1989–96. Ind. Mem., Essex Police Authy, 2001–05. Chm., Rory Peck Trust, 2001–10. Trustee, Media Legal Defence Initiative, 2013–. *Recreations:* walking, medieval art, opera. *Address:* Blue House Cottage, Maldon Road, Bradwell on Sea, Essex CM0 7MR. *T:* (01621) 776507.

JOBLING, Karen Elizabeth; *see* Todner, K. E.

JOBSON, Roy; Director of Children and Families Department, Edinburgh City Council, 2005–07; *b* 2 June 1947; *s* of James Jobson and Miriam H. Jobson; *m* 1971, Maureen Scott; one *s* two *d. Educ:* Bedlington Grammar Sch.; Univ. of Durham; Newcastle and Sunderland Polytechnics. Teacher: King's Sch., Tynemouth, 1970–73; Norham High Sch., 1973–74; Asst Sec., E Midland Regional Examining Bd, 1974–80; Asst Dir of Educn, Gateshead Metropolitan Borough Council, 1980–84; Dep. Chief Educn Officer, 1984–88, Chief Educn Officer, 1988–98, Manchester City Council; Dir of Education, Edinburgh CC, 1998–2005. Adviser: AMA, 1993–97; LGA, 1997–98. Member: Jt Council for GCSE, 1989–93; NEAB, 1992–93; Soc. of Educn Officers, 1988–2007; Chm., ACEO, 1997–98; Pres., Assoc. of Dirs of Educn in Scotland, 2004–05 (Vice-Pres., 2003–04). FRSA 1994. Hon. DS Heriot-Watt, 2010. *Recreations:* children, family, church, music, dogs. *Address:* 4 Buckstone View, Edinburgh EH10 6PE. *T:* (0131) 469 3322.

JOCELYN, family name of **Earl of Roden.**

JOCELYN, Viscount; Shane Robert Henning Jocelyn; *b* 9 Dec. 1989; *s* and *heir* of Earl of Roden, *qv. Educ:* London Business Sch. CFA. Worked for Hiscox, Brewin Dolphin, BCM & Partners, Key Capital and Dollarhane. *Recreations:* business, ice hockey, travelling, Rugby.

JODRELL, Prof. Duncan Ian, DM; FRCPE; Professor of Cancer Therapeutics, University of Cambridge, since 2008; Researcher, Cancer Research UK Cambridge Institute, since 2008; *b* Warrington, 8 Oct. 1958; *s* of Ian and Joyce Jodrell. *Educ:* Univ. of Southampton (BM 1982; DM 1990); Univ. of London (MSc 1989). FRCPE 1999. Registrar, Royal Marsden Hosp., London, 1986–87; Clinical Fellow, Inst. of Cancer Res., Univ. of London, 1987–90; Vis. Asst Prof., Univ. of Maryland at Baltimore, 1990–91; Sen. Registrar and Lectr, Beatson Oncol. Centre, Univ. of Glasgow, 1991–94; University of Edinburgh: Sen. Lectr, 1994–98; Reader, 1998–2006; Prof. of Cancer Therapeutics, 2006–08. *Recreations:* golf, hill-walking. *Address:* Cancer Research UK Cambridge Institute, Li-Ka Shing Centre, University of Cambridge, Robinson Way, Cambridge CB2 0RE. *T:* (01223) 769750. *E:* duncan.jodrell@cruk.cam.ac.uk. *Club:* Gog Magog (Cambridge).

JOEL, William Martin, (Billy); singer, pianist and songwriter, since 1972; *b* 9 May 1949; *s* of Howard Joel and Rosalind Joel (*née* Nyman); *m* 1st, 1971, Elizabeth Weber (marr. diss. 1982); 2nd, 1985, Christie Brinkley (marr. diss. 1994); one *d*; 3rd, 2004, Kate Lee. Albums include: Cold Spring Harbor, 1972; Piano Man, 1973; Streetlife Serenade, 1974; Turnstiles, 1976; The Stranger, 1977; 52nd Street, 1978; Glass Houses, 1980; The Nylon Curtain, 1982; An Innocent Man, 1983; The Bridge, 1986; Storm Front, 1989; River of Dreams, 1993; Fantasies and Delusions, 2001. *Publications:* Goodnight, My Angel: a lullabye, 2004; New York State of Mind, 2005. *Address:* c/o Maritime Music, 34 Audrey Avenue, Oyster Bay, NY 11771–1559, USA.

JOFFE, family name of **Baron Joffe**.

JOFFE, Baron *cr* 2000 (Life Peer), of Liddington in the County of Wiltshire; **Joel Goodman Joffe,** CBE 1999; *b* 12 May 1932; *s* of Abraham Joffe and Dena Joffe (*née* Idelson); *m* 1962, Vanetta Pretorius; three *d*. *Educ:* Marist Brothers' Coll., Johannesburg; Univ. of Witwatersrand (BCom, LLB). Admitted Solicitor, Johannesburg, 1956; called to the Bar, S Africa, 1962; Human Rights lawyer, 1958–65; Dir and Sec., Abbey Life Assurance Co., 1965–70; Dir, Jt Man. Dir and Dep. Chm., Allied Dunbar Life Assurance Co., 1971–91. Chairman: Swindon Private Hosp., 1982–87; Swindon HA, 1988–93; Swindon and Marlborough NHS Trust, 1993–95. Mem., Royal Commn on Long Term Care for the Elderly, 1997–98. Special Advr to S African Minister of Transport, 1997–98. Trustee, 1980–2000, Hon. Sec., 1982–85, Chm., 1985–93 and 1995–2001, Oxfam; Chm., The Giving Campaign, 2000–04; numerous other charitable organisations. Mem., H of L, 2000–15. *Publications:* The Rivonia Trial, 1995, 2nd edn as The State vs Nelson Mandela, 2007. *Recreations:* tennis, voluntary work.

JÓHANNSSON, Kjartan, PhD; Icelandic Ambassador to the European Union, 2002–05; *b* 19 Dec. 1939; *s* of Jóhann and Astrid Dahl Thorsteinsson; *m* 1964, Irma Karlsdottir; one *d*. *Educ:* Reykjavík Coll.; Royal Inst. of Technol., Sweden; Univ. of Stockholm; Illinois Inst. of Technol., Chicago. Consulting Engr, Reykjavik, 1966–78; University of Iceland: Teacher, Faculty of Engrg and Sci., 1966–74; Prof., Faculty for Econs and Business Admin, 1974–78 and 1980–89. Mem., Municipal Council, Hafnarfjördur, 1974–78; Mem. (SDP), Althing (Parlt of Iceland), 1978–89; Speaker, Lower Hse, 1988–89; Minister of Fisheries, 1978–80, also of Commerce, 1979–80; Ambassador and Perm. Rep. to UN and other internat. orgns, Geneva, 1989–94; Sec. Gen., EFTA, 1994–2000; Ambassador, Ministry for Foreign Affairs, Reykjavik, 2000–02. Social Democratic Party: Mem., Party Council and Exec. Council, 1972–89; Vice-Chm., 1974–80; Chm., 1980–84.

JOHANSEN, Lindsay; *see* Nicholson, L.

JOHANSEN-BERG, Rev. John; Founder Member, since 1984, and International Director, since 2001, Community for Reconciliation (Leader, 1986–2001); Moderator, Free Church Federal Council, 1987–88; *b* 4 Nov. 1935; *s* of John Alfred and Caroline Johansen-Berg, Middlesbrough; *m* 1971, Joan, *d* of James and Sally Ann Parnham, Leeds; two *s* one *d*. *Educ:* Acklam Hall Grammar Sch., Middlesbrough; Leeds Univ. (BA Hons Eng. Lit., BD); Fitzwilliam Coll., Cambridge Univ. (BA Theol Tripos, MA); Westminster Theol Coll. (Dip. Theol.). Tutor, Westminster Coll., Cambridge, 1961; ordained, 1962; pastoral charges: St Ninian's Presbyterian Church, Luton, 1962–70 (Sec., Luton Council of Churches); Founder Minister, St Katherine of Genoa Church, Dunstable (dedicated 1968); The Rock Church Centre, Liverpool (Presbyterian, then United Reformed), 1970–77, work begun in old public house, converted into Queens Road Youth Club, new Church Centre dedicated 1972, a building designed for youth, community and church use; Minister: St Andrew's URC, Ealing, 1977–86; Rubery URC, 1992–2001. Convener, Church and Community Cttee of Presbyterian C of E, 1970–72; Chm. Church and Society Dept, URC, 1972–79; Moderator of the Gen. Assembly of the URC, 1980–81. British Council of Churches: Mem., Assembly, 1987–90; formerly Member: Div. of Internat. Affairs; Div. of Community Affairs; Chm. Gp on Violence, Non-violence and Social Change (for Britain Today and Tomorrow Programme, 1977); Convenor, Commission on Non-Violent Action (report published 1973); Mem., Forum of Churches Together in England, 1990–97; Chairman: Reflection Gp, 2000–05, Mgt Gp, 2003–05, Project Gp, 2005–10, CTBI Living Spirituality Network. Chm., Christian Fellowship Trust, 1981–87; Trustee, Nat. Assoc. of Christian Communities and Networks, 1989–2001; Mem., Exec., CCJ, 1989–97; Mem. Council, Centre for Study of Judaism and Jewish Christian Relns, 1989–96; Trustee, Fellowship of Reconciliation, England, 2000– (Chm., 2005–12). Co-Convenor, Methodist/URC Gp Report, Peacemaking: A Christian Vocation, 2005–06. Founder Mem. and Sponsor, Christian Concern for Southern Africa, 1972–94; Founder Sponsor, Clergy Against Nuclear Arms, 1982– (Chm., 1986–90); Founder: Romania Concern, 1990; United Africa Aid, 1996; Ecumenical Order of Ministry, 1990; initiated Village India Aid, 2006; Jt Leader, Ecumenical Festivals of Faith in: Putney and Roehampton, 1978; Stroud, 1980; Banstead, 1983; North Mymms, 1985; Guildford, 1986; Jesmond, 1987; Worth Abbey, 1988; Palmers Green, 1990; Poole, and Ballyholme, 1991; Finchley, 1992; South Wallasey, 1994; Rye, 2003. Jt Editor, Jl of Presbyterian Historical Soc. of England, 1964–70. Pro Ecclesia Millennium Award, 2001. *Publications:* Arian or Arminian? Presbyterian Continuity in the Eighteenth Century, 1969; Prayers of the Way, 1987, rev. edn 1992; Prayers of Pilgrimage, 1988; Prayers of Prophecy, 1990; Prayers for Pilgrims, 1993; A Celtic Collection, 1996; Pilgrims on the Edge, 1997. *Recreations:* mountain walking, golf, drama. *Address:* 84 Ravencroft, Bicester, Oxon OX26 6YQ.

JOHANSON, Capt. Philip, OBE 2002; International Secretary, Church Army International, 2007–12; Chaplain to Mayor of Bournemouth, since 2014; *b* 10 April 1947; *s* of late Stanley Theodore Johanson and Betty Johanson. *Educ:* Alderman Cogan Sch., Hull; Wilson Carlile Coll. of Evangelism, London. Missioner, dio. of Coventry, 1972–75; Church Army: Head of Missions, 1975–83; Dir of Evangelism, 1983–90; Chief Sec., 1990–2006. Patron, African Pastors Trust, 2000–12 (Chm., 1981–97); Member: C of E Partnership for World Mission Cttee, 1990–2006; Portman House Trust, 1990–2006; Council, Evangelical Alliance, 1991–2003; C of E Board of Mission, 1997–2003; Council, Wilson Carlile Coll. of Evangelism, 2002–06; Council, Christian Enquiry Agency, 2003–07. Chm., Bournemouth Nightclub Outreach Work Trust, 2012–. Mem., Royal Commonwealth Soc., 1980–; Mem., Boscombe and Southbourne Rotary Club, 2011–. *Recreations:* theatre, music, travel, reading. *Address:* 10 Ditton Lodge, 8 Stourwood Avenue, Bournemouth BH6 3PN. *T:* (01202) 416917. *E:* p.johanson@btinternet.com. *Clubs:* Royal Over-Seas League, Nikaean.

JOHN, Rt Rev. Andrew Thomas Griffith; *see* Bangor, Bishop of.

JOHN, Sir David (Glyndwr), KCMG 1999; Chairman: BSI Group (formerly British Standards Institution), 2002–12; Royal Society for Asian Affairs, since 2009; *b* 20 July 1938; *o s* of William Glyndwr John and Marjorie John (*née* Gaze); *m* 1964, Gillian Edwards; one *s* one *d*. *Educ:* Llandovery Coll., Carms; Christ's Coll., Cambridge (MA); Columbia Univ., NY (MBA); Harvard Univ. (ISMP). 2nd Lieut, RA, 1957–59. United Steel Co., 1962–64; Rio Tinto Zinc Corp., 1966–73 (RTZ Consultants, Hardman & Holden); Redland plc, 1973–81 (Land Reclamation Co., Redland Indust. Services, Redland Purle); Inchcape, 1981–95; Main Bd Dir, 1988–95; Develt Dir, later Chief Exec., Gray Mackenzie & Co., Middle East, 1981–87; Chairman: Inchcape Bhd, Singapore, 1990–95 (Chief Exec., 1987–90); Inchcape Middle East, 1991–94; Inchcape Toyota, 1994–95; BOC Group, 1996–2002 (non-exec. Dir, 1993–96); Premier Oil plc, 1998–2009; Balfour Beatty, 2003–08 (non-exec. Dir, 2000–03). Non-executive Director: British Biotech plc, 1996–99; The St Paul Cos Inc., Minn, USA, 1996–2003. Dir, WDA, 2001–02; Vice Chm., British Trade Internat., 1999–2002. Vice Pres. and Mem. Bd, POW Business Leaders Forum, 1996–99; Member: President's Cttee, and Chm. Internat. Cttee, CBI, 1996–2002; CBI Internat. Adv. Bd, 2002–11; Dir and Trustee, Council for Industry and Higher Educn, 1996–2002; Mem., Wilson Cabinet Cttee on Export Promotion, 1998–99. Gov., SOAS, 1993–2008; Mem. Bd of Overseers, Columbia Business Sch., NY, 1996–2002; Trustee: Asia House, 2000–04; Llandovery Coll., Carms, 2003–11. Chm., Cotswold Water Park Trust, 2011–. Freeman, City of London, 1997; Liveryman, Scientific Instrument Makers' Co., 1997–. DUniv Glamorgan, 2003. *Recreations:* walking, gardening, reading. *Address:* c/o C. Hoare & Co., 37 Fleet Street, EC4P 4DQ. *Clubs:* Oxford and Cambridge, Oriental, Travellers.

JOHN, Dr David Thomas, (Dai), PhD; Vice Chancellor, University of Luton, 1998–2003; *b* 31 Oct. 1943; *s* of Trevor John and Violet Gwyneth; *m* 1966, Jennifer Christine Morris; one *s* two *d*. *Educ:* Portsmouth (BSc ext. London Univ.); Birkbeck Coll., London (PhD). Kingston Polytechnic: Asst Lectr, 1966–67; Lectr, 1967–70; Sen Lectr, 1970–74; Principal Lectr, 1974–84; Hd of Applied Sci. and Associate Dean of Sci., 1984–86; Vice Principal, NE Surrey Coll. of Technology, 1987–89; Dep. Dir, Luton Coll. of Higher Educn, 1989–93, Dep. Vice-Chancellor, Univ. of Luton, 1993–98. *Publications:* several books and chapters on geology and geomorphology; various sci. papers on Tertiary and Quaternary history of SE England and on soils. *Recreations:* music, reading, travel, squash, Rugby, fly-fishing, painting. *E:* johndaijen@btinternet.com.

JOHN, Sir Elton (Hercules), Kt 1998; CBE 1996; musician; *b* Pinner, Middlesex, 25 March 1947; *s* of late Stanley Dwight and of Sheila (now Farebrother); *né* Reginald Kenneth Dwight; changed name to Elton Hercules John; *m* 1984, Renate Blauel (marr. diss. 1988); civil partnership 2005, *m* 2014, David Furnish; two *s*. *Educ:* Pinner County Grammar Sch.; Royal Acad. of Music, London. Singer, songwriter, musician, began playing piano 1951; joined group, Bluesology, 1965; since 1969 has toured across the world consistently as solo performer and with the Elton John Band; played to over 2 million people across 4 continents, 1984–86; first popular Western singer to perform in USSR, 1979. Appeared: (film) Tommy, 1975; Live Aid, 1985; Freddie Mercury Tribute concert, 1992; Live 8, 2005. Voice (films): The Lion King, 1994; The Road to El Dorado, 2000. Pres., Watford Football Club, 1990– (Chm., 1976–90). Established Elton John AIDS Foundn, 1992; Patron: Amnesty International, 1997–; Internat. AIDS Vaccine Initiative, 1999–; Terrence Higgins Trust; Globe Theatre; Elton John Scholarship Fund, RAM, 2004–. Chm., Old Vic Trust, 2000–. *Composer: albums:* Empty Sky, 1969; Elton John, Tumbleweed Connection, 1970; 11.17.70, Friends, Madman Across the Water, 1971; Honky Chateau, 1972; Don't Shoot Me, I'm Only the Piano Player, Goodbye Yellow Brick Road, 1973; Caribou, Greatest Hits, 1974; Captain Fantastic and the Brown Dirt Cowboy, Rock of the Westies, 1975; Here and There, Blue Moves, 1976; Greatest Hits vol. II, 1977; A Single Man, 1978; Victim of Love, 1979; 21 at 33, 1980; The Fox, 1981; Jump Up, 1982; Too Low for Zero, 1983; Breaking Hearts, 1984; Ice on Fire, 1985; Leather Jackets, 1986; Live in Australia, 1987; Reg Strikes Back, 1988; Sleeping with the Past, 1989; To Be Continued, 1990; The One, 1992; Duets, 1993; Made in England, 1995; Love Songs, 1996; The Big Picture, 1997; Elton John and Tim Rice's Aida, The Muse, 1999; One Night Only, 2000; Songs From the West Coast, 2001; Greatest Hits—1970–2002, 2002; Peachtree Road, 2004; The Captain & the Kid, 2006; (with Leon Russell) The Union, 2010; The Diving Board, 2013; *musical scores:* (film) The Lion King, 1994 (Acad. Award for Best Original Song—Can You Feel the Love Tonight?); Broadway musicals: The Lion King, 1998 (6 Tony Awards); Aida, 2000 (Tony Award for Best Original Score); Lestat, 2006; (West End) Billy Elliot the Musical, 2005; *singles:* co-writer of many international hit songs with Bernie Taupin (and others) including Your Song, Rocket Man, Crocodile Rock, Daniel, Goodbye Yellow Brick Road, Candle in the Wind, Don't Let the Sun Go Down On Me, Philadelphia Freedom, Someone Saved My Life Tonight, Don't Go Breaking My Heart (duet with Kiki Dee), Sorry Seems to be the Hardest Word, The Bitch is Back, Song for Guy, I Guess that's Why They Call It the Blues, I'm Still Standing, Nikita, Sacrifice, Blue Eyes, Circle of Life, Are You Ready for Love?, I Want Love, Electricity. Biggest selling single of all time, Candle in the Wind, re-released 1997 (over 33,000,000 copies sold). Fellow, British Acad. of Songwriters and Composers, 2004. Hon. RAM 1997; Hon. Dr RAM, 2002. Awards include: 11 Ivor Novello Awards, 1973–2000; Brit Award (Best British Male Artist), 1991; inducted into Rock 'n Roll Hall of Fame, 1994; 5 Grammy Awards, 1986–2000; Grammy Legend Award, 2001; Kennedy Center Honor, 2004; Brits Icon Award, 2013. *Publications:* Love is the Cure: on life, loss and the end of AIDS, 2012. *Address:* Rocket Music Entertainment LLP, 1 Blythe Road, W14 0HG. *T:* (020) 7348 4800.

JOHN, Geoffrey Richards, CBE 1991; Chairman, Food From Britain, 1993–99; *b* 25 March 1934; *s* of Reginald and Mabel John; *m* 1st, 1961, Christine Merritt (*d* 2002); two *d*; 2nd, 2004, Eiluned Davies (*née* Edmunds). *Educ:* Bromsgrove School, Worcs; University College Cardiff (BA 1st cl. Hons Econs). Flying Officer, RAF, 1955–57; Cadbury Schweppes, 1957–74; Man. Dir, Spillers Foods, 1974–80; Chief Exec., Foods Div., Dalgety-Spillers, 1980–82; Chm. and Chief Exec., Allied Bakeries, 1982–87; Chm., Dairy Crest, 1988–94; Director: Associated British Foods, 1982–87; Frizzell Gp, 1991–92; Morland plc, 1993–99; NFU Services Ltd, 1999–2004. Mem., ARC, 1980–82; Chm., Meat and Livestock Commn, 1987–93. Dir, Hereford Hosps NHS Trust, 1994–99. Bromsgrove School: Pres., 1994–2010; Gov., 1965–94 (Chm., 1982–91); Governor: Inst. of Grassland and Envmtl Res., 1996–98; Hereford Cathedral Sch., 1997–2003; Aston Univ., 1999–2003 (Pro-Chancellor, 2003–08). Hon. DLitt Aston, 2010. *Recreations:* Rugby Football, music. *Address:* 71 Adventurers Quay, Cardiff Bay, Cardiff CF10 4NQ. *Clubs:* Royal Air Force, Harlequin FC.

JOHN, Very Rev. Jeffrey Philip Hywel, DPhil; Dean of St Albans, since 2004; *b* 10 Feb. 1953; *s* of late Howell John and of Dulcie John; civil partnership 2006, Rev. Grant Holmes. *Educ:* Tonyrefail Grammar Sch.; Hertford Coll., Oxford (BA Classics and Modern Langs 1975); St Stephen's House, Oxford (BA Theol. 1977, MA 1978); Brasenose Coll., Oxford; DPhil Oxon 1984. Ordained deacon, 1978, priest, 1979; Curate, St Augustine, Penarth, 1978–80; Asst Chaplain, Magdalen Coll., Oxford, 1980–82; Chaplain and Lectr, Brasenose Coll., Oxford, 1982–84; Fellow and Dean of Divinity, Magdalen Coll., Oxford, 1984–91; Vicar, Holy Trinity, Eltham, 1991–97; Canon Theologian and Chancellor, Dio. of Southwark, 1997–2004; nominated Bishop Suffragan of Reading, 2003. *Publications:* Living Tradition, 1990; Living the Mystery, 1995; This is Our Faith, 1995, 2nd edn 2001; Permanent, Faithful, Stable, 2000, extended edn as Permanent, Faithful, Stable: Christian same-sex marriage, 2012; The Meaning in the Miracles, 2002. *Recreation:* modern European languages. *Address:* The Deanery, Sumpter Yard, St Albans, Herts AL1 1BY.

JOHN, Lindsey Margaret; *see* Bareham, L. M.

JOHN, Maldwyn Noel, FREng, FIEEE, FIET; Consultant, Kennedy & Donkin, 1994–97 (Chairman, 1987–94); *b* 25 Dec. 1929; *s* of Thomas Daniel John and Beatrice May John; *m* 1953, Margaret Cannell; two *s*. *Educ:* University College Cardiff. BSc 1st Cl. Hons, Elec. Eng. Metropolitan Vickers Elec. Co. Ltd, Manchester, 1950–59; Atomic Energy Authy, Winfrith, 1959–63; AEI/GEC, Manchester, as Chief Engineer, Systems Dept, Chief Engineer, Transformer Div., and Manager, AC Transmission Div., 1963–69; Chief Elec. Engineer, 1969–72, Partner, 1972–86, Kennedy & Donkin. President: IEE, 1983–84; Convention of Nat. Socs of Elec. Engineering of Western Europe, 1983–84; Dir Bd, Nat. Inspection Council for Electrical Installation Contractors, 1988–91; Mem., Overseas Projects Bd, 1987–91. FIEE 1969, Hon. FIET (Hon. FIEE 1998); FIEEE 1985; FREng (FEng 1979). Freeman, City of London, 1987. *Publications:* (jtly) Practical Diakoptics for Electrical Networks, 1969; (jtly)

Power Circuit Breaker Theory and Design, 1975, 2nd edn 1982; papers in IEE Procs. *Recreation:* golf. *Address:* 65 Orchard Drive, Horsell, Woking, Surrey GU21 4BS. *T:* (01483) 825755.

JOHN, Martin Anthony; Deputy Director, Operations, Major Projects Authority, Cabinet Office, since 2015; *b* Kingston-upon-Thames, 15 Aug. 1970; *s* of Tony and Monika John; *m* 2007, Lisa Sadler (*née* Ennis); one *s. Educ:* Open Univ. (MBA). Sen. Policy Asst, DSS, 1998–2000; Planning and Corporate Services Manager, 2000–01, Expansion Programme Manager, 2001–02, Court Service, Immigration Appellate Authy; Director: Tribunal Ops, 2002–05; Asylum and Immigration Tribunals Service, 2005–07; Business Develt Tribunals Service, 2007–08; Public Guardian and Chief Exec., Office of the Public Guardian, MoJ, 2008–12; Hd of Civil Family and Tribunals, HM Courts and Tribunals Service, 2012–14; Dep. Dir, Programme, Assurance and Testing, Transforming Rehabilitation, MoJ, 2014–15. *Address:* Cabinet Office, 70 Whitehall, SW1A 2AS.

JOHN, Prof. Peter David, PhD; Vice-Chancellor and Chief Executive, University of West London (formerly Thames Valley University), since 2007; *b* Bridgend, S Wales, 15 Aug. 1957; *s* of Douglas and Pamela John; *m* 1984, Lydia Jones; three *d. Educ:* University Coll., Swansea (BA Hons Hist. 1978); Univ. Coll. of Wales, Aberystwyth (PGCE 1980); Birkbeck Coll., London (MA Victorian Studies 1988); Jesus Coll., Oxford (MSc Educn); Univ. of Bristol (PhD 1998). Lectr, Univ. of Reading, 1989–90; Lectr, 1990–96, Sen. Lectr, 1996–2003, Univ. of Bristol; University of Plymouth: Prof. and Dean, Faculty of Education, 2004–06; Pro Vice-Chancellor, 2005–06; Dep. Vice-Chancellor, 2006–07. FHEA; FRSA; MInstD. Hon. DEd Plymouth, 2008. Global Excellence Award, Amity Univ. *Publications:* (with P. Lurbe) Civilization Britannique, 1992, 8th edn 2010; Lesson Planning for Teachers, 1993, 2nd edn 1997; (with E. Hoyle) Professional Knowledge and Professional Practice, 1996; (with S. Wheeler) The Digital Classroom, 2006; (jtly) Interactive Education, 2008; (jtly) Improving Classroom Learning with ICT, 2009. *Recreations:* painting, reading, Rugby Union, France and French life, politics. *Address:* Somerset Villa, 33 Bloomfield Road, Bath BA2 2AD. *Club:* Oxford and Cambridge.

JOHN, Stephen Alun; His Honour Judge John; a Circuit Judge, since 2008; *b* London, 1 Feb. 1953; *s* of late S. Beynon John and of A. Sybil John; *m* 1985, Fiona Rosalind Neale; two *d. Educ:* Varndean Grammar Sch., Brighton; Jesus Coll., Oxford (Open Exhibnr 1971; Viscount Sankey Schol. 1972; BA Juris. 1974; MA 1979). Called to the Bar, Middle Temple, 1975; practised in common law and crime, 1975–2001; specialised in criminal law, 2001–08; Asst Recorder, 1999–2000; Recorder, 2000–08. *Recreations:* music, history (especially biography), Burgundy (the area and the wine). *Address:* Reading Crown Court, Old Shire Hall, The Forbury, Reading, Berks RG1 3EH. *T:* (0118) 967 4400, *Fax:* (0118) 967 4444. *E:* HHJudgeStephen.John@judiciary.gsi.gov.uk.

JOHN, Stewart Morris, OBE 1992; FREng, FRAeS; Director, Taikoo Aircraft Engineering Company, Xiamen, China, 1992–2013; *b* 28 Nov. 1938; *s* of Ivor Morgan John and Lilian John; *m* 1961, Susan Anne Cody; one *s* one *d. Educ:* Porth Co. Grammar Sch.; N Staffs Tech. Coll.; Southall Tech. Coll. CEng 1977; FREng (FEng 1990); FRAeS 1977. BOAC: apprentice, 1955–60; on secondment to: Kuwait Airways, 1960–63; Malaysia-Singapore Airlines, as Chief Engr, Borneo, 1963–67; Develt Engr, 1967–70; Workshop Superintendent/Manager, 1970–73; Manager Maintenance, American Aircraft Fleet, 1973–77; Cathay Pacific Airways: Dep. Dir, Engrg, Hong Kong, 1977–80; Engrg Dir (Main Bd Mem.), 1980–94; Dep. Chm., Hong Kong Aircraft Engrg Co., 1982–94; Director: Rolls-Royce Commercial Aero Engines Ltd, 1994–98; British Aerospace Aviation Services, 1994–98; British Midland Aviation Services, 1995–2000; Hong Kong Aero Engine Services Ltd, 1996–98. Non-executive Director: Green Dragon Gas, 2006–; Greka Drilling Ltd, 2011–; Mem., Adv. Bd, Kingfisher Airlines, 2006–09. President: Internat. Fedn of Airworthiness, 1993–96; RAeS, 1997–98 (Pres., Weybridge Br., 2004–). Trustee, Brooklands Mus., 1994–. Pres., Rolls-Royce Enthusiasts' Club, 2009– (Chm., Surrey Sect., 2000–09). Liveryman, GAPAN, 1996–2008. *Recreations:* golf, classic cars, Rugby. *Address:* Taipan, 5 Pond Close, Burwood Park, Walton-on-Thames, Surrey KT12 5DR. *Clubs:* Burhill Golf; Rolls Royce Enthusiasts; Hong Kong, Shek O Golf (Hong Kong).

JOHN, Dame Susan (Elizabeth), DBE 2011; Headteacher, Lampton School, since 1997 (Deputy Headteacher, 1987–97); *b* 1953; *m* 1975, Richard John. Dir, London Leadership Strategy. Non-exec. Dir, DfE. Mem., Future Leaders' Project Bd. Hon. Fellow, Brunel Univ., 2000. *Address:* Lampton School, Lampton Avenue, Hounslow, Middx TW3 4EP.

JOHN, His Honour Terence Aneurin; a Circuit Judge, 2009–14; a Designated Family Judge, Swansea Civil Justice Centre, 2012–14; *b* Wolf's Castle, Pembrokeshire; *s* of Joseph Aneurin John and Elizabeth May John; *m* 1971, Susan Helen Jones; one *s* one *d. Educ:* Haverfordwest Grammar Sch.; Univ. of Wales Inst. of Sci. and Technol. (BSc Econ.); Crewe Coll. of Educn (Cert Ed 1971). Solicitor, Eaton, Evans and Morris, Haverfordwest, 1976–94; Dep. District Judge, 1992–94; District Judge, 1994–2009. President: Pembrokeshire Law Soc., 1984–85; West Wales Law Soc., 1988–89; Assoc. of District Judges, 2006–07.

JOHNS, Vice Adm. Sir Adrian (James), KCB 2008; CBE 2001; DL; Governor and Commander-in-Chief, Gibraltar, 2009–13; *b* 1 Sept. 1951; *m* 1976, Susan Lynne; one *s* three *d. Educ:* Imperial Coll., London (BSc). In command: HMS Yarnton, 1981–83; HMS Juno and HMS Ariadne, 1989–90; HMS Campbeltown, 1995–96; Captain, RN Presentation Team, 1996–97; Asst Dir, Naval Plans, 1997–98; Principal Staff Officer to CDS, 1998–2000; i/c HMS Ocean, 2001–03; ACNS, MoD, 2003–05; Head, FAA, 2003–08; Second Sea Lord and C-in-C Naval Home Comd, 2005–08; Flag ADC to the Queen, 2005–08. Younger Brother, Trinity Hse, 2007–. Freeman, City of London, 2002; Liveryman, Hon. Co. of Air Pilots (formerly GAPAN), 2006–; Freeman, Co. of Farriers, 2002. DL Gtr London, 2015. QCVS 2003. KStJ 2011. *Recreations:* music, cycling.

JOHNS, Prof. David John, CBE 1998; FREng; Vice Chairman, Lay Advisory Group, Faculty of General Dental Practice, Royal College of Surgeons of England, since 2009; *b* 29 April 1931. *Educ:* Univ. of Bristol (BSc Eng, MSc Eng, Aeronautical Engineering); Loughborough Univ. of Technology (PhD, DSc). FREng (FEng 1990); FRAeS, FAeSI, FHKIE. Bristol Aeroplane Co., 1950–57 (section leader); Project Officer, Sir W. G. Armstrong Whitworth Co., 1957–58; Lectr, Cranfield Inst. of Technology, 1958–63; Loughborough University of Technology: Reader, 1964–68; Prof. in Aeronautics, 1968–83; Hd, Dept of Transport Technology, 1972–82; Senior Pro-Vice-Chancellor, 1982–83; (Foundation) Dir, City Polytechnic of Hong Kong, 1983–89; Vice-Chancellor and Principal, Univ. of Bradford, 1989–98. Chairman: Prescription Pricing Authy, 1998–2001; N and E Yorks and Northern Lincs Strategic HA, 2002–06; Genetics and Insce Cttee, DoH, 2002–09; Lay Mem., Exec. Cttee, e-learning for Dental Health, DoH, 2008–13. Dir, British Bd of Agrément, 1997–2006. Comr, Commonwealth Scholarships Commn, 2002–08. Member, Council: British Acoustical Soc., 1980–83; Hong Kong Instn of Engrs, 1985–88; RAEng, 2000–03; RAeS, 2002–05. Unofficial JP Hong Kong, 1987–89. *Publications:* Thermal Stress Analyses, 1965; 126 tech. articles and papers on educn and training in learned jls. *Recreations:* bridge, theatre, music, art appreciation. *Clubs:* Harrogate; Harrogate Men's Forum; Hong Kong; Hong Kong Jockey.

JOHNS, Derek Ernest; art dealer; *b* 22 July 1946; *s* of late Ernest Edward Johns and Evelyn May Johns (*née* Pays); *m* 1st, 1971, Annie Newman; one *s* one *d*; 2nd, 1981, Daphne Ellen Hainworth; one *s* one *d. Educ:* City of London Freemen's Sch., Ashtead Park. Dir, and Hd, Old Master Paintings, Sotheby's, London, 1966–81; Chm., Derek Johns Ltd, Fine Paintings, 1981–. Winner, Masterchef, BBC, 1997. Mem., Chirton Parish Council, Wilts, 2003–07. *Recreations:* horticulture, shooting, travel, languages, opera. *Address:* Conock Old Manor, Devizes, Wilts SN10 3QQ; Derek Johns Ltd, 12 Duke Street, St James's, SW1Y 6BN. *T:* (020) 7839 7671, *Fax:* (020) 7930 0986. *E:* fineart@derekjohns.co.uk. *Clubs:* East India, Beefsteak, Garrick.

JOHNS, Glynis; actress; *b* Pretoria, South Africa; *d* of late Mervyn Johns and Alice Maude (*née* Steel-Payne); *m* 1st, Anthony Forwood (marr. diss.); one *s*; 2nd, David Foster, DSO, DSC and Bar (marr. diss.); 3rd, Cecil Peter Lamont Henderson; 4th, Elliott Arnold. *Educ:* Clifton and Hampstead High Schs. First stage appearance in Buckie's Bears as a child ballerina, Garrick Theatre, London, 1935. Parts include: Sonia in Judgement Day, Embassy and Strand, 1937; Miranda in Quiet Wedding, Wyndham's, 1938 and in Quiet Weekend, Wyndham's, 1941; Peter in Peter Pan, Cambridge Theatre, 1943; Fools Rush In, Fortune; The Way Things Go, Phœnix, 1950; Gertie (title role), NY, 1952; Major Barbara (title role), NY, 1957; The Patient in Too True to Be Good, NY, 1962; The King's Mare, Garrick, 1966; Come as You Are, New, 1970; A Little Night Music, New York, 1973 (Tony award for best musical actress); Ring Round the Moon, Los Angeles, 1975; 13 Rue de l'Amour, Phœnix, 1976; Cause Célèbre, Her Majesty's, 1977 (Best Actress Award, Variety Club); Hayfever, UK; The Boy Friend, Toronto; The Circle, NY, 1989–90. Entered films as a child. *Films include:* South Riding, 49th Parallel, Frieda, An Ideal Husband, Miranda (the Mermaid), State Secret, No Highway, The Magic Box, Appointment with Venus, Encore, The Card, Sword and the Rose, Personal Affair, Rob Roy, The Weak and the Wicked, The Beachcomber, The Seekers, Poppa's Delicate Condition, Cabinet of Dr Caligari, Mad About Men, Josephine and Men, The Court Jester, Loser Takes All, The Chapman Report, Dear Bridget, Mary Poppins, Zelly and Me, Nuki, While You Were Sleeping. Also broadcasts; television programmes include: Star Quality; The Parkinson Show (singing Send in the Clowns); Mrs Amworth (USA); All You Need is Love; Across a Crowded Room; Little Gloria, Happy at Last; Sprague; Love Boat; Murder She Wrote; The Cavanaughs; starring role, Coming of Age (series). *Address:* Catalyst Group, 715 Navy Street, Santa Monica, CA 90405, USA.

JOHNS, Jasper; painter; *b* 15 May 1930; *s* of Jasper Johns and Jean Riley. *Educ:* Univ. of South Carolina. Works in collections of Tate Gall., NY Mus. of Modern Art, Buffalo, Cologne, Washington, Amsterdam, Stockholm, Dallas, Chicago, Baltimore, Basle, Cleveland, Minneapolis; one-man exhibitions principally in Leo Castelli Gallery, NY; others in UK, USA, Canada, France, Germany, Italy, Japan, Switzerland; retrospective exhibns, NY Mus. of Modern Art, 1996, Scottish Nat. Gall. of Modern Art, 2004. Hon. RA; Mem., Amer. Acad. of Arts and Letters (Gold Medal, 1986); Pittsburgh Internat. Prize, 1958; Wolf Foundn Prize, 1986; Venice Biennale, 1988; Nat. Medal of Arts, 1990; Praemium Imperiale Award, Japan, 1993. Officier, Ordre des Arts et des Lettres (France), 1990. *Address:* c/o Matthew Marks Gallery, 523 West 24th Street, New York, NY 10011, USA.

JOHNS, Michael Alan, CB 2000; Chief Executive, Valuation Office Agency and a Commissioner of Inland Revenue, 1997–2004; *b* 20 July 1946; *s* of John and Kathleen Johns. *Educ:* Judd School, Tonbridge; Queens' College, Cambridge (MA Hist.). Inland Revenue, 1967–79; Central Policy Review Staff, 1979–80; Inland Revenue, 1980–84; seconded to Orion Royal Bank, 1985; Inland Revenue, 1986–; Under Sec., 1987; Dir, Oil and Financial Div., 1988–91; Dir, Central Div., 1991–93; Dir, Business Ops Div., 1993–97. Treasurer, Working Men's College, 1986–90. Hon. RICS 2003. *Recreations:* trekking, teaching adults, moral philosophy.

JOHNS, Rev. Patricia Holly, MA; Headmistress, St Mary's School, Wantage, 1980–94; Priest in charge, Mildenhall, Marlborough, 1996–99; *b* 13 Nov. 1933; *d* of William and Violet Harris; *m* 1958, Michael Charles Bedford Johns (*d* 1965), MA; one *s* one *d. Educ:* Blackheath High Sch.; Girton Coll., Cambridge (BA 1956, MA 1959, CertEd with distinction 1957). Assistant Maths Mistress: Cheltenham Ladies' Coll., 1957–58; Macclesfield Girls' High Sch., 1958–60; Asst Maths Mistress, then Head of Maths and Dir of Studies, St Albans High Sch., 1966–75; Sen. Mistress, and Housemistress of Hopeman House, Gordonstoun, 1975–80. Ordained deacon, 1990, priest, 1994; non-stipendiary Curate, Marlborough Team Ministry, 1994–99. *Recreations:* choral singing, walking, travel. *Address:* Flat 1, Priory Lodge, 93 Brown Street, Salisbury, Wilts SP1 2BX. *T:* (01722) 328007.

JOHNS, Paul; public speaker; Co-founder, 1994, and Director, since 1998, SANA, development agency in Bosnia and Herzegovina; *b* 13 March 1934; *s* of Alfred Thomas Johns and Margherita Johns; *m* 1st, 1956, Ruth Thomas (marr. diss. 1973); two *s* one *d*; 2nd, 1984, Margaret Perry (marr. diss. 1986). *Educ:* Kingswood School, Bath; Oriel College, Oxford (MA Hons Modern Hist.); Univ. of Wales (MTh 2010). Personnel Management, Dunlop Rubber Co., 1958–63 and Northern Foods Ltd, 1963–68; Senior Partner, Urwick Orr & Partners, 1968–83; Dir, Profile Consulting, 1983–89; Man. Dir, Traidcraft, 1988–91; Chief Exec., Fairtrade Foundn, 1992–94. Chairperson, 1985–87, Vice-Chairperson, 1987–88, CND. Consultant, FA Premier League, 1994–2000. Dir, Coll. of Preachers, 2007–. Lay preacher, Methodist Church. *Recreations:* story telling, listening to music, watching football (keen supporter of Nottingham Forest). *Address:* 33 Burleigh Road, West Bridgford, Nottingham NG2 6FP.

JOHNS, Air Chief Marshal Sir Richard (Edward), GCB 1997 (KCB 1994; CB 1991); KCVO 2007 (LVO 1972); CBE 1985 (OBE 1978); FRAeS; Constable and Governor of Windsor Castle, 2000–08; *b* Horsham, 28 July 1939; *s* of late Lt-Col Herbert Edward Johns, MBE, RM and of Marjory Harley Johns (*née* Everett); *m* 1965, Elizabeth Naomi Anne Manning; one *s* two *d. Educ:* Portsmouth Grammar Sch.; RAF College, Cranwell. FRAeS 1997. Commissioned 1959; Night Fighter and Fighter/Reconnaissance Sqns, UK, Cyprus, Aden, 1960–67; Flying Instructional duties, 1968–71; Flying Instructor to Prince of Wales, 1970–71; OC 3 (Fighter) Sqn (Harrier), 1975–77; Dir, Air Staff Briefing, 1979–81; Station Comdr and Harrier Force Comdr, RAF Gütersloh, 1982–84; ADC to the Queen, 1983–84; RCDS 1985; SASO, HQ RAF Germany, 1985–88; SASO, HQ Strike Comd, 1989–91; AOC No 1 Gp, 1991–93; COS and Dep. C-in-C, Strike Comd and UK Air Forces, 1993–94; AOC-in-C Strike Comd, 1994; C-in-C, Allied Forces NW Europe, 1994–97; Chief of Air Staff, 1997–2000; Air ADC to the Queen, 1997–2000. Hon. Col, 73 Engr Regt (V), 1994–2002; Hon. Air Cdre, RAF Regt, 2000–13. Patron, Labrador Lifeline Trust, 2001–; Pres., Hearing Dogs for Deaf People, 2005–. Vice-Pres., Royal Windsor Horse Show, 2000–. Chm., Bd of Trustees, RAF Mus., 2000–06. Pres., Chitterne Cricket Club, 2012–; Vice-Pres., Royal Household Cricket Club, 2006–. Gov., Dauntsey's Sch., 2008–. Freeman, City of London, 1999; Liveryman, Hon. Co. of Air Pilots (formerly GAPAN), 1999–. *Recreations:* military history, Rugby, cricket, equitation. *Address:* Dolphin House, Warminster Road, Chitterne, Wilts BA12 0LH. *T:* (01985) 850039. *Club:* Royal Air Force.

JOHNSON, Rt Hon. Alan (Arthur); PC 2003; MP (Lab) Kingston-upon-Hull West and Hessle, since 1997; *b* 17 May 1950; *s* of late Lillian May and Stephen Arthur Johnson; *m* 1st, 1968, Judith Elizabeth Cox (marr. diss.); one *s* one *d* (and one *d* decd); 2nd, 1991, Laura Jane Patient; one *s. Educ:* Sloane Grammar School, Chelsea. Postman, 1968; UCW Branch Official, 1976; UCW Exec. Council, 1981; UCW National Officer, 1987–93; Gen. Sec., UCW, 1993–95; Jt Gen. Sec., CWU, 1995–97. PPS to Financial Sec. to the Treasury, 1997–99, to Paymaster General, 1999; Parly Under-Sec. of State, 1999–2001, Minister of State, 2001–03, DTI; Minister of State, DFES, 2003–04; Secretary of State: for Work and Pensions, 2004–05; for Trade and Industry, 2005–06; for Educn and Skills, 2006–07; for Health, 2007–09; for Home Dept, 2009–10; Shadow Sec. of State for Home Dept, 2010; Shadow Chancellor of the Exchequer, 2010–11. Mem., Trade and Industry Select Cttee,

1997. Mem. Gen. Council, TUC, 1994–95; Exec. Mem., Postal, Telegraph and Telephone Internat., 1994–97; Mem., Labour Party NEC, 1995–97; Dir, Unity Trust Bank plc. Duke of Edinburgh Commonwealth Study Conf., 1992. Gov., Ruskin Coll., 1992–97. *Publications:* This Boy: a memoir of a childhood, 2013 (Orwell Prize, 2014; Ondaatje Prize, 2014); Please, Mister Postman: a memoir, 2014. *Recreations:* music, tennis, reading, football, cookery, radio. *Address:* House of Commons, SW1A 0AA.

JOHNSON, Air Vice-Marshal Alan Taylor, FRAeS; Director of Occupational Health and Chief Medical Officer, Metropolitan Police, 1991–96; *b* 3 March 1931; *s* of Percy and Janet Johnson; *m* 1954, Margaret Ellen Mee; two *s* three *d* (and one *s* decd). *Educ:* Mexborough Grammar Sch.; Univ. of Sheffield (MB, ChB); DAvMed; FFOM, MFCM. Commnd RAF, 1957; MO, RAF Gaydon, 1957–59; Princess Mary's RAF Hosp., Akrotiri, Cyprus, 1959–61; No 1 Parachute Trng Sch., RAF Abingdon, 1961–65; RAF Changi, Singapore, 1965–67; RAF Inst. of Aviation Medicine, 1967–71; RAF Bruggen, Germany, 1971–74; Med. SO (Air) HQ RAF Support Comd, 1974–77; RAF Brize Norton, 1977–78; Chief of Aerospace Medicine HQ SAC Offutt AFB, USA, 1978–81; Dep. Dir of Health and Res. (Aviation Medicine), 1981–84; OC Princess Alexandra Hosp., RAF Wroughton, 1984–86; Asst Surg.-Gen. (Environmental Medicine and Res.), MoD, 1986; PMO, HQ RAF, Germany, 1986–88; PMO, HQ Strike Comd, RAF High Wycombe, 1988–91; retired. QHS 1986–91. OStJ 1976. *Recreations:* sport parachuting, music, cricket. *Address:* 6 Ivelbury Close, Buckden, St Neots, Cambs PE19 5XE. *Club:* Royal Air Force.

JOHNSON, (Alexander) Boris (de Pfeffel); Mayor of London (C), 2008–May 2016; MP (C) Uxbridge and South Ruislip, since 2015; *b* 19 June 1964; *s* of Stanley Patrick Johnson, *qv* and Charlotte Maria Johnson (*née* Fawcett); *m* 1st, 1987, Allegra Mostyn-Owen (marr. diss. 1993); 2nd, 1993, Marina Wheeler; two *s* two *d*. *Educ:* Eton (King's Schol.); Balliol Coll., Oxford (Brackenbury Schol.; Pres., Oxford Union). LEK Partnership, one week, 1987; The Times, 1987–88; Daily Telegraph, 1988–99: EC Correspondent, 1989–94; Asst Ed. and Chief Pol Columnist, 1994–99; Ed., The Spectator, 1999–2005. MP (C) Henley, 2001–June 2008. Opposition frontbench spokesman on higher educn, 2005–07. Jt Vice-Chm., Cons. Party, 2003–04. Commentator of the Year, 1997, Columnist of the Year, 2005, What the Papers Say Awards, 1997; Editors' Editor of the Year, 2003; Columnist of the Year, British Press Awards, 2004; Politician of the Year, Spectator Parliamentarian of the Year Awards, 2008, 2012; Politician of the Year, Political Studies Assoc., 2008; Politician of the Year, GQ Men of the Year Awards, 2008, 2012. *Publications:* Friends, Voters, Countrymen, 2001; Lend Me Your Ears: the essential Boris Johnson, 2003; Seventy Two Virgins (novel), 2004; The Dream of Rome, 2006; Life in the Fast Lane: the Johnson guide to cars, 2007; The Perils of the Pushy Parents, 2007; Johnson's Life of London, 2011; The Churchill Factor: how one man made history, 2014. *Recreations:* painting, cricket. *Address:* (until May 2016) Greater London Authority, City Hall, Queen's Walk, SE1 2AA; House of Commons, SW1A 0AA. *Club:* Beefsteak.

See also J. E. Johnson, L. F. Johnson, R. S. Johnson.

JOHNSON, Alistair; *see* Johnson, F. A.

JOHNSON, Andrew Robert; Headmaster, Stonyhurst College, since 2006; *b* Lytham St Annes, 1 April 1967; *s* of Robert and Josephine Johnson; *m* 1993, Dawn Bridger; two *s*. *Educ:* Univ. of Bristol (BA Hons Mod. Langs). Asst Teacher, Douai Sch., 1991–93; Winchester College: Asst Teacher, 1993–98; Hd, Mod. Langs, 1998–2002; Dep. Headmaster, Birkdale Sch., Sheffield, 2002–06. *Recreations:* hill-walking, theatre, music. *Address:* Stonyhurst College, Lancs BB7 9PZ. *T:* (01254) 826345. *E:* headmaster@stonyhurst.ac.uk. *Club:* Lansdowne.

JOHNSON, Anna S.; *see* Sylvester Johnson.

JOHNSON, Dame Anne (Mandall), DBE 2013; MD; FFPH, FRCP, FRCGP, FMedSci; Professor of Infectious Disease Epidemiology (formerly of Epidemiology), UCL Medical School (formerly University College London Medical School, then Royal Free and University College Medical School), since 1996, and Vice Dean for External Relations, Faculty of Population Health Sciences, since 2014, University College London; *b* 30 Jan. 1954; *d* of Gordon Trevor Johnson and Helen Margaret Johnson; *m* 1996, John Martin Watson; one *s* one *d*. *Educ:* Newnham Coll., Cambridge (BA 1974; MA 1979; Associate, 1996–); Univ. of Newcastle upon Tyne (MB BS 1978; MD with commendation 1992); LSHTM (MSc 1984); MRCGP 1982, FRCGP 2002; FFPH (FFPHM 1993); MRCP 1998, FRCP 2005. House Officer, Newcastle upon Tyne, 1978–79; Sen. House Officer, vocational trng in Gen. Practice, Northumbria, 1979–83; Registrar in Community Medicine, NE Thames RHA, 1983–84; Lectr, Middlesex Hosp. Med. Sch., 1985–88; University College London Medical School, subseq. Royal Free and University College Medical School, University College London: Sen. Lectr in Epidemiology and Hon. Consultant in Public Health Medicine, 1988–94; Reader in Epidemiology, 1994–96; Hd, Dept of Primary Care and Population Studies, 2002–07; Dir, Div. of Popn Health, UCL, 2007–10; Co-Dir, Institute for Global Health, UCL, 2008–13; Chair: UCL Populations and Lifelong Health Domain, 2011–12; UCL Grand Challenge for Global Health, 2012–14. Hon. Sen. Lectr, 1990–99, Vis. Prof., 1999–, LSHTM; Hon. Consultant in Public Health Medicine, Central and NW London NHS Trust (formerly Camden and Islington, subseq. Camden Primary Health Care) NHS Trust, 1995–. Non-exec. Dir, Whittington Hosp. NHS Trust, 2005–08. Dir, MRC UK Co-ordinating Centre for Epidemiol Study of HIV and AIDS, 1989–99. Chm., Prison Health Res. Ethics Cttee, 1999–2001 (Mem., 1996–); Member: Council, Inst. of Drug Dependency, London, 1990–98; Specialist Adv. Cttee on antimicrobial resistance, DoH, 2001–; MRC Physiological Medicine and Infections Bd, 2002–04; MRC Infections and Immunity Bd, 2004–06; Public Health Ethical Issues Wkg Party, Nuffield Council on Bioethics, 2006–07; Populations and Public Health Funding Cttee, 2008–, Bd of Govs, 2011–, Wellcome Trust; Adaptation Sub-cttee, Climate Change Cttee, DEFRA, 2009–; Expert Adv. Gp on AIDS, DoH, 2013–. Chairman: MRC Population Health Scis Gp, 2009–10; Health of the Public 2040 Working Gp, Acad. of Med. Scis, 2014–. Sen. Investigator, NIHR, 2009–. Vis. Scholar, Univ. of Sydney, 1998. Editor, AIDS, 1994–2000. FMedSci 2001. *Publications:* (jtly) Sexual Attitudes and Lifestyles, 1994; Sexual Behaviour in Britain, 1994; articles on HIV/AIDS, sexually transmitted diseases and infectious disease epidemiology. *Recreation:* singing. *Address:* Faculty of Population Health Sciences, University College London, Mortimer Market Centre, off Capper Street, WC1E 6JB.

JOHNSON, Anthony Smith Rowe; High Commissioner of Jamaica in the United Kingdom, 2010–12; *b* St Andrew, Jamaica, 14 June 1938; *s* of Cecil T. Johnson and Grethel Hairs (*née* Monfries); *m* 1969, Pamela Rosalie Casserly; one *s* two *d*. *Educ:* Kingston Coll.; Univ. of Calif, Los Angeles (BA Econs 1964; MA Internat. Trade and Finance 1965). Senior Economist: Min. of Finance, Jamaica, 1965–67; Central Planning Unit, 1967–70; Gen. Manager and Dir, Jamaica Frozen Food, 1970–75; Exec. Dir, Private Sector Orgn of Jamaica, 1976–80. Lectr, 1989–93, Sen. Lectr, 1993–2008, UWI. Parliament of Jamaica: Senator, 1980–83 and 1993–2008; Minister of State, 1983–89; MP, 1983–93. Ambassador of Jamaica to USA, 2008–10. *Publications:* The Economy: how it works, 1976; J. A. G. Smith, 1988; Kingston: portrait of a city, 1993; Jamaican Leaders, 1995; Ocho Rios: portrait of the garden parish, 1997; Ethical Business, 1997. *Recreation:* historical research. *Address:* 23 Plymouth Avenue, Kingston 6, Jamaica, West Indies. *T:* 9278001. *E:* ajohnson566@gmail.com.

JOHNSON, (Arthur) Keith; Vice Lord-Lieutenant for Orkney, since 2014; *b* Kirkwall, Orkney, 1 Feb. 1944; *s* of Robert Johnson and Lalla Johnson; *m* 1967, Jean Flett. *Educ:* Kirkwall Grammar Sch.; Aberdeen Nautical Coll. (Master Mariner); Glasgow Nautical Coll. (Extra Master Mariner). Ben Line Steamers, 1962–67; Shell Tankers UK, 1968–75; Shell International Marine: Asiatic Petroleum Corp., 1976–78; Qatar General Petroleum Corp., 1978–82; various posts, UK, 1982–93. Mem., Orkney Is Council, 1994–2007. Mem., Climatological Observers Link, 2004–. Chm., Birdsay Heritage Trust, 2010–. Mem., RMetS 2004. *Recreations:* gardening, walking, running water mill, voluntary work, climate observer for Met Office. *Address:* Hundasaeter, Twatt, Orkney KW17 2JD. *T:* (01865) 771328, 07788 418396. *E:* ak.johnson@btinternet.com.

JOHNSON, WO1 Barry, GC 1990; RAOC; Warrant Officer 1 (Staff Sergeant Major), 1986, retired 1992; *b* 25 Jan. 1952; *s* of Charles William Johnson and Joyce Johnson; *m* 1971, Linda Maria Lane; one *s* one *d*. Mem., Inst. of Explosives Engineers. Army Apprentices College, Chepstow, 1967; Royal Army Ordnance Corps, 1970; served in UK, BAOR, NI, Canada and Belize. *Club:* Victoria Cross and George Cross Association.

JOHNSON, Boris; *see* Johnson, A. B. de P.

JOHNSON, Prof. Brian Frederick Gilbert, PhD; FRS 1991; FRSE; FRSC; Professor of Inorganic Chemistry, University of Cambridge, 1995–2005; Master of Fitzwilliam College, Cambridge, 1999–2005; *b* 11 Sept. 1938; *s* of Frank and Mona Johnson; *m* 1962, Christine Draper; two *d*. *Educ:* Northampton Grammar Sch.; Univ. of Nottingham (BSc, PhD). FRSE 1992; FRSC 1992. Lecturer: Univ. of Manchester, 1965–67; UCL, 1967–70; Cambridge University: Lectr, 1970–78; Reader, 1978–90; Fitzwilliam College: Fellow, 1970–90, and 1995–99, Hon. Fellow, 2005; Pres., 1988–89; Vice Master, 1989–90; Crum Brown Prof. of Inorganic Chem., Univ. of Edinburgh, 1991–95. Mem., EPSRC, 1994–99 (Chm., Public Understanding of Sci., Engrg and Technol. Steering Gp, 1998–). Fellow, European Soc. *Publications:* Transition Metal Clusters, 1982. *Recreations:* chemistry, walking, cycling, travel.

JOHNSON, Sir Bruce Joseph F.; *see* Forsyth-Johnson.

JOHNSON, Christopher Edmund; Director General, Defence Accounts, Ministry of Defence, 1984–89; *b* 17 Jan. 1934; *s* of late Christopher and Phyllis Johnson; *m* 1956, Janet Yvonne Wakefield (*d* 2007); eight *s* three *d*. *Educ:* Salesian Coll., Chertsey; Collyer's Sch., Horsham. Sub Lt, RNVR, 1952–54. Exec. Officer, 1954–58, Higher Exec. Officer, 1959–65, War Office; Principal, MoD, 1965–71; UK Jt Comd Sec., ANZUK Force, Singapore, 1971–74; Ministry of Defence: Asst Sec., 1974–84; Asst Under Sec. of State, 1984. *Recreations:* gardening, reading. *Address:* 3 Cedric Close, Bath BA1 3PQ. *T:* (01225) 314247.

JOHNSON, Most Rev. Colin Robert; *see* Toronto, Archbishop of.

JOHNSON, Sir (Colpoys) Guy, 8th Bt *cr* 1755, of New York in North America; Director, ClearLine Communications Ltd, since 2002; *b* 13 Nov. 1965; *s* of Sir Peter Colpoys Paley Johnson, 7th Bt and his 1st wife, Clare (*née* Bruce); *S* father, 2003; *m* 1990, Marie-Louise, *d* of John Holroyd; three *s*. *Educ:* Winchester; King's Coll., London (BA Hons); Henley Mgt Coll. (MBA). Midland Bank plc, 1988–90; HSBC Capital Markets, 1990–98; Eurospend.com Ltd, 1999–2001. Hon. Col Comdt, King's Royal Yorkers, Canada, 2003. FRGS. *Recreations:* yacht racing, fly fishing. *Heir:* *s* Colpoys William Johnson, *b* 28 Dec. 1993. *Address:* Hollygate, Sleepers Hill, Winchester, Hants SO22 4ND. *T:* (01962) 869769. *Club:* Royal Ocean Racing.

JOHNSON, Daniel, GOQ 2008; PhD; Counsel, McCarthy Tétrault, Barristers and Solicitors LLP, since 1998; *b* Montreal, 24 Dec. 1944; *s* of Daniel Johnson (Premier of Quebec, 1966–68) and Reine (*née* Gagné); *m* 1993, Suzanne Marcil; one *s* one *d* from former marriage. *Educ:* Stanislas Coll., Montreal; Saint-Laurent Coll. (BA Univ. of Montreal); Univ. of Montreal (LLL); University Coll. London (LLM, PhD); Harvard Business Sch. (MBA). A lawyer. Corp. Sec., 1973–81, Vice-Pres., 1978–81, Power Corp. of Canada. Director: Bombardier Inc., 1999–; IGM Financial Inc., 1999–; Investors Gp, 2003–; Mackenzie Financial, 2003–; Bank of Canada, 2008–13; exp Global Inc. (formerly TROW Global Hldgs Inc.), 2009–14; Ezeflow Inc., 2014–. Mem. (L) Vaudreuil, Quebec Nat. Assembly, 1981–98; Minister of Industry and Commerce, 1985–88; Dep. House Leader, 1985–94; Chm., Treasury Bd, 1988–94; Minister responsible for Admin, 1988–89, for Admin and CS, 1989–94; Prime Minister and Pres. Exec. Council, Jan.–Sept. 1994; Leader of Official Opposition, 1994–98. Leader, Quebec Liberal Party, 1993–98. Chm., Quebec Judges Remuneration Cttee, 2007–10. Hon. Consul for Sweden in Montreal, 2002–. Ordre de la Pléiade (Francophonie); Order of the North Star (Sweden). *Address:* (office) Suite 2500, 1000 rue de La Gauchetière W, Montreal, QC H3B 0A2, Canada. *E:* djohnson@mccarthy.ca.

JOHNSON, Daniel Benedict; Editor, Standpoint, since 2008; *b* 26 Aug. 1957; *s* of Paul Bede Johnson, *qv*; *m* 1988, Sarah Thompson, *d* of late John William McWean Thompson, CBE; two *s* two *d*. *Educ:* Langley Grammar Sch.; Magdalen Coll., Oxford (BA 1st Cl. Hons Hist.). Res. Student, Peterhouse, Cambridge, 1978–81; Shakespeare Scholar, Berlin, 1979–80; taught German hist., QMC, 1982–84; Dir of Pubns, Centre for Policy Studies, 1983–84; Daily Telegraph: Leader Writer, 1986–87; Bonn Corresp., 1987–89; Eastern Europe Corresp., 1989; The Times: Leader Writer, 1990–91; Literary Editor, 1991–95; an Asst Editor, 1995–98; an Associate Editor, Daily Telegraph, 1998–2005; a Contrib. Editor, NY Sun, 2005–. *Publications:* White King and Red Queen: how the Cold War was fought on the chessboard, 2007; co-edited: German Neo-Liberals and the Social Market Economy, 1989; Thomas Mann: Death in Venice and other stories, 1991; Collected Stories, 2001; contrib. to Amer. and British newspapers and jls. *Recreations:* family, antiquarian book-collecting, music, chess. *Address:* c/o Georgina Capel Associates Ltd, 29 Wardour Street, W1D 6PS.

See also L. O. Johnson.

JOHNSON, Darren Paul; Member (Green), London Assembly, Greater London Authority, since 2000; *b* 20 May 1966; *s* of late Alan Johnson and of Joyce Johnson (*née* Abram, now Reynolds). *Educ:* Goldsmiths' Coll., Univ. of London (BA 1st Cl. Hons Politics and Econs 1997). Finance and admin posts, 1987–93. Envmt Advr to Mayor of London, 2000–01; Chm., Envmt Cttee, 2004–08, Housing Cttee, 2013–15, London Assembly, GLA; Dep. Chair, 2008–09 and 2012–13, Chair, 2009–10 and 2013–14, GLA. Mem. (Green) Lewisham BC, 2002–14 (Leader, Green Gp, 2006–10). Contested (Green) Lewisham Deptford, 2001, 2005, 2010. Mem., Green Party, 1987–; Elections Co-ordinator, Nat. Exec., 1993–95; Principal Speaker, 2001–03. *Recreations:* walking, cycling, music. *Address:* Greater London Authority, City Hall, Queen's Walk, SE1 2AA. *T:* (020) 7983 4000.

JOHNSON, Ven. David Allan G.; *see* Gunn-Johnson.

JOHNSON, David Gordon, CBE 2003; Director of Financial Planning and Analysis, Defence Equipment and Support, since 2013; *b* 1 Aug. 1966; *s* of Gordon Alexander Johnson and Margaret Edith Johnson (*née* Bangay); *m* 1995, Salimata Ouattara; two *s* one *d*. *Educ:* Chesterfield Sch.; Pembroke Coll., Oxford (BA Hons Classics, MA 1992). Ministry of Defence: various posts, 1989–95; Assistant Director: Housing Project Team, 1995–97; Defence Policy, 1997–98; Defence and Overseas Secretariat, Cabinet Office, 1998–2001; Asst Dir, Defence Resources and Plans, 2001–02; Director: Iraq, 2002–04; Human Resources Devel t, 2004–06; Dir-Gen., Logistics (Resources), 2006–07; Dir, later Dep. Command Sec. (Secretariat), 2007–10, Command Sec. (Secretariat), 2010, HQ Land Forces; Hd, Plans and Progs, then Resources and Plans, Defence Equipment and Support, 2011–13. *Recreations:* studying and teaching karate, coaching young cricketers. *Address:* Defence Equipment and Support, Maple 2C #2219, Ministry of Defence, Abbey Wood, Bristol BS34 8JH.

JOHNSON, David Robert W.; *see* Wilson-Johnson.

JOHNSON, David Timothy; Vice-President for Strategic Development and Washington Operations, Sterling Global Operations Inc., since 2014; *b* 28 Aug. 1954; *s* of Weyman T. Johnson and Dixie P. Johnson; *m* 1981, Scarlett M. Swan; one *s* two *d*. *Educ:* Emory Univ. (BA Econs 1976). United States Foreign Service, 1977–2011: Consul Gen., Vancouver, 1990–93; Dir, State Dept Press Office, 1993–95; Dep. Press Sec., The White House, and Spokesman for Nat. Security Council, 1995–97; Ambassador to OSCE, 1998–2001; Afghan Co-ordinator for US, 2002–03; Dep. Chief of Mission, US Embassy, London, 2003–07; Asst Sec. of State, Bureau of Internat. Narcotics and Law Enforcement Affairs, US, 2007–11. Sen. Advr (non-resident), Americas Prog., Center for Strategic and Internat. Studies, 2011–14. Mem., Internat. Narcotics Control Bd, 2012–.

JOHNSON, Diana Ruth; MP (Lab) Kingston upon Hull North, since 2005; *b* 25 July 1966; *d* of late Eric Johnson and Ruth Johnson. *Educ:* Northwich Co. Grammar Sch. for Girls, later Leftwich High Sch.; Sir John Deane's Sixth Form Coll., Cheshire; Queen Mary Coll., Univ. of London (LLB 1988). Volunteer/locum lawyer, Tower Hamlets Law Centre, 1991–94; lawyer: N Lewisham Law Centre, 1995–99; Paddington Law Centre, 1999–2002. Member (Lab): Tower Hamlets LBC, 1994–2002; London Assembly, GLA, March 2003–2004. Mem., Metropolitan Police Authy, 2003–04. Non-executive Director: Newham Healthcare Trust, 1998–2001; Tower Hamlets PCT, 2001–05. Vis. Legal Mem., Mental Health Act Commn, 1995–98. Contested (Lab) Brentwood and Ongar, 2001. PPS to Minister of State, DWP, 2005–06, to Chief Sec. to HM Treasury, 2006–07; an Asst Govt Whip, 2007–10; Parly Under-Sec. of State, DCSF, 2009–10; Shadow Minister for Health, 2010, for Home Office, 2010–15. *Recreations:* cinema, books, theatre, fan of Hull City Football Club, walking. *Address:* (office) Sycamore Suite, Community Enterprise Centre, Cottingham Road, Hull HU5 2DH. *E:* johnsond@parliament.uk. *W:* www.dianajohnson.co.uk, www.twitter.com/DianaJohnsonMP; House of Commons, SW1A 0AA.

JOHNSON, Edwin Geoffrey; QC 2006; barrister; *b* 11 May 1963; *s* of Colin Johnson and Fiona Johnson; *m* 1991, Mary Ann Thorne; two *s* one *d*. *Educ:* Lancing Coll.; Christ Church Coll., Oxford (BA Hons Jurisprudence 1986). Called to the Bar, Lincoln's Inn, 1987; in practice as a barrister, 1988–, specialising in real property and professional negligence. *Publications:* (ed) Snell's Equity, 31st edn 2005. *Recreations:* travel, running, hill walking, scuba diving, ski-ing, reading. *Address:* Maitland Chambers, 7 Stone Buildings, WC2A 3SZ. *T:* (020) 7406 1200, *Fax:* (020) 7406 1300. *E:* ejohnson@maitlandchambers.com.

JOHNSON, Emma Louise, MBE 1996; solo clarinettist; *b* 20 May 1966; *d* of Roger and Mary Johnson; *m* 1997, Chris West; one *d* (one *s* decd). *Educ:* Newstead Wood Sch.; Sevenoaks Sch.; Pembroke Coll., Cambridge (MA English Lit. and Music 1992; Hon. Fellow, 1999). Concerts and tours in Europe, USA, Far East, Australia and Africa; guest appearances with major orchestras world-wide; compositions commnd from several leading British composers. Dir, chamber music gp; Prof. of Clarinet, RCM, 1997–2002. Numerous recordings, including the concertos of Mozart, Crusell, Weber, Finzi, Arnold and Berkeley. Winner, BBC Young Musicians, 1984; Bronze Medal, Eurovision Young Musicians Competition, 1984; Winner, Young Concert Artists Auditions, NY, 1991. *Publications:* "Encore!": compositions and transcriptions for clarinet and piano, 1994; The Emma Johnson Collection, 2008. *Recreations:* theatre, literature, art, gardening, bird watching, travel. *Address:* c/o Nick Curry, Clarion Seven Muses, 47 Whitehall Park, N19 3TW. *T:* (020) 7272 4413.

JOHNSON, (Frederick) Alistair, PhD; FInstP; consultant, active vibration isolation, BAE Systems, since 2003; *b* Christchurch, NZ, 9 April 1928; *s* of Archibald Frederick Johnson and Minnie, *d* of William Frederick Pellew; *m* 1952, Isobel Beth, *d* of Horace George Wilson; two *d*. *Educ:* Christchurch Boys' High Sch.; Univ. of Canterbury, New Zealand (MSc, PhD). Rutherford Meml Fellow, 1952; Lectr, Univ. of Otago, 1952; post graduate research, Bristol Univ., 1953–55. Royal Radar Establishment, 1956–74: Individual Merit Promotion, 1964; Head of Physics Dept, 1968–72; Dep. Director, 1973–74; Dep. Dir, Royal Armament Research & Development Estabt, 1975–76; Dir of Scientific and Technical Intell., MoD, 1977–80; Chief Scientist (Royal Navy) and Dir Gen. Research A, MoD, 1981–84; Dir, Marconi Maritime Applied Res. Lab., and Chief Scientist, Marconi Underwater Systems Ltd, 1985–86; Technical Dir, GEC Research, later GEC-Marconi Res. Centre, 1987–94; Dir, Special Projects, GEC-Marconi, subseq. BAE Systems Res. Centre, 1995–99; consultant, active vibration isolation, 2000–02. Visiting Professor, Massachusetts Inst. of Technology, 1967–68; Hon. Prof. of Physics, Birmingham Univ., 1969–75. *Publications:* numerous physics papers on spectroscopy, optics and lattice dynamics in Proc. Physical Soc. and Proc. Royal Soc.; numerous energy papers on ocean thermal energy conversion and active vibration isolation. *Recreations:* opera, music, travel. *Address:* Otia Tuta, Grassy Lane, Sevenoaks, Kent TN13 1PL. *Clubs:* Athenæum; St Julians (Sevenoaks).

JOHNSON, Frederick James Maugham M.; *see* Marr-Johnson.

JOHNSON, Gareth Alan; MP (C) Dartford, since 2010; *b* Bromley, 12 Oct. 1969; *s* of Alan and Ruth Johnson; *m* 1997, Wendy Morris; one *s* one *d*. *Educ:* Dartford Grammar Sch.; Coll. of Law. Admitted solicitor, 1997; Solicitor, Thomas Boyd Whyte, Solicitors, 1997–2003. Contested (C) Dartford, 2005. *Recreation:* cricket. *Address:* House of Commons, SW1A 0AA. *E:* gareth.johnson.mp@parliament.uk.

JOHNSON, Gen. Sir Garry (Dene), KCB 1990; OBE 1977 (MBE 1971); MC 1965; Chairman, International Security Advisory Board, since 1995; *b* 20 Sept. 1937; *m* 1962, Caroline Sarah Frearson; two *s*. *Educ:* Christ's Hospital. psc, ndc, rcds. Commissioned 10th Princess Mary's Own Gurkha Rifles, 1956; Malaya and Borneo campaigns, 1956–67; Royal Green Jackets, 1970; command, 1st Bn RGJ, 1976–79; Comdr, 11 Armoured Brigade, 1981–82; Dep. Chief of Staff, HQ BAOR, 1983; ACDS (NATO/UK), 1985–87; Comdr, British Forces Hong Kong, and Maj.-Gen., Bde of Gurkhas, 1987–89; MEC, Hong Kong Govt, 1987–89; Comdr Trng and Arms Dirs, 1989–91; Inspector Gen. Doctrine and Trng, 1991–92; C-in-C, AFNORTH, 1992–94. Colonel, 10th PMO Gurkha Rifles, 1985–94; Col Comdt, Light Div., 1990–94. Chm., TEC Nat. Council, 1995–99; Vice-Pres., Nat. Fedn of Enterprise Agencies, 1996–99. Chairman: Ogilby Trust, 1991–2009; Need in Nepal, 1997–2005; Trustee, Gurkha Welfare Trust, 1985–2007 (Chm., 1987–89). Patron, Nat. Malaya & Borneo Veterans Assoc., 2002–. Pres., De Burght Foundn, 2001–07; Member: NACETT, 1995–99; Adv. Council, Prince's Youth Business Trust, 1995–99; NCIHE, 1996–99; Adv. Bd, Centre for Leadership Studies, Exeter Univ., 1998–2005; Chm., Adv. Bd, Internat. Centre for Defence Studies, Tallinn, 2008–. Treas. and Chm., Christ's Hosp. Foundn, 2007–13. FRGS 1993; FRAS 1994; FRSA 1994; FRUSI 1999. Hon. DSc Soton 1999. Order of Terra Mariana (Estonia), 1997; Order of Grand Duke Gediminas (Lithuania), 1999; Medal of Merit (Latvia), 2000; Order of Orange Nassau (Netherlands), 2008; Order of Honour (Georgia), 2010. *Publications:* Brightly Shone the Dawn, 1979; Inland from Gold Beach, 1999. *Club:* Army and Navy.

JOHNSON, Prof. Garth Roston, PhD; FREng, FIMechE; Professor of Rehabilitation Engineering, University of Newcastle upon Tyne, 1995–2008, now Emeritus; *b* 23 Jan. 1945; *s* of Daniel Cowan Johnson and Vera Olive Johnson; *m* 1978, Katherine Zaida Cooke; one *s*. *Educ:* Univ. of Leeds (BSc Hons; PhD 1974). CEng 1991, FIMechE 1991; FREng 2000. Res. engr, Adcock & Shipley, machine tool manufrs, Leicester, 1961–71; Res. Fellow, Rheumatology Res. Unit, Dept of Medicine, Univ. of Leeds, 1971–75; Tech. Dir, Orthotics and Disability Res. Centre, Derbys Royal Infirmary, 1975–81; University of Newcastle upon Tyne: William Leech Reader in Biomed. Engrg, Dept of Mechanical, Materials and Manufg Engrg, 1981–95; Tech. Dir, Centre for Rehabilitation and Engrg Studies, 1991–2008. Head of Res., ADL Smartcare Ltd, 2008–13. *Publications:* (ed with M. P. Barnes) Upper Motor Neurone Syndrome and Spasticity, 2001; contrib. to learned jls incl. Proc. IMechE, Jl Biomechanics, Clin. Biomechanics. *Recreation:* music. *Address:* c/o Centre for Rehabilitation and Engineering Studies, University of Newcastle upon Tyne, Stephenson Building, Newcastle upon Tyne NE1 7RU. *T:* (0191) 222 6196.

JOHNSON, Dr Gordon; President, Wolfson College, 1993–2010, and Deputy Vice-Chancellor, 2002–10, University of Cambridge; Chairman, Comberton Academy Trust, since 2011; *b* 13 Sept. 1943; *s* of Robert Johnson and Bessie (*née* Hewson); *m* 1973, Faith Sargent Lewis, New Haven, Conn; three *s*. *Educ:* Richmond Sch., Yorks; Trinity Coll., Cambridge (BA 1964; MA, PhD 1968). Fellow, Trinity Coll., Cambridge, 1966–74; Selwyn College, Cambridge: Fellow, 1974–94; Tutor, 1975–92; Hon. Fellow, 1994; University of Cambridge: Lectr in History of S Asia, 1974–2005; Dir, Centre of S Asian Studies, 1983–2001; Chairman, Faculty of: Oriental Studies, 1984–87; Architecture and History of Art, 1985–2008; Educn, 1994–2005; Member: Library Syndicate, 1978–2008; Press Syndicate, 1981–2010 (Chm., 1993–2009; Chm., Publishing Cttee, 2009–10); Syndicate on Govt of Univ., 1988–89; Statutes and Ordinances Revision Syndicate, 1990; Gen. Bd of Faculties, 1979–82 and 1985–90; Council, Senate, 1985–92 and 1999–2000; Sandars Reader in Bibliography, 2010. Lady Margaret Preacher, Univ. of Cambridge, 2006. Provost, Gates Cambridge Trust, 2000–10; Trustee: Cambridge Commonwealth Trust, 1983–2015; Cambridge Overseas Trust, 1989–2015; Malaysian Commonwealth Studies Centre, 1999–2011. Pres., RAS, 2009–12, 2015–. Governor: Comberton Village Coll., 1991–2001 (Chm., 1992–2001; Chm., Comberton Educnl Trust, 2008–); Gresham's Sch., 2006–10; Stephen Perse Foundn, 2012–. Liveryman, Stationers' Co., 2003–. Editor, Modern Asian Studies, 1971–2008; Gen. Editor, The New Cambridge History of India, 1979–. *Publications:* Provincial Politics and Indian Nationalism, 1973; University Politics: F. M. Cornford's Cambridge and his advice to the young academic politician, 1994; Cultural Atlas of India, 1995; Printing and Publishing for the University: three hundred years of the press syndicate, 1999. *Recreations:* reading, taking exercise. *Address:* Wolfson College, Cambridge CB3 9BB.

JOHNSON, Gordon Arthur; DL; Chief Executive, Lancashire County Council, 1998–2000; *b* 30 Aug. 1938; *y s* of Annie Elizabeth Johnson and William Johnson; *m* 1963, Jennifer Roxane Bradley; two *d*. *Educ:* Bournemouth Sch.; University College London (BA Hons Hist.). Solicitor. Kent CC, 1962–64; Staffs CC, 1964–73; Dep. Dir of Admin, W Yorks MCC, 1973–76; Dep. Clerk, 1977–90, Chief. Exec. Clerk, 1991–98, Lancs CC. Lancs County Electoral Returning Officer, 1991–2000; Clerk: Lancs Lieutenancy, 1991–2000; Lancs Police Authy, 1995–2000; Lancs Combined Fire Authy, 1998–2000; Secretary: Lancs Adv. Cttee, 1991–2000; Lord Chancellor's Adv. Cttee on Gen. Comrs of Income Tax, 1991–2000; Lancs Probation Cttee; Lancs Cttee, Prince's Trust-Action; Co. Sec., Lancs County Enterprises Ltd, 1991–2000; Mem., MSC Area Manpower Bd, 1986–88; Chm., Soc. of County Secretaries, 1987–88 (Hon. Treasurer, 1977–86); Dir, LAWTEC, 1991–98. Adviser: LGA Policy and Strategy Cttee, 1997–2000; Assoc. of Police Authorities, 1997–2000. Mem. Court, 1991–2000, Dep. Pro-Chancellor, 2002–10, Univ. of Lancaster. Constable, Lancaster Castle, 2004–13. DL Lancs, 2000. *Recreations:* travel, reading. *Address:* Beech House, 72 Higher Bank Road, Fulwood, Preston, Lancs PR2 8PH.

JOHNSON, Graham Rhodes, OBE 1994; concert accompanist; Senior Professor of Accompaniment, Guildhall School of Music, since 1986; *b* 10 July 1950; *s* of late John Edward Donald Johnson and of Violet May Johnson (*née* Johnson). *Educ:* Hamilton High Sch., Bulawayo, Rhodesia; Royal Acad. of Music, London. FRAM 1984; FGS (FGSM 1988). Concert début, Wigmore Hall, 1972; has since accompanied Elisabeth Schwarzkopf, Jessye Norman, Victoria de los Angeles (USA Tour 1977), Dame Janet Baker, Sir Peter Pears, Dame Felicity Lott, Dame Margaret Price (USA Tour 1985), Peter Schreier, John Shirley Quirk, Mady Mesplé, Thomas Hampson, Robert Holl, Tom Krause, Sergei Leiferkus, Brigitte Fassbaender, Matthias Goerne, Christine Schäfer. Work with contemporaries led to formation of The Songmakers' Almanac (Artistic Director); has devised and accompanied over 150 London recitals for this group since Oct. 1976. Tours of US with Sarah Walker, Richard Jackson, and of Australia and NZ with The Songmakers' Almanac, 1981. Writer and presenter of major BBC Radio 3 series on Poulenc songs, and BBC TV programmes on Schubert songs (1978) and the songs of Liszt (1986). Lectr at song courses in Savonlinna (Finland), US and at Pears-Britten Sch., Snape; Artistic advr and accompanist, Alte Oper Festival, Frankfurt, 1981–82; Song Adviser, Wigmore Hall, 1992–; Chm. Jury, Wigmore Hall Internat. Singing Competition, 1997, 1999 and 2001. Festival appearances in Aldeburgh, Edinburgh, Munich, Hohenems, Salzburg, Bath, Hong Kong, Bermuda. Many recordings incl. those with Songmakers' Almanac, Martyn Hill, Elly Ameling, Arleen Auger, Janet Baker, Philip Langridge, Marjana Lipovsek, Ann Murray, Sarah Walker, Anthony Rolfe Johnson, and of complete Schubert, Schumann and Brahms Lieder and Fauré and Poulenc mélodies, with various artists, 1987–. Hon. Member: Royal Swedish Acad. of Music, 2000; Royal Philharmonic Soc., 2010. Hon. DMus: Durham, 2013; New England Conservatory, Boston, USA 2013. Gramophone Award, 1989, 1996, 1997 and 2001; Royal Philharmonic Prize for Instrumentalist, 1998; Edison Prize, 2006; Walter Wilson Cobbett Chamber Music Medal, 2009; Wigmore Hall Medal, 2013. Chevalier, Ordre des Arts et des Lettres (France), 2002. *Publications:* (contrib.) The Britten Companion, ed Christopher Palmer, 1984; (contrib.) Gerald Moore, The Unashamed Accompanist, rev. edn 1984; (contrib.) The Spanish Song Companion, 1992; The Songmakers' Almanac: reflections and commentaries, 1996; A French Song Companion, 2000; Britten, Voice and Piano, 2003; Gabriel Fauré: the songs and their poets, 2009; Franz Schubert: the complete songs (3 vols), 2014; reviews in TLS, articles for music jls. *Address:* c/o Askonas Holt Ltd, Lincoln House, 300 High Holborn, WC1V 7JH.

JOHNSON, Sir Guy; *see* Johnson, Sir C. G.

JOHNSON, Heather Jean; *see* Mellows, H. J.

JOHNSON, Hugh Eric Allan, OBE 2007; author, editor and broadcaster; *b* 10 March 1939; *s* of late Guy Francis Johnson, CBE and Grace Kittel; *m* 1965, Judith Eve Grinling; one *s* two *d*. *Educ:* Rugby Sch.; King's Coll., Cambridge (MA; Fellow Commoner, 2001). Staff writer, Condé Nast publications, 1960–63; Editor, Wine & Food, and Sec., Wine and Food Soc., 1963–65; Wine Corresp., 1962–67, and Travel Editor, 1967, Sunday Times; Editor, Queen, 1968–70; Wine Editor, Gourmet, NY, 1971–72. President: The Sunday Times Wine Club, 1973–; Circle of Wine Writers, 1997–2006. Founder Mem., Tree Council, 1974. Chairman: Saling Hall Press, 1975–2013; Conservation Cttee, Internat. Dendrology Soc., 1979–86 (Vice Chm., 2014–); Winestar Productions Ltd, 1984–2006; The Hugh Johnson Collection Ltd, 1985–2014; Director: Société Civile de Château Latour, 1986–2001; Coldstream Winemakers Ltd, 1991–94; Exbury Gardens Ltd, 2013–. Editorial Director: Jl of RHS, 1975–89, Editl Cons., 1989–2006; The Plantsman, 1979–94. Wine Editor, Cuisine, New York, 1983–84; Wine Consultant: to Jardine Matheson Ltd, Hong Kong and Tokyo, 1985–2001; to British Airways, 1987–2002; to the Royal Tokaji Wine Co., 1990–; Hon. Trustee, Amer. Center for Wine, Food and the Arts, Calif, 2000–11; Hon. Pres., Internat. Wine and Food Soc., 2002–08; Hon. Pres., Wine and Spirit Educn Trust, 2009–11. Gardening Correspondent, New York Times, 1986–87; Columnist, Trad's Diary, 1975– (www.tradsdiary.com), Hortus mag. Editl Advr, The World of Fine Wine, 2004–. Video, How to Handle a Wine, 1984 (Glenfiddich Trophy, 1984; reissued as Understanding Wine, 1989); TV series: Wine—a user's guide (KQED, San Francisco), 1986; Vintage—a history of wine (Channel 4 and WGBH, Boston), 1989. Hon. Chm., Wine Japan (Tokyo exhibn), 1989–94. Pres., Metropolitan Public Gardens Assoc., 2012–; Vice-Pres., Essex Gardens Trust, 1997–2013. Hon. Liveryman, Vintners' Co., 2003. Docteur ès Vins, Acad. du Vin de Bordeaux, 1987. DUniv Essex, 1998. Hon. Citizen of Hungary, 2014. Carl-Friedrich von

Rumor Gold Award, German Gastronomic Acad., 1998; Veitch Meml Medal, RHS, 2000. Chevalier, Ordre Nat. du Mérite (France), 2003. *Publications:* Wine, 1966, rev. edn 1974; (ed) Frank Schoonmaker's Encyclopedia of Wine, English edn, 1967; The World Atlas of Wine, 1971, 7th edn (with Jancis Robinson) 2013; The International Book of Trees, 1973, 2nd edn as Trees: a lifetime's journey through forests, woods and gardens, 2010; (with Bob Thompson) The California Wine Book, 1976; Hugh Johnson's Pocket Wine Book, annually 1977–; The Principles of Gardening, 1979, rev. edn as Hugh Johnson's Gardening Companion, 1996; Understanding Wine, 1980; (with Paul Miles) The Pocket Encyclopedia of Garden Plants, 1981; Hugh Johnson's Wine Companion, 1983, 6th edn (with Stephen Brook), 2009; How to Enjoy Your Wine, 1985, 2nd edn 1998; The Hugh Johnson Cellar Book, 1986; The Atlas of German Wines, 1986, rev. edn (with Stuart Pigott) 1995; Hugh Johnson's Wine Cellar, (US) 1986; (with Jan Read) The Wine and Food of Spain, 1987; (with Hubrecht Duijker) The Wine Atlas of France, 1987, rev. edn 1997; The Story of Wine, 1989 (ten awards, incl. Glenfiddich Wine Award, 1990, Grand Prix de la Communication de la Vigne et du Vin, 1992), new illus. edn, 2004; Hugh Johnson's Pop-up Wine Book, 1989; (with James Halliday) The Art and Science of Wine, 1992, new edn 2006; Hugh Johnson on Gardening: the best of Tradescant's Diary, 1993; Tuscany and its Wines, 2000; Wine: a life uncorked, 2005; Hugh Johnson in The Garden, 2009; Wine Journal, 2011; articles on gastronomy, travel and gardening. *Recreations:* trees, staying at home, travelling, gardening, wine, lunch and dinner. *Address:* 70 Scarsdale Villas, W8 6PP. *Clubs:* Garrick, Brooks's, Saintsbury, Beefsteak; Essex (Pres., 2012); Keyhaven Yacht.

JOHNSON, Rt Rev. James Nathaniel; Bishop of St Helena, 1985–91, now Bishop Emeritus; Hon. Assistant Bishop, Diocese of Oxford, since 2004; *b* 28 April 1932; *s* of William and Lydia Florence Johnson; *m* 1953, Evelyn Joyce Clifford; one *s* one *d*. *Educ:* Primary and Secondary Selective School, St Helena; Church Army College; Wells Theol Coll. Deacon 1964, priest 1965; Curate of St Peter's, Lawrence Weston, Dio. of Bristol, 1964–66; Priest-in-charge of St Paul's Cathedral, St Helena, 1966–69, Vicar 1969–71; Domestic Chaplain to Bishop of St Helena, 1967–71; USPG Area Sec. for Dio. of Exeter and Truro, 1972–74; Rector of Combe Martin, Dio. of Exeter, 1974–80; Hon. Canon of St Helena, 1975–; Vicar of St Augustine, Thorpe Bay, Dio. of Chelmsford, 1980–85; Rector of Byfield with Boddington and Aston-le-Walls, and Hon. Asst Bishop, Dio. of Peterborough, 1991–92; Vicar of Hockley, Essex, 1992–97; Asst Bishop, 1992–97, Hon. Asst Bishop, 1997–2004, Dio. of Chelmsford. Non-residentiary Canon, Chelmsford Cathedral, 1994–97, Canon Emeritus, 1997. Permission to officiate, Dio. of Europe, 1998. *Recreations:* music, gardening, walking, cycling. *Address:* St Helena, 28 Molyneux Drive, Bodicote, Oxon OX15 4AP. *T:* (01295) 255357.

JOHNSON, James North, MD; FRCS, FRCP; FDSRCS; Consultant Surgeon: Halton General Hospital, Runcorn, 1985–2010; Royal Bolton Hospital, 2011–12; Chairman of Council, British Medical Association, 2003–07; *b* 13 Nov. 1946; *s* of Edwin Johnson and Elizabeth Marjorie Johnson (*née* North); *m* 1st, 1972, Dr Gillian Christine Markham (marr. diss. 2002); one *s* one *d*; 2nd, 2006, Fiona Helen Simpson. *Educ:* Liverpool Univ. Med. Sch. (MB ChB 1970, MD 1980). FRCS 1977; FRCP 2000; FDSRCS 2000. Demonstrator, then Lectr in Anatomy, Univ. of Liverpool, 1971–74; Fellow, Merseyside Assoc. for Kidney Res., 1974–75; Registrar and Sen. Registrar trng posts, Mersey Reg., 1975–85; Clinical Lectr in Surgery, Liverpool Univ., 1987–. Vis. Prof. in Anatomy, Univ. of Texas, 1973. British Medical Association: Mem. Council, 1975–80 and 1992–2007; Chairman: Hosp. Jun. Staffs Cttee, 1979–80; Central Consultants and Specialists Cttee, 1994–98 (Vice-Chm., 1990–94). Chm., Jt Consultants Cttee, 1998–2003 (Vice-Chm., 1994–98); Mem., Standing Med. Adv. Cttee, DoH, 1998–2004. Mem., Mgt Cttee, Nat. Counselling Service for Sick Doctors, 1985–2004. Hon. Consultant Surgeon, Guy's and St Thomas' NHS Trust, 2009–10. *Publications:* contrib. articles on surgical, vascular surgical and medico-political topics, incl. the future rôle of consultant, hospital configuration and appraisal. *Recreations:* travel, fine wine, medical politics, modern languages. *Address:* Talgarth, 66 View Road, Rainhill, Prescot, Merseyside L35 0LS. *T:* (0151) 426 4306, *Fax:* (0151) 493 0024. *E:* jnjohnson33@hotmail.com. *Clubs:* Athenæum; XX, Artists (Liverpool).

JOHNSON, Sir John (Rodney), KCMG 1988 (CMG 1981); HM Diplomatic Service, retired; Chairman, Countryside Commission, 1991–95; Visiting Fellow, Kellogg College, Oxford, 2000–15; *b* 6 Sept. 1930; *s* of Edwin Done Johnson, OBE and Florence Mary (*née* Clough); *m* 1956, Jean Mary Lewis; three *s* one *d*. *Educ:* Manchester Grammar Sch.; Oxford Univ. (MA). HM Colonial Service, Kenya, 1955–64; Dist Comr, Thika, 1962–64; Administrator, Cttee of Vice-Chancellors and Principals of UK Univs, 1965; First Sec., FCO, 1966–69; Head of Chancery, British Embassy, Algiers, 1969–72; Dep. High Comr, British High Commn, Barbados, 1972–74; Counsellor, British High Commn, Lagos, 1975–78; Head of W African Dept, FCO, and Ambassador (non-resident) to Chad, 1978–80; High Comr in Zambia, 1980–84; Asst Under Sec. of State (Africa), FCO, 1984–86; High Comr in Kenya, 1986–90; Dir, Foreign Service Prog., and specially elected Fellow, Keble Coll., Oxford Univ., 1990–95. Mem., Jt Nature Conservation Cttee, 1991–95. Chairman: Kenya Soc., 1992–98; Chilterns Conservation Bd, 2001–10; President: Friends of Lake Dist, 1995–2005; Long Distance Walkers Assoc., 1995–2015; Vice-President: Royal African Soc., 1995–2005; YHA, 1995–2008; Chiltern Soc., 1995–; Vice-Chm., Chilterns Conf., 1996–2001. *Publications:* (ed) Colony to Nation: British administrators in Kenya, 2002; Kenya: the land and the people, 2010. *Recreations:* walking, reaching remote places. *Address:* The Gables, 27 High Street, Amersham, Bucks HP7 0DP. *Clubs:* Travellers, Alpine; Climbers'; Mombasa.

JOHNSON, Joseph Edmund; MP (C) Orpington, since 2010; Minister of State (Minister for Universities and Science), Department for Business, Innovation and Skills, since 2015; *b* London, Dec. 1971; *s* of Stanley Patrick Johnson, *qv* and Charlotte Maria Fawcett; *m* 2005, Amelia Gentleman; one *s* one *d*. *Educ:* Eton Coll.; Balliol Coll., Oxford (MA 1st cl. Mod. Hist.); Inst. d'Etudes Européennes, Brussels (Licence Spéciale); INSEAD, Fontainebleau (MBA 2000). Corporate financier, Investment Banking Div., Deutsche Bank, 1996–97; Financial Times: Lex columnist, 1997–99; Paris corresp., 2001–05; S Asia Bureau Chief, 2005–08; Associate Ed. and Ed., Lex column, 2008–10. PPS to Mark Prisk, Minister of State for Business and Enterprise, 2010–12; an Asst Govt Whip, 2012–14; Hd of No 10 Policy Unit, and Chair, Policy Adv. Bd, 2013–15; Parly Sec., 2013–14, Minister of State, 2014–15, Cabinet Office. *Publications:* (with Martine Orange) The Man Who Tried to Buy the World, 2003; (ed jtly) Reconnecting Britain and India: ideas for an enhanced partnership, 2011. *Recreations:* trekking, writing, tennis. *Address:* House of Commons, SW1A 0AA. *E:* jo.johnson.mp@parliament.uk.

See also A. B. de P. Johnson, L. F. Johnson, R. S. Johnson.

JOHNSON, Keith; *see* Johnson, A. K.

JOHNSON, Kenneth James, OBE 1966; colonial administrator and industrialist; *b* 8 Feb. 1926; *s* of Albert Percy Johnson and Winifred Florence (*née* Coole); *m* 1951, Margaret Teresa Bontoft Jenkins; three *s* two *d*. *Educ:* Rishworth School, near Halifax; Wadham Coll., Oxford; LSE; SOAS. Indian Army (14 Punjab Regt), 1945–47. Colonial Admin. Service, Nigeria, 1949–61, Provincial Admin. (Dist Officer), Northern Region and senior appts in Min. of Finance and Min. of Commerce and Industry; Head of Economic Dept, later Dir of Industrial Affairs, CBI, 1961–70; Courtaulds Ltd, 1970–73: Chm. and Man. Dir, various subsidiary cos; Dep. Chm., Pay Board, 1973–74; Dunlop Group, 1974–85: Personnel Dir, 1974–79; Overseas Dir, Dunlop Holdings plc, 1979–84; Chm., Dunlop International AG, 1984–85; Chm., Crown Agents Pensions Trust, 1984–96. Member: Bd of Crown Agents for Oversea Govts and Administrations, 1980–88; Crown Agents Hldg and Realisation Bd, 1980–88. Chm., Farlington Sch. Trust, 1990–2000. FRSA 1972; FIPM 1976. *Recreation:* book-collecting. *Address:* Snappers Field, Shipley Road, Southwater, Horsham, West Sussex RH13 9BQ. *Club:* Oriental.

JOHNSON, Prof. Kenneth Langstreth, PhD; FRS 1982; FREng; Professor of Engineering, Cambridge University, 1977–92, now Emeritus; Fellow of Jesus College, Cambridge, 1957–92, now Emeritus; *b* 19 March 1925; *s* of Frank Herbert Johnson and Ellen Howorth Langstreth; *m* 1954, Dorothy Rosemary Watkins; one *s* two *d*. *Educ:* Barrow Grammar Sch.; Manchester Univ. (MScTech, MA, PhD). FIMechE; FREng (FEng 1987). Engr, Messrs Rotol Ltd, Gloucester, 1944–49; Asst Lectr, Coll. of Technology, Manchester, 1949–54; Lectr, then Reader in Engrg, Cambridge Univ., 1954–77. Hon. FUMIST, 1993. Tribology Trust Gold Medal, IMechE, 1985; Mayo Hersey Award, ASME, 1991; William Prager Medal, Amer. Soc. Engrg Sci., 1999; Royal Medal, Royal Soc., 2003; Timoshenko Medal, ASME, 2006. *Publications:* Contact Mechanics, 1985; contrib. scientific and engrg jls, and Proc. IMechE. *Recreations:* mountain walking, swimming. *Address:* 1 New Square, Cambridge CB1 1EY. *T:* (01223) 355287.

JOHNSON, Leo Fenton; Partner, PricewaterhouseCoopers Sustainability and Climate Change, since 2008 (Co-Founder and Director, Sustainable Finance Ltd, 2003–08); *b* London, 26 Sept. 1967; *s* of Stanley Patrick Johnson, *qv* and Charlotte Maria Johnson (*née* Fawcett); *m* 1996, Taies Nezam, *d* of Amanullah Nezam and Malal Moosa; two *d*. *Educ:* New Coll., Oxford (Stephens Schol.; BA); University Coll. London (MSc Resource and Envmtl Econs); INSEAD (MBA). Consultant, Envmt Dept, IFC, 1993–2003. Dir, Handbag Pictures, 1997–2003. Vis. Business Fellow, Smith Sch. of Enterprise and Envmt, Univ. of Oxford, 2010–. Presenter, Down to Business prog., BBC World News. Sustainability Advr and Judge, Prix Pictet for photography on sustainability; Judge, FT Boldness in Business Awards. Writer and dir, film, Eating and Weeping, 2002. Trustee: New Econs Foundn; Green Alliance. *Publications:* Beyond Risk, 2002; contribs to FT, Wall St Jl. *Recreation:* time with my wife and daughters. *Address:* c/o JLA Agency, 14 Berners Street, W1T 3LJ. *T:* (020) 7907 2800. *E:* leojohnson1@gmail.com.

See also A. B. de P. Johnson, J. E. Johnson, R. S. Johnson.

JOHNSON, Luke Oliver; Chairman: Risk Capital Partners, since 2001; StartUp Britain, since 2012; Brainspark, since 2012; TellTheChef, since 2014; Co-founder and Chairman, Centre for Entrepreneurs, since 2013; *b* 2 Feb. 1962; *s* of Paul Bede Johnson, *qv*; *m* 2004, Liza Pickrell; two *s* one *d*. *Educ:* Langley Grammar Sch.; Magdalen Coll., Oxford. Stockbroking Analyst, Grieveson Grant, then Kleinwort Benson, 1983–88; Director: AoD, 1989–92; ICD, 1989–92; Crabtree Gp, 1992–94; PizzaExpress, 1992–95 and 1998–99 (Chm., 1996–98); My Kinda Town, 1994–96; American Port Services, 1995–98; Abacus Recruitment, 1995–99; Integrated Dental Hldgs, 1996–2006; Whittards of Chelsea, 1998–2001; NewMedia SPARK, 1999–2001; Nightfreight, 1999–2001; Acquisitor, 1999–2004; Manager, Intrinsic Value, 1999–2001; Chairman: Belgo Gp, subseq. Signature Restaurants Ltd, 1997–2005; Grand Union, 2013–; Red Hot World Buffet, 2013–. Chairman: Channel 4 TV, 2004–09; Royal Soc. of Arts, 2009–12. Mem., Govt Adv. Panel on public library service in England, 2014–. Chm. of Trustees, Action on Addiction, 2012–. Gov., Univ. of the Arts, London (formerly London Inst.), 2000–06. Columnist: Sunday Telegraph, 1997–2006; FT, 2007–. *Publications:* How to Get a Highly Paid Job in the City, 1987; Betting to Win, 1990, 2nd edn 1997; The Maverick: dispatches from an unrepentant capitalist, 2007; Start It Up: why running your own business is easier than you think, 2011. *Recreations:* writing, tennis, swimming. *Address:* Risk Capital Partners, 31 North Row, W1K 6DA. *T:* (020) 7016 0700. *Clubs:* Royal Automobile, Groucho, Lansdowne.

See also D. B. Johnson.

JOHNSON, Prof. Margaret Anne, MD, FRCP; Consultant Physician in Thoracic Medicine and HIV Medicine, since 1989, and Clinical Director, HIV/AIDS, since 1992, Royal Free Hampstead NHS Trust; Professor of HIV Medicine, University College London, since 2005; *b* 7 Feb. 1952; *d* of Dr Frederick W. Johnson and Dr Margaret Rosemary Johnson; *m* 1980, Prof. John William Winston Studd, *qv*; one *s* two *d*. *Educ:* Convent of the Sacred Heart, Woldingham; Royal Free Hosp. Sch. of Medicine, Univ. of London (MD 1987). FRCP 1993. House Physician, 1976, House Surgeon, 1976–77, Royal Free Hosp.; Senior House Officer: Postgrad. Trng Scheme in Medicine, Whittington Hosp., 1977–78; London Chest Hosp., 1978; Nat. Hosp. for Nervous Diseases, 1978–79; Registrar Rotation in Gen. Medicine, St Mary's Hosp., W2, 1979–81; Res. Registrar, Royal Brompton Hosp., 1981–83; Sen. Registrar Rotation in Gen. Medicine and Thoracic Medicine, Royal Free Hosp./Royal Brompton Hosp., 1983–89; Med. Dir, Royal Free Hampstead NHS Trust, 2002–06. Chm., British HIV Assoc., 2004–08. *Publications:* An Atlas of HIV and AIDS, 1995, 2nd edn 2004; articles concerning clinical mgt of HIV in learned jls. *Address:* Department of HIV Medicine, Royal Free Hospital, Pond Street, NW3 2QG. *T:* (020) 7941 1820, *Fax:* (020) 7941 1830. *Club:* Athenæum.

JOHNSON, Prof. Mark Henry, PhD; FBA 2011; Professor of Psychology, and Director, Centre for Brain and Cognitive Development, Birkbeck, University of London, since 1997; *b* London, 4 June 1960; *s* of James Johnson and Krystyna Johnson; *m* 2001, Prof. Annette Dionne Karmiloff-Smith, *qv*. *Educ:* Univ. of Edinburgh (BSc Biol Scis 1981); King's Coll., Cambridge (PhD Zool. 1985). Res. Scientist, MRC Cognitive Devlt Unit, London, 1985–90; Associate Prof. of Psychol., Carnegie-Mellon Univ., 1991–95; Sen. Res. Scientist, MRC Cognitive Devlt Unit, London, 1994–98. *Publications:* (with J. Morton) Biology and Cognitive Development: the case of face recognition, 1991; Brain Development and Cognition: a reader, 1993, 2nd edn (jtly) 2002; (jtly) Rethinking Innateness: a connectionist perspective on development, 1996; Developmental Cognitive Neuroscience: an introduction, 1997, 3rd edn (with Michelle de Haan) 2010; (ed jtly) The Cognitive Neuroscience of Development, 2003; (ed jtly) Attention and Performance XXI: processes of change in brain and cognitive development, 2006; (jtly) Neuroconstructivism, vol. 1: how the brain constructs cognition, 2007, vol. 2: perspectives and prospects, 2007; (ed jtly) The Handbook of Face Perception, 2011. *Recreations:* gardening, whisky, science. *Address:* Centre for Brain and Cognitive Development, Department of Psychological Science, Birkbeck, University of London, WC1E 7HX. *T:* (020) 7631 6226. *Club:* Hanbury Manor (Ware, Herts).

JOHNSON, Martin; Sports Feature Writer, Sunday Times, since 2008; *b* 23 June 1949; *s* of late Basil Johnson and of Bridget Johnson; *m* 1985, Teresa Mary Wright; one *s* one *d*. *Educ:* St Julian's High Sch., Newport, Mon.; Monmouth Sch. Ronald French Advertising Agency, Liverpool, 1970; South Wales Argus, Newport, 1970–73; Leicester Mercury, 1973–86; Cricket Corresp., The Independent, 1986–95; Sports Feature Writer, Daily Telegraph, 1995–2008. *Publications:* (ed) The Independent World Cup Cricket, 1987; (jtly) Gower: the autobiography, 1992; Rugby and All That: an irreverent history, 2000. *Recreation:* golf. *Address:* The Old Chapel House, Chapel Road, Ross-on-Wye HR9 5PR. *Club:* Ross on Wye Golf.

JOHNSON, Prof. Martin Hume, PhD; FMedSci; FRS 2014; Professor of Reproductive Sciences, University of Cambridge, 1992–2012, now Emeritus; Life Fellow, Christ's College, Cambridge, since 1969 (Vice-Master, 2007–09; President, 2009–10; Tutor, 2013–14); *b* 19 Dec. 1944; *s* of late Reginald Hugh Ben Johnson and of Joyce Florence Johnson. *Educ:* Cheltenham Grammar Sch.; Christ's Coll., Cambridge (MA, PhD). Jun. Res. Fellow, Christ's Coll., Cambridge, 1969; MRC Jun. Res. Fellow, 1970; Harkness Fellow, 1971; University of Cambridge: Lectr in Anatomy, 1974–84; Reader in Exptl Embryology, 1984–92; Head of Dept of Anatomy, 1995–99. Hon. Sen. Lectr in Obstetrics and Gynaecology, UMDS,

1991–95; Distinguished Vis. Fellow, La Trobe Univ., 1993, 2006; Vis. Prof., Sydney Univ., 1999–2004; Hon. Academic Fellow, St Paul's Coll., Sydney Univ., 2005. Chm., Brit. Soc. for Developmental Biol., 1984–89; Mem., HFEA, 1994–99. Special Advr to Jt Lords and Commons Inquiry Cttee on the Human Tissue and Embryos (Draft) Bill, 2007. Chief Exec., Edwards and Steptoe Charitable Trust, 2010. Ed., Reproductive Medicine OnLine, 2010. Lectures: Hammond, Soc. for Study of Fertility, 1992; Haliburton, Dept of Physiol., KCL, 1994; S. T. Huang-Chan Meml, Hong Kong Univ., 1997; Ver Heyden de Lancey, Univ. of Cambridge, 2007; A. E. Szulman, Univ. of Pittsburg, 2007; Robert G. Edwards Nobel, Lisbon, 2012; Historical Lectr, Eur. Soc. for Human Reproduction, Istanbul, 2012. Hon. FRCOG (FRCOG 2005); FMedSci 2012. Albert Brachet Prize, Belgian Royal Acad. Scis, Letters and Fine Arts, 1989; Prize for Innovation in Med. Educn, King's Fund, 1993; Marshall Medal, Soc. for Reproduction and Fertility, 2014. *Publications:* Essential Reproduction, (with B. J. Everitt) 1980, 7th edn 2013 (BMA Book Prize in Obstetrics and Gynaecol., 2008); (ed jtly) Sexuality Repositioned: diversity and the law, 2004; (ed jtly) Death Rites and Rights, 2007; (ed jtly) Birth Rites and Rights, 2011; contrib. to numerous scientific pubns. *Recreations:* opera, music. *Address:* Anatomy School, Department of Physiology, Development and Neuroscience, Downing Street, Cambridge CB2 3DY. *T:* (01223) 333777.

JOHNSON, Martin Osborne, CBE 2004 (OBE 1998); Rugby Union football player, retired; Team Manager, England Rugby Football Union Team, 2008–11; *b* Solihull, 9 March 1970; *s* of David Johnson and late Hilary Johnson; *m* 2000, Kay Gredrig; one *s* one *d. Educ:* Robert Smyth Sch., Market Harborough. Joined Leicester RFU Club Youth team, 1988; played for College Old Boys, King Country, NZ and NZ Under 21s, 1989–90; joined Leicester Tigers, 1989: Captain, 1997–2003, 2004–05; Premiership Champions, 1999, 2000, 2001, 2002; winners, European Cup, 2001, 2002. 1st cap for England, 1993; Capt., 1999–2003; 84 caps, 39 as Capt.; captained Grand Slam side, 2003; has played in 3 World Cup teams, two as Capt.; winners, Rugby World Cup, Australia, 2003; Member, British Lions tours: NZ, 1993; S Africa, 1997 (Capt.); Australia, 2001 (Capt.). *Publications:* Agony and Ecstasy, 2001; Martin Johnson: the autobiography, 2003.

JOHNSON, Matthew Alfred; HM Diplomatic Service; UK Permanent Representative to Council of Europe, Strasbourg (with personal rank of Ambassador), 2012–summer 2016; *b* Rochford, Essex, 11 June 1970; *s* of late Alfred James Johnson and of Mary Theresa Johnson (*née* Slattery); *m* 1993, Heidi Suzanne Burton; one *s* one *d. Educ:* Westcliff High Sch. for Boys. Joined FCO, 1988; FCO, 1988–90; Pretoria and Cape Town, 1990–93; Third Sec., Middle E Dept, FCO, 1993; Vice-Consul, Osaka, 1994–96; Third, then Second Sec., Eastern Dept, FCO, 1996–99; Private Sec. to Hd of Policy Unit, Prime Minister's Office, 10 Downing St, 1999–2000; Second Sec., UK Mission to UN, NY, 2000–03; First Sec., Afghanistan Gp, FCO, 2003–06; First Sec. and Dep. Hd, Conflict Gp, FCO, 2006–08; Counsellor and Dep. High Comr, Accra, 2008–12. *Recreations:* sports (cricket, tennis, Rugby), history, music (piano and singing), films. *Address:* c/o Foreign and Commonwealth Office, King Charles Street, SW1A 2AH. *E:* matthew.johnson@fco.gov.uk. *W:* www.twitter.com/mjohnsonFCO.

JOHNSON, Melanie Jane; JP; *b* 5 Feb. 1955; *d* of David Guyatt Johnson and Mary Angela Johnson; one *s* twin *d* by William Jordan. *Educ:* University Coll. London (BA Jt Hons Phil. and Ancient Greek); King's Coll., Cambridge (postgrad. res.). Mem. Relns Officer, 1981–88, Retail Admin Manager, 1988–90, Cambridge Co-op. Soc.; Asst Gen. Manager (Quality Assurance), Cambs FHSA, 1990–92; Schools Inspector, 1993–97. Mem. (Lab) Cambs CC, 1981–97. MP (Lab) Welwyn Hatfield, 1997–2005; contested (Lab) same seat, 2005. PPS to Financial Sec., HM Treasury, 1999; Economic Sec., HM Treasury, 1999–2001; Parly Under-Sec. of State, DTI, 2001–03; Parly Under-Sec. of State (Minister for Public Health), DoH, 2003–05. Member: Public Admin. Select Cttee, 1997–98; Home Affairs Select Cttee, 1998–99; Chm., All Party Parenting Gp, 1998–2005. Chairman: Customer Impact Panel, ABI, 2006–11; UK Cards Assoc., 2009–. Contested (Lab) Cambs, EP elecn, 1994. JP Cambridge, 1994. *Recreations:* family, films, gardening. *E:* melaniejohnson@ntlworld.com.

JOHNSON, Melinda Jane; Director of Group Commercial Services, Department for Transport, since 2015; *b* Wakefield, 13 Nov. 1965; *d* of Henry and June Johnson; *m* 2004, Philip James Considine. *Educ:* Univ. of York (BSc Hons Psychol. 1988); Univ. of Durham (MBA (Dist.) 1996). DipM, MCIM 2003. Product buyer, BT, 1988–89; buyer, GSPK Electronics, 1989–90; Sen. Buyer, IT, Nat. Power plc, 1990–93; Head: Procurement, Univ. of Durham, 1993–99; Policy and Representation, Chartered Inst. of Purchasing and Supply, 1999–2003; Principal Procurement Consultant, Improvement and Develt Agency, 2003–05; Deputy Director: Centre for Procurement Performance, DfES, subseq. DCSF, 2005–08; Commercial, DCSF, subseq. DFE, 2008–11; Dep. Finance and Commercial Dir, DFE, 2011–12; Dir, Gp Procurement and Property, DfT, 2012–15. Chair, Extended Procurement Exec. Bd for Central Govt, 2011–12. Chartered Institute for Purchasing and Supply: Member: Council, 2008–11; Bd of Mgt, 2010–11; Disciplinary Cttee, 2011–14; Global Bd of Trustees, 2012–14; Chm., Global Congress, 2012–14. Mem. Council, 1995–98, Chair, 1998, Assoc. of Univ. Purchasing Officers. FCIPS 2003 (MCIPS 1992); MCMI 1996; MBPsS 2010. *Recreations:* travel, art, cinema, reading. *Address:* Department for Transport, Great Minster House, 33 Horseferry Road, SW1P 4DR. *T:* 07920 266375. *E:* melinda.johnson@dft.gsi.gov.uk.

JOHNSON, Michael Robert; graphic designer; Founder, 1992, and Creative Director, since 1992, Johnson Banks Design, graphic design consultancy; *b* 26 April 1964; *s* of late Charles Beverley Johnson and of Shirley Anne Johnson (*née* Fowler); *m* 1995, Elisabeth Schoon; one *s* one *d. Educ:* Ecclesbourne Sch., Duffield, Derby; Univ. of Lancaster (BA 1st Cl. Jt Hons Design and Mktg 1985). Junior consultant, Wolff Olins, London, 1985–86; designer, Billy Blue Gp, Sydney, 1986–87; freelance designer, Tokyo, 1987; designer, Emery Vincent Design, Melbourne and Sydney, 1988; Art Dir, Omon Advertising, Sydney, 1988; Sen. Designer, Sedley Place Design, London, 1988–89; Gp Art Dir, Smith and Milton, London, 1990–92. D&AD: Mem., 1991–; Cttee Mem., 1999–2003; Educn Chm., 2001–02; Pres., 2003; Chm., Design Week Awards, 1989, 1999. External Examiner: Glasgow Sch. of Art, 2001–04; Kingston Univ., 2006–; Mem., Re-validation Cttee, Communications course, RCA, 1998. Visiting Lecturer: Kingston Univ.; Nottingham Univ.; Northumbria Univ.; Middlesex Univ.; Falmouth Coll. of Art; Glasgow Sch. of Art; Central St Martins. *Exhibitions* include: *group*: The Power of the Poster (contrib. curator), 1998, Rewind: 40 Years of Design and Advertising (co-curator), 2002, V&A; European Design Biennial, Design Mus., 2003, 2005; Communicate: Independent British Graphic Design since the Sixties, Barbican Gall., 2004–05; *solo*: Words & Pictures, the design work of Michael Johnson + johnson banks, 2004, Jeans Shop Ginza, 2005, Creation Gall., Tokyo. Seven Silver Awards, one Gold Award, D&AD; 13 Design Week Awards; Gold Award, 1991, 2008, Silver Award, 2004, NY Art Dirs. *Publications:* Problem Solved: a primer in design and communication, 2002; (contrib.) Rewind: 40 years of design and advertising, 2002. *Recreations:* playing and collecting guitars, music. *Address:* Johnson Banks Design Limited, Crescent Works, Crescent Lane, SW4 9RW. *T:* (020) 7587 6400, *Fax:* (020) 7587 6411. *E:* Michael@johnsonbanks.co.uk.

JOHNSON, Michael York-; *see* York, M.

JOHNSON, Neil Anthony, OBE (mil.) 1989; TD 1985, bar 1992; DL; Chairman, Motability Operations Group plc (formerly Motability Finance Ltd), since 2001; *b* 13 April 1949; *s* of Anthony and Dilys Johnson, Glamorgan; *m* 1st, 1971 (marr. diss. 1996); three *d*; 2nd, 1996, Elizabeth Jane Hunter Johnston (*née* Robinson); one *d*, and three step *d. Educ:* Canton High Sch., Cardiff; RMA Sandhurst. Graduate Trainee, Lex Gp, 1971–73; British Leyland Motor Corp., 1973–82; Dir, Sales and Marketing, Jaguar Cars, 1982–86; MoD, 1986–89; Main Bd Dir, Rover Gp, British Aerospace, resp. for European Ops, 1989–92; Dir-Gen., EEF, 1992–93; Gen. Sec., 1994–99, Chief Exec., 1996–99, RAC; Chief Exec., British and Amer. Chamber of Commerce, 2000–01. Chairman: Hornby plc, 2000–13; Cybit plc, 2001–10; Tenon plc, 2003–06 (Dir, 2000–06); Autologic plc, 2006–07; Umeco plc, 2009–12; Synthomer (formerly Yule-Catto) plc, 2011–; Dir, Business Growth Fund, 2011–. Chm., Speedway Control Bd, 1994–96. Territorial Army: Pembroke Yeomanry, 1971; 4th Bn RGJ, 1973; CO, 1986–89; ADC to the Queen, 1990; Hon. Col, 157 Transport Regt, RLC, 1993–2001; Trustee RGJ TA Trust, 1994–; Hon. Col, F Co., London Regt, RGJ, 2000–07. Member: Prime Minister's Panel of Advrs on Citizen's Charter, Cabinet Office, 1995–2003; UK Round Table on Sustainable Develt, 1997–98; Cleaner Vehicles Task Force, 1997–99. Member: Nat. Employers' Liaison Cttee for the Reserve Forces, 1992–98; Nat. Employers' Adv. Bd, 2006–. Ind. Mem., Metropolitan Police Authy, 2008–12. Trustee, Jaguar Daimler Heritage Trust, 1994–99. FIMI; CCMI (CIMgt 1995); FRSA. Freeman, City of London, 1985. DL Greater London, 1993; Rep. DL, City of Westminster, 1993–2007. Ordre de l'Encouragement Publique (France), 1987. *Recreations:* town and country pursuits, fast British cars, slow Italian lunches. *Address:* 22 Southwark Bridge Road, SE1 9HB. *Clubs:* Army and Navy, Royal Green Jackets, Royal Automobile, Beefsteak, Cavalry and Guards; Cardiff and County (Cardiff); Woodroffe's; Midland Automobile (Shelsley Walsh); Arlberg Ski.

JOHNSON, Prof. Newell Walter, CMG 2011; MDSc, PhD; FDSRCS, FRACDS, FRCPath, FMedSci, FFOP (RCPA), FICD, FHEA; Honorary Professor of Dental Research, Menzies Health Institute Queensland at Griffith University (formerly Griffith Institute for Health and Medical Research, then Griffith Health Institute), Queensland, 2009–12, now Emeritus Professor; Professor of Oral Health Sciences, GKT Dental Institute, King's College London, 2003–05, now Emeritus; specialist in oral medicine, oral pathology and periodontics; *b* 5 Aug. 1938; *s* of Otto Johnson and Lorna (*née* Guy); *m* 1st, 1965, Pauline Margaret Trafford (marr. diss. 1984); two *d*; 2nd, 2003, Jeannette Giblin. *Educ:* University High Sch., Melbourne; Univ. of Melbourne (BDSc Hons 1960; MDSc 1963); Univ. of Bristol (PhD 1967). FDSRCS 1964; FRACDS 1966; FRCPath 1982; FMedSci 1995; FFOP (RCPA) 1996; FICD 2006. Res. Fellow in Pathology, Univ. of Melbourne, 1961–63; Lectr in Dental Surgery, UCL, 1963–64; Scientific Officer, MRC Dental Res. Unit, Bristol, 1964–67; London Hospital Medical College: Reader in Experimental Oral Path., 1968–76; Prof. of Oral Path., 1976–83; Hon. Dir, MRC Dental Res. Unit, 1983–93; Governor, 1983 (Chm., Academic Div. of Dentistry, 1983); Chm., London Hosp. Div. of Dentistry, 1981–83; Nuffield Res. Prof. of Dental Science, RCS, 1984–2003; Dir of Res. and Univ. Postgrad. Educn, Dental Inst., KCL, 1994–95; Prof. of Oral Pathology, King's Coll. Sch. of Medicine and Dentistry, subseq. GKT Dental Inst. of KCL, Univ. of London, 1994–2003; Foundn Dean and Hd, Sch. of Dentistry and Oral Health, Griffith Univ., Qld, 2005–09. Hon. Consultant Dental Surgeon: Royal London (formerly London) Hosp., 1968–; King's Healthcare NHS Trust, 1993–2005. Consultant, Fédération Dentaire Internationale, 1984– (Comr, 1996–); Academician, Argentine Acad. of Medicine, 2004. Consultant in Oral Health, WHO, 1984–; Dir, WHO Collaborating Centre for Oral Cancer and Precancer, 1995–2005. Pres., British Soc. of Periodontology, 1992–93. Chairman: UK Cttee, Royal Australasian Coll. of Dental Surgeons, 1981–83; Australasian Council of Dental Schs, 2006–10; Faculty of Oral Pathology, Royal Coll. of Pathologists, Australasia, 2008–10; FRSocMed (Mem. Council, 2001–; Mem. Council, Section of Odontology, 1972–91 (Pres., 1988–89 and 2004–05)); Founder FMedSci 1998; Fellow, NH&MRC, 2009. Member, Editorial Board: Jl of Oral Pathology, 1982–93; Jl of Periodontal Research, 1986–96 (Associate Ed., 1993–); Jl of Clin. Periodontology, 1990–; Oral Oncology, 1992–; Editor in Chief, Oral Diseases, 1994–2005. Hon. Mem., British Soc. for Oral Medicine, 2011. John Tomes Medal, BDA, 2005; Dist. Scientist Award, Oral Medicine and Pathology, IADR, 2005. *Publications:* (jtly) The Oral Mucosa in Health and Disease, 1975; (jtly) The Human Oral Mucosa: structure, metabolism and function, 1976; (jtly) Dental Caries: aetiology, pathology and prevention, 1979; (ed jtly) Oral Diseases in the Tropics, 1992; (ed) Detection of High Risk Groups for Oral Diseases, 3 vols, 1991; Oral Cancer, 2000; (ed jtly) Oral Cancer, 2003, 2nd edn 2015; (contrib.) Head and Neck Cancer: multimodality management, 2011, 2nd edn 2015; (contrib.) Oral Cancer: a comprehensive approach, 2015; articles in scientific jls. *Recreations:* music, theatre, visual arts, the environment, global health inequalities, multicultural studies. *E:* n.johnson@griffith.edu.au.

JOHNSON, Nichola, OBE 2013; FSA; Director of Museology, 1993–2010, Director, Museum Leadership Programme, 1994–2012, and Director, Sainsbury Centre for Visual Arts, 1996–2010, University of East Anglia; *b* 21 May 1945; *d* of John Nicholas Healey and Jessica (*née* Horrocks); *m* 1965, M. D. Johnson (marr. diss. 1971); one *s* one *d. Educ:* Ipswich High Sch.; Univ. of Sheffield (BA); Univ. of Essex (MA). FSA 2011. Lectr, Dept of Art History, Univ. of Essex, 1980–83; Hd, Dept of Later London History, Mus. of London, 1983–93. Chair: mda, 1998–2003; Univ. Museums Gp, 2003–09; Clore Leadership Prog., 2004–09 (Trustee, 2009–); Ruskin Foundn, 2009–12; E Anglia Art Fund, 2013–. Trustee: Dulwich Picture Gall., 2006–; Norfolk and Norwich Fest., 2009–; Brantwood Trust, 2009–; Nat. Trust, 2010–; Pallant House Gall., 2010–14; Sir John Soane's Mus., 2014–. Vis. Prof., Norwich Univ. of Arts, 2014–. *Publications:* University Museums in the United Kingdom, 2004; contribs to professional jls and edited volumes. *Recreations:* music-making, lurcher shows, long-distance walking. *Address:* The Lodging House, Church Street, Reepham, Norfolk NR10 4JW.

JOHNSON, Nicholas; Deputy Chief Executive, Urban Splash Group Ltd, 1999–2012; *b* Bolton, 10 Jan. 1966; *s* of Derek Johnson and Valerie Johnson; partner, Jenny; four *d. Educ:* Sheffield Hallam Univ. (BSc Hons). Principal, Johnson Urban Develt Consultants, 1991–99. Chm., Marketing Manchester, 2006–13; Mem., CABE, 2007–11. Dist. Vis. Fellow, Yale Sch. of Architecture, 2007–08. FRSA. *Recreations:* cycling, canal boats.

JOHNSON, Nicholas Robert; QC 2006; a barrister, since 1987; *b* 28 Aug. 1964; *s* of late Rev. Robin E. H. Johnson and of Joyce Verry Johnson; *m* 2001, JaneWoodfine; one *s* two *d. Educ:* St Paul's Cathedral Choir Sch.; Manchester Grammar Sch.; Leeds Univ. (BA Hist. 1985; played Rugby League for British Students, 1985); Poly. of Central London (Dip. Law 1986). Called to the Bar, Inner Temple, 1987. *Recreation:* catching up. *Address:* 7 Harrington Street, Liverpool L2 9YH. *T:* (0151) 236 0707. *Club:* John Mc's (Liverpool).

JOHNSON, Sir Patrick Eliot, 8th Bt *cr* 1818, of Bath; *b* 11 June 1955; *s* of Sir Robin Eliot Johnson, 7th Bt and of Barbara Alfreda, *d* of late Alfred T. Brown; *S* father, 1989, but his name does not appear on the Official Roll of the Baronetage; *m* 1980, Rose (marr. diss. 1989), *d* of Olav Alfhein; twin *s. Heir: s* Richard Eliot Johnson, *b* 8 Jan. 1983.

JOHNSON, Prof. Paul A., DPhil; Vice-Chancellor, University of Western Australia, since 2012; *b* Bath, 26 Nov. 1956; *s* of Alan and Joyce Johnson; *m* Dr Susannah Morris; one *s* one *d. Educ:* St John's Coll., Oxford (BA); Nuffield Coll., Oxford (DPhil). Res. Fellow, Nuffield Coll., Oxford, 1981–84; London School of Economics: Lectr in Social Hist., 1984–94; Reader in Econ. Hist., 1994–99; Prof. of Econ. Hist., 1999–2007; Dep. Dir, 2004–07; Vice-Chancellor and Pres., La Trobe Univ., Australia, 2007–11. *Publications:* Saving and Spending, 1985; Ageing and Economic Welfare, 1992; Twentieth Century Britain, 1994; Old Age: from antiquity to post-modernity, 1998; Cambridge Economic History of Modern Britain, 2004, 4th edn 2014; Making the Market, 2010. *Recreation:* my family. *Address:* University of Western Australia, 35 Stirling Highway, Crawley, WA 6009, Australia.

JOHNSON, Paul Antony; Deputy Editor, since 2008, and Editor, Sport, since 2010, Guardian News and Media; *b* Aldershot, 21 Nov. 1953; *s* of Alfred Johnson and Myrtle Johnson; *m* 2007, Fionnuala Cosgrove; one *s* one *d*. *Educ:* Cardiff Univ. (BSc; Postgrad. Dip. Journalism). The Guardian: reporter, 1979–87; News Ed., 1987–92; Asst Ed., 1992–95; Dep. Ed., 1995–2008. *Recreations:* football, running, cinema, cooking. *Address:* Guardian News and Media, Kings Place, 90 York Way, N1 9GU. *T:* (020) 3353 3802. *E:* paul.johnson@guardian.co.uk. *Clubs:* Middlesex County Cricket; Wolverhampton Wanderers Football.

JOHNSON, Paul (Bede); author; *b* 2 Nov. 1928; *s* of William Aloysius and Anne Johnson; *m* 1957, Marigold Hunt, MBE; three *s* one *d*. *Educ:* Stonyhurst; Magdalen Coll., Oxford. Asst Exec. Editor, Réalités, 1952–55; Editorial Staff, New Statesman, 1955, Dir, Statesman and Nation Publishing Co., 1965, Editor of the New Statesman, 1965–70. Member: Royal Commn on the Press, 1974–77; Cable Authority, 1984–90. *Publications:* The Suez War, 1957; Journey into Chaos, 1958; Left of Centre, 1960; Merrie England, 1964; Statesmen and Nations, 1971; The Offshore Islanders, 1972; (with G. Gale) The Highland Jaunt, 1973; Elizabeth I, 1974; A Place in History, 1974; Pope John XXIII, 1975 (Yorkshire Post Book of the Year Award, 1975); A History of Christianity, 1976; Enemies of Society, 1977; The National Trust Book of British Castles, 1978; The Recovery of Freedom, 1980; British Cathedrals, 1980; Ireland: Land of Troubles, 1980; Pope John Paul II and the Catholic Restoration, 1982; A History of the Modern World from 1917 to the 1980s, 1983, rev. edn 1991; The Pick of Paul Johnson, 1985; Oxford Book of Political Anecdotes, 1986; A History of the Jews, 1987; Intellectuals, 1988; The Birth of the Modern: world society 1815–30, 1991; Wake Up Britain! A Latterday Pamphlet, 1994; The Quest for God: a personal pilgrimage, 1996; To Hell With Picasso!: essays from the Spectator, 1996; A History of the American People, 1997; The Renaissance, 2000; Napoleon, 2002; Art: a new history, 2003; Washington, 2003; The Vanished Landscape: a 1930s childhood in the Potteries, 2004; Heroes: from Alexander the Great to Mae West, 2008; Churchill, 2009; Brief Lives, 2010; Darwin, 2010; Stalin, 2012; Socrates, 2013; Mozart, 2013; Eisenhower, 2014. *Recreations:* hill-walking, painting. *Address:* 29 Newton Road, W2 5JR.

See also D. B. Johnson, L. O. Johnson.

JOHNSON, Paul Gavin; Director, Institute for Fiscal Studies, since 2011 (Research Fellow, 2007–11); *b* 5 Jan. 1967; *s* of Robert and Joy Johnson; partner, Lorraine Dearden; four *s*. *Educ:* Keble Coll., Oxford (BA 1st. Cl. Hons PPE); Birkbeck Coll., London (MSc Econs). Inst. for Fiscal Studies, 1988–98 (Dep. Dir, 1996–98); Hd, Econs of Financial Regulation, FSA, 1999–2000; Chief Economist, and Dir, Analytical Services, DFEE, subseq. DFES, 2000–04; Dir, Public Services, and Chief Micro-Economist, HM Treasury, 2004–07; Dep. Hd, Govt Econ. Service, 2005–07; Sen. Associate, Frontier Economics Ltd, 2007–11. Vis. Prof., Dept of Econs, UCL, 2013–. Member: ESRC, 2002–07; Committee on Climate Change, 2012–; Actuarial Council, 2012–. *Publications:* (jtly) Inequality in the UK, 1996; (jtly) Pension Systems and Retirement Incomes Across OECD Countries, 2001; (ed) Tax by Design: the Mirrless review, 2011; contrib. numerous articles to econs jls and in press. *Address:* Institute for Fiscal Studies, 7 Ridgmount Street, WC1E 7AE. *E:* pjohnson@ifs.org.uk.

JOHNSON, Penelope Jane, CBE 2010; Director, Government Art Collection, since 1997; *b* Wimbledon, 23 June 1956; *d* of Dennis George Johnson and June Anne Johnson (*née* Wilkinson). *Educ:* St Helen's Sch., Northwood, Middx; Univ. of E Anglia (BA Fine Arts 1978); Univ. of Manchester (Postgrad. Dip. Gall. and Mus. Studies 1980); Dip. Mus Assoc. 1984. Catalogue asst and researcher, Art Nouveau Collection, Sainsbury Centre for Visual Arts, UEA, 1978–79; Asst Keeper of Fine Art, Stoke-on-Trent City Mus. and Art Gall., 1981–86; Curator, Towner Art Gall. and Local Mus., Eastbourne, 1987–97. Tutor (pt-time), UEA, 1981; asst (pt-time), Communications Dept, Mus. of London, 1981. *Publications:* (contrib.) Art Power Diplomacy. Government Art Collection: the untold story, 2011. *Recreations:* theatre, literature, film, walking, sailing, travel. *Address:* Government Art Collection, Queen's Yard, 179a Tottenham Court Road, W1T 7PA. *T:* (020) 7580 9120, *Fax:* (020) 7580 9130. *E:* penny.johnson@culture.gsi.gov.uk. *Club:* Chelsea Arts.

JOHNSON, Peter Michael; Chairman, Electrocomponents plc, since 2010; *b* 3 July 1947; *s* of late James and Nancy Johnson; *m* 1972, Janet Esther Ashman (*d* 2012); two *s* one *d*. *Educ:* Bromley Grammar Sch.; St Edmund Hall, Oxford (MA PPE, BPhil Econs). With Unilever PLC, 1970–73; Redland PLC, 1973–96: Gp Treas., 1978–81; Dir of Planning, 1981–84; Man. Dir, Redland Bricks Ltd, 1984–88; Dir, Redland PLC, 1988–96; Chief Executive: Rugby Gp PLC, 1996–2000; George Wimpey Plc, 2000–06. Chm., David S. Smith Hldgs, later DS Smith plc, 2007–12 (Dir, 1999–2012); Mem., Supervisory Bd, Wienerberger AG, 2005– (Vice-Chm., 2013–); Dir, SSL International Plc, 2008–10. President: Fédération Européene des Fabricants de Tuiles et de Briques, 1994–96; Nat. Council of Building Material Producers, 1997–2000; Mem., Council for Industry and Higher Educn, 2001–06. *Recreations:* music, tennis, cricket, sailing.

JOHNSON, Peter Michael; Headmaster, Millfield School, 1998–2008; *b* 21 Dec. 1947; *s* of Joseph William (Johnnie) Johnson and Dorothy Johnson; *m* 1969, Christine Anne Rayment; two *s*. *Educ:* Bec Grammar Sch.; Mansfield Coll., Oxford (Army Scholarship; MA Geog.; PGCE; Rugby Blue, 1968, 1969, 1970, Judo Blue, 1968, 1969). Commnd Royal Army Educn Corps, 1970; transf. to RA, 1972; served 7 Parachute Regt, RHA, 1971–76 (emergency tours in NI, 1972 and 1974 (GSM)); retd in rank of Captain. Radley College: Asst Master, 1976–91; Housemaster, 1983–91; Headmaster, Wrekin Coll., 1991–98. Educn Advr, London Chamber Orch., 2011–. Oxford Univ. Rep. on RFU Council, 1987–98; Trustee: Nat. Centre for Schs and Youth Rugby, 1992–98; Raleigh Internat., 2003–05; Wells Cathedral, 2004– (Chm. Trustees, 2009–); Pres., England Rugby Football Schs' Union, 2009–12. Governor: Blundell's Sch., 2008–; Sherborne Girls, 2008–12; Christ's Hospital, 2011–. Capt., Northampton FC, 1978–79. FRSA. *Recreations:* gardening, music, oenology. *Address:* Borrowdale, Mill Hill, Stoke Gabriel, Devon TQ9 6RY. *Clubs:* East India; Vincent's (Oxford); Free Foresters.

JOHNSON, Peter William; Chairman, Rank plc, 2007–11; *b* 2 Nov. 1947; *s* of Alfred and Emily Johnson; *m* 1973, Ann Gillian Highley; one *s* one *d*. *Educ:* Hull Univ. (BSc Hons Econs). Mgt trainee, 1969, sen. mgt posts, 1970–79, British Leyland; Sales Dir, Austin-Morris, 1980–84; Export Dir, Austin-Rover, 1984–86; Sales Dir, Rover Gp, 1986–88; Chief Executive: Applied Chemicals, 1988–90; Marshall Gp, 1990–94; Inchcape Motors International, 1994–99; Chief Exec., 1999–2005, Chm., 2006–09, Inchcape plc. Non-executive Director: Wates Gp, 2002–06, 2011–13; Bunzl plc, 2006–15; Chm., Automotive Skills Ltd, 2003–06. Vice Pres., Motor Agents Assoc., 1992–95. FIMI 1984 (Chm., 1991–95); MInstD 1990. *Recreations:* golf, reading, travel. *Clubs:* Royal Automobile; Redditch Golf.

JOHNSON, Prof. Peter William Montague, MD; FRCP; FMedSci; Professor of Medical Oncology, University of Southampton, since 1998; Chief Clinician, Cancer Research UK, since 2008; *b* Walton-on-Thames, 4 May 1961; *s* of Alan Montague and Bobbie Johnson; *m* 1987, Maria Susanna Alkema; one *s* one *d*. *Educ:* Sherborne Sch., Dorset; Gonville and Caius Coll., Cambridge (BA 1982; MB BChir 1985; MA 1986; MD 1994); St Thomas's Med. Sch., London. FRCP 1998. ICRF Clin. Res. Fellow, St Bartholomew's Hosp., London, 1989–94; Sen. Lectr, Univ. of Leeds, 1994–98. FMedSci 2014. *Publications:* contrib. papers on cancer res., malignant lymphoma, cancer immunol. *Recreations:* theatre, opera, wine, sleeping through the news. *Address:* Somers Cancer Research Building, Southampton General Hospital, Tremona Road, Southampton SO16 6YD. *T:* (023) 8120 6186. *E:* johnsonp@soton.ac.uk.

JOHNSON, Rachel Sabiha; journalist and novelist; columnist, Mail on Sunday, since 2012; *b* London, 3 Sept. 1965; *d* of Stanley Patrick Johnson, *qv* and Charlotte Maria Johnson (*née* Fawcett); *m* 1992, Ivo Nicholas Payan Dawnay; two *s* one *d*. *Educ:* Winsford First Sch., Exmoor; Primrose Hill Primary Sch., Camden; European Sch., Brussels; Ashdown Hse, Sussex; Bryanston Sch., Dorset (Schol.); St Paul's Girls' Sch., London; Davidson Coll., N Carolina (Dean Rusk Schol., 1984); New Coll., Oxford (MA Lit.Hum. 1988). Financial Times: grad. trainee, 1989–90; reporter, 1990–94; on secondment to FCO, 1992–93; sen. broadcast journalist, BBC Radio Four, 1994–96; columnist: Sunday Telegraph, 1996–98; FT, 1998–2000; Daily Telegraph and Evening Standard, 2000–06; contributing ed., Spectator, 2006–07; columnist, Sunday Times, 2007–09; Ed., 2009–12, Ed.-in-Chief, 2012, The Lady mag. *Publications:* (ed) The Oxford Myth, 1988; The Mummy Diaries, 2005; Notting Hell, 2006; Shire Hell, 2008; The Diary of a Lady: my first year as Editor, 2010; The Diary of a Lady: my first year and a half, 2011; Winter Games, 2012; Notting Hill, Actually, 2013; Fresh Hell, 2015. *Recreations:* tennis, parties, long walks, ski-ing. *Address:* 1 Rosmead Road, W11 2JG. *E:* racheljohnson11@btinternet.com. *Club:* Campden Hill Lawn Tennis.

See also C. J. P. Dawnay, A. B. de P. Johnson, J. E. Johnson, L. F. Johnson.

JOHNSON, Richard; National Hunt jockey; *b* 21 July 1977; *m* 2007, Fiona, *d* of Noel Chance; one *d*. Equal 10th in list of winning jockeys while still an apprentice, 1995–96; 2nd, 1996–07, 1997–98, 1998–99, 1999–2000, 2000–01, 2001–02, 2002–03, 2005–06, 2006–07, 2007–08, 2008–09, 2009–10, 2010–11, 2011–12 and 2013–14 seasons; 3rd, 2012–13 season; winner: Cheltenham Gold Cup on Looks Like Trouble, 2000; Queen Mother Champion Chase on Flagship Uberalles, 2002; Champion Hurdle on Rooster Booster, 2003. Rode 2,000th winner, Newbury, 2009. *Publications:* (with Alan Lee) Out of the Shadows, 2002. *Address:* c/o Nicholas Whittle, Bucklow Hill, Knutsford, Cheshire WA16 6PP.

JOHNSON, Richard John M.; *see* McGregor-Johnson.

JOHNSON, Sir Robert (Lionel), Kt 1989; a Justice of the High Court, Family Division, 1989–2004; *b* 9 Feb. 1933; *er s* of late Edward Harold Johnson, MSc, FRIC, and of Ellen Lydiate Johnson, Cranleigh; *m* 1957, Linda Mary, *er d* of late Charles William Bennie and Ena Ethel Bennie, Egglescliffe; one *d* (and one *s* one *d* decd). *Educ:* Watford Grammar Sch. (1940–51); London Sch. of Econs and Pol Science. 5th Royal Inniskilling Dragoon Guards, 1955–57, Captain; ADC to GOC-in-C Northern Comd, 1956–57; Inns of Court Regt, 1957–64. Called to the Bar, Gray's Inn, 1957, Bencher, 1986; QC 1978; a Recorder, 1977–89. Jun. Counsel to Treasury in Probate Matters, 1975–78; Legal Assessor, GNC, 1977–82. Chairman: Bar Fees and Legal Aid Cttee, 1984–86 (Vice-Chm., 1982–84); Family Law Bar Assoc., 1984–86; Family Law Cttee, Justice, 1990–93; Mem., Bar Council, 1981–88; Vice Chm., 1987, Chm., 1988, Gen. Council of Bar. Member: Supreme Court Procedure Cttee, 1982–87; Law Soc. Legal Aid Cttee, 1981–87; No 1 Legal Aid Area Cttee, 1980–87; Co-Chm., Civil and Family Cttee, Judicial Studies Bd, 1989–94. Pres., English Chapter, Internat. Acad. of Matrimonial Lawyers, 1986–89. Sec., Internat. Cystic Fibrosis Assoc., 1984–90; Trustee: Cystic Fibrosis Res. Trust, 1964–2009; Robert Luff Charitable Foundn, 1977–. *Publications:* (with James Comyn) Wills & Intestacies, 1970; Contract, 1975; (with Malcolm Stitcher) Atkin's Trade, Labour and Employment, 1975. *Recreations:* charitable work, gardening. *Address:* Forest Gate, Pluckley, Kent TN27 0RU.

JOHNSON, Robin Peter; His Honour Judge Johnson; a Circuit Judge, since 2009; *b* London, 28 June 1954; *s* of Peter and Kathleen Joan Johnson. *Educ:* Exeter Univ. (BA). Called to the Bar, Gray's Inn, 1979; Recorder, 2003–09. *Address:* Isleworth Crown Court, 36 Ridgeway Road, Isleworth, Surrey TW7 5LP.

JOHNSON, Prof. Roger Paul, FREng; Professor of Civil Engineering, University of Warwick, 1971–98, now Emeritus; *b* 12 May 1931; *s* of Norman Eric Ernest Johnson and Eleanor Florence (*née* Paul); *m* 1958, Diana June (*née* Perkins); three *s*. *Educ:* Cranleigh Sch., Surrey; Jesus Coll., Cambridge (BA 1953; MA 1957). FIStructE 1972; FICE 1979; FREng (FEng 1986). Holloway Bros (London), Civil Engineering Contractor, 1953–55; Ove Arup and Partners, Consulting Engineers, 1956–59; Lectr in Engineering, Cambridge Univ., 1959–71. Visiting Professor: Univ. of Sydney, 1982–83; Univ. of Adelaide, 1995, 1999. Gold Medal, IStructE, 2006. *Publications:* Structural Concrete, 1967; Composite Structures of Steel and Concrete, vol. 1, 1975, 3rd edn 2004, vol. 2 (with R. J. Buckby), 1979, 2nd edn 1986; (with D. Anderson) Designers' Handbook to Eurocode 4, 1994; Designers' Guide to Eurocode 4, Pt 1-1 (with D. Anderson), 2004, 2nd edn 2012, Pt 2 (with C. R. Hendy), 2006; contribs to learned jls. *Recreations:* music, travel, mountain walking. *Address:* School of Engineering, University of Warwick, Coventry CV4 7AL. *T:* (024) 7652 3129.

JOHNSON, Samantha T.; *see* Taylor-Johnson.

JOHNSON, Stanley Patrick; author and environmentalist; *b* 18 Aug. 1940; *s* of Wilfred Johnson and Irène (*née* Williams); *m* 1st, 1963, Charlotte Offlow Fawcett (marr. diss.); three *s* one *d*; 2nd, 1981, Mrs Jennifer Kidd; one *s* one *d*. *Educ:* Sherborne Sch.; Exeter Coll., Oxford (Trevelyan Schol., Sen. Classics Schol.; Newdigate Prize for Poetry, 1962; MA 1963; Dip. Agric. Econs 1965); Harkness Fellow, USA, 1963–64. World Bank, Washington, 1966–68; Project Dir, UNA-USA Nat. Policy Panel on World Population, 1968–69; Mem. Conservative Research Dept, 1969–70; Staff of Internat. Planned Parenthood Fedn, London, 1971–73; Consultant to UN Fund for Population Activities, 1971–73; Mem. Countryside Commn, 1971–73; Head of Prevention of Pollution and Nuisances Div., EEC, 1973–77; Adviser to Head of Environment and Consumer Protection Service, EEC, 1977–79; MEP (C) Wight and Hants E, 1979–84; Advr to Dir Gen. for Envmt, Civil Protection and Nuclear Safety, EEC, 1984–90; Dir for Energy Policy, EEC, 1990; Special Advr, Coopers & Lybrand, Deloitte, 1991; Dir, Envmtl Resources Mgt, 1992–94. Contested (C) Teignbridge, 2005. Hon. Ambassador, UNEP Convention on Migratory Species, 2005–. Chm., Gorilla Orgn, 2010–. Richard Martin Award, RSPCA, 1982; Greenpeace Award, 1984; Silver Medal, WWF, 2013. *Publications:* Life Without Birth, 1970; The Green Revolution, 1972; The Politics of the Environment, 1973; (ed) The Population Problem, 1973; The Pollution Control Policy of the EEC, 1979, 3rd edn 1989; Antarctica—the last great wilderness, 1985; (jtly) The Environmental Policy of the EEC, 1989, 2nd edn 1995; The Earth Summit: the United Nations Conference on Environment and Development, 1993; World Population—turning the tide, 1994; The Politics of Population, 1995; Stanley I Presume, 2009; (jtly) Survival: saving endangered migratory species, 2010; Where the Wild Things Were: travels of a conservationist, 2012; UNEP: the first forty years, 2013; Stanley I Resume, 2014; *novels:* Gold Drain, 1967; Panther Jones for President, 1968; God Bless America, 1974; The Doomsday Deposit, 1980; The Marburg Virus, 1982; Tunnel, 1984; The Commissioner, 1987; Dragon River, 1989; Icecap, 1999. *Recreations:* writing, travel. *Address:* Nethercote, Winsford, Minehead, Somerset TA24 7HZ; 34 Park Village East, NW1 7PZ. *T:* (020) 7380 0989. *Clubs:* Beefsteak, Garrick.

See also A. B. de P. Johnson, J. E. Johnson, L. F. Johnson, R. S. Johnson.

JOHNSON, Terry; playwright and director; *b* 20 Dec. 1955; *s* of Harry Douglas Johnson and Winifred Mary Johnson (*née* Wood); one *d* by Marion Bailey. *Educ:* Birmingham Univ. (BA 2nd cl. Drama and Th. Arts). Actor, 1971–75; *playwright:* Amabel, Bush Th., 1972; Insignificance, Royal Court (Most Promising Playwright, Evening Standard Award), 1982 (screenplay, 1985); Unsuitable for Adults, Bush, Cries from the Mammal House, Royal Ct, 1984; (jtly) Tuesday's Child, Stratford Th. Royal, 1986; Imagine Drowning, Hampstead (John Whiting Award), 1991; Hysteria, Royal Ct, 1993 (Meyer-Whitworth Award, 1993; Best Comedy, Olivier Award, and Best Play, Writers' Guild, 1994); (also dir.) Dead Funny, Savoy, 1994 (Best Play, Writers' Guild, 1994; Best New Play, Critics' Circle, and Playwright of the

Year, Lloyds Pvte Banking, 1995); adaptation (also dir.), The London Cuckolds, 1997, (also dir.) Cleo, Camping, Emmanuelle and Dick, 1998 (Best Comedy, Olivier Award, 1999), RNT; adaptation (also dir.), The Graduate, Gielgud, 2000; Hitchcock Blonde, Royal Court, 2003; (also dir.) Hysteria, Th. Royal, Bath, 2012, Hampstead Th., 2013; (also dir.) Mrs Henderson Presents, Th. Royal, Bath, 2015; plays also performed in USA, Europe, Australia, Canada and NZ; other *plays directed* include: The Memory of Water, Vaudeville, 1996; The Libertine, Chicago, 1996; Elton John's Glasses, Queen's, 1997; Sparkleshark, RNT, 1999; Entertaining Mr Sloane, Arts, 2001; One Flew Over the Cuckoo's Nest, Gielgud, 2004; Dumb Show, Royal Court, 2004; Piano/Forte, 2006; Whipping It Up, 2006; La Cage aux Folles, Menier Chocolate Factory, transf. Playhouse, 2008, NY, 2010 (Best Dir, Tony Awards, 2010); The Prisoner of Second Avenue, Vaudeville, 2010; End of the Rainbow, Trafalgar Studios, 2010; La Cage aux Folles, US tour, 2012; Race, Hampstead Th., 2013; The Duck House, Vaudeville, 2013; Oh What a Lovely War, Th. Royal, Stratford E, 2014; Fings Ain't Wot They Used T'Be, Th. Royal, Stratford E, 2014; Seminar, Hampstead Th., 2014; *television:* (dir.) Way Upstream, 1988; wrote and directed: Blood and Water, 1995; Cor Blimey!, 2000; Not Only But Always, 2004; The Man Who Lost His Head, 2007; screenplay, The Bite, 1994. *Publications:* Insignificance, 1982; Cries from the Mammal House, 1984; Unsuitable for Adults, 1985; Tuesday's Child, 1987; Imagine Drowning, 1991; Hysteria, 1993; Dead Funny, 1994; Johnson: Plays One, 1993; The London Cuckolds, 1997; Johnson: Plays Two, 1998; Cleo, Camping, Emmanuelle and Dick, 1998; The Graduate, 2000; Hitchcock Blonde, 2003; Piano/Forte, 2006.

JOHNSON, Wendy Rosalind; *see* James, W. R.

JOHNSON, Zoe Elisabeth; QC 2012; a Recorder, since 2010; *b* Poole, 27 March 1967; *d* of William Clifford Johnson and Jean Violetta Johnson; *m* 2014, Peter Eric Kyte, *qv*. *Educ:* Corfe Hills, Corfe Mullen; St Hilda's Coll., Oxford (BA Hons Eng. Lit.); City Univ. (DipLaw). Called to the Bar, Inner Temple, 1990; Jun. Treasury Counsel, 2004–11, Sen. Treasury Counsel, 2011–, Central Criminal Court. *Recreations:* travel to South East Asia, theatre, gardens, reading novels and comparative history. *Address:* QEB Hollis Whiteman Chambers, 1–2 Laurence Pountney Hill, EC4R 0EU. *T:* (020) 7933 8855, *Fax:* (020) 7929 3732. *E:* zoe.johnson@qebhw.co.uk.

JOHNSON-FERGUSON, Sir Ian (Edward), 4th Bt *cr* 1906, of Springkell, Dumfries, of Kenyon, Newchurch-in-Culceth, Lancaster, and of Wiston, Lanark; *b* 1 Feb. 1932; *s* of Sir Neil Edward Johnson-Ferguson, 3rd Bt, TD and Sheila Marion (*d* 1985), *er d* of Col H. S. Jervis, MC; *S* father, 1992; *m* 1964, Rosemary Teresa, *yr d* of late C. J. Whitehead; three *s*. *Educ:* Ampleforth Coll.; Trinity Coll., Cambridge (BA 1953); Imperial Coll., London (DIC Geophysics 1954). Royal Dutch Shell, 1954–62; IBM UK Ltd, 1963–90. *Heir: s* Lt-Col Mark Edward Johnson-Ferguson, RE [*b* 14 Aug. 1965; *m* 1995, Dr Julia Catherine, *d* of T. D. Getley; three *d*].

JOHNSON-LAIRD, Prof. Philip Nicholas, FRS 1991; FBA 1986; Stuart Professor of Psychology, Princeton University, 1994–2012, now Emeritus (Professor of Psychology, 1989–2012); Visiting Scholar, New York University, since 2012; *b* 12 Oct. 1936; *s* of Eric Johnson-Laird and Dorothy (*née* Blackett); *m* 1959, Maureen Mary Sullivan; one *s* one *d*. *Educ:* Culford Sch.; University Coll. London (Rosa Morison Medal, 1964; James Sully Schol., 1964–66; BA (Hons) 1964; PhD 1967; Fellow, 1994). MBPsS 1962. 10 years of misc. jobs, as surveyor, musician, hosp. porter (alternative to Nat. Service), librarian, before going to university. Asst Lectr, then Lectr, in Psychol., UCL, 1966–73; Reader, 1973, Prof., 1978, in Exptl Psychol., Univ. of Sussex; Asst Dir, MRC Applied Psychology Unit, Cambridge, 1983–89; Fellow, Darwin Coll., Cambridge, 1984–89. Vis. Mem., Princeton Inst. for Advanced Study, 1971–72; Vis. Fellow, Stanford Univ., 1980; Visiting Professor: Stanford Univ., 1985; Princeton Univ., 1986. Member: Psychol. Cttee, SSRC, 1975–79; Linguistics Panel, SSRC, 1980–82; Adv. Council, Internat. Assoc. for Study of Attention and Performance, 1984. Member: Linguistics Assoc., 1967; Exptl Psychol. Soc., 1968; Cognitive Sci. Soc., 1980; Assoc. for Computational Linguistics, 1981; Amer. Philosophical Soc. 2006; Nat. Acad. of Scis, 2007. Fellow, Assoc. of Psychol Sci., 2007. Hon. DPhil: Göteborg, 1983; Padua, 1997; Madrid, 2000; Dublin, 2000; Ghent, 2002; Palermo, 2005; Hon. DSc Sussex, 2007; Laurea *hc* Univ. Ca' Foscari, Venice, 2008. Spearman Medal, 1974, President's Award, 1985, BPsS; International Prize, Fondation Fyssen, 2002. *Publications:* (ed jtly) Thinking and Reasoning, 1968; (with P. C. Wason) Psychology and Reasoning, 1972; (with G. A. Miller) Language and Perception, 1976; (ed jtly) Thinking, 1977; Mental Models, 1983; The Computer and the Mind, 1988; (with Ruth Byrne) Deduction, 1991; Human and Machine Thinking, 1993; How We Reason, 2006; contribs to psychol, linguistic and cognitive sci. jls, reviews in lit. jls. *Recreations:* talking, arguing, laughing, composing music.

JOHNSON SIRLEAF, Ellen Eugenia, President of Liberia, since 2006; *b* Monrovia, Liberia, 29 Oct. 1938; *née* Johnson; *m* James Sirleaf (marr. diss.); four *s*. *Educ:* Coll. of W Africa, Monrovia; Madison Business Coll., Wisconsin (accounting degree); Univ. of Colorado; Kennedy Sch. of Govt, Harvard Univ. (MPA 1971). Joined Treasury Dept, Liberia, 1965; Asst Minister of Finance, 1972–73; Minister of Finance, 1979–80; Pres., Liberian Bank for Develt and Investment, 1980; forced to flee Liberia and travelled to Kenya, 1980; Vice-Pres., Africa Regl Office, Citicorp, Nairobi, 1980–85; Sen. Loan Officer, World Bank; Vice Pres., Equator Bank; Asst Adminr and Dir, Regl Bureau for Africa, UNDP, 1992–97; returned to Liberia, 1997; contested Presidential election, 1997; self-imposed exile in Côte d'Ivoire, 1997–2003; estabd Kormah Develt and Investment Corp., Abidjan; Chair, Governance Reform Commn, Nat. Transitional Govt of Liberia, 2003–05. Founding Mem., Internat. Inst. for Women in Political Leadership. Mem. Cttee to investigate Rwanda genocide, Orgn for African Unity, 1999. Former Member, Advisory Board: Internat. Crisis Gp; Women Waging Peace; Synergos Inst.; Open Soc. Inst. for W Africa (Chair); Chair, African Peer Rev. Mechanism, African Union Summit, 2013. Freedom Award, Internat. Republican Inst., 2006; Gold Medal, Pres. of Italian Republic, 2006; Freedom Award, Nat. Civil Rights Mus., 2007; Presidential Medal of Freedom, USA, 2007; Internat. Women's Leadership Award, 2008; CERES Medal, FAO, 2008; African Gender Award, PanAfrican Center for Gender, Peace and Develt, 2011; (jtly) Nobel Prize for Peace, 2011; Martin Luther King Peace Medal and Alpha Award of Honor, 2012; Indira Gandhi Prize for Peace, Disarmament and Develt, 2012; Grand Croix, Légion d'Honneur (France), 2012; Lifetime Humanitarian Award for Healthcare, Nat. Med. Assoc. of USA, 2013. *Publications:* This Child Will be Great (memoir), 2008. *Address:* Ministry of State for Presidential Affairs, Executive Mansion, PO Box 9001, Capitol Hill, Monrovia, Republic of Liberia.

JOHNSTON; *see* Campbell-Johnston.

JOHNSTON; *see* Lawson Johnston.

JOHNSTON, Alexander Dewar Kerr, (Alistair), CMG 2011; Global Vice Chairman, KPMG, 2007–10; *b* Giffnock, Scotland, 28 June 1952; *s* of Kerr Johnston and Elizabeth Alexandra Johnston (*née* Dewar); partner, Christina Maria Nijman. *Educ:* Hutchesons' Sch., Glasgow; Trinity Sch. of John Whitgift; London Sch. of Econs and Pol Sci. (BSc Hons Econs 1973). Chartered Accountant 1976; FCA 1976. Peat Marwick Mitchell, later KPMG: joined, 1973; San Francisco, 1977–79; Partner, 1986–2010; Internat. Office, 1987–89; Partner in Charge, UK Mktg, 1990–93; Hd, UK Insce Practice, 1994–97; Internat. Man. Partner, Global Mkts, 1998–2003; UK Vice Chm., 2004–10. Mem. Bd, FCO, 2005–10. Non-exec. Dir, Prudential plc, 2012–. Trustee: Design Mus., 2012–; Create, 2014–; Kate's Home Nursing, 2014–; Royal Acad., 2014–. Vis. Prof., Cass Business Sch., 2005– (Mem., Strategy and Develt Bd, 2009–14). *Recreations:* design, restoration, art, music. *T:* 07802 610102. *E:* adkjohnston@gmail.com. *Club:* Athenæum.

JOHNSTON, (Alexander) Graham; Sheriff of Strathkelvin at Glasgow, 1985–2005; part-time Sheriff, 2005–13; *b* 16 July 1944; *s* of Hon. Lord Kincraig; *m* 1st, 1972, Susan (marr. diss. 1982); two *s*; 2nd, 1982, Angela; two step *d*. *Educ:* Edinburgh Acad.; Strathallan Sch.; Univ. of Edinburgh (LLB); University Coll., Oxford (BA). Admitted as solicitor and Writer to the Signet, 1971; Partner, Hagart and Burn-Murdoch, Solicitors, Edinburgh, 1972–82. Sheriff of Grampian, Highland and Isles, 1982–85. Editor, Scottish Civil Law Reports, 1987–92. *Recreations:* photography, computing and IT, bridge, puzzles. *Address:* 1 The Courtyard, Elie House, Elie, Fife KY9 1ER. *E:* ag_johnston@btinternet.com. *Clubs:* Oxford and Cambridge Golfing Society; Vincent's (Oxford); Elie Golf House.

JOHNSTON, Alistair; *see* Johnston, A. D. K.

JOHNSTON, Angela Maureen Howard-; *see* Huth, A. M.

JOHNSTON, Callum William; Secretary and Chief Executive, Central Arbitration Committee, 1999–2002; *b* 15 Sept. 1946; *s* of James Johnston, OBE, and Mary Johnston; *m* 1974, Sarah Motta; one *s* one *d*. *Educ:* Westcliff High Sch.; King Edward VII Sch., Lytham; Durham Univ. (BA Econs and Law 1968); Indiana Univ. (MBA 1970). Financial journalist and broadcaster, 1970–73; DTI, 1973–79 (Private Sec., 1975–79); Cabinet Office, 1979–86; Department of Trade and Industry: British Steel privatisation, 1986–89; UK and EU Co. Law Policy, 1989–90; on secondment to Leyland DAF plc, 1990–92; UK and EU Technol. and IT Security Policy, 1992–95; Pay Dir, 1995–98; Dir, Small Business Policy, 1998–99. *Recreations:* music, walking, cycling, black and white photography. *Address:* 10 Wontner Road, SW17 7QT.

JOHNSTON, Carey Ann; QC 2003. *Educ:* Univ. of Warwick (LLB, LLM). Called to the Bar, Middle Temple, 1977, Bencher, 2009. Specializes in criminal law. *Address:* Red Lion Chambers, 18 Red Lion Court, EC4A 3EB. *T:* (020) 7520 6000.

JOHNSTON, Catherine Elizabeth, CB 2000; Parliamentary Counsel, since 1994; *b* 4 Jan. 1953; *d* of Sir Alexander Johnston, GCB, KBE and Betty Joan Johnston (*née* Harris), CBE; *m* 1989, Brendan Patrick Keith; one *s* one *d*. *Educ:* St Paul's Girls' Sch.; St Hugh's Coll., Oxford (Scholar 1970; BA 1974). Admitted as solicitor, 1978; joined Parliamentary Counsel Office, 1980; with Law Commn, 1983–85 and 1990–92; on secondment to Office of Parly Counsel, Canberra, 1987–88. *Address:* Office of the Parliamentary Counsel, Cabinet Office, 1 Horse Guards Road, SW1A 2HQ.

JOHNSTON, Christopher George; QC 2011; *b* Ballymena, 1967; *s* of Harry and Isobel Johnston; *m* 1996, Joanna Warwick; two *d*. *Educ:* Ballymena Acad.; Trinity Hall, Cambridge (BA Law 1989). Called to the Bar, Gray's Inn, 1990; in practice as a barrister, specialising in clinical negligence. *Publications:* (ed) Medical Treatment Decisions and the Law, 2001, 2nd edn 2010. *Recreations:* watching Rugby, playing football and tennis, reading Tintin. *Address:* Serjeants' Inn Chambers, 85 Fleet Street, EC4Y 1AE. *T:* (020) 7427 5000. *E:* cjohnston@serjeantsinn.com.

JOHNSTON, Claire Lizbeth, CB 2014; Director General, Government Legal Department (formerly Treasury Solicitor's Department), since 2014; *b* Edinburgh, 19 Feb. 1960; *d* of Ronald Johnston and Margaret Johnston (*née* Rae); *m* 1991, Chris Miele; one *d*. *Educ:* Clare Coll., Cambridge (BA Hons English 1981); Columbia Univ., NY (MA English and Comparative Lit. 1982); City of London Poly. (CPE and Law Soc. Finals). Admitted as solicitor: England and Wales, 1987; Scotland, 1993; Solicitor, T. V. Edwards & Co., 1985–92; Lawyer: Law Commn, 1992–96; Official Solicitor's Office, 1997–2001; Sen. Civil Service Lawyer, Lord Chancellor's Dept, 2001–06; Gp Hd, HMRC, 2006–07; Legal Dir, DFE, 2007–14. *Recreations:* dance, hill walking. *Address:* Government Legal Department, 1 Kemble Street, WC2B 4TS. *T:* (020) 7210 3090.

JOHNSTON, Prof. Clare Frances; Professor and Course Director of Textiles, and Business Fellow of Innovation, Royal College of Art, 2000–15; *b* Whitby, Yorks, 7 Aug. 1951; *d* of Rev. Alan and Joan Johnston; partner, Paul Notley. *Educ:* Birmingham Coll. of Art (DipAD Textile Design). Design asst to Pat Albeck, 1973–74; design partnership with Veronica Marsh, 1974–78; own design co. working with internat. fashion cos, 1978–80; Sen. Designer, Walker & Rice Fabrics, 1980–82; Design Consultant, Nigel French Enterprises, 1982–86; Principal Lectr, Brighton Coll. of Art, 1986–90; colour and textiles designer, Marks & Spencer, 1990–98; Hd of Design, Liberty of London, 1998–2003. *Recreations:* walking, yoga, contemporary dance.

JOHNSTON, Prof. David, MD, ChM; FRCS, FRCSE, FRCSGlas; Professor of Surgery and Head of Department, University of Leeds at Leeds General Infirmary, 1977–98, now Professor Emeritus; *b* Glasgow, 4 Sept. 1936; *s* of Robert E. and Jean Johnston; *m* (marr. diss); three *s* one *d*; *m* 1987, Dr Maureen Teresa Reynolds; two *s*. *Educ:* Hamilton Acad.; Glasgow Univ. (MB, ChB Hons; MD Hons, ChM). FRCSE 1963; FRCSGlas 1964; FRCS 1979. House Surgeon, Western Infirmary, Glasgow, 1961–62; Res. Asst and Registrar, Univ. Dept of Surg., Leeds Gen. Infirm., 1962–64; Lectr in Surg., Univ. of Sheffield, 1965–68; Sen. Lectr, then Reader, and Consultant, Univ. Dept of Surg., Leeds Gen. Infirm., 1968–75; Prof. of Surg. and Head of Dept, Univ. of Bristol (Bristol Royal Infirm.), 1975–77. *Publications:* papers on physiology and surgery of the stomach, colon and rectum, and on obesity. *Recreations:* reading, walking, tennis, fishing. *Address:* 3 The Coppice, Middleton, Ilkley, W Yorks LS29 0EZ. *T:* (01943) 816349, 07799 791545.

JOHNSTON, David Carr; education consultant, since 2002; Chief Education Officer, Manchester City Council, 1998–2002; *b* 18 March 1944; *s* of William and Sarah Johnston; *m* 1969, Jennifer Anne Hopkinson; two *d*. *Educ:* Didsbury Coll. of Educn (Teacher's Cert. 1965); Sheffield Univ. (DipASE 1971); Sheffield Poly. (Dip Educn Mgt 1975); Leicester Univ. (MEd 1982). Asst Teacher, Trafford, Lancs, 1965–67, Sheffield primary schs, 1967–69; Dep. Hd, Park Hill Jun. Sch., Sheffield, 1969–72; Headteacher: Shirebrook Middle Sch., Sheffield, 1972–74; Ballifield Nursery, First and Middle Sch., Sheffield, 1974–79; School Advr, Derbys CC, 1979–84; Sen. Sch. Inspector, 1984–88, Dep. Chief Educn Officer, 1988–92, Manchester City Council; Dir of Educn and Leisure, Salford City Council, 1992–98. *Publications:* Managing Primary Schools, 1985; Managing Primary Schools in the 1990s, 1990. *Recreations:* music appreciation, fell walking, supporting Manchester City FC. *Address:* Totley Hall Croft, Totley, Sheffield S17 4BE.

JOHNSTON, Dr David Eric Lothian; QC (Scot.) 2005; advocate, since 1992; *b* 10 March 1961; *e s* of late Thomas Lothian Johnston and of Joan (*née* Fahmy). *Educ:* Daniel Stewart's and Melville Coll., Edinburgh; St John's Coll., Cambridge (BA 1982; MA 1986; PhD 1986; LLD 2001). Research Fellow, 1985–89, Fellow, 1993–99, Christ's Coll., Cambridge; Regius Prof. of Civil Law, Univ. of Cambridge, 1993–99. Visiting Fellow: Univ. of Freiburg, 1985–86; Univ. of Michigan Law Sch., 1987; Univ. of Calif, Berkeley, Law Sch., 1996, 1998; Visiting Professor: Paris I, 1999; Paris V, 2000–03; Univ. of Osaka, 2000; Hon. Prof., Edinburgh Univ. Law Sch., 2000–. Comr (pt-time), Scottish Law Commn, 2015–. *Publications:* On a Singular Book of Cervidius Scaevola, 1987; The Roman Law of Trusts, 1988; Roman Law in Context, 1999; Prescription and Limitation, 1999, 2nd edn 2012; (ed with R. Zimmermann) Unjustified Enrichment: key issues, 2002; (contrib.) Gloag and Henderson, The Law of Scotland, 11th edn 2001; (ed with A. Burrows and R. Zimmermann)

Judge and Jurist: essays in memory of Lord Rodger of Earlsferry, 2013; (ed) The Cambridge Companion to Roman Law, 2015; articles in learned jls mainly on Roman law and legal history. *Recreations:* music, travel, wine and food. *Address:* Advocates' Library, Parliament House, Edinburgh EH1 1RF. *T:* (0131) 226 5071.

JOHNSTON, David Lawrence, OBE 1997; CEng, FIET; RCNC; Director General, National Inspection Council for Electrical Installation Contracting, 1989–2001; Chairman, National Quality Assurance Ltd, 1993–2001 (Director, 1989–93); *b* 12 April 1936; *s* of late Herbert David Johnston and Hilda Eleanor Johnston (*née* Wood); *m* 1959, Beatrice Ann Witten; three *d. Educ:* Lancastrian Sch., Chichester; King's Coll., Durham (BSc). FIET (FIEE 1980). Electrical Fitter Apprentice, HM Dockyard, Portsmouth, 1951–56; Short Service Commn (Lieut), RN, 1959–62; joined Ministry of Defence, 1962; Overseeing, Wallsend, 1962–63; switchgear design, Bath, 1963–66; Production and Project Mgt, Devonport Dockyard, 1966–73; Dockyard Policy, Bath, 1973–76; Warship System Design, Bath, 1976–79; Production and Planning, Portsmouth Dockyard, 1979–81; Planning and Production, Devonport Dockyard, 1981–84; Asst Under-Sec. of State, and Man. Dir, HM Dockyard, Devonport, 1984–87; Chm., Devonport Dockyard Ltd, Mgt Buy-out Co., 1985–87; Dep. Chm., Devonport Mgt Ltd, 1987–88; mgt consultant, 1988–89. Dep. Chm., NQA, USA Inc., 1998–2001 (Dir, 1993–98); Dir, UK Accreditation Service, 2000–06. Dir, Nat. Supervisory Council, Intruder Alarms Ltd, subseq. Nat. Approval Council, Security Systems Ltd, 1989–96. Chairman: BASEEFA Adv. Council, subseq. Electrical Equipment Certification Service Product Adv. Cttee, HSE, 1990–2002; BASEEFA 2001 Ltd, 2003–; Electrical Equipment Certification Adv. Bd, HSE, 1990–2002; Member: HSE Open Govt Complaints Panel, 1995–2002; IEE Wiring Regulations Policy Cttee, 2001–04. *Recreations:* home, hearth and garden, novice golf, watercolour painting. *Address:* Weirside Mill, 8 Greenland Mills, Bradford-on-Avon, Wilts BA15 1BL. *T:* (01225) 938977. *E:* davidjohnston999@talktalk.net.

JOHNSTON, David Lloyd, CC 1997 (OC 1988); CMM 2010; Governor General of Canada, since 2010; *b* 28 June 1941; *s* of Lloyd Johnston and Dorothy Stonehouse Johnston; *m* 1963, Sharon Downey; five *d. Educ:* Harvard Univ., Cambridge, Mass; Cambridge Univ.; Queen's Univ. at Kingston, Ont. Asst Prof., Faculty of Law, Queen's Univ., Kingston, 1966–68; Faculty of Law, Univ. of Toronto: Asst Prof., 1968–69; Associate Prof., 1969–72; Prof., 1972–74; Dean and Prof., Faculty of Law, Univ. of Western Ont, 1974–79; Prof. of Law, 1979–99, Principal and Vice-Chancellor, 1979–94, McGill Univ.; Pres. and Vice-Chancellor, Univ. of Waterloo, 1999–2010. Chairman: Nat. Round Table on Envmt and the Economy, 1988–92; Information Highway Adv. Council, 1994–97; Canadian Inst. for Advanced Res., 1994–99; NeuroScience Network, 1994–98. LLD *hc* Law Soc. of Upper Canada, 1980. *Publications:* Computers and the Law (ed), 1968; Canadian Securities Regulation, 1977; (jtly) Business Associations, 1979, 2nd edn 1989; (with R. Forbes) Canadian Companies and the Stock Exchange, 1980; (jtly) Canadian Securities Regulation, Supplement, 1982; (jtly) Partnerships and Canadian Business Corporations, 1989; (jtly) If Quebec Goes, 1995; (jtly) Getting Canada Online: understanding the information highway, 1995; (jtly) Cyberlaw and Communication Law, 1997; articles and reports. *Recreations:* jogging, ski-ing, tennis. *Address:* Government House, 1 Sussex Drive, Ottawa, ON K1A 0A1, Canada. *Clubs:* University (Toronto); University (Waterloo); Westmount Golf.

JOHNSTON, Hon. Donald (James); PC (Can.) 1980; OC 2008; QC (Can.) 1985; Secretary-General, Organisation for Economic Co-operation and Development, 1996–2006; *b* 26 June 1936; *s* of Wilbur Austin Johnston and Florence Jean Moffat Tucker; *m* 1965, Heather Bell Maclaren; four *d. Educ:* McGill Univ. (BA, BCL; Gold Medallist 1958); Univ. of Grenoble (schol.). Joined Strikeman & Elliott, 1961; founder of law firm, Johnston, Heenan and Blaikie; Counsel, Heenan Blaikie, 1988–96; Lectr, Fiscal Law, McGill Univ., 1963–76; MP (L) St Henri-Westmount, 1978–88; Pres., Treasury Bd of Canada, 1980–82; Minister for Econ. Develt, and Minister of State for Sci. and Tech., 1982–83; Minister of State for Econ. Develt and Tech., 1983–84; Minister of Justice and Attorney-Gen., Canada, 1984. Pres., Liberal Party, 1990–94. Chair, Internat. Risk Governance Council, 2006–10. Vis. Prof., Yonsei Univ., Seoul, S Korea, 2006–10. Hon. dr: King's Coll., Halifax, 1999; Econs Univ. of Bratislava, 2000; McGill, 2003; McMaster, 2008; Bishop's, 2010. Grand Cordon, Order of the Rising Sun (Japan), 2006; Commander's Cross with Star of the Order of Merit (Hungary), 2006; Order of White Double Cross, First Class (Slovak Republic), 2006; Grand-Croix de l'Ordre de Léopold II (Belgium), 2007; Officier, Légion d'Honneur (France), 2011. *Publications:* How to Survive Canada's Tax Chaos, 1974; Up the Hill (political memoirs), 1986; (ed) With a Bang, Not a Whimper: Pierre Trudeau speaks out, 1988. *Recreations:* writing, tennis, piano. *Clubs:* Mount-Royal (Montreal); Montreal Indoor Tennis.

JOHNSTON, Frederick Patrick Mair, CBE 1993; Chairman, Johnston Press plc (formerly F. Johnston & Co. Ltd), 1973–2001 (Director, 1959–2010); *b* Edinburgh, 15 Sept. 1935; *e s* of late Frederick M. Johnston and Mrs M. K. Johnston, Falkirk; *m* 1961, Elizabeth Ann Jones; two *s. Educ:* Morrison's Acad., Crieff; Lancing Coll., Sussex; New Coll., Oxford (MA, Mod. Hist.). Commissioned in Royal Scots Fusiliers, 1955; served in E Africa with 4th (Uganda) Bn, KAR, 1955–56. Joined Editorial Dept of Liverpool Daily Post & Echo, 1959; joined The Times Publishing Co. Ltd, as Asst Sec., 1960–62; F. Johnston & Co. Ltd, subseq. Johnston Press plc: Asst Manager, 1962; Company Sec., 1969–73; Managing Dir, 1973–80; Chief Exec., 1980–91; Exec. Chm., 1991–97. Chm., Dunn & Wilson Ltd, 1976–97; Director: Scottish Mortgage and Trust plc, 1991–2002; Lloyds TSB Bank Scotland plc, 1996–2003; The Press Association Ltd, 1997–2001. Dir, FIEJ, 1990–96. President: Young Newspapermen's Assoc., 1968–69; Forth Valley Chamber of Commerce, 1972–73; Scottish Newspaper Proprietors' Assoc., 1976–78; Newspaper Soc., 1989–90; Chm., Newspapers Press Fund Appeal, 1995; Chm., Central Scotland Manpower Cttee, 1976–83; Mem., Press Council, 1974–88; Treasurer: Soc. of Master Printers of Scotland, 1981–86; CPU, 1987–91. Chm., Edinburgh Internat. Book Fest. (formerly Edinburgh Book Fest.), 1996–2001. Chm., Scotland in Europe, 2001–04. Regent, RCSE, 2001–10. FRSA 1992. Liveryman, Stationers' and Newspapermakers' Co., 2004–. *Recreations:* reading, travelling. *Address:* Johnston Press plc, 108 Holyrood Road, Edinburgh EH8 8AS. *Clubs:* Caledonian; New (Edinburgh).

JOHNSTON, Gordon MacKenzie, OBE 1996; HM Diplomatic Service, retired; *b* 24 June 1941; *s* of William Johnston and Betty Isabel Lamond (*née* MacKenzie); *m* 1963, Barbara Glenis Christie; one *s* one *d. Educ:* Robert Gordon's Coll., Aberdeen; Dingwall Acad. Joined HM Foreign, later Diplomatic, Service, 1959; FO, 1959–63; Berne, 1963–65; Pro-Consul, Tamsui, 1966–67; FCO, 1967–71; Entry Clearance Officer, Islamabad, 1971; FCO, 1972–74; Commercial Attaché, Paris, 1974–77; Second Sec., Georgetown, 1978–81; Press Officer, FCO, 1981–84; First Secretary: Commercial, Belgrade, 1984–88; Economic, Dublin, 1989–90; FCO, 1990–92; Ambassador, Slovenia, 1992–97; Counsellor (Commercial and Econ.), Stockholm, 1997–98. *Recreations:* golf, tennis, reading.

JOHNSTON, Graham; *see* Johnston, A. G.

JOHNSTON, Lt Col Grenville Shaw, OBE 1986; TD (2 clasps) 1975; CA; Senior Partner, W. D. Johnston & Carmichael, 1975–2001 (Consultant, 2001–05); Lord-Lieutenant of Moray, since 2005 (Vice Lord-Lieutenant, 1996–2005); *b* 28 Jan. 1945; *s* of Lt Col William Dewar Johnston, OBE, TD, CA and Margaret Raynor Adeline Johnston (*née* Shaw); *m* 1972, Marylyn Jean Picken; two *d. Educ:* Seafield Primary Sch., Elgin; Blairmore Prep. Sch., Huntly; Fettes Coll., Edinburgh. CA 1968. Apprentice with Scott-Moncrieff Thomson & Sheils, Edinburgh, 1963–68; Asst, Thomson McLintock & Co., Glasgow, 1968–70; with W. D. Johnston & Carmichael, 1970–2005. Mem. Council, ICA Scotland, 1993–98 (Jun. Vice Pres., 1998; Sen. Vice Pres., 1999–2000; Pres., 2000–01). Chm., Grampian & Shetland Cttee, Royal Jubilee and Prince's Trusts, 1980–91; Mem., Grampian Cttee, Prince's Scottish Youth Business Trust, 1989–97. Sec., Moray Local Health Council, 1975–91; Board Member: Moray Enterprise Trust, 1985–93; Moray Badenoch & Strathspey Local Enterprise Co. Ltd, 1990–93; Cairngorm Mountain Ltd, 1999–2014 (Chm., 2008–14); Highlands and Is Airports Ltd, 2001–08 (Chm., 2009–); Chm., Caledonian Maritime Assets Ltd, 2007–14. Trustee: Nat. Museums of Scotland, 1998–2006; Knockando Woolmill Trust, 2004–14; Chm., Fresson Trust, 2010–. Vice-Chm., Gordonstoun Sch., 1985–99. Highland Area, TAVRA Association, later Highland Reserve Forces and Cadets Association: Mem., 1980–; Chm., Northern Area, 1999–2001; Chm., 2001–05; Vice Pres., 2005–06 and 2012–; Pres., 2007–12; Vice Chm. (Army), RFCA, 2003–07. Lt Col, TA, 1982; Hon. Col, 3rd Highlanders, 1997–99. Pres., Moray Scouts, 2005–; Hon. Pres., Moray Soc., 2009–. DL Moray, 1979. KCSG 1982; OStJ 2011. *Recreations:* fishing, ski-ing, shooting, singing tenor. *Address:* Spynie Kirk House, Quarrywood, Elgin, Moray IV30 8XJ. *T:* (01343) 542578, 07774 120202. *Clubs:* New, Royal Scots (Edinburgh); Elgin Rotary (Hon. Mem., 2008–).

JOHNSTON, Henry Butler M.; *see* McKenzie Johnston.

JOHNSTON, Hugh Philip, CB 1977; FREng; Deputy Secretary, Property Services Agency, Department of the Environment, 1974–87; *b* 17 May 1927; *s* of late Philip Rose-Johnston and Dora Ellen Johnston; *m* 1949, Barbara Frances Theodoridi; one *s* three *d. Educ:* Wimbledon Coll.; Faraday House. DFH (Hons). Air Ministry Works Dept: Asst Engr, 1951; Engr, 1956; Ministry of Public Buildings and Works: Prin. Engr, 1964; Asst Dir, 1969; Dir (Under-Sec.), Dept of Environment and Property Services Agency, Engrg Services Directorate, 1970. Pres., CIBSE, 1987–88. FREng (FEng 1989). *Recreations:* motoring, music. *Address:* 9 Devas Road, Wimbledon, SW20 8PD. *T:* (020) 8946 2021.

JOHNSTON, Sir Ian; *see* Johnston, Sir W. I. R.

JOHNSTON, Ian Alistair, CB 1995; PhD; Vice Chancellor and Principal, Glasgow Caledonian University, 1998–2006; *b* 2 May 1944; *s* of late Donald Dalrymple Johnston and Muriel Joyce Johnston; *m* 1973, Mary Bridget Lube; one *s* one *d. Educ:* Royal Grammar Sch., High Wycombe; Birmingham Univ. (BSc, PhD). Joined Dept of Employment as Assistant Principal, 1969; Private Sec. to Permanent Secretary, Sir Denis Barnes, 1972–73; Principal, 1973; First Sec. (Labour Attaché), British Embassy, Brussels, 1976–77; Asst Sec. (Director, ACAS), 1978; Under-Sec. (Dir of Planning and Resources, MSC), 1984; Chief Exec., Vocational Educn Trng Gp, MSC, 1985; Dep. Dir Gen., MSC, subseq. Training Commn, then Training Agency, then Training Enterprise and Education Directorate of Department of Employment, 1987–92; Dir of Resources and Strategy (Dep. Sec.), Dept of Employment, 1992; Dir Gen., TEED, Dept of Employment, 1992–95; Dep. Principal, Sheffield Hallam Univ., 1995–98. Director: Glasgow Chamber of Commerce, 1998–2005; CAPITB plc, 1999–2002. Hon. Treas. and Council Mem., Industrial Soc., 1991–2002. Mem., European Commn Expert Study Gp on Educn and Trng, 1995–2000. Member, Council: BTEC/Univ. of London Exam. Bd, 1995–98; Council for Industry and Higher Educn, 2001–06; Mem., Jt Nat. Council for Higher Educn Staff, 2002–06. Director: Qualification for Industry, 1996–99; Univs and Colls Employers Assoc., 2001–06; Board Member: Scottish Enterprise Glasgow, 2004–06; Lifelong Learning UK, 2005–06. Consultant, Young Foundn, 2008–10. Gov. and Dep. Chm., Sheffield Hallam Univ. (formerly Sheffield City Poly.), 1988–95; Chief. Exec., Transition, 1998, Bd Mem., then Dep. Chm., 1998–2003, Univ. for Industry; Trustee, Carnegie Trust for Univs of Scotland, 1998–2006. Chm., Buxton Fest. Foundn, 2010–15. Mem., Merchants House of Glasgow, 2005. Hon. Life Mem., Work Foundn, 2002. DL City of Glasgow, 2004–06. CCMI (CIMgt 1993); FCIPD (FIPD 1993); FRSA 1995. DUniv: Glasgow Caledonian, 2006; Sheffield Hallam, 2010. Lord Provost's Medallist for Educn, 2005. *Publications:* contribs to learned jls on atomic structure of metals, 1966–69, and subseq. on public admin and educn and trng strategy, incl. virtual educn and apprenticeships. *Recreations:* birding, fishing, travel, cooking, bridge, gardening. *Address:* Stonecroft, 18 Eaton Drive, Baslow, Bakewell, Derbys DE45 1SE.

JOHNSTON, Prof. Ian Alistair, PhD; FRSE; Chandos Professor, School of Biology, since 1997, and Director, Scottish Oceans Institute, since 2012, University of St Andrews; *b* 13 April 1949. *Educ:* Univ. of Hull (BSc 1st cl. Hons Biological Chem. and Zoology 1970; PhD 1973). NERC Res. Fellow, Univ. of Bristol, 1973; University of St Andrews: Lectr, 1976–84, Reader, 1984, in Physiology; Prof., 1985–95; Dir, Gatty Marine Lab., 1985–2008; Founding Chm., Dept of Biology and Preclin. Medicine, 1987–91; Head, Sch. of Biological and Med. Scis, 1991–92; Mem. Court, 1997–2002; Founding Head, Div. of Envmtl and Evolutionary Biol., Sch. of Biology, 1997–2004; Dir of Res., Sch. of Biology, 2003–06. Co-founder and CEO, Xelect Ltd, 2013–. Vis. Prof., Univ. of Nairobi, 1993. Mem. Council, NERC, 1995–2000. Pres., Soc. for Experimental Biol., 2007–09. FRSE 1987. Scientific Medal, Zool Soc., 1984. *Publications:* (contrib.) Essentials of Physiology, 3rd edn 1991 (trans. Spanish 1987, trans. Italian 1989, trans. French 1990); (ed jtly) Phenotypic and Evolutionary Adaptation of Animals to Temperature, 1996; (jtly) Environmental Physiology of Animals, 2000. *Address:* School of Biology, University of St Andrews, Scottish Oceans Institute, St Andrews KY16 8LB. *T:* (01334) 463440.

JOHNSTON, Jennifer, (Mrs David Gilliland), FRSL; author; *b* 12 Jan. 1930; *d* of late (William) Denis Johnston, OBE; *m* 1st, 1951, Ian Smyth; two *s* two *d*; 2nd, 1976, David Gilliland, *qv. Educ:* Park House Sch., Dublin; Trinity Coll., Dublin. FRSL 1979. Mem., Aosdána. Plays: Indian Summer, performed Belfast, 1983; The Porch, prod Dublin, 1986. Hon. DLitt: Ulster, 1984: TCD, 1992; QUB, 1993; UCD 2005. *Publications:* The Captains and the Kings, 1972; The Gates, 1973; How Many Miles to Babylon?, 1974; Shadows on Our Skin, 1978 (dramatised for TV, 1979); The Old Jest, 1979 (filmed as The Dawning, 1988); (play) The Nightingale and not the Lark, 1980; The Christmas Tree, 1981; The Railway Station Man, 1984; Fool's Sanctuary, 1987; The Invisible Worm, 1991; The Illusionist, 1995; (contrib.) Finbar's Hotel, 1997; Two Moons, 1998; The Gingerbread Woman, 2000; This Is Not a Novel, 2002; Grace & Truth, 2005; Foolish Mortals, 2007; Truth or Fiction, 2009. *Recreations:* theatre, cinema, gardening, travelling. *Address:* Brook Hall, Culmore Road, Derry, N Ireland BT48 8JE. *T:* (028) 7135 1297.

JOHNSTON, Mark Steven; racehorse trainer, since 1987; Trainer and Managing Director, Mark Johnston Racing Ltd, since 1988; *b* 10 Oct. 1959; *s* of Ronald and Mary Johnston; *m* 1985, Deirdre Ferguson; two *s. Educ:* Glasgow Univ. Vet. Sch. (BVMS 1983). MRCVS 1983. Veterinary practice, 1983–86. MRSocMed 1999. *Recreation:* cycling. *Address:* Kingsley House, Middleham, Leyburn, N Yorks DL8 4PH. *T:* (01969) 622237, *Fax:* (01969) 622484. *E:* mark@markjohnstonracing.com.

JOHNSTON, Lt-Gen. Sir Maurice (Robert), KCB 1982; CVO 2005; OBE 1971; Lord-Lieutenant of Wiltshire, 1996–2004; Deputy Chief of Defence Staff, 1982–83, retired 1984; *b* 27 Oct. 1929; *s* of late Brig. Allen Leigh Johnston, OBE, and Gertrude Geraldine Johnston (*née* Templer); *m* 1960, Belinda Mary Sladen; one *s* one *d. Educ:* Wellington College; RMA Sandhurst. rcds, psc. Commissioned RA, 1949; transf. The Queen's Bays, 1954; served in Germany, Egypt, Jordan, Libya, N Ireland, Borneo. Instr, Army Staff Coll., 1965–67; MA to CGS, 1968–71; CO 1st The Queen's Dragoon Guards, 1971–73; Comdr 20th Armoured Brigade, 1973–75; BGS, HQ UKLF, 1977–78; Senior Directing Staff, RCDS, 1979; Asst Chief of Gen. Staff, 1980; Dep. Chief of Defence Staff (Op. Reqs), 1981–82. Col, 1st The Queen's Dragoon Guards, 1986–91. Chairman: Secondary Resources plc, 1988–91; Detention Corp., 1988–94; Managing Director: Freshglen Ltd, Wraxall Gp, 1984–85; Unit Security Ltd, 1985–88; Director: HIAB (formerly Partek Cargotec), 1984–2010; Shorrock

Guards Ltd, 1988–91. Governor: Dauntsey's Sch., Wilts, 1987–2004, St Mary's Sch., Calne, 1988–94. DL Wilts, 1990, High Sheriff, 1993–94. *Recreations:* fishing, shooting, gardening, music, glass engraving. *Address:* The Paddock, Reeves Piece, Bratton, Wilts BA13 4TH.

JOHNSTON, Nicholas; *see* Johnston, P. N.

JOHNSTON, Paul Charles; HM Diplomatic Service; Deputy Permanent Representative, UK Joint Delegation to NATO, since 2015; *b* 29 May 1968; *s* of late Charles Johnston and of Muriel (*née* Hall); *m* 2004, Nicola Carol Maskell. *Educ:* Galashiels Acad.; Univ. of Glasgow (MA Hons). MoD, 1990–93; HM Diplomatic Service, 1993–: Desk Officer, Eastern Adriatic Unit, 1993–95 (Private Sec. to Lord Owen at Internat. Conf. on Former Yugoslavia, 1994); Private Sec. to Ambassador to France, 1995–97; 2nd Sec. (Political), Paris, 1997–99; Foreign and Commonwealth Office: Head: Kosovo Policy Section, 1999–2000; European Defence Section, 2000–01; Dep. Hd, EU Ext. Dept, 2001–02; Hd, Security Policy Dept, FCO, 2002–04; Counsellor (Political), UK Mission to the UN, NY, 2005–08; Dir, Internat. Security, FCO, 2008–11; Ambassador to Sweden, 2011–15. *Recreations:* cinema, music, walking, idling. *Address:* c/o Foreign and Commonwealth Office, King Charles Street, SW1A 2AH.

JOHNSTON, (Paul) Nicholas, FIMI; *b* 5 Jan. 1948; *s* of Joseph Leo Johnston and Winifred Vera Neale or Johnston; *m* 1st, 1972, Catherine MacPhee (marr. diss. 1993); one *s* two *d*; 2nd, 1993, Anna Jiménez-Olive; two *s*. *Educ:* North Kesteven Grammar Sch.; RMA Sandhurst. Dir, Eastern Hldgs Ltd, 1972. Mem. (C) Scotland Mid and Fife, Scottish Parlt, 1999–2001. *Recreations:* cookery, history, gardening.

JOHNSTON, Peter Henry; Director (formerly Controller), BBC Northern Ireland, since 2006; *b* 20 Jan. 1966; *s* of Tommy and Edna Johnston; *m* 1991, Jill McAlister; one *s* one *d*. *Educ:* Imperial College, London (MEng Chem. Engrg 1988). Business Consultant, Shell Internat., London, 1988–90; Sen. Associate, Price Waterhouse Coopers Mgt Consultants, Belfast, 1990–94; BBC Northern Ireland, Belfast: Res. and Special Projs Exec., 1994–97; Hd, Mktg and Develt, 1997–2001; Hd, New Media, BBC Nations and Regions, London, 2001–03; Hd, Broadcasting, BBC NI, Belfast, 2003–06. *Recreations:* no longer playing but watching Rugby, being at the North Coast of Northern Ireland, socialising, playing golf badly. *Address:* BBC Northern Ireland, Broadcasting House, Ormeau Avenue, Belfast BT2 8HQ. *T:* (028) 9033 8200, *Fax:* (028) 9033 8800. *E:* peter.johnston@bbc.co.uk.

JOHNSTON, Peter William; consultant, International Federation of Accountants (Chief Executive, 1999–2002, Director, 2002–03, Adviser, 2003–05); *b* 8 Feb. 1943; *s* of late William Johnston and of Louisa Alice Johnston (*née* Pritchard); *m* 1967, Patricia Sandra Macdonald; one *s* one *d*. *Educ:* Univ. of Glasgow (MA, LLB). Partner, MacArthur & Co., Solicitors, Inverness, 1971–76; Procurator Fiscal Depute, Dumfries, 1976–78; Procurator Fiscal, Banff, 1978–86; Senior Procurator Fiscal Depute, Crown Office, Edinburgh, 1986–87; Asst Solicitor, Crown Office, 1987–89; Chief Exec. and Sec., ICAS, 1989–99. Mem. Bd, Risk Management Authy, 2006– (Convenor, 2008–). Trustee, Friends of Duff House, 2006–. *Recreations:* music, foreign languages. *Address:* 13 Scotstown, Banff AB45 1LA.

JOHNSTON, Robert Alan, AC 1986; Governor, Reserve Bank of Australia, 1982–89; *b* 19 July 1924; *m* 1st, 1948, Verna (*d* 1999), *d* of H. I. Mullin; two *s* two *d*; 2nd, 2000, Judith Ann, *d* of P. A. Lazzarini. *Educ:* Essendon High School; University of Melbourne. BCom. Commonwealth Bank of Australia, 1940–60; RAAF, 1943–46; Reserve Bank of Australia, 1960–89: Dep. Manager and Manager, Investment Dept, 1964–70; Chief Manager, Internat. Dept, 1970–76; Adviser, 1973–82; Chief Representative, London, 1976–77; Exec. Dir, World Bank Group, Washington, 1977–79; Secretary, Reserve Bank of Aust., 1980–82. Director: Australian Mutual Prov. Soc., 1989–97; John Fairfax Gp Pty, 1989–90; Westpac Banking Corp., 1992–96. Pres., Cttee for Econ. Develt of Australia, 1990–94. Hon. DCom Melbourne, 1992.

JOHNSTON, Robert Gordon Scott, CB 1993; Executive Director, United Kingdom Major Ports Group, 1993–99; *b* 27 Aug. 1933; *s* of late Robert William Fairfield Johnston, CMG, CBE, MC, TD; *m* 1960, Jill Maureen Campbell; one *s* one *d*. *Educ:* Clifton; Clare Coll., Cambridge (1st Cl. Hons Classical Tripos, MA). 2/Lieut Scots Guards (National Service), 1955–57. Entered Air Min. as Asst Principal, 1957; Private Sec. to Parly Under Sec. of State for Air, 1959–62; transf. to MPBW, Def. Works Secretariat, 1963; Sec., Bldg Regulation Adv. Cttee, 1964; Principal Private Sec. to successive Ministers of Public Bldg and Works, 1965–68; seconded to Shell Internat. Chemical Co., Finance Div., 1968–70; Asst Dir of Home Estate Management, Property Services Agency, 1970–73; seconded to Cabinet Office, 1973–75; Asst Sec., Railways Directorate, Dept of Transport, 1975–79; Under Sec., DoE, 1979–93; seconded to Price Commn, 1979; Dir of Civil Accommodation, 1979–88, Dir, Defence Services, 1988–90, PSA; Man. Dir, PSA Internat., 1990–93. Rep. of Sec. of State for Envmt on Commonwealth War Graves Commn, 1988–93. Lay Chm., NHS Complaints Panels, 2000–05; Mem., Ind. Review Panel, Healthcare Commn, 2004–07. Coronation Medal, 1953. *Address:* 5 Methley Street, SE11 4AL.

JOHNSTON, Prof. Ronald John, OBE 2011; PhD; FBA 1999; FAcSS; Professor of Geography, Bristol University, since 1995; *b* 30 March 1941; *s* of Henry Louis Johnston and Phyllis Joyce (*née* Liddiard); *m* 1963, Rita Brennan; one *s* one *d*. *Educ:* Commonweal County Secondary Grammar Sch., Swindon; Univ. of Manchester (BA 1962; MA 1964); Monash Univ. (PhD 1967). Department of Geography, Monash University: Teaching Fellow, 1964; Sen. Teaching Fellow, 1965; Lectr, 1966; University of Canterbury, New Zealand: Lectr, 1967–68; Sen. Lectr, 1969–72; Reader, 1973–74; University of Sheffield: Prof. of Geography, 1974–92; Pro-Vice-Chancellor for Acad. Affairs, 1989–92; Vice-Chancellor, Essex Univ., 1992–95. FAcSS (AcSS 1999). DU Essex, 1996; Hon. LLD Monash, 1999; Hon. DLitt: Sheffield, 2002; Bath 2006. Murchison Award, 1985, Victoria Medal, 1990, RGS; Honors Award for Distinction in Res., Assoc. Amer. Geographers, 1991; Prix Vautrin Lud, Fest. Internat. de Geographie, 1999; Lifetime Achievement Award, Assoc. Amer. Geographers, 2010; Political Communicator of the Year, Political Studies Assoc., 2011. *Publications:* (with P. J. Rimmer) Retailing in Melbourne, 1970; Urban Residential Patterns: an introductory review, 1971; Spatial Structures: an introduction to the study of spatial systems in human geography, 1973; The New Zealanders: how they live and work, 1976; The World Trade System: some enquiries into its spatial structure, 1976; (with B. E. Coates and P. L. Knox) Geography and Inequality, 1977; Multivariate Statistical Analysis in Geography: a primer on the general linear model, 1978; Political, Electoral and Spatial Systems, 1979; (with P. J. Taylor) Geography of Elections, 1979; Geography and Geographers: Anglo-American human geography since 1945, 1979, 6th edn 2004; City and Society: an outline for urban geography, 1980; The Geography of Federal Spending in the United States of America, 1980; The American Urban System: a geographical perspective, 1982; Geography and the State, 1982; Philosophy and Human Geography: an introduction to contemporary approaches, 1983, 2nd edn 1986; Residential Segregation, the State and Constitutional Conflict in American Urban Areas, 1984; The Geography of English Politics: the 1983 General Election, 1985; On Human Geography, 1986; Bell-Ringing: the English art of change-ringing, 1986; Money and Votes: constituency campaign spending and election results, 1987; (jtly) The United States: a contemporary human geography, 1988; (with C. J. Pattie and J. G. Allsopp) A Nation Dividing?: the electoral map of Great Britain 1979–1987, 1988; Environmental Problems: nature, economy and state, 1989, 2nd edn 1996; (jtly) An Atlas of Bells, 1990; A Question of Place: exploring the practice of human geography, 1991; (ed) The Dictionary of Human Geography, 1989, 4th edn 2000; (with D. J. Rossiter and C. J. Pattie) The Boundary Commissions, 1999; (jtly) From Votes to Seats, 2001; (with C. J. Pattie) Putting Voters in Their Place, 2006; (with S. Hix and I. McLean) Choosing an Electoral System, 2010; (jtly) Drawing a New Constituency Map for the United Kingdom, 2010; (with C. J. Pattie) Money and Electoral Politics: local parties and funding in general elections, 2014; contrib. chapters in ed vols and numerous papers in learned jls. *Recreation:* bell-ringing. *Address:* School of Geographical Sciences, University of Bristol, Bristol BS8 1SS. *T:* (0117) 928 9116, *Fax:* (0117) 928 7878. *E:* r.johnston@bristol.ac.uk.

JOHNSTON, Prof. Sebastian Lennox, PhD; FRCP; FRSB; Asthma UK Clinical Professor, National Heart and Lung Institute, Imperial College London, since 2011; Director, MRC and Asthma UK Centre in Allergic Mechanisms of Asthma, since 2011 (Deputy Director, 2010–11); *b* London, 30 March 1959; *s* of Ivor Johnston and Marlo Johnston; *m* 1997, Dr Tea Endeladze; four *s* two *d*. *Educ:* Guy's Hosp., London (MB BS 1982); Univ. of Southampton (PhD 1993). MRCP 1985, FRCP 2000; FRSB (FSB 2011). MRC Travelling Res. Fellow, Univ. of Iowa, 1994–95; University of Southampton: Lectr in Medicine and Respiratory Medicine, 1992–96; Sen. Lectr in Medicine, Respiratory Medicine and Respiratory Infection, 1996–99; National Heart and Lung Institute, Imperial College London: Professorial Fellow in Respiratory Medicine, 1999–2000; Prof. of Respiratory Medicine, 2000–11. NIHR Sen. Investigator, 2009–13; Eur. Res. Council Advanced Investigator, 2009–13. Member: BMA, 1982; British Thoracic Soc., 1988; Eur. Respiratory Soc., 1992; Amer. Thoracic Soc., 1995; Assoc. of Physicians of GB and Ire., 2000; British Soc. of Allergy and Clin. Immunol., 2000; Eur. Acad. of Allergology and Clin. Immunol., 2001; Amer. Acad. of Asthma, Allergy and Immunol., 2002. *Publications:* (ed jtly) Asthma: critical debates, 2001; (ed jtly) Respiratory Infections in Allergy and Asthma, 2003; (jtly) Medicine and Surgery: a concise textbook, 2005; (ed jtly) Asthma Exacerbations, 2006; (ed) An Atlas of Asthma, 2007; contrib. book chapters and approx. 300 papers in jls. *Recreations:* opera, football, Rugby. *Address:* National Heart and Lung Institute, Imperial College London, Norfolk Place, W2 1PG.

JOHNSTON, Sir Thomas Alexander, 14th Bt *cr* 1626, of Caskieben; *b* 1 Feb. 1956; *s* of Sir Thomas Alexander Johnston, 13th Bt, and of Helen Torry, *d* of Benjamin Franklin Du Bois; *S* father, 1984. *Heir: cousin* William Norville Johnston, *b* 25 Dec. 1955.

JOHNSTON, Ven. William Francis, CB 1983; Rector, Winslow with Great Horwood and Addington, Diocese of Oxford, 1991–95; *b* 29 June 1930; *m* 1963, Jennifer Morton; two *s* one *d*. *Educ:* Wesley Coll., Dublin; Trinity Coll., Dublin (BA 1955; MA 1969). Ordained 1955; Curate of Orangefield, Co. Down, 1955–59; commissioned into Royal Army Chaplains Dept, 1959; served, UK, Germany, Aden, Cyprus; ACG South East District, 1977–80; Chaplain-Gen. to the Forces, 1980–86; QHC 1980–86; Priest-in-charge, Winslow with Addington, 1987–91. *Recreations:* golf, fishing, gardening. *Address:* Lower Axehill, Chard Road, Axminster, Devon EX13 5ED. *T:* (01297) 33259.

JOHNSTON, Sir (William) Ian (Ridley), Kt 2009; CBE 2001; QPM 1995; DL; Director of Security, London Organising Committee of the Olympic and Paralympic Games, 2009–13; *b* 6 Sept. 1945; *s* of late William and Alice Johnston; *m* 1968, Carol Ann Smith; two *s*. *Educ:* Enfield Grammar Sch.; LSE (BSc 1st Cl. Hons). Joined Metropolitan Police 1965; ranks of PC to Chief Supt, 1965–88; Staff Officer to Sir Peter Imbert, 1988–89; Senior Command Course, 1989; Asst Chief Constable, Kent, 1989–92; Dep. Asst Comr, 1992–94, Asst Comr, 1994–2001, Met Police; Chief Constable, British Transport Police, 2001–09. Non-exec. Dir, SIA, 2013–. Mem. Bd, Canterbury Christ Church Univ., 2014–. Trustee, Suzy Lamplugh Trust, 2004–. DL Gtr London, 2007. *Recreations:* jogging, tennis, football, squash. *E:* carolian.johnston@me.com. *Club:* Orpington Rovers Football.

JOHNSTON, Sir William Robert Patrick K.; *see* Knox-Johnston.

JOHNSTONE; *see* Hope Johnstone, family name of Earl of Annandale and Hartfell.

JOHNSTONE, VANDEN-BEMPDE-, family name of **Baron Derwent**.

JOHNSTONE, Lord; David Patrick Wentworth Hope Johnstone; Master of Annandale and Hartfell; *b* 13 Oct. 1971; *s* and *heir* of Earl of Annandale and Hartfell, *qv*; *m* 2001, Penny, *d* of late John Macmillan; one *s* two *d*. *Educ:* Stowe; St Andrews Univ. (BSc 1994). Chairman: Scottish Land & Estates, 2014–; Haffal Town Hall Redevelt Trust, 2013–; Vice Chm., Johnstonebridge Develt Trust, 2012–; Dir, Dumfries & Galloway Small Community Housing Trust, 2007–. *Heir: s* Percy John Wentworth Hope Johnstone, Master of Johnstone, *b* 16 Feb. 2002.

JOHNSTONE, Alexander; Member (C) North East Scotland, Scottish Parliament, since 1999; *b* 31 July 1961; *m* 1981, Linda; one *s* one *d*. *Educ:* Mackie Acad., Stonehaven. Farmer, 1981–. Contested (C): W Aberdeenshire and Kincardine, 2005, 2010; Banff and Buchan, 2015. *Address:* 25 Evan Street, Stonehaven, Kincardine AB39 2EQ.

JOHNSTONE, Catherine, (Mrs Martin Holt); Chief Executive, Samaritans, since 2009; *b* Beckenham, Kent, 6 June 1964; *d* of Ernest Arthur and Mavis Ann Clemson; *m* 2008, Martin Holt; two *s* three *d*. *Educ:* Highams Park Sen. Sch.; Highams Park 6th Form Coll.; W Essex Sch. of Nursing (RGN 1985). Nursing posts with NHS, 1986–96; Chief Executive: Crossroads Caring for Carers, 1996–2000; Bucks Community Action, 2000–03; Regl Action and Involvement SE, 2003–07; Capacitybuilders, 2007–09. Lay Rep., Aylesbury Vale Primary Care Gp, 1999–2001. Accredited Nat. Social Enterprise Advr, Small Firms Enterprise Develt Initiative, 1985–2000; non-deptl public body Accounting Officer, 2007–09. *Address:* The Samaritans, The Upper Mill, Kingston Road, Ewell, Surrey KT17 2AF. *T:* (020) 8394 8302, *Fax:* (020) 8394 8301. *E:* c.johnstone@samaritans.org.

JOHNSTONE, Vice Adm. Clive Charles Carruthers, CB 2015; CBE 2007; Commander Maritime Command HQ Northwood, since 2015; *b* Kampala, Uganda, 6 Sept. 1963; *s* of Charles and Patricia Johnstone; *m* 1990, Alison Duguid; two *d* (one *s* decd). *Educ:* Royal Shrewsbury Sch.; Durham Univ. (BA Hons Anthropol.); Britannia Royal Naval Coll. Joined RN, 1985; Commanding Officer: HMS Iron Duke, 1998–99; HMS Bulwark, 2005–06; Director: Naval Personnel Strategy, 2007; Naval Staff, 2008; HCSC, 2008; Principal Staff Officer to CDS, 2008–10; rcds, 2011; FOST, 2011–13; ACNS (Policy), 2013–15. Younger Brother, Trinity House, 2009–. *Recreations:* swimming, fishing, gardening, wine, enjoying family time in our cottage in Argyll. *Address:* Atlantic Building, Northwood Headquarters, Sandy Lane, Northwood, Middlx HA6 3HP. *Club:* Naval.

JOHNSTONE, David; Interim Director of Health and Social Care, Bristol City Council, 2010–11; *b* 9 May 1951; *s* of David Armour Johnstone and Veronica Johnstone; *m* 1974, Andra Newton; one *s* two *d*. *Educ:* Middlesex Poly. (BA Hons Social Sci.); Newcastle upon Tyne Univ. (MBA). Joined Social Services Dept, Newcastle upon Tyne, 1974, Asst Dir, 1990–95; Director of Social Services: Stockton on Tees, 1995–99; Devon CC, 1999–2009; Dir of Ops, Care Quality Commn, 2009. *Recreations:* sport, rare breed animal husbandry. *Club:* Teign Corinthian Yacht.

JOHNSTONE, Debbie; *see* Alder, D.

JOHNSTONE, Prof. Eve Cordelia, CBE 2002; MD; FRCPsych, FRCPGlas, FRCPE, FMedSci; FRSE; Professor of Psychiatry, 1989–2010, now Emeritus, and Honorary Assistant University Principal for Mental Health Research and Development, since 2010, University of Edinburgh (Head, Department of Psychiatry, 1989–2010); *b* 1 Sept. 1944; *d* of late William Gillespie Johnstone and Dorothy Mary Johnstone. *Educ:* Park Sch., Glasgow; Univ. of Glasgow (MB ChB 1967; DPM 1970; MD 1976). MRCP 1971; MRCPsych 1972, FRCPsych 1984; FRCPE 1992. House officer posts, 1967–68, trng posts in Psychiatry,

1968–72, Glasgow Hosp.; Lectr in Psychological Medicine, Glasgow Univ., 1972–74; Mem., Scientific Staff, MRC, Clin. Res. Centre and Northwick Park Hosp., Harrow, 1974–89 (Hon. Consultant, 1979–89). Mem., MRC, 1996–2002 (Chm., Neuroscience and Mental Health Bd, 1999–2002). Founder FMedSci 1998; FRSE 2005. *Publications:* Searching for the Causes of Schizophrenia, 1994; (ed) Biological Psychiatry, 1996; (ed jtly) Schizophrenia: concepts and management, 1999; (ed jtly) Companion to Psychiatric Studies, 6th edn 1998 to 8th edn 2010; (with C. Frith) Schizophrenia: a very short introduction, 2003; (ed jtly) Schizophrenia: from neuroimaging to neuroscience, 2004; numerous contribs to learned jls mainly relating to schizophrenia and other serious psychiatric disorders. *Recreations:* card-playing, gardening, listening to opera, foreign travel. *Address:* Department of Psychiatry, University of Edinburgh, Kennedy Tower, Royal Edinburgh Hospital, Edinburgh EH10 5HF. *T:* (0131) 650 9221.

JOHNSTONE, Sir Geoffrey (Adams Dinwiddie), KCMG 2002 (CMG 1994); Ambassador (non-resident) of The Bahamas to Chile, Argentina, Uruguay and Brazil, 1995–2002; *b* 19 Sept. 1927; *s* of Bruce Eric Johnstone and Wilhelmina Johnstone; *m* 1954, Winifred Anne Duncombe. *Educ:* Queen's Coll., Nassau, Bahamas; Inns of Court Sch. of Law, London. Called to the Bar: Middle Temple, 1950; Bahamas, as Counsel and Attorney-at-Law, 1950; in practice, 1950–98. MHA (United Bahamian) Bahamas, 1962–72; Cabinet Minister, 1964–67; Leader of Opposition, 1970–71; Dep. to Gov. Gen. of Bahamas on numerous occasions, 1995–2001. Chm., Hotel Corp. of The Bahamas, 1992–94. Silver Jubilee Award (Bahamas), 1998. *Recreations:* shooting, fishing. *Address:* 3 Commonwealth Avenue, Blair Estate, PO Box N3247, Nassau, Bahamas. *T:* 3932586, *Fax:* 3941208. *Club:* Royal Nassau Sailing.

JOHNSTONE, Sir (George) Richard (Douglas), 11th Bt *cr* 1700, of Westerhall, Dumfriesshire; *b* 21 Aug. 1948; *er s* of Sir Frederic Allan George Johnstone, 10th Bt and of Doris Johnstone (*née* Shortridge); *S* father, 1994; *m* 1976, Gwyneth Susan Bailey (marr. diss. 2003); one *s* one *d*. *Educ:* Leeds Grammar Sch.; Magdalen Coll., Oxford (MA; Dip. Physical Anthropology). *Recreations:* travel, computing. *Heir: s* Frederic Robert Arthur Johnstone, *b* 18 Nov. 1981.

JOHNSTONE, Iain Gilmour; author and broadcaster; *b* 8 April 1943; *s* of Jack and Gilly Johnstone; *m* 1980, Mo Watson; one *s* two *d*. *Educ:* Campbell College, Belfast; Bristol Univ. (LLB Hons). Newscaster, ITN, 1966–68; Producer, BBC TV, 1968–74; Prof. of Broadcasting, Boston Univ., 1975; Man. Dir, DVD Prodns Ltd (formerly Kensington TV), 1977–2015; BBC presenter, Film 1983, 1984; film critic, The Sunday Times, 1983–93. Accredited Mediator, ADR Gp. Screenplays: Fierce Creatures (with John Cleese), 1996; The Evening News, 2001; The Bank of San Benedetto, 2002; Elsinore: The Year Before; documentaries: John Wayne and his films, 1969; Muhammad Ali, 1977; The Pythons, 1979; Snowdon on Camera, 1981; Steven and Stanley, 2001; Making Connections: the Weizmann Institute, 2010. *Publications:* The Arnhem Report, 1977; The Man With No Name, 1980; Cannes: The Novel, 1990; Wimbledon 2000, 1992; The James Bond Companion, 1999; (contrib.) British Comedy Greats, 2003; Tom Cruise: all the world's a stage, 2006; (with Kathryn Apanowicz) Richard by Kathryn, 2006; Streep: a life in film, 2009; Pirates of the Mediterranean, 2009; Close Encounters: a media memoir, 2013. *Recreations:* lawn tennis, theatre, playing with Ralph. *Address:* 16 Tournay Road, SW6 7UF. *E:* iain.j@uk.com. *Clubs:* Garrick, Queen's.

See also Baron Tollemache.

JOHNSTONE, Isobel Theodora, PhD; painter and art consultant; Curator, Arts Council Collection, 1979–2004; *b* 1944. *Educ:* James Gillespie's High School; Edinburgh Univ.; Edinburgh Coll. of Art (MA Hons Fine Art); Glasgow Univ. (PhD). Lectr in History of Art, Glasgow School of Art, 1969–73; Scottish Arts Council, 1975–79. Painter. *Publications:* (as Isobel Spencer): Walter Crane, 1975; articles on late 19th century and 20th century British art. *Address:* 28 Elgin Crescent, W11 2JR.

JOHNSTONE, Sir (John) Raymond, Kt 1993; CBE 1988; Managing Director, Murray Johnstone Ltd, Glasgow, 1968–89 (Chairman, 1984–94; President, 1994–97); Chairman, Forestry Commission, 1989–94; *b* 27 Oct. 1929; *s* of Henry James Johnstone of Alva, Captain RN and Margaret Alison McIntyre; *m* 1979, Susan Sara Gore, DL; five step *s* two step *d*. *Educ:* Eton Coll.; Trinity Coll., Cambridge (BA Maths). CA. Apprenticed Chiene & Tait, Chartered Accts, Edinburgh, 1951–54; Robert Fleming & Co. Ltd, London, 1955–59; Partner in charge of investment management, Brown Fleming & Murray CA (becoming Whinney Murray CA, 1965), Glasgow, 1959–68; a Founder of Murray Johnstone Ltd, Glasgow to take over investment management dept of Whinney Murray, 1968. Chairman: Summit Gp, 1989–98; Atrium (formerly Lomond) Underwriting plc, 1994–2003; Director: Shipping Industrial Holdings, 1964–75; Scottish Amicable Life Assce Soc., 1971–97 (Chm., 1983–85); Dominion Insurance Co. Ltd, 1973–95 (Chm., 1978–95); Scottish Financial Enterprise, 1986–91 (Chm., 1989–91); Kiln plc, 1995–2002. Hon. Pres., Scottish Opera, 1986–98 (Dir, 1978–86; Chm., 1983–85); Chm., Patrons, Nat. Galls of Scotland, 1996–2003. Member: Scottish Adv. Cttee, Nature Conservancy Council, 1987–89; Scottish Econ. Council, 1987–95; Chm., Historic Buildings Council for Scotland, 1995–2002. Trustee, Nuclear Trust, 1996–2007; Dir, Nuclear Liabilities Fund (formerly Nuclear Generation Decommissioning Fund) Ltd, 1996–2007 (Chm., 1996–2003). *Recreations:* fishing, music, farming. *Address:* 32 Ann Street, Edinburgh EH4 1PJ. *T:* (0131) 311 7100.

JOHNSTONE, Paul William, FFPH; Regional Director, Public Health England North, since 2013; *b* 12 Feb. 1960; *s* of Peter and Pamela Johnstone; *m* Caroline; one *s* two *d*. *Educ:* Southampton Univ. (BM); Liverpool Univ. (DTM&H); LSHTM (MSc Public Health); Glasgow Univ. (DCH). MRCGP 1990; FFPH (FFPHM 2001). Overseas health volunteer, 1988–90; Officer, ODA, 1991–93; public health consultant, 1996–99; Dir of Public Health, Teesside, 2002; Medical Dir, Co. Durham Tees Valley, 2002; Regl Dir of Public Health, Yorks and Humberside, 2002–11; Dir of Public Health, NHS N of England, 2011–13. Visiting Professor: Nuffield Inst. for Health, Univ. of Leeds, 2002–; Leeds Beckett (formerly Leeds Metropolitan) Univ., 2004–. MRSocMed 1990. *Publications:* Management Support for Primary Care, 1994; around 40 peer reviewed articles and monographs. *Recreations:* ski-ing, walking. *Address:* 16 Almsford Avenue, Harrogate, N Yorks HG2 8HD.

JOHNSTONE, Peter, CMG 2004; HM Diplomatic Service, retired; Governor of Anguilla, 2000–04; *b* 30 July 1944; *m* 1969, Diane Claxton; one *s* one *d*. Joined FO, 1962; served: Berne, 1965–66; Benin City, 1966–68; Budapest, 1968–69; Maseru, 1969–72; FCO, 1973–77; Dacca, 1977–79; First Sec., Dublin, 1979–82; FCO, 1983–86; First Sec. (Commercial), Harare, 1986–89; Consul Gen., Edmonton, 1989–91; FCO, 1991–95; Counsellor (Commercial Develt), Jakarta, 1995–98; FCO, 1999.

JOHNSTONE, Sir Raymond; *see* Johnstone, Sir J. R.

JOHNSTONE, Sir Richard; *see* Johnstone, Sir G. R. D.

JOHNSTONE, Rev. Prof. William, DLitt; Professor of Hebrew and Semitic Languages, University of Aberdeen, 1980–2001; *b* 6 May 1936; *s* of Rev. T. K. Johnstone and Evelyn Hope Johnstone (*née* Murray); *m* 1964, Elizabeth Mary Ward; one *s* one *d*. *Educ:* Hamilton Academy; Glasgow Univ. (MA 1st Cl. Hons Semitic Langs, BD Distinction in New Testament and Old Testament; DLitt 1998); Univ. of Marburg. University of Aberdeen: Lectr 1962, Sen. Lectr 1972, in Hebrew and Semitic Languages; Dean, Faculty of Divinity, 1984–87; Hd of Dept, Divinity with Religious Studies, 1998–2000. Member, Mission archéologique française: Ras Shamra, 1963, 1964, 1966; Enkomi, 1963, 1965, 1971; Member, Marsala Punic Ship Excavation, 1973–79. Pres., SOTS, 1990. *Publications:* Exodus, 1990; 1 and 2 Chronicles, 1997; Exodus and Chronicles, 1998; Exodus (2 vols), 2014; (ed and contrib.) William Robertson Smith: essays in reassessment, 1995; (ed and contrib.) The Bible and the Enlightenment: a case study - Dr Alexander Geddes (1737–1802), 2004; *translation:* Fohrer: Hebrew and Aramaic Dictionary of the Old Testament, 1973; *contributions to:* Ugaritica VI, 1969, VII, 1978, Alasia I, 1972; Dictionary of Biblical Interpretation, 1990; Cambridge Companion to Biblical Interpretation, 1998; Eerdmans Commentary on the Bible, 2003; New Interpreter's Dictionary of the Bible, 2006; Festschriften for: W. McKane, 1986; R. Davidson, 1992; G. W. Anderson, 1993; C. H. W. Brekelmans, 1997; E. W. Nicholson, 2003; A. G. Auld, 2006; G. I. Davies, 2011; articles in Aberdeen Univ. Review, Atti del I Congresso Internazionale di Studi Fenici e Punici, Bibliotheca Ephemeridum Theologicarum Lovaniensium, Expository Times, Kadmos, Notizie degli Scavi, Palestine Exploration Qly, Trans. Glasgow Univ. Oriental Soc., Scottish Jl of Theology, Studia Theologica, Theology, Vetus Testamentum, Zeitschrift für die Alttestamentliche Wissenschaft, etc. *Recreation:* alternative work. *Address:* 9/5 Mount Alvernia, Edinburgh EH16 6AW; Makkevet Bor, New Galloway, Castle Douglas DG7 3RN.

JOHNSTONE, William Neill, RDI 1989; Founder Chairman: Neill Johnstone Ltd, 1986–2009; Fabric Design Consultants International, 1988–2009; *b* 16 May 1938; *s* of Harry McCall Johnstone and Ethel Mary Neill; *m* 1st, (marr. diss.); two *d*; 2nd, 1991, Mara Lukic; one *s* one *d*. *Educ:* Forfar Acad.; Edinburgh Acad.; Univ. of Edinburgh; Scottish Coll. of Textiles; RCA. Designer, then Design Dir, R. G. Neill & Son, 1961–70; Man. Dir and Design Dir, Neill of Langholm, 1970–85; Design Dir, Illingworth Morris Gp and Co-ordinator of design training programme, 1982–85; Internat. Wool Secretariat Design Consultant, 1978–90. Chm., Confedn of British Wool Textiles Ltd Steering Cttee, 1982–85; Industrialist on Selection Panel, Designer Graduate Attachment Scheme, 1982–85. *Recreations:* climbing, hill walking, collecting Inuit carvings, painting.

JOHNSTONE-BURT, Vice Adm. Charles Anthony, (Tony), CB 2013; OBE 1997; Master of HM Household, since 2013; *b* 1 Feb. 1958; *s* of Comdr Charles Leonard Johnstone-Burt, OBE, RN and Margaret Hilary Johnstone-Burt; *m* 1981, Rachel Ann Persson; three *s* two *d*. *Educ:* Wellington Coll.; Durham Univ. (BA Jt Hons Psychol. and Anthropol. 1980); US Naval War Coll., Rhode Is (MA Internat. Relns and Strategic Studies 1997; UK Res. Fellow). Chartered FCIPD 2002; FRAeS 2009; CCMI 2012. HMS Active, Falklands War, 1982; helicopter pilot, Fleet Air Arm, and Anti-submarine Warfare Officer; CO HMS Brave, 1994–96; Captain 6th Frigate Sqdn and CO HMS Montrose, 2000–02; Cdre, BRNC, 2002–04; CO HMS Ocean, 2004–05; Dep. Comdr and COS, Jt Helicopter Comd, 2005–06; FO Scotland, England, Wales and NI and FO Reserves, 2006–08; Comdr, Jt Helicopter Comd, 2008–11; ISAF Dir of Counter Narcotics, Kabul, 2011; COS to Supreme Allied Comdr Transformation, 2011–13. Mem., Windsor Leadership Trust, 1999–. Mem., Royal Co. of Archers, 2010. Younger Brother, Trinity House, 2005–. Freeman: City of London, 1998; Co. of Haberdashers, 1998; City of Glasgow, 2007; Mem., Incorporation of Wrights, Trades House, Glasgow, 2007. *Recreations:* all sports, reading, hill walking, fly fishing, running, longbow archery. *Address:* Buckingham Palace, SW1A 1AA.

JOICEY, family name of **Baron Joicey**.

JOICEY, 5th Baron *cr* 1906, of Chester-le-Street, Co. Durham; **James Michael Joicey;** DL; Bt 1893; *b* 28 June 1953; *s* of 4th Baron and Elisabeth Marion Joicey, MBE (*née* Leslie Melville); *S* father, 1993; *m* 1984, Agnes Harriet Frances Mary, *yr d* of Rev. and Mrs W. M. D. Thompson; two *s* two *d*. *Educ:* Eton Coll.; Christ Church, Oxford. DL Northumberland, 2006. *Heir: s* Hon. William James Joicey, *b* 21 May 1990. *Address:* Etal Manor, Berwick-upon-Tweed TD15 2PU.

JOICEY, Nicholas Beverley; Director General, Strategy, International and Biosecurity, Department for Environment, Food and Rural Affairs, since 2014; *b* Guisborough, 11 May 1970; *s* of Harold Beverley and Wendy Joicey. *Educ:* Wintringham Sch., Grimsby; Univ. of Bristol (BA Hons Hist.); Peterhouse, Cambridge (PhD 1996). Journalist, The Observer, 1995–96; HM Treasury: Asst Private Sec. to Chief Sec., 1996–98; Hd, Internat. Instns Br., 1998–99; Private Sec. and Speechwriter to Chancellor of the Exchequer, 1999–2001; Advr, UK Delegn to IMF and World Bank, Washington, 2001–03 (on secondment); Head: EU Policy Team, 2004–06; EU Coordination and Strategy, 2006–07; Dir, Europe, 2007–08; Dir, Internat., 2008–12. *Recreations:* modern history, film. *Address:* Department for Environment, Food and Rural Affairs, Nobel House, 17 Smith Square, SW1P 3JR.

JOINER, Hon. Sarah Louise; Deputy Chairman, Multiple Sclerosis Trust, since 2012 (Patron, 2007–12); Chairman of Trustees, Gardening for the Disabled Trust, since 2009 (Trustee, since 2006); *b* London, 3 March 1960; *d* of late Kevin Gardner and of Baroness Gardner of Parkes, *qv*; *m* 1991, Timothy M. Joiner (marr. diss. 2003). *Educ:* City of London Sch. for Girls; Birkbeck, Univ. of London (CertHE 2013). Jun. Sec., Cons. Central Office, 1979; PA to Dir, Saatchi & Saatchi Garland Compton Ltd, 1979–86; PA to Chief Exec., C F Anderson & Son Ltd, 1986–89; Business Manager, S Thames RHA, 1991–94; Hd, Office of Chm., SE NHS Exec., 1994–2001; Hd, Office of Chm., NHS Appts Commn, 2001–05, Hd, Private Office for Dir of Develt, 2005–07, DoH. Lady Mayoress of Westminster, 2005–06. Mem., All Party Osteoporosis Gp, 1996–2000. Member: N Westminster Lay (Police) Visitors Panel, 1987–94; Bd of Visitors, HMP Wormwood Scrubs, 1995–98. Member: Westminster Youth Cttee, 1978–85; Mgt Cttee, Nat. Youth Agency, 1989–93. Various county rôles, Girl Guides Assoc., 1979–91. Mem., N London Regl Steering Cttee, MS Soc., 1997–2002. Member: Access Focus Gp, Royal Opera Hse, 1996–2000; Self-Help Panel, Thames TV Trust, 1985–86; Bd, Habinteg Housing Assoc., 2014–. Mem. Cttee, RHS, 2013– (Trustee, 2010–13). Chm., Cook Soc., 2009–10. Gov., St Edward's Primary Sch., London, 1984–90. Volunteer counsellor, St John and St Elizabeth Hospice, London, 1987–90. *Recreations:* gardening, the arts, entertaining at home, garden history.

JOLL, James Anthony Boyd, FSA; Chairman: Pearson Group Pension Trustee, since 1988; Advisory Board, White Cloud Capital Advisors, since 2009; *b* 6 Dec. 1936; *s* of late Cecil Joll, FRCS and Antonia (*née* Ramsden); *m* 1st, 1963, Thalia Gough (marr. diss. 1973); one *s* two *d*; 2nd, 1977, Lucilla Kingsbury (marr. diss. 2007); two *s*. *Educ:* Eton (Oppidan Scholar); Magdalen Coll., Oxford (BA 1st Class Hons PPE 1960; MA). FSA 2000. 2nd Lieut, 4th Queen's Own Hussars, 1955–57. Editorial staff, Financial Times, 1961–68, Jt Ed., Lex column, 1965–68; N. M. Rothschild & Sons, 1968–80, Dir, 1970–80; Exec. Dir, 1980–96, Finance Dir, 1985–96, Pearson plc. Chairman: AIB Asset Mgt Hldgs, 1997–2004; Atrium Underwriting plc, 2006–07; Dep. Chm., Jarvis Hotels, 1990–2004; Director: The Economist Newspaper, 1995–99; Equitas Hldgs, 1996–2007. Chm., Museums and Galls Commn, 1996–2000; Mem., Urgent Issues Task Force, Accounting Standards Bd, 1991–95. Chairman: Sir Winston Churchill Archive Trust, 2000–10; S. J. Noble Trust, 2004–13. Trustee: Wallace Collection, 1990–2000; Design Museum, 1992–2005; Henry Moore Foundn, 2003–11; Royal Sch. of Needlework, 2006–11. Mem. Council, RCM, 2000–07. Robinson Medallist, V&A Museum, 2004. *Recreations:* painting, learning, the gothic revival. *Address:* White Cloud Capital Advisors, 20 Manchester Square, W1U 3PZ. *Club:* Boodle's.

JOLLIFFE, family name of **Baron Hylton**.

JOLLIFFE, Sir Anthony (Stuart), GBE 1982; Senior Partner, Cork Gully LLP, since 2012; *b* Weymouth, Dorset, 12 Aug. 1938; *s* of late Robert and Vi Dorothea Jolliffe. *Educ:* Portchester Sch., Bournemouth. Qualified chartered accountant, 1964; articled to Morison

Rutherford & Co.; commenced practice on own account in name of Kingston Jolliffe & Co., 1965, later, Jolliffe Cork & Co., Sen. Partner, 1976. Chairman: Jolliffe Internat.; CMS Ltd, 2005–; Dir, General Mediterranean Holdings. Chm., Stoke Mandeville NHS Trust, 1994–95. Alderman, Ward of Candlewick, 1975–84; Sheriff, City of London, 1980–81; Lord Mayor of London, 1982–83. Pres., London Chamber of Commerce, 1985–88. Formerly Treasurer: Relate; Britain in Europe. Pres., Soc. of Dorset Men, 1982–2011, Dep. Pres., 2011–. DL Dorset, 2006–13. KStJ 1983. *Recreations:* yachting, classic cars. *Clubs:* Garrick, City Livery (Pres., 1979–80), Saints and Sinners (Chm., 2011); Phyllis Court (Henley).

JOLLIFFE, Maj.-Gen. David Shrimpton, CB 2003; FRCP; Director General, Army Medical Services, 2000–03; *b* 20 March 1946; *s* of John Hedworth Jolliffe and Gwendoline Florence Angela Jolliffe (*née* Shrimpton); *m* 1969, Hilary Dickinson; two *d. Educ:* Ratcliffe Coll., Leicester; King's Coll. Hosp., London (MB). FRCP 1987. Regl MO, 23 Para Field Amb., 1971–73, 2 Para, 1973–74; Cons. Dermatologist, Queen Elizabeth Mil. Hosp., 1980–82; Consultant Advr in Dermatology to the Army, 1982–86; Commanding Officer: British Mil. Hosp., Hong Kong, 1986–89; Cambridge Mil. Hosp., Aldershot, 1993–94; COS, Army Medical Directorate, 1996–99; Comdr, Med. HQ, Land Command, 1999–2000. QHP 1999–2003. Hon. Med. Advr, Royal Commonwealth Ex-Services League, 2003–. Trustee: Hong Kong Locally Enlisted Personnel Trust, 2001– (Chm., 2001–11); Blind Veterans UK (formerly St Dunstan's), 2004–; RBL, 2012–. Gov., Ratcliffe Coll., Leicester, 2001–08; Mem., Council and Ct, LSHTM, 2006–14 (Chairman: Audit Cttee, 2001–12; Ct, 2009–14). Mem., Yorks and Humber Veterans Adv. and Pensions Cttee, 2010–. Hon. Col, 207 (Manchester) Field Hosp. (V), 2003–09. *Publications:* contrib. papers on general and tropical dermatology to professional jls. *Recreations:* carpentry, computer technology. *Address:* Ness House, 75 Eastgate, Pickering, North Yorkshire YO18 7DY. *E:* red@pennswood.demon.co.uk.

JOLLY, Baroness *cr* 2010 (Life Peer), of Congdon's Shop in the County of Cornwall; **Judith Anne Jolly;** Chairman, Digital Services Cornwall CIC, since 2009; *b* Leamington Spa; *m*; two *s. Educ:* Univ. of Leeds; Univ. of Nottingham (PGCE). Teacher of Maths and IT, 1974–97; Chief of Staff to MEP for Cornwall, 1997–99; teacher of English with British Council Oman. Chm., Exec. Cttee, Lib Dems, Devon and Cornwall, 2007–10. A Baroness in Waiting (Govt Whip), 2013–15. *Address:* House of Lords, SW1A 0PW.

JOLLY, Sir (Arthur) Richard, KCMG 2001; PhD; development economist; Hon. Professorial Fellow, Institute of Development Studies, University of Sussex; *b* 30 June 1934; *s* of late Arthur Jolly and Flora Doris Jolly (*née* Leaver); *m* 1963, Alison Bishop, PhD (*d* 2014); two *s* two *d. Educ:* Brighton Coll.; Magdalene Coll., Cambridge (BA 1956, MA 1959; Hon. Fellow, 2001); Yale Univ. (MA 1960, PhD 1966). Community Develt Officer, Baringo Dist, Kenya, 1957–59; Associate Chubb Fellow, Yale Univ., 1960–61; Res. Fellow, E Africa Inst. of Social Res., Makerere Coll., Uganda, 1963–64; Res. Officer, Dept of Applied Econs, Cambridge Univ., 1964–68 (seconded as Advr on Manpower to Govt of Zambia, 1964–66); Fellow, 1968–71, Professorial Fellow, 1971–81, Dir, 1972–81, Inst. of Develt Studies, Univ. of Sussex; Dep. Exec. Dir, Programmes, 1982–95, Actg Exec. Dir, 1995, UNICEF, NY; Special Advr to Adminr, UNDP, NY, 1996–2000; Co-Dir, UN Intellectual History Project, Graduate Center, City Univ., NY, 2000–10. Advr on Manpower Aid, ODM, 1968; Sen. Economist, Min. of Develt and Finance, Zambia, 1970; Advr to Parly Select Cttee on Overseas Aid and Develt, 1974–75; ILO Advr on Planning, Madagascar, 1975; Member: Triennial Rev. Gp, Commonwealth Fund for Tech. Co-operation, 1975–76; UK Council on Internat. Develt, 1974–78; UN Cttee for Develt Planning, 1978–81; Special Consultant on N-S Issues to Sec.-Gen., OECD, 1978; UN Sec.-Gen.'s Eminent Persons Gp Panel on Least Developed Countries, 2011; sometime member and chief of ILO and UN missions, and consultant to various governments and international organisations. Hon. Chairman: Water Supply and Sanitation Collaborative Council, 1997–2005 (Hon. Lifetime Patron, 2005); UNA-UK, 2001–05. Trustee, Oxfam, 2001–06. Pres., British Assoc. of Former UN Civil Servants, 2007–11. Sec., British Alpine Hannibal Expedn, 1959. Member: Founding Cttee, European Assoc. of Develt Insts, 1972–75; Governing Council, 1976–85, and N-S Round Table, SID, 1976– (Vice-Pres., 1982–85; Chm., N-S Round Table, 1988–96). Mem., Editorial Bd, World Development, 1973–90. Master, Curriers' Co., 1977–78. Hon. LittD E Anglia, 1988; Hon. DLitt Sussex, 1992; Hon. Dr Inst. of Social Studies, The Hague, 2007. *Publications:* (jtly) Cuba: the economic and social revolution, 1964; Planning Education for African Development, 1969; (ed) Education in Africa: research and action, 1969; (ed jtly) Third World Employment, 1973; (jtly) Redistribution with Growth, 1974 (trans. French 1977); (ed) Disarmament and World Development, 1978, 3rd edn 1986; (ed jtly) Recent Issues in World Development, 1981; (ed jtly) Rich Country Interests in Third World Development, 1982; (ed jtly) The Impact of World Recession on Children, 1984; (ed jtly) Adjustment with a Human Face, 1987 (trans. French 1987, Spanish 1987); (ed jtly) The UN and the Bretton Woods Institutions, 1995; (ed jtly) Human Development Report, annually 1996–2000 (trans. French, Spanish); (ed jtly) Development with a Human Face, 1998; (jtly) Ahead of the Curve, 2001; (ed) Jim Grant - UNICEF visionary, 2001; (jtly) UN Contributions to Development Thinking and Practice, 2004; (jtly) UN Ideas that Changed the World, 2009; (jtly) Be Outraged: there are alternatives, 2012; UNICEF: global governance that works, 2014; articles in professional and develt jls. *Recreations:* billiards, croquet, nearly missing trains and planes. *Address:* Institute of Development Studies, University of Sussex, Brighton, Sussex BN1 9RE. *T:* (01273) 606261. *E:* r.jolly@ids.ac.uk.

JOLLY, James Falcon; Editor-in-Chief, Gramophone, since 2006 (Editor, 1989–2005); Presenter, BBC Radio 3, since 2007; *b* 12 Feb. 1961; *s* of late Gordon Jolly, FRCOG and Enid Jolly; *m* 2006, Christopher Peter Davies. *Educ:* Pinewood Sch., Bourton; Bradfield Coll.; Univ. of Bristol (BA Hons); Univ. of Reading (MA). Asst Editor, Gramophone, 1985–88; Producer, BBC Radio 3, 1988–89. *Publications:* contrib. British Music Yearbook, 1986–88, Good CD Guide, Gramophone, Independent, Le Monde de la Musique, New Grove Dictionary of Opera. *Recreations:* food, wine, travel, cinema, gardening. *Address:* Downs Farm Barn, Baunton, Cirencester, Glos GL7 7BB. *T:* ((01285) 654865; Mark Allen Group, St Jude's Church, Dulwich Road, SE24 0PB.

JOLLY, Michael Gordon, CBE 2001; Director, Bluestone National Park Resort, Wales, 2009–13; *b* 21 Sept. 1952; *s* of Ron and Joy Jolly; *m* 1975, Julia Catherine Gordon Sharp; one *s* one *d. Educ:* Henley-on-Thames Grammar Sch. Marketing and other positions, Cadbury-Schweppes plc, 1972–83; Tussaud's Group: Head, Marketing, 1983–87; Bd Dir, 1987–91; Chief Operating Officer, 1991–94; CEO, 1994–2000; Chm., 1994–2001; Chief Exec., Penna Consulting plc, 2001–03; Chairman: Star Parks SA Europe, 2004–06; Park Holidays UK (formerly Cinque Ports Leisure Ltd), 2006–12. Comr, English Heritage, 2002–10. Trustee, Alnwick Garden Trust, 2009–12. *Recreations:* golf, the Arts.

JOLLY, Sir Richard; *see* Jolly, Sir A. R.

JONAH, Samuel Esson, Hon. KBE 2003; Chairman, Jonah Capital; *b* 19 Nov. 1949; *s* of Thomas Jonah and Beatrice Sampson; *m* 1973, Theodora (marr. diss.); three *s* two *d*; *m* 2009, Giselle. *Educ:* Camborne Sch. of Mines (ACSM 1973); Imperial Coll. of Sci. and Technol. (MSc Mine Mgt). CEO, Ashanti Goldfields Co. Ltd, 1986–2005 (non-exec. Dir, AngloGold Ashanti, 2004–07). Exec. Chm., Equator Exploration Co.; Director: Lonmin plc, 1992–2004; Anglo American Corp. of SA; Amplats; Standard Banking Gp. Member, International Advisory Council: Pres. of S Africa; Pres. of Ghana; Pres. of Nigeria; Member: Adv. Council of Pres. of African Develt Bank; Adv. Council, IFC; Global Compact Adv. Council of UN Sec.-Gen.; Togo Presidential Adv. Council; Co-Chm., World Econ. Forum, Durban, 2003. Vis. Prof. of Business, Univ. of Witwatersrand Business Sch. of Johannesburg. Trustee, Nelson Mandela Legacy Trust, UK. Hon. DSc Camborne Sch. of Mines and Univ. of Exeter, 1994. Lifetime Achievement Award, Mining Jl, 2004. *Relevant publication:* Sam Jonah and the Remaking of Ashanti, by A. A. Taylor. *Recreations:* fishing, golfing. *Address:* PO Box 551, Melrose Arch, 2076 Johannesburg, South Africa. *T:* (11) 5892000, *Fax:* (11) 5892019. *E:* sam.jonah@jonahcapital.com.

JONAS, Christopher William, CBE 1994; FRICS; President, Royal Institution of Chartered Surveyors, 1992–93; Chairman, Henderson International Income Trust plc, since 2011; *b* 19 Aug. 1941; *s* of late Philip Griffith Jonas, MC and Kathleen Marjory Jonas (*née* Ellis); *m* 1st, 1968, Penny Barker (marr. diss. 1997); three *s* one *d*; 2nd, 2003, Dame Judith Mayhew (*see* Dame Judith Mayhew Jonas). *Educ:* Charterhouse; Coll. of Estate Management; London Business Sch. (Sloan Fellow). TA Inns of Court Regt, 1959–66. Jones Lang Wootton, 1959–67; Drivers Jonas: Partner, 1967–82; Managing Partner, 1982–87; Sen. Partner, 1987–95. Property Adviser, Staffs County Council, 1982–2005. Director: SFA, 1988–91; BITC, 1999–2006; Railtrack Gp plc, 1994–2001; Canary Wharf Gp plc, 1994–2004; England Bd, Bank of Scotland, 1998–2000; Sunrise Senior (formerly Assisted) Living, 1998–2012; ECNlive (formerly Executive Channel Europe) Ltd, 2011–14; Chairman: Tate Modern develt, 1997–2000, and 2nd stage develt, 2006–; Education Capital Finance plc, 2000–03; Glasgow Harbour Ltd, 2001–03; Henderson Global Property Cos Ltd, 2006–11; Sen. Advr, Lazard & Co., 2007–13; Board Member: PLA, 1985–99; British Rail Property Bd, 1991–94; BR, 1993–94. Founder, ProHelp, 1989; Mem., FEFC, 1992–98. Chm., Economics Research Associates, USA, 1987–93; Mem., Counselors of Real Estate, USA, (Gold Medal 2007). Dir, ENO, 1999–2007; Trustee, Westminster Abbey Pension Fund, 2001–; Chm. Trustees, Contemporary Art Soc., 2014–. Governor: Charterhouse, 1995–2006; UCL, 1997–2005 (Vice-Chm., 2000–04); Chairman of Council: Roedean, 2004–11; Goldsmiths Univ. of London (formerly Goldsmiths Coll.), 2006–12. Second career as street photographer (www.cwjpix.org); exhibitions of photographs: Goldsmiths 2012; Tate Modern, 2013; RA, 2013; Garsington Opera, Wormsley, 2013; Nat. Churches Trust, 2013; Canary Wharf Gp Atrium, 2014; Peltz Gall., 2015. Liveryman, Clothworkers' Co. (Master, 2007–08). Hon. DSc De Montfort, 1997. *Recreations:* photographing the general public, English church music, lieder. *Address:* 25 Victoria Square, SW1W 0RB. *T:* (020) 7828 9977. *E:* cwj@kingslodge.com. *Club:* Queen's.

See also R. W. Jonas.

JONAS, Dame Judith M.; *see* Mayhew Jonas.

JONAS, Sir Peter, Kt 2000; CBE 1993; opera company and orchestra director; university lecturer; General Director (Staatsintendant), Bavarian State Opera, 1993–2006; *b* 14 Oct. 1946; *s* of late Walter Adolf Jonas and Hilda May Jonas; *m* 1st, 1989, Lucy (marr. diss. 2001), *d* of Christopher and Cecilia Hull; 2nd, 2012, Barbara, *d* of Eckhard and Karin Burgdorf. *Educ:* Worth School; Univ. of Sussex (BA Hons); Royal Northern Coll. of Music (LRAM; FRNCM 2000); Royal Coll. of Music (CAMS; Fellow, 1989); Eastman Sch. of Music, Univ. of Rochester, USA. Asst to Music Dir, 1974–76, Artistic Administrator, 1976–85, Chicago Symphony Orch.; Dir of Artistic Admin, Orchestral Assoc. of Chicago (Chicago Symph. Orch., Chicago Civic Orch., Chicago Symph. Chorus, Allied Arts Assoc., Orchestra Hall), 1977–85; Man. Dir, subseq. Gen. Dir, ENO, 1985–93. Member: Adv. Bd, Hypo-Vereinsbank, 1994–2005; Bd of Governors, Bayerische Rundfunk, 1999–2006; Chm., German Speaking Opera Intendants Conf., 2000–06; Lectr, Faculty, Univ. of St Gallen, Switzerland, 2003–; Visiting Lecturer: Univ. of Zürich, 2004–; Bavarian Theatre Acad., Munich, 2006–14. Mem., Adv. Bd, Tech. Univ., Munich, 2006–12. Member: Bd of Management, Nat. Opera Studio, 1985–93; Council, RCM, 1988–95; Council, London Lighthouse, 1990–94; Supervisory Bd, City of Berlin Opera Trust, 2005–12; Supervisory Bd, Netherlands Nat. Opera and Ballet (formerly Netherlands Opera), Amsterdam, 2009–; Governing Bd, Univ. of Lucerne, 2009–; Kuratorium and Governing Bd, Wissenschaftszentrum für Sozialforschung, Berlin, 2015–. FRSA 1989. Fellow: Bavarian Acad. of Fine Arts, 2005–; Univ. of Sussex, 2012–. Hon. DMus Sussex, 1994. Munich Prize for Culture, 2003; German-British Forum Award, 2006. Bavarian Constitutional Medal, 2001; Bayerische Verdienstorden, 2001, Maximiliansorden, 2008. *Publications:* (with Mark Elder and David Pountney) Power House, 1992; (jtly) Eliten und Demokratie, 1999; Wenn Musik der Liebe Nahrung ist, spielt weiter..., 2006. *Recreations:* cinema, old master paintings, cricket, long-distance hiking, Crystal Palace FC, epic TV series. *Address:* Scheuchzerstrasse 36, 8006 Zürich, Switzerland. *Clubs:* Athenæum; Surrey County Cricket.

JONAS, Richard Wheen, FRICS; Senior Partner, Cluttons, 1992–2003; *b* 10 April 1943; *s* of late Philip Griffith Jonas, MC and of Kathleen Marjory (*née* Ellis); *m* 1973, Bettina Banton; two *d. Educ:* Charterhouse; Royal Agricl Coll. Strutt & Parker, 1965–70; Carter Jonas, 1970–73; Cluttons, 1973–2003: Partner, 1978–2003. Dir, Babraham Bioscience Technologies Ltd, 2003–. Mem. Council, Roedean Sch., 2000–05; Gov., Sutton's Hospital in Charterhouse, 2002–13. Liveryman, Clothworkers' Co., 1965– (Master, 2010). Gold Medal, RASE, 1967. *Recreations:* shooting, golf, ornithology.

See also C. W. Jonas.

JONES; *see* Allen-Jones.

JONES; *see* Armstrong-Jones, family name of Earl of Snowdon.

JONES; *see* Clement-Jones, family name of Baron Clement-Jones.

JONES; *see* Duncan-Jones.

JONES; *see* Garel-Jones.

JONES; *see* Griffith-Jones.

JONES; *see* Gwynne Jones, family name of Baron Chalfont.

JONES; *see* Hugh-Jones.

JONES; *see* Idris Jones.

JONES; *see* Lloyd Jones and Lloyd-Jones.

JONES; *see* Neville-Jones.

JONES; *see* Owen-Jones.

JONES; *see* Rhys Jones.

JONES, family name of **Barons Jones** and **Jones of Cheltenham**.

JONES, Baron *cr* 2001 (Life Peer), of Deeside in the County of Clwyd; **Stephen Barry Jones;** PC 1999; Chancellor, Glyndŵr University, 2008–12; *b* 1937; *s* of late Stephen and Grace Jones, Mancot, Flintshire; *m* Janet Jones (*née* Davies); one *s*. MP (Lab): Flint East, 1970–83; Alyn and Deeside, 1983–2001. PPS to Rt Hon. Denis Healey, 1972–74; Parly Under-Sec. of State for Wales, 1974–79; Opposition spokesman on employment, 1980–83; Chief Opposition spokesman on Wales, 1983–87, 1988–92; Mem., Labour Shadow Cabinet, 1983–87 and 1988–92. Member: Speaker's Panel of Chairmen, 1993–2001; Prime Minister's Intelligence and Security Cttee, 1994–2001; Dep. Speaker, Westminster Hall, 2001–; Chm., Speaker's Adv. Cttee on political parties, 1999; Mem., Speaker's Cttee on Electoral Commn, 2001. Mem., WEU and Council of Europe, 1971–74. Member: Govs, Nat. Mus., Wales,

1992–; Court, Univ. of Wales, 1992–; Nat. Liby of Wales, 1992–; Bd, Clwyd Theatr Cymru, 2012–. Chm., St Asaph Diocesan Bd of Educn and Lifelong Learning, 2004–. President: Deeside Hosp., 2000–; Flintshire Br., Alzheimer's Soc., 2001–; Wrexham-Birkenhead Rail Users Assoc., 2001–; Chester and E Clwyd Advanced Motorists, 2003–; Arthritis Care Flintshire, 2006–; NE Wales Inst. for Higher Educn, 2007–08; Flintshire Neighbourhood Watch Assoc., 2008–; Deeside Industrial Park Forum, 2011–; Army Cadet Forces Assoc. Wales, 2012–; Sain Clwyd Sound; N Wales Exporters' Council; Training Ship Tuscan (Flintshire); Vice Pres., Attend (League of Friends) UK, 2013–. Trustee, Bodelwyddan Castle Trust, 2008–. Patron: Gap Quay Nomads AFC, 1985–; Brain Injury Rehabilitation and Develt Learning Centre, 1990–; Welsh Assoc. of ME and CFS Support, 2011–; N Wales and Chester News Centre. A Dementia Champion Wales, 2013. Hon. Fellow: Gladstone Liby, 2000–; Bangor Univ., 2012. *Address:* House of Lords, SW1A 0PW.

JONES OF BIRMINGHAM, Baron *cr* 2007 (Life Peer), of Alvechurch and of Bromsgrove in the county of Worcestershire; **Digby Marritt Jones,** Kt 2005; broadcaster, business adviser and author; Business Ambassador, UK Trade & Investment, 2008–12; *b* 28 Oct. 1955; *s* of late Derek Alwyn Jones and of Bernice Joyce Jones; *m* 1990, Patricia Mary Moody. *Educ:* Bromsgrove Sch. (Foundn Scholar); UCL (LLB Hons 1977; Fellow, 2004). Midshipman, RN, 1974–77. Admitted Solicitor, 1980. Joined Edge & Ellison, Solicitors, 1978; articled clerk, 1978–80; Asst Solicitor, 1980–81; Associate, 1981–84; Partner, 1984–98; Head of Corporate, 1987; Dep. Sen. Partner, 1990–95; Sen. Partner, 1995–98; Vice-Chm., Corporate Finance, KPMG Business Advisors, 1998–99; Dir Gen., CBI, 2000–06; Minister of State, UK Trade and Investment, BERR and FCO, 2007–08. Mem., CRE, 2003–07. Senior Advr to Exec., Deloitte, Barclays Capital, JCB, 2006–07; Corporate Advr to Ford of Europe, 2006–07; Corporate Affairs Advr to Bucknall Austin Ltd, 2006–07; Special Advisor: Monitise plc (formerly Monitise Ltd), 2006–07 (Global Ambassador, 2011–); Harvey Nash, 2009–; Mem., Adv. Bd, Thales (UK) Ltd, 2006–07; Chairman: Internat. Business Adv. Bd, HSBC, 2009–11 (Sen. Advr, 2012); Internat. Business Adv. Bd, British Airways, 2011–12; Grove Industries Ltd, 2012– (Business Advr, 2009–11); Business Advr, Barberry Develts Ltd, 2009–; Adviser: Birmingham Assay Office, 2009–; Babcock Internat. Gp plc, 2010– (Chm., Emergency Services Bd, 2012–14); Argentex LLP, 2012–; BP plc, 2013–. Non-executive Director: Alba plc, 2004–07; Leicester Tigers Rugby Club, 2005–; Flybe, 2012–13; Spicers Ltd, 2012–14; Grafton Fields Ltd, 2013–; G-Labs Ltd, 2015–; Dep. Chm., Unipart Expert Practices, 2013–; Chairman: Triumph Motorcycles Ltd, 2009–; Neutrino Concepts Ltd, 2009–15; SHP Ltd, 2014–; Cell Therapy Ltd, 2015–. Chm., Tourism Alliance, 2001–05; Dir, VisitBritain, 2003–06. Dir, BITC, 2000–06; Mem., Nat. Learning and Skills Council, 2003–06. UK Skills Envoy, 2006–07. Corporate Ambassador: Jaguar Cars, 2009–; JCB, 2009–; Cancer Res. UK, 2010–; Aon, 2014–. Vice-Pres., UNICEF, 2002–06 (Fellow, 2006). Special Advr to the Duke of York, 2006–07 and 2009–10. Chm., Adv. Bd, Birmingham Univ. Business Sch., 2005–. Trustee: Millennium Point, Birmingham, 2009–11; UK Community Foundn, 2014–; Temple Grafton Village Hall Trust. Mem., RSC, 2012–. Patron, Ladies Fighting Breast Cancer, 2010–. Presenter, TV series, The New Troubleshooter, 2014; winner, Celebrity Mastermind, 2010. CCMI. DUniv: UCE, 2002; Birmingham, 2002; Herts 2004; Hon. DLitt UMIST, 2003; Hon. Dr: London; Cardiff; Manchester; Middlesex; Sheffield Hallam; Aston; Hull; Warwick; Bradford; Thames Valley; Wolverhampton; QUB; Loughborough; Nottingham. *Recreations:* Rugby, ski-ing, military history, keeping fit by swimming, cycling (cycled from John O'Groats to Lands End in June 1998) and running (London Marathon in 5 hours 58 minutes and 26 seconds, 2005), theatre, Aston Villa FC. *Address:* House of Lords, SW1A 0PW.

JONES OF CHELTENHAM, Baron *cr* 2005 (Life Peer), of Cheltenham in the county of Gloucestershire; **Nigel David Jones;** *b* 30 March 1948; *m* 1981, Katy Grinnell; one *s* twin *d. Educ:* Prince Henry's Grammar Sch., Evesham. With Westminster Bank, 1965–67; computer programmer, ICL Computers, 1967–70; systems analyst, Vehicle and Gen. Insce, 1970–71; systems programmer, Atkins Computing, 1971; systems designer and consultant, ICL Computers, 1971–92. Contested (L) Cheltenham, 1979. MP (Lib Dem) Cheltenham, 1992–2005. Lib Dem spokesman on England, local govt and housing, 1992–93, science and technology, 1993–99, consumer affairs, 1995–97, culture, media and sport, 1997–99, internat. develt, 1999–2005. Mem., H of L Information Cttee, 2006–09. *Address:* House of Lords, SW1A 0PW.

JONES OF MOULSECOOMB, Baroness *cr* 2013 (Life Peer), of Moulsecoomb, in the County of East Sussex; **Jennifer, (Jenny), Helen Jones;** Member (Green), London Assembly, Greater London Authority, since 2000; *b* 23 Dec. 1949; *d* of Percy and Christine Jones; *m* (marr. diss.); two *d. Educ:* Westlain Grammar Sch., Brighton; Inst. of Archaeol., Univ. of London (BSc Envmtl Archaeol.). Archaeologist, 1990–99; Financial Controller, Metro Inspection Services, 1999–2000. Dep. Mayor of London, 2003–04; Greater London Authority: Chm., Standards Cttee, 2000–03; London Mayor's Road Safety Ambassador, 2002–08; London Mayor's Green Transport Advr, 2006–08; Chm., Planning and Housing Cttee, 2009–10, 2011–12; Dep. Chm., Police and Crime Cttee, 2012–; Mem., Metropolitan Police Authy, 2000–12; Chair: London Food, 2004–08; Mayor of London's Walking Adv. Panel (formerly Walking Forum), 2003–08. Mem. (Green), Southwark LBC, 2006–10. Contested (Green) Camberwell and Peckham, 2010; London Mayoral candidate, 2012. *Recreations:* yoga, cinema, family and friends. *Address:* Greater London Authority, City Hall, Queen's Walk, SE1 2AA. *T:* (020) 7983 4358.

JONES OF WHITCHURCH, Baroness *cr* 2006 (Life Peer), of Whitchurch in the County of South Glamorgan; **Margaret Beryl Jones;** Director of Policy and Public Affairs, UNISON, 1995–2006; *b* 22 May 1955; *d* of Bill and Audrey Jones. *Educ:* Whitchurch High Sch., Cardiff; Sussex Univ. (BA Hons Sociol. 1976). Regl Official, 1979–89, Nat. Officer, 1989–95, NUPE, later UNISON. Member, Board: Circle (formerly Circle Anglia), 2006–; Waste and Resources Action Prog., 2007–; Ombudsman Services, 2013–. Mem., Fitness to Practise Panel, GMC, 2006–13. Chm., RICS Ombudsman Scheme, 2007–13. Contested (Lab) Blaenau Gwent, 2005. *Address:* House of Lords, SW1A 0PW.

JONES, Hon. Lord; Michael Scott Jones; a Senator of the College of Justice in Scotland, since 2012; *b* Edinburgh, 18 Feb. 1948; *s* of Norman Rae Jones and Catherine Jones; *m* 1973, Linda Ann (marr. diss. 1995); *m* 1995, Fiona Elisabeth Craddock; two *s* four *d. Educ:* Royal High Sch., Edinburgh; RAF Coll., Cranwell; Univ. of Dundee (LLB). Commnd RAF, 1968; Gen. Duties (Flying) Br., 1968–73. Admitted Faculty of Advocates, 1977; Standing Jun. Counsel to Dept of Industry in Scotland, 1981–82; Advocate Depute (Crown Counsel), 1983–86; called to the Bar, Lincoln's Inn, 1987; QC (Scot.) 1989; Chm. (pt-time), Police Appeals Tribunal, 1997–2012; Ordinary Judge of Appeal, Jersey and Guernsey, 2005–12. Vis. Prof., Univ. of Strathclyde, 1999–2013. *Recreations:* hill-walking, running, ski-ing. *Address:* Court of Session, Parliament House, Parliament Square, Edinburgh EH1 1RF.

JONES, Adam M.; *see* Mars-Jones.

JONES, Adrianne Shirley, (Ann), CBE 2014 (MBE 1969); Women's Team Captain, Lawn Tennis Association, 1990–97; BBC tennis commentator, since 1970; *b* 17 Oct. 1938; *d* of Adrian Arthur Haydon and Doris (*née* Jordan); *m* 1962, Philip Frank Jones (*d* 1993); two *s* one *d. Educ:* King's Norton Grammar Sch., Birmingham. Finalist, World Table Tennis Championships: Ladies Doubles, 1954; Singles, Ladies Doubles, Mixed Doubles, 1957; Tennis Championships: Winner, French Open, 1961, 1966; Winner, Italian Open, 1966; Finalist, US, 1961, 1967; Wimbledon: Finalist, Ladies Singles, 1967; Winner, 1969; semi-finalist nine times. Chm., Women's Internat. Professional Tennis Council, 1977–84; Dir, European Ops, Women's Tennis Assoc., 1976–84. Member: Cttee of Mgt, Wimbledon Championships, 1991–; Internat. and Professional Tennis Bd, LTA, 1993–2004. *Publications:* Tackle Table Tennis My Way, 1957; Tennis: a game to love, 1970. *Recreations:* all sports, reading, music. *Address:* 101 Knightlow Road, Harborne, Birmingham B17 8PX. *T:* (0121) 247 5644. *Clubs:* All England Lawn Tennis; Edgbaston Priory.

JONES, Alan; consultant; Chief Executive, Somerset County Council, 2003–09; *b* 22 Sept. 1952; *s* of Thomas Jones and Ellen Jones; *m* 1974, Susan Fiona Dawn Lovell; two *d. Educ:* Univ. of Kent at Canterbury (BA 1st cl. Hons (Sociol.) 1974); Univ. of Liverpool (MCD 1st cl. 1976); Kent Coll. (Dip. Mgt Studies (Distn) 1982). Res. Asst, Merseyside MCC, 1975–76; Area Planning Officer, Maidstone BC, 1976–83; Prin. Planner, Gravesham BC, 1983–84; Develt Control Manager, Reading BC, 1984–86; Hd, Develt and Planning, Stevenage BC, 1986–88; Corporate Dir, Develt Services, Newbury DC, 1988–96; Chief Exec., Test Valley BC, 1996–2003; Interim Change Manager, Watford Council, 2002–03. Founder and Owner: Future Communities Ltd; AJAPlanning.com; Civic Cloud Ltd; non-exec. Dir, Public-i Gp Ltd, 2009–. *Recreations:* cycling, golf, canoeing, watercolour painting, photography, gardening.

JONES, Alan David, OBE 1996; Founder Chairman, Team Excellence Ltd, since 2004; *b* 16 June 1947; *s* of late Sydney Jones and Yvette Jones; *m* 1996, Juliet Louise Nance-Kivell Berrisford; one *s* three *d. Educ:* Holly Lodge Grammar Sch. for Boys; Staffordshire Coll. of Commerce. CTA 1968; FCCA 1973; FCILT (FCIT 1990); FCIPS 1992. Man. Dir, TNT UK Ltd, 1984–99; Gp Man. Dir, TNT Express, 1999–2003; Mem. Bd of Mgt, TPG NV, 1999–2003; Chief Exec., GSL, 2005–08. Founder Chairman, Midlands Excellence, 1996–2011; Chm., Investors in Excellence, 2011–. Director: Ardent Productions Ltd, 1994–2002; British Quality Foundn, 1995–99; Services Bd, DTI, 2001–04. Member: Ministerial Adv. Bd for Defence Procurement, 1996–2006; Employment Tribunal System Taskforce, 2002–04. Special Prof., Nottingham Univ. Business Sch., 2003–09. Founder, Faculty of Freight, Chartered Inst. of Transport, 1990, Chm., 1990–91, CIT; Mem. Council, Inst. of Logistics, 1992–94. Mem., Eastern Reg. Council, 1977–78, Nat. Council, 1989–91, CBI; Dep. Chm., Coventry and Warwicks TEC, 1992–99. Freeman, City of London, 1994; Liveryman, Co. of Carmen, 1994–2012. Guardian, Assay Office, Birmingham, 1998–2000. Chm., In Kind Direct, 1997–2004; Chm., European, Mediterranean and Arab States Regl Adv. Bd, and Trustee, Duke of Edinburgh's Award Internat. Foundn, 2004–. Mem. Ct, Warwick Univ., 1992–96. Invited Gov., European Foundn for Quality Mgt, 2000–09. CCMI (CIMgt 1993); CCQI (CIQA 2004). Chm., Upper Glyme Valley Br., W Oxfordshire Cons. Assoc., 2013–. Hon. MA Coventry, 1996; Hon. DSc Aston, 2002; DUniv UCE 2004. *Recreations:* reading, walking, jazz. *Address:* Cherwell House, Little Tew, near Chipping Norton, Oxon OX7 4JE. *Club:* Athenæum.

JONES, Sir Alan (Jeffrey), Kt 2005; CEng; Chairman, Toyota Motor Manufacturing (UK) Ltd, 2003–06, now Chairman Emeritus; Executive Vice-President, Toyota Motor Engineering and Manufacturing Europe, 2003–06, now Senior Executive Adviser. *Educ:* Luton Coll. of Higher Educn. Manufacturing Dir, Vauxhall Motors, 1987–90; Dir of Manufacturing, 1990–96, Dep. Man. Dir, 1996–2001, Man. Dir, 2001–03, Toyota Motor Manufacturing (UK) Ltd. Chairman: SMMT Industry Forum, 2002 (Founder Mem. Bd, 1997); Sci., Engrg and Manufg Technologies Alliance, 2006–10, now Chm. Emeritus; Mem. Bd, EngineeringUK.

JONES, Alan John P.; *see* Pateman-Jones.

JONES, Aled, MBE 2013; singer; television and radio presenter; musical theatre performer; *b* 29 Dec. 1970; *s* of Derek Jones and Nêst Jones; *m* 2001, Claire Fossett; one *s* one *d. Educ:* Royal Acad. of Music (ARAM); Bristol Old Vic Theatre Sch. Presenter: Songs of Praise, Escape to the Country, Cash in the Attic, BBC TV; Daybreak, 2012–14, Weekend, 2014–, ITV1; various progs on BBC Radio 2, Radio 3, Radio Wales, Classic FM. Musical theatre lead roles: Joseph and the Amazing Technicolour Dreamcoat, 2001; Chitty Chitty Bang Bang, Cardiff, 2008; White Christmas, Plymouth and Manchester, 2009, Southampton, Dublin and Liverpool, 2011, Dominion Th., London, 2014. UK concert tour, 2013. Recordings include: Walking in the Air, 1985; 30 albums include: Aled Jones; Ave Maria; Hear My Prayer; Whenever God Shines His Light, 2002; From the Heart, 2002; Aled, 2002; Higher, 2003; Morning Has Broken, 2003; Sacred Songs, 2004; The Christmas Album, 2004; New Horizons, 2005; You Raise Me Up: the best of Aled Jones, 2006; Forever, 2011. *Publications:* Aled: the autobiography (with Darren Henley), 2005; Forty Favourite Hymns, 2009; Favourite Christmas Carols, 2010; My Story (autobiog.), 2013. *E:* wendi.batt@sky.com. *W:* www.twitter.com/realaled, www.facebook.com/realaledjones.

JONES, Dr Aled Gruffydd; Chief Executive and Librarian, National Library of Wales, since 2013; *b* Bangor, Gwynedd, 9 Aug. 1955; *s* of John Edwin Jones and Ellen Jones; *m* 1994, Yasmin Ali. *Educ:* Ysgol Ardudwy, Harlech; Univ. of York (BA 1st Cl. Hist. 1977); Univ. of Warwick (MA 1978; PhD 1982). Aberystwyth University: Lectr, 1979–92; Sen. Lectr, 1992–95; Hd, Dept of Hist. and Welsh Hist., 1994–2002; Sir John Williams Prof. of Welsh Hist., 1995–2013; Dean, Faculty of Arts, 2004–05; Pro Vice-Chancellor, 2005–13. Joint Editor: Llafur, Jl of Welsh Labour Hist., 1985–92; Welsh Hist. Rev., 2003–11; Literary Dir (Modern), RHistS, 2000–04. *Publications:* Press, Politics and Society: a history of journalism in Wales, 1993; Powers of the Press: newspapers, power and the public in nineteenth-century England, 1996. *Recreations:* mountains, visual art. *Address:* Gwynfa, Heol y Llan, Llanbadarn Fawr, Aberystwyth, Ceredigion SY23 3SA. *T:* (01970) 612836. *E:* aledgjones@yahoo.co.uk.
See also R. M. Jones.

JONES, Alexander Martin, (Sandy); Chief Executive, Professional Golfers' Association, since 1991; *b* 9 Dec. 1946; *s* of Henry and Catherine Jones. *Educ:* Stow Coll., Glasgow (qualif. Structl Engr 1968). Structural engineer/computer programmer, 1969–80; Scottish Regl Sec., PGA, 1980–91; Director: Ryder Cup, 1991–; Golf Foundn, 1991–; Chm., PGA of Europe, 1995–. CCMI 2006. DUniv Birmingham, 2009. *Recreations:* golf, football (watching). *Address:* Professional Golfers' Association, Centenary House, The Belfry, Sutton Coldfield, W Midlands B76 9PT. *T:* (01675) 470333. *E:* sandy.jones@pga.org.uk. *Clubs:* Caledonian; Loch Lomond Golf, Little Aston Golf.

JONES, Allan William, MBE 2000; Owner and Director, Allan Jones Energy and Climate Change, 2008–09 and since 2014; *b* 23 Dec. 1948; *s* of Leonard John William Jones and Joan Violet Jones; *m* 1989, Margaret Jane Deeks; one *s* one *d*, and one step *s. Educ:* Guildford County Coll. of Technology (CNAA HNC Electrical and Electronic Engrg). IEng, FIET. From Design Engr to Sen. Manager, Dept of Mech. and Elec. Engrg, GLC, 1971–86; Sen. Manager, Dept of Bldg and Property Services, ILEA, 1986–89; Energy Services Manager, Woking BC, 1989–2004; Dir, Thameswey Ltd (Woking BC's energy and envmtl services co.), 1999–2004; Chief Develt Officer, then CEO, London Climate Change Agency, 2004–08; Chief Technologist, London Development Agency, 2007–08; Dir and Trustee, Sustainable Envmt Foundn, 2007–09; Mem. Bd, Nat. Climate Change Adaption Res. Facility, 2011–13; Chief Develt Officer, Energy and Climate Change, City of Sydney, 2009–14. Director: London ESCO Ltd, 2006–08; Better Building Partnership, 2008. Pres., Internat. Energy Adv. Council, 2014–; Mem., Seoul Internat. Energy Adv. Council, 2013–. FRSA 2005. *Publications:* Woking Park - fuel cell combined heat and power system, 2003; Moving London towards a Sustainable Low-carbon City, 2007; (contrib.) Cut Carbon, Grow Profits, 2007; (contrib.) Planning for Climate Change, 2009; (contrib.) City of Sydney Decentralised Water Master Plan, 2013; (contrib.) City of Sydney Decentralised Energy Master Plan - Renewable Energy, 2013; (contrib.) City of Sydney Decentralised Energy

Master Plan - Advanced Waste Treatment, 2014; numerous papers incl. for IEE, IMechE, CIBSE, Combined Heat and Power Assoc., Fuel Cell Europe, Renewable Power Assoc., Connecticut Clean Energy Fund, Forum for the Future, Parly Renewable and Sustainable Energy and Warm Homes Gps, London Hydrogen Partnership. *Recreations:* nature, the environment, walking, photography, the family.

JONES, Allen, RA 1986 (ARA 1981); artist; *b* 1 Sept. 1937; *s* of William Jones and Madeline Jones (*née* Aveson); *m* 1st, 1964, Janet Bowen (marr. diss. 1978); two *d*; 2nd, 1994, Deirdre Morrow. *Educ:* Ealing Grammar Sch. for Boys; Hornsey Sch. of Art (NDD; ATD); Royal Coll. of Art. Teacher of Lithography, Croydon Coll. of Art, 1961–63; Teacher of Painting, Chelsea Sch. of Art, 1966–68; Tamarind Fellow in Lithography, Los Angeles, 1968; Guest Professor: Hochschule für Bildenden Kunst, Hamburg, 1968–70, Univs of S Florida, 1970, Calif at Irvine, 1973, Los Angeles, 1977; Hochschule für Kunst Berlin, 1983; has travelled extensively. Sec., Young Contemporaries exhibn, London, 1961. First internat. exhibn, Paris Biennale, 1961 (Prix des Jeunes Artistes); first professional exhibn (with Howard Hodgkin), Two Painters, ICA, 1962; first UK mus. exhibn, Decade of Painting and Sculpture, Tate Gall., 1964; *museum and group exhibitions* in UK and abroad include: New Generation, Whitechapel, 1964; London, The New Scene, Minneapolis, 1965; British Drawing/New Generation, NY, 1967; Documenta IV, Kassel, 1968; Pop Art Redefined, Hayward Gall., 1969; British Painting and Sculpture, Washington, 1970; Metamorphosis of Object, Brussels, and tour, 1971; Seibu, Tokyo, 1974; Hyperealist/Realistes, Paris, 1974; Arte Inglese Oggi, Milan, 1976; El color en la pintura británica, British Council S American tour, 1977; British Painting 1952–77, Royal Academy, 1977; Arts Council sponsored exhibn tour, UK, 1978, Wales, 1992; British Watercolours, British Council tour, China, 1982; The Folding Image, Washington and Yale, 1984; Pop Art 1955–1970, NY, then Aust. tour, 1985; 40 Years of Modern Art, Tate Gall., 1986; British Art in the Twentieth Century, Royal Academy, then Stuttgart, 1987; Pop Art, Tokyo, 1987; Picturing People, British Council tour, Hong Kong, Singapore, Kuala Lumpur, 1990; New Acquisitions, Kunstmus., Dusseldorf, 1990; Seoul Internat. Art Fest., 1991; BM, 1991, 1997; Pop Art, Royal Academy, 1991, then Cologne, Madrid and Montreal, 1992; From Bacon to Now, Florence; Nat. Portrait Gall., 1994; Centre Georges Pompidou, Paris, 1995; Treasure Island, Gulbenkian Foundn, Lisbon, 1997; The Pop '60s, Centro Cultural de Belém, Lisbon, 1997; Pop Impressions Europe/USA, MoMA NY, 1999; Pop Art: US/UK Connections 1956–1966, Menil Foundn, Houston, 2001; Les années pop, Centre Georges Pompidou, Paris, 2001; Transition: the London art scene in the Fifties, Barbican, 2002; Out of Line: drawings from the Arts Council collection, 2002; Den Haag Sculptuur, 2002; Blast to Freeze, Wolfsburg, 2002; Thinking Big: concepts for 21st century British Sculpture, Peggy Guggenheim Collection, Venice, 2002; Phantom der Lust, Stadtmus., Graz, 2002; Mike Kelley - The Uncanny, Tate Liverpool, 2004; Art and the Sixties: This Was Tomorrow, Tate Britain, 2004 and Birmingham Mus. and Art Gall., 2004–05; Pop Art Portraits, NPG, 2007; Gagosian Gall., London, 2007, 2010; Kunsthalle Vienna, 2007–08; Raue, 2008; Grand Théâtre, Angers, 2008; Tate Liverpool, 2009; Musée D'Orsay, Paris, 2009–10; Samuel Freeman Gall., Los Angeles, 2009; Crash, Gagosian Gall., 2010; 60's Design, Möbelmuseum, Vienna, 2012; Glam, Tate Liverpool, 2012; You Inspire Me, Wolverhampton Art Gall. and Cartwright Hall, Bradford, 2012; Pop to Popism, Art Gall. of NSW, Sydney, 2012; Pop Art Design, Vitra Design Mus., Germany, 2012; Louisiana MOMA, Denmark, 2013; Moderna Museet, Stockholm, 2013; Oltre l'Informale verso la Pop Art, Guggenheim Collection, Vercelli, 2013; Pop Culture, Mana Fine Arts, Jersey City, 2013; Pop Art Myth, Museo Thyssen-Bornemisza, Madrid, 2014; The Wish List, London Design Fest., V&A Mus., 2014; The Artist's Eye, LWL-Museum für Kunst und Kultur, Münster, 2014; Ludwig Goes Pop, Museum Ludwig, Cologne, 2014; Pop Europe!, Wolverhampton Art Gall., 2014–15; exhibited annually at Royal Acad., 1981–; *one-man exhibitions* include: Arthur Tooth and Sons, London, 1963, 1964, 1967, 1970; Richard Feigen Gall., NY, Chicago and LA, 1964, 1965, 1970; Marlborough Fine Art, London, 1972; Arts Council sponsored exhibn tour, UK, 1974; Waddington Galls, London, 1976, 1980, 1982, 1983, 1985, 1993; James Corcoran Gall., LA, 1977, 1987; UCLA Art Galls, LA, 1977; Graphic Retrospective 1958–78, ICA, 1978; first Retrospective of Painting, 1959–79, Walker Art Gall., Liverpool, and tour of England and Germany, 1979; Thorden Wetterling, Gothenburg, 1983; Gall. Kammer, Hamburg, 1983, 1984; Gall. Wentzel, Cologne (sculpture), 1984; Gall. Patrice Trigano, Paris, 1985, 1986, 1989, 1998; Gall. Kaj Forsblom, Helsinki, 1985, 1999; Gall. Hete Hunermann, Dusseldorf, 1987, 1994; Charles Cowles Gall., NY, 1988; Heland Wetterling Gall., Stockholm, 1989; Gall. Wentzel, Cologne, 1992; Gall. Punto, Valencia, 1992; Gall. Levy, Hamburg and Madrid, 1993, 1995, 1997, 1999, 2003; Galerie Hilger, Vienna, 2004; Galerie Terminus, Munich, 2004, 2010; Print Retrospective, Barbican Centre and tour, 1995–98; Kunsthalle, Darmstadt, 1996; Galeria Civica, Modena, 1996; Thomas Gibson Fine Art, London, 1997; Trussardi, Milan, 1998; Ars Nova Mus. of Contemp. Art, Turku, 1999; Summerstage (sculpture), Vienna, 1999; Gall. d'Arte Maggiore, Bologna, 1999; Palazzo dei Sette, Orvieto, 2002; Norddeutschen Landesbank, Hanover, 2002; Landeshauptstadt, Schwerin, 2003; Galerie Trigano, Paris, 2006; Galerie Levy, Hamburg, 2006; Lorenzelli Arte, Milan, 2010; Wetterling Gall., Stockholm and Gothenburg, 2011–12; Off The Wall, Tübingen, Chemnitz and Völklinger Hutte, Ruhr, 2012–13; Galerie Terminus, 2014; Kunsthaus Hannover, 2014; Royal Acad., 2014–15; Gibson Fine Arts, 2014; Galerie Forsblom, Helsinki, 2014; *dedicated rooms:* RA Summer Exhibn, 2002; paintings and drawings, Tate Britain, 2007–08; water colours, Royal Acad., 2007–08; Galeria Prates, Lisbon, 2007; Alan Cristea Gall., London, 2007; Marlborough Fine Art, London, 2008; Galerie Hilger, Vienna, 2008; *murals and sculptures for public places* include: Fogal, Basel and Zurich; Liverpool Garden Fest., 1984; Citicorp/Canadian Nat. Bank, London Bridge City, 1987; Milton Keynes, 1990; BAA, Heathrow, 1990; Ivy Restaurant, London, 1990; Chelsea/Westminster Hosp., 1993; LDDC, 1994; Swire Properties, Hong Kong, 1997; Sculpture at Goodwood, 1998; Chatsworth House, 2000; GlaxoSmithKline, London, 2001; Swire Properties, Hong Kong, 2002; Yuzi Paradise Sculpture Parks, Guilin and Shanghai, China, 2006; television and stage sets include: O Calcutta!, for Kenneth Tynan, London and Europe, 1970; Manner Wir Kommen, WDR, Cologne, 1970; Understanding Opera, LWT, 1988; Cinema/Eric Satie, for Ballet Rambert, 1989; Signed in Red, for Royal Ballet, 1996. Television films have been made on his work. Trustee, British Mus., 1990–99. Hon. DArts Southampton Solent, 2007. *Publications:* Allen Jones Figures, 1969; Allen Jones Projects, 1971; Waitress, 1972; Sheer Magic, 1979, UK 1980; Allen Jones, 1993; Allen Jones Prints, 1995; Allen Jones, 1997; Allen Jones Works, 2005; articles in various jls. *Recreation:* gardening. *Address:* 41 Charterhouse Square, EC1M 6EA. *Fax:* (020) 7600 1204. *E:* aj@allenjonestheartist.com.

JONES, Alun; *see* Jones, R. A.

JONES, Dr Alun Denry Wynn, OBE 2001; FInstP; Chief Executive, Institute of Physics, 1990–2002; *b* 13 Nov. 1939; *s* of Thomas D. and Ray Jones; *m* 1964, Ann Edwards; two *d*. *Educ:* Amman Valley Grammar Sch.; Christ Church, Oxford (MA, DPhil). FInstP 1973; CSci 2004–10. Sen. Student, Commission for Exhibn of 1851, 1964–66; Sen. Research Fellow, UKAEA, 1966–67; Lockheed Missiles and Space Co., California, 1967–70; Tutor, Open Univ., 1971–82; joined Macmillan and Co., Publishers, 1971; Dep. Editor, Nature, 1972–73; British Steel Corp., 1974–77; British Steel Overseas Services, 1977–81; Asst Dir, Technical Change Centre, 1982–85; Dep. Dir, 1986–87, Dir, 1987–90, Wolfson Foundn. British Association for Advancement of Science, later British Science Association: Sec. of working party on social concern and biological advances, 1972–74; Mem., Section X Cttee, 1981–92; Council Mem., 1999–2005; Mem., Exec. Cttee, 2001–05; Mem., Audit Cttee, 2005–14. British Library: Adv. Council, 1983–85; Document Supply Centre Adv. Cttee, 1986–89; Mem. Council, Nat. Library of Wales, 1987–94 (Gov., 1986–94). Dir, Sci. Council (formerly Council for Sci. and Technol. Insts), 1990–2002 (Chair, Registration Authority, 2005–09); Mem. Council, Assoc. of Schs' Sci., Engrg & Technol. (formerly Standing Conf. on Schs' Sci. & Technol.), 1992–2000 (Dep. Chm., 1996–2000). Gov., 1990–92 and 2002–05, Council Mem., 2002–05, UCW, Aberystwyth; Governor: City Univ., 1991–2001; Sir William Perkins's Sch., Chertsey, 2002–12 (Chair of Govs, 2005–12). Fellow, Univ. of Wales, Aberystwyth, 2000. *Publications:* (with W. F. Bodmer) Our Future Inheritance: choice or chance, 1974. *Recreations:* gardening, theatre, cricket. *Address:* 4 Wheatsheaf Close, Woking, Surrey GU21 4BP.

JONES, Alun Ffred; Member (Plaid Cymru) Arfon, National Assembly for Wales, since 2007 (Caernarfon, 2003–07); *b* 29 Oct. 1949; *s* of Rev. Gerallt and Elizabeth Jane Jones; *m* 1981, Alwen Roberts (*d* 2005); two *s* one *d*. *Educ:* University Coll. of N Wales, Bangor (BA). Teacher: Deeside High Sch., 1971–75; Alun High Sch., Mold, 1975–79 (Head of Dept); TV journalist, 1979–81; TV director/producer, 1981–2003. Member: Arfon Borough DC, 1992–96; Gwynedd Council, 1996–2004; Leader, Gwynedd UA, 1996–2003. National Assembly for Wales: Minister for Heritage, 2008–11; Chairman: Envmt, Agric. and Planning Cttee, 2003–07; Envmt and Sustainability Cttee, 2014–. *Address:* Plaid Cymru, 8 Stryd y Castell, Caernarfon, Gwynedd LL55 1SE. *T:* (01286) 672076. *E:* alunffred.jones@assembly.wales.

JONES, Andrew Hanson; MP (C) Harrogate and Knaresborough, since 2010; Parliamentary Under-Secretary of State, Department for Transport, since 2015; *b* Leeds, 28 Nov. 1963; *s* of Richard and Jean Jones. *Educ:* Bradford Grammar Sch.; Leeds Univ. (BA English 1985). Marketing Manager: Kingfisher plc, 1985–88, 1996–98; Going Places, 1989–96; Account Dir, M&C Saatchi, 1998–2000; The Mktg Store, Leeds, 2000–05; Mktg consultant, 2005–10, incl. Bettys and Taylors of Harrogate, 2006–08. Mem. (C) Harrogate BC, 2003–11 (Cabinet Mem., Finance and Resources, 2006–10). Contested (C) Harrogate and Knaresborough, 2001. Mem., Regulatory Reform Select Cttee, 2010–15. Apprenticeship Ambassador, 2012–15. Chm., Bow Gp, 1999–2000. *Recreations:* cricket, walking. *Address:* 57 East Parade, Harrogate, N Yorks HG1 5LQ. *T:* (01423) 529614. *E:* andrew.jones.mp@parliament.uk. *Clubs:* Carlton, MCC; Yorkshire CC.

JONES, Prof. Andrew Malcolm, PhD; FRGS; Professor of Economic Geography and Dean, School of Art and Social Sciences, City University, since 2012; *b* Chester, 3 Nov. 1973; *s* of Radleigh and Pauline Jones; *m* 2011, Fay Sullivan; one *d*. *Educ:* King's Sch., Chester; St John's Coll., Cambridge (BA Geog. 1995; PhD Geog. 2001); Bristol Univ. (MSc Society and Space); Inst. of Educn, Univ. of London (Postgrad. DipEd). Birkbeck College, University of London: Lectr, 2000–06; Hd, Dept of Geog., Envmt and Develt Studies, 2006–12. Mem. (Lab), Hammersmith and Fulham LBC, 2002–06 and 2010– (Cabinet Mem. for Econ. Develt and Regeneration, 2014–). Contested (Lab) Eastbourne, 2005. FAcSS (AcSS 2011). *Publications:* Management Consultancy and Banking in an Era of Globalization, 2003; Dictionary of Globalization, 2006; (ed with N. Coe) The Economic Geography of the UK, 2010; Globalization: key thinkers, 2010; Human Geography: the basics, 2012. *Recreations:* politics, ski-ing, rowing coach. *Address:* City University, Northampton Square, EC1V 0HB. *T:* (020) 7040 3840. *E:* andrew.jones@city.ac.uk.

JONES, Angela; *see* Jones, S. A. M.

JONES, Ann; *see* Jones, Adrianne S.

JONES, Ann; Member (Lab) Vale of Clwyd, National Assembly for Wales, since 1999; *b* 4 Nov. 1953; *d* of Charles and Helen Sadler; *m* 1973, Adrian Jones; two *c*. *Educ:* Rhyl Grammar, then High, Sch. Fire Service Emergency Call Operator, 1976–99. Nat. Official, Fire Brigades Union, 1982–99. Member (Lab): Rhyl Town Council, 1991–99 (Mayor of Rhyl, 1996–97); Denbighshire CC, 1995–99 (Lab spokesman on educn, 1995–98). Mem., N Wales Fire Authy, 1995–99. Welsh Assembly: Chm., Lab Mems, 1999–2000; Member: Econ. Develt Cttee, 1999–2003; N Wales Regl Cttee, 1999–2007; Health and Social Services Cttee, 2000–03; Finance Cttee, 2011–; Chair: Equality of Opportunity Cttee, 2007–11; Communities, Equality and Local Govt Cttee, 2011–13; Assembly Labour Gp, 2011–; Children, Young People and Educn Cttee, 2013–. *Address:* 25 Kinmel Street, Rhyl LL18 1AH. *T:* (01745) 332813.

JONES, (Ann) Camilla; *see* Toulmin, A. C.

JONES, Anna Louise; *see* Bradley, A. L.

JONES, Prof. Anne; Professor of Lifelong Learning, Brunel University, 1995–2001, now Professor Emeritus; *b* 8 April 1935; *d* of Sydney Joseph and Hilda Pickard; *m* 1958, C. Gareth Jones (marr. diss. 1989); one *s* two *d*. *Educ:* Harrow Weald County Sch.; Westfield Coll., London (BA; Fellow, QMW, 1992); DipSoc, PGCE London. Assistant Mistress: Malvern Girls' Coll., 1957–58; Godolphin and Latymer Sch., 1958–62; Dulwich Coll., 1964; Sch. Counsellor, Mayfield Comprehensive Sch., 1965–71; Dep. Hd, Thomas Calton Sch., 1971–74; Head: Vauxhall Manor Sch., 1974–81; Cranford Community Sch., 1981–87; Under Sec. (Dir of Educn), Dept of Employment, 1987–91; management consultant, 1991–93; Brunel University: Prof. of Continuing Educn, 1991–97; Dir of Contg Educn, 1991–93; Hd of Dept of Contg Educn, 1993–97; Dir, Centre for Lifelong Learning, 1995–2001; Mem. of Ct, 2001–; Founder and Man. Dir, Lifelong Learning Systems Ltd, 2000–09. Vis. Prof. of Educn, Sheffield Univ., 1989–91. OFSTED Registered Inspector, 1993–2003. Chm., W London Area Manpower Bd, Manpower Services Commn, 1983–87. Chm., Parents in a Learning Soc., RSA, 1992–95. Director: CRAC, 1983–94; Grubb Inst. of Behavioural Studies, 1987–94. Occasional Mem., Selection Panel, Cabinet Office, 1993–. Advr, European Trng Foundn, 1995–2002. Ind. Lay Chair, Complaints, NHS, 1996–2003. Member Council: QMW, 1991–2002; W London Inst. of Higher Educn, 1991–95; NICEC, 1991–95. Chm., Boathouse Reach Mgt, 2005–10. Gov., Abbey Sch., Reading, 2004–12. Trustee: The Westfield Trust, 1992–2010; Menerva Educnl Trust, 1993–2004 (Chm., 1993–99). FRSA 1984 (Mem. Council, 1986–94); FCMI (FIMgt 1992) (Chm., Reading Br., 2004–08); FICPD 1998. Hon. FCP 1990. *Publications:* School Counselling in Practice, 1970; Counselling Adolescents in School, 1977, 2nd edn as Counselling Adolescents, School and After, 1984; Leadership for Tomorrow's Schools, 1987; The Education Roundabout, 2015; (with Jan Marsh and A. G. Watts): Male and Female, 1974, 2nd edn 1982; Living Choices, 1976; Time to Spare, 1980; contribs to various books. *Recreations:* travel, boating, gardening, theatre, opera, singing in Henley Choral Society (Chm., 2005–08). *Address:* 8 Boathouse Reach, Henley-on-Thames, Oxfordshire RG9 1TJ. *T:* (01491) 578672. *E:* annepickardjones@googlemail.com. *Club:* Phyllis Court (Henley-on-Thames) (Dir, 2009–15).

JONES, Prof. Anthony Edward, CBE 2003; FRCA; President, School of the Art Institute of Chicago, 1986–92 and 1996–2012, now Chancellor and President Emeritus (Co-Chief Executive Officer, Corporation of the Art Institute of Chicago, 1996–2012); Interim President, Kansas City Art Institute, since 2014; *b* 3 Aug. 1944; *s* of late Edward and Violet Jones; *m* 1st, 1972, Gwen Brandt (marr. diss. 1978); one *s*; 2nd, 1989, Patricia Jon Carroll. *Educ:* Goldsmiths' Coll., Univ. of London; Newport Coll. of Art, Newport (DipAD, BA); Tulane Univ., New Orleans (MFA). Artist-in-Residence, Loyola Univ., 1967–68; Teaching Fellow, Gloucester Coll. of Art, Cheltenham, 1968–69; Sen. Lectr and Dep. Head of Sculpture, Glasgow Sch. of Art, 1969–72; Chm., Dept of Art and Art Hist., Texas Christian Univ., 1972–80; Dir, Glasgow Sch. of Art, 1980–86 (Hon. Vice-Chm. of Govs, 2009); Rector, Royal Coll. of Art, 1992–96. Fulbright Scholar, USA, 1966–68. Hon. Prof., Univ.

of Wales, 2000; Hon. Dir, Osaka Univ. of the Arts, 2002. Exhibn, Liberty Style, Japan tour, 1999–2000, and catalogue, 1999; Exhibn, Painting the Dragon, Nat. Mus. of Wales, 2000 (presenter, BBC TV series, 2001). Chm., James Dyson America Foundn, 2011–; Co-Chm., Amer. Friends of RCA. FRCA 1993; FRSA 1994; Hon. AIA 1991; Hon. Fellow, Univ. of Wales, 2012. Hon. DFA Memphis Coll. of Art, 2002; Hon. Dr: Maryland Inst., 2009; Art Inst. of Chicago, 2011; LLD Lincoln, 2008; DLitt Glasgow, 2010. Newbery Medal, Glasgow Univ., 1986; US Nat. Council of Art Administrators Award, 2001; Austrian Cross of Honour for Sci. and the Arts, 2002. *Publications:* Chapel Architecture in the Merthyr Valley, 1964; Welsh Chapels (Capeli Cymru), 1984, 1996; Charles Rennie Mackintosh, 1990; Painting the Dragon, 2000; Living in Wales: David Hurn, 2003; Archibald Knox (essays), 2003; Robert Stewart Design (essays), 2003. *Recreation:* travel, reluctantly!

JONES, His Honour Anthony Graham Hume; a Circuit Judge, 1993–2015; Deputy Senior Judge, Sovereign Base Areas, Cyprus, 1999–2015; *b* 16 Aug. 1942; *s* of Rt Hon. Sir Edward Jones, PC and Margaret Anne Crosland (*née* Smellie); *m* 1966, Evelyn Ann Brice Smyth (*d* 1998), *o d* of Brice Smyth, Belfast; two *s* one *d*. *Educ:* Trinity Coll., Glenalmond; Trinity Coll., Dublin (BA 1966). Mardon, Son & Hall Ltd, 1966–71; called to the Bar, Gray's Inn, 1971; called to the Bar, NI, 1981; a Recorder, 1990–93; Resident Judge, Taunton Crown Court, 2003–13. Vice-Pres., Avon Br., SSAFA, 1993–; Mem. Council, RNLI, 2003–13. Master, Antient Soc. of St Stephen's Ringers, 1999–2000. *Recreations:* sailing, golf. *Address:* Yeowood, Wrington, Bristol BS40 5NS; Craig-y-Mor, Trearddur Bay, Holyhead, Anglesey LL65 2UP. *Clubs:* Royal Ocean Racing; Trearddur Bay Sailing (Cdre, 1994–96); Royal County Down Golf, Burnham and Berrow Golf, Holyhead Golf.

JONES, Anthony W.; *see* Whitworth-Jones.

JONES, Rt Rev. Arthur Lucas Vivian, OAM 2006; PhD; Interim Rector, then Rector, Holy Trinity Episcopal, Makati City, Manila, 2008–14; *b* 11 Dec. 1934; *s* of Arthur Edmond Jones and Mona Emily Jones; *m* 1979, Valerie Joan Maxwell; one *s* three *d*. *Educ:* St John's Coll., Morpeth, NSW (ThL); ACT (ThSchol); London Univ. (BD ext); Deakin Univ. (BA); Newcastle Univ., NSW (MA Classics); Adelaide Coll. of Adv. Educn (Grad. DipRE); Geneva Theol Coll. (ThD); Lambeth Diploma; La Trobe Univ. (PhD 1998; MCounsHS 2003). Deacon 1966, priest 1967; Curate, Holy Trinity, Orange, NSW, 1966–69; Missionary, Panama, 1970–73 and 1977–80; Rector, St Barnabas, Orange, NSW, 1973–77; Vicar, Corangamite, Vic, 1980–82; Lectr in NT, St John's Coll., Morpeth, 1982–85; Rector, Woy Woy, NSW, 1985–89; Dean, St Paul's Cathedral, Sale, 1989–94; Diocesan Theologian, Gippsland, 1989–94; Bishop of Gippsland, 1994–2001; Rector, Holy Trinity, Dubbo, NSW, 2004–07. Lectr in New Testament, Singapore, India, Manila, Peru, PNG, 2001–14. Hon. Res. Associate, Monash Univ., Vic, 2003. *Recreations:* golf, writing. *Address:* 151 Phillip Street, Orange, NSW 2800, Australia; 48 McKinley Road, Makati City 1219, Metro Manila, Philippines.

JONES, Prof. Arthur Stanley, CBE 1997; CBiol, FRSB; consultant to agricultural and food industries, since 1997; Principal, Royal Agricultural College, Cirencester, 1990–97; *b* 17 May 1932; *s* of John Jones and Anne Jones (*née* Hamilton); *m* 1962, Mary Margaret Smith; three *s* one *d*. *Educ:* Gosforth Grammar Sch.; Durham Univ. (BSc); Aberdeen Univ. (PhD). Commnd Army, 2nd Lieut, 1955–57; Pilot Officer, RAFVR, 1958–62. Rowett Research Institute: Res. Scientist, 1959; Hd, Applied Nutrition Dept, 1966; Chm., Applied Scis Div., 1975; Dep. Dir, 1983; Governor, 1986–90; Strathcona-Fordyce Prof. of Agriculture, Univ. of Aberdeen, 1986–90; Head, Sch. of Agriculture, Aberdeen, and Principal, N of Scotland Coll. of Agriculture, 1986–90; Gov., Aberdeen Centre for Land Use, 1987–90. Mem., House of Lords Rural Econ. Gp, 1992–94. Chairman: Scottish Beef Develts Ltd, 1988–91; RAC Enterprises Ltd, 1992–97; Member: Council, RASE, 1991–97; Bd, Arable Res. Centres, 1992–96. Gov., Henley Coll. of Management, 1996–2003 (Chm. Acad. Adv. Council, 1996–2001). Dir, Clan Grant Centre Trust Ltd, 1998–2006; Mem. Council and Hon. Treas., Clan Grant Soc., 1998–2006. Trustee: Trehane Trust, 1993–2007; Geoffrey Cragghill Meml Scholarship Trust, 1993–99; Ceres Foundn, 1996–2008. Hon. Prof., Univ. of Prague, 1994–2012. FRSA; FCMI; FIAgrM; FRAgS. *Publications:* Nutrition of Animals of Agricultural Importance (vol. 17, Internat. Encyc. of Food and Nutrition) (ed D. P. Cuthbertson), 1967; 115 articles in learned jls. *Recreations:* yachting, flying, gardening. *Address:* Begsdell, Caskieben, Kinellar, Aberdeenshire AB21 0TB. *Club:* Royal Air Force.

JONES, Benedict L.; *see* Llewellyn-Jones.

JONES, Brinley; *see* Jones, Robert B.

JONES, Bryn Terfel, (Bryn Terfel), CBE 2003; opera singer; bass baritone; *b* 9 Nov. 1965; *s* of Hefin and Nesta Jones; *m* Lesley Halliday (marr. diss. 2014); three *s*. *Educ:* Guildhall Sch. of Music and Drama (AGSM). Opera performances in major venues: WNO, 1990–; ENO, 1991–; Salzburg, 1992–; Covent Garden, 1992–; Vienna State Opera, 1993–; NY Metropolitan, 1994–; La Scala, Milan, 1997–; Sydney Opera House, 1999–; rôles include: Guglielmo, Jochanaan in Salome, Balstrode, Leporello, Figaro, Falstaff, Don Giovanni, Nick Shadow in The Rake's Progress, Wolfram in Tannhauser, Four Villains in Les Contes d'Hoffmann, Dulcamara in L'Elisir d'Amore, Mephistopheles in Gounod's Faust, Wotan in Der Ring des Nibelungen, The Flying Dutchman, Scarpia in Tosca, Sweeney Todd, Gianni Schicchi, Hans Sachs in Die Meistersinger von Nürnberg, Tevye in Fiddler on the Roof. Hon. Mem., Gorsedd, Royal Nat. Eisteddfod of Wales, 1992; Hon. RAM 2000. Hon. Fellow, Univ. of Wales, Bangor, 1994, Aberystwyth, 1995, Cardiff, 2009; Hon. FRWCMD (Hon. FWCMD, 1995). Hon. DMus: Glamorgan, 1997; Univ. of Wales, Cardiff, 2000. Queen's Medal for Music, 2006. *Recreations:* golf, supporting Manchester United, collecting fob watches. *Address:* c/o Harlequin Agency, 5th Floor, Gloworks, Porth Teigr, Cardiff CF10 4GA. *T:* (029) 2075 0821.

JONES, Caroline; *see* Dean, C.

JONES, Rt Hon. Carwyn (Howell); PC 2010; Member (Lab) Bridgend, National Assembly for Wales, since 1999; First Minister of Wales, since 2009; *b* 21 March 1967; *s* of Caron Wyn Jones and late (Katherine) Janice Jones; *m* 1994, Lisa Josephine Murray. *Educ:* Aberystwyth Univ. (LLB). Called to the Bar, Gray's Inn, 1989. Tutor, Centre for Professional Legal Studies, Cardiff, 1997–99. National Assembly for Wales: Sec. for Agric. and Rural Develt, 2000; Minister: for Rural Affairs, 2000–02; for Open Govt and Assembly Business, 2002–03; for Envmt, Planning and Countryside, 2003–07; for Educn, Culture and the Welsh Language, 2007; Counsel Gen., Leader of the House and Minister for Assembly Business and Communications, 2007–09. *Recreations:* sport, reading, travel. *Address:* National Assembly for Wales, Cardiff Bay, Cardiff CF99 1NA. *T:* 0300 200 7095. *Clubs:* Bridgend United Services; Brynamman Rugby, Bridgend Rugby.

JONES, Ceri Jayne, (Mrs T. C. Cuthbert); business and financial journalist; *b* 3 July 1958; *d* of David and Julie Jones; *m* 1984, Thomas Charles Cuthbert; three *s* one *d*. *Educ:* Keele Univ.; Liverpool Univ. (BA Hons 1982). Ed., Pensions & Employees Benefits, 1986; Ed., Pensions Management, 1986–87, Financial Advr, 1987–94, Financial Times magazines; Ed., Investors Chronicle, 1994–2002; Ed.-in-Chief, Personal Finance Div., Financial Times Business, 1997–2002. *Publications:* Guide to Alternative Investments, 2006; business and financial commentary in various newspapers and magazines. *Recreations:* natural history, travel.

JONES, (Charles) Ian (McMillan); education consultant, since 1995; *b* 11 Oct. 1934; *s* of Wilfred Charles Jones and Bessie Jones (*née* McMillan); *m* 1962, Jennifer Marie Potter; two *s*. *Educ:* Bishop's Stortford Coll.; St John's Coll., Cambridge (CertEd 1959; MA 1962). 2nd Lieut RA, 1953–55. Head of Geog. Dept, Bishop's Stortford Coll., 1960–70, Asst to Headmaster, 1967–70; Vice-Principal, King William's Coll., IoM, 1971–75; Head Master, Bedford School, 1975–86; Dir of Studies, BRNC, Dartmouth, 1986–88; Centre for British Teachers, subseq. CfBT Education Services: Project Dir, Brunei Darussalam, 1988–91, Malaysia, 1990–91; Regl Dir, Educn Services, SE Asia, 1991–94; Grants Adminr, UK, 1995–97. OFSTED Trained Inspector, 1996–2002; ISI Trained Reporting Inspector, 2000–05; Tutor for Nat. Professional Qualification for Head Teachers, 1998–2008. FCMI; FRSA. Man., England Schoolboy Hockey XI, 1967–74; Man., England Hockey XI, 1968–69; Pres., English Schoolboys Hockey Assoc., 1980–88; Mem. IoM Sports Council, 1972–75. Ed., Service Parents' Guide to Boarding Schs, 2007–12 (Chair, Adv. Bd, 2012–). *Publications:* articles in Guardian. *Recreations:* hockey (Captain Cambridge Univ. Hockey XI, 1959; England Hockey XI, 1959–64, 17 caps; Gt Britain Hockey XI, 1959–64, 28 caps), cricket (Captain IoM Cricket XI, 1973–75), golf. *Address:* 9 Phillipa Flowerday Plain, Norwich, Norfolk NR2 2TA. *Clubs:* MCC; Hawks (Cambridge); Royal Norwich Golf; Pantai Mentiri Golf (Brunei).

JONES, Chris; Director-General, City & Guilds, since 2008; *b* Berks, 15 July 1965; *s* of Phillip and Barbara Jones; *m* 1989, Judi Dixon; one *s* one *d*. Reed Business Publishing and EMAP plc, 1986–96; Gp Dir, FT Electronic Publishing, 1997–99; Senior Vice-President: LexisNexis Gp, 2000–01; LexisNexis Risk Mgt Gp, 2001–04; CEO, Harcourt Educn Internat., Reed Elsevier, later Pearson plc, 2004–08. Mem., Talent and Skills Leadership Team, BITC, 2011–. Gov., Activate Learning Gp, 2011–. Mem., Tallow Chandlers' Co. *Recreations:* keen reader and sports enthusiast, travel, music and film. *Address:* City & Guilds, 1 Giltspur Street, EC1A 9DD. *T:* (020) 7294 2569, *Fax:* (020) 7294 2408. *E:* chris.jones@cityandguilds.com.

JONES, Christine L.; *see* Lee-Jones.

JONES, Most Rev. Christopher, DD; Bishop of Elphin, (RC), 1994–2014, now Bishop Emeritus; *b* 3 March 1936; *s* of Christopher Jones and Christina Hanley. *Educ:* Maynooth Coll. (BA Classics 1958); UC Galway, NUI (Higher DipEd 1963); UC Dublin, NUI (DipSoc 1973). Ordained priest, 1962; Teacher, St Muireadach's, Ballina, 1962–65; Teacher, 1965–71, Spiritual Dir, 1972–79, Summerhill Coll., Sligo; Archivist, Diocesan Office, 1971–72; Dir, Sligo Social Service Council, 1973–87; Curate, Rosses Point, Sligo, 1979–87; Administrator, Cathedral Parish, Sligo, 1987–94. Freeman, Sligo City, 1995. *Publications:* Child, Adolescent and Adult in Family and Community, 1976, 2nd edn 1978. *Recreations:* walking, golfing, music, reading. *Address:* St Mary's, Sligo, Ireland. *T:* (71) 9162670, (71) 9150106. *Clubs:* Strandhill Golf; Co. Sligo Golf.

JONES, Sir Christopher L.; *see* Lawrence-Jones.

JONES, Clive Lawson, CBE 1997; Secretary General, European Energy Charter Conference, 1991–95; *b* 16 March 1937; *s* of Celyn John Lawson Jones and Gladys Irene Jones; *m* 1961, Susan Brenda (*née* McLeod); one *s* one *d*. *Educ:* Cranleigh School; University of Wales. BSc (Chemistry). With British Petroleum, 1957–61; Texaco Trinidad, 1961–68; Principal, Min. of Power, 1968–69; Min. of Technology, 1969–70; DTI, 1970–73; Asst Sec., Oil Emergency Group, 1973–74; Department Energy: Asst Sec., 1974–77; Under Sec., Gas Div., 1981–82; Counsellor (Energy), Washington, 1977–81; Dir for Energy Policy, EC, 1982–86; Dep. Dir Gen. for Energy, EC, 1987–94. Chm., European Consultative Cttees on Electricity and Gas Markets, 1990–91. *Recreation:* ephemera.

JONES, Clive William, CBE 2007; Chairman: Disasters Emergency Committee, since 2011; Runnymede Trust, since 2009 (Trustee, since 2004); London Metropolitan University, since 2010; Procam TV, since 2013; *b* 10 Jan. 1949; *s* of Kenneth David Llewellyn Jones and Joan Muriel Jones (*née* Withers); *m* 1st, 1971, Frances Mawer (marr. diss. 1988); two *s* one *d*; 2nd, 1988, Fern Britton (marr. diss. 2000); two *s* one *d*; 3rd, 2004, Victoria Mary Taylor Heywood, *qv*. *Educ:* Newbridge Grammar Sch.; LSE (BSc Econ.). Journalist, until 1978; with Yorks TV, 1978–82; Man. Editor, Editor, then Editor-in-Chief, TV-am Ltd, 1982–84; TVS: Controller, News, Current Affairs and Sport, 1984–87; Dep. Dir of Programmes, 1987–91; Dep. Man. Dir, 1991–92; Founding Man. Dir, London News Network, 1992–94; Man. Dir, Central Independent Television PLC, April–Dec. 1994; Man. Dir, Carlton UK Broadcasting Ltd, 1995; Chief Exec., Carlton Television, 1996–2004; Chairman: Westcountry Television, 1998–2001 (Dir, 1998–2007); HTV, 2000–07; GMTV, 2005–10 (Dir, 2001–10); Two Way TV, 2007–09 (Dir, 2007–09); Netplay TV, 2009–14; Jt Man. Dir, ITV, 2002–04; Chief Exec., ITV News and Regions, 2004–07; Dir, S4C, 2007–12. Chm., Energetic Communications, NY, 2007–. Dep. Chair, ITV Pension Fund, 2012– (Trustee, 2005–). Dir, Skills Develt Agency, 2006–08. Chairman: Skillset, 2002–10; YCTV, 2002–08; Wales IP Fund, 2005–11; Mediabox, 2007–. Dir, Young Vic Th., 2003–. Governor, Nat. Film and Television Sch., 1998–2012. FRTS 2000; FRSA 2000. *Recreations:* Rugby, golf, films, theatre. *Address:* 48 Church Crescent, N10 3NE. *Club:* Reform.

JONES, Prof. Colin David Hugh, CBE 2014; DPhil; FBA 2008; FRHistS; Professor of History, Queen Mary University of London, since 2006; *b* Isleworth, 12 Dec. 1947; *s* of Lawrence and Frances Joyce Jones; *m* 1996, Josephine McDonagh; three *s* one *d* from previous marriage. *Educ:* St Mary's C of E Primary Sch., Twickenham; Hampton Grammar Sch.; Jesus Coll., Oxford (Edwin Jones Schol.; BA Modern Hist. and Modern Langs (French) 1971); St Antony's Coll., Oxford (DPhil 1978). Temp. Lectr in Hist., Univ. of Newcastle upon Tyne, 1972–73; University of Exeter: Lectr in Hist., 1974–87; Sen. Lectr, 1987–90; Prof. of Hist., 1991–95; Prof. of Hist., Univ. of Warwick, 1996–2006. Fellow, Columbia Univ. Inst. of Scholars at Reid Hall (Paris), 2001–02; Kratter Vis. Prof. in Eur. Hist., Stanford Univ., 1993–94, 2000, 2005; Vis. Prof., Coll. de France, Paris, 2003; Visiting Fellow: Shelby Cullom Davis Center for Histl Studies, Princeton Univ., 1986; Nat. Liby of Medicine, Washington, 2004. Member: Steering Cttee, Hist. at Univ. Defence Gp, 1995–2001; Hist. of Medicine Panel, Wellcome Trust, 1999–2003 (Vice-Chm., 2001–03); Res. Panel for Hist., AHRC, 2004–08 (Convenor, 2006–08). Royal Historical Society: Fellow 1984; Vice Pres., 2000–03; Pres., 2009–12. Officier, Ordre des Palmes académiques (France), 2008. *Publications:* Charity and Bienfaisance: the treatment of the poor in the Montpellier Region, 1740–1815, 1982; The Longman Companion to the French Revolution, 1988; The Charitable Imperative: hospitals and nursing in Ancien Régime and Revolutionary France, 1989; (with J. Ardagh) Cultural Atlas of France, 1991; Cambridge Illustrated History of France, 1994; (with L. Brockliss) The Medical World of Early Modern France, 1997; The Great Nation: France from Louis XV to Napoleon (1715–99), 2002; Madame de Pompadour and her Image, 2002; Paris: biography of a city, 2004; The Smile Revolution in Eighteenth Century Paris, 2014; edited books, articles and book chapters on French hist., esp. 17th–19th centuries, incl. French Revolution and hist. of medicine. *Recreations:* music, wine, cooking, cycling, Paris. *Address:* History Department, Queen Mary University of London, Mile End Road, E1 4NS. *E:* c.d.h.jones@qmul.ac.uk.

JONES, Courtney John Lyndhurst, OBE 1989 (MBE 1980); President, National Ice Skating Association, 1987–95; *b* 30 April 1933; *s* of Reginald Jones and Inez Jones (*née* Wilsher). *Educ:* Ringwood Grammar Sch.; Bournemouth Coll. of Art (NDD). NSA Gold Medals for Ice Dance and for Pair Skating, 1957; British Ice Dance Champion, with June Markham, 1956–57, with Doreen Denny, 1958–60; European Ice Dance Champion, with June Markham, 1957–58, with Doreen Denny, 1959–61; World Ice Dance Champion, with June Markham, 1957–58, with Doreen Denny, 1959–60. Free-lance fashion designer, 1977–. Hon. Mem., Internat. Skating Union, 2010– (Mem., Council, 2002–10). Mem., US Figure Skating

Hall of Fame, 1987; George Hasler Medal, Internat. Skating Union, 1991. *Recreations:* reading, music, the arts. *Address:* Flat 3, Rameslie House, 61 Cinque Ports Street, Rye, E Sussex TN31 7AN. *T:* 07795 976597. *E:* c.jones912@btinternet.com, courtandbobskate@hotmail.com.

JONES, Prof. David, OBE 1986; FRCN; Professor, School of Nursing and Midwifery, University of Sheffield, 1995–2000, now Emeritus (Foundation Dean, 1995–98); *b* 27 July 1940; *s* of John Evan Jones and Edith Catherine (*née* Edwards); *m* 1962, Janet Mary Ambler; two *s* two *d*. *Educ:* Boys' Grammar Sch., Bala, N Wales; Univ. of Wales (BEd). SRN; RMN; RNT; FRCN 1998. Divl Nursing Officer, Gwynedd, 1974–78; Chief Admin. Nursing Officer, Gwynedd HA, 1979–87; first Chm., Welsh Nat. Bd for Nursing, Midwifery and Health Visiting, 1979–86; Chief Exec., English Nat. Bd for Nursing, Midwifery and Health Visiting, 1987–89; Principal, Sheffield and N Trent Coll. of Nursing and Midwifery, 1990–95. Trustee, Denbighshire Voluntary Services Council, 2008– (Chm., 2008–13). Board Mem., Clwyd Alyn Housing Assoc. Ltd, 2006–12. Hon. DSc Sheffield, 2005. *Recreations:* public affairs, countryside, family. *Address:* 7 Afon Glas, Llangollen, Denbighshire LL20 8AZ. *T:* (01978) 253081.

JONES, Sir David A.; *see* Akers-Jones.

JONES, Sir David (Charles), Kt 2009; CBE 1999; FCCA, FCIS; Chairman, CWM 2001 Ltd, since 2001; *b* 2 Feb. 1943; *s* of Frederick Charles Thomas Jones and Annie Marcella Jones; *m* 1968, Jeanette Ann Crofts; two *s* one *d*. *Educ:* King's Sch., Worcester. FCIS 1974; FCCA 1975. Joined Kays Mail Order Co. (part of Great Universal Stores), 1960, Finance Dir, 1971–77; Man. Dir, BMOC, 1977–80; Chief Exec., Grattan Plc, 1980–86; Next Plc: Dep. Chief Exec., 1986–88; Chief Exec., 1988–2001; Dep. Chm., 2001–02; Chm., 2002–06. Dir, JJB Sports plc, 2007–10 (Dep. Chm., 2008–09; Chm., 2009–10). *Publications:* Next to Me (autobiog.), 2005. *Recreations:* golf, snooker.

JONES, David George; Director General (formerly Assistant Under Secretary of State), Financial Management, Ministry of Defence, 1996–2001; *b* 31 May 1941; *s* of Frederick George Jones and Dorothy Jones (*née* Steele); *m* 1962, Leonie Usherwood Smith; three *s*. *Educ:* High Storrs Grammar Sch., Sheffield. Joined War Office as Exec. Officer, 1960; Asst Private Sec. to Army Minister, 1970–71; Principal, MoD Central Financial Planning Div., 1973–77; Private Sec. to Minister of State for Defence, 1977–80; Regl Marketing Dir, Defence Sales Organisation, 1980–84; Asst Sec., Air Systems Controllerate, 1984–85; Dep. Dir Gen., Al Yamamah Project Office, 1985–88; Dir Gen. Aircraft 2, Air Systems Controllerate, MoD (PE), 1988–89; Civil Sec., British Forces Germany, 1989–92; Dir Gen. Supplies and Transport (Naval), 1993–95, Dir Gen. Naval Bases and Supply, 1995–96, MoD. FCILT (FILog 1994). *Recreations:* gardening, travel.

JONES, (David) Huw; Chairman, S4C Authority (Welsh Fourth Channel), since 2011; *b* 5 May 1948; *s* of Idris Jones and Olwen Mair Lloyd Jones; *m* 1972, Sian Marylka Miarczynska; one *s* one *d*. *Educ:* Cardiff High Sch. for Boys; Jesus Coll., Oxford (BA, MA). Singer and TV presenter, 1968–76; Dir, Sain (Recordiau) Cyf, 1969–81; Man. Dir, Teledu'r Tir Glas, 1982–93; Director: Sgrin Cyf, 1996–2005; S4C Masnachol Cyf, 1999–2005; SDN Ltd, 1999–2005; Chief Exec., S4C (Welsh Fourth Channel), 1994–2005. Chairman: Barcud Cyf, 1981–93; TAC, 1984–86; Arianrhod Cyf, 1988–93; Celtic Film and TV Fest. Ltd, 2001–04; Portmeirion Ltd, 2007–; Cyfle Cyf, 2007–11; Dir, Nant Gwrtheyrn Cyf, 2007–. Member: FEFC for Wales, 1992–95; Investors in People Adv. Bd, UK Commn for Employment and Skills, 2010–11; Dir, Skillset Ltd, 2001–05 (Patron, 2006–08); Chair, Skillset Cymru Cyf, 2002–05; Vice-Chm., Wales Employment and Skills Bd, 2008–12. Welsh Government (formerly Welsh Assembly Government): Chm., Broadcasting Adv. Gp, 2008; Mem., Digital Wales Adv. Bd, 2010–11; Welsh-lang. educn strategy Ministerial Adv. Gp, 2011. Member: Welsh Lang. Bd, 2007–12; Adv. Cttee for Wales, RSPB, 2007–12; Council, RSPB, 2008–13. Trustee, RTS, 2012–. FRTS 1999. Hon. Fellow: Univ. of Wales, Aberystwyth, 1997; Bangor Univ., 2013. Gov., Coleg Llandrillo Cymru, 2010–12. *Recreations:* reading, cycling, walking, ski-ing. *Address:* Y Bwlan, Llandwrog, Caernarfon, Gwynedd LL54 5SR.

JONES, Rt Rev. David Huw; Bishop of St Davids, 1996–2001; *b* 1 July 1934; *s* of Joseph Elfed and Ethel Jones; *m* 1959, Gwyneth Jones; two *d*. *Educ:* Pontardawe Grammar Sch.; University Coll. of North Wales, Bangor (BA); University Coll., Oxford (MA). Curate: Aberdare, 1959–61; Neath, 1961–65; Vicar: Crynant, 1965–69; Michaelstone-super-Avon, 1969–73; Sub-Warden, St Michael's Coll., Llandaff, 1973–78; Lectr in Sch. of Theology, Univ. of Wales, Cardiff, 1973–78 (Asst Dean, 1977–78); Vicar of Prestatyn, 1978–82; Dean of Brecon, Vicar of Brecon, Battle and Llanddew, 1982–93; Asst Bishop, dio. of St Asaph, 1993–96. *Publications:* (ed jtly and contrib.) This Land and People, 1979; Guide to Brecon Cathedral, 1988. *Recreations:* reading, visiting historic gardens and homes, studying history of art, following Welsh Rugby. *Address:* 31 Cathedral Green, Llandaff, Cardiff CF5 2EB.

JONES, Rev. Dr (David) Huw, FRCR, FRCP; Dean, Postgraduate Medical and Dental Education for East of England, 2002–09; *b* 20 Feb. 1949; *s* of David and Nansi Jones; *m* 1984, Siân Davies; two *d*. *Educ:* Welsh Nat. Sch. of Medicine (MB BCh Hons 1972; MD 1979); MSc London 1978; MA Cantab 1987; E Anglian Ministerial Trng Course. FRCR 1983; FRCP 1996. Univ. Hosp. of Wales, Cardiff, 1972–75; MRC Fellow in Clin. Pharmacol., RPMS, Hammersmith Hosp., 1975–79; MRC Clin. Scientist, Clin. Oncology Unit, Cambridge, 1979–84; Consultant in Clinical Oncol., Addenbrooke's Hosp., Cambridge, 1984–2002; Associate Dean, Postgrad. Med. Educn, E Anglian Reg., 1998–2002. Vis. Prof. in Med. Educn, Anglia Ruskin Univ., 2003–09. Ordained deacon 1998, priest 1999; NSM, Trumpington, 1998–2002; permission to officiate, dio. Ely, 2002–07; Dean's Vicar, Gonville and Caius Coll., Cambridge, 2006–; Rural Dean, Cambridge South, 2011–; Hon. Canon, Ely Cathedral, 2014–. Hon. FFPM 2007. *Publications:* contribs on clinical pharmacol. and oncol. to peer-reviewed med. jls. *Recreations:* classical music, organ, gardening, carpentry.

JONES, Rt Hon. David (Ian); PC 2012; MP (C) Clwyd West, since 2005; *b* 22 March 1952; *s* of Bryn and Elspeth Savage Jones; *m* 1982, Sara Eluned Tudor; two *s*. *Educ:* Ruabon Grammar Sch.; University Coll. London (LLB); Coll. of Law. Admitted Solicitor, 1976; Sen. Partner, David Jones & Co., Llandudno, 1985–2009. Mem. (C) N Wales, Nat. Assembly for Wales, 2002–03. Parly Under-Sec. of State, Wales Office, 2010–12; Sec. of State for Wales, 2012–14. Contested (C): Conwy, 1997; City of Chester, 2001. *Recreation:* travel. *Address:* House of Commons, SW1A 0AA. *T:* (020) 7219 8070. *E:* david.jones.mp@parliament.uk.

JONES, Rev. David Ian Stewart; Headmaster, Bryanston School, 1974–82; *b* 3 April 1934; *s* of Rev. John Milton Granville Jones and Evelyn Moyes Stewart Jones (formerly Chedburn); *m* 1967, Susan Rosemary Hardy Smith; twin *s* and *d*. *Educ:* St John's Sch., Leatherhead; Selwyn Coll., Cambridge (MA); Westcott House, Cambridge. Commnd Royal Signals, 1952–54. Curate at Oldham Parish Church, 1959–62; Vicar of All Saints, Elton, Bury, 1963–66; Asst Conduct and Chaplain of Eton Coll., 1966–70; Conduct and Sen. Chaplain of Eton Coll., 1970–74; Rector-designate of Bristol City, 1982–85; Dir, 1985–97, Consultant, 1997–99, Lambeth Endowed Charities; Hon. Priest Vicar, Southwark Cath., 1985–94. Chm., Inner Cities Young People's Proj., 1988–98. *Recreations:* reading, music, politics. *Address:* 33 St Lucian's Garden, St Lucian's Lane, Wallingford, Oxon OX10 9ER. *Club:* East India, Devonshire, Sports and Public Schools.

JONES, Maj. Gen. David John R.; *see* Rutherford-Jones.

JONES, Sir David John Walter P.; *see* Prichard-Jones.

JONES, David le Brun, CB 1975; Director, Long Term Office, International Energy Agency, 1982–88; *b* 18 Nov. 1923; *s* of Thomas John Jones and Blanche le Brun. *Educ:* City of London Sch.; Trinity Coll., Oxford. Asst Principal, Min. of Power, 1947; Principal, MOP, 1952; Asst Sec., Office of the Minister for Science, 1962; Asst Sec., MOP, 1963; Under-Sec., MOP, later Min. of Technology and DTI, 1968–73; Dep. Sec., DTI, later DoI, 1973–76; Cabinet Office, 1976–77; Dept of Energy, 1978–82. Trustee, Nat. Energy Foundn, 1989–99. *Recreations:* walking, reading, chess. *Club:* Oxford and Cambridge.

JONES, Rt Hon. Sir David Lloyd, Kt 2005; PC 2012; **Rt Hon. Lord Justice Lloyd Jones;** a Lord Justice of Appeal, since 2012; Chairman, Law Commission, 2012–15; *b* 13 Jan. 1952; *s* of William Elwyn Jones and Annie Blodwen Jones (*née* Lloyd-Jones); *m* 1983, Annmarie Harris; one *s* one *d*. *Educ:* Pontypridd Boys' Grammar Sch.; Downing Coll., Cambridge (MA, LLB, Whewell Scholar; Hon. Fellow, 2012). Called to the Bar, Middle Temple, 1975, Bencher, 2005; Fellow, Downing Coll., Cambridge, 1975–91; Asst Recorder, 1989–94; a Recorder, 1994–2005; Junior Crown Counsel (Common Law), 1997–99; QC 1999; a Dep. High Court Judge, 2001–05; a Judge of the High Court, QBD, 2005–12; Presiding Judge of Wales, 2008–11. Asst Comr, 1996–2005, Dep. Chm., 2006–12, Parly Boundary Commn for Wales; Mem., Lord Chancellor's Adv. Cttee on Private Internat. Law, 1997–; Chm., Lord Chancellor's Standing Cttee on the Welsh Lang., 2008–11. Mem., Council of Legal Educn, 1991–96; Governor, Inns of Court Sch. of Law, 1996–2002. Vice Pres., Admin. Law Bar Assoc., 2012. Vis. Prof., City Univ., 1999–2005. Hon. Fellow, Aberystwyth Univ., 2012. Hon. LLD: Glamorgan, 2010; Swansea, 2014. *Publications:* articles in legal jls. *Recreations:* music, hill walking. *Address:* Royal Courts of Justice, Strand, WC2A 2LL.

JONES, David M.; *see* Mansel-Jones.

JONES, David Martin, FRSB; Director, North Carolina Zoological Park, since 1994; *b* 14 Aug. 1944; *s* of John Trevor Jones and Mair Carno Jones; *m* 1969, Janet Marian Woosley; three *s*. *Educ:* St Paul's Cathedral Choir Sch.; St John's Sch., Leatherhead; Royal Veterinary Coll., London (BSc, BVetMed). MRCVS. Veterinary Officer, Whipsnade, 1969; Sen. Veterinary Officer, 1975, Asst Dir of Zoos, 1981, Dir of Zoos, 1984, Gen. Dir, 1991, Dir, Conservation and Consultancy Div., 1992, Zoological Soc. of London. Trustee, WWF UK, 1986–92, 1993–96 (Chm., Conservation Review Gp, subseq. Conservation Cttee, 1990–94); Member Council: WWF UK, 1994–2005; WWF US, 1996–2002; Chm., Fauna and Flora Internat., 1987–94. Chairman: Brooke Hosp. for Animals, 1990–98, 2000–02 (Vice-Chm., 1973–90); Central Park NC (formerly Yadkin Pee-Dee Lakes Project), 1998–; Board Member: Uwharrie Capital Corps, 1998–2004; Nat. Audubon (N Carolina), 2002–07; Environmental Defense Fund (formerly Environmental Defense) (N Carolina), 2003– (Vice-Chm., 2012–14; Chm., 2015–); Pfeiffer Univ., 2004–10; Governor of N Carolina's Adv. Council on China, 2010–; Mem., Uwharrie Regl Resources Commn, 2010–13. *Publications:* over 100 papers on wildlife medicine, management and conservation, in veterinary, medical and zoological jls. *Recreations:* field conservation, travel, antiquarian books, driving, gardening. *Address:* North Carolina Zoological Park, 4401 Zoo Parkway, Asheboro, NC 27205, USA.

JONES, David Robert; Global Chief Executive Officer: Havas Worldwide (formerly Euro RSCG Worldwide), 2005–14; Havas, 2011–14; Co-Founder, One Young World, 2009; *b* Altrincham, Cheshire, 9 Nov. 1966; *s* of Robert Cyril Jones and Jennifer Ann Denise Studley Jones; *m* 1997, Karine Marie Bernard; two *s* one *d*. *Educ:* Middlesex Business Sch. (BA Hons Eur. Business Admin); Reutlingen Fachhochschule (Dip. Europaische Betriebswirtschaftslehre). Bd Account Dir, Abbott Mead Vickers BBDO, 1994–98; Euro RCSG: CEO, Partnership Sydney, 1998–2002; Pres., Global Brands, Worldwide, 2002–04; CEO, NY, 2004–05. Young Global Leader, WEF, 2008. *Publications:* Who Cares Wins: why good business is better business, 2011. *Recreations:* family, tennis, Rugby, wine. *Clubs:* Soho House, Stone.

JONES, Dr (David) Timothy; Deputy Chairman, Education and Learning Wales (formerly Education and Training Wales), 2001–06; non-executive Director: Orpar SA, since 2002; Rémy-Cointreau, since 2008; *b* 21 Aug. 1944; *s* of David Percy Jones and Elvair (*née* Evans); *m* 1968, Jean Margaret Whitehead; four *d*. *Educ:* Leeds Univ. (PhD Physical Chem.); INSEAD, Fontainebleau (MBA with Dist.). MRSC 1967. Gen. Manager, Deutsche BP, 1985–88; Dir, BP France, 1988–89; Chief Exec., BP Oil Supply and Trading, 1990; Dir, BP Oil Europe, 1990–93; Dep. Chm., 1993–2000, Chief Exec., 1996–2000, Lloyd's Register. Chm., Marine Panel, Foresight Initiative, DTI, 1999–2002. Mem. Exec. Cttee, Envmt, Sustainability and Energy Div., RSC, 2010–. *Recreations:* watching Rugby, walking, golf.

JONES, Deborah Elizabeth Vavasseur B.; *see* Barnes Jones.

JONES, Deborah Mary, PhD; Editor, The Ark (Catholic Concern for Animals), 1999–2014; Deputy Editor, Priests & People, 1991–96 and 1999–2004; *b* 5 April 1948; *d* of Thomas Jones and Glenys Jones. *Educ:* W Kirby Grammar Sch. for Girls; University Coll. of S Wales, Cardiff (BA Gen. Hons); Leeds Univ. (PGCE); Regina Mundi Pontifical Inst., Rome; Margaret Beaufort Inst. of Theol.; Anglia Poly. Univ. (MA); Univ. of Wales, Lampeter (PhD 2008). Teacher of English and Classical Studies, Clacton Co. High Sch., 1972–78; Dir, Adult Educn, dio. E Anglia, 1980–96 (pt-time, 1992–96); Lectr in Religious Studies, Suffolk Coll., 1987–92; Editor, Catholic Herald, 1996–98. *Publications:* Focus on Faith, 1987, 2nd edn 1996; This is My Body, 1989; The School of Compassion: a Roman Catholic theology of animals, 2009; contrib. articles to The Tablet, Priests & People, Ecotheology. *Recreations:* Baroque opera, playing 'cello, 18th century women's literature.

JONES, Della Louise Gething; mezzo-soprano; *d* of Eileen Gething Jones and late Cyril Vincent Jones; *m* 1988, Paul Vigars; one *s*. *Educ:* Neath Girls' Grammar School; Royal College of Music. GRSM; LRAM (singing), ARCM (piano); Kathleen Ferrier Scholarship. Mem., ENO, 1977–82, leading roles, 1982–: guest artist, ENO and Royal Opera House; sings with major British opera companies; overseas concert and operatic appearances in all major European countries, also Russia, Japan and USA; radio and TV; prolific recordings with all major recording cos. Hon. FRWCMD (Hon. FWCMD 1995). Hon. Fellow, Univ. of Wales Swansea, 1999. *Recreations:* writing cadenzas, art galleries, animal welfare, reading, piano. *Address:* c/o Music International, 13 Ardilaun Road, Highbury, N5 2QR. *T:* (020) 7359 5183.

JONES, Denise; Director: Eastside Arts and Eastside Books, since 1983; Brick Lane Bookshop, since 2004; *b* Farnham, 18 April 1945; *d* of Leslie William Turner and Stella Ethel May Turner (*née* Wright); *m* 1967, Daniel Elwyn Jones, MBE; two *s* one *d*. *Educ:* Rye Grammar Sch.; Brighton Coll. of Art; Avery Hill Coll., London (Teachers Cert. 1969). Primary sch. teacher, E London, 1960–76; community publisher, Stepney Books, 1974–2001. Mem. (Lab) Tower Hamlets LBC, 1994– (Chm., Culture, 1994–99; Mayor, 1999–2000; Dep. Leader, 2002–06; Leader, 2006–08). Chm. Bd, Mile End Partnership, 1997–; Vice Chm., NHS Tower Hamlets, 2006–11; Dir, Tower Hamlets Homes, 2008–10. Director: Arts Council London Regl Bd, 1998–2006; Trinity Buoy Wharf Trust, 1998–; Aldgate and Allhallows Foundn, 1998–; Wellclose Square Bldg Preservation Trust, 2000–; Wilton's Music Hall, 2000–; (Founder Mem.) Rich Mix Cultural Foundn, 2002–; V&A Nat. Mus. of Childhood, 2002–; Greenwich & Docklands Fest., 2002–06; VisitLondon, 2003–11; Heritage of London Trust, 2003–; TourEast London, 2004–10; Half Moon Young People's Theatre, 2004–06; Mus. of London and Mus. of London Docklands, 2005–09; St Katharine's & Shadwell Trust, 2006–08; 5 Borough Leaders' Olympics 2012 Bd, 2006–08; Whitechapel Art Gall., 2008–12; Cultural Industries Develt Agency, 2009–13; East End Community Trust, 2009–13; Lee Valley Regl

Park Authy, 2010–; Mem. Council, Women's Liby, 2008–13. Gov., Mulberry Sch. for Girls, 2002–. FRSA 2014. Freeman, City of London, 2002. Hon. DLitt East London, 2008. *Recreations:* arts and heritage, visiting galleries, theatre, cinema, reading, gym, swimming. *Address:* 196 Cable Street, E1 0BL. *T:* and *Fax:* (020) 7790 6420. *E:* denisejones196@hotmail.com.

JONES, Denise Idris; Member (Lab) Conwy, National Assembly for Wales, 2003–07; *b* 7 Dec. 1950; *d* of James and Rhona Woodrow; *m* 1984, John Idris Jones; two *s*. Teacher in English and French, Grango Secondary Sch., Rhos, Wrexham, 1972–2003. Contested (Lab) Aberconwy, Nat. Assembly for Wales, 2007. *Recreations:* travelling, literature, arts, golf. *Address:* Borthwen, Llanfair Road, Ruthin, Denbs LL15 1DA.

JONES, Sir Derek (William), KCB 2014 (CB 2009); Permanent Secretary, Welsh Government, since 2012; *b* 8 Dec. 1952; *o s* of William Jones and Patricia Mary Jones (*née* Gill); *m* 1976, Fiona Christine Anne Laidlaw; two *s*. *Educ:* UC Cardiff, Univ. of Wales (BA Hons). Regional policy, company law and privatisation, DTI, 1977–82; HM Treasury: Public Expenditure Control, 1982–84; Head, Financial Instns and Markets, 1984–87; Head, Japan Desk and Overseas Trade Policy Div., DTI, 1987–89; Welsh Office: Asst Sec., 1989; Head, Industrial Policy Div., 1989–92; Head, Finance Progs Div., 1992–94; Under Sec., 1994; Dir, Industry and Trng Dept, 1994–99; Dir, Economic Affairs, 1999–2003, Sen. Dir, 2003–08, Welsh Assembly Govt; Dir, Business and Strategic Partnerships, Cardiff Univ., 2008–12. Chairman: Membership Selection Panel, Welsh Water, 2011–12 (Mem., 2010–12); SE Wales Econ. Forum, 2011–12. Member: Bd, EADS Foundn Wales, 2011–12; Ministerial Adv. Bd (Business, Enterprise, Technology and Sci.), Welsh Govt, 2012. Chm. and Mem., Royal Anniversary Trust Awards Council for Queen's Anniversary Prizes. Pres., Civil Service Sports and Social Cttee. Hon. Prof., Cardiff Univ., 2008. *Recreations:* reading, blues guitar, surfing, watching Rugby. *Address:* Welsh Government, Cathays Park, Cardiff CF10 3NQ.

JONES, Diane C.; *see* Cellan-Jones.

JONES, Dylan, OBE 2013; Editor, GQ magazine, since 1999; Editor-in-Chief, GQ Style, since 2005; *b* 18 Jan. 1960; *s* of Michael and Audrey Jones; *m* 1997, Sarah Walter; two *d*. *Educ:* Chelsea Sch. of Art; St Martin's Sch. of Art (BA Hons Design and Photography). Ed., i-D mag., 1984–87; Contributing Ed., The Face, 1987–88; Ed., Arena, 1988–92; Associate Editor: Observer Mag., 1992–93; Sunday Times Mag., 1993–96; Gp Ed., The Face, Arena, Arena Homme Plus, 1996–97; Ed.-at-Large, Sunday Times, 1997–99. Chm., BSME, 2005. Chm., Fashion Rocks for Prince's Trust, 2005; Vice Pres., Hay Fest.; Member, Board: Norman Mailer Center; Norman Mailer Writers Colony. Editor of Year Award, BSME, 1993, 2001, 2002, 2004, 2007, 2008. *Publications:* Dark Star, 1990; Sex, Power and Travel, 1996; Meaty, Beaty, Big and Bounty, 1997; iPod, Therefore I Am, 2005; Mr Jones' Rules, 2006; (with David Cameron) Cameron on Cameron: conversations with Dylan Jones, 2008; (with David Bailey) British Heroes in Afghanistan, 2010; When Ziggy Played Guitar, 2012; (ed) The Biographical Dictionary of Popular Music, 2012; The Eighties: one day, one decade, 2013; Elvis Has Left the Building: the day the king died, 2014. *Address:* GQ Magazine, Vogue House, Hanover Square, W1S 1JU. *T:* (020) 7499 9080. *E:* dylan.jones@condenast.co.uk. *Clubs:* Chelsea Arts, Groucho, Soho House, Ivy, George.

JONES, Edward Bartley; QC 1997; a Recorder, since 2000; a Deputy High Court Judge, since 2002; *b* Oswestry, 24 Dec. 1952; *s* of Meurig Bartley Jones and late Ruby Jones (*née* Morris). *Educ:* Cardiff High Sch.; Balliol Coll., Oxford (BA Hons Modern Hist. 1973). Called to the Bar, Lincoln's Inn, 1975, Bencher, 2007; in practice as a Chancery/Commercial Barrister in Liverpool, 1976– (Hd, Commercial Dept, Exchange Chambers, Liverpool and Manchester, 1994–); Asst Recorder, 1996–2000. Part-time Lectr in Law, Liverpool Univ., 1977–81. Member: Northern Chancery Bar Assoc. (former Chm.); Chancery Bar Assoc. *Recreations:* ski-ing, opera, travel, golf, shooting. *Address:* Exchange Chambers, Pearl Assurance House, Derby Square, Liverpool L2 9XX. *T:* (0151) 236 7747; 13 Old Square, Lincoln's Inn, WC2A 3UA. *T:* (020) 7831 4445; Flat 2, Hardwicke Building, Lincoln's Inn, WC2A 3UJ. *Clubs:* Oxford and Cambridge; Portal (Tarporley).

JONES, Edward David Brynmor, CBE 2011; RIBA; architect in private practice, since 1973; Principal, Dixon Jones Ltd (formerly Jeremy Dixon·Edward Jones), since 1989; *b* 20 Oct. 1939; *s* of David Jones and Margot Derricourt; *m* 1st; one *s* two *d*; 2nd, Margot Griffin; one *s* two *d*. *Educ:* Haileybury and ISC; AA Sch. of Architecture (AADip Hons 1963); RIBA 1968; RAIC and Ont. Assoc. of Architects, Canada, 1983–89. Tutor, AA, PCL and UC Dublin, 1968–72; Sen. Tutor, Sch. of Environmental Design, RCA, 1973–83; Vis. Prof., 1973–82, Adjunct Prof., 1983–89, Univ. of Toronto; Visiting Professor: Cornell, Harvard, Princeton, Yale, Pennsylvania, Rice, Syracuse, Waterloo and Kent State (Florence) Univs, 1973–; Portsmouth Univ., 1994–98; Hon. Prof., Cardiff Univ. (formerly Univ. of Wales, Cardiff), 2003–. RIBA External Examiner: AA 1985; Portsmouth Univ., Kingston Univ., Heriot-Watt Univ., 1990–93; Univ. of Wales, 1995–97; Univ. of Technol., Kingston, Jamaica, 1997–2000; Mackintosh Sch., Glasgow, 2007–10. Member: RIBA President's Gold Medal Cttee, 1993, 1994; AA Council, 1993–99 (Vice Pres., 1995); RIBA Stirling Interim Award Cttee, 2004–08; RIBA Stirling Final Cttee, 2010; Hon. Librarian, AA, 1994–95. Competitions, first prize: Northampton County Offices, 1973; Mississauga City Hall, Canada, 1982–87; Bus Stn, Venice, 1990; other projects include: Royal Opera House, Covent Garden, 1983–99; buildings for: Henry Moore Foundn at Leeds, 1989–93 and Perry Green, 1989–; Darwin Coll., Cambridge, 1989, 1994; Robert Gordon Univ., Aberdeen, 1991; superstore for J. Sainsbury at Plymouth, 1991–94; Portsmouth Univ. (Dept of Sci.), 1992–96; housing in New Delhi, 1994; Nat. Portrait Gall., 1994–2000; Saïd Business Sch., Oxford Univ., 1996–2001, Phase 2, Centre for Exec. Educn, 2007–12; Somerset House, south terrace and central courtyard, 1998–2000; Kensington and Chelsea Coll., 2000–11; Student Centre, QUB, 2001; Panopticon Bldg, UCL, 2001–; Magna Carta Bldg, Salisbury Cathedral, 2001–; Portrait Gall. of Canada, 2003–; private houses in Bargemon, France, 2005, W London, 2012, and Georgian Bay, Canada, 2013; master plans for: Nat. Gall., 1998–2006; Somerset House, 1998–; Exhibition Road, 2003–; Chelsea Barracks Housing, 2009–; office developments: King's Cross for Parabola, 2001; Regent's Palace for Crown Estates, 2005–12; 5–6 St James's Square for Rio Tinto, 2006–; Edinburgh Park for Parabola, 2013–; housing developments: 35 Marylebone High St for Royalton Estates, 2011–; Chelsea Apartments for Manhattan lofts, 2003–11; Cheval properties, 55–91 Knightsbridge, 2006–; Moxon Street for Howard de Walden Estate, 2010. Rep. Britain at Biennale: Venice, 1980, 2002; Paris, 1981; Santiago, 1982. Chairman Jury: Laban Dance Sch. Competition, Deptford, 1987; Google's Line of Site Competition, 2008, 2009; Jury Member: Diana Princess of Wales Fountain Competition, London, 2002; new Parliament Bldg, Ottawa, 2003; Barbara Hepworth Gall. Competition, Wakefield, 2003; Univ. Boulevard Competition, UBC, 2005; Victoria Embankment Competition, 2005–; Europan Ireland, 2009; Mem., Design Review Panel, 2012 Olympics, 2006–; Vice Chair, Quality Review Panel, London Legacy Develt Corp., 2012. Trustee, Portsmouth Naval Base Property Trust, 2005–08. FRSA. Hon. FRIAI 2011. Hon. Fellow, Cardiff Univ., 2001; Hon. DLitt Portsmouth, 2001. Governor-General's Award for Architecture (Canada), 1988. *Publications:* A Guide to the Architecture of London (with C. Woodward), 1983, 5th edn 2013; (contrib.) Jeremy Dixon·Edward Jones Buildings and Projects, 1959–2002, 2002; contribs to arch. jls. *Recreations:* drawing, planting trees, looking out of the window in France, Staffordshire bull terriers. *Address:* 41 Gloucester Crescent, NW1 7DL. *T:* (020) 7267 7015.

See also B. J. Goldsmith.

JONES, Edward W.; *see* Wilson Jones.

JONES, Edwina Currie; *see* Currie, E.

JONES, Eleri Wynne; Member, Independent Television Commission, with special responsibility for Wales, 1990–98; *b* 9 Aug. 1933; *d* of Ellis Edgar and Elen Mary Griffith; *m* 1960, Bedwyr Lewis Jones (*d* 1992); two *s* one *d*. *Educ:* Howell's Sch., Denbigh (Foundn Schol.); University Coll. of Wales, Aberystwyth; University Coll., Cardiff. BA (Wales); DipIPM. Journalist, Canada, 1956–57; Careers Officer, Gwynedd, 1957–64; Tutor, Marr. Guidance Council, 1978–87; Lectr, Gwynedd Technical Coll., 1980–84; Member: Welsh Fourth Channel Authy, 1984–91; Bd of Channel Four, 1987–90. Dir, Cais Ltd, 1993–2001. Member: Staff Commn for Local Govt Reorgn (Wales), 1994–97; HEFCW, 2000–05; Rees Review into Devolution of Student Support System and Tuition Fees in Wales, 2004–05. Mem., Council, Univ. of Wales, Aberystwyth, 1995–98, Univ. of Wales, Bangor, 1998–2002 (Hon. Fellow, 2001). Formerly trainer and practitioner in psychotherapy and counselling. *Recreations:* walking, travel, television, films. *Address:* 3 Y Berllan, Lôn Las, Menai Bridge, Anglesey LL59 5BT. *T:* (01248) 714021.

JONES, Elin; Member (Plaid Cymru) Ceredigion, National Assembly for Wales, since 1999; *b* 1 Sept. 1966; *d* of John and Avril Jones. *Educ:* Llanwnnen Primary Sch.; Lampeter Comprehensive; UC Cardiff (BScEcon); Univ. of Wales, Aberystwyth (MSc). Research Officer, Dept of Agric. Econs, UCW, Aberystwyth, 1988–91; Econ. Develt Officer, Develt Bd for Rural Wales, 1991–98; Regl Develt Manager, WDA, 1998–99. Mayor of Aberystwyth, 1997–98. Chm., Plaid Cymru, 2000–02. Minister for Rural Affairs, Nat. Assembly for Wales, 2007–11. *Recreations:* music, Welsh culture. *Address:* (constituency office) Ty Goronwy, 32 Heol y Wig, Aberystwyth, Ceredigion SY23 2LN.

JONES, Elisabeth A.; *see* Arfon-Jones.

JONES, Elizabeth Jane; *see* Butler, E. J.

JONES, Elizabeth Sian; QC 2000; *b* 24 March 1960; *d* of John Oswald Jones and Margrette Rachel Jones; *m* 1997, John Clark; one *s* two *d*. *Educ:* Howell's Sch., Llandaff; Ryde Sch., IoW; King's Coll., Cambridge. Called to the Bar, Middle Temple, 1984; Bencher, Lincoln's Inn, 2007; in practice at the Bar, 1984–. *Recreations:* singing, opera, yoga, family. *Address:* Serle Court, 6 New Square, Lincoln's Inn, WC2A 3QS. *T:* (020) 7242 6105.

JONES, Prof. (Elphin) Wynne, OBE 2009; PhD; FRAgS, FIAgrE, FIAgrM, FCGI, FRSB; Principal, Harper Adams University College (formerly Harper Adams Agricultural College), 1996–2009; *b* 29 March 1949; *s* of Elphin and Eluned Jones; *m* 1977, Irfana Siddiqi; two *d*. *Educ:* University Coll. of N Wales, Bangor (BSc Hons); Univ. of Reading (PhD 1976). MIBiol 1978; FRAgS 1994; FIAgrE 2003; FIAgrM 2008; FCGI 2009; FRSB (FIBiol 2009). Lectr in Animal Prodn, 1975–78, Hd, Dept of Animal Prodn, 1978–88, Welsh Agricl Coll.; Vice Principal and Dir, Acad. Affairs, Harper Adams Agricl Coll., 1988–96. Mem., Bd of Mgt, BASIS, 2004–07. Chm., Trehane Trust, 2007–; Member, Board: of Trustees, Lantra, 2001–09; of Mgt, AMTRA, 2007–10; of Mgt, Shrewsbury Sch., 2007–; Mem. Council, Aberystwyth Univ., 2009–. Pres., Future Farmers of Wales, 2009–. Fellow, Inst. of Welsh Affairs, 2006. Hon. DSc Cranfield, 2006. Nat. Agricl Award, RASE, 2005. *Recreations:* travel, walking, reading. *Club:* Farmers.

JONES, Eurfron Gwynne; Director of Education, BBC, 1992–94; *b* 24 Sept. 1934; *d* of William Gwynne Jones and Annie (*née* Harries); *m* 1968, Michael Coyle; one *s*. *Educ:* Aberdare Girls' Grammar Sch.; University Coll., Cardiff, Univ. of Wales (BSc (Zoology); PhD). Teaching Asst, Mount Holyoke Coll., Mass, 1955–56; joined BBC as gen. trainee, 1959; Producer, BBC Sch. Radio, Sch. Television and Continuing Educn, TV, 1959–75; freelance broadcaster, writer and cons., Media Cons. Internat. Children's Centre, Educn Commn of the States, 1975–83; Asst Hd, Sch. Radio, 1983–84; Hd of Sch. Television, 1984–87; Controller, Educnl Broadcasting, BBC, 1987–92. Member: Wyatt Commn on Violence, 1986; OU Council, 1987–94; Open Coll. Council, 1987–89; Council, Royal Instn, 1989–92, and 1994–97; COPUS, 1992–94; Educn Adv. Cttee, Nat. Museums and Galls of Wales, 1995–99; Res. Panel, Inst. of Welsh Affairs, 1996–2002; Chm., Digital Coll. for Wales, 1997–2001. Vis. Prof., Inst. of Educn, Univ. of London, 1994–97. Chm., Friends of Glynn Vivian Art Gall., 2006–08. FRTS 1994 (Mem., 1984–94; Vice Pres., 1996–2002). Fellow, Univ. of Wales Cardiff, 1996. Hon. LLD Exeter, 1990; DUniv Open, 1996. *Publications:* Children Growing Up, 1973; The First Five Years, 1975; How Did I Grow?, 1977; Television Magic, 1978; Lifetime I, Lifetime II, 1982; numerous articles on children and educn. *Recreations:* photography, swimming.

JONES, Felicity; actress; *b* Bournville, Birmingham, 17 Oct. 1983; *d* of Gareth Jones and Julia Hadley. *Educ:* Wadham Coll., Oxford (BA Eng. Lit. and Lang. 2006). *Films:* The Treasure Seekers, 1996; Northanger Abbey, 2007; Brideshead Revisited, 2008; Soulboy, 2010; The Tempest, 2010; Like Crazy, 2011; Chalet Girl, 2011; Breathe In, 2013; The Invisible Woman, 2013; The Theory of Everything, 2014; *television series:* The Worst Witch, 1998–99; Weirdsister College, 2001–02; The Diary of Anne Frank, 2009; *theatre:* That Face, Royal Court, 2007; The Chalk Garden, Luise Miller, Donmar Warehouse, 2008. *Recreations:* reading, theatre, cinema, family, friends, swimming.

JONES, Fielding; *see* Jones, Norman F.

JONES, Gareth; *see* Jones, John Gareth.

JONES, Gareth, OBE 1991; Commissioner, Isle of Anglesey County Council, 2011–12; Chairman, C6 Creative Industries North Wales, since 2013; *b* 14 May 1939. *Educ:* UC, Swansea (BA Hons Geography). Former Headmaster; educnl consultant. Chm., Univ. of Wales Bd for Welsh Lang. Teaching, 2003–06. National Assembly for Wales: Mem. (Plaid Cymru) Conwy, 1999–2003; contested same seat, 2003; Mem. (Plaid Cymru) Aberconwy, 2007–11. Chm., Enterprise and Learning Cttee, Nat. Assembly for Wales, 2007–11. Mem. (Plaid Cymru), Conwy CBC, 1997–2008, 2012–. *Address:* Dolarfon, 21 Roumania Drive, Craig y Don, Llandudno LL30 1UY.

JONES, Gareth, OBE 2003; Director General for Natural Resources (formerly Sustainable Futures), Welsh Government, 2012–15; *b* 13 Aug. 1957; *s* of late Hubert John Jones and Audrey Margaret Jones; *m* 1979, Susan (*née* Brown); one *s* one *d*. *Educ:* Open Univ. (BA Hons Hist.). Civil Servant, 1979–2015; Private Sec. to Sec. of State for Trade and Ind., 1988–90; Welsh Assembly Government: Hd, CAP Mgt Div., Agric. and Rural Affairs Dept, 1999–2003; Dir, Dept for Envmt, Planning and Countryside, 2003–07; Registrar of Cos and Chief Exec., Companies House, 2007–12. CCMI 2011. FRSA. *Address:* Cyncoed, Cardiff. *Club:* Cardiff and County.

JONES, Gareth Daryl; His Honour Judge Gareth Jones; a Circuit Judge, since 2009; a Deputy High Court Judge, Family Division, since 2008; Designated Family Judge for North Wales, since 2011; *b* Swansea, 24 Nov. 1961; *s* of Marshall Stanley Jones and Esther Elizabeth Avril Jones; *m* 1989, Rosamund Ann, *d* of late Thomas Richard Lloyd and Marion Lloyd. *Educ:* Ysgol Gyfun Ystalyfera; University Coll. of Wales, Aberystwyth (LLB Hons 1983). Called to the Bar, Gray's Inn, 1984; Recorder, Wales and Chester Circuit, 2003–09. *Address:* Rhyl County Court, Clwyd Street, Rhyl, Denbighshire LL18 3LA. *T:* (01745) 352940.

JONES, Prof. Gareth (Hywel); QC 1986; FBA 1982; Fellow of Trinity College, Cambridge, since 1961; Downing Professor of the Laws of England, Cambridge University, 1975–98; *b* 10 Nov. 1930; *oc* of late B. T. Jones, FRICS, and late Mabel Jones, Tylorstown, Glam; *m* 1959, Vivienne Joy (*d* 2004), *o d* of late C. E. Puckridge, FIA, Debden Green, Loughton; two *s* one *d*. *Educ:* Rhondda County Sch. for Boys; University Coll. London (PhD; Fellow 1988); St Catharine's Coll., Cambridge (Scholar); Harvard Univ. (LLM). LLB London 1951; MA, LLB 1953, LLD 1972, Cantab. Choate Fellow, Harvard, 1953; Yorke Prize, 1960. Called to Bar, Lincoln's Inn, 1955 (Scholar); Hon. Bencher 1975. Lecturer: Oriel and Exeter Colls, Oxford, 1956–58; KCL, 1958–61; Trinity College, Cambridge: Lectr, 1961–75; Tutor, 1967; Sen. Tutor, 1972; Vice-Master, 1986–92 and 1996–99; Univ. Lectr, Cambridge, 1961–75; Chm., Faculty of Law, 1978–81; Chm., Fitzwilliam Mus. Syndicate, 1987–2001. Visiting Professor: Harvard, 1966 and 1975; Chicago, 1976–95; California at Berkeley, 1967 and 1971; Indiana, 1971, 1975; Michigan, 1983, 1997, 1999, 2001, 2002; Georgia, 1983; Texas, 1993. Lectures: Harris, Indiana, 1981; Wright, Toronto, 1984; Lionel Cohen, Hebrew Univ., 1985; Butterworth, QMC, 1987; Nambyar, India, 1991; Richard O'Sullivan, Thomas More Soc., 1991; Hochelaga, Hong Kong, 2000; Tory, Halifax, NS, 2001; Lansdowne, Victoria, BC, 2003. Mem., American Law Inst.; For. Mem., Royal Netherlands Acad. of Arts and Scis, 1991. Hon. LLD Glamorgan, 2008. *Publications:* (with Lord Goff of Chieveley) The Law of Restitution, 1966, 7th edn 2007; The History of the Law of Charity 1532–1827, 1969; The Sovereignty of the Law, 1973; (with Lord Goodhart) Specific Performance, 1986, 2nd edn 1996; various articles. *Address:* Trinity College, Cambridge CB2 1TQ; 9B Cranmer Road, Cambridge CB3 9BL; Clay Street, Thornham Magna, Eye, Suffolk IP23 8HE. *Club:* Oxford and Cambridge.

JONES, Gareth S.; *see* Stedman Jones.

JONES, Gemma; *see* Jones, Jennifer.

JONES, Geoffrey M.; *see* Melvill Jones.

JONES, George Quentin; freelance broadcaster and writer; Multi-media Political Correspondent, Press Association, 2007–10; *b* 28 Feb. 1945; *s* of (John) Clement Jones, CBE; *m* 1st, 1972, Diana Chittenden (marr. diss. 1989); one *s* one *d*; 2nd, 1990, Teresa Grace Rolleston. *Educ:* Highfields Sch., Wolverhampton. Trainee journalist, Eastern Daily Press, 1963–67; journalist, S Wales Argus and Western Mail, 1967–69; Reuters, London, 1969; Parly Staff, The Times, 1969–73; Parly and Political Corresp., Scotsman, 1973–82; Political Correspondent: Sunday Telegraph, 1982–85; Sunday Times, 1985–86; Political Corresp., 1986–88, Political Ed., 1988–2007, Daily Telegraph. Regular broadcaster, BBC News and current affairs programmes, Sky News. Chairman: Parly Lobby Journalists, 1987–88; Parly Press Gallery, 1996–97. Assessor, Leveson Public Inquiry into Culture, Practices and Ethics of the Press, 2011–13. Judge, Spectator Parliamentarian of the Year Awards, 1993–2006. Dir, North Curry Community Ltd, 2011–13. Mem., North Curry Parish Council, 2011–14. *Recreations:* walking (completing Offa's Dyke long distance path), cycling, bellringing, travelling, time with family, enjoying a long-awaited escape to the country after 40 years reporting parliament and politics. *Address:* Helland House, Helland, North Curry, Taunton, Som TA3 6DU. *T:* (01823) 491035.

JONES, Prof. George William, OBE 1999; Professor of Government, University of London, 1976–2003, now Emeritus; *b* 4 Feb. 1938; *er s* of George William and Grace Annie Jones; *m* 1963, Diana Mary Bedwell; one *s* one *d*. *Educ:* Wolverhampton Grammar Sch.; Jesus Coll., Oxford (BA 1960, MA 1965); Nuffield Coll., Oxford; DPhil Oxon 1965. Univ. of Leeds: Asst Lectr in Govt, 1963; Lectr in Govt, 1965; London School of Economics and Political Science: Lectr in Pol Sci., 1966; Sen. Lectr in Pol Sci., 1971; Reader in Pol Sci., 1974; Chm., Graduate Sch., 1990–93; Vice-Chm., Appts Cttee, 1996–99; Hon. Fellow, 2009. Sec., 1965–68, Mem. Exec. Cttee, 1969–75, Pol Studies Assoc. of the UK; Mem., Exec. Council, Hansard Soc., 1968–70; Member, Editorial Committee: Local Government Studies, 1970–98, 2003–; The London Journal, 1973–80; Governance, 1987–92; Korean Jl of Public Policy, 1988–; Studies in Law and Politics, 1989–; Nonprofit Management and Leadership, 1989–; Hong Kong Jl of Public Admin, 1992–. Member: Layfield Cttee of Inquiry into Local Govt Finance, 1974–76; Exams Cttee, and Admin. Staff Qualifications Council, Local Govt Trng Bd, 1977–80; Political Science and Internat. Relns Cttee, SSRC, 1977–81; Jt Working Party on Internal Management of Local Authorities, 1992–93; Chm., Central-Local Govt Relations Panel, SSRC, 1978–81; Special Adviser, Select Cttee on Welsh Affairs, 1985–87. Vis. Prof., Queen Mary, London, 2004–14; Hon. Prof., Birmingham Univ., 2003–; Vis. Res. Fellow, De Montfort Univ., 2007–. Member: Governing Council, Wolverhampton Polytechnic, 1978–83 (Hon. Fellow, 1986); Council, RIPA, 1984–90; Nat. Consumer Council, 1991–99 (Chm., Public Services Cttee, 1992–98); Beacon Councils Adv. Panel, 1999–2002; Vice-Pres., Assoc. of Councillors, 1980–. Associate, Centre for Public Service Partnerships, 2010–12. Hon. Member: CIPFA, 2003–; SOLACE, 2003–. FRHistS 1980. Hon. Fellow, Inst. of Local Govt Studies, Birmingham Univ., 1979. *Publications:* Borough Politics, 1969; (with B. Donoughue) Herbert Morrison: portrait of a politician, 1973, repr. 2001; (ed with A. Norton) Political Leadership in Local Authorities, 1978; (ed) New Approaches to the Study of Central-Local Government Relationships, 1980; (with J. Stewart) The Case for Local Government, 1983, 2nd edn 1985; (ed jtly) Between Centre and Locality, 1985; (ed) West European Prime Ministers, 1991; (with Tony Travers *et al*) The Government of London, 1991; Local Government and the Social Market, 1991; (with Tony Travers *et al*) The Impact of Population Size on Local Authority Costs and Effectiveness, 1993; Local Government: the management agenda, 1993; (with Tony Travers) Attitudes to Local Government in Westminster and Whitehall, 1994; (with Tony Travers *et al*) The Role of the Local Authority Chief Executive in Local Governance, 1997; The New Local Government Agenda, 1997; (jtly) At the Centre of Whitehall, 1998; (jtly) Regulation Inside Government, 1999; (with A. Blick) Premiership, 2010; (with A. Blick) At Power's Elbow, 2013; contribs to Political Studies, Public Admin, Political Qly, Parliamentary Affairs, Government and Opposition, Jl of Admin Overseas; Local Govt Chronicle; Internat. Jl Public Sector Mgt; Public Money and Mgt; Public Finance; The MJ; History and Policy. *Recreations:* cinema, politics. *Address:* Department of Government, London School of Economics, Houghton Street, WC2A 2AE. *T:* (020) 7955 7179. *E:* g.w.jones@lse.ac.uk. *Club:* Beefsteak.

JONES, Geraint Anthony; QC 2001; a Recorder, since 2009; *b* 5 April 1953; *s* of John and Lydia Jones; *m* 1976, Pauline Julia Gibson; two *d*. *Educ:* Christ Coll., Brecon; Jesus Coll., Cambridge (MA). MCIArb 2002. Called to the Bar, Middle Temple, 1976; in practice as barrister, specialising in chancery, commercial and professional negligence law, Cardiff, 1976–, and London, 2001–. Mem., Judicial Panel, World Rugby (formerly Internat. Rugby Bd), 2002–. *Recreations:* hill walking, sailing. *Address:* Devonshire House, Fairbourne, Cobham, Surrey KT11 2BT.

JONES, Geraint Stanley, CBE 1993; international broadcasting consultant and producer, 1994–2012; *b* 26 April 1936; *s* of Olwen and David Stanley Jones; *m* 1961, Rhiannon Williams; two *d*. *Educ:* Pontypridd Grammar Sch.; University Coll. of N Wales (BA Hons; DipEd; Hon. Fellow 1988). BBC-Wales: Studio Manager, 1960–62; Production Asst, Current Affairs (TV), 1962–65; TV Producer: Current Affairs, 1965–69; Features and Documentaries, 1969–73; Asst Head of Programmes, Wales, 1973–74; Head of Programmes, Wales, 1974–81; Controller, BBC Wales, 1981–85; Dir of Public Affairs, BBC, 1986–87; Man. Dir, Regl Broadcasting, BBC, 1987–89; Chief Exec., S4C, 1989–94. Director: WNO, 1985–94; Welsh Film Council, 1992–97; Screen Wales, 1992–96; Wales Millennium Centre, 1999–2005 (Vice-Pres., 2008–); Chm., Sgrîn, Media Agency for Wales, 1999–2004. Mem., Arts Council of Wales, 1994–2000. Chm., EBU Television Commn, 1990–96. Chm., Ryan Davies Trust, 1977–2008; Member: UK Freedom from Hunger Campaign Cttee, 1978–97; BT Wales Adv. Forum, 1994–2001; British Council Film and TV Cttee, 1995–2002; UNA (Welsh Centre) Trust, 1999–2005; Bd, Clwyd Theatr Cymru, 2006–09. Vice Pres., RWCMD (formerly WCMD), 2000– (Chm., Bd of Govs, 1990–2000); Mem., Court and Council, Univ. of Wales, Aberystwyth, 1990–96. Chm., Welsh Nat. Lang. Centre, 1994–97. Pres., Welsh Music Guild, 2008–. Vis. Prof., Internat. Acad. of Broadcasting, Montreux, 1994–2001. Trustee: Pendyrus Trust, 2001–09; Wales Video Gall., 2001–14; Clwyd Theatr Cymru Develt Trust, 2004–. FRSA 1989; FRTS 1992. FRWCMD (FWCMD 2000). Hon. LLD Wales, 1998; Hon. DLitt Glamorgan, 1999. *Recreations:* music, memories. *Address:* 12 Lady Mary Road, Roath Park, Cardiff CF23 5NS. *Clubs:* Royal Over-Seas League; Cardiff and County (Cardiff).

JONES, Dr Gerald, FRCP; Senior Principal Medical Officer, Department of Health (formerly of Health and Social Security), 1984–95; *b* 25 Jan. 1939; *s* of John Jones and Gladys Jones (*née* Roberts); *m* 1st, 1964, Anne Heatley (*née* Morris) (marr. diss. 1987); one *s* two *d*; 2nd, 1990, Jutta Friese. *Educ:* Swansea Grammar School; Merton College, Oxford; London Hosp. Med. Coll. (BA, BM, BCh, PhD, MSc). Appointments in hosp. medicine, 1965–69; research with MRC, 1969–73; pharmaceutical industry, 1974–75; medical staff, DHSS, later DoH, 1975–95. *Publications:* papers on cardiopulmonary physiology, respiratory medicine, cellular immunology and drug regulation. *Recreations:* music, gardening, mathematics. *Address:* 58 Palace Road, N8 8QP.

JONES, Gerald; MP (Lab) Merthyr Tydfil and Rhymney, since 2015; *b* Caerphilly, 21 Aug. 1970; *s* of Colin and Patricia Jones; partner, Tyrone Powell. *Educ:* Bedwelly Comprehensive Sch.; Ystrad Mynach Coll. Grants Liaison Officer, Cardiff CC, 1999–2000; Community Develt Officer, Gwent Assoc. of Voluntary Orgns, 2001–05 and 2009–12. Mem. (Lab) Caerphilly CBC, 1995–2015 (Dep. Leader, 2004–08 and 2012–15). *Recreations:* cinema, reading, music. *Address:* House of Commons, SW1A 0AA. *T:* (020) 7219 5874. *E:* gerald.jones.mp@parliament.uk.

JONES, Gerald Kenneth; Chief Executive, Wandsworth Borough Council, 1986–2010; *b* 16 June 1943; *s* of Sir Kenneth Jones, CBE, QC and of Menna (*née* Jones); *m* 1976, Janet Norma Dymock; three *s* one *d*. *Educ:* Royal Grammar Sch., Guildford; St John's Coll., Cambridge (MA 1965); Brunel Univ. (MTech 1972). Operational Res. Scientist, NCB, 1966–69; Mgt Consultant, RTZ Corp., 1969–72; Corporate Planner, Haringey Council, 1972–74; Wandsworth Council: Asst Dir, Admin, 1974–81; Dir, Admin, 1981–83; Dep. Chief Exec., 1983–86. *Publications:* contrib. technical and professional jls. *Recreations:* collecting antiquarian books, triathlon. *Address:* 9 McKay Road, Wimbledon, SW20 0HT.

JONES, Glyn Parry, FCA; Chairman: Aldermore Group plc, since 2014; Aldermore Bank plc, since 2014; *b* 17 March 1952; *m* 1976, Catherine Anne King; two *s* one *d*. *Educ:* Birkenhead Sch.; Gonville and Caius Coll., Cambridge (MA Econs and Social and Pol Scis). FCA 1976. Deloitte Haskins and Sells: Auditor, London, 1973–76; Consultant, Financial Mgt Consultancy, London, 1977–80; Man. Dir, Kenyan Consultancy, Nairobi, 1980–83; Partner, Midlands Consulting Practice, Birmingham, 1983–85; Partner in Charge, Financial Services Consulting, London, 1986–89; European Sector Leader, Financial Services, London, Coopers & Lybrand Mgt Consultants, 1989–91; Standard Chartered Bank: Divl Dir, Standard Chartered Equitor, Hong Kong, 1991–92; Gen. Manager, Internat. Private Banking, Hong Kong, 1993–97; Commercial Dir, NatWest Wealth Mgt, London, March–Oct. 1997; Chief Executive: Coutts Gp, 1997–2000; Gartmore Investment Mgt plc, 2000–04; Thames River Capital LLP, 2005–06; Chairman: Aspen Insurance Hldgs Ltd, 2007–; Hermes Fund Managers, 2008–12; Towry Gp (formerly Towry Law Gp), 2006–12. Sen. Ind. Dir, Direct Line Gp plc, 2012–. *Recreations:* travel, tennis, squash, theatre.

JONES, Rev. Canon Glyndwr; Secretary General, Mission to Seafarers (formerly Missions to Seamen), 1990–2000; a Chaplain to the Queen, 1990–2005; *b* 25 Nov. 1935; *s* of late Bertie Samuel Jones and of Elizabeth Ellen Jones; *m* 1st, 1961, Cynthia Elaine Jenkins (*d* 1964); 2nd, 1966, (Marion) Anita Morris; one *s* one *d*. *Educ:* Dynevor Sch., Swansea; St Michael's Theol Coll., Llandaff, Univ. of Wales (DipTh); MA Wales 2005. Nat. Service, 1954–56: RAPC, attached 19 Field Regt RA; served Korea, Hong Kong; demobbed Sgt AER. Deacon 1962, priest 1963; Curate: Clydach, 1962–64; Llangyfelach with Morriston, 1964–67; Sketty, 1967–70; Rector, Bryngwyn with Newchurch and Llanbedr, Painscastle with Llanddewi Fach, 1970–72; The Missions to Seamen: Port Chaplain, Swansea and Port Talbot, 1972–76; Sen. Chaplain, Port of London, 1976–81; Auxiliary Ministries Sec., Central Office, 1981–85; Asst Gen. Sec., 1985–90. Hon. Chaplain, Royal Alfred Seafarers Soc., 1987–93; Chaplain to Lay Sheriff of London, 1993–94, 1999–2000; Hon. Canon, St Michael's Cathedral, Kobe, Japan, 1988–. Commissary to Bp of Cyprus in the Gulf, 1996–2000. Mem., Eddie Baird Meml Trust, 2003–08 (Treas., 2007–08). Gov., Treetops Sch., Grays, 2008–12. Hon. Mem., Co. of Master Mariners, 1990–2000; Freeman, City of London, 1990; Chaplain: Co. of Information Technologists, 1989–2000; Co. of Innholders, 1990–2002; Co. of Farriers, 1990–2004 (Liveryman, 1999–); Co. of Carmen, 1990–2004 (Liveryman, 1995–). Sec. to Trustees, Orsett Churches Centre, 2003–07. President: Probus Club, Grays Thurrock, 2005–06; Batti-Wallahs' Soc., 2006–07. *Recreations:* sport, music, reading, theatre, travel. *Address:* 5 The Close, Grays, Essex RM16 2XU. *Clubs:* Little Ship (Hon. Chaplain, 1996–2000); Thurrock Rugby Football (Chaplain, 1999); Grays Thurrock Rotary (Pres., 2007–08; Sec., 2009–12).

JONES, Prof. Glynis Eleanor May, PhD; FBA 2013; Professor of Archaeology, University of Sheffield, since 2004; *b* Kenfig Hill, 4 Feb. 1950; *d* of Cyril Nelson and Phyllis Nelson (*née* Powell); one *s* by a previous marriage. *Educ:* Cynffig Comprehensive Sch.; University Coll. of Cardiff (BSc Hons Zool.; Cert Ed); Darwin Coll., Cambridge (MPhil Archaeol. 1979; PhD 1984). Teacher of Biol., Barry Comprehensive Sch., 1972–73; res. asst, Fitch Lab., British Sch. at Athens, 1974–78; Envmtl Archaeologist, Dept of Urban Archaeol., Mus. of London, 1983–84; Lectr, 1984–93, Sen. Lectr, 1993–2000, Reader, 2000–04, Dept of Archaeol., Univ. of Sheffield. *Publications:* (ed jtly) Fodder: archaeological, historical and ethnographic studies, 1998; (ed jtly) Archaeology of Plants, 2001; contrib. papers to learned jls. *Recreations:* walking, theatre, local conservation group. *Address:* Department of Archaeology, University of Sheffield, Northgate House, West Street, Sheffield S1 4ET. *T:* (0114) 222 2904. *E:* g.jones@sheffield.ac.uk.

JONES, Gordon Frederick; architect; *b* 25 Aug. 1929; *s* of Harold Frederick and Rose Isabel Jones; *m* 1954, Patricia Mary (*née* Rowley); one *s* one *d*. *Educ:* Saltley Grammar Sch.; The School of Architecture, Birmingham (DipArch 1950), and subseq. by BBC; Sch. of Planning, UCL (Cert. Landscape Design, 1963). RIBA 1950. FRSA. Architect: in local government, 1952; War Office, 1959; Asst City Architect, Sheffield, 1966; private practice, London, 1968; Property Services Agency, DoE: Architect, 1970; Head of Student Training Office, 1976; Head of Architectural Services, 1979–85; Res. Dir, 1985–90, Editor, 1990–93, Product Design Review. Dir, Building Centre, London, 1984–87. Chm. of Standards, BDB/–, BSI, 1984–87. *Recreations:* watching cats, listening to music, re-building houses. *Address:* Cartref, Monkleigh, Bideford, Devon EX39 5JT.

JONES, Graham Edward, MA; Headmaster, Repton School, 1987–2003; *b* 22 Sept. 1944; *s* of late Edward Thomas Jones and Dora Rachel Jones; *m* 1976, Vanessa Mary Heloise (*née* Smith). *Educ:* Birkenhead Sch.; Fitzwilliam Coll., Cambridge (schol.; 1st cl. Hons Econs Tripos 1966). Asst Master, Hd of Economics and Politics, Housemaster, Charterhouse, 1967–87; secondment to British Petroleum, 1981. Awarder in Economics, Oxford and Cambridge Schs Examination Bd, 1979–91; Reviser in Economics, JMB, 1981–91; Chm. Examrs, Oxford and Cambridge and RSA Examinations, 1996–2001; Chm., Ind. Schs Examinations Bd, 1998–2006. Governor: Birkenhead Sch., 2004–; Royal GS, Worcester,

2004–07; Malvern Coll., 2005 (Vice-Chm., 2011–). FRSA 1988. *Publications:* various articles on economics and teaching economics. *Recreations:* painting, walking, music, cooking, the classics. *Address:* Tilton House, Sutton St Nicholas, Hereford HR1 3BB. *T:* (01432) 882075.

JONES, His Honour Graham Julian; a Senior Circuit Judge, 2002–05 (a Circuit Judge, 1985–2005; authorised to sit as a Judge of the High Court, 1994–2005); a Judge of Technology and Construction Court (formerly a Circuit Official Referee), 1993–2005; Resident and Designated Judge, Cardiff County Court, 1994–98; Designated Civil Judge, Cardiff, 1998–2000, South and West Wales, 2000–05; Deputy High Court Judge, 2005–11; acting Designated Civil Judge for Wales, 2008; *b* 17 July 1936; *s* of late David John Jones, CBE, and Edna Lillie Jones; *m* 1961, Dorothy, *o d* of late James Smith and Doris Irene Tickle, Abergavenny; two *s* one *d. Educ:* Porth County Grammar Sch. (state scholarship); St John's Coll., Cambridge. MA, LLM (Cantab). Admitted Solicitor, 1961; Partner, Morgan Bruce and Nicholas, 1961 (represented Parents and Residents Assoc., Aberfan Disaster, 1966). Dep. Circuit Judge, 1975–78; a Recorder, 1978–85. Pres., Pontypridd Rhondda and Dist Law Soc., 1973–75; Member Council: Cardiff Law Soc., 1975–78, 1984–85; Associated Law Socs of Wales, 1974–85 (Pres., 1982–84); Member: Lord Chancellor's Legal Aid Adv. Cttee, 1980–85; Adv. Bd, Centre for Professional Legal Studies, Cardiff Law Sch., 1995–; Civil Justice Council, 2004–12 (Chm., Comparative Law Cttee and Collective Redress Working Gp, 2006–11); Judicial Estates Adv. Gp, 2004–10. Chairman: Swansea Intervention Bd, Welsh Assembly Govt, 2009–10; Pembrokeshire Ministerial Bd, 2011–13. Mem. Court, UWCC, 1995–; Gov., Univ. of Glamorgan, 1999–2006. Council Mem., RNLI, 2002–05 (Vice Pres., 2005–). *Publications:* papers and presentations in Europe on collective redress. *Recreations:* golf, boats. *Clubs:* Cardiff and County (Cardiff), Radyr Golf, Royal Porthcawl Golf.

JONES, Graham Peter; MP (Lab) Hyndburn, since 2010; *b* 2 March 1966; partner, Kimberley Whitehead; one *s* one *d. Educ:* BA (Hons) Applied Social Studies. Graphic Designer, 1992–2010. Member (Lab): Hyndburn BC, 2002–10; Lancs CC, 2009–10. *Address:* House of Commons, SW1A 0AA.

JONES, Gregory Dennis T.; *see* Treverton-Jones.

JONES, Gregory Percy; QC 2011; *b* Dartford, Kent, 4 Jan. 1968; *s* of late Colin Frederick Jones and of Jeannette Bridget Jones (*née* McDonald); *m* 1997, Rosali Margaretha Pretorius; two *d. Educ:* Colfe's Sch.; New Coll., Oxford (MA; Pres., Oxford Univ. Law Soc. 1986; Treas., Oxford Union Soc. 1986; New Coll. 1st XV Rugby); University Coll. London (LLM). ESU debating tour, USA, 1989; Stagiaire, EC, Brussels, 1990. Called to the Bar: Lincoln's Inn, 1991 (Hardwicke Schol.; Thomas More Bursar); King's Inns, Dublin, 1997; Inn of Court, NI, 2008; in practice as a barrister, 1993–. Pt-time Sen. Lectr in EU Law, South Bank Univ., 1993–97; Jean Pierre Warner Scholar, Eur. Court of Justice, Luxembourg, 1995; Fellow, Centre for Eur. Law, KCL, 2008–. Legal Associate, RTPI 2003. Deputy Chancellor: Dio. of Truro, 2008–; Dio. of Exeter, 2008–; Dio. of Ely, 2010–12. Governor: Colfe's Sch., 2008–13; Leathersellers' Fedn of Schs, 2012–. Member: Bar Council, 2008–; Governing Council, St Stephen's House, Univ. of Oxford, 2011–; Ct of Common Council, City of London (Farringdon Without), 2013–. FRSA 2013; FRGS 2014. Freeman, City of London, 1999; Liveryman, Leathersellers' Co., 2003. *Publications:* (jtly) Statutory Nuisance, 2001, 3rd edn 2011; (jtly) Environmental Law in Property Transactions, 3rd edn 2009; (ed and contrib.) The Habitats Directive: a developer's obstacle course?, 2012; (ed jtly and contrib.) The Strategic Environmental Assessment Directive: a plan for success?, 2014; (Asst Ed.) National Infrastructure Planning Articles, 2013–. *Recreations:* history (esp. military and Irish), 20th century South African art, scuba diving, watching Rugby, cricket and football. *Address:* Francis Taylor Building, Temple, EC4Y 7BY. *T:* (020) 7353 8415. *E:* clerks@ftb.eu.com. *Clubs:* Athenæum, Oxford and Cambridge; Surrey County Cricket; Old Colfeians Rugby Football.

JONES, Guy Charles L.; *see* Lloyd-Jones.

JONES, Gwilym Haydn; management consultant, 1997–2007; *b* 20 Sept. 1947; *s* of late Evan Haydn Jones and Mary Elizabeth Gwenhwyfar Jones (*née* Moseley); *m* 1974, Linda Margaret (*née* John); one *s* one *d.* Dir, Bowring Wales Ltd, 1980–92. Councillor, Cardiff CC, 1969–72 and 1973–83. MP (C) Cardiff North, 1983–97; contested (C) same seat, 1997. PPS to Minister of State, Dept of Transport, 1991–92; Parly Under-Sec. of State, Welsh Office, 1992–97. Secretary: Welsh Cons. Members Gp, 1984–92; All Party Gp for Fund for Replacement of Animals in Medical Experiments, 1987–92. Mem. Exec. Cttee, Assoc. of Former Members of Parlt, 2001–10. Founder Chm., Friendship Force in Wales, 1978–81; Chm., St John Ambulance Council for Cardiff and Vale of Glamorgan, 2013–; Vice Pres., Kidney Res. Unit for Wales Foundn, 1986–92. Rowed for Wales in Speaker's Regatta, 1986. Liveryman, Welsh Livery Guild, 1993–2010. Officer: United Grand Lodge of England, 2010–; Supreme Grand Chapter of England, 2012–; Grand Lodge of Mark Master Masons, 2015–. OStJ 1997. *Recreation:* watching Wales win at Rugby. *Clubs:* County Conservative, Cardiff and County (Cardiff).

JONES, Gwyn; *see* Jones, Miah G.

JONES, Gwyn; a District Judge (Magistrates' Courts), since 2013; *b* Trawsfynydd, 22 July 1960; *s* of Edgar and Lowri Jones; *m* 1986, Margaret Macmillan; one *s* one *d. Educ:* Ysgol Y Moelwyn, Blaenau Ffestiniog; Liverpool Poly. (BA Hons Law); Coll. of Law, Chester. Leo Abse & Cohen Solicitors: articled clerk, 1982–84; asst solicitor, 1984–86; Partner, 1986–96; Partner, Gamlins Solicitors, 1996–2013; Dep. Dist Judge (Magistrates' Courts), 2000–13. Chair, Llamau Housing Soc. Ltd, 1989–92. *Recreations:* gardening, mountain biking, travelling, eating out. *Address:* Llandudno Magistrates' Court, The Court House, Conwy Road, Llandudno, Conwy LL30 1GA. *T:* (01492) 863854.

JONES, Gwyn, FRAgS; farmer; Member, Agriculture and Horticulture Development Board, since 2014; Chairman, DairyCo, since 2014; *b* Dolgellau, 10 March 1954; *s* of Humphrey Lloyd Jones and Eirlys Lloyd Jones; *m* 1973, Lorayne; two *d. Educ:* Ysgol Y Gader, Dolgellau. Engrg apprentice, Rolls Royce, 1970. Chm., Dairy Bd, 2004–10, Vice Pres., 2010–12, NFU. Chairman: Eur. Platform for Responsible Use of Medicines in Animals, 2012–; Responsible Use of Medicines in Agric., 2013–; Vice Chm., COPA-Gogeca Animal Health and Welfare Wkg Gp, 2010–. Dir, Anaerobic Digestion and Bioresources Assoc., 2010–14. Nuffield Scholar. *Address:* Moores Green Cottage, Kirdford, Billingshurst, W Sussex RH14 0LE. *T:* 07730 001387. *E:* wealdclay@btinternet.com. *Club:* Farmers.

JONES, Gwyn Idris M.; *see* Meirion-Jones.

JONES, Dame Gwyneth, DBE 1986 (CBE 1976); a Principal Dramatic Soprano: Royal Opera House, Covent Garden, since 1963; Vienna State Opera, since 1966 (Hon. Member, 1989); Deutsche Oper Berlin, since 1966; Bavarian State Opera, since 1967; *b* 7 Nov. 1936; *d* of late Edward George Jones and late Violet (*née* Webster); one *d*; *m* 2008, Adrian Mueller. *Educ:* Twmpath Sec. Mod. Sch., Pontypool, Mon; Royal College of Music, London; Accademia Chigiana, Siena; Zürich Internat. Opera Studio. Maria Carpi Prof., Geneva. Guest Artiste: La Scala, Milan; Berlin State Opera; Munich State Opera; Bayreuth Festival; Salzburg Festival; Verona; Orange; Tokyo; Zürich; Metropolitan Opera, New York; Paris; Geneva; Dallas; San Francisco; Los Angeles; Teatro Colon, Buenos Aires; Edinburgh Festival; Welsh National Opera; Rome; Hamburg; Cologne; Maggio Musicale, Florence; Chicago; Seoul; Peking; Hong Kong. Many opera roles including: Leonora in Il Trovatore; Desdemona in Otello; Aida; Leonore in Fidelio; Senta in The Flying Dutchman; Medea (Cherubini); Sieglinde in Die Walküre; Lady Macbeth; Elizabeth in Don Carlos; Madame Butterfly; Tosca; Donna Anna in Don Giovanni; Salome/Herodias; Kundry in Parsifal; Isolde; Helena in Die Ägyptische; Färberin/Kaiserin in Die Frau ohne Schatten; Chrysothemis/Elektra/Klytaemnestra in Elektra; Elizabeth/Venus in Tannhäuser; Octavian/Marschallin in Der Rosenkavalier; Brünnhilde in Der Ring des Nibelungen; Ortrud in Lohengrin; Minnie in Fanciulla del West; Norma; Erwartung (Schoenberg); La voix humaine (Poulenc); Esmeralda in Notre Dame (Schmidt); Leokadia Begvick in Aufstieg und Fall der Stadt Mahagonny (Brecht/Weil); Kusterin Buryja in Jenufa (Janáček); Kabanicha in Katia Kabanowa (Janáček); Queen of Hearts in Alice in Wonderland (Unsuk Chin); Claire Zachanassian in Der Besuch der alten Dame (Gottfried von Einem); Cosima Wagner in Wagnerin; oratorio and recitals. Numerous recordings, radio and TV appearances; film, Quartet, 2013. Début as Opera Dir, Der Fliegende Holländer, Deutsches Nat. Th., Weimar, 2003. Pres., Richard Wagner Soc., 1990–. FRCM. Kammersängerin, Austria and Bavaria. Hon. Member: RAM, 1980; Vienna State Opera, 1989; Hon. FRWCMD 1992. Hon. DMus: Wales; Glamorgan. Shakespeare Prize, FVS Hamburg, 1987; Golden Medal of Honour, Vienna, 1991; Ehrenkreuz für Wissenschaft und Kunst, I Klasse, Austria, 1992; Premio Puccini, 2003; Cymru for the World Honours, 2004. Bundesverdienstkreuz (FRG), 1988; Comdr, Ordre des Arts et des Lettres (France), 1992. *Address:* PO Box 2000, 8700 Küsnacht, Switzerland.

JONES, Gwynoro Glyndwr; Director, EPPC Severn Crossing Ltd, 1999–2012; Lay Inspector of Schools, 1994–2012; *b* 21 Nov. 1942; *s* of late J. E. and A. L. Jones, Minyrafon, Foelgastell, Cefneithin, Carms; *m* 1967, A. Laura Miles (marr. diss. 1991); two *s* one *d. Educ:* Gwendraeth Grammar Sch.; Cardiff Univ. BSc Econ (Hons) Politics and Economics. Market Research Officer, Ina Needle Bearings Ltd, Llanelli, 1966–67; Economist Section, Wales Gas Bd, 1967–69; Public Relations Officer, Labour Party in Wales, March 1969–June 1970; West Glamorgan County Council: Dir of Res., 1974–77; Asst Educn Officer, Develt Forward Planning, 1977–92. Advr/Assessor, Investors in People, 1999–2007; External Assessor: Performance Mgt of Headteachers, 2000–06; for EFQM and Lexcel standards, 2003–06; Best Value Assessor, Audit Commn, 2003–05. Vice-Pres., Dist Council Assoc., 1974; Mem., Council of European Municipalities, 1975–77; first Chm., Welsh Council of European Movt, 1995–97. Broadcaster and television interviewer, S4C, 1993–95. MP (Lab) Carmarthen, 1970–Oct. 1974; Member: House of Commons Expenditure Cttee, 1972–74; Council of Europe and WEU, 1974; PPS to Home Sec., 1974. Pres., Nat. Eisteddfod of Wales, 1974. Co-ordinator, Wales in Europe campaign, 1975; Sponsor, Wales Lab and TU Cttee for Europe, 1975; joined SDP, May 1981; contested: (SDP) Gower, Sept. 1982; (SDP/Alliance) Carmarthen, 1987; (Lib Dem) Hereford, 1992; (Ind) Mid and W Wales, Nat. Assembly for Wales, 2007. Chairman: SDP Council for Wales, 1982–85, 1987–88; Alliance Cttee for Wales, 1983–88; Interim Chm., Welsh Soc & Lib Dem Exec., 1988; Member: Council for Social Democracy, 1982–88; SDP Nat. Cttee, 1982–85; SDP Orgn Cttee, 1987–88; Lib Dem Federal Exec., 1988–90; Vice Chm., Lib Dem Policy Cttee, 1988–89; rejoined Labour Party, 1997. *Publications:* booklets: The Record Put Straight, 1973; SDP and the Alliance in Wales 1981–1986, 1986; SLD Golden Opportunities, 1988; A Movement in Crisis, 1989. *Recreation:* sport (played Rugby for both 1st and 2nd class teams). *Address:* 180 West Street, Gorseinon, Swansea SA4 4AQ.

JONES, Sir Harry (George), Kt 2000; CBE 1995; Member (Lab), Newport County Borough Council, since 1995 (Leader of Council, 1995–2003); *b* 29 April 1927; *s* of Edward and Alice Jones; *m* 1956, Hazel Kembrey; three *s. Educ:* St Woolos Sch.; Newport Tech. Coll. Officer, Merchant Navy, 1948. Apprentice engr, 1943; worked in aluminium ind., 1970s. Member (Lab), Newport DC, 1973–96 (Shadow Mem., 1973–74; Leader of Council, 1987–96; Mayor, 1990–91). Leader, Welsh LGA, 1986–; Vice-Chm., LGA, 1995–; Chm., Local Govt Mgt Bd, 1994. Mem., Welsh NEC, 1990–, and Nat. Policy Forum, 1997–, Labour Party. Hon. Mem. Council, NSPCC, 1993–; Patron, Prince's Trust, 1995–; Trustee, Firebrake Wales, 2005–. Freeman, Newport City and County, 2003. Hon. Mem., RSA, 2000. Hon. Fellow, UCW, Newport, 1999. *Recreations:* swimming, art, gardening. *Address:* 8 Beaufort Place, Newport, S Wales NP19 7NB. *T:* (01633) 769538, (office) (01633) 232121.

JONES, Helen Mary; MP (Lab) Warrington North, since 1997; *b* 24 Dec. 1954; *d* of late Robert Edward Jones and of Mary Scanlan; *m* 1988, Michael Vobe; one *s. Educ:* Ursuline Convent, Chester; UCL; Chester Coll.; Univ. of Liverpool; Manchester Metropolitan Univ. BA, PGCE, MEd, CPE, LSF. Teacher of English; Develt Officer, Mind; Justice and Peace Officer, Liverpool; Solicitor. Contested (Lab): Shropshire N, 1983; Lancashire Central, EP elecn, 1984; Ellesmere Port and Neston, 1987. An Asst Govt Whip, 2008–09; Vice-Chamberlain of HM Household, 2009–10. Chm., Petitions Select Cttee, 2015–. *Address:* House of Commons, SW1A 0AA; 67 Bewsey Street, Warrington, Cheshire WA2 7JQ.

JONES, Helen Mary; Chief Executive, Youth Cymru, since 2011; public affairs consultant, since 2011; *b* 29 June 1960; *d* of late John Mervyn Jones and Daphne Lyle Stuart; one *d. Educ:* Colchester County High Sch. for Girls, Essex; Llanfair Caereinion High Sch.; UCW Aberystwyth (BA Hist.). Special Educn Teacher, Gwent, 1982–87; Orgnr for Wales, ActionAid, 1987–91; various positions in youth, community and social work, 1991–96; Sen. Develt Manager (Dep. Dir), EOC, Wales, 1996–99. Former Mem., Nat. Assembly Adv. Gp. National Assembly for Wales: Mem. (Plaid Cymru) Llanelli, 1999–2003 and 2007–11, Mid and W Wales, 2003–07; Plaid Cymru spokesman on educn and equality, 2002–03, on the environment, planning and countryside, 2003–05, on educn, 2005–07, on health and social services, 2007–11; Chair, Children and Young People's Cttee, 2007–11. Contested (Plaid Cymru): Islwyn, 1992; Montgomery, 1997; Llanelli, Nat. Assembly for Wales, 2011. Chair, Plaid Cymru, 2011–13. Mem. Bd, Ministerial Intervention Pembrokeshire, Welsh Govt, 2011–13. *Address:* Youth Cymru, Unit D, Upper Boat Business Centre, Treforest, Rhondda Cynon Taf CF37 5BP.

JONES, (Henry) John (Franklin); writer; *b* 6 May 1924; *s* of late Lt-Col James Walker Jones, DSO, IMS, and Doris Marjorie (*née* Franklin); *m* 1949, Jean Verity Robinson (*d* 2012); one *s* one *d. Educ:* Blundell's Sch.; Colombo Public Library; Merton Coll., Oxford. Served War, Royal Navy: Ordinary Seaman, 1943; Intell. Staff, Eastern Fleet, 1944. Merton Coll., Oxford: Harmsworth Sen. Scholar, 1948; Fellow and Tutor in Jurisprudence, 1949; Univ. Sen. Lectr, 1956; Fellow and Tutor in Eng. Lit., 1962; Prof. of Poetry, Univ. of Oxford, 1979–84. Dill Meml Lectr, QUB, 1983. Football Correspondent, The Observer, 1956–59. TV appearances include The Modern World, 1988. *Publications:* The Egotistical Sublime, 1954, 5th edn 1978; (contrib.) The British Imagination, 1961; On Aristotle and Greek Tragedy, 1962, 5th edn 1980; (contrib.) Dickens and the Twentieth Century, 1962; (ed) H. W. Garrod, The Study of Good Letters, 1963; John Keats's Dream of Truth, 1969, 2nd edn 1980; (contrib.) The Morality of Art, 1969; The Same God, 1971; Dostoevsky, 1983, 3rd edn 2002; Shakespeare at Work, 1995, 3rd edn 2002. *Address:* Garden Flat, 41 Buckland Crescent, NW3 5DJ. *T:* (020) 7586 1808; Yellands, Brisworthy, Shaugh Prior, Plympton, Devon PL7 5EL. *T:* (01752) 839310.

JONES, Sir Hugh; *see* Hugh-Jones, Sir W. N.

JONES, His Honour Hugh Duncan Hitchings, DL; a Circuit Judge, 1991–2004; a Deputy Circuit Judge, 2004–12; *b* 25 May 1937; *s* of Norman Everard Jones and Ann Jones (*née* Hitchings); *m* 1966, Helen Margaret Payne; three *d. Educ:* Mountain Ash Grammar School (State Scholarship); University College London (LLB). Admitted Solicitor, 1961; Registrar, Cardiff County Court and Dist Registrar of the High Court, Cardiff Dist Registry, 1978; a Recorder, 1988–91; Designated Family Judge, 1996–2004. Mem., County Court Rules Cttee, 1994–97. Vice-Pres., Disciplinary Tribunal, Church in Wales, 1996–2004. DL Mid

Glamorgan, 2007. *Recreations:* cricket, gardening, holidays in France. *Address:* The Cottage, Cwmpennar, Mountain Ash, Mid Glamorgan CF45 4DB. *Clubs:* MCC; Cardiff and County; Mountain Ash Golf.

JONES, Ven. Hughie; *see* Jones, Ven. T. H.

JONES, Huw; *see* Jones, David H.

JONES, Rev. Huw; *see* Jones, Rev. David H.

JONES, Hywel Ceri, CMG 1999; Chairman of Board, Wales Governance Centre, University of Cardiff, 2012–15; *b* 22 April 1937; *m* 1967, Morwenna Armstrong; one *s* one *d. Educ:* UCW, Aberystwyth (BA French and Classics, DipEd; Hon. Fellow, 1990). Admin. appts, Sussex Univ., 1962–73; joined EC, 1973; Head, Dept for Educn and Youth Policies, 1973–79; Dir for Educn, Vocational Trng and Youth Policy, 1979–88; Dir, Task Force for Human Resources, Educn, Trng and Youth, 1989–93; Acting Dir-Gen., 1993–95, Dep. Dir-Gen., 1995–98, Employment, Social Policy and Indust. Relns. Vis. Fellow in Educn and Contemp. European Studies, Sussex Univ., 1973–80. Eur. Advr to Sec. of State for Wales, 1998–99. Chm., Governing Bd, European Policy Centre, Brussels, 2000–07; Dir, Network of European Foundns, 2004–09; Governor: Eur. Cultural Foundn, Amsterdam, 1999–2007; Federal Trust for Educn and Research, 2004–; Eur. Funding Ambassador to Welsh Govt, 2014–. Board Member: Franco-British Council, 2004–10; Supervisory Bd, ECORYS Gp, 2006–14. Trustee: Tomorrow's Wales, 2008–; Equal Rights Trust, 2011–; Nat. Mus. of Wales, 2014–. Hon. Fellow: NE Wales Inst. of Higher Educn, 1992; Swansea, 1992; Aberystwyth, 1993; Glamorgan, 1994; Westminster, 1994; Trinity Univ. Coll., Carmarthen, 2008. DUniv: Sussex, 1991; Leuven, 1992; Open, 2000; Free Univ. Brussels, 2002; Univ. of Wales, 2013; Hon. LLD NCEA, Ireland, 1992. Gold Medal, Republic of Italy, 1987. *Recreations:* Rugby, cricket, snooker, theatre, travel, golf. *Address:* 38 Plymouth Road, Penarth CF64 3DH. *Clubs:* Reform; Fondation Universitaire (Brussels); Glamorganshire Golf.

JONES, Hywel Francis; Commissioner for Local Administration in Wales, 1985–91; *b* 28 Dec. 1928; *s* of late Brynmor and Beatrice Jones, Morriston, Swansea; *m* 1959, Marian Rosser Craven; one *d. Educ:* Bishop Gore Grammar School, Swansea; St John's College, Cambridge (BA 1949, MA 1953). IPFA 1953. Borough Treasurer's Dept, Swansea, 1949–56; Nat. Service, RAPC, 1953–55; Dep. County Treasurer, Breconshire, 1956–59; Asst County Treasurer, Carmarthenshire, 1959–66; Borough Treasurer, Port Talbot, 1966–75; Sec., Commn for Local Administration in Wales, 1975–85. Mem., Public Works Loan Board, 1971–75; Financial Adviser, AMC, 1972–74. Mem., Lord Chancellor's Adv. Cttee for West Glamorgan, 1990–97. Treasurer, Royal National Eisteddfod of Wales, 1975–95; Druid Mem., Gorsedd of Bards, 1977 (Treasurer, 1992–2007). *Recreations:* music, reading, gardening. *Address:* Godre'r Rhiw, 1 Lon Heulog, Baglan, Port Talbot, West Glam SA12 8SY. *T:* (01639) 813822.

JONES, Ian; *see* Jones, C. I. McM.

JONES, Ian; Chief Executive Officer, S4C, since 2012; *b* Swansea, 14 Jan. 1959; *s* of Lyle Jones and Margaret Jones; two *s. Educ:* Ysgol Gyfun Ystalyfera; University Coll. of Wales, Aberystwyth (BSc Econ.). Commng Exec., S4C, 1982–85; Unit Manager, Entertainment, ITV, 1986–87; Ind. Prod., 1987–89; Dir Business and S4C Internat., 1990–96; Dir, Internat., STV, 1997–99; Chief Operating Officer, ITEL, 2000; Dep. Man. Dir, Internat., Granada, 2000–04; Pres., Internat., National Geographic TV, 2004–07; Man. Dir, Target, 2007–09; Man. Dir, Content Distribution and Commercial Develt, A&E TV Networks Internat., 2010–11. *Recreation:* all forms of sport. *Address:* S4C, Park Ty Glas, Llanishen, Cardiff CF14 5DU. *T:* (029) 2074 1400. *E:* ian.jones@s4c.co.uk.

JONES, Ian Michael; Director, Office of Manpower Economics, 2007–10; *b* 5 Sept. 1949; *s* of Derek and Jean Jones; *m* 1976, Vivien Hepworth; two *s. Educ:* St Bartholomew's Grammar Sch., Newbury; Fitzwilliam Coll., Cambridge (BA Econs and Politics 1972). Home Office, 1972–83; DTI, 1983–85, Grade 5, 1985; Dept of Employment, 1985–89; Sec., BOTB, 1989–90; Department of Trade and Industry, 1989–2000: Regl Dir, SE Reg., 1990–94; Leader, London City Action Team, 1992–94; Grade 3, 1994; Head, Textiles and Retail Div., 1994–96; Head, Post, Retail and Textiles Directorate, 1996; Chief Exec., Employment Tribunals Service, 1997–2000; Dir, Regl Gp, British Trade Internat., 2000–01; Dep. Chief Exec., British Trade Internat., subseq. UK Trade and Investment, 2001–04; Dir, Efficiency Prog., 2004–05, Ops Directorate, 2005–07, DTI. Chm., RH7 History Gp, 2012–; Director: Lingfield and Dormansland Community Centre 2014–; Pennies from Heaven Distribn, 2015–. Trustee, William Buckwell Almshouses, 2011–. *Recreation:* cricket. *T:* (01342) 832907. *E:* ian@cyderbarn.com.

JONES, Rt Rev. Dr Idris; National Spiritual Director, Anglican Cursillo UK, since 2011; Director, Scottish Episcopal Church, since 2014; Bishop of Glasgow and Galloway, 1998–2009; Primus of the Episcopal Church in Scotland, 2006–09; *b* 2 April 1943; *s* of Edward Eric Jones and Alice Gertrude (*née* Burgess); *m* 1973, Alison Margaret Williams; two *s. Educ:* St David's Coll., Lampeter, Univ. of Wales (BA; Hon. Fellow 2007); Univ. of Edinburgh (LTh); NY Theol Seminary (DMin 1987); Dip. Person Centred Therapy 1994. Curate, St Mary, Stafford, 1967–70; Precentor, Dundee Cathedral, 1970–73; Team Vicar, St Hugh, Gosforth, 1973–80; Chaplain, St Nicholas Hosp. (Teaching), 1975–80; Rector, Montrose with Inverbervie, 1980–89; Canon, St Paul's Cathedral, Dundee, 1984–92; Anglican Chaplain, Dundee Univ. and Priest-in-Charge, Invergowrie, 1989–92; Team Rector, Ayr, Girvan, Maybole, 1992–98; Dir, Pastoral Studies, Theol Inst., Edinburgh, 1995–98. Lay Psychotherapist: Dundee, 1990–92; Ayr, 1995–98. Dir, Merchants House of Glasgow, 2010–; Collector, Trades House of Glasgow, 2012–13; Convenor, Incorporated Trades of Glasgow, 2014–15. Gov., Hutcheson's Educnl Trust, 2002–09; Patron, Hutcheson's Hosp., Glasgow, 2002–09. Mem., Incorpn of Skinners & Glovers of Glasgow, 1999–. Paul Harris Fellow, Rotary Internat., 2011. *Recreations:* walking, golf, music. *Address:* 27 Donald Wynd, The Rise, Largs KA30 8TH.

JONES, Ieuan Wyn; Director, Menai Science Park, since 2013; *b* 22 May 1949; *s* of late John Jones and of Mair Elizabeth Jones; *m* 1974, Eirian Llwyd (*d* 2014); two *s* one *d. Educ:* Pontardawe Grammar School; Ysgol-y-Berwyn, Y Bala, Gwynedd; Liverpool Polytechnic. LLB Hons. Qualified Solicitor, 1973; Partner in practice, 1974–87. Plaid Cymru: National Vice-Chm., 1975–79; National Chm., 1980–82, 1990–92; Pres., 2000–03; Leader, Assembly Gp, 2003–12. MP (Plaid Cymru) Ynys Môn, 1987–2001. Mem. Select Committee: on Welsh Affairs, 1990–92, 1997–2001; on Agriculture, 1992–97. Contested (Plaid Cymru) Ynys Môn (Anglesey), 1983. Mem. (Plaid Cymru) Ynys Môn, Nat. Assembly for Wales, 1999–2013. Dep. First Minister and Minister for the Economy and Transport, Nat. Assembly for Wales, 2007–11. Leader, Plaid Cymru, 2000–12. *Publications:* Europe: the challenge for Wales, 1996; Thomas Gee (biog.), 1998. *Recreations:* sport, local history. *Address:* Menai Science Park, Management Centre, Bangor University, College Road, Bangor, Gwynedd LL57 2DG. *T:* (01248) 365917. *E:* i.w.jones@bangor.ac.uk.

JONES, Iona Elisabeth Lois, (Mrs Timothy Wilson); Chief Executive, S4C, 2005–10; *b* 15 Jan. 1964; *d* of John Stuart Roberts and Verina Roberts (*née* Gravelle); *m* 1st, 1990, Wynford Jones (marr. diss. 2008); one *s* two *d*; 2nd, 2013, Timothy Wilson. *Educ:* Ysgol Gyfun Llanhari; Univ. of Exeter (BA Hons Econ. and Social Hist.); Cardiff Univ. (Postgrad. Dip. Journalism). Journalist, BBC Wales, 1986–95; Director, Corporate Affairs: S4C, 1995–2000; HTV Gp, 2000–03; Dir of Progs, S4C, 2003–05.

JONES, Jacqui; *see* Lait, J.

JONES, Prof. James Eirug Thomas, FRCPath, FRCVS; Courtauld Professor of Animal Health, Royal Veterinary College, University of London, 1984–93, now Emeritus Professor; *b* 14 June 1927; *s* of David John and Mary Elizabeth Jones; *m* 1953, Marion Roberts (*d* 2001); one *s* one *d. Educ:* Ystalyfera County Sch.; Royal Vet. Coll. PhD 1973. MRCVS 1950, FRCVS 1994; FRCPath, 1984. Gen. vet. practice, 1950–53; vet. officer, Birmingham Corp., 1953–54; Lectr in Path., RVC, 1954–58; Res. Officer, Animal Health Trust, 1958–63; Fulbright Scholar, Univ. of Pennsylvania, 1963–64; vis. worker, 1964, Sen. Lectr, 1967, Reader in Animal Health, 1975–84, RVC. J. T. Edwards Meml Medal, RCVS, 1985; Bledisloe Vet. Award, RASE, 1994. *Publications:* papers in sci. jls on infectious diseases of farm animals. *Recreations:* travel, Celtic history, National Portrait Gallery. *Address:* 19 West Park, SE9 4RZ. *T:* (020) 8299 7142.

JONES, (James) Roger; Head of Antiques Department, since 1994, and Director, since 1996, Sibyl Colefax & John Fowler; *b* 30 May 1952; *s* of late Albert James Jones and Hilda Vera Jones (*née* Evans); civil partnership 2007, Gregory John Ellis Chambers. *Educ:* Shrewsbury; St Catharine's Coll., Cambridge (Sen. Schol.; Double First, History and Law Triposes; MA). Called to the Bar, Middle Temple, 1974 (Lloyd Jacob Meml Exhibnr; Astbury Schol.); practised Oxford and Midland Circuit, 1975–83. Joined Office of Parly Counsel, 1983; with Law Commn, 1988–91; Dep. Parly Counsel, 1991–94. *Recreation:* walking the dog. *Address:* Sibyl Colefax & John Fowler, 39 Brook Street, W1K 4JE.

JONES, Rt Rev. James Stuart; Bishop of Liverpool, 1998–2013; Hon. Assistant Bishop in the Diocese of York, since 2014; *b* 18 Aug. 1948; *s* of Major James Stuart Anthony Jones and Helen Jones; *m* 1980, Sarah Caroline Rosalind Marrow; three *d. Educ:* Duke of York's Royal Mil. Sch., Dover; Exeter Univ. (BA Hons Theol.); Wycliffe Hall, Oxford. Teacher, Sevenoaks Sch., 1970–74; Producer, Scripture Union, 1975–81; ordained deacon, 1982, priest, 1983; Curate, Christ Church, Clifton, 1982–90; Vicar, Emmanuel Church, S Croydon, 1990–94; Bishop Suffragan of Hull, 1994–98; Bishop to HM Prisons, 2007–13. Took his seat in H of L, 2003. Visitor, St Peter's Coll., Oxford, 2007–13. Chairman: Hillsborough Ind. Panel, 2009–12; Ind. Panel on Future of Forestry, 2011–12; Adv. Bd on Corporate Social Responsibility, Waitrose, 2013–; Gosport Ind. Panel, 2013–. Advr to Home Sec. on Hillsborough, 2013–. Vice Pres., TCPA, 2008–. Fellow: Soc. of the Envmt, 2014; Inst. of Chartered Foresters, 2014. Ambassador, WWF, 2006–14 (Fellow, 2014–). Hon. Fellow, Liverpool John Moores, 2013. Hon. DD Hull, 1999; Hon. DLitt Lincolnshire and Humberside, 2001; Hon PhD: Liverpool Hope, 2009; Liverpool, 2013; Exeter, 2013; Gloucester, 2013. *Publications:* Finding God, 1987; Why do people suffer?, 1993; The Power and the Glory, 1994; A Faith that touches the World, 1994; People of the Blessing, 1999; The Moral Leader, 2002; Jesus and the Earth, 2003; With My Whole Heart, 2012. *Address:* Mount Pleasant Cottage, Burythorpe, Malton YO17 9LJ. *T:* (01653) 658325.

JONES, Janet Ann L.; *see* Lewis-Jones.

JONES, Jennifer, (Gemma); actress; *b* 4 Dec. 1942; *d* of late Griffith Jones and Irene Jones (*née* Isaac); one *s* by Sebastian Graham Jones. *Educ:* Royal Acad. of Dramatic Art (Gold Medal). *Theatre* includes: Hamlet, Birmingham Rep., 1968; Getting On, Queen's, 1972; A Streetcar Named Desire, Nottingham Playhouse, 1978; Unfinished Business, 1994; The Master Builder, Haymarket, 1995; Cat on a Hot Tin Roof, Lyric, 2001; And Then There Were None, Gielgud, 2005; On Religion, Soho Th., 2006; The Family Reunion, Donmar Warehouse, 2008; Richard III, Old Vic, 2011; The Turn of the Screw, Almeida, 2013; The Rivals, Arcola, 2014; Royal Shakespeare Co.: Julius Caesar, Twelfth Night, Henry VIII, The Winter's Tale; A Midsummer Night's Dream, 1970; *films* include: The Devils, 1971; Sense and Sensibility, 1995; Wilde, 1997; The Theory of Flight, 1998; The Winslow Boy, 1999; Captain Jack, 1999; Cotton Mary, 1999; Bridget Jones's Diary, 2001; Harry Potter and the Chamber of Secrets, 2002; Shanghai Knights, 2003; Kiss of Life, 2003; Bridget Jones: The Edge of Reason, 2004; Harry Potter and the Half-Blood Prince, 2009; You Will Meet a Tall Dark Stranger, 2011; Harry Potter and the Deathly Hallows, Pt 2, 2011; *television* includes series: The Duchess of Duke Street, 1976; Chelworth, 1989; Devices and Desires, 1991; The Phoenix and the Carpet, 1997; Spooks, 2007, 2008; The Lady Vanishes, 2013; Marvellous, 2014 (Best Supporting Actress, BAFTA, 2015). *Recreation:* hill-walking. *Address:* c/o Conway van Gelder Grant Ltd, 8–12 Broadwick Street, W1F 8HW. *T:* (020) 7287 0077, *Fax:* (020) 7287 1940.

JONES, Jennifer Grace; international election adviser and observer, 2003–08; *b* 8 Feb. 1948; *d* of Ernest Bew and Ivy Blake; *m* 1974, John Alun Charles Jones; one *s. Educ:* Bradford Univ. (BA Hons, CQSW 1972); Birmingham Univ. (MSocSc 1987); Wolverhampton Univ. (ITD). Legal Sec., ICI, 1968–69; Social Worker, Oxford CC, 1972–74; Housing Advr, Oxford Housing Aid Centre and Birmingham Housing Dept, 1974–77; Trng Officer, Birmingham Housing Co-op., 1980–85; Researcher, Wolverhampton Council, 1985–87; Business Advr, Black Country CDA, 1987–97. Trng Manager and Co. Dir, 1995–97. Mem. (Lab) Wolverhampton BC, 1991–97. MP (Lab) Wolverhampton SW, 1997–2001. Election advr, OSCE/UN Mission in Kosovo, 2002–03. Tutor, Open Univ., 2003–. *Recreations:* swimming, gardening, keeping cats, writing.

JONES, Joanne; *see* Elvin, J.

JONES, John; *see* Jones, H. J. F.

JONES, John Elfed, CBE 1987; DL; CEng, FIET; Chairman: International Greetings plc, 1996–2006; Eclectica Ltd, since 2007; *b* 19 March 1933; *s* of Urien Maelgwyn Jones and Mary Jones; *m* 1957, Mary Sheila (*née* Rosser); two *d. Educ:* Blaenau Ffestiniog Grammar Sch.; Denbighshire Technical Coll., Wrexham; Heriot-Watt Coll., Edinburgh. Student apprentice, 1949–53, graduate trainee, 1953–55, CEGB; National Service, RAF, 1955–57 (FO); Rock Climbing Instr, Outward Bound Sch., Aberdyfi, 1957; Technical Engr with CEGB, 1957–59; Dep. Project Manager, Rheidol Hydro-Electric Project, 1959–61; Sen. Elec. Engr, Trawsfynydd Nuclear Power Station, 1961–63; Deputy Manager: Mid Wales Gp of Power Stations, 1963–67; Connah's Quay Power Station, 1967–69; Anglesey Aluminium Metal Ltd: Engrg Manager, 1969–73; Production Manager, 1973–76; Admin. Director, 1976–77; Dep. Man. Dir, 1977–79; Industrial Dir, Welsh Office (Under Sec. rank), 1979–82. Chairman: Welsh Water Authy, later Welsh Water plc, 1982–93; British Water International Ltd, 1983–88. Dep. Chm., HTV Gp, 1991–96; Director: HTV Cymru/Wales Ltd, 1990–96 (Chm., 1992–96); W Midlands and Wales Regl Adv. Bd, National Westminster Bank, 1990–91; BMSS plc, 1993–96; Cwmni Rheilffordd Beddgelert Cyf., 1994–98; Cwmni Rheilffordd Caernarfon Cyf., 1994–99; Chairman: Menter Mantis Cyf., 1999–2004; Awen Cymru Ltd, 2009–12. Chm. Adv. Gp, Nat. Assembly of Wales, 1997–99. Treasurer, Urdd Gobaith Cymru, 1964–67; Chm., Welsh Language Bd, 1988–93; Mem., Royal National Eisteddfod of Wales, 1981–90; Member: BBC Broadcasting Council for Wales, 1979–83; Council, Food from Britain, 1985–87; Prince of Wales Cttee, 1986–90. Mem., British/Irish Encounter, 2000–05. Pres., Univ. of Wales, Lampeter, 1992–98; Member: Court and Council: UCNW, Bangor, 1978–89; Nat. Library of Wales, 1983–88; Coleg Harlech, 1983–88; Court, Univ. Coll., Aberystwyth, 1984–93. Mem., Civic Trust for Wales, 1982–88; President: CPRW, 1995–2001; Cwlwm Busnes Caerdydd a'r Cylch, 2009–; Cantorian Coety, 2009–. FRSA 1984; CCMI (CBIM 1990). DL Mid Glam, 1989. Hon. Fellow: Univ. of Wales, Aberystwyth, 1990; NE Wales Inst., 1996; Trinity St Davids Univ. (Trinity Univ. Coll., 2007); Glyndwr Univ., 2009. Hon. Dr Glamorgan, 1997; Hon. LLD Wales, 2000.

Hon. Col, Commonwealth of Kentucky, 1976. *Recreations:* fishing for salmon and trout, reading, attending Eisteddfodau, golf. *Address:* Ty Mawr, Coity, Bridgend, Mid Glamorgan CF35 6BN.

JONES, Sir John (Francis), Kt 2003; Educational Consultant and Managing Director, JFJ Training Ltd; *b* 20 Nov. 1950; *s* of late Thomas Jones and of Joan Jones (now Hogg); two *s* one *d*; partner, Rachel Glazebrook. *Educ:* Univ. of Wales, Bangor (BA Hons French and Latin; PGCE); Liverpool Univ. (MEd). Teacher, 1974–89; Res. Fellow, Lancaster Univ., 1988–89; Headteacher: Rivington High Sch., St Helens, 1989–91; Ruffwood Sch., Knowsley, 1991–99; Maghull High Sch., Sefton, 1999–2004. Member: Policy Action Team, Social Exclusion Unit, 1998–99; Task Gp, Truancy and Exclusion in Cities, DFES, 1998–2002; Leadership Develt Unit, Manchester Univ., DFES and Nat. Coll. for Sch. Leadership, 2002–03. Non-exec. Dir, Aintree Hosps Trust, 1994–98. Chm., Everton in the Community, 2010–. *Recreations:* reading, keeping fit, golf, playing guitar, theatre, fell-walking. *Address:* Waterside House, 135A The Green, Worsley, Manchester M28 2PA. *E:* jfjtraining@hotmail.com.

JONES, John Francis A.; *see* Avery Jones.

JONES, Prof. (John) Gareth, MD; FRCP; FRCA; Professor of Anaesthesia, Cambridge University, 1990–99; *b* 20 Aug. 1936; *s* of late Dr John and Catherine Jones; *m* 1964, Susan Price; three *d*. *Educ:* Canton High Sch., Cardiff; Welsh Nat. Sch. of Medicine, Univ. of Wales (MB BCh 1960); MD Birmingham, 1967. MRCP 1963, FRCP 1983; FRCA (FFARCS 1970). Res. Fellow, Dept of Medicine, 1964–68, Lectr, Anaesthesia, 1968–70, Univ. of Birmingham; North Sen. Fellow, Cardiovascular Res. Inst., Univ. of California, San Francisco, 1970–74; Scientific Staff, MRC, Northwick Park, 1974–86; Prof. of Anaesthesia, Univ. of Leeds, 1986–91. Vis. Scientist, Chest Service, Univ. of California, San Francisco, 1977–78; Consultant, Baragwanath Hosp., Soweto, South Africa, 1986. Royal College of Anaesthetists: Mem. Council, 1996–99; Ed., Bulletin, 1997–99. Ed., Cardiff Med. Grads Jl, 1999–2001. Ext. Examr, Center for Sensory-Motor Interaction, Aalborg Univ., Denmark, 2010–11. Member: York Model Engrg Soc., 1999–2009; Crusoe Soc., 2003–; Yorks Philosophical Soc., 2005–12 (Mem. Council, 2006–09); Friends of York Minster, 2012–14. Hon. FANZCA 1992. *Publications:* Effects of Anaesthesia and Surgery on Pulmonary Mechanisms, 1984; (jtly) Aspects of Recovery from Anaesthesia, 1987; Depth of Anaesthesia, 1989, 2nd edn 1993; (jtly) The Upper Airway, 1995; Thomas Graham Brown (1882–1965): behind the scenes at the Cardiff Institute of Physiology, 2011; (jtly) The Brenva Feud: Graham Brown vs Frank Smythe, 2014; res. papers on hypoxaemia at altitude, oxygen delivery in neonates, the effect of gen. anaesthetics on cognitive function, the effect of fatigue and sedation on saccadic eye movements, and computer methods for non-invasive measurement of oxygen exchange in infants. *Recreations:* writing, aeroplanes, gyrocopters, model engineering (1/3 scale replica Bugatti 35). *Address:* Woodlands, Rufforth, York YO23 2QF. *Clubs:* Royal Society of Medicine; Sherburn Aero, York Gliding.

JONES, John Knighton C.; *see* Chadwick-Jones.

JONES, John Lloyd, OBE 1995; DL; farmer; Examining Inspector for Nationally Significant Infrastructure Projects, Planning Inspectorate (formerly Infrastructure Planning Commission), since 2010; *b* 10 Nov. 1949; *s* of late Arthur Egryn Jones and Elizabeth Jones (*née* Owen); *m* 1972, Anne Tudor Lewis; three *d*. *Educ:* Tywyn Primary Sch.; Llandovery Coll. Chairman: NFU Wales, 1993–98; NFU Parly Land Use and Envmt Cttee, England and Wales, 1998–2000. Chairman: Welsh Adv. Cttee, Forestry Commn, 1994–2000; Countryside Council for Wales, 2000–10; Member: Bd, Inst. of Grassland and Envmtl Res., 2002–08; Rural Economy and Land Use Prog. Adv. Cttee, 2004–12; Welsh Nat. Cttee, Forestry Commn, 2009–13; Ext. Adv. Bd, Inst. of Biol, Envmtl and Rural Scis, 2009–; Bd, Cambrian Mountains Initiative, 2010–; Welsh Designated Landscapes Review Panel, 2014–15. Mem. Council, National Trust, 2009–15. Pres., Snowdonia Soc., 2013–. Lay Rep. for Disciplinary Hearings, Councils of Inns of Court, 2005–07. Mem., Gorsedd of Bards, 2002. DL Gwynedd, 2013. FRSA 1995; ARAgS 2009. Hon. Fellow, Univ. of Wales, Bangor, 2003. *Recreations:* woodland creation, gardening. *Address:* Hendy, Tywyn, Gwynedd LL36 9RU. *T:* (01654) 710457.

JONES, (John) Lynton; Chairman, Bourse Consult LLP, 2002–13, now Emeritus; *b* Prestatyn, N Wales, 12 Nov. 1944; *s* of Frank and Eileen Jones; *m* 1968, Judith Mary Coop; one *s* two *d*. *Educ:* Rhyl Grammar Sch.; University Coll. of Wales, Aberystwyth (BSc Econ 1st Cl. Hons Internat. Politics). VSO, India, 1963–64; HM Diplomatic Service: Third Secretary: FCO, 1968–69; Lusaka, 1969–70; Second Secretary: Bangkok, 1970–74; SE European Dept, FCO, 1974–76; Pte Sec. to Minister of State, FCO, 1976–79; First Sec., Commercial and Financial, Paris, 1979–83; Hd of Public Affairs, London Stock Exchange, 1983–87; Man. Dir, NASDAQ Internat., 1987–92; Chief Executive: OM London Exchange, 1992–96; Internat. Petroleum Exchange, 1996–99; Chairman: Jiway Hldgs Ltd, 2000–01; Dubai Internat. Financial Exchange, 2003–05; Digiservex Ltd, 2014–. Board Member: Futures & Options Assoc., 1995–97; London Clearing House, 1996–99; Kenetics Gp Ltd, 2006–11; Aseana plc, 2007–. Trustee, Horniman Mus., 2005–13. FCSI (Fellow, Securities and Investment Inst., 2008). MInstD 1996. Freeman, City of London, 2005. *Publications:* contribs to City of London Corporation research reports and to financial pubns. *Recreations:* photography, astronomy, Darwinism, secularism and the promotion of rationality. *E:* jlj@bourse-consult.com.

JONES, John Richard; QC 2002; a Recorder, since 1999; *b* 8 Feb. 1959; *s* of Harold Jones and Barbara Jones (*née* Jerstice); *m* 2000, Heather Billam; one *s*. *Educ:* Shevington High Sch.; Upholland Grammar Sch.; Liverpool Univ. (LLB Hons). Called to the Bar, Middle Temple (Winston Churchill Scholar), 1981. Mem., Very High Cost Cases Appeals Panel, Legal Services Commn, 2009–. *Recreations:* golf, fell-walking, music. *Address:* Carmelite Chambers, 9 Carmelite Street, EC4Y 0DR. *T:* (020) 7936 6300, *Fax:* (020) 7936 6301. *E:* johnrjonesqc@carmelitechambers.co.uk; Exchange Chambers, 1 Derby Square, Liverpool L2 9XX. *T:* 0845 300 7747, *Fax:* (0151) 236 3433. *E:* johnrjonesqc@exchangechambers.co.uk. *Clubs:* Royal Lytham and St Annes Golf; Formby Golf; Hindley Hall Golf; St Andrews Golf; Phoenician Golf (Arizona, USA).

JONES, John Richard William Day; QC 2013; barrister; *b* Wimbledon, 14 June 1967; *s* of Dr Hugh F. Jones and Margaret Day Jones; *m* 2007, Dr Miša Zgonec-Rožej; two *s*. *Educ:* Mander Portman Woodward; St Edmund Hall, Oxford (Open Exhibnr; BA); City Univ. (MA Law); George Washington Univ. (LLM). Called to the Bar, Lincoln's Inn, 1992; in practice as barrister, Doughty Street Chambers. Immigration Judge (pt-time), First-tier Tribunal (Immigration and Asylum Chamber), 2003–; Legal Officer: Internat. Criminal Tribunal for the former Yugoslavia, 1995–99; Internat. Criminal Tribunal for Rwanda, 1998; Actg Principal Defender, Special Court for Sierra Leone, 2003. Dir, Orangutan Protection Foundn, 2011–. *Publications:* International Criminal Practice, 1998, 3rd edn 2003; Extradition and Mutual Legal Assistance Handbook, 2005, 2nd edn 2010. *Recreations:* orangutan conservation, squash, ragtime guitar. *Address:* Doughty Street Chambers, 53–54 Doughty Street, WC1N 2LS. *T:* (020) 7404 1313, *Fax:* (020) 7404 2283/4. *E:* J.Jones@doughtystreet.co.uk. *Club:* Frontline.

JONES, (John) Stanley, MBE 2009; Director, Curwen Studio, 1959–2012; President and Director, Curwen Print Study Centre, since 2013; *b* 10 June 1933; *s* of George White Jones and Elizabeth Jones; *m* 1961, Jennifer Frances Stone; one *s* one *d*. *Educ:* Wigan Grammar Sch.; Wigan Art Sch. (NDD); Slade Sch. of Fine Art, UCL (Dip. Fine Art). Lectr in Lithography, Slade Sch. of Fine Art, 1958–98. Pres., Printmakers' Council, 1981–96. Hon. RE 2004. Hon. DLitt Southampton, 1999. *Publications:* Lithography for Artists, 1967 (Italian edn 1981); (contrib.) Elizabeth Frink Original Prints, ed C. Wiseman, 1998; (autobiog.) Stanley Jones and the Curwen Studio, 2010; contribs to Printmaking Today, Graphion. *Recreations:* black and white photography (analogue), country walking, weather observation, appreciation of music (contemporary). *Address:* Curwen Print Study Centre, Chilford Hall, Linton, Cambs CB21 4LE. *T:* (01223) 892380, *Fax:* (01223) 893638. *E:* enquiries@curwenprintstudy.co.uk. *Club:* Double Crown.

JONES, Prof. (John) Stephen, PhD, DSc; FRS 2012; Professor of Genetics, University College London, 1992–2011, now Senior Research Fellow (Head, Department of Genetics, Evolution and Environment, 2008–10); *b* 24 March 1944; *s* of Thomas Gwilym Jones and Lydia Anne Jones; *m* 2004, Norma Percy. *Educ:* Wirral Grammar Sch.; Univ. of Edinburgh (BSc, PhD 1971, DSc 2005). Postdoctoral Fellow, Univ. of Chicago, 1969–71; Lectr in Genetics, Royal Free Hosp. Med. Sch., 1971–78; Lectr then Reader in Genetics, UCL, 1978–92; Head of Dept of Genetics and Biometry, 1989–94. Reith Lectr, 1991. Columnist, Daily Telegraph, 1992–. Trustee, British Council, 2007–13. Pres., Assoc. for Sci. Educn, 2011. FRSL 2011; FLSW 2011; Fellow, Amer. Philosophical Soc., 2011. Faraday Medal, Royal Soc., 1996; Charter Medal, Inst. of Biology, 2002; Tercentenary Medal, Linnean Soc., 2007. *Publications:* (ed) Cambridge Encyclopedia of Human Evolution, 1992; The Language of the Genes, 1993 (Science Book Prize, 1994); In the Blood, 1996; Almost Like a Whale: the Origin of Species updated, 1999; Y: The Descent of Men, 2002; The Single Helix, 2005; Coral: a Pessimist in Paradise, 2007; Darwin's Island: the Galapagos in the garden of England, 2009; The Serpent's Promise: the Bible retold as science, 2013; scientific papers in learned jls. *Recreation:* not administrating. *Address:* Department of Genetics, Evolution and Environment, University College London, Gower Street, WC1E 6BT. *T:* (020) 3108 4095.

JONES, Jonathan Arthur David; QC 2013; *b* Cardiff, 12 March 1970; *s* of Peter Wingate Jones and Mary Catherine Jones; *m* 1998, Sally Ann Tudor; three *d*. *Educ:* Bedford Sch.; Univ. of St Andrews (MA Econs); City Univ. (Dip. Law); Inns of Court Sch. of Law. Called to the Bar, Gray's Inn, 1994. *Recreations:* tennis, ski-ing, sailing, golf. *Address:* No 5 Chambers, Fountain Court, Steelhouse Lane, Birmingham B4 6DR. *T:* (0121) 606 0500. *E:* jjo@no5.com.

JONES, Jonathan D.; *see* Davies-Jones.

JONES, Jonathan Dallas George, PhD; FRS 2003; Senior Scientist, Sainsbury Laboratory, John Innes Centre, since 1988; *b* 14 July 1954; *s* of George Ronald Jones and Isabel Dallas Orr (*née* Pinkney); one *d*; *m* 1991, Caroline Dean, *qv*; one *s* one *d*. *Educ:* Univ. of Cambridge (BSc Nat. Scis 1976; PhD 1980). Post-doctoral Fellow, Harvard, 1981–82; Res. Scientist, Advanced Genetic Scis Inc., Oakland, Calif, 1983–88. Mem., EMBO, 1998. *Publications:* contribs to Cell, Science, Plant Cell, Plant Jl, Genetics, Plant Physiol., etc. *Recreations:* sailing, wind-surfing, children. *Address:* Sainsbury Laboratory, Norwich Research Park, Colney Lane, Norwich NR4 7UH. *T:* (01603) 450327.

JONES, Jonathan Guy; HM Procurator General, Treasury Solicitor and Head of Government Legal Service, since 2014; *b* 21 May 1962; *s* of Leonard Martell Jones and Margaret Eleanor Jones (*née* Jones). *Educ:* Llandovery Coll.; Univ. of Durham (BA Law 1984). Called to the Bar: Middle Temple, 1985, Bencher, 2007; NI, 2006. Legal Advr, Motor Agents Assoc., 1986–89; Legal Div., OFT, 1989–93; Dept of Transport Adv. Div., Treasury Solicitor's Dept, 1993–94; Attorney General's Chambers, Legal Secretariat to the Law Officers, 1994–98; Dep. Legal Advr, HM Treasury, 1998–2002; Legal Dir, DFES and Dir, Treasury Solicitor's Dept, 2002–04; Dir Gen., Attorney General's Office, 2004–09; Dep. Treasury Solicitor, Treasury Solicitor's Dept, 2009–12; Dir Gen., Legal, Home Office, 2012–14. *Recreation:* music. *Address:* Government Legal Department, 1 Kemble Street, WC2B 4TS.

JONES, Jonathan Owen; *b* 19 April 1954; *s* of Gwynfor Owen Jones and Dorothy Mary (*née* Davies); *m* 1989, Allison Clement; two *s* one *d*. *Educ:* Univ. of East Anglia (BSc Hons Ecology); Cardiff Univ. (PGCE). Science and biology teacher, 1977–92. MP (Lab and Co-op) Cardiff Central, 1992–2005; contested (Lab and Co-op) same seat, 2005. An Opposition Whip, 1993–97; a Lord Comr of HM Treasury (Govt Whip), 1997–98; Parly Under-Sec. of State, Welsh Office, 1998–99. A Forestry Comr, 2007. *Recreations:* cooking, walking, watching Rugby, my family, caravanning. *Address:* 19 Ty Draw Road, Roath, Cardiff CF23 5HB. *Club:* Roath Labour.

JONES, Julia P.; *see* Peyton-Jones.

JONES, Julie, CBE 2010 (OBE 2003); Chief Executive, Social Care Institute for Excellence, 2007–12; *b* 17 March 1948; *d* of Peter and Kitty Clark; *m* 1970, Alan Richard Watson Jones; two *d*. *Educ:* Benenden C of E Primary Sch.; Tunbridge Wells Grammar Sch. for Girls; University Coll., Cardiff (BSc Econ. Hons Sociology 1969); Brunel Univ. (MA Public and Soc. Admin 1980). Dep. Hd, Soc. Services Planning Unit, Camden, 1972–76; Westminster City Council: Principal Res. and Planning Officer for Soc. Services, 1982–85; Dep. Dir, 1992–96, Dir, 1996–2005, Soc. Services; Dep. Chief Exec., 2000–07; Dir, Children and Community Services, 2005–07. Non-exec. Dir, Look Ahead Housing and Care, 2012–. Pres., Assoc. of Dirs of Social Services, 2005–06 (Vice Pres., 2004–05; Chm., London Assoc., 2001–04). Mem., Governance Bd, Centre for Workforce Intelligence, 2012–13. Lay Mem. Council, Inst. of Educn, 2007– (Vice Chair, Council and Chair, Audit Cttee, 2013–14); Comr, Future of Social Services in Wales, 2009–. Mem., C of E Nat. Safeguarding Panel, 2014–. Mem. Council, Queen's Coll., London, 1993–98. Trustee, Sir Simon Milton Foundn, 2013–. FRSA 2006; FCGI 2009 (Mem., Fellowship Adv. Cttee, 2013–). *Recreations:* reading, travel, opera, theatre, family and friends (3 granddaughters), Rugby Union. *Address:* 18 The Grove, N3 1QL. *T:* (020) 8349 1359. *E:* juliejonesuk@hotmail.co.uk.

JONES, Karen Elisabeth Dind, (Mrs Hamish Easton), CBE 2006; company director; Co-Founder, Food and Fuel Ltd, since 2006; *b* Billinge, 29 July 1956; *d* of Eric and Margaret Jones; *m* 1990, Hamish Easton; one *s* two *d*. *Educ:* Univ. of E Anglia (BA 1st Cl. English and American Lit.); Wellesley Coll., Mass. Account planner, Boase Massimi Pollitt, 1980–81; Ops Dir, Theme Hldgs plc, 1981–88; Man. Dir and Co-Founder, Pelican Gp plc, 1989–97; Punch Group Ltd: CEO, Punch Retail, 2000–02; Chief Exec., Spirit Gp Ltd, 2002–06. Chm., Hawksmoor, 2013–; non-executive Director: EMAP, 1997–2006; Gondola Hldgs plc, 2005–07 (Chm., Remuneration Cttee); HBOS plc, 2006–08 (Chm., Remuneration Cttee, 2007–08); Virgin Active Gp, 2008–11 (Chm., Remuneration Cttee, 2009–11); ASOS plc, 2009– (Chm., Remuneration Cttee; Mem., Audit Cttee); Booker plc, 2009– (Chm., Remuneration Cttee; Mem., Audit Cttee, 2009–12); Cofra Hldg AG, 2008– (Chm., HR Cttee; Mem., Audit Cttee); Firmenich Internat. SA, 2011– (Chm., Governance and Compensation Cttee); Corbin and King Restaurants Ltd, 2012– (Chm., Remuneration Cttee). Member: Bd, RNT, 1996–2002; Bd, RNT Enterprises, 2004–; Industrial Develt Adv. Bd, DTI, 2004–10. Mem., Rebuilding Childhoods Bd, NSPCC, 2006–13 (Chm., 2007–12). Gov., Ashridge Business Sch., 2005–15. Hon. DCL E Anglia, 2013. *Recreations:* my children, food and wine, theatre, contemporary American and English literature, art. *Address:* Paddock House, 9 Spencer Park, SW18 2SX. *T:* 07768 010030. *E:* karenj@foodandfuel.co.uk. *Clubs:* Hurlingham, Groucho.

JONES, Kathryn P.; *see* Pritchard-Jones.

JONES, Very Rev. Keith Brynmor; Dean of York, 2004–12, now Emeritus; permission to officiate, Diocese of St Edmundsbury and Ipswich, since 2013; *b* 27 June 1944; *s* of John Brynmor Jones and Mary Emily Jones; *m* 1973, Viola Mary, *d* of late Henry Leigh Jenkyns; three *d*. *Educ:* Selwyn Coll., Cambridge (BA 1965; MA 1969); Cuddesdon Coll., Oxford. Ordained deacon, 1969, priest, 1970; Asst Curate, Limpsfield with Titsey, Surrey, 1969–72; Dean's Vicar, Cathedral and Abbey Church of St Alban, 1972–76; Priest-in-charge, 1976–79, Team Vicar, 1979–82, St Michael's, Boreham Wood; Vicar of St Mary-le-Tower, Ipswich, 1982–95; Rural Dean of Ipswich, 1992–95; Hon. Canon, St Edmundsbury Cathedral, 1993–95; Dean of Exeter, 1996–2004. Mem., Gen. Synod of C of E, 1999–2005. Chm., Pilgrims Assoc., 2001–08. Affiliated to Order of Carmelites, 2011. *Publications:* Adam's Dream, 2008; (with L. Hampson and R. Shephard) York Minster: a living legacy, 2008. *Recreations:* playing the piano, looking out of the window. *Address:* 7 Broughton Road, Ipswich, Suffolk IP1 3QR. *Club:* Army and Navy.

JONES, Dr Keith Howard, CB 1997; FRCP, FRCPE; Chairman, European Medicines Evaluation Agency, 2000–03 (Member, 1995–2000); Chief Executive, Medicines Control Agency, Department of Health, 1989–2002; retired; *b* 14 Oct. 1937; *s* of Arthur Leslie Jones and Miriam Emily Jones; *m* 1962, Dr Lilian, (Lynne), Pearse; three *s*. *Educ:* Welsh Nat. Sch. of Medicine, Cardiff (MB, BCh 1960; MD 1966). FFPM 1989; FRCPE 1990; FRCP 1993. Posts in clinical and academic medicine, Cardiff, Edinburgh and Cambridge, 1960–67; Chief Toxicologist, Fisons Agrochemicals, 1967–70; Head, Safety Assessment, Beecham Res. Labs, 1970–79; Exec. Dir, Medical Affairs, Merck & Co., USA, 1979–89. Adjunct Prof. of Medicine, Thomas Jefferson Med. Sch., Philadelphia, 1985–89; Vis. Prof. of Pharmacology, Sch. of Pharmacy, Univ. of London, 1995–2002. UK Representative: EC Cttee for Pharmaceutical Medical Products, 1989–95; EC Pharmaceutical Cttee, 1989–2003; Chairman: EC Scientific Cttee for Medicinal Products and Med. Devices, 1997–2000; Expert Mem., EC Scientific Steering Cttee on Consumer Health and Food Safety, 1997–2003. *Publications:* contribs to learned jls on issues of metabolic medicine, toxicology, drug develt and regulatory matters. *Recreations:* sailing, tennis. *Address:* Shelford, Headley Road, Leatherhead, Surrey KT22 8PT. *T:* (01372) 376747.

JONES, Keith O.; *see* Orrell-Jones.

JONES, Sir Kenneth Lloyd, (Sir Ken), Kt 2009; QPM 2000; consultant; Defence and Security Adviser, British Embassy, Washington DC, since 2013; *b* Welshpool, 13 June 1952; *s* of John and Joan Jones; *m* 1985, Kaye Firth; three *d*. *Educ:* Welshpool High Sch.; Univ. of Sheffield (BA Hons, MBA). Joined Sheffield and Rotherham Constabulary, 1971; served ICAC, Hong Kong, 1985–88; Chief Constable, Sussex Police, 2001–06; Pres., ACPO, 2006–09; Dep. Comr, Victoria Police, Australia, 2009–11; Counter Terrorism Advr, ITN London, 2012. Fulbright Scholar, UCLA, 1996. *Recreations:* reading, cycling, running, aviation (glider and helicopter). *E:* homeward1@hotmail.com.

JONES, Kevan David; MP (Lab) North Durham, since 2001; *b* 25 April 1964. *Educ:* Univ. of Southern Maine, USA; Newcastle upon Tyne Poly. (BA). Political Officer, 1989–2001, Regl Organiser, 1992–99, Sen. Organiser, 1999–2001, GMB. Newcastle upon Tyne City Council: Mem. (Lab), 1990–2001; Chair of Public Health, 1993–97; Chief Whip, 1994–2000; Chair and Cabinet Mem. for Develt and Transport, 1997–2001. Parly Under-Sec. of State and Minister for Veterans, MoD, 2008–10; Shadow Minister for Armed Forces, 2010–15. Mem., Select Cttee on Defence, 2001–09. Chair, 1998–2000, Vice-Chair, 2000–01, Northern Regl Lab. Party. Mem., Commonwealth War Graves Commn, 2010–. *Address:* c/o House of Commons, SW1A 0AA; (office) Fulforth Centre, Front Street, Sacriston, Co. Durham DH7 6JT. *T:* (0191) 371 8834. *Club:* Sacriston Workmen's.

JONES, Kim Niklas; menswear designer; Men's Artistic Director, Louis Vuitton Malletier, since 2011; *b* London, 11 Sept. 1979. *Educ:* Central St Martins Sch. of Art and Design (MA Menswear). First catwalk collection, London Fashion Week, 2003; Paris collections, 2004–08; Creative Dir, Alfred Dunhill, 2008–11 (presented 8 collections, incl. NY Men's Collection, 2007); has designed for cos incl. Uniqlo, Topman, Umbro, Mulberry, Alexander McQueen, Hugo Boss and Iceberg; has presented short films, incl. Everywhere, with Alasdair McLellan, for London Fashion Week, 2006. Exhibn, Mus. of London, 2004. Menswear Designer of Year Award, British Fashion Council, 2006, 2009, 2011; Menswear Designer of Year, British Fashion Awards, 2012. *Relevant publication*: Kim Jones, by Luke Smalley, 2004. *Address:* Louis Vuitton, 2 rue du Pont-Neuf, 75001 Paris, France.

JONES, Kirsty Jackson; *see* Young, K. J.

JONES, Laura Anne; Member (C) South Wales East, National Assembly for Wales, 2003–07; *b* 21 Feb. 1979; *d* of John Dilwyn Jones and Penelope Anne Jones. *Educ:* Univ. of Plymouth (BSc Politics). Chm., SE Wales Cons. Future Area, 2000–02. Opposition spokesman on Sports, Nat. Assembly for Wales, 2003–07. Girl Guiding Ambassador, 2004–. Hon. Mem., Cardiff Business Club. *Recreations:* swimming, hockey, ski-ing, horse riding, cycling, Girl Guides. *Address:* Llanusk Cottage, Llanbadoc, Usk, Monmouthshire NP15 1TA; 105 Sovereign Quay, Cardiff Bay, Cardiff CF10 6SE. *Club:* Lord's Taverners.

JONES, Luke B.; *see* Bradley-Jones.

JONES, Sir Lyndon (Hugh), Kt 1999; Principal and Chief Executive, Harris City Technology College, 1990–99; *b* 2 Feb. 1943; *s* of late David Hugh Jones and Victoria Maud (*née* Elias); *m* 1st, 1965, Gillian Fortnum (marr. diss. 1981); two *s* one *d*; 2nd, 1990, Sandra Lees; two step *d*. *Educ:* Cardiff High Sch. for Boys; UC Cardiff (BA); Univ. of Reading (Postgrad. DipEd); Birmingham Univ. (MEd). Hd of Music Dept, Pool Hayes Comprehensive Sch., 1965–70; Sen. Lectr in Music and Educn, Bingley Teacher Trng Coll., 1970–76; Hd, Arts Faculty, Doncaster Inst. Higher Educn, 1976–78; Dir of Arts, Richmond Tertiary Coll., 1978–82; Dep. Principal, Westminster Further Educn Coll., 1982–85; Principal, S London Further Educn Coll., 1985–90. Chief Examr, GCE Music, London Univ., 1978–83. Tutor, Nat. Professional Qualification for Headship, 1998; Trainer, Leadership Prog. for Serving Head Teachers, 1999; Sch. Improvement Partner, Nat. Coll. for Sch. Leadership, 2006. Chm., E Surrey Carers Support Assoc., 2015–. Volunteer interviewer, Pecan jobs project; Volunteer, Crawley Open House, 2013. Mem., NAHT, 1990. Composer, The Prince and the Pauper, 1992. *Recreations:* playing the piano, composing, Rugby, mountaineering, opera, amateur chef and wine taster.

JONES, Dr Lynne Mary; Vice President, British Association for Counselling and Psychotherapy, 2009–14; *b* 26 April 1951; two *s*. *Educ:* Birmingham Univ. (BSc, PhD Biochem.); Birmingham Polytechnic (Dip. Housing Studies). Joined Labour Party, 1974; ASTMS, then MSF, subseq. Amicus, 1972–. Mem. (Lab) Birmingham City Council, 1980–94 (Chair, Housing Cttee, 1984–87). Former Exec. Mem., Labour Housing Gp. MP (Lab) Birmingham, Selly Oak, 1992–2010. Member: Select Cttee on science and technology, 1992–2001; Select Cttee on envmt, food and rural affairs, 2005–10. *W:* www.lynnejones.org.uk.

JONES, Lynton; *see* Jones, J. L.

JONES, Prof. Malcolm Lang, PhD; FDSRCSE, FDSRCS; Professor of Child Dental Health and Orthodontics, Cardiff University (formerly University of Wales College of Medicine), 1992–2010, Emeritus Professor, 2011 (Pro-Vice-Chancellor (Health and Estates), 2006–10); Hon. Consultant in Orthodontics, Dental Hospital, Cardiff and Vale NHS Trust, 1987–2010; *b* Surbiton, 28 June 1950; *s* of Derek Lang Jones and Ellen Joan Jones; *m* 1976, Rhona Marie Logue; one *s* one *d*. *Educ:* King's Coll. Sch., Wimbledon; Welsh Nat. Sch. of Medicine (BDS 1973; PhD 1987); Univ. of London (MSc 1979). DOrthRCS 1979; FDSRCSE 1980; FDSRCS 2003. Community Dental Officer, Derbys, 1973–74; Resident Hse Officer, Oral and Maxillofacial Surgery, Cardiff Dental Hosp., 1974–75; SHO, Chepstow Hosp., 1975; Registrar, Middlesex Hosp., 1976–77; Registrar, Orthodontics, Royal Dental Hosp., 1977–79; Lectr, 1979–84, Sen. Lectr, 1984–92, in Orthodontics; Head, Child Dental Health, Univ. of Wales Coll. of Medicine, 1992–99; Dean and Hd of Sch. of Dentistry, Cardiff Univ., 1999–2006; Gen. Manager, Dental Services, Cardiff & Vale NHS Trust, 1999–2006. Non-exec. Dir, Swansea NHS Trust, 2004–08; Ind. Mem. Bd, Cardiff and Vale NHS Trust, 2009–10. Ed., British Jl Orthodontics, subseq. Jl Orthodontics, 1995–2000. Exec. Sec., UK Council of Deans and Heads of Dental Schs, 2005–08; Founder Chm., Forum of Eur. Heads and Deans of Dental Schs, 2007–08; Pres., Assoc. for Dental Educn in Europe, 2008–09. Mem., Dental Council, RCSE, 2005–09 (Dental Faculty Gold Medal, 2009). Hon. Fellow, Hong Kong Coll. of Surgeons, 2007. Hon. MD Riga Stradins, Latvia, 2002; Hon. DDS Malmo 2004. Special Service Award, British Orthodontic Soc., 2002. *Publications:* (with K. G. Isaacson) Orthodontic Radiography Guidelines, 1994; (with R. G. Oliver) Walther and Houston's Orthodontic Notes, 5th edn, 1995, 6th edn, 2000; (with J. Middleton and G. N. Pande) Computer Methods in Biomechanics and Biomedical Engineering, 1996; (with J. Middleton and N. G. Shrive) Computer Methods in Biomechanics and Biomedical Engineering: book 4, 2003; numerous contribs to scientific jls mostly in areas of clinical trials, applied computational biomechanics and dental education. *Recreations:* sailing, Morgan sports cars, reading as widely as time allows. *Address:* Vice Chancellor's Office, Cardiff University, Main Building, Park Place, Cardiff CF10 3AT. *T:* (029) 2074 2075, *Fax:* (029) 2074 5306. *E:* JonesML@cf.ac.uk.

JONES, Marcus Charles; MP (C) Nuneaton, since 2010; Parliamentary Under-Secretary of State, Department for Communities and Local Government, since 2015; *b* 5 April 1974; *s* of Brian and Jean Jones; *m* 2004, Suzanne Clarke; one *s* one *d*. *Educ:* St Thomas More Sch., Nuneaton; King Edward VI Coll., Nuneaton. Conveyancing Manager, Tustain Jones & Co., Solicitors, 1999–2010. Mem. (C) Nuneaton and Bedworth BC, 2005–10 (Leader, 2008–09). *Address:* House of Commons, SW1A 0AA.

JONES, Dr Margaret Anne, OBE 2001; Chief Executive, Brook Advisory Centres, 1988–2001; *b* 30 Oct. 1940; *d* of Cecil Newton Collard and Rita Ross Collard (*née* White); *m* 1974, Hugh Vaughan Price Jones. *Educ:* Methodist Ladies' Coll., Burwood, Australia; Univ. of New South Wales (BSc, MSc); University College London (PhD); Dip. Mus. Open 2004. Postdoctoral Res. Fellow, Univ. of Cambridge, 1970–71; Res. Fellow, Univ. of Bath, 1971–74; Resources Officer, Health Education Council, 1974–88. Lay Mem., Chiltern and S Bucks Primary Care Gp, 1999–2002; non-exec. Dir, Chiltern and S Bucks Primary Care Trust, 2002–06. Mem., Ind. Adv. Gp, Teenage Pregnancy Unit, DoH, 2000–03. Hon. DSc Southampton, 2000. *Recreations:* music, cooking.

JONES, Sir Mark (Ellis Powell), Kt 2010; Master, St Cross College, Oxford, since 2011; *b* 5 Feb. 1951; *s* of John Ernest Powell-Jones, CMG and of Ann Paludan; *m* 1983, (Ann) Camilla Toulmin, *qv*; two *s* two *d*. *Educ:* Eton College; Worcester College, Oxford (MA; Hon. Fellow, 2015); Courtauld Inst. of Art. Asst Keeper, 1974–90, Keeper, 1990–92, Dept of Coins and Medals, BM; Dir, Nat. Mus of Scotland, 1992–2001; Dir, V&A Mus., 2001–11. Scottish Cultural Resources Access Network: Co-Founder, 1994–96; Mem. Bd, 1996–2003, 2013–; Chm., 2004–06. Director: Scottish Museums Council, 1992–2001; Edinburgh and Lothians Tourist Bd, 1998–2000. Member: Royal Mint Adv. Cttee, 1994–2006; Arts and Humanities Data Service Steering Cttee, 1997–99; Focus Gp, Nat. Cultural Strategy, 1999–2000; Bd, MLA, 2000–05; Council, RCA, 2001– (Hon. Sen. Fellow, 2014); Chancellor's Forum, Univ. of the Arts, London, 2002–06; Council, Crafts Council, 2002–06; Chm., Nat. Mus. Dirs' Conf., 2006–09. President: Fédn Internat. de la Médaille, 1994–2000; British Art Medal Soc., 1998–2004 (Sec., 1982–94); Corresp. Mem., Amer. Numismatic Soc., 1990. Trustee: Gilbert Collection, 2001–11; NT, 2005–12; Pilgrim Trust, 2006– (Chm., 2015–); Design Council, 2011–12; Tullie House Mus. and Art Gall., 2011–; Auckland Castle Trust, 2012–15; Grimsthorpe and Drummond Trust, 2012–; Watts Gall., 2012–. Gov., Compton Verney, 2013–. Hon. Prof., Univ. of Edinburgh, 1997. Editor, The Medal, 1983–97. FSA 1992; FRSE 1999. Hon. DLit London, 2002; Hon. DArts Abertay, 2009; Hon. LLD Dundee, 2012; Hon. DLitt UEA, 2012. Chevalier, Ordre des Arts et des Lettres (France), 2005. *Publications:* The Art of the Medal, 1977; Impressionist Painting, 1979; Catalogue of French Medals in the British Museum, I, 1982, II, 1988; Contemporary British Medals, 1986; (ed) Fake?: the art of deception, 1990; (ed) Why Fakes Matter, 1992; (ed) Designs on Posterity, 1994; contrib. Sculpture Jl and Museums Jl. *Address:* St Cross College, Oxford OX1 3LZ.

JONES, Prof. Martin Kenneth, DPhil; FSA; George Pitt-Rivers Professor of Archaeological Science, University of Cambridge, since 1990; Vice Master, Darwin College, Cambridge, since 2012; *b* 29 June 1951; *s* of John Francis Jones and Margaret Olive (*née* Baldwin); *m* 1985, Lucy Walker; one *s* one *d*. *Educ:* Eltham Coll.; Univ. of Cambridge (MA); Univ. of Oxford (DPhil 1985). FSA 1991. Oxford Archaeological Unit, 1973–79; Res. Asst, Oxford Univ., 1979–81; Lectr, 1981–89, Sen. Lectr, 1989–90, Durham Univ. MAE 2013. DUniv Stirling, 1999. *Publications:* The Environment of Man: the Iron Age to the Anglo-Saxon period, 1981; Integrating the Subsistence Economy, 1983; England before Domesday, 1986; Archaeology and the Flora of the British Isles, 1988; Molecular Information and Prehistory, 1999; The Molecule Hunt: archaeology and the search for ancient DNA, 2001; Conflict, 2006; Feast: why humans share food, 2007; Archaeology Meets Science, 2008. *Recreation:* dancing. *Address:* Department of Archaeology, Downing Street, Cambridge CB2 3DZ. *T:* (01223) 333520.

JONES, Martyn David; *b* 1 March 1947; *m* 1974, Rhona Bellis (marr. diss. 1991); one *s* one *d*. *Educ:* Liverpool and Trent Polytechnics. MRSB. Microbiologist, Wrexham Lager Beer Co., 1968–87. Mem., Clwyd CC, 1981–89. MP (Lab) Clwyd SW, 1987–97, Clwyd S, 1997–2010. An Opposition Whip, 1988–92; Opposition spokesman on food, agric. and rural affairs, 1994–95; Mem., Chairmen's Panel, 1992–94, 2005–10. Member: Select Cttee on Agriculture, 1987–94 and 1996–97; Select Cttee on Welsh Affairs, 1997–2010 (Chm., 1997–2005); Chm., Parly Labour Party Agriculture Cttee, 1987–94. *E:* jonesm47@hotmail.com.

JONES, Martyn Eynon, FCA; advisor and consultant, since 2012; President, Institute of Chartered Accountants in England and Wales, 2013–14 (Vice President, 2011–12; Deputy President, 2012–13); *b* Killay, Gower, Wales, 1951; *s* of James Cledwyn Jones and Megan Jones; *m* 1973, Doreen Judith Long; two *s*. *Educ:* Dynevor Grammar Sch., Swansea; Denbigh Grammar Sch.; Denbigh High Sch.; Swansea Univ. (BSc Hons). ACA 1976, FCA 1981. Chartered Accountant, Robson Rhodes, W Yorks and Deloitte Haskins & Sells, 1972–77; Lectr in Accounting and Auditing, then Hd, Accountancy Tuition Centre, Newcastle upon Tyne, 1977–81; Under-Sec., then Sec., Auditing Practices Cttee, Consultancy Cttee of Accounting Bodies, 1981–84; Sen. Manager, 1984–87, Nat. Audit Tech. Partner, 1987–2012, Nat. Accounting and Auditing, Nat. Audit Tech. Dept, Touche Ross & Co., subseq. Deloitte LLP. Member: Deloitte Touche Tohmatsu Global Service Innovation Adv. Bd, 1999–2002; Deloitte Touche Tohmatsu Global Tech. Policy and Methodol. Gp, then Audit Task Force Leaders, later Audit Tech. Adv. Bd, 1999–2012; Deloitte LLP: Chm., Corporate Governance Services Gp, 2007–12; Chm., Quality of Assce Services on sustainability and greenhouse gas emissions, 2010–12. Provision of adv. services on risk mgt, internal control and governance to entities incl. H of C, H of L, public sector bodies, corporate bodies and mutuals, 1998–2012; provision of advice to Sen. Policy Advr, 10 Downing St on going concern, 2009. UK and Irish Tech. Advr to Internat. Auditing Practices Cttee, 1983–84. Auditing Practices

Board: Mem., Internat. Cttee, 2002–12; Member Working Group: on going concern issues during current econ. conditions, 2008; on Clarified Internat. Standards on Auditing, 2009. CCAB Ltd (Consultative Committee of Accounting Bodies): Chm., Ethics Standards Gp, 2006–11; Mem., Takeover Panel, 2013–14; Mem. Bd, 2013–14. Institute of Chartered Accountants in England and Wales: Mem., Business Law Cttee, 1993–2006; Chairman: Special Reports of Accountants Sub-Cttee, then Panel, 1993–2000; Accountants Reports on Internal Controls over Financial Service Orgns, 1997–2013; Centre for Business Perf., 2002–06; Internat. Standards on Auditing Implementation Sub-Gp, 2003–11; Ethics Standards Cttee, 2006–11; Wkg Gp developing audit insights on manufg sector, 2013; Vice Chm., Tech. and Practical Auditing Cttee, 1995–2006; Member: Res. Bd, 1995–99; Tech. Strategy Bd, 2002–11; Corporate Governance Cttee, 2005–06; Council, 2006–; Nominating Cttee, 2011–13; Bd, 2011–14. Confederation of British Industry: Member: City Regulatory Panel, 1993–96; Corporate Law Panel, 1996–2003; Companies Cttee, 2003–12. Mem., Adv. Bd, 2009–12, Hon. Lectr, 2010–12, Swansea Univ. Sch. of Business and Econs; Chm., Adv. Bd, Dept of Econs and Finance, Brunel Univ. London, 2014–. FRSA 1997. Liveryman, Co. of Chartered Accountants in England and Wales, 2012 (Freeman, 2008; Court Asst, 2011–14). *Publications:* (jtly) Safely Past the Perils: the new investment business accounting requirements, 1987; (jtly) The Finance Director and the Audit Committee, 1992; (jtly) The Audit Committee and its Chairman, 1993; (Consultant Ed.) Corporate Governance Handbook, 1996–2003; (jtly) Taking Fraud Seriously, 1996; (jtly) Implementing Turnbull: a boardroom briefing, 1999; (jtly) Audit Committees: a framework for assessment, 1997. *Recreations:* gardening, appreciating Georgian architecture, watching Rugby, relaxing in Gower, S Wales and Cumbria. *Address:* Lorne Cottage, 23 Highland Road, Amersham, Bucks HP7 9AU. *E:* martyn.e.jones@btinternet.com.

JONES, Maude Elizabeth, CBE 1973; Deputy Director-General, British Red Cross Society, 1970–77; *b* 14 Jan. 1921; 2nd *d* of late E. W. and M. E. H. Jones, Dolben, Ruthin, North Wales. *Educ:* Brynhyfryd Sch. for Girls, Ruthin. Joined Foreign Relations Dept, Jt War Organisation BRCS and OStJ, 1940; Dep. Dir, Jun. Red Cross, BRCS, 1949; Dir, Jun. Red Cross, 1960; Dep. Dir-Gen. for Branch Affairs, BRCS, 1966. Member: Jt Cttee (and Finance and Gen. Purposes Sub-Cttee) OStJ and BRCS, 1966–77; Council of Nat. Council of Social Service; Council of FANY, 1966–77. Governor, St David's Sch., Ashford, Middx. SSStJ 1959. *Recreations:* music, gardening, reading. *Address:* Dolben, Ruthin, Denbighshire, North Wales LL15 1RB. *T:* (01824) 702443. *Club:* New Cavendish.

JONES, Medwyn; Partner, Wiggin, since 2014; *b* Bangor, 13 Sept. 1955; *s* of Ieuan Glyn du Platt Jones and Margaret Jones; *m* 1990, Rita Bailey; one *s* one *d*. *Educ:* Scorton Grammar Sch.; Chester Grammar Sch.; Univ. of Sheffield (LLB Hons); Coll. of Law. Articled clerk, 1978–80, solicitor, 1980–81, Theodore Goddard; solicitor, 1981–92, Partner, 1983–92, Walker Martineau; Partner, Cameron Markby Hewitt, 1992–94; Partner, 1994–2013, Hd, Television Gp, 1998–2013, Harbottle & Lewis LLP. Mem., BAFTA, 2002. *Recreations:* skiing, gym, cycling.

JONES, Merfyn; *see* Jones, Richard M.

JONES, Mervyn C.; *see* Colenso-Jones.

JONES, Mervyn Thomas; HM Diplomatic Service, retired; Partnership Development Officer, Diocese of Winchester, 2004–10; *b* 23 Nov. 1942; *s* of William Clifford Jones and Winifred Mary Jones (*née* Jenkins); *m* 1965, Julia Mary Newcombe; two *s*. *Educ:* Bishop Gore Grammar Sch., Swansea; University Coll., Swansea (BA Hons Eng.). Entered HM Diplomatic Service, 1964: FCO, 1964–66; Calcutta, 1966; Bonn, 1966–70; Warsaw, 1970–73; FCO, 1973–77; Oslo, 1977–80; First Sec. (Mgt), then Hd of Chancery, Bangkok, 1981–85; jsdc, RNC Greenwich, 1985; on secondment to Commonwealth Secretariat as Asst Dir, Internat. Affairs Div., 1985–90; Dep. Consul Gen. and Consul (Commercial), LA, 1990–94; Asst Hd, Migration and Visa Dept, FCO, 1994–96; Counsellor (Commercial and Econ.), Brussels, and co-accredited to Luxembourg, 1996–99; Consul-Gen. and Dep. Head of Mission, Brussels, 1999–2000; Governor, Turks and Caicos Is, 2000–02. *Recreations:* reading, cinema, music, walking, Rugby (Welsh).

JONES, Miah Gwynfor, (Gwyn Jones), PhD; Director, Corporate Technologies, since 1989; *b* 2 Dec. 1948; *s* of Robert John and Jane Irene Jones (*née* Evans); *m* 1976, Maria Linda Johnson; two *d*. *Educ:* Ysgol Eifionydd, Porthmadog; Univ. of Manchester (BSc 1st Cl. Hons); Univ. of Essex (PhD). FBCS 1987. British Steel Corp., 1974–77; ICL, 1977–81; Chm., Business Micro Systems, 1981–85; Chm. and Chief Exec., Corporate Technology Gp plc, 1985–87; Chm., L. G. Software, 1985–87; Director: ACT Computers PLC, 1989–95; Welsh Water Enterprises Ltd, 1990–93; Tesco plc, 1992–98; Invesco English and Internat. Trust plc, 1993–2010; HBO (formerly HBOL) (UK) Ltd, 1996–97; Real Radio Ltd, 2000–02; RMR plc, 2001–02; Si Corporate Devel Ltd, 2004–07 (Chm., 2006–07); Unit Superheaters Ltd, 2005–10; Dep. Chm., Agenda Television Ltd, 1997–2000; Partner, Quayside Properties, 1997–; Chairman: Agenda Multimedia Ltd, 2000–01; Press Red Ltd, 2003–05; Oxford English Trng Ltd, 2004–06; RogenSi, 2006–10. Chm., Adv. Cttee, NW Equity Fund, 2005–08. Chm., Welsh Devel Agency, 1988–93; BBC Nat. Gov. for Wales, 1992–96; Dir, S4C Authy, 1992–96; Pres., Royal Welsh Agric. Soc., 1993. Director: Univ. of Essex Knowledge Gateway Ltd, 2013–; Univ. of Essex Knowledge Gateway Hldgs Ltd, 2013–. Member: Council, Univ. of Wales, 1989–95; Court, UC of Swansea, 1989–95; Prince of Wales Cttee, 1989–92; Prince's Youth Business Trust, 1989–92. Chm., Adv. Bd, 2009–13, Vis. Prof., 2010–15, Dir, 2013–15, Essex Business Sch., Univ. of Essex; Ext. Academic, Global MBA, Manchester Business Sch., 2012–; Dean of Business, Univ. of Gloucestershire, 2015–. Hon. Fellow, Poly. of Wales, 1991. *Recreations:* cycling, reading, boats, mountain walking.

JONES, Michael Abbott; communications consultant; *b* 3 May 1944; *s* of Ronald and Irene Jones; *m* 1973, Wendy (*née* Saward); twin *d*. *Educ:* Felsted; Magdalen Coll., Oxford (BA, DipEd). Joined Life Offices' Assoc., 1968, Jt Sec. 1982; transf. to Assoc. of British Insurers on its formation, as Manager, Legislation, 1985, Chief Exec., 1987–93; Hd of Corporate Affairs, Sun Alliance, 1993–96; Hd of Gp Corporate Affairs, Royal & Sun Alliance Insurance Gp plc, 1996–98. *Recreations:* reading, photography, theatre. *Address:* 10 Parkhill Road, E4 7ED.

JONES, Michael Frederick; Associate Editor (Politics), The Sunday Times, 1995–2002; *b* 3 July 1937; *s* of late Glyn Frederick Jones and of Elizabeth (*née* Coopey); *m* 1959, Sheila Joan Dawes; three *s*. *Educ:* Crypt Grammar Sch., Gloucester. Reporter: Maidenhead Advertiser, 1956–59; Northern Echo, Darlington, 1959–61; Manchester Evening News, 1961–64; Labour reporter, Financial Times, 1964–65; Industrial reporter, Daily Telegraph, 1965–67; News Editor, later Asst Editor, Times Business News, 1967–70; Managing Editor, The Asian, Hong Kong, 1971; Sunday Times: Associate News Editor, 1972–75; political correspondent, 1975–84; Political Editor, 1984–95; Associate Editor, 1990–2002. Chm., Parly Press Gallery, 1989–91. Parly Researcher to Baroness Boothroyd, 2002–. Vis. Fellow, Goldsmiths Coll., London, 2000–02. Exec. Mem., Meml to Women of World War 2 Fund, 2004–05. *Publications:* (jtly) Strike: Thatcher, Scargill and the miners, 1985; (with Betty Boothroyd) Betty Boothroyd: the autobiography, 2001. *Address:* 43 Hillview Road, Orpington, Kent BR6 0SE. *T:* (01689) 820796.

JONES, Rt Rev. Michael Hugh Harold B.; *see* Bedford-Jones.

JONES, Michael Scott; *see* Jones, Hon. Lord.

JONES, Dr Nevin Campbell H.; *see* Hughes Jones.

JONES, Nicholas Graham; His Honour Judge Nicholas Jones; a Circuit Judge, since 2001; *b* 13 Aug. 1948; *s* of late Albert William Jones and Gwendolen Muriel Taylor-Jones; *m* 1976, Shelagh Ann Farror; one *s*. *Educ:* Latymer Upper Sch.; St Catherine's Coll., Oxford (MA). Film editing and prodn, BBC, 1969–73; called to the Bar, Inner Temple, 1975; S Eastern Circuit; a Recorder, 1994–2001. *Recreations:* sailing, walking, music. *Address:* Kingston Crown Court, 6–8 Penrhyn Road, Kingston-upon-Thames, Surrey KT1 2BB. *T:* (020) 8240 2500, *Fax:* (020) 8240 2675. *Clubs:* Royal London Yacht (Rear Cdre Yachting, 2014–), Royal Ocean Racing, Bar Yacht (Cdre, 2008–11).

JONES, Nicholas Keith Arthur; restaurateur; Chief Executive Officer (formerly Managing Director), Soho House, since 1991; *b* 22 Sept. 1963; *s* of Keith and Anna Jones; *m* 1999, Kirsty Jackson Young, *qv*; two *d*, and one *s* one *d* from former marriage. *Educ:* Shiplake Coll. Opened: Café Bohème, London W1, 1992; Soho House, 1995; Babington House, Som, 1998; Bohème Kitchen Bar, London W1, 1999; Electric Cinema, House and Brasserie, London W11, 2002; Soho House New York, 2003; Balham Kitchen and Bar, 2003; Cecconi's, London W1, 2005; Cowshed, Clarendon Cross, 2005; High Road House, Chiswick, 2006; Shoreditch House, 2007; Pizza East, London E1, 2009; Dean Street Townhouse, 2009; Cecconi's, LA, 2009; Soho House West Hollywood, 2010; Soho House Berlin, 2010; Soho Beach House, and Cecconi's, Miami, 2010; Pizza East, London W10, 2011; UK Little House, 2012; Soho House Berlin Apartments, 2012; Soho House Toronto, 2012; Pizza East, Chicken Shop, and Dirty Burger, London NW5, 2012. *Publications:* (jtly) Eat, Drink, Nap: bringing the house home, 2014. *Recreations:* cooking, eating, drinking, napping. *Address:* Soho House, Royalty House, 72–74 Dean Street, W1D 3SG. *T:* (020) 7851 1171, *Fax:* (020) 7851 1198.

JONES, Nicholas Michael Houssemayne, FCA; Director, British Horseracing Authority, 2011–14; Steward, Jockey Club, since 2011; *b* London, 27 Oct. 1946; *s* of Henry and Patricia Jones; *m* 1st, 1971, Veronica Anne Hamilton-Russell (marr. diss. 1999); one *s* one *d*; 2nd, 2002, Cherry Victoria Smart. *Educ:* Winchester Coll.; London Business Sch. (MBA). FCA 1969. Peat, Marwick, Mitchell & Co., 1965–73; J. Henry Schroder Wagg & Co. Ltd: Exec., 1975–83; Dir, 1983–87; Lazard: Man. Dir, 1987–2010; Vice-Chm., 1999–2010. Chm., Nat. Stud, 1991–2000. Director: Hilton Gp plc, 2002–06; Ladbroke Gp plc, 2006–10 (Dep. Chm., 2009–10); Newbury Racecourse plc, 2007–10; Candover Investments plc, 2008–10. Mem., Adv. Bd, London Business Sch., 1996–2010. Governor: James Allen Girls' Sch., 1989–93; Birkbeck Coll., Univ. of London, 1996–99. *Recreations:* racing, bridge, tennis, gardening, stalking. *Address:* The Manor, Coln St Dennis, Cheltenham, Glos GL54 3JU. *E:* colnvalleystud@hotmail.com. *Clubs:* Turf, Jockey.

JONES, (Nicholas) Rory C.; *see* Cellan-Jones.

JONES, Prof. Nicholas Spencer, MD; FRCS; Consultant Ear, Nose and Throat Surgeon, Queen's Medical Centre, Nottingham, since 1991; Honorary Professor, University of Nottingham, 1999–2014; *b* Davos, Switzerland, 12 Sept. 1953; *s* of John Spencer Jones and Philis Helen Jones (*née* Gibson); *m* 1984, Jean Margaret Shaw; one *s* one *d*. *Educ:* Epsom Coll.; Guy's Hosp. Dental Sch. (BDS 1975); Guy's Hosp. Med. Sch. (MB BS 1982); Univ. of London (MD 1997). FRCSEd 1986; FRCS 1986; FRCS (Otol) 1987. Sen. Registrar, Royal Nat. Throat, Nose and Ear Hosp., Gt Ormond St Hosp. and Royal Berks Hosp., 1989–91. Platinum Clin. Excellence Award, 2010. *Publications:* (with D. Simmen) A Manual of Endoscopic Sinus Surgery, 2005 (trans German, Spanish, Portuguese, Greek, Turkish, Mandarin); (ed jtly) Scott-Brown's Otorhinolaryngology, 7th edn 2008; Practical Rhinology, 2010; contribs to jls. *Recreations:* etching, golf. *Address:* Department of Otorhinolaryngology, Head and Neck Surgery, Queen's Medical Centre, University Hospital, Nottingham NG7 2UH. *T:* (0115) 924 9924, ext. 64848.

JONES, Nigel John I.; *see* Inglis-Jones.

JONES, Nigel Michael; Global Chief Strategy Officer, FCB (Foote, Cone & Belding) (formerly Draftfcb), since 2013; *b* Wolverhampton, 23 Sept. 1960; *s* of Ralph Michael Jones and Patricia May Jones; *m* (marr. diss.); two *s* one *d*. *Educ:* Wolverhampton Grammar Sch.; Keble Coll., Oxford (BA Hons Maths). BMP DDB, 1984–99, Hd, Account Planning, 1991–99; Founder, Jones Mason Barton Antenen, 1999–2001; CEO, Claydon Heeley Jones Mason, 2001–05; CEO, FCB London, later Draft FCB, 2005–08; CEO and Chm., Publicis Gp UK, 2008–13. *Recreations:* music, www.abarrelofnails.com, Wolverhampton Wanderers FC. *Address:* 11 St James's Drive, SW17 7RN. *T:* 07979 808771. *E:* nmjonesuk@yahoo.co.uk.

JONES, Dr (Norman) Fielding, FRCP; Consultant Physician, St Thomas' Hospital, London, 1967–93, now Emeritus; *b* 3 May 1931; *s* of William John and Winifred Jones; *m* 1958, Ann Pye Chavasse; three *s*. *Educ:* Christ Coll., Brecon; King's Coll., Cambridge (MA 1957; MD 1966); St Thomas' Hosp., London. FRCP 1970. Rockefeller Fellow, Univ. of N Carolina, 1963–64. Physician, King Edward VII's Hosp. for Officers, 1977–95; Consulting Physician, Metropolitan Police, 1980–92; Hon. Consulting Physician: to the Army, 1980–93; to Royal Hosp., Chelsea, 1987–93; CMO, Equitable Life Assurance Soc., 1985–97. Vice Chm., West Lambeth HA, 1989–90. Royal College of Physicians: Sen. Censor and Vice Pres., 1989–90; Treasurer, 1991–96; Chm., Cttee on Renal Disease, 1980–92; Chm., Cttee on Legal Aspects of Medicine, 1990–93. Medical Mem., Ind. Public Inquiries: Gulf War Illnesses, 2004; NHS Supplied Blood and Blood Products, 2007–09. Special Trustee, St Thomas' Hosp., 1990–94; Treas., Royal Medical Benevolent Fund, 1996–2002. Member: Med. Res. Soc., 1962–2011; Assoc. of Physicians of GB and Ire., 1968–. *Publications:* (ed) Recent Advances in Renal Disease, 1975; (ed with Sir Douglas Black) Renal Disease, 1979; (ed with D. K. Peters) Recent Advances in Renal Medicine, 1982. *Recreations:* icons, music. *Address:* The Old Coach House, Forest Park Road, Brockenhurst, Hants SO42 7SW.

JONES, His Honour Norman Henry; QC 1985; a Circuit Judge, 1992–2007 (a Senior Circuit Judge, 2000–07); *b* 12 Dec. 1941; *s* of late Henry Robert Jones and Charlotte Isabel Scott Jones; *m* 1970, Trudy Helen Chamberlain; two *s* one *d*. *Educ:* Bideford Grammar School; North Devon Tech. Coll.; Univ. of Leeds (LLB, LLM). Called to the Bar, Middle Temple, 1968 (Harmsworth Schol.). A Recorder, 1987–92. Recorder of Leeds and Resident Judge at Leeds, 2001–07; Asst Surveillance Comr, 2007–. *Recreations:* reading, walking, boating. *Address:* c/o The Crown Court, Oxford Road, Leeds LS1 3BG.

JONES, Owen Griffith Ronald, (Ron), CBE 2012; Founder and Executive Chairman, Tinopolis Ltd (formerly Agenda Television Ltd), since 1990; *b* Carmarthen, 11 Dec. 1948; *s* of William Tascar Jones and Eirlys Jones (*née* Jenkins); *m* 1970, Cheryl Noble (*d* 2009); one *d*; *m* 2015, Kim Morgans; one *s*. *Educ:* Amman Valley Grammar Sch.; Cardiff Univ. (BSc Econ 1970). FCA 1975. Joined Arthur Andersen as trainee, 1970, Partner, 1983–89. Chm., Real Radio Ltd, 1998–2000. Hon. Treas., Glamorgan CCC, 1989–97; Dir, Llanelli RFC, 1997– (Chm., 1997–98). Mem., Sports Council for Wales, 1994–2004; Chm., Sportlot Wales, 2000–04. Mem., Welsh Lang. Bd, 1985–2001. Chm., Welsh Govt Creative Industries Panel, 2010–. Former Mem. Council and Ct of Govs, Swansea Univ. Hon. Fellow: Univ. of Wales Trinity St David, 2009; Swansea Univ., 2011. *Address:* Coed, Ferryside, Carmarthen SA17 5TP. *T:* (01554) 880880. *E:* ron.jones@tinopolis.com.

JONES, Sir (Owen) Trevor, Kt 1981; Member (Lib Dem), Liverpool City Council, 2003–10; *b* 1927; *s* of Owen and Ada Jones, Dyserth; *m* Doreen. Mem., Liverpool City Council, 1968, Liverpool Metropolitan District Council, 1973–91 (Leader, 1981–83). Pres., Liberal Party, 1972–73; contested (L): Liverpool, Toxteth, Feb. 1974 and Gillingham, Oct. 1974.

JONES, Peter, CBE 2009; entrepreneur, philanthropist and author; Founder: Peter Jones Foundation, 2005; Peter Jones Enterprise Academy (formerly National Enterprise Academy), 2009; *b* 18 March 1966; *s* of David and Eileen Jones; five *c. Educ:* Haileybury Jun. Sch.; Windsor Boys' Sch. Dir, Siemens Nixdorf, 1996–97. Founder, Peter Jones TV Ltd, 2006; investor, various industries ranging from telecoms and fast moving consumer goods brands to property and publishing. Appeared in BBC TV business series, Dragons' Den, 10 series, 2005–12; creator, presenter and judge, American Inventor, US, 2006, 2007; creator, presenter and mentor, Tycoon, 2007; Peter Jones Meets…, 2012. Emerging Entrepreneur of Year, Ernst & Young/Times Nat. Awards, 2001. *Publications:* Tycoon: how to turn dreams into millions, 2006. *Recreations:* tennis, golf, karate. *Address:* Network House, Globe Park, Marlow, Bucks SL7 1EY. *E:* enquiries@peterjones.tv.

JONES, Peter Anthony; Chairman, Port of Milford Haven, since 2013; *b* 8 Jan. 1955. The Mersey Docks and Harbour Co.: Dir, 1993; Port Ops Dir, 1997–99; Dep. Chief Exec., 1999–2000; Chief Exec., 2000–06; Gp Chief Exec., Associated British Ports Hldgs Ltd, 2007–12.

JONES, Peter B.; *see* Bennett-Jones.

JONES, Peter Benjamin Gurner, CB 1991; Under Secretary; Director of Personnel, Board of Inland Revenue, 1984–92; *b* 25 Dec. 1932; *s* of Gurner Prince Jones and Irene Louise Jones (*née* Myall); *m* 1962, Diana Margaret Henly; one *s* one *d. Educ:* Bancroft's Sch.; St Catherine's Society, Oxford (BA (Hons) English Language and Literature). Inspector of Taxes, 1957; Inspector (Higher Grade), 1963; Sen. Inspector, 1969; Principal Inspector, 1975; Sen. Principal Inspector, 1980; Dir of Data Processing, Bd of Inland Revenue, 1981–84. Hon. Nat. Chm., CS Retirement Fellowship, 1994–2000 (Vice-Pres., 2001–). *Clubs:* Hampshire Rugby Union, Swanage and Wareham RFC.

JONES, Prof. Peter Brian, PhD; FMedSci; Professor of Psychiatry, since 2000, and Deputy Head, School of Clinical Medicine, since 2014, University of Cambridge (Head, Department of Psychiatry, 2000–14); *b* 24 Jan. 1960; *s* of Owen Trevor Jones and Amy M. Anita Jones; *m* 1986, Caroline Lea-Cox; two *s. Educ:* Northampton Grammar Sch.; King's Coll., London (BSc Neuroanatomy); Westminster Med. Sch. (MB BS); London Sch. of Hygiene and Tropical Medicine (MSc Dist.); Inst. of Psychiatry (PhD 1997). MRCP 1987, FRCP 2002; MRCPsych 1990, FRCPsych 2007. House physician, Westminster Hosp., 1984; house surgeon, E Surrey Hosp., 1985; Casualty Officer, Westminster Hosp., 1985; SHO, Whittington Hosp., 1986–87; Med. Registrar, KCH, 1987; Registrar, Bethlem Royal and Maudsley Hosps, 1987–90; Sen. Registrar in Psychiatry, KCH, 1991; MRC Trng Fellow, 1991–93; Sen. Lectr, Inst. of Psychiatry, 1993–95 (Hon. Lectr, 1991–93); Hon. Consultant Psychiatrist, Bethlem Royal and Maudsley Hosps, 1993–95; University of Nottingham: Sen. Lectr in Psychiatric Epidemiol., 1995–96; Prof. of Psychiatry and Community Mental Health, 1997–2000; Head, Div. of Psychiatry, 1997–2000. SMO (part-time), R&D Div., DoH, 1994–96. Hon. Consultant Psychiatrist: and Dir, R&D, Nottingham Healthcare Trust, 1995–2000; Addenbrooke's NHS Trust, 2000–; Cambs and Peterborough NHS Foundn Trust (formerly Cambs and Peterborough Mental Health Partnership NHS Trust), 2002– (Dir, 2003–05). Director: NIHR Collaboration in Applied Health Res. and Care, 2008–; Cambridge Univ. Health Partners, 2009–. FMedSci 2003. Hon. MD Oulu, Finland, 2006. *Publications:* contribs to learned jls on causation, clinical features, epidemiology and treatment of adult mental illness, the psychoses, in particular. *Recreations:* playing the flute, fell walking, salmon fishing (anywhere). *Address:* Department of Psychiatry, University of Cambridge, Herchel Smith Building, Robinson Way, Cambridge Biomedical Centre, Cambridge CB2 0SZ. *T:* (01223) 336960.

JONES, Peter Derek; Deputy Chairman, Civil Service Appeal Board, 1992–2001; Secretary: Council of Civil Service Unions, 1980–92; Civil Service National Whitley Council (Trade Union Side), 1963–92; *b* 21 May 1932; *s* of Richard Morgan Jones and Phyllis Irene (*née* Lloyd); *m* 1st, 1962, Noreen Elizabeth (*née* Kemp) (*d* 2001); 2nd, 2006, Delwin Ann Kirkstone Hunter (*née* Wood); one step *d. Educ:* Wembley County Grammar School. National Service and TA, Green Jackets/Parachute Regt, 1950–56; Civil Service, Nat. Assistance Bd, 1952–59; Asst Sec., Civil Service Nat. Whitley Council, 1959–63. Chm., Civil Service Housing Assoc. Ltd, 1988–97 (Dir, 1963–81; Vice Chm., 1981–88, 1997–99); Dir, Civil Service Building Soc., 1963–87. Vice-Pres., RIPA, 1991–92 (Chm., 1987–90; Vice-Chm., 1986–87; Mem. Exec. Council, 1981–85); Member: Adv. Council, Civil Service Coll., 1982–92; Tourism and Leisure Industries EDC, 1987–92; Adv. Council, CS Occupational Health Service, 1988–92; Employment (formerly Industrial) Tribunals, 1992–2002; Security Vetting Appeals Panel, 1997–2009; Chm., CIPFA Disciplinary Investigations Cttee, 2001–08. Trustee: Inst. of Contemporary Brit. History, 1985–; CS Benevolent Fund, 1992–99. Editor: Whitley Bulletin, 1963–83; CCSU Bulletin, 1984–92. *Publications:* articles in RIPA and personnel management jls; contrib. Oxford DNB. *Recreations:* relaxing, reading, painting. *Address:* Chaseview, Rowlands Hill, Wimborne, Dorset BH21 2QQ. *T:* (01202) 888824; Fern Cottage, Paradise Road, Lower Rowe, Holt, Wimborne, Dorset BH21 2DZ. *T:* (01202) 883578. *Clubs:* Belfry; Mansion House (Poole); Wimborne Cricket.

JONES, Peter Edward; HM Diplomatic Service; Director, Defence and International Security, Foreign and Commonwealth Office, since 2014; *b* Liverpool, 28 Aug. 1961; *s* of William Jones and Dorothy Jones; *m* 1998, Sumita Biswas. *Educ:* King Edward VI Sch., Southampton; Pembroke Coll., Oxford (MA Mod. Hist.). IBM UK Ltd, 1983–85; joined FCO, 1985; Second, then First Sec., UK Delegn to Vienna, 1989–92; First Sec., Bonn, 1994–98; Asst Dir, Personnel, 1998–2001, Afghanistan Emergency Unit, 2001, FCO; Counsellor, Rome, 2002–07; Dep. Dir, 2007–09, Dir, 2009–11, Migration, FCO; High Comr to Ghana, and Ambassador (non-res.) to Togo and Burkina Faso, 2011–14. *Recreations:* football and cricket (watching), cycling and walking (doing), history. *Address:* c/o Foreign and Commonwealth Office, King Charles Street, SW1A 2AH.

JONES, Peter H.; *see* Heaton-Jones.

JONES, Peter Henry Francis; His Honour Judge Peter Jones; a Circuit Judge, since 2001; *b* 25 Feb. 1952; *s* of late Eric Roberts Jones, MBE and Betty Irene Jones (*née* Longhurst); *m* 1978, Anne Elizabeth (*née* Jones); two *d. Educ:* Bishop Gore Grammar Sch., Swansea; Newport High Sch., Gwent; Balliol Coll., Oxford (MA (Hons) Lit.Hum.). Admitted Solicitor of Supreme Court, 1977. Partner: Darlington and Parkinson, Solicitors, London, 1978–87; J. Howell and Co., Solicitors, Sheffield, 1987–95; Asst Recorder, 1993–97; a Stipendiary Magistrate, then Dist Judge (Magistrates' Courts), S Yorks, 1995–2001; a Recorder, 1997–2001. Member: Lord Chancellor's Legal Aid Adv. Cttee, 1983–92; Legal Aid Bd, 1992–95; Sentencing Adv. Panel, 1999–2005; Magistrates' Cts Rules Cttee, 2001–04. *Recreations:* tennis, books, watching Rugby Union. *Address:* c/o Sheffield Combined Court Centre, 50 West Bar, Sheffield S3 8PH. *Clubs:* Dethreau Boat; Scorpions Cricket; Druidstone (Dyfed).

JONES, Prof. Peter (Howard), FRSE, FSAScot; Director and Trustee, Foundation for Advanced Studies in the Humanities, 1997–2002; Professor of Philosophy, 1984–98, now Emeritus, and Director, Institute for Advanced Studies in the Humanities, 1986–2000, University of Edinburgh; *b* 18 Dec. 1935; *s* of Thomas Leslie Jones and Hilda Croesora (*née* Parkinson); *m* 1st, 1960, (Elizabeth) Jean (*d* 2009), *yr d* of R. J. Roberton, JP; two *d*; 2nd, 2011, Dr Diana M. Henderson, *yr d* of Edna Henderson. *Educ:* Highgate Sch.; Queens' Coll., Cambridge. British Council, 1960–61; Asst Lectr in Philosophy, Univ. of Nottingham, 1963–64; Lectr, then Reader in Philosophy, 1964–84, Associate Dean of Arts, 1975–78 and 1986–89, Univ. of Edinburgh. Visiting Professor of Philosophy: Univ. of Rochester, NY, 1969–70; Dartmouth Coll., NH, 1973, 1983; Carleton Coll., Minn, 1974; Oklahoma Univ., 1978; Baylor Univ., 1978; Univ. of Malta, 1993; Belarusian State Univ., 1997; Jagiellonian Univ., Cracow, 2001–13; Mid-America Dist. Vis. Prof., 1978; Visiting Fellow: Humanities Res. Centre, ANU, 1984, 2002; Calgary Inst. for Humanities, 1992. Lothian Lectr, Edinburgh, 1993; Gifford Lectr, Univ. of Aberdeen, 1994–95; Loemker Lectr, Emory Univ., 1995–96; Lectures: Polish Acad. of Arts and Scis, 1998, 2013; St Petersburg Acad. of Scis, 1999; Hungarian Acad. of Sci., 2000. Mem., Spoliation Adv. Panel, 2000–. Trustee: Nat. Museums of Scotland, 1987–99 (Chm., Mus. of Scotland Client Cttee, 1991–99); Univ. of Edinburgh Develt Trust, 1990–98; AMAR Internat. Charitable Foundn, 1994–99; Charlemagne Inst., 1995–99; Policy Inst., 1999–2008; Scots at War, 1999–2014; Morrison's Acad., 1984–98; Fettes Coll., 1995–2005; MBI Al Jaber Foundn, 2005–. Member: UNESCO forum on tolerance, Tbilisi, 1995; UNESCO dialogue on Europe and Islam, 1997. Member: Court, Univ. of Edinburgh, 1987–90; Council, RSE, 1992–95. Founder Mem., Hume Soc., 1974. FRSE 1989; FSAScot 1993. *Publications:* Philosophy and the Novel, 1975; Hume's Sentiments, 1982; (ed) A Hotbed of Genius, 1986, 2nd edn 1996; (ed) Philosophy and Science in the Scottish Enlightenment, 1988; (ed) The Science of Man in the Scottish Enlightenment, 1989; (ed) Adam Smith Reviewed, 1992; (ed) Investigation of the Principles of Knowledge, by James Hutton, 1999; (ed) The Enlightenment World, 2004, 2nd edn 2006; (ed) The Reception of David Hume in Europe, 2005, 2nd edn 2012; (ed) Elements of Criticism, by Henry Home, Lord Kames, 2005; Ove Arup Master Builder of the Twentieth Century, 2006, 2nd edn 2008; The Reception of Edmund Burke in Europe, 2015; over 150 articles on philosophy, literature and culture. *Recreations:* opera, 18th century music and culture, boxing, gardens, clavichords. *Club:* New (Edinburgh).

JONES, Peter Ivan, CBE 2008; Director, Goodwood Racecourse, since 2008; *b* 14 Dec. 1942; *s* of Glyndwr and Edith Evelyn Jones; *m* 1st, 1964, Judith Watson (marr. diss. 1969); one *s* one *d*; 2nd, 1970, Elizabeth Gent; one *s* one *d. Educ:* Gravesend Grammar Sch.; London School of Economics (BSc Econs 1964). MIPA 1967. Chief Executive: Boase Massimi Pollitt, 1988–89; Omnicom UK plc, 1989–93 (Dir, Omnicom Inc., 1989–97); Pres., Diversified Agency Services, 1993–97. Dir, Sutton Gp Hldgs, 2005–. Dir, British Horseracing Bd, 1993–97; Mem., Horserace Betting Levy Bd, 1993–95; Chm., Horserace Totalisator Bd, 1997–2007 (Dir, 1995–97). Chm., Dorset Police Authy, 1997–2003. Chm., Goodwood Estate Pension Fund, 2010–. Pres., Racehorse Owners Assoc., 1990–93. Gov., LSE, 2007–; Chm., LSE Annual Fund, 2010–. Trustee, Animal Health Trust, 2010–. *Publications:* Trainers Record, annually 1973 to 1987 (Editor, 1982–87); (ed) Ed Byrne's Racing Year, annually 1980 to 1983. *Recreations:* horse racing, computer programming, watching sport, theatre. *Address:* Melplash Farmhouse, Melplash, Bridport, Dorset DT6 3UH. *T:* (01308) 488383. *Club:* Bridport and West Dorset Golf.

JONES, Maj.-Gen. (Peter) John R.; *see* Russell-Jones.

JONES, Prof. Philip Alan; Vice-Chancellor, Sheffield Hallam University, since 2007; *b* 26 Nov. 1950; *s* of Jean Keir; partner, Hilary Bloor. *Educ:* Poly. of Central London (LLB Hons (ext.) 1972); London Sch. of Econs (LLM 1973); Univ. of Essex (MA Sociol. 1979); Univ. of Surrey (Postgrad. Dip. Practice of Higher Educn). Lectr, Manchester Poly., 1973–75; Polytechnic of Central London, later University of Westminster: Lectr, then Sen. Lectr, 1975–87; Principal Lectr, 1987–91; Dep. Hd and Actg Hd, 1991–92; University of Sheffield: Dir, Legal Practice Course, 1993–97; Dean, Faculty of Law, 1996–98; Pro Vice Chancellor, 1998–2004; Dep. Vice-Chancellor and Sub-Warden, Durham Univ., 2004–07. Vis. Lectr, Brunel Univ., 1988; Vis. Prof., DC Sch. of Law, Washington, 1991. Ed.-in-Chief, Legal Practice Guides, 1993–2000; Exec. Ed., Internat. Jl Legal Profession, 1993–2004; Mem., Editl Bd, Jl Professional Legal Educn, 1995–2004. Member: Bd of Studies and Consultant, Council of Legal Educn, 1993–96; NCVQ Policy Cttee, 1996–98; S Yorks Learning and Skills Council, 2001–04; Quality Assce Cttee, UK eUniv., 2001–04; Quality Assce, Learning and Teaching Cttee, HEFCE, 2003–08; All Party Parly Univ. Gp, 2007–; Univ. Alliance, 2007–; Teacher Educn Adv. Gp, UUK, 2007–; Student Policy Network (formerly Student Experience Policy Cttee, then Students, Quality and Participation Policy Network), UUK, 2008–; Chm., Quality Assce System in Higher Educn Gp, UUK/GuildHE/HEFCE/Dept for Employment and Learning NI, 2010–; Advr to Higher Educn Quality Council, 1996–97; various QCA posts, 1998–2003, incl. Mem., Vocational Qualifications and Occupational Standards Cttee, 1998–2000 and Qualification Cttee, 2000–03. Director: Creative Sheffield, 2007–11; Nat. Sci. Learning Centre (Myscience), 2007–; Yorkshire Univs, 2007–. Mem., Sheffield City Region Local Enterprise Partnership, 2010–. Trustee, ENTHUSE Charitable Trust, 2008–. Hon. LittD Sheffield, 2014. *Publications:* (ed jtly) Politics and Power, vol. 1 1980, vol. 2 1980, vol. 3 1981; (contrib.) Problems in Labour Politics, 1980; (contrib.) Law, Politics and Justice, 1982; Lawyers' Skills, 1993, 4th edn 1996, then reprints annually; (contrib.) Examining the Law Syllabus: beyond the core, 1993; Competences, Learning Outcomes and Legal Education, 1994; (contrib.) Teaching Lawyers' Skills, 1996; (contrib.) An Agenda for Comparative Legal Skills Research: the European Community and the Commonwealth, 1996; (contrib.) The Development of the NVQ Framework at the Higher Levels, 1997; (contrib.) NVQs and Higher Education, 1997; contribs to jls incl. Law Teacher, Modern Law Rev., Jl Law and Soc., New Law Jl, Internat. Jl Legal Profession; numerous conf. papers and res. reports. *Recreations:* rock climbing and biking, road and mountain. *Address:* Sheffield Hallam University, City Campus, Howard Street, Sheffield S1 1WB. *T:* (0114) 225 2050, *Fax:* (0114) 225 2042. *Clubs:* Dark Peak Fell Running; Crosstrax Cycling.

JONES, Vice Adm. Sir Philip (Andrew), KCB 2014 (CB 2012); Fleet Commander and Deputy Chief of Naval Staff, since 2012; *b* 14 Feb. 1960; *s* of Edgar Jones and Edna Lilian Jones (*née* Peers); *m* 1987, Elizabeth Collins; one *s* two *d. Educ:* Birkenhead Sch.; Mansfield Coll., Oxford (BA Geog. 1981; MA 1985). HMS Fearless, Falklands War, 1982; Watchkeeping and Navigation Officer, Frigates and HMY Britannia, 1983–88; Prin. Warfare Officer, Frigates and Maritime Battle Staff, 1989–93; CO HMS Beaver, 1994–96; Directorate Navy Plans and Progs, MoD, 1997–99; CO HMS Coventry, 1999–2001; Chief of Defence Logistics Office, MoD, 2002–03; Dir, Jt Maritime Operational Trng Staff, 2003–04; ACOS C4ISTAR Fleet HQ, 2004–06; Comdr Amphibious Task Gp, 2006–08; FO Scotland, England, Wales and NI, and FO Reserves, 2008; Comdr UK Maritime Forces and Rear Adm., Surface Ships, 2008–09; Asst Chief of Naval Staff, 2009–11; Dep. C-in-C Fleet, COS Navy Comd HQ, and Chief Naval Warfare Officer, 2011–12. Mem., Windsor Leadership Trust, 2008–. Pres., RN Rugby Union, 2012– (Vice-Pres., 2008–12). Younger Brother, Trinity House, 2009. Freeman, City of Glasgow, 2009. *Recreations:* watching and following most sports (especially Rugby Union), supporting Liverpool FC, reading, hill walking. *Address:* Navy Command Headquarters, Leach Building, Whale Island, Portsmouth, Hants PO2 8BY. *E:* philip.jones586@mod.uk.

JONES, Lt Gen. Philip David, CB 2015; CBE 2012 (MBE 1994); Chief of Staff to Supreme Allied Commander Transformation, since 2013; *b* Maldon, Essex, 23 July 1961; *s* of Michael York Jones and Vivien Jones; *m* 1984, Denise Anne Spong; one *s* one *d*. *Educ:* King Edward VI Grammar Sch., Chelmsford; RMA, Sandhurst. Royal Anglian Regiment: Platoon Comdr, 3rd Bn, 1981–83, Inf. Jun. Leaders Bn, 1983–85; Anti-Tank Platoon Comdr, 3rd Bn, 1985–87; Adjt, 1st Bn, 1987–89; SO3 G3 Ops HQ, 8th Inf. Bde, Londonderry, 1989–92; Army Staff Coll., 1993; Comdr, Rifle Co., 1st Bn, Royal Anglian Regt, 1993–95; COS, HQ 24 Airmobile Bde, 1995–97; MA to C-in-C Allied Forces Northwest Europe, 1997–99; CO, 1st Bn, Royal Anglian Regt, 1999–2003; Chief of Plans: Combined Jt Task Force 180, Afghanistan, 2003; HQ ARRC, 2003–05; Comdr, 8th Inf. Bde, NI, 2005–06; MA to Special Rep. of Sec. Gen., UN Assistance Mission Afghanistan, 2006–07; Mil. Attaché, Washington DC, 2007–10; Dir Force Reintegration, HQ ISAF, Afghanistan, 2010–11; COS Jt Forces Comd, 2011–13. MInstD 1992. QCVS 2002. *Recreations:* family, dogs, reading, running, cycling.

JONES, Philip David Simon; Editor, The Bookseller, since 2012; *b* Manchester, 12 Oct. 1971; *s* of Barrie Jones and Jean Wright (*née* Healy); *m* 2005, Amy Lankester-Owen; three *s*. *Educ:* Wem Adams Sch.; Univ. of Reading (BA Hons Eng. Lang. and Lit.). The Bookseller: Financial Reporter, 1996–99; Web Ed., 2002–08; Man. Ed., 2008–10; Dep. Ed., 2010–12; Ed., Futurebook.net, 2010–. *Recreations:* cricket, reading, family. *Address:* The Bookseller, 56–58 Southwark Street, SE1 1UN. *T:* (020) 3358 0364. *E:* philip.jones@thebookseller.com. *Club:* Hospital.

JONES, Prof. Philip Douglas, PhD; FRMetS; Professor, since 1998, and Director, since 2003, Climatic Research Unit, School of Environmental Sciences, University of East Anglia; *b* 22 April 1952; *s* of late Douglas Idris Jones and Peggy Rita Yvonne Jones; *m* 1973, Ruth Anne Shackleton; one *s* one *d*. *Educ:* Univ. of Lancaster (BA Envmtl Scis 1973); Univ. of Newcastle upon Tyne (MSc Engrg Hydrol. 1974; PhD Hydrol. 1977). FRMetS 1992. Sen. Res. Associate, 1976–94, Reader, 1994–98, Co-Dir, 1998–2003, Climatic Res. Unit, Sch. of Envmtl Scis, UEA. Member, Editorial Board: Internat. Jl Climatol., 1989–94; Climatic Change, 1992–. Sec., Internat. Commn for Climatol., 1987–95. MAE 1998; Mem., 2001, Fellow, 2006, Amer. Meteorol. Soc.; Fellow, Amer. Geophys. Union, 2009. Hon. Dr Univ. Rovira i Virgili, Tarragona, Spain, 2012. Hugh Robert Mill Medal, 1995, Internat. Jl Climatol. Prize, 2002, RMetS; Hans Oeschger Medal, Eur. Geophysical Soc., 2002. *Publications:* (ed with R. S. Bradley) Climate since AD 1500, 1992, 2nd edn 1995; (ed Jtly) Climatic Variations and Forcing Mechanisms of the Last 2000 Years, 1996; (contrib.) Climate and Climate Impacts: the last 1000 years, 2001; (ed with D. Camuffo) Improved Understanding of Past Climatic Variability from Early Daily European Instrumental Sources, 2002; chapters in peer reviewed in books; contrib. Climate Change. *Recreation:* playing bridge for local club and for Norfolk. *Address:* Climatic Research Unit, University of East Anglia, Norwich NR4 7TJ. *T:* (01603) 592090, *Fax:* (01603) 507784. *E:* p.jones@uea.ac.uk.

JONES, Philip E.; *see* Edgar-Jones.

JONES, Philip Graham, CEng, FIChemE, FIExpE; occasional part-time safety adviser, since 1995; Deputy Director of Technology and Health Sciences Division, Health and Safety Executive, 1986–95; *b* 3 June 1937; *s* of Sydney and Olive Jones; *m* 1961, Janet Ann Collins; one *s* three *d*. *Educ:* Univ. of Aston in Birmingham (BSc). Eur Ing 1989. Professional positions in UK explosives industry, 1961–68 and 1972–76; service with Australian Public Service, 1969–71, with UK Civil Service, 1976–95; HM Chief Inspector of Explosives, 1981–86. Mem., Accreditation Bd, 1987–90, Professional Develt Cttee, 1988–91, IChemE. Chairman: Nat. Certification Scheme for Inservice Inspection Bodies, 1995–98; Engrg Inspection Technical Cttee, UK Accreditation Service, 1996–2001. Safety Advr, Severn Valley Rly, 1995–. Chm., Wenlock Olympian Soc., 2004–07. *Publications:* articles in The Chemical Engineer, Explosives Engineer, and railway jls. *Recreations:* walking, reading, curling.

JONES, Ven. Philip Hugh; Archdeacon of Hastings (formerly of Lewes and Hastings), since 2005; *b* 13 May 1951; *m* 1979, Anne Atkinson; two *s* two *d*. *Educ:* Leys Sch., Cambridge; Chichester Theol Coll. Admitted solicitor, 1975; in private practice, 1975–92. Ordained deacon, 1994, priest, 1995; Curate, Horsham, 1994–97; Vicar, Southwater, 1997–2005. RD Horsham, 2002–05. *Recreations:* ornithology, medieval history, music (esp. choral). *Address:* The Archdeaconry, High Street, Maresfield, E Sussex TN22 2EH. *T:* (01825) 763326.

JONES, Philip John; QC 2006; *s* of Colin and Sally Jones; *m* 1990, Philippa Seal; one *s* one *d*. *Educ:* Ynysawdre Comprehensive Sch.; Hertford Coll., Oxford (BCL, MA); Dalhousie Univ., Canada (LLM). Called to the Bar, Lincoln's Inn, 1985, Bencher, 2013; Jun. Counsel to the Crown, 1994–2006. Mem., YMCA. *Address:* 6 New Square, Lincoln's Inn, WC2A 3QS. *T:* (020) 7242 6105, *Fax:* (020) 7405 4004. *E:* pjones@serlecourt.co.uk.

JONES, (Piers) Nicholas L.; *see* Legh-Jones.

JONES, Raymond Francis, OBE 1986; HM Diplomatic Service, retired; Chairman, CPM Ltd, 2010–12; *b* 15 Nov. 1935; *s* of late Hugh and Jessie Jones; *m* 1957, Maurag Annat (*d* 1994); two *d*. *Educ:* Liverpool Collegiate Sch. Nat. Service, RAF, 1954–56. Joined Foreign Office, 1953; served Amman, Tokyo, Cairo, Accra, 1956–70; Second Sec., FCO, 1970–73; Consul, Seattle, 1973–78; First Sec., 1978; on loan to DoI, 1978–82; New Delhi, 1982–86; Dep. Consul-Gen., Chicago, 1986–91; High Comr, Honiara, Solomon Is, 1991–95. Dir, 1996–2002, Chm., 2001–02, Holywell Hook Heath Ltd. *Recreations:* music, sport, reading. *Address:* Flat 168, Centrium, Station Approach, Woking, Surrey GU22 7PE.

JONES, Prof. Raymond Leonard, PhD; FAcSS; Professor of Social Work, Kingston University and St George's, University of London, since 2008; *b* 21 Oct. 1949; *s* of Leonard and Pauline Jones; *m* 1973, Mary Elaine Abbott; one *s* one *d*. *Educ:* Redruth Grammar Sch.; Univ. of Bath (BSc 1st Cl. Hons Sociol. 1972; MSc 1981; PhD 1983). CQSW 1972. Asst Warden, Mental Health Hostel, Cornwall CC, 1967–68; Social Worker, then Sen. Social Worker, Social Services, Berks CC, 1972–75; Lectr in Social Work, Univ. of Bath, 1975–80; Area Team Leader, Social Services, Wilts CC, 1981–84; Asst Divl Dir, Barnardo's, 1984–87; Divl Dir, Social Services, Surrey CC, 1987–89; Dep. Dir, Social Services, Berks CC, 1989–92; Chief Exec., Social Care Inst. for Excellence, 2001–02; Dir, Social Services, 1992–2001 and 2002–06, Adult and Community Services, 2002–06, Wiltshire CC. Chm., Marlborough Brandt Gp, 2003–07. Dep. Chm., then Chm., BASW, 2005–06. Chairman: Bristol Safeguarding Children Bd, 2009–13; Salford Safeguarding Children Improvement Bd, 2010–13; Torbay Safeguarding Children Improvement Bd, 2012–14; IoW Safeguarding Children Bd, 2013–; Devon Safeguarding Children Bd, 2013–; Sandwell Children's Performance Accountability Bd, 2013–. Vis. Prof. (formerly Vis. Fellow), Univ. of Bath, 1993–; Vis. Prof. (formerly Univ. Fellow), Univ. of Exeter, 1997–2004. Trustee: Quarriers, 2006–11; Wytham Hall, 2011–14. FCMI (FIMgt 1992); FRSA 1996; FAcSS (AcSS 2002). Hon. Fellow, Univ. of Glos (formerly Cheltenham and Gloucester Coll.), 1995. Chm., Social Worker of the Year Awards, 2014–. *Publications:* Fun and Therapy, 1979; Intermediate Treatment and Social Work, 1979; Social Work with Adolescents, 1980; From Resident to Community Worker, 1983; Like Distant Relatives, 1987; The Story of Baby P: setting the record straight, 2014; chapters in books and papers on social work and social policy. *Recreations:* Rugby, fell walking. *Club:* Redruth Rugby Football.

JONES, Rhiannon; QC 2015; *b* Stockport, Cheshire, 7 April 1970; *d* of Geraint and Nina Jones; *m* 1996, Dominic Happé; two *s*. *Educ:* King's Coll. London (BMus; AKC; MA Med. Law and Ethics). Called to the Bar, Inner Temple, 1993; in practice as barrister, 1993–. *Recreations:* sport, music. *Address:* Farrars Building, Temple, EC4Y 7BD. *T:* (020) 7583 9241, *Fax:* (020) 7583 0090. *E:* rjones@farrarsbuilding.co.uk.

JONES, Richard, CBE 2015; operatic and theatrical director; *b* London. *Opera productions* include: English National Opera: The Love for Three Oranges, Die Fledermaus, 1993; Pelleas and Melisande (also for Opera North), 1995; From Morning to Midnight (David Sawer), 2001; Lulu, 2002; The Trojans, 2003 (Olivier Award); The Bitter Tears of Petra von Kant, 2005; Cavalleria Rusticana, Pagliacci, 2008; The Tales of Hoffman, 2012; Julietta, 2012; Rodelinda, 2014; The Girl of the Golden West, 2014; The Mastersingers of Nuremberg, 2015 (Best New Opera Production, Olivier Awards, 2015); Royal Opera: Der Ring des Nibelungen, 1994–95 (Evening Standard Award); Lady Macbeth of Mtsensk, 2004 (Olivier Award); L'Heure Espagnol, and Gianni Schicchi, 2007; The Gambler, 2010; Anna Nicole, 2011; Il Trittico, 2011; Gloriana, 2013; Welsh National Opera: Hansel and Gretel, 1998 (Olivier Award); The Queen of Spades, 2000; Wozzeck, 2005; Die Meistersinger, 2010; Glyndebourne: Flight (Jonathan Dove), 1998; Euryanthe, 2002; Macbeth, 2007; Falstaff, 2009; Der Rosenkavalier, 2014; Der fliegende Holländer, 1993, Jenufa, 1997, The Cunning Little Vixen, 2006, Amsterdam; Julius Caesar (Opernwelt Prodn of Year), 1994, The Midsummer Marriage, 1998, The Cunning Little Vixen, 2006, Lohengrin, 2009, The Tales of Hoffman, 2011, Munich; L'enfant et les Sortilèges, and Der Zweig, 1998, Julietta, 2012, Paris; Un ballo in maschera, 1999 ((jtly) Designer of the Year, 2000), La Bohème, 2001, Bregenz Fest.; The Fiery Angel, Brussels, 2007; Billy Budd, 2007, Makropulos Case, 2012, Frankfurt; Hansel and Gretel, Metropolitan Opera, 2007; Rusalka, Copenhagen, 2008; Skin Deep, Opera North, 2009; Peter Grimes, Milan, 2012; Gloriana, Hamburg, 2013; *theatre productions* include: Too Clever by Half (Olivier Award); The Illusion (Evening Standard Award), A Flea in Her Ear, 1989, Old Vic; Into the Woods, Phoenix, 1990 (Olivier and Evening Standard Awards); Le Bourgeois Gentilhomme, 1992, Tales from the Vienna Woods, 2003, NT; Holy Mothers, Royal Court, 1999; Six Characters Looking for an Author, 2001, Hobson's Choice, 2003, The Good Soul of Szechuan, 2008, Annie Get Your Gun, 2009, Government Inspector, 2010, Public Enemy, 2013, The Trial, 2015, Young Vic; A Midsummer Night's Dream, RSC, 2002; David Sawer's Rumpelstiltskin, Birmingham Contemporary Music Gp, 2009; in New York: La Bête, 1991; Black Snow, 1992; All's Well That Ends Well; Titanic, 1997; Wrong Mountain, 1999. *Address:* c/o Judy Daish Associates, 2 St Charles Place, W10 6EG.

JONES, Prof. Richard Anthony Lewis, PhD; FRS 2006; Professor of Physics, since 1998, and Pro-Vice-Chancellor for Research and Innovation, since 2009, University of Sheffield; *b* 7 March 1961; *s* of Rev. Robert Cecil Jones and Sheila Howell Jones; *m* 1998, Dulcie Anne Jordan; one *s* one *d*. *Educ:* Denstone Coll.; St Catharine's Coll., Cambridge (BA Natural Scis 1983; PhD Physics 1987). Postdoctoral Res. Associate, Cornell Univ., 1987–89; Asst Lectr, 1989–94, Lectr, 1994–98, Univ. of Cambridge. Mem., EPSRC, 2013–. *Publications:* Polymers at Surfaces and Interfaces (with R. W. Richards), 1999; Soft Condensed Matter, 2002; Soft Machines: nanotechnology and life, 2004; more than 100 papers in learned jls. *Recreations:* rock climbing, mountain walking. *Address:* University of Sheffield, Firth Court, Western Bank, Sheffield S10 2TN. *T:* (0114) 222 9820. *E:* r.a.l.jones@sheffield.ac.uk.

JONES, Rev. Richard Granville; Chairman of East Anglia District, Methodist Church, 1983–93; President of the Methodist Conference, 1988–89; *b* 26 July 1926; *s* of Henry William and Ida Grace Jones; *m* 1955, Kathleen Stone; three *d*. *Educ:* Truro School, Cornwall; St John's Coll., Cambridge (MA); Manchester Univ. (BD). Instructor Officer, RN, 1947–49. Methodist Minister in Plymouth East, 1949–50; Area Sec., SCM, 1953–55; Minister: Sheffield North Circuit, 1955–59; Sheffield Carver Street, 1959–64; Birkenhead, 1964–69; Tutor, Hartley Victoria Coll., Manchester, 1969–78, Principal 1978–82; Minister, Fakenham and Wells Circuit, 1982–83. Editor, Epworth Review, 1991–2005. Hon. DD Hull, 1988. *Publications:* (ed) Worship for Today, 1968; (with A. Wesson) Towards a Radical Church, 1972; How goes Christian Marriage?, 1978; Groundwork of Worship and Preaching, 1980; Groundwork of Christian Ethics, 1984; What to Do?: Christians and ethics, 1999; Michael's War, 2010. *Recreations:* walking, reading, writing. *Address:* 35 Davies Road, West Bridgford, Nottingham NG2 5JE. *T:* (0115) 914 2352.

JONES, Richard Henry; QC 1996; a Recorder, since 2000; *b* 6 April 1950; *s* of Henry Ingham Jones and Betty Marian Jones; *m* 1989, Sarah Jane Wildsmith; one *s* one *d*. *Educ:* Moseley Grammar Sch., Birmingham; St Peter's Coll., Oxford (MA Jurisp.). Called to the Bar, Inner Temple, 1972; in practice, 1973–80; Legal Adviser: Crown Life Insurance Gp, 1980–82; Financial Times Gp, 1982–86; in practice, 1986–. *Publications:* Investigations and Enforcement, 2001. *Recreations:* cricket and Rugby (spectating), reading, walking. *Address:* 5 Fountain Court, Steelhouse Lane, Birmingham B4 6DR. *T:* (0121) 606 0500. *Clubs:* Royal Automobile, MCC; London Scottish Football.

JONES, Richard Hugh Francis; HM Diplomatic Service; European External Action Service; Head of European Union Delegation to Switzerland and Principality of Liechtenstein, since 2012; *b* 28 Sept. 1962; *s* of late Lynn and Audrey Jones. *Educ:* Dulwich Coll.; Merton Coll., Oxford (MA). Joined FCO, 1983; Arabic lang. trng, 1984–86; Third, later Second Sec., Abu Dhabi, 1986–89; FCO, 1989–94; First Sec., UK Perm. Rep. to EU, Brussels, 1994–98; Dep. Hd, Common Foreign and Security Policy Dept, FCO, 1998–2000; Counsellor, Dep. Hd, EU Dept (Internal), FCO, 2000–03; Albanian lang. trng, 2003; Ambassador to Albania, 2003–06; Consul-Gen., Basra, 2007–08; Political Counsellor and Dep. Hd of Mission, UK Perm. Rep. to EU, Brussels, 2008–11. *Recreations:* music, places, words, the past, food. *Address:* c/o Foreign and Commonwealth Office, King Charles Street, SW1A 2AH.

JONES, Richard Mansell M.; *see* Mansell-Jones.

JONES, Prof. R(ichard) Merfyn, CBE 2011; PhD; FRHistS; Professor of Welsh History, 1994–2010, Vice-Chancellor, 2004–10, Bangor University (formerly University of Wales, Bangor); *b* 16 Jan. 1948; *s* of John Edwin Jones and Ellen Jones; *m* 1st, 1969, Dr Jill Lovecy (marr. diss. 2003); two *s*; 2nd, 2004, Dr Nerys Patterson (*née* Thomas) (*d* 2007); 3rd, 2009, Dr Catrin Hughes (*née* Richards). *Educ:* Univ. of Sussex (BA 1st cl. Hons 1968); Univ. of Warwick (MA; PhD 1976). Sen. Researcher, ESRC Coalfield Hist. Project, UC, Swansea, 1971–74; Lectr, then Sen. Lectr in Mod. Hist., Dept of Continuing Educn, Univ. of Liverpool, 1975–90; Sen. Lectr, Dept of Hist. and Welsh Hist., Univ. of Wales, Bangor, 1990–94. Chairman: Higher Educn Wales, 2006–08; Review of Higher Educn in Wales Task and Finish Gp (Jones Review), 2008–09; N Wales Branch, Inst. of Welsh Affairs, 2009–14; Vice-Pres., UUK, 2006–08. Ind. Mem., Betsi Cadwaladr Univ. Health Bd, 2009–13 (Chm., 2011–13). Writer and presenter of TV historical documentaries. Gov., BBC, 2002–06. Trustee, Sir Clough William-Ellis Foundn, 2010–; Chm., Coleg Cymraeg Cenedlaethol (Nat. Welsh Coll.) 2011–14. Hon. Patron, Bevan Foundn, 2005–. FRHistS 1996. *Publications:* The North Wales Quarrymen 1874–1922, 1981; Cymru 2000: Hanes Cymru yn yr Ugeinfed Ganrif (History of Wales in the Twentieth Century), 1999; numerous articles in specialist jls. *Recreations:* mountaineering, cooking, Rugby. *Clubs:* Athenæum; Royal Welsh Yacht (Trustee, 2011–).

See also A. G. Jones.

JONES, Riel Meredith K.; *see* Karmy-Jones.

JONES, (Robert) Alun; QC 1989; *b* 19 March 1949; *s* of late Owen Glyn Jones and Violet Marion Jones (*née* Luxton); *m* 1974, Elizabeth Clayton; one *s* three *d*. *Educ:* Oldershaw Grammar Sch., Wallasey, Cheshire; Bristol Univ. (BSc 1970). Called to the Bar, Gray's Inn, 1972. Asst Recorder, 1988–92; Recorder, 1992–96. *Publications:* Jones on Extradition, 1995, 2nd edn 2001, (jtly) 3rd edn, as Jones and Doobay on Extradition and Mutual Assistance, 2005. *Recreations:* gardening, rural conservation, local history, chess. *Address:* 37 Great James Street, WC1N 3HB. *T:* (020) 7440 4949.

JONES, Dr (Robert) Brinley, CBE 2000; FSA; President: National Library of Wales, 1996–2007 (Member, Court and Council, 1974–82); University of Wales Trinity Saint David (formerly University of Wales, Lampeter), since 2007; *b* 27 Feb. 1929; *yr s* of John Elias Jones and Mary Ann Jones (*née* Williams); *m* 1971, Stephanie Avril Hall; one *s*. *Educ:* Tonypandy Grammar Sch.; University Coll. Cardiff (BA Wales 1st cl. Hons 1950; DipEd 1951; Fellow 1984); Jesus Coll., Oxford (DPhil 1960); Internat. Inst. for Advanced Studies, Clayton, Mo (MA 1984). FSA 1971. Commissioned RAF, 1955; Educn Officer, RAF Kidlington and Bicester, 1955–58. Asst Master, Penarth Grammar Sch., 1958–60; Lectr, UC Swansea, 1960–66; Asst Registrar, Univ. of Wales, 1966–69; Dir, Univ. of Wales Press, 1969–76; Warden, Llandovery Coll., 1976–88. Member: Literature Cttee, Welsh Arts Council, 1968–74, 1981–87; Bd, British Council, 1987–96 (Chm., Welsh Cttee, 1987–96); Broadcasting Standards Council, 1988–91. Chairman: European Assoc. of Teachers, 1965; Dinefwr Tourism Gp, 1988–96; Carmarthenshire Tourist Forum, 1998–2007. Chm., Mgt Cttee, Univ. of Wales Centre for Advanced Welsh and Celtic Studies, 2002–07. Member: Council: St David's UC (later Univ. of Wales), Lampeter, 1977–95 (Hon. Fellow 1987); Trinity Coll., Carmarthen, 1984–2003 (Vice-Chm., 1998–2003; Hon. Fellow, 2003); Court: UC Swansea (later Univ. of Wales, Swansea), 1983–2007 (Hon. Fellow 2002); Univ. of Wales, 1997–2007; Univ. of Wales, Aberystwyth, 1997–2007; Univ. of Wales, Cardiff, 1997–2007; Governing Body, Church in Wales, 1981–2004 (Chairman: Provincial Validating Bd for Ministerial Educn, 1990–2012; Cathedrals and Churches Commn, 1994–2004; Church in Wales Publications, 1998–2001); Managing Trustee, St Michael's Theol Coll., 1982–94. Hon. Mem., Druidic Order, Gorsedd of Bards, 1979–; Mem., Welsh Acad., 1981–; Vice-Pres., Llangollen Internat. Musical Eisteddfod, 1989–. Hon. Pres., Assoc. of Friends of Nat. Liby of Wales, 2011–. Fellow, Royal Commonwealth Soc., 1988–91. Editor, The European Teacher, 1964–69. Hon. Series Editor, Writers of Wales, 2009–. Hon. DD Faraston Theol Seminary, Longview, WA, 1993; Hon. DLitt: Greenwich, 1997; Glamorgan, 2008; DUniv Wales, 2006. *Publications:* The Old British Tongue, 1970; (ed and contrib.) Anatomy of Wales, 1972; (ed with M. Stephens) Writers of Wales, 1970–2008 (100 titles published); (ed with R. Bromwich) Astudiaethau ar yr Hengerdd: studies in old Welsh poetry, 1978; Introducing Wales, 1978, 3rd edn 1988; Prifysgol Rhydychen a'i Chysylltiadau Cymreig, 1983; Certain Scholars of Wales, 1986; (ed with D. Ellis Evans) Cofio'r Dafydd, 1987; (contrib.) C. N. D. Cole, The New Wales, 1990; (introd.) Songs of Praises: the English hymns and elegies of William Williams Pantycelyn 1717–1791, 1991, 2nd edn 1995; Prize Days: a headmaster remembers his school 1976–1987, 1993; William Salesbury, 1994; A Lanterne to their Feete: remembering Rhys Prichard 1579–1644, 1994; Floreat Landubriense, 1998; The Particularity of Wales, 2001; World-Wide Wales, 2005; Sir John Williams *Bart*, MD, 1840–1926, 2007; Rhamant Rhydychen, 2015; articles and reviews in learned jls. *Recreations:* music, farming. *Address:* Drovers Farm, Porthyrhyd, Llanwrda, Dyfed SA19 8DF. *T:* (01558) 650649.

JONES, Robert David T.; *see* Trevor-Jones.

JONES, Sir Robert (Edward), Kt 1989; author; sporting and political commentator; Founder, Robt Jones Holdings Ltd, 1961 (Chairman, 1982–92); *b* 24 Nov. 1939; *s* of Edward Llewyllan and Joyce Lillian Jones; three *s* five *d*. *Educ:* Victoria Univ. of Wellington. Leader, New Zealand Party, Gen. Elect., 1984. Chm., NZ Winter Olympics Cttee, 1988. New Zealand Commemoration Medal, 1990. *Publications:* New Zealand Boxing Yearbooks, 1972 and 1973; Jones on Property, 1977, 6th edn 1979; NZ The Way I Want It, 1978; Travelling, 1980; Letters, 1981; Wimp Walloping, 1989; Prancing Pavonine Charlatans, 1990; 80's Letters, 1990; Punchlines, 1991; A Year of It, 1992; Wowser Whacking, 1993; Prosperity Denied—How the Reserve Bank Harms New Zealand, 1996; Memories of Muldoon, 1997; My Property World, 2005; Jones on Management, 2008; Fighting Talk: boxing and the modern lexicon, 2013; No Punches Pulled, 2013; *novels:* The Permit, 1984; Full Circle, 2000; Ogg, 2002; True Facts, 2003; Degrees For Everyone, 2004. *Recreations:* reading, writing, gardening, trout-fishing, tennis, travel, golf, wind-surfing. *Address:* Melling, Lower Hutt, New Zealand; Darling Point, Sydney, Australia.

JONES, Ven. Robert George; Archdeacon of Worcester, since 2014; *b* Birmingham, 30 Oct. 1955; *s* of Kenneth and Dorothy Jones. *Educ:* King Edward's Sch., Birmingham; Hatfield Coll., Durham (BA Modern Langs 1977); Ripon Coll., Cuddesden, Oxford (MA Theol. 1987); Ecumenical Inst., Geneva. Ordained deacon, 1980, priest, 1981; Curate, Holy Innocents, Kidderminster, 1980–84; Vicar, St Francis, Dudley, 1984–92; Rector, St Barnabas with Christ Church, Worcester, 1992–2006; Proctor in Convocation, 1995–2005; Rural Dean, Worcester East, 1999–2006. Hon. Canon, Worcester Cathedral, 2003–. *Recreations:* walking, choral singing, friends, German culture. *Address:* Archdeacon's House, Walkers Lane, Whittington, Worcester WR5 2RE. *T:* (01905) 773301. *E:* archdeacon.worcester@cofe-worcester.org.uk.

JONES, Prof. Robert Maynard, FBA 1993; FLSW; Fellow, Yr Academi Gymreig, 1995; Professor of Welsh Language and Literature, University of Wales, 1980–89, now Professor Emeritus; *b* 20 May 1929; *s* of Sydney Valentine Jones and Mary Edith Jones; *m* 1952, Anne Elizabeth James; one *s* one *d*. *Educ:* Univ. of Wales (BA 1949; MA 1951; PhD 1965; DLitt 1979); Univ. of Ireland; Laval Univ., Québec. Teaching in Llanidloes and Llangefni, 1952–56; Lectr, Trinity Coll., Carmarthen, 1956–58; University of Wales, Aberystwyth: Lectr in Educn, 1958–66; Lectr, Sen. Lectr, Reader, Prof. and Head of Dept of Welsh Language and Literature, 1966–89. Chm., Yr Academi Gymreig (Welsh Acad. of Letters), 1975–79, Pres., 2010–; Vice-President, UCCF, 1990–95. FLSW 2010. *Publications:* Y Gân Gyntaf, 1957; Crwydro Môn, 1957; Nid yw Dŵr yn Plygu, 1958; I'r Arch, 1959; Y Tair Rhamant, 1960; Bod yn Wraig, 1960; Rhwng Taf a Thaf, 1960; Graddio Geirfa, 1962; Emile, 1963; Cyflwyno'r Gymraeg, 1964; Cymraeg i Oedolion, I & II, 1965–66; Y Dyn na Ddaeth Adref, 1966; Yr Ŵyl Ifori, 1967; Ci wrth y Drws, 1968; Highlights in Welsh Literature, 1969; Daw'r Pasg i Bawb, 1969; System in Child Language, 1970; Pedwar Emynydd, 1970; Sioc o'r Gofod, 1971; Allor Wydn, 1971; Traed Prydferth, 1973; Tafod y Llenor, 1974; (with M. E. Roberts) Cyfeiriadur i'r Athro Iaith I–III, 1974–79; Llenyddiaeth Gymraeg 1936–1972, 1975; Gwlad Llun, 1976; Llên Cymru a Chrefydd, 1977; Pwy laddodd Miss Wales, 1977; Seiliau Beirniadaeth, 4 vols, 1984–88; Hunllef Arthur, 1986; (with Gwyn Davies) The Christian Heritage of Welsh Education, 1986; (with Gwyn Thomas) The Dragon's Pen, 1986; Llenyddiaeth Gymraeg 1902–1936, 1987; Selected Poems (trans. Joseph P. Clancy), 1987; Blodeugerdd Barddas o'r 19 Ganrif, 1988; (with Rhiannon Ifans) Gloywi Iaith I–III, 1988; Casgliad o Gerddi, 1989; Crio Chwerthin, 1990; Dawn Gweddwon, 1991; Language Regained, 1993; Cyfriniaeth Gymraeg, 1994; Canu Arnaf, Vol. I, 1994, Vol. II, 1995; Crist a Chenedlaetholdeb, 1994; Epistol Serch a Selsig, 1997; Tair Rhamant Arthuraidd, 1998; Ysbryd y Cwlwm, 1998; Ynghylch Tawelwch, 1998; O'r Bedd i'r Crud, 2000; Mawl a'i Gyfeillion, 2000; Mawl a Gelynion ei Elynion, 2002; Ôl Troed, 2003; Dysgu Cyfansawdd, 2003; Beirniadaeth Gyfansawdd, 2003; Rhy Iach, 2004; Y Fadarchen Hudol, 2005; Meddwl y Gynghanedd, 2005; Yr Amhortreadwy, 2009; Bratiau Budron, vol. I 2011, vol. II, 2012, vol. III, 2013, vol. IV, 2015; Breuddwydion Maxine, 2011; Y Cynllun Sy'n Canu, 2011; A Fydd y Cymry Cymraeg newn Pryd, 2011; Palu'r Ardd, 2011; Canu Gwirebol a Wittgenstein, 2011; Right as Rain (trans. Joseph P. Clancy), 2012; Storïau, 2012; Hanes Beirniadaeth Lenyddol Ddiweddar, 2012; Gobaith ac Anobaith Waldo ac R. S., 2012; (with Huw Walters) Llyfryddiaeth, 2012; Awdur y Beibl, 2014; Problemau with Adennill Iaith, 2014; Canalfon Ymchwil i Adennill Iaith, 2014. *Recreation:* walking. *Address:* Tandderwen, Ffordd Llanbadarn, Aberystwyth SY23 1HB. *T:* and *Fax:* (01970) 623603.

JONES, Robyn Anne, OBE 2011; Co-Founder, CH&Co Catering Ltd (formerly Charlton House Catering), since 1991; *b* Sutton Coldfield, 20 Aug. 1961; *d* of David and Patricia Lardge; *m* 1986, Timothy John Jones, *qv*; one *s* one *d*. *Educ:* Buxton Coll. (OND Hotel Catering and Instnl Mgt). Asst Cook, Compass Catering, 1981–83; Catering Manager, Gardner Merchant, 1983–85; Catering Adv. Officer, Potato Mktg Bd, 1985–87; Ops Manager, High Table Ltd, 1987–88; Ops Manager, Compass Catering, 1988–90; Business Develt Manager, Gazeway Catering, 1990–91. FIH (FHCIMA 1992; MHCIMA 1985). *Address:* Bryants Farm, Kiln Road, Dunsden, Reading, Berks RG4 9PB. *E:* Robyn.jones@chandco.net. *Club:* Phyllis Court (Henley on Thames).

JONES, Roger; *see* Jones, James R.

JONES, Rear-Adm. Roger Charles M.; *see* Moylan-Jones.

JONES, Prof. Roger Hugh, DM; FRCP, FRCGP, FRCPE, FMedSci; Editor, British Journal of General Practice, since 2010; Wolfson Professor of General Practice, 1993–2010, now Emeritus, and Head, Department of General Practice and Primary Care, 1993–2010, King's College London School of Medicine (formerly Guy's, King's and St Thomas's Medical School, King's College London); Chairman, Royal Medical Benevolent Fund, since 2013; *b* 11 Nov. 1948; *s* of (Sydney Elsom) Vernon Jones and Phyllis Marion Elsie Jones (*née* Yemm); *m* 1998, Prof. Janice Rymer; one *s* one *d* (and one *s* decd). *Educ:* Monmouth Sch.; St Peter's Coll., Oxford (MA 1973); St Thomas's Hosp. Med. Sch. (BM BCh 1973); Univ. of Southampton (DM 1990). MRCP 1976, FRCP 2000; FRCGP 1990; FRCPE 1992. House Surgeon and House Physician, St Richard's Hosp., Chichester, 1973–74; Registrar and Res. Fellow, Royal Sussex Co. Hosp., Brighton, and KCH, London, 1974–79; GP, Andover, 1979–84; Sen. Lectr in Primary Health Care, Univ. of Southampton, 1984–91; William Leech Prof. of Primary Health Care, Univ. of Newcastle upon Tyne, 1991–93; Dean for Ext. Affairs, 2001–07, Dean for Teaching, 2002–06, KCL. FMedSci 1998; FHEA 2007. FRSA 1996. Editor, Family Practice, 1990–2004. *Publications:* (Ed. in Chief) Oxford Textbook of Primary Medical Care, 2003. *Recreations:* literature, travel, golf, bridge. *Address:* 56 Scotts Sufferance Wharf, 5 Mill Street, SE1 2DE. *T:* (020) 7394 9586. *E:* roger.jones@kcl.ac.uk. *Club:* Athenæum.

JONES, Roger Kenneth; Secretary, Co-operative Wholesale Society, 1996–98; *b* 10 Sept. 1947; *s* of George Ephraim Jones and Winifred Annie Jones; *m* 1972, Caroline Ruth Proctor; three *d*. *Educ:* Abbeydale Grammar Sch., Sheffield; Manchester Univ. (BA Hons Econs 1969). Called to the Bar, Gray's Inn, 1977; Asst Sec., Manchester Ship Canal Co., 1977–83; Dep. Sec., CWS Ltd, 1983–96; Secretary: Unity Trust Bank, PLC, 1984–92; Co-operative Bank PLC, 1992–96. Mem., UK Co-operative Council, 1991–98. Hon. Pres., Co-operative Law Assoc., 1999–2007. Hon. Chm., Manchester Cathedral Country Home, 2002–07.

JONES, Sir Roger (Spencer), Kt 2005; OBE 1996; Chairman, ZooBiotic Ltd, since 2005; *b* 2 July 1943; *s* of Richard David Jones and Gwladys Jones; *m* 1970, Ann Evans; one *s* one *d*. *Educ:* Bala Boys' Grammar Sch.; Univ. of Wales (BPharm); Univ. of Bradford (MSc). FRPharmS 2009 (MRPharmS 1968). Area Manager, then Marketing Planning Manager, Wellcome Foundn Ltd, 1968–82; Man. Dir, Nigeria, Smith Kline & French Ltd, 1982–83; with Penn Pharmaceuticals Ltd, 1983–2000 (Chm., 1986–2000). Nat. Gov. for Wales, BBC, 1997–2003; Mem., S4C Broadcasting Authy, 2004–11. Chairman: Gwent TEC, 1993–98; TEC SE Wales, 1998–2000; Council of Welsh TECs, 1995–2001; Welsh Develt Agency, 2002–06. Non-exec. Dir, Powys Healthcare NHS Trust, 1993–2000. Chm., Wales Inst. of Dirs, 1995–2002. Chairman: Children in Need, 1999–2003; Carmarthen Heritage Regeneration Trust, 2004–11; Chm., Nat. Trust Wales Cttee, 2006–12 (Dep. Chm., 2005–06); Bd Mem., Botanic Gdns of Wales, 2005–. Pres., YMCA Wales, 2000–. Chm. Council, Swansea Univ. (formerly Univ. of Wales, Swansea), 2005– (Pro-Chancellor, 2009–). DUniv Glamorgan, 1997; Hon. DSc Wales, 2000. *Recreations:* salmon and trout fishing, shooting, nature conservation. *Address:* Battle House, Battle, Brecon LD3 9RW. *T:* (01874) 611777. *Club:* Athenæum.

JONES, Ron; *see* Jones, O. G. R.

JONES, Prof. Ronald Mervyn, MD; FRCA; Director of Continuing Education and Professional Development, and Editor of Bulletin, Royal College of Anaesthetists, 1999–2002; *b* 24 April 1947; *s* of Comdr Glyn Owen Jones, RN and Doris Woodley Jones; *m* 1st, 1970, Angela Christine Parsonage (marr. diss.); one *s* one *d*; 2nd, 1989, Caroline Ann Marshall; two *d*. *Educ:* Devonport High Sch., Plymouth; Univ. of Liverpool (MB ChB 1971; MD 1990). FRCA 1978. Karolinska Inst., Stockholm, 1978; Univ. of Michigan, 1979–80; Consultant, Nottingham Hosps, 1981–82; Sen. Lectr and Hon. Consultant, Guy's Hosp. and Med. Sch., 1982–90; Foundn Prof. of Anaesthetics and Hd of Dept, ICSM at St Mary's, London, 1990–99. Mem. Council, Royal Coll. of Anaesthetists, 1997–2002. Academician, European Acad. Anaesthesiologists, 1984; Hon. Life Mem., Australian Soc. Anaesthetists, 1988. *Publications:* (ed jtly) Medicine for Anaesthetists, 3rd edn 1989; (ed jtly) Clinical Anaesthesia, 1996. *Recreations:* art history, sailing. *Address:* Kermolet, Treverec, 22290 Côtes d'Armor, France. *Club:* Royal Naval Sailing Assoc.

JONES, Prof. Ronald Samuel, OBE 1998; DVSc; FRCVS; FRSB; JP; Professor of Veterinary Anaesthesia, 1991–2001, now Emeritus, and Head of Department of Anaesthesia, 1995–2000, University of Liverpool; *b* 29 Oct. 1937; *s* of Samuel and Gladys Jane Jones; *m* 1962, Pamela Evans; two *d*. *Educ:* High Sch. for Boys, Oswestry; Univ. of Liverpool (BVSc 1960; MVSc; DVA); DVetMed Berne, 1980; DVSc Pretoria, 1991. FRCVS 1981; FRSB (FIBiol 1987). University of Glasgow: house surgeon, 1960–61; Asst, 1961–62; University of Liverpool: Lectr, 1962–77; Sen. Lectr, 1977–86; Reader, 1986–90; Dean, Faculty of Vet. Sci., 1989–93. Visiting Professor: Univ. of Zurich, 1975; Cornell Univ., 1980, 1993; Univ. of Pretoria, 1994; Univ. of Valdivia, 2001, 2002, 2003; Univ. of Vienna, 2002, 2003. Member: Home Office Adv. Council on the Misuse of Drugs, 1994–2001; Medicines Commn, 1997–2005; Chm., Farriers' Registration Council, 2010–12. Royal College of Veterinary Surgeons: Mem. Council, 1986–98; Treas., 1993–95; Jun. Vice-Pres., 1995–96; Pres., 1996–97; Sen. Vice-Pres., 1997–98. Mem., EC Adv. Cttee of Vet. Trng, 1990–93. FLS 2003; FRSA 1996. JP Liverpool City, 1981–2007. Hon. FRCA 2001. John Henry Steele Medal, RCVS, 1989; Coll. Medal, Royal Coll. Anaesthetists, 1996. *Publications:* (jtly) Principles of Veterinary Therapeutics, 1994; contrib. chapters to books and vet. and med. jls. *Recreations:* horse-racing, fly-fishing, vegetable gardening, philately. *Address:* 7 Birch Road, Prenton, Merseyside CH43 5UF. *T:* (0151) 653 9008. *Clubs:* Farmers, Royal Society of Medicine.

JONES, Samuel, CBE 1996; DL; Chairman, Heathrow Airport Consultative Committee, 1997–2014; *b* 27 Dec. 1939; *s* of late Samuel Jones and Sarah Johnston Jones (*née* McCulloch); *m* 1964, Jean Ann Broadhurst; two *d*. *Educ:* Morpeth Grammar Sch.; Manchester Univ. (LLB); Kent Univ. (MA). Admitted Solicitor, 1964. Asst Solicitor, Macclesfield Bor. Council, 1964–67; Asst Town Clerk, Bedford Bor. Council, 1967–71; Head of Legal Div., Coventry CBC, 1971–73; Head of Admin and Legal Dept, Sheffield Dist Council, 1973–76; Chief Exec. and County Clerk, Leics CC, and Clerk of Lieutenancy, 1976–91; Town Clerk, Corp.

of London, 1991–96. Mem., Council on Tribunals, 1996–2002. Chairman: N Devon Marketing Bureau, 1996–98; Westcountry Ambulance Service NHS Trust, 1996–2004; N Devon NHS PCT, 2004–06; non-exec. Dir, Northern Devon Healthcare NHS Trust, 2006–10. Mem., Adjudication Panel for England, 2002–09. DL Leics, 1992. *Recreation:* dog walking. *Address:* Glenfield, Raleigh Park, Barnstaple, Devon EX31 4JD. *T:* (01271) 345010.

JONES, Sandy; *see* Jones, Alexander M.

JONES, Sarah Jane V.; *see* Vaughan Jones.

JONES, Sarah Louise R.; *see* Rowland-Jones.

JONES, Schuyler, CBE 1998; DPhil; Director (formerly Curator and Head of Department of Ethnology and Prehistory), Pitt Rivers Museum, 1985–97, and Fellow of Linacre College, 1970–97, now Emeritus Professor, Oxford University; *b* 7 Feb. 1930; *s* of Schuyler Jones, Jr and Ignace Mead Jones; *m* 1st, 1955, Lis Margit Søndergaard Rasmussen; one *s* one *d*; 2nd, 1998, Dr Lorraine Christine Da'Luz Vieira. *Educ:* Edinburgh Univ. (MA Hons Anthropology); Oxford Univ. (DPhil Anthropology). Anthropological expeditions to: Atlas Mountains, Southern Algeria, French West Africa, Nigeria, 1951; French Equatorial Africa, Belgian Congo, 1952; East and Southern Africa, 1953; Morocco High Atlas, Algeria, Sahara, Niger River, 1954; Turkey, Iran, Afghanistan, Pakistan, India, Nepal, 1958–59; ten expeditions to Nuristan in the Hindu Kush, 1960–70; to Chinese Turkestan, 1985; Tibet and Gobi Desert, 1986; Southern China, Xinjiang, and Pakistan, 1988; Western Greenland, 1991; Greenland and E Africa, 1993. Asst Curator, Pitt Rivers Mus., 1970–71; Asst Curator and Univ. Lectr in Ethnology, 1971–85. Mem. Council, Royal Anthropological Inst., 1986–89. Trustee, Horniman Mus., 1989–94. *Publications:* Sous le Soleil Africain, 1955 (Under the African Sun, 1956); Annotated Bibliography of Nuristan (Kafiristan) and The Kalash Kafirs of Chitral, pt 1 1966, pt 2 1969; The Political Organization of the Kam Kafirs, 1967; Men of Influence in Nuristan, 1974; (jtly) Nuristan, 1979; Afghanistan, 1992; Tibetan Nomads: environment, pastoral economy and material culture, 1996; A Stranger Abroad: a memoir, 2007; numerous articles. *Recreation:* travel in remote places. *Address:* The Prairie House, 1570 N Ridgewood Drive, Wichita, KS 67208, USA.

JONES, Simon Alan, LVO 1998; Senior Partner, Gardiner & Theobald, since 2001; Managing Director, Gardiner & Theobald Management Services, since 1986; *b* 28 March 1956; *s* of Alan Reginald Walter Jones, MBE and Kathleen Jones; *m* 1998, Hon. Caroline Lucy, *d* of Baroness Billingham, *qv*; two *s*. *Educ:* King Edward VII Sch., Lytham; Reading Univ. (BSc Quantity Surveying). Joined Gardiner & Theobald, 1977: Project Dir on behalf of the Royal Household, Windsor Castle Fire Restoration, 1993–97. Trustee, Historic Royal Palaces, 1998–. Lt Col, Engrg and Logistics Staff Corp., 2001–. *Recreations:* tennis, golf, squash. *Address:* 10 South Crescent, WC1E 7BD. *T:* (020) 7209 3000. *E:* s.jones@gardiner.com. *Clubs:* All England Lawn Tennis (Mem. Cttee, 2012–); Cumberland Lawn Tennis (Chm.); Highgate Golf.

See also Z. A. Billingham.

JONES, Ven. Simon David B.; *see* Burton-Jones.

JONES, Simon Martin Dedman; Policy and Public Affairs Director, Wales, Marie Curie, since 2015 (Head of Policy and Public Affairs, 2012–15); *b* 10 June 1958; *s* of Rev. Canon William David Jones and Sheila Mary Jones; *m* 2005, Lesley Ann Bird; one *s* two *d*. *Educ:* Mexborough Grammar Sch.; Durham Wearside Secondary Sch.; Exeter Univ. (BA Hons Politics). Business Manager, Rebecca, News Mag. of Wales, 1982–83; Research officer: TGWU, 1985–89; Wales TUC, 1989–93; Chief Exec., Wales Co-op. Centre, 1994–2004. Chair: Cardiff and Vale NHS Trust, 2003–08; NHS Wales Confedn, 2006–08; Lead Chair, NHS Trusts in Wales, 2004–07. Hd of Public Sector, Wales, Odgers Berndtson, 2009–12. Mem. Bd, Charities Commn, 2007–12. Member: S Glamorgan HA, 1989–96; Bro Taf HA, 1996–2003 (Chm., 2000–03). Chm., Welsh Assembly and Govt Commn to Review Voluntary Sector Scheme, 2003–04. Ind. Mem. Bd, RCT Homes, 2007–. Presenter, On the Fly, Radio Wales, 2005, 2006, 2007. *Recreations:* fly fishing and fly tying, cooking, gardening. *Address:* Marie Curie Hospice, Bridgeman Road, Penarth CF64 3YR. *E:* simon.jones57@ntlworld.com.

JONES, Sir Simon (Warley Frederick) Benton, 4th Bt *cr* 1919; JP; *b* 11 Sept. 1941; *o s* of Sir Peter Fawcett Benton Jones, 3rd Bt, OBE, and Nancy Benton Jones (*d* 1974); *S* father, 1972; *m* 1966, Margaret Fiona (OBE 1995, DL), *d* of David Rutherford Dickson; three *s* two *d*. *Educ:* Eton; Trinity College, Cambridge (MA). JP Lincolnshire, 1971 (Chm., Lincs Magistrates' Courts Cttee, 1996–2000); High Sheriff, Lincs, 1977. *Heir: s* James Peter Martin Benton Jones [*b* 1 Jan. 1973; *m* 2008, Leila Reuter; one *s* one *d*]. *Address:* Irnham Hall, Grantham, Lincs NG33 4JD. *T:* (01476) 550212; 19 Sopley, Christchurch, Dorset BH23 7AX.

JONES, Stanley; *see* Jones, John Stanley.

JONES, Stephen; *see* Jones, John Stephen.

JONES, Stephen Charles Ion; Warden, St Edward's School, Oxford, since 2011; *b* Shropshire, 11 Feb. 1959; *s* of Alfred Jones and Ann Jones (*née* Duff-Jones, now Clements); *m* 1983, Katie Ann Hannam; one *s* two *d*. *Educ:* Hurstpierpoint Coll.; Lord Wandsworth Coll.; Univ. of Durham (BA 1981; MLitt 1997); Open Univ. (BA 1987; MSc 1991). Assistant Master: Orley Farm Sch., 1981–82; Dragon Sch., 1983–85; Cheltenham Coll., 1985–90; Hd of Maths, Berkhamsted Sch., 1990–94; Housemaster, Radley Coll., 1994–2004; Headmaster, Dover Coll., 2004–11. *Recreations:* fives, sailing. *Address:* St Edward's School, Woodstock Road, Oxford OX2 7NN. *T:* (01865) 319323, *Fax:* (01865) 319242. *E:* warden@stedwardsoxford.org. *Clubs:* East India, Jesters; Royal Cinque Ports Yacht; Band of Brothers.

JONES, Stephen John Moffat, OBE 2010; RDI 2009; milliner; Designer, Stephen Jones Millinery Ltd, since 1980; *b* W Kirby, Cheshire, 31 May 1957; *s* of John Gordon Jones and Margaret Jones (*née* Moffat). *Educ:* Liverpool Coll.; St Martin's Sch. of Art (BA Hons Fashion Design). Hon. Prof., Univ. of the Arts, 2008–. Collaborations with Comme des Garçons, John Galliano and Christian Dior; hats in permanent collections: V&A Mus.; La Louvre; Metropolitan Mus. of Art, NY; Kyoto Costume Inst., Japan; Australian Nat. Gall., Canberra; curator, Hats: an anthology by Stephen Jones, V&A Mus., 2009. FRSA. Outstanding Achievement in Fashion Design Award, British Fashion Awards, 2008. *Publications:* (jtly) Hats: an anthology by Stephen Jones, 2009; *relevant publication:* Stephen Jones and the Accent of Fashion, by Hamish Bowles, 2010. *Recreations:* adventure, Rococo. *Address:* Stephen Jones Millinery, 36 Great Queen Street, WC2B 5AA.

JONES, Stephen Morris, CBE 2005; Senior Partner, The In Practice Partnership, management consultants, since 2005; *b* 12 March 1948; *s* of late Owain Morus Jones and Sylvia Blanche Jones (*née* Moss); *m* 1970, Rosemary Diana Pilgrim; one *s* two *d*. *Educ:* Univ. of Manchester (BA Hons Town Planning, 1970). MRTPI 1972. Asst Chief Exec., Bolton MBC, 1978–85; Chief Executive: Blackburn BC, 1985–90; Wigan MBC, 1990–2005. Chairman: Leigh Sports Village Co., 2005–; Shop 4 Support, 2008–14; Lancs Care NHS Foundn Trust, 2010–13. Dir, iMPOWER, 2006–. Mem., Soc. of Local Govt Chief Execs, 1985–. *Recreations:* family, walking, sport, reading, S Africa, New Hall Monday Club. *Address:* The In Practice Partnership, 5 Lostock Park Drive, Bolton BL6 4AH.

JONES, Stephen O.; *see* Oliver-Jones.

JONES, Stephen Roger Curtis; Chairman of Governors, Centre for Information on Language Teaching and Research, 1996–2003; *b* 31 March 1944; *s* of Roger Henry Curtis Jones and Kate Alice Jones (*née* Pearson); *m* 1973, Janet Corkett; two *d*. *Educ:* Brentwood Sch., Essex; Univ. of Southampton (BA Hons French 1967; MA French 1968); Cambridge/RSA Cert. TEFLA, 1996. MoD, 1968–71; UK Delegn to NATO, 1971–73; DES, 1973–81 (Private Sec. to Sec. of State, Rt Hon. Shirley Williams, 1976–78); Asst Dir, City of London Poly., 1982–85; Department of Education and Science: Staff Inspector, HM Inspectorate, 1986–88; Head, Internat. Relations Div., 1988–92; Head of Internat. Relns, Youth and Gen. Br., DFE, 1992–94. Trustee, Employability Forum, 2003–09. Mem., Guild of Voluntary Guides, Winchester Cath., 2010–. Comenius Fellow, CILT, the Nat. Centre for Langs, 2004. *Recreations:* walking, choral singing. *Address:* Hussle Cottage, Winton Hill, Stockbridge, Hants SO20 6HL. *T:* (01264) 810935. *E:* jstjones@btinternet.com.

JONES, Stephen William, CB 2007; Director of Finance and Resources (formerly Director, Finance and Performance, then Group Finance Director), Local Government Association, 2007–12. *Educ:* King's Sch., Macclesfield; Balliol Coll., Oxford (BA 1976). FCMA 2006; CPFA 2008. Inland Revenue, subseq. HM Revenue & Customs, 1976–2006: Dir, Large Business Office, 2000–03; Finance Dir, 2003–06. Chm., Adv. Bd, Public Sector Deposit Fund, 2011–.

JONES, Stewart Elgan; QC 1994; a Recorder, since 1990; *b* 20 Jan. 1945; *s* of late Gwilym John Jones and Elizabeth (*née* Davies); *m* 1979, Jennifer Anne (*née* Syddall); two *d*, and one step *s* one step *d*. *Educ:* Cheltenham Coll.; Queen's Coll., Oxford (MA Mod. Langs). Called to the Bar, Gray's Inn, 1972, Bencher, 2002; Mem., Western Circuit. *Recreations:* painting, home, hearth, the great outdoors. *Address:* 3 Paper Buildings, Temple, EC4Y 7EU. *T:* (020) 7583 8055. *W:* www.stew-art.fr.

JONES, Rev. Canon Stewart William; Rector, St Martin-in-the-Bullring, Birmingham, with St Andrew's, Bordesley, since 2005; *b* 17 March 1957; *s* of William Jones and Nettie Jean Jones; *m* 1st, 1982, Susan Kathleen Griffith (*d* 1990); one *d*; 2nd, 1992, Julie Marie Perkin; one *s* one *d*. *Educ:* Heriot-Watt Univ. (BA Hons Business Orgn); Bristol Univ. (Dip. Social Admin); Trinity Coll., Bristol (BA Hons Theol.). Grad. mgt trainee, National Westminster Bank, 1979–80; worker, Bristol Cyrenians, 1980–81; Supervisor, Bristol Churches Community Prog., 1983–85; ordained deacon 1988, priest 1989; Curate, St Mary's, Stoke Bishop, Bristol, 1988–92; Priest-in-charge, St Luke's, Brislington, Bristol, 1992–97; Archbp of Canterbury's Diocesan Chaplain and Tait Missioner, 1997–2003; Priest-in-charge, All Saints', Canterbury, 2001–05; Area Dean, Canterbury, 2002–05. Hon. Provincial Canon, Canterbury Cathedral, 2002–06; Hon. Canon, Birmingham Cathedral, 2011–. *Publications:* The Teaching of Jesus, 1994; The Touch of Jesus, 1995; Albert the Forgetful Angel, 2011; The Amazing Kindness of Obadiah, 2013. *Recreations:* cooking, sport on TV, films, reading. *Address:* St Martin's Rectory, 37 Barlows Road, Edgbaston, Birmingham B15 2PN.

JONES, Susan Elan; MP (Lab) Clwyd South, since 2010; *b* Wrexham, 1 June 1968; *d* of Richard James and Margaret Eirlys Jones. *Educ:* Grango Comprehensive Sch., Rhosllannerchrugog; Ruabon Comprehensive Sch.; Univ. of Bristol (BA 1989); Univ. of Wales, Cardiff (MA 1992). English teacher: Tomakomai English Sch., Japan, 1990–91; Atsuma Bd of Educn, Japan, 1992–94; Corporate Develt Fundraiser, Muscular Dystrophy Campaign, 1995–96; fundraiser, USPG, 1997–2002; Dir, CARIS Haringey, 2002–05; Fundraising Exec., Housing Justice, 2005–10. Mem. (Lab) Southwark LBC, 2006–09 (Dep. Opposition Leader, 2007–09). *Publications:* (contrib.) The Red Book of the Voluntary Sector, 2014. *Recreation:* classical music. *Address:* House of Commons, SW1A 0AA. *E:* susan.jones.mp@parliament.uk.

JONES, Very Rev. Dr Susan Helen; Director of Mission and Ministry, Diocese of Derby, since 2015; *b* Barry, S Wales, 29 Oct. 1960; *d* of Gwylim Jones and Joan Jones. *Educ:* Trinity Coll., Carmarthen (BEd 1992; MPhil 1994); Ripon Coll., Cuddesdon (Dip. Min. 1995); Univ. of Wales, Bangor (PhD 2002). Bank Clerk, Midland Bank; ordained deacon, 1995, priest, 1997; Chaplain, Univ. of Wales Swansea, 1995–98; Hon. Curate, Sketty, Swansea, 1995–98; Dir of Pastoral Studies, St Michael's Coll., Llandaff, 1998–2000; Lectr, Univ. of Wales, Cardiff, 1998–2000; Team Vicar, Rectorial Benefice of Bangor, 2000–10; Dir, Ministry Course, Bangor Dio., 2000–09; Area Dean, Ogwen, 2007–10; Dean of Bangor, 2011–15. Dir, St Seiriol Centre, Bangor, 2009–; Canon Missioner and Cursal Canon, Bangor Cathedral, 2010–11. Mem., Presidium and Central Cttee, Conf. of Eur. Churches, 1997–2009. Hon. Lectr, Univ. of Wales, Bangor, 2000–09; Vis. Res. Fellow, Glyndwr Univ., 2009–; Res. Associate, Religion and Psychol., Albert and Jesse Danielson Inst., Boston Univ., 2009–. *Publications:* (ed jtly) Psychological Perspectives on Christian Ministry, 1996; Listening for God's Call, 2014. *Address:* 25 Church Lane, Darley Abbey, Derby DE22 1EX. *T:* (01332) 554949. *Club:* Soroptimist Internat. (Bangor).

JONES, Dr (Sybil) Angela (Margaret), (Mrs Michael Pearson), FFPH; Consultant in Public Health Medicine, North (formerly North West) Thames Regional Health Authority, 1985–96; *b* 23 Aug. 1940; *d* of Cyril and Ida Jones; *m* 1964, Dr Michael Pearson; three *s* one *d*. *Educ:* Cranford House Sch.; King's College London (AKC); King's Coll. Hosp. (MB BS). Dist MO, Victoria Health Authy, 1982–85. Member: Tech. Sub-Gp of Achieving a Balance, 1988–92; Standing Cttee on Postgrad. Med. Educn, 1989–96 (Chm., working gp on Health of the Nation); Jt Planning Adv. Cttee, 1988–92; Chm., Regl Med. Manpower and Personnel Gp, 1988–92. *Publications:* articles on med. manpower and public health issues in learned jls. *Recreations:* opera, dining with friends.

JONES, Tecwyn, CMG 2002; OBE 1974; FRES, CBiol, FRSB; Chairman, BioNET-INTERNATIONAL Consultative Group, since 2000; Life President, BioNET-INTERNATIONAL, since 2002; consultant; *b* 7 Feb. 1929; *s* of Owen and Lily Jones; *m* 1952, Joan Peggy, (Joy), Edwards; three *s*. *Educ:* Aberaeron Co. Sch.; Imperial Coll., London (BSc Hons; ARCS). FRES 1952 (Hon. FRES 2001); FRSB (FIBiol 1974); CBiol 1979. Entomologist i/c W African Timber Borer Res. Unit, Gold Coast/Ghana, 1952–59; Hd, Biol. and Forestry Divs, Dep. Dir, then interim Dir, E African Agric. and Forestry Res. Orgn, Kenya, 1959–74; Dep. Dir, Centre for Overseas Pest Res. and Natural Resources Inst., ODA, 1974–89; pest mgt and quarantine consultant, FAO, Africa and Asia, 1989–92; Dir, Internat. Inst. of Entomol., CAB Internat., UK, 1992–95; Founder, 1993, and Dir, Technical Secretariat, BioNET-INTERNAT., 1993–2000. Ed., E African Agric. and Forestry Jl, 1963–74. Chm. Council, Internat. Bee Res. Assoc., 1977–90. Hon. Prof. of Entomol., Sch. of Pure and Applied Biol./Bioscis, Univ. of Cardiff (formerly UC, Cardiff), 1987–2002. Trustee, 2003–, Vice-Pres., 2004–07, Royal Entomol Soc. of London; Mem., Internat. Trust for Zool Nomenclature, 2006– (Mem., Mgt Cttee, 2006–). Trustee, Age Cymru (formerly Age Concern), Ceredigion, 2003–11 (Chm., 2003–10); Chairman: Chairs and Vice-Chairs Cttee, Age Concern, All Wales, 2005–07; Age Concern Partnership, Wales, 2006–09 (Mem., 2004–06, Chm., 2006–09, Exec. Cttee). Chairman: Senior Citizens' Club, Aberaeron, 2001–; Cross Inn and Maenygroes Retirement Assoc., 2004–10. *Publications:* contrib. numerous scientific and technical papers, reports and bulletins on tropical pests of agric. and forestry, plant quarantine and R&D, incl. networking; conceptual papers on BioNET-INTERNAT., a global network for taxonomy to support sustainable develt and implement the Convention on Biol Diversity. *Recreations:* amateur dramatics, the countryside, gardening, walking. *Address:* Weston, South Road, Aberaeron, Ceredigion SA46 0DP. *T:* and *Fax:* (01545) 571208.

JONES, Prof. Terence Valentine, FREng; Donald Schultz Professor of Turbomachinery, 1988–2004, and Director, Technology Centre in Aerodynamics and Heat Transfer, 1993–2004, Oxford University; Professorial Fellow, St Catherine's College, Oxford, 1988–2004, now Emeritus Fellow; *b* 14 Feb. 1939; *s* of Albert Duncalf Jones and Frances Jones; *m* 1962, Lesley Lillian (*née* Hughes); one *s* one *d*. *Educ:* William Hulme's Grammar School, Manchester; Lincoln College, Oxford (MA, DPhil 1966). Lecturer: Keble College, Oxford, 1971–77; Lincoln College, Oxford, 1976–80; Jesus College, Oxford, 1977–86; Rolls Royce Tutorial Fellow, St Anne's College, Oxford, 1979–88. Senior Academic Visitor, NASA Lewis Research Center, Ohio, 1986. FREng 2000. Royal Soc. Esso Energy Award, 1996; Silver Medal, RAeS, 2011. *Publications:* articles on turbomachinery, heat transfer and fluid dynamics in NATO, ASME and ARC jls and conf. procs. *Recreations:* hiking, paragliding. *Address:* Department of Engineering Science, Parks Road, Oxford OX1 3PJ. *T:* (01865) 288734.

JONES, Terry, (Terence Graham Parry Jones); writer, film director and occasional performer; *b* 1 Feb. 1942; *s* of Alick George Parry Jones and Dilys Louisa Newnes; *m* 1st, Alison Telfer (marr. diss.); one *s* one *d*; 2nd, 2012, Anna Söderström; one *d*. *Educ:* Esher C of E Primary Sch.; Royal Grammar Sch., Guildford; St Edmund Hall, Oxford. *Television and radio:* wrote for various TV shows, 1966–68; wrote and performed in series: Do Not Adjust Your Set, 1968–69; The Complete and Utter History of Britain, 1969; Monty Python's Flying Circus, 1969–75; wrote (with Michael Palin): Secrets (play), 1974; Ripping Yarns, 1976–79; presented: Paperbacks; Victorian Values, (radio); wrote and directed The Rupert Bear Story (documentary), 1981; wrote, directed and presented, So This Is Progress, 1991; co-wrote and presented: Crusades, 1995; Ancient Inventions, 1999; Gladiators, the Brutal Truth, 2000; Hidden History of Ancient Egypt/Ancient Rome, 2002/03; The Anti-Renaissance Show (radio), 2002; wrote and presented: Terry Jones's Medieval Lives, 2004; The Story of One, 2005; Terry Jones' Barbarians, 2006; In Charlie Chaplin's Footsteps, 2015. *Films:* And Now For Something Completely Different, 1971; directed (with Terry Gilliam), co-wrote and performed, Monty Python and the Holy Grail, 1975; directed, co-wrote and performed: Monty Python's Life of Brian, 1978; Monty Python's Meaning of Life, 1983 (Grand Prix Spécial du Jury, Cannes); directed Personal Services, 1986; wrote, directed and performed: Erik the Viking, 1989; The Wind in the Willows, 1996; Asterix and Obelix (English version), 2000; wrote (with Gavin Scott) and directed, Absolutely Anything, 2015. *Live show:* Monty Python Live (Mostly), 02 Arena, 2014. Wrote libretto and directed: musical play, Evil Machines, São Luiz, Lisbon, 2008; The Doctor's Tale, Royal Opera House, 2011; wrote libretto, The Owl and the Pussycat, ROH2 (touring), 2012. *Publications:* Chaucer's Knight, 1980, 3rd edn 1984; Fairy Tales, 1981, 4th edn 1987; The Saga of Erik the Viking, 1983, 3rd edn 1986; Nicobobinus, 1985, 2nd edn 1987; Goblins of the Labyrinth, 1986; The Curse of the Vampire's Socks, 1988; Attacks of Opinion, 1988; Fantastic Stories, 1992; (with Brian Froud) Lady Cottington's Pressed Fairy Book, 1994; (with Alan Ereira) Crusades, 1994; The Knight and the Squire, 1997; (with Brian Froud) Lady Cottington's Pressed Fairy Journal, 1998; The Lady and the Squire, 2000; Who Murdered Chaucer?, 2003; (with Alan Ereira) Medieval Lives, 2004; Terry Jones' War on the War of Terror, 2005; (with Alan Ereira) Terry Jones' Barbarians, 2006; (contrib.) Fourteenth Century England, 2008; Animal Tales, 2011; Trouble on The Heath, 2011; Evil Machines (short stories), 2011; (with Michael Palin): Dr Fegg's Encyclopeadia (sic) of all World Knowledge, etc; Ripping Yarns, etc; contrib. to the various Monty Python books. *Recreation:* sleeping.

JONES, Terry; Founding Editor-in-Chief, Creative Director and Publisher, i-D magazine, 1980–2013; *b* Northampton, 1945; *m* 1968, Patricia Sandra, (Tricia); one *s* one *d*. *Educ:* West of England Coll. of Art, Bristol (Nat. Dip. Graphics). Asst to Ivan Dodd, 1965–68; Asst Art Dir, Good Housekeeping, 1968–70; Art Director: Vanity Fair, 1970–71; British Vogue, 1972–77; Sportswear Europe, 1978–80. Advertising Consultant, Lurzep/Conrad Agency, 1978–80; Consultant Art Director: German Vogue, 1979–80; DONNA, 1979–80; Vogue Gioello, 1979–80; Music Video Co-Dir, Careless Memories, Duran Duran, 1981; Image Dir, Fiorucci, 1982–85; Image Consultant, Mexx, 1985–89; Ad Campaign and Catalogue Consultant, Charro, Fila, Mexx mag., Lorenzini, St Moritz, Fooks, Neos, Fiorucci, Swatch, Brylcreem and Mr Joe, 1985–88; Ad Campaign Consultant, Chipie, 1989–90. Eur. Art Dir, Espirit, 1989–90; Art Dir, Fire and Ice. (Jtly) Outstanding Achievement in Fashion Award, British Fashion Awards, 2013. *Publications:* The MGM Story, 1978; Women on Women, 1978; Not Another Punk Book, 1980; Masterpieces of Erotic Photography, 1980; The Tree; Wink; Private Viewing, 1983; A Decade of Ideas, 1990; Instant Design: a manual of graphic techniques, 1990; Catching the Moment, 1997; SMILE i-D, Fashion and Style: the best from 20 years of i-D, 2001; (ed) Fashion Now, 2003; (ed) Fashion Now II, 2005; SOUL i-D, 2008 (Chinese edn 2012); (ed) 100 Contemporary Fashion Designers, 2009; i-D Covers: 1980–2010, 2010; Vivienne Westwood, 2012; Rei Kawakubo, 2012; Yohji Yamamoto, 2012; Rick Owens, 2013; Raf Simons, 2013. *E:* instantdesignltd@gmail.com.

JONES, Ven. (Thomas) Hughie; Archdeacon of Loughborough, 1986–92, now Emeritus; *b* 15 Aug. 1927; *s* of Edward Teifi Jones and Ellen Jones; *m* 1949, Beryl Joan Henderson; two *d*. *Educ:* William Hulme's Grammar School, Manchester; Univ. of Wales (BA, LLM); Univ. of London (BD); Univ. of Leicester (MA; PhD 2002). Warden and Lectr, Bible Trng Inst., Glasgow, 1949–54; Minister, John Street Baptist Church, Glasgow, 1951–54; RE specialist, Leicester and Leics schs, 1955–63; Sen. Lectr in RE, Leicester Coll. of Educn, 1964–70; deacon 1966, priest 1967; Vice-Principal, Bosworth Coll., 1970–75; Principal, Hind Leys College, Leics, 1975–81; Rector, The Langtons and Stonton Wyville, 1981–86. Hon. Canon of Leicester Cathedral, 1983–86. Bishop's Officer, Clergy Widows and Retired Clergy, Ecclesiastical Law Soc., 1996–2003 (Vice-Chm., 1990; Hon. Exec. Officer, 1993–96; Hon. Life Mem., 2010); Member: Selden Soc., 1991; Canon Law Soc. of GB and Ireland, 1993. *Publications:* (contrib. OT articles) New Bible Dictionary, 1962, 2nd edn 1980; Old Testament, religious education and canon law articles in relevant jls. *Recreations:* entomology, genealogy, Welsh interests, canon law. *Address:* 2 Leigh Court, Moor Pond Piece, Ampthill, Beds MK45 2GR. *Club:* Carlton.

JONES, Timothy; *see* Jones, David T.

JONES, Timothy Aidan; *see* Marschall Jones, T. A.

JONES, Timothy John; Co-Founder and Chairman, CH&Co Catering Ltd (formerly Charlton House Catering), since 1991; *b* Newport, Gwent, 17 Nov. 1959; *s* of John Samuel Jones and Margaret Rose Jones (*née* Bull); *m* 1986, Robyn Anne Lardge (*see* R. A. Jones); one *s* one *d*. *Educ:* Croesyceiliog Sch.; Univ. of Bristol (BSc Hons Econs). ACA 1985. Asst Manager, Price Waterhouse, 1981–85; Financial Controller, Marvel Comics, 1985–90; Finance Dir, RWS Gp plc, 1990–2000. *Recreations:* golf, cycling, swimming, food and wine, travel, jukeboxes. *Address:* Bryants Farm, Kiln Road, Dunsden, Reading, Berks RG4 9PB. *T:* (0118) 946 6300, *Fax:* (0118) 946 6301. *E:* Tim.jones@chandco.net. *Club:* Huntercombe Golf.

JONES, Dr Timothy Rhys; continuo player, pianist and musicologist; Deputy Principal (Programmes and Research), Royal Academy of Music, since 2008; *b* Cardiff, 18 Jan. 1967; *s* of Wyndham Jones and Florence Jones (*née* Thomas). *Educ:* Porth Co. Comprehensive Sch.; Christ Church, Oxford (BA 1988; MA 1992; DPhil 1992). LTCL 1984. Lecturer: in Music, St Peter's Coll., Oxford, 1992–95; St Edmund Hall, Oxford, 1992–95; Keble Coll., Oxford, 1994–95; Univ. of Exeter, 1995–2005; RNCM, 2005–08; Reader, Univ. of London, 2009–. Trustee, Eur. String Teachers' Assoc., 2010–13. Hon. RAM 2014. *Publications:* Beethoven: The Moonlight and other sonatas Op. 27 and Op. 31, 1999; (contrib.) The Oxford Companion to Music, 2002; (contrib.) French Music since Berlioz, 2006; completion of fragments by Mozart, including: Concerto for piano and violin, 2008; Requiem, 2010; String Quintets, 2013; String Quartets, 2013; String Trio, 2013; Clarinet Quintets, 2014; Violin Sonatas, 2014. *Recreations:* cricket, Scrabble, Anglican liturgy. *Address:* Royal Academy of Music, Marylebone Road, NW1 5HT. *T:* (020) 7873 7309. *E:* t.jones@ram.ac.uk. *Club:* Athenæum.

JONES, Sir Tom; *see* Woodward, Sir T. J.

JONES, Tracey Anne; *see* Angus, T. A.

JONES, Sir Trevor; *see* Jones, Sir O. T.

JONES, Trevor; Deputy Chairman, NHS Direct NHS Trust, 2008–13 (Director, 2007–13); *b* 23 Dec. 1950; *s* of John Jones and Florence Mary Jones (*née* Rogerson); *m* 1974, Hazel Oliver. Local Govt Finance, 1969–78; Sen. Asst Regl Treas., Northern RHA, 1978; Dep. Treas., S Manchester HA, 1983; Waltham Forest Health Authority: Dir of Finance, 1986; Dist Gen. Manager, 1989–92; Chief Exec., Forest Healthcare NHS Trust, 1992–95; Gen. Manager, then Chief Exec., Lothian Health Bd, 1995–2000; Chief Exec., NHS Scotland and Hd of Health Dept, Scottish Exec., 2000–04; Chief Exec., Avon, Glos and Wilts Strategic HA, 2004–06. Chm., Gen. Managers' Gp, Scottish Health Bd, 1998–2000. Director: Pinnacle Staffing Gp plc, 2006–08; Patient Safety Agency, 2007–. Dir, Sport England SW, 2005–09. Trustee: WellChild, 2006–; Royal Voluntary Service, 2009–. Regl FRSocMed, 2004. CPFA, FCCA, CCMI. *Recreations:* golf, photography. *Address:* The Granary, Culkerton, Tetbury, Glos GL8 8SS. *Clubs:* Royal Society of Medicine; Durham CC.

JONES, Trevor Charles B.; *see* Bish-Jones.

JONES, Trevor David K.; *see* Kent-Jones.

JONES, Trevor Mervyn, CBE 2003; PhD; Director, Allergan Inc., since 2004; *b* 19 Aug. 1942; *s* of Samuel James Jones and Hilda May Jones (*née* Walley); *m* 1966, Verity Ann Bates; one *s* one *d*. *Educ:* Wolverhampton Grammar Sch.; King's Coll. London (BPharm Hons 1964; PhD 1967; FKC 1994). CChem 1975; FRSC 1978; FPS 1987; MCPP 1982. Lectr, Univ. of Nottingham, 1967–72; Hd of Pharmaceutical Develt, Boots Co. Ltd, 1972–76; Develt Dir, Wellcome Foundation Ltd, 1976–87; R&D Dir and Mem. Bd, Wellcome plc, 1987–94; Dir-Gen., Assoc. of British Pharmaceutical Industry, 1994–2004. Director: Wellcome Biotechnology Ltd, 1983–93; Wellgen Inc. USA, 1990–93; Merlin Partners, 1996–2012 (Chm., Scientific Adv. Bd, 1996–2012); Sen. R&D Advr, Esteve SA, 2004–08. Visiting Professor: KCL, 1984– (Vice Chm. Council, 2001–08); Univ. of Strathclyde, 1988–93; Adjunct Prof., Univ. of N Carolina, 1985–90. Non-executive Chairman: Health Reform Investment Trust plc, 1996–98; ReNeuron, 2000–11; Synexus Ltd, 2008–11; Simbec Res. Ltd, 2013–; Chairman: Kinetique Biomedical Seed Fund, 2001–08; Director: Next Pharma Ltd, 2004–11; BAC bv, 2005–08; People in Health, 2006–09; Verona Pharma plc, 2007–; Sigma-Tau Finanziaria SpA, 2008–13; Sigma-Tau SpA, 2010–11; Tecnogen SpA, 2010–11; Aegate Ltd, 2010–13; Pres., Sigma-Tau Pharmaceuticals Inc., 2012–14. Member: Expert Cttees, British Pharmacopoeia, 1976–89; Pharmacy Res. Bd, CNAA, 1978–83; UK Govt Medicines Commn, 1982–94; Adv. Bd on Human Genome, Cabinet Office, 1991–96; Expert Wkg Party on Use of Tissues, Nuffield Council for Bioethics, 1992–97; Exec. Cttee, Internat. Fedn of Pharmaceutical Manufrs, 1994–2004; Bd of Mgt, European Fedn of Pharmaceutical Industry Assoc., 1994–2004; Nat. Biological Standards Bd Review, 1995–97; Advisory Board: MRC, 2001–04; MRC Social, Genetic and Develtl Psychiatric Res. Centre, Inst. of Psych., 2002–; MRC Centre for Neurodegeneration Res., 2006–; Prime Minister's Task Force on Competitiveness of Pharmaceutical Industry, 2001; Bevan Commn, Welsh Govt, 2014–; Chm., Adv. Gp on Genetics Res., 2003–07. Pres., Internat. Commn on Technology, 1979–83, Member: Pharmaceut. Scis Bd, 1980–84, 1996–, Fédn Internat. Pharmaceutique; WHO Commn on Intellectual Property Rights, Innovation and Public Health, 2004–06; Senate, Eur. Fedn for Pharmaceutical Scis, 2014–. Founder and Mem. Bd, Medicines for Malaria Venture, 1999–2007. Trustee: Epilepsy Res. Foundn, 1996–2004; Northwick Park Inst. of Med. Res., 1998–2004; British Urological Foundn, 2005–07. Life Sci. Advr, Fleming Family and Partners, 2006–08. Liveryman, Co. of Apothecaries, 1989–. FRSocMed 2007. Hon. FFPM 1995; Hon. FRCP 2005; Hon. Fellow: London Sch. of Pharmacy, 1998; British Pharmacol. Soc., 2005. For. Mem., Acad. Nat. de Pharmacie, 2005–. Hon. PhD Athens, 1993; Hon. DSc: Strathclyde, 1994; Nottingham, 1998; Bath, 2000; Bradford, 2003. Harrison Meml Medal, 1987, Charter Gold Medal, 1996, RPSGB; Gold Medal, Comenius Univ., 1992. *Publications:* Drug Delivery to the Respiratory Tract, 1987; Advances in Pharmaceutical Sciences, 1993. *Recreations:* golf, gardening, Wales RU. *Address:* Woodhyrst House, Friths Drive, Reigate, Surrey RH2 0DS. *Club:* Athenæum.

JONES, Ven. Dr Trevor Pryce; Archdeacon of Hertford, since 1997; *b* 24 April 1948; *s* of John Pryce Jones and Annie (*née* Jepson); *m* 1976, Susan Diane Pengelley; one *s* one *d*. *Educ:* Dial Stone Sch., Stockport; St Luke's Coll., Exeter; Univ. of Southampton (BEd, BTh); Salisbury and Wells Theol Coll.; Univ. of Wales, Cardiff Law Sch. (LLM); St John's Coll., Univ. of Durham (DThMin). Asst Teacher and Lay Chaplain, Shaftesbury Grammar Sch., 1969–73; ordained deacon, 1976, priest, 1977; Asst Curate, Gloucester St George, Lower Tuffley, 1976–79; Warden, Bishop Mascall Centre, Ludlow, and Mem., Hereford Diocesan Educn Team, 1979–84; Diocesan Communications Officer, Hereford, 1981–86; Team Rector, Hereford S Wye Team Ministry, 1984–97. OCF, 1985–97. Prebendary, Hereford Cathedral, 1993–97; Hon. Canon, Cathedral and Abbey Church of St Alban, 1997. Chm., St Alban's and Oxford Ministry Course, 1998–2007; Vice-Chairman: E Anglia Ministerial Trng Course, 2005–07; Eastern Reg. Ministerial (formerly E Anglia Ministerial Trng) Course, 2007–. Bishops' Selector, 2001–08. Mem., Gen. Synod of C of E, 2000–05 and 2005–10 (Mem., Legal Adv. Commn, 2006–11; Mem., Rule Cttee, 2013–). Chairman: Reach Out Plus (formerly Reach Out Projects), 1998–2012; Rural Strategy Gp, dio. St Albans, 2001–. Chm., Hockerill Educnl Foundn, 2005–12. Mem., Royal Commonwealth Soc. *Recreations:* country walks, vintage buses and trains, film and theatre, biography. *Address:* Glebe House, St Mary's Lane, Hertingfordbury, Hertford SG14 2LE. *T:* (01727) 818159. *E:* archdhert@stalbans.anglican.org. *Club:* Royal Over-Seas League.

JONES, Prof. Tudor Bowden, MBE 2011; DSc; FInstP; Professor of Ionospheric Physics, 1980–98, Head of Department of Physics and Astronomy, 1993–98, University of Leicester, now Professor Emeritus; *b* 8 Nov. 1934; *s* of Idris Jones and Tydvil Ann Jones (*née* Bowden); *m* 1960, Patricia Brown; two *s*. *Educ:* County Grammar Sch., Ystradgynlais; University Coll. of Wales, Swansea (BSc Hons, PhD, DSc). FInstP 1975; CEng 1987; FIET (FIEE 1987). Res. Asst, UCW, Aberystwyth, 1959; University of Leicester: Lectr in Physics, 1960–69; Sen. Lectr, 1969–75; Reader, 1975–80. PPARC Nat. Co-ordinator for Solar Terrestrial Physics, 1998–2001. Guest Res. Scientist at various Govt estabts in UK and overseas, 1970–; Sen. Resident Associate, Nat. Oceanic and Atmospheric Admin Lab., Boulder, Colo, 1971–72. Leverhulme Emeritus Fellowship, 2001–02. Appleton Lectr, IEE, 1997. Appleton Prize, Internat. Union of Radio Sci. and Royal Soc., 1993; Charles Chree Prize and Medal, Inst. of Physics, 1995. *Publications:* (ed) Oblique Incidence Radio Wave Propagation, 1966; numerous papers in scientific jls on ionospheric physics and radio wave propagation. *Recreation:* classical music. *Address:* Department of Physics and Astronomy, University of Leicester, University Road, Leicester LE1 7RH. *T:* (0116) 252 3561.

JONES, Prof. Vaughan Frederick Randal, DCNZM 2002; FRS 1990; Professor of Mathematics, University of California, Berkeley, 1985–2011, now Emeritus; Distinguished Professor of Mathematics, Vanderbilt University, Nashville, since 2011; *b* Gisborne, NZ, 31 Dec. 1952; *s* of J. H. Jones and J. A. Goodfellow (*née* Collins); *m* 1979, Martha Weare Jones (*née* Myers); one *s* two *d. Educ:* St Peter's Sch., Cambridge, NZ; Auckland Grammar Sch.; Univ. of Auckland (schol.; Gillies schol.; Phillips Industries Bursary; BSc, MSc 1st Cl. Hons); Ecole de Physique, Geneva (Swiss Govt schol.; F. W. W. Rhodes Meml schol.); Ecole de Mathématiques, Geneva (DèsSc Mathematics); Vacheron Constantin Prize, Univ. de Genève. Asst, Univ. de Genève, 1975–80; E. R. Hedrick Asst Prof., UCLA, 1980–81; University of Pennsylvania: Vis. Lectr, 1981–82; Asst Prof., 1981–84; Associate Prof., 1984–85. Alfred P. Sloan Res. Fellowship, 1983; Guggenheim Fellowship, 1986. Hon. Vice Pres., Internat. Guild of Knot-tyers, 1991. Fields Medal, 1990. *Publications:* Coxeter graphs and Towers of algebras, 1989. *Recreations:* music, tennis, squash, ski-ing. *Address:* Department of Mathematics, 1326 Stevenson Center, Vanderbilt University, Nashville, TN 37240, USA.

JONES, Victoria Mary Taylor; *see* Heywood, V. M. T.

JONES, Walter; *see* Jones, William W. A.

JONES, Wilfred, CMG 1982; HM Diplomatic Service, retired; *b* 29 Nov. 1926; *m* 1952, Millicent Beresford; two *s.* Joined Foreign Office, 1949; served in Tamsui, Jedda, Brussels, Athens and FCO, 1950–66; First Sec. (Admin), Canberra, 1966–68; FCO, 1968–71; Copenhagen, 1971–74, Blantyre, 1974–75; Lilongwe, 1975–77; FCO, 1977–81; High Comr to Botswana, 1981–86. *Recreations:* sailing, golf, tennis.

JONES, William George Tilston; independent telecommunications consultant, 1990–2004; *b* 7 Jan. 1942; *s* of late Thomas Tilston Jones and Amy Ethel Jones; *m* 1965, Fiona Mary; one *d. Educ:* Portsmouth Grammar School; Portsmouth Polytechnic (BSc; Hon. Fellow 1989). Post Office Engineering Dept, 1960; Head, Electronic Switching Gp, 1969; Head, System X Develt Div., 1978; Dir, System Evolution and Standards, 1983; Chief Exec., Technology, BT, 1984; seconded as Exec. in Residence, Internat. Management Inst., Geneva, 1987; Sen. Strategy Adviser, BT, 1988. Member: IEE Electronics Divl Bd, 1984–89; Parly IT Cttee, 1985–87; Chairman: IT Adv. Bd, Polytechnic of Central London, 1984–87; Adv. Gp, Centre of Communication and Information Studies, 1988–89; SE Centre, IEE, 1989–90; Dir, Technology Studies, British Telecom, 1988–90. Governor, Polytechnic of Central London, 1985–89. *Publications:* contribs on telecommunications to learned jls. *Recreations:* theatre, camping, making furniture, landscape gardening.

JONES, William Michael Roger B.; *see* Bankes-Jones.

JONES, William Pearce A.; *see* Andreae-Jones.

JONES, (William) Walter (Alexander); Principal, Kolej Tuanku Ja'afar, Malaysia, 2005–11; *b* 11 Sept. 1949; *s* of Rev. Eric Jones and Elizabeth Jones; *m* 1974, Frances Linda Grant; one *s* two *d. Educ:* Campbell Coll., Belfast; Queens' Coll., Cambridge (MA; PGCE); Inst. of Education, Univ. of London (MA). Asst Teacher, St Edward's C of E Comprehensive, Romford, 1973–75; Head of Economics, King's Coll. Sch., Wimbledon, 1976–87; Second Master, King's Sch., Bruton, 1987–93; Headmaster, Royal Grammar Sch., Worcester, 1993–2005. *Publications:* contrib. to British Economic Survey. *Recreations:* Rugby, walking. *Address:* 4 Padwick's Field, Fittleworth, W Sussex RH20 1HJ.

JONES, Wynne; *see* Jones, Elphin W.

JONES-EVANS, Prof. Dylan, OBE 2013; PhD; Professor of Entrepreneurship and Strategy, Bristol Business School, University of the West of England, since 2013; *b* Bangor, Gwynedd, 16 May 1966; *s* of Cyril Jones-Evans and Carys Jones-Evans; *m* 1993, Dr Angela Sullivan; two *s. Educ:* Ysgol Glan y Mor, Pwllheli; University Coll. Cardiff (BSc Hons Physics 1987); Univ. of Manchester (MSc Tech. Change and Industrial Strategy 1988); Aston Univ. (PhD Entrepreneurship 1994). Res. Fellow, Durham Univ., 1992–94; Marie Curie Postdoctoral Res. Fellow, UCD, 1994–96; Prof. of Entrepreneurship and Small Business Mgt, Univ. of Glamorgan, 1996–2000; Dep. Dir, Sch. of Business and Regl Develt, Univ. of Wales, Bangor, 2000–04; Dir, Enterprise, NE Wales Inst. of Higher Educn, 2004–05; Dep. Dir, Centre for Advanced Studies, Cardiff Univ., 2005–08; Dir, Enterprise and Innovation, Univ. of Wales, 2008–13. Chm., Outlook Expeditions, 2001–08. Chm., Community Enterprise Wales, 1999–2003; Dir, Wales Fast Growth 50, 1999–. Chm., Star for Burton Appeal, 2012–13; Trustee, Prime Cymru, 2012–. Mem., Cardiff Business Club; MInstD. Columnist: Daily Post, 2003–; Western Mail, 2004–. FRSA 2002. *Publications:* Technology, Enterprise and Innovation: the European experience, 1997; Creating an Entrepreneurial Wales, 2001; Enterprise and Small Business: principles, policy and practice, 2012; articles in jls on entrepreneurship, innovation and business. *Recreations:* reading biographies, walking the dog, cinema. *Address:* Bristol Business School, University of the West of England, Coldharbour Lane, Bristol BS16 1QY. *T:* 07776 166361. *E:* dylan.jones-evans@uwe.ac.uk. *Clubs:* Cardiff and County; Rygbi Pwllheli; Crawshays Rugby.

JONES PARRY, Sir Emyr, GCMG 2007 (KCMG 2002; CMG 1992); PhD; FInstP; HM Diplomatic Service, retired; President: Aberystwyth University, since 2008; Learned Society of Wales, since 2014; Chairman: Redress, since 2008; Wales Millennium Centre, since 2010; *b* 21 Sept. 1947; *s* of Hugh Jones Parry and Eirwen Jones Parry (*née* Davies); *m* 1971, Lynn Noble; two *s. Educ:* Gwendraeth Grammar Sch.; University Coll. Cardiff (BSc, Dip Crystallography); St Catharine's Coll., Cambridge (PhD; Hon. Fellow, 2008). FInstP 2004. FO, 1973–74; First Sec., Ottawa, 1974–79; FO, 1979–82; First Sec., UK Rep. to EC, Brussels, 1982–86; Dep. Head, Office of Pres. of European Parlt, 1987–89; Head, EC Dept (External), FCO, 1989–93; Minister, British Embassy, Madrid, 1993–96; Dep. Pol Dir, FCO, 1996–97; Dir, EU, FCO, 1997–98; Political Dir, FCO, 1998–2001; UK Perm. Rep., UK Delegn to NATO, 2001–03; UK Perm. Rep. to UN, 2003–07. Chm., All Wales Convention, 2007–09. Hon. Fellow: Univ. of Cardiff, 2003; Univ. of Wales Aberystwyth, 2006; Trinity Coll., Carmarthen, 2007. Hon. Dr Laws Wales, 2005. *Publications:* various scientific articles. *Recreations:* gardening, theatre, reading, sport. *Address:* c/o Aberystwyth University, Visualisation Centre, Penglais Campus, Aberystwyth SY23 3BF. *Club:* Glamorgan County Cricket.

JONES-PARRY, Tristram, MA; Head Master, Westminster School, 1998–2005; *b* 23 July 1947; *s* of Sir Ernest Jones-Parry and late Mary (*née* Powell). *Educ:* Westminster Sch.; Christ Church, Oxford (MA). Operational Researcher, NCB, 1968–70; Maths Teacher, Dulwich Coll., 1970–73; Head of Maths, Housemaster and Under Master, Westminster Sch., 1973–94; Headmaster, Emanuel Sch., 1994–98. *Recreations:* reading, walking, cycling, travelling. *Address:* 4 Bainton Road, Oxford OX2 7AF. *Club:* Athenæum.

JONSSON, Lars Ossian; artist, author, ornithologist; *b* 22 Oct. 1952; *s* of Sven and May Jonsson; *m* 1985, Ragnhild Erlandson; two *s* two *d. Educ:* autodidact. Wildlife artist, mainly specialising in birds; debut show at age 15, Nat. Mus. of Natural Hist., Stockholm, 1968. Hon. Dr Uppsala, 2002. Master Wildlife Artist, Leigh Yawkey Wordson Art Mus., Wis, USA, 1988. *Publications:* Birds of Sea and Coast, 1978; Birds of Lake, River, Marsh and Field, 1978; Birds of Wood, Park and Garden, 1978; Birds of Mountain Regions, 1980; Bird Island, 1984; Birds of Europe: with North Africa and the Middle East, 1992; Birds and Light: the art of Lars Jonsson, 2002; Birds: paintings from a near horizon, 2009. *Recreations:* guitar music, travelling, art. *Address:* Hamra, Norrgårde 311, 620 10 Burgsvik, Sweden.

JOPLING, family name of **Baron Jopling**.

JOPLING, Baron *cr* 1997 (Life Peer), of Ainderby Quernhow in the co. of N Yorkshire; **Thomas Michael Jopling;** PC 1979; farmer; *b* 10 Dec. 1930; *s* of Mark Bellerby Jopling, Masham, Yorks; *m* 1958, Gail, *d* of Ernest Dickinson, Harrogate; two *s. Educ:* Cheltenham Coll.; King's Coll., Newcastle upon Tyne (BSc Agric. Durham). Mem., Thirsk Rural District Council, 1958–64; Mem. National Council, National Farmers' Union, 1962–64. Contested (C) Wakefield, 1959. MP (C): Westmorland, 1964–83; Westmorland and Lonsdale, 1983–97. PPS to Minister of Agriculture, 1970–71; an Asst Govt Whip, 1971–73; a Lord Comr, HM Treasury, 1973–74; an Opposition Whip, March–June 1974; an Opposition spokesman on agriculture, 1974–79; Shadow Minister of Agriculture, 1975–76; Parly Sec. to HM Treasury, and Chief Whip, 1979–83; Minister of Agriculture, Fisheries and Food, 1983–87. Mem., Select Cttee on Foreign Affairs, 1987–97; Chm., Select Cttee on Sittings of the House (Jopling Report), 1991–92; Member: H of L Select Cttee on European Legislation, 2000–04, 2007–12 (Mem. Sub-Cttee (D) Agric., 1998–2000, (C) Defence and Foreign Policy, 2000–04, 2010–15 (Chm., 2001–04), (F) Home Office, 2006–10 (Chm., 2007–10)); H of L Select Cttee on Merits of Statutory Instruments, 2003–07; Jt Sec., Cons. Parly Agric. Cttee, 1966–70. Hon. Sec., British Amer. Parly Gp, 1987–2001 (Vice Chm., 1983–86). Mem., UK Delegn to NATO Assembly, 1987–97, 2001– (Chairman: Civilian Aspects of Security Cttee, 2011–14; Democratic Governance Cttee, 2014–; Vice Pres., 2014–). Member, UK Executive: CPA, 1974–79, 1987–97 (Vice Chm., 1977–79); IPU, 1997–. Pres. Councils, EEC Agric. and Fishery Ministers, July–Dec. 1986; Leader, 1990–97, Mem., 2000–01, UK Delegn to OSCE Parly Assembly. Mem. Cttee, Assoc. of Cons. Peers, 1997–2000. Pres., Auto Cycle Union, 1989–2004. DL Cumbria, 1991–97, N Yorks, 1998–2005. Hon. DCL Newcastle, 1992. *Address:* Ainderby Hall, Thirsk, North Yorks YO7 4HZ. *T:* (01845) 567224. *Clubs:* Buck's (Hon.); Royal Automobile (Hon.).

See also J. Jopling.

JOPLING, Jeremy Michael Neal, (Jay); Founder, White Cube, art gallery, 1993; *s* of Lord Jopling, *qv*; *m* 1997, Samantha Taylor-Wood (*see* S. Taylor-Johnson) (marr. diss. 2009); two *d. Educ:* Eton; Univ. of Edinburgh (MA Art Hist. 1984). *Address:* White Cube, 144–152 Bermondsey Street, SE1 3TQ. *T:* (020) 7930 5373, *Fax:* (020) 7749 7480.

JORDAN, family name of **Baron Jordan**.

JORDAN, Baron *cr* 2000 (Life Peer), of Bournville in the co. of West Midlands; **William Brian Jordan,** CBE 1992; General Secretary, International Confederation of Free Trade Unions, 1995–2001; *b* 28 Jan. 1936; *s* of Walter and Alice Jordan; *m* 1958, Jean Ann Livesey; three *d. Educ:* Secondary Modern Sch., Birmingham. Convener of Shop Stewards, Guest Keen & Nettlefolds, 1966; full-time AUEW Divl Organiser, 1976; Pres., AEU, then AEEU, 1986–95. Mem., TUC General Council, 1986–95 (Chm., Cttee on European Strategy, 1988–95). A Gov., BBC, 1988–98. Member: NEDC, 1986–92; Engrg Industry Training Bd, 1986–91; Council, Industrial Soc., 1987–95; RIIA, 1987–; ACAS, 1987–95; Nat. Trng Task Force, 1989–92; Engrg Trng Authy, 1991–95; NACETT, 1993–95; English Partnerships, 1993–2002 (Chm., Pension Scheme, Homes and Communities Agency, 2004–). President: European Metal-Workers Fedn, 1986–95; Exec., Internat. Metalworkers Fedn, 1986–95; RoSPA, 2009–. Member: UN High Level Panel on Youth Employment; UN Global Compact Adv. Council; Victim Support Adv. Bd, 1990–2007; Steering Bd, Nat. Contact Point, 2007–. Fellow, World Econ. Forum. Governor: London School of Economics, 1987–2002; Manchester Business School, 1987–92; Ashridge Management Coll., 1992–; Mem. Ct of Govs, Henley Coll., 1991–. Hon. CGIA 1989. DUniv Central England, 1993; Hon. DSc Cranfield, 1995. *Recreations:* reading, keen supporter of Birmingham City FC. *Address:* 352 Heath Road South, Northfield, Birmingham B31 2BH.

JORDAN, Andrew; a Judge of the Upper Tribunal (Immigration and Asylum Chamber) (formerly a Vice President, Immigration Appeal Tribunal, later a Senior Immigration Judge, Asylum and Immigration Tribunal), since 2003; *b* 30 Nov. 1949; *s* of Norman and Muriel Jordan; *m* 1978, Susan Jennifer Young; one *s* two *d. Educ:* Univ. of Warwick (LLB); Univ. of Wales, Cardiff (LLM Canon Law). Called to the Bar, Lincoln's Inn, 1973; in practice as barrister, 1973–2000 (specialized in gen. common law); Immigration Adjudicator, 2000–03. Dep. Chancellor, 2001–02, Chancellor, 2002–, Dio. Guildford. *Recreations:* music, London. *Address:* Upper Tribunal (Immigration and Asylum Chamber), Field House, 15 Breams Buildings, EC4A 1DZ.

JORDAN, Anthony; television script writer and producer; Managing Director, Red Planet Pictures, since 2005; *b* Southport, Merseyside, 21 July 1957; *s* of Anthony and Lily Jordan; *m* 1995, Tracy Tyler; two *s* four *d. Educ:* Broadlands, Bristol. Lead writer, Eastenders, 1990–2007; series creator: City Central, 1995; Hustle, 2002–12; Moving Wallpaper, 2007; series co-creator, Life on Mars, 2005; writer: Nativity, 2011; Death in Paradise, 2011, 2012; The Passing Bells, 2014; The Ark, 2015. *Recreations:* music, swimming, boating, golf, hiking. *Address:* Red Planet Pictures Ltd, Axtell House, 23–24 Warwick Street, W1B 5NQ. *E:* tonyjordan@redplanetpictures.co.uk. *Club:* Century.

JORDAN, Dame Carole, DBE 2006; PhD; FRS 1990; Professor of Physics, University of Oxford, 1996–2008, now Emeritus; Wolfson Tutorial Fellow in Natural Science, Somerville College, Oxford, 1976–2008, now Emeritus Fellow; *b* 19 July 1941; *d* of Reginald Sidney Jordan and Ethel May Jordan. *Educ:* Harrow County Grammar School for Girls; University College London (BSc 1962; PhD 1965; Fellow 1991). FInstP 1973, Hon. FInstP 2011. Post-Doctoral Research Associate, Jt Inst. for Lab. Astrophysics, Boulder, Colorado, 1966; Asst Lectr, Dept of Astronomy, UCL, attached to Culham Lab., UKAEA, 1966–69; Astrophysics Research Unit, SRC, 1969–76; Oxford University: Lectr in Physics, 1976–94; Reader, Dept of Physics (Theoretical Physics), 1994–96. Member: SERC, 1985–90 (Chm., Solar System Cttee, 1983–86; Mem., Astronomy, Space and Radio Bd, 1979–86; Mem., Astronomy and Planetary Sci. Bd, 1986–90); PPARC, 1994–97. Pres., Royal Astronomical Soc., 1994–96 (Sec., 1981–90; Vice-Pres., 1990–91, 1996–97). DUniv Surrey, 1991; Hon. DSc QUB, 2008. *Publications:* scientific papers on astrophysical plasma spectroscopy and structure and energy balance in cool star coronae, in learned jls. *Address:* Department of Physics (Theoretical Physics), 1 Keble Road, Oxford OX1 3NP. *T:* (01865) 273983.

JORDAN, Craig; *see* Jordan, V. C.

JORDAN, Edmund Patrick, (Eddie), Hon. OBE 2012; Chief Executive Officer, Jordan Grand Prix, 1991–2004; *b* 30 March 1948; *s* of Patrick Jordan and Eileen Jordan; *m* 1979, Marie McCarthy; two *s* two *d. Educ:* Synge Street Sch., Dublin; Coll. of Commerce, Dublin. Winner, Irish Kart Championship, 1971; single seater racing in FF1600, 1974; winner, Irish Formula Atlantic Championship, 1978; teamed up with Stefan Johannson, Marlboro Team Ireland, for British Formula 3 Championship, 1978; Formula 2, 1979; test drove McLaren F1 car, 1979; retired from single seater racing, 1980; Founder: Eddie Jordan Racing, 1979; Jordan Grand Prix, 1991. Irish Sporting Ambassador, 1999. *Publications:* An Independent Man: the autobiography, 2007. *Recreations:* golf, music, ski-ing. *Clubs:* Sunningdale Golf, Oxfordshire Golf, Wentworth.

JORDAN, Gerard Michael, CEng; Site Director, AEA Technology Dounreay (formerly Director, Dounreay Nuclear Power Establishment, United Kingdom Atomic Energy Authority), 1987–92; *b* 25 Sept. 1929; *s* of Arthur Thomas and Ruby Eveline Jordan; *m* 1955, Vera Peers (*d* 2008); one *s* one *d. Educ:* Grange Sch., Birkenhead; Univ. of Liverpool. BEng; CEng, MIMechE, 1974. Marine Engrg Officer, 1950–55; Gp Engr, Messrs Thomas Hedley Ltd, 1956–59; United Kingdom Atomic Energy Authority: Principal Professional and Technical Officer, 1959–73; Band Grade Officer, 1973–80; Asst Dir (Safety and Reliability

Div.), 1980; Asst Dir (Engrg and Safety Dounreay), 1980–84; Dep. Dir (Engrg Northern Div.), 1984–85; Dir of Engrg (Northern Div.), 1985–87. *Publications:* Handbook on Criticality Data, 1974, 2nd edn 1979; various papers in Trans IMechE, Trans IChemE, Trans INucE. *Recreations:* hobby electronics, DIY, fishing.

JORDAN, Graham Harold Ben, CB 2004; Science and Technology Director, Ministry of Defence, 2001–03; Senior Science and Technology Adviser, since 2004, and Associate Fellow, since 2007, Royal United Services Institute; *b* 1 April 1945; *s* of Harold Jordan and Violet Emily Jordan (*née* Wakefield); *m* 1977, Jean Anne Swale. *Educ:* Chislehurst and Sidcup Grammar Sch.; Downing Coll., Cambridge (Schol.; BA 1966 Nat. Scis and Chem. Eng; MA 1970); Brunel Univ. (MTech 1974 Op. Res.). DOAE, 1967–77; Dept of Chief Scientist, RAF, 1977–78; Supt, Land Air Studies Div., DOAE, 1978–82; Royal Aircraft Establishment: Supt, Air to Air Weapons Div., 1982–85; Head, Defensive Weapons Dept, 1985–87; Head, Civil Service Personnel Policy Div., HM Treasury, 1987–90; Scientific Advr (Command Inf. Systems), MoD, 1990–91; Asst Chief Scientific Advr (Capabilities), MoD, 1991–95; Dep. Chief Scientist (Scrutiny and Analysis), MoD, 1995; Dir of Central IT Unit, Cabinet Office (OPS), 1995–97; Dep. Under-Sec. of State (Science and Technol.), MoD, 1997–2001. Member: Technol. Bd, DSAC, 2004–07; European Security Res. Adv. Bd, 2005–07; NATO Sci. Cttee, 2006–13. *Publications:* RUSI reports and articles in RUSI Jl and RUSI Defence Systems. *Recreations:* small scale farming, home maintenance, music, walking.

JORDAN, Marc Lowis Aron, FSA; Founder and Chief Executive, Creative Education Trust, since 2010; *b* 12 July 1955; *s* of late Philip Jordan, MICE and Dr Louise Jordan (*née* Jackson); *m* 2000, Olivia, *d* of late Terence Kilmartin, CBE and Joanna Kilmartin; one *s*. *Educ:* William Ellis Sch.; Univ. of Exeter (BA Hons English Lit.); Courtauld Inst. of Art (MA Hist. of Art); London Business Sch. (MBA). Res. Assistant, Nat. Portrait Gallery, 1979–80; Cataloguer, Dept of Watercolours and Drawings, Phillips Auctioneers, 1981–82; Grove Dictionary of Art: Area Editor, 1985–88; Dep. Editor, 1988–92; Commissioning Editor, Phaidon Press, 1992–95; Publisher, Harvey Miller Publishers, 1998–99; Man. Dir, Acoustiguide Ltd, 1999–2003; Mgt Consultant, AEA Consulting, 2003–06; Interim Dir, Contemporary Art Soc., 2006–07; mgt consultant, 2007–10. Trustee: Hackney Historic Buildings Trust, 2000–04; Bishopsgate Foundn, 2009–15; Member: London Regl Cttee, Heritage Lottery Fund, 2001–07; Adv. Panel on European Capital of Culture 2008, 2002–03. Mem. Council, Univ. of Exeter, 2007–13; Gov., Midhurst Rother Coll., 2008–12. Jt author, Arts Council England Rev. of Presentation of Contemporary Visual Arts, 2005. FSA 2007. *Publications:* contribs to Apollo, Burlington Magazine, The Times, NY Times, TLS. *Recreations:* gardening, old houses, sailing. *Address:* Creative Education Trust, 35 Old Queen Street, SW1H 9JA. *Clubs:* Athenæum; Beaulieu River Sailing.

JORDAN, Michael Anthony; Chairman and Senior Partner, Cork Gully, Chartered Accountants, 1983–93; Partner, Coopers & Lybrand, Chartered Accountants, 1980–93; *b* 20 Aug. 1931; *s* of Charles Thomas Jordan and Florence Emily (*née* Golder); *m* 1st, 1956, Brenda Gee (marr. diss. 1989); one *s* one *d*; 2nd, 1990, Dorothea Rosine Estelle Coureau (*d* 2000). *Educ:* Haileybury. FCA 1956. Joined R. H. March Son & Co., 1958, Partner, 1959–68; Partner: Saker & Langdon Davis, 1963–93; W. H. Cork Gully & Co., 1968–80. Principal insolvency appointments: Acrow, Barlow Clowes, Capper Neill, Homfray Carpets, Learfan, Lines Bros, Lyon Gp, Mitchell Construction, Norton Villiers Triumph Manufacturing, Norvic Shoes, Polly Peck, Savings & Investment Bank, Wolverhampton Wanderers FC; Jt Inspector for High Court of IoM into the affairs of the Savings & Investment Bank, 1983. Gen. Comr of Income Tax, City of London, 1970–2006 (Chm., 1998–2006). Gov., Royal Shakespeare Co., 1979–2001. Freeman, City of London; Master, Tower Ward, 1979–80; Liveryman, Bakers' Co. *Publications:* (jtly) Insolvency, 1986. *Recreations:* opera, DIY, gardening. *Address:* 8 Clifton Place, W2 2SN.

JORDAN, Richard James; theatrical producer, since 1998; Director, Richard Jordan Productions Ltd, since 2001; *b* Norwich, 28 Oct. 1974; *s* of Anthony Frederick Richard Jordan and Diane Jane Jordan (*née* Wiley); *m* 2005, Tammy Dale. *Educ:* Cringleford First and Middle Sch., Norfolk; Hethersett High Sch., Norfolk; Oxford Sch. of Drama (Stage Mgt and Th. Admin). Wanted to be a producer from age 12; wrote to Cameron Mackintosh for advice, encouraged by his reply, began career in theatre at age 16 as stagehand on West End musical, Cats, 1990; joined tech. team, Stephen Joseph Th., Scarborough, 1993; mgt team, Wycombe Swan Th., High Wycombe, Nederlander Theatres (London), Michael Codron Ltd, 1994–97; Line Manager, Cottesloe Th. for RNT, 1997–98. Creative Consultant, Teatros Artes, Brazil, 2001–11; Director: New Wolsey Th., Ipswich, 2003–11; Oxford Playhouse, 2008–11; Associate: Theatre Royal Haymarket, London, 2005– (Creative Dir, 2006–09); Perry St Theater, NYC, 2005–11; UK Associate, Primary Stages, NYC, 2007–09; Associate Artist, Bush Th., London, 2006–13; Internat. Associate, Illawarra Performing Arts Centre, Wollongong, Australia, 2009–; Internat. producing Partner, Chicago Shakespeare Th., 2011–. Artistic Consultant for creation and inaugural season of Theatre Royal Haymarket Co., 2007–08. Trustee, Youth Music Th. UK, 2003–11; Patron: Norwich Theatre Royal 250 Appeal; Norwich Playhouse; Brighton Fringe. Voting Mem., BAFTA, 2002–. Columnist, Stage newspaper; theatre contributor for BBC and ABC. First London prodn, Shylock, Hampstead Th., 1999; first NY prodn, Rum and Vodka, Ohio Th., 2002. Other productions include: Of Thee I Sing, Anna Weiss, 1999; Sweeney Todd - Demon Barber of Fleet St, God's Official, Troilus and Cressida, Rum and Vodka, The Good Thief, Almost Forever But, 2000; Kissing Sid James, St Nicholas, 2001; Smoking with Lulu, Love Songs, The Life of Galileo, Dust to Dust, Single Spies, 2002; Miriam Margolyes: Dickens' Women, 2002, 2012; Larkin with Women, 2002, 2003, 2005; The Lady in the Van, 2002, 2009, 2010, 2011, 2012; Protection, This Lime Tree Bower, Nine Parts of Desire, Miguel Street, Roald Dahl's The Twits, 2003; Third Finger Left Hand, Ladies and Gents, 2004; Dylan Thomas: Return Journey, A Mobile Thriller, The Broken Road, 2005; Monsieur Ibrahim and the Flowers of the Qur'an, Lunch with the Hamiltons, Killing Castro, Marlon Brando's Corset, Insomnobabble, Bussmann's Holiday, In the Continuum, The Truman Capote Talk Show, Goodness, an Oak Tree, 2006; Believe, Victor Spinetti: A Very Private Diary… Revisited!, Exits and Entrances, Get Your War On, Hamlet (solo), 2007; Life and Beth, Haunting Julia, Snake in the Grass, Falstaff, Once and For All We're Gonna Tell You Who We Are so Shut Up and Listen, Itsoseng, Berkoff's Women, Basic Training, 2008; Dumbshow, Under the Influence, Stefan Golaszewski is a Widower, Internal, The Smile Off Your Face, East 10th Street, Edwyn Collins - A Casual Introduction, Heroin(e) for Breakfast, Stefan Golaszewski Speaks about a Girl He Once Loved, Die Roten Punkte, Impressionism, MacHomer: the Simpsons do Macbeth!, 2009; A Game of You, Teenage Riot, Double Booked, Jordan, The Friendship Experiment, The Uber Hate Gang, en route, 2010; Roadkill, 2010, 2011, 2013, A Behanding in Spokane, 2010; Funk It Up About Nothin', Audience, Alphonse, Kafka and Son, Penny Dreadfuls Etherdome, Bette and Joan, My Filthy Hunt, Laundry Boy, Bigger Than Jesus, 2011; Midsummer (a play with songs), A History of Everything, All That is Wrong, XXXO, Othello: The Remix, Razing Eddie, 2012; Glasgow Girls, 2012, 2014, An Audience with the Duke of Windsor, 2012; Cadre, Bitch Boxer, Chapel Street, Bigmouth, Beeston Rifles, The Vanishing Inquisition, Vanya and Sonia and Masha and Spike, Fight Night, Ali J, The Adventure, Whatever Gets You Through the Night, Hirsch, Bonanza, Tourniquet, Freeze, La Merda, Parkin'Son, The Q Brothers, A Christmas Carol, 2013; Landscape with Skiproads, Looking for Paul, Sirens, Where the World is Going, That's Where We're Going, Live Forever, The Art of Falling Apart, Janis Joplin: Full Tilt, Small War, Since I Suppose, GRIT - the Martyn Bennett Story, Mush and Me, 2014; Mark Thomas' Bravo Figaro!, Pardon/In Cuffs, The Great Downhill Journey of Little Tommy, Are We Not Drawn Onward to New Era, The History of the World Through Banalities, Gary Busey's Hamlet, A Reason to Talk, Tristero, UpsideDownInsideOut, Forever Young, Night + Daze, 2015. Has also produced and presented prodns in Canada, Argentina, Australia, NZ, Iceland, S Africa, Zimbabwe, Belgium, France, Spain, Germany, Israel, Singapore, Italy, Ireland, UAE, Hong Kong, Sweden, Denmark, India, Holland, Portugal, Brazil, S Korea and theatres across UK and USA; associations with many of world's leading theatres and producing orgns. Lucille Lortel Award; John Gassner Award for Best New American Play; 2 Herald Angel Awards; 2 Helen Hayes Awards; 3 Obie Awards; 2 Jeff Awards; 8 Scotsman Fringe First Awards; Carol Tambor Award; 7 Total Theatre Awards; 3 Musical Th. Matters UK Awards; Spirit of the Fringe Award; Icelandic Mask Theatre Award; Tap Award; US Black Alliance Award; Time Out Lisbon Award; Adelaide Fest. Award; Off West End Award; Stage Award; Drama Desk Award; Outer Critics Circle Award; Drama League Award; TheaterMania Award; Emmy Award; TIF/Soc. of London Th. Producers Award; Laurence Olivier Award; Tony Award. *Recreations:* going to the theatre, collecting theatrical memorabilia and musical cast recordings, cinema, playing tennis, travelling. *Address:* Richard Jordan Productions Ltd, Mews Studios, 16 Vernon Yard, W11 2DX. *T:* (020) 7243 9001, *Fax:* (020) 7313 9667. *E:* info@richardjordanproductions.com. *Club:* Groucho.

JORDAN, Robert Anthony; His Honour Judge Jordan; a Circuit Judge, since 2015; *b* Dewsbury, 16 Aug. 1952; *s* of Neil Jordan and Maureen Jordan; *m* 1984, Helen Dorothy; three *s* two *d*. *Educ:* St Thomas Acquinas Grammar Sch., Leeds; Park Lane Coll., Leeds; Anglia Ruskin Univ.; Coll. of Law, London. Admitted solicitor, 1978; NP 1981; solicitor: Joynson-Hick, 1978–81; Jordans, 1981–99; Dep. Dist Judge, 1995–99; Dist Judge, 1999–2015; Recorder, 2008–15; Dep. High Court Judge, 2015–. Mem., Civil Justice Council, 2006–12. Pres., Assoc. of HM's District Judges, 2014–15. *Recreations:* sailing, fly fishing, hill walking, family, cycling. *Address:* Manchester County Court and Family Court Hearing Centre, Manchester Civil and Family Justice Centre, 1 Bridge Street West, Manchester M60 9DJ.

JORDAN, Prof. (Virgil) Craig, OBE 2002; PhD, DSc; Professor of Breast Medical Oncology and Molecular and Cellular Oncology, M. D. Anderson Hospital and Cancer Center, Houston, Texas, since 2014; *b* New Braunfels, Texas, 25 July 1947; *s* of Geoffrey Webster Jordan and Sybil Cynthia Jordan (*née* Mottram); two *d* by a previous marriage. *Educ:* Moseley Hall Grammar Sch., Cheadle; Leeds Univ. (BSc 1969; PhD 1972; DSc 1984). FMedSci 2009; FRSB (FSB 2009). Vis. Scientist, Worcester Foundn for Experimental Biol., Mass, 1972–74; Lectr in Pharmacol., Leeds Univ., 1974–79; Hd, Endocrine Unit, Ludwig Inst., Univ. of Berne, 1979–80; University of Wisconsin: Asst Prof. of Human Oncol., 1980–82; Associate Prof., 1982–85; Prof., 1985–93; Dir, Breast Cancer Res. and Treatment Prog., Wisconsin Comprehensive Cancer Center, 1988–93; Prof. of Cancer Pharmacol., 1993–2004, Diana Princess of Wales Prof. of Cancer Res., 1999–2004, Northwestern Univ. Med. Sch., Ill, and Dir, Breast Cancer Res., Lurie Cancer Center, Chicago, 1993–2004; Alfred G. Knudson Prof. of Cancer Res., and Res. Dir for Med. Scis, Fox Chase Cancer Center, Philadelphia, 2004–09; Scientific Dir, Vincent T. Lombardi Prof. of Translational Cancer Res. and Prof. of Oncol. and Pharmacol., and Vice Chm., Dept of Oncol., Lombardi Comprehensive Cancer Center, Georgetown Univ. Med. Center, Washington DC, 2009–14. Vis. Prof. in Molecular Medicine, Leeds Univ., 2012–. Pres., RSocMed Foundn, USA, 2010–. Commnd Leeds Univ. OTC, 1969; Captain: Intelligence Corps TAVR, 1970–75; 23 SAS TAVR, 1975–79; SAS RARO, 1980–97; SAS Reg. Assoc., 2007–; Hon. Col, Leeds Univ. OTC, 2014–. MNAS 2009. Hon. Mem., RPSGB, 2008. Hon. Faculty Fellow, Univ. Coll., Dublin, 2000; Hon. FRSocMed 2009; Fellow, Amer. Assoc. for Cancer Res. Acad., 2013; FCGI 2013. Hon. DM: Leeds, 2001; Crete, 2009; Hon. DSc: Mass, 2001; Bradford, 2005. Caine Award, Amer. Assoc. for Cancer Res., 1989; 1st Brinker Internat. Breast Cancer Award for Basic Sci., Susan G. Komen Foundn, 1992; Award for Experimental Therapeutics, Amer. Soc. for Pharmacol. and Experimental Therapeutics, 1993; Cameron Prize for Therapeutics, Edinburgh Univ. Med. Sch., 1993; Gaddum Meml Award, British Pharmacol Soc., 1993; 12th Award for Scientific Excellence in Medicine, Amer. Italian Foundn for Cancer Res., 1995; Laureate of 6th Cino del Duca Award for Oncol., Paris, 1997; Bristol-Myers Squibb Award for Cancer Res., 2001; 3rd Annual Breast Cancer Award, Eur. Inst. of Oncol., 2001; Medal of Honor, Amer. Cancer Soc., 2002; Avon Med. Advancement Award, Avon Foundn, 2002; Landon Prize, Amer. Assoc. for Cancer Res., 2002; Kettering Prize, Gen. Motors Cancer Res. Foundn, 2003; N Amer. Menopause Soc. and Eli Lilly SERM Res. Award, 2003; 3rd George and Christine Sosnovsky Award, RSC, 2004; Amer. Cancer Soc. Award for Chemoprevention, Amer. Soc. of Clin. Oncol., 2006; Gregory J. Pincus Award and Medal, Worcester Foundn for Biomed. Res., 2007; Karnofsky Award, Amer. Soc. of Clin. Oncol., 2008; Jephcott Medal, RSocMed, 2009; Susan G. Komen for the Cure Scientific and Medical Dist. Award, Susan G. Komen Foundn, 2010; St Gallen Breast Cancer Award, 2011; Goodman and Gilman Award, Amer. Soc. for Pharmacol and Exptl Therapeutics, 2012; 50 Luminaries, Amer. Soc. of Clin. Oncol., 2014; Sir James Black Award for Contribns to Drug Discovery, British Pharmacol Soc., 2015. *Publications:* Estrogen and Antiestrogen Action and Breast Cancer Therapy, 1985; Long Term Adjuvant Tamoxifen Therapy, 1992; Tamoxifen for the Treatment and Prevention of Breast Cancer, 1999; Tamoxifen: a pioneering medicine for breast cancer, 2013; Estrogen Action SERMs and Women's Health, 2013; over 750 res. articles in professional med. jls on receptor pharmacol. and breast cancer. *Recreations:* London, Germany, collecting mountains, English longbow, target pistol, military history, antique weapons collecting, my library, bookshops, Falkland Island stamps. *E:* VCJordan@mdanderson.org. *Clubs:* Royal Society of Medicine; Union League (Philadelphia).

JORDANOVA, Prof. Ludmilla Jane, PhD; FRHistS; Professor of History and Visual Culture, University of Durham, since 2013; *b* 10 Oct. 1949; *d* of Ivan Nicholov Jordanov and Phyllis Elizabeth Jordanova (*née* Brown); *m* 1970, Simon Thomas Emmerson (marr. diss. 1974); two *d* by Karl Michael Figlio. *Educ:* Oxford High Sch. for Girls; New Hall, Cambridge (BA 1971; MA, PhD 1977); Univ. of Essex (MA 1987). FRHistS 1989. Res. Fellow, New Hall, Cambridge, 1975–78; Res. Officer, Wellcome Unit for History of Medicine, Univ. of Oxford, 1978–79; Lectr, 1980–88, Sen. Lectr, 1988–91, Prof., 1991–93, Dept of Hist., Univ. of Essex; Prof., Dept of Hist., Univ. of York, 1993–96; Prof. of Visual Arts, 1996–2005 and Dean, Schs of World Art Studies and Music, 1999–2002, UEA; Dir, Centre for Res. in the Arts, Social Scis and Humanities, Univ. of Cambridge and Fellow, Downing Coll., Cambridge, 2003–05 (on secondment); Prof. of Modern Hist., KCL, 2006–13. Mem., Educn Honours Cttee, 2005–07. President: British Soc. for Hist. of Sci., 1998–2000; Hist. of Sci. Sect., BAAS, 2006; Mem. Council, 1993–97, Vice-Pres., 2001–04, RHistS. Trustee, Science Mus. Gp, 2011–. FRSocMed 1999. Trustee, Nat. Portrait Gall., 2001–09. *Publications:* Lamarck, 1984; Sexual Visions: images of gender in science and medicine between the Eighteenth and Twentieth Centuries, 1989; Nature Displayed: gender, science and medicine 1760–1820, 1999; Defining Features: scientific and medical portraits 1660–2000, 2000; History in Practice, 2000, 2nd edn 2006; The Look of the Past, 2012; several edited vols, book reviews, contribs to learned jls. *Recreations:* grandparenting, friendship, Edinburgh, travel, listening to music, art, museums, galleries. *Address:* Black Rose House, 19 Raven Court, Esh Winning, Durham DH7 9JS; 24 Lower Granton Road, Edinburgh EH5 3RT. *E:* ludmilla.jordanova@durham.ac.uk.

JORDON, William Eddy, CBE 2004; Executive Director, North Shore and Grangefield Academies, Stockton, since 2014 (Principal, North Shore Academy, 2012–14); Regional Director, North East, Future Leaders Charitable Trust, since 2012; *b* 17 Dec. 1947; *s* of John and Kathleen Jordon; *m* 1971, Doreen Thompson; one *s*. *Educ:* Newcastle upon Tyne Univ. (BPhil, MEd, DAES); Sunderland Polytech. (Teachers' Cert.). Hd, Phys. Educn, Marton Boarding Sch., Cheshire, 1969–73; Community Tutor and Dep. Hd (Community), Blyth

Ridley High Sch., 1973–78; Hd, Referral Unit, 1978–81, Hd of House, 1981–83, Slatyford Comprehensive Sch., Newcastle upon Tyne; Sen. Teacher, Redewood Comprehensive Sch., 1983–89; Dep. Hd, Ralph Gardner High Sch., N Tyneside, 1989–93; Headteacher, 1993–2011, Exec. Headteacher, 2011–12, Dyke House Sch., Hartlepool; Exec. Headteacher, Brierton Community Sch., Hartlepool, 2007–09. FRSA 2004. *Recreations:* running, walking the dog, reading, fell-walking, listening to music. *Address:* Rosemount, Ovingham, Prudhoe, Northumberland NE42 6DE. *T:* (01661) 832431; North Shore Academy, Talbot Street, Stockton on Tees TS20 2AY.

JORY, Richard Norman; QC 2013; *b* Bristol, 22 April 1967; *s* of William and Carolyn Jory; *m* 2002, Stephanie Suzanne Evans; two *s* one *d*. *Educ:* Sherborne Sch.; Reading Univ. (BA Hons Modern Hist. and Internat. Relns). Called to the Bar, Middle Temple, 1993; in practice as barrister, specialising in serious crime and fraud; Standing Counsel to Revenue and Customs Prosecutions Office, 2008–11. *Recreations:* theatre, cricket, competing in marathons and triathlons, dancing with my children, impersonating Elvis, badger conservation. *Address:* 9–12 Bell Yard, WC2A 2JR. *T:* (020) 7400 1800. *E:* r.jory@912by.com. *Club:* MCC.

JOSCELYNE, Richard Patrick; British Council Director, Japan, 1991–94; *b* 19 June 1934; *s* of Dr Patrick C. Joscelyne and Rosalind Whitcombe; *m* 1st, 1961, Vera Lucia Mello (marr. diss. 1988); one *s* one *d*; 2nd, 1988, Irangani Dias. *Educ:* Bryanston; Queens' Coll., Cambridge. Teaching posts in France, Brazil and Britain, 1958–62. British Council: Montevideo, 1962; Moscow, 1967; Madrid, 1969; Director, North and Latin America Dept, 1973; Representative, Sri Lanka, 1977; Controller, Overseas Div. B (America, Pacific and Asia Div.), 1980; Controller, Finance Div., 1982; Representative, Spain, 1987. *Address:* 4 Alexandra Close, Cam, Glos GL11 4GN.

JOSEPH, Cedric; *see* Joseph, His Honour T. J. C.

JOSEPH, David Philip; QC 2003; *b* 22 April 1961; *s* of late Dr Joe Joseph and of Judith Joseph (*née* Lobl); *m* 1990, Denise Bass; three *s*. *Educ:* St Paul's Sch., London; Pembroke Coll., Cambridge (BA 1982). Called to the Bar, Middle Temple, 1984; in practice specialising in internat. arbitration and commercial law. *Publications:* Jurisdiction and Arbitration Agreements and their Enforcement, 2005. *Recreations:* tennis, opera, singing, mountain walking. *Address:* Essex Court Chambers, 24 Lincoln's Inn Fields, WC2A 3ED. *E:* djoseph@essexcourt.net.

JOSEPH, (Hon. Sir) James Samuel, (3rd Bt *cr* 1943, of Portsoken, City of London); *b* 27 Jan. 1955; *o s* of Baron Joseph, CH (Life Peer) and Hellen Louise (*née* Guggenheimer); *S* to baronetcy of father, 1994, but does not use the title and his name does not appear on the Official Roll of the Baronetage; *m* 1990, Sarah Jane Thwaites; two *s*. *Heir: s* Sam Nathan Joseph, *b* 7 Aug. 1991.

JOSEPH, Jenny, (Mrs C. A. Coles), FRSL; writer, lecturer and reader; *b* 7 May 1932; *d* of Louis Joseph and Florence Joseph (*née* Cotton); *m* 1961, Charles Anthony Coles (*d* 1985); one *s* two *d*. *Educ:* St Hilda's Coll., Oxford (BA Hons English). Newspaper reporter; part-time lectr for WEA and Cambridge Univ. Extra-Mural Dept, later for Bristol Univ. Extra-Mural Dept. *Publications:* The Unlooked-for Season, 1960; Rose in the Afternoon, 1974; The Thinking Heart, 1978; Beyond Descartes, 1983; Persephone, 1986; The Inland Sea, 1989; Beached Boats (with Robert Mitchell's photographs), 1991; Selected Poems, 1992; Ghosts and Other Company, 1995; Warning, 1997; Extended Similes, 1997; All the Things I See, 2000; Led by the Nose, 2002; Extreme of Things, 2006; Nothing Like Love, 2009. *Address:* c/o Johnson & Alcock, Clerkenwell House, 45–47 Clerkenwell Green, EC1R 0HT. *T:* (020) 7251 0125, *Fax:* (020) 7251 2172. *E:* info@johnsonandalcock.co.uk.

JOSEPH, Julian; jazz pianist and composer; *b* London, 11 May 1966. *Educ:* Berklee Sch. of Music, Boston, Mass (BA). Founder: own quartet, 1990; Julian Joseph Trio; Forum Project (8 piece); Electric Project; All Star Big Band; tours of Europe, USA, Canada, Asia, Australia and appearances at festivals. Presenter, TV series, Jazz with Julian Joseph, 1999, 2000; writer and presenter, Jazz Legends, Radio 3, 2000–07. Composer: Bridgetower - A Fable of 1807 (jazz opera), UK tour, 2007; Shadowball (children's jazz opera), 2010. Patron, Jazz Develt Trust, 1998–. *Recordings:* The Language of Truth, 1991; Reality, 1993; Universal Traveller, 1996. *Address:* c/o James Joseph Music Management, 85 Cicada Road, SW18 2PA.

JOSEPH, Leslie; QC 1978; *b* 13 Aug. 1925; *s* of Benjamin Francis Joseph and Sarah Edelman; *m* 1st, 1964, Ursula Mary Hamilton (*d* 1988); one *s* two *d*; 2nd, 2001, Hedwig Erna Lydia Swan (*née* Pesendorfer). *Educ:* Haberdashers' Aske's, Hampstead; University Coll. London (LLB Hons). Served Army, 1943–47: Infantry, 1943–45 (Sgt); Chindits, Jan. 1945; AEC, 1945–47. Called to the Bar, Middle Temple, 1953, Bencher, 1986; Master of the Revels, 1989–2000; Autumn Reader, 2003. Mem., Common Professional Examn Bd, 1989–2001 (Chm., 1996–98); Chairman: Bar Vocational Stage Sub-Cttee, 1996; Bar Vocational Course Validation Panel, 1996–97. Gov., Inns of Court Sch. of Law, 1994–96. *Recreations:* wine, water, cooking for friends. *Address:* Rose Lodge, 1b Southway, Totteridge, N20 8EB. *T:* (020) 8445 3681; Church Cottage, Buckhorn Weston, Dorset SP8 5HS.

JOSEPH, Richard David; Chief Executive Officer, Arcadia Publishing International Inc. and Arcadia Publishing Inc., since 2002; *b* 6 June 1956; *s* of Philip and Pamela Joseph; *m* 1987, Nicole Beauchamp; three *s*. *Educ:* King Edward VII Sch., Johannesburg; Univ. of Witwatersrand (BCom). Higher Dip. in Accountancy, Public Accountants and Auditors Bd, SA. Articled clerk, Coopers & Lybrand, SA, 1978–80; Man. Dir, Books Etc Ltd, 1981–97; CEO, Borders (UK) Ltd, 1997–2000; Officer, Borders Gp Inc., 1997–2000. Member: Soc. of Bookmen, London, 1980–2008; Cttee, Book Sellers' Assoc. of GB and Ireland, 1983–2000. *Recreations:* family, vacation, swimming, books, flying, boating. *Address:* 420 Wando Park Boulevard, Mount Pleasant, SC 29464, USA. *E:* rjoseph@arcadiapublishing.com. *Club:* Groucho.

JOSEPH, Robert Edward; Editor-at-Large, Meininger's Wine Business International, since 2006; Co-owner: Le Grand Noir, since 2005; Greener Planet Wines, since 2005; commentator, consultant and speaker; *b* London, 15 Feb. 1955; *s* of Alfred and Vivienne Joseph; partner, Catharine Lowe; one *s* one *d*. *Educ:* St Paul's Sch., London. Ed., 1983–85, Publishing Ed., 1985–2005, Wine Internat. mag.; Wine corresp., Sunday Telegraph, 1984–99; Partner, Hugh, Kevin & Robert, 2005–. Publisher, Joseph Report, 2005–. Chm., Internat. Wine Challenge London, 1984–2005. Chm., Wine Inst. of Asia, 1997–. Dir, DoILikeIt? Ltd, 2010–; Partner, Winestars World, 2013–. Chevalier du Tastevin, 2004; Mem., Commanderie du Bontemps de Médoc et des Graves, Sauternes et Barsac. *Publications:* The Wine Lists, 1985; The Art of the Wine Label, 1987; The Good Wine Guide, annually, 1988–2004; The White Wines of France, 1989; The Essential Guide to Wine, 1989; The Wines of the Americas, 1990; Complete Encyclopedia of Wine, 1996, 2nd edn 2006; French Wines, 1999, 2nd edn 2005; (with M. Rand) Kiss Guide to Wine, 2000; Bordeaux and Its Wines, 2003; Wine Buyer's Guide, 2005, 2nd edn 2006; The Wine Travel Guide to the World, 2006; The Wine Sales and Marketing Toolkit, 2015. *Recreations:* travel, photography, cooking, collecting irony, tortoise husbandry. *Address:* 8 Herndon Road, Wandsworth, SW18 2DG. *T:* (020) 8870 2094. *E:* robertjoseph@unforgettable.com. *Club:* Chelsea Arts.

JOSEPH, Stephen Francis Waley, OBE 1996; Chief Executive, Campaign for Better Transport (formerly Transport 2000), since 1988; *b* London, 20 April 1956; *s* of Peter and Margaret Joseph; *m* 1986, Dr Jill Bartlett; three *d*. *Educ:* University Coll. Sch., Hampstead; Queen's Coll., Oxford (BA Hons Modern Hist.). Co-ordinator, Youth Envmtl Action, 1977–78; Director: Youth Unit, Council for Envmtl Conservation, 1978–82; Youth Participation Unit, British Youth Council, 1982–85; Jt Co-ordinator, London Planning Aid Service, TCPA, 1986–88. Member: Standing Adv. Cttee on Trunk Rd Assessment, 1996–99; Commn for Integrated Transport, 1999–2005. FRSA. Hon. DSc Hertfordshire, 2010. Lifetime Achievement Award, Nat. Transport Awards, 2005. *Publications:* Waking up Dormant Land, 1981; Urban Wasteland Now, 1989; contrib. articles and papers on aspects of transport to jls and newspapers. *Recreations:* family life, music, walking, exploring cities. *Address:* c/o Campaign for Better Transport, 16 Waterside, 44–48 Wharf Road, N1 7UX. *T:* (020) 7566 6481. *E:* stephen.joseph@bettertransport.org.uk.

JOSEPH, His Honour (Thomas John) Cedric; a Circuit Judge, 1994–2008; *b* 25 Aug. 1938; *s* of Thomas Rees Joseph and Katherine Ann Joseph; *m* 1960 Mary Weston; three *d*. *Educ:* Cardigan GS; LSE (LLB). Called to the Bar, Gray's Inn, 1960; Crown Counsel, Nyasaland, 1962–64; practised at the Bar, 1964–94; Asst Recorder, 1987–92; Recorder, 1992–94; Resident Judge, Croydon Crown Court, 1998–2006. Mem., Adv. Council on Misuse of Drugs, 2001–07. *Recreations:* music, travel, collecting old wine glasses and using them. *Address:* c/o Lewes Crown Court, The Law Courts, High Street, Lewes, East Sussex BN7 1YB.

JOSEPH, Wendy Rose; QC 1998; **Her Honour Judge Wendy Joseph;** a Senior Circuit Judge, since 2012; *b* 11 March 1952; *d* of late Norman Joseph and Carole Joseph (*née* Marks). *Educ:* Cathays High Sch., Cardiff; Westridge Sch. for Girls, Pasadena, Calif; New Hall, Cambridge (MA). Called to the Bar, Gray's Inn, 1975, Bencher, 2003; Asst Recorder, 1995–99; Recorder, 1999–2007; a Circuit Judge, 2007–12. A Pres., Mental Health Review Tribunal, 2001–12. *Recreations:* gardening, reading, Tudor history. *Address:* Central Criminal Court, Old Bailey, EC4M 7EH.

JOSEPHSON, Prof. Brian David, FRS 1970; Professor of Physics, Cambridge University, 1974–2007, now Emeritus; Fellow of Trinity College, Cambridge, since 1962; *b* 4 Jan. 1940; *s* of Abraham Josephson and Mimi Josephson; *m* 1976, Carol Anne Olivier; one *d*. *Educ:* Cardiff High School; Cambridge Univ. BA 1960, MA, PhD 1964, Cantab. FInstP. Asst Dir of Res. in Physics, 1967–72, Reader in Physics, 1972–74, Univ. of Cambridge. Res. Asst Prof., Illinois Univ., 1965–66; Vis., Fellow, Cornell Univ., 1971; Vis. Faculty Mem., Maharishi European Res. Univ., 1975; Visiting Professor: Wayne State Univ., 1983; Indian Inst. of Sci., Bangalore, 1984. Fellow, Sci. Mus., 2009. Hon. MIEEE, 1982; For. Hon. Mem., Amer. Acad. of Arts and Scis, 1974. Hon. DSc: Wales, 1974; Exeter, 1984. Awards: New Scientist, 1969; Research Corp., 1969; Fritz London, 1970; Nobel Prize for Physics, 1973; Casys, 2000. Medals: Guthrie, 1972; van der Pol, 1972; Elliott Cresson, 1972; Hughes, 1972; Holweck, 1973; Faraday, 1982; Sir George Thomson, 1984. *Publications:* Consciousness and the Physical World, 1980 (ed jtly); The Paranormal and the Platonic Worlds (in Japanese), 1997; research papers on physics and theory of intelligence, paranormal phenomena, Platonism, the convergence of science and religion; musical composition, Sweet and Sour Harmony, 2005. *Recreations:* mountain walking, ice skating, music, astronomy. *Address:* Cavendish Laboratory, J. J. Thomson Avenue, Cambridge CB3 0HE. *T:* (01223) 337260, *Fax:* (01223) 337356. *E:* bdj10@cam.ac.uk. *W:* www.tcm.phy.cam.ac.uk/~bdj10, www.myspace.com/josephsonmusic.

JOSHI, Bharat Suresh; HM Diplomatic Service; Deputy High Commissioner, Chennai, India, since 2013; *b* Croydon, 23 Aug. 1969; *s* of Suresh Kantilal Joshi and Geeta Suresh Joshi; *m* 1997, Bhakti, *d* of Navinchandra Umashankar Oza and Pravina Navinchandra Oza; two *d*. *Educ:* Middlesex Univ. (BSc Hotel and Restaurant Admin). Dep. High Comr, Gambia, 1999–2001; Team Leader, Policy Sect., then Hd, Correspondence Sect., UK Visas, 2001–04; Private Sec. to Parly Under-Sec. of State, FCO, 2004–06; Dir, Visa Services, Dhaka, 2006–07; Regl Manager for Gulf and Iran, Qatar, Doha, UK Border Agency, 2007–09; High Comr to Cameroon and Ambassador (non-resident) to Chad, Gabon, Equatorial Guinea and Central African Republic, 2009–13. *Recreations:* cricket, reading, watching old musicals, jogging, swimming, cooking, listening to motown, playing piano. *Address:* c/o Foreign and Commonwealth Office, King Charles Street, SW1A 2AH. *E:* bharat.joshi@fco.gov.uk, beebeeje@yahoo.com.

JOSHI, Prof. Heather Evelyn, CBE 2015 (OBE 2002); FBA 2000; FAcSS; Professor of Economic and Developmental Demography in Education, Institute of Education, London University, 1998–2011, now Emeritus (Director (formerly Principal Investigator), Millennium Cohort Study, 2000–11; Director, Centre for Longitudinal Studies, 2003–10); *b* 21 April 1946; *d* of Guy Malcolm Spooner, MBE and Molly Florence Spooner, MBE; *m* 1st, 1969, Vijay Ramchandra Joshi (marr. diss. 1977); 2nd, 1982, Gregory Hans David Martin; one *d* (one *s* decd), and two step *d*. *Educ:* St Hilda's Coll., Oxford (BA 1967, MA); St Antony's Coll., Oxford (MLitt 1970). Jun. Res. Officer, Oxford Inst. of Econs and Statistics, 1969–73; Econ. Advr, Govt Econ. Service, 1973–79; Res. Fellow, 1979–83, Sen. Res. Fellow, 1983–88, LSHTM; Sen. Res. Fellow, Birkbeck Coll., 1988–90; Sen. Lectr, LSHTM, 1990–93; Sen. Res. Fellow, subseq. Prof., City Univ., 1993–98; Dep. Dir, Centre for Longitudinal Studies, Inst. of Educn, London Univ., 1998–2003. Co-Dir, Eur. Child Cohort Network, 2008–13. President: Eur. Soc. for Population Econs, 1996; British Soc. for Population Studies, 1999–2001; Soc. for Longitudinal and Lifecourse Studies, 2010–12. *Publications:* (with V. R. Joshi) Surplus Labour and the City, 1976; (ed) The Changing Population of Britain, 1989; (with P. Paci) Unequal Pay for Women and Men, 1998; Children of the 21st Century: vol. 1, from birth to nine months (ed with S. Dex), 2005; vol. 2, the first five years (ed with K. Hansen and S. Dex), 2010; articles in economics, demography and social policy jls. *Recreations:* family life, listening to classical music. *Address:* Centre for Longitudinal Studies, UCL Institute of Education, 20 Bedford Way, WC1H 0AL. *T:* (020) 7612 6874.

JOSIPOVICI, Prof. Gabriel David, FRSL; FBA 2001; Research Professor, School of Graduate Studies, University of Sussex, since 1998; *b* 8 Oct. 1940; *s* of Jean Josipovici and Sacha (*née* Rabinovitch) (*d* 1996). *Educ:* Victoria Coll., Cairo; Cheltenham Coll.; St Edmund Hall, Oxford (BA 1st Cl. Hons 1961). FRSL 1998. School of European Studies, University of Sussex: Asst Lectr in English, 1963–65; Lectr, 1965–74; Reader (part-time), 1974–84; Prof. of English, 1984–98. Lord Northcliffe Lectr, UCL, 1980–81; Weidenfeld Vis. Prof. in Eur. Comparative Lit., Univ. of Oxford, 1996–97. *Plays:* Dreams of Mrs Fraser, 1972; Evidence of Intimacy, 1973; Playback, 1973; A Life, 1974; Vergil Dying, 1976; A Moment, 1977; AG, 1977; Kin, 1982; Mr Vee, 1987; A Little Personal Pocket Requiem, 1989. *Publications: fiction:* The Inventory, 1968; Words, 1971; Mobius the Stripper, 1974; The Present, 1975; Migrations, 1977; The Air We Breathe, 1981; Conversations in Another Room, 1984; Contre-Jour, 1987; The Big Glass, 1989; In the Fertile Land, 1991; Steps, 1992; In a Hotel Garden, 1993; Moo Pak, 1994; Now, 1998; Goldberg: Variations, 2002; Everything Passes, 2006; After, 2009; Making Mistakes, 2009; Heart's Wings, 2010; Only Joking, 2010; Infinity: the story of a moment, 2012; Hotel Andromeda, 2014; *non-fiction:* The World and the Book, 1971, 3rd edn 1994; The Lessons of Modernism, 1977, 2nd edn 1986; Writing and the Body, 1982; The Mirror of Criticism, 1983; The Book of God, 1987, 2nd edn 1989; Text and Voice, 1992; Touch: an essay, 1996; On Trust, 1999; A Life, 2001; The Singer on the Shore, 2006; Whatever Happened to Modernism?, 2010. *Recreations:* walking, swimming. *Address:* 60 Prince Edward's Road, Lewes, Sussex BN7 1BH.

JOSLIN, Peter David, QPM 1983; DL; Chief Constable of Warwickshire, 1983–98; *b* 26 Oct. 1933; *s* of Frederick William Joslin and Emma Joslin; *m* 1960, Kathleen Josephine Monaghan; one *s* one *d* (and one *s* decd). *Educ:* King Edward VI Royal Grammar School, Chelmsford; Essex University. BA Hons. Joined Essex Police, 1954–74 (Police Constable to Superintendent); Chief Superintendent, Divl Comdr, Leicestershire Constabulary, 1974–76; Asst Chief Constable (Operations), Leics Constab., 1976–77; Dep. Chief Constable,

Warwicks Constabulary, 1977–83. Chm., Traffic Cttee, ACPO, 1989–92. Pres., Warwickshire Assoc. for the Blind, 1993–. DL Warwickshire, 1999. *Recreations:* sport (now mainly as a spectator), house renovation, good wines, after dinner speaking. *Address:* Nash House, 41 High Street, Kenilworth, Warks CV8 1LY. *T:* (01926) 511517.

JOSPIN, Lionel Robert; Prime Minister of France, 1997–2002; *b* 12 July 1937; *s* of late Robert Jospin and Mireille Jospin (*née* Dandieu); *m*; one *s* one *d*; *m* 1994, Prof. Sylviane Agacinski; one step *s*. *Educ:* Institut d'Etudes Politiques, Paris; Ecole Nationale d'Administration. French Foreign Office, 1965–70; Prof. of Economics, Technical Univ. Inst., Paris-Sceaux, 1970–81; MP 1981–88; MEP 1984–88; French Socialist Party: Nat. Sec., various divs, 1973–81; First Sec., 1981–88 and 1995–97; Minister of State, Nat. Educn and Sports, 1988–92; Minister plenipotentiary, Foreign Office, 1992. Member: Conseil général, Haute-Garonne, 1988–2002; Conseil régional, Midi-Pyrénées, 1992–97. Grand-Croix, Ordre National du Mérite (France), 1997; Grand Officier, Légion d'Honneur (France), 2008. *Publications:* L'invention du Possible, 1991; Propositions pour la France 1995–2000, 1995; Le Temps de Répondre, 2002; Le Monde comme je le vois, 2005; L'Impasse, 2007; Lionel raconte Jospin, 2010. *Recreation:* tennis. *Address:* c/o Parti Socialiste, 10 Rue de Solferino, 75007 Paris, France.

JOSS, Vivienne Mary Hunt; *see* Parry, V. M. H.

JOSSE, David Benjamin; QC 2009; *b* London, 22 July 1961; *s* of S. E. Josse, OBE and Lea Harris; *m* 1995, Natalie Poplar. *Educ:* King's Coll. London (BA Hist.); City Univ. (Dip. Law). Called to the Bar, Middle Temple, 1985; in practice at Criminal Bar, 1985–2005, 2010–; Defence Counsel, Internat. Criminal Tribunal for former Yugoslavia, 2005–09. *Recreations:* watching most sports (in particular cricket), politics, Scotland. *Address:* 5 St Andrew's Hill, EC4V 5BZ. *T:* (020) 7332 5400. *E:* davidbjosse@yahoo.com. *Clubs:* MCC; Middlesex CC.

JOST, H. Peter, CBE 1969; DSc; CEng; CSci; FIM; Hon. FIET; Chairman, Engineering & General Equipment Ltd, 1977–2006; Director of overseas companies; Hon. Industrial Professor, Liverpool John Moores University (formerly Liverpool Polytechnic), since 1983; Hon. Professor of Mechanical Engineering, University of Wales, since 1986; *b* 25 Jan. 1921; *o s* of late Leo and Margot Jost; *m* 1948, Margaret Josephine, *o d* of late Michael and Sara Kadesh, Norfolk Is, S Pacific; two *d*. *Educ:* City of Liverpool Techn. Coll.; Manchester Coll. of Technology. Apprentice, Associated Metal Works, Glasgow and D. Napier & Son Ltd, Liverpool; Methods Engr, K & L Steelfounders and Engrs Ltd, 1943; Chief Planning Engr, Datim Machine Tool Co. Ltd, 1946; Gen. Man. 1949, Dir 1952, Trier Bros Ltd; Man. Dir, 1955–89, Chm., 1973–2000, K. S. Paul Products Ltd; Lubrication Consultant: Richard Thomas & Baldwins Ltd, 1960–65; August Thyssen Hütte AG, 1963–66; Chairman: Bright Brazing Ltd, 1969–76; Peppermill Brass Foundry Ltd, 1970–76; Centralube Ltd, 1974–77 (Man. Dir, 1955–77); Associated Technology Gp Ltd, 1976–; Director: Williams Hudson Ltd, 1967–75; Stothert & Pitt plc, 1971–85; Fuchs Lubritech International, 2000–03. Chairman: Lubrication Educn and Res. Working Gp, DES, 1964–65; Cttee on Tribology, DTI, 1966–74; Industrial Technologies Management Bd, DTI, 1972–74; Dep. Chm., Cttee for Industrial Technologies, DTI, 1972–74; Member: Adv. Council on Technology, 1968–70; Cttee on Terotechnology, 1971–72; Consultative Gp on Sci. and Technol., FCO, 1994–99. Hon. Associate, Manchester Coll. of Science and Technology, 1962; University of Salford: Privy Council's Nominee to Ct, 1970–83; Mem. Council, 1974–84; Mem. Court, Middlesex Univ., 1996–2000. Mem. Council: IProdE, 1973–91 (Vice-Pres., 1975–77, Pres., 1977–78; Chm., Technical Policy Bd and Mem., Exec. Policy Cttee, 1974; Hon. Fellow, 1980); IMechE, 1974–92 (Member: Technical Bd, 1975; Finance Bd, 1979– (Chm., 1988–91); Disciplinary Bd, 1979–; Vice-Pres., 1987–92); Council of Engineering Institutions: Mem. Bd, 1977–83; Mem. Exec., 1979–83 (Mem. External Affairs Cttee, 1974–80; Chm. Home Affairs Cttee, 1980–83); Mem., Parly and Scientific Cttee, 1973– (Hon. Sec., 1990–93; Vice-Pres., 1993–95 and 1998–2001; Vice Chm., 1995–98; Mem., Gen. Purposes Cttee, 1991–; Mem. Council (formerly Steering Cttee), 1983–; Life Mem., 2002). President: Internat. Tribology Council, 1973–; Manchester Technology Assoc., 1984–85; Chm., Manchester Technology Assoc. in London, 1976–90. Hon. Ed., Friction, Tsinghua Univ., China, 2013–. Chm. Trustees, Michael John Trust, 1986–. Rutherford Lectr, Manchester Technology Assoc., 1979; James Clayton Lectr, IMechE, 1981. Freeman, City of London, 1984; Liveryman, Engineers' Co., 1984. CCMI (CBIM 1984); Fellow, 1970, Life Fellow, 1986, ASME; FSME, USA, 1988 (Hon. Mem., 1977); Hon. MIPlantE, 1969; Hon. Member: Société Française de Tribologie, 1972; Gesellschaft für Tribologie, 1972; Chinese Mech. Engrg Soc., 1986; Russian (formerly USSR) Acad. of Engrg, 1991; Nat. Tribology Council of Bulgaria, 1991; Japanese Soc. of Tribologists, 1992; Slovak Tribology Soc., 1993; Ukrainian Acad. of Transport, 1994; Polish Tribolog. Soc., 1995; Belarus Acad. of Engrg and Technol., 1996; Fellow and Hon. Life Mem., Soc. of Tribologists and Lubrication Engrs, USA, 1997 (Internat. Award, 1997); Hon. FIMechE 2011; Hon. Fellow, Univ. of Central Lancs, 2003. Hon. DSc: Salford, 1970; Slovak Technical Univ., 1987; Bath, 1990; Technical Univ. of Budapest, 1993; Belarus Acad. of Scis, 2000; Hon. DTech CNAA, 1987; Hon. DEng: Leeds, 1989; UMIST 2004; Sheffield, 2011; DUniv Sofia. San Fernando Valley Engineers Council (USA) Internat. Achievement Award, 1978; State of California State Legislature Commendation, 1978; Georg Vagelpohl Insignia, Germany, 1979. Sir John Larking Medal 1944, Derby Medal 1955, Liverpool Engrg Soc.; Hutchinson Meml Medal 1952, Silver Medal for Best Paper 1952–53, 1st Nuffield Award 1981, IProdE; Merit Medal, Hungarian Scientific Soc. of Mech. Engrs, 1983; Gold Medal, Slovak Tech. Univ., 1984; Colclough Medal and Prize, Inst. of Materials, 1992; Louwe Alberts Award, S African Inst. of Tribology, 1992; Gold Medal, Chinese Tribology Instn, 2009; Sustained Achievement Award, RAEng, 2013. Gold Insignia, Order of Merit of Poland, 1986; Officer Cross, Order of Merit (Germany), 1992; Officier, Palmes Académiques (France), 1995; Decoration of Honour for Science and Art, 1st cl. (Austria), 2001; Order of Rising Sun, Gold Rays with Neck Ribbon (Japan), 2011. *Publications:* Oil-free Steam Cylinder Lubrication (Trans. of Liverpool Engrg Soc.), 1955; Lubrication (Tribology) Report of DES Cttee, 1966 (Jost Report); The Introduction of a New Technology, Report of DTI Cttee, 1973; Technology *vs* Unemployment, 1986; various papers in Proc. IMechE, Proc. IProdE, technical jls, etc. *Recreations:* music, opera, gardening. *Address:* Angel Lodge Chambers, Nicholas House, River Front, Enfield EN1 3FG. *T:* (020) 8959 3355. *Club:* Athenæum.

JOULWAN, Gen. George Alfred; Adjunct Professor, National Defense University, 2000–01; Olin Professor of National Security Studies, United States Military Academy, West Point, 1998–2000; Supreme Allied Commander, Europe, 1993–97; Commander-in-Chief, United States European Command, 1993–97; *b* 16 Nov. 1939; *m* Karen E. Jones; three *d*. *Educ:* US Mil. Acad., West Point (BS 1961); Loyola Univ. (Master of Pol Sci. 1968); US Army War Coll., Washington. Joined US Army, 1961; served Europe, US and Vietnam, 1962–73; Special Assistant: to the Pres., 1973–74; to Supreme Allied Comdr, SHAPE, 1974–75; Bn Comdr, Europe, 1975–77; US Army War College: student, 1977–78; Dir, Pol and Econ. Studies, 1978–79; Bde Comdr, Europe, 1979–81; COS, 3 Inf. Div., Europe, 1981–82; Exec. Officer to Chm., Jt Chiefs of Staff, Washington, 1982–86; US Army Europe and Seventh Army: DCS for Ops, 1986–88; Commanding General: 3rd Armoured Div., 1988–89; V Corps, 1989–90; C-in-C, US Southern Comd, Quarry Heights, Panama, 1990–93. Pres., One Team Inc. Defense Distinguished Service Medal, with two Oak Leaf Clusters (USA); Distinguished Service Medal (USA); Silver Star (with Oak Leaf Cluster) (USA). Foreign orders include: Grand Cross, Order of Merit, Hessian Order of Merit (Germany); Legion of Honour, Legion of Merit (France); Cross of Gallantry with three Gold Stars (Vietnam). *Address:* 2107 Arlington Ridge Road, Arlington, VA 22202–2120, USA.

JOURDAN, Dr Martin Henry, FRCS; Consultant Surgeon, Guy's Hospital, 1977–2011, and St Thomas' Hospital, 1982–2011; Reader in Surgery, University of London, 1982–2011; *b* 7 Oct. 1941; *s* of Henry George Jourdan and Jocelyn Louise (*née* Courteney); *m* 1966, May McElwain (*d* 2012); two *s* two *d*. *Educ:* Bishopshalt Sch., Hillingdon; Guy's Hosp. Med. Sch. (MB BS; PhD 1970; MS 1980). LRCP 1966; FRCS 1974. Lectr in Physiol., Guy's Hosp., 1967–70; MRC Travelling Fellow, Univ. of Calif, Berkeley, 1971–72; Registrar, then Sen. Registrar in Surgery, Guildford, Norwich and Guy's Hosp., 1974–77. Chm., Examrs in Surgery, Univ. of London, 1989–91; Mem., Court of Examrs, RCS, 1987–2000. Master, Soc. Apothecaries, 2001–02. *Publications:* (contrib.) The New Aird's Companion in Surgical Studies, 2000; papers on surgical nutrition and bowel disease. *Recreations:* tennis, theatre, gardening, opera. *Address:* 55 Shirlock Road, Hampstead, NW3 2HR. *T:* (020) 7267 1582.

JOURDAN, Stephen Eric; QC 2009; a Recorder, since 2010; a Deputy High Court Judge, since 2013; Judge First-tier Tribunal (Property Chamber), since 2013; *b* Hammersmith, 13 Nov. 1962; *s* of Werner Jourdan and Rita Jourdan; *m* 1986, Nicola Ann Gamble (marr. diss. 2011); one *s* two *d*. *Educ:* Haberdashers' Aske's Sch., Elstree; Trinity Coll., Cambridge (BA Law 1984; MA). Solicitor, Theodore Goddard, 1985–89; called to the Bar, Gray's Inn, 1989. Dep. Adjudicator, HM Land Registry, 2008–13. *Publications:* Adverse Possession, 2002, 2nd edn 2010. *Recreations:* jazz, walking, sailing. *Address:* Falcon Chambers, Falcon Court, EC4Y 1AA. *T:* (020) 7353 2484, *Fax:* (020) 7353 1261. *E:* jourdan@falcon-chambers.com.

JOVINE, Dame Nemat; *see* Shafik, Dame N.

JOWELL, Sir Jeffrey (Lionel), KCMG 2011; barrister; Director, Bingham Centre for the Rule of Law, British Institute of International and Comparative Law, since 2010; Professor of Law, University College London, 2006–10, now Emeritus (Professor of Public Law, 1975–2006); *b* 4 Nov. 1938; *s* of Jack and Emily Jowell, Cape Town; *m* 1963, Frances Barbara, *d* of late Dr M. M. Suzman and Helen Suzman, OM, Hon. DBE; one *s* one *d*. *Educ:* Cape Town Univ. (BA, LLB 1961); Hertford Coll., Oxford (BA 1963, MA 1969), Pres., Oxford Union Soc., 1963; Harvard Univ. Law Sch. (LLM 1966, SJD 1971). Called to Bar, Middle Temple, 1965 (Hon. Bencher, 1999, Bencher 2013); in practice as barrister, Blackstone Chambers. Research Asst, Harvard Law Sch., 1966–68; Fellow, Jt Center for Urban Studies of Harvard Univ. and MIT, 1967–68; Associate Prof. of Law and Admin. Studies, Osgoode Hall Law Sch., York Univ., Toronto, 1968–72; Leverhulme Fellow in Urban Legal Studies, 1972–74, and Lectr in Law, 1974–75, LSE; University College London: Dean, Faculty of Laws, 1979–89 and 1998–2002; Head of Dept, 1982–89 and 1998–2002; Vice Provost, 1992–99; Hon. Fellow, 1997. Chm., Rev. into Devolution in UK, 2015. Mem., Foreign Sec.'s Adv. Cttee on Human Rights, 2015–. UK Mem., 2000–11 and Mem., Governing Bd, 2001–11, Venice Commn (Eur. Commn on Democracy through Law) (Vice-Pres., 2003–05). Chairman, Social Sciences and The Law Cttee, 1981–84, and Vice-Chm., Govt and Law Cttee, 1982–84, Social Science Res. Council; Asst Boundary Comr, 1976–85; Chm., Cttee of Heads of University Law Schools, 1984–86; Member: Cttee of Management, Inst. of Advanced Legal Studies, 1978–89; Standing Cttee, Oxford Centre for Socio-Legal Studies, 1980–84; Gp for Study of Comparative European Admin, 1978–86; Nuffield Cttee on Town and Country Planning, 1983–86; Council, Justice, 1997–2013; Lord Chancellor's Review of Crown Office List, 1999–2000; Internat. Adv. Bd, Freedom Under Law, 2008–. UK deleg., Cttee of Experts, CSCE, Oslo, 1991. Mem., Royal Commn on Envmtl Pollution, 2003–10. Convenor of numerous internat. workshops and confs on constitutional law and human rights. Assisted with drafting of various nat. constitutions. Non-executive Director: UCL Press, 1993–95; Camden and Islington Community Health Services NHS Trust, 1994–97; Bd, Office of Rail Regulation, 2004–07; Chm., British Waterways Ombudsman Cttee, 2004–13. Trustee: John Foster Meml Trust, 1986–; Internat. Centre for Public Law, 1992–98; Bd, Inst. of Commonwealth Studies, 1994–99; Prince of Wales's Foundn (formerly Inst. of Architecture), 1997–99; Chairman: Inst. of Philanthropy, 2000–04; Friends of S African Constit. Court Trust, 2003–. Lionel Cohen Lect., Jerusalem, 1988; JUSTICE, Tom Sargent Meml Lect., Judicial Studies Bd of NI, 2008; Annual Lect., Constitutional and Admin. Law Bar Assoc., 2010; Eason Weinmann Lect., Univ. of Tulane, 2010; Visiting Professor: Univ. of Paris II, 1991; Univ. of Aix-Marseilles, 2002; Columbia Law Sch., NY, 2002; Hon. Prof., 1999–2005, Vis. Prof. and Rabinowitz Fellow, 2010, Univ. of Cape Town. Corresp. Mem., Acad. of Athens, 2009. Hon. QC 1993. Hon. DJur Athens, 1987; Hon. LLD: Ritsumeikan, 1988; Cape Town, 2000; Hon. Dr Univ. of Paris II, 2010. Member Editorial Bds: Public Law, 1977–93; Policy and Politics, 1976–83; Urban Law and Policy, 1978–83; Jl of Environmental Law, 1988–92; Public Law Review, 1995–; Judicial Review, 1996–; S African Law Jl, 2003–; Jt Editor, Current Legal Problems, 1984–89. *Publications:* Law and Bureaucracy, 1975; (ed jtly) Welfare Law and Policy, 1979; (ed jtly) Lord Denning: the Judge and the Law, 1984; (ed jtly) The Changing Constitution, 1985, 8th edn 2015; (ed jtly) New Directions in Judicial Review, 1988; (ed with H. Woolf) de Smith, Judicial Review of Administrative Action, 5th edn 1995 to 7th edn (jtly) as de Smith's Judicial Review, 2013; (ed jtly) Principles of Judicial Review, 1999; (ed jtly) Understanding Human Rights Principles, 2001; (ed jtly) Delivering Rights, 2003; articles and reviews on public law, human rights and planning law. *Recreations:* tennis, London, Exmoor. *Address:* Blackstone Chambers, Middle Temple, EC4Y 9BW. *T:* (020) 7583 1770.

JOWELL, Rt Hon. Dame Tessa (Jane Helen Douglas), DBE 2012; PC 1998; *b* 17 Sept. 1947; *d* of Kenneth and Rosemary Palmer; *m* 1st, 1970, Roger Mark Jowell, (Sir Roger Jowell, CBE) (marr. diss. 1977; he *d* 2011); 2nd, 1979, David Mills; one *s* one *d*. *Educ:* St Margaret's Sch., Aberdeen; Aberdeen Univ. (MA); Edinburgh Univ. (DSA); Goldsmiths Coll., Univ. of London (CQSW 1972). Child Care Officer, Lambeth, 1969–71; psychiatric social worker training, Goldsmiths' Coll., London Univ., 1971–72; Psychiatric Social Worker, Maudsley Hosp., 1972–74; Asst Dir, Mind, 1974–86; Dir, Community Care Special Action Project, Birmingham, and Sen. Vis. Fellow, PSI, 1986–90; Dir, Community Care Prog., Joseph Rowntree Foundn, and Sen. Vis. Fellow, King's Fund Inst., 1990–92. Councillor, Camden, 1971–86. Chair, Social Services Cttee, AMA, 1984–86; Mem., Mental Health Act Commn, 1985–90. MP (Lab) Dulwich, 1992–97, Dulwich and W Norwood, 1997–2015. An Opposition Whip, 1994–95; frontbench Opposition spokesperson on health, and on women, 1995–97; Minister of State (Minister for Public Health), DoH, 1997–99; Minister for Women, 1998–2001, 2005–06; Minister of State (Minister for Employment, Welfare to Work and Equal Opportunities), DfEE, 1999–2001; Sec. of State for Culture, Media and Sport, 2001–07; Minister for the Olympics, 2005–10; Paymaster Gen., 2007–10; Minister for London, 2007–08 and 2009–10; Minister for the Cabinet Office, 2009–10; Shadow Minister for the Cabinet Office and for London, 2010, for the Olympics, 2010–12, for Cabinet Office, 2011. Non-exec. Chair, Chime Specialist Gp, 2015–. Vis. Fellow, Nuffield Coll., Oxford, 1995; Sen. Fellow, Inst. for Govt, 2011–; Sen. Menschel Fellow in Advanced Leadership, Sch. of Public Health, Harvard Univ., 2015. Hon. FFPH, RCP, 2014. Trustee, Tennis Foundn, 2013–. Gov. and Trustee, Ditchley Park Foundn, 2011–; Chair, City Safe Foundn, 2011–. Freeman, City of London, 2014; Freedom, Bor. of Southwark, 2012. *Publications:* articles and contribs in political social work and social policy jls. *Recreations:* hill walking, reading, music.

[Created a Baroness (Life Peer) 2015 but title not yet gazetted at time of going to press.]

JOWITT, Sir Edwin (Frank), Kt 1988; a Justice of the High Court, Queen's Bench Division, 1988–2000; *b* 1 Oct. 1929; *s* of Frank and Winifred Jowitt; *m* 1959, Anne Barbara Dyson (*d* 2008); three *s* two *d*. *Educ:* Swanwick Hall Grammar Sch.; London Sch. of Economics. LLB London 1950. Called to Bar, Middle Temple, 1951, Bencher 1977; Member Midland and Oxford Circuit, 1952–80. Dep. Chm. Quarter Sessions: Rutland, 1967–71; Derbyshire,

1970–71; QC 1969; a Recorder of the Crown Court, 1972–80; a Circuit Judge, 1980–88; a Sen. Circuit Judge, 1987–88; Hon. Recorder, Birmingham, 1987–88; Presiding Judge, Midland and Oxford Circuit, 1996–99. Chm., Robert Hamill Inquiry, 2004–11. *Recreations:* walking, cycling. *Address:* Church House, Desborough, Northants NN14 2NP.

JOWITT, Juliet Diana Margaret, (Mrs Thomas Jowitt); DL; Member, Independent Broadcasting Authority, 1981–86; Director, Yorkshire Television, 1987–94; *b* 24 Aug. 1940; *yr d* of late Lt-Col Robert Henry Langton Brackenbury, OBE and Eleanor Trewlove (*née* Springman); *m* 1963, Frederick Thomas Benson Jowitt; one *s* one *d*. *Educ:* Hatherop Castle; Switzerland and Spain. Associate Shopping Editor, House and Garden and Vogue, 1966–69; Proprietor, Wood House Design (Interior Design) (formerly Colour Go Round), 1971–2002. Director: YTV Holdings PLC, 1988–92; Dancers Career Develt Trust Ltd, 2005–09; Northern Ballet Theatre, 2001–10. Member: Domestic Coal Consumers' Council, 1985–95; Potato Marketing Bd, 1986–90. Fellow, IDDA, 1995 (Mem., 1985; Mem. Council, 1989). Trustee, Great North Art Show, 2010–. Gov., Barnardo's, Ripon, 2002–10. JP North Yorks, 1973–89; DL N Yorks, 2004. *Address:* Thorpe Lodge, Littlethorpe, Ripon, N Yorkshire HG4 3LU.

JOWITT, Prof. Paul William, CBE 2011; PhD; CEng, FICE, CEnv, FREng; FRSE; Professor of Civil Engineering Systems, Heriot Watt University, since 1987; Executive Director, Scottish Institute of Sustainable Technology, 1999–2014; *b* Doncaster, 3 Aug. 1950; *s* of Stanley Jowitt and Joan Jowitt (*née* Goundry); *m* 1973, Jane Urquhart; one *s* one *d*. *Educ:* Maltby Grammar Sch.; Imperial Coll., London (BSc (Eng); PhD; DIC). CEng 1988; MICE 1988, FICE 1994; CEnv 2005. Lectr, Imperial Coll., London, 1974–86; Hd, Dept of Civil and Offshore Engrg, 1989–99, Dir, Inst. of Offshore Engrg, 1996–99, Heriot-Watt Univ. CEO and Chm., Tynemarch Systems Engrg Ltd, 1983–86. Mem. Bd, Edinburgh Envmtl Partnership Grants Scheme Ltd, 2000–04; non-executive Board Member: E of Scotland Water Authy, 1999–2002; Scottish Water, 2002–08; non-exec. Mem., E Regl Bd, Scottish Envmt Protection Agency, 2000–04. Non-exec. Dir, United Utilities Water, 2009–11. Warden, Falmouth-Keogh Hall, Imperial Coll., London, 1980–86. Pres., ICE, 2009–10. FRSE 2005; FCGI 2005; FIPENZ 2008; FREng 2012. FRSA 1996. Trustee: Forth Bridges Visitor Centre Trust, 2003–12; Steamship Sir Walter Scott Trust, 2005–14; Engrs Against Poverty, 2005– (Chm., 2011–). *Publications:* Bootstrapping Infrastructure: the driving forces for sustainable development, 2008; A Systems Journey - with the Systems Boys, 2010; Now is the Time, 2010; Decisions, Decisions, 2013; contribs to Proc. ICE. *Recreations:* Morgan cars, sculpture, painting, digging at the allotment (Dean Gallery allotments), making cider, canal cruising on a narrow boat. *Address:* 14 Belford Mews, Edinburgh EH4 3BT; Heriot Watt University, Edinburgh EH14 4AS. *E:* p.w.jowitt@hw.ac.uk. *Clubs:* Morgan Three Wheeler, Morgan Sports Car.

JOXE, Pierre Daniel, Hon. KBE; lawyer at the Bar, Paris, since 2010; *b* 28 Nov. 1934; *s* of Louis Joxe and Françoise-Hélène Joxe (*née* Halévy); *m* 4th, Laurence Fradin; two *s* two *d* from previous marriages. *Educ:* Lycée Henri-IV; Faculté de droit de Paris; Ecole Nat. d'Administration. Started career in Audit Office, 1962; elected Deputy for Saône-et-Loire, 1973, 1978, 1981, 1986, 1988; Mem., European Parlt, 1977–79; Minister of Industry, 1981; Minister of the Interior, 1984–86, 1988–91; Minister of Defence, 1991–93; Auditor General, Audit Office, Paris, 1993–2001; Mem., Constitutional Court, Paris, 2001–10. Mem. Exec., Socialist Party, 1971–. *Publications:* Parti socialiste, 1973; A propos de la France, 1997; L'Edit de Nantes: une histoire pour aujourd'hui, 1998; Pourquoi Mitterrand?, 2006; Cas de conscience, 2010; Pas de Quartier?, 2012; Soif de Justice, 2014. *Address:* (office) 39 Quai de l'Horloge, 75001 Paris, France.

JOY, David, CBE 1983; HM Diplomatic Service, retired; *b* 9 Dec. 1932; *s* of late Harold Oliver Joy and Doris Kate Buxton; *m* 1957, Montserrat Morancho Saumench, *o d* of late Angel Morancho Garreta and Josefa Saumench Castells, Zaragoza, Spain; one *s* one *d*. *Educ:* Hulme Grammar Sch., Oldham, Lancs; St Catharine's Coll., Cambridge (MA). HMOCS, Northern Rhodesia, 1956–64; Zambia, 1964–70: Cabinet Office, 1964; Under Sec. (Cabinet), 1968–70; joined HM Diplomatic Service, 1971; FCO, 1971–73; First Sec. (Inf.), Caracas, 1973–75; Head of Chancery, Caracas, 1975–77; Asst Head, Mexican and Caribbean Dept, FCO, 1977–78; Counsellor and Head of Chancery, Warsaw, 1978–82; Counsellor and Head of British Interests Section, Buenos Aires, 1982–84; Head of Mexico and Central America Dept, FCO, 1984–87; Ambassador to Honduras and El Salvador, 1987–89; Consul Gen., Barcelona, 1989–92. *Recreations:* golf, tennis, music, reading. *E:* dmmjoy@telefonica.net. *Clubs:* Oxford and Cambridge; Cercle del Liceu (Barcelona); Rotary, La Peñaza Golf (Zaragoza); Key Biscayne Yacht (Florida).

JOY, (Henry) Martin; His Honour Judge Joy; a Circuit Judge, since 2007; *b* Fleet, Hants, 18 April 1948; *s* of Henry and Margaret Joy; *m* 1977, Hilary Ann Smyth; one *s* one *d*. *Educ:* Bradfield Coll., Berks; Univ. of Southampton (LLB Hons). Called to the Bar, Lincoln's Inn, 1971; in practice as barrister, 1971–2007; Recorder, 1993–2007. *Recreations:* family, gardening, golf, Catholicism. *Address:* c/o Maidstone Combined Court Centre, Barker Road, Maidstone ME16 8EQ. *T:* (01622) 202000.

JOY, Peter, OBE 1969; HM Diplomatic Service, retired; *b* 16 Jan. 1926; *s* of late Neville Holt Joy and Marguerite Mary Duff Beith; *m* 1953, Rosemary Joan Hebden; two *s* two *d*. *Educ:* Downhouse Sch., Pembridge; New Coll., Oxford. Served with RAF, 1944–47. Entered Foreign (subseq. Diplomatic) Service, 1952; 1st Sec., Ankara, 1959; 1st Sec., New Delhi, 1962; FO, 1965; 1st Sec., Beirut, 1968; FCO, 1973; Counsellor, Kuala Lumpur, 1979–80; Counsellor, FCO, 1980–86. *Recreations:* gardening, fishing. *Address:* The Old Rectory, Stoke Bliss, near Tenbury, Worcs WR15 8QJ. *T:* (01885) 410342; Carrick House, Eday, Orkney KW17 2AB.

See also R. H. N. Joy.

JOY, Rupert Hamilton Neville; HM Diplomatic Service; Ambassador and Head, European Union Delegation to Morocco, since 2013; *b* London, 5 Sept. 1963; *s* of Peter Joy, *qv*; *m* 2004, Kirsteen Hall; two *s* one *d*. *Educ:* New Coll., Oxford (BA Modern Hist. 1985); Dijon Business Sch. (Master's Dip. in Internat. Wine and Spirits Trade 2004). English teacher, British Council, Hong Kong, 1986–87; editor: Macmillan Publishers, Hong Kong, 1987–88; Mitchell Beazley Publishers, 1988–90; entered FCO, 1990; Soviet Dept, FCO, 1990–91; Arabic lang. trng, 1991–93; Second Sec., Sana'a, 1994–95; First Sec., Riyadh, 1995–96; Counter-Terrorism Dept, FCO, 1996–99; Kosovo Unit, FCO, 1999; Dep. Hd of Mission, Rabat, 2000–03; Dep. Consul-Gen., Basra, 2005; S America Team, FCO, 2005–08; Ambassador to Uzbekistan, 2009–12. *Publications:* contribs to UK wine mag., Decanter. *Recreations:* wine, archaeology, Islamic history, tennis. *Address:* c/o European External Action Service, 1046 Brussels, Belgium.

JOYCE, Prof. Bruce Arthur, DSc; FRS 2000; CPhys, FInstP; Professor of Semiconductor Materials, Department of Physics, Imperial College, London, 1988–2000, now Emeritus Professor of Physics and Senior Research Investigator; *b* 17 Oct. 1934; *s* of Frederick Charles James Joyce and Dorothy Joyce (*née* Crouch); *m* 1956, Beryl Ann Mead; three *s* one *d*. *Educ:* Birmingham Univ. (BSc 1956; DSc 1973). CPhys, FInstP 1973. Nat. Service Commn, RAF, 1956–58. Sen. Scientist, Allen Clark Res. Centre, Plessey Co., 1958–69; Sen. Principal Scientist, Philips Res. Labs, Redhill, 1969–88; Dir, Univ. of London IRC for Semiconductor Materials, ICSTM, 1988–99. *Publications:* contrib. numerous papers to learned jls. *Recreations:* hill-walking, athletics (track and road running), Rugby football, cricket, crosswords, gardening. *Address:* 15 Tennyson Rise, East Grinstead, W Sussex RH19 1SQ. *T:* (01342) 323059.

JOYCE, Prof. Dominic David, DPhil; FRS; Professor of Mathematics, University of Oxford, since 2006; Senior Research Fellow, Lincoln College, Oxford, since 2006; *b* Cambridge, 8 April 1968; *s* of David Joyce and Dawn Joyce; *m* 1994, Jayne Clare Douglas; three *d*. *Educ:* Queen Elizabeth's Hospital Sch., Bristol; Merton Coll., Oxford (BA Maths 1989; DPhil Maths 1992). Jun. Res. Fellow, Christ Church Coll., Oxford, 1992–95; Lectr in Maths, Univ. of Oxford, 1995–2006; Tutorial Fellow in Pure Maths, Lincoln Coll., Oxford, 1995–2006; EPSRC Advanced Res. Fellow, 2001–06. *Publications:* Compact Manifolds with Special Holonomy, 2000; (jtly) Calabi-Yau Manifolds and Related Geometries, 2003; Riemannian Holonomy Groups and Calibrated Geometry, 2007. *Recreations:* family, walking, gardening. *Address:* Mathematical Institute, University of Oxford, Andrew Wiles Building, Radcliffe Observatory Quarter, Woodstock Road, Oxford OX2 6GG.

JOYCE, Eric Stuart; *b* 13 Oct. 1960; *s* of Leslie Joyce and Sheila Joyce (*née* Christie); *m* 1991, Rosemary Jones; twin *d*. *Educ:* Univ. of Stirling (BA Hons 1986); W London Inst. (PGCE 1987); Univ. of Bath (MA 1994); Univ. of Keele (MBA 1995). Served Army, 1978–99: Black Watch, 1978–81; RMA Sandhurst, 1987; commnd RAEC, 1987; served AGC; Maj. 1992. Public Affairs Officer, CRE, 1999–2000. MP Falkirk W, Dec. 2000–2005, Falkirk, 2005–15 (Lab, 2000–12, Ind 2012–15). PPS to Minister for Trade, Investment and Foreign Affairs, 2003–05, to Minister of State for Work, 2005–07, to Sec. of State for Business, Enterprise and Regulatory Reform, 2007–08, to Sec. of State for Defence, 2008–09, to Shadow Sec. of State for NI, 2010. *Publications:* Arms and the Man: renewing the armed services, 1997; (ed) Now's the Hour!: new thinking for Holyrood, 1999. *Recreations:* climbing, judo, most sports. *Club:* Camelon Labour (Falkirk).

JOYCE, Peter Robert, CB 2000; FCCA; Director General, Insolvency Practitioners Association, 2003–10; *b* 14 Jan. 1942; *s* of George Henry Joyce and Edith Doris Joyce; *m* 1st, 1965 (marr. diss. 1988); one *s* one *d*; 2nd, 1988, Marian Neal. *Educ:* Westwood's Grammar Sch., Northleach, Glos. FCCA 1970. Insolvency Service, Board of Trade, subseq. Department of Trade and Industry, 1960–2001: Examr, 1960–69; Sen. Examr, 1969–76; Asst Official Receiver and Chief Examr, 1976–82; Official Receiver and Principal Examr, 1982–85; Dep. Inspector General, 1985–89; Inspector General and Agency Chief Exec., 1989–2001. Consultant, World Bank, 2004–08. Chm., 1995–2001, Exec. Dir, 2002–08, Internat. Assoc. of Insolvency Regulators; World Bank Wkg Gp on Insolvency Regulatory Frameworks, 1999–2001. Mem. Council, Central Govt NTO, 1999–2001. Hon. FCIM 2000; Hon. FIPA 2010. *Recreations:* watching cricket, theatre, dining out. *Club:* Gloucestershire County Cricket.

JOYCE, Robert, FREng, FIMechE; Executive Director, Product Creation and Delivery, Jaguar Land Rover, since 2013; *b* Littlehampton, 24 May 1958; *s* of Charles and Audrey Joyce; *m* 1981, Amanda West; two *s* one *d*. *Educ:* Leicester Univ. (BSc Hons Engrg 1979); Warwick Univ. (MBA 1992). FIMechE 1991; FREng 2013. Austin Rover Group, then Rover Group: Manager: Engrg Performance Develt, 1987–90; Petrol Engine Design, 1990–91; Chief Engr, Small Engines, 1991–94; Director: Vehicle Engrg, 1994–95; Body and Trim, 1996–97; Dir, Prodn Engrg, 1997–98, Sen. Vice Pres., Mini Rover, 1998–2000, BMW; Jaguar Land Rover: Dir, Prodn Engrg, 2000–03; Gp Dir, Engrg, 2003–13. Hon. Dr Leicester, 2015. *Recreations:* motorbikes, Rugby. *E:* bjoyce2@jaguarlandrover.com.

JOYCE, Lt-Gen. Sir Robert John H.; *see* Hayman-Joyce.

JOYNSON-HICKS, family name of **Viscount Brentford**.

JUCKES, Robert William Somerville; QC 1999; **His Honour Judge Juckes;** a Circuit Judge, since 2007; Resident Judge, Worcester Crown Court, since 2011; *b* 1 Aug. 1950; *s* of late Dr William Renwick Juckes and Enid Osyth Juckes (*née* Hankinson); *m* 1974, Frances Anne MacDowel; three *s*. *Educ:* Marlborough Coll.; Exeter Univ. (BA Hons Sociol. and Law 1972). Called to the Bar, Inner Temple, 1974; in practice, Birmingham, 1975; Hd of Chambers, 2000–03. Asst Recorder, 1992–95; Recorder, 1995–2007; Hon. Recorder of Worcester, 2012–. *Recreations:* golf, tennis, cricket, novels of Patrick O'Brian, culturing three sons, one grandson and two granddaughters. *Address:* Worcester Combined Court, The Shirehall, Foregate Street, Worcester WR1 1EQ.

JUDD, family name of **Baron Judd**.

JUDD, Baron *cr* 1991 (Life Peer), of Portsea in the County of Hampshire; **Frank Ashcroft Judd;** Trustee, Saferworld, since 2002 (Senior Fellow, 1994–2002); Member, Advisory Board, Centre for Human Rights, since 2007, and Commission on Diplomacy, since 2014, London School of Economics; *b* 28 March 1935; *s* of late Charles Judd, CBE and Helen Judd, JP; *m* 1961, Christine Elizabeth Willington; two *d*. *Educ:* City of London Sch.; London Sch. of Economics. Short Service Commn, RAF (Educn Br.), 1957–59; Sec.-Gen., IVS, 1960–66. Contested (Lab): Sutton and Cheam, 1959; Portsmouth West, 1964; MP (Lab) Portsmouth W, 1966–74, Portsmouth N, 1974–79; PPS: to Minister of Housing and Local Govt, 1967–70; to the Leader of the Opposition, 1970–72; Mem., Opposition's Front Bench Defence Team, 1972–74; Parliamentary Under-Secretary of State: for Defence (Navy), MoD, 1974–76; ODM 1976; Minister of State: for Overseas Develt, 1976–77; FCO, 1977–79; Mem., British Parly Delegn to Council of Europe and WEU, 1970–73, 1997–2005; Rapporteur to Parly Assembly of Council of Europe on Chechnya, 1999–2004; Opposition front bench spokesperson, H of L, on for. affairs, 1991–92, on defence, 1995–97; principal spokesperson, on educn, 1992–94, on overseas develt co-operation, 1994–97; Member: Procedure Cttee, H of L, 2001–04; Ecclesiastical Cttee, H of C and H of L, 2001–; Human Rights Cttee, H of C and H of L, 2003–07; Sub Cttee F (Home Affairs), H of L Select Cttee on EU, 2010–; IPU Middle East Cttee, 2012–. Ind. Advr to UK Delegn to UN Special Session on Disarmament, 1982. Associate Dir, Internat. Defence Aid Fund for Southern Africa, 1979–80; Director: VSO, 1980–85; Oxfam, 1985–91. Sen. Fellow, De Montfort Univ., 1999 (Professional Advr, 1993–2012). Chairman: Centre for World Development Educn, 1980–85; Internat. Council of Voluntary Agencies, 1985–90; World Econ. Forum Conf., Geneva, on the future of S Africa, 1990 and 1991; Member: Steering Cttee, World Bank—NGO Cttee, 1989–91; Internat. Commn on Global Governance, 1992–2001; WHO Task Force on Health and Develt, 1994–98; Internat. Working Gp on Human Duties and Responsibilities in the New Millennium, 1997–99. Pres., European-Atlantic Gp, 1999–2001. Past Chm., Fabian Soc. Chm., Oxford Diocesan Bd for Social Responsibility, 1992–95; Convenor, Social Responsibility Forum, Churches Together in Cumbria, 1999–2005. Mem., NW Regl Cttee, Nat. Trust, 1996–2003; Dir (non-exec.), Portsmouth Harbour Renaissance Bd, 1998–2006; Vice-President: Council for Nat. Parks, 1998–; Lakeland Housing Trust, 2007–; UN Assoc.; Nat. Pres., YMCA England, 1996–2005; Pres., Friends of RN Mus., 2002–12, now Hon. Life Vice-Pres.; Pres., 2005–12, Patron, 2012–, Friends of the Lake Dist, 2005; Hon. Pres., Hospice at Home, W Cumbria, 2008–. Trustee: Internat. Alert, 1994–2000 (Chm., 1997–2000); Selly Oak Colls, Birmingham, 1994–97 (Chm. Council, 1994–97); Ruskin Foundn, 2002–11. University of Lancaster: Mem. Council, 1996–2002; Mem. Court, 2002–11; Life Mem., 2011; Hon. Fellow, 2013; Mem. Court, Univ. of Newcastle upon Tyne, 2004–13, Life Mem., 2013; Governor: LSE, 1982–2012, now Gov. Emeritus; Westminster Coll., Oxford, 1991–98. Member: Unite; GMB. Freeman, City of Portsmouth, 1995. Hon. Fellow: Univ. of Portsmouth (formerly Portsmouth Poly.), 1978; Univ. of Lancaster, 2015. Hon. DLitt: Bradford Univ., 1987; Portsmouth, 1997; De Montfort, 2006; Hon. LLD Greenwich, 1999. FRSA 1988. *Publications:* (jtly) Radical Future, 1967; Fabian International Essays, 1970; Purpose in Socialism, 1973; (jtly) Our Global Neighbourhood, 1995; (jtly) Imagining Tomorrow: rethinking the global challenge, 2000; various papers and articles on current affairs. *Recreations:* relaxing in the countryside, family holidays, enjoying music, opera, theatre and film. *Address:* House of Lords, SW1A 0PW. *Club:* Royal Over-Seas League.

JUDD, Clifford Harold Alfred, CB 1987; Under Secretary, HM Treasury, 1981–87; *b* 27 June 1927; *s* of Alfred Ernest and Florence Louisa Judd; *m* 1951, Elizabeth Margaret Holmes; two *d. Educ:* Christ's Hospital; Keble Coll., Oxford. National Service, RA, 1946–48 (to 2/Lt). HM Treasury: Executive Officer, 1948, through ranks to Principal, 1964, Sen. Prin., 1969, Asst Sec., 1973. *Recreations:* cricket, golf, do-it-yourself. *Address:* 17 Elgin Road, Lilliput, Poole, Dorset BH14 8QT. *Clubs:* Forty; Sevenoaks Vine; Knole Park Golf.

JUDD, Lt-Gen. David Leslie, CB 2003; CEng, FIMechE; Deputy Commander Allied Joint Force Command Brunssum (formerly Deputy Commander-in-Chief, Allied Forces North), 2004–07; *b* 26 Jan. 1950; *s* of Leslie and Jean Judd; *m* 1973, Margot Hazell Patterson; one *s* one *d. Educ:* RMCS (BSc Hons Engrg). CEng 1976, MIMechE 1976, FIMechE 2006. Commnd 13th/18th Royal Hussars (Queen Mary's Own), 1970; 22 Air Defence Regt RA Workshop, REME, 1974; Life Guards, 1976; Adjt Comd, Maintenance Corps Troops, REME, 1978–81; Army Staff Coll., 1981–83; Dep. COS, 33 Armd Bde, 1983–85; OC, 5 Armd Workshop, REME, 1985–87; SO1 Directing Staff, Staff Coll., 1987–88; Comdr Maintenance, 1st Armd Div., 1988–90; Col QMG, 1990–92; Chief Maintenance, HQ ARRC, 1992–94; rcds 1994; Dep. COS, G1/G4 HQ ARRC, 1994–98; Dir, Equipt Support Change Mgt Prog., 1998–99; Dir Gen., Equipt Support (Land), 1999–2002, and QMG, 2000–02; GOC 4th Div., 2003–04. *Recreations:* anything mechanical, Rugby, furniture restoration. *Club:* Army and Navy.

JUDD, Prof. Denis, PhD; FRHistS; Professor of British and Imperial History, London Metropolitan University (formerly North London Polytechnic, then University of North London), 1990–2004, now Emeritus; Professor of British Imperial History, New York University in London, since 2006; *b* 28 Oct. 1938; *s* of Denis and Joan Judd; *m* 1964, Dorothy Woolf; three *s* one *d. Educ:* Magdalen Coll., Oxford (BA Hons Mod. Hist.); Birkbeck Coll., London (PhD; PGCE). Poly., then Univ., of N London, later London Metropolitan Univ., 1964–2004. Visiting Professor: Univ. of California, 2002–05; NY Univ., 2007–. Series Editor, Traveller's History Series, 1989–; Advr, BBC History Mag., 2000–; writer and presenter, BBC Radio. *Publications:* Balfour and the British Empire, 1968; The Victorian Empire, 1970; Posters of World War Two, 1972; Livingstone in Africa, 1973; George V, 1973, 5th edn 1993; The House of Windsor, 1973; Someone has Blundered: calamities of the British army in the Victorian age, 1973, 3rd edn 2007; Edward VII, 1975; Palmerston, 1975, new edn 2015; The Crimean War, 1976; Eclipse of Kings, 1976; Radical Joe: a life of Joseph Chamberlain, 1977, 3rd edn 2010; The Adventures of Long John Silver, 1977 (Russian edn 2015); Return to Treasure Island, 1978 (Russian edn 2015); Prince Philip, 1980, 3rd edn 1991; (with Peter Slinn) The Evolution of the Modern Commonwealth 1902–80, 1982; Lord Reading, 1982, 2nd edn 2013; King George VI, 1982, 2nd edn 2012; Alison Uttley: the life of a country child, 1986, 3rd edn 2010; Jawaharlal Nehru, 1993; Empire: the British imperial experience from 1765 to the present, 1996, 4th edn 2012; (with Keith Surridge) The Boer War, 2002, 3rd edn 2013; The Lion and the Tiger: the rise and fall of the British Raj, 2004, 2nd edn 2005; (ed) The Diaries of Alison Uttley, 2009, 2nd edn 2011; regular contribs and reviews for nat. press. *Recreations:* reading, writing, film, theatre, sport (supports QPR), gardening, talking, listening, food and wine, travel, the Suffolk coast, playing with grandchildren, fixing things. *Address:* 20 Mount Pleasant Road, Brondesbury Park, NW10 3EL. *T:* and *Fax:* (020) 8459 1118. *E:* denisjudd@ntlworld.com. *W:* www.denisjudd.com.

JUDD, Frances Jean, (Mrs D. Pritchard); QC 2006; a Recorder, since 2002; a Deputy High Court Judge, since 2011; *b* 13 Feb. 1961; *d* of Christopher and Jean Judd; *m* 1985, David Pritchard; two *s. Educ:* King's Sch., Canterbury; New Hall, Cambridge (BA Hons Hist. 1982). Called to the Bar, Middle Temple, 1984; in practice at the Bar, 1984–, specialising in family law. Hd, Harcourt Chambers, Oxford, 2009–. *Publications:* (jtly) Contact: The New Deal, 2006. *Recreations:* cycling, walking, swimming outdoors. *Address:* Harcourt Chambers, 3 St Aldates Courtyard, Oxford OX1 1BN. *T:* (01865) 791559, *Fax:* (01865) 791585. *E:* fjudd@harcourtchambers.law.co.uk. *Club:* QI (Oxford).

JUDD, Judith Margaret; Editor-at-Large, Times Educational Supplement, 2007–09 (Associate Editor, 2001–05; Editor, 2005–07); *b* 18 April 1949; *d* of John Berry and Joan Berry (*née* Edge); *m* 1973, Very Rev. Peter Somerset Margesson Judd, *qv*; one *s* one *d. Educ:* Bolton Sch.; St Anne's Coll., Oxford (BA Modern History). Reporter, 1972–74, Educn Reporter, 1974–75, Birmingham Post and Birmingham Mail; joined THES, 1975, News Editor, 1977–79; Reporter, 1979–82, Educn Correspondent, 1982–90, Observer; Education Correspondent: Independent on Sunday, 1990–93; Independent, 1991–93; Educn Ed., The Independent and The Independent on Sunday, 1993–2001. Mem. Council, Essex Univ., 2010– (Pro-Chancellor, 2012–). Mem., Adv. Council, Whole Educn. *Recreations:* gardening, reading, walking, singing.

JUDD, Very Rev. Peter Somerset Margesson; Dean (formerly Provost) of Chelmsford Cathedral, 1997–2013; *b* 20 Feb. 1949; *s* of William Frank Judd and Norah Margesson Judd (*née* Margesson); *m* 1973, Judith Margaret Berry (*see* J. M. Judd); one *s* one *d. Educ:* Charterhouse Sch.; Trinity Hall, Cambridge (MA Architecture); Cuddesdon Coll., Oxford (Cert. Theol.). Ordained deacon, 1974, priest, 1975; Asst Curate, St Philip with St Stephen, Salford, 1974–76; Chaplain, 1976–81, Fellow, 1980–81, Clare Coll., Cambridge; Team Vicar of Hitcham and Dropmore, Burnham Team Ministry, Dio. of Oxford, 1981–88; Vicar, St Mary the Virgin, Iffley, 1988–97; Rural Dean of Cowley, 1995–97. DL Essex, 2009–13. *Recreations:* architecture, art, listening to music, literature, drawing, cooking, fell walking. *Address:* 18 Baycliffe Close, Cambridge CB1 8EE.

JUDGE, family name of **Baron Judge**.

JUDGE, Baron *cr* 2008 (Life Peer), of Draycote in the County of Warwickshire; **Igor Judge,** Kt 1988; PC 1996; Chief Surveillance Commissioner, since 2015; Lord Chief Justice of England and Wales, 2008–13; *b* 19 May 1941; *s* of Raymond and Rosa Judge; *m* 1965, Judith Mary Robinson; one *s* two *d. Educ:* Oratory Sch., Woodcote; Magdalene Coll., Cambridge (Exhbnr, MA; Hon. Fellow). Harmsworth Exhibnr and Astbury Scholar, Middle Temple. Called to the Bar, Middle Temple, 1963, Bencher, 1987; a Recorder, 1976–88; Prosecuting Counsel to Inland Revenue, 1977–79; QC 1979; a Judge of the High Court, QBD, 1988–96; Leader, 1988, Presiding Judge, 1993–96, Midland and Oxford Circuit; a Lord Justice of Appeal, 1996–2005; Sen. Presiding Judge for England and Wales, 1998–2003; Dep. Chief Justice of England and Wales, 2003–05; Pres., QBD, High Ct of Justice, 2005–08. Member: Senate, Inns of Court and the Bar, 1980–83, 1984–86; Bar Council, 1987–88; Judicial Studies Bd, 1984–88, 1991–94 and 1996–98 (Chm. Criminal Cttee, 1991–93 and 1996–98). Pres., Selden Soc., 2009–15. Hon. LLD Cantab, 2012. *Recreations:* history, music, cricket. *Address:* House of Lords, SW1A 0PW.

JUDGE, Hon. Barbara Singer T.; *see* Thomas Judge.

JUDGE, Harry George, MA Oxon, PhD London; Fellow of Brasenose College, Oxford, since 1973; Senior Research Fellow, University of Oxford Department of Educational Studies, since 1988 (Director, 1973–88); *b* 1 Aug. 1928; *s* of George Arthur and Winifred Mary Judge; *m* 1956, Elizabeth Mary Patrick; one *s* two *d. Educ:* Cardiff High Sch.; Brasenose Coll., Oxford; University Coll. London. Served RAF, 1946–48. Asst Master, Emanuel Sch. and Wallington County Grammar Sch., 1954–59; Dir of Studies, Cumberland Lodge, Windsor, 1959–62; Head Master, Banbury Grammar Sch., 1962–67; Principal, Banbury Sch., 1967–73. Visiting Professor: MIT, 1977 and 1980–82; Carnegie-Mellon Univ., 1984–86; Univ. of Virginia, 1987; Michigan State Univ., 1988–93; Pennsylvania State Univ., 1995–96; Visiting Scholar: Harvard Univ., 1985–87; Carnegie Foundn, 1998–2000; Sachs Lectr, Teachers' Coll., Columbia Univ., 1993; Read Distinguished Chair Lectr, Kent State Univ., 1996. Member: Public Schools Commission, 1966–70; James Cttee of Inquiry into Teacher Training, 1971–72; Educn Sub-Cttee, UGC, 1976–80; Oxon Educn Cttee, 1982–87. Chairman: School Broadcasting Council, 1977–81; RCN Commn on Education, 1984–85. Gen. Editor, Oxford Illus. Encyclopedia, 1985–93. *Publications:* Louis XIV, 1965; School Is Not Yet Dead, 1974; Graduate Schools of Education in the US, 1982; A Generation of Schooling: English secondary schools since 1944, 1984; The University and the Teachers: France, the United States, England, 1994; Faith-Based Schools and the State, 2002; (ed and contrib.) The University and Public Education: the contribution of Oxford, 2006; contribs on educational and historical subjects to collective works and learned jls. *Recreation:* canals. *Address:* Brasenose College, Oxford OX1 4AJ.

See also S. P. Judge.

JUDGE, Ian; international opera and theatre director; *b* 21 July 1946; *s* of Jack and Marjorie Judge. *Educ:* King George V Grammar Sch., Southport; Guildhall Sch. of Music and Drama (Prodn Prize). Joined RSC as an asst dir, 1975; productions include: The Wizard of Oz, 1987; The Comedy of Errors, 1990; Love's Labour's Lost, 1993; Twelfth Night, 1994; A Christmas Carol, 1994; The Relapse, 1995; Troilus and Cressida, 1996; The Merry Wives of Windsor, 1996; *opera:* English National Opera: Faust, 1985; Cavalleria Rusticana and Pagliacci, 1987; Don Quichotte, 1994; La Belle Vivette, 1995; Mephistopheles, 1999; Sir John in Love, 2006; Opera North: Macbeth, 1987; Tosca, 1988; Boris Godunov, 1989; Attila, 1990; Show Boat, 1990 (also at London Palladium); Scottish Opera: Falstaff, 1991; Norma, 1993; Royal Opera House: The Flying Dutchman, 1992; Simon Boccanegra (1857), 1997; Simon Boccanegra (1881), 2008; Los Angeles: Tosca, 1989; Madama Butterfly, 1991; Le Nozze di Figaro, 2004, 2014–15; Roméo et Juliette, 2005; Don Carlo, 2006; Tannhäuser, 2007; Die Gezeichneten, 2010; Melbourne and Sydney: Faust, 1990; Tales of Hoffman, 1992; Kirov, St Petersburg: La Bohème, 2001; Der fliegende Holländer, 2008; Macbeth, Cologne, 1992; Così Fan Tutte, Garsington, 1997; Eugene Onegin, Grange Park Opera, 2000; Falstaff, Paris, 2001; Ernani, Holland, 2002; Salome, NY, 2002; Tannhäuser, Teatro Real, Madrid, 2009; Simon Boccanegra, Canadian Opera Co., Toronto, 2009; A Midsummer Night's Dream, Britten Th., 2009; *theatre:* The Rivals and King Lear, Old Vic, 1977; Chichester: Henry VIII, 1991; Love for Love, 1996; Macbeth, Sydney Th. Co., 1999; *musical:* Merrily We Roll Along, London, Bloomsbury, 1983; Chichester: Oh! Kay, 1984; A Little Night Music, 1990 (also Piccadilly Theatre); West Side Story (Sydney and Melbourne), 1994–96; The Mikado, Savoy Theatre, 2000. *E:* ijudge1@mac.com.

JUDGE, Sir Paul (Rupert), Kt 1996; Sheriff, City of London, 2013–14; Chairman, Schroder Income Growth Fund plc, 2005–13 (Director, 1995–2013); *b* 25 April 1949; *s* of late Rupert Cyril Judge and Betty Rosa Muriel Judge (*née* Daniels), Forest Hill; *m*; two *s*; *m* 2002, Hon. Barbara Singer Thomas (*see* Hon. Barbara Thomas Judge). *Educ:* St Dunstan's Coll.; Trinity Coll., Cambridge (MA, Open Scholar); Wharton Business Sch., Univ. of Pennsylvania (MBA, Thouron Schol.). Cadbury Schweppes, 1973–86 (Group Planning Dir, 1984–86); Premier Brands: Man. Dir, 1986–87; Chm., 1987–89; Mem., Milk Marketing Bd, 1989–92; Chm., Food from Britain, 1990–92; Director: Grosvenor Development Capital plc, 1989–93; Boddington Group plc, 1989–93; WPP plc, 1991–97; Standard Bank Group Ltd (Johannesburg), 2003–12; Tempur-Sealy (formerly Pedic) Internat. Inc. (Kentucky), 2004–; ENRC plc, 2007–13; Abraaj Capital, 2010–; Mem., Adv. Bd, Barclays Private Bank Ltd, 2001–10. Dir Gen., Cons. Party, 1992–95; Ministerial Advr, Cabinet Office, 1995–96. Dir, UK Accreditation Service, 2006–. Chm., Adv. Bd, Judge Inst. of Management, Cambridge Univ., 1991–2002; Mem., Adv. Council, Inst. of Business Ethics, 2003–; Chairman: Wharton European Bd, 2000–09; British-N American Cttee, 2001–14; British-Serbian Chamber of Commerce, 2010–; Special Advr, RIIA, 2009–; Mem., Pres. of Togo's Internat. Adv. Council, 2011–. Chm. Trustees, Royal Soc. of Arts, 2003–06 (Dep. Chm., 2006–08); Trustee: Cambridge Foundn, 1991–2000 (Emeritus, 2000–); British Food Heritage Trust, 1997–2007; Imperial Soc. of Kts Bachelor, 1997–2012; Understanding Industry, later Businessdynamics, then Enterprise Educn Trust, 1998– (Chm. Trustees, 1999–); Royal Instn, 1999–2005; Amer. Mgt Assoc., 2000–12 (Dep. Chm., 2004–12). President: Assoc. of MBAs, 1997–; Chartered Mgt Inst., 2004–05 (Chm. Bd of Companions, 2001–04); CIM, 2008–14; Vice President: Mkting Council, 2001–07. Chm., Mus. of Packaging and Advertising, 2003–; Member: Finance Cttee, Trinity Coll., Cambridge, 1992–; Shakespeare's Globe Develt Council, 1999–2007 (Dep. Chm., 2000–06); Bd, HEFCE, 2008–10. Governor: Bromsgrove Sch., 1991–96; St Dunstan's Coll., 1997– (Chm., 2001–). FRSA 1971; FCIM; Fellow, Marketing Soc. Alderman, City of London, 2007–; Freeman: City of London, 1970; Educators' Co., 2009–; Guild of Entrepreneurs, 2014– (Foundn Master, 2014–15); Master, Marketors' Co., 2005–06 (Liveryman, 1993; Sen. Warden, 2004–05); Liveryman, Clothworkers' Co., 2008–. Hon. LLD: Cantab, 1995; South Bank, 2014; LittD Westminster, 2006; ScD City, 2007. *Recreations:* family, travel. *Address:* 152 Grosvenor Road, SW1V 3JL. *Clubs:* Athenæum; Mombasa (Kenya).

JUDGE, Richard, PhD; CEng, FIMechE; Chief Executive, Health and Safety Executive, since 2014; *b* 2 Nov. 1962; *s* of Peter Judge and Elspeth Judge; *m* 1998, Susan Thompson; one *d. Educ:* Elizabeth Coll., Guernsey; Durham Univ. (BSc Hons Engrg Sci. 1984; PhD 1987). CEng 1990, FIMechE 2006. Various roles, AEA Technology, 1987–2000; Man. Dir, AEA Technol. Rail BV, 2000–03; Gp Dir, AEA Envmt, 2003–05; an Interim Manager, 2005–07; Chief Exec., CEFAS, 2007–12; Inspector Gen. and Chief Exec., Insolvency Service, 2012–14. CDir 2011. FInstD 2011. *Address:* Health and Safety Executive, Redgrave Court, Merton Road, Bootle, Merseyside L20 7HS.

JUDGE, Simon Patrick; Finance Director, Department for Education, since 2012; *b* 10 Nov. 1959; *s* of Harry George Judge, *qv* and Elizabeth Mary Judge; *m* 1985, (Isobel) Jane Cox; three *s. Educ:* Banbury Sch.; Oxford Sch.; Clare Coll., Cambridge (BA 1981; MMath 2011). Warwick Business Sch. (Dip. 2008). CPFA 2009. Joined HM Treasury, 1985; Private Sec. to Paymaster Gen., 1987–88; Asst Sec., 1994; various posts, incl. Hd of Inf. Systems, 1995–97; Planning and Finance Div., DSS, subseq. Welfare to Work Directorate, DWP, 1999–2005; Dir of Financial Strategy, DCA, later MoJ, 2005–08; Finance Dir, DCMS, 2009–12. *Recreations:* canal boating, choral singing. *E:* simon.judge@education.gsi.gov.uk.

JUDSON, Air Vice-Marshal Robert William, FRAeS; Director Joint Warfare, 2013–14; *b* Harlington, Middx, 4 June 1962; *s* of Alan Sheffield Judson and Brenda Jane Judson; *m* 2006, Saab Benning. *Educ:* Christ's Hosp., Horsham. FRAeS 2007. Officer Cadet, RAF Coll., Cranwell, 1980; jsdc 1997; Officer Commanding: No 6 Sqdn, 1992–2002; RAF Coningsby, 2004–06; HCSC 2007; rcds 2007; Comdr, Kandahar Airfield, Afghanistan, 2008; Hd, Targeting and Information Ops, MoD, 2008–10; Liaison Officer of CDS to US Chm., Jt Chiefs, 2011; ACDS (Ops), 2011–13. FCMI. *Recreations:* ski-ing, scuba diving, poor quality golf! *Club:* Royal Air Force.

JUGNAUTH, Rt Hon. Sir Anerood, GCSK 2003; KCMG 1988; PC 1987; Grand Comdr, Order of Star and Key of Indian Ocean, 2003; QC (Mauritius) 1980; Prime Minister of Mauritius, 1982–95, 2000–03 and since 2014; Minister of Defence, Home Affairs and Minister for Rodrigues and National Development Unit, since 2014; *b* 29 March 1930; *m* Sarojini Devi Balla; one *s* one *d. Educ:* Roman Catholic Aided Sch., Palma, Mauritius; Regent Coll., Quatre Bornes. Called to the Bar, Lincoln's Inn, 1954 (Hon. Bencher, 2011). Teacher,

New Eton Coll., 1948; worked in Civil Service, 1949. MLA Rivière du Rempart, 1963–67, Piton-Rivière du Rempart, 1976, 1982, 1983, 1987, 1991 and 2000; Town Councillor, Vacoas-Phoenix, 1964; Minister of State for Develt, 1965–67; Minister of Labour, 1967; Leader of the Opposition, 1976–82; Minister of Finance, 1983–84 and 1990–91; Pres. of Mauritius, 2003–12. Dist Magistrate, 1967–69; Crown Counsel, 1969; Sen. Crown Counsel, 1971. Attended London Constitutional Conf., 1965. Pres., Mouvement Militant Mauricien, 1973–82; Leader, Mouvement Socialiste Militant, 1983–2003. Dr *hc* Aix-en-Provence, 1985; Hon. DCL Mauritius, 1985; Dr of Law *hc* Chennai, 2001; Hon. Dr Middx, 2009. Grand Prix, Order of La Pléiade, Assemblée parlementaire de la Francophonie, 1984. Order of Rising Sun (1st cl.) (Japan), 1988; Grand Officier, Ordre de la Légion d'Honneur (France), 1990. *Address:* La Caverne No 1, Vacoas, Mauritius.

JULIAN, Prof. Desmond Gareth, CBE 1993; MD, FRCP; Consultant Medical Director, British Heart Foundation, 1987–93; *b* 24 April 1926; *s* of Frederick Bennett Julian and Jane Frances Julian (*née* Galbraith); *m* 1st, 1956, Mary Ruth Jessup (decd); one *s* one *d*; 2nd, 1988, Claire Marley. *Educ:* Leighton Park Sch.; St John's Coll., Cambridge; Middlesex Hosp. MB BChir (Cantab) 1948; MA 1953; MD 1954; FRCPE 1967; FRCP 1970; FRACP 1970; FACC 1985. Surgeon Lieut, RNVR, 1949–51. Med. Registrar, Nat. Heart Hosp., 1955–56; Res. Fellow, Peter Bent Brigham Hosp., Boston, 1957–58; Sen. Reg., Royal Inf., Edinburgh, 1958–61; Cons. Cardiologist, Sydney Hosp., 1961–64, Royal Inf., Edinburgh, 1964–74; Prof. of Cardiology, Univ. of Newcastle upon Tyne, 1975–86. Mem., MRC Systems Bd, 1980–84. Pres., British Cardiac Soc., 1985–87; Second Vice-Pres., RCP, 1990–91. Hon. MD: Gothenburg, 1987; Edinburgh, 1997. Gold Medal, European Soc. of Cardiology, 1998; Mackenzie Medal, British Cardiac Soc., 2003; Internat. Service Award, Amer. Coll. of Cardiol., 2005. Editor, European Heart Jl, 1980–88. *Publications:* Cardiology, 1972, 8th edn 2004; (ed) Angina Pectoris, 1975, 2nd edn 1984; Acute Myocardial Infarction, 1967; (ed) Diseases of the Heart, 1989, 2nd edn 1995; Coronary Heart Disease: the facts, 1991; contribs to med. jls, particularly on coronary disease. *Recreations:* walking, writing. *Address:* Flat 1, 7 Netherhall Gardens, NW3 5RN. *T:* (020) 7435 8254. *Club:* Garrick.

JULIEN, Michael Frederick, FCA; FCT; Chairman, First Choice Holidays PLC (formerly Owners Abroad Group plc), 1993–97; *b* 22 March 1938; *s* of late Robert Auguste François and Olive Rita (*née* Evans); *m* 1963, Ellen Martinsen; one *s* two *d*. *Educ:* St Edward's Sch., Oxford. Price Waterhouse & Co., 1958–67; other commercial appts, 1967–76; Gp Finance Dir, BICC, 1976–83; Exec. Dir, Finance and Planning, Midland Bank, 1983–86; Man. Dir, Finance and Administration, Guinness PLC, 1987–88 (non-exec. Dir, 1988–97); Gp Chief Exec., Storehouse PLC, 1988–92. Director (non-executive): Littlewoods Orgn plc, 1981–86; Medeva PLC, 1993–98. *Recreations:* family, travel. *E:* michael@julienco.com.

JULIUS, Dr Anthony Robert; Deputy Chairman, Mishcon de Reya, since 2009 (Consultant, 1998–2009); *b* 16 July 1956; *s* of Morris and Myrna Julius; *m* 1st, 1979, Judith Bernie (marr. diss. 1998); two *s* two *d*; 2nd, 1999, Dina Rabinovitch (*d* 2007); one *s*; 3rd, 2009, Katarina Lester; one *s*. *Educ:* City of London Sch.; Jesus Coll., Cambridge (MA); University Coll. London (PhD 1992). Admitted Solicitor, 1981; Mishcon de Reya: Partner, 1984–98; Head of Litigation, 1988–98. Institute of Jewish Policy Research: Dir, 1996–2000; Mem. Council, 2000–04; Chair, Law Cttee, 1998–2000; Mem., Appeals Cttee, Dermatrust, 1999–2004; foreword, report on holocaust denial and UK law, 2000; Member: Adv. Bd, Community Security Trust, 2007–; Mayor of London's Race and Faith Inquiry, 2009–10; Advancing Human Rights, 2011–. Chairman: London Consortium, 2005–13; Jewish Chronicle, 2011–13; City and Guards Gp, 2012–; Oxera LLP, 2014–. Chair, Diana, Princess of Wales Meml Fund, 1997–99, Vice Pres., 2002–13; Mem., Fest. Council, The Word. Vis. Prof., Birkbeck, Univ. of London, 2005–. Chm. Mgt Bd, Centre for Cultural Analysis, Theory and History, Univ. of Leeds, 2001–05. Trustee: Beit Halochem, 2012–; Swarowski Foundn, 2013–; Phenomen Trust, 2015–. Hon. PhD Haifa, 2005. *Publications:* T. S. Eliot, anti-Semitism, and literary form, 1995, 2nd edn 2002; (contrib.) Law and Literature, 1999; Idolizing Pictures, 2001; Transgressions: the offences of art, 2002; Trials of the Diaspora: a history of anti-Semitism in England, 2010. *Recreation:* cinema. *Address:* (office) Summit House, 12 Red Lion Square, WC1R 4QD. *T:* (020) 7440 7000.

JULIUS, Dame DeAnne (Shirley), DCMG 2013; CBE 2002; PhD; Chairman: Council, University College London, since 2014; Royal Institute of International Affairs, 2003–12 (Member Council, 2000–03); *b* 14 April 1949; *d* of Marvin G. Julius and Maxine M. Julius; *m* 1976, Ian Harvey; one *s* one *d*. *Educ:* Iowa State Univ. (BSc Econs 1970); Univ. of Calif at Davis (MA 1974; PhD Econs 1975). Economic Analyst, US CS, 1970–71; Lectr, Univ. of Calif at Santa Barbara, 1975; project economist, then econ. advr, World Bank, 1975–82; Man. Dir, Logan Associates Inc., 1983–86; Prog. Dir for Econs, RIIA, 1986–89; Chief Economist: Shell Internat., 1989–93; British Airways, 1993–97; Chm., British Airways Pension Investment Mgt Ltd, 1995–97. Mem., Monetary Policy Cttee, 1997–2001, Mem. of Court, 2001–04, Bank of England. Chairman: Banking Code Review Gp, 2000–01; Public Services Industry Review, 2007–08. Non-executive Director: BP, 2001–11; Lloyds TSB, 2001–07; Serco, 2001–07; Roche, 2002–; Jones Lang LaSalle, 2008–; Deloitte LLP, 2011–14; Sen. Advr, Fathom Financial Consultants, 2008–11; Mem., Internat. Panel, Temasek, 2010–. Vice Chm., Inst. Develt Studies, 2000–03. Vice Pres., Soc. of Business Economists, 2002–. *Publications:* (jtly) Appropriate Sanitation Alternatives: a technical and economic appraisal, 1982; (jtly) The Monetary Implications of the 1992 Process, 1990; Global Companies and Public Policy: the growing challenge of foreign direct investment, 1990; (with A. Mashayekhi) Economics of Natural Gas: pricing, planning and policy, 1990; (contrib.) Beyond the Dollar, 2010. *Recreations:* ski-ing, sailing, tending bonsai. *Address:* University College London, Gower Street, WC1E 6BT.

JUMA, Prof. Calestous, DPhil; FRS 2006; Professor of the Practice of International Development, and Director, Science, Technology and Globalization Project, Belfer Center for Science and International Affairs, Harvard Kennedy School (formerly John F. Kennedy School of Government), Harvard University, since 2002; *b* Kenya; *m*; one *s*. *Educ:* Univ. of Sussex (DPhil 1987). Sci. and envmt reporter, Daily Nation, 1978–79; Ed., Ecoforum mag., Envmt Liaison Centre Internat., Nairobi, 1979–82. Founding Director, African Centre for Technol. Studies, Nairobi, 1988–95; Exec. Sec., UN Convention on Biol Diversity, 1995–98. Co-Chm., African Panel on Biotechnol., African Union and New Partnership for Africa's Develt, 2005–08; Co-ordinator, Task Force on Sci., Technol. and Innovation, UN Millennium Project, 2001–06; Mem., Nat. Econ. and Social Council, Kenya, 2004–06. Special Advr, Internat. Whaling Commn, 2007–08. Dir, Internat. Diffusion of Biotechnol. Prog., Internat. Fedn of Insts of Advanced Studies, 1989–91. Chancellor, Univ. of Guyana, 2002–03. Member: NAS; African Acad. of Scis; Acad. of Scis for the Developing World. Hon. FREng 2007. Hon. DSc: Sussex, 2006; Univ. of Educn, Winneba, Ghana, 2007. Order of the Elder of the Burning Spear (Kenya), 2006. *Publications:* articles in jls. *Address:* Harvard Kennedy School, Harvard University, 79 John F. Kennedy Street, Cambridge, MA 02138–5801, USA.

JUMAN, Curtis Mark; Chief Resources Officer, Equality and Human Rights Commission, since 2012; *b* London, 28 March 1968; *s* of Christopher and Nazina Juman; *m* 1990, Heather Revnell; one *s* two *d*. *Educ:* Kingsmead Comprehensive Sch.; Univ. of Birmingham (BSc Hons Chem.). CPFA 1994. Sen. Auditor, Nat. Audit Office, 1989–97; Sen. Manager, Deloitte, 1997–2000; Dep. Dir, Finance, Ofgem, 2000; Audit Dir, 2000–02, Dir, Finance Strategy, 2002–04, DTI; Change Dir, Finance, DWP, 2004–06; Dir, Finance Control, DTI, subseq. BERR, 2006–07; Dir of Finance, UKTI, 2007–12. Mem. Bd and Chm., Gp Audit Cttee, LHA-ASRA Housing Gp, 2006–12; Mem., Audit Cttee, Open Univ., 2010–12. Mem. Council, 2004–10, Chm., Central Govt Panel, 2005–10, CIPFA. *Recreations:* spending time with my young family, contributing to the life of Warlingham Methodist Church, watching sci-fi movies. *Address:* Equality and Human Rights Commission, Fleetbank House, 2–6 Salisbury Square, EC4Y 8JX.

JUNCKER, Dr Jean-Claude; President, European Commission, since 2014; *b* Redange-Attert, 9 Dec. 1954; *m* 1979, Christiane Frising. *Educ:* Secondary Sch., Clairefontaine, Belgium; Univ. of Strasbourg (Dr Public Law 1979). Parly Sec., Christian Social Party, 1979–82; State Sec. for Labour and Social Affairs, 1982–84; Mem., Chamber of Deputies, Luxembourg, 1984; Minister of: Labour and Minister i/c Budget, 1984–89; Labour and of Finance, 1989–95; Labour and Employment, 1995–99; Prime Minister, Minister of State and Minister for the Treasury (formerly Minister of Finance), 1995–2013. Pres., Christian Social Party, 1990–95. Pres., Eurogroup, 2005–13. *Address:* European Commission, 200 Rue de la Loi, 1049 Brussels, Belgium.

JUNG, Prof. Roland Tadeusz, MD; FRCP, FRCPE; Consultant Physician in Endocrinology and Diabetes, Ninewells Hospital, Dundee, 1982–2008; Chief Scientist, Scottish Government (formerly Executive) Health Department, 2001–07; *b* 8 Feb. 1948; *s* of Tadeusz Jung and Margaret (Pearl) Jung; *m* 1974, Felicity Helen King; one *d*. *Educ:* Pembroke Coll., Cambridge (BA 1969, MA 1972; MB, BChir 1972, MD 1980); St Thomas's Hosp. Med. Sch., London. FRCPE 1985; FRCP 1989. MRC Clinical Scientific Officer, Dunn Nutrition Unit, Cambridge, 1977–79; Sen. Registrar in Endocrinol. and Diabetes, RPMS, Hammersmith Hosp., 1980–82. Ext. Examr in Medicine, Univ. of Oxford, 2002–08. Rowett Institute of Nutrition and Health, University of Aberdeen: Mem., Prog. Mgt Cttee, 2007–12 (Chm., 2010–12); Mem., Scientific Consultative Gp, 2010–12. Hon. Prof. of Medicine, Univ. of Dundee, 1998–; Vis. Prof., Univ. of Southampton, 2009–. Newton-Jung Diabetes Lect., Univ. of Dundee, 2012. *Publications:* Colour Atlas of Obesity, 1990; chapters in books, original papers and reviews. *Recreations:* gardening, walking, volunteer guide for NT and HHA.

JUNGELS, Dr Pierre Jean Marie Henri, Hon. CBE 1989; Director, Baker Hughes Inc., since 2006; *b* 18 Feb. 1944; *s* of Henri and Jeanne Jungels; *m* 1988, Caroline Benc; one step *s* one step *d*; one *s* one *d* from former marriage. *Educ:* Univ. of Liège (Ing. Civ. 1967); California Inst. of Technology (PhD 1973). Petroleum Engr, Shell, 1973–74; Dist Manager, 1975–77, General Manager and Chief Exec., 1977–80, Petrangol (Angola); Man. Dir and Chief Exec., Petrofina UK, 1980–89; Exec. Dir, Downstream, Petrofina Gp, 1989–92; Exec. Dir, Exploration and Production, Petrofina Group, 1992–95; Man. Dir, Exploration and Production, British Gas, 1996; Chief Exec., Enterprise Oil plc, 1997–2001. Chairman: OHM plc, 2003–08; Rockhopper Exploration plc, 2005–; Velocys (formerly Oxford Catalysts) plc, 2006–; Director: Imperial Tobacco plc, 2002–12; Woodside Petroleum Ltd, 2002–12. Pres., Inst. of Petroleum, 1986–88 and 2002–03 (Jt Pres., Energy Inst., 2003). *Recreations:* tennis, shooting. *Address:* Enborne Chase, Enborne, Newbury, Berks RG20 0HD.

JUNGIUS, Vice-Adm. Sir James (George), KBE 1977; Supreme Allied Commander Atlantic's Representative in Europe, 1978–80, retired; Vice Lord-Lieutenant of Cornwall, 1995–98; *b* 15 Nov. 1923; *s* of Major E. J. T. Jungius, MC; *m* 1949, Rosemary Frances Turquand Matthey (*d* 2005); two *s* (and one *s* decd). *Educ:* RNC, Dartmouth. Served War of 1939–45 in Atlantic and Mediterranean; Commando Ops in Adriatic (despatches). Specialised in Navigation in 1946, followed by series of appts as Navigating Officer at sea and instructing ashore. Comdr, Dec. 1955; CO, HMS Wizard, 1956–57; Admty, 1958–59; Exec. Officer, HMS Centaur, 1960–61; Captain, 1963; Naval Staff, 1964–65; CO, HMS Lynx, 1966–67; Asst Naval Attaché, Washington, DC, 1968–70; CO, HMS Albion, 1971–72; Rear-Adm., 1972; Asst Chief of Naval Staff (Operational Requirements), 1972–74; Vice-Adm., 1974; Dep. Supreme Allied Comdr Atlantic, 1975–77. County Pres., Cornwall, RBL, 1995–2004. Vice-Chm., SW War Pensions Cttee, 1996–2000. Fellow, Woodard Corp., 1988–95. Gov., Grenville Coll., 1981–96. CCMI. DL Cornwall, 1982. CStJ 1995 (Chm., St John Council for Cornwall, 1987–95).

JUNIPER, Anthony Thomas; Special Adviser, Prince of Wales' International Sustainability Unit, since 2010; Fellow, University of Cambridge Institute (formerly Programme) for Sustainability Leadership (formerly for Industry), since 2013 (Senior Associate, 2008–13); Founding Member, Robertsbridge Group, since 2010; *b* 24 Sept. 1960; *s* of late Austin Wilfred Juniper and Constance Margaret Juniper; *m* 1990, Susan Jane Sparkes; two *s* one *d*. *Educ:* Bristol Univ. (BSc Zool./Psychol. 1983); University Coll. London (MSc Conservation 1988). Worked with school children on nature conservation, S Oxon Countryside Educn Trust, 1984–85; Parrot Conservation Officer, Internat. Council for Bird Preservation, 1989–90; Friends of the Earth: Sen. Tropical Rainforest Campaigner, 1990–93; Sen. Biodiversity Campaigner, 1993–97; Campaign Dir, 1997–98; Policy and Campaigns Dir, 1998–2003; Exec. Dir, England, Wales and NI, 2003–08; Vice Chm., Friends of the Earth Internat., 2000–08; Ed.-in-Chief, GREEN Mag. (formerly Nat. Geographic Mag. Green Supplement), 2009–12. Mem., ACEVO, 2001–08. Special Advr, Prince of Wales' Rainforests Project, 2008–10. Member, Advisory Board: BBC Wildlife mag., 1998–; NCC, 2002–05; Ecologist mag., 2008–; Sandbag, 2008–. Columnist, Sunday Times, 2009–10; regular contributor: The Guardian, 1995–; The Independent, 1995–; Resurgence and Ecologist, 2000–. Advr on Climate Change, Sci. Mus., 2009–; Chm., Adv. Bd, Action for Renewables, 2011–. Mem. Council, FFI, 2013–. Pres., Soc. for the Envmt, 2012–. Founding Trustee and Bd Mem., Stop Climate Chaos, 2005–08; Mem. Bd, Climate for Ideas, 2008–; Trustee: Beds, Cambs and Northants Wildlife Trust, 2009–; Ecologist-Resurgence Mag., 2012–. Patron, Inst. for Ecology and Envmtl Mgt, 2012–. Contested (Green) Cambridge, 2010. FRSA 2013. Hon. FIEnvSc 2009. Hon. DSc: Bristol, 2013; Plymouth, 2013. Rothschild Medal, 2009. *Publications:* (with Mike Parr) Parrots: a guide to the parrots of the world, 1998 (McColvin Medal, LA, 1999); Spix's Macaw, 2002; How many light bulbs does it take to change a planet?, 2007; Saving Planet Earth, 2007; (with HRH The Prince of Wales and Ian Skelly) Harmony, 2010; What Has Nature Ever Done For Us?: how money really does grow on trees, 2013; What Nature Does for Britain, 2015; contrib. to various scientific pubns. *Recreations:* natural history, fishing. *Address:* University of Cambridge Institute for Sustainability Leadership, 1 Trumpington Street, Cambridge CB2 1QA. *W:* www.tonyjuniper.com.

JUNKIN, (William) Roy, CB 2008; Deputy Director of Public Prosecutions for Northern Ireland, 1998–2008 (Acting Director, Jan.–July 2007); *b* 29 May 1948; *o s* of William John Junkin and Elizabeth Margaret Junkin (*née* Parker); *m* 1972, Valerie Ann Elizabeth Barbour; two *s*. *Educ:* Rainey Endowed Sch.; Queen's Univ. Belfast (LLB); Univ. of Ulster (BA Public Sector Mgt). Called to the Bar of NI, 1971 (Jt 1st, Bernard J. Fox Prize); called to the Bar, Gray's Inn, 1985, Bencher, 2006. Tutor in Law, QUB, 1970; Lectr in Law and Jurisp., QUB, and Asst Parly Draftsman, Parlt of NI, 1971–72; Lectr in Law, Univ. of Ulster, 1973; Government Legal Service, Northern Ireland, Department of Public Prosecutions: Professional Officer, 1974; Asst Sec., 1977; Under Sec., 1989. Part-time Vis. Lectr, Sch. of Public Admin, Univ. of Ulster, 1981–82. Mem., Exec. Bureau, Consultative Council of Prosecutors Gen. of Europe, Council of Europe, 2006–08. Member: Internat. Bar Assoc.; Human Rights Inst., Internat. Bar Assoc., 1998–2008; Eurojustice, 1998–2008; Internat. Assoc. of Prosecutors, 1998–2008 (Mem., Rev. Gp on Standards for Prosecutors, 2006–08); Statutory Cttee, Pharmaceutical Soc. of NI, 2008–12. Gov., Castlereagh Coll. of Further Educn, 2002–07. *Publications:* (jtly) Council of Europe, Budapest Guidelines: European guidelines on ethics and conduct for Public Prosecutors; contribs to Eurojustice and CCPE, notes and reviews in legal periodicals. *Recreations:* fly fishing, golf, cooking. *Address:* c/o Public Prosecution Service, 93 Chichester Street, Belfast BT1 3JR.

JUNOR, Penelope Jane, (Penny); journalist, writer and broadcaster; *b* 6 Oct. 1949; *d* of Sir John Junor and Pamela Mary (*née* Welsh); *m* 1970, James Stewart Leith; three *s* one *d*. *Educ:* Benenden Sch.; Univ. of St Andrews. Feature writer, 19 mag., 1970–71; reporter, Londoner's Diary, Evening Standard, 1971–74; freelance, 1974–; columnist, Private Eye, 1977–82; television: reporter, Collecting Now, 1981; Presenter: 4 What It's Worth, 1982–89; The Afternoon Show, 1984–85; The Travel Show, 1988–97. Gen. Ed., John Lewis Partnership, 1993–99. Patron: Women's Health Concern, 2002–; Cirencester beat Self-Help Gp, 2005–. Trustee: beat, 2006–12; Central London Samaritans, 2008–10. *Publications:* Newspaper, 1979; Diana, Princess of Wales, 1982; Babyware, 1982; Margaret Thatcher: wife, mother, politician, 1983; Burton, the Man Behind the Myth, 1985; Charles, 1987; (ed) What Every Woman Needs to Know, 1988; Queen Elizabeth II: a pictorial celebration of her reign, 1991; Charles and Diana: portrait of a marriage, 1991; The Major Enigma, 1993; Charles: victim or villain?, 1998; Home Truths: life around my father, 2002; The Firm: the troubled life of the House of Windsor, 2005; Pattie Boyd: wonderful today, 2007; (with Sir Cliff Richard) My Life, My Way, 2008; The Man Who Lives With Wolves, 2010; Prince William: born to be King, 2012; Prince Harry: brother, soldier, son, 2014. *Recreations:* walking, dogs and cats. *Address:* c/o Jane Turnbull, Barn Cottage, Veryan, Truro, Cornwall TR2 5QA. *T:* (01872) 501317. *E:* jane.turnbull@btinternet.com; Hilary Knight Management, Grange Farm, Church Lane, Old, Northants NN6 9QZ. *T:* (01604) 781818. *E:* hilary@hkmanagement.co.uk. *Clubs:* Groucho, Century.

JUPE, George Percival; Under Secretary, Ministry of Agriculture, Fisheries and Food, 1979–90; *b* 6 April 1930; *s* of Frederick Stuart Jupe and Elizabeth (*née* Clayton); unmarried. *Educ:* Sandown Grammar Sch., IoW; Hertford Coll., Oxford. Ministry of Agriculture, Fisheries and Food: Asst Principal, 1955; Principal, 1960; Asst Sec., 1970–79: Eggs and Poultry, and Potatoes Divs, 1970–74; Internat. Fisheries Div., 1975–78; Emergencies, Food Quality and Pest Controls Gp, 1979–85; Dir, ADAS Admin, 1985–88; Horticulture, Seeds, Plant Health and Flood Defence Gp, 1988–90. *Recreations:* hill walking, gardening, music. *Address:* 29 Belmore Road, Lymington, Hants SO41 3NU.

JUPP, Elisabeth Anne; an Upper Tribunal Judge (Administrative Appeals Chamber) (formerly a Social Security and Child Support Commissioner), 2001–11; a Deputy Upper Tribunal Judge (part-time) (Administrative Appeals Chamber), since 2012; *b* 4 April 1944; *d* of Alfred Barrett Tebb and Sarah Tebb (*née* Burnham); *m* 1968, Rev. Dr Peter Creffield Jupp; two *s*. *Educ:* Easingwold Sch.; King's Coll. London (LLB 1966). Admitted Solicitor, 1969; Partner, Alexanders, London, 1972–2001. Dep. Social Security and Child Support Comr, 1997–2001; Chm. (pt-time), Pensions Appeal Tribunal, 2001–14. Chm., Ministerial Trng Cttee, URC, 1987–92. Member: Council, Mansfield Coll., Oxford, 1984–88; Mgt Cttee, Westminster Coll., Cambridge, 2010–13; Trustee, Homerton Coll., Cambridge, 1992–2010. *Recreations:* gardening, reading, poetry, theatre.

See also M. H. B. Jupp.

JUPP, Miles Hugh Barrett; actor and writer; *b* London, 8 Sept. 1979; *s* of Rev. Dr Peter Creffield Jupp and Elisabeth Anne Jupp, *qv*; *m* 2008, Rachel Boase; four *s* one *d*. *Educ:* Univ. of Edinburgh (MA Hons Divinity 2005). *Television* includes: Rev, 2010–14; Spy, 2012; In and Out of the Kitchen, 2015; *films* include: Made in Dagenham, 2010; The Monuments Men, 2013; The Look of Love, 2014; Rosewater, 2015; *radio* includes: In and Out of the Kitchen, 2011–15; host, The News Quiz, Radio 4, 2015–; *theatre* includes: A Day in the Death of Joe Egg, Citizen's, Glasgow, 2011; People, NT, 2012–13; Neville's Island, Duke of York's, 2014; Rules for Living, NT, 2015. *Publications:* Fibber in the Heat, 2012, 2nd edn 2014. *Recreations:* watching cricket, walking, drinking cider in the bath. *Address:* c/o Molly Wansell, 42 Management, 8 Flitcroft Street, WC2H 8DL. *T:* (020) 7292 0554.

JUPPÉ, Alain Marie; Minister of Foreign and European Affairs, France, 2011–12; Mayor of Bordeaux, 1995–2004 and since 2006; *b* 15 Aug. 1945; *s* of Robert Juppé and Marie Darroze; *m* 1st, 1965, Christine Leblond (marr. diss.); one *s* one *d*; 2nd, 1993, Isabelle Bodin; one *d*. *Educ:* Lycées Victor-Duruy, Mont-de-Marsan and Louis-le-Grand, Paris; Ecole Normale Superieure (Dr in Classical Langs); Inst. of Political Studies; Nat. Sch. of Admin. Finance Inspector, 1972; Asst to Prime Minister Jacques Chirac, 1976; Advr to Minister for Co-operation, 1976–78; MEP, 1984–86; Deputy for Paris, 1988–93, for Bordeaux, 1997–2004, National Assembly; Dep. Minister of Finance, and Govt Spokesman, 1986–88; Minister of Foreign Affairs, France, 1993–95; Prime Minister of France, 1995–97; Minister of Environment, Energy and Transport, 2007; Minister of Defence and Veterans Affairs, 2010–11. Rassemblement pour la République: Nat. Deleg., 1976–78; Nat. Sec., 1984–86; Gen. Sec., 1988–95; Pres., 1995–97. Adviser to Mayor of Paris, 1978; Dir of Finance and Economic Affairs, City of Paris, 1980–81; Mem., Paris City Council, 1983–95; Dep. Mayor of Paris, i/c Finance, 1983–95. Chm., Union for a Popular Movt, 2002–04. *Publications:* La Tentation de Venise, 1993; Entre Nous, 1996; Montesquieu le Moderne, 1999; Entre Quatre-Yeux, 2001; France mon pays: lettres d'un voyageur, 2006; Je ne mangerai plus de cerises en hiver, 2009; La Politique, telle qu'elle meurt de ne pas être, 2011. *Address:* Mairie de Bordeaux, Place Pey-Berland, 33000 Bordeaux, France.

JUROWSKI, Vladimir; conductor; Chief Conductor, London Philharmonic Orchestra, since 2007; Artistic Director, Russian State Academic Symphony Orchestra, since 2011; *b* Moscow, 1972; *s* of Mikhail Jurowski, conductor. *Educ:* Music Coll., Moscow Conservatory; High Sch. of Music, Dresden; High Sch. of Music, Berlin. Internat. début, Wexford Fest., 1995; débuts: Royal Opera Hse, Covent Gdn, 1995; Metropolitan Opera, NY, 1999; joined Komische Oper, Berlin, 1996, First Kapellmeister, 1997–2001; Music Dir, Glyndebourne Fest. Opera, 2001–13. Principal Guest Conductor: Orch. Sinfonica Verdi, Milan; Teatro Comunale, Bologna, 2000–03; LPO, 2003–06; Russian Nat. Orch., 2005–09; Principal Artist, Orch. of the Age of Enlightenment, 2006–. Guest Conductor: Royal Opera Hse, Covent Gdn; Teatro La Fenice, Venice; Opéra Bastille, Paris; Th. de la Monnaie, Brussels; Maggio Music Fest., Florence; Rossini Opera Fest., Pesaro; Edinburgh Fest.; Semperoper, Dresden; WNO; Metropolitan Opera, NY; Berlin Philharmonic; Royal Concertgebouw Orch.; Philadelphia Orch.; LA Philharmonic; Chamber Orch. of Europe; Chicago Symphony; Tonhalle Orchester, Zurich; Dresden Staatskapelle. *Address:* c/o IMG Artists, The Light Box, 111 Power Road, Chiswick, W4 5PY.

JUSS, Prof. Satvinder Singh, PhD; Professor of Law, King's College London, since 2008; Deputy Judge of the Upper Tribunal (Immigration and Asylum Chamber), since 2010 (Immigration Judge, since 2000); *b* Moshi, Tanzania, 11 May 1958; *s* of Sardar Dhian Singh Juss and Sardarni Joginder Kaur Juss; *m* 1990, Ravinder Kaur; two *s*. *Educ:* Emmanuel Coll., Cambridge (PhD Law 1986); Harvard Law Sch. (Harkness Fellow 1996). Fellow and Coll. Lectr, Emmanuel Coll., Cambridge, 1985–88; called to the Bar, Gray's Inn, 1989; in practice as barrister, 1989–; pupillage at 4–5 Gray's Inn Sq., 1990; Law Lectr, Univ. of Wales Coll., Cardiff, 1991–93; Human Rights Fellow, Harvard Univ., 1997; Vis. Prof. of Law, Indiana Univ., Bloomington, 1998; Certified Lectr for Law Soc. of England and Wales, and Consultant, Coll. of Law, 1998–2001; Lectr in Law. 2000–03, Reader in Law, 2003–08, KCL. Vis. Fellow, Georgetown Univ., 1996–97. Alice Tay Lect., ANU, 2013; Annual Human Rights Lect., NZ Centre of Human Rights, 2014. Advocate: for Govt of Wales, Panel A, 2012–Sept. 2016; for Equality and Human Rights Commn of England and Wales, 2015–. Mem. Council, 2004, Migration Comr, 2005, RSA. Life Mem. and Mem. Council, Indian Council of Arbitration, 2010–. FRSA. *Publications:* Immigration, Nationality and Citizenship, 1993; Discretion and Deviation in the Administration of Immigration Control, 1998; International Migration and Global Justice, 2007; Contemporary Issues in Refugee Law, 2013; Ashgate Research Companion on Migration Law, Theory and Policy, 2014; Toward a Refugee Oriented Reform of Refugee Law, 2015; (ed with M. Sunkim) Landmark Cases in Public Law, 2016; (ed with C. Walker) Human Rights and the War on Terror, 2016; (ed) India and Human Rights, 2016; contrib. King's Law Jl. *Recreations:* cricket, tennis, swimming, long-distance walking, running, ghazal singing, delving in dusty shelves of arcane bookstores, keeping up with my children. *Address:* Dickson Poon School of Law, Somerset House, East Wing, King's College London, Strand, WC2R 2LS. *T:* (020) 7848 1189. *E:* satvinder.juss@kcl.ac.uk; 3 Hare Court, Temple, EC4Y 7BJ. *T:* (020) 7415 7800, 07931 728328, *Fax:* (020) 7415 7811. *E:* simonhamilton@3harecourt.com.

K

KABERRY, Hon. Sir Christopher Donald, (Hon. Sir Kit), 2nd Bt *cr* 1960, of Adel cum Eccup, City of Leeds; FCA; Director and Company Secretary, London & Continental Railways Ltd, 2011–14; *b* 14 March 1943; *s* of Lord Kaberry of Adel (Life Peer) and Lily Margaret (*d* 1992), *d* of Edmund Scott; *S* to baronetcy of father, 1991; *m* 1967, Gaenor Elizabeth Vowe, *d* of C. V. Peake; two *s* one *d*. *Educ:* Repton Sch. FCA 1967. Various overseas positions, Costain Group PLC, 1969–80; Financial Manager, United Buildings Factories, Bahrain, 1980–82; Resources Manager, Balfour Beatty Group, Indonesia and Bahamas, 1983–90; Hd of Finance, Union Railways, and CTRL Project, 1990–2007. Director: HSI (formerly Union Railways (North)) Ltd, 2004–10; CTRL (UK) Ltd, 2004–10; Channel Tunnel Rail Link Ltd, 2005–11. Trustee: W. H. Baxter Charity, 1990–; Rhino Ark (UK), 2011–; Zamcog, 2012–. *Recreations:* walking, gardening, Land Rover driving. *Heir:* *s* James Christopher Kaberry [*b* 1 April 1970; *m* 1989, Juliet Clare Hill (marr. diss. 1995); two *s* one *d*]. *Address:* Rock View, Chiddingstone Hoath, Kent TN8 7BT.

KABUI, Sir Frank (Utu Ofagioro), GCMG 2009 (CMG 1996); CSI 2002; OBE 1988; Governor General, Solomon Islands, since 2009; *b* Suluagwari, North Malaita, Solomon Is, 20 April 1946; *s* of late Michael Frank Kabui and Namaah Angialatha; *m* 1st, 1978, Maryanne (marr. diss. 1993; she *d* 2005); three *s* three *d*; 2nd, 1993, Grace Delight; one *s* one *d*. *Educ:* Elementary Sch., Malu'u, N Malaita; Aligegeo Sen. Prim. Sch., Auki, Malaita; King George VI Nat. Sec. Sch.; Univ. of Papua New Guinea (LLB 1974); Australian National Univ. (Grad. Dip. Internat. Law 1985). Joined Solomon Is Public Service as Crown Counsel, 1975; Asst Attorney-Gen., 1977–80; Attorney-Gen., 1980–94; first Chm., Law Reform Commn, 1995–98; a Puisne Judge, High Court, Solomon Is, 1998–2006; Chm., Law Reform Commn, 2006–09. Jt Sec., Constitutional Cttee, 1976; former mem. of numerous govt cttees. Mem., Investment Corp. of Solomon Is, 1979–94. Former Director: Solomon Taiyo Ltd; Sasape Marina Ltd; Solomon Airlines Ltd; Mendana Hotel Ltd; Nat. Bank of Solomon Is. Pres., Solomon Is Bar Assoc., 2007–09. *Publications:* contrib. to Jl of Pacific Studies. *Recreations:* table tennis, lawn tennis, squash, soccer, darts, golf. *Address:* Government House, PO Box 252, Honiara, Solomon Islands. *T:* 21777, 21778, *Fax:* 22533.

KACELNIK, Prof. Alejandro, DPhil; FRS 2011; Professor of Behavioural Ecology, University of Oxford, since 1997; E. P. Abraham Fellow of Pembroke College, Oxford, since 1990; *b* Buenos Aires, 14 Dec. 1946; *s* of Meyer Kacelnik and Lisa Kacelnik (*née* Kogan); *m* 1971, Lidia Estela Rapaport; one *s*. *Educ:* Univ. of Buenos Aires (Licenciado en Ciencias Biológicas); Wolfson Coll., Oxford (DPhil 1979). Post Doctoral Researcher: Univ. of Groningen, 1980–82; Univ. of Oxford, 1982–86; Sen. Res. Fellow, King's Coll., Cambridge, 1986–90; University of Oxford: Lectr in Zool., 1990–97; Founder and Dir, Behavioural Ecol. Res. Gp, 1990–. Fellow, Inst. for Advanced Studies, Berlin, 2001–03. Visiting Professor: Univ. of Leiden, 1988; Indiana Univ., 1995; Univ. Claude Bernard, Lyon, 1997; Univ. of Buenos Aires, 1999; Princeton Univ., 2005; Univ. Pompeu Fabra, Barcelona, 2009. MAE 2003. Cogito Prize (jtly), Cogito Foundn, 2004; Eduardo de Robertis Prize, Argentinian Soc. for Res. in Neuroscis, 2009; Raíces Prize, Argentinian Govt, 2011. *Publications:* (ed jtly) Quantitative Analyses of Behavior, vol. 6, Foraging, 1987; over 170 articles in major scientific jls. *Recreations:* cycling, rowing in the Paraná Delta, reading, cooking, gardening. *Address:* Department of Zoology, University of Oxford, South Parks Road, Oxford OX1 3PS. *T:* (01865) 271164, *Fax:* (01865) 271120. *E:* alex.kacelnik@zoo.ox.ac.uk. *Club:* Rowing Club Argentino.

KADOORIE, Hon. Sir Michael (David), Kt 2005; GBS 2003; Chairman: CLP Holdings Ltd (formerly China Light & Power Co. Ltd), since 1996 (Director, 1967–96); Hongkong & Shanghai Hotels Ltd, since 1985 (Director, 1964–85); *b* Hong Kong, 19 July 1941; *s* of Baron Kadoorie, CBE and Muriel Kadoorie (*née* Gubbay); *m* 1984, Betty Tamayo; one *s* two *d*. *Educ:* King George V Sch., Hong Kong; Le Rosey, Switzerland. Chairman: Heliservices (Hong Kong) Ltd, 1979–; Metrojet Ltd, 1996–; Dir, Sir Elly Kadoorie & Sons Ltd, 1988–; chairman, director and trustee of many other cos. Hon. LLD Hong Kong, 2004; Hon. DSc Imperial Coll. London, 2007. Commandeur: Ordre de Léopold II (Belgium), 1995; Ordre des Arts et des Lettres (France), 1998; Commandeur, Légion d'Honneur, 2014 (Chevalier, 1995; Officier, 2003). *Recreations:* world travel, flying, motor cars, photography. *Address:* 24th Floor, St George's Building, 2 Ice House Street, Central, Hong Kong SAR. *T:* 25249221, *Fax:* 28459133. *Clubs:* Hong Kong, Hong Kong Aviation, Hong Kong Jockey (Hong Kong).

KADRI, Sibghatullah; QC 1989; barrister-at-law; President, Standing Conference of Pakistani Organisations in UK, 1978–90 (Secretary General, 1975–78); *b* 23 April 1937; *s* of Haji Maulana Firasat Ullah Kadri and Begum Tanwir Fatima Kadri; *m* 1963, Carita Elisabeth Idman; one *s* one *d*. *Educ:* S. M. Coll., Karachi; Karachi Univ. Called to the Bar, Inner Temple, 1969, Bencher, 1997. Sec. Gen., Karachi Univ. Students Union, 1957–58; jailed without trial, for opposing military regime of Ayub Khan, 1958–59; triple winner, All Pakistan Students Debates, 1960; Gen. Sec., Pakistan Students' Fedn in Britain, 1961–62, Vice Pres., 1962–63; Pres., Inner Temple Students Assoc., 1969–70. Producer and broadcaster, BBC Ext. Urdu Service, 1965–68, and Presenter, BBC Home Service Asian Prog., 1968–70. In practice at the Bar, 1969– (former Hd of Chambers, 6 King's Bench Walk; Hd of Chambers, 2 King's Bench Walk). Chm., Soc. of Afro-Asian and Caribbean Lawyers, UK, 1979–83. Vis. Lectr in Urdu, Holborn Coll., London, 1967–70. Org. Pakistani Def. Cttees during wave of 'Paki-bashing', 1970; active in immigrant and race-relations activities, 1970–; led Asian delegn to Prime Minister, June 1976; attended UN Conf., Migrant Workers in Europe, Geneva, 1975; led Pakistan delegn to 3rd Internat. Conf., Migrant Workers in Europe, Turin, 1977; Mem., Race Relations Cttee of the Bar, 1983–85, 1988, 1989; Chm., UK Lawyers Cttee of Human Rights and Justice in Pakistan, 2007–. Gen. Sec., Pakistan Action Cttee, 1973; Convenor, Asian Action Cttee, 1976. Vice Chm., All Party Jt Cttee Against Racism, 1978–80. Publisher, Scopo News, London, until 1984. FRSA 1991. Lifetime Achievement Award, Soc. of Asian Lawyers, 2008; Lifetime Achievement Award, Third World Solidarity, 2008; Role Model of the Year, Pakistan Achievement Award UK and Europe, 2012. *Publications:* articles in ethnic minority press on immigration and race relations. *Recreations:* family, reading. *Address:* Kadri's Chambers, 2 King's Bench Walk, Temple, EC4Y 7DE.

KAHAN, George; Director of Conciliation and Arbitration, Advisory, Conciliation and Arbitration Service, 1988–91; *b* 11 June 1931; *er s* of late Joseph Kahan and Xenia (*née* Kirschner); *m* 1959, Avril Pamela Cooper (*d* 2004); one *s*. *Educ:* St Paul's Sch. Nat. Service, RAF, 1950–51. Park Royal Woodworkers Ltd, 1951–74 (Dir, 1960–74); Principal: Dept of Employment, 1975–76; Health and Safety Executive, Health and Safety Commn, 1976–80; Asst Sec., Dept of Employment, 1980–88. *Recreations:* lazing in the sun, reading, listening to music. *Address:* Half Timbers, The Thatchway, Rustington, Sussex BN16 2BN. *T:* (01903) 784070.

KAHN, (Jacob) Meyer; Group Chairman, SABMiller (formerly South African Breweries) plc, 1999–2012; *b* 29 June 1939; *s* of late Ben and Sarah Kahn; *m* 1968, Lynette Sandra Asher; two *d*. *Educ:* Univ. of Pretoria (BA, MBA). Joined South African Breweries Ltd, 1966; Man. Dir, Amrel, 1972–77; Man. Dir, 1977–80, Chm., 1980–83, OK Bazaars (1929) Ltd; Dir, 1981–2012, Man. Dir, 1983–90, Exec. Chm., 1990–97, South African Breweries, later SABMiller plc; Chief Exec., South African Police Service, 1997–99 (on secondment). *Address:* SABMiller plc, PO Box 6335, Johannesburg 2000, South Africa.

KAHN, Paul Emmanuel, CEng, FIET, FRAeS, FIMechE; President, Airbus Group UK, since 2014; *b* 27 Jan. 1966; *s* of Robert E. Kahn and Sylvia M. Kahn; *m* 1990, Sarah Burland; two *s* one *d*. *Educ:* Cardinal Vaughan Memorial Sch., Kensington; Brunel Univ. (BSc Hons, MEng Engrg and Mgt Systems); London Business Sch. (MBA). CEng 1992; FIET 2002; FRAeS 2004; FIMechE 2013. Undergrad., Ford Motor Co., 1984–88; Principal, MoD, 1988–95; Vice Pres., Thales (formerly Thomson-CSF), 1995–2010; Pres. and CEO, Thales Canada Inc., 2010–14. FAPM 2013. *Recreations:* family, ski-ing, running, hill walking, canoeing. *Address:* Airbus Group UK, Wellington House, 125–130 Strand, WC2R 0AP. *Club:* Royal Automobile.

KAHN, Paula; Chair, Metropolitan Housing Trust, since 2013; *b* 15 Nov. 1940; *d* of Cyril Maurice Kahn and Stella Roscoe. *Educ:* Chiswick County High Sch.; Bristol Univ. (BA Hons). Teacher, administrator, 1962–66; Longman Group, 1966–94: editor, publisher, Publishing Director, Divl Man. Dir, 1966–79; Managing Director: ELT Div., Dictionaries Div. and Trade and Ref. Div., 1980–85; Internat. Sector, 1986–88; Chief Exec. (Publishing), 1988–89; Chief Exec. and Chm., 1990–94; Vice-Pres., Publishers Assoc., 1994–95; Project Dir, World Learning Network, 1995–96; Man. Dir, Phaidon Press, 1996–97. Non-executive Director: Inst. of Internat. Visual Arts, 1994–2008; Focus Central London, TEC, 1998–2001; English Languages Services Internat. Ltd, 1998–2006; New Ways to Work, 1998–2001; ITDG Publishing, 1999–2004; Stonewall, 2000–06; Chairman: Equality Works, 2000–08; Hidden Art, 2007–12. Member: English Teaching Adv. Cttee, British Council, 1990–98; Educn and Training Sector Gp, DTI, 1993–98. Mem., Islington CHC and PCG, 1998–2001; Chair: Islington PCT, 2002–13; North Central London NHS Cluster, 2011–13. Mem., Governing Body, SOAS, 1993–95. Chm., Camden Arts Centre, 2008–14. Governor: Elizabeth Garrett Anderson Sch., Islington, 1997–2000; Cripplegate Foundn, 2000– (Chair, 2005–07); Trustee, Assoc. of Charitable Foundns, 2012–. FRSA 1993; CCMI (CIMgt 1992). *Recreations:* visual arts, cinema, theatre, reading. *Address:* 4 Mica House, Barnsbury Square, N1 1RN.

KAHNEMAN, Anne Marie; *see* Treisman, A. M.

KAHNEMAN, Prof. Daniel, PhD; Eugene Higgins Professor of Psychology, and Professor of Public Affairs, Woodrow Wilson School, Princeton University, 1993–2007, now Emeritus and Senior Scholar; *b* 1934; *m* 1st, Irah; 2nd, 1978, Prof. Anne Marie Treisman, *qv*. *Educ:* Hebrew Univ. (BA 1954); Univ. of Calif, Berkeley (PhD 1961). Lectr, 1961–66, Sen. Lectr, 1966–70, Associate Prof., 1970–73, Prof. of Psychol., 1973–78, Hebrew Univ.; Professor of Psychology: Univ. of BC, 1978–86; Univ. of Calif, Berkeley, 1986–94. Corresp. FBA 2008. Nobel Prize in Econ. Scis (jtly), 2002; Presidential Medal of Freedom (USA), 2013. *Publications:* Attention and Effort, 1973; (ed jtly) Well-Being: Foundations of Hedonic Psychology, 1999; (ed jtly) Choices, Values and Frames, 2000; (ed jtly) Heuristics and Biases: the psychology of intuitive judgement, 2002; Thinking, Fast and Slow, 2011; contrib. learned jls. *Address:* 322 Wallace Hall, Woodrow Wilson School of Public and International Affairs, Princeton University, Princeton, NJ 08544–1013, USA.

KAIN, Prof. Roger James Peter, CBE 2005; PhD, DLit; FSA; FBA 1990; Dean and Chief Executive, School of Advanced Study, University of London, since 2010; *b* 12 Nov. 1944; *s* of Peter Albert Kain and Ivy Kain; *m* 1970, Annmaree Wallington; two *s*. *Educ:* Harrow Weald County Grammar Sch.; University College London (BA; PhD 1973; DLit 1998; Fellow 2002). FSA 1992. Tutor, Bedford Coll., London, 1971–72; Exeter University: Lectr, 1972–88; Montefiore Reader in Geography, 1988–91; Montefiore Prof. of Geography, 1991–2010; Hd, Sch. of Geog. and Archaeol., 1999–2001; Dep. Vice-Chancellor, 2002–10. British Academy: Vice-Pres., 1997–99; Chm. Grants Cttee, 1999–2002; Treas., 2002–10; Vice Pres., Res. and Higher Educn Policy, 2014–. Mem., AHRC, 2008–14. Gill Meml Medal, RGS, 1990; Kenneth Nebenzahl Prize, Newberry Liby, Chicago, 1991. *Publications:* Planning for Conservation: an international perspective, 1984; The Tithe Surveys of England and Wales, 1985, repr. 2006; An Atlas and Index of the Tithe Files of Mid-Nineteenth-Century England and Wales, 1986; (jtly) Cadastral Mapping in the Service of the State: a history of property mapping, 1992; (jtly) The Tithe Maps of England and Wales: a cartographic analysis and county-by-county catalogue, 1995 (McColvin Medal, LA, 1996), repr. 2011; (jtly) English Cartography, 1997; (jtly) English Maps: a history, 1999; (ed) Historical Atlas of South-West England, 1999; (jtly) Tithe Surveys for Historians, 2000; Historic Parishes of England and Wales, 2001; (jtly) Enclosure Maps of England and Wales, 2004, repr. 2011; (ed) England's Landscape: the South-West, 2006; (jtly) British Town Maps: a history, 2015. *Recreations:* mountain walking, gardening. *Address:* School of Advanced Study, University of London, Senate House, Malet Street, WC1E 7HU. *T:* (020) 7862 8736. *Club:* Athenæum.

KAISER, Martin S.; *see* Seeleib-Kaiser, M.

KAISER, Michael Martin; Co-Chairman, IMG Artists, since 2014; *b* 27 Oct. 1953; *s* of Harold and Marion Kaiser. *Educ:* Brandeis Univ. (BS); Sloan Sch., MIT (MSM). Pres., Kaiser Associates, 1981–85; Exec. Dir, Kansas City Ballet, 1985–87; Associate Dir, Pierpoint

Morgan Library, 1987–91; Exec. Dir, Alvin Ailey American Dance Theatre, 1991–93; Pres., Kaiser-Engler Gp, 1994–95; Executive Director: American Ballet Theatre, 1995–98; Royal Opera House, 1998–2000; Pres., John F. Kennedy Center for Performing Arts, Washington, 2001–14. *Address:* IMG Artists, 7 West 54 Street, New York, NY 10019, USA.

KAISER, Prof. Nicholas, PhD; FRS 2008; Astronomer, Institute for Astronomy, University of Hawaii, since 1997; *b* 15 Sept. 1954; *s* of late Prof. Thomas Reeve Kaiser and of Pamela Kaiser. *Educ:* Leeds Univ. (BSc Physics 1978); Clare Coll., Cambridge (Pt III Maths Tripos 1979; PhD Astronomy 1982). Lindemann Fellow, Univ. of Calif, Berkeley, 1983; Post Doctoral Fellow: UCSB, 1984; Univ. of Calif, Berkeley, 1984; SERC Sen. Visitor, Univ. of Sussex, 1985; Post Doctoral Fellow, 1985–86, SERC Advanced Fellow, 1986–88, Univ. of Cambridge; Prof., Canadian Inst. for Theoretical Astrophysics, Univ. of Toronto, 1988–97. Ontario Fellow, Canadian Inst. Advanced Res. Cosmol. Prog., 1988; Steacie Fellow, NSERC, 1991–92. Helen Warner Prize, Amer. Astronomical Soc., 1989; Herzberg Medal, Canadian Assoc. Physicists, 1993; Rutherford Medal, RSC, 1997. *Publications: contributor:* Inner Space - Outer Space, 1986; Large Scale Motions in the Universe, 1989; The Epoch of Galaxy Formation, 1989; After the First 3 Minutes, 1991; contribs to learned jls incl. Astrophysical Jl, Bull. AAS, Monthly Notices of RAS, Nature, Contemporary Physics. *Address:* Institute for Astronomy, 2680 Woodlawn Drive, Honolulu, HI 96822, USA.

KAJUMBA, Ven. Daniel Steven Kimbugwe; Archdeacon of Reigate, since 2001; *b* 20 Nov. 1952; *s* of Prince Adonia Kajumba, Buganda royal clan, and Lady Esther Kajumba; family exiled to UK, 1971; *m* 1974, Tina Carole Hewlett; one *s* one *d*. *Educ:* school in Uganda; Southwark Ordination Course; HND 1977; Dip. Inst Municipal Bldg Mgt, 1981; DipTh London 1985; BA (Open) 1987; Postgrad. Cert. Preaching (Univ. of Wales), 2007. Employment before ordination included: Auxiliary Nurse, Bournemouth; Youth Officer, West Cliff Baptist Ch; Dep. Warden, Christian Alliance Centre; Prop., Poole Parkside and Edward Russell Residential Homes for the Elderly. Ordained deacon, 1985, priest, 1986; Curate, Goldington, Dio. St Albans, 1985–87; employment in Uganda, 1987–98, included: Man. Dir, Transocean; Gen. Mgr, Rio Hldgs Internat.; Kingdom of Buganda: Sec. Gen.; Minister for Public Relns, Functions and Protocol, and Foreign Affairs; Team Vicar, Horley St Francis, Dio. Southwark, 1999–2001. *Address:* (home) 84 Higher Drive, Purley, Surrey CR8 2HJ. *T:* (020) 8660 9276; (office) St Matthew's House, 100 George Street, Croydon CR0 1PE. *T:* (020) 8681 5496, *Fax:* (020) 8686 2074. *E:* daniel.kajumba@southwark.anglican.org.

KAKABADSE, Prof. Andrew, PhD; Professor of Governance and Leadership, Henley Business School, University of Reading, since 2013; *b* Athens, 30 March 1948; *s* of George Kakabadse and Elfrieda Kakabadse; *m* Patricia Sweetman (decd); one *d*; *m* 1995, Nada Korac (*see* N. Kakabadse); one *s*. *Educ:* Altrincham Grammar Sch.; Salford Univ. (BSc 1970); Brunel Univ. (MA 1973); Manchester Univ. (PhD 1977). Derbyshire CC, 1970–71; RBK&C, 1971–73; Dept of Mgt, Manchester Univ., 1973–77; WS Atkins Gp of Internat. Consultants, 1977–78; Prof. of Internat. Mgt Develt, Cranfield Univ., 1978–2012, now Emeritus. Vis. Professor: Sorbonne, 2009–; Univ. of Ulster, 2010–; Hon. Prof., Coll. of Social Scis, Kazakhstan, 2011–. Specialist Advr, Public Admin Select Cttee, 2011–. FBPsS; Fellow, Soc. of Internat. Business Leaders. Fellow, Windsor Leadership Trust, 2010–. *Publications:* (ed jtly) Leadership and Organisation Development, 1980; Culture of the Social Services, 1982; People and Organisations, 1982; Stress, Change and Organisation, 1982; Politics of Management, 1983; (ed jtly) Power, Politics and Organisations, 1984; (ed jtly) Future of Management Education, 1984; (jtly) Privatisation and the NHS, 1985; (with S. Tyson) Cases in Human Resource Management, 1987, 2nd edn 1994; Working in Organisations, 1988, 2nd edn 2004; Management Development and the Public Sector, 1989; The Wealth Creators, 1991; (with F. Analoui) Sabotage, 1991; (jtly) Japanese Business Leaders, 1996; (jtly) Success in Sight: visioning, 1998; (jtly) Designing World Class Corporate Strategies, 2005; (with L. Okazaki-Ward) Corporate Governance in Japan, 2005; (ed jtly) Corporate Social Responsibility, 2006; (jtly) Extraordinary Performance from Ordinary People, 2007; (jtly) Spiritual Motivation, 2007; (jtly) Leading for Success, 2008; (jtly) The Elephant Hunters, 2008; (jtly) Leadership Teams, 2009; (jtly) Citizenship, 2009; (jtly) Leading Smart Transformation, 2011; (jtly) Bilderberg People, 2011; (jtly) From Battlefield to Boardroom, 2012; with N. Korac-Kakabadse: Leadership in Government, 1998; Essence of Leadership, 1999; Creating Futures, 2000; The Geopolitics of Governance, 2001; Smart Sourcing, 2002; Intimacy, 2004; Governance, Strategy and Policy, 2005; CSR in Practice, 2007; Leading the Board, 2008; Global Boards, 2009; Rice Wine with the Minister, 2010; Global Elites, 2012; The Success Formula, 2015; over 220 articles. *Recreation:* walking. *Address:* Henley Business School, University of Reading, Greenlands, Henley-on-Thames, Oxon RG9 3AU. *T:* (01491) 418770. *E:* a.kakabadse@henley.ac.uk. *Club:* Athenæum.

KAKABADSE, Prof. Nada, PhD; Professor of Policy, Governance and Ethics, Henley Business School, University of Reading, since 2013; *b* 31 Jan. 1953; *d* of Dmitar and Mila Lisa Korac; *m* 1995, Prof. Andrew Kakabadse, *qv*; one *s*. *Educ:* Univ. of Canberra (BSc Maths and Computing; Grad. Dip. Mgt Sci.; MPA); Univ. of Western Sydney Nepean (PhD 1998); Inst. of Learning and Teaching, UK (Cert.). Cartographer/programmer, Australian Public Service, Dept of Minerals and Resources, Canberra, 1973–78; Regl Manager, Alfa-Laval AB, Lund, Sweden, 1978–84; Sen. IT Officer, Australian Public Service, Dept of Employment, Educn and Trng, 1985–95; on leave as Financial Officer, Dept of Ext. Affairs and Trade, Ottawa, 1989–91; Cranfield School of Management: Res. Fellow, HR Gp, 1995–97; Sen. Res. Fellow, Information Systems Res. Centre, 1997–2002; Northampton Business School, University of Northampton: Prof. of Mgt and Business Res., Hd, Doctoral Prog. and Res. Leader, 2002–13. Mem. and UK Rep., Eur. Acad. Scis and Arts. *Publications:* Overload: explaining, diagnosing and dealing with techno-addiction, 2007; (jtly) Leading for Success: seven sides to leadership, 2008; (jtly) The Elephant Hunters: chronicles of the moneymen, 2008; (jtly) Leadership Teams: developing and sustaining high performance, 2009; (ed jtly) Citizenship: a reality far from ideal, 2009; Leadership in the Public Sector, 2010; (jtly) Bilderberg People: inside the exclusive global elite, 2011 (trans. Mandarin, Chinese edn 2013); with A. Kakabadse: Leadership in Government: study of the Australian Public Service, 1998; Essence of Leadership, 1999; Creating Futures: leading change through information systems, 2000; Geopolitics of Governance, 2000; Smart Sourcing: international best practice, 2001; Intimacy: international survey of the sex lives of people at work, 2004; Governance, Strategy and Policy: seven critical essays, 2006; (ed) CSR in Practice: delving deep, 2007; Leading the Board: the six disciplines of world-class chairmen, 2008; (ed) Global Boards: one desire, many realities, 2009; Rice Wine with the Minister: distilled wisdom to manage, lead and succeed on the global stage, 2010; (ed) Global Elites: the opaque nature of transnational policy determination, 2012; contrib. chapters to internat. vols and articles. *Recreations:* long walks, swimming, classical music. *Address:* Henley Business School, University of Reading, Greenlands, Room EH 500, Henley-on-Thames, Oxon RG9 3AU. *T:* (01491) 418786. *E:* n.kakabadse@henley.ac.uk.

KAKKAR, family name of **Baron Kakkar**.

KAKKAR, Baron *cr* 2010 (Life Peer), of Loxbeare in the County of Devon; **Ajay Kumar Kakkar;** PC 2014; PhD; FRCS, FRCPE; Professor of Surgery, University College London, since 2011; Consultant Surgeon, University College London Hospitals NHS Foundation Trust, since 2006; Director, Thrombosis Research Institute, London, since 2009; *b* Dartford, Kent, 28 April 1964; *s* of Prof. Vijay Vir Kakkar, *qv*; *m* 1993, Nicola Susan Lear; two *d*. *Educ:* Alleyn's Sch., Dulwich; King's Coll., Univ. of London (BSc 1985; MBBS (Hons) 1988); Imperial Coll. London (PhD 1998). FRCS 1992; FRCPE 2011. Jun. surgical trng, King's Coll. Hosp., Brompton Hosp., Hammersmith Hosp. and Royal Sussex County Hosp., Brighton, 1988–92; Hammersmith Hospital, London: Registrar in Surgery, 1992–93; MRC Clinical Trng Fellow, 1993–96; MRC Clinician Scientist and Hon. Sen. Registrar, 1996–99; Sen. Lectr and Consultant Surgeon, Hammersmith Hosp. and Imperial Coll. London, 1999–2004; Prof. of Surgical Scis, Barts and the London Sch. of Medicine and Dentistry, QMUL, 2004–11; Consultant Surgeon, St Bartholomew's Hosp., 2004–11; Chm., UCL Partners Academic Health Scis System, 2014– (Chm., Clin. Quality Directorate, 2009–14). Chairman: Health Honours Cttee, 2013–; H of L Appts Commn, 2013–. UK Business Ambassador, Healthcare and Life Sci., 2013–. Mem., GMC, 2013–. Comr, Royal Hosp. Chelsea, 2012–. Trustee and Gov., King Edward VII Hosp. for Officers Sister Agnes, 2014–. Fellow, S African Soc. on Thrombosis and Haemostasis, 2009; Hon. Fellow, Assoc. of Surgeons of India, 2010. Hon. Fellow, Harris Manchester Coll., Oxford, 2010. Hunterian Prof., RCS, 1996; Wellcome Lectr, RSM, 2009; 12th Varma Lect., St George's, Univ. of London, 2011. James IV Assoc. of Surgeons Fellowship, 2006. David Patey Prize, Surgical Res. Soc., 1996; Knoll William Harvey Prize, Internat. Soc. on Thrombosis and Haemostasis, 1997. *Publications:* articles on prevention and treatment of venous thromboembolism and cancer associated thrombosis. *Recreation:* family. *Address:* House of Lords, SW1A 0PW. *T:* (020) 7351 8309, *Fax:* (020) 7351 8317. *E:* kakkara@parliament.uk. *Club:* Athenæum.

KAKKAR, Prof. Vijay Vir, OBE 2010; FRCS, FRCSE; Professor of Surgical Science, Guy's, King's and St Thomas' School of Medicine of King's College London (formerly King's College School of Medicine and Dentistry), 1975–97, and National Heart and Lung Institute, 1990–97, University of London, now Emeritus Professor, King's College London, and University of London; Founder, Chairman and Managing Trustee, TRI India, since 2004; *b* 22 March 1937; *s* of Dr H. B. and Mrs L. W. Kakkar; *m* 1962, Dr Savitri Karnani; two *s*. *Educ:* Vikram Univ., Ujjain, India (MB, BS 1960). FRCS 1964; FRCSE 1964. Junior staff appts, 1960–64; Lectr, Nuffield Dept of Surgery, Univ. of Oxford, 1964–65; Dept of Surgery, King's College Hospital, London: Pfizer Res. Fellow and Hon. Sen. Registrar, 1965–68; Sen. Registrar, 1968–69; Lectr and Hon. Sen. Registrar, 1969–71; Sen. Lectr and Hon. Consultant Surgeon, 1972–76; Dir, Thrombosis Res. Unit, 1975–97; Hon. Consultant Surgeon: King's Coll. Hosp. Gp, 1972–97; Mayday Hosp., Croydon, 1984–97; Hon. Cons. Vascular Surgeon, Royal Brompton Nat. Heart and Lung Hosps, 1990–97; Dir, Thrombosis Res. Inst., 1990–2009. Vis. Prof., Harvard Univ. Med. Sch., Boston, 1972. Pres., British Soc. for Haemostasis and Thrombosis, 1984–85 (Founder Mem., 1980, Sec., 1982–83); Member: Eur. Thrombosis Res. Orgn; Concerted Action Cttee on Thrombosis, EEC; Internat. Soc. on Thrombosis and Haemostasis (Chm., Cttee on Venous Thromboembolism); Internat. Surg. Soc.; Assoc. of Surgeons of GB and NI; Vascular Surg. Soc. of GB; Pan-Pacific Surg. Assoc.; Internat. Soc. for Haematology; Internat. Soc. for Angiology; Surg. Res. Soc. of GB; Hon. Mem., Assoc. of Surgeons of India; Hon. Fellow: Acad. of Medicine of Singapore; Hellenic Surgical Soc. Hunterian Prof., RCS, 1969; Lectures: Gunnar Bauer Meml, Copenhagen, 1971; James Finlayson Meml, RCPGlas, 1975; Cross Meml, RCS, 1977; Wright-Schulte, Internat. Soc. on Thrombosis and Haemostasis, 1977; Freyer Meml, RCSI, 1981; Dos Santos, 1994. David Patey Prize, Surg. Soc. of GB and Ireland, 1971. Member Editorial Board: Haemostasis, 1982; Clinical Findings, 1982; Internat. Angiology, 1982; Thrombosis Research, 1990. *Publications:* (jtly) Vascular Disease, 1969; (jtly) Thromboembolism: diagnosis and treatment, 1972; (jtly) Heparin: chemistry and clinical usage, 1976; (jtly) Chromogenic Peptide Substrates: chemistry and clinical usage, 1979; Atheroma and Thrombosis, 1983; 500 pubns in jls on thromboembolism and vascular disease. *Recreations:* golf, ski-ing, cricket. *Address:* Chalet Savi, Chemin de la Palaz, 1885 Chesieres, Villars-sur-Ollon, Switzerland. *Club:* Athenæum.

See also Baron Kakkar.

KALAMBEKOVA, Baktygul R.; Ambassador of the Kyrgyz Republic to the Court of St James's, 2010–12; *b* Batken, Kyrgyzstan, 18 Oct. 1961; *d* of Rysbay and Minavar; one *s*. *Educ:* Kyrgyz State Univ. (BA 1982); High Komsomol Sch.; Moscow Inst. of Youth (PhD Econs 1993); Inst. of Diplomacy, Turkey; Inst. of Internat. Relns and Diplomacy, Malaysia. Sen. Economist, Batken State Exec. Admin Agricl Sector, 1982–84; Sec., State Special Farm's Komsomol Cttee, 1984–85; First Sec., Batken Br., Leninist Young Communist League of the Soviet Union, 1985–90; First Sec., Central Asia and Caucasus Dept, and Mem., negotiation gp on border problems, Min. of Foreign Affairs, Kyrgyz Republic, 1993–95; Third Sec., Kyrgyz Embassy, Turkey, 1995–97; Second Sec., 1997–98, First Sec., 1998–2001, Western Countries Dept, Min. of Foreign Affairs, Kyrgyz Republic; Minister Counsellor, Kyrgyz Embassy, Turkey, 2001–04; Dep. Hd, Foreign Policy Planning and Multilateral Econ. Cooperation Dept, 2004–05, Advr to Minister, 2005–09, Vice-Minister, 2009–10, Min. of Foreign Affairs, Kyrgyz Republic; Foreign Policy Advr to Hd of Interim Govt and to Pres. of Kyrgyz Republic, 2010. Hon. Diploma, Foreign Min., Kyrgyzstan; Laureate of Internat. Award for merits before the Turkic World; Gold Medal and Diploma, Internat. Fund of Sci. and Culture Mustafa Kemal Ataturk. *Publications:* Agrarian Overpopulation in Kyrgyzstan (monograph), 2004; trans. six books from Kyrgyz, Russian and Turkish langs; 40 articles on regl and world econs. *Address:* c/o Embassy of the Kyrgyz Republic, 119 Ascot House, Crawford Street, W1U 6BJ.

KALETSKY, Anatole; Columnist, Reuters, since 2012; Co-Founder and Chief Economist, GaveKal Research, since 2001; Vice-Chairman and Chief Economist, GaveKal Dragonomics, Hong Kong; *b* Moscow, 1 June 1952; *s* of Jacob and Esther Kaletsky; *m* 1985, Fiona Murphy; two *s* one *d*. *Educ:* Melbourne High Sch., Australia; Westminster City Sch.; King's Coll., Cambridge (BA Maths); Harvard Univ. (MA Econs). Financial Writer, The Economist, 1976–79; Financial Times: Leader Writer, 1979–81; Washington Corresp., 1981–83; Internat. Econs Corresp., 1984–86; NY Bureau Chief, 1986–90; Moscow Assignment, 1990; The Times: Econs Ed., 1990–96; Associate Ed., 1992–2009; Ed. at Large, 2009–12. Hon. Sen. Scholar, King's Coll., Cambridge, 1973–74; Kennedy Scholar, Harvard Univ., 1974–76. Mem., Adv. Bd, UK Know-How Fund for E Europe and former Soviet Union, 1991–; Dir, Kaletsky Economic Consulting, 1997–2003. Mem. Council, REconS, 1999–2004. Trustee, New Europe Res. Trust, 1999–. Hon. DSc Buckingham, 2007. Specialist Writer of Year, British Press Awards, 1980, 1992; Commentator of the Year, What the Papers Say, 1996; Financial Journalist of the Year, Wincott Foundn Award, 1997. *Publications:* The Costs of Default, 1985; In the Shadow of Debt, 1992; Capitalism 4.0: the birth of a new economy, 2010. *Recreations:* playing the violin, cinema, family life.

KALLAGHE, Peter Allan; High Commissioner for United Republic of Tanzania in the United Kingdom, since 2010; *b* Korogwe, Tanzania, 31 Aug. 1959; *m* Joyce Daniel; two *s* two *d*. *Educ:* Kiev State Univ. (MA Internat. Relns 1982). Min. of Foreign Affairs, Tanzania, 1983–97; Dep. Private Sec. to President of Tanzania, 2001–06; Dir of Communications, President's Office, 2003–07; High Comr to Canada and Cuba, 2007–10. *Address:* High Commission for Tanzania, 3 Stratford Place, W1C 1AS. *T:* (020) 7569 1471, 07500 703388. *E:* pkallaghe@gmail.com.

KALLAS, Siim; Member and a Vice-President, European Commission, 2004–14; *b* 2 Oct. 1948; *s* of Udo Kallas and Rita Kallas; *m* 1972, Kristi Kartus; one *s* one *d*. *Educ:* Tartu State Univ. Chief Specialist, Min. of Finance, Estonia, 1975–79; Gen. Manager, Estonian Savings Bank, 1979–86; Dep. Ed., Rahva Hääl, 1986–89; Chm., Estonian Assoc. of Trade Unions, 1989–91; Pres., Bank of Estonia, 1991–95. MP, Estonia, 1995–2004; Minister: of Foreign Affairs, 1995–96; of Finance, 1999–2002; Prime Minister, 2002–03. Founder and Chm., Estonian Reform Party, 1994–2004. Vis. Prof. of Internat. Econs, Univ. of Tartu, 2015–. *Publications:* articles on econ. affairs, foreign policy and politics.

KALLASVUO, Olli-Pekka; President and Chief Executive Officer, 2006–10, Chairman of the Group Executive Board, 2006–10 (Member, 1990–2010) and Member of the Board of Directors, 2007–10, Nokia; *b* Lavia, Finland, 13 July 1953. *Educ:* Univ. of Helsinki (LLM). Various positions, Union Bank of Finland; Nokia: joined as Corporate Counsel, 1980; Asst Vice Pres., Legal Dept, 1987–88; Asst Vice Pres., 1988–90, Sen. Vice Pres., 1990–92, Finance; Exec. Vice Pres. and Chief Financial Officer, 1992–97; Corp. Exec. Vice Pres., Nokia Americas, 1997–98; Chief Financial Officer, 1999–2004; Exec. Vice Pres. and Gen. Manager, Mobile Phones, 2004–05; Pres. and Chief Operating Officer, 2005–06; Chm., Bd of Dirs, Nokia Siemens Networks, 2007–11. Chm., World Design Capital Helsinki 2012 Cttee, 2011–13. Member, Board: SRV Group plc, 2011– (Vice-Chm., 2012–); TeliaSonera, 2012–; Chm., Zenterio, 2013–. Member: Bd, Confedn of Finnish Industries, 2009–; Eur. Round Table of Industrialists, 2009–; EU-Russia Industrialists' Round Table, 2010–. Hon. LLD. *Recreations:* golf, tennis, reading about political history.

KALLIPETIS, Michel Louis; QC 1989; a Recorder, 1989; a Deputy High Court Judge, 1990; independent civil and commercial mediator, Independent Mediators Ltd, since 2006; *b* 29 Aug. 1941; *s* of late Takis George Kallipetis and Sheila Gallally; *m* 2009, Caroline Sarah (*née* Ball). *Educ:* Cardinal Vaughan Sch.; University Coll., London. FCIArb; Chartered Arbitrator, 2002. Exchequer and Audit Dept, 1960–66. Called to the Bar, Gray's Inn, 1968, Bencher, 1997. Registered and accredited mediator, 1996. *Recreations:* opera, cooking, travel. *Clubs:* Reform, Garrick.

KALMS, Baron *cr* 2004 (Life Peer), of Edgware in the London Borough of Barnet; **Harold Stanley Kalms,** Kt 1996; President, Dixons Retail (formerly Dixons Group, then DSG International) plc, 2002–14 (Chairman, 1972–2002); Treasurer, Conservative Party, 2001–03; *b* 21 Nov. 1931; *s* of Charles and Cissie Kalms; *m* 1954, Pamela Jimack (MBE 1995); three *s*. *Educ:* Christ's College, Finchley. Whole career with Dixons Group: started in 1948 in one store owned by father; went public, 1962; Man. Dir, 1962–72; Dir, British Gas, 1987–97. Chairman: Volvere plc, 2002–11; NMT Gp plc, 2005–08; Acorn Brands, 2006–07. Chm., King's Healthcare NHS Trust, 1993–96. Director: Centre for Policy Studies, 1991–2001 (Treas., 1993–98); Business for Sterling, 1998–2001; Founder, Centre for Social Cohesion, 2007; Chm., Henry Jackson Soc., 2011. Vis. Prof., Business Sch., Univ. (formerly Poly.) of N London, 1991–. Mem., Funding Agency for Schs, 1994–97. Governor: Dixons Bradford City Technol. Coll., 1988–2002; NIESR, 1995–2001. Trustee: Industry in Educn, 1993–2003; Economic Educn Trust, 1993–2002. Hon. FCGI 1991; Hon. Fellow, London Business Sch., 1995. Hon. DLitt: CNAA, 1991; Sheffield 2002; DUniv N London, 1994; Hon. DEcon Richmond, 1996; Hon. DSc Buckingham, 2002. *Recreations:* communal activities, opera, ballet. *Address:* House of Lords, SW1A 0PW. *T:* (020) 7629 1427.

KALMUS, Prof. George Ernest, CBE 2000; FRS 1988; Associate Director, 1986–94, Director, 1994–97, Particle Physics, Rutherford Appleton Laboratory; Visiting Professor, Physics and Astronomy Department, 1984–2000, Fellow, 1998, University College London; *b* 21 April 1935; *s* of late Hans Kalmus and Anna Kalmus; *m* 1957, Ann Christine Harland; three *d*. *Educ:* St Albans County Grammar Sch.; University Coll. London (BSc Hons, PhD). Res. Asst, Bubble Chamber Gp, UCL, 1959–62; Research Associate, Powell-Birge Bubble Chamber Gp, Lawrence Radiation Lab., Univ. of California, Berkeley, 1962–63 and 1964–67; Lectr, Physics Dept, UCL, 1963–64; Sen. Physicist, Lawrence Rad. Lab., 1967–71; Gp Leader, Bubble Chamber and Delphi Gps, Rutherford Appleton Lab., 1971–86. Mem., various Programme Cttees at CERN, 1974–; Mem., CERN Scientific Policy Cttee, 1990–96 (Chm., 1999–2001). *Publications:* numerous articles on experimental particle physics in Phys. Rev., Phys. Rev. Letters, Nuclear Phys., etc. *Recreations:* ski-ing, reading. *Address:* 16 South Avenue, Abingdon, Oxon OX14 1QH. *T:* (01235) 523340.

See also P. I. P. Kalmus.

KALMUS, Prof. Peter Ignaz Paul, OBE 2001; PhD; CPhys, FInstP; Professor of Physics, 1978–98, and Head of Physics Department, 1992–97, Queen Mary and Westfield (formerly Queen Mary) College, University of London, now Emeritus Professor, Queen Mary University of London (Hon. Fellow 2003); *b* 25 Jan. 1933; *s* of late Hans and Anna Kalmus; *m* 1957, Felicity (Trixie) Barker; one *s* one *d*. *Educ:* University Coll. London (BSc, PhD; Hon. Fellow 2001). CPhys, FInstP 1967. Res. Associate, University Coll. London, 1957–60; Lectr (part-time), Northern Poly. and Chelsea Poly., 1955–60; Physicist, Argonne Nat. Lab., USA, 1960–64; Queen Mary College, University of London: Lectr, 1964–66; Reader, 1966–78. Visiting Scientist: CERN, Geneva, 1961–62, 1970–71, 1981–82; Univ. of Chicago, 1965. Scientific Advr, UK Delegn to CERN, 1978–81; Member: SERC Nuclear Physics Bd, 1979–82, 1989–93; SERC Astronomy and Planetary Sci. Bd, 1990–93; PPARC Educn & Trng Cttee, 1994–98; PPARC Public Understanding of Sci. Panel, 1994–98. Member Council: Inst. of Physics, 1993–2000 (Vice-Pres., 1996–2000; Chairman: High Energy Physics Gp, 1989–93; London & SE Br., 2005–09; Hon. Fellow, 2010); Royal Instn, 1996–99 (MRI 1989–; Vice-Pres., 1997–99; Chm., Davy Faraday Lab. Res. Cttee, 1998–99); Member: Amer. Phys. Soc., 1963 (Fellow, 1995); European Phys. Soc., 1970 (Mem., High Energy Particle Physics Bd, 1994–98); BAAS, 1986 (Pres., Physics Sect., 1990–91; Hon. Fellow, 2002); International Union of Pure and Applied Physics: Vice Pres., 1999–2002; Mem., 1993–2002, Hon. Sec., 1996–99, Chm., 1999–2002, Commn on Particles and Fields. Active in physics outreach to schs and public. Rutherford Medal and Prize, 1988, Kelvin Medal and Prize, 2002, Branches Prize, 2010, Inst. Physics. Outreach Prize, Eur. Physical Soc., 2005. *Publications:* numerous papers in scientific jls. *Recreations:* photography, swimming, listening to jazz. *Address:* School of Physics and Astronomy, Queen Mary University of London, Mile End Road, E1 4NS. *T:* (020) 7882 6168. *E:* p.i.p.kalmus@qmul.ac.uk.

See also G. E. Kalmus.

KALVĪTIS, Aigars; Prime Minister of the Republic of Latvia, 2004–07; *b* Riga, 27 June 1966; *s* of Edmunds Kalvītis and Velta Kalvite; *m* Kristine Kalvite; three *s*. *Educ:* Riga Sec. Sch. No 41; Latvian Univ. of Agriculture (Bachelors degree 1992, Masters degree Agricl Economy 1995); University Coll. Cork (Masters course Food Ind. Bus. Admin, 1993). Milkman and tractor driver on farm, Sweden, 1990–91; Dir, Agro Biznesa Centrs, 1992–94; Chm. Bd, Zemgales Piens, jt stock co., 1994; Chm. Commn, Central Union of Latvian Dairying, 1994–98; in-service training, Holstein Assoc., Univ. of Wisconsin, 1995. Mem., 7th Saeima, 1998–99, Member: Budget and Finance (Taxation) Cttee; Public Expenditure and Audit Cttee; Minister: for Agriculture, 1999–2000; for Economics, 2000–02; Mem., 8th Saeima, 2002–04; Chm., parly gp of People's Party, 2002–04; Mem., 9th Saeima, 2007–09. Chairman: Supervisory Bd, Latvijas Balzams, 2009–; Bd, Dinamo Riga, 2010–.

KAMALL, Syed Salah, PhD; Member (C) London Region, European Parliament, since May 2005; *b* 15 Feb. 1967; *m* Sandira Beekoo; two *c*. *Educ:* Latymer Sch.; Univ. of Liverpool (BEng 1988); London Sch. of Econs and Pol Sci. (MSc 1989); City Univ. (PhD 2004). Business systems analyst, NatWest Bank Overseas Dept, 1989–91; Mgt Fellow, Sch. of Mgt, Univ. of Bath, 1994–96; Mgt Res. Fellow, Business Sch., Univ. of Leeds, 1996–97; Associate Dir and Consultant, Omega Partners, 1997–2001; Consultant, SSK Consulting, 2001–05. Contested (C) West Ham, 2001. *Publications:* Telecommunications Policy, 1996. *Address:* (office) 161 Brigstock Road, Croydon CR7 7JP; European Parliament, Rue Wiertz, 1047 Brussels, Belgium.

KAMEN, Ruth H(ope), MBE 2007; Director, and Sir Banister Fletcher Librarian, British Architectural Library, Royal Institute of British Architects, 1988–2004; *b* NYC, 19 April 1944; *d* of Markus M. Epstein and Hilda W. Epstein (*née* Winner); *m* 1964, Dr Robert I. Kamen (marr. diss. 1985). *Educ:* Univ. of Wisconsin (BA 1964); Smith Coll., Northampton, Mass (MAT 1965); Simmons Coll., Boston (MSLS 1967). FCLIP (FLA 1993; ALA 1986). Ref. Librarian, Fine Arts Dept, Res. Div., Boston Public Liby, 1965–70; Royal Institute of British Architects, British Architectural Library: Cataloguer, Handley-Read Collection, 1973; Loans, Serials and Ref. Librarian, 1974; Sen. Inf. Librarian, 1974–76; Hd of Liby Inf. Services, 1976–88. Sec., British Architectural Liby Trust, 1988–2001, 2003–04. Chm., ARLIS UK and Ireland, 1982–86 (Hon. Mem., ARLIS, 2005). FRSA 1989. Hon. FRIBA 2002. *Publications:* British and Irish Architectural History: a bibliography and guide to sources of information, 1981 (Besterman Award, LA); contrib. to books, jls and websites on architecture and librarianship. *Recreations:* art and architecture, painting, theatre, photography, shopping (especially antiques). *Address:* 15 Bingham Place, W1U 5AZ. *T:* (020) 7935 8975. *Club:* Architecture.

KAMIL, His Honour Geoffrey Harvey, CBE 2009; a Circuit Judge, 1993–2010; *b* 17 Aug. 1942; *s* of Peter and Sadie Kamil; *m* 1968, Andrea Pauline Kamil (*née* Ellis); two *d*. *Educ:* Leeds Grammar Sch.; Leeds University (LLB). Admitted as solicitor of the Supreme Court, 1968; Partner with J. Levi & Co., solicitors, Leeds, 1968–87; Asst Stipendiary Magistrate, 1986–87; Stipendiary Magistrate, W Midlands, 1987–90, W Yorks, 1990–93; Asst Crown Court Recorder, 1986–91; Recorder, 1991–93; Ethnic Minority Liaison Judge, Leeds and Bradford, 1998–2006; Liaison Judge, Wakefield and Pontefract, 1998–2007; Chm., Immigration Appeals Tribunal, 1998–2000; Lead Diversity and Community Relations Judge, 2006–10. Judicial Studies Board: Member: Magisterial Cttee, 1991–93; Equal Treatment Adv. Cttee, 2000–10; Family Cttee, 2004–10. Member: Centre for Criminal Justice Studies, Leeds Univ., 1992–; W Yorks Race Issues Adv. Gp, 1998–; Parole Bd, 2000– (Mem., Learning and Develt Cttee, 2012–); Race Issues Adv. Cttee, NACRO, 2003–10; Equality and Diversity Cttee, Law Soc., 2009–10. Leeds Law Society: Mem. Cttee, 1983–87; Chm., Courts Cttee, 1983–87; Mem., Duty Solicitor Cttee, 1986–87; Mem., Leeds Bar/Law Soc. Liaison Cttee, 1983–87. Sec., Kirkstall Lodge Hostel for Ex-Offenders, 1976–87. *Recreations:* golf, swimming, pumping iron, the Dales, classic cars, TV soap addict. *Address:* 52 High Ash Avenue, Alwoodley, Leeds, W Yorks LS17 8RG. *Club:* Moor Allerton Golf (Leeds) (Captain, 2015–).

KAMILL, Louise Naima Rachelle, (Mrs Max Lightwood); Her Honour Judge Kamill; a Circuit Judge, since 2008; *b* London, 9 March 1951; *d* of Dr Mostapha Kamill, GM and Joan Mary Kamill (*née* Hirst); *m* 1978, Max Lightwood; two *d*. *Educ:* St Paul's Girls' Sch.; University Coll. London (LLB Hons). Called to the Bar, Inner Temple, 1974; Recorder, 1986–2008. Mem., Parole Bd, 2010–. *Recreations:* chamber music, birdwatching, painting, golf, tennis, cycling. *Address:* Snaresbrook Crown Court, 75 Hollybush Hill, E11 1QW. *Clubs:* Sunningdale Golf, Campden Hill Lawn Tennis.

KAMIT, Sir (Leonard) Wilson (Fufus), Kt 2009; CBE 2002; Governor and Chairman of Board, Bank of Papua New Guinea, 1999–2009; Registrar, Savings and Loan Societies, Papua New Guinea, 1999–2009; Alternate Executive Director, Asian Development Bank, since 2010; Director, Kamchild Ltd; *b* Tufi, PNG, 19 Nov. 1953; *s* of John Caswell Kamit and Naomi Taroben Kamit; *m* 1976, Winifred Pakalmat Tare; one *s* one *d*. *Educ:* Univ. of Papua New Guinea (BEc 1975); Univ. of New England (Dip. Corp. Dirs). Bank of Papua New Guinea: sponsored scholarship student, 1972–75; res. officer, 1975–80; various mgt roles, 1980–90; Dep. Gov., 1991–99. Trustee: Anglican Ch of PNG; Sir Anthony Siaguru Foundn. *Recreations:* reading, watching sport, crossword puzzles, fishing. *Address:* Kamchild Ltd, PO Box 1569, Port Moresby, National Capital District, Papua New Guinea. *Club:* Royal Papua Yacht.

KAMPFNER, John Paul; Chief Executive, Creative Industries Federation, since 2014; *b* 27 Dec. 1962; *s* of Dr Fred Kampfner and Betty Kampfner (*née* Andrews); *m* 1992, Lucy Ash; two *d*. *Educ:* Westminster Sch.; Queen's Coll., Oxford (BA Hons Modern Hist. and Russian). Reuters, 1984–89 (Correspondent, Moscow, 1985–86, Bonn, 1987–89); Daily Telegraph: Berlin and Eastern Europe corresp., 1989–91; Moscow corresp., 1991–94; Chief Political Corresp., Financial Times, 1995–98; Political Corresp., Today prog., BBC Radio, 1998–2000; documentary maker, BBC, 2000–02; Political Ed., 2002–05, Ed., 2005–08, New Statesman; Chief Exec., Index on Censorship, 2008–12 (Trustee, 2012–13); Ext. Advr on freedom of expression and culture for EMEA, Google, 2012–14. Columnist: Daily Telegraph, 2007–08; Independent, 2012–13. Chairman: Turner Contemporary, 2008–; Clore Social Leadership Prog., 2014–. Mem. Council, KCL, 2012–15. FRSA 2003. Journalist of Year, For. Press Assoc., 2002; Ed. of Year, Current Affairs, BSME, 2006. *Publications:* Inside Yeltsin's Russia, 1994; Robin Cook, 1998; Blair's Wars, 2003; Freedom for Sale, 2009; The Rich: from slaves to super-yachts, a 2000-year history, 2014. *Recreations:* tennis, theatre, travel. *E:* john@jkampfner.net. *W:* www.jkampfner.net.

KAN, Prof. Yuet Wai, FRCP 1983; FRS 1981; Louis K. Diamond Professor of Hematology, University of California, San Francisco, since 1984; *b* 11 June 1936; *s* of Kan Tong Po and Kan Li Lai Wan; *m* 1964, Alvera L. Limauro; two *d*. *Educ:* Univ. of Hong Kong (MB, BS, DSc). Research Associate, Children's Hosp. Medical Center, Dept of Pediatrics, Harvard Medical Sch., Boston, Mass; Asst Prof. of Pediatrics, Harvard Medical Sch., 1970–72; Associate Prof. of Medicine, Depts of Medicine and Laboratory Medicine, Univ. of California, San Francisco, 1972–77; Chief, Hematology Service, San Francisco General Hospital, 1972–79; Investigator, Howard Hughes Med. Inst. Lab., 1976–2003; Prof. of Lab. Medicine and Medicine, 1977–, Hd of Div. of Molecular Medicine and Diagnostics, Dept of Lab. Medicine, 1989–2003, Univ. of California. Dir, Molecular Biology Inst., Univ. of Hong Kong, 1990–94 (Hon. Dir, 1988–90). Trustee, Croucher Foundn, 1992–2011 (Chm., 1997–2011). Member: Nat. Acad. of Scis, USA, 1986; Academia Sinica, Taiwan, 1988; Foreign Mem., Chinese Acad. of Scis, 1996. Hon. MD Univ. of Cagliari, Sardinia, 1981; Hon. DSc: Chinese Univ. of Hong Kong, 1981; Univ. of Hong Kong, 1987; Open Univ. of Hong Kong, 1998. *Publications:* contribs to: Nature, Genetics, Proc. of Nat. Academy of Sciences, Jl of Clinical Investigation, Blood, British Jl of Haematology, and others. *Address:* HSW 901, University of California, 513 Parnassus Avenue, San Francisco, CA 94143–0793, USA. *T:* (415) 4765841, *Fax:* (415) 4762956.

KANDEL, Prof. Eric Richard, MD; University Professor, since 1983, Fred Kavli Professor, Director, Kavli Institute for Brain Science, since 2004, and Co-Director, Mortimer B. Zuckerman Mind Brain Behavior Institute, Columbia University; Senior Investigator, Howard Hughes Medical Institute, since 1984; *b* 7 Nov. 1929; *s* of Herman and Charlotte Kandel; *m* 1956, Denise Bystryn; one *s* one *d*. *Educ:* Harvard Coll. (BA 1952); New York Univ. Sch. of Medicine (MD 1956). Intern, Montefiore Hosp., NY, 1956–57; Associate in Res., Lab. of Neurophysiol., Nat. Inst. of Mental Health, Bethesda, 1957–60; Resident in Psychiatry, 1960–64, Staff Psychiatrist, 1964–65, Massachusetts Mental Health Center, Harvard Med. Sch., Boston (Milton Res. Fellow, 1961–62); Instructor, Dept of Psychiatry, Harvard Med. Sch., 1963–65; Associate Prof., then Prof., Depts of Physiol. and Psychiatry, NY Univ. Sch. of Medicine, 1965–74; Chief, Dept of Neurobiol. and Behavior, Public Health Res. Inst. of City of NY, 1968–74; College of Physicians and Surgeons, Columbia University: Prof., Depts of Physiol. and Psychiatry, 1974–, and Dept of Biochem. and Molecular Biophysics, 1992–; Dir, Center for Neurobiol. and Behavior, 1974–83. Associate Editor: Annual Rev. of Neurosci., 1977–82; Jl Neurophysiol., 1977–80; Jl Neurosci., 1981–83; Learning and Memory, 1993–; Reviews Ed., Neuron, 1988–; Mem., Editl Bd, Proc. NAS, 1991–97. Pres., Soc. for Neurosci., 1980–81. Member: Bd of Trustees, Cold Spring Harbor Labs, 1985–90; Bd of Dirs, McKnight Foundn, 1986–98; Bd of Scientific Advrs, Merck Foundn, 1991–94. Mem., numerous professional socs. For. Mem., Royal Soc., 2013. Holds numerous hon. degrees, including: Hon. DSc: Edinburgh, 1999; (Medicine)

UCL, 2001. Numerous prizes and awards, including: Internat. Award for Outstanding Achievement in Med. Sci., Gairdner Foundn, Canada, 1987; Nat. Medal of Sci., NAS, 1988; NY Acad. of Medicine Award, 1996; Gerard Prize, Soc. of Neurosci., 1997; Wolf Prize in Biol. and Medicine, Israel, 1999; (jtly) Nobel Prize for Physiol. or Medicine, 2000. *Publications:* Cellular Basis of Behavior: an introduction to behavioral neurobiology, 1976; (ed) Handbook of Physiology: The Nervous System, Vol. 1, Cellular Biology of Neurons, 1977; A Cell-Biological Approach to Learning, 1978; The Behavioral Biology of Aplysia: a contribution to the comparative study of opisthobranch molluscs, 1979; (ed jtly) Principles of Neural Science, 1981, 4th edn 2000; (ed jtly) Molecular Aspects of Neurobiology, 1986; (ed) Molecular Neurobiology in Neurology and Psychiatry, 1987; (ed jtly) Essentials of Neural Science and Behavior, 1995; (with L. Squire) From Mind to Molecules, 1999; In Search of Memory, 2006; The Age of Insight; the quest to understand the unconscious in art, mind and brain, from Vienna 1900 to the present, 2012; contrib. numerous papers to learned jls incl. Jl Neurophysiol., Amer. Jl Physiol., Jl Physiol., Nature, Science, Brain Res., Scientific American. *Recreations:* tennis, opera. *Address:* Kavli Institute for Brain Science, New York State Psychiatric Institute, 1051 Riverside Drive, New York, NY 10032, USA. *T:* (212) 3054143, *Fax:* (212) 5435474. *E:* erk5@Columbia.edu.

KANE, Adam Vincent; QC 2015; *b* Cardiff, 19 June 1969; *s* of Vincent Kane, OBE and Mary Kane; *m* 2000, Emma Nott; one *s* two *d. Educ:* De La Salle Sch.; Radyr Sch.; University Coll., Oxford (BA); Wolverhampton Univ. (CPE). Called to the Bar, Gray's Inn, 1993; in practice as barrister, specialising in civil and criminal fraud, and commercial crime, 1993–. *Recreations:* extreme gardening, vintage champagne. *Address:* Voronzoff Gate, Savernake Forest, Marlborough, Wilts SN8 3HT. *T:* (020) 7936 6300. *E:* avkane@hotmail.com.

KANE, Archie Gerard, CA; Governor, Bank of Ireland, since 2012; *b* 16 June 1952; *s* of Archie and Rose Kane; *m* 1986, Diana Muirhead; two *d. Educ:* Glasgow Univ. (BAcc); City Univ. (MBA); Harvard Business Sch. (AMP). CA 1977. FCIBS 2005. Student CA, Mann Judd, 1974–77; Asst Manager, Price Waterhouse, 1978–80; General Telephone & Electronics Corporation, 1980–85: Sen. Mgt Auditor, Sylvania, 1980–82; Asst Financial Controller, 1982–83, Finance Dir, 1983–85, Directories Corp.; Finance Dir, British Telecom Yellow Pages Sales Ltd, 1986; Gp Finance Controller, TSB Commercial Hldgs Ltd, 1986–89; TSB Bank plc: Financial Controller, then Dir, Financial Control, Retail Banking Div., 1989–91; Dir, Financial Control, 1991–92, Ops Dir, 1992–94, Retail Banking and Insce; Gp Strategic Develt Dir, 1994–96; Lloyds TSB Group, later Lloyds Banking Group plc: Project Dir, Post-Merger Integration, then Retail Financial Services Dir, 1996; Dir, Gp IT and Ops, 1997–99; Dir, 2000–11; Gp Exec. Dir, IT and Ops, 2000–03; Gp Exec. Dir, Insurance and Investments, 2003–11; Chief. Exec., Scottish Widows plc, 2003–11; Gp Exec. Dir, Insce and Scotland, 2009–11; Dir of various cos in the Lloyds Banking (formerly Lloyds TSB) and Scottish Widows Gp, 2000–11. Chm., APACS (Admin) Ltd, 2001–03; Dir, Hill Samuel Asset Mgt Internat. Ltd, 2003–06. Chm., ABI, 2007–10 (Mem. Bd, 2004); Member: Takeover Panel, 2007; Retail Financial Services Gp, 2007–09; Insce Industry Working Gp, 2008–09; Financial Services Adv. Bd, 2009; TheCityUK, 2010. FCIBS 2005. *Recreations:* golf, tennis, ski-ing.

KANE, Christopher John; Creative Director, Christopher Kane, since 2006; *b* Bellshill, N Lanarkshire, 26 July 1982; *s* of Thomas Kane and Christine Kane. *Educ:* Central Saint Martin's Coll. of Art and Design (BA Womenswear; MA Womenswear). Launched Christopher Kane label, 2006; womenswear designer for Versus, Versace, 2009. Lancôme Colour Award, 2005; Young Designer of the Yr, Scottish Fashion Awards, 2006; New Generation Designer, 2007, British Collection of the Yr, 2009, Designer of the Year, 2013, British Fashion Awards; British Designer of the Yr, Elle Style Awards, 2011. *Recreations:* drawing, going to exhibitions, music concerts, theatre, travel, collecting books. *Address:* The Communications Store, 2 Kensington Square, W8 5EP. *T:* (020) 7938 1010.

KANE, Michael Joseph Patrick; MP (Lab) Wythenshawe and Sale East, since Feb. 2014; *b* Wythenshawe, 9 Jan. 1969; *s* of Joseph Kane and Kathleen Kane (*née* McGirl); *m* 1996, Sandra Bracegirdle. *Educ:* St Paul's RC High Sch.; Manchester Metropolitan Univ. (BA Social Scis 1997; PGCE 1999). Teacher, Springfield Primary Sch., 2000–08; Parliamentary Assistant: to Rt Hon. James Purnell, MP, 2008–10; to Jonathan Reynolds, MP, 2010–11; Sen. Exec. Asst, Tameside Council, 2011–14. Mem. (Lab) Manchester CC, 1991–2008. Nat. Chair, 2010–13, Actg Chief Exec., 2014, Movement for Change. *Recreations:* playing flute and bagpipes, Manchester City FC. *Address:* House of Commons, SW1A 0AA. *T:* (constituency office) (0161) 499 7900. *E:* mike.kane.mp@parliament.uk. *Club:* Stretford Wheelers.

KANE, Peter Ronald, PhD; Chamberlain, City of London Corporation, since 2014; *b* 24 Nov. 1956; *s* of Ronald Kane and Katherine Kane; *m* 1989, Jan Evans; two *d. Educ:* St Edmund Hall, Oxford (BA 1st Cl. Hons PPE); London Sch. of Econs (MSc Econs 1979; PhD Econs 1982). Economist, TUC, 1981–88; Chief Econ. Advr, London Bor. of Hackney, 1988–92; Principal, 1992–99, Team Leader, 1999–2001, HM Treasury; Director: Office of Public Service Reform, Cabinet Office, 2002–05; Finance and Performance, Home Office, 2006–14. *Recreations:* travelling the globe, ski-ing, tennis, cinema, reading, current affairs. *Address:* City of London Corporation, Guildhall, PO Box 270, EC2P 2EJ. *E:* peter.kane@cityoflondon.gov.uk.

KANE, Rosie; Member (Scot Socialist) Glasgow, Scottish Parliament, 2003–07. Scot Socialist spokesman for envmt and transport, Scottish Parlt, 2003–07. Contested: (Scot Socialist Alliance) Glasgow, Rutherglen, 1997; (Scot Socialist) Glasgow Shettleston, Scottish Parlt, 1999.

KANI, Wasfi, OBE 2001; Founder and Chief Executive Officer: Grange Park Opera, since 1998; Pimlico Opera, since 1987; *b* Cable Street, London, 7 March 1956; *d* of Khawaja Mohammed Kani and Jaria Kani. *Educ:* Burlington Grammar Sch., Shepherds Bush; St Hilda's Coll., Oxford (BA Hons). Computer programmer, then systems analyst, specialising in financial systems, 1980–90; initiated prog. of work in prisons, 1991; CEO, Garsington Opera, 1992–97. Trustee: Royal Court Th., 2008–14; Mayor's Fund for London, 2008–10; British Mus., 2013–. *Recreations:* stopping time fly, collecting rainwater. *Address:* Grange Park Opera, 24 Broad Street, Alresford SO24 9AQ. *E:* wasfikani@gmail.com.

KAO, Sir Charles (Kuen), KBE 2010 (CBE 1993); PhD; FRS 1997; FREng, FIET, FIEEE; Chairman and Chief Executive Officer, ITx (formerly Transtech) Services Ltd, 2000–09; Vice Chancellor, Chinese University of Hong Kong, 1987–96, Hon. Professor, since 1996; *b* Shanghai, 4 Nov. 1933; holds dual US/UK nationality; *s* of Chun-Hsian Kao and late Tsiung-Fong Ming; *m* 1959, May-Wan Wong; one *s* one *d. Educ:* Woolwich Poly. (BSc London); UCL (PhD 1965). FIEEE 1978; FIET (FIEE 1979); FREng (FEng 1989). Engr, Standard Telephone & Cables Ltd, 1957–60; Res. Scientist, then Res. Manager, Standard Telecom Labs Ltd, ITT Central Eur. Lab., 1960–70; Hd, Electronics Dept, Chinese Univ. of Hong Kong, 1970–74; Chief Scientist, 1974–81, Vice-Pres. and Dir of Engrg, 1982–83, Electro-Optical Products Div., ITT, Va; Exec. Scientist and Corporate Dir of Res., ITT Advanced Tech. Centre, Conn, 1983–87. Fellow: Royal Swedish Acad. of Engrg Sci., 1989; US Nat. Acad. of Engrg, 1990; Eur. Acad. Scis and Art; Academia Sinica, Taiwan, 1994; Chinese Acad. of Sci., 1996. Hon. DSc: Chinese Univ. of Hong Kong, 1985; Sussex, 1990; Durham, 1994; Hull, 1998; Yale, 1999; Dr *hc* Soka, 1991; Hon. DEng Glasgow, 1992; Padova, 1996. Numerous awards and prizes including: Alexander Graham Bell Medal, IEEE, 1985; Marconi Internat. Fellowship, 1985; Faraday Medal, IEE, 1989; Japan Prize, 1996; Prince Philip Medal, Royal Acad. of Engrg, 1996; Charles Stark Draper Prize, Nat. Acad. of Engrg, USA, 1999; (jtly) Nobel Prize in Physics, 2009. *Publications:* Optical Fiber Technology II, 1981; Optical Fiber Systems: technology, design and applications, 1982; Optical Fiber, 1988; A Choice Fulfilled: the business of high technology, 1991. *Recreations:* tennis, hiking, pottery-making. *Address:* c/o S. K. Yee Medical Foundation, Unit 1708 Office Tower, Convention Plaza, 1 Harbour Road, Wanchai, HKSAR. *E:* ckao@ie.cuhk.edu.hk.

KAPLAN, Neil Trevor, CBE 2001; QC (Hong Kong) 1982; arbitrator, mediator; *b* 1 Sept. 1942; *s* of Leslie Henry Kaplan and Sybil Sylvia Kaplan (*née* Gasson); *m* 1st, 1971, Barbara Jane Spector (marr. diss. 1997); one *s* one *d*; 2nd, 1998, Paula White (marr. diss. 2009); 3rd, 2013, Sue Lesser. *Educ:* St Paul's Sch.; King's College London (LLB). FCIArb. Called to the Bar, Inner Temple, 1965, Bencher 1991; practised London, 1965–80; Dep. Principal Crown Counsel, Hong Kong, 1980, Principal Crown Counsel, 1982; private practice, Hong Kong Bar, 1984–90; Solicitor-barrister, Victoria, NSW, 1983; NY Bar, 1986; High Court Judge, Hong Kong, 1990–94; Judge in charge of Construction and Arbitration List, 1990–94. Vis. Prof., City Univ. of Hong Kong, 1995–97 (Hon. Prof., 2001–). Pres., CIArb, 1999–2000 (Chm., Hong Kong Branch, 1984–87 and 1989–90); Chairman: Hong Kong Internat. Arbitration Centre, 1991–2004; Disputes Rev. Bd, new Hong Kong airport, 1995–99; Post-Release Supervision Bd, 1996–2006; WTO Rev. Body, Hong Kong, 2000–04; Hong Kong Telecommunications Appeal Tribunal, 2007–13 (Dep. Chm., 2001–07); Deputy Chairman: Justice, Hong Kong, 1988–90; Mem., Judicial Studies Bd, 1994–. Member: Council, ICCA, 1995–; Court of Arbitration, ICC, 2012–. Liveryman, Arbitrators' Co., 1982–. JP Hong Kong, 1984. Silver Bauhinia Star (HKSAR), 2007. *Publications:* (jtly) Hong Kong Arbitration—Cases and Materials, 1991; (jtly) Arbitration in Hong Kong and China, 1994; (jtly) Model Law Decisions, 2002; articles on arbitration. *Recreations:* golf, travel, food and wine, films, theatre, walking. *Address:* 13th Floor, Gloucester Tower, The Landmark, Hong Kong. *T:* 34431050. *E:* neilkaplan@btconnect.com. *Clubs:* Athenæum, Oriental, Old Pauline; Hong Kong, Hong Kong Cricket.

KAPOOR, Sir Anish, Kt 2013; CBE 2003; Padma Bhushan 2012; RA 1999; artist and sculptor; *b* Bombay, 12 March 1954; *s* of Rear Adm. D. C. Kapoor and Mrs H. Kapoor; *m* 1995, Susanne Spicale; one *s* one *d. Educ:* Hornsey Coll. of Art; Chelsea Sch. of Art. Lectr, Wolverhampton Polytechnic, 1979–83. Artist in Residence, Walker Art Gall., Liverpool, 1982–83. Mem., Arts Council England (formerly Arts Council of England), 1998–; Trustee, Tate Britain, 2006–09. One-man exhibitions include: Lisson Gall., London, 1982, 1984, 1985, 1988, 1989–90, 1993, 1998, 2000, 2003, 2006; Walker Art Gall., Liverpool, 1982, 1983; Gladstone Gall., NY, 1984, 1986, 1989, 1990, 1998, 2001, 2004, 2007; Tate Gall., London, 1990–91, Tate Modern, 2002; San Diego Mus. Contemporary Art, 1992; Tel Aviv Mus. of Art, 1993; Nat. Gall. of Canada, Ottawa, 1993; Rockefeller Center, NY, 2006; RA, 2009; Manchester Art Gall., 2011; Pinchuk Art Centre, Kiev, 2012; retrospective exhibitions: Hayward Gall., 1998; Lisson Gall., 2015; and others in Europe, USA, Australia, Japan and India; contrib. numerous group exhibns in Britain, Europe, USA, Canada, Australia and Japan, incl. Tate Gall., London, 1983, 1991, 1994; Art Inst., Chicago, 1990; Expo '92, Seville, 1992; public works include: Sky Mirror, Nottingham, 2001; Sky Mirror, Rockefeller Center, NY, 2006; Cloud Gate, Millennium Park, Chicago, 2006; Turning the World Upside Down, Israel Mus., Jerusalem, 2010; (with C. Balmond and A. Agu) Orbit, Olympic Tower, London, 2012. Hon. Fellow, Univ. of Wolverhampton, 1999; Hon. FRIBA 2001. Hon. Dr: London Inst., 1997; Leeds, 1997. Premio Duemila, Venice Biennale, 1990; Turner Prize, 1991; Praemium Imperiale, 2011. *Address:* c/o Lisson Gallery, 52–54 Bell Street, NW1 5BU.

KAPPLER, David John; Deputy Chairman, Shire plc, since 2008 (non-executive director, since 2004); *b* Winchester, 24 March 1947; *s* of Alec and Hilary Kappler; *m* 1970, Maxine Lea; three *d. Educ:* Lincoln Sch. FCMA 1975. Finance Director: Jeyes Gp, 1977–85; Trebor Gp, 1985–89; Cadbury Ltd, 1989–91; Cadbury Confectionery, 1991–93; Cadbury Schweppes plc: Corporate Finance Dir, 1993–94; Chief Financial Officer, 1995–2004. Chm., Premier Foods plc, 2004–10; non-executive Director: Camelot plc, 1995–2001; HMV plc, 2001–06; Intercontinental Hotels plc, 2004–14; Flybe plc. *Recreations:* playing golf, watching other sports, wine. *Address:* Willow House, 147 High Street, Old Amersham, Bucks HP7 0EB. *T:* 07785 714468, (office) (01727) 815897, *Fax:* (01727) 815979. *E:* djkappler@me.com. *Clubs:* Royal Automobile, MCC (Associate); Harewood Downs Golf.

KARABITS, Kirill; Principal Conductor, Bournemouth Symphony Orchestra, since 2009; Artistic Director, I, Culture Orchestra, since 2014; *b* Kiev, Ukraine, 26 Dec. 1976; *s* of Ivan Karabits and Marianna Kopytsa; partner, Coline Vandenberghe; one *s* one *d. Educ:* Lysenko Music Sch., Kiev; Tchaikovsky Nat. Acad. of Music, Kiev; Hochschule für Musik, Vienna. Asst Conductor, Budapest Fest. Orch., 1996–99; Associate Conductor, Orchestre Philharmonique de Radio France, 2002–05; Principal Guest Conductor, Orchestre Philharmonique de Strasbourg, 2005–07. *Address:* c/o HarrisonParrott Ltd, 5–6 Albion Court, Albion Place, W6 0QT. *T:* (020) 7229 9166. *E:* info@harrisonparrott.co.uk.

KARAMANLIS, Konstantinos A., (Kostas); MP (NDP) Thessaloniki A, Greece, since 1989; Prime Minister of Greece, 2004–09; President, New Democracy Party, 1997–2009; *b* 14 Sept. 1956; *s* of Alexandros and Ageliki Karamanlis; *m* 1998, Natasa Pazaiti; one *s* one *d* (twins). *Educ:* Sch. of Law, Univ. of Athens; Fletcher Sch. of Law and Diplomacy, Tufts Univ., Boston, USA. In practice as lawyer, 1984–89. Minister of Culture, 2004–06. Vice-President: EPP, 1999–2009 (Hd, Western Balkan Democracy Initiative, 2001–03; Chm., SE European Forum, 2003–05); Internat. Democrat Union, 2002; Co-Chm., Party Leaders Conf., European Democrat Union, 2003. *Publications:* Eleftherios Venizelos and Greek Foreign Relations, 1986; (ed) Spirit and Era of Gorbachev, 1987. *Address:* Hellenic Parliament, Vas. Sophias 2, 100 21 Athens, Greece.

KARAS, Jonathan Marcus; QC 2006; *b* 18 Sept. 1961; *s* of Arie Karas and Enid Novello Karas (*née* Owens); *m* 1989, Tracey Ann Elliott (marr. diss. 2012); three *d. Educ:* Brentwood Sch.; Trinity Coll., Oxford (Ford Student; MA Hons Lit.Hum.); City Univ. (Dip. Law). Called to the Bar, Middle Temple, 1986; Supplementary Panel, 1995–99, B Panel, 1999–2000, A Panel, 2000–06, of Jun. Counsel to the Crown. Subject Ed., Hill & Redman's Law of Landlord and Tenant, 1987–. *Publications:* (jtly) Elvin & Karas's Unlawful Interference with Land, 1995, 2nd edn 2002; (jtly) Commonhold and Leasehold Reform Act 2002, 2002; (jtly) Swinesend: Britain's greatest public school, 2006; Halsbury's Laws of England, 4th edn: (jtly) Compulsory Purchase, 1996 (reissue); Distress, 2000 (reissue, consultant ed.), 2007 (reissue); Forestry, 2007 (reissue, consultant ed.); (jtly and consultant ed.) Perpetuities, 2013. *Recreations:* writing, embarrassing my daughters. *Address:* Falcon Chambers, Falcon Court, EC4Y 1AA. *T:* (020) 7353 2484, *Fax:* (020) 7353 1261. *Club:* Travellers.

KARASIN, Grigory Borisovich; State Secretary and Deputy Minister of Foreign Affairs, Russian Federation, since 2005; *b* 23 Aug. 1949; *m* 1971, Olga V. Karasina; two *d. Educ:* Coll. of Oriental Langs, Moscow State Univ. Joined USSR Diplomatic Service, 1972: served: Senegal, 1972–76; Australia, 1979–85; UK, 1988–92; Dir, Dept of Africa, 1992–93, Dept of Inf. and Press, 1993–96, Min. of Foreign Affairs; Dep. Minister of Foreign Affairs, Russian Fedn, 1996–2000; Ambassador to UK, 2000–05.

KARET, Ian Albert Nathan; Partner, Linklaters LLP, since 1997; *b* London, 3 April 1963; *s* of Jerome Karet and Patricia Karet; *m* 1993, Sara Hoffbrand; three *d. Educ:* University College Sch., Hampstead; Worcester Coll., Oxford (MA Chem.). Linklaters LLP, London: articled clerk, 1987–89; admitted solicitor, 1990; Asst Solicitor, 1990–97. Trustee: Leo Baeck Coll., 2009–; Royal Botanic Gardens, Kew, 2014–. *Publications:* (contrib.) The Modern Law of Patents, 2010. *Recreations:* singing, cooking. *Address:* Linklaters LLP, One Silk Street, EC2Y 8HQ. *T:* (020) 7456 5800. *E:* ian.karet@linklaters.com.

KARIA, Chirag Vrajlal; QC 2012; *b* Nakuru, Kenya, 26 May 1965; *s* of Vrajlal Vallabhdas Karia and Vimlaben Vrajlal Karia; *m* 1995, Jagruty Topan; twin *s* one *d.* *Educ:* Sidney Sussex Coll., Cambridge (BA 1st Cl. Hons Law 1987; Slaughter & May Prize); Boalt Hall Sch. of Law, Univ. of Calif, Berkeley (LLM 1990). Denning Schol., Lincoln's Inn, 1987; Council of Legal Educn Studentship, 1987; Harkness Fellow, Commonwealth Fund of NY, 1989–90. Called to the Bar, Lincoln's Inn, 1988; called to State Bar of Calif as Attorney at Law, 1991; in practice as Attorney in commercial litigation and corporate law, Calif, 1991–2000; in practice as barrister, specialising in commercial law, London, 2000–. Examr of the Court, 2004–. *Publications:* (Jt Gen. Ed.) Butterworths Commercial Court and Arbitration Pleadings, 2005. *Recreations:* reading, music, ski-ing, theatre. *Address:* Quadrant Chambers, Quadrant House, 10 Fleet Street, EC4Y 1AU. *T:* (020) 7583 4444, *Fax:* (020) 7583 4455. *E:* chirag.karia@quadrantchambers.com.

KARIM, Sajjad Haider; Member for North West England, European Parliament, since 2004 (Lib Dem, 2004–07; C, since 2007); Partner, Marsdens Solicitors, since 2001; *b* 11 July 1970; *s* of Fazal Karim and Shamshad Karim; *m* 1997, Zahida Chaudhary; one *s* one *d.* *Educ:* London Guildhall Univ. (LLB Hons Business Law); Coll. of Law, Chester. Admitted solicitor, 1997. Mem. (Lib Dem) Pendle BC, 1994–2002. *Address:* 14b Wynford Square, West Ashton Street, Salford M50 2SN. *E:* info@sajjadkarim.eu.

KARK, Thomas Victor William; QC 2010; a Recorder, since 2000; *b* London, 12 Dec. 1960; *s* of Leslie and Evelyn Kark; *m* 1989, Judith Cornes; one *s* one *d.* *Educ:* Eton Coll.; Univ. of Buckingham (LLB). Called to the Bar, Inner Temple, 1982; in practice as barrister specialising in crime, inquiries, inquests and professional regulation; Standing Counsel to HM Customs and Excise, 2002–10; Asst Recorder, 1999–2000. Lead Counsel, Mid Staffs NHS Foundn Trust Public Inquiry, 2010–13. *Recreations:* martial arts, cooking. *Address:* QEB Hollis Whiteman Chambers, 1–2 Laurence Pountney Hill, EC4R 0EU. *Club:* 606 Jazz.

KARMAN, Tawakkol, journalist and human rights activist; *b* Taiz, Yemen, 7 Feb. 1979; *m* Mohamed al-Nahmi; three *c.* *Educ:* Univ. of Sci. and Technol., Sana'a; Univ. of Sana'a. Co-founder, Women Journalists Without Chains, 2005; organized weekly protests in Sana'a against government repression, corruption, and social and legal injustice, 2007–11. Sen. Mem., Al-Islah party. (Jtly) Nobel Peace Prize, 2011. *Address:* Women Journalists Without Chains, 12702 Daeery Street, Sana'a, Yemen.

KARMILOFF-SMITH, Prof. Annette Dionne, CBE 2004; FBA 1993; FMedSci; Professorial Research Fellow, Centre for Brain and Cognitive Development, Department of Psychological Sciences, Birkbeck, University of London, since 2006; *b* 18 July 1938; *d* of late Jack Smith and Doris Ellen Ruth Smith (*née* Findlay); *m* 1st, 1966, Igor Alexander Karmiloff (marr. diss. 1991); two *d*; 2nd, 2001, Prof. Mark Henry Johnson, *qv.* *Educ:* Edmonton County GS; Inst Français de Londres; Holborn Coll. of Law and Langs (Dip. Internat. Conf. Interpreting); Geneva Univ. (Dr of exptl and genetic psychol.). Internat. Conf. Interpreter, UN, 1966–70; Res. Consultant, UNWRA-UNESCO Inst. of Educn, Beirut, 1970–72; Res. Collaborator, Internat. Centre for Genetic Epistemiol., Geneva, 1972–76; Vis. Res. Associate, Max Planck Inst. for Psycholinguistics, Nijmegen, 1978–83; Sen. Res. Scientist (with Special Appt status), MRC Cognitive Development Unit, 1982–98; Hd, Neurocognitive Develt Unit, UCL Inst. Child Health, 1998–2006. Visiting Professor: Univs of Sussex, Brussels, Munich, Chicago, Tel-Aviv and Barcelona, 1979–88; of Psychol., UCL, 1982–2006. Sloan Fellow: Yale Univ., 1978; Univ. of Berkeley, 1981; Dist. Fellow, Cognitive Sci. Soc., 2008. MAE 1991; FMedSci 1999. FRSA 1997. Hon. FBPsS 2012. Dr *hc* Louvain, 2002; Amsterdam, 2010. BPsS Book Award, 1995; ESF Latsis Prize for Cognitive Science, 2002; Lifetime Achievement Award, BPsS, 2009; Mattei Internat. Prize for Psychol Scis, Internat. Union Psychol Sci., 2012. *Publications:* A Functional Approach to Child Language, 1979, 2nd edn 1981; (jtly) Child Language Research in ESF Countries, 1981; Beyond Modularity: a developmental perspective on cognitive science, 1992; Baby It's You, 1994; (jtly) Rethinking Innateness: connectionism in a developmental framework, 1996; (jtly) Everything Your Baby Would Ask, 1999; (jtly) Pathways to Language: from foetus to adolescent, 2001; (jtly) Getting to Know your Baby, 2010; (jtly) Neurodevelopmental Disorders Across the Lifespan, 2012; many chapters, and articles in learned jls. *Recreations:* writing/reading poetry, working out, going on multiple diets, writing a satire (Powerful Minds in Flabby Bodies). *Address:* River Quin Barn, Gravelly Lane, Braughing, Ware, Herts SG11 2RD. *T:* (01920) 821414, (work) (020) 7079 0767.

KARMY-JONES, Riel Meredith; QC 2015; *b* USA, 16 Dec. 1965; *d* of Prof. William John Jones and Leila Karmy; *m* 1990, Mark Major; one *s* one *d.* *Educ:* Tempo Sch., Edmonton; Univ. of Alberta, Edmonton (BA Drama and Eng. 1986); Drama Studio, London (Dip. Theatre Directing 1987); University Coll. London (LLB Hons 1994). Called to the Bar, Lincoln's Inn, 1995; in practice as a criminal barrister. Trustee, Pan Intercultural Arts, 2015–; Patron, GR8 AS U R, 2014–. *Publications:* (contrib.) Rock and Ward on Sexual Offences, 5th edn, 2015. *Recreations:* theatre, cinema, walking, gardening, family, reading, art. *Address:* c/o Red Lion Chambers, 18 Red Lion Court, EC4A 3EB. *T:* (020) 7520 6000. *E:* clerks@18rlc.co.uk.

KARP, Rachel Vivienne; Her Honour Judge Karp; a Circuit Judge, since 2013; *b* Liverpool, 4 June 1961; *d* of David Karp and Shirley Karp; *m* Stephen Adler; one *s* two *d.* *Educ:* King David High Sch., Liverpool; Univ. of Bristol. Partner, Daniel and Harris Solicitors, 1986–2004; a District Judge, 2004–13. *Address:* Willesden County Court, 9 Acton Lane, NW10 8SB. *T:* (020) 8963 8200.

KARPINSKI, Marek Romuald K.; *see* Korab-Karpinski.

KARPLUS, Prof. Martin, PhD; Theodore William Richards Research Professor, Harvard University, 1999–2004, now Professor Emeritus of Chemistry; Professeur Conventionné, Université de Strasbourg (formerly Université Louis Pasteur), since 1995; *b* Vienna, 15 March 1930; moved to USA, 1938; naturalized US citizen, 1945; *m* Marci; three *c.* *Educ:* Harvard Coll. (BA 1950); California Inst. of Technol. (PhD 1953). NSF Postdoctoral Fellow, Oxford Univ., 1953–55; instructor, 1955–57, Asst, then Associate Prof., 1957–60, Univ. of Illinois; Associate Prof., 1960–63, Prof., 1963–66, Columbia Univ.; Prof., 1966–79, Theodore William Richards Prof. of Chem., 1979–99, Harvard Univ. Professeur Associé: Univ. de Paris-Sud, 1972–73 and 1980–81; Univ. Louis Pasteur, Strasbourg, 1992, 1994–95; Professeur: Univ. de Paris VII, 1974–75; Coll. de France, Paris, 1980–81, 1987–88; Eastman Prof., Oxford Univ., 1999–2000; Linnett Vis. Prof., Cambridge Univ., 2003. Member: Amer. Acad. Arts and Scis; NAS; Internat. Acad. Quantum Molecular Sci.; Foreign Member: Netherlands Acad. Arts and Sci.; Royal Soc. Dr *hc* Sherbrooke, 1998; Ehrendoktorat Zurich, 2006; Bar-Ilan, 2014; Hon. MA Oxon, 1999. American Chemical Society: Harrison Howe Award, Rochester Section, 1967; Theoretical Chem. Award, 1993; Computers in Chem. and Pharmaceutical Res. Award, 2001; Pauling Award, Northwest Section, 2004; Award for Outstanding Contribn to Quantum Biol., Internat. Soc. for Quantum Biol., 1979; Irving Langmuir Award, Amer. Physical Soc., 1987; Anfinsen Award, Protein Soc., 2001; Lifetime Achievement Award in Theoretical Biophysics, Internat. Assoc. of Schs and Insts of Admin, 2008; Antonio Feltrinelli Internat. Prize for Chem., Accademia Nazionale dei Lincei, 2011; (jtly) Nobel Prize in Chemistry, 2013. *Publications:* (with R. N. Porter) Atoms & Molecules: an introduction for students of physical chemistry, 1970; (with O. M. Becker) A Guide to Biomolecular Simulations, 2006; Images of the 1950s (photography), 2011; Martin Karplus, La Couleur des Années 1950 (photography), 2013; contribs to scientific jls incl. Advanced Chem. Physics. *Recreations:* photography, cooking. *Address:* Department of Chemistry and Chemical Biology, Harvard University, 12 Oxford Street, Cambridge, MA 02138, USA.

KARRAN, Graham, QFSM 1985; Managing Director, Blundell, Benson & Co. Ltd, planning and safety consultants, 2004; *b* 28 Nov. 1939; *s* of Joseph Karran and Muriel Benson; *m* 1960, Thelma Gott; one *s* one *d.* *Educ:* Bootle Grammar Sch.; Liverpool College of Building. Estate Management, 1958–60; Southport Fire Bde, 1960–63; Lancashire County Fire Bde, 1963–74; Greater Manchester Fire Service, 1974–78; Cheshire County Fire Service, 1978–80; Chief Fire Officer, Derbyshire Fire Service, 1980–83; Chief Fire Officer, W Yorks Fire Service, and Chief Exec., W Yorks Fire and Civil Defence Authy, 1983–90. FIFireE 1980. *Publications:* articles in English and Amer. Fire jls. *Recreations:* music, beachcombing, sailing.

KARSTEN, His Honour Ian George Francis; QC 1990; a Circuit Judge, 1999–2014; *b* 27 July 1944; *s* of late Dr Frederick Karsten and Edith Karsten; *m* 1984, Moira Elizabeth Ann O'Hara (marr. diss. 2002); one *s* two *d.* *Educ:* William Ellis School, Highgate; Magdalen College, Oxford (MA, BCL); Diplôme, Hague Acad. of Internat. Law. Called to the Bar, Gray's Inn, 1967; Midland and Oxford Circuit; commenced practice 1970; Lectr in Law, Southampton Univ., 1966–70, LSE, 1970–88; a Recorder, 1994–99. UK Deleg. to Hague Conf. on Private Internat. Law (Convention on the Law Applicable to Agency) (Rapporteur), 1973–77; Leader, UK Delegn to Unidroit Conf. on Agency in Internat. Sale of Goods, Bucharest, 1979, Geneva, 1983. *Recreations:* opera, travel, chess.

KARSTEN, Rear Adm. Thomas Michael; Chief Executive, Centre for Environment, Fisheries and Aquaculture Science, since 2015; *b* Gorseinon, 22 Sept. 1961; *s* of Peter Karsten and Barbara Karsten; *m* 1993, Sarah Rees; one *s* two *d.* *Educ:* Charterhouse; Univ. of Exeter (BA Hist.). FRICS 2012. Entered RN, 1979; Commands: HMS Bicester, 1993–94; HMS Sheffield, 1995–96; HMS Endurance, 2003–05; Dir, Maritime Warfare Centre, 2005–07; Dep. Comdr Ops, Navy Comd, 2007; RN Sen. Hudson Fellow, Univ. of Oxford, 2009; Comdr British Forces Gibraltar, 2010–12; Nat. Hydrographer and Dep. Chief Exec., UK Hydrographic Office, 2012–15. *Recreation:* sport.

KARUNAIRETNAM, Nadesalingam, (Lee Karu); QC 2010; *b* Sri Lanka, 1 July 1954; *s* of Tharmalingam Karunairetnam and Malar Karunairetnam; *m* 1987, Usha Gupta (*see* U. Karunairetnam); two *s.* *Educ:* St Michael's Coll.; Univ. of Westminster (BA Hons Social Scis; DipLaw). Called to the Bar, Lincoln's Inn, 1985. *Recreations:* marlin fishing, cricket, tennis, golf, dining. *Address:* 9 Bedford Row, WC1R 4AZ. *T:* (020) 7489 2727. *E:* leekaru@9bedfordrow.co.uk.

KARUNAIRETNAM, Usha; Her Honour Judge Karu; a Circuit Judge, since 2005; *b* 18 Dec. 1958; *d* of Dharamchandra Gupta and Saroj Gupta; *m* 1987, Nadesalingam Karunairetnam, (Lee Karu), *qv*; two *s.* Called to the Bar, Middle Temple, 1984, Bencher, 2012; specialist criminal practitioner, SE Circuit; Asst Recorder, 1998–2000; Recorder, 2000–05; Judicial Mem., Mental Health Rev. Tribunal, 2010–; Circuit Judge Comr, Judicial Appts Commn, 2014–. *Recreations:* gardening, spending time with family, theatre. *Address:* Inner London Crown Court, Sessions House, Newington Causeway, SE1 6AZ. *T:* (020) 7234 3100, *Fax:* (020) 7234 3203.

KASER, Prof. Arthur, MD; Professor of Gastroenterology, University of Cambridge, since 2011; Hon. Consultant Physician, Cambridge University Hospitals NHS Foundation Trust, since 2011; *b* 1 May 1973; *s* of Dr Artur Kaser and Eva Kaser; *m* 2005, Dr Nicole C. Kaneider; one *s* two *d.* *Educ:* Anton-von-Eiselsberg Prim. Sch., Steinhaus bei Wels, Austria; Anton Bruckner Bundesrealgymnasium, Wels; Leopold-Franzens Univ., Innsbruck (MD 1996); Medical Univ. Innsbruck (Univ.-Doz. 2003). Postdoctoral Fellow, Dept of Medicine, 1996–98, Univ. Asst, 1998–2003, Leopold-Franzens Univ., Innsbruck; Consultant Physician, Innsbruck Univ. Hosp., 2002–10; Associate Prof. of Medicine, Medical Univ. Innsbruck, 2003–10. Max Kade Fellow, Mucosal Immunol. Lab., Brigham and Women's Hosp., Harvard Med. Sch., 2003–06. Vis. Prof. (pt-time), Dept of Medicine, Univ. of Oslo, 2009–12. *Publications:* articles on immunology and medicine. *Recreations:* reading, music, hiking, ski-ing. *Address:* Division of Gastroenterology and Hepatology, Department of Medicine, Addenbrooke's Hospital, Level 5, Box 157, Hills Road, Cambridge CB2 0QQ. *T:* (01223) 768308, *Fax:* (01223) 336846. *E:* ak729@cam.ac.uk.

KASER, Prof. Michael Charles, DLitt; Hon. Professor and Senior Research Fellow, Institute for German Studies, University of Birmingham, since 1994; Reader in Economics, University of Oxford, and Professorial Fellow of St Antony's College, 1972–93 (Sub-Warden, 1986–87), now Reader Emeritus and Emeritus Fellow; *b* 2 May 1926; *er s* of Charles Joseph Kaser and Mabel Blunden; *m* 1954, Elisabeth Anne Mary, *er d* of Cyril Gascoigne Piggford; four *s* one *d.* *Educ:* King's Coll., Cambridge (Exhibr); DLitt Oxon 1993. Economic Sect., Min. of Works, 1946–47; Foreign Service, London and Moscow, 1947–51; UN Secretariat, Econ. Commn for Europe, Geneva, 1951–63; Faculty Fellow, St Antony's Coll., Oxford, 1963–72; Institute of Slavonic Studies (formerly Institute of Russian, Soviet and East European Studies), University of Oxford: Dir, 1988–93; Sen. Res. Assoc., 1997–2004; Mem., Cttee on SE European Studies (formerly Prog. on Contemporary Turkey) in Oxford, 2000–. Associate Fellow, Green Templeton Coll. (formerly Templeton Coll.), Oxford, 1983–. Hon. Fellow, Divinity Faculty, Univ. of Edinburgh, 1993–96. Visiting Professor of Economics: Inst. Universitaire des Hautes Etudes Internats, Geneva, 1959–63; Univ. of Michigan, 1966; Vis. Faculty (formerly Fellow), Henley Management Coll., 1987–2002; Vis. Lectr, Cambridge Univ., 1967–68, 1977–78 and 1978–79; Vis. Lectr, INSEAD, Fontainebleau, 1959–82, 1988–92. Gen. Ed. Internat. Econ. Assoc., 1986–2007. Specialist Advr, Foreign Affairs Cttee, H of C, 1985–87. Oxford Univ. Latin Preacher, 1982. Convenor/Chm., Nat. Assoc. for Soviet and East European Studies, 1965–73, Chm., Jt Cttee with BUAS, 1980–84; Vice-Chm., Internat. Activities Cttee (Vice-Chm., Area Studies Panel, SSRC) ESRC, 1980–84; Chm., Co-ordinating Council, Area Studies Assocs, 1986–88 (Mem., 1980–93 and 1995; Sec., 1980–84, Vice-Chm., 1984–86); Governor, Plater Coll., Oxford, 1968–95, Emeritus Governor, 1995–2006; Chairman: Acad. Council, Wilton Park (FCO), 1986–92 (Mem., 1985–2001); Acad. Cttee, St Catharine's, Cumberland Lodge, 1991–2001 (Mem., 1973–2001); Sir Heinz Koeppler Trust, 1992–2001 (Mem., 1987–2001). President: British Assoc. for Slavonic and East European Studies, 1988–91 (Vice-Pres., 1991–93); British Assoc. of Former UN Civil Servants, 1994–2001; Chairman: Standing Cttee on E European Affairs, European Econ. Assoc., 1990–93; Keston Inst., 1994–2002. Member: Council, Royal Econ. Soc., 1976–86, 1987–90; Council, RIIA, 1979–85, 1986–92; Internat. Soc. Sci. Council, UNESCO, 1980–91; Council, SSEES, 1981–87; E Europe Cttee, CAFOD, 2001–05; Project Evaluation Gp, Univ. of Halle, 2002–05. Sec., British Acad. Cttee for SE European Studies, 1988–93 (Mem., 1970–75, 1983–93). Steering Cttee, Königswinter Anglo-German Confs, 1969–90 (Chm., Oxford Organizing Cttee, 1975–78). Hon. Mem., Eur. Assoc. Comparative Econs, 2006. Pres., Albania Soc. of Britain, 1992–95; Trustee, King George VI and Queen Elizabeth Foundn, 1987–2006. Missions for various internat. agencies, 1955–, incl. EC to Moscow, 1991, UNICEF to Albania, 1991, Turkmenistan and Uzbekistan, 1992, and IMF to Kyrgyzstan, 1998. Editorial Boards: Member: Central Asian Survey; Slavonic and East European Rev.; former Member: Econ. Jl; Jl of Industrial Econs; Soviet Studies; Oxford Rev. of Educn; CUP E European Monograph Series; World Develt; European Econ. Rev.; Energy Econs. Hon. DSocSc Birmingham, 1994. KSG 1990. Knight's Cross, Order of Merit (Poland), 1999; Order of Naim Frashëri (Albania), 1999. *Publications:* Comecon: Integration Problems of the Planned Economies, 1965, 2nd edn 1967; (ed) Economic Development for Eastern Europe, 1968; (with J. Zielinski) Planning in East Europe, 1970; Soviet Economics, 1970; (ed, with R. Portes) Planning and Market Relations, 1971; (ed, with H. Höhmann and K. Thalheim) The New Economic Systems of Eastern Europe, 1975; (ed, with A. Brown) The Soviet Union since the Fall of Khrushchev, 1975, 2nd edn 1978; Health Care in the

Soviet Union and Eastern Europe, 1976; (ed with A. Brown) Soviet Policy for the 1980s, 1982; (ed jtly) The Cambridge Encyclopaedia of Russia and the Soviet Union, 1982, revd edn as The Cambridge Encyclopaedia of Russia and the Former Soviet Union, 1994; Gen. Ed., The Economic History of Eastern Europe 1919–1975, vols I and II (1919–49), vol. III (1949–75), 1985–86; (ed with E. A. G. Robinson) Early Steps in Comparing East-West Economies, 1992; (ed with D. Phillips) Education and Economic Change in Eastern Europe and the Former Soviet Union, 1992; (with S. Mehrotra) The Central Asian Economies after Independence, 1992; Privatization in the CIS, 1995; The Economies of Kazakhstan and Uzbekistan, 1997; papers in economic jls and symposia. *Address:* 31 Capel Close, Oxford OX2 7LA. *T:* (01865) 515581. *E:* michael.kaser@economics.ox.ac.uk. *Club:* Reform.

KASMIN, John; art dealer, since 1960; *b* 24 Sept. 1934; *s* of Vera d'Olszewski and David Kosminsky (known as Kaye); *m* 1959, Jane Nicholson (marr. diss.); two *s. Educ:* Magdalen College School, Oxford. Adventurous and varied jobs in New Zealand, 1952–56; art gallery assistant, London, 1956–60; Founder Director: Kasmin Ltd, 1961– (in partnership with late Marquess of Dufferin and Ava); Knoedler Kasmin Ltd, 1977–92. *Recreations:* reading, walking in landscapes, museums, cities, collecting old postcards. *Address:* c/o Kasmin Ltd, 34 Warwick Avenue, W9 2PT.

KASPAROV, Garry Kimovich; chess player, retired; public speaker on strategy, decision-making, innovation and geopolitics, since 2004; *b* Baku, Azerbaijan, 13 April 1963; *né* Garry Weinstein; *s* of Kim Moiseyevich Weinstein and Klara Kasparova; *m* 1st, 1989, Maria Arapova (marr. diss. 1994); one *d*; 2nd, 1996, Yulia Vovk; one *s*; 3rd, 2005, Dasha; one *d*. Youngest world chess champion, 1985; retained title, 1986, 1987, 1990, 1993, 1995; lost title, 2000. Introduced (with Nigel Short) Rapid Chess, 1987; won first title, 1993; won PCA World Championship, NY, 1995. Played supercomputer Deep Blue, Philadelphia, 1996 and NY, 1997, series drawn; played first Advanced chess against Topolov, Spain, 1998; played The World, 1999. Founded Kasparov Chess Foundn USA, 2002, Europe, 2011, Africa, 2012, Asia-Pacific, 2013, Latin America, 2014. Chm., United Civil Front, 2005–; Russian Opposition Leader. Chm., Human Rights Foundn, NYC, 2012–. *Publications:* Kasparov Teaches Chess, 1985; New World Chess Champion, 1985; Fighting Chess, 1985; The Test of Time, 1986; London-Leningrad Championship Games, 1987; (with Donald Trelford) Child of Change, 1987; Unlimited Challenge, 1990; (with Daniel King) Kasparov Against the World, 2000; Garry Kasparov on My Great Predecessors: Part I and Part II, 2003, Part III and Part IV, 2004, Part V, 2006; Checkmate: my first chess book, 2004; How Life Imitates Chess, 2007; Garry Kasparov on Modern Chess: Part I, 2007, Part II, 2008, Part III, 2009, Part IV, 2010; Garry Kasparov on Garry Kasparov, Part 1, 2011, Part II, 2013, Part III, 2014; Trading in Fear (in Russian), 2015; Winter is Coming, 2015. *E:* office@kasparov.com. *W:* www.kasparov.com.

KASPI, Prof. Victoria Michelle, PhD; FRS 2010; FRSC; Professor of Physics, McGill University, since 2006; *b* Austin, Texas, 30 June 1967; *m*; three *c*. *Educ:* McGill Univ. (BSc Hons Physics 1989); Princeton Univ. (MA Physics 1991; PhD 1993). Higgins Instructor, Physics Dept, Princeton Univ., 1994; Vis. Associate, Astronomy Dept, CIT, 1994–96; Hubble Postdoctoral Fellow: Jet Propulsion Lab., Infrared Processing and Analysis Center, CIT, 1994–96; Center for Space Res., MIT, 1997; Asst Prof., Physics Dept, MIT, 1997–2002; Associate Prof., Physics Dept, McGill Univ., 1999–2006. Alfred P. Sloan Res. Fellow, 1998. Vis. Scientist, Space Scis Div., Canadian Space Agency, 2008–09. FRSC 2008. Rutherford Medal in Physics, Royal Soc. of Canada, 2007; John C. Polanyi Award, NSERC, 2011; Diamond Jubilee Medal, 2013. *Address:* Department of Physics, McGill University, Rutherford Physics Building, 3600 University Street, Montreal, QC H3A 2T8, Canada.

KATKHUDA, His Honour Samih Suleiman; a Circuit Judge, 1995–2010; *b* 15 Dec. 1941; *s* of Dr S. M. Katkhuda and U. Katkhuda (*née* Ciĉiĉ); *m* 1968, Suzanne Gundred de Warrenne Crews; two *s*. *Educ:* King's Sch., Bruton, Som; Inns of Court Sch. of Law. Court Admin, CCC, Old Bailey, 1964–73; called to the Bar, Gray's Inn, 1974; in practice as barrister, 1974–95; a Recorder, 1994–95. *Publications:* Forms of Indictment, 1990; (jtly) Crown Court Index, 2005–10; (contrib.) Witness Testimony, 2006. *Recreations:* music, travel, reading. *Club:* Savage.

KATKOWSKI, Christopher Andrew Mark; QC 1999; *b* 16 Jan. 1957; *s* of Edward and Maria Katkowski; *m* 1976, Anna Thérèse Louise Gunstone. *Educ:* Fitzwilliam Coll., Cambridge (BA Law 1978; LLB 1979). Lectr in Law, City of London Poly., 1979–83; called to the Bar, Gray's Inn, 1982, Bencher, 2007; in practice at the Bar, 1984–; Jun. Counsel to the Crown (Common Law), 1992–99; Hd of Chambers, 2006–09. Mem., Attorney-Gen.'s Supplementary Panel, 1988–92. *Recreation:* spending time with Anna and our dogs. *Address:* Landmark Chambers, 180 Fleet Street, EC4A 2HG. *T:* (020) 7430 1221.

KATONA, Nisha Sujata; barrister; *b* 23 Oct. 1971; *d* of Dr Nityendra Mohan Biswas and Dr Meena Biswas (*née* Chakrabarty); *m* 1999, Zoltan Katona; two *d*. *Educ:* Scarisbrick Hall Sch., Lancs; Liverpool John Moores Univ. (LLB Hons); Inns of Court Sch. of Law. Called to the Bar, Lincoln's Inn, 1996; in practice as barrister, specialising in family law, 1996–. Trustee, Nat. Museums Liverpool, 2008–. Ambassador for Diversity in Public Appts, 2009–. *Recreations:* horse-riding, theatre, reading, classical music, opera, gardening, teacher of Indian cookery. *Address:* Chavasse Court Chambers, 18 Queen Avenue, Liverpool L2 4TX. *E:* nisha@nishakatona.com.

KATSAV, Moshe; President of the State of Israel, 2000–07; *b* Iran, 5 Dec. 1945; emigrated to Israel, 1951; *m* Gila; four *s* one *d*. *Educ:* Hebrew Univ. of Jerusalem. Newspaper reporter, Yediot Aharonot, 1966–68; Member of Knesset, 1977–2000; Mem., Interior and Educn Cttees, Knesset, 1977–81; Dep. Minister of Housing and Construction, 1981–84; Minister: of Labour and Social Affairs, 1984–88; of Transportation, and Mem., Ministerial Cttee on Defence, 1988–92; Chm., Parly Cttee of Chinese-Israeli Friendship League, 1992–96; Dep. Prime Minister, Minister of Tourism, and Minister for Israeli-Arab Affairs, 1996–99; Chm., Ministerial Cttee for Nat. Events and Mem., Ministerial Cttee on Defence, 1996–99; Mem., Foreign Affairs and Defence Cttee, 1999–2000. Mem., Commn on adoptive children, 1978; Chm., Commn to determine higher educn tuition, 1982. Chairman, Likud Party: at Hebrew Univ., Jerusalem, 1969; in Knesset, 1992–96. Pres., B'nai B'rith Youth, 1968. Mayor, Kiryat Malachi, 1969 and 1974–81. Mem., Bd of Trustees, Ben-Gurion Univ., 1978. Hon. Dr: Nebraska, 1998; George Washington, 2001; Hartford, Connecticut, 2001; Yeshiva, 2002; Bar Ilan, 2003; China Agricl Univ., Beijing, 2003; Sorbonne, 2004; ELTE Univ. of Budapest, 2004. Bene Merito Medal, Acad. of Sci., Australia, 2004. *Publications:* contrib. articles in newspapers, Maariv and Yediot Aharonot. *Address:* c/o Office of the President, 3 Hanassi Street, Jerusalem, 92188 Israel.

KATZ, Ian Alexander; Editor, Newsnight, BBC, since 2013; *b* 9 Feb. 1968; *s* of John Katz and Adrienne (*née* Karnovsky); *m* 1997, Justine Roberts; two *s* two *d*. *Educ:* University College Sch., London; New Coll., Oxford (BA PPE 1989). Reporter, Sunday Correspondent, 1989–90; The Guardian: reporter, 1991–94; NY Corresp., 1994–97; Internet Editor, 1997–98; Features Ed., 1998–2006; Saturday Ed., 2006–08; Dep. Ed. and Hd of News, 2008–13. *Recreation:* sailing. *Address:* Newsnight, BBC Broadcasting House, Portland Place, W1A 1AA.

KATZ, Philip Alec Jackson; QC 2000; **His Honour Judge Katz;** a Circuit Judge, since 2014; *b* 8 May 1953; *s* of Stanley Zeb Jackson (*née* Katz) and Anita Jackson; adopted patronymic Katz, 1976. *Educ:* Roundhay Grammar Sch., Leeds; University Coll., Oxford (MA). Called to the Bar, Middle Temple, 1976, Bencher, 2008; a Recorder, 2000–14; Hd of Chambers, 9–12 Bell Yard, 2008–11. *Address:* Woolwich Crown Court, 2 Belmarsh Road, SE28 0EY. *T:* (020) 8312 7000.

KATZMAN, Silvia Suzen Giovanna; *see* Casale, S. S. G.

KAUFFMANN, Prof. C. Michael, MA, PhD; FBA 1987; FMA; FSA; Professor of History of Art and Director, Courtauld Institute of Art, University of London, 1985–95, now Professor Emeritus; *b* 5 Feb. 1931; *s* of late Arthur and late Tamara Kauffmann; *m* 1954, Dorothea (*née* Hill); two *s*. *Educ:* St Paul's Sch.; Merton Coll., Oxford (Postmaster); Warburg Inst., London Univ. (Jun. Research Fellow). Asst Curator, Photographic Collection, Warburg Inst., 1957–58; Keeper, Manchester City Art Gall., 1958–60; Victoria and Albert Museum: Asst Keeper, 1960–75, Keeper, 1975–85, Dept of Prints & Drawings and Paintings; Asst to the Director, 1963–66; Visiting Associate Prof., Univ. of Chicago, 1969. Mem. Exec. Cttee, NACF, 1987–2005; Trustee, Nat. Museums and Galls on Merseyside, 1986–99. *Publications:* The Baths of Pozzuoli: medieval illuminations of Peter of Eboli's poem, 1959; An Altar-piece of the Apocalypse, 1968; Victoria & Albert Museum: Catalogue of Foreign Paintings, 1973; British Romanesque Manuscripts 1066–1190, 1975; Catalogue of Paintings in the Wellington Museum, 1982; John Varley, 1984; Studies in Medieval Art, 1992; Biblical Imagery in Medieval England 700–1550, 2003.

KAUFMAN, Rt Hon. Sir Gerald (Bernard), Kt 2004; PC 1978; MP (Lab) Manchester, Gorton, since 1983 (Manchester, Ardwick, 1970–83); Father of the House, since 2015; *b* 21 June 1930; *s* of Louis and Jane Kaufman. *Educ:* Leeds Grammar Sch.; The Queen's Coll., Oxford. Asst Gen.-Sec., Fabian Soc., 1954–55; Political Staff, Daily Mirror, 1955–64; Political Correspondent, New Statesman, 1964–65; Parly Press Liaison Officer, Labour Party, 1965–70. Parly Under-Sec. of State, DoE, 1974–75, Dept of Industry, 1975; Minister of State, Dept of Industry, 1975–79; Shadow Envmt Sec., 1980–83; Shadow Home Sec., 1983–87; Shadow Foreign Sec., 1987–92. Chm., Select Cttee on Nat. Heritage, 1992–97, on Culture, Media and Sport, 1997–2005. Chairman: All-Party Dance Gp, 2006–; All-Party Opera Gp, 2010–; Mem., Parly Cttee of PLP, 1980–92. Mem., Labour Party NEC, 1991–92. Mem., Royal Commn on H of L reform, 1999. Chm., Booker Prize Judges, 1999. HPk (Pakistan), 1999. *Publications:* (jtly) How to Live Under Labour, 1964; (ed) The Left, 1966; To Build the Promised Land, 1973; How to be a Minister, 1980, 2nd edn 1997; (ed) Renewal: Labour's Britain in the 1980s, 1983; My Life in the Silver Screen, 1985; Inside the Promised Land, 1986; Meet Me in St Louis, 1994. *Recreations:* travel, going to the pictures. *Address:* 87 Charlbert Court, Eamont Street, NW8 7DA. *T:* (office) (020) 7219 3000.

KAUFMANN, Julia Ruth, OBE 1997; freelance consultant for voluntary sector, since 2000; *b* 29 March 1941; *d* of Prof. Felix Kaufmann and Ruth (*née* Arnold); marr. diss.; two *s* one *d*. *Educ:* St George's Hosp., London (SRN); Sidney Webb Coll. (BEd London); Brunel Univ. (Dip. Social Policy and Admin). Advisory teacher, ILEA, 1974–76; Dir, Centre for Social Educn, 1976–78; Press Officer, 1978–79, Dir, 1979–87, Gingerbread; Dir, BBC Children in Need Appeal, 1987–2000. Mem., Employment Relns Adv. Panel on Public Appts, 2001–04; Comr, Postcomm, 2000–05. Chairman: Nat. Assoc. of Toy and Leisure Libraries, 2000–04; Whizz Kidz, 2006–08; Bd Mem., Capacity Builders, 2006–09; Vice-Pres., DEAFAX, 2000–; Trustee, Community Network, 2000–07. *Address:* 2 Carberry Road, SE19 3RU. *T:* (020) 8653 3877.

KAUL, Kalyani; QC 2011; a Recorder, since 2009; *b* New Delhi, 11 Dec. 1960; *d* of Mahendra Nath Kaul, *qv*; *m* 1988, Martin Lee (marr. diss.); one *s* one *d*. *Educ:* Heathfield Sch., Harrow; London Sch. of Econs and Pol Sci. (LLB Hons). Called to the Bar, Middle Temple, 1983. *Recreations:* travel, work, spending time with friends, shopping, surviving my children with my sense of humour intact, laughing. *Address:* 5 St Andrew's Hill, EC4V 5BZ.

KAUL, Mahendra Nath, OBE 1975; Chairman, India's Restaurants Ltd, since 1997; *b* 28 July 1922; *s* of Dina Nath Kaul and Gauri Kaul; *m* 1955, Rajni Kapur, MA, MLS; one *d*. *Educ:* Univ. of the Punjab, India (BA). Joined Radio Kashmir of All India Radio, as news reader, actor and producer of dramas, 1949; appeared in two feature films and assisted in producing several documentaries, 1950–52; news reader and actor in three languages, also drama producer, All India Radio, New Delhi, 1952–55; joined Indian service of Voice of America, Washington DC, 1955, later becoming Editor of the service; joined external service of BBC, as newscaster, producer and dir of radio plays; producer/presenter, BBC TV prog. for Asian Viewers in UK, 1966–82. OBE awarded for services to race relations in Gt Britain. Received The Green Pennant from HRH The Duke of Edinburgh, awarded by Commonwealth Expedition (COMEX 10), 1980. *Recreations:* golf, cooking, boating, classical and light classical music, reading political works. *Address:* 109 Clive Court, Maida Vale, W9 1SF. *T:* (020) 7286 8131.

See also K. Kaul.

KAUNDA, Kenneth David; President of Zambia, Oct. 1964–1991 (Prime Minister, N Rhodesia, Jan.–Oct. 1964); Chancellor of the University of Zambia, 1966–91; *b* 28 April 1924; *s* of late David Julizgia and Hellen Kaunda, Missionaries; *m* 1946, Betty Banda (*d* 2012); five *s* two *d* one adopted *s* (and two *s* decd). *Educ:* Lubwa Training Sch.; Munali Secondary Sch. Teacher, Lubwa Training Sch., 1943–44, Headmaster, 1944–47; Boarding Master, Mufulira Upper Sch., 1948–49. African National Congress: District Sec., 1950–52; Provincial Organising Sec., 1952–53; Sec.-Gen., 1953–58; Nat. Pres., Zambia African Nat. Congress, 1958–59; founded United Nat. Independence Party, 1958, Nat. Pres., 1960–91, re-elected, 1995–2000; Chm., Pan-African Freedom Movement for East, Central and South Africa, 1962; Minister of Local Government and Social Welfare, N Rhodesia, 1962–63. Chairman: Organization of African Unity, 1970, 1987; Non-aligned Countries, 1970. Hon. Doctor of Laws: Fordham Univ., USA, 1963; Dublin Univ., 1964; University of Sussex, 1965; Windsor Univ., Canada, 1966; University of Chile, 1966; Univ. of Zambia, 1974; Univ. of Humboldt, 1980; DUniv York, 1966. *Publications:* Black Government, 1961; Zambia Shall Be Free, 1962; Humanist in Africa, 1966; Humanism in Zambia and its implementation, 1967; Letter to My Children; Kaunda on Violence, 1980. *Recreations:* golf, music, table tennis, football, draughts, gardening and reading. *Address:* c/o UNIP, POB 30302, 10101 Lusaka, Zambia.

KAUR-STUBBS, Sukhvinder; Managing Director, Engage, since 2012; *b* Punjab, India, 25 Oct. 1962; *d* of S. Inderjit Singh Thethy and Charanjit Kaur; *m* 1985, David Brian Stubbs (marr. diss. 2008); one *d*. *Educ:* Hertford Coll., Oxford (MA Geography; Henry Oliver Becket Meml Prize). MCIM 1992. Lectr, Orpington Coll., 1984–85; Graduate Manager, British Telecom, 1985–86; Mktg Exec., Prisoners Abroad, 1986–87; Appeals Dir, British Dyslexia Assoc., 1987–90; Dir of Corporate Affairs, Community Develt Foundn, 1990–94; Community Develt Manager, English Partnerships, 1994–96; Chief Executive: Runnymede Trust, 1996–2000; Barrow Cadbury Trust, 2001–09. Chair: European Network Against Racism, 1998–2002; Young Enterprise (WM), 2002–05; Volunteering Britain, 2009–14; Taylor Bennett Foundn, 2015–. Non-executive Director: W Midlands Regl Develt Agency (Advantage W Midlands), 1998–2003; CPS, 2000–02; Severn Trent Water, 2002–06; Home Gp Housing Assoc., 2013–; Lewisham and Greenwich NHS Trust, 2015–; Dir, Swan Housing Assoc., 2015–. Member: Learning and Skills Res. Develt Unit, 2001–03; Cabinet Office Better Regulation Taskforce, 2002–06; Consumer Focus (formerly National Consumer Council), 2007–13; Land and Society Commn, 2011; Director: Office for Public Mgt, 2009–; Bd, Admin. Justice and Tribunals Council, 2010–13; Trustee, Social Care Inst. for Excellence, 2009– (Chm., Audit Cttee, 2009–). Council Mem., Britain in Europe Trust, 2000–05; Steering Gp Mem., UN Cttee on World Conf. against Racism, 2001. Chm., Birmingham Secondary Educn Commn, 1998; Mem., Birmingham Democracy Commn,

2000–01. Trustee, Demos, 1998–2006. Mem., Lunar Soc., 1999. FRSA 1996; MInstD; Mem., ACEVO, 2002–; MCMI 2009. *Publications:* (contrib.) Renewing Citizenship and Democracy, 1997; (contrib.) Mindfields, 1998; Fear and Loathing in the EU, 2000; Participation in Social Care Regulation, 2004; Islam, Race and Being British, 2005; Better Regulation for Civic Society, 2005; (with Joel Anderson) Engaged Europe - developing full, free and equal participation, 2010; papers, articles in jls. *Recreations:* singing, gardening, school fundraising. *Address:* (office) 629 Kings Road, Birmingham B44 9HW.

KAVANAGH, Prof. Dennis Anthony; Professor of Politics, 1996–2006, Emeritus Professor and Research Fellow in Politics and Communications, since 2007, University of Liverpool; *b* 27 March 1941; *s* of Patrick Kavanagh and Agnes Kavanagh; *m* 1966, Monica Anne Taylor; one *s* three *d*. *Educ:* St Anselm's Coll., Birkenhead; Univ. of Manchester (BA, MA Econ). Asst Lectr, Univ. of Hull, 1965–67; Lectr, then Sen. Lectr, Univ. of Manchester, 1967–81; Prof. of Politics, Univ. of Nottingham, 1982–95. Ford Foundn Fellow, Univ. of Stanford, Calif, 1969–70; Visiting Professor: European Univ. Inst., Florence, 1977; Univ. of Calif, San Diego, La Jolla, 1979; Hoover Instn, Stanford Univ., 1985. Mem. Council, 1991–94, Mem. Res. Grants Bd, 1994–97, ESRC; Aurora, 1999–2000. Mem. Editl Bd, political jls. FRSA. *Publications:* Constituency Electioneering in Britain, 1970; Political Culture, 1972; (with R. Rose) New Trends in British Politics: contemporary issues for research and discussions, 1977; The Politics of the Labour Party, 1982; Political Science and Political Behaviour, 1983; (ed) Comparative Politics and Government: essays in honour of S. E. Finer, 1984; British Politics, continuities and change, 1985, 4th edn 2000; Thatcherism and British Politics: the end of consensus?, 1987, 2nd edn 1990; Consensus Politics from Attlee to Thatcher, 1989, 2nd edn 1994; The Thatcher Effect, 1989; Personalities and Politics, 1990; Electoral Politics, 1992; (ed with A. Seldon) The Major Effect, 1995; Election Campaigning: the new marketing of politics, 1995; The Reordering of British Politics, 1997; (ed) Oxford Dictionary of Political Leadership, 1998; (with A. Seldon) The Powers Behind the Prime Minister, 1999; (ed with A. Seldon) The Blair Effect, 2005; (with P. Cowley) The British General Election of 2010, 2010; Philip Gould: an unfinished life, 2012; (with P. Cowley) The British General Election of 2015, 2015; with David Butler: The British General Election of October 1974, 1975; The British General Election of 1979, 1980; The British General Election of 1983, 1984; The British General Election of 1987, 1988; The British General Election of 1992, 1992; The British General Election of 1997, 1997; The British General Election of 2001, 2002; The British General Election of 2005, 2006; over 100 contribs to jls and books. *Recreations:* running, tennis, music, obituaries. *Address:* Lynton, Belgrave Road, Bowdon, Altrincham, Cheshire WA14 2NZ. *E:* dennis.kavanagh@talktalk.net. *Clubs:* Bowdon Lawn Tennis, Hale Lawn Tennis.

KAVANAGH, George Collins; Sheriff, Sheriffdom of North Strathclyde, 2010 (Sheriff of North Strathclyde at Paisley, 1999–2010); *b* 29 May 1940; *s* of George and Mary Kavanagh (*née* Donagher); *m* 1967, Rosaleen Anne-Marie McCrudden or Kavanagh; two *s* two *d*. *Educ:* St John's Sch., Cumnock; St Joseph's High Sch., Kilmarnock; Univ. of Glasgow. Home Office, 1961–71; Hughes Dowdall, Solicitors, 1971–99, Sen. Partner, 1991–99. Examr, Soc. of Apothecaries, 2000–. KCHS 2000 (KHS 1995). *Recreations:* reading, cricket, sailing.

KAVANAGH, Trevor Michael Thomas; Associate Editor and Chief Political Columnist, The Sun, since 2006; *b* 19 Jan. 1943; *s* of Bernard George Kavanagh and Alice Rose (*née* Thompson); *m* 1967, Jacqueline Gai Swindells; two *s*. *Educ:* Reigate Grammar Sch. The Sun, 1978–: Industrial Corresp., 1981–83; Political Ed., 1983–2006. Chairman: Parly Lobby Journalists, 1990; Parly Press Gall., 2000. Journalist of the Year, Specialist Reporter of the Year, 1997, Reporter of the Year, 2005, British Press Awards; Scoop of the Year, What the Papers Say, 2000, 2004; Print Story of the Year, For. Press Assoc., 2004; Political Journalist of the Year, Pol Studies Assoc., 2004. *Recreations:* golf, swimming, travel. *Address:* Press Gallery, House of Commons, SW1A 0AA. *Club:* Royal Automobile.

KAWCZYNSKI, Daniel; MP (C) Shrewsbury and Atcham, since 2005; *b* 24 Jan. 1972; *s* of Leonard and Halina Kawczynski; *m* 2000, Kate Lumb (marr. diss. 2011); one *d*. *Educ:* Univ. of Stirling (BA Hons Business Studies with French 1994). Internat. export consultant in telecommunications industry, Middle E, 1994–2004. Contested (C) Ealing Southall, 2001. PPS to Minister of State for Agriculture and Food, 2010–12, to Sec. of State for Wales, 2012–14. Member: Envmt, Food and Rural Affairs Select Cttee, 2005–07; Justice Select Cttee, 2007–09; Internat. Develt Select Cttee, 2008–10; Foreign Affairs Select Cttee, 2015–; Chairman: All Party Gp for Dairy Farmers, 2006; All Party Parly Gp for Saudi Arabia, 2007–15; All Party Parly Gp for Libya, 2008–; British Middle E and N Africa Council, 2012–. *Publications:* Seeking Gaddafi, 2010. *Address:* House of Commons, SW1A 0AA. *E:* kawczynskid@parliament.uk.

KAY, Anne Jacqueline; *see* Ridley, A. J.

KAY, Prof. Anthony Barrington, (Barry), PhD, DSc; FRCPE, FRCP, FRCPath, FMedSci; FRSE; Professor of Clinical Immunology and Head, Department of Allergy and Clinical Immunology, Imperial College, London University, 1980–2004, now Professor Emeritus; Senior Research Investigator, National Heart and Lung Institute Division, Imperial College London, since 2004; Hon. Consultant Physician, Royal Brompton Hospital, 1980–2009; Consultant Physician (Allergy), The London Clinic, 2005–12; *b* 23 June 1939; *s* of Anthony Chambers and late Eva Gertrude (*née* Pearcey; she *m* 2nd H. Kay; later Mrs E. G. Reuben); *m* 1966, Rosemary Margaret Johnstone; three *d*. *Educ:* King's Sch., Peterborough; Edinburgh Univ. (MB, ChB 1963; DSc 1976); Jesus Coll., Cambridge (MA 1966; PhD 1970); Harvard Med. Sch. FRCPE 1975; FRCP 1980; FRCPath 1989. T. K. Stubbins Res. Fellow, RCP, 1969; Res. Fellow, Harvard Med. Sch., 1970–71; Lectr in Respiratory Diseases, Univ. of Edinburgh, 1972–74; Dep. Dir and Consultant, Immunology Div., Blood Transfusion Service, Royal Infirmary, Edinburgh, 1974–76; Sen. Lectr, then Reader, in Exptl Pathology, Dept of Pathology, Univ. of Edinburgh, 1977–79. Specialist Advr, H of L Select Cttee Enquiry into Allergy, 2006–07. Co-founder and Consultant, Circassia Ltd, 1999–. President: European Acad. of Allergology and Clinical Immunology, 1989–92; Brit. Soc. of Allergy and Clinical Immunology, 1993–96 (Hon. Mem., 2009). Jt Editor, Clinical and Exptl Allergy, 1984–2007. FRSE 1993; FMedSci 1999. Hon. Fellow: Amer. Coll. of Allergy, 1986; Amer. Acad. of Allergy, Asthma and Immunology, 2004; Hon. Member: Amer. Assoc. of Physicians, 1988; Hungarian Soc. of Allergology and Clinical Immunology, 1990; Swiss Soc. of Allergology and Clinical Immunology, 1991; Belgian Soc. for Allergol. and Clin. Immunol., 1999. Hon. Dr Medicine and Surgery, Ferrara, 2000. Scientific Achievement Award, Internat. Assoc. of Allergology and Clinical Immunology, 1991; Paul Ehrlich Medal, Eur. Acad. of Allergology and Clin. Immunol., 2005. *Publications:* edited: Asthma: clinical pharmacology and therapeutic progress, 1986; Allergy and Inflammation, 1987; Allergic Basis of Asthma, 1988; Allergy and Asthma: new trends and approaches to therapy, 1989; Eosinophils, Allergy and Asthma, 1990; Eosinophils in Allergy and Inflammation, 1993; Allergy and Allergic Diseases, 1997, 2nd edn 2008; numerous scientific articles on allergy and asthma. *Recreations:* Baroque and modern bassoon, tennis, country walks. *Address:* 58 Madrid Road, Barnes, SW13 9PG. *Clubs:* Chelsea Arts, Hurlingham.

KAY, Brian Christopher; broadcaster and musician; *b* 12 May 1944; *s* of Noel Bancroft Kay and Gwendoline Mary (*née* Sutton); *m* 1st, 1970, Sally Lyne; one *s* one *d*; 2nd, 1983, Gillian Fisher. *Educ:* Rydal Sch.; King's Coll., Cambridge (MA 1966); New Coll., Oxford (DipEd 1967). Bass Singer: Westminster Abbey Choir, 1968–71; King's Singers, 1968–82; Chorus Master, Huddersfield Choral Soc., 1983–93; Conductor: Cecilian Singers of Leicester, 1984–92; Cheltenham Bach Choir, 1989–97; Leith Hill Musical Fest., 1996–; Mary Wakefield Westmorland Fest., 1996–2003; Burford Singers, 2002–; Musical Dir, Bradford Fest. Choral Soc., 1998–2002; Principal Conductor, The Really Big Chorus, 2010– (Associate Conductor, 2005–10). Presenter: Music in Mind, Radio 4, 1989–98; Brian Kay's Sunday Morning, Radio 3, 1992–2001; Comparing Notes, Radio 4, 1996–98; Brian Kay's Light Programme, Radio 3, 2001–07. Friday Night is Music Night, Radio 2, 1998–. President: Nottingham Choral Trust; Harrogate Choral Soc.; Market Harborough Singers; Derbys Singers; Bristol Bach Choir; English Arts Chorale; Vice Pres., Joyful Co. of Singers. Vice-Pres., Assoc. of British Choral Dirs; Patron, Stars Orgn for Scope. Vice-Pres., RSCM, 2005–. Hon. FTCL 2004. Music Presenter of the Year, Sony Gold Award, 1996. *Recreations:* gardening, reading. *Address:* Bell Cottage, Church Lane, Fulbrook, Burford, Oxon OX18 4BA.

KAY, Prof. Elizabeth Jane, PhD; FDSRCPSGlas; Professor of Dental Public Health, Hon. Academic Consultant in Dental Public Health (Public Health England, formerly NHS Plymouth) and Foundation Dean, Dental School, Plymouth University Peninsula Schools of Medicine and Dentistry, since 2012; *b* 10 March 1959; *d* of late Robert Brian Kay and Cynthia Kay (*née* Bianchi); partner, Stella Ruth Tinsley. *Educ:* Univ. of Edinburgh (BDS 1982); Univ. of Glasgow (MPH 1984; PhD 1991). FDSRCPSGlas 1988; FDSRCS *ad eundem* 2002; FFGDP *ad eundem* 2010. Res. Fellow in Dental Epidemiology, Univ. of Edinburgh, 1982–86; Lectr in Community Dental Health, Univ. of Glasgow, 1986–90; Sen. Lectr in Dental Public Health, Univ. of Dundee, 1990–92; Sen. Registrar in Dental Public Health, South Glamorgan HA, 1992–94; University of Manchester: Sen. Lectr in Dental Health Services Res., 1994–98; Prof. of Dental Health Services Res., 1998–2006; Prof. of Oral Health and Dean, Peninsula Dental Sch., 2006–12. Member: Expert Cttee, NICE, 2013–; Med. and Dental Adv. Cttee, Equality Challenge Unit, 2013–. Shadow Gov., Royal Cornwall Hosp. Trust, 2013–. *Publications:* (jtly) Communication for the Dental Team, 1996, 2nd edn 2004; (jtly) Clinical Decision Making: an art or a science, 1997; (jtly) A Review of Effectiveness of Oral Health Promotion, 1997; (ed) A Guide to Prevention in Dentistry, 2004; (jtly) Integrated Dental Treatment Planning, 2005; (ed) Dentistry at a Glance, 2015; 142 learned papers in acad. and professional jls. *Recreations:* all things equine, rural or historical. *Address:* Peninsula Dental School, Portland Square, Plymouth University, Drake Circus, Plymouth PL4 8AA. *T:* (01752) 586800.

KAY, Prof. Helen Sheppard, (Sarah), DPhil, LittD; FBA 2004; Professor of French, New York University, since 2011; *b* 12 Nov. 1948; *d* of Brian Wilfrid Kay and Dorothea Sheppard Kay; *m* John Williamson (marr. diss.); one *s* two *d*. *Educ:* Somerville Coll., Oxford (BA 1st cl. (Mod. Langs (French)) 1971; DPhil 1976); Univ. of Reading (MA (Linguistics) 1972); LittD Cantab 2005. Kathleen Bourne Res. Fellow, St Anne's Coll., Oxford, 1973–75; Lectr in French, Univ. of Liverpool, 1975–84; University of Cambridge: Lectr, Dept of French, 1984–95; Reader, 1995–2001; Prof. of French and Occitan Lit., 2001–05; Fellow, 1984–2005, Life Fellow, 2005, Girton Coll.; Prof., Dept of French and Italian, Princeton Univ., 2006–11. Visiting Professor: Dept of Romance Langs, Univ. of Pennsylvania, 1993; Centre for Medieval and Renaissance Studies, QMW, 1996–99; Center for Medieval and Renaissance Studies, UCLA, 1999; Dept of Comparative Lit., Stanford Univ., 2004; Prof. invité, Univ. d'Artois, 1999. Guggenheim Fellow, 2014–15. Chevalier, Ordre des Palmes Académiques (France). *Publications:* Subjectivity in Troubadour Poetry, 1990; (ed) Raoul de Cambrai, 1992; (ed with Miri Rubin) Framing Medieval Bodies, 1994; The Chanson de geste in the Age of Romance: political fictions, 1995; The Romance of the Rose, 1995; (ed with S. Gaunt) The Troubadours: an introduction, 1999; Courtly Contradictions: the emergence of the literary object in the twelfth century, 2001; Zizek: a critical introduction, 2003; (jtly) A Short History of French Literature, 2003; The Place of Thought: the complexity of one in late Medieval French didactic poetry, 2007; (ed with S. Gaunt) The Cambridge Companion to Medieval French Literature, 2008; (with A. Armstrong) Knowing Poetry: verse in medieval France from the Rose to the rhetoriqueurs, 2011; (jtly) Thinking Through Chrétien de Troyes, 2011; Parrots and Nightingales: troubadour quotations and the development of European poetry, 2013; numerous articles and chapters in books. *Recreations:* eating, drinking, walking, reading difficult books. *Address:* 100 Bleecker Street, Apt 16E, New York, NY 10012, USA. *E:* hsk8@nyu.edu.

KAY, Jervis; *see* Kay, R. J.

KAY, Prof. John Anderson, CBE 2014; FBA 1997; FRSE; economist; *b* 3 Aug. 1948; *s* of late James Scobie Kay and of Allison (*née* Anderson); *m* 1st, 1986, Deborah Freeman (marr. diss. 1995); 2nd, 2009, Mika Oldham. *Educ:* Royal High Sch., Edinburgh; Univ. of Edinburgh (MA); Nuffield Coll., Oxford. Fellow of St John's Coll., 1970–, and Lectr in Econs, 1971–79, Univ. of Oxford; Res. Dir, 1979–81, Dir, 1981–86, Inst. for Fiscal Studies; London Business School: Prof., 1986–96; Dir, Centre for Business Strategy, 1986–91; Prof. of Mgt and Dir, Saïd Business Sch., Univ. of Oxford, 1997–99. Vis. Prof. LSE, 2000–. Chairman: Undervalued Assets Trust, then SVM UK Active Fund, 1994–2005; Clear Capital Ltd, 2004–08; Director: London Econs Ltd, 1986–2000 (Chm., 1986–96); Halifax plc (formerly Halifax Building Soc.), 1991–2000; Foreign & Colonial Special Utilities Investment Trust Plc, 1993–2003; Value and Income Trust plc, 1994–; Law Debenture Corp. plc, 2004–14; Scottish Mortgage Investment Trust, 2008–; Buddi, 2012–. Member: Council and Exec. Cttee, NIESR, 1989–97; Council of Econ. Advrs, Scottish Govt, 2007–10. Mem., Corporate Governance Adv. Bd, Norges Bank Investment Mgt, 2013–. Vice-Pres., Econs & Business Educn Assoc., 1996–. FRSE 2007. *Publications:* (with L. Hannah) Concentration in Modern Industry, 1977; (with M. A. King) The British Tax System, 1978, 5th edn 1997; (jtly) The Reform of Social Security, 1984; (jtly) The Economic Analysis of Accounting Profitability, 1987; Foundations of Corporate Success, 1993; Why Firms Succeed, 1995; The Business of Economics, 1996; The Truth about Markets, 2003; Culture and Prosperity, 2004; Everlasting Light Bulbs, 2004; The Hare and the Tortoise, 2006; The Long and the Short of It, 2009; Obliquity, 2010; Other People's Money, 2015; contrib. articles in learned jls and columns in Financial Times. *Recreations:* walking, especially in France. *Address:* Erasmus Press Ltd, PO Box 4026, W1A 6NZ. *T:* (020) 7224 8797.

KAY, Jolyon Christopher; HM Diplomatic Service, retired; *b* 19 Sept. 1930; *s* of Colin Mardall Kay and Gertrude Fanny Kay; *m* 1956, Shirley Mary Clarke; two *s* two *d*. *Educ:* Charterhouse; St John's Coll., Cambridge (BA 1953; MEng 1993); Rose Bruford Coll. (BA Theatre Studies 2012). Chemical Engr, Albright and Wilson, 1954; UKAEA, Harwell, 1958; Battelle Inst., Geneva, 1961; Foreign Office, London, 1964; MECAS, 1965; British Interests Section, Swiss Embassy, Algiers, 1967; Head of Chancery and Information Adviser, Political Residency, Bahrain, 1968; FCO, 1970; Economic Counsellor, Jedda, 1974–77; Consul-Gen., Casablanca, 1977–80; Science, later Commercial, Counsellor, Paris, 1980–84; Counsellor and Consul-Gen., Dubai, 1985–90. Editl Dir, London Insurance Insider, 1996–98. Convenor, Transport Gp, Oxfordshire CPRE, 1995–97. Chm., Cyprus Third Age, 2011–13 (Vice Chm., Limassol Br., 2009–10). Chm., Southern Croquet Fedn, 1999–2003; Mem. Council, Croquet Assoc., 2001–04. *Recreations:* theatre, croquet, Go, Bananagrams. *Address:* 1 Anexartisias Street, 4603 Anogyra, Limassol District, Cyprus.

KAY, Prof. Lewis Edward, PhD; FRS 2010; FRSC; Professor of Biochemistry, Molecular Genetics and Chemistry, University of Toronto. *Educ:* Yale Univ. (PhD 1988). Lab. of Chem. Physics, NIH, 1988–92. FRSC 2006. *Publications:* contribs to jls incl. Science, Jl Magnetic Resonance, Biochem., Jl Molecular Biol., Jl Phys. Chem. B, Jl Amer. Chem. Soc. *Address:* Department of Biochemistry, University of Toronto, 1 King's College Circle, Toronto, ON M5S 1A8, Canada.

KAY, Rt Hon. Sir Maurice (Ralph), Kt 1995; PC 2004; a Lord Justice of Appeal, 2004–14; *b* 6 Dec. 1942; *s* of Ralph and Hylda Kay; *m* 1968, Margaret Angela Alcock; four *s*. *Educ:* William Hulme's Grammar Sch., Manchester; Sheffield Univ. (LLB, PhD). Called to the Bar, Gray's Inn, 1975; Bencher, 1995 (Vice-Treas., 2012; Treas., 2013). Lecturer in Law: Hull Univ., 1967–72; Manchester Univ., 1972–73; Prof. of Law, Keele Univ., 1973–82. Practising barrister, 1975–95; an Asst Recorder, 1987–88; a Recorder, 1988–95; QC 1988; a Judge of the High Ct of Justice, QBD, 1995–2003; Judge, Employment Appeal Tribunal, 1995–2003; Lead Judge, Administrative Ct, 2002–03. Vice Pres., Court of Appeal Civil Div., 2010–14. Chm., Judicial Studies Bd, 2007–10. Judicial Visitor, UCL, 2006–. Hon. Fellow, Robinson Coll., Cambridge, 2007. Hon. LLD: Sheffield, 2003; Keele, 2005. *Publications:* (author, contributor) numerous legal books and jls. *Recreations:* music, theatre, sport. *Club:* Reform.

KAY, Michael Jack David; QC 2002; **His Honour Judge Kay;** a Circuit Judge, since 2004; a Deputy High Court Judge, since 2007; *b* 13 Oct. 1959; *m* 1984, Victoria Reuben; two *s* one *d*. *Educ:* Manchester Grammar Sch.; Christ's Coll., Cambridge. Called to the Bar, Lincoln's Inn, 1981; an Assistant Recorder, 1998–2000, Recorder, 2000–04; pt-time Chm., Employment Tribunals, 2001–04. *Recreations:* service to the community, football, theatre, praying.

KAY, Nicholas Peter, CMG 2007; HM Diplomatic Service; on unpaid leave as United Nations Secretary-General's Special Representative for Somalia, since 2013; *b* 8 March 1958; *s* of Ralph Peter Kay and Josephine Alice Kay (*née* Poyner); *m* 1986, Susan Ruth Wallace; one *s* two *d*. *Educ:* Abingdon Sch., Oxon; St Edmund Hall, Oxford (BA Hons English Lang. and Lit.); Univ. of Reading (MA Applied Linguistics). English lang. teacher, Spain, Peru, Brazil, Saudi Arabia, Cyprus and UK, 1980–94; entered FCO, 1994; Hd, Pakistan and Afghanistan Section, FCO, 1994–96; 1st Sec. and Dep. Hd of Mission, Havana, 1997–2000; Dep. Hd, Policy Planning Staff (later Directorate for Strategy and Innovation), FCO, 2000–02; Counsellor and Dep. Hd of Mission, Madrid, 2002–06; UK Regl Co-ordinator, Southern Afghanistan, 2006–07; Ambassador: to the Democratic Republic of the Congo and to the Republic of Congo, 2007–09; to Sudan, 2010–12; Dir, Africa, FCO, 2012–13. *Recreations:* sailing, vegetarian cookery, travel. *Address:* c/o Foreign and Commonwealth Office, King Charles Street, SW1A 2AH. *E:* kayn@un.org.

KAY, (Robert) Jervis; QC 1996; Admiralty Registrar, and Master of the Senior (formerly Supreme) Court, Queen's Bench Division, since 2009; *b* 25 Feb. 1949; *s* of late Philip Jervis Kay, VRD and Pamela Kay; *m* 1988, Henrietta Kathleen Ward; one *s* three *d*. *Educ:* Wellington Coll.; Nottingham Univ. (LLB Hons). Called to the Bar, Lincoln's Inn, 1972 (Bencher 2005); in practice at the Bar, 1973–2009. *Publications:* (Ed.) Atkins Court Forms, Vol. 3 Admiralty, 1979, 1990, 1994, 2000, 2004, 2008. *Recreation:* sailing. *Address:* Royal Courts of Justice, WC2A 2LL. *Clubs:* Turf, MCC, Royal Ocean Racing.

KAY, Sarah; *see* Kay, H. S.

KAY, Steven Walton; QC 1997; *b* 4 Aug. 1954; *s* of late John Walton Kay and Eunice May Kay; *m* 1st (marr. diss.); one *s*; 2nd, 2000, Valerie (*née* Logan); one *d*. *Educ:* Epsom Coll.; Leeds Univ. (LLB). Called to the Bar, Inner Temple, 1977. Asst Recorder, 1997–2000; Recorder, 2000–13. Defence Counsel, first trial, Internat. Criminal Tribunal for former Yugoslavia, 1996; *Amicus Curiae*, 2001–04, Assigned Defence Counsel, 2004–06, trial of ex-Pres. Milosevic; Defence Counsel: Internat. Criminal Tribunal for Rwanda, trial of Musema, 1997–2001; Internat. Criminal Tribunal for former Yugoslavia, trial of Gotovina *et al*, 2007–11; Internat. Criminal Ct, case of Pres. of Kenya, Uhuru Kenyatta, 2010–. Sec., Criminal Bar Assoc., 1993–96. Founder: Eur. Criminal Bar Assoc., 1998; Internat. Criminal Law Bureau, 2008. Dir, Melbury House Music Ltd, 2012–. *Publications:* (contrib.) The Rome Statute of the International Criminal Court, ed Casese, Gaeta and Jones, 2002. *Recreations:* ski-ing, golf, gardening, music, managing Jason Isaacs. *Address:* 9 Bedford Row, WC1R 4AZ. *T:* (020) 7489 2727. *Clubs:* Hurtwood Park Polo; Drift Golf.

KAY, William John; writer and journalist; Money columnist, Sunday Times, 2005–13 (Money Editor, 2005–06); *b* 12 Sept. 1946; *s* of William Jarvie Kay and Agnes Sutherland Walker; *m* 1968 (marr. diss. 1986); two *s*; partner, 1987, Lynne Bateson. *Educ:* Westminster City Sch.; The Queen's Coll., Oxford (MA); Univ. of Calif, Los Angeles. London Evening News, 1968; London Evening Standard, 1972; Daily Telegraph, 1977; Features Editor, Financial Weekly, 1979; Dep. Business Editor, Now!, 1979; Sen. Writer, Sunday Times Business News, 1981; City Editor, The Times, 1984; freelance, 1986–95; Financial Editor, Independent on Sunday, 1995; City Editor, Mail on Sunday, 1995–99; freelance, 1999–2001; Personal Finance Ed., Independent, 2001–05. Member: American Cinematheque, 2007–; Huntington Liby, 2007–; Hollywood Heritage, 2010–. Wincott Foundn Personal Finance Journalist of the Year, 2002; Headlinemoney Columnist of the Year, 2005; Lifetime Achievement Award, ABI, 2005. *Publications:* A–Z Guide to Money, 1983; Tycoons, 1985; Big Bang, 1986; (ed) The Stock Exchange: a market place for tomorrow, 1986; Battle for the High Street, 1987; (ed) Modern Merchant Banking, 1988; The Bosses, 1994; Lord of the Dance: the story of Gerry Robinson, 1999; Pasadena Parade, 2009. *Recreations:* cricket, travel, cheese, ice cream, Chelsea FC. *E:* billkay111@gmail.com. *Club:* MCC.

KAY-SHUTTLEWORTH, family name of **Baron Shuttleworth**.

KAYE, Rev. Dr Bruce Norman, AM 2005; General Secretary, The Anglican Church of Australia General Synod, 1994–2004; *b* 30 June 1939; *s* of John Harold Kaye and Elsie Evelyn Kaye; *m* 1st, 1965, Rosemary Jeanette Hutchison (*d* 1979); one *s* one *d*; 2nd, 1983, Margaret Louise Mathieson. *Educ:* Sydney Boys' High Sch.; Moore Theol Coll. (ThL 1963); Univ. of London (BD 1964); Univ. of Sydney (BA 1966); Univ. of Basel (Dr Theol 1976). Professional Officer, Sydney Water Bd, NSW, 1955–60. Deacon 1964, priest 1965; Curate, St Jude's, Dural, NSW, 1964–66; St John's College, University of Durham: Asst Tutor, 1968; Tutor, 1969; Tutor-Librarian, 1970–75; Sen. Tutor, 1975–82; Vice-Principal, 1979–82; Lectr, Faculty of Divinity, Univ. of Durham, 1970–82; Master, New Coll., Univ. of NSW, 1983–94; Founding Dir, New Coll. Inst. for Values Research, 1987–92. Visiting Fellow: Deutsche Akademische Austauschdienst, Freiberg, 1974; Sch. of Sci. and Technol. Studies, 1984–94, Sch. of Hist., 2005–, Univ. of NSW; Fellow Commoner, Churchill Coll., and Vis. Schol., Faculty of Divinity, Univ. of Cambridge, 1991–92; Vis. Schol., Sch. of Theol. and Ministry, Seattle Univ., 2003; Professorial Associate, 2007–12, Adjunct Res. Prof., 2012–, Charles Sturt Univ. Consulting Ed., Jl of Anglican Studies, 2013– (Founding Ed., 2002–13). Hon. ThD Australian Coll. of Theol., 2006. *Publications:* Using the Bible in Ethics, 1976; The Supernatural in the New Testament, 1977; (ed) Obeying Christ in a Changing World, 1977; (ed) Law, Morality and the Bible, 1978; The Argument of Romans with Special Reference to Chapter 6, 1979; (ed) Immigration: what kind of Australia do we want?, 1989; A Church Without Walls: being Anglican in Australia, 1995; (ed) Authority and the Shaping of Tradition, 1997; Godly Citizens, 1999; Web of Meaning, 2000; (Gen. Ed.) Anglicanism in Australia, 2002; Reinventing Anglicanism, 2003; Introduction to World Anglicanism, 2008; Conflict and the Practice of Christian Faith: the Anglican experiment, 2009; contrib. numerous articles to theological and other learned jls. *Recreations:* theatre, golf, walking, reading. *Address:* 217 Hopetown Avenue, Watson's Bay, NSW 2030, Australia. *Club:* Australian (Sydney).

KAYE, Dr Elaine Hilda, FRHistS; Headmistress, Oxford High School, GPDST, 1972–81; *b* 21 Jan. 1930; *d* of late Rev. Harold Sutcliffe Kaye and Kathleen Mary (*née* White). *Educ:* Bradford Girls' Grammar Sch.; Milton Mount Coll.; St Anne's Coll., Oxford; Sheffield Univ. (PhD 1995). Assistant Mistress: Leyton County High Sch., 1952–54; Queen's Coll., Harley Street, 1954–59; South Hampstead High Sch., GPDST, 1959–65; Part-time Tutor, Westminster Tutors, 1965–67; Dep. Warden, Missenden Abbey Adult Coll., 1967–72. Project Dir, Oxford Project for Peace Studies, 1989–92 (Vice-Chair and Editor, 1984–89); (non-stipendiary) Lectr in Theology (Church History), Mansfield Coll., Oxford, 1996–99 (College Historian, 1990–95). President: URC History Soc., 1997–2002; Friends of Congregational Liby, 2010–13. FRHistS 2004. *Publications:* History of the King's Weigh House Church, 1968; History of Queen's College, Harley St, 1972; Short History of Missenden Abbey, 1973, 2nd edn 1992; (contrib.) Biographical Dictionary of Modern Peace Leaders, 1985; (ed) Peace Studies: the hard questions, 1987; C. J. Cadoux: theologian, scholar and pacifist, 1988; (with Ross Mackenzie) W. E. Orchard: a study in Christian exploration, 1990; Mansfield College, Oxford: its origin, history and significance, 1996; (contrib.) Oxford Dictionary of the Christian Church, 3rd edn 1997; For the Work of Ministry: Northern College and its predecessors, 1999; (contrib) Christian Thinking and Social Order, 1999; (contrib.) Modern Christianity and Cultural Aspiration, 2003; (with Janet Lees and Kirsty Thorpe) Daughters of Dissent, 2004. *Recreations:* music, walking, conversation. *Address:* 4 Fairlawn Flats, First Turn, Oxford OX2 8AP.

KAYE, Geoffrey John; President, Animal Shelter AC, Mexico, since 2001; *b* 14 Aug. 1935; *s* of Michael and Golda Kaye; two *d*. *Educ:* Christ's College, Finchley. Started with Pricerite Ltd when business was a small private company controlling six shops, 1951; apptd Manager (aged 18) of one of Pricerite Ltd stores, 1953; Supervisor, Pricerite Ltd, 1955; Controller of all stores in Pricerite Ltd Gp, 1958; Director, 1963; Chairman and Man. Dir, 1966–73. Pres., Allied Automotive Inc., 1992. *Recreations:* tennis, golf.

KAYE, Sir John Phillip Lister L.; *see* Lister-Kaye.

KAYE, Lindsey Joy, (Mrs D. N. Kaye); *see* Kushner, L. J.

KAYE, Maj. Sir Paul (Henry Gordon), 5th Bt *cr* 1923, of Huddersfield, Co. York; Australian Army, retired 2001; *b* 19 Feb. 1958; *s* of Sir David Alexander Gordon Kaye, 4th Bt and of Adelle Francis Kaye (*née* Thomas); *S* father, 1994; *m* 1st, 1984, Sally Ann Louise Grützner (marr. diss. 2000); 2nd, 2005, Bonita Bonife Yang (marr. diss. 2007); 3rd, 2010, Marlyn Bancure Arambala; one *s*. *Educ:* Downlands Coll., Toowoomba; Univ. of Queensland (Dip. Applied Science (Rural Technol.) 1978). Lieut, Australian Regular Army, 1982; Captain, 1986; Major, 1991. Australian Service Medal, 1995; Multi-National Force and Observers Medal, 1995; Defence Force Service Medal, 1998. *Recreations:* Rugby Union, horse riding, motorcycle riding, reading. *Heir:* *s* Lionel Gordon Arambala Kaye, *b* 6 Sept. 2012.

KAYE, Roger Godfrey, TD 1980 and Bar 1985; QC 1989; **His Honour Judge Kaye;** a Circuit Judge, since 2005; Specialist Chancery/Mercantile Judge, North Eastern Circuit, since 2005; *b* 21 Sept. 1946; *s* of late Anthony Harmsworth Kaye and Heidi Alice (*née* Jordy); *m* 1974, Melloney Rose, *d* of late Rev. H. M. Westall. *Educ:* King's Sch., Canterbury; Birmingham Univ. (LLB 1968). FCIArb 2004. Lectr in Law, Kingston Poly., 1968–73. Called to the Bar, Lincoln's Inn, 1970, Bencher, 1997; Jun. Treasury Counsel in Insolvency Matters, 1978–89; Dep. High Court Registrar in Bankruptcy, 1985–2001; Dep. High Court Judge, Chancery Div., QBD and Family Div., 1990–2005; a Recorder, 1994–2005. Dep. Chancellor, dio. of Southwark, 1995–99; Chancellor: dio. of Hereford, 2000– (Dep. Chancellor, 1997–2000); dio. of St Albans, 2002– (Dep. Chancellor, 1995–2002). Chairman: Fees Collection Cttee, Bar Council, 1991–93 (Dep. Chm., 1990–91); Bristol & Cardiff Chancery Bar Assoc., 1990–95. Member: Professional Conduct Cttee, Bar Council, 1995–97; Panel of Chairmen, City Disputes Panel, 1997–2005. Varied TA service in Europe, 1967–97; Hon. Colonel: Intelligence and Security Gp (Volunteers), 1998–99; 3rd (Volunteer) Mil. Intelligence Bn, 1999–2011; 5th (Volunteer) Mil. Intelligence Bn, 2008–11. FRSA 1995. *Recreation:* going home. *Address:* Leeds Combined Court Centre, 1 Oxford Row, Leeds LS1 3BG. *Clubs:* Athenæum, Army and Navy, Royal Automobile, Special Forces; Northern Counties (Newcastle upon Tyne).

KAYE, Rosalind Anne, (Mrs J. A. Kaye); *see* Plowright, R. A.

KAYE, Prof. Stanley Bernard, MD; FRCP; FRSE; FMedSci; Cancer Research UK (formerly Cancer Research Campaign) Professor of Medical Oncology, since 2000, and Senior Research Fellow, Institute of Cancer Research and Royal Marsden NHS Foundation Trust (formerly Hospital); *b* 5 Sept. 1948; *s* of Peter Kaye and Dora Kaye (*née* Thomas); *m* 1975, Anna Catherine Lister; two *s* one *d*. *Educ:* Charing Cross Hosp. Med. Sch., London (BSc Biochem. 1969); Univ. of London (MB BS 1972; MD 1980). FRCP 1990. University of Glasgow: Sen. Lectr in Med. Oncology, 1980–85; Prof. of Med. Oncology, 1985–2000; Hd, Div. of Clin. Studies (formerly Sect. of Medicine), 2000–13, Hd, Drug Develt Unit, 2000–12, Inst. Cancer Res., London. FRSE 2001; FMedSci 2004. *Publications:* (ed jtly) Textbook of Medical Oncology, 1997, 4th edn 2009; (ed jtly) Emerging Therapeutic Targets in Ovarian Cancer, 2011. *Recreations:* playing squash, tennis and golf to varying degrees of indifference. *Address:* Royal Marsden Hospital, Downs Road, Sutton, Surrey SM2 5PT. *T:* (020) 8661 3539, *Fax:* (020) 8661 3541. *E:* stan.kaye@rmh.nhs.uk; (home) 44 Burdon Lane, Sutton, Surrey SM2 7PT. *Club:* Royal Automobile.

KAYE, (William) John H.; *see* Holland-Kaye.

KEABLE-ELLIOTT, Dr (Robert) Anthony, OBE 1988; FRCGP; general practitioner, 1948–87; *b* 14 Nov. 1924; *s* of Robert Keable and Jolie Buck; *m* 1953, Gilian Mary Hutchison (*d* 2011); four *s*. *Educ:* Sherborne Sch., Dorset; Guy's Hosp., London, 1943–48 (MB BS London). FRCGP 1966. Founder Mem., Chiltern Medical Soc., 1956, Vice-Pres. 1958, Pres. 1964; Member, Faculty Board of Thames Valley, Faculty of Royal Coll. of General Practitioners, 1960; Upjohn Travelling Fellowship, 1962; Member: Bucks Local Med. Cttee, 1958–75 (Chm., 1964–68; Hon. Life Mem., 1975–); GMC, 1989–94. British Medical Association: Mem., 1948–; Mem. Council, 1974–94; Treasurer, 1981–87; Chm., Journal Cttee, 1987–93; Chm., Gen. Med. Services Cttee, 1966–72. Mem., Finance Corp. of General Practice, 1974–79. Mem., Soc. of Apothecaries, 1985–; Freeman, City of London, 1986. Asst Editor, Guy's Hospital Gazette, 1947–48. BMA Gold Medal, 1994. *Recreations:* sailing, golf, gardening. *Address:* Peels, Ibstone, near High Wycombe, Bucks HP14 3XX. *T:* (01491) 638385.

KEAL, Anthony Charles; Partner, Simpson Thacher & Bartlett LLP, 2005–09; *b* Aldershot, 12 July 1951; *s* of Kitchener Keal and Joan Marjorie Keal; *m* 1979, Janet Michele King; four *s*. *Educ:* New Coll., Oxford (BA Juris.). Admitted solicitor, 1976; Partner, Allen & Overy, 1982–2005. *Recreations:* sailing, ski-ing, walking, opera, theatre. *Address:* c/o Simpson Thacher & Bartlett LLP, One Ropemaker Street, EC2Y 9HU. *T:* (020) 7275 6500, *Fax:* (020) 7275 6502.

KEALEY, Gavin Sean James; QC 1994; a Deputy High Court Judge, Queen's Bench Division (Commercial Court), since 2002; *b* 2 Sept. 1953; *s* of Paul and Evelyn Kealey; *m* 1981, Karen Elizabeth Nowak; three *d*. *Educ:* Charterhouse; University Coll., Oxford (BA Jurisp.). Lectr in Law, King's Coll. London, 1976–77; called to the Bar, Inner Temple, 1977, Bencher, 2002; Commercial Barrister, 1978; Recorder, 2000–10; Head of Chambers, 2003–. *Address:* 7 King's Bench Walk, Temple, EC4Y 7DS. *T:* (020) 7910 8300.
See also G. T. E. Kealey.

KEALEY, Prof. (George) Terence (Evelyn), DPhil; Professor of Clinical Biochemistry, University of Buckingham, since 2011 (Vice-Chancellor, 2001–14, now Emeritus); *b* 16 Feb. 1952; *s* of Paul and Evelyn Kealey; *m* 1989, Sally Harwood Gritten, *d* of late Donald Meredith

Gritten and of Stella Harwood Gritten (now Huber); one *s* one *d. Educ:* Charterhouse Sch.; St Bartholomew's Hosp. Med. Sch. (MB BS 1975; BSc Biochem. 1976); Balliol Coll., Oxford (DPhil 1982); MA Cantab 1995. House physician, St Bartholomew's Hosp., 1976–77; MRC Trng Fellow, Nuffield Dept of Clinical Biochem., Oxford, 1977–82; Jun. Dean, Balliol Coll., Oxford, 1980–81; Sen. Registrar in Clinical Biochem. and Metabolic Medicine, Royal Victoria Infirmary, Newcastle upon Tyne, 1982–86; Wellcome Sen. Res. Fellow in Clinical Sci., Nuffield Dept of Clinical Biochem., Univ. of Oxford, 1986–88; Lectr, Dept of Clinical Biochem., Univ. of Cambridge, 1988–2001. Member, Academic Advisory Council: Globalization Inst., 2005–; Global Warming Policy Foundn, 2009–; Sen. Fellow in Educn, Adam Smith Inst., 2008–; Adjunct Schol., Center for Study of Sci., Cato Inst., Washington, 2014–. Trustee, Buckingham Centre for the Arts, 2005–; Gov., Royal Latin Sch., Buckingham, 2011–. Hon. Consultant Chemical Pathologist: Oxford HA, 1986–88; Cambridge HA, 1988–2001. Lectures incl. 16th Annual IEA Hayek Meml Lect., 2007. Caldwell Prize, Pope Center for Higher Educn Policy, USA, 2001; Free Enterprise Award, IEA, 2004. *Publications:* The Economic Laws of Scientific Research, 1996; Sex, Science and Profits, 2008; contrib. papers in the molecular cell biol. of human skin develt. *Address:* University of Buckingham, Hunter Street, Buckingham MK18 1EG. *T:* (01280) 820207. *Club:* Athenæum.

KEALY, Robin Andrew, CMG 1991; HM Diplomatic Service, retired; consultant, since 2004; *b* 7 Oct. 1944; *s* of Lt-Col H. L. B. Kealy, Royal Signals and Mrs B. E. Kealy; *m* 1987, Annabel Jane Hood; two *s. Educ:* Harrow Sch.; Oriel Coll., Oxford (Open Scholar; BA Lit. Hum. (1st Cl. Hons Mods); MA). Joined HM Diplomatic Service, 1967; FO, 1967; MECAS, 1968; Tripoli, 1970; Kuwait, 1972; ME Dept, FCO, 1975; Port of Spain, 1978; Commercial Sec., Prague, 1982; Asst, Aid Policy Dept, FCO, 1985; Counsellor and Consul Gen., Baghdad, 1987–90; Dir of Trade Promotion and Investment, Paris, 1990–95; Head, Aviation and Maritime Dept, FCO, 1995–97; Consul-Gen., Jerusalem, 1997–2001; Ambassador to Tunisia, 2002–04. Chairman: Welfare Assoc. (UK), 2006–09; Med. Aid to Palestinians, 2008–13 (Mem. Bd, 2004–13; Vice-Chm., 2006–08); Dir, Sir Harold Hillier Gardens, Romsey, 2006–08. Trustee, Arab-British Chamber Charitable Foundn, 2007–13. *Recreations:* music, theatre, ski-ing, cooking, gardening. *Club:* Travellers.

KEANE, Prof. Adrian Nigel; Professor of Law, City University London, since 2001; *b* Arundel, W Sussex, 12 July 1955; *s* of Michael and Mildred Keane; *m* 1st, 1981, Angela Stewart (marr. diss. 1990); 2nd, 1994, Rosemary Simon (*d* 2010). *Educ:* Chichester High Sch. for Boys; Univ. of Hull (LLB). Called to the Bar, Inner Temple, 1978; Lectr, Sch. of Law, Univ. of Hong Kong, 1981–82; Inns of Court School of Law: Lectr, 1984–87; Sen. Lectr, 1987–90; Reader, 1990–2001; Dean, 2001–08; Dir, Professional Progs, City Univ. London, 2008–11. Vis. Tutor, Wadham Coll., Oxford, 1987–88; Guest Lectr, Dept of Law, LSE, 1989–90. Consultant, Centre for Criminal Procedure Reform, Renmin Univ., Beijing, 2011. Chm. (pt-time), Employment Tribunals, 1996–2001. Mem., Educn and Trng Wkg Party, Bar Council, 1992, 2002–03. *Publications:* The Modern Law of Evidence, 1985, 10th edn 2014; (jtly) Blackstone's Criminal Practice, 1991, 26th edn 2015; (jtly) Advocacy, 1996, 10th edn 2005; (jtly) Blackstone's Civil Practice, 2000, 15th edn 2015; contrib. articles on evidence law to learned jls. *Recreations:* music, gardening, cooking, Arsenal FC. *Address:* City Law School, City University London, 4 Gray's Inn Place, WC1R 5DX. *T:* (020) 7404 5787, *Fax:* (020) 7831 3193. *E:* a.n.keane@city.ac.uk.

KEANE, Sir Charles; *see* Keane, Sir J. C.

KEANE, Fergal Patrick, OBE 1997; BBC Special Correspondent, since 1997; *b* 6 Jan. 1961; *s* of Eamon Patrick Keane and Maura Theresa (*née* Hassett); *m* 1986, Anne Frances Flaherty; one *s* one *d. Educ:* Terenure Coll., Dublin; Presentation Coll., Cork. Reporter: Limerick Leader, 1979–82; Irish Press, 1982–84; RTE, 1984–88; joined BBC, 1988: Ireland Corresp., 1988–90; Southern Africa Corresp., 1990–94; Asia Corresp., 1994–97. Writer and presenter, TV series, Story of Ireland, 2011. Professorial Fellow, Inst. of Irish Studies, Univ. of Liverpool, 2013–. Radio Journalist of Year, Sony, 1994; Journalist of Year, RTS, 1994. BAFTA award, TV documentary, 1997. *Publications:* The Bondage of Fear, 1994; Season of Blood, 1995; Letter to Daniel, 1996; Letters Home, 1999; A Stranger's Eye, 2000; All of These People, 2005; Road of Bones: the siege of Kohima 1944, 2010 (British Army Mil. Book of Year, 2011). *Recreations:* fishing, sailing, reading. *Address:* c/o BBC News Centre, Broadcasting House, Portland Place, W1A 1AA. *Clubs:* Foreign Correspondents' (Hong Kong); Royal Cork Yacht (Cork).

KEANE, Francis Joseph; Sheriff of Tayside, Central and Fife at Kirkcaldy, 1998–2004; *b* 5 Jan. 1936; *s* of Thomas and Helen Keane; *m* 1960, Lucia Corio Morrison; two *s* one *d. Educ:* Blairs Coll., Aberdeen; Gregorian Univ., Rome (PhL); Univ. of Edinburgh (LLB). Solicitor; Partner, McCluskey, Keane & Co., 1959; Depute Procurator Fiscal, Perth, 1961, Edinburgh, 1963; Senior Depute PF, Edinburgh, 1971; Senior Legal Asst, Crown Office, Edinburgh, 1972; PF, Airdrie, 1976; Regional PF, S Strathclyde, Dumfries and Galloway, 1980; Sheriff: of Glasgow and Strathkelvin, 1984–93; of Lothian and Borders at Edinburgh, 1993–98. Pres., PF Soc., 1982–84. *Recreations:* music, painting, tennis.

KEANE, Sir (John) Charles, 7th Bt *cr* 1801, of Cappoquin, Co. Waterford; *b* UK, 16 Sept. 1941; *er s* of Maj. Sir Richard Keane, 6th Bt and Olivia Dorothy (*née* Hawkshaw); *S* father, 2010; *m* 1977, Corinne Everard de Harzir; two *s* one *d. Educ:* Christ Church, Oxford (BA 1963; MA 1967). ACA. *Recreations:* farming, forestry, gardening. *Heir: er s* Richard Christopher Keane, *b* 21 Aug. 1981. *Address:* Cappoquin House, Cappoquin, Co. Waterford, Ireland. *T:* 54290; 26 avenue d'Houguemont, 1180 Brussels, Belgium. *T:* (2) 3755464. *E:* charles-keane@skynet.be. *Club:* Kildare Street and University.

KEANE, John Granville Colpoys; artist; *b* 12 Sept. 1954; *s* of Granville Keane and Elaine Violet Meredith Keane (*née* Doubble); *m* 1996, Rosemary Anne McGowan; one *s* one *d. Educ:* Hardenwick Sch., Harpenden; Cheam Sch., Berks; Wellington Coll.; Camberwell Sch. of Art, London (BA Fine Art). 62 solo exhibns in UK, Europe and USA, 1980–; official British War Artist, Gulf War, 1991; Artist in Residence: Independent on Sunday, 2000–01; Sch. of Internat. Relns, St Andrews Univ., 2014–; commnd portrait of Kofi Annan for UN, 2010. Vis. Prof., London Inst., 2000; Vis. Res. Fellow, Camberwell Coll. of Arts, 2000–11. FRSA 2005. *Publications:* Gulf, 1992; (with Duncan Green) Guatemala: burden of paradise, 1992; (with Mark Lawson) Conflicts of Interest, 1995; (with Mark Lawson) Troubles My Sight, 2015. *Recreations:* tennis, unpopular music, snooker. *Address:* c/o Flowers East, 82 Kingsland Road, E2 8DP. *T:* (020) 7920 7777, *Fax:* (020) 7920 7770. *E:* gallery@flowerseast.com. *Clubs:* Groucho, Chelsea Arts; Thorpeness Country.

KEANE, Ronan; Chief Justice of Ireland, 2000–04; *b* 20 July 1932; *s* of John Patrick Keane and Katherine Gertrude Keane (*née* Boylan); *m* 1st, 1962, Ann Therese O'Donnell (*d* 2008); one *s* two *d*; 2nd, 2010, Irene Garavan. *Educ:* Blackrock Coll., Co. Dublin; University Coll., Dublin (BA 1953). Called to the Irish Bar, King's Inns, Dublin, 1954 (Bencher, 1979); in practice at the Bar, 1954–79; Jun. Counsel, 1954–70; Sen. Counsel, 1970–79; Judge: High Court of Ireland, 1979–96; Supreme Court of Ireland, 1996–2000. Chm., Irish Bar Council, 1974–75; Pres., Law Reform Commn, 1987–92. Hon. Bencher: Lincoln's Inn, 2000; NI Inn of Court, 2000. Hon. Fellow, Univ. of Dublin, 2008. Hon. LLD UC Dublin, 2003. *Publications:* The Law of Local Government in the Republic of Ireland, 1982; Company Law in the Republic of Ireland, 1985, 4th edn 2007; Equity and the Law of Trusts in the Republic of Ireland, 1988, 2nd edn 2011. *Recreations:* music, theatre, reading. *Address:* 13 Leeson Park Avenue, Dublin 6, Ireland. *T:* (1) 6697008.

KEARL, Guy Alexander; QC 2002; **His Honour Judge Kearl;** a Circuit Judge, since 2011; *b* 29 Sept. 1959; *s* of Ian Alexander Kearl and Sheila Kearl; *m* 1985, Anea Jayne Ellison; two *s. Educ:* Millfield Sch.; Univ. of Central Lancashire (BA Hons Law); Inns of Court Sch. of Law. Called to the Bar, Middle Temple, 1982; in practice, specialising in serious crime law; Recorder, 2001–11. *Recreations:* ski-ing, marathon running, tennis, cycling. *Address:* Leeds Combined Court Centre, Court House, 1 Oxford Row, Leeds LS1 3BG.

KEARLEY, family name of **Viscount Devonport**.

KEARNEY, Brian; Sheriff of Glasgow and Strathkelvin, 1977–2007; Temporary Sheriff Principal, South Strathclyde, Dumfries and Galloway, 2007–08; *b* 25 Aug. 1935; *s* of late James Samuel and Agnes Olive Kearney; *m* 1965, Elizabeth Mary Chambers; three *s* one *d. Educ:* Largs Higher Grade Sch.; Greenock Academy; Glasgow Univ. (MA, LLB). Qualified solicitor, 1960; Partner, Biggart, Lumsden & Co., Solicitors, Glasgow, 1965–74. Sheriff of N Strathclyde at Dumbarton (floating sheriff), 1974–77. Sometime tutor in Jurisprudence, and external examr in legal subjects, Glasgow Univ.; Hon. Lectr, Social Work Dept, Dundee Univ., 1995–. Chm., Inquiry into Child Care Policies in Fife, 1989–92 (report published, 1992). Mem., Judicial Studies Cttee (Scotland), 1997–2005. Pres., Glasgow Juridical Soc., 1964–65; Chm., Glasgow Marriage Guidance Council, 1977–90; Hon. President: Glasgow Marriage Counselling Service, 1990–; Family Law Assoc., Scotland, 1999–. *Publications:* An Introduction to Ordinary Civil Procedure in the Sheriff Court, 1982; Children's Hearings and the Sheriff Court, 1987, 2nd edn 2000; (ed jtly) Butterworths' Scottish Family Law Service, 1995; The Scottish Children's Hearings System in Action, 2007; articles in legal jls. *Recreations:* cutting sandwiches for family picnics, listening to music, reading, writing and resting. *Club:* Glasgow Art.

KEARNEY, Martha Catherine; BBC broadcaster; presenter: The Review Show (formerly Newsnight Review), since 2005; The World at One, BBC Radio 4, since 2007; *b* 8 Oct. 1957; *d* of Hugh and Catherine Kearney; *m* 2001, Christopher Thomas Shaw, *qv. Educ:* George Watson's Ladies' Coll., Edinburgh; St Anne's Coll., Oxford. LBC Radio, 1981–87; A Week in Politics, Channel Four, 1987–88; BBC, 1988–: reporter, On the Record, 1988–94; Panorama, 1993; reporter, 1994–2000, Political Ed., 2000–07, Newsnight; presenter, Woman's Hour, Radio 4, 1999–2007. Year back packing, 1989–90. Hon. DLit Keele, 2007. *Recreations:* reading, cooking, travel, beekeeping. *Address:* c/o BBC News Centre, Broadcasting House, Portland Place, W1A 1AA. *T:* (020) 9743 8000. *E:* martha.kearney@bbc.co.uk. *Clubs:* Royal Over-Seas League, Soho House.

KEARNEY, Hon. Sir William (John Francis), Kt 1982; CBE 1976; Judge of the Supreme Court of the Northern Territory, 1982–99; *b* 8 Jan. 1935; *s* of William John Kilbeg Kearney and Gertrude Ivylene Kearney; *m* 1959, Jessie Alice Elizabeth Yung; three *d. Educ:* Univ. of Sydney (BA, LLB); University Coll. London (LLM). Legal Service of Papua New Guinea, 1963–75; Sec. for Law, 1972–75; dormant Commn as Administrator, 1972–73, and as High Comr, 1973–75; Judge, Supreme Ct of PNG, 1976–82; Dep. Chief Justice, 1980–82. Aboriginal Land Comr, 1982–86. *Recreations:* travelling, literature.

KEARNS, Dr William Edward, FFPH; consultancy in health policy and public health, 1993–2000; *b* 10 July 1934; *s* of William Edward Kearns and Kathleen Wolfenden; *m* 1954, Beryl Cross; four *s* one *d* (and one *s* decd). *Educ:* Liverpool Coll.; Univ. of Liverpool (MB ChB); Univ. of London (MSc; DipTh 1995). MRCS, LRCP. Hosp. posts in cardiorespiratory physiology, gen. medicine and pathology, United Liverpool Hosps, 1958–70; NW Metropolitan Regional Hospital Board: Asst SMO, 1970–73; Regional Sci. Officer, 1973–74; Dist Community Physician, Kensington and Chelsea and Westminster AHA (Teaching), 1974–82; Hon. Sen. Lectr in Community Medicine, St Mary's Hosp. Med. Sch., 1975–86; Dist MO, Paddington and N Kensington HA, 1982–86; Regional MO and Dir of Health Care Policy, 1986–90, Dir of Public Health, 1990–92, CMO, 1990–93, NE Thames RHA. Reader, Neasden Parish Church (S Catherine); Sec. for Readers, dio. of London, 1996–2003; Oblate Novice, Monastery of Our Lady and St Benedict, Elmore Abbey, 1996–98; Oblate, Monastery of St Mary at the Cross, Edgware Abbey, 1998–. FRSA 1997. *Publications:* The Health Report, North East Thames Health Region, 1990, 1991; contribs to med. jls. *Recreations:* gardening for wild life conservation, grandparenting. *Address:* Five Midholm, Barn Hill, Wembley Park, Middx HA9 9LJ. *T:* (020) 8908 1511, *Fax:* (020) 8904 3884. *Club:* Royal Society of Medicine.

KEARON, Rt Rev. Kenneth Arthur; *see* Limerick and Killaloe, Bishop of.

KEATES, Jonathan Basil; writer; teacher of English, City of London School, 1974–2013; *b* 7 Nov. 1946; *s* of Richard Herbert Basil Keates and Evangeline Sonia Wilcox. *Educ:* Bryanston Sch., Dorset (Schol.); Magdalen Coll., Oxford (MA); Exeter Univ. (PGCE). FRSL 1993; FSA 2009. Chm., Venice in Peril Fund, 2013– (Actg Chm., 2012–13). *Publications:* The Companion Guide to the Shakespeare Country, 1979; Allegro Postillions (James Tait Black Prize; Hawthornden Prize), 1984; Handel: the man and his music, 1985, 2nd edn 2008; The Strangers' Gallery, 1987; Italian Journeys, 1991; Stendhal, 1994 (Enid McLeod Prize, 1995); Henry Purcell, 1995; Soon To Be a Major Motion Picture, 1997; Smile Please, 2000; The Siege of Venice, 2005; The Portable Paradise, 2011; Robert Browning, 2012. *Recreations:* Venice, libraries, music, friendship. *Address:* 5 Houblon Road, Richmond, Surrey TW10 6DB. *T:* (020) 8940 9679. *Club:* Athenæum.

KEATING, Prof. Jonathan Peter, PhD; FRS 2009; Henry Overton Wills Professor of Mathematics, University of Bristol, since 2012; *b* Salford, 20 Sept. 1963; *s* of Albert Edward Keating and Sheila Keating; *m* 2009, Prof. Heidy Marita Mader; one *s* one *d* (and one *s* decd). *Educ:* New Coll., Oxford (BA 1st Cl.); Univ. of Bristol (PhD 1989). Lectr in Applied Maths, Univ. of Manchester, 1991–95; University of Bristol: Reader in Applied Maths, 1995–97; Prof. of Mathematical Physics, 1997–2012; Hd, Dept of Maths, 2001–04; Dean of Sci., 2009–13. EPSRC Sen. Res. Fellow, 2004–09. *Publications:* contrib. papers to mathematical and scientific jls. *Recreations:* cooking, cricket, running and (most importantly) my family. *Address:* School of Mathematics, University of Bristol, Bristol BS8 1TW.

KEATING, Kay Rosamond Blundell; a District Judge (Magistrates' Courts) (formerly Metropolitan Stipendiary Magistrate), 1987–2004; *b* 3 Oct. 1943; *d* of Geoffrey Blundell Jones and Avis Blundell Jones; *m* 1st, 1965, Edmund Deighton (decd); one *d* decd; 2nd, 1978, Donald Norman Keating, QC (*d* 1995); one *s. Educ:* St Hugh's College, Oxford (BA Jurisp. 1965; MA 1968). Called to the Bar, Gray's Inn, 1966. *Recreations:* travel, walking, tennis, riding, opera.

KEATING, Prof. Michael, PhD; FBA 2012; FRSE; FAcSS; Professor of Politics, University of Aberdeen, since 1999; Director, ESRC Scottish Centre on Constitutional Change, since 2013; *b* Hartlepool, 2 Feb. 1950; *s* of Michael Joseph Keating and Margaret Keating (*née* Lamb); *m* 1975, Patricia Ann McCusker; one *s. Educ:* St Aidan's Grammar Sch., Sunderland; Pembroke Coll., Oxford (BA 1971; MA 1975); Glasgow Coll. of Technol. (PhD 1975). Sen. Res. Officer, Univ. of Essex, 1975–76; Lectr, N Staffs Poly., 1976–79; Lectr, 1979–86, Sen. Lectr, 1986–88, Univ. of Strathclyde; Professor: Univ. of Western Ontario, 1988–99; European Univ. Inst., Florence, 2000–10; (pt-time) Univ. of Edinburgh, 2012–. MAE. FRSE 2005; FAcSS (AcSS 2009). Hon. Dr Louvain. *Publications:* Labour and Scottish Nationalism, 1979; The Government of Scotland, 1983; Labour and the British State, 1985; Decentralisation in Contemporary France, 1986; Remaking Urban Scotland, 1986; Glasgow: the politics of urban regeneration, 1988; State and Regional Nationalism, 1988; Politics and Public Policy in Scotland, 1991; Comparative Urban Politics, 1992; The Politics of Modern

Europe, 1993, 2nd edn 1999; Nations against the State, 1996, 2nd edn 2001; The New Regionalism in Western Europe, 1998; Plurinational Democracy, 2001; Culture, Institutions and Economic Development, 2003; The Government of Scotland, 2005, 2nd edn 2010; The Independence of Scotland, 2009; Rescaling the European State, 2013; Small Nations in a Big World, 2014. *Recreations:* hill walking, sailing, traditional music. *Address:* 27 Dundas Street, Edinburgh EH3 6QQ. *T:* 07758 329876. *E:* m.keating@abdn.ac.uk.

KEATING, Michael Ray; Director, Education and Lifelong Learning, Rhondda Cynon Taff County Borough Council, 2005–11; *b* 31 Aug. 1946; *s* of Raymond and Marion Keating; *m* 1967, Jacqueline Ann Pope; two *s*. *Educ:* Ifield Grammar Sch., Crawley; Nottingham Coll. of Educn (Teachers Cert. 1967); Univ. of Newcastle upon Tyne (BEd Hons 1976); Univ. of Warwick (Advanced Dip. Educn 1987). Primary sch. teacher, Breaston, Derbys, then St Albans, and Newcastle upon Tyne, 1967–78; Headteacher, S Benwell Jun. Sch., 1978–80, S Benwell Primary Sch., 1980–88, Newcastle upon Tyne; Primary Advr, 1988–91, Sen. Advr, 1991–96, Mid Glamorgan CC; Asst Dir, Educn, Rhondda Cynon Taff CBC, 1996–2005. Lectr (pt-time), Univ. of Newcastle upon Tyne, 1984–86; External Examr, Manchester Metropolitan Univ., 1990–94. *Recreations:* football, supporting Newcastle United, Alfa Romeo cars, steam trains, modern jazz and blues music, food and wine, caravanning. *Address:* Holly House, 1 Farfield Manor, Sedgefield, Stockton-on-Tees TS21 3NR.

KEATING, Dr Michael Stockton, AC 1996 (AO 1990); Director, Insight Economics, since 2011; *b* 25 Jan. 1940; *s* of Russell James Keating and Alice (*née* Skinner); *m* 1962, Rosemary Gardner; four *s*. *Educ:* Geelong Coll.; Univ. of Melbourne (BCom Hons); ANU (PhD). Hd, Growth Studies and Resource Allocation Div., OECD, 1976–78; First Asst Sec., Econ. Div., Dept of Prime Minister and Cabinet, Australia, 1979–82; Dep. Sec., Dept of Finance, 1982–83; Secretary: Dept of Employment and Industrial Relns, 1983–86; Dept of Finance, 1986–91; Dept of the PM and Cabinet, 1991–96. Adjunct Prof., Griffith Univ., 1997–2004; Fellow, Econs Dept, Res. Sch. of Soc. Scis, ANU, 1997–2008. Chm., Ind. Pricing and Regulatory Tribunal, NSW, 2004–09. Member: Econ. Develt Bd, SA, 2005–14; Trng and Skills Commn, SA, 2008–14; Bd, Australian Workforce and Productivity Agency (formerly Skills, Australia), 2008–14. Chm., Community and Clinical Experts Adv. Council, Health NSW, 2009–10. Board Member: Australia Post, 1996–2001; Fujitsu Australia, 1998–2003. Mem. Council, ANU, 1996–2004. DUniv Griffith, 2000. Centenary Medal (Australia), 2001. *Publications:* The Australian Workforce 1910–1911 to 1960–61, 1973; (jtly) The Making of Australian Economic Policy: 1983–88, 1989; (jtly) The Future of Governance, 2000; (jtly) Institutions on the Edge, 2000; Who Rules?: how government retains control of a privatised economy, 2004. *Recreations:* bushwalking, reading, golf. *Address:* 11/7 Bowen Drive, Barton, ACT 2600, Australia. *T:* (2) 62739405.

KEATING, Hon. Paul John; Prime Minister of Australia, 1991–96; *b* 18 Jan. 1944; *s* of Matthew and Minnie Keating; *m* 1975, Annita Johanna Maria Van Iersel; one *s* three *d*. *Educ:* De La Salle College, Bankstown, NSW. Research Officer, Federated Municipal and Shire Council Employees Union of Australia, 1967. MP (ALP) Blaxland, NSW, 1969–96; Minister for Northern Australia, Oct.–Nov. 1975; Shadow Minister for Agriculture, Jan.–March 1976, for Minerals and Energy, 1976–80, for Resources and Energy, 1980–83; Shadow Treasurer, Jan.–March 1983; Federal Treas. of Australia, 1983–91; Dep. Prime Minister, 1990–91. Member: Cabinet Expenditure Review Cttee (Dep. Chm.), 1987–91; Parly Structural Adjustment Cttee, 1987; Parly Social and Family Policy Cttee, 1983. Chm., Australian Loan Council, 1983–91. Hon. LLD: Keio, Tokyo, 1995; Nat. Univ. of Singapore, 1999; NSW, 2003; Hon. DLit Macquarie, 2012. *Publications:* Engagement: Australia faces the Asia Pacific, 2000; After Words: the post Prime Ministerial speeches, 2011. *Recreations:* classical music, architecture, fine arts, swimming. *Address:* PO Box 1265, Potts Point, NSW 1335, Australia.

KEATING, Roland Francis Kester, (Roly); Chief Executive, British Library, since 2012; *b* 5 Aug. 1961; *s* of Donald Norman Keating and Betty Katharine Keating (*née* Wells); *m* 1989, Caroline Marguerite Cumine Russell; one *s* two *d*. *Educ:* Westminster Sch.; Balliol Coll., Oxford (BA Hons). Joined BBC as gen. trainee, 1983: attachments to Radio Ulster, Kaleidoscope, Everyman, Newsnight progs; producer and dir, Music and Arts Dept, 1985–89; Editor: The Late Show, 1990–92; Bookmark, 1992–97; Executive Producer: (also devised and launched) One Foot in the Past, 1992; A History of British Art, 1996; The House Detectives, 1997; How Buildings Learn, 1997; Hd of Develt, Music and Arts, with special resp. for New Services, 1995; on secondment (part-time) to BBC Broadcast to develop new channel propositions for BBC Worldwide/Flextech jt venture, UKTV, 1996; Hd of Programming, UKTV, 1997–99; Controller, Digital Channels, 1999–2000, Controller of Arts Commissioning and Digital Channels, 2000–01, BBC TV; Controller, BBC4, 2001–04, on secondment as Jt Leader, BBC Charter Review, 2003; Controller, BBC2, 2004–08; Actg Controller, BBC1, 2007–08; Dir, Archive Content, BBC, 2008–12. Mem., Govt Adv. Panel on public library service in England, 2014–. Mem. Bd, Barbican Centre, 2009–. Trustee, Turner Contemporary, Margate, 2009–. Hon. Dr: Lincoln, 2013; York, 2014; Warwick, 2015. *Recreations:* family, reading, walking, being by the seaside. *Address:* British Library, 96 Euston Road, NW1 2DB. *Club:* Soho House.

KEATLEY, Robert Leland; Editor, The Hong Kong Journal, 2005–11; *b* 14 Feb. 1935; *s* of Robert L. Keatley and Eva S. Keatley; *m* 1st, 1970, Anne Greene (marr. diss.); one *s*; 2nd, 1982, Catharine Williams; two *d*. *Educ:* Univ. of Washington (BA); Stanford Univ. (MA). Diplomatic Corresp., Wall St Jl, Washington, 1969–77; Foreign Ed., Wall St Jl, NY, 1978; Editor: Asian Wall St Jl, Hong Kong, 1979–84; Wall St Jl Europe, Brussels, 1984–92; columnist and feature editor, Wall St Jl, Washington, 1992–98; South China Morning Post: Sen. Associate Editor, 1998–99; Editor, 1999–2001. Consultant, Nat. Cttee on US-China Relns, 2011–. Mem. Bd, Washington Inst. Foreign Affairs, 2006–. Contrib., www.nationalinterest.org, 2012–. *Publications:* China: behind the mask, 1974. *Recreations:* hiking, golf. *Address:* 3109 Cathedral Avenue NW, Washington, DC 20008, USA. *Clubs:* Hong Kong, China, Ladies Recreation (Hong Kong); Cosmos (Washington).

KEAY, Dr Anna Julia; Director, Landmark Trust, since 2012; *b* Oban, Argyll, 22 Aug. 1974; *d* of John Stanley Melville Keay, *qv*; *m* 2008, Simon John Thurley, *qv*; one *s* one *d* (twins). *Educ:* Bedales Sch., Hants; Magdalen Coll., Oxford (BA Hons Modern Hist. 1995); Queen Mary and Westfield Coll., Univ. of London (PhD 2004). Asst Curator, Historic Royal Palaces, 1995–2002; Curatorial Dir, English Heritage, 2002–12. Presenter, TV progs and history documentaries. Trustee, Leeds Castle Foundn, 2009–. Gov., Bedales Sch., 2013–. *Publications:* The Elizabethan Tower of London: the Haiward and Gascoyne plan, 2001; The Magnificent Monarch: Charles II and the ceremonies of power, 2008; (jtly) The White Tower, 2009; The Crown Jewels, 2011; The Elizabethan Garden at Kenilworth, 2013; (jtly) Landmark: a history of Britain in 50 buildings, 2015; contrib. articles to jls. *Recreations:* picnics, palaeography. *Address:* Landmark Trust, Shottesbrooke, Maidenhead, Berks SL6 3SW. *T:* (01628) 825920. *E:* akeay@landmarktrust.org.uk. *Club:* Soho House.

KEAY, John Stanley Melville; author and history writer, since 1971; *b* 18 Sept. 1941; *s* of Capt. Stanley Walter Keay and Florence Jessie Keay (*née* Keeping); *m* 1972, Julia Margaret Atkins (*d* 2011); two *s* two *d*; *m* 2014, Amanda Jane Douglas. *Educ:* Ampleforth Coll.; Magdalen Coll., Oxford (BA Hons Modern Hist.). Various jobs in advertising, printing, journalism (freelance, mostly as special corresp. on India for The Economist), 1963–71; writer and presenter of radio documentaries, mainly on Asia, 1981–95. Sykes Meml Medal, RSAA, 2009. *Publications:* Into India, 1973, 3rd edn 1999; When Men and Mountains Meet, 1977, The Gilgit Game, 1979, combined as The Explorers of the Western Himalayas, 1996; India Discovered, 1981, 3rd edn 2001; Eccentric Travellers, 1983, 2nd edn 2001; Highland Drove, 1984; Explorers Extraordinary, 1985, 2nd edn 2001; (Gen. Ed.) The Royal Geographical Society History of World Exploration, 1991; The Honourable Company: a history of the East India Company, 1991; (ed with Julia Keay) Collins Encyclopaedia of Scotland, 1994, 2nd edn 2000; Indonesia: from Sabang to Merauke, 1995; Last Post: the end of Empire in the Far East, 1997, 2nd edn 2000; India: a history, 2000; The Great Arc, 2000; Sowing the Wind: the seeds of conflict in the Middle East, 2003; Mad About the Mekong: exploration and empire in South East Asia, 2005; The Spice Route: a history, 2005; (ed with Julia Keay) The London Encyclopaedia, 3rd edn 2008; China: a history, 2008; Midnight's Descendants: South Asia from partition to the present day, 2014. *Recreations:* weeding, walking, the warmer parts of Asia. *Address:* Succoth, Dalmally, Argyll PA33 1BB. *T:* (01838) 200250.

See also A. J. Keay.

KEBEDE, Susan Michelle; a Judge of the Upper Tribunal, Immigration and Asylum Chamber, since 2011; *b* Hull, 2 July 1964; *d* of Ronald Gordon Field and late Esther Judith Field; *m* 1998, Dr Zelalem Kebede; one *s* one *d*. *Educ:* Wolfreton Comprehensive Sch.; Leeds Univ. (LLB Hons 1986). Articled clerk, Saunders, Sobell, Leigh & Dobin; admitted as solicitor, 1991; Caseworker, Refugee Legal Centre, 1993–2001; non-salaried Immigration Adjudicator, later Judge, 2001–03; Salaried Immigration Judge, 2003–11. *Recreations:* mother of two (therefore not much time for recreations), spending time with children, walking in countryside. *Address:* Upper Tribunal (Immigration and Asylum Chamber), Field House, 15 Breams Buildings, EC4A 1DZ.

KEDDIE, Dr Alistair William Carnegie, CB 2003; FRAS; Deputy Director General, Innovation Group, Department of Trade and Industry, 2002–03 (Acting Director General, 2002); part-time Principal Fellow, Warwick Manufacturing Group, University of Warwick, since 2003; *b* 1 Jan. 1943; *s* of late Stuart Keddie and Ethel Carnegie Keddie; *m* 1966, Marjorie Scott Masterton; one *s* one *d*. *Educ:* Breadalbane Acad., Aberfeldy; Univ. of Glasgow (BSc Hons; PhD 1970). FRAS 1969. Res. Asst, then Asst Lectr, Dept of Astronomy, Univ. of Glasgow, 1967–70; res. mgt posts, 1970–77; Hd, Air Pollution Div., Warren Spring Lab., Stevenage, 1977–84; Department of Trade and Industry: Mem., Policy Planning Unit, 1984–85; Dir, Sci. and Technol. Policy, 1985–89; Dir, Single Market Unit, 1989–91; Hd, Innovation Unit, 1991–99; Dir, Envmt, Innovation, 1999–2002. Member: EPSRC, 2001–03; Bd, Carbon Trust, 2001–04. Trustee, Green Alliance, 2003–. *Recreations:* walking, bird watching, music, gardening, voluntary work. *Address:* Pitully, Dull, Aberfeldy, Perthshire PH15 2JQ. *T:* (01887) 820367.

KEEBLE, Dame Reena (Kapur), DBE 2011; EdD; Headteacher, Cannon Lane First School, Harrow, 1992–2014; *b* New Delhi, 21 July 1955; *d* of Rabinder Nath Kapur and Enakshi Kapur; *m* 1980, Peter Weimer Keeble; one *s* one *d*. *Educ:* City of London Poly. (BSc Psychol. 1977); Roehampton Inst., Univ. of London (PGCE 1978); Inst. of Educn, Univ. of London (MSc Psychol. of Educn 1983); Univ. of Hull (EdD Educnl Leadership and Mgt 2006). Nursery teacher, 1981–84; Early Years Teacher, Brent Council, 1984–87; Hd of Nursery, Elsley Primary Sch., Harrow, 1987–89; Dep. Headteacher, Glebe Primary Sch., Harrow, 1989–92. Regl Leader for London, 2006–08. (Pt-time) Nat. Coll. for Sch. Leadership, 2006–08. *Recreations:* family, theatre, art, cooking, knitting. *E:* rkeeble@btinternet.com.

KEEBLE, Sally Curtis; Director, The Anglican Alliance: Development, Relief, Advocacy, 2010–13; *b* 13 Oct. 1951; *d* of Sir (Herbert Ben) Curtis Keeble, GCMG and Margaret Keeble; *m* 1990, Andrew Porter; one *s* one *d*. *Educ:* St Hugh's Coll., Oxford (BA Hons); Univ. of S Africa (BA Hons). Journalist, Daily News, Durban, SA, 1974–79; Reporter, Birmingham Post, 1979–83; Press Officer, Labour Party, 1983–84; Asst Dir, Ext. Relns, ILEA, 1984–86; Hd of Communications, GMB, 1986–90; Public Affairs Consultant, 1994–97. MP (Lab) Northampton N, 1997–2010; contested (Lab) same seat, 2010, 2015. Parly Under-Sec. of State, DTLR, 2001–02, DFID, 2002–03. Mem. (Lab) Southwark BC, 1986–94 (Leader, 1990–93). Hon. Fellow, S Bank Univ. *Publications:* Collectors' Corner, 1984; Conceiving Your Baby: how medicine can help, 1995. *Recreations:* walking, antiques, reading. *Address:* 8 Oakpark Close, Northampton NN3 5JG. *T:* (01604) 646310.

KEEFE, Denis Edward Peter Paul; HM Diplomatic Service; Ambassador to Serbia, since 2014; *b* 29 June 1958; *s* of late Dr John Victor Keefe and Dr Oonagh Rose Keefe (*née* McAleer); *m* 1983, Catherine Ann Mary Wooding; three *s* three *d*. *Educ:* Campion Sch., Hornchurch; Churchill Coll., Cambridge (MA Classics); Hertford Coll., Oxford; Malmö Univ. Joined HM Diplomatic Service, 1982; FCO, 1982–84; Second Sec., Prague, 1984–88; First Secretary: FCO, 1988–92; Nairobi, 1992–95; Dep. Hd, S Asian Dept, FCO, 1996–97; Hd, Asia-Europe Meeting Unit, 1997–98; Dep. Hd of Mission, Prague, 1998–2002; on secondment as Counter Terrorism Strategy Team Leader, Cabinet Office, 2002–03; Head, China Hong Kong Dept, 2003–04, Far Eastern Gp, 2004–06, FCO; Ambassador to Georgia, 2007–10; Dep. Head of Mission, Moscow, 2010–14. *Recreations:* singing, sailing, walking, learning languages. *Address:* c/o Foreign and Commonwealth Office, King Charles Street, SW1A 2AH. *E:* denis.keefe@fco.gov.uk.

KEEFFE, Barrie Colin; dramatist; *b* 31 Oct. 1945; *s* of late Edward Thomas Keeffe and Constance Beatrice Keeffe (*née* Marsh); *m* 1st, 1969, Dee Sarah Truman (marr. diss. 1979); 2nd, 1981, Verity Eileen Proud (*née* Bargate) (*d* 1981); Guardian of her two *s*; 3rd, 1983, Julia Lindsay (marr. diss. 1993); 4th, 2012, Jacky Stoller. *Educ:* East Ham Grammar School. Formerly actor with Nat. Youth Theatre; began writing career as journalist; Thames Television Award writer-in-residence, Shaw Theatre, 1977; Resident playwright, Royal Shakespeare Co., 1978; Associate Writer, Theatre Royal, Stratford East, 1986–91. Member: Board of Directors: Soho Theatre Co., 1978–95; Theatre Royal, Stratford E, 1988–91; Tutor, City Univ., London, 2002–05; Dir and Tutor, Collaldra Sch. of Writing, Venice, 2008–; Resident Writer, Kingston Univ., 2011–. Patron, Writing for Performance, Ruskin Coll., Oxford, 2010–. Edith J. Wilson Fellow, Christ's Coll., Cambridge, 2003–04. UN Ambassador, 1995. Hon. DLitt Warwick, 2010. French Critics Prix Revelation, 1978; Giles Cooper Best Radio Plays, 1980; Mystery Writers of America Edgar Allan Poe Award, 1982. *Theatre plays:* Only a Game, 1973; A Sight of Glory, 1975; Scribes, 1975; Here Comes the Sun, 1976; Gimme Shelter, 1977; A Mad World My Masters, 1977, 1984; Barbarians, 1977; Frozen Assets, 1978; Sus, 1979; Bastard Angel, 1980; She's So Modern, 1980; Black Lear, 1980; Chorus Girls, 1981; Better Times, 1985; King of England, 1988; My Girl, 1989; Not Fade Away, 1990; Wild Justice, 1990; I Only Want to Be With You, 1995; The Long Good Friday, 1997; Shadows on the Sun, 2001; Still Killing Time, 2006; My Girl 2, 2014; *television plays:* Substitute, 1972; Not Quite Cricket, 1977; Gotcha, 1977; Nipper, 1977; Champions, 1978; Hanging Around, 1978; Waterloo Sunset, 1979; King, 1984; *television series:* No Excuses, 1983; *films:* The Long Good Friday, 1981; SUS, 2010; also radio plays. *Publications: novels:* Gadabout, 1969; No Excuses, 1983; *plays:* Gimme Shelter, 1977; A Mad World My Masters, 1977; Barbarians, 1977; Here Comes the Sun, 1978; Frozen Assets, 1978; Sus, 1979; Bastard Angel, 1980; The Long Good Friday, 1984, new edn 1998; Better Times, 1985; King of England, 1988; My Girl, 1989; Wild Justice, Not Fade Away, Gimme Shelter, 1990; Barrie Keeffe Plays 1, 2001; My Girl 2, 2014. *Recreation:* origami. *Address:* 33 Brookfield, Highgate West Hill, N6 6AT.

KEEGAN, Sir Donal (Arthur John), KCVO 2012; OBE 1999; DPhysMed; FRCP, FRCPE, FRCPI; Lord-Lieutenant of Londonderry, 2002–13; *b* 8 Oct. 1938; *s* of Daniel McManus Keegan and Geraldine Keegan (*née* Halpin); *m* 1973, Doreen Elizabeth Nelson; one *d*. *Educ:* St Columb's Coll., Londonderry; Queen's Univ., Belfast (BSc Hons, MB BCh, BAO); DPhysMed. FRCPI 1973; FRCPE 1989; FRCP 1990. Consultant Physician: Highland and Western Isles Health Bd Areas, 1970–75; Altnagelvin Hosp., Londonderry,

1975–2003, now Emeritus. Chairman: Regl Adv. Cttee on Cancer, 1997–2005; NI Council for Postgrad. Med. and Dental Educn, 1998–2004; Central Med. Adv. Cttee, NI, 1999–2003; Mem., Cttee on Higher Med. Trng, RCPI, 2004–. Med. Dir, Distinction and Meritorious Service Awards Cttee, NI, 2001–04. Vis. Prof., Univ. of Ulster, 2009–13. Pres., RFCA for NI, 2009–13. Hon. Col, 204 (N Irish) Field Hosp. (V), 2004–11. Freeman, City of London, 2013. *Publications:* articles on cardiology and musculoskeletal disease. *Recreations:* fishing, shooting, bird migration. *Address:* Auskaird, 5 Greenwood, Culmore, Londonderry BT48 8NP. *T:* (028) 7135 1292. *Club:* Royal Society of Medicine.

KEEGAN, Dame (Elizabeth) Mary, DBE 2007; FCA; non-executive Director, National Audit Office, 2009–14; *b* 21 Jan. 1953; *d* of Michael Keegan and Elizabeth Keegan (*née* Sarginson); *m* 2011, Albert Prangnell. *Educ:* Brentwood County High Sch. for Girls; Somerville Coll., Oxford (Caroline Haslett Meml Scholar, Coombs Exhibitioner; rowing blue; BA Natural Sci. 1974; MA 1977; Hon. Fellow 2008). ACA 1977, FCA 1983. Price Waterhouse, subseq. PricewaterhouseCoopers: articled London, 1974; Paris, 1979; Chicago, 1982; Partner, 1985–2001; Nat. Technical Partner, 1991–96; Dir Professional Standards Europe, 1994–98; Hd Global Corporate Reporting Gp, 1998–2001; Mem. Supervisory Bd, European Financial Reporting Adv. Gp, 2001–04; Finance Dir, 2004–07, Hd Govt Finance Profession and Mem. Bd, 2004–08, HM Treasury. Chm., Accounting Standards Bd, 2001–04. Member: Urgent Issues Task Force, Accounting Standards Bd, 1993–99; Standing Interpretations Cttee, Internat. Accounting Standards Cttee, 1997–2001; Internat. Forum on Accountancy Develt, 1999–2001; Chm., Financial Reporting Cttee, 1994–97, Mem. Council, 1994–97, ICAEW; Vice-Pres. and Mem. Council, Chm. Auditing Working Party, FEE, 1997–2001; Mem., Financial Reporting Rev. Panel, Financial Reporting Council, 2007–13. Member: Audit Cttee, RHS, 2009–; Adv. Cttee, Univ. of Exeter Business Sch., 2009–. Gov., University Coll. Falmouth, 2007–12. FRSA. Hon. DBA Oxford Brookes, 2005; Hon. LittD Manchester, 2006; Hon. LLD Exeter, 2008. Outstanding Achievement Award, ICAEW, 2014. *Publications:* (jtly) The ValueReporting Revolution: moving beyond the earnings game, 2001. *Recreations:* gardening, classical music, sailing. *Address:* Old Matthews Farm, Kerswell, Cullompton, Devon EX15 2EL. *E:* mary.keegan@btinternet.

KEEGAN, Dame Geraldine (Mary Marcella), DBE 2000 (OBE 1995); part-time management consultant; Headmistress, St Mary's College, Londonderry, 1987–2006; *b* 17 Jan. 1941; *d* of Daniel Anthony McManus Keegan and Geraldine Catherine Veronica (*née* Halpin). *Educ:* St Mary's UC, Belfast (Cert Ed 1963); Univ. of Ulster (DipEd 1972); Univ. of Manchester (MEd 1975). Secondary sch. teacher of music, history and English, 1963–75; Sen. Lectr in Educnl Psychology, St Mary's UC, Belfast, 1975–85; Dep. Dir, NI Centre for Educn Mgt, 1985–87. Pro-Chancellor, 1997–2001, Vis. Prof., 2001–, Univ. of Ulster. Mem. Cttee, European Foundn for Quality Mgt, 2001–06; Board Member: Community of Practice (Educn) SENTINUS, 1996–2007; Centre for Migration Studies, 1997–; Museums and Art Galls of NI, 2002–; Optimus Approvals Cttee, Fáilte Ireland, 2005–; NW Regional Coll., 2007–; Ilex Urban Regeneration Co. NI representative: UK Bd, Investors in People, 2002–08; Leadership and Mgt Adv. Panel, 2007–. Member: Bd, President's Award, Ireland, 2002–; RUC George Cross Foundn, 2002–; Bd, Spirit of Enniskillen Trust, 2005–; Trustee, Scotch Irish Trust, 1994–. FRSA 1995. DUniv Ulster, 2006. *Recreations:* classical music, travel, fishing. *Address:* 7 Locarden, Culmore Point Road, Londonderry BT48 8RP.

KEEGAN, James Douglas; QC (Scot.) 2009; solicitor advocate; Senior Partner, Keegan Smith SSC, since 1998; *b* Glasgow; *s* of James Keegan and Susan Keegan; *m* Karen; three *d*. *Educ:* Our Lady's High Sch., Motherwell; Univ. of Strathclyde (LLB 1973); Univ. of Glasgow (DipFM 1994; MPhil 1998). FCIArb 1994; WS 2008. Notary Public, 1977; Partner, Drummond & Co., Edinburgh, 1978–87; Sen. Partner, Keegan Walker SSC, 1987–97. FRSA 2000. *Recreations:* football, music, Rugby. *Address:* Keegan Smith SSC, Ochil House, Almondvale, Livingston, West Lothian EH54 6QF. *T:* (01506) 497500, *Fax:* (01506) 497086. *E:* jdKeegan1@msn.com. *Club:* Livingston Rugby.

KEEGAN, (Joseph) Kevin, OBE 1982; professional footballer, 1966–84; *b* 14 Feb. 1951; *s* of late Joseph Keegan; *m* 1974, Jean Woodhouse; two *d*. Professional footballer with: Scunthorpe Utd, 1966–71; Liverpool, 1971–77; Hamburg, 1977–80; Southampton, 1980–82; Newcastle Utd, 1982–84. Internat. appearances for England, 1973–82, Captain, 1976–82. Manager, Newcastle Utd FC, 1992–97 and 2008; Chief Operating Officer, Fulham FC, 1997–99; Coach, England Football Team, 1999–2000; Manager, Manchester City FC, 2001–05. Formerly football expert, Thames TV. Winners' medals: League Championships, 1973, 1976; UEFA Cup, 1973, 1976; FA Cup, 1974; European Cup, 1977. European Footballer of the Year, 1978, 1979. *Publications:* Kevin Keegan, 1978; Against the World: playing for England, 1979; Kevin Keegan: my autobiography, 1997.

KEEGAN, Dame Mary; *see* Keegan, Dame E. M.

KEEGAN, William James Gregory, CBE 2009; Senior Economics Commentator, The Observer, since 2003 (Economics Editor, 1977–2003); *b* 3 July 1938; *s* of William Patrick Keegan and Sheila Julia Keegan (*née* Buckley); *m* 1st, 1967, Tessa (*née* Young, *widow* of John Ashton) (marr. diss. 1982); two *s* two *d*; 2nd, 1992, Hilary, *d* of late Maurice Frank Stonefrost, CBE; one *s* two *d*. *Educ:* Wimbledon Coll.; Trinity Coll., Cambridge (MA). National Service (Army), 1957–59 (commissioned). Journalist, Financial Times, Daily Mail and News Chronicle, 1963–67; Economics Correspondent, Financial Times, 1967–76; Economic Intell. Dept, Bank of England, 1976–77; The Observer: Asst Editor and Business Editor, 1981–83; Associate Editor, 1983–2003. Member: BBC Adv. Cttee on Business and Indust. Affairs, 1981–88; Council, Employment Inst., 1987–92; Adv. Bd, Dept of Applied Economics, Cambridge, 1988–92; Cttee for Soc. Scis, CNAA, 1991–92; Nat. Council, The Catalyst Forum, 1998–; Adv. Bd, Mile End Gp, QMUL, 2011–; Chm., Editl Bd, OMFIF, 2010–. Gov., NIESR, 1998–. Vis. Prof. of Journalism, 1989–, Hon. Res. Fellow, 1990–, Sheffield Univ.; Vis. Prof. of Econs and Finance, QMUL, 2012–. Hon. LittD Sheffield, 1995; Hon. DLitt City, 1998. *Publications:* Consulting Father Wintergreen, 1974; A Real Killing, 1976; (jtly) Who Runs the Economy?, 1978; Mrs Thatcher's Economic Experiment, 1984; Britain Without Oil, 1985; Mr Lawson's Gamble, 1989; The Spectre of Capitalism, 1992; 2066 and All That, 2000; The Prudence of Mr Gordon Brown, 2003; 'Saving the World'?: Gordon Brown reconsidered, 2012; Mr Osborne's Economic Experiment: austerity 1945–51 and 2010–, 2015; contribs to The Tablet. *Address:* 76 Lofting Road, Islington, N1 1JB. *T:* (020) 7607 3590; The Observer, Kings Place, 90 York Way, N1 9GU. *Clubs:* Garrick, MCC.

KEEHAN, Hon. Sir Michael (Joseph), Kt 2013; **Hon. Mr Justice Keehan;** a Judge of the High Court of Justice, Family Division, since 2013; *b* 31 March 1960; *s* of Michael and Alice Keehan; *m* 1988, Sarah Elizabeth Monk; two *d*. *Educ:* Birmingham Univ. (LLB). Called to the Bar, Middle Temple, 1982, Bencher, 2013; QC 2001; a Recorder, 2000–13. *Recreations:* family life, gardening, walking. *Address:* Royal Courts of Justice, Queen's Building, Strand, WC2A 2LL.

KEEL, Aileen Margaret, (Mrs Paul Dwyer), CBE 2008; FRCPath; FRCPGlas, FRCPE, FRCSE, FRCGP; Deputy Chief Medical Officer, Scottish Government (formerly Scottish Executive), since 1999; *b* Glasgow, 23 Aug. 1952; *d* of Walter and Everina Keel; *m* 1995, Paul Dwyer (*d* 2010); one *s*. *Educ:* Univ. of Glasgow (MB ChB 1976). MRCP 1979; MRCPath 1986, FRCPath 1995; FRCPGlas 1992; FRCPE 2005; MFPH 2004. Trng in gen. medicine and haematol., Glasgow Royal Infirmary, Royal Hosp. for Sick Children, Glasgow, Aberdeen Royal Infirmary, 1976–84; Consultant Haematologist and Dir of Pathol., Cromwell Hosp., London, 1987–89; Hon. Consultant Haematologist and Hon. Res. Fellow, Central Middx and Middx Hosp., London, 1988–92; SMO, 1992–98, PMO, 1998–99, Scottish Office. Founding Fellow, Inst. for Contemp. Scotland, 2000. *Recreations:* the arts in general, music, particularly opera, current affairs, good food and wine, evidence based arguing! *Address:* Scottish Government Health Department, St Andrew's House, Regent Road, Edinburgh EH1 3DG. *T:* (0131) 244 2799. *E:* aileen.keel@scotland.gsi.gov.uk.

KEELER, Walter Charles John; self-employed potter, since 1965; *b* 22 April 1942; *s* of Walter Stanley Keeler and Iris Eileen Keeler (*née* Callaghan); *m* 1964, Madoline; two *s* one *d*. *Educ:* Harrow Sch. of Art (Intermediate NDD); Hornsey Coll. of Art (Art Teachers Cert). Sen. Lectr in Studio Pottery, Harrow Sch. of Art, 1964–78; Bristol Polytechnic, subseq. University of West of England: Sen. Lectr in Ceramics, 1978–94; Reader, 1994–98; Prof. of Ceramics, 1998–2002. Pottery Studio: Bledlow Ridge, Bucks, 1965–76; Moorcroft Cottage, Penallt, Mons, 1976–. Associate Dir, Nat. Electronic and Video Archive of the Crafts, 1992–2002. Exhibitions include: Craft Potters Assoc., London, 1982; Contemp. Applied Arts, London, 1989, 1999; Leeds City Art Gall., 1993; Contemp. Ceramics, London, 2002; work in public collections including: V&A Mus.; Crafts Council Collection; Nat. Mus. of Wales, Cardiff; Fitzwilliam Mus., Cambridge, and worldwide. Fellow, Craft Potters Assoc., 1967; Mem., Contemp. Applied Arts (formerly British Crafts Centre), 1969–. *Relevant publication:* Walter Keeler, by E. Cooper and A. Fielding, 2004. *Recreations:* gardening, music, travel, cooking and eating. *Address:* Moorcroft Cottage, Penallt, Monmouthshire NP25 4AH. *T:* (01600) 713946, *Fax:* (01600) 712530. *E:* penalltpottery@gmail.com.

KEELEY, Barbara Mary; MP (Lab) Worsley and Eccles South, since 2010 (Worsley, 2005–10); *b* 26 March 1952; *d* of late Edward and Joan Keeley; *m* Colin Huggett. *Educ:* Univ. of Salford (BA 1st Cl. Hons Pols and Contemp. Hist.). Field Systems Engr and Systems Engrg Manager, IBM UK, until 1989; community regeneration advr, 1989–94; Area Manager, BITC, 1994–95; local govt and voluntary sector, 1995–2001; Consultant, researching policy issues, Princess Royal Trust for Carers, 2001–05. PPS to Parly Sec., Cabinet Office, then Minister of State, DWP, 2006–07, to Minister for Women and Equality, 2007–08; an Asst Govt Whip, 2008–09; Parly Sec., Leader of H of C, 2009–10; Shadow Minister: for Care Services, 2010; for Communities and Local Govt, 2010–11; for Treasury, 2015–. Mem., Health Select Cttee, 2011–15. Chair, PLP Women's Cttee, 2007–08. Mem., Trafford MBC, 1995–2004 (Cabinet Mem., 1999–2004). Dir, Pathfinder Children's Trust, 2002–04. *Recreations:* running, watching cricket, listening to live music. *Address:* c/o House of Commons, SW1A 0AA. *T:* (020) 7219 8025. *W:* www.barbarakeeley.co.uk.

KEELING, Maj.-Gen. Andrew Myles, CB 1994; CBE 1992 (OBE 1988); self-employed consultant, 1996–2013; *b* 4 July 1943; *s* of late Richard George Maynard Keeling, OBE and Audrey Stuart Baxter (*née* Frederick); *m* 1st, 1965, Ann Margaret Grey Dudley (*d* 2001); one *s* two *d*; 2nd, 2003, Woppy (*née* Brittan). *Educ:* Rugby School. Commissioned 2nd Lieut RM, 1961; served 41, 42 and 45 Commandos, and training jobs at BRNC, Dartmouth and RMA, Sandhurst, 1963–75; student, Canadian Forces Command and Staff Coll., 1975–76; HQ 3 Cdo Bde RM, 1976–78; 41 Cdo, 1978–80; Bde Major, HQ 3 Cdo Bde, 1980–81; Directing Staff, NDC and JSDC, 1982–83; Jt Force HQ, 1984–85; CO 45 Cdo, 1985–87; MoD, 1987–89; Comd, 3 Cdo Bde, 1990–92; COS to Comdt-Gen. RM, 1992–93; Maj.-Gen., RM, 1993–95, retired. Rep. Col Comdt, RM, 1998–2002. UK Rep., Saab Microwave Systems (formerly Ericsson Microwave Systems AB), 1997–2008. Sec., Salisbury Dio. Sudan Link, 2001–05; Lay Canon, Salisbury Cathedral, 2003–. Specialist Advr, Defence Select Cttee, H of C, 1997–98. Dir of Humanitarian Affairs, AMAR Internat. Charitable Foundn, 1995–96. Freeman, City of London, 1993. President: City of Winchester Br., RMA, 1996–2004; SBS Assoc., 2001–; Devon County RBL, 2005–08; Naval Vice-Pres., CCF Assoc., 1995–2001; Mem. Council, Blind Veterans UK (formerly St Dunstan's), 1995–2013 (Vice-Chm., 2004–08; Chm., 2008–13; Vice-Pres., 2014–); Vice-Pres., 2006–12, Pres., 2012–, St George's Day Club. *Recreations:* gardening, family, walking. *Clubs:* Special Forces; Royal Marines Sailing (Hon. Life Vice-Commodore).

KEEMER, Peter John Charles; Assistant Auditor General, National Audit Office, 1989–93; *b* 27 Jan. 1932; *s* of late Frederick and Queenie Keemer; *m* 1954, Yvonne Griffin (*d* 2002); one *s* one *d* (and one *s* decd). *Educ:* Price's Sch., Fareham; Univ. of Bath (MPhil). Exchequer and Audit Department: Asst Auditor and Auditor, 1950–62; Private Sec. to Comptroller and Auditor Gen., 1962–65; seconded to Parly Comr for Administration as Chief Exec. Officer, 1966–70; Chief Auditor, 1970; Dep. Dir, 1973; Dir, 1978–89 (seconded to European Court of Auditors as Director, 1978–86). External Auditor, European Univ. Inst., Florence, 1994–97. Mem., Conciliation Cttee, EC, 2001–06. Mem., CIPFA, 1982. Chm., 1995–2001, Trustee, 1995–2009, Dir, 1997–2009, Breakthrough Breast Cancer; Mem. Council, Inst. of Cancer Res., 1994–2000 (Hon. Treas., 1996–2000). *Address:* Highfield, Hazelwood Lane, Chipstead, Coulsdon CR5 3QW. *T:* (01737) 553711. *E:* pjckeemer@gmail.com. *Club:* Royal Thames Yacht.

KEEN, family name of **Baron Keen of Elie**.

KEEN OF ELIE, Baron *cr* 2015 (Life Peer), of Elie in Fife; **Richard Sanderson Keen;** QC (Scot.) 1993; Advocate General for Scotland, since 2015; *b* 29 March 1954; *s* of Derek Michael Keen and Jean Sanderson Keen; *m* 1978, Jane Carolyn Anderson; one *s* one *d*. *Educ:* King's Sch., Rochester; Dollar Acad.; Edinburgh Univ. (LLB Hons 1976; Beckman Schol.). Admitted Faculty of Advocates, 1980 (Treas., 2006–07; Dean, 2007–14); Standing Jun. Counsel in Scotland to DTI, 1986–93. Called to the Bar, Middle Temple, 2009, Bencher, 2011; Mem., Blackstone Chambers, London, 2011–. Chairman: Appeals Cttee, ICAS, 1996–2001; Police Appeals Tribunal, 2004–10. Chm., Scottish Cons. and Unionist Party, 2014–. *Recreations:* golf, ski-ing, shooting, opera. *Address:* The Castle, Elie, Fife KY9 1DN; 27 Ann Street, Edinburgh EH4 1PL. *Clubs:* New (Edinburgh); Golf House (Elie); Hon. Co. of Edinburgh Golfers (Muirfield).

KEEN, Ann Lloyd; *b* 26 Nov. 1948; *d* of late John Fox and Ruby Fox; one *s*; *m* 1980, (David) Alan Keen, MP (*d* 2011); one step *s* one step *d*. *Educ:* Elfed Secondary Modern Sch., Clwyd; Univ. of Surrey (PGCE). Formerly: Hd, Faculty of Advanced Nursing, Queen Charlotte's Coll., Hammersmith; Gen. Sec., Community and District Nursing Assoc. Contested (Lab) Brentford and Isleworth, 1987, 1992. MP (Lab) Brentford and Isleworth, 1997–2010; contested (Lab) same seat, 2010. Parly Under-Sec. of State, DoH, 2007–10. Hon. Professor of Nursing: Thames Valley Univ.; Florence Nightingale Sch. of Nursing, KCL. Hon. Sec., Imperial Coll. Global Initiative. Trustee: Florence Nightingale Foundn; Katie Piper Foundn. Hon. LLD Beds.

KEEN, His Honour Kenneth Roger; QC 1991; a Circuit Judge, 2001–13; *b* 13 May 1946; *s* of Kenneth Henry Keen and Joan Megan Keen (*née* Weetman); *m* Mary Lorraine Raeburn; one *s* one *d* by previous marriage. *Educ:* Doncaster Grammar School. Qualified Solicitor, 1968; called to the Bar, Gray's Inn, 1976; practice on NE circuit; a Recorder, 1989. Former Member: Mental Health Tribunal; Boundary Commn; Complaints and Disciplinary Cttee, Bar Council; Mem., Parole Bd, 2010–13. *Recreations:* tennis, travel, golf.

KEEN, Laurence John, OBE 2000; FSA, FRHistS; President, British Archaeological Association, 1989–2004; County Archaeological Officer, Dorset County Council, 1975–99; Consultant, John Stark & Crickmay Partnership, architects, 1999–2003; *b* 11 July 1943; *er s* of late John William Frederick Keen and Dorothy Ethel Keen (*née* French). *Educ:* Kilburn GS; St John's Coll., York (Cert Ed (Music) 1966); Inst. of Archaeology, Univ. of London (Postgrad. Dip. in European Archaeol. 1969; Gordon Childe Meml Prize); UCL (MPhil 1978). FRHistS 1974; FSA 1979; MCIfA (MIFA 1985); FSAScot 1995. Répétiteur, Lycée Mohammed V, Marrakech, 1962–63; Asst Master, Cundall Manor Sch., York, 1966–67; Dir,

Southampton Archaeol Res. Cttee, 1972–75. Archaeol Cons., MPBW, then DoE, then English Heritage, 1964–. Dir, Census of Medieval Tiles in Britain, 2004–. Director of excavations: Wardour Castle, Wilts; Blackfriars, Gloucester; Kingswood Abbey, Glos; Tattershall Coll., Lincs; Mountgrace Priory, Yorks; Beeston Castle, Cheshire; Prudhoe Castle, Northumberland; Sherborne Abbey, Dorset. Vis. Lectr in Archaeology, Univ. of Southampton, 1973–75. Winston Churchill Fellow, 1970; Hon. Research Fellow: Centre for South-Western Hist. Studies, Univ. of Exeter, 1995–98; York St John Univ. (formerly UC of Ripon and York St John, then York St John Coll.), 1995–. Member: DAC for Faculties, 1977–97, Re-use of Closed Churches Working Gp (formerly Diocesan Redundant Churches Cttee), 1985–97, 2005–, Salisbury; Paintings Cttee, Council for the Care of Churches, 1979–96; Fabric Advisory Committee: Gloucester Cath., 1991–; St George's Chapel, Windsor Castle, 1998–2013 (Chm., 1999–2009); Exeter Cath., 2006– (Chm., 2011–). Chairman: Dorset Local Hist. Gp, 1985–99; Dorset Archaeol Cttee, Dorset Nat. Hist. and Archaeol Soc., 2002–15; Member, Council: Soc. for Medieval Archaeology, 1973–76; British Archaeol Assoc., 1973–76, 1978–81, 1984–87 (Vice-Pres., 1988, 2004–; Reginald Taylor Essay Prize, 1969); Royal Archaeol Inst., 1982–85. Trustee, Oxford Archaeol., 2004–. Foreign Corresp. Associate Mem., Société Nat. des Antiquaires de France, 1990. Freeman, City of London, 1991; Freeman and Liveryman, Co. of Painter-Stainers, 1991. *Publications:* (jtly) William Barnes: the Dorset engravings, 1986 ((jtly) Mansel-Pleydell Essay Prize, Dorset Nat. Hist. & Archaeol. Soc., 1985), 2nd edn 1989; William Barnes: the Somerset engravings, 1989; (ed jtly) Historic Landscape of the Weld Estate, 1987; Dorset Domesday: an introduction, 1991; (ed jtly) Medieval Art and Architecture at Salisbury Cathedral, 1996; (ed) Almost the Richest City: Bristol in the Middle Ages, 1997; (jtly) Dorset from the Air, 1998; (ed) Studies in the Early History of Shaftesbury Abbey, 1999; (ed jtly) Windsor Castle: medieval archaeology, art and architecture of the Thames Valley, 2002; (jtly) Sherborne Abbey and School: excavations 1972–76 and 1990, 2005; (jtly) Mount Grace Priory: excavations of 1957–92, 2015; articles and reviews in nat. and county jls. *Recreations:* making music, entertaining, perfecting bread and butter pudding. *Address:* Hardye Chambers, 7 Church Street, Dorchester, Dorset DT1 1JN. *T:* (01305) 265460.

KEEN, Lady Mary; *see* Keen, Lady P. M. R.

KEEN, Nigel John, FCA, FIET; Chairman: Oxford Instruments plc, since 1999; Syncona Partners, since 2013; Oxford Academic Health Science Network, since 2013; Isis Innovation Ltd, since 2014; *b* 21 Jan. 1947; *s* of Peter and Margaret Keen; *m* 1972, Caroline Jane Cumming; two *s*. *Educ:* Charterhouse; Peterhouse, Cambridge (MA). FCA 1979; FIET 2012. Auditor, Touche Ross & Co., 1968–74; Dir, Eur. Banking Co. Ltd, 1974–83; Chm., Cygnus gp of cos, 1983–2001; Dep. Chm., 1999–2000, Chm., 2000–14, Laird (formerly Laird Gp) plc; Chairman: Axis-Shield plc, 1999–2010; Deltex Med. Gp plc, 2000–. Dir, Channel Is Develt Corp., 1996–2007; non-exec. Dir, 2008–09, Chm., 2009–, Bioquell plc. Trustee, David Shepherd Wildlife Foundn, 1999–. *Recreations:* opera, golf. *Address:* 19 Pembroke Square, W8 6PA. *T:* (020) 7937 6008. *Clubs:* HAC; Royal Mid Surrey Golf.

KEEN, Lady (Priscilla) Mary (Rose); garden designer, writer and lecturer; *b* 12 Feb. 1940; *d* of 6th Earl Howe and of Priscilla (*née* Weigall, who *m* 2nd, Harold Coriat); *m* 1962, Charles Keen; one *s* three *d*. *Educ:* Lawnside, Malvern; Lady Margaret Hall, Oxford. Gardening Columnist: Evening Standard, 1980–88; Perspectives, 1988–98; Independent on Sunday, 1988–98; freelance journalist: Gardening; Daily Telegraph; designed Glyndebourne Opera House new gardens, 1992–93, and many large private commissions, as Mary Keen and Pip Morrison, Designed Landscapes. National Trust: Member: Gardens Panel, 1982–2006; Thames and Chilterns Regl Cttee, 1982–92; Severn Regl Cttee, 1996–2002. Inspirational Garden Journalist of the Year, Garden Writer's Guild Awards, 1999. *Publications:* The Garden Border Book, 1987; The Glory of the English Garden, 1989; Colour Your Garden, 1991; Decorate Your Garden, 1993; Creating a Garden, 1996; Paradise and Plenty: a Rothschild family garden, 2015. *Recreation:* gardening. *Address:* The Old Rectory, Duntisbourne Rous, Cirencester, Glos GL7 7AP.

KEENAGHAN, Fiona Therese; Controller, Daytime and Lifestyle Features, ITV, 2008–13; *b* St Helens, Merseyside, 23 June 1969; *d* of James Keenaghan and Patricia Catherine Anne Keenaghan; partner, Paul Anthony Mottram; one *s* one *d*. *Educ:* Thames Valley Univ. (BA Hons Design and Media Mgt). Ed., Tonight with Trevor McDonald, 2005–06, Exec. Producer, 2006–08, ITV. *Recreations:* my children, theatre, opera, travel, books.

KEENAN, Rt Rev. John; *see* Paisley, Bishop of, (RC).

KEENAN, Paul; Chief Executive, Bauer Media, since 2008; *b* Shrewsbury, 29 Dec. 1963; *s* of Thomas Keenan and Bridget Keenan; *m* 1990, Sandra Scase. *Educ:* St Ignatius Coll., London. Reporter, Local Government Chronicle, 1986; joined Emap, 1992; Managing Director: Emap Fashion, 1995–98; Emap Elan, 1998–2000; Dir, Emap Digital, 2000–01; Chief Exec., Emap Consumer, 2001–08. Dir, PPA, 2002– (Chm., Mktg Bd, 2005–09). *Address:* Bauer Media, Endeavour House, 189 Shaftesbury Avenue, WC2H 8JG. *T:* (020) 7295 5000.

KEENE, Rt Hon. Sir David (Wolfe), Kt 1994; PC 2000; a Lord Justice of Appeal, 2000–09; Chairman, Qatar Financial Centre Regulatory Tribunal, since 2013; Arbitrator, Kuala Lumpur Regional Centre for Arbitration; *b* 15 April 1941; *s* of Edward Henry Wolfe Keene and Lilian Marjorie Keene; *m* 1965, Gillian Margaret Lawrance; one *s* one *d*. *Educ:* Hampton Grammar Sch.; Balliol Coll., Oxford (Winter Williams Prizewinner, 1962; BA 1st Cl. Hons Law, 1962; BCL 1963; Hon. Fellow, 2004). ACIArb. Called to the Bar, Inner Temple, 1964 (Eldon Law Scholar, 1965; Bencher, 1987; Treas., 2006); QC 1980; a Recorder, 1989–94; a Dep. High Court Judge, 1993–94; a Judge of High Court of Justice, QBD, 1994–2000; a Judge, Employment Appeal Tribunal, 1995–2000; Dep. Pres., Qatar Internat. Court, 2011–13. Chm. of Panel, Cumbria Structure Plan Examination in Public, 1980; conducted County Hall, London, Inquiry, 1987; Chairman: Planning and Envmtl Law Reform Working Gp, 1997–2009; Judicial Studies Bd, 2003–07 (Chm., Adv. Cttee on Equal Treatment, 1998–2003); Mem., QC Selection Panel, 2010–12. Chm., Planning Bar Assoc., 1994 (Vice-Chm., 1990–94). Non-exec. Chm., Argentum Capital Ltd, 2011–14. Mem. Bd, Sch. of Advanced Study, Univ. of London, 2008–10. Visitor, Brunel Univ., 1995–2000. Trustee: Oxford Philomusica, 2009–; Slynn Foundn, 2010–. Hon. Fellow, Soc. of Advanced Legal Studies, 1998. Hon. LLD Brunel, 2001. *Recreations:* walking, opera, jazz, gardening. *Address:* Royal Courts of Justice, Strand, WC2A 2LL. *Clubs:* Athenæum, Garrick.

KEENE, Prof. Derek John, DPhil; Leverhulme Professor of Comparative Metropolitan History, Institute of Historical Research, 2001–08, now Honorary Fellow and Professor Emeritus; *b* 27 Dec. 1942; *s* of Charles Henry Keene and Edith Anne Keene (*née* Swanston); *m* 1969, Suzanne Victoria Forbes (*see* S. V. Keene); one *s* one *d*. *Educ:* Ealing Grammar Sch.; Oriel Coll., Oxford (MA, DPhil). FRHistS. Researcher, 1968–74, Asst Dir, 1974–78, Winchester Research Unit; Institute of Historical Research: Dir, Social and Economic Study of Medieval London, 1987–99; Dir, Centre for Metropolitan History, 1987–2002; Actg Dir, 2008. Internat. Advr to Urban Society in the Low Countries, Belgian Sci. Policy Office, 2002–. Member: RCHM, 1987–99; Commn internat. pour l'histoire de villes, 1990–; Fabric Adv. Cttee, St Paul's Cathedral, 1991–; London Adv. Cttee, 1998–2004, Urban Panel, 2000–, English Heritage. *Publications:* Winchester in the Early Middle Ages (jtly), 1976; Survey of Medieval Winchester, 1985; Cheapside Before the Great Fire, 1985; (with V. Harding) A survey of documentary sources for property holding in London before the Great Fire, 1985; (with V. Harding) Historical Gazetteer of London before the Great Fire, 1987; (ed with P. J. Corfield) Work in Towns 850–1850, 1990; (jtly) A Medieval Capital and its Grain Supply: agrarian production and distribution in the London region *c* 1300, 1993; (ed jtly) St Paul's: the cathedral church of London 604–2004, 2004; (ed jtly) Integration—Assimilation: religious and ethnic groups in the medieval towns of Central and Eastern Europe, 2009; (ed jtly) Cities into Battlefields: metropolitan scenarios, experiences and commemorations of total war, 2011; (ed jtly) The Singularities of London, 1578, 2014; contribs to learned jls and to collections of essays. *Recreations:* metropolises, walking uphill, making and repairing things, wood-turning, woodland management. *Address:* 162 Erlanger Road, SE14 5TJ. *T:* (020) 7639 5371.

KEENE, Dr Suzanne Victoria, FIIC; Course Director, Museum Studies, Institute of Archaeology, University College London, 2001–09, now Reader Emeritus in Museum Studies; *b* 21 July 1944; *d* of late Lt-Comdr Lachlan Andrew Forbes, RN and Adelaide Talbot Suzanne Forbes; *m* 1969, Derek John Keene, *qv*; one *s* one *d*. *Educ:* various schools; University Coll. London (Dip. Archaeol Conservation; Gordon Childe Prize, Inst. of Archaeol., 1969; PhD 1993). FIIC 1985. Archaeol Asst, British Sch. at Rome, 1964–66; Winchester Research Unit: Archaeol Conservator, 1969–75; Ed., Medieval Finds pubn, 1975–77; Museum of London: Hd of Section, Archaeol Conservation, 1979–86; Hd of Conservation, 1986–92; Hd of Collections Mgt, Science Mus., 1992–2000. Member: Exec. Cttee, 1970–74, Gen. Sec., 1972–76, UK Inst. for Conservation; Panel on Archaeol Collections, Area Mus. for S Eastern England, 1976–90; UK Nat. Cttee, ICOM, 1993–99; Bd, Textile Conservation Centre, 1993–2000. Member: Working Parties, English Heritage and Mus and Galls Commn, 1988–90 and 1992; Working Gp on Mus and Nat. Grid for Learning, DCMS, 1998–99; Bd, London Museums Agency, 2001–04; Bd, Collections Trust (formerly Mus Documentation Assoc.), 2006–12. Mem. Cttee, S Wilts and N Dorset Gps, 2011–, Mem., Dorset Countryside Forum, 2013–, CPRE. Trustee, Tank Mus., 1998–2005. *Publications:* Managing Conservation in Museums, 1996, 2nd edn 2002; Digital Collections: museums in the information age, 1998; Fragments of the World, 2005; Collections for People, 2008; (with Francesca Monti) Museums and Silent Objects, 2013; contrib. numerous articles on museum digitisation and conservation. *Recreations:* beautiful country-side, reading novels, films, the internet.

KEENLYSIDE, Hilary Anne; Co-Founder and Director, Bonnar Keenlyside, since 1991; *b* Crawley, Sussex, 18 April 1955; *d* of Frederick Keenlyside and Hazel Keenlyside. *Educ:* Thomas Bennett Sch.; Dartington Coll. of Arts (BA Hons); City Univ. (Dip Arts Admin); London Business Sch. (Sloan Fellow); Univ. of London (MSc Mgt). Executive Director: Acad. of St Martin in the Fields, 1985–90; Almeida Th., 1990–91. Gov., City Literary Inst., 1999–2009 (Dep. Chm., 2007–09). Trustee, 2001–13, Chm. Bd, 2011–13, Barnardo's. Studying for BA Hons Modern Langs, Open Univ., 2009–. *Recreation:* sailing. *Address:* Bonnar Keenlyside, Toynbee Studios, 28 Commercial Street, E1 6AB. *E:* london@b-k.co.uk. *Club:* Bosham Sailing.

KEENLYSIDE, Simon John, CBE 2003; baritone; *b* London, 3 Aug. 1959; *s* of Raymond Keenlyside and Ann Leonie Hirsch; *m* 2006, Zenaida Yanowsky, ballerina; one *s* one *d*. *Educ:* St John's Coll., Cambridge (BA Zoology 1983; Hon. Fellow, 2008); Royal Northern Coll. of Music. With Scottish Opera, 1989–94 (rôles incl. Marcello, Danilo, Guglielmo, Figaro in Barber of Seville, Billy Budd, Papageno and Belcore); *débuts:* Royal Opera, Covent Garden, 1989 (Silvio in Pagliacci); ENO, 1990 (Guglielmo in Così fan tutte); WNO, 1991 (Falke); San Francisco, 1993 (Olivier in Capriccio); Geneva, 1993 (Papageno in Die Zauberflöte); Paris Opéra (Papageno), Australian Opera (Figaro) and La Scala, Milan, 1995; Glyndebourne, 1996 (Guglielmo); Metropolitan Opera, NY (Belcore in L'elisir d'amore); other rôles incl. Count Almaviva, Don Giovanni, Orfeo, Pelléas, Dandini in La Cenerentola, Wolfram in Tannhäuser, Yeletski in Queen of Spades, Oreste in Iphigénie en Tauride, Ubalde in Armide, Ford in Falstaff, title rôle in Hamlet, Prospero in The Tempest, Valentin in Gounod's Faust, Winston in 1984, title rôle in Eugene Onegin, title rôle in Wozzeck. Frequent concerts and recitals; recordings incl. operas, recitals of Schubert, Strauss and Mahler, and Schumann lieder. *Recreations:* a passion for all things zoological, diving, walking, painting, fly fishing. *Address:* c/o Askonas Holt, Lincoln House, 300 High Holborn, WC1V 7JH. *T:* (020) 7400 1700.

KEEP, Charles Reuben; Chairman and Managing Director, Resource Management Associates Ltd, since 1992; Chairman, Towergate Securities, since 1978; *b* 1932; *m*; one *d*. *Educ:* HCS, Hampstead. Joined Lloyds & Scottish Finance Ltd, 1956, Director, 1969; Man. Dir, International Factors Ltd, 1970; Group Man. Dir, Tozer Kemsley & Millbourn (Holdings) Ltd, 1973–77; Chm., Tozer Kemsley & Millbourn Trading Ltd, 1978–80; Director: Tozer Standard & Chartered Ltd, 1973–77; Barclays Tozer Ltd, 1974–77; Manufacturers Hanover Credit Corp., 1977–80; Chm., Export Leasing Ltd, Bermuda, 1974–77; Pres., France Motors sa Paris, 1974–81. *Address:* 23 Grovewood Place, Chigwell, Essex IG8 8PX. *T:* (020) 8504 3897. *Club:* Chigwell Golf.

KEETCH, Paul Stuart; political and historical consultant; *b* 21 May 1961; *s* of late John Norton Keetch and Agnes, (Peggy), Keetch; *m* 1991, Claire Elizabeth Baker; one *s*. *Educ:* Boys' High Sch., Hereford; Hereford Sixth Form Coll. With Midland Bank, 1978, then various water hygiene cos, 1979–95; Dir, MarketNet, 1996. Political and media advr to Lithuanian and Bosnian political parties, 1995–96. OSCE monitor to Albanian elections, 1996. Joined Liberal Party, 1975; Mem. (Lib Dem) Hereford CC, 1983–86. MP (Lib Dem) Hereford, 1997–2010. Lib Dem spokesman on: health, 1997; employment and training, 1997–99; defence, 1999–2005. Member: Educn and Employment Select Cttee, 1997–99; Armed Forces Bill Select Cttee, 2001; Envmtl Audit Select Cttee, 1999–2001; Foreign Affairs Select Cttee, 2005–10; Quadripartite (Strategic Arms Export Control) Cttee, 2005–10. All Party Groups: Pres., Cider Gp (Founder 1997); Founder and Co-Chm., British Lithuanian Gp; Vice-Chairman: Overseas Territories; Trinidad and Tobago; Childcare; Treasurer: Botswana; Serbia and Montenegro; Secretary: Albanian, 1997–2010; RN; Member: RM; Macedonia; Iraq; Bermuda; Bosnia; Czech and Slovak; Hungary; Madagascar; Netherlands; Montserrat; Channel Is; Turks and Caicos Is; Somaliland; Shipbuilding and Ship Repair; Racing and Bloodstock Issues. Dir, and Mem. Council, Electoral Reform Soc., 1997. Member: CPA, 1997–10; IPU. Patron, St Michael's Hospice, Hereford, 1997; President: Hereford Hosp. Radio, 1998–; Pegasus Juniors FC; Ross Sea Cadets; Vice-President: Nat. Childminding Assoc., 1998; Westfields FC, Hereford, 1997–; Hereford Young Europeans Gp; Ross-on-Wye Horticl Soc.; Hereford Amateur Operatic Soc.; Barrs Ct Sch., Hereford. Member: IISS; IPMS, 1998–; RUSI, 1999–. Hon. Mem., Falkland Is Assoc. *Recreations:* swimming, entertaining, building model warships. *E:* pkhereford@googlemail.com. *Clubs:* National Liberal; Herefordshire Farmers; Herefordshire County Cricket (Life Mem.), Surrey County Cricket.

KEHOE, Paul; Chief Executive Officer, Birmingham Airport Ltd (formerly International Airport Ltd), since 2008; *b* Liverpool, 21 April 1959; *s* of Reginald and Mary Kehoe; *m* 1983, Lesley Powell; one *s* one *d*. *Educ:* Univ. of Leicester (BSc Hons 1981); Warwick Business Sch., Univ. of Warwick (MBA 1990). Served RAF, Flt Lieut, Air Traffic Control, 1979–87. Manager, Airports, BAE Systems, 1990–93; Man. Dir, Serco-IAL Ltd, Serco Gp, 1993–97; TBI plc: Man. Dir, Belfast Internat. Airport, 1997–2000; Dir, Eur. Airports, 1999–2001; Man. Dir, London Luton Airport, 2001–05; Gp Ops Dir, 2001–05; Chief Executive Officer: DX Services plc, 2005–06; Bristol Internat. Airport, 2007–08. Hon. DBus Birmingham City, 2012. *Recreations:* flying (Private Pilots Licence), sailing (day skipper), reading. *T:* (0121) 767 7100. *E:* paul.kehoe@birminghamairport.co.uk.

KEIGHLEY, Prof. Michael Robert Burch, FRCS, FRCSE; Barling Professor of Surgery, University of Birmingham, 1988–2004, now Professor Emeritus; Managing Director, Keighleycolo Ltd, since 2009; *b* 12 Oct. 1943; *s* of late Dr Robert Arthur Spink Keighley and of Dr Jacqueline Vivian Keighley; *m* Dr Dorothy Margaret, MBE; one *s* one *d*. *Educ:* Monkton

Combe Sch.; St Bartholomew's Hosp., Univ. of London (MB BS 1967; MS 1976); Durham Univ. FRCS 1970; FRCSE 1970. Prof. of Surgery, General and Dental Hosps, Univ. of Birmingham, 1984–88. Boerhaave Prof. of Surgery, Univ. of Leiden, 1985; Eyber's Vis. Prof., Univ. of OFS, 1987; Vis. Prof., Harvard Univ., 1990; Penman Vis. Prof., Univ. of Cape Town, 1992; Vis. Prof., St Mark's Hosp., London, 1995; Rupert Turnbull Prof., Washington Univ., 1996; Vis. Prof., Karolinska Inst., 2000; Hon. Prof., Christian Med. Coll., Vellore, India, 2004–. Chairman: Public Affairs, United European Gastroenterol Fedn, 2000–05; Public Relns and Ethics, 2002–06, Assoc. of Coloproctol. of GB and Irc. (Pres., Res. Foundn, 2005–09). Mem., Christian Med. Fellowship, 1967–. Hon. Fellow: Brazilian Coll. of Surgeons, 1991; Sri Lankan Coll. of Surgeons, 2015; Hon. FRACS 1992; Hon. Mem., Portuguese Soc. of Surgery, 2004. Jacksonian Prize, RCS, 1979; Hunterian Prof., RCS, 1979. *Publications:* Antimicrobial Prophylaxis in Surgery, 1979; Inflammatory Bowel Diseases, 1981, 3rd edn 1995; Gastrointestinal Haemorrhage, 1983; Textbook of Gastroenterology, 1985, 2nd edn 1994; Surgery of the Anus, Rectum and Colon, 1994, 3rd edn 2008; Atlas of Colorectal Surgery, 1996. *Recreations:* painting, music, sailing, climbing. *Address:* Whalebone Cottage, Vicarage Hill, Tanworth in Arden, Warwicks B94 5AN. *T:* (01564) 742903, *Fax:* (01564) 742705. *E:* Keighleycolo@btinternet.com. *Clubs:* Athenæum, Royal Society of Medicine; Aston Martin Owners.

KEIGHLEY, Rev. Thomas Christopher, TSSF; FRCN; independent health care consultant, since 2001; Associate Priest, Hornchurch St Nicholas, Elm Park, since 2012; *b* 4 May 1951; *s* of late John Charles Keighley and Frances Louise Keighley (*née* Leary); *m* 1st, 1974, Anne Gibson (marr. diss. 1978); 2nd, 1979, Elizabeth Redfern (marr. diss. 1989); 3rd, 1990, Amanda Gunner; one step *s* one step *d*. *Educ:* St Michael's Coll., Kirkby Lonsdale; Preston Sch. of Nursing (SRN 1974; RMN 1976); Charles Frear Sch. of Nursing (NDN Cert. 1976); Huddersfield Polytechnic (RCNT 1979); Dip. Nursing, London Univ., 1981; BA Hons Open Univ. 1985; NE Oecumenical Course, Ushaw Coll., Durham (DipHE (Theol) 2003). FRCN 2004. Aux. Nurse, Deepdale Hosp., Preston, 1970; Staff Nurse, Preston Royal Infirmary, 1974; Community Charge Nurse, NW Leics, 1976; Clinical Teacher: Maidstone, 1977; Cambridge HA, 1979; RCN Adviser, Research, 1982; Dist Dir of Nursing, 1986, of Nursing and Quality, 1988, Waltham Forest; Regl Dir of Nursing, Yorkshire Health, 1990–95; Dir, Inst. of Nursing, Univ. of Leeds, 1993–96; Dir of Internat. Develt, Sch. of Healthcare Studies, Univ. of Leeds, 1997–2001. Associate Researcher, Lincoln Theol Inst., Sheffield Univ., 1998–2002. Lawrence S. Bloomberg Vis. Prof., Faculty of Nursing, Univ. of Toronto, 2012–13. Mem., EU Adv. Cttee on Training for Nursing, 1990–2000. Ordained deacon, C of E, 2003, priest, 2004; Curate, Upper Nidderdale, 2003–06; Assistant Priest: Dacre with Hartwith and Darley with Thornthwaite, dio. Ripon and Leeds, 2006–07; Christchurch and St John with St Luke, Isle of Dogs, 2007–12; Dean, Coll. of Self Supporting Ministers, Stepney Area, Dio. of London, 2008–12; Anglican Chaplain, St Joseph's Hospice, London, 2009–10. Winifred Raphael Meml Lecture, RCN Res. Soc., 1988; Ven. Catherine McAuley Meml Lecture, Mater Misericordiae Hosp., Dublin, 2002. TSSF, 2001–. Hon. Mem., American Orgn of Nurse Execs, 2010. Gran Cruz, Asociación Colombiana de Facultades de Medicina, 2001. Editor, Nursing Management, 1997–2004. *Publications:* articles on nursing, health care and theology. *Recreations:* opera, art, walking, rug making. *Address:* The Vicarage, 17 St Nicholas Avenue, Elm Park, Hornchurch RM12 4PT. *T:* (01708) 474639.

KEIGHTLEY, Maj.-Gen. Richard Charles, CB 1987; Chairman, Southampton University Hospitals NHS Trust, 2002–08; *b* 2 July 1933; *s* of General Sir Charles Keightley, GCB, GBE, DSO, and late Lady (Joan) Keightley (*née* Smyth-Osbourne); *m* 1958, Caroline Rosemary Butler, *er d* of Sir Thomas Butler, 12th Bt, CVO, DSO, OBE; three *d*. *Educ:* Marlborough Coll.; RMA, Sandhurst. Commissioned into 5th Royal Inniskilling Dragoon Guards, 1953; served Canal Zone, BAOR, N Africa, Singapore, Cyprus; sc Camberley, 1963; comd 5th Royal Inniskilling Dragoon Guards, 1972–75; Task Force Comdr, 3 Armd Div., 1978–79; RCDS 1980; Brigadier General Staff HQ UKLF, 1981; GOC Western Dist, 1982–83; Comdt, RMA Sandhurst, 1983–87. Col, 5th Royal Inniskilling Dragoon Guards, 1986–91. Defence Consultant, Portescap (UK), 1987–92. Chairman: W Dorset, subseq. Dorset, HA, 1988–95, 1998–2002; Dorset Healthcare NHS Trust, 1996–98. President: Dorset Br., Royal British Legion, 1990–2012; Dorset Relate, 2001–14; St John Ambulance Dorset, 2008–12 (Chm., St John Priory Gp, 2012–). Chm., Combined Services Polo Assoc., 1982–86. CStJ 2013 (OStJ 2004). *Recreations:* field sports, cricket, farming, horse racing. *Address:* Kennels Farmhouse, Tarrant Gunville, Blandford, Dorset DT11 8JQ. *Club:* Cavalry and Guards.

KEIR, Colin; Member (SNP) Edinburgh Western, Scottish Parliament, since 2011; *b* 9 Dec. 1959; *s* of John Keir and Catherine Keir (*née* Bonnar). *Educ:* Craigmount High Sch., Edinburgh. Mem. (SNP), Edinburgh CC, 2007–12 (Convener: Regulatory Cttee, 2007–11; Mgt Cttee, Pentland Hills Regl Park, 2007–11). *Recreations:* golf, fly fishing, Rugby. *Address:* Scottish Parliament, Edinburgh EH99 1SP. *T:* (0131) 348 5860. *E:* colin.keir.msp@scottish.parliament.uk. *Club:* RHC Cougars Rugby Football.

KEIR, Jane; Senior Partner, Kingsley Napley LLP, since 2013; *b* Skelton, Cumbria, 4 March 1962; *d* of Ronald John Keir, OBE and Audrie Jill Keir (*née* Curtis). *Educ:* Queen Elizabeth Grammar Sch., Penrith; Newcastle Poly. (LLB Hons); Coll. of Law, Chester. Admitted Solicitor, 1987; Asst Solicitor, Alexanders, 1987–89; Kingsley Napley LLP, 1989–: Sen. Equity Partner, 1997; Jt Man. Partner, 2004–07. Member: Law Soc., 1989–; Internat. Acad. of Matrimonial Lawyers, 2006–. Mem., Thoroughbred Breeders' Assoc., 2011–. *Recreations:* horseracing - breeding and owning, owner of Elkington Stud, Oxon. *Address:* Kingsley Napley LLP, Knights Quarter, 14 St John's Lane, EC1M 4AJ. *T:* (020) 7814 1273, 07887 571050. *E:* jkeir@kingsleynapley.co.uk.

KEITH, family name of **Earl of Kintore**.

KEITH, Hon. Sir Brian (Richard), Kt 2001; a Judge of the High Court, Queen's Bench Division, 2001–14; *b* 14 April 1944; *s* of late Alan Keith, OBE, broadcaster, and Pearl Keith (*née* Rebuck); *m* 1978, Gilly, *d* of late Air Cdre Ivan de la Plain, CBE; one *s* one *d*. *Educ:* University College School, Hampstead; Lincoln College, Oxford (MA). John F. Kennedy Fellow, Harvard Law School, 1966–67; called to the Bar, Inner Temple, 1968, Bencher, 1996; in practice, 1969–91; Assistant Recorder, 1988; QC 1989; a Recorder, 1993–2001. A Judge of the Supreme Court of Hong Kong, 1991–97; a Judge of the Court of First Instance, High Court of Hong Kong, 1997–99; Presiding Judge, Admin. Law List, High Court of Hong Kong, 1997–99; a Judge of the Court of Appeal, Hong Kong, 1999–2001; Judge of the Supreme Court of Fiji, 2015–. Hon. Lectr, Univ. of Hong Kong, 1994–2001. Mem., Judicial Studies Bd, Hong Kong, 1994–2001. Chm., Zahid Mubarek Inquiry, 2004–06. *Recreations:* travel, tennis, cinema. *E:* brkeith@blueyonder.co.uk. *Club:* Hong Kong.

KEITH, Hon. Hugo George; QC 2009; barrister; *b* Edinburgh, 6 Feb. 1967; *twin s* of Baron Keith of Kinkel, GBE, PC and of Alison Hope Alan Keith (*née* Brown); *m* 1999, Lottie Bulwer-Long; one *s* three *d*. *Educ:* Winchester Coll.; Magdalen Coll., Oxford (BA Juris.). Called to the Bar, Gray's Inn, 1989, Bencher, 2013; Treasury Counsel: Supplementary Panel, 1994–95; B Panel Civil, 1995–2000; A Panel Civil, 2000–08. Mem., Bar Council, 1995–98. *Recreation:* sailing. *Address:* 3 Raymond Buildings, Gray's Inn, WC1R 5BH. *T:* (020) 7400 6400, *Fax:* (020) 7400 6464.

See also R. S. Steedman.

KEITH, Rt Hon. Sir Kenneth (James), ONZ 2007; KBE 1988; PC 1998; a Judge of the International Court of Justice, 2006–15; Distinguished Fellow, Victoria University of Wellington; *b* 19 Nov. 1937; *s* of Patrick James Keith and Amy Irene Keith (*née* Witheridge); *m* 1961, Jocelyn Margaret Buckett; two *s* two *d*. *Educ:* Auckland Grammar Sch.; Auckland Univ.; Victoria Univ. of Wellington (LLM); Harvard Law Sch. Barrister and Solicitor, High Court of New Zealand; QC (NZ) 1994. NZ Dept of External Affairs, 1960–62; Victoria Univ. of Wellington, 1962–64, 1966–91, Prof. of Law, 1974–91, now Emeritus; UN Secretariat, NY, 1968–70; NZ Inst. of Internat. Affairs, 1972–74; Pres., NZ Law Commn, 1991–96; a Judge of NZ Court of Appeal, 1996–2003; a Judge of Supreme Ct, Fiji, 2003, NZ, 2004–05; a Judge of Court of Appeal: Western Samoa, 1982; Cook Is, 1982; Niue, 1995. Permanent Ct of Arbitration, 1985–2008. Mem., 1991–2006, Pres., 2002–06, Internat. Fact Finding Commn (Geneva Conventions). Mem., Inst de Droit Internat., 2003– (Assoc. Mem., 1997–2003). Hon. LLD: Auckland, 2001; Victoria, Wellington, 2004. *Publications:* (ed) Human Rights in New Zealand, 1968; The Extent of the Advisory Jurisdiction of the International Court, 1971; contrib. to Amer. Jl of Internat. Law, Internat. and Comparative Law Qly, NZ Univs Law Rev., etc. *Recreations:* walking, reading, music. *Address:* 11 Salamanca Road, Wellington 6012, New Zealand.

KEITH, Larry Bacon; Head of Conservation and Keeper, National Gallery, since 2010; *b* San Jose, Costa Rica, 18 April 1960; *s* of Clifford Keith and Shirley Keith; *m* 2006, Marie Louise Juel Sauerberg; one *s*. *Educ:* Oberlin Coll. (BA Art Hist. 1982); Royal Coll. of Music (LRCM 1988); Hamilton Kerr Inst., Univ. of Cambridge (DipCons 1988). Intern: with Herbert Lank, London, 1988–89; Metropolitan Mus., 1989–91; Conservator, Nat. Gall., 1991–. Mem. and ext. examnr, Internat. Adv. Bd of Studies, Dept of Conservation and Technol., Courtauld Inst. of Art, Univ. of London; ext. examnr, post-grad. easel painting conservation course, Hamilton Kerr Inst., Cambridge. Advisor: Bank of America Conservation Prog.; Heritage Conservation Trust; Mem., Adv. Bd, Reynolds Res. Proj., Wallace Collection. *Recreations:* music, cinema, sport. *Address:* National Gallery, Trafalgar Square, WC2N 5DN. *E:* larry.keith@ng-london.org.uk. *Club:* Blacks.

KEITH, Dame Penelope (Anne Constance), (Dame Penelope Timson), DBE 2014 (CBE 2007; OBE 1989); DL; actress; *b* 2 April; *d* of Frederick A. W. Hatfield and Constance Mary Keith; *m* 1978, Rodney Timson. *Educ:* Annecy Convent, Seaford, Sussex; Webber Douglas Sch., London. First prof. appearance, Civic Theatre, Chesterfield, 1959; repertory, Lincoln, Salisbury and Manchester, 1960–63; RSC, Stratford, 1963, and Aldwych, 1965; rep., Cheltenham, 1967; Maggie Howard in Suddenly at Home, Fortune Theatre, 1971; Sarah in The Norman Conquests, Greenwich, then Globe Theatre, 1974; Lady Driver in Donkey's Years, 1976; Orinthia in The Apple Cart, Chichester, then Phoenix Theatre, 1977; Epifania in The Millionairess, Haymarket, 1978; Sarah in Moving, Queen's Theatre, 1981; Maggie in Hobson's Choice, Haymarket, 1982; Lady Cicely Waynflete in Captain Brassbound's Conversion, Haymarket, 1982; Judith Bliss in Hay Fever, Queen's, 1983; The Dragon's Tail, Apollo, 1985; Miranda, Chichester, 1987; The Deep Blue Sea, Haymarket, 1988; Dear Charles, Yvonne Arnaud, Guildford, 1990; The Merry Wives of Windsor, Chichester, 1990; Lady Bracknell in The Importance of Being Earnest, UK tour, 1991; On Approval, UK tour, 1992; Glyn and It, Richmond, 1994; Monsieur Amilcar, Chichester, 1995; Mrs Warren's Profession, Richmond, 1997; Good Grief, nat. tour, 1998; Star Quality, Apollo, 2001; Time and the Conways, nat. tour, 2003; Madame Arcati in Blithe Spirit, Th. Royal, Bath, transf. Savoy Th., 2004; Entertaining Angels, Chichester, 2006; The Importance of Being Earnest, Vaudeville, 2008; Mrs Malaprop in The Rivals, Th. Royal, Bath, 2010; directed: Relatively Speaking, nat. tour, 1992; How the Other Half Loves, nat. tour, 1994; The Way of the World, Chichester, 2012; *film:* The Priest of Love, 1980. Television plays and series include: The Good Life, 1974–77; The Norman Conquests, 1977; To the Manor Born, 1979, 1980 and 1981; Sweet Sixteen, 1983; Moving, 1985; Executive Stress, 1986–88; No Job for a Lady, 1990–92; Next of Kin, 1995–97; Margery and Gladys, 2003; presenter: What's My Line?, 1988; Growing Places, 1989; The Manor Reborn, 2011; Penelope Keith's Hidden Villages, 2014, 2015. Mem., HFEA, 1990–96. President: The Actors' Benevolent Fund, 1990–; KeepOut, 2011–; S of England Agricultural Soc., 2012–13. Vice-Pres., Queen Elizabeth's Foundn for Disabled People (formerly Gov., Queen Elizabeth's Foundn for the Disabled), 1989–. Patron, Yvonne Arnaud Theatre, 1992–. High Sheriff, Surrey, 2002–03; DL Surrey, 2004. Awards: BAFTA, 1976 and 1977; SWET, 1976; Variety Club of GB, 1976 and 1979. *Recreation:* gardening. *Address:* c/o The Actors' Benevolent Fund, 6 Adam Street, WC2N 6AA. *T:* (020) 7439 1456.

KEITH, Shona; *see* McIsaac, S.

KEKIĆ, Dr Razia; a Judge of the Upper Tribunal (Immigration and Asylum Chamber) (formerly a Senior Immigration Judge, Asylum and Immigration Tribunal), since 2008; *b* London, 7 July 1956; *d* of Abdur Razzak Dada and Diane Dada; *m* 1983, Laza Kekić (marr. diss. 1996); two *d*. *Educ:* Convent of Jesus and Mary, Karachi; Karachi Grammar Sch.; Univ. of Kent, Canterbury (BA Hons Social Anthropol.); London Sch. of Econs (MSc; PhD Social Anthropol. 2000). Counsellor, 1978–83, Sen. Counsellor, 1983–88, UK Immigrants Adv. Service, Harmondsworth; caseworker, 1992–2000, Team Leader, 2001, Refugee Legal Centre; Immigration Judge (pt-time), 2001–02, (full-time), 2002–05; Designated Immigration Judge, 2005–08. *Recreations:* walking, exploring, travel, reading, particularly travel books, Scandinavian crime and ethnic books, cinema, painting, photography, vegetarian cookery and juicing. *Address:* Upper Tribunal (Immigration and Asylum Tribunal), Field House, 15–25 Breams Building, EC4A 1DZ. *T:* (020) 7073 4249, *Fax:* (020) 7073 4004. *E:* razia.kekic@judiciary.gsi.gov.uk.

KELBURN, Viscount of; courtesy title of heir of Earl of Glasgow, not used by current heir.

KELEHER, Paul Robert; QC 2009; *b* Ilford, Essex; *s* of Roy and Margaret Keleher; *m* 2001, Barbara Grzybowska; one *s* one *d*. *Educ:* Chigwell Sch.; Gonville and Caius Coll., Cambridge (BA 1978); Inns of Court Sch. of Law. Called to the Bar, Gray's Inn, 1980, Bencher, 2013. *Recreations:* walking, cycling, gardening, fine wine and real ale. *Address:* 25 Bedford Row, WC1R 4HD. *T:* (020) 7067 1500. *E:* paul.keleher@25bedfordrow.com.

KELL, Prof. Douglas Bruce, CBE 2014; DPhil; FRSB; FLSW; FAAAS; Professor of Bioanalytical Science, University of Manchester (formerly University of Manchester Institute of Science and Technology), since 2002; *b* 7 April 1953; *s* of William Howard Kell and Nancy Kell (*née* Finniston); *m* 1989, Dr Antje Wagner; one *s* two *d*. *Educ:* Bradfield Coll., Berks (Top Schol.); St John's Coll., Oxford (BA Hons Biochem. Upper 2nd Cl. with Dist. in Chem. Pharmacol.; Sen. Schol., 1975–76; MA, DPhil 1978). FRSB (FIBiol 1999). UCW, Aberystwyth, then University of Wales, Aberystwyth: SRC Postdoctoral Res. Fellow, 1978–80; SERC Advanced Fellow, 1981–83; New Blood Lectr, 1983–88; Reader, 1988–92; Prof. of Microbiology, 1992–2002, Dir of Res., 1997–2002, Inst. of Biol Scis; Dir, Manchester Centre for Integrative Systems Biology, 2005–08; Chief Exec. and Dep. Chm., BBSRC, 2008–13 (on secondment). Fleming Lectr, Soc. for Gen. Microbiol., 1986. Founding Director: Aber Instruments, 1988–2008 (Queen's Award for Export Achievement 1998); Predictive Solutions Ltd (formerly Aber Genomic Computing), 2000–08. Member: Council, 2000–06, Strategy Bd, 2001–06, BBSRC; numerous scientific cttees of SRC, SERC and BBSRC, incl.: Plant Scis and Microbiol., 1985–88, Biotech. Directorate, 1992–94, Chemicals and Pharmaceuticals Directorate, 1994–96, Engrg and Biol Systems, 1999–2000; Biosci. for Industry Panel, 2007–08; DTI LINK Prog. Mgt Cttees for Technol. for Analytical and Physical Measurement, 1992–94, Biochem. Engrg, 1994–98, Analytical Biotech. (Chm., 1995–99); Basic Technol. Strategic Adv. Cttee, Res. Councils UK, 2001–04; Sci. Bd, STFC, 2007–08; Adv. Bd, UK PubMed Central, 2007–08. FLSW 2012; FAAAS 2012. Fellow, Aberystwyth Univ., 2013. Hon. DSc: Cranfield, 2012; Aberdeen, 2015. Interdisciplinary Award, 2004, Chem. Biol. Award, 2005, SAC Gold Medal, 2006, RSC; Theodor Bücher

Medal, FEBS-IUBMB, 2005; Royal Soc./Wolfson Merit Award, 2005. *Publications:* numerous scientific pubns. *Recreation:* family. *Address:* School of Chemistry and Manchester Institute of Biotechnology, University of Manchester, 131 Princess Street, Manchester M1 7DN.

KELL, Michael Stuart; Director, Economic Analysis, National Audit Office, since 2010; *b* 27 Jan. 1965; *s* of Malcolm Kell and Jill Kell (*née* Wood); *m* 1995, Jane Morris; three *d*. *Educ:* St Edmund Hall, Oxford (BA Hons PPE 1986); Nuffield Coll., Oxford (MPhil Econs 1991). Res. Officer, Inst. for Fiscal Studies, 1986–89; Econ. Advr, HM Treasury, 1991–96; Advr to UK Exec. Dir, IMF and World Bank, 1996–98; Sen. Economist, Fiscal Affairs Dept, IMF, 1998–2002; Hd, Central Econ. Analysis, 2002–03, Chief Economist, 2003–07, ODPM, subseq. DCLG; Dir, Econ. Consulting, Deloitte and Touche LLP, 2008–10. *Recreations:* spending time with Ruby, Alice and Josie. *T:* 07931 738719. *E:* michael.kell@nao.gsi.gov.uk.

KELLAND, John William, LVO 1977; QPM 1975; Overseas Police Adviser and Inspector General of Dependent Territories' Police, Foreign and Commonwealth Office, 1985–91; *b* 18 Aug. 1929; *s* of William John Kelland and Violet Ethel (*née* Olsen); *m* 1963, Brenda Nancy (*née* Foulsham) (decd); *m* 1986, Frances Elizabeth (*née* Byrne); one step *d*; two *s* from a former marriage. *Educ:* Sutton High Sch.; Plymouth Polytechnic. FIMgt. RAF, 1947–49. Constable, later Insp., Plymouth City Police, 1950–67; Insp., later Supt, Devon & Cornwall Constabulary, 1968–72; Asst Chief Constable, Cumbria Constabulary, 1972–74; Dir, Sen. Comd Courses, Nat. Police Coll., Bramshill, 1974–75 and 1978–80; Comr, Royal Fiji Police, 1975–78; 1981–85: Management Consultant and Chm., CSSBs; Sen. Consultant, RIPA; Sen. Lectr, Cornwall Coll.; Facilitator, Interpersonal Skills, Cornwall CC Seminars. Mem., Cornwall & Isles of Scilly FHSA, 1992–93. Chm., Old Suttonian Assoc., 1993–2011 (Vice Pres., 2011–). *Publications:* various articles in learned jls. *Recreations:* Rugby football, choral singing. *Clubs:* Civil Service, Royal Air Force.

KELLAWAY, (Charles) William; Secretary and Librarian, Institute of Historical Research, University of London, 1971–84; *b* 9 March 1926; *s* of late Charles Halliley Kellaway, FRS; *m* 1952, Deborah (*d* 2006), *d* of late Sir Hibbert Alan Stephen Newton; one *s* two *d*. *Educ:* Geelong Grammar Sch.; Lincoln Coll., Oxford. BA Modern History, 1949, MA 1955. FCLIP, FRHistS. Asst Librarian, Guildhall Library, 1950–60; Sub-Librarian, Inst. of Historical Research, 1960–71. Hon. General Editor, London Record Society, 1964–83. *Publications:* The New England Company, 1649–1776, 1961; (ed jtly) Studies in London History, 1969; Bibliography of Historical Works Issued in UK, 1957–70, 3 vols, 1962, 1967, 1972; (ed jtly) The London Assize of Nuisance 1301–1431, 1973. *Address:* 18 Canonbury Square, N1 2AL. *T:* (020) 7354 0349.

KELLAWAY, Richard Edward, CBE 2005; FRGS; Director General, Commonwealth War Graves Commission, 2000–10; *b* 13 Aug. 1946; *s* of late Edward John Kellaway and Elsie May Kellaway (*née* Judd); *m* 1968, Ann Clarke; two *d*. *Educ:* Poole Grammar Sch. FRGS 2010. Commnd as Officer of Customs and Excise, 1966: Sen. Investigation Officer, 1975–79; Principal, VAT Admin, 1979–80; Asst Chief Investigation Officer, 1980–84; Chief Staff Inspector, 1984–87; Head: Customs Dept, Bermuda, 1987–90; Estates and Security, 1990–94; Chief Investigation Officer, 1994–99; on secondment as Drugs and Serious Crime Advr, FCO, 1999–2000. *Recreations:* industrial archaeology, cooking, gardening. *Address:* Cranford, Ridge Langley, Sanderstead, Surrey CR2 0AR. *E:* rekellaway@blueyonder.co.uk. *Clubs:* Royal Air Force; Automobile de l'Ouest (France).

KELLAWAY, William; *see* Kellaway, C. W.

KELLEHER, Dame Joan, (Joanna), DBE 1965; Hon. ADC to the Queen, 1964–67; Director, Women's Royal Army Corps, 1964–67; *b* 24 Dec. 1915; *d* of late Kenneth George Henderson, barrister-at-law, Stonehaven; *m* 1970, Brig. Mortimer Francis Howlett Kelleher (*d* 2006), OBE, MC, late RAMC. *Educ:* privately at home and abroad. Joined ATS, 1941; commissioned ATS, 1941; WRAC, 1949. *Recreation:* gardening.

KELLEHER, Patricia Mary; Principal, Stephen Perse Foundation (formerly Perse School for Girls and Stephen Perse Sixth Form College), since 2001; *b* 17 March 1962; *d* of Liam and Margaret Kelleher. *Educ:* Lady Margaret Hall, Oxford (MA Modern Hist. 1984); Univ. of Sussex (MA Renaissance Theory and Culture 1995); Univ. of Nottingham (PGCE 1985). History Teacher, Haberdashers' Aske's Sch. for Girls, Elstree, 1985–88; Hd of History and Hd of Year 7, Brighton and Hove High Sch. (GDST), 1988–97; Dep. Headmistress, Brentwood Sch., Essex, 1997–2001. *Recreations:* walking, travel, reading. *Address:* Stephen Perse Foundation, Union Road, Cambridge CB2 1HF. *T:* (01223) 454700, *Fax:* (01223) 467420. *E:* principal@stephenperse.com.

KELLENBERGER, Dr Jakob; President, International Committee of the Red Cross, 2000–12; *b* 19 Oct. 1944; *s* of Jakob and Klara Kellenberger; *m* 1973, Elisabeth Kellenberger-Jossi; two *d*. *Educ:* Univ. of Zurich (PhD 1975). Joined Swiss Diplomatic Service, 1974: served Madrid, EU (Brussels), London, 1974–84; Hd, Dept for European Integration, Berne, 1984–92 (Minister, 1984–88; Ambassador, 1988–92); State Sec. for Foreign Affairs, Switzerland, 1992–99. Teaching posts: Univ. of Salamanca; Grad. Inst., Geneva. Member, Board: Council for Future of Europe, 2011–; Centre for Humanitarian Dialogue, Geneva, 2012–; Pres., Swisspeace, 2013–. Hon. Councillor, Swiss Fed. Inst. of Technology, Zurich, 2007; Hon. Mem., Amer. Soc. of Internat. Law, 2012. Dr *hc* Basle, 2003; Catania, 2006. Grosses Verdienstkreuz mit Stern (Germany), 2012; Commandeur, Légion d'Honneur (France), 2013. *Publications:* Calderón de la Barca und das Komische, 1975; Humanitäres Völkerrecht, 2010; Wo liegt die Schweiz?, 2014; numerous articles, particularly on Swiss–EU relations. *Recreations:* reading (literature, philosophy), cross country ski-ing, jogging, tennis.

KELLETT, Sir Stanley Charles, 7th Bt *cr* 1801; *b* 5 March 1940; *s* of Sir Stanley Everard Kellett, 6th Bt, and of Audrey Margaret Phillips; *S* father, 1983, but his name does not appear on the Official Roll of the Baronetage; *m* 1st, 1962, Lorraine May (marr. diss. 1968), *d* of F. Winspear; 2nd, 1968, Margaret Ann (marr. diss. 1974), *d* of James W. Bofinger; 3rd, 1982, Catherine Lorna (marr. diss. 1991), *d* of W. J. C. Orr; two *d*; 4th, 1991, Yvonne Patricia (*d* 2001), *d* of Alan Blogg. *Heir: cousin* Maxwell Rex Kellett [*b* 1947; *m* 1968, Jennifer Maher; one *d*]. *Address:* 21 Debussy Place, Cranebrook, NSW 2749, Australia.

KELLETT-BOWMAN, Edward Thomas; JP; business and management consultant in private practice, since 1974; *b* 25 Feb. 1931; *s* of late R. E. Bowman and M. Bowman (*née* Mathers); *m* 1st, 1960, Margaret Patricia Blakemore (*d* 1970); three *s* one *d*; 2nd, 1971, (Mary) Elaine Kellett (Dame Elaine Kellett-Bowman, DBE). *Educ:* Reed's Sch.; Slough Coll. of Technol. (DMS 1973); Cranfield Inst. of Technol. (MBA 1974). Technical and management trng in textiles, 1951–53; textile management, 1953–55; pharmaceutical man., 1955–72. Mem. (C) Lancs East, European Parlt, 1979–84; contested same seat, 1984; MEP (C) Hampshire Central, Dec. 1988–1994, Itchen, Test and Avon, 1994–99; contested (C) SE Region, 1999. Freeman: City of London, 1978; Wheelwrights' Co., 1979. Hon. Citizen, New Orleans, 1960. FCMI. JP Middx, 1966. *Recreations:* shooting, tennis, swimming. *Address:* Endymion, Ampfield, Romsey, Hants SO51 9BD.

KELLEY, Joan, CB 1987; Member, Official Side Panel, Civil Service Appeal Board, 1987–96; *b* 8 Dec. 1926; *er d* of late George William Kelley and Dora Kelley. *Educ:* Whalley Range High Sch. for Girls, Manchester; London Sch. of Econs and Pol Science (BScEcon 1947). Europa Publications Ltd, 1948; Pritchard, Wood & Partners Ltd, 1949; joined Civil Service as Econ. Asst in Cabinet Office, 1949; admin. work in Treasury, 1954; Principal, 1956; Asst Sec., 1968; Under Sec., 1979; on secondment to NI Office, 1979–81; Under Sec., 1979–86, Principal Estabt Officer and Principal Finance Officer, 1984–86, HM Treasury. Mem. Council, Univ. of London Inst. of Educn, 1992–98. *Recreations:* gardening, map reading, drinking wine, foreign travel. *Address:* The Nook, The Street, Little Chart, Ashford, Kent TN27 0QB.

KELLNER, family name of **Baroness Ashton of Upholland**.

KELLNER, Peter Jon; President, YouGov, online polling and market research company, since 2007 (Chairman, 2001–07); *b* 2 Oct. 1946; *s* of Michael Kellner and Lily Agnes Samson Kellner (*née* McVail); *m* 1st, 1972, Sally Collard (marr. diss. 1988); one *s* two *d*; 2nd, 1988, Catherine Margaret Ashton (*see* Baroness Ashton of Upholland); one *s* one *d*. *Educ:* Minchenden Grammar Sch., Southgate, London; Royal Grammar Sch., Newcastle upon Tyne; King's Coll., Cambridge (BA 1st Cl. Hons 1969). Journalist, Sunday Times, 1969–80; Political Ed., New Statesman, 1980–87; political columnist: Independent, 1986–92; Sunday Times, 1992–96; Observer, 1996–97; Evening Standard, 1997–2003. TV political analyst and commentator: A Week in Politics, 1982–88; Newsnight and election progs, 1990–97; Powerhouse, 1999–2003; radio presenter, Analysis, 1995–98. Trustee: Royal Commonwealth Soc., 2007–13 (Chm., 2009–13); ASH, 2009–; Hansard Soc., 2012–; UpRising, 2013–. Mem. Council, NIESR, 2013–. Journalist of Year, BPA, 1978; Chairman of the Year, Quoted Company Awards, 2007; Special Recognition Award, Political Studies Assoc., 2011. *Publications:* (with C. Hitchens) Callaghan: the road to Number Ten, 1976; (with Lord Crowther-Hunt) The Civil Servants, 1980; Democracy, 2009; contribs to various jls, incl. Parly Affairs, Political Qly, British Journalism Rev., Internat. Jl Mkt Res. *Recreations:* reading, arguing, travel. *Address:* YouGov, 50 Featherstone Street, EC1Y 8RT. *T:* (020) 7012 6000.

KELLS, Ronald David, OBE 1999; DL; Group Chief Executive, Ulster Bank Ltd, 1994–98; *b* 14 May 1938; *s* of Robert Kells and Frances Elizabeth Kells; *m* 1964, Elizabeth Anne Kells; one *s* one *d*. *Educ:* Bushmills Grammar Sch.; Sullivan Upper Sch.; Queen's Univ., Belfast (BSc Econ). FCIS 1979; FIB 1985. Joined Ulster Bank, 1964; Investments Manager, 1969–76; Dep. Head, Related Banking Services, 1976–79; Head of Planning and Marketing, 1972–82; seconded to National Westminster Bank, 1982–84; Dir and Head, Retail Services (formerly Branch Banking Div.), 1984–94. Chm., Cunningham Coates Ltd, stockbrokers, 1998–2002; Non-exec. Director: United Drug Plc, 1999– (Chm., 2005–12); Readymix PLC, 1999–2009. Pres., Confedn of Ulster Socs, 1999–2004. Gov., BFI, 1998–2003. DL Belfast, 1998. Hon. DEcon QUB, 2012. *Recreations:* golf, ski-ing. *Address:* The Moyle, 10 Upper Knockbreda Road, Belfast BT6 9QA. *T:* (028) 9079 7912. *Clubs:* Ulster Reform (Belfast); Royal County Down Golf, Royal Belfast Golf, Portmarnock Golf.

KELLY, Dame Barbara (Mary), DBE 2007 (CBE 1992); DL; Convenor, Crichton Foundation, 2003–14; *b* 27 Feb. 1940; *d* of John Maxwell Prentice and Barbara Bain Adam; *m* 1960, Kenneth Archibald Kelly; one *s* two *d* (and two *s* decd). *Educ:* Dalbeattie High Sch.; Kirkcudbright Academy; Moray House Coll., Edinburgh. DipEd. Partner in mixed farming enterprise. Dir, Clydesdale Bank, 1994–98; Member: Scottish Adv. Bd, BP plc, 1990–2003; Scottish PO Bd, 1997–2003. Chairman: Area Manpower Bd, MSC, 1987–88; Scottish Consumer Council, 1985–90; Rural Forum, 1988–92 (Hon. Pres., 1992–99); Training 2000, 1991–97; Architects Registration Bd, 1997–2002; Member: Nat. Consumer Council, 1985–90; Scottish Enterprise Bd, 1990–95; Priorities Bd, MAFF, 1990–95; BBC Rural Affairs and Agric. Adv. Cttee, 1991–97; Scottish Econ. Council, 1991–98; Scottish Tourist Bd, 1993–97; Rathbone Community Industry Bd, 1993–98; Scottish Nat. Heritage Bd, 1995–2001; BBC Broadcasting Council for Scotland, 1997–2002; Comr, EOC, 1991–95. Convener, Millennium Forest for Scotland Trust, 1995–2008. Nat. Vice-Chm., Scottish Women's Rural Insts, 1983–86. Hon. Pres., Scottish Conservation Projects Trust. Chm., Scottish Adv. Cttee, and Mem., Nat. Adv. Cttee, Duke of Edinburgh's Award Scheme, 1980–85. Trustee: Scottish Community (formerly Caledonian) Foundn, 1995–2002; Strathclyde Foundn, 1997–2002; Robertson Trust, 2002– (Chm.); Royal Botanic Gdn, Edinburgh, 2002–11. Freeman, City of London, 2002. DL Dumfries, 1998. Fellow, Bell Coll., 2006; Hon. Fellow, Queen Margaret UC, 2005. Hon. FRIAS 2008; Hon. FRSGS 2008. Hon. LLD: Strathclyde, 1995; Aberdeen, 1997; Glasgow, 2002; DUniv: Glasgow, 2002; W of Scotland, 2010. *Recreations:* home and family, music, painting, the pursuit of real food, gardening of necessity. *Address:* Barncleugh, Irongray, Dumfries DG2 9SE. *T:* (01387) 730210.

KELLY, Prof. Ben, RDI 2007; interior designer; Principal, Ben Kelly Design, since 1976; Professor of Interior and Spatial Design, University of the Arts London, since 2014; *b* Welwyn Garden City, 1 April 1949; *s* of Herbert and Doreen Kelly; two *s*; *m* 2008, Clare Cumberlidge. *Educ:* Appletreewick Prim. Sch., N Yorks; Ermysted's Grammar Sch., Skipton; Lancaster Coll. of Art; Royal Coll. of Art (MA 1974). Notable projects include: Howie Shop, Covent Garden, 1977; Seditionaries, King's Rd, London, 1977; Sex Pistols rehearsal studio, Denmark St, London, 1978; The Haçienda, Manchester, 1982; Smile, King's Rd, London, 1983; DRY 201, Manchester, 1989; Factory Records HQ, 1990, and conversion into nightclub, FAC 251 The Factory, 2010; BAR TEN, Glasgow, 1991; The Basement, Sci. Mus., London, 1995; Design Council offices, Bow St, London, 1997; Borough Hotel, Edinburgh, 2001; Gymbox, St Martin's Lane, London, 2006; The Public, West Bromwich, 2008; Gymbox, Cornhill, City of London, 2008–09; Gymbox, Westfield, London, 2010; BIMM Manchester, 2013; exhibn design for V&A Mus., British Design 1948–2012 (incl. part re-build of Haçienda nightclub), 2012; Gymbox, Farringdon, 2012; Media Space, Sci. Mus., 2013; exhibn design for Mus. of London, Cheapside Hoard London's Lost Jewels, 2013. Solo exhibitions: International Orange, Kingston Univ., 2008; International Orange: Please Shut the Gate, Glasgow Sch. of Art, 2010. Vis. Prof. of Interior Design, RCA, 2015–. Res. Fellow, Kingston Univ., 2013–. Hon. DDes Kingston, 2000. *Publications:* (contrib.) Plans and Elevations: Ben Kelly Design, 1990; (cover design) Cut & Shut, 2012. *Recreations:* walking, looking at art, making art, studying the work of Marcel Duchamp, watching Finbar (my younger son) grow up, Pop culture, looking at the colour orange, looking out of my window at the sea, looking out of my window at the stars, making coracles, stiles, gates and dry-stone walls. *Address:* c/o Ben Kelly Design, 10 Stoney Street, SE1 9AD. *T:* (020) 7378 8116. *E:* ben@bkduk.co.uk.

KELLY, Bernadette Mary, CB 2010; Director General, Rail Executive, Department for Transport, since 2015; *b* 10 March 1964; *d* of Edward Kelly and Teresa Bridget Kelly (*née* Garvey); *m* 1998, Howard Ewing; one *s*. *Educ:* King Edward VI Camp Hill Sch. for Girls, Birmingham; Hull Univ. (BA Hons); Imperial Coll., London (MBA 1997). Department of Trade and Industry: Admin. trainee, 1987–91; Grade 7, 1991–97; Sen. Civil Servant, HM Treasury, 1998–2000 (on secondment); Principal Private Sec. to Sec. of State for Trade and Industry, 2000–02; on secondment to ICI, 2002–03; Dir, Corporate Law and Governance, DTI, 2003–05; Sen. Policy Advr, Policy Directorate, Prime Minister's Office, 2005–06; Dir, Planning Reform, Cabinet Office, 2006–07; Exec. Dir, Planning, 2007–09, Housing, 2009–10, DCLG; Dir Gen., Market Frameworks (formerly Fair Markets), 2010–12, Mkts and Local Growth, 2012–13, Business and Local Growth, 2013–15, BIS. Mem. Council, Inst. of Employment Studies, 2011–. *Address:* Department for Transport, Great Minster House, 33 Horseferry Road, SW1P 4DR. *Clubs:* Goodwood, Midhurst Cricket (Sussex).

KELLY, Most Rev. Brendan; *see* Achonry, Bishop of, (RC).

KELLY, Brendan Damien; QC 2008; barrister; a Recorder, since 2002; *b* Manchester, 14 Oct. 1965; *s* of John Bosco Kelly and Maureen Olive Kelly; *m* 1992, Sallie Ann Bennett-Jenkins, QC; six *c*. *Educ:* Leeds Poly. Called to the Bar, Gray's Inn, 1988. *Recreations:* Rugby, golf, fishing. *Address:* 2 Hare Court, Temple, EC4Y 7BH. *T:* (020) 7353 5324. *E:* brendankelly@2harecourt.com.

KELLY, Prof. Catriona Helen Moncrieff, DPhil; FBA 2007; Professor of Russian, and Co-Director, European Humanities Research Centre, University of Oxford, since 2002; Fellow, New College, Oxford, since 1996; *b* 6 Oct. 1959; *d* of late Alexander Kelly and (Helen) Margaret Kelly (*née* Moncrieff); *m* 1993, Prof. Ian Thompson. *Educ:* St Hilda's Coll., Oxford (BA 1st cl. Hons Mod. Langs (German and Russian)); DPhil Oxon 1986. Christ Church, Oxford: Sen. Schol., 1983–87; Jun. Res. Fellow, 1987–90; British Acad. Post-Doctoral Fellow, 1990–93; Lectr, SSEES, Univ. of London, 1993–96; Lectr in Russian, Univ. of Oxford, 1996–2002. Member, Judging Panel: Rossica Prize, 2007; Independent Prize for Foreign Fiction, 2011; Joseph Brodsky/Stephen Spender Prize, 2011, 2012. Gen. Ed., Cambridge Studies in Russian Lit., 1995–2000; Member, Editorial Board: Antropologicheskii forum (Forum for Anthropol. and Culture) (St Petersburg); Kritika; Slavic Review; Eurasia Past and Present. Pres., Assoc. for Slavic, E Eur., and Eurasian Studies, USA, 2015. *Publications:* (ed jtly) Discontinuous Discourses in Modern Russian Literature, 1989; Petrushka, the Russian Carnival Puppet Theatre, 1990; A History of Russian Women's Writing 1820–1992, 1994; (ed) An Anthology of Russian Women's Writing 1777–1992, 1994; (ed with D. Shepherd) Constructing Russian Culture in the Age of Revolution, 1998; (ed with D. Shepherd) Russian Cultural Studies: an introduction, 1998; (ed) Utopias: Russian modernist texts 1905–1940, 1999; (ed with S. Lovell) Russian Literature, Modernism and the Visual Arts, 2000; Refining Russia: advice literature, polite culture and gender from Catherine to Yeltsin, 2001; Russian Literature: a very short introduction, 2001; Comrade Pavlik: the rise and fall of a Soviet boy hero, 2005; Children's World: growing up in Russia 1890–1991, 2007 (Grace Abbott Prize, Soc. for History of Childhood and Youth, USA, 2009); (ed with V. Bezrogov) The Little Town in a Snuffbox: documents on the history of Russian childhood from Nicholas II to Boris Yeltsin, 2 vols, 2008; (ed with M. Bassin), Soviet and Post-Soviet Identities, 2012; (ed jtly) Russian Cultural Anthropology after the Collapse of Communism, 2012; St Petersburg: shadows of the past, 2014; *translations:* Leonid Borodin, The Third Truth, 1989; (contrib.) New Russian Fiction, ed O. Chukhontsev, 1989; Sergei Kaledin, The Humble Cemetery, 1990; (contrib.) Paradise, 1993; (contrib.) The Silk of Time, 1994; (contrib.) An Anthology of Contemporary Russian Women Poets, 2005; (contrib.) The Ties of Blood: Russian literature from the 21st century, 2008; contrib. numerous articles to professional jls and edited books, and reviews in TLS, Guardian, Evening Standard, etc. *Recreations:* freezing in the Atlantic, walking in St Petersburg. *Address:* New College, Oxford OX1 3BN. *T:* (01865) 279502. *E:* catriona.kelly@new.ox.ac.uk.

KELLY, Chris; *b* Wolverhampton, 1978. *Educ:* Wolverhampton Grammar Sch.; Oxford Brookes Univ. (BA Hons 1999); Imperial Coll., London (MBA 2003). Keltruck Ltd: Sales and Mktg Exec., 1999–2000; Mktg Manager, 2000–02; non-exec. Dir, 2004–06 and 2010–; Mktg Dir, 2006–10. MP (C) Dudley S, 2010–15. *Recreations:* swimming, squash, tennis, golf, ski-ing, running.

KELLY, Sir Christopher (William), KCB 2001; Chairman: Financial Ombudsman Service, 2005–12 (non-executive Director, 2002–12); Responsible Gambling Strategy Board, since 2013; *b* 18 Aug. 1946; *s* of late Reginald and Peggy Kelly; *m* 1970, Alison Mary Collens Durant; two *s* one *d*. *Educ:* Beaumont College; Trinity College, Cambridge (MA); Manchester University (MA (Econ)). HM Treasury, 1970; Private Sec. to Financial Sec., 1971–73; Sec. to Wilson Cttee of Inquiry into Financial Instns, 1978–80; Under Sec., 1987–97; Dir of Fiscal and Monetary Policy, 1994–95; Dir of Budget and Public Finances, 1995; Hd of Policy Gp, DSS, 1995–97; Permanent Sec., DoH, 1997–2000. Sen. Ind. Dir, Co-operative Gp, 2014–. Chairman: Cttee on Standards in Public Life, 2008–13; Rev. of Co-operative Bank, 2013–14. Chairman: NSPCC, 2002–10; The King's Fund, 2010–; TPO Foundn, 2012–. Mem. Bd, NCC, 2001–08. Gov., Acland Burghley Sch., 1991–98. *Recreations:* walking, grandchildren.

KELLY, Daniel; Sheriff of South Strathclyde, Dumfries and Galloway at Hamilton, since 2015 (at Airdrie, 2011–15); *b* Dunfermline, 22 Jan. 1958; *s* of Daniel and Madeline Kelly; *m* 1985, Christine Marie MacLeod; three *s* one *d*. *Educ:* Univ. of Edinburgh (LLB Hons); Coll. of Europe, Bruges (Cert. de Hautes Études Européennes). Solicitor, 1981–90; lawyer, Brussels, 1983–84; Procurator Fiscal Depute, 1984–90; Advocate, 1991–2007; Temp. Sheriff, 1997–99; Pt-time Sheriff, 2005–11; QC (Scot.) 2007–11. Chair, Scottish Child Law Centre, 2007–09. Ed., Scots Law Times Sheriff Court Reports, 1992–. *Publications:* Criminal Sentences, 1993; (contrib.) Green's Litigation Styles, 1994; (ed) Scottish Family Law Service, 2010–; various legal articles. *Recreations:* literature, travel, cycling, golf. *Address:* Hamilton Sheriff Court, 4 Beckford Street, Hamilton ML3 0BT. *T:* (01698) 282957, *Fax:* (01698) 201366. *E:* hamilton@scotcourts.gov.uk.

KELLY, Sir David (Robert Corbett), Kt 1996; CBE 1991; Chairman, Kelly Packaging Limited, 1962–99 (Managing Director, 1962–85); Chairman, Conservative Party Committee on Candidates, 1995–2000; *b* 10 Dec. 1936; *s* of late Col Robert Cecil Kelly, TD, DL, JP and Jean Haswell Kelly (*née* Bowran), JP; *m* 1969, Angela Frances Taylor; four *d*. *Educ:* Sedbergh; St John's Coll., Cambridge (Lamor Award; MA). Farm labourer, 1955–56; Nat. Service, Stick of Honour, Mons OCS, 1960; 2nd Lt, 2nd Bn, 7th DEO Gurkha Rifles, 1960–61; 17th (later 4th) Bn, Parachute Regt (9 DLI), TA, 1962–69 (Major); Mil. Mem., TA&VRA for N of England, 1969–75. Board Member: Regl Bd, Brit. Technol. Gp, 1980–84; Northumbrian Water Authy, 1983–89; Washington Develt Corp., 1984–88; NE Industrial Develt Bd, 1989–97. Chm., NE Reg., 1966–67, Industrial Relns Cttee, 1968–71, British Box and Packaging Assoc. Confederation of British Industry: Member: Smaller Firms Council, 1977–83; Regl Council, 1979–86; Council, 1981–83; Industrial Policy Cttee, 1981–83; Mem., Lord Chancellor's Adv. Cttee on Tax Comrs, Tyne and Wear, 1981–93. Contested (C) Gateshead W, 1979. Chm., Northern Area Conservatives, 1990–93; Vice Pres., 1992–95, Pres., 1995–96, Nat. Union of Cons. and Unionist Assocs; Chm., Cons. Pty Conf., 1995; Chm. Trustees, Cons. Agents Benevolent Fund, 2000–15; Trustee, Cons. Agents Superannuation Fund, 2000–15. Mem., Gateshead CHC, 1975–77. President: Gateshead Dispensary Housing Assoc., 1992–2011 (Chm., 1982–92 and 1993–2011); Craigielea Community Nursing Home, 1992–2011 (Chm., 1988–92, and 1993–2011); Gateshead Dispensary Nursing Home (Craigielea) Ltd, 2011–13; Chm., Gateshead Dispensary Trust, 1999–2011 (Trustee, 1965–2011); Trustee, Northumbrian Educnl Trust, 1981– (Chm., 1983–93). Vice Pres., Cancer Bridge, 1999–2001. Exec. Vice Chm., SCF Newcastle City Appeal, 1996–98; Patron, Spirit of Enterprise Appeal, 1997–2000. Chm. Govs, Westfield Sch., 1983–93. *Recreations:* family, country living. *Address:* Stanton Fence, Morpeth, Northumberland NE65 8PP. *T:* (01670) 772236. *E:* stantonfence@hotmail.com. *Club:* Northern Counties (Newcastle upon Tyne).

KELLY, Prof. Deirdre Anne, (Lady Byatt); DL; MD; FRCP, FRCPI, FRCPCH; Director, Liver Unit, Birmingham Children's Hospital, since 1989 (Medical Director, 2000–07); Hon. Professor of Paediatric Hepatology, University of Birmingham, since 2001; *b* 1 Feb. 1950; *d* of Frank Kelly and Kathleen Kelly (*née* Scannell); *m* 1st, 1973, Miles Parker (marr. diss. 1990); two *s*; 2nd, 1997, Sir Ian (Charles Rayner) Byatt, *qv*. *Educ:* Convent of Holy Child, Killiney, Dublin; TCD (MB BCh BAO 1973; MD 1979). FRCPI 1990; FRCP 1995; FRCPCH 1997. Lectr in Medicine, TCD, 1980–82; Wellcome Res. Fellow, Royal Free Hosp., London, 1982–84; Lectr in Child Health, St Bartholomew's Hosp., 1987; Asst Prof. in Pediatrics, Univ. of Nebraska, 1987–89. Chm., Nat. Adv. Commn (formerly Panel) for Enquiry into Child Health, 2004–09; Board Member: Healthcare Commn, 2007–09; Care Quality Commn, 2008–13; Member: Adv. Cttee on Safety of Blood, Tissues and Organs, 2008–12; Adv. Gp on Hepatitis, 2010–; Prog. Develt Gp, NICE, 2011–12; GMC, 2013–. Associate non-exec. Dir, Royal Wolverhampton NHS Trust, 2013–15; non-exec. Dir, Health Res. Authy, 2015–. President: Internat. Pediatric Transplant Assoc., 2002–05; British Soc. of Paediatric Gastroenterol., Hepatol. and Nutrition, 2004–07; Eur. Soc. of Paediatric Gastroenterol., Hepatol. and Nutrition, 2007–10; Eur. Fedn of Biliary Atresia Res., 2004–09. Chairman: Cttee of Hepatol., Eur. Soc. of Paediatric Gastroenterol., Hepatol. and Nutrition, 2001–04; Coll. Specialty Adv. Cttee, RCPCH, 2004–07; Lunar Soc., 2007–09. Gov., Health Foundn, 2008–. Gov., St Martin's Sch., Solihull, 2004–05. DL W Midlands, 2008. Hosp. Dr of the Year, 1991. *Publications:* Pediatric Gastroenterology and Hepatology, 1996; Diseases of the Liver and Biliary System in Children, 1999, 3rd edn 2008; Paediatric Solid Organ Transplantation, 2000, 2nd edn 2007; Practical Approach to Paediatric Gastroenterology, Hepatology and Nutrition, 2014; contribs on clinical and basic sci. related to paediatric liver disease. *Recreations:* gardening, hill-walking, opera, entertaining friends and family. *Address:* Liver Unit, Birmingham Children's Hospital, Steelhouse Lane, Birmingham B4 6NH. *T:* (0121) 333 8253, *Fax:* (0121) 333 8251. *E:* Deirdre.Kelly@bch.nhs.uk.

KELLY, Prof. Francis Patrick, (Frank), CBE 2013; FRS 1989; Professor of the Mathematics of Systems, University of Cambridge, since 1990; Master of Christ's College, Cambridge, since 2006 (Fellow, since 1976); *b* 28 Dec. 1950; *s* of Francis Kelly and Margaret Kelly (*née* McFadden); *m* 1972, Jacqueline Pullin; two *s*. *Educ:* Cardinal Vaughan Sch.; Van Mildert Coll., Durham (BSc 1971); Emmanuel Coll., Cambridge (Knight Prize 1975; PhD 1976; Hon. Fellow, 2007). Operational Research Analyst, Scicon, 1971–72; Cambridge University: Asst Lectr in Op. Res., Faculty of Engineering, 1976–78; Lectr in Statistical Lab., 1978–86; Reader in Faculty of Maths, 1986–90; Dir, Statistical Lab., 1991–93; variously Research Fellow, Dir of Studies, Tutor, Mem. College Council and Investments Cttee, Christ's Coll., 1976–. Vis. Prof., Stanford Univ., 2001–02. For. Associate, NAE, 2012. Chm., Lyndewode Research Ltd, 1987–2011. Non-exec. Dir, Autonomy Corp. plc, 2010–11. Chief Scientific Advr, DfT, 2003–06. Chm., Council for Mathematical Scis, 2010–13. Mem., Bd of Trustees, RAND Europe, 2008–. Clifford Paterson Lectr, Royal Soc., 1995; Blackett Lectr, ORS, 1996. CompOR 2006. Foreign Mem., NAE, 2012. Hon. DSc: Heriot-Watt, 2001; Eindhoven Univ. of Technol., 2011. Rollo Davidson Prize, Cambridge Univ., 1979; Guy Medal in Silver, Royal Statistical Soc., 1989; Lanchester Prize, ORS of Amer., 1992; Naylor Prize, London Math. Soc., 1996; Koji Kobayashi Award, 2005, Alexander Graham Bell Medal, 2015, IEEE; John von Neumann Theory Prize, INFORMS, 2008; Sigmetrics Achievement Award, ACM, 2009; Gold Medal, Assoc. of Eur. Operational Res. Socs, 2009; Beale Medal, ORS, 2011. *Publications:* Reversibility and Stochastic Networks, 1979, reissued 2011; (ed) Probability, Statistics and Optimization, 1994; (ed jtly) Stochastic Networks, 1995; Mathematical Models in Finance, 1995; Stochastic Networks: theory and application, 1996; (with E. Yudovina) Stochastic Networks, 2014; articles in math. and stat. jls. *Recreations:* golf, ski-ing. *Address:* Statistical Laboratory, Centre for Mathematical Sciences, Wilberforce Road, Cambridge CB3 0WB. *T:* (01223) 337963.

KELLY, Gerard Anthony; Partner, GK & Partners, since 2014; *b* Melton Mowbray, Leics, 10 Nov. 1960; *s* of Joseph Patrick Kelly and Ivy Kelly; civil partnership 2008, José Eduardo de Castro Oliveira. *Educ:* King Edward VII Upper Sch.; Univ. of Warwick (BA 1983). Times Higher Education Supplement: Journalist, 1991–2002; Dep. Ed., 2002–07; Ed., 2007–08; Ed., TES, 2008–13. Ed. of the Year, PPA, 2011. *Recreation:* food and drink. *Address:* (office) 39 Fairfax Road, NW6 4EL. *Clubs:* Hospital, Home House.

KELLY, Graham; *see* Kelly, R. H. G.

KELLY, Iain Charles MacDonald; HM Diplomatic Service, retired; Foreign and Commonwealth Office, 2009–14; *b* 5 March 1949; *s* of Walter John Kelly and Doreen Sylvia Wilkins; *m* 1981, Linda Clare McGovern; two *s*. *Educ:* Cathays High Sch. for Boys; UCW, Aberystwyth (BSc Econ); Univ. of London (DipLib 1974); Army Sch. of Langs. Joined HM Diplomatic Service, 1974; Russian Wing, Army Sch. of Languages, 1975–76; Moscow, 1976–79; Kuala Lumpur, 1979–82; Istanbul, 1986–88; Los Angeles, 1990–92; Moscow, 1992–95; Amsterdam, 1995–98; Sen. Mem., Jesus Coll., Oxford, 1998–99; Ambassador and Consul General, Belarus, 1999–2003; FCO, 2003–07; Sen. Mem., St Antony's Coll., Oxford, 2007; Ambassador to Uzbekistan, 2007–09. FRGS 1999. *Recreations:* early music, privacy. *Clubs:* Highland Soc. of London; Phyllis Court (Henley-on-Thames).

KELLY, Ian Francis; actor, historical biographer, dramatist; *b* Cambridge, 16 Jan. 1966; *s* of Prof. Donald Francis Kelly and Patricia Ann Kelly (*née* Holt); *m* 1998, Claire Janette Davies; one *s* one *d*. *Educ:* Backwell Sch., Avon; Calday Grange County Grammar Sch. for Boys, Wirral; Trinity Hall, Cambridge (BA Hist.; Open Exhibn Entrance Schol.); Film Sch., Univ. of Calif, Los Angeles (MA Film, Theater, TV; Schol.). Actor: *theatre* includes: The Changeling, LA, 1989; Pygmalion, Theatr Clywyd, 1991; Arsenic and Old Lace, Salisbury, 1992; A Busy Day, Bristol and King's Head, London, 1993–94, transf. Bristol Old Vic and Lyric, 2000; Arcadia, Manchester, 2000; Relative Values, UK tour, 2002; Cooking for Kings (also writer), NY, 2004, 2006; Beau Brummell, NY, 2006; The Pitmen Painters, Newcastle, transf. NT, NY and West End, 2008–12 (Performance of the Year, NE Culture Awards, 2009); Mr Foote's Other Leg, Hampstead Th., 2015; *films* include: Howards End, 1992; In Love and War, 1996; Voina, 2002; Admiral Kolchak, 2008; Creation, 2009; Harry Potter and the Deathly Hallows, Part 1, 2010, Part 2, 2011; Closed Circuit, 2013; *television* includes: Drop the Dead Donkey, 1998; In a Land of Plenty, 1999; Sensitive Skin, 2005; Beau Brummell, 2006; Downton Abbey, 2009. *Publications:* Cooking for Kings: the life of Antonin Carême, a biography with recipes, 2003; Beau Brummell, 2006 (filmed, 2006); Casanova (Sunday Times Biog. of the Year), 2008; Mr Foote's Other Leg: comedy, tragedy and murder in Georgian London, 2012 (Theatre Book of the Year, Soc. for Theatre Res., 2013); (with Dame Vivienne Westwood) Vivienne Westwood, 2014; Mr Foote's Other Leg (playscript), 2015. *Recreations:* my children, art, cooking, gym. *Address:* (literary agent) Ivan Mulcahy, First Floor, 7 Meard Street, W1F 0EW. *T:* (020) 7287 1170. *E:* ivanmulcahy@ma-agency.com. *Club:* Last Tuesday Society.

KELLY, James Anthony; Member (Lab) Rutherglen, Scottish Parliament, since 2011 (Glasgow Rutherglen, 2007–11); *b* 23 Oct. 1963; *s* of Frank and Lilian Kelly; *m* 1992, Alexandra Mullan; two *d*. *Educ:* Trinity High Sch., Cambuslang; Glasgow Coll. of Technol. (BSc Computer Information Systems 1985). CIMA 1994. Analyst/programmer, Argyll and Clyde Health Bd, 1985–88; Scottish Power: Analyst/Programmer, 1988–90; Computer Auditor, 1990–92; Analyst Programmer, 1992–93; Asset Mgt Proj., 1993–95; Finance Officer, 1995–99; Scottish Electricity Settlements, 1999–2004; Business Analyst, SAIC, 2004–07. *Recreations:* running, five-a-side football, golf. *Address:* Constituency Office, 51 Stonelaw Road, Rutherglen G73 3TN. *T:* (0141) 647 0707, *Fax:* (0141) 643 1491. *E:* james.kelly.msp@scottish.parliament.uk.

KELLY, Jane Maureen, (Mrs M. Blanckenhagen); Founder Patron, Mulberry Centre, West Middlesex University Hospital, since 2000 (Chairman, 2005–08; Trustee, since 2005); *b* 20 Sept. 1948; *d* of late Captain Adrian Morgan Kelly and of Monica Dallas Kelly (*née* Edwards); *m* 1994, Michael Blanckenhagen; three step *d*. *Educ:* Notre Dame High Sch., Sheffield; Univ. of Birmingham (LLB). Admitted solicitor, 1971; solicitor in private practice, England, Hong Kong and Brunei, 1971–79; AMI Healthcare Group plc, 1979–90: legal advr, 1979–83; Co. Sec., 1983–88; Dir, Corporate Health Services, 1988–90; Dir, 1987–90; independent mgt consultant, 1990–. Chairman: W Middx Univ. Hosp. NHS Trust, 1992–2002; NW London Strategic HA, 2002–03; NHS Bd Leadership Prog., 2001–04; London Regl Comr, NHS Appts Commn, 2003–05. Mem. Adv. Cttee, Clinical Excellence Awards, DoH, 2008–. Associate, Centre for Leadership and Mgt, Univ. of York, 1996–2006. Lay Mem., Gen. Council and Register of Osteopaths, 1990–95. Chm., Women in Mgt,

1987–89. Mem. Council, English Nature, 1992–2000. Mem. Council, Brunel Univ., 2006– (Dep. Chm., 2008–11; Chm., 2011–). *Recreations:* family life, wildlife holidays, walking in Italy, theatrical biographies. *Address:* Gable House, 18–24 Turnham Green Terrace, Chiswick, W4 1QP.

See also Baroness Hollins.

KELLY, Janis Mary; opera and concert singer (soprano); *b* Glasgow, 30 Dec. 1954; *d* of Peter Crossan Kelly and Maureen Kelly (*née* McCann); *m* 1983, William Ward Veazey; three *d* (triplets). *Educ:* Royal Acad., Inverness; Royal Scottish Acad. of Music and Drama (DRSAMD 1976); Royal Coll. of Music (FRCM 2015). Début, ENO, 1980; Principal Guest Artist: ENO, 1980–; Opera North, 1990–; Grange Park Opera, 1990–; Scottish Opera, 1990–; début: Royal Opera House, 2009; Metropolitan Opera, NY, 2011; LA Opera, 2012. Roles include: Mrs Nixon, in Nixon in China; Violetta, in La Traviata; Magda, in La Rondine; Romilda, in Xerxes; Marschallin, in Der Rosenkavalier; Elizabeth, in Maria Stuarda; title role in Alcina; Countess, in Le Nozze di Figaro; Lady Billows, in Albert Herring; Musetta, Mimi, in La Bohème; Governess, Miss Jessel, in The Turn of the Screw; Sarah, in Clemency; title role in Prima Donna (world premiere); Christine, in Intermezzo; Hazel, The Perfect American; Berta, in Il barbiere di Siviglia. Director, Così fan tutte, 2001, and Iolanthe, 2003, Grange Park Opera. Voice Prof., RCM, 2007–. Volunteer, Wormwood Scrubs Pony Centre. *E:* janismkelly@aol.com.

KELLY, John Philip, CMG 2000; LVO 1994; MBE 1984; HM Diplomatic Service, retired; Vice-President, Victoria League for Commonwealth Friendship, since 2007 (Chairman, 2002–07); *b* 25 June 1941; *s* of William Kelly and Norah Kelly (*née* Roche); *m* 1964, Jennifer Anne Buckler; one *s*. *Educ:* Oatlands Coll., Stillorgan, Dublin; Open Univ. (BA Hons 2013). Joined Foreign Office, 1959; Leopoldville, 1962–65; Cairo, 1965–68; Bonn, 1968–70; FCO, 1970–73; Canberra, 1973–77; Antwerp, 1977–78; FCO, 1978–81; seconded to Dept of Trade, 1981; Grenada, 1982–86; FCO, 1986–89; Dep. Gov., Bermuda, 1989–94; FCO, 1994–96; Gov., Turks and Caicos Islands, 1996–2000. *Recreations:* cruise lecturing, golf, walking, reading, Rotarian. *Address:* The Laurels, 56 Garden Lane, Royston, Herts SG8 9EH. *Club:* Royston Golf (Captain, 2003–04).

KELLY, Joseph Anthony; Managing (formerly Editorial) Director, Universe Media Group Ltd (formerly Gabriel Communications), since 1998; Editor, The Universe, since 1995; *b* 10 Aug. 1958; *s* of Terence Christopher Kelly and Catherine Ethel Kelly (*née* Walsh); *m* 1999, Catherine Jane, *d* of William and Margaret Brownlie; two *s*. *Educ:* Presentation Coll., Reading; Ruskin Coll., Oxford; Univ. of Manchester (MA Theol. 2004). Associate, Instn of Buyers, 1980. Sen. Buyer, Church & Co., Reading, 1979–81; Buyer, J. Sainsbury, Reading, 1981–82; freelance photo-journalist, 1984–91; Editor: Welsh Arts Council Lit. Rev., 1991–94; Deeside Midweek Leader, 1991–92; Dep. Editor, Wrexham Leader, 1992–93; Ed., Country Quest (mag. for Wales), 1993; Dep. Ed., The Universe, 1994; Editor: Catholic Life mag., 1995, 1998–2006; School Building mag., 2004–05; Urban Building mag., 2006; Church Building mag., 2006–. Chm., NW Region, Soc. of Editors, 1999; Vice Chm., Catholic Writers' Guild (North), 2002–03. Member: Historic Bldgs Adv. Council for Wales, 2008–10; Christian Assoc. of Business Execs, 2008–; MInstD 2009. Gov., RNLI, 1997–; Foundn Gov., St Richard Gwyn RC High Sch., Flint, 2002–10. Associate Mem., RIBA, 2008–. Photo-journalism Award, Irish Post, 1981. *Publications:* From Sulham Head, Collected Poems, 1980; The Pendulum, 1982. *Recreations:* hill-walking, ecclesiastical history, photography. *Address:* c/o Universe Media Group Ltd, Alberton House, 30 St Mary's Parsonage, Manchester M3 2WJ. *T:* (office) (0161) 214 1200. *Club:* Frontline.

KELLY, Judith Pamela, (Jude), CBE 2015 (OBE 1997); Artistic Director, South Bank Centre, since 2005; Chair, Metal, since 2005 (Artistic Director, 2002–05); *b* 24 March 1954; *d* of John Kelly and Ida Kelly; *m* 1993, Michael Bird (known professionally as Michael Birch); one *s* one *d*. *Educ:* Calder High Sch.; Birmingham Univ. (BA 2nd Cl. Hons). Freelance singer (folk and jazz), 1970–75; artistic director, 1975–76; Founder Dir, Solent People's Theatre, 1976–80; Artistic Dir, Battersea Arts Centre, 1980–85; Dir of Plays, Nat. Theatre of Brent, 1982–85; freelance dir, 1986–88; Festival Dir, York Fest. and Mystery Plays, 1986–88; Artistic Dir, 1988–2002, Chief Exec., 1993–2002, West Yorkshire Playhouse. Major productions include: West Yorkshire Playhouse: Merchant of Venice, 1994; Beatification of Area Boy, 1996 (also NY and Eur. tour); The Seagull, The Tempest, 1998; Singin' in the Rain, 1999, 2001 (also RNT, 2000; Olivier Award, 2001); Half a Sixpence, 2000; Sarcophagus, RSC, 1986; When We Are Married, Chichester Fest. Th., transf. Savoy, 1996; Othello, Shakespeare Th., Washington, 1997; English National Opera: The Elixir of Love, 1997; On the Town, 2005; The Wizard of Oz, RFH, 2008. British Rep. on culture for UNESCO, 1997–99. Visiting Professor of Drama: Leeds Univ.; Kingston Univ. Chair: Common Purpose Charitable Trust, 1997–2010; QCA, 2001–03. Chm., London 2012 Olympic Cttee for Culture, Educn and Ceremonies, 2004–09; Vice-Chm., Nat. Adv. Cttee on Creative and Cultural Educn, 1998–2000; Member: Council, RSA, 1998–2000; ITC, 1999–2004; Bd, British Council. Member Board: Liverpool Biennale, 2004–06; Cultural Olympiad; New Deal of the Mind; Mem., Dishaa Adv. Gp; Chair, World Book Night. Hon. Fellow, Dartington Coll. of Arts, 1999. Hon. Prof., York Univ., 2000. Hon. DLitt: Leeds Metropolitan, 1995; Bradford, 1996; Hon. LitD Leeds, 2000; DUniv Open, 2001; Hon. Dr: Birmingham, 2011; Loughborough, 2011; Goldsmiths, 2011. *Recreation:* wind-surfing. *Address:* South Bank Centre, SE1 8XX. *E:* jude.kelly@southbankcentre.co.uk.

KELLY, Julian Thomas; Director General, Public Spending and Finance, HM Treasury, since 2014; *b* London, 28 Dec. 1970; *s* of Justin and Valerie Kelly; *m* 1995, Katie Wilkins; four *d*. *Educ:* Lancaster Royal Grammar Sch.; Trinity Coll., Oxford (BA Hons Modern Langs). ACMA 2011. Policy Advr, HM Treasury, 1995–2000; on secondment, Treasury and Mkts Div., HSBC, 2000–02; Sen. Policy Advr, Prime Minister's Strategy Unit, Cabinet Office, 2002–03; Dep. Dir for Home Affairs, HM Treasury, 2003–07; Dir of Finance, UK Border Agency, Home Office, 2008–11; Finance Dir, 2011–12, Dir, Public Spending, 2012–14, HM Treasury. *Recreations:* running, tennis, family. *Address:* HM Treasury, 1 Horse Guards Road, SW1A 2HQ.

KELLY, Hon. Dame Kathryn Mary; *see* Thirlwall, Hon. Dame K. M.

KELLY, Laurence Charles Kevin, FRSL; FRGS; non-executive Director, 1972–93, and Vice-Chairman, 1988–93, Helical Bar PLC (Deputy Chairman, 1981–84; Chairman, 1984–88); *b* 11 April 1933; *s* of late Sir David Kelly, GCMG, MC, and Lady Kelly (*née* Jourda de Vaux); *m* 1963, (Alison) Linda McNair Scott; one *s* two *d*. *Educ:* Downside Sch.; New Coll., Oxford (Beresford Hope Schol.; MA Hons). Lieut, The Life Guards, 1949–52; served (temp.) Foreign Office, 1955–56; Guest, Keen and Nettlefolds, 1956–72; Director: GKN International Trading Ltd, 1972–77; Morganite International Ltd, 1984–91; KAE, subseq. Mintel, Ltd, 1980–2003; Chm., Queenborough Steel Co., 1980–89. Member: Northern Ireland Development Agency, 1972–78; Monopolies and Mergers Commn, 1982–89. Chairman, Opera da Camera Ltd (charity), 1981–87; Trustee: Apollo Foundn, 1984–2013; Choir of Carmelite Priory, Kensington (charity), 1997–2015. Vice-Chm., British Iron and Steel Consumers' Council, 1976–85. Sen. Associate Mem., St Antony's Coll., Oxford, 1985–91. FRGS 1972; FRSL 2003. Gen. Ed., Travellers' Companion series, 2004–. *Publications:* Lermontov, Tragedy in the Caucasus, 1978 (Cheltenham Literary Prize, 1979); (ed) St Petersburg, a Travellers' Anthology, 1981; (ed) Moscow, a Travellers' Anthology, 1983; Istanbul, a Travellers' Anthology, 1987; (with Linda Kelly) Proposals, 1989; Diplomacy and Murder in Teheran: Alexander Griboyedov and Imperial Russia's mission to the Shah of Persia, 2001; reviews, TLS, etc. *Recreation:* opera-going. *Address:* 44 Ladbroke Grove, W11 2PA. *T:* (020) 7727 4663; Lorton Hall, Low Lorton, near Cockermouth, Cumbria CA13 9UP. *T:* (01900) 85252. *Clubs:* Beefsteak, Brooks's, Turf; Kildare Street and University (Dublin).

KELLY, Linda Mary; Chief Executive, Lloyds TSB Foundation for England and Wales, 2006–12; *b* 2 Jan. 1955; *d* of John Nicholl Millar and Vicenta Amy Gibson Millar (*née* Smith); *m* 1987, Brian James Kelly; two *d*. *Educ:* Nottingham Univ. (BPharm Hons). MRPharmS. Basic grade pharmacist, 1977–78; various appts in med. information, clin. trials, mkt res. and product mgt, Merck Sharpe & Dohme Ltd, 1978–87; New Product Planning Manager, 1987–88, Mktg Dir, 1988–91, Smith Kline Beecham; Man. Dir, Bristol Myers Squibb (UK and Ireland), 1991–95; Pres., Astra Pharmaceuticals Ltd (UK), 1995–99; Chief Exec., Parkinson's Disease Soc., 2001–05. FRSA 2003. *Recreations:* the arts, walking.

KELLY, Dame Lorna (May) B.; *see* Boreland-Kelly.

KELLY, Mandi N.; *see* Norwood, M.

KELLY, Matthias John; QC 1999; SC (Ire.) 2005; a Recorder, since 2002; *b* 21 April 1954; *s* of Ambrose and Annie Kelly; *m* 1979, Helen Holmes; one *s* one *d*. *Educ:* St Patrick's Secondary Modern; St Patrick's Acad., Dungannon; Trinity Coll., Dublin (BA Mod., LLB). Called to the Bar, Gray's Inn, 1979, Bencher, 2002; in practice as Barrister, 1979–; called to Irish Bar, Belfast and Dublin, 1983; admitted Attorney: NY Bar, 1986; US Federal Bar, 1987; Consultant to EU Commn on UK Health and Safety Law, 1994–96. Mem., Inter-Disciplinary Wkg Pty on Actuarial Tables (Ogden Tables), 1997–2003. Chairman: Personal Injuries Bar Assoc., 2001–02; Bar Council (England and Wales), 2003 (Mem., 1998–2003; Vice Chm., 2002; Chm., Public Affairs Gp, 2001; Chm., Policy Gp, 2000). Chairman: End the Vagrancy Act Campaign, 1989–93; Alcohol Recovery Project, 1993–96. FRSA 2003. *Publications:* (ed jtly) Personal Injury Manual, 1997, 2nd edn 2001, (contrib.) 3rd edn 2007; (contrib.) Munkman Employer's Liability, 13th edn 2001; (contrib.) Personal Injury and Wrongful Death Damages Calculations: a transatlantic dialogue, 2009; articles in legal jls. *Recreations:* walking, reading, cycling, theatre, travel, life. *Address:* 39 Essex Street, WC2R 3AT. *T:* (020) 7832 1111; Merchants Quay Chambers, 25–26 Merchants Quay, Dublin 8, Ireland. *T:* (53) 17079031.

KELLY, Dr Michael, CBE 1983; JP; DL; Managing Director, Michael Kelly Associates, since 1984; columnist, Scotsman, 1996–2001 and 2011; *b* 1 Nov. 1940; *s* of David and Marguerite Kelly; *m* 1965, Zita Harkins; one *s* two *d*. *Educ:* Univ. of Strathclyde (BScEcon, PhD). FCIM (FInstM 1988). Asst Lectr in Economics, Univ. of Aberdeen, 1965–67; Lectr in Economics, Univ. of Strathclyde, 1967–84. Councillor: Anderston Ward Corp. of Glasgow, 1971–75 (Convener, Schools and Sch. Welfare; Vice-Convener, Transport); Hillington Ward, Glasgow Dist, 1977–84 (Chairman: General Purposes Cttee; Buildings and Property Cttee); Lord Provost of Glasgow, 1980–84 (masterminded "Glasgow's Miles Better" Campaign); Campaign Dir, Edinburgh—Count Me In, 1987–89. Rector, Univ. of Glasgow, 1984–87. Director: Celtic Football Club, 1990–94; Intelligent Land Investments Ltd, 2009–. Chm., Children 1st (formerly RSSPCC), 1987–96; Member: Scottish Cttee, NACF, 1990–93; ESRC External Relns Adv. Gp (formerly Media Relns Cttee), 2000–. Founding Editor, Jl Economic Studies, 1965. BBC Radio Scotland News Quiz Champion, 1986, 1987. Presenter, Clyde 2 Talk-In, 1997–2000; regular commentator: BBC Newsnight Scotland, 2010–; Scotland Tonight; Radio Scotland. Hon. Mem., Clan Donald, USA; Hon. Mayor, Tombstone, Ariz; Hon. Citizen: Illinois; San José; St Petersburg; Kansas City; Dallas; Fort Worth; Winnipeg. JP Glasgow 1973; DL Glasgow 1984. Hon. LLD Glasgow, 1984. Glasgow Herald Scot of the Year, 1983. OStJ 1983. Knight's Star, Order of Merit (Poland), 1998. *Publications:* Studies in the British Coal Industry, 1970; Paradise Lost: the struggle for Celtic's soul, 1994; London Lines, 1996. *Recreations:* photography, ski-ing, golf (Mem. Cttee, Pollok Golf Club, 2009–). *Address:* 50 Aytoun Road, Glasgow G41 5HE. *T:* (0141) 427 1627.

KELLY, Prof. Michael Joseph, FRS 1993; FREng; FInstP, FIET; Prince Philip Professor of Technology, University of Cambridge, since 2002; Fellow of Trinity Hall, Cambridge, 1974–81, 1989–92 and since 2002; *b* New Plymouth, NZ, 14 May 1949; *s* of late Steve and Mary Constance Kelly; *m* 1991, Ann Elizabeth Taylor, BA, *d* of late Dr Daniel Brumhall Cochrane Taylor; one *d*. *Educ:* Francis Douglas Meml Coll., New Plymouth, NZ; Victoria Univ. of Wellington (BSc Hons 1970; MSc 1971); Gonville and Caius Coll., Univ. of Cambridge (PhD 1974); Trinity Hall, Cambridge (MA 1975; ScD 1994). FInstP 1988; FIET (FIEE 1989); FREng (FEng 1998). IBM Res. Fellow, Univ. of Calif., Berkeley, 1975–76; SRC Advanced Fellow, Cavendish Lab., 1977–81; Mem., Research Staff, GEC Hirst Res. Centre, 1981–92, Co-ordinator, GEC Superlattice Res., 1984–92; University of Surrey: Prof. of Physics and Electronics, 1992–96; Hd of Dept of Electronic and Electrical Engrg, 1996; Hd of Sch. of Electronic Engrg, Inf. Technol. and Maths, then Sch. of Electronics, Computing and Maths, 1997–2001; Hd of Advanced Technol. Inst. and Dir, Centre for Solid State Electronics, 2001–02; Exec. Dir, Cambridge-MIT Inst., 2003–05; Chief Scientific Advr, DCLG, 2006–09. Vis. Scientist, Cavendish Lab., 1988–92; Royal Soc./SERC Industrial Fellow, 1989–91; Erskine Fellow, Univ. of Canterbury, NZ, 1999. Non-executive Director: Surrey Satellite Technol. Ltd, 1997–2002; Laird Gp, 2006–. Mem. Council, Royal Soc., 2001–02. Mem. Council, Univ. of Surrey, 1996–2002; Mem. Council, 1997–2001, Vice-Pres., 2001–05, Inst. of Physics. MAE 2009. Hon. FRSNZ 1999. Hon. ScD Victoria Univ. of Wellington, 2002. Royal Soc. Rutherford Meml Lectr, NZ, 2000. Paterson Medal and Prize, Inst. of Physics, 1989; GEC Nelson Gold Medal, 1991; Silver Medal, Royal Acad. Engrg, 1999; Hughes Medal, Royal Soc., 2006. *Publications:* (ed jtly) The Physics and Fabrication of Microstructures and Microdevices, 1986; Low Dimensional Semiconductors, 1995; numerous papers and review articles on semiconductor physics-for-devices in scientific jls. *Recreations:* music, literature. *Address:* Department of Engineering, University of Cambridge, Electronic Engineering Division, CAPE Building, 9 J. J. Thomson Avenue, Cambridge CB3 0FA. *T:* (01223) 748303, *Fax:* (01223) 748348. *E:* mjk1@cam.ac.uk.

KELLY, Owen, QPM 1987; Director, Webb Estate Ltd, since 2004; UK Director, Fairfax International Corporation, Virginia, USA, 1994–2001; *b* 10 April 1932; *s* of Owen Kelly and Anna Maria (*née* Hamill); *m* 1957, Sheila Ann (*née* McCarthy); five *s*. *Educ:* St Modan's High School, St Ninians, Stirlingshire. National Service, RAF, 1950–52; Metropolitan Police in all ranks from Police Constable to Commander, 1953–82; Asst and Dep. to Comr of Police for City of London, 1982–85; Comr of Police for City of London, 1985–93; created secure zone in City of London (Ring of Steel) for prevention of terrorist activity, July 1993, and scheme continues. 18th Senior Command Course, Nat. Police Coll., 1981; Graduate, 14th Session of Nat. Exec. Inst., FBI, USA, 1991. Mem., Police Disciplinary Appeals Bd, Home Office, 1994–2000. Mem. Panel, Ind. Enquiry into death of Christopher Edwards in HM Prison, Chelmsford, 1996; Special Advr to Ind. Enquiry into death of PC Nina MacKay, 1998. Hon. Sec., Chief Constables' Club, 1989–93. Chm., City of London Br., Leukaemia Res. Fund, 1985–93. Chm., Probus, Purley, 2013–14. Freeman, City of London, 1984. CStJ 1987 (OStJ 1986). Commendation, Order of Civil Merit, Spain, 1986; Ordre du Wissam Alouite Class III, Morocco, 1987; Ordre du Mérite, Senegal, 1988; Ordem do Merito, Class III (Portugal), 1993. *Publications:* contrib. Police Review and Policing. *Recreations:* enjoying the society of a large family, do-it-yourself house maintenance, reading, cycling, hill walking. *Address:* c/o City of London Police HQ, 37 Wood Street, EC2P 2NQ.

KELLY, Philip Charles; City Treasurer, then Director of Resources and Chief Finance Officer, Liverpool City Council, 1986–2000; *b* 23 Aug. 1948; *s* of late Charles and Irene May Kelly; *m* 1971, Pamela (*née* Fagan); one *s* two *d*. *Educ:* Inst. of Science and Technology, Univ. of Wales (BSc Econ). DipM; CIPFA. Market Research, British Steel Corp., 1970–72;

Economist, Coventry City Council, 1972–74; Technical Officer, 1974–78, Asst Dir of Finance, 1978–82, Kirklees MDC; Dep. City Treasurer, Liverpool City Council, 1982–86; Treas., Merseyside Fire and Civil Defence Authy, 1986–2003. *Recreations:* family, National Observer with Institute of Advanced Motorists, Sefton Gp.

KELLY, Philip John; journalist and political consultant; *b* 18 Sept. 1946; *s* of late William Kelly and Mary Winifred Kelly; *m* 1988, Dorothy Margaret Jones; two *s. Educ:* St Mary's Coll., Crosby; Leeds Univ. (BA Hons Politics). Freelance journalist and PR consultant, 1970–87; Editor, Tribune, 1987–91; Press Officer to Michael Meacher, MP, 1991–92. Director: Grandfield Public Affairs, 1995–98; Butler Kelly Ltd, 1998–2010. Co-Founder: Leveller, 1976; State Research, 1977; Chair, London Freelance Br., NUJ, 1983. Councillor (Lab) London Borough of Islington, 1984–86, 1990–98 (Chm., Educn Cttee, 1993–97; Dep. Leader, 1997–98), 2006–14 (Mayor of Islington, 2011–12). Contested (Lab) Surrey SW, 1992. *Recreations:* railways, model railways, Arsenal FC. *Address:* 56 Windsor Road, N7 6JL. *T:* (020) 7272 9093. *E:* philkelly46@gmail.com.

KELLY, (Robert Henry) Graham, FCIS; freelance writer and broadcaster; Chief Executive/ General Secretary of the Football Association, 1989–98; *b* 23 Dec. 1945; *s* of Thomas John Kelly and Emmie Kelly; *m* 1st, 1970, Elizabeth Anne Wilkinson (marr. diss. 1996); one *s* one *d*; 2nd, 1999, Romayne Armstrong (marr. diss. 2003); 3rd, 2004, Jeanette Bailey. *Educ:* Baines Grammar Sch., Poulton-le-Fylde. FCIS 1973. Barclays Bank, 1964–68; Football League, 1968–88, Sec., 1979–88. Trustee, Football Grounds Improvement Trust, 1985–88. Chm., Fylde and Wyre Older People's Strategic Partnership Bd, 2007–09.

KELLY, Rt Hon. Ruth (Maria); PC 2004; Global Head of Client Strategy, HSBC Global Asset Management, since 2012; *b* 9 May 1968; *d* of late Bernard James Kelly and of Gertrude Anne Kelly (*née* Murphy); *m* 1996, Derek John Gadd; one *s* three *d. Educ:* Queen's Coll., Oxford (BA PPE); London School of Economics (MSc Econs). Economics Writer, The Guardian, 1990–94; Bank of England: Dep. Head, Inflation Report Div., 1994–96; Manager, Special Projects Div., 1997. MP (Lab) Bolton W, 1997–2010. PPS to Minister of Agric., Fisheries and Food, 1998–2001; Economic Sec., 2001–02, Financial Sec., 2002–04, HM Treasury; Minister of State, Cabinet Office, 2004; Secretary of State: for Educn and Skills, 2004–06; for Communities and Local Govt, 2006–07; Minister for Women, 2006–07; Sec. of State for Transport, 2007–08; various roles, HSBC Global Asset Mgt, 2008–12. Mem., Treasury Select Cttee, 1997–98. Sen. Manager, Strategy for Global Businesses, HSBC, 2010. Non-exec. Dir, Nat. Grid, 2011–. *Recreations:* walking, family.

KELLY, Samuel Thomas, (Tom), CB 2008; Strategic Communications Adviser, HS2, since 2014; *b* Belfast, 8 July 1955; *s* of late Monty Kelly and of Mary Kelly; *m* 2003, Linda; two *s* two *d. Educ:* Royal Belfast Academical Instn; Univ. of Birmingham. Trainee journalist, Belfast Telegraph, 1979–81; Press Officer, NI Housing Exec., 1981–82; joined BBC, 1982: reporter, producer, asst ed., Radio and Current Affairs, NI, 1982–87; Producer, Newsnight, 1987–88; Political Ed., NI, 1988–91; Ed., NI News, 1992–95; Asst Ed., World at One, 1995–96; Actg Ed., Talkback prog., Radio Ulster, 1996–97; Dir of Communications, NI Office, 1998–2001; Prime Minister's Official Spokesman, 2001–07; Dir, Corporate Affairs, BAA Ltd, 2008–10; Director of Communications: FSA, 2010–11; Network Rail, 2011–14. Non-exec. Dir, DECC, 2014–. *Recreations:* spending time with my family, gardening, beach walking, reading, music, watching Rugby when I can.

KELLY, Stephen Paul; Chief Executive Officer, Sage Group plc, since 2014; *m* Siobhan; three *d. Educ:* Bath Univ. (BSc Hons). Chief Operating Officer, 1997–2001, Chief Exec. Officer, 2001–05, Chordiant Software Inc.; CEO, Microfocus Internat. Ltd, 2006–10; Chief Operating Officer for Govt and Hd, Efficiency and Reform Gp, Cabinet Office, 2012–15. *Address:* Sage Group plc, North Park, Newcastle upon Tyne NE13 9AA. *T:* (0191) 294 3000.

KELLY, Susan; *see* Hamilton, Her Honour S.

KELLY, Tom; *see* Kelly, S. T.

KELMAN, James; novelist, short story writer, occasional essayist and dramatist; *b* Glasgow, 9 June 1946. *Publications:* An Old Pub Near the Angel (short stories), 1973; (jtly) Three Glasgow Writers, 1975; Short Tales from the Nightshift, 1978; Not, Not While the Giro (short stories), 1983; The Busconductor Hines, 1984; A Chancer, 1985; (jtly) Lean Tales, 1985; Greyhound for Breakfast (Cheltenham Prize), 1987; A Disaffection (James Tait Black Meml Prize), 1989; The Burn (short stories), 1991; Hardie and Baird and Other Plays, 1991; Some Recent Attacks: essays cultural and political, 1992; How Late it Was, How Late (Booker Prize), 1994; The Good Times (short stories), 1998; Translated Accounts, 2001; Selected Stories, 2001; And the Judges Said… (essays), 2002; You have to be careful in the Land of the Free, 2004; Kieron Smith, Boy (Saltire Soc. Scottish Book of the Year Award), 2008; If It Is Your Life, 2010; Mo Said She Was Quirky (Saltire Soc. Scottish Book of the Year Award), 2012. *Address:* c/o Rodgers, Coleridge and White, 20 Powis Mews, W11 1JN.

KELNER, Simon; Chief Executive Officer, Seven Dials Ltd, since 2013; *b* 9 Dec. 1957; *m* 1st, 1988, Karen Bowden (marr. diss. 2001); one *d*; 2nd, 2001, Sally Ann Lasson (marr. diss. 2015). *Educ:* Bury Grammar Sch.; Preston Poly. Trainee reporter, Neath Guardian, 1976–79; sports reporter, Extel, 1979–80; Sports Ed., Kent Evening Post, 1980–83; Asst Sports Ed., Observer, 1983–86; Dep. Sports Ed., Independent, 1986–89; Sports Editor: Sunday Correspondent, 1989–90; Observer, 1990–91; Ed., Observer Mag., 1991–93; Sports Ed., Independent on Sunday, 1993–95; Night Ed., 1995, Features Ed., 1995–96, Independent; Ed., Night & Day mag., Mail on Sunday, 1996–98; Ed.-in-Chief, The Independent and The Independent on Sunday, 1998–2008 and 2010–11; Man. Dir and Ed.-in-Chief, The Independent, 2008–10; CEO, Journalism Foundn, 2011–13. Vis. Fellow, Univ. of Gloucestershire, 2008–. Hon. Fellow, Univ. of Central Lancashire, 1999. Hon. DLitt: Bolton, 2008; Ulster, 2013. Ed. of the Year, What the Papers Say Awards, 1999 and 2003; Edgar Wallace Award, London Press Club, 2000; Ed. of the Year, GQ Awards, 2004, 2010; Media Achiever of the Year, Campaign Media Awards, 2004; Marketeer of the Year, Marketing Week Effectiveness Awards, 2004; Editorial Intelligence Comment Award, 2010. *Publications:* To Jerusalem and Back, 1996. *Clubs:* Groucho; Swinton Rugby League Supporters; Kirtlington Golf.

KELSALL, Ian Maxwell, OBE 1982; DL; Principal, Ian Kelsall Development, since 2006; Chairman, Welsh Information Governance (formerly NHS Wales Informatics Service) Board, since 2010; *s* of Harry Kelsall and Elsie Kelsall (*née* Hansard); *m* 1983, Julia Ann Harding. *Educ:* Carre's Grammar Sch., Sleaford, Lincs; Nottingham Univ. (BA Hons Hist.). Dir, CBI Wales, 1966–94; Director: Merthyr Tydfil Business Forum Ltd, 1994–98; Business for Merthyr, 1998–2001; Chm., Informing Healthcare, 2004–10. Chairman: TSW Mgt Solutions Ltd, 1995–2006; TSW Ltd, 1995–2006; Welsh Risk Pool, 1998–2003; @teb, 2001–06; non-exec. Dir, Sedgewick Wales, 1994–97. Non-exec. Dir, Llandough NHS Trust, 1993–94; Chairman: E Glamorgan NHS Trust, 1994–99; Pontypridd and Rhondda NHS Trust, 1999–2004; Velindre NHS Trust, 2008–11. Chm., Welsh NHS Confedn, 1998–2001. Mem., Electoral Commn, 2008–12. DL Mid Glamorgan, 1991. *Recreations:* music (playing the organ), reading, current affairs, watching football, Rugby, cricket. *Address:* c/o Welsh Information Governance Board, Brunel House, 2 Fitzalan Road, Cardiff CF24 0HA. *T:* (029) 2050 2729.

KELSALL, John Arthur Brooks, MA; Headmaster, Brentwood School, Essex, 1993–2004; *b* 18 June 1943; *o s* of late Joseph Brooks Kelsall and Dorothy Kelsall (*née* Bee); *m* 1965, Dianne Scott Woodward, *o d* of Rev. William James Vaughan Woodward and Jean Ewart Woodward; one *s* one *d. Educ:* Royal Grammar Sch., Lancaster; Emmanuel Coll., Cambridge (BA 1965; MA 1969). Head of Economics, King Edward VII Sch., Lytham St Annes, 1965–68; Head of Geography, Whitgift Sch., Croydon, 1968–78; Dep. Headmaster, 1978–81, Headmaster, 1981–87, Bournemouth Sch.; Headmaster, Arnold Sch., Blackpool, 1987–93. *Recreations:* golf, fell-walking, opera, ornithology. *Club:* Cretingham Golf.

KELSEY, Maj.-Gen. John, CBE 1968; Director, Wild Heerbrugg (UK) Ltd, 1978–87; Director of Military Survey, 1972–77; *b* 1 Nov. 1920; *s* of Benjamin Richard Kelsey and Daisy (*née* Powell); *m* 1944, Phyllis Margaret (*d* 1995), *d* of Henry Ernest Smith, Chingford; one *s* one *d. Educ:* Royal Masonic Sch.; Emmanuel Coll., Cambridge; Royal Mil. Coll. of Science. BSc. Commnd in RE, 1940; war service in N Africa and Europe; Lt-Col 1961; Col 1965; Dep. Dir Mil. Survey; Brig. Dir Field Survey, Ordnance Survey, 1968; Dir of Mil. Survey, Brig. 1972; Maj.-Gen. 1974. *Recreations:* Rugby football (played for Cambridge Univ., Richmond, Dorset, Wilts; Mem. RFU, 1965–66); sailing.

KELSEY, Linda; journalist and author; *b* 15 April 1952; *d* of Samuel Cohen and Rhona (*née* Fox); *m* 1st, 1972 (marr. diss. 1980); 2nd, 1999, Christian Testorf; one *s. Educ:* Woodhouse Grammar Sch., N12; Birkbeck, Univ. of London (BA Arts and Humanities). Sub-editor, Good Housekeeping, 1970–72; Features Editor, Cosmopolitan, 1975–78; Deputy Editor: Company, 1978–81; Options, 1981–82; Cosmopolitan, 1983–85, Editor, 1985–89; Editor, She magazine, 1989–95; Editor at Large, Nat. Magazine Co., 1996–98; Consultant Ed., Parkhill Publishing, 1999–2000; Exec. Ed., In Style, 2000–02; freelance writer, 2002–; columnist, Daily Telegraph, 2008–, Daily Mail, 2009–. Editor of the Year Award: PPA, 1989, for Cosmopolitan; Brit. Soc. Mag. Editors, 1990, for She. *Publications:* Was it Good for You, Too?, 2003; Fifty is Not a Four-letter Word (novel), 2007; The Secret Lives of Sisters (novel), 2008; The Twenty Year Itch (novel), 2010. *Recreations:* reading, walking, theatre, film, family.

KELSEY, Timothy Claude; Commercial Director, Telstra Health, Melbourne, from Jan. 2016; *b* Welwyn Garden City, 7 May 1965; *s* of late Col Michael Kelsey, TD, ADC and of Dr Anthea Kelsey; four *s* with Alison Kelsey; two *s* with Hilary Rowell. *Educ:* Wellington Coll.; Magdalene Coll., Cambridge (BA Hons Hist. 1987; Exhibnr). Foreign corresp., Turkey, Independent, 1988–90; reporter, Independent on Sunday, 1990–95; Sunday Times: Insight Team, 1995–97; Focus Ed., 1997–98; News Ed., 1998–2000; CEO, Dr Foster, 2000–06; Chm., Exec. Bd, Dr Foster Intelligence, 2006–10; Sen. Expert, McKinsey & Co., 2010–12; on secondment as UK Govt advr on transparency and open data policy, Efficiency and Reform Gp, 2011; Exec. Dir, Transparency and Open Data, Efficiency and Reform Gp, Cabinet Office, 2012; Nat. Dir for Patients and Information, NHS England (formerly NHS Commissioning Bd), 2012–15; Nat. Information Dir and Chair, Nat. Information Bd for Health and Care in England, 2014–15. Prog. Dir, NHS Choices, 2006–08. Member: Nat. Quality Bd, 2009–12; 2020 Public Services Commn, 2009–11. Trustee, Nuffield Trust, 2008–14. *Publications:* Dervish: invention of modern Turkey, 1996. *Recreations:* my family, jazz, sailing, writing. *W:* www.twitter.com/tkelsey1. *Clubs:* Naval and Military; Royal Dart Yacht.

KELSON, Peter John; QC 2001; **His Honour Judge Kelson;** a Circuit Judge, since 2010; *b* 7 March 1959; *s* of Gordon Charles and Patricia Sylvia Kelson; *m* 1982, Rosalind Margaret Clark; two *s. Educ:* Sheffield Univ. (LLB Hons). Called to the Bar, Middle Temple, 1981; Recorder, 1997–2010; Hd of Chambers, 2004–10. *Recreations:* golf, piano, chess, travel, music. *Address:* Sheffield Combined Court Centre, The Law Courts, 50 West Bar, Sheffield S3 8PH. *Club:* Sickleholme Golf (Derbys).

KELTZ, Jennie, (Mrs James Keltz); *see* Bond, J.

KEMAKEZA, Hon. Sir Allan, Kt 2001; Speaker, Solomon Islands Parliament, since 2010; *b* 11 Oct. 1950; *m* Joycelyn; two *s* three *d. Educ:* Police Acad.; CID Course, W Yorks Metropolitan Police; VIP Protection Course, Fed. Police Coll., Canberra. Royal Solomon Is Police Force, 1972–88: Constable; Asst Superintendent of Police; ADC to Governor-Gen.; Hd of CID; Sen. SO to Comr of Police; Asst to Comr of Police Admin. MP (People's Alliance) Savo/Russel, Solomon Is, 1989–2010; Minister: for Police and Justice, 1989–90; for Housing and Govt Services, 1991–93; for Forests, Envmt and Conservation, 1995–96; for Nat. Unity, Reconciliation and Peace, and Dep. Prime Minister, 2000–01; Prime Minister, 2001–06; Dep. Speaker of Parlt, 2006–07; Minister of Forestry, 2007–10. Dep. Leader of Opposition, 1993–94, Leader, 1997–99. *Recreations:* reading, fishing, farming. *Address:* Parliament House, PO Box G19, Vavaya Ridge, Honiara, Solomon Islands.

KEMBALL, Air Marshal Sir (Richard) John, KCB 1990; CBE 1981; DL; FRAeS; Co-ordinator of British-American Community Relations, Ministry of Defence, 1994–2004; Chief Executive, Racing Welfare, 1995–2004; *b* 31 Jan. 1939; *s* of Richard and Margaret Kemball; *m* 1962, Valerie Geraldine Webster; two *d. Educ:* Uppingham; Open Univ. (BA 1990). Commissioned RAF, 1957; OC No 54 Squadron, 1977; OC RAF Laarbruch, 1979; Commandant, CFS, 1983–85; Comdr, British Forces, Falkland Islands, 1985–86; COS and Dep. C-in-C, Strike Command and UK Air Forces, 1989–93. ADC to HM The Queen, 1984–85. Chm., Essex Rivers Healthcare NHS Trust, 1993–95. Hon. Col, 77 Engr Regt (V), 1993–96. President: RAFA, 1995–98 (Vice-Pres., 1993–95; Life Vice-Pres., 1998); Corps of Commissionaires, 2002–08 (Gov., 1993–08). Pres., Southend Br., RAeS, 1999–2009. Freeman, City of London, 1995. DL 1999, High Sheriff, 2007–08, Suffolk. FRAeS 2003. *Recreations:* country pursuits, tennis, cricket, gardening. *Address:* c/o HSBC, 46 Market Hill, Sudbury, Suffolk CO10 6ES. *Club:* Royal Air Force.

KEMBER, Anthony Joseph, MA; Communications Adviser, Department of Health, 1989–92; *b* 1 Nov. 1931; *s* of Thomas Kingsley Kember and May Lena (*née* Pryor); *m* 1957, Drusilla Mary (*née* Boyce) (*d* 2013); one *s* two *d. Educ:* St Edmund Hall, Oxford (MA). MHSM, DipHSM. Deputy House Governor and Secretary to Bd of Governors, Westminster Hospital, 1961–69; Gp Secretary, Hillingdon Gp Hospital Management Cttee, 1969–73; Area Administrator, Kensington and Chelsea and Westminster AHA(T), 1973–78; Administrator, 1978–84, Gen. Man., 1984–89, SW Thames RHA. Mem., Lord Chancellor's Adv. Cttee on JPs for SW London (formerly SW London Area Adv. Cttee on Appointment of JPs), 1994–2002. Trustee, Disabled Living Foundn, 1981–2000 (Chm., 1993–2000); Founder Trustee, Charity Trust Networks, 1998–2000 (Vice-Chm., 1998–99). Chm., Richmond Art Soc., 1995–97 (Sec., 1992–95); Mem., Richmond upon Thames Arts Council, 2001–02. CCMI (CBIM 1988). *Publications:* The NHS—a Kaleidoscope of Care, 1994; various articles for professional jls. *Recreations:* painting, inside and out; tennis, royal and common-or-garden. *Address:* 16 Orchard Rise, Richmond, Surrey TW10 5BX. *Clubs:* Athenæum, Roehampton, Romney Street Group; Royal Tennis Court, Hamsters Real Tennis (Hampton Court).

KEMBER, William Percy, FCA; FCT; Group Financial Controller, British Telecommunications, 1981–92; *b* 12 May 1932; *s* of late Percy Kember and Mrs Q. A. Kember, Purley, Surrey; *m* 1982, Lynn Kirkham. *Educ:* Uppingham. Chartered Accountant; Corporate Treasurer. Various posts with Royal Dutch/Shell Group in Venezuela, 1958–63; British Oxygen Co., 1963–67; Coopers & Lybrand, 1967–72; Post Office (Telecommunications), 1972–81. Director: Centel Financial Systems Inc., 1983–86; Marshalls Finance, 1991–98. Visitor, Royal Institution, 1977–79, Chm., 1979. *Recreation:* bridge. *Address:* 83 Hillway, N6 6AB. *Clubs:* Royal Automobile; Highgate Golf, Royal Dornoch Golf.

KEMP, family name of **Viscount Rochdale**.

KEMP, Prof. Alexander George, OBE 2006; FRSE; Professor of Petroleum Economics, University of Aberdeen, since 1983; *b* Aberdeenshire, 27 Oct. 1939; *s* of Alexander Rae Kemp and Emily Kemp. *Educ:* Skene Primary Sch.; Robert Gordon's Coll., Aberdeen; Univ. of Aberdeen (MA 1st Cl. Hons Econ. Sci.). Economist, Shell Internat. Petroleum Co., 1962–64; Lectr in Econs, Univ. of Strathclyde, 1964–65; University of Aberdeen: Lectr, 1966–77; Sen. Lectr, 1977–81; Reader, 1981–83. Member: Energy Adv. Panel to Minister of Energy, 1993–2003; Council of Econ. Advrs to First Minister of Scotland, 2007–11. FRSE 2001. *Publications:* Petroleum Rent Collection Around the World, 1988; Official History of North Sea Oil and Gas, 2 vols, 2011; over 200 articles on petroleum econs in acad. jls. *Recreations:* following football and cricket (passively), traditional Scottish music and songs, poems of Robert Burns, current affairs. *Address:* University of Aberdeen, Department of Economics, King's College, Aberdeen AB24 3QY. *T:* (01224) 272168, *Fax:* (01224) 272181. *E:* a.g.kemp@abdn.ac.uk.

KEMP, Prof. Barry John, CBE 2011; FBA 1992; Professor of Egyptology, 2005–07, now Emeritus, and Fellow, McDonald Institute of Archaeological Research, since 2008, University of Cambridge; Fellow of Wolfson College, Cambridge, 1990–2007, now Emeritus; *b* 14 May 1940. *Educ:* Liverpool Univ. (BA); MA Cantab 1965. Lectr, 1969–90, Reader in Egyptology, 1990–2005, Univ. of Cambridge. Project Dir, Amarna Project, 2006–; Chm., Amarna Trust, 2006–. Corresponding Member: German Archaeological Inst., Berlin, 1982–; Archaeological Inst. of America, 2009–. *Publications:* Amarna Reports, Vols 1–6, 1984–95; Ancient Egypt: anatomy of a civilisation, 1989, 2nd edn 2005; (jtly) Survey of the Ancient City of El-Amarna, 1993; (jtly) The Ancient Textile Industry of Amarna, 2001; 100 Hieroglyphs, 2005; How to Read the Egyptian Book of the Dead, 2007; (jtly) Busy Lives at Amarna: excavations in the Main City, 2010; The City of Akhenaten and Nefertiti: Amarna and its people, 2012. *Address:* 4 Abu Hureiba Street, Darb el-Ahmar, Cairo, Egypt; (project office) No 1, Midan el-Tahrir, Flat 17, Floor 5, Downtown Cairo, Egypt. *E:* bjk2@cam.ac.uk.

KEMP, Prof. Bruce Ernest, PhD; FRS 2002; FAA; NHMRC Fellow, St Vincent's Institute of Medical Research, since 2008 (NHMRC Senior Principal Research Fellow and Deputy Director, 1989–2003; Hon. NHMRC Fellow, 2003–08); *b* 15 Dec. 1946; *s* of Norman Beck Kemp and Mary Frances Kemp (*née* Officer); *m* 1970, Alison Virginia Sanders; three *s. Educ:* Adelaide Univ. (BAgrSc Hons); Flinders Univ., SA (PhD 1975). Postdoctoral Fellow, Edwin G. Krebs Lab., Univ. of Calif, Davis, 1974–76; Nat. Heart Foundn Fellow, Flinders Med. Centre, 1977–78; Queen Elizabeth II Sen. Res. Fellow, Howard Florey Inst., Univ. of Melbourne, 1979–84; Sen. Res. Fellow, Dept of Medicine, Repatriation Gen. Hosp., Heidelberg, Vic, 1984–88; Fedn Fellow, CSIRO, 2003–08. FAA 2000. *Publications:* (ed and contrib.) Peptides and Protein Phosphorylation, 1990; chapters in books; contrib. conf. procs and learned jls incl. Nature, Science. *Recreations:* tennis, walking, bicycle riding. *Address:* St Vincent's Institute of Medical Research, 41 Victoria Parade, Fitzroy, Vic 3065, Australia. *T:* (3) 92882480, *Fax:* (3) 94162676. *Club:* University House (Melbourne).

KEMP, Charles James Bowring; His Honour Judge Kemp; a Circuit Judge, since 1998; *b* 27 April 1951; *s* of late Michael John Barnett Kemp and of Brigid Ann (*née* Bowring; now Vernon-Smith); *m* 1974, Fenella Anne Herring; one *s* one *d. Educ:* Shrewsbury Sch.; University Coll. London (LLB). Called to the Bar, Gray's Inn, 1973; in practice at the Bar, 1974–98; Asst Recorder, 1987–91; a Recorder, 1991–98; South Eastern Circuit. Member: Sussex Probation Bd, 2001–07; Sussex Courts Bd, 2004–07; Surrey and Sussex Courts Bd, 2007–10. Vice Pres., E Sussex Magistrates' Assoc., 2013–. *Recreations:* music, tennis, swimming, golf, country pursuits. *Address:* Law Courts, High Street, Lewes, E Sussex BN7 1YB. *T:* (01273) 480400. *E:* c.kemp2@me.com. *Clubs:* Piltdown Golf; Harbour (Portscatho).

KEMP, Prof. David Thomas, PhD; FRS 2004; Professor of Auditory Biophysics, University College London, 1990–2009, now Emeritus; Research Director and Chairman, Otodynamics Ltd (Director and Chief Executive Officer, 1989); *b* 24 Feb. 1945; *s* of Rev. Thomas Kemp and Alice Kemp (*née* Holliday); *m* 1970, Gillian Barbara Langford; one *s* one *d* (and one *s* one *d* decd). *Educ:* Southport Technical Coll.; KCL (BSc Hons (Physics) 1966; AKC; PhD (Radiophysics) 1970). Res. Scientist, CEGB, 1970; PSO, RNTNEH, London, 1971; Sen. Lectr, Inst. of Laryngol. and Otol., London, 1980–86; Reader in Auditory Biophysics, UCL, 1986–90. Discoverer of otoacoustic emissions; patented invention of otoacoustic emission hearing screening device, in widespread use (Queen's Award for Export Achievement, 1993, for Technol Achievement, 1998, Otodynamics Ltd; Queen's Award for Technol Achievement, Inst. of Laryngol. and Otol., UCL, 1998). Dr *hc* Claude-Bernard, Lyon, 2006. Award of Merit, Assoc. for Res. in Otol., 2003; Dist. Service Award, Amer. Speech and Hearing Assoc., 2003. *Publications:* articles in Jl of Acoustical Soc. of America and in jls concerned with hearing and geophysics; book chapters on otoacoustic emissions. *Recreations:* history of electronic technologies, astronomy, family history and genealogy, walking. *Address:* UCL Centre for Auditory Research, The Ear Institute, 332 Gray's Inn Road, WC1X 8EE; Otodynamics Ltd, 30–38 Beaconsfield Road, Hatfield, Herts AL10 8BB. *T:* (01707) 267540, *Fax:* (01707) 262327. *E:* d.kemp@ucl.ac.uk.

KEMP, Edward Thomas; freelance director, playwright, librettist, translator and dramaturg, since 1986; Director, Royal Academy of Dramatic Art, since 2008; Principal, Conservatoire for Dance and Drama, since 2014; *b* Oxford, 9 Oct. 1965; *s* of late Rt Rev. Eric Waldram Kemp and of (Leslie) Patricia Kemp (*née* Kirk); partner, Jane Heather; one *s* one *d. Educ:* King's Sch., Worcester; New Coll., Oxford (BA). Staff Dir, NT, 1991–97; Dramaturg, Chichester Fest. Th., 2003–05; Guest Dramaturg, Bern Ballet, 2006–13; Artistic Dir, RADA, 2007–08. Vis. Prof., Bennington Coll., Vermont, 2000–01. *Plays directed* include: Wanted Man, 1999, Missing Reel, 2001, NT Studio; Wild Orchids, Chichester Fest., 2002; The Accrington Pals, 2002, Dr Faustus, 2004, Office Suite, 2007, Minerva, Chichester; Savages, Royal Court, 2006; Macbeth, Regent's Park, 2007; Penthesilea, 2008; Company, 2010, The Young Idea, 2011, King Lear, 2012, Six Pictures of Lee Miller, The Sea, 2013, Andromaque, 2015, RADA; *adaptations* include: Le Malade Imaginaire, W Yorks Playhouse, 1996; The Mysteries, RSC, 1997 (Radio 3, 1998); Molière's Don Juan, W Yorks Playhouse, 1998; Faulkner's As I Lay Dying, Young Vic, 1998, Baton Rouge, 1999; Sebald's The Emigrants, Radio 3, 2001; Lessing's Nathan the Wise, Chichester and Radio 3, 2003, Hampstead, 2005; Bulgakov's Master and Margarita, Chichester, 2004; Brecht's Turandot, Hampstead, 2008; Kleist's Penthesilea, RADA, 2008; Racine's Athalie (unperformed); The King James Bible, NT, 2011; Bulgakov's Master and Margarita, Complicite, 2012; Goldoni's Holiday Trilogy, RADA, 2014; Racine's Andromaque, RADA, 2015; *lyric works* include: Ease, Donmar, 1993; Travels in the Arctic Circle, Royal Opera Hse at Riverside Studios, 1993; Ivan the Terrible, BBC Proms, 2003; Six Pictures of Lee Miller, Minerva, Chichester, 2005; Echo and Narcissus, Royal Opera Hse 2, 2007; The Ground Beneath Her Feet, Manchester Internat. Fest., 2007; The Yellow Sofa, Glyndebourne, 2009, 2012; How the Whale Became, Linbury Studio, ROH, 2013; *screenplay:* Chop Chop, 2015; *ballet scenarios* include: Ghosts, Royal Opera Hse, 2005; Tale of Two Cities, Northern Ballet, 2008; Sturmhohe, 2009, Juliet and Romeo, Clara, 2010, Ein Winternachtstraum, 2011, Hexenhatz, 2013, Bern; Blood Wedding, Helsinki, 2010; Swan Maidens, Koblenz, 2015. *Publications:* The Mysteries, 1997; Nathan the Wise, 2003; The Master and Margarita, 2004; 5/11, 2005. *Recreations:* music, art, reading, landscape, family, baking. *Address:* Royal Academy of Dramatic Art, 62–64 Gower Street, WC1E 6ED. *T:* (020) 7908 4713. *E:* edwardkemp@rada.ac.uk.

KEMP, Fraser; *b* 1 Sept. 1958; *s* of William and Mary Kemp; *m* 1989, Patricia Mary (marr. diss. 2002), *d* of Patrick and Patricia Byrne; two *s* one *d. Educ:* Washington Comp. Sch. Civil Servant (clerical asst/officer), 1975–81; Labour Party: Agent, Leicester, 1981–84; Asst Regl Organiser, E Midlands, 1984–86; Regl Sec., W Midlands, 1986–94; Nat. Gen. Election Co-ordinator, 1994–96. MP (Lab) Houghton and Washington E, 1997–2010. An Asst Govt Whip, 2001–05. Mem., Select Cttee on Public Admin, 1997–99. Chm., PLP Cabinet Office Cttee, 1997–2001; Vice-Chm., Labour Election Planning Gp, 2004–05. *Recreation:* people.

KEMP, Air Vice-Marshal George John, CB 1976; *b* 14 July 1921; *m* 1943, Elspeth Beatrice Peacock; one *s* two *d.* Commnd RAF, 1941; served in night fighter sqdns with spell on ferrying aircraft to Middle East; RAF Staff Coll., 1952; AHQ Iraq, 1953–54; Air Secretary's Dept, Air Ministry, 1955–57; jssc, 1958; MoD Secretariat, 1959; Far East Planning Staff, 1960–61; RAF Staff Coll. Directing Staff, 1962–63; UNISON Planning Staff, MoD, 1964; Dir of Personnel (Policy and Plans), RAF, 1965–67; Stn Comdr RAF Upwood, 1968–69; Dir of Manning (RAF), 1970–72; Dir-Gen. of Personnel Management, RAF, 1973–75. *Recreations:* working with wood, 20th century history, reading The Times. *Address:* Myatts, White Horse Square, Steyning, W Sussex BN44 3GQ. *T:* (01903) 813804. *Club:* Royal Air Force.

KEMP, Lindsay; Founder, Artistic Director and Principal Performer, Lindsay Kemp Co., since 1962; painter, designer, teacher; *b* 3 May 1938; *s* of Norman Kemp and Marie (*née* Gilmour). *Educ:* Sunshine Sch. of Dancing, Bradford; Royal Merchant Navy Sch., Bearwood; Bradford Coll. of Art; Sigurd Leeder Sch. of Modern Dance; Ballet Rambert Sch.; studied with Marcel Marceau. Lindsay Kemp Co. productions include: Illuminations, Lyric, Hammersmith, 1965; Turquoise Pantomime; Woyzeck; Salomé; Legends; Flowers, West End, 1974, later Broadway and world tour, 1974–94; Mr Punch's Pantomime; A Midsummer Night's Dream; Duende; Nijinsky; Façade; The Big Parade; Alice; Onnagata; Cinderella: a gothic operetta; Dreamdances, Peacock Th., 2002; Hoffman Tales, Santander, 2007. Dir, David Bowie's Ziggy Stardust concerts, 1972; created for Ballet Rambert: The Parade's Gone By, 1975; Cruel Garden, 1978; film appearances include: Savage Messiah, 1971; The Lindsay Kemp Circus, 1971; Wicker Man, 1972; Sebastian, 1974; Jubilee, 1977; Italian Postcards, 1986; Travelling Light, 1993. *Publications:* (with D. Haughton) Drawing and Dancing, 1988; *relevant publications:* Lindsay Kemp, by David Haughton, 1982; Flowers, 1987. *Recreation:* interior decorating.

KEMP, Prof. Martin John, FBA 1991; Professor of the History of Art, 1995–2007, Research Professor of the History of Art, 2007–08, Emeritus Professor, 2008, University of Oxford; Fellow of Trinity College, Oxford, 1995–2008, now Emeritus; British Academy Wolfson Research Professor, 1993–98; *b* 5 March 1942; *s* of Frederick Maurice Kemp and Violet Anne Tull; *m* 1966, Jill Lightfoot (marr. diss. 2005), *d* of Dennis William Lightfoot and Joan Betteridge; one *s* one *d. Educ:* Windsor Grammar Sch.; Downing Coll., Cambridge (MA Nat. Scis and Art History; Hon. Fellow, 1999); Courtauld Inst. of Art, London Univ. (Academic Dip.). Lectr in History of Art, Dalhousie Univ., Halifax, NS, Canada, 1965–66; Lectr in History of Fine Art, Univ. of Glasgow, 1966–81; Fellow, Inst. for Advanced Study, Princeton, 1984–85; University of St Andrews: Prof. of Fine Arts, subseq. of Hist. and Theory of Art, 1981–95; Associate Dean of Graduate Studies, Faculty of Arts, 1983–87; Mem. Court, 1988–91; Provost of St Leonard's Coll., 1991–95. Prof. of History and Hon. Mem., Royal Scottish Acad., 1985–; Slade Prof. of Fine Art, Cambridge Univ., 1987–88; Visiting Professor: Benjamin Sonnenberg, Inst. of Fine Arts, New York Univ., 1988; Wiley, Univ. of N Carolina, Chapel Hill, 1993; Lila Wallace—Reader's Digest, Villa I Tatti, Harvard Univ., 2010; Louise Smith Brosse Prof., Univ. of Chicago, 2000; Vis. Scholar, Getty Res. Inst., LA, 2002; Mellon Sen. Res. Fellow, Canadian Centre for Architecture, Montreal, 2004. Page-Barbour Lectr, Univ. of Virginia, 2012; Robert Janson La Palme *60 Lectr, Princeton Univ., 2013. Co-Founder, Wallace Kemp/Artakt, 2001; Res. Dir, Universal Leonardo, 2001–07. Chair, Assoc. of Art Historians, 1989–92; Member: Board, Scottish Museums Council, 1990–95; Res. Awards Adv. Cttee, Leverhulme Trust, 1991–98; Board, Mus. Trng Inst., 1993–99; Board, Interalia, 1993–99; Council, British Soc. for History of Sci., 1994–97. Pres., Leonardo da Vinci Soc., 1987–96. Trustee: National Gall. of Scotland, 1982–87; V&A Museum, 1985–89; BM, 1995–2005. Broadcasts, Radio 3 and TV. For. Mem., American Acad. of Arts and Scis, 1996. FRSA 1983–98; FRSE 1992. Hon. FRIAS 1988. Hon. Fellow, Glyndŵr Univ., 2009. Hon. DLitt: Heriot-Watt, 1995; Uppsala, 2009. Mitchell Prize for best first book in English on Art History, 1981; Armand Hammer Prize for Leonardo Studies, 1992; President's Prize, Italian Assoc. of America, 1998. *Publications:* Leonardo da Vinci, The Marvellous Works of Nature and Man, 1981; (jtly) Leonardo da Vinci, 1989; (jtly) Leonardo on Painting, 1989; The Science of Art, 1990; Behind the Picture, 1997; (ed) The Oxford History of Western Art, 2000; Visualizations, 2000; (with Marina Wallace) Spectacular Bodies, 2000; Leonardo, 2004, 2011; Seen/Unseen, 2006; Leonardo da Vinci: experience, experiment, design, 2006; The Human Animal, 2007; (with Pascal Cotte) La Bella Principessa: the story of the new masterpiece by Leonardo da Vinci, 2010; (with T. Wells) Leonardo da Vinci's Madonna of the Yarnwinder, 2011; Christ to Coke: how image becomes icon, 2011; Continuity, Change and Progress: a message from the visual arts?, 2014; Leonardo da Vinci, Ritratto di Bianca Sforza: la bella Principessa, 2014; Art in History: 600 BC–2000 AD, 2014; articles in Jl of Warburg and Courtauld Insts, Burlington Magazine, Art History, Art Bull., Connoisseur, Procs of British Acad., Jl of RSA, L'Arte, Bibliothèque d'Humanisme et Renaissance, Med. History, TLS, London Rev. of Books, Guardian, Nature, Sunday Times, etc. *Recreations:* keeping fit, avoiding academics, music (especially early music and modern dance).

KEMP, Neil Reginald, OBE 1990 (MBE 1980); PhD; international education consultant; Visiting Fellow, Institute of Education, University of London (Senior Adviser (International), 2005); *b* 18 March 1945; *s* of Harry Reginald Kemp and Ada Mary Kemp (*née* Roberts); *m* 1982, Elizabeth Jacob; two *s. Educ:* University College of Wales, Swansea (BSc; PhD Analytical Chem. 1971). Laboratory technician, 1961–63; VSO as Lectr, Gordon Coll., Rawalpindi, Pakistan, 1967–68; joined British Council, 1971: Jakarta, 1971–74; Calcutta, 1976–79; Res. Associate, Univ. of London Inst. of Educn, 1979–80; Head, Sci. and Technol. Dept, London, 1981–85; New Delhi, 1985–89; Colombo, 1990–91; Develt and Trng Services, Manchester, 1991–95; Director: Indonesia, 1995–2001; Educn UK Div., 2001–05. Board Member: Assoc. of Ind. Higher Educn, 2005–; Open Univ. Worldwide Ltd, 2005–13; Council for Educn in Commonwealth. *Recreations:* athletics, cycling, cricket and basketball, travelling, jazz and blues. *Address:* 37 Houndean Rise, Lewes, E Sussex BN7 1EQ.

KEMP, Prof. Peter Anthony, DPhil; Vice Dean (formerly Associate Director), Blavatnik School of Government, since 2011, and Professor of Public Policy, since 2013, University of Oxford; *b* 25 Dec. 1955; *s* of Ronald Percy James Kemp and Emilie Kemp; two *d. Educ:* Univ. of Southampton (BSc 1977); Univ. of Glasgow (MPhil 1979); Univ. of Sussex (DPhil 1984). Researcher, SHAC, 1983–85; Res. Fellow, Univ. of Glasgow, 1985–87; Lectr, Univ. of Salford, 1987–90; Joseph Rowntree Prof. of Housing Policy and Founder Dir, Centre for Housing Policy, Univ. of York, 1990–95; Prof. of Housing and Social Policy, Univ. of Glasgow, 1996–2002; Prof. of Social Policy and Dir, Social Policy Research Unit, Univ. of York, 2002–06; Barnett Prof. of Social Policy, Univ. of Oxford, 2006–13; Fellow, St Cross Coll., Oxford, 2006–13. FAcSS (AcSS 2011). *Publications:* The Private Provision of Rented Housing, 1988; Housing and Social Policy, 1990; Tax Incentives and the Revival of Private Renting, 1991; A Comparative Study of Housing Allowances, 1997; Private Renting in Transition, 2004; Sick Societies?: trends in disability benefits in post-industrial welfare states, 2006; Cash and Care: challenges in the welfare state, 2006; Housing Allowances in Comparative Perspective, 2007; Transforming Landlords: housing, markets and public policy, 2011; Private Rental Housing: comparative perspectives, 2014. *Recreations:* cycling, going to the gym, reading. *Address:* Blavatnik School of Government, University of Oxford, 10 Merton Street, Oxford OX1 4JJ.

KEMP, Richard Geoffrey Horsford, MA; Director, Langford Educational Ltd, since 2006; Head Master, Pate's Grammar School, Cheltenham, 2000–06; *b* 27 Oct. 1948; *s* of Athole Stephen Horsford Kemp and Alison Kemp (*née* Bostock); *m* 1st, 1970 (marr. diss. 1990); 2nd, 1996, Denise (*née* Fraser); one step *s* one step *d. Educ:* Westminster Sch.; Christ Church, Oxford (MA). Marketing and Advertising Manager, Unilever, 1970–73; Teacher: Eton Coll., 1973–74; Henry Box Sch., Witney, 1974–78; Lord Williams's Sch., Thame, 1978–84; res., Dept of Educn, Oxford Univ., 1984–85; Buckinghamshire LEA, 1985–92 (Sen. Educn Advr, 1989–92); Sen. Dep. Head, Actg Headmaster, Aylesbury Grammar Sch., 1992–99. *Publications:* various geography textbooks and atlases. *Recreations:* gardening, wine, travel, military history. *Address:* Kemp's Yard, Langford, Lechlade, Glos GL7 3LF. *T:* (01367) 860176.

KEMP-GEE, Mark Norman; non-executive Director: Murgitroyd Group plc, since 2001; Moncreiffe & Co. plc, since 1986; *b* 19 Dec. 1945; *s* of late Bernard Kemp-Gee and Ann Kemp-Gee (*née* Mackilligin); *m* 1980, Hon. Lucy Lyttelton, *d* of 10th Viscount Cobham, KG, GCMG, GCVO, TD, PC; three *s. Educ:* Marlborough Coll.; Pembroke Coll., Oxford (MA). Chm., Greig Middleton & Co. Ltd, 1978–99; Chief Exec., Exeter Investment Gp plc, 1999–2004. Director: King & Shaxson Hldgs plc, 1993–96; Gerrard Gp plc, 1996–99. Member (C): Lambeth BC, 1982–86; Hampshire CC, 2005–. Mem., S Downs Nat. Park Authy, 2011–. Chm., E Hampshire Cons. Assoc., 2009–12. *Recreations:* point-to-pointing, French animalier bronzes. *Address:* Park House, Upper Wield, Alresford, Hants SO24 9RU. *Clubs:* City of London; Oxford Union.

KEMP-WELCH, Sir John, Kt 1999; Director, HSBC Holdings, 2000–06; Chairman, London Stock Exchange, 1994–2000 (Director, 1991–2000); *b* 31 March 1936; *s* of late Peter Wellesbourne Kemp-Welch, OBE and Peggy Penelope Kemp-Welch; *m* 1964, Diana Elisabeth Leishman (*d* 2013); one *s* three *d. Educ:* Abberley Hall, Worcs; Winchester Coll. Hoare & Co., 1954–58; Cazenove & Co., 1959–94 (Jt Sen. Partner, 1980–94). Chairman: Scottish Eastern Investment Trust, 1994–99 (Dir, 1993–99); Lowland Investment Co., 1993–97 (Dir, 1963–97); Claridge's Hotel, 1995–97; Martin Currie Portfolio Investment Trust plc, 1999–2000; Director: Savoy Hotel PLC, 1985–98; Royal & Sun Alliance Insurance Gp (formerly Sun Alliance Gp), 1994–99; British Invisibles, 1994–98; Pro Share, 1995–97. Dep. Chm., Financial Reporting Council, 1994–2000; Director: SFA, 1994–97; Accountancy Foundn, 2000–01. Member: City Capital Markets Cttee, 1989–94; Panel on Takeovers and Mergers, 1994–2000. Mem., Stock Exchange, 1959–86. Vice Pres., Fedn of European Stock Exchanges, 1996–98; Mem. Exec. Cttee, Federation Internationale des Bourses de Valeurs, 1994–98; President: Investor Relations Soc., 1994–2000; Securities Industry Mgt Assoc., 1994–2000. Member: (Lord Mayor of London's) City No 1 Consultancy, 1994–2000; Council, London First, 1994–96. Pres., Reed's Sch. Foundn Appeal, 2003–04; Vice-Pres., Reed's Sch., 2005–; Governor: Ditchley Foundn, 1980–2012; North Foreland Lodge Sch., 1980–92; Chm., King's Med. Res. Trust, 1991–2006 (Trustee, 1984–2006); Trustee: KCH Special Trustees, 1997–99; KCH Charitable Trust, 1998–99; Trustee and Mem. Council, Game Conservancy Trust, 1990–94 (Hon. Res. Fellow, 1998–); Mem. Adv. Council, PYBT, 1996–2000; Pres., Cazenove Assoc., 2005–; Trustee: Stock Exchange Benevolent Fund, 1980–2000; Sandford St Martin Trust, 1994–99; Dulverton Trust, 1994– (Vice Chm., 2001–); Farmington Trust, 2002–; St Paul's Knightsbridge Foundn, 2002–; Chm., Lucy Kemp-Welch Meml Trust, 1965–. Mem., Highland Soc. of London, 1992–. Mem., Guild of Internat. Bankers, 2004–. Hon. FCSI (MSI 1992; FSI 1996). CCMI (CBIM 1984); FRSA 1989. Hon. DBA London Guildhall Univ., 1998. Joseph Nickerson Heather Award, Joseph Nickerson Heather Improvement Foundn, 1988. *Recreations:* the hills of Perthshire, City of London history, cricket nostalgia, champagne and claret, Lucy Kemp-Welch paintings, heather moorland management. *Address:* 74 Melton Court, Onslow Crescent, SW7 3JH. *Clubs:* White's, City of London, Pilgrims, MCC; Essex.

KEMPF, Frederick Albert, (Freddy); concert pianist and conductor; *b* Croydon, 14 Oct. 1977; *s* of Fritz Kempf and Yoshimi Kempf; *m* 2007, Katja; two *s* one *d. Educ:* St Edmund's Sch., Canterbury; Royal Acad. of Music. First public appearance, 1981; first professional engagement, 1983; concerto debut with RPO, 1985, conducting debut, 2011; many performances and collaborations worldwide. BBC Young Musician of the Year, 1992; Bronze Medal, Internat. Tchaikovsky Competition, Moscow, 1998; Classical Brit Award, 2001. *Recreations:* sport, mountaineering, ski-ing, languages, food and wine. *Address:* Munich, Germany. *E:* (agent) tmasi@imgartists.com.

KEMPNER, Prof. Thomas; Principal and Professor of Management Studies, Henley Management College (formerly Administrative Staff College), 1972–90, now Emeritus Professor; Director of Business Studies, Brunel University, 1972–90, now Emeritus Professor; Director, Henley Centre for Forecasting, 1974–2001 (Chairman, 1974–95); *b* 28 Feb. 1930; *s* of late Martin and Rosa Kempner; *m* 1st, 1958, June Maton (*d* 1980); two *d* (and one *d* decd); 2nd, 1981, Mrs Veronica Ann Vere-Sharp (*d* 2012); one step *s* two step *d. Educ:* Denstone Coll.; University Coll. London (BSc (Econ)). Asst Administrator, Hyelm Youth Hostels, 1948–49, and part-time, 1951–55; Research Officer, Administrative Staff Coll., Henley, 1954–59; Lectr (later Sen. Tutor) in Business Studies, Sheffield Univ., 1959–63; Prof. of Management Studies, Founder, and Dir of Management Centre, Univ. of Bradford, 1963–72. Chm., Henley Distance Learning Ltd, 1980–95. Member of various cttees, including: Social Studies and Business Management Cttees of University Grants Cttee, 1966–76; Management, Education and Training Cttee of NEDO, 1969–72 (Chm. of its Student Grants Sub-Cttee); Chm., Food Industry Manpower Cttee of NEDO, 1968–71; Jt Chm., Conf. of Univ. Management Schools, 1973–75. Chm. Council, Brunel Univ., 1997–99 (Vice-Chm., 1992–97). Trustee, Greenwich Foundn for RNC, 1997–2002. CCMI (FBIM 1971). Hon. DSc Cranfield, 1976; Hon. LLD Birmingham, 1983; DUniv Brunel, 1990. Burnham Gold Medal, 1970. *Publications:* editor, author, and contributor to several books, including: Bradford Exercises in Management (with G. Wills), 1966; Is Corporate Planning Necessary? (with J. Hewkin), 1968; A Guide to the Study of Management, 1969; Management Thinkers (with J. Tillet and G. Wills), 1970; Handbook of Management, 1971, 4th edn 1987; (with K. Macmillan and K. H. Hawkins) Business and Society, 1974; Models for Participation, 1976; numerous articles in management jls. *Recreation:* travel. *Address:* Garden House, Maidensgrove, Henley-on-Thames, Oxon RG9 6EZ. *T:* (01491) 638597.

KEMPSELL, Rosemary Ann, CBE 2014; Worldwide President, Mothers' Union, 2007–12 (Trustee, 2001–06); *b* 29 Sept. 1943; *d* of Laurence and Ada Harriet Jackson; *m* 1967, John Baron Kempsell; two *d. Educ:* Collingwood Sch., Wallington; Willows Co. Sch., Morden; Open Univ. (BA 1992; DipEurHum 1993). Examr, Estate Duty Office, 1963–71. Mem., Mgt Bd, S London Industrial Mission, 1993–2002. Pres., Southwark Dio., Mothers' Union, 1998–2000. Trustee: Traidcraft Foundn, 2012–; Us (formerly USPG), 2012–. *Recreations:* listening to opera, participating in choral singing, reading, swimming. *Address:* 3 All Saints Drive, South Croydon CR2 9ES. *E:* rosemary@kempsell.freeserve.co.uk. *Clubs:* Oriental; Purley Downs Golf.

KEMPSON, Prof. (Helen) Elaine, CBE 2007; Consultant, World Bank, since 2010; Director, Personal Finance Research Centre, 1998–2010, and Professor of Personal Finance and Social Policy Research, 2001–10, now Emeritus, University of Bristol; *b* Bideford, 1947; *d* of Robert and Doreen Hersey; *m* 1982, Nick Moore. *Educ:* Univ. of Sussex (BSc Biol.); Coll. of Librarianship, Univ. of Wales (Postgrad. Dip.). Librarian, Lambeth BC, 1972–77; Dir, Community Information Project, Liby Assoc., 1977–82; Hd of Res., Social Services Dept, Somerset CC, 1982–84; Partner, Acumen Res. and Consultancy Ltd, 1984–; Principal Res. Fellow, Policy Studies Inst., 1988–98. Mem., Social Security Adv. Cttee, 2003–12. Non-executive Director: Banking Codes Standards Bd, 2006–08; Financial Ombudsman Service, 2008–12. Member: Financial Inclusion Taskforce, HM Treasury, 2005–11; Bd, IFS Sch. of Finance, 2007–08; Sustainability Panel, Wessex Water, 2010–; Consumer Adv. Gp, Central Bank of Ireland, 2011–; Universal Credit Evaluation Gp, 2012–. *Publications:* (with M. Dee) A Future Age, 1987; Legal Advice and Assistance, 1989; *reports relating to research on personal finance include:* (with R. Berthoud) Credit and Debt in Britain, 1992; (with K. Rowlingson) Gas Debt and Disconnection, 1993; Household Budgets and Housing Costs, 1993; (with N. Moore) Designing Public Documents: a review of research, 1994; (with K. Rowlingson) Paying with Plastic: a study of credit card debt, 1994; (jtly) Hard Times?: how poor families make ends meet, 1994; Outside the Banking System: a review of households without a current account, 1994; (with A. Herbert) Water Debt and Disconnection, 1995; Money Advice and Debt Counselling, 1995; (jtly) Mortgage Arrears and Possessions, 1995; (jtly) Paying for Rented Housing, 1995; (with A. Herbert) Credit Use and Ethnic Minorities, 1996; Life on a Low Income, 1996; (with C. Callender) Student Finances, 1996; (jtly) Money Matters, 1997; (jtly) Paying for Peace of Mind: access to home contents insurance for low-income households, 1998; Kept Out or Opted Out?: understanding and combating financial exclusion, 1999; Banking without Branches, 2000; (jtly) In or Out? financial exclusion: a literature and research review, 2000; Tackling Financial Exclusion, 2001; Over-indebtedness in Britain, 2002; Independent Review of the Banking Codes, 2002 and 2004; (with S. McKay) Saving and Life Events, 2003; (jtly) Fair and Reasonable: an assessment of the Financial Ombudsman Service, 2004; (with S. Collard) Affordable Credit: the way forward, 2005; (jtly) Levels of Financial Capability in the UK, 2006; (jtly) Easy come, easy go: borrowing over the life cycle, 2007; (jtly) Genworth Index: measuring consumer financial vulnerability in 10 European markets, 2008; (with A. Finney) Consumer purchasing outcomes survey, 2008; (with A. Atkinson) Investigating Debt, 2008; (jtly) Debt and older people, 2008; (jtly) Financial services provision and prevention of financial exclusion, 2008; (jtly) Towards a common operational definition of over-indebtedness, 2008; Looking beyond our shores: consumer protection regulation lessons from the UK, 2008; (with A. Finney) Regression analysis of the unbanked, 2009; (jtly) Is a not-for-profit home credit business feasible?: building a business case, 2009; (with A. Finney) Saving in lower-income households, 2009; Framework for the development of financial literacy baseline surveys: a first international comparative analysis, 2010; (with S. Collard) Money Guidance Pathfinder, 2010; (jtly) The Child Trust Fund, 2011; (with S. Collard) Developing a vision for financial inclusion, 2012; (jtly) Impact on business and consumers of a cap on the total cost of credit, 2013; (jtly) Measuring Financial Capability, 2013. *Recreations:* gardening, walking, cooking, travel. *Address:* School of Geographical Sciences, University of Bristol, University Road, Bristol BS8 1SS.

KEMPSON, Martyn Rex; Principal Advisor to John Lyon's Charity, since 2002; *b* 31 July 1947; *s* of Horace and Winifred May Kempson; *m* 1986, Carole J. Kendall; two *s. Educ:* Luton Grammar Sch.; North-Western Poly. MCLIP (ALA 1968). Librarian: Luton Public Libraries, 1963–68; Buckinghamshire CC Libraries, 1968–71; London Borough of Sutton Libraries, 1971–91: Borough Librarian, 1987–88; Asst Dir of Leisure, 1988–91; Barnet London Borough Council, 1991–2002: Controller: Libraries and Arts, 1991–94; Recreation, Leisure and Arts, and Dep. Dir, Educn Services, 1995–98; Dir, Educnl Services, 1998–99; Strategic Dir of Educn and Children, 1999–2002. Chairman: British Judo Council, British Judo Foundn, 2011–. FRSA; FLS. *Publications:* I-Spy Football, 1991; contrib. poetry, First Time mag. *Recreations:* supporting Luton Town FC, poetry, tennis, judo.

KEMPSON, Prof. Ruth Margaret, (Mrs M. J. Pinner), FBA 1989; Professor of General Linguistics, King's College London, 1999–2009, now Emeritus; *b* 26 June 1944; *d* of Edwin Garnett Hone Kempson and late Margaret Cecilia Kempson; *m* 1973, Michael John Pinner; two *s. Educ:* Univ. of Birmingham (BA (2 ii) Music and English); Univ. of London (MA (with dist.) Mod. English Language 1969; PhD Linguistics 1972). Res. Asst to Survey of English Usage, UCL, 1969–70; School of Oriental and African Studies, University of London: Lectr in Linguistics, 1971–85; Reader in Gen. Linguistics, 1985–87; Prof. of Gen. Linguistics, 1987–99; Head of Linguistics Dept, 1992–96; Leverhulme Personal Res. Prof., KCL, 1999–2004. Vis. Prof. in Semantics, Univ. of Massachusetts, 1982–83. Pres., Linguistics Assoc. of GB, 1986–91. MAE 2000. *Publications:* Presupposition and the Delimitation of Semantics, 1975; Semantic Theory, 1977; Mental Representations: the interface between language and reality, 1988; (jtly) Dynamic Syntax: the flow of language understanding, 2001; The Dynamics of Language, 2005; Semantics: an introduction to meaning in language, 2009; (ed) The Handbook of Philosophy of Linguistics, 2012; articles in Linguistics and Philosophy, Jl of Linguistics and edited collections. *Address:* Philosophy Department, King's College London, Strand, WC2R 2LS.

KEMSLEY, 3rd Viscount *cr* 1945, of Dropmore, co. Bucks; **Richard Gomer Berry;** Bt 1928; Baron Kemsley 1936; *b* 17 April 1951; *o s* of Hon. Denis Gomer Berry, 2nd *s* of 1st Viscount Kemsley, GBE and Pamela Berry (*née* Wellesley); *S* uncle, 1999; *m* 1994, Elizabeth Jane Barker; two *s. Educ:* Eton. *Heir: s* Hon. Luke Gomer Berry, *b* 2 Feb. 1998. *Address:* Church Hill Farm, Church Lane, Brockenhurst, Hants SO42 7UB.

KENDAL, Felicity Ann, CBE 1995; actress; *d* of late Geoffrey and Laura Kendal; *m* (marr. diss.); one *s*; *m* 1983, Michael Rudman, *qv* (marr. diss. 1994); one *s. Educ:* six convents in India. First appeared on stage at age of 9 months, when carried on as the Changeling boy in A Midsummer Night's Dream; grew up touring India and Far East with parents' theatre co., playing pageboys at age of eight and graduating through Puck, at nine, to parts such as Viola in Twelfth Night, Jessica in The Merchant of Venice, and Ophelia in Hamlet; returned to England, 1965; made London debut, Carla in Minor Murder, Savoy, 1967; Katherine in Henry V, and Lika in The Promise, Leicester, 1968; Amaryllis in Back to Methuselah, Nat. Theatre, 1969; Hermia in A Midsummer Night's Dream, and Hero in Much Ado About Nothing, Regent's Park, 1970; Anne Danby in Kean, Oxford, 1970, London, 1971; Romeo and Juliet, 'Tis Pity She's A Whore, and The Three Arrows, 1972; The Norman Conquests, Globe, 1974; Viktosha in Once Upon a Time, Bristol, 1976; Arms and The Man, Greenwich, 1978; Mara in Clouds, Duke of York's, 1978; Constanze Mozart in Amadeus, NT, 1979; Desdemona in Othello, NT, 1980; Christopher in On the Razzle, NT, 1981; Paula in The Second Mrs Tanqueray, NT, 1981; The Real Thing, Strand, 1982; Jumpers, Aldwych, 1985; Made in Bangkok, Aldwych, 1986; Hapgood, Aldwych, 1988; Ivanov, and Much Ado About Nothing, Strand, 1989 (Best Actress Award, Evening Standard); Hidden Laughter, Vaudeville, 1990; Tartuffe, Playhouse, 1991; Heartbreak House, Haymarket, 1992; Arcadia, NT, 1993; An Absolute Turkey, Globe, 1994; Indian Ink, Aldwych, 1995; Mind Millie for Me, Haymarket, 1996; Waste, and The Seagull, Old Vic, 1997; Alarms and Excursions, Gielgud, 1998; Fallen Angels, Apollo, 2000; Humble Boy, Gielgud, 2002; Happy Days, Arts Th., 2003; Amy's View, Garrick, 2006; The Vortex, Apollo, 2008; The Last Cigarette, Minerva, Chichester, 2009; Mrs Warren's Profession, Comedy, 2010; Relatively Speaking, Th. Royal, Newcastle, 2012, transf. Wyndham's, 2013; Chin-Chin, UK tour, 2013; Hay Fever, Theatre Royal, Bath, 2014, Australia tour, 2014, transf. Duke of Yorks Th., 2015. *Television:* four series of The Good Life, 1975–77; Viola in Twelfth Night, 1979; Solo, 1980, 2nd series 1982; The Mistress, 1985, 2nd series 1986; The Camomile Lawn, 1992; Honey for Tea, 1994; How Proust Can Save Your Life, 1999; Rosemary and Thyme, 3 series 2003–05; plays and serials. *Films:* Shakespeare Wallah, 1965; Valentino, 1976. Variety Club Most Promising Newcomer, 1974, Best Actress, 1979, 2001; Clarence Derwent Award, 1980; Variety Club Woman of the Year Best Actress Award, 1984. *Publications:* White Cargo (memoirs), 1998. *Recreations:* reading, working. *Address:* c/o Dallas Smith, United Agents, 12–26 Lexington Street, W1F 0LE. *T:* (020) 3214 0800.

KENDALL, Bridget, MBE 1994; Diplomatic Correspondent, BBC News, since 1998; Presenter, The Forum, BBC World Service, since 2008; *b* 27 April 1956; *d* of Prof. David George Kendall, FRS. *Educ:* Lady Margaret Hall, Oxford (BA Hons; Hon. Fellow, 2015); Harvard Univ. (Harkness Fellow); Moscow State Univ.; St Antony's Coll., Oxford (Hon. Fellow, 2005). Joined BBC, 1983: trainee, World Service, 1983; presenter, Newsnight, 1983–84; producer/reporter, World Service, 1984–89; Moscow Corresp., 1989–93; Washington Corresp., 1994–98. Jubilee Lectr, St Antony's Coll., Oxford, 2000; Roskill Lectr, Churchill Coll., Cambridge, 2003; Darwin Coll. Lecture Series, Cambridge, 2013; Vis. Prof., Univ. of Lincoln, 2005–. Member, Advisory Boards: Russia and Eurasia Prog., Chatham House, 2000–06; RUSI Council, 2001–05; Mem. Adv. Council, Wilton Park, 2012–. Trustee, Asia Hse, 2010–14. DUniv UCE, 1999; Hon. LLD: St Andrews, 2001; Exeter, 2002. *Publications:* (jtly) David the Invincible, 1980; (contrib.) The Day that Shook the World, 2001; (contrib.) The Battle for Iraq, 2003; (contrib.) International News Reporting: frontlines and deadlines, 2008. *Recreations:* literature, cinema, tennis, hiking, gardening. *Address:* World Affairs Unit, The Bridge on the Third Floor, BBC Broadcasting House, Portland Place, W1A 1AA.

See also W. S. Kendall.

KENDALL, David William; Chairman, G-T-P Group Ltd, 2006–11; *b* 8 May 1935; *s* of William Jack Kendall and Alma May Kendall; *m* 1st, 1960, Delphine Hitchcock (marr. diss.); one *s* one *d*; 2nd, 1973, Elisabeth Rollison; one *s* one *d*. *Educ:* Enfield Grammar School; Southend High School. FCA. Elles Reeve, Shell-Mex & BP, Irish Shell & BP, 1955–70; British Petroleum Co.: Crude Oil Sales Manager, 1971–72; Manager, Bulk Trading Div., 1973–74; Organisation Planning Cttee, 1975; BP New Zealand: Gen. Manager, 1976–79; Man. Dir and Chief Exec., 1979–82; Chm., BP SW Pacific, 1979–82; BP Oil: Finance and Planning Dir, 1982–85; Man. Dir and Chief Exec., 1985–88; Director: BP Chemicals Internat., 1985–88; BP Oil Internat., 1985–88; Associated Octel Co., 1985–88. Chairman: Bunzl, 1990–93 (Dir, 1988–93); Ruberoid plc, 1993–2000; Whitecroft plc, 1993–2000; Blagden Industries plc, 1994–2000; Meyer Internat., 1994–95; Celtic Energy Ltd, 1994–2003; Wagon Industrial Hldgs, subseq. Wagon plc, 1997–2005; Danka Business Systems plc, 1998–2001 (Dir, 1993–2001); Dep. Chm., British Coal Corp., 1989–91; Director: STC plc, 1988–90; Gowrings plc, 1993–2005; South Wales Electricity plc, 1993–96; BSI, 2000–05. President: UK Petroleum Industries Assoc., 1987–88; Oil Industries Club, 1988. *Recreations:* golf, piano, France and its history. *Address:* 41 Albion Street, W2 2AU. *T:* (020) 7258 1955. *Club:* Royal Mid Surrey Golf.

KENDALL, Elizabeth Louise; MP (Lab) Leicester West, since 2010; *b* 1971. *Educ:* Watford Grammar Sch. for Girls; Queens' Coll., Cambridge (BA 1st Cl. Hons Hist. 1993). Special Advr to Harriet Harman, MP, 1997–98; Res. Fellow, King's Fund; Associate Dir, Health, Social Care and Children's Early Years, IPPR; Dir, Maternity Alliance; Special Advr to Patricia Hewitt, MP, 2004–07; Dir, Ambulance Service Network, 2008–10. Shadow Minister for Care and Older People, 2011–15. Mem., Educn Select Cttee, 2010. *Address:* House of Commons, SW1A 0AA.

KENDALL, Rev. Frank; Non-stipendiary Priest, since 2002, and Chairman, World Development Group, since 2007, Diocese of Blackburn; *b* 15 Dec. 1940; *s* of Norman and Violet Kendall; *m* 1965, Brenda Pickin; one *s* one *d*. *Educ:* Bradford Grammar School; Corpus Christi College, Cambridge (MA Classics); Southwark Ordination Course (London Univ. Dip. in Religious Studies). MPBW, 1962; DEA, 1967–68; MPBW, DoE and Dept of Transport, 1969–89; Under Secretary 1984; Chief Exec., St Helens MBC, 1989–91; Venue Develt Manager, British Olympic Bid, 1992; Inspector of Schs, 1993–2000. Mem., Northern Rent Assessment Panel, later Residential Property Tribunal Service, 1997–2010. Ordained deacon, 1974, priest, 1975; Hon. Curate: Lingfield, Dio. of Southwark, 1974–75 and 1978–82; Sketty, Dio. of Swansea and Brecon, 1975–78; Limpsfield, Dio. of Southwark, 1982–84; Licensed Preacher, Dio. of Manchester, 1984–89; Non-stipendiary Priest, 1989–2001 and Chm., Bd for Social Responsibility, 1996–2001, Dio. of Liverpool. FRSA 1990–2004. *Recreations:* painting: (i) pictures, (ii) decorating. *Address:* 52 Kingsway, Penwortham, Preston PR1 0ED. *T:* (01772) 748021.

KENDALL, Prof. Kevin, FRS 1993; Professor of Formulation Engineering, University of Birmingham, 2000–11, now Honorary Professor; Director, Adelan Ltd, since 1996; *b* 2 Dec. 1943; *s* of Cyril Kendall and Margaret (*née* Swarbrick); *m* 1969, Patricia Jennifer Heyes; one *s* one *d*. *Educ:* London Univ. (BSc Physics External); PhD Cantab. Joseph Lucas, 1961–66; Cavendish Lab., 1966–69; British Rail Research, 1969–71; Monash Univ., 1972–74 (QEII fellowship); Akron Univ., 1974; ICI Runcorn, 1974–93; Prof. of Materials Science, Keele Univ., 1993–2000. *Publications:* Molecular Adhesion and its Applications, 2001; (with S. C. Singhal) High Temperature Solid Oxide Fuel Cells, 2003; (jtly) Adhesion of cells, viruses and nanoparticles, 2012; papers in learned jls on adhesion, fracture, ceramics and materials. *Recreations:* walking, cycling. *Address:* Wycherley, Tower Road, Ashley Heath, Market Drayton, Shropshire TF9 4PY. *T:* (01630) 672665.

KENDALL, Sir Peter Ashley, Kt 2015; Chairman, Agriculture and Horticulture Development Board, since 2014; *b* Bedford, 8 May 1960; *s* of John and Jasmine Kendall; *m* 1999, Emma McAlley; two *s* one *d*. *Educ:* Nottingham Univ. (BA Agricl Econs). Farmer, family business, farming and contracting. Chm., Cereals, 2003, Dep. Pres., 2004–06, Pres., 2006–14, NFU; Pres., World Farmers Orgn, 2014. Mem., Rural Climate Change Panel, DEFRA, 2006–. Vice Pres., COPA, 2007–. Mem., Policy Issues Council, IGD, 2006–. *Recreations:* countryside, shooting, occasional veteran's Rugby, ski-ing. *Address:* Church Farm, Eyeworth, Sandy, Beds SG19 2HH. *T:* (01767) 631262, *Fax:* (01767) 631278.

KENDALL, Raymond Edward, QPM 1984; Secretary General, International Criminal Police Organization (Interpol), 1985–2000, now Hon. Secretary General; *b* 5 Oct. 1933; *m*. *Educ:* Simon Langton School, Canterbury; Exeter College, Oxford (MA Hons). RAF, 1951–53 (principally Malaya). Asst Supt of Police, Uganda Police, 1956–62; Metropolitan Police, New Scotland Yard, 1962–86 (principally Special Branch). Pres., Supervisory Cttee, EU Anti-Fraud Office, 2001–05. Exec. Chm., Brighterion. Mem., Forensic Sci. Soc. Editor-in-Chief: Counterfeits and Forgeries; Internat. Criminal Police Review. Chevalier de la Légion d'Honneur (France), 1997. *Recreations:* shooting, golf. *Address:* BP 202, 69657 Villefranche-Cedex, France. *Clubs:* Special Forces; Chief Constables.

KENDALL, Prof. Tim, DPhil; Professor of English Literature, since 2006, and Head of Department, since 2009, University of Exeter; *b* Plymouth, 11 Jan. 1970; *s* of Leslie and Susan Kendall; *m* 1995, Fiona Mathews; one *s* two *d*. *Educ:* Plymouth Coll.; Christ Church, Oxford (MA Hons 1991); Hertford Coll., Oxford (DPhil 1994). Lectr in English Lit., Christ Church, Oxford, 1994; Sir James Knott Res. Fellow, Univ. of Newcastle upon Tyne, 1995–97; Lectr, 1997–2001, Sen. Lectr, 2001–06, in English Lit., Univ. of Bristol. *Publications:* Paul Muldoon, 1996; Sylvia Plath: a critical study, 2001; Strange Land: poems, 2006; Modern English War Poetry, 2007; The Art of Robert Frost, 2012; Poetry of the First World War, 2013. *Recreations:* swimming, reading, writing poetry. *Address:* 2 Colybank, Rosemary Lane, Colyton, Devon EX24 6LR. *T:* (01297) 553222. *E:* t.kendall@exeter.ac.uk.

KENDALL, Prof. Wilfrid Stephen, DPhil; Professor of Statistics, University of Warwick, since 1994; *b* 5 Nov. 1954; *s* of Prof. David George Kendall, FRS; *m* 1984, Catherine Mary Usher; two *s* two *d*. *Educ:* Perse Sch., Cambridge; Queen's Coll., Oxford (BA 1975; MA 1986); Linacre Coll., Oxford (MSc 1976; DPhil 1979); Univ. of Warwick (DSc 2013). Lectr, in Mathematical Stats, Univ. of Hull, 1978–84; Sen. Lectr in Stats, Univ. of Strathclyde, 1984–88; University of Warwick: Lectr in Stats, 1988–91; Reader, 1991–94; Chm., Dept of Stats, 1999–2002. Co-Dir, Acad. for PhD Trng in Statistics, 2006–. Pres., Bernoulli Soc. for Mathematical Statistics and Probability, 2013–15 (Scientific Sec., 1996–2000). Member, Council: London Mathematical Soc., 2010–12; ISI, 2015–. *Publications:* (jtly) Stochastic Geometry and its Applications, 1985, 2nd edn 1995; (jtly) New Directions in Dirichlet Forms, 1998; (ed jtly) Markov chain Monte Carlo: innovations and applications, 2005; (ed jtly) New Perspectives in Stochastic Geometry, 2009; contrib. numerous papers to learned jls. *Recreations:* family, hill-walking. *Address:* Department of Statistics, University of Warwick, Coventry CV4 7AL. *T:* (024) 7652 3082, *Fax:* (024) 7652 4532. *E:* wsk@wilfridkendall.co.uk.

See also B. Kendall.

KENDRICK, Prof. Anthony Robert, MD; FRCGP; FRCPsych; Professor of Primary Care, University of Southampton, since 2013; *b* Dover, 26 Sept. 1956; *s* of Anthony Ivor Kendrick and Robina Philp Smith Kendrick; *m* 2013, Dr Helen Mander; one *s* one *d*. *Educ:* Dover Grammar Sch.; St George's Hospital Med. Sch., Univ. of London (BSc 1978, MB BS 1981; DRCOG 1983; DCH 1984; MD 1996). FRCGP 1997; FRCPsych 2001. GP, 1985–2013; Mental Health Foundn Res. Fellow, 1990–94; Sen. Lectr, 1994–97, Reader, 1997–98, in Gen. Practice, St George's Hosp. Med. Sch., Univ. of London; Prof. of Primary Med. Care, Univ. of Southampton, 1998–2010; Dean, Hull York Med. Sch., 2010–13. Non-exec. Dir, Hull and E Yorks NHS Trust, 2010–13. President's Medal, RCGP, 2009. *Publications:* The Prevention of Mental Illness in Primary Care, 1996; Child Mental Health in Primary Care, 2001; (contrib.) Oxford Handbook of General Practice, 2005; Primary Care Mental Health, 2009; over 100 articles in jls on primary care mental health. *Recreations:* marathon running, ski-ing, long distance walking. *Address:* Aldermoor Health Centre, Southampton SO16 5ST. *T:* (023) 8024 1083, *Fax:* (023) 8070 1125. *E:* A.R.Kendrick@soton.ac.uk. *Club:* Totton Running.

KENDRICK, Dominic John; QC 1997; *b* 23 Feb. 1955; *s* of late Anthony Kendrick and Joan Kendrick; *m* 1984, Marice Chantal; one *s* two *d*. *Educ:* St Ambrose Coll.; Trinity Coll., Cambridge (BA Hons, MA); City Univ. (Dip. Law); Inns of Court Sch. of Law. Called to the Bar, Middle Temple, 1981, Bencher, 2013. *Recreations:* theatre, restoration of old houses, reading. *Address:* 7 King's Bench Walk, Temple, EC4Y 7DS. *T:* (020) 7583 0404.

KENDRICK, Graham Andrew; song and hymn writer; *b* 2 Aug. 1950; *s* of Maurice and Olive Kendrick; *m* 1976, Jill Gibson; four *d*. *Educ:* Avery Hill Coll. of Educn (Cert Ed 1972). Music Dir, British Youth for Christ, 1976–80; Kendrick & Stevenson (music and mime duo), 1981–84; Mem., Leadership Team, Ichthus Christian Fellowship, 1984–2004; Co-founder, March for Jesus, 1987. Songs and hymns sung in many languages worldwide; has recorded numerous albums, 1971–. Hon. DD Brunel, 2000. *Publications:* Worship, 1984; Ten Worshipping Churches, 1987; March for Jesus, 1992; Shine Jesus Shine, 1992; Awakening our Cities for God, 1993. *Recreations:* family, walking, music. *Address:* c/o Make Way Music, PO Box 320, Tunbridge Wells, Kent TN2 9DE. *E:* info@makewaymusic.com.

KENEALLY, Thomas Michael, AO 1983; FRSL; FAAAS; author; *b* 7 Oct. 1935; *s* of Edmond Thomas Keneally; *m* 1965, Judith Mary Martin; two *d*. Studied for NSW Bar. Schoolteacher until 1965; Commonwealth Literary Fellowship, 1966, 1968, 1972; Lectr in Drama, Univ. of New England, 1968–69. Vis. Prof., Dept of English, Univ. of California, Irvine, 1985; Berg Prof., Dept of English, New York Univ., 1988; Distinguished Prof., Dept of English and Comparative Lit., Univ. of Calif, Irvine, 1991–95. Chm., Australian Republican Movement, 1991–94. Member: (inaugural) Australia-China Council, 1978–83; Adv. Panel, Australian Constitutional Commn, 1985–88; Literary Arts Bd, Australia, 1985–88; Chm., Aust. Soc. Authors, 1987–90 (Mem. Council, 1985–); Pres., Nat. Book Council Australia, 1985–89. FRSL 1973. Silver City (screenplay, with Sophia Turkiewicz), 1985. Hon. DLitt: Queensland, 1993; NUI, 1994; Fairleigh Dickinson, NJ, 1994; Western Sydney, 1997. *Publications:* The Place at Whitton, 1964; The Fear, 1965, 2nd edn 1973; Bring Larks and Heroes, 1967, 2nd edn 1973; Three Cheers for the Paraclete, 1968; The Survivor, 1969; A Dutiful Daughter, 1971; The Chant of Jimmie Blacksmith, 1972 (filmed 1978); Blood Red, Sister Rose, 1974; Gossip from the Forest, 1975 (TV film, 1979); The Lawgiver, 1975; Season in Purgatory, 1976; A Victim of the Aurora, 1977; Ned Kelly and the City of the Bees, 1978; Passenger, 1979; Confederates, 1979; Schindler's Ark, 1982, reissued as Schindler's List, 1994 (Booker Prize; LA Times Fiction Prize; filmed as Schindler's List, 1994); Outback, 1983; The Cut-Rate Kingdom, 1984; A Family Madness, 1985; The Playmaker, 1987 (stage adaptation, perf. Royal Court, 1988); Towards Asmara, 1989; Flying Hero Class, 1991 (also screenplay); The Place where Souls are born, 1992; Now and in Time to be, 1992; Woman of the Inner Sea, 1992 (also screenplay); Memoirs from a Young Republic, 1993; Jacko, 1993; The Utility Player (biog.), 1994; A River Town, 1995; Homebush Boy: a memoir, 1995; The Great Shame, 1998; Bettany's Book, 2000; American Scoundrel: the life of the notorious Civil War General Dan Sickles, 2002; The Office of Innocence, 2002; The Tyrant's Novel, 2003; Lincoln, 2003; The Widow and Her Hero, 2007; Searching for Schindler (memoir), 2008; The People's Train, 2009; The Daughters of Mars, 2012; Shame and the Captives, 2014; *non-fiction:* Australians: origins to eureka, 2009; Three Famines, 2010; Australians: eureka to the diggers, 2011. *Recreations:* swimming, crosswords, hiking, cross-country ski-ing. *Address:* c/o Deborah Rogers, Rogers, Coleridge & White, 20 Powis Mews, W11 1JN.

KENILOREA, Rt Hon. Sir Peter (Kauona Keninaraiso'ona), KBE 1982; PC 1979; Speaker, Solomon Islands Parliament, 2001–10; Ombudsman of the Solomon Islands, 1996–2001; Prime Minister of the Solomon Islands, 1978–81 and 1984–86; *b* Takataka, Malaita, 23 May 1943; *m* 1971, Margaret Kwanairara; two *s* two *d*. *Educ:* Univ. and Teachers' Coll., NZ (Dip. Ed.). Teacher, King George VI Secondary Sch., 1968–70. Asst Sec., Finance, 1971; Admin. Officer, Dist Admin, 1971–73; Lands Officer, 1973–74; Dep. Sec. to Cabinet and to Chief Minister, 1974–75; Dist Comr, Eastern Solomon Is, 1975–76; MLA, subseq. MP, East Are-Are, 1976–91; Chief Minister, Solomon Is, 1976–78; Leader of the Opposition, 1981–84; Dep. Prime Minister, 1987–89; Minister of Foreign Affairs, 1987–89, for Foreign Affairs and Trade Relations, 1990. Dir, Forum Fisheries Agency, 1991–94. Hon. Dr Queensland, 2008. Silver Jubilee Medal, 1977; Solomon Is Ind. Medal, 1978. *Publications:* Tell It As It Is (autobiog.), 2008; political and scientific, numerous articles.

KENILWORTH, 4th Baron *cr* 1937, of Kenilworth; **(John) Randle Siddeley;** Managing Director, Siddeley Landscapes, since 1976; Director, John Siddeley International Ltd; *b* 16 June 1954; *s* of John Tennant Davenport Siddeley (3rd Baron Kenilworth) and of Jacqueline Paulette, *d* of late Robert Gelpi; *S* father, 1981; *m* 1st, 1983, Kim (marr. diss. 1989), *o d* of Danie Serfontein, Newcastle upon Tyne; 2nd, 1991, Mrs Kiki McDonough (marr. diss. 2012); two *s*; 3rd, 2013, Catherine B. Bachand. *Educ:* Northease Manor, near Lewes, Sussex; West Dean College (studied Restoration of Antique Furniture); London College of Furniture. Worked at John Siddeley International as interior designer/draughtsman, 1975; formed own company, Siddeley Landscapes, as landscape gardener, 1976; formed Randle Siddeley Associates, as landscape designer, 1994. *Recreation:* ski-ing. *Heir:* *s* Hon. William Randle John Siddeley, *b* 24 Jan. 1992. *Address:* Randle Siddeley Associates, 3 Palmerston Court, Palmerston Way, SW8 4AJ. *Clubs:* St James's, Annabel's, Hertford Street.

KENNALLY, Katharine; Strategic Director of Communities (formerly Director, People), London Borough of Barnet, since 2013; *b* Amersham, 22 Feb. 1971; *d* of David Brown and Elizabeth Bateman; civil partnership 2009, Rachael Rothero; one *s* one *d*. *Educ:* Univ. of Leeds (BA Hons Pols and Social Policy). Exec. Manager, Integrated Commissioning, Bucks CC, 2002–04; Area Prog. Lead, Hampshire and IoW Strategic HA, 2004–06; London

Borough of Barnet: Asst Dir, 2006–08, Dep. Dir, 2008–10, Adult Social Services; Dir, Adult Social Care and Health, 2010–13. *Recreations:* cinema, walking, local history, travel. *T:* (020) 8359 4808. *E:* Kate.Kennally@barnet.gov.uk.

KENNARD, Prof. Christopher, PhD; FRCP, FMedSci; Professor of Clinical Neurology, and Head, Nuffield Department of Clinical Neurosciences (formerly Department of Clinical Neurology), University of Oxford, since 2008; Senior Kurti Fellow, Brasenose College, Oxford, since 2009; *b* 5 Jan. 1946; *s* of late Keith and Enid Kennard; *m* 1973, Cherry Fay Mortimer; two *d. Educ:* St Marylebone Grammar Sch., London; Charing Cross Hosp. Med. Sch., Univ. of London (MB BS Hons 1970; PhD 1978). FRCP 1988. Research Fellow: NIMR, 1973–76; Neuro-ophthalmology Unit, Univ. of Calif, San Francisco, 1980; Jun. hosp. appts, Charing Cross Hosp. and London Hosp., 1976–81; Consultant Neurologist, Royal London Hosp., 1981–91; Prof. of Clinical Neurology, Charing Cross and Westminster Med. Sch., 1991–97; Imperial College London: Prof. of Clinical Neurology, 1997–2008; Hd, Div. of Neurosci. and Psychol Medicine, 1997–2003; Dean, Charing Cross Campus, 2001–08; Dep. Principal, Faculty of Medicine, and Hd, Dept of Visual Neurosci., subseq. Dept of Clinical Neurosci., 2003–08; Chief of Service, 1995–98, Clinical Dir, 1998–2004, Neuroscis, Hammersmith Hosp. NHS Trust; Divl Dir, Neuroscis, Trauma and Specialist Surgery, Oxford Radcliffe Hosps NHS Trust, then Oxford Univ. Hosps NHS Trust, 2010–13. Non-exec. Mem., W London Mental Health NHS Trust, 2001–07. Chm., Cttee on Neurology, RCP, 1997–2005. Mem., MRC, 2006–08 (Mem., 2000–04, Chm., 2006–12, Neuroscience and Mental Health Bd). President: Assoc. of British Neurologists, 2003–05 (Asst Sec., 1990–92; Hon. Sec., 1992–95); European Neuro-ophthalmology Soc., 2011–15. Sec.-Gen., World Congress of Neurol., 2001. Trustee: Migraine Trust, 1991–2008; Brain and Spine Foundn, 1993–2005. Deleg., OUP, 2010–. Chm., Pubn Cttee, World Fedn of Neurology, 2010–. Ed., Jl Neurology, Neurosurgery and Psychiatry, 1997–2003. FMedSci 2001 (Mem. Council, 2004–07). *Publications:* editor, several books on clinical neurology; papers on cognitive neuroscience and neuro-ophthalmology. *Recreation:* music. *Address:* Nuffield Department of Clinical Neurosciences, Level 6, West Wing, John Radcliffe Hospital, Headley Way, Headington, Oxford OX3 9DU. *Club:* Athenæum.

KENNARD, Dr Olga, (Lady Burgen), OBE 1988; ScD; FRS 1987; Director, Cambridge Crystallographic Data Centre, 1965–97; *b* 23 March 1924; *d* of Joir and Catherina Weisz; *m* 1st, 1948, David William Kennard (marr. diss. 1961); two *d*; 2nd, 1993, Sir Arnold Burgen, *qv*. *Educ:* Newnham Coll., Cambridge (BA 1945, MA 1948); Lucy Cavendish Coll., Cambridge (ScD 1973; Fellow). Res. Asst, Cavendish Laboratory, Cambridge, 1944–48; MRC Scientific Staff: Inst. of Ophthalmology, London, 1948–51; Nat. Inst. for Med. Res., London, 1951–61; seconded to University Chemical Laboratory, Cambridge, 1961–71; MRC special appt, 1974–89. Mem. Council, Royal Soc., 1995–97. Trustee, British Mus., 2004–12. Hon. LLD Cantab, 2003. *Publications:* about 200 pubns in field of X-ray structure determination of organic and bioactive molecules and correlation between structure, chemical properties and biological activity, and technical innovations in X-ray crystallography; ed 20 standard reference books. *Recreations:* reading, walking, architecture. *Address:* Keelson, 8A Hills Avenue, Cambridge CB1 7XA. *T:* (01223) 415381.

KENNAWAY, Sir John (Lawrence), 5th Bt *cr* 1791; *b* 7 Sept. 1933; *s* of Sir John Kennaway, 4th Bt and Mary Felicity (*d* 1991), *yr d* of late Rev. Chancellor Ponsonby; *S* father, 1956; *m* 1961, Christina Veronica Urszenyi, MB, ChB (Cape Town) (marr. diss. 1976); one *s* two *d. Educ:* Harrow; Trinity Coll., Cambridge. *Heir: s* John Michael Kennaway [*b* 17 Feb. 1962; *m* 1988, Lucy Frances, *yr d* of Dr Jeremy Houlton Bradshaw-Smith; two *d*]. *Address:* Escot House, Escot Park, Ottery St Mary, Devon EX11 1LU.

KENNEDY, family name of **Marquess of Ailsa**.

KENNEDY OF CRADLEY, Baroness *cr* 2013 (Life Peer), of Cradley in the Metropolitan Borough of Dudley; **Alicia Pamela Kennedy;** *b* Birmingham, 22 March 1969; *d* of Frank and Mary Chater; *m* 2004, Roy Francis Kennedy (*see* Baron Kennedy of Southwark). *Educ:* Warwick Univ. (BSc Hons Psychol.). Labour Party: COS, 2001–03; Taskforce Leader, Field Ops, 2003–05 and 2009–10; Dep. Gen. Sec., 2006–11; Strategic Advr to Leader of Labour Party and of the Opposition, 2011–13. Member: Black Country Soc.; Child Poverty Action Gp; Amnesty Internat. Trustee, APT Action on Poverty, 2013–. MCIM. *Address:* House of Lords, SW1A 0PW. *T:* (020) 7219 6495. *E:* alicia.kennedy@parliament.uk.

KENNEDY OF THE SHAWS, Baroness *cr* 1997 (Life Peer), of Cathcart in the City of Glasgow; **Helena Ann Kennedy;** QC 1991; Principal, Mansfield College, Oxford, since 2011; *b* 12 May 1950; *d* of Joshua Patrick Kennedy and Mary Veronica (*née* Jones); partner, 1978–84, (Roger) Iain Mitchell; one *s*; *m* 1986, Dr Iain Louis Hutchison; one *s* one *d. Educ:* Holyrood Secondary Sch., Glasgow; Council of Legal Educn. Called to the Bar, Gray's Inn, 1972, Bencher, 1999; established chambers at: Garden Court, 1974; Tooks Court, 1984; Doughty St, 1990. Member: Bar Council, 1990–93; Cttee, Assoc. of Women Barristers, 1991–92; Nat. Bd, Women's Legal Defence Fund, 1989–91; Council, Howard League for Penal Reform, 1989– (Chm., commn of inquiry into violence in penal instns for children, report, 1995); CIBA Commn into Child Sexual Abuse, 1981–83; Exec. Cttee, NCCL, 1983–85; Bd, Minority Access to Legal Profession Project, Poly. of South Bank, 1984–85; British Council Law Adv. Cttee, 1995–98; Chairman: British Council, 1998–2004; Human Genetics Commn, 2000–07; Justice, 2011–; Co-Chm., IBA Inst. of Human Rights, 2012–. Chancellor, Oxford Brookes Univ., 1994–2001. Chairman: Haldane Soc., 1983–86 (Vice-Pres., 1986–); Charter '88, 1992–97; Standing Cttee for Youth Justice, NACRO, 1993–; Cttee on widening participation of FEFC, 1995–97 (report, Learning Works); Leader of inquiry into health, envmtl and safety aspects of Atomic Weapons Establishment, Aldermaston (report, 1993). Member: Adv. Council, World Bank Inst.; Internat. Task Force On Terrorism, IBA, 2001–02. Commissioner: BAFTA inquiry into future of BBC, 1990; Hamlyn Nat. Commn on Educn, 1991–93. Chm., London Internat. Fest. of Theatre, 1993–2002. Member Board: City Limits Magazine, 1982–84; Counsel Magazine, 1990–92; Hampstead Theatre, 1989–98; Chm., Arts and Business, 2006–10. Broadcaster: first female moderator, Hypotheticals (Granada) on surrogate motherhood and artificial insemination; presenter: Heart of the Matter, BBC, 1987; Putting Women in the Picture, BBC2, 1987; The Trial of Lady Chatterley's Lover, Radio 4, 1990; Raw Deal, series of progs on med. negligence, BBC2, 1990; co-producer, Women Behind Bars, Channel 4, 1990; presenter, The Maguires: forensic evidence on trial, BBC2, 1991; creator, drama series, Blind Justice, BBC, 1988; host, After Dark, Channel 4, 1988; presenter, Time Gentlemen Please, BBC Scotland, 1994; presenter, Capital Justice, Radio 4, 2012. Trustee: BM, 2004–12; Man Booker Prize, 2008–. FRSA; FCGI. Hon. Fellow, Inst. of Advanced Legal Studies, Univ. of London, 1997; Hon. FBA 2013; Hon. FRCPath; Hon. FRCPsych; Hon FRCPCH; Hon. FRSE 2014 (Royal Medal, 2011). Hon. Mem., Acad. Universelle des Cultures, Paris. Holds 37 hon. degrees. UK Woman of Europe Award, 1995. Cavaliere di Gran Croce, Order of Merit (Italy). *Publications:* (jtly) The Bar on Trial, 1978; (jtly) Child Abuse Within the Family, 1984; (jtly) Balancing Acts, 1989; Eve was Framed, 1992; Just Law, 2004; lectures; contribs on issues connected with law, civil liberties and women. *Recreations:* theatre, reading, spending time with family and friends. *Address:* House of Lords, SW1A 0PW. *T:* and *Fax:* (01708) 379482. *E:* hilary.hard@btinternet.com.

KENNEDY OF SOUTHWARK, Baron *cr* 2010 (Life Peer), of Newington in the London Borough of Southwark; **Roy Francis Kennedy;** Director of Finance, Labour Party, 2005–10; *b* Lambeth, 9 Nov. 1962; *s* of John Francis Kennedy and Frances Kennedy (*née* Hoban); *m* 2004, Alicia Chater (*see* Baroness Kennedy of Cradley). *Educ:* St Thomas the Apostle Sch., Peckham. Labour Party Official, 1990–2010: Organiser: London and SE, 1990–91; City of Coventry, 1991–93; Regl Officer, 1994–98, Regl Dir, 1998–2005, E Midlands. Election Agent to Harriet Harman, MP, 1985–87. Mem. (Lab) Southwark LBC, 1986–94 (Dep. Leader, 1990–92). An Opposition Whip, 2011–. Mem., Electoral Commn, 2010–. Chair, Council of People with Diabetes, Diabetes UK, 2012–. Governor: Morley Coll., 2013–; City of London Acad., Southwark, 2013–. Trustee, Mayor of Southwark's Common Good Trust, 2013–. Hon. Alderman, Southwark LBC, 2007. *Recreations:* reading, walking, travelling, films, theatre. *Address:* House of Lords, SW1A 0PW. *T:* (020) 7219 1772. *E:* kennedyro@parliament.uk.

KENNEDY, Maj.-Gen. Alasdair Ian Gordon, CB 1996; CBE 1991 (OBE); Secretary, Royal Automobile Club, 1998–2010 (Assistant General Secretary, 1997); *b* 6 Oct. 1945; *m* 1980, Meade Funsten; one *s* one *d. Educ:* RMCS. psc. Commnd Gordon Highlanders, 1966; Brig. 1988, Maj.-Gen. 1991. Comdr, HQ 24 Airmobile Bde, 1988–90; Dir Gen., Territorial Army, 1992–95; Sen. Army Mem., RCDS, 1995–96, retired 1997. Dir/Trustee, ABF: the Soldiers Charity. Hon. Col, Tayforth Univs OTC, 1991–97. *Address:* Tall Trees, Quarry Wood Road, Marlow, Bucks SL7 1RF.

KENNEDY, (Alastair) James; Director, International Office, University of Warwick, since 2008; *b* 6 May 1954; *s* of David Kennedy and Janet Farquahar Kennedy; *m* 1982, Kathryn Patricia Lawry; two *s* two *d. Educ:* Univ. of Exeter (BA Modern Langs); Inst. of Educn, Univ. of London (PGCE); Edinburgh Univ. (MSc Applied Linguistics). VSO, Laos, then Tanzania, 1978; British Council: Kuwait, 1982–84; Malaysia, 1984–86; London, 1986–90; Swaziland, 1990–94; Malaŵi, 1994–98; Manchester, 1998–2001; Kazakhstan, 2001–04; Regional Dir, Russia, 2004–08. Mem., Coventry Dio. Bd of Educn, 2010–. Trustee, UK Council for Internat. Student Affairs, 2011–. *Address:* University of Warwick, Coventry CV4 7AL.

KENNEDY, Alison Louise; writer; *b* 22 Oct. 1965; *d* of Robert Alan Kennedy and Edwardene Mildred Kennedy. *Educ:* Warwick Univ. (BA Hons Theatre Studies and Dramatic Arts). Community arts worker, Clydebank and Dist, 1980–89; Writer-in-Residence: Hamilton and E Kilbride Social Work Dept, 1989–91; Project Ability, 1989–95; Copenhagen Univ., 1995; Lectr (pt-time), Creative Writing Prog., St Andrews Univ., 2003–07; Associate Prof., Creative Writing Prog., Warwick Univ., 2007–. *Publications:* Night Geometry and the Garscadden Trains, 1990; Looking for the Possible Dance, 1993; Now That You're Back, 1994; So I Am Glad, 1995; The Life and Death of Colonel Blimp, 1997; Original Bliss, 1997; On Bullfighting, 1999; Everything You Need, 1999; Indelible Acts, 2002; Paradise, 2004; Day, 2007; What Becomes, 2009; The Blue Book, 2011; On Writing, 2013; All the Rage, 2014. *Recreations:* few. *Address:* c/o Antony Harwood, Antony Harwood Ltd, 103 Walton Street, Oxford OX2 6EB. *T:* (01865) 559615, *Fax:* (01865) 310660. *E:* ant@antonyharwood.com.

KENNEDY, Anthony McLeod; Associate Justice of the Supreme Court of the United States, since 1988; *b* 23 July 1936; *s* of Anthony J. Kennedy and Gladys Kennedy; *m* Mary Davis; two *s* one *d. Educ:* Stanford Univ. (AB 1958); LSE; Harvard Univ. (LLB 1961). Mem., Calif. Bar, 1962, US Tax Court Bar, 1971. Associate, Thelen Marrin Johnson & Bridges, San Francisco, 1961–63; sole practice, 1963–67; partner Evans, Jackson & Kennedy, 1967–75. Prof. of Constitutional Law, McGeorge Sch. of Law, Univ. of Pacific, 1965–88; Judge, US Court of Appeals, 9th Circuit, Sacramento, 1976–88. UN Commn on Legal Empowerment of the Poor, 2005–08. Hon. Fellow: Amer. Bar Assoc. (Medal for Dist. Service, 2007); Amer. Coll. of Trial Lawyers. Hon. Bencher, Inner Temple. *Address:* Supreme Court of the United States, 1 First Street NE, Washington, DC 20543, USA.

KENNEDY, Catherine Mary; *see* Law, C. M.

KENNEDY, Christopher Laurence Paul; QC 2010; *b* Sheffield, 10 Aug. 1966; *s* of Rt Hon. Sir Paul (Joseph Morrow) Kennedy, *qv*; *m* 1992, Rebecca McCarthy; two *s* two *d. Educ:* Ampleforth Coll.; Gonville and Caius Coll., Cambridge (BA Law 1988). Called to the Bar, Gray's Inn, 1989. *Address:* 9 St John Street, Manchester M3 4DN. *T:* (0161) 955 9000. *E:* christopher.kennedy@9sjs.com.

KENNEDY, Danny; *see* Kennedy, T. D.

KENNEDY, David, CMG 1997; Director-General, Commonwealth War Graves Commission, 1993–2000; *b* 7 Nov. 1940; *s* of Lilian Alice Kennedy; *m* 1964, Peta Jennifer Hatton; two *d. Educ:* Ryhope Robert Richardson Grammar Sch., Co. Durham. City of London Coll. Exchequer and Audit Dept, 1959–69; Commonwealth War Graves Commission: Higher Exec. Officer, 1969–71; Sen. Exec. Officer, 1971–74; Principal: Dir of Management Services, 1975–79; Dir, Outer Area, 1979–84; Senior Principal: Dir, France Area, 1984–86; Dir of Personnel, 1986–87; Dep. Dir-Gen., Admin, 1987–92; rcds 1992. Dir, Reading Golf Club, 2005–11. Mem., MENSA, 2002–; Licentiate, British Professional Photographers Assoc., 2004–. *Recreations:* golf, photography, hill-walking, travel. *Address:* March House, Blands Close, Burghfield Common, Berks RG7 3JY. *T:* (0118) 983 2941.

KENNEDY, David, CBE 2015; PhD; Director General for Economic Development, Department for International Development, since 2014; *b* Manchester, 29 Sept. 1969; *s* of Peter Kennedy and Anne Kennedy; *m* 2001, Philippa Stonebridge; two *s* one *d. Educ:* Sheffield Univ. (BA Economics/Econometrics); Univ. of Manchester (MA (Econ)); London Sch. of Economics (PhD Econs 1995). Res. Fellow, LSE, 1993–96; Consultant, Centre for Regulated Industries, 1996–97; Senior Economist: EBRD, 1997–2003; World Bank, 2003–06; Chief Exec., Cttee on Climate Change, 2008–14. *Publications:* Building a Low-carbon Economy (with Adair Turner), 2008; Meeting Carbon Budgets: the need for a step change, 2009; over 50 reports and articles on energy, infrastructure and climate change. *Recreations:* kids, classical clarinet, jazz saxophone, literature, Manchester City. *Address:* Department for International Development, 22 Whitehall, SW1A 2EG.

KENNEDY, David Patrick Leslie; Chief Executive, Northampton Borough Council, since 2007; *b* Cork, 21 Oct. 1959; *s* of Prof. Patrick Brendan Kennedy and Pamela Mary Kennedy; *m* 1998, Sarah Jacqueline Mela Sheehan. *Educ:* York Minster Song Sch.; Lord Wandsworth Coll.; Nunthorpe Grammar Sch., York; Newcastle Poly. (BA Hons Govt 1983); Univ. of Bristol (Masters Public Policy Studies 1987). Res. and Intelligence Asst, 1984–86, Res. and Analysis Officer, 1986–87, Arun DC; Performance Mgt Officer, 1987–89, Hd, Policy and Performance Services, 1989–90, City of York Council; Hd, Strategic Develt, Watford BC, 1990–96; Chief Exec., Gedling BC, 1996–2000; Dir, Envmt and Develt, 2001–03, Dir of Develt and Dep. Chief Exec., 2003–07, Barnsley MBC. Mem., SOLACE; Academician, Acad. of Urbanism. FRSA. *Recreations:* travel, photography, French wine, cricket and Rugby spectating, music, theatre. *Address:* c/o Northampton Borough Council, The Guildhall, St Giles Square, Northampton NN1 1DE. *T:* (01604) 837726. *E:* mail@dkennedy.co.uk.

KENNEDY, Her Honour Denise Margaret; a County Court Judge, Northern Ireland, 2000–12; *b* 13 April 1942; *d* of late David L. R. Halliday and Doris Halliday (*née* Molyneaux); *m* 1966, John Andrew Dunn Kennedy; two *s* one *d. Educ:* Cheltenham Ladies' Coll.; Exeter Univ. (BA Hons); Queen's Univ. of Belfast. Called to the Bar: NI, 1977; Ireland, 1985; in practice at the Bar, 1977–90; Legal Sec. to Lord Chief Justice of NI, 1990–93; Master, High Court, Supreme Court of Judicature of NI, 1993–2000; Dep. County Court Judge, 1993–2000; Dep. Clerk of Crown for NI, 1993–2000. Part-time Chm., Industrial Tribunals, NI, 1985–90; Mem., Independent Commn for Police Complaints, NI, 1988–90. Mem., Civil

Justice Reform Gp for NI, 1998–2000. *Recreations:* travel, gardening, cinema. *Address:* 2 Burnage Court, 6 Martello Park, Canford Cliffs, Poole, Dorset BH13 7BA. *Clubs:* Royal Over-Seas League; Royal North of Ireland Yacht.

KENNEDY, Sir Francis, KCMG 1986; CBE 1977 (MBE 1958); DL; HM Diplomatic Service, retired; Chancellor, University of Central Lancashire, 1995–2002; *b* 9 May 1926; *s* of late James Kennedy and Alice (*née* Bentham); *m* 1957, Anne O'Malley (*d* 2007); two *s* two *d*. *Educ:* Univs of Manchester and London. RN, 1944–46. Min. of Supply, 1951–52; HM Colonial Service, Nigeria, 1953–63; Asst Dist Officer, 1953–56; Dist Officer, 1956–59; Principal Asst Sec. to Premier E Nigeria, 1961–62; Provincial Sec., Port Harcourt, 1962–63; HM Diplomatic Service, 1964; First Sec., Commercial and Economic, Dar-es-Salaam, 1965; First Sec. and Head of Post, Kuching, 1967–69; Consul, Commercial, Istanbul, 1970–73; Consul-Gen., Atlanta, 1973–78; Counsellor later Minister Lagos, 1978–81; Ambassador to Angola, 1981–83; Dir-Gen., British Trade and Investment, and Consul-Gen., NY, 1983–86. Special Advr to Chm. and Bd, 1986–96, Dir, 1987–96, British Airways; Chairman: British Airways Regl, 1993–96 (Dir, 1993–2003); Fluor Daniel Ltd, 1989–96 (Dir, 1986–96); Director: Leslie & Godwin Ltd, 1986–91; Global Analysis Systems, 1986–88; Hambourne Development Co., 1987–94; Smith & Nephew, 1988–96; Fleming Overseas Investment Trust, 1988–96; Brunner Mond Hldgs, 1992–99; Magadi Soda Co., 1994–2001; Mem. Bd and Council, Inward, 1986–90; Advr, Brook Lowe Internat., 1999–2000. Chm., Africa Centre, 1999–2000; Mem., Nigeria British Consultative Process, 2002–04; Dir, Pan African Health Foundn, 2004–. Mem. Bd, Univ. of Central Lancs (formerly Lancashire Polytechnic), 1989–96. Governor, British Liver Foundn, 1990–93. Pres., Assoc. of Lancastrians in London, 2004–05. DL Lancs 1995. *Clubs:* Brooks's; Shaw Hill Golf and Country.
See also Rt Rev. Mgr J. Kennedy.

KENNEDY, Sir George Matthew Rae, 9th Bt *cr* 1836, of Johnstown Kennedy, Co. Dublin; *b* 9 Dec. 1993; *s* of Sir Michael Edward Kennedy, 8th Bt and of Helen Christine Jennifer (*née* Rae); *S* father, 2012, but his name does not appear on the Official Roll of the Baronetage.

KENNEDY, Heather Claire; *see* Lloyd, H. C.

KENNEDY, Prof. Hugh Nigel, PhD; FBA 2012; Professor of Arabic, School of Oriental and African Studies, University of London, since 2007; *b* Hythe, Kent, 22 Oct. 1947; *s* of David Kennedy and Janet Kennedy; *m* 1970, Hilary Wybar; one *s* two *d* (and one *d* decd). *Educ:* Pembroke Coll., Cambridge (BA 1969; PhD 1977). Lectr, 1972–97, Prof. of Middle Eastern Hist., 1997–2007, Dept of Mediaeval Hist., Univ. of St Andrews. *Publications:* The Early Abbasid Caliphate, 1981; The Prophet and the Age of the Caliphates, 600–1050, 1986 (trans. Hebrew), 2nd edn 2004; Al-Mansur and al-Mahdi: being an annotated translation of vol. xxix of the History of al-Tabari, 1990; Crusader Castles, 1994; Muslim Spain and Portugal, 1996 (trans. Portuguese); The Armies of the Caliphs, 2001; (ed) An Historical Atlas of Islam, 2nd edn 2002; Mongols, Huns and Vikings, 2003 (trans. French); The Court of the Caliphs, 2004 (trans. Arabic, Italian, Polish, Spanish); (ed jtly) Building Legitimacy, 2004; (ed) Muslim Military Architecture in Syria, 2006; The Great Arab Conquests, 2007 (trans. Arabic, Dutch, Italian, Spanish, Indonesian, Persian, Turkish); (ed) Al-Tabari, 2008. *Recreations:* visiting castles, hill walking, architectural history. *Address:* Faculty of Languages and Cultures, School of Oriental and African Studies, University of London, WC1H 0XG. *E:* hk1@soas.ac.uk.

KENNEDY, Sir Ian (Alexander), Kt 1986; Judge of the High Court of Justice, Queen's Bench Division, 1986–2000; *b* 7 Sept. 1930; *s* of late Gerald and Elizabeth Kennedy; *m* 1962, Susan Margaret, *d* of late Edward and Eileen Hatfield; three *s* one *d*. *Educ:* Wellington Coll., Berks; Pembroke Coll., Cambridge (BA). Called to the Bar, Middle Temple, 1953; Treas., 1999. Dep. Chm., IoW QS, 1971; a Recorder of the Crown Court, 1972; QC 1974. Judge, Employment Appeal Tribunal, 1990–2000. Mem., Parole Bd, 1991–94 (Vice-Chm., 1992–93). *Recreations:* theatre, walking, gardening. *Address:* c/o Messrs C. Hoare & Co., 37 Fleet Street, EC4P 4DQ.

KENNEDY, Sir Ian (McColl), Kt 2002; FBA 2002; Chairman, Independent Parliamentary Standards Authority, 2009–May 2016; Professor of Health Law, Ethics and Policy, School of Public Policy, University College London, 1997–2001, now Emeritus; *b* 14 Sept. 1941; *s* of late Robert Charles Kennedy and Dorothy Elizabeth Kennedy; two *s*. *Educ:* King Edward VI Sch., Stourbridge; University Coll. London (1st Cl. Hons LLB; Fellow, 1999); Univ. of Calif, Berkeley (LLM); LLD London. Called to the Bar, Inner Temple, 1974 (Hon. Bencher, 1996). Fulbright Fellow, 1963–65; Lectr in Law, UCL, 1965–71; Ford Foundn Fellow, Yale Univ. and Univ. of Mexico, 1966–67; Vis. Prof., Univ. of Calif, LA, 1971–72; King's College, London: Lectr in Law, 1973–78; Reader in English Law 1978–83; British Acad. Res. Fellow, 1978; Dir, Centre of Law, Medicine and Ethics, subseq. Centre of Med. Law and Ethics, 1978–93; Prof. of Med. Law and Ethics, 1983–97; Hd, Dept of Laws, 1986–89; Hd and Dean of Sch. of Law, 1989–92 and 1993–96; Pres., Centre of Med. Law and Ethics, 1993–97. FKC 1988. Vis. Prof., LSE, 2003–. Vice-Pres., Coll. of Medicine, 2010–. Chairman: Sec. of State for Health's Adv. Gp on Ethics of Xeno-transplantation, 1996–97; Minister of Agriculture's Adv. Gp on Quarantine, 1997–98; Public Inquiry into paediatric cardiac surgical services at Bristol Royal Infirmary, 1998–2001; Commn for Healthcare Audit and Inspection, 2004–09 (Shadow Chm., 2002–04); UK Panel for Res. Integrity in Health and Biomed. Sci., 2006–13; King's Fund Inquiry into quality of care in general practice, 2009–; Internat. Panel for Designation of Academic Health Sci. Centres, DoH, 2009; Assessment Panel, Paediatric Cardiac Surgery, DoH, 2010–11; Breast Surgery Review, Heart of England NHS Foundn Trust, 2013; Nat. Adv. Gp on Mortality Outliers, DoH, 2013; Member: Medicines Commn, 1984–91; GMC, 1984–93; Expert Adv. Gp on AIDS, DHSS, later Dept of Health, 1987–94; Gen. Adv. Council, BBC, 1987–91; Med. Ethics Cttee, BMA, 1990–98; Nuffield Council on Bioethics, 1991–2002 (Chm., 1998–2002); Archbishop of Canterbury's Adv. Gp on Med. Ethics, 1994–2003; Register of Ind. Mems, Defence Scientific Adv. Council, MoD, 1997–; Genetics Cttee, ABI, 1997–2001; Science in Society Cttee, Royal Soc., 2000–04; Adv. Gp on Human Remains, Natural Hist. Mus., 2006–; Adv. Cttee on Military Medicine, MoD, 2006–; Adv. Bd, NHS Staff Coll., 2011–; Expert Panel on PIP Breast Implants, DoH, 2011–12; Adv. Gp, Review of Cosmetic Surgery, DoH, 2012–13. Mem., Council, Open Section, RSM, 1978–88 (Vice-Pres., 1981–86; FRSocMed 1985); Regent, RCSE, 2006. Trustee, London Pathway - Healthcare for the Homeless, 2011–. Reith Lectr, 1980. Editor, Medical Law Review, 1993–98. Fellow, SLS, 2004. Hon. QC 2015. Hon. FRCGP 2002; Hon. FRCP 2003; Hon. FRCPCH 2004; Hon. FRCA 2004; Hon. FRCSE 2005; Hon. FIIA 2009; Hon. FRCS 2013. Hon. DSc Glasgow, 2003; Hon. DM Birmingham, 2006. *Publications:* The Unmasking of Medicine, 1981, rev. edn 1983; Treat Me Right, 1988; (with A. Grubb) Medical Law: cases and materials, 1989, 2nd edn as Medical Law: text with materials, 1994, 3rd edn 2000; (with A. Grubb) Principles of Medical Law, 1998; Appraising the Value of Innovation and Other Benefits, 2009; Getting it Right for Children and Young Persons: review of children's services in the NHS, 2010. *Recreations:* ballet, talking to my sons. *Address:* c/o Independent Parliamentary Standards Authority, 7th Floor, Portland House, Bressenden Place, SW1E 5BH. *Club:* Garrick.

KENNEDY, James; *see* Kennedy, A. J.

KENNEDY, Rt Hon. Jane (Elizabeth); PC 2003; Police and Crime Commissioner (Lab) for Merseyside, since 2012; *b* 4 May 1958; *d* of Clifford and Barbara Hodgson; *m* 1977, Robert Malcolm Kennedy (marr. diss. 1998); two *s*. *Educ:* Haughton Comprehensive Sch.; Darlington; Queen Elizabeth Sixth Form Coll.; Liverpool Univ. Child care residential worker 1979–84, Care Assistant 1984–88, Liverpool Social Services; Area Organiser, NUPE, 1988–92. MP (Lab) Liverpool Broadgreen, 1992–97, Liverpool, Wavertree, 1997–2010. An Asst Govt Whip, 1997–98; a Lord Comr of HM Treasury (Govt Whip), 1998–99; Parly Sec., LCD, 1999–2001; Minister of State: NI Office, 2001–04; DWP, 2004–05; DoH, 2005–06; Financial Sec., HM Treasury, 2007–08; Minister of State, DEFRA, 2008–09. Mem., Social Security Select Cttee, 1992–94. *Recreation:* dogs. *Address:* (office) Allerton Police Station, Rose Lane, Allerton, Liverpool L18 5ED.

KENNEDY, Jane Hope, (Mrs J. Maddison), RIBA; Partner, Purcell Architecture (formerly Purcell Miller Tritton (Architects)), since 1992 (Chairman, 2009–13); *b* 28 Feb. 1953; *d* of Thomas Brian Kennedy and Emily Hope Kennedy (*née* Bailey); *m* 1975, John Maddison; two *s*. *Educ:* Manchester Polytech. (DipArch). RIBA 1990; IHBC 1997; AABC 2000. Assistant: British Waterways Bd, 1978–80; David Jeffcoate, 1980–81; self-employed architect, 1981–86; Historic Bldgs Architect, Norwich CC, 1986–88; architect, 1988–90, Associate, 1990–92, Purcell Miller Tritton. Major projects include: repairs to North and South Fronts and re-presentation of interiors, Stowe House, Bucks, 1999–; repairs, 1997–2012, Processional Way, 2001, Ely Cathedral; restoration of Ballyfin, Central Eire, 2002–09; re-presentation of Kew Palace, 2004–. Surveyor to Fabric of Ely Cathedral, 1994–; Architect to Newcastle Cathedral, 2006–; refurbishment of Blue Boar Quad, Christ Church, Oxford, 2007–09; Architect to Foundn, Christ Church, Oxford, 2008–. Comr, English Heritage, 2006–14. Mem. Heritage Adv. Panel, Canal and River Trust, 2012–. Trustee, Historic Royal Palaces, 2015–. Sec., Cathedral Architects' Assoc., 2000–06. FRSA 1994. *Publications:* articles in conservation jls. *Recreations:* old buildings, walking, re-learning the violin, boating. *Address:* Purcell Architecture, 15 Bermondsey Square, SE1 3UN. *T:* (020) 7397 7171. *E:* jane.kennedy@purcelluk.com.

KENNEDY, Joanna Alicia Gore, OBE 1995; FREng, FICE; Director, 1996–2013, and Global Programme and Project Management Leader, 2010–13, Ove Arup and Partners; *b* 22 July 1950; *d* of late Captain G. A. G. Ormsby, DSO, DSC, RN and Susan Ormsby; *m* 1979, Richard Paul Kennedy, *qv*; two *s*. *Educ:* Queen Anne's School, Caversham; Lady Margaret Hall, Oxford (Scholar, 1969; BA 1st cl. Hons Eng. Sci. 1972; MA 1976). MICE 1979, FICE 1992; FREng (FEng 1997). Ove Arup and Partners, consulting engineers: Design Engineer, 1972; Sen. Engr, 1979; Arup Associates, 1987; Arup Project Management, 1990; Associate, 1992; Associate Dir, 1994; Leader, Arup Project Management Europe, 2006–10. Member: Engineering Council, 1984–86 and 1987–90; Council, ICE, 1984–87; Adv. Council, RNEC Manadon, 1988–94; Engrg, later Engrg and Technol. Bd, SERC, 1990–94; EPSRC, 2002–06 (Mem., Tech. Opportunities Panel, 1994–97); Dir, Engrg and Technol. Bd, 2002–05. Mem. Bd, PLA, 2000–09 (Vice-Chm., 2008–09); Dir, Port of London Properties Ltd, 2001–05. Comr, Royal Commn for Exhibn of 1851, 2003–12. Trustee: Nat. Mus. of Science and Industry, 1992–2002; Ove Arup Partnership, 1998–2005; Cumberland Lodge, 2001–11, 2013–; Ove Arup Foundn, 2010–. Member, Board: ERA Foundn, 2014–; NPG, 2015–. Member, Council: Univ. of Southampton, 1996–99; RCA, 2001–; Governor: Downe House Sch., 1985–89; Channing Sch., 1992–2002; Mem., Smeatonian Soc. of Civil Engineers, 2005–. Patron, Women into Sci. and Engrg, 2008–. Major, Engineer and Logistic Staff Corps, RE (V), 2004–14. Hon. DSc Salford, 1994. FRSA 1986. Woman of the Year, Inspire Awards for Built Environment, 2007; RCUK Woman of Outstanding Achievement Award, 2008; CBI/Real Business First Women Award for Engrg, 2013. *Address:* 9 Luscombe Road, Poole, Dorset BH14 8ST.

KENNEDY, Rt Rev. Mgr John; Parish Priest, Holy Family, Southport, 1991; *b* 31 Dec. 1930; *s* of James Kennedy and Alice Kennedy (*née* Bentham). *Educ:* St Joseph's College, Upholland; Gregorian University, Rome (STL); Oxford University (MPhil). Curate: St John's, Wigan, 1956–63; St Austin's, St Helens, 1963–65; St Edmund's, Liverpool, 1965–68; Lectr in Theology, Christ's College, Liverpool, 1968–84 (Head of Dept, 1976–84); Rector, Ven. English Coll., Rome, 1984–91; Asst Lectr in Theol., Gregorian Univ., Rome, 1984–91. *Recreations:* golf, squash.
See also Sir Francis Kennedy.

KENNEDY, Rev. Joseph, DPhil; Vicar of St Saviour's, Oxton, since 2011; *b* Edinburgh, 1 Jan. 1969; *s* of late Andrew Kennedy and of Margaret Anne Kennedy (*née* Lawson); *m* 2001, Emily Elizabeth Lyons Connell; one *s*. *Educ:* Edinburgh Univ. (BSc 1991; BD 1994); Moray House Inst. of Educn (PGCE 1997); St Stephen's House, Oxford; St Hugh's Coll., Oxford (MSt 2000); Keble Coll., Oxford (Gosden Scholar; DPhil 2006). Ordained deacon, 2002, priest, 2003; Assistant Curate: Mortimer, 2002–03; Abingdon, 2003–05; Dean of Chapel, Chaplain and Fellow, Selwyn Coll., Cambridge, 2005–08; Chaplain, Newnham Coll., Cambridge, 2005–08; Principal, Coll. of Resurrection, Mirfield, 2008–11. Hon. Canon, Wakefield Cathedral, 2010–11. *Recreations:* reading, travel, baking my own bread. *Address:* The Vicarage, 7 Willow Lea, Prenton, Wirral CH43 2GQ. *T:* (0151) 652 2402. *E:* revd.j.kennedy@gmail.com.

KENNEDY, Lulu, MBE 2012; Founder and Director, Fashion East, since 2000; Creative Director, Lulu & Co., since 2010; *b* Newcastle upon Tyne, 28 Dec. 1969; *d* of John Paul Kennedy and Dr Ruth Kennedy. *Educ:* Middlesex Univ. (BA). Events Manager, Old Truman Brewery, 1996–2000. Ed.-at-Large, Love mag., 2012–. *Address:* Fashion East, Old Truman Brewery, 91 Brick Lane, E1 6QL. *T:* (020) 7770 6150. *E:* info@fashioneast.co.uk.

KENNEDY, Dr Malcolm William, CBE 2000; FRSE; FREng, FIET; Chairman, PB Power (incorporating Merz and McLellan), 1999–2002 (Executive Chairman, Merz and McLellan, 1995–98); *b* 13 March 1935; *s* of William and Lily Kennedy; *m* 1962, Patricia Ann Forster; (one *d* decd). *Educ:* Durham Univ. (BSc 1961); Univ. of Newcastle upon Tyne (PhD 1964). FIET (FIEE 1974); FREng (FEng 1985); FRSE 2002. Apprentice, C. A. Parsons, 1951–56; Merz and McLellan, 1964–2002: Power Systems Design Engr, 1964; Head, Electrical Div., 1976; Sen. Partner, 1988–91; Chm. and Man. Dir, 1991–95. Mem. Electricity Panel, 1993–98, Water and Telecommunications Panel, 1998–2001, Monopolies and Mergers Commn. Non-exec. Director: Port of Tyne Authority, 1994–2001; New and Renewable Energy Centre, 2003–12; Renewable Energy Generation Ltd, 2007–. Advr, London Power Associates Ltd, 2011–. Vice Pres., Nat. Energy Action, 2007– (Chm., 2001–07). Pres., IEE, 1999–2000 (Henry Nimmo Premium, 1961; Chm., Power Div., 1986–87; Vice-Pres., 1994–96; Dep. Pres., 1996–99). Methodist local preacher. *Publications:* papers on electricity industry, UK and overseas. *Recreations:* cricket, railways. *Address:* 39 Princess Mary Court, Jesmond, Newcastle upon Tyne NE2 3BG. *Club:* National.

KENNEDY, His Honour Michael Denis; QC 1979; a Circuit Judge, 1984–2004; *b* 29 April 1937; *s* of Denis George and Clementina Catherine (*née* MacGregor); *m* 1964, Elizabeth June Curtiss; two *s* two *d*. *Educ:* Downside School; Gonville and Caius College, Cambridge (open Schol., Mod. Langs; MA). 15/19 King's Royal Hussars, 1955–57. Called to the Bar, Inner Temple, 1961; a Recorder, 1979–84; Designated Civil Judge for Sussex, 1999–2004. *Address:* Iford Court, Iford, Lewes, E Sussex BN7 3EU. *T:* (01273) 476432, *Fax:* (01273) 486092.

KENNEDY, Nigel Paul; solo concert violinist; Artistic Director, Polish Chamber Orchestra, 2002–08; founder, Orchestra of Life, 2010; *b* 28 Dec. 1956; *s* of John Kennedy and Scylla Stoner; one *s*; *m* Agnieszka Chowaniec. *Educ:* Yehudi Menuhin School; Juilliard School of Performing Arts, NY. ARCM. Début at Festival Hall with Philharmonia Orch., 1977; regular appearances with London and major orchestras throughout the world, 1978–; Berlin début with Berlin Philharmonic, 1980; Henry Wood Promenade début, 1981; New York début with BBC SO, 1987; tour of Hong Kong and Australia, with Hallé Orch., 1981; foreign tours, 1978–: India, Japan, S Korea, Turkey, USA, Europe, Scandinavia; many appearances as jazz violinist with Stéphane Grappelli, incl. Edinburgh Fest., 1974 and Carnegie Hall, 1976; many

TV and radio appearances, incl. Vivaldi's Four Seasons with ECO (Golden Rose of Montreux, 1990), and two documentaries. Pop, jazz and classical recordings, incl. Vivaldi's Four Seasons (best-selling album of a complete classical work; No 1 in UK Classical Chart for over one year (Guinness Book of Records, 1990)); Best Classical Record, British Record Industry Awards: for Elgar Violin Concerto, 1985; for Beethoven Violin Concerto, 1991; Best Recording, Gramophone mag., for Elgar Violin Concerto, 1985. Variety Club Showbusiness Personality of the Year, 1991. Hon. DLitt Bath, 1991. *Publications:* Always Playing, 1991. *Recreations:* football (watching and playing), cricket. *Address:* Terri Robson Associates, 63–64 Leinster Square, W2 4PS.

KENNEDY, Rt Hon. Sir Paul (Joseph Morrow), Kt 1983; PC 1992; a Lord Justice of Appeal, 1992–2005; Interception of Communications Commissioner, 2006–12; President, Court of Appeal of Gibraltar, 2011–15 (Member, since 2006); *b* 12 June 1935; *o s* of late Dr J. M. Kennedy, Sheffield; *m* 1965, Virginia, twin *d* of Baron Devlin, FBA and of Madeleine, *yr d* of Sir Bernard Oppenheimer, 1st Bt; two *s* two *d*. *Educ:* Ampleforth Coll.; Gonville and Caius Coll., Cambridge (MA, LLB; Hon. Fellow, 1998). Called to Bar, Gray's Inn, 1960, Bencher, 1982 (Vice Treas., 2001; Treas., 2002); a Recorder, 1972–83; QC 1973; Judge, High Court of Justice, QBD, 1983–92; Presiding Judge, N Eastern Circuit, 1985–89; Vice-Pres., QBD, High Ct of Justice, 1997–2002. Mem., Judicial Studies Bd, 1993–96 (Chm., Criminal Cttee, 1993–96). Hon. LLD Sheffield, 2000.

See also C. L. P. Kennedy.

KENNEDY, Prof. Peter Graham Edward, CBE 2010; MD, PhD, DSc; FRCP, FRCPath, FMedSci; FRSE; Burton Professor of Neurology, University of Glasgow, since 1987; Consultant Neurologist, Institute of Neurological Sciences, Southern General Hospital, Glasgow, since 1986; *b* 28 March 1951; *s* of Philip Kennedy and Trudy Sylvia Kennedy (*née* Summer); *m* 1983, Catherine Ann King; one *s* one *d*. *Educ:* University Coll. Sch.; University College London and UCH Med. Sch. (MB BS, MD, PhD, DSc); Univ. of Glasgow (MLitt, MPhil). FRCP 1988; FRCPath 1997. FRSE 1992. Med. Registrar, UCH and Whittington Hosps, 1977–78; Hon. Res. Asst, MRC Neuroimmunology Project, UCL, 1978–80; Registrar and Res. Fellow, Univ. of Glasgow, 1981; Registrar then Sen. Registrar, Nat. Hosp. for Nervous Diseases, 1982–84; Asst Prof. of Neurology, Johns Hopkins Univ. Hosp., USA, 1985; New Blood Sen. Lectr in Neurology and Virology, 1986–87, Hd, Div. of Clin. Neuroscis, 2004–10, Univ. of Glasgow. Chm., Scientist Panel on Infections incl. AIDS, European Fedn of Neurol Socs, 2000–07. Vis. Fellow in Medicine, Jesus Coll., Cambridge, 1992; Fogarty Internat. Scholar-in-Residence, NIH, 1993–94 (Fogarty Medal, 1994). Lectures: Fleming, 1990, Livingstone, 2004, RCPSG; Stevens, Univ. of Colorado, 1994; Brain Bursary, KCH, London, 1999; Richard T. Johnson Prize, Liverpool Univ., 2007; Dist. Lecture Series, Columbia Univ., NY, 2013. Founder FMedSci 1998; FRAS 2004; Fellow, Amer. Neurol Assoc., 1989 (Corresp. Mem., 1989). Member: Assoc. of British Neurologists, 1986; Assoc. of Physicians of GB and Ire., 1990. Pres., Internat. Soc. for Neurovirology, 2004–10 (Sec., 2000–03; Pres.-elect, 2003). Member Editorial Board: Jl of Neuroimmunology, 1988–; Jl of Neurovirology, 1994– (Sen. Associate Editor, 1996–); Jl of Neurological Scis, 1997–2013; Brain, 1998–2004; Neurocritical Care, 2004–; Scottish Med. Jl, 2004–. BUPA Med. Foundn Doctor of the Year Res. Award, 1990; Linacre Medal and Lectr, RCP, 1991; T. S. Srinivasan Gold Medal and Endowment Lectr, 1993; Dist. Service Award, 2010, Audrey Steinman Gilden Lectureship Award, 2012, Internat. Soc. for Neurovirol.; Sir James Black Medal (Sen. Prize in Life Scis), RSE, 2014. *Publications:* (with R. T. Johnson) Infections of the Nervous System, 1987; (with L. E. Davis) Infectious Diseases of the Nervous System, 2000; The Fatal Sleep, 2007; Reversal of David (novel), 2014; numerous papers on neurology, neurobiology, neurovirology and sleeping sickness. *Recreations:* philosophy, tennis, music, astronomy, walking in the country, reading, writing. *Address:* Glasgow University Department of Neurology, Institute of Neurological Sciences, Southern General Hospital, Glasgow G51 4TF. *T:* (0141) 201 2500, *Fax:* (0141) 201 2993. *E:* peter.kennedy@glasgow.ac.uk.

KENNEDY, Richard Paul, MA; Head Master of Highgate School, 1989–2006; *b* 17 Feb. 1949; *e s* of David Clifton Kennedy and Evelyn Mary Hall (*née* Tindale); *m* 1979, Joanna Alicia Gore Ormsby (*see* J. A. G. Kennedy); two *s*. *Educ:* Charterhouse; New College, Oxford (BA Maths and Phil. 1970; MA 1977). Assistant Master, Shrewsbury Sch., 1971–77, Westminster Sch., 1977–84; Dep. Headmaster, Bishop's Stortford Coll., 1984–89 (Acting Headmaster 1989). Headmasters' Conference: Mem., Sports Cttee, 1992–95; Mem., Cttee, 1995–96; Chm., London Div., 1996; Mem., Finance Steering Gp, 2001–04. Mem. Council, ISCO, 1995–2000. Governor: The Hall Sch., Hampstead, 1989–2006; Wycombe Abbey Sch., 1992–2002. GB internat. athlete (sprints), 1973–76. Mem., Acad. of St Martin-in-the-Fields Chorus, 1977–2000. *Recreations:* choral music, walking in Dorset. *Address:* Luscombe Hall, 9 Luscombe Road, Poole, Dorset BH14 8ST. *T:* (01202) 466810.

KENNEDY, Rosemary; *see* Foot, R. J.

KENNEDY, Seema Louise Ghiassi; MP (C) South Ribble, since 2015; *b* Blackburn, 1974; *m* 2003, Paul Kennedy; three *s*. *Educ:* Westholme Sch., Blackburn; Pembroke Coll., Cambridge (BA Oriental Studies 1997); Université Sorbonne Nouvelle (Licence 1996). Solicitor, Slaughter and May, 2000–03; Associate Solicitor, Bevan Brittan, 2003–06; Dir, Tustin Develts, 2006–. *Recreations:* walking, opera, family. *Address:* House of Commons, SW1A 0AA. *T:* (020) 7219 4412. *E:* seema.kennedy.mp@parliament.uk.

KENNEDY, Thomas Daniel, (Danny); Member (UU) Newry and Armagh, Northern Ireland Assembly, since 1998; *b* 6 July 1959; *s* of John Trevor Kennedy and Mary Ida Kennedy (*née* Black); *m* 1988, Karen Susan McCrum; two *s* one *d*. *Educ:* Bessbrook Primary Sch.; Newry High Sch. With BTNI, 1978–98. Mem., UU Party, 1974–; Mem., Newry and Mourne DC, 1985–2010 (Chm., 1994–95). Northern Ireland Assembly: Minister for Employment and Learning, 2010–11; Minister for Regl Develt, 2011–15; Chairman: Educn Cttee, 1999–2002; Cttee Office of First Minister and Dep. First Minister, 2007–10; Mem., Exec. Rev. Cttee, 2007–10; Dep. Leader, UU Assembly Party, 2005–10. Mem., NI Tourist Bd, 1996–98. Contested: (UU) Newry and Armagh, 1997, 2005, 2015; (UCUNF), 2010. Clerk of Kirk Session and Sabbath Sch. Superintendent, Bessbrook Presbyterian Church. *Recreations:* family, Church activities, sport (purely spectating), reading. *Address:* Parliament Buildings, Stormont, Belfast BT4 3XX. *T:* (028) 9052 1336; Ulster Unionist Advice Centre, 47 Main Street, Markethill, Co. Armagh BT60 1PH. *T:* (028) 3755 2831; 80 Market Street, Tandragee, Co. Armagh BT62 2BP. *T:* (028) 3884 1166.

KENNEDY, Thomas John, LVO 2004; Foreign and Commonwealth Office, 2011–13; *b* 3 Feb. 1957; *m* 1985, Clare Marie Ritchie; one *s*. Entered FCO, 1992; Second Sec. (Aid/ Information), Buenos Aires, 1994–97; First Sec., FCO, 1997–2002; Consul Gen., Bordeaux, 2002–06; Ambassador to Costa Rica and Nicaragua, 2006–11.

KENNEDY, William Andrew; His Honour Judge William Kennedy; a Circuit Judge, since 2001; Deputy Resident Judge, Snaresbrook Crown Court, since 2004; *b* 13 Feb. 1948; *s* of late Sidney Herbert and Kathleen Blanche Kennedy; *m* 1st, 1974, Alice Steen Wilkie (*d* 1987); 2nd, 1988, Lindsey Jane Sheridan; one *s* one *d*. *Educ:* Buckhurst Hill County High Sch.; College of Law, Lancaster Gate. Articled Clerk, Trotter Chapman & Whisker, Epping, Essex, 1966–72; admitted Solicitor, 1972; Partner 1972–75, Jt Sen. Partner 1975–91, Trotter Chapman & Whisker, later Whiskers; Notary Public, 1981; Metropolitan Stipendiary Magistrate, then Dist Judge (Magistrates' Courts), 1991–2001; Chm., Youth Courts, 1992–2001; an Asst Recorder, 1995–99; a Recorder, 1999–2001; part-time (Plate) Judge Advocate, 1995–2001. Judicial Mem., London Probation Bd, 2005–09; Judicial Dir, HM Court Service, 2010–12. Pres., W Essex Law Soc., 1983–84. *Recreations:* golf, gentle domestic pursuits. *Address:* c/o Snaresbrook Crown Court, Snaresbrook, E11 1QW. *Club:* Chigwell Golf.

KENNERLEY, Prof. (James) Anthony (Machell), CEng, CMath; Independent Commissioner, Stansted Airport, 2005–10, and Heathrow Airport, 2009–12, British Airports Authority; *b* 24 Oct. 1933; *s* of late William James Kennerley and Vida May (*née* Machell); *m* 1978, Dorothy Mary (*née* Simpson); one *s* one *d* (twins). *Educ:* Universities of Manchester (BSc; Silver Medallist, 1955) and London (MSc 1967; IMechE James Clayton Fellow). AFIMA, AFRAeS; MIMechE. Fourth Engr, Blue Funnel Line, Alfred Holt, 1954; Engineer, A. V. Roe, Manchester, 1955–58; Aerodynamicist, Pratt & Whitney, Montreal, Canada, 1958–59; Jet Pilot, RCAF, 1959–62; Asst Professor of Mathematics, Univ. of New Brunswick, Canada, 1962–67; Director of Graduate Studies, Manchester Business Sch., 1967–69; Associate Professor of Business Studies, Columbia Univ., New York, 1969–70; Director, Executive Programme, London Business Sch., 1970–73; Prof. of Business Admin, and Dir, Strathclyde Business Sch., 1973–83; Dir, InterMatrix Ltd, Management Consultants, 1984–92; Vis. Prof. of Management, City Univ., 1984–93; Prof. of Health Care Mgt, Univ. of Surrey, 1993–97. Complaints Comr, Channel Tunnel Rail Link, 1997–2007; Infrastructure Inf. Referee, Crossrail, 2002–09. Chm., London Region, Inland Waterways Assoc., 2010–11. Chm., Council for Professions Supplementary to Medicine, 1990–96. Tutor to sen. management courses in the public sector, Sunningdale, 1985–2000. Chairman: W Surrey and NE Hants, then NW Surrey, HA, 1986–95; W Surrey Health Commn, 1995–96. Chairman: Management Res. Gp, Scotland, 1981–82; Scottish Milk Marketing Scheme Arbitration Panel, 1981–83. Member: South of Scotland Electricity Bd, 1977–84; Management Studies Bd, CNAA, 1977–84; BIM Educn Cttee, 1982–92; Competition (formerly Monopolies and Mergers) Commn, 1992–2001; Adv. Bd, Meta Generics, Cambridge, 1992–95; Council, Inst. of Mgt, 1995–98. Chm., Conf. of Univ. Management Schs, 1981–83; Director: Business Graduates Assoc., 1983–86; First Step Housing Co., Waverley BC, 1990–94. Arbitrator, ACAS, 1976–2011. Mem., Trans-Turkey Highway World Bank Mission, 1982–83. Founder Mem., Bridgegate Trust, Glasgow, 1982–85. *Publications:* Guide to Business Schools, 1985; Arbitration: cases in industrial relations, 1994; articles, papers on business studies, on Public Sector management, and on applied mathematics. *Recreations:* flying, travelling. *Address:* 15 Stone Lodge Lane, Ipswich, Suffolk IP2 9PF. *T:* (01473) 603127. *Clubs:* Reform, Caledonian.

KENNET, 3rd Baron *cr* 1935, of the Dene, co. Wilts; **William Aldus Thoby Young;** writer and entrepreneur; Co-owner, Kennet Creative Ltd, 2009–11; *b* London, 24 May 1957; *o s* of 2nd Baron Kennet, (author, Wayland Young), and Elizabeth Ann Young (*née* Adams); *S* father, 2009; *m* 1987, Hon. Josephine Mary, *yr d* of 2nd Baron Keyes; two *s* one *d*. *Educ:* Marlborough Coll.; Dartington Hall Sch.; Sussex Univ. *Recreations:* music, art, travel. *Heir:* *s* Hon. Archibald Wayland Keyes Young, *b* 7 June 1992. *E:* thoby.kennet@gmail.com.

KENNETT, Prof. Brian Leslie Norman, PhD, ScD; FRS 2005; FAA; Professor of Seismology, Research School of Earth Sciences, Australian National University, since 1984 (Director, 2006–09); *b* 7 May 1948; *s* of Norman and Audrey Kennett; *m* 1971, Heather Margaret Duncan; one *s* one *d*. *Educ:* Dulwich Coll.; Emmanuel Coll., Cambridge (BA 1969; PhD 1973; ScD 1992). Fellow, Emmanuel Coll., Cambridge, 1972–84; Lectr, Univ. of Cambridge, 1976–84; Pro Vice Chancellor, 1994–97, Chm. Bd, Inst. of Advanced Studies, 1994–97 and 2001–03, ANU. Editor: Geophysical Jl Internat., 1979–99; Physics of the Earth and Planetary Interiors, 2003–06. Fellow, Amer. Geophysical Union, 1988; FAA 1994; Associate, RAS, 1996. Humboldt Foundn Res. Award, 2004; Jaeger Medal, 2005, Flinders Medal (Physical Sci.), 2011, Australian Acad. of Sci.; Murchison Medal, Geol Soc., 2006; Gutenberg Medal, Eur. Geoscis Union, 2007; Gold Medal for Geophysics, Royal Astronomical Soc., 2008. Centenary Medal (Australia), 2003. *Publications:* Seismic Wave Propagation in Stratified Media, 1983; IASPEI Seismological Tables, 1991; The Seismic Wavefield, Vol. I 2001, Vol. II 2002; (with H. P. Bunge) Geophysical Continua, 2008; Planning and Managing Scientific Research, 2014; numerous scientific contribs. *Recreations:* walking, photography, painting. *Address:* Research School of Earth Sciences, Australian National University, Canberra, ACT 2601, Australia. *T:* (2) 61254621, *Fax:* (2) 62572737. *E:* Brian.Kennett@anu.edu.au.

KENNETT, Hon. Jeffrey (Gibb), AC 2005; Chairman: Beyondblue, the National Depression Initiative, since 2000; Primary Opinion (formerly Jumbuck Entertainment) Ltd, since 2004; Open Windows Australia Pty Ltd, since 2005; CT Management Group Pty Ltd, since 2011; Amtek Corporation Pty Ltd, since 2012; Ledified Lighting Corp. Pty Ltd, since 2014 The Torch, since 2015; *b* 2 March 1948; *m* 1972, Felicity; three *s* one *d*. 2 Lt, Royal Australian Regt, 1968–70. Government of Victoria: MLA (L) Burwood, 1976–2000; Minister for Aboriginal Affairs, for Immigration and Ethnic Affairs, and for Housing, 1981–82; Leader of the Opposition, 1982–89, 1991–92; Premier of Victoria, 1992–99; Minister for Multicultural Affairs, 1992–99; Minister for the Arts, 1996–99. Dir, Equity Trustees Ltd, 2008–. Chairman: Australian Seniors Finance Ltd, 2004–08; Bd of Mgt, PFD Food Services Pty Ltd, 2006–. Mem. Adv. Bd, Singapore Tourism, 2000–06. Pres., Hawthorn Football Club, 2005–11. Chm., Enterprize Ship Trust, 2005–09.

KENNETT, Ronald John, FRAeS; Director, Royal Aeronautical Society, 1988–98; *b* 25 March 1935; *s* of William John and Phyllis Gertrude Kennett; *m* 1957, Sylvia Barstow; one *s* three *d*. *Educ:* Bradford Technical College (HNC Electrical Engrg 1956). Lucas Aerospace: joined 1956; Chief Engineer, 1978–86; Quality Assurance Manager, 1986–88. Non-exec. Dir, Beds and Herts Ambulance and Paramedic Service NHS Trust, 2000–06. Hero of Bradford College, 2008. *Recreations:* village life, reading, photography, music, pug fan. *Address:* Greenbanks, Toms Hill Road, Aldbury, Herts HP23 5SA. *Club:* Royal Air Force (Hon. Mem.).

KENNEY, Anthony, FRCS; FRCOG; Consultant Obstetrician and Gynaecologist: St Thomas' Hospital, 1980–2002; in independent sector, 1980–2007; *b* 17 Jan. 1942; *s* of late Eric Alfred Allen Kenney and Doris Winifred Kenney; *m* 1st, 1966, Elizabeth Dain Fielding (marr. diss.); two *s*; 2nd, 1973, Patricia Clare Newbery (*d* 2007); two *s* one *d*; 3rd, 2013, Jennifer Phillips. *Educ:* Brentwood School; Gonville and Caius College, Cambridge (MA 1967); London Hosp. Med. Coll. MB BChir 1966; FRCS 1970; MRCOG 1972, FRCOG 1987. House appts, London Hosp., Queen Charlotte's Hosp. and Chelsea Hosp. for Women, 1966–72; Registrar and Sen. Registrar, Westminster and Kingston Hosps, 1972–79. Teacher of Obstetric Life Saving Skills in Africa and Asia, 2008–12. Past Examiner: in Obstetrics and Gynaecology, RCOG; Univs of London, Liverpool and Cambridge. Mem., Higher Trng Cttee, RCOG, 1997–2000. Mus. Curator, RCOG, 2006–10. Co-founder and Trustee, Tommy's The Baby Charity (formerly Tommy's Campaign), 1989–2009; Trustee, Quit, 1995–. Chm. of Trustees, Med. Soc. of London, 2010– (Treas., 2002–07; Pres., 2007–08; Trans Ed., 2011–). *Publications:* contribs to med. jls. *Recreations:* canal cruising, foreign travel. *Address:* Field End, Greenways, Ovingdean, Brighton, E Sussex BN2 7BA. *T:* (01273) 307360, 07703 162277. *Club:* Royal Society of Medicine.

KENNEY, Prof. Edward John, FBA 1968; Kennedy Professor of Latin, University of Cambridge, 1974–82; Fellow of Peterhouse, Cambridge, 1953–91; *b* 29 Feb. 1924; *s* of George Kenney and Emmie Carlina Elfrida Schwenke; *m* 1955, Gwyneth Anne, *d* of late Prof. Henry Albert Harris. *Educ:* Christ's Hospital; Trinity Coll., Cambridge. BA 1949, MA 1953. Served War of 1939–45: Royal Signals, UK and India, 1943–46; commissioned 1944, Lieut 1945. Porson Schol., 1948; Craven Schol., 1949; Craven Student, 1949; Chancellor's Medallist, 1950. Asst Lectr, Univ. of Leeds, 1951–52; University of Cambridge: Research

Fellow, Trinity Coll., 1952–53; Asst Lectr, 1955–60, Lectr, 1960–70; Reader in Latin Literature and Textual Criticism, 1970–74; Peterhouse: Director of Studies in Classics, 1953–74; Librarian, 1953–82, Perne Librarian, 1987–91; Tutor, 1956–62; Senior Tutor, 1962–65; Domestic Bursar, 1987–88. James C. Loeb Fellow in Classical Philology, Harvard Univ., 1967–68; Sather Prof. of Classical Literature, Univ. of California, Berkeley, 1968; Carl Newell Jackson Lectr, Harvard Univ., 1980. President: Jt Assoc. of Classical Teachers, 1977–79; Classical Assoc., 1982–83; Horatian Soc., 2002–07. For. Mem., Royal Netherlands Acad. of Arts and Scis, 1976. Treasurer and Chm., Council of Almoners, Christ's Hosp., 1984–86. Jt Editor, Classical Qly, 1959–65; Jt Gen. Ed., Cambridge Greek and Latin Classics, 1966–. *Publications:* P. Ouidi Nasonis Amores etc (ed), 1961, 2nd edn 1995; (with Mrs P. E. Easterling) Ovidiana Graeca (ed), 1965; (with W. V. Clausen, F. R. D. Goodyear, J. A. Richmond) Appendix Vergiliana (ed), 1966; Lucretius, De Rerum Natura III (ed), 1971, 2nd edn 2014; The Classical Text, 1974 (trans. Italian 1995); (with W. V. Clausen) Latin Literature (ed and contrib.) (Cambridge History of Classical Literature II), 1982; The Ploughman's Lunch (*Moretum*), 1984; introd. and notes to Ovid, Metamorphoses, trans. A. D. Melville, 1986; Ovid, The Love Poems, 1990; Apuleius, Cupid & Psyche (ed), 1990; introd. and notes to Ovid, Sorrows of an Exile (*Tristia*), trans. A. D. Melville, 1992; Ovid, Heroides XVI–XXI (ed), 1996; (trans., with introd. and notes) Apuleius, The Golden Ass, 1998, 2nd edn 2004, Folio Soc. edn 2015; (ed) Ovidio, Metamorfosi, vol. IV (Libri VII–IX), 2011; articles and reviews in classical jls. *Recreations:* discursive reading, listening to the wireless. *Address:* 4 Belvoir Terrace, Trumpington Road, Cambridge CB2 7AA.

KENNEY, Rt Rev. William, CP; Auxiliary Bishop of Birmingham, (RC), since 2006; Titular Bishop of Midica, since 1987; *b* 7 May 1946; *s* of Leonard Kenney and Christine (*née* Farrell). *Educ:* Heythrop Coll., Oxon (STL 1969); Univ. of Gothenburg (Fil. Kand. 1973). Entered novitiate of Passionist Congregation, Broadway, Worcs, 1962; ordained priest, 1969; Researcher, Inst. for Sociology of Religion, Stockholm, 1973–77; Institute for Scientific Study of Religions, University of Gothenburg: Lectr, 1979–82; Dean of Studies, 1980–82; Lectr and Dean of Studies, 1984–87; Gen. Counsellor, Passionist Congregation, Rome, 1982–84; Superior, Passionists, Sweden, 1985–87; ordained bishop, 1987; Aux. Bishop of Stockholm, 1987–2006. Chair: Caritas Sweden, 1987–2006; Commn for Financing Religious Bodies, Swedish Govt, 1990–98 (Mem., 1988–98); Caritas Europe, 1991–99; Justice & Peace Commn, Stockholm, 1999–2006; Gothenburg Process, 2000–13 (Internat. Chair, 2007–13); Eur. Justice and Peace Network, 2011–14; Co-Chair, Lutheran RC Dialogue, 2013–; Vice-Chair, Caritas Internationalis, 1991–99 (Mem., Legal Affairs Commn, 1999–2011); Member: Bd for Religious Affairs, Swedish Govt, 1998–2006; Commn of the Bishops' Confs of the EC, Brussels, 2000–; Passionists Internat., NY, 2006–10; Internat. Adv. Bd, Life and Peace Inst., Uppsala, Sweden, 2011– (Mem. Governing Bd, 2008–11). Spokesperson on European questions, Cath. Bishops' Conf. of England and Wales, 2006–. Hon. PhD Gothenburg, 1988. KC★HS 2003. *Publications:* various articles on European, social and religious affairs. *Recreations:* listening to music, walking, reading (professionally but also history, biography and politics). *Address:* St Hugh's House, 27 Hensington Road, Woodstock, Oxon OX20 1JH. *T:* (01993) 812234. *E:* wk@sthughs.plus.com.

KENNICUTT, Prof. Robert Charles, Jr, PhD; FRS 2011; FRAS; Plumian Professor of Astronomy and Experimental Philosophy, since 2005, and Head, School of the Physical Sciences, since 2012, University of Cambridge (Director, Institute of Astronomy, 2008–11); Fellow, Churchill College, Cambridge, since 2006; *b* 4 Sept. 1951; *s* of Robert Charles Kennicutt and Joyce Ann Kennicutt; one *d*. *Educ:* Rensselaer Polytechnic Inst. (BS Phys 1973); Univ. of Washington (MS 1976, PhD Astronomy 1978). Carnegie Postdoctoral Fellow, Hale Observatories, 1978–80; Asst, then Associate Prof., Dept of Astronomy, Univ. of Minnesota, 1980–88; Associate, then Prof. and Astronomer, Steward Observatory, Univ. of Arizona, 1988–. Beatrice M. Tinsley Centennial Prof., Univ. of Texas, 1994; Adriaan Blaauw Prof., Univ. of Groningen, 2001. Member: AAS, 1979– (Vice-Pres., 1998–2001); IAU, 1981–; NAS, 2006–. Fellow, American Acad. of Arts and Scis, 2001. FRAS 2006. Dannie Heineman Prize in Astrophysics, AIP/AAS, 2007; (jtly) Cosmology Prize, Gruber Foundn, 2009. Editor-in-Chief, Astrophysical Jl, 1999–2006. *Publications:* Galaxies: interactions and induced star formation, 1998; Hubble's Science Legacy in Future Optical/Ultraviolet Astronomy from Space, 2003; papers in astronomical jls. *Recreations:* rock and mineral collecting, lapidary arts. *Address:* Institute of Astronomy, University of Cambridge, Madingley Road, Cambridge CB3 0HA. *T:* (01223) 765844, *Fax:* (01223) 339910. *E:* robk@ast.cam.ac.uk; School Office, 17 Mill Lane, Cambridge CB2 1RX.

KENNON, Andrew Rowland; Clerk of Committees, House of Commons, since 2011; *b* 15 July 1955; *y s* of Vice-Adm. Sir James Edward Campbell Kennon, KCB, CBE and Anne Kennon; *m* 1983, Mary Gamblin; one *s* two *d*. *Educ:* Stowe Sch.; Jesus Coll., Cambridge (exhibitioner; BA Law 1977). Called to the Bar, Gray's Inn, 1979. House of Commons: Asst Clerk, 1977; various procedural, cttee and internat. posts, 1977–87; Clerk of Select Committees: on Trade and Ind., 1987–92; on Procedure, 1992–95; on Defence, 1995–97; on Home Affairs, 1999–2002; seconded to Cabinet Office to advise on parly and constitutional reform, 1997–99; Hd, Scrutiny Unit, 2002–04; Prin. Clerk of Select Cttees, 2004–06; Sec., H of C Commn, 2006–08; Clerk of Jls, 2008–09; Principal Clerk, Table Office, 2009–11. *Publications:* (with R. Blackburn) Griffith and Ryle, Parliament: functions, practice and procedures, 2nd edn 2002. *Recreation:* sailing. *Address:* Committee Office, House of Commons, SW1A 0AA.

KENNY, Sir Anthony (John Patrick), Kt 1992; FBA 1974; Pro-Vice-Chancellor, Oxford University, 1984–2001 (Pro-Vice-Chancellor for Development, 1999–2001); Warden, Rhodes House, 1989–99; Professorial Fellow, St John's College, Oxford, 1989–99, now Emeritus Fellow; Master of Balliol College, Oxford, 1978–89; *b* Liverpool, 16 March 1931; *s* of John Kenny and Margaret Jones; *m* 1966, Nancy Caroline, *d* of Henry T. Gayley, Jr, Swarthmore, Pa; two *s*. *Educ:* Gregorian Univ., Rome (STL); St Benet's Hall, Oxford; DPhil 1961, DLitt 1980. Ordained priest, Rome, 1955; Curate in Liverpool, 1959–63; returned to lay state, 1963. Asst Lectr, Univ. of Liverpool, 1961–63; University of Oxford: Fellow, 1964–78, Sen. Tutor, 1971–72 and 1976–78, Balliol Coll.; Lectr in Philosophy, Exeter and Trinity Colls, 1963–64; University Lectr, 1965–78; Wilde Lectr in Natural and Comparative Religion, 1969–72; Speaker's Lectureship in Biblical Studies, 1980–83; Mem., Hebdomadal Council, 1981–93; Vice-Chm., Libraries Bd, 1985–88; Curator, Bodleian Library, 1985–88; Deleg., and Mem., Finance Cttee, OUP, 1986–93. Jt Gifford Lectr, Univ. of Edinburgh, 1972–73; Stanton Lectr, Univ. of Cambridge, 1980–83; Bampton Lectr, Columbia Univ., 1983. Visiting Professor: Univs of Chicago, Washington, Michigan, Minnesota and Cornell, Stanford and Rockefeller Univs. Chairman: British Liby Bd, 1993–96 (Mem., 1991–96); Soc. for Protection of Science and Learning, 1989–93; British Nat. Corpus Adv. Bd, 1990–95; British Irish Assoc., 1990–94; Bd, Warburg Inst., Univ. of London, 1996–2000. Pres., British Acad., 1989–93 (Mem. Council, 1985–88; Vice-Pres., 1986–88). MAE 1991; Member: Amer. Phil Soc., 1993; Norwegian Acad. of Scis, 1993; Amer. Acad. of Arts and Scis, 2003. Hon. Fellow, Harris Manchester Coll., Oxford, 1996. Hon. DLitt: Bristol, 1982; Liverpool, 1988; Glasgow, 1990; TCD, 1992; Hull, 1993; Sheffield, Warwick, 1995; Hon. DHumLitt: Denison Univ., Ohio, 1986; Lafayette Univ., Penn, 1990; Hon. DCL: Oxon, 1987; QUB, 1994; Hon. DLit London, 2002; Hon. DD Liverpool Hope, 2010. Hon. Bencher, Lincoln's Inn, 1999. Aquinas Medal, Amer. Catholic Philos. Assoc., 2006. Editor, The Oxford Magazine, 1972–73. *Publications:* Action, Emotion and Will, 1963, 2nd edn 2003; Responsa Alumnorum of English College, Rome, 2 vols, 1963; Descartes, 1968; The Five Ways, 1969; Wittgenstein, 1973, 2nd edn 2005; The Anatomy of the Soul, 1974; Will, Freedom and Power, 1975; The Aristotelian Ethics, 1978; Freewill and Responsibility, 1978; Aristotle's Theory of the Will, 1979; The God of the Philosophers, 1979; Aquinas, 1980; The Computation of Style, 1982; Faith and Reason, 1983; Thomas More, 1983; The Legacy of Wittgenstein, 1984; A Path from Rome (autobiog.), 1985; Wyclif, 1985; The Logic of Deterrence, 1985; The Ivory Tower, 1985; A Stylometric Study of the New Testament, 1986; The Road to Hillsborough, 1987; Reason and Religion, 1987; The Heritage of Wisdom, 1987; God and Two Poets, 1988; The Metaphysics of Mind, 1989; The Oxford Diaries of Arthur Hugh Clough, 1990; Mountains: an anthology, 1991; Aristotle on the Perfect Life, 1992; What is Faith?, 1992; Aquinas on Mind, 1993; (ed) Oxford Illustrated History of Western Philosophy, 1994; Frege, 1995; A Life in Oxford (autobiog.), 1997; A Brief History of Western Philosophy, 1998, 2nd illus. edn 2006; Essays on the Aristotelian Tradition, 2001; (ed) The History of the Rhodes Trust, 2001; Aquinas on Being, 2002; The Unknown God, 2004; A New History of Western Philosophy, vol. 1, 2004, vol. 2, 2005, vol. 3, 2006, vol. 4, 2007, single vol. edn 2010; Arthur Hugh Clough: the life of a poet, 2005; What I Believe, 2006; (with C. Kenny) Life, Liberty and the Pursuit of Utility, 2006; (with R. Kenny) Can Oxford be Improved?, 2007; From Empedocles to Wittgenstein, 2008; (with S. Perry) Balliol Poetry, 2011; (ed and trans.) Aristotle, the Eudemian Ethics, 2011; (ed and trans.) Aristotle, Poetics, 2013; (ed) Arthur Hugh Clough, Mari Magno, Dipsychus and other poems, 2014; (ed and trans. with Jonathan Barnes) Aristotle, the Ethical Works, 2014; Christianity in Review, 2015. *Address:* The Old Bakery, 1A Larkins Lane, Oxford OX3 9DW. *Clubs:* Athenæum, Oxford and Cambridge.

KENNY, Bernadette Joan; Chief Executive, Church of England Pensions Board, since 2011; Chair, Yarrow Housing, since 2011; *b* 10 Dec. 1956; *d* of James Francis Kenny and Mary Lourdes Kenny (*née* Carroll); *m* 1981, Jonathan Appleby; three *s* (incl. twins) (and twin *s* decd). *Educ:* Chichester High Sch. for Girls; Univ. of Manchester (LLB Hons 1978). DipLCM 2014. Called to the Bar, Lincoln's Inn, 1979; LCD, 1980–91 and 1993–95; Court Service: Dep. Circuit Administrator, 1991–93; Dir of Personnel and Training, 1995–98; Dir of Operational Policy, 1999–2002; Change Dir, LCD, subseq. DCA, 2002–05; Chief Exec., Royal Parks Agency, 2005; HM Revenue and Customs: Dir of Distributed Processes, 2005; Actg Dir Gen., 2005–06; Dir Gen., Customer Contact and Processing, subseq. Personal Taxes, 2006–10; Comr, 2008–10. *Recreations:* twins (Mem., Twins and Multiple Births Assoc.), gardening, ski-ing, music. *Address:* Church House, Great Smith Street, SW1P 3AZ. *Club:* Ski Club of GB.

KENNY, Gen. Sir Brian (Leslie Graham), GCB 1991 (KCB 1985); CBE 1979; Bath King of Arms, 1999–2009; *b* 18 June 1934; *s* of late Brig. James Wolfenden Kenny, CBE, and of Aileen Anne Georgina Kenny (*née* Swan); *m* 1958, Diana Catherine Jane Mathew; one *s* (and one *s* decd). *Educ:* Canford School. Commissioned into 4th Hussars (later Queen's Royal Irish Hussars), 1954; served BAOR, Aden, Malaya and Borneo; Pilot's course, 1961; Comd 16 Recce Flt QRIH; psc 1965; MA/VCGS, MoD, 1966–68; Instructor, Staff Coll., 1971–73; CO QRIH, BAOR and UN Cyprus, 1974–76; Col GS 4 Armd Div., 1977–78; Comd 12 Armd Bde (Task Force D), 1979–80; RCDS 1981; Comdr 1st Armoured Div., 1982–83; Dir, Army Staff Duties, MoD, 1983–85; Comdr 1st (British) Corps, BAOR, 1985–87; Comdr, Northern Army Gp, and C-in-C, BAOR, 1987–89; Dep. SACEUR, 1990–93. Gov., Royal Hosp., Chelsea, 1993–99. Col QRIH, 1985–93; Colonel Commandant: RAVC, 1983–95; RAC, 1988–93. Chm., Army Benevolent Fund, 1993–99. Non-exec. Dir, Dorset Ambulance Trust, 2000–07; Pres., Dorset and Somerset Air Ambulance Trust, 2009–12 (Trustee, 2000–08). Governor, Canford Sch., 1983–2006. *Recreations:* ski-ing, golf, shooting, racing. *Address:* c/o Lloyds Bank, Camberley, Surrey GU15 3SE. *Clubs:* MCC, I Zingari, Free Foresters.

KENNY, Enda; Member (FG) of the Dáil (TD) for Mayo, since 1975; Taoiseach (Prime Minister) of Ireland, since 2011; Leader, Fine Gael, since 2002; *b* Islandeady, Castlebar, Co. Mayo, 24 April 1951; *s* of Henry Kenny; *m* 1992, Fionnuala O'Kelly; two *s* one *d*. *Educ:* St Patrick's Coll. of Educn; University Coll., Galway. Primary sch. teacher. Mem., Mayo CC, 1975–95. Minister of State, Dept for Educn and Labour, 1986–87; Minister for Tourism and Trade, 1994–97; Leader of Opposition, 2002–11. *Address:* Department of the Taoiseach, Government Buildings, Upper Merrion Street, Dublin 2, Ireland.

KENNY, Mary Cecilia, (Mrs R. West); journalist and writer; *b* 4 April 1944; *d* of Patrick and Ita Kenny; *m* 1974, Richard West (*d* 2015); two *s*. *Educ:* Loreto Coll., Dublin; Birkbeck Coll., Univ. of London (BA Hons French Studies 1997). Journalist and broadcaster, 1966–: feature writer and European Corresp., London Evening Standard, 1966–69; Woman's Ed., Irish Press, Dublin, 1969–71; Features Ed. and writer, Evening Standard, 1971–73; freelance journalist, subseq. Columnist, Sunday Telegraph, 1976–96; TV Critic, Daily Mail, 1981–86; contributor: Daily Mail, The Tablet, Daily Telegraph, The Times, Guardian, Spectator, Listener, New Statesman, TLS, The Oldie, Irish Independent (also columnist), Sunday Independent, Irish Times, Studies (Dublin), Catholic Herald, Irish Catholic, and others; *TV and radio* including: panellist, Late, Late Show, RTE; Question Time, BBC; Any Questions, Radio 4; The Panel, RTE; presenter, and contrib. to, various documentaries in UK and Ireland. Master of The Keys, Catholic Writers' Guild (formerly Guild of Catholic Writers), 2010–12. *Publications:* Abortion: the whole story, 1986; A Mood for Love (short stories), 1989; Goodbye to Catholic Ireland: a social history, 1997; Death by Heroin, Recovery by Hope, 2001; Germany Calling: a personal biography of William Joyce, Lord Haw-Haw, 2003; Allegiance: Michael Collins and Winston Churchill 1921–1922, 2005; Crown and Shamrock: love and hate between Ireland and the British monarchy, 2009; A State of Emergency: a drama set in neutral Eire 1940, 2010; Something of Myself… and others (memoir), 2013; Conversation before a Hanging: William Joyce's last days, 2016. *Recreations:* cinema, theatre, reading in French, summer festivals in Ireland. *Address:* 84 West Street, Deal, Kent CT14 6AZ. *E:* mary@mary-kenny.com. *W:* www.mary-kenny.com, www.twitter.com/MaryKenny4; 15 Kildare Street, Dublin 2, Ireland. *Club:* Reform.

KENNY, Prof. Neil Francis, DPhil; FBA 2011; Professor of French, University of Oxford, since 2014; Senior Research Fellow, All Souls College, Oxford, since 2012; *b* Tolworth, 5 Nov. 1960; *s* of Alf and Maureen Kenny; *m* 2003, Dr Leslie Topp; one *s* one *d*. *Educ:* Gonville and Caius Coll., Cambridge (BA Modern and Medieval Langs 1981); St John's Coll., Oxford (DPhil French 1987). English Asst, Coll. Calvin, Geneva, 1981–82; Frances A. Yates Fellow, Warburg Inst., Univ. of London, 1985–87; Temp. Lectr in French, Birkbeck, Univ. of London, 1987; Stipendiary Lectr in French, New Coll., Oxford, 1987–89; Lectr in French, Queen Mary Coll., later Queen Mary and Westfield Coll., Univ. of London, 1989–94; University of Cambridge: Lectr in French, 1994–2000; Sen. Lectr in French, 2000–05; Reader in Early Modern French Literature and Thought, 2005–12; Fellow in French, Churchill Coll., Cambridge, 1994–2005. *Publications:* The Palace of Secrets: Béroalde de Vérville and Renaissance conceptions of knowledge, 1991; Curiosity in Early Modern Europe: word histories, 1998; The Uses of Curiosity in Early Modern France and Germany, 2004; An Introduction to Sixteenth-Century French Literature and Thought: other times, other places, 2008. *Recreations:* family, music, sport. *Address:* All Souls College, Oxford OX1 4AL.

KENNY, Siobhan Mary, (Mrs P. Pearson); Chief Executive Officer, RadioCentre, since 2014; *b* 15 Oct. 1959; *d* of late Patrick Kenny and of Della Kenny (*née* Raftery); *m* 1996, Pat Pearson. *Educ:* St Michael's Convent Grammar Sch., Finchley, London; Univ. of Manchester (BA English, French, German 1982); Birkbeck Coll., London (MA French 1988). Press Officer: TV-am, 1986–89; Govt Inf. Service, 1989–93; Attachée de Presse, Council of Europe, Strasbourg, 1993–94; Press Officer, then Strategy Advr, No 10 Downing Street, 1994–99; Dir of Communications, National Magazine Co., 1999–2002; Dir of Strategic

Communication, DCMS, 2002–05; Vice Pres., Communications, Europe, Middle E and Africa, Walt Disney TV, 2005–07; Gp Communications Dir, HarperCollins UK and Internat., 2007–13. *Recreations:* sailing, ski-ing, football, film. *T:* (020) 8307 4507. *E:* siobhan.kenny@radiocentre.org, siobhanmarykenny@gmail.com.

KENNY, Stephen Charles Wilfrid; QC 2006; *b* 12 Aug. 1964; *s* of late Charles John Michael Kenny and Gillian Beatrice Maud Kenny (*née* Shelford); *m* 1998, Anna Aida, *d* of Dr the Rt Hon. Sir (John) Vincent Cable, *qv*; one *s*. *Educ:* Farleigh House Sch.; Ampleforth Coll. (scholar); Worcester Coll., Oxford (Exhibnr; MA; BCL 1st Cl. Hons). Called to the Bar, Inner Temple, 1987; in practice as a barrister, 1987–, specialising in commercial law. *Recreations:* family and friends, music, literature, early medieval history, ski-ing, supporting hopefully Fulham FC. *Address:* 7 King's Bench Walk, Temple, EC4Y 7DS. *T:* (020) 7910 8300, *Fax:* (020) 7910 8400. *E:* skenny@7kbw.co.uk.

KENNY, Yvonne Denise, AM 1989; international opera singer; *b* Australia, 25 Nov. 1950; *d* of late Arthur Raymond Kenny and of Doris Jean (*née* Campbell). *Educ:* Sydney Univ. (BSc). Operatic début in Donizetti's Rosmonda d'Inghilterra, Queen Elizabeth Hall, 1975; joined Royal Opera House, Covent Garden as a principal soprano, 1976; roles include: Pamina in Die Zauberflöte; Ilia in Idomeneo; Marzelline in Fidelio; Susanna, and Countess, in Le Nozze di Figaro; Adina in L'Elisir d'Amore; Liu in Turandot; Aspasia in Mitridate; Alcina; Semele; Cleopatra in Giulio Cesare; Donna Anna in Don Giovanni; Fairy Queen; Countess in Capriccio; Die Feldmarshallin in Der Rosenkavalier; Alice Ford in Falstaff; international appearances include: ENO; Glyndebourne; Berlin Staatsoper; Vienna State Opera; La Scala, Milan; La Fenice, Venice; Paris; Munich; Zurich; Australian Opera, Sydney, etc; regular concert appearances with major orchs and conductors in Europe and USA. Has made numerous recordings. Hon. DMus Sydney, 2000. *Recreations:* swimming, walking, gardening.

KENSINGTON, 8th Baron *cr* 1776 (Ire.); **Hugh Ivor Edwardes;** Baron Kensington (UK) 1886; *b* 24 Nov. 1933; *s* of Hon. Hugh Owen Edwardes (*d* 1937) (2nd *s* of 6th Baron) and of Angela Dorothea (who *m* 1951, Lt Comdr John Hamilton, RN retd), *d* of late Lt-Col Eustace Shearman, 10th Hussars; *S* uncle, 1981; *m* 1961, Juliet Elizabeth Massy Anderson; two *s* one *d*. *Educ:* Eton. *Heir: s* Hon. William Owen Alexander Edwardes [*b* 21 July 1964; *m* 1991, Marie Hélène Anne Véronique, *d* of Jean-Alain Lalouette; one *s* two *d*]. *Address:* Friar Tuck, PO Box 549, Mooi River, Natal 3300, Republic of S Africa. *Clubs:* Boodle's; Victoria Country (Pietermaritzburg).

KENSINGTON, Area Bishop of, since 2015; **Rt Rev. Dr Graham Stuart Tomlin;** *b* Bristol, 1 Aug. 1958; *s* of Ivor Howard Tomlin and Anne Lilian Tomlin; *m* 1982, Janet Wynn; two *c*. *Educ:* Bristol Grammar Sch.; Lincoln Coll., Oxford (BA English 1980); Wycliffe Hall, Oxford (BA Theol. 1985); Exeter Univ. (PhD Theol. 1996). Ordained deacon, 1986, priest, 1987; Curate, St Leonard's, Exeter, 1986–89; part-time Chaplain, Jesus Coll., Oxford, 1989–94; Wycliffe Hall, Oxford: part-time, then full-time Tutor, 1989–98; Vice Principal, 1998–2005; Principal: St Paul's Theol Centre, 2005–15; St Mellitus Coll., 2007–15 (Pres., 2015–). *Publications:* The Power of the Cross, 1999; Walking in His Steps, 2001; The Provocative Church, 2002, 4th edn 2014; Luther and his World, 2002; The Responsive Church, 2006; Spiritual Fitness, 2007; The Seven Deadly Sins, 2007; The Prodigal Spirit, 2011; Philippians and Colossians: reformation commentary on scripture, 2013; Looking Through the Cross, 2013; The Widening Circle, 2014. *Recreations:* football, cricket, Rugby, guitar. *Address:* Dial House, Riverside, Twickenham TW1 3DT. *T:* (020) 7932 1180. *E:* bishop.kensington@london.anglican.org. *Club:* MCC.

KENSWOOD, 2nd Baron *cr* 1951; **John Michael Howard Whitfield;** *b* 6 April 1930; *o s* of 1st Baron Kenswood; *S* father, 1963; *m* 1951, Deirdre Anna Louise, *d* of Colin Malcolm Methven, Errol, Perthshire; four *s* one *d*. *Educ:* Trinity Coll. Sch., Ontario; Harrow; Grenoble Univ.; Emmanuel Coll., Cambridge (BA). FRSA. *Heir: s* Hon. Michael Christopher Whitfield, *b* 3 July 1955.

KENT, Alan Peter; QC 2009; *b* Billericay, 7 Aug. 1963; *s* of Peter Kent and late Linda Kent; *m* 1989, Barbara, *d* of John and Frances Mulhall; two *s* two *d*. *Educ:* Warden Park Comprehensive Sch., Cuckfield; Poly. of N London (LLB Hons). Called to the Bar, Inner Temple, 1986; in practice as barrister specialising in criminal law. Member: Criminal Bar Assoc.; Cttee, South Eastern Circuit, 2009–; Chm., Sussex Bar Mess, 2009–. *Recreations:* my family, football, doing the ironing, football hooliganism. *Address:* Carmelite Chambers, 9 Carmelite Street, EC4Y 0DR.

KENT, Brian Hamilton, FREng, FIET, FIMechE; Chairman: Wellington Holdings plc, 1993–2005; Hallmark Industries Ltd, 2006–14; President, Institution of Mechanical Engineers, 1994–95; *b* 29 Sept. 1931; *s* of Clarence Kent and Edyth (*née* Mitchell); *m* 1954, Margery Foulds; one *s* two *d*. *Educ:* Hyde Grammar Sch.; Salford Coll. of Technology (BSc Eng). FREng (FEng 1995). Instructor Lieut, RN Short Service Commn, 1954–57. Mather & Platt Ltd: graduate apprentice, 1952–54; Asst Technical Manager, Electrical Gp, then Gen. Manager, Mather & Platt Contracting Ltd, 1957–65; Morgan Crucible Co. Ltd, London, 1965–69; Man. Dir and Chief Exec., Alfa-Laval Ltd, 1969–78; Dir, Staveley Industries Ltd, 1978–80; Staveley Industries plc: Chief Exec., 1980–87; Chm., 1987–93; non-exec. Chm., 1993–94. Chm., British Printing Co. Ltd, 1996–98; Dep. Chm., Industrial Acoustics Corp. Ltd, 2000–12. Senator, Engrg Council, 1996–99. Chm., Management Cttee, Industry and Parlt Trust, 1988–90. Gov., Kingston Univ., 1996–2003 (Chm., Finance Bd). FInstD. Hon. FIMechE 2006. Hon. DSc Salford, 1995. *Recreation:* sailing. *Club:* Royal Automobile.

KENT, Bruce; campaigner for peace and disarmament; Hon. Vice President, Campaign for Nuclear Disarmament, since 1985 (General Secretary, 1980–85; Vice-Chairman, 1985–87; Chairman, 1987–90); *b* 22 June 1929; *s* of Kenneth Kent and Rosemary Kent (*née* Marion); *m* 1988, Valerie Flessati. *Educ:* Lower Canada Coll., Montreal; Stonyhurst Coll.; Brasenose Coll., Univ. of Oxford (BCL 1956; Hon. Fellow 2013). Ordination, Westminster, 1958; Curate, Kensington, North and South, 1958–63; Sec., Archbishop's House, Westminster, 1963–64; Chm., Diocesan Schools Commn, 1964–66; Catholic Chaplain to Univ. of London, 1966–74; Chaplain, Pax Christi, 1974–77; Parish Priest, Somers Town, NW1, 1977–80; retired from active Ministry, Feb. 1987. President: Internat. Peace Bureau, 1985–92; Nat. Peace Council, 1999–2000; Vice President: Pax Christi, 1986–; CND, 1989–; Movement for the Abolition of War, 2002–. Mem., Nat. Exec., UNA, 1993–97. Contested (Lab) Oxford West and Abingdon, 1992. Hon. LLD Manchester, 1987; DUniv Middx, 2002. *Publications:* Undiscovered Ends (autobiog.), 1992; essays and pamphlets on disarmament, Christians and peace. *Recreations:* friends, walking, peace/war history. *Address:* 11 Venetia Road, N4 1EJ.

KENT, Georgina; Her Honour Judge Georgina Kent; a Circuit Judge, since 2009; *b* Malaysia, 25 June 1966; *d* of Derek Kent and Beatrice Kent; *m* 1st, 1992, Dominic Kern Chambers, *qv* (marr. diss. 2009); one *s* two *d*; 2nd, 2013, Martin Hale Scott; one step *d*. *Educ:* King's Coll. London (LLB Hons). Called to the Bar, Gray's Inn, 1989, Bencher, 2014; Recorder, 2002–09. Gov., Kingswood House Sch., 2012–. *Address:* Crown Court, 6–8 Penrhyn Road, Kingston-upon-Thames, Surrey KT1 2BB. *T:* (020) 8240 2500.

KENT, Mark Andrew Geoffrey; HM Diplomatic Service; Ambassador to the Kingdom of Thailand, 2012–15; *b* Spilsby, 14 Jan. 1966; *s* of Geoffrey Kent and Patricia June Kent; *m* 1991, Martine Delogne; one *s* one *d*. *Educ:* Horncastle Grammar Sch.; Lincoln Coll., Oxford (BA Law 1986); Univ. Libre de Bruxelles (Licence Spéciale en Droit Européen 1987); Open Univ. (Postgrad. Cert. in Business Admin 2007). Joined HM Diplomatic Service, 1987; Nr East and N Africa Dept, FCO, 1987–89; Third Sec., later Second Sec., Brasilia, 1989–93; Second, later First Sec., UK Perm. Repn to EU, 1993–98; First Sec., News Dept, FCO, 1998–2000; First Sec., later Counsellor (Commercial) and Consul-Gen., Mexico City, 2000–04; on secondment to SHAPE, 2004–05; Hd, Migration Gp, FCO, 2005–07; Ambassador to Socialist Republic of Vietnam, 2007–10; language and other trng, London and Thailand, 2010–12. FInstLM 2011. *Recreations:* running, football (especially Arsenal), Michael Caine films, foreign languages. *Address:* c/o Foreign and Commonwealth Office, King Charles Street, SW1A 2AH. *E:* mark.kent@fco.gov.uk.

KENT, Michael Harcourt; QC 1996; a Recorder, since 2000; a Deputy High Court Judge, since 2010; *b* 5 March 1952; *s* of late Captain Barrie Harcourt Kent, RN and of Margaret Harcourt Kent; *m* 1977, Sarah Ann Ling; two *s*. *Educ:* Nautical Coll., Pangbourne; Sussex Univ. (BA Hons). Called to the Bar, Middle Temple, 1975, Bencher, 2012; SE Circuit; Supplementary Panel, Junior Counsel to the Crown, Common Law, 1988–96; Asst Recorder, 1999–2000. Member: London Common Law and Commercial Bar Assoc. (Chm., 2011–13); Admin. Law Bar Assoc.; TecBar; London Ct of Internat. Arbitration. *Recreation:* sailing. *Address:* Crown Office Chambers, 2 Crown Office Row, Temple, EC4Y 7HJ. *T:* (020) 7797 8100.

KENT, Nicolas; *see* Kent, R. N.

KENT, Paul Welberry; JP; DSc; FRSC; Student Emeritus of Christ Church, Oxford; *b* Doncaster, 19 April 1923; *s* of Thomas William Kent and Marion (*née* Cox); *m* 1952, Rosemary Elizabeth Boutflower, *y d* of Major C. H. B. Shepherd, MC; three *s* one *d*. *Educ:* Doncaster Grammar Sch.; Birmingham Univ. (BSc 1944, PhD 1947); Jesus Coll., Oxford (MA 1951, DPhil 1953, DSc 1966). Asst Lectr, subseq. ICI Fellow, Birmingham Univ., 1946–50; Vis. Fellow, Princeton Univ., 1948–49; Univ. Demonstrator in Biochem., Oxford, 1950–72; Lectr, subseq. Student, Tutor and Dr Lees Reader in Chem., 1955–72, Censor of Degrees, 2000–10, Christ Church, Oxford; Durham University: Master of Van Mildert Coll. and Dir, Glycoprotein Res. Unit, 1972–82; Mem. of Senate, 1972–82; Mem. of Council, 1976–80. Research Assoc., Harvard, 1967; Vis. Prof., Windsor Univ., Ont, 1971, 1980. Bodleian Orator, 1959. Mem., Oxford City Council, 1964–72; Governor: Oxford Coll. of Technology, subseq. Oxford Polytechnic, 1964–72, 1983–89 (Vice-Chm. 1966–69, Chm. 1969–70); Oxford Polytechnic Higher Educn Corp., 1988–92 (Dep. Chm., 1988–92); Oxford Brookes Univ., 1992–97 (Vice-Chm., 1992–94). Member: Cttee, Biochemical Soc., 1963–67; Chemical Council, 1965–70; Res. Adv. Cttee, Cystic Fibrosis Res. Trust, 1977–82; Commn on Religious Educn in School. Sec., Foster and Wills Scholarships Bd, 1960–72; Pres., Soc. for Maintenance of the Faith, 1974–99 (Vice-Pres., 2000–); Governor, Pusey House, 1983–2000 (Vice-Pres., 2003–); Chm., Patrons Consultative Gp, 1994–2012. JP Oxford, 1972. Hon. Fellow, Canterbury Coll., Ont, 1976. Hon. LHD Drury, 1973; Hon. DSc CNAA, 1991. Rolleston Prize, 1952; Medal of Société de Chemie Biologique, 1969; Verdienstkreuz (Germany), 1970. *Publications:* Biochemistry of Amino-sugars, 1955; (ed) Membrane-Mediated Information, Vols I and II, 1972; (ed) International Aspects of the Provision of Medical Care, 1976; (ed) New Approaches to Genetics, 1978; (ed with W. B. Fisher) Resources, Environment and the Future, 1982; Some Scientists in the life of Christ Church, Oxford, 2001; (ed with A. Chapman) Robert Hooke and The English Renaissance, 2005; articles in sci. and other jls. *Recreations:* music, travel. *Address:* 18 Arnolds Way, Cumnor Hill, Oxford OX2 9JB. *T:* (01865) 862087. *Club:* Athenæum.

KENT, Peter Humphreys, CMG 2001; President, European Intelligent Building Group, 2002–09; private sector government trade adviser; Associate, Harvey's of Edinburgh, since 2010; *b* 21 April 1937; *s* of Cosmo Weatherley Kent and Beatrice Humphreys Tordoff; *m* 1964, Noel Mary Curwen; one *s*. *Educ:* Denehurst Prep. Sch.; Royal Grammar Sch., Guildford. Commnd Queen's Royal Regt, 1956; seconded RWAFF, 1956; served: 5 Bn Queen's Own Nigeria Regt, 1956–57; 1st Bn Queen's Royal Regt, TA, 1957–60. Union Internat. Co. Ltd, London and Nigeria, 1958–61; I. H. S. Lotinga Ltd, Nigeria, 1961–64; Newton Chambers & Co. Ltd, 1964–73 (Man. Dir, Izal Overseas Ltd, and Dir, Izal Ltd); Mktg Dir, Europe, Sterling Winthrop Ltd, 1973–76; Arthur Guinness & Sons, 1975–78 (Internat. Mktg Dir, Jackel Ltd); Man. Dir, Steinerco (UK) Ltd, 1978–83; Dir, More O'Ferrall Plc, 1983–97. Chairman: Starlite Media LLC, NY, 2000–02; Starlite Media Internat. Ltd, UK, 2000–02; non-exec. Dir, GruppeM Investments plc, 2007–09. Dir, Taiwan Trade Centre (TAITRA (formerly CETRA)) Ltd, 1993–2009; Chm., Taiwan Advrs Gp, 1997–2006; Vice-Chm., Taiwan Britain Business Council, 1998–; Mem., Singapore Britain Business Council, 2003–12. Asia Pacific Advr, DTI/BTI/UK Trade & Investment (formerly Trade Partners UK), 1985–2012. Mem., CBI Internat. Cttee, 1998–2000. Dir, 1993–2003, Mem. Council, 2005–, Internat. Shakespeare Globe Centre; Dir, Shakespeare's Globe Centre (USA) Ltd, 2007–14. Trustee, 1992–2005, Vice-Chm., 2004–05, Colchester and Dist Visual Arts Trust; Mem., Noel Coward Soc., 2009–. Freeman, City of London, 1980; Liveryman, Co. of Launderers, 1980–. Member: RSAA, 2001; European-Atlantic Gp, 1993. FInstD 1968; Fellow, Inst. of Export, 1967. Friend of the Foreign Service Medal (Taiwan), 2000; Economic Medal (Taiwan), 2003. *Recreations:* film and theatre, travelling, socialising. *Address:* Cherry Ground, Holbrook, Suffolk IP9 2PS. *T:* and *Fax:* (01473) 328203; 202 Marlyn Lodge, Portsoken Street, E1 8RB. *E:* peterhkent1@btinternet.com. *Clubs:* Naval and Military; Jockey Club Rooms (Newmarket).

KENT, (Robert) Nicolas; director and producer, theatre, television and radio; Artistic Director, Tricycle Theatre, 1984–2012; *b* London, 26 Jan. 1945; *s* of Henry and Mary Kent. *Educ:* Stowe Sch.; St Catharine's Coll., Cambridge (BA Hons English 1967). ABC TV trainee dir, Liverpool Playhouse, 1967–68; Artistic Dir, Watermill Th., 1970; Associate Dir, Traverse Th., Edinburgh, 1970–72; Admin. Dir, Oxford Playhouse Co., 1976–82; freelance prodns at Royal Court Th., Young Vic, National Th., RSC and West End include: Ain't Misbehavin', Lyric, 1995; Colour of Justice, Victoria Palace, 1999; Guantanamo, New Ambassadors and NY, 2004; The Great Game: Afghanistan, USA nat. tour, incl. the Pentagon, 2010–11; The Nightmares of Carlos Fuentes, Arcola, 2014; Co-Producer: Before the Party, Queens, 1979; The Price, Apollo, 2003; 39 Steps, Criterion, 2006–; director of plays for TV including: Playboy of the West Indies, 1984; Pentecost, 1990; Justifying War, 2003. Member: Council, AA, 1998–2000; Mayor of London's Cultural Strategy Gp, 1998–2000; Council, Arts Council, London, 2002–06. Dir, Soc. of London Theatres, 2000–07. Hon. DLitt Westminster, 2007. Freedom, London Borough of Brent, 2012. Outstanding Individual Achievement Award, Theatre Managers' Assoc., 2009; Human Rights Arts Award, Liberty, 2010; Peter Brook Special Achievement Award, 2011. *Publications:* Srebrenica, 2005 (broadcast on BBC World Service); (contrib.) Verbatim Verbatim, 2008; (jtly) The Tricycle: collected Tribunal Plays 1994–2012, 2014. *Recreations:* country walks, tennis, African-American literature, art, architecture, politics, French films on winter afternoons, dead-heading roses in the sun. *Address:* 10 Alma Square, NW8 9QD. *T:* (020) 7286 1436. *E:* nicolas@nicolaskent.com.

KENT, Roderick David; Chairman, Caledonia Investments plc, since 2011; *b* 14 Aug. 1947; *s* of Dr Basil Stanley Kent, MB, BS, FFARCS and Vivien Margaret Kent (*née* Baker); *m* 1972, Belinda Jane Mitchell; three *d*. *Educ:* King's Sch., Canterbury; Corpus Christi Coll., Oxford (MA); INSEAD (MBA 1972). MCSI. Investment Div., J. Henry Schroder Wagg, 1969–71; Triumph Investment Trust, 1972–74; Dir, 1974–2002, Chm., 1990–2002, Close Brothers Ltd; Man. Dir, 1975–2002, non-exec. Dir, 2002–06, Chm., 2006–08, Close Brothers Gp plc. Chairman: Grosvenor Ltd, 2000–09; Bradford & Bingley Gp plc, 2002–08; BT Pension Scheme, 2008–11. Non-executive Director: Wessex Water plc, 1988–98; English and Scottish Investors plc, 1988–98; M & G Gp plc, 1995–99 (non-exec. Chm., 1998–99);

Grosvenor Group Ltd, 2000–12; Whitbread plc, 2002–08. Trustee, Esmée Fairbairn Foundn, 2001–08; Chm. Trustees, Calthorpe Estates, 2011–. Gov., Wellcome Trust (formerly Wellcome Foundn), 2008–12. Liveryman, Pewterers' Co., 1976–. *Recreations:* farming, antique furniture restoration, sports.

KENT, Thomas George, CBE 1979; CEng, MIMechE, FRAeS; aerospace and defence consultant; Director: Third Grosvenor Ltd, since 1987; Grosvenor General Partner, since 1995. *Educ:* Borden Grammar School; Medway College of Technology. Joined English Electric Co., 1951; Special Director, British Aircraft Corp., 1967; Dep. Man. Dir, 1974; Man. Dir, 1977; Director, Hatfield/Lostock Division and Stevenage/Bristol Div. of Dynamics Group, British Aerospace, 1977–79; Gp Dep. Chief Exec., BAe Dynamics Gp, 1980–85; Bd Mem., BAe, 1981–85; Director: BAe Australia Ltd, 1980–86 (Chm., 1984–86); Arab British Dynamics, 1980–85; BAJ Vickers Ltd, 1982–87 (non-exec.); Grosvenor Technol. Ltd, 1984–95; Grosvenor Develt Capital, 1993–95; Mercury Grosvenor Trust PLC, 1995–97.

KENT-JONES, His Honour Trevor David, TD; a Circuit Judge, 1991–2006; *b* 31 July 1940; *s* of late David Sandford Kent-Jones and Madeline Mary Kent-Jones (*née* Russell-Pavier); one *s* one *d. Educ:* Bedford Sch.; Liverpool Univ. (LLB; DIntLaw). Called to the Bar, Gray's Inn, 1962; Mem., NE Circuit, 1963–91, Junior, 1969; a Recorder, 1985–91. Commnd KOYLI TA, 1959; served 4th Bn KOYLI, 5th Bn Light Infantry, HQ NE Dist, 1959–85; Lt-Col 1977. Pres., Yorkshire RFU, 2011–12. *Recreations:* cricket, Rugby, travel, fell-walking. *Address:* Harrogate, N Yorks. *Club:* Naval and Military.

KENTFIELD, Graham Edward Alfred; Deputy Director, 1994–98, and Chief Cashier, 1991–98, Bank of England; *b* 3 Sept. 1940; *s* of late E. L. H. Kentfield and F. E. M. Kentfield (*née* Tucker); *m* 1965, Ann Dwelley Hewetson; two *d. Educ:* Bancroft's Sch., Woodford Green, Essex; St Edmund Hall, Oxford (BA 1st cl. Lit.Hum.). Entered Bank of England, 1963; seconded to Dept of Applied Econs, Cambridge, 1966–67; Editor, Bank of England Qly Bull., 1977–80; Adviser: Financial Stats Div., 1980–84; Banking Dept, 1984–85; Dep. Chief of Banking Dept and Dep. Chief Cashier, 1985–91; Chief of Banking Dept, 1991–94. Member: Bldg Socs Investment Protection Bd, 1991–2001; Financial Law Panel, 1994–98; Chm., Insolvency Practices Council, 2000–04. Trustee: CIB Pension Fund, 1994–2006 (Chm., 2000–06); Overseas Bishoprics Fund, 1999– (Chm., 2005–12). Vice-Pres., CIB, 2000–. Chm., Building Socs Trust Ltd, 2002–. Hon. Treas., Soc. for Promotion of Roman Studies, 1991–2010. Mem. Council, Univ. of London, 2000–08 (Mem., 2000–14, Chm., 2005–08, Investment Cttee). *Recreations:* Roman history, genealogy, philately.

KENTRIDGE, Sir Sydney (Woolf), KCMG 1999; QC 1984; *b* Johannesburg, 5 Nov. 1922; *s* of Morris and May Kentridge; *m* 1952, Felicia Geffen (*d* 2015); two *s* two *d. Educ:* King Edward VII Sch., Johannesburg; Univ. of the Witwatersrand (BA); Exeter Coll., Oxford Univ. (MA; Hon. Fellow, 1986). War service with S African forces, 1942–46. Advocate 1949, Senior Counsel 1965, South Africa; called to the English Bar, Lincoln's Inn, 1977, Bencher, 1986. Mem., Ct of Appeal, Botswana, 1981–88; Judge, Cts of Appeal, Jersey and Guernsey, 1988–92; acting Justice, Constitutional Court of S Africa, 1995–96. Roberts Lectr, Univ. of Pennsylvania, 1979. Hon. Mem., Bar Assoc., NY, 2001. Hon. Fellow, American Coll. of Trial Lawyers, 1999. Hon. LLD: Seton Hall Univ., NJ, 1978; Leicester, 1985; Cape Town, 1987; Natal, 1989; London, 1995; Sussex, 1997; Witwatersrand, 2000; Buckingham, 2009. Granville Clark Prize, USA, 1978. *Publications:* Free Country, 2012. *Recreation:* opera-going. *Address:* Brick Court Chambers, 7–8 Essex Street, WC2R 3LD. *T:* (020) 7379 3550. *Club:* Athenæum.

KENWARD, Michael Ronald John, OBE 1990; science writer and editorial consultant; *b* 12 July 1945; *s* of late Ronald Kenward and Phyllis Kenward; *m* 1969, Elizabeth Rice. *Educ:* Woolverstone Hall; Sussex Univ. Res. scientist, UKAEA, Culham Laboratory, 1966–68; Technical editor, Scientific Instrument Res. Assoc., 1969; various editorial posts, New Scientist, 1969–79, Editor, 1979–90; Science Consultant, The Sunday Times, 1990. Member: Royal Soc. COPUS, 1986–90; Public Affairs Cttee, 1989–93, Sci. and Industry Cttee, 1994–99, BAAS; Bd, Assoc. of British Editors, 1986–90; Royal Instn Task Force, 1995–96; Centre Cttee, Wellcome Centre for Med. Sci., 1997–98; Medicine in Society Panel, Wellcome Trust, 1998–2000; Adv. Cttee, AlphaGalileo Foundn (formerly AlphaGalileo electronic news service), 1999–. Writer in residence, OST Foresight Projects on Cognitive Systems, 2002–04, on Intelligent Infrastructure Systems, 2005. Internat. Rep., Assoc. of British Sci. Writers, 1993–97. Member: Editl Cttee, Science and Public Affairs, 1994–97; Editl Bd, Ingenia, Royal Acad. of Engrg, 2004–; Ed.-at-Large, Science|Business, 2005–. *Publications:* Potential Energy, 1976; articles on science, technology, and business. *Recreations:* walking, photography, collecting 'middle-aged' books, listening to baroque opera. *Address:* Grange Cottage, Staplefield, W Sussex RH17 6EL.

KENWAY-SMITH, Wendy Alison, FCA; Assistant Auditor General, National Audit Office, 2000–10; *b* 21 Feb. 1959; *d* of Derek Peter Kenway-Smith and Muriel Anne Kenway-Smith (*née* Stevens). *Educ:* Marist Sch., Ascot; Guildford Tech. Coll.; City of London Poly. (BA Hons Accountancy). ACA 1983, FCA 1993. Joined BDO Stoy Hayward, 1980, Partner, 1990–95; Dir, Nat. Audit Office, 1995–99. Freeman, City of London, 1993. *Recreations:* travel, gardening, good food, theatre, classical music.

KENWOOD, Diane, (Mrs Cary Zitcer); Editor, Woman's Weekly, since 2007; *b* London, 25 Jan. 1960; *d* of 2nd Baron Morris of Kenwood and of Hon. Ruth, *d* of Baron Janner; *m* 1981, Cary Zitcer; two *d. Educ:* St Paul's Girls' Sch.; Central Sch. of Speech and Drama (Dip. Stage Mgt). TV and radio presenter, 1986–99, incl. Travelog, Channel 4, On the Road, BBC 2, children's progs, BBC 1, Woman's Hour, Radio 4, sports on Sky News, Spectrum Radio; Features Ed., Having a Baby mag., then Ed., Health Supplement, Good Housekeeping mag., 1999–2001; Ed., Marks & Spencer mag., 2001–07. Chair, British Soc. of Magazine Editors, 2013 (Mem. Cttee, 2013–). Member: Council, Women of Year Lunch; Adv. Bd, Chai Cancer Care. JP Brent, 1997–2007. *Recreations:* sport, cinema, theatre, travel, DIY. *Address:* Woman's Weekly, Blue Fin Building, 110 Southwark Street, SE1 0SU. *T:* (020) 3148 6590. *E:* diane_kenwood@ipcmedia.com.

See also Baron Morris of Kenwood.

KENWORTHY, family name of **Baron Strabolgi**.

KENWORTHY, Duncan Hamish, OBE 1999; film producer; Managing Director, Toledo Productions Ltd, since 1995; *b* 9 Sept. 1949; *s* of Bernard Ian Kenworthy and Edna Muriel Kenworthy (*née* Calligan). *Educ:* Rydal Sch.; Christ's Coll., Cambridge (MA English 1975); Annenberg Sch., Univ. of Pennsylvania (MA Communications 1973). Children's Television Workshop, NY, 1973–76; Consulting Producer, Arabic Sesame Street, Kuwait, 1977–79; Prod. and Exec., Jim Henson Productions, London, 1979–95; Dir, DNA Films Ltd, 1997–2009. Associate Prod., The Dark Crystal (film), 1980; Producer: *television:* Fraggle Rock, 1982 (Outstanding Children's Programming, Internat. Emmy Award, 1983); The Storyteller, 1986–88 (Best Children's Prog. (Entertainment/Drama), BAFTA Children's Awards, 1988); Living with Dinosaurs, 1988 (Best Children's Prog., Internat. Emmy Award, 1990); Monster Maker, 1988; Greek Myths, 1990 (Best Children's Prog. (Fiction), BAFTA Children's Awards, 1991); Gulliver's Travels, 1996 (Outstanding Mini-series, Emmy Award, 1996); *films:* Four Weddings and a Funeral, 1994 (Best Film, and Lloyd's Bank Peoples' Choice Award, BAFTA, 1994; Best Comedy Film, British Comedy Awards, 1994; Best Foreign Film: Cesar Award, 1994; Australian Film Inst., 1994); Lawn Dogs, 1997; Notting Hill, 1999 (Orange Audience Award, BAFTA, 2000; Best Comedy Film, British Comedy Awards, 1999); The Parole Officer, 2001; Love Actually, 2003; The Eagle, 2011. Vice-Pres., BAFTA, 2009– (Chm., 2004–06; Chm., Film, 2002–04); Mem., Film Policy Review Gp, 1997–99; Dir, Film Council, 1999–2003; Chm., Film Adv. Cttee, British Council, 1999–2008; Mem., BAFTA Hong Kong Adv. Bd, 2013–. Fellow, Nat. Film and TV Sch., 2015 (Gov., 2001–14). British Producer of the Year, London Film Critics, 1994. FRSA 2000. *Recreations:* working out, hiking, visual arts, gardening, bee-keeping. *Address:* Toledo Productions, Suite 44, 10 Richmond Mews, W1D 3DD. *Club:* Garrick.

KENWORTHY, (Frederick) John; Adviser, University of Cambridge, 2008–10; Managing Director, Aktus (formerly Align) Consulting (UK) Ltd, 1997–2010; *b* 6 Dec. 1943; *s* of late Rev. Fred Kenworthy and of Mrs Ethel Kenworthy; *m* 1968, Diana Flintham; one *d. Educ:* William Hulme's Grammar Sch., Manchester; Manchester Univ. (BA Econ Hons, Politics). Entered Admin. Class, Home Civil Service, as Asst Principal, MoD (Navy), 1966; Treasury Centre for Admin. Studies, 1968–69; joined BSC, Sheffield, 1969; Principal, MoD, 1972; Royal Commn on the Press Secretariat, 1974; Asst Sec., Dir, Weapons Resources and Progs (Naval), MoD, 1979–83; Head of Resources and Progs (Navy) (formerly DS4), RN Size and Shape Policy, and Sec. to Navy Bd, MoD, 1983–86; Dir of Ops, Disablement Services Authy (formerly Div.), DHSS, 1986–88; Dir, IT Systems Directorate (Under Sec.), 1989–90, Chief Exec., IT Services Agency, 1990–93, Dept of Social Security; Management Consultant, ICL (Internat.), 1993–95; Prin. Consultant, Independent Management Consultants, 1996. Interim Dir of Mgt Inf. Services, 2001, Advr, Inf. Strategy, 2002–08, Univ. of Cambridge. Sen. Associate Mem., Hughes Hall, Cambridge, 2007–. MInstD. FBCS 2010. Freeman, Co. of Information Technologists, 1992. *Publications:* contribs on Hungarian revenue collection and pensions, and on social security in People's Republic of China. *Recreations:* music, history. *T:* 07831 580796. *E:* aktusconsulting@aol.com.

KENWORTHY, Joan Margaret, BLitt, MA; Principal, St Mary's College, University of Durham, 1977–99; *b* Oldham, Lancs, 10 Dec. 1933; *o d* of late Albert Kenworthy and Amy (*née* Cobbold). *Educ:* Girls Grammar Sch., Barrow-in-Furness; St Hilda's Coll., Oxford (BLitt, MA). Henry Oliver Beckit Prize, Oxford, 1955; Leverhulme Overseas Res. Scholar, Makerere Coll., Uganda, and E African Agriculture and Forestry Res. Org., Kenya, 1956–58; Actg Tutor, St Hugh's Coll., Oxford, 1958–59; Tutorial Res. Fellow, Bedford Coll., London, 1959–60; Univ. of Liverpool: Asst Lectr in Geography, 1960–63; Lectr, 1963–73; Sen. Lectr, 1973–77; Warden of Salisbury Hall, 1966–77 and of Morton House, 1974–77. Vis. Lectr, Univ. of Dar es Salaam, 1965; IUC short-term Vis. Lectr, Univ. of Sierra Leone, 1975; Vis. Lectr, Univ. of Fort Hare, Ciskei, 1983. Hon. Res. Associate, Dept of Geog., Univ. of Durham, 2009–15. Mem., NE England, Churches Regl Broadcasting Council, 1978–82; Bishop's Selector for ACCM, 1982–87. Member: Council, African Studies Assoc. of UK, 1969–71, 1994–97; Standing Cttee on Univ. Studies of Africa, 1994–98; Council, Inst. of Brit. Geographers, 1976–78; Cttee, Merseyside Conf. for Overseas Students Ltd, 1976–77; Council, RMetS, 1980–83 (Mem., Cttee, History Gp, 2001–12); Council, Friends of the Oriental Mus., 1995–98 and 2010–12; Treasurer, Assoc. of Brit. Climatologists, 1976–79. Northern Chm., Durham Univ. Soc., 1979–82. Gov., St Anne's Sch., Windermere, 1992–95. Member: Satley PCC, 2001–04 and 2009–12 (Treas., 2002–04); Stanhope Deanery Synod, 2001–04. A Dir (formerly Trustee), Wear Valley CAB, 2001–04. Hon. Fellow, Harris Manchester Coll., Oxford, 2009–. Jehuda Neumann Meml Prize, Royal Meteorol Soc., 2015. *Publications:* (contrib.) Geographers and the Tropics, ed R. W. Steel and R. M. Prothero, 1964; (contrib.) Oxford Regional Economic Atlas for Africa, 1965; (contrib.) Studies in East African Geography and Development, ed S. Ominde, 1971; (contrib.) An Advanced Geography of Africa, ed J. I. Clarke, 1975; (contrib.) Rangeland Management and Ecology in East Africa, ed D. J. Pratt and M. D. Gwynne, 1977; (contrib.) The Climatic Scene: essays in honour of Emeritus Prof. Gordon Manley, ed M. J. Tooley and G. Sheail, 1985; (ed with B. D. Giles) Observatories and Climatological Research, 1994; (ed with J. M. Walker) Colonial Observatories and Observations, 1997; articles in jls, encycs, reports of symposia and occasional papers on hist. of meteorology, RMetS. *Address:* 3 Satley Plough, Satley, Bishop Auckland, Co. Durham DL13 4JX. *T:* (01388) 730848. *Clubs:* Penn, Oxford and Cambridge.

KENWORTHY, John; *see* Kenworthy, F. J.

KENWRIGHT, Prof. John, MD; FRCS; FRCSE; Nuffield Professor of Orthopaedic Surgery, Oxford University, 1992–2001; Professorial Fellow, Worcester College, Oxford, 1992–2001, now Emeritus; *b* 2 May 1936; *s* of Cecil Kenwright and Norah (*née* Langley); *m* 1960, Vivien Mary Curtis; two *s. Educ:* University College Sch.; Nottingham High Sch.; St John's Coll., Oxford; University College Hosp. MA Oxon; BM, BCh; MD Stockholm 1972. FRCS 1966; FRCSE (*ad hominem*) 1998. Nuffield Surgical Res. Fellow, Oxford, 1968; Res. Fellow, Karolinska Inst., Stockholm, 1971; Consultant Orthopaedic Surgeon, Nuffield Orthopaedic Centre and John Radcliffe Hosp., Oxford, 1973–2001. Royal College of Surgeons of England: Hunterian Prof., 1991–92; Robert Jones Lectr, 1998; Res. Dir, Wishbone Trust, British Orthopaedic Assoc., 2002–03. President: Girdlestone Orthopaedic Soc., 1993–2002; Oxford Medico-legal Soc., 1998–; British Limb Reconstruction Soc., 1998–2000; British Orthopaedic Res. Soc., 1999–; Internat. Soc. for Fracture Repair, 2002–04. *Publications:* articles in scientific jls on factors which control fracture and soft tissue healing; also on leg lengthening and correction of post traumatic deformity. *Recreation:* sailing. *Address:* Nuffield Orthopaedic Centre, Headington, Oxford OX3 7LD. *T:* (01865) 862695, *Fax:* (01865) 862695. *E:* johnandvkenwright@gmail.com. *Club:* Oxford and Cambridge Sailing Society.

KENWRIGHT, William, (Bill), CBE 2001; theatre producer, since 1970; *b* 4 Sept. 1945; *s* of Albert Kenwright and Hope Kenwright (*née* Jones); partner, Jennifer Ann Seagrove, *qv. Educ:* Liverpool Inst. Actor, 1964–70; has produced more than 500 plays and musicals, including: Joseph and The Amazing Technicolor Dreamcoat; Evita; Cabaret; Jesus Christ Superstar; A Streetcar Named Desire; Stepping Out; Blood Brothers; Shirley Valentine; Travels with My Aunt; Piaf; Medea; A Doll's House; An Ideal Husband; Passion; Long Day's Journey into Night; Cat on a Hot Tin Roof, etc; *films:* Stepping Out; Don't Go Breaking My Heart; Die Mommie Die; The Purifiers; Cheri; Broken. Chm., Everton FC, 2004– (Dir, 1989–; Dep. Chm., 1998). Hon. Professor: Tameside Univ.; Liverpool Univ. Hon. Dr: Liverpool John Moores; West London; Hon. DLitt Nottingham Trent. Has won Tony, Olivier, Evening Standard, Variety Club and TMA Lifetime Achievement awards. *Address:* Bill Kenwright Ltd, BKL House, 1 Venice Walk, W2 1RR. *T:* (020) 7446 6200.

KENYON, family name of **Baron Kenyon**.

KENYON, 6th Baron *cr* 1788; **Lloyd Tyrell-Kenyon;** Bt 1784; Baron of Gredington, 1788; *b* 13 July 1947; *s* of 5th Baron Kenyon, CBE and of Leila Mary, *d* of Comdr John Wyndham Cookson, RN and *widow* of Hugh William Jardine Ethelston Peel; *S* father, 1993; *m* 1971, Sally Carolyn, *e d* of J. F. P. Matthews; two *s. Educ:* Eton; Magdalene Coll., Cambridge (BA). Mem. (C), Wrexham County (formerly Wrexham Maelor) BC, 1991–. Mem., EU Cttee of the Regions, 1994–97. High Sheriff, Clwyd, 1986. *Heir: s* Hon. Lloyd Nicholas Tyrell-Kenyon, *b* 9 April 1972. *Address:* Gredington, Whitchurch, Shropshire SY13 3DH.

KENYON, Eleanor Mary Henrietta; *see* Hill, E. M. H.

KENYON, Margaret; DL; Headmistress, Withington Girls' School, Manchester, 1986–2000; *b* 19 June 1940; *d* of Hugh Richard Parry and Aileen Cole (*née* Morgan); *m* 1962, Christopher George Kenyon (CBE 2003); two *s. Educ:* Merchant Taylors' Sch. for Girls, Crosby; Somerville Coll., Oxford (MA; Hon. Fellow, 1999). Asst French Mistress, Cheadle Hulme Sch., 1962–63 and 1974–83; Hd of French, Withington Girls Sch., 1983–85. Girls' School Association: Chm., NW Region, 1989–91; Pres., 1993–94. Mem. Adv. Council, Granada

Foundn, 1986–2012. Trustee, Mus. of Science and Industry, Manchester, 1998–2004. Mem. Court, Univ. of Manchester, 1991–2004 (Chair, Press Bd, 2001–10). Governor: Bolton Sch., 2001–12; Cheadle Hulme Sch., 2001–12; Haberdashers' Aske's Schs, Elstree, 2002–09. DL Greater Manchester, 1998. Medal of Honour, Manchester Univ., 2011. *Recreations:* reading, talking, family. *Address:* Alderley House, 33 Lemsford Road, St Albans, Herts AL1 3PP.

KENYON, Sir Nicholas (Roger), Kt 2008; CBE 2001; Managing Director, Barbican Centre, since 2007; *b* 23 Feb. 1951; *s* of late Thomas Kenyon and Kathleen Holmes; *m* 1976, Marie-Ghislaine Latham-Koenig; three *s* one *d*. *Educ:* Balliol College, Oxford (BA Hons 1972). Music critic: The New Yorker, 1979–82; The Times, 1982–85; The Observer, 1985–92; Music Editor, The Listener, 1982–87; Editor, Early Music, 1983–92; Controller, BBC Radio 3, 1992–98; Dir, BBC Promenade Concerts, 1996–2007; Controller, BBC Proms, Live Events and TV Classical Music, 2000–07. Member: AHRB, subseq. AHRC, 2004–08; Arts Council England, 2009–. Mem. Bd, Sage Gateshead. Trustee, Dartington Hall Trust. *Publications:* The BBC Symphony Orchestra 1930–80, 1981; Simon Rattle, 1987, 2nd edn 2001; The Faber Pocket Guide to Mozart, 2005; The Faber Pocket Guide to Bach, 2011; *edited:* Authenticity and Early Music, 1988; (jtly) The Viking Opera Guide, 1993; (jtly) The Penguin Opera Guide, 1995; BBC Proms Guide to Great Symphonies, 2003; BBC Proms Guide to Great Concertos, 2003; Musical Lives, 2003; BBC Proms Guide to Great Choral Works, 2004; BBC Proms Guide to Great Orchestral Works, 2004; The City of London: a companion guide, 2012. *Recreation:* family. *Address:* Barbican Centre, Silk Street, EC2Y 8DS. *T:* (020) 7382 7005.

KENYON-SLANEY, (William) Simon (Rodolph), OBE 2004; JP; Vice Lord-Lieutenant of Shropshire, 1996–2007; *b* 31 Jan. 1932; *s* of Major R. O. R. Kenyon-Slaney, Grenadier Guards, and Nesta, *d* of Sir George Ferdinand Forestier-Walker, 3rd Bt; *m* 1960, Mary Helena, *e d* of Lt-Col Hon. H. G. O. Bridgeman, DSO, MC, RA, and Joan, *d* of Hon. Bernard Constable Maxwell; three *s*. *Educ:* Eton. FLAS 1964; FRICS 1970. Grenadier Guards, 1950–52; formerly: Chartered Land Agent and Surveyor; farmer. Non-exec. Dir, South Staffs Gp PLC, 1988–02. Chm., Ludlow Cons. Assoc., 1989–91. Trustee, Ironbridge Gorge Museum, 1995–2012 (Dep. Chm., 2002–12; Vice Pres., 2012–). Former school governor. Shropshire: JP 1969 (Chairman: Probation Cttee, 1979–84; Staffs and Shropshire Magistrates' Assoc., 1982–87; Bridgnorth Bench, 1990–95; Magistrates' Courts Cttee, 1994–97); CC, 1977–85 (Chm., Planning and Transport Cttee, 1982–85); High Sheriff, 1979; DL 1986. Member: Council, Shropshire, SJAB, 1969–2012 (Chm., 1974–2002); Nat. Council, Magistrates' Assoc., 1982–92. KStJ 1993 (OStJ 1976; CStJ 1983; Mem., Chapter-General, 1990–99, Priory Chapter, 1999–2002). *Recreations:* gardening, travel, theatre, fishing. *Address:* Cedars House, 13 Victoria Road, Much Wenlock, Shropshire TF13 6AL. *T:* (01952) 726775.

KEOGH, Prof. Sir Bruce (Edward), KBE 2003; MD; FRCS, FRCSE; National Medical Director, NHS England (formerly NHS Commissioning Board), since 2012; *b* 24 Nov. 1954; *s* of Gerald Keogh and Marjorie Beatrice Keogh (*née* Craig); naturalised British citizen, 2004; *m* 1979, Ann Katherine (*née* Westmore); four *s*. *Educ:* St George's Coll., Zimbabwe; Charing Cross Hosp. Med. Sch., Univ. of London (BSc Hons 1977; MB BS 1980; MD 1989). MRCS 1980, FRCS *ad eundem* 2000; LRCP 1980; FRCSE 1985. Demonstrator in Anatomy, Charing Cross Hosp. Med. Sch., 1981–82; Registrar training: Northern Gen. Hosp., Sheffield, 1984–85; Hammersmith Hosp., 1985–89 (BHF Jun. Res. Fellow, 1987–88); Sen. Registrar in Cardiothoracic Surgery, St George's and Harefield Hosps, 1989–91; BHF Sen. Lectr in Cardiac Surgery, RPMS Hammersmith Hosp., 1991–95; Consultant in Cardiothoracic Surgery, 1995–2004, and Associate Med. Dir for Clinical Governance, 1998–2003, University Hosp. Birmingham NHS Trust; Prof. of Cardiac Surgery, 2004–07, Hon. Prof., 2008, UCL; Dir of Surgery, 2004–07, Consultant Cardiothoracic Surgeon, 2004–07, The Heart Hosp., UCL Hosps NHS Trust; NHS Medical Dir, DoH, 2007–13. Visiting Professor: Univ. of Tokyo, 2006; Chinese Univ. of HK, 2007; Univ. of Colorado, 2009; King James IV Prof., RCSE, 2005; RCS Tudor Edwards Lectr, 2007. Member: Commn for Health Improvement, 2002–04; Commn for Healthcare Audit and Inspection, 2004–07 (Chm., Clinical Adv. Gp, 2004–06); Chairman: Jt Commn for Health Improvement and Audit Commn Nat. Service Framework Prog. Bd, 2002–04; Jt DoH, Healthcare Commn and Soc. for Cardio Thoracic Surgery Central Cardiac Audit Database Oversight Cttee, 2004–07; Co-Chm., Nat. Quality Bd, 2014–. Member: NHS Nat. Taskforce for Coronary Heart Disease, 2000–06; NHS Standing Med. Adv. Cttee, 2002–04; Chairman: W Midlands NHS Regl Coronary Heart Disease and Tobacco Modernisation Gp, 2000–02; DoH Inf. Taskforce on Clinical Outcomes, 2006–07. Founder and Co-ordinator, Nat. Adult Cardiac Surgical Database, 1994–2007. Member: Intercollegiate Specialist Adv. Cttee on higher surgical trng in cardiothoracic surgery, 1999–2004; Intercollegiate Exam. Bd in Cardiothoracic Surgery, 1999–2004 (Examr, 1999–2004). Mem. Council, RCS, 2002–04, 2006–08; Cardiothoracic section, Royal Society of Medicine: Mem. Council, 1992–99; Hon. Sec., 1993–99; Pres., 2005–07; Society for Cardio Thoracic Surgery in GB and Ireland: Ronald Edwards Medal, 1991; Hon. Sec., 1999–2003; Pres., 2006–08; Sec.-Gen., European Assoc. for Cardio-Thoracic Surgery, 2004–08; Society of Thoracic Surgeons: Internat. Dir, 2005–11; Ferguson Lect., 2009; McKeown Medal Lect., RCSE, 2012; Hunterian Orator, RCS, 2013. Inaugural Judge, Hippocrates Prize for Poetry and Medicine, 2010. Fellow: European Soc. of Cardiology, 1992; European Bd of Thoracic and Cardiovascular Surgery, 1999. Member: Lunar Soc.; American Assoc. for Thoracic Surgery, 2007; Council, British Heart Foundn, 2008–13. Trustee, Healing Foundn, 2014–. Vice Patron, RBL Poppy Factory, 2011–. Hon. FRCP 2005; Hon. FRCGP 2009; Hon. FACS 2009; Hon. FRCSI 2011; Hon. FRCA 2011. Hon. MD: Birmingham, 2009; Sheffield, 2009; Hon. DSc: Toledo, 2009; Coventry, 2010. Member, Editorial Board: Jl RSocMed, 1994–99; CTSNet, 1999–2007; Heart, 2000–06. *Publications:* Normal Surface Anatomy, 1984; The Evidence for Cardiothoracic Surgery, 2004; National Adult Cardiac Surgical Database Report, 1999, 6th edn 2009; National Reports on: neonatal services, 2009; safety of breast implants, 2012; cosmetic interventions, 2013; trusts with high mortality, 2013; urgent and emergency care, 2013; articles in jls on cardiac surgery and measurement of health outcomes. *Recreations:* diving, photography. *Address:* Claremont House, 68 Oakfield Road, Selly Park, Birmingham B29 7EG.

KEOHANE, Desmond John, OBE 1991; consultant in education and training, retired; *b* 5 July 1928; *s* of William Patrick Keohane and Mabel Margaret Keohane; *m* 1960, Mary Kelliher; two *s* two *d*. *Educ:* Borden Grammar Sch., Sittingbourne; Univ. of Birmingham (BA and Baxter Prize in History, 1949); London Univ. (Postgrad. Cert in Educn). Postgrad. res., 1949–50; Nat. Service, Educn Officer, RAF, 1950–52; sch. teacher and coll. lectr, 1953–64; Head, Dept of Social and Academic Studies, 1964–68, and Vice-Principal, 1969–71, Havering Technical Coll.; Principal, Northampton Coll. of Further Educn, 1971–76; Principal, Oxford Coll. of Further Educn, 1976–90. Part-time Lectr in Educnl Management, Univ. of Leicester, 1990–93; Vis. Fellow (Educn), 1991–94, Hon. Fellow, 1991, Oxford Brookes Univ. (formerly Oxford Polytechnic). Member: Council, Southern Regional Council for Further Educn, 1977–90; Secondary Exams Council, 1983–86; Berks and Oxon Area Manpower Board, 1985–88; Special Employment Measures Adv. Gp, MSC, 1986–89; Northampton RC Diocesan Educn Commn, 1991–2002; E Midlands Panel, Nat. Lottery Charities Bd, 1995–98; Co-opted Mem. Educn Cttee, Northants CC, 1996–2002. Chm. Trustees, Stress at Work, 1987–2002. Formerly governor of various educnl instns; Chm. of Govs, Thomas Becket Sch., Northampton, 1983–98. Gen. Ed., series Managing Colleges Effectively, 1994–99. *Recreations:* enjoying family and friends, watching cricket. *Address:* 2 Neale Close, Weston Favell, Northampton NN3 3DB. *T:* (01604) 416474. *E:* desmond.keohane@btinternet.com.

KEPPEL, family name of **Earl of Albemarle**.

KER; *see* Innes-Ker, family name of Duke of Roxburghe.

KERBY, John Vyvyan; Chief Executive, National Talking Newspapers and Magazines, 2007–13 (Trustee, 2005–07); *b* 14 Dec. 1942; *s* of Theo Rosser Fred Kerby and Constance Mary (*née* Newell); *m* 1978, Shirley Elizabeth Pope (*d* 2012); one step *s* one step *d*. *Educ:* Eton Coll.; Christ Church, Oxford (MA). Temp. Asst Principal, CO, 1965; Asst Principal, ODM, 1967; Pvte Sec. to Parly Under-Sec. of State, FCO, 1970; Principal, ODA, 1971–74, 1975–77; CSSB, 1974–75; Asst Sec., ODA, 1977; Head of British Develt Div. in Southern Africa, 1983; Under Sec. and Prin. Establishment Officer, ODA, 1986–93; Hd, Asia and Pacific Div., ODA, subseq. Dir, Asia and Pacific, DFID, 1993–97; Dir, Eastern Europe and Western Hemisphere Div., DFID, 1997–2001; UK Dir, EBRD, 2001–03. Gov., subseq. Mem. Adv. Council, Centre for Internat. Briefing, 1986–2004. Mem., Heathfield and Waldron Parish Council, 2005–11. *Recreations:* gardening, cricket, music, entomology. *Address:* Crown Cottage, Groombridge Hill, Tunbridge Wells, Kent TN3 9QE. *T:* (01892) 864987.

KERE, Dr Sir Nathan Kumamusa, KCMG 2014; Medical Practitioner, since 1975; Infectious Disease Specialist and Malariologist, since 1994; *b* Sasamugga village, Choiseul Is., Solomon Is, 4 Aug. 1950; *s* of Nelson Kere and Nelly Zaoro; *m* 1984, Joy Finioa; three *s* four *d*. *Educ:* King George VI Sch.; Fiji Sch. of Medicine (DSM 1974); Otago Univ. (DPH 1978); Univ. of Liverpool (MCommH 1982); London Sch. of Hygiene and Tropical Medicine, Univ. of London (PhD Epidemiol. and Control of Infectious Diseases 1992). Solomon Islands: MO, then SMO, 1975–78; CMO (Communicable Diseases), 1979–83; Undersec. for Health Improvement, 1983–88; Dir, Solomon Is Medical Training and Res. Inst., and Govt Malariologist, 1988–93; Perm. Sec. for Health, 1993–94. Civil Aviation Authorised MO, 1994–, Maritime Authorised MO, 1994–, MO for Rotary, 1997–, Solomon Is. Hon. Consultant, Fiji Sch. of Medicine, 1993. Pres., Solomon Is Golf Fedn, 2010–. World Health Medal, 1988; Paul Harris Recognition, 2002, Service Above Self Medal, 2006, Sapphire Pin, 2011, Rotary Internat. *Publications:* articles in jls Health Policy and Planning, SE Asian Jl of Tropical Medicine and Public Health, Travel Medicine Internat. and Med. Veterinary Entomol. *Recreations:* golf, fishing, swimming, charity fund raising, cricket. *Address:* East Medical Centre Ltd, PO Box 1173, Honiara, Solomon Islands. *T:* 39220, 7475434, *Fax:* 39221. *E:* kere@solomon.com.sb. *Clubs:* Rotary (Honiara); Honiara Golf.

KEREVAN, George; MP (SNP) East Lothian, since 2015; *b* Glasgow, 28 Sept. 1949; *m* Angela. *Educ:* Univ. of Glasgow. Lectr in Econs, Napier Univ., Edinburgh; Associate Ed., Scotsman, 2000–09; Producer, What If Prodns (Television) Ltd, 2000–06; producer of documentary films for Discovery, Hist. Channel and PBS. Former Chm., Edinburgh Tourist Bd; Member, Board: Edinburgh Internat. Fest.; Edinburgh Internat. Film Fest; Founder, Edinburgh Sci. Fest.; Co-organiser, Prestwick World Fest. of Flight. Mem. (Lab) Edinburgh CC, 1984–96. Contested (SNP) Edinburgh E, 2010. *Address:* House of Commons, SW1A 0AA.

KERIN, Hon. John Charles, AM 2001; Chairman, Australian Meat and Livestock Corporation, 1994–97; Forestry Commissioner, New South Wales, 1998–2003; *b* 21 Nov. 1937; *s* of Joseph Sydney Kerin and Mary Louise Fuller; *m* 1st, Barbara Elizabeth Large (marr. diss.); one *d* and one step *s* two step *d*; 2nd, 1983, Dr June Raye Verrier. *Educ:* Univ. of New England (BA); ANU (BEc). Axeman and bricksetter, then farmer and businessman, 1952–71; Res. Economist, 1971–72, Principal Res. Economist, 1976–78, Bureau of Agricl Econs. MP (ALP) for Macarthur, NSW, 1972–75, for Werrina, 1978–93; Minister: for Primary Industry, 1983–87; for Primary Industries and Energy, 1987–91; Treas., 1991; Minister: for Transport and Communications, 1991; for Trade and Overseas Develt, 1991–93. Statutory office holder and businessman, 1993–. Chairman: Corporate Investment Australia Funds Management Ltd, 1994–99; John Kerin and Associates, 1994; Spire Technologies, 1998–2001; Chm., Coal Mines Australia Ltd, subseq. Mem. Bd, Billiton, 1995–2001. Chairman: NSW Water Adv. Council, 1995–2003; Reef Fisheries Management Adv. Cttee, 1995–2003; Stored Grain Res. Lab., 2002–05; Co-operative Research Centres: Sustainable Plantation Forestry (formerly Temperate Hardwood Forests), 1994–2002; Tropical Savannas, 1995–2008; Australian Weed Mgt (formerly Weed Mgt Systems), 1995–2008; Sensor Signals and Information Processing, 1996–2005; Poultry, 2010–. Chm., Qld Fisheries Mgt Authy, 1999–2000; Bd Mem., Southern Rivers Catchment Mgt Authy, 2004–11. Chm. Adv. Cttee, Nat. Ovine Johne's Prog., 2000–06; Mem., Safe Food Prodn Adv. Cttee, NSW, 2000–03. Dep. Pres., UNICEF (Australia), 1994–2008; Mem., Birds Australia Council, 2002–05. Mem. Bd, CSIRO, 2008–11. NSW Chm., 2000, ACT Chm., 2006–, Crawford Fund. Mem. Bd of Trustees, Univ. of Western Sydney, 1996–2006; Trustee, Clunies Ross Foundn, 2004. Fellow, Aust. Inst. of Agricl Sci., 1995; FTSE 2001. Hon. Dr Rural Sci., New England, 1993; Hon. DLitt Western Sydney, 1995; Hon. Dr Sci. Tasmania, 2001. *Recreations:* live arts, music, reading, walking. *Address:* 26 Harour Place, Garran, ACT 2605, Australia. *T:* (2) 62852480.

KERINS, Angela; Chief Executive, Rehab Group, 2007–14; *b* Waterford City, 29 May 1958; *m* 1983, Sean Kerins; one *s* one *d*. *Educ:* Basildon and Thurrock Sch. of Nursing and Midwifery (SRN 1979; SCM 1981). Cert IoD. Clinical and healthcare mgt posts, 1980–92; Dir, Public Affairs and Gp Develt, Rehab Gp, 1992–2007; Chief Exec., RehabCare, 1995–2007. Chair: TBG Learning, 2006–14; Momentum Scotland, 2007–14; Rehab JobFit, 2011–14. Chair: Nat. Disability Authy, Ire., 1999–2009; Equality Authy, 2007–12; Co-Chair, Nat. Disability Strategy Stakeholders Monitoring Gp, 2005–11; Mem., Health Information and Quality Authy, 2007–12. Pres., European Platform for Rehabilitation, 2012–14. Mem., Nat. Council, Irish Business and Employers Confedn, 2004–14. Hon. LLD NUI, 2003. *Publications:* contribs to The Irish Times, Comment and Analysis. *Club:* Royal Irish Automobile.

KERN, Karl-Heinz; Head of Arms Control Department, Ministry of Foreign Affairs, German Democratic Republic, 1987–90; research in international affairs, since 1990; *b* 18 Feb. 1930; *m* 1952, Ursula Bennmann; one *s*. *Educ:* King George Gymnasium, Dresden; Techn. Coll., Dresden (chem. engrg); Acad. for Polit. Science and Law (Dipl. jur., post-grad. History. Leading posts in diff. regional authorities of GDR until 1959; foreign policy, GDR, 1959–62; Head of GDR Mission in Ghana, 1962–66; Head of African Dept, Min. of For. Affairs, 1966–71; Minister and Chargé d'Affaires, Gt Britain, 1973; Ambassador to UK, 1973–80; Dep. Head of Western European Dept, Min. of Foreign Affairs, 1980–82; Ambassador to N Korea, 1982–86. Holds Order of Merit of the Fatherland, etc. *Recreations:* sport, reading, music. *Address:* Karl-Marx-Allee 70a, 10243 Berlin, Germany.

KERNAGHAN, Paul Robert, CBE 2005; QPM 1998; Commissioner for Standards, House of Lords, since 2010; *b* Dec. 1955; *s* of Hugh Kernaghan and Diane Kernaghan (*née* Herdman); *m* 1983, Mary McCleery; one *d*. *Educ:* Methodist Coll., Belfast; Queen's Univ., Belfast (LLB Hons); Univ. of Ulster (DPM); Univ. of Leicester (MA Public Order). MIPD 1991. Served UDR (part-time), 1974–77; commnd 1976, Second Lieut; served RUC, 1978–91: grad. entrant, Constable, 1978; served Belfast, Londonderry, Strabane and Warrenpoint, operational and staff appts; Superintendent, 1991–92, Detective Superintendent, 1992–95, W Midlands Police; Asst Chief Constable, 1995; Asst Chief Constable (Designated), 1996–99, N Yorks Police; rcds 1997; Chief Constable, Hampshire Constabulary, 1999–2008. Internat. affairs portfolio holder, ACPO, 2000–08; Hd of Mission, EU Police Co-ordinating Office for Palestinian Police Support, 2009. Member: UN Internat. Policing Adv. Council, 2006–08; Armed Forces Pay Review Body, 2011–; (non-exec.) Civil Nuclear Police Authy, 2013–. *Recreations:* family, walking, reading. *E:* p.kernaghan@btinternet.com.

KERR, family name of **Marquess of Lothian** and **Barons Kerr of Kinlochard, Kerr of Tonaghmore** and **Teviot**.

KERR OF KINLOCHARD, Baron *cr* 2004 (Life Peer), of Kinlochard in Perth and Kinross; **John Olav Kerr,** GCMG 2001 (KCMG 1991; CMG 1987); Director, Scottish American Investment Trust, since 2002; Deputy Chairman, Scottish Power, since 2012 (Director, since 2009); Member, Advisory Board, Edinburgh Partners, since 2012; *b* 22 Feb. 1942; *s* of late Dr J. D. O. Kerr; *m* 1965, Elizabeth, *d* of late W. G. Kalaugher; two *s* three *d*. *Educ:* Glasgow Academy; Pembroke Coll., Oxford (Hon. Fellow, 1991). HM Diplomatic Service, 1966–2002; HM Treasury, 1979–84: Principal Private Sec. to Chancellor of the Exchequer, 1981–84; Asst Under-Sec. of State, FCO, 1987–90; Ambassador and UK Perm. Rep. to the EU, 1990–95; Ambassador to USA, 1995–97; Perm. Under-Sec. of State, FCO, and Hd, Diplomatic Service, 1997–2002; Sec.-Gen., European Convention, 2002–03. Director: Shell Transport and Trading, 2002–05; Rio Tinto plc, 2003–15; Dep. Chm., Royal Dutch Shell plc, 2005–12. Indep. Mem., H of L, 2004–; Mem., EU Select Cttee, H of L, 2006–10, 2014–15. Mem. Council, Centre for Eur. Reform, 2004– (Chm., 2009–); Hon. Pres., UK/Korea Forum for the Future, 2007–13; Vice-Pres., Eur. Policy Centre, 2007–. Trustee: Rhodes Trust, Oxford, 1997–2010; Nat. Gall., 2002–10; Fulbright Commn, 2004–09; Carnegie Trust for Univs of Scotland, 2005– (Dep. Chm., 2013–). Chm., Ct and Council, 2005–11, Fellow, 2013, Imperial Coll. London. Hon. Pres., St Andrew's Clinics for Children, 2008–. Hon. FRSE 2006. Hon. LLD: St Andrews, 1996; Glasgow, 1999; Hon. DLitt Aston, 2010. *Address:* House of Lords, SW1A 0PW. *Clubs:* Garrick; Queen's Park Rangers Football.

KERR OF TONAGHMORE, Baron *cr* 2009 (Life Peer), of Tonaghmore in the County of Down; **Brian Francis Kerr,** Kt 1993; PC 2004; a Justice of the Supreme Court of the United Kingdom (formerly a Lord of Appeal in Ordinary), since 2009; *b* 22 Feb. 1948; *s* of late James William Kerr and Kathleen Rose Kerr; *m* 1970, Gillian Rosemary Owen Widdowson; two *s*. *Educ:* St Colman's College, Newry, Co. Down; Queen's Univ., Belfast (LLB 1969). Called to NI Bar, 1970, to the Bar of England and Wales, Gray's Inn, 1974 (Hon. Bencher, 1997); QC (NI) 1983; Bencher, Inn of Court of NI, 1990; Junior Crown Counsel (Common Law), 1978–83; Sen. Crown Counsel, 1988–93; Judge of the High Ct of Justice, NI, 1993–2004; Lord Chief Justice of NI, 2004–09. Chm., Mental Health Commn for NI, 1988. Member: Judicial Studies Bd, NI, 1995–2004; Franco British Judicial Co-operation Cttee, 1995–2001. Chm., Distinction and Meritorious Service Awards Cttee, NI, 1997–2001. Eisenhower Exchange Fellow, 1999. Hon. Bencher, King's Inns, 2004. Hon. Fellow, American Bd of Trial Advocates 2004. Hon. LLD: QUB, 2009; Ulster, 2014. *Recreation:* trying to be (and hoping to make my family) happy. *Address:* Supreme Court of the United Kingdom, Parliament Square, SW1P 3BD.

KERR, Alan Grainger, OBE 2000; FRCS, FRCSE; Consultant Otolaryngologist, Royal Victoria and Belfast City Hospitals, since 1968; *b* 15 April 1935; *s* of Joseph William and Eileen Kerr; *m* 1962, Patricia Margaret M'Neill (*d* 1999); two *s* one *d*. *Educ:* Methodist College, Belfast; Queen's Univ., Belfast (MB). DObst RCOG. Clinical and Res. Fellow, Harvard Med. Sch., 1967; Prof. of Otorhinolaryngology, QUB, 1979–81. Otolaryngology Mem. Council, RCS, 1987–92; President: Otorhinolaryngological Res. Soc., 1985–87; Internat. Otopathology Soc., 1985–88; Otology Sect., RSM, 1989–90; British Assoc. of Otorhinolaryngologists—Head and Neck Surgeons, 1993–96; Irish Otolaryngological Soc., 1997–99; Politzer Soc., 1998–2002. Master, British Academic Conf. in Otolaryngology, 2006. Lectures, UK, Europe and USA. Prizes: Jobson Horne, BMA; Harrison, RSocMed; Howells, Univ. of London. Gen. Editor, Scott-Brown's Otolaryngology, 1987–2008. *Publications:* papers on ear surgery. *Recreations:* tennis, ski-ing, hill walking, bowls. *Address:* 6 Cranmore Gardens, Belfast BT9 6JL. *T:* (028) 9066 9181. *Club:* Royal Society of Medicine.

KERR, Prof. Allen, AO 1992; FRS 1986; FAA; Professor of Plant Pathology, University of Adelaide, 1980–91, Professor Emeritus, since 1992; *b* 21 May 1926; *s* of A. B. Kerr and J. T. Kerr (*née* White); *m* 1951, Rosemary Sheila Strachan (*d* 2010); two *s* one *d*. *Educ:* George Heriot's Sch., Edinburgh; Univ. of Edinburgh. North of Scotland Coll. of Agric., 1947–51; University of Adelaide: Lectr, 1951–59; Sen. Lectr, 1959–67 (seconded to Tea Research Inst., Ceylon, 1963–66); Reader, 1968–80. FAA 1978. For. Associate, Nat. Acad. of Scis, USA, 1991. *Recreation:* golf. *Address:* 419 Carrington Street, Adelaide, SA 5000, Australia. *T:* (8) 82322325.

KERR, Andrew Cameron; Owner, Kerr Strategic Consultancy Ltd, since 2011; Chief Executive, Edinburgh City Council, since 2015; *b* Falkirk, 17 March 1959; *s* of James Scott Kerr and Sheana Kerr; *m* 1994, Edda Hermannsdottir; one *s* two *d*. *Educ:* Falkirk High Sch.; London Univ. (BEd PE and Hist.); Cardiff Business Sch. (MBA 1996). Leisure Officer, Falkirk DC, 1983–87; Principal Leisure Officer, Cardiff CC, 1987–90; Hd, Participation, Sports Council for Wales, 1990–96; Hd, Lifelong Learning and Leisure, Caerphilly CBC, 1996–2000; Lead Inspector, Audit Commn, 2000–01; Birmingham City Council: Dir, Leisure and Culture, 2001–03; Dir, Performance Improvement, 2003–05; Chief Executive: North Tyneside Council, 2005–10; Wiltshire Council, 2010–11; Chief Operating Officer, Cardiff CC, 2012–13; Chief Exec., Cornwall Council, 2014–15. Mem., Govt Efficiency Task Force, 2010. Pres., Inst. of Leisure and Amenity Mgt, 2003. British athletics international, 1977–83; British Under-20 Indoor and Outdoor Champion, 400m, 1977; Bronze Medal, Eur. Jun. Championships, 1977; 17 Scottish Championship medals; 12 AAA Championship medals. *Recreations:* fitness, golf, reading political and sports biographies, science fiction, music. *Address:* 10 Durley Park, Neston, Wilts SN13 9YG. *T:* (01225) 811775, 07766 924803.

KERR, Andrew Mark; Partner, Bell & Scott, WS, Edinburgh, 1969–99 (Senior Partner, 1987–96); Clerk to Society of Writers to HM Signet, 1983–2003; *b* Edinburgh, 17 Jan. 1940; *s* of William Mark Kerr and Katharine Marjorie Anne Stevenson; *m* 1967, Jane Susanna Robertson; one *d*. *Educ:* Edinburgh Acad.; Cambridge Univ. (BA); Edinburgh Univ. (LLB). Served RNR, 1961–76. British Petroleum, 1961–62; apprenticeship with Davidson & Syme, WS, Edinburgh, 1964–67; with Bell & Scott, Bruce & Kerr, WS, later Bell & Scott, WS, 1967–99. Vice-Chm., Edinburgh New Town Conservation Cttee, 1972–76; Chm., Edinburgh Solicitors' Property Centre, 1976–81. Chairman: Penicuik House Preservation Trust, 1985–2001; Arts Trust of Scotland, 1996–2015; Dunedin Concerts Trust, 1996–2009; Member: Council, Edinburgh Internat. Fest., 1978–82; Scottish Arts Council, 1988–94 (Chm., Drama Cttee, 1988–91, and 1993–94); Director: Edinburgh Fest. and King's Theatres, 1997–2003; Edinburgh World Heritage Trust, 1999–2010; Historic Scotland Foundn, 2001–06; Sec., Edinburgh Fest. Fringe Soc. Ltd, 1969–2002. Trustee: Usher Hall Conservation Trust, 1999–; Saltire Soc. Trust, 2014–. Mem. Council, St George's Sch. for Girls, Edinburgh, 1985–93; Gov., New Sch., Butterstone, 1995–2007. *Recreations:* architecture, hill walking, music, ships, ski-ing, theatre. *Address:* 16 Ann Street, Edinburgh EH4 1PJ. *T:* (home) (0131) 332 9857. *Club:* New (Edinburgh).

KERR, Andrew Palmer; Chief Executive Officer, Sense Scotland, since 2011; *b* 17 March 1962; *s* of William and May Kerr; *m* 1992, Susan Kealy; three *d* (incl. twins). *Educ:* Glasgow Coll. (BA Social Scis); Glasgow Caledonian Univ. (Postgrad. Cert. Mgt 2009; MBA 2010). Dep. Pres., Glasgow Coll. Students' Assoc., 1983–85; Convenor, Glasgow Area, NUS, 1985–86; Dep. Pres., NUS (Scotland), 1986–87; R&D Officer, Strathkelvin DC, 1987–90; Man. Dir, Achieving Quality, QA Consultancy, 1990–93; Strategy and Develt Manager, Cleansing Dept, Glasgow CC, 1993–99. Mem. (Lab) East Kilbride, Scottish Parlt, 1999–2011. Scottish Executive: Minister: for Finance and Public Services, 2001–04; for Health and Community Care, 2004–07; Shadow Cabinet Sec. for Finance and Sustainable Growth, 2007–11. Contested (Lab) East Kilbride, Scottish Parlt, 2011. *Recreations:* family, half marathon and 10K running, football, reading. *Address:* 6 Muirkirk Gardens, Strathaven ML10 6FS.

KERR, (Anne) Judith, OBE 2012; writer and illustrator, since 1968; *b* Berlin, 14 June 1923; *d* of Alfred and Julia Kerr; *m* 1954, Nigel Kneale (*d* 2006); one *s* one *d*. *Educ:* Ten different schs in four different countries; Central Sch. of Arts and Crafts, London (Schol.; failed Dip. in Book Illustration 1948). Painter, textile designer and art teacher, 1948–52; script reader, script ed., then script writer for BBC Television, 1952–57; full-time mum, 1958–65. Peter Pan Award, Action for Children's Arts, 2006. *Publications: for children:* The Tiger Who Came to Tea, 1968; Mog the Forgetful Cat, 1970; When Hitler Stole Pink Rabbit, 1971 (Jugendbuch Preis, Germany, 1974); When Willy Went to the Wedding, 1972; The Other Way Round, 1975, re-issued as Bombs on Aunt Dainty, 2002; Mog's Christmas, 1976; A Small Person Far Away, 1978; Mog and the Baby, 1980; Mog in the Dark, 1983; Mog and Me, 1984; Mog's Family of Cats, 1985; Mog's Amazing Birthday Caper, 1986; Mog and Bunny, 1988; Mog and Barnaby, 1991; How Mrs Monkey Missed the Ark, 1992; Mog on Fox Night, 1993; The Adventures of Mog, 1993; Mog in the Garden, 1994; Mog's Kittens, 1994; Out of the Hitler Time (trilogy: When Hitler Stole Pink Rabbit, The Other Way Round, A Small Person Far Away), 1994; Mog and the Granny, 1995; Mog and the Vee Ee Tee, 1996; The Big Mog Book, 1997; Birdie Halleluyah!, 1998; Mog's Bad Thing, 2000; The Other Goose, 2001; Goodbye Mog, 2002; Mog Time, 2004; Goose in a Hole, 2005; Twinkles, Arthur and Puss, 2007; One Night in the Zoo, 2009; My Henry, 2011; The Great Granny Gang, 2012; Judith Kerr's Creatures, 2013; The Crocodile Under the Bed, 2014; Mr Cleghorn's Seal, 2015. *Recreations:* walking across the river in the early morning, talking to cats, watching old films, remembering, staying alive. *Address:* c/o Society of Authors, 84 Drayton Gardens, SW10 9SB.

KERR, Calum Robert; MP (SNP) Berwickshire, Roxburgh and Selkirk, since 2015; *b* Galashiels, 5 April 1972; *m* Ros; three *c*. *Educ:* Peebles High Sch.; St Andrews Univ. (MA Hons Modern Hist. 1994). Account Manager, Philips Business Communications, 1995–98; Channel Account Manager, 1998–2003, High Touch Account Manager, 2004–09, Nortel Networks; Avaya: Named Account Manager, 2009–12; Practice Consultant - Sales Acceleration, 2012–13; Practice Leader - Sales Mgt Excellence, 2014–15. *Address:* House of Commons, SW1A 0AA.

KERR, Caroline; Media Consultant and Company Secretary, Millbank Media, since 2006; Independent Editorial Adviser, BBC Trust, since 2007; *b* 27 May 1962; *d* of John and Maureen Kerr; one *s* one *d*. *Educ:* Newnham Coll., Cambridge (MA English). Joined ITN, 1984: trainee, 1984–91; gen. reporter, 1991–94; Asia Corresp., 1994–98; Consumer Affairs Corresp., 1998–99; Business and Economics Ed., 1999–2004. *Address:* Millbank Media, 4 Millbank, SW1P 3JA.

KERR, David; *see* Kerr, M. D.

KERR, Prof. David James, CBE 2002; MD; DSc; FRCP, FRCPE, FMedSci; Professor of Cancer Medicine, University of Oxford, since 2009; Fellow, Harris Manchester College, Oxford, since 2012; *b* 14 June 1956; *s* of Robert James Andrew Kerr and Sarah Pettigrew Kerr (*née* Hogg); *m* 1st, 1980, Anne Miller Young (marr. diss.); one *s* two *d*; 2nd, 2013, Rachel Midgley; one *s* one *d*. *Educ:* Univ. of Glasgow (BSc 1st Cl. Hons 1977; MB ChB 1980; MSc 1985; MD 1987; PhD 1990; DSc 1997). FRCPGlas 1995; MRCP 1983, FRCP 1996; FRCPE 2009. Sen. Registrar (Med. Oncol.), Western Infirmary, Glasgow, 1985–89; Sen. Lectr, Glasgow Univ., 1989–92; Prof. of Clinical Oncol., and Clinical Dir, CRC Inst. For Cancer Studies, Univ. of Birmingham, 1992–2001; Rhodes Prof. of Therapeutics, Univ. of Oxford, 2001–09; Fellow, Corpus Christi Coll., Oxford, 2001–10. Visiting Professor: Univ. of Strathclyde, 1991–; Weill Cornell Med. Coll., NY, 2009–. FMedSci 2000. Hon. FRCGP 2007. *Publications:* (ed jtly) Regional Chemotherapy, 1999; Kerr Report on future of NHS in Scotland, 2005; Oxford Textbook of Oncology, 2014; contrib. numerous articles to peer reviewed med. and scientific jls. *Recreations:* football, busking. *Address:* Harris Manchester College, Mansfield Road, Oxford OX1 3TD; Nuffield Department of Clinical and Laboratory Sciences, Level 4, Academic Block, John Radcliffe Hospital, Oxford OX3 9DU. *Clubs:* Reform; Partick Thistle Supporters' (Glasgow).

KERR, Frith Zelda; graphic designer; Director, Studio Frith, since 2009; *b* 3 Oct. 1973; *d* of Peter and Jenny Kerr. *Educ:* Surbiton High Sch.; Kingston Poly.; Camberwell Coll. of Art (BA Hons); Royal Coll. of Art (MA). Vis. Lectr, Camberwell Coll. of Art, 1998–2003. Partner, Co-founder and Dir, Kerr/Noble, 1997–2008. Clients include Liberty, V&A Mus., RSA, Channel 4, David Chipperfield Architects, Chisenhale Gall. and Violette Editions. *Recreation:* reading in the bath. *Address:* Studio Frith, 10 Stoney Street, SE1 9AD. *E:* info@studiofrith.com.

KERR, Hugh; Press Officer, Solidarity, 2006–11; *b* 9 July 1944; *m*; one *s*. Former Sen. Lectr, Univ. of North London. Former Mem. (Lab) Harlow DC. MEP (Lab 1994–98, Ind. Lab 1998–99), Essex W and Herts E. Press officer for Scottish Socialist Party, 2000–04; Brussels corresp., The Scotsman, 2004.

KERR, James, QPM 1979; Chief Constable, Lincolnshire Police, 1977–83; *b* 19 Nov. 1928; *s* of William and Margaret Jane Kerr; *m* 1952, Jean Coupland (*d* 2009); one *d*. *Educ:* Carlisle Grammar School. Cadet and Navigating Officer, Merchant Navy, 1945–52 (Union Castle Line, 1949–52). Carlisle City Police and Cumbria Constabulary, 1952–74; Asst Director of Command Courses, Police Staff Coll., Bramshill, 1974; Asst Chief Constable (Operations), North Yorkshire Police, 1975; Deputy Chief Constable, Lincs, 1976. Officer Brother, OStJ, 1980. *Recreations:* music, squash. *Address:* 41/471 Maroondah Highway, Lilydale, Vic 3140, Australia. *Club:* Royal Automobile Club of Victoria (Victoria).

KERR, John, MBE 1986; Vice Lord-Lieutenant of Suffolk, 2003–14; *b* 19 Nov. 1939; *s* of William Kerr and Mary Laurie Kerr; *m* 1967, Gillian Hayward; two *s* two *d*. *Educ:* Framlingham Coll.; Writtle Coll. Farmer and company dir. Director: Wm Kerr (Farms) Ltd, 1971–2012; Grosvenor Farms Ltd, 1992–2005; Easton Events Ltd, 1994–; Suffolk Top Attractions Gp, 1997–2014; Grosvenor Farms Hldgs Ltd, 1999–2005; Anglian Pea Growers, 1999–2009; Cogent Breeding Ltd, 2002–05; Forum for Sustainable Farming, 2004–10; Chm., Rural East, Clydesdale Bank, 2005–12. Dir, Suffolk Agricl Assoc. Ltd, 1983–2008 (Chm., 1999–2002; Pres., 2006; Hon. Dir, Suffolk Show, 1982–84). Director: Ipswich Town FC, 1983–2008 (Chm., 1991–95); Ipswich Town plc, 2004–. Trustee, Farmers' Club Charitable Trust, 1995– (Chm., 1995–2014). Governor: Seckford Foundn, 1986–2002 (Chm., Finance, 1993–2000); Framlingham Coll., 1987–2010. Liveryman, Farmers' Co., 1985. JP 1972–93, DL 1988, High Sheriff 1997, Suffolk. DUniv Essex, 2002. *Address:* Blaxhall, Suffolk. *Clubs:* Farmers (Chm., 1994); Ipswich and Suffolk.

KERR, John Andrew Sinclair; Director, Kerr Consulting, since 2005; *b* 29 May 1958; *s* of Andrew Kerr and Frances Kerr; *m* 1979, Beverly Johnston; one *s* one *d*. *Educ:* Hutchesons' Grammar Sch., Glasgow; Univ. of Glasgow (LLB Hons). Contracts Lawyer, British Steel, 1979–83; film industry, 1983–88; Sen. Manager, Regulatory Affairs, Stock Exchange, 1988–98; Corporate Affairs Dir, 1998–2001, Chief Exec., 2001–05, Edexcel Ltd; Dir of Develt, Edge Foundn, 2005–10. FRSA. *Recreations:* gardening, running smallholding, film. *Address:* Holly Cottage, Water Lane, Cranbrook, Kent TN18 5AP.

KERR, Adm. Sir John (Beverley), GCB 1993 (KCB 1989); DL; FRIN; Commander-in-Chief, Naval Home Command, 1991–94; Flag Aide-de-Camp to the Queen, 1991–94; *b* 27 Oct. 1937; *s* of late Wilfred Kerr and Vera Kerr (*née* Sproule); *m* 1964, Elizabeth Anne, *d* of late Dr and Mrs C. R. G. Howard, Burley, Hants; three *s*. *Educ:* Moseley Hall County Grammar Sch., Cheadle; Britannia Royal Naval Coll., Dartmouth. Served in various ships, 1958–65 (specialized in navigation, 1964); Staff, BRNC, Dartmouth, 1965–67; HMS Cleopatra, 1967–69; Staff, US Naval Acad., Annapolis, 1969–71; NDC, Latimer, 1971–72; i/c HMS Achilles, 1972–74; Naval Plans, MoD, 1974–75; Defence Policy Staff, MoD, 1975–77; RCDS, 1978; i/c HMS Birmingham, 1979–81; Dir of Naval Plans, MoD, 1981–83; i/c HMS Illustrious, 1983–84; ACNS (Op. Requirements), 1984; ACDS (Op. Requirements) (Sea Systems), 1985–86; Flag Officer First Flotilla/Flotilla One, 1986–88; MoD, 1988–91. Member, Independent Review: of Armed Forces' Manpower, Career and Remuneration Structures, 1994–95; of Higher Educn Pay and Conditions, 1998–99. Mem., Museums and Galls Commn, 1994–2000. Mem., CWGC, 1994–2001 (Vice-Chm., 1998–2001). Cdre, RNSA, 1992–95; Member: Cttee of Management, RNLI, 1993–98; Cttee, Manchester Mus., 1994–2004 (Chm., 1996–2004); Central Council, Royal Over-Seas League, 2001–04. Member: Audit Cttee, 1994–98 (Chm., 1995–98), Council, 1995–98, Lancaster Univ.; Court and Council, Manchester Univ., 1998–2004; Court, UMIST, 2000–04; Pro-Chancellor, Univ. of Manchester, 2004–12. Mem., Lake District Nat. Park Authy, 2007–11 (Dep. Chm., 2008–11). CCMI (CIMgt 1993); FRIN 2008 (Associate FRIN 2006). DL Lancs 1995. Medal of Honour, Univ. of Manchester, 2012. *Recreations:* listening to music, sailing, hill walking, history.

KERR, Judith; *see* Kerr, A. J.

KERR, Malcolm James; Founder and Chief Executive Officer, DP9, planning consultants, since 2004; *b* Glasgow, 20 Oct. 1959; *s* of Michael and Evelyn Kerr; *m* 1989 (marr. diss. 2010); one *s* two *d*. *Educ:* Jordanhill College Sch., Glasgow; Univ. of Strathclyde (LLB 1980; Dip. Legal Studies 1981). ARICS 1986. Trainee solicitor, Shepherd and Wedderburn, WS, 1981–83; NP, 1983; Montagu Evans, Chartered Surveyors, 1983–2004. *Recreations:* countryside, walking, cycling, Roman history, architecture, Charlton Athletic. *Address:* DP9, 100 Pall Mall, SW1Y 5NQ. *T:* (020) 7004 1729. *E:* malcolm.kerr@dp9.co.uk. *Club:* Royal Automobile.

KERR, Rear-Adm. Mark William Graham; DL; freelance documentary photographer, since 2010; *b* 18 Feb. 1949; *s* of Captain M. W. B. Kerr, DSC, RN and Pat Kerr; *m* 1978, Louisa Edwards; two *s* one *d*. *Educ:* Marlborough Coll.; New Coll., Oxford (BA). FCIPD 2002–09. Joined RN, 1967; i/c HMS Alert, 1976; Principal Warfare Officer, HMS Charybdis, 1978–79; Staff Navigation Officer, Captain MinecounterMeasures, 1979–81; i/c HMS Beachampton, 1982–84; Officer i/c RN Schs Presentation Team, 1984–85; First Lieut, HMS Ariadne, 1985–88; i/c HMS Broadsword, 1988–90; MoD, 1990–94; i/c HMS Cumberland, 1994–95; Captain, RN Presentation Team, 1995–96; Dep. Flag Officer, Sea Trng, 1996–99; Commodore, BRNC, Dartmouth, 1999–2002; Naval Sec., 2002–04. Hon. Col, Powys ACF, 2006–11. Chief Exec., Powys County Council, 2004–09. Vice Chm., Soc. of Local Authy Chief Execs (Wales), 2008–09. Trustee: Nat. Botanical Garden of Wales, 2011– (Interim Dir, 2009–10; Chm., Steering Cttee, Regency Restoration Project, 2014–); Brecon Univ. Scholarship Fund, 2014–. President: Brecon Br., Royal Naval Assoc., 2010–11; Powys Br., SSAFA (formerly SSAFA Forces Help), 2012–; Vice-Pres., Friends of Gwent and Powys ACF, 2010–. Gov. and Mem. Council, RNLI, 2012–. DL Powys, 2013. *Recreations:* walking, ski-ing, history, photography. *Address:* Ty Llyn, Llangorse, Powys LD3 7UD. *W:* markkerr.co.uk.

KERR, (Michael) David; Chief Executive Officer, Bird & Bird, since 1996; *b* Gosforth, 28 April 1960; *s* of Douglas Kerr and Patricia Kerr; *m* 1985, Rebecca Spiro; one *s* one *d*. *Educ:* Sevenoaks Sch.; Jesus Coll., Cambridge (BA 1982); Chester Coll. of Law. Admitted Solicitor, 1985. Clifford Turner, 1983–85; Bird & Bird: Asst, 1985–87; Partner, 1987–. *Address:* Bird & Bird, 15 Fetter Lane, EC4A 1JP. *E:* david.kerr@twobirds.com.

KERR, Sir Ronald (James), Kt 2011; CBE 1998; Chief Executive, Guy's and St Thomas' NHS Foundation Trust, since 2007; *b* 2 Feb. 1950; *s* of James Boe Kerr and Margaret Catherine Kerr (*née* Robson); *m* 2005, Nicola Jane Martin; one step *s* one step *d*; one *d* from a previous marriage. *Educ:* Sandbach Sch., Cheshire; Cambridgeshire Coll. of Arts and Technol.; London Univ. (BSc Hons Geog. with Econs); London Business Sch. (MSc Business Studies). Sec., S Manchester CHC, 1974–77; Asst Sec., NE Thames RHA, 1977–79; Dep. House Gov., Moorfields Eye Hosp., 1979–80; Hosp. Sec., London Hosp., 1980–85; Dist Gen. Manager, N Herts HA, 1985–88; Dep. Dir of Financial Mgt, NHS Exec., 1988–90; Dist Gen. Manager, Lewisham and N Southwark HA and Chief Exec., SE London Commng Agency, 1990–93; Regl Gen. Manager, NW Thames RHA, 1993–94; Regl Dir, N Thames Regl Office, NHS Exec., 1994–98; Dir of Ops, NHS Exec., DoH, 1998–2001; Chief Executive: Nat. Care Standards Commn, 2001–04; United Bristol Healthcare NHS Trust, 2004–07. Chm., Assoc. of UK University Hosps, 2007–14. Mem. Council, Univ. of Bristol, 2010–. Hon. FKC 2010. *Recreations:* travel, reading, restaurants, music, Manchester City FC. *Address:* 17 Julian Road, Sneyd Park, Bristol BS9 1JZ.

KERR, Rose; Deputy Keeper, Asian Department (formerly Curator, then Chief Curator, Far Eastern Collections, subseq. Far Eastern Department), Victoria and Albert Museum, 1990–2003; Consultant, East Asian Art and Archaeology, since 2003; Museums Specialist Adviser, Hong Kong, since 2014; *b* 23 Feb. 1953; *d* of William Antony Kerr and Elizabeth Rendell; *m* 1990. *Educ:* SOAS, Univ. of London (BA Hons 1st Cl., Art and Archaeology of China); Languages Inst., Beijing. Fellow, Percival David Foundn of Chinese Art, 1976–78; joined Far Eastern Dept, V&A, 1978, Keeper, 1987–90. Hon. Associate, Needham Res. Inst., Cambridge, 2003. Member: Council, Oriental Ceramic Soc., 1987–2000 (Pres., 2000–03); GB-China Educnl Trust, 1995– (Chm., 2005–). Trustee: Worcester Porcelain Mus., 2008–; Sir Percival David Foundn, 2012–. Hon. Fellow, Univ. of Glasgow, 2004. *Publications:* (with P. Hughes-Stanton) Kiln Sites of Ancient China, 1980; (with John Larson) Guanyin: a masterpiece revealed, 1985; Chinese Ceramics: porcelain of the Qing Dynasty 1644–1911, 1986; Later Chinese Bronzes, 1990; (ed and contrib.) Chinese Art and Design: the T. T. Tsui Gallery of Chinese Art, 1991; (with Rosemary Scott) Ceramic Evolution in the Middle Ming Period, 1994; England's Victoria and Albert Museum: Chinese Qing Dynasty Ceramics (in Chinese), 1995; (with John Ayers *et al*) Blanc de Chine: porcelain from Dehua, 2002; Song Dynasty Ceramics, 2004; (with Nigel Wood) Science & Civilisation in China, vol. V, pt 12: Ceramic Technology, 2004; Song China through 21st Century Eyes, 2009; (with Luisa Mengoni) Chinese Export Ceramics, 2011; (jtly) East Asian Ceramics: the Laura collection, 2012; (with William R. Sargent) Treasures of Chinese Export Ceramics from the Peabody Essex Museum, 2012; (with John Johnston) Chinese Ceramics: the Leonora and Walter F. Brown Collection at the San Antonio Museum of Art, 2014; (contrib.) Asian Art, Rijksmuseum, 2014; articles in Oriental Art, Orientations, Apollo, Craft Magazine, V&A Album. *Recreation:* travel and research. *Address:* 14 St Joseph's Mews, Candlemas Lane, Beaconsfield HP9 1GA.

KERR, Simon Douglas O.; *see* Ofield-Kerr.

KERR, Hon. Sir Timothy Julian, Kt 2015; **Hon. Mr Justice Kerr;** a Judge of the High Court, Queen's Bench Division, since 2015; *b* 15 Feb. 1958; *s* of Rt Hon. Sir Michael Robert Emanuel Kerr, PC and of Julia Kerr; one *s*; *m* 1990, Nicola Mary Croucher; two *s*. *Educ:* Westminster Sch.; Magdalen Coll., Oxford (BA 1st Cl. Hons Juris.). Called to the Bar, Gray's Inn, 1983, Bencher, 2015; in practice as barrister, specialising in public law, sport, education and employment law, 1983–2015; QC 2001; a Recorder, 2008–15; a Dep. High Court Judge (Chancery Div.), 2013–15. Pt-time Chm., Employment Tribunals, 2001–06. Member: Sport Resolutions UK Arbitrators' Panel, 2000–; FA Premier League Arbitrators' Panel, 2007–. Chairman: Anti-Doping Tribunal, ICC, 2011–; Anti-Doping Tribunal, Bd of Control for Cricket in India, 2013–. *Publications:* (jtly) Sports Law, 1999, 2nd edn 2012; contrib. various articles to learned jls. *Recreations:* music, travel, reading, friends, family, running, supporting Chelsea Football Club, languages (French, German, Spanish). *Address:* Royal Courts of Justice, Rolls Building, Fetter Lane, EC4A 1NL.

KERR, William Andrew S.; *see* Scott-Kerr.

KERR-DINEEN, Peter Brodrick; Chairman: Howe Robinson Partners Pte Ltd, since 2015; Howe Robinson and Co. Ltd, since 2013 (Joint Chairman, 1994–2013); Howe Robinson Group (formerly Investments) Ltd, since 2013 (Joint Chairman, 1996–2013); Chairman, Baltic Exchange, 2003–05 (Member, since 1976; Director, 1998–2005, and since 2013); *b* 26 Nov. 1953; *s* of late Canon F. G. Kerr-Dineen and of Hermione Kerr-Dineen; *m* 1996, Dr Susan Dodd, FRCPath; one *s* one *d*. *Educ:* Marlborough Coll.; Gonville and Caius Coll., Cambridge (BA 1975, MA 1978). Mgt trainee, Ocean Transport and Trading, 1975–76; joined Howe Robinson, 1976; Director: Great Eastern Shipping Co. London Ltd, 1989–; P and M Consulting Services Ltd, 2010–; Chairman: Maritime Strategies Internat., 2008–; Shyvers Savoy Shipping Ltd, 2012–. Mem., Develt Campaign Bd, Gonville and Caius Coll., Cambridge. FRAI 1975. Liveryman, Shipwrights' Co., 2007–. *Recreations:* riding, fishing, drama, anthropology, painting. *Address:* Baltic Exchange Ltd, St Mary Axe, EC3A 8BH. *T:* (020) 7369 1621. *E:* kerrdineen@hotmail.com. *Clubs:* Hurlingham, Oxford and Cambridge.

KERRIDGE, Thomas; Chef Patron: The Hand and Flowers, Marlow, since 2005; The Coach, since 2014; *b* Salisbury, Wilts, 27 July 1973; *s* of late Michael John Kerridge and Jackie Kerridge; *m* 2000, Beth Cullen. *Educ:* Saintbridge Comprehensive Sch., Glos. Commis chef: Calcot Manor, Tetbury, 1991–92; Painswick Hotel, Gloucester, 1992–94; chef de partie: Country Elephant, Gloucester, 1994–96; Capital Hotel, London, 1996; sous chef: Stephen Bull, St Martins, London, 1996–99; Rhodes in the Square, London, 1999; Odettes Restaurant, London, 1999–2001; head chef: Bellamy's Dining Room, London, 2001; Gt Fosters Hotel, Surrey, 2001; sen. sous chef, Monsieur Max Restaurant, Hampton, 2001–03; hd chef, Adlards, Norwich, 2003–05. Television presenter: Tom Kerridge's Proper Pub Food (series), 2013; Tom Kerridge Cooks Christmas, 2013; Spring Kitchen with Tom Kerridge, 2014; Tom Kerridge's Best Ever Dishes (series), 2014. MIH (MHCIMA 2007). Michelin Star, 2006, 2nd Michelin Star, 2012; 3 AA Rosettes, 2007, 2008. *Publications:* Tom Kerridge's Proper Pub Food, 2013; Tom Kerridge's Best Ever Dishes, 2014. *Address:* The Hand and Flowers, 126 West Street, Marlow, Bucks SL7 2BP. *T:* (01628) 482277. *E:* contact@thehandandflowers.co.uk.

KERRIGAN, Greer Sandra, CB 2006; former Director of Legal Services, Department for Work and Pensions; *b* Port of Spain, Trinidad, 7 Aug. 1948; *d* of Wilfred M. Robinson and Rosina Robinson (*née* Ali); *m* 1974, Donal Brian Mathew Kerrigan; one *s* one *d*. *Educ:* Bishop Anstey High Sch., Trinidad; Coll. of Law, Inns of Court. Called to the Bar, Middle Temple, 1971. Legal Advr, Public Utilities Commn, Trinidad, 1972–74; Department of Health and Social Security, subseq. Department of Social Security, then Department for Work and Pensions: Legal Assistant, 1974–77; Sen. Legal Assistant, 1977–85; Asst Solicitor, 1985–91; Principal Asst Solicitor, subseq. Legal Dir (Health), then Legal Director (Work and Pensions), later Dir of Legal Services (Work and Pensions), 1991; Principal Asst Solicitor, then Legal Dir (Health), DoH, 1991–2004. *Recreations:* reading, music, bridge.

KERRIGAN, Herbert Aird; QC (Scot.) 1992; *b* 2 Aug. 1945; *s* of Herbert Kerrigan and Mary Agnes Wallace Hamilton or Kerrigan; one adopted *s*. *Educ:* Whitehill, Glasgow; Univ. of Aberdeen (LLB Hons 1968); Hague Acad. of Internat. Law; Keele Univ. (MA 1970); Oxford Univ. (Postgrad. Dip. in Applied Theol. 2002). Admitted Faculty of Advocates, 1970; Lectr in Criminal Law and Criminology, 1969–73, in Scots Law, 1973–74, Edinburgh Univ.; called to the Bar, Middle Temple, 1990; in practice, 1991–. Vis. Prof., Univ. of Southern Calif., 1979–. Mem., Longford Commn, 1972. Church of Scotland: Elder, 1967– (now at Greyfriars Tolbooth and Highland Kirk, Edinburgh); Reader, 1969; Mem., Assembly Council, 1981–85; Sen. Chaplain to Moderator, Gen. Assembly of Church of Scotland, 1999–2000; Convener, Cttee on Chaplains to HM's Forces, 2001– (Vice Convener, 1998–2001). Pres., Edinburgh Royal Infirmary Samaritan Soc., 1992– (Vice-Pres., 1989–92). *Publications:* An Introduction to Criminal Procedure in Scotland, 1970; (contrib.) Ministers for the 1980s, 1979; (contributing ed.) The Law of Contempt, 1982; (contrib.) Sport and the Law, 2nd edn 1995. *Recreation:* travel. *Address:* c/o Advocates' Library, Parliament House, Edinburgh EH1 1RF. *T:* (0131) 226 5071; 9–12 Bell Yard, WC2A 2JR. *T:* (020) 7400 1800, *Fax:* (020) 7400 1405; (home) 20 Edinburgh Road, Dalkeith, Midlothian EH22 1JY. *T:* (0131) 660 3007.

KERRIGAN, Prof. John Francis, FBA 2013; Professor of English 2000, University of Cambridge, since 2001; Fellow, St John's College, Cambridge, since 1982; *b* 16 June 1956; *s* of late Stephen Francis Kerrigan and of Patricia Kerrigan (*née* Baker); one *d*. *Educ:* St Edward's Coll., Liverpool (Christian Brothers); Keble Coll., Oxford (BA). Domus Sen. Schol., 1977–79, Jun. Res. Fellow, 1979–82, Merton Coll., Oxford; University of Cambridge: Asst Lectr in English, 1982–86; Lectr in English, 1986–98; Reader in English Lit., 1998–2001; Dir of Studies in English, St John's Coll., 1987–97; Chm., English Faculty Bd, 2003–06. Visiting Professor: Meiji Univ., Tokyo, 1986; UCLA, 2009. Visiting Fellow: Jadavpur Univ., Calcutta, 2008; Univ. of Delhi, 2008; Univ. of Auckland, 2011. Res. Reader, British Acad., 1998–2000; Leverhulme Res. Fellow, 2012–13. Lectures: Chatterton, British Acad., 1988; J. A. W. Bennett Meml, Perugia, 1998; Acad. for Irish Cultural Heritages, 2003; F. W. Bateson, Oxford, 2004; Nicholson and Poetics, Chicago, 2007; Shakespeare, British Acad., 2009; Andrew Lang, St Andrews, 2009; Alice Griffin, Auckland, 2011. Foundn Fellow, English Assoc., 1999; Fellow, Wordsworth Trust, 2001. Trustee, Dove Cottage, Wordsworth Trust, 1984–2001. Charles Oldham Shakespeare Prize, 1976, Matthew Arnold Meml Prize, 1981, Oxford Univ.; Truman Capote Award for Literary Criticism, 1998. *Publications:* (ed) Love's Labour's Lost, 1982; (ed) Shakespeare's Sonnets and A Lover's Complaint, 1986, 2nd edn 1995; (ed with J. Wordsworth) Wordsworth and the Worth of Words, by Hugh Sykes Davies, 1987; Motives of Woe: Shakespeare and Female Complaint, 1991; (ed jtly) English Comedy, 1994; Revenge Tragedy: Aeschylus to Armageddon, 1996; (ed with P. Robinson) The Thing about Roy Fisher: critical studies, 2000; On Shakespeare and Early Modern Literature: essays, 2001; Archipelagic English: literature, history and politics 1603–1707, 2008; Shakespeare's Binding Language, 2016; contrib. London Rev. of Books, TLS and poetry mags. *Recreation:* music. *Address:* St John's College, Cambridge CB2 1TP. *T:* (01223) 338620. *E:* jk10023@cam.ac.uk.

KERRY, Earl of; Simon Henry George Petty-Fitzmaurice; *b* 24 Nov. 1970; *s* and *heir* of Marquess of Lansdowne, *qv*. *Educ:* Eton; Jesus Coll., Cambridge.

KERRY, Knight of; *see* FitzGerald, Sir A. J. A. D.

KERRY, John Forbes, JD; Secretary of State, United States of America, since 2013; *b* 11 Dec. 1943; *s* of Richard John Kerry and Rosemary Kerry (*née* Forbes); *m* 1st, 1970, Julia S. Thorne (marr. diss. 1985); two *d*; 2nd, 1995, (Maria) Teresa (Thierstein) Heinz (*née* Simoes-Ferreira). *Educ:* Yale Univ. (BA 1966); Boston Coll. (MA; JD 1976). Served US Navy, 1966–70; Nat. Co-ordinator, Vietnam Veterans Against the War, 1969–71. Called to the Bar, Mass, 1976; Asst Dist Attorney, Middx Co., Mass, 1976–79; Partner, Kerry & Sragow, Boston, 1979–82; Lt Gov., Mass, 1982–84; US Senator from Mass, 1985–2013. Presidential cand. (Democrat),

US elections, 2004. *Publications:* The New Soldier, 1971; The New War: the web of crime that threatens America's security, 1997. *Address:* Department of State, 2201 C Street NW, Washington, DC 20520, USA.

KERSE, Dr Christopher Stephen, CB 2003; Second Counsel to Chairman of Committees and Legal Adviser to Select Committee on the European Union, House of Lords, 1995–2007; *b* 12 Dec. 1946; *s* of late William Harold Kerse and Maude Kerse; *m* 1st, 1971, Gillian Hanks (*d* 2007); one *s* one *d*; 2nd, 2008, Retha Coetzee. *Educ:* King George V Sch., Southport; Univ. of Hull (LLB; PhD 1995). Admitted Solicitor, 1972. Lecturer in Law: Univ. of Bristol, 1968–72; Univ. of Manchester, 1972–76; Asst Prof., Faculty of Law, Univ. of British Columbia, 1974–75; Sen. Legal Asst, OFT, 1976–81; Department of Trade and Industry: Sen. Legal Asst, 1981–82; Asst Solicitor, 1982–88; Head, Consumer Affairs Div., 1991–93; Under-Sec. (Legal), 1988–95; Prof. of Law, Univ. of Surrey, 2007–09. Vis. Prof., KCL, 1992–2010. *Publications:* The Law Relating to Noise, 1975; EC Antitrust Procedure, 1981, 5th edn 2005 (with N. Khan); (with J. C. Cook) EC Merger Control, 1991, 5th edn 2009; articles in various legal jls. *Recreations:* the double bass, orchestration, wood. *E:* kerse@btinternet.com.

KERSFELT, Anita Ingegerd; *see* Gradin, A. I.

KERSHAW, family name of **Baron Kershaw**.

KERSHAW, 4th Baron *cr* 1947; **Edward John Kershaw;** Chartered Accountant; business consultant; Partner, Bartlett Kershaw Trott, Chartered Accountants, 1996–2001; *b* 12 May 1936; *s* of 3rd Baron and Katharine Dorothea Kershaw (*née* Staines); *S* father, 1962; *m* 1963, Rosalind Lilian Rutherford; one *s* two *d*. *Educ:* Selhurst Grammar Sch., Surrey. Entered RAF Nov. 1955, demobilised Nov. 1957. Admitted to Inst. of Chartered Accountants in England and Wales, Oct. 1964. Mem., Acad. of Experts, 1995. Lay Governor, The King's Sch., Gloucester, 1986–95. JP Gloucester, 1982–95. *Heir: s* Hon. John Charles Edward Kershaw, *b* 23 Dec. 1971. *Address:* 1 Phillips Court, Baldock Street, Royston, Herts SG8 9DL.

KERSHAW, Andrew; broadcaster and journalist, since 1984; *b* 9 Nov. 1959; *s* of John (Jack) Kershaw and Eileen Kershaw (*née* Acton); one *s* one *d* by Juliette Banner. *Educ:* Hulme Grammar Sch., Oldham; Leeds Univ. Joined BBC, 1984: presenter: Whistle Test, 1984–87 (Live Aid, 1985); Andy Kershaw Prog., Radio 1, 1985–2000, Radio 3, 2001–07; Andy Kershaw's World of Music, World Service, 1987–2000; Music Planet (series), Radio 3, 2011; occasional foreign news reports for Radio 4, 1990 (incl. reports from Haiti, Angola, Rwanda, N Korea, Iraq); Travelog, Channel 4, 1991–97 (incl. first ever film made inside N Korea, 1995); freelance journalist, 1988–; Radio Critic, Independent, 1999. Hon. MusD: UEA, 2003; Leeds, 2005. Sony Radio Awards, 1987, 1989 (two), 1996, 2002 (three). *Publications:* No Off Switch (autobiog.), 2011. *Recreations:* music, motorcycle racing, travels to extreme countries, boxing, fishing.

KERSHAW, Dame Betty; *see* Kershaw, Dame J. E. M.

KERSHAW, David Andrew; Chief Executive, M&C Saatchi plc, since 2004 (Founding Partner, 1995–2004); *b* 26 Feb. 1954; *s* of Lawrence Kershaw and Rona Kershaw (now Lucas); *m* 1993, Clare Whitley; one *s* one *d*. *Educ:* Bedales Sch.; Univ. of Durham (BA Hons Pols 1977); London Business Sch. (MBA 1982). Account Exec., Wasey Campbell-Ewald, 1977–80; Saatchi & Saatchi UK: Account Dir, 1982–90; Man. Dir, 1990–94; Chief Exec., 1994–95. Trustee, Creative and Cultural Skills, 2005–09; Chm., Cultural Leadership Prog., 2006–11; Mem., Strategic Adv. Cttee, Clore Leadership Prog., 2011–. Gov., Southbank Centre, 2009–. *Recreations:* Arsenal, golf, opera, clarinet. *Address:* M&C Saatchi plc, 36 Golden Square, W1F 9EE. *T:* (020) 7543 4500. *E:* davidk@mcsaatchi.com. *Clubs:* Groucho, Ivy; Coombe Hill Golf.

KERSHAW, Helen Elizabeth, (Mrs W. J. S. Kershaw); *see* Paling, Her Honour H. E.

KERSHAW, Sir Ian, Kt 2002; DPhil; FBA 1991; Professor of Modern History, University of Sheffield, 1989–2008; *b* Oldham, 29 April 1943; *s* of late Joseph Kershaw and of Alice (*née* Robinson); *m* 1966, Janet Elizabeth Murray Gammie (*see* Dame J. E. M. Kershaw); two *s*. *Educ:* St Bede's Coll., Manchester; Univ. of Liverpool (BA 1965); Merton Coll., Oxford (DPhil 1969; Hon. Fellow, 2005). FRHistS, 1972–74, 1991. University of Manchester: Asst Lectr in Medieval Hist., 1968–70, Lectr, 1970–74; Lectr in Modern Hist., 1974–79, Sen. Lectr, 1979–87, Reader elect, 1987; Prof. of Modern History, Univ. of Nottingham, 1987–89. Vis. Prof. of Contemporary Hist., Ruhr-Univ., Bochum, 1983–84. Fellow: Alexander von Humboldt-Stiftung, 1976; Wissenschaftskolleg zu Berlin, 1989–90. Bundesverdienstkreuz (Germany), 1994. Hon. DLitt: Manchester, 2004; QUB, 2007; Sheffield, 2009; Oxford, 2010; Leeds, 2012; DUniv: Stirling, 2006; Huddersfield, 2013. Meyer-Struckmann Prize, Univ. of Düsseldorf, 2013. *Publications:* (ed) Rentals and Ministers' Accounts of Bolton Priory 1473–1539, 1969; Bolton Priory: the economy of a Northern monastery, 1973; Der Hitler-Mythos: Volksmeinung und Propaganda im Dritten Reich, 1980, Eng. trans. 1987; Popular Opinion and Political Dissent in the Third Reich: Bavaria 1933–1945, 1983; The Nazi Dictatorship: problems and perspectives of interpretation, 1985, 4th edn 2000; (ed) Weimar: why did German democracy fail?, 1990; Hitler: a profile in power, 1991, 2nd edn 2000; (ed with M. Lewin) Stalinism and Nazism, 1997; Hitler: vol. 1, 1889–1936: hubris, 1998, vol. 2, 1936–1945: nemesis, 2000 (Bruno Kreisky Prize (Austria), 2000; Wolfson Prize for History, 2000; British Acad. Prize, 2001); (ed with David M. Smith) The Bolton Priory Compotus 1286–1325, 2001; Making Friends with Hitler: Lord Londonderry and Britain's road to war, 2004 (Elizabeth Longford Historical Biog. Prize, 2005); Fateful Choices: ten decisions that changed the world 1940–1941, 2007; Hitler, the Germans and the Final Solution, 2008; Luck of the Devil: the story of Operation Valkyrie, 2009; The End: Hitler's Germany, 1944–45, 2011 (Leipzig Book Prize for European Understanding, 2012); To Hell and Back: Europe 1914–49, 2015; articles in learned jls. *Recreations:* Rugby League, football, cricket, music, real ale, outings in the Yorkshire dales. *Address:* 13 Fairfax Avenue, Didsbury, Manchester M20 6AJ.

KERSHAW, Dame Janet Elizabeth Murray, (Dame Betty), DBE 1998; FRCN; Education Adviser, Royal College of Nursing, 2008–11; Professor and Dean, School of Nursing and Midwifery, University of Sheffield, 1999–2006, now Dean Emeritus; *b* 11 Dec. 1943; *d* of Ian U. Gammie and Janet Gammie; *m* 1966, Ian Kershaw (*see* Sir Ian Kershaw); two *s*. *Educ:* Crossley and Porter Grammar Sch., Halifax; United Manchester Hosps (SRN; OND); Manchester Univ. (MSc Nursing; RNT). Dir of Educn, Royal Marsden Hosp., 1984–87; Principal, Stockport, Tameside and Glossop Coll. of Nursing, 1987–94; Dir of Nurse Educn, Coll. of Midwifery and Nursing, Manchester, 1994–97; Dir, Centre for Professional Policy Develt, Sch. of Nursing, Midwifery and Health Visiting, Univ. of Manchester, 1997–98. Visiting Professor: Manchester Metropolitan Univ., 2006; Birmingham City Univ., 2007–. Pres., RCN, 1994–98 (FRCN 2001). Chm., GNC Trust, 2007–. Chief Officer, Nursing and Social Care, St John Ambulance, 1998–2005. Hon. LLD Manchester, 1995. OStJ 1998. *Publications:* (with J. Salvage) Models For Nursing, 1986; (with J. Salvage) Models for Nursing 2, 1990; (with Bob Price) The Riehl Model of Care, 1993; (with J. Marr) Caring for Older People, 1998. *Recreations:* theatre, music, travel. *Address:* Royal College of Nursing, Cavendish Square, W1G 0RN.

KERSHAW, Jann Peta Olwen; *see* Parry, J. P. O.

KERSHAW, (Philip) Michael; QC 1980; DL; *b* 23 April 1941; *m* 1980, Anne (*née* Williams); one *s*. *Educ:* Ampleforth Coll.; St John's Coll., Oxford (MA). FCIArb 1991. Called to the Bar, Gray's Inn, 1963; in practice, 1963–90; a Recorder, 1980–90; Circuit Commercial Judge, 1990–91, Circuit Mercantile Judge, 1991–2006. Dir, Bar Mutual Insce Co. Ltd, 1988–90. Consulting Ed. and contrib., Atkin's Court Forms, 1997–2013. DL Lancs, 2007. *Publications:* Fraud and Misrepresentation, Injunctions, Bills of Sale, Bonds and Banking and Bills of Exchange, in Atkin's Court Forms; (contrib.) Interests in Goods, 1993. *Recreation:* choral singing.

KERSHAW, Stephen Edward; Senior Director for Strategy and Transformation, Immigration Enforcement, Home Office, since 2014; *b* 20 Sept. 1959; *s* of Barry Kershaw, railway signal engr, and Audrey Kathleen (*née* Breadmore). *Educ:* St Peter's C of E Primary Sch., Rickmansworth; William Penn Comprehensive Sch., Rickmansworth, Herts; Wadham Coll., Oxford (Open Schol.; BA 1st Cl. Hons Mod. Hist. 1981; MA; res., 1981–84). Lectr in Mod. Hist., Wadham Coll., Oxford, 1984–85; Cabinet Office, 1985–87 (Private Sec. to Second Perm. Sec., 1986–87); DES, 1987–89; Next Steps Team, Cabinet Office, 1989–92; DFE, later DfEE, 1992–99; on secondment as Hd, Strategic Planning, Manchester LEA, 1999–2000; Actg Dir, Pupil Support and Inclusion Gp, DfEE, 2000–01; Dir, Teachers' Gp, subseq. Sch. Workforce Unit, DfEE, later DfES, 2001–03; Finance Dir, DfES, 2003–06; Dir, Prime Minister's Delivery Unit, Cabinet Office, 2006–07; Home Office: Dir, Police Reform and Resources, 2007–12; Foreign Nat. Offenders Strategy, Internat. and Immigration Policy Gp. *Publications:* (contrib.) The Tudor Nobility, ed G. W. Bernard, 1992; contrib. reviews in various jls. *Recreations:* family history, Spain, Laurel and Hardy, indulging my niece and nephews.

KERSLAKE, family name of **Baron Kerslake**.

KERSLAKE, Baron *cr* 2015 (Life Peer), of Endcliffe in the City of Sheffield; **Robert Walter Kerslake,** Kt 2005; Chair, King's College Hospital NHS Foundation, since 2015; *b* 28 Feb. 1955; *m* Anne; one *s* one *d*. *Educ:* Univ. of Warwick (BSc Hons Maths). CPFA. Greater London Council, 1979–85: CIPFA trainee, 1979–82; Transport Finance, 1982–85; with ILEA, 1985–89; Dir of Finance, 1989–90, Chief Executive: London Borough of Hounslow, 1990–97; Sheffield CC, 1997–2008; Chief Exec., Homes and Communities Agency, 2008–10; Perm. Sec., DCLG, 2010–15; Hd of the Civil Service, 2012–14. Chairman: Peabody, 2015–; Centre for Public Scrutiny, 2015–. Pres., LGA, 2015–. *Recreations:* music, walking.

KERSLAKE, Deborah Ann; Chief Executive, Cruse Bereavement Care, since 2008; *b* Liverpool, 3 March 1958; *d* of Norman Thompson and Marjorie Thompson; *m* 1986, Michael Kerslake. *Educ:* Merchant Taylors' Sch. for Girls, Liverpool; Univ. of York (BA Hons Hist.); University Coll. Cardiff, Univ. of Wales (CQSW; DipSW); Univ. of Birmingham (Postgrad. Dip. Public Sector Mgt). Birmingham City Council: Social Worker, 1981–83; Sen. Social Worker Childcare, 1983–87; Sen. Social Worker Physical Disability, 1986–87; Actg Team Manager, 1988; Actg Principal Social Worker, 1988–89; Co-ordinator, 1989–93, Manager, 1993–99, Share Scheme; Cruse Bereavement Care: Proj. Manager, Quality in Bereavement Care, 1999–2002; Hd, Service Planning and Develt, 2002–08. *Publications:* articles in Bereavement Care and Grief Matters: the Aust. Jl of Grief and Bereavement. *Recreations:* running, theatre, opera, tennis, reading, travel. *Address:* Cruse Bereavement Care, PO Box 800, Richmond, Surrey TW9 1RG. *T:* (020) 8939 9532, *Fax:* (020) 8940 1671. *E:* debbie.kerslake@cruse.org.uk.

KERSLAKE, Rosaleen Clare; Chief Executive, Prince's Regeneration Trust, since 2006; *b* Bath, 8 March 1957; *d* of Robert James Kerslake and Maura Kerslake (*née* Moloney); partner, Stuart Sim; one *s* two *d*. *Educ:* Blue Sch., Wells, Som; Univ. of Keele (BA Law and Psychol.); Open Univ. Business Sch. (MBA). Admitted as solicitor, 1982; Chamberlins Solicitors, 1980–86, Partner, 1983–86; Legal Advr, Conoco Ltd, 1986–88; Dir, Gulf Oil, 1988–96; Internat. Hd, Gp Services, Booker plc, 1996–2000; Property Dir, Network Rail, 2000–03; Chief Exec., Regenco Urban Regeneration Co., 2003–06. Chair, Regeneration Leaders' Network, 2008–. Non-exec. Dir, Quintain plc, 2013–. Trustee, Heritage Alliance, 2014–. *Recreations:* gardening, walking, fostering children and bringing up my own. *Address:* Prince's Regeneration Trust, 14 Buckingham Palace Road, SW1W 0QP. *T:* (020) 3262 0560. *E:* ros.kerslake@princes-regeneration.org.

KERSWELL, Prof. Richard Rodney, PhD; FRS 2012; Professor of Applied Mathematics, University of Bristol. *Educ:* Emmanuel Coll., Cambridge (BA Maths 1987); Univ. of Calif (MA Applied Maths 1988); Massachusetts Inst. of Technol. (PhD 1992). *Publications:* articles in jls. *Address:* Department of Mathematics, University of Bristol, University Walk, Clifton, Bristol BS8 1TW.

KERTÉSZ, Imre; writer and translator, since 1953; *b* Budapest, 9 Nov. 1929; *m* Magda. With Világosság newspaper, Budapest, 1948–51; mil. service, 1951–53. Nobel Prize in Literature, 2002. Books translated into numerous languages, incl. English, German, Spanish, French, Czech, Russian, Swedish and Hebrew. *Publications: novels:* Sorstalanság, 1975 (Fateless, 1992); A nyomkeresö (The Pathfinder), 1977; A kudarc (Fiasco), 1988; Kaddis a meg nem született gyermekért, 1990 (Kaddish for a Child not Born, 1997); Az angol labogó (The English Flag), 1991; Gályanapló (Galley Diary), 1992; Jegyzökönyv, 1993; Valaki más: a változás krónikája (I, Another: chronicle of a metamorphosis), 1997; Felszámolás (Liquidation), 2003; *essays:* A holocaust mint kultúra (The Holocaust as Culture), 1993; A gondolatnyi csend, amíg kivégzöoztag újratölt (Moments of Silence while the Execution Squad Reloads), 1998; A számüzött nyelv (The Exiled Language), 2001; K. dosszié, 2006 (Dossier K., 2013). *Address:* c/o Magvetö Press, Dankó u. 4–8, 1086 Budapest, Hungary.

KERVIN, Alison; author; Sports Editor, Mail on Sunday, since 2013; *b* Birmingham, 1969; *d* of Peter and Christine Kervin; one *s*. *Educ:* Kings Norton Girls' Sch.; Univ. of Sussex (BSc Hons). Chief Sports Writer, Slough Observer, 1989; PR Manager and Rugby Develt Officer, England Rugby Team, 1991–95; Ed., Rugby World mag., 1995–98; publisher of sports titles, IPC Mags, 1998–99; Rugby Ed., 1999–2002, Chief Sports Feature Writer, 2002–05, The Times; Chief Sports Interviewer, Daily Telegraph, 2005–13. *Publications: non-fiction:* Sports Writing: a guide to the profession, 1997; A Guide to the 1999 Rugby World Cup, 1999; (ed) Denise Lewis: personal best, 2001; (with J. Leonard) Jason Leonard: autobiography, 2001, 2nd edn 2004; Clive Woodward: the biography, 2005; Thirty Bullies: a history of the Rugby World Cup, 2007; Phil Vickery: raging bull, 2010; *fiction:* Wags Diary, 2007; A Wag Abroad, 2008; Celebrity Bride, 2009; Wags at the World Cup, 2010; A Wags Guide to Euro 2012, 2012; Mother & Son, 2014. *Recreations:* theatre, ballet, literature, sports. *E:* ak@alisonkervin.co.uk.

KESCHNER, Catherine Mary; *see* Muirden, C. M.

KESSLER, Dinah Gwen Lison; *see* Rose, D. G. L.

KESSLER, Edward David, MBE 2011; PhD; Founder and Executive Director, Woolf Institute (formerly Woolf Institute of Abrahamic Faiths), Cambridge, since 1998; Fellow, St Edmund's College, Cambridge, since 2002; *b* 3 May 1963; *s* of William and Joanna Kessler; *m* 1989, Patricia Josephine Oakley; one *s* two *d*. *Educ:* Univ. of Leeds (BA Jt Hons 1985); Harvard Univ. (MTS 1987); Univ. of Stirling (MBA 1989); Univ. of Cambridge (PhD 1999). W. H. Smith, 1987–89; Kesslers Internat. Ltd, 1989–95. Sternberg Interfaith Award, 2006. Co-Ed., Studies in Jewish-Christian Relns, 2005–07. *Publications:* An English Jew: the life and writings of Claude Montefiore, 1989, 2nd edn 2002; (ed with J. Pawlikowski) Jews and Christians in Conversation: crossing cultures and generations, 2002; Bound by the Bible: Jews, Christians and the Sacrifice of Isaac, 2004; The Founders of Liberal Judaism: Israel Abrahams, Claude Montefiore, Israel Mattuck and Lily Montagu, 2004; (ed with D. Goldberg) Aspects of Liberal Judaism: essays in honour of Rabbi John D. Rayner, 2004; (ed with M. Wright) Themes in Jewish-Christian Relations, 2005; (ed with N. Wenborn) A Dictionary of Jewish-Christian Relations, 2005; (ed with J. Aitken) Challenges in Jewish-Christian Relations, 2006; What do Jews Believe?, 2006; An Introduction to Jewish-Christian Relations, 2010; Jews, Christians and Muslims, 2013. *Recreations:* family, supporting Arsenal, Mediterranean cycling. *Address:* 12–14 Grange Road, Cambridge CB3 9DU. *T:* (01223) 741048. *E:* edk21@cam.ac.uk. *Club:* Athenæum.

See also J. R. Kessler.

KESSLER, James Richard; QC 2003; *b* 1959; *s* of William and Joanna Kessler; *m* 1983, Jane Marie Pinto; two *s* one *d*. *Educ:* Brasenose Coll., Oxford (MA). FTII 1990. Called to the Bar: Gray's Inn, 1984; Northern Ireland, 2003; in practice at Revenue Bar; Bencher, Lincoln's Inn, 2013; Head, Tax Chambers, 2015–. Founder, Trusts Discussion Forum, 1999. Trustee: Phoenix Cinema Trust, 2009–; Purbeck Film Charitable Trust, 2009–. *Publications:* Tax Planning for the Foreign Domiciliary, 1987; Tax Planning and Fundraising for Charities, 1989, 10th edn as Taxation of Charities and Non-Profit Organisations, 2015; Drafting Trusts and Will Trusts, 1992, 12th edn 2014; Taxation of Foreign Domiciliaries, 2001, 13th edn as Taxation of Non-Residents and Foreign Domiciliaries, 2015; Drafting Trusts and Will Trusts in Canada, 2003, 3rd edn 2011; Drafting Trusts and Will Trusts in Northern Ireland, 2004, 3rd edn 2012; Drafting Cayman Island Trusts, 2007; Drafting Trusts and Will Trusts in the Channel Islands, 2007, 2nd edn 2013; Drafting Trusts and Will Trusts in Singapore, 2007, 2nd edn 2015; Drafting Trusts and Will Trusts in Australia, 2008; Drafting Trusts and Will Trusts in New Zealand, 2010; Drafting Trusts and Will Trusts in Scotland, 2013; Drafting BVI Trusts, 2014. *Recreations:* cinema, jogging. *Address:* 15 Old Square, Lincoln's Inn, WC2A 3UE. *T:* (020) 7242 2744. *E:* kessler@kessler.co.uk.

See also E. D. Kessler.

KESTELMAN, Sara; actor and writer; *d* of late Morris Kestelman, RA and Dorothy Mary (*née* Creagh). *Educ:* Hampstead Parochial Sch.; Camden Sch. for Girls; Cecchetti ballet trng; Central Sch. of Speech and Drama. Early rôles with Open Air Th., Regent's Park, Liverpool Playhouse, Manchester Liby Th., Castle Th., Farnham; Royal Shakespeare Co. includes: A Midsummer Night's Dream (dir. Peter Brooks), 1970–72, Broadway, 1971; Macbeth, 1982–83; King Lear, 1983; Lear (by Edward Bond), 1983; The Custom of the Country, 1983; Moscow Gold, 1990–91; Misha's Party, 1994; National Theatre, subseq. Royal National Theatre, includes: As You Like It, 1979; Love for Love; 3D Opera; American Clock, 1986; Bedroom Farce; Square Rounds, 1992; Copenhagen, 1998, transf. Duchess, 1999; Hamlet, 2000; other productions: The Way of the World, Chichester Festival, 1984; Waste, Lyric, 1985; Three Sisters, Greenwich, transf. Albery, 1987; Lettice and Lovage, Globe, 1989; Another Time, Wyndham's, 1990; The Cabinet Minister, Albery, 1991; The Cherry Orchard, Gate, Dublin, 1992; Cabaret, Donmar, 1993–94 (Olivier and Derwent Awards, for best supporting performance in a musical); Fiddler on the Roof, London Palladium, 1994; Three Tall Women, Wyndham's, 1995; A Two Hander (songwriter, jt writer, performer), Hampstead, 1996; Nine, Donmar, 1996–97; one woman cabaret show, All About Me! (tour), 1998–2003; The Shape of Metal, Abbey Th., Dublin, 2003; Flower Drum Song (musical), Lilian Baylis Th., 2006; My Child, Royal Court, 2007; Girl with a Pearl Earring, Haymarket, 2008; Coco, Lilian Baylis, 2011; Making Noise Quietly, Donmar, 2012; Torch Song Trilogy, Menier Chocolate Factory, 2012; 4,000 Miles, Theatre Royal, Bath and Print Room, 2013; Ignis, Print Room, 2014; The Summer Book, Unicorn, 2014; dir, Brass, Nat. Music Youth Th., 2014; *films:* Zardoz, 1973; Lisztomania, 1975; Break of Day, 1976; Lady Jane, 1984; Ex Memoria, 2006; *television* includes: Caucasian Chalk Circle, 1973; The Cafeteria, 1975; Crown Court; The Last Romantics, 1991; Casualty, 1996, 2003; Tom Jones, 1997; Kavanagh QC, 1997; Invasion Earth, 1998; Anna Karenina, 2000; Trial and Retribution, 2003, 2004; Midsomer Murders, 2004; Ultimate Force, 2004; Instinct, 2006; Rome, 2006; Holby City; From There to Here, 2014; narrations for documentaries; numerous radio plays, incl. Hitler in Therapy (Actress of the Year, World Air Awards, BBC World Service, 2005), Golda Meir in Payback, Life and Fate, 2011, A Small Person Far Away, 2012, and book readings; adapted Molly Keane's Full House for Book at Bedtime, 1991. Sen. Lectr, Central Sch. of Speech and Drama, 2007–10. Lead Reader, Interact Reading Service, for sufferers of stroke in hosps, hospices and stroke gps. Life Coach certificates, 2006 and 2007; Master practitioner in Neuro-linguistic programming, 2007. *Publications:* (with Susan Penhaligon) A Two Hander (poems), 1996. *Recreations:* writing - song writer and poet, tapestry, drawing, photography, dance. *Address:* c/o Shepherd Management Ltd, 3rd Floor, Joel House, 17–21 Garrick Street, WC2E 9BL.

KESTENBAUM, family name of **Baron Kestenbaum**.

KESTENBAUM, Baron *cr* 2011 (Life Peer), of Foxcote in the County of Somerset; **Jonathan Andrew Kestenbaum;** Chairman, Capital Holdings plc, since 2014; Chief Operating Officer, RIT Capital Partners plc, since 2010; *b* 5 Aug. 1959; *s* of late Ralph Kestenbaum and of Gaby Kestenbaum; *m* 1984, Deborah Zackon; three *s* one *d*. *Educ:* London Sch. of Econs (BA Hons 1982); Wolfson Coll., Cambridge; Hebrew Univ. (MA 1989); Cass Business Sch. (MBA 1994). Chief Executive: Office of Chief Rabbi, 1991–96; UJIA, 1996–2002; Portland Trust, 2002–06; COS to Sir Ronald Cohen, Chm. of Apax Partners, 2002–06; Chief Exec., NESTA, 2005–10; Chm., Five Arrows Ltd, 2010–13. Non-exec. Chm., Quest Ltd, 2002–06; Dir, Pershing Square Hldgs Ltd, 2014–. Non-executive Board Member: Enterprise Insight, 2005–08; Design Council, 2006–10; Profero Ltd, 2006–14. Mem., Technology Strategy Bd, 2006–13. Tutor, Cass Business Sch., 1999–2006; Adjunct Prof., Imperial Coll. Business Sch., 2011–. Trustee, London Community Centre, 2003–10; Gov. and Mem. Bd, RSC, 2007–12. Chancellor, Plymouth Univ., 2013–. CCMI 2008. *Recreations:* tennis, ski-ing. *Address:* RIT Capital Partners plc, Spencer House, 27 St James's Place, SW1A 1NR. *T:* (020) 7647 8565. *Club:* MCC.

KESTER, David Martin Albert; Chief Executive, Design Council, 2003–12; *b* 23 May 1964; *s* of Simon and Stephanie Kester; *m* 1992, Sophia Adamou; two *s*. *Educ:* Bristol Univ. (BA Hons). Friends of the Earth, 1990–93; Chartered Soc. of Designers, 1993–94; Chief Exec., British Design and Art Direction, 1994–2003. Member: Bd, Design Business Assoc., 2003; Bd, Kingston Rose Th., 2007–; Bd, Home Office Design and Technol. Alliance, 2007. Non-exec. Dir, Thames & Hudson, 2012–.

KESTING, Very Rev. Sheilagh Margaret; Secretary, Committee on Ecumenical Relations, Church of Scotland, 1993–2007 and since 2008; Moderator of the General Assembly of the Church of Scotland, 2007–08; *b* 10 June 1953; *d* of Douglas Norman Kesting and Joan Robertson Kesting (*née* Blair). *Educ:* Nicolson Inst., Stornoway; Edinburgh Univ. (BA 1974; BD Hons 1977). Ordained, C of S, 1980; Parish Minister: Overtown, Lanarkshire, 1980–86; St Andrew's High, Musselburgh, 1986–93. Hon DD Edinburgh, 2008. *Recreations:* gardening, photography, embroidery. *Address:* Church of Scotland Offices, 121 George Street, Edinburgh EH2 4YN. *T:* (0131) 225 5722, *Fax:* (0131) 240 2239. *E:* skesting@churchofscotland.org.uk.

KESWICK, Hon. Annabel Thérèse, (Tessa), (Hon. Lady Keswick); Deputy Chairman, Centre for Policy Studies, since 2004 (Director, 1995–2004); *b* 15 Oct. 1942; *d* of 17th Baron Lovat, DSO, MC and of Rosamond, *o d* of Sir Delves, (Jock), Broughton, 11th Bt; *m* 1st, 1964, 14th Lord Reay (marr. diss. 1978; he *d* 2013); two *s* one *d*; 2nd, 1985, Henry Neville Lindley Keswick (*see* Sir H. N. L. Keswick). *Educ:* Convent of the Sacred Heart, Woldingham. Trainee, J. W. Thompson, 1960–62; Dir, Cluff Investments, 1980–95. Special Advr to Rt Hon. Kenneth Clarke, 1989–95. Non-exec. Dir, Daily Mail and Gen. Trust plc, 2013–. Member: Corporate Adv. Gp, Tate; Internat. Strategy Cttee, British Mus. Mem. (C), Kensington Council, 1982–86. Chancellor, Univ. of Buckingham, 2014–. Contested (C), Inverness, Nairn and Lochaber, 1987. Hon. FKC 2007. *Recreation:* travelling. *Address:* 6 Smith Square, SW1P 3HT.

See also Lord Reay.

KESWICK, Sir Chippendale; *see* Keswick, Sir J. C. L.

KESWICK, Sir Henry (Neville Lindley), Kt 2009; Chairman: Matheson & Co. Ltd, since 1975; Jardine, Matheson Holdings Ltd, Hong Kong, 1972–75 and since 1989 (Director, since 1967); Jardine Strategic Holdings, since 1989 (Director, since 1988); *b* 29 Sept. 1938; *e s* of Sir William Keswick and Mary, *d* of Rt Hon. Sir Francis Lindley, PC, GCMG; *m* 1985, Tessa, Lady Reay (*see* Hon. A. T. Keswick). *Educ:* Eton Coll.; Trinity Coll., Cambridge (BA Hons Econs and Law; MA). Commnd Scots Guards, Nat. Service, 1956–58. Director: Sun Alliance and London Insurance, 1975–96; Robert Fleming Holdings Ltd, 1975–2000; Rothmans Internat., 1988–94; Hongkong Land Co., 1988–; Mandarin Oriental Internat., 1988–; Dairy Farm Internat. Hldgs, 1988–; Royal & Sun Alliance (formerly Sun Alliance) Gp, 1989–2000; The Telegraph, 1990–2001; Mem., Adv. Bd, Telegraph Gp Ltd, 2002–04; Rothschilds Continuation Hldgs AG, 2006–11. Member: London Adv. Cttee, Hongkong and Shanghai Banking Corp., 1975–92; 21st Century Trust, 1987–97. Proprietor, The Spectator, 1975–81. Trustee: Nat. Portrait Gall., 1982–2001 (Chm., 1994–2001); Royal Botanic Gdns, Kew, 2008–. Pres., RHASS, 2003–04; Mem. Council, NT, 2005–07, 2009–10. Chm., Hong Kong Assoc., 1988–2001. *Recreation:* country pursuits. *Address:* Matheson & Co. Ltd, 3 Lombard Street, EC3V 9AQ. *Clubs:* White's, Turf; Third Guards.

See also Sir J. C. L. Keswick, S. L. Keswick.

KESWICK, Sir (John) Chippendale (Lindley), Kt 1993; Director, De Beers SA, 2001–10; Chairman, Arsenal Football Club, since 2013 (Director, since 2005); *b* 2 Feb. 1940; 2nd *s* of Sir William Keswick and Mary, *d* of Rt Hon. Sir Francis Lindley, PC, GCMG; *m* 1966, Lady Sarah Ramsay, *d* of 16th Earl of Dalhousie, KT, GCVO, GBE, MC; three *s*. *Educ:* Eton; Univ. of Aix/Marseilles. Glyn Mills & Co., 1961–65; Jt Vice Chm., 1986, Jt Dep. Chm., 1990–97, Gp Chief Exec., 1995–97, Chm., 1997–98, Hambros PLC; Chief Exec., 1985–95, Chm., 1986–98, Hambros Bank. A Dir, Bank of England, 1993–2001. Sen. Banking and Capital Mkts Advr, Société Générale, 1998–2000. Director: Persimmon Plc, 1984–2006; Edinburgh Investment Trust, 1992–2001; De Beers Consolidated Mines, 1993–2006; De Beers Centenary AG, 1994–2005; IMI plc, 1994–2003; Anglo Amer. plc, 1995–2001; Investec Bank (UK) Ltd, 2000–10; Investec plc, 2002–10; Arsenal Hldgs plc, 2005–. Mem., Queen's Body Guard for Scotland, Royal Company of Archers, 1976. Chm., Test & Itchen Assoc., 1992–2009. *Recreations:* bridge, country pursuits. *Address:* E. Oppenheimer & Son Holdings Ltd, 1 Charterhouse Street, EC1N 6SA. *T:* (020) 7421 9823. *Clubs:* White's, Portland.

See also Sir H. N. L. Keswick, S. L. Keswick.

KESWICK, Simon Lindley; Director: Jardine Matheson Holdings Ltd, since 1972 (Chairman, 1983–89); Jardine Lloyd Thompson Group plc, since 2001; *b* 20 May 1942; *s* of Sir William Keswick and Mary, *d* of Rt Hon. Sir Francis Lindley, PC, GCMG; *m* 1971, Emma, *d* of Major David Chetwode; two *s* two *d*. *Educ:* Eton Coll. Director: Hong Kong and Shanghai Banking Corp., 1983–88; Matheson & Co. Ltd, 1982–; Jardine Strategic Hldgs Ltd, 1987– (Chm., 1987–89); Hanson plc, 1991–2005; Wellcome plc, 1995–96; Fleming Mercantile Investment Trust, 1988–2007 (Chm., 1990–2003). Director: Hongkong Land Hldgs Ltd, 1983– (Chm., 1983–2013); Mandarin Oriental Internat. Ltd, 1984– (Chm., 1984–2013); Dairy Farm Internat. Hldgs Ltd, 1984– (Chm., 1984–2013). Trustee: British Museum, 1989–99; Henry Moore Foundn, 2003–13. Patron, RCS, 1998–. *Recreations:* country pursuits, bridge, soccer. *Address:* May Tower 1, 5–7 May Road, Hong Kong; 7 Ennismore Gardens, SW7 1NL. *Clubs:* White's, Portland; Shek O (Hong Kong).

See also Sir H. N. L. Keswick, Sir J. C. L. Keswick.

KESWICK, Hon. Tessa; *see* Keswick, Hon. A. T.

KETT, Paul Michael; Director, Army Reform, British Army, since 2014; *b* Norwich, 25 Feb. 1980; *s* of Rosemary Kett. *Educ:* City of Norwich Sch.; Univ. of Leicester (BSc Hons Physics 2001); Univ. of Birmingham (MPhil Sci. and Engrg Materials 2002). DTI, 2002–04; Information Rights, DCA, 2005; Dep. Principal Private Sec. to Lord Chancellor and Sec. of State for Justice, 2006–08; Hd of Secretariat, Commn on Scottish Devolution, 2008–09; Prog. Dir, Implementation Prog., Ind. Parly Standards Authy, 2009–10; Dep. Dir, Strategy, 2010, Prog. Dir, 2010–11, Dir, Justice Reform, 2011–14, MoJ. *Recreations:* theatre, cooking, swimming, eating jamón. *Address:* Ministry of Defence, Main Building, Whitehall, SW1A 2HB. *T:* (020) 7218 7031. *E:* armyreform-comdgp-DAR@mod.uk.

KETTERLE, Prof. Wolfgang, PhD; John D. MacArthur Professor of Physics, Massachusetts Institute of Technology, since 1998; *b* Heidelberg, 21 Oct. 1957; German and US citizen; *m*; two *d*; two *s* one *d* from a former marriage. *Educ:* Univ. of Heidelberg (Vordiplom Physics 1978); Tech. Univ. Munich (Diplom Physics 1982); Ludwig Maximilians Univ. of Munich and Max-Planck Inst. for Quantum Optics (PhD 1986). Intern, Volkswagen Co., Puebla, Mexico, 1980; res. asst, 1982–85, staff scientist, 1985–88, Max-Planck Inst. for Quantum Optics, Germany; res. scientist, Dept of Physical Chem., Univ. of Heidelberg, 1989–90; Department of Physics, Massachusetts Institute of Technology: Res. Associate, 1990–93; Asst Prof. of Physics, 1993–97; Prof. of Physics, 1997–98. NATO/Deutscher Akademischer Austauschdienst Postdoctoral Fellow, 1990–91; David and Lucile Packard Fellow, 1996–2001; Dist. Traveling Lectr, Div. of Laser Sci., APS, 1998–99. Member: German Physical Soc.; Optical Soc. of America, 1997; Eur. Acad. of Scis and Arts, 2002; Acad. of Scis in Heidelberg, 2002; Eur. Acad. of Arts, Scis and Humanities, 2002; Bavarian Acad. of Scis, 2003; German Acad. of Natural Scientists Leopoldina, 2005; For. Associate, NAS, 2002; Fellow: APS, 1997; Amer. Acad. Arts and Scis, 1999; FInstP 2002. Hon. DSc: Gustavus Adolphus Coll., St Peter, 2005; Connecticut, 2007; Ohio State, 2007. Michael and Philip Platzman Award, MIT, 1994; I. I. Rabi Prize, APS, 1997; Gustav-Hertz Prize, German Physical Soc., 1997; Award for Technological Innovation, Discover Mag., 1998; Fritz London Prize in Low Temp. Physics, 1999; Dannie-Heineman Prize, Acad. of Scis, Göttingen, 1999; Benjamin Franklin Medal in Physics, 2000; (jtly) Nobel Prize in Physics, 2001; Killian Award, MIT, 2004. Kt Comdr's Cross (Badge and Star), Order of Merit (Germany), 2002; Medal of Merit, State of Baden-Württemberg (Germany), 2002; Officer, Legion of Honour (France), 2002. *Address:* Massachusetts Institute of Technology, 77 Massachusetts Avenue, Cambridge, MA 02139, USA. *T:* (617) 2536815, *Fax:* (617) 2534876. *E:* ketterle@mit.edu; 80 Clifton Street, Belmont, MA 02478, USA.

KETTLE, Captain Alan Stafford Howard, CB 1984; Royal Navy (retired); General Manager, HM Dockyard, Chatham, 1977–84; *b* 6 Aug. 1925; *s* of Arthur Stafford Kettle and Marjorie Constance (*née* Clough); *m* 1952, Patricia Rosemary (*née* Gander); two *s*. *Educ:* Rugby School. Joined RN, 1943; Comdr, Dec. 1959; Captain, Dec. 1968; retired, Sept. 1977. Entered Civil Service as Asst Under-Sec., Sept. 1977. *Address:* Woodside, 9 Roland Bailey Gardens, Tavistock, Devon PL19 0RB. *T:* (01822) 618721.

KETTLEWELL, Comdt Dame Marion M., DBE 1970 (CBE 1964); Director, Women's Royal Naval Service, 1967–70; *b* 20 Feb. 1914; *d* of late George Wildman Kettlewell, Bramling, Virginia Water, Surrey, and of Mildred Frances (*née* Atkinson), Belford, Northumberland. *Educ:* Godolphin Sch., Salisbury; St Christopher's Coll., Blackheath. Worked for Fellowship of Maple Leaf, Alta, Canada, 1935–38; worked for Local Council, 1939–41; joined WRNS as MT driver, 1941; commnd as Third Officer WRNS, 1942; Supt

WRNS on Staff of Flag Officer Air (Home), 1961–64; Supt WRNS Training and Drafting, 1964–67; Gen. Sec., GFS, 1971–78. Pres., Assoc. of Wrens, 1981–92. *Recreations:* needlework, walking, and country life. *Address:* Norton House, 10 Arneway Street, SW1P 2BG.

KEVERNE, Prof. Eric Barrington, (Barry), DSc; FRS 1997; Professor of Behavioural Neuroscience, 1998–2009, now Emeritus, and Fellow of King's College, since 1985, University of Cambridge. *Educ:* London Univ. (BSc, PhD); MA 1975, DSc 1993, Cantab. University of Cambridge: Lectr, Dept of Anatomy, then of Zoology, until 1990; Reader in Behavioural Neurosci., 1990–98. Chm., Healthy Organism Strategy Panel, BBSRC, 2005–07; Member: Royal Soc. Res. Fellowships Cttee, 1998–2003; Animals Res. Cttee, Royal Soc., 2004–; MRC Cross Bds Cttee, 2000–03. FMedSci 2005. Foreign Hon. Fellow, American Acad. of Arts and Scis, 1998. *Address:* Sub-Department of Animal Behaviour, University of Cambridge, High Street, Madingley, Cambridge CB23 8AA. *T:* (01223) 741801; King's College, Cambridge CB2 1ST.

KEVILL, Siân Louise; Founder and Director, MAKE World Media Ltd, since 2011; *b* Enfield, 29 Jan. 1961; *d* of David Courtney Kevill and Frances Morfydd Kevill; *m* 1987 (marr. diss. 1999); one *s* one *d.* *Educ:* Newnham Coll., Cambridge (BA 1st Cl. Hons Hist. 1982). Staff writer, Keesing's Contemp. Archives, Longman Publishing, 1983–84; BBC: Talks writer, BBC World Service, 1984–85; News Trainee, 1986–88; Asst Producer, 1988–90, Producer, 1990–92, Asst Ed., 1992–94, Newsnight; Dep. Ed., On the Record, 1994–95; Ed., Foreign Progs, BBC Radio, 1995–97; Dep. Hd, Political Progs, 1997–98; Ed., Newsnight, 1998–2003; Hd, Political Progs Rev., 2003–04; Editl Dir, 2004–08, Dir, 2008–10, BBC World News Ltd. *Publications:* Sino-Soviet Relations, 1984; Aquino and the Philippines, 1985. *Recreations:* sport, swimming, running, cinema, reading, socialising. *E:* sian@makeworldmedia.com.

KEY, Rear Adm. Benjamin John; Flag Officer Sea Training, 2013–15; *b* Rugby, 7 Nov. 1965; *s* of John and Loveday Key; *m* 1994, Eleanor Morton; two *s* one *d.* *Educ:* Bromsgrove Sch.; Royal Holloway Coll., Univ. of London (BSc Hons Physics 1988). Joined RN, 1984; Surface Fleet and Fleet Air Arm appts, 1988–99; Commanding Officer: HMS Sandown, 1999–2000; HMS Iron Duke, 2000–01; HMS Lancaster, 2001–02; Aviation Desk Officer, Navy Resources and Plans, MoD, 2003–05; Advr, Iraqi Jt HQ, Baghdad, 2006; Dep. Asst COS, UK Perm. Jt HQ, 2006–08; CO, HMS Illustrious, 2009–10; Cdre, Jt Air Maritime Orgn, 2010; Hd, Navy Resources and Plans, MoD, 2011; Principal Staff Officer to CDS, 2011–13. Gov., Stover Sch., 2005–. Younger Brother, Trinity Hse, 2011–. FCMI 2008. *Recreations:* talking about the many sports he can no longer play, jazz and classical music, outdoor activities, gardening. *Address:* c/o Naval Secretary, Navy Command Headquarters, Whale Island, Portsmouth PO2 8BY.

KEY, Brian Michael; Member (Lab) Yorkshire South, European Parliament, 1979–84; *b* 20 Sept. 1947; *s* of Leslie Granville Key and Nora Alice (*née* Haylett); *m* 1974, Lynn Joyce Ambler. *Educ:* Darfield County Primary Sch.; Wath upon Dearne Grammar Sch.; Liverpool Univ. (BA Hons). Careers Officer, West Riding County Council, 1970–73; Sen. Administrative Officer, South Yorkshire CC, 1973–79. Mem. (Lab), Barnsley MBC, 2011–15. *Address:* 25 Cliff Road, Darfield, Barnsley S73 9HR. *Clubs:* Darfield Working Men's; Trades and Labour (Doncaster).

KEY, Rt Hon. John Phillip; MP (Nat.) Helensville, New Zealand, since 2002; Leader, National Party, since 2006; Prime Minister of New Zealand, since 2008; *b* 9 Aug. 1961; *s* of George Key and Ruth (*née* Lazar); *m* 1984, Bronagh Dougan; one *s* one *d.* *Educ:* Canterbury Univ. (BCom Accounting 1981). Hd, Treasury, Bankers Trust of NZ, 1988–95; Merrill Lynch, 1995–2001: Asian Hd, Foreign Exchange, Singapore; Global Hd, Foreign Exchange, London; Eur. Hd, Bonds and Derivatives, London; Hd, Fixed Income, Australia. Leader of the Opposition, NZ, 2006–08. *Recreations:* spending time with family, cooking, watching Rugby. *Address:* Parliament of New Zealand, PO Box 18–041, Wellington, New Zealand. *T:* (4) 817 6800, *Fax:* (4) 427 2075. *E:* j.key@ministers.govt.nz.

KEY, Matthew David; Chairman and Chief Executive Officer, Telefónica Digital, 2011–14; Member, Executive Committee, Telefónica SA, 2008–14; *b* 3 March 1963; *s* of Kenneth Charles Key and Christina Mary Key; *m* 1990, Karen Lorraine Cook; two *s* one *d.* *Educ:* Sir Joseph Williamson's Mathematical Sch., Rochester; Univ. of Birmingham (BSocSc 1st cl. Hons Econs; 2nd Yr Undergraduate Prize). ACA 1987. Arthur Young, 1984–89; Grand Metropolitan Foods Europe, 1989–91; Coca-Cola & Schweppes Beverages Ltd, 1991–95; Woolworths, Kingfisher plc, 1995–99; appts in retail and network divs, 1999–2001, Finance Dir, 2001–02, Vodafone UK; Chief Financial Officer, 2002–05, CEO, 2005–07, O_2 UK Ltd, subseq. Telefónica O_2 UK Ltd; Chm. and CEO, Telefónica Europe plc, 2008–11. Non-exec. Dir, Burberry Gp plc, 2013–. Chm., Dallaglio Foundn, 2013–.

KEY, Dr Paul Anthony; QC 2013; *b* Christchurch, NZ, 8 Sept. 1967; *s* of Jack and Erene Key. *Educ:* Univ. of Auckland (LLB Hons); Gonville and Caius Coll., Cambridge (PhD 1994). Called to the Bar, Inner Temple, 1997; in practice as barrister, 1997–. *Address:* Essex Court Chambers, 24 Lincoln's Inn Fields, WC2A 3EG. *T:* (020) 7813 8000.

KEY, Very Rev. Robert Frederick; Dean of Jersey, since 2005; *b* 29 Aug. 1952; *s* of Frederick and Winifred Key; *m* 1974, Daphne Mary Manning; one *s* two *d.* *Educ:* Bristol Univ. (BA 1973); Oak Hill Coll. (DPS 1976). Ordained deacon, 1976, priest, 1977; Curate, St Ebbe's, Oxford, 1976–80; Minister, St Patrick's, Wallington, 1980–85; Vicar: Eynsham and Cassington, 1985–91; St Andrew's, Oxford, 1991–2001; Gen. Dir, CPAS, 2001–05. Canon Preacher, Dio. Rio Grande, 2004–. *Recreations:* civil aviation, detective fiction. *Address:* The Deanery, David Place, St Helier, Jersey JE2 4TE. *E:* deanofjersey@gov.je.

KEY, (Simon) Robert; *b* 22 April 1945; *s* of late Rt Rev. J. M. Key; *m* 1968, Susan Priscilla Bright Irvine, 2nd *d* of late Rev. T. T. Irvine; one *s* two *d* (and one *s* decd). *Educ:* Salisbury Cathedral Sch.; Forres Sch., Swanage; Sherborne Sch.; Clare Coll., Cambridge. MA; CertEd. Assistant Master: Loretto Sch., Edinburgh, 1967; Harrow Sch., 1969–83. Warden, Nanoose Field Studies Centre, Wool, Dorset, 1972–78; Governor: Sir William Collins Sch., NW1, 1976–81; Special Sch. at Gt Ormond Street Hosp. for Sick Children, 1976–81; Roxeth Sch., Harrow, 1979–82. Founder Chm., ALICE Trust for Autistic Children, 1977–82; Council Mem., GAP Activity Projects, 1975–84. Vice-Chm., Wembley Br., ASTMS, 1976–80. Contested (C) Camden, Holborn and St Pancras South, 1979. MP (C) Salisbury, 1983–2010. Political Sec. to Rt Hon. Edward Heath, 1984–85; PPS: to Minister of State for Energy, 1985–87; to Minister for Overseas Develt, 1987–89; to Sec. of State for the Envmt, 1989–90; Parly Under-Sec. of State, DoE, 1990–92, Dept of Nat. Heritage, 1992–93, Dept of Transport, 1993–94; Opposition front bench spokesman on defence, 1997–2001, on trade and industry, 2001–02, on internat. develt, 2002–03. Mem., Select Cttee on Educn, Science and the Arts, 1983–86, on Health, 1994–95, on Defence, 1995–97, on Science and Technology, 2003–05, on Defence, 2005–10; Chm., Select Cttee on Information, 2004–05; Sec., Cons. Parly Backbench Cttee on Arts and Heritage, 1983–84; Jt Parly Chm., Council for Educn in the Commonwealth, 1984–87; Vice-Chm., 1988–90, Chm., 1996–97, All-Party Gp on AIDS. Chm., Harrow Central Cons. Assoc., 1980–82; Vice-Chm., Central London Cons. Euro-Constit., 1980–82; Mem., Cons. Party Nat. Union Exec., 1981–83. Member: UK Nat. Commn for UNESCO, 1984–85; MRC, 1989–90 (Mem., AIDS Cttee, 1988–90). Director and Trustee: Wessex Archaeology, 2004–13 (Chm., 2011–13); Trussell Trust, 2014–; Mem. Council, Winston Churchill Meml Trust, 2004–07; Trustee, Salisbury and S Wilts Mus., 2010–13. Mem., Gen. Synod, C of E, 2005–15; Lay Canon, Salisbury Cathedral, 2008–; Chm., Salisbury Cathedral Magna Carta 2015 Project, 2010–15. Vice-Pres., Haemophilia Soc., 1988–90. Hon. FCollP, 1989. FSA 2007. *Recreations:* singing, cooking, country life.

KEYES, family name of **Baron Keyes**.

KEYES, 3rd Baron *cr* 1943, of Zeebrugge and of Dover, co. Kent; **Charles William Packe Keyes;** Bt 1919; *b* 8 Dec. 1951; *s* of 2nd Baron Keyes and Grizelda Mary Keyes (*née* Packe); *S* father, 2005, but does not use the title; *m* 1984, Sally Jackson; one *d.* *Educ:* Camberwell Sch. of Arts and Crafts (OND Conservation of Paper). Retained Firefighter, Suffolk Fire and Rescue Service, 1990–2006. Operational Postal Grade, Royal Mail, 2000–08. Warden, Aldham Roadside Nature Reserve. Queen's Golden Jubilee Medal, 2002. *Recreations:* bird watching, drawing, auctions, drinking coffee, Scotland, botany, gardening. *Heir:* *b* Hon. (Leopold Roger) John Keyes [*b* 8 June 1956; *m* 1988, Jane Owen (marr. diss. 1997); two *d*].

KEYES, Timothy Harold, MA; Headmaster, King's School, Worcester, 1998–2014; *b* 15 Dec. 1954; *s* of Alfred Edward Keyes and Mary Irene Keyes (*née* Mylchreest); *m* 1979, Mary Anne Lucas; two *s.* *Educ:* Christ's Hospital, Horsham; Wadham Coll., Oxford (BA 1st cl. Classics, MA, PGCE). Teacher: of classics and rowing, Tiffin Sch., Kingston upon Thames, 1979–83; of classics and hockey, Whitgift Sch., Croydon, 1983–88; Head of Classics, Perse Sch., Cambridge, 1988–93; Dep. Head, Royal Grammar Sch., Guildford, 1993–98. *Recreations:* choral singing, bell-ringing, walking, Yorkshire cricket. *Address:* 11 Bank Crescent, Ledbury, Herefordshire HR8 1AA.

KEYNES, Prof. Simon Douglas, PhD, LittD; FBA 2000; FSA, FRHistS; Elrington and Bosworth Professor of Anglo-Saxon, University of Cambridge, since 1999; Fellow, Trinity College, Cambridge, since 1976; *b* Cambridge, 23 Sept. 1952; *y s* of Prof. Richard Darwin Keynes, CBE, FRS and of Anne Pinsent Keynes, *e d* of 1st Baron Adrian, OM, FRS, and Dame Hester Agnes Adrian, DBE; one *s* with Tethys Lucy Carpenter. *Educ:* King's Coll. Choir Sch., Cambridge; Leys Sch., Cambridge; Trinity Coll., Cambridge (BA Hons 1973; MA 1977; PhD 1978; LittD 1992). FRHistS 1982; FSA 1985. University of Cambridge: Asst Lectr, Dept of Anglo-Saxon, Norse and Celtic, 1978–82; Lectr, 1982–92; Reader in Anglo-Saxon Hist., 1992–99; Head, Dept of Anglo-Saxon, Norse and Celtic, 1999–2006. British Acad. Res. Reader in Humanities, 1991–93. Member: British Acad./RHistS Jt Cttee on Anglo-Saxon Charters, 1982– (Sec., 1983–2013; Chm., 2013–14); British Acad. Cttee for Sylloge of Coins of British Isles, 1995– (Chm., 2003–); Chm., Sect. H8 (Medieval Studies: Hist. and Lit.), British Acad., 2005–08. Member, Editorial Board: Anglo-Saxon England, 1979– (Exec. Ed., 1982–); Cambridge Studies in Anglo-Saxon England, 1986–2005; Early English MSS in Facsimile, 1996–2002; Associate Ed., Oxford DNB, 1993–2004. Liveryman, Goldsmiths' Co., 1991–. *Publications:* The Diplomas of King Æthelred 'the Unready' 978–1016, 1980; (with M. Lapidge) Alfred the Great: Asser's Life of King Alfred and other contemporary sources, 1983; Anglo-Saxon History: a select bibliography, 1987, 8th edn, as Anglo Saxon England: a bibliographical handbook, 2010; Facsimiles of Anglo-Saxon Charters, 1991; The Liber Vitae of the New Minster and Hyde Abbey, Winchester, 1996; (ed jtly and contrib.) The Blackwell Encyclopaedia of Anglo-Saxon England, 1999, 2nd edn 2014; Quentin Keynes: explorer, film-maker, lecturer and book collector 1921–2003, 2004; (ed and contrib.) Ethiopian Encounters: Sir William Cornwallis Harris and the British mission to the Kingdom of Shewa (1841–3), 2007; contrib. articles in books and learned jls, incl. Anglo-Saxon England, Anglo-Norman Studies, English Hist. Rev. and Early Medieval Europe. *Recreation:* 19th-century travel and exploration. *Address:* Trinity College, Cambridge CB2 1TQ. *T:* (01223) 338421; Primrose Farm, Wiveton, Norfolk NR25 7TQ. *T:* (01263) 740317. *Club:* Roxburghe.

KEYNES, Stephen John, OBE 1993; FLS; Founder, 1999, and Chairman, since 2003, Charles Darwin Trust; *b* 19 Oct. 1927; 4th *s* of Sir Geoffrey Keynes, MD, FRCP, FRCS, FRCOG, and late Margaret Elizabeth, *d* of Sir George Darwin, KCB; *m* 1955, Mary, *o d* of late Senator the Hon. Adrian Knatchbull-Hugessen, QC (Canada), and late Margaret, *o d* of G. H. Duggan; three *s* two *d.* *Educ:* Oundle Sch.; King's Coll., Cambridge (Open Scholar; MA). Royal Artillery, 1949–51. Partner, J. F. Thomasson & Co., Private Bankers, 1961–65; Director: Charterhouse Japhet Ltd and Charterhouse Finance Corp., 1965–72; Arbuthnot Latham Holdings Ltd, 1973–80; Sun Life Assce Soc. plc, 1965–89; English Trust Co. Ltd, 1980–90; Hawkshead Ltd, 1987–91. Member: IBA (formerly ITA), 1969–74; Cttee and Treas., Islington and North London Family Service Unit, 1956–68; Adv. Cttee, Geffrye Museum, 1964–78; Trustee: Centerprise Community Project, 1971–75; Needham Research Inst. (formerly E Asian Hist. of Science Trust), 1984–2015; Chm., English Chamber Theatre, 1986–92; Chairman of Trustees: Whitechapel Art Gallery, 1979–96; William Blake Trust, 1981–2014; Mark Baldwin Dance Co., 1997–2001. Associate Producer, The Heart of the Dragon, 1981–84. FLS 1999. Hon. Fellow, Darwin Coll., Cambridge, 2010. *Recreations:* medieval, western and Ethiopian manuscripts, gardening, travelling. *Address:* 14 Canonbury Park South, Islington, N1 2JJ. *T:* (020) 7226 8170; Lammas House, Hall Lane, Brinkley, nr Newmarket, Suffolk CB8 0SB. *T:* (01638) 507268. *Clubs:* Cranium, Roxburghe, Ad Eundem.

KEYS, Stuart Cameron; Vice Lord-Lieutenant, City of Londonderry, since 2004; *b* Nottingham, 1946; *s* of Dr and Mrs Robin Keys; *m* 1969, Elizabeth Margaret Hosford; two *s* one *d.* *Educ:* Merchiston Castle Sch., Edinburgh; Stow Coll., Glasgow. Cert. Inst. Wood Sci. Works Dir, 1969–78, Man. Dir, 1978–91, Chm., 1991–99, Robert Keys Gp of Cos. Tutor, Sch. of Philosophy and Econ. Sci., St Columb's Park Hse Peace and Reconciliation Centre, 2004–. Port and Harbour Comr, Londonderry, 1986–92. Chairman: NI Builders Merchants Assoc., 1982–84; NI Timber Trade Assoc., 1989–91. Pres., NW Animal Welfare, 2009–. DL 1993, High Sheriff, 1997, Co. Bor. Londonderry. *Recreations:* practical philosophy, animal welfare, organic gardening, art. *Address:* Heronsway, 67 Ballougry Road, Molenan, Londonderry, Northern Ireland BT48 9XL. *T:* (028) 7126 0898. *E:* stuartckeys@gmail.com.

KEYSER, Andrew John; QC 2006; **His Honour Judge Keyser;** a Circuit Judge, since 2011; a Specialist Mercantile Circuit Judge, Wales Circuit, since 2012; *b* 19 Dec. 1963; *s* of late James William Keyser and of Elizabeth Jane Keyser (*née* Hall); *m* 1st, 1985 (marr. diss. 1998); two *s*; 2nd, 2011, Andrea Markham; one step *d.* *Educ:* Cardiff High Sch.; Balliol Coll., Oxford (BA 1st Cl. Hons 1985; MA 1989); Inns of Court Sch. of Law. Called to the Bar, Middle Temple, 1986; Recorder, 2002–11; Dep. High Ct Judge, 2008–; Principal Technol. and Construction Court Judge for Leeds, 2011–12, for Wales, 2012–. An Asst Boundary Comr for Wales, 2003–11. Dep. Chancellor, Dio. of Llandaff, 2007–11 and 2014–; Church in Wales: Mem., Disciplinary Tribunal, 2007–11; Mem., Governing Body, 2013–; Chm., Legal sub-cttee of Standing Cttee, 2013–. *Recreations:* reading, music. *Address:* Cardiff Civil Justice Centre, 2 Park Street, Cardiff CF10 1ET.

KEYWOOD, Richard David C.; *see* Collier-Keywood.

KHALIDI, Prof. Tarif, PhD; Sheikh Zayed Professor of Islamic and Arabic Studies, Centre for Arab and Middle Eastern Studies, American University of Beirut, since 2002; *b* 24 Jan. 1938; *s* of Ahmad Samih Khalidi, MBE and Anbara Salam; *m* 1st, 1960, Amal Saidi (decd); one *s* one *d*; 2nd, 2001, Magda Moussallem. *Educ:* Haileybury Coll., Hertford; University Coll., Oxford (BA; MA); Univ. of Chicago (PhD). Prof. of History, American Univ. of Beirut, 1970–96; Sir Thomas Adams's Prof. of Arabic, and Fellow of King's Coll., Cambridge Univ., 1996–2002. *Publications:* Islamic Historiography, 1975; (ed) Land Tenure and Social Transformation in the Middle East, 1983; Classical Arab Islam, 1984; Arabic Historical

Thought in the Classical Period, 1994; The Muslim Jesus: sayings and stories in Islamic literature, 2001; The Qu'ran: a new translation, 2008. *Recreations:* gliding, admiring trees. *Address:* American University of Beirut, PO Box 11–0236, Beirut, Lebanon.

KHALIL, Karim; QC 2003; a Recorder, since 2000; *b* 7 Jan. 1962; *s* of Dr Hassan and Anna Shakir-Khalil; *m* 1986, Sally Ann Boyle; two *s*. *Educ:* Cheadle Hulme Sch., Manchester; Queens' Coll., Cambridge (MA Hons Law). Called to the Bar, Lincoln's Inn, 1984, Bencher, 2013; in practice, specialising in criminal law, health and safety, and regulatory law; Asst Recorder, 1997–2000; Hd of Chambers, 2011–. Chairman: S Eastern Circuit Liaison Cttee, 2003–; Cambridge and Peterborough Bar Mess, 2003–; Member: SE Circuit Cttee, 2000–; Jt Advocate Selection Cttee, SE Circuit, 2011–. Ed., The Circuiteer; Co-Ed., news@One (electronic legal bull. of 1 Paper Bldgs), 2010–. *Publications:* (contrib. chapter) Fraud: law, practice and procedure, 2005. *Recreations:* tennis, golf, alto sax in The Eye, ski-ing, lacrosse (Mem., Cambridge Univ. Lacrosse XVI). *Address:* Drystone Chambers, 35 Bedford Row, WC1R 4JH. *Clubs:* Hawks, Gog Magog Golf; Okeford Duck Golf, Brocket Hall Golf.

KHALIQUE, Nageena; QC 2015; *b* Nottingham, 10 Dec. 1961; *d* of Abdul Khalique and Mumtaz Khalique; *m* 1992, Andrew Mark Sean Brown; one *s* one *d*. *Educ:* Nottingham High Sch. for Girls GPDST; University Coll. London (BDS 1987); Univ. of London (Dip. Vocational Trng 1988); City Univ. (DipLaw 1993); Inns of Court Sch. of Law (BVQ 1994). LDS 1987. Hosp. dentist, Birmingham Children's Hosp., 1987–90; Registrar in Oral and Maxillofacial Surgery, Selly Oak Hosp. and City Hosp., 1990–92; called to the Bar, Gray's Inn, 1994; in practice as a barrister, No5 Chambers, 1995–2007 and 2008–; Associate Barrister, Mills & Reeve LLP, 2007–08. Hon. Tutor in Med. Ethics, Univ. of Birmingham, 1992–2004; Postgrad. Lectr, Medico-Legal and Ethics, W Midlands Deanery, 2008–14. Chair, Court of Protection Practitioners Assoc. (Midlands), 2014–; Mem., Legal Panel, Assoc. of Child Psychotherapists, 2015–. *Publications:* contrib. to Lawtel, Law Reports, Kemp & Kemp, British Dental Jl, British Jl of Oral and Maxillofacial Surgery. *Recreations:* ballet, marathon runner and triathlete, opera, music, ski-ing. *Address:* No5 Chambers, Steelhouse Lane, Birmingham B4 6DR; No5 Chambers, 4–7 Salisbury Court, EC4Y 8AA. *T:* 0845 210 5555. *E:* nk@no5.com.

KHAMENEI, Ayatollah Sayyed Ali; religious and political leader of the Islamic Republic of Iran, since 1989; *b* Mashhad, Khorasan, 17 July 1939; *m* 1964; four *s* two *d*. *Educ:* Qom; studied under Imam Khomeini, 1956–64. Imprisoned six times, 1964–78; once exiled, 1978; Mem., Revolutionary Council, 1978 until its dissolution, 1979 (Rep. in Iranian Army and Assistant of Revolutionary Affairs in Min. of Defence); Rep. of First Islamic Consultative Assembly, and of Imam Khomeini in the Supreme Council of Defence, 1980; Comdr, Revolutionary Guards, 1980; Friday Prayer Leader, Teheran, 1980; Sec. Gen., and Pres. of Central Cttee, Islamic Republic Party, 1980–87; survived assassination attempt, June 1981; Pres., Islamic Republic of Iran, 1981–89. *Recreations:* reading, art, literature. *Address:* Office of Religious Leader, Tehran, Islamic Republic of Iran.

KHAMISA, Mohammed Jaffer; QC 2006; a Recorder, since 2003; *b* 16 Feb. 1962; *s* of Isak Ismail and Sugra Khamisa; *m* 1992, Roumana; two *s* one *d*. *Educ:* City of London Poly. (BA Hons Law). Called to the Bar, Middle Temple, 1985, Bencher, 2010. Pres., Mental Health Rev. Tribunals, 2002–11; Standing Counsel, DTI, 2005–; Special Advocate, Special Immigration Appeals Commn, 2005–; Chair, Summary Disciplinary Panels, Bar Standards Bd, 2006–12. Legal Assessor, GMC, 2007–10. *Recreations:* reading, cricket, Rugby, jazz and blues. *Address:* Thomas Bingham Chambers, 33 Bedford Row, WC1R 4JH.

KHAN, Akram Hossain, MBE 2005; dancer and choreographer; Artistic Director, Akram Khan Company, since 2000; *b* 29 July 1974; *s* of Mosharaf Hossain Khan and Anwara Khan. *Educ:* De Montfort Univ. (BA); Northern Sch. of Contemporary Dance (BPA Hons (Dance)). Performed in The Mahabharata, RSC, 1987–89; Associate Artist: RFH, 2003–05; Sadler's Wells Th., 2005–. Principal works include: Loose in Flight, Rush, 2000; Kaash, 2002; ma, 2004; Sacred Monsters, 2006; zero degrees, 2007; Confluence, 2009; Vertical Road, 2010; Gnosis, 2011; DESH, 2012 (Olivier Award for Best New Dance Prodn); iTMOi, 2013; Dust, 2014; (with Israel Galván) Torobaka, 2014; technê, 2015. Guest Artistic Dir, Nat. Youth Dance Co., 2013–. UK Critics' Circle Nat. Dance Award for Best Male Dancer, 2012. Hon. Fellow, Trinity Laban Conservatoire of Music and Dance, 2010. Hon. DArts De Montfort, 2004; Hon. DLitt Roehampton, 2010. *Recreations:* cinema, world music, Rugby. *Address:* Unit 232a, 35 Britannia Row, N1 8QH. *T:* (020) 7354 4333, *Fax:* (020) 7354 5554. *E:* office@akramkhancompany.net.

KHAN, Prof. Geoffrey Allan, PhD; FBA 1998; Regius Professor of Hebrew, University of Cambridge, since 2012; *b* 1 Feb. 1958; *s* of Clive and Diana Khan; *m* 1984, Colette Alcock; one *s* one *d*. *Educ:* Acklam Sixth Form Coll.; SOAS, London Univ. (BA Semitic Langs 1980; PhD 1984). Res. Asst, 1983–87, Res. Associate, 1987–93, Taylor-Schechter Genizah Res. Unit, Cambridge Univ. Liby; Cambridge University: Lectr in Hebrew and Aramaic, 1993–99; Reader in Semitic Philology, 1999–2002; Prof. of Semitic Philology, 2002–12. Fellow, Inst. for Advanced Studies, Jerusalem, 1990–91. Lidzbarski Gold Medal for Semitic Philology, Deutsche Morgenländische Ges., 2004. *Publications:* Studies in Semitic Syntax, 1988; Karaite Bible manuscripts from the Cairo Genizah, 1990; Arabic Papyri: selected material from the Khalili collection, 1992; Arabic Legal and Administrative Documents in the Cambridge Genizah collections, 1993; Bills, Letters and Deeds: Arabic papyri of the 7th–11th centuries, 1993; A Grammar of Neo-Aramaic, 1999; The Early Karaite Tradition of Hebrew Grammatical Thought, 2000; Early Karaite Grammatical Texts, 2000; Exegesis and Grammar in Medieval Karaite Texts, 2001; The Neo-Aramaic Dialect of Qaraqosh, 2002; The Karaite Tradition of Hebrew Grammatical Thought in its Classical Form, 2003; The Jewish Neo-Aramaic Dialect of Sulemaniyya and Halabja, 2004; Arabic Documents from Early Islamic Khurasan, 2007; The Neo-Aramaic Dialect of Barwar, 2008; Neo-Aramaic Dialect Studies, 2008; The Jewish Neo-Aramaic Dialect of Urmi, 2008. *Recreations:* mountain-walking, miniature carpentry. *Address:* Faculty of Asian and Middle Eastern Studies, Sidgwick Avenue, Cambridge CB3 9DA. *T:* (01223) 335114.

KHAN, Humayun; Chairman, Institute of Rural Management, Pakistan; Director, Commonwealth Foundation, 1993–99; *b* 31 Aug. 1932; *s* of K. B. Safdar Khan and Mumtaz Safdar; *m* 1961, Munawar; three *d*. *Educ:* Bishop Cotton Sch., Simla; Trinity College, Cambridge (MA); Univ. of Southern California (MPA, Dr PA). Called to the Bar, Lincoln's Inn, 1954; joined Pakistan CS, 1955; Sec. to Govt of NWPP, 1970–73; Jt Sec., Pakistan Govt, 1973–74; Minister, Pakistan Embassy, Moscow, 1974–77; Dep. Perm. Rep., UNO, Geneva, 1977–79; Ambassador to Bangladesh, 1979–82; Additional Sec., Min. of Foreign Affairs, Pakistan, 1982–84; Ambassador to India, 1984–88; Foreign Sec. of Pakistan, 1988–89; High Comr in UK, 1990–92. Former Member: Nat. Finance Commn, Pakistan; Bd, Nat. Rural Support Prog., Pakistan. *Publications:* Cross-Border Talks: Diplomatic Divide, 2004. *Recreations:* golf, cricket, shooting, fishing. *Club:* Islamabad.

KHAN, Imran, (Imran Ahmad Khan Niazi); Hilal-e-Imtiaz, Pakistan, 1993; Founder, 1997, and Chairman, Pakistan Teehreek-e-Insaf Party; MP (PTI) Mainwali, Pakistan, 2002–07; *b* Lahore, 25 Oct. 1952; *m* 1995, Jemima (marr. diss. 2004), *d* of Sir James Goldsmith; two *s*; *m* 2015, Reham Khan. *Educ:* Aitchison Coll.; Keble Coll., Oxford (BA Hons; cricket blue, 1973, 1974, 1975; Captain, Oxford XI, 1974; Hon. Fellow, 1988). Début for Lahore A, 1969; played first Test for Pakistan, 1970, Captain, 1982–84, 1985–87, 1988–89, 1992; with Worcs CCC, 1971–76 (capped, 1976); with Sussex CCC, 1977–88 (capped, 1978; Hon. Life Mem., 1988). Editor-in-Chief, Cricket Life Internat., 1989–90. Mem., Internat. Cricket Council, 1993–. Chancellor, Bradford Univ., 2005–. Special Sports Rep., UNICEF; Founder, Imran Khan Cancer Appeal (formerly Imran Khan Cancer Hosp. Appeal), 1991–; Chm., Bd of Govs, Shaukat Khanum Memorial Cancer Hosp. and Res. Centre. Pride of Performance Award, Pakistan. *Publications:* Imran, 1983; All-Round View (autobiog.), 1988; Indus Journey, 1990; Warrior Race, 1993; Pakistan: a personal history, 2011. *Recreations:* shooting, films, music.

KHAN, Imran; Partner, Imran Khan and Partners, Solicitors, since 2000; *b* 19 Nov. 1964; *s* of Habib Shah and Khursheed Shah. *Educ:* Univ. of East London (LLB Hons). Trainee Solicitor, Birnberg Pierce, 1989–91; Asst Solicitor, then Partner, J. R. Jones Solicitors, 1991–2000. Council Mem., Law Soc., 2002–03. Vis. Lectr, South Bank Univ., 2002. Vice Chm., Nat. Civil Rights Movement, 1999–. Trustee, Anne Frank Trust, 2002–06. Hon. Dr: East London; Staffordshire; DUniv Oxford Brookes, 2000. Lawyer of the Year, Lawyer Mag., 1999. *Address:* Imran Khan and Partners, 47 Theobald's Road, WC1X 8SP. *T:* (020) 7404 3004, *Fax:* (020) 7404 3005.

KHAN, Javed Akhtar; Chief Executive, Barnardo's, since 2014; *b* Amersham, Bucks, 31 July 1963; *s* of Jahan Dad Khan and Raj Begum Khan; *m* 1991, Aamirah Hussein; four *d*. *Educ:* Univ. of Salford (BSc Maths); Didsbury Sch. of Educn (PGCE). Teacher of Maths, Cadbury Sixth Form Coll., 1985–87; Lectr in Maths, 1988–95, Asst Principal, 1995–98, E Birmingham Coll.; Dir of Develt (Further Educn), City Coll., Birmingham, 1998–2000; Asst Dir of Educn, Birmingham CC, 2000–03; Harrow Council: Chief Educn Officer, 2003–06; Dir, Community and Cultural Services, 2006–09; Exec. Dir, London Serious Youth Violence Bd, 2009–10; Chief Exec., Victim Support, 2010–14. Mem., Sentencing Council for England and Wales, 2013–; Comr, Voluntary Sector and Ageing Commn, 2013–15; Mem., Adv. Bd, Children's Comr for England, 2014–. Mem., Hounslow CCG, 2013–. Member: Exec. Bd, Children's Workforce Develt Council, 2010–13; Bd, Skills for Justice, 2010–14; Bd, Criminal Justice Council, 2010–14; Bd, Victim Support Europe, 2010–14. *Publications:* (contrib.) Educational Leadership and the Community, 2003. *Recreations:* cricket, current affairs, voluntary work. *Address:* Barnardo's, Tanners Lane, Barkingside, Ilford, Essex IG6 1QG. *E:* javed.khan@barnardos.org.uk.

KHAN, Karim Asad Ahmad; QC 2011; barrister; *b* Edinburgh, 30 March 1970; *s* of Dr Saeed Ahmad Khan and Selma Khan; three *s*. *Educ:* Silcoates Sch., Wakefield; King's Coll. London (LLB Hons; AKC); Univ. of Nice (Dip. Internat. Relns); Abo Akademi, Turku Law Sch. (Adv. Dip. Internat. Human Rights Law); Wolfson Coll., Oxford (DPhil candidate). Called to the Bar, Lincoln's Inn, 1992; in practice as a barrister, 1992–; Sen. Crown Prosecutor, CPS, 1992–96; Lawyer: Law Commn of England and Wales, 1996–97; Office of the Prosecutor, UN Internat. Criminal Tribunal for former Yugoslavia and for Rwanda, 1997–2000; defence counsel in numerous internat. criminal cases. Sen. Res. Fellow, KCL, 1999–2002; Hon. Lectr, Sch. of Law, Univ. of Utrecht, 2010–11, 2012–; Dir, Peace and Justice Initiative, 2010–. Member: wkg gp on ICC Act 2001, Criminal Bar Assoc., 2000; Attorney Gen.'s Panel of Prosecution Advocates, 2001–04; Pro Bono Human Rights Panel, FCO, 2002–. International Criminal Tribunal for former Yugoslavia: Chm., Amicus Cttee, 2007–08, Mem., Disciplinary Council, 2007–10, Mem., Exec. Cttee, 2010–, Assoc. of Defence Counsel; Mem., Disciplinary Bd, 2009–10. Member: Internat. Legal Assistance Consortium, 2008; Disciplinary Appeals Bd, Internat. Criminal Court, The Hague, 2010–. Dr hc Fama University Coll., Pristina, Kosovo, 2012. Co-Editor, Internat. Criminal Law Reports, 2006–. *Publications:* (contrib.) A Commentary to the the Rome Statute on the ICC, 2000, 2nd edn 2008; (contrib.) Human Rights Practice, 2002–; (jtly) Archbold International Criminal Courts, 2003, 3rd edn 2009; (contrib.) Security Dimension to EU Enlargement, 2007; (ed jtly and contrib.) Principles of Evidence in International Criminal Justice, 2010. *Recreations:* tennis, driving, shooting, reading, travelling. *Address:* Temple Garden Chambers, 1 Harcourt Buildings, Temple, EC4Y 9DA. *T:* (020) 7583 1315, *Fax:* (020) 7353 3969. *E:* karimahmadkhan@hotmail.com. *Club:* Islamabad (Islamabad).

KHAN, (Mohammed) Afzal, CBE 2008; Member (Lab) North West Region, European Parliament, since 2014; *b* Jhelum, Pakistan, 5 April 1958; *m* Dr Shkeela Kayani; one *s* two *d*. *Educ:* Abraham Moss Coll.; Manchester Poly. (law degree). Admitted as Solicitor, 1996. Labourer; bus driver; police constable, Gtr Manchester Police, 1987; Sen. Partner, HSK Solicitors; Founder and Partner, Khan Solicitors, 2005–09; Partner, Mellor & Jackson Solicitors, Oldham, 2009–. Mem. (Lab), Manchester CC, 2000–15; Lord Mayor of Manchester, 2005–06. *Address:* European Parliament, Rue Wiertz, Brussels 1047, Brussels.

KHAN, Rt Hon. Sadiq (Aman); PC 2009; MP (Lab) Tooting, since 2005; *b* 8 Oct. 1970; *s* of late Amanullah Ahmad Khan and of Sehrun Nisa Khan; *m* 1994, Saadiya Ahmad; two *d*. *Educ:* Ernest Bevin Secondary Comprehensive Sch.; Univ. of N London (LLB Hons 1992); Coll. of Law, Guildford. Christian Fisher Solicitors: trainee solicitor, 1993–95; Solicitor, 1995–98; Partner, 1998–2000; Equity Partner: Christian Fisher Khan Solicitors, 2000–02; and Co-founder, Christian Khan Solicitors, 2002–04. Vis. Lectr, Univ. of N London and London Metropolitan Univ., 1998–2004. Mem. (Lab), Wandsworth BC, 1994–2006; Dep. Leader of Labour Gp, 1996–2001; Hon. Alderman, 2006. PPS to Lord Privy Seal and Leader of H of C, 2007; Govt Whip, 2007–08; Parly Under-Sec. of State, DCLG, 2008–09; Minister of State, DfT, 2009–10; Shadow Sec. of State for Transport, 2010; Shadow Lord Chancellor and Sec. of State for Justice, 2010–15; Shadow Minister for London, 2013–15. Chm., All-Party Parly Gp for Citizens Advice, 2006–08. Chair, Liberty, 2001–04; Founding Mem., Human Rights Lawyers Assoc., 2003. Exec. Mem., Fabian Soc., 2006– (Vice Chair, 2007; Chair, 2008–10); Vice Chair, Legal Action Gp, 1999–2004; Patron, Progress, 2005. *Publications:* Challenging Racism, 2003; Police Misconduct: Legal Remedies, 2005; Fairness not Favours, 2008; Punishment and Reform: how our justice system can help cut crime, 2011. *Recreations:* playing and watching sport, cinema, family, friends, local community. *Address:* House of Commons, SW1A 0AA. *T:* (020) 7219 6967, *Fax:* (020) 7219 6477. *E:* sadiqkhanmp@parliament.uk.

KHAN, Tahir Zaffar; QC 2011; a Recorder, since 2004; *b* Bradford, 25 April 1964; *s* of Muzaffar Khan and Khadija Begum; *m* 1988, Samina Tahir; two *s* one *d*. *Educ:* Liverpool Poly. (LLB Hons Law); Inns of Court Sch. of Law. Called to the Bar, Lincoln's Inn, 1986. *Recreations:* playing tennis for Bingley Tennis Club, enjoy playing badminton, avid reader. *Address:* Broadway House Chambers, 9 Bank Street, Bradford, West Yorks BD1 1TW. *T:* (01274) 722560, *Fax:* (01274) 370708. *E:* clerks@broadwayhouse.co.uk.

KHANBHAI, Bashir Yusufali Simba; Member (C) Eastern Region, England, European Parliament, 1999–2004; *b* 22 Sept. 1945; *s* of Yusufali Simba Khanbhai and Jenambai Khanbhai; *m* 1981, Maria Bashir Khanbhai (*née* Da Silva); one *s*. *Educ:* Sch. of Pharmacy, Univ. of London (BPharm Hons 1966); Balliol Coll., Oxford (MA Hons PPE 1969). Manufg industry, export and finance, 1970–97; Chief Executive Officer: Headlands Chemicals Ltd, 1970–76; Khanbhai Industries Ltd, 1977–84; Teqny Ltd, 1984–99. *Publications:* (ed) The Jowett Papers, 1970. *Recreations:* tennis, travel, theatre, music, food. *Address:* 20 Burntwood Road, Sevenoaks, Kent TN13 1PT. *E:* emailbashir@gmail.com.

KHARCHENKO, Ihor, PhD; Ambassador of Ukraine to Japan, since 2013; *b* 15 May 1962; *s* of Yuri and Raiisa; *m* 1986, Maria Rozhytsina; two *d*. *Educ:* Taras Shevchenko Kyiv State Univ. (Internat. Relns; PhD History). Lectr, then Asst Prof., Taras Shevchenko Kyiv State Univ., 1988–92; Ministry of Foreign Affairs, Ukraine: Policy Planning Staff, 1992–93; Dir, Policy Planning Staff, 1993–97; Ambassador-at-Large, Hd of Secretariat of Pres. of UN Gen. Assembly and Dep. Perm. Rep. of Ukraine to the UN, NY, 1997–98; Ambassador of Ukraine to Romania, 1998–2000; Dep. Foreign Minister of Ukraine, 2000–03, Special Rep. of Pres. of Ukraine to the Balkans, 2001–03; Ambassador of Ukraine to Poland, 2003–05; Ambassador of Ukraine to the Court of St James's, 2005–10; Perm. Rep. of Ukraine to Internat. Maritime Orgn, 2006–11; Special Rep. of Ukraine on Transdniestrian Settlement, 2010–13. Order of Merit (Ukraine), 2002. *Recreations:* family, literature, music. *Address:* 3–5–31 Nishi-Azabu, Minato-ku, Tokyo 106–0031, Japan.

KHARE, Prof. Chandrashekhar Bhalchandra, PhD; FRS 2012; Professor of Mathematics, University of California, Los Angeles, since 2007; *b* Mumbai, 1967; *m* Rajanigandha; one *s* one *d. Educ:* Trinity Coll., Cambridge (BA Maths 1989); Calif Inst. of Technol. (PhD 1995). Vis. Fellow, 1995–96, Fellow, 1996–2001, Associate Prof., 2001–07, Tata Inst. of Fundamental Res., Mumbai; Associate Prof. of Maths, Univ. of Utah, 2005–07. Guggenheim Fellow, 2008. Fermat Prize, 2007; Infosys Prize in Math. Scis, 2010; (jtly) Frank Nelson Cole Prize in Number Theory, Amer. Math. Soc., 2011. *Address:* Mathematics Department, University of California, Los Angeles, PO Box 951555, Los Angeles, CA 90095–1555, USA.

KHATAMI, Hojjatoleslam Seyed Mohammad; President of the Islamic Republic of Iran, 1997–2005; *b* 29 Sept. 1943; *s* of Ayatollah Sayyid Ruhollah Khatami, religious scholar; *m* 1974, Zohreh Sadeghi; one *s* two *d. Educ:* High Sch.; Qom Theol. Sch.; Isfahan Univ. (BA Philosophy); Tehran Univ. (MA); Qom Seminary. Head, Hamburg Islamic Centre, Germany, 1979; Mem. for Ardakan and Maybod, first Islamic Consultative Assembly, 1980–82; Dep. Hd of Jt Comd of Armed Forces, and Chm., War Propaganda HQ, Iran-Iraq War, 1980–88; Dir, Keyhan Newspaper Inst., 1981; Minister of Culture and Islamic Guidance, 1982–92; Advr to Pres. Rafsanjani, 1992–96. Mem., High Council for Cultural Revolution, 1996. Chm., 8th Session, Islamic Summit Conf., 1997–2000. *Publications:* From the World of the City to the City of the World, 1994; Fear of Wave, 1997; Faith and Thought Trapped by Despotism; contrib. articles to Arabic mags and newspapers.

KHAW, Prof. Kay-Tee, (Mrs Kay-Tee Fawcett), CBE 2003; FRCP; Professor of Clinical Gerontology, University of Cambridge, since 1989; Fellow, Gonville and Caius College, Cambridge, since 1991; *b* 14 Oct. 1950; *d* of Khaw Kai Boh and Tan Chwee Geok; *m* 1980, Prof. James William Fawcett, *qv*; one *s* one *d. Educ:* Girton Coll., Cambridge (BA, MA; MB BChir); St Mary's Hosp. Med. Sch., London; London Sch. of Hygiene and Tropical Med. (MSc). MRCP 1977, FRCP 1993; DCH 1978; MFPHM 1993. LTCL 1969. Wellcome Trust Research Fellow, LSHTM, St Mary's Hosp. and Univ. of California San Diego, 1979–84; Asst Adjunct Prof., Univ. of California Sch. of Med., San Diego, 1985; Sen. Registrar in Community Medicine, Univ. of Cambridge Sch. of Clinical Medicine, 1986–89. Member: NHS Central R&D Cttee, 1991–97; HEFCE, 1992–97; MRC Health Services and Public Health Res. Bd, 1999–2003; MRC Cross Bd Gp, 2001–05. Chair: Nutrition Forum, Food Standards Agency, 2002–09; World Heart Fedn Council on Epidemiology and Prevention, 2008–12 (Vice-Chair, 2002–07); Med. Protection Soc., 2012–. FMedSci 1999. Daland Fellow, Amer. Philosophical Soc., 1984. Trustee: Help the Aged, 1993–98; BHF, 2006–14. *Publications:* contribs to scientific jls on chronic disease epidemiology. *Address:* Clinical Gerontology Unit, Box 251, University of Cambridge School of Clinical Medicine, Addenbrooke's Hospital, Cambridge CB2 2QQ.

KHAW, Prof. Sir Peng Tee, Kt 2013; PhD; FRCP, FRCOphth; FRCPath; FMedSci; CBiol, FRSB; Professor of Glaucoma and Ocular Healing, UCL Institute of Ophthalmology, since 1997; Consultant Ophthalmic Surgeon, Moorfields Eye Hospital, since 1997; Director: National Institute for Health Research Biomedical Research Centre in Ophthalmology, Moorfields Eye Hospital and UCL Institute of Ophthalmology, since 2007; Research and Development, Moorfields Eye Hospital, since 2008; Programme Director, Eyes and Vision, UCL Partners, Academic Health Science Centre, since 2009; *b* 1957; *m. Educ:* Southampton Univ. (BM 1980); Royal Coll. of Surgeons (DO 1985); Univ. of London (PhD Cell and Molecular Biol. Healing 1994). MRCP 1983, FRCP 1999; FRCSGlas 1985; FRCOphth 1989; CBiol 2000; FRSB (FIBiol 2000); FRCPath 2002. SHO, then Registrar, Southampton Eye Hosp., 1984–85; Lectr in Ophthalmol., Southampton Eye Hosp. and Univ. of Southampton, 1985–87; Sen. Registrar, Moorfields Eye Hosp., 1987–89; Wellcome Trust Res. Fellow, 1989–92; Wellcome Trust Res. Fellow and Vis. Faculty, Inst. for Wound Res., Univ. of Florida, 1991–92; Wellcome Vision Res. Fellow, Inst. of Ophthalmol., UCL, 1992–93; Consultant Ophthalmic Surgeon, Moorfields Eye Hosp., 1993–98. FMedSci 2002; Fellow, ARVO (Pres., 2013; Gold Fellow 2014). Hon. FRCS 1996; Hon. FCOptom 2011. Hon. DSc Anglia Ruskin, 2012. *Publications:* (jtly) ABC of Eyes, 1988, 4th edn 2003; (jtly) Ophthalmology Revision Aid, 1989, 2nd edn 1995; (ed with R. Pitts-Crick) Textbook of Clinical Ophthalmology, 1997, 2nd edn 2000; (jtly) Ophthalmology: clinical examination techniques, 1999; (jtly) Eye Disease in Clinical Practice: a concise clinical atlas, 2000; (with I. Russell-Eggitt) Glaucoma in Babies and Children: a guide for parents, 2004, 2nd edn 2008; (jtly) Training Manual in Ophthalmology, 2008; some 450 pubns as papers, books, chapters and articles in jls. *Address:* University College London Institute of Ophthalmology and Moorfields Eye Hospital, 11–43 Bath Street, EC1V 9EL. *T:* and *Fax:* (020) 7608 6887. *E:* p.khaw@ucl.ac.uk.

KHAYAT, His Honour Georges Mario; QC 1992; a Circuit Judge, 2002–11; *b* 15 Aug. 1941; *s* of Fred Khayat and Julie Germain. *Educ:* Terra Sancta Coll., Nazareth; Prior Park Coll., Bath. Called to the Bar, Lincoln's Inn, 1967. A Recorder, 1987–2002. Head of Chambers, 1999–2002. Chm., Surrey and S London Bar Mess, 1995–98. *Recreations:* horse riding, reading, boating, music. *Address:* 2 Stephen Weiss, Haifa, Israel.

KHEMKA, Dame Asha, DBE 2014 (OBE 2009); Principal and Chief Executive, West Nottinghamshire College Group, since 2006; *b* Sitamarhi, India; *d* of late Mr and Mrs Agarwal; *m* 1967, Shankar Lal Khemka; two *s* one *d. Educ:* NE Wales Inst. of Higher Educn (BEd Hons, Cert Ed Cardiff Univ.). Lectr, Oswestry Coll., 1987–95; Dir of Quality and Dep. Hd of Faculty, Tamworth Coll., 1995–2001; Asst Principal, Stafford Coll., 2001–04; Dep. Principal, New Coll., Nottingham, 2004–06. Associate Inspector, Ofsted, 1996–2005. Member: Bd, Educn and Trng Foundn; Bd, D2N2 LEP; Educn Hons Cttee; Bd, Assoc. of Colls (Chair: Quality and Perf. Cttee; Assoc. of Colls India); Council, Univ. of Nottingham, 2009–. Founder and Trustee, Inspire and Achieve Foundn, 2008–. Dadabhai Naoroji Award for Educn, 2014. *Recreations:* travel, cinema, music, entertaining. *Address:* West Nottinghamshire College, Derby Road, Mansfield, Notts NG18 5BH. *T:* (01623) 627191. *E:* asha.khemka@wnc.ac.uk.

KHERAJ, Naguib; Senior Adviser, Aga Khan Development Network, since 2010; *b* London, 15 July 1964; *m* Nina Hirji Kheraj; one *s. Educ:* Dulwich Coll.; Robinson Coll., Cambridge (MA Econs 1990). Dir, Investment Banking, then Man. Dir and Chief Financial Officer, Salomon Bros, London, 1986–96; with Robert Fleming, 1996–97; with Barclays plc, 1997–2007: Chief Operating Officer, Investment Banking Div.; Global Hd of Investment Banking; Dep. Chm., Asset Mgt; Chief Exec., Private Clients; Gp Finance Dir, 2004–07; Sen. Advr, 2007; Dir and Mem., Gp Exec. Cttee; CEO, JPMorgan Cazenove Ltd, 2008–10; Vice Chm., Barclays Bank plc, 2011–12. Non-exec. Dir, NHS Commng Bd, 2012–13; Independent Director: Standard Chartered PLC, 2014– (Sen. Ind. Dir, 2015–); Rothesay Life, 2014–. Mem., Investment Cttee, Wellcome Trust, 2008–. Mem., Bd of Govs, Inst. of Ismaili Studies; Chm., Nat. Cttee, Aga Khan Foundn (UK); Trustee, Aga Khan Univ.

KHIYAMI, Dr Sami Madani; Ambassador of the Syrian Arab Republic to the Court of St James's, 2004–12; *b* Damascus, 28 Aug. 1948; *s* of Dr Madani and Jamila Khiyami; *m* 1978, Yamina Farhan; one *s* two *d. Educ:* American Univ. of Beirut (BE 1972); Univ. of Claude Bernard, Lyons, France (Dip. Electronics 1974; PhD 1979). Asst, Faculty of Mech. and Electrical Engrg, Damascus Univ., 1972–73; with Siemens-Karlsruhe, Germany, 1972–74; Asst Prof., Univ. of Damascus, and researcher and gp leader, Scientific Studies and Res. Centre, Damascus, 1979–85; Prof. of Computer Engrg and Electronic Measurements, Univ. of Damascus, 1985–94; Higher Institute of Applied Sciences and Technology, Damascus: Hd, Electronics Dept, Chief Researcher, then Dir of Res., 1986–95; Actg Dir, 1993; Vice-Dir for Res., 1993–95. Consultant, Systems Internat., Syria, 1993–94; Nat. Telecom and Technol. Consultant, 1999–2002. Board Member: Syrian Arab Airlines, 2004; Spacetel, 2004. Co-founder and Dir, Syrian Computer Soc., 1989. *Publications:* Electronic Measurements and Measuring Devices, 1982; Microprocessors and Microprocessor Based Systems, 1982; Algorithms and Data Structures, 1983; numerous contribs to scientific reviews on technol. and related econ. policies, IT and telecom strategies. *Recreations:* philately, gardening, music.

KHOKHAR, Mushtaq Ahmed; His Honour Judge Khokhar; a Circuit Judge, since 2006; *b* 2 Feb. 1956; *s* of Yousaf and Sakina Khokhar; *m* 1991, Dr Ramla Mumtaz; two *s. Educ:* Leeds Poly. (BA Hons Law 1980); Queen Mary Coll., London (LLM 1981). Called to the Bar, Lincoln's Inn, 1982; Asst Recorder, 1998–2000; a Recorder, 2000–06. Standing Counsel to HM Customs and Excise, then HMRC, 2001–06. *Recreations:* watching cricket and football, su doku, walking, theatre, eating out, reading biographies, playing snooker and squash. *Address:* Manchester Crown Court, Minshull Street, Manchester M1 3FS.

KHOO, Francis Kah Siang; writer; solicitor and advocate; *b* 23 Oct. 1947; *s* of late Teng Eng Khoo and Swee Neo Chew; *m* 1977, Dr Swee Chai Ang, MB BS, MSc, FRCS. *Educ:* Univ. of Singapore (LLB (Hons) 1970); Univ. of London (MA 1980). Advocate and Solicitor, Singapore, 1971. Lawyer, Singapore, 1971–77; journalist and political cartoonist, South magazine, and Mem., NUJ (UK), 1980–87; Gen. Sec. (Dir), War on Want, 1988–89; Solicitor, England and Wales, 1998. Founding Mem. and Trustee of British charity, Medical Aid for Palestinians, 1984–; Sec., RADICLE charity, 2000– (Chm., Trustees, 2004–); Trustee, Living Stones charity, 2004–. *Publications:* And Bungaraya Blooms All Day: collection of songs, poems and cartoons in exile, UK, 1978; Hang On Tight, No Surrender: tape of songs, 1984; Rebel and the Revolutionary (poems), 1995; (contrib.) Our Thoughts are Free: poems and prose on imprisonment and exile, 2009. *Recreations:* photography, hill-walking, singing and song-writing, camera designing and inventions, swimming. *Address:* 285 Cambridge Heath Road, Bethnal Green, E2 0EL. *T:* and *Fax:* (020) 7729 3994.

KHUSH, Dr Gurdev Singh, FRS 1995; consultant to Director General, International Rice Research Institute, Philippines, 2001–04 (Principal Plant Breeder, and Head, Division of Plant Breeding, Genetics and Biochemistry, 1989–2001); *b* 22 Aug. 1935; *s* of Kartar Singh and Pritam Kaur; *m* 1961, Harwant Kaur Grewal; one *s* three *d. Educ:* Punjab Univ., Chandigarh, India (BScAgr); Univ. of Calif, Davis (PhD Genetics 1960). University of California, Davis: Research Asst, 1957–60; Asst Geneticist, 1960–67; International Rice Research Institute, Philippines: Plant Breeder, 1967–72; Head, Dept of Plant Breeding, 1972–89. Adjunct Prof., Dept of Plant Scis (formerly Vegetable Crops), Univ. of Calif., Davis, 2003–. Hon. DSc: Punjab Agricl, 1987; Tamil Nadu Agricl, 1995; C. S. Azad Univ. of Agric. and Technol., 1995; G. B. Pant Univ. of Agric. and Technol., 1996; De Montfort, 1998; Cambridge, 2000; ND Univ. of Agric. and Technol., 2003. Borlaug Award in Plant Breeding, Coromandel Fertilizers Ltd, India, 1977; Japan Prize, Japan Sci. and Technol. Foundn, 1987; Fellows Award 1989, Internat. Agronomy Award 1990, Amer. Soc. of Agronomy; Emil M. Mrak Internat. Award, Univ. of California, Davis, 1990; World Food Prize, World Food Prize Foundn, 1996; Rank Prize, Rank Prize Funds, 1998; Wolf Prize, Wolf Foundn, Israel, 2000. *Publications:* Cytogenetics of Aneuploids, 1973; Host Plant Resistance to Insects, 1995; *edited:* Rice Biotechnology, 1991; Nodulation and Nitrogen Fixation in Rice, 1992; Apomix: exploiting hybrid vigor in rice, 1994; Rice Genetics III, 1996; Rice Genetics IV, 2001; contrib. chapters in books; numerous papers in jls. *Recreation:* reading world history. *Address:* 39399 Blackhawk Place, Davis, CA 95616–7008, USA.

KIBAKI, Mwai; President (Nat. Rainbow Coalition, 2002–07, Party of National Unity, 2007–13), and Commander in Chief of the Armed Forces, Kenya, 2002–13; UNESCO Goodwill Ambassador of Water in Africa, since 2014; *b* Othaya, Kenya, 1931; *m* Lucy Muthoni; three *s* one *d. Educ:* Makerere UC (BA); London Sch. of Econs (BSc Econs). Lectr in Econs, Makerere UC, 1959–60; Nat. Exec. Officer, Kenya African Nat. Union (KANU), 1960–64; Kenyan Rep. to E African Legislative Assembly of E African Common Services Orgn, 1962; Mem. (KANU) Nairobi Doonholm, House of Reps, 1963–74; Parly Sec. to Treasury, 1963–64; Asst Minister of Econ. Planning and Devélt, 1964–66; Minister: for Commerce and Industry, 1966–69; of Finance, 1969–70; of Finance and Econ. Planning, 1970–78; of Finance, 1978–82; of Home Affairs, 1978–88; of Health, 1988–91; Vice Pres. of Kenya, 1978–88; Leader, Official Opposition, 1998–2002. Vice-Pres., KANU, 1978–91; Leader: Democratic Party, 1991–2002; Party of Nat. Unity, 2008. Chief of the Golden Heart (Kenya), 2002. *Recreations:* reading, golf.

KIBBEY, Sidney Basil; Under-Secretary, Department of Health and Social Security, 1971–76; *b* 3 Dec. 1916; *y s* of late Percy Edwin Kibbey and Winifred Kibbey, Mickleover, Derby; *m* 1939, Violet Gertrude, (Jane), Eyre; (twin) *s* and *d. Educ:* Derby Sch. Executive Officer, Min. of Health, 1936; Principal, Min. of National Insurance, 1951; Sec., Nat. Insurance Adv. Cttee, 1960–62; Asst Sec., Min. of Pensions and Nat. Insurance, 1962. *Address:* 29 Beaulieu Close, Datchet, Berks SL3 9DD. *T:* (01753) 549101.

KIBBLE, Sir Thomas (Walter Bannerman), Kt 2014; CBE 1998; PhD; FRS 1980; Emeritus Professor of Theoretical Physics, and Senior Research Fellow, Imperial College, London, since 1998; *b* 1932; *s* of Walter Frederick Kibble and Janet Cowan Watson (*née* Bannerman); *m* 1957, Anne Richmond Allan; one *s* two *d. Educ:* Doveton-Corrie Sch., Madras; Melville Coll., Edinburgh; Univ. of Edinburgh (MA, BSc, PhD). Commonwealth Fund Fellow, California Inst. of Technology, 1958–59; Imperial College, London: NATO Fellow, 1959–60; Lecturer, 1961; Sen. Lectr, 1965; Reader in Theoretical Physics, 1966; Prof. of Theoretical Physics, 1970–98; Hd, Dept of Physics, 1983–91. Sen. Visiting Research Associate, Univ. of Rochester, New York, 1967–68; Lorentz Prof., Univ. of Leiden, 2007. Member: Nuclear Physics Bd, SERC, 1982–86; Astronomy, Space and Radio Bd, 1984–86; Physical Sciences Sub-cttee, UGC, 1985–89. Chairman: Scientists Against Nuclear Arms, 1985–91 (Vice-Chm., 1981–85); Martin Ryle Trust, 1985–96. Mem. Council, Royal Soc., 1987–89 (Vice-Pres., 1988–89). Hon. DSc: KCL, 2013; Edinburgh, 2013. (Jtly) Hughes Medal, 1981, Royal Medal, 2012, Royal Soc.; (jtly) Rutherford Medal, 1984, Guthrie Medal, 1993, Inst. of Physics; (jtly) J. J. Sakurai Prize, APS, 2010; Dirac Medal, Abdus Salam Internat. Centre for Theoretical Physics, Trieste, 2014. *Publications:* Classical Mechanics, 1966, 5th edn 2004; papers in Phys. Rev., Proc. Royal Soc., Nuclear Physics, Nuovo Cimento, Jl Physics, and others. *Recreations:* cycling, walking, destructive gardening. *Address:* Blackett Laboratory, Imperial College, Prince Consort Road, SW7 2AZ. *T:* (020) 7594 7845.

KIDD, Prof. Cecil; Regius Professor of Physiology, 1984–97, part-time Professor of Physiology, 1997–2000, now Emeritus, Marischal College, University of Aberdeen; *b* 28 April 1933; *s* of Herbert Cecil and Elizabeth Kidd; *m* 1956, Margaret Winifred Goodwill; three *s. Educ:* Queen Elizabeth Grammar School, Darlington; King's College, Newcastle upon Tyne, Univ. of Durham (BSc, PhD). FRSB; FRSA. Research Fellow then Demonstrator in Physiology, King's Coll., Univ. of Durham, 1954–58; Asst Lectr then Lectr in Physiol., Univ. of Leeds, 1958–68; Res. Fellow in Physiol., Johns Hopkins Univ., 1962–63; Sen. Lectr then Reader in Physiol., 1968–84, Sen. Res. Associate in Cardiovascular Studies, 1973–84, Univ. of Leeds. *Publications:* textbooks of physiology; scientific papers in physiological jls. *Recreations:* opera, walking, food, alpines, gardening. *Address:* c/o School of Medical Sciences, College of Life Sciences and Medicine, University of Aberdeen, Aberdeen AB25 2ZD. *T:* (01224) 273005.

KIDD, Charles William; Editor of Debrett's Peerage and Baronetage, since 1980; *b* 23 May 1952; *yr s* of late Charles Vincent Kidd and Marian Kidd, BEM (*née* Foster), Kirkbymoorside. *Educ:* St Peter's Sch., York; Bede Coll., Durham. Assistant Editor: Burke's Peerage, 1972–77; Debrett's Peerage and Baronetage, 1977–80. Mem., Friends of Margravine Cemetery. FSG 2000. *Publications:* Debrett's Book of Royal Children (jtly), 1982; Debrett Goes to Hollywood, 1986; articles in Genealogists' Mag. *Recreations:* cinema, researching film and theatre dynasties, tennis.

KIDD, Prof. Colin Craig, DPhil; FBA 2010; FRSE; Wardlaw Professor of Modern History, University of St Andrews, since 2012; *b* Ayr, 5 May 1964; *s* of George Kidd and Rine Kidd; *m* 1988, Lucy Isabelle Armstrong; one *s* one *d*. *Educ:* Glasgow Acad.; Gonville and Caius Coll., Cambridge (BA 1985); Univ. of Oxford (DPhil 1992). Vis. Choate Fellow, Harvard Univ., 1985–86; Fellow, All Souls Coll., Oxford, 1987–94; Lectr, then Reader, 1994–2003, Prof. of Modern Hist., 2003–10, Univ. of Glasgow; Prof. of Intellectual History and Political Thought, QUB, 2010–12. Fifty-pound Fellow, All Souls Coll., Oxford, 2005–. Gov., Glasgow Acad., 2002–08. FRSE 2002. *Publications:* Subverting Scotland's Past, 1993; British Identities Before Nationalism, 1999; The Forging of Races, 2006; Union and Unionisms, 2008. *Recreations:* Watergate, Galloway. *Address:* School of History, University of St Andrews, St Katharine's Lodge, The Scores, St Andrews, Fife KY16 9BA.

KIDD, Hon. Sir Douglas (Lorimer), KNZM 2009 (DCNZM 2000); Member, Waitangi Tribunal, since 2004; Speaker, House of Representatives, New Zealand, 1996–99; District Licensing Commissioner, Wellington City Council, since 2013; *b* 12 Sept. 1941; *s* of Lorimer Edward Revington Kidd and Jessie Jean Kidd (*née* Mottershead); *m* 1964, Jane Stafford Richardson; one *s* two *d*. *Educ:* Ohau Primary Sch.; Horowhenua Coll.; Victoria Univ., Wellington (LLB 1964). Mil. service, Territorial Service, Royal Regt of NZ Artillery, 1960–64. Admitted Barrister and Solicitor, 1964; Partner, Wisheart Macnab & Partners, 1964–78. MP (N) Marlborough, 1978–96, Kaikoura, 1996–99; List MP (N), 1999–2002. Minister of Fisheries, 1990–93, and of State-Owned Enterprises, 1990–91; Associate Minister of Finance, 1990–94; Minister of Maori Affairs, 1991–94; Minister of Energy and Fisheries, 1993–96; Minister of Accident Rehabilitation and Compensation, 1994–96. Chairman: Cabinet Revenue and Expenditure Cttee; Regulations Rev. Select Cttee, 1999–2002; Ministerial Aquaculture Review Cttee, 2009; Joint Chm., Parly Appropriations Review Cttee, 2010; Mem., Privileges and Maori Affairs Select Cttee, 1999–2002. Mem., Commonwealth Observer Gp, Pakistan Federal and Provincial Elections, 2002; Chm., Commonwealth Election Monitoring Mission to Pakistan, 2013. Dir and Partner, plantation forestry, marine farming and wine co. ventures, Marlborough, 1968–94. Hon. Mem., Canterbury/Nelson/Marlborough/W Coast Regt, 1980–97 (Hon. Col, 1997–2003). CGS's Commendation for outstanding service to NZ Army, 1999. NZ Commemoration Medal, 1990; NZ Defence Service Medal (Territorial), 2011. *Recreations:* walking, fishing, reading, travel. *Club:* Marlborough (Blenheim).

KIDD, (John Christopher William) Matthew; HM Diplomatic Service; High Commissioner, Cyprus, 2010–14; *b* Aberystwyth, 4 Feb. 1957; *s* of Captain John Franklin Kidd, RN and Gwenllian Anne Kidd (*née* Lewes); *m* 1995, Carine Celia Ann (*née* Coldwell), *widow* of Sir Richard John Maitland, 9th Bt; twin *d* and one step *s* one step *d*. *Educ:* Winchester Coll.; Jesus Coll., Oxford (BA). Entered FCO, 1978; Asst Desk Officer, S Asian Dept, 1978–79; Third, later Second Sec., Nicosia, 1980–83; UKMIS NY, 1983; Private Sec. to Ambassador to France, 1984–86; Head of Section: Western Eur. Dept, FCO, 1986–87; Security Policy Dept, FCO, 1987–90; Dep. Hd of Mission, Addis Ababa, 1990–93; Dep. Hd, Far Eastern and Pacific Dept, FCO, 1993–94; Dep. Hd, later Actg Hd, Policy Planning Staff, FCO, 1994–96; on secondment to Eur. Commn as Foreign Policy Advr, 1996–98; Head: Political and Public Affairs Section, Bonn, then Berlin, 1998–2001; Whitehall Liaison Dept, FCO, 2001–04; Dep. Perm. Rep., UK Delegn to NATO, 2004–08; Sec. Gen.'s Special Rep. for HQ Reform, NATO (on secondment), 2008–09. *Address:* c/o Foreign and Commonwealth Office, King Charles Street, SW1A 2AH.

See also C. A. Maitland.

KIDD, Paul Ashley; Head of Financial Services, Royal Borough of Kensington and Chelsea, 2008–11; *b* Gravesend, 6 Sept. 1951; *s* of Ronald William and Marion Kidd; *m* 1975, Jennifer Davies; one *s*. *Educ:* York Univ. (BA Hons Social Sci.). CPFA 1976. London Borough of Croydon: Finance trainee, 1973–75; Sen. Accountant, 1976–78; Royal Borough of Kensington and Chelsea: Sen. Accountant, 1978–81; Principal Accountant, 1981–82; Asst Chief Accountant, 1982–88; Chief Accountant, 1988–91; Hd, Accountancy Services, 1991–95; Hd, Financial Services, 1995–2008. *Recreations:* walking, gardening, DIY, digital photography, compiling quizzes, visiting France, sport (watching not playing), music (listening and playing badly), films, reading.

KIDDLE, Ven. John; Archdeacon of Wandsworth, since 2015; *b* 28 June 1958. *Educ:* Monkton Combe Sch., Bath; Ridley Hall, Cambridge; Queens' Coll., Cambridge (MA 1983); Heythrop Coll., London (MTh 2002). Maths Teacher, Bacon's C of E Sch., Bermondsey, 1980–81; ordained deacon, 1982, priest, 1983; Curate, St Peter and St Paul, Ormskirk, 1982–86; Vicar: St Gabriel, Huyton Quarry, Liverpool, 1986–91; St Luke, Watford, 1991–2008; Rural Dean, Watford, 1999–2004; Hon. Canon, 2005–10, Canon Residentiary, 2010–15, St Albans Cathedral; Diocesan Officer for Mission and Devel, 2008–15, Dir of Mission, 2011–15, Diocese of St Albans. *Publications:* (contrib.) Ready Steady Slow: thoughts for advent, 2010; (contrib.) Reflections for Daily Prayer, 2011. *Address:* 620 Kingston Road, Raynes Park, SW20 8DN. *T:* (020) 8545 2440.

KIDGELL, John Earle, CB 2003; consultant in economic statistics; Director of Economic Statistics, Office for National Statistics (formerly Head of Economic Accounts Division, Central Statistical Office), 1994–2002 (Grade 3, 1988–2002); *b* 18 Nov. 1943; *s* of Gilbert James Kidgell and Cicely Alice (*née* Earle); *m* 1968, Penelope Jane Tarry; one *s* two *d*. *Educ:* Eton House Sch., Southend-on-Sea; Univ. of St Andrews (MA); London School of Economics and Political Science (MSc). NIESR, 1967–70; Gallup Poll, 1970–72; Statistician, CSO and Treasury, 1972–79; Chief Statistician, DoE, 1979–86; Hd of Finance Div., PSA, 1986–88; Head of Directorate D, Central Statistical Office, 1989–91. *Publications:* articles in Nat. Inst. Econ. Rev., Econ. Trends, etc. *Recreations:* hill walking, tennis, golf, reading.

KIDMAN, Nicole Mary, AC 2006; actress; *b* Hawaii, 20 June 1967; *d* of late Dr Antony David Kidman, AM and of Janelle Ann Kidman (*née* Glenny); *m* 1990, Tom Cruise (*see* T. Cruise Mapother) (marr. diss. 2001); one adopted *s* one adopted *d*; *m* 2006, Keith Urban; two *d*. *Educ:* N Sydney High Sch. Worked at Phillip Street Th., Sydney. *TV mini-series:* Vietnam, 1986; Bangkok Hilton, 1989; *theatre:* The Blue Room, Donmar Warehouse, 1998, NY 1999; Photograph 51, Noël Coward Th., 2015; *films include:* Bush Christmas, 1983; Dead Calm, 1989; Days of Thunder, 1990; Billy Bathgate, 1991; Far and Away, Flirting, 1992; Malice, My Life, 1993; Batman Forever, To Die For, 1995; The Portrait of a Lady, 1996; The Peacemaker, 1997; Practical Magic, Eyes Wide Shut, 1999; Moulin Rouge, The Others, 2001; Birthday Girl, 2002; The Hours (Academy and BAFTA Awards for best actress, 2003), The Human Stain, Cold Mountain, 2003; Dogville, The Stepford Wives, Birth, 2004; The Interpreter, Bewitched, 2005; Fur: An Imaginary Portrait of Diane Arbus, The Invasion, The Golden Compass, 2007; Margot at the Wedding, Australia, 2008; Nine, 2009; Rabbit Hole, 2011; Hemingway & Gellhorn (TV film), 2012; The Paperboy, Stoker, 2013; The Railway Man, Grace of Monaco, Before I Go to Sleep, Paddington, 2014; Queen of the Desert, 2015; prod., In the Cut, 2003. *Address:* c/o 42West, 11400 W Olympic Boulevard, Suite 1100, Los Angeles, CA 90064, USA.

KIDNER, Rear-Adm. Peter Jonathan, CEng, FRAeS; Chief Executive, Defence Medical Education and Training Agency (formerly Defence Medical Training Organisation), 2002–04; *b* 21 July 1949; *s* of Col Peter Kidner and Patricia (*née* Bunyard); *m* 1973, Jean Caley; one *s* one *d*. *Educ:* Sherborne Sch.; RNEC (BSc). CEng 1992; FRAeS 1995. Air Engineer Officer: 849 B Flight, HMS Ark Royal, 1975–76; 899 Sqn, 1981; Dir, Helicopter Support, 1997–2000; CO, HMS Sultan, 2000–02. Local Corresp., Open Spaces Soc., 2007–; Mem., Ramblers' Assoc. *Recreations:* walking, Dolomites.

KIDNEY, David Neil; Chief Executive, UK Public Health Register, since 2013; *b* 21 March 1955; *s* of Neil Bernard Kidney and Doris Kidney; *m* 1978, Elaine Dickinson; one *s* one *d*. *Educ:* Bristol Univ. (LLB). Solicitor in private practice, Kenneth Wainwright & Co., then Wainwrights, subseq. Jewels & Kidney, 1977–97, Partner, 1983–97. Mem. (Lab) Stafford BC, 1987–97. Contested (Lab) Stafford, 1992. MP (Lab) Stafford, 1997–2010; contested (Lab) same seat, 2010. Team PPS, DEFRA, 2002–03; Parly Under-Sec. of State, DECC, 2009–10. Hd of Policy, Chartered Inst. of Envmtl Health, 2010–13. *Recreations:* bridge, chess. *Address:* 6 Beechcroft Avenue, Stafford ST16 1BJ.

KIDRON, Baroness *cr* 2012 (Life Peer), of Angel in the London Borough of Islington; **Beeban Kidron,** OBE 2012; film director, since 1982; *b* 2 May 1961; *d* of late Michael Kidron and of Nina Kidron; one *s* one *d*; *m* 2003, Lee Hall, *qv*. *Educ:* Camden Sch. for Girls; Nat. Film and Television Sch. Maker of films, documentaries, TV drama and features, 1982–: director: *television* includes: Oranges are not the Only Fruit, 1989; Antonia and Jane, 1990; Itch, 1991; Great Moments in Aviation, 1993; Texarkana, 1998; Cinderella, 2000; Murder, 2002; *documentaries:* Carry Greenham Home, 1983; Hookers Hustlers Pimps and their Johns, 1993; Eve Arnold in Retrospect, 1996; Antony Gormley: Making Space, 2007; Storyville: Sex, Death and the Gods, 2011; In Real Life, 2013; *films:* Vroom, 1990; Used People, 1992; To Wong Foo Thanks for Everything, Julie Newmar, 1995; Swept from the Sea, 1997; Bridget Jones: The Edge of Reason, 2004. Member: Directors Guild of America, 1990–; Directors UK; Acad. of Motion Picture Scis, 1992–; Council, ICA, 2011–. Trustee: UK Film Council, 2008–10; Paul Hamlyn Foundn, 2011–. Co-Founder, Into Film (formerly Film Club Educnl Charity), 2008 (Vice Chm., 2008). Gov., BFI, 2010–13. Hon. DEd Kingston, 2010; Hon. LittD UEA, 2015. *Recreations:* eating, reading, buying old crockery, shouting at the radio in exasperation. *Address:* House of Lords, SW1A 0PW. *E:* info@crossstreetfilms.com.

KIDSTON, Catherine Isabel Audrey, (Cath Kidston), MBE 2010; Founder and Creative Director, 1993–2014, and non-executive Director, since 2014, Cath Kidston Ltd; *b* London, 6 Nov. 1958; *d* of Archibald Martin Glen Kidston and Susan Myrtle Kidston; *m* 2012, Hugh Padgham; one step *d*. *Educ:* boarding sch. Interior designer to Nicky Haslam, 1984–87; Jt Proprietor, Curtainalia and interior design store, 1987–92. FRSA. *Publications:* Vintage Style, 1999; Tips for Vintage Style, 2004; Cath Kidston in Print, 2005; Make!, 2008; Sew!, 2009; Stitch!, 2010; Patch!, 2011; Coming Up Roses: the story of growing a business, 2013. *Recreations:* family, art exhibitions, car boot sales, travel. *Address:* Woodroffe House, Chiswick Mall, W4 2PJ. *E:* cathk@me.com.

KIERNAN, Prof. Kathleen Elizabeth, OBE 2006; PhD; FBA 2012; Professor of Social Policy and Demography, University of York, since 2004; *b* Leeds, 11 Feb. 1948; *d* of Patrick Joseph Kiernan and Julia Anne Kiernan (*née* Hastings); *m* 1971, John Hobcraft; one *s* one *d*. *Educ:* Notre Dame Grammar Sch., Leeds; Univ. of Liverpool (BA Soc. Studies); London Sch. of Econs and Pol Sci. (MSc Demography); Univ. of London (PhD 1987). Res. Officer, 1972–75, SO, 1975–78, Nat. Survey of Health and Develt, MRC; Res. Fellow, 1978–83, Sen. Res. Fellow, 1983–86, Centre for Popn Studies, LSHTM; Dep. Dir, Social Statistics Res. Unit, City Univ., 1986–89; Res. Dir, Family Policy Studies Centre, 1989–93; London School of Economics and Political Science: Sen. Res. Fellow in Demography, 1993–95; Reader in Social Policy and Demography, 1995–2001; Prof. of Social Policy and Demography, 2001–04; Co-Dir, ESRC Centre for Analysis of Social Exclusion, 1997–2008. Res. Associate, Center for Child Develt and Wellbeing, Office of Popn Res., Woodrow Wilson Sch. of Public and Internat. Affairs, Princeton Univ., 2014– (Vis. Res. Scholar, 2005–14). *Publications:* (with M. Wicks) Family Change and Future Policy, 1990; (with V. Estaugh) Cohabitation, Extramarital Childbearing and Social Policy, 1993; (jtly) Lone Motherhood in the Twentieth Century: from footnote to front page, 1998; (ed jtly) Human Development across Lives and Generations: the potential for change, 2004; articles in demography, social policy, medical and social sci. jls. *Recreations:* family life, art and design, travel, photography, theatre. *Address:* Department of Social Policy and Social Work, University of York, Heslington, York YO10 5DD. *T:* (01904) 321279. *E:* kathleen.kiernan@york.ac.uk.

KIERNAN, Peter Anthony; Chairman, European Investment Banking, Canaccord Genuity, since 2013 (Vice Chairman, 2012–13); *b* Watford, 11 Sept. 1960; *s* of Joseph Kiernan and Mary, (Molly), Kiernan; *m* 1991, Felicity Pearce; one *d*. *Educ:* St Michael's Comp. Sch., Watford; Downing Coll., Cambridge (BA Natural Scis 1982; MA). ACA 1986, FCA 2013. With Peat, Marwick Mitchell, 1982–86; Managing Director: S. G. Warburg, then Swiss Bank Corp., later UBS Warburg, 1986–2000; Goldman Sachs, 2000–04; Hd, UK Investment Banking, 2004–06, Man. Dir, 2004–11, Lazard. Mem., Adv. Bd, Bell Pottinger (formerly Pelham Bell Pottinger), 2012–; non-exec. Dir, Tungsten Corporation plc, 2012–; Sen. Advr, UK Bd of Practice, Hedrick and Struggles, 2015–. Mem. Adv. Bd, Masters Degree in Law and Finance, Oxford Univ., 2010–. Trustee, Ireland Fund of GB, until 2014. *Recreations:* family, friends, ski-ing, watching sports, supporting Watford FC.

KILBRACKEN, 4th Baron *cr* 1909, of Killegar, co. Leitrim; **Christopher John Godley;** *b* 1 Jan. 1945; *s* of 3rd Baron Kilbracken, DSC and Penelope Anne, *y d* of Rear-Adm. Sir Cecil Nugent Reyne, KBE; *S* father, 2006; *m* 1969, Gillian Christine, *yr d* of Lt-Comdr Stuart Wilson Birse, OBE, DSC, RN retd; one *s* one *d*. *Educ:* Rugby; Reading Univ. (BSc Agric. 1967). ICI: Agriculturalist, 1968–78; Gp Buyer, Hd Office, 1978–81; Countertrade Mgr, 1982–2000. Chm., London Countertrade Roundtable, 1997–2002. Patron, John Robert Godley Meml Trust, NZ; Vice Patron, Canterbury Assoc., NZ. *Recreations:* yachting, gardening. *Heir:* *s* Hon. James John Godley [*b* 3 Jan. 1972; *m* 2002, Anna Charlotte Weld-Forester; one *s* three *d*]. *Address:* Four Firs, Marley Lane, Haslemere, Surrey GU27 3PZ.

KILCLOONEY, Baron *cr* 2001 (Life Peer), of Armagh in the County of Armagh; **John David Taylor;** PC (NI) 1970; Member (UU) Strangford, Northern Ireland Assembly, 1998–2007; *b* 24 Dec. 1937; *er s* of George D. Taylor and Georgina Baird; *m* 1970, Mary Frances Todd; one *s* five *d*. *Educ:* Royal Sch., Armagh; Queen's Univ. of Belfast (BSc). AMInstHE, AMICEI. MP (UU) S Tyrone, NI Parlt, 1965–73; Mem. (UU), Fermanagh and S Tyrone, NI Assembly, 1973–75; Mem. (UU), North Down, NI Constitutional Convention, 1975–76; Parly Sec. to Min. of Home Affairs, 1969–70; Minister of State, Min. of Home Affairs, 1970–72; Mem. (UU), North Down, NI Assembly, 1982–86. Mem., Strangford, NI Forum, 1996–98. Mem. (UU) NI, Eur. Parlt, 1979–89. MP (UU) Strangford, 1983–2001 (resigned seat Dec. 1985 in protest against Anglo-Irish Agreement; re-elected Jan. 1986). Mem. Assembly, Council of Europe, 1997–2004. Resigned UU Party, 2007. Partner, G. D. Taylor and Associates, Architects and Civil Engineers, 1966–74; Director: West Ulster Estates Ltd, 1968–; Bramley Apple Restaurant Ltd, 1974–; West Ulster Hotels Co. Ltd, 1976–86; Gosford Housing Assoc. Ltd, 1977–2012; Tontine Rooms Ltd, 1978–; Ulster Gazette (Armagh) Ltd, 1983–; Cerdac (Belfast) Ltd, 1986–; Tyrone Printing Co. Ltd, 1986–; Tyrone Courier Ltd, 1986–; Sovereign Properties (NI) Ltd, 1989–; Tyrone Constitution Ltd, 1999–; Outlook Press Ltd, 1999–; Coleraine Chronicle Ltd, 2003–; Northern Constitution Ltd, 2003–; East Antrim Newspapers Ltd, 2003–; Northern Newspapers Ltd, 2003–; Midland Tribune Ltd, 2003–; Alpha Newspapers Ltd, 2003–; Northern Media Gp Ltd, 2003–14; BoL Pubs Ltd, 2006–;

Newry Democrat Ltd, 2012–. *Publications:* (jtly) Ulster—the facts, 1982. *Recreation:* foreign travel. *Address:* Mullinure, Portadown Road, Armagh, Northern Ireland BT61 9EL. *T:* (028) 3752 2409, (020) 7931 7211. *Clubs:* Farmers; Armagh County (Armagh).

KILDUFF, Prof. Martin James, PhD; Professor of Management, University College London, since 2012; *b* London, 16 July 1949; *s* of Michael Kilduff and Millicent Amy Kilduff (*née* Summerfield); *m* 1977, Constance Eleanor Johnson; one *s*. *Educ:* Quintin Grammar Sch., London; Washington State Univ. (BA, MBA); Cornell Univ. (MS; PhD 1988); MA Cantab 2009. Asst Prof., INSEAD, France, 1988–90; Penn State University: Asst Prof., 1990–94; Associate Prof., 1994–99; Prof., 1999–2006; King Ranch Centennial Prof. of Mgt, Univ. of Texas at Austin, 2006–08; Diageo Prof. of Mgt Studies, Judge Business Sch., Univ. of Cambridge, 2008–12; Fellow, Sidney Sussex Coll., Cambridge, 2008–12. *Publications:* Social Networks and Organizations, 2003; Interpersonal Networks in Organizations: cognition, personality, dynamics and culture, 2008; contribs to jls incl. Admin. Sci. Qly, Acad. of Mgt Jl. *Recreations:* running, walking, snorkelling. *Address:* Department of Management Science and Innovation, University College London, Gower Street, WC1E 6BT. *T:* (020) 3108 1001, *Fax:* (020) 3108 1009. *E:* mjkilduff@gmail.com.

KILFOIL, His Honour Geoffrey Everard; a Circuit Judge, 1987–2004; *b* 15 March 1939; *s* of Thomas Albert and Hilda Alice Kilfoil; *m* 1962, Llinos Mai Morris; one *s* one *d*. *Educ:* Acrefair Jun. Sch.; Ruabon Grammar Sch.; Jesus Coll., Oxford (BA Hons Jurisprudence; MA; Sankey Bar Schol., 1960). NCB underground worker, Gresford and Hafod Collieries, 1960–62; Lectr, English and Liberal Studies Dept, Denbs Tech. Coll. and Hd, English Dept, Gwersyllt Secondary Sch., 1962–66. Called to the Bar, Gray's Inn, 1966 (Holker Sen. Schol.); practised Wales & Chester Circuit; Dep. Circuit Judge, Asst Recorder then Recorder, 1974–87; pt-time *ad hoc* local Chm., Med. Appeals Tribunal (Wales) and Police Appeals Tribunals, 1976–87. Member (Lab), 1962–67: Cefn Mawr Parish Council (Chm., 1965–67); Wrexham RDC; Denbs CC; prospective parly cand. (Lab) Ludlow, 1965. Pres., Friends of Miners' Welfare Inst., Rhosllannerchrugog; Vice-Pres., Llangollen Internat. Musical Eisteddfod; Pres., Denbs Hist. Soc.

KILFOYLE, Peter; *b* 9 June 1946; *s* of Edward and Ellen Kilfoyle; *m* 1968, Bernadette (*née* Slater); two *s* three *d*. *Educ:* St Edward's Coll., Liverpool; Durham Univ.; Christ's Coll., Liverpool. Building labourer, 1965–70; student, 1970–73; building labourer, 1973–75; teacher/youth worker, 1975–85; Labour Party Organiser, 1985–91. MP (Lab) Liverpool, Walton, July 1991–2010. Parly Sec., Cabinet Office, 1997–99 (OPS, 1997–98); Parly Under Sec. of State, MoD, 1999–2000. *Publications:* Left Behind: lessons from Labour's heartlands, 2000; Lies, Damned Lies and Iraq, 2007; Labour Pains: how the party I love lost its soul, 2010. *Recreations:* reading, music, spectator sport, bonsai.

KILGALLON, William, OBE 1992; National Director, Office for Professional Standards, Catholic Church in Aotearoa, New Zealand, since 2013; *b* 29 Aug. 1946; *s* of William and Bridget Agnes Kilgallon (*née* Early); *m* 1978, Stephanie Martin (MBE 2012); two *s*, and one adopted *s*. *Educ:* Gregorian Univ., Rome (STL); London Sch. of Econs (Dip. Social Admin); Univ. of Warwick (MA); Univ. of Lancaster (MSc). RC Priest, Dio. Leeds, 1970–77; Asst Priest, St Anne's Cathedral, Leeds, 1970–74; Founder, and Chm., St Anne's Shelter & Housing Action, 1971–74; social work trng, 1974–76; Social Worker, Leeds Catholic Children's Soc., 1976–77; returned to lay state, 1977; Manager, St Anne's Centre, 1977–78; Chief Executive: St Anne's Shelter & Housing Action, 1978–2002; Social Care Inst. for Excellence, 2003–07; St Gemma's Hospice, Leeds, 2007–10. Leeds City Council: Mem. (Lab), 1979–92; Chairman: Housing Cttee, 1984–88; Social Services Cttee, 1988–90; Envmt Cttee, 1991–92; Lord Mayor, 1990–91. Member: Leeds FPC, 1978–80; Leeds AHA (T), 1980–82; Leeds E DHA, 1982–86; Yorks RHA, 1986–90 (non-exec. Dir and Vice Chm., 1990–92); Chairman: Leeds Community and Mental Health Services NHS Trust, 1992–98; Leeds Teaching Hosps NHS Trust, 1998–2002. Mem., W Yorks Police Authy, 2007–09. Member: Council, NHS Confedn, 1996–2002; CCETSW, 1998–2001. Leader: Ind. Inquiry into Abuse Allegations, Northumberland, 1994–95; Ext. Rev., Earls House Hosp., Durham, 1997–98; Ind. Rev. of Contracting for Neighbourhood Services, Leeds CC, 2010; Member: Cumberlege Commn reviewing protection of children and vulnerable adults in Catholic Ch in England and Wales, 2006–07; Joseph Rowntree Charitable Trust Commn of Inquiry into destitution among asylum seekers, 2006–07. Chair, Nat. Catholic Safeguarding Commn, 2008–10. Member: Ind. Ref. Gp on Mental Health, NSF, 1998–99; Nat. Task Force on Learning Disability, 2001–04; Pontifical Commn for Protection of Minors, 2014–. Non-exec. Dir, Places for People Gp, 2004–05. Mem. Council, Univ. of Leeds, 1992–2000; Gov., Park Lane FE Coll., 2000–02. Mem., Leeds & Dist Rugby League Referees Soc., 1992–2009. Hon. LLD Leeds, 1997; DUniv Leeds Metropolitan, 2000. *Recreations:* reading, travel, cricket, Rugby League. *Address:* 119 Hinemoa Street, Birkenhead, Auckland 0626, New Zealand.

KILGOUR, Rear Adm. Niall Stuart Roderick, CB 2005; Secretary and Chief Executive, Hurlingham Club, since 2005; *b* 4 March 1950; *s* of Leonard and Kathleen Kilgour; *m* 1974, Jane Birtwistle; one *s* two *d*. *Educ:* Pangbourne Coll. Commanding Officer: HMS Porpoise, 1980–82; HMS Courageous, 1986–88; Captain, 6th Frigate Sqdn, 1994–96; Commanding Officer: HMS Norfolk, 1994–95; HMS Montrose, 1995–96; Asst COS Ops C-in-C Fleet, 1996–98; Comdr, Amphibious Task Gp, 1998–2001; Comdr Ops to C-in-C Fleet and Rear Adm. Submarines, 2001–04. Younger Brother, Trinity House. QCVS 2000. *Recreations:* shooting, walking, history, sport. *Address:* The Cottage, Beercrocombe, Taunton TA3 6AG. *T:* (01823) 480251.

KILGOUR, Very Rev. Richard Eifl; General Secretary, International Christian Maritime Association, since 2015; *b* 26 Oct. 1957; *s* of Owen Frederick George Kilgour and Barbara Kilgour; *m* 1981, Janet Katharine Williams; three *d*. *Educ:* Eirias High Sch., Colwyn Bay; Hull Nautical Coll.; Edinburgh Univ. (BD Hons 1985); Univ. of Wales, Lampeter (MA Theol. 2010). Apprentice Navigation Officer, 1977–80, Serving Deck Officer, to 1981, Anchor Line, Glasgow; Jun. Officer, Trinity House Corp., 1981; 1st Officer, Fishery Protection Fleet, Dept of Agriculture and Fisheries, Scotland, 1981. Ordained deacon, 1985, priest, 1986, Church in Wales; Curate, Rectorial Benefice of Wrexham, 1985–88; Vicar, Whitford, and Industrial Chaplain, NE Wales, Industrial Mission for Council of Churches for Wales, 1988–97; Vicar/Rector, Newtown, Llanllwchaiarn, Aberhafesp, 1998–2003; Priest-in-charge, St Ninian, Aberdeen, 2003–06; Rector and Provost, Cathedral Church of St Andrew, Aberdeen, 2003–15. RD, Cedewain, Dio. of St Asaph, 2001–03. Hon. Canon, Christchurch Cathedral, Hartford, Conn, 2004. *Recreations:* sailing, foreign travel, dry-stone walling. *Address:* International Christian Maritime Association, Herald House, 15 Lambs Passage, EC1Y 8TQ.

KILLALEA, Stephen Joseph; QC 2006; barrister; *b* 25 Jan. 1959; *s* of Edward James Killalea and (Isabelle) Marie-Louise Killalea (*née* Elliott); *m* 1991, Catherine Marie Stanley (*d* 2011); two *d*. *Educ:* Bishopshalt Sch., Hillingdon; Univ. of Sheffield (LLB Hons). Called to the Bar, Middle Temple, 1981, Bencher, 2012; barrister in private practice specialising in catastrophic brain and spinal injuries and health and safety prosecutions. Advanced Advocacy Trainer, Middle Temple. *Publications:* (jtly) Health and Safety: the modern legal framework, 2nd edn 2001. *Recreations:* my girls, pubs, horse racing. *Address:* Devereux Chambers, Queen Elizabeth Building, Temple, EC4Y 9BS. *T:* (020) 7353 7534.

KILLANIN, 4th Baron *cr* 1900, of Galway, co. Galway; **George Redmond Fitzpatrick Morris;** Bt 1885; film producer; *b* 26 Jan. 1947; *e s* of 3rd Baron Killanin, MBE, TD and Mary Sheila Cathcart Morris (*née* Dunlop), MBE; *S* father, 1999; *m* 1st, 1972, Pauline Horton (marr. diss. 1999); one *s* one *d*; 2nd, 2000, Sheila Lynch; one *s* one *d*. *Educ:* Ampleforth Coll., York; Trinity Coll., Dublin. Films produced: The Miracle, 1991; Splitting Heirs, 1993; The Butcher Boy, 1998; co-producer: Interview with the Vampire, 1994; Michael Collins, 1996; In Dreams, 1999; The Reader, 2008. *Recreations:* film, theatre, music, Ireland. *Heir:* *s* Hon. Luke Michael Geoffrey Morris [*b* 22 July 1975; *m* 2010, Laura, 2nd *d* of Bernard Dewe Mathews]. *Address:* 9 Lower Mount Pleasant Avenue, Dublin 6, Ireland. *Club:* Groucho.

KILLEARN, 3rd Baron *cr* 1943, of Killearn, co. Stirling; **Victor Miles George Aldous Lampson;** Bt 1866; Director, AMP Ltd, 1999–2003; Chairman (non-executive), Henderson Global Investors (Holdings) Ltd, 2001–05; *b* 9 Sept. 1941; *s* of 1st Baron Killearn, GCMG, CB, MVO, PC and of his 2nd wife, Jacqueline Aldine Leslie, *o d* of Marchese Count Aldo Castellani; *S* half-brother, 1996; *m* 1971, Melita Amaryllis Pamela Astrid (*d* 2014), *d* of Rear-Adm. Sir Morgan Charles Morgan-Giles, DSO, OBE, GM; two *s* two *d*. *Educ:* Eton. Late Captain, Scots Guards. Partner, 1979–2001, Man. Dir, Corporate Finance, 2001–02, Cazenove & Co. Ltd. Non-executive Director: Maxis Communications Bhd, Malaysia, 2002–06; Shanghai Real Estate Ltd, 2002–07; Ton Poh Emerging Thailand Fund, 2005; Vietnam Dragon Fund, 2006–11. *Heir:* *s* Hon. Miles Henry Morgan Lampson [*b* 10 Dec. 1977; *m* 2008, Emily, *d* of Christopher Watkins; two *s* one *d*]. *Clubs:* White's; Hong Kong.

KILLEN, Prof. John Tyrrell, PhD; FBA 1995; Professor of Mycenaean Greek, Cambridge University, 1997–99, now Emeritus; Fellow, Jesus College, Cambridge, since 1969; *b* 19 July 1937; *e s* of John Killen and Muriel Caroline Elliott Killen (*née* Bolton); *m* 1964, Elizabeth Ann Ross; one *s* two *d*. *Educ:* High Sch., Dublin; Trinity Coll., Dublin (1st Foundn Schol. in Classics 1957; 1st Vice-Chancellor's Latin Medallist 1959; BA 1st Cl. 1960); St John's Coll., Cambridge (Gardiner Meml Schol. 1959; PhD 1964). Cambridge University: Asst Lectr in Classics, 1967–70; Lectr, 1970–90; Reader in Mycenaean Greek, 1990–97; Chm., Faculty Bd of Classics, 1984–86; Churchill College: Gulbenkian Res. Fellow, 1961–62; Fellow and Librarian, 1962–69 (initiated Churchill Archives Project, 1965); Jesus College: Lectr, 1965–97; acting Bursar, 1973; Sen. Bursar, 1979–89; Dir, Quincentenary Develt Appeal, 1987–90. *Publications:* (jtly) Corpus of Mycenaean Inscriptions from Knossos, 4 vols, 1986–98; (ed jtly) Studies in Mycenaean and Classical Greek, festschrift for John Chadwick, 1987; (with J.-P. Olivier) The Knossos Tablets, 1989; (ed with S. Voutsaki) Economy and Politics in the Mycenaean Palace States, 2001; Economy and Administration in Mycenaean Greece: collected papers on Linear B (ed M. Del Freo), 3 vols, 2015; articles in learned jls. *Recreations:* golf, watching sport on television, reading the FT, music. *Address:* Jesus College, Cambridge CB5 8BL.

KILLEN, Patrick, OBE 1991; Vice Lord-Lieutenant, County Tyrone, since 2013; independent business consultant, since 1995; *b* Co. Down, 25 Nov. 1945; *s* of James and Teresa Killen; *m* 1968, Gemma; two *s* three *d*. Salesman of agricl products, 1965–72; Chief. Exec., Tyrone Crystal Gp, 1972–95. Chm., NI Citizens' Charter Panel. Lay Mem., Industrial Tribunals; Panel Member: Criminal Injuries Appeal Panel for NI; Fair Employment Tribunals. Former Panel Mem., Wilson Cttee, examng and reporting on complaints procedure in UK Health Service. Formerly Member: Bd, Pigs Mktg Bd for NI; Bd, Health and Safety Agency for NI; NI Partnership Bd; Probation Bd for NI; Broadcasting Council, BBC NI. Gov., St Patrick's Coll., Dungannon. *Recreation:* walking. *T:* 07711 685997. *E:* patkillen@gmail.com.

KILLICK, Angela Margaret; Deputy Chairman, Children and Families Court Advisory and Support Service, 2001–03; *b* 18 May 1943; *o d* of late Tom Killick and Dora (*née* Jeffries); *m* 1983, Alec Grezo; one *s*. *Educ:* Watford Grammar Sch. for Girls. Various posts, incl. voluntary sector and abroad, until 1970; civil servant, incl. Hd, Res. Grants and Council Secretariat, SERC and AFRC; Hd, Radioactive Waste Policy Unit, DoE, 1970–91. Chairman: Hampstead HA, 1990–92; Enfield Community Care NHS Trust, 1992–98; Mt Vernon and Watford Hosps NHS Trust, 1998–2000. Member: Radioactive Waste Mgt Adv. Cttee, 1991–98; Lay Associate Mem., GMC, 2001–06. Lay Chm., NHS Ind. Review Panels, 2000–05; Lay Reviewer, Healthcare Commn, 2004–06. Mem. (C) Westminster CC, 1974–90. Trustee: Tennant Housing Assoc., 1976–85; Westminster Children's Soc., 1988–95 (Chm., 1993–95). Lay Visitor, Postgrad. Med. Educn Trng Bd, 2005–10. Ind. Custody Visitor, 2008–. Governor: St Clement Danes Sch., Covent Gdn, 1976–82; St Mary's Sch., Bryanston Sq., 1990–96; Russell Sch., Chorleywood, 1997– (Chm. of Govs, 1998–2002). Binney Award Certificate for Bravery, Binney Meml Trust, 1985. JP Camberwell, 1983–86. *Publications:* Council House Blues, 1976. *Recreations:* reading, gardening, family history, Private Pilot's licence, 1972.

KILLICK, Anthony John, (Tony), OBE 2007; consultant on economic development and aid policies, 1999–2011; Senior Research Associate, Overseas Development Institute, since 1999 (Director, 1982–87; Senior Research Fellow, 1987–99); *b* 25 June 1934; *s* of William and Edith Killick; *m* 1958, Ingeborg Nitzsche; two *d*. *Educ:* Ruskin and Wadham Colls, Oxford (BA Hons PPE). Lectr in Econs, Univ. of Ghana, 1961–65; Tutor in Econs, Ruskin Coll., Oxford, 1965–67; Sen. Econ. Adviser, Min. of Overseas Develt, 1967–69; Econ. Adviser to Govt of Ghana, 1969–72; Res. Fellow, Harvard Univ., 1972–73; Ford Foundn Vis. Prof., Econs Dept, Univ. of Nairobi, 1973–79; Res. Officer, Overseas Develt Inst., 1979–82. Vis. Fellow, Wolfson Coll., and Vis. Scholar, Dept of Applied Economics, Cambridge Univ., 1987–88. Vis. Prof., Dept of Economics, Univ. of Surrey, 1988–. Member: Commn of Inquiry into Fiscal System of Zimbabwe, 1984–86; Council, Royal Africa Soc. Chm. Bd of Dirs, African Econ. Res. Consortium, 1995–2001. Former consultant to various internat. orgns, and to Government of: Sierra Leone; Kenya; Republic of Dominica; Nepal; Ethiopia; Mozambique; Rwanda; Pakistan; Tanzania. Associate, Inst. of Develt Studies, Univ. of Sussex, 1986–94. Pres., Develt Studies Assoc., 1986–88. Hon. Res. Fellow, Dept of Political Economy, UCL, 1985–98. Editorial adviser: Journal of Economic Studies; Develt Policy Review; World Develt. *Publications:* The Economies of East Africa, 1976; Development Economics in Action: a study of economic policies in Ghana, 1978, 2nd edn 2010; Policy Economics: a textbook of applied economics on developing countries, 1981; (ed) Papers on the Kenyan Economy: structure, problems and policies, 1981; (ed) Adjustment and Financing in the Developing World: the role of the IMF, 1982; The Quest for Economic Stabilisation: the IMF and the Third World, 1984; The IMF and Stabilisation: developing country experiences, 1984; The Economies of East Africa: a bibliography 1974–80, 1984; A Reaction Too Far: the role of the state in developing countries, 1989; The Adaptive Economy: adjustment policies in low income countries, 1993; The Flexible Economy: causes and consequences of the adaptability of national economies, 1995; IMF Programmes in Developing Countries, 1995; Aid and the Political Economy of Policy Change, 1998; learned articles and contribs to books on Third World develt and economics. *Recreations:* gardening, music, Adviser at Citizens Advice Bureau. *Address:* 35 Pauls Lane, Hoddesdon, Herts EN11 8TR. *T:* (01992) 275093. *E:* tonykillick@outlook.com.

KILLIK, Paul Geoffrey; Senior Partner, Killik & Co., since 1989; *b* 24 Dec. 1947; *s* of Guy Frederick Killik and Rita Mildred (*née* Brewer); *m* 1981, Karen Virginia Mayhew; one *s* one *d*. *Educ:* Clayesmore Sch., Dorset. MSI (Dip.) 1969, FCSI. Hedderwick Borthwick, 1969–71; Killik Haley, 1971–74; Partner, Killik Cassel Haley, 1974–75; joined Quilter Goodison, 1975: Partner, 1977–85, Dir, 1985–88; Head, Private Client Dept, 1983–88. Mem., Stock Exchange, 1973. Mem. Bd, Wealth Mgt Assoc., 1997–. *Address:* (office) 46 Grosvenor Street, W1K 3HN. *T:* (020) 7337 0400.

KILMAINE, 8th Baron *cr* 1789 (Ire.); **John Francis Sandford Browne;** Bt 1636 (NS); *b* 4 April 1983; *o s* of 7th Baron Kilmaine and of Linda (*née* Robinson); *S* father, 2013.

KILMARNOCK, 8th Baron *cr* 1831; **Dr Robin Jordan Boyd;** Chief of Clan Boyd; *b* 6 June 1941; *s* of 6th Baron Kilmarnock, MBE, TD, and Hon. Rosemary Guest (*d* 1971), *er d* of 1st Viscount Wimborne; *S* brother, 2009; *m* 1st, 1977, Ruth Christine, *d* of Michael Fisher (marr. diss. 1986); two *s*; 2nd, 2000, Hilary Vivien, *d* of Peter Cox; one *d* by Catherine Hoddell. *Educ:* Eton; Keble Coll., Oxford (BA). MB BS (London) 1970; MRCS, LRCP, 1970; DCH 1973; AFOM, RCP, 1983. *Heir: s* Hon. Simon John Boyd [*b* 29 Oct. 1978; *m* 2004, Valeria Beatriz Matzkin; one *s* one *d*].

KILMARTIN, Dr John Vincent, FRS 2002; Staff Scientist, Medical Research Council Laboratory of Molecular Biology, Cambridge, 1969–2008, now Emeritus; *b* 22 July 1943; *s* of Vincent Kilmartin and Sadie (*née* Blake); *m* 1985, Margaret Scott Robinson, *qv*; one *d*. *Educ:* Mt St Mary's Coll., Spinkhill, Sheffield; St John's Coll., Cambridge (MA, PhD 1969). Visitor, Yale Univ., 1976–77. Mem., EMBO, 1995. *Publications:* contrib. papers to scientific jls on hemoglobin and yeast mitosis. *Recreations:* reading, wine, cooking, opera, walking. *Address:* MRC Laboratory of Molecular Biology, Francis Crick Avenue, Cambridge Biomedical Campus, Cambridge CB2 0QH. *T:* (01223) 267000.

KILMARTIN, Margaret Scott; *see* Robinson, M. S.

KILMISTER, (Claude Alaric) Anthony, OBE 2005; Founder, 1994, and President, 2004–12, Prostate Action (formerly Prostate Research Campaign UK); Vice President, Prostate Cancer UK, since 2012; *b* 22 July 1931; *s* of late Dr Claude E. Kilmister; *m* 1958, Sheila Harwood (*d* 2006). *Educ:* Shrewsbury Sch. National Service (army officer), 1950–52. NCB, 1952–54; Conservative Party Org., 1954–60; Asst Sec. 1960–61, Gen. Sec. 1962–72, Cinema & Television Benevolent Fund; Sec., Royal Film Performance Exec. Cttee, 1961–72; Exec. Dir, Parkinson's Disease Soc. of UK, 1972–91. Founding Cttee Mem., Action for Neurological Diseases, 1987–91. Founding Mem. and Dep. Chm., Prayer Book Soc. (and its forerunner, BCP Action Gp), 1972–89, Chm., 1989–2001, Vice-Pres., 2001–; Mem. Council, 1975–, Pres., 2007–, Anglican Assoc.; Member: Internat. Council for Apostolic Faith, 1987–93; Steering Cttee, Assoc. for Apostolic Ministry, 1989–96; St Alban's Diocesan Synod, 2006–09. Freeman, City of London, 2002. MA Lambeth, 2002. *Publications:* The Good Church Guide, 1982; When Will Ye be Wise?, 1983; My Favourite Betjeman, 1985; The Prayer Book and Ordination: a Prayer Book view of women bishops, 2006; contribs to jls, etc. *Recreations:* walking, writing. *Address:* 3 Homewood Court, Cedars Village, Chorleywood, Herts WD3 5GB. *T:* (01923) 824278.

KILMORE, Bishop of, (RC), since 1998; **Most Rev. Leo O'Reilly,** STD; *b* 10 April 1944; *s* of Terence O'Reilly and Maureen (*née* Smith). *Educ:* St Patrick's Coll., Maynooth (BSc, BD, HDipEd); Gregorian Univ., Rome (STD 1982). Ordained priest, 1969; on staff: St Patrick's Coll., Cavan, 1969–76; Irish Coll., Rome, 1976–81; Chaplain, Bailieborough Community Sch., 1981–88; missionary work, Nigeria: diocese of Minna, 1988–90; staff, St Paul's Seminary, Abuja, 1990–95; Parish Priest, Castletara, Cavan, 1995–97; Coadjutor Bishop of Kilmore, 1997–98. *Publications:* Word and Sign in the Acts of the Apostles: a study in Lucan theology, 1987. *Recreations:* walking, reading, golf. *Address:* Bishop's House, Cullies, Cavan, Co. Cavan, Ireland.

KILMORE, ELPHIN AND ARDAGH, Bishop of, since 2013; **Rt Rev. (Samuel) Ferran Glenfield;** *b* 1954; *m* 1979, Jean Glover; three *c*. *Educ:* Queen's Univ. Belfast (BA 1976); Trinity Coll. Dublin (MLitt 1990; MA 1994); Oxford Univ. (MTh 1999); Wycliffe Hall, Oxford. Teacher, Rainey Endowed Sch., 1978–88; ordained deacon, 1991, priest, 1992; Asst Curate, Douglas with Blackrock, Frankfield and Marmullane, 1991–94; Rector: Rathcooney Union of Parishes, 1994–96; Kill o'the Grange, Blackrock, 1996–2012; St Malachi, Hillsborough, 2012–13. *Address:* The See House, Kilmore, Cavan, Republic of Ireland.

KILMOREY, 6th Earl of, *cr* 1822; **Richard Francis Needham,** Kt 1997; PC 1994; Viscount Kilmorey 1625; Viscount Newry and Mourne 1822; Chairman: Tetra Strategy Ltd, since 2009; Rose Petroleum plc, since 2010; *b* 29 Jan. 1942; *e s* of 5th Earl of Kilmorey and Helen, *y d* of Sir Lionel Faudel-Phillips, 3rd Bt; *S* father, 1977; *m* 1965, Sigrid Juliane Thiessen-Gairdner; two *s* one *d*. *Educ:* Eton College. Chm., R. G. M. Print Holdings Ltd, 1967–85. CC Somerset, 1967–74. Contested (C): Pontefract and Castleford, Feb. 1974; Gravesend, Oct. 1974; MP (C): Chippenham, 1979–83; Wilts N, 1983–97. PPS to Sec. of State for NI, 1983–84, to Sec. of State for the Environment, 1984–85; Parly Under-Sec. of State, NI Office, 1985–92 (Minister for Health and Social Security, 1988–89, for Envmt, and for Economy, 1989–92); Minister of State (Minister for Trade), DTI, 1992–95. Mem., Public Accts Cttee, 1982–83. Chairman: GPT Ltd, 1996–97; Quantum Imaging Ltd, 1999–2003; Biocompatibles plc, 2000–06; Newfield IT Ltd, 2003–08; Director: GEC plc, 1995–97; NEC Europe Ltd, 1998– (Vice Chm., 1997–2010); Smarta.com, 2011– (Chm., 2009–11); Avon Rubber plc, 2012–13 (Chm., 2007–11); Independent Director: Dyson Ltd, 1995–2011 (Dep. Chm., 2000–04); Mivan Ltd, 1995–99; Meggitt PLC, 1997–2002; Tough Glass Ltd, 1997–2001; MICE plc, 1998–2003; Hansard Gp plc, 2003–04; deltaDOT Ltd, 2006–07; Adaptive Modules Ltd, 2015–; non-executive Director: Lonrho plc, 2011–12; Rank Gp plc, 2012–; Advr, Amec plc, 1998–2009. Chm., Gleneagles (UK) Ltd (formerly Nat. Heart Hosp.), 1995–2001; Hon. Chm., GW & Partners, 2015. Patron, Mencap (NI), 1996–2010. Pres., British Exporters Assoc., 1998–. Founder Member: Anglo-Japanese 21st Century (formerly 2000) Gp, 1984–; Anglo-Korean Forum for the Future, 1993–2000. Governor, British Inst. of Florence, 1983–85. Hon. Life Mem., British-Singapore Business Council, 2002. Hon. LLD Ulster, 2010. Gold and Silver Star, Order of the Rising Sun (Japan), 2004. *Publications:* Honourable Member, 1983; Battling for Peace, 1999. *Heir: s* Viscount Newry and Morne, *qv*. *Clubs:* Pratt's, Brooks's.

KILNER, Prof. John Anthony, PhD; CPhys, FInstP; FIMMM; B. C. H. Steele Professor of Energy Materials, Imperial College London (formerly Imperial College of Science, Technology and Medicine, London University), since 2006; Principal Investigator, International Institute for Carbon-Neutral Energy Research, Kyushu University, Japan, since 2011; *b* 15 Dec. 1946; *s* of Arnold and Edith Kilner; *m* 1973, Ana Maria del Carmen Sánchez; one *s* one *d*. *Educ:* Univ. of Birmingham (BSc Hons 1968; MSc 1971; PhD 1975). MInstP, CPhys 1987; FIMMM (FIM 2000); FInstP 2002; CSci 2007; CEng 2007. Res. Fellow and SERC Postdoctoral Res. Fellow, Univ. of Leeds, 1975–79; Department of Materials, Imperial College: Wolfson Res. Fellow, 1979–83; SERC Advanced Res. Fellow, IT, 1983–87; Lectr, 1987–91; Reader in Materials, 1991–95; Prof. of Materials Sci., 1995–2006; Head of Dept, 2000–06; Dean, RSM, 1998–2000. Gp Leader, Ceramic Electrolytes Gp, CIC Energigune, Vitoria, Spain, 2011–. Co-Founder, Ceres Power Ltd, 2001, now Consultant. Member: Polar Solids Discussion Gp, RSC, 1981–; European Materials Res. Soc., 1991–. An Associate Ed., Materials Letters, 1992–; European Ed., Solid State Ionics, 2004–. FCGI 2007. *Publications:* contribs to sci. jls. *Recreations:* travel, walking, food, drink. *Address:* 34 Castle Avenue, Ewell, Surrey KT17 2PQ. *T:* (020) 8224 7959. *Club:* Athenæum.

KILNER, Sarah-Jayne; *see* Blakemore, S.-J.

KILPATRICK, family name of **Baron Kilpatrick of Kincraig**.

KILPATRICK OF KINCRAIG, Baron *cr* 1996 (Life Peer), of Dysart in the district of Kirkcaldy; **Robert Kilpatrick,** Kt 1986; CBE 1979; President, General Medical Council, 1989–95 (Member, 1972–76 and 1979–95); *b* 29 July 1926; *s* of Robert Kilpatrick and Catherine Sharp Glover; *m* 1950, Elizabeth Gibson Page Forbes; two *s* one *d*. *Educ:* Buckhaven High Sch.; Edinburgh Univ. MB, ChB (Hons) 1949; Ettles Schol.; Leslie Gold Medallist; MD 1960; FRCP(Ed) 1963; FRCP 1975; FRCPSGlas 1991; FRSE 1998. Med. Registrar, Edinburgh, 1951–54; Lectr, Univ. of Sheffield, 1955–66; Rockefeller Trav. Fellowship, MRC, Harvard Univ., 1961–62; Commonwealth Trav. Fellowship, 1962; Prof. of Clin. Pharmacology and Therapeutics, Univ. of Sheffield, 1966–75; Dean, Faculty of Medicine, Univ. of Sheffield, 1970–73; Univ. of Leicester: Prof. and Head of Dept of Clinical Pharmacology and Therapeutics, 1975–83; Dean, Faculty of Medicine, 1975–89; Prof. of Medicine, 1984–89. Chairman: Adv. Cttee on Pesticides, 1975–87; Soc. of Endocrinology, 1975–78; Scottish Hosp. Endowment Res. Trust, 1996–2000. Pres., BMA, 1997–98. Hon. FRCS 1995; Hon. FRCPI 1995; Hon. FRCPath 1996; Hon. FRCSE 1996; Hon. FRCPE 1996. Dr *hc* Edinburgh, 1987; Hon. LLD: Dundee, 1992; Sheffield, 1995; Hon. DSc: Hull, 1994; Leicester, 1994. *Publications:* articles in med. and sci. jls. *Recreation:* golf. *Address:* 12 Wester Coates Gardens, Edinburgh EH12 5LT. *Clubs:* New (Edinburgh); Royal and Ancient (St Andrews).

KILPATRICK, Francesca; *see* Greenoak, F.

KILPATRICK, Helen Marjorie, CB 2010; HM Diplomatic Service; Governor, Cayman Islands, since 2013; *b* 9 Oct. 1958; *d* of Henry Ball and Nan Dixon Ball; one *s* one *d*. *Educ:* King's Coll., Cambridge (BA 1981). Mem. CIPFA 1986. Finance posts at GLC, London Bor. of Tower Hamlets and London Bor. of Southwark, 1982–89; Controller of Financial Services, London Bor. of Greenwich, 1989–95; Dir for Resources, Co. Treas. and Dep. Chief Exec., West Sussex CC, 1995–2005; Treas., Sussex Police Authy, 1995–2005; Dir Gen., Financial and Commercial, Home Office, 2005–13. *Address:* Governor's Office, Government Administration Building, Suite 101, KY1-9000, Grand Cayman.

KILPATRICK, Reginald M.; *see* Mitchell Kilpatrick.

KILROY-SILK, Robert; Chairman, The Kilroy Television Co., 1989; *b* 19 May 1942; *s* of William Silk (RN, killed in action, 1943) and Rose O'Rooke; *m* 1963, Jan Beech; one *s* one *d*. *Educ:* Saltley Grammar Sch., Birmingham; LSE (BScEcon). Lectr, Dept of Political Theory and Institutions, Liverpool Univ., 1966–74; television presenter: Day to Day, 1986–87; Kilroy, 1987–2004; Shafted, 2001. Contested (Lab) Ormskirk, 1970; MP (Lab): Ormskirk, Feb. 1974–1983; Knowsley N, 1983–86; PPS to Minister for the Arts, 1974–75; opposition frontbench spokesman on Home Office, 1984–85. Mem., Home Affairs Select Cttee, 1979–84; Vice-Chairman: Merseyside Gp of MPs, 1974–75; PLP Home Affairs Gp, 1976–86; Chairman: Parly All-Party Penal Affairs Gp, 1979–86; PLP Civil Liberties Gp, 1979–84; Parly Alcohol Policy and Services Group, 1982–83. Contested (Veritas) Erewash, 2005. MEP (UK Ind, then Veritas) E Midlands, 2004–09. Member: Council, Howard League for Penal Reform, 1979; Adv. Council, Inst. of Criminology, Cambridge Univ., 1984; Sponsor, Radical Alternatives to Prison, 1977–; Patron, APEX Trust; Chm., FARE, 1981–84. Governor, National Heart and Chest Hospital, 1974–77. Political columnist: Time Out, 1985–86; Police Review, 1983; columnist: The Times, 1987–90; Today, 1988–90; Daily Express, 1990–96; Sunday Express, 2001–04. *Publications:* Socialism since Marx, 1972; (contrib.) The Role of Commissions in Policy Making, 1973; The Ceremony of Innocence: a novel of 1984, 1984; Hard Labour: the political diary of Robert Kilroy-Silk, 1986; *novels*: Betrayal, 2011; Closure, 2011; Abduction, 2011; articles in Political Studies, Manchester School of Economic and Social Science, Political Quarterly, Industrial and Labor Relations Review, Parliamentary Affairs, etc. *Recreation:* gardening.

KIM, Young Sam; President, Republic of Korea, 1993–98; *b* 20 Dec. 1927; *m* 1951, Sohn Myoung Soon; two *s* three *d*. *Educ:* Coll. of Liberal Arts and Science, Seoul Nat. Univ. (BA). Mem., Nat. Assembly, 1954–93; Member: Liberal Party, 1954–60; Democratic Party, 1960–63; Civil Rule Party, 1963–65; Minjung Party, 1965–67 (also spokesman and floor leader); New Democratic Party, 1967–86 (floor leader, 1967–71, Pres., 1974–76 and 1979); Advr to New Korea Democratic Party, 1986–87; Pres., Reunification Democratic Party, 1987–90; Exec. Chm., 1990–92, Pres., 1992–96, Democratic Liberal Party; Pres., New Korea Party, 1996–97. Candidate for Pres., Republic of Korea, 1987. Chm., Council for the Promotion of Democracy, 1984–86. Averell Harriman Democracy Award, Nat. Democratic Inst. for Internat. Affairs, USA, 1993; Global Leadership Award, UNA, USA, 1995. Grand Order of Mugunghwa (Republic of Korea). *Publications:* We Can Depend on No One but Ourselves, 1964; Why our Country needs Standard-Bearers who are in their 40s, 1971; Government Power is Short, Politics is Long; Hoisting the Flag of Democracy; The True Reality of My Fatherland, 1984; My Resolution, 1987; Democratization, the Way of Salvation of My Country, 1987; Society which wins Honesty and Truth, 1987; New Korea 2000, 1992. *Address:* 7–6 Sangdo 1-dong, Dongjak-gu, Seoul, Korea 156–031.

KIMBER, Sir Rupert Edward Watkin, 5th Bt *cr* 1904, of Lansdowne Lodge, co. London; Principal, Tiburon Partners LLP, since 2009; *b* 20 June 1962; *s* of Sir Timothy Roy Henry Kimber, 4th Bt and Antonia Kathleen Brenda, *d* of Sir Francis John Watkin Williams, 8th Bt, QC; *S* father, 2012, but his name does not appear on the Official Roll of the Baronetage; *m* 1997, Lisa Caroline Samantha Cave; three *d*. *Educ:* Eton; Univ. of York (BA Politics). With Cazenove, 1984–2003 (Partner, 1997–2003); KBC Financial Products, 2003–05; Polar Capital, 2005–07; Belvedere Investment Partners, 2007–09. *Heir: b* Hugo Charles Kimber [*b* 4 April 1964; *m* 1996, Alexandra Sabine Joanna Hoogeweegen; two *s* one *d*]. *Address:* The Old Hall, Blickling Road, Aylsham, Norfolk NR11 6ND.

KIMBERLEY, 5th Earl of, *cr* 1866; **John Armine Wodehouse,** CEng; Bt 1611; Baron Wodehouse 1797; internet and computer consultant, since 2012; *b* 15 Jan. 1951; *s* of 4th Earl of Kimberley and his 2nd wife, Carmel June (*née* Maguire); *S* father, 2002; *m* 1973, Hon. Carol Palmer, (Rev. Canon Countess of Kimberley), MA (Oxon), PGCE, *er d* of 3rd Baron Palmer, OBE; one *s* one *d*. *Educ:* Eton; Univ. of East Anglia (BSc (Chemistry) 1973; MSc (Physical Organic Chemistry) 1974). CEng 1993; MBCS 1988; CITP 2004. Glaxo, subseq. Glaxo Wellcome: Research Chemist, 1974–79; Systems Programmer, 1979–86, Prin. Systems Programmer, 1987–95; Advanced Informatics and Tech. Specialist, Glaxo Wellcome, subseq. GlaxoSmithKline, 1996–2003; Sen. Internet Analyst, GlaxoSmithKline, 2003–12. Chm., UK Info Users Gp, 1981–83. Fellow, British Interplanetary Soc., 1984 (Associate Fellow, 1981–83). Reader, C of E, 2008–. FRSA. *Recreations:* interest in spaceflight, photography, computing, cats, walking, spirituality. *Heir: s* Lord Wodehouse, *qv*. *Address:* Fieldfares, Ferry Lane, Medmenham, Marlow, Bucks SL7 2EZ.

KIMMANCE, Peter Frederick, CB 1981; Chief Inspector of Audit, Department of the Environment, 1979–82; Member, Audit Commission for Local Authorities in England and Wales, 1983–87; *b* 14 Dec. 1922; *s* of Frederick Edward Kimmance, BEM, and Louisa Kimmance; *m* 1944, Helen Mary Mercer Cooke. *Educ:* Raine's Foundation, Stepney; University of London. Post Office Engineering Dept, 1939; served Royal Signals, 1943; District Audit Service, 1949; District Auditor, 1973; Controller (Finance), British Council, 1973–75; Dep. Chief Inspector of Audit, DoE, 1978. Mem. Council, CIPFA, 1979–83; Hon. Mem., British Council, 1975. *Recreations:* sailing, books, music. *Address:* 6 Laurel Court, Stanley Road, Folkestone, Kent CT19 4RL. *T:* (01303) 273773. *Clubs:* Royal Over-Seas League; Medway Yacht (Lower Upnor).

KIMMINS, Charles Dominic; QC 2010; *b* London, 1971; *s* of Malcolm Kimmins, CVO, DL and Jane Kimmins; *m* 2003, Talita De Brito e Cunha; one *s* two *d*. *Educ:* Eton Coll.; Trinity Coll., Cambridge (BA 1st Cl. Hons 1993). Called to the Bar, Inner Temple, 1994; in practice as barrister, specialising in commercial law. *Recreations:* horse racing, ski-ing, golf, theatre. *Address:* 20 Essex Street, WC2R 3AL. *T:* (020) 7842 1200, *Fax:* (020) 7842 1270. *E:* ckimmins@20essexst.com. *Clubs:* White's; Swinley Forest Golf; Derby.

KIMMINS, Simon Edward Anthony, VRD 1967; Lt-Comdr RNR; *b* 26 May 1930; *s* of late Captain Anthony Kimmins, OBE, RN, and Elizabeth Kimmins; three *s* three *d*; *m* 2007, Ingrid Jeanne Aleida Sickler. *Educ:* Horris Hill; Charterhouse. Man. Dir, London American Finance Corp. Ltd (originally BOECC Ltd), 1957–73; Dir, Balfour Williamson, 1971–74; Chief Exec., Thomas Cook Gp, 1973–75; Dir, Debenhams Ltd, 1972–85; Chief Exec., Delfinance SA Geneva, 1984–98; Chm., Associated Retail Develts Internat., 1980–85; Pres., Piguet Internat., 1986–91; Chief Exec., then Chm., Interoute Telecommunications (Switzerland) SA, 1996–99; Chief Exec., YoStream Holdings BV, Holland, 2000–05; Strategic Investment Dir, Ron Winter Gp, 2005–. Vice-Pres., British Export Houses Assoc., 1974–80 (Chm., 1970–72); Chm., Protelecom Carriers Cttee, 1998–2000. Governor, RSC, 1975–2007. *Recreations:* cricket (played for Kent), golf, writing. *Address:* 3 Westbourne House, Mount Park Road, Harrow on the Hill, Middx HA1 3JT. *Club:* Garrick.

KIMMONS, Rear Adm. Michael, CB 2008; Chief Executive, British Orthopaedic Association, since 2010; *b* 24 Dec. 1953; *s* of Robert Edward Kimmons and Patricia Kimmons (*née* Wyn); *m* 1979, Christine Joy Spittle (marr. diss. 2015); one *s* one *d*; *m* 2015, Susan Allen. *Educ:* Stamford Sch.; Heriot-Watt Univ. (BA Hons Modern Langs). Joined RN, 1972; served in HM Ships, Intrepid, Jupiter, Hermes, Active, Illustrious, Royal Yacht Britannia; Sec. to First Sea Lord, 1999–2001; rcds 2002; Director: Naval Personnel Corporate Programming, 2002–03; Naval Staff, 2003–05; COS to Second Sea Lord and COS (Support) to C-in-C Fleet, 2005–07; Chief Naval Logistics Officer, 2005–08; Sen. Directing Staff (Navy), RCDS, 2007–08. ADC to the Queen, 2004–05. Chief Exec., St Philips Chambers Ltd, Birmingham, 2008–09; Dir, Kimmons and Kimmons Ltd, 2009–12. NATO Medal 1995. *Publications:* (contrib.) Seaford House Papers, 2002. *Recreations:* golf, international relations. *Club:* Copthorne Golf (W Sussex).

KINAHAN, Daniel de Burgh; DL; MP (UU) South Antrim, since 2015; *b* Belfast, 14 April 1958; *s* of Sir Robert George Caldwell Kinahan and of Coralie Kinahan (*née* de Burgh); *m* 1991, Anna Marguerite Bence-Trower; one *s* three *d*. *Educ:* Stowe Sch., Bucks; Royal Military Acad., Sandhurst; Edinburgh Univ. (BCom). Served Blues and Royals, 1977–84. Asst PR Manager, Short Bros, 1985–88; Rep. for Ireland and NI, Christie's, 1988–2003; estabd Danny Kinahan Fine Art and Castle Upton Gall., 2003–. Mem. (UU) S Antrim BC, 2005–09. Mem. (UU) S Antrim, NI Assembly, 2009–June 2015. Sqdn Leader, N Irish Horse (TA), 1988–89 (Hon. Col, 2013–). High Sheriff, Antrim, 1996. *Recreations:* tennis, football, walking, all sport, history, travel, reading. *Address:* Castle Upton, Templepatrick, Co. Antrim BT39 0AH. *T:* (028) 9443 3480. *E:* danny@castleuptongallery.com. *Club:* Reform (Belfast).

KINAHAN, Maj.-Gen. Oliver John, CB 1981; Paymaster-in-Chief and Inspector of Army Pay Services, 1979–83; *b* 17 Nov. 1923; *m* 1950, Margery Ellis Fisher (*née* Hill) (*d* 2007); one *s* two *d*. Commissioned Royal Irish Fusiliers, 1942; served with Nigeria Regt, RWAFF, Sierra Leone, Nigeria, India, Burma, 1943–46; Instr, Sch. of Signals, 1947–49, Sch. of Infantry, 1950–51; transf. to RAPC, 1951; Japan and Korea, 1952–53; psc 1957; Comdt, RAPC Trng Centre, 1974–75; Chief Paymaster, HQ UKLF, 1975–76; Dep. Paymaster-in-Chief (Army), 1977–78. Col Comdt RAPC, 1984–87. FIMgt. *Recreation:* country pursuits. *Address:* c/o Drummonds Branch, Royal Bank of Scotland, 49 Charing Cross, SW1A 2DX.

KINCADE, James, CBE 1988; MA, PhD; Headmaster, Methodist College, Belfast, 1974–88; *b* 4 Jan. 1925; *s* of George and Rebecca Jane Kincade; *m* 1952, Elizabeth Fay, 2nd *d* of J. Anderson Piggot, OBE, DL, JP; one *d* (and one *s* decd). *Educ:* Foyle Coll.; Magee University Coll.; Trinity Coll. Dublin (Schol. and Gold Medallist, MA, Stein Research Prize); Oriel Coll., Oxford (MA, BLitt); Edinburgh Univ. (PhD). Served RAF, India and Burma, 1944–47 (commnd, 1945). Senior English Master, Merchiston Castle Sch., 1952–61; Vis. Professor of Philosophy, Indiana Univ., 1959; Headmaster, Royal Sch., Dungannon, 1961–74. Dir, Design Council, NI, 1990–93; Mem., Design Council, UK, 1993–94 (Chm., NI Cttee, 1993–94); Chairman: Fashion Business Centre, NI, 1992–94; NI Fashion & Design Centre, 1992–94. Nat. Gov. for NI, BBC, 1985–91. President, Ulster Headmasters' Assoc., 1975–77; Vice Pres., Assoc. for Art and Design Educn, 1991–; Mem., Council for Catholic Maintained Schools, 1987–90. Mem. of Senate, and Mem. Standing Cttee, QUB, 1982–98. Pres., Belfast Literary Soc., 2002–03. Trustee, Save the Homeless Fund, 1990–2007. Hon. LLD QUB, 2000. *Publications:* articles in Mind, Hermathena, Jl of Religion. *Recreation:* gardening. *Address:* 10A Harry's Road, Hillsborough BT26 6HJ. *T:* (028) 9268 3865.

KINCH, Carol Lesley; *see* Atkinson, C. L.

KINCH, Christopher Anthony; QC 1999; **His Honour Judge Kinch;** a Circuit Judge, since 2012; a Senior Circuit Judge, Resident Judge for Woolwich, since 2013; Hon. Recorder of Greenwich, since 2014; *b* 27 May 1953; *s* of late Anthony Alec Kinch, CBE and Barbara Patricia Kinch; *m* 1994, Carol Lesley Atkinson, *qv*; one *s* two *d*. *Educ:* Bishop Challoner Sch., Shortlands, Bromley; Christ Church, Oxford (MA Modern Hist.). Called to the Bar, Lincoln's Inn, 1976, Bencher, 2007; Stagiaire, EC Commn, 1976–77; in practice at the Bar, 1977–2012; Asst Recorder, 1994–98; Recorder, 1998–2012; Head of Chambers, 23 Essex Street, 2005–09. Mem., SE Circuit Cttee, 1992–95 and 1996–99. Dir of Educn, 2005–08, Vice-Chm., 2009–10, Chm., 2010–11, Criminal Bar Assoc. Chairman: Kent Bar Mess, 2001–04; Nat. Mock Trial for Schs Competition Working Party, 1999–2009. Trustee, Citizenship Foundn, 2006–15. *Recreations:* my family, Rugby, cricket. *Address:* Woolwich Crown Court, 2 Belmarsh Road, SE28 0EY. *Club:* Beckenham Rugby Football.

KINCHEN, Richard, MVO 1976; HM Diplomatic Service, retired; Ambassador to Belgium, 2003–07; *b* 12 Feb. 1948; *s* of Victor and Margaret Kinchen; *m* 1972, Cheryl Vivienne Abayasekera; one *s* two *d* (and one *d* decd). *Educ:* King Edward VI Sch., Southampton; Trinity Hall, Cambridge (BA). Entered FCO, 1970; attached British Commn on Rhodesian Opinion, 1972; MECAS, 1972; Kuwait, 1973; FCO, 1974; Luxembourg, 1975; Paris, 1977; FCO, 1980; Pvte Sec. to Parly Under-Sec. of State, 1982; Rabat, 1984; Counsellor, UK Mission to UN, 1988–93; Head: Regl Secretariat for British Dependent Territories in Caribbean, 1993–96; Resource Planning Dept, FCO, 1997–2000; Ambassador to Lebanon, 2000–03. Member: UN Adv. Cttee on Admin. and Budgetary Questions, 1991–93; UN Jt Staff Pension Bd, 1992–93. *Address:* 12 Windermere Way, Farnham, Surrey GU9 0DE.

KINCLAVEN, Hon. Lord; Alexander Featherstonhaugh Wylie; a Senator of the College of Justice in Scotland, since 2005; *b* 2 June 1951; *s* of Ian Hamilton Wylie and Helen Jane Mearns or Wylie; *m* 1975, Gail Elizabeth Watson Duncan; two *d*. *Educ:* Edinburgh Univ. (LLB Hons). ACIArb 1977, FCIArb 1991. Qualified Solicitor in Scotland, 1976; called to the Scottish Bar, 1978; called to the Bar, Lincoln's Inn, 1990. Standing Junior Counsel in Scotland to Accountant of Court, 1986–89; Advocate Depute, 1989–92; QC (Scot.) 1991; part-time Sheriff, 2000–05. Chm. (part-time), Police Appeals Tribunal, 2001–05. Jt Chm., Discipline Cttee, Inst. of Chartered Accountants of Scotland, 1994–2005; Member: (part-time), Scottish Legal Aid Bd, 1994–2002; Scottish Council of Law Reporting, 2001–05; Scottish Criminal Cases Review Commn, 2004–05. *Address:* Supreme Courts, Parliament House, Parliament Square, Edinburgh EH1 1RQ.

KINDERSLEY, family name of **Baron Kindersley**.

KINDERSLEY, 4th Baron *cr* 1941; **Rupert John Molesworth Kindersley;** Director, Investment Banking, Terastream Broadband Inc., Toronto, since 2014; *b* London, England, 11 March 1955; *s* of 3rd Baron Kindersley and Venice Marigold Kindersley (*née* Hill); *S* father, 2013; *m* 1975, Sarah Anne (*née* Warde); one *s* one *d*. *Educ:* Eton Coll.; Trinity Coll., Univ. of Toronto (BA Econs). Asst Branch Manager, Toronto Dominion Bank, 1977–80; Project Finance Exec. and Mem., EEC Advr's team, Midland Bank International, 1980–85; Director and Company Secretary: Allied Entertainments Gp, 1985–86; Daniels Gp, 1986–93; Dir, Edgecombe Gp/Edgemark Capital Gp, 1993–98; Dir, Commercial Credit, Elliot Lake & North Shore Corpn for Business Develt, 1998–99; stockbroker, Brawley Cathers Ltd, 1999–2002; Dir and Treas., InnLand Hospitality Inc. 2002–; corporate finance, Cityspace Inc., 2002–; investment banker, Union Securities Ltd, 2006, team moved to MGI Securities Inc., 2009, merged with IA Securities Inc., 2014. *Recreations:* walking dogs, reading, swimming, cross-country ski-ing. *Heir: s* Hon. Frederick Hugh Molesworth Kindersley, *b* 9 Jan. 1987. *Address:* 15 Falcon Street, Toronto, ON M4S 2P4, Canada. *T:* (home) (416) 4855103, (office) (416) 4855103. *E:* rupert@kindersley.us.

KINDERSLEY, Lydia Helena L. C.; *see* Lopes Cardozo Kindersley.

KINDERSLEY, Peter David; Chairman, Dorling Kindersley, publishers, 1974–2000; *b* 13 July 1941; *s* of late David Kindersley, MBE and of Christine Kindersley; *m* 1965, Juliet Elizabeth Martyn; one *s* one *d*. *Educ:* King Edward VI School, Norwich; Camberwell School of Arts and Crafts. Founding Art Director, Mitchell Beazley, 1969–74. Owner, Sheepdrove Organic Farm. Chm., Neal's Yard Remedies, 2005–. Fellow, Univ. of the Arts London (formerly London Inst.), 2001; FRSA 2000. DUniv Open 2002. *Recreations:* environment, biodiversity, interesting work.

KING, family name of **Earl of Lovelace** and **Baron King of Bridgwater**.

KING OF BOW, Baroness *cr* 2011 (Life Peer), of Bow in the London Borough of Tower Hamlets; **Oona Tamsyn King;** broadcaster, campaigner and political diarist; Head of Diversity, Channel 4, 2009–11; *b* 22 Oct. 1967; *d* of Prof. Preston King and Hazel King; *m* 1994, Tiberio Santomarco; one *s* and one adopted *s* two adopted *d*. *Educ:* Haverstock Comprehensive Secondary Sch.; York Univ. (BA 1st cl. Hons Politics); Univ. of Calif, Berkeley (Scholar). Stagiare for Socialist Gp, EP, 1991; Political Asst to Glyn Ford, MEP, 1991–93; Mem., John Smith's Campaign Team for leadership of Labour Party, 1992; Political Asst to Glenys Kinnock, MEP, 1994–95; Trade Union Organiser, Equality Officer, GMB Southern Region, 1995–97. MP (Lab) Bethnal Green and Bow, 1997–2005; contested (Lab) same seat, 2005. PPS to Sec. of State for Trade and Industry, 2003–05. Member, Select Committee: on Internat. Develt, 1997–2001; on Urban Affairs, 2001–03; founding Chair, All-Party Gp on Genocide Prevention, 1998–2005. Freelance journalist and television presenter, 2005–07; Dep. Asst Pol Sec., 2007–08, Sen. Advr, 2008–09, to Prime Minister. Vice-Chm., British Council, 1998–2001; founding Chair, Rich Mix Cultural Foundn, 1999–2009; Chair, Inst. of Community Cohesion, 2007–09. Gov., BFI. *Publications:* House Music, 2007. *Recreations:* cinema, music. *Address:* 129 Antill Road, E3 5BW.

KING OF BRIDGWATER, Baron *cr* 2001 (Life Peer), of Bridgwater in the County of Somerset; **Thomas Jeremy King,** CH 1992; PC 1979; *b* 13 June 1933; *s* of late J. H. King, JP; *m* 1960, Jane, *d* of late Brig. Robert Tilney, CBE, DSO, TD; one *s* one *d*. *Educ:* Rugby; Emmanuel Coll., Cambridge (MA). National service, 1951–53: commnd Somerset Light Inf., 1952; seconded to KAR; served Tanganyika and Kenya; Actg Captain 1953. Cambridge, 1953–56. Joined E. S. & A. Robinson Ltd, Bristol, 1956; various positions up to Divisional Gen. Man., 1964–69; Chairman: Sale, Tilney Co. Ltd, 1971–79 (Dir, 1965–79); London Internat. Exhibition Centre Ltd, 1994–2008 (Dir, 2008–); Dir, Electra Investment Trust, 1992–2008. MP (C) Bridgwater, March 1970–2001. PPS to: Minister for Posts and Telecommunications, 1970–72; Minister for Industrial Develt, 1972–74; Front Bench spokesman for: Industry, 1975–76; Energy, 1976–79; Minister for Local Govt and Environmental Services, DoE, 1979–83; Sec. of State for the Environment, Jan.–June 1983, for Transport, June–Oct. 1983, for Employment, 1983–85, for NI, 1985–89, for Defence, 1989–92. Chm., Parly Intelligence and Security Cttee, 1994–2001; Mem., Cttee on Standards in Public Life, 1994–97. *Recreations:* cricket, ski-ing. *Address:* House of Lords, SW1A 0PW.
See also S. R. Clarke.

KING OF LOTHBURY, Baron *cr* 2013 (Life Peer), of Lothbury in the City of London; **Mervyn Allister King,** KG 2014; GBE 2011; FBA 1992; Professor of Economics and Law, New York University, since 2014; Professor of Economics, London School of Economics and Political Science, since 2015; Governor, Bank of England, 2003–13; *b* 30 March 1948; *s* of Eric Frank King and Kathleen Alice Passingham; *m* 2007, Barbara Melander. *Educ:* Wolverhampton Grammar School; King's College, Cambridge (BA 1st cl. hons 1969, MA 1973; Hon. Fellow, 2004). Research Officer, Dept of Applied Economics, Cambridge, 1969–76; Kennedy Schol., Harvard Univ., 1971–72; Fellow, St John's Coll., Cambridge, 1972–77 (Hon. Fellow, 1997); Lectr, Faculty of Economics, Cambridge, 1976–77; Esmée Fairbairn Prof. of Investment, Univ. of Birmingham, 1977–84; Prof. of Economics, LSE, 1984–95; Bank of England: non-exec. Dir, 1990–91; Chief Economist and Exec. Dir, 1991–98; Dep. Gov., 1998–2003; Founder Mem., Monetary Policy Cttee, 1997, Chm., 2003–13; Chm., Interim Financial Policy Cttee, 2011–13. Vice Chm., European Systematic Risk Bd, 2011–13. Visiting Professor of Economics: Harvard Univ., 1982–83, 1990; MIT, 1983–84; LSE, 1996–; Visiting Fellow: Nuffield Coll., Oxford, 2002–; Council on For. Relns, 2013–. Co-Dir, LSE Financial Markets Gp, 1987–91. Member: City Capital Markets Cttee, 1989–91; Group of Thirty, 1997–. President: Eur. Econ. Assoc., 1993; Inst. for Fiscal Studies, 1999–2003 (Hon. Life Mem., 2006). Member: Meade Cttee, 1975–78; Council and Exec., Royal Economic Soc., 1981–86, 1992–97; Bd, The Securities Assoc., 1987–89. Fellow, Econometric Soc., 1982. Managing Editor, Review of Economic Studies, 1978–83; Associate Editor: Jl of Public Economics, 1982–98; Amer. Economic Review, 1985–88. Trustee: Kennedy Meml Trust, 1990–2000; Nat. Gall., 2005–09, 2014–. Mem., Adv. Council, LSO, 2001–. Patron, Worcs CCC, 2004– (Pres., 2015–). Hon. Foreign Mem., Amer. Acad. of Arts and Scis, 2000. Hon. Dr: London Guildhall, 2001; City, Birmingham, 2002; Wolverhampton, LSE, 2003; Worcester, 2008; Hon. DCL Kent, 2012; Dr *hc* Edinburgh, 2005; Helsinki, 2006; Hon. LLD Cambridge, 2006. Helsinki Univ. Medal, 1982. *Publications:* Public Policy and the Corporation, 1977; (with J. A. Kay) The British Tax System, 1978, 5th edn 1990; (with D. Fullerton) The Taxation of Income from Capital, 1984; numerous articles in economics jls. *Address:* House of Lords, SW1A 0PW. *Clubs:* Athenæum, Brooks's, Garrick; All England Lawn Tennis and Croquet.

KING, Alison Sarah; *see* Grief, A. S.

KING, Andrew; *b* 14 Sept. 1948; *s* of late Charles King and Mary King; *m* 1975, Semma Ahmet; one *d*. *Educ:* St John the Baptist Sch., Uddingston; Coatbridge Tech. Coll.; Missionary Inst., London; Hatfield Poly.; Stevenage Coll. (CQSW); Nene Coll., Northants (CMS). Labourer; Postal Officer; apprentice motor vehicle mechanic; Social Work Manager, Northants CC, 1989–97. Member: Warwickshire CC, 1989–98 (Chm., Social Services, 1993–96); Rugby BC, 1995–98. MP (Lab) Rugby and Kenilworth, 1997–2005; contested: (Lab) same seat, 2005; (Lab) Rugby, 2010. Member: Social Security Select Cttee, 1999–2001; Deregulation Select Cttee, 1999–2005. Member: Unison (formerly NALGO), 1978–; Co-op. Party, 1995–. *Recreations:* golf, dominoes. *Clubs:* Hillmorton Ex-Servicemen's; Bilton Social; Rugby Golf, Rugby Labour.

KING, Prof. Andrew John, PhD; FMedSci; Professor of Neurophysiology, since 2004, and Wellcome Trust Principal Research Fellow, since 2006, University of Oxford; Fellow, Merton College, Oxford, since 2002; *b* Greenford, Middx, 8 April 1959; *s* of Neville Douglas King and Audrey Kathleen King (*née* Manix); partner, Dr Scott Bryan. *Educ:* Eliot's Green Grammar Sch.; Northolt High Sch.; King's Coll. London (BSc Physiol.); King's Coll. London and Nat. Inst. for Med. Res. (PhD 1984). University of Oxford: Douglas McAlpine Jun. Res.

Fellow in Neurol., Green Coll., 1983–86; SERC Postdoctoral Fellow, Lab. of Physiol., 1984–86; E. P. Abraham Cephalosporin Jun. Res. Fellow in Med. Scis, Lincoln Coll., 1986–89; Lister Inst. Res. Fellow, 1986–91, Wellcome Trust Sen. Res. Fellow in Basic Biomed. Sci., 1991–2006, Lab. of Physiology; Res. Lectr, 1996–2000; Reader in Auditory Physiol., 2000–04; Sen. Res. Fellow in Med. Scis, Merton Coll., 2002–07. Vis. Prof., Univ. of Salamanca, 2012; Vis. Asst Scientist, Eye Res. Inst., Retina Foundn, Boston, Mass, 1988. Chief Scientific Advr, Deafness Res. UK, 2011–13. FMedSci 2011. Layton Sci. Res. Award, KCL, 1980; Wellcome Prize Medal and Lect. in Physiol., 1990. *Publications:* (jtly) Auditory Neuroscience: making sense of sound, 2011; contrib. book chapters; contribs to scientific jls. *Recreations:* gardening, cooking, Renaissance and Baroque music. *Address:* Department of Physiology, Anatomy and Genetics, Sherrington Building, University of Oxford, Parks Road, Oxford OX1 3PT. *E:* andrew.king@dpag.ox.ac.uk.

KING, Angela Audrey Mary; Founder Director and Joint Director, Common Ground, 1982–2012; freelance campaigner; *b* 27 June 1944; *d* of Dr George John Graham King and Audrey Thora Dorothee King. *Educ:* Queensmount Sch.; St Christopher Sch., Letchworth; Millfield Sch., Som; Mayer Sch. of Fashion Design, NY. Fashion designer and buyer, NY, 1965–70; Friends of the Earth: wildlife campaigner, 1971–75; campaigned for ban on imports of leopard, cheetah and tiger skins, implemented 1972; (jtly) drafted Wild Creatures and Wild Plants Bill (enacted 1975), and Endangered Species (Import and Export) Act (enacted 1976); Initiator: Save the Whale Campaign, 1972 (campaigned for import ban on baleen whale products, introduced 1973, and Internat. Whaling Commn's 10 year ban on commercial whaling, introduced 1982); (jtly) Otter Project, 1976 (campaigned for ban on otter hunting in England and Wales, introduced 1978); Jt Co-ordinator, Otter Haven Project, 1977–80; Consultant, Earth Resources Res., 1979–80; author of NCC report on wildlife habitat loss, 1981; founded (with Sue Clifford and Roger Deakin) Common Ground, 1982; initiator with Sue Clifford of several projects, including: New Milestones, 1985; Trees, Woods and the Green Man, 1986; Parish Maps Project, 1987; Campaign for Local Distinctiveness, 1990; Confluence, 1998; Orgnr, exhibns which link the arts and the envmt. *Publications:* (ed jtly) Second Nature, 1984; (jtly) Holding Your Ground: an action guide to local conservation, 1987; (ed jtly) Trees Be Company (poetry anthology), 1989, 2nd edn 2001; (jtly) The Apple Source Book, 1991, enlarged edn 2007; (ed jtly) Local Distinctiveness: place particularity and identity, 1993; (jtly) Celebrating Local Distinctiveness, 1994; (ed jtly) from place to PLACE: maps and Parish Maps, 1996; (ed jtly) Field Days: an anthology of poetry, 1998; (ed jtly) The River's Voice: an anthology of poetry, 2000; (ed jtly) The Common Ground Book of Orchards, 2000; (with Sue Clifford) England in Particular: a celebration of the commonplace, the local, the vernacular and the distinctive, 2006; (with Sue Clifford) Community Orchards Handbook, 2008, 2nd edn 2011; conservation guides, and pamphlets, for Friends of the Earth, Common Ground, etc. *Recreations:* gardening, walking, watching wildlife, reading. *Address:* c/o Common Ground, Lower Dairy, Toller Fratrum, Dorchester, Dorset DT2 0EL. *T:* (01300) 321778.

KING, Ann P.; *see* Francke, A. P.

KING, Annette, (Mrs Henry Stevens); Chief Executive Officer, Ogilvy and Mather Group UK, since 2014; *b* Farnborough, 29 Sept. 1968; *d* of Frank and Linda King; *m* 2005, Henry Stevens; one *s* one *d*. *Educ:* Oxford Brookes Univ. (BA Hons Business Studies; DipM). Account Dir, Wunderman London, 1992–96; Vice Pres. Account Dir, Wunderman NY, 1996–2000; Man. Partner, 2000–06, Man. Dir, 2006–08, CEO, 2008–12, CEO EMEA, 2012–14, OgilvyOne UK. Non-exec. Dir, London First, 2011–. Advr, Strategic Adv. Council, Royal Mail, 2011–. Mem. Council, IPA, 2010–. *Recreations:* collecting art, theatre, entertaining. *Address:* Ogilvy and Mather Group UK, 10 Cabot Square, Canary Wharf, E14 4GB. *T:* (020) 7566 7355. *E:* annette.king@ogilvy.com. *Clubs:* Women in Advertising and Communications London, Marketing Group of GB.

KING, Anthony James Langdale; Pensions Ombudsman, 2007–15; Lay Member, Office for Legal Complaints, since 2015; *b* Birmingham, 20 Feb. 1953; *s* of late Norman Edward King and Florence Elizabeth King; *m* Alvine Elizabeth Baltzars. *Educ:* St David's University Coll., Univ. of Wales (BA Hons 1976). Casework Dir for Pensions Ombudsman, 1994–2003; Financial Ombudsman Service: Ombudsman, 2003–05; Lead Ombudsman, Pensions and Securities, 2005–07. Chm., Ombudsman Assoc., 2012–14. *Recreations:* music (listening well and playing badly), walking, reading, beer.

KING, Prof. Anthony Stephen, FBA 2010; Professor of Government, University of Essex, since 1969; *b* 17 Nov. 1934; *o s* of late Harold and Marjorie King; *m* 1st, 1965, Vera Korte (*d* 1971); 2nd, 1980, Jan Reece. *Educ:* Queen's Univ., Kingston Ont. (1st Cl. Hons, Hist. 1956); Magdalen Coll., Oxford (Rhodes Schol.; 1st Cl. Hons, PPE, 1958). Student, Nuffield Coll., Oxford, 1958–61; DPhil (Oxon) 1962. Fellow of Magdalen Coll., Oxford, 1961–65; Sen. Lectr, 1966–68, Reader, 1968–69, Essex Univ. ACLS Fellow, Columbia Univ., NY, 1962–63; Fellow, Center for Advanced Study in the Behavioral Scis, Stanford, Calif., 1977–78; Visiting Professor: Wisconsin Univ., 1967; Princeton Univ., 1984. Member: Cttee on Standards in Public Life, 1994–98; Royal Commn on H of L Reform, 1999. Chm., RSA Commn on Illegal Drugs, Communities and Public Policy, 2005–07. Hon. Foreign Mem., Amer. Acad. of Arts and Scis, 1993; Hon. Life FRSA 2006. *Publications:* (with D. E. Butler) The British General Election of 1964, 1965; (with D. E. Butler) The British General Election of 1966, 1966; (ed) British Politics: People, Parties and Parliament, 1966; (ed) The British Prime Minister, 1969, 2nd edn 1985; (with Anne Sloman) Westminster and Beyond, 1973; British Members of Parliament: a self-portrait, 1974; (ed) Why is Britain Becoming Harder to Govern?, 1976; Britain Says Yes: the 1975 referendum on the Common Market, 1977; (ed) The New American Political System, 1978, 2nd edn 1990; (ed) Both Ends of the Avenue: the Presidency, the Executive Branch and Congress in the 1980s, 1983; (ed) Britain at the Polls 1992, 1992; (with Ivor Crewe) SDP: the birth, life and death of the British Social Democratic Party, 1995; Running Scared: why America's politicians campaign too much and govern too little, 1997; (ed) New Labour Triumphs: Britain at the polls, 1997; (ed) British Political Opinion 1937–2000: the Gallup polls, 2001; Does the United Kingdom still have a Constitution?, 2001; (ed) Britain at the Polls 2001, 2001; (ed) Leaders' Personalities and the Outcomes of Democratic Elections, 2002; (ed) Britain at the Polls 2005, 2005; The British Constitution, 2007; The Founding Fathers v. the People: paradoxes of American democracy, 2012; (with Ivor Crewe) The Blunders of Our Governments, 2013; Who Governs Britain?, 2015; frequent contributor to British and American jls and periodicals. *Recreations:* music, theatre, holidays. *Address:* Department of Government, University of Essex, Wivenhoe Park, Colchester, Essex CO4 3SQ. *T:* (01206) 873393; The Mill House, Lane Road, Wakes Colne, Colchester, Essex CO6 2BP. *T:* (01787) 222497.

KING, His Honour Anthony William Poole; a Circuit Judge, 1993–2012; *b* 18 Aug. 1942; *s* of late Edmund Poole King and Pamela Midelton King (*née* Baker); *m* 1971, Camilla Anne Alexandra Brandreth; two *s* one *d*. *Educ:* Winchester Coll.; Worcester Coll., Oxford (MA Jur.). Called to the Bar, Inner Temple, 1966; a Recorder, 1987–93; Midland and Oxford Circuit. *Recreations:* fishing, other people's gardens. *Address:* c/o Oxford Crown and County Court, St Aldate's, Oxford OX1 1TL.

KING, (Austin) Michael (Henry); Consultant Solicitor, Stone King LLP (formerly Stone King), since 2014 (Partner, 1975–2014; Chairman, 1997–2014); *b* Bath, 9 Feb. 1949; *s* of Gerald and Pauline King; *m* 1975, Frances-Anne Sutherland; three *s*. *Educ:* Stonyhurst Coll. Admitted Solicitor, 1974. Chm., Charity Law Assoc., 1997–2000. Trustee, Holburne Mus. of Art, 1999–2007, 2010–. Chm. Govs, Prior Park Coll., 2014–. *Publications:* (with A. Phillips) Charities Act 2006: a guide to the new law, 2005. *Recreations:* sailing, shooting, tennis, watching Rugby, family. *Address:* Stone King LLP, 13 Queen Square, Bath BA1 2HJ. *T:* 07977 517304. *E:* michaelking@stoneking.co.uk. *Club:* Lansdowne.

KING, Prof. Bernard, Hon. CBE 2003; PhD; FIWSc; CBiol, FRSB; Vice-Chancellor, University of Abertay Dundee, 1994–2011 (Principal, Dundee Institute of Technology, 1992–94); *b* 4 May 1946; *s* of Bernard and Cathleen King; *m* 1970, Maura Antoinette Collinge; two *d*. *Educ:* Synge St Christian Brothers Sch., Dublin; Coll. of Technology, Dublin; Univ. of Aston in Birmingham (MSc 1972; PhD 1975). FIWSc 1975; CBiol, FRSB (FIBiol 1987). Research Fellow, Univ. of Aston in Birmingham, 1972–76; Dundee Institute of Technology: Lectr, 1976–79; Sen. Lectr, 1979–83; Head, Dept of Molecular Life Scis, 1983–91; Dean, Faculty of Sci., 1987–89; Asst Principal, Robert Gordon Inst. of Technol., 1991–92. Chairman: Scottish Crop Res. Inst., 2003–08; Mylnefield Res. Services Ltd, 2003–08. Board Member: ACU, 2003–06 (Mem. Audit Cttee, 2006–08); Scottish Leadership Foundn, 2004–08; Higher Educn Acad., 2005–10 (Chm., Audit Cttee, 2009–10); Mem., Council for Industry and Higher Educn, 2008–11; Convenor, Universities Scotland, 2010–11 (Vice Convenor, 2006–10); Vice Pres., Universities UK, 2010–11; Mem. Exec., Million +, 2007–11. Gov., Unicorn Preservation Soc., 1993–. CCMI (CIMgt 1999). *Publications:* numerous scientific and tech. papers on biodeterioration with particular ref. to biodeterioration and preservation of wood. *Recreations:* reading, music, sailing. *Address:* 11 Dalhousie Place, Arbroath, Angus DD11 2BT.

KING, Billie Jean; professional tennis player, 1968–83; Chief Executive Officer, Team Tennis, 1981–91; Founder, WTT Charities Inc., 1987; *b* 22 Nov. 1943; *d* of Willard J. Moffitt; *m* 1965, Larry King (marr. diss.). *Educ:* Los Cerritos Sch.; Long Beach High Sch.; Los Angeles State Coll. Played first tennis match at age of eleven; won first championship, Southern California, 1958; coached by Clyde Walker, Alice Marble, Frank Brennan and Mervyn Rose; won first All England Championship, 1966, and five times subseq., and in 1979 achieved record of 20 Wimbledon titles (six Singles, ten Doubles, four Mixed Doubles); has won all other major titles inc. US Singles and Doubles Championships on all four surfaces, and 24 US national titles in all. Pres., Women's Tennis Assoc., 1980–81. Presidential Medal of Freedom (USA), 2009. *Publications:* Tennis to Win, 1970; Billie Jean, 1974; (with Joe Hyams) Secrets of Winning Tennis, 1975; Tennis Love (illus. Charles Schulz), 1978; (with Frank Deford) Billie Jean King, 1982; (with Cynthia Starr) We Have Come a Long Way: the story of women's tennis, 1989; (with Christine Brennan) Pressure is a Privilege, 2008. *Address:* c/o Mylan WTT, 1776 Broadway, Suite 600, New York, NY 10019, USA.

KING, Bradley Maurice; Executive Director, USS Massachusetts Memorial Committee Inc., and Battleship Cove Naval Heritage Museum, Battleship Cove, Fall River, since 2010; *b* 10 June 1955; *s* of Maurice Wilfrid King and June King (*née* Wright); *m* 1977, Linda Ann (*née* Baker); one *s*. *Educ:* Chigwell Sch.; Polytech. of North London (BA Hons 1988); Univ. of Greenwich (MA 1999). Imperial War Museum: joined as Clerical Officer, 1980; Public Services Officer, Film Archive, 1987–2000; on secondment as Mus. Project Officer, Bridport Mus., Dorset, 2000; Keeper, Photograph Archive, 2001–02; Dir, HMS Belfast, 2002–10. Historic Naval Ships Association: Bd Mem., 2006–; Internat. Co-ordinator, 2007–09; Vice Pres., 2009–11; Pres., 2011–13 (Internat. Leadership Award, 2006; William J. Diffley Award, 2010); Vice Pres., SE Mass Convention and Visitors Bureau, 2013–. Freeman, City of London, 2007; Liveryman, Shipwrights' Co., 2007. Adviser: World Ship Trust, 2003–13; Bridport Mus. Trust, 2010–13 (Trustee, 2003–10); Mem. Bd (ex Officio), Marine Mus. of Fall River, 2012–. *Publications:* Royal Naval Air Service 1912–1918, 1997. *Recreations:* history, genealogy, woodworking, cooking, flying, motoring. *Address:* c/o Battleship Massachusetts, Battleship Cove, 5 Water Street, Fall River, MA 02722–0111, USA. *E:* bradking@battleshipcove.org.

KING, Brenda; First Legislative Counsel, Northern Ireland, since 2012; *b* Belfast, 13 June 1964; *d* of Thomas and Margaret King; *m* 1999, James Sullivan. *Educ:* Queen's Univ. Belfast (LLB Hons 1986; CPLS 1987); Wolfson Coll., Cambridge (LLM Internat. Law 1990); Univ. of S Carolina. Admitted as solicitor, 1989; in private practice, 1987–89; NI Office, 1990–91; Asst Legislative Counsel, NI, 1991–94; Sen. Asst Legislative Counsel, 1994–2001; Legislative Counsel, 2001–12. *Recreations:* travel, wine, the arts. *Address:* Office of the Legislative Counsel, Parliament Buildings, Stormont, Belfast BT4 3XX. *E:* Brenda.King@ofmdfmni.gov.uk.

KING, Dr Brian Edmund; owner manager, King Innovations, since 1994; *b* 25 May 1928; *s* of Albert Theodore King and Gladys Johnson; *m* 1952 (marr. diss.); two *s*; *m* 1972, Eunice Wolstenholme; one *d*. *Educ:* Pocklington Sch.; Leeds Univ. TMM (Research) Ltd, 1952–57; British Oxygen, 1957–67; Dir, 1967–87, and Chief Exec., 1977–87, Wira Technology Group Ltd (formerly Wool Industries Research Assoc.); Dir and Chief Exec., Barnsley Business and Innovation Centre, 1987–93. *Recreations:* bridge, swimming, travel.

KING, Caradoc; literary agent; Partner, United Agents LLP, since 2012; *b* 19 Dec. 1946; *s* of late Joan Bartlett (*née* Richardson); *m* 1st, 1975, Jane Grant Morris (marr. diss. 2001); one *s* one *d*; 2nd, 2013, Ingrid Boeck; one *d*. *Educ:* Belmont Abbey; Exeter Coll., Oxford (MA). With Associated Book Publishers, 1968–70; Senior Editor: Allen Lane, Penguin Press, 1970–72; Penguin Books, 1970–75; joined A. P. Watt, 1976: Associate, A. P. Watt & Son, 1976–81; Dir, A. P. Watt Ltd, 1981–2013; Man. Dir and Chm., 1992–96; Jt Man. Dir and Chm., 1996–2012. *Publications:* Problem Child (memoir), 2011. *Recreations:* ski-ing, lunch, collecting wine, motor-biking. *Address:* c/o United Agents LLP, 12–16 Lexington Street, W1F 0LE. *Clubs:* Soho House, Quo Vadis.

KING, (Catherine) Mary; mezzo soprano; Director of Voicelab, Southbank Centre, since 2006. *Educ:* Univ. of Birmingham (BA English); St Anne's Coll., Oxford (PGCE); Guildhall Sch. of Music and Drama. Vocal career encompasses music theatre, opera and recital, with specialism in contemporary repertoire. Dir, The Knack, 1995–2006, Artistic Associate, Baylis Prog., 2004–06, ENO; Hd of Singing and Music, Millennium Performing Arts, Woolwich, 2006–. Mem., Music Council, Royal Philharmonic Soc. Trustee, Orpheus Centre, 1999–2004. Hon. ARAM; Hon. Fellow, Rose Bruford Coll.; Hon. FRNCM 2011. *Publications:* (with A. Legge) The Singer's Handbook, 2007; Boosey Voice Coach, vol. 1: Singing in English, 2007, vol. 2: Singing in French, 2009, vol. 3: Singing in German, 2010. *Recreation:* gardening.

KING, Prof. Christine Elizabeth, CBE 2007; DL; PhD; FRHistS; Vice-Chancellor and Chief Executive, 1995–2011, now Vice-Chancellor Emeritus, and Professor of History, 1991–2011, now Emeritus, Staffordshire University (formerly Staffordshire Polytechnic); *b* 31 Aug. 1944; *d* of late William Edwin King and Elizabeth Violet May King (*née* Coates). *Educ:* Birmingham Univ. (BA Hons Hist. and Theol. 1966; MA Theol. 1973; PhD Religious Hist. 1980). FRHistS 1994. Teaching, research and management posts in sch., further and higher educn sectors; Head, Sch. of Histl and Critical Studies, 1985–87, Dean, Faculty of Arts, 1987–90, Lancs Poly.; Staffordshire Polytechnic, subseq. Staffordshire University: Dean of Business, Humanities and Social Scis, 1990–92; Pro Vice-Chancellor, 1992–95. Pres., NIACE, 2001–06. FRSA; CCMI (CIMgt 1995; FIMgt 1993). DL Staffs, 1999. Hon. Fellow, Univ. of Central Lancs, 2001; Hon. DLitt: Birmingham, 1998; Portsmouth, 2001; DUniv Derby, 2001; Dr *hc* Edinburgh, 2005. *Publications:* The Nazi State and the New Religions, 1983; (ed) Through the Glass Ceiling: effective management development for women, 1993; articles and chapters on history of religion in Nazi Germany, women in management, higher educn and on Elvis Presley and his fans. *E:* dr.c.e.king@gmail.com.

KING, Christopher Peter Morgan; Headmaster, Leicester Grammar School, and Chief Executive, Leicester Grammar School Trust, since 2001; *b* Bristol, 3 Nov. 1955; *s* of Peter and Esme King; *m* 1982, Elizabeth; three *s*. *Educ:* Queen Elizabeth's Hosp., Bristol; Durham Univ. (BA, MA). Water Resource Planner, Wessex Water Authy, 1975–78; Teacher of Geog., Sutton Vallence Sch., 1979–83; Hd of Geog. and Sen. Housemaster, Rendcomb Coll., 1983–95; Dep. Hd, Kimbolton Sch., 1995–2001. Chm., HMC, 2015–Aug. 2016 (Chm., Professional Develt Cttee, 2001–14). Chief Exec., Leicester GS Trust. Hon. Principal, Blue Tassel Sch., Suzhou, China, 2014–15. Gov., King's Sch., Macclesfield, 2014–. *Recreations:* golf, hill walking, theatre, Rugby. *Address:* Leicester Grammar School, London Road, Great Glen, Leicester LE8 9FL. *T:* (0116) 259 1912. *E:* Kingc@leicestergrammar.org.uk.

KING, Sir David (Anthony), Kt 2003; FRS 1991; FRSC, FInstP; Director, Smith School of Enterprise and the Environment, University of Oxford, 2008–12; Fellow, University College, Oxford, 2009–12; Foreign Secretary's Special Representative on Climate Change, Foreign and Commonwealth Office, since 2013; Chairman, Future Cities Catapult, Clerkenwell, since 2013; *b* 12 Aug. 1939; *s* of Arnold King and Patricia (*née* Vardy), Durban; *m* Jane Lichtenstein; one *s* one *d*, and two *s* by previous marriage. *Educ:* St John's Coll., Johannesburg; Univ. of the Witwatersrand, Johannesburg (BSc; PhD 1963); ScD E Anglia, 1974; ScD Cantab, 1999. Shell Scholar, Imperial Coll., 1963–66; Lectr in Chemical Physics, Univ. of E Anglia, Norwich, 1966–74; Brunner Prof. of Physical Chemistry, Univ. of Liverpool, 1974–88; Cambridge University: 1920 Prof. of Physical Chemistry, 1988–2005; Head, 1993–2000, Dir of Research, 2005–11, Dept of Chemistry; Fellow, St John's College, 1988–95; Master, Downing Coll., 1995–2000, Hon. Fellow, 2001; Fellow, Queens' Coll., 2001–08. Chief Scientific Advr to the Govt, and Hd, Office of Sci. and Technol., then of Sci. and Innovation, subseq. Govt Office for Sci., 2000–07. Sen. Science Advr, UBS, 2008–13. Dir, Cambridge Kaspakas, 2011–. Member: Comité de Direction of Centre de Cinétique Physique et Chimique, Nancy, 1974–81; Nat. Exec., Assoc. of Univ. Teachers, 1970–78 (Nat. Pres., 1976–77); British Vacuum Council, 1978–87 (Chm., 1982–85); Internat. Union for Vacuum Science and Technology, 1978–86; Faraday Div., Council, Chem. Soc., 1979–82; Scientific Adv. Panel, Daresbury Lab., 1980–82; Res. Adv. Cttee, Leverhulme Trust, 1980–92 (Chm., 1995–2001); Beirat, Fritz Haber Inst., West Berlin, 1981–93. Pres., BAAS, 2007–08. Chairman: Gallery Cttee, Bluecoat Soc. of Arts, 1986–88; Kettle's Yard Gall., Cambridge, 1989–2000. Pres. Bd, Coll. Carlo Alberto, Turin, 2008–11. Chancellor, Univ. of Liverpool, 2010–13. Miller Vis. Res. Prof., Univ. of Calif, Berkeley, 1996. Chm. Jury, Prix Pictet, 2010–. Lectures: Tilden, Chem. Soc., 1989; Frontiers, Texas A & M Univ., 1993; Dupont Distinguished, Indianapolis Univ., 1993; Dow Chemical Canada, Univ. W Ont, 1994; Zuckerman, Foundn for Sci. and Technol., 2002; Plenary, AAAS, Seattle, 2003; Annual British Ecol Soc., 2004; Greenpeace Business, 2004; Pimentel, Berkeley, 2005; Magna Carta, Australian Parlt, 2005; ACU Centenary, Jamaica, Hong Kong, Brunei, Kuala Lumpur, 2013. Member Editorial Board: Jl of Physics C, 1977–80; Surface Science Reports, 1983–98; Surface Science, 2000–; Editor, Chemical Physics Letters, 1989–2001. Hon. FREng 2006; Hon. Fellow: Indian Acad. of Scis, 1998; Third World Acad. of Scis, 2000; Amer. Acad. of Arts and Scis, 2002; Hon. FRSSAf 2001; Hon. Life FRSA 2006. Hon. Fellow, Cardiff Univ., 2001. Hon. DSc: UEA, Liverpool, Cardiff, 2001; Leicester, Milan, Stockholm, 2002; Witwatersrand, York, St Andrews, 2003; La Trobe, QUB, 2005; Newcastle, Goldsmiths Coll. London, Turin, 2006; University Coll. London, 2009; Western Ontario, 2010; Warwick, 2012. Chem. Soc. Award for surface and colloid chemistry, 1978; British Vacuum Council medal and prize for research, 1991; Liversidge Lect. and Medal, 1997, Lewis Lect. and Medal, 2013, RSC; Rumford Medal and Prize, Royal Soc., 2002; WWF Awareness Award, 2004; Linnaeus Medal, Royal Swedish Acad. of Scis, 2007; Adamson Award for Surface Chem., Amer. Chem. Soc., 2009. Officier de la Légion d'Honneur (France), 2009. *Publications:* (with Gabrielle Walker) The Hot Topic, 2008; (with Oliver Inderwildi) Energy, Transport and the Environment, 2012; papers on the physics and chemistry of solid surfaces in Proc. Royal Soc., Surface Science, Science, Jl Chemical Physics, Physical Rev. Letters etc, and on science in govt, global warming etc in Nature and Science. *Recreations:* photography, art. *Address:* 20 Glisson Road, Cambridge CB1 2HD.

KING, David E., FCCA, Chartered FCSI; Chief Executive, DKI, 2009–12; *b* 18 Aug. 1945; *m* 1972, Jenny Hall; four *s*. *Educ:* Manchester Poly.; Cranfield Sch. of Mgt (MBA 1984). FCCA 1976. Qualified as Certified Accountant, 1976; sen. financial positions both overseas and in UK, 1976–; joined London Metal Exchange, 1987, Chief Exec., 1989–2001; Man. Dir, Supervision, later Acting CEO, Dubai Internat. Financial Centre, Dubai Financial Services Authy, 2003–05; Man. Dir, Business Develt, Global Banking, Middle East and N Africa, HSBC Middle East, and Sen. Exec. Officer, HSBC Middle East Leasing Partnership, 2005–09; Exec. Dir, Middle East Business Develt, China Construction Bank Internat., 2009–11; Chm., Gulf Region, FD Internat., 2009–11. Non-executive Director: IGI Co. (UK) Ltd, 2012– (Chm., Audit, Risk and Compliance Cttee, 2012–); IGI Hldgs, 2014– (Chm., Risk and Audit Cttee, 2014–); FXCM, 2014– (Chm., Audit Cttee, 2014–). Mem., Jersey Finance Gp, GCC, 2011–12. UAE Adv. Bd Mem., Chartered Inst. for Securities and Investment (formerly Securities and Investment Inst.), 2009–12; Mem., Middle E and N Africa Adv. Bd, Cass Business Sch., 2011–12. Judge, Platts Global Metals Awards, 2012–. *Recreations:* working and playing hard and, in the case of golf, playing badly; UK and international charitable and fundraising activities.

KING, (Denys) Michael (Gwilym), CVO 1989; FICE; Director, 1986–91, Assistant Chief Executive, 1991, BAA plc, retired (Member, British Airports Authority, 1980–86); *b* 29 May 1929; *s* of William James King, FCIS, and Hilda May King; *m* 1st, 1956, Monica Helen (marr. diss. 1973); three *d*; 2nd, 1985, Ann Elizabeth. *Educ:* St Edmund's Sch., Canterbury; Simon Langton Sch., Canterbury; Battersea Polytechnic, London (BScEng Hons London, 1949). MIMechE 1966; FICE 1977. Engr, J. Laing Construction Ltd, 1961–71, Dir, 1971–74; Engrg Dir, BAA, 1974–77; Dir, 1977–86, Man. Dir, 1986–88, Heathrow Airport; Man. Dir, Airports Div., BAA, 1988–91. *Recreations:* yachting, preserved railways.

KING, Deryk Irving; Chairman, iCON Infrastructure Management Ltd, since 2010; Managing Partner, iCON Infrastructure LLP, since 2011; *b* 20 Dec. 1947; *s* of Cyril Montford King and Irene Muriel King (*née* Irving); *m* 1971, Janet Lorraine Amos; one *d*. *Educ:* Arnold Sch., Blackpool; University Coll., Oxford (MA Chem.). Joined Air Products Ltd as sales engr, 1970; with Imperial Chemical Industries PLC, 1973–96: Product Manager, 1973–77; Asst Gen. Manager, Chemicals, ICI Japan Ltd, 1977–79; Sen. Product Manager, 1979–83; Export Sales Manager, Mond Div., 1983–84; Commercial Manager, ICI Soda Ash Products, and Dir, Magadi Soda Co., 1984–88; Dir, Ellis & Everard (Chemicals) Ltd, 1987–88; Commercial Manager, 1988–91, Gen. Manager, 1991–92, ICI Fertilizers; Chm., Scottish Agricl Industries and BritAg Industries, and Dir, Irish Fertilizer Industries, 1991–92; Man. Dir, ICI Polyester, 1992–96; Chm., ICI Far Eastern, 1995–96; Gp Man. Dir, PowerGen plc, 1996–98; Dir, Ellis & Everard plc, 1999–2001; Projects Dir, 1999–2000, Man. Dir, N America, 2000–09, Centrica plc; Chm. and CEO, Direct Energy Marketing Ltd, 2000–09; Chairman: Sutton and East Surrey Water plc, 2009–13; Firmus Energy Ltd, 2014–. Chairman: Centrica Pension Plan Trustees Ltd, 2010–; Centrica Trustees Ltd, 2010–; Centrica Engineers' Trustees Ltd, 2010–. Director: Kvaerner ASA, 1997–2001; Consumers' Waterheater Income Fund, 2002–09; Allstream (formerly AT&T Canada) Inc., 2003–04; Trustee, Coventry 2000, 1997–2000. Chm., W Midlands Regl Awards Cttee, and Mem., England Cttee, Nat. Lottery Charities Bd, 1998–2000. FCIM 1992; MInstD 2000. *Recreations:* travel, wine and food, watching sport. *Address:* iCON Infrastructure LLP, Pollen House, 10–12 Cork Street, W1S 3NP. *Clubs:* Oxford and Cambridge; Toronto.

KING, Prof. Desmond Stephen, DLitt; FBA 2003; FRHistS; Andrew W. Mellon Professor of American Government, University of Oxford, and Fellow, Nuffield College, Oxford, since 2002; *b* Dublin, 23 Oct. 1957; *s* of Desmond and Margaret King; *m* 1995, Dr Carolyn Cowey; one *s*. *Educ:* The High Sch., Dublin; Trinity Coll., Dublin (BA 1st cl. 1979; Bastable Prize, 1979); Northwestern Univ., Illinois (MA 1981; David Minar Prize, 1981; PhD 1985); DLitt Oxon 2015. Lectr in Politics, Univ. of Edinburgh, 1984–88; Lectr in Govt, LSE, 1988–91; University of Oxford: Lectr in Politics, 1991–2002; titular Prof., 1996–; Official Fellow and Tutor in Politics, St John's Coll., 1991–2002, Emeritus Fellow, 2002–. Nuffield Foundn Social Sci. Fellow, 1997–98; Res. Reader, British Acad., 2000–02; Leverhulme Major Res. Fellow, 2005–08. Delegate and Mem., Finance Cttee, OUP, 1999–2010. FRSA 2000; FAcSS (AcSS 2013); FRHistS 2015. Hon. MRIA 2015. *Publications:* (jtly) the State and the City, 1987; The New Right: politics, markets and citizenship, 1987; (ed jtly and contrib.) Challenges to Local Government, 1990; Separate and Unequal: Black Americans and the US Federal Government, 1995, rev. edn. as Separate and Unequal: African Americans and the US Federal Government, 2007; Actively Seeking Work?: the politics of unemployment and welfare policy in the US and Britain, 1995; (ed jtly and contrib.) Preferences, Institutions and Rational Choice, 1995; (ed jtly and contrib.) Rethinking Local Democracy, 1996; In the Name of Liberalism: illiberal social policy in the USA and Britain, 1999; Making Americans: immigration, race and the origins of the diverse democracy, 2000; The Liberty of Strangers: making the American nation, 2005; (ed jtly and contrib.) The Polarized Presidency of George W. Bush, 2007; (ed jtly and contrib.) The Unsustainable American State, 2009; (ed jtly and contrib.) Democratization in America, 2009; (jtly) Still a House Divided: race and politics on Obama's America, 2011; (ed jtly and contrib.) Obama at the Crossroads, 2012; (jtly) Sterilized by the State, 2013; (ed jtly) Forging a Discipline, 2014; articles in jls incl. Past and Present, World Politics, American Pol Sci. Rev. *Recreations:* walking, free jazz. *Address:* Nuffield College, Oxford OX1 1NF. *T:* (01865) 278500.

KING, Douglas Alexander, FREng; environmental engineer; Principal, Doug King Consulting Ltd, since 2008; *b* Stanton Drew, Avon, 10 April 1968; *s* of Ian King and Caroline King; *m* 2007, Alexandra Goloverova. *Educ:* Bideford Sch.; Imperial Coll. London (BSc ARCS Physics 1990). CPhys 1997; CEng 1997; CEnv 2009; FEI 2009; FCIBSE 2009; FInstP 2010; FREng 2012. Engr, Max Fordham and Partners, 1990–94; Partner, Max Fordham Associates, 1994–97; Associate Director: Capita Greatorex Ltd, 1997–98; Buro Happold Ltd, 1998–2002; Dir, King Shaw Associates, 2002–12. Building projects include: Sainsbury's, Greenwich, 2000 (Channel 4 Bldg of the Year; Design Council Millennium Product; RIBA Jl Sustainability Award); Genzyme Centre, Cambridge, Mass, 2002 (RIBA Worldwide Award); Rolls Royce Motor Cars, Goodwood, W Sussex, 2003 (Royal Fine Art Commn Bldg of the Year); RSC Courtyard Theatre, Stratford upon Avon, 2006 (RIBA Nat. Award; AIA Award); Innovate Green Office, Leeds, 2007 (British Construction Industry Envmtl Award; Construction News Green Bldg of the Year). Visiting Professor: Univ. of Bath, 2007–; Chongqing Univ., 2013–. Chief Sci. and Engrg Advr, BRE, 2012–13. Hon. FRIBA 2011. Edmund Hambley Medal, 2007, James Watt Medal, 2008, ICE; Silver Medal, RAEng, 2011. *Publications:* contrib. to jls incl. Sci. in Parliament and Energy; reports for RAEng. *Recreation:* experimenting with flavours. *T:* (01225) 839846. *E:* mail@dougking.co.uk.

KING, Edmund Valerian; President, Automobile Association, since 2008; *b* Aldershot, 6 March 1958; *s* of Michael Dominic King and Mary Angela King; *m* 2000, Deirdre Elizabeth Lavelle; two *s* one *d*. *Educ:* St Hugh's Coll., Tollerton; Chipping Norton Sch.; Santa Monica Coll.; Newcastle upon Tyne Univ. (BA Hons Politics). Wine taster and PR, Bouchard Aîné et fils, Beaune, 1976–77; Cttee Sec., SSRC, 1981–82; grad. trainee, Dept of Employment, 1982–84; Job Centre Manager, Hackney, 1983–84; proprietor, English antiques business, Los Angeles, 1984–86; reporter, KRTH radio, LA, 1985–87; Dir, Marathon Rent a Car, LA, 1985–88; Campaign Dir, British Rd Fedn, 1988–92; Hd of Campaigns, RAC, 1992–99; Exec. Dir, RAC Foundn, 1999–2007. Vis. Prof. of Transport, Newcastle Univ., 2009–. *Recreations:* mountain biking, running, football (with sons), cooking, fine wines, antiques auctions, driving. *Address:* Automobile Association, Fanum House, Basing View, Basingstoke, Hants RG21 4EA. *T:* (01256) 491538, *Fax:* (01256) 492090. *E:* edmund.king@theAA.com. *Club:* 2 Brydges Place.

KING, Rt Hon. Dame Eleanor (Warwick), DBE 2008; PC 2014; **Rt Hon. Lady Justice King;** a Lady Justice of Appeal, since 2014; *b* 13 Sept. 1957; *d* of Selby William Guy Hamilton and Dr Margaret Hamilton; *m* 1981, (David) Thomas King; four *d*. *Educ:* Queen Margaret's Sch., Escrick; Hull Univ. (LLB). Called to the Bar, Inner Temple, 1979; QC 1999; Asst Recorder, 1996–2000; Recorder, 2000–08; a Dep. High Court Judge, 2000–08; a Judge of the High Court of Justice, Family Div., 2008–14. Chm. Governors, Queen Margaret's Sch., 1992–2011; Mem. Chapter, York Univ. Fellow, Internat. Acad. of Matrimonial Lawyers, 2004. Hon. DLaws Hull, 2011. *Recreations:* walking, cycling, running. *Address:* Royal Courts of Justice, Strand, WC2A 2LL.

KING, Frances; Principal, Collège Alpin Beau Soleil, since 2013; *b* 26 Sept. 1960; *d* of Sir Colin Henry Imray, *qv*; *m* 1982, Timothy King; one *s* one *d*. *Educ:* Ashford Sch., Kent; St Hilda's Coll., Oxford (MA Theology); Heythrop Coll., London Univ. (MA); Hull Univ. (MBA). Actg Hd of RE, Lady Eleanor Holles Sch., Hampton, 1984–85; Head of Religious Education: Francis Holland Sch., London, 1985–90; Guildford Co. Sch., 1990–93; Tormead Sch., Guildford, 1993–2000; Dep. Headmistress, 2000–03, Headmistress, 2003–07, St Mary's Sch., Ascot, later Heathfield, Ascot; Headmistress, Roedean Sch., 2008–13. *Recreation:* walking. *Address:* Collège Alpin Beau Soleil, Route du Village 1, 1884 Villars-sur-Ollon, Switzerland. *Club:* Royal Over-Seas League.

KING, Graeme Crockatt; Chairman, Hydro Hotel Eastbourne plc, since 2004; Chairman, Audit Committee, Company Director and Board Consultant, Rank Foundation, since 2006; *b* 8 Sept. 1948; *s* of late William Ramsay Morrison King and Margaret Lowe Robertson (*née* Crockatt); *m* 1975, Dr Susan Margaret Hobbins; one *s* one *d*. *Educ:* High Sch. of Dundee; St Andrews Univ. (MA Science 1970). Member: ICAS, 1974; Inst. of Chartered Accts of Canada, 1976. Arthur Andersen, 1970–79; Finance Dir, Aurora Gp, 1979–81; Mintz and Partners, Toronto, 1982–84; Chief Acct, then Gen. Manager, Lloyd's of London, 1984–94; Principal, Binder Hamlyn/Arthur Andersen, 1994–96; Man. Dir, Insurance Captives, P & O, 1997–2000; Gen. Sec., SPCK, 2001–06. Chm., Hydro Hotel Eastbourne PLC, 2004–. Chm., Rochester Dio. Bd of Finance, 2000–12; Trustee: All Saints Educnl Trust, 2001–06; NCVO, 2002–08; Hon. Treas., Farnborough Hosp. Special Care Baby Fund, 1985–2012. Master, Insurers' Co., 2009–10 (Hon. Treas., 2002–08). *Recreations:* golf, climbing (Mem., Munro Soc.), ski-ing, outdoors. *E:* hobbinsking@btinternet.com. *Clubs:* Lloyds, Nikaean, Caledonian; Grampian; Wildernesse Golf (Sevenoaks), Rye Golf; Royal Queensland Golf (Brisbane).

KING, Harold Samuel; Founder and Artistic Director, London City Ballet, 1978–96; choreographer and lecturer; special events consultant; *b* Durban, 13 May 1949. *Educ:* Sea Point Boys' High Sch.; University Ballet Sch., Cape Town; Univ. of Cape Town (Teacher Trng Course). Soloist, Cape Performing Arts Bd Ballet Co., 1968–70; joined Western Th. Ballet, in GB, as dancer and choreographer, 1970; with Opera Ballet, Covent Gdn, 1976–77, incl. seasons with Nat. Ballet of Zimbabwe, as Guest Artist with Cape Performing Arts Bd, and Guest Teacher, Royal Acad. of Dance Summer Sch.; Artistic Co-ordinator, Victor Hochhauser Gala Ballet Season, RFH, 1978; asst, Rudolf Nureyev seasons at London Coliseum, 1978; toured with, newly-formed London City Ballet, 1978–96; founder, and Artistic Dir, City Ballet of London, 1996–2001, produced Dances from Napoli and choreographed Prince Igor, Nutcracker Suite and Carmen; Artistic Dir, Ballet de Zaragoza,

Spain, 2001; guest artist, Cape Town City Ballet (performed Madge, the witch, in La Sylphide), Cape Town, 2003; Artistic Co-ordinator, Cape Town City Ballet, 2005–08; teacher, adult jazz and ballet, 2008–12, Guest Teacher and fundraising co-ordinator for Ikapa Dance Th., 2008–10, Cape Town; choreographed: The Little Princess, 1995 and created Flowers for Mrs Harris, 1998, for London Children's Ballet; The Lion, the Witch and the Wardrobe for London Studio Centre, 1996; Requiem de Fauré for Ballet de Zaragoza, 2001; Shostakovich Suites for Univ. of Cape Town Sch. of Ballet, 2004; Habanera for Dance for All, township dance co., S Africa, 2005. Chief Trustee, David Blair Meml Trust, 2000–05. Fundraising Consultant: Union Dance Co., 2003; Mavin Khoo Dance, 2003; The Army Biehl Foundn, 2011; Dance for All, outreach project, Cape Town, 2012–13. Jazz dance instructor and lectr, 5 world cruises, Queen Mary 2, 2010–. Patron, London Ballet, 2014–.

KING, Helen Mary, QPM 2011; Assistant Commissioner, Territorial Policing, Metropolitan Police Service, since 2014; *b* Bishop's Stortford, Herts, 26 April 1965; *d* of Robert Shirley King, *qv* and late Mary King; *m* (marr. diss.); two *d. Educ:* Herts and Essex High Sch., Bishop's Stortford; Perse Sch. for Girls, Cambridge; St Anne's Coll., Oxford (BA 1986; MA); Univ. of Manchester (MA 1994); Univ. of Cambridge (Postgrad. Dip. 2003). Police Officer (Constable to Chief Superintendent), Cheshire Constabulary, 1986–2005; Asst Chief Constable, Merseyside Police, 2005–12; Dep. Chief Constable, Cheshire Constabulary, 2012–14. ACPO lead for cash and valuables in transit attacks, 2007–12; Nat. Policing lead for Horizon Scanning, 2012–14. Trustee, PSS, 2007–14. *Address:* Metropolitan Police Service, New Scotland Yard, 10 Broadway, SW1H 0BG. *T:* (020) 7230 1613. *E:* helen.king2@met.pnn.police.uk.

KING, Ian David; Business Presenter, Sky News, since 2014; *b* Poole, Dorset, 23 March 1967; *s* of John and Sylvia King; *m* 2010, Angela Jameson; two *s* one *d. Educ:* Park Sch., Barnstaple, Devon; N Devon Coll.; Univ. of Manchester (BA Hons); City Univ. (Postgrad. Dip. Newspaper Journalism). Graduate trainee, 1989, Business Analyst, 1990–93, Midland Bank; City Reporter, Daily Telegraph, 1994–95; City Reporter, 1995–97, Stock Market corresp., 1998, Guardian; Sen. Financial Corresp., Mail on Sunday, 1998–2000; Business Ed., The Sun, 2000–08; Dep. Business Ed., 2008–11, Business Ed., 2011–14, columnist, 2014–, The Times. *Recreations:* family, cricket, football. *Address:* Sky News, 15th Floor, 30 St Mary Axe, EC3A 8EP. *Club:* MCC.

KING, Isobel Wilson; *see* Buchanan, I. W.

KING, Sir James (Henry Rupert), 5th Bt *cr* 1888, of Campsie, Stirlingshire; Teacher of French, Aldro School, since 2002; *b* Westminster, 24 May 1961; *s* of Sir John Christopher King, 4th Bt and of Patricia Monica King (*née* Foster); *S* father, 2014; *m* 1995, Elizabeth Dora, *d* of late Richard Henry Ellingworth; two *s* one *d. Educ:* Sandroyd; Eton; Edinburgh Univ. (MA); Warwick Univ. (PGCE). Wine merchant, 1986–2002. *Recreations:* bee-keeping, sailing. *Heir: s* John Alasdair Ellingworth King, *b* 4 June 1996. *Address:* 12 Great Stuart Street, Edinburgh EH3 7TN. *Club:* Royal Cruising.

KING, Jane; author; organisational development and learning consultant; *b* 12 Dec. 1954; *d* of Tom and Mabel Scott; *m* 1st, 1978, Edward Isaacs (marr. diss. 2009); two *d*; 2nd, 2011, Reginald King. *Educ:* Edinburgh Univ. (MA); Wolverhampton Business Sch. (DMS, MBA); Open Univ. (Dip. Lit.). Associate Lectr, Open Univ. Business Sch., 1996–. Non-executive Director: Wolverhampton HA, 1994–98; Mid Staffordshire NHS Foundn Trust, 2011–15; Chm., Wolverhampton Healthcare NHS Trust, 1998–2001; Regl Appts Comr, W Midlands, NHS Appts Commn, 2001–05. Man. Partner, ATM Consulting, 2006–12. Chm., Wolverhampton Voluntary Sector Council, 1992–95; non-exec. Dir, Wolverhampton TEC, 1993–95; Consultant, Internat. Devel Office, Open Univ., 2014–. Mem., Regl Panel, Nat. Lottery Charities Bd, 1995–97. *Recreations:* writing, gardening, keeping chickens. *Address:* 40 Rowley Bank, Stafford ST17 9BA.

KING, Jean Mary; Under Secretary, Chief Executive, Employment Division of the Manpower Services Commission, 1979–82, retired; Member, Civil Service Appeal Board, 1984–93; *b* 9 March 1923; *d* of Edgar and Elsie Bishop; *m* 1st, 1951, Albert Robert Collingridge (*d* 1994); one *d*; 2nd, 1996, John Ernest Agar King (*d* 2000). *Educ:* County High School, Loughton, Essex; University College London (BSc Econ); LSE (Social Science Course). Asst Personnel Officer, C. and J. Clark, 1945–49; Personnel Manager, Pet Foods Ltd, 1949–50; Ministry of Labour/Department of Employment: Personnel Management Adviser and Industrial Relations Officer, 1950–65; Regl Industrial Relations Officer/Sen. Manpower Adviser, 1965–71; Assistant Secretary, Office of Manpower Economics 1971–73, Pay Board 1973–74, Dept of Employment HQ 1974–76; Dep. Chief Exec., Employment Service Div. of Manpower Services Commn, 1976–79. Chm., Kent Area Manpower Bd, 1983–88. Chm., Fareham Good Neighbours, 1999–2003. *Publications:* (jtly) Personnel Management in the Small Firm, 1953. *Recreation:* studying problems of ageing. *Address:* 16 Faregrove Court, Grove Road, Fareham, Hants PO16 7AS. *T:* (01329) 236340.

KING, Jeremy Richard Bruce, OBE 2014; restaurateur; *b* 21 June 1954; *s* of late Charles Henry King and Molly King (*née* Chinn); *m* 1st, 1982, Debra Hauer (marr. diss. 2007); one *s* two *d*; 2nd, 2012, Lauren Gurvich. *Educ:* Christ's Hosp., Horsham. Co-founder (with Christopher Corbin) and Director: Caprice Hldgs Ltd, 1982–2003; restaurants: Le Caprice, 1981–2003; The Ivy, 1990–2003; J. Sheekey, 1998–2003; The Wolseley, 2003–; The Delaunay, 2011–; Brasserie Zédel, 2012–; Colbert, 2012–; Fischer's, 2014–; Beaumont Hotel, 2014–. Dir, Tate Enterprises Ltd, 2006–14. Member, Council: Tate Gall. of Modern Art, 1999–2013; Tate Britain, 2014. Mem./Dir, Northbank BID, 2014–. Trustee: Artangel Trust, 1994–2005; Soho Th., 2008–. Hon. MSc London Sch. of Hospitality and Tourism, 2014. *Recreations:* contemporary art, theatre, cycling, solitude. *Clubs:* Garrick, Royal Automobile, Chelsea Arts (Trustee, 2014–), Groucho, MCC.

KING, John Arthur Charles; Chairman, Superscape plc (formerly Superscape VR), 1998–2003; *b* 7 April 1933; *s* of late Charles William King and Doris Frances King; *m* 1958, Ina Solavici; two *s. Educ:* Univ. of Bristol (BSc). IBM UK, 1956–70; Managing Director, Telex Computer Products UK Ltd, 1970–73; Dir, DP Div., Metra Consulting Gp, 1974–75; Marketing Dir, UK, later Europe (Brussels), ITT Business Systems, 1976–81; Commercial Dir, Business Communications Systems, Philips (Hilversum), 1981–83; Dir, Marketing and Corporate Strategy, subseq. Corporate Dir and Man. Dir, Overseas Div., BT plc, 1984–88; Man. Dir, Citicorp Information Business Internat., 1988–91; Chairman: Quotron Internat., 1988–91; Analysys Ltd, 1991–2001. Non-executive Director: olsy (formerly Olivetti) UK Ltd, 1991–98 (Chm., 1995–98); Leeds Permanent Building Society, 1991–95 (Vice-Chm., 1994–95); Knowledge Support Systems Ltd, 1997–2001 (non-exec. Chm., 1998–2001); TTP Capital Partners Ltd, 1999–2003. Non-exec. Dir, CSA, 1996–98; Mem. Supervisory Bd, FUGRO NV, 1997–2003; Advr, Enterprise First (formerly Surrey Business Advice), 2004–08. Sec. Gen., Eur. Foundn for Quality Management, 1993–94. Mem., Restrictive Practices Ct, 1995–2000. Freeman, City of London, 1987; Liveryman, Co. of Information Technologists, 1992. FBCS 1968; CCMI (CBIM 1986); FInstD 1986; FRSA 1993. *Recreations:* golf, bridge, music. *E:* jacking33@btinternet.com. *Club:* Wisley.

KING, Jonathan Colin Harmsworth; private intellectual, anthropologist and museum curator; Senior Research Fellow, Museum of Archaeology and Anthropology, University of Cambridge, since 2012; *b* 5 Jan. 1952; *s* of Michael King and Elizabeth King (*née* Hobhouse); *m* 1976, Fionn O'Beirne (marr. diss. 2011); one *s* one *d. Educ:* Eton; St John's Coll., Cambridge (MA 1975). British Museum: Curator, Native N American Collections, Dept of Ethnography, 1975–2005; Keeper, Dept of Africa, Oceania and the Americas, 2005–10; Keeper of Anthropology, 2010–12. *Publications:* Artificial Curiosities from the Northwest Coast of America, 1981; (ed with H. Lidchi) Imaging the Arctic, 1998; First Peoples First Contacts, 1999; (ed jtly) Arctic Clothing, 2005; (with H. Waterfield) Provenance, 2006; (with C. Feest) Woodlands Art, 2007; (with G. Were) Extreme Collecting, 2012; (ed jtly) Turquoise in Mexico and North America, 2012. *Recreations:* ephemera, reading, collecting, swimming. *Address:* Museum of Archaeology and Anthropology, Downing Street, Cambridge CB2 3DZ.

KING, Josanne Penelope Jeanne; *see* Rickard, J. P. J.

KING, Dame Julia (Elizabeth), DBE 2012 (CBE 1999); PhD; CEng, FREng, FIMMM, FRAeS, FIMarEST; FInstP; FEI; Vice Chancellor, Aston University, Birmingham, since 2006; Fellow, Churchill College, Cambridge, 1987–94 and since 2002; *b* 11 July 1954; *d* of Derrick Arthur King and Joan (*née* Brewer); *m* 1984, Dr Colin William Brown. *Educ:* Godolphin and Latymer Girls' Sch.; New Hall, Cambridge (BA 1975; MA 1978; PhD 1979). Rolls-Royce Res. Fellow, Girton Coll., Cambridge, 1978–80; Univ. Lectr, Nottingham Univ., 1980–87; Cambridge University: British Gas/FEng Sen. Res. Fellow, 1987–92; Univ. Lectr, 1992–94; Asst Dir, Univ. Technology Centre for Ni-Base Superalloys, 1993–94; Hd of Materials, Rolls-Royce Aerospace Gp, 1994–96; Dir of Advanced Engrg, Rolls-Royce Industrial Power Gp, 1997–98; Man. Dir, Fan Systems, Rolls-Royce plc, 1998–2000; Dir, Engrg and Technology-Marine, Rolls-Royce plc, 2000–02; Chief Exec., Inst. of Physics, 2002–04; Principal, Faculty of Engrg, Imperial Coll. London, 2004–06. Dir, Birmingham Technology Ltd, 2007–; non-executive Director: Green Investment Bank, 2012–; Angel Trains, 2012–. Mem., Green Commn, 2012–, Smart City Commn, 2013–, Birmingham CC. Chm., DSAC, 2003–07; Member: Technology Strategy Bd, 2004–09; BIS (formerly BERR) Ministerial Adv. Gp on Manufacturing, 2007–09; Higher Educn Statistics Agency Bd, 2007–12 (Chair, 2011–12); DIUS Strategic Bd, 2008–09; DECC (formerly DEFRA) Cttee on Climate Change, 2008–; Automotive Industry Council (formerly Global Agenda Council on Future of Transportation), World Economic Forum, 2008–12; Low Carbon Vehicle Partnership Bd, 2008–11; Interim Nat. Security Forum, 2009–10; BIS Mgt Bd, 2009–12; Independent Rev. Panel for Higher Educn Funding and Student Finance, 2009–10; Bd, Universities UK, 2011– (Chair, Innovation and Growth (formerly Employability, Business and Industry) Policy Network, 2011–); UK Airports Commn, 2012–. UK Low Carbon Business Ambassador, 2009–. Member: Council, and Hon. Sec. for Educn and Trng, Royal Acad. of Engrg, 2003–06; Council, Energy Inst., 2009–12; Nat. Centre for Univs and Business (formerly Council for Industry and Higher Educn), 2011– (Mem., Bd of Dirs, 2013–); EPSRC, 2012– (Chm., Fusion Adv. Bd, 2012); Gtr Birmingham and Solihull Local Enterprise Partnership, 2013–. Mem., Governing Body, European Inst. of Innovation and Technol., 2008–12. Member: Internat. Sci. Cttee, L'Oréal-UNESCO For Women in Science Awards, 2007–; Sci. and Technol. Honours Cttee, 2012–. Mem., Bd of Trustees, Cumberland Lodge, 2013–. Hon. Fellow: New Hall (later Murray Edwards Coll.), Cambridge, 2003; Cardiff Univ., 2003; Soc. for the Envmt, 2011; British Sci. Assoc., 2011; Polymer Processing Acad., India, 2012. FIMMM (FIM 1993); FREng (FEng 1997); FRAeS 1998; FIMarEST (FIMarE 2001); FInstP 2002; FCGI 2002; FEI 2009; FRSA. Hon. FSE 2011. Freeman, City of London, 1998; Liveryman, Co. of Goldsmiths, 2005–. Hon. DSc: QMUL, 2008; Manchester, 2014; Exeter, 2015. Grunfeld Medal, 1992, (jtly) Bengough Medal, 1995, Inst. of Materials; Kelvin Medal, ICE, 2001; John Collier Medal, IChemE, 2010; Lunar Soc. Medal, 2011; Constance Tipper Medal, ICF-World Acad. Structural Integrity, 2012; Erna Hamburger Prize, Swiss Federal Inst. Technol., 2012; President's Prize of Engrg, Professors' Council, 2012; LowCVP Low Carbon Champions Award, 2014; Leonardo da Vinci Medal, SEFI, 2014. *Publications:* (ed) Aerospace Materials and Structures, 1997; Educating Engineers for the 21st Century, 2007; King Review of Low Carbon Cars: part I, the potential for CO_2 reduction, 2007; part 2, recommendations for action, 2008; over 150 papers on fatigue and fracture in structural materials, aeroengine materials and marine propulsion technology. *Recreations:* people, growing orchids, collecting modern prints, gardening, walking. *Address:* Aston University, Aston Triangle, Birmingham B4 7ET. *T:* (0121) 204 4884.

KING, Sir Julian Beresford, KCVO 2014 (CVO 2011); CMG 2006; HM Diplomatic Service; Director General, Economic and Consular, Foreign and Commonwealth Office, since 2014; *b* 22 Aug. 1964; *s* of Brian Harold King and Barbara Mary King (*née* Beresford); *m* 1992, Lotte Vindelov Knudsen. *Educ:* Bishop Vesey's Grammar Sch.; St Peter's Coll., Oxford (BA). FCO, 1985; Ecole Nat. d'Admin, Paris, 1987–88; Paris, 1988–90; Luxembourg and The Hague, 1991; Second, later First, Sec., FCO, 1992; Private Sec. to Perm. Under-Sec. of State, FCO, 1995–98; UK Perm. Repn to EU, Brussels, 1998–2003; Counsellor and Hd of Chancery, UK Mission to UN, NY, 2003–04; UK Rep. to EU Pol and Security Cttee and UK Perm. Rep. to WEU, Brussels, 2004–07; Chef de Cabinet to Mem., EC, 2008–09 (on loan); Ambassador to Ireland, FCO, 2009–11; Dir Gen., NI Office, 2012–14. *Address:* c/o Foreign and Commonwealth Office, King Charles Street, SW1A 2AH.

KING, Justin Matthew, CBE 2011; Vice Chairman, Terra Firma Capital Partners, since 2015; *b* 17 May 1961; *s* of Alan and Elaine King; *m* 1990, Claire Andrea Simmons (marr. diss.); one *s* one *d. Educ:* Tudor Grange Sch.; Solihull Sixth Form Coll.; Bath Univ. (BSc Business Admin). Nat. Account Manager, Mars Confectionery, 1983–89; Sales and Mktg Dir, Egypt, Pepsi Internat., 1989–90; Man. Dir, UK, Haagen-Dazs, 1990–93; Man. Dir, Hypermkts, Asda Stores, 1993–2000; Exec. Dir, Food, Marks and Spencer plc, 2000–04; Chief Exec., J. Sainsbury plc, 2004–14. Mem. Bd, LOCOG, 2009–13. *Club:* Hayling Island Sailing.

KING, Kanya, MBE 1999; Founder and Chief Executive Officer, MOBO Organisation, since 1996; *b* London; *d* of Christian Ocloo and Mary Folan; one *s. Educ:* Goldsmiths Coll., Univ. of London (BA English Lit.). TV researcher, Carlton TV. Patron, Horniman Mus., 2000–. Hon. Fellow, Goldsmith's Coll., Univ. of London, 2004. Hon. DBA London Metropolitan, 2006; Hon. DMus Leeds Metropolitan, 2009. *Recreations:* walking, travelling, reading. *Address:* MOBO Organisation, 52 Oak Street, Manchester M4 5JA. *Clubs:* Home House, One Alfred Place.

KING, Mary; *see* King, C. M.

KING, Mary Elizabeth, MBE 2013; three-day event rider; *b* 8 June 1961; *d* of late Lt Comdr Michael Dillon Harding Thomson and of Patricia Gillian Thomson; *m* 1995, Alan David Henry King; one *s* one *d. Educ:* Manor House Sch., Honiton; King's Sch., Ottery St Mary; Evendine Court, Malvern (Distinction, Cordon Bleu, 1980). British Open Champion, 1990, 1991, 1997, 2007; Winner: Windsor Horse Trials, 1988, 1989, 1992; Badminton Horse Trials, 1992, 2000; Mem., Olympic Team, Barcelona, 1992, Atlanta, 1996, Sydney, 2000, Athens, 2004 (Team Silver Medal), Beijing, 2008 (Team Bronze Medal), London, 2012 (Team Silver Medal); European Championships: Team Gold Medal, 1991, 1994, 1997, 2007; World Equestrian Games: Team Gold Medal, 1995, 2010; Team Silver Medal, 2006. *Publications:* Mary Thomson's Eventing Year, 1993; All the King's Horses, 1997; William and Mary, 1998; Mary King: the autobiography, 2009; My Way, 2014. *Recreations:* tennis, snow and water ski-ing. *Address:* Thorn House, Salcombe Regis, Sidmouth, Devon EX10 0JH.

KING, Michael; *see* King, D. M. G.

KING, Michael; *see* King, A. M. H.

KING, Neil Gerald Alexander; QC 2000; *b* 14 Nov. 1956; *s* of late Joseph and of Leila King; *m* 1978, Matilda Magdalen Grenville (*née* Oppenheimer); four *d. Educ:* Harrow Sch.; New Coll., Oxford (MA). Called to the Bar, Inner Temple, 1980. Director: White Lodge

Properties Ltd, 1985–; Scarista House Ltd, 2000–; Garsington Opera Ltd, 2002–; Harrison Housing Ltd, 2004–; Univ. of York Music Press Ltd, 2014–. *Publications:* (ed jtly) Ryde on Rating and the Council Tax, 1990–2004. *Recreations:* classical music, golf, walking, Real tennis. *Address:* The White House, High Street, Whitchurch-on-Thames, Oxon RG8 7HA. *T:* (0118) 984 2915. *Clubs:* Army and Navy, Royal Automobile; Huntercombe Golf; Isle of Harris Golf; Royal Jersey Golf; Royal St George's Golf.

KING, Dr Paul Frederick; Transport Consultant, KPMG Passenger Transport Group, 1997–2004; *b* 4 Jan. 1946; *s* of Cedric Marcus King and Theresa Mary King; *m* 1980, Bertha Ines Avila de King; two *s*. *Educ:* Charterhouse Sch.; Queens' Coll., Cambridge (MA); Univ. of London (MSc, PhD). Lectr, Management Studies, Cambridge Univ., 1970–75; Dir, Special Assignments, TI Group, 1975–79; Sales and Marketing Dir, TI Raleigh, 1979–87; Planning and Marketing Dir, British Shoe Corp., 1987–90; Regional Railways, BR: Planning and Marketing Dir, 1990–93; Man. Dir, 1993–94; Gp Man. Dir, North and West, BRB, 1994–97. Non-executive Director: British Waterways, 1998–2001; Connex Rail Ltd, 1999–2003. *Recreation:* boat building. *Address:* 8 Steeple Close, SW6 3LE. *T:* (020) 7013 0818.

KING, Paul James; Managing Director, Sustainability, Lend Lease Europe, since 2015; *b* Cheshunt, Herts, 17 June 1967; *s* of Gordon King and Joyce King; partner, Gail Murray; two *s*. *Educ:* Goffs Sch., Cheshunt; Univ. of Warwick (BA Hist. 1988); Univ. of Reading (MBA 1999). Sales and mktg, Penguin Books, 1990–94; WWF-UK: Sponsorship Manager, 1994–98; Corporate Business Coordinator, 1998–99; Capacity Building secondment to WWF Bhutan, 1999–2000; Progs Sen. Manager and Campaigns Dir, WWF-UK, 2000–07; Chief Exec., UK Green Building Council, 2007–15. Chairman: Zero Carbon Hub, 2008–; Bldgs Wkg Gp, Green Construction Bd, 2011–; Sec., Bd, World Green Building Council, 2011–. Mem., Footprint Adv. Bd, Igloo Regeneration, 2006–. *Publications:* (with Pooran Desai) One Planet Living, 2006. *Recreations:* ocean and river rowing, a capella singing, writing, exotic travel, dog walking, exploring with my family.

KING, Paul William; Agent General for British Columbia in the United Kingdom and Europe, 1995–2002; *b* Srinagar, Kashmir, 6 Sept. 1943; *s* of late Rev. Canon Roderick King and of Kathleen King; *m* 1st, 1969, Susan Jane Glenny (*d* 2000); two *s*; 2nd, 2011, Mrs Jeni Sayer. *Educ:* Exeter Sch.; Univ. of Alberta (BA). With E. I. du Pont de Nemours, USA, 1964; Kodak Canada Ltd, 1965–77; Dir responsible for trade with Pacific Rim countries, Govt of Alberta, 1977–81; Director: European Ops, Alberta House, London, 1982–90; Trade and Investment, BC House, London, 1990–95. MInstD. Freeman, City of London, 1996. *Publications:* Climbing Maslow's Pyramid, 2009. *Recreations:* gardening, travel, motor-racing. *Address:* 22 Saffrons Park, Eastbourne, E Sussex BN20 7UX. *Club:* East India.

KING, Perry Allan, RDI 2000; Co-Founder and Partner, King & Miranda Design, since 1976; *b* Lambeth, London, 1938; *s* of Allan King and Kathleen King; *m* 1967, Daniela Garrone; two *d*. *Educ:* Ackworth Sch.; Birmingham Coll. of Art (NDD 1959). Nat. Service, Army, 1959–60. Designer, Wilkes and Ashmore, 1962–64; Consultant, Olivetti, Italy, 1965–70 and 1972–76; travelling in Asia, 1970–71. Visiting Professor: RCA, 1996–97; Univ. of the Arts, London, 2004. Fellow, UCE, 1995. Hon. Fellow, Glasgow Sch. of Art, 1998. *Recreations:* walking, drawing, carving, family. *Address:* King & Miranda Design srl, Via Savona 97, 20144 Milan, Italy. *T:* (02) 48953851, 335202700. *E:* king@kingmiranda.com.

KING, Peter Arthur, CBE 2009; sports management consultant, since 2010; Chair, England Athletics, since 2012; *b* Dorking, Surrey, 19 Oct. 1944; *s* of Arthur King and Alys King; *m* 1968, Judith Anne Lattimer; two *s* one *d*. *Educ:* Dorking Co. Grammar Sch. FCIS 1976; FCMA 1976; FCMI 2006; CGMA 2012. Chartered Sec. and Accountant, 1973–. Dir, Eur. Regions Airline Assoc., 1986–. CEO, British Fencing, 2012–14; CEO, 1997–2008, Exec. Dir, 2009–14, British Cycling; CEO, Pentathlon GB, 2010–11. Director: Sport and Recreation Alliance, 2008–14; Sport and Recreation Ventures Ltd, 2008–14; Commonwealth Games England, 2009–12; Mem. Bd, Sport Wales, 2012–. *Recreations:* cycling, walking, family activities, travelling. *Address:* (home) The Old Cottage, Lynwick Street, Rudgwick, Horsham, W Sussex RH12 3DN. *T:* (01403) 824073; (office) Jayes Park Courtyard, Ockley, Dorking, Surrey RH5 5RR. *T:* (01306) 621513, 07710 101801, *Fax:* (01306) 621514. *E:* peter@peteraking.co.uk. *Clubs:* Redhill Cycling, Dorking Cycling (Pres., 2013–).

KING, Rev. Peter Duncan, TD 1986; a Judge of the Upper Tribunal (Immigration and Asylum Chamber) (formerly a Vice President, Immigration Appeal Tribunal, later a Senior Immigration Judge, Asylum and Immigration Tribunal), since 2004; *b* 13 Feb. 1948; *s* of Clifford Norman King and Margaret Fraser King; *m* 1982, Maureen Diane Williams; one *s* one *d*. *Educ:* King's Coll., London (LLB 1970; AKC; MA 2011); Fitzwilliam Coll., Cambridge (MA); Westcott House, Cambridge. ACIArb 2004. Called to the Bar, Gray's Inn, 1970; Legal Officer, Army Legal Services, 1972–77; barrister in private practice, specialising in common law and crime, in London and Cambridge, 1977–2000; Plate Judge Advocate, 1995–2010, then Deputy; Special Immigration Adjudicator, 1995; Acting Stipendiary Magistrate, 1998–2000; Legal Mem., Immigration Appeals Tribunal, 1999; Dep. Dist Judge (Magistrates' Courts), 2000–; Immigration Adjudicator, 2000–04; Judge, Special Immigration Appeals Commn, 2013–. Pres., Council of Immigration Judges, 2007–09; Member: Internat. Assoc. of Refugee Law Judges, 2000–; Commonwealth Magistrates' and Judges' Assoc., 2005–. Ordained Minister in Secular Employment, C of E, 1980; Hon. Priest, Mortlake with E Sheen, 1982–; Dean for MSE, Kingston Episcopal Area, 1999–. Former Mem. Exec. and Moderator, CHRISM. Mem., Rotary Internat. (Dist Gov., 2002–03; Pres., RIBI, 2014–15. Liveryman, Co. of Arbitrators, 2004. RCT (TA) (Movt Control/Liaison), 1967–72 and 1977–97. *Recreations:* golf, bowls, Rotary International (Dist Gov., 2002–03). *Address:* Upper Tribunal (Immigration and Asylum Chamber), Field House, 15 Bream's Buildings, EC4A 1DZ.

KING, Air Vice-Marshal Peter Francis, CB 1987; OBE (mil.) 1964; FRCSE; The Senior Consultant, RAF, 1985–87; Air Vice-Marshal, Princess Mary's RAF Hospital, Halton, 1983–87; Consultant Otorhinolaryngologist, King Edward VII Hospital, Midhurst, 1988–96; *b* 17 Sept. 1922; *s* of Sqn Ldr William George King, MBE, RAF, and Florence Margaret King (*née* Sell); *m* 1945, Doreen Maxwell Aaröe (*d* 2006), 2nd *d* of Jorgen Hansen-Aaröe; one *d* (one *s* decd). *Educ:* Framlingham Coll.; King's Coll. London, 1940–42; Charing Cross Hosp., 1942–45; Univ. of Edinburgh, 1947. DLO; MRCS, LRCP; MFOM. Kitchener Med. Services Schol. for RAF, 1941; Ho. Phys., Ho. Surg., Charing Cross Hosp., 1945; commnd RAF, 1945; specialist in Otorhinolaryngology, employed Cosford, Ely, Fayid, Halton, CME; Cons. in Otorhinolaryngology, 1955; Hunterian Prof., RCS, 1964; Cons. Adviser in Otorhinolaryngology, 1966; Air Cdre 1976; Reader in Aviation Med., Inst. of Aviation Med., 1977; Whittingham Prof. in Aviation Med., IAM and RCP, 1979; QHS 1979–87; Dean of Air Force Medicine, 1983. Cons. to Herts HA, 1963, and CAA, 1973; Examiner for Dip. in Aviation Med., RCP, 1980. Littler Meml Lectr, British Soc. of Audiology, 2001. Pres., Sect. of Otology, RSocMed, 1977–78 (Sec., 1972–74); Chm., Brit. Soc. of Audiology, 1979–81 (Hon. Life Mem., 1998); Vice-Pres., RNID, 1990–2004 (Vice-Chm., 1980–88); Member: BMA, 1945– (Life Mem., 1996); Scottish Otological Soc., 1955–90; Royal Aeronaut. Soc., 1976– (FRAeS 1998); Council, Brit. Assoc. of Otorhinolaryngologists, 1960–89 (Hon. Life Mem., 1996); Editorial Bd, British Jl of Audiology, 1980–88. Fellow, Inst. of Acoustics, 1977. FRSocMed. CStJ 1987. Lady Cade Medal, RCS, 1967; (jtly) Howells Meml Prize, Univ. of London, 1992; recognised as co-descriptor of King-Kopetzky Syndrome, 1992. *Publications:* Noise and Vibration in Aviation (with J. C. Guignard), 1972; (with John Ernsting) Aviation Medicine, 1988; (jtly) Assessment of Hearing Disability, 1992; Peter Pilgrim's Progress, 2011; numerous articles, chapters, lectures and papers, in books and relevant jls on aviation otolaryngology, noise deafness, hearing conservation, tympanoplasty, facial paralysis, otic barotrauma, etc. *Recreations:* sculpture, looking at prints. *Address:* 5 Churchill Gate, Oxford Road, Woodstock, Oxon OX20 1QW. *T:* (01993) 813115. *Club:* Royal Air Force.

KING, Philip Henry Russell; QC 2002; *b* 15 Feb. 1949; *s* of Percy Sydney King and Patricia Maude (*née* Ball); *m* 2005, Jacqueline Riley (*née* Green). *Educ:* Clifton Coll.; Univ. of East Anglia (BA Hons). Called to the Bar, Inner Temple, 1974; in practice as barrister, 1976–. *Recreations:* history, food, the countryside, travel. *Address:* (chambers) 187 Fleet Street, EC4A 2AT.

KING, Phillip, CBE 1975; RA 1991 (ARA 1977); sculptor; President, Royal Academy of Arts, 1999–2004; Professor of Sculpture: Royal College of Art, 1980–90, Emeritus since 1991; Royal Academy Schools, 1990–99; *b* 1 May 1934; *s* of Thomas John King and of Gabrielle (*née* Liautard); *m* 1st, 1957, Lilian Odelle (marr. diss. 1987); (one *s* decd); 2nd, 1988, Judith Corbalis. *Educ:* Mill Hill Sch.; Christ's Coll., Cambridge Univ. (languages; Hon. Fellow, 2002); St Martin's Sch. of Art (sculpture). Teacher at St Martin's Sch. of Art, 1959–78; Asst to Henry Moore, 1959–60. Trustee: Tate Gallery, 1967–69; NPG, 1999–2004; Mem. Art Panel, Arts Council, 1977–79. Vis. Prof., Berlin Sch. of Art, 1979–81. *One-man exhibitions include:* British Pavilion, Venice Biennale, 1968; European Mus. Tour, 1974–75 (Kröller-Müller Nat. Mus., Holland; Kunsthalle, Düsseldorf; Kunsthalle, Bern; Musée Galliera, Paris; Ulster Mus., Belfast); UK Touring Exhibn, 1975–76 (Sheffield, Cumbria, Aberdeen, Glasgow, Newcastle, Portsmouth); Hayward Gall. (retrospective), 1981; Forte di Belvedere, Florence, 1997; Bernard Jacobson Gall., London, 1998, 2001, 2006 and 2008; Flowers Gall., London, 2011, 2012; Thomas Dane Gall., London, 2014. Commissions include: Cross Bend, European Patent Office, Munich, 1978; Hiroshima Mus. of Art, 1989. Hon. LittD Cambridge, 2012. First Prize, Socha Piestanskych Parkov, Piestany, Czechoslovakia, 1969; Lifetime Achievement Award, Internat. Sculpture Center, 2010. *Address:* c/o Bernard Jacobson Gallery, 6 Cork Street, W1S 3NX.

KING, Reyahn; Head of Heritage Lottery Fund, West Midlands, since 2012; *b* Edinburgh, 2 May 1965; *d* of Robert Bruce King and Jamela King (*née* Abrams); *m* 2008, Garry Morris; one step *s* one step *d*. *Educ:* Balliol Coll., Oxford (BA Hons Modern Hist.); Boston Univ. (MA Hist. of Art). AMA 1997. Archive Asst, NPG, 1990–91; Curatorial Asst, Boston Univ. Art Gall., Mass, 1991–93; Grad. Fellow, Photographic Resource Center, Boston (pt-time), 1992–93; Periodicals Librarian, National Gall., London, 1994–97; Guest Curator, Ignatius Sancho exhibn, NPG (pt-time), 1996–97; Curator, Prints and Drawings, Birmingham Mus and Art Gall., 1997–2001; Art Gall. and Mus. Develt Manager, Coventry Arts and Heritage, 2001–03; Hd, Interpretation and Exhibns, Birmingham Mus and Art Gall., 2003–07; Dir, Art Galleries, Nat. Museums Liverpool, 2007–12. Trustee, New Art Exchange, Nottingham, 2011– (Clore Fellow, 2010–11). FRSA. *Publications:* (ed) Ignatius Sancho: an African man of letters (1729–1780), 1997; Anwar Shenza, 1997; Varvara Shavrova: inscriptions, 2001; (ed) Aubrey Williams: Atlantic fire, 2010. *Recreations:* Tai Chi, seeing friends and family, enjoying food. *Address:* (office) Grosvenor House, 14 Bennetts Hill, Birmingham B2 5RS.

KING, Robert John Stephen; conductor; harpsichordist; Artistic Director, The King's Consort, since 1980; *b* 27 June 1960; *s* of Stephen King and Margaret Digby; *m* Viola Scheffel; one *s* one *d*. *Educ:* Radley Coll.; St John's Coll., Cambridge (MA). Writer; editor of much music *pre* 1750; broadcaster; conductor, orchestras and choirs, incl. New World SO, Houston SO, Minnesota SO, Atlanta SO, Seattle SO, Detroit SO, Nat. SO Washington, Stavanger SO, Aarhus SO, Norrköping SO, Danish Nat. Radio SO, Bergen Philharmonic, Malmö SO, Trondheim SO, Iceland SO, Zurich Chamber Orch., Netherlands Chamber Orch. and Chamber Choir, RAI Nat. SO, Orch. Verdi Milan, RTSI Orch., English Chamber Orch., Westdeutscher Rundfunk SO, Norddeutscher Rundfunk SO, Hamburg SO, Royal Seville SO, Orch. de Navarra, Granada SO, Swiss Radio Choir, BBC Singers, Danish Radio Choir, Buxton Fest. Opera. Work on Hollywood film scores incl. Da Vinci Code, Shrek 2, Pirates of the Caribbean, Chronicles of Narnia, Kingdom of Heaven. Artistic Director: Aldeburgh Easter Fest., 1998–2000; Nordic Baroque Music Fest., 2001–04; Internat. Organ Week Nuremberg, 2003–07. *Publications:* Henry Purcell, 1994; numerous musical edns incl. English Church Music, vol. 1, 2010, vol. 2, 2011. *Recreations:* ski-ing, cricket, lupin growing. *E:* info@tkcworld.org. *W:* www.tkcworld.org.

KING, Robert Shirley; Under Secretary, Department of Health and Social Security, 1976–80; *b* 12 July 1920; *s* of late Rev. William Henry King, MC, TD, MA, and Dorothy King (*née* Sharpe); *m* 1st, 1947, Margaret Siddall (*d* 1956); two *d*; 2nd, 1958, Mary Rowell (*d* 1996); one *s* two *d*; 3rd, 1998, Daphne Shercliff. *Educ:* Alexandra Road Sch., Oldham; Manchester Grammar Sch.; Trinity Coll., Cambridge (Schol., MA). Served War, RAF, 1940–45. Colonial Service, Tanganyika, 1949–62 (Dist Comr, Bukoba, 1956–58, Geita, 1959–62); Home Office: Principal, 1962–69 (seconded to Civil Service Dept, 1968–69); Asst Sec., 1969–70; transf., with Children's Dept, to DHSS, 1971; Asst Sec., DHSS, 1971–76; Sec., Wkg Party on Role and Tasks of Social Workers, Nat. Inst. for Social Work, 1980–82; part-time Asst Sec., Home Office, 1985–86. Sec., Health Promotion Res. Trust, 1984–89. Member Council: British and Foreign Sch. Soc., 1982–89; Shape, 1982–89. Governor: Cheshunt Foundn, 1976–83; Bell Educnl Trust, 1984–89. *Recreations:* walking, reading.

See also H. M. King.

KING, Ven. Robin Lucas Colin; Archdeacon of Stansted, since 2013; *b* Quebec, Canada, 15 Feb. 1959; *s* of Colin King and Alison King; *m* 1988, Katharine Mighall; two *s*. *Educ:* King's Sch., Canterbury; Dundee Univ. (MA Hons 1981); Ridley Hall Theol Coll. Ordained deacon, 1989, priest, 1990; Curate, St Augustine's, Ipswich, 1989–92; Vicar, St Mary's, Bures, 1992–2013; Rural Dean, Sudbury, 2006–13. Hon. Canon, St Edmundsbury Cath., 2009–13. *Recreations:* rowing, sailing, diving. *Address:* The House, The Street, Bradwell, Essex CM77 8EL. *T:* (01376) 563357. *E:* rlcking@hotmail.co.uk.

KING, Roger Douglas; Chief Executive, Road Haulage Association, 2000–09; *b* 26 Oct. 1943; *s* of Douglas and Cecilie King; *m* 1976, Jennifer Susan (*née* Sharpe); twin *s* one *d*. *Educ:* Solihull Sch. Served automobile engrg apprenticeship with British Motor Corp., 1960–66; sales rep., 1966–74; own manufg business, 1974–81; self-employed car product distributor, 1982–83; Dir of Public Affairs, 1992–99, Dep. Chief Exec., 1999–2000, SMMT. Director: Prince Michael Road Safety Awards Scheme, 1992–2009; Roadsafe, 2000–09. Non-executive Director: Nat. Express Hldgs, 1988–91; Coventry Bldg Soc., 1995–2007. Vice Chm., Internat. Road Transport Union Goods Transport Council, 2006–09. MP (C) Birmingham, Northfield, 1983–92. PPS to Minister for Local Govt, 1987–88, for Water and Planning, 1988, DoE, to Sec. of State for Employment, 1989–92. Mem., H of C Transport Select Cttee, 1984–87; Vice-Chm., All Party Motor Industry Gp, 1985–92; Jt Sec., Cons. Tourism Cttee, 1985–87. Volunteer, British Motor Industry Heritage Trust, 2012–. FIMI 1986–2009. Mem., Co. of Carmen, 2001–10. *Recreation:* classic car motoring. *Address:* 241 Tessall Lane, Northfield, Birmingham B31 5EQ. *T:* (0121) 476 6649.

KING, Prof. Roger Patrick; Vice-Chancellor, University of Lincolnshire and Humberside (formerly Humberside), 1992–2000; *b* 31 May 1945; *s* of late Timothy Francis King and Vera May King; *m* 1966, Susan Winifred Ashworth; one *d*. *Educ:* Wimbledon Coll.; Univ. of London (BSc Hons Econ.); Univ. of Birmingham (MSocSci). HM Civil Service, 1963; Sales Management Trainee, United Glass, 1964; Sales Manager, Marley Tiles, 1965; Lectr and Sen. Lectr in Social Scis, Manchester Polytechnic, 1970–75; Principal Lectr, later Head of Dept of Behavioural Scis, Huddersfield Poly., 1976–85; Dep. Dir, 1985–89, Dir and Chief Exec., 1989–92, Humberside Poly. Vis. Fellow, ACU, 2003–05; Visiting Professor: OU, 2003–11;

Univ. of Bath, 2010–; Adjunct Prof., Univ. of Queensland, 2010–; Res. Associate, LSE, 2007–. Co-Chm., Higher Educn Commn's Inquiry, 2013 (Report, Regulating Higher Educn, 2013). *Publications:* (with N. Nugent) The British Right, 1977; (with N. Nugent) Respectable Rebels, 1979; The Middle Class, 1981; Capital and Politics, 1983; The State in Modern Society, 1986; (with J. Simmie) The State in Action, 1990; (with G. Kendall) The State, Democracy and Globalization, 2004; The University in the Global Age, 2004; The Regulatory State in an Age of Governance, 2007; Governing Universities Globally, 2009; (jtly) Handbook of Globalization and Higher Education, 2011; (jtly) The Globalization of Higher Education, 2013. *Recreations:* reading, running, swimming. *Address:* Griffins, Hanging Birch Lane, Horam, Heathfield, E Sussex TN21 0BH. *T:* (01435) 813443.

KING, Sarah Penelope, RDI 2008; textile designer and consultant; designer, First Eleven Studio; designer and consultant, William Yeoward; *b* Welwyn Garden City, 1958; *d* of Hugh and Phoebe King. *Educ:* Goldsmith's Coll., London Univ. (BA Fine Art Textiles); Manchester Metropolitan Univ. (MA Textile Design). Textile design: for fashion, 1987–95; for furnishing fabrics, 1995–2009; exhibns with Crafts Council of GB, 1987–95. *Recreations:* walking, food, cinema. *Address:* 35 St Martins Road, SW9 0SP. *E:* sarah.king21@btinternet.com. *Club:* Two Brydges.

KING, Stephen Edwin; author; *b* Portland, Maine, 21 Sept. 1947; *s* of Donald King and Nellie Ruth King (*née* Pillsbury); *m* 1971, Tabitha Jane Spruce; two *s* one *d*. *Educ:* Lisbon Falls High Sch.; Univ. of Maine at Orono (BS 1970). Laundry worker, 1970; English Teacher, Hampden Acad., 1971–73; writer in residence, Univ. of Maine at Orono, 1978–79. *Screenplay,* Sleepwalkers, 1991; many of his stories have been filmed; writer, TV series, Kingdom Hospital, 2004; dir, Maximum Overdrive, 1986. *Publications:* Carrie, 1974; 'Salem's Lot, 1975; The Shining, 1976; The Stand, 1978; Night Shift (short stories), 1978; Firestarter, 1980; Danse Macabre, 1981; Cujo, 1981; Different Seasons, 1982; The Dark Tower: vol. 1, The Gunslinger, 1982, vol. 2, The Drawing of the Three, 1987, vol. 3, Waste Lands, 1991, vol. 4, Wizard and Glass, 1997, vol. 5, Wolves of the Calla, 2003, vol. 6, Song of Susannah, 2004, vol. 7, The Dark Tower, 2004; Christine, 1983; Pet Sematary, 1983; (jtly) The Talisman, 1984; Cycle of the Werewolf, 1985; It, 1986; Skeleton Crew (short stories), 1986; The Eyes of the Dragon, 1987; Misery, 1987; The Tommyknockers, 1987; The Dark Half, 1989; The Stand (unabridged edn), 1990; Four Past Midnight, 1990; (jtly) Dark Visions, 1990; Needful Things, 1991; Gerald's Game, 1992; Dolores Claiborne, 1992; Nightmares and Dreamscapes (short stories), 1993; Insomnia, 1994; Desperation, 1996; The Green Mile, 1996; Bag of Bones, 1998; The Girl Who Loved Tom Gordon, 1999; Hearts In Atlantis, 1999; On Writing: a memoir of the craft, 2000; Dreamcatcher, 2001; Everything's Eventual (short stories), 2002; From a Buick 8, 2002; (with Stewart O'Nan) Faithful: two diehard Boston Red Sox fans chronicle the historic 2004 season, 2004; Cell, 2006; Lisey's Story, 2006; Duma Key, 2008; Just After Sunset (short stories), 2008; Under the Dome, 2009; Full Dark, No Stars, 2010; 11.22.63, 2011; Joyland, 2013; Doctor Sleep, 2013; Mr Mercedes, 2014; Revival, 2014; Finders Keepers, 2015; (as Richard Bachman): Rage, 1977; The Long Walk, 1979; Roadwork, 1981; The Running Man, 1982; Thinner, 1984; The Regulators, 1996; Blaze, 2007. *Address:* c/o Hodder & Stoughton, 338 Euston Road, NW1 3BH.

KING, Hon. Sir Timothy (Roger Alan), Kt 2007; **Hon. Mr Justice King;** a Judge of the High Court of Justice, Queen's Bench Division, since 2007; *b* 5 April 1949; *s* of late Harold Bonsall King and Dorothy King; *m* 1986, Bernadette Goodman. *Educ:* Booker Avenue County Primary Sch., Liverpool; Liverpool Inst. High Sch.; Lincoln Coll., Oxford (MA, BCL). Called to the Bar, Lincoln's Inn, 1973 (Bencher, 2000); Mem., Northern Circuit, 1973; QC 1991; a Recorder, 1991–2007. *Recreations:* travel, Association football. *Address:* Royal Courts of Justice, Strand, WC2A 2LL. *Club:* Travellers.

KING, His Honour Timothy Russell; a Circuit Judge, 1995–2012; *b* 4 June 1946; *s* of late Charles Albert King and Elizabeth Lily King (*née* Alexander); *m* 1st, 1973, Christine Morison (marr. diss. 1979); two *s*; 2nd, 1989, Rotraud Jane (*née* Oppermann). *Educ:* St Mary's Coll., Bitterne Park, Southampton; Inns of Court Sch. of Law. HM Diplomatic Service (Colonial Office), 1966–67; called to the Bar, Gray's Inn, 1970; in practice, SE Circuit, 1970–86; Dep. Judge Advocate, 1986; AJAG, 1990–95; Asst Recorder, 1989–93; Recorder, 1993–95. Legal Mem., Restricted Patients Panel, Mental Health Review Tribunal, 2002–; Mem., Public Chairs Forum, 2010– (Mem., Mgt Cttee, 2011–13); Chm., Lord Chancellor's Adv. Cttee on Conscientious Objectors, 2008–13. Dir, Osborne GC Ltd, 2013–. Pres., St Leonard's Soc., 1998–2006. *Recreations:* sailing, ski-ing, classical music, reading, walking, cooking, golf. *Address:* c/o Judicial Office, Ministry of Justice, 102 Petty France, SW1H 9AJ. *Clubs:* Royal London Yacht, Osborne Golf (Cowes).

KING, Prof. Ursula, PhD; freelance lecturer and writer; Professor Emerita of Theology and Religious Studies, and Senior Research Fellow at Institute for Advanced Studies, University of Bristol, since 2002; Professorial Research Associate, Department of the Study of Religions (formerly Centre for Gender and Religions Research), School of Oriental and African Studies, University of London, since 2002; Fellow Heythrop College, University of London, since 2004; *b* 22 Sept. 1938; *d* of Hedwig and Adolf Brenke; *m* 1963, Prof. Anthony Douglas King; four *d*. *Educ:* Univs of Bonn, Munich, Paris (STL), Delhi (MA; Indian Philosophical Congress Gold Medal, 1969) and London (PhD). Lectr in Divinity, Coloma Coll. of Educn, 1963–65; Visiting Lecturer, 1965–70: Dept of Philosophy, Univ. of Delhi; Indian Inst. of Technology; Indian Social Inst.; Lectr and Sen. Lectr, Dept of Theology and Religious Studies, Univ. of Leeds, 1971–89; S. A. Cook Bye-Fellow, Newnham Coll. and Gonville and Caius Coll., Cambridge, 1976–77; Bristol University: Prof. of Theology and Religious Studies, 1989–2002; Head of Dept, 1989–97; Dir, Centre for Comparative Studies in Religion and Gender, 1996–2002. Pres., Catherine of Siena Virtual Coll., 2008–16. Visiting Professor: in Feminist Theology, Univ. of Oslo, 1999–2001; in Ecumenical Theology and Interreligious Dialogue, Xavier Univ., Cincinnati, 1999; Dist. Bingham Prof. of Humanities, Univ. of Louisville, Ky, 2005. Lectures include: Sri Aurobindo Meml, London, 1971; Cardinal Bea Meml, London, 1977; Sir Francis Younghusband Meml, London, 1978; Teilhard de Chardin Exhibn, London, 1983; Cardinal Heenan, London, 1984; Hibbert, London, 1984; Lambeth Interfaith, Lambeth Palace, 1985; Teape, Delhi, Calcutta, Santiniketan, 1986; Bampton, 1996, Whyte, 2000, Sir Alister Hardy, 2002, Oxford; Sir George Trevelyan, London, 2002; Anne Spencer, Bristol, 2002; Julian of Norwich, Norwich, 2007; Burke, UCSD, 2012; wide internat. lecturing in Europe, N America, Asia, Australasia, and S Africa. Past mem. of many editorial and adv. bds of jls; consultant to numerous internat. publishers. President: British Assoc. for the Study of Religions, 1991–94; European Soc. of Women in Theological Research, 1993–95; Vice-Pres., World Congress of Faiths, 1972–; Mem., Shap Working Party on World Religions in Educn, 1975–. Judge, Templeton Prize, 2015–. Life FRSA. Hon. DD: Edinburgh, 1996; Dayton, 2003; Hon. Dr Theol Oslo, 2000. Student awards from Germany and France. *Publications:* Towards a New Mysticism, 1980; The Spirit of One Earth, 1989; Women and Spirituality, 1989; (ed) Turning Points in Religious Studies, 1990; (ed) Feminist Theology from the Third World, 1994; (ed) Religion and Gender, 1995; Spirit of Fire: the life and vision of Teilhard de Chardin, 1996, new edn 2016; Christ in All Things: exploring spirituality with Teilhard de Chardin, 1997; (ed) Pierre Teilhard de Chardin: writings selected with an introduction, 1999; (ed) Spirituality and Society in the New Millennium, 2001; Christian Mystics: their lives and legacies throughout the ages, 2001; (ed with Tina Beattie) Gender, Religion and Diversity: crosscultural approaches, 2004; The Search for Spirituality, 2008; Teilhard de Chardin and Eastern Religions, 2011; contribs to acad. jls. *Recreations:* walking, reading, travelling, meeting old friends.

KING, Sir Wayne Alexander, 8th Bt *cr* 1815; Regional Program Manager, The Canadian Hearing Society, Sault Ste Marie, since 2009; *b* 2 Feb. 1962; *s* of Sir Peter Alexander King, 7th Bt, and Jean Margaret (who *m* 2nd, 1978, Rev. Richard Graham Mackenzie), *d* of Christopher Thomas Cavell, Deal; *S* father, 1973; *m* 1984 (marr. diss. 1990); one *s*; *m* 2003, Deborah Lynn, *d* of Douglas Arthur and Marilyn MacDougall, Sydney, NS. *Educ:* Sir Roger Manwood's Sch., Sandwich, Kent; Algonquin Coll., Ottawa, Ont (majored in Accounting and Retail Management). Canadian Hearing Society: Develt Co-ordinator, Toronto, 2004–06; Manager of Admin, Kitchener and Waterloo, 2006–08. *Recreation:* all sports. *Heir: s* Peter Richard Donald King, *b* 4 May 1988. *Address:* 64 Fields Square, Sault Ste Marie, P6B 6H2, Canada.

KING-HELE, Desmond George, FRS 1966; author; Deputy Chief Scientific Officer, Space Department, Royal Aircraft Establishment, Farnborough, 1968–88, retired; *b* 3 Nov. 1927; *s* of late S. G. and of B. King-Hele, Seaford, Sussex; *m* 1954, Marie Thérèse Newman (separated 1992); two *d*. *Educ:* Epsom Coll.; Trinity Coll., Cambridge. BA (1st cl. hons Mathematics) 1948; MA 1952. At RAE, Farnborough, 1948–88, working on space research from 1955. Mem., International Academy of Astronautics, 1961. Chairman: Satellite Optical Tracking Cttee, Royal Soc., 1972–97; History of Science Grants Cttee, Royal Soc., 1990–93; British Nat. Cttee for History of Science, Medicine and Technol., 1985–89; Adv. Panel for Culture of Sci., Technol. and Medicine, BL, 1992–2002. Pres., Birmingham and Midland Inst., 2002. Lectures: Symons, RMetS, 1961; Duke of Edinburgh's, Royal Inst. of Navigation, 1964; Jeffreys, RAS, 1971; Halley, Oxford, 1974; Bakerian, Royal Soc., 1974; Sydenham, Soc. of Apothecaries, 1981; H. L. Welsh, Univ. of Toronto, 1982; Milne, Oxford, 1984; Wilkins, Royal Soc., 1997. FIMA; FRAS. Hon. DSc Aston, 1979; DUniv Surrey, 1986. Eddington Medal, RAS, 1971; Charles Chree Medal, Inst. of Physics, 1971; Lagrange Prize, Acad. Royale de Belgique, 1972; Nordberg Medal, Internat. Cttee on Space Res., 1990. Editor, Notes and Records of Royal Soc., 1989–96. *Publications:* Shelley: His Thought and Work, 1960, 3rd edn 1984; Satellites and Scientific Research, 1960; Erasmus Darwin, 1963; Theory of Satellite Orbits in an Atmosphere, 1964; (ed) Space Research V, 1965; Observing Earth Satellites, 1966, 2nd edn 1983; (ed) Essential Writings of Erasmus Darwin, 1968; The End of the Twentieth Century?, 1970; Poems and Trixies, 1972; Doctor of Revolution, 1977; (ed) The Letters of Erasmus Darwin, 1981; (ed) The RAE Table of Earth Satellites, 1981, 4th edn 1990; Animal Spirits, 1983; Erasmus Darwin and the Romantic Poets, 1986; Satellite Orbits in an Atmosphere: theory and applications, 1987; A Tapestry of Orbits, 1992; (ed) John Herschel, 1992; (ed) A Concordance to the Botanic Garden, 1994; Erasmus Darwin: a life of unequalled achievement (Society of Authors' Medical History Prize), 1999; Antic and Romantic (poems), 2000; (ed) Charles Darwin's The Life of Erasmus Darwin, 2002; (ed) The Collected Letters of Erasmus Darwin, 2007 (ed jtly) The Shorter Poems of Erasmus Darwin, 2012; Erasmus Darwin and Evolution, 2014; *radio drama scripts:* A Mind of Universal Sympathy, 1973; The Lunaticks, 1978; over 400 papers in Proc. Royal Society, Nature, Keats-Shelley Meml Bull., New Scientist, Planetary and Space Science, and other scientific and literary jls. *Recreations:* tennis, reading, writing verse. *Address:* 7 Hilltops Court, 65 North Lane, Buriton, Hants GU31 5RS. *T:* (01730) 261646.

KING MURRAY, Ronald; *see* Murray, Rt Hon. Lord.

KING-REYNOLDS, Guy Edwin; Head Master, Dauntsey's School, West Lavington, 1969–85; *b* 9 July 1923; *er s* of late Dr H. E. King Reynolds, York; *m* 1st, 1947, Norma Lansdowne Russell (*d* 1949); 2nd, 1950, Jeanne Nancy Perris Rhodes; one *d*. *Educ:* St Peter's Sch., York; Emmanuel Coll., Cambridge (1944–47). LRAM (speech and drama) 1968. Served RAF, 1942–44. BA 1946, MA 1951. Asst Master, Glenhow Prep. Sch., 1947–48; Head of Geography Dept, Solihull Sch., Warwickshire, 1948–54; family business, 1954–55; Head of Geography, Portsmouth Grammar Sch., 1955–57; Solihull School: Housemaster, 1957–63, Second Master, 1963–69. Part-time Lecturer in International Affairs, Extra-Mural Dept, Birmingham Univ., 1951–55, 1957–62; Chm., Solihull WEA, 1957–62. Mem., BBC Regl Adv. Council, 1970–73. Headmasters' Conference: Mem., 1969–85; Mem. Cttee, 1977–78, Chm., SW Div., 1978; Member: Political and PR Cttee, 1971–79; Governing Council, ISIS, 1977–83; Editl Bd, Conference and Common Room, 1977–84. Mem., DES Assisted Places Cttee, 1980–93. Vice-Chm., Boarding Schs Assoc., 1975–76; Mem. Cttee, GBA, 1986–89, 1990–97. Governor: St Peter's Sch., York, 1984–97; Dean Close Sch., Cheltenham, 1985–94 (Vice Pres., 1994–99, and Life Gov., 1994); La Retraite, Salisbury, 1985–88. Mem., Bp of Salisbury's DAC, 1983–86. JP: Solihull, 1965–69; Wiltshire, 1970–91 (Chm., 1982–85, Vice-Chm., 1985–91, Devizes Bench); Avon (Bath), 1991–93. Freeman, City of London, 1988. *Recreations:* drama (director and actor); travel. *Address:* 14 Pulteney Mews, Great Pulteney Street, Bath BA2 4DS.

KING-TENISON, family name of **Earl of Kingston**.

KINGARTH, Rt Hon. Lord; Hon. Derek Robert Alexander Emslie; PC 2006; a Senator of the College of Justice in Scotland, 1997–2010; *b* 21 June 1949; *s* of Baron Emslie, PC, MBE; *m* 1974, Elizabeth Jane Cameron Carstairs, *d* of Andrew McLaren Carstairs; one *s* two *d*. *Educ:* Edinburgh Acad.; Trinity Coll., Glenalmond; Gonville and Caius Coll., Cambridge (Hist. Schol.; BA); Edinburgh Univ. (LLB). Advocate 1974; Standing Jun. Counsel, DHSS, 1979–87; Advocate Depute, 1985–88; QC (Scot.) 1987; part time Chairman: Pension Appeal Tribunal (Scotland), 1988–95; Medical Appeal Tribunal (Scotland), 1990–95. Vice-Dean, Faculty of Advocates, 1995–97. *Recreations:* golf, cinema, football. *Address:* 35 Ann Street, Edinburgh EH4 1PL. *T:* (0131) 332 6648.

See also Rt Hon. Lord Emslie.

KINGHAM, Teresa Jane, (Tess); Romney Marsh Partnership Co-ordinator, since 2013; *b* 4 May 1963; *d* of Roy Thomas Kingham and Patricia Ribian Kingham (*née* Murphy); *m* 1991, Mark Luetchford; one *s* two *d* (of whom one *s* one *d* are twins). *Educ:* Dartford Girls' Grammar Sch.; Royal Holloway Coll., Univ. of London (BA Hons German 1984); Univ. of East Anglia (PGCE Mod. Langs 1985); University Coll. London (MA Egyptian Archaeol. 2007). Appeals Dir, War on Want, 1986–90; Mktg and Communications Dir, Blue Cross (animal welfare), 1990–92; Editor, Youth Express, Daily Express, 1992–94; Communications Exec., Oxfam, 1994–96. Contested (Lab) Cotswolds, EP elecn, 1994. MP (Lab) Gloucester, 1997–2001. Chair, All Party Gp on Western Sahara, 1997–2001. Mem., Egypt Exploration Soc. *Publications:* (with Jim Coe) The Good Campaigns Guide, 2nd edn 2005. *Recreations:* international travel/affairs, archaeology, walking with family.

KINGHAN, Neil, CB 2005; public policy reviewer; student of United States History, University College London; *b* 20 Aug. 1951; *s* of late Derek Kinghan and of Esme Kinghan; *m* 1994, Dr Lilian Pusavat. *Educ:* Hertford Coll., Oxford (MA, MPhil); University Coll. London (MA US Hist. 2013). Department of the Environment: admin trainee, 1975; Private Sec. to Parly Under-Sec. of State, 1978–80; Principal, 1980; Private Sec. to Minister of State, 1984–87; Asst Sec., 1987; Head: Sport and Recreation Div., 1987–89; Homelessness Policy Div., 1989–92; Director: Housing Policy, 1992–94; DoE Mgt Review, 1994–96; Local Govt Finance, 1996–97; Local Government Association: Dir, Local Govt Finance, 1997–2002; Econ. and Envmtl Policy, 2002–03; Dir Gen., Local and Regl Govt, then Local Govt and Fire, ODPM, subseq. Local and Regl Governance, then Fire and Resilience, DCLG, 2003–07; Dir Gen., Equality and Human Rights Commn, 2009–10. Consultant, Essex CC, 2007–08; Advr, Assoc. of Chief Execs of Voluntary Orgns, 2011–13; Consultant, Executive Action, 2011–13; Independent Reviews: of Riot in Clapham Junction for Wandsworth BC, 2011; of Riot Damages Act 1886 for Home Sec., 2013. Chm., Policy Commn on Primary Sch. Orgn in Shropshire, 2008–09. Chm., Mgt Bd, Fire Service Coll., 2008–09. Trustee,

Naomi House Children's Hospice, 2005–. FRSA 2007. *Recreations:* ski-ing, cricket, watching ballet, cycling, trying to run a marathon in less than five hours. *E:* neil.kinghan@btinternet.com. *Clubs:* Athenæum; Surrey County Cricket.

KINGHORN, Prof. George Robert, OBE 2012; MD; FRCP, FRCPGlas; Clinical Director, NIHR South Yorkshire Comprehensive Local Research Network, 2011–15; Hon. Consultant in Genitourinary Medicine, Sheffield Teaching Hospitals NHS Foundation Trust, since 2013; *b* 17 Aug. 1949; *s* of Alan Douglas Kinghorn and Lilian Isabel Kinghorn; *m* 1973, Sheila Anne Littlewood; one *s* one *d*. *Educ:* Newburn Manor Sch.; Royal Grammar Sch., Newcastle upon Tyne; Univ. of Sheffield (MB ChB 1972; MD 1984). FRCP 1988; FRCPGlas 2003. Sen. Registrar, Royal Infirmary, Sheffield, 1976–79; Consultant Physician in Genitourinary Medicine: Leeds Gen. Infirmary, 1979; Sheffield, 1979–2013; Hon. Sen. Clinical Lectr, 1979–2006, Hon. Prof., 2006–, Univ. of Sheffield; Clinical Dir for Communicable Diseases, Sheffield Teaching Hosps NHS Foundn Trust, 1991–2010. Mem., Ind. Adv. Gp on Sexual Health and HIV, 2003–10. Mem., MRC Coll. of Experts, 2005–10. Fellow, BASHH (formerly Med. Soc. for Study of Venereal Diseases), 2001 (Mem., 1976; Pres., 1991–2001; Trustee, 2001–05; Lifetime Achievement Award, 2009; Hon. Life Fellow, 2011); Trustee, Med. Foundn for HIV and Sexual Health, 2003–. FRSocMed 1998. Freeman: Soc. of Apothecaries, 2007; City of London, 2011. Platinum Nat. Clinical Excellence Award, 2006. *Publications:* scientific papers and book chapters on genital tract infections, sexual health and HIV. *Recreations:* gardening, golf, travel, photography. *Address:* 3 Serlby Drive, Harthill, Sheffield, S Yorks S26 7UJ. *T:* (01909) 772610. *E:* george.kinghorn@sth.nhs.uk, g.r.kinghorn@sheffield.ac.uk, g.r.kinghorn@nihr.ac.uk.

See also M. A. Kinghorn.

KINGHORN, Myra Anne; Chair, Scheme Management Committee, European Payments Council, 2007–15; *b* 24 Jan. 1951; *d* of Alan Douglas Kinghorn and Lilian Isabel Kinghorn; *m* 1986, Richard John Haycocks; two *s*. *Educ:* La Sagesse High Sch., Newcastle upon Tyne; Univ. of Wales, Aberystwyth (BLib Jt Hons (Hist. and Librarianship) 1973). FCA (ACA 1977); CDir 2000. Exec. Manager, Ernst & Young, 1984–88; Chief Exec. and Company Sec., Investors Compensation Scheme, 1988–2001; non-exec. Dir, Serious Fraud Office, 2001–04; Chief Exec., Pension Protection Fund, 2004–06. Non-exec. Mem., OPRA, 2003–04. Mem., Architects Registration Bd, 2008–March 2016. Gov., Morley Coll., 2007– (Vice Chair, 2007–15); Mem., Develt Adv. Bd, Aberystwyth Univ., 2015– (Chair, 2010–15). *Recreations:* theatre visits, history, music, photography, French, cooking. *Address:* 10 Courtenay Drive, Beckenham, Kent BR3 6YE. *Club:* Institute of Directors.

See also G. R. Kinghorn.

KINGMAN, Sir John (Frank Charles), Kt 1985; FRS 1971; mathematician; Vice-Chancellor, University of Bristol, 1985–2001; *b* 28 Aug. 1939; *er s* of late Dr F. E. T. Kingman, FRSC and Maud (*née* Harley); *m* 1964, Valerie Cromwell, FSA, FRHistS (Dir, History of Parlt, 1991–2001; High Sheriff of Bristol, 2004–05), *d* of late F. Cromwell, OBE, ISO; one *s* one *d*. *Educ:* Christ's Coll., Finchley; Pembroke Coll., Cambridge (MA, ScD; Smith's Prize, 1962; Hon. Fellow, 1988). CStat 1993. Fellow of Pembroke Coll., 1961–65, and Asst Lectr in Mathematics, 1962–64, Lectr, 1964–65, Univ. of Cambridge; Reader in Maths and Stats, 1965–66, Prof. 1966–69, Univ. of Sussex; Prof. of Maths, Univ. of Oxford, 1969–85; Fellow, St Anne's Coll., Oxford, 1978–85, Hon. Fellow, 1985; N. M. Rothschild & Sons Prof. of Mathematical Scis, Dir of Isaac Newton Inst. for Mathematical Scis, and Fellow of Pembroke Coll., Univ. of Cambridge, 2001–06. Visiting appointments: Univ. of Western Australia, 1963, 1974; Stanford Univ., USA, 1968; ANU, 1978. Chairman: Science Bd, SRC, 1979–81; SERC, 1981–85; founding Chm., Statistics Commn, 2000–03; Vice-Pres., Parly and Scientific Cttee, 1986–89, 2002–05 (Vice-Chm., 1983–86); Mem. Bd, British Council, 1986–91. Chm., Cttee of Inquiry into the Teaching of English Language, 1987–88. Director: IBM UK Holdings Ltd, 1985–95; Beecham Group plc, 1986–89; SmithKline Beecham plc, 1989–90; Bristol United Press plc, 1989–2001 (Dep. Chm., 1998–2001); British Technology Group plc, 1992 (Mem. Council, British Technol. Gp, 1984–92); SW RHA, 1990–94; Avon HA, 1996–99. Chm., 1973–76, Vice-Pres., 1976–92, Inst. of Statisticians; President: Royal Statistical Soc., 1987–89 (Vice-Pres., 1977–79; Guy Medal in Silver, 1981, in Gold, 2013; Hon. Fellow, 1993); London Math. Soc., 1990–92; European Math. Soc., 2003–06. Mem., Brighton Co. Borough Council, 1968–71; Chm., Regency Soc. of Brighton and Hove, 1975–81. MAE 1995; AcSS 2000. For. Associate, US Nat. Acad. of Scis, 2007. Hon. Senator, Univ. of Hannover, 1991. Hon. DSc: Sussex, 1983; Southampton, 1985; West of England, 1993; Brunel, 2004; Hon. LLD: Bristol, 1989; Queen's Univ., Kingston, Ontario, 1999; Hon. DPhil Cheltenham and Gloucester, 1998; Dr *hc* St Petersburg Univ. of Humanities and Social Scis, 1994. Royal Medal, Royal Soc., 1983. Officier des Palmes Académiques, 1989. *Publications:* Introduction to Measure and Probability (with S. J. Taylor), 1966; The Algebra of Queues, 1966; Regenerative Phenomena, 1972; Mathematics of Genetic Diversity, 1980; Poisson Processes, 1993; papers in mathematical and statistical jls. *Address:* Harley Lodge, Clifton Down, Bristol BS8 3BP. *Clubs:* Lansdowne, Reform; Clifton (Bristol).

See also J. O. F. Kingman.

KINGMAN, John Oliver Frank; Second Permanent Secretary, HM Treasury, since 2012; *b* 24 April 1969; *s* of Sir John Frank Charles Kingman, *qv*. *Educ:* Dragon Sch., Oxford; Westminster Sch. (Queen's Schol.); St John's Coll., Oxford (Casberd Schol.; BA 1st Cl. Hons). HM Treasury, 1991–94, Private Sec. to Financial Sec., 1993–94; Prin. Private Sec. to Sec. of State, DNH, 1994–95; Lex Columnist, FT, 1995–97; Gp Chief Exec.'s Office, BP, 1997–98; Press Sec. to Chancellor of the Exchequer, 1999–2000; HM Treasury: Hd, Productivity and Structural Reform, 2000–02; Dir, Enterprise and Growth Unit, 2003–06; Man. Dir, Finance and Industry, 2006; Man. Dir, Public Services and Growth, 2006–08; Second Perm. Sec., 2007–08; Chief Exec., UK Financial Investments Ltd, 2008–09; Global Co-Hd, Financial Instns Gp, Rothschild, 2010–12. Dir, EIB, 2003–06; non-exec. Dir, Framestore CFC Ltd, 2004–06. Mem., Global Adv. Bd, Centre for Corporate Reputation, Univ. of Oxford, 2008–. Vis. Fellow, Inst. of Political and Econ. Governance, Univ. of Manchester, 2003–06; World Fellow, Yale Univ., 2004. Mem., Develt Trust Bd, St Martin-in-the-Fields, 2006–09; Trustee, Royal Opera Hse, 2014–. Freeman, Goldsmiths' Co., 2012–. *Address:* HM Treasury, 1 Horse Guards Road, SW1A 2HQ.

KINGS, Rt Rev. Dr Graham Ralph; Mission Theologian in the Anglican Communion, since 2015; an Honorary Assistant Bishop, Diocese of Southwark, since 2015; *b* Barkingside, 10 Oct. 1953; *s* of Ralph Norman Kings and Kathleen Eugenia Kings (*née* Warren); *m* 1977, Alison Audrey Britton; three *d*. *Educ:* Buckhurst Hill County High Sch.; RMA Sandhurst; Hertford Coll., Oxford (MA Theology 1980); Ridley Hall Theol Coll., Cambridge; Selwyn Coll., Cambridge (DipTh 1980); Utrecht Univ. (PhD 2002). 2nd Lt, 5th Royal Inniskilling Dragoon Guards, 1973; Caretaker, All Souls', Langham Place, 1977; ordained deacon, 1980, priest, 1981; Asst Curate, St Mark, Harlesden, 1980–84; CMS Mission Partner, Kenya, 1985–91; Dir of Studies, 1985–88, Vice Principal, 1989–91, St Andrew's Coll., Kabare; Overseas Advr, Henry Martyn Trust, Cambridge, 1992–95; Lectr, Mission Studies, 1992–2000, Dir, Henry Martyn Centre for Mission Studies and World Christianity, 1995–2000, Cambridge Theol Fedn; Affiliated Lectr, Univ. of Cambridge, 1996–2000; Vicar, St Mary's, Islington, 2000–09; Bishop Suffragan of Sherborne, 2009–15. Theol Sec., Fulcrum, 2003–. Honorary Curate: Holy Trinity, Cambridge, 1992–96; St Andrew's, Chesterton, 1996–2000. Select Preacher (Ramsden), Univ. of Cambridge, 1996; Hon. Fellow, Dept of Theology and Religion, Durham Univ., 2015–. *Publications:* (jtly) Offerings from Kenya to Anglicanism: liturgical texts and contexts, 2001; Christianity Connected: Hindus, Muslims and the world in the letters of Max Warren and Roger Hooker, 2002; Signs and Seasons: a guide for your Christian journey, 2008. *Recreations:* walking, swimming, tennis, cricket, poetry. *Address:* 483b Southwark Park Road, SE16 2JP. *E:* graham.kings@durham.ac.uk.

KINGSALE, 36th Baron *cr* 1223 (by some reckonings 31st Baron); **Nevinson Mark de Courcy;** Baron Courcy and Baron of Ringrone; Premier Baron of Ireland; *b* 11 May 1958; *s* of late Nevinson Russell de Courcy, and Nora Lydia de Courcy (*née* Plint); *S* cousin, 2005. *Educ:* Auckland Grammar Sch.; Univ. of Auckland; Emmanuel Coll., Cambridge. *Recreations:* reading, conservation, jigsaws. *Address:* 22 Armadale Road, Remuera, Auckland 1050, New Zealand. *T:* (9) 5248875. *E:* nmdecourcy@clear.net.nz.

KINGSBOROUGH, Viscount; Charles Avery Edward King-Tenison; *b* 18 Nov. 2000; *s* and *heir* of Earl of Kingston, *qv*.

KINGSBURY, Derek John, CBE 1988; FREng, FIET; Chairman: Fairey Group plc, 1987–96 (Group Chief Executive, 1982–91); David Brown Group plc, 1992–96; Goode Durrant plc, 1992–96; *b* 10 July 1926; *s* of late Major Arthur Kingsbury, BEM, Virginia Water and Gwendoline Mary Kingsbury; *m* 1st, 1959, Muriel June Drake; one *s* (and one *s* decd); 2nd, 1980, Sarah Muriel Morgan (*d* 2006); one *s*; 3rd, 2007, Wendy Christine Jacobs. *Educ:* Strode's Secondary Sch., City and Guilds Coll. BScEng Hons; DIC. FIET (FIEE 1968); FCGI 1977; FREng (FEng 1991). 2nd Lieut, REME, 1947–49. Apprentice, Metropolitan Vickers, 1949–51; Exch. Schol., Univ. of Pennsylvania, 1952–53; Associated Electrical Industries: Manager, E Canada, 1954–61; PA to Chm., 1961–63; Gen. Manager, AEI Distribution Transformers, 1963–66; Gen. Manager, Overseas Manufacturing Develt, 1966–69; Thorn Electrical Industries: Man. Dir, Foster Transformers, 1969–76; Man. Dir, Elect. & Hydr. Div., 1972–76, Exec. Dir, 1973–76; Dowty Group: Dep. Chief Exec., 1976–82. Chm., Ultra Electronics, 1977–82; industrial mission to China, 1978; non-executive Director: Vickers, 1981–91; ACAL plc, 1991–94. Institution of Electrical Engineers: Dir Peter Peregrinus, 1976–81; Mem., Finance Cttee, 1978–80; Confederation of British Industry: Mem. Council, 1980–86; Chm., Overseas Cttee, 1980–84; missions to Japan 1981, 1983, 1985; Defence Manufacturers Association: Mem. Council, 1985–92; Chm., 1987–90; Chm., F and GP Cttee, 1990–92; Vice-Pres., 1993–2002; Member: Review Bd for Govt Contracts, 1986–94; Engineering Council, 1990–93 (Chm., CET Pilot Scheme Steering Cttee, 1988–90); Council, BEAMA, 1973–75. Mem. Ct, Imperial Coll. London, 2012–. Freeman, City of London, 1994; Liveryman, Scientific Instrument Makers' Co., 1994. CCMI; FRSA 1994. President: BHF Horse Show, 1977–98; Aircraft Golfing Soc., 1995–2005. *Recreations:* golf, swimming, walking. *Address:* Trecaven, Rock, Cornwall PL27 6LB. *T:* (01208) 863608. *Clubs:* Royal Automobile, MCC, St Enodoc Golf (Vice-Captain, 1997–99; Captain, 1999–2001); Rock Sailing.

KINGSBURY, Sally Jane; *see* O'Neill, Sally J.

KINGSHOTT, (Albert) Leonard; Director: International Banking Division, Lloyds Bank Plc, 1985–89; Mutual Management Services, since 1993; Member, Monopolies and Mergers Commission, 1990–96; *b* 16 Sept. 1930; *s* of A. L. Kingshott and Mrs K. Kingshott; *m* 1958, Valerie Simpson; two *s* one *d*. *Educ:* London Sch. of Economics (BSc); ACIS 1958, FCIS 1983. Flying Officer, RAF, 1952–55; Economist, British Petroleum, 1955–60; Economist, British Nylon Spinners, 1960–62; Financial Manager, Iraq Petroleum Co., 1963–65; Chief Economist, Ford of Britain, 1965; Treas., Ford of Britain, 1966–67; Treas., Ford of Europe, 1968–70; Finance Dir, Whitbread & Co., 1972; Man. Dir, Finance, BSC, 1972–77; Dir, Lloyds Bank International, responsible for Merchant Banking activities, 1977–80, for European Div., 1980–82, for Marketing and Planning Div., 1983–84; Dep. Chief Exec., Lloyds Bank International, 1985. Exec. Dir, The Private Bank & Trust Co., 1989–91; Director: Bank of London and South America Ltd, 1977–89; Lloyds Bank International, 1977–89; Lloyds Bank (France) Ltd, 1980–89; Lloyd's Bank California, 1985–88; Rosehaugh plc, 1991–92 (Chm.); Shandwick plc, 1993–2000; Newmarket Foods Ltd, 1994–97; Man. Dir, Cypher Science Ltd, 1996–. Mem. Bd, Crown Agents for Oversea Govts and Admin, and Crown Agents Hldg and Realisation Bd, 1989–92. Associate Mem. of Faculty, 1978, Governor, 1980–91, Ashridge Management Coll. Chm., Oakbridge Counselling, 1990–. FCIS. *Publications:* Investment Appraisal, 1967. *Recreations:* golf, chess. *Address:* 4 Delamas, Beggar Hill, Fryerning, Ingatestone, Essex CM4 0PW. *T:* (01277) 352077.

KINGSHOTT, Air Vice-Marshal Kenneth, CBE 1972; DFC 1953; Royal Air Force, retired 1980; *b* 8 July 1924; *s* of Walter James Kingshott and Eliza Ann Kingshott; *m* 1st, 1948, Dorrie Marie (*née* Dent) (*d* 1978); two *s*; 2nd, 1990, Valerie Rosemary Brigden. Joined RAF, 1943; served: Singapore and Korea, 1950; Aden, 1960; Malta, 1965; MoD, London, 1968; OC RAF Cottesmore, 1971; HQ 2 Allied Tactical Air Force, 1973; HQ Strike Command, 1975; Dep. Chief of Staff Operations and Intelligence, HQ Allied Air Forces Central Europe, 1977–79. *Recreations:* golf, fishing, music. *Club:* Royal Air Force.

KINGSHOTT, Leonard; *see* Kingshott, A. L.

KINGSLAND, Camilla Anne MacNeill; *see* Campbell, C. A. M.

KINGSLAND, Dr James Patrick, OBE 2012; President, National Association of Primary Care, since 2008 (Chairman, 2004–08); National Clinical Commissioning Network Lead, Department of Health, 2009–13; *b* Nottingham, 20 April 1960; *s* of late Richard Alan Kingsland and of Noreen Monica Kingsland; *m* 1986, Sarah Elizabeth Higham; two *d*. *Educ:* Mundella Grammar Sch., Nottingham; Univ. of Liverpool (MB ChB 1984; DRCOG 1988; DFFP 1998). Sen. Partner, Gen. Practice, Wallasey, Merseyside, 1989–. Non-exec. Dir, Clatterbridge Centre for Oncology Foundn Trust, 2010–. GP Advr to DoH, 1998–2003, 2008–10. Chm., Jhoots Pharmacy Gp, 2014–. Resident Doctor, BBC Radio Merseyside. *Publications:* contrib. to numerous govt policy documents for NHS. *Recreations:* media, golf, football (Nottingham Forest supporter). *Address:* 7 Holm Hill, Wirral CH48 7JA. *T:* (0151) 625 5556. *E:* james.kingsland@nhs.net. *Club:* National Liberal (non-political Mem.).

KINGSLEY, Sir Ben, Kt 2002; actor; *b* 31 Dec. 1943; *s* of Rahimtulla Harji Bhanji and Anna Leina Mary Bhanji; surname changed to Kingsley by Deed Poll, 1982; *m* 2007, Daniela Lavender; three *s* one *d* from former marriages. *Educ:* Manchester Grammar Sch. Associate artist, Royal Shakespeare Co.; work with RSC includes, 1970–80; 1985–86: Peter Brook's Midsummer Night's Dream, Stratford, London, Broadway, NY; Gramsci in Occupations; Ariel in The Tempest; title role, Hamlet; Ford in Merry Wives of Windsor; title role, Baal; Squeers and Mr Wagstaff in Nicholas Nickleby; title role, Othello, Melons; National Theatre, 1977–78: Mosca in Volponë; Trofimov in The Cherry Orchard; Sparkish in The Country Wife; Vukhov in Judgement; additional theatre work includes: Johnny in Hello and Goodbye (Fugard), King's Head, 1973; Errol Philander in Statements After An Arrest (Fugard), Royal Court, 1974; Edmund Kean, Harrogate, 1981, Haymarket, 1983 (also televised); title role, Dr Faustus, Manchester Royal Exchange, 1981; Waiting for Godot, Old Vic, 1997; *television* 1974–, includes The Love School (series), 1974, Silas Marner (film), 1985, Murderers Amongst Us (mini-series), 1989, Anne Frank - the full story (Best Actor award, Screen Actors' Guild), 2001, and several plays; *films:* title role, Gandhi, 1980 (2 Hollywood Golden Globe awards, 1982; NY Film Critics' Award, 2 BAFTA awards, Oscar, LA Film Critics Award, 1983, Variety Club of GB Best Film Actor award, 1983); Betrayal, 1982; Turtle Diary, 1985; Harem, 1986; Testimony, Maurice, 1987; Pascali's Island, The Train, 1988; Without a Clue, 1989; Bugsy, Sneakers, Dave, 1992; Schindler's List, 1993; Innocent Moves, 1994; Death and the Maiden, Species, 1995; Twelfth Night, 1996; Photographing Fairies, 1997; The Assignment, Weapons of Mass Distraction, Sweeney Todd, Alice in Wonderland, Crime and

Punishment, Spookey House, 1998; The Confession, Rules of Engagement, What Planet are you from?, 1999; Sexy Beast, 2001; Tuck Everlasting, 2002; Suspect Zero, Sound of Thunder, House of Sand and Fog, 2003; Thunderbirds, Triumph of Love, 2004; Oliver Twist, 2005; Lucky Number Slevin, 2006; The Last Legion, You Kill Me, 2007; War, Inc., Transsiberian, Elegy, The Wackness, The Love Guru, 2008; Fifty Dead Men Walking, 2009; Shutter Island, Prince of Persia, 2010; Hugo, 2011; The Dictator, 2012; Iron Man 3, 2012; Ender's Game, 2013; (short) Marvel One-Shot: All Hail the King, 2014; Exodus: Gods and Kings, 2014; Night at the Museum: Secret of the Tomb, 2014; Life, 2015. Best Film Actor, London Standard Award, 1983; Best Actor: European Film Acad., 2001; British Ind. Film Award, 2001; Screen Actors Guild, 2002; Broadcast Critics Award, 2002. Medici Soc. Award, 1989; Simon Wiesenthal Humanitarian Award, 1989; Berlin Golden Camera Award, 1990; Albert R. Broccoli Britannia Award for Worldwide Contribn to Entertainment, BAFTA, LA Britannia Awards, 2013; Nat. Leadership Award, US Holocaust Meml Mus., 2014. Hon. MA Salford, 1984; Hon. DLitt: Sussex, 2008; Hull, 2008. Padma Shri (India), 1984. *Address:* c/o Independent Talent Group Ltd, 40 Whitfield Street, W1T 2RH.

KINGSLEY, Joy, (Mrs Michael Blackburn); Senior Partner, JMW Solicitors LLP, since 2010; *b* Manchester, 16 Jan. 1956; *d* of late Roger James Kingsley, OBE and of Valerie Marguerite Mary Kingsley (*née* Hanna); *m* 1991, Michael Blackburn; two *s*. *Educ:* Manchester High Sch.; Nottingham Univ. (LLB). Admitted Solicitor, 1980. With Pannone LLP (formerly: Goldberg Blackburn, Goldberg Blackburn and Howards, Pannone and Partners, Pannone Marsh Pearson, Pannone Pritchard Englefield, Pannone and Partners), 1978–2010: Partner, 1983; Hd, Private Client Dept, 1989–95; Man. Partner, 1993–2008; Sen. Partner, 2008–10. Non-executive Director: I-COM, 2006–; Legal Mktg Innovation Co., 2013–. Gov., Manchester GS, 1999–. *Recreations:* travel, reading, ski-ing, cinema and theatre, music. *Address:* JMW Solicitors LLP, 1 Byrom Place, Spinningfields, Manchester M3 3HG. *T:* (home) (0161) 941 1258, 07788 970020.

KINGSLEY, Nicholas William, FSA; Head, Archives Sector Development (formerly National Advisory Services), and Secretary, Historical Manuscripts Commission, National Archives, since 2005; *b* 14 Sept. 1957; *s* of Philip Francis Kingsley and Joan Rosamond Kingsley (*née* Holliday); *m* 1980, (Susan) Mary Summerhayes. *Educ:* St Paul's Sch., London; Keble Coll., Oxford (BA 1978, MA 1982). Archive trainee, Bodleian Liby, Oxford, 1978–79; Asst Archivist, 1979–82, Modern Records Archivist, 1982–89, Glos Record Office; City Archivist, Birmingham City Archives, 1989–96; Central Liby Manager, Birmingham Central Liby, 1996–2000; Co. and Diocesan Archivist, Glos Record Office, 2000–05. Member: Nat. Council on Archives, 1991–2010 (Sec., 1993–99; Vice-Chm., 2000–01; Chm., 2001–05); Govt Archives Taskforce, 2002–04; MLA, 2004–06. Dir and Trustee, Media Archive of Central England, 1994–2004; Chairman: Nat. Cttee, Victoria County History, 2005–11; EU Document Lifecycle Mgt Forum, 2006; Adv. Cttee, Victoria History Trust, 2011–13; Archives Accreditation Bd, 2011–13. Member: Working Gp on Literary Heritage, 2006–13; Exec. Cttee, Friends of Nat. Libraries, 2006–; Arts Adv. Panel, Nat. Trust, 2012–; Archives Accreditation Panel, 2013–. Trustee: Glos County History Trust, 2010–; Victoria Co. History Trust, 2013–. Gen. Ed., Phillimore & Co. English Country Houses series, 1994–2004. Author of blog, http://landedfamilies.blogspot.co.uk, 2013–. FSA 2003. Hon. DLitt Birmingham, 2006. *Publications:* Handlist of the Contents of the Gloucestershire Record Office, 1988, 4th edn 1998, Supplement, 2002; The Country Houses of Gloucestershire: 1500–1660, 1989, 2nd edn 2001, 1660–1830, 1992, 1830–2000 (with M. Hill), 2001; Archives Online, 1998; (jtly) Full Disclosure, 1999; Changing the Future of our Past, 2002; contribs and reviews for Country Life and professional jls. *Recreations:* architectural and historical research, photography, food. *Address:* Tor Bank, 38 Dial Hill Road, Clevedon, N Somerset BS21 7HN. *T:* (01275) 542263. *E:* nick.kingsley@blueyonder.co.uk; 45 Grosvenor Road, Brentford, Middx TW8 0NW. *E:* nickk2@globalnet.co.uk. *T:* (020) 8560 5392.

KINGSMILL, family name of **Baroness Kingsmill**.

KINGSMILL, Baroness *cr* 2006 (Life Peer), of Holland Park, in the Royal Borough of Kensington and Chelsea; **Denise Patricia Byrne Kingsmill,** CBE 2000; a Deputy Chairman, Competition (formerly Monopolies and Mergers) Commission, 1997–2003; *b* 24 April 1947; *d* of Patrick Henry Byrne and Hester Jean Byrne; *m* 1st, 1970, David Gordon Kingsmill (marr. diss. 2002); one *s* one *d*; 2nd, 2006, Richard Wheatly (*d* 2015). *Educ:* Girton Coll., Cambridge. Admitted Solicitor, 1980. With ICI Fibres, then Internat. Wool Secretariat, 1968–75; Robin Thompson & Partners, 1979–82; Russell Jones and Walker, 1982–85; Denise Kingsmill & Co., 1985–90; Partner, D. J. Freeman, 1990–93; Consultant, Denton Hall, 1994–2000. Chm., Optimum Health Services NHS Trust, 1992–99. Non-executive Director: Rainbow UK, 1993–94; MFI Furniture Gp, 1997–2001 (Dep. Chm., 1999–2001); Norwich and Peterborough Bldg Soc., 1997–2001; Telewest Communications, 2001–03; Manpower UK, 2001–03; British Airways, 2004–11; Korn/Ferry Internat., 2009–12; Betfair, 2011–12; IAG Internat. Airlines Gp, 2011–; E.ON AG, 2011–; Sen. Ind. Dir, APR Energy plc, 2011– (Vice Chm., 2014–); Chm. Adv. Forum, Laing O'Rourke, 2003–04; Sen. Advr, RBS, 2005–08; Chm., Eur. Adv. Bd, (24)7, 2011–; Mem., European Adv. Council, Microsoft, 2009–12; Dep. Chm., Adv. Bd, PwC, 2011–14. Chairman: Women's Employment and Pay Review, 2001; Accounting for People Taskforce, DTI, 2003–; Model Health Inquiry, 2007. Kingsmill Review: Taking Care, 2014. Trustee, Design Mus., 2000–10. Chm., Sadler's Wells Foundn, 2003–04. Member: Develt Cttee, Judge Business Sch. (formerly Judge Inst.), Cambridge Univ., 2000–06; Internat. Adv. Bd, IESE Business Sch., Univ. of Navarra, 2011–; Pro-Chancellor, Brunel Univ., 2002–06. Gov., Coll. of Law, 1992–2001. Columnist, Mgt Today, 2008–. Hon. Fellow, Univ. of Wales, Cardiff, 2000. Hon. LLD: Brunel, 2001; Stirling, 2003; Hon. DSc Cranfield, 2007. *Recreations:* trying to stay fit, fly fishing. *Address:* House of Lords, SW1A 0PW.

KINGSTON, 12th Earl of, *cr* 1768 (Ire.); **Robert Charles Henry King-Tenison;** Bt 1682; Baron Kingston 1764; Viscount Kingston of Kingsborough 1766; Baron Erris 1800; Viscount Lorton 1806; *b* 20 March 1969; *o s* of 11th Earl of Kingston and his 1st wife, Patricia Mary (*née* Killip); *S* father, 2002; *m* 1994, Ruth Margaret Buckner (marr. diss. 2012); one *s* one *d*. *Heir: s* Viscount Kingsborough, *qv*.

KINGSTON (Ontario), Archbishop of, (RC), since 2007; **Most Rev. Brendan Michael O'Brien;** *b* Ottawa, 28 Sept. 1943; *s* of Redmond and Margaret O'Brien (*née* Foran). *Educ:* Univ. of Ottawa (BA); St Paul Univ., Ottawa (BTh); Lateran Univ., Rome (Dr Moral Theology). Ordained priest, 1968; Pastor in several Ottawa parishes; ordained bishop, 1987; Auxiliary Bishop of Ottawa, 1987–93; Bishop of Pembroke, 1993–2000; Archbishop of St John's, 2000–07. *Address:* 390 Palace Road, Kingston, ON K7L 4T3, Canada. *T:* (613) 5484461, *Fax:* (613) 5484744. *E:* archbishop@romancatholic.kingston.on.ca.

KINGSTON, (William) Martin; QC 1992; a Recorder, 1991–99; *b* 9 July 1949; *s* of William Robin Kingston and Iris Edith Kingston; *m* 1972, Jill Mary Bache; one *s* two *d*. *Educ:* Middlewich Secondary Modern Sch.; Hartford Coll. of Further Educn; Liverpool Univ. (LLB). Called to the Bar, Middle Temple, 1972, Bencher, 2002; Asst Recorder, 1987. Dep. Chm., Agricl Lands Tribunal, 1985–. Asst Comr, Parly Boundary Commn for England, 1992–. *Recreations:* ski-ing, fishing, reading, going on holiday. *Address:* (chambers) Greenwood House, 4–7 Salisbury Court, EC4Y 8AA; Kemble House, Kemble, Cirencester, Glos GL7 6AD.

KINGSTON-upon-THAMES, Area Bishop of, since 2002; **Rt Rev. Dr Richard Ian Cheetham;** *b* 18 Aug. 1955; *s* of John Brian Margrave Cheetham and Mollie Louise Cheetham; *m* 1977, Felicity Mary Loving; one *s* one *d*. *Educ:* Kingston Grammar Sch.; Corpus Christi Coll., Oxford (MA, PGCE); Ripon Coll., Cuddesdon (Cert. Theol. 1987); King's Coll., London (PhD 1999; Hon. Res. Fellow, 2011). Science Teacher, Richmond Sch., N Yorks, 1978–80; Physics Master, Eton Coll., 1980–83; Investment Analyst, Legal & General, London, 1983–85; ordained deacon, 1987, priest 1988; Asst Curate, Holy Cross, Fenham, Newcastle upon Tyne, 1987–90; Vicar, St Augustine of Canterbury, Luton, 1990–99; RD of Luton, 1995–98; Archdeacon of St Albans, 1999–2002. Lead Bishop, Equipping Religious Leaders in an Age of Science, 2015–. Whitelands Professorial Fellow in Christian Theol. and Contemp. Issues, Univ. of Roehampton, 2013–. Chairman: Southwark Diocesan Bd of Educn, 2002–; Christian Muslim Forum, 2010–12 (Anglican Pres., 2012–); British Regl Cttee, St George's Coll., Jerusalem, 2013–. Pres., YMCA London SW; Patron: Fircroft Trust; Kingston Bereavement Service. Mem. Council, Roehampton Univ., 2006–12. Pres., Old Kingstonians Hockey Club, 2009–. *Publications:* Collective Worship: issues and opportunities, 2004. *Recreations:* hockey (England U19 hockey 1974; Oxford Hockey Blue, 1975; British Univs, 1975), squash, tennis, walking, theatre, cinema. *Address:* Kingston Episcopal Area Office, 620 Kingston Road, Raynes Park, SW20 8DN. *W:* www.bishoprichardcheetham.com.

KINGWELL, Rear Adm. John Matthew Leonard; Director, Development, Concepts and Doctrine Centre, Joint Force Command, since 2013; *b* London, 26 Aug. 1966; *s* of John and Diane Kingwell; *m* 1990, Alison Hogg; two *d*. *Educ:* Streatham Modern Sch.; Southwark Coll.; Loughborough Univ. (BA Hons Hist. 1988); King's Coll. London (MA Defence Studies 2000). Joined RN as Warfare Officer, 1984; served: HMS Edinburgh, 1989–90; HMS Sheraton, 1990–92; CO, HMS Pursuer and O i/c Sussex Univ. Royal Naval Unit, 1993–94; HMS Monmouth, 1995–96; jscsc, 1999–2000; CO, HMS Argyll, 2001–02; Advr to Hd of Iraqi Navy, Baghdad, 2005; MA to VCDS/2nd Perm. Under Sec., MoD, 2006–08; CO, HMS Albion, 2009–10; Comdr, UK Task Gp, Libya, 2011; Hd, Navy Resources and Plans, MoD, 2011–13. President: Newhaven and Seaford Sea Cadets, 2005–; Hastings Sea Cadets, 2010–. Liveryman, Shipwrights' Co., 2003. Younger Brother, Trinity House, 2011–. QCVS 2012. *Recreations:* military history, jogging, family. *Address:* Development, Concepts and Doctrine Centre, Shrivenham, Swindon, Wilts SN6 8RF. *E:* dcdc-director@mod.uk. *Club:* Army and Navy.

KINLOCH, Prof. Anthony James, PhD, DSc; FRS 2007; FREng, CEng; CChem, FRSC; FIMMM; FCGI; FIMechE; Professor of Adhesion, Imperial College London, since 1990; *b* 7 Oct. 1946; *s* of Nathan and Hilda May Kinloch; *m* 1969, Gillian Patricia Birch; two *s* one *d*. *Educ:* London Nautical Sch.; Queen Mary Coll., London (PhD 1972); DSc London 1989. CChem 1982; FRSC 1982; FIMMM (FIM 1982); FREng (FEng 1997); FIMechE 2009. RARDE, MoD, 1972–84; Reader, 1984–89, Chair, Mechanics of Materials Div., 2004–07, Imperial Coll., London. Visiting Professor: EPFL, Lausanne, 1986; Univ. of Utah, 1988. Lectures: C&G Centenary, 1995; Thomas Hawksley, IMechE, 1996. Mem. Council, Inst. Materials, 1997–2002; Chm., Soc. for Adhesion and Adhesives, 2000–02. Fellow, US Adhesion Soc., 1995 (Pres., 2002–04); FCGI 2001. Adhesion Soc. of Japan Award, 1994; Griffith Medal and Prize, 1996, Wake Meml Medal, 2002, Inst. of Materials; Thomas Hawksley Gold Medal, IMechE, 1997; Le Prix Dédale de la Société Française d'Adhesion, 2009; Armourers and Brasiers' Co. Prize for Excellence in Materials Sci. and Technol., Royal Soc., 2009. *Publications:* Adhesion and Adhesives: science and technology, 1987; (with R. J. Young) Fracture Behaviour of Polymers, 1983; (ed) Durability of Structural Adhesives, 1983; (ed jtly) Toughened Plastics: I 1993, II 1996; over 200 papers in learned jls. *Recreations:* opera, tennis, walking. *Address:* Imperial College London, Department of Mechanical Engineering, Exhibition Road, SW7 2AZ.

KINLOCH, Sir David, 13th Bt *cr* 1686, of Gilmerton; *b* 5 Aug. 1951; *s* of Sir Alexander Davenport Kinloch, 12th Bt and of Anna, *d* of late Thomas Walker, Edinburgh; *S* father, 1982; *m* 1st, 1976, Susan Middlewood (marr. diss. 1986); one *s* one *d*; 2nd, 1987, Maureen Carswell (marr. diss. 2009); two *s*. *Educ:* Gordonstoun. Career in research into, and recovery and replacement of, underground services. *Recreation:* treasure hunting. *Heir: s* Alexander Kinloch, *b* 31 May 1978. *Address:* Gilmerton House, North Berwick, East Lothian EH39 5LQ. *T:* (01620) 880207.

KINLOCH, Sir David Oliphant, 5th Bt *cr* 1873, of Kinloch, co. Perth; CA; Director, Caledonia Investments PLC, 1988–2004; *b* 15 Jan. 1942; *s* of Sir John Kinloch, 4th Bt and Doris Ellaline (*d* 1997), *e d* of C. J. Head; *S* father, 1992; *m* 1st, 1968, Susan Minette Urquhart (marr. diss. 1979), *y d* of Maj.-Gen. R. E. Urquhart, CB, DSO; three *d*; 2nd, 1983, Sabine Irene, *o d* of Philippe and Yolaine de Loës; one *s* one *d*. *Educ:* Charterhouse. *Heir: s* Alexander Peter Kinloch, *b* 30 June 1986. *Address:* House of Aldie, Kinross KY13 0QH; 29 Walpole Street, SW3 4QS.

KINLOCH, Henry, (Harry); Chairman, Quartermaine & Co., since 1989; *b* 7 June 1937; *s* of William Shearer Kinloch and Alexina Alice Quartermaine Kinloch; *m* 1st, 1966, Gillian Anne Ashley (marr. diss. 1979); one *s* one *d*; 2nd, 1987, Catherine Elizabeth Hossack. *Educ:* Queen's Park Sch., Glasgow; Univs of Strathclyde, Birmingham and Glasgow. MSc, PhD, ARCST, CEng, FIMechE. Lecturer in Engineering: Univ. of Strathclyde, 1962–65; Univ. of Liverpool, 1966; Vis. Associate Prof. of Engrg, MIT, 1967; Sen. Design Engr, CEGB, 1968–70; PA Management Consultants, 1970–73; Chief Exec., Antony Gibbs (PFP) Ltd, 1973–74; Chm. and Chief Exec., Antony Gibbs Financial Services Ltd, 1975–77; Man. Dir, British Shipbuilders, 1978–80; Dep. Man. Dir and Chief Exec., Liberty Life Assce Co., 1980–83; Associate, Lazard Brothers, 1980–84; Chm. and Chief Exec., Ætna Internat. (UK), 1984–89. Chm., Helm Investments Ltd, 1995–98; Gp Man. Dir, Ultraseal Internat. Ltd, 1997–98. Associate, AA Advrs, 2014–. Director: Barfoots of Botley Ltd, 2005–; ACM Envmtl (formerly ACM Waste Mgt) plc, 2009–13; Strata Technology Ltd, 2011–; WES Ltd, 2014–. Consultant, London Bridge Capital, 2010–13. Mem., Ct of Govs, Univ. of Westminster, 2013–. *Publications:* many publications on theoretical and applied mechanics, financial and business studies. *Recreations:* reading book reviews, opera, political biography, walking, sometimes with others! *Address:* AA Advisers LLP, Room 226, Linen Hall, 162–168 Regent Street, W1B 5TD. *Clubs:* Athenæum (Mem., Gen. and Exec. Cttees, 2003–08; Dep. Chm., 2005–08; Chm., 2009–12), Farmers; Worplesdon Golf; Hunstanton Golf.

KINLOSS, Lady (13th in line, of the Lordship *cr* 1602); **Teresa Mary Nugent Freeman-Grenville;** *b* Tanga, Tanganyika, 20 July 1957; *er d* of Lady Kinloss (12th in line) and Dr Greville Stewart Parker Freeman-Grenville (*d* 2005); *S* mother, 2012. *Educ:* Rye St Antony Sch., Oxford; York Art Sch. (C&G Cert. in Women's Light Clothing); Cert. in Fashion, Yorkshire and Humberside Council. Milk Recorder for Nat. Milk Records, 1992–. *Recreations:* goat keeper, dogs, spinning, crochet, weaving, etc. *Heir: sister* Hon. Hester Josephine Anne Haworth, Mistress of Kinloss [*b* 9 May 1960; *m* 1984, Peter Haworth; three *s*]. *Address:* North View House, Main Street, Sheriff Hutton, N Yorks YO60 6ST. *T:* (01347) 878447.

KINMONTH, Prof. Ann-Louise, (Mrs Ann-Louise Kinmonth-Davis), CBE 2002; MD; FRCP, FRCPCH, FRCGP, FMedSci; Professor of General Practice, 1997–2011, now Emeritus, and Honorary Director of Research, General Practice and Primary Care Research Unit, 2011–14, University of Cambridge; Fellow of St John's College, Cambridge, since 1997 (Member of Council, since 2013); *b* 8 Jan. 1951; *d* of late Maurice Henry Kinmonth and Gwendolyn Stella (*née* Phillipps); *m* 2005, Prof. John Allen Davis, *qv*. *Educ:* New Hall, Cambridge (MA); St Thomas' Hosp. Med. Sch. (MB, BChir, MSc, MD 1984). FRCGP 1992; FRCP 1994; FRCPCH 1997. House Officer, Lambeth and Salisbury Hosps, 1975–76; SHO, Oxford Hosps, 1976–78; Res. Fellow in Paediatrics, Oxford Univ., 1978–80; Oxfam

MO, Somalia, 1981; general practice trng, Oxford, 1981–82; Principal, Aldermoor Health Centre, Southampton, 1983–96; University of Southampton: Lectr, 1983–84; Sen. Lectr, 1984–91; Reader, 1991–92; Prof., 1992–96. Advr in Primary Care to MRC/DoH, 2004–05; Associate Dir (Primary Care), UK Clinical Res. Network, 2005–07; Ext. Associate, Inst. of Medicine (USA), 2007. Founder FMedSci 1998 (Mem. Council, 1998–2001). *Publications:* (ed with J. D. Baum) Care of the Child with Diabetes Mellitus, 1986; (ed with R. Jones) Critical Reading for Primary Care, 1995; (ed jtly) Evidence Base for Diabetes Care, 2002, 2nd edn 2010; contrib. papers on diabetes care and prevention of cardio-vascular disease in peer reviewed jls. *Address:* 1 Cambridge Road, Great Shelford, Cambridge CB22 5JE.

KINNAIR, Dame Donna, DBE 2008; Clinical Director for Emergency Medicine, Barking, Havering and Redbridge University Hospitals NHS Trust, since 2014; *b* London, 17 Feb. 1961; *d* of Victor and Dolores Nesbitt; *m* 1981, Stephen Kinnair; two *s* one *d. Educ:* Rushmore Prim. Sch.; Skinners' Company's Sch. for Girls; Princess Alexandra Sch. of Nursing; Univ. of E London (LLB 1996); King's Coll. London (Dip. Healthcare Ethics); Univ. of Greenwich (PGCE 1999); Univ. of Manchester (MA Ethics and Law 2006). Nurse: London Hosp., 1983–87; Antigua, WI, 1987; Health Visitor, London Boroughs of Newham, Tower Hamlets and Hackney, 1988–96; Child Protection Nurse Specialist, Optimum Health Services, Lewisham and Southwark, 1996–99; Strategic Comr, Children's Services, Lambeth, Southwark and Lewisham HA, 1999–2002; Dir of Nursing, 2002–11, Dir of Commissioning, 2008–11, Southwark PCT, later Southwark Health and Social Care; Dir of Nursing, NHS SE London, 2011–13; Dir of Governance and Special Projects, Barking, Havering and Redbridge Univ. Hosps NHS Trust, 2012–13 (on secondment). Nurse Advr, Victoria Climbié Inquiry, 2001. Vis. Prof. of Primary Care, London Southbank Univ., 2008–. Consultant Ed., Nursing Management, 2006–. *Recreations:* cycling, walking, theatre, cinema. *Address:* Barking, Havering and Redbridge University Hospitals NHS Trust, Queen's Hospital, Rom Valley Way, Romford, Essex RM7 0AG.

KINNAIRD, Alison Margaret, (Mrs R. Morton), MBE 1997; free-lance musician and artist, since 1970; *b* 30 April 1949; *d* of John and Margaret Kinnaird; *m* 1974, Robin Morton; one *s* one *d. Educ:* George Watson's Ladies' Coll.; Edinburgh Univ. (MA 1970). Artworks in public and private collections incl. V&A Mus., Scottish Nat. Portrait Gall., Corning Mus. of Glass, NY and Scottish Parlt; specialises in engraved glass. Has performed, playing Scottish harp, nationally and internationally; has made recordings. *Publications:* (with Keith Sanger) Tree of Strings: a history of the harp in Scotland, 1992; The Small Harp, 1989; The Lothian Collection, 1995. *Address:* Shillinghill, Temple, Midlothian EH23 4SH. *T:* (01875) 830328, *Fax:* (01875) 830392. *E:* alisonk@templerecords.co.uk. *W:* www.alisonkinnaird.com.

KINNEAR, Jonathan Shea; QC 2012; a Recorder, since 2009; *b* Ballymena, NI, 22 July 1971; *s* of John Brian Kinnear and Helga Louisa Kinnear; *m* 2006, Marlo Zoe Beaudet; two *s. Educ:* Methodist Coll., Belfast; Univ. of Newcastle upon Tyne (LLB Hons 1993). Called to the Bar: Gray's Inn, 1994; NI, 1996; a Dep. Dist Judge, 2004–09. Mem., Bar Standards Professional Conduct Cttee, 2008–13. *Recreations:* playing and coaching Rugby, crossfit. *Address:* 9–12 Bell Yard, WC2A 2JR. *T:* (020) 7400 1800. *E:* j.kinnear@9-12bellyard.com. *Clubs:* Wimbledon Rugby Football; Roehampton.

KINNELL, Ian; QC 1987; professional arbitrator; *b* 23 May 1943; *o s* of Brian Kinnell and Grace Madeline Kinnell; *m* 1970, Elizabeth Jane Ritchie; one *s* one *d. Educ:* Sevenoaks Sch., Kent. Called to the Bar, Gray's Inn, 1967. A Recorder, 1987–89; Immigration Appeal Adjudicator, 1990–91; part-time Chm., Immigration Appeal Tribunal, 1991–97. Mem., London Maritime Arbitrator's Assoc., 1991. *Recreation:* rural pursuits. *Address:* The Vineyard, Heyope, Knighton, Powys LD7 1RE. *T:* (01547) 520990.

KINNOCK, family name of **Baron Kinnock** and **Baroness Kinnock of Holyhead**.

KINNOCK, Baron *cr* 2005 (Life Peer), of Bedwellty in the County of Gwent; **Neil Gordon Kinnock;** PC 1983; Chairman, British Council, 2004–09; *b* 28 March 1942; *s* of Gordon Kinnock, labourer, and Mary Kinnock (*née* Howells), nurse; *m* 1967, Glenys Elizabeth Parry (*see* Baroness Kinnock of Holyhead); one *s* one *d. Educ:* Lewis Sch., Pengam; University Coll., Cardiff. BA in Industrial Relations and History, UC, Cardiff (Chm. Socialist Soc., 1963–66; Pres. Students' Union, 1965–66; Hon. Fellow, 1982). Tutor Organiser in Industrial and Trade Union Studies, WEA, 1966–70; Mem., Welsh Hosp. Bd, 1969–71. MP (Lab) Bedwellty, 1970–83, Islwyn, 1983–95. PPS to Sec. of State for Employment, 1974–75; Chief Opposition spokesman on educn, 1979–83; Leader of the Labour Party, and Leader of the Opposition, 1983–92. Mem., 1995–2004, and a Vice Pres., 1999–2004, EC. Non-exec. Dir, Data & Research Services plc, 2005–12. Member: Nat. Exec. Cttee, Labour Party, 1978–94 (Chm., 1987–88); Parly Cttee of PLP, 1980–92. Chm. Internat. Cttee, Labour Party, 1993–94; Vice-Pres., Socialist Internat., 1984–. Chm., Adv. Bd, Hds of the Valleys Circuit Develt Co., 2011–. Trustee, IPPR, 2002–. Pres., Univ. of Cardiff, 1998–2009. Hon. FIHT 1997. Hon. LLD: Wales, 1992; Glamorgan, 1996; Robert Gordon, 2002; Queen Margaret, 2007; Glasgow Caledonian, 2009; Aston, 2013. Alexis de Tocqueville Prize, European Inst. of Public Admin, 2003; Danish Shipowners' Assoc. Maritime Award, 2004. *Publications:* Making Our Way, 1986; Thorns and Roses, 1992; contribs to various jls. *Recreations:* music esp. opera and male choral, Rugby and Association football, cricket, theatre, being with family. *Address:* House of Lords, SW1A 0PW.

See also S. N. Kinnock.

KINNOCK OF HOLYHEAD, Baroness *cr* 2009 (Life Peer), of Holyhead in the County of Ynys Môn; **Glenys Elizabeth Kinnock;** *b* 7 July 1944; *m* 1967, Neil Gordon Kinnock (*see* Baron Kinnock); one *s* one *d. Educ:* Holyhead Comprehensive Sch.; University College of Wales, Cardiff. Teacher in secondary and primary schools, and special sch., 1966–93. MEP (Lab) S Wales E, 1994–99, Wales, 1999–2009. Co-Pres., EU-Africa, Caribbean, Pacific Jt Parly Assembly, 2001–09. Minister of State, FCO, 2009–10. Vice-Pres., Univ. of Wales, Cardiff, 1988–95. Member: Bd, European Centre for Develt Policy, 2009–; Council, Overseas Develt Inst., 2009–; Bd, Burma Campaign UK. Patron: Saferworld; Drop the Debt Campaign; Med. Foundn for Victims of Torture; Nat. Deaf Children's Soc. Hon. Fellow: Univ. of Wales Coll., Newport, 1998; Univ. of Cardiff, 2013. Hon. LLD Thames Valley, 1994; Hon. Dr: Brunel, 1997; Kingston, 2001. *Publications:* Eritrea: images of war and peace, 1988; (ed) Voices for One World, 1988; Namibia: birth of a nation, 1990; By Faith and Daring, 1993; Zimbabwe on the Brink, 2003. *Address:* House of Lords, SW1A 0PW.

See also S. N. Kinnock.

KINNOCK, Stephen Nathan; MP (Lab) Aberavon, since 2015; *b* Tredegar, 1 Jan. 1970; *s* of Baron Kinnock, *qv* and Baroness Kinnock of Holyhead, *qv*; *m* 1996, Helle Thorning-Schmidt; two *d. Educ:* Drayton Manor Comp. Sch.; Queens' Coll., Cambridge (BA Mod. Langs French and Spanish 1992); Coll. of Europe, Bruges. Policy Researcher for Gary Titley, MEP, 1993–94; Consultant, Lancashire Enterprises, 1994–96; British Council: Business Develt Manager, Dep. Dir, then Dir, Brussels, 1996–2003; Director: Contract Mgt Change Prog., 2003–05; St Petersburg, 2005–08; Sierra Leone, 2008; Dir, Hd of Europe and Central Asia, WEF, 2009–12; Man. Dir, Global Leadership and Technol. Exchange, Xyntéo AS, 2012–15. *Recreations:* football, gym. *Address:* (office) Unit 7, Water Street Business Centre, Water Street, Port Talbot SA12 6LF. *T:* (01639) 897660. *E:* stephen.kinnock.mp@parliament.uk.

KINNOULL, 16th Earl of, *cr* 1633 (Scot.); **Charles William Harley Hay;** Viscount Dupplin and Lord Hay of Kinfauns, 1627, 1633, 1697; Baron Hay (GB), 1711, MA; barrister; *b* 20 Dec. 1962; *s* of 15th Earl of Kinnoull and of Gay Ann, *er d* of Sir Denys Lowson, 1st Bt; *S* father, 2013; *m* 2002, Clare, *d* of His Honour William Hamilton Raymund Crawford, *qv*; one *s* three *d* (incl. twins). *Educ:* Summer Fields; Eton; Christ Church, Oxford (Scholar); City Univ. (Dip. in Law); Inns of Court Sch. of Law. Called to the Bar, Middle Temple, 1990. Associate, Credit Suisse First Boston Ltd, 1985–88; Underwriter, Roberts & Hiscox, then Hiscox Syndicates Ltd, 1990–95; Man. Dir (Europe), Hiscox Insce Co. Ltd, 1995–2000; Dir of Mergers and Acquisitions, Hiscox Ltd, 2000–14; Co. Sec., Hiscox Gp, 2009–12; CEO, Hiscox Insce Co. (Bermuda) Ltd, 2009–12. Non-executive Director: Construction & Gen. Guarantee Insce Co., 2001–; Amorphous Sugar Ltd, 2001–; HIM Capital Ltd, 2007–09; non-exec. Chm., Heritage Group Ltd, 2001–05. Dir, Assoc. of Bermuda Insurers and Reinsurers, 2009–12; Member, Board: Reinsce Assoc. of America, 2009–12; Assoc. of Bermuda Internat. Cos, 2011–12. Mem. Bd, Perth City Develt Bd, 2014–. Lieut, 1993–2008, Capt., 2008–, Atholl Highlanders. Mem., Queen's Bodyguard for Scotland (Royal Co. of Archers), 2000–. Pres., London Mems, NT for Scotland, 2007–12; Dir, Masterworks Mus. of Bermuda Art, 2012–; Mem. Bd, Fine Art Fund, 2008–. Pres., Royal Caledonian Charities Trust (formerly Royal Caledonian Ball), 2012– (Trustee, 1992–; Chm., 1996–2009; Vice-Pres., 2009–12); Chm., Red Squirrel Survival Trust, 2013–. Mem., Develt Cttee, Christ Ch, Oxford, 2004–09. Dir, Horsecross Arts Ltd, 2014–. Elected Mem., H of L, 2015. FRPSL 2006 (Mem., 2000). *Publications:* contrib. Jl of Chem. Soc. *Recreations:* cricket, Cresta Run, Real tennis, skiing, philately. *Heir: s* Viscount Dupplin, *qv*. *Address:* 17 Cumberland Street, SW1V 4LS. *T:* (020) 7976 6973; Pitkindie, Abernyte, Perthshire PH14 9RE. *T:* (01828) 686342. *Clubs:* White's, Turf, Pratt's, MCC; Royal Perth (Perth); Jockey (Vienna).

KINROSS, 5th Baron *cr* 1902; **Christopher Patrick Balfour;** Partner in HBJ Gateley Wareing, 2005–09; *b* 1 Oct. 1949; *s* of 4th Baron Kinross, OBE, TD, and Helen Anne (*d* 1969), *d* of A. W. Hog; *S* father, 1985; *m* 1st, 1974, Susan Jane (marr. diss. 2004), *d* of I. R. Pitman, WS; two *s*; 2nd, 2004, Catherine Ierenka, *d* of Stanislav Ostrycharz. *Educ:* Belhaven Hill School, Dunbar; Eton College; Edinburgh Univ. (LLB). Mem., Law Soc. of Scotland, 1975; WS 1975. Partner: Shepherd & Wedderburn, WS, Solicitors, 1977–97; Taylor Kinross Legal Partnership, 1997–2005. UK Treas., James IV Assoc. of Surgeons, 1981– (Hon. Mem., 1985–). Member, Queen's Body Guard for Scotland, Royal Company of Archers, 1980–. Member: Mil. Vehicle Trust; Scottish Land Rover Owners' Club. Golden Jubilee Medal, 2002; Diamond Jubilee Medal, 2012. Grand Baili, Grand Bailiwick of Scotland, Order of St Lazarus of Jerusalem, 2002–09. *Recreations:* rifle and shotgun shooting, stalking, motorsport. *Heir: s* Hon. Alan Ian Balfour [*b* 4 April 1978; *m* 2006, Lindsay Fiona Gourlay]. *Address:* 33/8 Orchard Brae Avenue, Edinburgh EH4 2UP.

KINSELLA, (Jonathan) Neil; Chief Executive Officer, Slater & Gordon Lawyers UK, since 2012 (Chief Executive and Managing Partner, Russell Jones and Walker Solicitors, 2003–12); *b* Leigh, Lancs, 17 May 1958; *s* of Donald John and Irene Kinsella; *m* 1982, Susan Elizabeth Cotterell; one *s* one *d. Educ:* Manchester Univ. (LLB Hons Law); Coll. of Law, Chester. Admitted Solicitor, 1983; trained at Goldberg Blackburn, 1981–83; Partner, Pannone Napier, 1986–91, specialising in conduct of disaster litigation, incl. Manchester Air Crash, Chinook Helicopter Disaster, Piper Alpha Disaster; joined Russell Jones and Walker, 1991. Law Soc. apptd rep. on Lord Chancellor's Adv. Gp on awards of damages in serious injury cases. Founder Mem., Claims Standards Council. Mem., MoJ review panels and discussion forums on changes to personal injury litigation and fee structures. Medal for work on internat. transport, Assoc. of Young Internat. Lawyers, 1988. *Publications:* contrib. articles on legal issues with particular interest in access to justice and alternative business structures in legal profession. *Recreations:* painting, wild swimming, tennis. *Address:* Slater & Gordon Lawyers, 50–52 Chancery Lane, WC2A 1HL.

KINSELLA, Thomas; poet; *b* 4 May 1928; *m* 1955, Eleanor Walsh; one *s* two *d*. Entered Irish Civil Service, 1946; resigned from Dept of Finance, 1965. Artist-in-residence, 1965–67, Prof. of English, 1967–70, Southern Illinois Univ.; Prof. of English, Temple Univ., Philadelphia, 1970–90. Elected to Irish Academy of Letters, 1965; Mem., Amer. Acad. of Arts and Scis, 2000. J. S. Guggenheim Meml Fellow, 1968–69, 1971–72; Hon. Sen. Fellow, Sch. of English, University Coll., Dublin, 2003–. Freeman, City of Dublin, 2007. Hon. PhD: NUI, 1984; Turin Univ., 2005. Ulysses Medal, Univ. Coll. Dublin, 2008. *Publications: poetry:* Poems, 1956; Another September, 1958; Downstream, 1962; Nightwalker and other poems, 1968; Notes from the Land of the Dead, 1972; Butcher's Dozen, 1972; A Selected Life, 1972; Finistère, 1972; New Poems, 1973; Selected Poems 1956 to 1968, 1973; Vertical Man and The Good Fight, 1973; One, 1974; A Technical Supplement, 1976; Song of the Night and Other Poems, 1978; The Messenger, 1978; Fifteen Dead, 1979; One and Other Poems, 1979; Poems 1956–73, 1980; Peppercanister Poems 1972–78, 1980; One Fond Embrace, 1981; Songs of the Psyche, 1985; Her Vertical Smile, 1985; St Catherine's Clock, 1987; Out of Ireland, 1987; Blood and Family, 1988; Personal Places, 1990; Poems from Centre City, 1990; Madonna, 1991; Open Court, 1991; From Centre City, 1994; Collected Poems 1956–1994, 1996; The Pen Shop, 1997; The Familiar, 1999; Godhead, 1999; Citizen of the World, 2000; Littlebody, 2000; Collected Poems 1956–2001, 2001; Marginal Economy, 2005; Man of War, 2007; Belief and Unbelief, 2007; Selected Poems, 2007; Fat Master, 2012; Love Joy Peace, 2012; Late Poems, 2013; *translations and general:* (trans.) The Táin, 1969; contrib. essay in Davis, Mangan, Ferguson, 1970; (ed) Selected Poems of Austin Clarke, 1976; An Duanaire—Poems of the Dispossessed (trans. Gaelic poetry, 1600–1900), 1981; (ed) Our Musical Heritage: lectures on Irish traditional music by Seán Ó Riada, 1982; (ed, with translations) The New Oxford Book of Irish Verse, 1986; The Dual Tradition: an essay on poetry and politics in Ireland, 1995; Readings in Poetry, 2005; A Dublin Documentary, 2006; Prose Occasions (1951–2006) - collected occasional prose, 2008.

KINSEY, Thomas Richard Moseley, FREng; Consultant, Delcam International (formerly Deltacam Systems), 2007 (Chairman, 1989–2007); *b* 13 Oct. 1929; *s* of late Richard Moseley Kinsey and Dorothy Elizabeth Kinsey; *m* 1953, Ruth (*née* Owen-Jones); two *s. Educ:* Newtown Sch.; Trinity Hall, Cambridge (MA). FIMechE; FREng (FEng 1982). ICI Ltd, 1952–57; Tube Investments, 1957–65; joined Delta plc, 1965: Director, 1973–77; Jt Man. Dir, 1977–82; Dir, 1980, Dep. Chief Exec., 1982–87, Mitchell Cotts plc, 1980–87. Chm., Birmingham Battery & Metal Co., 1984–89; Director: Gower Internat., 1984–89; Telcon, 1984–89; Unistrut Europe, 1989–92. CCMI. *Recreations:* golf, travel. *Address:* 6 Sutton Lodge, Blossomfield Road, Solihull, W Midlands B91 1NB. *T:* (0121) 704 2592. *Clubs:* Athenæum; Edgbaston Golf.

KINSKY, Cyril Norman Francis; QC 2010; *b* London, 4 Aug. 1954; *s* of Alfons and Monique Kinsky; *m* 1986, Natasha Farrant; two *s* two *d. Educ:* Ampleforth Coll.; Trinity Coll., Cambridge (BA 1975). Freelance theatre dir, 1976–86; called to the Bar, Middle Temple, 1988; in practice as barrister with wide commercial practice: Brick Court Chambers, 1988–2003; 3 Verulam Bldgs, 2003–. Chm., Ecole Française de Londres Jacques Prévert, 2003–06. Trustee, Cardinal Hume Centre, 2010–13. *Recreation:* designing and making marquetry furniture. *Address:* 3 Verulam Buildings, Gray's Inn, WC1R 5NT. *T:* (020) 7831 8441. *E:* ckinsky@3vb.com.

KINSMAN, Jeremy Kenneth Bell; writer; director; Regents' Lecturer, University of California, Berkeley, 2009–10; *b* Montreal, 28 Jan. 1942; *s* of Ronald Kinsman and Katharine Nixon Bell; *m* 1992, Hana Tallichova; two *d. Educ:* Princeton Univ.; Institut d'Etudes Politiques, Paris. Aluminium Co. of Canada, 1965–66; entered Foreign Service of Canada, 1966; Econ. Div., Ext. Affairs, 1966–68; Third, then Second, Sec. and Vice-Consul, Brussels/EEC, 1968–70; Central Secretariat, Ottawa, 1970–72; Commercial Div., 1972–73; First Sec., Algiers, 1973–75; Counsellor, then Minister and Dep. Perm. Rep., Perm. Mission of Canada to UN, NY, 1975–80; Chm., Policy Planning Secretariat, Ottawa, 1980–81; Minister, Pol Affairs, Washington, 1981–85; Assistant Deputy Minister: Cultural Affairs and Broadcasting,

Ottawa, 1985–89; Pol and Internat. Security Affairs, and Pol Dir, Ext. Affairs, 1990–92; Ambassador: to Russia and several other Repubs, 1993–96; to Italy, 1996–2000 (concurrently Ambassador to Albania and High Comr to Malta); High Comr in UK, 2000–02; Ambassador to the EU, 2002–06. Project Dir, The Diplomat's Handbook for Democracy Development Support, Council of a Community of Democracies, 2007–; Diplomat in Residence, Woodrow Wilson Sch. of Public and Internat. Affairs, Princeton Univ., 2007–08. Ind. Dir, Dundee Precious Metals Inc., 2007–; Mem. Bd, Byways, UK, 2004–. Commentator, Diplomatically Speaking, CBC News, 2006–. Gov., Victoria Conservatory of Music, 2007–. *Publications:* contrib. on foreign affairs in Policy Options; contrib. Globe, Mail, Internat. Herald Tribune. *Recreations:* tennis, running, ski-ing, hiking, books, theatre, music.

KINSMAN, Prof. Rodney William, RDI 1990; FCSD; Chairman and Design Director (formerly Managing Director), OMK Design Ltd, since 1966; *b* 9 April 1943; *s* of John Thomas Kinsman and Lilian Kinsman (*née* Bradshaw); *m* 1966, Lisa Sai Yuk; one *s* two *d*. *Educ:* Mellow Lane Grammar Sch.; Central Sch. of Art (NDD 1965). FCSD 1983. Founded: OMK Design Ltd, 1966; Kinsman Associates, 1981. Mem., British Furniture Council, 1995 (Exec. Mem., RDI Cttee). Numerous internat. exhibns; work in permanent collections incl. Omkstak Chair and other designs, in V&A, museums in USA, Spain, Germany. Broadcasts on TV and radio. Vis. Prof., 1985–86 and Ext. Examr, 1986–88, RCA; Vis. Prof., 1996–, Gov., 1996–2010, Univ. of the Arts (formerly London Inst.). Hon. FRCA 1988; FRSA 2012. Many internat. awards incl. Millennium Product, Design Council, 2000. *Recreations:* polo, ski-ing. *Address:* Kinsman Associates Ltd, Stephen Building, 30 Stephen Street, W1T 1QR. *T:* (020) 7631 1335. *Clubs:* Reform, Groucho, Chelsea Arts.

KINTORE, 14th Earl of, *cr* 1677 (Scot.); **James William Falconer Keith;** Lord Keith of Inverurie and Keith Hall, 1677 (Scot.); Bt 1897; Baron 1925; Viscount Stonehaven, 1938; *b* 15 April 1976; *s* of 13th Earl of Kintore and Mary Keith (*née* Plum); *S* father, 2004; *m* 2006, Carrie Fiona, *d* of Ian and Dr Fiona Paxton, Edinburgh; two *s*. *Heir: s* Lord Inverurie, *qv*.

KINVIG, Maj.-Gen. Clifford Arthur; Director, Educational and Training Services (Army) (formerly Director of Army Education, Ministry of Defence), 1990–93, retired; *b* 22 Nov. 1934; *s* of Frank Arthur Kinvig and Dorothy Maud (*née* Hankinson); *m* 1956, Shirley Acklam; two *s* one *d*. *Educ:* Waterloo Grammar Sch., Liverpool; Durham Univ. (BA 1956); King's Coll., London (MA War Studies 1969). Commnd, RAEC, 1957; educnl and staff appts in Lichfield, Beaconsfield and York, 1957–65; served FE, 1965–68; Sen. Lectr, RMA, Sandhurst, 1969–73; SO2 Educn, UKLF, 1973–75; Chief Educn Officer, W Midland Dist, 1976–79; SO1 Educn, MoD, 1979–82; Sen. Lectr and Head of Econs, Politics and Social Studies Br., RMCS, Shrivenham, 1982–86; Col AEd1, MoD, 1986; Comdt, RAEC Centre, 1986–90. Dep. Col Comdt, AGC, 1997–2000. Mem., Management Bd, NFER, 1990–93. Trustee and Sec., Gallipoli Meml Lect. Trust, 1990–92. *Publications:* Death Railway, 1973; River Kwai Railway, 1992; (contrib.) The Forgotten War, 1992; Scapegoat: General Percival of Singapore, 1996; (contrib.) Japanese Prisoners of War, 2000; Sixty Years On, 2002; Churchill's Crusade, 2006; contribs to books and jls on mil. hist. topics. *Recreations:* writing, gardening, reading, walking. *Address:* Toft Cottage, Perrotts Brook, Cirencester, Glos GL7 7BL.

KIOUSSIS, Dimitris, FRS 2009; FMedSci; Head, Division of Molecular Immunology, MRC National Institute for Medical Research, 1991–2010; *b* Athens, 3 Nov. 1949; *s* of Alexandros Kioussis and Maria Kioussis; partner, John W. Griffin. *Educ:* Athens University Medical Sch. (Med. Dr degree 1975); Temple Univ., Philadelphia (PhD Biochem. 1980). Mem., MRC Scientific Staff, Lab. of Gene Structure and Expression, NIMR, 1980–84; Lectr, Immunology Dept, Middlesex Hosp. Med. Sch., 1984–86; Mem., MRC Sen. Scientific Staff, Lab. of Gene Structure and Expression, NIMR, 1986–91. Mem., EMBO, 1997–. FMedSci 2002. *Publications:* research articles in Nature, Science, Cell, EMBO Jl, Procs of NAS, Jl of Immunology. *Recreations:* theatre, music, dance, film, books, translation of contemporary British theatre plays into Greek. *Address:* Division of Molecular Immunology, Francis Crick Institute, The Ridgeway, Mill Hill, NW7 1AA. *T:* (020) 8816 2501, *Fax:* (020) 8816 2248. *E:* dimitris.kioussis@crick.ac.uk.

KIRBY, Prof. Anthony John, PhD; FRS 1987; CChem, FRSC; Professor of Bioorganic Chemistry, University of Cambridge, 1995–2002, now Emeritus; Fellow, Gonville and Caius College, Cambridge, since 1962; *b* 18 Aug. 1935; *s* of Samuel Arthur Kirby and Gladys Rosina Kirby (*née* Welch); *m* 1962, Sara Sophia Benjamina Nieweg; one *s* two *d*. *Educ:* Eton College; Gonville and Caius College, Cambridge (MA, PhD 1962). NATO postdoctoral Fellow: Cambridge, 1962–63; Brandeis Univ., 1963–64; Cambridge University: Demonstrator, 1964–68, Lectr, 1968–85, Reader, 1985–95, in Organic Chemistry; Gonville and Caius College: Dir of Studies in Natural Scis and Coll. Lectr, 1968–2002; Tutor, 1966–74. Visiting Professor/Scholar: Paris (Orsay), 1970; Groningen, 1973 (Backer Lectr, 2003); Cape Town, 1987; Paris VI, 1987; Haifa, 1991; Queen's, Kingston, Ont, 1996; Toronto, 1997; Western Ontario, 1997. Co-ordinator, European Network on Catalytic Antibodies, 1993–96, on Gemini Surfactants, 1997–2001, on Artificial Nucleases, 2000–04. Fellow, Japan Soc. for Promotion of Science, 1986; Royal Society of Chemistry: Fellow, 1980; Award in Organic Reaction Mechanisms, 1983; Tilden Lectr, 1987; Chm., Organic Reaction Mechanisms Gp, 1986–90; Ingold Lectr, 1996–97. Marin Drinov Medal, Bulgarian Acad. of Scis 2003. Hon. DPhil Univ. of Turku, 2006. *Publications:* (with S. G. Warren) The Organic Chemistry of Phosphorus, 1967; The Anomeric Effect and Related Stereoelectronic Effects at Oxygen, 1983; Stereoelectronic effects, 1996; (with F. Hollfelder) From Enzyme Models to Model Enzymes, 2009; papers in Jls of RSC and Amer. Chem. Soc. *Recreations:* chamber music, walking. *Address:* University Chemical Laboratory, Cambridge CB2 1EW. *T:* (01223) 336370; 87 Holbrook Road, Cambridge CB1 7SX. *T:* (01223) 210403.

KIRBY, Carolyn; solicitor; President, Law Society of England and Wales, 2002–03; Chairman, Mental Health Review Tribunal for Wales, since 1999; *b* 24 May 1953; *d* of Cyril Treharne-Jones and Elaine Margaret Sanders; *m* 1977, Anthony Robert Kirby. *Educ:* Cheltenham Ladies' Coll.; University Coll., Cardiff (LLB Hons). Admitted solicitor, 1979; Partner, Kirby & Partners, Solicitors, Swansea, 1985–97. Legal Registrar to Archdeacon of Gower, 1997–; Church in Wales: Mem., Disciplinary Tribunal, 2001–; Lay Judge, Provincial Court, 2014–. Trustee, Swansea and Brecon Diocesan Trust, 2009–. Chm., Cancer Information and Support Services, 1995–. Chm., Council of Govs, Cheltenham Ladies' Coll., 2004–12. Hon. Fellow: Univ. of Wales, Lampeter, 2002; Cardiff Univ., 2004. Hon. LLD UWE, 2003. *Recreations:* walking, dogs, gardening, interior design. *Address:* Admirals Wood, Vennaway Lane, Parkmill, Swansea SA3 2EA. *T:* (01792) 234494. *E:* sxlawsoc@aol.com.

KIRBY, Dame Georgina (Kamiria), DBE 1994; QSO 1989; JP; Executive Director, Maori Women's Development Inc. (formerly Maori Women's Development Fund), 1978–2011; *b* 31 Jan. 1936; *d* of William Tawhiri Matea Smith and Tuhe Nga Tukemata Christie (*née* Thompson); *m* 1961, Brian Ian Kirby (*d* 2014); two *s* one *d*. *Educ:* Horohoro Sch., Rotorua; Rotorua High Sch.; Auckland Univ. Cert. Book-keeping; Cert. Practical Accounting. Jun. Asst Teacher, Rotorua, 1953–55; NZ PO Trng Officer, 1955–63; managed and partnered husband in service businesses, 1966–70; Personnel Officer, Stock & Station, 1971–76. Estabd Te Taumata Art Gall., 1991; Foundn Trustee, Maori Arts NZ (Toi Maori Aotearoa). Mem., Maori Women's Welfare League Inc., 1976– (Nat. Pres., 1983–87); formed Matatau Maori In Business (Maori Business and Professional Assoc.), 2006. NZ Vice Pres., Commonwealth Countries League, London, 1988–. JP NZ, 1981. Commemoration Medal (NZ), 1988; Women's Suffrage Medal (NZ), 1993. *Publications:* Liberated Learning, 1993; Vision Aotearoa Kaupapa New Zealand, 1994; contrib. NZ Maori Artists and Writers Mag., Koru. *Recreations:* reading, badminton, horse-riding. *Address:* 11A Northland Street, Grey Lynn, Auckland 1021, New Zealand. *T:* (9) 3767032, *T:* and *Fax:* (9) 3077014. *Club:* Zonta International (Auckland).

KIRBY, Jill; writer and policy analyst; *b* Bedford, 29 April 1957; *d* of Kenneth and Christine Fernie; *m* 1985, Richard Kirby; two *s* (and one *s* decd). *Educ:* Rugby High Sch.; Bristol Univ. (LLB). Admitted as solicitor, 1981; Solicitor: Speechly Bircham, 1979–84; Clifford Chance, 1984–86. Chairman: Full Time Mothers, 1998–2001; Family Policy Gp, Centre for Policy Studies, 2001–07; Dir, Centre for Policy Studies, 2007–11. Policy Advr, Renewing One Nation, 2001–03. Mem., Tax Reform Commn, 2005–06. *Publications:* Broken Hearts, 2002; Choosing to be Different, 2003; The Price of Parenthood, 2005; The Nationalisation of Childhood, 2006; Who Do They Think They Are?, 2008; The Reality Gap, 2009; contribs to newspapers and jls. *Recreations:* walking, gardening. *Address:* Yerdley House, Long Compton, Warwicks CV36 5LH.

KIRBY, Hon. Michael Donald, AC 1991; CMG 1983; jurist, arbitrator and mediator; Justice of the High Court of Australia, 1996–2009; Acting Chief Justice of Australia, 2007, 2008; Chair, UN Commission of Inquiry on Human Rights in North Korea, 2013–14; *b* 18 March 1939; *s* of late Donald Kirby and Jean Langmore Kirby; partner, since 1969, Johan van Vloten. *Educ:* Fort Street Boys' High Sch.; Univ. of Sydney (BA, LLM, BEc). Admitted Solicitor, 1962; admitted to the Bar of NSW, 1967; Mem., NSW Bar Council, 1974; Judge, Federal Court of Australia, 1983–84; President, Court of Appeal: NSW, 1984–96; Solomon Is, 1995–96; Actg Chief Justice of NSW, 1988, 1990, 1993. Dep. Pres., Aust. Conciliation and Arbitration Commn, 1975–83; Chairman: Australian Law Reform Commn, 1975–84; OECD Inter-govtl Gp on Privacy and Internat. Data Flows, 1978–80; OECD Inter-govtl Gp on Security of Information Systems, 1991–92; Member: Admin. Review Council of Australia, 1976–84; Council of Aust. Acad. of Forensic Scis, 1978–89 (Pres., 1987–89); Aust. National Commn for Unesco, 1980–83, 1996–2007; Aust. Inst. of Multi-cultural Affairs, 1981–84; Exec., CSIRO, 1983–86; NSW Ministerial Adv. Cttee on AIDS, 1987; Trustee, AIDS Trust of Australia, 1987–93; Commissioner: Global Commn on AIDS, WHO, Geneva, 1989–91; UNAIDS/Lancet Commn on Sustainable Health, 2013–15; UNDP Global Commn on HIV and Law, 2010–12; Chm., UN AIDS expert gp on HIV testing of UN peacekeepers, 2001–02, on human rights and access to treatment, 2002; Member: UN AIDS gp on AIDS and human rights, 2003–; UNODC Judicial Integrity Gp, 2002–; Eminent Persons Gp on future of Commonwealth of Nations, Commonwealth Secretariat, 2010–11; Adv. Council, Transparency Internat., 2011–; Global Fund to Fight Aids, Tuberculosis and Malaria, High Level Panel for Equitable Access to Healthcare, 2015–. Deleg., Unesco Gen. Conf., Paris, 1983; Chm., Unesco Expert Gp on Rights of Peoples, 1989 (Rapporteur, Budapest, 1991); Member: Unesco Expert Gps on Self-Determination and Rights of Peoples, 1984; Perm. Tribunal of Peoples, Rome, 1992; ILO Fact Finding and Conciliation Commn on S Africa, 1991–92; Ethics Cttee, Human Genome Orgn, 1995–2004; Internat. Bioethics Cttee, UNESCO, 1996–2005; Internat. Jury, UNESCO Prize for Teaching of Human Rights, 1994–96; Judicial Ref. Gp, UN High Comr for Human Rights, 2007–; Special Rep. of UN Sec.-Gen., for Human Rights in Cambodia, 1993–96; Ind. Chm., Malawi Constit. Conf., 1994, Chm. Constit. Seminar, 1997; Hon. Advr on bioethics to UN High Comr for Human Rights, 2001–03. International Commission of Jurists: Comr, 1984–2001; Mem. Exec. Cttee, 1989–95, Chm., 1992–95; Pres., 1995–98; Pres., Aust. Section, 1989–96. Internat. Consultant, Commn for Transborder Data Flow Develt, Intergovtl Bureau of Informatics, Rome, 1985–86; Member, Board: Internat. Trustees, Internat. Inst. for Inf. and Communication, Montreal, 1986–2000; Aust. Centre for Internat. Commercial Arbitration, 2009–14; Mem. Council, Human Rights Inst., IBA, London, 2009–; Counselor, Amer. Soc. of Internat. Law, 2009–. President: Criminology Sect., ANZAAS, 1981–82; Law Sect., ANZAAS, 1984–85. Granada Guildhall Lectr, 1984; Acting Prof., Fac. of Salzburg Seminar, Salzburg, 1985, 2000, 2015; Hon. Prof., Nat. Law Sch. of India Univ., Bangalore, 1995–; Visiting Professor of Law: Univ. of NSW, ANU and Southern Cross Univ., 2009–; Univ. of Melbourne, Deakin and Univ. of Tasmania, 2010–; Victoria Univ., 2011–; Univ. of Hong Kong, 2013–; Chinese Univ. of Hong Kong, 2015–. Sen. Anzac Fellow, NZ Govt, 1981; Fellow, NZ Legal Res. Foundn, 1985. Pres., Nat. Book Council of Australia, 1980–83; Member: Library Council of NSW, 1976–85; Council, Australian Opera, 1983–89; Patron: RSPCA, Australia, 2000–09; Voiceless, 2012–; Voiceless (Australia), 2013–. Fellow, Senate, Sydney Univ., 1964–69; Dep. Chancellor, Univ. of Newcastle, NSW, 1978–83; Chancellor, Macquarie Univ., Sydney, 1984–93. Mem. Bd of Governors, Internat. Council for Computer Communications, Washington, 1984–2000; Bd Mem., Kinsey Inst. for Res. in Sex, Gender and Reprodn, Indiana Univ., 2001–13; Adv. Bd Mem., Internat. Human Rights Law Inst., De Paul Univ., Chicago, 2002–. Fellow, Inst. of Arbitrators and Mediators, Aust., 2009 (Pres., 2009–10). Hon. Member: Amer. Law Inst., 2000; Soc. of Legal Scholars, 2006; Hon. Life Member: Aust. Bar Assoc., 2008; NSW Bar Assoc., 2009; Law Council of Aust., 2009. Fellow, Australian Acad. Law, 2009. Hon. FASSA 1997; Hon. Fellow, Australian Acad. of Humanities, 2006; Hon. Bencher, Inner Temple, 2006. Hon. DLitt: Newcastle, NSW, 1987; Ulster, 1998; James Cook, 2003; Hon. LLD: Macquarie, 1994; Sydney, 1996; Nat. Law Sch. of India Univ., 1997; Buckingham, 2000; ANU, 2004; NSW, 2008; Murdoch, Indiana, Melbourne, 2009; Bond, 2009; Univ. of Technol., Sydney, 2009; Colombo, 2010; Victoria, 2011; Deakin, 2012; Monash, 2015, Queen's, Ont, 2015; DUniv: S Australia, 2001; Southern Cross, 2007; Griffith, 2008; La Trobe, 2011; Central Queensland Univ., 2013. Australian Human Rights Medal, 1991; UNESCO Prize for Human Rights Educn, 1998; Gruber Justice Prize, 2010; Meritorious Service to Public Educn Award, Dept of Educn, NSW, 2012. *Publications:* Industrial Index to Australian Labour Law, 1978, 2nd edn 1983; Reform the Law, 1983; The Judges (Boyer Lectures), 1983; (ed jtly) A Touch of Healing, 1986; Through the World's Eye, 2000; Judicial Activism (Hamlyn Lectures), 2004; A Private Life, 2011; What Would Gandhi Do?, 2013; essays and articles in legal and other jls. *Recreation:* work. *Address:* Level 7, 195 Macquarie Street, Sydney, NSW 2000, Australia. *T:* (2) 92315800, *Fax:* (2) 92315811. *E:* mail@michaelkirby.com.au.

KIRBY, Maj.-Gen. Norman George, OBE 1971; FRCS; Consultant Accident and Emergency Surgeon, Guy's Nuffield House, 1994–2004, now Emeritus; Consultant Accident and Emergency Surgeon, 1982–93, Director, Clinical Services, Accidents and Emergencies, 1985–93, Guy's Hospital; *b* 19 Dec. 1926; *s* of George William Kirby and Laura Kirby; *m* 1949, Cynthia Bradley; one *s* one *d*. *Educ:* King Henry VIII Sch., Coventry; Univ. of Birmingham (MB, ChB). FRCS 1964, FRCSE 1980; FICS 1980; FRCEM (FFAEM 1993); DMCC 1997; FIFEM 2000. Surgical Registrar: Plastic Surg. Unit, Stoke Mandeville Hosp., 1950–51; Birmingham Accident Hosp., 1953–55; Postgraduate Med. Sch., Hammersmith, 1964. Regt MO 10 Parachute Regt, 1950–51; OC 5 Parachute Surgical Team, 1956–59 (Suez Landing, 5 Nov. 1956); Officer i/c Surg. Div., BMH Rinteln, 1959–60; OC and Surg. Specialist, BMH Tripoli, 1960–62; OC and Consultant Surgeon, BMH Dhekelia, 1967–70; Chief Cons. Surgeon, Cambridge Mil. Hosp., 1970–72; Cons. Surg. HQ BAOR, 1973–78; Dir of Army Surgery, Cons. Surg. to the Army and Hon. Surgeon to the Queen, 1978–82; Hon. Cons. Surgeon, Westminster Hosp., 1979–. Examr in Anatomy, RCSE, 1982–90; Mem., Court of Examiners, RCS, 1988–94. Chm., Army Med. Dept Working Party Surgical Support for BAOR, 1978–80; Member: MoD Med. Bds, 1978–82; Med. Cttee, Defence Scientific Adv. Council, 1979–82. Hon. Colonel: 308 (Co. of London) Gen. Hosp. RAMC, TA, 1982–87; 144 Para Field Sqdn (formerly Field Ambulance) RAMC (Volunteers), TA, 1985–96; Col Comdt, RAMC, 1987–92. Member: Council, Internat. Coll. of Surgeons; Airborne Med. Soc.; British Assoc. for Accident and Emergency Medicine (formerly Casualty Surgeons Assoc.), 1981–94 (Vice-Pres., 1988; Pres., 1990–93); Pres., Med. Soc. of London,

1992–93 (FMS 1981; Hon. Editor, 2003–12); Vice-Pres., British Assoc. of Trauma in Sport, 1982–88; Chm., Accidents & Emergencies Cttee, SE Thames RHA, 1984–88. Mem. Council, TAVRA, Gtr London, 1990–97. Liveryman, Soc. of Apothecaries of London, 1983–; Mem., HAC, 1988. Fellow, British Orthopaedic Assoc., 1967. Hon. Mem., Amer. Coll. of Emergency Physicians, 1993. McCombe Lectr, RCSE, 1979. Mem., Editl Bd, Brit. Jl Surg. and Injury, 1979–82. Mem., Surgical Travellers Club, 1979–2000. OStJ 1977 (Mem. Council, London, 1990–2005). Mitchener Medal, RCS, 1982. *Publications:* (ed) Field Surgery Pocket Book, 1981; Pocket Reference, Accidents and Emergencies, 1988, 2nd edn 1991; contrib. Brit. Jl Surg., Proc. RSocMed, etc. *Recreations:* travel, motoring, reading, archaeology. *Address:* 14 Hillview Crescent, Baldwin's Gate, Newcastle under Lyme, Staffs ST5 5DE. *T:* (01782) 680029.

KIRBY, Simon Gerard; MP (C) Brighton Kemptown, since 2010; an Assistant Government Whip, since 2015; *b* Hastings, 22 Dec. 1964; *m* 1992, Elizabeth Radford; four *s* two *d*. *Educ:* Hastings Grammar Sch.; Open Univ. (BSc Hons). Man. Dir, C-Side Ltd, 1989–2001. Member (C): E Sussex CC, 1992–93, 2005–09; Brighton BC, 1995–97; Brighton and Hove CC, 1996–99; Mid Sussex DC, 1999–2001. *Address:* House of Commons, SW1A 0AA. *T:* (020) 7219 7024. *E:* simon.kirby.mp@parliament.uk.

KIRBY-HARRIS, Robert, PhD; Secretary General, International Union of Pure and Applied Physics, 2008–12; Chairman, Cornwall Area of Outstanding Natural Beauty, since 2013; *b* 12 June 1952; *s* of Lionel George Harris and Enid Josephine Harris; adopted surname Kirby-Harris, adding family name, 1980; *m* 1979, Abigail Anne Mee; two *s*. *Educ:* Ashford Grammar Sch.; Univ. of Kent at Canterbury (BSc 1st Cl. Hons Theoretical Phys 1973); Clare Coll., Cambridge (MA (III) Applied Maths and Theoretical Phys 1974); Univ. of Sussex (PGCE Secondary Sci. 1975); Plymouth Poly. (DMS 1985); Lancaster Univ. (PhD Educnl Res. 2003). CPhys 1985, FInstP 2005; MIMA 1985, CMath 1999. Secondary Sci. Teacher, Wakeford Sch., Havant, 1975–77; RN Instructor Officer, Lt RN, 1977–82, Lt Comdr RN, 1982–85: Lectr in Electronics and Maths, RN Weapons Engrg Sch., Fareham, 1977–79; Sen. Instructor Officer, RN Supply and Secretariat Sch., Chatham, 1980–83; Sen. Lectr in Maths, RNEC Manadon, Plymouth, 1983–85; Exec. Dir, Poly Enterprise Plymouth, 1985–90; Dep. Vice-Chancellor (Resources), Middlesex Univ., 1991–95; Pro Vice-Chancellor (Admin and Finance), Univ. of Namibia, S Africa, 1996–2002; Corp. Dir, Ops and Finance, Royal Botanic Gardens, Kew, 2003–05; Chief Exec., Inst. of Physics, 2005–12. Mem. Bd, Science Council, 2008–12 (Vice Pres., 2006–08). Dir, Big Bang Fair Community Interest Co., 2010–13. Mem., SRHE, 1997–2007. *Publications:* contrib. Higher Educn jl. *Recreations:* hill walking, ski-ing, gardens, arts, family life. *Address:* Camel View House, St Breward, Bodmin, Cornwall PL30 4LU. *E:* r.kirby_harris@btinternet.com. *Club:* Naval.

KIRCH, Sir David (Roderick), KBE 2013; Senior Trustee, David Kirch Charitable Trust, since 1987; *b* Wimbledon, London, 23 July 1936; *s* of Leonard Kirch and Margaret Kirch. *Educ:* Tonbridge Sch. Property developments and property investments. Pres., Age Concern Jersey, 2007–. *Recreations:* golf when younger, now bridge. *Address:* The Octagon, Le Mont de Gouray, St Martin, Jersey JE3 6ET. *T:* (01534) 851339, *Fax:* (01534) 851120. *E:* admin@chapsjsy.net.

KIRCHNER, Prof. Emil Joseph, PhD; Professor of European Studies, Department of Government, University of Essex, since 1992; *b* 19 March 1942; *m* 1975, Joanna Bartlett; two *s*. *Educ:* Case Western Reserve Univ. (BA Econ 1970; MA 1971; PhD 1976, Pol Sci.). Essex University: Lectr and Sen. Lectr, Dept of Govt, 1974–92; Hon. Jean Monnet Prof. of European Integration, 1997–. Visiting Professor: Dept of Pol Sci., Univ. of Connecticut, 1986–87; Centre for Econ. Res. and Grad. Educn, Charles Univ., Prague, 1997–2000; Hon. Guest Prof., Renmin Univ. of China, 2001–; Dist. Vis. Scholar, Suffolk Univ., 2008; NATO Fellowship, 2001. Chm., Assoc. for Study of German Politics, 2002– (Mem., 1989–90). Gen. Series Editor, Europe in Change (Manchester Univ. Press), 1993; Exec. Ed., Jl of European Integration, 1997–2007. FAcSS (AcSS 2009). Lifetime Achievement Award in Contemp. Eur. Studies, University Assoc. of Contemp. Eur. Studies, 2012; Cross, Order of Merit (Germany), 2002. *Publications:* Decision Making in the European Community, 1992; (jtly) The Federal Republic of Germany and NATO: 40 years after, 1992; (jtly) The Future of European Security, 1994; (jtly) The Recasting of the European Order: security architectures and economic co-operation, 1996; (jtly) The New Europe: east, west, centre, 1997; Decentralization and Transition in the Visegrad, 1999; (jtly) Committee Governance in the EU, 2000; (jtly) Studies on Policies and Policy Processes of the European Union, 2003–; (ed with James Sperling) Global Security Governance, 2007; (with James Sperling) EU Security Governance, 2008; (ed with James Sperling) National Security Cultures, 2010; (ed with Roberto Dominguez) The Security Governance of Regional Organizations, 2011; (ed jtly) The Palgrave Handbook of EU Asia Relations, 2013. *Recreations:* music, sports, travel.

KIRCHSCHLAGER, Angelika; mezzo-soprano opera singer; *b* Salzburg, 24 Nov. 1965; *d* of Walter and Maria Kirchschlager; one *s*. *Educ:* Vienna Music Acad. (Singing Dip.). Opera début, Graz Opera, 1991; début, Vienna State Opera, 1993; major débuts include: NY Metropolitan Opera, 1997; Opéra Nat. de Paris, 1997; Teatro alla Scala, 1998; Bayerische Staatsoper Munich, 2001; Royal Opera Hse, Covent Gdn, 2002; Deutsche Oper Berlin, 2005. Guest Professor: Salzburg Mozarteum, 2007–11; Univ. of Graz, 2011–13. Kammersängerin, Vienna State Opera, 2007. Hon. Mem., Royal Acad. Music, 2009. ECHO Klassik Award, 2000, 2005, 2010; Grammy Award, 2004; BBC Music Mag. Award, 2013; Eur. Cultural Award, 2013. *Publications:* Was ich dir sagen möchte - Lass dir's gut gehen, 2005; Angelika Kirschschlager: liederreisebuch, 2012; Ich erfinde mich jeden Tag neu, 2013. *Address:* c/o Askonas Holt, Lincoln House, 300 High Holborn, WC1V 7JH.

KIRK, Anthony James Nigel; QC 2001; *b* 3 May 1958; *s* of late James Brian Kirk and of Lavinia Mary Kirk (*née* Kellow). *Educ:* Ipswich Sch.; King Edward VII Sch., Lytham St Anne's; King's Coll., London (LLB Hons; AKC). Called to the Bar, Gray's Inn, 1981 (Stuart Cunningham Macaskie and Lord Justice Holker Schol.; Bencher, 2006); in practice as barrister, 1982–. Chm., Family Law Bar Assoc., 2006–08 (Vice-Chm., 2003–05; Nat. Sec., 1999–2002); Member: Bar Council, 1996–99 (Mem., Professional Conduct and Complaints Cttee, 1999–2002); Bd, Family Mediators' Assoc., 1999–2002; ADR Cttee, 2002–; Internat. Family Law Cttee, 2002–. Fellow, Internat. Acad. of Matrimonial Lawyers. FRSocMed. Mem., RCO. *Publications:* (contrib.) Jackson & Davies Matrimonial Finance and Taxation, 6th edn 1996; (contrib.) Rayden & Jackson on Divorce, 19th edn. *Recreation:* classical music. *Address:* (chambers) 1 King's Bench Walk, Temple, EC4Y 7DB. *T:* (020) 7936 1500.

KIRK, Geoffrey Eric, RDI 2001; FREng, FIMechE; FRAeS; FIED; Chief Design Engineer, Civil Aerospace, Rolls-Royce, 1994–2007; *b* 24 Feb. 1945; *s* of Eric and Lily Kirk (*née* Melbourne); *m* 1966, Linda Jean Butcher. *Educ:* Bramcote Hills Tech. Grammar Sch.; Loughborough Tech. Coll.; Loughborough Univ. (Associateship). CEng 1973, FREng 2005; FIMechE 1993; FRAeS 1993; FIED 2002. Drawing office student apprentice, 1961–66, Design Draughtsman, 1966–68, Brush Electrical Engrg Co.; design engr, Rolls-Royce, 1968–73; adult trainee, Rolls-Royce/Loughborough Univ., 1971–72; Chief Design Engr, Ariel Pressings, 1973–75; Rolls-Royce: Sen. Tech. Designer, 1975–82; Chief Design Engr, RB211-535E4, 1982–85; Chief Engineer: V2500, 1985–87; Res. and Mfg Technol., 1987–89; Chief Design Engineer, Civil Engineers, 1989–92; Head of Powerplant Engineering, 1992–94. Visiting Professor: Queen Mary, Univ. of London (formerly QMW), 1996–2011 (Hon. Fellow, 2005); Nottingham Univ., 2003–; Cambridge Univ., 2006–12. Mem., Design Council, 2005–10. FRSA 2002. Hon. Pres., IED, 2006–10 (Gerald Frewer Meml Trophy, 2002; Founder's Prize, 2011). British Bronze Medal, RAeS, 1998; Prince Philip Designers' Prize, 2002; Sir Misha Black Medal, RCA, 2006. *Publications:* contribs to various confs and seminars, predominantly on design. *Recreations:* sport, photography, private flying.

KIRK, Matthew John Lushington; Group External Affairs Director, and Member, Executive Committee, Vodafone Group Plc, since 2009 (Director, External Relationships, 2006–09); *b* 10 Oct. 1960; *s* of Sir Peter Michael Kirk, MP and Elizabeth Mary Kirk (*née* Graham); *m* 1989, Anna Thérèse Macey, *d* of Rear-Adm. David Edward Macey, CB; two *d*. *Educ:* Vinehall Sch.; Coll. Joseph d'Arbaud; Felsted Sch.; St John's Coll., Oxford (MA Phil. and Theol.); Ecole Nat. d'Admin, Paris (Dip. Internat. d'Admin Public). Entered HM Diplomatic Service, 1982; UK Mission to UN, NY, 1982, Vienna, 1983; FCO, 1983–84; 3rd, later 2nd, Sec., Belgrade, 1984–87; FCO, 1987–88; Office of Governor of Gibraltar, 1988; FCO, 1989–92; 1st Secretary: Paris, 1993–97; FCO, 1997–98; Cabinet Secretariat (on secondment), 1998–99; FCO, 1999–2002; Ambassador to Finland, 2002–06. Alternate Dir, Vodafone Essar Ltd (India), 2007–09; Dir, UK-India Business Council, 2010–12. Trustee, Vodafone Gp Foundn, 2009–; Member: Adv. Council, World Wide Web Foundn, 2011–; WEF Global Agenda Council, 2014–. Mem., Koenigswinter Cttee, 2008–. Mem., BUPA Assoc., 2013–. Gov., Downe House Sch., 2009– (Chm., 2015–). FRGS 1989. *Recreations:* music, wine, walking, travel. *Address:* Vodafone Group Services Ltd, One Kingdom Street, Paddington, W2 6BY. *E:* matthew.kirk@vodafone.com. *Clubs:* Brooks's, Beefsteak.

KIRK, Prof. Raymond Maurice, FRCS; Honorary Professor of Surgery, Division of Surgery and Interventional Sciences, University College London (formerly Royal Free Hospital School of Medicine, then Royal Free and University College Medical School), since 2004 (part time Lecturer in Anatomy, 1989–2011); Hon. Consulting Surgeon, Royal Free Hospital (Consulting Surgeon, 1989); *b* 31 Oct. 1923; *m* 1952, Margaret Schafran; one *s* two *d*. *Educ:* Mundella Sch., Nottingham; County Secondary Sch., West Bridgford; King's College London; Charing Cross Hosp. MB BS, MS, London; LRCP. RN 1942–46; Lieut RNVR. Charing Cross Hosp., 1952–53; Lectr in Anatomy, King's Coll. London, 1953–54; Hammersmith Hosp., 1954–56; Charing Cross Hosp., 1956–60; Senior Surgical Registrar, Royal Free Hosp., 1961; Consultant Surgeon: Willesden Gen. Hosp., 1962–74; Royal Free Hosp. Group, 1964–89. Dir, Overseas Doctors' Trng Scheme, RCS, 1990–95; formerly Mem. Court of Examrs, RCS; formerly Examr to RCPSG, Univs of London, Liverpool, Bristol, Khartoum, Colombo, Kuwait; Mem. Council, RCS, 1983–91; FRSocMed (Pres., Surgical Section, 1986–87). Member: British Soc. of Gastroenterol.; Soc. of Academic and Res. Surgery; Med. Soc. of London (Pres., 1988–89); Hunterian Soc. (Pres., 1995–96); Soc. of Authors. Hon. Fellow: Assoc. of Surgeons of Poland; Coll. of Surgeons of Sri Lanka. Hon. Editor, Annals of RCS, 1983–92. *Publications:* Manual of Abdominal Operations, 1967; Basic Surgical Techniques, 1973, 6th edn 2010; (jtly) Surgery, 1974; General Surgical Operations, 1978, 6th edn as Kirk's General Surgical Operations, 2013; Complications of Upper Gastrointestinal Tract Surgery, 1987; (jtly) Clinical Surgery in General, 1993, 4th edn 2004; A Career in Medicine, 1998; (jtly) Essential General Surgical Operations, 2001, 2nd edn 2007; papers in sci. jls and chapters in books on peptic ulcer, oesophageal, gastric and general abdominal surgery and surgical trng. *Recreations:* opera, theatre, surgical history. *Address:* 10 Southwood Lane, Highgate Village, N6 5EE. *T:* (020) 8340 8575, *Fax:* (020) 7472 6444. *E:* r.kirk@ucl.ac.uk, rm.kirk.kirk@gmail.com. *Club:* Royal Society of Medicine.

KIRK, Richard Stanley, CBE 2006; Chief Executive, Poundstretcher Ltd, 2012; *b* 16 Nov. 1945; *s* of Charles Kirk and Margaret (*née* Green); *m* 1st, 1969 (marr. diss. 1988); two *s*; 2nd, 1995, Barbara Mount (marr. diss. 2005). *Educ:* Chesterfield Grammar Sch. Store Manager, then Area Manager, F. W. Woolworth, 1966–77; Iceland Frozen Foods, subseq. Iceland Gp, PLC, 1977–96: Stores Dir, 1982–86; Man. Dir, 1986–96; Chief Exec., Peacock's Stores, 1996–2012. *Recreations:* ski-ing, shooting, travel.

KIRK-GREENE, Anthony Hamilton Millard, CMG 2001; MBE 1963; FRHistS; Emeritus Fellow, St Antony's College, Oxford, since 1992; *b* 16 May 1925; *e s* of late Leslie and Helen Kirk-Greene; *m* 1967, Helen Margaret Martyn Sellar. *Educ:* Rugby Sch. (Open Schol.); Clare Coll., Cambridge (Open Schol.; MA); Edinburgh Univ. Served Indian Army, 8th Punjab Regt, 1943–47. Colonial Admin. Service, Northern Nigeria, 1950–66; Supervisor, Admin. Service Trng, 1957–60; Sen. Dist Officer, 1960–66; Reader in Govt, Ahmadu Bello Univ., 1962–66; Vis. Fellow, Clare Coll., Cambridge, 1967; Sen. Res. Fellow in African Studies, St Antony's Coll., Oxford, 1967–92; Special Lectr in Modern Hist. of Africa, Oxford Univ., 1981–92; Director: Oxford Colonial Records Project, 1980–84; Oxford Univ. Foreign Service Prog., 1986–90. Chm., Bd of Mgt, Beit Fund, 1987–92. ODA Consultant, E African Staff Coll., 1972; UK Election Supervisor, Rhodesia/Zimbabwe, 1980. Harkness Fellow, Northwestern Univ. and UCLA, 1958–59; Hans Wolff Lectr, Indiana Univ., 1973. Killam Vis. Prof., Calgary Univ., 1985; Leverhulme Emeritus Fellow, 1993; Adjunct Prof., Stanford Univ. in Oxford, 1992–99. Mem. Council, Britain-Nigeria Assoc., 1984–2008; Pres., African Studies Assoc., UK, 1988–90 (Distinguished Africanist Award, 2005); Vice-Pres., Royal African Soc., 1990–2006. Mem., Oral History Cttee, British Empire and Commonwealth Mus., 1998–. Gen. Ed., Methuen Studies in African History, 1970–80; Academic Consultant: Holmes and Meier African Series, 1980–85; Radcliffe Press, 1992–; Jt Ed., Hoover Colonial Series, 1985–90; Series Ed., Modern Revivals in Africa, Gregg Press, 1990–95; Reviews Editor: Corona Club Jl, 1990–2000; Britain-Nigeria Assoc. Newsletter, 2002–07; Associate Ed., Oxford DNB, 1996–2002. *Publications:* Adamawa Past and Present, 1958; Barth's Travels in Nigeria, 1962; Principles of Native Administration in Nigeria, 1965; (with S. J. Hogben) Emirates of Northern Nigeria, 1966; Hausa Proverbs, 1967; Crisis and Conflict in Nigeria 1966–1970, 1971; (with C. Kraft) Teach Yourself Hausa, 1975; A Biographical Dictionary of the British Colonial Governor, 1980; 'Stay by Your Radios': the military in Africa, 1981; (with D. Rimmer) Nigeria since 1970, 1981; A Biographical Dictionary of the British Colonial Service, 1991; Diplomatic Initiative: a Jubilee history, 1994; (with J. H. Vaughan) Hamman Yaji: diary of a Nigerian Chief, 1995 (Best Text Award, African Studies Assoc., USA, 1996); On Crown Service, 1999; (with D. Rimmer) Britain's Intellectual Engagement with Africa, 2000; Britain's Imperial Administrators, 2000; Glimpses of Empire, 2001; Symbol of Authority, 2005; Aspects of Empire, 2012; numerous monographs, chapters and articles on African and Imperial history. *Recreations:* reading, travel, controlled walking, wine tasting; played hockey for Cambridge Univ. 1948–50 (Capt., CU Wanderers, 1949–50). *Address:* c/o St Antony's College, Oxford OX2 6JF. *T:* (01865) 284700. *Club:* Hawks (Cambridge).

KIRKBRIDE, Julie; Consultant, Tetra Strategy, since 2010; *b* 5 June 1960; *d* of late Henry Raymond Kirkbride and of Barbara (*née* Bancroft); *m* 1997, Andrew James MacKay, *qv*; one *s*. *Educ:* Highlands Sch., Halifax; Girton Coll., Cambridge. Researcher, Yorkshire TV, 1983–86; Producer: BBC news and current affairs, 1986–89; ITN, 1989–92; Political Correspondent: Daily Telegraph, 1992–96; also Social Affairs Ed., Sunday Telegraph, 1996. MP (C) Bromsgrove, 1997–2010. Shadow Sec. of State for Culture, Media and Sport, 2003–04. Rotary Foundn Scholar, Yorkshire Area, 1982–83. *Recreations:* walking, travelling, opera.

KIRKBY, Dame (Carolyn) Emma, DBE 2007 (OBE 2000); freelance classical concert singer; soprano; *b* 26 Feb. 1949; *d* of late Capt. Geoffrey Kirkby, CBE, DSC, RN and of Daphne Kirkby; one *s* by Anthony Rooley, *qv*. *Educ:* Hanford School; Sherborne School for Girls; Somerville College, Oxford (BA Classics). FGS (FGSM 1991). Private singing lessons with Jessica Cash. Regular appearances with Taverner Choir and Players, 1972–; Member: Consort of Musicke, 1973–; Academy of Ancient Music, 1975–; numerous radio broadcasts, gramophone recordings, appearances at the Proms, 1977–. Hon. DLitt Salford, 1985; Hon. DMus: Bath, 1994; Sheffield, 2000; Oxford, 2008; Newcastle, 2010; York, 2011. Queen's Medal for Music, 2010. *T:* (Consort of Musicke) (020) 8444 6565. *E:* consort@easynet.co.uk.

KIRKHAM, family name of **Baroness Berners** and **Baron Kirkham**.

KIRKHAM, Baron *cr* 1999 (Life Peer), of Old Cantley in the county of South Yorkshire; **Graham Kirkham,** Kt 1996; CVO 2001; Partner, Black Diamond Investments LP, since 2010; *b* 14 Dec. 1944; *m* 1965, Pauline Fisher; one *s* one *d*. Founder, 1969, Chm., 1983–2010, Northern Furnishing, subseq. DFS Furniture Co. Ltd. Sen. Party Treas., Conservative Party, 1997–98. Trustee, Duke of Edinburgh's Award Scheme (Chm., Bd of Trustees, 2010–); Dep. Patron, Outward Bound, 2006–. Dep. Pres., Animal Health Trust, 2003–. Hon. Liveryman, Furniture Makers' Co., 2007. Hon. Dr Bradford, 1997. *Address:* Black Diamond Investments, 8 Ebor Court, Redhouse Interchange, Adwick-le-Street, Doncaster DN6 7FE.

KIRKHAM, Donald Herbert, CBE 1996; FCIS; Group Chief Executive, Woolwich Building Society, 1991–95 (Chief Executive, 1986–90); *b* 1 Jan. 1936; *s* of Herbert and Hettie Kirkham; *m* 1960, Kathleen Mary Lond; one *s* one *d*. *Educ:* Grimsby Technical Sch. Woolwich Equitable Building Society, later Woolwich Building Society: Representative, 1959; Branch Manager, 1963; Gen. Manager's Asst, 1967; Business Planning Manager, 1970; Asst Gen. Manager, 1972; Gen. Manager, 1976; Mem. Local Board, 1979; Dep. Chief Gen. Manager, 1981; Mem. Board, 1982; non-exec. Dir, 1996–97; Dir, Gresham Insurance Co. Ltd, 1995–96. President: Banque Woolwich SA, 1995–2001; Banca Woolwich SpA, 1995–2002. Director: Horniman Museum and Public Park Trust, 1989–2004 (Chm., 1996–2004); Building Socs Investor Protection Bd, 1995–97; Bexley and Greenwich HA, 1996–98 and 1999–2001; Oxleas NHS Foundn Trust, 2006–09. Chartered Building Societies Institute: Mem. Council, 1976; Dep. Pres., 1980; Pres., 1981; Vice-Pres., 1986–93, then Vice-Pres., CIB, 1993–98; Institute of Chartered Secretaries and Administrators: Mem. Council, 1979; Vice-Pres., 1985; Sen. Vice-Pres., 1990; Pres., 1991; Building Societies Association: Mem. Council, 1991–95; Dep. Chm., 1993–94; Chm., 1994–95. Trustee, Ranyard Meml Charitable Trust (formerly Ranyard Charitable Trust), 2001–10. Hon. DBA Thames Poly., 1991. *Address:* 2 Chaundrye Close, The Court Yard, Eltham, SE9 5QB. *T:* (020) 8859 4295. *Club:* Christchurch Sailing.

KIRKHAM, Elizabeth Anne, (Libby); *see* Wiener, E. A.

KIRKHAM, Her Honour Frances Margaret, CBE 2011; FCIArb; a Senior Circuit Judge, Technology and Construction Court, Birmingham, 2000–11; Judge, Qatar International Court, since 2013; Chartered Arbitrator, adjudicator and mediator; trainer of advocacy and advanced litigation skills; *b* 29 Oct. 1947; *d* of Brian Llewellyn Morgan Davies and Natalie May Davies (*née* Stephens); *m* 1971, Barry Charles Kirkham. *Educ:* King's Coll. London (BA Hons 1969; AKC 1969). FCIArb 1991. Bank of England, 1969–73; Lloyds Bank Internat., 1973–74; admitted solicitor, 1978; Pinsent & Co., 1976–84; Bettinsons, 1984–87; Edge & Ellison, 1987–95; Dibb Lupton Alsop, 1995–2000. Parly Boundary Comr, 2000; Mem., Judicial Appts Commn, 2006–11. Member: Wkg Party on Civil Justice Reform, Law Soc. and Bar Council, 1992–93; Civil Litigation Cttee, 1988–92, Litigation Casework Cttee, 1990–92, Law Soc.; Civil Litigation Cttee, Birmingham Law Soc., 1992–93; Council, CIArb, 1992–97, 2000 (Chm., W Midlands Br., 1994–97). Non-exec. Dir, Royal Orthopaedic Hosp. NHS Foundn Trust, 2011–. Founder Chm., W Midlands Assoc. Women Solicitors; Sec., UK Assoc. of Women Judges, 2003–06. Hon. Member: Arbrix, 2002–; Technol. and Construction Ct Solicitors' Assoc., 2005– (formerly Founder Cttee Mem.; Clare Edwards Award, 2008); Technol. and Construction Bar Assoc., 2011–; Member: Soc. of Construction Arbitrators, 2011–; Professional Conduct Cttee, CIArb, 2012–. Mem., Adv. Bd, Centre for Advanced Litigation, Nottingham Law Sch., 1992–97. Consultant, Qatar Internat. Ct and Dispute Resolution Centre, 2012. Hon. Bencher, Inner Temple, 2008. Gov., Heathfield Sch., Harrow, 1981–91 (Chm., 1984–91). Hon. Life Mem., Soc. of Construction Law, 2014. Lifetime Achievement Award, Birmingham Law Soc., 2011. *Recreations:* time with friends, sailing, ski-ing, walking, music, theatre. *Address:* Atkin Chambers, Gray's Inn, WC1R 5AT. *Club:* University Women's.

KIRKHAM, Rt Rev. John Dudley Galtrey; Assistant Bishop, Diocese of Salisbury, since 2001; *b* 20 Sept. 1935; *s* of late Rev. Canon Charles Dudley Kirkham and Doreen Betty Galtrey; *m* 1986, Mrs Hester Gregory. *Educ:* Lancing Coll.; Trinity Coll., Cambridge (BA 1959, MA 1963). Commnd, Royal Hampshire Regt, seconded to 23 (K) Bn, King's African Rifles, 1954–56. Trinity Coll., Cambridge, 1956–59; Westcott House, 1960–62; Curate, St Mary-le-Tower, Ipswich, 1962–65; Chaplain to Bishop of Norwich, 1965–69; Priest in Charge, Rockland St Mary w. Hellington, 1967–69; Chaplain to Bishop of New Guinea, 1969; Asst Priest, St Martin-in-the-Fields and St Margaret's, Westminster, 1970–72; Domestic Chaplain to Archbishop of Canterbury, and Canterbury Diocesan Director of Ordinands, 1972–76; Bp Suffragan, later Area Bp, of Sherborne, 1976–2001; Canon and Preb., Salisbury Cath., 1977–2001, and 2002–10; Bp to the Forces, 1992–2001. Archbishop of Canterbury's Advr to HMC, 1990–92. Commissary to Bp of Polynesia and Archbp of PNG. Hon. Chaplain: Princess of Wales Royal Regt, 1992–; KAR and EAF Assoc., 2001–. Provost, Western Region, Woodard Schs, 2002–10. ChStJ 1991; Chaplain to the Guild of the Nineteen Lubricators. Croix d'Argent de Saint-Rombaut, 1973. *Recreations:* walking, bicycling, gardening, woodwork. *Address:* Flamston House, Flamstone Street, Bishopstone, Salisbury, Wilts SP5 4BZ. *Clubs:* Army and Navy, Kandahar.

KIRKHAM, Keith Edwin, OBE 1987; PhD; Administrative Director, Clinical Research Centre, Medical Research Council, 1988–94; *b* 20 Oct. 1929; *s* of Thomas Kirkham and Clara Prestwich Willacy; *m* 1953, Dorothea Mary Fisher; two *s*. *Educ:* Kirkham Grammar Sch.; Birmingham Univ. (BSc); Fitzwilliam House, Cambridge (DipAgrSci; T. H. Middleton Prize); MA, PhD Cantab. National Service, 2nd Lieut RA, 1955–57. Asst in Res., Cambridge, 1951–54; Univ. Demonstr, Cambridge, 1954–60; Sci. Staff, Clin. Endocrinology Res. Unit, MRC, 1960–73; Asst Dir (Admin), Clin. Res. Centre, MRC, 1973–88. Sec., Soc. for Endocrinology, 1975–79. Governor: Harrow Coll. of Higher Educn, 1983–90 (Chm. of Govs, 1986–90); Univ. of Westminster (formerly Poly. of Central London), 1990–2000. Hon. DSc Westminster, 1999. *Publications:* contribs to sci. jls on endocrinology. *Recreations:* cruising, sport (watching).

KIRKHILL, Baron *cr* 1975 (Life Peer), of Kirkhill, Aberdeen; **John Farquharson Smith;** *b* 7 May 1930; *s* of Alexander F. Smith and Ann T. Farquharson; *m* 1965, Frances Mary Walker Reid; one step *d*. Lord Provost of the City and Royal Burgh of Aberdeen, 1971–75. Minister of State, Scottish Office, 1975–78. Chm., N of Scotland Hydro-Electric Bd, 1979–82. Deleg. to Parly Assembly of Council of Europe and WEU, 1987–2001 (Chm., Cttee on Legal Affairs and Human Rights, 1991–95). Hon. LLD Aberdeen, 1974. *Address:* 3 Rubislaw Den North, Aberdeen AB15 4AL. *T:* (01224) 314167.

KIRKHOPE, Timothy John Robert; Member (C) Yorkshire and the Humber Region, European Parliament, since 1999; solicitor; *b* 29 April 1945; *s* of late John Thomas Kirkhope and Dorothy Buemann Kirkhope (*née* Bolt); *m* 1969, Caroline (*née* Maling); four *s*. *Educ:* Royal Grammar School, Newcastle upon Tyne; College of Law, Guildford. Conservative Party: joined 1961 (N Area Vice-Chm. of YC and Mem., Nat. Cttee); Hexham Treasurer, 1982–85; Exec., N Area, 1975–87; Mem., Nat. Exec., 1985–87; Mem. Bd, 2005–07 and 2008–10; Mem., Northern Bd and Yorks Bd, 2007–. County Councillor, Northumberland, 1981–85. Mem., Newcastle Airport Bd, 1982–85; Mem., Northern RHA, 1982–86; Founder Lawyer Mem., Mental Health Act Commn, 1983–86. Contested (C): Durham, Feb. 1974; Darlington, 1979. MP (C) Leeds North East, 1987–97; contested (C) same seat, 1997. PPS to Minister of State for the Envmt and Countryside, 1989–90; an Asst Govt Whip, 1990–92; a Lord Comr of HM Treasury (Govt Whip), 1992–95; Vice Chamberlain, HM Household, 1995; Parly Under-Sec. of State, Home Office, 1995–97. Mem., Select Cttee on Statutory Instruments, 1987–90; Vice Chm., Backbench Legal Cttee, 1988–89; Jt Hon. Sec., Cons. Backbench Envmt Cttee, 1988–89. European Parliament: Chief Whip, 1999–2001, Leader, 2004–07 and 2008–10, UK Conservatives; Cons. spokesman: on justice and home affairs, 1999–2007, 2009–; on transport and tourism, 2007–09; Mem., Culture, Media, Arts, Youth and Educn Cttee, 1999–2002 (Substitute Mem., 2009–); Cons. Mem., Future of Europe Convention, 2002–04; Vice-Chm., EPP-ED, 2004–05; Vice-Pres., EP Const. Affairs Cttee, 2007–09; Dir, Movt for European Reform, 2007–09; Founder and Dep. Leader, European Cons. and Reformist Gp, 2009–11; Chm., EP Delegn to Australia and NZ, 2008–09; Mem., EP Delegn to USA, 2009–; Mem., Special Justice Home Affairs and Civil Liberties Cttee of Inquiry into Electronic Mass Surveillance of EU Citizens, 2013–14. Vice-Chm., Special Cttee on Organised Crime, 2012–14. Mem., Adv. Panel, Europarl TV, 2009–. Chm., Kirkhope Commn on Asylum, 2003, on Immigration, 2004, Cons Party. Dir, Bournemouth and W Hampshire Water Co., 1999–11. Dep. Chm., GBA, 1990–98. Trustee, Biwater Retirement and Security Scheme, 2011–. Gov., Royal Grammar Sch., Newcastle upon Tyne, 1989–99. MInstD 1998. *Recreations:* flying (holds private pilot's licence), tennis, golf, swimming, watching TV quiz shows, collecting and appreciating classic cars. *Address:* Beechwood Farm, Scotton, Knaresborough, N Yorks HG5 9HY; European Parliament, Rue Wiertz, Brussels 1047, Belgium. *Clubs:* Northern Counties (Newcastle upon Tyne); Dunstanburgh Castle Golf (Northumberland).

KIRKMAN, (John) Paul; Director, National Railway Museum, since 2012; *b* Bolton, 8 Aug. 1967; *s* of John Kevan Kirkman and Susan Elizabeth Kirkman (*née* Fell); *m* 2013, Lilly Shahravesh. *Educ:* Univ. of Edinburgh (MA Philos. 1989); Goldsmiths Coll., Univ. of London (MA Art Hist. 1998). HM Treasury, 1991–95; Private Sec. to Dir Gen. of CBI, 1995–96; Hd, Policy and Planning, Natural Hist. Mus., 1999–2001; HM Treasury, 2001–05; Department for Culture, Media and Sport: Hd, Mus, Libraries and Cultural Property, 2005–06; Hd, Arts, 2006–08; Dep. Dir, Progs, 2008–11; Hd, Arts, 2011–12; Hd, Arts and Creative Industries, 2012. *Recreations:* cycling, cooking. *Address:* National Railway Museum, Leeman Road, York YO26 4XJ. *T:* (01904) 686200. *E:* paul.kirkman@nrm.org.uk.

KIRKMAN, William Patrick, MBE 1993; Secretary: University of Cambridge Careers Service, 1968–92; Cambridge Society, 1992–2003; Administrator, American Friends of Cambridge University, 2000–01; Fellow, Wolfson College, (formerly University College), Cambridge, 1968–2000, now Emeritus; *b* 23 Oct. 1932; *s* of late Geoffrey Charles Aylward Kirkman and Bertha Winifred Kirkman; *m* 1959, Anne Teasdale Fawcett; two *s* one *d*. *Educ:* Churcher's Coll., Petersfield, Hants; Oriel Coll., Oxford. 2nd cl. hons, mod. langs, 1955; MA 1959; MA (Cantab) by incorporation, 1968. National Service, 1950–52, RASC (L/Cpl); TA, 1952–59, Intell. Corps (Lieut). Editorial staff: Express & Star, Wolverhampton, 1955–57; The Times, 1957–64 (Commonwealth staff, 1960–64, Africa Correspondent, 1962–64). Asst Sec., Oxford Univ. Appointments Cttee, 1964–68. Chm., Standing Conf. of University Appointments Services, 1971–73; Member: Management Cttee, Central Services Unit for Univ. Careers and Appointments Services, 1971–74, 1985–87; British Cttee, Journalists in Europe, 1985–97; Cambridge Univ. PR Co-ordinating Cttee, 1987–96; Trng Bd, ESRC, 1990–93; Non-service Mem., Home Office Extended Interview Bds, 1993–2002. Member: BBC South and East Regl Adv. Council, 1990–92, Midlands and E Regl Adv. Council, 1992–93, E Regl Adv. Council, 1994–96; Chm., BBC Radio Cambridgeshire Adv. Council, 1992–96. Wolfson College: Vice-Pres., 1980–84; Mem. Council, 1969–73, 1976–80, 1988–92, 1994–95; Dir, Press Fellowship Programme, 1982–96. Churchwarden, St Mary and All Saints Willingham, 1978–85, 1996–97. Vice-Chm., Assoc. of Charitable Foundns, 1994–97; Mem. Regl Cttee, RSA, 1997–2003; Mem. Council, U3A, Cambridge, 2007–10. Trustee: Sir Halley Stewart Trust, 1969–2009, now Emeritus (Hon. Sec., 1978–82; Vice-Chm., 1998–2002); Willingham British Sch. Trust, 1974–91; Homerton Coll., 1980–89; Lucy Cavendish Coll., 1989–97; Chaplaincy to People at Work in Cambs, 1999–2014; Mem. Cttee, Cambridge Soc., 1979–83. Editor: Cambridge, 1992–2003; CRAC Newsletter, 1997–98; Chm., CAMREAD, 2004–12. *Publications:* Unscrambling an Empire, 1966; contrib.: Policing and Social Policy, 1984; Models of Police/Public Consultation in Europe, 1985; Managing Recruitment, 4th edn 1988; Graduate Recruitment: a 25-year retrospective, 1993; Reflections on Change, 2007; contributor to journals incl. The Hindu (Chennai), The Round Table, Africa Contemporary Record, Cambridge Rev. and to BBC. *Recreations:* local and international politics, church activities, writing. *Address:* 14 George Street, Willingham, Cambridge CB24 5LJ. *T:* (01954) 260393. *E:* wpk1000@cam.ac.uk.

KIRKPATRICK, Sir Ivone Elliott, 11th Bt *cr* 1685; *b* 1 Oct. 1942; *s* of Sir James Alexander Kirkpatrick, 10th Bt and Ellen Gertrude, *o d* of Captain R. P. Elliott, late RNR; *S* father, 1954. *Educ:* Wellington Coll., Berks; St Mark's Coll., University of Adelaide. *Heir: nephew* Glen Sydney Kirkpatrick, *b* 1 April 1973.

KIRKPATRICK, Janice Mary, OBE 2013; Designer and Creative Director, Graven (formerly Graven Images), since 1985; Chairman, Lighthouse Trust, 2004–07 (Director, 1999–2007); *b* 16 April 1962; *d* of James Burns Kirkpatrick and Jane Henry Coupland Kirkpatrick (*née* Borthwick); *m* 2008, Ross Buchanan Hunter. *Educ:* Glasgow Sch. of Art (BA 1st Cl Hons Graphic Design 1984; MA Design 1985). Vis. Prof., Glasgow Sch. of Art, 2000– (Gov., 1999–2010; Vice Chm., 2008–10). Trustee, NESTA, 1999–2005. Hon. DLitt Glasgow, 2014. *Recreations:* riding and driving Clydesdale horses, breeding British Saddleback pigs, trying to be a horseman, beekeeper and gardener. *Address:* Graven, 175 Albion Street, Glasgow G1 1RU. *T:* (0141) 522 6626, *Fax:* (0141) 552 0433. *E:* janice@graven.co.uk.

KIRKUP, William, CBE 2008; FRCP, FRCOG, FFPH; Associate Chief Medical Officer, Department of Health, 2005–09 (Director General, Clinical Programmes, 2005–08; Associate NHS Medical Director, 2008); *b* 29 April 1949; *s* of late William Kirkup and Patience Kirkup (*née* Wilford); *m* 1972 (marr. diss. 1983); three *d*; *m* 2004, Denise Lambert; one *d*. *Educ:* Newcastle Royal Grammar Sch.; Worcester Coll., Oxford (MA, BM BCh 1974). MRCOG 1979, FRCOG 1993; MFPHM 1986, FFPH (FFPHM 1994); FRCP 2006. Obstetrics and gynaecology posts, Oxford, Sheffield and Newcastle, 1975–82; public health trng, 1982–86; Consultant, Newcastle, 1986–87; Sen. Lectr, Newcastle Univ., 1986–91; Dir of Public Health, N Tyneside, 1987–91; Dir posts, (Performance Review, Healthcare Devel̲t, NHS Trusts Div.), Northern Reg. and NHS Exec., 1991–99; Regl Dir of Public Health and Healthcare, Northern and Yorks, NHS Exec., DoH, 1999–2002; Regl Dir of Public Health, NE, DoH, 2002–05. *Publications:* contribs to learned jls. *Recreations:* Newcastle United FC, music, playing with computers.

KIRKWOOD, family name of **Barons Kirkwood** and **Kirkwood of Kirkhope**.

KIRKWOOD, 3rd Baron *cr* 1951, of Bearsden; **David Harvie Kirkwood;** Hon. Senior Lecturer and Metallurgical Consultant, 1987–2002, Sheffield University (Senior Lecturer in Metallurgy, 1976–87); *b* 24 Nov. 1931; *s* of 2nd Baron Kirkwood and Eileen Grace (*d* 1999), *d* of Thomas Henry Boalch; *S* father, 1970; *m* 1965, Judith Rosalie, *d* of late John Hunt; three *d*. *Educ:* Rugby; Trinity Hall, Cambridge (MA, PhD); CEng. Lectr in Metallurgy, Sheffield Univ., 1962; Warden of Stephenson Hall, Sheffield Univ., 1974–80. Mem., Select Cttee on Sci. and Technology, H of L, 1987–92, 1996–99. *Heir: b* Hon. James Stuart Kirkwood [*b* 19 June 1937; *m* 1965, Alexandra Mary, *d* of late Alec Dyson; two *d*]. *Address:* 56 Endcliffe Hall Avenue, Sheffield S10 3EL. *T:* (0114) 266 3107.

KIRKWOOD OF KIRKHOPE, Baron *cr* 2005 (Life Peer), of Kirkhope in Scottish Borders; **Archibald Johnstone Kirkwood,** Kt 2003; *b* 22 April 1946; *s* of David Kirkwood and Jessie Barclay Kirkwood; *m* 1972, Rosemary Chester; one *d* one *s*. *Educ:* Cranhill School; Heriot-Watt Univ. (BSc Pharmacy). Solicitor. MP Roxburgh and Berwickshire, 1983–2005 (L/Alliance 1983–88, Lib Dem 1988–2005). Lib Dem convenor and spokesman on welfare, 1988–92, on social security, 1992–94 and 1997–2001, on community care, 1994–97; Chief Whip, 1992–97. Chairman: Social Security Select Cttee, 1997–2001; Work and Pensions Select Cttee, 2001–05. Trustee, Joseph Rowntree Reform Trust, 1985–2007 (Chm., 1999–2006). *Address:* House of Lords, SW1A 0PW.

KIRKWOOD, Rt Hon. Lord; Ian Candlish Kirkwood; PC 2000; a Senator of the College of Justice in Scotland, 1987–2005; *b* 8 June 1932; *o s* of late John Brown Kirkwood, OBE, and Mrs Constance Kirkwood, Edinburgh; *m* 1970, Jill Ingram Scott; two *s*. *Educ:* George Watson's Boys' Coll., Edinburgh; Edinburgh Univ. (MA 1952; LLB 1954); Univ. of Michigan, USA (LLM 1956). Called to Scottish Bar, 1957; apptd Standing Junior Counsel to Scottish Home and Health Dept, 1963; QC (Scot.) 1970. Mem., Parole Bd for Scotland, 1994–97. Formerly Pres., Wireless Telegraphy Appeal Tribunal in Scotland. Chm., Med. Appeal Tribunal in Scotland, until 1987. *Recreations:* fishing, golf, chess, tennis. *Address:* 58 Murrayfield Avenue, Edinburgh EH12 6AY. *T:* (0131) 477 1994; Knockbrex House, near Borgue, Kirkcudbrightshire. *Club:* New (Edinburgh).

KIRKWOOD, Ian Candlish; *see* Kirkwood, Rt Hon. Lord.

KIRKWOOD, Dr James Kerr, OBE 2008; writer; Chief Executive and Scientific Director: Universities Federation for Animal Welfare, 2000–14; Humane Slaughter Association, 2000–14; *b* 8 Nov. 1951; *s* of late Andrew Kerr Kirkwood and of Patricia Mary Kirkwood (*née* Brown); *m* 1983, Julia Mary Christine Brittain; two *s* one *d*. *Educ:* Bradfield Coll., Berks; Bristol Univ. (BVSc 1975; PhD 1982). CBiol, FRSB (FIBiol 1997). Research Associate, later Res. Fellow, Dept of Pathology, Bristol Univ., 1981–84; Sen. Vet. Officer, Zoological Soc. of London, and Head of Vet. Sci. Gp, Inst. of Zoology, 1984–96; specialist in zoo and wildlife medicine, RCVS, 1992–2000; Scientific Dir, UFAW, and Hon. Dir, Humane Slaughter Assoc., 1996–2000. Ed.-in-Chief, Animal Welfare, 1996–2014. Dir, Master's Course in Wild Animal Health, RVC/Inst. of Zoology, 1994–96; Vis. Prof., Dept of Pathology and Infectious Diseases, RVC, 1997–; Hon. Res. Fellow, Inst. of Zoology, 1997–2003. Chm., Zoos Forum, 2005–11 (Mem., 1999–2011); Dep. Chm., Companion Animal Welfare Council, 2003–12 (Mem., 2000–12); Chm., DEFRA Ind. Wkg Gp on Snares, 2004–05; Member: IUCN Vet. Specialist Gp, 1990–; Council, Zool Soc. of London, 2004–07; TB Adv. Gp, 2006–09, Wildlife Health and Welfare Strategy Bd, 2006–08, DEFRA; Head of UK Delegn at Internat. Whaling Commn Workshop on Welfare, St Kitts, 2006. Mem., Lead Ammunition Gp, 2010–. Trustee, Zebra Foundn for Vet. Zool Educn, 1990–2012; Pres., British Vet. Zool Soc., 1994–96. Hon. FRCVS 2011. *Publications:* (with K. Stathatos) Biology, Rearing and Care of Young Primates, 1992; (ed jtly) Science in the Service of Animal Welfare, 2004; sundry publications in the scientific literature on aspects of the biology, diseases, conservation and welfare of animals. *Recreations:* music, cycling, literature, natural history. *Address:* c/o Universities Federation for Animal Welfare and Humane Slaughter Association, The Old School, Wheathampstead, Herts AL4 8AN. *T:* (01582) 831818.

KIRKWOOD, Michael James, CMG 2003; FCIB; Chairman, Circle Holdings plc (formerly Health Investment Holdings), since 2011; Senior Adviser, Ondra Partners LLP, since 2012 (Chairman, 2009–12); *b* Glasgow, 7 June 1947; *s* of James Kirkwood and June Alexandra Scott Kirkwood (*née* Peters); *m* 1969, Karen Marie Wolf; one *s* one *d*. *Educ:* Trinity Coll., Glenalmond; Stanford Univ., Calif. (BA Hons). FCIB 2001. Hongkong and Shanghai Banking Corp., 1965–68; Alt. Dir, Temenggong Securities Ltd, Singapore, 1973–76; Chief Exec., Temenggong Merchant Bankers Ltd, Singapore, 1974–76; Dir, Scotland, Ansbacher & Co. Ltd, 1976–77; Citigroup, 1977–2008: Country Senior Officer: Scotland, 1977–80; Denmark, 1981–83; CEO, Citicorp Investment Bank Switzerland SA, 1985–88; Gp COS, NY, 1988–91; Div. Hd, Continental Europe, 1991–92; Hd, UK Corporate Banking, 1993–2008; Chief Country Officer, Citigroup Inc., UK, 1999–2008. Mem. Bd, British American Business Inc. (Chm., 2001–03); non-executive Director: Kidde plc, 2001–05; UK Financial Investments Ltd, 2009–14; London Scottish International Ltd, 2009–; AngloGold Ashanti Ltd, 2012–; Dep. Chm. Adv. Bd, PricewaterhouseCoopers, 2009–11; Sen. Advr, 2009–12, non-exec. Dir, 2012–14, Eros International plc. Chairman: American Banks Assoc., 2000–02; Assoc. of Foreign Banks, 2004; Pres., Chartered Inst. of Bankers, 2003–04 (Dep. Pres., 2002–03); Vice Chm. (formerly Vice Pres.), British Bankers' Assoc., 2001–08; Mem. Adv. Bd, ACT. Chm., Habitat for Humanity GB, 2004–11; Dir and Trustee, Stone Foundn, 1996–2003. FRSA. HM Lieut for the City of London, 2004. Freeman, City of London, 2002; Mem. Ct, Co. of Internat. Bankers, 2001–11, now Ct Emeritus (Master, 2005–06). *Recreations:* Mediterranean horticulture, golf, Rugby, shooting and travel. *Address:* 125 Old Broad Street, EC2N 1AR. *Clubs:* Boodle's, Pilgrims; Denham Golf; Country (Johannesburg).

KIRKWOOD, Prof. Thomas Burton Loram, CBE 2009; PhD; FRCPE; Professor of Medicine, 1999–2013, Associate Dean for Ageing, 2011–13, and Scientific Director, NIHR Biomedical Research Centre on Ageing, 2007–13, University of Newcastle upon Tyne, now Distinguished Research Fellow; *b* 6 July 1951; *s* of late Kenneth Kirkwood; *m* 1973, Betty Rosamund Bartlett (marr. diss. 1995); one *s* one *d*; *m* 1995, Jane Louise Bottomley. *Educ:* Dragon Sch., Oxford; Magdalen Coll. Sch., Oxford; St Catharine's Coll., Cambridge (MA; PhD 1983); Worcester Coll., Oxford (MSc). FRCPE 2013. Scientist, Nat. Inst. for Biol Standards and Control, 1973–81; National Institute for Medical Research: Sen. Scientist, 1981–88; Head, Lab. of Mathematical Biol., 1988–93; Prof. of Biol Gerontology, Univ. of Manchester, 1993–99; University of Newcastle upon Tyne: Hd of Gerontology, 1999–2004; Co-Dir, 2004–06, Dir, 2006–11, Inst. for Ageing and Health; Dir, Centre for Integrated Systems Biol. of Ageing and Nutrition, 2005–11. Various distinguished lectures incl. Reith Lectures, 2001. Chm., Brit. Soc. for Research on Ageing, 1992–99; Dir, Jt Centre on Ageing, Univs of Manchester and Newcastle upon Tyne, 1996–99; Gov., 1998–2001, and Chm., Res. Adv. Council, 1999–2000, Research into Ageing; Chm., Foresight Task Force on Health Care of Older People, 1999–2001; Member: WHO Expert Adv. Panel on Biol Standardization, 1985–2004; UK Human Genome Mapping Project Cttee, 1991–93; Basic Scis Interest Gp, Wellcome Trust, 1992–97; BBSRC, 2001–04; Science and Industry Council, NE England, 2007–09. Specialist Advr, Inquiry into Scientific Aspects of Ageing, H of Lords Select Cttee on Sci. and Technol., 2004–06. Trustee, Cumberland Lodge, 2007–; Trustee Dir, Big Lottery Centre for Ageing Better, 2013–15. Co-Ed., Mechanisms of Ageing and Develt, 2000–06. President: Internat. Biometric Soc. (British Reg.), 1998–2000; (Biol.), Eur. Section, Internat. Assoc. of Gerontology, 2003–07; Scientific Bd, AXA Res. Fund, 2013–. Fellow, Inst. for Advanced Study, Budapest, 1997; Tower Fellow, NZ Inst. for Res. on Ageing, 2004. FMedSci 2001 (Mem. Council, 2002–06). Hon. FFA 2002. Hon. DSc Hull, 2003. Heinz Karger Prize, 1983; Fritz Verzár Medal, 1996; Dhole-Eddlestone Prize, British Geriatrics Soc., 2001; Henry Dale Prize, Royal Instn, 2002; Cohen Medal, British Soc. for Res. on Ageing, 2006; Longevity Prize, Ipsen Foundn, 2011. *Publications:* (jtly) Accuracy in Molecular Processes: its control and relevance to living systems, 1986; Time of Our Lives: the science of human ageing, 1999; (with C. E. Finch) Chance, Development and Aging, 2000; The End of Age, 2001; (jtly) Sex and Longevity: sexuality, gender, reproduction, parenthood, 2001; (jtly) Wellbeing in Later Life, 2014; many scientific articles. *Recreations:* travel, pottery, gardening. *Address:* Newcastle University Institute for Ageing, Newcastle University, Campus for Ageing and Vitality, Newcastle upon Tyne NE4 5PL. *T:* (0191) 208 1103, *Fax:* (0191) 208 1101. *E:* Tom.Kirkwood@newcastle.ac.uk.

KIRSHBAUM, Ralph; cellist; Gregor Piatgorsky Chair in Violoncello, University of Southern California, Los Angeles; *b* Texas, 4 March 1946; *m* 1982, Antoinette Reynolds; one *s*. Founder and Artistic Dir, RNCM Manchester Internat. Cello Fest., 1988–2007. Has performed with major orchestras including: BBC Symphony; Boston Symphony; Cleveland Orch.; London Symphony; Orchestre de Paris; Pittsburgh Symphony; San Francisco Symphony; Chicago Symphony; Tonhalle; Berlin Radio Symphony; Royal Danish; Stockholm Philharmonic. Festival appearances at Aspen, Bath, Edinburgh, Lucerne, New York, Santa Fe, Ravinia and Verbier. Chamber music collaboration with Gyorgy Pauk, Peter Frankl and Pinchas Zukerman. Recordings include: concertos: Barber; Elgar; Haydn D major; Tippett Triple; Walton; Beethoven Triple; Brahms Double; Barber, Shostakovich and Prokofiev sonatas; Ravel, Shostakovich and Brahms Trios, complete Bach suites. *Address:* c/o Ingpen & Williams, 7 St George's Court, 131 Putney Bridge Road, SW15 2PA.

KIRTON, Muriel Elizabeth; international consultant and teacher of Daoist philosophy and healing arts, management training and lifestyle, since 2002; *b* 4 July 1950; *d* of William Waddell Kirton and Belle Jane Kirton (*née* Barnett). *Educ:* Glasgow Univ. (MA Hons Eng. and French 1974); Kent Univ. (MA TEFL 1979); Edinburgh Univ. (DipEd 1975); Moray House Coll. of Educn (PGCE 1975). Teacher of French and English, Cornwall Coll., Montego Bay, Jamaica, 1975–77; teacher of French, Dane Court Tech. High Sch., Broadstairs, 1977–78; Lectr in ELT, Hilderstone Coll., Kent, 1978–79; Sen. Lectr in ELT, Nonington Coll., Kent, 1979–82; joined British Council, 1982: Project Manager, ELT, China, 1982–85; Projects Dir, Hong Kong, 1985–89; Educn Officer, Egypt, 1990–93; Director: Vietnam, 1993–96; Commonwealth Relations, 1996–2000; Cyprus, 2000–01; Yugoslavia, 2001–02. *Recreations:* scuba diving, alternative/complementary healing therapies, reading, cinema, theatre. *Address:* 15 Leven Terrace, Bruntsfield, Edinburgh EH3 9LW. *E:* murielkirton@gmail.com.

KIRTON-DARLING, Judith; Member (Lab) North East Region, European Parliament, since 2014; *b* Dar-es-Salaam, Tanzania, 2 June 1977; *d* of Hugh Fenwick Ridley Kirton-Darling and Janette Kirton Darling (*née* Kohn); *m* 2013, Benjamin Daune. *Educ:* Hall Garth Secondary Sch., Middlesbrough; Acklam 6th Form Coll., Middlesbrough; Univ. of Sheffield (BA Hons Social and Pol Studies); Univ. of Bath (MSc Eur. Social Policy Analysis). Prog. asst, Quaker Council for Eur. Affairs, 1999–2000; researcher, Eur. Trade Union Inst., 2001–03; Policy Advr, UNI Europa, 2003–06; Eur. Officer, Unite the Union, 2006–07; Industrial Policy Officer, Eur. Metalworkers' Fedn, 2007–11; Confederal Sec., ETUC, 2011–14. *Address:* Labour Party, Kings Manor, Newcastle upon Tyne NE1 6PA. *E:* jude.kirton-darling@europarl.europa.eu.

KIRUI, Nancy Chepkemoi; Permanent Secretary, Ministry of State for Defence, Kenya, 2008–13; *b* 4 June 1957; *d* of Isaiah Cheluget and Rael Cheluget; *m* 1993, Nicholas Kirui; two *d*, and three step *s* one step *d*. *Educ:* Alliance Girls' Sch., Kikuyu, Kenya; Univ. of Nairobi (LLB); Kenya Sch. of Law (Postgrad. Dip. Law). Legal Officer: Min. of Foreign Affairs, Nairobi, 1985–88; Perm. Mission of Kenya to UN, Geneva, 1988–91; Min. of Foreign Affairs, 1991–94; Kenya High Commn, London, 1994–98; Hd of Legal Div., then Hd, Americas Div., Min. of Foreign Affairs, 1998–2000; High Comr in London, 2000–03; Permanent Secretary: Min. of Gender, Sports, Culture and Social Services, Nairobi, 2003–04; Min. of Labour and Human Resource Develt, Nairobi, 2004–06; Office of the Vice-Pres. and Min. of Home Affairs, 2006–08. *Recreations:* sketching, painting, cooking. *Address:* c/o Ministry of State for Defence, Ulinzi House, Lenana Road, PO Box 40668–00100, Nairobi, Kenya.

KIRWAN, Sir John (James Patrick), KNZM 2012 (ONZM 2007); MBE 1987; Head Coach, Blues Rugby, Auckland, since 2013; *b* Auckland, 16 Dec. 1964; *s* of late Pat Kirwan and of Pat Kirwan; *m* Fiorella Tomasi; two *s* one *d*. *Educ:* De La Salle Coll., Auckland. Formerly butchers apprentice. Player: Rugby Union: Auckland and Marist team, 1983–94; NZ All Blacks, 1984–94 (35 tries in 63 Tests for NZ; Mem., winning team, Rugby World Cup, 1987); Benetton Treviso, 1986–90; NEC Green Rockets, Japan, 1997–99; Rugby League: Auckland Warriors, 1995–96. Coach, NEC Green Rockets, Japan, 1999–2001; asst coach, Auckland Blues, 2001; coach: Italian nat. Rugby team, 2002–05; Japanese nat. Rugby team, 2007–11; Barbarians, 2012. Spokesman and campaigner involved in mental health and depression awareness campaigns in NZ. *Publications:* Running on Instinct, 1992; Why I Am, 1999; All Blacks Don't Cry, 2010. *Recreation:* surfing. *Address:* c/o Auckland Blues Rugby, PO Box 56152, Dominion Road, Auckland 1446, New Zealand. *E:* john.kirwan@theblues.co.nz.

KIRYA, Prof. George Barnabas; High Commissioner for Uganda in the United Kingdom, 1990–2003, and Ambassador to Ireland, 1995–2003 (Senior High Commissioner at the Court of St James's, 1997); Dean of the Diplomatic Corps, 1999–2003; *b* 9 Feb. 1939; *m*; five *s* one *d*. *Educ:* Univ. of E Africa (MB ChB 1966); Birmingham Univ. (MSc Gen. Virology 1971); Manchester Univ. (Dip. Bacteriology 1974). Med. House Officer, Mulago Hosp., Uganda, 1966–67; Sen. House Officer, Dept of Paediatrics and Child Health, Makerere Fac. of Medicine, 1967; East Africa Virus Res. Inst., Entebbe: Virologist, 1967; Sen. Med. Res. Officer, 1968; Principal Med. Res. Officer and Head, Dept of Arbovirology, 1969; Hon. Lectr, Dept of Med. Microbiol., Makerere Univ., 1970; Consultant on Yellow Fever Epidemics, WHO, 1970; Department of Microbiology, Faculty of Medicine, Makerere University: Sen. Lectr, 1973–75; Associate Prof. and Hd of Dept, 1975–78; Prof. and Hd of Dept, 1978; Makerere University: Mem. Senate, 1977–90; Mem. Univ. Council, 1981–90; Vice Chancellor, 1986–90. Chairman: Commonwealth Finance Cttee, 1993–2003; African Union (formerly OAU) Heads of Mission Gp, London, 1997–2003; Commonwealth Heads of Mission Gp, 1997–2003; Commonwealth Africa Gp, 1997–2003; Commonwealth People's Assoc. of Uganda, 2006–. Mem., WHO Scientific and Technical Adv. Gp, serving as WHO Temp. Advr, 1990–93. Dir, Central Public Health Labs in Uganda supported by WHO, UNICEF and Min. of Health, 1980–86; Chairman: Disease Surveillance Sub-Cttee, Min. of Health; Uganda Health Service Commn, 2007–11; Uganda Nat. Health Consumers' Orgn, 2010– (Chm., Exec. Bd, 2006); Adv. Council, Amref Health Africa Uganda, 2011–; Member: Nat. Cttee for Prevention of Blindness in Uganda; Adv. Cttee for Res. of Viruses in Uganda; E and Central African Physicians Assoc.; Founder Mem., Uganda Health Mktg Gp, 2006–; Uganda Medical Association: Treas., 1978–82; Pres., 1982–86; Chm., CPD, 2005–08. Chm., Advocates for Professionalism and Quality in Health. Chancellor, Lugazi Univ., 2007–10; Mem. Gov. Council, Ernest Cook Ultrasound Research and Educn Inst., 2005–. Teaching and supervising undergrad. and post-grad. med. students, med. lab. technologists, nurses and midwives and health visitors. Internal examr and external examr for several univs incl. Univ. of Ibadan, Lagos Univ. and Univ. of Nairobi. Member, Editorial Bd: E African Jl for Med. Res.; Uganda Med. Jl. Hon. LLD Birmingham, 2001. *Address:* PO Box 5406, Kampala, Uganda. *Club:* Africa Cricket (Kampala).

KISIN, Prof. Mark, PhD; FRS 2008; Professor of Mathematics, Harvard University, since 2009; *b* Lithuania. *Educ:* Monash Univ. (BSc 1991); Princeton Univ. (MSc 1995; PhD 1998). Postdoctoral Fellow, Australian Res. Council, 1998–2001; res. at Westfälischen Wilhelms Univ., Germany, 1998–2003; Asst Prof., 2003–05, Prof., 2005–09, Univ. of Chicago. Editor: Inventiones; Mathematische Annalen; Jl Number Theory. *Publications:* contribs to jls incl. Jl Amer. Maths Soc., Invent. Maths, Current Develts in Maths, Annals of Maths. *Address:* Department of Mathematics, Harvard University, 1 Oxford Street, Cambridge, MA 02138, USA.

KISSACK, Paul; Director-General, Children's Services, Department for Education, since 2014; *b* Douglas, IOM, 3 April 1976; *s* of Frederick and Carole Kissack; *m* 2006, Emma Jane Lindsell; one *s* two *d*. *Educ:* Queen Elizabeth II High Sch., Peel, IOM; Univ. of Warwick (BA Hons Hist. 1997); Jesus Coll., Cambridge (MPhil Histl Studies 1998). HM Treasury: Hd of Communications and Press Spokesman for Chancellor of Exchequer, 2004–06; Hd of Productivity and Reform, 2006–08; Hd, Commng, Delivery and Service Improvement, Children's Services, Richmond upon Thames LBC, 2008–10; Principal Private Sec. to Cabinet Sec., 2010–11; Dir, DFE, 2011–14. *Address:* Department for Education, Sanctuary Buildings, Great Smith Street, SW1P 3BT. *E:* paul.kissack@education.gsi.gov.uk.

KISSIN, Evgeny Igorevich; concert pianist; *b* 10 Oct. 1971; *s* of Igor Kissin and Emilia Kissina. *Educ:* Gnessin Special Sch. of Music, Moscow; Gnessin Russian Acad. of Music, Moscow. Début, Moscow State Philharmonic Orch., conducted by Dmitry Kitaenko, Great Hall, Moscow Conservatoire, 1984; toured Japan, 1986; European début with Berlin Radio Orch., 1987; UK début with BBC Manchester Orch., Lichfield Fest., 1987; USA début with NY Philharmonic Orch., 1990. Has made numerous recordings. Hon. RAM 2005. Hon. DMus Manhattan Sch. of Music, 2001; Hon. DLitt Hong Kong, 2009; Hon. Dr Hebrew Univ., Jerusalem, 2010. Musician of the Year, Chigiana Music Acad., Italy, 1991; Instrumentalist of the Year, Musical America mag., 1994; Triumph Award for outstanding contrib. to Russian culture, Triumph Ind. Charity Foundn, 1997; various awards for recordings in UK, France, Holland, incl. Grammy Award, 2006. *Recreations:* reading, long and fast walks, getting together with friends. *Address:* c/o Askonas Holt Ltd, Lincoln House, 300 High Holborn, WC1V 7JH. *T:* (020) 7400 1700.

KISSINGER, Henry Alfred, Hon. KCMG 1995; Bronze Star (US); Chairman, Kissinger Associates Inc., since 1982; Counselor to Center for Strategic and International Studies, since 1977 and Trustee, since 1987; *b* Germany, 27 May 1923; *s* of late Louis Kissinger and Paula (*née* Stern); *m* 1st, 1949, Anne Fleischer (marr. diss. 1964); one *s* one *d*; 2nd, 1974, Nancy Maginnes. *Educ:* George Washington High Sch., NYC; Harvard Univ., Cambridge, Mass (BA 1950, MA 1952, PhD 1954). Emigrated to United States, 1938; naturalised, 1943. Served Army, 1943–46. Teaching Fellow, Harvard Univ., 1950–54; Study Director: Council on Foreign Relations, 1955–56: Rockefeller Bros Fund, 1956–58; Associate Professor of Govt, Harvard Univ., 1958–62, Prof. of Govt, 1962–71, and Faculty Mem., Center for Internat. Affairs, Harvard; Director: Harvard Internat. Seminar, 1951–69; Harvard Defense Studies Program, 1958–69; Asst to US President for Nat. Security Affairs, 1969–75; Secretary of State, USA, 1973–77. Chm., Nat. Bipartisan Commn on Central America, 1983–84; Member: President's Foreign Intelligence Adv. Bd, 1984–90; Commn on Integrated Long-Term Strategy of the National Security Council and Defense Dept, 1986–88; Dir, Internat. Rescue Cttee, 1987–; Hon. Gov., Foreign Policy Assoc., 1985–. Chm., Internat. Adv. Bd, American Internat. Group, Inc., 1988–; Counselor and Mem., Internat. Adv. Cttee, JP Morgan Chase & Co. (formerly Chase Manhattan Bank, then Chase Manhattan Corp.), 1977–; Advr to Bd of Dirs, American Express Co.; Dir, ContiGroup Cos Inc.; Dir Emeritus, Freeport-McMoRan Copper and Gold Inc.; formerly Dir, Hollinger Internat. Inc. Trustee, Metropolitan Mus. of Art, 1977, now Emeritus. Syndicated writer, Los Angeles Times, 1984–. (Jtly) Nobel Peace Prize, 1973; Presidential Medal of Freedom, 1977; Medal of Liberty, 1986. *Publications:* A World Restored: Castlereagh, Metternich and the Restoration of Peace, 1957; Nuclear Weapons and Foreign Policy, 1957 (Woodrow Wilson Prize, 1958; citation, Overseas Press Club, 1958); The Necessity for Choice: Prospects of American Foreign Policy, 1961; The Troubled Partnership: a reappraisal of the Atlantic Alliance, 1965; Problems of National Strategy: A Book of Readings (ed), 1965; American Foreign Policy: three essays, 1969, 3rd edn 1977; White House Years (memoirs), 1979; For the Record: selected statements 1977–1980, 1981; Years of Upheaval (memoirs), 1982; Observations: selected speeches and essays 1982–1984, 1985; Diplomacy, 1994; Years of Renewal, 1999; Does America Need a Foreign Policy?, 2001; Ending the Vietnam War, 2003; Crisis, 2003; On China, 2011; World Order, 2014. *Address:* Suite 400, 1800 K Street NW, Washington, DC 20006, USA; 350 Park Avenue, New York, NY 10022, USA. *Clubs:* Century, River, Brook (New York); Metropolitan (Washington); Bohemian (San Francisco).

KISZELY, Lt-Gen. Sir John (Panton), KCB 2004; MC 1982; DL; defence and security consultant, since 2008; *b* 2 April 1948; *s* of Dr John Kiszely and Maude Kiszely; *m* 1984, Hon. Arabella Jane, *d* of 3rd Baron Herschell; three *s*. *Educ:* Marlborough Coll.; RMA Sandhurst. Commnd into Scots Guards, 1969; Co. Comdr, 2nd Bn Scots Guards, 1981–82; Bde Major, 7 Armd Bde, 1982–85; CO 1st Bn Scots Guards, 1986–88 (mentioned in dispatches); Comdr, 22 Armd Bde, 1991–92; Comdr, 7 Armd Bde, 1993; Dep. Comdt, Staff Coll., Camberley, 1993–96; GOC 1st (UK) Armd Div., 1996–98; ACDS (Resources and Plans), MOD, 1998–2001; Dep. Comdr, NATO Force, Bosnia, 2001–02; Comdr Regl Forces, Land Comd, 2002–04; Dep. Comdr, Multinat. Force, Iraq, 2004–05; Dir Gen., Defence Acad. of the UK, 2005–08. Regtl Lt-Col, Scots Guards, 1995–2001; Col Comdt, Intelligence Corps, 2000–08. Vis. Prof. in War Studies, King's Coll. London, 2008–13; Mem., Adv. Bd, Baltic Defence Coll., 2011–. Trustee, Imperial War Mus., 2008– (Dep. Chm., 2011–). Nat. Pres., RBL, 2009–12. Vice Patron, Disabled Sailors Assoc., 2010–. CRAeS 2006. Hon. Col, Univ. of London OTC, 2003–09. Liveryman, Painter-Stainers' Co., 2008. DL Glos, 2010. QCVS 1997. Officer, Legion of Merit (USA), 2005. *Publications:* (contrib.) The Science of War: back to first principles, 1993; Military Power: land warfare in theory and practice, 1997; The Falklands Conflict Twenty Years On, 2004; (contrib.) The Past as Prologue: history and the military profession, 2006; (contrib.) The Impenetrable Fog of War, 2008; Coalition Command in Contemporary Operations, 2008; (contrib.) British Generals in Blair's Wars, 2013; numerous articles in military jls. *Recreations:* sailing, shooting, fishing, music. *Address:* c/o Headquarters Scots Guards, Wellington Barracks, Birdcage Walk, SW1E 6HQ. *Clubs:* Cavalry and Guards; Royal Solent Yacht.

KITAMURA, Hiroshi, Hon. KBE 2003; Corporate Advisor to Mitsubishi Corporation, 1994–99; President, Shumei University, 1998–2001; *b* 20 Jan. 1929; *s* of Teiji and Fusako Kitamura; *m* 1953, Sachiko Ito; two *d*. *Educ:* Univ. of Tokyo (LLB 1951); Fletcher School of Law and Diplomacy, Medford, USA, 1952. Joined Min. of Foreign Affairs, Tokyo, 1953; postings to Washington DC, New York, New Delhi, London; Dir, Policy Planning Div., Res. and Planning Dept, Tokyo, 1974; Private Sec. to Prime Minister, 1974–76; Dep. Dir-Gen., Amer. Affairs Bureau, 1977–79; Consul-Gen., San Francisco, 1979–82; Dir-Gen., American Affairs Bureau, 1982–84; Dep. Vice Minister for Foreign Affairs, 1984–87; Dep. Minister, 1987–88; Ambassador: to Canada, 1988–90; to UK, 1991–94. *Publications:* Psychological Dimensions of US-Japanese Relations, 1971. *Recreations:* traditional Japanese music, culinary arts, golf. *Address:* 1–15–6 Jingumae, Shibuya-ku, Tokyo 150–0001, Japan.

KITCHEN, Rev. Dr Martin; Priest-in-Charge, South Rodings, 2008–11; *b* 18 May 1947; *s* of Reginald Thomas Kitchen and Alice Kitchen (*née* Johnson); *m* 1971, Sheila Solveig Pettersen; one *s*. *Educ:* Sir Walter St John's Sch., Battersea; Poly. of N London (BA London Univ. 1971); King's Coll. London (BD 1976; AKC 1977); Univ. of Manchester (PhD 1988). Ordained deacon, 1979, priest, 1980; Lectr, Church Army Trng Coll., and Curate, St James, Kidbrooke, 1979–83; Chaplain, Manchester Poly., 1983–88; Team Vicar, 1983–86, Team Rector, 1986–88, Whitworth, Manchester; Diocese of Southwark: Advr, In-Service Trng, 1988–95; Co-ordinator of Trng, 1995–97; Residentiary Canon, Southwark Cathedral, 1988–97; Durham Cathedral: Residentiary Canon, 1997–2005; Sub-Dean, 1998–99; Vice Dean, 1999–2004; Dean of Derby, 2005–07. Permission to officiate: Dio. of Europe, 2011; Dio. of Newcastle, 2012. Theol Consultant, Ministry Div., Archbishop's Council, 2008–09. Sec., 1996–2001, Dir, 2001–, Archbishop's Exam. in Theol.; Sec., Anglo-Nordic-Baltic Theol Conf., 1997–2009; Consultant, C of E Doctrine Commn, 1999–2005. *Publications:* Ephesians, 1994; Guide to Durham Cathedral, 2000; A Talent for Living, 2003; editor and co-author: Word of Life, 1997; Word of Promise, 1998; Word of Truth, 1999; Word in Our Time, 2000; Word Among Us, 2001; various articles and translations in bks and jls. *Recreations:* music, poetry, good food and wine, astronomy, needlepoint. *Address:* 4 Town Farm Close, Wall, Hexham NE46 4DH. *T:* (01434) 689696.

KITCHEN, Michael; actor; *b* 31 Oct. 1948; *s* of Arthur and Betty Kitchen; partner, Rowena Miller; two *s*. *Educ:* City of Leicester Boys' Grammar School. Entered acting profession, 1970; *stage includes:* seasons at Belgrade Theatre, Coventry, National Youth Theatre; Royal Court, 1971–73; Big Wolf, Magnificence, Skyvers; Young Vic, 1975: Othello, Macbeth, As You Like It, Charley's Aunt; National Theatre: Spring Awakening, 1974; Romeo and Juliet, 1974; State of Revolution, 1977; Bedroom Farce, 1977; No Man's Land, 1977; The Homecoming, 1978; Family Voices, 1981; On the Razzle, 1981; The Provok'd Wife, 1981; Rough Crossing, 1984; Royal Shakespeare Company: Romeo and Juliet, Richard II, 1986; The Art of Success, 1987; *films include:* The Bunker; Breaking Glass; Towards the Morning; Out of Africa; Home Run; The Russia House; Fools of Fortune; The Dive; Goldeneye; Mrs Dalloway; The Last Contract; The World is not Enough; My Week With Marilyn; *television series:* Steven Hind; Divorce; Freud, 1983; The Justice Game, 1989; The Guilty, 1992; To Play the King, 1993; Dandelion Dead, 1994; The Hanging Gale, 1995 (Best Actor Award, Internat. Fest. of Audiovisual Progs, Biarritz, 1996); Reckless, 1997; Oliver Twist (serial), 1999; Foyle's War, 2002–15 (9 series); Alibi, 2003; The Life of Rock, 2014; *television films and plays include:* Caught on a Train; Benefactors; Ball-Trap; Pied Piper; The Enchanted April; Hostage; Falling; Mobile, Hacks; numerous other TV and radio performances. *Recreations:* piano, guitar, sailing, writing, tennis, riding. *Address:* c/o Curtis Brown, Haymarket House, 28–29 Haymarket, SW1Y 4SP.

KITCHENER-FELLOWES, family name of **Baron Fellowes of West Stafford**.

KITCHIN, Rt Hon. Sir David (James Tyson), Kt 2005; PC 2011; **Rt Hon. Lord Justice Kitchin;** a Lord Justice of Appeal, since 2011; *b* 30 April 1955; *s* of late Norman Tyson Kitchin and Shirley Boyd Kitchin (*née* Simpson); *m* 1989, Charlotte Anne Cadbury, *d* of Comdr David Jones; one *s* one *d*. *Educ:* Oundle Sch. (schol.); Fitzwilliam Coll., Cambridge (MA; Hon. Fellow, 2012). Called to the Bar, Gray's Inn, 1977, Bencher, 2003; pupilled to Robin Jacob, 1978; entered chambers of Thomas Blanco White, 1979; QC 1994; a Dep. High Ct Judge, 2001–05; apptd to hear Trade Mark Appeals, 2001–05; a Judge of the High Court, Chancery Div., 2005–11; Chancery Supervising Judge for Wales, Western and Midland Circuits, 2009–11 Mem., Enlarged Bd of Appeal, European Patent Office, 2009–11. Chm., Vet. Code of Practice Cttee, Nat. Office of Animal Health, 1995–2001. Chm., Intellectual Property Bar Assoc., 2004–05; Mem., Bar Council, 2004–05 (Mem., European Cttee, 2004–05). Mem. Council, Queen Mary, Univ. of London, 2006–11. *Publications:* (ed jtly) Patent Law of Europe and the United Kingdom, 1979; (ed jtly) Kerly's Law of Trade Marks and Trade Names, Supplement to 12th edn 1994, 13th edn, 2001, 14th edn 2005; (jtly) The Trade Marks Act 1994 (text and commentary), 1995. *Recreations:* golf, tennis, theatre. *Address:* Royal Courts of Justice, Strand, WC2A 2LL. *Clubs:* Hawks (Cambridge); Leander (Henley); Walton Heath Golf.

KITCHING, Alan, RDI 1994; Typographer and Proprietor, The Typography Workshop, since 1989; *b* 29 Dec. 1940; *s* of Walter Kitching and Kathleen (*née* Davies); *m* 1962, Rita Haylett (*d* 1984); two *s*; *m* 2007, Celia Stothard (*d* 2010). Apprentice compositor, 1955–61; Asst, Exptl Printing Workshop, Watford Coll. of Technol. Sch. of Art, 1963–68; Vis. Tutor in Typography, Central Sch. of Art and Design, 1968–72; Established freelance design practice, working in magazine, book and exhibition design, 1971; Partner, Omnific Studios (Graphic Design), 1977–88; established Typography Workshop, Printroom and Studio (with Celia Stothard), 2005; Vis. Tutor in Typography, RCA, 1988–2006; Vis. Prof., Univ. of the Arts London (formerly London Inst.), 2001–. Retrospective Exhibn, Alan Kitching and Celia Stothard: The Typography Workshop - twenty years of new letterpress prints, London, 2009; exhibited, RA, 2011, 2012; solo exhibn, Advanced Graphics, London, 2012, 2015; exhibited at The Discerning Eye, Mall Gall., London, 2013; solo exhibn, Alan Kitching and Monotype, London Coll. of Communication, 2014; solo exhibn, Alan Kitching on Press at The Guardian, King's Place, 2015. AGI 1994. Hon. FRCA 2006 (FRCA 1998). *Publications:* Typography Manual, 1970; Alan Kitching's A-Z of Letterpress, 2015. *Recreations:* reading, cooking, accordion. *Address:* 19 Cleaver Street, SE11 4DP. *Club:* Chelsea Arts.

KITCHING, Christopher John, CBE 2004; PhD; FSA, FRHistS; Secretary, Historical Manuscripts Commission, National Archives (formerly Royal Commission on Historical Manuscripts), 1992–2004; *b* 5 Aug. 1945; *s* of Donald Walton Kitching and Vera (*née* Mosley); *m* 1976, Hilary Mary Ruth Horwood; two *s*. *Educ:* Durham Univ. (BA Mod. Hist. 1967; PhD 1970). Registered Mem., Soc. of Archivists, 1987. Asst Keeper, PRO, 1970–82; Asst Sec., Royal Commn on Historical MSS, 1982–92. Asst Editor, Archivum, 1984–92. Hon. Treasurer, 1980–85, Vice-Pres., 2002–05, RHistS; Mem., Archives Task Force, MLA, 2002–04. Council Mem., Canterbury and York Soc., 1974–2004; Mem., Adv. Cttee, Durham Cath. Library, 2011–. Chm., Trustees, St Mary-the-Virgin, Primrose Hill, 1998–; Trustee: Miss E. M. Johnson's Charitable Trust, 1997–2005; Lambeth Palace Library, 2009–. Mem. Editl Bd, Jl of Soc. of Archivists, 1992–2004. Hon. Sec., Essay Club, 2009–15. Alexander Prize, RHistS, 1973. *Publications:* The Royal Visitation of 1559, 1975; Survey of the Central Records of the Church of England, 1976; London and Middlesex Chantry Certificate 1548, 1980; Surveys of historical manuscripts in the United Kingdom: a select bibliography, 1989, 3rd edn 1997; The impact of computerisation on archival finding aids, 1990; Archive Buildings in the United Kingdom 1977–1992, 1993; Archives: the very essence of our heritage, 1996; Archive Buildings in the United Kingdom 1992–2005, 2007; articles and reviews. *Recreations:* music, historical research, Freedom-pass exploration. *Address:* 11 Creighton Road, NW6 6EE. *T:* (020) 8969 6408.

KITCHING, Peter Marshall; Chairman, Baltic Exchange, 2000–03 (Member, 1961–2003); *b* 24 June 1938; *s* of Horace and Clare Kitching; *m* 1961, Anna; one *s* one *d*. *Educ:* Stowe Sch. Sen. Partner, Simpson Spence & Young, 1992–2001. *Recreations:* golf, travel, music. *Address:* 59 Crown Lodge, Elystan Street, Chelsea, SW3 3PR. *Club:* Effingham Golf.

KITNEY, Prof. Richard Ian, OBE 2001; PhD, DSc(Eng); FREng; Professor of Biomedical Systems Engineering, Imperial College London (formerly Imperial College of Science, Technology and Medicine), since 1997; *b* 13 Feb. 1945; *s* of Leonard Walter Richard Kitney and Gladys Simpson Kitney; *m* 1977, Vera Baraniecka; two *s*. *Educ:* Enfield Grammar Sch.; Univ. of Surrey (MEng 1969); Imperial Coll., London Univ. (PhD, DIC 1972; DSc(Eng) 1993). FREng 1999. Electronics Engr, Thorn Electrical Industries, 1963–72; Lectr in Biophysics, Chelsea Coll., London Univ., 1972–78; Imperial College, London: Lectr, 1975–85; Reader, 1985–89; Dir, Centre for Biol and Med. Systems, 1991–97; Hd, Dept of Biol and Med. Systems, 1997–2001; Dean, 2003–06, Sen. Dean, 2007–11, Faculty of Engrg; Dir, Graduate Sch. of Engrg and Physical Scis, 2006–11; Chm., Inst. of Systems & Synthetic Biology, 2007–; Co-Dir, EPSRC Centre for Synthetic Biology and Innovation, 2010–; Co-Dir, UK Nat. Centre for Industrial Translation of Synthetic Biology, 2013–; Gov., 1995–98, 2006–; Gov., RPMS, 1995–98. Visiting Professor: Georgia Inst. of Technology, 1981–90; MIT, 1991–. Tech. Dir, Intravascular Res. Ltd, 1987–94; Dir, St Mary's Imaging plc, 1991–96; Dep. Chm. and Tech. Dir, comMedica Ltd, 1999–2006; Chm., Visbion Ltd, 2006–; Trustee, Smith and Nephew Foundn, 1996–2003. Mem., Adv. Cttee on Technology in Medicine, DTI, 1995; Chm., RAEng Inquiry on Synthetic Biology, 2008–09; Mem., Govt's

Leadership Council for Synthetic Biology, 2012–. FIAMBE 2003; FAIMBE 2005. FRSocMed 1994; FRSA 2001; FCGI 2005; Hon. FRCS 2006; Hon. FRCP 2006; Hon. FRCPE. Freeman, City of London, 1996; Liveryman, Co. of Engineers, 1995. Regular contributor, BBC Radio. Nightingale Prize, Internat. Fedn of Biol Engrg Socs, 1975. *Publications:* (jtly) Recent Advances in the Study of Heart Rate Variability, 1980; (jtly) The Beat-by-Beat Investigation of Cardiac Function, 1987; (jtly) The Coming of the Global Healthcare Industry, 1998; conf. proceedings, papers in learned jls. *Recreations:* history, cooking, France. *Address:* Department of Bioengineering, Imperial College London, South Kensington Campus, SW7 2AX. *T:* (020) 7594 6226. *Club:* Athenæum.

KITSON, Gen. Sir Frank (Edward), GBE 1985; (CBE 1972; OBE 1968; MBE 1959); KCB 1980; MC 1955 and Bar 1958; DL; *b* 15 Dec. 1926; *s* of late Vice-Adm. Sir Henry Kitson, KBE, CB and Lady (Marjorie) Kitson (*née* de Pass); *m* 1962, Elizabeth Janet (OBE 2015; DL), *d* of late Col C. R. Spencer, OBE, DL; three *d. Educ:* Stowe. 2nd Lt Rifle Bde, 1946; served BAOR, 1946–53; Kenya, 1953–55; Malaya, 1957; Cyprus, 1962–64; CO 1st Bn, Royal Green Jackets, 1967–69; Defence Fellow, University Coll., Oxford, 1969–70; Comdr, 39 Inf. Bde, NI, 1970–72 (CBE for gallantry); Comdt, Sch. of Infantry, 1972–74; RCDS, 1975; GOC 2nd Division, later 2nd Armoured Division, 1976–78; Comdt, Staff College, 1978–80; Dep. C-in-C, UKLF, and Inspector-Gen., TA, 1980–82; C-in-C, UKLF, 1982–85. ADC Gen. to the Queen, 1983–85. 2nd Bn, The Royal Green Jackets: Col Comdt, 1979–87; Rep. Col Comdt, 1982–85; Hon. Col, Oxford Univ. OTC, 1982–87. DL 1989. *Publications:* Gangs and Counter Gangs, 1960; Low Intensity Operations, 1971; Bunch of Five, 1977; Warfare as a Whole, 1987; Directing Operations, 1989; Prince Rupert: portrait of a soldier, 1994; Prince Rupert: Admiral and General-at-sea, 1998; Old Ironsides: the military biography of Oliver Cromwell, 2004; When Britannia Ruled the Waves, 2007. *Address:* c/o Lloyds Bank, Farnham, Surrey GU9 7LT. *Club:* Boodle's.

KITSON, Richard David; a District Judge (Magistrates' Courts), since 2002; *b* 30 Dec. 1954; *s* of Stanley Kitson and Maisie Kitson; *m* 1980, Barbara Ann Kitching; one *s* one *d. Educ:* Doncaster Grammar Sch.; Newcastle upon Tyne Poly. (BA Hons 1976; Maxwell Prize). Admitted solicitor, 1979; Partner, Ward Bracewell & Co., then Taylor Bracewell, Solicitors, Doncaster, 1981–2002. Chairman: Doncaster FHSA, 1994–96 (non-exec. Mem., 1985–94); Doncaster Royal and Montagu Hosp. NHS Trust, 1996–2001; Doncaster Central Primary Care Trust, 2001–02. *Recreations:* hill walking, running, tennis, gardening, Rugby Union. *Address:* Leeds District Magistrates' Court, PO Box No 97, Westgate, Leeds LS1 3JP. *T:* (0113) 245 9653.

KITSON, Sir Timothy (Peter Geoffrey), Kt 1974; *b* 28 Jan. 1931; *s* of late Geoffrey H. and of Kathleen Kitson; *m* 1959, Diana Mary Fattorini; one *s* two *d. Educ:* Charterhouse; Royal Agricultural College, Cirencester. Farmed in Australia, 1949–51. Chairman: Provident Financial Gp, later Provident Financial plc, 1983–95; London Clubs Internat. plc, 1995–2002; Vice Chm., Halifax Bldg Soc., 1995–98; Director: Leeds Permanent Bldg Soc., 1983–95; Alfred McAlpine plc, 1983–94; SIG plc, 1995–2002. Member: Thirsk RDC, 1954–57; N Riding CC, 1957–61. MP (C) Richmond, Yorks, 1959–83; PPS to Parly Sec. to Minister of Agriculture, 1960–64; an Opposition Whip, 1967–70; PPS to the Prime Minister, 1970–74, to Leader of the Opposition, 1974–75. Chm., Defence Select Cttee, 1982–83. *Recreations:* shooting, hunting, racing. *Address:* Ulshaw Farm, Middleham, Leyburn, N Yorks DL8 4PU.

KITTMER, John; Ambassador to the Hellenic Republic, since 2013; *b* Cuckfield, Sussex, 6 July 1967; *s* of Roy Kittmer and Jean Kittmer; civil partnership 2007, David Bates. *Educ:* Christ's Coll., Cambridge (BA 1988); King's Coll. London (MA 2007); Magdalen Coll., Oxford. Various posts, DFEE, 1993–98; First Sec., UK Perm. Repn to EU, Brussels, 1998–2002; Hd of Section, FCO, 2002–04; Hd of Section, DEFRA, 2005–06; Dep. Dir, Cabinet Office, 2006–07; Dep. Dir, Exotic Animal Diseases, DEFRA, 2008; Principal Private Sec. to Sec. of State, 2008–10, Dep. Dir, Inland Waterways, 2011–12, DEFRA. *Recreations:* walking, music, things Greek. *Address:* c/o Foreign and Commonwealth Office, King Charles Street, SW1A 2AH. *E:* john.kittmer@fco.gov.uk.

KITZINGER, Uwe, CBE 1980; Affiliate, Lowell House and Centre for European Studies, Harvard University, since 2003 (Visiting Scholar, 1993–2003); Senior Research Fellow, Atlantic Council, since 1993; *b* 12 April 1928; *o s* of late Dr G. and Mrs L. Kitzinger, Abbots Langley, Herts; *m* 1952, Sheila Helena Elizabeth Webster, (Sheila Kitzinger, MBE) (*d* 2015); five *d. Educ:* Watford Grammar Sch.; Balliol Coll. and New Coll. (Foundn Schol.), Oxford (1st in Philosophy, Politics and Economics, MA, MLitt; Pres., Oxford Union, 1950; Ed., University). Economic Section, Council of Europe, Strasbourg, 1951–58; Nuffield College, Oxford: Research Fellow, 1956–62, Official Fellow, 1962–76, Emeritus Fellow, 1976; Acting Investment Bursar, 1962–64; Investment Bursar, 1964–76; Mem., Investment Cttee, 1962–88; Assessor of Oxford University, 1967–68; leave of absence as Adviser to Sir Christopher (later Lord) Soames, Vice-Pres. of the Commn of the European Communities, Brussels, 1973–75; Dean, INSEAD (European Inst. of Business Admin), Fontainebleau, 1976–80 (Mem. Board, 1976–83); Dir, Oxford Centre for Management Studies, 1980–84; Founding Pres., Templeton Coll. (now Green Templeton Coll.), Oxford, 1984–91 (sabbatical, 1991–93; Hon. Fellow, 2001–). Visiting Professor: of Internat. Relations, Univ. of the West Indies, 1964–65; of Government, Harvard, 1969–70; Univ. of Paris 1970–73. Member: ODM Cttee for University Secondment, 1966–68; British Universities Cttee of Encyclopædia Britannica, 1967–98; Nat. Council of European Movement, 1974–76; Council, RIIA, 1973–85; Court, Cranfield Inst. of Technology, 1984–85. Founding Chm., Cttee on Atlantic Studies, 1967–70. Co-Founder, Lentils for Dubrovnik, 1991–. Founding Pres., 1987–92, Pres., 1996–, Internat. Assoc. of Macro-Engrg Socs. Member: Oxfam Council, 1981–84; Major Projects Assoc., 1981–91 (Founding Chm., 1981–86); Adv. Bd, Pace Univ., NY, 1982–92; Berlin Science Centre, 1983–90; Acad. Adv. Bd, World Management Council, 1989–; Bd, Jean Monnet Foundn, Lausanne, 1990–; Tufts Inst. for Global Leadership, 2006–. Chair, GARIWO Campaign for Civil Courage Sarajevo, 2001–12. Pres., Féd. Britannique des Alliances Françaises, 1999–2004. Trustee: European Foundn for Management Educn, Brussels, 1978–80; Oxford Trust for Music and the Arts, 1986–91. Patron, Asylum Welcome, 2005–. Chm., Oxford Radio Consortium, 1988. Founding Editor, Jl of Common Market Studies, 1962–. Hon. LLD Buena Vista, 1986. Order of the Morning Star (Croatia), 1997. Documents, books and articles on Britain's relationship with emergent EU 1945–76 deposited Histl Archives of EU, Eur. Univ. Inst., Florence, 2012. *Publications:* German Electoral Politics, 1960 (German edn 1960); The Challenge of the Common Market, 1961 (Amer. edn, The Politics and Economics of European Integration, 1963, et al); Britain, Europe and Beyond, 1964; The Background to Jamaica's Foreign Policy, 1965; The European Common Market and Community, 1967; Commitment and Identity, 1968; The Second Try, 1968; Diplomacy and Persuasion, 1973 (French edn 1974); Europe's Wider Horizons, 1975; (with D. E. Butler) The 1975 Referendum, 1976, 2nd edn 1996; (ed with E. Frankel) Macro-Engineering and the Earth, 1998. *Recreations:* sailing, travel, old buildings. *Address:* Standlake Manor, near Witney, Oxon OX29 7RH. *T:* (01865) 300266, 300438; La Rivière, 11100 Bages, France. *T:* (4) 68417013. *E:* uwe_kitzinger@yahoo.com. *Club:* Royal Thames Yacht.

KIYOTAKI, Prof. Nobuhiro, PhD; FBA 2003; Professor, Department of Economics, Princeton University, since 2006; *b* 24 June 1955. *Educ:* Univ. of Tokyo (BA 1978); Harvard Univ. (PhD 1985). Asst Prof., Dept of Econs, Univ. of Wisconsin-Madison, 1985–91; Lectr, Dept of Econs, LSE, 1989–91; Associate Prof., Dept of Econs, Univ. of Minnesota, 1991–97; Cassel Prof. of Econs, LSE, 1997–2006; Sen. Economist and Resident Schol., Fed. Reserve Bank of NY, 2005–06. Visiting Professor: LSE, 1995–96 and 2010–; Dept of Econs, MIT, 2000–01. Mem., Monetary Policy Panel, Federal Reserve Bank of NY, 2006–. *Address:* Department of Economics, Princeton University, 112 Fisher Hall, Princeton, NJ 08544–1021, USA.

KLAUS, Prof. Václav; President of Czech Republic, 2003–13; *b* 19 June 1941; *s* of Václav Klaus and Marie Klausová; *m* 1968, Livia Klausová; two *s. Educ:* Prague Sch. of Economics (Hon. Dr 1994); Cornell Univ. Researcher, Inst. of Econs, Czechoslovak Acad. of Scis, to 1970; Czechoslovak State Bank, 1971–86 (Head, Dept of Macroeconomic Policy); Inst. of Forecasting, Czechoslovak Acad. of Scis, 1987; founder, Civic Forum Movt (Chm., 1990–91); Minister of Finance, Czech Republic, 1989–92; Dep. Prime Minister, 1991–92; Prime Minister, 1992–97; Pres., Chamber of Deputies, 1998–2003. Chm., Civic Democratic Party, Czech Republic, 1991–2002. Vice-Chm., European Democratic Union, 1996–. Prof. of Finance, Prague Sch. of Economics, 1994–. Hon. doctorates from Univs in USA, Canada, Guatemala, Mexico, Argentina, France, UK, Czech Republic, Germany; numerous awards from USA, Germany, France, Denmark, Austria, Switzerland, Czech Republic. *Publications:* A Road to Market Economy, 1991; Tomorrow's Challenge, 1991; Economic Theory and Economic Reform, 1991; Signale aus dem Herzen Europas, 1991; I Do Not Like Catastrophic Scenarios, 1991; Dismantling Socialism, 1992; Why Am I a Conservative?, 1992; The Year: how much is it in the history of the country?, 1993; The Czech Way, 1994; Rebirth of a Country, 1994; Summing Up to One, 1995; Tschechische Transformation & Europäische Integration, 1995; Economic Theory and Reality of Transformation Processes, 1995; Between the Past and the Future, 1996; Renaissance, 1997; The Defence of Forgotten Ideas, 1997; Thus Spoke Václav Klaus, 1998; Why I Am not a Social Democrat, 1998; The Country without Governing, 1999; The Way out of the Trap, 1999; From the Opposition Treaty to the Tolerance Patent, 2000; Europe from the Point of View of a Politician and an Economist, 2001; Conversations with Václav Klaus, 2001; The First Year, 2004; Europe of Václav Klaus, 2004; The Second Year, 2005; On the Road to Democracy, 2005. *Recreations:* tennis, ski-ing. *Address:* c/o Office of the President, Pražský hrad, 11908 Prague 1, Czech Republic.

KLEIN, Anita, RE 1995 (ARE 1992); artist; President, Royal Society of Painter Printmakers, 2003–06; *b* Sydney, 14 Feb. 1960; *d* of Prof. Anthony George Klein and Mavis Klein; *m* 1984, Nigel Swift; two *d. Educ:* Chelsea Sch. of Art (Foundn Cert. 1979); Slade Sch. of Fine Art (Henrique Schol. 1982 and 1983; BA Hons Painting 1983; Higher Dip. Fine Art (Printmaking) 1985). *Solo exhibitions* include: paintings and prints: Creaser Gall., London, 1986; Printworks, Colchester, 1990; Wilson Hale, London, 1991; Royal Pavilion Contemp. Gall., Brighton, 1992; Woodlands Art Gall., 1993; Cambridge Contemp. Art, 1996, 1998, 2000; Advanced Graphics, London, 2010; Fine Art Partnership, London, 2010; Bankside Gall. and Menier Gall., London, 2010; prints: Leigh Gall., London, 1987; Tall House Gall., London, 1990; Victorian Artists Soc., Melbourne, 1992; Brighton Fest., Brighton Marina Arts Index, 1993; two person show (with Paula Rego), Gateway Arts Centre, Shrewsbury, 1995; CCA, Oxford, 1996; Leeds City Art Gall., 1997; New Ashgate Gall., Farnham, 1998; Old Town Gall., Tustin, Calif, 1999; Port Jackson Press, Melbourne, 1999, 2000; Pyramid Gall., York (and ceramics), 1999; Advanced Graphics, London, 2002 (retrospective exhibn, 20 Years of Printmaking), 2004; paintings: Royal Exchange Th., Manchester, 1994; Eur. Art Fair, Ghent, 1995; Beaux Arts, Bath, 1996, 1998; Helen Gory Gall., Melbourne, 2003; paintings, drawings and watercolours: Boundary Gall., London, 2001 (and ceramics), 2002, 2004, 2006, 2009 (and stained glass); Advanced Graphics, London, 2006, 2008; Bankside Gall., London, 2006, 2009; Royal Commonwealth Club, 2007; Chelsea and Westminster Hosp., 2008; *group exhibitions* include: Hayward Gall.; RA; ICA; Blond Fine Art; Contemp. Arts Soc.; Christies; Discerning Eye Exhibn, Mall Galls, London; Hunting Art Prizes, RCA; Cleveland Drawing Biennale; Glasgow Print Studio; London Art Fair; Barbican Concourse Gall.; *works in public collections* include: Collection of Prints and Drawings, BM; BL; Arts Council England. Trustee, Paintings in Hosps, 2007–. Joseph Webb Award, Royal Soc. of Painter Printmakers, 1984; John Purcell Award: for an outstanding print, Bankside Open, 1991; Nat. Print Exhibn, London, 1995; Univ. of Wales Purchase Prize, Nat. Print Exhibn, London, 2003. *Publications:* Anita Klein, Painter Printmaker, 2006; Anita Klein: Italian angels, 2009; Through the Looking Glass, 2011. *Recreations:* walking, cinema, visiting Italy, laughing, drinking red wine. *E:* anita@anitaklein.com. *T:* (020) 7407 5471, 07780 682841, (Italy) 0575749224. *W:* www.anitaklein.com. *Club:* Chelsea Arts.

KLEIN, Calvin Richard; fashion designer; *b* 19 Nov. 1942; *s* of Leo Klein and Flore (*née* Stern); *m* 1st, 1964, Jayne Centre (marr. diss. 1974); one *d*; 2nd, 1986, Kelly Rector (marr. diss. 2006). *Educ:* Fashion Inst. of Technology, NY; High Sch. of Art and Design. Started own fashion business, 1968; Vice Chm., 1969, Consulting Creative Dir, 2003, Calvin Klein Inc. Dir, Fashion Inst. of Technology, 1975–. Numerous awards.

KLEIN, Deborah; Joint Chief Executive, Engine Group, since 2008; Chairman, WCRS, since 2008; *b* Zimbabwe, 10 Aug. 1968; *d* of Len and Audrey Klein; *m* 2002, Max Cantor; one *s* one *d. Educ:* Brooklyn Primary Sch.; Pretoria High Sch. for Girls; Univ. of Cape Town (BBus Sci. (Econs and Mktg)). AC Nielson, 1990–92; strategic planner, Saatchi & Saatchi, 1993–97 (Dir, 1996–97); WCRS: Hd of Planning, 1997–2003; Chief Exec., 2004–08. Member: WACL; Mktg Gp of GB. *Publications:* Women in Advertising, 2000. *Recreations:* yoga, cooking, walking, my children. *Address:* Engine, 60 Great Portland Street, W1W 7RT. *E:* debbie.klein@theenginegroup.com.

KLEIN, Prof. Jacob, PhD; FRSC; FInstP; Dr Lee's Professor of Physical Chemistry, University of Oxford, 2000–07, Professor Emeritus, since 2010; Professor, Weizmann Institute of Science, Israel, since 1987; *b* 20 Aug. 1949; *s* of Moshe Klein and Edna Klein (*née* Lipper); *m* 1974, Michele Castle; two *s* two *d. Educ:* in Israel; Whittinghame Coll., Brighton; St Catharine's Coll., Cambridge (BA 1st Cl. Hons Physics 1973; MA, PhD 1977). FRSC 2011. Mil. Service, Israel, 1967–70; Post-doctoral res., Weizmann Inst., Israel, 1977–80; Demonstrator, Cavendish Lab., and Fellow of St Catharine's Coll., Cambridge, 1980–84; Weizmann Institute, Israel: Sen. Scientist, 1980–84; Associate Prof., 1984–87; Chairman: Polymer Res. Dept, 1989–91; Scientific Council, 1998–2000; University of Oxford: Hd, Dept of Chemistry, 2000–05; Professorial Res. Fellow, 2008–10. MAE 2013. FAPS 2003; FInstP 2004. Somach Sacks Prize, Weizmann Inst., 1983; Charles Vernon Boys Prize, Inst. Physics (GB), 1984; Jeanett and Samuel Lubel Prize, 1989; Internat. Kao Fellow (Japan), 1994; Ford Prize for Polymer Physics, APS, 1995; Kolthoff Prize, Technion Israel Inst. of Technology, 2007; Prize of Excellence, Israel Chem. Soc., 2010; Soft Matter and Biophysical Chem. Prize, RSC, 2011; Tribology Gold Medal, Tribology Trust/IMechE, 2012. *Publications:* contrib. numerous papers to scientific jls, etc. *Recreations:* reading, family holidays, hiking. *Address:* 1 Ruppin Street, Rehovot 76353, Israel; Materials & Interfaces Department, Weizmann Institute of Science, Rehovot 76100, Israel; Physical and Theoretical Chemistry Laboratory, South Parks Road, Oxford OX1 3QZ.

KLEIN, Jonathan David; Co-Founder, since 1995 and Chairman, since 2015, Getty Images Inc. (Chief Executive Officer, 1995–2015); *b* 13 May 1960; *s* of Louis and Hilda Klein; *m* 1988, Deborah Ann Hunter; three *s. Educ:* Trinity Hall, Cambridge (MA). Hambros Bank Ltd, 1983–98: Dir, 1989–93; non-exec. Dir, 1993–98. *Recreations:* all sports, global health, movies, theatre, the Third World. *Address:* c/o Getty Images Inc., 75 Varick Street, Suite 500, New York, NY 10013, USA.

KLEIN, Prof. Michael Lawrence, PhD; FRS 2003; Laura H. Carnell Professor of Science, and Director, Institute for Computational Molecular Science, Temple University, Philadelphia, since 2009; *b* 13 March 1940; *s* of Jack Klein and Bessie Klein (*née* Bloomberg); *m* 1962, Brenda Woodman; two *d. Educ:* Bristol Univ. (BSc Hons 1961; PhD Chemistry

1964). Assoc. Res. Officer, 1968–74, Sen. Res. Officer, 1974–85, Prin. Res. Officer, 1985–87, Chemistry Div., NRCC, Ottawa; University of Pennsylvania, Philadelphia: Prof. of Chemistry, 1987–91; William Smith Prof. of Chemistry, 1991–93; Earle Hepburn Prof. of Physical Sci., and Dir, Lab. for Res. on the Structure of Matter, 1993–2009. Fellow Commoner, Trinity Coll., Cambridge, 1985–86; Louis Néel Prof., Ecole Normale Supérieure, Lyon, 1988; Guggenheim Fellow, 1989–90; Sen. Humboldt Fellow, Max Planck Inst., Stuttgart, 1995; Miller Prof., Univ. of Calif., Berkeley, 1997; Linnett Vis. Prof., Univ. of Cambridge, 1998; Schlumberger Prof., Oxford and Cambridge, 2003. Associate Fellow, Acad. of Scis for the Developing World, 2004–. FInstP 2003; FRSCan 1984; FCIC 1979; Fellow, American Acad. of Arts and Scis, 2003; Mem., NAS, 2009. Honorary Fellow: Indian Acad. of Scis, 2006; Trinity Coll., Cambridge, 2013. Computational Physics Prize, APS, 1999; CECAM Prize, 2004; Physical Chemistry Prize, ACS, 2008; Boys-Rahman Award, RSC, 2011. *Publications:* over 600 articles in scientific jls and books. *Address:* Institute for Computational Molecular Science, SERC Building 704E, Temple University, 1925 North 12th Street, Philadelphia, PA 1922, USA. *E:* mlklein@temple.edu.

KLEIN, Richard Henry; Director of Factual, ITV, since 2013; *b* Burwash Common, Sussex, 12 Oct. 1958; *s* of Hans Joachim Klein and Bernadine Klein (*née* Thorne); one *d. Educ:* Prior Park Coll.; Aberdeen Univ. (MA Hons English 1983); City Univ. (Dip. Journalism 1985). Bank clerk, Lloyds Bank; researcher, reporter, then Dir, Weekend World, LWT, 1987–90; joined BBC TV as series producer, 1996; Commng Ed., Documentaries, 2005–07; Hd, Ind. Commng, Factual TV, 2007–08; Controller, BBC Four, 2008–13. *Recreations:* cycling, reading, rock music, hill walking, theatre. *Address:* 83 Chesson Road, W14 9QS.

KLEIN, Prof. Rudolf Ewald, CBE 2001; FBA 2006; Professor of Social Policy, University of Bath, 1978–98, now Emeritus; *b* 26 Aug. 1930; *o s* of Robert and Martha Klein; *m* 1st, 1957, Josephine Parfitt (*d* 1996); one *d*; 2nd, 2012, Ans Ankone. *Educ:* Bristol Grammar Sch.; Merton Coll., Oxford (Postmaster) (Gibbs Schol. 1950; MA). Leader Writer, London Evening Standard, 1952–62; Editor, 'The Week', Leader Writer, Home Affairs Editor, The Observer, 1962–72; Research Associate, Organisation of Medical Care Unit, London Sch. of Hygiene and Tropical Medicine, 1972–73; Sen. Fellow, Centre for Studies in Social Policy, 1973–78; Professorial Fellow, then Sen. Associate, King's Fund, 1995–2001. Visiting Professor: LSE, 1996–2013; LSHTM, 2001–. Member: Wiltshire AHA, 1980–82; Bath DHA, 1982–84. Jt Editor, Political Quarterly, 1981–87. Foreign Associate, Inst. of Medicine, NAS, USA, 2001. FMedSci 2006. Hon. DArts Oxford Brookes, 1998. Margaret E. Mahoney Award, Commonwealth Fund, NY, 1999. *Publications:* Complaints Against Doctors, 1973; (ed) Social Policy and Public Expenditure, 1974; (ed) Inflation and Priorities, 1975; (with Janet Lewis) The Politics of Consumer Representation, 1976; The Politics of the NHS, 1983; (ed with Michael O'Higgins) The Future of Welfare, 1985; (with Patricia Day) Accountabilities, 1987; (with Linda Challis *et al*) Joint Approaches to Social Policy, 1988; (with Patricia Day) Inspecting the Inspectorates, 1990; (with Neil Carter and Patricia Day) How organisations measure success, 1991; (with Patricia Day and David Henderson) Home Rules, 1993; The New Politics of the NHS, 1995, 7th edn 2013; (with Patricia Day and Sharon Redmayne) Managing Scarcity, 1996; papers on public policy, health policy and public expenditure in various jls. *Recreations:* opera, cooking, football. *Address:* 12A Laurier Road, NW5 1SG. *T:* (020) 7428 9767.

KLEIN, Suzy; broadcaster and writer; *b* London, 1 April 1975; *d* of Barry and Alison Klein; *m* 2005, James Fischelis; one *s* one *d. Educ:* S Hampstead High Sch., London; St Hugh's Coll., Oxford (BA 1st Cl. Hons Music); City Univ., London (Postgrad. Dip. Broadcast Journalism). Researcher, BBC Radio 4, 1997–98; BBC Television: Asst Producer, Arts, 1998–2000; Producer, Classical Music, 2001–08. Presenter: Proms, BBC TV; The Review Show, BBC2; Saturday Live, BBC Radio 4; Sky Arts TV; Leeds Piano Competition, BBC TV, In Tune, BBC Radio 3; Rule Britannia! (series), BBC TV, 2014. Feature writer and reviewer for The Guardian, New Statesman, BBC Music Mag. *Publications:* (jtly) What's That? Contemporary Arts for Children, 2011; (jtly) What is Contemporary Art? A Children's Guide, 2012. *Recreations:* walking, opera, concerts, wine, explaining complex existential matters to inquisitive 4 year-olds. *Address:* BBC Broadcasting House, W1A 1AA. *E:* suzy.klein@bbc.co.uk.

KLEINMAN, Mark Daniel; City Editor, Sky News, since 2009; *b* London, 25 April 1977; *s* of Louis Kleinman and Jacqueline Kleinman (*née* Cooper-Smith); partner, Barbara Serra. *Educ:* Eaglesfield Sch.; Univ. of York (BA Hons Eng. 1998). Reporter: Leisure Week, 1998–99; Precision Marketing, 1999–2000; Reporter, then Chief Reporter, Marketing, 2000–03; Business Correspondent: Sunday Express, 2004; Sunday Times, 2004–06; Asia Business Editor, Daily Telegraph and Sunday Telegraph, 2006–08; City Editor, Sunday Telegraph, 2008–09. Business Journalist of the Year, London Press Club, 2011. *Recreations:* football (supporter of Charlton Athletic), tennis, film, travel. *Address:* Sky News, 2nd Floor, 4 Millbank, SW1P 3JA. *T:* (020) 7032 2833. *E:* Mark.Kleinman@bskyb.com. *Club:* Soho House.

KLEINPOPPEN, Prof. Hans Johann Willi, FRSE; Professor of Experimental Physics, 1968–96, now Emeritus, and Head, Unit of Atomic and Molecular Physics, 1982–96, University of Stirling; *b* Duisburg, Germany, 30 Sept. 1928. *Educ:* Univ. of Giessen (Dipl. Physics 1955); Univ. of Tübingen; Dr rer. nat. 1961. Habilitation, Tübingen, 1967. Head, Physics Dept, 1971–73, Dir, Inst. of Atomic Physics, 1975–81, Univ. of Stirling. Vis. Fellow, Univ. Colorado, 1967–68; Vis. Associate Prof., Columbia Univ., 1968; Fellow, Center for Theoretical Studies, Univ. of Miami, 1972–73; Bielefeld University: Guest Prof., 1978–79; Vis. Fellow, Zentrum für interdisziplinäre Forschung, 1979–80; Sen. Res. Fellow, 1980–98; Res. Visitor, Fritz Haber Inst., Berlin, 1991–; Leverhulme Emeritus Fellow, 1998–2000. Chairman: Internat. Symposium on Physics of One- and Two-Electron Atoms (Arnold Sommerfeld Centennial Meml Meeting, Munich 1968); Internat. Symposium on Electron and Photon Interactions with Atoms, in honour of Ugo Fano, Stirling, 1974; Internat. Workshop on Coherence and Correlation in Atomic Collisions, dedicated to Sir Harrie Massey, UCL, 1978; Internat. Symp. on Amplitudes and State Parameters in Atomic Collisions, Kyoto, 1979; Org Cttee on Workshops on Polarized Electron and Polarized Photon Physics, SERC, 1993, 1994; Co-Chm. (with D. M. Campbell), Peter Farago Symposium on Electron Physics, RSE, 1995; Co-Dir, Advanced Study Inst. on Fundamental Processes in Energetic Atomic Collisions, Maratea, Italy, 1982; Dir, Advanced Study Inst. on Fundamental Processes in Atomic Collision Physics, S Flavia, Sicily, 1984; Co-Dir, Advanced Study Inst. on Fundamental Processes on Atomic Dynamics, Maratea, Italy, 1987. FInstP 1969; Fellow Amer. Physical Soc. 1969; FRAS 1974; FRSE 1987; FRSA 1990. *Publications:* edited: (with F. Bopp) Physics of the One- and Two-Electron Atoms (A. Sommerfeld centennial meml conf.), 1969; (with M. R. C. McDowell) Electron and Photon Interactions with Atoms, 1976; Progress in Atomic Spectroscopy, (with W. Hanle) Vol. A 1978, Vol. B 1979, (with H. J. Beyer) Vol. C 1984, Vol. D 1987; (with J. F. Williams) Coherence and Correlations in Atomic Collisions, 1980; (with D. J. Fabian and L. H. Watson) Inner-Shell and X-Ray Physics of Atoms and Solids, 1981; (with J. S. Briggs and H. O. Lutz): Fundamental Processes in Energetic Atomic Collisions, 1983; Fundamental Processes in Atomic Collision Physics, 1985; Fundamental Processes in Atomic Dynamics, 1988; (with W. R. Newell) Polarized Electron/Polarized Photon Physics, 1995; (with D. M. Campbell) Selected Topics on Electron Physics, 1996; series editor (with P. G. Burke), Physics of Atoms and Molecules (about 50 monographs and conf. proceedings); (contrib.) McGraw-Hill Yearbook of Science/Technology, 2005; about 200 papers in Zeitschr. f. Physik, Z. f. Naturf., Z. f. Angew Physik, Physikalische Blätter, Physical Review, Physical Review Letters, Jl of Physics, Physics Letters, Internat. Jl of Quantum Chemistry, Physics Reports, Advances of Atomic, Molecular and Optical Physics, Applied Physics, Physica, Philosophical Trans of Royal Soc.; *festschriften:* (for 60th birthday) (ed H.-J. Beyer, K. Blum and R. Hippler) Coherence in Atomic Collision Physics, 1988; (for 70th birthday) (ed U. Becker and A. Crowe) Hans Kleinpoppen Symposium on Complete Scattering Experiments, 1998. *Address:* Orberstrasse 12, 14193 Berlin, Germany.

KLEINWORT, Sir Richard (Drake), 4th Bt *cr* 1909, of Bolnore, Cuckfield, Sussex; DL; Chairman, Richard Kleinwort Consultancy Group, since 2001; *b* 4 Nov. 1960; *s* of Sir Kenneth Drake Kleinwort, 3rd Bt and his 1st wife, Lady Davina Pepys (*d* 1973), *d* of 7th Earl of Cottenham; *S* father, 1994; *m* 1989, Lucinda, *d* of William Shand Kydd; three *s* one *d. Educ:* Stowe; Exeter Univ. (BA). Kleinwort Benson, Geneva, 1979; Banco General de Negocios, Buenos Aires, 1983; Deutsche Bank AG, Hamburg and Frankfurt, 1985–88; Biss Lancaster plc, 1988–89; Grandfield Rork Collins Financial, 1989–91; Partner, 1991–94, Dir, 1994–2000, Cardew & Co.; Head of Financial PR, Ogilvy PR Worldwide, 2000–01. Non-exec. Dir, RDF Gp plc, 2008–10; non-exec. Chm., Hungry Hamsters Ltd, film prodn co., 2009–11; Vice Chm., Cubitt Consulting, 2010–. Mem., Adv. Bd, Kleinwort Benson Private Bank, 2011–. President: Haywards Heath Hospital, 1991–97; The Little Black Bag Housing Assoc., 1991–. Dir, Steppes East Gp, 1998–. Life Mem., British Field Sports Soc., 1981; Member: WWF (1001) Club, 1979– (Mem., Council of Ambassadors, WWF, 2005–); S of England Agricl Soc., 1988–; RHS, 1991–; Sussex Club, 1996–; Countryside Alliance, 1997–; Compagnie Internat. de la Chasse, 1998–. Chm., Knepp Castle Polo Club, 1997–2006. Fellow, World Scout Foundn, Geneva, 1989. Mem., Instn of King Edward VII Hosp., Midhurst, 1992–2000; Trustee: Ernest Kleinwort Charitable Trust, 1988–; Patron: Cuckfield Soc., 1995–; Ackroyd Trust, 1995– (Trustee); Vice Patron, Sussex Young Cricketers Educn Trust, 2008–; Vice Pres., Chichester Cathedral Millennium Endowment Appeal, 1998–2005. Ambassador, The Prince's Trust, 1998–. Gov., Stowe Sch., 1999–2004 (Chairman: Foundn Appeal; Stowe Sch. Foundn, 1999–; Campaign for Stowe, 1999–2004). DL 2005, High Sheriff 2008–09, W Sussex. *Recreations:* travel, my family, laughter, shooting, gardening, farming, watching England winning any sport. *Heir: s* Rufus Drake Kleinwort, *b* 16 Aug. 1994. *Clubs:* White's, MCC, Turf, Arts.

KLEISTERLEE, Gerard Johannes; Chairman, Vodafone Group plc, since 2011; *b* Ludwigsburg, 28 Sept. 1946; *m* 1971, Annemieke Berdina Gerarda Janssen; one *s* two *d. Educ:* Eindhoven Tech. Univ. (Masters Electronic Engrg). Philips Electronics NV: various posts, 1974–96; Country Chm., Taiwan/China and Regl Pres., Philips Components Asia Pacific, 1996–99; CEO, Philips Components, 1999–2000; Exec. Vice Pres. and Chief Operating Officer, 2000–01; Chm. and CEO, 2001–11. Ind. Dir, Vivendi, 2002–05; non-executive Director: Dutch Central Bank, 2006–12; Daimler AG, 2009–14; Royal Dutch Shell, 2010–; Dell, 2011–13; IBEX Global Solutions, 2014–. Member: Asia Business Council, 2002–; World 50 Prog., 2011–. Chm., Cancer Foundn Amsterdam, 2002–11. Hon. Dr Catholic Univ. of Leuven, 2005. Eur. Businessman of Year, Fortune mag., 2007. *Recreation:* opera. *Address:* Vodafone Group plc, Vodafone House, The Connection, Newbury, Berks RG14 2FN.

KLEMPERER, Prof. Paul David, PhD; FBA 1999; Edgeworth Professor of Economics, University of Oxford, since 1995; Fellow, Nuffield College, Oxford, since 1995; *b* 15 Aug. 1956; *s* of late Hugh G. Klemperer and Ruth M. M. Klemperer (*née* Jordan); *m* 1989, Margaret Meyer; two *s* one *d. Educ:* King Edward's Sch., Birmingham; Peterhouse, Cambridge (BA Engrg, 1st Cl. Hons with Dist., 1978); Stanford Univ. (MBA 1982 (Top Student Award); PhD Econs 1986). Consultant, Andersen Consulting, 1978–80; Harkness Fellow, Commonwealth Fund, 1980–82; Oxford University: Univ. Lectr in Operations Res. and Mathematical Econs, 1985–90; Reader in Econs, 1990–95; John Thomson Fellow and Tutor, St Catherine's Coll., 1985–95. Visiting positions: MIT, 1987; Berkeley, 1991, 1993; Stanford, 1991, 1993; Yale, 1994; Princeton, 1998. Mem., UK Competition Commn, 2001–05. Consultant: UK Radiocommunications Agency (principal auction theorist for UK 3G auction, 2000), 1997–2000; US Federal Trade Commn, 1999–2001; Bank of England, 2007–; US Treasury, 2008–09; Bank of Canada, 2009; Advr to EU, US, UK, and other govts and private firms. Mem., Council, Royal Econ. Soc., 2001–05. Foreign Hon. Mem., Amer. Acad. of Arts and Scis, 2005; Hon. Mem., Argentine Economic Assoc., 2006. Fellow: Econometric Soc., 1994 (Mem. Council, 2001–06); European Economic Assoc., 2004 (Mem. Council, 2002–07). Hon. Fellow, ESRC Centre for Econ. Learning and Social Evolution, 2001. Editor, RAND Jl of Econs, 1993–99; Associate Editor or Member, Editorial Board: Rev. of Econ. Studies, 1989–97; Jl of Industrial Econs, 1989–96; Oxford Econ. Papers, 1986–2000; Internat. Jl of Industrial Orgn, 1993–2000; Eur. Econ. Rev., 1997–2001; Rev. of Econ. Design, 1997–2000; Econ. Policy, 1998–99; Econ. Jl, 2000–04; Frontiers in Econs, 2000–; BE Jl of Econ. Analysis and Policy, 2001–; Jl of Competition Law and Econs, 2004–. *Publications:* The Economic Theory of Auctions, 2000; Auctions: theory and practice, 2004; articles in econs jls on industrial organization, auction theory, and other econ. theory and policy. *Address:* Nuffield College, Oxford OX1 1NF. *T:* (01865) 278588. *E:* paul.klemperer@economics.ox.ac.uk.

KLENERMAN, Prof. David, PhD; FRS 2012; Professor of Biophysical Chemistry, University of Cambridge; Fellow, Christ's College, Cambridge, since 1994; *s* of late Leslie Klenerman and Naomi Klenerman. *Educ:* Christ's Coll., Cambridge (BA 1982); Churchill Coll., Cambridge (PhD 1986). Fulbright Schol., Stanford Univ.; Laser Spectroscopy Gp, BP Research; Univ. of Cambridge. Co-founded, Solexa, 1998. *Publications:* contribs to learned jls incl. Proc. NAS, Biophysics Jl, Nature Methods, Jl Biol Chem., Nature Structural and Molecular Biol. *Address:* Department of Chemistry, University of Cambridge, Lensfield Road, Cambridge CB2 1EW.

KLENERMAN, Prof. Paul, DM, DPhil; FRCP, FRCPath; Professor of Immunology, University of Oxford; *b* London, 26 March 1963; *s* of late Leslie Klenerman and Naomi Klenerman; *m* 1999, Sally Morse; one *s* one *d. Educ:* Clare Coll., Cambridge (BA 1985); Univ. of Oxford (BM BCh Clin. Medicine 1988; DPhil 1995; DM 2003). MRCP 1991; MRCPath 2001. Univ. of Oxford, 1992; Univ. Zurich; Wellcome Trust Sen. Res. Fellow, Nuffield Dept of Medicine, Univ. of Oxford, 2000–. Hon. Consultant Physician, Oxford, 2001–. FMedSci 2013. *Publications:* articles in gen. biosci., med. and immunol. jls. *Recreations:* fencing, triathlon, IMMposters (sax and fiddle). *Address:* Peter Medawar Building for Pathogen Research, University of Oxford, South Parks Road, Oxford OX1 3SY. *T:* (01865) 281885. *E:* paul.klenerman@ndm.ox.ac.uk.

KLEOPAS, Myrna Y.; Member, Committee against Torture, Office of the High Commissioner for Human Rights, 2008–11 (Rapporteur, 2008); *b* Nicosia, 23 Aug. 1944; *m* Yiangos P. Kleopas; one *s* one *d*. Called to the Bar; practised law in Cyprus, 1971–77; Legal Advr, Min. of Foreign Affairs, Cyprus, 1977–79; entered Cyprus Foreign Service, 1979; Pol Affairs Div., Min. of Foreign Affairs, 1979–80; Counsellor, 1980–86, Consul-Gen., 1981–86, London; Pol Affairs Div., 1986–90; Rep. of Min. of Foreign Affairs to Central Agency for Women's Rights, Cyprus, 1988; Rep. of Cyprus to UN Commn on Status of Women, 1989; Dir, Office of Perm. Sec., Min. of Foreign Affairs, 1990–93; Ambassador to China, and also to Japan, Pakistan, Mongolia and the Philippines, 1993–96; Dir, Pol Affairs Div. (Cyprus Question), Min. of Foreign Affairs, 1996–97; Ambassador to Italy, and also to Switzerland, Malta and San Marino, 1997–2000; High Comr in the UK, 2000–04. *Recreations:* reading, the arts, swimming, walking. *Address:* Office of the High Commissioner for Human Rights, Palais des Nations, 1211 Geneva 10, Switzerland.

KLOOTWIJK, Jaap; Managing Director, Shell UK Oil, and Joint Managing Director, Shell UK, 1983–88; *b* 16 Nov. 1932; *s* of J. L. Klootwijk and W. J. Boer. *Educ:* Rotterdam Grammar Sch.; Technological Univ., Delft (MSc Mech. Eng, 1956). Lieut Royal Netherlands Navy, 1956–58. Joined Royal Dutch/Shell Gp, 1958; worked in various capacities in Holland, UK, France, Switzerland, Sweden, Algeria, Kenya; Area Co-ordinator, SE Asia, 1976–79; Man. Dir, Shell Internat. Gas Ltd, 1979–82; Chm., UK Oil Pipelines, 1983–88. Pres., UK Petroleum Industry Assoc., 1985–87. Director: The Flyfishers' Co. Ltd, 1985–94; Grove Hldgs Ltd, 1991–2001. *Recreations:* shooting, fishing, reading. *Address:* 46 Oak Lodge, Chantry Square, W8 5UL. *T:* (020) 7937 6099. *Club:* Flyfishers' (Pres., 1985–87).

KLOSE, Hans-Ulrich; Member (SPD), Bundestag, Germany, 1983–2013; *b* 14 June 1937; *m* 1992, Dr Anne Steinbeck-Klose; two *s* two *d* by former marriages. *Educ:* Bielefeld; Clinton, Iowa; Freiburg Univ., Hamburg Univ. (Law graduate 1965). Joined SPD 1964; Dep. Chm., Young Socialists, 1966; Dep. Chm., SPD, 1968; Mayor of Hamburg, 1974–81; Treasurer, SPD, 1987–91. Bundestag: Leader of the Opposition, 1991–94; Vice-Pres., 1994–98; Chm., 1998–2002, Vice-Chm., 2002–13, Cttee on Foreign Affairs; Chm., German-American Parly Gp, 2003–13. *Publications:* Altern der Gesellschaft, 1993; Altern hat Zukunft, 1993; poetry (3 vols), 1997, 1999, 2007. *Address:* Schloßstrasse 67A, 14059 Berlin, Germany.

KLUG, Sir Aaron, OM 1995; Kt 1988; ScD (Cantab); FRS 1969; Director, Medical Research Council Laboratory of Molecular Biology, Cambridge, 1986–96 (member of staff, since 1962, Joint Head, Division of Structural Studies, 1978–86); President, Royal Society, 1995–2000; Hon. Fellow of Peterhouse, since 1993 (Fellow, 1962–93); *b* 11 Aug. 1926; *s* of Lazar Klug and Bella Klug (*née* Silin); *m* 1948, Liebe, *o d* of Alexander and Annie Bobrow, Cape Town, SA; one *s* (and one *s* decd). *Educ:* Durban High Sch.; Univ. of the Witwatersrand (BSc); Univ. of Cape Town (MSc). Junior Lecturer, Cape Town, 1947–48; 1851 Exhibn Overseas Fellow from SA to Cambridge; Research Student, Cavendish Laboratory, Cambridge, 1949–52; Rouse-Ball Research Studentship, Trinity Coll., Cambridge, 1949–52; Colloid Science Dept, Cambridge, 1953; Nuffield Research Fellow, Birkbeck Coll., London, 1954–57; Head, Virus Structure Research Group, Birkbeck Coll., 1958–61. Mem., Council for Sci. and Technology, 1993–2000. Hon. Prof., Univ. of Cambridge, 1989. Lectures: Carter-Wallace, Princeton, 1972; Leeuwenhoek, Royal Soc., 1973; Dunham, Harvard Medical Sch., 1975; Harvey, NY, 1979; Lane, Stanford Univ., 1983; Silliman, Yale Univ., 1985; Nishina Meml, Tokyo, 1986; Pauli, ETH Zürich, 1986; Cetus, Univ. of California, Berkeley, 1987; Konrad Bloch, Harvard, 1988; Steenbock, Univ. of Wisconsin, 1989; National, US Biophysical Soc., Washington, 1993; William and Mary, Leiden, 1996. Founder FMedSci 1998. For. Associate, Nat. Acad. of Scis, USA, 1984; Foreign Member: Max Planck Soc., Germany, 1984; Japan Acad., 1996; For. Hon. Mem., Amer. Acad. of Arts and Scis, 1969; For. Associate, Acad. des Scis, Paris, 1989. Hon. FRCP 1987; Hon. FRCPath 1991. Hon. Fellow: Trinity Coll., Cambridge, 1983; Amer. Phil Soc., 1996. Hon. DSc: Chicago, 1978; Columbia Univ., 1978; Witwatersrand, 1984; Hull, 1985; St Andrews, 1987; Western Ontario, 1991; Warwick, 1994; Cape Town, 1997; Weizmann Inst., 1997; Stirling, 1998; London, 2000; Oxford, 2001; Dr *hc* Strasbourg, 1978; Hon. PhD Jerusalem, 1984; Hon. Dr Fil. Stockholm, 1980; Hon. LittD Cantab, 1998. Heineken Prize, Royal Netherlands Acad. of Science, 1979; Louisa Gross Horwitz Prize, Columbia Univ., 1981; Nobel Prize in Chemistry, 1982; Gold Medal of Merit, Univ. of Cape Town, 1983; Copley Medal, Royal Soc., 1985; Harden Medal, Biochem. Soc., 1985; Baly Medal, RCP, 1987; William Bate Hardy Prize, Cambridge Phil. Soc., 1996; Croonian Prize Lect., Royal Soc., 2007. Order of Mapungubwe (Gold) (S Africa), 2005. *Publications:* papers in scientific jls. *Recreations:* reading, ancient history. *Address:* MRC Laboratory of Molecular Biology, Francis Crick Avenue, Cambridge CB2 0QH. *T:* (01223) 248011.

KLUG, Francesca Marilyn Simone, OBE 2002; Professorial Research Fellow, London School of Economics, since 2001; *b* 16 Dec. 1953; *d* of Isaac and Bertha Klug; *m* 1993, Michael Shew; one *d*. *Educ:* London Sch. of Econs (BSc Sociol.). Res. and Information Officer, Runnymede Trust, 1980–84; Policy Advr, Hackney Council, 1984–89; Dir, Civil Liberties Trust, 1989–92; Res. Fellow, Human Rights Centre, Essex Univ., 1992–96; Sen. Res. Fellow, Law Sch., KCL, 1996–2001. Mem., Commn for Equality and Human Rights, 2007–09. *Publications:* (jtly) The Three Pillars of Liberty, Political Rights and Freedoms in the UK, 1996; Values for a Godless Age: the history of the Human Rights Act and its political and legal consequences, 2000; A Magna Carta for All Humanity: homing in on human rights, 2015; contribs to national press, various anthologies and jls incl. Public Law, Eur. Human Rights Law Rev., Policy and Politics. *Recreations:* reading, walking our dog Ruby with my daughter Tania, having fun with friends. *Address:* London School of Economics, Houghton Street, WC2A 2AE. *T:* (020) 7955 6429. *E:* f.m.klug@lse.ac.uk.

KLYBERG, Rt Rev. Mgr Charles John; *b* 29 July 1931; *s* of late Captain Charles Augustine Klyberg, MN and Ivy Lilian Waddington, LRAM; unmarried. *Educ:* Eastbourne College. Eaton Hall OCS, 1953; 2nd Lieut, 1st Bn The Buffs, Kenya Emergency, 1953–54; Lieut 1955. MRICS. Asst Estates Manager, Cluttons, 1954–57. Lincoln Theological Coll., 1957–60. Curate, S John's, East Dulwich, 1960–63; Rector of Fort Jameson, Zambia, 1963–67; Vicar, Christ Church and S Stephen, Battersea, 1967–77; Dean of Lusaka Cathedral, Zambia, and Rector of the parish, 1977–85, Dean Emeritus, 1985; Vicar General, 1978–85; Bishop Suffragan of Fulham, 1985–96; first Archdeacon of Charing Cross, 1989–96. Received into RC Ch and ordained priest, 1996; Prelate of Honour, 2000. UK Commissary for Anglican Church in Zambia, 1985–89. Chairman: Church Property Development Gp, 1978–85; Fulham Palace Museum Trust, 1991–96. Pres., Guild of All Souls, 1988–95. Guardian, Shrine of Our Lady of Walsingham, 1991–96. Warden, Quainton Hall Sch., Harrow, 1992–96. *Recreations:* reading, music, travel. *Club:* Athenæum.

KNAPMAN, Dr Paul Anthony; DL; FRCP, FRCS, FFFLM; HM Coroner for Westminster, 1980–2011 (Jurisdiction of Inner West London); *b* 5 Nov. 1944; *s* of Frederick Ethelbert and Myra Knapman; *m* 1970, Penelope Jane Cox; one *s* three *d*. *Educ:* Epsom Coll.; King's Coll., London; St George's Hosp. Med. Sch. (MB, BS 1968). MRCS, LRCP 1968; DMJ 1975; FRCP 1998; FRCS 1999; FFFLM 2003. Called to the Bar, Gray's Inn, 1972. Dep. Coroner for Inner W London, 1975–80. Hon. Lectr in Med. Jurisprudence, St George's Hosp. Med. Sch., 1978–2004; Hon. Clinical Teacher (Forensic Medicine), Royal Free and UC (formerly Middlesex and UCH) Med. Sch., 1981–2004; Hon. Clinical Sen. Lectr, ICSTM (formerly Westminster and Charing Cross Med. Sch.), 1987–2006. Langdon-Brown Lectr, RCP, 1998; Christmas Lectr, ICSTM, 1999. Legal Member: Mental Health Rev. Tribunal, 1978–88; Med. Appeal Tribunal, 1982–88; Disability Appeal Tribunal, 1988–89; Coroner Mem., Nat. Confidential Enquiry into Peri-Operative Deaths, 1995–2001. Chm., Mgt Cttee, Coroner's Ct Support Service, 2004–11 (Trustee, 2004–11). Member: Medicolegal Soc., 1971–; Chelsea Clin. Soc., 1977–; British Acad. of Forensic Scis, 1980– (Mem. Council, 1983–86); Soc. of Doctors of Law, 1989–; Exams Bd, Soc. of Apothecaries, 1994–2012. President: S Eastern England Coroners' Soc., 1980; Sect. of Clinical Forensic Medicine, RSocMed, 1995–97; Coroners' Soc. of England and Wales, 2008–09 (Mem., 1975–; Mem. Council, 1989–). Trustee: David Isaacs Fund, 1980–2011. Fellow, Med. Soc. of London, 2002–. Gov., London Nautical Sch., 1981–99 (Chm., 1995–99); Pres., Old Epsomian Club, 1999–2000. Liveryman, 1982–, and Mem., Ct of Assistants, 1993–, Soc. of Apothecaries (Master, 2006–07). DL Greater London, 2007; Rep. DL for City of Westminster (Commn of Gtr London), 2013–. Specialist Editor (Coroners Law), JP Reports, 1990–. *Publications:* (jtly) Coronership: the law and practice on coroners, 1985; Medicine and the Law, 1989; Casebook on Coroners, 1989; Sources of Coroners' Law, 1999; contributor to: Medical Negligence, 1990, 3rd edn 2000; Atkin's Court Forms, vol. 13, 1992, 3rd edn 2000; papers on medico-legal subjects. *Recreations:* boating, beagling, travel and family life. *Clubs:* Athenæum, Garrick; RNVR Yacht; Thurlestone Golf.

KNAPMAN, Roger Maurice; Leader, UK Independence Party, 2002–06 (Political Adviser, 2000–02); *b* 20 Feb. 1944; *m* 1967, Carolyn Trebell (*née* Eastman); one *s* one *d*. *Educ:* Royal Agricl Coll., Cirencester. FRICS 1967. MP (C) Stroud, 1987–97; contested (C) same seat, 1997; contested (UK Ind): N Devon, 2001; Totnes, 2005. PPS to Minister of State for Armed Forces, 1991–93; an Asst Govt Whip, 1995–96; a Lord Comr of HM Treasury (Govt Whip), 1996–97. Vice-Chm., Cons. backbench European Affairs Cttee, 1989–90; Mem., Select Cttee on Agric., 1994–95. MEP (UK Ind) SW Reg., 2004–09. Mem., AFRC, 1991–94. *Address:* Lower Crockers, Crockers Hele, Meeth, Okehampton, Devon EX20 3QN.

KNAPP, (John) David, OBE 1986; Director of Conservative Political Centre, 1975–88; an Assistant Director, Conservative Research Department, 1979–88; *b* 27 Oct. 1926; *s* of late Eldred Arthur Knapp and Elizabeth Jane Knapp; *m* 1st, 1954, Dorothy Ellen May (*née* Squires) (marr. diss.); one *s*; 2nd, 1980, Daphne Monard, OBE, *widow* of Major S. H. Monard. *Educ:* Dauntsey's Sch., Wilts; King's Coll., London (BA Hons). Dir, Knapp and Bates Ltd, 1950–54. Vice-Chm., Fedn of University Conservative and Unionist Assoc., 1948–49; Conservative Publicity and Political Educn Officer, Northern Area, 1952–56; Political Educn Officer, NW Area, 1956–61, and Home Counties N Area, 1961; Dep. Dir, Conservative Political Centre, 1962–75. Member (C), Hampshire CC, 1989–93. *Recreations:* philately, walking cavalier spaniels. *Address:* Greenway, Yaverland Road, Yaverland, Isle of Wight PO36 8QP. *T:* (01983) 401045.

KNAPP, Trevor Frederick William Beresford; Director, KADE, since 1997; *b* 26 May 1937; *s* of Frederick William Knapp and Linda Knapp (*née* Poffley); *m* 1st, 1964, Margaret Fry; one *s* one *d*; 2nd, 2013, Eileen Poole. *Educ:* Christ's Hospital; King's College London (BSc 1958). MRSC (ARIC 1960), CChem. Ministry of Aviation, 1961; Sec., Downey Cttee, 1965–66; Sec., British Defence Research and Supply Staff, Canberra, 1968–72; Asst Sec., MoD, 1974; GEC Turbine Generators Ltd, 1976; Central Policy Review Staff, 1977–79; Ministry of Defence: Under-Sec., 1983; Dir Gen. (Marketing), 1983–88; Asst Under Sec. of State (Supply and Organisation) (Air), 1988–91; Asst Under-Sec. of State (Infrastructure and Logistics), 1992–96. Member Board: Waltham Abbey Royal Gunpowder Mills Co., 1997–2012 (Chm., 1998–2012); Waltham Abbey Trust, 1997–; Trustee: Bromley Voluntary Sector Trust, 1999–2014 (Chm., 2003–14); Bromley MIND, 2006–14. *Address:* c/o National Westminster Bank, Strand, WC2H 5JB.

KNATCHBULL, family name of **Countess Mountbatten of Burma** and **Baron Brabourne**.

KNATCHBULL, Hon. Philip Wyndham Ashley; Chief Executive Officer, Curzon World Ltd (formerly Curzon Cinemas Ltd), since 2006; *b* London, 2 Dec. 1961; *s* of 7th Baron Brabourne, CBE and of Countess Mountbatten of Burma, *qv*; *m* 1st, 1991 (marr. diss.); one *d*; 2nd, 2002, Wendy Wills; two *s*. *Educ:* Dragon Sch.; Gordonstoun Sch. CEO, Front Page Films, 1983–94; Chm., Showcase Cinemas, 1989; Dir, Silicon Media Gp (formerly Network Media Television), 1997–2001; CEO, Knatchbull Communications Gp, 1997–2006. *E:* info@knatchbull.com.

See also Baron Brabourne, A. A. S. Zuckerman.

KNEALE, (Anne) Judith; *see* Kerr, A. J.

KNEALE, (Robert) Bryan (Charles), RA 1974 (ARA 1970); sculptor; Professor of Drawing, Royal College of Art, 1990–95; *b* 19 June 1930; *m* 1956, Doreen Lister (*d* 1998); one *d* (one *s* decd). *Educ:* Douglas High Sch.; Douglas Sch. of Art, IOM; Royal Academy Schools: Rome prize, 1949–51; RA diploma. Tutor, RCA Sculpture Sch., 1964–; Head of Sculpture Sch., Hornsey, 1967; Assoc. Lectr, Chelsea Sch. of Art, 1970. Fellow RCA, 1972, Sen. Fellow, 1995; Head of Sculpture Dept, RCA, 1985–90 (Sen. Tutor, 1980–85); Royal Academy: Master of Sculpture, 1982–85; Prof. of Sculpture, 1985–90; Trustee, 1995–2007. Member: Fine Art Panels, NCAD, 1964–71, Arts Council, 1971–73, CNAA, 1974–82; Chm., Air and Space, 1972–73. *Organised:* Sculpture '72, RA, 1972; Battersea Park Silver Jubilee Sculpture, 1977 (also exhibited); Sade Exhibn, Cork, 1982. *Exhibitions:* Redfern Gallery, 1954, 1956, 1958, 1960, 1962, 1964, 1967, 1970, 1976, 1978, 1981; 1983; John Moores, 1961; Sixth Congress of Internat. Union of Architects, 1961; Art Aujourd'hui, Paris, 1963; Battersea Park Sculpture, 1963, 1966; Profile III Bochum, 1964; British Sculpture in the Sixties, Tate Gall., 1965; Whitechapel Gall. 1966 (retrospective), 1981; Structure, Cardiff Metamorphis Coventry, 1966; New British Painting and Sculpture, 1967–68; City of London Festival, 1968; Holland Park, Sculpture in the Cities, Southampton, and British Sculptors, RA, 1972; Holland Park, 1973, 2000; Royal Exchange Sculpture Exhibition, 1974; New Art, Hayward Gallery, 1975; Sculpture at Worksop, 1976; Taranman Gall., 1977, 1981; Serpentine Gall., 1978; Compass Gall., Glasgow, 1981; 51 Gall., Edinburgh, 1981; Bath Art Fair, 1981; Henry Moore Gall., RCA (retrospective), 1986; Fitzwilliam Mus., 1987; Sala Uno, Rome, 1988; Chichester Fest., 1988; New Art Centre, 1990; Nat. History Mus., 1991; Manx Mus., 1992; RWA (retrospective), 1995; Angela Flowers Gall., 1998; 70th Birthday Exhibn, Roche Court, 2000; Eye of the Storm, Turin, 2000; Hart Gall., 2002, 2004; Cass Sculpture Foundn, London, 2005; Royal British Sculptors Gall., 2010; Aspects of Drawing, RA, 2011; Phoenix Beaux Arts Gall., Cork St, 2011; Martini Arte Internazionale, Parco Culturale Le Serre, Turin, 2011; Crucible Exhibn, Gloucester Cathedral, 2012, 2014; Gall. Pangolin, 2015; *commissions:* LCC, Fenwick Place, 1961; Loughborough campus, 1962; Camberwell Beauty Liby, Old Kent Rd, 1964; Hall Caine Meml, Douglas, 1971; King Edward Sch., Totnes, 1972; Woodside Sculpture, Gloversville, NY, 1972–73; Monumental Sculpture for Manx Millennium, Ronaldsway, IOM, 1979; Wall Sculpture for Govt Bldgs, Douglas, IOM, 1996; Sculpture at Goodwood Sculpture Park, 1996; Bronze doors, Portsmouth Cathedral, 1997; Relief Sculpture for Westminster Cath., 1999; Sculpture for Villa Marina, Douglas, IOM, 2003; Sculpture for New Nobles Hosp., IOM, 2004; Trafalgar Meml Sculpture, Castletown, IOM, 2005; Meml to Illiam Dhone, Malew Ch, IOM, 2006; Sculpture for Rio Tinto Zinc HQ, Paddington, 2008. Arts Council Tours, 1966–71. *Collections:* Arts Council of GB; Contemp. Art Soc.; Manx Museum; Leics Educn Authority; Nat. Galls of Victoria, S Australia and New Zealand; City Art Galls, York, Nottingham, Manchester, Bradford and Leicester; Tate Gall.; Beaverbrook Foundn, Fredericton; Museum of Modern Art, São Paulo, Brazil; Bahia Museum, Brazil; Oriel Coll., Oxford; Museum of Modern Art, New York; City Galleries, Middlesbrough, Birmingham, Wakefield; Fitzwilliam Museum, Cambridge; W Riding Educn Authority; Unilever House Collection; Walker Art Gallery; Nat. History Mus., Taiwan; Nat. History Mus., London. Marsh Award for Public Sculpture, Public Monuments and Sculpture Assoc., 2007. *Address:* Pangolin London, Kings Place, 90 York Way, N1 9AG; Hart Gallery, 113 Upper Street, N1 1QN.

KNEBWORTH, Viscount; Philip Anthony Scawen Lytton; *b* 7 March 1989; *s* and *heir* of Earl of Lytton, *qv*.

KNEEBONE, Prof. Roger Lister, PhD; FRCS, FRCSE, FRCGP; Professor of Surgical Education and Engagement Science, Imperial College London, since 2011; Wellcome Trust Engagement Fellow, 2013–15; *b* London, 1 Feb. 1954; *s* of Geoffrey Thomas Kneebone and Eileen Margaret Kneebone (*née* Lister); *m* 1979, Danuta Sarah McKay; two *d*. *Educ:* Westminster Sch.; St Andrews Univ. (BSc Med. Sci. 1974); Univ. of Manchester (MB ChB 1977); Univ. of Bath (PhD 2002). DRCOG 1981; FRCSE 1985; FRCS 1986; MRCGP 1987, FRCGP 2006. House Surgeon and Physician, Wrexham, 1977; Anatomy

Demonstrator, Univ. of Manchester, 1978–79; SHO, in Orthopaedics and A&E, 1979–80, in Obstetrics and Gynaecol., 1980–81, Nottingham Univ. Hosp.; Surgical Registrar: Baragwanath Hosp., Johannesburg, 1981–84; Groote Schuur Hosp., Cape Town, 1984–86; Consultant Surgeon and Hd, Trauma Unit, Red Cross Children's Hosp., Cape Town, 1986; GP Trainee, St Chad Health Centre, Lichfield, 1986–87; GP Principal, Lovemead Gp Practice, Trowbridge, 1987–2003; Imperial College London: Clinical Sen. Lectr, 2003–08, Reader, 2008–11, in Surgical Educn. Hon. Lectr, 1997–2000, Hon. Sen. Lectr, 2000, Univ. of Bath; Visiting Professor: Univ. of Toronto, 1998; Lee Kong Chian Sch. of Medicine, Singapore, 2012; Affiliated Schol., Wilson Centre for Surgical Educn, Toronto, 2007. FHEA (ILTM 2000); FAcadMEd 2009. Mem., Art Workers' Guild, 2012. Nat. Teaching Fellowship Award, Higher Educn Acad., 2011. *Publications:* (with J. Schofield) Skin Lesions, 1996; (with H. Fry) Surgical Education: theorising an emerging domain, 2011; 12 book chapters; 130 papers in scientific, social sci. and humanities jls. *Recreations:* playing the harpsichord, listening to jazz, walking in high and lonely places, exploring unexpected connections. *Address:* Centre for Engagement and Simulation Science, Imperial College London, Academic Surgery (3rd Floor), Chelsea and Westminster Hospital, 369 Fulham Road, SW10 9NH. *T:* (020) 3315 8470. *E:* r.kneebone@imperial.ac.uk.

KNIBB, Prof. Michael Anthony, PhD; FBA 1989; Samuel Davidson Professor of Old Testament Studies, 1997–2001, now Emeritus, and Head, School of Humanities, 2000–01, King's College London; *b* 14 Dec. 1938; third *s* of Leslie Charles Knibb and Christian Vera Knibb (*née* Hoggar); *m* 1972, Christine Mary Burrell. *Educ:* Wyggeston Sch., Leicester; King's Coll. London (BD, PhD; FKC 1991); Union Theol Seminary, NY (STM); Corpus Christi Coll., Oxford. King's College London: Lectr in OT Studies, 1964–82; Reader, 1982–86; Prof. of OT Studies, 1986–97; Head, Dept of Theology and Religious Studies, 1989–93, 1998–2000; Dep. Head, Sch. of Humanities, 1992–97. British Academy: Res. Reader, 1986–88; Mem. Council, 1992–95; Schweich Lectr, 1995; Mem., Humanities Res. Bd, 1995–98 (Chm., Postgrad. Cttee, 1996–98). Editor: Book List of SOTS, 1980–86; Guides to the Apocrypha and Pseudepigrapha, 1995–2004. Hon. Sec., Palestine Exploration Fund, 1969–76. Member, Governing Body: Watford GS for Girls, 1993–2002; SOAS, 2000–10 (Vice-Chm., 2006–10); Chm., Remuneration Cttee, Corpus Christi Coll., Oxford, 2008–14. FRAS 1993. *Publications:* The Ethiopic Book of Enoch: a new edition in the light of the Aramaic Dead Sea Fragments, 2 vols, 1978; Het Boek Henoch, 1983; Cambridge Bible Commentary on 2 Esdras, 1979; (ed jtly) Israel's Prophetic Tradition: essays in honour of P. R. Ackroyd, 1982; The Qumran Community, 1987; (ed with P. W. van der Horst) Studies on the Testament of Job, 1989; Translating the Bible: the Ethiopic version of the Old Testament, 1999; (ed) The Septuagint and Messianism, 2006; Essays on the Book of Enoch and Other Early Jewish Texts and Traditions, 2009; The Ethiopic Text of the Book of Ezekiel: a critical edition, 2015; reviews and articles in books and learned jls. *Recreation:* hill walking. *Address:* 6 Shootersway Park, Berkhamsted, Herts HP4 3NX. *T:* (01442) 871459. *Club:* Athenæum.

KNIBBS, Kevin; Headmaster, Hampton School, since 2013; *b* Billericay, 18 Jan. 1972; *s* of Graham Arthur Knibbs and Jean Pamela Knibbs (*née* Robbins); *m* 2007, Jacqueline Francesca Taylor. *Educ:* King Edward VI Grammar Sch., Chelmsford; St Edmund Hall, Oxford (Exhibnr; BA Mod. Hist. 1993; MA); Univ. of Oxford (PGCE 1995). Bolton School: Hist. Master, 1995–98; Head: First Year, 1998–2003; Lower Sch., 2003–06; Sen. Master, 2006–07; Dep. Headmaster, Hampton Sch., 2007–13. *Recreations:* ski-ing, cycling, reading, football coaching, theatre, film, following the fortunes of Arsenal FC. *Address:* Hampton School, Hanworth Road, Hampton, Middx TW12 3HD. *T:* (020) 8979 5526, *Fax:* (020) 8783 4035. *E:* headmaster@hamptonschool.org.uk.

KNIGHT, family name of **Baroness Knight of Collingtree** and **Baron Knight of Weymouth**.

KNIGHT OF COLLINGTREE, Baroness *cr* 1997 (Life Peer), of Collingtree in the co. of Northamptonshire; **Joan Christabel Jill Knight,** DBE 1985 (MBE 1964); *m* 1947, Montague Knight (*d* 1986); two *s*. *Educ:* Fairfield Sch., Bristol; King Edward Grammar Sch., Birmingham. Mem., Northampton County Borough Council, 1956–66. MP (C) Birmingham, Edgbaston, 1966–97. Member: Select Cttee on Race Relations and Immigration, 1969–72; Select Cttee for Home Affairs, 1980–83, 1992–97; Chairman: Lords and Commons All-Party Child and Family Protection Gp, 1978–97; Cons. Back Bench Health and Social Services Cttee, 1982–97; Member: Exec. Cttee, 1922 Cttee, 1979–97 (Sec., 1983–87; Vice-Chm., 1987–88, 1992–97); Council of Europe, 1977–88, 1999–2011; WEU, 1977–88, 1999–2011 (Chm., Cttee for Parly and Public Relations, 1984–88); Exec. Cttee, IPU, 1991–97 (Chm., 1994–97). Mem., Select Cttee on EU, 1999–2001. Vice-Chm., Assoc. of Cons. Peers, 2002–05. Pres., West Midlands Conservative Political Centre, 1980–83. Vice-Pres., Townswomen's Guilds, 1986–95. Director: Computeach International plc, 1991–2006; Heckett Multiserv, 1999–2006. Pres., Sulgrave Manor Trust, 2012– (Chm., 2007–12). Hon. DSc Aston, 1999. Kentucky Colonel, USA, 1973; Nebraska Admiral, USA, 1980; Texas Ranger, 2014–. *Publications:* About the House, 1995. *Recreations:* music, reading, tapestry work, theatre-going, antique-hunting. *Address:* c/o House of Lords, SW1A 0PW.

KNIGHT OF WEYMOUTH, Baron *cr* 2010 (Life Peer), of Weymouth in the County of Dorset; **James Philip Knight;** PC 2008; Managing Director, Online Learning, TES Global (formerly TSL Education) Ltd, since 2014; *b* 6 March 1965; *s* of Philip Knight and Hilary Howlett; *m* 1989, Anna Wheatley; one *s* one *d*. *Educ:* Eltham Coll., London; Fitzwilliam Coll., Cambridge (BA Hons Geog. and Social and Pol Sci.). Worker, Works Theatre Co-operative Ltd, 1986–88; Manager, Central Studio Arts Centre, 1988–90; Dir, W Wilts Arts Centre Ltd, 1990–91; Dentons Directories Ltd: Sales Exec., 1991–96; Gen. Manager, 1997–98; Dir, 1998–2000; Prodn Manager, 2000–01. MP (Lab) S Dorset, 2001–10; contested (Lab) same seat, 2010. PPS to Minister of State, DoH, 2003–04; Parly Under-Sec. of State, DEFRA, 2005–06; Minister of State, DFES, later DCSF, 2006–09; Minister of State (Minister for Employment and Welfare Reform), DWP, and Minister for the SW, 2009–10. Dir, Egale Ltd. Vis. Prof., London Knowledge Lab., UCL Inst. of Educn (formerly Inst. of Educn, Univ. of London), 2013–. Trustee: Tinder Foundn Ltd; Nominet Trust. *Recreations:* Arsenal Football Club, English literature, tennis, walking. *Address:* House of Lords, SW1A 0PW. *E:* knightja@parliament.uk. *W:* www.twitter.com/jimpknight.

KNIGHT, Dr Alan Paul, OBE 1998; General Manager for Corporate Social Responsibility and Sustainable Development, Arcelor Mittal, since 2014; *b* London, 17 May 1964; *s* of Ernest Owen Knight and Anita Mavis Knight; civil partnership, Tim Stainton. *Educ:* Univ. of Southampton (BSc Geol.); Royal Holloway and Bedford New Coll., Univ. of London (PhD Marine Biol.). Head of Sustainability: B&Q, 1990–2000; Kingfisher plc, 2000–03; SABMiller plc, 2003–06; Ind. Advr (formerly Special Advr), Virgin Gp on Sustainable Devel, 2007–12; Sustainability Dir, BITC, 2012–14. Non-executive Director: WRAP, 2011–; Virgin Earth Challenge, 2012–. Visiting Professor: Exeter Univ., 2009–; Southampton Univ., 2013–; Vis. Fellow, Cambridge Prog. of Sustainability Leadership, 2006–. Chm., Adv. Cttee for Consumer Products and the Envmt, 1998–2004; Mem., Sustainable Devel Commn, 2000–09; Co-Chm., Roundtable of Sustainable Consumption, 2003–05; Chairman: Global Assoc. of Corp. Sustainability Officers, 2010–; Sustainable Growing Media Task Force, 2011–. Dir, Forest Stewardship Council, 1991–93 and 2006–09. Founder, Single Planet Living, 2007–. Mem., Ind. Panel of UK Forestry. Chm., Cornwall and Isles of Scilly Local Nature Partnership, 2013–. *Publications:* I Will If You Will, 2005. *Recreations:* walking on Perranporth Beach, surfing, kayaks, taking photos, collecting fossils, masks, riding bicycles. *Address:* Silverstone, Northants. *T:* 07774 830087. *E:* Alan@DrAlanknight.com. *W:* www.dralanknight.com.

KNIGHT, Prof. Alan Sydney, DPhil; Professor of the History of Latin America, University of Oxford, 1992–2013, now Emeritus; Fellow of St Antony's College, Oxford, 1992–2013, now Emeritus; *b* 6 Nov. 1946; *s* of William Henry Knight and Eva Maud Crandon; *m* 1st, 1969, Carole Jones (marr. diss. 1979); one *d*; 2nd, 1985, Lidia Lozano; two *s*. *Educ:* Balliol Coll., Oxford (BA Modern Hist. 1968); Nuffield Coll., Oxford (DPhil 1974). Research Fellow, Nuffield Coll., Oxford, 1971–73; Lectr in Hist., Essex Univ., 1973–85; Worsham Centennial Prof. of History, Univ. of Texas at Austin, 1986–92. *Publications:* The Mexican Revolution (2 vols), 1986; US-Mexican Relations 1910–40, 1987; Mexico, vol. 1, From the Beginning to the Conquest, 2002, vol. 2, The Colonial Era, 2002; contrib. Jl of Latin American Studies, Bull. of Latin American Res., etc. *Recreation:* kayaking. *Address:* c/o St Antony's College, Oxford OX2 6JF.

KNIGHT, Very Rev. Alexander Francis, OBE 2006; Dean of Lincoln, 1998–2006, now Emeritus; *b* 24 July 1939; *s* of late Rev. Benjamin Edward Knight and of Dorothy Mary Knight; *m* 1962, Sheelagh Elizabeth (*née* Faris); one *s* three *d*. *Educ:* Taunton Sch.; St Catharine's Coll., Cambridge (MA). Curate, Hemel Hempstead, 1963–68; Chaplain, Taunton Sch., 1968–74; Dir, Bloxham Project, 1975–81; Dir of Studies, Aston Training Scheme, 1981–83; Priest-in-charge, Easton and Martyr Worthy, 1983–90; Archdeacon of Basingstoke and Canon Residentiary of Winchester Cathedral, 1990–98. Dean of the Priory of England and the Islands of Hosp. of St John of Jerusalem, 2007–. Hon. DLitt Lincoln, 2004. KStJ 2011 (CStJ 2009). *Publications:* contrib. SPCK Taleteller series. *Recreations:* hill walking, theatre, reading, gardening. *Address:* Shalom, Clay Street, Whiteparish, Salisbury SP5 2ST.

KNIGHT, Andrew Stephen Bower; company director and farmer in Warwickshire and Dannevirke; *b* 1 Nov. 1939; *s* of late M. W. B. Knight and S. E. F. Knight; *m* 1st, 1966, Victoria Catherine Brittain (marr. diss.); one *s*; 2nd, 1975, Sabiha Rumani Malik (marr. diss. 1991); two *d*; 3rd, 2006, Marita Georgina Phillips Crawley. *Educ:* Ampleforth Coll.; Balliol Coll., Oxford (MA). Editor, The Economist, 1974–86; Chief Exec., 1986–89, Editor-in-Chief, 1987–89, Daily Telegraph plc; Chairman: News Internat. plc, 1990–94; Times Newspapers Hldgs, 1990–94 and 2012– (Dir, 1990–). Dir, The News Corporation Ltd, 1991–2012; Dep. Chm., Home Counties Newspapers Hldgs, 1996–98; Dir, Rothschild Investment Trust CP, 1996–2008 (Mem. Adv. Bd, 2013–); Chm., 2008–11, Dir, 2011–13, J. Rothschild Capital Mgt. Member: Steering Cttee, Bilderberg Meetings, 1980–98; Adv. Bd, Center for Economic Policy Research, Stanford Univ., 1981–; Adv. Council, Inst. of Internat. Studies, Stanford Univ., 1990–. Chm., Harlech Scholars' Trust, 2001–10 (Trustee, 1986–10). Governor and Mem. Council of Management, Ditchley Foundn, 1982–2014. Founder Chm., Shipston Home Nursing, 1997–2004; Founder Trustee, Spinal Muscular Atrophy Trust, 2003–14; Trustee: Mariinsky Theatre Trust, 1999–; Centre for Policy Studies, 2010–. *Address:* Compton Scorpion, Warwicks. *Clubs:* Beefsteak, Brooks's, Royal Automobile; Tadmarton Heath Golf.

KNIGHT, Angela Ann, CBE 2007; Chief Executive, Energy UK, 2012–14; *b* 31 Oct. 1950; *d* of late Andrew McTurk Cook and Barbara Jean (*née* Gale); *m* 1981, David George Knight (marr. diss.); two *s*. *Educ:* Penrhos Coll., N Wales; Sheffield Girls' High Sch.; Bristol Univ. (BSc Hons Chem. 1972). Management posts with Air Products Ltd, 1972–77; Man. Dir and Chm., Cook & Knight (Metallurgical Processors) Ltd, 1977–84; Chm., Cook & Knight (Process Plant), 1984–91. Chief Executive: Assoc. of Private Client Investment Managers and Stockbrokers, 1997–2006; BBA, 2007–12. Non-executive Director: PEP and ISA (formerly PEP) Managers Assoc., 1997–99; Scottish Widows, 1997–2006; Saur Water Services and South East Water plc (formerly Saur Water Services), 1997–2004; Mott MacDonald, 1998–2001; Logica, 1999–2003; Logica CMG plc, 2003–08; Lloyds TSB, 2003–06; Brewin Dolphin plc, 2008–; Tullett Prebon, 2011–. Member Board: PLA, 2002–08; Financial Services Skill Council, 2008–. MP (C) Erewash, 1992–97; contested (C) same seat, 1997. PPS to Minister for Industry, 1993–94, to Chancellor of the Exchequer, 1994–95; Econ. Sec. to HM Treasury, 1995–97. Governor: Gayhurst Sch., 2000–02; Bradfield Coll., 2001–07. *Recreations:* walking, ski-ing, music, books. *Clubs:* London Capital; Goodwood Road Racing.

KNIGHT, Prof. Bernard Henry, CBE 1993; MD, FRCPath; novelist; consultant in forensic medicine; Consultant Pathologist to Home Office, 1965–96; Professor of Forensic Pathology, University of Wales College of Medicine, 1980–96, now Emeritus; *b* 3 May 1931; *s* of Harold Ivor Knight and Doris (*née* Lawes); *m* 1955, Jean Gwenllian Ogborne; one *s*. *Educ:* Univ. of Wales (BCh, MD); MRCPath 1964, FRCPath 1966; DMJ (Path) 1967; MRCP 1983. FHKCPath 1993. Called to the Bar, Gray's Inn, 1967. Captain RAMC, Malaya, 1956–59. Lecturer in Forensic Medicine: Univ. of London, 1959–61; Univ. of Wales, 1961–65; Sen. Lectr, Forensic Med., Univ. of Newcastle, 1965–68; Sen. Lectr, then Reader of Forensic Pathology, Univ. of Wales Coll. Med., 1968–80. Hon. Consultant Pathologist, Cardiff Royal Infirmary, 1968–96. Vis. Prof., Univs of Hong Kong, Kuwait, Malaya and Guangzhou (China). Mem., Home Office Policy Adv. Cttee in Forensic Pathology; Chm., Forensic Sub-Cttee and Bd Examnrs, RCPath, 1990–93; Mem., GMC, 1979–94. President: Brit. Assoc. Forensic Med., 1991–93; Forensic Science Soc., 1988–90; Vice-Pres., Internat. Acad. Legal Med., 1980–. Hon. FRSocMed 1994. Hon. Mem., German, Finnish and Hungarian Socs of Forensic Med. Hon. DSc Glamorgan, 1995; Hon. LLD Wales, 1998; Hon. MD Turku, Finland, 2000; Hon. PhD: Tokyo, 2000; Coimbra, 2009. GSM Malaya, 1956. *Publications: fiction:* The Lately Deceased, 1961; The Thread of Evidence, 1963; Russian Roulette, 1968; Policeman's Progress, 1969; Tiger at Bay, 1970; Deg y Dragwyddoldeb (Welsh), 1972; Edyfyn Brau (Welsh), 1973; Lion Rampant, 1973; The Expert, 1975; Prince of America, 1977; The Sanctuary Seeker, 1998; The Poisoned Chalice, 1998; Crowner's Quest, 1999; The Awful Secret, 2000; The Tinner's Corpse, 2000; The Grim Reaper, 2001; Fear in the Forest, 2003; Brennan, 2003; The Witch Hunter, 2004; Figure of Hate, 2005; The Tainted Relic, 2005; The Elixir of Death, 2006; The Sword of Shame, 2006; The Noble Outlaw, 2007; The House of Shadows, 2007; The Manor of Death, 2008; The Lost Prophesies, 2008; Crowner Royal, 2009; King Arthur's Bones, 2009; Where Death Delights, 2010; A Plague of Heretics, 2010; The Sacred Stone, 2010; According to Evidence, 2010; Hill of Bones, 2011; Grounds for Appeal, 2011; Dead in the Dog, 2012; The First Murder, 2012; Crowner's Crusade, 2012; The False Virgin, 2013; The Deadliest Sin, 2014; *biography:* Autopsy: the memoirs of Milton Helpern, 1977; *non-fiction:* Murder, Suicide or Accident, 1965; Discovering the Human Body, 1980; *medical textbooks:* Legal Aspects of Medical Practice, 1972, 5th edn 1992; Forensic Radiology, 1982; Sudden Infant Death, 1982; Post-mortem Technician's Handbook, 1983; Forensic Medicine for Lawyers, 1984, 2nd edn 1998; Forensic Medicine, 1985; (ed) Simpson's Forensic Medicine, 9th edn 1985, 11th edn 1996; Coroner's Autopsy, 1985; Forensic Pathology, 1991, 3rd edn 2004; Estimation of the Time of Death, 1995, 2nd edn 2002. *Recreation:* writing. *Address:* 26 Millwood, Llysfaen, Cardiff CF14 0TL. *T:* (029) 2075 2798.

KNIGHT, His Honour Brian Joseph; QC 1981; a Senior Circuit Judge, 1998–2011; Mercantile Judge, London Mercantile Court, and Judge in charge of the Technology and Construction Court List at Central London Civil Justice Centre (formerly Business List Judge, Central London County Court), 1998–2011; *b* 5 May 1941; *s* of Joseph Knight and Vera Lorraine Knight (*née* Docksey); *m* 1967, Cristina Karen Wang Nobrega de Lima (*d* 2003); *m* 2010, Lyn Christine Thornton. *Educ:* Colbayns High Sch., Clacton; University Coll. London. LLB 1962, LLM 1963. FCIArb 1995–2015. Called to the Bar, Gray's Inn, 1964, *ad eundem*

Lincoln's Inn, 1979; called to the Bar of Hong Kong, 1978, of Northern Ireland, 1979; a Recorder, 1991–98. Asst Parly Boundary Comr, 1992. Mem., HK Internat. Arbitration Centre, 2011–14. *Club:* Garrick.

KNIGHT, Brigid Agnes; a District Judge (Magistrates' Courts), since 2002; *m*; one *s* two *d*. *Educ:* Liverpool Univ. (LLB Hons); Coll. of Law, Guildford. Solicitor in private practice, 1975–2002. *Recreations:* family, theatre, ballet, contemporary dance, drawing and sketching. *Address:* Cheshire Magistrates' Courts, Justices' Clerks' Office, Winmarleigh Street, Warrington WA1 1PB. *T:* (01925) 236250.

KNIGHT, Rt Hon. Sir Gregory, Kt 2013; PC 1995; MP (C) East Yorkshire, since 2001; writer, consultant solicitor; *b* 4 April 1949; *s* of late George Knight and Isabella Knight (*née* Bell). *Educ:* Alderman Newton's Grammar School, Leicester; College of Law, Guildford. Self employed solicitor, 1973–83. Member: Leicester City Council, 1976–79; Leicestershire County Council, 1977–83 (Chm., Public Protection Cttee). MP (C) Derby North, 1983–97; contested (C) same seat, 1997. PPS to the Minister of State: Home Office, 1987; Foreign Office, 1988–89; an Asst Govt Whip, 1989–90; a Lord Comr of HM Treasury, 1990–93; Dep. Govt Chief Whip and Treas. of HM Household, 1993–96; Minister of State, DTI, 1996–97; Shadow Dep. Leader, H of C, 2001–03; Opposition front bench spokesman: on transport and envmt, 2003–05; on transport, 2005–06; Vice-Chamberlain of HM Household (Govt Whip), 2012–13. Chm., H of C Procedure Select Cttee, 2005–12. Vice Chm., Cons. Candidates' Assoc., 1998–2001. Dir, Leicester Theatre Trust, 1979–85 (Chm., Finance Cttee, 1982–83). *Publications:* (jtly) Westminster Words, 1988; Honourable Insults: a century of political insult, 1990; Parliamentary Sauce: more political insults, 1992; Right Honourable Insults, 1998; Naughty Graffiti, 2005; Dishonourable Insults, 2011; pamphlets and articles for law, motoring and entertainment publications. *Recreations:* driving classic cars and making music. *Address:* House of Commons, SW1A 0AA. *Club:* Bridlington Conservative.

KNIGHT, Sir Harold (Murray), KBE 1980; DSC 1945; *b* 13 Aug. 1919; *s* of W. H. P. Knight, Melbourne; *m* 1951, Gwenyth Catherine Pennington; four *s* one *d*. *Educ:* Scotch Coll., Melbourne; Melbourne Univ. Commonwealth Bank of Australia, 1936–40. AIF (Lieut), 1940–43; RANVR (Lieut), 1943–45. Commonwealth Bank of Australia, 1946–55; Asst Chief, Statistics Div., Internat. Monetary Fund, 1957–59; Reserve Bank of Australia: Research Economist, 1960–62; Asst Manager, Investment Dept, 1962–64, Manager, 1964–68; Dep. Governor and Dep. Chm. of Board, 1968–75; Governor and Chm. of Bd, 1975–82. Chairman: Mercantile Mutual Hldgs, 1985–89; IBJ Australia Bank Ltd, 1985–92; Dir, Western Mining Corp., 1982–91. Mem., Police Bd of NSW, 1988–89, 1991–93. Mem. Council, Macquarie Univ., 1990–92. Pres., Scripture Union, NSW, 1983–2002. *Publications:* Introducción al Análisis Monetario (Spanish), 1959.

KNIGHT, Henrietta Catherine, (Mrs T. W. Biddlecombe); licensed racehorse trainer, 1989–2012; *b* 15 Dec. 1946; *d* of late Maj. Guy Knight, MC and Hester Knight; *m* 1995, Terence Walter Biddlecombe (*d* 2014). *Educ:* Didcot Girls' Grammar Sch.; Westminster Coll. of Educn, Oxford (BEd Oxon); Berkshire Coll. of Agric. (Advanced NCA). Schoolteacher, hist. and biol., St Mary's Sch., Wantage, 1970–74; ran private livery Point to Point yard, 1974–84 (trained over 100 Point to Point winners). Chm., Sen. Selection Cttee, British Horse Soc. (Three Day Eventing), 1984–88. National Hunt winners include: Stompin, Glenlivet Hurdle, Aintree, 1995; Karshi, Stayers Hurdle, Cheltenham, 1997; Edredon Bleu, Grand Annual Chase, Cheltenham, 1998; Lord Noelie, Sun Alliance Chase, Edredon Bleu, Queen Mother Champion Chase, Cheltenham, 2000; Best Mate, 2002, Edredon Bleu, 2003, King George VI Steeplechase, Kempton; Somersby, Victor Chandler Chase, Grade 1, Ascot, 2012; Best Mate, 3 Cheltenham Gold Cups, 2002, 2003, 2004. *Publications:* Best Mate: Chasing Gold, 2003; Best Mate: Triple Gold, 2004. *Recreations:* farming, breeding Connemara ponies, judging at major horse shows each summer. *Address:* West Lockinge Farm, Wantage, Oxon OX12 8QF. *T:* (01235) 833535, *Fax:* (01235) 820110. *E:* hen@westlockinge.co.uk.

KNIGHT, Jeffrey Russell, FCA; Chief Executive, The Stock Exchange, 1982–89; *b* 1 Oct. 1936; *s* of Thomas Edgar Knight and Ivy Cissie Knight (*née* Russell); *m* 1959, Judith Marion Delver Podger; three *d* (and one *d* decd). *Educ:* Bristol Cathedral Sch.; St Peter's Hall, Oxford (MA). Chartered Accountant, 1966; The Stock Exchange, London, 1967–90: Head of Quotations Dept, 1973; Dep. Chief Executive, 1975. Member: City Company Law Cttee, 1974–80; Dept of Trade Panel on Company Law Revision, 1980–84; Accounting Standards Cttee, 1982–89; Special Adviser to Dept of Trade, 1975–81; Adviser to Council for the Securities Industry, 1978–85; UK Delegate: to EEC Working Parties; to Internat. Fedn of Stock Exchanges, 1973–90 (Chm., Task Force on Transnational Settlement, 1987–91); to Fedn of Stock Exchanges in EEC, 1974–90 (Chm., Wking Cttee, 1980–90); to Internat. Orgn of Securities Commns, 1987–91 (Chm. Wkg Party on Capital Adequacy). *Recreations:* cricket, music. *Address:* Lordsmeade, Hurtmore Road, Godalming, Surrey GU7 2DY. *T:* (01483) 424399. *Clubs:* Brooks's, MCC; Woking Golf.

KNIGHT, Julian Carlton; MP (C) Solihull, since 2015; *b* Chester, 5 Jan. 1972; *s* of Carlton and Valerie Knight; *m* 2014, Philippa Harrison. *Educ:* Chester Catholic High Sch.; Hull Univ. (BA Hons). Field sales exec., News Internat., 1995–98; staff writer, Reader's Digest, 1998–2002; personal finance and consumer affairs reporter, BBC News, 2002–07; Money and Property Ed., Independent, 2007–15. *Publications:* Wills, Probate and Inheritance Tax for Dummies, 2004, 2nd edn 2008; Retiring Wealthy, 2005; Cricket for Dummies, 2006, 2nd edn 2013; (with M. Pattison) British Politics for Dummies, 2010, 2nd edn 2015; Eurocrisis for Dummies, 2012. *Recreations:* tennis, cricket, golf, football, cycling, the arts. *Address:* House of Commons, SW1A 0AA. *T:* (020) 7219 3577. *E:* julian.knight.mp@parliament.uk.

KNIGHT, Sir Kenneth John, (Sir Ken), Kt 2006; CBE 2001; QFSM 1992; DL; Chief Fire and Rescue Adviser, Department for Communities and Local Government, 2007–13; *b* 3 Jan. 1947; *s* of Dennis and Nancy Knight. MIFireE 1970, FIFireE 2008. Westminster Bank, Reigate, 1964–66; joined Surrey Fire Bde, 1966; Home Office, 1985–87; Asst Chief Officer, London Fire Bde, 1987–92; Dep. Chief Officer, Devon Fire Bde, 1992–94; Chief Fire Officer: Dorset, 1994–98; W Midlands, 1998–2003; Comr for Fire and Emergency Planning, London Fire Bde, 2003–07. Efficiencies Review of Fire Service (reviews of N Iraq, Ireland, Bermuda, Gibraltar, England), 2013–. Master, Worshipful Co. of Firefighters, 1998. DL Greater London, 2006 (Rep. DL London Borough of Richmond upon Thames, 2007). CCMI 2005. OStJ 2005. *Recreations:* theatre, walking. *Address:* Coaxdon Farm, Axminster, Devon EX13 7LP. *Club:* East India.

KNIGHT, Malcolm Donald; Visiting Professor, London School of Economics and Political Science; Distinguished Fellow, Centre for International Governance Innovation, Waterloo, Ontario; *b* 11 April 1944; *s* of Gordon James Knight and Muriel Edith Knight (*née* McGregor); *m* 1972, Amy W. Crumpacker; three *d*. *Educ:* Amherstburg District High Sch. (Sen. Matric. 1963); Univ. of Toronto (BA Hons Pol Sci. and Econs 1967); London Sch. of Econs and Pol Sci. (MSc Econ. 1968; PhD 1972). Asst Prof. of Econs, Univ. of Toronto, 1971–72; Lectr in Econs, LSE, 1972–75; International Monetary Fund: economist, 1975–83, Chief, Ext. Adjustment Div., 1983–87, Res. Dept; Div. Chief, 1987–89, Asst Dir, 1989–91, ME Dept; Asst Dir, Res. Dept, 1991–93; Sen. Advr, 1993–95, and Dep. Dir, 1995–96, ME Dept; Dep. Dir, Monetary and Exchange Affairs Dept, 1996–98; Dep. Dir, European I Dept, 1998–99; Sen. Dep. Gov., Bank of Canada, 1999–2003; Gen. Manager and CEO, Bank for Internat. Settlements, 2003–08; Vice Chm., 2008–12, Advr, 2012–14, Deutsche Bank AG. Mem. Bd of Dirs, Swiss Reinsurance Inc., 2010–14. Adjunct Professor: Virginia Poly. and State Univ. Grad. Prog., Northern Virginia, 1978–85; Sch. of Advanced Internat. Studies, Johns Hopkins Univ., 1980–96; Vis. Prof. in Finance, LSE, 2008–. Trustee: Internat. Accounting Standards Cttee Foundn, 2003–07; Per Jacobsson Foundn, 2003–; Internat. Valuation Standards Council, 2010–; Member: IMF Capital Markets Consultative Gp, 2003–08; Financial Stability Forum, 2005–08; Markets Monitoring Gp, Inst. of Internat. Finance, 2009–; Ext. Panel to Review IMF's Risk Mgt Framework, 2011; Bd of Dirs, Global Risk Inst. in Financial Services, Toronto, 2011–; Internat. Adv. Panel, Risk Mgt Inst., Univ. of Singapore, 2011–; Observer, IMF Internat. Monetary and Financial Cttee, 2003–08; Chm., Bd of Patrons, European Assoc. of Banking and Financial Hist., 2008– (Mem., Bd of Patrons, 2005–). Member: Soc. of Scholars, Johns Hopkins Univ., 2006–; Bd of Dirs, New Jersey Center for Visual Arts, 2011–. Mem., Hon. Senate, Lindau Nobel Prize Winners' Foundn, 2006–. Woodrow Wilson Nat. Fellow, 1967; Canada Council Doctoral Fellow, 1968–70. Hon. Dr Toronto, 2006. *Publications:* (ed jtly) Transforming Financial Systems in the Baltics, Russia and Other Countries of the Former Soviet Union, 1999; The Canadian Economy, 1989, rev. edn 1996; (contrib.) Financial Crisis Management and Bank Resolution, 2009; contrib. numerous articles to learned jls on internat. finance, stabilization progs in developing countries, monetary policy, empirical aspects of growth theory and financial system structure and regulation. *Recreations:* tennis, ski-ing, bicycling, hiking, swimming, windsurfing, golf, watercolour. *Address:* 28 Fairview Avenue #2, Summit, NJ 07901, USA. *T:* (917) 3277266. *E:* malcolm.knight100@gmail.com.

KNIGHT, Maureen R.; *see* Rice-Knight.

KNIGHT, Sir Michael (William Patrick), KCB 1983 (CB 1980); AFC 1964; Life Vice-President, The Air League, since 2004 (Member of Council, 1990–2004; Chairman, 1992–98; President, 1998–2004; Founders' Medal, 2005); *b* 23 Nov. 1932; *s* of William and Dorothy Knight; *m* 1967, Patricia Ann (*née* Davies) (*d* 2008); one *s* two *d*. *Educ:* Leek High Sch.; Univ. of Liverpool (BA Hons 1954; Hon. LittD 1985). Univ. of Liverpool Air Sqn, RAFVR, 1951–54; commnd RAF, 1954; served in Transport and Bomber Comds, and in Middle and Near East Air Forces, 1956–63; Comd No 32 Sqn, RAF Akrotiri, 1961–63; RAF Staff Coll., 1964; Min. of Aviation, 1965–66; Comd Far East Strike Wing, RAF Tengah, 1966–68; Flying Wing, 1968–69; Head of Secretariat, HQ Strike Comd, 1969–70; Mil. Asst to Chm., NATO Mil. Cttee, 1970–73; Comd RAF Laarbruch, 1973–74; RCDS, 1975; Dir of Ops (Air Support), MoD, 1975–77; SASO, HQ Strike Command/DCS (Ops & Intelligence) HQ UK Air Forces, 1977–80; AOC No 1 Gp, 1980–82; Air Mem. for Supply and Organisation, 1983–86; UK Military Rep. to NATO, 1986–89; Air ADC to the Queen, 1986–89 (ADC, 1973–74); retd in rank of Air Chief Marshal, 1989; commnd Flying Officer, RAFVR (Trng Br.), 1989–2004. Adjunct Prof., Internat. Peace and Security, Carnegie Mellon Univ., Pittsburgh, 1989–95. Dep. Chm., 1994–95, Chm., 1995–2001, Cobham plc; Chairman: Page Gp Hldgs Ltd, 1996–2000; Cranfield Aerospace Ltd, 2000–03; Director: Craigwell Research, 1990–97; RAFC Co. Ltd, 1993–2003; SBAC (Farnborough) Ltd, 1996–98; non-executive Director: FR Group plc, 1990–94; Page Aerospace Gp, 1991–96; Smiths Industries Aerospace and Defence Systems Group, 1992–95; Associate, JGW Associates Ltd, 1989–2002; Chm., Northern Devon Healthcare NHS Trust, 1991–94. Mem., Internat. Adv. Bd, British/Amer. Business Council, 1995–2001. Mem., IISS, 1968–2002; Member Council: RUSI, 1984–87; SBAC, 1995–99; Exmoor Calvert Trust, 2000–09 (Chm., 2000–09; Hon. Vice-Pres., 2011); Pres., Council, NAAFI, 1984–86; Vice-Pres., Atlantic Council of UK, 1994–2008. Chm., N Devon Family Support Service, Leonard Cheshire Foundn, 1989–91; Devon County Rep., RAF Benev. Fund, 1990–; RAF Pres., 1991–97, Sen. Pres., 1997–2000, Officers' Assoc.; President: Aircrew Assoc., 1992–97; Buccaneer Aircrew Assoc., 1994–2014; No 32 (The Royal) Sqn Assoc., 1997–; Royal Internat. Air Tattoo, 2005–08 (Vice-Pres., 1991–2002; Vice-Patron, 2003–04; Hon. Vice-Patron, 2008–; Spirit of the Meet Award, 2008); Vice-Pres., The Youth Trust, 1994–98; Chm., 2003–07, Life Pres., 2007–, Vulcan to the Sky Trust (Patron, Vulcan Restoration Appeal, 2000–03); Chm., RAF Charitable Trust, 2005–08. Trustee: RAF Central Fund, 1983–86; RAF Mus., 1983–86. Pres., Mortehoe Mus. Trust (formerly Mortehoe Heritage Trust), 2009–. Patron, Guild of Aviation Artists, 2005–09 (Vice-Pres., 1997–2005); Vice-Patron, Yorks Air Mus., 1997–. Gov. and Council Mem., Taunton Sch., 1987–2000; Mem., Univ. of Liverpool Develt Team, 1986–. Rugby Football Union: Mem. Cttee, 1977–92; Mem. Exec. Cttee, 1989–92; Chm., Internat. Sub Cttee, 1987–90; Chm., Forward Planning Sub Cttee, 1990–92; Privilege Mem., 1992– (Chm., Privilege Members Assoc., 2011–). President: RAF Rugby Union, 1985–89 (Chm., 1975–78); Combined Services RFC, 1987–89 (Chm., 1977–79); RAF Lawn Tennis Assoc., 1984–86; Vice-President: Leek RUFC, 1959–; Crawshay's Welsh RFC, 1997–; Penguin Internat. RFC, 2001–. Hon. Air Cdre, No 7630 (VR) Intelligence Sqn, RAuxAF, 2001–07. FRAeS 1985; FRGS 1994 (Mem. Council, 1995–97); FRSA 1994. Freeman, City of London, 1989; Liveryman, Hon. Co. of Air Pilots (formerly GAPAN), 1993– (Upper Freeman, 1990–93; Guild Award of Honour, 2007). *Publications:* (contrib.) War in the Third Dimension, 1986; Strategic Offensive Air Power and Technology, 1989; articles in prof. pubns, 1975–. *Recreations:* Rugby football, lesser sports, music, writing, travel, public speaking. *Address:* c/o National Westminster Bank, Leek, Staffs. *Clubs:* Royal Air Force (Vice-Pres., 1983–2003), Colonels (founder).

KNIGHT, Nicholas David Gordon, OBE 2010; photographer; Director: N. K. Image Ltd, since 1998; Showstudio Ltd, since 2000; *b* 24 Nov. 1958; *s* of Michael A. G. Knight and Beryl Rose Knight; *m* 1995, Charlotte Esme Wheeler; one *s* two *d*. *Educ:* Hinchingbrooke Comprehensive Sch., Huntingdon; Chelsea Coll., London Univ.; Bournemouth and Poole Coll. of Art (PQE Dip. in Art and Design (Distinction) 1982; Hon. Fellow, 1998). Commissioning Picture Editor, ID magazine, 1990; Photographer, Vogue, 1995–. Hon. MA Anglia Poly. Univ., 2000. *Publications:* Skinhead, 1982; Nicknight, 1994; Flora, 1997; Nick Knight, 2009. *Recreations:* architecture, natural history. *T:* (020) 8940 1086.

KNIGHT, Dr Peter Clayton, CBE 1995; DL; Vice-Chancellor, University of Central England in Birmingham, 1992–2006 (Director, Birmingham Polytechnic, 1985–92); *s* of Norman Clayton Knight and Vera Catherine Knight; *m* 1977, Catherine Mary (*née* Ward); one *s* one *d*. *Educ:* Univ. of York (BA 1st cl. Hons Physics; DPhil). SRC Studentship, 1968; Asst Teacher, Plymstock Comprehensive Sch., 1971; Plymouth Polytechnic: Lectr, 1972; Sen. Lectr, 1974; Head of Combined Studies, 1981; Dep. Dir, Lancashire Polytechnic, 1982–85. Nat. Pres., NATFHE, 1977; Chm., SRHE, 1987–89; Member: Burnham Cttee of Further Educn, 1976–81; Working Party on Management of Higher Educn, 1977; Nat. Adv. Body on Public Sector Higher Educn, 1982–85; PCFC, 1989–93; Polytechnic and Colleges Employers Forum, 1989–94; Teacher Training Agency, 1994–2000. Member: Armed Forces Pay Review Bd, 2004–10; Boundary Cttee for England, 2007–10; Local Govt Boundary Commn for England, 2010–; Chair, Prison Service Pay Review Body, 2011–. Mem., Focus Housing Assoc., 1991–; Chm., Prime Focus Regeneration Gp (formerly Focus Housing Gp), 1996–2006; Mem. Bd, Wolverhampton Homes, 2008–. DL W Midlands, 2008. DUniv: York, 1991; Middlesex, 2006; Birmingham City, 2007; Hon. DSc Aston, 1997. *Publications:* articles, chapters and reviews in learned jls on educnl policy, with particular ref. to higher educn. *Recreation:* flying and building light aircraft. *Address:* Sandy Lodge, Sandy Lane, Brewood, Staffs ST19 9ET.

KNIGHT, Prof. Sir Peter Leonard, Kt 2005; DPhil; FRS 1999; FInstP; Professor of Quantum Optics, 1988–2010, now Emeritus, Senior Principal, 2008–09, and Deputy Rector (Research), 2009–10, Imperial College of Science, Technology and Medicine; Senior Fellow in Residence (formerly Principal), Kavli Royal Society International Centre, Chicheley Hall, since 2010; *b* 12 Aug. 1947; *s* of Joseph and Eva Knight; *m* 1965, Christine Huckle; two *s* one *d*. *Educ:* Bedford Modern Sch.; Sussex Univ. (BSc, DPhil). FInstP 1991. Research Associate, Univ. of Rochester, NY, 1972–74; SRC Res. Fellow, Sussex Univ., 1974–76; Jubilee Res.

Fellow, 1976–78, SERC Advanced Fellow, 1978–79, RHC; Imperial College, London: SERC Advanced Fellow, 1979–83; Lectr, 1983–87; Reader, 1987–88; Head, Laser Optics and Spectroscopy, then Quantum Optics and Laser Sci., Physics Dept, 1992–2001; Head, Physics Dept, 2001–05; Acting Principal of Physical Scis, 2004–05; Principal, Faculty of Natural Scis, 2006–08. Chief Scientific Advr, 2002–05, Chm., Quantum Measurement Inst., 2014–, Mem., Sci. and Technol. Adv. Cttee, 2015–, NPL; Chm., Defence Scientific Adv. Council UK, MoD, 2007–10. Mem., SERC Atomic and Molecular Physics Sub Cttee, 1987–90; Co-ordinator, SERC Nonlinear Optics Initiative, 1989–92 (Chm., Prog. Adv. Gp, 1992–95). Member Council: Royal Soc., 2005–07; STFC, 2009–12 (Chm., Sci. Bd, 2007–08). Chm., Quantum Electronics Div., European Physical Soc., 1988–92; President: Physics Sect., BAAS, 1994–95; Optical Soc. of America, 2004 (Fellow 1996; Dir, 1999–2001); Inst. of Physics, 2011–13. Mem. Council, Sussex Univ., 2013–. Corresp. Mem., Mexican Acad. of Scis, 2000. Hon. DSc: Nat. Inst. for Astronomy, Optics and Electronics, Mexico, 1998; Slovak Acad. of Scis, 2000; Sussex, 2010; Heriot-Watt, 2010; Royal Holloway, 2013; Macquarie, 2014; Glasgow, 2015; Huddersfield, 2015. Parsons Meml Lectr, Royal Soc. and Inst. of Physics, 1991; Humboldt Res. Award, Alexander von Humboldt Foundn, 1993; Einstein Medal and Prize for Laser Science, Soc. of Optical and Quantum Electronics and Eastman Kodak Co., 1996; Thomas Young Medal and Prize, 1999, Glazebrook Medal, 2009, Inst. of Physics; Ives Medal, Optical Soc. of America, 2008; Royal Medal, Royal Soc., 2010. Editor: Jl of Modern Optics, 1987–2006; Contemporary Physics, 1993–. *Publications:* Concepts of Quantum Optics, 1983; (with Chris Gerry) Introductory Quantum Optics, 2004; papers in Phys. Rev., Phys. Rev. Letters and other jls. *Recreations:* traditional music, walking. *Address:* Blackett Laboratory, Imperial College London, Prince Consort Road, SW7 2AZ. *T:* (020) 7584 7727. *Club:* Athenæum.

KNIGHT, Roger David Verdon, OBE 2007; Secretary & Chief Executive, Marylebone Cricket Club, 2000–06 (Secretary, 1994–2000); *b* 6 Sept. 1946; *s* of late David Verdon Knight and Thelma Patricia Knight; *m* 1971, Christine Ann McNab (*née* Miln); one *s* one *d*. *Educ:* Dulwich Coll.; St Catharine's Coll., Cambridge (BA Modern and Medieval Langs 1969; MA 1972; DipEd 1970). Assistant Master: Eastbourne Coll., 1970–78; Dulwich Coll., 1978–83; Housemaster, Cranleigh Sch., 1983–90; Headmaster, Worksop Coll., 1990–93. Professional cricketer (summers only): Gloucestershire, 1971–75; Sussex, 1976–77; Surrey, 1978–84 (Captain, 1978–83). Vice-Chm., SE Region, Sports Council, 1985–90; Chm. Management Cttee, SE Region, Centres of Excellence, 1987–90; Member: Cricket Cttee, Surrey CCC, 1987–90 (Pres., 2008–09); MCC Cttee, 1989–92; HMC Sports Sub-Cttee, 1991–93; ICC Develt Cttee, 1996–2006, 2007–10; Mgt Bd, ECB, 1997–2006; Council, London Playing Fields Soc., 1998–2002; European Cricket Council, 1998–2011 (Chm., 2006–11); Chm., ECB Assoc. of Cricket Officials, 2009–; President: European Cricket Fedn, 1994–97; Cambridge Univ. CC, 2009–; MCC, 2015–. Trustee, MCC Foundn, 2006–. Governor: TVS Trust, 1987–92; Rendcomb Coll., 1995–99; King's Coll., Taunton, 1998– (Chm., Educn Cttee, 2005–10; Custos, King's Schs, 2010–); Dulwich Coll., 2004–10; Millfield, 2008–09. *Recreations:* cricket, tennis, bridge, piano music, 17th Century French literature, walking, Real Tennis, travel.

KNIGHT, Dr Roger John Beckett, FRHistS; Professor of Naval History, University of Greenwich, 2006–09 (Visiting Professor, 2001–06 and 2009–14); Senior Research Fellow, Institute of Historical Research, University of London, since 2014; *b* 11 April 1944; *s* of John Beckett Knight and Alyson Knight (*née* Nunn); *m* 1st, 1968, Elizabeth Magowan (marr. diss. 1980); two *s*; 2nd, 1998, Jane Hamilton-Eddy. *Educ:* Tonbridge Sch.; Trinity Coll., Dublin (MA); Sussex Univ. (PGCE); University Coll. London (PhD). FRHistS 1988. Asst Master, Haberdashers' Aske's Sch., Elstree, 1972–73; National Maritime Museum: Dep. Custodian of Manuscripts, 1974–77, Custodian, 1977–80; Dep. Head, Printed Books and Manuscripts Dept, 1980–84; Head, Inf. Project Gp, 1984–86; Head, Documentation Div., 1986–88; Chief Curator, 1988–93; Dep. Dir, 1993–2000. Trustee, Nat. Maritime Mus., Cornwall, 1998–2002. Member Council: Soc. for Nautical Research, 1977–81 (Vice-Pres., 1993–2006); Navy Records Soc., 1974–2009 (Vice-Pres., 1980–84, 2003–07). Caird Medal, Nat. Maritime Mus., Greenwich, 2014. *Publications:* Guide to the Manuscripts in the National Maritime Museum, vol. 1, 1977, vol. 2, 1980; (with Alan Frost) The Journal of Daniel Paine 1794–1797, 1983; Portsmouth Dockyard Papers 1774–1783: the American War, 1987; (ed jtly) British Naval Documents 1204–1960, 1993; The Pursuit of Victory: the life and achievement of Horatio Nelson, 2005 (Mountbatten Maritime Prize, British Maritime Charitable Foundn, 2005; Duke of Westminster's Medal, RUSI, 2006); (with Martin Wilcox) Sustaining the Fleet, 1793–1815: war, the British navy and the contractor state, 2010; Britain Against Napoleon: the organization of victory, 1793–1815, 2013; articles, reviews in jls. *Recreations:* walking, music. *Address:* Institute of Historical Research, University of London, Senate House, WC1E 7HU. *Club:* Athenæum.

KNIGHT, Stephen John; Member (Lib Dem) London Assembly, Greater London Authority, since 2012; Leader of the Opposition, London Borough of Richmond upon Thames, since 2010; *b* Roehampton, 15 May 1970; *s* of Dr David Knight and Ruth Knight; partner, 2004, Jennifer Churchill; two *d*; one step *d* from previous marriage. *Educ:* Teddington Sch.; Richmond upon Thames Coll.; Univ. of Southampton (BSc Physics). Pres., Southampton Univ. Students Union, 1992–93; PR Officer, Jubilee Sailing Trust, 1994–95; Consultant, Argyll Public Relns, 1995–96; Political Advr to Lib Dem Gp, Assoc. of London Govt, subseq. London Councils, 1996–2008. Mem. (Lib Dem), Richmond upon Thames LBC, 1998– (Dep. Leader, 2006–10). Mem., Standards Bd for England, 2009–12; Vice Chairman: Workforce Bd, LGA, 2011–13; Nat. Employers' Orgn for Sch. Teachers, 2011–13. Chm. Govs, St Mary's and St Peter's Primary Sch., 2002–12. FRSA. *Recreations:* family, cinema, sailing. *Address:* 73 Harrowdene Gardens, Teddington TW11 0DJ. *T:* (020) 7983 7362, *Fax:* (020) 7983 4417. *E:* stephen.knight@london.gov.uk.

KNIGHT, Steven; writer, since 1989; *b* 5 Aug. 1959; *s* of George and Ida Knight. *Educ:* University Coll. London (BA Hons English). Writer, producer, Capital Radio, 1983–87; writer for television, 1990–: Detectives; Canned Carrott; Ruby Wax Show; Commercial Breakdown; All About Me; Peaky Blinders, 2013, 2014; Co-creator, Who Wants To Be a Millionaire?, 1998; screenwriter: Gypsy Woman, 2000; Dirty Pretty Things, 2003 (awards include: Best British Screenwriter, London Film Critics' Circle Awards, 2003; Humanitas Award, 2004; Edgar Award for Best Motion Picture Screenplay, 2004); Amazing Grace, 2007 (Epiphany Prize, John Templeton Foundn, 2008); Eastern Promises, 2007 (Cadillac People's Choice Award, Tribeca Film Fest., 2007; Genie Award, Acad. of Canadian Cinema and TV, 2008); (also Dir) Hummingbird, 2013; Closed Circuit, 2013; The Hundred-Foot Journey, 2014; (also Dir) Locke, 2014; Seventh Son, 2015; writer for theatre: The President of an Empty Room, NT, 2005. *Publications:* The Movie House, 1994; Alphabet City, 1998; Out of the Blue, 1999; The Last Words of Will Wolfkin, 2010. *Recreations:* writing, fishing, Birmingham City FC. *Address:* c/o Natasha Galloway, United Agents, 12–26 Lexington Street, W1F 0LE.

KNIGHT, Terence Gordon, FRICS; *b* 1 June 1944; *s* of Albert Henry and Eileen Doris Knight; *m* 1968, Gillian Susan West; two *s*. *Educ:* St Paul's Sch. FRICS 1976. Joined Weatherall Green & Smith, Chartered Surveyors, 1962; Partner, 1976–2001; Sen. Partner, 1992–98. Liveryman, Chartered Surveyors' Co., 1988 (Master, 2004–05). *Recreations:* golf, walking. *Clubs:* St Enodoc Golf, Worplesdon Golf.

KNIGHT, Veronica Lesley; *see* Hammerton, V. L.

KNIGHT, Warburton Richard, CBE 1987; Director of Educational Services, Bradford Metropolitan District Council, 1974–91; *b* 2 July 1932; *s* of late Warburton Henry Johnston and Alice Gweneth Knight; *m* 1961, Pamela Ann (*née* Hearmon); two *s* one *d*. *Educ:* Trinity Coll., Cambridge (MA). Teaching in Secondary Modern and Grammar Schs in Middlesex and Huddersfield, 1956–62; joined West Riding Educn Authority, 1962; Asst Dir for Secondary Schs, Leics, 1967; Asst Educn Officer for Sec. Schs and later for Special and Social Educn in WR, 1970. Hon. DLitt Bradford, 1992. *Recreations:* walking, choral music, travel. *Address:* Thorner Grange, Sandhills, Thorner, Leeds LS14 3DE. *T:* (0113) 289 2356. *Club:* Royal Over-Seas League.

KNIGHT, William John Langford, OBE 2012; Chairman, Financial Reporting Review Panel, 2004–12; Senior Partner, Simmons & Simmons, 1996–2001; photographer of theatre and opera; *b* 11 Sept. 1945; *s* of William Knight and Gertrude Alice Knight; *m* 1973, Stephanie Irina Williams; one *s* one *d*. *Educ:* Sir Roger Manwood's Sch., Sandwich; Bristol Univ. (LLB). Admitted solicitor, 1969; joined Simmons & Simmons, 1967; Partner, 1973; i/c Hong Kong Office, 1979–82; Head, Corporate Dept, 1994–96. Chairman: London Weighting Adv. Panel, GLA, 2002; Enforcement Cttee, Gen. Insce Standards Council, 2002–05; Member: Financial Reporting Council, 2004–07 (Dir, 2008–12); Gaming Bd for GB, 2004–05; Gambling Commn, 2005–12. Specialist Advr to Treasury Select Cttee in reln to report by FSA on failure of Royal Bank of Scotland, 2011–12. Trustee: Common Purpose Internat., 2008–10; National Life Stories, 2011–. Mem. Council, Lloyd's, 2000–08 (Dep. Chm., 2003–08). Liveryman, Solicitors' Co., 1983 (Master, 2007–08). FRSA. Photographic exhibn, The Refugee's Gift, St Martin-in-the-Fields, 2014; Portrait of Elsbeth Juda, NPG, 2014. *Publications:* The Acquisition of Private Companies and Business Assets, 1975, 7th edn 1997. *Recreations:* tennis, Arsenal FC. *W:* www.knightsight.co.uk. *Clubs:* Travellers; Hong Kong (Hong Kong).

KNIGHT-SANDS, Catherine; HM Diplomatic Service; Ambassador to Montenegro, 2009–13. British Council: Sen. Teaching Advr, Naples, 1984–87; Asst Dir of Studies, Jakarta, 1987–89; Dir of Studies, Milan, 1990–94; entered FCO, 1994; Desk Officer: France, Switzerland, Italy, Western Eur. Dept, FCO, 1994–96; Eur. Defence Section, Security Policy Dept, FCO, 1996–98; Hd, France/Italy Section, Western Eur. Dept, FCO, 1998–99; First Sec. Political (Balkans), UK Delegn to OSCE, Vienna, 1999–2003; Dep. Hd of Mission, Sarajevo, 2004–07; Political Counsellor, Baghdad, 2007–09. *Address:* c/o Foreign and Commonwealth Office, King Charles Street, SW1A 2AH.

KNIGHT SMITH, Ian; *see* Smith, Ian K.

KNIGHTLEY; *see* Finch-Knightley, family name of Earl of Aylesford.

KNIGHTLEY, Sharman; *see* Macdonald, S.

KNIGHTON, Dr Tessa Wendy; writer; ICREA Research Professor, Institució Milà i Fontanals (CSIC), Barcelona, since 2011; Fellow, Clare College, Cambridge, 1996–2011, now Emeritus; *b* 31 March 1957; *d* of Geoffrey Morris Knighton and (Margaret) Wendy Knighton; *m* 1984, Ivor Bolton, *qv*; one *s*. *Educ:* Felixstowe Coll., Suffolk; Clare Coll., Cambridge (MA 1980; PhD 1984). Jun. Res. Fellow, Lady Margaret Hall, Oxford, 1982–84; freelance writer and editor, 1984–; Asst Ed., 1988–91, Ed., 1992–2009, Early Music; Lectr, Faculty of Music, Cambridge Univ., 1991–93; Res. Associate, RHBNC, Univ. of London, 1993–99; Leverhulme Res. Asst, Faculty of Music, Univ. of Cambridge, 2000–03. Artistic Dir, Lufthansa Fest. of Baroque Music, 1986–97; Early Music Critic: Gramophone, 1988–; The Times, 1995–; radio broadcasts. Series Ed., Studies in Medieval and Renaissance Music, 2004–. *Publications:* (ed jtly) Companion to Medieval and Renaissance Music, 1992; Música y Músicos en la Corte de Fernando de Aragón 1474–1516, 2000; (jtly) Felipe II y la Música, 2001; Early Music Printing and Publishing in the Iberian World, 2007; Devotional Music in the Iberian World, 1450–1800, 2008; Music and Urban Society in Colonial Latin America, 2011; Pure Gold: sacred music of the Iberian Renaissance, 2011; articles in Music and Letters, Early Music History, Early Music, Plainsong and Medieval Music, Revista de Musicología, Renaissance Studies, Artigrama, etc. *Recreations:* wine, walking, whippets, song. *Address:* Institució Milà i Fontanals (CSIC), Calle Egipcíaques 15, 08001 Barcelona, Spain.

KNIGHTON, William Myles, CB 1981; Principal Establishment and Finance Officer, Department of Trade and Industry, 1986–91; *b* 8 Sept. 1931; *s* of late George Harry Knighton, OBE, and Ella Knighton (*née* Stroud); *m* 1957, Brigid Helen Carrothers; one *s* one *d*. *Educ:* Bedford School; Peterhouse, Cambridge (MA). Asst Principal, Min. of Supply, 1954; Principal, Min. of Aviation, 1959; Cabinet Office, 1962–64; Principal Private Sec. to Minister of Technology, 1966–68; Asst Sec., Min. of Technology, subseq. DTI and Dept of Trade, 1967–74; Under Sec., 1974–78, Dep. Sec., 1978–83, Dept of Trade; Dep. Sec., Dept of Transport, 1983–86. *Publications:* (with D. E. Rosenthal) National Laws and International Commerce, 1982. *Recreations:* gardening, hill-walking, music, painting, reading. *Address:* Court Green, St Anne's Hill, Midhurst, W Sussex GU29 9NN. *T:* (01730) 817860. *Club:* Oxford and Cambridge.

KNIGHTS, Laurence James W.; *see* West-Knights.

KNIGHTS, Martin Christopher, FREng, FICE; Senior Vice President, and Managing Director and Senior Fellow of Technology, Tunnelling and Earth Engineering Practice, CH2MHill, since 2013; *b* Watford, 16 May 1948; *s* of Anthony and Rita Knights; *m* 1970, Jennifer Anne Gleeson; one *s* one *d*. *Educ:* St Gabriel's, Bury, Lancs; Bolton Inst. of Technol.; Univ. of Manchester Inst. of Sci. and Technol. (BSc Hons 1970). FREng 2013. Site and Design Engr, Mott Hay and Anderson, 1970–76; Researcher, UMIST, 1972–73; Design Engr, Saudi Arabia, Yemen and UK, 1976–77; Project Design and Site Mgr, Sir Alexander Gibb and Partners, SA, 1977–81; Design Mgr, WS Atkins, 1981–89; Dir, KBR (UK), 1989–2005; Hd of Profession for Tunnelling, Jacobs Babtia (UK), 2005–10; Dir, Tunnelling and Earth Engrg, CH2MHill, 2010–13. Industrial Tutor, Univ. of Oxford, 1996–99. Pres., Internat. Tunnelling Assoc., 2007–10. Hon. Pres., Croatian Tunnelling Assoc., 2010–. Trustee, Brunel Mus., Rotherhithe, 2008–. James Clarke Medal, ICE, 2010. *Publications:* The Story of Tunnels, 1989; contrib. tech. papers and guidelines on tunnel design. *Recreations:* family, music, travel, walking. *Address:* CH2MHill-Halcrow, 44 Brook Green, W6 7EF. *T:* (020) 7493 8000. *E:* martin.knights@ch2m.com.

KNIGHTS, Peter David; Co-Founder and Chief Executive Officer, WildAid, since 2000; *b* Birmingham, 9 Feb. 1964; *s* of James and Ruth Knights; *m* 2002, Corie Eva Henniger; two *d*. *Educ:* King Edward's Sch., Birmingham; London Sch. of Econs and Pol Sci. (BSc Econs 1987). Investigator and campaigner, Envmtl Investigation Agency, 1989–95; prog. dir of illegal wildlife trade, Global Survival Network, 1995–98; Dir, Barbara Delano Foundn, 1998–2000. *Address:* WildAid US, 744 Montgomery Street, Suite 300, San Francisco, CA 94111, USA. *T:* (415) 8343174. *E:* knights@wildaid.org. *Club:* Battery (San Francisco).

KNIGHTS, Rosemary Margaret; *see* Steven, R. M.

KNILL, Sir Thomas (John Pugin Bartholomew), 5th Bt *cr* 1893, of The Grove, Blackheath, Kent; *b* 23 Aug. 1952; *er s* of Sir John Kenelm Stuart Knill, 4th Bt and Violette Maud Florence Martin (*née* Barnes; *d* 1983); *S* father, 1998; *m* 1977, Kathleen Muszynski (marr. diss. 1996); three *d*. Gov., Lucton Sch., Herefordshire, 2010–. Member: Pugin Soc.; Old Luctonians Assoc. *Recreations:* reading, cinema, theatre, riding, country pursuits, art, Rugby, history, public affairs. *Heir:* *b* Jenkyn Martin Benedict Stuart Knill [*b* 19 Jan. 1954; *m* 1978, Helen Marguerite Gulliver; two *s* one *d*].

KNIVETON, Patrick Edward, CEng, FIMechE, FIET; Head, Engineering Skills and Knowledge Management, Rolls-Royce Marine Power, since 2014; President, Institution of Mechanical Engineers, 2013–14; *b* Scarborough, 29 July 1954; *s* of Edward George Kniveton and Winifred Mary Kniveton (*née* Hopwood); *m* 1988, Melanie Lucas; one *s* two *d*. *Educ:* Scarborough High Sch. for Boys; Univ. of Leeds (BSc Hons Mech. Engrg 1976); Univ. of Newcastle upon Tyne (MBA Dist. 1999). CEng 1985; MIMechE 1985, FIMechE 1993; FIET 2004. Tech. Asst, NEI Reyrolle, 1976–79; Asst Manager, Quality Control, Grubb Parsons, 1979–85; Sen. Applications Engr, SKF Engrg Products, 1985–87; Engrg Manager, Rotawing Fans, 1987–89; Sen. Design Engr, NEI Controls, 1989–92; Asst Chief Engr, RR Industrial Controls, 1992–98; Divl Engrg Manager, Rolls-Royce Materials Handling, 1998–99; Hd, Business Mgt, Rolls-Royce GT Ops Engrg, 1999–2007; Hd, Infrastructure, 2007–09, Hd, Engrg Improvement, 2009–14, Rolls-Royce Marine Power. Vis. Prof., Univ. of Derby, 2014–. Dir, Rolls-Royce (Pension Trustees) Ltd, 1998–. Institution of Mechanical Engineers: Mem. Council, 1992–2002; Mem., Trustee Bd, 2002–07; Vice Pres., 2004–07; Dep. Pres., 2011–13. MCMI (MIMgt 1994), FCMI (FIMgt 2001); CMgr 2003; CCMI 2014. *Recreations:* theatre, Romano-British history, badminton, swimming, walking, ski-ing, cycling. *Address:* Rolls-Royce Submarines, RAY-SUBS HQ, Raynesway, Derby DE21 7XX.

KNOLLYS, family name of **Viscount Knollys**.

KNOLLYS, 3rd Viscount *cr* 1911, of Caversham; **David Francis Dudley Knollys;** Baron *cr* 1902; *b* 12 June 1931; *s* of 2nd Viscount Knollys, GCMG, MBE, DFC, and Margaret (*d* 1987), *o d* of Sir Stuart Coats, 2nd Bt; *S* father, 1966; *m* 1959, Hon. Sheelin Virginia Maxwell (*see* Viscountess Knollys); three *s* one *d*. *Educ:* Eton. Lt, Scots Guards, 1951. *Heir: s* Hon. Patrick Nicholas Mark Knollys [*b* 11 March 1962; *m* 1998, Mrs Sarah Wright, *o d* of Michael Petch; one *s* one *d*]. *Address:* The Bailiff's House, Bramerton Hall Farm, Norwich, Norfolk NR14 7DN.

KNOLLYS, Viscountess; Sheelin Virginia Knollys, OBE 2005; Vice Lord-Lieutenant, Norfolk, 2005–12; *b* 5 Dec. 1937; *d* of late Hon. Somerset Maxwell, MP and Susan Maxwell (*née* Roberts); *m* 1959, Hon. David Francis Dudley Knollys (*see* Viscount Knollys); three *s* one *d*. *Educ:* Hatherop Castle Sch.; Sorbonne. Partner in dried flower business, 1975–97. Mem., E Anglian Tourist Bd, 1988–91; Chairman: Norwich Area Tourism Agency, 1993–2005; English Rural Housing Assoc., 1996–2009; Inland Waterways Amenity Adv. Council, 1997–2006; Norfolk and Suffolk Broads Authy, 1997–2003 (Mem., 1987–2003). Non-exec. Dir, E Norfolk HA, 1990–99; Dir, VisitNorwich Ltd, 2005–. Vice Pres., Inland Waterways Assoc., 2004–. Branch Pres., Arthritis Care, 1965–2005. Trustee: How Hill Trust, 2000–14 (Vice Chm., 2000–14); S Norfolk Buildings Preservation Trust, 2000–11 (Chm., 2000–08); Norfolk Partners Against Crime Taskforce, 2008–. Mem. (C) S Norfolk DC, 1983–2003 (Chm., 1996–97). DL 1996, High Sheriff 2008–09, Norfolk. Gov., Wymondham Coll., 1989–97 (Visitor, 2014–); Lay Mem., Council, UEA, 1997–2006. *Recreations:* gardening, golf. *Address:* The Bailiff's House, Bramerton Hall Farm, Norwich, Norfolk NR14 7DN.

See also Baron Farnham.

KNOPF, His Honour Elliot Michael; a Circuit Judge, 2002–15; a Deputy High Court Judge, 2008–15; *b* 23 Dec. 1950; *s* of Harry and Clara Knopf; *m* 1976, Elizabeth Carol Lieberman; one *s* one *d*. *Educ:* Bury Grammar Sch.; University Coll. London (LLB Hons); Coll. of Law, Chester. Admitted solicitor, 1976; Partner, Pannone and Partners, Manchester, 1979–91; a District Judge, 1991–2002; Asst Recorder, 1996–2000; a Recorder of the Crown Court, 2000–02. *Recreations:* foreign travel, reading, entertaining friends and being entertained by them, the family.

KNORPEL, Henry, CB 1982; QC 1988; Counsel to the Speaker, House of Commons, 1985–95; *b* 18 Aug. 1924; 2nd *s* of late Hyman and Dora Knorpel; *m* 1953, Brenda Sterling; two *d*. *Educ:* City of London Sch.; Magdalen Coll., Oxford. BA 1945, BCL 1946, MA 1949. Called to Bar, Inner Temple, 1947, Entrance Scholar, 1947–50, Bencher, 1990; practised 1947–52; entered Legal Civil Service as Legal Asst, Min. of Nat. Insce, 1952; Sen. Legal Asst, Min. of Pensions and Nat. Insce, 1958; Law Commn, 1965; Min. of Social Security, 1967; Dept of Health and Social Security: Asst Solicitor, 1968; Principal Asst Solicitor (Under-Sec.), 1971; Solicitor (also to OPCS and Gen. Register Office), 1978–85. Vis. Lecturer: Kennington Coll. of Commerce and Law, 1950–58; Holborn Coll. of Law, Languages and Commerce, 1958–70; Univ. of Westminster (formerly Polytechnic of Central London), 1970–. *Publications:* articles on community law. *Recreation:* relaxing. *Address:* Conway, 32 Sunnybank, Epsom, Surrey KT18 7DX. *T:* (01372) 721394.

KNOTT, (Graeme) Jonathan; HM Diplomatic Service; Ambassador to Hungary, 2012–15; *b* 2 Nov. 1966; *s* of Daniel Wilfred Knott and Anne Lesley Knott; *m* 2005, Angela Susan Jepson; two *s* one *d*. *Educ:* Portsmouth Grammar Sch.; Mansfield Coll., Oxford (MA Law); MSP. ACMA 2007. Entered FCO, 1988; Dep. Eur. Corresp. to EU, 1995–96; Hd, Political/Econ. Section, Mexico City, 1996–2000; UK Trade and Finance negotiator, OECD, 2000–04; Prog. Dir, FCO Services Trading Fund, 2005–06; Hd, Financial Planning and Perf., FCO, 2006–08; Dep. Hd of Mission and Minister Counsellor, Seoul, S Korea, 2008–11. *Recreations:* tennis, golf, travel. *Address:* c/o Foreign and Commonwealth Office, King Charles Street, SW1A 2AH.

KNOTT, Prof. John Frederick, OBE 2004; ScD; FRS 1990; FREng; Professor of Metallurgy and Materials, University of Birmingham, since 1990 (Head, School of Metallurgy and Materials, 1990–96; Feeney Professor, 1994–2004; Dean of Engineering, 1995–98); *b* Bristol, 9 Dec. 1938; *s* of Fred Knott and Margaret (*née* Chesney); *m* 1st, 1963, Christine Mary Roberts (marr. diss. 1986); two *s*; 2nd, 1990, Susan Marilyn Cooke (*née* Jones); two step *s*. *Educ:* Queen Elizabeth's Hosp., Bristol; Sheffield Univ. (BMet 1st cl. Hons 1959); Cambridge Univ. (PhD 1963; ScD 1991). FIMMM (FIM 1974); FWeldI 1985; FREng (FEng 1988); FIMechE 1994. Res. Officer, Central Electricity Res. Labs, Leatherhead, 1962–67; Cambridge University: Lectr, Dept of Metallurgy, 1967–81; Reader in Mechanical Metallurgy, 1981–90; Churchill College: Goldsmiths' Fellow, Coll. Lectr and Dir of Studies in Metallurgy and Materials Sci., 1967–90; Tutor, 1969–79; Tutor for Advanced Students, 1979–81; Vice-Master, 1988–90; Extra-Ordinary Fellow, 1991–2006. Member: Materials, Manufacturing and Structures Adv. Bd (formerly Materials and Processing Adv. Bd), Rolls-Royce plc, 1987–2015 (Chm., 2000–11); Technical Adv. Gp on Structural Integrity, Nuclear Power Industries, 1988– (Chm., 2010–); Res. Bd, Welding Inst., 1989–; Nuclear Safety Adv. Cttee (formerly Adv. Cttee on the Safety of Nuclear Installations), HSE, 1990–2005 (Acting Chm., 2004); Graphite Technical Adv. Cttee, 2004–; Defence Nuclear Safety Cttee, 2006–. Pres., Internat. Congress on Fracture, 1993–97. Editor, Materials Sci. and Technology, 2003–14. Hon. Professor: Beijing Univ. of Aeronautics and Astronautics, 1992; Xian Jiaotong Univ., 1995; Hatfield Lecture, IMMM, 2006. Mem. Governing Body, Shrewsbury Sch., 1996–2001. FRSA. Foreign Member: Acad. of Scis of the Ukraine, 1993; Japan Inst. of Metals, 2005; Foreign Associate, NAE, USA, 2003; Foreign Fellow, Indian NAE, 2006. Hon. DEng: Glasgow, 2004; Sheffield, 2010. L. B. Pfeil Prize, 1973, Rosenhain Medal, 1978, Metals Soc.; Leslie Holliday Prize, Materials Sci. Club, 1978; Griffith Medal, 1999; Robert Franklin Mehl Award, Metals, Materials and Minerals Soc., USA, 2005; Leverhulme Medal, Royal Soc., 2005; Brooker Medal, Welding Inst., 2008; Platinum Medal, IMMM, 2009; Cottrell Gold Medal, Internat. Congress on Fracture, 2013. *Publications:* Fundamentals of Fracture Mechanics, 1973, 2nd edn 1979; (with P. A. Withey) Fracture Mechanics: worked examples, 1993; many scientific papers in Acta Met., Metal Sci., Materials Sci. and Technology, Met. Trans, Engrg Fracture Mechanics, etc. *Recreations:* bridge, cryptic crosswords, traditional jazz, playing the tenor recorder with enthusiasm rather than skill. *Address:* 43 West Street, Stratford-upon-Avon, Warwickshire CV37 6DN.

KNOTT, Jonathan; *see* Knott, G. J.

KNOWLAND, Raymond Reginald, CBE 1992; Managing Director, British Petroleum, 1990–92; *b* 18 Aug. 1930; *s* of Reginald George Knowland and Marjorie Doris Knowland (*née* Alvis); *m* 1956, Valerie Mary Higgs; three *s*. *Educ:* Bristol Grammar Sch.; Sir John Cass College London. CChem, FRSC 1972. BP Chemicals: specialty plastics and PVC Plant Management, Barry Works, 1957–69; Works Gen. Manager, Barry Works, 1969–75, Baglan Bay Works, 1975–78; Man. Dir, Belgium, 1978–80; Dir, London, 1980–90; Chief Exec. Officer, London, 1983–90. Non-executive Director: BSI plc, 1992–99; Laporte plc, 1992–99; Sterling Chemicals Inc., 1992–96; BNFL, 1993–97; Sentrachem Internat. Holdings Ltd, 1992–96; Reaction Systems Engineering Ltd, 2006–08. President: British Plastics Fedn, 1983–84; Assoc. of Petrochemical Producers in Europe, 1985–88; CIA, 1990–92; Vice Pres., SCI, 1993–96. Chm., European Chemical Industry Ecology and Toxicology Centre, 1986–90. Liveryman, Horners' Co., 1987 (Master, 2000, Dep. Master, 2001). *Recreations:* sailing, photography, Rugby football (spectator). *Address:* Buoys, The Quay, Appledore, Bideford, N Devon EX39 1QS. *T:* (01237) 471489. *Clubs:* Athenæum, Savage.

KNOWLES, Ann; *see* Knowles, P. A.

KNOWLES, Ben; Director of Music, Marketing and Communications, War Child, since 2014; *b* 29 Aug. 1973; *s* of John and Pat Knowles; *m* 2010, Charlotte Saxe; two *s*. *Educ:* Beverley Grammar Sch.; Hertford Coll., Oxford (BA Hons Hist.). Writer: Daily Mirror, 1994–95; Smash Hits, 1995–97; Melody Maker, 1998–2000; Ed., New Musical Express, 2000–02; Dep. Ed., Zoo mag., 2003–06; Jt Dep. Ed., Daily Star, 2006–08; Music and Entertainment Dir, 2008–11, Dir of Fundraising, 2011–14, War Child. Mem., Cultural Strategy Gp for London, GLA, 2000–04. Dir, War Child Music, 2004–. *Recreations:* Fulham FC, pubs, rock 'n' roll, cooking, photography, spending time with my family. *Address:* War Child, Linton House, 39–51 Highgate Road, NW5 1RT. *E:* benk@warchild.org.uk.

KNOWLES, Sir Charles (Francis), 7th Bt *cr* 1765; architect in private practice, since 1984; *b* 20 Dec. 1951; *s* of Sir Francis Gerald William Knowles, 6th Bt, FRS, and of Ruth Jessie, *d* of late Rev. Arthur Brooke-Smith; *S* father, 1974; *m* 1979, Amanda Louise Margaret, *d* of late Lance Lee Bromley (marr. diss. 2003); two *s*. *Educ:* Marlborough Coll.; Oxford Sch. of Architecture (DipArch 1977; RIBA 1979). Director: Charles Knowles Design Ltd (architects); Richmond Knowles Architects; works include: new Battersea Dogs Home, London and Old Windsor; refurbishment of Bank of England, historic country houses and listed London properties. FRSA. *Recreations:* photography, shooting, travel, piloting light aircraft. *Heir: s* (Charles) William (Frederick Lance) Knowles [*b* 27 Aug. 1985; *m* 2011, Holly Koch]. *Address:* c/o Charles Knowles Design Ltd, 5 The Powerhouse, 70 Chiswick High Road, W4 1SY.

KNOWLES, Colin George, PhD; feudal title, Lord Knowles of Houghton and Burnett, 2006; Director of Development and Public Relations, University of Bophuthatswana, 1985–95; Secretary and Trustee, University of Bophuthatswana Foundation, 1985–95; *b* 11 April 1939; *s* of late George William Knowles, Tarleton, Lancs; three *d* by former marriages. *Educ:* King George V Grammar Sch., Southport; CEDEP, Fontainebleau, France; Trinity Coll., Delaware, USA (MA 1991; PhD 1994). MInstM 1966; MCIPR (MIPR 1970); Mem. BAIE 1972; FPRISA 1993 (MPRISA 1983); APR 1987; AAArb 1991; MSAAIE 1993. Appointed Comr of Oaths, 1991. Joined John Player & Sons, 1960; sales and marketing management appts; Head of Public Relations, 1971–73; joined Imperial Tobacco Ltd, 1973; Hd of Public Affairs, 1973–80; Company Sec., 1979–80. Chairman: Griffin Associates Ltd, 1980–83; Concept Communications (Pty) Ltd (S Africa), 1983–84; Dir, TWS Public Relations (Pty) Ltd (S Africa), 1984–85. Mem. Council, Tobacco Trade Benevolent Assoc., 1975–80; Chm., Bophuthatswana Reg., PRISA, 1988–91. Dir, Bophuthatswana Council for Consumer Affairs, 1991–94. Director: Nottingham Festival Assoc. Ltd, 1969–71; English Sinfonia Orchestra, 1972–80; Midland Sinfonia Concert Soc. Ltd, 1972–80; (also co-Founder) Assoc. for Business Sponsorship of The Arts Ltd, 1975–84 (Chm., 1975–80); Bristol Hippodrome Trust Ltd, 1977–81; Bath Archaeological Trust Ltd, 1978–81; The Palladian Trust Ltd, 1979–82; Mem., Chancellor of Duchy of Lancaster's Cttee of Honour on Business and the Arts, 1980–81. Arts sponsorship initiatives include responsibility for: Internat. Cello Competition (with Tortelier), Bristol, 1975 and 1977; Internat. Conductors Awards, 1978; Pompeii Exhibn, RA, 1976–77; new prodns at Royal Opera House, Covent Garden, at Glyndebourne, and at National Theatre. Governor: Manning Grammar Sch., Nottingham, 1972–73; Clayesmore Sch., Dorset, 1975–85. Chm., St John Ambulance Foundn in Bophuthatswana, 1989–94; Mem. Chapter, Priory of St John, S Africa, 1992–99. Liveryman, Worshipful Co. of Tobacco Pipe Makers and Tobacco Blenders, 1973; Freeman, City of London, 1974. FCMI (FBIM 1972); FRSA 1975; FRCSoc 1976. KStJ 1995 (CStJ 1991; OStJ 1977). *Recreations:* reading, travel, country pursuits. *E:* lkhb@talktalk.net. *Clubs:* Carlton, MCC, XL.

KNOWLES, Sir Durward (Randolph), Kt 1996; OBE 1964; OM (Bahamas) 1996; President, Caribbean Towing Company, since 1982; *b* 2 Nov. 1917; *s* of late Harry Knowles and Charlotte Knowles; *m* 1947, Holly; one *s* two *d*. *Educ:* Queen's Coll., Nassau, Bahamas. Captain of freighters plying in Caribbean, 1942–46; various Captain appts, 1946–52; Harbour Pilot, Nassau, 1952–96. Pres., Island Sand; Vice-Pres., Island Shipping. Star Class Yacht Racing World Champion, 1947; competed in eight Olympic Games in Star Class: 1948, 1952, 1956 (Bronze Medal), 1960, 1964 (Gold Medal), 1968, 1972 and 1988. *Relevant publication:* Driven by the Stars: the story of Durward Knowles, by Douglas Hanks, Jr, 1992. *Recreation:* yachting. *Address:* Winton Highway, PO Box N–1216, Nassau, Bahamas. *Clubs:* Nassau Yacht; Coral Reef Yacht (Coconut Grove, Florida).

KNOWLES, Eric; independent fine art valuer and broadcaster; *b* Nelson, Lancs, 19 Feb. 1953; *s* of James and June Knowles; *m* 1976, Anita Whiting; two *s*. *Educ:* Edge End Sch., Nelson; Nelson and Colne Coll. of Further Educn. Reservations Clerk, Lyons Tours, 1970–71; Cataloguer, Herbert Sutcliffe Antique Dealers, 1971–72; Quality Controller, Pioneer Weston Engrg, 1972–75; joined Bonham's Auctioneers, 1976; porter, then Hd, Ceramics Dept, 1981–2001; Dir, 1984–2005. Non-exec. Dir, W. Moorcroft Ltd, 2002–. Consultant: Dreweatt Neate Fine Art, 2013–15; Swan Fine Art Auctions, 2015–. *Television* programmes include: expert: in ceramics, Antiques Roadshow, 1981–; Great Antiques Hunt, 1995–99; Antique Inspectors, 1997–98; (resident) Going for a Song, 1997–2000; The Really Useful Show, 1997; 20th Century Roadshow, 2004; (resident) Antique Master, 2010–11; presenter: Crimewatch UK, 1988–98; Noel's House Party, 1993–99; Good Morning with Anne and Nick, 1994–95; The Great House Game, 1998–99; Celebrity Ready Steady Cook, 1998, 2007; You Can't Take it with You, 1999; It's a Gift, 2000; Selling the Family Silver, 2000; Restoration Roadshow, 2010; Put Your Money Where Your Mouth Is, 2012–; panellist: Call My Bluff, 1994–2004; Going, Going Gone, 1995–96; various roles: Dictionary Corner, Countdown, 1998–2004; Pointless, 2014. Resident antiques expert, Jimmy Young Show, BBC Radio 2, 1993–2003; regular contrib., Homes and Antiques Mag., 1993–; resident antiques expert, Sunday Times, 2005–. Freeman, City of London, 2000. Hon. Fellow, Univ. of Central Lancs, 1999. Hon. MA Nottingham Trent, 1997. FRSA 1996. *Publications:* Victoriana, 1991, 2nd edn 2000; Art Deco, 1991, 2nd edn 2000; Art Nouveau, 1992, 2nd edn 2000; (contrib.) Treasures in your Home, 1993; Victoriana to Art Deco, 1993, repr. as 100 Years of Decorative Arts, 1994; Royal Memorabilia, 1994; Discovering Antiques, 1996; (contrib.) Miller's Understanding Antiques, 1997; Eric Knowles Antiques: a beginner's guide,

2006; (consultant ed.) English Furniture, 2010; Lalique, 2011; Art Deco, 2014. *Recreations:* country walking, jazz, soul and classical music, family, cinema, theatre, football, Roman Britain, visiting National Trust and English Heritage sites, historic buildings and museums. *T:* 07833 246453. *E:* eric@ericknowles.co.uk.

KNOWLES, George Peter; Registrar of the Province and Diocese of York, and Archbishop of York's Legal Secretary, 1968–87; *b* 30 Dec. 1919; *s* of Geoffrey Knowles and Mabel Bowman; *m* 1948, Elizabeth Margaret Scott; one *s* two *d. Educ:* Clifton Coll., Bristol; Queens' Coll., Cambridge. MA, LLM. Served war, Royal Artillery, 1939–46 (Lieut). Admitted a solicitor, 1948; Chm., York Area Rent Tribunal, 1959; Mem., Mental Health Review Tribunal for Yorkshire Regional Health Authority Area, 1960. *Recreations:* gardening, fishing, wildlife. *Address:* 11 Lang Road, Bishopthorpe, York YO23 2QJ. *T:* (01904) 706443. *Club:* Yorkshire (York).

KNOWLES, Rt Rev. Graeme Paul, CVO 2012; Dean of St Paul's, 2007–11; an Honorary Assistant Bishop: Diocese of St Edmundsbury and Ipswich, since 2012; Diocese of Ely, since 2012; *b* 25 Sept. 1951; *s* of Grace and Stanley Knowles; *m* 1973, Susan Gail Marsden. *Educ:* Dunstable Grammar Sch., 1963–70; King's Coll. London, 1970–73 (AKC; FKC 2011). Ordained deacon, 1974, priest, 1975; Asst Curate, St Peter in Thanet, 1974–79; Precentor and Sen. Curate, Leeds Parish Church, 1979–81; Chaplain and Precentor, 1981–87, Chapter Clerk, 1985–87, Portsmouth Cathedral; Vicar of Leigh Park, 1987–93; Rural Dean of Havant, 1990–93; Archdeacon of Portsmouth, 1993–99; Dean of Carlisle, 1999–2003; Bishop of Sodor and Man, 2003–07. Chm., Church Buildings Council (formerly Council for the Care of Churches), 2003–09 (Mem., 1991–2000); Mem., Gen. Synod of C of E, 2002–07. Registrar, Sons and Friends of the Clergy, 2012–. Hon. Chaplain, RNR, 2008–13. *Recreations:* Victorian and Edwardian songs, the books of E. F. Benson, wine and food. *Address:* 102A Barons Road, Bury St Edmunds, Suffolk IP33 2LY. *Club:* Garrick.

KNOWLES, Graham Roy; QC 2009; **His Honour Judge Knowles;** a Circuit Judge, since 2010; *b* Manchester, 20 Feb. 1968; *s* of late Roy Knowles and of Margaret Knowles; *m* 1999; two *s* two *d. Educ:* Queen Elizabeth II High Sch., Peel, IOM; King's Coll., Cambridge (BA 1989; MA 1993). Called to the Bar, Middle Temple, 1990 (Astbury Law Scholar); in practice as a barrister, 1990–2010; Junior, N Circuit, 1994; Recorder, 2005–10. Member: Gen. Council of the Bar, 1995–97; Professional Conduct Cttee of the Bar, 1997–99. *Recreations:* family life, Venice. *Address:* Law Courts, Openshaw Place, Ring Way, Preston, Lancs PR1 2LL. *T:* (01772) 844700.

KNOWLES, Rev. John Geoffrey; Warden of Readers, Diocese of Chester, since 2005; Associate Minister, Handforth, since 2013; *b* 12 June 1948; *s* of Geoffrey and Jean Knowles; *m* 1974, Roey Wills; three *d. Educ:* St Bees Sch.; Univ. of Manchester (BSc Physics); Worcester Coll., Oxford (CertEd); Univ. of London (MSc Nuclear Physics); W Midlands Ministerial Trng Course. Assistant Master: Mill Hill Sch., 1970–75; Wellington Coll., 1975–76; Head of Physics, Watford GS, 1976–84; Vice Master, Queen Elizabeth's GS, Blackburn, 1984–90; Headmaster, King Edward VI Five Ways Sch., Birmingham, 1990–99; Rector, Hutchesons' GS, 1999–2004. Ordained deacon 1998, priest 1999; Non-Stipendiary Curate, Holy Trinity, The Lickey, 1998–99; Vicar, Woodford, 2005–12. Chief Examr, A-Level Physics (Nuffield), 1990–99. Vice-Chm., 1996–98, Chm., 1998–99, Assoc. Heads of Grant Maintained Schools. Chm. Governors, Kingsmead Sch., 1986–92; Mem., Gen. Convocation, Univ. of Strathclyde, 2003–04. Treas., 1976–84, Vice-Chm., 1991–95, Elgar Soc. *Publications:* Elgar's Interpreters on Record, 1978, 2nd edn 1985; (contrib.) Elgar Studies, 1988; (contrib.) This is the Best of Me, 1999. *Recreation:* music. *Address:* 15 Clare Avenue, Handforth, Wilmslow SK9 3EQ. *T:* (01625) 526531. *E:* john.knowles92@btinternet.com.

KNOWLES, Julian Bernard; QC 2011; a Recorder, since 2009; *b* Manchester, 26 Jan. 1969; *s* of Leo and Patricia Knowles; *m* 2011, Dr Nicola Levitt; one *s. Educ:* St John Plessington High Sch.; Xaverian Coll.; Balliol Coll., Oxford (BA 1990). Called to the Bar, Inner Temple, 1994. *Publications:* The Law of Extradition and Mutual Assistance, 2002, 3rd edn 2013. *Recreations:* electronic dance music, looking in bookshops, lager. *Address:* Matrix Chambers, Griffin Building, Gray's Inn, WC1R 5LN. *T:* (020) 7404 3447, *Fax:* (020) 7404 3448. *E:* jknowles@matrixlaw.co.uk. *Clubs:* Oxford and Cambridge; Manchester City Football.

KNOWLES, Michael; independent governance consultant, since 1992; *b* 21 May 1942; *s* of Martin Christopher and Anne Knowles; *m* 1965, Margaret Isabel Thorburn; three *d. Educ:* Clapham Coll. RC Grammar Sch. Sales Manager, Export & Home Sales. Mem. (C), 1971–83, Leader, 1974–83, Kingston upon Thames Borough Council. MP (C) Nottingham East, 1983–92; PPS to Minister for Planning and Regional Affairs, 1986, to Minister for Housing and Planning, 1987–88, DoE; Member: Select Cttee on European Legislation, 1984; Select Cttee on Defence, 1990. Governance consultant in Africa, 1992–2003, and in Iraq, 2003–12. *Recreations:* walking, history. *Address:* 2 Ditton Reach, Portsmouth Road, Thames Ditton, Surrey KT7 0XB.

KNOWLES, Michael Ernest, PhD; CChem, FRSC; FIFST, FIAFoST; consultant in food science and regulatory affairs, Belgium, since 2013; *b* 6 May 1942; *s* of late Ernest Frederick Walter Knowles and Lesley (*née* Lambert); *m* 1st, 1965, Rosalind Mary Griffiths (marr. diss. 1975); two *s*; 2nd, 1994, Alexandra Knowles (*née* Hadjiyianni). *Educ:* Nottingham Univ. (BPharm 1st cl. Hons; PhD). CChem 1969; FRSC 1982; FIFST 1983; FIAFoST 2012. ICI Postdoctoral Fellow, Nottingham Univ., 1967–69; Ministry of Agriculture, Fisheries and Food: Food Sci. Unit, Norwich, 1969–74; Scientific Advr, Food Sci. Div., 1974–79; Head, Food Sci. Lab., 1979–85; Head, Food Sci. Div., 1985–89; Chief Scientist (Fisheries and Food), 1989–91; Dir, Scientific and Regulatory Affairs, EMEA, 1992–97, Gtr Europe, 1997–2008, Coca-Cola International; Vice Pres., Global Scientific and Regulatory Affairs, Coca-Cola Co., Brussels, 2009–13. Liveryman, Soc. of Apothecaries; Freeman, City of London, 2011. FRSA. *Publications:* series of papers on chemical aspects of food safety in learned jls. *Recreations:* clay pigeon and practical pistol shooting, walking, gardening. *Address:* Rue General Lotz 103/bte 15, 1180 Brussels, Belgium. *T:* (2) 497052452. *E:* mek59100@gmail.com. *Clubs:* Royal Over-Seas League; Strangers (Norwich).

KNOWLES, Sir Nigel (Graham), Kt 2009; Global Co-Chairman, DLA Piper International LLP, since 2015; *b* 1956; *m*; two *s* one *d. Educ:* Sheffield Univ.; Chester Coll. of Law. Broomhead & Neals, Yorkshire: articled clerk, 1978–80; Asst Solicitor, 1980–84; Partner, 1984–90; Dibb Lupton Broomhead, later Dibb Lupton Alsop, then DLA, subseq. DLA Piper Internat. LLP: Hd, Commercial Gp, 1990–95; Partner, 1993; Dep. Man. Partner, 1995–96; Man. Partner, 1996–2005; Jt CEO and Man. Partner for Europe and Asia, 2005–14. Non-executive Chairman: Blenheim Capital Services Ltd, 2010–; LawVest, 2011–; Zeus Capital, 2014–. Chairman: Managing Partners' Forum, 2004–13; Legal Sector Alliance, 2008–14. Member: Envmtl Leadership Team, Business in the Community; Steering Cttee, Prince of Wales Rainforest Initiative; Chm., Prince's Trust Internat., 2014–. Vis. Prof., Univ. of Sheffield, 2010. Fellow, Harris Manchester Coll., Oxford. Hon. DCL Sheffield, 2011. *Address:* DLA Piper International LLP, 3 Noble Street, EC2V 7EE.

KNOWLES, (Patricia) Ann, (Mrs P. A. Knowles-Foster); Director, Emirates Project, Marriage Care, 2006–10; *b* 31 Oct. 1944; *d* of John and Margaret Miller; *m* 1st, 1964, Leslie John Knowles (*d* 1996); two *s* one *d*; 2nd, 2000, Malcolm Foster. *Educ:* Our Lady's Prep. Sch., Barrow-in-Furness; Our Lady's Convent Sch.; Open Univ. (BA); CENTRA (Dip. Therapeutic Counselling, 1999); St John's Coll., Leeds Univ. (Cert. Couple Counselling, 2000). Reporter: North Western Evening Mail, Barrow, 1962–68; North Somerset Mercury, Clevedon, 1969–70; Western Daily Press, Bristol, 1970–72; Theatre Critic, Evening Star, Burnley, 1973–77; Sub-Editor, Dep. Chief Sub-Editor, News Editor, Burnley Express, 1977–84; Asst Editor, Citizen Publications, Blackburn, 1985–87; Sub-Editor, Keighley News, 1987–89; Group Editor, Herald and Post, Burnley, 1989–90; Editor, The Universe, 1990–95. NW Regl Develt Worker, 1997–2001, Dir, Marriage Support, 2001–05, Marriage Care. Member: Nat. Assoc. of Tangent Clubs, 1984–2010; Soroptimists International, Burnley, 1990–92; Catholic Union of GB, 1991–99; Nat. Bd of Catholic Women, 1994–98; Rimington WI, 2011–. *Publications:* (with Mgr John Furnival) Archbishop Derek Worlock—His Personal Journey, 1997. *Recreations:* gardening, interior decoration, family interests, travel. *Address:* 2 Horton Lodge, Horton in Craven, Skipton, N Yorks BD23 3JX.

KNOWLES, Peter Francis Arnold, CB 1996; Parliamentary Counsel, 1991–2008; *b* 10 July 1949; *s* of Sidney Francis Knowles and Patricia Anette Knowles; *m* 1972, Patricia Katharine Clifford; two *s. Educ:* Whitgift School, Croydon; University College, Oxford (MA). Called to the Bar, Gray's Inn, 1971. In practice at Chancery Bar, 1973–75; joined Parliamentary Counsel Office, 1975; with Law Commission, 1979–81, 1993–96; with Tax Law Rewrite Project, 2001–03. *Publications:* (contrib.) Halsbury's Laws of England; The Giulia Coupés 1963–1976, 1998. *Recreations:* music, walking, ski-ing, bird watching, classic car restoration.

KNOWLES, Peter William; Controller, BBC Parliament, since 2006; Editor: Today in Parliament, since 2003; Democracy Live, since 2010; *b* Bolton, Lancs, 17 May 1961; *s* of Alan and Mary Knowles; *m* 1988, Kaye Barker; two *s. Educ:* Bolton Sch.; St Catherine's Coll., Oxford (BA Hons English Lang. and Lit. 1983); Univ. of Bradford (MBA 1997); Univ. of Chester (FdA Contextual Theol. 2013). Reporter, Carlisle News Agency, 1984; BBC: news trainee, 1984–86; journalist, BBC Manchester, 1986–87; sen. journalist, BBC Leeds, 1987–89; Prod., Nine O'Clock News, 1989–91; Asst Ed., BBC World Service TV News, 1991–96; News Ed., BBC World News, 1997–99; Man. Ed., BBC TV News, 2000–01; Channel Ed., BBC Parlt, 2001–06. Dir, Parly Broadcasting Unit Ltd, 2003–11. Trustee: Hansard Soc., 2010–; Pitzhanger Manor and Gall., 2013–; Chm. Trustees, St Andrew's Ch Centre, Ealing, 2013–. Lay Preacher, URC, 2013–. Convener, Gen. Assembly Communications and Editl Cttee, URC, 2015–. *Recreations:* long distance walks, architectural conservation. *Address:* BBC Parliament, 4 Millbank, SW1P 3JQ. *E:* peter.knowles@bbc.co.uk. *Club:* Players.

KNOWLES, Hon. Sir Robin St John, Kt 2014; CBE 2006; **Hon. Mr Justice Knowles;** a Judge of the High Court, Queen's Bench Division, since 2014; *b* 7 April 1960; *s* of Norman Richard Knowles and Margaret Mary Knowles (*née* Robinson); *m* 1987, Gill Adams; one *d. Educ:* Sir Roger Manwood's Grammar Sch.; Trinity Coll., Cambridge (MA). Called to the Bar: Middle Temple, 1982, Bencher 2004; Gray's Inn (*ad eundem*); in practice at the Bar, 1983–; Asst Recorder, 1998–2000; QC 1999; a Recorder, 2000–14; a Deputy High Court Judge, 2006–14. Member: Exec., Commercial Bar Assoc., 1999– (Chm., 2005–07; Chm., N American Cttee, 2000–); various Bar Council and Commercial Bar Assoc. and Inn cttees and working parties; and Trustee, Mgt Cttee, Bar Pro Bono Unit, 1996– (Chm., 2005–); Trustee: Solicitors Pro Bono Gp, 2001–; Bar in the Community, 2001–; Advice Bureau, RCJ, 1999–. *Recreations:* the East End of London, and being with friends and family. *Address:* Royal Courts of Justice, Rolls Building, Fetter Lane, EC4A 1NL.

KNOWLES, Tanya; *see* Barron, T.

KNOWLES, Timothy; Director, Welsh Water, then Hyder, plc, 1989–99; *b* 17 May 1938; *s* of Cyril William Knowles and Winifred Alice Knowles (*née* Hood); *m* 1967, Gaynor Hallett; one *d. Educ:* Bishop Gore Grammar Sch., Swansea. Chartered Accountant. Company Sec./Accountant, Louis Marx & Co. Ltd, 1960–68; Controller, Modco Valenite, 1968–69; HTV Ltd: Company Sec., 1969–78; Financial Dir, 1975–81; Asst Man. Dir, 1981–86; HTV Group plc: Financial Dir, 1976–86; Gp Man. Dir, 1986–88; Finance Dir, Insurance Services Gp, ECGD (for privatisation), 1990–91; Dir, Frost & Reed (Holdings) Ltd, 1985–88. Member: S Wales Electricity Bd, 1981–82; Welsh Water Authority, 1982–89; Disciplinary Cttee, 1993–2002 (Chm. Tribunals, 1996–2002), Appeal Cttee, 2002–09, ICAEW. Dir, University Hosp. of Wales Healthcare NHS Trust, 1995–99. Chm., CG90, 1994–97 (Treas., 2000–). Contested (C) Swansea East, 1966. Mem., Livery Co. of Wales (formerly Welsh Livery Guild), 1994– (Treas., 2001–05; Emeritus Treas., 2006–). *Recreations:* travel, watching cricket, golf, genealogy, challenging bureaucracy. *Address:* Cae Ffynnon, 12 Ger-y-Llan, St Nicholas, Cardiff CF5 6SY. *T:* (01446) 760726. *Clubs:* Cardiff and County (Cardiff); Glamorgan CC; Cottrell Park Golf.

KNOWLES-FOSTER, (Patricia) Ann; *see* Knowles, P. A.

KNOX, family name of **Earl of Ranfurly.**

KNOX, Sir David (Laidlaw), Kt 1993; *b* 30 May 1933; *s* of late J. M. Knox, Lockerbie and Mrs C. H. C. Knox (*née* Laidlaw); *m* 1980, Mrs Margaret Eva Maxwell, *d* of late A. McKenzie. *Educ:* Lockerbie Academy; Dumfries Academy; London Univ. (BSc (Econ) Hons). Management Trainee, 1953–56; Printing Executive, 1956–62; O&M Consultant, 1962–70. Contested (C): Stechford, Birmingham, 1964 and 1966; Nuneaton, March 1967. MP (C) Leek Div. of Staffs, 1970–83, Staffordshire Moorlands, 1983–97. PPS to Ian Gilmour, Minister of State for Defence, 1973, Sec. of State for Defence, 1974. Member: Select Cttee on European Legislation, 1976–97; House of Commons Chairmen's Panel, 1983–97; Secretary: Cons. Finance Cttee, 1972–73; Cons. Trade Cttee, 1974; Vice-Chm., Cons. Employment Cttee, 1979–80; Chairman: W Midlands Area Young Conservatives, 1963–64; W Midlands Area Cons. Political Centre, 1966–69; a Vice Chairman: Cons. Party Organisation, 1974–75; Cons. Gp for Europe, 1984–87. Editor, Young Conservatives National Policy Group, 1963–64. Chm., London Union of Youth Clubs, 1998–99; Dep. Chm., Fedn of London Youth Clubs, 1999–2008 (Vice Pres., 2011–). Vice President: Commercial Travellers' Benevolent Instn, 1998–; One World Trust, 2004–. Mem., Drama Panel, Buxton Opera House, 2007–. *Recreations:* watching association football and cricket, reading, theatre, walking. *Address:* The Mount, Alstonefield, Ashbourne, Derbys DE6 2FS.

KNOX, James Peter Witherow; Partner, Berwin Leighton Paisner LLP, since 2010; *b* Redhill, 30 Sept. 1961; *s* of Peter and Georgina Knox; *m* 1988, Dee Pilgrim; three *s. Educ:* Reigate Grammar Sch.; Bristol Univ. (LLB Hons 1984). Articled clerk, Druces & Attlee, 1985–87; Solicitor, 1987–99, Partner, 1999–2010, Linklaters. *Recreations:* running, scuba diving, tennis, hill walking, clay pigeon shooting. *Address:* Berwin Leighton Paisner LLP, Adelaide House, London Bridge, EC4R 9HA. *T:* (020) 3400 1000, *Fax:* (020) 3400 1111. *E:* james.knox@blplaw.com. *Clubs:* Royal Automobile; Canterbury Tennis.

KNOX, James Richard Dunsmuir, FSAScot; Managing Director, The Art Newspaper, since 2005; Director, Fleming Wyfold Art Foundation, since 2015; *b* Kilwinning, Ayrshire, 18 Oct. 1952; *s* of Sir Bryce Muir Knox, KCVO, MC, TD and Patricia Mary Knox (*née* Dunsmuir); *m* 1983, Caroline Angela Owen; one *s* one *d. Educ:* Eton Coll.; Trinity Coll., Cambridge (BA 1974); INSEAD (MBA). FSAScot 1975. Writer, Antique Collector, 1975–77; Associate Publisher: Ebury Press, 1977–78; Illustrated London News Gp, 1980–82; Publisher, The Spectator, 1983–92; Founder, Art for Work Consultancy, 1992–2005. Curator, The Genius of Osbert Lancaster, Wallace Collection, 2008. Chm., Ayr Renaissance, 2014–. Trustee: Great Steward of Scotland's Dumfries House Trust, 2007–; Nat. Galls of Scotland, 2007–13; NT for Scotland, 2011–; Chm., Boswell (formerly Boswell Mus. and Mausoleum) Trust, 2010–. *Publications:* The Trinity Foot Beagles, 1978; Robert Byron, 2003;

Cartoons and Coronets: the genius of Osbert Lancaster, 2008; The Scottish Country House, 2012. *Recreations:* architecture, the visual arts. *Address:* Martnaham Lodge, by Ayr, Ayrshire KA6 6ES.

KNOX, John Andrew; Deputy Director, Serious Fraud Office, 1990–96; *b* 22 July 1937; *s* of late James Telford Knox and Mary Knox; *m* 1964, Patricia Mary Martin; one *s* one *d*. *Educ:* Dame Allan's Sch., Newcastle upon Tyne; Merton Coll., Oxford (MA). ACA 1964, FCA 1974. Cooper Brothers & Co. Chartered Accountants, 1961–65; Vickers Ltd, 1966–72; entered CS as a Sen. Accountant, 1972; Chief Accountant, 1973; Asst Sec., 1976; Head of Accountancy Services Div., 1977–85; Grade 3, 1979–96; Hd of Industrial Financial Appraisal Div., DTI, 1985–87; Chief Accountant, Serious Fraud Office, 1987–90. Board Member: Criminal Cases Review Commn, 1997–2003; Mental Health Act Commn, 2006–09; Member: Disciplinary Panel, Actuarial Profession, 2004–; Audit Cttee, Criminal Injuries Compensation Authy, 2004–08. Leonard Shaw Award for Management Accountancy, Leonard Shaw Meml Fund, 1973.

KNOX, Prof. John Henderson, FRS 1984; FRSE 1971; University Fellow and Emeritus Professor of Physical Chemistry, University of Edinburgh, since 1984; *b* 21 Oct. 1927; *s* of John Knox and Elizabeth May Knox (*née* Henderson); *m* 1957, Josephine Anne Wissler; four *s*. *Educ:* George Watson's Boys' Coll.; Univ. of Edinburgh (BSc 1949, DSc 1963); Univ. of Cambridge (PhD 1953). University of Edinburgh: Lectr in Chemistry, 1953–66; Reader in Physical Chemistry, 1966–74; Director of Wolfson Liquid Chromatography Unit, 1972–92; Personal Prof. of Phys. Chem., 1974–84. Sen. Vis. Research Scientist Fellow, Univ. of Utah, 1964. *Publications:* Gas Chromatography, 1962; Molecular Thermodynamics, 1971, 2nd edn 1978; Applications of High Speed Liquid Chromatography, 1974; High Performance Liquid Chromatography, 1978, 3rd edn 1983. *Recreations:* sailing, hill walking. *Address:* 67 Morningside Park, Edinburgh EH10 5EZ. *T:* (0131) 447 5057.

KNOX, (John) Robert, FSA; cultural consultant, since 2007; *b* Port Alberni, BC, Canada, 4 June 1946; *s* of John Arthur Knox and Rosalind Knox (*née* Kingscote); *m* 1981, Helen Elizabeth Irène Zarb; three *d*. *Educ:* Univ. of Victoria, BC (BA Hons); Emmanuel Coll., Cambridge (MA). Department of Oriental Antiquities, later Department of Asia, British Museum: Asst Keeper, 1978–92; Dep. Keeper, 1992–94; Keeper, 1994–2006. Museum strategic planning and educn work, Afghanistan, Indonesia and Timor Leste, 2007–. Mem. Council, Britain-Nepal Academic Council, 2000–. Mem. Bd Dirs, UK Br., Global Heritage Fund, 2009–11. Trustee, Gurkha Mus., 2000–. FSA 1991 (Vice Pres., 1994–97). *Publications:* Ancient China, 1978; (jtly) India: past into present, 1982; (jtly) Explorations and Excavations in Bannu District, North-West Frontier Province, Pakistan 1985–88, 1991; Amaravati, Buddhist Sculpture from the Great Stupa, 1992; (jtly) Akra, the First Capital of Bannu (NWFP Pakistan), 2000; (jtly) Sheri Khan Tarakai and Early Village Life in the Borderlands of North-West Pakistan: Bannu archaeological project surveys and excavations 1985–2001, 2010; Practical Guide for Museum Revitalisation in Indonesia, 2011; articles in learned jls on archaeol. of India and Pakistan. *Recreations:* walking, music, theatre, classical 78s and vinyl. *E:* jrknox57@gmail.com.

KNOX, Lesley Mary; Chairman, Grosvenor Group Ltd, since 2011; *b* South Africa, 19 Sept. 1953; *d* of Dr Eric Samuel and Vera Samuel; *m* 1991, Brian Knox; one *d*. *Educ:* Churchill Coll., Cambridge (BA Law 1975). Admitted solicitor, 1979. With Slaughter and May, 1976–79; solicitor: Sherman & Sterling, 1979–80; Slaughter and May, 1980–81; Kleinwort Benson, 1981–96: Corp. Finance Dir, 1986; Hd, Instnl Asset Mgt, Kleinwort Benson Investment Mgt, 1991–96; Dir, 1996; Dep. Gov., 1997–98, Gov., 1999, British Linen Bank; Founder Dir, British Linen Advrs, 2000–03; Chm., Alliance Trust, 2004–12. Non-executive Director: Turcan Connell Asset Mgt, 2010–; SAB Miller plc, 2011–; Centrica plc, 2012–. Mem. Adv. Bd, Reform Scotland. Chm., Design Dundee Ltd, 2010–. Hon. DLaws Abertay, 2012. *Recreations:* contemporary art, textile art, opera. *Address:* 10A Circus Lane, Edinburgh EH3 6SU. *E:* lesley.knox@grosvenor.com. *Clubs:* Athenæum; New (Edinburgh).

KNOX, Peter; *see* Knox, S. C. P.

KNOX, Robert; *see* Knox, J. R.

KNOX, Prof. Selby Albert Richard, PhD, DSc; Pro-Vice-Chancellor, University of Bristol, 2004–08; *b* 24 Sept. 1944; *s* of George Henry Knox and Elsie (*née* Stobbart); *m* 1979, Julie Dawn Edwards; one *s* two *d*. *Educ:* Univ. of Bristol (BSc; PhD 1967; DSc 1985). CChem 1990, FRSC 1990. University of Bristol: Prof. of Inorganic Chem., 1990–96, Alfred Capper Pass Prof. of Chem., 1996–2004; Hd, Sch. of Chem., 1992–2001; Hd of Inorganic and Materials Chem., 2001–04. Non-exec. Dir, Univ. Hosps Bristol NHS Foundn Trust, 2008–12. *Publications:* numerous contribs on organometallic chemistry to learned jls. *Recreations:* fly fishing, golf, ski-ing.

KNOX, (Simon Christopher) Peter; QC 2006; *b* London, 21 Jan. 1957; *s* of Oliver Arbuthnot and Patricia Knox; *m* 1987, Teresa (separated 2003); one *s* two *d*. *Educ:* Westminster Sch., London; Wadham Coll., Oxford (BA Hons). Called to the Bar, Middle Temple, 1983. *Recreations:* music, wine. *Address:* 3 Hare Court, Temple, EC4Y 7BJ. *T:* (020) 7415 7800, *Fax:* (020) 7415 7811. *E:* peterknox@3harecourt.com.

KNOX, Timothy Aidan John, FSA; Director, Fitzwilliam Museum, Cambridge, since 2013; Fellow, Gonville and Caius College, Cambridge, since 2013; *b* 9 Aug. 1962; *s* of Andrew Knox and Margaret Barbara Knox (*née* Allen); civil partnership 2006, Robert Todd Longstaffe-Gowan. *Educ:* Ratcliffe Coll., Leics; Courtauld Inst. of Art, Univ. of London (BA Hons). Liby Asst, King's Fund Inst. Liby, 1987–88; Photographic Librarian, Press Assoc., 1988–89; Res. Asst, 1989–91, Asst Curator, 1991–95, RIBA Drawings Collection; Architectural Historian, 1995–2002, Head Curator, 2002–05, NT; Dir, Sir John Soane's Mus., 2005–13. Mem. Editl Bd, 2002–04, Mem. Consultative Cttee, 2005–, Sculpture Jl: Jl of Public Monuments and Sculpture Assoc. Historic Bldgs Advr to FCO, 2005–. Member: Reviewing Cttee on Export of Works of Art, 2002–10; Conseil scientifique de l'Etablissement public du musée et du domaine nat. de Versailles, 2005–09; Adv. Cttee on Design of Coins, Medals, Seals and Decorations, Royal Mint, 2008–; Chm., Acceptance in Lieu Panel, 2011–13. Chm. and Trustee, Mausolea and Monuments Trust, 1997–2004 (Patron, 2008–). Trustee: Monument 85 Trust, 1996–2005; Hall Bequest (Stowe Sch.), 1998–2009; Spitalfields Historic Bldgs Trust, 1999–2005; Pilgrim Trust, 2006–; Stowe House Preservation Trust, 2006–09; Vice-Patron, Public Monuments and Sculpture Assoc., 2012–. Member, Advisory Committee: Moggerhanger House Preservation Trust, 1998–2002; Strawberry Hill Trust, 2007–10; Welbeck Abbey, 2013–; Nat. Heritage Meml Fund, 2014–; Member: Council, Attingham Trust, 2006–14; Soc. of Dilettanti, 2008–; Adv. Bd, Kettle Yard, 2013–. Curator of exhibn, The Return of the Gods: Neoclassical Sculpture in Britain, Tate Britain, 2008. Mem., Editl Bd, Georgian Gp Jl, 2009–. FSA 2006. *Publications:* (contrib.) Artifici d'Aque e Giardini: la cultura delle grotte e dei ninfei in Italiae in Europa, 1999; (contrib.) Enlightenment: discovering the world in the eighteenth century, 2003; (contrib.) Collecting Sculpture in Early Modern Europe, 2008; (contrib.) Follies of Europe: architectural extravaganzas, 2008; Sir John Soane's Museum, London, 2009; The British Ambassador's Residence, Paris, 2011; numerous country house guidebooks; contribs to Apollo, Country Life, Sculpture Jl, Architectural Hist., Georgian Gp Jl, London Gardener. *Recreations:* art and architecture, collecting, smooth-haired miniature dachshunds. *Address:* Malplaquet House, 137–9 Mile End Road, Stepney, E1 4AQ; Grove Lodge, Trumpington Street, Cambridge CB2 1RB.

KNOX-JOHNSTON, Sir William Robert Patrick, (Sir Robin), Kt 1995; CBE 1969; RD (and bar) 1983; Chairman, Clipper Ventures plc, since 1996; *b* 17 March 1939; *s* of late David Robert Knox-Johnston and Elizabeth Mary Knox-Johnston (*née* Cree); *m* 1962, Suzanne (*née* Singer) (*d* 2003); one *d*. *Educ:* Berkhamsted School. Master Mariner; FRIN. Merchant Navy, 1957–69. First person to sail single-handed non-stop Around the World, 14 June 1968 to 22 April 1969, in yacht Suhaili; won Sunday Times Golden Globe, 1969; won Round Britain Race, Ocean Spirit, 1970; won round Britain Race, British Oxygen, 1974; set British transatlantic sailing record, from NY to the Lizard, 11 days 7 hours 45 mins, 1981; established new record of 10 days 14 hours 9 mins, 1986; set world sailing record for around Ireland, 76 hours 5 mins 34 secs, May 1986; World Class II Multihull Champion, 1985; completed Guardian Columbus voyage, 1989; with Peter Blake, set non-stop around the world sailing record, 74 days, 22 hours, 17 mins 22 secs, 1994; Velux 5-Oceans Race, 2006–07; Route du Rhum Race, 2014. Marina consultant, 1974–96; Man. Dir, St Katharine's Yacht Haven Ltd, 1975–76; Director: Mercury Yacht Harbours Ltd, 1970–73; Rank Marine International, 1973–75; Troon Marina Ltd, 1976–83; National Yacht Racing Centre Ltd, 1979–86; Knox-Johnston Insurance Brokers Ltd, 1983–92; St Katherine's Dock, 1975–93 (Man. Dir, 1991–93); Caversham Lake Trust Ltd, 2001–03. Pres., British Olympic Yachting Appeal, 1972–77; Pres. (formerly Chm.), STA, 1993–2001; Pres., Cruising Assoc., 2008–10 (Patron, 2009–); Vice Pres., RNLI, 2009–. Member: Sports Council Lottery Panel, 1995–99; Sport England Council, 1999–2002. Trustee: Nat. Maritime Mus., Greenwich, 1993–2002; Nat. Maritime Mus., Cornwall, 1997–2006; Cutty Sark Trust, 2011–. Younger Brother, Trinity House, 1973. Freeman: Borough of Bromley, Kent, 1969; City of London, 1992. Liveryman, Co. of Master Mariners, 1975. Lt-Comdr RNR 1971, retired. Hon. Life Rear Cdre, RNSA. Fellow, Liverpool John Moores Univ., 2006. Hon. DSc Maine Maritime Acad., 1989; Hon. DTech Nottingham, 1993; Hon. Dr Hull, 2012. Yachtsman of the Year, Yachting Journalists' Assoc., 1969, 1995, 2007, 2015; Silk Cut Seamanship Award, 1990; Seamanship Foundn Trophy, RYA, 1991; Gold Medal, RIN, 1992; ISAF Sailor of the Year, 1994; Blue Water Medal, Cruising Club of America, 2010. *Publications:* A World of my Own, 1969; Sailing, 1975; Twilight of Sail, 1978; Last but not Least, 1978; Bunkside Companion, 1982; Seamanship, 1986; The BOC Challenge 1986–1987, 1988; The Cape of Good Hope, 1989; History of Yachting, 1990; The Columbus Venture, 1991 (Book of the Sea Award); Sea, Ice and Rock, 1992; Cape Horn, 1994; Beyond Jules Verne, 1995; Force of Nature, 2007; Knox-Johnston on Sailing, 2009. *Recreations:* sailing, maritime history. *Address:* 1 Tower Street, Old Portsmouth, Hampshire PO1 2JR. *Clubs:* Little Ship (Pres.); Royal Yacht Squadron (Hon. Mem.) (Cowes); Royal Harwich Yacht (Hon. Mem.); Royal Western Yacht (Hon. Mem.); Royal Southampton Yacht (Hon. Mem.); Royal Southern Yacht (Hon. Mem.); Benfleet Yacht (Hon. Mem.); Liverpool Yacht (Hon. Mem.); Royal Irish Yacht (Hon. Life Mem., 1969) (Dublin); Howth Yacht (Hon. Mem.) (Eire); Royal Bombay Yacht (Hon. Mem.); Nat. Yacht (Hon. Mem.) (Dublin); Royal North of Ireland Yacht (Hon. Mem.); Royal Southern Yacht (Hon. Mem.); Island Sailing Yacht (Hon. Mem.); Portsmouth Sailing; Erith Yacht (Hon. Mem.); Royal St George Yacht (Hon. Mem.) (Dublin); RNVR Yacht (Hon. Mem.); Cruising Assoc. (Hon. Mem.); Ocean Cruising; Royal Ocean Racing.

KNOX-LECKY, Maj.-Gen. Samuel, CB 1979; OBE 1967; BSc(Eng); CEng, FIMechE; Director-General, Agricultural Engineers Association, 1980–88; *b* 10 Feb. 1926; *s* of late J. D. Lecky, Coleraine; *m* 1947, Sheila Jones (*d* 2015); one *s* two *d*. *Educ:* Coleraine Acad.; Queen's Univ., Belfast (BSc). Commnd REME, 1946; served Egypt, 1951–52; Kenya, 1953–54; jssc 1964; AA&QMG HQ 1(BR) Corps, 1965–66; CREME 4 Div., 1966–68; Sec., Principal Personnel Officers, MoD, 1968–70; RCDS, 1971; Comdt, SEME, 1972–74; DEME, BAOR, 1975; Dir, Military Assistance Office, MoD, 1976–77; Minister (DS), British Embassy, Tehran, 1977–79. Hon. Col, QUB OTC, 1978–83; Col Comdt, REME, 1980–86. *Recreations:* fishing, sailing.

KNUSSEN, (Stuart) Oliver, CBE 1994; composer and conductor; Music Director, London Sinfonietta, 1998–2002, now Conductor Laureate; *b* Glasgow, 12 June 1952; *s* of Stuart Knussen and Ethelyn Jane Alexander; *m* 1972, Susan Freedman (*d* 2003); one *d*. *Educ:* Watford Field Sch.; Watford Boys' Grammar Sch.; Purcell Sch. Private composition study with John Lambert, 1963–68; Countess of Munster Awards, 1964, 1965, 1967; Peter Stuyvesant Foundn Award, 1965; début conducting Symph. no 1 with LSO, 1968; Watney-Sargent award for Young Conductors, 1969; Fellowships to Berkshire Music Center, Tanglewood, 1970, 1971, 1973; Caird Trav. Schol., 1971; Margaret Grant Composition Prize (Symph. no 2), Tanglewood, 1971; study with Gunther Schuller in USA, 1970–73; Koussevitzky Centennial Commn, 1974; Composer-in-residence: Aspen Fest., 1976; Arnolfini Gall., 1978; Instr in composition, RCM Jun. Dept, 1977–82; BBC commn for Proms 1979 (Symph. no 3); Co-Artistic Dir, Aldeburgh Fest., 1983–98; Berkshire Music Center, Tanglewood: Guest Teacher, 1981; Composer-in-residence, 1986; Co-ordinator of Contemporary Music Activities, 1986–90. Arts Council Bursaries, 1979, 1981; winner, first Park Lane Gp Composer award (suite from Where the Wild Things Are), 1982; BBC commn for Glyndebourne Opera, 1983. Frequent guest conductor, Philharmonia Orch., many other ensembles, UK and abroad, 1981–; Dir, Almeida Ensemble, 1986; Associate Guest Conductor, 1989–, Artist in Association, 2009–12, BBC SO; Artist in Association, Birmingham Contemp. Music Gp, 2006; Associate Artist, S Bank Centre, 2006. Mem. Exec. Cttee, SPNM, 1978–85; Member: Leopold Stokowski Soc.; International Alban Berg Soc., New York; Hon. Mem., AAAL, 1994. RPS Conductor Award, 2010. *Publications* include: Symphony no 1 op. 1, 1966–67; Symphony no 2 op. 7, 1970–71; Symphony no 3 op. 18, 1973–79; Where the Wild Things Are—opera (Maurice Sendak), op. 20, 1979–83 (staged, Glyndebourne at NT, 1984); Higglety Pigglety Pop!—opera (Sendak), op. 21, 1983–85 (staged Glyndebourne, 1984 and 1985); Horn Concerto, 1994 (commnd for Barry Tuckwell); numerous orchestral, chamber, vocal works; articles in Tempo, The Listener, etc. *Recreations:* cinema, record collecting, record producing, visual arts. *Address:* c/o Faber Music Ltd, Bloomsbury House, 74–77 Great Russell Street, WC1B 3DA; c/o HarrisonParrott Ltd, 5–6 Albion Court, Albion Place, W6 0QT.

KNUTSFORD, 6th Viscount *cr* 1895; **Michael Holland-Hibbert;** Bt 1853; Baron 1888; *b* 27 Dec. 1926; *s* of Hon. Wilfrid Holland-Hibbert (*d* 1961) (2nd *s* of 3rd Viscount) and of Audrey, *d* of late Mark Fenwick; *S* cousin, 1986; *m* 1951, Hon. Sheila, *d* of 5th Viscount Portman; two *s* one *d*. *Educ:* Eton College; Trinity Coll., Cambridge (BA). Welsh Guards, 1945–48. SW Regional Director, Barclays Bank, 1956–86. National Trust: Chm. Cttee for Devon and Cornwall, 1973–86; Mem. Exec. Cttee, 1973–86; Mem. Council, 1979–85; Mem. Finance Cttee, 1986–99. DL 1977, High Sheriff 1977–78, Devon. *Heir: er s* Hon. Henry Thurstan Holland-Hibbert [*b* 6 April 1959; *m* 1988, Katherine, *d* of Sir John Ropner, Bt, *qv*; two *s* two *d*]. *Address:* Munden, Watford, Herts WD25 8PZ. *Club:* Brooks's.

KOBAYASHI, Prof. Makoto, PhD; Professor, 1985–2003, Professor Emeritus, 2006, and Director, Institute of Particle and Nuclear Science, 2003–06, High Energy Accelerator Research Organisation, Tsukuba, Japan (formerly National Laboratory for High Energy Physics); *b* Nagoya, Japan, 7 April 1944; *s* of Hisashi Kobayashi and Ai Kobayashi (*née* Kaifu); *m* 1st, 1975, Sachiko Enomoto (decd); one *s*; 2nd, 1990, Emiko Nakayama; one *d*. *Educ:* Nagoya Univ. (BS 1967; PhD 1972). Res. Associate, Physics Dept, Kyoto Univ., 1972–79; Associate Prof., 1979–85, Hd of Physics Div. II, 1989–2003, Nat. Lab. for High Energy Physics, later High Energy Accelerator Res. Exec. Dir, Japan Soc. for the Promotion of Sci., 2007. Orgn. Nishina Meml Prize, Nishina Foundn, 1979; J. J. Sakurai Prize, Amer. Physical Soc., 1985; Japan Acad. Prize, 1985; Person of Cultural Merit, 2001, Order of Culture, 2008,

Japan; High Energy Particle Physics Prize, Eur. Phys. Soc., 2007; (jtly) Nobel Prize in Physics, 2008. *Address:* c/o High Energy Accelerator Research Organisation (KEK), 1–1 Oho, Tsukuba, Ibaraki 305–0801, Japan.

KOBBORG, Johan; ballet dancer; Director, Romanian National Ballet, since 2014; *b* Odense, Denmark; *s* of Martinus Vedel Kobborg and Käthe Kobborg. *Educ:* Royal Danish Ballet Sch. Joined Royal Danish Ballet, 1991, Principal, 1994–99; Principal, Royal Ballet, 1999–2013. Guest dancer with Mariinsky Ballet, Bolshoi Ballet, La Scala Ballet, Nat. Ballet of Canada, Stuttgart Ballet, Hamburg Ballet and Teatro San Carlo, Naples. Performances include main rôles in La Sylphide, Swan Lake, The Nutcracker, Coppélia, Romeo and Juliet, Giselle, Sleeping Beauty, Don Quixote, Onegin, Cinderella, Anastasia, The Dream, Masquerade and Manon. *Address:* c/o Romanian National Ballet, Bucharest National Opera House, Boulevard Mihail Kogălniceanu 70–72, Section 5, Bucharest, Romania.

KOBILKA, Prof. Brian Kent, MD; Professor of Medicine, Cardiology and Molecular and Cellular Physiology, since 1989, and Helene Irwin Fagan Chair in Cardiology, Stanford University School of Medicine; *b* Little Falls, Minnesota, 30 May 1955; *s* of Franklyn Kobilka and Elisabeth Kobilka; *m* 1978, Tong Sun Thian; one *s* one *d*. *Educ:* Univ. of Minnesota (BS Biol. and Chem. 1977); Yale Univ. (MD 1981). Clin. trng as Sen. Resident in Internal Medicine, Barnes Hosp., Washington Univ. Med. Center, St Louis, Missouri, 1981–84; Cardiol. Res. Fellow, 1984–89, Asst Prof., 1988–89, Dept of Medicine, Duke Univ. Med. Center; Investigator, Howard Hughes Med. Inst., 1987–2003. Co-Founder, ConfometRX. Mem., NAS, 2011. (Jtly) Nobel Prize in Chemistry, 2012. *Publications:* contribs to learned jls incl. Nature. *Address:* School of Medicine, Stanford University, 157 Beckman Center, 279 Campus Drive, Stanford, CA 94305–5345, USA.

KOCIENSKI, Prof. Philip Joseph, PhD; FRS 1997; FRSE; FRSC; Professor and Head of Department of Organic Chemistry, University of Leeds, 2000–09, now Emeritus Professor; *b* 23 Dec. 1946; *s* of Philip Joseph Kocienski and Marian Edyth (*née* Peters); *m* 1st, 1967, Anna Petruso (marr. diss. 1987); one *s* one *d*; 2nd, 1987, Joanna Davie. *Educ:* Brown Univ., Providence, RI (PhD 1973). FRSC 1995; FRSE 1998. Lectr, Leeds Univ., 1979–85; Prof. of Chemistry, Southampton Univ., 1985–97. Regius Prof. of Chemistry, Glasgow Univ., 1997–2000. Mem., EPSRC, 1999. For. Mem., Polish Acad. of Sci., 2000. Hon. Dr Univ. Paul Cézanne, Aix-Marseille, 2009. Marie Sklodowska Curie Medal, Polish Chem. Soc., 1997. *Publications:* Protecting Groups, 1994; numerous res. papers in learned jls. *Recreations:* Russian and Eastern European music, violin. *Address:* Department of Chemistry, Leeds University, Leeds LS2 9JT. *T:* (0113) 343 6555.

KOFFMANN, Pierre; chef, Koffmann's, since 2010; *b* 21 Aug. 1948; *s* of Albert and Germaine Koffmann; *m* 1972, Annie Barrau (decd); one *d*. *Educ:* Ecole Jean Jacques Rousseau, Tarbes. Mil. Service, 1967–69. Commis: L'Aubette, Strasbourg, 1966; Grand Hôtel Palais, Juan les Pins, 1967; Le Provençal, La Ciotat, 1969–70; La Voile d'Or, Lausanne, 1970; Le Gavroche, 1970–71; Chef: Brasserie Benoist, London, 1971; Waterside Inn, Bray, 1971–77; Proprietor, La Tante Claire, 1977–2002. *Publications:* Memories of Gascony, 1990, 2012; La Tante Claire: recipes from a master chef, 1992.

KOHL, Dr Helmut; Grosskreuz Verdienstorden, 1979; Member, Bundestag, 1976–2002; Chancellor, Federal Republic of Germany, 1982–98 (re-elected, 1991, as Chancellor of reunited Germany); *b* 3 April 1930; *s* of Hans and Cäcilie Kohl; *m* 1960, Hannelore Renner (*d* 2001); two *s*; *m* 2008, Maike Richter. *Educ:* Frankfurt Univ.; Heidelberg Univ. (Dr phil 1958 Heidelberg). On staff of a Trade Assoc., 1958–59; Mem., Parlt of Rhineland Palatinate, 1959–76; Leader, CDU Parly Party in Rhineland Palatinate Parlt, 1963–69; Mem., Federal Exec. Cttee of CDU at federal level, 1964–98; Chairman: CDU, Rhineland Palatinate, 1966–74; CDU, 1973–98; Minister-President, Rhineland Palatinate, 1969–76; Leader of the Opposition, Bundestag, 1976–82. Numerous foreign decorations. *Publications:* Die politische Entscheidung in der Pfalz und das Wiedererstehen der Parteien nach 1945, 1958; Hausputz hinter den Fassaden, 1971; Zwischen Ideologie und Pragmatismus, 1973; Die CDU: Porträt einer Volkspartei, 1981; Der Weg zur Wende, 1983; Reden 1982–1984, 1984; Die Deutsche Einheit, 1992; Der Kurs der CDU, 1993; Mein Tagebuch 1998–2000, 2000. *Address:* Büro Bundeskanzler a. D. Dr Helmut Kohl, Deutscher Bundestag, Unter den Linden 71, 10117 Berlin, Germany.

KÖHLER, Dr Horst; President, Federal Republic of Germany, 2004–10; *b* 22 Feb. 1943; *s* of Eduard and Elisa Köhler; *m* 1969, Eva Luise Bohnet; one *s* one *d*. *Educ:* Tübingen Univ. (PhD Econs and Pol Sci. 1977). Inst. for Applied Econ. Res., 1969–76; economist, German Federal Min. of Econs, 1976–80; Advr to Ministerpräsident, Chancellery, Schleswig-Holstein, 1981–82; German Federal Min. of Finance, 1982–93 (Permanent Under Sec., 1990–93); Pres., German Savings Banks Assoc., 1993–98; Pres., EBRD, 1998–2000; Man. Dir, IMF, 2000–04.

KOHLHAUSSEN, Martin; Chairman, Supervisory Board, Commerzbank AG, 2001–08; *b* 6 Nov. 1935; *m*; three *c*. *Educ:* Univs of Frankfurt (Main), Freiburg, Marburg (Law). Worked domestically in banking, Frankfurt and Hanau (Br. Manager), 1965–76; worked internationally in banking (Br. Manager), Tokyo and New York, 1976–81. Mem., 1982–2001, Chm., 1991–2001, Bd of Man. Dirs, Commerzbank AG. *Address:* c/o Commerzbank AG, 60261 Frankfurt, Germany. *T:* (69) 13620.

KOHLI, Jitinder; Director, Deloitte Consulting, since 2012; *b* 2 Feb. 1973; *s* of Inder Pal and Swarn Kohli. *Educ:* Univ. of Oxford (BA Hons PPE 1995); Southampton Univ. (BSc Sociol. and Soc. Policy 1996). Co-ordinator, Oxford Access Scheme, 1992–93; DTI, 1996–98; Cabinet Office: Econ. and Domestic Secretariat, 1998–99; Prime Minister's Strategy Unit, 1999–2000; Productivity and Structural Reform Team, HM Treasury, 2000–02; Hd, Community Cohesion Unit, Home Office, 2002–03; Hd, Productivity and Structural Reform Team, HM Treasury, 2003–04; Dir, Active Communities, Home Office, 2004–05; Chief Exec., Better Regulation Exec., Cabinet Office, later at BERR, then BIS, 2005–09; Dir Gen., Strategy and Communications, BIS, 2009. Non-exec. Dir, Circle Anglia Housing Gp, 2003–09; Chm. of Trustees, EPIC Trust, 2005–09; Trustee, Adventure Capital Fund, 2008–09. Sen Fellow, Center for American Progress, 2009–; Fellow: Young Foundn, 2009–; Nat. Acad. of Public Admin, 2012. Mem., Editl Bd, Public Admin Rev., 2013–. *Address:* Deloitte Consulting, 1919 North Lynn Street, Arlington, VA 22209, USA.

KOHN, David; Director, David Kohn Architects, since 2007; *b* Cape Town, SA, 3 Oct. 1972; *s* of Richard and Gerda Kohn; *m* 2011, Margherita Laera; one *d*. *Educ:* Loughborough Grammar Sch.; Jesus Coll., Cambridge (BA 1994; DipArch). Associate, Caruso St John Associates, 2002–06. Projects include: Stable Acre, 2010; Thomas Dane Gall., 2011; The White Building, 2012; A Room for London, 2012; Sotheby's S|2 Gall., 2013; Apartment on Carrer Avinyó, 2013. *Recreations:* contemporary art, travel. *Address:* David Kohn Architects, 39–51 Highgate Road, NW5 1RT. *T:* (020) 7424 8596.

KOHN, Sir Ralph, Kt 2010; Chairman, Harley Street Holdings Ltd, since 1998; medical scientist, musician and baritone; *b* Leipzig, 9 Dec. 1927; *s* of Marcus Kohn and Lena Kohn (*née* Aschheim); *m* 1963, Zahava Kanarek; three *d*. *Educ:* primary sch., Amsterdam; Manchester Univ. (BSc, MSc; WildPrize for Pharmacol., 1953; PhD 1954); Princeton Univ. FRPharmS (FPS 1952). Charter Travelling Fellow, 1954–56, Paterno Fellow, 1956–57, Inst. of Health, Rome; Riker Fellow, Albert Einstein Coll. of Medicine, NY, 1957–58; Head, exploratory pharmacology, Smith Kline & French Labs, UK, 1958–65; Man. Dir, UK subsid. of Robapharm AG, 1965–71; estabd Adv. Services (Clinical and Gen.) Ltd, first co. in Adv. Services Hldgs Gp, 1971; Man. Dir, Adv. Services Hldgs Gp, 1971–98 (Queen's Award for Export Achievement, to Gp, 1990). Bynum Tudor Lectr and Vis. Fellow, Kellogg Coll., Oxford, 2008. Med. Advr, Nat. Osteoporosis Soc., 1986– (Founder Mem., 1986; Mem., Med. Adv. Gp, 1994–); Mem. Exec. Cttee, Brit. Digestive Foundn, 1997–. Chm. Cttee, Sir John Eliot Gardiner's Millennium Bach Cantata Pilgrimage, 2000. Member: President's Circle, Royal Soc., 1997– (Mem., Royal Soc. 350th Anniv. Campaign Bd, 2007); Cttee, Sir Henry Dale Prize, Royal Instn, 2003–; RSocMed; RPSGB; Brit. Pharmacol Soc.; RSH; CRUK, 2004–; Vice-Chancellor's Circle, Univ. of Oxford, 2015–. Has given numerous recitals and performances with orchestras in UK and abroad, incl. concerts at Wigmore Hall, Purcell Room, St John's, Smith Sq., Queen Elizabeth Hall and Royal Albert Hall; orchestral broadcasts for radio; has made numerous recordings; lectures on medical, scientific and musical topics incl. Council for Assisting Refugee Academics 75th Anniv. Lect., Royal Soc., 2008; Lect., Imperial Coll., 2009; A. V. Hill Lect., Manchester Univ., 2009; Lect., Harvard Univ., 2010. Chairman: Cttee, Wigmore Hall Internat. Song Comp., 1997–2004; Wigmore Hall/ Kohn Foundn Internat. Song Comp., 2006–. Founder Mem., Jewish Music Inst., 2000–; Member: Curatorium Bach Archiv, Leipzig, 2003–; Cttee, RAM Annual Bach Prize, 2006; Cttee, Imperial Coll. Annual Sir Ernst Chain Prize, 2003; Cttee, Royal Soc. Kohn Award for Excellence in Engaging the Public with Science, 2006. Chm. Trustees, Kohn Foundn, 1991–; Trustee: Rudolf Kempe Soc., 1998–; Foundn for Liver Res., Inst. of Hepatology, 2011–; Wigmore Hall, 2015–; Hon. Trustee, 2001–, Patron, 2015–, Monteverdi Choir and Orch. Pres., Birmingham and Midland Inst., 2011– (Pres. Elect, 2009–11). Hon. FRAM 2003; Hon. FMedSci 2003; Hon. FRS 2006; Hon. FBPhS (Hon. FBPharmacolS 2008); Hon. FRCP 2009; Hon. Life Fellow, Royal Instn, 2002. Hon. Fellow, Chorherren Foundn, St Thomas's, Leipzig, 2003. Hon. MAE 2008. Hon. MusD Manchester, 2009; Hon. DMus London, 2014; Hon. DSc: Salford, 2009; Buckingham, 2014. Medal of Honour of City of Leipzig, 2011; Cross, Order of Merit (Germany), 2014. *Recreations:* music, chess, literature. *Address:* 50 West Heath Road, NW3 7UR. *T:* (020) 8458 2037, (office) (020) 7436 6001. *Club:* Athenæum.

KOHN, Prof. Walter, PhD; Professor of Physics, 1984–91, now Emeritus, and Research Professor, since 1991, University of California at Santa Barbara; *b* Vienna, 9 March 1923; *s* of Salomon and Gittel Kohn; *m* 1st, 1948, Lois Mary Adams; three *d*; 2nd, 1978, Maia Schiff. *Educ:* Univ. of Toronto (BA Math. and Physics 1945; MA Applied Math. 1946); Harvard Univ. (PhD Physics 1948; Lehman Fellow). Indust. Physicist (pt-time), Sutton Horsley Co., 1941–43; Geophysicist (pt-time), Koulomzine, Quebec, 1944–46; Instr, Dept of Physics, Harvard Univ., 1948–50; Asst Prof., 1950–53, Associate Prof., 1953–56, Prof., 1956–60, Dept of Physics, Carnegie Mellon Univ.; Prof., 1960–79, and Chm., 1961–63, Dept of Physics, UCSD; Dir, Inst. of Theoretical Physics, UCSB, 1979–84. Consultant: Westinghouse Res. Lab., 1953–57; Bell Telephone Labs, 1953–66; Gen. Atomic, 1960–72; IBM, 1978. Oersted Fellow, Copenhagen, 1951–52; Sen. NSF Fellow, Imperial Coll., London, 1958; Guggenheim Fellow, Paris, 1963. Member: Amer. Acad. of Arts and Scis, 1963–; NAS, 1969–; Reactor Div., Nat. Inst. of Sci. and Technol., 1946–98; Bd of Govs, Tel Aviv Univ.; Bd of Govs, Weizmann Inst., 1996–. Numerous hon. doctorates. Buckley Medal, 1960, Davisson-Germer Prize, 1977, APS; Feenberg Medal, 1991; Nobel Prize for Physics, 1998; Niels Bohr Medal, UNESCO, 1998. *Publications:* more than 200 articles and reviews in Phys. Review, Phys. Review Letters, Review of Modern Phys., etc. *Recreations:* listening to classical music, reading, going for walks, roller blading. *Address:* Department of Physics, Broida Hall, University of California at Santa Barbara, Santa Barbara, CA 93106–9530, USA. *T:* (805) 8933061.

KOK, William, (Wim); Prime Minister and Minister for General Affairs, the Netherlands, 1994–2002; Member, International Commission on Missing Persons, since 2002; *b* 29 Sept. 1938. *Educ:* Nijenrode Business Sch. Mil. Service, 1959–60. Netherlands Federation of Trade Unions: Asst Internat. Officer, Construction Div., 1961–65; Mem. for Econ. Affairs, 1965–67; Union Sec., 1967–69; Sec., 1969–72; Dep. Chm., 1972–73; Chm., 1973–85. Leader, Parly Labour Party, and Mem., Lower House, Netherlands, 1986–89, re-elected 1994, and 1998; Dep. Prime Minister and Minister of Finance, 1989–94. Vice Chm. of Bd, Netherlands Bank. Member, Supervisory Board: ING Gp, 2003–09; PostNL (formerly TNT NV), 2003–; Royal Dutch Shell plc, 2003–05 (non-exec. Dir, 2004–11); KLM Royal Dutch Airlines, 2003–. Chm., ETUC, 1979–82. Mem., Adv. Bd, Eur. Assoc. History Educators (Euroclio).

KOLADE, Christopher Olusola, CON 2000; Pro-Chancellor, Pan-Atlantic (formerly Pan-African) University, 2009–15; *b* 28 Dec. 1932; *s* of Abraham and Lydia Kolade; *m* Beatrice; two *d*. *Educ:* Fourah Bay Coll., Sierra Leone (BA, DipEd). Educn Officer, 1955–60; Controller, 1960–72, Dir-Gen., 1972–78, Nigerian Broadcasting Corp.; Dir, 1978–89, CEO, 1989–93, Chm., 1993–2002, Cadbury Nigeria; High Comr for Nigeria in UK, 2002–07. Lectr, Lagos Business Sch., 1995. Hon. DCL 1976. *Recreations:* church music, lawn tennis, walking. *Address:* c/o Pan-Atlantic University, Km 22 Lekki-Epe Expressway, Ajah, Lagos, Nigeria.

KOLANKIEWICZ, Prof. Jerzy, (George), PhD; Professor of Sociology with special reference to Central Europe, 1999–2011, now Emeritus, and Director, 2001–06, School of Slavonic and East European Studies, University College London; Managing Director, ESRC/ AHRC/HEFCE Centre for East European Language Based Area Studies, 2006–11; *b* 10 April 1946; *s* of late Józef and of Janina Kolankiewicz; *m* 1977, Danuta Elzbieta Manthey; one *s* one *d*. *Educ:* Salesian Coll., Farnborough; Univ. of Leeds (BA 1st cl. Hons 1968); Univ. of Essex (PhD 1984). Res. Officer, Univ. of Essex, 1969–71; Lecturer in Sociology: UC, Swansea, 1971–72; Univ. of Essex, 1972–99. Fellow, Woodrow Wilson Internat. Center for Scholars, Smithsonian Instn, Washington, DC, 1986–87. Dir, E-W Prog., ESRC, 1990–96; Member: Econ. and Social Cttee on Overseas Res., DFID, 1994–2000; HEFCE Chief Executive's Strategically Important Subjects Adv. Gp, 2005. Mem. Governing Body, British Assoc. for Central and Eastern Europe, 2002–08. Dep. Pres., Polish Educnl Soc., 2002–11. Member: Internat. Adv. Bd, Inst. of Global and Eur. Integration, Corvinus Univ., Budapest, 2010–; Excellence Initiative Review Panel, Humanities and Social Scis, German Res. Foundn, Bonn, 2012; Speaker, XXI Economic Forum, Krynica-Zdroj, Poland, 2011; Centenary MB Grabowski Meml Lect., Sch. of Slavonic and E Eur. Studies, UCL, 2015. Mem., Hon. Cttee, V Jubilee Edn, Internat. Fest. of Music, Music on the Peaks, Zakopane, Poland, 2013–15. Diploma of Polish Min. of Foreign Affairs, 2007. Comdr's Cross and Star, Order of Merit (Poland), 2004; Officer's Cross, Order of Merit (Hungary), 2006. *Publications:* (with D. Lane) Social Groups in Polish Society, 1973; (with P. Lewis) Poland: politics, economics and society, 1988; Towards a Sociology of the Transition: rights, resources and social integration in Poland, 2000; (ed with T. Zarycki) Regional Issues in Polish Politics, 2003; (contrib.) Oxford Companion to Comparative Politics, 2012; contribs to British Jl Sociol., Internat. Affairs, Daedalus, E European Politics and Societies, Sociologia Ruralis. *Recreations:* walking (Lake District, Tatras), swimming, opera. *E:* george.kolankiewicz@btinternet.com.

KOLBERT, His Honour Colin Francis; Assistant Surveillance Commissioner, 2001–13; Deputy Chairman, Regulatory Decisions Committee, Financial Services Authority, 2001–06; *b* 3 June 1936; *s* of late Arthur Richard Alexander Kolbert and Dorothy Elizabeth Kolbert (*née* Fletcher); *m* 1959, Jean Fairgrieve Abson; two *d*. *Educ:* Queen Elizabeth's, Barnet; St Catharine's Coll., Cambridge (Harold Samuel Schol., 1959; BA 1959; PhD 1962; MA 1963). FCIArb 1997. RA, 1954–56. Called to the Bar, Lincoln's Inn, 1961, Bencher, 2005; a Recorder, SE Circuit, 1985–88; a Circuit Judge, 1988–95. Oxford University: Fellow and Tutor in Jurisprudence, St Peter's Coll., 1964–68 (MA, DPhil (Oxon) by incorp., 1964); CUF Lectr, Faculty of Law, 1965–68; Cambridge University: Fellow, Magdalene Coll., 1968–

(Tutor, 1969–88); Univ. Lectr in Law, Dept of Land Economy, 1969–88; Sec., Faculty of Music, 1969–75; Coll. Rugby Administrator, CURUFC, 1982–88 (Trustee, 1989–2012); Mem. CUCC Cttee, 1996–. Vis. Prof. and Moderator, Univs of Ife, Lagos, Enugu, and Ahmadu Bello, Nigeria, 1970–80. Ind. Bd Mem., 1995–2000, Chm., Disciplinary Tribunal, 1995–2001, SFA. Mem., Cambridge City Council, 1970–74. Member: Istituto di Diritto Agrario Internazionale e Comparato, Florence, 1964–; Secretariat, World Conf. on Agrarian Reform and Rural Develt, FAO Rome, 1978–79 (Customary Land Tenure Consultant, 1974–80). Freeman, City of London, 1998; Liveryman, Wax Chandlers' Co., 1999– (Master, 2009–10). Governor: Wellingborough Sch., 1970–80; Cranleigh Sch., 1970–88; Glenalmond Coll., 1978–89; Hurstpierpoint Coll., 1978–89; Wisbech GS, 2001–10; Feoffee, Chetham's Hosp. and Library, 1993–2010. Violin music critic, Records and Recording, 1972–78. *Publications:* (trans. and ed) The Digest of Justinian, 1979, 4th edn 1993; various legal and musical. *Recreations:* music (especially playing the violin), cricket, Rugby, military history, cooking, walking in London and Yorkshire. *Address:* Magdalene College, Cambridge CB3 0AG; Outer Temple Chambers, 222 Strand, Temple, WC2R 1BA. *Clubs:* MCC, Farmers; Hawks (Cambridge); Cambridge University Rugby Union Football; Colonsay Golf.

KOLTAI, Ralph, CBE 1983; RDI 1984; freelance stage designer; designer for Drama, Opera and Dance, since 1950; Associate Designer, Royal Shakespeare Company, 1963–66 and since 1976; *b* 31 July 1924; Hungarian-German; *s* of Dr(med) Alfred Koltai and Charlotte Koltai (*née* Weinstein); *m* 1st, 1956, Annena Stubbs (marr. diss. 1976); 2nd, 2008, Jane Alexander. *Educ:* Central Sch. of Art and Design (Dip. with Dist.). Served British Intelligence, Nuremberg Trials and War Crimes Interrogation Unit, 1946–47. Early work entirely in field of opera. First production, Angelique, for London Opera Club, Fortune Theatre, 1950. Designs for The Royal Opera House, Sadler's Wells, Scottish Opera, National Welsh Opera, The English Opera Group. First of 7 ballets for Ballet Rambert, Two Brothers, 1958. Head, Sch. of Theatre Design, Central Sch. of Art & Design, 1965–72. *Productions:* RSC: The Caucasian Chalk Circle, 1962; The Representative, 1963; The Birthday Party, Endgame, The Jew of Malta, 1964; The Merchant of Venice, Timon of Athens, 1965; Little Murders, 1967; Major Barbara, 1970; Too True To Be Good, 1975; Old World, 1976; Wild Oats, 1977; The Tempest, Love's Labour's Lost, 1978; Hippolytus, Baal, 1979; Romeo and Juliet, Hamlet, 1980; The Love Girl and the Innocent, 1981 (London Drama Critics Award); Much Ado About Nothing, Molière, 1982; Custom of the Country, Cyrano de Bergerac (SWET Award), 1983; Troilus and Cressida, Othello, 1985; They Shoot Horses, Don't They?, 1987; for National Theatre: an "all male" As You Like It, 1967; Back to Methuselah, 1969; State of Revolution, 1977; Brand (SWET Award), The Guardsman, 1978; Richard III, The Wild Duck, 1979; Man and Superman, 1981; *other notable productions include: opera:* for Sadler's Wells/English National Opera: The Rise and Fall of the City of Mahagonny, 1963; From the House of the Dead, 1965; Bluebeard's Castle, 1972; Wagner's (complete) Ring Cycle, 1973; Seven Deadly Sins, 1978; Anna Karenina, 1981; Pacific Overtures, 1987; for The Royal Opera House: Taverner, 1972; The Ice Break, 1977; Tannhäuser, Sydney, 1973; Wozzeck, Netherlands Opera, 1973; Fidelio, Munich, 1974; Verdi's Macbeth, Edinburgh Festival, 1976; Les Soldats, Lyon Opera, 1983; Italian Girl in Algiers, 1984, Tannhäuser, 1986, Geneva; (also dir.) Flying Dutchman, Hong Kong, 1987; La Traviata, Hong Kong, 1990, Stockholm, 1993; The Makropulos Affair, Oslo, 1991; Otello, Essen, 1994; Madam Butterfly, Tokyo, 1995; Simon Boccanegra, WNO, and Carmen, Royal Albert Hall, 1997; Dalibor, Scottish Opera and Nabucco, Chorégie Orange, 1998; Don Giovanni, Kirov, 1999; Genoveva, Opera North, 2000; Katya Kabanova, Venice, 2003; Simon Boccanegra, Tel Aviv, 2003, Prague, 2013; The Barber of Seville, The Marriage of Figaro, Figaro Gets a Divorce, WNO, 2016; *theatre:* Pack of Lies, Lyric, 1983; Across from the Garden of Allah, Comedy, 1986; Twelfth Night, Theatre Royal, Copenhagen, 1996; Midsummer Night's Dream, and Macbeth, Teater Gladsaxe, Copenhagen, 1998; (also dir.) Suddenly Last Summer, Nottingham Playhouse, 1998; The Romans in Britain, Crucible Th., Sheffield, 2006; An English Tragedy, Watford, 2008; Erwartung (workshop), Nicosia, 2009; for Aalborg Theatre, Denmark: Threepenny Opera, 1979; The Love Girl and the Innocent, 1980; Terra Nova, 1981; The Carmelites, 1981; Mahagonny, 1984; *musicals:* Billy, Drury Lane, 1974; Bugsy Malone, Her Majesty's, 1983; Dear Anyone, Cambridge Theatre, 1983; Carrie, Stratford, NY, 1988; Metropolis, Piccadilly, 1989; My Fair Lady, NY, 1993; *ballet:* The Planets, Royal Ballet, 1990; Cruel Garden, 1992; has worked in most countries in Western Europe, also Bulgaria, Argentine, USA, Canada, Australia, Japan. Retrospective exhibition, London, Beijing, HK, Taipei, Prague, 1997–99; exhibitions: Landscapes of the Theatre, Tokyo, 2003; Designer for the Stage, NT, 2004; Metal Collages/Sculptures, NT, 2010; Ralph Koltai State II, Royal Welsh College of Music and Drama, 2016. Workshop and public lecture, Hong Kong Acad. for Performing Arts, 2013; lectures, Nat. Acad. of Chinese Th. Arts, Beijing, 2013. Fellow: London Inst., 1996; Hong Kong Acad. for Performing Arts, 2010; Rose Bruford Coll.; FRSA. London Drama Critics Award, Designer of the Year, 1967 (for Little Murders and As You Like It); (jtly) Gold Medal, Internat. Exhibn of Stage Design, Prague Quadriennale, 1975, 1979; Individual Silver Medal, Prague Quadriennale, 1987; Special Award for Dist. Service to the Theater, USA, 1993. *Publications:* Ralph Koltai: designer for the stage, 1997. *Recreation:* wildlife photography. *Address:* c/o Berlin Associates, 7 Tyers Gate, SE1 3HX. *T:* (020) 7836 1112.

KOLVIN, Philip Alan; QC 2009; barrister; *b* Edinburgh, 4 Aug. 1961; *s* of Prof. Israel Kolvin and Rona Kolvin; *m* 1991, Dr Laurie Ann Johnston; two *d*. *Educ:* Balliol Coll., Oxford (BA Juris. 1983; MA 2004). Called to the Bar, Inner Temple, 1985; Cornerstone Barristers (formerly Chambers of Mark Lowe, QC), 1994–, Hd of Chambers, 2014–; Associate Mem., Kings Chambers, Manchester, 2011–14. Co-opted expert, Commn for a Sustainable London, 2010–12. Chairman: Inst. of Licensing, 2004–11 (Patron, 2011–); Purple Flag, 2007–. Chairman: Crystal Palace Campaign, 1998–2004; Civic Trust, 2007–09; Best Bar None, 2012–; Trustee, CPRE, 2004–07. FRSA 2010. *Publications:* Saving Open Space, 2004; Licensed Premises: law, practice and policy, 2005, 2nd edn 2013; Gambling for Local Authorities: licensing, planning and regeneration, 2007, 2nd edn 2010; Sex Licensing, 2010; (ed) Atkins Court Forms (Licensing), 2011; (ed) Encyclopedia of Forms and Precedents (Licensing), 2014; (ed) Cornerstone on Councillors' Conduct, 2015; (ed) Cornerstone on Anti-social Behaviour, 2015. *Recreations:* Everton, the Blues, walking, cooking, the allotment. *Address:* Cornerstone Barristers, 2–3 Gray's Inn Square, WC1R 5JH. *T:* (020) 7242 4986, *Fax:* (020) 7405 1166. *E:* philipk@cornerstonebarristers.com.

KOMISARENKO, Prof. Serhiy Vassiliovych, MD; PhD; Director, Palladin Institute of Biochemistry, since 1998; Academician-Secretary, Ukrainian National Academy of Sciences, since 2004; *b* 9 July 1943; *s* of late Prof. Vassiliy Komisarenko and Lubov Drosovska-Komisarenko; *m* 1970, Natalia Ignatiuk; one *d*. *Educ:* Ukrainian-English Sch., Kiev; Kiev Med. Inst. (MD with dist. 1966); Kiev Univ.; Inst. of Biochem., Kiev (PhD 1970); Inst. of Molecular Biology, Kiev (DSc 1989). Palladin Institute of Biochemistry, Ukrainian Academy of Sciences, Kiev: Jun., then Sen. Scientific Researcher, 1969–75; Scientific Sec., 1972–74; Hd of Dept, 1975–92; Prof. of Biochem., 1989; Dir, 1989–92; Dep. Prime Minister, Ukraine, 1990–92; Ambassador of Ukraine to UK, 1992–98, and to Ireland, 1995–98. Visiting Scientist: Pasteur Inst., Paris, 1974–75; Sloan-Kettering Cancer Inst., NY, 1981. Chairman: Nat. Commn on Biosafety, 2007–; Bd, Internat. Foundn of the Ukrainian Nat. Heritage, 2007–; Mem., Bd of Dirs, British-Ukrainian Chamber of Commerce, 2010–. President: Ukrainian Biochem. Soc., 1999–; Ukrainian Inst. for Peace and Democracy, 1999–; Special Olympics, Ukraine, 2002–; Ukrainian Biosafety Assoc., 2013–. Hon. Prof., Odesa Nat. Univ., 2010. Member: Ukrainian Nat. Acad. of Scis, 1991; Ukrainian Acad. of Med. Scis, 1993. Hon. DSc: Kingston, 1997; N London, 1997. Ukrainian State Award, 1979; Ukrainian State Order of Merit (III degree), 1996, (II degree), 1998, (I degree), 2013; Ukrainian State Order of Yaroslav the Wise (V degree), 2005. *Publications:* Radiation and Human Immunity, 1994; Structure and Biological Activity of Bacterial Biopolymers, 2003; Molecular Mechanisms of Foundation and Degradation of Fibzin, 2013; Biochemistry and Biotechnology for Modern Medicine, 2013; numerous articles on biochem. and immunology; also articles on Ukrainian culture and politics. *Recreations:* music, ski-ing, clay pigeon shooting, lawn tennis, windsurfing. *Address:* Palladin Institute of Biochemistry, 9 Leontovicha Street, Kiev, 01601, Ukraine. *T:* (44) 2345974. *E:* svk@biochem.kiev.ua.

KON, Stephen David; Senior Partner, since 2012 and Co-Deputy Global Chairman, since 2013, King & Wood Mallesons (formerly SJ Berwin) LLP; *b* London, 26 Sept. 1949; *s* of Teddy and Lillian Kon; *m* 1980, Sue Kamlish; three *d*. *Educ:* Harrow Co. Sch. for Boys; Univ. of Sussex (BA Law and Eur. Studies); Coll. of Europe, Brussels (Dip. Supérieur d'Hautes Études). Accredited Mediator, Centre for Effective Dispute Resolution. Admitted as solicitor, 1980, and as solicitor advocate, 2003; Lecturer in Law: Univ. of Reading, 1976–79; Univ. of Sussex, 1979–82; SJ Berwin, later King & Wood Mallesons LLP, 1982–, Partner and Hd of EU Competition and Regulatory Dept, 1984–2012. Member, Editorial Board: Competition Law Insight; Jl Competition Law and Econs. *Publications:* (ed) The Competition Act 1998, 1998. *Recreations:* family, cinema, theatre, Watford FC, cricket, horseracing. *Address:* King & Wood Mallesons LLP, 10 Queen Street Place, EC4R 1BE. *T:* (020) 7111 2237, *Fax:* (020) 7111 2000. *E:* stephen.kon@eu.kwm.com.

KONG, Janis Carol, OBE 2002; Chairman, Bristol Airport, since 2014. *Educ:* Univ. of Edinburgh (BSc Psychol.); Harvard Business Sch. Joined BAA, Edinburgh Airport, 1973; Mktg Manager, Scottish Airports; Gen. Manager, Terminal 4, Heathrow Airport; Ops Dir, 1994–97, Man. Dir, 1997–2001, Gatwick Airport Ltd; Chm., Heathrow Airport Ltd, 2001–06; Dir, BAA plc, 2002–06. Chm., Heathrow Express, 2006. Non-executive Director: Portmeirion Hldgs plc, 2000–; RBS plc, 2006–09; Kingfisher plc, 2006–; Network Rail, 2010–; TUI Travel plc, 2012–; Copenhagen Airports, 2012–. Former Mem., SE England Develt Agency; Mem. Bd, VisitBritain, 2006–. Chm. Trustees, Forum for the Future, 2007–12. DUniv Open.

KONIGSBERG, Allen Stewart; *see* Allen, Woody.

KONSTANT, Rt Rev. David Every; Bishop of Leeds, (RC), 1985–2004, now Emeritus; *b* 16 June 1930; *s* of Antoine Konstant and Dulcie Marion Beresford Konstant (*née* Leggatt). *Educ:* St Edmund's College, Old Hall Green, Ware; Christ's College, Cambridge (MA); Univ. of London Inst. of Education (PGCE). Priest, dio. Westminster, 1954; Cardinal Vaughan School, Kensington, 1959; Diocesan Adviser on Religious Educn, 1966; St Michael's School, Stevenage, 1968; Dir, Westminster Religious Educn Centre, 1970; Auxiliary Bishop of Westminster (Bishop in Central London) and Titular Bishop of Betagbara, 1977–85. Chm., Dept for Catholic Educn and Formation (formerly Dept for Christian Doctrine and Formation), 1984–99, Dept for Internat. Affairs, 1999–2004, Bishops' Conf. of Eng. and Wales; Chm., Catholic Educn Service, 1991–99. FRSA 1996. Freeman, City of London, 1984. Hon. DLaws Leeds Metropolitan, 2004; DUniv Bradford, 2006. *Publications:* various books on religious education and liturgy. *Recreation:* music. *Address:* Ashlea, 62 Headingley Lane, Leeds LS6 2BU.

KONZOTIS, Sotiroula Maria, (Roula); Director, Roula Konzotis Associates, since 2011; *b* Eastbourne, 11 June 1953; *d* of Polychronis Konzotis and Evangelia Konzotis (*née* Michou); *m* 1988, Nicholas Jonathan Wood; two *s*. *Educ:* Burlington Grammar Sch. for Girls; Manchester Univ. (BEd 1st cl. Hons Drama 1976; Cert Ed (Dist.) 1976); City Univ. (Postgrad. Dip. Arts Admin 1983). Hd of Drama and English, Cardinal Newman Sch., Sussex, 1976–79; English teacher, Kostea-Geitonas Sch., Athens, 1979–80; Press and PR Officer, Ballet Rambert, 1983–85; Touring Mktg Officer, Arts Council of GB, 1985–88; Dir of Mktg and Press, English Nat. Ballet, 1988–89; freelance contracts, 1989–94; Sen. Consultant, Bonnar Keenlyside, London, 1994–98; Dir of Communications, RIBA, 1999–2011. UK Trade & Investment: Member: Creative Industries Mktg Strategy Bd, 2006–11; Design Partners, adv. gp on design, 2008–11. Governor: English Nat. Ballet, 2005–11; Belmont Primary Sch., Chiswick, 2011–14. Trustee, Dancers' Career Develt, 2006–11. *Recreations:* the arts, architecture, attending major sporting events, swimming, collecting Rupert annuals. *Address:* 28 Linden Gardens, Chiswick, W4 2EQ. *T:* 07771 715332. *E:* roula@konzotis.com.

KOOLHAAS, Prof. Remment; Joint Founder and Partner, Office for Metropolitan Architecture, since 1975; Professor in Practice of Architecture and Urban Design, Graduate School of Design, Harvard University, since 1995; *b* Rotterdam, 17 Nov. 1944. *Educ:* Architectural Assoc. Sch. of Architecture (DipArch 1972). Journalist and script writer, 1962–72; taught at: Sch. of Architecture, UCLA, 1975; AA, 1976; Professor of Architecture: Technical Univ., Delft, 1988–89; Rice Univ., Houston, 1991–92; Arthur Rotch Adjunct Prof. of Architecture, Graduate Sch. of Design, Harvard Univ., 1990–95. Projects include: Netherlands Dance Theatre, The Hague, 1987; Nexus World Housing, Fukuoka, 1991; Kunsthal, Rotterdam, 1992; Grand Palais and city centre masterplan, Lille, 1994; Educatorium, Univ. of Utrecht, 1997; house in Bordeaux, 1998; Second Stage Theatre, NY, 1999; Prada stores, NY, 2001, LA, 2004; McCormick Tribune Campus, Illinois Inst. of Technol., Chicago, 2003; Seattle Central Library, 2004; Casa da Musica, Porto, 2005; Netherlands Embassy, Berlin, 2005 (Mies van der Rohe Award, EU, 2005); China Central Television, Beijing, 2008. Pritzker Prize, 2000; Praemium Imperiale, Japan Art Assoc., 2003; Royal Gold Medal, RIBA, 2004; Golden Lion for Lifetime Achievement, Venice Biennale, 2010. Co-founder, Volume Magazine, 2005. *Publications:* Delirious New York: a retroactive manifesto for Manhattan, 1978; (jtly) S,M,L,XL, 1997; OMA Rem Koolhaas Living, Vivre, Leben, 1999; OMA 30: 30 Colours, 1999; Content, 2004; Lagos: how it works, 2007. *Address:* Office for Metropolitan Architecture, Heer Bokelweg 149, 3032 AD Rotterdam, Netherlands; Department of Architecture, Harvard Design School, 48 Quincy Street, Cambridge, MA 02138, USA.

KOONER, Prof. Jaspal Singh, MD; FRCP, FMedSci; Professor of Clinical Cardiology, Imperial College London, since 2004; Consultant Cardiologist: Imperial College Healthcare Trust (formerly Royal Postgraduate Medical School and Hammersmith Hospital), since 1995; Ealing Hospital NHS Trust (formerly Ealing Hospital), since 1995; *b* Nairobi, 10 April 1956; *s* of Dhanna Singh Kooner and Bhagwant Kaur Kooner; *m* 1993, Ravinder Kaur; two *s* two *d*. *Educ:* Gillingham Grammar Sch.; St Thomas's Hosp. Med. Sch., Univ. of London (MB BS 1981; MD 1990). MRCP 1985, FRCP 1992. Sen. Lectr in Cardiovascular Medicine, RPMS, 1990–95; Consultant Cardiologist: Hammersmith Hosp., 1990–95; Ealing Hosp., 1990–95. Dir, Lolipop Res. Prog., 1995–. FMedSci 2012. *Publications:* over 30 papers in Nature and Nature Genetics on genetics of coronary artery disease, type-2 diabetes, obesity and other common diseases; papers on coronary heart disease and diabetes in Indian Asians. *Recreations:* research, keeping fit, Gurbani Kirtan, family. *Address:* 7 Alexandra Gardens, Hounslow, Middx TW3 4HT. *T:* (020) 3330 0030, *Fax:* (020) 8196 2273. *E:* j.kooner@imperial.ac.uk.

KOONS, Jeff; artist; *b* York, Penn, 21 Jan. 1955; *s* of Henry and Gloria Koons; one *d*; *m* 1991, Ilona Staller (marr. diss. 1994); one *s*; *m* 1995, Justine Wheeler; four *s*. *Educ:* Sch. of Art, Inst. of Chicago; Maryland Inst. Coll. of Art, Baltimore (BFA 1976). Wall St commodities broker, 1980; estabd studio to produce his work, 1980s; *solo exhibitions* include: New Mus. of Contemporary Art, NY, 1980; Equilibrium, NY and Chicago, 1985; Luxury and Degradation, NY and Daniel Weinberg Gall., LA, 1986; Banality, Chicago, Cologne and Sonnabend Gall., NY, 1988; Made in Heaven, Cologne and Sonnabend Gall., NY, 1991; Easyfun, Sonnabend Gall., NY, 1999; Puppy, Rockefeller Center, NY, 2000; Easyfun-

Ethereal, Fruitmarket Gall., Edinburgh, 2001, Guggenheim Mus., NY and Sao Paulo Biennial, 2002; Popeye, Sonnabend Gall., NY, 2003; (retrospective) Astrup Fearnley MOMA, Oslo and Helsinki City Art Mus., 2004–05; Diamond, V&A Mus., 2006; Cracked Egg, 2006, Hulk Elvis, 2007, Gagosian Gall., London; Metropolitan Mus. of Art, NY, 2008; (retrospective) Château de Versailles, 2008; Gagosian Gall., LA, 2008–09, 2012–13; Popeye Series, Serpentine Gall., London, 2009; Nat. Galls Scotland, 2011; Brighton Mus. and Art Gall., 2013; Gagosian Gall., NY, 2013; Gagosian Gall., HK, 2014–15; Pompidou Centre, Paris (retrospective), 2015; *group exhibitions* include: Whitney Mus., NY, 1985, 1987, 1989, 1990; ICA, Boston, 1988; Sonnabend Gall., NY, 1886; Saatchi Collection, London, 1987; Centre Georges Pompidou, 1987; MOMA, NY, 1990, 2001; Venice Biennale, 1990; Biennial, Sydney, 1990; Royal Acad., 1993, 2000, 2011; Hayward Gall., London, 1992; Mus. Contemp. Art, Sydney, 1995; Serpentine Gall. and V&A Mus., London, 2001; Guggenheim, Bilbao, 2007; Tate Gall., 2009–10; *work in collections* includes: MOMA, Whitney Mus. of American Art, Guggenheim Mus., NY; National Gall. and Hirshhorn Mus., Washington; MOMA, San Francisco; Tate Gall., London; Tokyo Metropolitan Mus.; *public works* include: Balloon Flower (Blue), Potsdamer Platz, Berlin, 1992; Puppy, 1992, Bad Arolsen, Germany, re-erected Mus. of Contemporary Art, Sydney, 1995, subseq. at Guggenheim Mus., Bilbao, 1997; Split-Rocker, Avignon, 2000; Balloon Flower (Red), 7 World Trade Center, NYC, 2006. Dir, Internat. Center for Missing and Exploited Children, 2002–. Fellow, Amer. Acad. Arts and Scis, 2005. Hon. RA 2010. Officier, Légion d'Honneur (France), 2007 (Chevalier, 2001). *Address:* Jeff Koons LLC, 601 W 29th Street, New York, NY 10001–1109, USA; c/o Gagosian Gallery, 17–19 Davies Street, W1K 3DE.

KOOPMAN, Prof. Antonius Gerhardus Michael, (Ton); harpsichordist, organist and conductor; Founder and Conductor, Amsterdam Baroque Orchestra, since 1978, and Choir, 1992–2013; Professor: of Harpsichord, Royal Conservatory, The Hague, since 1989; for Musicology, Leiden University, since 2003; *b* 10 Oct. 1944; *m* 1975, Tini Mathot; three *d*. *Educ:* Amsterdam Conservatory; Univ. of Amsterdam (degree in musicology 1968). Professor: of Harpsichord and Performance Practice, Early Music, Conservatory of Zwolle, 1968–73; of Harpsichord, Conservatory of Groningen, 1973–79; of Harpsichord, Conservatory of Amsterdam, 1979–89. Principal Conductor, Netherlands Radio Chamber Orch., 1994–2001; Principal Guest Conductor, Lausanne Chamber Orch., 1999–; guest conductor with orchestras in USA, Europe and Japan. Established: chamber ensemble, Musica da Camera, 1966; baroque orch., Musica Antiqua Amsterdam, 1968. Hon. RAM 1985. Hon. Dr Utrecht, 2000. Prix de l'Académie du Disque Lyrique, 1994; Prix Hector Berlioz, Paris, 1995; Deutsche Schallplattenpreis Echo Klassik, 1997. *Publications:* Barokmuziek: theorie en praktijk, 1985; (contrib.) The World of the Bach Cantatas, ed Christopher Wolff, 1997; contrib. Early Music, Mens en Melodie, etc. *Address:* Meerweg 23, 1405 BC Bussum, The Netherlands. *T:* (35) 6926006, *Fax:* (35) 6926008. *E:* dagmar@tonkoopman.nl.

KOOPS, Hon. Dame Mary Claire; *see* Hogg, Hon. Dame M. C.

KOPELMAN, Prof. Michael David, PhD; FBPsS, FRCPsych, FMedSci, FRSB; Professor of Neuropsychiatry, Institute of Psychiatry, King's College London (formerly Guy's, King's and St Thomas's School of Medicine), since 1998; *b* London, 8 Feb. 1950; *s* of late Dr Harry Kopelman and Joan Margaret Kopelman (*née* Knowlman); *m* 1985, Dr Sophie Janine Thomson; two *d*. *Educ:* Felsted Sch.; Univ. of Keele (BA Psychol. and Econs 1972); Middx Hosp. Med. Sch., UCL (MB BS 1978); Inst. of Psychiatry, Univ. of London (PhD 1988). FBPsS 1990; FRCPsych 1993; FRSB (FSB 2009). Sen. Lectr, 1988–93, Reader, 1994–97, UMDS, Guy's and St Thomas's Sch. of Medicine. Expert witness in criminal extradition, death row and civil liberties cases, Criminal Appeal Court. President: British Neuropsychol Soc., 2004–06; Internat. Neuropsychiatric Assoc., 2011–13; British Acad. of Forensic Scis, 2011–13. FMedSci 2008. *Publications:* (jtly) Handbook of Memory Disorders, 2002; (jtly) Lishman's Organic Psychiatry, 4th edn 2009; (jtly) Forensic Neuropsychology in Practice, 2009; contribs to scientific jls. *Recreations:* enjoying a good book or a proper newspaper in print you can touch, feel and smell. *E:* michael.kopelman@kcl.ac.uk.
See also Prof. P. G. Kopelman.

KOPELMAN, Prof. Peter Graham, MD; FRCP, FFPH; Principal, St George's, University of London, since 2008; Hon. Consultant Physician, St George's Hospital NHS Trust, since 2008; *b* London, 23 June 1951; *s* of late Dr Harry Kopelman and Joan Kopelman (*née* Knowlman); *m* 1981, Susan Mary Sarah Lewis; one *s* two *d*. *Educ:* Felsted Sch.; St George's Hosp. Med. Sch., London (MB BS 1974; MD 1982). FRCP 1992; FFPH 2005. Sen. Lectr in Medicine, 1986–97, Reader in Medicine, 1997–99, Prof. of Clinical Medicine, 1999–2006, London Hosp. Med. Coll., subseq. St Bartholomew's and Royal London Sch. of Medicine and Dentistry, then Barts and The London Sch. of Medicine and Dentistry, QMUL; Deputy Warden and Vice Principal, QMUL, 2001–06; Consultant Physician, Newham Gen. Hosp., 1986–95; Hon. Consultant Physician, Barts and The London NHS Trust, 1999–2006; Dean, Fac. of Health, UEA, 2006–08; Hon. Prof. of Medicine, Norfolk and Norwich Hosp., Norwich, 2006–08. Non-executive Director: NE London Strategic HA, 2003–06; St George's Healthcare NHS Trust, 2012–. Member: Scientific Adv. Cttee on Nutrition, DoH/Food Standards Agency, 2001–10; HEFCE Res. Strategy Cttee, 2007–13; Bd, Med. Educn England, 2009–12; Exec. Cttee, Med. Schs Council, 2009–; Bd, Centre for Workforce Intelligence, 2010–13; Steering Gp, Future Hosps Commn, 2011–13; Chairman: MRCP(UK) Clin. Examining Bd, RCP, 2004–08; NIHR Clin. Acad. Careers Panel, DoH, 2005–08; London Medicine Gp, London Higher, 2010–; UCEA Clinical Academic Staff Adv. Gp, 2010–; Faculty Bd, Royal Pharmaceutical Soc., 2013–; Health Educn England Pharmacist Educn and Trng Reforms Delivery Pricing Gp, 2015–; Dep. Chm., Health Educn Res. Policy Gp, UUK, 2012–. Pres., Eur. Assoc. for the Study of Obesity, 2003–06. Censor, RCP, 2010–14; Mem., Bd of Trustees, Univ. of London, 2011–13. *Publications:* (ed jtly) Clinical Obesity, 1998, 3rd edn 2009; scientific articles and book chapters on obesity, its causes, complications, treatment and prevention. *Recreations:* all sports, music, drawing, modern literature, political biographies. *Address:* Principal's Office, St George's, University of London, Cranmer Terrace, SW17 0RE. *T:* (020) 8725 5008, *Fax:* (020) 8672 6940. *E:* pkopelman@sgul.ac.uk. *Club:* Athenæum.
See also Prof. M. D. Kopelman.

KOPELOWITZ, Dr (Jacob) Lionel (Garstein), MBE 2015; JP; General Medical Practitioner, 1953–2010; *b* 9 Dec. 1926; *s* of Maurice and Mabel Kopelowitz; *m* 1980, Sylvia Waksman (*née* Galler). *Educ:* Clifton Coll., Bristol; Trinity Coll., Cambridge (MA 1947); University Coll. Hosp. London. MRCS, LRCP 1951; MRCGP 1964. Resident MO, London Jewish Hosp., 1951–52; Flying Officer, RAF Med. Branch, 1952–53. Member: General Medical Council, 1984–94; General Optical Council, 1979–93; Standing Med. Adv. Cttee, DHSS, 1974–78; British Medical Association: Fellow, 1980; Mem. Council, 1982–94; Chm., Newcastle Div., 1968–69; Pres., Northern Regional Council, 1984–88; Mem., Gen. Med. Services Cttee, 1971–90 (Past Chm., Maternity Services Sub-Cttee); Chm., Central Adv. Cttee, Deputising Services, 1980–90; Dep. Chm., Private Practice Cttee, 1972–89; Chairman: St Marylebone and Bloomsbury Div., 1992–; London Regl Council, 2001–04. Chm., Newcastle upon Tyne FPC, 1979–85; Pres., Soc. of FPCs of England and Wales, 1978–79; Mem. Council, RCGP, 1995–. Vice-Pres., Trades Adv. Council, 1988–. President: Board of Deputies of British Jews, 1985–91; Nat. Council for Soviet Jewry, 1985–91; European Jewish Congress, 1986–91; Vice President: Conf. on Jewish Material Claims Against Germany, 1988–; Conf. on Jewish Material Claims Against Austria, 1988–; Council of Christians and Jews, 2009–. Member: Exec. Cttee, Meml Foundn for Jewish Culture, 1988–; United Synagogue, 1991–96. Vice-Pres., Assoc. of Baltic Jews, 1995–; Mem., Chm., Pres., numerous med. bodies and Jewish organisations, UK and overseas. Vice-Pres., British Council, Share Zedek Med. Centre, 1990–. Mem. Bd of Govs, Clifton Coll., Bristol, 1988–; Pres., Old Cliftonian Soc., 1991–93; Mem., Cambridge Union Soc. Liveryman, Apothecaries' Co., 1969. JP Northumberland, 1964. Grand Cross, Order of Merit (Germany), 1993. *Publications:* articles in med. jls; contrib. to Med. Annual. *Recreations:* foreign travel, contract bridge. *Address:* 10 Cumberland House, Clifton Gardens, W9 1DX. *T:* (020) 7289 6375. *Club:* Athenæum.

KOPERNICKI, Jan Marceli, CMG 2012; CBiol, FRSB; Director, 1994–95 and 1998–2011, and Shell Group Function Head for Shipping, 1998–2011, Shell International Trading and Shipping Co. Ltd (Member, Executive Committee, Shell Trading, 1998–2011); Director, Wangaratta Consulting Ltd, since 2011; *b* Overton, 15 Nov. 1948; *s* of Tadeusz Marceli Kopernicki and Irena Kopernicka; *m* 1976, Jennifer Gail Lack; one *s* one *d*. *Educ:* King Edward's Sch., Birmingham; Univ. of Leicester (BSc Hons Biol Scis 1971). CDipAF 1975; CBiol, FRSB (FSB 2009). Posts with Shell Internat. and Shell Oil Co. (USA), 1971–98. Director: Shell Tankers (UK) Ltd, 1996–2004; Shell Response Ltd, 1998–2011. Chamber of Shipping of UK: Dir, 1998–2014; Pres., 2010–11; Dir, Supervisory Bd, 2014–. Non-executive Director: Nordic Tankers Hldgs AB, 2012–; J & J Denholm Ltd, 2012–; BMT Gp Ltd, 2014. Jt Chm., UK Shipping Defence Adv. Cttee, 2005–11; Mem., Internat. Business Adv. Bd, British Airways, 2007–12. Pres., Maritime UK, 2010–11; Chairman: Oil Cos Internat. Marine Forum, 2002–11; Nat. Cttee, Det Norske Veritas UK. Dir, Internat. Tank Owners' Pollution Fedn Ltd, 1998–2011. Mem. Bd, UK P&I Club. Chm., Exec. Bd, World Maritime Univ., 2010–11. Dir, UK Mutual Steam Ship Assce Assoc. (Bermuda) Ltd, 1998–2011. Vice Chm., RNLI, 2012–13; Dir, RNLI Heritage Trust, 2012–13. Pres., Shell Pensioners Assoc., 2012–. Trustee: Royal Mus at Greenwich, 2003–11; Lloyd's Register Foundn, 2008–13. Hon. Captain, RNR, 2012. Freeman, City of London; Liveryman, Shipwrights' Co. Younger Brother of Trinity House. *Recreations:* photography, computing, science fiction, museums, travel.

KOPIECZEK, Aloysius Michael, (Louis); a Judge of the Upper Tribunal, Immigration and Asylum Chamber, since 2011; *b* Putney, 27 July 1959; *s* of Jozef Karol Kopieczek and Bernadette Marie Kopieczek (*née* Culhane); *m* 1990, Alison Patricia Hammond; two *s* one *d*. *Educ:* St Augustine's Coll., Westgate; Bristol Poly. (LLB Hons Law); Inns of Court Sch. of Law. Called to the Bar, Gray's Inn, 1983; in practice as a barrister, 1984–2002; Immigration Adjudicator: pt-time, 1999–2002; salaried, 2002–05; Immigration Judge, Asylum and Immigration Tribunal, 2005–08; Judge of First-tier Tribunal (Health, Educn and Social Care Chamber), 2008–10; Immigration Judge, First-tier Tribunal (Immigration and Asylum Chamber), 2010–11. Legal Mem., Mental Health Rev. Tribunal, 1996–2008; Mem., First-tier Tribunal (Mental Health), 2008–. Mem., Soc. of Old Augustinians. Mem., Traditional Internat. Shotokan Karate Assoc. *Recreations:* family, karate (3rd Dan Black Belt Shotokan Karate). *Address:* Upper Tribunal (Immigration and Asylum Chamber), Field House, 15 Breams Buildings, EC4A 1DZ.

KORAB-KARPINSKI, Marek Romuald, FRCS, FRCSE; Consultant Orthopaedic and Spinal Surgeon, Hull and East Yorkshire Hospitals NHS Trust, since 1987; *b* 29 Jan. 1950; *s* of Lt Col Marian Korab-Karpinski, MC, VM and Zofia Korab-Karpinska; *m* 1999, Dr Malgorzata Szymanska, orthopaedic surgeon; two *s* one *d* by previous marriage. *Educ:* Univ. of Nottingham (BMedSci 1977; BM BS); Univ. of Liverpool (MChOrth 1985). FRCS 1981; FRCSE 1981 (FRCSE (Orth) 1985). Higher surgical orthopaedic trng, Birmingham, 1981–83, Nottingham, 1983–87. Hon. Vis. Prof., Poznan Acad. of Orthopaedics, Poland, 1997. Fellow, Brit. Orthopaedic Assoc., 1985. Patron, PPA Internat., 1997. Hon. Fellow, Univ. of Hull, 1996. Computer Assisted Operative Surgery Prize, BCS, 1996. Designated co-inventor, Computer Assisted Robotic Surgery Technique, 1997. *Publications:* Posterior Lumbar Interbody Fusion and Cages, 1977; (contrib.) Current Concepts in Lumbar Spine Disorders, Vol. 2, 1997; various articles related to orthopaedics and computers, incl. robotic surgery; res. papers. *Recreations:* tennis, snow ski-ing, travel, charity work of a surgical nature. *Address:* 10 Harley Street, W1N 1AA. *T:* (020) 7436 5252. *Club:* Kandahar.

KORALEK, Paul George, CBE 1984; RA 1991 (ARA 1986); RIBA; consultant architect; Founding Partner, Ahrends Burton and Koralek, architects, 1961 (Consultant, until 2012); *b* 7 April 1933; *s* of late Ernest and Alice Koralek; *m* 1958, Jennifer Chadwick; two *d* (one *s* decd). *Educ:* Aldenham School; Architectural Assoc. School of Architecture. RIBA 1957; AA Dip. Hons. Architect: with Powell & Moya, London, 1956–57; with Marcel Breuer, New York, 1959–60. Part-time teaching, Sch. of Arch., Leicester Polytechnic, 1982–84. *Major projects include: public buildings:* Maidenhead Libr., 1972; Roman Catholic Chaplaincy, Oxford, 1972; Nucleus Low Energy Hosp., IoW, 1982; winning entry, Nat. Gall. Extension Hampton Site Comp., 1982; Dover Heritage Centre, 1988–90 (Civic Trust Award, 1992); British Embassy, Moscow, 1993–99; Dublin Dental Hosp., Trinity Coll., 1994–98 (RIBA Arch. Award; RIAI Award); Techniquest Science Centre, Cardiff, 1995 (RIBA Arch. Award); Offaly County Council offices, 2002–; County Offices, Neneagh, Tipperary, 2004; *educational buildings:* Chichester Theol Coll., 1965; Berkeley Liby, TCD, 1967 (1st Prize, Internat. Comp., 1961); Templeton Coll., Oxford, 1967; Arts Faculty Bldg, TCD, 1975–79; Portsmouth Poly. Liby, 1975–79; Residential bldg, Keble Coll., Oxford, 1976 (RIBA Arch. Award, 1978); Selly Oak Colls Learning Resources Centre, 1997; Insts of Technol. at Tralee, Waterford and Blanchardstown, 1997–2002; Loughborough Univ. Business Sch., 1998; Innovation Centre, TCD, 2001; John Wheatley Coll., Glasgow, 2007–; *residential buildings:* houses, Dunstan Rd, Oxford, 1969; Nebenzahl House, Jerusalem, 1972; Chalvedon Housing, 1975–77; Whitmore Court Housing, Basildon, 1975 (RIBA Good Design in Housing Award, 1977); Felmore Housing, 1975–80; *commercial/industrial buildings:* Habitat Warehouse, Showroom and Offices, Wallingford, 1974 (Financial Times Indust. Arch. Award, and Structl Steel Design Award (Warehouse), 1976); factory bldgs and refurbishment, Cummins Engine Co., Shotts, Scotland, 1975–83 (Structl Steel Design Award, 1980); J. Sainsbury supermarket, Canterbury, 1984 (Structl Steel Design Award, 1985; FT Arch. at Work Award Commendation, 1986); W. H. Smith Offices, Greenbridge, 1985 and 1996 (FT Arch. at Work Award Commendation, 1987); John Lewis Dept Store, Kingston-upon-Thames, 1987 (Civic Trust Commendation, 1991). *Exhibitions of drawings and works:* RIBA Heinz Gall., 1980; Douglas Hyde Gall. Dublin, 1981; Technical Univ. of Braunschweig and Tech. Univ. of Hanover, Germany, Mus. of Finnish Arch., Helsinki, Univ. of Oulu, and Alvar Aalto Mus., Jvasklya, Finland, 1982; HQ of AA, Oslo, 1983. Chm., SE Regl Design Panel, 2002–. Member: Develt Adv. (formerly Design and Architectural Rev.) Panel, Cardiff Bay Develt Corp., 1988; ARCUK Bd of Architectural Educn, 1987–93; Trustee, Bldg Industry Youth Trust, 1981–95. External Examiner: Sch. of Arch., Univ. of Manchester, 1981–85; Plymouth Poly., 1988; Assessor: RIBA competitions, incl. Toyota UK HQ, 1997; Irish Dept of Educn Schs competition; Civic Trust Awards; Advr, Cardiff Bay Opera House, 1994–95. Papers and lectures, UK and abroad, 1964–. *Publications:* paper and articles in RIBA and other prof. jls. *Recreations:* drawing, walking, gardening. *Address:* 3 Rochester Road, NW1 9JH.
See also C. L. Ricks.

KORNBERG, Prof. Sir Hans (Leo), Kt 1978; MA, DSc, ScD, PhD; FRS 1965; FRSB; University Professor and Professor of Biology, Boston University, since 1995 (Director, University Professors Program, 2002–05 and 2007–11); Sir William Dunn Professor of Biochemistry, University of Cambridge, 1975–95, and Fellow of Christ's College, Cambridge, since 1975 (Master, 1982–95); *b* 14 Jan. 1928; *o s* of Max Kornberg and Margarete Kornberg (*née* Silberbach); *m* 1st, 1956, Monica Mary King (*d* 1989); twin *s* two *d*; 2nd, 1991, Donna, *d* of William B. Haber and Ruth Haber. *Educ:* Queen Elizabeth Grammar Sch.,

Wakefield; Univ. of Sheffield (BSc, PhD); MA 1958, DSc 1961, Oxon; ScD Cantab 1975. FIBiol 1965, Hon. FRSB (Hon. FIBiol 2004). Commonwealth Fund Fellow of Harkness Foundation, at Yale University and Public Health Research Inst., New York, 1953–55; Mem. of scientific staff, MRC Cell Metabolism Res. Unit, University of Oxford, 1955–60; Lectr, Worcester Coll., Oxford, 1958–61 (Hon. Fellow 1980); Prof. of Biochemistry, Univ. of Leicester, 1960–75. Visiting Instructor, Marine Biological Lab., Woods Hole, Mass, 1964–66, 1981–85, Trustee, 1982–93. Dir, UK Nirex Ltd, 1986–95. Member: SRC, 1967–72 (Chm., Science Bd, 1969–72); UGC Biol. Sci. Cttee, 1967–77; NATO Adv. Study Inst. Panel, 1970–76 (Chm., 1974–75); Kuratorium, Max-Planck Inst., Dortmund, 1979–90 (Chm., Sci. Adv. Cttee); AFRC (formerly ARC), 1980–84; Priorities Bd for R & D in Agriculture, 1984–90; BP Venture Res. Council, 1981–91; ACARD, 1982–85; Adv. Council on Public Records, 1984–86; UK Cttee on Eur. Year of the Environment, 1986–88; Vice-Chm., EMBO, 1978–81; Chairman: Royal Commn on Environmental Pollution, 1976–81; Adv. Cttee on Genetic Modification, 1986–95; Co-ordinating Cttee on Environmental Res., Res. Councils, 1986–88; Sci. Adv. Cttee, Inst. for Mol. Biol. and Medicine, Monash Univ., 1987–; President: BAAS, 1984–85 (Hon. Mem., 2003); Biochemical Soc., 1990–95; IUBMB, 1991–94 (Dist. Service Award, 2003); Assoc. for Science Educn, 1991–92; Vice-Pres., Inst. of Biol., 1971–73. A Managing Trustee, Nuffield Foundn, 1973–93; Trustee, 1990–92, Gov., 1992–95, Wellcome Trust; Academic Governor, Hebrew Univ. of Jerusalem, 1976–97 (Hon. Gov., 1997–); Governor: Weizmann Inst., 1980–97 (Hon. Gov., 1997–); Lister Inst., 1990–95. Hon. Fellow: Brasenose Coll., Oxford, 1983; Wolfson Coll., Cambridge, 1990. FRSA 1972. Fellow, Amer. Acad. of Microbiol., 1992. For. Associate, Nat. Acad. of Sciences, USA, 1986; Foreign Member: Amer. Philosoph. Soc., 1993; Accademia Nazionale dei Lincei, 1997; Hon. For. Mem., Amer. Acad. of Arts & Scis, 1987; Member: Leopoldina German Acad. of Scis, 1982; Acad. Europaea, 1989; Hon. Member: Amer. Soc. Biol Chem., 1972; Biochem. Soc., FRG, 1973; Japanese Biochem. Soc., 1981; Biochem. Soc. (UK), 2001; Phi Beta Kappa, 1996; Hon. FRCP 1989. Hon. ScD Cincinnati, 1974; Hon. DSc: Warwick, 1975; Leicester, 1979; Sheffield, 1979; Bath, 1980; Strathclyde, 1985; South Bank, 1994; Leeds, 1995; La Trobe, 1997; DUniv Essex, 1979; Hon. Dr med Leipzig, 1984; Hon. LLD Dundee, 1999. Colworth Medal of Biochemical Soc., 1963; Otto Warburg Medal, Biochem. Soc. of Federal Republic of Germany, 1973. *Publications:* (with Sir Hans Krebs) Energy Transformations in Living Matter, 1957; articles in scientific jls. *Recreations:* cooking and conversation, playing the cello (badly). *Address:* Biology Department, Boston University, 5 Cummington Mall, Boston, MA 02215, USA; (home) 134 Sewall Avenue, # 2, Brookline, MA 02446, USA.

KORNBERG, Prof. Roger David, PhD; Mrs George A. Winzer Professor in Medicine, Stanford University School of Medicine, since 2003; *b* St Louis, Mo, 24 April 1947; *s* of late Prof. Arthur Kornberg (jtly, Nobel Prize in Physiology or Medicine, 1959) and Sylvy Ruth Kornberg (*née* Levy); *m* 1984, Yahli Lorch; two *s* one *d*. *Educ:* Harvard Univ. (BS 1967); Stanford Univ. (PhD 1972). Postdoctoral Fellow and Mem. of Scientific Staff, MRC Lab. of Molecular Biol., Cambridge, 1972–75; Asst Prof. in Biol Chem., Harvard Medical Sch., 1976–78; Prof. of Structural Biol., Stanford Univ. Sch. of Medicine, 1978– (Chair, Dept of Structural Biol., 1984–92). Foreign Mem., Royal Soc., 2009. Nobel Prize in Chemistry, 2006. *Publications:* articles in learned jls. *Address:* Department of Structural Biology, Stanford University School of Medicine, Fairchild Building, 299 Campus Drive, Stanford, CA 94305–5126, USA.

KORNER, Joanna Christian Mary, CMG 2004; QC 1993; **Her Honour Judge Korner;** a Circuit Judge, since 2012; *b* 1 July 1951; *d* of late John Hugh George Korner and of Martha (*née* Tupay von Isertingen). *Educ:* Queensgate Sch.; Inns of Court Sch. of Law. Called to the Bar, Inner Temple, 1974, Bencher, 1996; Recorder, 1995–2012. Member: Bar Council, 1994–97; Crown Court Rules Cttee, 1994–2000; Hd, Internat. Section, Advocacy Trng Council, 2008–12. Sen. Prosecuting Counsel, Internat. Criminal Tribunal (formerly Internat. War Crimes Tribunal) for former Yugoslavia, 1999–2004, 2009–12. Chair, Adv. Cttee for Conscientious Objectors, 2013–. Dir, Internat. Course, Judicial Coll., 2014–. *Recreations:* collecting books and porcelain, cinema, tennis. *Address:* Snaresbrook Crown Court, 75 Hollybush Hill, Snaresbrook, E11 1QW. *Club:* Reform.

KORNICKI, Prof. Peter Francis, DPhil, DLitt; FBA 2000; Professor of Japanese Studies and Head, Department of East Asian Studies, University of Cambridge, 2012–14, now Professor Emeritus; Fellow, since 1986, and Deputy Warden, since 2008, Robinson College, Cambridge; *b* 1 May 1950; *er s* of Sqn Leader Franciszek Kornicki, VM and Patience Ceridwen Kornicka (*née* Williams); *m* 1st, 1975, Catharine Olga Mikolaski (*d* 1995); one *s* one *d*; 2nd, 1998, Francesca Orsini. *Educ:* St George's Coll., Weybridge; Lincoln Coll., Oxford (BA 1972; MSc 1975; Hon. Fellow, 2004); St Antony's Coll., Oxford (DPhil 1979); DLitt Oxon 2011. Lectr, Univ. of Tasmania, 1978–82; Associate Prof., Kyoto Univ., 1982–84; Cambridge University: Lectr, 1985–95; Reader in Japanese History and Bibliography, 1995–2001; Prof. of Japanese History and Bibliography, 2001–07; Sandars Reader in Bibliography, 2007–08; Prof. of East Asian Studies, 2007–12; Chm., Faculty Bd of Oriental Studies, 1993–95, 2004–05. Chm., African and Oriental Studies sect., 2006–09, E Asia Panel, 2009–, British Acad. Pres., European Assoc. for Japanese Studies, 1997–2000. MAE 2012. Special Prize, Japan Foundn, 1992; Yamagata Banto Prize, Osaka Prefecture, 2013. *Publications:* The Reform of Fiction in Meiji Japan, 1982; Early Japanese Books in Cambridge University Library, 1991; (jtly) Cambridge Encyclopedia of Japan, 1993; The Book in Japan: a cultural history, 1998; Early Japanese Books in the Russian State Library, 1999; The Iwakura Embassy, vol. 4, 2002; (jtly) The Female as Subject: reading and writing in early modern Japan, 2010; (jtly) Catalogue of the Japanese Coin Collection (pre-Meiji) at the British Museum, 2011; (jtly) F. V. Dickins' Letters to Ernest M. Satow, Kumagusu Minakata and others, 2011; (jtly) The History of the Book in East Asia, 2013; numerous articles and reviews in jls. *Recreations:* travel, cooking, languages. *Address:* Robinson College, Cambridge CB3 9AN. *T:* (01223) 339156.

KOSCIUSZKO, Stefan Henry; Managing Director, Head of Distribution, Asia Pacific, CQS Ltd, since 2013; *b* 2 June 1959; *s* of late Konstanty Kosciuszko and of Elisabeth Kerr Kosciuszko (*née* Havelock); *m* 1985, Takako Yamaguchi; two *d*. *Educ:* Gordonstoun Sch.; Divine Mercy Coll., Henley-on-Thames; Keele Univ. (Josiah Wedgwood Meml Award for Hist.; BA Hons (Internat. Relns) 1980). National Westminster Bank, 1980–82; Sumitomo Bank, London/Tokyo, 1982–85; Chemical Bank, London/Tokyo, 1985–88; Schroders: Gen. Manager, Tokyo, 1988–91; Asst Dir, Internat. Finance Dept, London, 1992–95; Director, 1995–98; Hd, Asia-Pacific Equity Capital Markets Regl Investment Banking Cttee and Asian Securities Mgt Cttee, 1995–97; Hd, Corporate Finance, Indonesia, 1997–98; Man. Dir, Gavin Anderson & Co., 1999–2000; Dir, Credit Suisse First Boston, 2000–02; Chief Exec., Asia House, 2002–07; Chief of Staff, Hinduja Group, 2007–09; Dir and Sen. Advr, Asia Pacific, Praetoria Ltd, 2010–13; Chm., TwoFoldTwenty, 2010–13; Dir of Marketing and Communications, fibre GarDen, 2010–14. Consultant, BTG Pactual, 2010–11. Executive Director: Pakistan Britain Trade and Investment Forum, 2003–07; Korea Forum for the Future, 2007–09; Sec., Indo-British Partnership Network, 2005–07. Mem. Cttee, 48 Gp Club, 2010– (Chief Exec., 2012–13). Gov., Gainsborough House Mus., 2002–06. Sec., Sudbury Soc., 2002–06; Pres., Sudbury Girls' Football Club, 2003–07. FRSA 2006. *Recreations:* sports, chess, fine wine, antiques, Asian culture, history, hard work and my two daughters—living life to fullest extent possible. *Address:* Abbas Hall, Cornard Tye, Great Cornard, Suffolk CO10 0QD. *E:* stefan@kosciuszko.com. *Club:* Naval and Military.

KOSHIBA, Prof. Masatoshi, PhD; Professor, Department of Physics, 1970–87, now Emeritus, and Director, International Centre for Elementary Particle Physics, 1984–87, now Senior Counsellor, University of Tokyo; *b* 19 Sept. 1926; *m* 1959, Kyoko Kato. *Educ:* Univ. of Tokyo; Univ. of Rochester, NY (PhD 1955). Res. Associate, Dept of Physics, Univ. of Chicago, 1955–58; Associate Prof., Inst. of Nuclear Study, Univ. of Tokyo, 1958–63; Sen. Res. Associate, Dept of Physics, Univ. of Chicago, 1959–62 (on secondment); Associate Prof., Dept of Physics, Univ. of Tokyo, 1963–70. Founding Chm., Heisei Foundn for Basic Science, Tokyo, 2003. (Jtly) Nobel Prize in Physics, 2002. *Address:* International Centre for Elementary Particle Physics, University of Tokyo, 7–3–1 Hongo, Bunkyo-ku, Tokyo 113–0033, Japan.

KOSMINSKY, Peter; freelance film director and writer, since 1995; *b* London, 21 April 1956; *s* of Leon and Erika Kosminsky; two *d*. *Educ:* Haberdashers' Aske's Sch., Herts; Worcester Coll., Oxford (BA Hons Chem. 1980; MA). Gen. trainee, 1980–82, Asst Producer, 1982–85, BBC; producer and dir, Documentaries Dept, Yorkshire TV, 1985–95; programmes include: The Falklands War: the untold story (UK Broadcast Press Guild Award, BFI Special Award, 1987); Cambodia: children of the killing fields (One World Broadcasting Trust Award, 1988); director: Shoot to Kill, 1990 (UK Broadcast Press and RTS Awards); (film) Wuthering Heights, 1992; dir and producer, The Dying of the Light, 1994; freelance, 1995–: *film:* White Oleander, 2002; *television:* producer and director: No Child of Mine, 1997 (BAFTA Award); Walking on the Moon, 1999; Innocents, 2000; director: Warriors, 1999 (BAFTA and RTS Awards); The Project, 2002; Wolf Hall, 2015; writer and director: The Government Inspector, 2005 (BAFTA and RTS Awards); Britz, 2007 (BAFTA and RTS Awards); The Promise, 2011 (Best Drama Prize, One World Media Awards). Member: Council, BAFTA, 2003–07; Council, Liberty, 2008–13; Bd, Directors UK, 2008–11; Bd, First Light, 2011–12; Gov., BFI, 2012–. Mem., Consultative Cttee, Worcester Coll., Oxford, 2009–. FRSA 2005; FRTS 2006; Hon. Fellow, Univ. Coll. Falmouth, 2011. Hon. Mem., UN Internat. Criminal Tribunal for the former Yugoslavia Staff Union, 2009. Hon. DArt Bournemouth, 2009. Special Award for TV Achievement, BFI, 1989; Alan Clarke Award, BAFTA, 1999; EuroFipa d'Honneur, Biarritz, 2005. *Recreations:* photography, cinema, being a daddy. *Address:* c/o United Agents, 12–26 Lexington Street, W1F 0LE. *E:* ajones@unitedagents.co.uk. *Clubs:* Groucho, Century.

KOTCH, Laurie, (Mrs J. K. Kotch); *see* Purden, R. L.

KOUCHNER, Bernard Jean, Hon. KBE 2005; Minister of Foreign and European Affairs, France, 2007–10; *b* Avignon, 1 Nov. 1939; *s* of Georges Kouchner and Léone Mauric; *m* Evelyne Pisier (marr. diss.); three *c*; one *s* with Christine Ockrent. *Educ:* Faculté de Médicine de Paris (Cert. d'études spéciales in gastroenterology); Dip. digestive endoscopy. Co-founder, Evènement, 1965–69; Mem., Red Cross med. mission to Biafra, 1968–69; humanitarian missions to help victims in most of major natural and industrial disasters and political crises, 1968–; Co-founder, Actuel jl, 1970; Co-founder and Pres., Médecins Sans Frontières, 1971–79; Gastroenterologist, Cochin Hosp., Paris, 1975–87. Minister of State: with resp. for Social Integration, 1988; with resp. for Humanitarian Action, 1988–92; Minister: for Health and Humanitarian Action, 1992–93; MEP (Réunir/Socialiste), 1994–97; Pres., Commn for Develt and Co-operation, Eur. Parlt, 1994–96; Minister of State for Health, 1997–98, for Health and Social Action, 1998–99; UN Sec. Gen.'s Special Rep. for Kosovo, 1999–2001; Minister Delegate for Health, 2001–02. Mem., Socialist Party, 1997–2007. Prof. of Health and Develt, Conservatoire national des arts et métiers, 2002–07. Lectr, Harvard Sch. of Public Health, 2003. Founder Chm., BK Consultants. Mem., Bd of Dirs, PlaNet Finance. Founder, 1980, Pres., 1980–84, Hon. Pres., 1984–88, Médecins du Monde; Founder, Volontaires européens du développement, 1988. Chm., ESTHER public interest gp, 2001–07. Pres., then Hon. Pres., Réunir, 1993–2007. Member: Hon. Cttee, Children Action; Bd of Dirs, Internat. Women's Coalition. Founder Mem., La chaîne de l'espoir. Writer, TV series, under pseudonym Bernard Gridaine: Médecins de nuit, 1978; Hôtel de police, 1985. Prix Dag Hammarskjöld, 1979; Prix Athinai de la fondation Alexandre Onassis, 1981; Prix Europa, 1984; Prix européen des Droits de l'homme, 2005. *Publications:* (jtly) La France sauvage, 1970; (jtly) Les Voraces, 1974; L'Ile de lumière, 1979 (Prix Louise Weiss, Eur. Parlt); Charité business, 1986; (jtly) Le Devoir d'ingérence, 1988; Les Nouvelles solidarités, 1989; Le Malheur des autres, 1991; (jtly) Dieu et les hommes, 1993; Ce que je crois, 1995; Vingt idées pour l'an 2000, 1995; La Dictature médicale, 1996; Le Premier qui dit la vérité, 2002; Les Guerriers de la paix: du Kosovo à l'Irak, 2004; (jtly) Quand tu seras président, 2004; Deux ou trois choses que je sais de nous, 2006; articles.

KOUMI, Margaret, (Maggie); freelance editorial consultant, since 2001; *b* 15 July 1942; *d* of Yiasoumi Koumi and Melexidia Paraskeva; *m* 1980, Ramon Sola. *Educ:* Buckingham Gate Sch., London. Sec., Thomas Cook Travel, 1957–60; Sub-Editor and writer, Boyfriend and Trend magazines, 1960–66; Sub-Editor, TV World, 1967–68; Production Editor, 1968–70, Editor, 1970–86, 19 magazine; Man. Editor, Practical Parenting and Practical Health, 1986–87; Jt Ed., 1988–93, Ed., 1993–2001, Hello! mag. (the magazine has won several awards). *Publications:* Claridges: within the image, 2004. *Recreations:* reading, travel.

KOURTZI, Prof. Zoe, PhD; Professor of Experimental Psychology, University of Cambridge, since 2013; *b* Athens, 12 Aug. 1971; *d* of Dimitrios Kourtzis and Maria Kourtzi; *m* 2004, Andrew Edward Welchman; two *s*. *Educ:* Univ. of Crete (BS Psychol. 1993); Rutgers Univ. (PhD Cognitive Psychol. 1998). Postdoctoral Fellow: Vision Sci. Lab., Harvard Univ., 1998–99; Dept of Brain and Cognitive Sci., MIT, 1998–2002; Vis. Scientist, 2000–02, Sen. Res. Scientist, 2002–05, Max Planck Inst. for Biol Cybernetics, Germany; Professor: of Brain Imaging, Birmingham Univ., 2005–13; Lab. for Neuro- and Psychophysiol., Catholic Univ. of Leuven, Belgium, 2011–13. *Publications:* contribs to learned jls. *Recreations:* dance, theatre. *Address:* Department of Psychology, University of Cambridge, Downing Street, Cambridge CB2 3EB. *T:* (01223) 766558. *E:* zk240@cam.ac.uk.

KOUZARIDES, Prof. Tony, FRS 2012; Royal Society Napier Research Professor of Cancer Biology, since 2002, and Deputy Director, Wellcome Trust/Cancer Research UK Gurdon Institute, since 2004, University of Cambridge; *b* 17 Jan. 1958; *s* of Takis and Annie Kouzarides; *m* 1984, Penny Hall; one *s* one *d*. *Educ:* Univ. of Leeds (BSc Genetics 1981); Univ. of Cambridge (PhD Virology 1984). Postdoctoral Fellow: MRC Lab. of Molecular Biology, Cambridge, 1984–86; New York Univ. Med. Center, 1986–89; Res. Associate, Dept of Pathology, Univ. of Cambridge, 1989–91; Wellcome Trust/Cancer Research UK (formerly Cancer Research Campaign) Institute, University of Cambridge: Sen. Res. Associate, 1991–96; Reader, 1996–99; Prof. of Molecular Cancer Biology, 1999–2001; Hd of CRUK Labs, 2002–04. Co-founder and Director: Abcom Ltd, 1998–; Chroma Therapeutics, 2001–. Novartis Medal and Prize, Biochem. Soc., 2012. *Publications:* various articles in many scientific jls. *Recreations:* films, music. *Address:* The Wellcome Trust/Cancer Research UK Gurdon Institute, Henry Wellcome Building of Cancer and Developmental Biology, University of Cambridge, Tennis Court Road, Cambridge CB2 1QN. *T:* (01223) 334112, *Fax:* (01223) 334089. *E:* tk106@cam.ac.uk.

KOVACEVICH, Stephen; pianist and conductor; *b* 17 Oct. 1940; *s* of Nicholas Kovacevich and Loreta (*née* Zuban, later Bishop). *Educ:* studied under Lev Shorr and Myra Hess. Solo and orchestral debut, San Francisco, USA 1951; London debut, Nov. 1961. First known professionally as Stephen Bishop, then as Stephen Bishop-Kovacevich, and since 1991 as Stephen Kovacevich. Concert tours: in England, Europe and USA, with many of the world's leading orchestras, incl. New York Philharmonic, Los Angeles Philharmonic, Israel Philharmonic, Amsterdam Concertgebouw, London Symphony, London Philharmonic, and

BBC Symphony. Has appeared at Edinburgh, Bath, Berlin and San Sebastian Festivals. Gave 1st performance of Richard Rodney Bennett's Piano Concerto, 1969 (this work is dedicated to and has been recorded by him, under Alexander Gibson). Performed all Mozart Piano concertos, 1969–71; recorded all Beethoven sonatas, 2003. Principal Guest Conductor: Australian Chamber Orch., 1987–91; Zagreb Philharmonic Orch.; Music Dir, Irish Chamber Orch., 1990–93. Edison Award for his recording of Bartok's 2nd Piano Concerto and Stravinsky's Piano Concerto, with BBC Symphony Orch., under Colin Davis; Gramophone Award, 1993 and Stereo Review Record of the Year for Brahms' Piano Concerto No 1 with LPO, under Wolfgang Sawallisch. *Recreations:* snooker, chess, films, tennis. *Address:* c/o International Classical Artists, Dunstan House, 14a St Cross Street, EC1N 8XA. *T:* (020) 7902 0520.

KOVACH, Catherine Anne; *see* Duigan, C. A.

KOVÁCS, László; MP (MSzP) Hungary (formerly Republic of Hungary), 2010–14; *b* 3 July 1939; *m*; one *d*. *Educ:* Petrik Lajos Tech. Sch. for Chem. Industry, Budapest; Univ. of Econ. Scis, Budapest; Coll. of Politics. Chem. Technician, Medicolor, and Kőbánya Pharmaceutical Works, 1957–66; Consultant and Dep. Hd, Dept for Internat. Relns, Hungarian Socialist Workers' Party, 1975–86; Dep. Foreign Minister, Hungary, 1986–89; Sec. of State, Min. of Foreign Affairs, 1989–90; MP, 1990–2004; Minister for Foreign Affairs, 1994–98, 2002–04; Mem., Eur. Commn, 2004–10. Leader, Hungarian Socialist Party, 1998–2004.

KOVATS, Steven Laszlo; QC 2010; a Recorder, since 2010; a Deputy High Court Judge, since 2013; *b* London, 1 Feb. 1966; *s* of Laszlo Joseph Kovats and Joan Kovats; *m* 1999, Michelle Ewing; one *d*. *Educ:* Christ's Hosp.; Trinity Hall, Cambridge (BA Hons Law 1988). Called to the Bar, Middle Temple, 1989. Attorney Gen.'s Civil Litigation 'A' Panel, 2001–10. *Recreations:* running marathons, cooking. *Address:* 39 Essex Street, WC2R 3AT. *T:* (020) 7832 1111, *Fax:* (020) 7353 3978. *E:* steven.kovats@39essex.com.

KOVOOR, Rev. George Iype; Principal, Trinity College, Bristol, 2005–13; Chaplain to the Queen, since 2003; *b* 6 June 1957. *Educ:* Delhi Univ. (BA 1977); Serampore Univ. (BD 1980); Christian Medical Assoc. of India (Dip. Counselling and Hosp. Chaplaincy 1985); Union Biblical Seminary, Yavatmal. Ordained deacon and priest, 1980, Ch of N India; Curate, Shanti Niwas Ch, Faridabad, 1980–82; Presbyter: Santokh Majra Ch, 1982–83; St Paul's Cathedral, Ambala, 1984–88; Nat. Youth Dir, Ch of N India, 1987–90; Principal Chaplain, St Stephen's Hosp., Delhi, 1988–90; Curate, St Augustine's, Derby, and Minister, Derby Asian Christian Ministry Project, 1990–94; Tutor, 1994–97, Principal, 1997–2004, Crowther Hall CMS Trng Coll.; Mission Educn Dir, CMS, 1997–2005; Dir, Centre for Anglican Communion Studies, Selly Oak. Canon Theologian, Province of Niger Delta North, 2010; Canon Missiologist, Dio. of Sabah, 2010. Hon. Canon, Worcester Cathedral, 2001–.

KOWALSKI, Gregor; Parliamentary Counsel, 2005–09; consultant legislative drafter, since 2011; *b* 7 Oct. 1949; *s* of Mieczyslaw Kowalski and Jeanie Hutcheson Kowalski (*née* MacDonald); *m* 1974, Janet McFarlane Pillatt; two *s*. *Educ:* Airdrie Academy; Strathclyde Univ. (LLB 1971). Apprentice, then Asst Solicitor, Levy & McRae, Glasgow, 1971–74; Procurator Fiscal Depute, Glasgow, 1974–78; Asst, later Deputy Parly Draftsman for Scotland and Asst Legal Sec. to Lord Advocate, 1978–87; seconded to Govt of Seychelles as Legal Draftsman, 1982–83; Scottish Parly Counsel and Asst Legal Sec. to Lord Advocate, 1987–99; Scottish Parly Counsel to UK Govt, 1999–2000; Dep. Parly Counsel, 2000–05. Chm., Holywell Hook Heath Ltd, 2012–. Vice-Chm., London Symphony Chorus, 2012–14. *Recreations:* singing, opera, travel. *Address:* 10 Holywell, Hook Heath Road, Woking, Surrey GU22 0LA.

KRAEMER, (Thomas Whilhelm) Nicholas; conductor; *b* 7 March 1945; *s* of William Paul Kraemer and Helen Bartrum; *m* 1984, Elizabeth Mary Anderson; two *s* two *d* (and one *s* decd). *Educ:* Edinburgh Acad.; Lancing Coll.; Dartington Coll. of Arts; Nottingham Univ. (BMus 1967). ARCM. Harpsichordist with Acad. of St Martin in the Fields, 1972–80, with Monteverdi Choir and Orchestra, 1970–80; Musical Director: Unicorn Opera, Abingdon, 1971–75; West Eleven Children's Opera, 1971–88; Founder and Dir, Raglan Baroque Players, 1978–2003; Principal Conductor, Divertimenti, 1979–89; Permanent Guest Conductor: Manchester Camerata, 1995– (Principal Conductor, 1992–95); Music of the Baroque, Chicago, 2002–; Guest Conductor, English Chamber Orch., 1975–84; Conductor, Glyndebourne, 1980–82; Musical Dir, Opera 80, 1980–83; Associate Conductor, BBC Scottish SO, 1983–85; Artistic Director: London Bach Orch., 1985–93; Irish Chamber Orch., 1985–90; Guest Conductor: Scottish Chamber Orch.; Northern Sinfonia; BBC Philharmonic; BBC Nat. Orch. of Wales; Hallé Orch.; St Paul Chamber Orch. (USA); Berlin Philharmonic; ENO; Bergen Philharmonic; Gothenburg SO; Kristiansand SO; Chicago SO; Detroit SO; Colorado SO; Toronto SO; W Australian SO; Minnesota Orch.; Orch. ensemble Kanazawa; Musikkollegium Winterthur; Iceland SO; Aalborg SO; Auckland Philharmonia; Lapland Chamber Orch.; Irish Chamber Orch.; Collegium Musicum Bergen; Principal Guest Conductor, Kristiansand SO; Conductor of Opera at Grange Park, 2012; Conductor of Opera at Buxton, 2013; Associate Artist: Trinity Coll. of Music, 2012–; Orquesta Metropolitana di Lisboa, 2014–; Civic Orch., Chicago, 2015–. Prog. Dir, Bath Fest., 1994. Recordings include works by Vivaldi, Locatelli, Mozart, Handel, Thea Musgrave. *Recreation:* keeping fit. *Address:* c/o Caroline Phillips Management, 11 Pound Pill, Corsham, Wilts SN13 9HZ.

KRAMER, family name of **Baroness Kramer**.

KRAMER, Baroness *cr* 2010 (Life Peer), of Richmond Park in the London Borough of Richmond upon Thames; **Susan Veronica Kramer;** PC 2014; *b* 21 July 1950; *m* 1972, John Davis Kramer (*d* 2006); one *s* one *d*. *Educ:* St Hilda's Coll., Oxford (BA PPE, MA 1972); Illinois Univ. (MBA Business/Finance 1982). Staff Associate, Nat. Acad. of Engrg, 1972–73; Second Vice-Pres., Continental Bank, USA, 1982–88; Vice-Pres., Corporate Finance, Citibank/Citicorp, USA, 1988–92; Chief Operating Officer, Future Water Internat., 1992–95; Partner, Kramer & Associates, 1995–99. Board Mem., CAIB Infrastructure Project Advrs, 1997–99; Director: Infrastructure Capital Partners Ltd, 1999–2007; Speciality Scanners plc, 2001–11. Mem. Bd, Transport for London, 2000–05. London Mayoral candidate, 2000. MP (Lib Dem) Richmond Park, 2005–10; contested (Lib Dem) same seat, 2010. Minister of State, DfT, 2013–15. Lib Dem Spokesperson for economics, 2015–. *Publications:* (contrib.) Harnessing the Markets to Achieve Environmental Goals, 2004. *Recreations:* theatre, reading, rowing. *Address:* House of Lords, SW1A 0PW. *Club:* National Liberal.

KRAMER, Prof. Ivor Robert Horton, OBE 1984; MDS; DSc (Med); FDSRCS, FFDRCSI, Hon. FRACDS, FRCPath; Emeritus Professor of Oral Pathology, University of London; *b* 20 June 1923; *yr s* of late Alfred Bertie and Agnes Maud Kramer; *m* 1st, 1946, Elisabeth Dalley (*d* 1978); one *s*; 2nd, 1979, Mrs Dorothy Toller (*d* 1985); 3rd, 1991, Mrs Virginia Webster. *Educ:* Royal Dental Hosp. of London Sch. of Dental Surgery; MDS 1955; DSc (Med) London 1993. FDSRCS 1960 (LDSRCS 1944); FRCPath 1970 (MRCPath 1964); FFDRCSI 1973. Asst to Pathologist, Princess Louise (Kensington) Hosp. for Children, 1944–48; Wright Fleming Inst. of Microbiol., 1948–49; Instr in Dental Histology, Royal Dental Hosp. Sch. of Dental Surgery, 1944–50; Asst Pathologist, Royal Dental Hosp., 1950–56; Institute of Dental Surgery: Lectr in Dental Path., 1949–50, Sen. Lectr, 1950–57; Reader in Oral Path., 1957–62; Prof. of Oral Path., 1962–83; Sub-dean, 1950–70; Dean and Dir of Studies, 1970–83; Head, Dept of Path., Eastman Dental Hosp., 1950–83. Civilian Cons. in Dental Path., RN, 1967–83. Member: WHO Expert Adv. Panel on Dental Health, 1975–97; Bd of Faculty of Dental Surgery, RCS, 1964–80, Council, RCS, 1977–80; GDC, 1973–84; Mem., Council for Postgrad. Med. Educn in Eng. and Wales, 1972–77 (Chm., Dental Cttee, 1972–77); Pres., Odontological Section, RSocMed, 1973–74; Pres., British Div., Internat. Assoc. for Dental Res., 1974–77. Hon. Pres. of the Assoc., 1974–75. Editor, Archives of Oral Biology, 1959–69. Lectures: Wilkinson, Manchester, 1962; Charles Tomes, 1969, Webb Johnson, 1981, RCS; Holme, UCH, 1969; Elwood Meml, QUB, 1970; Hutchinson, Edinburgh, 1971; Wilkinson, IDS, 1987. Hon. FRACDS 1978. Howard Mummery Prize, BDA, 1966; Maurice Down Award, Brit. Assoc. of Oral Surgeons, 1974; Colyer Gold Medal, FDS, RCS, 1985. Dr *hc* Helsinki, 2000. *Publications:* (with R. B. Lucas) Bacteriology for Students of Dental Surgery, 1954, 3rd edn 1966; (with J. J. Pindborg and H. Torloni) World Health Organization International Histological Classification of Tumours: Odontogenic Tumours, Jaw Cysts and Allied Lesions, 1972 (2nd edn, with J. J. Pindborg and M. Shear, as World Health Organisation Histological Typing of Odontogenic Tumours, 1992); (with B. Cohen) Scientific Foundations of Dentistry, 1976; numerous papers in med. and dental jls. *Address:* 11 Sheepcote Close, Beaconsfield, Bucks HP9 1SX. *T:* (01494) 680306.

KRAMER, Prof. Jeffrey, PhD; FREng; Professor of Distributed Computing, Imperial College London (formerly Imperial College of Science, Technology and Medicine, London), since 1995; *b* 7 Jan. 1949; *s* of Dr Bobby Kramer and Joyce Kramer (*née* Feitelberg); *m* 1981, Nitza Omer; one *s* one *d*. *Educ:* Univ. of Natal (BSc Eng Electrical Engrg 1971); Imperial College, London (MSc Computing 1972; PhD Computing 1979). CEng 1986; FIET (FIEE 1992). Department of Computing, Imperial College, London: programmer, 1973–75; Res. Asst, 1975–76; Lectr, 1976–87; Sen. Lectr, 1987–90; Reader in Distributed Computing, 1990–95; Head of Dept, 1999–2004; Dean, Faculty of Engineering, 2006–09; Sen. Dean, 2009–12. Ernest Oppenheimer Meml Trust/W. D. Wilson Vis. Fellow, S Africa, 1995. Computing Expert, World Bank Project for Provincial Univs, Peoples Republic of China, 1991. Founding Mem., Wkg Gp on Requirements Engrg, IFIP, 1995; Chm., Steering Cttee, 2000–02, Gen. Chm., 2010, Internat. Conf. on Software Engrg. Ed.-in-Chief, IEEE Trans on Software Engrg, 2006–10. FACM 2000; FCGI 2007; FREng 2008. (Jtly) Outstanding Res. Award, 2005, Distinguished Service Award, 2011, ACM Special Interest Gp on Software Engrg. *Publications:* (with M. S. Sloman) Distributed Systems and Computer Networks, 1986 (trans. Japanese and German); (ed jtly) Software Process Modelling and Technology, 1994; (with J. Magee) Concurrency: state models & Java programs, 1999, 2nd edn 2006; contrib. over 200 papers to learned internat. jls on software engrg, distributed computing, requirements engrg, software architectures, model checking and self-managed adaptive systems. *Recreations:* fanatical about films and music, travel, tennis, ski-ing, mountain walking, diving and surfing, whenever the opportunity arises. *Address:* Department of Computing, Imperial College London, SW7 2AZ. *T:* (020) 7594 8271, *Fax:* (020) 7594 8282.

KRAMER, Prof. Dame Leonie (Judith), AC 1993; DBE 1983 (OBE 1976); DPhil; Professor of Australian Literature, University of Sydney, 1968–89, now Professor Emeritus; Chancellor, University of Sydney Senate, 1991–2001 (Deputy Chancellor, 1989–91); *b* 1 Oct. 1924; *d* of Alfred and Gertrude Gibson; *m* 1952, Harold Kramer (*d* 1988); two *d*. *Educ:* Presbyterian Ladies Coll., Melbourne; Univ. of Melbourne (BA 1945); St Hugh's Coll., Oxford Univ. (DPhil 1953; Hon. Fellow, 1994); MA Sydney, 1989. FAHA; FACE. Tutor and Lectr, Univ. of Melb., 1945–49; Tutor and Postgrad. Student, St Hugh's Coll., Oxford, 1949–52; Lectr, Canberra University Coll., 1954–56; Lectr, subseq. Sen. Lectr and Associate Prof., Univ. of NSW, 1958–68. Chm., Quadrant Mag., 1986–99. Member: Univs Council, 1974–86; NSW Bd of Studies, 1990–; Adv. Bd, World Book Encyclopaedia, 1989–99; Internat. Adv. Cttee, Encyc. Brit., 1991–98; Council, Sci. Foundn for Physics, Univ. of Sydney, 2002–. Director: Australia and NZ Banking Gp, 1983–94; Western Mining Corp., 1984–96. Mem., NSW Council, Aust. Inst. of Co. Dirs, 1992–2001. Comr, Electricity Commn, NSW, 1988–95. Chairman: ABC, 1982–83; Operation Rainbow Aust. Ltd, 1996–2001; Chm., 1987–91, Dep. Chm., 1991–95, Bd of Dirs, Nat. Inst. of Dramatic Art. Dir, St Vincent's Hosp., Sydney, 1988–93. Mem. Council, Nat. Roads & Motorists Assoc., 1984–95; National President: Australia-Britain Soc., 1984–93; Order of Australia Assoc., 2001–04; Member Council: Asia Soc., 1991–2000; Foundn for Young Australians, 1989–. Sen. Fellow, Inst. of Public Affairs, 1988–96. Hon. Fellow: St Andrew's Coll., Univ. of Sydney, 2002; Janet Clarke Hall, Univ. of Melbourne, 2005. Hon. DLitt: Tasmania, 1977; Queensland, 1991; New South Wales, 1992; Sydney, 2009; Hon. LLD: Melbourne, 1983; ANU, 1984. Britannica Award, 1986. *Publications:* as L. J. Gibson: Henry Handel Richardson and Some of Her Sources, 1954; as Leonie Kramer: A Companion to Australia Felix, 1962; Myself when Laura: fact and fiction in Henry Handel Richardson's school career, 1966; Henry Handel Richardson, 1967, repr. as contrib. to Six Australian Writers, 1971; (with Robert D. Eagleson) Language and Literature: a synthesis, 1976; (with Robert D. Eagleson) A Guide to Language and Literature, 1977; A. D. Hope, 1979; (ed and introd) The Oxford History of Australian Literature, 1981; (ed with Adrian Mitchell) The Oxford Anthology of Australian Literature, 1985; (ed and introd) My Country: Australian poetry and short stories—two hundred years, 1985; (ed and introd) James McAuley, 1988; (ed) Collected Poems of David Campbell, 1989; (ed) Collected Poems of James McAuley, 1995; Broomstick: personal reflections of Leonie Kramer, 2012. *Recreations:* gardening, music. *Address:* 12 Vaucluse Road, Vaucluse, NSW 2030, Australia. *T:* (2) 93514164.

KRAMER, Prof. Matthew Henry, JD, PhD, LLD; FBA 2014; Professor of Legal and Political Philosophy, University of Cambridge, since 2002; Fellow of Churchill College, Cambridge, since 1994; *b* Boston, Mass, 9 June 1959; *s* of Alton Marshall Kramer and Alma Eunice Kramer (*née* Bixon). *Educ:* Cornell Univ. (BA 1981); Harvard Law Sch. (JD 1985); Trinity Coll., Cambridge (PhD 1989; LLD 2004). Jun. Res. Fellow, Darwin Coll., Cambridge, 1989–91; Vis. Fellow, Inst. for Res. in Humanities, 1991–94; Lectr in Legal Philos., 1994–99, Reader in Legal and Pol Philos., 1999–2002, Univ. of Cambridge. *Publications:* Legal Theory, Political Theory, and Deconstruction, 1991; Critical Legal Theory and the Challenge of Feminism, 1995; Hobbes and the Paradoxes of Political Origins, 1997; John Locke and the Origins of Private Property, 1997; (jtly) A Debate over Rights, 1998; In Defense of Legal Positivism, 1999; In the Realm of Legal and Moral Philosophy, 1999; Rights, Wrongs, and Responsibilities, 2001; The Quality of Freedom, 2003; Where Law and Morality Meet, 2004; Objectivity and the Rule of Law, 2007; (ed jtly) Freedom: a philosophical anthology, 2007; (ed jtly) The Legacy of H. L. A. Hart, 2008; Moral Realism as a Moral Doctrine, 2009; (ed jtly) Hillel Steiner and the Anatomy of Justice, 2009; The Ethics of Capital Punishment, 2011; (ed jtly) Crime, Punishment and Responsibility, 2011; Torture and Moral Integrity, 2014. *Recreations:* biblical commentary, Shakespearean drama, classical music, long-distance running. *Address:* Churchill College, Cambridge CB3 0DS. *T:* (01223) 336231, *Fax:* (01223) 336180. *E:* mhk11@cam.ac.uk.

KRAMER, Stephen Ernest; QC 1995; **His Honour Judge Kramer;** a Senior Circuit Judge at the Central Criminal Court, since 2005 (a Circuit Judge 2003–05); *b* 12 Sept. 1947; *s* of late Frederic Kramer and of Lotte Karoline Kramer (*née* Wertheimer); *m* 1978, Miriam Leopold; one *s* one *d*. *Educ:* Hampton Grammar Sch.; Keble Coll., Oxford (BA 1969; MA 1987); Université de Nancy. Called to the Bar, Gray's Inn, 1970, Bencher, 2002; Standing Counsel to HM Customs and Excise (Crime), S Eastern Circuit, 1989–95; a Recorder, 1991–2003; Hd of Chambers, 2 Hare Court, 1996–2003. Chm., Liaison Cttee, Bar Council/Inst. of Barristers' Clerks, 1996–99; Criminal Bar Association: Chm., 2000–01; Vice-Chm., 1999–2000; acting Vice-Chm., 1998–99. Contested (L), Twickenham, Feb. and Oct. 1974. Gov., Hampton Sch., 2005–. *Recreations:* swimming, walking, theatre, watching Rugby Union. *Address:* Central Criminal Court, Old Bailey, EC4M 7EH.

KRAYE, Prof. Jill Adrian; Professor of the History of Renaissance Philosophy, 2004–13, now Professor Emeritus, and Librarian, 2002–13, Warburg Institute, University of London (Hon. Fellow, 2014); *b* 27 Aug. 1947; *d* of Philip M. and Frances B. Kraye; *m* 1986, Martin Charles Davies. *Educ:* Univ. of Calif, Berkeley (BA Hist. 1969); Columbia Univ. (MA Hist. 1970; PhD 1991). Warburg Institute: Asst Librarian (Acad.), 1974–86; Lectr in Hist. of Philos., 1987–96; Sen. Lectr, 1996–98; Reader in Hist. of Renaissance Philos., 1999–2004. Vis. Prof., Seminar für Geistesgeschichte und Philosophie der Renaissance, Ludwig-Maximilians Univ., Munich, 2002. Vice-Pres., European Soc. for Early Modern Philosophy, 2007–10. Joint-Editor: Jl Warburg and Courtauld Insts, 1997–; Internat. Jl of Classical Tradition, 2012–; Mem., Editl Bd (Renaissance and 16th Century), Stanford Encyclopedia of Philosophy, 2002–; Mem., Bd of Assoc. Editors, History of Humanities, 2014–. *Publications:* (ed) The Cambridge Companion to Renaissance Humanism, 1996 (trans. Spanish 1998); (ed) Cambridge Translations of Renaissance Philosophical Texts, 2 vols, 1997; Classical Traditions in Renaissance Philosophy, 2002; (ed jtly) Conflicting Duties: science, medicine and religion in Rome, 1550–1750, 2009; (ed jtly) Fourteenth-Century Classicism: Petrarch and Bernat Metge, 2012; contrib. articles to Jl Hist. of Philosophy, Renaissance Studies, Rinascimento, Common Knowledge and other jls. *Recreations:* reading, cinema, feeding squirrels, avoiding writing book reviews. *Address:* Warburg Institute, Woburn Square, WC1H 0AB. *T:* (020) 7862 8916, *Fax:* (020) 7862 8955. *E:* Jill.Kraye@sas.ac.uk.

KREBS, Baron *cr* 2007 (Life Peer), of Wytham in the county of Oxfordshire; **John Richard Krebs,** Kt 1999; DPhil; FRS 1984; Principal, Jesus College, Oxford, 2005–15; *b* 11 April 1945; *s* of Sir Hans Adolf Krebs, FRCP, FRS and Margaret Cicely Krebs; *m* 1st, 1968, Katharine Anne Fullerton (marr. diss. 2012); two *d*; 2nd, 2013, Sarah Margaret Phibbs. *Educ:* City of Oxford High School; Pembroke College, Oxford (BA 1966; MA 1970; DPhil 1970). Asst Prof., Univ. of British Columbia, 1970–73; Lectr in Zoology, UCNW, 1973–75; University of Oxford: Univ. Lectr in Zoology, 1976–88; Royal Soc. Res. Prof., Dept of Zoology, 1988–2005 (on leave of absence, 1994–99); Fellow, Pembroke Coll., 1981–2005 (E. P. Abraham Fellow, 1981–88; Hon. Fellow, 2005). Dir, AFRC Unit of Ecology and Behaviour, NERC Unit of Behavioural Ecology, 1989–94; Chief Exec., NERC, 1994–99; Chm., Food Standards Agency, 2000–05. Storer Lectr, Univ. of Calif, 1985; Croonian Lectr, Royal Soc., 2004. Mem., AFRC, 1988–94 (Animals Res. Cttee, 1990–94; sen. scientific consultant, 1991–94). Mem., Sci. and Technol. Select Cttee, H of L, 2010–. President: Internat. Soc. for Behavioral Ecology, 1988–90; Assoc. for the Study of Animal Behaviour, 1993–94; Campden BRI, 2011–; British Sci. Assoc., 2012–13. Scientific Member: Max Planck Soc., 1985–; Council, Zoological Soc. of London, 1991–92; Academia Europæa, 1995; Leopoldina, German Nat. Acad. Scis, 2013. FMedSci 2004. Hon. Mem., British Ecol Soc., 1999; Internat. Mem. (formerly Foreign Mem.), Amer. Philosophical Soc., 2000; Hon. Foreign Mem., Amer. Acad. Arts and Scis, 2000; Hon. Fellow, German Ornithologists' Union, 2003; Foreign Associate, US Nat. Acad. of Scis, 2004. Hon. Fellow: Cardiff Univ., 1999; UWIC, 2006; Univ. of Wales, Bangor, 2006; Assoc. for Nutrition, 2012; Hon. FZS 2006. Hon. DSc: Sheffield, 1993; Wales, Birmingham, 1997; Exeter, 1998; Warwick, 2000; Cranfield, Kent, Plymouth, 2001; QUB, Heriot-Watt, 2002; South Bank, 2003; Lancaster, 2005; Guelph, 2006; Aberdeen, 2010; Newcastle, 2012; Western, 2015; DUniv Stirling, 2000. Scientific Medal, Zool Soc., 1981; Bicentenary Medal, Linnaean Soc., 1983; Frink Medal, Zool Soc., 1997; Elliott Coues Award, Amer. Ornithol Union, 1999; Medal, Assoc. for Study of Animal Behaviour, 2000; Benjamin Ward Richardson Gold Medal, RSH, 2002; Wooldridge Medal, BVA, 2003; Lord Rayner Medal, RCP, 2005; Outstanding Achievement Award, Soc. for Food Hygiene Technology, 2005; Harben Gold Medal, RIPH, 2006. *Publications:* Behavioural Ecology, 1978, 4th edn 1997; Introduction to Behavioural Ecology, 1981, 4th edn 2012; Foraging Theory, 1986; Behavioural and Neural Aspects of Learning and Memory, 1991; Food: a very short introduction, 2013; articles in Animal Behaviour, Jl of Animal Ecology. *Recreations:* gardening, tennis, running, walking, cooking. *E:* john.krebs@zoo.ox.ac.uk.

KREMER, Gidon; violinist; founder and Artistic Director, Kremerata Baltica, since 1997; *b* 27 Feb. 1947. *Educ:* Riga Sch. of Music; Moscow Conservatory. First Prize, Internat. Tchaikovsky Competition, Moscow, 1970. Has played with most major internat. orchestras including: Berlin Philharmonic; Boston Symphony; Concertgebouw; London Philharmonic; LA Philharmonic; NY Philharmonic; Philadelphia; Royal Philharmonic; Vienna Philharmonic. Founded Lockenhaus Fest., Austria, 1981. *Address:* c/o Opus 3 Artists, 470 Park Avenue South, 9th Floor North, New York, NY 10016, USA.

KREMER, Lorraine; *see* Sutherland, L.

KRESTOVNIKOFF, Miranda Jane; television and radio broadcaster; author; President, Royal Society for the Protection of Birds, since 2014; *b* Taplow, Bucks, 29 Jan. 1973; *d* of F. D. and J. A. M. Harper-Jones; *m* 1998, Nicholas Krestovnikoff; one *s* one *d*. *Educ:* Abbey Sch., Reading; Univ. of Bristol (MSc Zool. 1994). Runner, then researcher, BBC Bristol, 1993–2001; television presenter: World Gone Wild, 1998–2000; Water Warriors, 2000; The Nature of Shopping, 2001; Smile, 2002; Hidden Treasure, 2003; Wreck Detectives, 2003–04; Time Trail, 2004; Coast, 2004–15; History Mysteries, How to Holiday Greener, Countrylives, Thames Wildlife Superhighway, Nature of Britain, 2007; One Show, 2008–; Big British Wildlife Revival, 2013; Inside Out, 2014–15; reporter, Costing the Earth, Living World, BBC Radio 4, 2012–14; presenter, Tweet of the Day, BBC Radio 4, 2013–14. Patron: Whale and Dolphin Conservation, 2008–; Alderney Wildlife Trust, 2008–. *Publications:* (with M. Halls) Scuba Diving, 2006; Best British Beaches, 2009. *Recreations:* walking the dog, scuba diving, singing, playing flute (flautist, New Bristol Sinfonia), charity, travel, cycling, keeping one step ahead of the children. *Address:* c/o Jo Sarsby Management, 58 St John's Road, Clifton, Bristol BS8 2HG. *T:* (0117) 927 9423. *E:* jo@josarsby.com.

KRETZMER, Herbert, OBE 2011; journalist and lyricist; *b* Kroonstad, S Africa, 5 Oct. 1925; *s* of William and Tilly Kretzmer; *m* 1st, 1961, Elisabeth Margaret Wilson (marr. diss., 1973); one *s* one *d*; 2nd, 1988, Sybil Sever. *Educ:* Kroonstad High Sch.; Rhodes Univ., Grahamstown. Entered journalism, 1946, writing weekly cinema newsreel commentaries and documentary films for African Film Productions, Johannesburg. Reporter and entertainment columnist, Sunday Express, Johannesburg, 1951–54; feature writer and columnist, Daily Sketch, London, 1954–59; Columnist, Sunday Dispatch, London, 1959–61; feature writer and theatre critic, Daily Express, 1962–78; TV critic, Daily Mail, 1979–87. TV Critic of the Year, Philips Industries Award, 1980; commended in British Press Awards, 1981. As lyric writer, contributed weekly songs to: That Was The Week…, Not So Much A Programme…, BBC 3, That's Life. Wrote lyrics of Goodness Gracious Me, 1960 (Ivor Novello Award) and Yesterday When I was Young, 1969 (ASCAP award); Gold record for She, 1974; Our Man Crichton, Shaftesbury Theatre, 1964 (book and lyrics); The Four Musketeers, Drury Lane, 1967 (lyrics); Les Misérables, RSC, 1985 (lyrics (Tony Award, 1987; Grammy Award, 1988)); Marguerite, Haymarket Th., 2008 (lyrics); Kristina, Carnegie Hall, NY, 2009 (co-lyricist with Björn Ulvaeus); *film:* Can Heironymus Merkin Ever Forget Mercy Humppe And Find True Happiness?, 1969 (lyrics); Les Miserables, 2012 (lyrics and co-writer, screenplay) (Satellite Award for Best Original Song in Motion Picture for 'Suddenly', Internat. Press Acad., 2012); has also written lyrics for other films, and for TV programmes. Hon. Dr of Letters, Richmond Coll., Amer. Internat. Univ. in London, 1996; Hon. DLaws Rhodes, 2011. Jimmy Kennedy Award, British Acad. of Songwriters, Composers and Authors, 1989. Chevalier de l'Ordre des Arts et des Lettres, 1988. *Publications:* Our Man Crichton, 1965; (jointly) Every Home Should Have One, 1970; Snapshots: encounters with 20th century legends, 2014. *Address:* c/o Berlin Associates, 7 Tyers Gate, SE1 3HX. *Clubs:* Garrick, Royal Automobile.

KRIER, Léon; architecture, urbanism and design consultant; *b* Luxembourg, 7 April 1946. *Educ:* Univ. of Stuttgart. Asst to James Stirling, London, 1968–70, 1973–74; Project Partner, J. P. Kleihues, Berlin, 1971–72; private architectl practice, London, 1974–97, Claviers, 1998–2002, Luxembourg, 2003–. Lecturer: Architectl Assoc. Sch., 1973–76; Princeton Univ., 1977; RCA, 1977; Jefferson Prof. of Architecture, Univ. of Virginia, 1982; Vis. Prof., 1990–2013, Inaugural Robert A. M. Stern Vis. Prof., 2015, Yale Sch. of Architecture. *Projects* include: Spitalfields Market, 1987; New Town of Poundbury develt (also masterplan), 1988–; Justice Palace, Luxembourg, 1995; Village Hall, Windsor, Fla, 1997; Krier House, Seaside, Fla, 1997 (extension, 2000); Archaeol Mus., Sintra, Portugal, 1999; Heulebrug Urban Develt, Knokke, Belgium (also masterplan), 1998; Citta Nuova Urban Centre Alessandria, Italy, 1999; tower block restyling, Alessandria, Italy, 2000; Sch. of Architecture Auditorium, Miami Univ., 2002; Brasserie Val d'Europe, Eurodisney, 2003; Market Tower, Seaside, Fla, 2003–; Oro Trend Factory restyling, Valenza, Italy, 2003; Cayala, Guatemala City (also masterplan), 2003–; Palazzo Saggini, Alessandria, Italy, 2005; Georgetown develt, Corbianca, Romania, 2008; Paralimni oceanside resort, Cyprus, 2009–; Mason House, Uzés, France, 2009; Béguin House, Sanilhac, France, 2009; Queen Mother Monument, Dorset, 2009–15; EBSCO model house, Alys Beach, Fla, 2015–; *Masterplans* include: Area Fiat, Novoli, Italy, 1993; Hardelot, France, 2000; Noordwijk, Holland, 2002; Meriam Park, Chico, Calif, 2003; Newquay Growth Area, for Duchy of Cornwall, 2004–06; New Educnl Campus and Urban Centre, Osio Sotto, Bergamo, Italy, 2005–; New Urban Centre, Val d'Europe, France, 2006–11; Renovation Piazza Marconi EUR, Rome, 2008; Abu-Sidra, Qatar, 2009; Poundbury NE Quarter, 2009–11; Tor Bella Monaca, Rome, 2010; High Malton Village develt, Malton, Yorks, 2014; New Urban Quarter El Socorro, Guatemala City, 2015–; *Designs* include: Rita Wolff exhibn, Fondation de l'Architecture, Brussels, 1990; furniture for Giorgetti, Italy, 1991–; garden furniture for the Prince of Wales, Duchy Originals, 1995–2003; urban furniture for Poundbury, 1998–; urban furniture for Cayala, Guatemala City, 2011–. *Exhibitions* include: Triennale, Milan, 1973; Rational Architecture, London, Barcelona, 1975; Inst. for Architecture and Urban Studies, NY, 1976 and 1978; Roma Interrotta, Rome, 1978; Léon Krier La Ricostruzione Della Citta Europea, Museo di Castelvecchio, Verona, 1980; La Presenza del Passato, Venice Biennale of Architecture, 1980; Drawings, Max Protetch Gall., NY, 1981, 1984; Model Futures, ICA, 1983; (with R. Bofill) Architecture, Urbanism and History, MOMA, NY, 1985; Léon Krier and the Plan of Washington, Amer. Architectl Foundn Octagon, Washington DC, 1987; Atlantis Project, DAM, Frankfurt, 1987; Imago Luxemburgi, Amsterdam, 1991, Prague, 1993, Lisbon, 1995; Vision of Europe, Bologna, 1992; Biennale di Arte Sacra, Venice, 1992; Sensori del Futuro, Venice Biennale of Architecture, 1996; At the End of the Century, Mus. of Contemporary Art, LA, 2000; Furniture Designed by Léon Krier, Kunstgewerbemuseum, Berlin, 2000; Eisenman-Krier: two ideologies, Yale, 2003; Genialidad Krier, Univ. Francisco Marroquin, Guatemala City, 2010. City of Berlin Architecture Prize, 1977; Jefferson Meml Medal, 1985; Chicago AIA Award, 1987; Eur. Culture Prize, 1995; Silver Medal, Acad. Française, 1997; Richard Driehaus Prize, 2003; Lifetime Achievement Award, Congress of New Urbanism, 2006. *Publications* include: (ed) James Stirling: Buildings and Projects, 1974; (ed) Cities Within the City, 1977; (ed) Rational Architecture Rationelle, 1978; Houses, Palaces, Cities, 1984; Albert Speer: architecture 1932–42, 1985, rev. edn 2013; The Completion of Washington DC, 1986; Atlantis, 1987; (ed) New Classicism, 1990; Architecture and Urban Design 1967–1992, 1992; Architecture: choice or fate, 1997; Eisenman-Krier: two ideologies, 2005; (jtly) Get Your House Right, 2007; The Architectural Turning of Settlements, 2008; The Architecture of Community, 2009; Drawings for Architecture, 2009; articles in jls.

KRIKLER, Dennis Michael, MD; FRCP; Consultant Cardiologist, Hammersmith Hospital, and Senior Lecturer in Cardiology, Royal Postgraduate Medical School, 1973–94, now Emeritus; *b* 10 Dec. 1928; *s* of late Barnet and Eva Krikler; *m* 1955, Anne (*née* Winterstein); one *s* one *d*. *Educ:* Muizenberg High Sch.; Univ. of Cape Town, S Africa. Ho. Phys. and Registrar, Groote Schuur Hosp., 1952–55; Fellow, Lahey Clinic, Boston, 1956; C. J. Adams Meml Travelling Fellowship, 1956; Sen. Registrar, Groote Schuur Hosp., 1957–58; Consultant Physician: Salisbury Central Hosp., Rhodesia, 1958–66; Prince of Wales's Hosp., London, 1966–73; Consultant Cardiologist, Ealing Hosp., 1973–89. Expert Clinicien en Cardiologie, Ministère des Affaires Sociales, Santé, France, 1983. Visiting Professor: Baylor, Indiana and Birmingham Univs, 1985; Boston, Los Angeles and Kentucky, 1988; Lectures: Internat., Amer. Heart Assoc., 1984 (Paul Dudley White Citation for internat. achievement); George Burch Meml, Assoc. of Univ. Cardiologists, 1989; Joseph Welker Meml, Univ. of Kansas, 1989; Denolin, Eur. Soc. of Cardiology, 1990; Hideo Ueda, Japanese Soc. of Electrocardiology, 1990; Howard Burchell, Univ. of Minnesota, 1991. Member, British Cardiac Soc., 1971– (Treasurer, 1976–81); Hon. Member: Soc. Française de Cardiologie, 1981–; Soc. di Cultura Medica Vercellese, Italy; Soc. de Cardiologia de Levante, Spain. Editor, British Heart Journal, 1981–91 (Editor Emeritus, 1992–); Member, Editorial Committee: Cardiovascular Res., 1975–91; Archives des Maladies du Coeur et des Vaisseaux, 1980–; Revista Latina de Cardiologia, 1980–; ACCEL Audiotape Jl, 1987–2000. Mem. Scientific Council, Revista Portuguesa de Cardiologia, 1982–. FACC 1971; Fellow, Eur. Soc. of Cardiology, 1988 (Medal of Honour, 1990). Hon. Fellow, Council on Clin. Cardiol., Amer. Heart Assoc., 1984. Freeman: Soc. of Apothecaries, 1989; City of London, 1990. McCullough Prize, 1949; Sir William Osler Award, Miami Univ., 1981; Silver Medal, British Cardiac Soc., 1992. Chevalier, Legion of Honour (France), 1999. *Publications:* Cardiac Arrhythmias (with J. F. Goodwin), 1975; (with A. Zanchetti) Calcium antagonism in cardiovascular therapy, 1981; (with D. A. Chamberlain and W. J. McKenna) Amiodarone and arrhythmias, 1983; (jtly) 20th Century British Cardiology, 2000; papers on cardiology in British, American and French jls. *Recreations:* reading (and also writing), especially history (contemporary and cardiological); photography. *Address:* 2 Garden Court, Grove End Road, NW8 9PP. *E:* dennis.krikler@sky.com.

KRIKLER, His Honour Leonard Gideon; a Circuit Judge, 1984–2001; *b* 23 May 1929; *s* of late Major James Harold Krikler, OBE, ED, and Tilly Krikler; *m* 1st, 1955, Dr Thilla Krikler (*d* 1973); four *s*; 2nd, 1975, Lily Shub; one *s*, and one step *s* two step *d*. *Educ:* Milton Sch., Bulawayo, S Rhodesia (Zimbabwe). Called to Bar, Middle Temple, 1953. Crown Counsel, Court Martial Appeals Court, 1968; Dep. Circuit Judge, 1974; a Recorder, 1980–84; Dep. Circuit Judge, SE and Midland Circuits, 2001–04. Head of Chambers, London and Cambridge, 1975–84. *Recreations:* cartooning, drawing and painting.

KRIVANEK, Dr Ondrej Ladislav, PhD; FRS 2010; Founder, 1997, and President, Nion Co.; Affiliate Professor, Arizona State University. *Educ:* Leeds Univ.; Trinity Coll., Cambridge (PhD 1976). Postdoctoral res. at Kyoto Univ., Bell Labs and Lawrence Berkeley Lab., Univ. of Calif, Berkeley; Consultant, then Dir, R&D, Gatan Inc., 1983; Arizona State University: Asst Prof., Center for Solid State Sci. and Associate Dir, Center for High Resolution Electron Microscopy; Adjunct Prof., Dept of Physics, 1985–95. *Publications:* contribs to Nature, Ultramicroscopy, Science, Phys. Rev. Letters. *Address:* Nion Co., 1102 8th Street, Kirkland, WA 98033, USA.

KROEMER, Prof. Herbert, PhD; Professor of Electrical and Computer Engineering, University of California at Santa Barbara, 1976–2013, now Professor Emeritus; *b* Weimar, Germany, 25 Aug. 1928. *Educ:* Univ. of Göttingen (PhD 1952). Semiconductor research: Central Telecommunications Laboratory, Germany, 1952; RCA Labs, Princeton, NJ, 1954–57; Varian Associates, Palo Alto, Calif, 1959–66; Prof. of Physics, Univ. of Colorado, 1968–76. (Jtly) Nobel Prize for Physics, 2000. Grand Cross, Order of Merit (Germany), 2001.

Publications: Quantum Mechanics: for engineering, materials science and applied physics; (jtly) Thermal Physics; articles in jls. *Address:* c/o Electrical and Computer Engineering Department, University of California, Santa Barbara, CA 93106–9560, USA.

KROES, Neelie; Member, 2004–14, and a Vice-President, 2010–14, European Commission; Special Envoy for Startups, Ministry of Economic Affairs, Netherlands, 2014–16; *b* 19 July 1941. *Educ:* Erasmus Univ., Rotterdam (MSc 1965). Asst Prof. of Transport Econs, Erasmus Univ., Rotterdam, 1965–71; Mem., Rotterdam Municipal Council, 1969–71; MP (VVD), Netherlands, 1971–77; Dep. Minister of Transport, Public Works and Telecommunications, 1977–81; Minister of Transport and Public Works, then of Transport and Waterways, 1982–89; Advr, European Transport Comr, Brussels, 1989–91; Pres., Nijenrode Univ., 1991–2000; Chm., Supervisory Bd, MeyerMonitor, until 2004. Non-executive Director: Ballast Nedam, 1990–2004; New Skies Satellites, 1999–2004; mmO_2, 2001–04; Volvo Gp, 2003–04; Royal P&O Nedlloyd, 2004. Trustee, Prologis, 2002–04.

KROLL, Prof. (John) Simon, FRCP, FRCPCH; FMedSci; Professor of Paediatrics and Molecular Infectious Diseases, and Head, Molecular Infectious Diseases Group, Department of Paediatrics, Imperial College London, since 1993; Hon. Consultant in Paediatrics, Imperial College Healthcare NHS Trust, St Mary's Hospital (formerly St Mary's Hospital), since 1993; *b* London, 29 Nov. 1952; *s* of late Alexander Kroll and Maria Kroll (*née* Wolff); *m* 1978, Mary Eileen Soothill; one *s* one *d*. *Educ:* Bousfield Primary Sch.; St Paul's Sch., London; Balliol Coll., Oxford (BA 1st Cl. Natural Scis (Chem.) 1975; MA 1980; BM BCh 1980; Hon. Fellow 2009). FRCP 1995; FRCPCH 1997. University of Oxford: Clin. Lectr in Paediatrics, 1984–89; Lister Inst. Res. Fellow, 1986–89; Lectr in Paediatrics, 1989–93; Fellow, Corpus Christi Coll., Oxford, 1989–93; Hon. Consultant in Paediatrics, John Radcliffe Hosp., Oxford, 1989–93. Campus Dean and non-exec. Dir, St Mary's Hosp. NHS Trust, 2004–06. Mem., Lister Inst. of Preventive Medicine, 1991–. Hon. Med. Dir, Meningitis Trust, 2009–. FMedSci 2001. *Publications:* Meningitis: a guide for families, 1997; chapters on meningitis in med. textbooks; contribs to scientific jls on molecular basis of virulence of bacterial pathogens, especially Haemophilus influenzae and Neisseria meningitidis. *Recreation:* clarinet playing (jazz and classical). *Address:* Department of Paediatrics, Faculty of Medicine, Wright Fleming Institute, Imperial College London, St Mary's Campus, Norfolk Place, W2 1PG. *T:* (020) 7594 3695, *Fax:* (020) 7594 3984. *E:* s.kroll@imperial.ac.uk.
See also N. J. Kroll.

KROLL, Nicholas James, CB 2002; Director, BBC Trust, 2007–14; *b* 23 June 1954; *s* of late Alexander Kroll and Maria Kroll (*née* Wolff); *m* 1981, Catherine Askew; one *s* one *d* (and one *d* decd). *Educ:* St Paul's Sch.; Corpus Christi Coll., Oxford. Entered Civil Service, 1977: DoE/ Dept of Transport, 1977–86; HM Treasury, 1986–93; Department of National Heritage, then Department for Culture, Media and Sport, 1993–2004: Dir, Creative Industries Media and Broadcasting Gp, 1996–2000; Corporate Services Dir, 2000–02 (acting Perm. Sec., 2001); Chief Operating Officer and Dep. to Perm. Sec., 2002–04; Dir of Governance, BBC, 2004–06. Member: Bd, NYO, 2005–11; Council, Hellenic Soc., 2010–11. *Recreation:* music.
See also J. S. Kroll.

KROLL, Simon; *see* Kroll, J. S.

KROLL, Rev. Dr Una (Margaret Patricia), CJC; writer and broadcaster, since 1970; *b* 15 Dec. 1925; *d* of George Hill, CBE, DSO, MC, and Hilda Hill; *m* 1957, Leopold Kroll (*d* 1987); one *s* three *d*. *Educ:* St Paul's Girls' Sch.; Malvern Girls' Coll.; Girton Coll., Cambridge; The London Hosp. MB, BChir (Cantab) 1951; MA 1969. MRCGP 1967. House Officer, 1951–53; Overseas service (Africa), 1953–60; General Practice, 1960–81; Clinical MO, 1981–85, Sen. Clinical MO, 1985–88, Hastings Health Dist Theological trng, 1967–70; worker deaconess, 1970–88; ordained deacon, 1988, priest, 1997, Church in Wales; Sister, Soc. of the Sacred Cross, 1991–94; political work as a feminist, with particular ref. to status of women in the churches in England and internationally, 1970–89. *Publications:* Transcendental Meditation: a signpost to the world, 1974; Flesh of My Flesh: a Christian view on sexism, 1975; Lament for a Lost Enemy: study of reconciliation, 1976; Sexual Counselling, 1980; The Spiritual Exercise Book, 1985; Growing Older, 1988; In Touch with Healing, 1991; Vocation to Resistance, 1995; Trees of Life, 1997; Forgive and Live, 2000; Anatomy of Survival, 2001; Living Life to the Full, 2006; Bread Not Stones: the autobiography of an eventful life, 2014; contrib. Cervical Cytology (BMJ), 1969. *Recreation:* doing nothing. *Address:* 6 Hamilton House, 57 Hanson Street, Bury, Lancs BL9 6LR.

KROOK, (Elizabeth) Jane; *see* Maher, E. J.

KROTO, Sir Harold (Walter), Kt 1996; FRS 1990; Frances Eppes Professor, Department of Chemistry and Biochemistry, Florida State University, since 2004; *b* 7 Oct. 1939; *s* of Heinz and Edith Kroto; *m* 1963, Margaret Henrietta Hunter; two *s*. *Educ:* Bolton Sch.; Univ. of Sheffield (BSc, PhD). Res. in fullerenes, spectroscopy, radioastronomy, clusters and nanotechnology; Res. student, Sheffield Univ., 1961–64; Postdoctoral Fellow, NRCC, 1964–66; Res. scientist, Bell Telephone Labs, NJ, 1966–67; University of Sussex: Tutorial Fellow, 1967–68; Lectr, 1968–77; Reader, 1977–85; Prof. of Chemistry, 1985–91 and 2001–04, now Emeritus; Royal Soc. Res. Prof., 1991–2001. Visiting Professor: UBC 1973; USC 1981; UCLA, 1988–92; Univ. of Calif, Santa Barbara, 1996–2004. Chm., Vega Sci. Trust, 1995–. Pres., RSC, 2002–04. Longstaff Medal, RSC, 1993; (jtly) Nobel Prize for Chemistry, 1996; Erasmus Medal, Acad. Europaea, 2002; Michael Faraday Prize, 2001, Copley Medal, 2004, Royal Soc. *Publications:* Molecular Rotation Spectra, 1975, 2nd edn 1983; 350 papers in chemistry, chem. physics and astronomy jls. *Recreations:* art and graphic design, tennis. *Address:* Department of Chemistry and Biochemistry, Florida State University, Tallahassee, FL 32306–4390, USA; School of Chemistry, Physics and Environmental Science, University of Sussex, Brighton BN1 9QJ.

KRUGER, Prudence Margaret, (Mrs Rayne Kruger); *see* Leith, P. M.

KRUGMAN, Prof. Paul Robin, PhD; Professor of Economics and International Affairs, Woodrow Wilson School of Public and International Affairs, Princeton University, since 2000; Centenary Professor, London School of Economics and Political Science; *b* New York, 28 Feb. 1953; *m* Robin Wells. *Educ:* Yale Univ. (BA 1974); Massachusetts Inst. of Technol. (PhD 1977). Asst Prof., Yale Univ., 1977–80; Associate Prof., 1980–83, Prof. of Econs, 1983–94 and 1996–2000, MIT; Prof. of Econs, Stanford Univ., 1994–96. Sen. Internat. Economist, US President's Council of Econ. Advrs, 1982–83. Consultant: Federal Reserve Bank of NY; World Bank; IMF; UN. Columnist, NY Times, 1999–. Res. Associate, Nat. Bureau of Econ. Res., 1979–. Fellow, Econometric Soc. John Bates Clark Medal, AEA, 1991; Asturias Award (Spain), 2004; Nobel Prize in Economics, 2008. *Publications:* Exchange Rate Instability, 1988; The Age of Diminished Expectations, 1990; Rethinking International Trade, 1990; Geography and Trade, 1991; Currencies and Crises, 1992; Peddling Prosperity, 1994; Development, Geography and Economic Theory, 1995; The Self-Organizing Economy, 1996; Pop Internationalism, 1996; The Accidental Theorist and Other Dispatches from the Dismal Science, 1998; Fuzzy Math: the essential guide to the Bush Tax Plan, 2001; The Great Unraveling, 2003; The Conscience of a Liberal, 2007; The Return of Depression Economics and the Crisis of 2008, 2009; End This Depression Now!, 2012; (with R. Wells) Microeconomics, 2004, 2nd edn, 2008; (with R. Wells) Macroeconomics, 2005, 2nd edn, 2009; International Economics, 2011; Essentials of Economics, 2011; articles in jls. *Address:* Woodrow Wilson School of Public and International Affairs, Princeton University, 414 Robertson Hall, Princeton, NJ 08544–1013, USA.

KRZNARIC, Dr Roman Alexander; cultural thinker and writer on the art of living; *b* Sydney, Australia, 21 Dec. 1970. *Educ:* Pembroke Coll., Oxford (BA Hons PPE 1992); Inst. of Latin American Studies, Univ. of London (MSc Latin American Politics 1996); Essex Univ. (PhD 2003). Lecturer and Tutor in Sociology and Politics: Essex Univ., 1996–99; Cambridge Univ., 1999–2001; City Univ., 2003; Policy Consultant for Oxfam, UNDP, Commonwealth Secretariat, 2002–08; Project Dir, Oxford Muse, 2003–07; Founding Faculty Mem., Sch. of Life, 2008–. *Publications:* (with T. Zeldin) Guide to an Unknown University, 2006; The First Beautiful Game: stories of obsession in Real Tennis, 2006; The Wonderbox: curious histories of how to live, 2011; How to Find Fulfilling Work, 2012; Empathy: a handbook for revolution, 2014. *Recreations:* fanatical Real Tennis player, obsessive symbolic gardener, greenwood furniture maker, struggling singer. *W:* www.romankrznaric.com.

KUBEKOV, Susannah Kate; *see* Simon, S. K.

KUBIŠ, Ján; United Nations Special Representative and Head of the UN Assistance Mission in Afghanistan, 2012–14; *b* Bratislava, 12 Nov. 1952; *m*; one *d*. *Educ:* Jura Hronca High Sch., Bratislava; Moscow State Inst. for Internat. Affairs. Internat. Econ. Orgns Dept, Min. of Foreign Affairs, Prague, 1976–77; Office of the Minister, 1978–80; Attaché and Third Sec., Addis Ababa, 1980–85; Second Sec., 1985–87, Hd of Section, Security and Arms Control, 1987–88, Main Political Questions Dept, Min. of Foreign Affairs, Prague; First Sec. and Counsellor, Moscow, 1989–90; Dep. Hd of Embassy and Hd of Political Section, Moscow, 1990–91; Dir-Gen., Euro-Atlantic Section, Min. of Foreign Affairs, Prague, and Ambassador-at-large, 1991–92; Chm., Cttee of Sen. Officials, CSCE, 1992; Perm. Rep. of Czechoslovakia, 1992, of Slovak Republic, 1993–94, to UN and GATT, Geneva; Special Ministerial Envoy and Slovak Chief Negotiator on Pact for Stability in Europe, 1994; Dir, Conflict Prevention Centre, OSCE, 1994–98; Special Rep. of UN Sec.-Gen. for Tajikistan and Head, UN Mission of Observers to Tajikistan, 1998–99; Sec. Gen., OSCE, 1999–2005; EU Special Rep. for Central Asia, 2005–06; Minister of Foreign Affairs, Slovak Republic, 2006–09; Exec. Sec., UN Economic Commn for Europe, 2009–11. Mem., Adv. Bd, Geneva Centre for Security Policy. OSCE Medal, 1998. *Publications:* contrib. learned jls.

KUCHMA, Leonid Danylovych; President of Ukraine, 1994–2004; *b* 1938. *Educ:* Dnipropetrovsk State Univ. Constructor, Research-Production Union, Pirdenny Machine-Bldg Plant, 1960–75; Sec., Party Cttee, 1975–82; Dep. Dir Gen., 1982–86; Dir Gen., 1986–92; Chm., Ukrainian Union of Industrialists and Entrepreneurs, 1993–94. Deputy, Ukraine Parlt, 1991–94; Prime Minister, Ukraine, 1992–93. Mem., Central Cttee, Ukraine Communist Party, 1981–91; Mem., CPSU, 1960–91. *Address:* c/o Office of the President, Bankova Street 11, 01220 Kyiv, Ukraine.

KUENSSBERG, Joanna Kate; HM Diplomatic Service; High Commissioner to Mozambique, since 2014; *b* Lima, Peru, 1973; *d* of Nicholas Christopher Kuenssberg, *qv*; *m* 1997; three *s*. *Educ:* New Coll., Oxford (BA Hons Modern Langs 1995). Desk Officer, DoE, 1995–96; Project Manager (EU enlargement), EC, 1996–97; entered FCO, 1997; Dep. Hd, Enlargement Section, EU Dept, FCO, 1997–99; on secondment: to Min. of Foreign Affairs, Hungary, 1999–2000; to Quai d'Orsay, EU Directorate, 2000–01; First Sec. (EU/Econ.), Paris, 2001–04; Business Team Leader, Global Business/Sustainable Develt and Business Gp, FCO, 2004–07; Project Manager, Consular Strategy Prog., FCO, 2008–09; Russian lang. trng, 2009–10; Policy Unit, FCO, 2010; Portuguese lang. trng, 2010; Dep. Hd of Mission, 2010–14, Chargé d'Affaires, 2011, Lisbon. *Address:* British High Commission, Avenue Vladimir Lenine 310, Maputo, Mozambique.

KUENSSBERG, Nicholas Christopher, OBE 2004; Principal, Horizon Co-Invest, since 1995; *b* 28 Oct. 1942; *s* of late Ekkehard von Kuenssberg, CBE; *m* 1965, Sally Robertson (CBE 2000); one *s* two *d*. *Educ:* Edinburgh Acad.; Wadham Coll., Oxford (BA Hons), FCIS. Worked overseas, 1965–78; Dir, J. & P. Coats Ltd, 1978–91; Chm., Dynacast International Ltd, 1978–91; Director: Coats Patons Plc, 1985–91; Coats Viyella plc, 1986–91; Dawson International PLC, 1991–95. Chairman: David A. Hall Ltd, 1996–98; GAP Gp Ltd, 1996–2005; Stoddard Internat. PLC, 1997–2000; Canmore Partnership Ltd, 1999–; Iomart Gp Plc, 2000–08; Keronite PLC, 2005–07; eTourism Ltd, 2007–08; Scott and Fyfe Ltd, 2008–; mLED Ltd, 2010–; Social Investment Scotland, 2013–; Klik2Learn Ltd, 2013–; Director: Scottish Power plc (formerly S of Scotland Electricity Bd), 1984–97; W of Scotland Bd, Bank of Scotland, 1984–88; Standard Life Assce Co., 1988–97; Baxi Partnership, 1996–99; Chamberlin & Hill plc, 1999–2006; Citizens Theatre Glasgow Ltd, 2000–03; RingProp plc, 2002–06; Amino Technols plc, 2004–07. Member: Scottish Legal Aid Bd, 1996–2004; SEPA, 1999–2007 (Dep. Chm., 2003–07); Scottish Cttee, British Council, 1999–2008; QAA Scotland, 2004–10 (Chm., 2007–10); Council, ICAS, 2008–11; Dir, QAA, 2007–10. Chm., Assoc. of Mgt Educn & Trng in Scotland, 1996–98. Strathclyde Business School: Hon. Res. Fellow, 1986–88; Vis. Prof., 1988–91; Ext. Examr, Aberdeen Business Sch., 1998–2003; Hon. Prof., Univ. of Glasgow, 2008–. Chairman: Scottish Networks Internat., 2001–08; ScotlandIS, 2001–03; Scotland the Brand, 2002–04; Glasgow Sch. of Art, 2003–10. Gov., Queen's Coll., Glasgow, 1989–91. Trustee: David Hume Inst., 1994–2008; Pitlochry Fest. Th., 2010–. CCMI; FInstD (Chm., Scotland, 1997–99); FRSA. DUniv Glasgow, 2011. *Publications:* (ed) The First Decade: the first ten years of the David Hume Institute, 1996; (ed) Arguments Amongst Friends: twenty five years of sceptical enquiry, 2010; contrib. articles to business and policy jls. *Recreations:* sport, travel, opera, languages, employee ownership, social enterprise. *Address:* 6 Cleveden Drive, Glasgow G12 0SE. *T:* (0141) 339 8345.
See also J. K. Kuenssberg.

KUFUOR, John Agyekum, Hon. GCB 2007; President, Republic of Ghana, 2001–09; Ambassador Against Hunger, United Nations World Food Programme, since 2009; Founder, The John A. Kufuor Foundation, 2011; *b* 8 Dec. 1938; *m* Theresa Mensah; five *c*. *Educ:* Prempeh Coll., Kumasi; Univ. of Oxford (BA 1964). Called to the Bar, Lincoln's Inn, 1961. Chief Legal Officer and Town Clerk of Kumasi, 1967; Mem., Constituent Assembly, Ghana, 1968–69, 1979; formerly MP and a Dep. Foreign Minister; imprisoned after mil. coup, 1972–73; returned to law practice; Sec. for Local Govt, 1982. Founding Member: Progress Party, 1969; Popular Front Party, 1979; New Patriotic Party, 1992 (Leader, 1996–2007). Member: High Level Commn on Modernization of World Bank Gp Governance, 2009; Internat. Adv. Bd, SNV Netherlands Develt Orgn, 2009–. Chairman: Governing Council, Interpeace, 2009–; Sanitation and Water for All, 2011–. Hon. Fellow, Exeter Coll., Oxford, 2002. World Food Prize, 2011.

KUH, Prof. Diana Jane Lewin, PhD; Professor of Life Course Epidemiology, University College London, since 2003; Director, MRC National Survey of Health and Development, since 2007; Director, MRC Unit for Lifelong Health and Ageing at UCL (formerly MRC Unit for Lifelong Health and Ageing), since 2008; *b* Chichester, 23 Feb. 1953; *d* of Allan and Doris Lewin; *m* 1974, Peter Michael Kuh; one *s* one *d*. *Educ:* King Edward VI Camp Hill Sch. for Girls, Birmingham; New Hall Coll., Cambridge (BA Econs 1974); London Sch. of Econs (PhD 1993). Res. scientist, Inst. of Biometry and Community Medicine, 1975–81, Res. Fellow, Paediatric Res. Unit, 1982–87, Univ. of Exeter; Scientist, 1987–93, Sen. Scientist, 1994–2006, MRC Nat. Survey of Health and Develt, UCL. FFPH 2007. *Publications:* (with Prof. Y. Ben-Shlomo) A Life Course Approach to Chronic Disease Epidemiology, 1997, 2nd edn 2004; (with Dr R. Hardy) A Life Course Approach to Women's Health, 2002; (jtly) A Life Course Approach to Healthy Ageing, 2014; contrib. over 300 articles to learned jls.

Recreations: country walking, relaxing and having fun with my grandchildren (Finn, Owen and Martha), family and friends. *Address:* MRC Unit for Lifelong Health and Ageing at UCL, 33 Bedford Place, WC1B 5JU. *T:* (020) 7670 5700, *Fax:* (020) 7580 1501. *E:* d.kuh@ucl.ac.uk.

KUHN, Prof. Annette Frieda, PhD; FBA 2004; Senior Professorial Fellow in Film Studies, Queen Mary University of London, since 2009 (Professor of Film Studies, 2006–09, now Emeritus); *b* 29 Sept. 1945; *d* of Henry Philip Kuhn and Minnie Alice, (Betty), Cowley; *m* 1967, Peter Robert Brodnax Moore (marr. diss. 1982). *Educ:* Twickenham County Grammar Sch.; Univ. of Sheffield (BA (Econ.) 1969; MA 1975); Inst. of Educn, Univ. of London (PhD 1986). Adult Educn Tutor, Open Univ. and Univ. of London, 1971–88; pt-time Lectr in Film Studies, Polytech. of Central London, 1977–88; Lectr, 1989–91, Reader, 1991–98, in Film and TV Studies, Univ. of Glasgow; Reader in Cultural Res., 1998–2000, Prof. of Film Studies, 2000–06, Lancaster Univ. *Publications:* (ed with AnnMarie Wolpe) Feminism and Materialism, 1978; (ed jtly) Ideology and Cultural Production, 1979; Women's Pictures: feminism and cinema, 1982, 2nd edn 1994; The Power of the Image, 1985; Cinema, Censorship and Sexuality 1909 to 1925, 1988; (ed) The Women's Companion to International Film, 1990; (ed) Alien Zone: cultural theory and contemporary science fiction cinema, 1990; Family Secrets, 1995, rev. edn 2002; (ed) Queen of the Bs: Ida Lupino behind the camera, 1995; (ed with Jackie Stacey) Screen Histories, 1998; (ed) Alien Zone II: the spaces of science fiction cinema, 1999; An Everyday Magic: cinema and cultural memory, 2002; (ed with Catherine Grant) Screening World Cinema, 2006; (ed with Kirsten Emiko McAllister) Locating Memory: photographic acts, 2006; Ratcatcher, 2008; (ed) Screen Theorizing Today, 2009; (with Guy Westwell) Oxford Dictionary of Film Studies, 2012; (ed) Little Madnesses: Winnicott, transitional phenomena and cultural experience, 2013. *Recreations:* vermiculture, housekeeping, rail travel. *Address:* School of Languages, Linguistics and Film, Queen Mary University of London, Mile End Road, E1 4NS.

KUHN, Michael Ashton; Chairman, Qwerty Films, since 1999; *b* 7 May 1949; *s* of George and Bea Kuhn; *m* 1995, Caroline Burton; two *s*. *Educ:* Dover Coll.; Clare Coll., Cambridge (BA 1971); Coll. of Law. Admitted Solicitor, 1974. Denton, Hall & Burgin, 1971–72; Legal Advr, Polygram UK, 1972–74; Asst Solicitor, Field, Fisher & Martineau, 1974–75; Sen. Legal Advr, Polygram Internat., 1975–98 (Gen. Counsel, 1975–77, Pres., Polygram Filmed Entertainment, 1990–98, Bd Mem., 1998). Chairman: Nat. Film and TV Sch., 2002–10 (Hon. Fellow, 2010); Ind. Cinema Office, 2004–; AudioGo Ltd, 2011–13; Member, Board: Northern Ireland Screen, 2012–; UK Jewish Film. Mem. Council, BAFTA, 2006–09. Producer: The Duchess, 2008; Last Days on Mars, 2013; Suite Française, 2014; Florence Foster Jenkins, 2015. FRSA. Michael Balcon Award, BAFTA, 1998. *Publications:* 100 Films and a Funeral, 2001. *Recreation:* playwriting. *Address:* Qwerty Films, 2nd Floor, 29 Poland Street, W1F 8QR. *T:* (020) 7439 9524. *E:* info@qwertyfilms.com. *Club:* Groucho.

KÜHNL, Karel; Agent for Expatriate Affairs, Ministry of Foreign Affairs, Czech Republic, since 2013; *b* 12 Sept. 1954; *s* of Karel Kühnl and Marie Kühnlova (*née* Větrovcová); *m* 1983, Daniela Kusin; one *s* one *d*. *Educ:* Charles Univ., Prague (BA Law 1978); Univ. of Vienna (BA Econs 1983). Left Czechoslovakia in 1980 for political reasons; free-lance journalist, Vienna and Munich, 1983–87; editor and analyst, Radio Free Europe, Munich (Czech and Slovak broadcasting), 1987–91; returned to Czechoslovakia, 1991, after fall of communism in 1989; Sen. Lectr, Law Faculty, Charles Univ., Prague, 1991–93; Chief Advr to Prime Minister of Czech Republic, 1991–93; Ambassador to UK, 1993–97; Minister of Industry and Trade, 1997–98; Mem. (Civic Democratic Alliance, 1997–98, Freedom Union, 1998–2004), Chamber of Deputies, Czech Republic; Minister of Defence, 2004–06; Ambassador to Croatia, 2007–12. Chm., Freedom Union Party, 1999–2001. Hd of Bd, Czech TV, 1992–93. *Publications:* numerous articles in Czech, German and Austrian newspapers and jls. *Recreations:* family, history, archaeology, architecture.

KUHRT, Prof. Amélie Thekla Luise, FBA 2001; Professor of Ancient Near Eastern History, University College London, 1997–2010, now Emeritus; *b* 23 Sept. 1944; *d* of Edith Woodger and Ernest Woodger (adoptive father); *m* 1965, David Alan Kuhrt (marr. diss. 1977); two *d*. *Educ:* King's Coll., London; University Coll. London; Sch. of Oriental and African Studies (BA Hons Ancient Hist.). Lectr in Near Eastern Hist., 1979–89, Reader, 1989–97, UCL. James Henry Breasted Prize, Amer. Historical Assoc., 1997. *Publications:* (with A. Cameron) Images of Women in Antiquity, 1983, 2nd edn 1993; (with H. Sancisi-Weerdenburg) Achaemenid History II–IV, 1987–90, VI, 1991, VIII, 1994; (with S. Sherwin-White) Hellenism in the East, 1987; From Samarkhand to Sardis, 1992; The Ancient Near East, 2 vols, 1995 (trans. Spanish, Persian, Hungarian, Turkish); The Persian Empire: a corpus of sources for the Achaemenid period, 2 vols, 2007 (World Prize Book of the Year, Iran, 2010). *Recreations:* music, literature. *Address:* Department of History, University College London, Gower Street, WC1E 6BT. *T:* (020) 7679 3634.

KUHRT, Ven. Dr Gordon Wilfred; Archdeacon Emeritus, Diocese of Southwark, since 1996; *b* 15 Feb. 1941; *s* of late Wilfred and Doris Kuhrt; *m* 1963, Olive Margaret Powell; three *s*. *Educ:* Colfe's Grammar School; London Univ. (BD Hons); Oak Hill Theol Coll.; Middx Univ. (Dr Professional Studies 2001). Religious Education teacher, 1963–65; Curate: Illogan, Cornwall, 1967–70; Wallington, Surrey, 1970–74; Vicar: Shenstone, Staffs, 1974–79; Emmanuel, South Croydon, Surrey, 1979–89; RD, Croydon Central, 1981–86; Hon. Canon, Southwark Cathedral, 1987–89; Archdeacon of Lewisham, 1989–96; Chief Sec., ABM, Gen. Synod of C of E, 1996–98; Dir of Ministry, Archbishops' Council, C of E, 1999–2006; Associate Minister, Tredington and Darlingscott with Ilmington with Stretton-on-Fosse, and Ditchford with Preston-on-Stour with Whitchurch and Atherstone-on-Stour, 2006–12. Permission to officiate, Dio. of Oxford, 2012–. Mem., C of E Gen. Synod, 1986–96 (Mem., Bd of Ministry, 1991–96). Fellow, Coll. of Preachers (Mem. Council, 1992–97). Theological Lectr, London Univ. Extra-Mural Dept, 1984–89. Trustee, Church Pastoral-Aid Soc., 2008–13 (Vice-Chm., 2010–13). *Publications:* A Handbook for Council and Committee Members, 1985; Believing in Baptism, 1987; (contrib.) The Church and its Unity, 1992; (ed and contrib.) Doctrine Matters, 1993; (contrib.) Growing in Newness of Life: Christian initiation in Anglicanism today, 1993; (ed) To Proclaim Afresh, 1995; (contrib.) Church Leadership, 1997; Issues in Theological Education and Training, 1997; Clergy Security, 1998; An Introduction to Christian Ministry, 2000; Ministry Issues for the Church of England: mapping the trends, 2001; (ed) Bridging the Gap: Reader ministry today, 2002; Life's not always easy, 2011; contrib. reviews and articles to Anvil, Fulcrum. *Address:* 87 Churchway, Haddenham, Aylesbury, Bucks HP17 8DT. *T:* (01844) 698358.

KULKARNI, Prof. Shrinivas Ramachandra, PhD; FRS 2001; McArthur Professor of Astronomy and Planetary Science, California Institute of Technology, Pasadena, since 2001; Director, Caltech Optical Observatories, since 2006; *b* 4 Oct. 1956; *s* of Dr Ramachandra H. Kulkarni and Vimala Kulkarni; *m* 1985, Dr Hiromi Komiya; two *d*. *Educ:* Indian Inst. of Technology, New Delhi (MS Physics 1978); Univ. of California at Berkeley (PhD Astronomy 1983). Post-doctoral Fellow, Radio Astronomy Lab., Univ. of California at Berkeley, 1983–85; California Institute of Technology: Robert A. Millikan Fellow in Radio Astronomy, 1985–87; Asst Prof. of Astronomy, 1987–90; Associate Prof. of Astronomy, 1990–92; Prof. of Astronomy, 1992–95; Prof. of Astronomy and Planetary Scis, 1996–2001; Exec. Officer, Astronomy, 1997–2000; Sen. Fellow, Mount Wilson Inst., Pasadena, 1998–2001. A. D. White Prof.-at-Large, Cornell Univ., 2007–13. Mem., US Nat. Acad. of Scis, 2003. Helen B. Warner Prize, 1991, Alan T. Waterman Prize, 1992, NSF. *Publications:* (contrib.) Interstellar Processes, 1987; contrib. Nature in fields of pulsers, brown dwarfs and gamma-ray bursters. *Address:* Department of Astronomy, California Institute of Technology, 1200 East California Boulevard, Pasadena, CA 91125, USA. *T:* (626) 395 4010. *E:* srk@astro.caltech.edu.

KULUKUNDIS, Sir Eddie, Kt 1993; OBE 1988; Chairman, Ambassadors Theatre Group, 1992–2010, now Life President; Director, Rethymnis & Kulukundis Ltd, since 1964; Member of Lloyd's, 1964–95 (Member Council, 1983–89); *b* 20 April 1932; *s* of late George Elias Kulukundis and Eugénie (*née* Diacakis); *m* 1981, Susan Hampshire, *qv*. *Educ:* Collegiate Sch., New York; Salisbury Sch., Connecticut; Yale Univ. Mem., Baltic Exchange, 1959–2001. Chairman: Sports Aid Foundn Ltd, 1988–93 (Gov., 1977–2006); London Coaching Foundn, 1990–2009; British Athletics Charitable Trust (formerly British Athletics Field Events Charitable Trust), 1996–2009; Vice-Pres., UK Athletics, 1998–2003. Governor: Royal Shakespeare Theatre, 1976–2003; The Raymond Mander and Joe Mitchenson Theatre Collection Ltd, 1981–2001; Vice-Pres., Traverse Theatre, 1988–; Director: Hampstead Theatre Ltd, 1969–2004; Hampstead Theatre Trust, 1980–2003. Mem., Richmond Theatre Trust, 2001–. Mem. Bd, SOLT, 1973–2003 (Hon. Vice-Pres., 2003). Trustee: Theatres Trust, 1976–95; Salisbury Sch., Connecticut, 1983–2007. FRSA. Theatrical Producer, 1969–96; London productions include (some jtly): Enemy, 1969; The Happy Apple, Poor Horace, The Friends, How the Other Half Loves, Tea Party and The Basement (double bill), The Wild Duck, 1970; After Haggerty, Hamlet, Charley's Aunt, Straight Up, 1971; London Assurance, Journey's End, 1972; Small Craft Warnings, A Private Matter, Dandy Dick, 1973; The Waltz of the Toreadors, Life Class, Pygmalion, Play Mas, The Gentle Hook, 1974; A Little Night Music, Entertaining Mr Sloane, The Gay Lord Quex, What the Butler Saw, Travesties, Lies, The Sea Gull, A Month in the Country, A Room With a View, Too True to Be Good, The Bed Before Yesterday, 1975; Dimetos, Banana Ridge, Wild Oats, 1976; Candida, Man and Superman, Once A Catholic, 1977; Privates on Parade, Gloo Joo, 1978; Bent, Outside Edge, Last of the Red Hot Lovers, 1979; Beecham, Born in the Gardens, 1980; Tonight At 8.30, Steaming, Arms and the Man, 1981; Steafel's Variations, 1982; Messiah, Pack of Lies, 1983; Of Mice and Men, The Secret Diary of Adrian Mole Aged 13¾, 1984; Camille, 1985; The Cocktail Party, 1986; Curtains, 1987; Separation, South Pacific, Married Love, 1988; Over My Dead Body, 1989; Never the Sinner, 1990; The King and I, Carmen Jones, 1991; Noël and Gertie, A Slip of the Tongue, Shades, Making it Better, 1992; The Prime of Miss Jean Brodie, 1994; New York productions (jtly): How the Other Half Loves, 1971; Sherlock Holmes, London Assurance, 1974; Travesties, 1975; The Merchant, 1977; Players, 1978; Once a Catholic, 1979. *Address:* c/o Ambassadors Theatre Group, 39–41 Charing Cross Road, WC2R 0AR. *T:* (020) 7534 6100. *Club:* Garrick.

KUMAR, Harpal Singh; Chief Executive, Cancer Research UK, since 2007 (Chief Operating Officer, 2004–07); *b* London, 13 Jan. 1965; *s* of Mohinder Singh and Prem Kaur Kumar; *m* 1998, Benita Sokhey; one *s* one *d*. *Educ:* St John's Coll., Cambridge (BA Chem. Engrg 1986; MEng 1987); Harvard Grad. Sch. of Business Admin (MBA 1991). Associate Engagement Manager, McKinsey & Co. Inc., 1987–89, 1991–93; Chief Executive: Papworth Trust, 1993–97; Nexan Gp plc, 1997–2002; Cancer Research Technology, 2002–07. Hon. DSc Manchester, 2011. *Recreations:* theatre, opera, football. *Address:* Cancer Research UK, Angel Building, 407 St John Street, EC1V 4AD. *T:* (020) 3469 8469. *E:* harpal.kumar@cancer.org.uk.

KUMAR, Prof. Parveen June, (Mrs David Leaver), CBE 2001; MD; FRCP, FRCPE; Professor of Medicine and Education, Barts and the London School of Medicine and Dentistry, Queen Mary University of London, since 2004 (Professor of Clinical Medical Education, 1999–2004); Hon. Consultant Physician and Gastroenterologist, Barts Health NHS Trust (formerly St Bartholomew's Hospital, then Barts and the London NHS Trust) and Homerton University Hospital Foundation NHS Trust (formerly Homerton Hospital), since 1983; Consultant Gastroenterologist, London Digestive Health, London Clinic, since 2000; *b* 1 June 1942; *d* of Cyril Proshuno Fazal Kumar and Grace Nazira Kumar; *m* 1970, Dr David Leaver (*d* 2003); two *d*. *Educ:* Lawrence Sch., Sanawar, India; Maida Vale High Sch., London; St Bartholomew's Hosp. Med. Coll., London (BSc Hons 1963; MB BS; MD 1976). FRCP 1987; FRCPE 1998. Consultant Physician, 1982–, Sen. Lectr, 1985–94, Reader in Gastroenterology, 1994–99, Sub Dean for Undergrad. Educn, 1995–98, Barts and the London, Queen Mary Sch. of Medicine and Dentistry, Univ. of London; Dir of Postgrad. Med. Educn, Royal Hospital NHS Trust, 1994–96; Hd, Acad. Unit of Gastroenterology, Homerton Hosp., 1998–2002; Associate Med. Dir, 1998–2000, non-exec. Dir, 1999–2003, Barts and the London NHS Trust. Mem., 1994–2005, Chm., 2002–05, Medicines Commn; non-exec. Dir, NICE, 1999–2002. Mem., Internat. Adv. Bd, Southern African Consortium for Res. Excellence, 2010–. Royal College of Physicians: Dep. Regl Advr, Coll. and Clinical Tutor, 1989–96; Censor, 1996–98; Dir, Continual Professional Develt, 1998–2002; Vice-Pres. (Acad.), 2003–05. President: BMA, 2006–07 (Acting Pres., 2007–08); RSM, 2010–12 (Mem. Council, 2008–); Royal Med. Benevolent Fund, 2013–; Vice Pres., 2013–14, Pres., May 2016–, Medical Women's Fedn; Mem. Council, British Soc. of Gastroenterology, 2001–04 (Trustee, 2009–); Mem., Wesleyan Nat. Adv. Bd, 2008–; Vice Chm., Galien Awards, 2008–; Member: NI Medical Distinction Awards Cttee, 2000–10; Queen's Anniv. Awards Cttee, 2007–; Member, External Advisory Board: Fac. of Health and Med. Sci., Univ. of Surrey, 2008–12; Warwick Univ., 2013–. Sen. examr for undergrad. and postgrad. med. degrees at home and abroad. Chm., e-learning Adv. Bd, BMJ Publishing, 2009–12. Erasmus Vis. Prof., Univ. Sapienza, Rome, 1992. Trustee: St Bartholomew's Hosp. Med. Coll. Trust, 2002–10; CancerBackup, 2003–08; Tropical Health and Educn Trust, 2009–; British Youth Opera, 2013–; Gov., BUPA Foundn, 2007–13 (Chm., 2011–13). FCGI 2007; Fellow, Internat. Med. Acad., 2011; Hon. FAPI; Hon. FRCPath 2010. Hon. Fellow, Mansfield Coll., Oxford, 2011. Hon. DM: Nottingham, 2006; Sussex, 2011; Plymouth, 2014; Hon. DSc: Hull, 2012; Glasgow, 2014; Hon. DEd Trinity Coll. Dublin, 2011. Gold Medal for Services to Med. Educn, BMA, 2008; British Assoc. for Physicians of Indian Origin Distinction Award, 2009; MDI Distinction Award, 2009. *Publications:* Kumar and Clark's Clinical Medicine: a textbook for students and doctors (with Michael Clark), 1987, 8th edn 2012; Acute Clinical Medicine, 2000, 2nd edn 2006; Kumar and Clark's Handbook of Medical Management and Therapeutics, 2012; Kumar and Clark's Cases in Clinical Medicine, 2013 (BMA Prize, 2014); series co-editor, 6 pocket essentials; other books; res. articles mainly on coeliac disease and small bowel disorders in med. jls. *Recreations:* opera, ski-ing, walking, reading. *Address:* Wingate Institute, Barts and the London School of Medicine, 26 Ashfield Street, E1 2AJ. *T:* (020) 7882 7191. *E:* p.j.kumar@qmul.ac.uk. *Clubs:* Royal Automobile, Forum.

KUMAR, Surendra, FRCGP; general medical practitioner, since 1971; *b* 15 Sept. 1945; *m* 1971, Dr Santosh Kumar; two *d*. *Educ:* Univ. of Delhi (MB BS). Mem., 1999–2003, Assoc. Mem., and Chair, Fitness to Practise Panel, 2003–, GMC; Mem., GPs' Cttee, BMA, 1993–; Pres., British Internat. (formerly Overseas) Doctors Assoc., 2003–09 (Nat. Chm., 1993–99). SBStJ 1991. *Recreation:* medical politics. *Address:* 11 Churchfields, Widnes WA8 9RP.

KUMARATUNGA, Chandrika Bandaranaike; President of Sri Lanka, 1994–2005; Chairman: CBK Foundation for Democracy and Justice; South Asia Policy and Research Institute; *b* Colombo, 29 June 1945; *d* of late Solomon W. R. D. Bandaranaike, former Prime Minister of Ceylon, and Sirimavo R. D. Bandaranaike, former Prime Minister of Sri Lanka; *m* 1978, Wijaya Kumaratunga, film actor and political leader (*d* 1988); one *s* one *d*. *Educ:* St Bridget's Convent, Colombo; Inst. of Pol Studies, Paris; Ecole Pratique des Hautes Etudes, Paris. Chm. and Man. Dir, Dinakara Sinhala newspaper, 1975–85. Dir, Land Reform Commn, 1972–75; Chair, Janawasa Commn, 1975–77; Expert Consultant, FAO, 1978–81; Res. Fellow, Univ. of London, 1988–91. Guest Lecturer: Univ. of Bradford, 1989; Jawaharlal

Nehru Univ., India, 1991; Virginia and Harvard Law Schs; Harvard Univ.; KCL; Oxford Univ. Debating Soc. Chief Minister and Minister for Law and Order, W Provincial Council, 1993–94; Prime Minister of Sri Lanka, Aug.–Nov. 1994; Minister of Finance and Planning, of Nat. Integration and Reconciliation, of Defence, of Educn and of Buddha Sasana, 1994–2005. Sen. Vice-Pres., 1993–2000, Pres., 2000–06, Sri Lanka Freedom Party; Pres., Sri Lanka Mahajana Party, 1988. Advr on poverty alleviation, Clinton Global Initiative, 2007–; Mem., Bd of Dirs, Club of Madrid, 2009–; Chm., Sri Lanka Chapter, S Asia Foundn, 2007–; Mem., Global Leadership Forum, 2012. *Publications:* research papers on land reform, food policies, poverty alleviation, democracy and good governance, political violence and conflict management. *Recreations:* swimming, Kandyan dance, music, reading, art and sculpture, drama, cinema. *Address:* (office) 27 Independence Avenue, Colombo 10, Sri Lanka. *T:* (1) 2694372. *E:* officecbk@gmail.com.

KUNDERA, Milan; writer; *b* Brno, 1 April 1929; *s* of Dr Ludvik Kundera and Milada Kunderova-Janosikova; *m* 1967, Věra Hrabánková. *Educ:* Film Faculty, Acad. of Music and Dramatic Arts, Prague, later Asst Prof. and Prof. there, 1958–69; Prof., Univ. of Rennes, 1975–80; Prof., Ecole des hautes études en sciences sociales, Paris, 1980. Mem., Union of Czechoslovak Writers, 1963–69. Member: Editl Bd, Literárni noviny, 1963–67, 1968; Editl Bd, Listy, 1968–69. Czechoslovak Writers' Publishing House Prize, 1969; Commonwealth Award, 1981; Prix Europa-Littérature, 1982; Jerusalem Prize, 1985; Nelly Sachs Preis, 1987; Österreichische Staatspreis, 1988; London Independent Prize, 1991; State Prize for Literature (Czech Republic), 2007; Grand Prix de la Bibliothèque Nat. de France, 2012. *Publications:* The Joke, 1967; Laughable Loves (short stories), 1970; Jacques et son maître (drama), 1971–81; Life is Elsewhere, 1973 (Prix Médicis); The Farewell Waltz, 1976 (Prem. lett. Mondello); The Book of Laughter and Forgetting, 1979; The Unbearable Lightness of Being, 1984 (LA Times Prize); The Art of the Novel, 1987; Immortality, 1990; Les testaments trahis, 1993; Slowness, 1996; Francis Bacon, 1996; Identity, 1998; La Ignorancia, 2000; Le Rideau (essays), 2005 (English trans., The Curtain: an essay in seven parts, 2007); Une Rencontre (essays), 2009 (English trans., Encounter: essays, 2010); The Festival of Insignificance, 2014.

KUNEVA, Meglena Shtilianova, PhD; Chairman, Governing Board, European Policy Centre, since 2010; Member, European Commission, 2007–10; *b* Sofia, 22 June 1957. *Educ:* Sofia Univ. St Kliment Ohridski (MA Law 1981; PhD Envmtl Law 1984); Georgetown Univ., Washington, DC (Postgrad. PEW Econ. Prog. 1995; Postgrad. Prog. Law Sch. 2000). Ed. and Radio Anchor, Bulgarian Nat. Radio, 1987–90; Asst Prof., Sofia Univ. St Kliment Ohridski, 1987–89; Prof., Bourgas Free Univ., 1992–94. Sen. Legal Advr, Council of Ministers, 1990–2001; legal consultant, 1992–98. Member: Supervisory Bd, Privatization Agency, 1994–95; Bulgarian Delegn, 4th Session Commn for Sustainable Develt, UN, 1995. Founder Mem. and Mem. Pol Council, Nat. Movement Simeon II. MP (Nat. Movement Simeon II), 2001, 2005. Dep. Minister of For. Affairs and Chief Negotiator with EU, 2001–02; Minister for Eur. Affairs, 2002–06, and Chief Negotiator with EU, 2002–05; Special Rep. of Bulgaria to Convention on Future of EU, 2002–03. Dir, BNP Paribas, 2010–13. Member: Bd Trustees, Berlin Conf. 'A Soul for Europe'; Internat. Council of Envmtl Law, UN; Access to Information Prog. Foundn; Adv. Bd and Steering Cttee, TIME Eco-projects Foundn; Atlantic Club, Bulgaria (Gold distinction, 2005); Union of Bulgarian Jurists. Writer of screenplay, Stories of Murders (documentary film), 1993. Order of Civil Merit (Spain), 2002; Legion d'Honneur (France), 2003; Order of Prince Enrique (Portugal), 2004; Order of Star of Italian Solidarity (Italy), 2005. *Publications:* articles in jls and newspapers.

KÜNG, Prof. Dr Hans; Ordinary Professor of Ecumenical Theology, 1980–96 and Director of Institute for Ecumenical Research, 1963–96, University of Tübingen, now Professor Emeritus; *b* Sursee, Lucerne, 19 March 1928. *Educ:* schools in Sursee and Lucerne; Papal Gregorian Univ., Rome (LPhil, LTh); Sorbonne; Inst. Catholique, Paris. DTheol 1957. Further studies in Amsterdam, Berlin, Madrid, London. Ordained priest, 1954. Pastoral work, Hofkirche, Lucerne, 1957–59; Asst for dogmatic theol., Univ. of Münster, 1959–60; Ord. Prof. of fundamental theol., 1960–63, Ord. Prof. of dogmatic and ecumenical theol., 1963–80, Univ. of Tübingen. Official theol. consultant (peritus) to 2nd Vatican Council, 1962–65; Guest Professor: Union Theol. Seminary, NYC, 1968; Univ. of Basle, 1969; Univ. of Chicago Divinity Sch., 1981; Univ. of Michigan, 1983; Toronto Univ., 1985; Rice Univ., Texas, 1987, 1989; guest lectures at univs in Europe, America, Asia and Australia; Hon. Pres., Edinburgh Univ. Theol Soc., 1982–83. Pres., Foundn Global Ethic, Germany, 1995–2013, Switzerland, 1997–2013, Hon. Pres., 2013. Editor series, Theologische Meditationen; co-Editor series, Ökumenische Forschungen and Ökumenische Theologie; Associate Editor, Jl of Ecum. Studies. Mem., Amer. and German PEN Clubs. Holds hon. doctorates. *Publications:* (first publication in German) The Council and Reunion, 1961; That the World may Believe, 1963; The Living Church, 1963; The Changing Church, 1965; Justification: the doctrine of Karl Barth and a Catholic reflection, 1965; Structures of the Church, 1965; (contrib.) Theologische Meditationen, 1965 (Amer. edn as Freedom Today, 1966); The Church, 1967; (contrib.) Christian Revelation and World Religions, ed J. Neuner, 1967; Truthfulness: the future of the Church, 1968; Infallible? an inquiry, 1971 (paperback 1972); Why Priests?, 1972; 20 Thesen zum Christsein, 1975; On Being a Christian, 1977 (abridged as The Christian Challenge, 1979); Was ist Firmung?, 1976; Jesus im Widerstreit: ein jüdisch-christlicher Dialog (with Pinchas Lapide), 1976; Brother or Lord?, 1977; Signposts for the Future, 1978; Freud and the Problem of God, 1979; The Church—Maintained in Truth?, 1980; Does God Exist?, 1980; Art and the Question of Meaning, 1981; Eternal Life?, 1984; (jtly) Christianity and World Religions, 1986; The Incarnation of God, 1986; Church and Change: the Irish experience, 1986; Why I am still a Christian, 1987; (with Julia Ching) Christianity and Chinese Religions, 1989; Reforming the Church Today: keeping hope alive, 1990; Theology for the Third Millennium: an ecumenical view, 1991; Global Responsibility: in search of a new world ethic, 1991; Judaism: the religious situation of our time, 1992; Mozart: traces of transcendence, 1992; Credo: the Apostles' Creed explained for today, 1993; Great Christian Thinkers, 1994; Christianity: essence and history, 1995; (jtly) A Dignified Dying: a plea for personal responsibility, 1995; Yes to a Global Ethic, 1996; A Global Ethic for Global Politics and Economics, 1997; (ed with Helmut Schmidt) A Global Ethic and Global Responsibilities: two declarations, 1998; The Catholic Church: a short history, 2001; (ed with G. Picco and R. v. Weizsäcker) Crossing the Divide: dialogue among civilisations, 2001; Tracing the Way, 2002; Women in Christianity, 2002; My Struggle for Freedom (memoirs), 2003; Islam: History, Present, Future, 2007; The Beginning of All Things, 2007; Disputed Truth (memoirs, vol. 2), 2008; (with Rabbi Walter Homolka) How to do Good and Avoid Evil: a global ethic from the sources of Judaism, 2009; What I Believe, 2010; Can We Save the Catholic Church? We Can Save the Catholic Church!, 2013. *Address:* Waldhäuserstrasse 23, 72076 Tübingen, Germany.

KUNKEL, Edward Thomas; Director, President and Chief Executive Officer, Foster's Group Ltd, 1992–2004; Chairman, Billabong International Ltd, 2005–12 (Director, 2002–12); *b* 22 May 1943; *s* of Francis James Kunkel and Doris Kunkel (*née* Baulcombe). *Educ:* Auckland Univ. (BSc Chem. and Zool.). Joined Carlton & United Breweries, Melbourne, 1968 as Asst Brewer; sen. positions throughout Group, 1968–84; Gen. Manager, NSW, 1985–87; Pres. and Chief Exec. Officer, Carling O'Keefe Breweries of Canada Ltd, 1987–89; Exec. Chm., Molson Breweries, N America, 1989–92; Chm., Molson Breweries, Canada, 1996–98. *Recreation:* golf. *Clubs:* Huntingdale Golf (Vic); Sanctuary Cove Country (Qld).

KUPER, Prof. Adam Jonathan, PhD; FBA 2000; Professor of Social Anthropology, Brunel University, 1985–2008; Centennial Professor of Anthropology, London School of Economics and Political Science, 2014–Sept. 16; *b* 29 Dec. 1941; *s* of Simon Meyer Kuper and Gertrude (*née* Hesselson); *m* 1966, Jessica Sue Cohen; two *s* one *d*. *Educ:* Univ. of Witwatersrand (BA 1961); King's Coll., Cambridge (PhD 1966). Lecturer: in Social Anthropol., Makerere Univ., Kampala, 1967–70; in Anthropol., UCL, 1970–76; Prof. of African Anthropol. and Sociol., Univ. of Leiden, 1976–85. Vice-Pres., British Acad., 2006–07. MAE 1993. Hon. DFil Gothenburg, 1978. Rivers Meml Medal, 2000, Huxley Medal, 2007, RAI. *Publications:* Kalahari Village Politics: an African democracy, 1970; (ed with A. Richards) Councils in Action, 1971; Anthropologists and Anthropology: the British School 1922–1972, 1973, 3rd edn 1996; Changing Jamaica, 1976; (ed) The Social Anthropology of Radcliffe-Brown, 1977; Wives for Cattle: bridewealth and marriage in Southern Africa, 1982; (ed with J. Kuper) The Social Science Encyclopedia, 1985, 3rd edn 2004; South Africa and the Anthropologist, 1987; The Invention of Primitive Society: transformations of an illusion, 1988; (ed) Conceptualising Society, 1992; The Chosen Primate: human nature and cultural diversity, 1994; Culture: the anthropologists' account, 1999; Among the Anthropologists: history and context in anthropology, 1999; Incest and Influence: the private life of bourgeois England, 2009. *Address:* 16 Muswell Road, N10 2BG. *T:* (020) 8883 0400. *Club:* Hampstead Golf.

KUREISHI, Hanif, CBE 2008; writer; *b* 5 Dec. 1954; *s* of Rafiushan Kureishi and Audrey Buss. *Educ:* King's College London. PEN/Pinter Prize, 2010. *Filmscripts:* My Beautiful Laundrette, 1984; Sammy and Rosie Get Laid, 1987; (also dir.) London Kills Me, 1991; My Son the Fanatic, 1998; The Mother, 2003; Venus, 2007; Weddings and Beheadings, 2007; Le Week-End, 2013. *Publications: plays:* Outskirts, 1981; Borderline, 1981; Birds of Passage, 1983; Outskirts and Other Plays, 1992; Sleep With Me, 1999; When the Night Begins, 2004; *novels:* The Buddha of Suburbia, 1990 (televised 1993); The Black Album, 1995; Intimacy, 1998 (adapted as a film, 2000); Gabriel's Gift, 2001; Something to Tell You, 2008; The Last Word, 2014; *short stories:* Love in a Blue Time, 1997; Midnight All Day, 1999; Collected Stories, 2010; *novella and short stories:* The Body, 2002; *short stories and essays:* Love + Hate, 2015; *non-fiction:* (ed jtly) The Faber Book of Pop, 1995; Dreaming and Scheming: reflections on writing and politics, 2002; My Ear at his Heart (memoir), 2004; The Word and The Bomb (essays), 2005. *Recreations:* pop music, cricket, sitting in pubs. *Address:* c/o Deborah Rogers, Rogers, Coleridge & White Ltd, 20 Powis Mews, W11 1SN.

KURTH, Air Vice-Marshal Nicholas Julian Eugene, CBE 2006 (OBE 1996; MBE 1990); Chairman of Trustees, Ulysses Trust, since 2013 (Vice Patron, 2013); Chairman, BMC Access Management Group, since 2013; *b* 13 Sept. 1955; *s* of Heinz Kurth and Renate Kurth; *m* 1984, Sandra Johnson; two *s* one *d*. *Educ:* Archbishop Tenison's Grammar Sch.; Open Univ. Business Sch. (MBA 1991); King's Coll. London (MA Internat. Studies 2001). CEng 1999. Joined RAF as apprentice, RAF Halton, 1972; commnd 1978; Jun. Engrg Officer 3(F) Sqdn, 1980–83; Sen. Engrg Officer XI(F) Sqdn, 1988–90; RAF advanced staff course, 1991; Support Mgt Develt, 1991–95; OC Engrg and Supply Wing, RAF Leuchars, 1995–97; Aircraft Logistics Policy, 1997–2000, Dep. Dir Support Mgt Airworthiness, 2000–01, HQ Logistics Comd; rcds, 2001; Ministry of Defence: Jt Warfare, 2002–03; Dir of Progs, Defence Estates, 2003–06; Dir Logistics (Strike) Plans/Future, Defence Logistics Orgn, 2006–07; COS Support Air Comd, 2007–10. Rail Business Dir, Amey, 2012. FRGS 1997; FRAeS 1999. *Recreations:* rock climbing, mountaineering (Pres., RAF Mountaineering Assoc., 2005–10 (Hon. Vice-Pres., 2011–); responsible for British Services Makalu Expedition, 2008), fencing (President: RAF Fencing Union, 2002–10 (Hon. Vice-Pres., 2010–); Combined Services' Fencing Assoc., 2008–10), road cycling (Chm., Berkhamsted Cycling Club), painting, playing the electric guitar (badly). *Clubs:* Royal Air Force, Geographical.

KUSHNER, Lindsey Joy; QC 1992; **Her Honour Judge Kushner;** a Circuit Judge, since 2000; *b* 16 April 1952; *d* of Harry Kushner and Rita Kushner (*née* Alexander); *m* 1976, David Norman Kaye; one *s* one *d*. *Educ:* Manchester High Sch. for Girls; Liverpool Univ. (LLB). Called to the Bar, Middle Temple, 1974; part time Chm., Medical Appeal Tribunal, 1989–2000, Disablement Appeal Tribunal, 1992–99; Asst Recorder, 1989–93; a Recorder, 1993–2000. Mem., Ethnic Adv. Cttee, Lord Chancellor's Dept, 1994–99. *Recreations:* cooking, cinema. *Address:* c/o Northern Circuit Administrator, Oriel Chambers, 18 Ribblesdale Place, Preston PR1 3NA.

KUTNER, Kay Elizabeth; *see* Burley, K. E.

KVERNDAL, Simon Richard; QC 2002; *b* 22 April 1958; *s* of late Ole Sigvard and of Brenda Kverndal; *m* 1997, Sophie Rowsell; two *s*. *Educ:* Haileybury; Sidney Sussex Coll., Cambridge (MA). Called to the Bar, Middle Temple, 1982; barrister, specialising in maritime and commercial law, 1983–. Lloyd's Open Form Salvage Arbitrator, 2006–. Mem., Ct of Assts, Co. of Shipwrights, 1999–. Comdr d'Honneur, Commanderie du Bontemps de Medoc et Graves, 1994. *Recreations:* Real tennis, rackets, wine-tasting. *Address:* Quadrant Chambers, Quadrant House, 10 Fleet Street, EC4Y 1AU. *T:* (020) 7583 4444, *Fax:* (020) 7583 4455. *E:* info@quadrantchambers.com. *Clubs:* Garrick, Queen's, MCC, Jesters; Hawks (Cambridge); Mjolnirs Rackets.

KWARTENG, Dr Kwasi Alfred Addo; MP (C) Spelthorne, since 2010; *b* London, 26 May 1975; *s* of Alfred and Charlotte Kwarteng. *Educ:* Eton Coll. (King's Schol.; Newcastle Schol.); Trinity Coll., Cambridge (BA 1996; MA; PhD 2000); Harvard Univ. (Kennedy Schol.). Financial Analyst: JP Morgan, then WestLB, 2000–04; Odey Asset Mgt, 2004–06; journalist and author, 2006–10. Member: Transport Cttee, 2010–13; Work and Pensions Cttee, 2013–15. Chm., Bow Gp, 2005–06. Trustee, History of Parliament Trust, 2011–. Contested (C): Brent E, 2005; London Assembly, GLA, 2008. *Publications:* Gridlock Nation (with J. Dupont), 2011; Ghosts of Empire, 2011; War and Gold, 2014; Thatcher's Trial, 2015. *Recreations:* music, history. *Address:* House of Commons, SW1A 0AA.

KWIATKOWSKA, Prof. Marta Zofia, PhD; FBCS; Professor of Computing Systems, University of Oxford, since 2007; Fellow, Trinity College, Oxford, since 2007; *b* Gorlice, Poland, 26 Feb. 1957; *d* of Jan Kwiatkowski and Teresa Kwiatkowska; *m* 1990, Paul Warren; one *d*. *Educ:* Univ. of Kraków (BSc Computer Sci. *summa cum laude*, MSc 1980); Univ. of Leicester (PhD Computer Sci. 1989). Asst Prof., Jagiellonian Univ., Kraków, 1980–88; University of Leicester: Res. Schol., 1984–86; Lectr in Computer Sci., 1986–94; University of Birmingham: Lectr in Computer Sci., 1994–98; Reader in Semantics for Concurrency, 1998–2001; Prof. of Computer Sci., 2001–07. Visiting Professor: Centrum voor Wiskunde en Informatica, Amsterdam, 1991; Lab. for Specification and Verification, Ecole Normale Supérieure de Cachan, Paris, 2002; Nuffield Sci. Foundn Res. Fellow, Imperial Coll., London, 1992–93. Associate Ed., IEEE Trans on Software Engrg, 2010–12; Mem., Editl Bd, Philosophical Trans Royal Soc. A, 2010–12. FBCS 2008. Professional Mem., ACM, 2009–. *Publications:* (ed jtly) Semantics for Concurrency, 1990; contribs to Philosophical Trans Royal Soc. A and CRM Monograph Series. *Address:* Trinity College, Oxford OX1 3BH.

KYDD, Ian Douglas; HM Diplomatic Service, retired; *b* 1 Nov. 1947; *s* of late Alexander Henry John Kydd and Sheila Doreen Riley Kydd (*née* Kinnear); *m* 1968, Elizabeth Louise Pontius; one *s* one *d*. *Educ:* Melville Coll., Edinburgh. DSAO, later FCO, 1966; Attaché, New Delhi, 1970–74; Dep. Dir, later Dir, Radio and TV Div., British Inf. Services, NY, 1974–79; FCO, 1979; Press Officer to Prime Minister, 1981–83; First Sec., Lagos, 1984–88, Ottawa, 1988–92; Dep. Head, News Dept and Head of Newsroom, FCO, 1993–95; Consul-Gen. and Counsellor (Mgt), Moscow, 1995–98; Consul-Gen., Vancouver, 1998–2002; Counsellor (Mgt), New Delhi, 2003–06; Counsellor: Beirut, 2006; Kabul, 2006–07. Sen. Advr, Rainmaker Global Business Develt Ltd, Calgary, 2006–10. Trng Consultant, 2008–11. Trustee, UK Foundn, Univ. of British Columbia, 2009–. Games Maker, London Olympics and Paralympics, 2012. Parish Clerk, Great Shelford, 2014–. *Recreations:* all sport, esp. downhill ski-ing, golf. *E:* ian@kydd.com. *Clubs:* Gog Magog Golf (Cambridge); Tuesday Lunch (New Delhi).

KYDLAND, Prof. Finn Erling, PhD; Jeffrey Henley Professor, University of California, Santa Barbara, since 2004; Richard P. Simmons Distinguished Professor, Tepper School of Business, Carnegie Mellon University, since 2007; *b* 1943; *s* of Martin Kydland and Johanna Kydland; *m* 1968, Liv Kjellevold (marr. diss.); two *s* two *d*; *m* Tonya Schooler. *Educ:* Norwegian Sch. of Econs and Business Admin (BS 1968); Carnegie Mellon Univ. (PhD 1973). Norwegian Sch. of Econs and Business Admin, 1973–76; Associate Prof., then Prof. of Econs, Carnegie Mellon Univ., 1977–2004. (Jtly) Nobel Prize in Economics, 2004. *Publications:* contrib. learned jls. *Address:* Department of Economics, 2127 North Hall, University of California, Santa Barbara, CA 93106, USA.

KYLE, Barry Albert; freelance director, since 1991; Hon. Associate Director, Royal Shakespeare Company, since 1991 (Associate Director, 1978–91); *b* 25 March 1947; *s* of Albert Ernest Kyle and Edith Ivy Bessie Gaskin; *m* 1st, 1971, Christine Susan Iddon (marr. diss. 1988); two *s* one *d*; 2nd, 1990, Lucy Joy Maycock (marr. diss. 2003); one *d*. *Educ:* Birmingham Univ. (BA, MA). Associate Dir, Liverpool Playhouse, 1970–72; joined RSC as Asst Dir, 1973; first Artistic Dir, Swan Theatre, Stratford-upon-Avon, 1987; numerous RSC productions and directing abroad, incl. Australia, Israel, USA, Czechoslovakia, Japan, Italy and Asia; founding Artistic Dir, Swine Palace Productions, La, USA; Dir, Theatre for a New Audience, NYC, 1995–96; Shakespeare's Globe, London: Master of Play, 2001; Dir, Women's Co., 2003. Director: The Coventry Mysteries, 2006 (Daily Mail Dir of the Year); Cymru Theatr Clwyd, 2006 and 2008. Vis. Dir, Czechoslovak Nat. Theatre, Prague (first Briton to direct there). *Publications:* Sylvia Plath: a dramatic portrait, 1976; contribs to Literary Review. *Recreation:* foreign travel. *Address:* Flat 5, 20 Charing Cross Road, WC2H 0HU. *T:* (020) 7836 5911.

KYLE, David William, CBE 2006; Member, Criminal Cases Review Commission, 1997–2005; *b* 30 March 1951; *s* of William and Judy Kyle; *m* 1st, 1975, Rosemary Elizabeth Bazire (marr. diss. 2006); two *d*; 2nd, 2007, Glenys Stacey. *Educ:* Monkton Combe Sch.; Queens' Coll., Cambridge (BA). Called to the Bar, Inner Temple, 1973; Office of Director of Public Prosecutions: Legal Asst, 1975–79; Sen. Legal Asst, 1979–86; Crown Prosecution Service: Branch Crown Prosecutor, 1986–89; Head of Div., HQ Casework, 1989–93; Head of HQ Casework, then Chief Crown Prosecutor, Central Casework, 1993–97. Member: Fitness to Practise Panel, GMC, later MPTS, 2006–; Conduct (formerly Disciplinary) Cttee, RICS, 2007–09; Professional Conduct Bd, BPsS, 2007–09; Conduct and Competence Cttee, 2008–, Health Cttee, 2009–, NMC. *Recreations:* music, walking, cycling, canal boating.

KYLE, Francis Ferdinand; Founder and Director, Francis Kyle Gallery, 1978–2014; *b* 20 Jan. 1944; *s* of Ferdinand and Dilys Kyle; *m* 1996, Christine Ann Caddick. *Educ:* Harrow; Jesus Coll., Oxford (Schol.; MA). Foreign Rights: George Rainbird Publishers, 1968–71; William Heinemann Publishers, 1972–73; Dir, Thumb Gall., 1974–78. *Publications:* (with R. Ingrams) The Ridgeway, Europe's Oldest Road: paintings from Francis Kyle Gallery, 1988; Lair of the Leopard: twenty artists go in search of Lampedusa's Sicily, 2006; numerous exhibn catalogues. *Recreations:* reading, walking, theatre, museums. *E:* franciskylecollection@gmail.com. *Club:* Garrick.

KYLE, James, CBE 1989; FRCSE; FRCSI; FRCS; Chairman, Raigmore Hospital NHS Trust, 1993–97; *b* 26 March 1925; *s* of John Kyle and Dorothy Frances Kyle; *m* 1950, Dorothy Elizabeth Galbraith; two *d*. *Educ:* Queen's Univ., Belfast. MB BCh BAO 1947 (Gold Medal in Surgery); MCh 1956 (Gold Medal); DSc 1972. FRCSI 1954; FRCS 1954; FRCSEd 1964. Mayo Clinic, USA, 1950; Tutor in Surgery, QUB, 1952; Lectr in Surgery, Univ. of Liverpool, 1957; Aberdeen University: Sen. Lectr, Surgery, 1959; Mem., Univ. Senatus, 1970; Consultant Surgeon, Aberdeen Royal Infirmary, 1959–89; Chm., Grampian Health Bd, 1989–93 (Mem., 1973). Mem., GMC, 1979–94; Chairman: Scottish Cttee for Hosp. Med. Services, 1977–81; Rep. Body, BMA, 1984–87; Scottish Jt Consultants' Cttee, 1984–89. British Council lectr, SE Asia, S America, 1963–74. Ext. Examr, Belfast, Dublin, Dundee, Edinburgh, Sydney, West Indies. Pres., Aberdeen Medico-Surgical Soc. Bicentenary, 1989–90; Member: Council, Surgical Res. Soc., 1972–74; Internat. Soc. of Surgery, 1971–84; Cons. Med. Soc., 1988–93. Regl Rep., War Memls Trust, 2004–. Patron, Royal Scottish Nat. Orch. FRPSL; FRAS. Burgess of Aberdeen, 1990. *Publications:* Peptic Ulceration, 1960; Pye's Surgical Handicraft, 21st edn, 1962; Scientific Foundations of Surgery, 4th edn, 1989; Crohn's Disease, 1973; papers on surgery, history, philately. *Recreations:* astronomy, amateur radio (callsign GM4 CHX), philately. *Address:* Grianan, 7 Fasaich, Gairloch, Ross-shire IV21 2DH. *T:* (01445) 712398. *Club:* Royal Northern (Aberdeen).

KYLE, (James) Terence; General Counsel, Nomura International plc, 2004–07; *b* 9 May 1946; *s* of James Kyle and Elizabeth Kyle (*née* Cinnamond); *m* 1975, Diana Jackson; one *s* two *d*. *Educ:* Royal Belfast Academical Instn; Christ's Coll., Cambridge (MA). Linklaters & Paines, later Linklaters & Alliance, subseq. Linklaters: Articled Clerk, 1970–72; Solicitor, 1972–79; Partner, 1979–89; Head, Internat. Finance, 1989–95; Managing Partner, 1995–98; Chief Exec., 1998–2001; Managing Partner, Americas, 2001–03. *Recreations:* cricket, golf.

KYLE, Dr Peter; MP (Lab) Hove, since 2015; *b* Rustington, 9 Sept. 1970; *s* of Leslie Kyle and Joanna Murrell (*née* Davies). *Educ:* Felpham Community Coll.; Sussex Univ. (BA Hons Geog., Envmtl Studies and Internat. Devlt 1999; DPhil Community Econ. Devlt 2003). Dir, Children on the Edge, 1992–96; Co-Founder, Fat Sand Films, 2003–06; Dep. CEO, ACEVO, 2007–13; Chief Exec., Working for Youth, 2013–15. Non-exec. Dir, CAF Bank, 2011–. *Address:* House of Commons, SW1A 0AA; (office) 99 Church Road, Hove BN3 2BA. *E:* peter.kyle.mp@parliament.uk.

KYLE, Peter William, OBE 2011; Director-General, English-Speaking Union of the Commonwealth, 2011–14; *b* 21 Nov. 1948; *s* of late Robert Kyle and Evelyn Kyle (*née* Palliser-Bosomworth); *m* Kathryn Anna Grundy; two *d*. *Educ:* Rambert Sch. of Ballet; Bretton Hall Coll., Yorks; Inst. für Bühnen Tanz, Cologne. Former ballet dancer; soloist: Northern Ballet Theatre, 1971–73; Royal New Zealand Ballet, 1973–75; Dance Advr, Leics Educn Authy, 1975–81; Dance Officer, Arts Council of GB, 1981–83; Artistic Dir, Queen's Hall Arts Centre, Hexham, 1983–88; Chief Exec., Scottish Ballet, 1988–95; arts consultant and choreographer, 1995–97; Dean, Arts Educational Sch., London, 1997–98; Gen. Dir, Internat. Shakespeare Globe Centre, later Chief Exec., The Shakespeare Globe Trust, 1998–2010. CCMI 2002. Hon. Fellow, London South Bank Univ., 2005.

KYLE, Air Vice-Marshal Richard Henry, CB 1997; LVO 2013; MBE 1977; an Extra Gentleman Usher to the Queen, since 2013 (a Gentleman Usher, 2002–13); *b* 4 Jan. 1943; *s* of Air Chief Marshal Sir Wallace Hart Kyle, GCB, KCVO, CBE, DSO, DFC and Lady (Molly) Kyle; *m* 1971, Anne Weatherup; two *s* two *d*. *Educ:* Cranbrook Sch., Kent; RAF Tech. College, Henlow; Southampton Univ. (BSc Eng 1964). CEng 1971. FRAeS 1993. Served RAF stations: Syerston, 1965–67; Acklington, 1967–68; Ternhill, 1968–69; Changi, 1969–71; MoD, 1971–73; No 1 (F) Sqn, RAF Wittering, 1973–76; MoD, 1976–78; RAF Staff Coll., 1978; RAF Gütersloh, 1979–81; MoD, 1982–84; RAF Halton, 1984–86; RCDS, 1987; MoD, 1988–89; RAF St Athan, 1990–92; Dir Gen. Support Services (RAF), 1992–93; AOC Maintenance Units, RAF Logistics Comd, 1993–97. *Recreations:* orienteering, golf, offshore sailing, hill walking. *Club:* Royal Air Force.

KYLE, Terence; *see* Kyle, J. T.

KYLES, Raymond William; HM Diplomatic Service; Deputy High Commissioner, Lagos, since 2015; *b* 10 March 1956; *s* of William and Elizabeth Kyles; *m* 2007, Kate Short; two *s*. *Educ:* Glasgow Acad.; Univ. of Strathclyde (BA Business Admin 1980). Joined HM Diplomatic Service, 1980: FCO, 1980–82; UKMIS Geneva, 1982–85; UKREP Brussels, 1985–87; FCO, 1987–91; First Sec., Pretoria, 1991–95; Dep. Press Sec. to Sec. of State, 1996–98 and 2000–01; Dep. Perm. Rep. to OECD, 1998–2000; Pol Advr, Unilever UK, 2001–03 (on secondment); Deputy High Commissioner: Kenya, 2003–07; Islamabad, Pakistan, 2008–09; Kuala Lumpur, 2010–14. *Recreations:* indie music, football, golf, Rugby, films, travel. *Address:* c/o Foreign and Commonwealth Office, King Charles Street, SW1A 2AH. *E:* ray.kyles@fco.gov.uk.

KYLIÁN, Jiří; Resident Choreographer and Adviser, Nederlands Dans Theater, 1999–2009 (Artistic Director, 1975–99); *b* Prague, 21 March 1947; *s* of Vaclav Kylián and Marketá Pestová. *Educ:* Ballet Sch., Nat. Theatre, Prague; Prague Conservatory; Royal Ballet Sch., London. Stuttgarter Ballett, Germany; Guest Choreographer, Nederlands Dans Theater, 1973–75; *works choreographed* include: Viewers, 1973; Stoolgame, 1974; La cathédrale engloutie, 1975; Return to a Strange Land, 1975; Sinfonietta, 1978; Symphony of Psalms, 1978; Forgotten Land, 1981; Svadebka, 1982; Stamping Ground, 1983; L'Enfant et les Sortilèges, 1984; No More Play, 1988; Falling Angels, 1989; Sweet Dreams, 1990; Sarabande, 1990; Petite Mort, 1991; As If Never Been, 1992; No Sleep Till Dawn of Day, 1992; Whereabouts Unknown, 1993; Double You, 1994; Arcimboldo, 1995; Tears of Laughter, 1996; Wings of Wax, 1997; A Way a Lone, 1998; Indigo Rose, 1998; Half Past, 1999; Doux Mensonges, 1999; Study from Blackbird, 2002; Toss of a Dice, 2005; Vanishing Twin, 2008; Gods and Dogs, 2008, Last Touch First, Mémoires d'Oubliettes, 2009. Has worked with numerous cos, incl. Royal Swedish Ballet, Royal Danish Ballet, Royal Ballet, London, Finnish Nat. Ballet, Aust. Ballet, Nat. Ballet of Canada, Amer. Ballet Theatre, Wiener Staatsoper, Tokyo Ballet, Opéra de Paris, Rambert Dance Co. Hon. Dr, Juilliard Sch., NY, 1997. Critics' Award for Dance, Edinburgh Fest., 1996, 1997; Joost van den Vondel Preis, 1997. Officier: Ordre des arts et des lettres (France); Order of Oranje Nassau (Netherlands), 1995; Golden Medal for Outstanding Merits (Czech Republic); Chevalier de la Légion d'Honneur (France), 2004; Golden Lion, Venice Biennale, 2008; Medal for Art and Sci. (Netherlands), 2008; Medal of Honour, Order of House of Orange (Netherlands), 2008. *Address:* Kylián Productions, Acaciastraat 14, 2565 KB The Hague, Netherlands.

KYME, Rt Rev. Brian Robert; Director, Institute of Anglican Studies at St George's Cathedral, Perth, WA, since 2006; *b* 22 June 1935; *s* of John Robert Kyme and Ida Eileen Benson; *m* 1961, Doreen Muriel Williams; one *s* one *d*. *Educ:* Melbourne High School; Ridley Theological Coll., Melbourne; Aust. Coll. of Theology (ThL 1956); Melbourne Coll. of Divinity (Dip RE 1958); WA Coll. of Advanced Educn (BA 1989); Edith Cowan Univ. (MA 2005). MACE 1991. Ordained deacon, 1958, priest, 1960; Curate: St John's, E Malvern, 1958–60; Glenroy and Broadmeadows, 1960–61; Morwell, 1961–63; Vicar, St Matthew's, Ashburton, 1963–69; Dean, Holy Cross Cathedral, Geraldton, WA, 1969–74; Rector, Christ Church, Claremont, Perth, 1974–82; Archdeacon of Stirling, 1977–82; Asst Bishop of Perth, 1982–93; Nat. Dir, Australian Bd of Missions, later Anglican Bd of Mission-Australia, 1993–2000; Episcopal Asst to Primate of Australia, 2000–05. ChLJ, WA, 1985–93; ChLJ, NSW, 1998–99. *Recreations:* reading, music. *Address:* 153 Carr Street, West Perth, WA 6005, Australia. *T:* (home) (8) 93286065, (office) (8) 9325 5766, *Fax:* (8) 93256741.

KYNASTON, Dr David Thomas Anthony; historian, since 1973; *b* Aldershot, 30 July 1951; *s* of Arthur Kynaston and Gisela Hunt (*née* Siedbürger); *m* 1985, Lucy Robbins; two *s* one *d*. *Educ:* New Coll., Oxford (BA Modern Hist. 1973); London Sch. of Econs and Pol Sci. (PhD 1983). Hon. Prof., Kingston Univ., 2001–. *Publications:* King Labour, 1976; The Secretary of State, 1978; The Chancellor of the Exchequer, 1980; Bobby Abel: professional batsman, 1982; Archie's Last Stand, 1984; The Financial Times, 1988; WG's Birthday Party, 1990; Cazenove & Co., 1991; The City of London, vol. 1, 1994, vol. 2, 1995, vol. 3, 1999, vol. 4, 2001; (ed jtly) The Bank of England, 1995; LIFFE: a market and its makers, 1997; (with W. J. Reader) Phillips & Drew: professionals in the City, 1998; (with Richard Roberts) City State, 2001; Siegmund Warburg, 2002; Austerity Britain, 2007; Family Britain, 2009; Modernity Britain, Book One, 2013, Book Two, 2014; (with Richard Roberts) The Lion Wakes: a modern history of HSBC, 2015. *Recreations:* cricket, football (Aldershot Town), music (Dylan *et al*), reading. *Address:* c/o Rogers, Coleridge & White, 20 Powis Mews, W11 1JN. *Club:* MCC.

KYNASTON, Nicolas; freelance organist, since 1971; Professor of Organ, Royal Academy of Music, 2002–14; *b* 10 Dec. 1941; *s* of late Roger Tewkesbury Kynaston and Jessie Dearn Caecilia Kynaston (*née* Parkes); *m* 1st, 1961, Judith Felicity Heron (marr. diss. 1989); two *s* two *d*; 2nd, 1989, Susan Harwood Styles. *Educ:* Westminster Cathedral Choir Sch.; Downside; Accademia Musicale Chigiana, Siena; Conservatorio Santa Cecilia, Rome; Royal Coll. of Music. Organist of Westminster Cathedral, 1961–71; concert career, 1971–, travelling throughout Europe, North America, Asia and Africa; Organist, Athens Concert Hall, 1995–2010. Début recital, Royal Festival Hall, 1966; Recording début, 1968. Artistic Dir, Athens Organ Fest., 1997, 1999. Consultant, J. W. Walker & Sons Ltd, 1982–83 (Artistic Dir, 1978–82); Organ Consultant: Bristol Cathedral, 1986–91; St Chad's Cathedral, Birmingham, 1989–94; Bath Abbey, 1989–97; Tewkesbury Abbey, 1993–97; City of Halle, Germany, 1997–2000; Rugby Sch., 1998–2001. Mem., Westminster Abbey Fabric Commn, 2000–04. Jury member: Grand Prix de Chartres, 1971; St Albans Internat. Organ Festival, 1975. Pres., Incorp. Assoc. of Organists, 1983–85; Chm., Assoc. of Ind. Organ Advrs, 1997–2000. Chm., Nat. Organ Teachers' Encouragement Scheme, 1993–95. Hon. FRCO 1976. Hon. RAM 2010. Records incl. 6 nominated Critic's Choice; EMI/CFP Sales Award, 1974; MTA nomination Best Solo Instrumental Record of the Year, 1977; Deutscher Schallplattenpreis, 1978; Preis der Deutschen Schallplattenkritik, 1988. *Publications:* Transcriptions for Organ, 1997. *Recreations:* walking, church architecture. *Address:* 28 High Park Road, Kew Gardens, Richmond-upon-Thames, Surrey TW9 4BH. *T:* (020) 8878 4455, *Fax:* (020) 8392 9314.

KYNOCH, George Alexander Bryson, OBE 2013; Drumduan Associates, since 1997; *b* 7 Oct. 1946; *s* of late Lt Col Gordon Bryson Kynoch, CBE and Nesta Alicia Janet Thora (*née* Lyon); *m* 1st, 1971, Dr Rosslyn Margaret McDevitt (*d* 2002); one *s* one *d*; 2nd, 2008, Dorothy Anne Stiven. *Educ:* Cargilfield Sch., Edinburgh; Glenalmond Coll., Perthshire; Univ. of Bristol (BSc Hons Mech. Engrg). Plant Engr Silicones Plant, ICI Ltd, Nobel Div., 1968–71; G. and G. Kynoch, subseq. Kynoch Group, 1971–92; Finance Dir, then Jt Man. Dir; Chief Exec., 1981–90; Gp Exec. Dir, 1990–92; non-exec. Dir, 1992–95. Non-executive Director: Aardvark Holdings Ltd, 1992–95; PSL Holdings, 1998; Premisys Technologies (formerly WML Gp, then Premisys Gp) plc, 1998–2001; Talent Gp plc, 2003–14; tecc-IS plc, 2003–04; non-executive Chairman: Silvertech Internat., 1997–2000; London Marine Gp, 1998–2004; Muir Matheson, 1998–2007; Benson Gp, 1998–2005; Jetcam Internat. Hldgs, 1999–2003; TEP Exchange Gp plc, 2001–13; RDF Gp plc (formerly Eurolink Managed Services plc), 2003–06; Toluna plc, 2005–11; OCZ Technology Inc., 2006–09; Madwaves (UK) Ltd, 2006–08; Mercury Group plc, 2007–08; ITWP Acquisitions Ltd, 2011–; Red Squirrel Wine Ltd, 2014–. Chm., Scottish Woollen Publicity Council, 1983–90; Pres., Scottish Woollen Industry, 1990–91; Mem., Aberdeen and Dist MMB, 1988–92; Dir, Moray Badenoch and Strathspey Local Enterprise Co. Ltd, 1991–92. MP (C) Kincardine and Deeside, 1992–97; contested (C) Aberdeenshire West and Kincardine, 1997. Parliamentary Private Secretary: to Minister of State, FCO, 1992–94; to Sec. of State for Educn, 1994–95; Parly Under Sec. of State, Scottish Office (Minister for Industry and Local Govt), 1995–97. Mem., Scottish Affairs Select Cttee, 1992–95. Dep. Chm., Scottish Cons. and Unionist Party, 2008–12. Chm.,

Moray and Banff Cons. and Unionist Assoc., 1990–92; Vice-Chm., Northern Area, Scottish Cons. and Unionist Assoc., 1991–92. *Recreations:* golf, travel. *Address:* Wallflowers, Queen Street, Bloxham, Oxon OX15 4QQ. *Club:* Carlton (Dep. Chm., 2012–).

KYPRIANOU, Markos; Deputy Chairman, Democratic Party, since 2014; *b* 22 Jan. 1960. *Educ:* Univ. of Athens; Trinity Coll., Cambridge (LLM 1983); Harvard Law Sch. Associate, Antis Triantafyllides & Sons, law firm, 1985–91; Partner, Kyprianou & Boyiadjis, subseq. George L. Savvides & Co., 1991–2003. Mem., Nicosia Municipal Council, 1986–91. MP (Democratic) Nicosia, Cyprus, 1991–2003; Minister of Finance, 2003–04; Minister of Foreign Affairs, 2008–12. Mem., EC, 2004–08.

KYRIAZIDES, Nikos Panayis; Comdr, Order of George I of Greece; Deputy Minister, Ministry of Finance, Greece, 1994–96; *b* 3 Sept. 1927; *m* 1960, Ellie Kyrou; one *s* one *d*. *Educ:* Exeter Coll., Oxford Univ. (MA); Chicago Univ. Min. of Co-ordination, 1949; Head, Monetary Policy Div., 1950–51; Dir, External Payments and Trade, 1951–54; Alternate Economic Advr, Bank of Greece, 1956–60; Mem., Greek Delegn, negotiations for EFTA and assoc. of Greece to EEC, 1957–61; seconded to Min. of Co-ordination as Dir Gen., relations with EEC, 1962–64; Economic Advr, Nat. Bank of Greece, 1964–67; Sen. Economist, IMF, 1968–70; Advr to Cyprus Govt, negotiations for assoc. of Cyprus to EEC, 1971–72; Dep. Governor, Bank of Greece, 1974–77; Head of Greek delegn to Accession negotiations to the EEC, 1974–77; Advr to Cyprus Govt on relations with EEC, 1979–82; Ambassador to UK, and to Republic of Iceland, 1982–85; Alternate Exec. Dir, IMF, 1986–92. Knight Commander: Order of Merit (Italy); Order of Leopold II (Belgium); Comdr, Order of Merit (FRG). *Address:* 28 Loukianou Street, Athens 10675, Greece. *Club:* Athens (Athens).

KYTE, Peter Eric; QC 1996; a Recorder, since 1991; *b* 8 May 1945; *s* of late Eric Frank Kyte and Cicely Evelyn Leslie Kyte; *m* 1969, Virginia Cameron Cornish-Bowden; one *s* one *d*; *m* 2014, Zoe Elisabeth Johnson, *qv*. *Educ:* Wellington Coll.; Trinity Hall, Cambridge (MA Law). Called to the Bar, Gray's Inn, 1970; in business, 1970–74; Asst Recorder, 1988. *Recreations:* tennis, motorcycling, scuba diving, watching England perform on the sports field. *Address:* QEB Hollis Whiteman Chambers, 1–2 Laurence Pountney Hill, EC4R 0EU. *Club:* Aula (Cambridge).

KYUCHUKOV, Lyubomir Nedkov; Chief Executive Officer, Economics and International Relations Institute, Sofia, since 2012; *b* Sofia, 14 June 1955; *s* of Nedko Georgiev Kyuchukov and Evgenia Pancheva Kyuchukova; *m* 1983, Rumyana Laleva Baeva; one *s* one *d*. *Educ:* English Lang. Secondary Sch., Varna; Moscow State Univ. (MA Internat. Relns 1981); Georgetown Univ., Washington, DC (Specialization 2002). Mem., Embassy of Bulgaria, Bucharest, 1981; desk officer, Romania and Poland, E Europe Dept, Min. of Foreign Affairs, Bulgaria, 1981–84; Hd of Dept, Internat. Youth Movt, 1984–90; Researcher, Sofia Univ., 1991; political analyst, BBSS Gallup Internat., 1992–94; Chief Advr, Secretariat for Eur. Integration, Council of Ministers, 1996–97; Manager, Consultancy Co., 1997–2005; Mem., Council for Eur. and Euro-Atlantic Integration to Pres. of Bulgaria, 2001–05; Dep. Minister, 2005–09, Actg Minister, 2009, of Foreign Affairs; Mem., Nat. Security Council, 2005–09; Ambassador to the Court of St James's, 2009–12. Permanent Representative of Bulgaria to: Internat. Mobile Satellite Orgn, 2010–12; IMO, 2010–12. Participant in Nat. Round Table and Public Council on Nat. Issues, 1990; Vice-Chairman: Supreme Council, Bulgarian Socialist Party, 1990–91; Social Democratic Pol Movt, 2005–07. Founder Mem., Governing Council, Inst. of Econs and Internat. Relns, 2003–05; Mem. Bd, Diplomatic Inst. of Bulgaria, 2005–09. Mem., Nat. Council, UN Assoc. of Bulgaria, 1988–91. Founder, 1997, Mem. Bd, 2012–, Bulgarian Diplomatic Soc. Mem. Editl Bd, Internat. Relns mag., 2005–10. *Publications:* Regional Cooperation in Southeast Europe, 2009; New Regionalism in Southeast Europe, 2009; articles. *Recreations:* reading, walking, tourism. *E:* lyubomir@kyuchokov.com.

L

LAAJAVA, Jaakko; Commander First Class, Order of the Lion of Finland, 2004; Hon. CMG 1995; Under-Secretary of State for Foreign and Security Policy, Ministry for Foreign Affairs, Finland, since 2010; *b* Joensuu, Finland, 23 June 1947; *s* of Erkki Laajava and Aune Laajava; *m* 1971, Pirjoriitta, (Rita), Väyrynen; one *s* two *d*. *Educ:* Stockholm Univ. (BA 1972); Helsinki Univ. (MA 1972). Entered Finnish Foreign Service, 1972; assignments in Geneva, Paris, Warsaw, Belgrade, Madrid and Washington, DC, 1973–90; Dir-Gen. for Political Affairs, 1992; Ambassador to the US, 1996–2001; Under-Sec., 2001–05; Ambassador to the Court of St James's, 2005–10. Fellow, Harvard Univ., 1985. *Publications:* several articles on foreign and security policy. *Recreations:* music, golf. *Address:* Ministry for Foreign Affairs, PO Box 412, 00023 Government, Finland. *T:* (9) 16055030. *E:* jaakko.laajava@formin.fi. *Clubs:* Travellers, Royal Automobile; Harvard Club of Finland.

LABANYI, Prof. Jo(sephine), FBA 2005; Professor of Spanish, New York University, since 2006; *b* 28 March 1946; *d* of Cyril and Louisa Wood; *m* 1969, Peter Labanyi (marr. diss. 1975). *Educ:* Lady Margaret Hall, Oxford (BA Hons 1st cl. Spanish 1967). Birkbeck Coll., London, 1971–2000: Lectr, 1971–85, Sen. Lectr, 1985–92, Reader, 1992–95, in Spanish; Prof. in Spanish Cultural Studies, 1995–2000; Dir, Inst. of Romance Studies, Sch. of Advanced Study, London, 1997–2002; Prof. of Spanish and Cultural Studies, Univ. of Southampton, 2001–06. Vis. King Juan Carlos I Prof. of Spanish Culture and Civilization, NY Univ., 2002. An Ed., Jl of Spanish Cultural Studies, 2000– (Founding Ed., 2000); Mem. Adv. Bd, Jl of Romance Studies, 2003– (Founding Ed., 2001). *Publications:* Ironía e historia en 'Tiempo de silencio', 1985; Myth and History in the Contemporary Spanish Novel, 1989; (ed) Galdós, 1992; (ed and trans) Benito Pérez Galdós, Nazarín, 1993; (ed jtly) Spanish Cultural Studies: an introduction, 1995; (ed jtly) Culture and Gender in Nineteenth-century Spain, 1995; Gender and Modernization in the Spanish Realist Novel, 2000; (ed) Constructing Identity in Contemporary Spain, 2002; Spanish Literature: a very short introduction, 2010; (ed jtly) Europe and Love in Cinema, 2012; (ed jtly) Companion to Spanish Cinema, 2012. *Recreations:* classical music, walking round cities. *Address:* Department of Spanish and Portuguese, New York University, 13–19 University Place, New York, NY 10003–4556, USA. *T:* (212) 9987570, *Fax:* (212) 9954149. *E:* jo.labanyi@nyu.edu.

LABORDE, Prof. Cécile, DPhil; FBA 2013; Professor of Political Theory, University College London, since 2009; *b* Dax, France, 16 April 1971; *d* of Jacques and Pierrette Laborde; partner, 1995, Mark Hewitson; two *d*. *Educ:* Inst. d'Études Politiques, Bordeaux; Hull Univ. (MA 1993); St Antony's Coll., Oxford (DPhil 1996). Lecturer in Political Theory: Univ. of Exeter, 1996–98; KCL, 1998–2003; University College London: Lectr in Pol Theory, 2003–05; Sen. Lectr, 2005–09; Reader, 20009. Fellow, Inst. for Advanced Study, Princeton, 2010–11. *Publications:* Pluralist Thought and the State in Britain and France, 2000; (ed with J. Maynor) Republicanism and Political Theory, 2007; Critical Republicanism, 2008; Français encore un effort pour être républicains!, 2010. *E:* c.laborde@ucl.ac.uk.

LACEY, Prof. (John) Hubert, MD; FRCPsych; Professor of Psychiatry, St George's, University of London, 1991–2011, now Emeritus; Clinical Director and Head of Eating Disorders, Nightingale Hosptial (formerly Capio Nightingale Hospital), London, since 2007; Medical Director, Newbridge House, Birmingham, since 2006; *b* 4 Nov. 1944; *s* of Percy Hubert Lacey and Sheila Margaret Lacey (*née* Neal); *m* 1976, Susan Millicent Liddiard; two *s* one *d*. *Educ:* Loughborough Grammar Sch.; Univ. of St Andrews (MB ChB 1969); Univ. of London (MPhil 1974); Univ. of Dundee (MD 1988); DRCOG 1972. MRCPsych 1974, FRCPsych 1985. Jun. hosp. appts, Dundee, St Thomas' and St George's Hosps, London, 1969–78; Sen. Lectr, Middlesex Hosp. Med. Sch., London, 1978–80; Sen. Lectr, 1980–87, Reader, 1987–91, Chm., 1991–2003, St George's, Univ. of London. Clinical Director and Consultant: St George's Eating Disorders Service, 1980–2011; Yorkshire Centre for Eating Disorders, Leeds, 2003–07; Peninsula Eating Disorder Service, Exeter, 2004–08; Medical Adviser: BUPA, 1994–99; Priory Hosp. Gp, 1990–2008; Surrey NHS Trust, 2004–09; Consultant, Eating Disorder Unit, Priory Hosp., 1989–2008. Non-exec. Dir, various NHS Trusts, 1991–99. Mem., Court of Electors, 1991–2006, Council, 2002–06, RCPsych. Chm., Eur. Council on Eating Disorders; Past Pres., Internat. Coll. of Psychosomatic Medicine. Patron, Eating Disorders Assoc. Freeman, City of London, 1986; Liveryman, Co. of Plaisterers, 1986– (Master, 2010–11; Dep. Master, 2011–12; Chm., Charity Cttee, 2012–). *Publications:* Psychological Management of the Physically Ill, 1989; Overcoming Anorexia Nervosa, 2007; Bulimia, Binge-Eating and Their Treatment, 2010; over 180 contribs in books and learned jls on anorexia nervosa, bulimia nervosa, obesity, psychosomatic illnesses. *Recreations:* art, jazz, hill walking, seven (and counting) grandchildren! *Address:* 5 Atherton Drive, Wimbledon, SW19 5LB. *E:* jhubertlacey@hotmail.com; Eating Disorders Service, Nightingale Hospital, 11–19 Lisson Grove, NW1 6SH. *T:* (020) 7535 7927. *E:* hlacey@sgul.ac.uk. *Club:* Athenæum.

LACEY, Prof. Nicola Mary, FBA 2001; Professor of Law, Gender and Social Policy, London School of Economics and Political Science, since 2013; *b* 3 Feb. 1958; *d* of John McAndrew and Gillian Wroth; *m* 1991, David William Soskice, *qv*. *Educ:* University Coll. London (LLB 1979); University Coll., Oxford (BCL 1981; Hon. Fellow, 2010). Lectr in Law, UCL, 1981–84; Fellow in Law, New Coll., Oxford, and CUF Lectr, Univ. of Oxford, 1984–95; Prof. of Law, Birkbeck Coll., Univ. of London, 1995–97; Prof. of Criminal Law and Legal Theory, LSE, 1998–2010; Prof. of Criminal Law and Legal Theory, Univ. of Oxford, 2010–13; Sen. Res. Fellow, All Souls Coll., Oxford, 2010–13. Guest Prof., Humboldt Univ., 1995; Adjunct Prof., Res. Sch. of Social Scis, ANU, 1998–2007; Fellow, Wissenschaftskolleg zu Berlin, 1999–2000; Leverhulme Trust Major Res. Fellowship, 2006–09; Visiting Professor: Global Law Sch., New York Univ., 2001–; Center for Ethics, Politics and Economics, Yale Univ., 2004; Harvard Law Sch., 2013; Vis. Fellow, Center for European Studies, Harvard Univ., 2007; Dist. Global Fellow, Hauser Global Law Sch. Prog., NY Univ. Sch. of Law, 2014. Hon. Fellow, New Coll., Oxford, 2007–. Hon. Bencher, Inner Temple, 2011. Hans Sigrist Prize, Univ. of Bern, 2011. *Publications:* State Punishment: political principles and community values, 1988; (with Celia Wells and Oliver Quick) Reconstructing Criminal Law, 1990, 3rd edn, 2003; (with Elizabeth Frazer) The Politics of Community, 1993; Criminal Justice: a reader, 1994; Unspeakable Subjects: feminist essays in legal and social theory, 1998; A Life of H. L. A. Hart: the nightmare and the noble dream, 2004; The Prisoners' Dilemma: political economy and punishment in contemporary democracies, 2008; Women, Crime and Character: from Moll Flanders to Tess of the D'Urbervilles, 2008. *Address:* Department of Law, London School of Economics and Political Science, Houghton Street, WC2A 2AE. *E:* N.M.Lacey@lse.ac.uk.

LACEY, Air Vice-Marshal Richard Howard, CBE 2004; a Gentleman Usher to the Queen, since 2013; Consultant to Sodexo Defence Ltd, 2012–13 (Strategy Director, 2009–12); Commander British Forces and Administrator of the Sovereign Base Areas, Cyprus, 2006–08; *b* 11 Dec. 1953; *s* of Henry Howard Lacey and Mary Elliot Lacey; *m* 1980, Catherine Helen Brown; one *s* one *d*. *Educ:* John Ruskin Grammar Sch.; Peterhouse, Cambridge (BA 1975); RCDS. RAF Coll., Cranwell, 1975–77; Flying Instr, 1984–85; Flight Comdr, 72 Sqn, 1985–87; RAF Staff Coll., 1988; PSO to Dep. C-in-C, later C-in-C, HQ STC, 1989–91; OC 33 Sqn, 1992–94; Station Comdr, RAF Benson, 1997–99; Dir NATO Policy, MoD, 2000–03; Comdr British Forces Falkland Is, 2003–05; UK Nat. Mil. Rep. to SHAPE, 2005–06. *Recreations:* photography, model engineering, industrial archaeology. *E:* lacey.richardh@gmail.com. *Club:* Royal Air Force.

LACEY, Prof. Richard Westgarth, MD, PhD; FRCPath; Professor of Medical Microbiology, University of Leeds, 1983–98, now Emeritus; Consultant to Leeds Health Authority, 1983–98; *b* 11 Oct. 1940; *s* of Jack and Sybil Lacey; *m* 1972, Fionna Margaret Stone; two *d*. *Educ:* Felsted Sch., Essex; Cambridge Univ. (BA, MB, BChir; MD 1969); London Hosp.; Univ. of Bristol (PhD 1974). FRCPath 1985; DCH 1966. House Officer, London and Eastbourne, 1964–66; Sen. House Officer, 1966–67, Registrar, 1967–68, Bristol Royal Infirmary; Lectr, 1968–73, Reader in Clinical Microbiology, 1973–74, Univ. of Bristol; Consultant in Microbiology, 1974–83, and Consultant in Chemical Pathology, 1975–83, Queen Elizabeth Hosp., King's Lynn; Consultant in Chem. Path., E Anglian RHA, 1974–83. Consultant, WHO, 1983–. Evian Health Award, 1989; Caroline Walker Award, 1989; Freedom of Information Award, 1990. *Publications:* Safe Shopping, Safe Cooking, Safe Eating, 1989; Unfit for Human Consumption, 1991; Hard to Swallow, 1994; Mad Cow Disease: a history of BSE in Britain, 1994; Poison on a Plate, 1998; 210 contribs to learned scientific jls. *Recreations:* antique furniture, gardening, chess, sleeping, walking, eating (not recently).

LACEY, Robert (David Weston); author and broadcaster; *b* 3 Jan. 1944; *s* of late Leonard John Lacey and Vida Ivy Pamela (*née* Winch); *m* 1st, 1971, Alexandra Jane Avrach (marr. diss. 2010); two *s* one *d*; 2nd, 2012, Lady Jane Antonia Frances Rayne, *er d* of 8th Marquess of Londonderry and *widow* of Baron Rayne (Life Peer). *Educ:* Clifton Nat. Infants' Sch.; Bristol Grammar Sch.; Selwyn Coll., Cambridge (MA, DipEd). Reporter and columnist, Johannesburg Sunday Times, 1967; ed. and compiler, Jackdaw collections of historical documents for children, 1967–74; writer, Illustrated London News, 1968; writer and Asst Ed., Sunday Times mag., 1969–73; Ed., Look! pages, Sunday Times, 1973–74; Guest Ed., The Court Historian, 2003, 2004; book reviewer, Oxford Jl of Islamic Studies; royal commentator, ITN, CNN, Good Morning America, ABC; writer and presenter: Aristocrats, BBC2 series, 1983; BBC Radio 4 series: The Year 1000, 2000; The Year 1901, 2001; Crown and People, 2002; The Year 1953, 2003; 1914: The Diaries of King George V, 2004; Rehab for Terrorists (TV film), 2009; contrib., Sands of Time, BBC Radio 4 series, 2015. Mem., Cttee, Soc. for Court Studies, 2001–09. Sec., Careers Cttee, Old Bristolians' Soc., 2002–06. Pres., Selwyn Coll. Assoc., 2014–15. Al-Rawabi Holding Award for contribns to Saudi-British relations, Saudi-British Soc., 2011. *Publications:* Robert, Earl of Essex, 1971; The Life and Times of Henry VIII, 1972; The Queens of the North Atlantic, 1973; Sir Walter Ralegh, 1973; Majesty: Elizabeth II and the House of Windsor, 1977; The Kingdom: Arabia and the House of Saud, 1981; (with M. Rand) Princess, 1982; Aristocrats, 1983; Ford: the men and the machine, 1986; God Bless Her!, 1987; Little Man: Meyer Lansky and the gangster life, 1991; Grace, 1994; Sotheby's: bidding for class, 1998; (with D. Danziger) The Year 1000, 1999; (with M. Rand) The Queen Mother's Century, 1999; Royal: Her Majesty Queen Elizabeth II, 2002 (US edn as Monarch: the life and reign of Elizabeth II); series Great Tales from English History: vol. 1, Cheddar Man to the Peasants' Revolt, 2003; vol. 2, Chaucer to the Glorious Revolution, 2004; vol. 3, Battle of the Boyne to DNA, 2006; 3 vol. omnibus edn, Great Tales from English History, 2007, Folio Soc. edn 2008; Inside the Kingdom: kings, clerics, modernists, terrorists and the struggle for Saudi Arabia, 2009; A Brief Life of the Queen, 2012; (ed jtly) Gulf Charities and Islamic Philanthropy in the 'Age of Terror' and Beyond, 2014; Model Woman: Eileen Ford and the business of beauty, 2015. *Recreations:* swimming, meditating, yoga. *Address:* c/o Jonathan Pegg Literary Agency, 32 Batoum Gardens, W6 7QD. *E:* robert@robertlacey.com. *Clubs:* Chelsea Arts, Frontline; Italian (Jeddah).

LACEY, Stephen Charles David Lloyd; gardener, author, journalist and broadcaster; *b* 6 May 1957; *s* of late Charles Leslie Lacey and Myra Lloyd Lacey (*née* Lloyd Williams). *Educ:* Trearddur House Prep. Sch.; Shrewsbury Sch.; Trinity Coll., Oxford (MA Mod. Langs). Early career in property investment; gardening columnist and feature writer, Daily Telegraph, 1989–; a presenter, Gardeners' World, BBC TV, 1992–2002; freelance horticultural lectr in UK, USA and Canada. *Publications:* The Startling Jungle, 1986; Scent in Your Garden, 1991, rev. edn as RHS Companion to Scented Plants, 2014; Lawns and Ground Cover, 1991; Gardens of the National Trust, 1996, 3rd edn 2011; Real Gardening, 2002. *Recreations:* adventurous travel, tropical birdwatching, collecting, ski-ing. *Address:* 37 Rosary Gardens, SW7 4NQ. *T:* (020) 7244 8111.

LACHMANN, Sir Peter (Julius), Kt 2002; FRCP, FRCPath; FRS 1982; FMedSci; Sheila Joan Smith Professor of Immunology (formerly Tumour Immunology), University of Cambridge, 1977–99, now Emeritus Professor; Fellow of Christ's College, Cambridge, 1962–71 and since 1976; Head, Microbial Immunology Group, Centre for Veterinary Science, Cambridge, 1997–2006; *b* 23 Dec. 1931; *s* of late Heinz Lachmann and Thea (*née* Heller); *m* 1962, Sylvia Mary, *d* of Alan Stephenson; two *s* one *d*. *Educ:* Christ's Coll., Finchley; Trinity Coll., Cambridge (Hon. Fellow, 2007); University College Hosp. MA, MB BChir, PhD, ScD (Cantab). FRCP 1973; FRCPath 1981. John Lucas Walker Student, Dept of Pathology, Cambridge, 1958–60; Vis. Investigator, Rockefeller Univ., New York, 1960–61; Empire Rheumatism Council Res. Fellow, Dept of Pathology, Cambridge, 1962–64; Asst Dir of Res. in Pathology, Univ. of Cambridge, 1964–71; Prof. of

Immunology, Royal Postgraduate Med. Sch., 1971–75; Hd, 1976–77, Hon. Hd, 1977–80, MRC Gp on Mechanisms in Tumour Immunity; Hon. Dir, MRC Mechanisms in Tumour Immunity Unit, later MRC Molecular Immunopathology Unit, 1980–97; Hon. Clin. Immunologist, Cambridge HA, 1976–99. Member: Systems Bd, MRC, 1982–86; Med. Adv. Cttee, British Council, 1983–97; Council, RCPath, 1982–85, 1989–93 (Pres., 1990–93); Gene Therapy Adv. Cttee, 1993–96; UNESCO Internat. Bioethics Cttee, 1993–98; Med. Educn Res. Co-ordinating Cttee, 1994–98; Scientific Adv. Bd, SmithKline Beecham, 1995–2000; Chm. Scientific Adv. Bd, Adprotech plc, 1997–2004; non-exec. Dir, Synovis plc, 2001–05. Chairman: Med. Res. Cttee, Muscular Dystrophy Gp, 1987–91; Sci. Cttee, Assoc. Medical Res. Charities, 1988–92; Res. Adv. Cttee, CORE, 2003–09. Trustee: Darwin Trust, 1991–2001; Arthritis Res. Campaign, 2000–06. President: Henry Kunkel Soc., 2003–05; European Fedn of Academies of Medicine, 2004–05. Vis. Investigator, Scripps Clinic and Research Foundn, La Jolla, 1966, 1975, 1980, 1986, 1989; Vis. Scientist, Basel Inst. of Immunology, 1971; RSM Vis. Prof. in USA (various centres), 1983; Smith Kline & French Vis. Prof. in Australia (various centres), 1987; Vis. Prof., Dept of Medicine, RPMS, London, 1986–89 (Fellow, 1995; FIC 2001). Meyerhoff Vis. Prof., Weizmann Inst., Rehovoth, 1989; Prof., Collège de France, 1993; RCS Sir Arthur Sims Travelling Prof., India, 1994; Lectures: Foundn, RCPath, 1983; Langdon-Brown, RCP, 1986; first R. R. Porter Meml, 1986; Heberden Oration, 1986; Prathap Meml, Malaysia, 1991; Charnock Bradley Meml, Royal (Dick) Vet. Sch., Edinburgh, 1994; Frank May Med. Scis, Univ. of Leicester, 1994; Vanguard Medica, Univ. of Surrey, 1998; Lloyd Roberts, Med. Soc. of London, 1999; first Jean Shanks, Acad. Med. Scis, 2001; Ver Heyden de Lancey, Faculty of Law, Univ. of Cambridge, 2011. Biological Sec., and a Vice-Pres., Royal Soc., 1993–98; Founder FMedSci 1998 (Pres., 1998–2002). Foreign Fellow, Indian Nat. Sci. Acad., 1997; Foreign Member: Norwegian Acad. of Science and Letters, 1991; Academia Europea, 1992. Hon. Fellow, Faculty of Pathology, RCPI, 1993; Hon. Member: Assoc. of Physicians, 1998; Czech Med. Acad., 2012. Hon. DSc Leicester, 2005. Gold Medal, Eur. Complement Network, 1997; Medicine and Europe Sen. Prize, Acad. des Scis de la Santé, 2003. Associate Editor, Clinical and Experimental Immunology, 1989–2001. *Publications:* co-ed, Clinical Aspects of Immunology, 3rd edn 1975, 4th edn 1982, 5th edn 1993; First Steps: a personal account of the formation of the Academy of Medical Sciences, 2010; papers in sci. jls on complement, microbial immunology, immunopathology, cultural evolution, religion and ethical aspects of biosci. *Recreations:* visiting mountains, keeping bees. *Address:* Conduit Head, 36 Conduit Head Road, Cambridge CB3 0EY. *T:* (01223) 354433. *Club:* Athenæum.

LACKEY, Mary Josephine, CB 1985; OBE 1966; former Under Secretary, Department of Trade and Industry; *b* 11 Aug. 1925; *d* of William and Winifred Lackey. *Educ:* King Edward VI High Sch., Birmingham; Lady Margaret Hall, Oxford (MA). Board of Trade, 1946; Asst Principal, Central Land Bd, 1947–50; BoT, 1950–61; UK Delegn to EFTA and GATT, 1961–66; BoT, subseq. DTI and Dept of Trade, 1966–85; Asst Sec., 1968; Under Sec., 1974. *Club:* Oxford and Cambridge.

LACLOTTE, Michel René; Commandeur de la Légion d'honneur; Commandeur de l'ordre national du Mérite; Hon. CBE 1994; Director, The Louvre Museum, Paris, 1987–94; *b* 27 Oct. 1929; *s* of Pierre Laclotte, advocate, and Huguette (*née* de Kermabon). *Educ:* Lycée Pasteur, Neuilly; Institut d'art et d'archéologie, l'Université de Paris; Ecole du Louvre. Inspector, Inspectorate General of provincial museums, 1955–66; Chief Conservator: Dept of Paintings, Louvre Mus., 1966–87; Collections of Musée d'Orsay, 1978–86. *Publications:* works on history of art, catalogues, articles in art reviews, esp. on Italian paintings of 14th and 15th centuries and French primitives. *Address:* 10 bis rue du Pré-aux-Clercs, 75007 Paris, France.

LACON, Sir (Edmund) Richard (Vere), 9th Bt *cr* 1818, of Great Yarmouth, Norfolk; *b* 2 Oct. 1967; *o s* of Sir Edmund Vere Lacon, 8th Bt and of Gillian Lacon (*née* Middleditch); *S* father, 2014; *m* 1997, Natalie, *o d* of Joginder Shinh; one *s. Heir: s* Luke Edmund Lacon, *b* 28 May 2001.

LACROIX, Christian Marie Marc; Commandeur de l'Ordre des Arts et des Lettres, 1998; Chevalier de la Légion d'Honneur, 2002; designer; launched Christian Lacroix haute couture, 1987; *b* 16 May 1951; *s* of Maxime Lacroix and Jeannette Bergier; *m* 1989, Françoise Roesenstiehl. *Educ:* Paul Valéry Univ., Montpellier; Sorbonne. History of Art degree. Assistant at Hermès, 1978; Asst for Guy Paulin, 1980; designer for Patou, 1981–86; Creative Dir, Pucci, 2002–05. Artistic Advr, La Monnaie de Paris, 2010. Pres., Centre National du Costume de Scène, 2006–08, now Hon. Pres. Golden Thimble Award, 1986 and 1988; CFDA Award, NY, 1987; Prix Balzac, 1989; Goldene Spinnrad, Krefeld, Germany, 1990; Molière Theatre Award, 1996, 2007. *Publications:* Pieces of a Pattern (autobiog.), 1992; The Diary of a Collection, 1996; Qui est là?, 2004; illustrator of albums, Styles d'aujourd'hui, 1995; Christian Lacroix on Fashion, 2006.

LACROIX, Prof. Robert, CM 2000; OQ; PhD; FRSC; Fellow, Centre for Interuniversity Research and Analysis on Organisations, Montreal; Rector, University of Montreal, 1998–2005; *b* 15 April 1940; *s* of Léo Lacroix and Léonne Galarneau; *m* 1962, Ginette Teasdale; three *d. Educ:* Univ. of Montreal (BA, BSc, MA Econs); Univ. of Louvain, Belgium (PhD Econs 1970). University of Montreal: Asst Prof., 1970, Prof., 1979, Dept of Econs; Chm., Dept of Econs, 1977–83; Dir, Centre for R&D in Econs, 1985–87; Dean, Faculty of Arts and Scis, 1987–93; Pres. and CEO, Centre for Interuniv. Res. and Analysis on Orgns, 1994–98. Project Dir, Econ. Council of Canada, 1976–78. Member, Board of Directors: Assoc. of Univs and Colls of Canada, 1998–2004 (Pres., 2001–03); Conf. of Rectors and Principals of Quebec Univs, 1998–2000; Ecole Polytechnique de Montréal, 1998–2005; Ecole des Hautes Etudes Commerciales, 1998–2005; Bd of Trade, Metropolitan Montreal, 2001–04; CAE, 2006–13; Groupe Jean Coutu; Pomerleau. Mem., Academic Adv. Cttee, Inst. of Canadian Bankers, 1999–2003; Mem. Bd of Govs, Foundn for Educnl Exchange between Canada and USA, 2003–06. *Publications:* (with J. M. Cousineau) Wage Determination in Major Collective Agreements in the Private and Public Sectors, 1977; (with Y. Rabeau) Politiques nationales, Conjonctures régionales: la stabilisation économique, 1981; (with F. Martin) Les conséquences de la décentralisation régionale des activités de R&D, 1987; (with M. Huberman) Le partage de l'Emploi: solution au chômage ou frein à l'emploi, 1996; (with L. Maheu) Le CHUM, une tragédie québécoise, 2010; (with L. Maheu) Leading Research Universities in a Competitive World, 2015. *Address:* CIRANO, 1130 Sherbrooke Ouest, Suite 1400, Montreal, QC H3A 2M8, Canada.

LACY, Very Rev. David William; DL; Moderator of the General Assembly of the Church of Scotland, 2005–06; Minister, Kay Park (formerly Henderson) Church, Kilmarnock, since 1989; *b* 26 April 1952; *s* of Peter and Nan Lacy; *m* 1974, Joan Stewart Robertson; one *s* one *d. Educ:* Univ. of Strathclyde (BA 1972); Univ. of Glasgow (BD 1975). Asst Minister, St George's West Church, Edinburgh, 1975–77; Minister, St Margaret's, Knightswood, Glasgow, 1977–89. Convener: Bd of Practice and Procedure, 2000–04; Gen. Assembly Business Cttee, 2000–04. Hon. DLitt Strathclyde, 2006. DL Ayrshire and Arran, 2013. *Recreations:* sailing, choral singing. *Address:* 52 London Road, Kilmarnock, Ayrshire KA3 7AJ. *T:* (01563) 523113. *E:* thelacys@tinyworld.co.uk. *Club:* Kilmarnock.

LACY, Sir Patrick Bryan Finucane, 4th Bt *cr* 1921, of Ampton, co. Suffolk; *b* 18 April 1948; *s* of Sir Maurice John Pierce Lacy, 2nd Bt and his 2nd wife, Nansi Jean (*née* Evans); *S* brother, 1998; *m* 1971, Phyllis Victoria James; one *s* one *d. Educ:* Downside. *Heir: s* Finian James Pierce Lacy, *b* 24 Sept. 1972.

LADDIE, James Matthew Lang; QC 2012; *b* London, 25 Oct. 1972; *s* of Prof. Sir Hugh Ian Lang Laddie and Stecia Elizabeth Laddie; *m* 1999, Emma Louise Robinson; one *s* three *d. Educ:* St Paul's Sch.; Sidney Sussex Coll., Cambridge (BA 1994). Called to the Bar, Middle Temple, 1995. *Recreations:* bird watching, blues, cricket, crosswords, cycling. *Address:* Matrix Chambers, Gray's Inn, WC1R 5LN. *T:* (020) 7404 3447.

LADDS, Rt Rev. Robert Sidney, SSC; Bishop Suffragan of Whitby, 1999–2008; an Hon. Assistant Bishop, Diocese of London, since 2009; Honorary Curate, St Peter's, London Docks, since 2015; *b* 15 Nov. 1941; *s* of late Sidney Ladds and of Joan Dorothy Ladds (*née* Cant); *m* 1964, Roberta Harriet Sparkes; three *s. Educ:* Christ Church Coll., Canterbury (CertEd 1970, BEd Hons 1971, London Univ.); Canterbury Sch. of Ministry. LRSC 1972; FRSC (FCS 1972). Industrial res. chemist, 1959–68; schoolmaster, 1971–80; ordained deacon, 1980, priest, 1981; Asst Curate, St Leonard, Hythe, 1980–83; Rector of Bretherton, 1983–91; Chaplain, Bishop Rawstorne Sch., 1983–86; Bishop of Blackburn's Chaplain for Ministry, 1986–90; Bishop's Audit Officer, 1990–91; Rector of Preston, 1991–97; Hon. Canon, Blackburn, 1993–97; Archdeacon of Lancaster, 1997–99; House-for-duty Priest, St Mary and Christ Church, Hendon, 2009–15. Fellow, 2010, and Provost (Eastern Region), 2014–, Woodard Corp. (Asst Provost, 2010–14). Commissary for Northern Province to Bp of Taejon, S Korea, 1997–99; Vice-Pres., Korea Mission Partnership, 1999–. Superior-Gen., Soc. of Mary, 2000–. *Recreations:* gardening, fell-walking, bonsai, church architecture. *Address:* Christ Church House, 76 Brent Street, NW4 2ES. *T:* (020) 8202 8123. *E:* episcopus@ntlworld.com.

LADE, Hilary Jane; Director, Plymouth Culture Board, since 2014; *b* 11 June 1957; *d* of Herbert Alfred Lade and Margaret (*née* Clark); *m* 2002, Mark Wilson. *Educ:* Selwyn Coll., Cambridge (MA Oriental Studies (Chinese)); Harvard Univ. (MA E Asian Langs and Civilisations); Univ. of Calif, Berkeley (MA Internat. Relns). Oil trader, Shell Internat., 1984–87; Man. Dir, Shell Gas Ltd, Shell UK, 1987–91; Estate Manager, Fountains Abbey and Studley Royal, NT, 1991–93; Dir of Historic Properties, English Heritage, 1993–97; Hd of Business Improvement, Shell, 1997–99. Chm., Royal Parks Adv. Bd, 1999–2002. Director: Nat. Forest Co., 1998–2002; Southern Arts Bd, 1998–2002; YHA, 1999–2001; BTA, 2000–03; Oxford Inspires, 2003–09; Dir and Trustee, Heritage Lottery Fund, 2008–14. Trustee, Nat. Trust, 2001–06. Mem., Bd of Visitors, Ashmolean Mus., 2011–14. Gov., Plymouth Coll. of Art, 2014–. Winston Churchill Travelling Fellow, 1978; Harkness Fellow, 1980. *Recreations:* music (violin player), travel, ski-ing, mountaineering. *E:* hilary.lade@live.co.uk.

LADENIS, Nicholas Peter; Chef Patron, Chez Nico Restaurants, 1973–2000; *b* 22 April 1934; *s* of Peter and Constandia Ladenis; *m* 1963, Dinah-Jane Zissu; two *d. Educ:* Prince of Wales Sch., Nairobi; Regent Street Poly.; LSE; Hull Univ. (BSc Econs 1958). Appts with various cos, incl. Caltex, Ford Motor Co., Sunday Times, up to 1970; entered catering trade, 1971; opened restaurants (with wife and business partner): Chez Nico, 1973; Simply Nico, 1986; Nico Central, 1989; Consultant: Incognico, 2000–04; Deca, 2002–04. Awarded 3 Michelin Stars, 1995; first restaurateur to achieve full marks in Good Food Guide. Hon. DSc(Econ) Hull, 1997. *Publications:* My Gastronomy, 1987; Nico, 1996. *Recreations:* food, family, home, travel, expensive cars.

LADER, Prof. Malcolm Harold, OBE 1996; MD, PhD, DSc; FRCPsych, FMedSci; Professor of Clinical Psychopharmacology, Institute of Psychiatry, University of London, 1978–2001, now Emeritus; *b* 27 Feb. 1936; *s* of Abe and Minnie Lader; *m* 1961, Susan Ruth Packer; three *d. Educ:* Univ. of Liverpool (BSc 1956; MB ChB 1959; MD 1964); University Coll. London (PhD 1963; DSc 1976); DPM 1966; Open Univ. (LLB 2006). FRCPsych 1976. Res. Asst, UCL, 1960–63; Registrar in Psychiatry, 1963–66, Hon. Consultant, 1970–2001, Maudsley Hosp.; Mem., MRC External Staff, 1966–2001. Trustee, Psychiatry Res. Trust, 2002–. FRSocMed 1963; FMedSci 1999. Hon. Fellow: Amer. Coll. of Psychiatrists, 1993; Soc. for Study of Addiction, 1998; British Assoc. for Psychopharmacology, 1994. *Publications:* Psychiatry on Trial, 1978; (ed jtly) Psychiatry and General Practice, 1982; (jtly) Role of Neurotransmitter Systems in Anxiety Modulation, 1984; (contrib.) Patterns of Improvement in Depressed In-patients, 1987; (ed) Psychopharmacology of Addiction, 1988; Biological Treatments in Psychiatry, 1990, 2nd edn 1996; (ed jtly) Nature of Alcohol and Drug-related Problems, 1992; (jtly) Anxiety, Panic and Phobias, 1997; 670 articles in scientific jls. *Recreations:* antiques, eating too much. *Address:* 16 Kelsey Park Mansion, 78 Wickham Road, Beckenham, Kent BR3 6QH. *T:* (020) 8650 0366.

LADER, Philip, JD; Chairman, WPP Group, 2001–15; Senior Adviser, Morgan Stanley International, since 2001; *b* 17 March 1946; *s* of Phil and Mary Tripoli Lader; *m* 1980, Linda LeSourd; two *d. Educ:* Duke Univ. (BA 1966); Univ. of Michigan (MA History 1967); Pembroke Coll., Oxford (Hon. Fellow, 1994); Harvard Law Sch. (JD). Admitted to Bar: Florida, 1972; District of Columbia, 1973; S Carolina, 1979; Associate, Sullivan & Cromwell, 1972; Law Clerk to US Circuit Judge, 1973; President: Sea Pines Co., 1979–83; Winthrop Univ., 1983–86; GOSL Land Assets Mgt, 1986–88; Business Execs for Nat. Security, 1990; Exec. Vice-Pres., Sir James Goldsmith's US Hldgs, 1986–89; Pres. and Vice Chancellor, Bond Univ., Australia, 1991–92; Dep. Dir for Mgt, Office of Mgt and Budget, US Govt, 1993; White House Dep. Chief of Staff and Asst to the Pres., 1993–94; Adminr, Small Business Admin, and Mem., President's Cabinet, 1994–97; Ambassador of the USA to the UK, 1997–2001. West Prof. of Internat. Studies, The Citadel, 2001–07. Partner, Nelson Mullins Law Firm, 2001–; Director: American Red Cross, 1995–96; AES Corp., 2001–; Marathon Oil, 2001–; Songbird Estates, 2006–10; UC RUSAL, 2007–. Mem. Council, Lloyd's, 2004–10. Trustee: British Museum, 2001–06; RAND Corp., 2001–11, 2013–; St Paul's Cathedral Trust, 2002–07; Windsor Leadership Trust, 2002–06; Salzburg Global Seminar, 2004–; Smithsonian Mus. of American Hist., 2006–. Chm., Amer. Assoc., Royal Acad. of Arts Trust, 2001–04; Founder, Renaissance Inst., 1981. Mem., Council on Foreign Relns, Chief Execs' Orgn; Member, Advisory Board: British-American Business Council, 2000–; The Prince's Trust, 2001–06. John C. Whitehead Lecture, RIIA, 1998. Hon. Bencher, Middle Temple, 1998. Hon. Fellow: Liverpool John Moores Univ., 1998; London Business Sch., 2000. Fourteen hon. doctorates. Benjamin Franklin Medal, RSA, 2001; Global Service to Humanity Award, Rotary Internat. Foundn, 2007. *Recreations:* walking, tennis. *Address:* (office) 20 Bank Street, Canary Wharf, E14 4AD. *Clubs:* Harvard (New York); Metropolitan (Washington); Lost Tree (Florida).

LADYMAN, Dr Stephen John; Chairman, Somerset Partnership NHS Foundation Trust, since 2013; *b* 6 Nov. 1952; *s* of Frank Ladyman and Winifred Ladyman; *m* 1st, 1975 (marr. diss. 1994); 2nd, 1995, Janet Ann Baker; one *d*, and one step *s* one step *d* (and one step *s* decd). *Educ:* Liverpool Poly. (BSc Hons Applied Biol. 1975); Strathclyde Univ. (PhD 1982). Res. scientist, MRC Radiobiol. Unit, 1979–84; Head: of Computing, Mathilda and Terence Kennedy Inst. of Rheumatology, 1984–90; of Computer-User Support, Pfizer Central Res., 1990–97. Mem. (Lab) Thanet DC, 1995–99 (Chm., Finance and Monitoring, 1995–97). Contested (Lab) Wantage, 1987. MP (Lab) S Thanet, 1997–2010; contested (Lab) same seat, 2010. PPS to Minister for the Armed Forces, 2001–03; Parly Under-Sec. of State, DoH, 2003–05; Minister of State, DfT, 2005–07. Mem., Select Cttee on Envmt, Transport and the Regs, 1999–2001 (Mem., Transport Sub-Cttee, 1999–2001); Chm., SE Reg. Select Cttee, 2009–10. Chairman: All Party Parly Gp on Autism, 2000–03; All-Party British-Netherlands Parly Gp, 2001–03; All Party Major Infrastructure Projs Gp, 2009–10. Vice Chm. with responsibility for SE England, Labour Party, 2007–10. Chief Exec., Retirement Security Ltd, 2010–12; Dir, Oak Retirement Ltd, 2010–; Chair, Retirement Housing Gp, 2013–. Strategic Advr, Clearview Traffic Gp, 2012–. *Publications:* Natural Isotopic Abundances in Soil Studies,

1982; various learned articles. *Recreations:* occasional golf, walking the dog, watching soccer, house renovations. *Address:* Manzano, St Mary's Lane, Pilton, Somerset BA4 4BD. *T:* (01749) 890224.

LAFFERTY, Austin Joseph Aloysius; President, Law Society of Scotland, 2012–13 (Vice-President, 2011–12); *b* Cambuslang, 3 June 1959; *s* of Austin Lafferty and Ada Lafferty (*née* Paterson); *m* 1983, Yvonne McCabe; one *s* one *d. Educ:* St Aloysius Coll., Glasgow; Univ. of Glasgow (LLB). Admitted solicitor, 1981; NP 1981; solicitor in private practice, 1981–. Broadcaster on TV and radio incl. BBC and STV; journalist with various newspapers and mags; web blogger. *Publications:* It's the Law, 2004. *Recreations:* karate (2nd dan black belt), drawing, painting. *Address:* 213 Fenwick Road, Glasgow G46 6JD. *T:* (0141) 621 2212, *Fax:* (0141) 621 1342. *E:* alafferty@laffertylaw.com. *Clubs:* Glasgow Art; Bushido Karate.

LAFFERTY, John; His Honour Judge Lafferty; a Circuit Judge, since 2007; *b* Baillieston, 26 Dec. 1949; *s* of James and Susannah Lafferty. *Educ:* Univ. of Strathclyde (BA Hons English and Hist.); Nottingham Trent Univ. (LLM); Univ. of Glasgow (MPhil); Jordan Hill Coll. of Educn (Cert Ed); Leeds Poly. (CPE and Solicitors' Finals). Adminr/instructor, W Africa, 1974–76; English teacher, Our Lady's High Sch., Motherwell, 1976–80; Edward Fail, Bradshaw and Waterson: Articled clerk, 1983–85; Solicitor, 1985–87; Partner, 1987–90; Man. Partner, 1990–2005; Consultant, 2005–07; Recorder, 2000–07. Trustee: Disability Law Service, 2004–12; Sightsavers Internat., 2004–15. *Recreations:* walking, reading history, literature, theatre, music, travel. *Address:* Snaresbrook Crown Court, 75 Hollybush Hill, E11 1QW.

LAFONTAINE, Oskar; Member of Bundestag, 1990–94, 1998–99 and 2005–10; Minister of Finance, Germany, 1998–99; *b* 16 Sept. 1943; *m* 1993, Christa Müller; one *s*, and one *s* from a former marriage. *Educ:* Bonn Univ.; Saarbrücken Univ. Social Democratic Party (SPD), Germany: joined, 1966; officer, Saarland, 1970–75; Chm., Saarland Reg., 1977–96; Mem., Nat. Exec., 1994–2005; Chm., SPD, 1995–99; Left Party (Die Linke): Parly Leader, 2005–09; Chm., 2007–10. Mem., 1970–75 and 1985–98, Premier, 1985–98, Saarland Regl Parlt; Mayor, 1974–76, Lord Mayor, 1976–85, Saarbrücken; Pres., Bundesrat, 1995–96; Chm., Jt Cttee of Bundesrat and Bundestag, 1995–96. *Publications:* Angst vor den Freunden: die Atomwaffen-Strategie der Supermächte Zerstört die Bündnisse, 1983; Der andere Fortschritt: Verantwortung statt Verweigerung, 1985; Die Gesellschaft der Zukunft, 1988; Das Lied vom Teilen, 1989; Deutsche Wahrheiten, 1990; Das Herz schlägt links (autobiog.), 1999; Die Wut wächst, 2002.

LA FRENAIS, Ian, OBE 2007; writer, screenwriter and producer; *b* 7 Jan. 1937; *s* of Cyril and Gladys La Frenais; *m* 1984, Doris Vartan; one step *s. Educ:* Dame Allan's School, Northumberland. *Television:* writer or co-writer (with Dick Clement): The Likely Lads, 1965–68; The Adventures of Lucky Jim, 1968; Whatever Happened to the Likely Lads, 1971–73; Thick as Thieves, 1974; Porridge, 1974–77; Going Straight, 1978; Further Adventures of Lucky Jim, 1983; Auf Wiedersehen Pet, 1983–84, 2002–04; Mog, 1985; Lovejoy, 1986; Spender, 1990; Freddie and Max, 1990; Old Boy Network, 1991; Full Stretch, 1993; Over the Rainbow, 1993; The Rotters' Club (adaptation), 2005; Archangel (adaptation), 2005; Spies of Warsaw (adaptation), 2013; *US television:* On The Rocks, 1976–77; Billy, 1979; Sunset Limousine, 1983; Tracy Ullman Special, 1993; Tracy Takes On, 1995–99; *films:* writer or co-writer (with Dick Clement): The Jokers, 1967; The Touchables, 1968; Otley, 1968; Hannibal Brooks, 1969; The Virgin Soldiers, 1969; Villain, 1970; Catch Me a Spy, 1971; The Likely Lads, 1975; Porridge, 1979; To Russia with Elton, 1979; Prisoner of Zenda, 1981; Water, 1984; writer-producer, Vice Versa, 1987; co-writer (with Dick Clement): The Commitments, 1991; Excess Baggage, 1997; Still Crazy, 1998 (also Exec. Prod.); Honest, 2000; Goal!, 2005; Flushed Away, 2006; Across the Universe, 2007; The Bank Job, 2008; Killing Bono, 2011; *stage:* writer, Billy, 1974; co-producer, Anyone for Denis?, 1982; writer: Gwen, 2001; The Likely Lads, 2008; Porridge, 2009. Partner (with Dick Clement and Allan McKeown), Witzend Productions; producer, co-producer, director, numerous productions. Hon. DCL Northumbria, 2006. Awards from BAFTA, Broadcasting Guild, Screen Writers' Guild, Soc. of TV Critics, Writers' Guild of America, London Film Critics' Circle, Acad. of Television Arts and Scis, Nat. Television Awards, British Comedy Awards.

LAGARDE, Christine Madeleine Odette; Chevalier de la Légion d'Honneur (France), 2000; Commandeur du Mérite agricole (France); Managing Director, International Monetary Fund, since 2011; *b* 1 Jan. 1956; *d* of Robert Lallouette and Nicole Lallouette (*née* Carre); *m* (marr. diss.); two *s. Educ:* Université Paris X (BA Eng.; BA Law; MPhil Law; JD); Institut d'Études Politiques Aix-en-Provence (MA Pol Sci.). Lawyer, Baker & McKenzie, 1981–2005: Partner, 1987–95; Hd of Western Europe, 1995–99; Chm., 1999–2005; Pres., Global Strategic Cttee, 2004–05; Minister: of Commerce and Industry, 2005–07; of Agric. and Fisheries, 2007; of Economy, Finance and Industry, 2007–11. *Recreations:* swimming, scuba diving, opera, ballet. *Address:* International Monetary Fund, 700 19th Street, NW, Washington, DC 20431, USA. *T:* (202) 6237000. *E:* publicaffairs@imf.org.

LAGARDÈRE, Arnaud Georges André; General and Managing Partner, Lagardère SCA, since 2003 (Co-Managing Director, 1998–2003); Chairman and Chief Executive Officer: Lagardère Media (formerly Hachette SA), since 1999; Arjil Commanditée Arco, since 2004; *b* Boulogne-Billancourt, 18 March 1961; *s* of late Jean-Luc Lagardère. *Educ:* Univ. of Paris-Dauphine (DEA Econs). Dir, 1986, then CEO, 1989–92, Multi Média Beaujon; Vice-Chm., Supervisory Bd, Arjil & Cie, 1987–2005; Mem. Bd, 1988–2003, CEO, 1988–, Chm., 2003–, Lagardère Capital and Mgt (formerly Arjil Gp); manager of emerging activities and media, Mem. Mgt and Strategic Cttee, Lagardère Gp, 1989–92; Dep. Chm. and Chief Operating Officer, Arjil Commanditée Arco, 1992–2004; Chairman: Grolier Inc., USA, 1994–98; Lagardère Active Broadband (formerly Grolier Interactive Europe), 1994–2008; Chm., Europe 1 Communication, subseq. Lagardère Active Broadcast, 1999–2007; Chm. and CEO, 1999–2001, Man. Dir, 2001–03, Europe Régies, subseq. Lagardère Publicité; Chairman, Supervisory Board: Lagardère Active (Chm., 2001–06); Lagardère Services; Chm., Exec. Cttee, Lagardère Unlimited. Man. Dir, Nouvelles Messageries de la Presse Parisienne, 1999–2003; Member Board: Société d'Agences et de Diffusion, 2000–03; CanalSatellite, 2001–03; Lagardère-Sociétés, 2002–03; France Telecom, 2003–08; Moët Hennessy Louis Vuitton, 2003–09; Eur. Aeronautic Defence and Space Co. (EADS NV), 2003–13 (Chm., 2012–13); Fimalac, 2003–06; Hachette Livre; Lagardère Ressources; Member Supervisory Board: Aérospatiale Matra, 1999–2000; Daimler (formerly DaimlerChrysler) AG, 2005–10; Le Monde, 2005–08; Virgin Stores, 2005–08. Member: France Galop Cttee, 2003–06; Conseil Stratégie des Technologies de l'Information, 2004–. Chm., Jean-Luc Lagardère (formerly Hachette) Foundn, 2003– (Pres.). Chairman: Club des Entreprises Paris 2012, 2004–06; Assoc. des Amis de Paris Jean-Bouin, 2004–10; Nouvel Elan Croix Catelan Assoc., 2006–; Lagardère Paris Racing Assoc. *Address:* Lagardère SCA, 4 rue de Presbourg, 75116 Paris, France. *T:* (1) 40691640. *E:* secretariatal@lagardere.fr.

LAGNADO, Prof. Leon, PhD; FMedSci; Professor of Neuroscience and Director, Sussex Neuroscience, University of Sussex, since 2013; *b* London, 26 Sept. 1963; *s* of Maurice Lagnado and Fortunée Lagnado (*née* Yaluz); *m* 1990, Dr Ruth Murrell; three *d. Educ:* Whitefield Comprehensive Sch.; University Coll. London (BSc 1985); Gonville and Caius Coll., Cambridge (PhD 1988). Human Frontier Sci. Prog. Long-term Fellow, Stanford Univ., 1990–93; MRC Prog. Leader (tenure track), 1993–99, MRC Prog. leader, 1999–2013, MRC Lab. of Molecular Biol., Cambridge. FMedSci 2014. *Publications:* contribs to scientific jls, esp. dealing with neurosci. of vision. *Recreations:* reading, football, building microscopes, hoping for the best. *Address:* School of Life Sciences, University of Sussex, Falmer, Brighton BN1 9QG. *T:* (01273) 877431. *E:* l.lagnado@sussex.ac.uk. *Club:* Fulbourn Institute Sports and Social.

LAGOS ESCOBAR, Ricardo, PhD; Professor at Large, Watson Institute for International Studies, Brown University, USA, since 2007; President of Chile, 2000–06; *b* 2 March 1938; *s* of Froilán Lagos and Emma Escobar; *m* 1971, Luisa Durán; five *c. Educ:* Sch. of Law, Univ. of Chile; Duke Univ., N Carolina (PhD 1962). University of Chile, 1963–72: Prof., and Hd, Sch. of Pol and Admin. Scis; Dir, Inst. of Econs; Sec. Gen., 1969–72; Sec. Gen., Latin American Faculty of Social Scis (UNESCO initiative), 1972–74; Vis. Prof., Univ. of N Carolina, 1974–75; Econ. Hd, Regl Prog. for Latin America and the Caribbean, UN, 1978–84. Chairman: Alianza Democrática, 1983–84; Partido por la Democracia, 1987–90; Minister of Educn, 1990–92, of Public Works, 1994–98. UN Special Envoy on Climate Change, 2007–10. Founder and Pres., Foundn for Democracy and Develt, 2006–. *Publications:* Población, Pobreza y Mercado de Trabajo en América Latina, 1997; books and articles on econs and politics. *Address:* c/o Palacio de la Moneda, Santiago, Chile.

LA GRENADE, Dame Cécile (Ellen Fleurette), GCMG 2013; OBE 2005; PhD; Governor General of Grenada, since 2013; *b* Grenada, 30 Dec. 1952; *d* of Alan La Grenade and Sibyl La Grenade (*née* Sylvester). *Educ:* St Joseph's Convent, St George's, Grenada; Univ. of West Indies, Trinidad (BSc 1978); Univ. of Maryland (MSc 1986; PhD 1990). Teacher, Holy Faith Convent, Couva, Trinidad, 1978–79; Produce Chemist, Min. of Agric., 1979–82; res. asst (pt-time), US Dept of Agric., 1987–90; res. biologist, US Food and Drug Admin, 1990–91; Man. Dir, De La Grenade Industries, 1991–2013. Member: Grenada Orchid Soc., 1998–; Horticulture Soc. of Grenada, 2005–13. *Recreations:* gardening, orchid cultivation. *Address:* Office of the Governor General, PO Box 369, St George's, Grenada, West Indies. *T:* 4402401, *Fax:* 4406688. *E:* patogg@spiceisle.com.

LAHIRI, Prof. Aditi, DPhil; FBA 2010; Professor of Linguistics, University of Oxford, since 2007; Fellow, Somerville College, Oxford, since 2007; *b* Calcutta, 14 July 1952; *d* of Haranath and Arundhati Roy; *m* 2003, Prof. Henning Reetz. *Educ:* Univ. of Calcutta (BA Maths and Econs 1971; MA Comparative Philol. 1973; DPhil Comparative Philol. and Linguistics 1979); Brown Univ. (PhD 1982). Postdoctoral Res. Asst, Dept of Linguistics, Brown Univ., 1982–83; Vis. Asst Prof., Dept of Linguistics, UCLA, 1983–84; Adjunct Asst Prof., Bd of Studies in Linguistics, Univ. of Calif, Santa Cruz, 1984–85; Sen. Res. Scientist, Max Planck Inst. for Psycholinguistics, Nijmegen, 1985–92; Prof. of Gen. Linguistics, Univ. of Konstanz, 1992–2007. Hon. Life Mem., Linguistic Soc. of America, 2013. Max Planck Forschungspreis für internationale kooperation, 1994; Leibniz Prize, Deutsche Forschungsgemeinschaft, 2000; Prof. Sukumar Sen Gold Medal for Excellence in Res., 2009. *Publications:* contrib. to Jl Acoustical Soc. of America, Cognitive Brain Res., Jl Cognitive Neurosci., Trans Philological Soc., Jl Phonetics. *Recreations:* visiting the Cotswolds, reading crime fiction. *Address:* Centre for Linguistics and Philology, University of Oxford, Walton Street, Oxford OX1 2HG. *T:* (01865) 280400, *Fax:* (01865) 280412. *E:* aditi.lahiri@ling-phil.ox.ac.uk.

LAÏDI, Ahmed; Algerian Ambassador to Mexico, 1988–89; *b* 20 April 1934; *m* 1964, Aicha Chabbi-Lemsine; one *s* one *d* (and one *s* decd). *Educ:* Algiers Univ. (BA); Oran Univ. (LLB). Counsellor to Presidency of Council of Algerian Republic, 1963; Head of Cabinet of Presidency, 1963–64; Dir Gen. of Political and Economic Affairs, Min. of Foreign Affairs, 1964–66; Chm., Prep. Cttee, second Afro-Asian Conf., 1964–65; Special Envoy to Heads of States, Senegal, Mali, Ivory Coast and Nigeria, 1966; Ambassador to Spain, 1966–70; Head, Delegn to Geneva Conf. of non-nuclear countries, 1968; Wali (Governor): province Médea, 1970–74; province Tlemcen, 1975–78; Ambassador to Jordan, 1978–84; Special Envoy to Heads of States and govts, Zambia, Malaŵi, Botswana, Zimbabwe, 1985; Ambassador to UK, 1984–88, and to Ireland, 1985–88. Member: Algerian Football Fedn, 1964–66; Algerian Nat. Olympic Cttee, 1965–72. Foreign Orders: Liberia, 1963; Bulgaria, 1964; Yugoslavia, 1964; Spain, 1970; Jordan, 1984. *Recreations:* theatre, cinema, football.

LAIDLAW, Baron *cr* 2004 (Life Peer), of Rothiemay in Banffshire; **Irvine Alan Stewart Laidlaw;** founder Chairman, IIR Holdings Ltd, 1974–2005; *b* 22 Dec. 1942; *s* of Roy Alan and Margaret Laidlaw; *m* 1987, (Marie) Christine Laidlaw. *Educ:* Merchiston Castle Sch.; Univ. of Leeds (BA Hons); Columbia Univ. (MBA). Chm., Abbey Business Centres Ltd, 1998–2010. Chm., Laidlaw Youth Trust, 2003–09. Sponsor, Excelsior Acad., Newcastle upon Tyne, 2004–; founder and sponsor, Laidlaw Schs Trust, 2011–. Mem., H of L, 2004–10. Hon. LLD St Andrews, 2003; Hon. DHC Aberdeen, 2007. *Recreations:* historic motor racing, sailing, opera, piloting helicopters. *Address:* 11 Avenue President J F Kennedy, MC 98000, Monaco. *E:* irvine.laidlaw@rothiemay.net. *Clubs:* Royal Thames Yacht; New York Yacht; Monaco Yacht; Costa Smeralda Yacht.

LAIDLAW, (Henry) Renton; golf correspondent, Evening Standard, 1973–98; *b* 6 July 1939; *s* of late Henry Renton Laidlaw and Margaret McBeath Laidlaw (*née* Raiker). *Educ:* James Gillespie's Boys' School, Edinburgh; Daniel Stewart's College, Edinburgh. Golf corresp., Edinburgh Evening News, 1957–67; news presenter and reporter, Grampian Television, Aberdeen, 1968–69; BBC news presenter, Edinburgh, 1970–72; BBC Radio golf reporter, 1976–90; presenter: BBC Radio Sport on 2, 1986, 1987; ITV Eurosport, 1988; golf presenter: BSB, 1989–91; Golf Channel, US, 1995–; Chief Commentator, PGA European Tour Prodns, 1988–2013. Pres., Assoc. of Golf Writers, 2004–15. Jack Nicklaus Meml Journalism Award, 2000; PGA of America Lifetime Achievement Award in Journalism, 2003; PGA Lifetime Achievement Award, 2012; Augusta Masters Achievement Award, 2013. *Publications:* Play Golf (with Peter Alliss), 1977; Jacklin—the first 40 years, 1984; (ed) Johnnie Walker Ryder Cup '85, 1985; Play Better Golf, 1986; (ed) Johnnie Walker Ryder Cup '87, 1987; Ten Years—the history of the European Open, 1988; Golf Heroes, 1989; (ed) Johnnie Walker Ryder Cup '89, 1989; (with Bernard Gallacher) Captain at Kiawah, 1991; Wentworth: a host of happy memories, 1993; (ed) The Royal and Ancient Golfer's Handbook, annually, 1998–; (ed) The Golfers' Guide to Scotland, 2000–01. *Recreations:* theatre, golf. *T:* (c/o Mrs Kay Clarkson) (01707) 275639, 07768 746605. *Clubs:* Caledonian; Royal & Ancient (St Andrews); Sunningdale Golf, Wentworth, Royal Burgess Golf, Ballybunion Golf.

LAIDLAW, Jonathan James; QC 2008; a Recorder, since 1998; *b* 28 Feb. 1960. *Educ:* Univ. of Hull (LLB). Called to the Bar, Inner Temple, 1982. Jun. Treasury Counsel, 1995–2001; Sen. Treasury Counsel, 2001–08; First Sen. Treasury Counsel, Central Criminal Court, 2008–10. *Address:* 2 Hare Court, Temple, EC4Y 7BH.

LAIDLAW, Renton; *see* Laidlaw, H. R.

LAIDLAW, William Samuel Hugh, (Sam); Chief Executive, Neptune Oil and Gas, since 2015; *b* 3 Jan. 1956; *s* of Sir Christophor Charles Fraser Laidlaw and Nina Mary (*née* Prichard); *m* 1989, Deborah Margaret Morris-Adams; three *s* one *d. Educ:* Eton College; Gonville and Caius College, Cambridge (MA); MBA. Admitted Solicitor, 1980; Insead, Fontainebleau, 1981. Soc. Françaises Pétroles BP, 1980; Amerada Hess: Manager, corporate planning, NY, 1981–83; Vice-Pres., London, 1983–85, Sen. Vice-Pres., 1986–90, Man. Dir, 1986–95, London; Exec. Vice-Pres., NY, 1990–95; Pres. and CEO, NY, 1995–2001; Chm., London, 1995–2001; Chief Exec., Enterprise Oil plc, 2001–02; Exec. Vice-Pres., ChevronTexaco Corp., 2003–06; Chief Exec., Centrica plc, 2006–14. Non-executive Director: Premier Oil, 1995; Yes Television plc, 2000–03; Hanson plc, 2003–07; HSBC Hldgs plc, 2008–; Lead non-exec. Dir, DfT, 2010–; Chm., Sponsorship Consulting Ltd, 2002–07. Dir, Business Council of Internat. Understanding, 1998–. Member: Govt Energy Adv. Panel, 1994–98; Prime Minister's Business Adv. Gp, 2010–12. Chm., Petroleum Sci. and Tech. Inst., 1993–94;

NEL, 1993–95. Pres., UKOOA, 1991. Chm., CBI Higher Educn Task Force, 2008–09. Mem. Council, Radley Coll., 2008–. FInstPet (Vice-Pres., 1994–95); FRSA 1990. *Clubs:* Buck's; Royal Thames Yacht, Royal Yacht Squadron.

LAINÉ, Christopher Norman; Chairman, Allied Textile Companies plc, 1999–2000 (Director, 1998–2000); Partner, Coopers & Lybrand, 1971–98; President, Institute of Chartered Accountants in England and Wales, 1997–98; *b* 12 Oct. 1936; *s* of James Norman Balliol Lainé and Sybil Mary Lainé (*née* Fuge); *m* 1967, Sally Outhwaite; one *s* one *d. Educ:* King's Sch., Canterbury (Scholar); Trinity Coll., Oxford (Exhibnr; MA). FCA. Nat. Service, RA, 1955–57; commnd 1956. Cooper Brothers & Co., later Coopers & Lybrand: joined 1960; Partner i/c S Coast, 1971–90; Sen. Partner, S Coast, 1990–98. Pres., Southern Soc. of Chartered Accountants, 1986–87; Institute of Chartered Accountants in England and Wales: Mem. Council, 1990–2000; Chm., 1999–2000; Chm., Dist Socs Cttee, 1991–95; Exec., 1993–98; Vice-Pres., 1995–96; Dep. Pres., 1996–97; Dir, Accountancy and Actuarial Discipline (formerly Accountancy Investigation and Discipline) Bd, 2001–09. Gov., Canford Sch., 1990–2004. *Recreations:* cricket, golf, classical music, painting. *Clubs:* Hampshire CC; Stoneham Golf; Hampshire Hogs Cricket, Forty.

LAINE, Dame Clementine Dinah, (Dame Cleo), (Lady Dankworth), DBE 1997 (OBE 1979); vocalist, actress; *b* 28 Oct. 1927; British; *m* 1st, 1947, George Langridge (marr. diss. 1957); one *s*; 2nd, 1958, Sir John Philip William Dankworth, CBE; one *s* one *d.* Joined Dankworth Orchestra, 1953; with John Dankworth estabd Performing Arts Centre, Wavendon Stables, 1969. Melody Maker and New Musical Express Top Girl Singer Award, 1956; Moscow Arts Theatre Award for acting role in Flesh to a Tiger, 1958; Top place in Internat. Critics Poll by Amer. Jazz magazine, Downbeat, 1965. Lead, in Seven Deadly Sins, Edinburgh Festival and Sadler's Wells, 1961; acting roles in Edin. Fest., 1966, 1967, Cindy-Ella, Garrick, 1968; film, Last of the Blonde Bombshells, 2000. Many appearances with symphony orchestras performing Façade (Walton), Pierrot Lunaire and other compositions; played Julie in Show Boat, Adelphi, 1971; title role in Colette, Comedy, 1980; Hedda Gabler; Valmouth; A Time to Laugh; The Women of Troy; The Mystery of Edwin Drood, 1986; Into the Woods (US nat. tour), 1989; Noyes Fludde (Proms), 1990. Frequent TV appearances. Hon. Freeman, Musicians' Co., 2002. Freedom of Bor. of Milton Keynes, 2011. Hon. MA Open, 1975; Hon. DMus: Berklee Sch. of Music, 1982; York, 1993; Cambridge, 2004; Brunel, 2007. Woman of the Year, 9th annual Golden Feather Awards, 1973; Edison Award, 1974; Variety Club of GB Show Business Personality Award (with John Dankworth), 1977; TV Times Viewers Award for Most Exciting Female Singer on TV, 1978; Grammy Award for Best Female Jazz Vocalist, 1985; Theatre World Award, 1986; NARM Presidential Lifetime Achievement Award, 1990; British Jazz Awards Vocalist of the Year, 1990; Distinguished Artists Award, Internat. Soc. for the Performing Arts, 1999; Bob Harrington Lifetime Achievement Award (with John Dankworth), Back Stage, 2001; Lifetime Achievement Award, BBC Radio Jazz Awards (with John Dankworth), 2002. Gold Discs: Feel the Warm; I'm a Song; Live at Melbourne; Platinum Discs: Best Friends; Sometimes When We Touch. *Publications:* Cleo (autobiog.), 1994; You Can Sing If You Want To, 1997. *Recreation:* painting. *Fax:* (01908) 584414.

LAING, Alastair David, FSA; Curator of (formerly Adviser on) Pictures and Sculpture, National Trust, 1986–2013; *b* 5 Aug. 1944; *s* of late Malcolm Strickland Laing and Margaret Clare Laing (*née* Briscoe); *m* 1979, Hana Novotná; one *s. Educ:* Chafyn Grove Sch.; Bradfield Coll.; Corpus Christi Coll., Oxford (BA Hons 1966; Dip. Hist. Art 1967); Courtauld Inst. of Art, Univ. of London. FCO, 1967–68; translator, 1969–76; Night Operator, Internat. Telephone Exchange, 1973–76; Researcher, Heim Gall., 1976–83; Researcher and Jt Curator, François Boucher exhibn, NY, Detroit and Paris, 1983–85; Area Editor, Macmillan Dictionary of Art, 1985–86. Member: Adv. Council, Hamilton Kerr Inst., 1986–; Paintings Panel, Council for the Care of Churches, 1993–2006; Academic Cttee, Waddesdon Manor, 1993–; Acceptance in Lieu Panel, 1994–2005; Export Reviewing Cttee, 1996–2002; Old Master Paintings Vetting Cttee, The European Fine Art Fair, Maastricht, 1996–; Sci. Cttee for restoration of The Apotheosis of Hercules, Versailles, 1999–2001; Sci. Cttee, Arthéna, 1999–; Adv. Panel, Apsley House, 2005–09; Conservation Cttee, Chatsworth House, 2008–; Adv. Bd, A. G. Leventis Gall., Nicosia, 2013–. Trustee: Holburne Mus., Bath, 1998–2007; Mausolea and Monuments Trust, 2008–10; Art Fund, 2012–; Heritage Conservation Trust, 2012–; Trustee and Dir, Burlington Mag., 2001–. Thaw Sen. Fellow, Morgan Library, NY, 2015. Chevalier, l'Ordre des Arts et des Lettres (France), 1988. *Publications:* (with Anthony Blunt) Baroque & Rococo, 1978; Lighting, 1982; (with Richard Walker) Portrait Miniatures in National Trust Houses: vol. 1, Northern Ireland, 2003; vol. II, Cornwall, Devon and Somerset, 2005; (jtly) The James A. de Rothschild Bequest at Waddesdon Manor: drawings for architecture, design and ornament, 2006; exhibition catalogues include: François Boucher, 1986; In Trust for the Nation, 1995; The Drawings of François Boucher, 2003; Oil Paintings in National Trust Properties, 6 vols, 2013; articles in Country Life, Apollo, Burlington Mag., Umění, etc. *Recreation:* church- and tomb-crawling. *Address:* 24 Aberdeen Road, N5 2UH. *Club:* Travellers.

LAING, Andrew; HM Inspector of Constabulary for Scotland, 2010–13; Director, Optimise Design and Build Ltd, since 2013; *b* Edinburgh, 9 Aug. 1963; *s* of John Harvey Laing and Agnes Stirling Laing (*née* Wightman); partner, June Kennedy Russell; two *s. Educ:* Leith Acad. Primary Sch., Edinburgh; Portobello High Sch., Edinburgh; Napier Univ., Edinburgh (BA Hons Business Studies 1996). Dip. IoD. Lothian and Borders Police, 1982–2004 (Superintendent, 2002–04); Fife Constabulary: Chief Superintendent, 2004–09; Dep. Chief Constable, 2009–10. Dir, Scottish Business Resilience Centre (formerly Scottish Business Crime Centre), 2011–15. FRSA. *Recreations:* squash, badminton, golf, cooking.

LAING, Christine Katherine; QC 2006; **Her Honour Judge Laing;** a Circuit Judge, since 2014; *b* 4 Nov. 1961; *d* of Ludovic Baillie Laing and Christina (*née* Easton). *Educ:* St Thomas of Aquinas RC High Sch., Edinburgh; Univ. of Newcastle-upon-Tyne (LLB Hons 1983). Called to the Bar, Lincoln's Inn, 1984; criminal practitioner, 1984–2014; a Recorder, 2004–14. *Recreations:* travel, music, arts, rich friends, inexpensive wine. *Address:* Woolwich Crown Court, 2 Belmarsh Road, SE28 0EY. *E:* c.laing957@btinternet.com.

LAING, David Eric, RIBA; FZS; Lord-Lieutenant of Northamptonshire, since 2014; *b* Budleigh Salterton, Devon, 28 March 1945; *s* of Sir (William) Kirby Laing and Joan Laing; *m* 1968, Frances Mary Underwood; four *s* one *d. Educ:* St Lawrence Coll., Ramsgate; Bartlett Sch. of Architecture, University Coll. London (BA Arch. 1967; MA Hons Arch. 1969). RIBA 1971. With Spence, Bonnington and Collins, Architects, 1969–72; Partner: Bryant Laing Partnership, 1972–2001; G. H. M. Rock Townsend Architects, 1985–98. Chm., Country and Metropolitan Homes plc, 1996–2005; Dir, Eskmuir Properties, 2003–. Chairman: Rural Develt Commn, Herts and Beds, 1988–96; Northants Community Foundn, 2005–14; Vice Chm., Northants Enterprise Partnership, 2008–13. Chm., St John Ambulance, Herts, 1998–2005, Northants, 2010–14. Chairman: David Laing Foundn, 1979–; Sir Kirby Laing Foundn, 2007–; Adrenaline Alley, 2010–. Trustee: Grove Hse Hospice, St Albans, 1988–95; St Andrew's Hosp., 2010– (Chm., Pension Fund, 2011–); Youth Sports Trust, 1998–2010; Nat. Hockey Foundn, 2002–; Northants Assoc. Youth Clubs, 2006– (Pres., 2005–); Church Schs Trust, 2009–12; Educn Fellowship Foundn, 2012–14; Northants Historic Churches Trust, 2015–. FZS 1995. Mem. Court, Paviors' Co., 1993– (Master, 2006). *Recreations:* motor racing, rallying, hockey, ski-ing, sailing, music. *Address:* The Manor House, Grafton Underwood, Northants NN14 3AA. *T:* (01536) 330404. *E:* david@david-laing.co.uk, david.laing@mhqu.org. *Clubs:* Farmers; Aston Martin Owners, Vintage Sports Car, Lawn Tennis Association.

LAING, Eleanor Fulton; MP (C) Epping Forest, since 1997; First Deputy Chairman of Ways and Means, and a Deputy Speaker, House of Commons, since 2013; *b* 1 Feb. 1958; *d* of late Matthew and Betty Pritchard; *m* 1983, Alan Laing (marr. diss. 2003); one *s. Educ:* St Columba's Sch., Kilmacolm; Edinburgh Univ. (Pres., Union, 1980–81; BA, LLB 1982). Solicitor, Edinburgh and London, 1983–89; Special Advr to Rt Hon. John MacGregor, MP, 1989–94. Contested (C) Paisley N, 1987. An Opposition Whip, 1999–2000; frontbench opposition spokesman on constitutional affairs, 2000–01, on educn, 2001–03, on women and equality, 2004–07; Shadow Sec. of State for Scotland, 2005; Shadow Minister for Justice, 2007–10. *Recreations:* theatre, music, golf, Agatha Christie Society. *Address:* House of Commons, SW1A 0AA.

LAING, Ian Michael, CBE 2004; DL; Chairman, MEPC Milton Park Ltd, 1993–2006; *b* 24 Dec. 1946; *s* of Anthony and Ruth Laing; *m* 1973, Caroline Pender Cudlip; two *s* one *d. Educ:* Bedford Sch.; St Edmund Hall, Oxford (MA); London Business Sch. (MSc). Dir, English Property Corp. plc, 1972–85; Man. Dir, Lansdown Estates Gp Ltd, subseq. MEPC Milton Park Ltd, 1984–93. Non-executive Director: Oxford Radcliffe NHS Trust, 1992–99; Stanhope plc, 2006–12; Adaptimmune Therapeutics plc, 2008–; Immunocore Ltd, 2008–; Aegate Hldgs Ltd, 2013–. Nuffield Medical Trustee, 2004–. Governor: London Business Sch., 1996–2005; Royal Shakespeare Co., 1998–2005 and 2006–. Hon. Bencher, Inner Temple, 2004; Fellow, Green Templeton Coll., Oxford, 2013–. DL 1998, High Sheriff, 2005–06, Oxon. *Recreations:* sailing, ski-ing, opera, theatre, farming. *T:* (01865) 559092. *E:* ianlaing@cix.co.uk. *Clubs:* Boodle's; Royal Yacht Squadron; New York Yacht; Royal Norwegian Yacht; Kandahar Ski.

LAING, James Findlay; Under Secretary, Scottish Office Environment Department (formerly Scottish Development Department), 1988–93; *b* 7 Nov. 1933; *s* of Alexander Findlay Laing and Jessie Ross; *m* 1969, Christine Joy Canaway; one *s. Educ:* Nairn Academy; Edinburgh Univ. MA (Hons History). Nat. Service, Seaforth Highlanders, 1955–57. Asst Principal and Principal, Scottish Office, 1957–68; Principal, HM Treasury, 1968–71; Asst Sec., Scottish Office, 1972–79; Under Sec., Scottish Econ. Planning Dept, later Industry Dept for Scotland, 1979–88. *Recreations:* squash, chess. *Address:* 6 Barnton Park Place, Edinburgh EH4 6ET. *T:* (0131) 336 5951. *Club:* Edinburgh Sports.

LAING, Jennifer Charlina Ellsworth; Associate Dean, External Relations, London Business School, 2002–07; Chairman and Chief Executive Officer, North American Operations, Saatchi & Saatchi, 1997–2000; *b* 1947; *d* of late James Ellsworth Laing, FRCS, and Mary McKane (*née* Taylor); *m* John Henderson (marr. diss.). Joined Garland-Compton, 1969; Dir, Saatchi & Saatchi Garland-Compton, 1977; Dep. Chm., 1983, Jt Chm., 1987, Saatchi & Saatchi Advertising UK; Chm. and CEO, Aspect Hill Holliday (later Laing Henry Ltd), 1988, which was acquired by Saatchi & Saatchi Advertising UK, 1995; Chm., Saatchi & Saatchi Advertising UK, 1995–97. Non-executive Director: Hudson Highland Gp Inc., 2003–14 (Chm., Compensation Cttee, 2011–14); InterContinental Hotels Gp, 2005– (Chm., Corporate Responsibility Cttee, 2009–); Premier Foods plc, 2012–. Former non-executive Director: Remploy; Great Ormond Street Hosp. for Children NHS Trust.

LAING, Sir (John) Martin (Kirby), Kt 1997; CBE 1991; DL; Chairman, 1985–2001, non-executive Director, 2001–04, Hon. President, 2004–06, John Laing plc; non-executive Chairman, NHP plc, 1999–2005; *b* 18 Jan. 1942; *s* of Sir (William) Kirby Laing; *m* 1965, Stephanie Stearn Worsdell; one *s* one *d. Educ:* St Lawrence College, Ramsgate; Emmanuel College, Cambridge (MA). FRICS. Joined Laing Group 1966; Dir, John Laing, 1980. Chairman: BOTB, 1995–99; Construction Industry Employers Council, 1995–2000; Vice-Chm., British Trade Internat., 1999; Member: Major Contractors Gp, 1985 (Chm., 1991–92); CBI Council, 1986–2002; CBI Overseas Cttee, 1983–96 (Chm., 1989–96); CBI Task Force on Business and Urban Regeneration, 1987–88; Cttee for Middle East Trade, 1982–86; SE Asia Trade Adv. Group, 1985–89; UK Adv. Cttee, British American Chamber of Commerce, 1985–2002; Council, World Economic Forum, 1986–2002; NEDO Construction Industry Sector Gp, 1988–93; Business in the Community, 1986–2002 (Mem. Bd, 1995–2000); World Business Council for Sustainable Develt, 1991–2002; UK-Japan 2000 Gp, 1988–2002; British Council, 1997–; Council, BESO, 1999–2003; Corporate Finance Adv. Bd, PricewaterhouseCoopers, 2003–05; Chm., British Urban Develt, 1988–90; Dep. Chm., Building Experience Trust, 1992–95. Chairman: Americas Advrs, Trade Partners UK, 2000–03; Ecologic Malta, 2007–; BioRem Internat., Malta, 2007–. Member: Council, London First, 1992–2002; Valletta Alive Foundn, 2007–. Non-executive Director: Parsons Brinckerhoff Inc., USA, 2003–06; Eskmuir Properties Ltd, 2003–; Lam Investments Internat., Malta, 2010–. Member: Home Office Parole Review Cttee, 1987–88; Archbishop's Council, Church Urban Fund, 1987–94; Trilateral Commn, 1993–99. President: Construction Confedn, 1997–2000; Inst. of Export, 2001–08. Dir, City of London Sinfonia, 1988–95. Dir, Herts Groundwork Trust, 1986–91; Trustee: Nat. Energy Foundn, 1988–99; WWF Internat., 1991–97; Marine Stewardship Council, 1998–2006; Trustee Emeritus, WWF (UK), 1998– (Trustee, 1988–97; Chm., 1990–97). Adv., RP&C Internat. Ltd, 2006–07. Crown Mem., Court of Univ. of London, 1987–95; Member: Council, United World Coll. of the Atlantic, 1996–; Board of Governors, Papplewick School, Ascot, 1983–93; Governor: St Lawrence Coll., Ramsgate, 1988–95; NIESR, 1999–. Trustee, RICS Foundn, 2001–04. Master, Paviors' Co., 1995–96. CIEx 1987; FICE 1993; FCIOB 1995. DL Hertford, 1987. Hon. DSc: City, 1996; Birmingham, 2002; Kingston, 2004. Hon. DEng UWE, 1997. *Recreations:* gardening, music, travel.

LAING, (John) Stuart; Master, Corpus Christi College, Cambridge, since 2008; *b* 22 July 1948; *s* of late Dr Denys Laing and Dr Judy Laing (*née* Dods); *m* 1972, Sibella Dorman, *d* of Sir Maurice Dorman, GCMG, GCVO; one *s* two *d. Educ:* Rugby Sch.; Corpus Christi Coll., Cambridge (MA, MPhil). Joined HM Diplomatic Service, 1970; FCO, 1970–71; MECAS, Lebanon, 1971–72; 2nd Sec., Jedda, 1973–75; First Secretary: UK Perm. Rep. to EC, 1975–78; FCO, 1978–83; Cairo, 1983–87; FCO, 1987–89; Counsellor, Prague, 1989–92; Dep. Hd of Mission and HM Consul-Gen., British Embassy, Riyadh, 1992–95; Hd, Know How Fund for Central Europe, FCO, later DFID, 1995–98; High Comr to Brunei, 1998–2002; Ambassador: to Oman, 2002–05; to Kuwait, 2005–08. Trustee, CfBT Educn Trust, 2008–. *Publications:* (with Robert Alston) Unshook Till the End of Time: a history of relations between Britain and Oman, 2012. *Recreations:* playing music, hill-walking, desert travel. *Address:* Corpus Christi College, Cambridge CB2 1RH.

LAING, Sir Martin; *see* Laing, Sir J. M. K.

LAING, Richard George, FCA; Chair, Miro Forestry, since 2014 (non-executive Director, since 2012); *b* 24 Feb. 1954; *s* of George Denys Laing, MB BChir and Julian (Judy) Ursula Laing (*née* Dods), MB ChB; *m* 1979, Susan Pamela Mills, MA, MSc, PhD; four *s. Educ:* Rugby Sch.; Corpus Christi Coll., Cambridge (BA 1975; MA). FCA 1980. Asst Manager, Marks & Spencer, 1975–76; Manager, Price Waterhouse, 1976–81; Analyst, Booker Agric. Internat., 1981–84; Analyst, De la Rue Plc, 1984–86; De la Rue Brazil: Finance Dir, 1986–89; Gp Financial Controller, 1989–96; Gp Finance Dir, 1996–99; Finance Dir, 2000–04, Chief Exec., 2004–11, Advr, 2011–12, Commonwealth Develt Corp., then CDC Gp plc. Non-executive Director: Camelot, 1997–99; Pacific Rim Palm Oil, 2001–06; Aureos Capital, 2005–10; London Metal Exchange, 2011–12; Perpetual Income and Growth Investment Trust plc, 2012–; Madagascar Oil plc, 2013–15; JP Morgan Emerging Markets Investment Trust plc, 2015–. Trustee: ODI, 2004–; Plan UK, 2010–; Leeds Castle Foundn, 2012–. *Recreations:* classical music, gardening, Munro bagging, and much else that involves being outside. *Club:* Athenæum.

LAING, Sophie Henrietta T.; *see* Turner Laing.

LAING, Stuart; *see* Laing, J. S.

LAIRD, family name of **Baron Laird**.

LAIRD, Baron *cr* 1999 (Life Peer), of Artigarvan in the county of Tyrone; **John Dunn Laird;** Chairman, John Laird Public Relations Ltd, 1976–2001; *b* Belfast, 23 April 1944; *s* of late Dr Norman Davidson Laird, OBE, sometime NI MP, and Margaret Laird; *m* 1971, Caroline Ethel Ferguson; one *s* one *d*. *Educ:* Royal Belfast Academical Institution. Bank Official, 1963–67; Bank Inspector, 1967–68; Computer Programmer, 1968–73. MP (UU) St Anne's, Belfast, NI Parlt, 1970–73; Member (UU) West Belfast: NI Assembly, 1973–75; NI Constitutional Convention, 1975–76. Vis. Prof. of Public Relns, Univ. of Ulster, 1993–. Chm., Ulster Scots Agency, 1999–2004. Mem. Bd Govs, Royal Belfast Academical Instn, 1993–2004. FCIPR (FIPR 1991); FRSA 2011; FBCS 2012. Freeman, City of London, 2012. Lifetime Achievement Award, CIPR, 2011. *Publications:* A Struggle to be Heard, 2010. *Recreations:* history, railways, travel. *Address:* House of Lords, SW1A 0PW. *T:* (020) 7219 8626.

LAIRD, David Logan, OBE 2000; JP, DL; WS; FRICS; solicitor; Partner, Thorntons WS, 1985–2002; chartered surveyor; *b* 13 April 1937; *s* of William Twaddle Laird and Janet Nicolson (*née* MacDonald); *m*; two *s* one *d*. *Educ:* Bell Baxter Sch., Cupar; Edinburgh and East of Scotland Coll. of Agriculture. Chartered surveyor and land agent, 1963; Partner, Clark Oliver Dewar & Webster, SSC, 1971–85. Mem., and Chm. NE Region, NCC Scotland, now Scottish Natural Heritage, 1990– (Chm., E Area Bd, 1997–2000); Chm. Bd, Cairngorms Partnership, 1994–97. JP 1968, DL 1989, Angus. *Recreations:* stalking, gardening, shooting, fishing. *Address:* West Memus, Forfar, Angus DD8 3TY. *T:* (01307) 860251. *Club:* New (Edinburgh).

LAIRD, Francis Joseph; QC 2011; **His Honour Judge Laird;** a Circuit Judge, since 2015; *b* Middlesbrough, 18 March 1964; *s* of Christopher Laird and Carmel Laird; *m* 2004, Linda Jones (marr. diss. 2013); two *d*. *Educ:* St George's Catholic Secondary Sch., Middlesbrough; Acklam Coll., Middlesbrough; University of Newcastle upon Tyne (LLB Hons 1985); Inns of Court Sch. of Law (Bar Finals 1986). Called to the Bar, Gray's Inn, 1986; 3 Fountain Court Chambers, 1989–2006; St Philips Chambers, 2006–15; a Recorder, 2009–15. *E:* HHJ.LairdQC@judiciary.gsi.gov.uk.

LAIRD, Sir Gavin (Harry), Kt 1995; CBE 1988; General Secretary, AEU Section, Amalgamated Engineering and Electrical Union, 1992–95; Chairman, Greater Manchester Buses North, 1994–97; *b* 14 March 1933; *s* of James and Frances Laird; *m* 1956, Catherine Gillies Campbell; one *d*. *Educ:* Clydebank High School. Full-time Trade Union Official, 1972–95; Mem. Exec. Council, 1975–95, Gen. Sec., 1982–94, AUEW, subseq. AEU, then AEEU. Mem., TUC Gen. Council, 1979–82; Mem. Exec., CSEU, 1975–95. Director: BNOC, 1976–86; Bank of England, 1986–94; non-exec. Director: Scottish Media Group plc (formerly Scottish TV), 1986–99; FS Assurance, then Britannia Life, 1988–99; GEC Scotland, 1991–99; Edinburgh Investment Trust, 1994–2003; Britannia, then Britannic, Investment Managers, 1996–2001; Chm., Murray VCT 4, 2000–03; Mem. Adv. Cttee, Murray Johnstone Pvte Equity Partnerships 1 & 2, 1995–. Pt-time Mem., SDA, 1987–92. Member: Arts Council of GB, 1983–86; London Cttee, Scottish Council for Devlt and Industry, 1984–95; President's Cttee, Business in the Community, 1988–90; Forestry Commn, 1991–94; Envmtl Council, BNFL, 1993–96; Adv. Bd, Know How Fund, 1988–95; Armed Forces Pay Review Body, 1995–98; Employment Appeal Tribunal, 1996–2003. Chm., Trade Union Friends of Israel, 1980–96. Dir, Westminster Foundn for Democracy, 1992–96. Mem. Governing Council, 1987–91, Gov., 1991–97, Atlantic Coll.; Trustee, Anglo-German Foundn, 1994–2002. Pres., Kent Active Retirement Assoc., 1996–2003. Fellow, Paisley Coll. of Technol., 1991. Hon. DLitt: Keele, 1994; Heriot-Watt, 1994. *Recreations:* hill walking, reading, music, bowls. *Address:* 9 Clevedon House, Holmbury Park, Bromley BR1 2WG. *T:* and *Fax:* (020) 8464 2376.

LAIT, Jacqui; *b* 16 Dec. 1947; *d* of Graham Harkness Lait and Margaret Stewart (*née* Knight); *m* 1974, Peter Jones. *Educ:* Paisley Grammar Sch.; Univ. of Strathclyde. Public relations posts: jute trade, Dundee; Visnews, internat. TV news agency; with Govt Inf. Service, in Scottish Office, Privy Council Office and Dept of Employment, 1974–80; Parly Advr, Chemical Inds Assoc., 1980–84; Parly Consultancy, 1984–92. Contested (C): Strathclyde W, Euro-election, 1984; Tyne Bridge, Dec. 1985. MP (C) Hastings and Rye, 1992–97; contested (C) same seat, 1997; MP (C) Beckenham, Nov. 1997–2010. An Asst Govt Whip, 1996–97; Opposition Whip, 1999–2000; Opposition spokesman on pensions, 2000–01; Shadow Scottish Sec., 2001–03; Shadow Minister for Home, Constitutional and Legal Affairs, 2003–05, for London, 2005–07, for Planning, 2007–10. Chm., City and E London FHSA, 1988–91. Chm., British Section, European Union of Women, 1990–92; Vice-Chm., Cons. Women's Nat. Cttee, 1990–92. Chairman: of Patrons, Rye Studio Sch., 2012–; Rye Academy Trust, 2015–; Mem. Bd, Five Villages Housing Assoc., 2012–. *Recreations:* walking, theatre, food and wine.

LAIT, His Honour Leonard Hugh Cecil, (Josh); a Circuit Judge, 1987–2003; *b* 15 Nov. 1930; *m* 1967, Cheah Phaik Teen; one *d*. *Educ:* John Lyon School, Harrow; Trinity Hall, Cambridge (BA). Called to the Bar, Inner Temple, 1959; Mem., SE circuit; a Recorder, 1985–87. *Recreations:* music, gardening.

LAITHWAITE, Anthony Hugh Gordon; Founder, Bordeaux Direct, subsequently Laithwaite's Wine, 1969; Chairman, Direct Wines Ltd, since 1972; *b* 22 Dec. 1945; *s* of late Eric and Winneth Laithwaite; *m* 1975, Barbara Anne Hynds; three *s*. *Educ:* Windsor Boys' Grammar Sch.; Bishop Vesey's Grammar Sch., Sutton Coldfield; Univ. of Durham (BA Hons (Geog.) 1968). Founded first shop, Windsor, 1969; Co-founder, Sunday Times Wine Club, 1973. FRGS 1999. Hon. DCL Durham, 2014. Chevalier, Ordre Nat. du Mérite Agricole (France), 2011. *Publications:* Laithwaite's Great Wine Trek, 1984. *Recreation:* wine. *Address:* The Old Brewery House, 86 New Street, Henley-on-Thames, Oxon RG9 2BT. *T:* (01491) 844780, *Fax:* (01491) 410562. *E:* tonylaithwaite@directwines.co.uk. *Club:* Royal Automobile.

LAITTAN, James S.; *see* Smith-Laittan.

LAITY, Mark Franklyn; Chief Strategic Communications, Supreme Headquarters Allied Powers Europe, since 2007; *b* 18 Dec. 1955; *s* of Frank and Pamela Laity. *Educ:* Redruth Co. Grammar Sch.; Univ. of York (BA Hons Hist./Politics; MA Southern African Studies). Reporter, Western Mail, 1978–81; BBC Radio: Producer: Radio Wales, 1981–82; Today prog., 1982–86; Sen. Producer, Analysis prog., 1986–88; Dep. Ed., The World This Weekend, 1988–89; Defence Corresp., BBC, 1989–2000; Dep. Spokesman and Personal Advr, subseq. Special Advr to NATO Sec.-Gen., 2000–03; Special Advr, later Chief of Public Inf., SACEUR, 2004–06; NATO spokesman in Kabul, Afghanistan, 2006–07, 2008; Advr to NATO Sen. Civilian Rep., 2010. Meritorious Service Medal, NATO, 2007. *Publications:* Preventing War in Macedonia: pre-emptive diplomacy for the 21st century, 2008; (contrib.) Strategy in NATO: preparing for an imperfect world, 2014. *Recreation:* sailing. *Address:* Rue Fetis 17, Bte C1, Mons 7000, Belgium. *E:* markflaity@hotmail.com. *Clubs:* Royal Air Force; Thames Sailing.

LAKE, (Charles) Michael, CBE 1996; Director, Royal Commonwealth Society, since 2014 (Interim Director, 2013–14); *b* 17 May 1944; *s* of Stanley Giddy and late Beryl Giddy (*née* Heath); step *s* of late Percival Redvers Lake; *m* 1970, Christine Warner; three *d*. *Educ:* Humphry Davy Grammar Sch., Penzance; RMA, Sandhurst. FILog 1995. SCLI 1963; commnd RCT, 1965; Regtl appts, Germany, Hong Kong, NI, Oman; attached Commandant-Gen., RM, 1977–78; Directing Staff, Staff Coll., 1982–83; Comd, 1st Div. Transport Regt, 1983–86; Comdr Transport, HQ British Forces Riyadh, Gulf War, 1990–91; Regtl Col, RLC, 1992–96; retired 1997. Dir Gen., Help the Aged, 1996–2009; Dir-Gen., English-Speaking Union of the Commonwealth, 2009–11 (Sec. Gen., Internat. Council, 2009–11); Chm., Morley Coll., 2011–12. Member: Bd, HelpAge Internat., 1996–2004; Benevolent and Strategy Cttee, RBL, 1997–2000 (External Advr, RBL, 1999); Council, Occupational Pensions Adv. Service, 1997–2001; Bd, Network Housing Assoc., 1999–2001; Council, Oxford Inst. of Ageing, 2000–; Bd, CAF, 2006–09; Bd, Charity Bank, 2007–10; Bd, Cornwall Care, 2010–; Bd, Orchard Care Homes, 2012–; Lay Mem., Lord Chancellor's Adv. Cttee on Conscientious Objectors, 2002–; Dep. Dir, Charities, 2009, Consultant, 2009–10, Prince's Charity Foundn; Special Advr, Charities Benevolent Fund, 2010–13. Mem. Bd, Golden Charter Ltd, 2009–14. Vice-Chm., Air Ambulance Foundn, 2003–04; Chm., Internat. Longevity Centre UK, 2009–13; Trustee: Disasters Emergency Cttee, 1999–2009; Pensions Policy Inst., 2001–09; Chm., British Gas Energy Trust, 2005–10. Chm. Bd, Chelsea Arts Club Ltd, 1997–2011. Freeman: City of London, 1995; Carmen's Co., 1995. *Recreations:* sports, avid golfer, cricketer, Rugby; Post Impressionism, Penzance and Newlyn school. *Address:* c/o Holt's Bank, Royal Bank of Scotland, Farnborough, Hants GU14 7NR. *Clubs:* MCC, Sloane (Hon. Life Mem.), Chelsea Arts (Life Mem.); Penguin International Rugby; W Cornwall Golf, North Hants Golf.

LAKE, Sir Edward Geoffrey, 11th Bt *cr* 1711, of Edmonton, Middlesex; *b* 17 July 1928; *y s* of Captain Sir Atwell Henry Lake, 9th Bt, CB, OBE, RN and Kathleen Marion Lake (*née* Turner); *S* brother, 2013; *m* 1965, Judith Ann, *d* of John Fox; one *s* one *d*. *Educ:* Eton. *Heir:* *s* Mark Winter Lake, *b* 26 Oct. 1968.

LAKE, Michael; *see* Lake, C. M.

LAKE, Robert Andrew; Independent Chairman, Walsall Safeguarding Children Board, since 2012; *b* 14 April 1948; *s* of Rev. William Henry Lake and Ruth Lake (*née* Hammond); *m* 1975, Celia Helen Probert; one *s* two *d*. *Educ:* Hull Grammar Sch.; Univ. of Coventry (CQSW). Welfare Asst, Bolton Welfare Dept, 1968–70; various posts, Coventry Social Services Dept, 1972–80; Area Manager, 1980–82, Principal Asst, 1982–84, Newcastle upon Tyne Social Services; Asst Dir, 1984–91, Dir, 1991–96, Humberside Social Services Dept; Dir of Social Services, Staffs CC, 1996–2005; Chm., Staffordshire Ambulance Service, 2005–07; Dir of Social Care, NHS Information Centre, 2007–11. Non-exec. Dir (Care and Support), Midland Heart Housing Assoc., 2008–. FRSocMed 2006. Vis. Fellow, Keele Univ., 1997. *Recreations:* music, D-I-Y, the family. *E:* ralake1@btinternet.com.

LAKE, Very Rev. Stephen David; Dean of Gloucester, since 2011; *b* 17 Dec. 1963; *s* of David Lake and Heather Lake; *m* 1986, Carol Waltham; two *s* one *d*. *Educ:* Chichester Theol Coll. (BTh Southampton Univ.); King's Coll. London (MA 2013). Ordained deacon, 1988, priest, 1989; Asst Curate, Sherborne Abbey, 1988–92; Priest-in-charge, 1992–96, Vicar, 1996–2001, St Aldhelm, Branksome; Rural Dean, Poole, 2000–01; Canon Res. and Sub-Dean, St Albans Cathedral, 2001–11; Chaplain to Lord Lieut of Glos, 2012–. Proctor in Convocation, 2003–10. Chm., Gloucester City Regeneration Adv. Bd, 2013–; Mem., Glos Dio. Academies Trust, 2014–. Trustee, Scout Assoc., 2010–. Queen's Scout, 1982; Scout Medal of Merit, 2010. *Publications:* Using Common Worship: marriage, 2000; Confirmation Prayer Book, 2002; Let the Children Come to Communion, 2006; Prayer Book for Lay People, 2008; Welcoming Marriage, 2009; Rethinking Confirmation, 2011. *Recreation:* hill-walking. *Address:* The Deanery, 1 Miller's Green, Gloucester GL1 2BP. *T:* (01452) 524167.

LAKE-TACK, Dame Louise (Agnetha), GCMG 2007; Governor-General, Antigua and Barbuda, 2007–14; *b* Long Lane Estate, Antigua, 26 July 1944; *m* (decd); two *c*. *Educ:* Antigua Girls' High Sch. Nurse, Charing Cross Hosp., Nat. Heart Hosp. and Harley Street Clinic, London. JP 1995. *Address:* c/o Governor-General's Residence, St John's, Antigua, West Indies.

LAKEY, Dr John Richard Angwin, CEng, FEI; CPhys, FInstP, CRadP; President, International Radiation Protection Association, 1988–92 (Publications Director, 1979–88); *b* 28 June 1929; *s* of late William Richard Lakey and Edith Lakey (*née* Hartley); *m* 1955, Dr Pamela Janet, *d* of late Eric Clifford Lancey and Florence Elsie Lancey; three *d*. *Educ:* Morley Grammar Sch.; Sheffield Univ. BSc (Physics) 1950, PhD (Fuel Technology) 1953. R&D posts with Simon Carves Ltd, secondment to AERE Harwell and GEC, 1953–60; Royal Naval College, Greenwich: Asst Prof., 1960–80; Prof. of Nuclear Sci. and Technol., 1980–89; Dean, 1984–86, 1988–89. Reactor Shielding Consultant, DG Ships, 1967–89; Radiation Consultant, WHO, 1973–74; Mem. and Vice-Chm., CNAA Physics Board, 1973–82; Mem., Medway Health Authy, 1981–90; Chm., UK Liaison Cttee for Scis Allied to Medicine and Biology, 1984–87. Founder, 1989, independent consultant, 1989–2000, John Lakey Associates. University of Surrey: External Examr, 1980–86; Hon. Vis. Prof., 1987–94; Vis. Lectr, Harvard Univ., 1984–2004; Vis. Prof., Univ. of Greenwich, 1998–2004. Mem. Editl Bd, Physics in Medicine and Biology, 1980–83; News Editor, Health Physics, 1980–88. Pres., Instn of Nuclear Engrs, 1988–90 (Vice-Pres., 1983–87); Vice-President: London Internat. Youth Sci. Forum, 1988–2010; European Nuclear Soc., 1989–95. Liveryman, Engineers' Co., 1988–. CRadP 2008. Hon. FSRP 1992. G. William Morgan Award, US Health Physics Soc., 1997. *Publications:* Protection Against Radiation, 1961; Radiation Protection Measurement: philosophy and implementation, 1975; (ed) ALARA principles and practices, 1987; (ed) IRPA Guidelines on Protection Against Non-Ionizing Radiation, 1991; (ed) Off-site Emergency Response to Nuclear Accidents, 1993; (jtly) Radiation and Radiation Protection: a course for primary and secondary schools, 1995; Radiation Protection for Emergency Workers, 1997; papers on nuclear safety, radiological protection and management of emergencies. *Recreations:* photography, sketching, travel. *Address:* 5 Pine Rise, Meopham, Gravesend, Kent DA13 0JA. *T:* (01474) 812551. *Clubs:* Athenæum; Royal Naval Sailing Association.

LAKHA, (Gulam) Abbas; QC 2003; *b* 2 Oct. 1962; *s* of Hassan Lakha and Leila (*née* Alibhai); *m* 1992, Shamira Fazal; one *s* two *d*. *Educ:* Stowe Sch.; Leeds Poly. (BA Hons Law). Called to the Bar, Inner Temple, 1984, Bencher, 2007; *ad eundem* Mem., Gray's Inn, 2002; in practice as barrister, specialising in all areas of serious and complex litigation, 1984–. Inspector, DTI, 1997–99. Mem., N London Bar Mess Cttee, 1998–. *Recreations:* travel, fast cars, modern architecture, work. *Address:* 9 Bedford Row, WC1R 4AZ. *T:* (020) 7489 2727, *Fax:* (020) 7489 2828. *E:* abbaslakha@9bedfordrow.co.uk.

LAKHANI, Kamlesh, (Mrs N. Lakhani); *see* Bahl, K.

LAKHANI, Mayur Keshavji, CBE 2007; FRCP, FRCPE, FRCGP; Principal in General Practice, Highgate Medical Centre, Sileby, Loughborough, since 1991; *b* 20 April 1960; *s* of Keshavji Vithaldas. Lakhani and Shantaben Keshavji Lakhani; *m* 1988, Mayuri Jobanputra; one *s* two *d*. *Educ:* Univ. of Dundee (MB ChB 1983). DFFP 1997; FRCGP 1998; FRCPE 2002; FRCP 2006. Vis. Prof., Dept of Health Scis, Leicester Univ. Sch. of Medicine, 2006–. Chairman: RCGP, 2004–07; Nat. Council for Palliative Care, 2008–15. *Publications:* (ed jtly) Evidence Based Audit in General Practice, 1998; (ed) A Celebration of General Practice, 2003; (ed jtly) Recent Advances in Primary Care, 2005; various articles on quality in health care and health policy. *Recreation:* tennis (Mem., Rothley Ivanhoe Tennis Club). *Address:* Highgate Medical Centre, 5 Storer Close, Sileby LE12 7UD. *E:* mklakhani@aol.com.

LAKIN, His Honour Peter Maurice; a Circuit Judge, 1995–2014; Resident Judge, Manchester Crown Court, 2006–14; *b* 21 Oct. 1949; *s* of late Ronald Maurice Lakin and of Dorothy Kathleen Lakin (*née* Cowlishaw); *m* 1971, Jacqueline Jubb; one *s* one *d. Educ:* King Henry VIII Sch., Coventry; Manchester Univ. (LLB). Articled Clerk, Conn Goldberg, solicitors, Manchester, 1971–74; Goldberg Blackburn, solicitors, Manchester (later Pannone & Partners): Asst Solicitor, 1974–76; Partner i/c of Corporate Defence and Forensic Unit, 1976–95; Asst Recorder, 1989–93; Recorder, 1993–95. Hon. Sec., Manchester and Dist Medico-Legal Soc., 1989–95. *Recreations:* fell-walking, opera, gardening, local history, grandchildren.

LAKIN, Sir Richard Anthony, 5th Bt *cr* 1909, of The Cliff, Borough of Warwick; *b* 26 Nov. 1968; *s* of Sir Michael Lakin, 4th Bt and of Felicity Ann Lakin (*née* Murphy); *S* father, 2014; *m* 1997, Lara Maryanne Rose (marr. diss. 2009); one *s* one *d. Educ:* Treverton Coll., Natal, SA. *Heir: s* Henry Anthony Lakin, *b* 22 June 1999. *Address:* c/o Lowesmoor Farm, Cherington, Tetbury, Glos GL8 8SP.

LALANNE, Bernard Michel L.; *see* Loustau-Lalanne.

LALL, Vikram, CBE 2005; Director, Heriot Services Ltd, since 1996; *b* 5 Dec. 1946; *s* of late Jag Mohan Lall and Dr Shuki Lall; *m* 1981, Carol Anne Ask; one *s* one *d. Educ:* Doon Sch., Dehra Dun; St Stephen's Coll., Delhi (BA Hons Econs 1966). CA 1972. Executive Director: Noble Grossart Ltd, 1975–77; Vikram Lall & Co. Ltd, 1977–82; McNeill Pearson Ltd, 1982–85; Heriot & Co. Ltd, 1985–87; Bell Lawrie White & Co., 1987–2003; Brewin Dolphin Hldgs plc, 1989–2003 (non-exec. Dir, 2003–08). Non-executive Director: Isis Property Trust, 2003–13; Crown Place VCT, 2006–12; Ramco Hldgs Ltd, 2005–13; Corsie Gp plc, 2006–08; Elephant Capital plc, 2010– (Chm., 2011–); F&C Real Estate Investments Ltd, 2013–; non-exec. Chm., Ryden LLP, 2005–09. Chm., Scottish Industrial Develt Adv. Bd, 2002–07 (Mem., 2000–07). Member: Bd, Royal Lyceum Th. Co., 2002–07; Governing Body, Queen Margaret UC, Edinburgh, 2003–09; Finance and Develt (formerly Finance and Investments) Cttee, RCSE, 2005–. *Recreations:* golf, travel, mind exercise. *Address:* Newmains House, Drem, East Lothian EH39 5BL. *T:* 07739 800223. *E:* vikramlall@macace.net. *Club:* Luffness New Golf.

LALLY, Patrick James; DL; Lord Provost and Lord-Lieutenant of Glasgow, 1995–99; Chairman, Scottish Senior Citizens Unity Party, 2008–09; *s* of Patrick James Lally and Sarah Joyce Lally; *m* 1967, Margaret Beckett McGuire (*d* 2007); two *s*. Former Dir, Retail Clothing Co. Member: Glasgow Corp., 1966–75 (Dep. Leader, 1972–75); Glasgow DC, 1975–77, 1980–96 (Treas., 1984–86; Leader, 1986–92, 1994–96). Contested (Ind.) Glasgow Cathcart, Scottish Parly elecns, 2003, 2005. Chairman: Gtr Glasgow Tourist Bd, 1989–96; Gtr Glasgow and Clyde Valley Tourist Bd, 1996–99; Director: Glasgow Internat. Jazz Fest. (Chm., 1989–99); Glasgow Develt Agency, 1990–92; Scottish Exhibn Centre Ltd, 1994–99; Glasgow 1999 Co. Ltd, 1996–99; Castlemilk Pensioners' Action Centre, 2008–. Mem., RGI, 1989–. Hon. Mem., Royal Faculty of Procurators in Glasgow. Member: Merchants House of Glasgow, 1997–; Incorporation of Tailors, Glasgow, 1990–; Incorporation of Gardiners, Glasgow, 1990–. JP Glasgow, 1970–2007, DL Glasgow, 1986. Hon. FRIAS 2009. Hon. Citizen, Dalian, China, 1995. OStJ 1997. Hon. LLD Strathclyde 1996. Silver Thistle Award, Scottish Tourist Bd, 1999. Comdr, Ordre Nat. du Mérite (France), 1996. *Publications:* Lazarus Only Done it Once (autobiog.), 1999. *Recreations:* enjoying the arts, reading, watching TV, football. *Address:* 2 Tanera Avenue, Simshill, Glasgow G44 5BU. *Club:* Glasgow Art.

LALONDE, Hon. Marc; PC (Can.) 1972; OC 1989; QC 1971; sole law practitioner, since 2006; *b* 26 July 1929; *s* of late J. Albert Lalonde and Nora (*née* St Aubin); *m* 1955, Claire Tétreau; two *s* two *d. Educ:* St Laurent Coll., Montreal (BA 1950); Univ. of Montreal (LLL 1954; MA Law 1955); Oxford Univ. (Econ. and Pol Science; MA 1957); Ottawa Univ. (Dip. of Superior Studies in Law, 1960). Prof. of Commercial Law and Econs, Univ. of Montreal, 1957–59; Special Asst to Minister of Justice, Ottawa, 1959–60; Partner, Gelinas, Bourque Lalonde & Benoit, Montreal, 1960–68; Lectr in Admin. Law for Doctorate Students, Univ. of Ottawa and Univ. of Montreal, 1961–62; Policy Advisor to Prime Minister, 1967; Principal Sec. to Prime Minister, 1968–72; MP (L) Montreal-Outremont, 1972–84; Minister of National Health and Welfare, 1972–77; Minister of State for Federal-Provincial Relations, 1977–78; Minister resp. for Status of Women, 1975–78; Minister of Justice and Attorney-Gen., 1978–79; Minister of Energy, Mines and Resources, 1980–82; Minister of Finance, 1982–84. Law Partner, 1984–2003, Sen. Counsel, 2003–06, Stikeman Elliott, Montreal. *Ad hoc* Judge, Internat. Court of Justice, 1985–. Counsel before several Royal Commns inc. Royal Commn on Great Lakes Shipping and Royal Commn on Pilotage. Mem., Cttee on Broadcasting, 1964; Dir, Canadian Citizenship Council, 1960–65; Member, Bd of Directors: Inst. of Public Law, Univ. of Montréal, 1960–64; Citibank Canada, 1985–2011; O&Y Properties, 1993–2005; Sherritt Power, subseq. Sherritt International, Inc., 1998–2013; Oxbow Equities Corp., 2000–07. Dr *hc*: Limburg, Maastricht, 1992; Western Ontario, 1996. Dana Award, Amer. Public Health Assoc., 1978. *Publications:* The Changing Role of the Prime Minister's Office, 1971; New Perspectives on the Health of Canadians (working document), 1974. *Recreations:* ski-ing, jogging, sailing, reading. *Address:* 1155 René-Lévesque Boulevard West, B–1, Montreal, QC H3B 3V2, Canada.

LALUMIÈRE, Catherine; French politician; President: Maison de l'Europe, Paris, since 2003; Fédération Français des Maisons de l'Europe, since 2008; European Association of Schools of Political Studies, Council of Europe, since 2008; *b* Rennes, 3 Aug. 1935. Dr in Public Law; degree in Pol Scis and History of Law. Asst, Univ. of Bordeaux I, and Bordeaux Inst. of Pol Studies, 1960–71; Sen. Lectr, Univ. of Paris I, 1971–81. Mem., National Assembly for Gironde, 1981, and 1986–89: Vice-Pres., Cttee of For. Affairs; Vice-Pres., Delegn to EC. Sec. of State i/c Public Service, 1981; Minister of Consumer Affairs, 1981–84; Sec. of State, resp. for Eur. Affairs, Min. of For. Affairs, 1984–86; Mem., Parly Assembly, Council of Europe, 1987–89; Sec. Gen., Council of Europe, 1989–94; Mem., 1994–2004, a Vice-Pres., 2001–04, Eur. Parlt; Pres., Eur. Radical Alliance Gp, 1994–2004. Mem., Parti Radical de Gauche (Vice Pres., 1994); Vice-President: Eur. Movement, France; Eur. Movement Internat.; Pres., Relais-Culture Europe. Regl Councillor, Ile de France, 1998–2004. *Recreation:* walking. *Address:* Maison de l'Europe de Paris, 35–37 rue des Francs-Bourgeois, 75004 Paris, France.

LALVANI, Prof. Ajit, DM; FRCP, FMedSci, FRSB; Professor of Infectious Diseases and Director, Tuberculosis Research Centre, National Heart and Lung Institute, since 2007, and Director, NIHR Health Protection Research Unit in Respiratory Infections, since 2014, Imperial College London; Hon. Consultant Physician, St Mary's Hospital, Imperial College Healthcare NHS Trust, since 2007; *b* New Delhi, 1 Dec. 1963; *s* of Dr Kartar Lalvani and Dr Mira Lalvani; *m* 2002, Maria-Jesus Ordoñana San Vicente. *Educ:* University Coll. Sch., London; St Peter's Coll., Oxford (BA Physiol Scis 1986; MA 1991); Royal Free Hosp. Sch. of Medicine, Univ. of London (MB BS Dist. 1989); Balliol Coll., Oxford (DM 1999). FRCP 2006; FRSB (FSB 2011); FMedSci 2012. SHO, Royal Brompton Hosp., London and Addenbrooke's Hosp., Cambridge, 1990–91; Specialist Registrar, Universitaetsspital, Basel and Churchill Hosp., Oxford, 1992–93; University of Oxford: MRC Clin. Res. Fellow, Weatherall Inst. Molecular Medicine and Sen. Res. Associate, Balliol Coll., 1993–96; Clin. Lectr in Gen. Medicine and Infectious Diseases, Nuffield Dept of Clin. Medicine, John Radcliffe Hosp., 1997–2001; Sherrington Lectr in Medicine, Magdalen Coll., 1999–2005; Wellcome Trust Sen. Res. Fellow in Clin. Sci. and Hon. Consultant Physician in Infectious Diseases and Gen. Medicine, Nuffield Dept of Clin. Medicine, John Radcliffe Hosp., 2001–06; Wellcome Trust Sen. Res. Fellow in Clin. Sci., Imperial Coll. London, 2007–13. Vis. Prof. of Medicine, Nuffield Dept of Medicine, Univ. of Oxford, 2012–. Sen. Investigator, NIHR, 2009–. Snell Meml Lectr, British Thoracic Soc., 2008. Mem., Academic Medicine Cttee, RCP, 2012–. Mem., Assoc. of Physicians, 2000. FRSocMed 2010. Chair, Bromley-by-Bow Centre, 2014–. Scientific Prize, Internat. Union against Tuberculosis and Lung Disease, 2005; Weber-Parkes Medal, RCP, 2008. *Publications:* contrib. res. articles, reviews, editls and book chapters on infectious diseases (tuberculosis, HIV, malaria, influenza), immunol., epidemiol. and public health. *Recreations:* gardening, philosophy, walking, cycling, cinema, architecture. *Address:* Tuberculosis Research Centre, National Heart and Lung Institute, Imperial College London, St Mary's Campus, Norfolk Place, W2 1PG. *E:* a.lalvani@imperial.ac.uk.

LAM, Martin Philip; *b* 10 March 1920; *m* 1953, Lisa Lorenz (*d* 2008); one *s* one *d. Educ:* University College Sch.; Gonville and Caius Coll., Cambridge (Scholar). Served War of 1939–45, Royal Signals and Special Ops Mediterranean. Asst Principal, Board of Trade, 1947; Nuffield Fellowship (Latin America), 1952–53; Asst Sec., 1960; Counsellor, UK Delegn to OECD, 1963–65, Advr, Commercial Policy, 1970–74, Leader UNCTAD Delegn, 1972; Under-Sec. (Computer Systems and Electronics), DoI, 1974–78; Associate of BIS Mackintosh, and of General Technology Systems, 1979–90; on contract to Directorate-Gen. XIII, European Commn, 1986–88; consultant: Scaneurope, 1989–90; KCL, 1991–92. *Publications:* (jtly) Kanji from the Start, 1995; contrib. Jl of World Trade, Knowledge Engrg Review. *Address:* 44 York Lodge, Pegasus Court, Park Lane, Tilehurst, Reading RG31 5DB.

LAMB, family name of **Baron Rochester**.

LAMB, Sir Albert Thomas, (Sir Archie), KBE 1979 (MBE 1953); CMG 1974; DFC 1945; HM Diplomatic Service, retired; *b* 23 Oct. 1921; *s* of R. S. Lamb and Violet Lamb (*née* Haynes); *m* 1944, Christina Betty Wilkinson; one *s* two *d. Educ:* Swansea Grammar Sch. Served RAF 1941–46. FO 1938–41; Embassy, Rome, 1947–50; Consulate-General, Genoa, 1950; Embassy, Bucharest, 1950–53; FO 1953–55; Middle East Centre for Arabic Studies, 1955–57; Political Residency, Bahrain, 1957–61; FO 1961–65; Embassy, Kuwait, 1965; Political Agent in Abu Dhabi, 1965–68; Inspector, 1968–70, Sen. Inspector, 1970–73, Asst Under-Sec. of State and Chief Inspector, FCO, 1973–74; Ambassador to Kuwait, 1974–77; Ambassador to Norway, 1978–80. Mem., BNOC, 1981–82; Dir, Britoil plc, 1982–88; Member Board: British Shipbuilders, 1985–87; Nat. Bank of Kuwait (Internat.), 1994–2008; Sen. Associate, Conant and Associates Ltd, Washington DC, 1985–93; Adviser, Samuel Montagu and Co. Ltd, 1986–88. Clerk to Parish Councils of Zeals and Stourton with Gasper, 1991–97. Hon. Fellow: Swansea Inst. of Higher Educn, 2004; Univ. of Wales Swansea, 2005. *Publications:* A Long Way from Swansea, 2003; Abu Dhabi 1965–1968, 2003; The Last Voyage of SS Oronsay, 2004. *Address:* White Cross Lodge, Zeals, Wilts BA12 6PF. *T:* (01747) 840321. *Club:* Royal Air Force.

See also R. D. Lamb.

LAMB, (Emma) Harriet, CBE 2006; Chief Executive Officer, Fairtrade International, since 2012; *b* 3 June 1961; *d* of late Gilbert and Sarah Lamb; partner, Steve Percy; one *s* one *d. Educ:* Trinity Hall, Cambridge (BA Social and Pol Sci. 1982); Inst. of Develt Studies Univ. of Sussex (MPhil Develt Studies 1986). Volunteer, village co-operatives, India, 1982–84; researcher, Northern Reg. Low Pay Unit, 1987–90; Co-ordinator, NE Refugee Service, 1990–92; Campaigns Co-ordinator, World Develt Movt, 1992–99; Interim Dir/Banana Co-ordinator, Fairtrade Labelling Orgns Internat., Germany, 1999–2001; Exec. Dir, Fairtrade Foundn, 2001–12. *Publications:* Working for Big Mac, 1987; Fighting the Banana Wars and Other Fairtrade Battles: how we took on the corporate giants to change the world, 2008; (contrib.) The Fair Trade Revolution, 2011. *Recreations:* cycling slowly, gardening badly, chatting loudly, playing with my kids, walking Northumbrian hills, swimming. *Address:* Fairtrade International, Bonner Talweg 177, 53129 Bonn, Germany.

LAMB, Air Vice-Marshal George Colin, CB 1977; CBE 1966; AFC 1947; Chairman, Yonex (UK) Ltd, 1995–97 (Managing Director, 1990–95); *b* 23 July 1923; *s* of late George and Bessie Lamb, Hornby, Lancaster; *m* 1st, 1945, Nancy Mary Godsmark; two *s*; 2nd, 1981, Mrs Maureen Margaret Mepham (*d* 2015). *Educ:* Lancaster Royal Grammar School. War of 1939–45: commissioned, RAF, 1942; flying duties, 1942–53; Staff Coll., 1953; Air Ministry, special duties, 1954–58; OC No 87 Sqdn, 1958–61; Dir Admin. Plans, MoD, 1961–64; Asst Comdt, RAF Coll., 1964–65; Dep. Comdr, Air Forces Borneo, 1965–66; Fighter Command, 1966; MoD (Dep. Command Structure Project Officer), 1967; HQ, Strike Command, 1967–69; OC, RAF Lyneham, 1969–71; RCDS, 1971–72; Dir of Control (Operations), NATS, 1972–74; Comdr, Southern Maritime Air Region, RAF Mount Batten, 1974–75; C of S, No 18 Gp Strike Comd, RAF, 1975–78. RAF Vice-Pres., Combined Cadet Forces Assoc., 1978–94. Chief Exec., Badminton Assoc. of England, 1978–89; Gen. Sec., London Inst. of Sports Medicine, 1989–90. Consultant, Television, Sport and Leisure Ltd, 1989–90. Chairman: Lilleshall Nat. Sports Centre, 1984–2005; British Internat. Sports Develt Aid Trust, 1995–2005; Member: Sports Council, 1983–88 (Mem., Drug Abuse Adv. Gp, 1988–92); Sports Cttee, Prince's Trust, 1985–88; British Internat. Sports Cttee, 1989–2005; Privilege Mem. of RFU, 1985– (Mem., RFU Cttee, 1973–85). Dir (non-exec.), Castle Care-Tech. Security, 1993–2005. President: St George's Day Club, 1994–2012; Assoc. of Lancastrians in London, 1999. Vice-Pres., British Berlin Airlift Assoc., 1998–2009. Internat. Rugby referee, 1966–71. FCMI. *Recreations:* Rugby football, cricket (former Pres., Adastrian Cricket Club), gardening, walking. *Address:* Hambleden, 17 Meadway, Berkhamsted HP4 2PN. *T:* (01442) 862583. *Club:* Royal Air Force.

LAMB, Lt-Gen. Sir Graeme (Cameron Maxwell), KBE 2009 (OBE 1991; MBE 1988); CMG 2003; DSO 2004; Commander, Field Army, 2007–09; *b* 21 Oct. 1953. *Educ:* Rannoch Sch.; Royal Mil. Acad. Sandhurst. Commnd Queen's Own Highlanders, 1973; Comdr, 81 Army Youth Team, Inverness, 1975–77; Northern Ireland (despatches, 1981); Staff Coll., Camberley, 1985; Comdr, B Co., 1st Bn, 1988–90; jsdc, 1989–90; Comdr, 1st Bn, 1991–93; Mil. Ops, MoD, 1993–94; HCSC, 1996; Comdr, 5th Airborne Bde, 1996–97; rcds, 1998; Asst Comdt (Land), JSCSC, 1999–2001; MoD, 2001–03; GOC 3rd (UK) Div., 2003–05; Dir Gen., Trng Support, MoD, 2005–06; Dep. Comdg Gen., Multinat. Force, Iraq, 2006–07. Special Advr to Gen. McChrystal, Comdr ISAF, 2009–10; consultant in defence and security, 2009–10. Chm., Army Snowboarding Assoc., 2001–09. QCVS 1994. Officer, Legion of Merit (USA), 2009.

LAMB, Harriet; *see* Lamb, E. H.

LAMB, Prof. Joseph Fairweather, PhD; FRCPE; FRSE; Chandos Professor of Physiology, St Leonard's College, University of St Andrews, 1969–93, now Professor Emeritus; *b* 18 July 1928; *s* of Joseph and Agnes May Lamb; *m* 1st, 1955, Olivia Janet Horne (marr. diss. 1989); three *s* one *d*; 2nd, 1989, Bridget Cecilia Cook; two *s. Educ:* Auldbar Public Sch.; Brechin High School (Dux, 1947); Edinburgh Univ. (MB ChB, BSc, PhD). FRCPE 1985. National Service, RAF, 1947–49. House Officer, Dumfries and Edinburgh, 1955–56; Hons Physiology Course, 1956–57; Univ. Junior Res. Fellow, 1957; Lectr in Physiology, Royal (Dick) Vet. Sch., 1958–61; Lectr, Sen. Lectr in Physiol., Glasgow, 1961–69. Sec., Physiol. Soc., 1982–85; Chm., Save British Science Soc., 1986–97; Chm./Organiser, Gas Greed Campaign, 1994–95. Gov., Rowett Res. Inst., Aberdeen, 1998–2004. Editor: Jl of Physiol., 1968–74; Amer. Jl of Physiol., 1985–88. FRSA; FRSE 1985. *Publications:* Essentials of Physiology, 1980, 3rd edn 1991; articles in learned jls. *Recreations:* reading, NHS voluntary work.

LAMB, Juliet; *see* Warkentin, J.

LAMB, Martin James; Chairman: Evoqua Water Technologies, since 2014; Rotork plc, since 2015; Senior Independent Director, Severn Trent plc, since 2008; *b* 7 Jan. 1960; *s* of Dr Trevor Lamb and Shirley Lamb; *m* 1983, Jayne Louise Bodenham; four *d*. *Educ:* Bradford Grammar Sch.; Solihull Sixth Form Coll.; Imperial Coll., London (BSc Mech. Eng. 1982); Cranfield Business Sch. (MBA 1990). Grad. Trainee, IMI Cornelius Inc., USA, 1982–83; Project Engr, IMI Air Conditioning, UK, 1983–85; R&D Manager, Coldflow Ltd, 1985–87; Mktg Dir, 1987–91, Man. Dir, 1991–96, IMI Cornelius (UK) Ltd; Exec. Dir, 1996–2000, Chief Exec., 2001–13, IMI plc. Non-executive Director: Spectris plc, 1999–2006; Mercia Technologies plc, 2014–. Trustee, City Technol. Coll., Birmingham, 1997–2008. *Recreations:* tennis, golf.

LAMB, Prof. Michael Ernest, PhD; Professor of Psychology, University of Cambridge, since 2004; *b* Lusaka, N Rhodesia, 22 Oct. 1953; *s* of Frank Lamb and Michelle Lamb (*née* de Lestang); *m* 2005, Hilary S. Clark; four step *d*, and three *s* one *d* from previous marriage. *Educ:* Univ. of Natal, S Africa (BA Psychol. and Econs); Johns Hopkins Univ. (MA Psychol.); Yale Univ. (MS, MPhil; PhD 1976). Assistant Professor of Psychology: Univ. of Wisconsin, 1976–78; Univ. of Michigan, 1978–80; Prof. of Psychol., Psychiatry and Pediatrics, Univ. of Utah, 1980–87 (Dist. Res. Award, 1986); Sen. Scientist and Section Chief, Nat. Inst. of Child Health and Human Develt, USA, 1987–2004. Mem., ESRC, 2006–11. Mem., REF 2014 sub-panel 4, 2011–. Hon. PhD Goteborg, 1995; Hon. DCL UEA, 2006; Hon. DSc Abertay, 2015. Cattell Award for Lifetime Contribn to Psychol., Assoc. for Psychol. Sci., 2004; Dist. Contribns Award, American Psychology-Law Soc., 2013; Tom Williamson Award, Internat. Investigative Interviewing Res. Gp, 2013; Stanley Hall Award, 2014, Dist. Scientific Award for Applications of Psychol. and Award for Dist. Contribns to Sci. in the Public Interest, 2015, Amer. Psychol Assoc. *Publications:* (ed) The Role of the Father in Child Development, 1976, trans. Japanese 1981, 5th edn 2010; (ed) Social and Personality Development, 1978; (ed jtly) Social Interaction Analysis, 1979; (ed jtly) Developmental Science: an advanced textbook, 1981, 7th edn 2015; (jtly) Child Psychology Today, 1982, 2nd edn 1986; (ed jtly) Advances in Developmental Psychology, vol. 1, 1981, vol. 2, 1982, vol. 3, 1984, vol. 4, 1986; (ed jtly) Infant Social Cognition, 1982; (jtly) Development in Infancy: an introduction, 1982, 4th edn 2002; (jtly) Socialization and Personality Development, 1982; (ed) Nontraditional Families, 1982, trans. Japanese 1998; (jtly) Infant-Mother Attachment, 1985; (ed) The Father's Role: applied perspectives, 1986; (ed jtly) Adolescent Fatherhood, 1986; (ed) The Father's Role: cross-cultural perspectives, 1987; (ed jtly) Adolescent Problem Behaviours, 1994; (ed jtly) Images of Childhood, 1996; (jtly) Investigative Interviews of Children, 1998; (ed) Parenting and Child Development in Nontraditional Families, 1999; (ed jtly) Hunter-gatherer Childhoods, 2005; (ed jtly) Child Sexual Abuse, 2007; (jtly) Tell Me What Happened: structured investigative interviews of child victims and witnesses, 2008; (ed jtly) Children's Testimony, 2011; (ed jtly) Children and Cross-Examination: time to change the rules?, 2012; (ed jtly) Fathers in Cultural Context, 2013; (ed jtly) Handbook of Child Psychology and Development Science, 7th edn, vol. 3: social, emotional, and personality development, 2015. *Recreations:* travel, family, performing arts, literature. *Address:* Department of Psychology, Free School Lane, University of Cambridge, Cambridge CB2 3RQ. *T:* (01223) 334523, *Fax:* (01223) 334550. *E:* mel37@cam.ac.uk.

LAMB, Rt Hon. Norman (Peter); PC 2014; MP (Lib Dem) North Norfolk, since 2001; *b* 16 Sept. 1957; *s* of late Hubert Horace Lamb and of Beatrice Moira Lamb; *m* 1984, Mary Elizabeth Green; two *s*. *Educ:* Wymondham Coll., Norfolk; Leicester Univ. (LLB). Sen. Asst Solicitor, Norwich CC, 1984–86; Solicitor, 1986–87, Partner, 1987–2001, Steele & Co. Lib Dem spokesman for health, 2007–10; an Asst Govt Whip, and Chief Parly and Political Advr to the Dep. Prime Minister, 2010–12; Parly Under-Sec. of State (Minister for Employment Relns, Consumer and Postal Affairs), BIS, 2012; Minister of State, DoH, 2012–15. *Publications:* Remedies in the Employment Tribunal, 1998. *Recreations:* football, walking. *Address:* House of Commons, SW1A 0AA. *T:* (020) 7219 0542; (office) Unit 4, The Garden Centre, Nursery Drive, Norwich Road, North Walsham, Norfolk NR28 0DR.

LAMB, Robin David; HM Diplomatic Service, retired; Director General, Libyan British Business Council, since 2009; Executive Director, Egyptian British Business Council, since 2009; *b* 25 Nov. 1948; *s* of Sir Albert Thomas Lamb, *qv*; *m* 1977, Susan Jane Moxon; two *s* one *d*. *Educ:* St John's, Leatherhead; Brasenose Coll., Oxford (MA Oriental Studies). Mgt asst, Abu Dhabi Cement Mktg Assoc., 1966–67; Mgt Develt Prog., Barclays Bank, 1970–71; joined FCO, 1971: lang. trng, MECAS, 1974–75; Res. Officer, FCO, 1975–79; Second Sec., Jedda, 1979–82; Principal Res. Officer, FCO, 1982–85; First Secretary: Riyadh, 1985–87; FCO, 1988–93; Hd, Pol Section, Cairo, 1993–96; FCO, 1996–99; British Trade Internat., 1999–2001; Counsellor and Dep. Hd of Mission, Kuwait, 2001–03; Ambassador, Bahrain, 2003–06; Consul-Gen., Basra, April–Aug. 2006. Hd, Business Develt, Arab British Chamber of Commerce, 2007–09. Mem., Ahtisaari Leadership Fund Wkg Gp, 2013–. Dir, BESO, 1999–2001. Trustee, British Univ. in Egypt, 2014–. Fellow, British Soc. for ME Studies, 1992. Bahrain Medal (1st cl.) (Bahrain), 2006; Iraq Reconstruction Service Medal, 2007. *Recreations:* family, reading. *E:* robinlamb@lbbc.org.uk.

LAMB, Shona Hunter; *see* Dunn, S. H.

LAMB, Hon. Timothy Michael; Chief Executive: England and Wales Cricket Board (formerly Test and County Cricket Board), 1996–2004; Sport and Recreation Alliance (formerly Central Council of Physical Recreation), 2005–14; *b* 24 March 1953; *s* of Baron Rochester, *qv*; *m* 1978, Denise Ann Buckley; one *s* one *d*. *Educ:* Shrewsbury Sch.; Queen's Coll., Oxford (MA Modern Hist.). Professional cricketer: with Middx CCC, 1974–77 (Hon. Life Mem.); with Northants CCC, 1978–83 (Hon. Life Mem.); Sec. and Gen. Manager, Middx CCC, 1984–88; Cricket Sec., 1988–96, Dep. Chief Exec., May–Oct. 1996, TCCB. Director: TML Sports Connections Ltd, 2014–; Sports Mktg Intelligence Gp, 2015–. Chair, Sports Betting Gp, 2010–14. Mem., Sport Hons Cttee, Cabinet Office, 2011–. Hon. Life Mem., Cricket Writers' Club. *Recreations:* golf, travel, walking, photography. *Clubs:* MCC (Hon. Life Mem.); Durham CC (Hon. Life Mem.).

LAMB, Timothy Robert; QC 1995; **His Honour Judge Lamb;** a Circuit Judge, since 2008; *b* 27 Nov. 1951; *s* of Stephen Falcon Lamb and Pamela Elizabeth Lamb (*née* Coombes); *m* 1978, Judith Anne Ryan; one *s* one *d*. *Educ:* Brentwood Sch.; Lincoln Coll., Oxford (MA Jurisp.). Called to the Bar, Gray's Inn, 1974, Bencher, 2003. Asst Recorder, 1998–2000; Recorder, 2000–08. Jt Head of Chambers, 3 Paper Buildings, Temple, 2004–08. Bar Council: Western Circuit Rep., 2005–08; Circuits Rep., Law Reform Cttee, 2005–08. Legal Assessor, GDC, 2002–08; Legal Adviser: Royal Pharmaceutical Soc., 2006–08; General Optical Council, 2006–08. Member: Restricted Patients Panel, Mental Health Review Tribunal, 2009–12; Lord Chancellor's N and E London Magistrates' Adv. Cttee, 2012–. Accredited mediator and adjudicator. FCIArb. *Recreations:* family, travel, water sports. *Address:* Kingston-upon-Thames Crown Court, 6–8 Penrhyn Road, Kingston-upon-Thames, Surrey KT1 2BB.

LAMB, Prof. Trevor David, FRS 1993; FAA; Distinguished Professor, 2008–11, now Emeritus Professor, and Research Director, ARC Centre of Excellence in Vision Science, 2006–10, John Curtin School of Medical Research, Australian National University (ARC Federation Fellow, 2003–07); *b* 20 Sept. 1948; *s* of Arthur and Margaret Lamb; *m* 1979, (Janet) Clare Conway; two *s* one *d*. *Educ:* Melbourne Grammar Sch.; Univ. of Melbourne (BE 1st Cl. Hons 1969); Univ. of Cambridge (PhD 1975; ScD 1988). University of Cambridge: Wellcome Sen. Res. Fellow, 1978–80, Royal Soc. Locke Res. Fellow, 1980–84, Physiological Lab.; Univ. Lectr in Physiol., 1984–91; Reader in Neuroscience, 1991–94; Prof. of Neurosci., 1994–2002; Fellow, Darwin Coll., 1985–2002. FAA 2005. *Publications:* articles on photoreceptors, sensory transduction and eye evolution in Jl Physiol. and other learned jls. *Address:* Department of Neuroscience, John Curtin School of Medical Research, Australian National University, Canberra, ACT 2601, Australia. *T:* (2) 61258929, *Fax:* (2) 61259532. *E:* trevor.lamb@anu.edu.au.

LAMBART, family name of **Earl of Cavan**.

LAMBECK, Prof. Kurt, AO 2009; DPhil, DSc; FRS 1994; FAA; Professor of Geophysics, Australian National University, since 1977; *b* 20 Sept. 1941; *s* of Jacob and Johanna Lambeck; *m* 1967, Bridget Marguerite Nicholls; one *s* one *d*. *Educ:* Univ. of NSW (BSurv. Hons); Hertford Coll., Oxford (DPhil, DSc). Geodesist, Smithsonian Astrophysical Observatory and Harvard Coll. Observatory, Cambridge, Mass, 1967–70; Directeur Scientifique, Observatoire de Paris, 1970–73; Prof. of Geophysics, Univ. of Paris, 1973–77; Dir, Res. Sch. of Earth Scis, ANU, 1984–93. Tage Erlander Prof., Swedish Res. Council, 2001–02; Blaise Pascal Chair, École Normale Supérieure, Paris, 2011–12. Pres., Aust. Acad. Sci., 2006–10 (Vice Pres., 1998–2000; Foreign Sec., 2000–04). Fellow, Amer. Geophysical Union, 1976; FAA 1984. Foreign Member: Royal Netherlands Acad. of Arts and Scis, 1993; Norwegian Acad. of Science and Letters, 1994; Foreign MAE, 1999; Associé étranger, Institut de France, Académie des Sciences, 2005; For. Associate, NAS, 2009; For. Hon. Mem., Amer. Acad. of Arts and Scis, 2011; Hon. Mem., European Geophysical Soc., 1987. Hon. DEng Nat. Tech. Univ., Athens, 1994; Hon. DSc: NSW, 1999; Wollongong, 2015. Macelwane Medal, 1976, Whitten Medal, 1993, Amer. Geophysical Union; Jaeger Medal, Aust. Acad. of Sci., 1995; Alfred Wegener Medal, Eur. Union of Geoscis, 1997; Georges Lemaître Prize, Catholic Univ. of Louvain, 2001; Federation Medal, 2003; Balzan Prize, Internat. Balzan Foundn, 2012; Wollaston Medal, Royal Geol Soc., 2013; Matthew Flinders Medal, Australian Acad. of Sci., 2015. Chevalier, Légion d'Honneur (France), 2011; Cavaliere, Ordine al Merito della Repubblica Italiana, 2013. *Publications:* The Earth's Variable Rotation, 1980; Geophysical Geodesy: the slow deformations of the earth, 1988; numerous articles in fields of geodesy, geophysics and geology. *Address:* Research School of Earth Sciences, Australian National University, Canberra, ACT 0200, Australia; 31 Brand Street, Hughes, ACT 2605, Australia.

LAMBERT, Anne; *see* Lambert, G. M. A.

LAMBERT, David Arthur Charles; General President, National Union of Knitwear, Footwear and Apparel Trades, 1991–94 (General Secretary, 1975–82, General President, 1982–90, National Union of Hosiery and Knitwear Workers); President, International Textile, Garment and Leather Workers' Federation, Brussels, 1992–96 (Vice-President, 1984–92); *b* 2 Sept. 1933; *m* Beryl Ann (*née* Smith); two *s* one *d*. *Educ:* Hitchin Boys' Grammar Sch., Herts. Employed as production worker for major hosiery manufr; active as lay official within NUHKW; full-time official, NUHKW, 1964–90. Member: Employment Appeal Tribunal, 1978–2004; TUC Gen. Council, 1984–94; CRE, 1987–93. Gov., Welbeck Coll., 2001–09.

LAMBERT, David George; Registrar, Diocese of Llandaff, 1986–2013; *b* 7 Aug. 1940; *s* of George and Elsie Lambert; *m* 1966, Diana Mary Ware; one *s* one *d*. *Educ:* Barry Grammar Sch.; UCW, Aberystwyth (LLB). Notary Public; Solicitor in private practice, 1965; Welsh Office: Legal Officer, 1966–74; Asst Legal Adviser, 1974–91; Solicitor and Legal Advr, 1991–99; Legal Advr, Presiding Office, Nat. Assembly for Wales, 2000–04. Res. Fellow, Cardiff Univ., 2000–12. Dep. Chapter Clerk, Llandaff Cath., 1980–. *Recreation:* Baroque music. *Address:* 9 The Chantry, Llandaff, Cardiff CF5 2NN. *T:* (029) 2056 8154.

LAMBERT, (Gillian Mary) Anne, CMG 2006; a Panel Deputy Chair, Competition and Markets Authority, since 2014; *b* 11 July 1956; *d* of late Roy and of Joyce Lambert. *Educ:* St Anne's Coll., Oxford (BA Hons Exptl Psychol. 1977). Joined Department of Trade and Industry, 1977: Telecommunications Div., 1982–84; Industrial Policy Div. (Grade 7), 1984–86; Insce Div., 1986–88; Personnel Div. (Grade 6), 1989–90; Insce Div. (Grade 5), 1990–93; on secondment to FCO as Counsellor (Industry), UK Perm. Repn to EU, Brussels, 1994–98; Dep. Dir Gen., Oftel, 1998–2002; Hd of Nuclear Liabilities, DTI, 2002–03; UK Dep. Perm. Rep. to EU, Brussels, 2003–08; Dir, Govt and Eur. Affairs, NATS, 2008–14. Trustee, Woodland Trust, 2009–. Gov., Portsmouth Univ., 2012–. *Recreations:* theatre, squash, horse racing, walking. *E:* gmalambert@gmail.com.

LAMBERT, Jean Denise; Member (Green) London Region, European Parliament, since 1999; *b* 1 June 1950; *d* of Frederick John and Margaret Archer; *m* 1977, Stephen Lambert; one *s* one *d*. *Educ:* Palmers Grammar Sch. for Girls, Grays, Essex; University Coll., Cardiff (BA Modern Langs); St Paul's Coll., Cheltenham (PGCE). ADB(Ed). Secondary sch. teacher, Waltham Forest, 1972–89 (examr in spoken and written English, 1983–88). Green Party: joined 1977 (then Ecology Party); London Area Co-ordinator, 1977–81; Co-Chm. Council, 1982–85, 1986–87; Rep. to European Green Parties, 1985–86, 1988–89; UK rep. to Green Gp in European Parlt, 1989–94; Green Party Speaker, 1988–, Jt Principal Speaker, 1992–93; Chair of Executive, 1993–94. Vice-Pres., Green/EFA Gp, 2002–. Contested (Green Party): GLC, 1981; local Council, 1986; London NE, European Parlt, 1984, 1989, 1994; Walthamstow, Gen. Elecn, 1992. Founder Member: Ecology Building Soc., 1981 (Bd, 1981–84; Chm., 1982–83; now Patron); Play for Life, 1984; Member: Council, Charter 88, 1990; Cttee, Voting Reform Gp, 1995. Trustee, London Ecology Centre, 1995–97. Radio and TV broadcaster. *Publications:* (contrib.) Into the 21st Century, 1988; No Change? No Chance!, 1996; Refugees and the Environment, 2002; articles to magazines. *Recreations:* reading (esp. detective fiction), cooking, dance. *Address:* European Parliament, Rue Wiertz, 1047 Brussels, Belgium. *E:* jeanlambert@greenmeps.org.uk.

LAMBERT, Jenni Cecily; *see* Russell, J. C.

LAMBERT, John Sinclair; Chairman, Friends of the Peak District (Campaign to Protect Rural England South Yorkshire), since 2014; executive coach and mentor; *b* 8 April 1948; *s* of late Norman and Doris Lambert; *m* 1971, Ann Dowzell (*d* 2011); two *s*. *Educ:* Denstone Coll.; Selwyn Coll., Cambridge (MA); Sheffield Hallam Univ. (MSc 2005). Department of Employment, subseq. Department for Education and Employment, 1970–2000: Private Sec. to Perm. Sec., 1973–74; on secondment to Marconi Space and Defence Systems, 1977–78; Dep. Chief Conciliation Officer, ACAS, 1982–83; Head of European Communities Branch, 1983–85; Dir of Field Ops, MSC, 1987–90; Dir of Ops (N and W), 1990–92; Dir, Adult Learning Div., 1992–93; Dir, Sheffield First Partnership, 1993–97 (on secondment); Regl Dir, Govt Office for Eastern Reg., 1997–98; Dir, Learning Ops, Univ. for Industry, 1998–99. Partner, John Lambert Associates, 2000–13. Dep. Chm., Govs, 2007–09, Trustee, Students' Union, 2010–, Sheffield Hallam Univ. Chm., Save Longstone Edge, 2008–13. *Recreations:* birdwatching, music, mountain walking. *Address:* 1 Calver Mill, Calver, Hope Valley, Derbys S32 3YU.

LAMBERT, Rear Adm. Nicholas Richard; Director: Nick Lambert Associates Ltd, since 2012; LW Partners Ltd, since 2014; *b* Isleworth, Middx, 27 April 1958; *s* of Michael and Anne Lambert; *m* 1989, Beverly Slim; one *s* one *d*. *Educ:* Devizes Sch.; Durham Univ. (BA Hons Geog.); BRNC Dartmouth; Henley Business Sch., Univ. of Reading (Cert. Coaching). Entered RN, 1977; in command: HMS Brazen, 1996; HMS Newcastle, 1996–98; Dep. Asst Dir, Above Water Warfare, MoD, 1998–99; Chief Maritime and Amphibious Ops, NATO Regl HQ, Brunssum, 1999–2002; COS, UK Maritime Battlestaff, 2002–05; i/c HMS Endurance, 2005–07; Comdr, Task Force 158, 2007; Talent Mgt Study Team Leader, Staff of Naval Sec., 2007–08; Dep. FOST, 2008–09; ACOS (Ops and Capability Integration), 2009–10. Nat. Hydrographer and Dep. CEO, UK Hydrographic Office, 2010–12. Non-exec.

Dir, ECDIS Ltd, 2013–. Younger Brother, Corp. of Trinity House, 2010–. MInstD. Friend, Cttee Mem. and Chm., Friends of Scott Polar Res. Inst., 2010–. Pres., RN Gliding and Soaring Assoc., 2014– (Chm., 2004–13); Life Mem., Portsmouth Naval Gliding Centre, 2003–. Freeman, Master Mariners' Co., 2000. FRGS 2011. Legionnaire, Legion of Merit (USA), 2004. *Recreations:* family, unfulfilled ambition to manage the construction of a house, passionate glider pilot, cookery, gardening, sailing.

LAMBERT, Nigel Robert Woolf; QC 1999; a Recorder, since 1996; *b* 5 Aug. 1949; *s* of Dr E. Vivian Lambert, MB BS, MRCS, LRCP, and Sadie Lambert (*née* Woolf); *m* 1975, Roamie Elisabeth Sado; one *s* one *d*. *Educ:* Cokethorpe Sch., Oxford; Coll. of Law, London. Called to the Bar, Gray's Inn, 1974, Bencher, 2004; *ad eundem* Mem., Inner Temple, 1986. In practice, SE Circuit, 1974–; Asst Recorder, 1992–96; Dep. Hd of Chambers, 2004–09; Hd of Chambers, 2009–14. Member: Bar Council, 1993–2000 (Member: Professional Standards Cttee, 1993–95, 1997–99; Public Affairs Cttee, 1994; Finance Cttee, 1994; Legal Aid and Fees Cttee, 1996); S Eastern Circuit Cttee, 1992–2007 (Mem. Exec. Cttee, 2001–07; Chm., S Eastern Circuit/Inst. of Barristers' Clerks Cttee, 2001–07); Inner Temple Bar Liaison Cttee, 2002–03; Inner Temple Circuit Cttee, 2002–03. Member: Criminal Bar Assoc. (Mem., Cttee, 1993–2000); Justice. Chm., N London Bar Mess, 2001–07. Gov., Cokethorpe Sch., 1971–78 (Life Vice Pres., Cokethorpe Old Boys' Assoc., later Cokethorpe Soc.). *Recreations:* supervising, organising, gossiping. *Address:* (chambers) Carmelite Chambers, 9 Carmelite Street, EC4Y 0DR. *T:* (020) 7936 6300. *E:* nlambertqc@carmelitechambers.co.uk. *Clubs:* Garrick, MCC.

LAMBERT, Vice Adm. Sir Paul, KCB 2012 (CB 2008); Secretary-General, Order of St John, since 2012; *b* 17 Nov. 1954; *s* of Ernest Harry Lambert and Lillian Lambert (*née* Rutten); *m* 2012, Enid Wynn Pugh (*née* Rogers); one step *s*, and three *s* one *d* from a previous marriage. *Educ:* City Univ., London (BSc 1978); Darwin Coll., Cambridge (MPhil 1989); DipFM, ACCA 2002. Joined RN, 1974; Commanding Officer: HMS Onyx, 1989–91; HMS Tireless, 1991–92; submarine comd course, 1992–94; CO, HMS Coventry, 1996–98; Capt. Submarine Sea Trng, 1998–99; rcds 2000; hcsc 2001; Dir, Equipment Capability (Underwater Battlespace), MoD, 2001–04; Comdr Ops to C-in-C Fleet, Comdr Submarines and Allied Naval Force N and Rear Adm. Submarines, 2004–06; Capability Manager (Precision Attack), 2006–09; Controller of the Navy, 2007–09; DCDS (Equipment Capability), 2009–12. Pres., Merseyside Submarine Assoc., 2008–. *Recreations:* walking, modern history, politics. *Address:* St John House, 3 Charterhouse Mews, EC1M 6BB. *Club:* Royal Navy of 1765 and 1785.

LAMBERT, Paul Julian Lay; His Honour Judge Lambert; a Circuit Judge, since 2004; a Deputy High Court Judge, since 2010; *b* 24 Aug. 1961; *s* of late Arnold Michael Lay Lambert and Rowena Lambert; *m* 2003, Sharon Dawn Curzon; two *s*. *Educ:* LSE (LLB). Called to the Bar, Middle Temple, 1983; in practice as barrister, 1983–2004, specialising in fraud and corporate crime. Mem., Professional Conduct Cttee, Bar Council, 1998–2001. *Recreation:* urbane pursuits. *Address:* Bristol Crown Court, Small Street, Bristol BS1 1DA.

LAMBERT, Sir Peter John Biddulph, 10th Bt *cr* 1711, of London; teacher; *b* 5 April 1952; *s* of John Hugh Lambert (*d* 1977) (*g s* of 5th Bt) and of Edith May, *d* of late James Bance; *S* kinsman, Sir Greville Foley Lambert, 9th Bt, 1988, but his name does not appear on the Official Roll of the Baronetage; *m* 1989, Leslie Anne, *d* of R. W. Lyne; one *s* one *d*. *Educ:* Upper Canada Coll., Toronto; Trent Univ. (BSc 1975); Univ. of Manitoba (MA 1980); Univ. of Toronto (BEd). *Heir: s* Thomas Hugh John Lambert, *b* 14 March 1999.

LAMBERT, Captain Richard Edgar, CBE 1982; RN; Vice Lord-Lieutenant, County of Powys, 1997–2004; *b* 24 Oct. 1929; *s* of Joseph Edgar Hugo Lambert and Mildred Lambert (*née* Mason); *m* 1954, Eleanor Ruth Owen; two *s* one *d*. *Educ:* RNC, Dartmouth; BA Hons Open 1994. RN 1943–82; RCDS 1977; CO, HMS Raleigh, 1978–79. Marconi Underwater Systems, 1982–88. Non-exec. Dir, S and E Wales Ambulance NHS Trust, 1993–97. Dir, Machynlleth Tabernacle Trust, 1986–. President: Côr Meibion Powys, 1989–2008; Montgomeryshire Area Scout Council, 1997–2004. DL Powys, 1993. *Recreations:* gardening, music, art, ornithology. *Address:* Felin Rhisglog, Glaspwll, Machynlleth, Powys SY20 8TU. *T:* (01654) 702046. *Club:* Army and Navy.

LAMBERT, Sir Richard (Peter), Kt 2011; Director General, Confederation of British Industry, 2006–11; *b* 23 Sept. 1944; *s* of late Peter and Mary Lambert; *m* 1973, Harriet Murray-Browne; one *s* one *d*. *Educ:* Fettes Coll.; Balliol Coll., Oxford (BA). Staff of Financial Times, 1966–2001: Lex Column, 1972; Financial Editor, 1978; New York Correspondent, 1982; Dep. Editor, 1983; Editor, 1991–2001. Mem., Monetary Policy Cttee, Bank of England, 2003–06; Lead Ind. Dir, FCO, 2011–. Ind. non-exec. Dir, EY (formerly Ernst & Young), 2011–; Mem. Adv. Panel, EDF Energy, 2011–. UK Business Ambassador, 2011–. Chairman: Big Society Trust, 2011–15; Fair Educn Alliance, 2015–. Chancellor, Univ. of Warwick, 2008–. Trustee, BM, 2003–11 (Chm., Bd of Trustees, 2014–). Hon. Fellow, Liverpool John Moores Univ., 2011. Hon. DLitt: City, 2000; Herts, 2010; Hon. LLD: Warwick, 2004; Brighton, 2005; DUniv York, 2007; Hon. DSc: Cranfield, 2008; (Econs) QUB, 2008; Aston, 2011; Hon. DLaws Exeter, 2010.

LAMBERT, Sophia Jane, CB 2004; *b* 15 May 1943; *d* of Michael Lambert and Florence Lambert (*née* Macaskie). *Educ:* Univ. of Paris; LSE (BSc). Entered FCO, 1966; Second Secretary: Bonn, 1968–72; FCO, 1972–76; First Secretary: Pretoria, 1976–80; FCO, 1980–82; Counsellor, Cabinet Office, 1982–85; Department of Transport: Head: Internat. Div., 1985–87; Public Transport (Metropolitan) Div., 1987–91; Channel Port Link Div., 1991–92; Director: Road and Vehicle Safety, 1992–98; Wildlife and Countryside, DETR, then DEFRA, 1998–2003 (also Dir, Flood Mgt, 2001–03). Chair, Standards Cttee, RBKC, 2006–12. Lay Mem., Gen. Council of the Inns of Court, 2005–12. Mem. Bd, London TravelWatch, 2009–12. Trustee: NOVA New Opportunities, 2012–; Kensington Soc., 2014–. *E:* s@sophialambert.com.

LAMBERT, Stephen; Chief Executive, Studio Lambert Ltd, since 2008; Chairman, All3Media America LLC, since 2013; *b* 22 March 1959; *s* of Roger Lambert and Monika Lambert (*née* Wagner); *m* 1988, Jenni Cecily Russell, *qv*; one *s* one *d*. *Educ:* Univ. of East Anglia; Nuffield Coll., Oxford. Joined BBC Television, 1983; Producer and Dir, BBC Documentary Features Dept, 1986–94, prog. series incl. 40 Minutes (East Side Story, Dolebusters, Greenfinches, Who'll win Jeanette?, Crack Doctors, Hilary's in Hiding, Malika's Hotel), Inside Story (Children of God, The Missing, Suicide Killers, Dogs of War), and True Brits; Exec. Producer, BBC Documentaries Dept, 1994–99, progs incl. The System (Best Factual Series, RTS, 1996), 42 Up (Best Documentary, BAFTA, 1998), The Mayfair Set (Best Factual Series, BAFTA, 1999), Mersey Blues, The Clampers, Lakesiders, Premier Passions, The Day the Guns Fell Silent; Editor: Modern Times, BBC TV, 1994–98; Real Life, ITV, 1998–2001; RDF Television, later RDF Media: Dir of Progs, 1998–2005; Exec. Producer, 1999–2007; Chief Creative Officer, RDF Media Gp, 2005–07; progs incl. Faking It (Best Popular Arts Prog., Internat. Emmy Awards, 2002; Best Features Prog., BAFTA, 2002 and 2003; Best Primetime Features Prog., RTS, 2002; Golden Rose, Montreux, 2003), Perfect Match (Silver Rose, Montreux, 2002), The Century of the Self (Best Documentary Series, Broadcast Awards, 2003), Wife Swap (Best Features Prog., BAFTA, 2004; Golden Rose, Lucerne, 2004; Golden Nymph, Monte Carlo, 2004), The Power of Nightmares (Best Factual Series, BAFTA, 2005; Best Documentary Series, RTS, 2005), The Secret Millionaire (Best Reality Prog., Golden Rose, Lucerne, 2007), The Hip Hop Years, Shipwrecked, Going Native; Studio Lambert progs incl. Undercover Boss (Best Reality Prog., Primetime Emmy Awards, 2012, 2013), Gogglebox (Best Reality and Constructed Factual Prog., BAFTA, 2014; Best Popular Factual and Features Prog., RTS, 2014), Four in a Bed, How to Get a Council House, The Great Interior Design Challenge, The Flaw, The Fairy Jobmother, Seven Days, The Pitch, Supermarket Superstars, Outlaw Empires. Trustee: RSA, 2009–11; Impetus Trust, 2009–12. Mem. Exec. Cttee, Edinburgh Internat. TV Fest., 2002; Dir, Sheffield Internat. Documentary Fest., 2003–05. Mem. Council, BAFTA, 1996–98. FRSA. Best Commissioning Editor, Broadcast Awards, 1996. *Publications:* Channel Four: television with a difference?, 1982. *Recreations:* sailing, ski-ing, walking, cinema, my children. *Address:* Studio Lambert Ltd, 1 Denmark Street, WC2H 8LP. *T:* (020) 3040 6800. *E:* stephen.lambert@studiolambert.com.

LAMBERT, Prof. Susan Barbara, (Mrs J. D. W. Murdoch); Professor, since 2014, and Head, Museum of Design in Plastics, since 2007, Arts University Bournemouth (formerly Arts Institute, Bournemouth, then Arts University College at Bournemouth); *b* 24 Jan. 1944; *d* of Alan Percival Lambert and Barbara May Lambert (*née* Herbert); *m* 1990, John Derek Walter Murdoch, *qv* (marr. diss. 2007). *Educ:* Downe House; Courtauld Inst. of Art, London Univ. (BA). Victoria and Albert Museum: Department of Prints and Drawings, subseq. Prints, Drawings and Paintings: Res. Asst, 1968–75; Asst Keeper, 1975–79; Dep. Keeper, 1979–89; Chief Curator, 1989–2002; Keeper, Word & Image Dept, 2002–05. *Publications:* Printmaking, 1983; Drawing, Technique and Purpose, 1984; The Image Multiplied, 1987; Form Follows Function?, 1993; Prints, Art and Technique, 2001. *Address:* Brick Hill, Burghclere, Berks RG20 9HJ. *T:* (01635) 278295.

LAMBETH, Archdeacon of; *see* Gates, Ven. S. P.

LAMBIE, David; *b* 13 July 1925; *m* 1954, Netta May Merrie; one *s* four *d*. *Educ:* Kyleshill Primary Sch.; Ardrossan Academy; Glasgow University; Geneva University. BSc, DipEd. Teacher, Glasgow Corp., 1950–70. Chm., Glasgow Local Assoc., Educnl Inst. for Scotland, 1958–59; Chm., Scottish Labour Party, 1964; Chief Negotiator on behalf of Scottish Teachers in STSC, 1969–70; Sec., Westminster Branch, Educnl Inst. of Scotland, 1985–88, 1991–92. MP (Lab) Ayrshire Central, 1970–83, Cunninghame South, 1983–92. Chm., Select Cttee on Scottish Affairs, 1981–87; Sec., Parly All-Party Cttee for Energy Studies, 1980–92; Chm., PLP Aviation Cttee, 1990–92. Chm., Saltcoats Labour Party, 1993–95, 2000–03; Member: Cunninghame N Constituency Labour Party, 1993–2004; N Ayrshire and Arran Constituency Labour Party, 2004–. Chm. Develt Cttee, Cunninghame Housing Assoc., 1992–. Dir, Galloway Training Ltd, 1997–2011. Member: Council of Europe, 1987–92; WEU, 1987–92. FEIS 1970. *Recreation:* watching football. *Address:* 11 Ivanhoe Drive, Saltcoats, Ayrshire KA21 6LS. *T:* (01294) 464843. *Club:* North Ayrshire and Arran Constituency Labour Social (Saltcoats).

LAMBIE-NAIRN, Martin John, RDI 1987; FCSD; consultant creative director, since 2011; *b* 5 Aug. 1945; *s* of Stephen John and Joan Lois Lambie-Nairn; *m* 1970, Cordelia Margot Summers; one *s* two *d*. *Educ:* King Ethelbert Sch., Birchington, Kent; Canterbury Coll. of Art. NDD. Asst Designer, Graphic Design Dept, BBC, 1965; Designer, Rediffusion, 1966; freelance graphic designer, 1967; Art Dir, Conran Associates, 1968; Dep. to Sen. Designer, ITN, overseeing changeover from black and white to colour TV, 1968; Designer, LWT, working on light entertainment, drama and current affairs progs, 1970; Founder and Creative Director, Robinson Lambie-Nairn Ltd, later Lambie-Nairn, design consultancy producing film and TV graphics, corporate identity, packaging and financial lit., 1976–2008 (Chm., 1976–97); work included Channel 4 TV corporate identity, 1982, develt of original idea for Spitting Image, 1984, Anglia TV corporate identity, 1988, TFI (France) corporate identity, 1989, BBC1 and BBC2 channel identities, 1991, Carlton Television corporate identity, 1993, Orange (Sky NZ) channel identity, and ARTE corporate identity, 1995, BBC corporate identity, 1997–, New Millennium Experience corporate identity, 1998, BAE SYSTEMS corporate identity, 1999; Founder and Partner, ML-N Branding Consultancy, 2008–09, 2011–. Creative Director: NTL, 2001–03; Heavenly, 2010–11. Mem. Cttee, D & AD, 1985– (Pres., 1990–91; Chm., Corporate Identity Jury, 2000); Chm., Graphics Jury, BBC Design Awards, 1987. Visiting Prof., Lincoln Univ., 2006–10. FCSD (FSIAD 1982); FRTS 2004. Hon. Fellow, Kent Inst. of Art and Design, 1994. Hon. DArts: Lincoln, 2004; Northampton, 2010. Jt winner, BAFTA Craft Awards (for excellence in craft of graphics), 1991; RTS Judges' Award, 1996; President's Award, D&AD, 1997; Prince Philip Designers' Prize, 1998; Lion d'Or, Cannes (for brand identity), 2009. *Publications:* Brand Identity for Television with Knobs On, 1997. *Recreations:* opera, family, France.

LAMBIRTH, Mark Nicholas; Director of Corporate Strategy, Department for Transport, 2008–09; *b* 30 May 1953; *s* of late Peter Mabson Lambirth and of Jean Margaret Lambirth; *m* 1986, Anne Catherine Wood. *Educ:* St Albans Sch.; Queens' Coll., Cambridge. Price Commn, 1975; entered Civil Service, 1977; Department of Transport, 1983–95: Ministerial speechwriter and Dep. Head, Inf. Div., 1988–89; Asst Sec., 1989; Head, Public Transport in London Div., 1989–92; Head, Central Finance Div., 1992–95; Under-Sec., 1995; Dir of Planning and Transport, Govt Office for London, 1995–98; Dir of Local Govt Finance Policy, DETR, then of Local Govt Finance, DTLR, 1998–2002; Dir of Railways, then of Rail Strategy and Resources, DTLR, then DfT, 2002–05; Dir of Rail Strategy and Finance, subseq. of Rail Strategy, 2005–07, Dir of Planning and Perf., 2007–08, DfT. *Recreations:* poetry, cooking, wine. *Address:* 13, 28 Oktovriou Street, Mesa Chorio, Paphos 8290, Cyprus. *Club:* MCC.

LAMBTON, family name of **Earl of Durham.**

LAMBTON, Viscount; Frederick Lambton; environmental campaigner; *b* 23 Feb. 1985; *s* and *heir* of Earl of Durham, *qv*. *Educ:* Bedales; Stowe.

LAMBTON, Lucinda; photographer and writer, since 1960; broadcaster, since 1983; *b* 10 May 1943; *e d* of Viscount Lambton (disclaimed Earldom, 1970; *d* 2006), *s* of 5th Earl of Durham, and Belinda, *d* of Major D. H. Blew-Jones; *m* 1st, 1965, Henry Mark Harrod (marr. diss. 1973); two *s*; 2nd, 1986, Sir Edmund Fairfax-Lucy, *qv* (marr. diss. 1989); 3rd, 1991, Sir Peregrine Worsthorne, *qv*. *Educ:* Queensgate Sch., London. Television series include: Hurray for Today, 1989; Hurray for Today, USA, 1990; Lucinda Lambton's Alphabet of Britain (3 series), 1990; Old New World, 2001; Lucinda Lambton's Jamaican Adventure, 2004. Gives talks throughout Britain. Hon. FRIBA 1997. *Publications:* Vanishing Victoriana, 1976; Temples of Convenience, 1978, Chambers of Delight, 1983, combined 3rd edn, 2007; Beastly Buildings, 1985; An Album of Curious Houses, 1988; (ed) Magnificent Menagerie (anthology), 1992; Lucinda Lambton's Alphabet of Britain, 1996; Old New World, 2000; The Queen's Doll House, 2010; Palaces for Pigs, 2011. *Recreations:* looking at buildings, talking to dogs and taking them for walks. *Address:* The Old Rectory, Hedgerley, Bucks SL2 3UY. *T:* (01753) 646167. *Clubs:* Chelsea Arts, City University.

LAMDIN, Rev. Canon Keith Hamilton; Principal, Sarum College, Salisbury, 2008–15; Non-residentiary Canon, Salisbury Cathedral, 2009–15; *b* Eastbourne, 4 Feb. 1947; *s* of Ronald Lamdin and Joan Lamdin; *m* 1970, Ruth Mary Turpin; three *s*. *Educ:* Monkton Combe Sch., Bath; Bristol Univ. (BA 1969). Chaplain, Bristol Univ., 1969–73; Minister, Devizes Baptist Church, 1973–80; Trng Officer, Guisborough Deanery, 1980–83; ordained deacon, 1986, priest, 1987; Diocese of Oxford: Adult Educn Officer, 1983–86; Dir of Trng, 1986–90; Dir, Dept of Stewardship Trng, Evangelism and Ministry, 1990–2008. Honorary Canon: Christ Church, Oxford, 1997–2008, now Emeritus; St Cyprians, Kimberley, SA, 2008–. *Publications:* Ready for Action, 1988; Monday Matters, 1995; Supporting New Ministers in the Local Church, 2007; Finding Your Leadership Style, 2012. *Recreations:* walking, gardening. *Address:* 2 Forge Close, West Overton, Marlborough, Wilts SN8 4PG. *T:* (01672) 861550. *E:* khlamdin@gmail.com.

LAMEY, Steven; Managing Director, Chessdale Ltd, since 2014; *b* 26 Dec. 1955; *s* of Kenneth Gordon Lamey and Sylvia Patricia Lamey; *m* 1981, Ann Williams; one *s* one *d*. *Educ:* UC Cardiff (BSc Mining and Mineral 1978). BOC Group, 1978–99: Proj. Manager; Sen. Ops Manager; European Infrastructure Manager; Inf. Mgt Dir, Global User Service; British Gas Gp, 1999–2004: Vice Pres., Inf. Mgt; Chief Inf. Officer; HM Revenue and Customs: Chief Inf. Officer and Dir Gen., 2004–07; Chief Operating Officer and Dir Gen., 2007–08; Dir Gen., Benefits and Credits, 2008–12; Comr, 2008–12; Chief Operating Officer, Kelway, 2012. *Recreations:* music—Bruce Springsteen/Marillion through to classical/opera, Rugby.

LAMING, Baron *cr* 1998 (Life Peer), of Tewin in the co. of Hertfordshire; **William Herbert Laming,** Kt 1996; CBE 1985; PC 2014; DL; Chief Inspector, Social Services Inspectorate, Department of Health, 1991–98; *b* 19 July 1936; *s* of William Angus Laming and Lillian Laming (*née* Robson); *m* 1962, Aileen Margaret Pollard (*d* 2010). *Educ:* Univ. of Durham (Applied Social Scis); Rainer House (Home Office Probation Trng, 1960–61); LSE (Mental Health Course, 1965–66). Notts Probation Service: Probation Officer, 1961–66; Sen. Probation Officer, 1966–68; Asst Chief Probation Officer, Nottingham City and Co. Probation Service, 1968–71; Dep. Dir, 1971–75, Dir, 1975–91, Social Services, Herts CC. Pres., Assoc. of Dirs Social Services, 1982–83. Chairman: Ind. Inquiry into care and treatment of Ms Justine Cummings, 2000; Modernising the Management of the Prison Service, 2000; Victoria Climbié Inquiry, 2001–03; Progress Report on the Protection of Children, 2009. Convenor, Crossbench Peers, 2011–15. DL Herts, 1999. *Publications:* Lessons from America: the balance of services on social care, 1985. *Address:* House of Lords, SW1A 0PW.

LAMMER, Dr Peter; non-executive Director, Sophos Ltd, since 2006 (Joint Chief Executive Officer, 2000–05); *b* 18 Dec. 1958; *s* of Alfred Ritter von Lammer and Benedicta (*née* Countess Wengersky); one *d*. *Educ:* Alleyn's Sch.; Univ. of Warwick (BSc (Eng) 1981); St John's Coll., Oxford (DPhil 1986). Co-founder, 1985, Man. Dir, 1985–2000, Sophos Ltd. KM 2004. *Recreations:* music, bridge, forestry, old sports cars. *Address:* c/o Sophos Ltd, The Pentagon, Abingdon Science Park, Abingdon, Oxon OX14 3YP. *T:* (01235) 559933. *Club:* Travellers'.

LAMMY, Rt Hon. David (Lindon); PC 2008; MP (Lab) Tottenham, since June 2000; *b* 19 July 1972; *s* of David and Rosalind Lammy; *m* 2005, Nicola Green; two *s*. *Educ:* King's Sch., Peterborough; SOAS, London Univ. (LLB Hons 1993); Harvard Law Sch. (LLM 1997). Called to the Bar, Lincoln's Inn; Attorney, Howard Rice, Calif, 1997–98; with D. J. Freeman, 1998–2000. Mem. (Lab), London Assembly, GLA, May–June 2000. PPS to Sec. of State for Educn and Skills, 2001–02; Parliamentary Under-Secretary of State: DoH, 2002–03; DCA, 2003–05; DCMS, 2005–07; DIUS, 2007–08; Minister of State, DIUS, then BIS, 2008–10. Member: Procedure Cttee, 2001; Public Admin Cttee, 2001; Chair, All Party Parly Gp on Fatherhood, 2013–, on Crossrail2, 2013–, on Race and Equality, on Wellbeing Economics, on London-Stansted-Cambridge Corridor. Member: Gen. Synod, C of E, 1999–2002; Archbishops' Council, 1999–2002. Trustee, ActionAid, 2001–06. *Publications:* Out of the Ashes: Britain after the riots, 2011. *Recreations:* film, theatre, live music, Spurs FC. *Address:* c/o House of Commons, SW1A 0AA. *T:* (020) 7219 0767.

LAMOND, Prof. Angus Iain, PhD; FRS 2010; FRSE; FMedSci; Wellcome Principal Research Fellow and Professor of Biochemistry, Centre for Gene Regulation and Expression, University of Dundee, since 1995; Co-founder, Dundee Cell Products, since 2006. *Educ:* Univ. of Glasgow (BSc Molecular Biol. 1981); Christ's Coll. and St John's Coll., Cambridge (PhD 1984). Postdoctoral trng, MIT, 1984–87; Gp Leader, Eur. Molecular Biol. Lab., Heidelberg, 1987–95. Molecular and Proteomics Prize Lect. in Proteomics, 2012. FRSE 1996; FMedSci 2014. Novartis Medal and Prize, Biochem. Soc., 2011. *Publications:* contribs to jls incl. Current Biol., Jl Cell Biol., EMBO Reports, Molecular & Cellular Proteomics, Molecular Biol. of the Cell, Molecular Cell, Proteomics. *Address:* College of Life Sciences, University of Dundee, Dundee DD1 5EH.

LAMOND, Jilly; *see* Forster, J.

LAMONT, family name of **Baron Lamont of Lerwick.**

LAMONT OF LERWICK, Baron *cr* 1998 (Life Peer), of Lerwick in the Shetland Islands; **Norman Stewart Hughson Lamont;** PC 1986; politician, writer and company director; *b* Lerwick, Shetland, 8 May 1942; *s* of late Daniel Lamont and of Helen Irene; *m* 1971, Alice Rosemary White; one *s* one *d*. *Educ:* Loretto Sch. (scholar); Fitzwilliam Coll., Cambridge (BA; Hon. Fellow 2014). Chm., Cambridge Univ. Conservative Assoc., 1963; Pres., Cambridge Union, 1964. PA to Rt Hon. Duncan Sandys, MP, 1965; Conservative Research Dept, 1966–68; Merchant Banker, N. M. Rothschild & Sons, 1968–79; Dir, Rothschild Asset Mgt, 1978. Non-exec. Dir, N. M. Rothschild & Sons, 1993–95; Director: Balli Gp Plc, 1995–2012; RAB Capital, 2004–11; Jupiter Second Split Trust, 2005–15; Small Companies Dividend Trust, 2008–. Pres., British-Romanian Chamber of Commerce, 2003–; Chm., British-Iranian Chamber of Commerce, 2004–; Adviser to: Romanian Govt, on privatisation, 1995–97; Monsanto Corp., 2006–07; Western Union Corp., 2007–08; Abraaj Gp, 2012–; Stanhope Capital, 2013–. Contested (C) East Hull, Gen. Election, 1970. MP (C) Kingston-upon-Thames, May 1972–97; contested (C) Harrogate and Knaresborough, 1997. PPS to Norman St John-Stevas, MP, Minister for the Arts, 1974; an Opposition Spokesman on: Prices and Consumer Affairs, 1975–76; Industry, 1976–79; Parly Under Sec. of State, Dept of Energy, 1979–81; Minister of State, DTI (formerly DoI), 1981–85; Minister of State for Defence Procurement, 1985–86; Financial Sec. to HM Treasury, 1986–89; Chief Sec. to HM Treasury, 1989–90; Chancellor of the Exchequer, 1990–93. Chairman: G7 Gp of Finance Ministers, 1991; EU Finance Ministers, 1992; Mem., H of L Select Cttee on EU, 1999–2003, EU Sub-Cttee on Economic Affairs, 2005–08, EU Sub-Cttee on External Affairs, 2010–15. Chairman: Coningsby Club, 1970–71; Bow Group, 1971–72; Vice Pres., Bruges Gp; Pres., Economic Res. Council, 2008–. Mem. Adv. Bd, Iran Heritage Foundn, 2011–; Pres., British Inst. for Study of Iraq, 2011–. Pres., Clan Lamont Soc., 2006–08. Commander, Order of Faithful Service (Romania), 2010. *Publications:* Sovereign Britain, 1995; In Office, 1999. *Recreations:* books, ornithology, theatre. *Address:* House of Lords, SW1A 0PW. *T:* (020) 7219 3000. *Clubs:* Garrick, Beefsteak, White's.

LAMONT, Donald Alexander; HM Diplomatic Service, retired; *b* 13 Jan. 1947; *s* of Alexander Lamont and Alexa Lee Lamont (*née* Will); *m* 1981, Lynda Margaret Campbell; one *s* one *d*. *Educ:* Aberdeen Grammar Sch.; Aberdeen Univ. (MA Russian Studies). British Leyland Motor Corp., 1970; Second Sec., subseq. First Sec., FCO, 1974; First Sec., UNIDO/IAEA, Vienna, 1977; First Sec. (Commercial), Moscow, 1980; First Sec., FCO, 1982; Counsellor on secondment to IISS, 1988; Political Advr and Head of Chancery, British Mil. Govt, Berlin, 1988–91; Ambassador to Uruguay, 1991–94; Hd of Republic of Ireland Dept, FCO, 1994–97; COS and Dep. High Rep., Sarajevo, 1997–99; Gov., Falkland Is, and Comr for S Georgia and S Sandwich Is, 1999–2002; Ambassador to Venezuela, 2003–06. Chief Exec., Wilton Park, 2007–09. Mem. Bd, Sistema Scotland, 2007–. Dep. Chm., British Venezuelan Soc., 2011–13; Chm., British Uruguayan Soc., 2014– (Dep. Chm., 2012–14). Chairman: UK Antarctic Heritage Trust, 2013– (Trustee, 2008–); Friends of Falkland Is Mus. and Jane Cameron Nat. Archives, 2013–; Falklands Maritime Heritage Trust, 2014–. Gov., Steyning Grammar Sch., 2010–. *Address:* 3 Southdown Terrace, Steyning, W Sussex BN44 3YJ. *Club:* Caledonian.

LAMONT, Graham William; Chief Executive, Lamont Pridmore, since 1979; *b* Workington, Cumbria, 7 May 1952; *s* of Gordon and Marjorie Lamont; *m* 1986, Maggie Rudd; one *s*. *Educ:* Workington Tech. Sch.; W Cumbria Coll. Chartered Sec. 1973; FCA 1978; FCCA (ACCA 1985). Home Sec.'s Rep., Selection Panel for Ind. Mems, Cumbria Police Authy, 1998–2004. Mem., Cumbria Foot and Mouth Task Force, 2001. Vice Chm., Cumbria Sub-Regl Assembly, 1999–2002; Business Mem., Cumbria Strategic Partnership, 2002–07; Vice Chm., W Cumbria Strategic Partnership, 2007–10; Chair, Cumbria Employment and Skills Bd, 2008–11. Non-executive Member: W Cumbria Healthcare Trust, 1993–2001 (Chm., Audit Cttee); Govt Taskforce to merge Business Link Cumbria, 1996–97 (non-exec. Dir, Activ8: Business Link Cumbria, 2001–05); Enterprise Cumbria, 1998–2001; Cumbria LSC, 2001–08 (Chm., 2006–08); NW LSC, 2006–09. Mem., Cumbria Panel, Rural Develt Commn, 1995–97; Private Sector Mem. Bd, Cumbria LEP, 2013–. Ind. Mem., Cumbria Vision, 2004–05. Founding Pres., Cumbria Chamber of Commerce, 1998–2008. Institute of Chartered Accountants of England and Wales: Member: Financial Services Authorisation Cttee, 1997–98; nat. taskforce on How to Create the Modern Gen. Accountancy Practice, 2001–03; Ed., Adding Value newsletter, 2000–05; Mem. Cttee, 1987–94, Courses Chm., 1990–93, Chm., 1992–93, Cumberland Soc. Chartered Accountants; Mem. Cttee, 1991–93, Mem., Tech. Adv. Cttee, 1993–94, Northern Soc. of Chartered Accountants. Jt Chair, Theatre by the Lake, Keswick, 1984–. Governor: St Bees Sch., 1997–2002; Lakes Coll., W Cumbria, 2001–04; Carlisle Coll., 2002–04. MCMI 1990; MIMC 2002. FRSA 2007. High Sheriff Cumbria, 2008–09. *Publications:* 57 Ways to Grow Your Business, 2013. *Recreations:* theatre, art, reading, jogging, golf. *Address:* Bank Farm, Lorton, Cockermouth, Cumbria CA13 0RQ. *T:* (01900) 85617. *E:* bank.farm@virgin.net.

LAMONT, Johann MacDougall; Member (Lab) Glasgow Pollok, Scottish Parliament, since 1999; *b* 11 July 1957; *y d* of Archie Lamont and Effie Lamont (*née* Macleod); *m* Archie Graham; one *s* one *d*. *Educ:* Univ. of Glasgow (MA Hons); Jordanhill Coll. of Educn (postgrad. secondary teaching qualification). Secondary School teacher, 1979–99. Dep. Minister for Communities, 2004–06, for Justice, 2006–07, Scottish Exec. Dep. Leader, 2008–11, Leader, 2011–14, Labour Party, Scottish Parlt. Mem., EIS, 1979–. *Recreations:* running, watching football, doing crosswords, enjoying time with my children. *Address:* Scottish Parliament, Edinburgh EH99 1SP.

LAMONT, John; Member (C) Ettrick, Roxburgh and Berwickshire, Scottish Parliament, since 2011 (Roxburgh and Berwickshire, 2007–11); *b* 15 April 1976; *s* of Robert Lamont and Elizabeth Lamont. *Educ:* Kilwinning Acad.; Univ. of Glasgow. Solicitor: Freshfields, 2000–04; Bristows, 2004–05; Brodies, 2005–07. Contested (C) Berwickshire, Roxburgh and Selkirk, 2005, 2010, 2015. *Recreations:* travel, running, swimming, cycling. *Address:* Scottish Parliament, Edinburgh EH99 1SP. *T:* (0131) 348 6533, *Fax:* (0131) 348 5932; 25 High Street, Hawick, Roxburghshire TD9 9BU. *E:* john.lamont.msp@scottish.parliament.uk.

LAMONTAGNE, Hon. (J.) Gilles; PC (Can.) 1978; OC 1990; CQ 2000; CD 1980; Lieutenant-Governor of Quebec, 1984–90; *b* 17 April 1919; *s* of Trefflé Lamontagne and Anna Kieffer; *m* 1949, Mary Katherine Schaefer (*d* 2006); three *s* one *d*. *Educ:* Collège Jean-de-Bréboeuf, Montréal, Québec (BA). Served RCAF, 1941–45 (despatches, 1945). Businessman in Québec City, 1946–66. Alderman, Québec City, 1962–64, Mayor, 1965–77. MP (L) Langelier, 1977–84; Parly Sec. to Minister of Energy, Mines and Resources, 1977; Minister without Portfolio, Jan. 1978; Postmaster Gen., Feb. 1978–1979; Actg Minister of Veterans Affairs, 1980–81; Minister of National Defence, 1980–83. Dir, Québec City Chamber of Commerce and Industry; Member: Econ. Council of Canada; Br. 260, Royal Canadian Legion (Grand Pres., 1991–94). Special Counsel, GPC Internat. (formerly GPC Consilium, then GPC Relations gouvernementales), 2002 (Consultant, 1992; Sen. Counsel, 1995). Mem. Bd, Canadian Centre of Substance Abuse, 1991–95. Chm. Bd of Govs, Royal Mil. Coll., Kingston, Canada, 1995–2002. Hon. Col, Tactical Aviation Wing (Montreal), 1987. KStJ 1985. Hon. LLD Kingston Royal Mil. Coll., 1986; Hon. DAdmin St Jean Royal Mil. Coll., 1989. UN Medal 1987. Croix du Combattant de l'Europe; Chevalier, Légion d'honneur (France), 2006. *Address:* 8 Jardins Mérici # 1405, Quebec, QC G1S 4N9, Canada. *Clubs:* Cercle de la Garnison de Québec, Royal Québec Golf.

LAMONTE, Air Vice Marshal Dr Jonathan; DL; Chief Executive, Transport for Greater Manchester, since 2013; *b* London, 30 Dec. 1959; *s* of late Jack Lamonte and of Sheila Lamonte. *Educ:* Southgate Sch., Cockfosters, Herts; Keele Univ. (BSc Maths and Geol.); King's Coll. London (MA Defence Studies); Birmingham Univ. (PhD History 2011). CMath, FIMA 1993; CDipAF 2001; FRIN 2002; FRICS 2013; FCILT 2013. Hercules navigator, No 24 Sqdn, 1984–86; Instructor, No 6 Flying Trng Sch., RAF Finningley, 1986–87; Gen. Duties, Aerosystems Course, 1987–88; Flt Comdr, No 115 (Andover) Sqdn, RAF Benson, 1988–92; SO, MoD, 1993–96; OC No 30 (Hercules) Sqdn, RAF Lyneham, 1996–98; Strategic Defence Rev. Implementation, MoD, 1998–99; Dep. Dir, Resources and Plans Centre, MoD, 1999–2001; Detachment Comdr, Ali-Al-Salem Air Base, Kuwait, 2001; OC, RAF Brize Norton, 2002–04; Dir, Resources and Prog. Mgt, Defence Logistics Orgn, 2005–07; Dir, Material Progs, 2007–08, Dir Gen. Finance, 2008, Defence Equipment and Support Orgn; COS for Strategy, Policy and Plans, RAF, 2009–10; Chief Exec., Tube Lines Ltd, 2011–12. Slessor Fellow, Univ. of Birmingham, 2008. CCMI 2012 (FCMI 2005); Fellow and Chartered Dir, IoD, 2007. FRSA 2013. President: Southgate and Wood Green RAFA, 1998–2014; No 2267 Sqdn ATC, 2002–14; No 2473 Sqdn ATC, 2009–14. Freeman, City of London, 1996. Liveryman, Hon. Co. of Air Pilots (formerly GAPAN), 2002–. DL Gtr Manchester, 2014. *Address:* Transport for Greater Manchester, 2 Piccadilly Place, Manchester M1 3BG.

LAMPARD, Kathryn Felice, (Kate), (Mrs John Leigh-Pemberton), CBE 2015; DL; Vice Chairman, NHS South of England, 2011–13; *b* London, 20 April 1960; *d* of Martin Robert Lampard and Felice Lampard; *m* 1986, Hon. John Leigh-Pemberton; two *s* one *d*. *Educ:* Exeter Univ. (BA Hons); City Univ. (Dip. Law); Inns of Court Sch. of Law. Called to the Bar, Lincoln's Inn, 1984; in practice as barrister, 1984–97; non-exec. Dir, W Kent HA, 1997–2000; Chairman: Invicta Community Care NHS Trust, 2000–02; Kent and Medway Strategic HA, 2002–06; Consultant to NHS and other public bodies, 2006–09; Chm., SE Coast Strategic HA, 2009–11. Overseer, DoH and NHS investigations into activities of Jimmy Savile, 2012–. Non-executive Director: Ind. Housing Ombudsman, 1997–2000 (Chm., 2000–02); Financial Ombudsman Service Ltd, 2002–12. Non-exec. Dir, RHS Enterprises Ltd, 2008–11. Trustee, Esmée Fairbairn Foundn, 2000–. DL Kent, 2002. *Recreations:* gardens and gardening, family life, sea bathing. *Address:* Yokes Court, Frinsted, Sittingbourne, Kent ME9 0ST.

LAMPERT, Catherine Emily; independent curator; Director, Whitechapel Art Gallery, 1988–2001; *b* 15 Oct. 1946; *d* of Emily F. Schubach and Chester G. Lampert; *m* 1st, 1971, Robert Keith Mason (marr. diss. 1994); one adopted *d*; 2nd, 2006, (James) Andrew Dempsey, *qv*. *Educ:* Brown Univ. (BA); Temple Univ. (MFA). UCL, 1966–67; Asst Curator, RI Sch. of Design, Mus. of Art, 1968–69; Studio Internat., 1971–72; Sen. Exhibn Organiser, Hayward Gall., 1973–88. Vis. Prof., Univ. of the Arts, 2007–. Curator: Frank Auerbach: painting and drawing 1954–2001, RA, 2001–02; Nan Goldin, Centre Pompidou and tour, 2001; Lucian Freud, Dublin, Humlebaek, The Hague, 2007–08; Miquel Barceló, CaixaForum, Madrid, CaixaForum Barcelona, 2010; Francis Alÿs, Dublin 2010; Daumier, RA, 2013; Co-curator: Rodin, RA, 2006; Bare Life: London artists working from life 1950–80, LWL-Mus. für Kunst und Kultur, Münster, 2014. *Publications:* Rodin: sculpture and drawings, 1986; Lucian Freud: recent work, 1993; The Prophet and the Fly: Francis Alÿs, 2003; Euan Uglow: the complete paintings, 2007. Peter Doig, 2011; The Mystery of Appearance: conversations between ten post-war British painters, 2011; Frank Auerbach: speaking and painting, 2015; numerous catalogue essays on Frank Auerbach, Barry Flanagan, Tony Cragg, Francisco Toledo and other subjects of Twentieth Century art. *Address:* 92 Lenthall Road, E8 3JN. *T:* (020) 7249 7650.

LAMPL, Sir Peter, Kt 2003; OBE 2000; Chairman: Sutton Trust, since 1997; Education Endowment Foundation, since 2011; *b* 21 May 1947; *s* of Frederick and Margaret Lampl; *m* 1st, 1976, Janet Clowes (marr. diss. 1980); 2nd, 1994, Karen Gordon (marr. diss. 2010; she *d* 2013); one *s* two *d*; 3rd, Susan. *Educ:* Reigate Grammar Sch.; Cheltenham Grammar Sch.; Corpus Christi Coll., Oxford (BA, MA; Hon. Fellow, 1998); London Business Sch. (MBA). Mktg Exec., Beecham Gp, London, 1970–71; Mgt Consultant, Boston Consulting Gp, Boston, Paris, Munich, 1973–77; Dir, Planning and Business Develt, Internat. Paper, NY, then Pres., Internat. Paper Realty, 1977–83; Founder, Pres., then Chm., Sutton Co. (private equity firm), NY, London, Munich, 1983–97; Founder, Sutton Trust, 1997 (provides educnl opportunities for young people from non-privileged backgrounds). Ind. Advr to Sec. of State for Educn, 2000–. Member: Bd, Specialist Schs and Academies Trust, 1999–2008; Council for Industry and Higher Educn, 2002–09; Social Mkt Foundn, 2002–; Teach First, 2002–05. Mem. Council, KCL, 2001–04; Chm., Develt Bd, Corpus Christi Coll., Oxford, 2002–06. Hon. Fellow: Birkbeck Coll., London, 2007; LSE, 2008; London Business Sch., 2009. Hon. DSc: Nottingham, 1999; Imperial Coll. London, 2004; City, 2007; Hon. Dr jur Bristol, 2001; DUniv: Birmingham, 2003; Brunel, 2004; Hon. LLD Exeter, 2010; Hon. DLaws Coll. of Law, 2010; Hon. DCL Durham, 2013. *Recreations:* golf, tennis, ski-ing, swimming, body surfing, opera. *Address:* The Sutton Trust, 9th Floor, Millbank Tower, 21–24 Millbank, SW1P 4QP. *T:* (020) 7802 1660. *Clubs:* Athenæum, Queen's, Hurlingham, Royal Automobile, Roehampton; Wisley Golf (Surrey); Queenwood Golf (Surrey); Westchester Country (NY); Pine Tree Golf (Palm Beach).

LAMPORT, Sir Stephen (Mark Jeffrey), KCVO 2002 (CVO 1999); DL; Chapter Clerk and Receiver General, Westminster Abbey, since 2008; *b* 27 Nov. 1951; *s* of Eric and late Jeanne Lamport; *m* 1979, Angela Vivien Paula Hervey; two *s* one *d*. *Educ:* Dorking Co. Grammar Sch.; Corpus Christi Coll., Cambridge (Schol., MA); Sussex Univ. (MA). HM Diplomatic Service, 1974–2002: UK Mission to UN, 1974; Tehran, 1975–79; FCO, 1979–84; Private Secretary to Minister of State, 1981–84; First Sec., Rome, 1984–88; FCO, 1988–93; Dep. Private Sec. to the Prince of Wales, 1993–96; Private Sec. and Treas. to the Prince of Wales, 1996–2002; Gp Dir, RBS, 2002–07. Non-exec. Dir, Brewin Dolphin Holdings plc, 2007–15. Member: Exec. Cttee, British Red Cross Queen Mother Meml Fund, 2003–06; Court, Royal Foundn of St Katharine, 2004–; Council of Mgt, Arvon Foundn, 2004–08; Council, Guildford Cathedral, 2006–10; Chm., British Red Cross Flood Relief Adv. Panel, 2007–08. Trustee, Community Foundn for Surrey (formerly Surrey Community Foundn), 2006–10 (Vice-Pres., 2010–). DL Surrey, 2006. *Publications:* (with D. Hurd) The Palace of Enchantments, 1985. *Address:* Westminster Abbey, SW1P 3PA. *Clubs:* Royal Automobile (Mem., Bd of Dirs, 2012–), Grillion's.

LAMPSON, family name of **Baron Killearn.**

LAMY, Pascal Lucien Fernand; Director General, World Trade Organisation, 2005–13; *b* 8 April 1947; *s* of Jacques Lamy and Denise (*née* Dujardin); *m* 1972, Geneviève Luchaire; three *s*. *Educ:* Ecole des Hautes Etudes Commerciales; Inst d'Etudes Politiques, Paris; Ecole Nat. d'Admin. Inspector-Gen. of Finances, 1975–79; French Treasury, 1979–81; Advr to Minister for Econ. Affairs and Finance, 1981–83; Dep. Hd, Prime Minister's Pvte Office, 1983–84; Head, Pvte Office of Pres. of EC, 1985–94; with Crédit Lyonnais, 1994–99, Dir Gen., 1997; Mem., European Commn, 1999–2004. Mem. Steering Cttee, Socialist Party of France, 1985–94. Member: Global Ocean Commn; UNAIDS; Lancet Commn. Trustee Dir, Thomson Reuters, 2009–. President: World Cttee of Tourism Ethics; Conseil d'Admin des Musiciens du Louvre-Grenoble, 2009–; Vice-Pres., Foundn for European Progressive Studies; Hon. Pres., Notre Europe, Jacques Delors Inst. Dr *hc*: Geneva, 2009; Warwick, 2009; Montréal, 2010; Dhaka, 2012; Edinburgh, 2012. Officier, Légion d'Honneur, 1999; Grosses Verdienstkreuz (Germany), 1991; Commandeur de l'Ordre Nat. du Mérite (Luxembourg), 1995; Officer, Order of Merit (Gabon), 2000; Order of Aztec Eagle (Mexico), 2003; Médaille de la Fraternité (Vietnam), 2007. *Publications:* (jtly) L'Europe de nos Volontes, 2000; L'Europe en Première Ligne, 2002; La Démocratie-monde, 2004; The Geneva Consensus, 2013; Quand la France s'éveillera, 2014. *Address:* Jacques Delors Institute, 19 rue de Milan, 75009 Paris, France.

LAN, David Mark, CBE 2014; PhD; playwright, producer, director and social anthropologist; Artistic Director, Young Vic Theatre, since 2000; Consulting Artistic Director, Performing Arts Center, World Trade Center, New York, since 2013; *b* 1 June 1952; *s* of Joseph Lan and Lois Lan (*née* Carklin). *Educ:* Univ. of Cape Town (BA 1972); London Sch. of Econs (BSc; PhD 1984). Writer in Residence, Royal Court Th., 1995–97. *Plays:* Painting a Wall, Almost Free Th., 1974; Bird Child, 1974, Homage to Been Soup, Paradise, The Winter Dancers, 1975, Royal Ct Th. Upstairs; Red Earth, ICA, 1976; Not in Norwich, Royal Ct Young People's Th. Scheme, 1977; Sergeant Ola and His Followers, Royal Ct, 1979; (with C. Churchill) A Mouthful of Birds, Jt Stock Th. Gp, 1986; Flight, RSC, 1986; Ghetto (English trans. of play by Joshua Sobol), NT, 1989; Desire, 1990, Hippolytos (version of Euripides' play), 1991, Almeida; Ion (version of Euripides' play), RSC, 1994; The Ends of the Earth, NT, 1996; Uncle Vanya (new version), RSC at Young Vic, 1998; La Lupa (English version of play by Giovanni Verga), RSC, 2000; Cherry Orchard (new version), NT, 2000; *television:* BBC 2: The Sunday Judge, 1985; The Crossing, 1988; Welcome Home Comrades, Dark City, 1989; *film:* (jtly) Streets of Yesterday, 1988; *radio:* Charley Tango, Radio 4 and World Service, 1995; *libretti:* Tobias and the Angel, 1999, Ion, 2000, The Magic Flute (trans.), 2008, Almeida Opera; *director:* Artist Unknown, 1995, Royal Court Diaries, 1996, BBC 1; The Glass Menagerie, Palace Th., Watford, 1998; for Young Vic: Tis Pity She's a Whore, 1999; Julius Caesar, 2000; A Raisin in the Sun, 2001, tour 2005; Dr Faustus, The Daughter-in-Law, 2002; The Skin of Our Teeth, 2004; As You Like It, Wyndham's, 2005; The Soldier's Fortune, 2007; Joe Turner's Come and Gone, 2010; Blackta, 2012. Chm., Belarus Free Theatre, 2012–; Mem. Bd, Motley Theatre Design Sch., 2013–. Hon. DLitt London South Bank, 2009. John Whiting Award, Arts Council, 1975; George Orwell Award, 1980; Zurich Internat. TV Award, 1989; Laurence Olivier Award, 2004. *Publications:* Guns and Rain: guerillas and spirit mediums in Zimbabwe, 1985; all plays published. *Address:* c/o Judy Daish Associates, 2 St Charles Place, W10 6EG. *T:* (020) 8964 8811.

LANCASHIRE, Sarah Jane Abigail, (Mrs P. Salmon); actress; *b* 10 Oct. 1964; *d* of late Geoffrey Lancashire and of Hilda Lancashire (*née* McCormack); *m* 1st, 1987, Gary Hargreaves (marr. diss. 1997); two *s*; 2nd, 2001, Peter Salmon, *qv*; one *s*. *Educ:* Werneth Private Prep. Sch., Oldham; Hulme Grammar Sch. for Girls, Oldham; Oldham Coll. of Technol.; Guildhall Sch. of Music and Drama. Lectr (pt-time), Salford Univ. Coll., 1987–90. *Theatre:* professional début, The Beauty Game and Pacific Overtures, Manchester Liby Th., 1986; Educating Rita, Hornchurch, 1991; The Little Shop of Horrors, Oldham, 1993; West End début, Blood Brothers, Albery, 1990; Betty Blue Eyes, Novello, 2011; *television:* Coronation Street, 1991–96 (Best Actress Award, RTS (NW), 1996); Where the Heart Is, 1996–99; Blooming Marvellous, 1997; Clocking Off, 1999; Seeing Red, 1999 (Best Actress, Nat. TV Awards, 2000; Drama TV Performer of Year, TV and Radio Industry Awards, 2001); Chambers, 2000; Gentleman's Relish, 2000; My Fragile Heart, 2000; The Cry, 2000 (Best Actress, Monte Carlo TV Fest., 2002); The Glass, 2000; The Birthday Girl, 2001; Sons and Lovers, 2002; Rose & Maloney, 2002–05; Rotters' Club, 2004; Cherished, 2004; All the Small Things, 2009; Wuthering Heights, 2009; Five Daughters, 2010; The Paradise, 2012, 2013; Last Tango in Halifax, 2012–15; Happy Valley, 2014; Dir, Viva las Blackpool, 2003 (Best New Talent, RTS (Midlands), 2004). Hon. MA Salford, 2002. *Recreations:* gardening, family, cinema. *Address:* c/o Independent Talent Group Ltd, 40 Whitfield Street, W1T 2RH.

LANCASTER, Bishop Suffragan of, since 2006; **Rt Rev. Geoffrey Seagrave Pearson;** *b* 18 July 1951; *m* 1973, Jean Richardson; one *s* two *d*. *Educ:* St John's Coll., Durham (BA 1972); Cranmer Hall, Durham. Ordained deacon, 1974, priest, 1975; Asst Curate, Kirkheaton, 1974–77; Curate-in-charge, 1977–82, Incumbent, 1982–85, Ch of the Redeemer, Blackburn; Asst Home Sec., Gen. Synod Bd for Mission and Unity, and Hon. Curate, Forty Hill, 1985–89; Vicar, Roby, 1989–2006. Exec. Sec., BCC Evangelism Cttee, 1986–89; Area Dean, Huyton, 2002–06; Hon. Canon, Liverpool Cathedral, 2003–06. *Address:* Shireshead Vicarage, Forton, Preston PR3 0AE.

LANCASTER, Bishop of, (RC), since 2009; **Rt Rev. Michael Gregory Campbell,** OSA; *b* Larne, NI, 2 Oct. 1941. *Educ:* Campion House, Osterley; University Coll. Dublin (BA); Gregorian Univ., Rome; King's Coll. London (MA Biblical Studies). Entered Augustinian Order, Clare Priory, 1962; ordained priest, 1971; Teacher/Chaplain, Christ the King Sch., Southport; Parish Curate, St John Stone's, 1972–75; Prior of the Community, St Monica's, Hoxton, 1972–85; Teacher/Chaplain, Bishop Challoner Girls' Sch., London, 1972–85; Lectr, St Augustine's Major Seminary, Jos, Nigeria, 1985–89; Episcopal Vicar, Dio. of Lancaster, 1990–99; Prior and Parish Priest, St Augustine's, Hammersmith. *Address:* Bishop's Office, The Pastoral Centre, Balmoral Road, Lancaster LA1 3BT.

LANCASTER, Archdeacon of; *see* Everitt, Ven. M. J.

LANCASTER, Anthony Trevor; His Honour Judge Lancaster; a Circuit Judge, since 2001; Designated Diversity and Community Relations Judge for Cumbria, since 2011; *b* 26 June 1948; *s* of late Thomas William Lancaster and of Jean Margaret Lancaster (*née* Grainger); *m* 2012, Louise Askins; four *s* two *d* by previous marriage. *Educ:* Austin Friars Sch., Carlisle; Univ. of Leeds (LLB Hons 1970). Admitted solicitor, 1973; in private practice, 1973–88; County Court Registrar, 1988–91; a Dist Judge, 1991–2001; Asst Recorder, 1995–99; a Recorder, 1999–2001. Pt-time Chm., Social Security Appeals Tribunal, 1985–88. Pres., Assoc. of Dist Judges, 2000–01. *Recreations:* cooking, music. *Address:* Lancaster County Court, Mitre House, Church Street, Lancaster LA1 1UZ. *T:* (01524) 68112.

LANCASTER, (Charles) Roy, CBE 2014 (OBE 1999); freelance author, lecturer, plant explorer and dendrologist, since 1980; *b* 5 Dec. 1937; *s* of Charles and Norah Lancaster; *m* 1977, Susan Lloyd; one *s* one *d*. *Educ:* Castle Hill Co. Secondary Sch., Bolton; Cambridge Univ. Botanic Garden. Curator, Hillier Arboretum, 1970–80. Member: Mgt Cttee, Sir Harold Hillier Gardens and Arboretum, 1990–2007 (Patron, 2007–); Arboreta Adv. Cttee, Nat. Arboreta (formerly Consultative Cttee, Westonbirt Nat. Arboretum), 1990–; Gardens Panel, NT, 2000–09; Vice Chm., Woody Plant Cttee (formerly Floral Cttee B), RHS, 1998–2010. Vice Pres., RHS, 2005–; Pres., The Hardy Plant Soc., 2007–. Trustee, Tree Register of British Isles, 2001–; Patron, Soc. of Floral Painters, 2008–. Veitch Meml Medal, RHS, 1972; VMH 1989; Inst. of Horticulture Award, 1996; TV Gardening Presenter of the Year, 1993, Lifetime Achievement Award, 2002, Garden Writers' Guild; Journalist of the Year, Garden Media Guild, 2008. *Publications:* Trees for your Garden, 1974; (with Vicomte Noailles) Mediterranean Gardens and Plants, 1977; A Plantsman in Nepal, 1981; In Search of the Wild Asparagus, 1983; Garden Plants for Connoisseurs, 1987; Travels in China: a plantsman's paradise, 1989; Garden Shrubs Through the Seasons, 1991; What Plant Where, 1995; What Perennial Where, 1997; (with Matthew Biggs) What House Plant Where, 1998; Perfect Plant Perfect Place, 2001; contribs to Gdn Jl of RHS. *Recreations:* bird watching, walking, travel, gardening, music. *Address:* 58 Brownhill Road, Chandlers Ford, Hants SO53 2EG. *Club:* Farmers.

LANCASTER, (John) Mark, TD 2002; DSc; MP (C) Milton Keynes North, since 2010 (Milton Keynes North East, 2005–10); Parliamentary Under-Secretary of State, Ministry of Defence, since 2015; *b* 12 May 1970; *s* of Rev. Ronald Lancaster, *qv*; *m* (marr. diss.); one *d*; *m* 2014, Caroline Dinenage, *qv*; two step *s*. *Educ:* Kimbolton Sch., Cambs; Buckingham Univ. (BSc 1992; DSc 2007); Exeter Univ. (MBA 1993). Served Army, RE, 1988–90; Officer, TA, RE, 1990–. Dir, Kimbolton Fireworks Ltd, 1993–2005. PPS to Sec. of State for Internat. Develt, 2010–12; a Lord Comr of HM Treasury (Govt Whip), 2012–15. Mem. (C) Huntingdon DC, 1995–99. Consultant, Palmer Capital Partners, 2010–12. *Publications:* (contrib.) Fireworks Principles and Practice, 3rd edn 1998. *Recreations:* collector and restorer of classic British motorcycles, avid football supporter. *Address:* House of Commons, SW1A 0AA. *E:* lancasterm@parliament.uk.

LANCASTER, Rev. Ronald, MBE 1993; Founder, 1964, Managing Director, 1986–2006, Director and Chairman, since 2007, Kimbolton Fireworks Limited; *b* 9 March 1931; *s* of Jack and Kathleen Lancaster; *m* 1966, Kathleen Smith; one *s* one *d*. *Educ:* Durham Univ. (BA 1953; MA 1956); Cuddesdon Coll., Oxford. Ordained deacon, 1957, priest, 1958; Curate: St Peter, Morley, Yorks, 1957–60; St Peter, Harrogate, 1960–63; Chaplain, Kimbolton Sch., Huntingdon, 1963–88. Hon. CChem, FRSC 1983. Hon. MSc Durham, 2009. *Publications:* Fireworks Principles and Practice, 1972, 4th edn 2006. *Recreations:* gardening, organist. *Address:* 7 High Street, Kimbolton, Huntingdon, Cambs PE28 0HB. *T:* (01480) 860498, *Fax:* (01480) 861277. *E:* ron@kimboltonfireworks.co.uk.

See also J. M. Lancaster.

LANCASTER, Roy; *see* Lancaster, C. R.

LANCE, Seán Patrick; Chairman, African Leadership Institute, since 2003; *b* 4 Aug. 1947; *s* of James Lance and Kathleen (*née* Carmody); *m* 1st, 1969, Pamela Joan Gray (marr. diss. 1990); two *s* two *d*; 2nd, 1990, Patricia Anne (*née* Bungay). *Educ:* Christian Brothers Coll., Pretoria. Noristan Gp, S Africa, 1967–82; Chm., Boots Co., S Africa, 1982–85; Man. Dir, Glaxo, S Africa, 1985–87; Regl Dir (London), Glaxo Hldgs plc, 1987–89; Man. Dir, Glaxo Pharms UK Ltd, 1989–93; Dir, Glaxo Hldgs plc, 1993–97; Chief Operating Officer, Glaxo Wellcome plc, 1997; Chief Exec. and Pres., 1998–2003, Chm., Bd of Dirs, 1998–2004, Chiron Corp. Mem., Supervisory Bd, Crucell, 2004–10. President: Proprietary Assoc. of S Africa, 1983–84; Pharmaceutical Manufacturers Assoc. of S Africa, 1987–88; Internat. Fedn of Pharmaceut. Manufacturers Assoc., 1996–2000; Vice-Pres., Assoc. of British Pharmaceutical Industry, 1993–94. Special Forces, S Africa, 1965–75. *Recreations:* hockey, golf, football, cricket, Kyukoshin karate (2nd Dan). *Clubs:* Special Forces; Harlequins, Pretoria Country (Pretoria); Richmond Hockey.

LANCELOT, James Bennett, FRCO; Master of the Choristers and Organist, Durham Cathedral, since 1985; *b* 2 Dec. 1952; *s* of late Rev. Roland Lancelot; *m* 1982, Sylvia Jane (*née* Hoare); two *d*. *Educ:* St Paul's Cathedral Choir Sch.; Ardingly Coll.; Royal College of Music (ARCM); King's Coll., Cambridge (Dr Mann Organ Student; MA; BMus). Asst Organist, St Clement Danes and Hampstead Parish Ch., 1974–75; Sub-Organist, Winchester Cath., 1975–85; Asst Conductor, Winchester Music Club, 1983–85; Conductor, Durham Univ. Choral Soc., 1987–2013; Organist, Durham Univ., 2002–. Member: Council, RCO, 1988–99, 2002–06; Cathedrals Liturgy Gp, 1993–2003. President: Cathedral Organists' Assoc., 2001–03; Darlington and Dist Organists' and Choirmasters' Assoc., 2004–05; IAO, 2013–15. Lay Canon, Durham Cathedral, 2002–. Hon. FGCM 2002; Hon. FRSCM 2008; Hon. Fellow, St Chad's Coll., Durham, 2006. Hon. DMus Durham, 2014. Has played or conducted premières, incl. Mathias' Berceuse, Tavener's Ikon of St Cuthbert, Josephs' Mass for St Cuthbert, MacMillan's Missa Dunelmi, Casken Magnificat and Nunc dimittis. Organ recitals and broadcasts in UK; concerts in Germany, Denmark, France, Norway, Sweden, Poland, Belgium, Russia, Brazil, Canada, USA, NZ. Recordings with choirs of King's Coll., Cambridge, Winchester Cath., Durham Cath., and as soloist. *Publications:* (with R. Hird)

Durham Cathedral Organs, 1991; (contrib.) The Sense of the Sacramental, 1993. *Recreations:* railways, the works of John Buchan. *Address:* 6 The College, Durham DH1 3EQ. *T:* (0191) 3864766.

LANCHESTER, John Henry, FRSL; writer; *b* Hamburg, 25 Feb. 1962; *s* of G. W., (Bill), Lanchester and Julie Lanchester; *m* 1994, Miranda Carter; two *s*. *Educ:* Gresham's Sch., Holt; St John's Coll., Oxford (BA 1st cl. Hons; Violet Vaughan Morgan Award, Charles Oldham Shakespeare Prize). Asst Ed., London Review of Books, 1987–91; Ed., Penguin Books, 1991–92; Dep. Ed., London Review of Books, 1993–96. FRSL 2003. *Publications:* The Debt to Pleasure, 1996 (Whitbread First Novel Award, Betty Trask Prize, 1996; Hawthornden Prize, Julia Child Award, 1997); Mr Phillips, 2000; Fragrant Harbour, 2002 (Premi Llibreter, 2005); Family Romance, 2007 (E. M. Forster Award, AAAL, 2008); Whoops!: why everyone owes everyone and no one can pay, 2010; Capital, 2012; How to Speak Money, 2014. *Recreation:* watching television. *Address:* c/o A. P. Watt Ltd, United Agents, 12–26 Lexington Street, W1F 0LE. *T:* (020) 3214 0800, *Fax:* (020) 3214 0801. *E:* apw@apwatt.co.uk.

LANCHIN, Gerald, OBE 2001; consultant; *b* 17 Oct. 1922; *o s* of late Samuel Lanchin, Kensington; *m* 1st, 1951, Valerie Sonia Lyons (*d* 2009); one *s* two *d*; 2nd, 2010, Anne Robinson. *Educ:* St Marylebone Grammar Sch.; London Sch. of Economics. BCom 1st cl. hons 1951; Leverhulme Schol. 1950–51. Min. of Labour, 1939–51; served with Army, RAOC and REME, 1942–46; Board of Trade (subseq. DTI and Dept of Trade): Asst Principal, 1952; Principal 1953; 1st Sec., UK Delegn to OEEC, Paris, 1955–59; Principal, Estabt and Commercial Relations and Exports Divs, 1959–66; Asst Sec., Finance and Civil Aviation Divs, 1966–71; Under-Sec., Tariff, Commercial Relations and Export, Shipping Policy, General and Consumer Affairs Divs, 1971–82. Chairman: Packaging Council, 1983–84; Direct Mail Services Standards Bd, 1983–89; Member: Council, Consumers' Assoc., 1983–88; Data Protection Tribunal 1985–98; Consumer Panel, PIA, 1994–98; Financial Services Consumer Panel, 1998–2000. A Vice-Pres., Nat. Fedn of Consumer Gps, 1984–2002. Mem., Berkhamsted Town Council, 1997–2007. FRSA. *Publications:* Government and the Consumer, 1985. *Recreations:* photography, reading, music. *Address:* 28 Priory Gardens, Berkhamsted, Herts HP4 2DS. *T:* (01442) 875283.

LAND, Alastair; *see* Land, W. M. A.

LAND, Dame Gillian; *see* Lynne, Dame Gillian.

LAND, Prof. Michael Francis, FRS 1982; PhD; Professor of Neurobiology, University of Sussex, since 1984; *b* 12 April 1942; *s* of late Prof. Frank William Land and of Nora Beatrice Channon; *m* 1980, Rosemary (*née* Clarke); one *s* one *d* (and one *d* decd). *Educ:* Birkenhead Sch., Cheshire; Jesus Coll., Cambridge (MA); University Coll. London (PhD). Asst Lectr in Physiology, UCL, 1966–67; Miller Fellow, 1967–79, and Asst Prof. of Physiology-Anatomy, 1979–81, Univ. of Calif, Berkeley; Lectr in Biol Sciences, 1971–77, Reader, 1977–84, Univ. of Sussex. Vis. Prof., Univ. of Oregon, 1980; Sen. Res. Fellow, ANU, 1982–84. Frink Medal, Zool Soc. of London, 1994; Rank Prize for Optoelectronics, 1998. *Publications:* (with D. E. Nilsson) Animal Eyes, 2002, 2nd edn 2012; (with B. W. Tatler) Looking and Acting, 2009; A Very Short Introduction to the Eye, 2014; numerous papers on animal and human vision in learned jls. *Recreations:* photography, music. *Address:* Dart Cottage, 1 The Elms, Ringmer, East Sussex BN8 5EZ. *T:* (01273) 813911.

LAND, Nicholas Charles Edward, FCA; Chairman, Ernst & Young, 1995–2006; *b* 6 Feb. 1948; *s* of Charles and Norma Land; *m* 1975, Sonia Tan; one *s*. *Educ:* Steyning Grammar Sch. FCA 1971. Articled Spain Brothers Dalling & Co., 1967–71; joined Turquand Young, later Ernst & Young, 1971: Partner, 1978–2006; Managing Partner, London Office, 1986–92; Managing Partner, 1992–95; Mem., Global Exec. Bd, 1992–2006; Chm., Northern Europe, Middle East, India and Africa Area, 2001–06. Non-executive Director: Royal Dutch Shell plc, 2006–10; BBA Aviation plc (formerly BBA Gp plc), 2006–; Ashmore Gp plc, 2006–; Vodafone Gp plc, 2006–; Alliance Boots GmbH, 2008–15; Financial Reporting Council, 2011– (Chm., Codes and Standards Cttee, 2015–); Advisory Board Member: Three Delta LLP, 2006–11; Aecus Ltd (formerly Alsbridge plc), 2010–14. Chairman: Practice Adv. Bd, ICAEW, 2006–10; Audit and Assurance Council (formerly Auditing Practices Bd), 2012–15; Guidelines Monitoring Gp, BVCA, 2013–; Advr to Bd, Dentons UKEMEA (formerly Denton Wilde Sapte, later SNR Denton), 2008–; Advr, Silicon Valley Bank, London, 2013–. Member: Adv. Bd, Cambridge Judge Business Sch., 2005–07; Finance and Audit Cttees, Nat. Gall., 2005–13. Chairman, Board of Trustees: Farnham Castle, 2007–; Vodafone Gp Foundn, 2009– (Trustee, 2007–). CCMI 1992; FRSA 1995. Hon. Chartered Dir, IoD, 2009. *Recreations:* carpentry, ballet. *Address:* (office) Sheil Land Associates Ltd, 52 Doughty Street, WC1N 2LS.

LAND, (William Martin) Alastair; Deputy Head Master, Harrow School, 2012–April 2016; Headmaster, Repton School, from April 2016; *b* Manchester, 24 Sept. 1971; *s* of Martin Land and Elaine Land; *m* 2010, Madeleine Copin; one *s*. *Educ:* Manchester Grammar Sch.; Trinity Coll., Cambridge (BA Nat. Scis 1st Cl. 1993; PGCE 1994). Asst Master, Eton Coll., 1994–2003; Master in Coll., Winchester Coll., 2003–12. FLS 2003; FRSB (FSB 2014). *Recreations:* CCF officer, endurance running, antiquarian natural history books. *Address:* (until April 2016) Harrow School, 5 High Street, Harrow on the Hill HA1 3HP; (from April 2016) The Hall, Repton, Derbys DE65 6FH. *E:* alastairland@gmail.com. *Club:* Royal Society of Medicine.

LANDALE, Sir David (William Neil), KCVO 1993; DL; company director; *b* 27 May 1934; *s* of David Fortune Landale and Louisa (*née* Forbes); *m* 1961, Melanie Roper; three *s*. *Educ:* Eton Coll.; Balliol Coll., Oxford (MA Hist. 1958). Served Black Watch, RHR, 1952–54. Joined Jardine Matheson & Co. Ltd, Hong Kong, 1958; served in Thailand, Hong Kong, Taiwan and Japan, 1960–71; Director: Jardine Matheson and Co. Ltd, 1966–75; Matheson & Co. Ltd, 1975–96; Pinneys of Scotland, Annan, 1982–87; Duchy Originals Ltd, 1992–95. Chm., T. C. Farries & Co. Ltd, 1982–97. Regl Chm., Timber Growers, Scotland, 1983–85; Chm., Timber Growers UK Ltd, 1985–87. Chairman: Scottish Forestry Trust, 1995–2001; Ingliston Develt Trust, 1996–; Nith Dist Fisheries Bd, 2000–. Member: Exec. Cttee and Council, NT for Scotland, 1980–85; Exec. Cttee, Scottish Landowners Fedn, 1980–87. Sec. and Keeper of Records, Duchy of Cornwall, 1987–93. Chairman: Sargent Cancer Care, Scotland (formerly Cttee for Scotland, Malcolm Sargent Cancer Fund for Children), 1994–96; Crichton Foundn (formerly Crichton Coll. Endowment Trust), 1998–2000, Convenor, 2001, Pres., 2006–. Mem., Royal Co. of Archers, Queen's Body Guard for Scotland, 1966–. FRSA 1990. DL Nithsdale/Annandale Dumfries, 1988. *Recreations:* all countryside pursuits, theatre, reading, history. *Address:* Bankhead, Dalswinton, Dumfries DG2 0XT. *T:* (01387) 740208. *Clubs:* Boodle's, Pratt's; New (Edinburgh).

LANDALE, Tina Jeanette; Her Honour Judge Landale; a Circuit Judge, since 2015; *b* Hebden Bridge, 25 Nov. 1965; *d* of John Barry Landale and Marjorie Landale; *m* 2002, Christopher Rainham; one *s* one *d*. *Educ:* Calder High Sch., Mytholmroyd; Wolverhampton Poly. (LLB Hons). Called to the Bar, Middle Temple, 1988; a Recorder, 2009–15. *Recreations:* theatre, art, family, travel, music. *Address:* Peterborough Combined Court Centre, Crown Buildings, Rivergate, Peterborough PE1 1EJ.

LANDAU, Dr David, Hon. CBE 2007; Chairman, Saffron Hill Investors (Guernsey), since 2000; *b* 22 April 1950; *s* of Aharon Landau and Evelyne Conti; *m* 2001, Marie-Rose Kahane; one *s* one *d* (twins). *Educ:* Univ. of Pavia, Italy (MD 1978); Wolfson Coll., Oxford (MA 1979). Print Curator, The Genius of Venice, RA, 1983; Chm., Steering Cttee, Andrea Mantegna exhibn, RA and Metropolitan Mus. of Art, NY, 1992. Founder and Jt Man. Dir, Loot, 1985–95; Chm., Loot Gp of Cos, 1995–2000. Founder and Editor, Print Qly, 1984–2010 (Trustee, 2010–); Founder, FAPIA (Free-ad Papers Internat. Assoc.), 1986, Chm., 1990–91; Dir, Nat. Gall. Co. (formerly Nat. Gall. Pubns), 1995–2003 (Chm., 1998–2003); Dir, Getty Images, 2003–06. Director: Yad Hanadiv (Rothschild Foundn), 2012–; Yad Hanadiv Israel, 2012–; Trustee: British Friends of Art Museums of Israel, 1995–2007; Nat. Gall. Trust, 1995–; NACF (The Art Fund), 1996–2010; Nat. Gall., 1996–2003; Venice in Peril Fund, 1996–2012 (Treas., 1997–2010); NGT Foundn, 1997–; Rothschild Foundn (Hanadiv) Europe (formerly Rothschild Foundn Europe), 2001–; Warburg Charitable Trust, 2001–09; Borletti-Buitoni Charitable Trust, 2002–; Courtauld Inst., 2002–12; Fondazione dei Musei Civici di Venezia, 2010. Supernumerary Fellow, Worcester Coll., Oxford, 1980–2009. Commendatore dell'Ordine al Merito della Repubblica Italiana, 2007. *Publications:* Georg Pencz, 1978; Federica Galli, 1982; (with Prof. P. Parshall) The Renaissance Print, 1994; articles in Print Qly, Master Drawings, Burlington Mag., etc. *Recreations:* looking at and collecting art, opera, Venice. *Address:* Chesa Carla, 7505 Celerina, Switzerland. *T:* (81) 8321550.

LANDAU, Sir Dennis (Marcus), Kt 1987; Chief Executive, Co-operative Wholesale Society Ltd, 1980–92 (Deputy Chief Executive Officer, 1974–80); *b* 18 June 1927; *s* of late Michael Landau, metallurgist; *m* 1992, Mrs Pamela Garlick; two step *s*. *Educ:* Haberdashers' Aske's Hampstead Sch. Schweppes Ltd, 1952; Man. Dir, Schweppes (East Africa) Ltd, 1958–62; Chivers-Hartley: Prodn Dir, 1963; Man. Dir, 1966–69; Chm., Schweppes Foods Div., 1969; Dep. Chm. and Man. Dir, Cadbury Schweppes Foods, 1970; Controller, Food Div., Co-operative Wholesale Society Ltd, 1971. Chairman: CWS (India) Ltd, 1980–92; Unity Trust Bank plc, 1992–2000 (Dir, 1984–2000); Dep. Chm., Co-operative Bank plc, 1989–92; Vice-Chm., Lancashire Enterprises plc, 1989–97; Director: Co-operative Retail Services Ltd, 1980–91; CWS (NZ Hldgs) Ltd, 1980–91; Co-operative Insce Soc. Ltd, 1980–92. Chm., Social Economy Forum, 1993–2001; Member: Metrication Bd, 1972–80; Exec. Cttee, Food & Drink Fedn (formerly Food Manufacturers' Fedn Inc.), 1972–92. Member: Council, Manchester Business Sch., 1982–93 (Chm., 1991–93); Court, Manchester Univ., 1992–2000. FIGD 1977 (Pres. 1982–85); CCMI (CBIM 1980). FRSA 1992. *Recreations:* Rugby, cricket, music. *Clubs:* MCC, Royal Over-Seas League; Lancashire CC (Hon. Treas., 1997–2003; Pres., 2003–07; Vice Pres., 2008–).

LANDAU, Toby Thomas; QC 2008; FCIArb; *b* London, 9 Oct. 1967; *s* of late Dr Thomas L. Landau and of Marianne Landau; *m* 1998, Nudrat B. Majeed; one *d*. *Educ:* University Coll., Sch., Hampstead; Merton Coll., Oxford (BA 1st Cl. Hons Juris; BCL 1st Cl.); Harvard Law Sch. (LLM); Inns of Court Sch. of Law. FCIArb 2000; Chartered Arbitrator, 2000. Called to the Bar, Middle Temple, 1993; Member: NY State Bar, 1994; NI Bar, 2000; BVI Bar, 2011; in private practice as barrister and arbitrator, 1993–. Vis. Prof., KCL, 2009– (Vis. Sen. Lectr, 2005–09). Dir, London Court of Internat. Arbitration, 2000–; Mem. Bd, Arbitration Inst., Stockholm Chamber of Commerce, 2012–. Trustee, CIArb, 2004–08. Advr and Asst on drafting of English Arbitration Act, 1996. Member, Editorial Board: Global Arbitration Rev., 2005–; Jl Internat. Arbitration, 2007–. *Publications:* contrib. articles to ICCA Congress series and other law jls. *Address:* c/o Essex Court Chambers, 24 Lincoln's Inn Fields, WC2A 3EG.

LANDE, Prof. Russell Scott, PhD; FRS 2012; Royal Society Research Professor in Natural Sciences, Imperial College London, since 2007; *b* Mississippi, USA, 1951. *Educ:* Univ. of Calif, Irvine (BS 1972); Univ. of Chicago; Harvard Univ. (PhD 1976). Post-doctoral work, Univ. of Wisconsin, 1976–78; Asst Prof., Dept of Biophys and Theoretical Biol., 1978–82, Associate Prof. of Ecol. and Evolution, 1982–89, Louis Block Prof., Dept of Ecol. and Evolution, 1989–90, Univ. of Chicago; Professor of Biology: Univ. of Oregon, 1990–99; UCSD, 1999–2007. Adjunct Prof., Centre for Conservation Biol., Norwegian Univ. of Sci. and Technol. Guggenheim Meml Fellow, 1996; MacArthur Foundn Fellow, 1997–2002. Pres., Soc. for Study of Evolution, 1997. Fellow, Amer. Acad. Arts and Scis, 1997. Sewall Wright Award, Amer. Soc. Naturalists, 1992; Weldon Meml Prize and Medal, Univ. of Oxford, 2010; Balzan Prize, Balzan Prize Foundn, 2011. *Publications:* (jtly) Stochastic Population Dynamics in Ecology and Conservation, 2003; articles in jls. *Address:* Division of Biology, Imperial College London, Silwood Park, Ascot, Berks SL5 7PY.

LANDEG, Frederick John, CBE 2008; Deputy Chief Veterinary Officer, 2004–07, Interim Chief Veterinary Officer, 2007–08, Department for Environment, Food and Rural Affairs; *b* 16 Jan. 1948; *s* of Frederick Henry Landeg and Ivy May Landeg; *m* 1973, Sandra Stagg; three *s*. *Educ:* Sir Walter St John's Sch., Battersea; Royal Veterinary Coll., London (BVetMed; MSc). MRCVS. Gen. veterinary practice, 1971–75; Ministry of Agriculture, Fisheries and Food: Vet. Officer, 1975–83; Sen. Vet. Officer, 1983–87; Div. Vet. Officer, Preston, 1987–90; Dep. Regl Vet. Officer, Reading, 1990–93; Hd, Vet. Resources Div., 1993–2000; Hd, Vet. Exotic Diseases Div., 2000–04, MAFF, subseq. DEFRA. *Recreations:* reading, walking. *Address:* 6 Oak Tree Copse, Tilehurst, Reading RG31 6PX.

LANDELS, William, (Willie); painter, typographer; *b* Venice, 14 June 1928; *s* of late Reynold Landels and Carla Manfredi; *m* 1st, 1958, Angela Ogden (marr. diss. 1986); two *d*; 2nd, 2002, Josephine Grever. *Educ:* privately. Apprentice stage designer at La Scala, Milan, 1947; Art Director: J. Walter Thompson, 1950; Queen Magazine, 1965; Editor, Harpers & Queen, 1970–86; Editor, Departures, 1989–90. One-man Exhibitions: Hamburg, 1992; Rebecca Hossack Gall., London, 1993, 1995, 1998, 2013; Olsen-Carr Gall., Sydney, 1994; Gallery 482, Brisbane, 1997; Pasricha Fine Arts, London, 2002. Designer, carpets, furniture and books. *Publications:* (with Alistair Burnet) The Best Years of Our Lives, 1981. *Address:* 292 South Lambeth Road, SW8 1UJ.

LANDER, Nicholas Laurence; Restaurant Correspondent, The Financial Times, since 1989; foodservice consultant; *b* 8 April 1952; *s* of Israel Lennard and Pauline Lander; *m* 1981, Jancis Mary Robinson, *qv*; one *s* two *d*. *Educ:* Manchester Grammar Sch.; Jesus Coll., Cambridge (MA); Manchester Business Sch. (DipBA). Restaurateur, 1980–88; Foodservice Consultant: South Bank Centre, 1993–; Royal Opera House, Covent Garden, 1999–; St Pancras, 2007–; Ashmolean, Oxford, 2007; Barbican, 2008–; Chiswick House Trust, 2009. *Publications:* Dinner for a Fiver, 1994; Harry's Bar London, 2005; The Art of the Restaurateur, 2012. *Recreations:* cooking, reading, sitting round a table with friends. *E:* nick@jancisrobinson.com. *Club:* Manchester United.

LANDER, Sir Stephen (James), KCB 2000 (CB 1995); Lay Member, Special Immigration Appeals Commission, since 2011; Member, Solicitors Regulation Authority (formerly Regulation Board, Law Society), 2006–09 (Independent Commissioner, 2002–05); Chairman, Serious Organised Crime Agency, 2004–09; *b* 1947; *s* of John N. B. Lander and (Eleanor) Tessa Lander (*née* Heanley); *m* 1972, Felicity Mary Brayley; one *d* (one *s* decd). *Educ:* Bishop's Stortford Coll.; Queens' Coll., Cambridge (BA, MA, PhD). Inst. of Historical Research, Univ. of London, 1972–75; Security Service, 1975–2002, Dir Gen., 1996–2002; non-exec. Dir, HM Customs and Excise, 2002–05. Non-executive Director: Northgate Information Solutions, 2004–08; Streamshield Networks, 2004–07. Panel Chair, Judicial Appts Commn, 2008–12. Trustee, Dawes Trust, 2012–. Gov., Bishop's Stortford Coll., 2002–. Hon. LLD Hertfordshire, 2005; Hon. DSc Cranfield, 2007. *Address:* PO Box 12378, SW1P 1XU.

LANDERER, John, CBE 1997; AM 1990; lawyer; Senior Partner, Landerer & Co., since 1979; *b* 3 May 1947; *s* of William and Felicia Landerer; *m* 1986, Michelle H. Sugar; one *s* one *d*. *Educ:* Sydney Univ. (LLB 1969). Chairman: FAI Insurances Ltd, 1989–99 (Actg Chm., 1988); Tiger Investment Co. Ltd, 1994–99; Goldsearch Ltd, 1995–; Nat. Hire Gp Ltd,

1997–2004; Terrace Tower Gp, 1997–2007; Director: TNT Ltd, 1985–93; Internat. Distillers Hldgs Ltd, 1986–99; Advance Bank Aust. Ltd, 1989–97; Goodman Fielder Ltd, 1989–94; Aust. Nat. Industries Ltd, 1989–96; Bridge Oil Ltd, 1991–94; Gandel Gp Pty Ltd, 1995–98; D. W. Gp of Cos, 1996–. Chm., NSW Govt Home Purchase Assistance Authy, 1994–2001. University of Sydney: Hon. Fellow, 1990; Hon. Gov., Law Sch. Foundn, 1990–; Mem. Bd, Asia Pacific Law Centre, 1994; Chm., Endocrinol. and Diabetes Res. Foundn, 2008– (Councillor, 2006–); Macquarie University: Chm., Adv. Bd, Business Law Dept, 1994–; Vis. Prof., 1998–. Trustee, WWF Australia, 1992–99. Councillor, Sydney Conservatorium of Music Foundn, 1994–96. Vice Pres., Temora Aviation Mus., 1998–; Board Member: Sydney Jewish Mus., 2004 (Pres., 2005–10); Life Educn Aust., 2004–; JewishCare Foundn, 2004–; Garvan Res. Foundn, 2007–. Dir, Royal Inst. of Deaf and Blind Children, 2005–. Member: Fundraising Cttee, 1989–93, Victor Chang Cardiac Centre Appeal Cttee, 1993–96, St Vincent's Hosp.; Red Shield Appeal Cttee, Salvation Army, 1991–98. Vice Chm., Bd of Govs, Tel Aviv Univ., 2000– (Hon. Fellow, 2008). Hon. LLD Macquarie, 1999. B'nai B'rith Internat. Award, 2001. Commendatore dell'Ordine della Stella della Solidarietà Italiana, 2008. *Recreations:* reading, walking, swimming. *Address:* (office) Level 31, 133 Castlereagh Street, Sydney, NSW 2000, Australia. *T:* (612) 92614242, *Fax:* (612) 92618523. *Clubs:* Carlton; American, Tattersalls (Sydney).

LANDERS, Brian James; author; Chairman, Companies House, since 2012; *b* 21 April 1949; *s* of James Jocelyn Landers, OBE and Beatrice Edith Landers (*née* Western); *m* 1st, 1975, Elsa Louise Dawson (marr. diss.); 2nd, 1986, Thérèse Doumit (marr. diss.); one *s*; 3rd, 1993, Sarah Catherine Cuthbert; two *d*. *Educ:* Univ. of Exeter (BA); London Business Sch. (MSc). With Commercial Union, 1973–79; Internat. Planned Parenthood Fedn, 1979–82; Tenneco Automotive, 1982–83; Chief Internal Auditor, then Retail Financial Controller, J. Sainsbury plc, 1985–88; Price Waterhouse, 1988–90; UK Finance Dir, then Gp Finance Dir, Habitat, 1990–93; Finance Director: HM Prison Service, 1993–96; W. H. Smith Retail, 1996–97; with Waterstone's Ltd, 1997–98; Gp Finance Dir, 2000, Chief Operating Officer, 2000–03, Pearson Education; Finance and Ops Dir, Penguin Gp, 2003–09. Dep. Chm., Financial Ombudsman Service, 1999–2005; Member: Audit Commn, 2010–15; Competition Appeal Tribunal, 2011–. Trustee: Royal Armouries, 1999–2002; Refugee and Migrant Justice, 2009–10. Treas., Amnesty Internat. UK, 2010–13. *Publications:* Empires Apart, 2009. *Address:* 63 Elm Quay Court, Nine Elms Lane, SW8 5DF.

LANDERS, Dr John Maxwell; Principal, 2005–11, Senior Research Fellow, since 2011, Hertford College, Oxford; *b* 25 Jan. 1952; *s* of William Maxwell Landers and Muriel Landers; *m* 1991, Diana Clare Parker, *qv*. *Educ:* Southgate Tech. Coll.; Hertford Coll., Oxford (MA; LittD 2006); Churchill Coll., Cambridge (PhD 1984). Oil demand analyst, Shell UK Ltd, 1979–80; Lectr in Biol Anthropol., UCL, 1980–90; Lectr in Histl Demography, and Fellow, All Souls Coll., Oxford, 1991–2005. *Publications:* Death and the Metropolis: studies in the historical demography of London 1670–1830, 1993; The Field and the Forge: population, production and power in the pre-industrial West, 2003. *Address:* Hertford College, Oxford OX1 3BW. *Clubs:* Athenæum, Oxford and Cambridge.

LANDON, Prof. David Neil; Professor of Neurocytology, University of London, 1991–2001, now Emeritus Professor; Dean, and Member Committee of Management, Institute of Neurology, London, 1987–95; *b* 15 May 1936; *er s* of late Christopher Guy Landon and Isabella Catherine (*née* Campbell); *m* 1960, Karen Elizabeth, LRCP, MRCS, *yr d* of late John Copeland and Else Margrethe Poole, Bolney, Sussex; two *s* one *d*. *Educ:* Lancing Coll.; Guy's Hospital Med. Sch. (BSc Hons Anat. 1957, MB BS 1960). LRCP, MRCS 1959. Ho. Officer, Guy's Hosp., 1959–60; Lectr in Anatomy, Guy's Hosp. Med. Sch., 1961–64; Lectr, later Sen. Lectr, in Neurobiology, MRC Res. Gp in Applied Neurobiology, 1964–77; Reader in Neurocytology, Inst. of Neurology, 1977–91. Hon. Cons. in Morbid Anatomy, National Hosps, Queen Square, 1974–2001. University of London: Member: Senate and Academic Council, 1992–94; Univ. Council, 1996–2001; Mem., Med. Cttee, 1996–98; Convenor, Subject Panel in Anatomy, 1996–2001. Vis. Prof., Coll. of Medicine, Lagos, 1975. Gov., National Hosps for Nervous Diseases SHA, 1988–95; Appointed Mem., GMC, 1988–94. Member: Res. Cttee, World Fedn of Neurology, 1987–2001; Cttees of Management, Inst. of Child Health, 1987–96, Inst. of Dental Surgery, 1993–95; Chm., Med. Res. Ethics Cttee, 1987–93, Chm., Med. Cttee, 1998–2000, Nat. Hosp. for Neurology and Neurosurgery. Mem. Grants Council, 1999–2001, Mem. Adv. Council, 2001–05, Charities Aid Foundn; Trustee, Brain Res. Trust, 2004–10. FLS 2013; Hon. Fellow, Inst. of Child Health, London Univ., 1996. Freeman, 2001, Liveryman, 2009, Pewterers' Co.; Freeman, City of London, 2009. Editorial Cttee, Jl of Anatomy, 1981–94; Associated Editor: Jl of Neurocytol., 1980–83; Neuromuscular Disorders, 1990–94; Muscle and Nerve, 1997–2001. *Publications:* The Peripheral Nerve, 1976; contribs to learned jls on the fine structure, develt and pathology of nerve and muscle. *Recreations:* gardening, travel. *Address:* Woodmans, Wallcrouch, Wadhurst, East Sussex TN5 7JG.

LANDRY, Prof. (Jean-) Bernard, GOQ 2008; Professor of Business Studies, University of Quebec at Montreal, since 2005; *b* 9 March 1937; *s* of Bernard Landry and Thérèse Landry (*née* Granger); *m* 1963, Lorraine Jacquemin (*d* 1999); one *s* two *d*; *m* Chantal Renaud. *Educ:* Acad. Saint Louis, Saint-Jacques, Québec; Séminaire de Joliette; Univ. de Montréal; Inst. d'Etudes Politiques, Paris. Tech. Advr, Min. of Natural Resources, Quebec, Co-ordinator for Quebec, Canadian Council of Resource Ministers and chargé de mission, Min. of Educn, 1964–68; called to the Bar, Quebec, 1965; Min. of Finance and Econ. Affairs, Paris, 1965–67; in practice as lawyer, Joliette and Montréal, 1969–76. Associate Prof., Dept of Admin, Univ. du Québec à Montréal, 1986–94. National Assembly of Quebec: contested Joliette, 1970, Joliette-Montcalm, 1973; Mem. (Parti Québécois) for Fabre, 1976–81, for Laval-des-Rapides, 1981–85, for Verchères, 1994–2005; Minister of State for Econ. Develt, 1977–82; Minister: for External Trade, 1982–84; of Internat. Relations, 1984–85; of Finance, 1985; Dep. Prime Minister, 1994–2001; Prime Minister, 2001–03; Leader of the Opposition, 2003–05. Mem. Nat. Exec., Parti Québécois, 1974–2005 (Vice-Chm., 1989–94; Chm., 2001–05).

LANDSHOFF, Prof. Peter Vincent, PhD; Professor of Mathematical Physics, University of Cambridge, 1994–2004; Fellow, Christ's College, Cambridge, since 1963 (Vice-Master, 1999–2002); Consultant, Cambridge-MIT Institute, 2004–07; *b* 22 March 1937; *m* 1962, Pamela Carmichael; three *s*. *Educ:* City of London Sch.; St John's Coll., Cambridge (MA, PhD). FInstP 1999. Cambridge University: Fellow, St John's Coll., 1961–63; Reader in Mathematical Physics, 1974–94. Instructor, Princeton Univ., 1961–62; Scientific Associate, CERN, Geneva, 1975–76, 1984–85, 1991–92. Chairman, Management Committee: Isaac Newton Inst. for Mathematical Scis, 1990–94 and 2001–06; Cambridge eScience Centre, 2001–04; Nat. Inst. for Envmtl eScience, 2002–04; Cambridge Computational Biol. Inst., 2003–04; Council, Sch. of Physical Scis, Cambridge Univ., 2004. Trustee, Cambridge Past, Present and Future (formerly Cambridge Preservation Soc.), 2007–14; Chairman: E of England Assoc. of Civic Trust Socs, 2008–15; E of England RSA, 2010–12 (Vice-Chm., 2009–10); Cam Catchment Partnership, 2013–; Leader, E of England Transport Information project, 2009–. Hon. Vice-Chm., Cambridge Ahead, 2013–. Editor, Physics Letters B (Elsevier Science), 1982–2005. FRSA. *Publications:* (jtly) The Analytic S-Matrix, 1966; (jtly) Simple Quantum Physics, 1979, 2nd edn 1997; Pomeron Physics and QCD, 2002; research papers on theoretical high-energy physics. *Address:* Department of Applied Mathematics and Theoretical Physics, Centre for Mathematical Sciences, Wilberforce Road, Cambridge CB3 0WA. *T:* (01223) 337880. *E:* pvl@damtp.cam.ac.uk. *W:* www.damtp.cam.ac.uk/user/pvl.

LANDSMAN, David Maurice, OBE 2000; PhD; Executive Director, Tata Ltd, since 2013; *b* 23 Aug. 1963; *s* of Sidney Landsman and Miriam Landsman (*née* Cober); *m* 1990, Catherine Louise Holden; one *s*. *Educ:* Chigwell Sch.; Oriel Coll., Oxford (BA Lit. Hum. 1985; MA 1988); Clare Coll., Cambridge (MPhil 1986; PhD 1989). Univ. of Cambridge Local Exams Syndicate, 1988–89; entered FCO, 1989; Second Secretary: (Econ.) Athens, 1991–94; FCO, 1994–97; Dep. Hd of Mission, Belgrade, 1997–99; FCO, 1999; Hd of Office, Banja Luka, and concurrently First Sec., Budapest, 1999–2000; Hd, British Interests Section, Embassy of Brazil, and subseq. Chargé d'Affaires, British Embassy Belgrade, 2000–01; Ambassador to Albania, 2001–03; Hd, Counter-Proliferation Dept, FCO, 2003–06; on secondment as Internat. Affairs Advr, De La Rue Identity Systems, 2006–08; Balkans Dir, FCO, 2008; Ambassador to Greece, 2009–13. MInstD. *Publications:* contrib. occasional articles on the Greek lang. *Recreations:* travel, languages, music, food, visiting zoos. *Address:* Tata Ltd, 18 Grosvenor Place, SW1X 7HS. *Club:* Athenæum.

LANDY, John Michael, AC 2001; CVO 2005; MBE 1955; Governor of Victoria, Australia, 2001–06; *b* 12 April 1930; *s* of Clarence Gordon Landy and Elva Katherine Ashton; *m* 1971, Lynne (*née* Fisher); one *s* one *d*. *Educ:* Malvern Grammar Sch.; Geelong Grammar; Univ. of Melbourne (BAgrSc). Holder: 1500m World Record, 1954–55; one mile World Record, 1954–57; Olympic and Commonwealth Games medals; second man to run the mile in under 4 mins. ICI Australia, 1962–82, R&D Manager, Biological Gp, 1971–82. Comr Gen., Australian Pavilion Expo 86, Vancouver, 1986. Chairman: Wool R&D Corp., 1989–94; Clean-up Australia, 1990–94; Australia Day Cttee (Victoria), 1990–93; Coode Is. (major chemical spill) Review Panel, 1991–92; Athletics Task Force, 1992–93; Meat Res. Corp., 1995–98; Dir, Australian Sports Drug Agency, 1998–2000. Chairman: Bd Governors, Australian Nat. Insect Collection, 1995–2000; Aust. Wool Testing Authy Ltd Wool Educn Trust, 1997–2000; Athletics Internat. Trust, 1997–2000; Pres., Greening Australia (Victoria), 1998–2000; Member: Land Conservation Council of Victoria, 1971–79; Reference Areas Cttee, Victoria's system of Scientific Reference Areas, 1979–86; Bd Dirs, Australian Inst. of Sport, 1985–87; External Earnings Review Working Party, Aust. Sci. and Technol. Council, 1993–94. Chm., Adv. Panel, Victorian Bushfire Appeal Fund, 2009. Hon. LLD: Victoria, BC, 1994; Melbourne, 2003; Deakin, 2004; Hon. D Rural Sci. New England, 1997. *Publications:* Close to Nature, 1985 (C. J. Dennis Award); A Coastal Diary, 1993.

LANDY, Michael Anthony Andrew, RA 2008; artist; Associate Artist in Residence, National Gallery, 2010–12; *b* London, 13 May 1963; *s* of John and Ethel Landy; partner, Gillian Wearing, *qv*. *Educ:* Goldsmiths' Coll., Univ. of London (BA 1st Cl. Hons Fine Art 1988). Solo exhibitions include: Market, 1990; Nourishment, 2002; Saints Alive, 2013; works include, Break Down, 2001; Semi-Detached, 2004; Art Bin, 2010; Acts of Kindness, 2010–11. Sir Roland Penrose Meml Lect., Tate Modern, 2013. *Publications:* Michael Landy: everything must go, 2008. *Recreation:* running. *Address:* c/o National Gallery, Trafalgar Square, WC2N 5DN. *T:* (020) 7925 2505, *Fax:* (020) 7925 2506. *E:* michael.landy@ng-london.org.uk. *Club:* Ivy.

LANE, Anthony John, CB 1990; Deputy Secretary, Department of Trade and Industry, 1987–96; *b* 30 May 1939; *s* of late Eric Marshall Lane and Phyllis Mary Lane; *m* 1967, Judith Sheila (*née* Dodson); two *s* one *d*. *Educ:* Caterham Sch.; Balliol Coll., Oxford (BA PPE, MA). Investment Analyst, Joseph Sebag & Co., 1964–65; joined Civil Service as Asst Principal, 1965; various appts in DTI, Dept of Transport, DoE and OFT; Prin. Pvte Sec. to several Ministers; Asst Sec., 1975; Under Sec., 1980; Head of Internat. Trade Policy, DTI, 1984–87; Dep. Dir Gen., OFT, 1987–90; Dir Gen. for Industry, DTI, 1990–94; Chief Exec., PSA, 1994–96. Associate Dir, Maxwell Stamp plc, econ. consultants, 1997–2009. Brighton University: Mem., Bd of Govs, 1997–2006 (Dep. Chm., 1999–2002); Chm., Univ. Property Cttee, 1998–99. *Recreations:* music, gardens, travel. *Address:* Fountain House, Dulcote, Wells, Som BA5 3NU.

LANE, Maj.-Gen. Barry Michael, CB 1984; OBE 1974 (MBE 1965); Chief Executive, Cardiff Bay Development Corporation, 1987–92; *b* 10 Aug. 1932; *m* 1st, 1956, Eveline Jean (*d* 1986), *d* of Vice-Adm. Sir Harry Koelle, KCB and Enid (*née* Corbould-Ellis); one *s* one *d*; 2nd, 1987, Shirley Ann, *d* of E. V. Hawtin. *Educ:* Dover Coll. Commissioned, 1954; served Somerset LI, 1954–59, Somerset and Cornwall LI, 1959–68, LI, 1968–75; Instructor, Staff Coll. Camberley, 1970–72; CO, 1st Bn, LI, 1972–75; Comd, 11 Armoured Bde, 1977–78; RCDS, 1979; Dep. Dir, Army Staff Duties, MoD, 1980–81; Dir, Army Quartering, 1981–82; VQMG, 1982–83; GOC SW Dist, 1984–87. Col, The LI, 1982–87. Hon. Colonel: 6th Bn, LI, 1987–97; Bristol Univ., OTC, 1988–99. Pres. of Council, and Chm. of Govs, Taunton Sch., 1997–2001; Vice Pres., St Margaret's Somerset Hospice, 2003–. *Club:* Army and Navy.

LANE, Clive Nicholas; a Judge of the Upper Tribunal (Immigration and Asylum Chamber), since 2009; *b* Worcester, 16 Nov. 1957; *s* of late Frank Henry Lane and of June Maureen Lane (*née* Moore); *m* 1985, Heather Elizabeth Owen; one *d*. *Educ:* St Stephen's Primary Sch., Worcester; Royal Grammar Sch., Worcester; New Coll., Oxford (BA Hons Mod. Hist. 1979); City of Birmingham Poly. (Law Soc. Final Exam. 1983). Admitted solicitor, 1985; Partner, Ginn & Co. solicitors, Cambridge, 1986–2001, Sen. Partner, 2000–01; Dep. Dist Chm., Social Security Tribunal (Appeals Service), 1999–2007; a Dep. District Judge, 2001–; Immigration Judge (formerly Adjudicator), Asylum and Immigration Tribunal (formerly Immigration Appellate Authy), 2001–09; Legal Mem., Special Immigration Appeals Commn, 2014–. Mem., Friends of Ilkley Lido. *Publications:* contribs to legal jls incl. Family Law. *Recreations:* hill walking, ornithology, 'cello, theatre, opera, Worcestershire County Cricket Club, urban vinyl, seeking out doom paintings in English churches. *Address:* Upper Tribunal (Immigration and Asylum Chamber), Phoenix House, Rushton Avenue, Bradford BD7 3BH. *T:* (01274) 267063. *E:* clive.lane@judiciary.gsi.gov.uk. *Club:* Oxford and Cambridge.

See also P. R. Lane.

LANE, David Goodwin; QC 1991; a Recorder of the Crown Court, since 1987; *b* 8 Oct. 1945; *s* of James Cooper Lane and Joyce Lilian Lane; *m* 1991, Jacqueline Elizabeth Cocks. *Educ:* Crypt Sch., Gloucester; King's College London (LLB, AKC). Lord Justice Holker Junior Exhibnr; Lee Essay Prizeman, H. C. Richard Ecclesiastical Law Prizeman; Albion Richardson Scholar. Called to the Bar, Gray's Inn, 1968; Asst Recorder, 1982. Freeman, City of London. *Address:* St Johns Buildings, 24a–28 St John Street, Manchester M3 4DJ. *T:* (0161) 214 1500.

LANE, David Ian, (David Ian); theatre producer, since 1991; Chairman: Global Theatre, Live Nation, 2005–07; David Ian Productions Ltd, since 2006; *b* 15 Feb. 1961; *s* of Reg and Jean Lane; *m* 1994, Tracy Carter; one *s* one *d*. *Educ:* Ilford County High Grammar Sch. Joined Live Nation (formerly Clear Channel Entertainment), 2000. Actor: title rôle, Joseph and the Amazing Technicolor Dreamcoat; Pirates of Penzance, London Palladium; Time, Dominion. Producer, 1991–: Ain't Misbehavin', Lyric, 1995; Saturday Night Fever, London Palladium, 1998; Defending the Caveman, Apollo, 1999; The King and I, London Palladium, 2000; Grease (revival), Dominion, 2001, transf. Cambridge Th. and Victoria Palace; Daisy Pulls It Off, Lyric, 2002; Anything Goes, 2003, The Producers, 2004, Drury Lane Th. Royal; Guys and Dolls, Piccadilly, 2005; The Sound of Music, London Palladium, 2006; Grease, Piccadilly, 2007; La Cage aux Folles, Playhouse; Shawshank Redemption, Wyndhams; Sweet Charity, Haymarket; Flashdance, Shaftesbury; The Bodyguard, Adelphi; also many UK tours and productions in USA and Australia. Writer of play, Stalin's Daughter, Tobacco Factory, Bristol, 2014. *Recreations:* sport, marathon running, theatre. *Address:* (office) David Ian Productions Ltd, 53 Parker Street, 5th Floor, WC2B 5PT.

LANE, David Neil, CMG 1983; HM Diplomatic Service, retired; *b* 16 April 1928; *er s* of late Clive and Hilda Lane, Bath; *m* 1968, Sara, *d* of late Cecil Nurcombe, MC; two *d*. *Educ:* Abbotsholme Sch.; Merton Coll., Oxford. Army, 1946–48; Foreign (later Foreign and Commonwealth) Office: 1951–53, 1955–58, 1963–68, 1972–74; British Embassy, Oslo, 1953–55; Ankara, 1959–61, 1975–78; Conakry, 1961–63; UK Mission to the United Nations, New York, 1968–72, 1979; NI Office, 1978–79; High Comr in Trinidad and Tobago, 1980–85; Ambassador to the Holy See, 1985–88. Pres., UN Trusteeship Council, 1971–72; UK Delegate, Internat. Exhibns Bureau, 1973–74. Asst Sec.-Gen., 1989–92, Sec., 1990–92, Order of St John; OStJ 1990. Chm., Anglo-Turkish Soc., 1995–2001. *Publications:* Three Carols for chorus and orchestra, 2000. *Address:* 6 Montagu Square, W1H 2LB. *T:* (020) 7486 1673.

LANE, Sir David (Philip), Kt 2000; PhD; FRCPath, FMedSci; FRS 1996; FRSE; Chief Scientist, Agency for Science, Technology and Research, Singapore, since 2009 (Executive Director, Institute of Molecular and Cell Biology, 2004–07 (on sabbatical); Chairman, Biomedical Research Council, 2007–09); Scientific Director, Ludwig Institute, since 2013; *b* 1 July 1952; *s* of John Wallace Lane and Cecelia Frances Evelyn Lane (*née* Wright); *m* 1975, Ellen Birgitte Muldal; one *s* one *d*. *Educ:* John Fisher Sch., Purley; University College London (BSc 1973, PhD 1976; Fellow). FRCPath 1996. FRSE 1992. Res. Fellow, ICRF, 1976–77; Lectr, Imperial Coll., 1977–85; Staff Scientist, ICRF, 1985–90; Prof. of Molecular Oncology, Univ. of Dundee, 1990–2009; CEO, Experimental Therapeutic Centre, Singapore, 2007–09; Chief Scientist, CRUK, 2007–10. Vis. Fellow, Cold Spring Harbor Labs, NY, 1978–80; Gibb Fellow, Cancer Res. UK (formerly CRC), 1990–. Founder, Dir and Chief Scientific Officer, Cyclacel Pharmaceuticals Inc., 1996–2004; Chm., Chugai Pharmabody, 2013–. Mem., EMBO, 1990. Founder FMedSci 1998. Hon. DSc: Abertay Dundee, 1999; Stirling, 2000; Aberdeen, 2002; Birmingham, 2002; Hon. MD Nottingham, 2006; Dr *hc* Univ. Paul Sabatier, Toulouse, 2007. Prize, Charles Rodolphe Brupbacher Foundn, 1993; Prize, Joseph Steiner Foundn, 1993; Howard Hughes Internat. Scholar, Howard Hughes Med. Inst., 1993; Yvette Mayent Prize, Inst. Curie, 1994; Medal, Swedish Soc. of Oncology, 1994; Prize, Meyenburg Foundn, 1995; Black Prize, Jefferson Hosp., 1995; Silvanus Thompson Medal, British Inst. of Radiol., 1996; Henry Dryerre Prize, 1996; Paul Ehrlich Prize, 1998; Tom Connors Prize, 1998; Bruce-Preller Prize, 1998; SCI Medal, 2003; Anthony Dipple Carcinogenesis Award, 2004; Buchanan Medal, Royal Soc., 2004; Biochem. Soc. Award, 2004; Internat. Agency for Res. on Cancer Medal, 2005; Sergio Lombroso Award for Cancer Research Work, 2005; INSERM Medal d'Etranger, 2006; Gregor Mendel Medal, Masaryk Cancer Inst., Czech Republic, 2006; Colin Thomson Medal, Beatson Inst., Glasgow, 2007; David Hungerford Medal, Bangalore, 2007; Royal Medal, RSE, 2008; CRUK Lifetime Achievement Award, 2013. *Publications:* Antibodies: a laboratory manual, 1988; numerous papers in learned jls. *Recreations:* tennis, motor cycles, old cars, walking. *Address:* Agency for Science, Technology and Research, 8A Biomedical Grove, #06–06 Immunos, Singapore 138648, Republic of Singapore.

LANE, David Stuart, PhD, DPhil; FAcSS; Reader in Sociology, 1992–2000, now Reader Emeritus, and Fellow of Emmanuel College, 1974–80 and 1990–2000, now Emeritus Fellow, Senior Research Associate, 2001–07, University of Cambridge; *b* Monmouthshire (now Gwent), 24 April 1933; *s* of Reginald and Mary Lane; *m* 1962, Christel Noritzsch; one *s* one *d*. *Educ:* Univ. of Birmingham (BSocSc); Univ. of Oxford (DPhil); PhD Cantab. Graduate student, Nuffield Coll., Oxford, 1961–62, 1964–65. Formerly engrg trainee, local authority employee, sch. teacher; univ. teacher, Birmingham, Essex (Reader in Sociology) and Cambridge Univs; Prof. of Sociology, Univ. of Birmingham, 1981–90; Lectr in Sociology, Cambridge Univ., 1990–92. Visiting Professor: Lund Univ., 1985; Cornell Univ., 1987; Univ. of Graz, 1991, 1996; Harvard Univ., 1993, 2001; Kennan Inst., Washington, 1986, 1996; Sabanci Univ., 2000–02. Member: Exec. Cttee, British Sociol Assoc., 1987–92; Exec. Cttee, European Social Assoc., 1999–2001 (Vice Pres.); Vice Pres., Soc. for Co-operation in Russian and Soviet Studies, 2013–; Co-Chair, first European Conf. of Sociology, 1992. Vice-Chm., Birmingham Rathbone, 1986–90; Vice-Chm., Down's Children's Assoc., 1981–82; Chm., W Midlands Council for Disabled People, 1983–86. ESRC res. award to study Soviet and Russian political elites, 1991–95, econ. elites, 1996–98, and financial business elite, 1999–2002; Leverhulme Trust res. award to study transformation of state socialism, 2004–07; British Acad. network award for study of strategic elites and European enlargement, 2004–08, award to study coloured revolutions, 2009–10, res. award to study unemployment in Ukraine and China, 2012; Mem., EU Inter-Univs Consortium to study new modes of governance within the EU, 2004–08. FAcSS (AcSS 2011). Participates in meetings of Valdai Discussion Club (Russian Fedn), Moscow Econ. Forum, and Assoc. for Slavic, E Eur. and Eurasian Studies. Member, Editorial Boards: Sociology, 1985–88; Disability, Handicap and Society, 1987–90; Perspectives on European Politics and Soc., 1990–; Mir Rossii, 2006–. *Publications:* Roots of Russian Communism, 1969, 2nd edn 1975; Politics and Society in the USSR, 1970, 2nd edn 1978; The End of Inequality?, 1971; (with G. Kolankiewicz) Social Groups in Polish Society, 1973; The Socialist Industrial State, 1976; (with F. O'Dell) The Soviet Industrial Worker, 1978; The Work Needs of Mentally Handicapped Adults, 1980; Leninism: a sociological interpretation, 1981; The End of Social Inequality?: class status and power under state socialism, 1982; State and Politics in the USSR, 1985; Soviet Economy and Society, 1985; (ed jtly and contrib.) Current Approaches to Down's Syndrome, 1985; (ed) Employment and Labour in the USSR, 1986; Soviet Labour and the Ethic of Communism, 1987; (ed and contrib.) Political Power and Elites in the USSR, 1988; Soviet Society under Perestroika, 1990, 2nd edn 1992; (ed and contrib.) Russia in Flux, 1992; (ed and contrib.) Russia in Transition, 1995; The Rise and Fall of State Socialism, 1996, trans. Russian, 2006, Japanese, 2007; (with C. Ross) The Transition from Communism to Capitalism: ruling elites from Gorbachev to Eltsin, 1998; (ed and contrib.) Political Economy of Russian Oil, 1999; (ed and contrib.) The Legacy of State Socialism and the Future of Transformation, 2002; (ed and contrib.) Russian Banking: evolution, problems and prospects, 2002; (ed with M. Myant and contrib.) Varieties of Capitalism in Post-Communist Countries, 2007; (ed and contrib.) The Transformation of State Socialism: system change, capitalism or something else?, 2007; (ed jtly and contrib.) Revolution in the Making of the Modern World, 2007; (ed jtly) Restructuring of Economic Elites after State Socialism: recruitment, institutions and attitudes, 2007; (ed with A. Gamble and contrib.) European Union and World Politics, 2009; (ed jtly) Migration and Mobility in Europe, 2009; (ed with S. White and contrib.) Rethinking the 'Coloured Revolutions', 2010; (ed and contrib.) Elites and Identities in Post-Soviet Space, 2011; Elites and Classes in the Transformation of State Socialism, 2011; The Capitalist Transformation of State Socialism, 2013; The Capitalist Transformation of State Socialism: the making and breaking of state socialist society and what followed, 2014; (contrib.) Political Elites in the Transatlantic Crisis, 2014; (ed with V. Samokhvalov and contrib.) The Eurasian Project and Europe: regional discontinuities and geopolitics, 2015; contribs to jls incl. Perspectives on European Politics and Society, Pol Studies, Europe-Asia Studies, Sociology, Jl of Communist Studies and Transition Politics, Political Qly, Studies in Comparative Econ. Devclt, British Jl of Pols and and Internat. Relns, New Pol Economy, Comparative Econ. Studies, Eur. Societies, Mir Rossii, Sotsiologicheski Zhurnal, Sotsiologicheskie Issledovaniya, Revue Française de Sci. Politique, POLIS (Moscow), Mir Peremen (Moscow), Russian Analytical Digest (Zurich), Alternativy (Moscow). *Recreations:* soccer, squash, films, TV, theatre, watching Arsenal FC. *Address:* Emmanuel College, Cambridge CB2 3AP. *T:* (01223) 359113, *Fax:* (01223) 334426. *E:* dsl10@cam.ac.uk.

LANE, Rt Rev. Elizabeth Jane Holden; *see* Stockport, Bishop Suffragan of.

LANE, Ian Francis, DM; FRCS, FRCSE; vascular surgeon; Consultant Surgeon: University Hospital of Wales, 1988–2012; Spire Hospital, since 1988; Medical Director, Cardiff and Vale NHS Trust, 1999–2009; *b* 14 May 1952; *s* of Frank Ernest Lane and Teresa Ellen Lane (*née* Wallace); *m* 1980, Carol Myhill Morris; one *s* one *d*. *Educ:* Downside Sch.; Lincoln Coll., Oxford (BA (Physiol.) 1973; BM BCh 1976; MA 1979; DM 1987; MCh 1988); St Thomas' Hosp. Med. Sch. MRCS 1976, FRCS 1981; FRCSE 1981. Lectr in Surgery, Charing Cross and Westminster Med. Sch., 1981–88; Hon. Teacher in Vascular Surgery, Univ. of Wales Coll. of Medicine, 1988–. Dir, Ethics Cttee, Dr Foster Research, 2006–. Mem. Council, Vascular Surgical Soc. of GB and Ireland, 1999–2002; Sec., Venous Forum, RSocMed, 2000–03. Non-exec. Dir, Time for Medicine, 2010–. Mem., Ct of Examrs, RCS, 1995–2001. *Publications:* res. and teaching articles in peer-reviewed jls on aspects of arterial and venous disease. *Recreations:* fine arts, travel to remote areas, exotic cars, wine. *Address:* Spire Hospital, Croescadarn Road, Cardiff CF23 8XL. *T:* (029) 2073 6011, *Fax:* (01446) 781970.

LANE, Jane; *see* Tewson, J.

LANE, John Bristowe; Partner, Linklaters, since 2000; *b* Johannesburg, 18 May 1965; *s* of William and Elizabeth Lane; *m* 1990, Karen Ann Maher; three *s*. *Educ:* St John's Coll., Johannesburg; Univ. of Cape Town (BA 1985; LLB 1987); Trinity Hall, Cambridge (LLM 1991). Qualified as Attorney, Webber Wentzel, Johannesburg, 1989; Linklaters: trainee, 1991–93; admitted Solicitor, 1993; Asst Solicitor, Corporate Dept, London, 1993–99. *Recreations:* walking, cycling, tennis, the Listing Rules. *Address:* Linklaters LLP, One Silk Street, EC2V 8HQ. *T:* (020) 7456 3542, *Fax:* (020) 7456 2222. *E:* john.lane@linklaters.com.

LANE, Rev. John Ernest, OBE 1994; charity consultant; Associate: Craigmyle & Co., 2001–05; Bill Bruty Associates, since 2001; Fundraising Training Co., since 2001; Director, Corporate Affairs, St Mungo Community Housing Association Ltd, 1996–2001; *b* 16 June 1939; *s* of Ernest William Lane and Winifred (*née* Lloyd); *m* 1st, 1962, Eileen Williams (marr. diss. 1988); three *d*; 2nd, 2001, Ishbel Margaret, *d* of late William Curr and of Jean Curr (*née* Payne). *Educ:* Burnley Grammar Sch.; Handsworth Coll., Birmingham; City of London Polytechnic (DMS); Cranfield Inst. of Technol. (MSc). Methodist Minister: Llanharan, 1962–64; Great Harwood, 1964–67; Lewisham and Peckham, 1967–72; Dir, Peckham Settlement, 1972–77; Nat. Public Relns Officer, YWCA of GB, 1977–80; Dir and Sec., St Mungo Community Housing Assoc. Ltd, 1980–96; Sec., 1980–96, Dir, 1994–96, St Mungo Assoc. Charitable Trust. Ordained deacon and priest, 1980; Hon. Curate, St John and St Andrew, Peckham, 1980–95; permission to officiate: dio. of Southwark, 1995–98; Lichfield Cathedral, 2002–; NSM, St Alfege with St Peter, Greenwich, 1998–2000. Administrateur, European Fedn of Nat. Orgns Working with the Homeless, 1991–95. Dir, Nat. Sleep Out Week, 1990–94. Trustee: Newton's Trust, 2006–; Dr Milley's Hosp., 2008–12. *Publications:* (ed) Homelessness in Industrialised Countries, 1987. *Recreations:* politics, social affairs, cooking, washing up, cricket, travel, arts, persuading Yvonne not to support Arsenal, vetting Vanessa's boyfriends, following Alison around the world, doting on Sophie. *Address:* 2 Tregony Rise, Lichfield, Staffs WS14 9SN. *T:* (01543) 415078.

LANE, Jonathan Stewart, OBE 2015; FRICS; Chairman, Shaftesbury PLC UK, since 2013 (Deputy Chairman, 2011–13); *b* Camborne, Cornwall, 10 Nov. 1945; *s* of Thurstan Tregoning Lane and Mary Lane (*née* Marriott); *m* 1969, Kerry Grant; two *d*. *Educ:* Clifton Coll., Bristol; Oriel Coll., Oxford (MA Modern Hist. 1967). FRICS 1971. Cadet valuer, Valuation Office, Inland Revenue, 1968–71; Stock Conversion plc: Exec., 1971–78; Dir, 1978–82; Gen. Manager, 1982–84; Man. Dir, 1984–86; Chief Exec., Shaftesbury PLC UK, 1986–2011. Non-executive Director and Chairman: Porthminster Hotel Ltd, 1979–2008; Tregarthen's Hotel (Scilly) Ltd, 1980–; non-exec. Chm., EasyHotel plc, 2015– (non-exec. Dir, 2014–15). Member: Property Cttee, Art Fund (formerly NACF), 2006–10; Property Panel, Oriel Coll., Oxford, 2010–; 2020 Strategy Gp, Royal Botanic Gdns, Kew, 2014–. Trustee and Deputy Chairman: Crafts Council, 1988–98; Theatres Trust, 1994–2003 (Consultant, 2003–); Trustee: Royal Shakespeare Trust, later Royal Th. Support Trust, 2008–; Oppenheim-John Downes Meml Trust, 2013–. Gov., RSC, 1997–2009. Councillor, LTA, 1997–; Chm., Tennis Foundn, 2007–. *Recreations:* family, theatre, music, walking, fishing. *Address:* c/o Shaftesbury PLC UK, 22 Ganton Street, W1F 7FD, W1S 3DL. *T:* (020) 7333 8118.

LANE, Kenneth Frederick; former mining consultant; Director, RTZ Consultants, 1988–97; *b* 22 March 1928; British; *m* 1950, Kathleen Richards; one *s* two *d*. *Educ:* Emmanuel Coll., Cambridge. Degree in Maths. Steel Industry in Sheffield, 1951–59; North America, 1959–61; Rio Tinto-Zinc Corp., 1961–65; Man. Dir, RTZ Consultants Ltd, 1965–70; Dir, RTZ Corp., 1970–75. Vis. Prof., RSM, 1979–85. *Publications:* The Economic Definition of Ore, 1988. *Recreations:* bridge, boat building, sailing. *Address:* 4 Towerdene, 16 Tower Road, Poole, Dorset BH13 6HZ. *T:* (01202) 751958.

LANE, Dr Nancy Jane, OBE 1994; CBiol, FRSB; FZS; Senior Research Associate, Zoology Department, University of Cambridge, since 1990; Lecturer, since 1970, Fellow, 1970–2006, now Life Fellow, Girton College, Cambridge; *d* of Temple Haviland Lane and Frances de Forest Gilbert Lane; *m* 1969, Prof. Richard Nelson Perham, FRS (*d* 2015); one *s* one *d*. *Educ:* Dalhousie Univ., Nova Scotia (BSc, MSc); Lady Margaret Hall, Oxford (DPhil 1963); Girton Coll., Cambridge (PhD 1968; ScD 1981). CBiol 1991, FRSB (FIBiol 1991); FZS 1986. Res. Asst Prof., Albert Einstein Coll. of Medicine, NY, 1964–65; Res. Staff Biologist, Yale Univ., 1965–68; University of Cambridge: SSO, 1968–73, PSO, 1973–82, SPSO, 1982–90, AFRC Unit, Zoology Dept; Tutor, Girton Coll., 1975–98; Project Dir, Women in Science, Engrg and Technology Initiative, 1999–2006. Editor-in-Chief, Cell Biol. Internat., 1995–98; Chm., Editl Cttee, People and Science (formerly Science and Public Affairs), 2001–13. Vis. Lectr, British Council, 1999–2004. Non-executive Director: Smith & Nephew plc, 1991–2000; Peptide Therapeutics plc, 1995–98. Mem., PM's Adv. Panel for Citizen's Charter, 1991–93; Chairman: BTEC's Adv. Bd for Sci. and Caring, 1991–94; Wkg Party for Women in Sci. and Engrg (OST), Cabinet Office, 1993–94. Member: Forum UK, 1994–2008; All Souls Gp, Oxford, 1994–2005; CVCP's Commn on Univ. Career Opportunities (CUCO), 1996–2000; UNESCO's Sci. Cttee for Women, Sci. and Technol., 1997–; Scientific, Engrg and Envmt Adv. Cttee, British Council, 2003–07; Dep. Chm., Steering Cttee for CUCO/OST/HEFCE Athena Project, 1998–2003; UNESCO Cttee for Natural Scis, 2005–10. Chm., Athena Project, 2003–07. Dir, 1997–2004, Mem. Council, 2005–, Women of the Year Lunch and Assembly; Partner, UK Resource Centre for Women in Sci., DTI, 2004–08; Chm., UK Resource Centre Experts Database, 2005–07; Gender Equality Champion, Zoology Dept, Cambridge Univ., 2013–. Pres., Inst. of Biology, 2002–04; Member: Council, Zool Soc. of London, 1998–2001 (Vice-Pres., 1999–2001); Brit. Soc. Cell Biol., 1980– (Sec., 1982–90); Exec. Council, Biosciences Fedn, 2002–06. Co-author, SET Fair, Greenfield Report, 2002. Mem., Selection Bd, Vanier/Banting Canada Grad. Scholarships Prog., 2009–11. FRSA 1992; MInstD 1991. Hon. Fellow, BAAS, 2005. Hon. LLD Dalhousie, 1985; Hon. ScD: Salford, 1994; Sheffield Hallam, 2002; Oxford Brookes, 2003; Surrey, 2005. Elected to Nova Scotia Hall of Fame for Sci. and Technology, 2006. *Publications:* contrib. numerous scientific papers and chapters on cell-cell junctions, cellular structures and interactions, in field of cell biology, and on women in science, in a range of learned scientific jls. *Recreations:* theatre and opera, 20th century art, travelling. *Address:* Department of Zoology, University of Cambridge, Downing Street, Cambridge CB2 3EJ. *T:* (01223) 336609/336600/363710, *Fax:* (01223) 336676. *E:* njl1@cam.ac.uk.

LANE, Peter Alfred; artist potter, photographer and author; *b* 26 April 1932; *s* of late Alfred John Lane and Freda Margaret Lane; *m* 1958, Margaret Jean Edwards (*d* 2009); two *d. Educ:* Bath Acad. of Art (Art Teacher's Cert.); Cert Ed Bristol 1956. Art teacher: Botley Co. (All-Age) Sch., Berks, 1956–58; Head, Art Department: Matthew Arnold Secondary Sch., Cumnor, Berks, 1958–60; Andover GS, 1961–64; Lectr/Organiser, Somerset Coll. of Art, Taunton, 1964–66; Keswick Hall College of Education, Norwich: Lectr in Art Educn and Ceramics, 1966–70; Sen. Lectr, 1970–80; Hd, Art Dept, 1980–81; University of E Anglia: Sen. Lectr and Hd, Dept of Art Educn and Ceramics, 1981–84; Sen. Fellow in Art Educn, 1984–87. Examr/Assessor at various art colls, 1980–88. Judge, ceramics exhibns in UK, 1964–; Judge, international ceramics exhibitions: 2nd Biennale Canadian Ceramics, 1986; Fletcher Challenge Ceramics Award, NZ, 1989; 1st Taiwan Ceramics Biennale, 2004; Zelli Porcelain Award, 2005. Has exhibited, lectured and demonstrated ceramics widely throughout the world; individual ceramics in many public collections in UK, Australia, Canada, Europe, Korea, USA. Co-founder, Norfolk Contemporary Crafts Soc., 1971. Fellow: Craft Potters' Assoc. of GB, 1962 (Hon. Fellow 2004); Soc. of Designer Craftsmen, 1976. Member: Devon Guild of Craftsmen, 2013; Internat. Acad. Ceramics, Geneva, 1997. Centennial Silver Medal, Soc. Designer Craftsmen, 1981. *Publications:* Studio Porcelain, 1980; Studio Ceramics, 1983; Ceramic Form, 1988, new enlarged edn 1998; (consultant ed and contrib.) Ceramics Manual, 1990; Contemporary Porcelain, 1995; Contemporary Studio Porcelain, 2003; contrib. numerous mag. articles on ceramics; book and exhibn reviews, 1970–. *Recreations:* fell-walking, painting, foreign travel, theatre. *Address:* Tavistock, Devon. *W:* www.studioporcelain.co.uk.

LANE, Peter Richard; a Judge of the Upper Tribunal (Immigration and Asylum Chamber) (formerly a Vice President, Immigration Appeal Tribunal, later a Senior Immigration Judge, Asylum and Immigration Tribunal), since 2003; Legal Member, Special Immigration Appeals Commission, since 2005; President, General Regulatory Chamber of the First-tier Tribunal, since 2014; *b* 26 April 1953; *s* of late Frank Henry Lane and of June Maureen Lane (*née* Moore); *m* 1980, Shelley Ilene Munjack (*see* S. I. M. Lane); one *s* one *d. Educ:* St Stephen's Primary Sch., Worcester; Worcester Royal Grammar Sch.; Hertford Coll., Oxford (BA 1st cl. (Jurisprudence) 1974); Univ. of Calif, Berkeley (LLM 1975). Called to the Bar, Middle Temple, 1976; re-qualified as Solicitor, 1985. In practice at Bar, 1977–80; Lectr in Laws, QMC, 1978–80; Asst Parly Counsel, 1980–85; Solicitor and Parly Agent, 1985–2001, Partner, 1987–2001, Rees & Freres; Immigration Adjudicator, pt-time, 1996–2001, full-time, 2001–03. *Publications:* (jtly) Blackstone's Guide to the Transport and Works Act 1992, 1992; (jtly) Blackstone's Guide to the Environment Act 1995, 1995; (contrib.) Douglas & Geen on the Law of Harbours, Coasts and Pilotage, 5th edn 1997; articles on, and reviews of, film music. *Recreations:* hill-walking, opera, American and British film music 1930–1975. *Address:* Upper Tribunal (Immigration and Asylum Chamber), Field House, 15 Bream's Buildings, EC4A 1DZ. *T:* (020) 7073 4056. *E:* peter.lane@judiciary.gsi.gov.uk.
See also C. N. Lane.

LANE, Philip Anthony, OBE 2009; Strategic Head of Sport Development, Greenwich Leisure Ltd, since 2011; *b* Ruardean, Glos, 2 Sept. 1953; *s* of Ronald Lane and Vanda Lane; *m* 1999, Emma; three *s* one *d. Educ:* Royal Forest of Dean Grammar Sch.; Shoreditch Coll., London (MSc, BEd 1st Cl., CertEd). Headteacher, 1990–2001. Hd Coach, England Under 18 Rugby Team, 1999–2001; Chef de Mission, GB Paralympic Team, 2002, 2004, 2006, 2008, 2010. Director: Paralympic World Cup, 2005–11; Team 2012, 2009–11; Chm., Pro-Active E London, 2006–08; CEO, British Paralympic Assoc., 2001–11. Visiting Lecturer: Hull Univ., 2002–05; Reading Univ., 2005–07; Vis. Prof., UEL, 2007–. Hon. DBA London Metropolitan, 2007; Hon. PhD Middlesex. *Recreations:* sport, music (playing and listening), literature.

LANE, Dr Richard Paul, OBE 2011; Director of Science, Natural History Museum, 2003–11; *b* 16 May 1951; *s* of Alfred George Lane and Patricia Ann Lane (*née* Trotter); *m* 1972, Maureen Anne Grogan; two *s* one *d. Educ:* Imperial Coll., Univ. of London (BSc, ARCS, DIC, PhD). Dept of Entomology, British Museum (Natural History), 1974–85, Head of Med. Insects Sect., 1983–85; Sen. Lectr, LSHTM, Univ. of London, 1985–92, Head of Vector Biology and Transmission Dynamics Unit, 1989–92; Keeper of Entomology, Natural History Mus., 1992–97; Internat. Prog. Dir, Wellcome Trust, 1997–2004. Vis. Prof., Imperial Coll., London, 2005–11. Member: Council, RSTM&H, 1985–89, 1999–2003; Biological Council, 1985–89; Wellcome Trust Panels, 1986–97; Expert Adv. Panel on Parasitic Diseases, WHO, 1988–; Steering Cttee on Leishmaniasis, WHO, 1988–93; Bd of Trustees, Biosis, Philadelphia, 1993–98; Steering Cttee on research ethics related to healthcare in developing countries, Nuffield Council on Bioethics, 2001–08; Exec. Cttee and Founding Mem., Consortium for DNA Barcode of Life, 2005–09; Institutional Council and Governance Bd, Encyclopaedia of Life, 2007–11; Chairman: Sci. Collections Internat., OECD Global Sci. Forum, 2005–08. Member, External Scientific Advisory Board: Leibniz-Institut für Evolutions und Biodiversitätsforschung, Berlin, 2007–10; Netherlands Centre for Biodiversity Naturalis, Leiden, 2010–; Natural History Museum of Denmark, 2010–13. Royal Entomological Society: Mem. Council, 1980–83, 1989–92; Vice-Pres., 1991–92; Pres., 1994–96. Mem. Council, Internat. Congress of Entomology, 1992–2008. Trustee, Against Malaria Foundn, 2004–. Hon. DSc Kingston, 2010. *Publications:* (ed jtly) Medical Insects and Arachnids, 1993; papers on insects of medical importance in sci. jls, esp. on sandflies and transmission of leishmaniasis. *Recreations:* natural history, gardening.

LANE, Robert Charles, CBE 2001; Partner, since 1990, and Head of Regulated Industries, since 2000, CMS Cameron McKenna LLP (formerly McKenna & Co.); *b* London, 29 Aug. 1958; *s* of Sidney Lane and Eileen Lane (*née* Cleave); *m* 1986, Margaret Stubbs; two *s* one *d. Educ:* Buckhurst Hill Sch.; University Coll. London (LLB Hons 1979). Admitted as solicitor, 1982; Solicitor: Slaughter and May, 1982–88; McKenna & Co., 1988–90. Chm., Govt Power Sector Adv. Gp, 2004–13; Executive Member: British Energy Assoc./Energy Inst., 2003–; Parly Gp for Energy Studies, 2004–. Mem. Bd, Energy Industries Club, 2004–. Chm., Energy Cttee, City of London Solicitors' Co., 2010–. Chm. Trustees, Orchid Cancer Charity, 2014– (Trustee, 2008–). *Recreations:* theatre, opera, music, Rugby, cricket, family. *Address:* CMS Cameron McKenna LLP, Cannon Place, 78 Cannon Street, EC4N 6HL. *T:* (020) 7367 3000, *Fax:* (020) 7367 2000. *E:* robert.lane@cms-cmck.com. *Clubs:* Garrick, Royal Automobile, City of London.

LANE, Maj.-Gen. Roger Guy Tyson, CBE 2003 (OBE 1994); Managing Director, Roger Lane Consulting Ltd, since 2007; *b* 23 Feb. 1954; *s* of Capt. and Mrs M. E. Lane; *m* 1981, Nichola J. Redrobe; one *s* one *d. Educ:* Christ's Hospital, Horsham. Joined RM, 1972; OC, HMS Zulu, 1977–79; Intelligence Security Gp, NI, 1979–80 (despatches 1981); Adjutant, 1982–84; Canadian Comd and Staff Coll., 1985–86; Co. Comdr 42 Commando, 1988–90 (despatches 1990); Staff Officer (Grade 2), Mil. Ops 2 Br., resp. for NI Ops Policy, MoD, 1991–94; RM Rep., US Marine Corps Combat and Develt Comd, USA, 1994–96; CO 42 Commando, 1996–98; CSO Ops HQ RM, 1998–99; rcds, 2000; HCSC, 2001; Comdr 3 Commando Bde, 2001–02; Dir, HCSC, 2002–03; Dep. Comdr, HQ NATO Rapid Deployable Corps, Italy, 2003–06; Dep. Comdr Ops, HQ ISAF, Kabul, 2005–06. NATO Sen. Mentor, 2008–14. FCMI. Bronze Star, USA, 2002; Commendatore, Order of Merit (Italy), 2006; Baryal Medal, 1st Grade (Afghanistan), 2007. *Publications:* articles on NATO, leadership, empowerment and stabilisation. *Recreations:* ski-ing, sailing, gardening, fly fishing, genealogy, writing.

LANE, Shelley Ilene Munjack; an Upper Tribunal Judge (Administrative Appeals Chamber) (formerly a Social Security and Child Support Commissioner), since 2008; *b* Brooklyn, New York; *d* of late Morris Munjack and Helen Munjack; *m* 1980, Peter Richard Lane, *qv*; one *s* one *d. Educ:* Case Western Reserve Univ., Cleveland (BA magna cum laude, phi beta kappa); Queen Mary Coll., Univ. of London (LLB Hons). Called to the Bar, Gray's Inn, 1977; Lectr, then Sen. Lectr in Laws, QMUL, 1978–99; immigration adjudicator (pt-time), 1997–99; Dist Chm., Social Security and Child Support Appeals Tribunals, 1999–2008; Mem. (pt-time), Gender Recognition Panel, 2004. *Publications:* The Status of Licensing Common Law Marks, 1991; (jtly) Video Law, 1992; Intellectual Property (study guides), 1994, 2nd edn 1997; (jtly) Readings in Intellectual Property, 1998; (contrib.) Yearbook of Copyright and Media Law, 1999; numerous pubns in field of intellectual property. *Recreations:* opera, theatre, gardening. *Address:* Upper Tribunal, Administrative Appeals Chamber, 5th Floor, Rolls Building, 7 Rolls Buildings, Fetter Lane, EC4A 1NL.

LANE, Shirley Christine; *see* Price, S. C.

LANE-FOX OF SOHO, Baroness *cr* 2013 (Life Peer), of Soho in the City of Westminster; **Martha Lane Fox,** CBE 2013; *b* Oxford, 10 Feb. 1973; *d* of Robin James Lane Fox, *qv. Educ:* Westminster Sch.; Magdalen Coll., Oxford (BA). Former Consultant, Spectrum Strategy; Co-Founder, Man. Dir, 1997–2003, non-exec. Dir, 2003–05, lastminute.com; Founder and Chairman: Lucky Voice Gp Ltd, 2005–; Go On UK, 2012–; Chm., MakieLab, 2012–. Non-executive Director: Channel 4, 2006–12; mydeco.com, 2007–; Marks & Spencer plc, 2007–; Women's Prize for Fiction, 2011–. UK Digital Champion, 2009–13. Chancellor, Open Univ., 2014–. Mem. Bd, Founders Forum for Good; Founder and Chm., Antigone Foundn, 2007–; Patron, Reprieve (Founding Trustee, 2000–10). *Address:* House of Lords, SW1A 0PW.

LANE FOX, Robin James, FRSL; Tutorial Fellow, 1977–2014, now Emeritus Fellow, and Garden Master, since 1981, New College, Oxford; Reader in Ancient History, Oxford, 1990–2014; *b* 5 Oct. 1946; *s* of James Henry Lane Fox and Anne (*née* Loyd); *m* 1970, Louisa Caroline Mary (marr. diss. 1993), *d* of Charles and Lady Katherine Farrell; one *s* one *d. Educ:* Eton; Magdalen Coll., Oxford (Craven and de Paravicini scholarships, 1966; Passmore Edwards and Chancellors' Latin Verse Prize, 1968). FRSL 1974. Fellow by examination, Magdalen Coll., Oxford, 1970–73; Lectr in Classical Lang. and Lit., 1973–76, Res. Fellow, Classical and Islamic Studies, 1976–77, Worcester Coll., Oxford; Lectr in Ancient Hist., Oxford Univ., 1977–90. Writer and presenter, Greek Myths and Tales of Travelling Heroes, BBC4, 2010. Weekly gardening correspondent, Financial Times, 1970–. *Publications:* Alexander the Great, 1973, 3rd edn 1978 (James Tait Black, Duff Cooper, W. H. Heinemann Awards, 1973–74); Variations on a Garden, 1974, rev. edn 1986; Search for Alexander, 1980; Better Gardening, 1982; Pagans and Christians, 1986; The Unauthorized Version, 1991; The Making of 'Alexander', 2004; (ed and contrib.) The Long March: Xenophon and the Ten Thousand, 2004; The Classical World: an epic history from Homer to Hadrian, 2005 (Runciman prize, 2006); Travelling Heroes: Greeks and their myths in the epic age of Homer, 2008; Thoughtful Gardening, 2010; (ed and contrib.) Brill's Companion to Ancient Macedon, 2011; Augustine: convert and confessor, 2015. *Recreations:* gardening, remembering fox-hunting. *Address:* New College, Oxford OX1 3BN. *Club:* Beefsteak.
See also Baroness Lane-Fox of Soho.

LANE-FOX-PITT-RIVERS, Valerie; *see* Pitt-Rivers, V.

LANE-NOTT, Rear Adm. Roger Charles, CB 1996; FCMI; Director General and Chief Executive Officer, Agricultural Engineers Association, Milking Equipment Association, and National Sprayer Testing Scheme, since 2007; *b* 3 June 1945; *s* of John Henry Lane-Nott, MBE and Kathleen Mary Lane-Nott; *m* 1968, Roisin MacQuillan; one *s* two *d. Educ:* Pangbourne Coll.; BRNC, Dartmouth. Joined RN, 1963: qualified submarines, 1966; served in HM Submarines: Andrew, Opossum, Otus, Revenge (Starboard), Conqueror, Aeneas, 1966–74; commanded HM Submarines: Walrus, 1974–76; Swiftsure, 1979; Splendid, 1979–82 (mentioned in despatches, Falklands, 1982); US Naval War Coll., 1983; Captain SM, Third Submarine Sqdn, 1985–86; Asst Dir, Defence Concepts, MoD, 1986–89; RCDS 1989; Captain First Frigate Sqdn and in comd HMS Coventry, 1990–91; Sen. Naval Officer, ME, 1991; Chief of Staff to Flag Officer Submarines, 1992–93; Flag Officer Submarines, and Comdr Submarines (NATO), Eastern Atlantic and Northwest, 1993–96; COS (Ops) to C-in-C Fleet, 1994–96; RN retd, 1996. Formula One Race Dir and Safety Delegate, Fédn Internat. de l'Automobile, 1996–97; Chief Exec., Centre for Marine and Petroleum Technol., 1997–99; Sec., British Racing Drivers' Club, 1999–2007; Dir Gen. and CEO, Assoc. of Manufacturers of Power Generating Systems, 2007–14. Chm. of Trustees, RN Submarine Mus., 2005–10; Bd Dir, Nat. Mus. of RN, 2008–10. MRIN 1976; MNI 1991; FCMI (FIMgt 1983); FIAgrE 2008–14; MInstPet 1997. *Recreations:* watching sport (Rugby, cricket, motor racing), unusual stationery, lighthouses. *Address:* The Hawthorns, 5 Dudley Hill, Shenley Church End, Bucks MK5 6LL. *Clubs:* Oriental, British Racing Drivers'.

LANE-SMITH, Roger; Senior Partner, DLA (formerly Dibb Lupton Alsop), Solicitors, 1998–2005; Senior Consultant, DLA Piper, since 2005; Chairman, Lomond Capital Partners, since 2009; *b* 19 Oct. 1945; *s* of Harry Lane-Smith and Dorothy Lane-Smith; *m* 1969, Pamela; one *s* one *d. Educ:* Stockport Grammar Sch.; Guildford Coll. of Law. Admitted Solicitor, 1969; founded Lee Lane-Smith, 1977; Lee Lane-Smith merged with Alsop Stevens, 1983; Alsop Stevens merged with Wilkinson Kimbers to form Alsop Wilkinson, 1988; Chm. and Sen. Partner, Alsop Wilkinson, 1993–96; Alsop Wilkinson merged with Dibb Lupton to form Dibb Lupton Alsop, 1996; Dep. Sen. Partner, Dibb Lupton Alsop, 1996–98. Non-executive Director: JJB Sports, 1998–2009 (Chm., 2005–09); MS Internat., 1983–; Timpson, 1984–; Dolphin Capital Investors, 2006–; WH Ireland, 2007–14. *Publications:* A Fork in the Road: from single partner to largest legal practice in the world, 2014. *Recreations:* golf, shooting. *Club:* Mark's.

LANG, family name of **Baron Lang of Monkton**.

LANG OF MONKTON, Baron *cr* 1997 (Life Peer), of Merrick and the Rhinns of Kells in Dumfries and Galloway; **Ian Bruce Lang;** PC 1990; DL; Chairman, Marsh & McLennan Companies Inc., since 2011 (Director, since 1997); *b* 27 June 1940; *y s* of late James Fulton Lang, DSC, and Maude Margaret (*née* Stewart); *m* 1971, Sandra Caroline, *e d* of late John Alastair Montgomerie, DSC; two *d. Educ:* Lathallan Sch., Kincardineshire; Rugby Sch.; Sidney Sussex Coll., Cambridge (BA 1962). Insurance Broker, 1962–79. Director: CGU (formerly General Accident) plc, 1997–2000; Lithgows Ltd, 1997–2008; Automobile Assoc., 1998–99; Charlemagne Capital Ltd, 2006–. Trustee: Savings Bank of Glasgow, 1969–74; West of Scotland Trustee Savings Bank, 1974–83. Member, Queen's Body Guard for Scotland (Royal Company of Archers), 1974–. Contested (C): Central Ayrshire, 1970; Glasgow Pollok, Feb. 1974; MP (C) Galloway, 1979–83, Galloway and Upper Nithsdale, 1983–97; contested (C) Galloway and Upper Nithsdale, 1997. An Asst Govt Whip, 1981–83; a Lord Comr of HM Treasury, 1983–86; Parliamentary Under Secretary of State: Dept of Employment, 1986; Scottish Office, 1986–87; Minister of State, Scottish Office, 1987–90; Sec. of State for Scotland and Lord Keeper of the Great Seal of Scotland, 1990–95; Pres., Board of Trade, and Sec. of State for Trade and Industry, 1995–97. Member: Constitution Cttee, H of L, 2001–05 and 2012– (Chm., 2014–); Special Cttee on the Barnett Formula, H of L, 2008–09; Chm., Prime Minister's Adv. Cttee on Business Appts, 2009–14. Chm., Patrons of Nat. Galls of Scotland, 1999–2007. Gov., Rugby Sch., 1997–2007. DL Ayrshire and Arran, 1998. OStJ 1974. *Publications:* Blue Remembered Years, 2002. *Address:* House of Lords, SW1A 0PW. *Clubs:* Pratt's; Prestwick Golf.

LANG, Alistair Laurie, MBE 1970; Chief Executive, Drugs Abuse Resistance Education (DARE) UK Ltd, 2002–05; *b* 9 Sept. 1943; *s* of late Comdr John Robert Lang, RN (retd) and Jennifer Douglas Lang; *m* 1979, Ilona Augusta Avery; one *s* one *d*. *Educ:* Hurstpierpoint Coll.; BRNC; University Coll., Oxford (BA 1979); Internat. Management Inst., Geneva (MBA 1989). Served Royal Navy, 1962–75: in HM Ships Wizard, Salisbury, Devonshire, Malcolm, Plymouth and Kent; loan service to: Kenya Navy (Kenya Navy Ship Chui), 1966; Royal Malaysian Navy (i/c Kapel di-Raja Sri Sarawak and Fleet Ops Officer), 1968–70; Imperial Iranian Navy, 1974. Hong Kong Civil Service, 1979–90: Asst Sec. for Security, 1980–82; City Dist Officer, Kowloon City, 1982–83; support to Governor during negotiation with China on future of Hong Kong, 1983–85; Clerk of Councils (Sec. to Exec. and Legislative Councils), 1985–88; attached British Embassy, Beijing (on secondment), 1989; UK Rep., Hong Kong Exec. and Legislative Councils, 1990–92. Clerk to Drapers' Co., 1993–2000; Chief Exec., Canine Partners for Independence, 2000–02. *Recreations:* swimming, walking, reading, theatre. *Address:* Little Mead, Home Lane, Sparsholt, Winchester, Hants SO21 2NN. *T:* (01962) 776204.

See also Rear-Adm. J. S. Lang.

LANG, Dame Beverley Ann Macnaughton, DBE 2011; **Hon. Mrs Justice Lang;** a Judge of the High Court, Queen's Bench Division, since 2011; *b* 13 Oct. 1955; *d* of William Macnaughton Lang and Joan Margaret Mantua Lang (*née* Utting); one *d*. *Educ:* Wycombe Abbey Sch., Bucks; Lady Margaret Hall, Oxford (BA Hons Jurisprudence 1977; Hon. Fellow, 2011). Called to the Bar, Inner Temple, 1978, Bencher, 2006; Lectr, UEA, 1978–81; in practice at the Bar, 1981–2011; QC 2000; a Recorder, 2006–11. Chm. (part-time), Employment Tribunals, 1995–2001; Chm. (part-time), later Judge (part-time), Special Educnl Needs and Disability Tribunal, 2004–09. *Address:* Royal Courts of Justice, Strand, WC2A 2LL.

LANG, Dr Brian Andrew; Principal and Vice-Chancellor, University of St Andrews, 2001–08, now Principal Emeritus; *b* 2 Dec. 1945; *s* of Andrew Ballantyne Lang and Mary Bain Lang (*née* Smith); *m* 1st, 1975 (marr. diss. 1982); one *s*; 2nd, 1983 (marr. diss. 2000); one *s* one *d*; 3rd, 2002, Tari Hibbitt (*see* Tari Lang). *Educ:* Royal High Sch., Edinburgh; Univ. of Edinburgh (MA, PhD). Social anthropological field research, Kenya, 1969–70; Lectr in social anthropology, Aarhus Univ., 1971–75; Scientific Staff, SSRC, 1976–79; Scottish Office (Sec., Historic Buildings Council for Scotland), 1979–80; Sec., Nat. Heritage Meml Fund, 1980–87; Dir of Public Affairs, Nat. Trust, 1987–91; Chief Exec. and Dep. Chm., British Library, 1991–2000; Chairman: Eur. Nat. Libraries Forum, 1993–2000; Heritage Image Partnership (formerly Nat. Heritage Image Liby), 2000–02; Internat. Adv. Council, Internat. Leadership Sch. (Glasgow), 2011–. Member: Bd, Scottish Enterprise, Fife, 2003–08; Scottish Exec. Cultural Commn, 2004–05; Cttee for Scotland, Heritage Lottery Fund, 2004–11 (Chair, 2005–11). Member: Liby and Inf. Services Council (England), 1991–94; Liby and Inf. Commn, 1995–2000. Vis. Prof., Edinburgh Napier (formerly Napier) Univ., 1999–; Vis. Scholar, Getty Inst., Calif, 2000. Pforzheimer Lecture, Univ. of Texas, 1998. Trustee: 21st Century Learning Initiative, 1995–99; Hopetoun House Preservation Trust, 2001–05; Nat. Heritage Meml Fund, 2005–11; Nat. Museums of Scot., 2014–. Chm., Royal Scottish Nat. Orch., 2008–. Chm. Trustees, Newbattle Abbey Coll., 2004–08. Member, Council: Nat. Trust for Scotland, 2001–04; St Leonard's Sch., 2001–08. Pres., Inst. of Information Scientists, 1993–94 (Hon. Fellow, 1994). FRSE 2006. Hon. FCLIP (Hon. FLA 1997). Dr *hc* Edinburgh, 2008; Hon. LLD St Andrews, 2008. *Publications:* numerous articles, contribs etc to professional jls. *Recreations:* music, museums and galleries, pottering. *Address:* 4 Manor Place, Edinburgh EH3 7DD. *Club:* New (Edinburgh).

LANG, David Geoffrey, CMG 2007; CBE 1992; QC (Turks and Caicos) 1985; Attorney General, Falkland Islands, 1987–2006; *b* Scarborough, 4 Nov. 1941; *s* of Alexander and Nora Lang; *m* 1975, Theresa Margaret Hurt; one *s* three *d*. *Educ:* St Edmund's Sch., Canterbury; College of Law, London. Admitted solicitor, 1965; Asst Solicitor, Bognor Regis UDC, 1965–68; Partner, Wintle & Co. Solicitors, Bognor Regis, 1968–69; Asst Solicitor, 1969–71, Partner, 1971–76, Hedges & Mercer Solicitors, Oxon; Sec. for Justice, Rep. of Nauru, 1977–82; Attorney General, Turks and Caicos Is, 1982–87. *Recreations:* bridge, computer strategy games, science fiction, amateur dramatics. *Address:* 28 Goss Road, Stanley, Falkland Islands FIQQ 1ZZ.

LANG, Rt Rev. Declan; *see* Clifton, Bishop of, (RC).

LANG, Hugh Montgomerie, CBE 1978; Chairman, Acertec Holdings Ltd, 1999–2006; *b* Glasgow, 7 Nov. 1932; *s* of John Montgomerie Lang and Janet Allan (*née* Smillie); *m* 1st, 1959, Marjorie Jean Armour (marr. diss. 1981); one *s* one *d*; 2nd, 1981, Susan Lynn Hartley (*née* Russell). *Educ:* Shawlands Acad., Glasgow; Glasgow Univ. (BSc). ARCST 1953; CEng 1967; FIET (FIProdE 1976); FIMC 1970. Officer, REME, 1953–55 (National Service). Colvilles Ltd, 1955–56; Glacier Metal Co. Ltd, 1956–60; L. Sterne & Co. Ltd, 1960–61; P-E Consulting Group, 1961–92: Manager for ME, 1965–68; Scottish Reg. Manager, 1968–72; Man. Dir, 1974–77; Chm., P-E Internat., 1980–92 (Dir, 1972–92; Chief Exec., 1977–92). Chairman: Brammer plc, 1990–98; Manganese Bronze Hldgs, 1992–2000; Victaulic, 1995; Albion Automotive, 1997–98; Director: Redman Heenan Internat., 1981–86 (Chm., 1982–86); Fairey Holdings Ltd, 1978–82; UKO International, 1985–86; B. Elliott, 1986–88; Siebe, 1987–91; Strong & Fisher (Hldgs), 1988–90; Co-ordinated Land and Estates, 1988–93; OGC International, 1993–94; Ericsson Ltd, 1993–99. Chairman: Food, Drink and Packaging Machinery Sector Working Party, 1976–81; Technology Transfer Services Adv. Cttee, 1982–85 (Mem., 1978–85); Member: Business Educn Council, 1980–81; CBI Industrial Policy Cttee, 1980–83; Design Council, 1983–90 (Dep. Chm., 1986–90); Engrg Council, 1984–86. *Recreations:* fishing, gardening, golf, reading, walking. *Address:* Welders Wood, Chalfont St Peter, Bucks SL9 8TT. *Club:* Denham Golf.

LANG, Jack Mathieu Emile, Chevalier de la Légion d'Honneur; Hon. GCVO 1992; Deputy (Soc.) for Pas de Calais, National Assembly, France, 2002–12; President, Institut du Monde Arabe, since 2013; *b* 2 Sept. 1939; *s* of Roger Lang and Marie-Luce Lang (*née* Bouchet); *m* 1961, Monique Buczynski; one *d* (and one *d* decd). *Educ:* Inst. d'Etudes Politiques; Dr of Public Law. Founder and Producer, World Fest. Univ. Theatre, Nancy, 1963–72; Dir, Nancy Univ. Theatre, 1963–72; Dir, Palais de Chaillot Théâtre, 1972–74; Prof. of Internat. Law, 1971–81; Dir, teaching and research unit in legal and econ. scis, Nancy, 1977–80; Prof., Univ. of Paris X, 1986–88. Paris councillor, 1977–89; nat. deleg. for cultural affairs, Socialist Party, 1979–81; Minister of Culture, 1981–83 and 1984–86; Deputy, Loir-et-Cher, 1986–88 and 1997–2000; Minister of Culture and Communication, 1988–92; Govt Spokesman, 1991–92; Minister of State, and Minister of Nat. Educn and Culture, 1992–93; Minister for Educn, 2000–02. Pres., Foreign Affairs Cttee, French Nat. Assembly, 1997–2000. Mayor of Blois, 1989–2001; Conseiller Général de Blois, 1992–93. Order of Orange Nassau (Netherlands), 1991; Order of the Crown of Belgium, 1992. *Publications:* L'Etat et le Théâtre, 1968; Le plâteau continental de la mer du nord, 1970; Les politiques culturelles comparée en Europe; La jonction au fond des exceptions préliminaires devant la cour, 1971; (with J.-D. Bredin) Éclats, 1978; Demain les femmes, 1995; Lettre à Malraux, 1996; François 1er ou le rêve italien, 1997; (jtly) La politique, d'où ça vient?, 2000; Laurent le Magnifique, 2002; (with C. Lang) Anna au Muséum, 2002; (with C. Bretécher) Qu'apprend-on au collège?, 2002; Une école élitaire pour tous, 2003; Un nouveau régime politique pour la France, 2004; Nelson Mandela: leçon de vie pour l'avenir, 2005; Changer, 2005; (with H. Le Bras) Immigration Positive, 2006; Faire la révolution fiscale, 2006; L'école abandonnée: lettre à Xavier Darcos, 2008; (with J.-M. Helvig) Demain comme hier, 2009; Le Choix de Versailles, 2009; contribs to newspapers.

LANG, Jacqueline Shelagh; Headmistress, Walthamstow Hall, Sevenoaks, 1984–2002; *b* 17 June 1944; *d* of James Wicks and Mary Mills Wicks (*née* Green); *m* 1965, Andrew Lang; two *d*. *Educ:* Walthamstow Hall; St Anne's Coll., Oxford (Schol.; MA). Res., mediaeval French literature, KCL, 1964–66; Ursuline Convent School, Wimbledon: Asst Mistress, 1970–76; Head of Langs, 1976–83; Foundn Gov., 1984–93. Chairman: London and SE Region, ISIS, 1991–95; Assisted Places Cttee, ISC, 1998–2002; Pres., GSA, 1997. *Recreations:* history of architecture, gardens, visiting archaeological sites. *Address:* 82 Richmond Road, SW20 0PD.

LANG, Rear-Adm. John Stewart; DL; Royal Navy, retired; Chief Inspector of Marine Accidents, Marine Accident Investigation Branch, Department for Transport, Local Government and the Regions (formerly Department of Transport, then Department of the Environment, Transport and the Regions), 1997–2002; *b* 18 July 1941; *s* of late Comdr John Robert Lang, RN and Jennifer Douglas Lang; *m* 1971, Joanna Judith Pegler; two *d*. *Educ:* Cheltenham Coll. Jun. Sch.; Nautical Coll., Pangbourne. FNI 1986; FRIN 1997. Navigating Officer Apprentice, P&OSN Co., 1959–62; RN 1962; served HM Ships Chilcompton, Totem, Auriga, Oberon, Revenge, Opossum, 1964–71; qualified Submarine Command, 1971; commanded: HMS Walrus, 1971–72; HMS Renown, 1976–78; HMS Beaver, 1983–85; Captain, Royal Naval Presentation Team, 1986–87; ACOS (Ops) to C-in-C Fleet, 1987–89; Dir, Naval Ops and Trade, 1989–91; Dep. Chief of Defence Intelligence, 1992–95. Chm., EC Marine Accident Investigation Wkg Gp, 2004–06. President: Inst. of Seamanship, 2001–; Assoc. of Sail (formerly Sea) Trng Orgns, 2003–; Winchester Sea Cadets TS Itchen, 2003–. Mem., Yachtmaster Qualification Panel, RYA, 2008–; Vice Pres., RNLI, 2012– (Mem. Council, 2006–12). Patron, Sea Safety Gp, 2002–04; Trustee: Shipwrecked Mariners Soc., 2003–11 (Chm., 2008–11); Royal Nat. Mission to Deep Sea Fishermen, 2003– (Dep. Chm., 2009–); Chm., Nautical Inst. Fellowship Cttee, 2002–; Trustee Dir, Nautilus Internat. (formerly NUMAST, then Nautilus UK), 2003– (Mem., Nautilus Internat. Welfare Cttee, 2009–). Younger Brother, Trinity House, 1982–. Gov., Southampton Solent Univ. (formerly Southampton Inst.), 2004–10. DL Hants, 2008. Hon. DTech Nottingham Trent, 2002. *Publications:* Titanic: a fresh look at the evidence by a former Chief Inspector of Marine Accidents, 2012. *Recreations:* sailing, photography, oil painting, writing, lecturing. *Address:* Wangfield House, Martyr Worthy, Winchester, Hants SO21 1AT.

See also A. L. Lang.

LANG, Tari; advisor and non-executive director; Partner, Lang Consultancy, since 2009; *b* Prague, 18 June 1951; *d* of late Suwondo Budiardjo and of Carmel Budiardjo; *m* 1st, 1971, Roger Hibbitt (marr. diss. 1996); one *s* one *d*; 2nd, 2002, Dr Brian Andrew Lang, *qv*. Founder and Dir, Clasma Software, 1980–86; Man. Dir, Rowland Co., 1988–95; UK CEO, Edelman PR, 1995–2002; Founding Partner, Reputation Inc., 2002–09. Member, Board: National Th. of Scotland, 2008–; Edinburgh Internat. Fest., 2012–; Nat. Galls of Scotland, 2014–. Mem., Nominating Council, Women of Year, 2002–. *Recreations:* theatre, cinema. *T:* 07785 307933. *E:* tari@lang-uk.com.

LANG, Prof. Timothy Mark, PhD; FFPH; Professor of Food Policy, and Director, Centre for Food Policy, City University London, since 2002; *b* Lincoln, 7 Jan. 1948; *s* of Robert Antony Lang and Katharine Margaret Lang (*née* Alcock); *m* 2004, Valerie Elizabeth Castledine; one step *s* one step *d*. *Educ:* Leeds Univ. (BA Hons Psychol. and Sociol. 1970; PhD Psychol. 1974). Lectr, Trinity and All Saints Coll., Horsforth, Leeds, 1973–74; Partner, Simfield & Ramsclough Farms, Slaidburn, Clitheroe, Lancs, 1973–80; Sen. Lectr, Preston Poly., 1975–82; Sen. Lectr, and Dir, Food Policy Unit, Manchester Poly., 1982–84; Director: London Food Commn, 1984–90; Parents for Safe Food, 1990–94; Prof. of Food Policy, Thames Valley Univ., 1994–2002. Chair, Scottish Diet Action Plan Rev., Scottish NHS Exec., 2005–06; Member: Expert Adv. Gp for Healthy Weight Healthy Lives prog., DoH, 2008–10; Council of Food Policy Advrs to Sec. of State for Envmt, Food and Rural Affairs, 2008–10; Adviser to Parliamentary Select Committee inquiries: Agric. (Globalisation), 2000; Health and Agric. (Food Standards), 2000; Health (Obesity), 2003–04. Tech. Advr, Food and Nutrition Initiative, French Presidency of EC, 1999–2000; Advr, Prime Minister's Strategy Unit Review of Food and Food Policy, 2007–08; Mem., Mayor of London's Food Bd, 2010–. Natural Resources and Land Use Comr, Sustainable Develt Commn, 2006–11. Consultant, WHO, Geneva and Copenhagen, 1996–2002. Mem. Council, Public Health Alliance, 1987–99 (Sec., 1987–88). Chair, Sustain, 1999–2005. Vice-Pres., Chartered Inst. of Envmtl Health, 1999–. Trustee, Friends of the Earth, 1994–2001; President: Caroline Walker Trust, 2005–; Garden Organic, 2008–. FFPH 2001 (Hon. Mem. 1999); FRSA 1998. Hon. Fellow, UWIC, 2008. Hon. Freeman, Cooks' Co., 2008. Hon. DSc Lincoln, 2009. Derek Cooper Award, Food and Farming Awards, BBC Radio 4, 2004. *Publications:* (with C. Clutterbuck) More Than We Can Chew, 1982; (with A. Webb) Food Irradiation, 1987, 2nd edn 1990 (trans. 5 langs); Food Adulteration and How to Beat It, 1988; (with C. Clutterbuck) P is for Pesticides, 1991; (with C. Hines) The New Protectionism, 1993 (trans. 7 langs); (with Y. Gabriel) The Unmanageable Consumer, 1995, 2nd edn 2006; (with E. Millstone) The Atlas of Food, 2003 (André Simon Food Book of Year, 2003), 2nd edn 2008; (with M. Heasman) Food Wars, 2004; (jtly) Food Policy, 2009; (with G. Rayner) Ecological Public Health, 2012. *Recreations:* trying to grow fruit and vegetables in my London garden, thinking, reading the papers, riding my bike around London, talking with family and friends, eating home-cooking in our summerhouse at the end of the garden, collecting family pottery. *Address:* Centre for Food Policy, City University London, Northampton Square, EC1V 0HB. *T:* (020) 7040 8798. *E:* t.lang@city.ac.uk.

LANG LANG; concert pianist; *b* Shenyang, China, 14 June 1982. *Educ:* Central Music Conservatory, Beijing; Curtis Inst. of Music, Philadelphia. Began piano lessons, aged 3; winner, Shenyang Piano Comp. and first recital, aged 5; winner, Internat. Tchaikovsky Comp. for Young Musicians, 1995. Has performed with major orchestras in USA and worldwide, incl. Vienna Philharmonic, Berlin Philharmonic and Shanghai SO; work with conductors incl. Zubin Mehta, Sir Simon Rattle, Daniel Barenboim and Seiji Ozawa; world tour, 2009, with Herbie Hancock. Has held masterclasses at instns incl. Curtis Inst. of Music, Juilliard Sch., Manhattan Sch. of Music, Hanover Conservatory and conservatories in China. Founder, Lang Lang Internat. Music Foundn, NY, 2008. Chm., Montblanc de la Culture Arts Patronage Award Project; Member: Adv. Cttee, Weill Music Inst., 2004–; Bd of Trustees, Carnegie Hall, 2007–. Goodwill Ambassador, UNICEF, 2004–. Hon. DMus RAM, 2011; Hon. Dr Musical Arts Manhattan Sch. of Music, 2012. Presidential Merit Award, 2007, Cultural Ambassador to China, 2008, Recording Acad. Order of Merit (Germany), 2012. *Publications:* Journey of a Thousand Miles (autobiog.), 2008; Playing with Flying Keys (autobiog. for young readers), 2008. *Address:* Columbia Artists Music LLC, 5 Columbus Circle, 1790 Broadway, 16th Floor, New York, NY 10019, USA. *T:* (212) 8419564, *Fax:* (212) 8419719. *E:* jcesbron@camimusic.com.

LANGAN, His Honour Peter St John Hevey; QC 1983; a Circuit Judge, 1991–2013; Specialist Mercantile Circuit Judge, North Eastern Circuit, 2004–13; acting Puisne Judge, Gibraltar, since 2013; practising mediator and arbitrator, since 2014; *b* 1 May 1942; *s* of late Frederick Hevey Langan and Myrrha Langan (*née* Jephson), Mount Hevey, Hill of Down, Co. Meath; *m* 1st, 1976, Oonagh May Winifred McCarthy (marr. diss.); 2nd, 2003, Alison Felicity Tuffnell; one step *d*. *Educ:* Downside School; Trinity College, Dublin (MA, LLB); Christ's College, Cambridge (PhD). Lectr in Law, Durham Univ., 1966–69. In practice at the Bar, 1970–91; a Recorder, 1989–91; Designated Civil Judge, Norwich and Cambridge, 1998–2001; Mercantile and Chancery Judge, NE Circuit, 2001–04. Legal Assessor: GMC, 1990–91; GDC, 1990–91. Mem., Legal Commn, Caritas Internationalis, Rome, 1991–93; Trustee, CAFOD, 1993–99 (Mem., Management Cttee, 1984–91). *Publications:* Maxwell on

Interpretation of Statutes, 12th edn 1969; Civil Procedure and Evidence, 1st edn 1970, 3rd edn (with L. D. J. Henderson) as Civil Procedure, 1983; (with P. V. Baker) Snell's Principles of Equity, 28th edn 1982, 29th edn 1990. *Address:* 6 Catley Grove, Long Ashton, Bristol BS41 9NH. *T:* (01275) 394235; Enterprise Chambers, 9 Old Square, Lincoln's Inn, WC2A 3SR. *T:* (020) 7405 9471.

LANGDALE, Prof. Jane Alison, PhD; FRS 2015; Professor of Plant Development, University of Oxford, since 2006; Senior Research Fellow, Queen's College, Oxford, since 2006; *b* Coventry, 25 Aug. 1960; *d* of Edwin S. and Jean M. Langdale. *Educ:* Barrs Hill Grammar Sch., Coventry; Univ. of Bath (BSc Applied Biol. 1982); Univ. of London (PhD Human Genetics 1985). Postdoctoral Res. Associate, Biol. Dept, Yale Univ., 1985–90; University of Oxford: Department of Plant Sciences: SERC Res. Fellow, 1990–93; Royal Soc. Res. Fellow, 1993–94; Lectr, 1994–2006; Hd of Dept, 2007–12; Founding Dir, Plants for 21st Century Inst., 2008–13; Associate Hd, Maths, Physical and Life Scis Div., 2009–13; Tutorial Fellow, Queen's Coll., Oxford, 1994–2006. *Publications:* (jtly) How to Succeed as a Scientist: from postdoc to professor, 2011; contribs to learned jls incl. Nature, Sci., Current Biol., Develt, EMBO Jl, Genes & Develt, Plant Cell, Plant Jl. *Recreations:* gardening, cooking, Airedale Terriers. *Address:* Department of Plant Sciences, University of Oxford, South Parks Road, Oxford OX1 3RB. *T:* (01865) 275099. *E:* jane.langdale@plants.ox.ac.uk.

LANGDALE, Rachel; QC 2009; *b* Coventry, 1965; *d* of Edwin and Jean Langdale; *m* 1999, Simeon Andrew Maskrey, QC; one *s* one *d*. *Educ:* Bristol Poly. (LLB Hons); Darwin Coll., Cambridge (MPhil Criminol.). Called to the Bar, Middle Temple, 1990, Bencher, 2011; in practice as barrister specialising in public and regulatory law, and child and family law. *Recreation:* family life. *Address:* 7 Bedford Row, WC1R 4BU. *T:* (020) 7242 3555.

LANGDALE, Simon John Bartholomew; Director of Grants and Special Projects (formerly Educational and General Grants), The Rank Foundation, 1988–2002; Chairman, Arthur Rank Training, 2001–08; *b* 26 Jan. 1937; *s* of late Geoffrey Ronald Langdale and Hilda Joan Langdale (*née* Bartholomew); *m* 1962, Diana Marjory Hall; two *s* one *d*. *Educ:* Tonbridge Sch.; St Catharine's Coll., Cambridge. Taught at Radley Coll., 1959–73 (Housemaster, 1968–73); Headmaster: Eastbourne Coll., 1973–80; Shrewsbury Sch., 1981–88. *Recreations:* reading, gardening, golf. *Address:* Park House, Culworth, Banbury, Oxon OX17 2AP. *T:* (01295) 760222. *Clubs:* Hawks (Cambridge); Free Foresters, Jesters.

See also T. J. Langdale.

LANGDALE, Timothy James; QC 1992; a Recorder, 1996–99; *b* 3 Jan. 1940; *m* twice; two *d*; *m* 3rd, 2001, Susan Smith (*née* Hare). *Educ:* Sevenoaks Sch.; St Andrews Univ. (MA). Called to the Bar, Lincoln's Inn, 1966. Res. Assistant, Community Justice Center, Watts, Los Angeles, 1969–70; Jun. Prosecuting Counsel to the Crown, 1979–87, Sen. Prosecuting Counsel, 1987–92, CCC. Appeal Steward, BBB of C, 2002– (Chm., 2012–). *Recreations:* reading, the arts. *Address:* Cloth Fair Chambers, 39–40 Cloth Fair, EC1A 7NT. *T:* (020) 7710 6444.

See also S. J. B. Langdale.

LANGDON, Andrew Dominic; QC 2006; a Recorder, since 2002; *b* 23 July 1963; *s* of Michael and Phillipa Langdon; *m* 1989, Caroline; one *s* three *d*. *Educ:* Bristol Univ. (LLB). Called to the Bar, Middle Temple, 1986. *Recreations:* music, tennis, swimming, fishing. *Address:* Guildhall Chambers, 23 Broad Street, Bristol BS1 2HG. *T:* (0117) 927 3366. *E:* andrew.langdon@guildhallchambers.co.uk.

LANGDON, Anthony James; Deputy Under Secretary of State, Home Office, 1989–95; *b* 5 June 1935; *s* of Dr James Norman Langdon and Maud Winifred Langdon; *m* 1969, Helen Josephine Drabble, *y d* of His Honour J. F. Drabble, QC; one *s* one *d*. *Educ:* Kingswood Sch., Bath; Christ's Coll., Cambridge. Entered Home Office, 1958; Office of Minister for Science, 1961–63; Treasury, 1967–69; Under Sec., Cabinet Office, 1985–89. *Publications:* (with Ian Dunbar) Tough Justice, 1998; A Guide to Baroque Rome: the palaces, 2015.

LANGDON, Janet Mary; Director and Secretary, Water Services Association of England and Wales, 1992–98; *b* 5 March 1940; *d* of late Geoffrey Harry Langdon and Iris Sarah Langdon. *Educ:* St Hilda's Coll., Oxford (BSc, MA). Asst Lectr, Wellesley Coll., Mass, 1962–63; Distillers' Co. Ltd, 1963–68; NEDO, 1968–71; Shell Chemicals UK Ltd and Shell Internat. Chemical Co. Ltd, 1971–82; Projects and Export Policy Div., DTI, 1982–85; Director: Asia, Gp Exports, GEC PLC, 1985–89; Export Div., GEC ALSTHOM Ltd, 1989–92. Member: Sch. Teachers' Rev. Body, 1996–2002; POUNC, 1998–2000. *Recreations:* walking, tennis, travel, theatre. *Address:* 43 Fairfax Place, NW6 4EJ. *T:* (020) 7624 3857.

LANGDON, Prof. John Dudley, FDSRCS, FRCSE, FMedSci; Professor of Oral and Maxillofacial Surgery, King's College London, 1992–2004; *b* 24 March 1942; s of Jack Langdon and Daphne Irene Heloise Liebsch. *Educ:* London Hosp. Med. Coll., Univ. of London (BDS, MB BS, MDS). LDSRCS 1965, FDSRCS 1971; FRCSE 1985. Sen. Lectr in Oral and Maxillofacial Surgery, KCL, 1983–92; Consultant Oral and Maxillofacial Surgeon, Queen Mary's Hosp., Roehampton and Ashford Gen. Hosp., Middx, 1977–83; Hon. Consultant: St George's Hosp., 1984–2000; Royal Surrey Co. Hosp., Guildford, 1993–2003; Epsom Gen. Hosp., 1994–2004. Dean of Dental Scis, Baqai Medical Univ., Karachi, 2006–08. FMedSci 1998; FKC 2002. *Publications:* Malignant Tumours of the Mouth, Jaws and Salivary Glands, 1985, 2nd edn 1995; Surgical Pathology of the Mouth and Jaws, 1996; Operative Maxillofacial Surgery, 1998; The Infratemporal Fossa, 2002; Operative Oral and Maxillofacial Surgery, 2010. *Recreations:* opera, ballet, gardening, antiques. *Address:* The Old Rectory, Limington, Somerset BA22 8EQ.

LANGER, Bernhard, Hon. OBE 2006; golfer; *b* Germany, 27 Aug. 1957; *m* 1984, Vikki Lopez; two *s* two *d*. Major championships include: US Masters, 1985, 1993; German Open 5 times; US Senior Open, 2010; Senior British Open, 2010; 10 Ryder Cup appearances for Europe, 1981–97, and 2002, Europe Captain, 2004. Founder, Bernhard Langer Foundn, 2003. Order of Merit (Bavaria), 2012. *Publications:* (with Bill Elliott) While the Iron is Hot (autobiog.), 1988; (with Stuart Weir) Bernhard Langer: the autobiography, 2002. *Address:* PO Box 40, 86416 Diedorf-Anausen, Germany.

LANGFORD, 9th Baron *cr* 1800; **Colonel Geoffrey Alexander Rowley-Conwy,** OBE (mil.) 1943; DL; RA, retired; Constable of Rhuddlan Castle and Lord of the Manor of Rhuddlan; *b* 8 March 1912; *s* of late Major Geoffrey Seymour Rowley-Conwy (killed in action, Gallipoli, 1915), Bodrhyddan, Flints, and Bertha Gabrielle Rowley-Conwy, JP (*d* 1984), *d* of late Lieutenant Alexander Cochran, Royal Navy, Ashkirk, Selkirkshire; *S* kinsman, 1953; *m* 1st, 1939, Ruth St John (marr. diss. 1956; she *d* 1991), *d* of late Albert St John Murphy, The Island House, Little Island, County Cork; 2nd, 1957, Grete (*d* 1973), *d* of late Col E. T. C. von Freiesleben, formerly Chief of the King's Adjutants Staff to the King of Denmark; three *s*; 3rd, 1975, Susan Winifred Denham, *d* of C. C. H. Denham, Chester; one *s* one *d*. *Educ:* Marlborough; RMA Woolwich. Served War of 1939–45, with RA (2nd Lieut, 1932; Lieut, 1935; Captain, 1939; Major 1941); Singapore, 1942 (POW escaped) and with Indian Mountain Artillery in Burma (Arakan, Kohima), 1941–45 (despatches, OBE); Staff Coll., Quetta, 1945; Berlin Airlift, Fassberg, 1948–49; GSO I 42 Inf. Div., TA, 1949–52; Lt-Col 1945; retired 1957; Colonel (Hon.), 1967. Freeman, City of London, 1986–. DL Clwyd, 1977. *Heir: s* Hon. Owain Grenville Rowley-Conwy [*b* 27 Dec. 1958; *m* 1st, 1986, Joanna (marr. diss. 1993), *d* of Jack Featherstone; one *s* one *d*; 2nd, 2008, Lorraine Hennequin]. *Address:* Bodrhyddan, Rhuddlan, Denbighshire LL18 5SB. *Club:* Army and Navy.

LANGFORD, Anthony John, CB 1996; FRICS; Chief Executive, Valuation Office Agency, 1994–96; *b* 25 June 1936; *s* of Freeman and Ethel Langford; *m* 1958, Joan Winifred Barber; one *s* one *d*. *Educ:* Soham Grammar School. FRICS 1978. Joined Valuation Office, Inland Revenue, 1957; District Valuer, Camden, 1976; Superintending Valuer, Northern Region, 1981; Asst Chief Valuer, 1983; Dep. Chief Valuer, then Dep. Chief Exec., Valuation Office Agency, 1988–94. *Recreations:* walking, gardening, bowls.

LANGHAM, Sir John (Stephen), 16th Bt *cr* 1660, of Cottesbrooke, Northampton; *b* 14 Dec. 1960; *s* of Sir James Michael Langham, 15th Bt, TD and of Marion Audrey Eleanor Langham (*née* Barratt); *S* father, 2002; *m* 1991, Sarah Jane Verschoyle-Greene; one *s* two *d*. Farmer and landowner. Web media and internet consultant. *Heir: s* Tyrone Denis James Langham, *b* 13 Aug. 1994. *Address:* Tempo Manor, Demesne, Tempo, Co. Fermanagh BT94 3PA. *T:* (028) 8954 1953.

LANGHAM, Patricia Anne, CBE 2009; Principal, Wakefield Grammar School Foundation, 2000–09; Headmistress, Wakefield Girls' High School, 1987–2009; Chairman, Independent and State Schools Partnership Forum, 2011–14 (Co-Chairman, 2008–11); *b* Carlisle, 1 Jan. 1951; *d* of Andrew and Mary Lowrie; *m* 2008, Nev Hanley; one step *s* two step *d*. *Educ:* Carlisle and County High Sch. for Girls; Univ. of Leeds (BA English and Russian; MEd). Ilkley Grammar Sch., 1973–78; Brigshaw Comp. Sch., 1978–82; Dep. Head, Woodkirk High Sch., 1982–87. Pres., GSA, 2007. Trustee, Royal Armouries, 2004–13, now Emeritus. *Recreations:* literature, gardening, travel, dog walking, collecting flying ducks. *E:* patlangham@aol.com.

LANGHORNE, Prof. Richard Tristan Bailey, FRHistS; Professor of Global Politics, and Director, Centre for Global Studies, University of Buckingham, 2010–14, now Honorary Professor; *b* 6 May 1940; *s* of late Eadward John Bailey Langhorne and Rosemary Scott-Foster; *m* 1971, Helen Logue (*d* 2005), *o d* of William Donaldson, CB and Mary Donaldson; one *s* one *d*. *Educ:* St Edward's Sch., Oxford; St John's Coll., Cambridge (Exhibnr). BA Hist. Tripos, 1962; Certif. in Hist. Studies, 1963; MA 1965. Tutor in History, Univ. of Exeter, 1963–64; Research Student, St John's Coll., Cambridge, 1964–66; Lectr in History, 1966–74 and Master of Rutherford Coll., 1971–74, Univ. of Kent at Canterbury; St John's College, Cambridge: Steward, 1974–79; Junior Bursar, 1974–87; Fellow, 1974–93; Dir, Centre of Internat. Studies, Univ. of Cambridge, 1987–93; Dir and Chief Exec., Wilton Park, FCO, 1993–96; Prof. of Political Sci., 1996–2010, Dir, 1996–2008, Center for Global Change and Governance, later Division of Global Affairs, Rutgers Univ., NJ. Vis. Prof., Univ. of Southern Calif, 1986; Hon. Prof. of Internat. Relns, Univ. of Kent at Canterbury, 1994–97; Vis. Prof., Canterbury Christchurch Univ., 2006; Hon. Prof. of Global Pols, Univ. of Buckingham, 2007–10. Freeland K. Abbott Meml Lectr, Tufts Univ., 1990; Queen Beatrix Lectr, Royal Foundn, Amsterdam, 1998. *Publications:* The Collapse of the Concert of Europe, 1890–1914, 1980; (ed) Diplomacy and Intelligence during the Second World War, 1985; (with K. Hamilton) The Practice of Diplomacy, 1994, 2nd edn 2010; The Coming of Globalization, 2000; (ed) Guide to International Relations and Diplomacy, 2002; (with C. Jönsson) Diplomacy (3 vols), 2004; The Essentials of Global Politics, 2006; reviews and articles in Historical Jl, History, Review of International Studies, and Diplomacy and Statecraft. *Recreations:* music, railways. *Address:* May Cottage, South Street, Castle Cary, Somerset BA7 7EW. *Club:* Athenæum.

LANGLANDS, Sir Alan; *see* Langlands, Sir R. A.

LANGLANDS, Allister Gordon; Chairman, John Wood Group PLC, 2012–14 (Chief Executive, 2007–12); *b* 31 March 1958; *s* of John and Diana Langlands; *m* 1993, Helen Shoreman; four *s* one *d*. *Educ:* Forfar Acad.; Univ. of Edinburgh (MA Hons Econs 1980); Harvard Univ. (AMP 1999). CA. Deloitte Haskins & Sells: Trainee Chartered Accountant, 1980–83; Manager Corporate Finance/Audit, 1984–89; Partner, 1989–91; John Wood Group PLC: Gp Finance Dir, 1991–99; Dep. Chief Exec., 1999–2006. *Recreations:* family, golf, racquet sports, gardening.

LANGLANDS, Sir (Robert) Alan, Kt 1998; Vice-Chancellor, University of Leeds, since 2013; *b* 29 May 1952; *s* of James Langlands and May Langlands (*née* Rankin); *m* 1977, Elizabeth McDonald; one *s* one *d*. *Educ:* Allan Glen's Sch.; Univ. of Glasgow (BSc Pure Sci). FRSE 2002. Grad. Trainee, NHS Scotland, 1974–76; Argyll and Clyde Health Bd, 1976–78; Simpson Meml Maternity Pavilion, Elsie Inglis Hosp., 1978–81; Unit Administrator, Middx and University Coll. Hosps and Hosp. for Women, Soho, 1981–85; Dist Gen. Manager, Harrow HA, 1985–89; Practice Leader, Health Care, Towers Perrin, 1989–91; Gen. Manager, NW Thames RHA, 1991–92; Dep. Chief Exec., 1993–94, Chief Exec., 1994–2000, NHS Executive; Principal and Vice-Chancellor, Dundee Univ., 2000–09; Chief Exec., HEFCE, 2009–13. Member: Central R&D Cttee, NHS, 1991–92; Nat. Forum R&D, 1994–99; Health Sector Gp, BOTB, 1998–2000. Chairman: UK Biobank, 2004–12; Commn on Good Governance, 2004–05; Health Foundn, 2009–. Non-executive Director: Office for Strategic Coordination of Health Research, 2007–; UK Statistics Authy, 2008–09; Medicines and Healthcare Products Regulatory Agency, 2012. Trustee, Nuffield Trust, 2007–09. Hon. Prof., 1996, and Mem. Bd, Univ. of Warwick Business Sch., 1999–2000; Member: Council and Court, Univ. of York, 1998–2000; Adv. Bd, INSEAD, 1999–2003; US Nat. Adv. Bd, Johns Hopkins Univ. Bioethics Inst., 2000–04. Hon. FFPH (Hon. FFPHM 1994); FIA 1999; FCGI 2000; CCMI (CIMgt 2000); Hon. FRCP 2001; Hon. FRCGP 2001; Hon. FRCSE 2001; Hon. FRCPSGlas 2002. DUniv Glasgow, 2001; LLD Dundee, 2010; Dr *hc* Edinburgh, 2010. *Recreation:* living and walking in Scotland and Yorkshire. *Address:* Vice-Chancellor's Office, University of Leeds, Leeds LS2 9JT.

LANGLANDS, Prof. Robert Phelan, FRS 1981; Professor of Mathematics, Institute for Advanced Study, Princeton, New Jersey, 1972–2007, now Emeritus; *b* 6 Oct. 1936; *s* of Robert Langlands and Kathleen Johanna (*née* Phelan); *m* 1956, Charlotte Lorraine Cheverie; two *s* two *d*. *Educ:* Univ. of British Columbia (BA 1957, MA 1958); Yale Univ. (PhD 1960). FRSC 1972. Princeton University: Instructor, 1960–61; Lectr, 1961–62; Asst Prof., 1962–64; Associate Prof., 1964–67; Prof., Yale Univ., 1967–72. Associate Prof., Ortadoğu Teknik Universitesi, 1967–68; Gast Prof., Universität Bonn, 1980–81. Mem., Nat. Acad. of Scis, USA, 1993; Foreign Member: Russian Acad. of Scis, 2012; Turkish Bilim Akademesi, 2013. Hon. DSc: British Columbia, 1985; McMaster, 1985; CUNY, 1985; Paris VII, 1989; McGill, 1991; Toronto, 1993; Montreal, 1997; Laval, 2002; Madras, 2005; Chicago, 2011; Hon. DMath Waterloo, 1988. Wilbur L. Cross Medal, Yale Univ., 1975; Cole Prize, 1982, Steele Prize, 2005, Amer. Math. Soc.; Common Wealth Award, Sigma Xi, 1984; Maths Award, Nat. Acad. of Scis, 1988; Wolf Prize in Maths, Wolf Foundn of Israel, 1996; Grande Médaille d'Or, Acad. des Scis, Paris, 2000; Frederic Esser Nemmers Prize, Northwestern Univ., 2006; Shaw Prize, Shaw Foundn, Hong Kong, 2007. *Publications:* Automorphic Forms on GL(2) (with H. Jacquet), 1970; Euler Products, 1971; On the Functional Equations satisfied by Eisenstein Series, 1976; Base Change for GL(2), 1980; Les débuts d'une formule des traces stable, 1983; contrib. Canadian Jl Maths, Proc. Amer. Math. Soc. Symposia, Springer Lecture Notes. *Address:* Institute for Advanced Study, School of Mathematics, 1 Einstein Drive, Princeton, NJ 08540, USA. *T:* (609) 7348106.

LANGLEY, Sir (Julian Hugh) Gordon, Kt 1995; Chairman, Panel on Takeovers and Mergers, since 2010 (a Deputy Chairman, 2009–10); *b* 11 May 1943; *s* of late Gordon Thompson Langley and of Marjorie Langley; *m* 1968, Beatrice Jayanthi Langley; two *d*. *Educ:* Westminster School; Balliol College, Oxford (MA, BCL). Called to the Bar, Inner Temple,

1966, Bencher, 1996; QC 1983; a Recorder, 1986–95; a Judge of the High Ct of Justice, QBD, 1995–2007. *Recreations:* music, sport. *Address:* c/o Fountain Court Chambers, Temple, EC4Y 9DH.

LANGLEY, Ven. Robert; Archdeacon of Lindisfarne, 2001–07, now Archdeacon Emeritus; *b* 25 Oct. 1937; *s* of Maurice and Kathleen Langley; *m* 1961, Elisabeth Hart; one *s* two *d. Educ:* Worksop Coll.; St Catherine's Coll., Oxford (BA Maths 1961). Ordained deacon, 1963, priest, 1964; Asst Curate, Aston cum Aughton, Sheffield, 1963–68; Midlands and HQ Sec., Christian Educn Movt, 1968–74; Principal: Ian Ramsay Coll., Brasted, 1974–77; St Albans Dio. Ministerial Trng Scheme, 1977–85; Canon Missioner, Newcastle Dio., 1985–98; Dir, Ministry and Trng, Newcastle Dio., 1998–2001. Chm., Northumberland Strategic Partnership, 2008–11. Chairman: William Temple Foundn, 1994–2006; Community Action Northumberland, 2005–08; Vice Chm., SE Northumberland and N Tyneside Regeneration Initiative, 2006–09. *Recreations:* cycling, walking, music, furniture restoration. *Address:* Brook House, Middlewood Lane, Fylingthorpe, Whitby, N Yorks YO22 4TT.

LANGLEY, Prof. Robin Stewart, PhD; FRAeS; Professor of Mechanical Engineering, since 1998, and Head, Division of Mechanics, Materials and Design, Department of Engineering, since 2008, Cambridge University; Fellow of Fitzwilliam College, Cambridge, since 1998; *b* 5 April 1957; *s* of Robert Langley and Marie Langley (*née* Lewins); *m* 1st, 1982, Pamela Heath (marr. diss. 1997); 2nd, 2007, Elizabeth Nachapkina. *Educ:* Univ. of Leicester (BSc 1978); Cranfield Univ. (MSc 1981; PhD 1983). CMath, FIMA 1989; CEng, MRAeS 1990. Accountant, Armitage and Norton, 1978–79; Teaching Associate, 1983–84, Lectr in Structural Dynamics, 1984–91, Cranfield Univ.; Sen. Lectr in Aerospace Structures, 1991–95, Prof. of Structural Dynamics, 1995–98, Southampton Univ.; Dep. Hd (Grad. Studies), Dept of Engrg, Cambridge Univ., 1999–2002. Fellow: Acoustical Soc. of Amer., 2000; Internat. Inst. of Acoustics and Vibration, 2005; Royal Aeronautical Soc., 2011. *Publications:* articles in academic jls, mainly on random vibration, structural dynamics, and acoustics. *Recreations:* walking, literature, family and friends. *Address:* Department of Engineering, University of Cambridge, Trumpington Street, Cambridge CB2 1PZ. *T:* (01223) 748242.

LANGRIDGE, Stephen Maitland; conductor; Artistic Director, Gothenburg Opera, since 2013; *b* London, 28 May 1963; *s* of Philip Langridge, CBE and Hilary Holloway (*née* Davidson); *m* 1996, Denise L. Mellion; two *d. Educ:* John Lyon Sch., Harrow; Exeter Univ. (BA Hons Drama). Asst Dir, Opera Factory, 1985–90; freelance opera dir, 1990–, incl. prodns for Glyndebourne, Lyric Opera Chicago, Opera di Roma, Salzburg Festspiele, Bregenzer Festspiele, Royal Opera Hse, Covent Gdn, Kunlinga Operan Stockholm, Den Norske Opera, Malmö Opera, Gothenburg Opera. Occasional lectr in opera and music th., 1985–2013. A dir, Share Music (has devised music theatre with integrated gps of people with and without disabilities), 1989–. Leader: creative music projects with professional and non-professional gps in schs, prisons, hosps and in wider community; trng courses for teachers, singers, instrumentalists, composers and librettists. Mem., Gothenburg Beekeeping Gp. *Recreation:* running. *Address:* c/o Rayfield Allied, Southbank House, Black Prince Road, SE1 7SJ. *W:* www.stephenlangridge.com.

LANGRISH, Rt Rev. Michael Laurence; Bishop of Exeter, 2000–13; an Honorary Assistant Bishop, Diocese of Chichester, since 2014; *b* 1 July 1946; *s* of Douglas Frank and Brenda Florence Langrish; *m* 1968, Esther Vivien (*née* Rudd); one *s* two *d. Educ:* King Edward Sch., Southampton; Birmingham Univ. (BSocSc 1967; PGCE 1968); Fitzwilliam Coll., Cambridge (BA 1973; MA 1978); Ridley Hall, Cambridge. Lectr in Educn, Mid-West State Coll. of Educn, Nigeria, 1969–71. Ordained deacon, 1973, priest, 1974; Asst Curate, Stratford-upon-Avon with Bishopston, 1973–76; Chaplain, Rugby Sch., 1976–81; Vicar, Offchurch and Diocesan Dir of Ordinands, 1981–87; Team Rector, Rugby Team Ministry, 1987–93; Bishop Suffragan of Birkenhead, 1993–2000. Chm., Rural Strategy Gp (formerly Rural Affairs Cttee), C of E Bd of Mission, 2001–09. Chairman: Devon Strategic Partnership, 2002–07; Melanesian Mission (UK), 2003–09; Churches' Legislation Advisory Service, 2009–13; Mem. Bd, Christian Aid, 2003–11. Mem. Council, Univ. of Exeter, 2001–10. Entered House of Lords, 2005. Hon. DD: Birmingham, 2006; Exeter, 2007. *Recreations:* gardening, local history, theatre, railways, music. *Address:* 39 The Meadows, Walberton, Arundel, W Sussex BN18 0PB. *Clubs:* Athenæum, Farmers.

LANGRISHE, Sir James Hercules, 8th Bt *cr* 1777, of Knocktopher Abbey, Kilkenny; *b* 3 March 1957; *o s* of Sir Hercules Ralph Hume Langrishe, 7th Bt and of Hon. Grania Sybil Enid Wingfield, *o d* of 9th Viscount Powerscourt; *S* father, 1998; *m* 1985, Gemma Mary Philomena (marr. diss. 2010), *e d* of Patrick O'Daly; one *s* one *d. Heir: s* Richard James Hercules Langrishe, *b* 8 April 1988. *Address:* Arlonstown, Dunsany, Co. Meath, Ireland.

LANGSHAW, George Henry; Managing Director, UK Regions, British Gas, 1992; *b* 6 Dec. 1939; *s* of George Henry and Florence Evelyn Langshaw; *m* 1962, Maureen Cosgrove; one *s* two *d. Educ:* Liverpool Inst. High Sch. FCMA; ACIS. Various accountancy appts, Wm Crawford & Sons, 1957–63, Littlewoods Orgn, 1963–67; British Gas: Accountant, NW, 1967–70; Devolt Accountant, Southern, 1970–73; Prin. Financial Analyst, HQ, 1973–76; Chief Accountant, Wales, 1976–78; Dir of Finance, Southern, 1978–82; Dep. Chm., NW, 1982–87; Regional Chm., British Gas (Wales), 1987–89; Gp Dir of Personnel, 1989–90; Man. Dir, Global Gas, 1990–92. Chm., BG Corporate Ventures, 1990. Director: British Gas Deutschland GmbH, 1991; British Gas Holdings (Canada), 1992; BG Holdings Inc., 1992. Dir, Bd of Gas Consumers, Canada, 1990. CIGEM (CIGasE 1988); CCMI (CBIM 1991). *Recreations:* soccer, reading, golf.

LANGSLOW, Derek Robert, CBE 2000; PhD; Acting Chairman, Marine Management Organisation, 2010–11; *b* 7 Feb. 1945; *s* of Alexander Frederick Langslow and Beatrice Bibby Langslow (*née* Wright); *m* 1969, Helen Katherine (*née* Addison); one *s* one *d. Educ:* Ashville College, Harrogate; Queens' College, Cambridge (MA, PhD). Post-Doctoral Fellow, Cambridge and Univ. of Kansas; Lectr, Univ. of Edinburgh, 1972–78; Nature Conservancy Council: Senior Ornithologist, 1978–84; Asst Chief Scientist, 1984–87; Dir, Policy and Planning, 1987–90; Chief Scientist, 1990; Chief Exec., English Nature, 1990–2000; Chm., Rail Passenger Cttee for Eastern England, 2000–05; Chm., East of England Tourism, 2006–10. Director: British Waterways, 2000–06; Harwich Haven Authy, 2001–09 (Dep. Chm., 2007–09); Marine Mgt Orgn, 2010–. Member: Agriculture and Envmt Biotechnol. Commn, 2000–05; Passenger Focus, 2005–11. Trustee: Heritage Lottery Fund, 2002–08; Natural History Mus., 2008–May 2016; Beds, Cambs, Northants and Peterborough Wildlife Trust, 2009– (Chm., 2013–). *Publications:* numerous papers in learned jls. *Recreations:* badminton, hill-walking, sheep, bird watching, music. *Address:* 4 Engaine, Orton Longueville, Peterborough PE2 7QA. *T:* (01733) 232153.

LANGSTAFF, Hon. Sir Brian (Frederick James), Kt 2005; **Hon. Mr Justice Langstaff;** a Judge of the High Court, Queen's Bench Division, since 2005; Liaison Judge (with responsibility for the Administrative Court) for the North of England, 2009–11; President, Employment Appeal Tribunal, 2012–15 (Judge, 2000–03); *b* 30 April 1948; *s* of Frederick Sidney Langstaff and Muriel Amy Maude Langstaff (*née* Griffin); *m* 1975, Deborah Elizabeth Weatherup; one *s* one *d. Educ:* George Heriot's Sch.; St Catharine's Coll., Cambridge (BA); Inns of Court Sch. of Law. VSO, Sri Lanka, 1966–67. Called to the Bar, Middle Temple, 1971 (Harmsworth Schol., 1975), Bencher, 2001. Called to the Bar of NI, 1999. Lectr and Sen. Lectr in Law, Mid-Essex Technical Coll. and Sch. of Art, Chelmsford, 1971–75; Asst Recorder, SE Circuit, 1991–95; QC 1994; a Recorder, 1995–2005. Hd of Cloisters Chambers, 2002–05. Leading Counsel, Bristol Royal Infirmary Inquiry, 1998–2000. Chairman: Personal Injury Bar Assoc., 1999–2001 (Hon. Pres., 2011–); Exec. Cttee, Industrial Law Soc., 1997–2005 (Hon. Vice-Pres., 2005–); Law Reform Cttee, Bar Council, 2001–03 (Vice-Chm., 1999–2001); Master of Rolls' working party on structured settlements, 2001–02; Serious Injury and Clinical Negligence Cttee, Civil Justice Council, 2003–06; Tribunals Procedure Cttee, 2012–; Exec. Mem., Judicial Studies Bd, 2008–11 (Chm., Tribunals Cttee, 2008–11). Gov., local primary sch., 1986– (Chm. Govs, 1991–98). Adv. Editor, Occupational Health, Safety & Environment, 1997–2000. *Publications:* Concise College Casenotes: equity and trusts, 1975; Health and Safety at Work: Halsbury's Laws vol. 20, 4th edn 1994; (ed and contrib.) Personal Injury Handbook, 2000, 3rd edn 2007; Bullen, Leake and Jacobs, Precedents of Pleading, (adv. ed.) 14th edn 2001 to (gen. ed.) 18th edn 2015; (contrib.) Munkman's Employers' Liability, 13th edn 2001 to 16th edn 2013; Personal Injury Schedules: calculating damages, 2001, (Adv. Ed.) 3rd edn 2010; (contrib.) Butterworths Personal Injury Litigation Service, part 1, 2004–; (contrib.) Occupational Illness Litigation, 2010; legal articles. *Recreations:* sport, current affairs, mowing the lawn, bell-ringing, solving sudoku, cooking and eating, travel. *Address:* Royal Courts of Justice, Strand, WC2A 2LL.

LANGSTAFF, Rt Rev. James Henry; *see* Rochester, Bishop of.

LANGSTON, Group Captain John Antony S.; *see* Steff-Langston.

LANGTON; *see* Temple-Gore-Langton, family name of Earl Temple of Stowe.

LANGTON, Bryan David, CBE 1988; Director, Bass plc, 1985–96; Chairman and Chief Executive Officer, Holiday Inn Worldwide, 1990–96; *b* 6 Dec. 1936; *s* of Thomas Langton and Doris (*née* Brown); *m* 1960, Sylva Degenhardt; two *d. Educ:* Accrington Grammar Sch.; Westminster Tech. Coll. (Hotel Operation Dip.); Ecole Hôtelière de la SSA, Lausanne (Operations Dip.). Dep. Manager, Russell Hotel, London, 1959–63; General Manager: Victoria Hotel, Nottingham, 1964–66; Grand Hotel, Manchester, 1966–71; Crest Hotels: Divl Manager, 1971–73; Ops Dir UK, 1973–75; Ops Dir Europe, 1975–77; Divl Managing Dir, Europe, 1977–81; Managing Dir, Ops, 1981–82; Man. Dir, 1982–88; Chairman, 1985–90. Chairman: Holiday Inns International, 1988–90; Toby Restaurants, 1988–90; Fairfield Communities Inc., 1999–2002 (non-exec. Dir, 1996–99); Dir, Caribiner Internat. Inc., 1996–2001; Vice Chm., E Suites LLC, 2007–; Member: Adv. Bd, Mote Marine Sarasota, 1997–2001; Bd, Florida West Coast Symphony, 1997–2008 (Pres., 2005–06). Vice Pres., Internat. Hotel Assoc., 1990. Trustee, Educnl Inst., Amer. Hotel and Motel Assoc., 1990–97. Member, Board of Trustees: Woodruff Arts Center, Atlanta, 1990–97; Northside Hosp. Foundn Bd, 1990–97; YMCA, Sarasota, Fla, 1999–2002. Trustee, Bd of Visitors, Emory Univ., 1990–97. Hon. Fellow, Manchester Poly., later Manchester Metropolitan Univ., 1990–99. *Recreations:* golf, cricket, reading, theatre.

LANGTRY, (James) Ian; Education Officer, Association of County Councils, 1988–96; *b* 2 Jan. 1939; *s* of late Rev. H. J. Langtry and I. M. Langtry (*née* Eagleson); *m* 1st, 1959, Eileen Roberta Beatrice (*née* Nesbitt) (*d* 1999); one *s* one *d*; 2nd, 2007, Alison Mitchell Burgoyne (*née* Mann). *Educ:* Coleraine Academical Instn; Queen's Univ., Belfast (Sullivan Schol.; BSc 1st Cl., Physics). Assistant Master, Bangor Grammar Sch., 1960–61; Lectr, Belfast College of Technology, 1961–66; Asst Director of Examinations/Recruitment, Civil Service Commission, 1966–70; Principal, Dept of Educn and Science, 1970–76, Asst Sec., 1976–82, Under Sec., 1982–87; Under Sec., DHSS, 1987–88. *Address:* 7 Bucklerburn Drive, Peterculter, Aberdeen AB14 0XJ.

LANIGAN, Audrey Cecelia; *see* Slaughter, A. C.

LANKESTER, Patricia; consultant in the arts, heritage, social justice and learning; *b* 28 July 1946; *d* of Leo Cockcroft and Jennie Cockcroft; *m* 1968, Sir Timothy Patrick Lankester, *qv*; three *d. Educ:* King's Coll., London (BA 1967); Inst. of Educn, London (PGCE 1976). Hd of Hist., Barnsbury Sch., Islington, 1980–83; Hd of Humanities, Islington VI Form Centre, 1983–85; Hd of Educn, Nat. Trust, 1988–96; Dir, Paul Hamlyn Foundn, 1998–2004. Member: Learning Panel, RSC, 2009–; Council, Tate Britain, 2013–. Trustee: Heritage Lottery Fund, 1998–2003 (Mem., Expert Panel, 2008–11); Tate, 2005–13; Nat. Gall., 2007–13. Trustee: Open Coll. of the Arts, 1988–96; Farms for City Children, 1996–99; Villiers Park Educnl Trust, 2000–07; Eureka!, Halifax, 2004–09; Foundling Mus., 2005–14; The Hanover Foundn, 2006–10; Sage Music Centre, Gateshead, 2007–; Chelsea Physic Gdn, 2009–; Clore Social Leadership Prog., 2010–; Bristol Museums Devolt Trust, 2010–11; Holburne Mus., Bath, 2014–. Adviser to: Clore Duffield Foundn, 2005–; Heritage Lottery Fund, 2008–. *Recreations:* art, theatre, historic buildings, fiction, walking. *E:* patricia.lankester@btinternet.com. *Club:* Academy.

LANKESTER, Richard Shermer; Clerk of Select Committees, House of Commons, 1979–87; Registrar of Members' Interests, 1976–87; *b* 8 Feb. 1922; *s* of late Richard Ward Lankester; *m* 1950, Dorothy, *d* of late Raymond Jackson, Worsley; two *s* one *d* (and one *s* decd). *Educ:* Haberdashers' Aske's Hampstead Sch.; Jesus Coll., Oxford (MA). Served Royal Artillery, 1942–45. Entered Dept of Clerk of House of Commons, 1947; Clerk of Standing Cttees, 1973–75; Clerk of Expenditure Cttee, 1975–79. Co-Editor, The Table, 1962–67.

LANKESTER, Sir Timothy Patrick, (Sir Tim), KCB 1994; President, Corpus Christi College, Oxford, 2001–09, Honorary Fellow, 2010; *b* 15 April 1942; *s* of late Preb. Robin Prior Archibald Lankester and Jean Dorothy (*née* Gilliat); *m* 1968, Patricia Cockcroft (*see* P. Lankester); three *d. Educ:* Monkton Combe Sch.; St John's Coll., Cambridge (BA; Hon. Fellow 1995); Jonathan Edwards Coll., Yale (Henry Fellow, MA). Teacher (VSO), St Michael's Coll., Belize, 1960–61; Fereday Fellow, St John's Coll., Oxford, 1965–66; Economist, World Bank, Washington DC, 1966–69; New Delhi, 1970–73; Principal 1973, Asst Sec. 1977, HM Treasury; Private Secretary to Rt Hon. James Callaghan, 1978–79; to Rt Hon. Margaret Thatcher, 1979–81; seconded to S. G. Warburg and Co. Ltd, 1981–83; Under Sec., HM Treasury, 1983–85; Economic Minister, Washington and Exec. Dir, IMF and World Bank, 1985–88; Dep. Sec., HM Treasury, 1988–89; Perm. Sec., ODA, FCO, 1989–94; Perm. Sec., Dept for Educn, 1994–95; Dir, SOAS, London Univ., 1996–2000. Dep. Chm., British Council, 1997–2003. Non-executive Director: CGU plc, 1997–2002; London Metal Exchange, 1997–2002; Smith and Nephew plc, 1997–2003; Mitchells and Butler plc, 2003–10; Actis Capital LLP, 2004–09. Chm., Council, LSHTM, 2006–15. Gov., Asia-Europe Foundn, 1997–2011; Member: UK-India Round Table, 1997–; UK Nat. Cttee, Aga Khan Foundn, 2000–. Chm., Contemporary Dance Trust, 2007–13. *E:* tim.lankester@ccc.ox.ac.uk.

LANNON, Frances, DPhil; FRHistS; Principal, Lady Margaret Hall, University of Oxford, 2002–15; *b* 22 Dec. 1945; *d* of Martin Lannon and Margaret (*née* O'Hare). *Educ:* Sacred Heart Grammar Sch., Newcastle upon Tyne; Lady Margaret Hall, Oxford (BA 1st Cl. Hons Mod. Hist., MA 1972); St Antony's Coll., Oxford (DPhil Mod. Spanish Hist. 1976). FRHistS 1986. Lectr in Hist., QMC, London, 1975–77; Fellow and Tutor in Mod. Hist., LMH, Oxford, 1977–2002. Vis. Prof., Univ. of South Carolina, 1986. Mem., Commonwealth Scholarship Commn, 1982–91; Fellow, Woodrow Wilson Center, Washington, 1992. *Publications:* Privilege, Persecution and Prophecy: the Catholic Church in Spain 1875–1975, 1987; (ed with Paul Preston) Elites and Power in Twentieth-Century Spain, 1990; The Spanish Civil War, 2002; contrib. Oxford DNB, TLS, Jl of Contemporary Hist., other learned jls. *Recreations:* Spain, visual arts, contemporary fiction. *E:* frances.lannon@lmh.ox.ac.uk.

LANSBURY, Dame Angela (Brigid), DBE 2014 (CBE 1994); actress; *b* London, England, 16 Oct. 1925; *d* of Edgar Lansbury and late Moyna Macgill (with one *s* 1st, Reginald Denham); *m* 1st, Richard Cromwell; 2nd, 1949, Peter Shaw (*d* 2003); one *s* one *d* and one step *s. Educ:* South Hampstead High Sch. for Girls; Webber Douglas Sch. of Singing and Dramatic Art,

Kensington; Feagin Sch. of Drama and Radio, New York. With Metro-Goldwyn-Mayer, 1943–50; *films:* Gaslight, 1944; National Velvet, 1944; The Picture of Dorian Gray, 1945; The Harvey Girls, 1946; The Hoodlum Saint, 1946; Till the Clouds Roll By, 1946; The Private Affairs of Bel-Ami, 1947; If Winter Comes, 1948; Tenth Avenue Angel, 1948; State of the Union, 1948; The Three Musketeers, 1948; The Red Danube, or Storm over Vienna, or Vespers in Vienna, 1949; Samson and Delilah, 1949; Kind Lady, 1951; Mutiny, 1952; Remains to be Seen, 1953; A Life at Stake, or Key Man, 1955; The Purple Mask, 1956; The Court Jester, 1956; A Lawless Street, 1956; Please Murder Me, 1956; The Long Hot Summer, 1958; The Reluctant Debutante, 1958; Breath of Scandal, 1960; The Dark at the Top of the Stairs, 1960; Season of Passion, 1961; Blue Hawaii, 1961; All Fall Down, 1962; The Manchurian Candidate, 1962; In the Cool of the Day, 1963; The World of Henry Orient, 1964; Dear Heart, 1964; The Greatest Story Ever Told, 1965; Harlow, 1965; The Amorous Adventures of Moll Flanders, 1965; Mister Buddwing, or Woman Without a Face, 1966; Something for Everyone, or Black Flowers for the Bride, 1970; Bedknobs and Broomsticks, 1971; Death on the Nile, or Murder on the Nile, 1978; The Lady Vanishes, 1980; The Mirror Crack'd, 1980; The Pirates of Penzance, 1982; The Company of Wolves, 1983; Beauty and the Beast, 1991; Nanny McPhee, 2005; Mr Popper's Penguins, 2011; *plays:* appearances include: Hotel Paradiso (Broadway debut), 1957; Helen, in A Taste of Honey, Lyceum Theatre, New York, 1960; Anyone Can Whistle (Broadway musical), 1964; Mame (Tony Award for best actress in a Broadway musical), Winter Garden, NYC, 1966–68; Dear World (Broadway), 1969 (Tony Award); Pretty Belle, 1971; All Over, RSC, 1971; Gypsy (Broadway Musical), Piccadilly, 1973, US tour, 1974 (Tony Award; Chicago, Sarah Siddons Award, 1974); Gertrude, in Hamlet, Nat. Theatre, 1975; Anna, in The King and I (Broadway), 1978; Mrs Lovett, in Sweeney Todd (Broadway), 1979 (Tony Award); A Little Family Business, 1983; Deuce, NY, 2007; Blithe Spirit (Broadway), 2009 (Tony Award), Gielgud Th., 2014 (Best Supporting Actress, Olivier Awards, 2015); A Little Night Music (Broadway), 2009; The Best Man (Broadway), 2012; Driving Miss Daisy (Australia tour), 2013; *television includes:* series, Murder She Wrote, 1984–95 (Golden Globe Award, 1984, 1986, 1991, 1992); Little Gloria, Happy At Last, 1982; The Gift of Love: a Christmas Story, 1983; A Talent for Murder (with Laurence Olivier), 1984; Lace, 1984; The First Olympico-Athens 1896, 1984; Rage of Angels II, 1986; Shootdown, 1988; The Shell Seekers, 1989; The Love She Sought, 1990; Mrs Arris Goes to Paris, 1992; Mrs Santa Claus, 1996; South by Southwest, 1997; The Unexpected Mrs Pollifax, 1998; A Story to Die for, 2000. NY Drama Desk Award, 1979; Sarah Siddons Award, 1980 and 1983; inducted Theatre Hall of Fame, 1982; Silver Mask for Lifetime Achievement, BAFTA, 1991; Lifetime Achievement Award, Screen Actors' Guild, 1997; Nat. Medal of the Arts, USA, 1997; Hon. Acad. Award, 2013.

LANSDOWN, Gillian Elizabeth, (Mrs Richard Lansdown); *see* Tindall, G. E.

LANSDOWNE, 9th Marquess of, *cr* 1784 (GB); **Charles Maurice Petty-Fitzmaurice,** LVO 2002; 30th Baron of Kerry and Lixnaw, 1181; Viscount Clanmaurice and Earl of Kerry, 1722; Baron Dunkeron and Viscount Fitzmaurice, 1751; Earl of Shelburne, 1753; Baron Wycombe (GB), 1760; Viscount Calne and Calston and Earl of Wycombe (GB), 1784; Vice Lord-Lieutenant, Wiltshire, since 2012; *b* 21 Feb. 1941; *s* of 8th Marquess of Lansdowne, PC and Barbara, *d* of Harold Stuart Chase; *S* father, 1999; *m* 1st, 1965, Lady Frances Eliot, *o d* of 9th Earl of St Germans; two *s* two *d*; 2nd, 1987, Fiona Merritt, *d* of Lady Davies and Donald Merritt. *Educ:* Eton. Page of Honour to The Queen, 1956–57. Served with Kenya Regt, 1960–61; with Wiltshire Yeomanry (TA), amalgamated with Royal Yeomanry Regt, 1963–73. Pres., Wiltshire Playing Fields Assoc., 1965–74; Wiltshire County Councillor, 1970–85; Mem., South West Economic Planning Council, 1972–77; Chairman: Working Committee Population & Settlement Pattern (SWEPC), 1972–77; North Wiltshire DC, 1973–76; Mem., Calne and Chippenham RDC, 1964–73. Mem., Historic Bldgs and Monuments Commn, 1983–89; President: HHA, 1988–93 (Dep. Pres., 1986–88); South West Tourism, 1989–2006; Wiltshire Historic Bldgs Trust, 1994–; Wilts & Berks Canal Partnership, 2001–. Mem., Prince's Council, Duchy of Cornwall, 1990–2001; President: Wiltshire Assocs Boys Clubs and Youth Clubs, 1976–2003; North-West Wiltshire District Scout Council, 1977–88; N Wilts Cons. Assoc., 1986–89. Contested (C) Coventry North East, 1979. DL Wilts, 1990. *Heir: s* Earl of Kerry, *qv*. *Address:* Bowood House, Calne, Wiltshire SN11 0LZ. *T:* (01249) 813343. *Clubs:* Turf, Brooks's.

LANSLEY, family name of **Baron Lansley**.

LANSLEY, Baron *cr* 2015 (Life Peer), of Orwell in the County of Cambridgeshire; **Andrew David Lansley,** CBE 1996; PC 2010; *b* 11 Dec. 1956; *s* of late Thomas Lansley and of Irene Lansley; *m* 1st, 1985, Marilyn Jane Biggs (marr. diss. 2001); three *d*; 2nd, 2001, Sally Anne Low; one *s* one *d*. *Educ:* Univ. of Exeter (BA). Administration trainee, Dept of Industry, 1979; Private Sec. to Sec. of State for Trade and Industry, 1984–85; Principal Private Sec. to Chancellor of Duchy of Lancaster, 1985–87; Dir, Policy, 1987–89, Dep. Dir-Gen., 1989–90, ABCC; Director: Cons. Res. Dept, 1990–95; Public Policy Unit, 1995–97. MP (C) S Cambridgeshire, 1997–2015. Shadow Minister for the Cabinet and Shadow Chancellor of the Duchy of Lancaster, 1999–2001; Shadow Sec. of State for Health, 2003–10; Sec. of State for Health, 2010–12; Lord Privy Seal and Leader of H of C, 2012–14. Member: Select Cttee on Health, 1997–98; Trade and Industry Select Cttee, 2001–04. A Vice-Chm., Cons. Party, 1998–99. *Publications:* A Private Route?, 1988; Conservatives and the Constitution, 1997. *Recreations:* travel, cricket, films, history.

LANTOS, Prof. Peter Laszlo, PhD, DSc; FRCPath, FMedSci; Professor of Neuropathology, Institute of Psychiatry, King's College, London, 1979–2001, now Professor Emeritus; *b* 22 Oct. 1939; *s* of late Sandor Leipniker and Ilona Leipniker (*née* Somlo); name changed by deed poll to Lantos, 1961. *Educ:* Medical Univ. Szeged, Hungary (MD 1964); Middlesex Hosp. Sch. of Medicine, Univ. of London (PhD 1973, DSc 1992). FRCPath. Wellcome Res. Fellow, 1968–69; Lectr, 1969–75, Sen. Lectr and Hon. Consultant, 1976–79, in Neuropathol., Middx Hosp. Sch. of Medicine; Hon. Consultant in Neuropathology: Bethlem Royal and Maudsley Hosp., 1979–2001; KCH, 1984–2002; St Thomas' Hosp., 1992–2002; Dir, Neuropathol. Service, King's Neurosci. Centre, 1995–2001. Advr, German Fed. Ministry for Educn and Res., 2000–02. Chairman: Bd of Examrs in Neuropathol., RCPath, 1983–89; Scientific Adv. Panel, Brain Res. Trust, 1985–91; Samantha Dickson Res. Trust, 2003–; Trustee: Psychiatry Res. Trust, 1996–; Alzheimer Res. UK (formerly Alzheimer Res. Trust), 2001–14. FMedSci 2001. *Publications:* (ed) Greenfield's Neuropathology, 6th edn 1997, 7th edn 2002; Parallel Lines (autobiog.), 2006; Closed Horizon (novel), 2012; The Visitor (play), 2013; Distorting Mirrors (play), 2014; contrib. numerous book chapters and scientific and med. papers and rev. articles to jls incl. Lancet and Nature. *Recreations:* travel, languages, theatres, fine arts. *T:* (020) 7487 5275. *E:* peter.lantos@btinternet.com. *Club:* Athenæum.

LANYON, (Harry) Mark; Regional Director, Government Office for East Midlands, 1994–98; *b* 15 July 1939; *s* of late Henry Lanyon and Heather Gordon (*née* Tyrrell); *m* 1970, Elizabeth Mary Morton; one *s* one *d*. *Educ:* Ardingly Coll.; St Andrews Univ. (BSc Hons 1962). CEng 1965; MIMechE 1965. Ministry of Aviation: Engr Cadet, 1963–65; Aeronautical Inspectorate, 1965–68; Concorde Div., Min. of Technol., 1968–75; Department of Trade and Industry: Shipbuilding Policy Div., 1975–77; Dep. Dir, SW Region, 1977–82; Regl Dir, W Midlands, 1982–85; Hd of Br., Mechanical and Electrical Engrg Div., 1985–90; Asst Dir, Consumer Affairs, OFT, 1990–93; Regl Dir, Yorks and Humberside, DTI, 1993–94.

See also L. E. Lanyon.

LANYON, Prof. Lance Edward, CBE 2001; Principal, Royal Veterinary College, 1989–2004; Pro-Vice-Chancellor, University of London, 1997–99; *b* 4 Jan. 1944; *s* of late Henry Lanyon and Heather Gordon (*née* Tyrrell); *m* 1st, 1972, Mary Kear (marr. diss. 1997); one *s* one *d*; 2nd, 2003, Joanna Price. *Educ:* Christ's Hospital; Univ. of Bristol (BVSC, PhD, DSc). MRCVS. Lectr, 1967, Reader in Vet. Anatomy, 1967–79, Univ. of Bristol; Associate Prof., 1980–83, Prof., 1983–84, Tufts Sch. of Vet. Medicine, Boston, Mass; Prof. of Vet. Anatomy, Royal Vet. Coll., Univ. of London, 1984–89, personal title, 1989–2004, now Prof. Emeritus (Head, Dept of Vet. Anatomy, 1984–87, of Vet. Basic Scis, 1987–88). Vis. Prof., Univ. of Bristol, 2010–. Almoner, Christ's Hosp., 1998–2009. Chm., Governing Body, Christ's Hosp. Sch., 2007–09. Founder FMedSci 1998; FRVC 2005. Hon. FRCVS 2012. Hon. DSc Bristol, 2004. *Publications:* chapters in books on orthopaedics, osteoporosis, and athletic training; articles in professional jls. *Recreations:* building, home improvements, sailing. *Address:* 5 Cotham Road, Bristol BS6 6DG. *T:* (0117) 909 0363.

See also H. M. Lanyon.

LANYON, Mark; *see* Lanyon, H. M.

LAPIDGE, Prof. Michael, PhD, LittD; FBA 1994; Fellow of Clare College, Cambridge, since 1990; *b* 8 Feb. 1942; *s* of Rae H. Lapidge and Catherine Mary Lapidge (*née* Carruthers). *Educ:* Univ. of Calgary (BA 1962); Univ. of Alberta (MA 1965); Univ. of Toronto (PhD 1971); LittD Cantab 1988. Cambridge University: Lectr, 1974–88; Reader in Insular Latin Literature, 1988–91; Elrington and Bosworth Prof. of Anglo-Saxon, 1991–98; Notre Dame Prof. of English, Univ. of Notre Dame, Indiana, 1999–2004. Corresponding Fellow: Bayerische Akademie der Wissenschaften, 1997; Accad. dei Lincei, 2001. Hon. DLitt Toronto, 2011. *Publications:* Aldhelm: the prose works, 1979; Alfred the Great, 1983; Aldhelm: the poetic works, 1985; A Bibliography of Celtic Latin Literature 400–1200, 1985; Wulfstan of Winchester: the life of St Ethelwold, 1991; Anglo-Saxon Litanies of the Saints, 1991; Anglo-Latin Literature 900–1066, 1993; Biblical Commentaries from the Canterbury School of Theodore and Hadrian, 1994; Archbishop Theodore, 1995; Byrhtferth's Enchiridion, 1995; Anglo-Latin Literature 600–899, 1996; The Cult of St Swithun, 2003; The Anglo-Saxon Library, 2006; Beda: storia degli Inglesi, vol. 1, 2008, vol. 2, 2010; Byrhtferth of Ramsey: the lives of St Oswald and St Ecgwine, 2009; (with H. Gneuss) Anglo-Saxon Manuscripts, 2014; articles in learned jls. *Recreation:* hill-walking. *Address:* 143 Sturton Street, Cambridge CB1 2QH. *T:* (01223) 363768.

LA PLANTE, Lynda, CBE 2008; writer and producer; Founder and Chairman: La Plante Productions, since 1994; La Plante Global, since 2014; *m* Richard La Plante (marr. diss.). *Educ:* RADA (schol.). Former actress. Writer: *television: series:* Widows, 1983; Prime Suspect, 1991, series 3, 1993; Civvies, 1992; Seekers, 1993; The Lifeboat, 1994; The Governor, 1995, series 2, 1996; The Prosecutors (US); Supply and Demand, 1996, series 2, 1998; Trial and Retribution, annual series, 1997–2009; Killer Net, 1998; Mind Games, 2000; The Commander, 2003, 2005; Above Suspicion, 2009; The Red Dahlia, 2010; *play:* Seconds Out. Hon. Fellow, Forensic Sci. Soc., 2013. *Publications:* The Legacy, 1988; The Talisman, 1989; Bella Mafia, 1991 (televised, US); Entwined, 1992; Framed, 1993; Seekers, 1993; Widows, 1994; Cold Shoulder, 1994; Prime Suspect, 1995; Prime Suspect 3, 1995; She's Out, 1995; The Governor, 1995; Cold Blood, 1986; Cold Heart, 1998; Trial and Retribution, no 1, 1997, no 2, 1998, no 3, 1999, no 4, 2000; Sleeping Cruelty, 2000; Royal Flush, 2002; Above Suspicion, 2004; The Red Dahlia, 2006; Clean Cut, 2007; Deadly Intent, 2008; Silent Scream, 2009; Blind Fury, 2010; Blood Line, 2011; The Little One, 2012; Backlash, 2012; Wrongful Death, 2013; Twisted, 2014. *Address:* c/o Simon & Schuster, 222 Gray's Inn Road, WC1X 8HB.

LAPLI, Sir John Ini, GCMG 1999; Governor General, Solomon Islands, 1999–2004; baptized 24 June 1955; *s* of Christian Mekope and Ellen Lauai; *m* 1985, Helen; three *s* one *d*. *Educ:* Nabakaenga Jun. Primary Sch., Solomon Is; Lueslemba Sen. Primary Sch., Solomon Is; Selwyn Coll., Guadalcanal; Bp Patterson Theol Coll., Guadalcanal (Cert. Theol.); St John's Theol Coll., Auckland (LTh, Dip. and Licentiate in Theol.). Tutor, Theol Coll., 1982–83; teacher, Catechist Sch., Rural Trng Centre, 1985; parish priest, 1986; Bible translator, 1987–88; Premier, Temotu Province, Solomon Is, 1988–99. *Recreations:* gardening, before taking up public office. *Address:* c/o Government House, PO Box 252, Honiara, Solomon Islands.

LAPOTAIRE, Jane Elizabeth Marie; actress; *b* 26 Dec. 1944; *d* of unknown father and Louise Elise Lapotaire; *m* 1st, 1965, Oliver Wood (marr. diss. 1967); 2nd, 1974, Roland Joffé (marr. diss. 1982); one *s*. *Educ:* Northgate Grammar Sch., Ipswich; Old Vic Theatre Sch., Bristol. Bristol Old Vic Co., 1965–67; Nat. Theatre Co., 1967–71, incl. Measure for Measure, Flea in Her Ear, Dance of Death, Way of the World, Merchant of Venice, Oedipus, The Taming of the Shrew; freelance films and TV, 1971–74; RSC, 1974–75 (roles included Viola in Twelfth Night, and Sonya in Uncle Vanya); Prospect Theatre Co., West End, 1975–76 (Vera in A Month in the Country, Lucy Honeychurch in A Room with a View); freelance films and TV, 1976–78; Rosalind in As You Like It, Edin. Fest., 1977; RSC, 1978–81: Rosaline in Love's Labours Lost, 1978–79; title role in Piaf, The Other Place 1978, Aldwych 1979, Wyndhams 1980, Broadway 1981 (SWET Award 1979, London Critics Award and Variety Club Award 1980, and Broadway Tony Award 1981); National Theatre: Eileen, Kick for Touch, 1983; Belvidera, Venice Preserv'd, Antigone, 1984; Saint Joan (title rôle), Compass Co., 1985; Double Double, Fortune Theatre, 1986; RSC, 1986–87: Misalliance, 1986; Archbishop's Ceiling, 1986; Greenland, Royal Court, 1988; Shadowlands, Queen's, 1989–90 (Variety Club Best Actress Award); RSC, 1992–94: Gertrude in Hamlet, 1992; Mrs Alving in Ghosts, 1993; Katharine of Aragon in Henry VIII, RSC, UK and USA tour, 1996–98 (Helen Hayes Award, USA, 1998); one-woman show, Shakespeare as I knew her, Bristol, 1996, Stratford and USA, 1997; Duchess of Gloucester in Richard II, RSC, 2013–14; *television:* Marie Curie (serial), 1977; Antony and Cleopatra, 1981; Macbeth, 1983; Seal Morning (series), 1985; Napoleon and Josephine, 1987; Blind Justice (serial), 1988 (British Press Guild Best Actress Award); The Dark Angel, 1989; Love Hurts (series), 1992, 1993; The Big Battalions (series), 1992; Johnny and the Dead (series), 1994; He Knew He Was Right, 2004; Trial and Retribution, 2008; Lucan, 2013; *films* include: Eureka, 1983; Lady Jane, 1986; Surviving Picasso, 1996; There's Only One Jimmy Grimble, 2000. Vis. Fellow, Sussex Univ., 1986–2002. Mem., Marie Curie Meml Foundn Appeals Cttee, 1986–88. Pres., Bristol Old Vic Theatre Club, 1985–2009; Hon. Pres., Friends of Shakespeare's Globe, 1986–2002. Hon. Associate Artist, RSC, 1992. Hon. Fellow, Exeter Univ., 2007. Hon. DLitt: Bristol, 1997; East Anglia, 1998; Warwick, 2000; Exeter, 2005. *Publications:* Grace and Favour (autobiog.), 1989 (repubd as Everybody's Daughter, Nobody's Child, 2007); Out of Order: a haphazard journey through one woman's year, 1999; Time Out of Mind: recovering from a brain haemorrhage, 2003. *Recreation:* walking. *Address:* c/o Gardner Herrity, 24 Conway Street, W1T 6BG. *T:* (020) 7388 0088.

LAPPIN, Prof. Shalom, PhD; FBA 2010; Professor of Computational Linguistics, King's College London, since 2005. *Educ:* York Univ., Toronto (BA Philosophy 1970); Brandeis Univ. (MA 1973; PhD 1976). Lectr in Philosophy, Ben Gurion Univ., 1974–80; Lecturer in Linguistics: Univ. of Ottawa, 1980–84 (Chair, Linguistics Dept, 1981–84); Univ. of Haifa, 1984–88; Tel Aviv Univ., 1988–89; Res. Staff Mem., Natural Lang. Gp, Computer Sci. Dept, IBM T. J. Watson Res. Center, 1989–93; Linguistics Dept, SOAS, Univ. of London, 1993–99; Philosophy, then Computer Sci. Dept, KCL, 1999–2005 (Hd, Natural Lang. Processing Gp, 2000–05). Member, Linguistics Panel: RAE 2001, 1999–2001; RAE 2008, 2005–08. *Publications:* Linguistic Nativism and the Poverty of the Stimulus, 2010; (ed jtly and contrib.) Handbook of Computational Linguistics and Natural Language Processing, 2010;

contribs to jls incl. Linguistic Analysis, Computational Linguistics, Jl Linguistics, Computational Modelling. *Address:* Department of Philosophy, King's College London, Strand, WC2R 2LS.

LAPPING, Anne Shirley Lucas, CBE 2005; independent television producer; Founder Director, Brook Lapping Productions (formerly Brook Associates), 1982–2008; *b* 10 June 1941; *d* of late Frederick Stone and of Dr Freda Lucas Stone; *m* 1963, Brian Michael Lapping, *qv*; three *d. Educ:* City of London Sch. for Girls; London Sch. of Econs. New Society, 1964–68; London Weekend TV, 1970–73; writer on The Economist, 1974–82. Other writing and broadcasting. Director: Channel Four, 1989–94; NW London Mental Health NHS Trust, 1992–99; Scott Trust, 1994–2004; Interights, 2006–12; Vice-Chm., Central and NW London Mental Health Trust, 1999–2004. Member: SSRC, 1977–79; Nat. Gas Consumers' Council, 1978–79; Bd, IPSO, 2014– (Dep. Chm., 2015–). Trustee, openDemocracy, 2006–. Gov., LSE, 1994– (Mem. Council, 2004–; Vice Chm., 2008–14). *Recreations:* reading, cooking, arguing. *Address:* 61 Eton Avenue, NW3 3ET. *T:* (020) 7586 1047.

LAPPING, Brian Michael, CBE 2005; television producer; Chairman, Brook Lapping Productions Ltd; *b* 13 Sept. 1937; *s* of Max and Doris Lapping; *m* 1963, Anne Shirley Lucas Stone (*see* A. S. L. Lapping); three *d. Educ:* Pembroke Coll., Cambridge (BA). Reporter, Daily Mirror, 1959–61; reporter and Dep. Commonwealth Corresp., The Guardian, 1961–67; Ed., Venture (Fabian Soc. monthly jl), 1963–68; feature writer, Financial Times, 1967–68; Dep. Ed., New Society, 1968–70; Granada TV, 1970–88: Producer: What the Papers Say; Party confs; This is Your Right; Executive Producer: World in Action; Hypotheticals; End of Empire; Apartheid; Breakthrough at Reykjavik, etc; Dir, Brian Lapping Associates, subseq. Brook Lapping Productions, 1988–: executive producer: Countdown to War, 1989; The Second Russian Revolution, 1991; Question Time, 1991–94; Watergate, 1993; The Death of Yugoslavia, 1995; Fall of the Wall, Death of Apartheid, 1996; The 50 Years' War—Israel and the Arabs, 1998; Hostage, Playing the China Card, Finest Hour, 1999; Endgame in Ireland, 2001; Tackling Terror, 2002; The Fall of Milosevic, 2003; Elusive Peace, Israel and the Arabs, 2005; Iran and the West, 2009; The Day that Changed the World, 2011; Putin's Russia and the West, 2012; The Iraq War, 2013. Awards include: RTS Awards, 1978, 1991, 1995, 2006, 2010; Emmy Award, 1994; BPG Awards, 1986, 1991, 1995, 2003; Gold Medal, NY Internat. Film and TV Fest., 1986, 1990, 1995; Silver/Gold Batons, du Pont/Columbia Awards, 1994, 1996 and 2007; History-Makers, 2010; The Indie, Producers Alliance for Cinema and Television, 1996; BAFTA Lifetime Achievement Award, 2003. *Publications:* (with G. Radice) More Power to the People, 1962; The Labour Government 1964–70, 1970; End of Empire, 1985; Apartheid: a history, 1987. *Recreation:* tending vines. *Address:* 61 Eton Avenue, NW3 3ET. *T:* (020) 7586 1047.

LAPPING, Peter Herbert; Headmaster of Sherborne, 1988–2000; *b* 8 Aug. 1941; *s* of late Dr Douglas James Lapping, MBE and Dorothy Lapping (*née* Horrocks) of Nhlangano, Swaziland; *m* 1967, Diana Dillworth, *d* of late Lt-Col E. S. G. Howard, MC, RA; one *s* one *d. Educ:* St John's College, Johannesburg; Univ. of Natal, Pietermaritzburg (BA Hons *cum laude*); Lincoln College, Oxford (MA). Asst Master, Reed's Sch., Cobham, 1966–67; Head of History, Loretto Sch., 1967–79 (Housemaster, Pinkie House, 1972–79); Headmaster, Shiplake Coll., Oxon, 1979–88. Governor: Sherborne Prep. Sch., 1998–; King's Sch., Gloucester, 2008–. *Recreations:* cricket and other games, cooking, walking, basking in the beauty of the Cotswolds. *Address:* Lower Bubblewell, Minchinhampton, Glos GL6 9DL. *Clubs:* MCC, Victory Services; Vincent's (Oxford); Glos County Cricket (Life Mem.).

LAPSLEY, Angus Charles William; HM Diplomatic Service; Ambassador (Political and Security), UK Permanent Representation to European Union, Brussels, since 2015; *b* Cheltenham, 16 March 1970; *s* of Howard and Susan Lapsley; *m* 1999, Georgina Power; two *s. Educ:* Warwick Sch.; Corpus Christi Coll., Oxford (BA Hons English Lit. and Lang. 1991). HEO, DoH, 1991–94; Second Sec., UK Representation to EU, 1994–95; Private Sec. (Home Affairs) to Prime Minister, 1996–99; entered FCO, 1999; Hd, EU Institutions Unit, FCO, 1999–2001; First Sec., Paris, 2001–05; Dep. Hd, Western Balkans Gp, FCO, 2005–06; Counsellor, UK Representation to EU, 2006–10; Dir, The Americas, FCO, 2010–12; Dir, Eur. and Global Issues Secretariat, Cabinet Office, 2012–15. *Recreations:* touch Rugby, motorsport, French food and wine. *Address:* UK Permanent Representation to European Union, 10 avenue d'Auderghem, Brussels 1040, Belgium. *E:* angus.lapsley@fco.gov.uk. *Club:* Royal Automobile.

LAPTHORNE, Sir Richard (Douglas), Kt 2010; CBE 1997; Chairman, Cable and Wireless Communications plc (formerly Cable and Wireless plc), since 2003; *b* 25 April 1943; *s* of Eric Joseph Lapthorne and Irene Ethel Lapthorne; *m* 1967, Valerie Waring; two *s* two *d. Educ:* Calday Grange GS, West Kirby; Liverpool Univ. (BCom). FCMA, FCCA, FCT. Unilever plc: Audit, 1965–67; Lever Brothers, Zambia, 1967–69; Central Pensions Dept, 1969–71; Food Industries, 1971–75; Synthetic Resins, 1975–77; Sheby, Paris, 1978–80; Crosfield Chemicals, 1980–83; Gp Financial Controller, 1983–86, Gp Finance Dir, 1986–92, Courtaulds plc; Gp Finance Dir, 1992–98, Vice Chm., 1998–99, British Aerospace plc; Chm., 1996–97, 1999–2003, Dep. Chm., 1997–99, Nycomed Amersham, subseq. Amersham plc; Chairman: Morse Hldgs plc, 1998–2008; Avecia Ltd, 1999–2005; Tunstall Ltd, 2000–04; TI Automotive Systems plc, 2001–03; Arlington Securities Ltd, 2005; New Look Retailers Ltd, 2005–07; McLaren Gp, 2009–10; Vice-Chm., JP Morgan Investment Bank, 2001–05. Non-executive Director: Orange plc, 1992–99; Oasis Internat. Leasing (Abu Dhabi), 1998–2006; Robert Fleming, 2001–; Sherritt Internat. (Toronto), 2011–. Mem., Public Interest Body, PricewaterhouseCoopers, 2010– (Chm., 2011–). Dir, Working Age Project, HM Treasury, 2000; Ext. Advr, Navy Bd, 2000–03; Chm., Lead Expert Gp, Govt Foresight Study on Future of UK Manufacturing, 2012–13. Trustee: Royal Botanic Gdns, Kew, 1998–2009 (Chm., Foundn and Friends, 1997–2004; HM the Queen's Trustee, 2004–09); Calibre, 1999–2008; Tommy's Campaign, 2003–14. CCMI. Hon. CRAeS 1997. *Recreations:* gardening, opera, travel.

LAQUEUR, Walter; historian, political commentator and writer; Chairman, Research Council, Center for Strategic and International Studies, Washington, 1978–2001; Academic Adviser, Institute of Contemporary History and Wiener Library, London, 1964–92; *b* 26 May 1921; *s* of late Fritz Laqueur and Else Laqueur; *m* 1st, 1941, Barbara (*d* 1995), *d* of Prof. Richard Koch and Maria Koch (*née* Rosenthal); two *d*; 2nd, 1996, Christa Susi Wichmann (*née* Genzen). Agricultural labourer during War, 1939–44. Journalist, free lance author, 1944–55; Editor of Survey, 1955–65; Co-editor of Journal of Contemporary History, 1966–2005. Prof., History of Ideas, Brandeis Univ., 1967–71; Prof. of Contemporary History, Tel Aviv Univ., 1970–; Vis. Professor: Chicago Univ.; Johns Hopkins Univ.; Harvard Univ. Hon. Dr: Hebrew Union Coll., NY, 1988; Adelphi Univ., 1990; Brandeis Univ., 1991. Grand Cross of Merit, FRG, 1986. *Publications:* Communism and Nationalism in the Middle East, 1956; Young Germany, 1961; Russia and Germany, 1965; The Road to War, 1968; Europe Since Hitler, 1970; Out of the Ruins of Europe, 1971; Zionism, a History, 1972; Confrontation: the Middle East War and World Politics, 1974; Weimar: a Cultural History, 1918–33, 1974; Guerrilla, 1976; Terrorism, 1977; The Missing Years, 1980; (ed jtly) A Reader's Guide to Contemporary History, 1972; (ed) Fascism: a reader's guide, 1978; The Terrible Secret, 1980; Farewell to Europe, 1981; Germany Today: a personal report, 1985; World of Secrets: the uses and limits of intelligence, 1986; The Long Road to Freedom, 1989; Stalin: the glasnost revelations, 1991; Europe in Our Time, 1992; Thursday's Child Has Far to Go, 1994; Generation Exodus, 2001; The Last Days of Europe, 2007; Best of Times, Worst of Times: memoirs of a political education, 2009; Harvest of One Decade, 2011. *Recreations:* swimming, motor-boating. *E:* walterlaqueur@gmail.com.

LARA, Brian Charles, TC 1994; OCC 2008; cricketer; Ambassador for Sport, Trinidad and Tobago; *b* Trinidad, 2 May 1969; *s* of late Bunty and Pearl Lara; two *d* with Leasal Rovedas. *Educ:* San Juan Secondary Sch.; Fatima Coll., Port of Spain. Started playing cricket aged 6; left-handed batsman; played for: WI Under-19s (Captain, WI Youth XI against India); Trinidad and Tobago, 1987–2008 (Captain, 1993); Warwickshire, 1994, 1998 (Captain) (world record 1st cl. score of 501 not out, *v* Durham at Edgbaston, 1994); West Indies, 1990–2007 (played in 131 Test Matches, scoring 11,953 runs; Captain, 1997, 1998–99, 2000, 2003–04, 2007; world record score of 400 in a Test Match, St John's, Antigua, 2004); 34 Test, 65 1st class, centuries. Founded charity, Pearl and Bunty Lara Foundn. Ambassador, Chittagong Kings, Bangladesh Premier League, 2013–. Hon. Dr Sheffield, 2007; Hon. LLD UWI, 2011. Hon. AM 2009. *Publications:* Beating the Field (autobiog.), 1995. *Recreations:* golf, horse-racing. *Address:* c/o West Indies Cricket Board, PO Box 616 W, St John's, Antigua.

LARCOMBE, Brian Paul; Chief Executive, 3i Group plc, 1997–2004; *b* 27 Aug. 1953; *s* of John George Larcombe and Joyce Lucille Larcombe (*née* Westwood); *m* 1983, Dr Catherine Bullen. *Educ:* Bromley Grammar Sch.; Univ. of Birmingham (BCom). Joined 3i Gp, 1974: Local Dir, 1982; Regl Dir, 1988; Finance Dir, 1992–97. Non-executive Director: Smith and Nephew plc, 2002–; F&C Asset Management, 2005–10; Party Gaming plc, 2005–06; Gallaher Gp plc, 2006–07; gategroup Hldg AG (formerly Gate Gourmet Gp Hldg LLC), 2008–; Incisive Media Hldgs Ltd, 2010–14; Kodak Alaris Hldgs, 2014–. Chm., Bramdean Alternatives Ltd, 2007–09. Member: Council, British Venture Capital Assoc., 1989–96 (Chm., 1994–95); UK Council, INSEAD, 1997–2006; Singapore British Business Council, 1997–2004; Exchange Markets Gp, London Stock Exchange, 2001–03. *Recreations:* golf, biographies, modern paintings. *Address:* 32 Fife Road, East Sheen, SW14 7EL.

LARGE, Sir Andrew (McLeod Brooks), Kt 1996; Deputy Governor, Bank of England, 2002–06; Founding Partner, Systemic Policy Partnership, since 2012; adviser on systemic policy issues, since 2008; *b* 7 Aug. 1942; *s* of late Maj.-Gen. Stanley Eyre Large, MBE and Janet Mary Large (*née* Brooks); *m* 1967, Susan Mary Melville; two *s* one *d. Educ:* Winchester Coll.; Corpus Christi Coll., Cambridge (BA Hons Econ; MA); INSEAD, Fontainebleau (MBA). BP, 1964–71; Man. Dir, Orion Bank, 1971–79; Exec. Bd Mem., Swiss Bank Corp., 1980–89; Large, Smith & Walter, 1990–92; Chairman: SIB, 1992–97; IOSCO, 1992; a Dep. Chm., Barclays Bank, 1998–2002. Chm., Euroclear, 1998–2000; non-executive Director: Nuclear Electric, 1990–94; Rank Hovis McDougall, 1990–92; Phoenix Securities, 1990–92; Dowty Gp, 1991–92; English China Clays, 1991–96; London Fox, 1991–92 (Chm.); Luthy Baillie Dowsett Pethick, 1990–92 (Chm.); Axis Capital, Bermuda, 2006–; MW Tops Ltd, 2006–09 (Chm.); Oliver Wyman, 2006– (Chm., Sen. Adv. Bd); Marshall Wace, 2009–12 (Chm., Adv. Cttee). Chm., Securities Assoc., 1986–87; Member: Council, Stock Exchange, 1986–87; Panel on Takeovers and Mergers, 1987–88; Lloyds Council, 1992–93; Bd of Banking Supervision, 1996–97; Sen. Advr, Hedge Fund Standards Bd, 2008– (Chm., Wkg Gp, 2007–08). Member Board: Inst. of Internat. Finance, Washington, 1998–2001; INSEAD, 1998–2010 (Chm. UK Council, 1997–2002; Chm., Adv. Council, 2011–). Governor: Abingdon Sch., 1991–98; Winchester Coll., 1998–2008 (Warden, 2003–08); Christ Coll., Brecon, 1998–2010. *Recreations:* old apple trees, ski-ing, walking, photography, music. *Club:* Brooks's.

LARKCOM, Joy Kerr, (Mrs D. A. Pollard); garden writer, since 1973; *b* Farnborough, Hants, 16 Nov. 1935; *d* of Eric Herbert Jacobs-Larkcom and Dorothy Primrose Kerr Jacobs-Larkcom (*née* Tasker); *m* 1967, Donald Aloysius Pollard; one *s* one *d. Educ:* Ancaster House Sch.; Wye Coll., Univ. of London (BSc Hort.). Teacher at sch. for American children, Thailand, 1958–59; Library Asst, Sci. and Med. Div., Toronto Univ. Library, 1959–61; Journalist, Discovery and Personnel mags, 1961–64; Ed., Personnel Mag., 1964–67; careers columnist, Observer newspaper, 1967–68, then freelance journalist. Veitch Meml Medal, RHS, 1993; Lifetime Achievement Award, Garden Writers' Guild, 2003. *Publications:* Vegetables from Small Gardens, 1977, 3rd edn 1995; Salads the Year Round, 1980; RHS Vegetable Garden Displayed, 1982, rev. edn 1992; Sainsbury's Homebase Guide to Vegetable Gardening, 1983; The Salad Garden, 1984; Oriental Vegetables, 1991, 2nd edn 2007; Salads for Small Gardens, 1995; Creative Vegetable Gardening, 1997, 4th edn 2008; The Organic Salad Garden, 2001; Grow Your Own Vegetables, 2002; Just Vegetating, 2012; contribs to RHS Jl. *Recreations:* photography, music, omnivorous reading, gardening by outwitting West Cork's wind, languages, swimming, fighting off Old Father Time, letter writing, mildly malicious gossip. *Address:* c/o Frances Lincoln Ltd, Aurum Press, 74–77 White Lion Street, Islington, N1 9PF. *T:* (020) 7284 9300, *Fax:* (020) 7485 0490. *E:* publicity@frances-lincoln.com. *Club:* Wye College Agricola.

LARKEN, Comdt Anthea, CBE 1991; Director and Company Secretary, Operational Command Training Organisation Ltd, 1991–96; *b* 23 Aug. 1938; *d* of Frederick William Savill and Nance (*née* Williams); *m* 1987 (marr. diss. 1997). *Educ:* Stafford Girls' High Sch. Joined WRNS as Range Assessor, 1956; commnd, 1960; qualified: as Photographic Interpreter, 1961; as WRNS Secretarial Officer, 1967; Staff Officer in Singapore, 1964–66; i/c WRNS Officers' Training, BRNC Dartmouth, 1976–78; NATO Military Agency for Standardisation, Brussels, 1981–84; CSO (Admin) to Flag Officer Plymouth, 1985–86; RCDS, 1987; Dir, WRNS, 1988–91. ADC to the Queen, 1988–91. Lady Pres., Not Forgotten Assoc., 1995–; Pres., Assoc. of Wrens, 1999–. Hon. LLD Greenwich, 2000. *Recreations:* theatre, music, reading, home, family and friends. *Club:* Army and Navy.

LARKEN, Rear Adm. (Edmund Shackleton) Jeremy, DSO 1982; Managing Director, OCTO, since 1991; advisory consultant in corporate crisis and emergency management and leadership; *b* 14 Jan. 1939; *s* of Rear Adm. Edmund Thomas Larken, CB, OBE and Eileen Margaret (*née* Shackleton); *m* 1st, 1963, Wendy Nigella Hallett (marr. diss. 1987); two *d*; 2nd, 1987, Anthea Savill (*see* Comdt Anthea Larken) (marr. diss. 1997); 3rd, 1997, Helen Shannon; one *s* one *d. Educ:* Bryanston Sch.; BRNC, Dartmouth. Joined RN as Cadet, 1957; qualified: in Submarines, 1960; in Navigation, 1965; in Submarine Comd, 1960; served HMS Tenby, Finwhale, Tudor, Ambush and Narwhal; Navigation Officer, HMS Valiant; First Lieut, HMS Otus; commanded HMS Osiris, Glamorgan and Valiant, Third Submarine Sqn, and HMS Fearless (including Falklands Campaign, 1982); exchange with USN (Submarines), 1971–73; Naval Plans; Dir, Naval Staff Duties, 1985; Cdre Amphibious Warfare, 1985–87; ACDS (Overseas), 1988–90. Mem., RUSI, 1970–2006. Governor, Bryanston Sch., 1988–99. FInstD 2003 (MInstD 1996). *Publications:* papers and articles in professional books and periodicals. *Recreations:* defence, maritime and aviation interests, strategy, travel, sailing, theatre, reading, home, family and friends. *Address:* OCTO, Caerlleon House, 142 Boughton, Chester CH3 5BP. *E:* Jeremy.Larken@octo.uk.com. *Club:* Reform.

LARKIN, Sean; QC 2010; *b* London, 29 April 1963; *s* of James Larkin and Joan Larkin; *m* 1998, Ann Walsh; two *s. Educ:* Salesian Coll.; Queen Mary Coll., London (LLB). Called to the Bar, Inner Temple, 1987. *Publications:* (contrib.) Fraud: law, practice and procedure. *Recreations:* sport, music (listening and performing). *Address:* QEB Hollis Whiteman, 1–2 Laurence Pountney Hill, EC4R 0EU. *T:* (020) 7933 8855, *Fax:* (020) 7929 3732. *E:* sean.larkin@qebholliswhiteman.co.uk.

LARKINS, Prof. Richard Graeme, AO 2002; MD, PhD; FTSE; Vice-Chancellor and President, Monash University, 2003–09; Chair, Universities Australia, 2008–09; *b* 17 May 1943; *s* of Graeme Larkins and Margaret Larkins (*née* Rosanove, now Lusink); *m* 1966,

Caroline Cust; three *d*. *Educ:* Univ. of Melbourne (MB BS 1966; MD 1972); RPMS London (PhD 1974). FRACP 1975; FRCP 1990; FRCPI 2000. Resident, Sen. Resident, then Med. Registrar, 1967–69, Asst Endocrinologist, 1970–72, Royal Melbourne Hosp.; Res. Fellow (Churchill Fellow and MRC Fellow), Endocrine Unit, RPMS, Hammersmith Hosp., London, 1972–74; Physician to Endocrine Lab., and to Outpatients, Royal Melbourne Hosp., 1974–77; University of Melbourne: First Asst, 1978–83, Reader in Medicine, 1983, Dept of Medicine, and Dir, Endocrine and Metabolic Unit, 1979–83, Repatriation Gen. Hosp., Heidelberg, Vic; James Stewart Prof. of Medicine, and Hd, Dept of Medicine, Royal Melbourne Hosp./Western Hosp., 1984–97; Associate Dean, Planning, 1996–97, Dean, 1998–2003, Fac. of Medicine, Dentistry and Health Scis; Royal Melbourne Hospital: Endocrinologist, 1984; Dir, Dept of Diabetes and Endocrinology, 1989–93; Chm., Div. of Medicine, 1991–94; Med. Dir, Clinical Business Unit, Internal Medicine, 1994–96. Chairman: Accreditation Cttee, Australian Med. Council, 1991–95; NH&MRC, Australia, 1997–2000; EMBL Australia Council, 2009–; Chair, Victorian Comprehensive Cancer Centre, 2009–; Member: Prime Minister's Sci., Engrg and Innovation Council, 1997–2000; Nat. Aboriginal and Torres Strait Islander Health Council, 1997–2000. President: Endocrine Soc. of Aust., 1982–84; RACP, 2000–02; Nat. Stroke Foundn, 2009–15; Australian Univ. Sport, 2009–13. Chair, Council, Melbourne Grammar Sch., 2010–15; Mem., Council, LaTrobe Univ., 2014–. FTSE 2008; Fellow: Academy of Medicine: Malaysia; Singapore; Australian Acad. of Health and Med. Scis. Honorary Fellow: Royal Coll. of Physicians of Thailand; Ceylon Coll. of Physicians; Hon. FACP. Hon. LLD: Melbourne; Monash. Eric Susman Prize for Med. Res., RACP, 1982; Sir William Upjohn Medal, Univ. of Melbourne, 2002; Centenary of Federation Medal, Acad. of Technol Scis and Engrg, 2003. *Publications:* (jtly) A Textbook of Clinical Medicine: an approach to patients' major problems, 1983; A Practical Approach to Endocrine Disorders, 1985; (jtly) Problems in Clinical Medicine, 1989; (ed jtly) Diabetes 1988, 1989; (with R. A. Smallwood) Clinical Skills, 1993; New Tricks, 2014; many scientific articles. *Recreations:* golf, reading, rowing. *Address:* PO Box 33061, Melbourne, Vic 3004, Australia. *T:* (3) 99038002, (0) 413433000. *E:* richard.larkins@monash.edu. *Clubs:* Melbourne; Royal Melbourne Golf; Barwon Heads Golf; 13th Beach Golf; Melbourne Univ. Boat.

LaROCQUE, Judith Anne, CVO 1992; Ambassador and Permanent Representative of Canada to the Organisation for Economic Co-operation and Development, 2011–15; *b* Hawkesbury, Ontario, 27 Sept. 1956; *d* of Olier LaRocque and Elizabeth (*née* Murray); *m* 1991, André Roland Lavoie. *Educ:* Carleton Univ. (BA Pol Sci. 1979; MA Public Admin 1992). Admin. Asst, Internal Audit Directorate, Public Service Commn, 1979; writer/researcher, Prime Minister's Office, 1979; Special Asst, Office of Leader of Opposition, 1980–82; Cttee Clerk, Cttees and Private Legislation Br., H of C, 1982–84; Legislative Asst to Govt House Leader, 1984–85; Head of House Business, Office of Govt House Leader, Pres. Queen's Privy Council for Canada and Minister Responsible for Regulatory Affairs, 1985–86; Exec. Asst to Minister of Justice and Attorney Gen. of Canada, 1986–89; COS to Govt Leader in Senate and Minister of State for Federal-Provincial Relns, 1989–90; Sec. to Gov. Gen. of Canada, 1990–2000; Sec. Gen., Order of Canada and Order of Military Merit, and Herald Chancellor of Canada, 1990–2000; Associate Dep. Minister, 2000–02, Dep. Minister, 2002–10, of Canadian Heritage. OStJ 1990. *Recreations:* gardening, cross-country ski-ing. *Address:* 3715 Front Road, Hawkesbury, ON K6A 2W5, Canada.

LAROSIÈRE de CHAMPFEU, Jacques Martin Henri Marie de; *see* de Larosière de Champfeu.

LARPENT, Andrew Lionel Dudley de H.; *see* de Hochepied Larpent.

LARSON, Gary; cartoonist; *b* 14 Aug. 1950; *s* of Vern and Doris Larson; *m* 1988, Toni Carmichael. *Educ:* Washington State Univ. (BA Communications). Cartoonist: The Far Side syndicated panel (1900 newspapers worldwide), 1980–95 (Best Syndicated Panel Award, 1985); The Far Side syndicated panel (syndicated internationally in 40 countries), 1995–2009. *Films:* Gary Larson's Tales From The Far Side, 1994; Gary Larson's Tales From The Far Side II, 1998. Reuben Award for Outstanding Cartoonist of Year, 1991 and 1994; Max and Moritz Prize, Best Internat. Cartoon, 1993; Grand Prix, Annecy Film Fest., 1995; Internat. Comics Fest. Award, for French lang. edn of Hound of The Far Side, 1997. *Publications:* The Far Side, 1982; Beyond The Far Side, 1983; In Search of The Far Side, 1984; Valley of The Far Side, 1985; Bride of The Far Side, 1985; It Came From The Far Side, 1986; Hound of The Far Side, 1987; The Far Side Observer, 1987; Night of The Crash-Test Dummies, 1988; Wildlife Preserves, 1989; Wiener Dog Art, 1990 (Wheatley Medals Award, Liby Assoc., 1991); Unnatural Selections, 1991; Cows of Our Planet, 1992; The Chickens are Restless, 1993; The Curse of Madame C, 1994; Last Chapter and Worse, 1996; There's a Hair in My Dirt! A Worm's Story, 1998; *anthologies:* The Far Side Gallery, 1, 2, 3, 4, 5; The PreHistory of The Far Side, 1989; The Complete Far Side, 2 vols, 2003. *Recreations:* jazz guitar, pick-up basketball. *Address:* c/o Andrews McMeel Publishers, 1130 Walnut Street, Kansas City, MO 64106–2109, USA. *T:* (816) 5817500.

LARSSON, Gen. John; General of The Salvation Army, 2002–06; *b* 2 April 1938; *s* of Sture and Flora Larsson; *m* 1969, Freda Turner; two *s*. *Educ:* London Univ. (BD). Commnd as Salvation Army Officer, 1957, in corps, youth and trng work; Chief Sec., S America West, 1980–84; Principal, William Booth Meml Trng Coll., 1984–88; Admin. Planning, 1988–90; Territorial Commander: UK and Republic of Ireland, 1990–93; NZ and Fiji, 1993–96; Sweden and Latvia, 1996–99; COS, Salvation Army Internat. HQ, 1999–2002. *Publications:* Doctrine Without Tears, 1974; Spiritual Breakthrough, 1983; The Man Perfectly Filled with the Spirit, 1986; How Your Corps can Grow, 1988; Saying Yes to Life (autobiog.), 2007; 1929—A Crisis That Shaped The Salvation Army's Future, 2009; Inside a High Council, 2013; Those Incredible Booths, 2015. *Recreations:* music, walking, reading. *Address:* 3 Oakbrook, 8 Court Downs Road, Beckenham, Kent BR3 6LR.

LARTER, Prof. Stephen Richard, PhD; FRS 2009; FRSC; FGS; J. B. Simpson Professor of Geology, University of Newcastle upon Tyne, since 1989; Canada Research Chair in Petroleum Geology, University of Calgary, since 2004; Co-Director, Alberta Ingenuity Center for In situ Energy, Calgary, 2004–10; *b* Christchurch, Cambs, 31 Jan. 1953; *s* of Jack and Jean Larter; *m* 1982, Karen Cullen; three *s*. *Educ:* Peterhouse, Cambridge (BA Natural Scis 1974); Univ. of Newcastle upon Tyne (MSc 1975; PhD 1978). Res. Geochemist, Sen. Res. Geochemist, then Res. Associate, Unocal Corp., USA, 1979–86; Nordisk Ministeraad Prof. of Geochem., Univ. of Oslo, 1987–89; University of Newcastle upon Tyne: Founder and Hd, Fossil Fuels and Envmtl Geochem., Postgrad. Inst., 1989–94 and 1997–99; Dean of Res., Faculty of Sci., Agric. and Engrg, 2002–04; Mem., Univ. Res. Cttee, 1997–2003 (Chm., 2000–02). CEO and Chief Scientific Officer, Gushor Inc., 2008–13; Scientific Dir, Carbon Mgt Canada, 2010–14. Dist. Lectr, Amer. Assoc. Petroleum Geologists, 2005–06. Chm., Gordon Conf. in Organic Geochem., 2006. Foreign Mem., Norwegian Acad. Sci. and Letters, 2004. William Smith Medal, Geol Soc., 1998. FRSC 2012. Friendship Medal (China), 2000; Medal of Merit, Canadian Soc. of Petroleum Geologists, 2012 and 2014; Treibs Medal, Geochemical Soc., 2014. *Recreations:* walking, playing the bagpipes and yoga… not simultaneously! *Address:* Department of Geosciences, University of Calgary, 2500 University Drive NW, Calgary AB T2N 1N4, Canada. *E:* slarter@ucalgary.ca. *Club:* Cowtown Yeast Wranglers (Calgary).

LASCELLES, family name of **Earl of Harewood**.

LASCELLES, Viscount; Alexander Edgar Lascelles; *b* 13 May 1980; *s* and *heir* of Earl of Harewood, *qv*.

LASH, Prof. Nicholas Langrishe Alleyne, DD; Norris-Hulse Professor of Divinity, University of Cambridge, 1978–99, now Emeritus; Fellow, Clare Hall, Cambridge, since 1988; *b* 6 April 1934; *s* of late Henry Alleyne Lash and Joan Mary Lash (*née* Moore); *m* 1976, Janet Angela Chalmers; one *s*. *Educ:* Downside Sch.; Oscott Coll.; St Edmund's House, Cambridge. MA, PhD, BD, DD. Served RE, 1952–57. Oscott Coll., 1957–63; Asst Priest, Slough, 1963–68; Fellow, 1969–85, Dean, 1971–75, St Edmund's House, Cambridge; Univ. Asst Lectr, Cambridge, 1974–78. Hon. DD: London, 2002; Durham, 2011; Sacred Heart, Fairfield, Conn, 2012. *Publications:* His Presence in the World, 1968; Change in Focus, 1973; Newman on Development, 1975; Voices of Authority, 1976; Theology on Dover Beach, 1979; A Matter of Hope, 1982; Theology on the Way to Emmaus, 1986; Easter in Ordinary, 1988; Believing three ways in one God, 1992; The Beginning and the End of 'Religion', 1996; Holiness, Speech and Silence, 2004; Seeing in the Dark: university sermons, 2005; Theology for Pilgrims, 2008. *Address:* 4 Hertford Street, Cambridge CB4 3AG.

LASKEY, Prof. Ronald Alfred, CBE 2011; FRS 1984; FMedSci; FLSW; Charles Darwin Professor, University of Cambridge, 1983–2011, now Emeritus; Fellow of Darwin College, Cambridge, since 1982; Hon. Director, 1999–2006, Joint Hon. Director, 2006–10, MRC Cancer Cell Unit; *b* 26 Jan. 1945; *s* of Thomas Leslie and Bessie Laskey; *m* 1971, Margaret Ann Page; one *s* one *d*. *Educ:* High Wycombe Royal Grammar Sch.; Queen's Coll., Oxford (MA, DPhil 1970; Hon. Fellow, 2011). Scientific Staff: Imperial Cancer Research Fund, 1970–73; MRC Lab. of Molecular Biology, 1973–83; Co-Dir, Molecular Embryology Group, Cancer Research Campaign, 1983–91; CRC Dir, Wellcome Cancer Res. UK (formerly CRC) Inst., 1991–2001. Mem. Bd, UK Panel for Res. Integrity, 2005–11. Member, Scientific Advisory Committee: EMBL, 1999–2004; Max-Planck Inst. for Biochem., 2000–11 (Chm., 2002–10); CRUK London Res. Inst., 2006–13; Louis Jeantet Foundn, 2008– (Vice-Pres., 2010–). Pres., British Soc. of Cell Biology, 1996–99. Vice-Pres., Acad. of Med. Scis, 2007–12; Pres., Biochemical Soc., 2012–14. Mem., Academia Europaea, 1989; Founder FMedSci 1998. Trustee: Strangeways Res. Lab., 1993–2010; ICRF, 2000–02; Inst. of Cancer Res., 2007–12. Croonian Lect., Royal Soc., 2001; Werner Heisenberg Lect., Bavarian Acad., 2010. FLSW 2013. Hon. LLD Dundee, 2014; Hon. DMedSci London, 2014. Colworth Medal, Biochem. Soc., 1979; CIBA Medal, Biochem. Soc., 1997; Feldberg Foundn Prize, 1998; Louis Jeantet Prize for Medicine, Jeantet Foundn, Geneva, 1998; Medical Futures Health Innovation Award, 2007; Royal Medal, Royal Soc., 2009; Lifetime Achievement in Cancer Res. Prize, Cancer Res. UK, 2014. *Publications:* articles on cell biology in scientific jls; Songs for Cynical Scientists and Selected Songs for Cynical Scientists. *Recreations:* music, mountains. *Address:* Department of Zoology, University of Cambridge, Downing Street, Cambridge CB2 3EJ. *T:* (01223) 334106, 334107.

LASOK, (Karol) Paul (Edward); QC 1994; PhD; a Recorder, 2000–12; *b* 16 July 1953; *s* of Prof. Dominik Lasok, QC; *m* 1991, Karen Bridget Morgan Griffith; two *d*. *Educ:* St Mary's Sch., Clyst St Mary; Jesus Coll., Cambridge (MA); Exeter Univ. (LLM, PhD). Called to the Bar, Middle Temple, 1977, Bencher, 2002; Legal Sec., Court of Justice of the EC, 1980–84 and (*locum tenens*) 1985; private practice, 1985–. Chairman: Bar European Gp, 2007–09; VAT Practitioners' Gp, 2009–11. FIIT. Consultant Editor, Butterworths European Court Practice; Jt Editor, Common Market Law Reports, 1996–2010. *Publications:* The European Court of Justice: practice and procedure, 1984, 2nd edn 1994; (jtly) Judicial Control in the EU, 2004; contribs to: Halsbury's Laws of England, 4th edn, vols 51 and 52; Law of European Communities (ed D. Vaughan); Law and Institutions of the European Union, 7th edn 2001; Atkin's Court Forms, vol. 10, 2009, vol. 17, 2011; (contrib. and Gen. Ed.) Value Added Tax: commentary and analysis, 2009; Weinberg and Blank on Takeovers and Mergers; legal periodicals. *Recreation:* amusing daughters. *Address:* 1 & 2 Raymond Buildings, Gray's Inn, WC1R 5NR. *T:* (020) 7405 7211.

LAST, Maj.-Gen. Christopher Neville, CB 1990; OBE 1976; health management consultant, 1998–2000; *b* 2 Sept. 1935; *s* of late Jack Neville Last, MPS, FSMC, FBOA and Lorna (*née* Goodman), MPS; *m* 1961, Pauline Mary Lawton, BA; two *d*. *Educ:* Culford Sch.; Brighton Tech. Coll. psc†, ndc. Commnd Royal Signals, 1956; Germany, Parachute Bde, Borneo, Singapore, 1956–67; OC 216 Para. Signal Sqdn, 1967; RMCS and Staff Coll., Logistics Staff 1 (BR) Corps, 1968–71; NDC, 1972; Lt-Col, Signal Staff HQ, BAOR, 1973; CO Royal Signals NI, 1974; Staff, MoD Combat Develt, 1976, Mil. Ops, 1977; Col, Project Manager MoD (PE) for Army ADP Comd and Control, 1977; CO (Col) 8 Signal Regt Trng, Royal Signals, 1980; Brig., Comd 1 Signal Bde 1 (BR) Corps, 1981; Dir, Mil. Comd and Control Projects, MoD (PE), 1984; Head of Defence Procurement Policy (Studies Team), on Chief of Defence Procurement Personal Staff, MoD (PE), 1985; Maj.-Gen. 1986; Vice Master Gen. of the Ordnance, 1986–88; Mil. Dep. to Head of Defence Export Services, 1988–90; Chief Exec., Clwyd FHSA, 1990–96; Dir of Business Management, Clwyd and Oswestry Tissue Bank, 1996–97; Advr and Chm. (designate), 2002–05, UK Human Tissue Bank. Col Comdt, RCS, 1990–96. Chairman: Royal Signals Instn, 1994–98; Bd of Trustees, Royal Signals Mus., 1994–2004. Mem., RFCA for Wales, 1996–. President: BRCS N Wales, 1996–2004, 2007–13 (Chm., 2004–07); Airborne Signals Assoc., 2013–; Vice-Pres., BRCS Wales, 2000–04. Chm., Kigezi Foundn, 2001–02; Trustee, The Community Foundn in Wales, 2002–09. Liveryman, Co. of Information Technologists, 1988 (Chm., Med. and Health Panel, 1998–2002); Freeman, City of London, 1988. *Recreations:* travel, theatre, ballet, sailing, ski-ing, shooting and country pursuits. *Address:* Regimental HQ Royal Signals, Griffin House, Blandford Camp, Blandford Forum, Dorset DT11 8RH. *Clubs:* Special Forces, Fadeaways.

LAST, John; *see* Last, R. J.

LAST, John William, CBE 1989; Director, Public Affairs, United Utilities plc (formerly North West Water Group), 1993–98; Chairman, Museums Training Institute, 1990–97; *b* 22 Jan. 1940; *s* of late Jack Last (sometime Dir of Finance, Metrop. Police) and Freda Last (*née* Evans); *m* 1967, Susan Josephine, *er d* of late John and Josephine Farmer; three *s*. *Educ:* Sutton Grammar Sch., Surrey; Trinity Coll., Oxford (MA 1965). Littlewoods Organisation, Liverpool, 1969–93. Chairman: Dernier Properties Ltd, 1996–2009; Bute Communications Ltd, 2004–08; Director: Boom, 1990–93; Inward, investment agency for NW, 1992–96; sparesFinder.com Ltd, 1999–2002. Mem., Merseyside CC, 1973–86 (Chm., Arts Cttee, 1977–81). Prospective Parly Cand. (L), Ilkeston, 1963; contested (C) Liverpool, West Derby, Feb. and Oct. 1974, Stockport N, 1979. Hon. Treas., 2002–03, Chm., 2008–13, Pres. 2013–, Welsh Lib Dem Party; UK Lib Dem Party: Dep. Treas., 2003–05; Welsh Mem., UK Exec., 2007–09; Federal Vice Pres., 2009–. Vis. Prof., 1987–98, Prof. of Museum Studies, 1998–2006, City Univ., London. Bd Mem., Royal Liverpool Philharmonic Soc., 1973–93 (Chm., 1977–81, 1986–92); Founder Chairman: Merseyside Maritime Museum, 1977; Empire Theatre (Merseyside) Trust, 1979–81 (Bd Mem., 1986–); Chairman: Walker Art Gall., Liverpool, 1977–81; Library Assoc./Arts Council Wkg Party on Art in Libraries, 1982–84; Wkg Party to form Merseyside TEC, 1989–90; Enquiry into Local Authorities and Museums, 1989–91; Develt Bd, Nat. Mus. of Wales, 2006–; Nat. Chm., Area Museums Councils of GB, 1979–82; Vice-Pres., NW Museum and Art Gall. Service, 1992– (Chm., 1977–82, 1987–92); Vice-Chm., Merseyside Arts, 1985–88; Member: Museums Assoc. Council, 1978–86 (Vice-Pres., 1983); Arts Council of GB, 1980–84 (Chm., Housing the Arts Cttee, 1981–84; Chm., Regional Cttee, 1981–84); Museums and Galleries Commn, 1983–95 (Mem., Scottish Wkg Pty, 1984–85); Enquiry into Tyne and Wear Service, 1988–89; Bd, Northern Ballet Theatre, 1986–98 (Vice Chm., 1986–88); Merseyside Tourism Bd, 1986–92; NW Industrial Council, 1985–98; Calcutt Cttee on Privacy and Intrusion by the Press, 1989–90; Video Appeals Cttee, BBFC, 2002–11; Lay Member: Press Council, 1980–86; Bar

Standards Bd, 2008–14. Advr on Local Govt to Arts Council, 1984–91; Chm., Arts, Initiative and Money Cttee, Gulbenkian Foundn, 1980–83. Mem. Bd, Charities Trust, 1990–94; Trustee: Norton Priory Museum, 1983–87; V&A Museum, 1984–86 (Mem., Adv. Council, 1978–84; Mem., Theatre Museum Cttee, 1983–86); Nat. Museums and Galls on Merseyside, 1986–99; Community Foundn in Wales, 2004–06; Governor: NYO, 1985–93; Nat. Mus. of Wales, 1994–97 and 2003–12. Member Court: Liverpool Univ., 1973–96 (Mem., Council, 1977–81, 1986–96); Univ. of Wales, 2005–08; Vice-Chm. Council, NE Wales Inst., 2002–08 (Mem., 1999–2008). Mem., Peel Gp, 2002–. Vice Pres., N Wales Music Festival, subseq. N Wales Internat. Music Festival, 2000– (Patron, 1994–). Chm., Centenary Develt Trust, Sutton Grammar Sch., 1998–2005. FRSA 1988. Hon. FMA, 1987. Hon. Fellow, Liverpool John Moores Univ. (formerly Liverpool Polytechnic), 1989; Hon. Fellow, Glyndwr Univ., 2009. Freedom of City of London, 1985; Barber Surgeons' Co.: Freeman, 1985; Liveryman, 1987–; Mem., Ct of Assts, 1999–; Master, 2005–06; Freeman, Guild of Educators, 2006–08. Hon. DLitt City, 1995. Merseyside Gold Medal for Achievement, 1991. *Publications:* A Brief History of Museums and Galleries, 1986; The Last Report on Local Authorities and Museums, 1991; reports: (jtly) Arts: the way forward, 1978; (jtly) A Future for the Arts, 1987. *Recreations:* swimming, music, memorabilia of Edward VIII. *Address:* Llannerch Hall, near St Asaph, Denbighshire LL17 0BD. *Club:* Garrick.

LAST, Prof. (Richard) John; Vice-Chancellor, Norwich University of the Arts (formerly Norwich University College of the Arts), since 2009; *b* Peterborough, 23 Dec. 1953; *s* of Frederick and Vera Last; one *d. Educ:* Abbey Grammar Sch., Ramsey; Univ. of Sussex (BA Hons 1975; MA (Ed) 1984); Univ. of Leeds (PGCE 1977). Croydon College: Lectr, 1976–79; Principal Lectr, 1979–94; Asst Principal and Hd, Croydon Sch. of Art, 1994–98; Dep. Principal, Arts UC Bournemouth, 1998–2008. Member, Board: Higher Educn Stats Agency, 2009–; GuildHE, 2011–; Dir, Higher Educn Acad., 2015–. Member, Board: Norwich Heritage and Regeneration Trust, 2009–; Forum Trust, 2010–. Trustee, Norwich Sch., 2014–. FRSA. *Recreations:* visual arts, opera, jazz, watching cricket. *Address:* Norwich University of the Arts, Francis House, 3–7 Redwell Street, Norwich NR2 4SN. *T:* (01603) 756224, *Fax:* (01603) 615728. *E:* j.last@nua.ac.uk. *Clubs:* Athenæum, MCC.

LATASI, Rt Hon. Sir Kamuta, KCMG 2007; OBE 1982; PC 1996; MP for Funafuti, Tuvalu, since 2000; Speaker of Parliament of Tuvalu, 2006–14; *b* 4 Sept. 1936; *s* of Latasi and Malili; *m* 1966, Naama (*d* 2012); two *s* two *d* (and one *d* decd). *Educ:* South Devon Tech. Coll., Torquay (Dip. Public and Soc. Admin). Gilbert and Ellice Islands Colony: Admin. Officer (Cadet), 1960–64; Lands Officer, 1965–66; Secretary: Min. of Natural Resources, 1967; Min. of Works and Utilities, 1968–70; Dist Officer, Funafuti, Ellice Is, 1972; Dist Comr, Ocean Is., 1972–75; Magistrate, Criminal and Civil Courts, 1965–75; Tuvalu Government: Asst Sec. to Chief Minister's Office, 1975; Sec., Min. of Natural Resources, 1976–77; First High Comr of Tuvalu to Fiji, also accredited to PNG and Perm. Rep. to S Pacific Commn, Noumea, New Caledonia and S Pacific Forum, Suva, 1978–83; Dean, Diplomatic Corps, Fiji, 1981–83; Manager, SW Pacific, British Petroleum Co., Tuvalu, 1983–93. MP, Tuvalu, 1983–97; Prime Minister of Tuvalu, 1993–96. *Recreations:* fishing, gardening. *Address:* Parliament of Tuvalu, Vaiaku, Funafuti, Tuvalu. *T:* 20252, 20254.

LATCHMAN, Prof. David Seymour, CBE 2010; Professor of Genetics, and Master of Birkbeck College, University of London, since 2003; Professor of Human Genetics, University College London, since 1999; *b* 22 Jan. 1956; *s* of Emanuel Latchman and Ella Latchman (*née* Wohl); *m* 2002, Hannah Garson; one *s. Educ:* Haberdashers' Aske's Sch.; Queens' Coll., Cambridge (BA 1978; MA 1981; PhD 1981); DSc London 1994. FRCPath 1999. Lectr in Molecular Genetics, Dept of Biology, UCL, 1984–88; Dir, Med. Molecular Biology Unit and Reader in Molecular Biology, Dept of Biochemistry, UCL and Middlesex Sch. of Medicine, 1988–91; University College London: Prof. of Molecular Pathology, 1991–99; Head, Div. of Pathol., 1995–99; Dir, Windeyer Inst. of Med. Scis, 1996–99; Dep. Hd, UCL Graduate Sch., 1998–99; Dean, Inst. of Child Health, UCL and Great Ormond Street Hosp. for Children, 1999–2002. Chm., Sci. Expert Adv. Cttee, Univ. of London, 1988–97. External Examiner: Brunel Univ., 1993–97; Nottingham Univ., 1999–2002; Mem., Examng Panel in Genetics, RCPath, 1999–. Member: Med. Adv. Panel, Parkinson's Disease Soc., 1995–2008 (Dep. Chm., 1997–2008); MRC Adv. Bd, 1997–2004; Project Grants Cttee, BHF, 1998–2002; Sci. Policy Adv. Cttee, 1998–2009 (Chm., 2003–09), Nat. Biol Standards Bd, 2002–09, Nat. Inst. for Biol Standards and Control; Home Office Nat. DNA Database Ethics Gp, 2011–; DoH Genetics and Insurance Cttee, 2002–09; Health Protection Agency Bd, 2003–07; HEFCE Res. Strategy Cttee, 2003–06; MRC Coll. of Experts, 2004–; UUK Res. Strategy Cttee, 2004–; Bd, UUK, 2013– (Mem., England and NI Council, 2007–11). Non-exec. Dir, Gt Ormond St Hosp. for Children NHS Trust, 2001–02; Chairman: London 'Ideas' Genetic Knowledge Park, 2002–09; London Higher, 2006–10. Member, Council: Lifelong Learning UK, 2005–11; CBI London, 2009–13; Promote London, 2009–10; Member, Board: London Skills and Employment Bd, 2009–10; London First, 2009–; Bd Observer, LDA, 2006–12; Governor: SOAS, 2004–09; LSHTM, 2004–09 (Mem. Bd of Mgt, 2004–09); Mem., Bd of Trustees, Univ. of London, 2011–. Pres., The Maccabaeans, 2007–. FRSA 2003; FKC 2014. Haldane Lectr, 1994, Crabtree Orator, 1997 (Pres., 2008), Sainer Lectr, 2007, Roth Lectr, 2011, UCL. Dep. Chm., Editl Bd, Biochemical Jl, 1995–97. *Publications:* Gene Regulation, 1990, 5th edn 2005; Eukaryotic Transcription Factors, 1991, 5th edn 2008; (ed) Transcription Factors: a practical approach, 1993, 2nd edn 1999; (ed) From Genetics to Gene Therapy, 1994; (ed) PCR applications in Pathology, 1995; (ed) Genetic Manipulation of the Nervous System, 1995; (ed) Basic Molecular and Cell Biology, 1997; (ed) Landmarks in Gene Regulation, 1997; (ed) Stress Proteins, 1999; (ed) Viral Vectors for Treating Diseases of the Nervous System, 2003; Gene Control, 2010, 2nd edn 2015. *Recreations:* book collecting, opera. *Address:* Birkbeck College, Malet Street, WC1E 7HX. *Club:* Athenæum.

LATHAM, family name of **Baron Latham.**

LATHAM, 2nd Baron *cr* 1942, of Hendon; **Dominic Charles Latham;** Senior Telecommunications Engineer, Aurecon Australia Pty Ltd, since 1994; *b* 20 Sept. 1954; *s* of Hon. Francis Charles Allman Latham (*d* 1959) and Gabrielle Monica (*d* 1987), *d* of Dr S. M. O'Riordan; *S* grandfather, 1970. *Educ:* Univ. of New South Wales, Australia (BEng (civil), 1977, Hons I; MEngSc 1981). Civil Engr, Electricity Commn, NSW, 1979–88; Structl Engr, Rankine & Hill, Consulting Engrs, 1988–91; Sen. Structl Engr, Gerard Barry Associates, 1992; Teacher, Rock around the Clock Dancing, 1993–94. *Recreations:* rock-'n'-roll/ballroom dancing, electronics, personal computing, sailboarding. *Heir: yr* twin *b* Anthony Michael Latham [*b* 20 Sept. 1954; *m* Margot].

LATHAM, Alison Mary; editor and writer; *b* 13 July 1948; *d* of John Llewellyn Goodall and Patricia Anne Goodall (*née* Tapper); *m* 1972, Richard Brunton Latham, *qv*; three *s. Educ:* Univ. of Birmingham (BMus Hons). Associate Editor, The Musical Times, 1977–88; Publications Editor, Royal Opera House, Covent Garden, 1989–2000; Commng Ed., Edinburgh Internat. Fest. progs, 2003–. FRSA 1999. *Publications:* (ed with S. Sadie) The Cambridge Music Guide, 1985; (ed with R. Parker) Verdi in Performance, 2001; The Oxford Companion to Music, 2002; (ed) Sing, Ariel: essays and thoughts for Alexander Goehr's seventieth birthday, 2003. *Address:* c/o The Oxford Companion to Music, Oxford University Press, Great Clarendon Street, Oxford OX2 6DP. *E:* Alison.Latham@btinternet.com.

LATHAM, Arthur Charles; Member (Lab), Havering Council (formerly Romford Borough Council), 1952–78 and 1986–98; *b* Leyton, 14 Aug. 1930; *m* 1st, 1951, Margaret Green (*d* 2000); one *s* two *d*; 2nd, 2001, Caroline Warren. *Educ:* Romford Royal Liberty Sch.; Garnett Coll. of Educn; LSE. Further Educn Coll. Lectr, 1967–. Havering Council (formerly Romford Borough Council): Leader, Labour Gp, 1962–70 and 1986–98; Leader of the Opposition, 1986–90; Leader of Council, 1990–96; Alderman, 1962–78. Mem., NE Regional Metropolitan Hosp. Bd, 1966–72; non-exec. Dir, London Transport Bd, 1983–84. MP (Lab) Paddington N, Oct. 1969–1974, City of Westminster, Paddington, 1974–79; Founder, and Jt Chm., All Party Gp for Pensioners, 1971–79; Chm., Tribune Gp, 1975–76 (Treasurer, 1977–79). Contested (Lab): Woodford, 1959; Rushcliffe, Notts, 1964; City of Westminster, Paddington, 1979; Westminster N, 1983. Chm., Greater London Lab. Party, 1977–86; Vice-Chm., Nat. Cttee, Labour League of Youth, 1949–53; Vice-President: Labour Action for Peace; AMA; Treasurer, Liberation (Movement for Colonial Freedom), 1969–79; Member: British Campaign for Peace in Vietnam; Campaign for Nuclear Disarmament. Vegetarian. Resigned from Labour Party, May 2003 over Iraq War and other issues, rejoined, 2007. *Recreations:* bridge, chess, cricket, country music, walking, theatre, Chelsea Football Club, pet rats. *Address:* 9 Cotleigh Road, Romford, Essex RM7 9AS.

LATHAM, Christopher George Arnot; Chairman, James Latham PLC, 1988–95; *b* 4 June 1933; *s* of late Edward Bryan Latham and Anne Arnot Duncan; *m* 1963, Jacqueline Cabourdin; three *s. Educ:* Stowe Sch.; Clare Coll., Cambridge (MA). FCA. Articled Fitzpatrick Graham, chartered accountants, 1955; joined James Latham Ltd, timber importers, 1959, Dir 1963. A Forestry Comr, 1973–78. Dir, CILNTEC, 1991–97. Pres., Inst. of Wood Sci., 1977–79; Chairman: Timber Res. and Develt Assoc., 1972–74; Commonwealth Forestry Assoc., 1975–77; Psychiatric Rehabilitation Assoc., 1983–91. Mem., Co. of Builders Merchants, 1985– (Master, 1999–2000; Almoner, 2002–07; Trustee, 2008–11). *Recreations:* forestry, classic cars. *Address:* Marlow.

LATHAM, David John; President, Employment Tribunals (England and Wales), 2009–14; *b* 21 April 1946; *s* of William and Edna Latham; *m* 1969, Cherill Disley; one *s* one *d. Educ:* Quarry Bank Sch., Liverpool; Hull Univ. (LLB Hons). Admitted solicitor, 1971; Partner, Chambers Thomas, Solicitors, Hull, 1972–85; Principal, D. J. Latham & Co., Solicitors, Hull, 1986–87; Partner, Sandersons, Solicitors, Hull, 1988–96. Chm., Employment Tribunals, (pt-time), 1992–96, (full-time), 1996–2001; Regl Chm., Employment Tribunals, later Regl Employment Judge, London Central Reg., 2001–08; Dir, Nat. Trng Employment Tribunals, Judiciary, 1998. Chm., Hull FC, 1993–95. *Recreations:* sport, particularly basketball and Rugby, walking, gardening, theatre, opera, Rotary member. *E:* djl.froburn@yahoo.co.uk. *Club:* Reform.

LATHAM, Rt Hon. Sir David (Nicholas Ramsay), Kt 1992; PC 2000; Chairman, Parole Board of England and Wales, 2009–12; a Lord Justice of Appeal, 2000–09; Vice-President, Court of Appeal (Criminal Division), 2006–09; *b* 18 Sept. 1942; *s* of late Robert Clifford Latham, CBE, FBA and Eileen (*née* Ramsay); *m* 1967, Margaret Elizabeth (*née* Forrest); three *d. Educ:* Bryanston; Queens' Coll., Cambridge (MA). Called to the Bar, Middle Temple, 1964, Bencher, 1989; QC 1985; one of the Junior Counsel to the Crown, Common Law, 1979–85; Junior Counsel to Dept of Trade in export credit matters, 1981–85; a Recorder, 1983–92; a Judge of the High Court, QBD, 1992–2000; Presiding Judge, Midland and Oxford Circuit, 1995–99. Vice-Chm., Council of Legal Educn, 1992–97 (Mem., 1988–97); Member: Gen. Council of the Bar, 1987–92; Judicial Studies Bd, 1988–91. Trustee, Slynn Foundn, 2013–. Gov., Warminster Sch., 2009–. *Recreations:* reading, music, travel. *Address:* 3 Manor Farm Close, Pimperne, Blandford Forum, Dorset DT11 8XL. *Clubs:* Travellers, Beefsteak, Pilgrims; Leander.

LATHAM, Derek James, RIBA; Chairman, Derek Latham & Co., (Lathams), since 1989 (Managing Director, 1989–2010); *b* 12 July 1946; *s* of late James Horace Latham and Mary Pauline Latham (*née* Turner); *m* 1968, Pauline Elizabeth Tuxworth; two *s* one *d. Educ:* King Edward VI Grammar Sch., Retford; Leicester Sch. of Architecture (DipArch 1970); Nottingham Trent Poly. (DipTP 1974, DipLD 1977). RIBA 1972; MRTPI 1975; AABC 2003. Clifford Wearden & Associates (architects and planners), London, 1968–70; Housing Architect and Planner, Derby CC, 1970–73; Design and Conservation Officer, Derbys CC, 1974–78; Principal, Derek Latham and Associates, 1980–89; Man. Dir, Michael Saint Develts Ltd, 1984–96; Dir, Acanthus Associated Architectural Practices Ltd, 1984–98 (Chm., 1987–89). RIBA Client Design Advr, 2005–. Chairman: Church Converts Ltd, 1996–; Opun (Architecture and Built Envmt Centre for E Midlands), 2002–04, 2009–10 (Mem. Cttee, 2010–); Urban Partnership Gp, 2008–; Dir, Regeneration E Midlands, 2004– (Chm., 2006–10). Tech. Advr, Derbys Historic Bldgs Trust, 1978–98; Member: Exec. Cttee, Council for Care of Churches, 1985–91; Cttee, SPAB, 1993–2001. Regl Ambassador, 2001–11, Educn Enabler, 2002–11, CABE. Vis. Prof., Univ. of Derby, 2014–. Chm., RSA at Dean Clough, 1995–98. Member: Regl Cttee, Heritage Lottery Fund, 2001–06; Urban Panel, English Heritage, 2011–. MLI 1979; IHBC 1999–; Member: AHI, 1976–; IEMA, 1991–2006. Founder Academician, Acad. of Urbanism, 2002–. FRSA. Hon. PrD Derby, 2008. *Publications:* Creative Re-use of Buildings, 2000; various tech. articles on urban design and conservation. *Recreations:* racquet ball, sailing, ski-ing, rambling, cycling, swimming, painting, horse riding. *Address:* Lathams, St Michael's, Derby DE21 5EA. *T:* (01332) 365777, *Fax:* (01332) 290314. *E:* d.latham@lathamarchitects.co.uk. *Clubs:* Duffield Squash and Lawn Tennis, Little Eaton Lawn Tennis (Pres., 1991–2003).

LATHAM, Ian; Founder and Publishing Editor, Architecture Today, since 1989; Director, Rightangle Publishing, since 1998; *b* Dover, Kent, 20 March 1956; *s* of Michael and Brenda Latham; *m* 1985, Christine Watson; one *s* one *d. Educ:* St Olave's Grammar Sch., Orpington; Oxford Poly. (BA; DipArch). Tech. Ed., Architectural Design, 1979–83; Dep. Ed., Building Design, 1983–89. Hon. FRIBA 2015. *Publications:* Joseph Maria Olbrich, 1980; (ed) Dixon Jones, 2002; (ed) Feilden Clegg Bradley, 2007; (ed) van Heyningen and Haward, 2010; (ed) MacCormac Jamieson Prichard, 2010; (ed) Allies and Morrison, 2011; Peter Ahrends, 2015; Richard Burton, 2015. *Recreation:* Hellenic studies. *Address:* Architecture Today, 34 Pentonville Road, N1 9HF. *T:* (020) 8883 4207. *E:* watson.latham@virgin.net.

LATHAM, John; Vice-Chancellor and Chief Executive Officer, Coventry University, since 2014; *b* St Asaph, Denbighshire, 22 Feb. 1960; *s* of John and Barbara Latham; one *d. Educ:* Coventry Univ. (BSc Hons Computer Sci. 1983; MBA 1998). Software engr, Plessey Telecoms Ltd, Liverpool, 1981–84; Coventry Polytechnic, later Coventry University: Lectr, then Sen. Lectr, Dept of Computer Sci., 1984–92 (on secondment: researcher, GEC Electrical Projects Ltd, 1986; Res. Fellow, British Telecom, Martlesham, 1989); Principal Lectr and Hd of Trng Consultancy, 1992–95, Business Develt Manager, 1995–97, Commercial Develt Unit (on secondment: Business Develt Dir, JHP Gp Ltd, Coventry, 1994–95; Fire Service Coll., Moreton-in-Marsh, Home Office, 1995–97; Competitiveness Unit, Govt Office for W Midlands, 1997–2000; Competitiveness Team, Advantage W Midlands RDA, 1999–2001); Asst Dir, 1997–99, Dir/Man. Dir, 1999–2006, Commercial Affairs Dept/Coventry Univ. Enterprises Ltd; Pro-Vice-Chancellor, then Dep. Vice-Chancellor (Business Develt), 2005–13. Extraordinary Prof., Stellenbosch Univ., SA, 2014–. Mem., UK Govt Measurement Bd, 2007–14. Dir, UK Nat. Animation and Dissemination Unit, EC EUROTECNET Prog., 1993–94; IT Advr, Coventry HA, 1993–2000; Project Advr, Heart of England Tourist Bd, 1998–99; Evaluator and Prog. Advr, FP7/Horizon 2020, 2010–. Director: Midlands Assoc. for Skills and Trng using Educnl Resources, Univ. Enterprise Trng Partnership, 1997–99; SW Innovation Relay Centre, 1997–2000. Non-executive Director: Membrasense Ltd, 2004–06; Coventry UC Ltd, 2005–; Coventry Univ. London Campus Ltd, 2005–; CUE Ltd, 2005–; CU Social Enterprise CIC, 2005–; CU Services Ltd, 2005–; UK Plugged Ltd, 2008–10; ACUA Ltd, 2010–13; ACUA Solutions Ltd, 2010–13; Serious Games Internat. Ltd, 2012–; Serious Games (Singapore) Ltd, 2012–. Board Member: EBN SA, 2003–10; UKBi Ltd,

2004–13; Business Link W Midlands, 2007–10; Coventry and Warwickshire LEP, 2010–. Member: Adv. Bd, Centre for Carbon Measurement, 2012–; Adv. Bd, Design Council, 2013–; Advr Network, Connected Digital Econ. Catapult, 2014–; Res. and Knowledge Exchange Cttee, HEFCE, 2014–. Mem., Innovation and Growth Policy Network, Univs UK, 2014–; Mem., Leadership Council, Nat. Centre for Univs and Business, 2014–. Mem., Stratford-upon-Avon Coll. Corp., 2001–10 (Chm., 2004–09). Gov., Chipping Camden Acad. Sch., 2009–14. *Recreations:* travel and exploring new parts of the world, widening my skills knowledge and competence through new challenges; with a background in engineering, looking to keep abreast of the latest technological developments; a keen interest in company, financial markets and current affairs, keeping fit through swimming and walking. *Address:* Vice-Chancellor's Office, Coventry University, Priory Street, Coventry CV1 5FB. *T:* (024) 7688 8212. *E:* j.latham@coventry.ac.uk.

LATHAM, Sir Michael (Anthony), Kt 1993; DL; Partnering Advisor, Willmott Dixon Ltd, 2010–12 (Chairman, 1999–2002; Deputy Chairman, 2002–09); *b* 20 Nov. 1942; *m* 1969, Caroline Terry (*d* 2006); two *s*. *Educ:* Marlborough Coll.; King's Coll., Cambridge; Dept of Educn, Oxford. BA Cantab 1964, MA Cantab 1968, CertEd Oxon 1965. Housing and Local Govt Officer, Conservative Research Dept, 1965–67; Parly Liaison Officer, Nat. Fedn of Building Trades Employers, 1967–73; Dir, House-builders Fedn, 1971–73. Westminster City Councillor, 1968–71. Contested (C) Liverpool, West Derby, 1970; MP (C) Melton, Feb. 1974–1983, Rutland and Melton, 1983–92. Chairman: Jt Govt/Industry Rev. of Procurement and Contractual Problems in Construction Industry, 1993–94; Govt Review of 1996 Construction Act, 2004. Mem., Adv. Council on Public Records, 1985–91. Vice-Pres., Building Socs Assoc., 1981–91. Mem. Exec. Cttee, 1987–2000, Dir, 1992, Jt Hon. Treas., 1996–2000, Vice-Pres., 2000–, CCJ. Visiting Professor: Northumbria Univ., 1995–2000; Bartlett Sch. of Architecture, UCL, 1997–2001; UCE, 2001–08; Univ. of Leeds, 2009–. C of E Lay Reader, 1988–. Liveryman Emeritus, Constructors' Co., 2012 (Liveryman, 2005). Hon. Mem. RICS, 1996; Hon. FCIPS 1994; Hon. FCIOB 1995; Hon. FICE 1995; Hon. FREng (Hon. FEng 1997); Hon. FLI 1997; Hon. FRIAS 1998; Hon. FRIBA 2000; Hon. CIBSE 2003. DL Leics, 1994. Hon. LLD Nottingham Trent, 1995; Hon. DEng Birmingham, 1998; Hon. DCL Northumbria, 1999; Hon. DTech Loughborough, 2004. *Publications:* Trust and Money, 1993; Constructing the Team, 1994; articles on housing, land, town planning and building. *Recreations:* gardening, fencing, listening to classical music, cricket. *Address:* Rosary Farm, 10 Arnhill Road, Gretton, Northants NN17 3DN. *Club:* Carlton.

LATHAM, Paul Robert; Chief Operating Officer, Live Nation Entertainment (International) (formerly Live Nation Europe), since 2009; *b* Crewe, 24 Sept. 1960; *s* of Norman and Iris Latham; marr. diss.; two *s*. *Educ:* Brierley St Sch., Crewe. Joined Apollo Leisure as Manager, 1984; Pres., Live Nation UK, 2002–09. Chm., Nat. Skills Acad. for Creative and Cultural Skills, 2008–. Mem. Bd, UK Music, 2011– (Chm., UK Music (Live), 2011–). *Recreations:* vice in Miami, Arsenal FC, NFL and Chicago Bears in particular (visited all 32 NFL teams at home, now for 119 1A colleges), the adoration of Alan Ball, punting ponies, Hooters and Tilted Kilts, going from juvenile to senile without anyone noticing the difference. *Address:* Live Nation UK, 3rd Floor, Regent Arcade House, 19–25 Argyll Street, W1F 7TS. *T:* (020) 7009 3333. *E:* paul.latham@livenation.co.uk.

LATHAM, Pauline, OBE 1992; MP (C) Mid Derbyshire, since 2010; *b* Lincs, 4 Feb. 1948; *m* 1968, Derek Latham; two *s* one *d*. *Educ:* Bramcote Hills Tech. Grammar Sch. Proprietor, Humble Pie, 1976–87; Dir, Michael St Develt, 1982–. Member (C): Derbys CC, 1987–93; Derby CC, 1992–96 and 1998–2010 (Mayor, 2007–08). Contested (C): Broxtowe, 2001; E Midlands, EP, 1999, 2004. Mem., Internat. Develt Select Cttee, 2010–. *Address:* House of Commons, SW1A 0AA.

LATHAM, Air Vice-Marshal Peter Anthony, CB 1980; AFC 1960; *b* 18 June 1925; *s* of late Oscar Frederick Latham and Rhoda Latham; *m* 1953, Barbara Mary; two *s* six *d*. *Educ:* St Philip's Grammar Sch., Birmingham; St Catharine's Coll., Cambridge. psa 1961. Joined RAF, 1944; 1946–69: served No 26, 263, 614, and 247 Sqdns; CFE; Air Min.; Comd No 111 Sqdn; RAF Formation Aerobatic Team (Leader of Black Arrows, 1959–60); MoD Jt Planning Staff; Comd NEAF Strike and PR Wing; Coll. of Air Warfare; Ops No 38 Gp; Comd RAF Tengah, 1969–71; MoD Central Staff, 1971–73; Comd Officer and AOC, Aircrew Selection Centre, Biggin Hill, 1973–74; SASO No 38 Gp, 1974–76; Dir Def. Ops, MoD Central Staff, 1976–77; AOC No 11 Group, 1977–81. Principal, Oxford Air Trng Sch., and Dir, CSE Aviation Ltd, 1982–85; Sen. Air Advr, Short Bros, 1985–90. Cdre, RAF Sailing Assoc., 1974–80; Pres., Assoc. of Service Yacht Clubs, 1978–81; Mem. Bd, RAF Heraldry Trust, 1996–. Pres., British Horological Inst., 1996. Hon. Pres., 2507 (Bicester) Sqdn, 2000–. Liveryman, Clockmakers' Co., 1987 (Mem., Ct of Assts, 1990–; Master, 1996). *Recreations:* sailing, horology. *Address:* c/o Lloyds Bank, 134 New Street, Birmingham B2 4QZ. *Club:* Royal Air Force.

LATHAM, His Honour Peter Heaton; a Circuit Judge, 1997–2008; *b* 3 June 1938; *s* of Tom Heaton Latham and Dorothy Latham (*née* Williams). *Educ:* The Grammar Sch., Ashton-in-Makerfield, Lancs; Pembroke Coll., Oxford (BA Juris 1962). Nat. Service, 2nd Lieut, RA, 1957–59. Instructor, Univ. of Pennsylvania Law Sch., 1962–64; called to the Bar Gray's Inn, 1965 (James Mould Schol., 1965; Lee Essay Prize, 1965); in practice, 1965–97.

LATHAM, Richard Brunton; QC 1991; a Recorder, 1987–2010; *b* 16 March 1947; *s* of Frederick and Joan Catherine Latham; *m* 1972, Alison Mary Goodall (*see* A. M. Latham); three *s*. *Educ:* Farnborough Grammar School; Univ. of Birmingham (LLB 1969). Called to the Bar, Gray's Inn, 1971; Bencher, 2000; practice in London and on Midland Circuit. *Recreations:* sailing, opera. *Address:* 7 Bedford Row, WC1R 4BS. *T:* (020) 7242 3555.

LATHAM, Sir Richard Thomas Paul, 3rd Bt *cr* 1919, of Crow Clump; *b* 15 April 1934; *s* of Sir (Herbert) Paul Latham, 2nd Bt, and Lady Patricia Doreen Moore (*d* 1947), *o d* of 10th Earl of Drogheda; *S* father, 1955; *m* 1958, Marie-Louise Patricia, *d* of Frederick H. Russell, Vancouver, BC; two *d*. *Educ:* Eton; Trinity Coll., Cambridge. *Address:* 2125 Birnam Wood Drive, Santa Barbara, CA 93108, USA.

LATHAM, Roger Alan; Chief Executive, Nottinghamshire County Council, 2002–08; *b* 3 May 1950; *s* of Edward and Florrie Latham; *m* 1973, Angela Judith Warwick (*née* Pearce); one *s*. *Educ:* Bristol Univ. (BSc Econs with Stats); Birmingham Univ. (MSocSc); Liverpool Polytechnic. CPFA; CStat. Economic Assistant, National Westminster Bank, 1972–76; Economist, 1976–85, Asst Chief Finance Officer, 1985–90, Dudley MBC; Dep. County Treasurer, 1990–91, County Treasurer, 1991–2002, Notts CC. Vis. Fellow, Nottingham Trent Univ., 2008–. Pres., CIPFA, 2009–10 (Vice Pres., 2008–09). Methodist Local Preacher. *Recreations:* photography, gardening, computers, reading, dinosaurs, Japanese films, t'ai chi. *Address:* 25 Potters Lane, East Leake, Loughborough, Leics LE12 6NQ. *T:* (01509) 856562.

LA THANGUE, Prof. Nicholas Barrie, PhD; FRSE; FMedSci; Professor of Cancer Biology, University of Oxford, since 2005; Fellow, Linacre College, Oxford, since 2005; *b* Manchester, 29 Nov. 1957; *s* of David. L. Easty and Patricia A. La Thangue (*née* Mayhew). *Educ:* Cheadle Hulme Sch.; Birmingham Univ. (BSc); Reading Univ. (MSc); University Coll. London (PhD 1983); Oxford Univ. (MA). Jenner Fellow, Lister Inst., MRC NIMR, London, 1987–95; Cathcart Prof. of Biochem., Univ. of Glasgow, 1995–2005. Chief Scientific Officer: Prolifix Ltd, 1993–2001; Topo Target A/S, 2001–06. Mem., EMBO, 2003. FRSE 2004; FMedSci 2008. *Publications:* (ed) Seminars in Cancer Biology: cell cycle regulation and cancer, 1995; Targets for Cancer Chemotherapy, 2002; contribs to learned scientific and med. jls. *Recreations:* fishing, music, wine. *Address:* Department of Oncology, University of Oxford, Old Road Campus Research Building, off Roosevelt Drive, Oxford OX3 7DQ. *T:* (01865) 617090. *E:* nick.lathangue@oncology.ox.ac.uk.

LATHE, Dr Richard Frank; Director, Pieta Research, since 2002; Associate Professor, Institute of Bio-Organic Chemistry, University of Pushchino, Russia, since 2011; *b* 23 April 1952; *s* of late Prof. Grant Henry Lathe; one *s* four *d*. *Educ:* Univ. of Edinburgh (BSc Molecular Biol. 1973); Free Univ. of Brussels (DSc 1976). Research Scientist: Univ. of Heidelberg, 1977–79; Univ. of Cambridge, 1979–81; Asst Sci. Dir, Transgene SA, Strasbourg, 1981–84; Principal Sci. Officer, Animal Breeding Res. Orgn, 1984–85; Prof. of Genetics and Genetic Engrg, Lab. of Eukaryotic Molecular Genetics, and Co-Dir, Ecole Supérieure de Biotechnologie, Univ. of Strasbourg, 1985–89; University of Edinburgh: Dir, Centre for Genome Res., 1989–95; Res. Prof., 1989–2002. *Publications:* Autism, Brain, and Environment, 2006. *Address:* Pieta Research, PO Box 27069, Edinburgh EH10 5YW. *T:* (0131) 478 0684.

LATIMER, Sir Graham (Stanley), KBE 1980; Hon. President, New Zealand Maori Council, since 2012 (Delegate, 1964; Vice-President, 1969–72; President, 1972–2012); *b* Waiharara, N Auckland, 7 Feb. 1926; *s* of Graham Latimer and Lillian Edith Latimer (*née* Kenworthy); *m* 1948, Emily Patricia Moore; two *s* two *d*. *Educ:* Pukenui and Kaitaia District High School. Dairy farmer, 1961–95. Chairman: Aotearoa Fisheries, 1991; Crown Forestry Rental Trust, 1991–2012, now Patron; Moana Pacific, 1991–98; Dep. Chm., Maori Fisheries Commn, 1989–90; Negotiator, NZ Maori Fisheries. Member: Tai Tokerau Dist Maori Council, 1962– (Sec. 1966–75; Chm., 1976–); Otamatea Maori Exec., 1959– (Sec. Treas. 1962–72, Chm. 1975–); Otamatea Maori Cttee, 1955–62; Arapaoa Maori Cttee, 1962– (Chm. 1962–69 and 1972–); N Auckland Power Bd, 1977; Waitangi Tribunal, 1976. Chairman: (since inception) Northland Community Coll.; Tai Tokerau Maori Trust Bd, 1979– (Mem., 1975–); Pacific Foundn, 1990–; Trustee: Kohanga Reo Nat. Trust, 1979; Maori Education Foundn; Member: Ngatikahu Trust Bd, 1976; Cttee, Nat. Art Gall. Museum and War Memorial; NZ Maori Arts and Crafts Inst., 1980–; Tourist Adv. Council; Northland Regional Develt Council, 1980–; Alcoholic Liquor Adv. Council, 1980–. Lay Canon, Auckland Anglican Cathedral, 1978; Mem. Gen. Synod. JP. *Relevant publication:* Graham Latimer: a biography, 2002. *Recreations:* Rugby football, tennis. *Address:* PO Box 661, Kaitaia, New Zealand.

LATNER, Stephen; Managing Director, Warburg Dillon Read, 1998–99; *b* 23 July 1946; *s* of late Julius Latner and Anita Latner; *m* 1971, Jennifer Keidan; three *s*. *Educ:* Grocers' Sch.; Queen Mary Coll., London (BSc); Manchester Business Sch. (MBA). With ICL, 1968–71; joined S. G. Warburg, 1973: Dir, 1983–96; Dep. Chm., 1993–96; UK Country Hd, SBC Warburg, then Warburg Dillon Read, 1996–98. Chm. Council, Bobath Centre for Children with Cerebral Palsy, 2002– (Mem. Council, 1999–). *Recreations:* music, cinema, theatre, reading, sport.

LA TROBE-BATEMAN, Richard George Saumarez; structures designer/maker; *b* 17 Oct. 1938; *s* of late John La Trobe-Bateman and of Margaret (*née* Schmid); *m* 1969, Mary Elizabeth Jolly (OBE 2000); one *s* two *d*. *Educ:* Westminster Sch.; St Martin's Sch. of Art; Royal Coll. of Art (MDesRCA). Set up workshop, 1968. Member: Council of Management, British Crafts Centre, 1975–86; Council, Contemporary Applied Arts, 1987–94; Crafts Council: Mem., 1984–86; Index Selector, 1972–73; Chm., Index Selection Cttee, 1980–82. Work in: V&A Collection, 1979; Crafts Council Collection, 1981 and 1984; Keble Coll., Oxon, 1981; Temple Newsam Collection, 1983; Southern Arts Collection, 1983; Pembroke Coll., Oxon, 1984; Crafts Study Centre Collection, Bath, 1985; Northern Arts Collection, 1988; Royal Soc. of Arts, 1994; work presented by Crafts Council to the Prince of Wales, 1982; Longlands footbridge, Cumbria, 1995; Nat. Pinetum footbridge, Kent, 1999; swing-lift opening bridge, Glos (Wood Award), 2003; Langport footbridge, Somerset, 2005–06; Tassajara footbridge, Calif, 2005–06; Rolling drawbridge, Buscot, Oxon, 2010–11; series of truss bridges, Napa Valley, Calif, 2011–12. Vis. Prof., San Diego State Univ., 1986–87. *Publications:* Making Triangles, 2012; articles in Crafts, American Crafts. *Recreations:* listening to music, hill-walking. *Address:* Elm House, Batcombe, Shepton Mallet, Somerset BA4 6AB. *T:* (01749) 850442. *Club:* Contemporary Applied Arts.

LATTER, (Henry) James (Edward); a Judge of the Upper Tribunal (Immigration and Asylum Chamber) (formerly a Vice President, Immigration Appeal Tribunal, later Senior Immigration Judge, Asylum and Immigration Tribunal), 2001–15; *b* 19 April 1950; *s* of Henry Edward Latter and Hilda Bessie Latter; *m* 1978, Penelope Jane Morris; one *s* one *d*. *Educ:* Reigate Grammar Sch.; Trinity Hall, Cambridge (BA 1971; MA 1974). Called to the Bar, Middle Temple, 1972; in practice as Barrister, 1972–95; full-time Immigration Adjudicator, 1995–96; Regl Adjudicator, Hatton Cross, 1996–98; Dep. Chief Adjudicator, 1998–2001.

LATTO, Prof. Jennifer Elizabeth; Provost, Liverpool John Moores University, 1994–2002; *b* 3 Aug. 1944; *d* of Prof. Sir Henry Clifford Darby, CBE, FBA, and Eva Constance Darby (*née* Thomson); *m* 1967, Richard Matheson Latto; one *s*. *Educ:* Berkhamsted Sch. for Girls; Newnham Coll., Cambridge (BA Exptl Psychol. 1966); Homerton Coll., Cambridge (PGCE 1967); University Coll. London (Dip. Educnl Psychol. 1969). Educnl Psychologist, Essex CC, 1968–72; Lectr in Educnl Psychol., Homerton Coll., Cambridge, 1970–73; SSRC Studentship, Dept of Education, Univ. of Cambridge, 1972–75; Educnl Psychologist, Cheshire CC, 1978–79; Sen. Lectr, then Hd, Educn Dept, Liverpool Poly., 1979–92; Prof. of Educnl Psychol., 1992–2002, Dir, Sch. of Educn and Community Studies, 1992–94, Liverpool John Moores Univ.; Adviser: on Higher Educn, Govt Office NW, 2002–05; on Higher Educn Strategy, NW Develt Agency, 2003–07. Chm., NW Heritage Lottery Fund, 2005–11. Dir, Liverpool City of Learning, 2000–02. Chm., Univs Council for Educn of Teachers, 1993–95. Trustee, Tate, and Chm. Council, Tate Liverpool, 1998–2007. Mem., Adv. Cttee, 2004–11, Trustee, 2011–, Granada Foundn. *Publications:* (with Richard Latto) Study Skills for Psychology Students, 2009. *Recreations:* modern design, opera. *Address:* Monksferry House, Grassendale Park, Liverpool L19 0LS.

LATYMER, 9th Baron *cr* 1431; **Crispin James Alan Nevill Money-Coutts;** *b* 8 March 1955; *s* of 8th Baron Latymer and Hon. Penelope Ann Clare (*née* Emmet); *S* father, 2003; *m* 1st, 1978, Hon. Lucy Rose (marr. diss. 1995), *y d* of Baron Deedes, KBE, MC, PC; one *s* two *d*; 2nd, 1995, Mrs Shaunagh Heneage. *Educ:* Eton Coll.; Keble Coll., Oxford. E. F. Hutton & Co., 1977–81; Bankers Trust, 1981–84; European Banking Co., 1984–86; Coutts & Co., 1986–99; Cazenove & Co., 2000–08. Director: Manek Investment Mgt, 1994–; Throgmorton Trust, 2007– (Chm., 2012–). Trustee: Astor Foundn, 1993–; UCLH Charity (formerly Charities), 2005–15 (Chm., 2008–15). *Publications:* Where the Ocean Meets the Sky, 2009. *Recreations:* travelling, sailing. *Heir:* *s* Hon. Drummond William Thomas Money-Coutts, *b* 11 May 1986. *Address:* 8 Turner House, Erasmus Street, SW1P 4DZ. *E:* crispin@latymer.org. *Clubs:* House of Lords Yacht, Ocean Cruising; Velo Rocacorba.

LAU-WALKER, Anthony Stanley, CBE 2013; Chief Executive Officer, Eastleigh College, 2002–14; Member, UK Commission for Employment and Skills, since 2011; *b* Shipley, W Yorks, 3 May 1951; *s* of Benjamin Meek and Vera Meek (*née* Killip, later Walker); *m* 1987, Margaret Lau; one *s* one *d*. *Educ:* Hanson's Boys' Grammar Sch., Bradford; University Coll. of Swansea (BA Politics); University Coll. of Wales, Aberystwyth (MSc Strategic Studies); Thames Valley Coll. of HE (Dip. Mgt); Surrey Univ. (Dip. Counselling). Hd, Teacher Trng and Staff Develt, 1977–87, Hd of Div., 1987–97, Guildford Coll. of Further and Higher

Educn; Curriculum Dir, Eastleigh Coll., 1997–2002. Chm., Windsor Gp of Colls, 2009–14. Trustee, Awarding Body, Vocational Trng Charitable Trust, 2007–. *Recreations:* theatre, cinema, art, walking, foreign travel, family.

LAUDER, Desmond Michael Frank Scott; Programme Manager, International Expansion, Cambridge International Examinations, 2013–15; *b* 28 July 1947; *s* of late Col Philip Lauder and Frances Lauder; *m* 1975, Xanthe Aristidou Theodosiadou; one *s* one *d. Educ:* Magdalene Coll., Cambridge (BA, MA); Inst. of Education, Univ. of London (PGCE). Teacher: Royal Grammar School, Guildford, 1970–72; Saint Ignatius Coll., Enfield, 1972–73; British Council: Asst Dir, Salonika, Greece, 1973–76; Asst Dir, Rio de Janeiro, Brazil, 1976–79; Asst Sec., CNAA, 1979–83; British Council: service in Czechoslovakia and Singapore, 1983–87; Corporate Planning Dept, 1987–91; Dir, Ecuador, 1991–93; Regl Dir, Asia Pacific, 1994–97; Director: Hong Kong, 1997–2003; Greece, 2003–07; Acting Dir, Marketing and Customer Services, 2007–08; Hd, Contracts and Projects Delivery, 2008–10; Asst Chief Exec., VSO, 2010–11. *Recreations:* walking, reading. *Address:* 44 Lings Coppice, Dulwich, SE21 8SX.

LAUDER, Prof. Ian, FRCPath; FMedSci; Dean of Medicine, 2000–08, and Dean, Faculty of Medicine and Biological Sciences, 2003–08, University of Leicester; *b* 17 June 1946; *s* of late Thomas William Lauder and of Joan Lauder; *m* 1969, Patricia Christine Purvis; one *s* one *d. Educ:* King James 1st Grammar Sch., Bishop Auckland; Univ. of Newcastle upon Tyne (MB BS 1969). FRCPath 1985. Lectr in Pathol., Univ. of Newcastle upon Tyne, 1970–78; Sen. Lectr, Pathol., Univ. of Leeds, 1978–84; Prof. of Pathol., Univ. of Leicester, 1984–2000, Prof. Emeritus, 2008; Dean: Leicester Warwick Med. Schs, 2000–07; Faculty of Medicine, Univ. of Warwick, 2002–04. Hon. Prof. of Pathology, Univs of Leicester and Warwick, 2008–. Chairman: Adv. Cttee on Assessment of Lab. Standards, DoH, 1990–95; Armed Services Consultants Appts Bd Pathology, 2003–08. Non-exec. Dir, Univ. Hosps of Leicester NHS Trust, 2000–08; Mem., GMC, 2002–03. Treas., Council of Hds of Med. Schs, 2000–05. Mem. (Liberal), Gateshead MDC, 1976–78. Sec., British Lymphoma Pathol. Gp, 1980–90; Royal College of Pathologists: Chm., Speciality Adv. Cttee, 1990–93; Vice-Pres., 1996–99. Pres., 1942 Club, 2008–10. Vice-Chm., Hope Against Cancer, 2006–. FMedSci 1998 (Treas., 2005–10). Chancellor's Medal, Univ. of Warwick, 2007. *Publications:* Lymphomas other than Hodgkin's Disease, 1981; Malignant Lymphomas, 1988; contrib. numerous papers on malignant lymphomas, cancer pathol. and quality assurance in pathol. *Recreations:* fly-fishing, hill-walking, marathon running, ballroom dancing. *Address:* Paddock House, Illston on the Hill, Leicester LE7 9EG. *T:* (0116) 259 6511. *E:* prof_lauder@hotmail.com.

LAUDER, Sir Piers Robert Dick-, 13th Bt *cr* 1688; *S* father, 1981.

LAUDERDALE, 18th Earl of, *cr* 1624; **Ian Maitland;** Baron Maitland, 1590; Viscount Lauderdale, 1616; Viscount Maitland, Baron Thirlestane and Boltoun, 1624; Bt (NS), 1680; Hereditary Bearer of the National Flag of Scotland, 1790 and 1952; Chief of the Clan Maitland; Marketing Adviser, London School of Economics and Political Science, 1995–2001; *b* 4 Nov. 1937; *er s* of 17th Earl of Lauderdale and Stanka (*née* Lozanic); *S* father, 2008; *m* 1963, Ann Paule, *d* of Geoffrey Clark; one *s* one *d. Educ:* Radley Coll., Abingdon; Brasenose Coll., Oxford (MA Modern History). Various appointments since 1960; with Hedderwick Borthwick & Co., 1970–74; National Westminster Bank, 1974–95: Regl Manager, Maghreb, 1986, ME and N Africa, 1989–91; Sen. Regl Manager, Africa and ME, 1991–95. Dir, Maitland Consultancy Services Ltd, 1995–2009. Lecturer: NY Inst. of Finance, 1997–2000; Euromoney Instnl Investor (formerly Euromoney Publications) PLC, 1998–2006; LSE Gurukul Scholarship Course, 1999. Royal Naval Reserve (Lieutenant), 1963–73; Mem., Queen's Body Guard for Scotland, Royal Co. of Archers, 1986–. Freeman, City of London, 1998; Liveryman, Fanmakers' Co., 1998–2004. *Recreations:* photography, sailing. *Heir: s* The Master of Lauderdale, Viscount Maitland, *qv. Address:* 150 Tachbrook Street, SW1V 2NE; Newlands Barn, By Thornhill, Dumfriesshire DG3 5EE. *Clubs:* Royal Ocean Racing; New, Puffin's (Edinburgh).

See also Lady H. O. Maitland.

LAUDERDALE, Master of; *see* Maitland, Viscount.

LAUENER, Peter Rene, CB 2004; Chief Executive: Education Funding Agency, since 2012; Skills Funding Agency, since 2014; *b* 29 Sept. 1954; *s* of Rene George Lauener and Anne McLean Lauener (*née* Ross); *m* 1976, Angela Margaret Mulliner; one *s* two *d. Educ:* George Watson's Coll., Edinburgh; Univ. of Durham (BA Hons Econs 1975). Economic Assistant, Scottish Office, 1975–82; Manpower Services Commission: Economic Advr, 1982–85; Hd of Strategy, Evaluation and Res., 1986–87; Area Manager, Manchester, 1987–89; Dept of Employment, 1989–92, 1995–96; Dir, Skills & Enterprise, Govt Office for E Midlands, 1992–95; Head of Resources & Budget Mgt, DfEE, 1996–2000; Dir, Learning, Delivery and Standards Gp, DfEE, subseq. DfES, 2000–04; Dir, Qualifications and Young People's Gp, 2004–05, Acting Dir Gen. for Lifelong Learning, 2005, DfES; Dir of Local Transformation, DfES, later DCSF, 2006–09; Chief Exec., Young People's Learning Agency, 2009–12; Mem. Bd, DFE, 2012–. Trustee, Educators Internat., 2012–. *Recreations:* being enchanted by granddaughter since 2013, reading, walking, wine. *Address:* 82 Pingle Road, Sheffield S7 2LL. *T:* (0114) 236 2188.

LAUGHARNE, Albert, CBE 1983; QPM 1978; Deputy Commissioner, Metropolitan Police, 1983–85; *b* 20 Oct. 1931; *s* of Reginald Stanley Laugharne and Jessica Simpson Laugharne; *m* 1st, 1954, Barbara Thirlwall (*d* 1994); two *d*; 2nd, 1999, Margaret Ann Blackmore; four step *s. Educ:* Baines' Grammar Sch., Poulton-le-Fylde; Manchester Univ. Detective Inspector, Manchester City Police, 1952–66; Supt, Cumbria Constab., 1966–70; Chief Supt, W Yorks Constab., 1970–73; Asst Chief Constable, Cheshire Constab., 1973–76; Chief Constable: Warwicks, 1977–78; Lancashire, 1978–83. RCDS, 1975. *Publications:* Seaford House Papers, 1975. *Recreations:* gardening, painting.

LAUGHLIN, Prof. Robert Betts, PhD; Anne T. and Robert M. Bass Professor of Physics, School of Humanities and Sciences, Stanford University, since 1992; *b* 1 Nov. 1950; *s* of David H. and Margaret B. Laughlin; *m* 1979, Anita R. Perry; two *s. Educ:* Univ. of Calif, Berkeley (AB Maths 1972); Massachusetts Inst. of Technol. (PhD Physics 1979). Post-doctoral res., Bell Telephone Labs, 1979–81; post-doctoral res., then Res. Physicist, Lawrence Livermore Nat. Lab., 1981–84; Associate Prof. of Physics, 1984–89, Prof., 1989–, Stanford Univ. Member: Amer. Acad. Arts and Scis, 1990–; NAS, 1994–. E. O. Lawrence Award for Physics, US Dept of Energy, 1985; Oliver E. Buckley Prize, APS, 1986; Franklin Medal for Physics, 1998; (jtly) Nobel Prize for Physics, 1998. *Publications:* A Different Universe: remaking physics from the bottom down, 2005; The Crime of Reason: and the closing of the scientific mind, 2008; contrib. numerous articles in Physical Rev. Letters, Physical Rev., Advances in Physics, etc. *Recreations:* hiking, ski-ing, computers, music. *Address:* Department of Physics, Stanford University, Stanford, CA 94305, USA. *T:* (650) 7234563, *Fax:* (650) 72565411. *E:* rbl@large.stanford.edu.

LAUGHLIN, Prof. Simon Barry, PhD; FRS 2000; Professor of Neurobiology, Department of Zoology, University of Cambridge, since 2004; Fellow, Churchill College, Cambridge, since 1991; *b* 19 Dec. 1947; *s* of Peter and Margaret Laughlin; *m* 1980, Barbara Frances Howard; two *s* one *d. Educ:* Clare Coll., Cambridge (BA, MA); Australian Nat. Univ. (PhD Neurobiol. 1974). Fellow, Res. Sch. of Biol Scis, ANU, 1976–84; Cambridge University: Lectr in Zool., 1984–96; Reader in Sensory Neuroscience, 1996–99; Rank Res. Prof. in Opto-electronics, 1999–2004. *Publications:* contribs on vision, neural processing and energy efficiency to learned jls. *Recreation:* classical bassoon. *Address:* Department of Zoology, Downing Street, Cambridge CB2 3EJ. *T:* (01223) 336608.

LAUGHTON, Sir Anthony Seymour, Kt 1987; FRS 1980; oceanographic consultant; Director, Institute of Oceanographic Sciences, 1978–88; *b* 29 April 1927; *s* of Sydney Thomas Laughton and Dorothy Laughton (*née* Chamberlain); *m* 1st, 1957, Juliet Ann Chapman (marr. diss. 1962); one *s*; 2nd, 1973, Barbara Clare Bosanquet; two *d. Educ:* Marlborough Coll.; King's Coll., Cambridge (MA, PhD). RNVR, 1945–48. John Murray Student, Columbia Univ., NY, 1954–55; Nat. Inst. of Oceanography, later Inst. of Oceanographic Sciences, 1955–88: research in marine geophysics in Atlantic and Indian Oceans, esp. in underwater photography, submarine morphology, ocean basin evolution, midocean ridge tectonics; Principal Scientist of deep sea expedns. Member: Co-ordinating Cttee for Marine Sci. and Technol., 1987–91; nat. and internat. cttees on oceanography and geophysics. President: Challenger Soc. for Marine Sci., 1988–90; Soc. for Underwater Technol., 1995–97 (Mem. Council, 1986–92; President's Award, 1998); Hydrographic Soc., 1997–99. Member Council: Royal Soc., 1986–87; Marine Biology Assoc., 1980–83, 1988–92. Mem. Cttee, 1966–2003, Chm., 1987–2003, Gen. Bathymetric Chart of the Oceans. Member: Governing Body, Charterhouse Sch., 1981–2000 (Chm., 1995–2000); Council, University Coll. London, 1983–93; Adv. Council, Ocean Policy Inst., Hawaii, 1991–93. Trustee, Natural Hist. Mus., 1990–94. Pres., Haslemere Musical Soc., 1997–. Silver Medal, RSA, 1958; Cuthbert Peek grant, RGS, 1967; Prince Albert 1er Monaco Gold Medal for Oceanography, 1980; Founders Medal, RGS, 1987; Murchison Medal, Geol. Soc., 1989. *Publications:* (ed jtly) Of Seas and Ships and Scientists, 2010; papers on marine geophysics and oceanography. *Recreations:* music, gardening, sailing. *Address:* Okelands, Pickhurst Road, Chiddingfold, Surrey GU8 4TS. *T:* (01428) 683941.

LAUGHTON, Prof. Michael Arthur, PhD, DSc(Eng); FREng, FIET, FIEEE; Professor of Electrical Engineering, Queen Mary and Westfield (formerly Queen Mary) College, University of London, 1977–2000, now Emeritus; *b* 18 Dec. 1934; *s* of William Arthur Laughton and Laura (*née* Heap); *m* 1960, Margaret Mary Coleman (marr. diss. 1994); two *s* two *d. Educ:* King Edward's Five Ways Sch., Birmingham; Etobicoke Collegiate Inst., Toronto; Toronto Univ. (BASc 1957); Univ. of London (PhD 1965; DSc(Eng) 1976). FREng (FEng 1989); FIET (FIEE 1977); FIEEE 2010; CEng 1965. GEC, Witton, 1957–61; Queen Mary, later Queen Mary and Westfield, College, London University: Res. Student, Dept of Elect. Engrg, 1961–64; Lectr, 1964–72; Reader, 1972–77; Dean, Faculty of Engrg, 1983–85; Pro-Principal, 1985–89; Dean of Engrg, London Univ., 1990–94. Visiting Professor: Purdue Univ., USA, 1966; Tokyo Univ., 1977; ICSTM, 2002–. Sec. and Dir, Unicom Ltd, 1971–74; Dir, QMC Industrial Res. Ltd, 1979–91 (Chm., 1988–91); Chm., Tower Shakespeare Co. Ltd, 1985–93. Organising Sec., 1963–81, Chm., Exec. Cttee, 1981–2014, Pres. of Council, 2014–, Power Systems Computation Confs; Science and Engineering Research Council: Chm., Machines and Power Educn and Trng Cttee, 1983–86; Member: Elect. Engrg Cttee, 1982–84; Wind Energy Panel, 1985–86; Institution of Electrical Engineers: Chm., Wkg Gp on New Electronic Technol. in Publishing, 1983–87; Member: Council, 1990–94; Governing Cttee, Benevolent Fund, 1990–93; Mem. Exec., Watt Cttee on Energy, 1986– (Chm., Wkg Gp on Renewable Energy Sources, 1986–88); Mem., Inf. Cttee, 1988–92, Mem., Energy Policy Adv. Gp, 2001–, Royal Soc.; Mem., Internat. Cttee, Royal Acad. of Engrg, 2002–06. Specialist Adviser: Sub-Cttee B (Energy, Transport and Technol.), H of L Select Cttee on Eur. Communities, 1987–89; H of C Select Cttee on Welsh Affairs, 1993–94. Member: Fulbright Commn Scholarships Cttee, 1991–; Council, Cranfield Inst. of Technol., 1991–96. Freeman: City of London, 1990; Liveryman: Barbers' Co., 1995; Engineers' Co., 2009. Founder and Jt Ed., Internat. Jl of Electrical Power and Energy Systems, 1978–; Ed., Procs of Power System Computation Confs 5–8, 1975–84. Career Achievement Medal, IEE, 2002. *Publications:* edited: Energy Policy Planning, 1979; Electrical Engineers Reference Book, 14th edn 1985, 15th edn 1993, 16th edn 2002; Renewable Energy Sources, 1990; Expert System Applications in Power Systems, 1990; numerous papers and contribs in the fields of control systems, electrical power systems, energy economics, electrical machines, computational techniques and modelling theory. *Recreations:* painting, music, cricket, Rugby. *Address:* 28 Langford Green, Champion Hill, SE5 8BX. *T:* (020) 7326 0081. *E:* michael.laughton1@btinternet.com. *Club:* Athenæum.

LAUGHTON, Roger Froome, CBE 2000; Chairman, Arts University Bournemouth, since 2012; *b* 19 May 1942; *s* of late Eric Laughton and Elizabeth Laughton (*née* Gibbons); *m* 1967, Suzanne Elizabeth Taylor; one *d. Educ:* King Edward VII Sch., Sheffield; Merton Coll., Oxford (Postmaster; BA 1st Cl. Hons Modern Hist.); Inst. of Educn, Oxford Univ. (DipEd (Dist)). Royal Insce Co. Fellow, Stanford Univ., USA, 1964–65; BBC, 1965–90: Producer, 1965–77; Editor, Features, Manchester, 1977–80; Head: Network Features, 1980–85 (Jt Series Producer, River Journeys (BAFTA Award for best documentary series), 1984); Daytime Programmes, 1985–87; Dir, Co-prodns and BBC Enterprises, 1987–90; Man. Dir, MAI Media, 1990–96; Chief Executive: Meridian Broadcasting, 1991–96; United Broadcasting and Entertainment, 1996–99; Hd, Media Sch., Bournemouth Univ., 1999–2005. Chm., ITV Broadcast Bd, 1995–97; Director: ITV, 1992–99; United News and Media, 1996–2000; ITN, 1997–99. Laughton Media Associates, 2003–11; Chm., South West Screen, 2004–10; Member, Board: Metfilm, 2006–10; Services Sound and Vision Corp., 2007–14. Chm., DCMS/Skillset Audio-Visual Industries Trng Gp, 1999–2001. Chm., Screen Heritage Prog. Bd, 2008–11. Visiting Professor: Bournemouth Univ., 2005–; Univ. of Lincoln, 2010–. Governor: BFI, 2002–08 (Dep. Chair, 2006–08); Arts Univ. Coll. of Bournemouth (formerly Arts Inst. at Bournemouth), 2006–12. Mem., Internat. TV Acad., 1994; FRTS 1994 (Gold Award, 1999). Hon. DA Lincoln, 2009. *Recreations:* walking, cricket, reading, allotment. *Address:* 6 Lawn Crescent, Richmond, Surrey TW9 3NR. *T:* (020) 8948 0231. *Club:* Royal Automobile.

LAUNDER, Prof. Brian Edward, FRS 1994; FREng, FIMechE, FRAeS; Research Professor, School of Mechanical, Aerospace and Civil Engineering, University of Manchester (formerly Department of Mechanical, Aerospace and Manufacturing Engineering, UMIST), since 1998; *b* 20 July 1939; *s* of Harry Edward Launder and Elizabeth Ann Launder (*née* Ayers); *m* 1967, Dagny Simonsen; one *s* one *d. Educ:* Enfield Grammar Sch.; Imperial Coll., London (BScEng Mech Engrg 1961); MIT (SM 1963; ScD 1965 Mech Engrg). Res. Asst, MIT, 1961–64; Lectr, 1964–71, Reader in Fluid Mechanics, 1971–76, Imperial Coll.; Prof. of Mech. Engrg, Univ. of California, Davis, 1976–80; University of Manchester Institute of Science and Technology: Prof. of Mech. Engrg, 1980–98; Head, Thermo-Fluids Div., 1980–90; Head, Dept of Mech. Engrg, 1983–85 and 1993–95; Regl Dir (North), Tyndall Centre for Climate Change Res., 2000–06; Dir, Mason Centre for Envmtl Flows, 2003–06. Hon. Prof., Nanjing Aeronautics Inst., 1993. FREng (FEng 1994); FASME. Dr *hc:* Inst Nat. Polytechnique de Toulouse, 1999; Thessaloniki, 2005; Univ. Paul Cézanne, Aix-en-Provence, 2008; Hon. Dip. Russian Acad. of Sci., 2013. Nusselt-Reynolds Prize in Fluid Mechanics, Assembly of World Confs on Experimental Heat, Transfer, Fluid Mechanics and Thermodynamics, 2013. *Publications:* (with D. B. Spalding) Mathematical Models of Turbulence, 1972; (ed) Turbulent Shear Flows, vol. 1, 1978–vol. 9, 1994; (ed with N. D. Sandham) Closure Strategies for Turbulent and Transitional Flows, 2002; (ed with J. M. T. Thompson) Geo-engineering Climate Change: environmental necessity or Pandora's Box?, 2010; (with K. Hanjalic) Modelling Turbulence in Engineering and the Environment: second-moment routes to closure, 2011; numerous articles on turbulent flow in learned jls. *Recreations:* vacationing in France, photography, country walking. *Address:* School of Mechanical, Aerospace and Civil Engineering, University of Manchester, George Begg Building, Sackville Street, Manchester M13 9PL. *T:* (0161) 306 3801.

LAURANCE, Anthony John, CBE 2005; Chief Executive Officer, Medical Aid for Palestinians, since 2013; *b* 11 Nov. 1950; *s* of Dr Bernard Laurance and Margaret Audrey Laurance (*née* Kidner); *m* 1981, Judith Allen; two *d. Educ:* Bryanston Sch.; Clare Coll., Cambridge (MA). Drum Publications, Zambia, 1973–74; News Training Scheme, BBC, 1975; joined DHSS, 1975; Admin. Trainee, subseq. HEO(D), 1975–80; Mgt Services, 1980–81; Policy Strategy Unit, 1981–83; Finance Div., 1983–85; Prin. Private Sec. to Sec. of State for Social Services, 1985–87; Newcastle Central Office, 1987–90; Territorial Dir, Benefits Agency, 1990–95; Regl Gen. Manager/Regl Dir, South and West RHA, 1995; Regl Dir, SW, NHS Exec., DoH, 1995–2002; Prog. Dir, NHSU, DoH, 2002–04; Iraq: Health Team Leader, Coalition Provisional Authy, 2004; Sen. Advr to Minister of Health, 2004–05; Adviser to Centre of Govt, 2005–06; Advr, Public Admin Develt Prog., Libya, 2006–07; Technical Officer, WHO, Geneva, 2007–08; Hd, WHO, West Bank and Gaza, 2008–13. *Recreations:* modern fiction, tennis, walking, building rocket mass heaters. *Address:* 26A Lowman Road, N7 6DE.

LAUREN, Ralph; fashion designer; Chairman, Ralph Lauren Corporation (formerly Polo Ralph Lauren Corporation) (Chief Executive, until 2015); *b* 14 Oct. 1939; *s* of Frank and Frieda Lifschitz; changed name to Lauren, 1955; *m* 1964, Ricky Beer; three *s*. Salesman, New York: Bloomingdale's; Brooks Bros; Asst Buyer, Allied Stores; Rep., Rivetz Necktie Manufrs; Neckwear Designer, Polo Div., Beau Brummel, 1967–69; creator of designer and ready-to-wear clothing, accessories, fragrances, home furnishings, etc; Founder: Polo Menswear Co., 1968; Ralph Lauren's Women's Wear, 1971; Polo Leathergoods, 1978; Polo Ralph Lauren Luggage, 1982; Ralph Lauren Home Collection, 1983. Numerous fashion awards. *Address:* Ralph Lauren Corporation, 625 Madison Avenue, New York, NY 10022, USA.

LAURENCE, Ven. Christopher; *see* Laurence, Ven. J. H. C.

LAURENCE, George Frederick; QC 1991; *b* 15 Jan. 1947; *s* of Dr George Bester Laurence and Anna Margaretha Laurence; *m* 1st, 1976, (Ann) Jessica Chenevix Trench (*d* 1999); one *s* one *d*, and one step *s*; 2nd, 2000, (Anne) Jacqueline Baker; one *s* one *d. Educ:* Pretoria High Sch. for Boys; Univ. of Cape Town (Smuts Meml Scholarship; BA); University College, Oxford (Rhodes Scholar; MA). Called to the Bar, Middle Temple, 1972 (Harmsworth Law Scholar; Bencher, 1999); Asst Recorder, 1993–2000; Dep. High Court Judge, 1997–2004; a Recorder, 2000–04. Mem. Council, S African Inst. of Race Relns, 1998–2008. Fellow, Soc. for Advanced Legal Studies, 1998. Patron, Sir John Soane's Mus., 2007–14. *Publications:* articles in Jl of Planning and Envmt Law and Rights of Way Law Review. *Recreations:* theatre, access to the countryside, cricket, tennis. *Address:* 12 New Square, Lincoln's Inn, WC2A 3SW. *T:* (020) 7419 8000.

LAURENCE, Ven. (John Harvard) Christopher; Archdeacon of Lindsey, Diocese of Lincoln, 1985–94, now Archdeacon Emeritus; *b* 15 April 1929; *s* of Canon H. P. Laurence and Mrs E. Laurence; *m* 1952, E. Margaret E. Chappell (*d* 2014); one *s* one *d. Educ:* Christ's Hospital; Trinity Hall, Cambridge (MA); Westcott House, Cambridge. Nat. service commn, Royal Lincolnshire Regt, 1948–50. Asst Curate, St Nicholas, Lincoln, 1955–59; Vicar, Crosby St George, Scunthorpe, 1959–73; St Hugh's Missioner, Lincoln Diocese, 1974–79; Bishops' Director of Clergy Training, London Diocese, 1979–85. *Recreation:* sculpture. *Address:* 5 Haffenden Road, Lincoln LN2 1RP. *T:* (01522) 531444.

LAURENCE, Vice Adm. Sir Timothy (James Hamilton), KCVO 2011 (MVO 1989); CB 2007; ADC(P) 2004; company director and adviser, since 2010; *b* 1 March 1955; *s* of Guy Stewart Laurence and Barbara Alison Laurence (*née* Symons); *m* 1992, HRH The Princess Royal. *Educ:* Sevenoaks Sch.; Durham Univ. (BSc Geog.). Joined RN, 1973; in command: HMS Cygnet, 1979–80; HMS Boxer, 1989–91; MoD, 1992–95; in command: HMS Cumberland, 1995–96; HMS Montrose and 6th Frigate Sqdn, 1996–97; MoD, 1997–98; Hudson Vis. Fellow, St Antony's Coll., Oxford, 1999; Asst Comdt (Maritime), JSCSC, Shrivenham, 1999–2001; Dir, Navy Resources & Plans, MoD, 2001–04; ACDS (Resources and Plans), MoD, 2004–07; Chief Exec., Defence Estates, 2007–10; RN retd, 2010. Dir, Saturn Land, 2011–14; non-exec. Dir, Capita (P&I) (formerly Capita Symonds), 2011–14; Chairman: Dorchester Regeneration, 2011–; Major Projects Assoc., 2013–; Purfleet Centre Regeneration Ltd, 2014–; Sen. Advr, PA Consulting, 2011–. Commissioner: Commonwealth War Graves Commn, 2011–; English Heritage, 2011–15; Chm., English Heritage Trust, 2015–; Dir, HMS Victory Preservation Co., 2011–; Chm., Ops Commn, 2013–. Mem. Council, 2004–, Trustee, 2011–, RNLI; Pres., Craft Club, 2012–. Hon. Fellow, Nautical Inst., 2008–; Younger Brother, Trinity House, 2008–; Hon. MRICS 2009. Master, Coachmakers' and Coach Harness Makers' Co., 2010–11. *Recreation:* most sporting and outdoor activities. *Address:* c/o Buckingham Palace, SW1A 1AA.

See also under Royal Family.

LAURENCE SMYTH, Liam Cledwyn; Acting Clerk of Legislation, House of Commons, since 2014; *b* 2 Sept. 1955; *s* of Wing Comdr William Laurence Smyth, MBE, RAF, retired, and late Joan Laurence Smyth (*née* Davies); *m* 1st, 1983, Helen Susan Elizabeth Kingham (marr. diss. 1988); one step *d*; 2nd, 1990, Sally Anne de Ste Croix (*née* Coussins); one *s*, and one step *s* one step *d. Educ:* Plymouth Coll.; New Coll., Oxford (Scholar; MA PPE). A Clerk, House of Commons, 1977–: Clerk: Social Security Cttee, 1994–99; Educn and Employment Cttee, 1999–2001; Educn and Skills Cttee, 2001–02; Delegated Legislation, 2003–05; Overseas Office, 2005–08; of Bills, 2008–09; of Journals, 2009–14. *Recreation:* Gascony in August. *Address:* Public Bill Office, House of Commons, SW1A 0AA. *T:* (020) 7219 3255.

LAURENS, André Antoine; Editor-in-Chief of Le Monde, 1982–84; *b* 7 Dec. 1934; married. Journalist: L'Eclaireur méridional, Montpellier, 1953–55; l'Agence centrale de la presse, Paris, 1958–62; joined Le Monde, 1963; Home Affairs reporter, 1969; Associate Editor, Home Affairs, 1979; Dir, 1982–85; Médiateur, 1992–96; Vice-Pres. Dir Gen. L'Indépendant du Midi, 2000–07; Vice-Pres., Directoire des Journaux du Midi (Midi-Libre, L'Indépendant, Centre Presse), 2004–07. Vice-Pres., Société des Rédacteurs. *Publications:* Les nouveaux communistes, 1972; D'une France à l'autre, 1974; Le métier politique, 1980.

LAURENSON, James Tait; Managing Director, Adam & Company Group, 1984–93 (founder Director and Deputy Chairman, 1983); Chairman, Adam & Company plc, 1985–93; *b* 15 March 1941; *s* of James Tait Laurenson, FRCS and Vera Dorothy Kidd; *m* 1969, Hilary Josephine Thompson (*d* 2009); one *s* three *d. Educ:* Eton; Magdalene College, Cambridge (MA). FCA. Ivory & Sime, investment managers, 1968–83, Partner 1970, Dir 1975; Tayburn Design Group: Man. Dir, 1983–84; Chm., 1984–89; Man. Dir, Hillhouse Investments Ltd, 1993–2005. Director: Alvis, 1971–95; ISIS (formerly I & S UK) Smaller Companies Trust, 1983–2005; The Life Association of Scotland, 1991–93; Fidelity Special Values, 1994–2005. Chairman: Hopetoun House Preservation Trust, 1999–2004; Hohepa Auckland Regl Bd, 2009–; Helensville Birthing Trust, 2009–14; Governing Council, Erskine Stewart's Melville, 1994–99; Trustee, Hohepa Trust Bd, 2009–. *Recreations:* family, golf, gardening, travel. *Address:* Woodhill House, 38 Kaipara View Road, RD2, Helensville 0875, New Zealand. *T:* (9) 4207195. *Club:* Hon. Company of Edinburgh Golfers.

LAURIE, Sir Bayley; *see* Laurie, Sir R. B. E.

LAURIE, (James) Hugh (Calum), OBE 2007; actor, comedian, writer; *b* 11 June 1959; *s* of late Dr (William George) Ranald (Mundell) Laurie; *m* 1989, Jo Green; two *s* one *d. Educ:* Dragon Sch., Oxford; Eton Coll.; Selwyn Coll., Cambridge (Rowing Blue; Pres., Footlights). *Television series:* Alfresco, 1982–84; Blackadder II, 1985; Blackadder the Third, 1987; Blackadder Goes Forth, 1989; A Bit of Fry and Laurie, 1989–95; Jeeves and Wooster, 1990–92; All or Nothing at All; Fortysomething, 2003; House, 2005–12 (Best Actor, Golden Globes, 2006, 2007); *television film:* The Young Visiters, 2003; *films:* Plenty, 1985; Peter's Friends, 1992; Sense and Sensibility, 1996; 101 Dalmatians, 1996; Cousin Bette, 1998; Maybe Baby, 2000; Stuart Little, 2000; That Girl from Rio, 2001; Stuart Little 2, 2002; Flight of the Phoenix, 2003; Street Kings, 2008; The Oranges, 2012; *theatre:* Gasping, Theatre Royal, Haymarket, 1990. Blues albums: Let Them Talk, 2011; Didn't It Rain, 2013. *Publications:* The Gun Seller, 1996; Paper Soldiers, 2009. *Address:* Hamilton Hodell Ltd, 20 Golden Square, W1F 9JL. *T:* (020) 7636 1221.

LAURIE, Sir (Robert) Bayley (Emilius), 7th Bt *cr* 1834; *b* 8 March 1931; *s* of Maj.-Gen. Sir John Emilius Laurie, 6th Bt, CBE, DSO, and Evelyn Clare, (*d* 1987), *d* of late Lt-Col Lionel James Richardson-Gardner; *S* father, 1983; *m* 1968, Laurelie, *d* of Sir Reginald Lawrence William Williams, 7th Bt, MBE, ED; two *d. Educ:* Eton. National Service, 1st Bn Seaforth Highlanders, 1949–51; Captain, 11th Bn Seaforth Highlanders (TA), 1951–67. Lloyd's, 1951–92, Mem., 1955–; with C. T. Bowring & Co. Ltd, 1958–89; Chief Exec., C. T. Bowring (Underwriting Agencies) Ltd, 1974–83; Chm., Bowring Members' Agency, 1983–89; Dir, Murray Lawrence Members' Agency, 1989–92. *Heir: cousin* Andrew Ronald Emilius Laurie [*b* 20 Oct. 1944; *m* 1970, Sarah Anne, *e d* of C. D. Patterson; two *s*]. *Address:* Holly House, Church Road, Stockcross, Newbury, Berks RG20 8LN. *T:* (01488) 658306.

LAURIE, His Honour Robin; a Circuit Judge, 1986–2003; a Deputy Circuit Judge, 2003–10; *b* 26 Jan. 1938; *s* of J. R. Laurie and Dr W. Metzner; *m* 1965, Susan Jane (*neé* Snelling); two *d. Educ:* Fettes Coll.; Geneva Univ.; Jesus Coll., Oxford (MA). Called to the Bar, Inner Temple, 1961; practice at the Bar (South Eastern Circuit), 1961–86. Pres., later Tribunal Judge, Mental Health Rev. Tribunals (restricted patients panel), 1994–2010. *Recreations:* mountaineering, mycology. *Club:* Alpine.

LAURITZEN, Prof. Steffen Lilholt; Knight, Order of Dannebrog (Denmark), 1999; FRS 2011; Professor of Statistics, University of Oxford, 2004–14, now Emeritus; Fellow of Jesus College, Oxford, 2004–14, now Emeritus; Professor of Statistics, University of Copenhagen, since 2014; *b* Frederiksberg, Denmark, 22 April 1947; *m* 1967, Kirsten Bodil Larsen; three *d. Educ:* Univ. of Copenhagen (candidatus statisticae 1972; licentiatus statisticae 1975; dr scientarum 1982); Univ. of Oxford (MA 2004). Lectr, Univ. of Copenhagen, 1972–81; Prof., Univ. of Aalborg, 1981–2004. *Publications:* Graphical Models, 1996; Thiele: pioneer in statistics, 2001; articles in learned jls. *Address:* Department of Mathematical Sciences, University of Copenhagen, Universitetsparken 5, 2100 Copenhagen, Denmark. *E:* lauritzen@math.ku.dk.

LAUTENBERG, Alexis Peter; Senior Policy Advisor, Steptoe & Johnson LLP, Brussels, since 2010; President, British Swiss Chamber of Commerce, since 2010; Chairman, Swiss Finance Council, since 2014; *b* Zürich, 28 Oct. 1945; *s* of Anatole Lautenberg and Nelly Schnapper-Lautenberg; *m* 1972, Gabrielle Feik; one *s* two *d. Educ:* Univ. of Lausanne (BA Pol Sci.). Entered Swiss Diplomatic Service, 1974; Attaché, CSCE, Geneva and Stockholm, 1974–75; Dep. Hd of Mission, Warsaw, 1976; Mem., Swiss Delegn to EFTA and GATT, Geneva, 1977–81; Econ. Counsellor, Bonn, 1981–85; Dep. Dir of Internat. Orgns, Berne, 1985–86; Hd, Econ. and Finance Div., Fed. Dept of Foreign Affairs, Berne, 1986–93; Ambassador and Hd, Mission to EC, Brussels, 1993–99; Ambassador to Italy and Malta, in Rome, 1999–2004; Ambassador to the Court of St James's, 2004–10. Mem. Bd, Sisal SpA, Milano, 2011–. Chairman: Gp for negotiations on financial services during Uruguay Round, GATT, 1990–91; Financial Action Task Force on Money Laundering, OECD, 1991–92. Mem. Bd, Foundn for Res. in Internat. Banking and Finance, at Calif Univ., Riverside, 1987–94. Mem. Bd, Coll. of Europe, Bruges, 1994–99. *Recreations:* golf, ski-ing. *Address:* Steptoe & Johnson LLP, Avenue Louise 240, Box 5, 1050 Brussels, Belgium. *T:* (2) 6404084; Swiss Finance Council, Square de Meeûs, 1000 Brussels, Belgium. *Club:* Athenæum.

LAUTERPACHT, Sir Elihu, Kt 1998; CBE 1989; QC 1970; Fellow of Trinity College, Cambridge, since 1953; Director, Research Centre for International Law, 1983–95, now Director Emeritus, and Hon. Professor of International Law, since 1994, University of Cambridge; practising international lawyer and arbitrator; *b* 13 July 1928; *o s* of late Sir Hersch Lauterpacht, QC and Rachel Steinberg; *m* 1955, Judith Maria (*d* 1970), *er d* of Harold Hettinger; one *s* two *d*; *m* 1973, Catherine Daly; one *s. Educ:* Phillips Acad., Andover, Mass; Harrow; Trinity Coll., Cambridge (Entrance Schol.). 1st cl. Pt II of Law Tripos and LLB; Whewell Schol. in Internat. Law, 1950; Holt Schol. 1948 and Birkenhead Schol. 1950; LLD 2011. Gray's Inn; called to Bar, 1950, Bencher, 1983. Joint Sec., Interdepartmental Cttee on State Immunity, 1950–52; Cambridge University: Asst Lectr in Law, 1953; Lecturer, 1958–81; Reader in Internat. Law, 1981–88. Founding Sec., Internat. Law Fund, 1955–85; Dir of Research, 1959–60, Lectr 1976 and 1996, Hague Academy of Internat. Law; Vis. Prof. of Internat. Law, Univ. of Delhi, 1960. Chm., East African Common Market Tribunal, 1972–75; Consultant to Central Policy Review Staff, 1972–74, 1978–81; Legal Adviser, Australian Dept of Foreign Affairs, 1975–77; Consultant on Internat. Law, UN Inst. for Training and Res., 1978–79; mem. arbitration panel, Internat. Centre for Settlement of Investment Disputes; Chm., North Atlantic Free Trade Area Dispute Settlement Panels, 1996 and 1997; Panel Chm., UN Compensation Commn, 1998–99; Pres., Eritrea-Ethiopia Boundary Commn, 2001–08; Deputy Leader: Australian Delegn to UN Law of the Sea Conf., 1975–77; Australian Delegn to UN Gen. Assembly, 1975–77. Judge *ad hoc*, Internat. Court of Justice (Bosnia *v* Yugoslavia), 1993–2002. Pres., Eastern Reg., UNA, 1991–2001; Pres., World Bank Admin. Tribunal, 1996–98 (Mem., 1980–98; Vice-Pres., 1995–96); Chm., Asian Develt Bank Admin. Tribunal, 1991–95; Member: Social Sciences Adv. Cttee, UK Nat. Commn for Unesco, 1980–84; Panel of Arbitrators, Internat. Energy Agency Dispute Settlement Centre; Panel of Arbitrators, UN Law of the Sea Convention, 1998–; Inst. of Internat. Law, 1983– (Associate, 1979); Trustee, Internat. Law Fund, 1983. Editor: British Practice in International Law, 1955–68; International Law Reports, 1960–. Hon. Fellow, Hebrew Univ. of Jerusalem, 1989. Hon. Mem., Amer. Soc. of Internat. Law, 1993 (Annual Cert. of Merit, 1972; Hudson Medal, 2005). Comdr, Order of Merit (Chile), 1969; Order of Bahrain, 2001; Datuk (Malaysia), 2005. Hague Prize for Internat. Law, 2013. *Publications:* Jerusalem and the Holy Places, 1968; (ed) International Law: the collected papers of Sir Hersch Lauterpacht, vol I, 1970, vol. II, 1975, vol. III, 1977, vol. IV, 1978, vol. V, 2004; The Development of the Law of International Organization, 1976; (ed) Individual Rights and the State in Foreign Affairs, 1977; Aspects of the Administration of International Justice, 1991; Life of Sir Hersch Lauterpacht, 2010; various articles on international law. *Address:* Lauterpacht Centre for International Law, 5 Cranmer Road, Cambridge CB3 9BL. *T:* (01223) 335358; 20 Essex Street, WC2R 3AL. *T:* (020) 7583 9294, *Fax:* (020) 7842 1200. *Club:* Garrick.

LAVELLE, Roger Garnett, CB 1989; financial executive; Hon. Vice-President, European Investment Bank, since 1993 (Vice-President, 1989–93); *b* 23 Aug. 1932; *s* of Henry Allman Lavelle and Evelyn Alice Garnett; *m* 1956, Elsa Gunilla Odeberg; three *s* one *d. Educ:* Leighton Park; Trinity Hall, Cambridge (BA, LLB). Asst Principal, Min. of Health, 1955; Principal, HM Treasury, 1961; Special Assistant (Common Market) to Lord Privy Seal, 1961–63; Private Sec. to Chancellor of the Exchequer, 1965–68; Asst Secretary, 1968, Under Sec., 1975, Dep. Sec., 1985, HM Treasury; Dep. Sec., Cabinet Office, 1987. Dir, EBRD, 1993–2000. *Recreations:* music, gardening. *Address:* 36 Cholmeley Crescent, Highgate, N6 5HA. *T:* (020) 8340 4845.

LAVENDER, Anuja Ravindra; *see* Dhir, A. R.

LAVENDER, Rt Rev. Mgr Gerard; Vicar General, Diocese of Hexham and Newcastle, 2009–13; Parish Priest, Cullercoats and Tynemouth, 2009–13; *b* 20 Sept. 1943; *s* of Joseph and Mary Lavender. *Educ:* Ushaw Coll., Durham. Ordained, 1969; Asst Priest, St Mary Cath., Newcastle upon Tyne, 1969–75; loaned to Royal Navy as Chaplain, 1975; completed All Arms Commando Course, 1976; served with RM, 1976–79; sea going, 1979–80, 1987–89; Exchange Chaplain to San Diego, with US Navy, 1981–83; Chaplain in: Scotland (Rosyth), 1983–85; Portsmouth, 1985–87; Plymouth, 1989–90; Prin. RC Chaplain (Navy), MoD, 1990–93, retired. Parish Priest, Holy Family, Darlington, 1993–2009; Diocesan Episcopal Vicar, 2005–09. GSM, NI, 4 visits 1977–79. *Recreations:* golf, hill walking.

LAVENDER, Nicholas; QC 2008; a Recorder, since 2010; a Deputy High Court Judge, since 2013; *b* Barnsley, 7 Aug. 1964; *s* of Brian and Betty Lavender; *m* 2002, Anuja Ravindra Dhir, *qv*; two *s* one *d*. *Educ:* Queen Elizabeth Grammar Sch., Wakefield; Corpus Christi Coll., Cambridge (BA 1987); Oriel Coll., Oxford (BCL). Called to the Bar, Inner Temple, 1989. Chm., Bar Council, 2014 (Vice Chm., 2013). *Publications:* (ed jtly) Barristers, Vol. 3(1) of Halsbury's Laws of England, 2005. *Address:* Serle Court, 6 New Square, Lincoln's Inn, WC2A 3QS. *Clubs:* Garrick, MCC; Yorkshire County Cricket.

LAVENDER, Dame Tina, DBE 2012; PhD; Professor of Midwifery, and Director, Centre for Global Women's Health, University of Manchester; *m* Jay; one *s* one *d*. *Educ:* Roby Comp. Sch. RGN 1987; RM 1990; MSc 1995; PhD 1999. Clinical midwife, Oxford Street and Mill Lane Maternity Hosps; Prof. of Midwifery and Women's Health, Univ. of Central Lancashire; Hon. Consultant Midwife: Liverpool Women's Hosp.; St Mary's Hosp., Manchester. Vis. Prof., Univ. of Nairobi. Advr, WHO. Co-ed. in Chief, Brit. Jl of Midwifery; Associate Ed., African Jl of Midwifery and Women's Health. Hon. Fellow: Royal Coll. of Midwives; Eur. Acad. of Nurse Sci. *Publications:* articles in jls. *Address:* School of Nursing, Midwifery and Social Work, University of Manchester, Jean McFarlane Building, University Place, Oxford Road, Manchester M13 9PL.

LAVER, Gillian Margaret; Independent Member, Audit and Governance Committee, Human Fertilisation and Embryology Authority, since 2013; *b* 10 Jan. 1949; *d* of Alfred Robert Mansbridge and Doris Edna Mansbridge; *m* 1999, Barry Charles Laver. *Educ:* Horsham High Sch. for Girls; Univ. of Keele (BA Hons 1971). CA 1977. Sen. Consultant, Strategy Div., PA Management Consultants, 1986–89; Finance Dir, Wedgwood Div., Waterford Wedgwood plc, 1989–94; Gp Finance and IT Dir, GEC Avery Ltd, 1994–98; Nat. Dir of Finance, Eversheds, 1998–2000; Cogenza Consulting Ltd, 2001–05; Dir of Finance and Central Services, Archbishops' Council, 2005–06. Non-executive Director and Chairman, Audit Committee: W Midlands Strategic HA, 2006–10; Nat. Treatment Agency for Substance Misuse, 2009–13. Chm., Adv. Cttee on Clinical Excellence Awards, W Midlands Region, 2008–. Member: Auditing Practices Bd, 2001–06; Audit Cttee, Arts Council England, 2004–10; Council, Univ. of Keele, 2009–10. Trustee and Hon. Treas., Diabetes UK, 2001–05. *Recreations:* tennis, golf, ski-ing, gardening.

LAVER, Prof. John David Michael Henry, CBE 1999; FBA 1990; FRSE; Emeritus Professor of Speech Sciences, Queen Margaret University (formerly Queen Margaret University College) (Research Professor, 2001–04, Vice-Principal, 2002–03, Deputy Principal, 2003–04); *b* 20 Jan. 1938; *s* of Harry Frank Laver and Mary Laver; *m* 1st, 1961, Avril Morna Anel Macqueen Gibson; two *s* one *d*; 2nd, 1974, Sandra Traill; one *s*. *Educ:* Churcher's Coll., Petersfield; RAF Coll., Cranwell; Univ. of Edinburgh (MA Hons; Postgrad. Dip. in Phonetics; PhD; DLitt). Asst Lectr and Lectr in Phonetics, Univ. of Ibadan, 1963–66; University of Edinburgh: Lectr, Sen. Lectr, Reader in Phonetics, 1966–85; Prof. of Phonetics, 1985–2000; Dir, 1984–89, Chm., 1989–94, Centre for Speech Technology Research; Associate Dean, Faculty of Arts, 1989–92; Vice-Principal, 1994–97. Pres., Internat. Phonetic Assoc., 1991–95 (Mem. Council, 1986–); Member: Board, European Speech Communication Assoc., 1988–92; Council, Philological Soc., 1994–97; Council, British Acad., 1998–2001 (Chm., Humanities Res. Bd, 1994–98); Board of Governors: Edinburgh Univ. Press, 1999–2000; Caledonian Res. Foundn, 1999–2006; Chm., Bd of Governance, Trinity Long Room Hub, Trinity Coll. Dublin, 2008–10. FRSE 1994 (Vice-Pres., 1996–99; Fellowship Sec., 1999–2002; Bicentenary Medal, 2004; Royal Medal, 2007); Fellow, Inst. of Acoustics, 1988–2001. Hon. FRCSLT 2003. Hon. DLitt: Sheffield, 1999; De Montfort, 1999; Queen Margaret UC, 2006; Hon. LittD Trinity Coll. Dublin, 2013. *Publications:* Communication in Face to Face Interaction, 1972; Phonetics in Linguistics, 1973; The Phonetic Description of Voice Quality, 1980; The Cognitive Representation of Speech, 1981; Aspects of Speech Technology, 1988; The Gift of Speech, 1991; Principles of Phonetics, 1994; The Handbook of Phonetic Sciences, 1997, 2nd edn 2010. *Recreations:* reading, birdwatching, lexicography. *Address:* Queen Margaret University, Queen Margaret University Drive, Musselburgh EH21 6UU.

LAVERCOMBE, Dr Brian James; Honorary Member, British Council, since 1997 (Regional Director for the Americas, 1994–96); *b* 17 Dec. 1938; *s* of Ralph Lavercombe and Doris (*née* Hawkins); *m* 1966, Margaret Jane Chambers; one *s* one *d*. *Educ:* Barnstaple Grammar Sch.; Imperial Coll., London (BSc Hons Physics, ARCS, MSc, DIC; PhD 1966); Reading Univ. (MA Medieval Studies 2001). Post-doctoral Fellow and Asst Prof. in Residence, UCLA, 1966–68; British Council: Science Officer: Chile, 1968–72; Spain, 1972–77; Israel, 1977–80; Projects Officer, Science and Technol. Div., 1980–81; Dir, Science Dept, 1981–84; Rep., Colombia, 1984–87; Dep. Controller, Sci., Technol. and Educn Div., 1987–90; Dir, Mexico, 1990–94. Advr, Earthwatch, 1997–2002. *Publications:* papers on scientific co-operation and technology transfer; research papers in Nature and Accoustica; articles on ornithology. *Recreations:* cricket, ornithology, painting, mediaeval history. *Address:* 37 Playfield Road, Kennington, Oxford OX1 5RS. *T:* (01865) 739659. *Clubs:* Whiteditch Wanderers Cricket (Basingstoke); Isis Probus (Oxford).

LAVERICK, David John; Principal Judge, First-tier Tribunal, Local Government Standards in England, since 2010; *b* 3 Aug. 1945; *s* of Wilfred Henry Laverick and I. M. Doreen Laverick (*née* Lockhart); *m* 1968, Margaret Elizabeth Myatt; three *s*. *Educ:* Sir William Turner's Sch., Redcar; King's Coll. London (LLB Hons 1967); Coll. of Law. Admitted solicitor, 1970; Asst Solicitor, Beds and Lincs CC, 1970–73; Dir of Admin, E Lindsey DC, 1973–75; Dir, Local Govt Ombudsman Service, 1975–95; Chief Exec., Family Health Services Appeal Authy, 1995–2001; Pensions Ombudsman, 2001–07; Pres., Adjudication Panel for England, 2001–10. Legal Mem., Mental Health Rev. Tribunals, 1999–2002. *Recreation:* Scottish country dancing.

LAVERS, Richard Douglas; HM Diplomatic Service, retired; Ambassador to Guatemala, 2001–06, and concurrently non-resident Ambassador to El Salvador, 2003–06 and to Honduras, 2004–06; *b* Nairobi, 10 May 1947; *s* of Douglas Arthur Lavers and Edyth Agnes (*née* Williams); *m* 1986, Brigitte Anne Julia Maria Moers, *e d* of late Robert Moers, Turnhout, Belgium; two *s*. *Educ:* Hurstpierpoint Coll.; Exeter Coll., Oxford (MA). Joined HM Diplomatic Service, 1969; Third Sec., Buenos Aires, 1970–72; Second, later First Sec., Wellington, 1973–76; FCO, 1976–81; First Sec., Pol and Econ., Brussels, 1981–85; on secondment to Guinness Mahon, 1985–87; FCO, 1987–89; NATO Defence Coll., Rome, 1989; Dep. Hd of Mission and HM Consul General, Santiago, 1990–93; Ambassador to Ecuador, 1993–97; FCO, 1997–99; Hd of Research Analysts, FCO, 1999–2001. Non-exec. Dir, PetroLatina, 2006–07; Dir, FORO Consulting, 2011–. Chairman: Anglo-Ecuadorian Soc., 2007–12; Anglo-Central American Soc., 2008–12. Vis. Res. Fellow, Inst. of Latin American Studies, 2001. *Recreations:* books, pictures, travel, fishing, golf. *Club:* Oxford and Cambridge.

LAVERTY, Ashley; *see* Page, Ashley.

LAVERY, (Charles) Michael; QC (NI) 1971; Chairman, Standing Advisory Commission on Human Rights, 1995–99; *b* 10 June 1934; *s* of Charles Lavery and Winifred (*née* McCaffrey); *m* 1962, Anneliese Gisela Lehmann (*d* 2008); three *s* two *d*. *Educ:* Queen's Univ., Belfast (LLB 1954); Trinity Coll., Dublin (BA 1956). Member of the Bar: NI, 1956– (Bencher, 1974, Treas., 1987, Inn of Court); Ireland, 1974–. Chm., Gen. Council of Bar, NI, 1987–89. *Recreations:* walking, reading, cooking. *Address:* c/o The Bar Library, 91 Chichester Street, Belfast BT1 3JQ.

LAVERY, Gerald; Senior Finance Director, Department of Agriculture and Rural Development, Northern Ireland, since 2013; *b* 9 April 1952; *s* of David and Mary Lavery; *m* 2002, Kathy McClurg; one *s* two *d*. *Educ:* Christian Brothers' Grammar Sch., Belfast; Queen's Univ., Belfast (BA Hons Italian Lang. and Lit. 1974). Joined NI Civil Service, 1974; Dept of Manpower Services, 1974–81; Dept of Econ. Develt, 1982–89; Trng and Employment Agency, 1990; NI Office, 1991–94; Sen. Civil Service, 1995; Department of Agriculture and Rural Development, 1995–: Fisheries Sec., 1996–2000; Finance Dir, 2000–03; Sen. Finance Dir, 2003–10; Permanent Sec., 2010–13. *Recreations:* prayer and Christian life, choral singing, keeping fit, enjoyment of all arts. *Address:* Department of Agriculture and Rural Development, Dundonald House, Upper Newtownards Road, Belfast BT4 3SB. *T:* (028) 9052 4638, *Fax:* (028) 9052 4813.

LAVERY, Ian; MP (Lab) Wansbeck, since 2010; *b* Newcastle upon Tyne, 6 Jan. 1963; *s* of John Robert Lavery and Patricia Lavery; *m* 1986, Hilary Baird; two *s*. *Educ:* New Coll., Durham (HNC Mining Engrg). Miner, National Coal Board: Lynemouth Colliery, 1980; Ellington Colliery, 1981–92; National Union of Mineworkers: Mem., Nat. Exec. Cttee, 1992–2010; Gen. Sec., Northumberland Area, 1992–2002; Pres., 2002. Mem. (Lab) Wansbeck DC, 1995–2002. Member, Select Committee: on NI Affairs, 2010–11; on Regulatory Reform, 2010–15; on Energy and Climate Change, 2010–. *Address:* House of Commons, SW1A 0AA.

LAVERY, Dr Kevin Gregory; Chief Executive, Wellington City Council, New Zealand, since 2013; *b* Newcastle upon Tyne, 9 May 1960; *s* of Matthew and Kathleen Lavery; *m* 1986, Catherine Wilkey; two *s*. *Educ:* Manchester Univ. (BA Hons); Kent Univ. (PhD 1987); Univ. of Southern Calif (Harkness Fellow). Graduate trainee, Assoc. of Dist Councils, 1984–86; Gen. Asst to Chief Exec., London Bor. of Bexley, 1986–87; Corporate Policy Manager, Kent CC, 1987–91; Hd of Corporate Team, City of Westminster, 1991–93; Sen. Manager, Price Waterhouse, 1993–97; Chief Executive Officer: City of Newcastle upon Tyne, 1997–2001; Agilisys, 2001–03; Managing Director: Enterprise plc, 2004–05; BT Local and Regl Govt, 2005–06; CEO, Serco Solutions, 2006–08; Chief Exec., Cornwall Council (formerly Cornwall CC), 2008–13. *Publications:* Smart Contracting for Local Government, 1999. *Recreations:* running, watching Newcastle United. *Address:* Wellington City Council, 101 Wakefield Street, PO Box 2199, Wellington 6140, New Zealand. *T:* (4) 8013462. *E:* Kevin.Lavery@wcc.govt.nz. *Club:* Lansdowne.

LAVERY, Michael; *see* Lavery, C. M.

LAVIGNE, Marc T.; *see* Tessier-Lavigne.

LAVIN, Deborah Margaret; Principal, Trevelyan College, 1980–95 (Hon. Fellow, 1997), Principal-elect of new college, 1995–97, and President, Howlands Trust, 1993–97, University of Durham; *b* 22 Sept. 1939. *Educ:* Roedean Sch., Johannesburg, SA; Rhodes Univ., Grahamstown, SA; Lady Margaret Hall, Oxford (MA, DipEd). Asst Lectr, Dept of History, Univ. of the Witwatersrand, 1962–64; Lectr, 1965–78, Sen. Lectr, 1978–80, Dept of Mod. Hist., The Queen's Univ. of Belfast. Sen. Associate, St Antony's Coll., Oxford, 2001–. Trustee: Westlakes Research Ltd, 1995–2001; UK Friends of South African Peace Quartet Trust, 2013–; Peace Quartet Trust (UK), 2013–. Chm., East Hendred Heritage Trust, 2005–. Member: Council, Benenden Sch., 1998–2009; Ct of Govs, Truro Coll., 2005–09. Hon. Life Mem., Nat. Maritime Mus. Cornwall, 2003–. Assoc. Fellow, RIIA, 1997–2000. *Publications:* South African Memories, 1979; The Making of the Sudanese State, 1990; The Transformation of the Old Order in the Sudan, 1993; From Empire to International Commonwealth: a biography of Lionel Curtis, 1995; Friendship and Union: the South African correspondence of Patrick Duncan and Lady Maud Selborne, 1907–1943, 2010; articles in learned jls. *Recreations:* the arts, gardening, tennis. *Address:* Hickmans Cottages, Cat Street, East Hendred, Oxon OX12 8JT. *T:* (01235) 833408. *Club:* Reform.

LAVOIE, Judith Anne, (Mrs A. R. Lavoie); *see* LaRocque, J. A.

LAW, family name of **Barons Coleraine** and **Ellenborough**.

LAW, Andrew Jonathan Parker; Executive Chairman, SuperCommunications, since 2014; Director, Parity Group plc, since 2014; *b* Bromley, 25 May 1956; *s* of Peter Leslie Law and Audrey Iris Law; *m* 2015, Alessandra Lemma; one *s* two *d*, and one step *s*. *Educ:* Portsmouth Grammar Sch.; Univ. of Bristol (BA Jt Hons Classics 1978). Dir, Collett Dickenson Pearce, 1982–89; CEO/Business Develt Dir, Chiat/Day, London, 1990–95; Founder and Chairman: St Luke's, 1995–2003; The Law Firm, 2003–12; Chm., Fearlessly Frank, 2012–14. Entrepreneur of the Year, Ernst & Young, 2003. *Publications:* Open Minds, 1998; Experiment at Work, 2003; Implosion, 2013. *Recreations:* Latin, Greek, ancient history, Italy. *Address:* SuperCommunications, 48 Warwick Street, W1B 5AW. *T:* (020) 7300 3555. *E:* a.law@supercommunications.com.

LAW, Prof. Catherine Mary, CBE 2014 (OBE 1999); MD; FRCP, FRCPCH; FMedSci; Professor of Public Health and Epidemiology, Institute of Child Health, University College London, since 2007; *b* Northampton, 26 Oct. 1954; *d* of Thomas and Margaret Law; *m* 1983, Colin Kennedy; two *s*. *Educ:* Eggars Grammar Sch., Alton, Hants; London Hosp. Med. Coll., Univ. of London (MB BS 1979; MD 1989). MRCP 1981, FRCP 1996; MFPHM 1991, FFPH 2001; FRCPCH 1997. Jun. doctor, various London hosps, 1979–82; Lectr, Inst. of Child Health, 1983–85; Res. Fellow, Johns Hopkins Sch. of Hygiene and Public Health, Baltimore, 1985–87; Sen. Res. Fellow, 1987–92, Sen. Lectr, 1992–2003, Univ. of Southampton Med. Sch.; Consultant in Public Health Medicine, Wessex RHA, 1992–97; Reader in Children's Health, Inst. of Child Health, subseq. Inst. of Child Health, University Coll. London, 2003–07. Hon. Consultant, Gt Ormond St Hosp. for Children NHS Foundn Trust, 2003–. Prog. Dir, NIHR Public Health Res. Prog., 2008–14. Chair, Public Health Adv. Cttee, NICE, 2005–15. FMedSci 2015. *Publications:* contrib. scientific papers on epidemiol. and public health to peer-reviewed jls. *Recreations:* gardening, watching Southampton Football Club, sailing, reading, feeling guilty. *Address:* UCL Institute of Child Health, 30 Guilford Street, WC1N 1EH. *T:* (020) 7905 2304. *E:* catherine.law@ucl.ac.uk.

LAW, Christopher Murray Alexander; MP (SNP) Dundee West, since 2015; *b* Edinburgh, 21 Oct. 1969; *s* of John and Jean Law. *Educ:* Madras Coll., St Andrews; Dundee Coll. of Further Educn (C&G Catering); Univ. of St Andrews (MA 1st Cl. Hons Social Anthropol.; postgrad. dip. in IT). Raleigh Internat., Namibia; organiser, motorbike expeditions in Himalayas; proprietor, Freewheeling Tours; businessman in financial sector. Mem., Scottish Affairs Cttee, 2015–; Vice Chm., All Party Parly Gp on Canada, 2015–, on Wine and Spirits, 2015–, on Whisky, 2015–. *Recreations:* reading, travel, motorcycles. *Address:* (office) 2 Marshall Street, Lochee, Dundee DD2 3BR. *T:* (01382) 848906. *E:* chris.law.mp@parliament.uk.

LAW, Prof. Colin Nigel, PhD; Head of Laboratory, Cambridge Laboratory, Institute of Plant Science Research, John Innes Centre, Norwich, 1989–92; *b* 18 Nov. 1932; *s* of Joseph and Dorothy Mildred Law; *m* 1964, Angela Patricia Williams; three *d. Educ:* Queen Elizabeth's Grammar Sch., Blackburn; Univ. of Birmingham (BSc Hons Genetics); UCW, Aberystwyth (PhD). Nat. Service, RA, 1955–57. Res. worker, Plant Breeding Inst., Cambridge, 1956–87, Head of Cytogenetics Dept, 1972–87; Divl Head, Plant Genetics and Breeding, Inst. of Plant Sci. Res., 1987–89. Sen. Foreign Res. Fellow, Nat. Sci. Foundn, N Dakota State Univ., 1969. Hon. Prof., Univ. of East Anglia, 1990–. Prix Assinsel, Assoc. Internationale des Sélectionneurs, 1982. *Publications:* papers and articles on chromosome manipulation techniques to identify genes of agric. importance in crop plants, esp. wheat; genetic control of cereal plant responses to envmtl stress, particularly salinity. *Recreations:* fishing, painting. *Address:* 41 Thornton Close, Girton, Cambridge CB3 0NF. *T:* (01223) 276554.

LAW, (David) Jude; actor; *b* 29 Dec. 1972; *s* of Peter Law and Maggie Law; *m* 1997, Sadie Frost (marr. diss. 2003); two *s* one *d. Educ:* Alleyn's Sch., Dulwich. Co-founder and Dir, Natural Nylon, prodn co., 2000–03. *Theatre includes:* Les Parents Terribles, NT, 1994; Death of a Salesman, W Yorks Playhouse; Ion, Royal Court, 1995; 'Tis a Pity She's a Whore, 1999, Doctor Faustus, 2002, Young Vic; Hamlet, Wyndham's Th., transf. NY, 2009; Anna Christie, Donmar Warehouse, 2011; Henry V, Noël Coward, 2013. *Films include:* Shopping, 1994; Gattaca, Wilde, Midnight in the Garden of Good and Evil, Bent, 1997; Music From Another Room, Final Cut, The Wisdom of Crocodiles, 1998; eXistenZ, The Talented Mr Ripley (Best Supporting Actor, BAFTA, 2000), 1999; Love, Honour and Obey, 2000; Enemy at the Gates, A. I. Artificial Intelligence, 2001; Road to Perdition, 2002; Cold Mountain, 2003; I Heart Huckabees, (also prod.) Sky Captain and the World of Tomorrow, Alfie, 2004; Closer, The Aviator, 2005; All The King's Men, Breaking and Entering, The Holiday, 2006; Sleuth, 2007; My Blueberry Nights, 2008; The Imaginarium of Dr Parnassus, Sherlock Holmes, 2009; Repo Men, 2010; Contagion, Sherlock Holmes: A Game of Shadows, 2011; 360, 2012; Anna Karenina, 2012; Side Effects, Dom Hemingway, 2013; The Grand Budapest Hotel, Black Sea, 2014. Chevalier des Arts et des Lettres (France), 2007; Variety Award, BIFA, 2012. *Address:* Julian Belfrage Associates, 3rd Floor, 9 Argyll Street, W1F 7TG.

LAW, George Llewellyn; Vice Chairman, Morgan Grenfell Group plc, 1987–89; *b* 8 July 1929; *s* of late George Edward Law and Margaret Dorothy Law, OBE (*née* Evans); *m* 1960, Anne Stewart, *d* of late Arthur Wilkinson and Ness Wilkinson (*née* Muir); one *d. Educ:* Westminster Sch. (Schol.); Clare Coll., Cambridge (Schol.; BA). ACIArb. Solicitor. Slaughter and May, Solicitors, 1952–67, Partner 1961–67; Dir, Morgan Grenfell & Co. Ltd, 1968–91; Dir, Morgan Grenfell Gp plc, 1971–89. Deputy Chairman: Baker Perkins plc, 1986–87 (Dir, 1981–87); Blackwood Hodge plc, 1988–90 (Dir, 1968–90); Director: Bernard Sunley Investment Trust, 1968–75; Sidlaw Group, 1974–82; APV, 1987–90. Mem., Arbitration Panel, SFA Consumer Arbitration Scheme, 1988–2001. Member of Council: Furniture Hist. Soc., 1978–85; Ancient Monuments Soc., 1992– (Actg Hon. Treas., 2008); British-Italian Soc., 1994–97; Vice-Pres., Kensington and Chelsea Decorative and Fine Arts Soc., 2013–. Chm., Council of Mgt, Spitalfields Fest., 2002–06 (Mem., Trustee, and Chm., Fest. Patrons' Cttee, 1995–2006; Hon. Life Patron, 2001; Hon. Advr, 2006). Trustee and Hon. Treas., Nat. Assoc. for Gambling Care, Educnl Resources and Trng, 1998–2004. Trustee, Opera Holland Park Friends, 2003. FRSA. *Recreations:* history of furniture and decorative arts, architectural history, music, reading, swimming, cricket. *Address:* 6 Phillimore Gardens Close, W8 7QA. *T:* (020) 7937 3061. *Clubs:* Brooks's, MCC, Surrey County Cricket.

LAW, Jude; *see* Law, D. J.

LAW, Prof. Malcolm Ross, FRCP, FFPH, FMedSci; Professor of Epidemiology and Preventive Medicine, Wolfson Institute of Preventive Medicine, Barts and The London, Queen Mary's School of Medicine and Dentistry, since 2001; *b* 9 May 1946; *s* of Harold Palmer Law and Jessie Maud Law; *m* 1976, Amelia Anne McRedmond; one *s. Educ:* Adelaide High Sch.; Univ. of Adelaide (MB BS 1970; MSc 1984). MRCP, FRCP 1995; FFPH 2002. Jun. med. posts, Adelaide, London and Cardiff, 1971–78; Lectr and Sen. Registrar, Royal Brompton Hosp., London, 1979–83; Lectr, 1984–87, Sen. Lectr, 1987–94, Reader, 1994–2001, in Epidemiology and Preventive Medicine, Wolfson Inst. of Preventive Medicine, Barts and The London, Queen Mary's Sch. of Medicine and Dentistry. FMedSci 2006. *Publications:* contrib. to learned jls on prevention of cardiovascular disease by drugs and diet. *Address:* Wolfson Institute of Preventive Medicine, Barts and The London, Queen Mary's School of Medicine and Dentistry, Charterhouse Square, EC1M 6BQ. *T:* (020) 7882 6268.

LAW, Patricia; Member (Ind) Blaenau Gwent, National Assembly for Wales, June 2006–2011; *m* 1976, Peter John Law, MP (*d* 2006); two *s* three *d. Educ:* Glanyravon Secondary Modern Sch.; Ebbw Vale Coll. Former Nursing Asst, Gwent Healthcare NHS Trust.

LAW, Prof. Robin Christopher Charles, PhD; FBA 2000; FRSE; FRHistS; Professor of African History, Stirling University, 1993–2009, now Emeritus; *b* 7 Aug. 1944. *Educ:* Balliol Coll., Oxford (BA 1st cl. Hons Lit.Hum. 1966); PhD (Hist. and African Studies) Birmingham 1971. Res. Asst to Dir of African Studies, Lagos Univ., 1966–69; Res. Fellow, Centre of W African Studies, Birmingham Univ., 1970–72; Stirling University: Lectr in Hist., 1972–78; Sen. Lectr, 1978–83; Reader, 1983–93. Visiting posts: Ilorin Univ., Nigeria, 1978; Leiden Univ., Netherlands, 1993–94; York Univ., Canada, 1996–97; Hebrew Univ. of Jerusalem, 2000–01; Vis. Prof., Sch. of History, Univ. of Liverpool, 2008, now Hon. Sen. Res. Fellow. FRHistS 1997; FRSE 2002. UK Distinguished Africanist Award, African Studies Assoc. of UK, 2010. *Publications:* The Oyo Empire *c*1600–*c*1836, 1977; The Horse in West African History, 1980; The Slave Coast of West Africa 1550–1750, 1991; (ed) From Slave Trade to Legitimate Commerce: the commercial transition in 19th century West Africa, 1995; (with Paul Lovejoy) The Biography of Mahommah Gardo Baquaqua, 2001; Ouidah: the social history of a West African slaving 'port' 1727–1892, 2004. *Address:* History and Politics Division, Stirling University, Stirling FK9 4LA.

LAW, Roger, RDI 2000; artist and caricaturist; *b* 6 Sept. 1941; *m* 1960, Deirdre Amsden; one *s* one *d. Educ:* Littleport Secondary Mod. Sch.; Cambridge Sch. of Art (expelled 1960). Cartoonist and illustrator, The Observer, 1962–65; illustrator, Sunday Times, 1965–67; Artist in Residence, Reed Coll., Oregon, and first puppet film, 1967; freelance illustrator, Pushpin Studios, NY, 1968–69; caricaturist and features editor, Sunday Times, 1971–75; with Peter Fluck: formed Luck & Flaw, 1976; founder, Spitting Image, 1982 (first series televised, 1984, 18th series, 1996); Creative Dir, Spitting Image Productions Ltd, 1983–97; first American show for NBC TV, 1986; TV series, The Winjin' Pom, 1991; presenter of radio programmes including: Nasty, Brutish and Short: the History of Mr Punch, 1997; Spitting Images, Art Made in China, 2008; Whatever Happened to the Teapots?, 2009; Spitting in Russian, The Secrets of the Art and the Artist Caravaggio, Archive on 4: Satire the Great British Tradition, I'm a Celebrity Get Me Into Here, 2010; The New Silk Road, Roger's Rabbits, 2011; Roger Law and the Chinese Curiosities, 2012; South Africa Spits Back, 2013; Wow! How Did They Do That?, 2013. Artist in residence, Nat. Art Sch., Sydney, 1998; film, Potshots, 1999; TV film, Arena: whatever happened to Spitting Image, 2014. Major installation for Barbican art gall., 1992; ceramic exhibitions with Janice Tchalenko: V&A, 1993; Richard Dennis Gall., 1996; puppet installation, RA, 1997; gp exhibn, Porcelain City: Jingdezhen, V&A, 2011; Her Maj - 60 Years of Unofficial Portraits of the Queen, Cartoon Mus., 2012; Spitting Image, From Start to Finish, Cartoon Mus., 2014; Internat. Art Fair for Contemp. Objects, Saatchi Gall.; one-man exhibitions: Aussie Stuff, Hossack Gall., 2000; The Land of Oz, Fine Art Soc., 2005; Travelling Light, Mary Place Gall., Sydney, 2012; Roger Law - Porcelain, Sladmore Contemporary Gall., 2014; retrospective exhibn, Still Spitting at Sixty, Newsroom Archive and Visitor Centre, 2005; work in collections: V&A Mus., British Council, 1993; Norwich Castle Mus., 1995; Print Collection of Nat. Gall. of Australia, 2008. Mem., AGI, 1993; Fellow, Internat. Specialised Skills, Melbourne, 1997. Hon. FRCA 2004. Hon. DLitt Loughborough, 1999. DAAD Award, 1967; Assoc. of Illustrators Award (to Luck & Flaw), 1984; BPG TV Award for Best Light Entertainment Prog., 1984; DAAD Award (to Luck and Flaw), 1984; Internat. Emmy Award (for Spitting Image), 1986; Grammy Award, 1987; Emmy Award (for Peter and the Wolf), 1994; Lifetime Achievement Award, Cartoon Art Trust, 1998. *Publications:* The Appallingly Disrespectful Spitting Image Book, 1985; Spitting Images, 1987; The Spitting Image Giant Komic Book, 1988; (with L. Chester) A Nasty Piece of Work, 1992; Goodbye, 1992; Thatcha: the real Maggie memoirs, 1993; Still Spitting at Sixty (autobiog.), 2005; illustrator with Peter Fluck: A Christmas Carol, 1979; Treasure Island, 1986. *Recreation:* making mischief.

LAWES, Glenville Richard; Chairman: Darwin Birthplace Society, 2005–13; Shropshire Tourism, 2011–13; Director, Robert Jones and Agnes Hunt Orthopaedic Hospital Foundation Trust, 2009–13; *b* 28 May 1945; *s* of Eric Lawes and Phyllis (*née* Witchalls); *m* 1969, Isobel Prescott Thomas; one *s* two *d. Educ:* Univ. of Birmingham (BSc Eng). Technol. Editor, New Scientist, 1967–70; HM Diplomatic Service, 1970–80: served Moscow, Geneva and Paris; First Sec., FCO, 1976; with British Petroleum Co. plc, 1980–91; Sen. Analyst, BP Internat., 1980–86; Gen. Manager, BP Middle East, 1986–90; Regl Manager, BP Oil Internat., 1990–91. Chief Exec., Ironbridge Gorge Mus. Trust, 1991–2006; Mem. Bd, MLA, 2009–12 (Chm, W Midlands MLA, 2006–09). FRSA 1999. *Recreations:* music, reading, theatre, renovating old houses. *Address:* 10 Church Street, Bathford, Bath BA1 7TU. *E:* glenlawes@btopenworld.com.

LAWES, William Patrick Lagan; Partner, since 1994, and Senior Partner, since 2011, Freshfields Bruckhaus Deringer (formerly Freshfields) LLP; *b* Swanage, Dorset, 2 Jan. 1964; *s* of Colin Lawes and Paddy Lawes (*née* Lagan); *m* 1995, Rebecca Yongman; three *s* one *d. Educ:* Victoria Univ., Wellington (LLB Hons); Gonville and Caius Coll., Cambridge (LLM 1986). Law Clerk, NZ Court of Appeal and the High Court, Wellington, 1984–85; joined Freshfields, 1986. Vis. Fellow, Centre for Corporate Reputation, Univ. of Oxford, 2008–. Mem., Soc. of Merchants Trading to the Continent, 2007–. *Recreations:* golf, sailing, ski-ing, Real tennis. *Address:* c/o Freshfields Bruckhaus Deringer LLP, 65 Fleet Street, EC4Y 1HS. *T:* (020) 7832 7029, *Fax:* (020) 7832 7645. *E:* william.lawes@freshfields.com. *Clubs:* Hurlingham, City Law; Brancaster Golf, Berkshire Golf, Royal Worlington Golf, Royal North Devon Golf.

LAWLER, Geoffrey John; Managing Director, The Public Affairs Company (GB) Ltd (formerly Lawler Associates), since 1987; Vice-President, International Access Inc., 1987–94; *b* 30 Oct. 1954; *s* of late Major Ernest Lawler, RAEC and Enid Lawler; *m* 1989, Christine (marr. diss. 1998), *d* of Carl Roth, Cheyenne, Wyoming. *Educ:* Richmond Sch., N Yorks; Hull Univ. (BSc (Econ); Pres., Students' Union, 1976–77). Trainee chartered accountant, 1977–78. Community Affairs Dept, 1978–80, Research Dept, 1980–82, Cons. Central Office; Public Relations Exec., 1982–83; Dir, publicity co., 1983. Contested (C) Bradford N, 1987. MP (C) Bradford N, 1983–87. EC Observer for Russian elections, 1993, 1995, 1996, for Liberian election, 1997; UN Observer for S African elections, 1994; OSCE Observer, Ukraine, 2014. Dir, Democracy Internat. Ltd, 1995–2006. Mem. Council, UKIAS, 1987–93. Hon. Pres., British Youth Council, 1983–87; Pres., W Yorks Youth Assoc., 1995–2004 (Vice-Pres., 1986–95). *Recreations:* cricket, music, travel. *Address:* 1 Moorland Leys, Leeds LS17 5BD. *T:* (0113) 278 0211.

LAWLER, Sir Peter (James), Kt 1981; OBE 1965; retired 1987; Australian Ambassador to Ireland and the Holy See, 1983–86; *b* 23 March 1921; *m*; six *s* two *d. Educ:* Univ. of Sydney (BEc). Prime Minister's Dept, Canberra, 1949–68 (British Cabinet Office, London, 1952–53); Dep. Secretary: Dept of the Cabinet Office, 1968–71; Dept of the Prime Minister and Cabinet, 1972–73; Secretary: Dept of the Special Minister of State, 1973–75; Dept of Admin. Services, Canberra, 1975–83. *Recreation:* writing. *Clubs:* Melbourne (Melbourne); University House, Wine & Food (Canberra).

LAWLER, Simon William; QC 1993; **His Honour Judge Lawler;** a Circuit Judge, since 2002; *b* 26 March 1949; *s* of Maurice Rupert Lawler and Daphne Lawler (*née* Elkins); *m* 1985, Josephine Sallie Day; two *s. Educ:* Winchester County Secondary Sch.; Peter Symonds, Winchester; Univ. of Hull (LLB Hons). Called to the Bar, Inner Temple, 1971; in practice at the Bar, 1972–2002; Asst Recorder, 1983–89; a Recorder, 1989–2002. A Pres., Mental Health Rev. Tribunal, 2002–07. *Recreations:* cricket, gardening, opera, wine. *Address:* The Crown Court, 50 West Bar, Sheffield S3 8PH. *T:* (0114) 281 2400.

LAWLEY, Dr Leonard Edward; Director of Kingston Polytechnic, 1969–82; *b* 13 March 1922; *yr s* of late Albert Lawley; *m* 1944, Dorothy Beryl Round; one *s* two *d. Educ:* King Edward VI Sch., Stourbridge; Univs of Wales and Newcastle upon Tyne. BSc, PhD; FInstP. Served with RAF, 1941–46; Lectr, Univ. of Newcastle upon Tyne, 1947–53; Sen. Lectr, The Polytechnic, Regent Street, 1953–57; Kingston Coll. of Technology: Head of Dept of Physics and Maths, 1957–64; Vice-Principal, 1960–64; Principal, 1964–69. *Publications:* various papers in scientific jls on transmission ultrasonic sound waves through gases and liquids and on acoustic methods for gas analysis.

LAWLEY, Susan, (Sue), OBE 2001; broadcaster, since 1970; *b* 14 July 1946; *d* of late Thomas Clifford and Margaret Jane Lawley; *m* 1st, 1975, David Ashby (marr. diss. 1985); one *s* one *d*; 2nd, 1987, Hugh Williams. *Educ:* Dudley Girls' High Sch., Worcs; Bristol Univ. (BA Hons Modern Languages). Thomson Newspapers' graduate trainee, Western Mail and South Wales Echo, Cardiff, 1967–70; BBC Plymouth: sub-editor/reporter/presenter, 1970–72; presenter, BBC Television: Nationwide, 1972–75; Tonight, 1975–76; Nationwide, 1977–83; Nine O'Clock News, 1983–84; Six O'Clock News, 1984–88; Here and Now, 1995–97; Presenter, Desert Island Discs, BBC Radio Four, 1988–2006; Chair, Reith Lectures, BBC, annually, 2001–. Board Member: English Tourism Council, 2000–03; ENO, 2001–05. Hon. LLD Bristol, 1989; Hon. MA Birmingham, 1989; Hon. DLitt CNAA, 1991. *Publications:* Desert Island Discussions, 1989. *Recreations:* family, walking, golf, bridge. *Address:* c/o BBC, Broadcasting House, W1A 1AA.

LAWRANCE, Cynthia; *see* Lawrance, J. C.

LAWRANCE, Prof. Jeremy Norcliffe Haslehurst, DPhil; FBA 2011; Professor of Spanish Golden Age Studies, University of Nottingham, since 2006; *b* Jinja, Uganda, 12 Dec. 1952; *s* of Jeremy Charles Dalton Lawrance and Elizabeth Ann Lawrance; *m* 1975, Martha María de las Mercedes Camargo Álvarez; one *d. Educ:* King's Sch., Canterbury; Balliol Coll., Oxford (MA 1978; DPhil 1983). Fellow, Magdalen Coll., Oxford, 1978–85; University of Manchester: Lectr in Spanish, 1985–93; Prof. of Spanish, 1993–2006. Pres., Assoc. of Hispanists of GB and Ire., 2004–06. *Publications:* (ed and trans. with Anthony Pagden) Francisco de Vitoria: political writings, 1991; (ed and trans. with Brian Tate) Alfonso de Palencia: Gesta Hispaniensia, vol. 1, 1998, vol. 2, 1999; Spanish Conquest, Protestant Prejudice: Las Casas and the Black Legend, 2009; approx. 60 articles in learned jls. *Recreations:* searching for stone circles with daughter, entertaining friends, evading capture by elephants, loud music, geriatric football, Bologna. *Address:* School of Languages, Cultures and Area Studies, University of Nottingham, Nottingham NG7 2RD. *E:* jeremy.lawrance@nottingham.ac.uk.

LAWRANCE, John Ernest; Under Secretary, Director, Technical Division 1, Inland Revenue, 1982–88, retired; *b* 25 Jan. 1928; *s* of Ernest William and Emily Lewa Lawrance; *m* 1956, Margaret Elsie Ann Dodwell; two *s* one *d*. *Educ:* High School for Boys, Worthing; Southampton Univ. (BA Hons Modern History). Entered Inland Revenue as Inspector of Taxes, 1951; Principal Inspector, 1968; Senior Principal Inspector on specialist technical duties, 1974. *Address:* 71A Alderton Hill, Loughton, Essex IG10 3JD. *T:* (020) 8508 7562.

LAWRANCE, Mrs (June) Cynthia; Headmistress of Harrogate Ladies' College, 1974–93; *b* 3 June 1933; *d* of late Albert Isherwood and Ida Emmett; *m* 1957, Rev. David Lawrance, MA, BD (*d* 1999); three *d*. *Educ:* St Anne's Coll., Oxford (MA). Teaching appts: Univ. of Paris, 1954–57; Cyprus, 1957–58; Jordan, 1958–61; Oldham, Lancs, 1962–70; Headmistress, Broughton High Sch., Salford, 1971–73. *Recreations:* music, French literature. *Address:* Kinver House, The Green, Kirklington, Bedale DL8 2NQ.

LAWRANCE, Keith Cantwell; Deputy Chairman, Civil Service Appeal Board, 1981–89 (Member 1980–89); Vice-President, Civil Service Retirement Fellowship, since 1988 (Chairman, 1982–88); *b* 1 Feb. 1923; *s* of P. J. Lawrance; *m* 1952, Margaret Joan (*née* Scott); no *c*. *Educ:* Latymer Sch., N9. Clerical Officer, Admiralty, 1939. Served War, RNVR, 1942–46; Sub-Lt (A), 1945. Exec. Officer, Treasury, 1947; Asst Principal, Post Office, 1954; Principal, Post Office, 1959; Asst Sec., Dept of Economic Affairs, Dec. 1966; Under-Sec., Civil Service Dept, 1971–79. Vice-Chm., Inst. of Cancer Research, 1989–95. *Recreations:* model engineering, music. *Address:* White Gables, 35 Fairmile Avenue, Cobham, Surrey KT11 2JA. *T:* (01932) 863689.

LAWRENCE, family name of **Barons Lawrence** and **Trevethin and Oaksey**, and **Baroness Lawrence of Clarendon**.

LAWRENCE, 5th Baron *cr* 1869; **David John Downer Lawrence;** Bt 1858; *b* 4 Sept. 1937; *s* of 4th Baron Lawrence and Margaret Jean (*d* 1977), *d* of Arthur Downer, Kirdford, Sussex; *S* father, 1968. *Educ:* Bradfield College. *Address:* c/o Bird & Bird, 15 Fetter Lane, EC4A 1JP.

LAWRENCE OF CLARENDON, Baroness *cr* 2013 (Life Peer), of Clarendon in the Commonwealth Realm of Jamaica; **Doreen Delceita Lawrence,** OBE 2003; rights campaigner; Founder, Stephen Lawrence Charitable Trust, 1998; *b* Jamaica, 24 Oct. 1952; *d* of Ruby Howe and Blandford Graham; *m* 1972, Neville Lawrence (marr. diss. 1999); one *s* one *d* (and one *s* decd). *Educ:* Univ. of Greenwich (BA Hons Humanities 1995; Postgrad. prog. in Counselling Skills 1997; Dip. Therapeutic Counselling 1999). Emigrated to UK, 1961. Bank worker; Student Financial Advr, Univ. of Greenwich, 1996–2002. Mem. Exec. Cttee, Liberty, 2005– (Mem. Council, 2012–14). Patron, Stop Hate UK. Hon. Dr Greenwich, 2006; Hon. DEd E London, 2012. Lifetime Achievement Award, Pride of Britain Awards, 2012. *Publications:* And Still I Rise: seeking justice for Stephen, 2006. *Address:* c/o Stephen Lawrence Charitable Trust, The Stephen Lawrence Centre, 39 Brookmill Road, Deptford, SE8 4HU.

LAWRENCE, Prof. Andrew, PhD; FRAS; Regius Professor of Astronomy, University of Edinburgh, since 1994 (Head, Institute for Astronomy, 1994–2004; Head, School of Physics, 2003–08); *b* 23 April 1954; *s* of Jack Lawrence and Louisa Minnie (*née* Sandison); partner, Debbie Ann Capel; three *s* one *d*. *Educ:* Chatham House Grammar Sch., Ramsgate; Univ. of Edinburgh (BSc Hons 1976); Univ. of Leicester (PhD 1980). FRAS 1983. Exchange scientist, MIT, 1980–81; Sen. Res. Fellow, Royal Greenwich Observatory, 1981–84; PDRA, QMC, 1984–87; Queen Mary and Westfield College, London: SERC Advanced Fellow, 1987–89; Lectr, 1989–94. Vis. Scientist, SLAC, 2008–09. Mem., various res. councils and internat. cttees, panels, etc, 1983–99; Mem., PPARC, 2000–03. FRSE 1997. *Publications:* (ed) Comets to Cosmology, 1987; numerous contribs to professional astronomy jls. *Recreations:* acting, painting electrons, teasing publishers. *Address:* Edinburgh Institute for Astronomy, University of Edinburgh, Royal Observatory Edinburgh, Blackford Hill, Edinburgh EH9 3HJ. *T:* (0131) 668 8346.

LAWRENCE, Andrew Steven; Director of Corporate Affairs, Hutchison Whampoa Europe Ltd, since 2012; *b* Epsom, 26 Jan. 1973; *s* of Keith Lawrence and Val Long; *m* 2001, Nicolette Sanders; three *d*. *Educ:* Corpus Christi Coll., Cambridge (BA Modern Langs 1995; MA); Imperial Coll. Bus. Sch. (MBA 2002). Ministry of Agriculture, Fisheries and Food, subseq. Department for Environment, Food and Rural Affairs: EU Policy Team, Veterinary Medicines Directorate, 1995–96; Envmt, Fisheries and Internat. Sci. Div., 1996–97; Stagiaire DG XIV (Fisheries), EC, Brussels, 1997–98 (on secondment); Pvte Sec. to Perm. Sec., 1998–99; Hd, EU Enlargement Unit, 1999–2001; Manager, Waste Implementation Prog., 2002–03; Dep. Dir, CAP Reform and EU Strategy, 2003–07; Dir, Delivery Transformation (formerly Customer Focus and Regulation), 2007–08; Dir, Transition, DECC, 2008–09; Dir, Green Economy and Strategy (formerly Strategy and Sustainability), DEFRA, 2009–12. *Recreations:* spending time with family, enjoying the great outdoors, armchair sports expert - cricket and Rugby in particular, admiring others' gardens and beautiful buildings, travelling, very amateur ornithology. *Address:* Hutchison Whampoa Europe Ltd, Hutchison House, 5 Hester Road, SW11 4AN.

LAWRENCE, Sir Aubrey Lyttelton Simon, 6th Bt *cr* 1867, of Ealing Park, Middlesex; *b* 22 Sept. 1942; *s* of Peter Stafford Hayden Lawrence and Helena Francis Lawrence (*née* Lyttelton); *S* cousin, 2015, but his name does not appear on the Official Roll of the Baronetage; *m* 1984, Danielle de Froidment; one *s*. *Heir: s* Thomas Lyttelton de Froidment Lawrence, *b* 12 April 1985.

LAWRENCE, (Barbara) Jane; *see* Elliott, B. J.

LAWRENCE, Most Rev. Caleb James; Archbishop of Moosonee, and Metropolitan of Ontario, 2004–10; Interim Incumbent (part-time), St Mary's Parish, Nanoose Bay, Diocese of British Columbia, since 2014; *b* 26 May 1941; *s* of James Otis Lawrence and Mildred Viola Burton; *m* 1966, Maureen Patricia Cuddy; one *s* two *d*. *Educ:* Univ. of King's College; BA Dalhousie Univ. 1962; BST 1964. Deacon 1963, priest 1965; Missionary at Anglican Mission, Great Whale River, Quebec, 1965–75; Rector of St Edmund's Parish, Great Whale River, 1975–79; Canon of St Jude's Cathedral, Frobisher Bay, Diocese of The Arctic, 1974; Archdeacon of Arctic Quebec, 1975–79; Bishop Coadjutor, Jan.–Nov. 1980, Bishop, 1980–2010, Diocese of Moosonee; Asst Bishop and Diocesan Administrator, Diocese of British Columbia, 2013–14. Hon. DD: Univ. of King's Coll., Halifax, NS, 1980; Huron University Coll., 2010. *Recreations:* reading, photography.

LAWRENCE, Hon. Carmen (Mary), PhD; Professorial Fellow, Institute of Advanced Studies, University of Western Australia, since 2008; *b* 2 March 1948; *d* of Ern and Mary Lawrence; *m* (marr. diss.); one *s*. *Educ:* Univ. of Western Australia (BPsych 1st cl. Hons 1968; PhD 1983). Univ. lectr, tutor, researcher, consultant, 1968–83; Research Psychologist, Psychiatric Services Unit, Health Dept, 1983–86. MLA (ALP): Subiaco, WA, 1986–89; Glendalough, WA, 1989–94; Fremantle, WA, 1994–2007; Minister for Education, 1988–90; Premier of WA, 1990–93; Leader of the Opposition, WA, 1993–94; Minister for Human Services and Health, and Minister assisting the Prime Minister for the Status of Women, Australia, 1994–96; Shadow Minister: for the Envmt, for the Arts, and assisting the Leader of the Opposition on the Status of Women, Australia, 1996–97; for Industry, Innovation and Technol., 2000–01; for the Arts and Status of Women, 2000–02; for Reconciliation, Aboriginal and Torres Strait Islander Affairs, 2001–02. *Publications:* psychological papers. *Recreations:* literature, theatre, music. *Address:* Institute of Advanced Studies, Mail Bag M021, University of Western Australia, 35 Stirling Highway, Crawley, WA 6009, Australia.

LAWRENCE, Christopher Nigel, NDD, FTC; FIPG; goldsmith, silversmith; modeller, medallist, industrial and graphic designer; *b* 23 Dec. 1936; *s* of late Rev. William W. Lawrence and Millicent Lawrence; *m* 1958, Valerie Betty Bergman; two *s* two *d*. *Educ:* Westborough High Sch.; Central School of Arts and Crafts. Apprenticed, C. J. Vander Ltd; started own workshops, 1968. *One man exhibitions:* Galerie Jean Renet, 1970, 1971; Hamburg, 1972; Goldsmiths' Hall, 1973; Ghent, 1975; Hasselt, 1977. Major commissions from Royalty, British Govt, City Livery cos, banks, manufacturing cos; official silversmith to Bank of England. Judge and external assessor for leading art colleges; specialist in symbolic presentation pieces and limited edns of decorative pieces, e.g. silver mushrooms; large commissions for Middle East palaces. Chm., Goldsmiths, Craft and Design Council, 1976–77; Liveryman, Goldsmiths' Co., 1978–; television and radio broadcaster. Jacques Cartier Meml award for Craftsman of the Year, 1960, 1963, 1967 (unique achievement); Lifetime Achievement Award, Goldsmiths' Craft and Design Council, 2013. *Recreations:* badminton, tennis, bowls, carpentry, painting. *Address:* 44 St Johns Road, Westcliff-on-Sea, Essex SS0 7JZ. *T:* (01702) 338443.

LAWRENCE, Prof. Clifford Hugh, FRHistS; Professor of Medieval History, 1970–87, now Emeritus (Head of the Department of History, Bedford College, Royal Holloway and Bedford New College (formerly at Bedford College), University of London, 1981–85); *b* 28 Dec. 1921; *s* of Ernest William Lawrence and Dorothy Estelle; *m* 1953, Helen Maud Curran; one *s* five *d*. *Educ:* Stationers' Co.'s Sch.; Lincoln Coll., Oxford (BA 1st Cl. Hons Mod. Hist. 1948; MA 1953; DPhil 1956). FRHistS 1960; FSA 1984. War service in RA and Beds and Herts: 2nd Lieut 1942, Captain 1944, Major 1945. Asst Archivist to Co. of Gloucester, 1949. Bedford Coll., London: Asst Lectr in History, 1951; Lectr, 1953–63; Reader in Med. History, 1963–70. External Examr, Univ. of Newcastle upon Tyne, 1972–74, Univ. of Bristol, 1975–77, Univ. of Reading, 1977–79; Chm., Bd of Examnrs in History, London Univ., 1981–83. Mem., Press Council, 1976–80; Vice-Chm. of Govs, Governing Body, Heythrop Coll., Univ. of London; Mem. Council, Westfield Coll., Univ. of London, 1981–86. *Publications:* St Edmund of Abingdon, History and Hagiography, 1960; The English Church and the Papacy in the Middle Ages, 1965, 2nd edn 1999; Medieval Monasticism, 1984, 4th edn 2015; The Friars: the impact of the early mendicant movement on western society, 1994; (trans. and ed) Matthew Paris, The Life of St Edmund, 1996; The Letters of Adam Marsh, vol. 1, 2006, vol. 2, 2010; contribs to: Pre-Reformation English Spirituality, 1967; The Christian Community, 1971; The History of the University of Oxford, Vol. I, 1984; The Oxford Companion to Christian Thought, 2000; The Medieval World, 2001; articles and reviews in Eng. Hist. Review, History, Jl Eccles. Hist., Oxoniensia, Encyc. Brit., Lexicon für Theol u Kirche, etc. *Recreations:* gardening, painting. *Address:* 11 Durham Road, SW20 0QH. *T:* (020) 8946 3820.

LAWRENCE, Sir Clive Wyndham, 4th Bt *cr* 1906, of Sloane Gardens, Chelsea; *b* 6 Oct. 1939; *yr s* of Sir Roland Lawrence, 2nd Bt, MC and Susan, 3rd *d* of Sir Charles Addis, KCMG; *S* brother, 2002; *m* 1st, 1966, Sophia Annabel Stuart (marr. diss. 2003), *d* of late (Ian) Hervey Stuart Black, TD; three *s*; 2nd, 2007, Susan Jane St Pierre, *d* of late Denis John Neal Smith. *Heir: s* James Wyndham Stuart Lawrence, *b* 25 Dec. 1970.

LAWRENCE, Craig; *see* Lawrence, J. C.

LAWRENCE, David Kenneth, DPhil; non-executive Director and Chairman, Science and Technology Advisory Board, since 2009, and Member, Audit Committee, since 2013, Syngenta AG (Head, Research, 2000–03; Head, Research and Development, 2003–09); *b* 9 March 1949; s of Ken and Dorothy Lawrence; *m* 1971, Elizabeth Ann Robertson; two *d*. *Educ:* Highbury Avenue Jun. Sch., Salisbury; Bishop Wordsworth Grammar Sch., Salisbury; Keble Coll., Oxford (BA Hons Chem. 1971; DPhil 1974). ICI: Scientist, 1974–86; Manager, Biochemistry, 1986–90; Proj. Leader, 1990–95; Hd, Plant Scis, Zeneca, 1995–2000; Hd, Projects, Syngenta, 2000–02. Member: Council, BBSRC, 2008–14 (Mem., Biomolecular Scis Panel, 1991–94; Chm., Industrial Biotechnol. Strategy Adv. Panel, 2012–14); UK Industrial Biotechnol. Leadership Forum, 2009–; Agri-tech Strategy Leadership Council, 2013–; Nuffield Council for Bioethics, 2014–; Dir, Bioscis Knowledge Transfer Network, 2010–13; Chair, Industrial Biotechnol. Sector Gp, 2010–14. Chm., Plastid AS, 2012– (non-exec. Dir, 2009–12); Dir, KTN Ltd, 2014–. Mem. Adv. Bd, Krebs Inst., 1990–95. Dir and Trustee, Rothamsted Research Ltd, 2007–. Mem., Biotechnol. Council, WEF, 2012–14. *Recreations:* trying to understand how things work, photography, music including choral singing as a tenor, travel, gadgets, anything else which stimulates the mind and avoids boredom but is suitable for an introvert. *E:* davelaw2@btinternet.com.

LAWRENCE, Sir Edmund (Wickham), GCMG 2013 (KCMG 2010); OBE 1998; CSM 2009; JP; Managing Director, St Kitts-Nevis-Anguilla National Bank Ltd Group of Companies, since 1972; Governor General, St Christopher and Nevis, since 2013 (Deputy Governor General, 1997–2013); *m* Hulda; one *s* six *d*. *Educ:* Basseterre Boys' Sch., St Kitts; Univ. of London (BSc Econ). Teacher, elementary schs, St Kitts, 1951–54; Lectr, Walbrook Coll., London, 1967–69; estabd St Kitts-Nevis-Anguilla Nat. Bank Ltd, 1970, Man. Dir, 1971–72; Gp Man. Dir, 1972–80, Chm. and Gp Man. Dir, 1980–82, Nat. Bank Gp of Cos. Director: Cable Bay Hotel Develt Co. Ltd; Digicel (St Kitts-Nevis) Ltd; Develt and Finance Corp., St Kitts; Nat. Agricl Corp., St Kitts; Central Housing Authy, St Kitts; Caribbean Credit Card Corp.; Republic Bank (Grenada) Ltd; E Caribbean Financial Hldgs Ltd; Eastern Caribbean Currency Union Bankers Assoc. Mem., Electoral Commn, St Kitts-Nevis. Consultant for establishment of: Nat. Commercial Bank of Dominica Ltd, 1977; Nat. Commercial Bank of St Vincent Ltd, 1978; Nat. Bank of Anguilla Ltd, 1985 (Advr, 1985–90); Nat. Investment Co. of Anguilla Ltd and Anguilla Nat. Insce Co. Ltd, 1990; Anguilla Mortgage Co. Ltd, 1991; Gen. Business Services Ltd, St Kitts, 1992; Ind. Consultant on Banking and Finance, Caribbean Develt Bank, to Govts of Antigua, 1977, St Kitts-Nevis, 1979 and Montserrat, 1980. *Recreations:* football, cricket, chess, bridge. *Address:* Government House, PO Box 41, Springfield, St Kitts, West Indies. *E:* govgen@sisterisles.kn.

LAWRENCE, Felicity; journalist, The Guardian, since 1995; *b* London, 15 Aug. 1958; *d* of Prof. Hugh Lawrence and Helen Lawrence (*née* Curran); *m* 1989, Matthew Bullard; three *d*. *Educ:* St Anne's Coll., Oxford (BA Hons Lit. Hum. 1980). Trainee, then Editor, Haymarket Publishing, 1981–86; Ed., Sunday Telegraph mag., 1986–88; aid work, North West Frontier Province, Pakistan, 1989–91. *Publications:* Not on the Label, 2004; Eat Your Heart Out, 2008. *Address:* c/o The Guardian, King's Place, 90 York Way, N1 9GU.

LAWRENCE, Sir Henry (Peter), 7th Bt *cr* 1858, of Lucknow; Deputy Head, Radiotherapy Physics, Ipswich Hospital, 2012; *b* 2 April 1952; *s* of late George Alexander Waldemar Lawrence and Olga Lawrence (*née* Schilovsky); *S* uncle, 1999; *m* 1st, 1979, Penny Maureen Nunan (marr. diss. 1993); one *s* one *d*; 2nd, 2001, Elena Jennie Norman, theatre designer. *Educ:* Eton Coll.; Hackney Coll. BSc Physics with Astronomy, MSc Radiation Physics, London Univ. Builder and scaffolder, 1970–79; Physicist, Royal London Hosp., 1981–86; Sen. Physicist, Cheltenham Gen. Hosp., 1986–90; Head, Radiation Metrology (formerly Dosimetry), Bristol Haematology and Oncology Centre (formerly Bristol Oncology Centre), 1991–2012. Author of Europlan radiotherapy treatment planning system. Mem., Inst. of Physics and Engineering in Medicine. Hon. Mem., Romanian Assoc. of Medical Physics. *Publications:* Physics in Medicine and Biology, 1990. *Recreations:* songwriter, musician, juggler. *Heir: s* Christopher Cosmo Lawrence, *b* 10 Dec. 1979. *Address:* 24 Perfect View, Bath BA1 5JY.

LAWRENCE, (Henry) Richard (George); writer and lecturer on music; *b* 16 April 1946; *s* of late George Napier Lawrence, OBE, and Peggy Neave (*née* Brey). *Educ:* Westminster Abbey Choir Sch.; Haileybury (music schol.); Worcester Coll., Oxford (Hadow Schol.; BA 1967). Overseas Dept, Ginn & Co., educational publishers, 1968–73; Music Officer, 1973–83, Music Dir, 1983–88, Arts Council of GB; Chief Exec., RSCM, 1990–94; Acting Ed., 1994–95, Ed., 1995–96, Early Music News; Ed., Leading Notes, 1997–99. Tutor at various adult educn colls and for WEA, 1997–; lectr abroad on opera, 2000–. Qualif. London Registered Blue Badge Guide, 2001. Occasional broadcaster, 1989–. Chm., Arts Council Staff Assoc., 1974–76. Voluntary work, Friends of the Earth Trust, 1989–90. *Publications:* (contrib.) Collins Classical Music Encyclopedia, 2000; revs and articles in TLS, Church Times, Opera Now, BBC Music Mag, Jl of RAS, Early Music Today, The Gramophone, Amadeus (Milan). *Recreations:* travelling in Asia, pre-1914 Baedekers. *Address:* 1 Claverton Street, SW1V 3AY. *T:* (020) 7834 9846.

LAWRENCE, Sir Ivan (John), Kt 1992; QC 1981; barrister-at-law; broadcaster, author, law and politics lecturer and after-dinner speaker; *b* 24 Dec. 1936; *o s* of late Leslie Lawrence and Sadie Lawrence, Brighton; *m* 1966, Gloria Hélène; (one *d* decd). *Educ:* Brighton, Hove and Sussex Grammar Sch.; Christ Church, Oxford (MA). Nat. Service with RAF, 1955–57. Called to Bar, Inner Temple, 1962 (Yarborough-Anderson Schol.; Bencher, 1991); S Eastern Circuit; Asst Recorder, 1983–87; a Recorder, 1987–2002; Hd of Chambers, 1 Essex Ct, 1997–2000. Contested (C) Peckham (Camberwell), 1966 and 1970. MP (C) Burton, Feb. 1974–1997; contested (C) same seat, 1997. Mem., Select Cttee on Foreign Affairs, 1983–92; Chm., Select Cttee on Home Affairs, 1992–97; Chairman: Cons. Parly Legal Cttee, 1987–97; Cons. Parly Home Affairs Cttee, 1988–97; All-Party Parly Anti-Fluoridation Cttee; All-Party Parly Barristers Gp, 1987–97; Member: Parly Expenditure Select Sub-Cttee, 1974–79; Jt Parly Cttee on Consolidation of Statutes, 1974–87. Mem. Exec., 1922 Cttee, 1988–89, 1992–97. Chm., Exec. Cttee, UK CPA, 1994–97 (Mem., 1989–97). Member: Council of Justice, 1989–95; Council, Statute Law Soc., 1985–95; Exec., Soc. of Conservative Lawyers, 1989–97 and 1999–2012 (Chm., Criminal Justice Cttee, 1997–); Bar Council, 2004–10. Fellow, Soc. of Advanced Legal Studies, 2002–. Visiting Professor of Law: Univ. of Buckingham, 2004–; BPP Univ., 2015–. Vice-Pres., Fed. of Cons. Students, 1980–82; Mem., W Midlands Cons. Council, 1985–97; Pres., Spelthorne Cons. Assoc., 2013–; Vice-Pres., Soc. of Cons. Lawyers, 2015–. Vice Chm., Cons. Friends of Israel, 1994–97; Mem. Bd of Deputies of British Jews, 1979–. Chm., Burton Breweries Charitable Trust, 1979–97; Trustee, Holocaust Educnl Trust, 2002–. Pres., Past and Present Assoc., Brighton, Hove and Sussex Grammar Sch., 1999–. Freeman, City of London, 1993. Hon. LLD Buckingham, 2013. *Publications:* My Life of Crime (memoir), 2010, 2nd edn 2012; pamphlets (jointly): Access to Justice; Correcting the Scales; The Conviction of the Guilty; Towards a New Nationality; Financing Strikes; Trial by Jury under attack; nat. newspaper and magazine articles on law and order and foreign affairs. *Recreations:* piano, squash, travel, friends. *Address:* 5 Pump Court Chambers, Temple, EC4Y 7AP. *Club:* Burton (Burton-on-Trent).

LAWRENCE, Jacqueline Rita, (Jackie); *b* 9 Aug. 1948; *d* of Sidney and Rita Beale; *m* 1968, David Lawrence; two *s* one *d*. *Educ:* Upperthorpe Sch., Darlington, Co. Durham; Upperthorpe Coll.; Open Univ. With TSB Bank plc, until 1992. Member (Lab): Dyfed CC, 1993–96; Pembs CC, 1995–97 (Leader, Lab Gp). MP (Lab) Preseli Pembrokeshire, 1997–2005. PPS to Dep. Minister for Women and Equality, DTI, 2003–05. Member, Select Committee: on Welsh Affairs, 1997–99; on Trade and Industry, 2001–03; Chm., All Pty Parly Gp on Nat. Parks, 2001–05. Hon. Sec., Welsh Gp of Labour MPs, 2000–05.

LAWRENCE, Maj. Gen. (John) Craig, CBE 2013 (MBE 1997); Chief of Staff Joint Warfare Development, since 2014; *b* Wakefield, Yorks, 18 Oct. 1963; *s* of Michael Edmund Lawrence and Vera Veronica Lawrence; *m* 2001, Laura-Jo Newton; two *d*, and three step *s*. *Educ:* St Peter's Sch., York; Durham Univ. (BSc Engrg Sci.); Cranfield Univ. (MSc Inf. Systems Design); King's Coll. London (MA Conflict, Security and Develt). Commnd 2nd King Edward VII's Own Gurkha Rifles, 1987; Command: 1st Bn, Royal Gurkha Rifles, 2003; 52 Inf. Bde, 2008; COS Force Develt and Trng Comd, 2009. Col, Royal Gurkha Rifles, 1999–. QCVS 2005. *Publications:* The Gurkhas: 200 years of service to the Crown, 2015; The Legacy (novel), 2015. *Recreations:* scuba-diving, running, writing, climbing. *Club:* Army and Navy.

LAWRENCE, Air Vice-Marshal John Thornett, CB 1975; CBE (mil.) 1967 (OBE (mil.) 1961); AFC 1945; *b* 16 April 1920; *s* of late T. L. Lawrence, JP, and Mrs B. M. Lawrence; *m* 1951, Hilary Jean (*née* Owen); three *s* one *d*. *Educ:* The Crypt School, Gloucester. RAFVR 1938. Served War of 1939–45 in Coastal Command (235, 202 and 86 Squadrons); Directing staff, RAF Flying Coll., 1949–53; CO 14 Squadron, 1953–55; Group Captain Operations, HQ AFME, 1962–64; CO RAF Wittering, 1964–66; AOC, 3 Group, Bomber Command, 1967; Student, IDC, 1968; Dir of Organisation and Admin. Plans (RAF), 1969–71; Dir-Gen. Personnel Management (RAF), 1971–73; Comdr N Maritime Air Region and AOC Scotland and NI, 1973–75, retired 1975. Vice-Pres., Glos County SSAFA, 1990– (Chm., 1980–90); Mem., Nat. Council, SSAFA, 1987–90. Order of Leopold II, Belgium, 1945; Croix de Guerre, Belgium, 1945. *Recreations:* travel, reading. *Address:* The Coach House, Wightfield Manor, Apperley, Glos GL19 4DP. *Club:* Royal Air Force.

LAWRENCE, John Wilfred, RE 1987; book illustrator and wood engraver; *b* 15 Sept. 1933; *s* of Wilfred James Lawrence and Audrey Constance (*née* Thomas); *m* 1957, Myra Gillian Bell; two *d*. *Educ:* Salesian Coll., Cowley, Oxford; Hastings Sch. of Art; Central Sch. of Art. Visiting Lecturer in Illustration: Brighton Polytech., 1960–68; Camberwell Sch. of Art, 1960–94; Visiting Professor in Illustration: London Inst., 1994–2000; Cambridge Sch. of Art, Anglia Ruskin Univ., 2006–15; External Assessor in Illustration: Bristol Polytech., 1978–81; Brighton Polytech., 1982–85; Duncan of Jordanstone Coll. of Art, 1986–89; Exeter Coll. of Art, 1986–89; Kingston Polytechnic, 1989–93; Edinburgh Coll. of Art, 1991–94. Member: Art Workers Guild, 1972 (Master, 1990); Soc. of Wood Engravers, 1984; Wynken de Worde Soc., 2013–. Work represented in Ashmolean Mus., V&A Mus., Nat. Mus. of Wales, Manchester Metropolitan Univ. Special Collections, and collections abroad. *Publications:* The Giant of Grabbist, 1968; Pope Leo's Elephant, 1969; Rabbit and Pork Rhyming Talk, 1975 (Francis Williams Book Illustration Award, 1977); Tongue Twisters, 1976; George, His Elephant and Castle, 1983; A Selection of Wood Engravings, 1986; Good Babies, Bad Babies, 1987; *illustrated:* more than 250 books, incl.: Colonel Jack, 1967 (Francis Williams Book Illustration Award, 1971); Diary of a Nobody, 1969; The Blue Fairy Book, 1975; The Illustrated Watership Down, 1976; Everyman's Book of English Folk Tales, 1981; The Magic Apple Tree, 1982; The Cranks Recipe Book, 1982; Mabel's Story, 1984; Entertaining with Cranks, 1985; Emily's Own Elephant, 1987; Christmas in Exeter Street, 1989; A New Treasury of Poetry, 1990; The Sword of Honour trilogy, 1990; Treasure Island, 1990, 2009; Shades of Green, 1991 (Signal Prize for Poetry); Poems for the Young, 1992; King of King's, 1993; The Twelve Days of Christmas, 1994; The Christmas Collection, 1994; Memoirs of a Georgian Rake, 1995; Robin Hood, 1995; Poems for Christmas, 1995; Collected Poems for Children by Charles Causley, 1996; (with Allan Ahlberg) The Mysteries of Zigomar, 1997; A Year and a Day, 1999; This Little Chick, 2002 (NY Times Cert. of Excellence); The Once and Future King, 2003; Lyra's Oxford, by Philip Pullman, 2003; Tiny's Big Adventure, 2004; Sea Horse: the shyest fish in the sea, 2006; Once Upon a Time in the North, by Philip Pullman, 2008; The Arthur Trilogy, by Kevin Crossley-Holland, 2010; Wayland The Smith, by Tony Mitton, 2013; Beware of the Crocodile, by Martin Jenkins, 2016. *Address:* 6 Worts Causeway, Cambridge CB1 8RL. *Club:* Double Crown (Pres., 2005).

LAWRENCE, Josie; actress; *b* 6 June 1959; *d* of Bert and Kathleen Lawrence. *Educ:* Dartington Coll. of Arts (BA Hons Theatre). Professional acting début, 1983; joined Comedy Store Players, 1986; *theatre* includes: Painting Churches, 1988; Tatyana, 1992, Eliza in Pygmalion, 1994, Nottingham Playhouse; Moll Flanders, Lyric Hammersmith, 1993; The Cherry Orchard, Faust and Kate in The Taming of the Shrew, RSC, 1995; The Alchemist, NT, 1996; Alarms and Excursions, Gielgud, 1998; Anna in The King and I, Palladium, 2001; Frozen, NT, 2002; Much Ado About Nothing, Globe, 2004; Acorn Antiques - The Musical, Th. Royal, Haymarket, 2005; Hapgood, 2008, The Cherry Orchard, 2010, Birmingham Rep.; *films* include: Enchanted April, 1992; The Sin Eater, 1999; Bonobo, 2014; *television* includes: Friday Night Live, 1988; Whose Line Is It Anyway?, 1988–97; Not With a Bang, 1990; Josie, 1991; Downwardly Mobile, 1994; Maggie in Outside Edge, 3 series, 1994–96; A Many Splintered Thing, 2000; Fat Friends, 2000; Easy Peasy, 2006; Robin Hood, 2007; The Old Curiosity Shop, 2007; Minder, 2008; Eastenders, 2009–10; Beat the Brain, 2015. Hon. Dr Plymouth; Hon. DLitt Wolverhampton; Hon. DA Aston. Best Actress Award, Manchester Evening News; Globe Award for Best Actress; Dame Peggy Ashcroft Prize, Shakespeare Golden Globe Awards, 1997. Charity walks for breast cancer research in Cuba, Peru, Africa and China; climbed Kilimanjaro for Sunfield Sch., 2005 (Patron, 1995–). *Recreations:* painting, walking.

LAWRENCE, Michael John, PhD; Chief Executive, London Stock Exchange, 1994–96; *b* 25 Oct. 1943; *s* of Geoffrey Frederick Lawrence and Kathleen (*née* Bridge); *m* 1967, Maureen Joy Blennerhassett; two *s* one *d*. *Educ:* Exeter Univ. (BSc 1st Cl. Hons Physics); Bristol Univ. (PhD Mathematical Physics). FCA 1972. With Price Waterhouse, 1969–87, Partner 1978; Finance Dir, Prudential Corp., 1988–93. Non-executive Director: PLA, 1983–89; London Transport, 1994–99; Yattendon Investment Trust, 1998–. Chm., 100 Gp of Finance Dirs, 1991–93. Mem. (C), Royal Borough of Windsor and Maidenhead Unitary Council, 1996–2004 (Leader, 2000–04). Freeman, City of London, 1974; Liveryman, Tin Plate Workers' Co., 1974– (Master, 2000–01). *Recreations:* sailing, bridge, tennis, opera. *Address:* Springmead, Bradcutts Lane, Cookham Dean, Berks SL6 9AA.

LAWRENCE, Murray; *see* Lawrence, W. N. M.

LAWRENCE, Nigel Stuart; QC 2014; *b* Heswall, Wirral, 4 Nov. 1965; *s* of Dr T. L. J. Lawrence and E. R. D. Lawrence; *m* 1994, Jane C. E.; two *s* three *d*. *Educ:* Kingsmead Sch., Wirral; Rydal Sch., Colwyn Bay; Univ. of Leicester (LLB Hons); Inns of Court Sch. of Law. Called to the Bar, Lincoln's Inn, 1988; in practice as barrister, specialising in regulatory crime and enforcement, particularly health and safety, manslaughter, personal injury and criminal negligence, 1988–; Standing Counsel: to HSE, 2004–; to Office of Rail and Road (formerly Rail Regulation), 2007–. *Recreations:* sport, wine, travel. *Address:* 7 Harrington Street Chambers, 7 Harrington Street, Liverpool L2 9YH. *T:* (0151) 242 0707. *E:* n.lawrence4@ntlworld.com.

LAWRENCE, Peter Anthony, PhD; FRS 1983; Staff Scientist, Medical Research Council Laboratory of Molecular Biology, Cambridge, 1969–2006, now emeritus researcher, Department of Zoology, University of Cambridge, supported by Wellcome Trust; *b* 23 June 1941; *s* of Ivor Douglas Lawrence and Joy Lawrence (*née* Liebert); *m* 1971, Birgitta Haraldson. *Educ:* Wennington Sch., Wetherby, Yorks; Cambridge Univ. (MA, PhD). Harkness Fellowship, 1965–67; Dept of Genetics, Univ. of Cambridge, 1967–69. *Publications:* Insect Development (ed), 1976; The Making of a Fly, 1992; (jtly) Principles of Development, 1998, 5th edn 2015; scientific papers. *Recreations:* Ascalaphidae, fungi, gardening, golf, theatre, trees. *Address:* Department of Zoology, University of Cambridge, Cambridge CB2 3EJ; MRC Laboratory of Molecular Biology, Hills Road, Cambridge CB2 0QH.

LAWRENCE, Richard; *see* Lawrence, H. R. G.

LAWRENCE, His Honour Timothy; a Circuit Judge, 1986–2006; *b* 29 April 1942; *s* of late A. Whiteman Lawrence, MBE, and Phyllis G. Lawrence (*née* Lloyd-Jones). *Educ:* Bedford School; Coll. of Law. Admitted Solicitor, 1967; with Solicitor's Dept, New Scotland Yard, 1967–70; Partner with Claude Hornby & Cox, Solicitors, 1970–86 (Sen. Partner, 1977–86). An Asst Recorder, 1980; a Recorder, 1983–86; Pres., Industrial Tribunals for Eng. and Wales (as Sen. Circuit Judge), 1991–97. Legal Mem., Mental Health Review Tribunals, 1989–2015; Mem., Parole Bd, 1998–2004, 2005–11; Chm., No 14 Area, Regional Duty Solicitor Cttee, 1984–86; Mem., No 13 Area, Legal Aid Cttee, 1983–86. Pres., London Criminal Courts Solicitors' Assoc., 1984–86 (Sec., 1974–84); Member: Law Society's Criminal Law Cttee, 1980–86; Council, Westminster Law Soc., 1979–82; Judicial Studies Bd, 1984–88, 1991–96; British Academy of Forensic Sciences, 1972– (Pres., 1992–93); Dep. Chm., Adv. Cttee on Conscientious Objectors, 2003–12. Legal Assessor: Professions Supplementary to Medicine, 1976–86; Insurance Brokers Registration Council, 1983–86. Jt Editor, Medicine, Science and the Law, 1996–2002. FRSA 1991. *Publications:* various articles in legal jls. *Recreations:* walking, wine, travel. *Address:* 8 Slaidburn Street, SW10 0JP; Hill Cottage, Great Walsingham, Norfolk NR22 6DR. *Clubs:* Reform, Hurlingham.

LAWRENCE, Vanessa Vivienne, CB 2008; FRICS; Chair, UN Committee of Experts on Global Geospatial Information Management, since 2011; *b* 14 July 1962; *d* of Leonard Walter Sydney Lawrence and Margaret Elizabeth Lawrence. *Educ:* St Helen's Sch., Northwood, Middx; Sheffield Univ. (BA (Soc. Sci.) Hons Geography); Dundee Univ. (MSc Remote Sensing, Image Processing and Applications). CGeog 2002; FRICS 2003. Longman Group UK Ltd: Publisher, 1985–89; Sen. Publisher, 1989–91; Publishing Manager, 1991–92; Tech. Dir, GeoInformation Internat. (Pearson Gp), 1993–96; Regl Business Develt Manager, UK, ME, Africa, GIS Solutions Div., Autodesk Ltd, 1996–2000; Global Manager, Strategic Mktg and Communications, GIS Solutions Div., Autodesk Inc., 2000; Dir Gen. and Chief Exec., Ordnance Survey, 2000–14. Non-exec. Dir, DCLG (formerly ODPM), 2002–06. Hon. Res. Associate, Manchester Univ., 1990–; Visiting Professor: Southampton Univ., 2000–; Kingston Univ., 2003–. Mem. Court, Southampton Univ., 2001–12 (Mem. Council, 2002–09); Mem. Council, Univ. of Cambridge, 2009–12. Member: RGS, 1987– (Mem. Council, 2002–); Assoc. for Geographic Inf., 1992– (Mem. Council, 1995–2000; Chm., 1999); Bd, Open Geospatial Consortium, 2005–; Hon. Vice-Pres., Geographical Assoc., 2006–. Chm., ACE, 2003–08; Patron: MapAction, 2006–; Cure Parkinson's Trust, 2007–. CCMI 2003. Hon. FInstCES 2001; Hon. FREng 2008. Hon. Fellow, UCL, 2003. Hon. Col, 135 Independent Geographic Squadron, Royal Engineers (Volunteers), 2009–. Hon. DSc: Sheffield, 2001; Southampton Inst., 2002; Kingston, 2002; Glasgow, 2005; Southampton, 2014; DUniv: Oxford Brookes, 2001; RHUL, 2014; Hon. LLD Dundee, 2003. Scottish Geographical Medal, RSGS, 2006; SE Dir of the Year, IoD, 2008; Geospatial Personality of the Decade Award, Geospatial World Forum, 2011. *Publications:* contrib. many books and jls on Geographical Inf. Systems. *Recreations:* scuba diving, sailing, tennis, collecting antique maps. *Clubs:* Rickmansworth Sailing; Horsley Sports.

LAWRENCE, Vernon John; freelance television producer; *b* 30 April 1940; *m* 1960, Jennifer Mary Drewe; two *s* one *d*. *Educ:* Dulwich Coll.; Kelham Coll. BBC Studio Manager, 1958; BBC Radio Producer, 1964; BBC TV Producer and Dir, 1967; Yorkshire Television: Exec. Producer, 1973; Controller, Entertainment, 1985; Controller, Network Drama and Entertainment, ITV, 1993–95; Man. Dir, 1995–97, Chm., 1997–2000, MAI Prodns, subseq. United Film & TV Prodns, then United Prodns. *Productions* include: Rising Damp, 1978 (also dir); Duty Free, 1984–86 (also dir, 1984); The Darling Buds of May, 1991–93; A Touch of Frost, 1992; Hornblower, 1998–99; New Statesman, 1987–92; dir, Song by Song, 1978–80. FRTS 1995. *Recreations:* oil painting, fishing, walking, gardening.

LAWRENCE, (Walter Nicholas) Murray; Chairman of Lloyd's, 1988–90 (a Deputy Chairman 1982, 1984–87; Member: Committee of Lloyd's, 1979–82; Council of Lloyd's, 1984–91); Chairman, Murray Lawrence Holdings Ltd, 1988–94; *b* 8 Feb. 1935; *s* of Henry Walter Neville Lawrence and Sarah Schuyler Lawrence (*née* Butler); *m* 1961, Sally Louise O'Dwyer (*d* 2008); two *d*. *Educ:* Winchester Coll.; Trinity Coll., Oxford (BA, MA). C. T. Bowring & Co. (Ins.) Ltd, 1957–62; Asst Underwriter, H. Bowring & Others, 1962–70, Underwriter, 1970–84; Director: C. T. Bowring (Underwriting Agencies) Ltd, 1973–84; C. T. Bowring & Co. Ltd, 1976–84; Murray Lawrence Members Agency Ltd, 1988–94 (Chm., 1988–93); Murray Lawrence & Partners Ltd, 1989–95 (Sen. Partner, 1985–89; Chm., 1989–92); Chm., Fairway (Underwriting Agencies) Ltd, 1979–85. Mem., Lloyd's Underwriters Non-Marine Assoc., 1970–84 (Dep. Chm., 1977; Chm., 1978). *Recreations:* golf, opera, travelling. *Clubs:* Boodle's, MCC; Royal & Ancient (St Andrews), Royal St George's (Sandwich), Rye, Pine Valley Golf, Merion Golf.

LAWRENCE-JONES, Sir Christopher, 6th Bt *cr* 1831; *S* uncle, 1969; *m* 1967, Gail Pittar, Auckland, NZ; two *s*. *Educ:* Sherborne; Gonville and Caius Coll., Cambridge; St Thomas' Hospital. MA Cantab 1964; MB, BChir Cantab 1964; DIH Eng. 1968. MFOM 1979, FFOM 1987; FRCP 1991. Medical adviser to various orgns, 1967–94; CMO, Imperial Chemical Industries PLC, 1985–93; Chm., Medichem, 1986–92. Pres., Section of Occupational Medicine, RSM, 1990–91. *Heir: s* Mark Christopher Lawrence-Jones, *b* 28 Dec. 1968. *Club:* Royal Cruising.

LAWRENSON, Mark Thomas; football pundit, BBC Television, 1997; *b* Preston, 2 June 1957; *s* of Thomas and Theresa Lawrenson; *m* 2001, Suzanne; one *s* one *d*. *Educ:* Preston Catholic Coll. Professional footballer: Preston N End, 1974–77; Brighton & Hove Albion, 1977–81; Republic of Ireland, 1977–87 (39 Caps); Liverpool, 1981–88; Barnet, 1988–89; Tampa Bay Rowdies, 1989; Corby Town, 1990–91; Manager: Oxford United, 1988; Peterborough United, 1989–90. Hon. Citizen of Preston, 2002. *Recreations:* cricket, golf.

LAWRENSON, Prof. Peter John, DSc; FRS 1982; FREng, FIET, FIEEE; Founder Chairman, Switched Reluctance Drives Ltd, 1981–97 (Managing Director, 1986–94; Director, 1997–2002); Professor of Electrical Engineering, Leeds University, 1966–91, now Emeritus; *b* 12 March 1933; *s* of John Lawrenson and Emily (*née* Houghton); *m* 1958, Shirley Hannah Foster; one *s* three *d*. *Educ:* Prescot Grammar Sch.; Manchester Univ. (BSc, MSc; DSc 1971). FIET (FIEE 1974); FIEEE 1975; FREng (FEng 1980). Duddell Scholar, IEE, 1951–54; Res. Engr, Associated Electrical Industries, 1956–61; University of Leeds: Lectr, 1961–65; Reader, 1965–66; Head, Dept of Electrical and Electronic Engrg, 1974–84; Chm., Faculty of Science and Applied Science, 1978–80; Chm., Faculty of Engrg, 1981. Dir, major internat. equipment exhibns integrated with confs, in UK, Dusseldorf, Paris and Hong Kong, 1980–99. Science and Engineering Research Council: Mem., Electrical and Systems Cttee, 1971–77; Chm., Electrical Engrg Sub-Cttee, 1981–84; Mem., Machines and Power Cttee, 1981–84; Mem., Engrg Bd, 1984–87; Organiser, National Initiative, Integrated Drive Systems, 1984–86. Tech. Dir, Internat. Drives, Motors, Controls Conf. and Exhibn, 1981–88. Director: Allenwest Ltd, 1988–91; Dale Electric Internat., 1988–94; Consultant: Emerson Electric Co., 1994–97; Rolls-Royce, 2000–02. Institution of Electrical Engineers: Mem. Council, 1966–69 and 1981–98; Chm., Accreditation Cttee, 1979–83; Chm., Power Divisional Bd, 1985–86; Dep. Pres., 1990–92; Pres., 1992–93. Mem. of cttees, Engrg Council, 1983–89 and 1997–2000; Mem. Council, Buckingham Univ., 1987–93. IEE Awards: Premia-Crompton, 1957 and 1967; John Hopkinson, 1965; The Instn, 1981; Faraday Medal, 1990; James Alfred Ewing Medal, ICE and Royal Soc., 1983; Royal Soc. Esso Energy Award, 1985; Edison Medal, IEEE, 2005; Sir Frank Whittle Medal, Royal Acad. of Engrg, 2005. *Publications:* (with K. J. Binns) Analysis and Computation of Electromagnetic Field Problems, 1963, 2nd edn 1973; (with M. R. Harris and J. M. Stephenson) Per Unit Systems, 1970; (with K. J. Binns and C. W. Trowbridge) The Analytical and Numerical Solution of Electric and Magnetic Fields, 1992; papers and patents in areas of electromagnetism, electromechanics and control. *Recreations:* lawn tennis, chess, bridge, jewellery design, gardening, music. *Address:* Cornerways, 1 Garth Avenue, Collingham, Wetherby LS22 5BJ.

LAWREY, Keith; JP; Learned Societies' Liaison Officer, Foundation for Science and Technology, since 1997; *b* 21 Aug. 1940; *s* of George William Bishop Lawrey and Edna Muriel (*née* Gass); *m* 1969, Helen Jane Marriott, BA; two *s* two *d*. *Educ:* Colfe's Sch.; Birkbeck Coll., Univ. of London (MSc Econ; LLB); Heythrop Coll., Univ. of London (MA). Barrister-at-Law; called to Bar, Gray's Inn, 1972 (Sec. to Seniors-in-Hall, 1997–). Education Officer, Plastics and Rubber Inst., 1960–68; Lectr and Sen. Lectr, Bucks Coll. of Higher Educn, 1968–74; Head of Dept of Business Studies, Mid-Kent Coll. of Higher and Further Educn, 1974–78; Sec.-Gen., Library Assoc., 1978–84; Dean, Faculty of Business and Management, Harrow Coll. of Higher Educn, subseq. Head, Sch. of Business and Management, Polytechnic of Central London/Harrow Coll., 1984–90; Sec. and Registrar, RCVS, 1990–91; Headmaster, Cannock Sch., 1992–95; Clerk (pt-time) to Corp. of S Kent Coll., 1996–99. Member: Social Security Appeal Tribunal, 1996–99; Registration Authy, Sci. Council, 2004–10; Privy Council and Governance Panel (formerly Privy Council Panel, subseq. Privy Council and Regulations Panel), Engrg Council, 2004–; Exec. Cttee, Fellowship of Clerks, 2010–15; Dep. Chm., Chartered Security Professionals Registration Authy, 2012–. FCollT (FCollP 1982), Hon. FCollT 2012 (Hon. Treas., Coll. of Preceptors, then Coll. of Teachers, 1987–2010); FCIS. Associate, Engrg Council, 2010–. Gov., Cannock Sch., 1976–92; Mem. Court, City Univ., 2004–. Mem., Orpington Rotary Club, 1993–2007 (Pres., 1999–2000); Trustee, Carers Bromley (formerly Carers Support and Information Service), 2001–05; Sec., Alice Shepherd Foundn, 2002–05; Trustee: and Hon. Treas., Trust for Educn and Care of Child Workers in Ecuador, 2003–06; Hosp. Saturday Fund, 2007–10 (Mem., Grant-Making Cttee, 2006–). Hon. Mem., RPS, 2004 (Fenton Medallist, 2004); Hon. MCIL 2005; Hon. FRIN 2007; Hon. FCIPHE 2009; Hon. FAcadMed 2010; Hon. Fellow: Security Inst., 2011; Chartered Assoc. of Building Engrs, 2013. Liveryman, Chartered Secretaries and Administrators' Co., 1976; Hon. Liveryman: Hackney Carriage Drivers' Co., 2014; Livery Co. of Wales, 2014; Educators' Co., 2015 (Hon. Clerk, Guild of Educators, subseq. Co. of Educators, 1997–2013; Hon. Foundn Clerk, 2013–15); Hon. Freeman, Master Mariners' Co., 2014. JP Inner London, 1974–2009 (Supplemental List, 2009–). Mem. Editl Bd, Graya, 1976– (Sec., 1992–); Ed., Foundn Sci. Technol. Newsletter (bi-monthly), 1997–. Medal of Appreciation, IED, 2012. *Publications:* papers in Law Soc. Gazette, Educn Today, Jl Assoc. of Law Teachers, Trans and Jl of Plastics Inst., Graya, Graya News. *Recreations:* preaching, sailing, swimming, theatre, gardening. *Clubs:* Old Colfeians; Dell Quay Sailing; City Livery.

LAWS, Rt Hon. David (Anthony); PC 2010; *b* 30 Nov. 1965; *s* of David Anthony, (Tony), Laws and Maureen Teresa Laws. *Educ:* St George's Coll., Weybridge (Observer Mace Schs Debating Champion 1984); King's Coll., Cambridge (schol.; Double 1st Cl. Hons Econs 1987). Vice Pres., Treasury Dept, J. P. Morgan and Co., 1987–92; Man. Dir, Hd of Sterling and US Dollar Treasury, Barclays de Zoete Wedd, 1992–94; Econs Advr, Lib Dem Parly Party, 1994–97; Dir of Policy and Res., Lib Dems, 1997–99; drafted first Partnership Agreement for Lib Dem-Lab Coalition in Scottish Parlt, 1999. Contested (Lib Dem) Folkestone and Hythe, 1997. MP (Lib Dem) Yeovil, 2001–15; contested (Lib Dem) same seat, 2015. Lib Dem Dep. Treasury spokesman, 2002–05; Lib Dem spokesman for work and pensions, 2005–07, for children, schools and families, 2007–10; Chief Sec. to the Treasury, 2010; Minister of State, DfE and Cabinet Office, 2012–15. Mem., Treasury Select Cttee, 2001–03. *Publications:* 22 Days in May: the birth of the Lib Dem-Conservative Coalition, 2010. *Recreations:* running, watching Rugby, visiting desert regions.

LAWS, Eleanor Jane, (Mrs C. L. D. Nelson); QC 2011; *b* Manchester, 10 Nov. 1966; *d* of David Laws and Barbara Laws; *m* 1998, Cairns Louis David Nelson, *qv*; two *s* two *d*. *Educ:* North London Collegiate Sch.; Univ. of Birmingham (BA Hons Hist. 1988; DipLaw 1989). Called to the Bar, Inner Temple, 1990; in practice as a barrister, specialising in crime, 5 King's Bench Walk, 1991–2001, 6 Pump Court, 2001–. *Publications:* The Sexual Offences Referencer, 2007. *Recreations:* reading, tennis, ballet. *Address:* 6 Pump Court, Temple, EC4Y 7AR. *T:* (020) 7797 8401, *Fax:* (020) 7797 8406. *E:* eleanor.laws@6pumpcourt.co.uk.

LAWS, Rt Hon. Sir John (Grant McKenzie), Kt 1992; PC 1999; **Rt Hon. Lord Justice Laws;** a Lord Justice of Appeal, since 1999; *b* 10 May 1945; *s* of late Dr Frederic Laws and Dr Margaret Ross Laws, *d* of Prof. John Grant McKenzie; *m* 1973, Sophie Susan Sydenham Cole Marshall, MLitt, MA; one *d*. *Educ:* Durham Cathedral Choir Sch.; Durham Sch. (King's Scholar); Exeter Coll., Oxford (Sen. Open Classical Scholar; BA 1967, Hon. Sch. of Lit. Hum. 1st Cl.; MA 1976; Hon. Fellow, 2000). Called to the Bar, Inner Temple, 1970, Bencher, 1985, Reader, 2009, Treas., 2010; practice at Common Law Bar, 1971–92; First Junior Treasury Counsel, Common Law, 1984–92; Asst Recorder, 1983–85; Recorder, 1985–92; a Judge of the High Court of Justice, QBD, 1992–98; admitted to Bar: New South Wales, 1987; Gibraltar, 1988. President: Bar European Gp, 1994–; Proceeds of Crime Law Assoc., 2010–; Constitutional and Admin. Law Bar Assoc., 2012–. An Hon. Vice-Pres., Administrative Law Bar Assoc., 1992. Vis. Prof., Northumbria Univ., 2011–14. Judicial Visitor, UCL, 1997–; Visitor, Cumberland Lodge, 2004–. Hon. Fellow, Robinson Coll., Cambridge, 1992. *Publications:* contributor to: Dict. of Medical Ethics, 1977; Supperstone and Goudie, Judicial Review, 1992, 2nd edn 1997; Importing the First Amendment, 1998; The Golden Metwand and the Crooked Cord, 1998; Cicero the Advocate, 2004; The Common Law Constitution, 2014; reviews for Theology, Law & Justice; contribs to legal jls. *Recreations:* Greece, living in London, philosophy. *Address:* Royal Courts of Justice, WC2A 2LL. *Club:* Garrick.

LAWS, Simon Reginald; QC 2011; *b* 16 May 1966; *s* of Alfred Reginald Laws and Mary Margaret Laws (*née* Jones); *m* 1994, Sarah Anne Conlon; two *d*. *Educ:* Univ. of York (BA English and Related Lit.); City Univ. (DipLaw); Inns of Court Sch. of Law. Called to the Bar, Inner Temple, 1991; in practice as barrister, London, 1991–98, Exeter, 1999–; Trial Attorney, Office of Prosecutor, Internat. Criminal Tribunal for Former Yugoslavia, 2008–10. Consultant: TWL Legal Consulting Ltd, 2014–; to govt depts and NGOs overseas. Hon. Fellow, Exeter Centre for Ethno-Political Studies, Univ. of Exeter, 2010–. *Recreations:* hiking, running, books. *Address:* Walnut House, 63 St David's Hill, Exeter EX4 4DW. *Club:* Devon and Exeter Institution.

LAWS, Sir Stephen (Charles), KCB 2011 (CB 1996); First Parliamentary Counsel, 2006–12; *b* 28 Jan. 1950; *s* of late Dennis Arthur Laws, MC and Beryl Elizabeth Laws (*née* Roe); *m* 1st, 1972, Angela Mary Deardon (*d* 1998); two *s* three *d*; 2nd, 2001, Elizabeth Ann Owen (*née* Williams). *Educ:* St Dunstan's College, Catford; Bristol Univ. (LLB Hons 1972). Called to the Bar, Middle Temple, 1973, Bencher, 2008. Asst Lectr, Univ. of Bristol, 1972; Legal Asst, Home Office, 1975; Asst, Sen. Asst, then Dep. Parly Counsel, 1976–91; Parly Counsel, 1991–2006. Chm., Civil Service Benevolent Fund, 2009–12. Member: Exec. Cttee, Commonwealth Assoc. of Legislative Counsel, 2009–11; Exec. Council, Statute Law Soc., 2012–; McKay Commn on consequences of devolution for H of C, 2012–13; Chm., Adv. Bd, Big Data for Law Project, 2014–. Sen. Associate Res. Fellow, Inst. of Advanced Legal Studies, Univ. of London, 2012–; Hon. Sen. Res. Associate, UCL, 2013–. Mem., Adv. Bd, Univ. of Bristol Law Sch., 2013–. Member: Thomas More Soc., 1976–; Soc. of Legal Scholars, 2012–. Study of Parlt Gp, 2013–. Hon. QC 2011. Hon. LLD: Bristol, 2012; London, 2014. *Publications:* (with Peter Knowles) Statutes title in Halsbury's Laws of England, 4th edn, 1983; (contrib.) Drafting Legislation: a modern approach, 2008; (contrib.) Statute Law Review, 2011; (contrib.) Law in Politics, Politics and Law, 2013; contrib. to Eur. Jl Law Reform. *Recreations:* Italy, medieval and constitutional history, gadgets, cricket watching, golf. *Club:* Canterbury Golf.

LAWSON, family name of **Barons Burnham** and **Lawson of Blaby**.

LAWSON OF BLABY, Baron *cr* 1992 (Life Peer), of Newnham in the County of Northamptonshire; **Nigel Lawson;** PC 1981; *b* 11 March 1932; *o s* of Ralph Lawson and Joan Elisabeth Lawson (*née* Davis); *m* 1st, 1955, Vanessa Salmon (marr. diss. 1980; she *d* 1985); one *s* two *d* (and one *d* decd); 2nd, 1980, Thérèse Mary Maclear (marr. diss. 2012); one *s* one *d*. *Educ:* Westminster; Christ Church, Oxford (Scholar; 1st class hons PPE, 1954). Served with Royal Navy (Sub-Lt RNVR, CO HMMTB Gay Charger), 1954–56. Mem. Editorial Staff, Financial Times, 1956–60; City Editor, Sunday Telegraph, 1961–63; Special Assistant to Prime Minister (Sir Alec Douglas-Home), 1963–64; Financial Times columnist and BBC broadcaster, 1965; Editor of the Spectator, 1966–70; regular contributor to: Sunday Times and Evening Standard, 1970–71; The Times, 1971–72; Fellow, Nuffield Coll., Oxford, 1972–73; Special Pol Advr, Cons. Party HQ, 1973–74. Contested (C) Eton and Slough, 1970; MP (C) Blaby, Leics, Feb. 1974–1992. An Opposition Whip, 1976–77; an Opposition Spokesman on Treasury and Economic Affairs, 1977–79; Financial Sec. to the Treasury, 1979–81; Sec. of State for Energy, 1981–83; Chancellor of the Exchequer, 1983–89. Chairman: Central Europe Trust Co. Ltd, 1990–2012; Oxford Investment Partners (OXIP), 2006–13; Dir, Barclays Bank, 1990–98. Founding Chm., Global Warming Policy Foundn, 2009–. Pres., British Inst. of Energy Econs, 1995–2003. Mem., Governing Body, Westminster Sch., 1999–2005. Hon. Student, Christ Church, Oxford, 1996. Hon. DSc Buckingham, 2011. IEA Nat. Free Enterprise Award, 2008. Mousquetaire d'Armagnac, 2010. *Publications:* (with Jock Bruce-Gardyne) The Power Game, 1976; The View from No 11, 1992, rev. edn as Memoirs of a Tory Radical, 2010; (with Thérèse Lawson) The Nigel Lawson Diet Book, 1996; An Appeal to Reason: a cool look at global warming, 2008. *Address:* House of Lords, SW1A 0PW. *Clubs:* Beefsteak, Garrick, Pratt's.

See also Hon. D. R. C. Lawson, N. L. Lawson.

LAWSON, Sir Charles (John Patrick), 4th Bt *cr* 1900, of Weetwood Grange, West Riding of Yorks; *b* 19 May 1959; *o s* of Sir John Charles Arthur Digby Lawson, 3rd Bt, DSO, MC and Tresilla Anne Elinor (*née* Buller-Leyborne-Popham); *S* father, 2001; *m* 1987, Lady Caroline Lowther, *d* of 7th Earl of Lonsdale; three *s* one *d*. *Educ:* Harrow; Univ. of Leeds; RAC Cirencester. MRICS. Director: Jackson-Stops & Staff, Exeter, 1992– (Mem., Exec. Cttee, 2011–); JSS Development Land and New Homes Co. Ltd, 2010–. *Heir: s* Jack William Tremayne Lawson, *b* 6 Dec. 1989. *Address:* Heckwood, Sampford Spiney, Yelverton, Devon PL20 6LG. *T:* (office) (01392) 214222. *E:* charlielawson@outlook.com.

LAWSON, Christopher John; Chief Executive, Meat Hygiene Service, Food Standards Agency, 2001–07; *b* 16 March 1947; s of late John Hedley Lawson and of Joyce Patricia Lawson (*née* Robson); *m* 1969, Janice Ray Langley; two *s* one *d* (and one *d* decd). *Educ:* Ascham House Sch.; Rossall Sch.; Univ. of Newcastle upon Tyne (BSc Hons Agric.). Livestock Husbandry Advr, NAAS, 1970–72, ADAS, 1972–73; MAFF, 1973–2000: Dir of Policy, Vet. Medicines Directorate, 1991–96; Hd, Meat Hygiene Div., 1996–2000; Food Standards Agency, 2000–07. Member: NE Rly Assoc.; NE Locomotive Preservation Gp; Vintage Carriage Trust. *Recreations:* steam railway preservation, fell walking, photography, DIY, industrial archaeology, supporting Newcastle United, sport generally, the North East. *Address:* 67 The Mount, York YO24 1AX. *Club:* Gateshead RU.

LAWSON, Prof. Colin James, PhD, DMus; FRCM, FLCM, FRNCM; international clarinet soloist; Director, Royal College of Music, since 2005; *b* 24 July 1949; *s* of Eric William and Edith Mary Lawson; *m* 1982, Aileen Hilary Birch; one *s*. *Educ:* Keble Coll.,

Oxford (MA); Univ. of Birmingham (MA); Univ. of Aberdeen (PhD 1976); Univ. of London (DMus 2000). ARCM 1967, FRCM 2005; FLCM 2005; FRNCM 2009. Lectr in Music, Aberdeen Univ., 1973–77; Sheffield University: Lectr, 1978–90; Sen. Lectr, 1991–96; Reader, 1996–97; Prof. of Performance Studies, Goldsmiths Coll., Univ. of London, 1998–2001; Pro-Vice Chancellor, Thames Valley Univ., 2001–05. Concert appearances as clarinet soloist include: Carnegie Hall; Lincoln Center, NY; Principal Clarinet: Hanover Band, 1987–2006; English Concert, 1991–2006. Recordings incl. Mozart Clarinet Quintet and fragments (with the Revolutionary Drawing Room), 2012. Hon. RAM. *Publications:* The Chalumeau in Eighteenth-Century Music, 1981; (ed) Cambridge Companion to the Clarinet, 1995; Mozart Clarinet Concerto, 1996; Brahms' Clarinet Quintet, 1998; (with R. Stowell) The Historical Performance of Music, 1999; The Early Clarinet, 2000; (ed) Cambridge Companion to the Orchestra, 2003; (ed with R. Stowell) Cambridge History of Musical Performance, 2012. *Recreations:* travel, acquisition of early clarinets. *Address:* Royal College of Music, Prince Consort Road, SW7 2BS. *T:* (020) 7591 4363, *Fax:* (020) 7591 4356. *Club:* Athenæum.

LAWSON, Prof. David Hamilton, CBE 1993; Hon. Consultant Physician, Glasgow Royal Infirmary, since 2003 (Consultant Physician, 1973–2003); *b* 27 May 1939; *s* of David Lawson and Margaret Harvey Lawson (*née* White); *m* 1st, 1963, Alison Diamond (*d* 1996); three *s*; 2nd, 2010, Avril Eleanor Yarrow Meighan (*née* Scott). *Educ:* High Sch. of Glasgow; Univ. of Glasgow. MB, ChB 1962; MD 1973. FRCPE 1975; FRCPGlas 1986; FFPM 1989; FRCP 2001; FFPH (FFPHM 2001). Junior medical posts in Royal Infirmary and Western Infirmary, Glasgow; Boston Collaborative Drug Surveillance Prog., Boston, Mass, 1970–72; Attending Physician, Lemuel Shattuck Hosp., Boston, 1971; Adviser on Adverse Drug Reactions, Wellcome Foundn, 1975–87; Vis. Prof., Faculty of Sci., Univ. of Strathclyde, 1976–2005; Hon. Prof. of Medicine, Univ. of Glasgow, 1993–. Chairman: Medicines Commn, 1994–2001; Scottish Medicines Consortium, 2000–04; Bd Trustees, Drug Safety Research Unit, Univ. of Southampton, 2010–; Member: Health Services Res. Cttee of Chief Scientist Office, SHHD, 1984–88; Cttee on Safety of Medicines, Dept of Health (formerly DHSS), 1987–93; Mem., 1979–91, Chm., 1987–91, Cttee on Review of Medicines, Dept of Health (formerly DHSS). Mem. Council, RCPE, 1992–99 (Vice-Pres., 1997–99; Trustee, 2005–). Examiner, Final MB, Univs of Glasgow, Dundee, Birmingham, London, Kota Bharu, Malaysia. Pres., Antonine Probus Club, Bearsden and Milngavie, 2008–09. Hon. DSc: Hertfordshire, 2000; Strathclyde, 2001. *Publications:* Clinical Pharmacy and Hospital Drug Management (ed with R. M. E. Richards), 1982; Current Medicine 2, 1990; (ed jtly) Risk Factors for Adverse Drug Reactions: epidemiological approaches, 1990; Current Medicine 3, 1991; Current Medicine 4, 1994; papers on clinical pharmacol, haematol and renal topics. *Recreations:* hill-walking, photography, bird-watching. *Address:* 5 Tannoch House, 138 Mugdock Road, Milngavie, Glasgow G62 8NP. *T:* (0141) 956 2766.

LAWSON, Denis; actor and director; *b* 27 Sept. 1947; *s* of Laurence and Phyllis Lawson; *m* 2004, Sheila Gish (*d* 2005); one *s*, and two step *d*. *Educ:* Crieff Primary Sch.; Morrison's Acad., Crieff; Royal Scottish Acad. of Music and Drama, Glasgow. *Productions*: as *actor*: *theatre* includes: Pal Joey, Albery, 1980 (Most Promising New Actor, Drama Critics' Award); Mr Cinders, Fortune, 1983; (Best Actor in a Musical Award, SWET, 1984); Lend Me a Tenor, Globe, 1986; The Importance of Being Earnest, Royalty, 1987; Volpone, Almeida, 1990; Lust, Haymarket, 1993; La Cage aux Folles, Playhouse, 2008; Acid Test, Royal Court, 2011; *films* include: Providence, The Man in the Iron Mask, 1977; Local Hero, 1983; The Chain, 1984; Perfect Sense, 2011; Broken, The Machine, 2013; *television* includes: The Kit Curran Radio Show, 1984; That Uncertain Feeling, Dead Head, 1986; The Justice Game, 1989; Natural Lies, 1992; Hornblower, The Ambassador, 1998; Bob Martin, Other People's Children, 2000; The Fabulous Bagel Boys, 2001; Holby City, 2002–04; Sensitive Skin, Bleak House, 2005; Jekyll, 2006; Criminal Justice, 2009; Marchlands, 2011; New Tricks, 2012–; as *director*: *theatre*: Little Malcolm and His Struggle Against the Eunuchs, Comedy, 1998; The Anniversary, Garrick, 2004; *films*: The Bass Player, 1998; Solid Geometry, 2002. *Recreations:* vodka martinis, jazz. *Address:* c/o Claire Maroussas, Independent Talent Group Ltd, 40 Whitfield Street, W1T 2RH. *T:* (020) 7636 6565, *Fax:* (020) 7323 0101.

LAWSON, Hon. Dominic Ralph Campden; journalist and broadcaster; *b* 17 Dec. 1956; *s* of Baron Lawson of Blaby, *qv* and late Vanessa Mary Addison Lawson (*née* Salmon); *m* 1st, 1982, Jane Whytehead (marr. diss.); 2nd, 1991, Hon. Rosamond Mary Monckton, *qv*; two *d*. *Educ:* Westminster Sch.; Christ Church, Oxford (exhibnr; Hons PPE). Researcher, BBC TV and radio, 1979–81; Financial Times: joined 1981; energy corresp., 1983–86; columnist (Lex), 1986–87; The Spectator: Dep. Editor, 1987–90; Editor, 1990–95; Editor, Sunday Telegraph, 1995–2005; columnist: Sunday Correspondent, 1990; Financial Times, 1991–94; Daily Telegraph, 1994–95; Independent, 2006–13; Sunday Times, 2008–; Standpoint, 2008–; Daily Mail, 2013–. Presenter, BBC Radio series: Across the Board, 2013–15; Why I Changed My Mind, 2015. Mem., Press Complaints Commn, 1998–2002. Vis. Schol., Green Templeton (formerly Green) Coll., Oxford, 2007–08. Pres., English Chess Fedn, 2014–. FRSA 1993. Harold Wincott Prize for financial journalism, 1987; Columnist of the Year, British Press Awards, 2014. *Publications:* (with Raymond Keene) Kasparov-Korchnoi, the London Contest, 1983; (jtly) Britain in the Eighties, 1989; The Inner Game, 1993; (ed) Snake Oil and Other Preoccupations, 2001. *Recreation:* chess. *Address:* Cox's Mill, Dallington, Heathfield, East Sussex TN21 9JG. *Club:* MCC.

See also N. L. Lawson.

LAWSON, Prof. Donald Douglas; Professor of Veterinary Surgery, University of Glasgow, 1974–86; *b* 25 May 1924; *s* of Alexander Lawson and Jessie Macnaughton; *m* 1949, Barbara Ness (*d* 1998); one *s* one *d* (and one *s* one *d* decd). *Educ:* Whitehill Sch., Glasgow; Glasgow Veterinary Coll. MRCVS, BSc, DVR. Asst in Veterinary Practice, 1946–47; Asst, Surgery Dept, Glasgow Vet. Coll., 1947–49; Glasgow Univ.: Lectr, Vet. Surgery, 1949–57; Sen. Lectr, 1957–66; Reader, 1966–71; Titular Prof., 1971–74. *Publications:* many articles in Veterinary Record and Jl of Small Animal Practice. *Recreations:* gardening, motoring. *Address:* 5 Hewlings Place, Temuka 7920, New Zealand.

LAWSON, Elizabeth Ann; QC 1989; a Recorder, since 1998; *b* 29 April 1947; *d* of Alexander Edward Lawson, FCA, and Helen Jane Lawson (*née* Currie). *Educ:* Croydon High School for Girls (GPDST); Nottingham Univ. (LLB). Called to Bar, Gray's Inn, 1969, Bencher, 1999. Chm., Family Law Bar Assoc., 1995–97. Chm., Leeways Enquiry for London Borough of Lewisham, 1985; Chm., Liam Johnson Review for Islington Area Child Protection Cttee, 1989. *Recreations:* knitting, reading, cake decoration.

LAWSON, Prof. Gerald Hartley; Professor of Business Finance, Manchester Business School, University of Manchester, 1969–88, now Emeritus; financial and economic consultant; *b* 6 July 1933; of English parents; *m* 1957, Helga Elisabeth Anna Heine; three *s*. *Educ:* King's Coll., Univ. of Durham. BA (Econ), MA (Econ); Univ. of Manchester (MBA; PhD 1994); FCCA. Accountant in industry, 1957–59; Lectr in Accountancy and Applied Economics, Univ. of Sheffield, 1959–66; Prof. of Business Studies, Univ. of Liverpool, 1966–69. British Council Scholar, Hochschule für Welthandel, Vienna, 1967, and Univ. of Louvain, 1978. Visiting Professor: Univ. of Augsburg, Germany, 1971–72; Univ. of Texas, 1977, 1981; Ruhr Univ., Bochum, 1980; Southern Methodist Univ., Dallas, 1989–93; Nanyang Technological Univ., Singapore, 1989; Martin Luther Univ., Halle-Wittenberg, 1993–96; Otto-von-Guericke-Univ. of Magdeburg, 1998–2001; Vis. Erskine Fellow, Univ. of Canterbury, NZ, 1997. Dir, Dietsmann (UK), 1984–89. Lifetime Achievement Award, BAA, 2008. *Publications:* (with D. W. Windle): Tables for Discounted Cash Flow, etc, Calculations, 1965 (6th repr. 1979); Capital Budgeting in the Corporation Tax Regime, 1967; (with M. Schweitzer and E. Trossman) Break-Even Analyses: basic model, variants, extensions, 1991; Studies in Cash Flow Accounting, 1992 (repr. 2013); Aspects of the Economic Implications of Accounting, 1997; many articles and translations. *Recreations:* cricket, ski-ing, opera. *Address:* 1702 Woodcreek Drive, Richardson, TX 75082, USA. *E:* gerrylawson@tx.rr.com. *Club:* Manchester Business School.

LAWSON, Sir John Philip H; *see* Howard-Lawson.

LAWSON, Lesley, (Twiggy); actress, singer and model; *b* 19 Sept. 1949; *y d* of late (William) Norman Hornby and of Nell (Helen) Hornby (*née* Reeman); *m* 1st, 1977, Michael Whitney Armstrong (*d* 1983); one *d*; 2nd, 1988, Leigh Lawson. Started modelling in London, 1966; toured USA and Canada, 1967; world's most famous model, 1966–71. *Films:* The Boy Friend, 1971 (most promising newcomer and best actress in a musical or comedy, Golden Globe Awards); W, 1973; There Goes the Bride, 1979; Blues Brothers, 1981; The Doctor and the Devils, 1986; Club Paradise, 1986; Madame Sousatzka, 1989; Harem Hotel, Istanbul, 1989; Woundings, 1998; *stage:* Cinderella, 1976; Captain Beaky, 1982; My One and Only, 1983, 1984; Blithe Spirit, Chichester, 1997; Noel and Gertie, NY, 1998; If Love Were All, NY, 1999; Blithe Spirit, NY, 2002; Mrs Warren's Profession (UK tour), 2003; *television:* numerous appearances and series, UK and USA, incl. The Taming of the Shrew, 2005; judge on America's Next Top Model, 2005–08; Twiggy's Frock Exchange, 2008; numerous recordings, incl. Romantically Yours, 2011. Exhibn, Twiggy: a life in photographs, NPG, 2009–10. Many awards and honours including Hon. Col, Tennessee Army, 1977. *Publications:* Twiggy, 1975; An Open Look, 1985; Twiggy in Black and White (autobiog.), 1997; Twiggy: a guide to looking and feeling fabulous over forty, 2008; (contrib.) Twiggy: a life in photographs, 2009. *Recreations:* daughter Carly, music, dressmaking. *Address:* c/o Peters, Fraser & Dunlop, Drury House, 34–43 Russell Street, WC2B 5HA. *T:* (020) 7344 1010, *Fax:* (020) 7836 9544.

LAWSON, Mark Gerard; journalist, broadcaster and author; *b* 11 April 1962; *s* of late Francis Lawson and of Teresa Lawson (*née* Kane); *m* 1990, Sarah Bull; two *s* one *d*. *Educ:* St Columba's Coll., St Albans; University College London (BA Hons English). Junior reporter and TV critic, The Universe, 1984–85; TV previewer, Sunday Times, 1985–86; TV critic and parly sketchwriter, The Independent, 1986–89; feature writer, Independent Magazine, 1988–95; columnist, The Guardian, 1995–; theatre critic, The Tablet, 2006–; presenter for radio and TV, 1990–, including: Late Review, later Review, subseq. Newsnight Review (BBC2), 1994–2005; Front Row (Radio 4), 1998–2014; Mark Lawson Talks To... (BBC4), 2006–; Never Ending Stories (BBC2); scriptwriter for radio and TV, including: The Vision Thing (BBC2), 1993; The Man Who Had 10,000 Women (Radio 4), 2002; St Graham and St Evelyn, Pray for Us (Radio 4), 2003; Absolute Power (BBC2), 2003–05; The Third Soldier Holds His Thighs (Radio 4), 2005; London, this is Washington (Radio 4), 2006; Expand This (Radio 4), Sex After Death (Radio 4), 2007; The Number of the Dead (Radio 3), 2009; Reading Between the Lines (Radio 4), 2009; Suspicion for 10 Voices (Radio 4), 2013; Foreign Bodies (Radio 4), 2013–14. British Press Award, 1987; TV critic of the Year, 1989, 1990. *Publications:* Bloody Margaret, 1991; The Battle for Room Service, 1993; Idlewild, 1995; John Keane, 1995; Going Out Live, 2001; Enough Is Enough, 2005; The Deaths, 2013. *Recreations:* theatre, cricket, tennis, wine, reading. *Address:* c/o Cat Ledger Literary Agency, 20–21 Newman Street, W1T 1PG. *E:* cat.ledger@virgin.net.

LAWSON, Ven. Michael Charles; Archdeacon of Hampstead, 1999–2010; Rector, St Saviour's, Guildford, 2010–12; *b* 23 May 1952; *s* of Gerald Simon Lawson and Myrtle Helena Lawson; *m* 1978, Claire Mary MacClelland; three *d*. *Educ:* Hove Grammar Sch.; Guildhall Sch. of Music; Ecoles d'Art Américaines, Fontainebleau; Univ. of Sussex (BA); Trinity Coll., Bristol (BCTS). Composer and pianist, 1970–75. Deacon 1978, priest 1979; Curate, St Mary the Virgin, Horsham, 1978–81; Dir of Pastoring, All Souls, Langham Place, W1, 1981–86; Vicar, Christ Church, Bromley, 1987–99. Permission to officiate, dio. of Ely, 2013–. Maker of documentaries: Aids Orphans, Mozambique, 2002; India's Broken People, 2005; India's Hidden Slavery, 2007; India's New Beginnings, 2009; India's Forgotten Women, 2010. Member and Fellow, Inst. of Videography. *Publications:* Sex and That, 1985, 2nd edn 1992; Facing Anxiety and Stress, 1986, 2nd edn 1995; The Unfolding Kingdom, 1987; Facing Depression, 1989, 2nd edn 1997; Facing Conflict, 1990; The Better Marriage Guide, 1998; Conflict, 1999; Living by God's Master Plan, 2000; D is for Depression, 2006. *Recreations:* my wife and children, friends, music, writing, video production, photography, computers, theatre, cookery, lots of things.

LAWSON, Michael Henry; QC 1991; **His Honour Judge Michael Lawson;** a Circuit Judge, since 2004; *b* 3 Feb. 1946; *s* of late Dr Richard Pike Lawson, MC and Margaret Haines (*née* Knight); *m* 1969, Ann Pleasance Symons Brisker; two *d*. *Educ:* Monkton Combe School, Bath; London Univ. (LLB). Called to the Bar, Inner Temple, 1969, Bencher, 1993; a Recorder, 1987–2004. Leader, SE Circuit, 1997–2000. Mem., Bar Council, 1997–2003. Ct Asst, Curriers' Co., 2011– (Master, 2007–08). *Publications:* (jtly) Professional Conduct (Inns of Court School of Law Manual), annually, 1989–2000; (contrib.) Refocus on Child Abuse, 1994. *Recreations:* opera, music, wine, walking. *Address:* Crown Court, 182 High Street, Lewes, E Sussex BN7 1YB.

LAWSON, Nigella Lucy; freelance journalist and broadcaster, since 1982; *b* 6 Jan. 1960; *d* of Baron Lawson of Blaby, *qv* and late Vanessa Mary Addison Lawson (*née* Salmon); *m* 1st, 1992, John Diamond (*d* 2001); one *s* one *d*; 2nd, 2003, Charles Saatchi, *qv* (marr. diss. 2013). *Educ:* Lady Margaret Hall, Oxford (BA (Hons) Medieval and Mod. Langs). Presenter, television series: Nigella Bites, 2000; Nigella Bites II, 2001; Forever Summer with Nigella, 2002; Nigella's Christmas Kitchen, 2006, 2008; Nigella Express, 2007; Nigella Kitchen, 2010; Nigellissima, 2012; mentor, The Taste, 2013–15. *Publications:* How to Eat, 1998; How to be a Domestic Goddess, 2000; Nigella Bites, 2001; Forever Summer, 2002; (contrib.) Oxford Companion to Italian Literature, 2002; Feast, 2004; Nigella Express, 2007; Nigella Christmas, 2008; Kitchen: recipes from the heart of the home, 2010; Nigellissima: instant Italian inspiration, 2012; Simply Nigella: feel good food, 2015. *Address:* c/o Ed Victor Ltd, 6 Bayley Street, Bedford Square, WC1B 3HB. *T:* (020) 7304 4100.

See also Hon. D. R. C. Lawson.

LAWSON, Gen. Sir Richard (George), KCB 1980; DSO 1962; OBE 1968; Commander-in-Chief, Allied Forces Northern Europe, 1982–86; *b* 24 Nov. 1927; *s* of John Lawson and Florence Rebecca Lawson; *m* 1956, Ingrid Lawson (*d* 2006); one *s*. *Educ:* St Albans Sch.; Birmingham Univ. CO, Independent Squadron, RTR (Berlin), 1963–64; GSO2 MoD, 1965–66; C of S, South Arabian Army, 1967; CO, 5th RTR, 1968–69; Comdr, 20th Armoured Bde, 1972–73; Asst Military Deputy to Head of Defence Sales, 1975–77; GOC 1st Armoured Div., 1977–79; GOC Northern Ireland, 1980–82. Col Comdt, RTR, 1980–82. Leopold Cross (Belgium), 1963; Knight Commander, Order of St Sylvester (Vatican), 1964. *Publications:* Strange Soldiering, 1963; All the Queen's Men, 1967; Strictly Personal, 1972. *Address:* c/o Drummonds, 49 Charing Cross, SW1A 2DX.

LAWSON, Robert John; QC 2009; *b* Burnham, 7 Nov. 1964; *s* of Alan and Katherine Lawson; *m* 1992, Rachel Claire Stanton; two *s* two *d*. *Educ:* Sheredes Comprehensive Sch.; Queen's Coll., Oxford (BA Hons PPE); City Univ., London (DipLaw). Called to the Bar, Inner Temple, 1989; in private practice, 1989–, specialising in aviation, travel and professional discipline. Fellow, Internat. Acad. of Trial Lawyers, 2006. MRAeS 1998, FRAeS 2010; MCIArb 2005. *Publications:* contrib. on aviation, Halsbury's Laws of England, Vol. 2 (3), 4th edn reissue, 2003; contrib. articles on issues of aviation law. *Recreations:* sport, classical music.

Address: Quadrant Chambers, Quadrant House, 10 Fleet Street, EC4Y 1AU. *T:* (020) 7583 4444, *Fax:* (020) 7583 4455. *E:* robert.lawson@quadrantchambers.com. *Club:* Corkscrew (Herts).

LAWSON, Roger Hardman; Director Resource, 3i plc, 1993–2002; *b* 3 Sept. 1945; *s* of Harold Hardman Lawson and Mary Doreen Lawson; *m* 1974, Jenniferjane Grey; three *d. Educ:* Bedford School. ACA 1967; FCA. Articled Wilson de Zouche & Mackenzie, 1963–67; joined ICFC, subseq. 3i, 1968; Manager, UK Regions, 1968–84; Dir, 3i International (USA, Asia and Pacific), 1984–92. Dir, Zotefoams plc, 2002–12. Mem., Takeover Panel, 1994–95. Chm., London Soc. of Chartered Accountants, 1985–86; Pres., ICAEW, 1994–95. Trustee: Thalidomide Trust, 2001–14; St Paul's Cathedral Staff Pension Fund, 2003–14. *Recreations:* food, family, fun. *Address:* 62 Thurleigh Road, SW12 8UD. *Clubs:* Royal Wimbledon Golf; Rye Golf.

LAWSON, Hon. Rosa(mond) Mary; *see* Monckton, Hon. R. M.

LAWSON, Sonia, RA 1991 (ARA 1982); RWS 1988 (ARWS 1985); artist; Visiting Lecturer, Royal Academy Schools, 1985–2003; *b* 2 June 1934; *d* of Frederick Lawson and Muriel (*née* Metcalfe), artists; *m* 1969, C. W. Congo; one *d. Educ:* Leyburn; Southwick Girls' Sch.; Doncaster Sch. of Art; Royal Coll. of Art (ARCA 1st cl. 1959). Postgraduate year, RCA; Travelling Scholarship, France, 1960. *Annual exhibitions:* RA, 1961–; RWS, 1983–. *Solo exhibitions:* Zwemmer, London, 1960; New Arts Centre, London, 1963; Queen's Sq. Gall., Leeds, 1964; Trafford Gall., London, 1967; Bradford New Liby, 1972; Middlesbrough and Billingham, 1977; Open Univ., Darlington and Harrogate Art Galls, 1979; Harrogate Northern Artists, 1980; Manchester City Art Gall., 1987; Wakefield City Art Gall., 1988, 2008; Cartwright Hall, Bradford, 1989; Boundary Gall., London, 1989, 1995, 1998, 2000, 2003, 2005; Univ. of Birmingham, 1994, 2006; Shire Hall, Stafford, 1999; RWA, Bristol, 2000; Carlow Arts Fest., Ireland, 2001; Vertigo Gall., London, 2002; *retrospectives:* Shrines of Life, toured 1982–83, Sheffield (Mappin), Hull (Ferens), Bradford (Cartwright), Leicester Poly., Milton Keynes (Exhibn Gall); Dean Clough Gall., Halifax, 1996; Aylesbury Art Gall. and Mus., 2006; *mixed exhibitions:* Arts Council of GB Touring Exhibns (Fragments against Ruin, The Subjective Eye); Tolly Cobbold National Exhibns; Moira Kelly Fine Art; Hayward Annual; Soho, New York (8 in the 80s); Fruitmarket Gall., Edinburgh; London Gp; RCA (Exhibition Road, to celebrate 150 years of RCA), 1988; Smith Gall., London, 1988, 1989; Faces of Britain, China (British Council Touring Exhibn), 1989–90; Glasgow Royal Inst. of Fine Art, 1990; Galerie zur alten deutschen Schule, Thun, Switzerland, 1990; Royal Academy (The Infernal Method, etchings by Academicians), 1991; John Moores, Liverpool, 1991; Bonnington Gall., Nottingham Trent Univ. (Representing Lives), 1997. Works in public collections: Arts Council of GB; Graves Art Gall., Sheffield; Huddersfield, Bolton, Carlisle, Belfast, Middlesbrough, Bradford, Dewsbury, Rochdale, Wakefield, and Harrogate Art Galls; Imperial War Mus.; Min. of Educn; Min. of Works; Leeds Univ.; Open Univ.; Cranfield Univ.; RCA; St Peter's Coll., Oxford; Nuffield Foundn; Royal Acad.; Univ. of Qld; Augustine (commissioned), presented by Archbishop of Canterbury to Pope John Paul II, Vatican Collection, Rome, 1989; private collections in UK, Germany, Australia, USA. BBC TV, Monitor, 1960, John Schlesinger's doc. "Private View". Visual records of Exercise Lionheart, BAOR, Germany, 1984 (Imperial War Mus. commn). Hon. RWA 2005. Rowney Prize, Royal Acad., 1984; Gainsborough House Drawing Prize, Eastern Arts, 1984; Lorne Scholarship, Slade Sch. of Fine Art, 1986; Lady Evershed Drawing Prize, Eastern Arts Open, 1990. *Publications:* (illustrator) Look At It This Way: poems for young people, by James Kirkup, 1994; (illustrator) New Year's Eve, by Fay Weldon, 1995. *Address:* c/o Royal Academy of Arts, Burlington House, Piccadilly, W1J 0BD. *T:* (020) 7300 5680. *E:* art@sonialawson.co.uk. *W:* www.sonialawson.co.uk. *Club:* Arts.

LAWSON JOHNSTON, family name of **Baron Luke**.

LAWSON-ROGERS, (George) Stuart; QC 1994; a Recorder, since 1990; *b* 23 March 1946; *s* of late George Henry Roland Rogers, CBE, sometime MP and Mary Lawson; *m* 1969, Rosalind Denise Leach; one *s* one *d. Educ:* LSE (LLB Hons). Called to the Bar, Gray's Inn, 1969; Asst Recorder, 1987–89. Asst Comr, Parly and Local Govt Boundary Commns, 1981, 1983; Chm., Structure Plan Exams in Public, DoE, 1984; Legal Assessor, GMC and GDC, 1988–2005; Standing Counsel (Crime, SE Circuit) to HM Customs and Excise, 1989–94; DTI Inspector, Insider Dealing, 1989; Dept of Transport Inspector, Merchant Shipping Act 1988, 1989–90. Dir, Watford AFC Ltd, 1990–96. *Recreations:* theatre, music, opera, reading, gardening.

LAWSON-TANCRED, Sir Andrew (Peter), 11th Bt *cr* 1662, of Boroughbridge, Yorks; Chairman, Northern Aldborough Festival, since 2010; *b* Wetherby, Yorks, 18 Feb. 1952; *e s* of Sir Henry Lawson-Tancred, 10th Bt and Jean Veronica (*d* 1970), 4th and *y d* of late G. R. Foster; *S* father, 2010; *m* 2003, Julia Francesca, *d* of John Murray; one *s* one *d. Educ:* Eton Coll.; Univ. of Leeds; Inns of Court Sch. of Law. Called to the Bar, Middle Temple, 1977; in practice as a barrister, 1977–84. Director: Legal and Business Affairs, WH Smith TV, 1990–94; TV Corp. Plc, 1995–99. Chair: Ripon Cathedral Music Trust; Friends of Roman Aldborough. *Recreations:* flying, music. *Heir: s* Thomas Alexander Claude Lawson-Tancred, *b* 17 June 2006. *Address:* Aldborough Manor, Boroughbridge, York YO51 9EP. *E:* andrew@aldborough.com.

LAWTON, Prof. Denis; Professor of Education, University of London Institute of Education, 1974–2003, now Emeritus; *b* 5 April 1931; *s* of William Benedict Lawton and Ruby (*née* Evans); *m* 1953, Joan Weston; two *s. Educ:* St Ignatius Coll.; Univ. of London Goldsmiths' Coll. (BA); Univ. of London Inst. of Education (PhD). Asst Master, Erith Grammar Sch., 1958–61; Head of English/Housemaster, Bacon's Sch., SE1, 1961–63; University of London Institute of Education: Research Officer, 1963–64; Lectr in Sociology, 1964–67; Sen. Lectr in Curriculum Studies, 1967–72; Reader in Education, 1972–74; Dep. Dir, 1978–83; Dir, 1983–89. Chairman: Univ. of London Sch. Exams Bd, subseq. Sch. Exams and Assessment Council, 1984–96; Consortium for Assessment and Testing in Schools, 1989–91; Jt Council for GCSE, 1996–99; Acad. Sec., UCET, 2000–02. Hon. Fellow, College of Preceptors, 1983. *Publications:* Social Class, Language and Education, 1968; Social Change, Education Theory and Curriculum Planning, 1973; Class, Culture and the Curriculum, 1975; Social Justice and Education, 1977; The Politics of the School Curriculum, 1980; An Introduction to Teaching and Learning, 1981; Curriculum Studies and Educational Planning, 1983; (with P. Gordon) HMI, 1987; Education, Culture and the National Curriculum, 1989; Education and Politics in the 1990s, 1992; The Tory Mind on Education, 1994; Beyond the National Curriculum, 1996; Royal Education Past, Present and Future, 1999; (with P. Gordon) A History of Western Educational Ideas, 2002; Education and Labour Party Ideologies 1900–2001 and Beyond, 2004. *Recreations:* walking German Shepherd dogs, photographing bench-ends, sampling real ale, music. *Address:* Laun House, Laundry Lane, Nazeing, Essex EN9 2DY.

LAWTON, Sir John (Hartley), Kt 2005; CBE 1997; FRS 1989; Chairman, Royal Commission on Environmental Pollution, 2005–11 (Member, 1989–96); Chief Executive, Natural Environment Research Council, 1999–2005; *b* 24 Sept. 1943; *s* of Frank Hartley Lawton and Mary Lawton; *m* 1966, Dorothy (*née* Grimshaw); one *s* one *d. Educ:* Balshaw's Grammar Sch., Leyland, Lancs; University Coll. and Dept of Zoology, Univ. of Durham (BSc, PhD). Res. Student, Univ. of Durham, 1965–68; Deptl Demonstrator in Animal Ecology, Oxford Univ., 1968–71; College Lectr in Zoology, St Anne's and Lincoln Colls, Oxford, 1970–71; University of York: Lectr, 1971–78; Sen. Lectr, 1978–82; Reader, 1982–85; Personal Chair, 1985–89; Dir, NERC Centre for Population Biology, ICSTM, 1989–99. Mem., NERC, 1995–99. Hon. Vis. Res. Fellow, Nat. Hist. Mus., 1990–2005; Adjunct Scientist, Inst. of Ecosystem Studies, NY Botanic Garden, 1991–2000. Vice-President: RSPB, 1999– (Chm. Council, 1993–98); British Trust for Ornithology, 1999–2008. Foreign Member: US NAS, 2008; Amer. Assoc. of Arts and Scis, 2008. FIC 2006. Hon. DSc: Lancaster, 1993; Birmingham, York, 2005; East Anglia, Aberdeen, 2006. *Publications:* Insects on Plants: community patterns and mechanisms (with D. R. Strong and T. R. E. Southwood), 1984; (ed jtly) The Evolutionary Interactions of Animals and Plants, 1991; (ed jtly) Extinction Rates, 1996; (ed jtly) Linking Species and Ecosystems, 1996; Community Ecology in a Changing World, 2000; over 300 sci. papers in specialist jls. *Recreations:* bird watching, natural history photography, travel, gardening, walking, cooking. *Address:* The Hayloft, Holburns Croft, Heslington, York YO10 5DP.

LAWTON, Julie Grace; Headmistress, Wolverhampton Girls' High School, 2004–12; *b* 2 April 1958; *d* of Arthur and Audrey Barber; *m* 1979, Mark Lawton. *Educ:* Univ. of Hull (BA; PGCE); Univ. of Birmingham (MEd); NPQH 2002. Teacher: of French and German, Newland High Sch. for Girls, Hull, 1980–83; i/c German, Parkfield Sch., Wolverhampton, 1983–86; Hd, Modern Langs, Kingswinford Sch., Dudley, 1987–94; Vice Principal and Dir, Sixth Form Studies, St Peter's Collegiate Sch., Wolverhampton, 1995–2003. *Recreations:* walking, travelling abroad, foreign languages.

LAWTON, Paul Anthony; His Honour Judge Lawton; a Circuit Judge, since 2014; *b* Stoke on Trent, 12 July 1964; *s* of George Lawton and Joan Lawton; *m* 1991, Andrea Walker; three *d. Educ:* Alsager Sch.; Manchester Poly. (LLB Hons 1986). Called to the Bar, Lincoln's Inn, 1987; a Recorder, 2005–14. Mem., Bar Disciplinary Tribunal, 2012–14; Visitor, Inns of Court, 2013. *Recreations:* kitchen gardening, fly fishing, walking.

LAXTON, Robert; *b* 7 Sept. 1944; *s* of Alan and Elsie Laxton; *m*; one *s. Educ:* Woodlands Secondary Sch.; Derby Coll. of Art and Technology. Branch Officer, CWU, 1974–97; Telecommunications Engr, BT plc, 1961–97. Mem., Derby CC, 1979–97 (Leader, 1986–88, 1994–97). MP (Lab) Derby North, 1997–2010. PPS to Minister of State: DTI, 2001–03; DFES, 2003–04; PPS to Secretary of State: DWP, 2004–05; DTI, 2005. Mem., Trade and Industry Select Cttee, 1997–2001. Vice Chairman: Trade Union Gp of Lab. MPs; PLP DTI Deptl Cttee. Chm., E Midlands Local Govt Assoc., 1995–97; Vice Pres., LGA.

LAY, Richard Neville, CBE 2001; Chairman, 1999–2015, Trustee, since 1999, Portman Estate; Chairman, DTZ (formerly Debenham Tewson & Chinnocks) Holdings plc, 1987–2000; President, Royal Institution of Chartered Surveyors, 1998–99; *b* 18 Oct. 1938; *s* of late Edward John Lay; *m* 1st, 1964; one *s* one *d*; 2nd, 1991; 3rd, 2003, Veronica Anne Jones (*née* Hamilton-Russell). *Educ:* Whitgift School. FRICS. Partner, Debenham Tewson & Chinnocks, 1965–87. Vice Chm., 1992–2001, Chm., 2001–, Central London Board, RSA (formerly Sun Alliance and London, then Royal and Sun Alliance) Insurance Group. Dir, Nat. House Building Council, 2001–07. Chairman: cttee advising RICS on market requirements of the profession, 1991; Commercial Property Panel, RICS, 1992–95; Member: Council, British Property Fedn, 1992–99; General Council, RICS, 1994–2000; Bank of England Property Forum, 1994–99; Chm., Commercial Property Gp, DCLG (formerly Wkg Party on Commercial Property Issues, ODPM), 2004–10; Mem., Adv. Panel on Standards in Planning Inspectorate, 1993–2000. Co-Chm., Corby Regeneration Co. Ltd, 2003–06; Chm., N Northants Develt Co. Ltd, 2006–08. Chm., London Underwriting Centre, 2005–. Trustee, Tate Gall. Foundn, 1989–94. Master, Armourers' and Brasiers' Co., 2003–04 (Surveyor, 1983–98; Mem., Ct of Assts, 1998–). Governor, Belmont Sch., Surrey, 1983–88; Mem. Bd, Coll. of Estate Mgt, 2000–05. Property Person of the Year, Property Week, 1999. *Recreations:* gardening, walking. *Address:* Meadow Cottage, Winderton, Banbury OX15 5JF. *T:* (01608) 685458.

LAYARD, Baron *cr* 2000 (Life Peer), of Highgate in the London Borough of Haringey; **Peter Richard Grenville Layard,** FBA 2003; Director, Well-Being Programme, Centre for Economic Performance, London School of Economics, since 2003 (Professor of Economics, 1980–99, now Emeritus); *b* 15 March 1934; *s* of Dr John Layard and Doris Layard; *m* 1991, Molly Meacher (*see* Baroness Meacher). *Educ:* Eton Coll.; King's Coll., Cambridge (BA); London School of Economics (MScEcon; Hon. Fellow, 2004). History Master: Woodberry Down Sch., 1959–60; Forest Hill Sch., 1960–61; Senior Research Officer, Robbins Cttee on Higher Educn, 1961–63; London School of Economics: Dep. Director, Higher Educn Research Unit, 1964–74 (part-time from 1968); Lectr in Economics, 1968–75; Reader in the Economics of Labour, 1975–80; Hd, Centre for Labour Econs, 1974–90; Dir, Centre for Econ. Performance, 1990–2003. Chm., Employment Inst., 1987–92. Mem., UGC, 1985–89. Econ. Consultant to Russian Govt, 1991–97; Consultant: DfEE, 1997–2001; Cabinet Office, 2001; DoH, 2006–. Co-founder, Action for Happiness, 2011. Chair, Global Agenda Council on Wellbeing and Mental Health, WEF, 2012. Fellow: Econometric Soc., 1986; Eur. Econ. Assoc., 2004; Soc. of Labor Economists, 2008. Leontief Medal, Russian Acad. of Natural Scis, 2005; President's Medal, RCPsych, 2010; (jtly) IZA Prize in Labor Econs, 2008. *Publications:* (jtly) The Causes of Graduate Unemployment in India, 1969; (jtly) The Impact of Robbins: Expansion in Higher Education, 1969; (jtly) Qualified Manpower and Economic Performance: An Inter-Plant Study in the Electrical Engineering Industry, 1971; (ed) Cost-Benefit Analysis, 1973, 2nd edn 1994; (jtly) Microeconomic Theory, 1978; (jtly) The Causes of Poverty, 1978; More Jobs, Less Inflation, 1982; How to Beat Unemployment, 1986; (jtly) Handbook of Labour Economics, 1986; (jtly) The Performance of the British Economy, 1988; (jtly) Unemployment: Macroeconomic Performance and the Labour Market, 1991; (jtly) Reform in Eastern Europe, 1991; (jtly) East-West Migration: the alternatives, 1992; (jtly) Post-Communist Reform: pain and progress, 1993; Macroeconomics: a text for Russia, 1994; (jtly) The Coming Russian Boom, 1996; What Labour Can Do, 1997; Tackling Unemployment, 1999; Tackling Inequality, 1999; (ed) What the Future Holds, 2002; Happiness: lessons from a new science, 2005, 2nd edn, 2011; (jtly) A Good Childhood: searching for values in a competitive age, 2009; (jtly) World Happiness Report, 2012, 2013, 2015; (jtly) Thrive: the power of evidence-based psychological therapies, 2014. *Recreations:* tennis, sailing. *Address:* London School of Economics, Houghton Street, WC2A 2AE. *T:* (020) 7955 7048.

LAYARD, Adm. Sir Michael (Henry Gordon), KCB 1993; CBE 1982; Second Sea Lord, and Chief of Naval Personnel (Member of Admiralty Board, Defence Council), 1993–95; Commander-in-Chief Naval Home Command, 1994–95; Flag Aide-de-Camp to the Queen, 1994–95; *b* Sri Lanka, 3 Jan. 1936; *s* of late Edwin Henry Frederick and Doris Christian Gordon (*née* Spence); *m* 1966, Elspeth Horsley Fisher; two *s. Educ:* Pangbourne Coll.; RN Coll., Dartmouth. Joined RN, 1954; specialised in aviation, 1958; Fighter Pilot, 1960–72; Air Warfare Instructor, 1964; Commanded: 899 Naval Air Sqn, in HMS Eagle, 1970–71; HMS Lincoln, 1971–72; ndc, 1974–75; Directorate, Naval Air Warfare, MoD, 1975–77; Comdr (Air), HMS Ark Royal, 1977–78; CSO (Air), FONAC, 1979–82; Sen. Naval Officer, SS Atlantic Conveyor, Falklands conflict, 1982 (CBE); Commanded: RNAS Culdrose, 1982–84; HMS Cardiff, 1984–85; Task Gp Comdr, Persian Gulf, 1984; Dep. Dir, Naval Warfare (Air), MoD, 1985–88; Flag Officer Naval Aviation (formerly Air Comd), 1988–90; Dir Gen., Naval Manpower and Trng, 1990–92; Leader of RN Officers Study Gp, MoD, 1992–93; Adm. Pres., RNC, Greenwich, 1993–94. Gentleman Usher to the Sword of State, 1997–2005. Non-exec. Dir, Taunton & Somerset NHS Trust, 1996–2000. Trustee, FAA Mus., 1995–2006 (Life Vice Pres., 2010–). Mem., FAA Officers' Assoc., 1964–; Member Council: White Ensign Assoc., 1996–2006 (Chm., 1996–99); Royal Patriotic Fund, 1995–2010. Governor: Pangbourne Coll., 1995–2014; King's Coll., Taunton, 1997–2005; King's Hall, Taunton, 1997–2005. Chevalier Bretvin, 1984. Freeman, City of London, 1994. *Recreations:*

painting, sailing, music, history, collecting experiences. *Address:* Harwood House, Aller, Somerset TA10 0QN. *Clubs:* Royal Navy of 1765 and 1785; Royal Naval Sailing Association; Royal Navy Golfing Society (Pres., 1988–94).

LAYCRAFT, Hon. James Herbert, OC 2002; Chief Justice of Alberta, 1985–92; *b* 5 Jan. 1924; *s* of George Edward Laycraft and Hattie Cogswell Laycraft; *m* 1948, Helen Elizabeth Bradley; one *s* one *d. Educ:* University of Alberta (BA, LLB 1951). Admitted to Bar, 1952; law practice, 1952–75; Trial Div. Judge, Supreme Court of Alberta, 1975; Judge, Court of Appeal, Alberta, 1979–85. Hon. LLD Calgary, 1986. *Publications:* articles in Canadian Bar Review and Alberta Law Review. *Recreation:* outdoor activities. *Address:* 200 Lincoln Way SW, Apt 419, Calgary, AB T3E 7G7, Canada. *Club:* Ranchman's (Calgary).

LAYDEN, Anthony Michael, CMG 2009; HM Diplomatic Service, retired; *b* 27 July 1946; *s* of Sheriff Michael Layden, SSC, TD and Eileen Mary Layden; *m* 1969, Josephine Mary McGhee; three *s* one *d. Educ:* Holy Cross Academy, Edinburgh; Edinburgh Univ. (LLB Hons Law and Econ. 1968). Lieut, 15th (Scottish Volunteer) Bn, Parachute Regt, 1966–69. Foreign Office, 1968; MECAS, Lebanon, 1969; Jedda, 1971; Rome, 1973; FCO, Middle East, Rhodesia, Personnel Ops Depts, 1977–82; Head of Chancery, Jedda, 1982–85; Hong Kong Dept, FCO, 1985–87; Counsellor and Head of Chancery, Muscat, 1987–91; Counsellor (Economic and Commercial), 1991–95, and Dep. Hd of Mission, 1994–95, Copenhagen; Head of Western European Dept, FCO, 1995–98; Ambassador to Morocco and (non-resident) to Mauritania, 1999–2002; Ambassador to Libya, 2002–06. Special Rep. for Deportation with Assurances, FCO, 2006–13. *Recreations:* sailing, walking, music, bridge. *Club:* Travellers (Chm., 2010–14).

See also P. J. Layden.

LAYDEN, Patrick John, TD 1981; QC (Scot.) 2000; Commissioner, Scottish Law Commission, 2008–14; *b* 27 June 1949; *s* of Sheriff Michael Layden, SSC, TD and Eileen Mary Layden; *m* 1984, Patricia Mary Bonnar; three *s* one *d. Educ:* Holy Cross Acad., Edinburgh; Edinburgh Univ. (LLB Hons). Called to the Scottish Bar, 1973; Lord Advocate's Department: Dep. Scottish Parly Counsel and Asst Legal Sec., 1977–87; Scottish Parly Counsel and Sen. Asst Legal Sec., 1987–99; Legal Sec. to Lord Advocate, 1999–2003; Dep. Solicitor, Office of the Solicitor to the Scottish Exec., later Govt, 2003–08. Univ. of Edinburgh OTC, 1967–71; 2/52 Lowland Vol., TA, 1971–77; 1/51 Highland Vol., 1977–81 (OC London Scottish, 1978–81); OC 73 Ord. Co. (V), 1981–84. *Recreations:* reading, walking.

See also A. M. Layden.

LAYER, Prof. Geoffrey Mark, OBE 2003; DL; Professor and Vice Chancellor, University of Wolverhampton, since 2011; *b* Corbridge, 31 Oct. 1955; *s* of John Layer and Winifred Layer; two *s* one *d. Educ:* Newcastle Royal Grammar Sch.; Soham Grammar Sch.; City of Ely Sixth Form Coll.; Newcastle Poly. (LLB Hons). Sheffield City Polytechnic, later Sheffield Hallam University: Lectr, Sheffield Business Sch., 1983–89; Hd of Access, 1989–99; Prof. of Lifelong Learning, 1996–99; University of Bradford: Dean, 1999–2004; Pro Vice Chancellor, 2004–08; Dep. Vice Chancellor, 2008–11. Dir, Action on Access, 2000–05. DL W Midlands, 2014. *Publications:* (ed) Closing the Equity Gap, 2005; (ed jtly) Widening Participation: which way forward for English higher education, 2005. *Recreations:* playing cricket for Sheffield Collegiate, watching Sunderland Football Club, cinema, friends. *Address:* Vice Chancellor's Office, University of Wolverhampton, Wulfruna Street, Wolverhampton WV1 1LY. *T:* (01902) 322102. *E:* geoff.layer@wlv.ac.uk.

LAYMAN, Rear-Adm. Christopher Hope, CB 1991; DSO 1982; LVO 1977; Commander, British Forces, Falkland Islands, 1986–87; *b* 9 March 1938; *s* of late Captain H. F. H. Layman, DSO, RN and Elizabeth Hughes; *m* 1964, Katharine Romer Ascherson (*d* 2008); one *s* one *d. Educ:* Winchester. Joined Royal Navy, 1956; specialised Communications and Electronic Warfare, 1966; commanded HM Ships: Hubberston, 1968–70; Lynx, 1972–74; Exec. Officer, HM Yacht Britannia, 1976–78; Captain, 7th Frigate Sqn, 1981–83; commanded HM Ships: Argonaut, 1981–82; Cleopatra, 1982–83; Invincible, 1984–86; Asst Dir (Communications and Information Systems), IMS, NATO HQ, Brussels, 1988–91, retd. Consultant in communications and inf. systems and maritime affairs, 1991–2001. Gentleman Usher of the Green Rod, Order of the Thistle, 1997–. *Publications:* Man of Letters, 1990; The Falklands and the Dwarf, 1995; The Wager Disaster, 2015. *Recreations:* fishing, archaeology. *Club:* New (Edinburgh).

LAYTON, family name of **Baron Layton.**

LAYTON, 3rd Baron *cr* 1947, of Danehill; **Geoffrey Michael Layton;** Director: Imperial Aviation Group, 1992–96; Historical Aviation Group, 1992–96; Wellington International Ltd, 1992–96; Historical Aviation Mail Order Ltd, 1996; *b* 18 July 1947; *s* of 2nd Baron Layton and Dorothy Rose (*d* 1994), *d* of Albert Luther Cross; *S* father, 1989; *m* 1st, 1969, Viviane Cracco (marr. diss. 1971); 2nd, 1989, Caroline Jane Soulis (marr. diss. 1999). *Educ:* St Paul's School; Stanford Univ., California; Univ. of Southern California. Partner, Layton Antiques, 1979–96; Director: The Toxbox Co. Ltd, 1986–93; Westminster and Whitehall Environmental Consultants Ltd, 1990–92. PA to Chm., Eurobridge Study Gp, 1983–85. Trustee, Historical Aviation Foundn, 1995–96. *Recreations:* riding, shooting. *Heir: cousin* Jonathan Francis Layton [*b* 16 Feb. 1942; *m* 1971, Julia Goodwin; two *s* one *d*].

See also Hon. C. W. Layton.

LAYTON, Alexander William; QC 1995; barrister; a Recorder, since 2000; a Deputy High Court Judge, since 2007; *b* 23 Feb. 1952; *s* of Paul Henry Layton and Frances Evelyn Layton (*née* Weekes); *m* 1988, Sandy Forshaw (*née* Matheson); two *d. Educ:* Marlborough Coll.; Brasenose Coll., Oxford (MA); Ludwig-Maximilian Univ., Munich. Called to the Bar, Middle Temple, 1976 (Astbury Law Scholar), Bencher, 2004; Asst Recorder, 1998–2000. Chairman: British-German Jurists Assoc., 1988–93; Bar European Gp, 2005–07; Bd of Trustees, Brit. Inst. of Internat. and Comparative Law, 2005–11. Trustee: Allachy Trust, 1979–2008; Rivendell Trust, 1979–2004; Lincoln Clinic and Centre for Psychotherapy, 2003–06; Frensham Heights Sch., 2008–11; Acad. of Eur. Law, 2012–. Mem., Adv. Bd, Bingham Centre for Rule of Law, 2011–; Adv. Council, Inst. of European and Comparative Law, Oxford Univ., 2014–. Vis. Fellow, NYU, 2011. FCIArb 2000. *Publications:* (contrib.) The Bar on Trial, 1977; (jtly) European Civil Practice, 1989, 2nd edn 2004; (contrib.) Practitioners' Handbook of EC Law, 1998; (contrib.) Forum Shopping in the European Judicial Area, 2007; (contrib.) The Brussels I Review Proposal Uncovered, 2012; (contrib.) Extraterritoriality and Collective Redress, 2012; (contrib.) Forum Shopping in the International Arbitration Context, 2013. *Recreation:* family. *Address:* 20 Essex Street, WC2R 3AL. *T:* (020) 7842 1200, *Fax:* (020) 7842 1270. *E:* alayton@20essexst.com.

LAYTON, Hon. Christopher Walter; Trustee (formerly Director), Action for a Global Climate Community, since 2008 (Chairman, 2003–08); *b* 31 Dec. 1929; *s* of 1st Baron Layton, CH, CBE; *m* 1st, 1952, Anneliese Margaret, *d* of Joachim von Thadden, Hanover (marr. diss. 1957); one *s* one *d*; 2nd, 1961, Margaret Ann, *d* of Leslie Moon, Molesey, Surrey (marr. diss. 1995); two *d* (and one *d* decd); 3rd, 1995, Wendy Daniels (*d* 2009), *d* of Kenneth Bartlett, Hemel Hempstead; one *d. Educ:* Oundle; King's Coll., Cambridge. Intelligence Corps, 1948–49; ICI Ltd, 1952; The Economist Intelligence Unit, 1953–54; Editorial writer, European affairs, The Economist, 1954–62; Economic Adviser to Liberal Party, 1962–69; Dir, Centre for European Industrial Studies, Bath Univ., 1968–71; Commission of European Communities: Chef de Cabinet to Commissioner Spinelli, 1971–73; Dir, Computer Electronics, Telecomms and Air Transp. Equipment Manufg, Directorate-Gen. of Internal Market and Industrial Affairs, 1973–81, now Hon. Dir-Gen.; Editor, Alliance, 1982–83, Associate Editor, New Democrat, 1983–85. Dir, World Order Project, Federal Trust, 1987–90; Fellow, Findhorn Foundn, 1987–; Trustee: One World Trust, 1986–2007; Peace Building UK, 2006–11 (Chm., 2006–08); Founder Mem., Grimstone Community, 1990–2007; Jt Founder and Vice Chm., Moor Trees, 1996–2006. Contested: (L) Chippenham, Nov. 1962, 1964, 1966; (SDP) London W, European Parly Elecn, 1984. *Publications:* Transatlantic Investment, 1966; European Advanced Technology, 1968; Cross-frontier Mergers in Europe 1970; (jtly) Industry and Europe, 1971; (jtly) Ten Innovations: International Study on Development Technology and the Use of Qualified Scientists and Engineers in Ten Industries, 1972; Europe and the Global Crisis, 1987; A Step Beyond Fear, 1989; The Healing of Europe, 1990; A Climate Community: a European initiative with the South, 2001, 3rd edn 2006. *Recreations:* painting, sculpture, writing. *Address:* Wrey Cottage, Madge Lane, Tavistock, Devon PL19 0DY.

LAYTON, Matthew Robert; Managing Partner, Clifford Chance LLP, since 2014; *b* Leeds, 27 Feb. 1961; *s* of Prof. D. Layton; *m* 2002, Emma-Marie Brown; two *s* two *d. Educ:* Leeds Grammar Sch.; Univ. of Leeds (LLB). Admitted as Solicitor, 1986. With Clifford Chance LLP, 1983–: Partner, 1991–; Global Hd, Corporate Practice, 2008–14. *Recreations:* theatre, Cornish artists, music. *Address:* Clifford Chance LLP, 10 Upper Bank Street, E14 5JJ. *T:* (020) 7006 1000, *Fax:* (020) 7006 5555. *E:* matthew.layton@cliffordchance.com.

LAYTON, Peter Stephen; Founder and Managing Director: London Glassblowing, since 1976; Peter Layton & Associates Ltd, since 1992; *b* 21 June 1937; *s* of Freddie Layton (*né* Löwe) and Edith Beatrice Layton (*née* Hecht); *m* 1st, 1966, Tessa Schneideman (marr. diss. 1982; she *d* 2001); one *s*; 2nd, 1984, Ann Ashmore; one *s* one *d. Educ:* Belle Vue Grammar Sch. for Boys, Bradford; Bradford Coll. of Art; Central Sch. of Art and Design (Dip.). Various lectureships and professorships including: Univ. of Iowa, Sacramento State Univ., Univ. of Calif, Davis and Art Inst. of Chicago, 1966–68; Stoke on Trent Coll. of Art, Hornsey Coll. of Art, Camberwell Coll. of Art, Croydon Coll. of Art and Sir John Cass Coll. of Art, 1968–78. Chairman: British Artists in Glass, 1983–85; Contemp. Glass Soc., 1997–99 (Hon. Life Mem.); Member: Glass Circle; Glass Assoc.; Glass Art Soc. With Ann Layton, created Emerging Talent Award for British Glass Biennale, 2015. Freeman: City of London; Glass Sellers' Co. Hon. DLitt Bradford, 2003. *Publications:* Glass Art, 1996; Neues Glas, 2003; Peter Layton and Friends, 2006; Past and Present: Peter Layton and London Glassblowing, 2012. *Recreations:* art, travel, beachcombing, theatre, film, food, country living. *Address:* London Glassblowing, 62–66 Bermondsey Street, SE1 3UD. *T:* (020) 7403 2800, *Fax:* (020) 7403 7778. *E:* peter@londonglassblowing.co.uk.

LAYTON, Prof. Robert Hugh, DPhil; FBA 2012; Professor of Anthropology, Durham University, 1991, now Emeritus; *b* Welwyn Garden City, 1 Dec. 1944. *Educ:* University Coll. London (BSc Anthropol. 1966; MPhil (Dist.) 1968); Univ. of Sussex (DPhil 1971). Lectr in Anthropol., UCL, 1970–74; res. consultant in social anthropol., Australian Inst. of Aboriginal and Torres Strait Islander Studies, Canberra, 1974–79; anthropologist resp. for land claims, Northern (Aboriginal) Land Council, Darwin, 1979–81; Reader in Anthropol., Durham Univ., 1982–91. High-End For. Expert, Chinese Nat. Acad. Arts, 2013–. Rivers Medal, RAI, 2003. *Publications:* The Anthropology of Art, 1981, 2nd edn 1991; Uluru: an aboriginal history of Ayers Rock, 1986, re-issued 2001; (ed) Conflict in the Archaeology of Living Traditions, 1989; Australian Rock Art: a new synthesis, 1992; An Introduction to Theory in Anthropology, 1997; (ed with P. Ucko) The Archaeology and Anthropology of Landscape, 1999; (ed jtly) Destruction and Conservation of Cultural Property, 2000; Anthropology and History in Franche Compté: a critique of social theory, 2000; (ed jtly) Hunter-gatherers: an interdisciplinary perspective, 2001; Order and Anarchy: civil society, social disorder and war, 2006; articles in jls. *Address:* c/o Department of Anthropology, Durham University, Dawson Building, South Road, Durham DH1 3LE.

LAYTON, Stephen David, FRCO; conductor; Fellow and Director of Music, Trinity College, Cambridge, since 2006; *b* 23 Dec. 1966; *s* of David Layton and Hazel Layton (*née* Bestwick); *m* 2005, Christine Counsell (*née* Watts). *Educ:* Pilgrim's Sch., Winchester; Eton Coll. (Music Schol.); King's Coll., Cambridge (A. H. Mann Organ Schol.; BA 1988; MA 1991). FRCO 1985. Asst Organist, Southwark Cathedral, 1988–97; Dir of Music, 1997–2006, Organist, 1997–2004, Temple Church, London; Founder and Music Dir, Polyphony, 1986–; Music Dir, Holst Singers, 1993–; Artistic Dir and Principal Conductor, City of London Sinfonia, 2010–. Conductor, BBC Promenade Concerts, 1995–; Chief Guest Conductor, Danish Nat. Choir, 1999–2012; Chief Conductor, Netherlands Kammerchor, 2001–05 (Guest Conductor, 1998–2001); Guest Conductor: Orch. of the Age of Enlightenment, 1999–; ENO, 2000, 2002; Australian Chamber Orch., 2000, 2001; Irish Chamber Orch., 2001, 2008; Britten Sinfonia, 2001–; Acad. of Ancient Music, 2002–; Scottish Chamber Orch., 2002, 2004; English Chamber Orch., 2003, 2004, 2009–; London Sinfonietta, 2004; Odense SO, 2004, 2007, 2010; LPO, 2005; Philadelphia Orch., 2005; Minnesota Orch., 2007; Aalborg SO, 2007, 2011, 2013; Melbourne SO, Qld Orch., 2009; Opera North, 2013; *tours* as conductor include: USA, 1989, 1994, 1996, 2004, 2005, 2007, 2009, 2012; Brazil, 1995, 1998; Estonia, 1993, 1995, 2009; Australia, 2000, 2001, 2009, 2010, 2012, 2014; Poland, 2005, 2006, 2008, 2013; Latvia, 2007, 2013; Korea, 2009; Hong Kong, 2012; New Zealand, 2012, 2014. Recordings incl. premières of Pärt, Tavener, Adès, Macmillan, Jackson, Lukaszewski, Whitacre, Lauridsen, Esenvalds, Tormis, Briggs and Praulins. Hon. Bencher, Middle Temple, 2007. Gramophone Award, 2001, 2012. *Recreations:* food, cyberspace, kite flying, gadgets. *Address:* Trinity College, Cambridge CB2 1TQ. *Club:* Athenaeum.

LAYZELL, Prof. Paul John, PhD; CEng; FBCS; Principal, Royal Holloway, University of London, since 2010; *b* London, 23 July 1957; *s* of Andrew and Celia Layzell; *m* 1982, Pamela Margaret Seymour. *Educ:* Univ. of Manchester (BA Econ. 1978); Univ. of Manchester Inst. of Technol. (MSc Computation 1979; PhD Computation 1982). CEng 1990; FBCS 1990. University of Manchester Institute of Science and Technology: Lectr, 1982–92; Sen. Lectr, 1992–95; Prof. of Computer Sci., 1995–2004; Pro-Vice-Chancellor, 2000–04; Vice-Pres. (Univ. Develt), Univ. of Manchester, 2004–06; Dep. Vice-Chancellor, Univ. of Sussex, 2006–10. Chair: Eduserv, 2008–13; Assessment and Qualifications Alliance, later AQA, 2009–. FHEA 2007. *Publications:* COBOL 85 Reference Summary, 1986; (with P. Loucopoulos) Systems Analysis and Development, 1986; (ed with K. Spurr) CASE on Trial, 1990; (ed with K. Spurr) CASE: current practice, future prospects, 1992; (with C. G. Davies) The Jackson Approach to System Development: an introduction, 1993; (ed jtly) Software Assistance for Business Process Re-Engineering, 1993; (ed jtly) Computer Support for Co-operative Work, 1994; (ed jtly) Business Objects: software solutions, 1994; contribs to learned business, computing and IT jls and articles in conf. proceedings. *Recreations:* walking, gardening, travel. *Address:* Royal Holloway, University of London, Egham, Surrey TW20 0EX. *T:* (01784) 443033. *E:* principal@royalholloway.ac.uk.

LAZARE, Philippe Henri; Chief Executive Officer, since 2007, and Chairman, since 2010, Ingenico Group (Board Member, since 2005); *b* Neuilly-sur-Seine, 30 Oct. 1956; *s* of Robert Lazare and Suzanne (*née* Legallo); *m* 2010, Mrs Nathalie Rouvet; four *s* from previous marriages. *Educ:* Lycée Marcel Roby, Saint-Germain-en-Laye; École Supérieure d'architecture, Paris-la-Défense (Architect Govt Dip.). Industrial buyer, 1983–87; Project Manager for 605 Peugeot, 1987–89; Peugeot Planning Manager, Soc. Gén. d'achats PSA gp, 1989–90; Groupe Sextant Avionique: Industrial sub-contracting Manager, 1990–91; Site Industrial Manager, 1991–93; Site Dir at Châtellerault, 1993–94; Dir, Peat Marwick Consultants, 1994–95; Air France: Dir, Maintenance Result Centre, 1995–96; Man. Dir,

Industries Profit Centre, and Dep. Manager i/c industrial logistics, 1996; Chm. and CEO, Servair Gp and Cie de réparation de moteurs d'avion (CRMA), 1997–98; Man. Dir, Lucien Barrière Gp, 1998–2000; Man. Dir, 2000–01, CEO, 2001–02, Eurotunnel; Dir of Buying, Property and Cost-Reduction, Groupe La Poste, 2003–06; Chm. and CEO, Poste Immo, 2004–07; Dep. Dir, Territorial Develt, Groupe La Poste. *Recreations:* sports: Rugby, show jumping. *Address:* Ingenico Group, 28–32 boulevard de Grenelle, 75015 Paris, France.

LAZAREV, Alexander Nikolaevich; Principal Conductor, Japan Philharmonic Orchestra, since 2008; *b* 5 July 1945; *m* Tamara Lazareva; one *d. Educ:* St Petersburg Conservatory; Moscow Conservatory. Bolshoi Theatre: Founder, Ensemble of Soloists, 1978; Chief Conductor and Artistic Dir, 1987–95; UK début with Royal Liverpool Philharmonic Orch., 1987; Principal Guest Conductor: BBC SO, 1992–95; Royal Scottish Nat. Orch., 1994–97; Principal Conductor, Royal Scottish Nat. Orch., 1997–2005. Hon. Prof., Univ. of Glasgow, 2005–. 1st Prize and Gold Medal, Karajan Comp., Berlin, 1972; People's Artist of Russia, 1982; Glinka Prize, 1986. Commendatore dell'Ordine al Merito della Repubblica Italiana, 2004; Order of Merit for the Fatherland (Russia), 2010. *Address:* c/o Tennant Artists, Unit 2, 39 Tadema Road, SW10 0PZ.

LAZAROWICZ, Marek Jerzy, (Mark); *b* 8 Aug. 1953; *m* 1992, Caroline Elizabeth Johnston; three *s* one *d. Educ:* Univ. of St Andrews (MA); Univ. of Edinburgh (LLB; Dip. Legal Practice). Member (Lab): City of Edinburgh DC, 1980–96; City of Edinburgh Council, 1999–2001. MP (Lab) Edinburgh N and Leith, 2001–15; contested (Lab) same seat, 2015. Special Rep. of the Prime Minister on carbon trading, 2008–10; Shadow Minister for Internat. Develt, 2010–11. Member: Modernisation of H of C Select Cttee, 2005–10; Envmtl Audit Select Cttee, 2007–15. *Publications:* (jtly) The Scottish Parliament: an introduction, 1999, 3rd edn 2003; various articles and papers on legal and political matters.

LAZARUS, Mary Helen; Her Honour Judge Lazarus; a Circuit Judge, since 2015; *b* Bristol, 27 Sept. 1966; *d* of Peter Lazarus and Joanna Brown (*née* Smijth-Windham); *m* 2001, Nicholas Cooper; one *s* two *d. Educ:* Downs Sch., Wraxall; Malvern Girls' Coll.; Marlborough Coll.; Newnham Coll., Cambridge (BA 1988; MA 1992). Called to the Bar, Middle Temple, 1991; in practice as barrister, 1991–2015; Fee-paid Judge of First-tier Tribunal (Health, Educn and Social Care Chamber (Mental Health)), 2002–; a Recorder, 2012–15. *Recreations:* avid reader, keen art lover, occasional singer, knitter, cinema and theatre goer, and frequent efforts to combine delight in nature, keeping fit and having fun with the family, Member of Cloud Appreciation Society. *Address:* Medway County Court and Family Court Hearing Centre, Anchorage House, 47–67 High Street, Chatham, Kent ME4 4DW. *E:* family@medway.countycourt.gsi.gov.uk.

LAZENBY, Prof. Alec, AO 1988; FTSE, FRSB, FAIAST; consultant on agricultural research and development and higher education, 1991–2011; *b* 4 March 1927; *s* of G. and E. Lazenby; *m* 1957, Ann Jennifer, *d* of R. A. Hayward; one *s* two *d. Educ:* Wath on Dearne Grammar Sch.; University Coll. of Wales, Aberystwyth. BSc 1949, MSc 1952, Wales; MA 1954, PhD 1959, ScD 1985, Cantab. Scientific Officer, Welsh Plant Breeding Station, 1949–53; Demonstr in Agricultural Botany, 1953–58, Lectr in Agricultural Botany, 1958–65, Univ. of Cambridge; Fellow and Asst Tutor, Fitzwilliam Coll., Cambridge, 1962–65; Foundation Prof. of Agronomy, Univ. of New England, NSW, 1965–70, now Professor Emeritus; Vice-Chancellor, Univ. of New England, Armidale, NSW, 1970–77; Dir, Grassland Res. Inst., 1977–82; Vice-Chancellor, Univ. of Tasmania, 1982–91. Principal Consultant, Internat. Develt Prog., Aust. Univs, 1985–99. Vis. Prof., Reading Univ., 1978. Hon. Professorial Fellow, Univ. of Wales, 1979; Hon. Prof., Victoria Univ. of Technol., 1992–97. Hon. DRurSci New England, NSW, 1981; Hon. LLD Tasmania, 1992. Centenary Medal, Australia, 2003. *Publications:* (ed jtly) Intensive Pasture Production, 1972; (ed jtly) Australian Field Crops, vol. I, 1975, vol. II, 1979; Australia's Plant Breeding Needs, 1986; (ed jtly) The Grass Crop, 1988; (jtly) The Story of IDP, 1999; (ed jtly) Competition and Succession in Pastures, 2001; papers on: pasture plant breeding; agronomy; weed ecology, in various scientific jls. *Recreations:* golf, gardening, public affairs, reading. *Address:* 16/99 Groom Street, Hughes, ACT 2605, Australia.

LEA OF CRONDALL, Baron *cr* 1999 (Life Peer), of Crondall in the county of Hampshire; **David Edward Lea,** OBE 1978; Assistant General Secretary of the Trades Union Congress, 1977–99; *b* Tyldesley, Lancs, 2 Nov. 1937; *s* of Edward Cunliffe Lea and Lilian May Lea. *Educ:* Farnham Grammar Sch.; Christ's Coll., Cambridge (MA). Pres., CU Liberal Club, 1960; Nat. Pres., Union of Liberal Students, 1961; Inaugural Chair, Cambridge Univ. Students' Representative Council, 1961. Nat. Service, RHA, 1955–57. Economist Intelligence Unit, 1961; Economic Dept, TUC, 1964, Asst Sec., 1967, Sec. 1970. Jt Sec., TUC-Labour Party Liaison Cttee, 1972–86; Secretary: TUC Cttee on European Strategy, 1989–99; Envmt Action Gp, 1989–99; Task Force on Representation at Work, 1994–99; Chm., Econ. Cttee, 1980–91, Mem. Steering Cttee, 1991–99, Vice Pres., 1997–98, ETUC; Member: Royal Commn on the Distribution of Income and Wealth, 1974–79; Adv. Gp on Channel Tunnel and Cross-Channel Services, 1974–75; Cttee of Inquiry on Industrial Democracy, 1975–77; Energy Commn, 1977–79; Retail Prices Index Adv. Cttee, 1977–99; Delors Cttee on Economic and Social Concepts in the Community, 1977–79; NEDC Cttee on Finance for Investment, 1978–92; Kreisky Commn on Unemployment in Europe, 1986–89; Franco-British Council, 1982–99; EU Steering Cttee on Social Dialogue, 1992–99; Central Arbitration Cttee, 2000–; UK Round Table on Sustainable Develt, 1995–99; Chm., Round Table Gp on Greening Business, 1997–98; Expert Adviser, UN Commn on Transnational Corporations, 1977–81; Hon. Mem., UK Delegn, Earth Summit on Envmt and Develt, Rio, 1992. Mem., Sub Cttee A, EU Cttee, 1999–, Sub Cttee C, Foreign Affairs, Defence and Develt, 2003–, H of L; Chairman: All Party Parly Gp on Bolivia, 2005–09; All Party Parly Gp on Madagascar, 2006–; Vice-Chairman: All Party Gp on Africa, 2003–; PLP Gp on Transport, 2003–; Anglo-Swiss Parly Gp, 2003–; Franco-British Parly Gp, 2004–; Vice-Pres., All Party Gp on Arts and Heritage, 2003–; Secretary: All Party Parly Gp on Algeria, 2007–; All Party Gp on Faroe Is, 2010–; Treas., All Party Parly Gps on Serbia and Macedonia, 2003–. Governor, NIESR, 1981–; Trustee, Employment Policy Inst., 1992–99. Chairman: Farnham Roads Action, 1986–; Hammarskjold Inquiry Trust, 2012–14; Mem. Cttee, Tilford Bach Soc., 1995–99; Patron, Third Age Trust, 1991–97. Joined Labour Party, 1963. FRSA 1993. Mem. Editl Bd, New Economy (IPPR review), 1993–2000. *Publications:* Trade Unionism, 1966; (contrib.) The Multinational Enterprise, 1971; (jtly) Industrial Democracy (TUC), 1974; Keynes Plus: a participatory economy (ETUC), 1979; (jtly) Europe and Your Rights at Work, 2006; The Labour Social Democracy Project, 2010. *Address:* South Court, Crondall, Hants GU10 5QF. *T:* (01252) 850711; 17 Ormonde Mansions, 106 Southampton Row, WC1B 4BP. *T:* (020) 7405 6237. *Club:* Bourne (Farnham).

LEA, Jeremy Hugh Chaloner; His Honour Judge Lea; a Circuit Judge, since 2005; Designated Family Judge, Nottingham County Court, since 2013; *b* 29 March 1954; *s* of Henry Hugh Edgar Lea and Teresa Lea (*née* Baker); *m* 1992, Jane Elizabeth Turrill; one *s* one *d. Educ:* John Fisher Sch., Purley; Univ. of Sussex (BA 1976; LLB 1977); Univ. de Strasbourg. Called to the Bar, Middle Temple, 1978; a barrister, Midland Circuit, 1979–2005; a Recorder, 2001–05; Designated Family Judge, Leicester County Court, 2008–12. *Recreations:* coarse ski-ing, real ale, watching cricket. *Address:* c/o Nottingham County Court, 60 Canal Street, Nottingham NG1 7EJ. *T:* (0115) 910 3500.

LEA, Judith Elizabeth; *see* Hackitt, J. E.

LEA, Lyndon; Co-founder and Partner, Lion Capital, since 2004; *b* Morecambe, 13 Jan. 1969; *s* of David and Sylvia Lea; one *s* one *d. Educ:* Univ. of Western Ontario (BA Business Admin 1990). Investment banker: Goldman Sachs, 1990–92; Schroders, 1992–94; Glenisla, 1994–98; Partner, Hicks Muse Tate & Furst, 1998–2004. Mem. Bd, Not For Sale charity. *Recreations:* polo, jiujitsu, family time. *Club:* Guards Polo.

LEA, Ruth Jane, CBE 2015; Economic Adviser, Arbuthnot Banking Group, since 2007 (non-executive Director, since 2005); *b* 22 Sept. 1947; *d* of Thomas Lea and late Jane (*née* Brown). *Educ:* Lymm Grammar Sch.; York Univ. (BA); Bristol Univ. (MSc). Asst Statistician, later Sen. Economic Assistant, HM Treasury, 1970–73; Lectr in Econs, Thames Poly., 1973–74; Statistician: CS Coll., 1974–77; HM Treasury, 1977–78; CSO, 1978–84; Statistician, 1984–87, Dep. Dir, Invest in Britain Bureau, 1987–88, DTI; Sen. Economist, 1988–90, Chief Economist, 1990–93, Mitsubishi Bank; Chief UK Economist, Lehman Bros, 1993–94; Econs Ed., ITN, 1994–95; Hd of Policy Unit, Inst. of Dirs, 1995–2003; Director: Centre for Policy Studies, 2004–07; Global Vision, 2007–10. Member: Retail Prices Adv. Cttee, 1992–94; NCC, 1993–96; Nurses' Pay Rev. Body, 1994–98; Bd, ESRC Res. Priorities (formerly ESRC Res. Centres), 1996–97. ONS Stats Adv. Cttee, 1996–97. Member Council: REconS, 1995–2000; Univ. of London, 2001–06. Gov., LSE, 2003–08. Freeman, City of London, 2014; Freeman: Curriers' Co., 2014; World Traders' Co., 2014. Hon. DBA: Greenwich, 1997; BPP Univ. Coll., 2010. *Publications:* numerous research papers and articles on economic issues. *Recreations:* music, natural history and countryside, heritage, philately. *Address:* 25 Redbourne Avenue, N3 2BP. *T:* (020) 8346 3482. *Club:* Reform.

LEA, Sir Thomas (William), 5th Bt *cr* 1892, of The Larches, Kidderminster and Sea Grove, Dawlish; *b* 6 Sept. 1973; *s* of Sir Julian Lea, 4th Bt and of Gerry Valerie, *d* of late Captain Gibson C. Fahnestock; *S* father, 1990. *Educ:* Uppingham Sch. *Heir: b* Alexander Julian Lea, *b* 28 Oct. 1978.

LEACH, family name of **Baron Leach of Fairford**.

LEACH OF FAIRFORD, Baron *cr* 2006 (Life Peer), of Fairford in the County of Gloucestershire; **(Charles Guy) Rodney Leach,** MA; Director, Jardine Matheson Holdings Ltd, since 1984; Deputy Chairman, Jardine Lloyd Thompson Group plc, since 1997; *b* 1 June 1934; *s* of late Charles Harold Leach and Nora Eunice Ashworth; *m* 1st, 1963, Felicity Ballantyne (marr. diss. 1989); two *s* three *d*; 2nd, 1993, Mrs Jessica Violet Douglas-Home, *qv. Educ:* Harrow; Balliol Coll., Oxford (MA 1st Cl. Hon. Mods, 1st Cl. Lit. Hum.). DSc. N. M. Rothschild & Sons, 1963–76: Partner, 1968; Dir, 1970; Director: Trade Development Bank, 1976–83; Matheson & Co., 1983–; Hongkong Land, 1985–; Dairy Farm, 1987–; Mandarin Oriental, 1987–; Robert Fleming Hldgs Ltd, 1999–2000; Paris Orléans (formerly Rothschild Continuation AG), 2006–. Chairman: Business for Sterling, 1999–; Open Europe, 2005–. Mem. Bd, British Library, 1996–2004. *Publications:* Europe: a concise encyclopedia of the European Union, 1998, 4th edn 2004. *Recreations:* the humanities, sport, bridge. *Address:* 3 Lombard Street, EC3V 9AQ. *T:* (020) 7816 8100; House of Lords, SW1A 0PW. *Clubs:* White's, Portland.

LEACH OF FAIRFORD, Lady; *see* Douglas-Home, J. V.

LEACH, Allan William, FCLIP; Director-General and Librarian, National Library for the Blind, 1982–95; *b* 9 May 1931; *yr s* of Frank Leach, MBE and Margaret Ann Bennett; *m* 1962, Betty (*d* 2004), *e d* of William George Gadsby and Doris Cree; one *s* one *d. Educ:* Watford Grammar Sch.; Loughborough Coll. BA Open; DPA London. Various posts with Hertfordshire County Library, 1948–59; Librarian, RAF Sch. of Educn, 1949–51; Regional Librarian, Warwickshire County Libr., 1959–65; County Librarian, Bute County Libr., 1965–71; Librarian and Curator, Ayr Burgh, 1971–74; Dir of Library Services, Kyle and Carrick District, 1974–82. Vice-Chm., UK Assoc. of Braille Producers, 1994–96 (Chm., 1991–94); Member: Standing Cttee, Section of Libraries for the Blind, IFLA, 1983–95 (Chm., 1985–87; Ed., Newsletter, 1985–92); Nat. Steering Cttee, Share the Vision, 1992–95. Chm., Ulverscroft Foundn, 1999–2010 (Trustee, 1993–2013). Editor: Rickmansworth Historian, 1961–66; Ayrshire Collections, 1973–82. *Publications:* Begin Here, 1966; Rothesay Tramways, a brief history, 1969; Round old Ayr (with R. Brash and G. S. Copeland), 1972; Libraries in Ayr, 1975; Looking Ahead, 1987; articles on libraries, local history, literature, braille and educn. *Recreations:* music, painting, the countryside, people, books, University of the Third Age (U3A). *Address:* 4 Windsor Road, Hazel Grove, Stockport, Cheshire SK7 4SW. *T:* (0161) 285 1287.

LEACH, Clive William, CBE 2000; Chairman: YFM (formerly Yorkshire Enterprise) Group Ltd, 1995–2008; Universe Media Group Ltd (formerly Gabriel Communications Ltd), since 1997; Durham County Cricket Club (Holdings) Ltd, since 2004; *b* 4 Dec. 1934; *s* of Stanley and Laura Leach; *m* 1st, 1958, Audrey (*née* Parker) (*d* 1978); three *s*; 2nd, 1980, Stephanie (*née* McGinn); one *s. Educ:* Sir John Leman Grammar Sch., Beccles, Suffolk. Professional cricketer, Warwickshire CCC, 1955–58. Gen. Sales Manager, Tyne Tees Television, 1968–74; Sales Dir, 1974–79, Dir of Sales and Marketing, 1979–82, Trident Television; Man. Dir, Link Television, 1982–85; Dir of Sales and Marketing, 1985–88, Man. Dir, 1988–93, Yorkshire Television; Man. Dir, 1985–88, Chm., 1988–93, Yorkshire Television Enterprises. Chairman: Yorkshire Television Internat., 1988–93; Yorkshire-Tyne Tees Television Holdings, 1993 (Gp Chief Exec., 1992–93); Dir, ITN, 1988–93. Chairman: Yorkshire Fund Managers Ltd, 1996–2008; Serene Pavilions (Sri Lanka) Ltd; Dir, British Small Cos Venture Capital Trust plc, 1996–2004. Dep. Chm., Regl Chamber, subseq. Regl Assembly, for Yorks and Humber, 2001–05. Chairman: Leeds TEC, 1991–2000; Leeds HA, 1996–2000; W Yorks Learning and Skills Council, 2000–09; Yorks Cultural Consortium, 2001–; Dir, Opera North Ltd, 1992–2003. FRSA; MCIM 1994. *Recreations:* golf, cricket, travel. *Address:* The White House, Barkston Ash, Tadcaster, N Yorks LS24 9TT. *Clubs:* Reform, MCC; Alwoodley Golf.

LEACH, Jennifer Irene, CBE 2006; Chief Guide, Girlguiding UK (Guide Association), 2001–06 (Vice President, since 2008); Chief Commissioner, Commonwealth Girl Guides Associations, 2001–06; *b* 11 Oct. 1944; *d* of Arthur and Beatrice Garner; *m* 1966, Arthur John Leach; one *s* one *d.* Guide Association: Unit Guider, 1974–87; Dist Comr, 1980–86; Co. Comr, W Yorks, 1987–92; Chief Comr, NE England, 1994–99 (Vice Pres., 2000). FRSA 2002. *Recreations:* four grandsons, cooking, France. *Address:* Laithe Croft, Rastrick, Brighouse, W Yorks HD6 3HL. *T:* (01484) 714950.

LEACH, Katherine Jane; HM Diplomatic Service; Ambassador to Armenia, 2014–15 (Joint Ambassador, 2012–14); *m* Jonathan James Aves, *qv*; three *c.* Joined FCO, 2000; Desk Officer, EU Trade and Develt Policy, FCO, 2000–01; Hd, External Pol Section, 2002–03, First Sec. (Internal Pol), 2003–04, Moscow; Dep. Hd, Passports and Documentary Services, Consular Directorate, FCO, 2005; Japanese lang. trng, FCO, 2005–07; Hd, Energy and Envmt Team, Tokyo, 2007–11. *Address:* c/o Foreign and Commonwealth Office, King Charles Street, SW1A 2AH.

LEACH, Penelope, PhD; psychologist and writer on childcare; *b* 19 Nov. 1937; 2nd *d* of late Nigel Marlin Balchin and Elisabeth Balchin; *m* 1963, Gerald Leach (*d* 2004); one *s* one *d. Educ:* Newnham Coll., Cambridge (BA Hons 1959); LSE (Dip. in Soc. Sci. Admin 1960; MA Psychol. 1962; PhD Psychol. 1964). Home Office, 1960–61; Lectr in Psychol., LSE, 1965–67; Res. Officer and Res. Fellow, MRC, 1967–76; Ext Med. Ed., Penguin Books, 1970–78; Founder and Dir, Lifetime Productions (childcare videos), 1985–87; Res. Consultant, Internat. Centre for Child Studies, 1984–90. Dir, Families, Children and Child Care Project,

1997–2005, and Hon. Sen. Res. Fellow, 1997–2002, Royal Free and UCL Med. Sch., Univ. of London. Hon. Senior Research Fellow: Tavistock Centre, 2000–; Inst. for the Study of Children, Families and Social Issues, Birkbeck Coll., Univ. of London, 2002–; Hon. Prof., Dept of Educn, Univ. of Winchester, 2014–. Member: Voluntary Licensing Authy on IVF, 1985–89; Commn on Social Justice, 1993–95; Commn on Children and Violence, 1993–95; Mental Health Rev., Social Justice Commn, 2010–. Founder and Parent-Educn Co-ordinator, End Physical Punishment for Children, 1989–; Chm., Child Develt Soc., 1993–95 (Pres., 1992–93); Advr, Assoc. for Infant Mental Health, 2000– (Mem., Founding Cttee, 2005–); non-exec. Dir, Mindful Policy Gp, 2010–. Pres., Nat. Child Minders' Assoc., 1999–; Vice-President: Pre-School Playgroups Assoc., 1977; Health Visitors Assoc., 1982–99. Mem. Adv. Council, Amer. Inst. for Child, Adolescent and Family Studies, 1993–. Mem., professional socs and assocs; FBPsS 1988; Hon. Fellow, Dept of Mental Health, Bristol Univ., 1988. Hon. DEd Kingston, 1996. *Publications:* Babyhood, 1974; Baby and Child, 1977, 2nd edn 1989; Who Cares?, 1979; The Parents' A–Z, 1984; The First Six Months, 1987; The Babypack, 1990; Children First, 1994; Your Baby and Child, 1997, 4th edn 2010; Child Care: what we know and what we need to know, 2009; The Essential First Year, 2010; Family Breakdown: helping children hang on to both their parents, 2014. *Recreations:* cooking, family and friends, gardening, travel. *Address:* 2 Bull Lane, Lewes, E Sussex BN7 1UA. *T:* (01273) 474702.

LEACH, Philippa Mary; *see* McAtasney, P. M.

LEACH, Dr Renny Philip; Chief Executive, South West Academic Health Science Network, since 2013; *b* Brighton, 9 April 1956; *s* of Robert and Marie-Hélène Leach; *m* 1975, Karin Eneberg; one *s* one *d* (and one *d* decd). *Educ:* Univ. of Sussex (BSc Hons Biochem. 1982; DPhil 1986). Sen. Scientist, MRC, 1989–90; Dir of Res., Action Res., 1990–94; Dir, R&D, Gt Ormond St Hosp. and Inst. of Child Health, 1994–98; Chief Executive: Intercern, 1998–2003; iResearch, 2003–09. Mem., Clin. Medicine Sub-Panel, REF 2014, 2012–. Sen. Ind. Dir, Queen Victoria Hosp. NHS Foundn Trust, 2008–13. Hon. Med. Dir, Sparks, 2007–13. Chm., Snowden Trust, 2010–. *Recreations:* cycling, family. *Address:* South West Academic Health Science Network, Innovation Centre, Exeter University, Rennes Drive, Exeter, Devon EX4 4RN. *E:* renny.leach@swahsn.com. *Club:* Royal Society of Medicine.

LEACH, Stephen James, CB 2007; Director of Criminal Justice, Northern Ireland Office, and Chairman, Criminal Justice Board, 2000–09; Commissioner, Criminal Cases Review Commission, since 2014; *b* 12 Feb. 1951; *s* of late Edward Stephen Leach and Mollie Leach (*née* O'Hara); *m* 1982, Jane Williams; one *s* two *d*. *Educ:* De La Salle Coll., Jersey; Peterhouse, Cambridge (1st cl. Hons English Tripos). NI Office, 1975–84; Dept of Energy, 1984–87; Prin. Private Sec. to Sec. of State for NI, 1988–90; Humphrey Fulbright Fellow, Univ. of Minnesota, 1990–91; Northern Ireland Office: responsibilities in policing, security and personnel policy and political development, 1991–96; Associate Political Dir, then Associate Policing and Security Dir, 1996–2000. Lay Mem., Nat. Security Certificate Appeals Tribunal, 2012–. A Parole Comr for NI, 2009–. Non-exec. Dir, Health and Social Care Bd, NI, 2009–. *Recreations:* reading, tennis, watching Rugby.

LEADBEATER, Charles Richard; independent writer, since 1996; *b* Preston, Lancs, 9 Jan. 1959; *s* of William Leadbeater and Olive Leadbeater; *m* 1997, Geraldine Claire Bedell; two *s*, and one step *s* one step *d*. *Educ:* Vyne Comp. Sch., Basingstoke; Queen Mary's Sixth Form Coll., Basingstoke; Balliol Coll., Oxford (BA PPE 1st Cl. 1981). Researcher, Weekend World, LWT, 1983–85; Financial Times: journalist, 1985–89; Labour Ed., 1989–91; Industrial Ed., 1991–92; Tokyo Bureau Chief, 1992; Asst Ed., 1992–95; Asst Ed., Independent, 1995–96. Co-Founder, Participle, 2007. Associate, Demos, 1996; Mem., Policy Adv. Council, IPPR, 2010. Trustee: Apps for Good, 2010; Nominet Trust, 2011. Mem., Tate. *Publications:* In Search of Work (with John Lloyd), 1987; The Rise of the Social Entrepreneur, 1997; Living on Thin Air, 1998; The Independents, 1998; Up the Down Escalator, 2000; The Pro-Am Revolution, 2004; We-Think, 2008; Innovation in Education, 2012; The Frugal Innovator: creating change on a shoestring budget, 2014. *Recreations:* reading, cooking, walking. *W:* www.charlesleadbeater.net.

LEADBETTER, Alan James, CBE 1994; DSc; Directeur Adjoint, Institut Laue Langevin, Grenoble, France, 1994–99; *b* 28 March 1934; *s* of Robert and Edna Leadbetter; *m* 1957, Jean Brenda Williams; one *s* one *d*. *Educ:* Liverpool Univ. (BSc 1954; PhD 1957); Bristol Univ. (DSc 1971). CPhys 1972; FInstP 1972; CChem 1980; FRSC 1980. Fellow, NRCC, 1957–59; Res. Asst, Lectr and Reader, Univ. of Bristol, 1959–74; Prof. of Phys. Chem., Univ. of Exeter, 1975–82; Associate Dir, Science, Rutherford Appleton Lab., SERC, 1982–88; Dir, Daresbury Lab., SERC, 1988–94. Chairman: Internat. Scientific Adv. Bd, Vestale project, French Atomic Energy Commn, 2002–06; Evaluation Panels for EC Sixth Framework Programme: Res. Infrastructures action, 2002–06; Marie-Curie actions, 2004–07, 2011–12; Member: Divl Review Cttee, Los Alamos Nat. Lab., 1999–2003; Technical Adv. Cttee, Australian Nuclear Sci. and Technol. Orgn, 2000–06. Hon. Professor: Univ. of Manchester, 1989–94; Univ. of Hull, 1992–2005; Vis. Prof., De Montfort Univ., 1994–2001; Hon. Vis. Prof., Univ. of Exeter, 2002–05. Hon. DSc De Montfort, 2000. *Publications:* 150 papers in various scientific jls, 1959–88. *Recreations:* gardening, cooking. *Address:* 23 Hillcrest Park, Exeter EX4 4SH.

LEADER-WILLIAMS, Prof. Nigel, PhD, ScD; Director, Conservation Leadership, University of Cambridge, since 2009; Fellow, Churchill College, Cambridge, since 2009; *b* Hatton, Ceylon, 24 Nov. 1949; *s* of Geoffrey and Honor Leader-Williams (*née* Tindall); *m* 1982, Alison Mary Rosser; two *s*. *Educ:* Blundell's Sch., Tiverton; Liverpool Univ. (BVSc; MRCVS 1972); Corpus Christi Coll., Cambridge (PhD 1981; ScD 2011). Practising veterinary surgeon, 1972; research: S Georgia with British Antarctic Survey, Cambridge, 1973–80; Zambia, with Dept of Zool., Univ. of Cambridge, 1980–90; Chief Tech. Advr to Dept of Wildlife, Tanzania, 1991–95; University of Kent: Prof. of Biodiversity Mgt, 1995–2009 (Hon. Prof., 2010–); Dir, Durrell Inst. of Conservation and Ecol., 1999–2009. Leverhulme Res. Fellow, 1987; Research Fellow: Wildlife Conservation Soc., NY, 1993–95; Inst. of Zool., London, 1995 (Hon. Res. Fellow, 1996–99); Prog. Fellow, Envmtl Planning Gp, Internat. Inst. for Envmt and Develt, London, 1996–99. Mem., Organising Cttee, Student Conf. on Conservation Sci., 1999–. Member: Council, Fauna and Flora Internat., 1998–2006 and 2008– (Vice-Chm., 2012–); Council, Zool Soc. of London, 2001–04. Sec., Durrell Trust for Conservation Biol., 2001–09; Mem., Bd of Trustees, Zeitz Trust (formerly Resource Africa), 2001–. Mem., Darwin Expert Cttee (formerly Darwin Adv. Cttee), 2006–12. Mem. Council, Churchill Coll., Cambridge, 2012–. *Publications:* Reindeer on South Georgia: the ecology of an introduced population, 1988; The World Trade in Rhino Horn: a review, 1992; (ed jtly) The Live Bird Trade in Tanzania, 1996; (ed jtly) Tourist Hunting in Tanzania, 1996; (ed jtly) Community-based Conservation in Tanzania, 1996; (ed jtly) Mining in Protected Areas in Tanzania, 1996; (jtly) Take Only Photographs, Leave Only Footprints: the environmental impacts of wildlife tourism, 1997; (ed jtly) Wildlife and People: conflict and conservation in Masai Mara, Kenya, 2003; (ed jtly) Trade-offs in Conservation: deciding what to save, 2010; contrib. book chapters and papers to learned jls, incl. Nature and Science. *Recreations:* snow and mountains, sights, smells and sounds of Africa, young minds, Liverpool FC. *Address:* Department of Geography, University of Cambridge, Downing Place, Cambridge CB2 3EN. *T:* (01223) 333397, *Fax:* (01223) 333392. *E:* nigel.leader-williams@geog.cam.ac.uk.

LEADLAY, Prof. Peter Francis, DPhil, PhD; FRS 2000; FRSC; Herchel Smith Professor of Biochemistry, University of Cambridge, since 2006; Fellow of Clare College, Cambridge, since 1979; Co-Founder and Director, BIOTICA Technology Ltd, 1996–2013; *b* 13 Dec. 1949; *s* of late Kenneth Rupert Simpson Leadlay, RN and Ellen Theresa Leadlay (*née* Coleman); *m* 1974, Christina Maria Peake; three *d*. *Educ:* St Joseph's Coll., London; New Coll., Oxford (Gibbs Schol.; BA 1971); Corpus Christi Coll., Oxford (Sen. Schol.; DPhil 1974; MA 1974); Clare Coll., Cambridge (PhD 1979). FRSC 2006. Royal Soc. European Res. Fellow, ETH, Zürich, 1974–76; Demonstr, Dept of Biochemistry, and Jun. Res. Fellow, Wolfson Coll., Univ. of Oxford, 1976–79; University of Cambridge: Demonstr in Biochemistry, 1979–84; Lectr, 1984–95; Reader, 1995–99; Prof. of Molecular Enzymology, 1999–2006; Sen. Res. Fellow, BBSRC, 1999–2004. Blaise Pascal Res. Prof., Institut Pasteur, Paris, 2002–03; Smets Prof., Univs of Leuven and Louvain-la-Neuve, 2009; Hon. Prof., Univ. of Wuhan, 2011. Remsen Award, Amer. Chem. Soc., 2007; Humboldt Res. Prize, Alexander von Humboldt Foundn, 2011; Inhoffen Medal, Helmholtz Centre for Infection Res. and Tech. Univ. Braunschweig, 2012; Wolfson Merit Award, Royal Soc., 2014. *Publications:* Enzyme Chemistry, 1969; articles in scientific jls, particularly on enzymes and antibiotic biosynthesis. *Recreations:* reading, walking, sailing, identifying plants. *Address:* Department of Biochemistry, University of Cambridge, 80 Tennis Court Road, Cambridge CB2 1GA. *T:* (01223) 766041.

LEADSOM, Andrea Jacqueline; MP (C) South Northamptonshire, since 2010; Minister of State, Department of Energy and Climate Change, since 2015; *b* Aylesbury, 13 May 1963; *d* of Richard Salmon and Judy Crompton (*née* Kitchin); *m* 1993, Ben Leadsom; two *s* one *d*. *Educ:* Tonbridge Girls' Grammar Sch.; Warwick Univ. (BA Hons). Fixed Interest and Treasury, BZW, 1987–91; Financial Instns Dir, Barclays Bank, 1993–97; Man. Dir, DPFM Ltd, 1997–99; Sen. Investment Officer, Invesco Perpetual, 1999–2009. Mem. (C) S Oxfordshire DC, 2003–07. Econ. Sec., HM Treasury, 2014–15. Contested (C) Knowsley S, 2005. *Address:* House of Commons, SW1A 0AA. *T:* (020) 7219 7149. *E:* andrea.leadsom.mp@parliament.uk.

LEAFE, Richard Neil, FRGS; Chief Executive, Lake District National Park Authority, since 2007; *b* Nottingham, 26 Jan. 1965; *s* of Leonard and Kathleen Leafe. *Educ:* Fernwood Comprehensive Sch., Nottingham; Bilborough Coll., Nottingham; Univ. of Sheffield (BSc Hons Geog. 1987; MPhil 1990). FRGS 1991. Res. asst, Dept of Geog., Univ. of Sheffield, 1987–90; tour leader, Explore Worldwide, 1990; coastal geomorphologist, NCC/English Nature, 1990–94; English Nature: Hd, Coastal Initiative and coastal geomorphologist, Maritime Team, 1994–96; Eur. and Internat. Relns Manager, 1996–99; Team Manager, Ext. Relns Team, 1999–2003; Gen. Manager and Regl Dir, E Midlands, 2003–06; Dir, NW Reg., Natural England, 2006–07. Winston Churchill Meml Trust Travelling Fellow, 1992. Member: Res. Tech. Adv. Gp on policy issues, Flood and Coastal Defence Div., DEFRA, 2000–03; Panel, Making Space for Nature rev. of England's wildlife sites, 2009–10; Bd, Envmt Agency, 2012–. Chair, Scientific Council, Eur. Centre for Nature Conservation, Netherlands, 2000–05. Mem., NW Regl Cttee, RGS, 2011–. *Publications:* contrib. papers on marine and coastal mgt. *Recreations:* ski-ing, ski mountaineering, fell walking and running, cycling, wild swimming, climbing, performing arts and film. *Address:* Lake District National Park Authority, Murley Moss, Oxenholme Road, Kendal LA9 7RL.

LEAFE, Susannah Mary; Director, Reform, since 2013; *b* King's Lynn, 28 Dec. 1971; *d* of David Henderson Cowie and Alison Margaret Graham Cowie; *m* 1997, Daniel John Leafe. *Educ:* Wimbledon High Sch.; Univ. of Bristol (BSc Geog.); Univ. of Nottingham (PGCE). Hd of Geography, Clifton High Sch., 1997–2008; Women's Worker, Fowey Parish Church, 2008–13. Family Life and Marriage Educn Co-ord., Dio. of Truro, 2008–09. *Recreations:* tennis, sailing. *Address:* 6 Troy Court, Daglands Road, Fowey PL23 1JX. *E:* ds.leafe@gmail.com.

LEAHY, Helen Blodwen R.; *see* Rees Leahy.

LEAHY, Sir John (Henry Gladstone), KCMG 1981 (CMG 1973); HM Diplomatic Service, retired; *b* 7 Feb. 1928; *s* of late William Henry Gladstone and late Ethel Leahy; *m* 1954, Elizabeth Anne, *d* of late J. H. Pitchford, CBE; two *s* two *d*. *Educ:* Tonbridge Sch.; Clare Coll., Cambridge; Yale University. RAF, 1950–52; FO, 1952–54 (Asst Private Sec. to Minister of State, 1953–54); 3rd, later 2nd Sec., Singapore, 1955–57; FO, 1957–58; 2nd, later 1st Sec., Paris, 1958–62; FO, 1962–65; Head of Chancery, Tehran, 1965–68; Counsellor, FCO, 1969; Head of Personnel Services Dept, 1969–70; Head of News Dept, FCO, 1971–73; Counsellor and Head of Chancery, Paris, 1973–75; seconded as Under Sec., NI Office, 1975–76; Asst Under-Sec. of State, FCO, 1977–79; Ambassador to South Africa, 1979–82; Dep. Under-Sec. of State, FCO, 1982–84; High Comr, Australia, 1984–88. Chm., Lonrho, 1994–97 (Dir, 1993–98; Vice-Chm., 1994); Dir, The Observer, 1989–93. Chm., Urban Foundn (London), 1991–94 (Exec. Dir, 1989–91). Pro-Chancellor, City Univ., 1991–97. Chm., British-Australia Soc., 1994–97. Mem., Franco-British Council (Chm., 1989–93). Master, Skinners' Co., 1993–94. Hon. DCL City, 1997. Officier, Légion d'Honneur (France), 1996. *Publications:* A Life of Spice, 2006. *Address:* 16 Ripley Chase, The Goffs, Eastbourne, East Sussex BN21 1HB. *T:* (01323) 725368.

LEAHY, Michael James, OBE 2004; General Secretary, Community (formerly Iron and Steel Trades Confederation), 1999–2014; *b* 7 Jan. 1949; *s* of Michael James Cyril Leahy, ISM, and Iris Jarrett Leahy; *m* 1974, Irene Powell; two *s*. *Educ:* Twmpath Secondary Modern Sch., Pontypool. Chargehand, Cold Rolling Dept, Panteg Works, Richard Thompson & Baldwins Ltd, 1965–77; Iron and Steel Trades Confederation, later Community: Mem., 1965–; Organiser, 1977–86; Sen. Organiser, 1986–92; Asst Gen. Sec. Elect, 1992–93; Asst Gen. Sec., 1993–98; Gen. Sec. Elect, 1998–99. Various posts, British Steel/Corus Gp plc, 1995– (Employees' Sec., Eur. Works Council, 1998–). Chm., Communitas (formerly Steel Partnership Trng Ltd, later Knowledge Skills Partnership), 2000–; Member Board: Unions Today Ltd, 1999–2002; UK Steel Enterprise Ltd, 2003–. Mem., 1992–, Chm., 1998–, Steel Co-ordinating Cttee, Nat. Trades Union; Mem. Exec. Council, CSEU, 1994–99; Mem., 1995–2002, Mem., Sub-cttee for Mkts and Forward Studies, 1995–2002, Consultative Cttee, ECSC; General Federation of Trade Unions: Mem., Exec. Council, 1996–2003; Mem., Educnl Trust, 1996–2003 (Trustee, 1999–); Vice Pres., 1999–2001; Pres., 2001–03; Trades Union Congress: Mem. Gen. Council, 1999–; Mem., Exec. Cttee, 2000–; Pres., 2010–11; Mem., Consultative Commn on Industrial Change, Eur. Econ. and Social Cttee, 2002–. Hon. Sec., British Section, 1999–, Pres., Iron, Steel and Non-Ferrous Metals Dept, 1999–, Internat. Metalworkers Fedn; European Metalworkers' Federation: Member: Exec. Cttee, 1999– (Steering Gp, 2003–); Industrial Policy Cttee, 1999–; Steel Cttee, 1999–. Mem., Central Arbitration Cttee, 2002–. Labour Party: Mem., 1966–; Member: NEC, 1996; Nat. Policy Forum, 1996–99; Auditor, 2002–13. Chairman: Bevan Foundn, 2000–02 (Mem., Bd of Dirs, 2002–; Chm. Trustees, 2002–; Hon. Vice-Pres., 2009); TUFI, 2014–. Pres., Welsh Trust for Prevention of Abuse, 2005–. FRSA. *Recreations:* golf, Rugby.

LEAHY, Sir Terence Patrick, (Sir Terry), Kt 2002; Chief Executive, Tesco plc, 1997–2011; *s* of Terence and Elizabeth Leahy; *m* Alison; two *s* one *d*. *Educ:* St Edward's Coll., Liverpool; UMIST (BSc Hons Mgt Scis). Joined Tesco, 1979, as Mktg Exec.; Marketing Dir, 1984–86; Dir, 1992–2011; Dep. Man. Dir, 1995–97. Sen. Advr, Clayton Dubilier & Rice LLP, 2011–; Chm., B&M Retail (formerly Bargains), 2012–; Dir, Motor Fuel Gp, 2015–. *Publications:* Management in 10 Words, 2012. *Recreations:* sport, reading, theatre, architecture.

LEAKE, Prof. Bernard Elgey, PhD, DSc, FRSE, FGS; Hon. Research Fellow, School of Earth and Ocean Sciences (formerly School of Earth, then Earth, Ocean and Planetary Sciences), Cardiff University, since 1998; Leverhulme Emeritus Fellow, 2000–02; Professor of Geology, Department of Geology and Applied Geology (formerly Department of Geology), and Keeper of Geological Collections in Hunterian Museum, University of Glasgow, 1974–97, now Professor Emeritus (Head, Department of Geology and Applied Geology (formerly Department of Geology), 1974–92); *b* 29 July 1932; *s* of late Norman Sidney Leake and Clare Evelyn (*née* Walgate); *m* 1955, Gillian Dorothy Dobinson; five *s*. *Educ:* Wirral Grammar Sch., Bebington, Cheshire; Liverpool Univ. (1st Cl. Hons BSc, PhD); Bristol Univ. (DSc 1974); Glasgow Univ. (DSc 1998). Leverhulme post-doctoral Res. Fellow, Liverpool Univ., 1955–57; Asst Lectr, subseq. Lectr in Geology, Bristol Univ., 1957–68, Reader in Geol., 1968–74. Res. Associate, Berkeley, Calif, 1966; Gledden Sen. Vis. Fellow, Univ. of W Australia, 1986; Erskine Vis. Res. Fellow, Univ. of Canterbury, NZ, 1999. Chm., Cttee on amphibole nomenclature, Internat. Mineral Assoc., 1982–2006 (Sec., 1968–79); Member: NERC, 1978–84 (Chm., Vis. Gp to Brit. Geol Survey, formerly Inst. of Geological Sciences, 1982–84; Chm., Isotope Facilities Prog. Cttee, 1981–85, 1987–91); Council, Mineral Soc., 1965–68, 1978–80, 1996–99 (Vice-Pres., 1979–80, 1996–97; Pres., 1998–99; Managing Trustee, 1997–98, 2000–04; Hon. Life Mem., 2004); Council, Geol Soc., 1979–85, 1989–96, 2002–05 (Vice-Pres., 1980; Treasurer, 1981–85, 1989–96; Pres., 1986–88; Lyell Medal, 1977); Council, RSE, 1988–90; publication cttees, Mineral Soc., 1970–85, Geol Soc., 1970–85, and 1986–96; Geol Soc. Publication Bd, 1987–2005 (Chm., 1987–96); Geologists' Association: (Treas., 1997–2009; Hon. Life Mem., 2009; Foulerton Award, 2010). Mem. Ct, Cardiff Univ., 2001–14. FRSE 1978. Hon. Life Mem., Liverpool Geol Soc., 2007. Sodic amphibole mineral, leakeite, named by Internat. Mineral Assoc., 1992. Editor: Mineralogical Magazine, 1970–83; Jl of Geol Soc., 1973 and 1974. *Publications:* A Catalogue of analysed calciferous and sub-calciferous amphiboles, 1968; The Geology of South Mayo, 1989; The Geology of the Dalradian and associated rocks of Connemara, W Ireland, 1994; The Life of Frank Coles Phillips (1902–82) and the Structural Geology of the Moine Petrofabric Controversy, 2002; The Life and Work of Professor J. W. Gregory FRS (1864–1932): geologist, writer and explorer, 2011; over 160 papers in geol, mineral and geochem. jls on geol. of Connemara, study of amphiboles, X-ray fluorescence anal. of rocks and use of geochem. in identifying origins of highly metamorphosed rocks; geological maps: Connemara, 1982; South Mayo, 1985; Slyne Head, 1985; Errismore, 1990; Clifden, 1997; Central Galway granite and its northern margin, Oughterard, 2006; The Western Galway Granite, 2011; Camus, Co. Galway, 2012; Joyces Country, Co. Galway, 2014. *Recreations:* reading, theatre, museums, genealogy, study of railway and agricultural development. *Address:* School of Earth and Ocean Sciences, Cardiff University, Main Building, Park Place, Cardiff CF10 3AT. *T:* (029) 2087 6421; The Chippings, Bridge Road, Llanblethian, Cowbridge, Vale of Glamorgan CF71 7JG. *Club:* Geological Society.

LEAKE, Rt Rev. David, CBE 2003; Bishop of Argentina, 1990–2002; an Hon. Assistant Bishop, Diocese of Norwich, since 2002; *b* 26 June 1935; *s* of Rev. Canon William Alfred Leake and Dorothy Violet Leake; *m* 1961, Rachel Yarham; two *s* one *d*. *Educ:* St Alban's Coll., Buenos Aires; London Coll. of Divinity. ALCD 1959 (LTh). Deacon 1959, priest 1960; Assistant Bishop: Paraguay and N Argentina, 1969–73; N Argentina, 1973–79; Bishop of Northern Argentina, 1979–89; Presiding Bishop, Province of Anglican Ch of Southern Cone of America, 1982–89. *Publications:* Under an Algarrobo Tree, 2012. *Recreations:* observing people's behaviour at airports, railway stations and bus terminals. *Address:* The Anchorage, Lower Common, East Runton, Cromer, Norfolk NR27 9PG. *T:* (01263) 513536.

LEAKE, Nicholas Howard; HM Diplomatic Service; Counsellor, EU/Economic, Berlin, since 2014; *b* Wordsley, 15 Jan. 1972; *s* of John Howard Leake and Karen Leake; *m* 2013, Oana Maria Bucsa; one *s*. *Educ:* Univ. of Warwick (LLB); Univs of Warwick, Lille and Saarbrücken (Integrated Common Prog. Eur. Law); Open Univ. (MBA). Entered FCO, 1994; Second Sec., Budapest, 1996–2000; First Sec., UK Perm. Repn to EU, 2000–02; Hd of Public Sector Preparations and Consumer Protection, Eur. Preparations Unit, HM Treasury (on secondment), 2002–04; Economy Theme Manager, Commn for Africa, 2004; Private Sec. to Minister for Europe, and Minister for Trade, 2005; Dep. Hd of Mission, Sofia, 2006–10; Chargé d'Affaires, Madagascar, 2010–12; High Comr to Mauritius and Ambassador to The Comoros, 2010–14. *Recreations:* cricket, cycling, travel, food and wine. *Address:* British Embassy, Berlin, Germany; c/o Foreign and Commonwealth Office, King Charles Street, SW1A 2AH. *E:* nick.leake@fco.gov.uk.

LEAKEY, Lt Gen. (Arundell) David, CMG 2006; CBE 1997; Gentleman Usher of the Black Rod and Serjeant-at-Arms, House of Lords, and Secretary to the Lord Great Chamberlain, since 2011; *b* 18 May 1952; *s* of Maj.-Gen. (Arundell) Rea Leakey, CB, DSO, MC and Muriel Irene Le Poer Trench; *m* 1983, Shelagh Jane Lawson; two *s*. *Educ:* Sherborne Sch.; Fitzwilliam Coll., Cambridge (MA Law); RMA Sandhurst. CO 2nd RTR, 1991; Comdr 20 Armoured Bde, 1996; Dir Mil. Ops, MoD, 1997–99; COS HQ NI, 1999–2001; Dir Gen., Army Trng and Recruiting, and Chief Exec., Army Trng and Recruiting Agency, 2001–04; Comdr, EU Force in Bosnia and Herzegovina, 2004–05; MoD, 2006–07; Dir Gen., EU Mil. Staff, 2007–10. Col Comdt, RTR, 2006–10 (Dep. Col Comdt, 1999–2006); Col, Dorset Yeomanry, 2008–. Hon. Col, ACF Music, 2004–11. Chm., Wyke Hall (Management) Ltd, 1996–2010 (Dir, 1993–2010). Mem. Adv. Bd, Security Defence Agenda, 2008–. Trustee, Nat. Children's Orch., 2001–14 (Vice Chm., 2012–13; Chm., 2013–14). President: Army Squash Rackets Assoc., 1997–2010; Tank Memorial Ypres Salient, 2008–; Sherborne Pilgrims, 2012–. *Recreations:* music, field sports, squash, tennis, sailing, ski-ing, golf, chain-sawing. *Address:* Black Rod, House of Lords, SW1A 0PW. *E:* davidleakey@aol.com. *Clubs:* Hawks (Cambridge); Jesters; Escorts; GB Veterans Squash.

LEAKEY, Richard Erskine Frere, FRS 2007; Permanent Secretary, Secretary to the Cabinet and Head of the Public Service, Kenya, 1999–2001; *b* 19 Dec. 1944; *s* of late Louis Seymour Bazett Leakey, FBA, and Mary Douglas Leakey, FBA; *m* 1970, Dr Meave (*née* Epps); three *d*. *Educ:* Nairobi Primary Sch.; Lenana (formerly Duke of York) Sch., Nairobi. Self employed tour guide and animal trapper, 1961–65; Dir, Photographic Safaris in E Africa, 1965–68; Administrative Dir, 1968–74, Dir, 1974–89, Nat. Museums of Kenya; Dir, Wildlife and Conservation Management Service, Kenya, 1989–90; Chm., 1989–93, Dir, 1993–94 and 1998–99, Kenya Wildlife Service; Man. Dir, Richard Leakey and Associates, wildlife consultancy, 1994–98; Sec. Gen. SAFINA, 1995–98. MP Kenya, 1998. Co-leader, palaeontol expedn to Lake Natron, Tanzania, 1963–64; expedn to Lake Baringo, Kenya, in search of early man, 1966; Co-leader, Internation Omo River Expedn, Ethiopia, in search of early man, 1967; Leader, E Turkana (formerly E Rudolf) Res. Proj. (multi-nat., interdisciplinary sci. consortium investigation of Plio/Pleistocene, Kenya's northern Rift Valley), 1968–. Chairman: Foundn for Res. into Origin of Man (FROM), 1974–81; E African Wild Life Soc., 1984–89 (Vice-Chm., 1978–84); Kenya Cttee, United World Colls, 1987; Bd of Governors and Council, Regent's Coll., London, 1985–90; Nat. Museums of Kenya, 1999–; Trustee: Nat. Fund for the Disabled; Wildlife Clubs of Kenya, 1980–; Rockford Coll., Illinois, 1983–85. Presenter: The Making of Mankind, BBC TV series, 1981; Earth Journal, US TV series, 1991. Mem., Selection Cttee, Beyond War Award, 1985–; Juror: Kalinga Prize, Unesco, 1986–88; Rolex Awards, 1990. Hon. Mem., Bd of Dirs, Thunderbird Res. Corp., USA, 1988–. Hon. degrees from Wooster Coll., Rockford Coll., SUNY, Univs of Kent, Ohio, Aberdeen, Washington and Bristol. Golden Ark Medal for Conservation, 1989. *Publications:* (contrib.) General History of Africa, vol. 1, 1976; (with R. Lewin) Origins, 1978; (with R. Lewin) People of the Lake, 1979; (with M. G. Leakey) Koobi Fora Research Project, vol. I, 1979; The Making of Mankind, 1981; Human Origins, 1982; One Life, 1984; (with R. Lewin) Origins Reconsidered, 1992; (with R. Lewin) The Origins of Humankind, 1995; (with R. Lewin) The Sixth Extinction: biodiversity and its survival, 1996; articles on palaeontol. in Nature, Jl of World Hist., Science, Amer. Jl of Phys. and Anthropol. *Address:* PO Box 24926, Nairobi 00502, Kenya.

LEAMAN, Rear Adm. Richard Derek, CB 2010; OBE 1993; Chief Executive, Guide Dogs for the Blind, since 2010; *b* Lynton, Devon, 29 July 1956; *s* of Derek Alan Leaman and Jean Rita Leaman; *m* 1999, Suzanne Clarke (separated). *Educ:* Britannia Royal Naval Coll.; Manchester Business Sch. (Advanced Mgt Achievement Course 2010). Joined RN, 1975; navigation and gunnery duties in ships deployed worldwide, 1976–90; in command: HMS Dumbarton Castle, 1991–92; HMS Cardiff, 1993–94; ops and trng appts, 1995–98; HMS Cumberland, 1999–2000; HCSC, 2000; Dir, RN Communications, 2000–01; Comdr, UK Maritime Task Gp, 2002–03; Defence Strategic Leadership Course, 2004; Dir, HCSC, 2003–05; COS, Maritime HQ, Naples, 2005–07; Dep. COS, NATO Strategic Comd, Norfolk, Va, 2007–09. Trustee: Vision 2020 UK, 2010–13; NCVO, 2012–. Chm., Assoc. of RN Officers, 2013–. *Recreations:* swimming, listening to music, theatre, dog walking. *Address:* Guide Dogs for the Blind Association, Reading, Berks RG7 3YG. *T:* (0118) 983 8555. *E:* richard.leaman@guidedogs.org.uk.

LEAN, Very Rev. (David) Jonathan Rees; Dean and Precentor, St Davids Cathedral, since 2009; *b* Fishguard, 29 May 1952; *s* of late David Samuel Lean and of Sylvia Patricia Lean. *Educ:* St Davids Univ. Coll., Lampeter (DipTh 1974); Coll. of the Resurrection, Mirfield. Ordained deacon, 1975, priest, 1976; Asst Curate, Rectorial Benefice of Tenby, 1975–81; Vicar: Llanrhian, Llanhowell and Llanrheithan, 1981–88; St Martin's, Haverfordwest with Lambston, 1988–2000; Area Dean of Rhoose, 1999–2000; Canon Residentiary, St Davids Cathedral, 2000–09. *Recreations:* music, gardening. *Address:* The Deanery, The Close, St Davids, Pembrokeshire SA62 6RD. *T:* (01437) 720202. *E:* dean@stdavidscathedral.org.uk.

LEAN, Geoffrey; Contributing Editor, Environment, Daily Telegraph, since 2009; *b* 21 April 1947; *s* of late Garth Dickinson Lean and Margaret Mary Lean (*née* Appleyard); *m* 1972, Judith Eveline Wolfe; one *s* one *d*. *Educ:* Sherborne Sch.; St Edmund Hall, Oxford (BA (Hons) Mod. Hist). Grad. Trainee, Yorkshire Post Newspapers, 1969–72; reporter, Goole Times, 1969; Yorkshire Post: reporter, 1969–72; Feature Writer, 1972–77; Envmt Correspondent, 1973–77; Reporter, 1977–79, Envmt Correspondent, 1979–93, The Observer; Dir, Central Observer, 1990–93; Envmt Correspondent, 1993–2000, Envmt Editor, 2000–09, Independent on Sunday; Columnist, Grist.org, 2009–10. Contrib. Editor, Fairness Radio, USA, 2010–13. Editor, Our Planet, 1994–, Tunza, 2003–11, UNEP; Mem., Exec. Cttee, Stakeholder Forum for Our Common Future (formerly UNED Forum), 1989–95. Trustee, European Sect., Internat. Inst. of Energy Conservation, 1995–98; UK rep. to Commn IV, Gen. Conf. of UNESCO, 1997; Mem. Bd, Leadership in Envmt and Develt Internat., 1998–2003; Trustee, LEAD UK, 2000–06. Consultancies for UNEP, UNDP, UNICEF, World Bank, FAO and WMO. Clerk, Yorkshire Post and Yorkshire Evening Post jt chapels, NUJ, 1975–77; Vice Chm., Leeds Branch, NUJ, 1977. Chair of Judges, Andrew Lees Meml Award, 1994–2009; Juror, Goldman Envmtl Prize, 1996–. Yorkshire Council for Social Services Press Award, 1972; Glaxo Science Fellowship, 1972; World Envmt Fest. Rose Award, 1986; Communication Arts Award of Excellence, 1986; UN Global 500, 1987; Awareness Award, 1991, Journalist of the Year, 1993, 2002, British Envmt and Media Awards; Schumacher Award, 1994; Foundn Award to launch IUCN/Reuters press awards, 1998; Scoop of the Year, London Press Club Awards, 2000, British Press Awards, 2001; Martha Gellhorn Prize, Martha Gellhorn Trust Cttee, 2002. *Publications:* Rich World, Poor World, 1978; (jtly) The Worst Accident in the World, 1986; (jtly) Chernobyl: the end of the nuclear dream, 1987; (gen. ed.) Atlas of the Environment, 1990, revd edn 1994; (ed) Radiation: doses, effects, risks, 1985; (ed) Action on Ozone, 1988, revd edn 1990; (contrib. ed.) Dimensions of Need: a world atlas of food and agriculture, 1995; (ed) Down to Earth, 1995; (ed) Human Development Report, 1998; (ed) Progress of Nations Report, 1999; (ed) A Sea of Troubles, 2001; (ed) Protecting the Oceans from Land-Based Activities, 2001. *Recreations:* family, garden, West Cork, bad puns. *Address:* c/o Daily Telegraph, 111 Buckingham Palace Road, SW1W 0DT. *T:* (020) 7931 2000. *E:* geoffrey.lean@telegraph.co.uk.

LEAN, Very Rev. Jonathan; *see* Lean, Very Rev. D. J. R.

LEAR, Joyce, (Mrs W. J. Lear); *see* Hopkirk, Joyce.

LEAR, Peter; *see* Lovesey, P. H.

LEARMONT, Gen. Sir John (Hartley), KCB 1989; CBE 1980 (OBE 1975); Quarter Master General, Ministry of Defence, 1991–94, retired; *b* 10 March 1934; *s* of Captain Percy Hewitt Learmont, CIE, RIN and Doris Orynthia Learmont; *m* 1957, Susan (*née* Thornborrow); three *s*. *Educ:* Fettes College; RMA Sandhurst. Commissioned RA, 1954; Instructor, RMA, 1960–63; student, Staff Coll., 1964; served 14 Field Regt, Staff Coll. and 3 RHA, 1965–70; MA to C-in-C BAOR, 1971–73; CO 1 RHA, 1974–75 (despatches 1974); HQ BAOR, 1976–78; Comdr, 8 Field Force, 1979–81; Dep. Comdr, Commonwealth Monitoring Force, Rhodesia, Nov. 1979–March 1980; student RCDS, 1981; Chief of Mission, British Cs-in-C Mission to Soviet Forces in Germany, 1982–84; Comdr Artillery, 1 (British) Corps, 1985–87; COS, HQ UKLF, 1987–88; Comdt, Staff Coll. Camberley, 1988–89; Mil. Sec., MoD, 1989–91. Conducted review (Learmont Inquiry) of Prison Service security in Eng. and Wales, 1995. Colonel Commandant: Army Air Corps, 1988–94; RA, 1989–99; RHA, 1990–99; Hon. Colonel: 2nd Bn Wessex Regt (Vols), 1990–95; 2nd (Vol.) Bn, Royal Gloucestershire, Berkshire and Wiltshire Regt, 1995–97. Patron: Glider Pilot Regtl Assoc., 1996–; Air OP Officers' Assoc., 2000–. *Recreations:* fell walking, golf, theatre.

LEARY, Brian Leonard; QC 1978; FCIArb; *b* 1 Jan. 1929; *o s* of late A. T. Leary; *m* 1965, Myriam Ann Bannister, *d* of Kenneth Bannister, CBE, Mexico City. *Educ:* King's Sch., Canterbury; Wadham Coll., Oxford (MA). Called to the Bar, Middle Temple, 1953; Harmsworth Scholar; Bencher, 1986. Senior Prosecuting Counsel to the Crown at Central Criminal Court, 1971–78. Chm., British-Mexican Soc., 1989–92. *Recreations:* travel, sailing, growing herbs. *Address:* Calle Reforma, No. 13, San Angel, Mexico DF 01000, Mexico. *T:* (55) 55508270.

LEASK, Maj.-Gen. Anthony de Camborne Lowther, CB 1996; CBE 1990 (OBE 1984; MBE 1979); *b* 4 Jan. 1943; *s* of Lt-Gen. Sir Henry Leask, KCB, DSO, OBE, and Zoë Leask (*née* Paynter); *m* 1974, Heather Catherine Moir; one *s* two *d*. *Educ:* Wellington Coll.; RMA, Sandhurst. Commnd Scots Guards, 1963; mentioned in despatches, 1974; CO Bn, 1981–83; attached US Army, 1983–85; Col Mil. Ops 2, MoD, 1986–89; in Comd, 15 Inf. Bde, 1989–91; rcds 1992; Dir, Defence Commitments, Far East and Western Hemisphere, 1993–94; Maj.-Gen. 1994; Comdr Land Forces NI, 1994–95; retd 1996. Director: Nat. Assoc. of Almshouses, 1996–2004; Corps of Commissionaires Mgt Ltd, 1999–2010 (Chm., 2001–10). Mem., Queen's Bodyguard for Scotland, Royal Co. of Archers, 1976–. *Publications:* Sword of Scotland, 2006. *Recreations:* wildlife, country pursuits. *Address:* c/o Bank of Scotland, Aberfoyle, by Stirling. *Club:* Cavalry and Guards.

See also Earl of Clarendon.

LEASK, Derek William; High Commissioner for New Zealand in the United Kingdom, 2008–12; *b* Wellington, NZ, 29 Feb. 1948; *s* of Lloyd Samuel Leask and Judith Leask (*née* Poynter); *m* 1972, Annabel E. Murray (marr. diss.); one *s* one *d*; partner, Patricia D. Stevenson. *Educ:* Victoria Univ. of Wellington (BCA); Univ. of Canterbury, NZ (MComm Hons).

Entered NZ Diplomatic Service, 1969; Counsellor, London, 1985–89; Ambassador to EC, 1995–99; Dep. Sec., NZ Ministry of Foreign Affairs and Trade, 2005–08. *Recreations:* golf, NZ history (19th century wars in NZ). *Clubs:* Wellington; Royal Wellington Golf.

LEASK, Prof. Nigel James, PhD; FBA 2012; FRSE; FEA; Regius Professor of English Language and Literature, since 2004, and Head, School of Critical Studies, 2010–13, University of Glasgow; *b* Glasgow, 29 Sept. 1958; *s* of F. Reay Mackay Leask and M. Anne Leask (*née* Boyd); *m* 1994, Evelyn Arizpe; two *d. Educ:* Edinburgh Acad.; University Coll., Oxford (BA 1980); Trinity Coll., Cambridge (PhD 1987). FEA 2006; FRSE 2008. Jun. Res. Fellow, 1986–89, Fellow and Dir of Studies in English, 1989–2004, Queens' Coll., Cambridge; Lectr, Faculty of English, 1989–2004, Lectr, then Reader in Romantic Lit., 2004, Univ. of Cambridge. *Publications:* British Romantic Writers and the East: anxieties of Empire, 1992 (Indian imprint 1994); Curiosity and the Aesthetics of Travel Writing, 1770–1840: from an antique land, 2002; (ed jtly) Land, Nation and Culture, 1740–1840: thinking the republic of taste, 2004; (ed with Dr P. Connell) Romanticism and Popular Culture in Britain and Ireland, 2009; Robert Burns and Pastoral: poetry and improvement in late 18th century Scotland, 2010 ((jtly) Saltire/Nat. Liby of Scotland Prize for Best Res. Book of Year). *Recreations:* hill-walking, fiddle-playing, pre-Hispanic Mexico. *Address:* 2 Hamilton Drive, Glasgow G12 8DR; School of Critical Studies, 4 University Gardens, University of Glasgow, Glasgow G12 8QQ. *E:* nigel.leask@glasgow.ac.uk.

LEATES, Margaret; freelance parliamentary draftsman, since 1990; *b* 30 March 1951; *d* of Henry Arthur Sargent Rayner and Alice (*née* Baker); *m* 1973, Timothy Philip Leates; one *s* one *d. Educ:* Lilley and Stone Girls' High Sch., Newark; King's Coll., London (LLB 1st cl. hons, LLM distinction; undergrad. and postgrad. schol.; AKC); MA (Theol) distinction, Univ. of Kent. Admitted Solicitor, 1975; joined Office of Parliamentary Counsel, 1976; with Law Commn, 1981–83 and 1987–89; Dep. Parly Counsel, 1987–90; drafting for Tax Law Rewrite, 1997–2010. *Publications:* When I'm 64: a guide to pensions law; Review of Planning Law of States of Guernsey. *Recreations:* hermeneutics, junk, other people's gardens, walking, reading. *Address:* Crofton Farm, 161 Crofton Lane, Petts Wood, Orpington, Kent BR6 0BP. *T:* (01689) 820192; Nyanza, 87 Bennell's Avenue, Whitstable, Kent CT5 2HR. *T:* (01227) 272335. *E:* ml@leates.org.uk.

LEATHAM, Dorian; Chief Executive, Arhag Housing Association, since 2011; Special Adviser, Homes and Communities Agency, since 2008; *b* 2 Aug. 1949; *s* of Robert Clement Leatham and Anna Ismay Leatham; partner, Janet Patrick; one *s* one *d. Educ:* High Wycombe Coll. of Technol. (BSc Sociol. (ext.) London); Brunel Univ. (MA Public and Social Admin). Various posts, 1970–75; Allocations Manager, Lambeth, 1975–77; District Housing Manager: City of Westminster, 1977–83; Camden, 1983–87; Dep. Dir of Housing, Brent, 1987–92; Dir, Housing Mgt, Circle 33 Housing Trust, 1992–93; Asst Dir of Housing, Hounslow, 1993–95; Dir of Housing, Croydon, 1995–98; Chief Exec., London Bor. of Hillingdon, 1998–2006; Chair, Nottingham Housing Strategic Partnership, 2007–09; Interim Exec. Dir, Housing and Develt, London Bor. of Lambeth, 2009–11. *Recreations:* watching cricket, going to cinema and theatre, cooking, reading, supporting voluntary groups. *Address:* Arhag Housing Association, Unit B, Ground Floor, Mary Brancker House, 54–74 Holmes Road, Kentish Town, NW5 3AQ.

LEATHER, Dame Susan Catherine, (Dame Suzi), DBE 2006 (MBE 1994); DL; Chair, Charity Commission for England and Wales, 2006–12; *b* 5 April 1956; *d* of late Dr Hugh Moffat Leather and of Dr Catherine Margaret Leather (*née* Stephen); *m* 1986, Prof. Iain Hampsher-Monk; one *s* two *d. Educ:* Exeter Univ. (BA Hons Politics 1977; BPhil Dist. Social Work 1986); Leicester Univ. (MA Eur. Politics 1978). CQSW 1986. Lectr, Politics Dept, Trent Poly. and Tutor, Leicester Univ., 1977–78; Mkt res. exec., AMR, 1978–79; Res. Officer, then Sen. Res. Officer, Consumers in Europe Gp, 1979–84; trainee Probation Officer, 1984–86; freelance consumer consultant, 1988–97; Chair: Exeter and Dist Community NHS Trust, 1997–2001; Human Fertilisation and Embryology Authy, 2002–06. Chair: Sch. Meals Rev. Panel, 2005; Sch. Food Trust, 2005–06; Council of Food Policy Advrs, 2008–10; Ethics Cttee, RCOG, 2011–; Lankelly Chase Foundn, 2012–; Plymouth Fairness Commn, 2013–; Dep. Chair, Food Standards Agency, 2000–02. Board Member: Human Tissue Authy, 2004–06; UK Accreditation Service, 2006–; Consumer Focus, 2008–13; Mem., GMC, 2013–. Member: Council, Exeter Univ., 2004–13; State Hons Cttee, 2008–14; Bd, SW Min. Trng Course, 2014–. Vice Pres., Hospicare, 2012–. Trustee, StepChange, 2015–. DL Devon, 2009. FRCOG *ad eund* 2004. Hon. FRSPH (Hon. FRSH 2006). Hon. DLitt Exeter, 2003; Hon. DCL Huddersfield, 2005; DLaws Leicester, 2007; DUniv Aberdeen, 2007. *Publications:* The Making of Modern Malnutrition, 1996; contrib. articles on consumer, food and health policy. *Recreations:* keeping fit, walking, running, cinema, family discussions.

LEATHERBARROW, Prof. Robin John, DPhil, DSc; CChem, FRSC, FRSB; Pro-Vice-Chancellor (Scholarship, Research and Knowledge Transfer), Liverpool John Moores University, since 2013; *b* Farnworth, 14 Jan. 1959; *s* of John and Dorothy Leatherbarrow; *m* 1988, Marcella Mary Beale; two *d. Educ:* St John's C of E Primary Sch., Mosley Common; Leigh Grammar Sch.; Eccles Sixth Form Coll.; Liverpool Univ. (BSc Hons Biochem.); Exeter Coll., Oxford (DPhil 1983); Imperial Coll. London (DSc 2014). CChem 2004, FRSC 2004; FRSB (FSB 2010). Res. Lectr, Christ Church, Oxford, 1982–84; Imperial College London: MRC Postdoctoral Fellow, 1984; Royal Soc. Pickering Res. Fellow, 1984; Lectr, 1984–99; Reader, 1999–2002; Prof. and Hd of Biol and Biophysical Chem., then Chemical Biol., Dept of Chem., 2002–13; Dir, 2001–13, Co-Chm., 2010–13, Chemical Biol. Centre, then Inst. of Chemical Biol.; Dean, Faculty of Natural Scis, 2010–13. Man. Dir, Erithacus Software Ltd, 1989–. Hon. Treas., British Biophysical Soc., 1993–99; Chm., Peptide and Protein Sci. Gp, RSC, 2009–. *Publications:* scientific contribs to learned jls; computer progs. *Recreations:* playing cricket and squash, watching Manchester United on TV, programming computers, refurbishing old houses. *Address:* Liverpool John Moores University, Egerton Court, 2 Rodney Street, Liverpool L1 2UA.

LEATHERBARROW, Prof. William John; Professor of Russian, University of Sheffield, 1994–2007, now Emeritus; *b* 18 Oct. 1947; *s* of William and Lily Leatherbarrow; *m* 1968, Vivien Jean Burton; one *s* one *d. Educ:* Univ. of Exeter (BA Hons 1969; MA 1972). University of Sheffield: Lectr, 1970–90; Sen. Lectr, 1990–92; Reader in Russian, 1992–94; Dean, Faculty of Arts, 1997–99; Chm., Sch. of Modern Langs, 2001–04, 2005–06. Mem. Council and Dir, Lunar Section, British Astronomical Assoc., 2009– (Pres., 2011–13; Vice Pres., 2013–). *Publications:* Fedor Dostoevsky, 1981; (with D. C. Offord) A Documentary History of Russian Thought, 1987; Fedor Dostoevsky: a reference guide, 1990; Dostoyevsky: The Brothers Karamazov, 1992; Dostoevsky and Britain, 1995; Dostoevsky's "The Devils", 1999; The Cambridge Companion to Dostoevskii, 2002; A Devil's Vaudeville: the demonic in Dostoevsky's major fiction, 2005; (with D. C. Offord) A History of Russian Thought, 2010; many edns and articles in scholarly jls. *Recreations:* wine, hiking, cricket, astronomy. *Address:* Department of Russian and Slavonic Studies, University of Sheffield, Sheffield S10 2TN. *E:* w.leatherbarrow@sheffield.ac.uk.

LEATHERS, family name of **Viscount Leathers.**

LEATHERS, 3rd Viscount *cr* 1954, of Purfleet, Co. Essex; **Christopher Graeme Leathers;** Baron Leathers, 1941; *b* 31 Aug. 1941; *er s* of 2nd Viscount Leathers and his 1st wife, Elspeth Graeme Stewart (*d* 1985); *S* father, 1996; *m* 1964, Maria Philomena, *yr d* of late Michael Merriman, Charlestown, Co. Mayo; one *s* one *d. Educ:* Rugby Sch.; Open Univ. (BA Hons). New Zealand Shipping Co. Ltd, 1961–63; Wm Cory & Son Ltd, 1963–84; Mostyn Docks Ltd, 1984–88; with Dept of Transport, then DETR, subseq. DTLR, then DfT, 1988–2003. MICS 1965; MCMI (MIMgt 1987). Liveryman, Shipwrights' Co., 1969–. JP Clwyd, 1993. *Heir: s* Hon. James Frederick Leathers, *b* 27 May 1969. *Address:* 53 Daisy Avenue, Bury St Edmunds, Suffolk IP32 7PG.

LEATHWOOD, Barry, OBE 1998; National Secretary, Rural, Agricultural and Allied Workers National Trade Group, Transport and General Workers' Union, 1987–2002; *b* 11 April 1941; *s* of Charles and Dorothy Leathwood; *m* 1963, Veronica Ann Clarke; one *d.* Apprentice Toolmaker, 1956–62; Toolmaker/Fitter, 1962–73; District Organiser, Nat. Union of Agric. and Allied Workers, 1973–83; Regional Officer, TGWU Agric. Group, 1983–87. Member: British Potato Council, 2002–; Nat. Access Forum, 1999–. UK Delegate/Expert to ISO Wkg Gp on Social Responsibility, 2005. Patron, Community Council for Somerset, 2001–; CAB Voluntary Advr, 2004–. FRSA 1996. *Recreations:* socialist politics, reading, walking, photography. *Address:* 32 Nursery Close, Combwich, Bridgwater, Som TA5 2JB.

LEATT, Allen Frederick, FREng, CEng, FICE; Senior Vice President, Subsea 7, since 2011; *b* Cullompton, 13 April 1954; *s* of Leslie and Dorothy Leatt; *m* 1981, Carol Ann Shillabeer; one *s. Educ:* Aston Univ. (BSc Hons); Cranfield Univ. (MBA). CEng 1981; FICE 2010; FREng 2012. Civil engr, John Laing Construction, 1977–81; offshore engr, Subsea Offshore, 1982–87; Commercial Manager, Stena Offshore, 1988–89; Gen. Manager, Stena Drilling, 1990–93; Strategy Director: Stena Offshore, 1994–95; Coflexip Stena Offshore, 1995–96; CEO, Perry Tritech, 1997–2000; Chm. and CEO, Perry Slingsby Systems, 2000–02; Exec. Vice Pres., Technip, 2002–03; Chief Technol. Officer, Acergy, 2003–11. Mem., Smeatonian Soc., 2015–. *Recreations:* modern art, technology, golf. *Address:* Subsea 7, 200 Hammersmith Road, W6 7DL. *T:* (020) 8210 5500. *E:* allen.leatt@gmail.com.

LEAVER, Sir Christopher, GBE 1981; JP; director of private and public companies; Vice Chairman, Thames Water Plc, 1994–2000 (Deputy Chairman, 1989–93; Chairman, 1993–94); *b* 3 Nov. 1937; *s* of Dr Robert Leaver and Mrs Audrey Kerpen; *m* 1975, Helen Mireille Molyneux Benton; one *s* two *d. Educ:* Eastbourne Coll. Commissioned (Army), RAOC, 1956–58. Member, Retail Foods Trades Wages Council, 1963–64. JP Inner London, 1970–83, City, 1974–92; Member: Council, Royal Borough of Kensington and Chelsea, 1970–73; Court of Common Council (Ward of Dowgate), City of London, 1973; Alderman (Ward of Dowgate), City of London, 1974–2002; Sheriff of the City of London, 1979–80; Lord Mayor of London, 1981–82; one of HM Lieutenants, City of London, 1982–2002. Chm., London Tourist Bd, 1983–89; Dep. Chm., Thames Water Authority, 1983–89; Chm., Thames Line Plc, 1987–89; Director: Bath & Portland Gp, 1983–85; Thermal Scientific plc, 1986–88; Unionamerica Holdings Plc, 1994–97. Advr on Royal Parks to Sec. of State for Nat. Heritage, 1993–96. Member: Bd of Brixton Prison, 1975–78; Court, City Univ., 1978–2002 (Chancellor, 1981–82); Council of the Missions to Seamen, 1983–95; Council, Wine and Spirit Benevolent Soc., 1983–88; Finance Cttee, London Diocesan Fund, 1983–86; Transitional Council, St Paul's Cathedral, 1999; Trustee: Chichester Festival Theatre, 1982–97; LSO, 1983–91; Vice-President: Bridewell Royal Hosp., 1982–89; NPFA, 1983–99; Governor: Christ's Hospital Sch., 1975–2002; City of London Girls' Sch., 1975–78; City of London Freemen's Sch., 1980–81; Chm., Council, Eastbourne Coll., 1989–2005 (Mem., 1988–2005); Almoner Trustee, St Paul's Cathedral Choir Sch. Foundn, 1986–90. Trustee, Music Therapy Trust, 1981–89; Chairman, Young Musicians' Symphony Orch. Trust, 1979–81; Hon. Mem., Guildhall Sch. of Music and Drama, 1982–. Church Warden, St Olave's, Hart Street, 1975–90 (Patronage Trust, 1990–96); Church Comr, 1982–93, 1996–99. Mem., Ct of Assistants, Carmen's Co., 1973 (Master, 1987–88); Hon. Liveryman: Farmers' Company, 1980; Water Conservators' Co., 2000 (Hon. Freeman, 1995); Freeman, Co. of Watermen and Lightermen, 1988; Hon. Freeman, Co. of Environmental Cleaners, 1983; Hon. Col, 151 (Greater London) Tpt Regt RCT (V), 1983–88; Hon. Col Comdt, RCT, 1988–91. Hon. DMus City, 1981. KStJ 1982. Order of Oman Class II. *Recreations:* gardening, music.

LEAVER, Prof. Christopher John, CBE 2000; FRS 1986; FRSE; Sibthorpian Professor of Plant Sciences, 1990–2007, now Professor Emeritus, and Head, Department of Plant Sciences, 1991–2007, University of Oxford; Fellow, St John's College, 1989–2007, now Emeritus; *b* 31 May 1942; *s* of Douglas Percy Leaver and Elizabeth Constance Leaver; *m* 1971, Anne (*née* Huggins); one *s* one *d. Educ:* Lyme Regis Grammar Sch. (State Scholarship); Imperial College, University of London (BSc, ARCS, DIC, PhD); MA (Oxon) 1990. Botanist, Imperial Coll., London: Hornsund Expedition, Spitzbergen, 1962; Beerenberg Expedition, Jan Mayen, 1963; Fulbright Scholar, Purdue Univ., 1966–68; Scientific Officer, ARC Plant Physiology Unit, Imperial Coll., 1968–69; University of Edinburgh: Lectr, Dept of Botany, 1969–80; Reader, 1980–86; SERC Sen. Res. Fellow, 1985–89; Prof. of Plant Molecular Biol., 1986–89. Dir, ISIS Innovations Ltd, 1996–2002. EMBO Sen. Fellow, Biozentrum Basel, 1980; Vis. Prof., Univ. of WA, Perth, 2002–. Member: AFRC, 1990–94; Priorities Bd for R&D to advise MAFF, 1990–94 (Chm., Arable Crops Adv. Sectoral Gp, 1990–94); Council, EMBO, 1991–97 (Chm., 1996–97); ACOST for HM Govt, 1992–93; Council, Royal Soc., 1992–94; BBSRC, 2000–03 (Mem., Individual Merit Promotion Panel, 1996–2005; Mem., Scientific CS Personal Merit Promotion Panel, 2005–10); Govt GM Sci. Review Panel, 2002–04; Scientific Adv. Bd, Australian Res. Council Centre of Excellence in Plant Energy Biol., Perth, 2005–13; Internat. Adv. Panel, Nat. Univ. of Singapore Graduate Sch., 2006– (Chm., 2009–); Chairman: Sci. Adv. Bd, IACR, Rothamsted, 1995–2000; Scientific Adv. Bd, Inst. for Molecular and Cell Biology, Porto, 2000–; Mem., Cttee of Scientific Planning and Rev., ICSU, Paris, 2006–12. Advr in Biol Scis, Carnegie Trust for Univs of Scotland, 1995–2014; Scientific Advr in Bioscis, Farming in Africa, 2011–. Biochemical Society: Mem. Council, 1995–99; Chm., Nucleic Acids and Molecular Biol. Gp, 1995–2000; Vice Chm., 2002–04, Chm., 2005–07, Exec. Cttee; Trustee, 2005–07; Mem., Educn Cttee, 2005–12. Curator, Oxford Botanic Garden, 1991–98. Mem. Gov. Council, John Innes, 1984–2012; Trustee: John Innes Foundn, 1987–; Nat. History Mus., 1997–2006; Sense About Sci., 2002–13. Deleg., OUP, 2002–07. Corresp. Mem., Amer. Soc. of Plant Biologists, 2003, Fellow, 2007. FRSE 1987; MAE 1988. T. H. Huxley Gold Medal, Imperial Coll., 1970; Tate & Lyle Award, Phytochem. Soc. of Europe, 1984; Humboldt Prize, Alexander von Humboldt Foundn, Bonn, 1997; Sibthorp Medal, Univ. of Oxford, 2007. *Publications:* numerous papers in internat. sci. jls. *Recreation:* walking and talking in Upper Coquetdale. *Address:* St John's College, Oxford OX1 3JP. *E:* chris.leaver@plants.ox.ac.uk.

LEAVER, David; *see* Leaver, J. D.

LEAVER, Elaine Kildare; *see* Murray, E. K.

LEAVER, Prof. (John) David, PhD; CBiol, FRSB; FRAgS, FIAgrE, FRASE; Principal, Royal Agricultural College, Cirencester, 2002–07, now Professor Emeritus; *b* 5 Jan. 1942; *s* of John and Elsie Leaver; *m* 1969, Sally Ann Posgate; two *s* one *d. Educ:* Univ. of Durham (BSc Agric.); Wye Coll., Univ. of London (PhD 1967). CBiol, FRSB (FIBiol 1988); FRAgS 1986; FIAgrE 2003; FRASE 2009. PSO, Nat. Inst. for Res. in Dairying, 1967–76; Hd, Dept of Animal Prodn and Farm Dir, Crichton Royal W of Scotland Agricl Coll., 1976–87; Prof. of Agriculture and Vice Principal, Wye Coll., Univ. of London, 1987–2000; Vice Provost, Wye, Imperial Coll., 2000–02. Dir, UCAS, 2006–07. Dir, NMR plc, 1994–97. Member: Adv. Cttee, BSE, the Cost of a Crisis, Nat. Audit Office, 1997; Prog. Mgt Cttee, DEFRA Sustainable Livestock Prog., 2002–12 (Chm., 2007–12); Council of Food Policy Advrs, 2008–10; Chief Scientific Advr's Food Res. Partnership, 2009–15. Chm., Practice with Sci. Adv. Gp, RASE, 2009–13. Mem., Wilson Cttee, Nat. Cattle Genetic Database, 1989–90;

Scientific Advr, Internat. Foundn for Science, 1994–2014. President: British Soc. of Animal Sci., 1995–96; British Grassland Soc., 2000–01; British Inst. of Agricl Consultants, 2009–; Wye Coll. Agricola Club, 2009–; Royal Assoc. of British Dairy Farmers, 2012–. Trustee: Frank Parkinson Agricl Trust, 1994– (Chm., 1999–2011); Frank Parkinson Yorks Trust, 1999– (Chm., 2008–11); Sir Emrys Jones Meml Trust, 2005–; Stapledon Meml Trust, 2010–; Wye Coll. Meml Trust, 2011–. *Publications:* Herbage Intake Handbook, 1982; Milk Production, Science and Practice, 1983; over 250 articles in peer-reviewed jls and conf. papers on dairy systems res. *Recreations:* sport, music, poetry, countryside. *Address:* Sole Street Farm, Crundale, Canterbury, Kent CT4 7ET. *E:* jdleaver@gmail.com. *Club:* Farmers.

LEAVER, Marcus Edward; Chief Executive Officer, Quarto Group Inc., since 2012; *b* 1 April 1970; *s* of Peter Lawrence Oppenheim Leaver, *qv*; *m* 1997, Anna Gwendoline Morgan; one *s* three *d*. *Educ:* Eton Coll.; UEA (BA Hons (Hist. of Art and Architecture) 1992); London Business Sch. (MBA 1999). Corporate Develt Dir, Chrysalis Gp plc, 2001–03; Chief Exec., Chrysalis Books Gp plc, 2003–05; Exec. Vice-Pres. and Chief Operating Officer, 2005–08, Pres., 2008–12, Sterling Publishing Co. Inc.; Chief Operating Officer, Quarto Gp Inc., 2012. *Recreations:* Tottenham Hotspur, New York Yankees, cricket, CrossFit. *Address:* Quarto Group Inc., The Old Brewery, 6 Blundell Street, N7 9BH. *T:* (020) 7700 9004. *E:* marcus.leaver@quarto.com. *Clubs:* MCC, Soho House.

LEAVER, Parveen June; *see* Kumar, P. J.

LEAVER, Peter Lawrence Oppenheim; QC 1987; a Recorder, since 1994; *b* 28 Nov. 1944; *er s* of Marcus Isaac Leaver and Lena Leaver (*née* Oppenheim); *m* 1969, Jane Rachel, *o d* of Leonard and Rivka Pearl; three *s* one *d*. *Educ:* Aldenham Sch., Elstree; Trinity Coll., Dublin. Called to the Bar, Lincoln's Inn, 1967, Bencher, 1995. Chairman: Bar Cttee, 1989; Internat. Practice Cttee, 1990; Member: Gen. Council of the Bar, 1987–90; Cttee on the Future of the Legal Profession, 1986–88; Council of Legal Educn, 1986–91. Chief Exec., FA Premier League, 1997–99. Dir, IMRO Ltd, 1994–2000. Chm., London Court of Internat. Arbitration, 2008–12. Pres., UK Nat. Anti-Doping Panel, 2008–15. *Recreations:* sport, theatre, wine. *Address:* 1 Essex Court, Temple, EC4Y 9AR. *T:* (020) 7583 2000. *Clubs:* Garrick, MCC.

See also M. E. Leaver.

LEAVEY, Thomas Edward, PhD; Director General, International Bureau of Universal Postal Union, 1995–2005; *b* Kansas City, 10 Nov. 1934; *s* of Leonard J. Leavey and Mary (*née* Horgan); *m* 1968, Anne Roland. *Educ:* Josephinium Coll., Columbus, Ohio (BA 1957); Institut Catholique, Paris; Princeton Univ. (MA 1967; PhD 1968). Sch. administrator and teacher, Kansas City, Mo, 1957–63; Prof., Fairleigh Dickinson Univ., NJ and George Washington Univ., Washington, 1968–70; United States Postal Service: Prof., Trng and Develt Inst., Bethesda, Md, 1970–72; Dir, Postal Service Trng and Develt Mgt Trng Center, LA, 1973–75; Gen. Manager, Employment and Placement Div., HQ, 1976–78; Dir, Postal Career Exec. Service, HQ, 1979; Postmaster/Sectional Manager, Charlottesville, Va, 1980; Regl Dir of Human Resources, Central Reg., Chicago, 1981; Controller, HQ, 1982; Gen. Manager, Internat. Mail Processing Div., HQ, 1982–87; Asst PMG and Sen. Dir, Internat. Postal Affairs, HQ, 1987–94. Universal Postal Union: Chairman: Customs Co-operation Council Contact Cttee, 1987–89; Private Operators Contact Cttee, 1991–94; Postal Develt Action Gp, 1991–94; Provident Scheme Mgt Bd, Internat. Bureau, 1989–94; Exec. Council, 1989–94. USPS Special Achievement Awards for Distinguished Service, 1970–90; John Wanamaker Award, USPS, 1991. *Publications:* numerous articles on business and postal matters in postal and trade jls. *Recreations:* golf, tennis, ski-ing. *Address:* 13978 Siena Loop, Lakewood Ranch, FL 34202–2443, USA.

LEBRECHT, Andrew John, CB 2006; Deputy Permanent Representative, UK Permanent Representation to the European Union, 2008–12; *b* 13 Dec. 1951; *s* of late Heinz Martin Lebrecht and Margaret Lebrecht (*née* Cardis); *m* 1976, Judit Catan; two *d*. *Educ:* De La Salle Coll., Hove; Leeds Univ. (BA Econs); Reading Univ. (MSc Agricl Econs). Ministry of Agriculture, Fisheries and Food, 1977–2001: Private Sec. to Parly Sec., 1980–82; on secondment to HM Diplomatic Service as First Sec. (Fisheries and Food), UK Rep. Brussels, 1985–89; Principal Private Sec. to Minister of Agriculture, 1989–91; Head: Sheep and Livestock Subsidies Div., 1991–93; Review of Animal Health and Veterinary Gp, 1993–94; EU Div., 1994–98; EU and Internat. Policy, 1998–2001; Dir Gen., Food, Farming and Fisheries, then Sustainable Farming, Food and Fisheries, then Sustainable Farming and Food, subseq. Food and Farming, DEFRA, 2001–07. *Recreations:* family life, the countryside, reading.

LEBRECHT, Norman; writer and broadcaster; *b* 11 July 1948; *s* of late Solomon and Marguerite Lebrecht; *m* 1977, Elbie Spivack; three *d*. *Educ:* Hasmonean Grammar Sch. Radio and TV producer, 1970–79; specialist contributor: Sunday Times, 1982–91; Independent mag., 1991–92; Music Columnist, Daily Telegraph, 1993–2002; Asst Ed. and Arts Columnist, Evening Standard, 2002–09. Owner and publisher, Slipped Disc, 2008–. Contributor: Bloomberg, 2010–14; Wall St Jl, 2010–; Standpoint mag., 2011–. Contributor, The Late Show, BBC TV, 1994–95; Presenter, Lebrecht Live, BBC Radio 3, 2000–15. *Publications:* Discord, 1982; Hush, Handel's in a Passion, 1985; The Book of Musical Anecdotes, 1985; Mahler Remembered, 1987; The Book of Musical Days, 1987; The Maestro Myth, 1991; The Companion to 20th Century Music, 1992; When the Music Stops, 1996; The Complete Companion to 20th Century Music, 2000; Covent Garden: the untold story, 2000; Maestros, Masterpieces and Madness, 2007; Why Mahler?, 2010; *novels:* The Song of Names (Whitbread First Novel Award), 2002; The Game of Opposites, 2009. *Recreations:* reading, prayer, listening to music, watching cricket, vigorous disputation, deltiology. *Address:* 3 Bolton Road, NW8 0RJ. *E:* norman@normanlebrecht.com.

LE BRETON, David Francis Battye, CBE 1978; HM Diplomatic Service, retired; Secretary, Overseas Service Pensioners Association and Benevolent Society, since 1992; *b* 2 March 1931; *e s* of late Lt-Col F. H. Le Breton, MC, and Elisabeth, (Peter), Le Breton (*née* Trevor-Battye), Endebess, Kenya; *m* 1961, Patricia June Byrne; one *s* two *d*. *Educ:* Winchester; New Coll., Oxford. Colonial Administrative Service, Tanganyika, 1954; Private Sec. to Governor, 1959–60; Magistrate, 1962; Principal, CRO, 1963; HM Diplomatic Service, 1965; First Sec., Zanzibar, 1964; Lusaka, 1964–68; FCO, 1968–71; Head of Chancery, Budapest, 1971–74; HM Comr in Anguilla, 1974–78; Counsellor and Head of Chancery, Nairobi, 1978–81; High Comr in The Gambia, 1981–84; Head of Commonwealth Co-ordination Dept, FCO, 1984–86; Head of Nationality and Treaty Dept, FCO, 1986–87. Financial Advr/Sales Associate, Allied Dunbar Assurance, 1987–91. *Publications:* (ed) I Remember It Well: Colonial Service reminiscences, 2010. *Recreations:* country living, African and colonial affairs. *Address:* Brackenwood, French Street, near Westerham, Kent TN16 1PN.

LE BRUN, Christopher Mark, RA 1997; artist; President, Royal Academy, since 2011 (Professor of Drawing, 2000–02); *b* 20 Dec. 1951; *s* of late John Le Brun, BEM and Eileen Betty (*née* Miles); *m* 1979, Charlotte Eleanor Verity; two *s* one *d*. *Educ:* Portsmouth Southern Grammar Sch.; Slade Sch. of Fine Art (DFA); Chelsea Sch. of Art (MA). Lecturer: Brighton Coll. of Art, 1975–82; Wimbledon Coll. of Art, 1982–84; Vis. Lectr, Slade Sch. of Fine Art, 1984–90. Deutscher Akademischer Austauschdienst Fellowship, Berlin, 1987–88. Designer, Ballet Imperial, Royal Opera Hse, Covent Gdn, 1984. Designed stained glass window, LSE, 2014. One man exhibitions include: Nigel Greenwood Gall., London, 1980, 1982, 1985, 1989; Gillespie-Laage-Salomon, Paris, 1981; Sperone Westwater, NY, 1983, 1986, 1988; Fruitmarket Gall., Edinburgh, 1985; Arnolfini Gall., Bristol, 1985; Kunsthalle, Basel, 1986; Daadgalerie, Berlin, 1988; Galerie Rudolf Zwirner, Cologne, 1988; Art Center, Pasadena, Calif, 1992; LA Louver Gall., Venice, Calif, 1992; Marlborough Fine Art, 1994, 1998, 2001, 2003; Galerie Fortlaan 17, Ghent, 1994, 2002; Astrup Fearnley Mus. of Modern Art, Oslo, 1995; Fitzwilliam Mus., Cambridge, 1995; Marlborough Chelsea, NY, 2004; New Art Gall., Walsall, 2008; Hohenthal und Bergen, Berlin, 2009; New Art Centre, E Winterslow, Salisbury, 2010; Friedman Benda, NY, 2014; group exhibitions include: Milan, 1980; Berlin, 1982; Tate Gall., 1983; Mus. Modern Art, NY, 1984, 2005; The British Show, toured Australia and NZ, 1985; Oxford, Budapest, Prague, Warsaw, 1987; LA County Mus., 1987; Cincinnati Mus. and American tour, 1988–89; Setagaya Art Mus. and Japanese tour, 1990–91; Scottish Nat. Gall. Modern Art, 1995; Yale Center for British Art, New Haven, 1995; Nat. Gall., 2000; Tate Britain, 2011; work in public collections includes: Arts Council of GB, British Council, BM, NY Mus. Modern Art, Scottish Nat. Gall. Modern Art, Tate Gall., Walker Art Gall., Liverpool, Whitworth Art Gall., Manchester and Fitzwilliam Mus., Cambridge. Trustee: Tate Gall., 1990–95; Nat. Gall., 1996–2003; Dulwich Picture Gall., 2000–05; NPG, 2012–; Member: Slade Cttee, 1992–95; Develt Cttee, Tate Gall. of British Art, 1995–97. Chm., Royal Acad. Masterplan Briefing Gp, 2005–11. Advr, Prince of Wales's Drawing Studio, Shoreditch, 2000–03; Trustee and Chm., Academic Bd, Royal Drawing Sch. (formerly Prince of Wales's Drawing Sch.), 2004–. Hon. Fellow, Univ. of the Arts, London, 2010. Prizewinner, John Moores Liverpool Exhibns, 1978 and 1980; Gulbenkian Foundn Printmakers Award, 1983. *Relevant publication:* Christopher Le Brun, by Charles Saumarez Smith and Bryan Robertson, 2001. *Address:* c/o Royal Academy of Arts, Piccadilly, W1J 0BD.

LE CARRÉ, John; *see* Cornwell, David John Moore.

LE CHEMINANT, Air Chief Marshal Sir Peter (de Lacey), GBE 1978; KCB 1972 (CB 1968); DFC 1943, and Bar, 1951; Lieutenant-Governor and Commander-in-Chief of Guernsey, 1980–85; *b* 17 June 1920; *s* of Lieut-Colonel Keith Le Cheminant and Blanche Etheldred Wake Le Cheminant (*née* Clark); *m* 1st, 1940, Sylvia (*d* 1998), *d* of J. van Bodegom; one *s* two *d*; 2nd, 2007, Norma Gardiner, MVO. *Educ:* Elizabeth Coll., Guernsey; RAF Coll., Cranwell. Flying posts in France, UK, N Africa, Malta, Sicily and Italy, 1940–44; comd No 223 Squadron, 1943–44; Staff and Staff Coll. Instructor, 1945–48; Far East, 1949–53; comd No 209 Sqn, 1949–51; Jt Planning Staff, 1953–55; Wing Comdr, Flying, Kuala Lumpur, 1955–57; jssc 1958; Dep. Dir of Air Staff Plans, 1958–61; comd RAF Geilenkirchen, 1961–63; Dir of Air Staff Briefing, 1964–66; SASO, HQ FEAF, 1966–67, C of S, 1967–68; Comdt Joint Warfare Estabt, MoD, 1968–70; Asst Chief of Air Staff (Policy), MoD, 1971–72; UK Mem., Perm. Mil. Deputies Gp, CENTO, Ankara, 1972–73; Vice-Chief of Defence Staff, 1974–76; Dep. C-in-C, Allied Forces, Central Europe, 1976–79. FRUSI 2001. KStJ 1980. *Publications:* The Royal Air Force - A Personal Experience, 2001; Ridiculous Rhymes, 2005; *as Desmond Walker:* Bedlam in the Bailiwicks, 1987; Task Force Channel Islands, 1989. *Recreations:* writing, reading. *Address:* La Madeleine De Bas, Ruette de la Madeleine, St Pierre du Bois, Guernsey, CI. *Club:* Royal Air Force.

LECHLER, Sir Robert (Ian), PhD; Kt 2012; FRCP, FRCPath; FMedSci; Professor of Immunology, since 2004, Vice-Principal for Health, since 2005 and Dean, School of Medicine and Dental Institute, Guy's, King's College and St Thomas' Hospitals (formerly Guy's, King's and St Thomas' Schools of Medicine and Dentistry), since 2005, King's College London; Executive Director, King's Health Partners Academic Health Science Centre, since 2009; Hon. Consultant, Department of Renal Medicine and Transplantation, Guy's Hospital, since 2004; *b* 24 Dec. 1951; *s* of Ian Lechler and Audrey Lechler (*née* Wilson); *m* 1st, 1975, Valerie Susan Johnston (separated 1990; marr. diss. 2007); two *s* one *d*; 2nd, 2008, Giovanna Lombardi; one *s* one *d*. *Educ:* Monkton Combe Sch.; Victoria Univ. of Manchester (MB ChB 1975); Royal Postgrad. Med. Sch., Univ. of London (PhD 1983). FRCP 1990; FRCPath 1996. Postgrad. med. trng in internal medicine and renal medicine, Manchester Royal Infirmary, Wythenshawe Hosp. and St Bartholomew's Hosp., London, 1975–79; Med. Res. Trng Fellow, Dept of Immunol., RPMS, 1979–82; Renal Registrar, 1982–83, Sen. Renal Registrar, 1983–84, Professorial Med. Unit, Hammersmith Hosp.; Wellcome Trust Travelling Fellow, Lab. of Immunol., NIH, Bethesda, USA, 1984–86; Royal Postgraduate Medical School: Sen. Lectr in Immunol., 1986–98; Reader in Immunol., 1989–92; Prof. of Molecular Immunol., 1992–94; Hon. Consultant in Medicine, 1986–94; Consultant Transplant Physician, Hammersmith Hosps NHS Trust, 1986–2004; Imperial College, University of London: Prof. of Immunol., 1994–2004; Dean of Hammersmith Campus, 2001–04; Hd, Div. of Medicine, 2003–04; Dean, GKT Sch. of Medicine, KCL, 2004–05. Internat. Advr to NIH Immune Tolerance Network, 2000–. Chairman: Scientific Adv. Bd, Embryonic Stem Cell Internat., 2003–; Expert Adv. Gp, Cttee for Safety of Medicines, 2007–. Councillor, Internat. Xenotransplantation Assoc., 2001–05; Mem. Exec., Council of Hds of Med. Schs, 2006–. Mem., Scientific Cttee, Inst de transplantation et de recherche en transplantation, Nantes, 2000–06; Dir, Ruggero Ceppellini Sch. of Immunol., Naples, 2001–. Chm., Chairs and Prog. Grants Cttee, 2003–07, Trustee, 2010–, BHF. FMedSci 2000 (Council Mem., 2006–). *Publications:* HLA in Health and Disease, 1994, 2nd edn 2000; numerous contribs to leading jls on transplantation and immune tolerance. *Recreations:* theatre, music, sketching. *Address:* (home) 78 Woodstock Road, W4 1EQ; King's Health Partners Academic Health Sciences Centre Headquarters, Ground Floor, Counting House, Guy's Hospital Campus, St Thomas' Street, SE1 9RT. *E:* robert.lechler@kcl.ac.uk.

LECHMERE, Sir Nicholas Anthony Hungerford, 8th Bt *cr* 1818, of The Rhydd, Worcs; *b* 24 April 1960; *e s* of Sir Reginald Lechmere, 7th Bt and Anne Jennifer (*née* Dind); *S* father, 2010; *m* 1991, Caroline Gahan; three *s* one *d*. *Heir: s* Frederick Patrick Hungerford, *b* 9 Dec. 1992.

LECKEY, Mark; artist; *b* Birkenhead, 25 June 1964; *s* of Bruce and Carole Leckey; *m* 2012, Lizzie Carey-Thomas; one *d*. *Educ:* Whitby Comprehensive Sch., Ellesmere Port; Newcastle Poly. (BA Fine Art 1990). Prof. of Film Studies, Städelschule, Frankfurt, 2005–09. *Solo exhibitions* include: Gavin Brown's enterprise, NY, 2000, 2002, 2004, 2006, 2010; Migros Mus., Zurich, 2003; Tate Britain, 2003, 2008; Portikus, Frankfurt, 2005; Industrial Light and Magic, Consortium, Dijon, 2007; Guggenheim Mus., NY, Kölnischer Kunstverein, Cologne, 2008; ICA, London, 2009; Milton Keynes Gall., 2010; Serpentine Gall., 2011; Walter Phillips Gall., Banff Centre, Alberta, Canada, Galerie Buchholz, Berlin, 2012; The Bluecoat, Liverpool, Nottingham Contemp., De La Warr Pavilion, Bexhill-on-Sea, 2013; *group exhibitions* include: ICA, London, 1990, 2000, 2001; Tate Modern, 2001, 2011; Tate Liverpool, 2002; Manifesta 5, Eur. Biennial of Contemp. Art, San Sebastian, Spain, 2004; 9th Istanbul Biennial, 2005; Mus. of Contemp. Art, Chicago, 2007; Contemp. Art Gall., Vancouver, 2009; 8th Gwangju Biennale, S Korea, 2010; Venice Biennale, 2013; *work in public collections* including: Centre Georges Pompidou, Paris; Mus. of Contemp. Art, LA; MOMA, NY; Tate Gall., London; Trussardi Foundn, Milan; Walker Art Center, Minneapolis. Winner, Turner Prize, 2008; Central Art Award, Kölnischer Kunstverein, 2008. *Recreation:* walking. *Address:* 32 Wallace House, Caledonian Road, N7 8TL. *T:* 07894 711830. *E:* mark.leckey@hotmail.com.

LECKIE, Carolyn; Member (Scot Socialist) Scotland Central, Scottish Parliament, 2003–07; *b* 5 March 1965. Midwife. Contested (Scot Socialist), Springburn, 2001. Scot Socialist spokesperson for Health and Community Care, Scottish Parlt, 2003–07.

LECKY, Maj.-Gen. Samuel K.; *see* Knox-Lecky.

LE CLÉZIO, Jean-Marie Gustave; writer; *b* Nice, 13 April 1940; *s* of Raoul Le Clézio; *m* 1975, Jémia Jean; one *d*; one *d* from a previous marriage. *Educ:* Bristol Univ.; Institut d'Études Littéraires, Nice; Univ. of Aix-en-Provence (MA 1964); Univ. of Perpignan (PhD 1983). Prix Théophraste Renaudot, 1963; Nobel Prize for Literature, 2008. *Publications:* Le procès-verbal, 1963 (The Interrogation, 1964); Le jour où Beaumont fit connaissance avec sa douleur, 1964; La fièvre, 1965 (Fever, 1966); Le déluge, 1966 (The Flood, 1967); L'extase matérielle, 1967; Terra Amata, 1967 (Terra Amata, 1969); Le livre des fuites, 1969 (The Book of Flights, 1971); La guerre, 1970 (War, 1973); Haï, 1971; Mydriase, 1973; Les géants, 1973 (The Giants, 1975); Voyages de l'autre côté, 1975; L'inconnu sur la terre, 1978; Vers les icebergs, 1978; Voyage au pays des arbres, 1978; Mondo et autres histoires, 1978; Désert, 1980; Trois villes saintes, 1980; Lullaby, 1980; La ronde et autres faits divers, 1982 (The Round & Other Cold Hard Facts, 2002); Celui qui n'avait jamais vu la mer, La montagne du dieu vivant, 1982; Balaabilou, 1985; Le chercheur d'or, 1985 (The Prospector, 1993); Villa Aurore, Orlamonde, 1985; Voyage à Rodrigues, 1986; Le rêve mexicain ou la pensée interrompue, 1988 (The Mexican Dream or The Interrupted Thought of Amerindian Civilizations, 1993); Printemps et autres saisons, 1989; La grande vie, Peuple du ciel, 1990; Onitsha, 1991 (Onitsha, 1997); Étoile errante, 1992 (Wandering Star, 2004); Pawana, 1992; Diego et Frida, 1993; La quarantaine, 1995; Poisson d'or, 1996; La fête chantée, 1997; Hasard, Angoli Mala, 1999; Coeur brûlé et autres romances, 2000; Révolutions, 2003; L'Africain, 2004; Ourania, 2005; Raga: approche du continent invisible, 2006; Ballaciner, 2007; Ritournelle de la faim, 2008; Histoire du pied et autres fantaisies, 2011; Les musées sont des mondes, 2011. *Address:* c/o Éditions Gallimard, 5 rue Gaston-Gallimard, 75328 Paris cedex 07, France.

LE COCQ, Timothy John; QC (Jersey) 2008; Deputy Bailiff for Jersey, since 2015; *b* Jersey, 9 Dec. 1956; *s* of Bernard Reginald Le Cocq and Janet Le Cocq (*née* Gibbs); *m* 1st, 1988, Elizabeth Case (marr. diss. 1994); one *s*; 2nd, 1994, Ruth Iona Leighton; two *s* one *d*. *Educ:* De La Salle Coll., Jersey; Univ. of Keele (BA Hons Law and Psychol. 1980). Called to the Bar, Inner Temple, 1981; called to Jersey Bar, 1985; in practice as Jersey Advocate, 1985–2008; Crown Advocate, Jersey, 1996–2008; HM Solicitor Gen. for Jersey, 2008–09; HM Attorney Gen. for Jersey, 2009–15. *Address:* c/o Bailiff's Chambers, Royal Court House, St Helier, Jersey JE1 1BA. *T:* (01534) 441103, *Fax:* (01534) 441137. *E:* DeputyBailiff@gov.je. *Clubs:* Oriental; United (Jersey).

LECONFIELD, Baron; *see* Egremont.

LEDERER, Peter Julian, CBE 2005 (OBE 1994); Chairman, Gleneagles Hotels Ltd, 2007–14 (Managing Director, 1984–2007); Chairman: Taste Communications, since 2011; Hamilton & Inches Ltd (Director, since 2008); Applecrate; *b* 30 Nov. 1950; *s* of Thomas F. Lederer and Phoebe J. Lederer; *m* 1981, Marilyn R. MacPhail; two *s*. *Educ:* City of London Sch.; Middlesex Poly. (Nat. Dip. Hotelkeeping and Catering); INSEAD (AMP 1994). Manager, Four Seasons Hotels, 1972–79; Partner and Vice Pres., Wood Wilkings Ltd, 1979–81; Gen. Manager, Plaza Hotels Ltd, 1981–83. Hon. Prof., Univ. of Dundee, 1994. Director: Leading Hotels of the World, 1998–2012; Diageo Scotland, 2008–14; Baxters Food Gp; Pod Global Solutions; Royal Edinburgh Military Tattoo. Chairman: Scottish Tourist Bd, later VisitScotland, 2001–10; Saltire Foundn, 2009–14; Internat. Leadership Sch., 2010–14. Patron: Hospitality Industry Trust Scotland, 2004– (Chm., 1992–2003); Queen Margaret UC Foundn, 1998. FIH (FHCIMA 1987; Pres., Inst. of Hospitality, 2007–12); CCMI 2002. Liveryman, Co. of Innholders, 1999–. Hon. DBA Queen Margaret UC, 1997; DUniv Stirling, 2009. Master Innholder, 1988. *Recreations:* motor racing, current affairs, travel. *Address:* 18 Great Stuart Street, Edinburgh EH3 7TN. *T:* 07803 855421. *E:* pjlederer@icloud.com.

LEDERMAN, David; QC 1990; a Recorder, 1987–2014; *b* 8 Feb. 1942; *s* of late Eric Kurt Lederman and Marjorie Alice Lederman; *m* 2003, Jennifer Oldland; one *s* two *d* from a previous marriage. *Educ:* Clayesmore School, Dorset; Gonville and Caius College, Cambridge. Called to the Bar, Inner Temple, 1966; criminal practice, fraud, murder, etc. *Recreations:* tennis, horses, France, family.

LEDERMAN, Dr Leon Max, FInstP; Director, Fermi National Accelerator Laboratory, 1979–89, Director Emeritus, since 1989; Pritzker Professor of Science, Illinois Institute of Technology, since 1992; *b* 15 July 1922; *s* of Minnie Rosenberg and Morris Lederman; *m* 1st, Florence Gordon; one *s* two *d*; 2nd, 1981, Ellen. *Educ:* City College of New York (BS 1943); Columbia Univ. (AM 1948; PhD 1951). FInstP 1998. US Army, 1943–46. Columbia University: Research Associate, Asst Prof., Associate Prof., 1951–58; Prof. of Physics, 1958–89; Associate Dir, Nevis Labs, 1953, Director, 1962–79. Resident Scholar, Ill Maths and Sci. Acad., 1998–. Ford Foundn Fellow, 1958–59; John Simon Guggenheim Foundn Fellow, 1958–59; Ernest Kempton Adams Fellow, 1961. Fellow, Amer. Physical Soc.; Mem., Nat. Acad. of Scis, 1965. Numerous hon. degrees. Nat. Medal of Science, 1965; (jtly) Nobel Prize in Physics, 1988; Enrico Fermi Prize, DOE, US, 1992. *Publications:* From Quarks to the Cosmos, 1989; The God Particle, 1992; Symmetry and the Beautiful Universe, 2004; papers and contribs to learned jls on high energy physics. *Recreations:* mountain hiking, ski-ing, jogging, piano, riding, gardening. *Address:* c/o Fermi National Accelerator Laboratory, PO Box 500, Batavia, IL 60510–5011, USA. *T:* (630) 8402856, (312) 5678920.

LEDGER, Frank, CBE 1992 (OBE 1985); FREng; Deputy Chairman, Nuclear Electric plc, 1990–92, retired; *b* 16 June 1929; *s* of Harry and Doris Ledger; *m* 1953, Alma Moverley; two *s*. *Educ:* Leeds College of Technology (BSc Eng). FREng (FEng 1990); FIMechE; FIET. Student Apprentice, Leeds Corp. Elect. Dept, 1947; appts in power station construction and generation operation in CEA then CEGB, 1955–65; Station Manager, Cottam Power Station, 1965; Central Electricity Generating Board: Group Manager, Midlands Region, 1968; System Operation Engineer, 1971; Dir, Resource Planning, Midlands Region, 1975; Dir of Computing, 1980; Dir of Operations, 1981; Exec. Bd Mem. for Prodn, 1986. Sen. Associate, Nichols Associates Ltd, 1992–98. Member: Council, IEE, 1987–92; British Nat. Cttee, UNIPEDE, 1981–90; Council, British Energy Assoc., 1990–92; Vice-Pres., Energy Industries Club, 1988–92. *Publications:* (jtly) Crisis Management in the Power Industry: an inside story, 1994. *Recreations:* music, photography, gardening, walking. *Address:* 3 Barns Dene, Harpenden, Herts AL5 2HH. *T:* (01582) 762188.

LEDINGHAM, Prof. John Gerard Garvin, DM; FRCP; May Reader in Medicine, 1974–95, Professor of Clinical Medicine, 1989–95, and Director of Clinical Studies, 1977–82 and 1991–95, University of Oxford; Fellow of New College, Oxford, 1974–95, Emeritus, 1995–2000, Hon. Fellow, since 2000; Hon. Clinical Director, Biochemical and Clinical NMR Unit, Medical Research Council, Oxford, 1988–95; *b* 19 Oct. 1929; *s* of late John Ledingham, MB BCh, DPH, and late Una Ledingham, MD, FRCP, *d* of J. L. Garvin, CH, Editor of The Observer; *m* 1961, Elaine Mary, *d* of late R. G. Maliphant, MD, FRCOG, and of Dilys Maliphant, Cardiff; four *d*. *Educ:* Rugby Sch.; New Coll., Oxford; Middlesex Hosp. Med. Sch. (1st Cl. Physiol. 1954; BM BCh 1957; DM 1966). FRCP 1971 (MRCP 1959). Junior appts, Middlesex, London Chest, Whittington, and Westminster Hospitals, London, 1957–64; Travelling Fellow, British Postgraduate Med. Fedn, Columbia Univ., New York, 1965–66; Consultant Physician, Oxford AHA(T), 1966–82, Hon. Consultant Physician, Oxfordshire HA, 1982–. Chm., Medical Staff Council, United Oxford Hosps, 1970–72. Chm., Medical Res. Soc., 1988–92; Hon. Sec., Assoc. of Physicians of Gt Britain and Ireland 1977–82, Hon. Treas., 1982–88; Pro-Censor, RCP, 1983–84, Censor, 1984–85. Member: Commonwealth Scholarship Commn, ACU, 1993–98; Nuffield Council on Bioethics, 2000–03. Governing Trustee, Nuffield Trust (formerly Nuffield Provincial Hosps Trust), 1978–2002; Trustee, Beit Trust, 1989–2008. Osler Meml Medal, Oxford Univ., 2000. Distinguished Friend of Univ. of Oxford, 2011. *Publications:* (ed jtly) Oxford Textbook of Medicine, 1982, 3rd edn 1995; (ed with Mark Pottle) We Hope to Get Word Tomorrow: the Garvin family letters 1914–16, 2009; contribs to med. books and scientific jls in the field of hypertension and renal diseases. *Recreations:* music, golf. *Address:* 124 Oxford Road, Cumnor, Oxford OX2 9PQ. *T:* (01865) 865806. *E:* jeled@btinternet.com. *Club:* Vincent's (Oxford).

LEDLIE, John Kenneth, CB 1994; OBE 1977; Director, Peter Harrison Foundation, 2002–11; *b* 19 March 1942; *s* of late Reginald Cyril Bell Ledlie and Elspeth Mary Kaye; *m* 1st, 1965, Rosemary Julia Allan (marr. diss. 2006); three *d*; 2nd, 2011, Elisabeth Leader. *Educ:* Westminster School (Hon. Schol.); Brasenose Coll., Oxford (Triplett Exhibnr; MA Lit Hum); Open Univ. (BA Hons 2011). Solicitor of the High Court; articles with Coward Chance, 1964–67; Min. of Defence, 1967; Asst Private Sec. to Minister of State for Equipment and Sec. of State for Defence, 1969–70; First Sec., UK Delegn to NATO, Brussels, 1973–76; Dep. Chief, Public Relations, 1977–79; NI Office and Cabinet Office, 1979–81; Procurement Exec., MoD, 1981–83; Head, Defence Secretariat 19, MoD, 1983; Regional Marketing Dir, Defence Sales Orgn, 1983–85; Chief of PR, MoD, 1985–87; Fellow, Center for Internat. Affairs, Harvard Univ., 1987–88; Asst Under-Sec. of State, MoD, 1988–90; Dep. Sec., NI Office, 1990–93; Dep. Under Sec. of State (Personnel and Logistics), MoD, 1993–95; Partnership Sec., Linklaters & Paines, subseq. Linklaters, 1995–2002. *Recreations:* ornithology, cricket, tennis, theatre, opera. *Address:* 1030 Mission Ridge Road, Santa Barbara, CA 93103, USA.

Le DRIAN, Jean-Yves; Minister of Defence, France, since 2012; *b* Lorient, 30 June 1947. *Educ:* Univ. of Rennes. Mem., Lorient Town Council, 1977 (Mayor, 1981–98). Mem. (Soc.) for Morbihan, Nat. Assembly, 1978–91 and 1992–2007; Sec. of State for Sea, Min. of Works, Housing and Transport and Space, 1991–92. Pres., Regl Council, Brittany, 2004–. Nat. Sec. i/c defence matters, Socialist Party, 2004–12. Hon. Inspector Gen., Nat. Educn Dept. *Address:* Ministère de la Défense, 14 rue St Dominique, 75007 Paris, France.

LEDSOME, Neville Frank, CB 1988; Deputy Chairman, Civil Service Appeal Board, 1994–99; Under Secretary, Personnel Management Division, Department of Trade and Industry, 1983–89, retired; *b* 29 Nov. 1929; *s* of late Charles Percy Ledsome and Florence Ledsome; *m* 1953, Isabel Mary Lindsay; three *s*. *Educ:* Birkenhead Sch. Exec. Officer, BoT, 1948; Monopolies Commn, 1957; Higher Exec. Officer, BoT, 1961; Principal, 1964; DEA, 1967; HM Treasury, 1969; DTI, 1970; Asst Sec., 1973; Under Sec., 1980. *Recreations:* gardening, theatre.

LEE, family name of **Baron Lee of Trafford**.

LEE OF TRAFFORD, Baron *cr* 2006 (Life Peer), of Bowdon in the County of Cheshire; **John Robert Louis Lee;** DL; FCA; company director, investor and financial journalist; *b* 21 June 1942; *s* of late Basil and Miriam Lee; *m* 1975, Anne Monique Bakirgian; two *d*. *Educ:* William Hulme's Grammar Sch., Manchester. Accountancy Articles, 1959–64; Henry Cooke, Lumsden & Co., Manchester, Stockbrokers, 1964–66; Founding Dir, Chancery Consolidated Ltd, Investment Bankers; non-executive Director: Paterson Zochonis (UK) Ltd, 1974–75; Paterson Zochonis PLC, 1990–99; Emerson Developments (Hldgs), 2000–; Chm., WMC Retail Partners (formerly Wellington Market) plc, 2006–. Contested (C) Manchester, Moss Side, Oct. 1974; MP (C) Nelson and Colne, 1979–83, Pendle, 1983–92; contested (C) Pendle, 1992. PPS to Minister of State for Industry, 1981–83, to Sec. of State for Trade and Industry, 1983; Parly Under Sec. of State, MoD, 1983–86, Dept of Employment, 1986–89 (Minister for Tourism, 1987–89). Chm., All-Party Tourism Cttee, 1991–92. Jt Sec., Conservative Back Benchers' Industry Cttee, 1979–80. Lib Dem spokesman on Defence, H of L, 2007–12. Mem., Jt Cttee on Nat. Security Strategy, 2010–. Chm., Christie Hosp. NHS Trust, 1992–98. Chairman: ALVA, 1990–; Mus. of Sci. and Industry in Manchester, 1990–2001; Mem., English Tourist Bd, 1992–99. Vice-Chm., NW Conciliation Cttee, Race Relations Bd, 1976–77; Chm. Council, Nat. Youth Bureau, 1980–83. DL 1995, High Sheriff 1998, Greater Manchester. *Publications:* How to Make a Million - Slowly, 2014. *Recreations:* golf, fly fishing, collecting. *Address:* House of Lords, SW1A 0PW.

LEE, Alan John; book illustrator, since 1972; film conceptual designer, since 1983; *b* 20 Aug. 1947; *s* of George James Lee and Margaret Lee (*née* Cook); *m* 1979, Marja Kruyt (marr. diss.); one *s* one *d*. *Educ:* Manor Secondary Modern Sch., Ruislip; Ealing Sch. of Art. Conceptual designer of films: Legend, 1985; Erik the Viking, 1989; The Hobbit: An Unexpected Journey, 2012; The Desolation of Smaug, 2013; The Battle of the Five Armies, 2014; conceptual designer and set decorator of films: The Fellowship of the Ring, 2001; The Two Towers, 2002; The Return of the King, 2003 (Academy Award for Art Direction, 2004). *Publications: illustrator:* The Importance of Being Ernest, 1972; Faeries, 1978, 2nd edn 2003; The Mabinogion, 1982, 2nd edn 2002; Castles, 1984; Michael Palin, The Mirrorstone, 1986; Joan Aiken, The Moon's Revenge, 1987; Peter Dickinson, Merlin Dreams, 1988; J. R. R. Tolkien, The Lord of the Rings, 1992; Rosemary Sutcliff, Black Ships Before Troy (Kate Greenaway Medal), 1993; Rosemary Sutcliff, The Wanderings of Odysseus, 1995; J. R. R. Tolkien, The Hobbit, 1997; J. R. R. Tolkien, The Children of Hurin, 2007; J. R. R. Tolkien, Tales from the Perilous Realm, 2008; Adrian Mitchell, Shapeshifters, 2009; *written and illustrated:* The Lord of the Rings Sketchbook, 2005. *Recreation:* tango dancing. *E:* alanlee@dircon.co.uk. *Club:* Pudding (Chagford).

LEE, Alan Peter; racing correspondent, The Times, since 1999; *b* 13 June 1954; *s* of Peter Alexander Lee and Christina Carmichael; *m* 1980, Patricia Drury; one *s* one *d*. *Educ:* Cavendish Grammar Sch., Hemel Hempstead. With Watford Observer, 1970–74; Hayters Agency, 1974–78; freelance, 1978–82; cricket correspondent: Mail on Sunday, 1982–87; The Times, 1988–99. Racing Journalist of the Year, HWPA Derby Awards, 2001, 2004, 2014. *Publications:* A Pitch in Both Camps, 1979; Diary of a Cricket Season, 1980; Lambourn, Village of Racing, 1983; Raising the Stakes: the modern cricket revolution, 1996; The Course Inspector: racecourse guide to Britain, 2001; *biographies:* (with Tony Greig) My Story, 1978; (with David Gower) With Time to Spare, 1980; (with Graham Gooch) Out of the Wilderness, 1985; Fred (biog. of Fred Winter), 1991; (with Pat Eddery) To Be A Champion, 1992; Lord Ted: the Dexter enigma, 1995; (with David Lloyd) David Lloyd: the autobiography, 2000; (with Richard Johnson) Out of the Shadows: the Richard Johnson story, 2002. *Recreations:* National Hunt racing (has owned or part-owned ten horses), tennis, wine. *Address:* 8 The Courtyard, Montpellier Street, Cheltenham, Glos GL50 1SR. *T:* (01242) 572637. *Club:* Cricketers'.

LEE, Allen; *see* Lee Peng-Fei, A.

LEE, Dr Anne Mary Linda; independent academic consultant, since 2010; Senior Academic Development Adviser, University of Surrey, 2005–10; *b* 14 Oct. 1953; *d* of Cecil and Eugenie Covell; *m* 1973, Anthony Mervyn Lee, *qv*; one *s* one *d*. *Educ:* Shenfield High Sch.; Open Univ. (BA); Univ. of Surrey (PhD). FCIPD; GMBPS; FHEA 2007; FSEDA 2009, SFSEDA 2011. Inf. Officer, Unilever, 1972–74; Trng Officer, G. D. Searle & Co., 1974–76; Management and Trng Advr, Industrial Soc., 1976–78; Head of Trng, Morgan Guaranty Trust Co., 1978–81; Dir, Anne M. Lee (Training) Ltd, 1983–94; Headmistress, Malvern Girls' Coll., 1994–96. Dir, Next Chapter Ltd, 1998–2006. Mem., Huhne Commn on Future of Public Services, 2001–02. Mem. (Lib Dem), Guildford BC, 1997–2001. Contested (Lib Dem): Norfolk S, 2001; Woking, 2005. Member Board/Trustee: Guildford CAB, 1998–2001; Merrow Sunset Homes, 1998–2001; Guildford and Waverly PCT, 1999–2001; Lay Chm., Guildford Deanery Synod, 2012–. Gov., Queenswood Sch., 1996–2005.

Publications: Supervision Teams: making them work, 2008; Helping New Postgraduates: a guide for academics, 2009; (with M. Pettigrove) Preparing to Teach in Higher Education, 2010; Successful Research Supervision, 2012; contribs to educnl, personnel and management jls and The Times. *Recreations:* singing, walking, friendship, words and music. *Address:* The Post House, West Clandon, Guildford, Surrey GU4 7ST. *T:* (01483) 222610. *W:* www.drannelee.wordpress.com.

LEE, Anthony Mervyn; Chief Executive (formerly Director), Age Concern Surrey, 2001–10; *b* 21 Feb. 1949; *s* of Sydney Ernest Lee and Evelyn May Lee; *m* 1973, Anne Mary Linda Lee, *qv*; one *s* one *d*. *Educ:* Romford Sch.; Cranfield Sch. of Mgt (MBA). FCCA 1971; FCMA 1975. Financial trng, Eastern Electricity Bd, 1967–72; Finance Manager, ITT SemiConductors, 1972–74; Financial Controller, Mars Confectionery, 1974–77; Managing Director: Am Bruning Ltd, 1978–82; Citibank Trust, 1982–86; Chief Exec., Access (JCCC Ltd), 1987–91; Ops Dir, Natwest Card Services, 1991–97; Exec. Dir, Muscular Dystrophy Campaign, 1998–2001. Trustee: Age Concern Mole Valley North, 2009–; Age Concern Dorking, 2009–14; Homestart, 2011– (Treas., 2011–). *Recreations:* keep fit, gardening, politics. *Address:* The Post House, The Street, West Clandon, Surrey GU4 7ST. *T:* (01483) 222610.

LEE, Christopher Robin James, RD 1981 (Bar 1991); historian, writer and broadcaster; *b* 13 Oct. 1941; *s* of James Thomas Lee and Winifred Lee (*née* Robertson); *m* 1st, 1969, Christine Elizabeth Adams (marr. diss. 2010); two *d*; 2nd, 2011, Fiona Margaret Graham-Mackay (*née* Bain). *Educ:* Dartford Tech. Sch.; Wilmington Grammar Sch.; Goldsmiths' Coll., London; Birkbeck Coll., London (MA History of Ideas). Deck apprentice, 1958–59; freelance writer, 1962–67; journalist, Daily Express, 1967–76 (Asst Ed., 1975–76); Defence and Foreign Affairs Corresp., BBC radio, 1976–86; Quatercentenary Fellow in Contemporary Hist., Emmanuel Coll., Cambridge, 1986–91; lecturer, author and scriptwriter, 1991–; various BBC radio drama and comedy series incl. The Archers, The House, Colvil and Soames, The Trial of Walter Ralegh, Our Brave Boys, A Pattern in Shrouds, 1987–2009; Kicking the Habit, 2007–08; Air Force One, 2013; This Sceptred Isle, hist. of Britain, 1995–96, This Sceptred Isle, 90-pt hist. series, 2005–06, Radio 4. Dir, Sceptred Isle Publishing Ltd, 2006–; Editl Adv. Bd, BBC History Mag., 2001–; Historical Advr to NT production of Saint Joan, 2007. Sen. Tutor, Creative Writing, Bayford Studios, 2008–; global politics analyst, Limehouse Gp of Commentators, 2001–; defence and foreign affairs analyst, British Forces Broadcasting Services, 2010–; internat. politics analyst on climate change, Fort Foundn, 2014–. Vis. Lectr, Univ. of Utah, 1986; Gomes Lectr, Emmanuel Coll., Cambridge, 2001. FRSA 2008. Royal Naval Reserve: Services Intelligence Wing, 1966–82; OC Public Affairs Br., 1982–86; CO, HMS Wildfire, 1988–90. Trustee, Sail Trng Assoc., 1994–2001. Younger Brother, Trinity House, 2002–. *Publications:* Seychelles: political castaways, 1976; Final Decade, 1981; (with Bhupendra Jasani) Countdown to Space War, 1984; War in Space, 1987; (ed) Nicely Nurdled Sir, 1988; From the Sea End, 1989; The Madrigal, 1993; The House, 1994; The Bath Detective, 1995; (ed) Through the Covers, 1996; Killing of Sally Keemer, 1997; This Sceptred Isle 55 BC–1901, 1997; (ed) History of the English-speaking Peoples, 1998; The Killing of Cinderella, 1998; The 20th Century, 1999; Eight Bells and Topmasts, 2001; Dynasties, 2002; 1603: a turning point in English history, 2003; This Sceptred Isle: Empire, 2005; Nelson & Napoleon: the long haul to Trafalgar, 2005; This Sceptred Isle: the making of the British, 2012; Monarchy: past, present… future?, 2013; Royal Ceremonial, 2015; The Viceroys, 2016. *Recreations:* opera, sailing. *Address:* Woodside, Beckley, E Sussex TN31 6UE. *Clubs:* Athenæum, Eccentrics, MCC; Royal Naval Sailing Association.

LEE, Colin Geoffrey; Principal Clerk, Committee Office, House of Commons, since 2013; *b* Petts Wood, 18 Sept. 1965; *s* of Geoffrey and Susan Lee; *m* 2006, Brenda Barker. *Educ:* Trinity Sch., Croydon; Pembroke Coll., Cambridge (BA 1988). House of Commons: procedural, cttee and internat. posts, 1988–97; Clerk: Culture, Media and Sport Cttee, 1997–2001; Public Bill Office, 2001–05; Treasury Cttee, 2005–08; Dir, Departmental Services, 2008–10; Clerk, Table Office, 2010–11; on secondment to Cabinet Office as Parly Advr, 2011–12; Clerk, Parly Commn on Banking Standards, 2012–13. *Recreations:* theatre, watching Chelsea FC. *Address:* House of Commons, SW1A 0AA. *T:* (020) 7219 3000.

LEE, Ven. David John, PhD; Archdeacon of Bradford, 2004–Jan. 2016; *b* 31 Jan. 1946; *s* of John and Sheila Lee; *m* 1989, Janet Mary Strong; two *s*. *Educ:* Bristol Univ. (BSc Mech. Eng 1967); London Univ. (DipTh 1973); Fitzwilliam Coll., Cambridge (BA (Theol.) 1976, MA 1979); Birmingham Univ. (PhD (NT Studies) 1996). Schoolmaster: Lesotho, Southern Africa, 1967; Walsall, 1968. Ordained deacon, 1977, priest, 1978; Curate, St Margaret's, Putney, 1977–80; Lecturer: in Theol., Bp Tucker Coll., Mukono, Uganda, 1980–86; in Missiology, Selly Oak Colls, Birmingham, 1986–91; Rector, Middleton and Wishaw, Birmingham, 1991–96; Dir of Mission, Dio. Birmingham, and Canon Residentiary, Birmingham Cathedral, 1996–2004. Non-exec. Dir, Bradford Churches for Dialogue and Diversity, 2005–; Director and Chairman: Wellsprings Together Bradford, 2011–; Bradford Diocese Acads Trust, 2012–; Chm., Bradford Diocesan Adv. Cttee, 2012–. *Publications:* Discovering Science (jtly), 1970; Jesus in the Stories of Luke, 1999; (ed) Ministry and Mission in a Multifaith Context, 2001. *Recreations:* conversation, music, walking, motoring, multi-media, DIY in its better manifestations, redeeming the vocation of property landlords. *Address:* 47 Kirkgate, Shipley, W Yorks BD18 3EH. *T:* (01274) 200698, 07711 671351. *E:* david.lee@westyorkshiredales.org.

LEE, Prof. David Morris, FInstP; James Gilbert White Distinguished Professor of Physical Sciences, Cornell University, 1997–2009, now Emeritus; Professor of Physics, Texas A&M University, since 2009; *b* 20 Jan. 1931; *s* of Marvin and Annette Lee; *m* 1960, Dana Thorangkul; two *s*. *Educ:* Harvard Univ. (AB 1952); Connecticut Univ. (MS 1955); Yale Univ. (PhD Physics 1959). FInstP 1998. US Army, 1952–54. Cornell University: Instructor in Physics, 1959–60; Asst Prof., 1960–63; Associate Prof., 1963–68; Prof. of Physics, 1968–. Guggenheim Fellow, 1966, 1974; Fellow, Japan Soc. for Promotion of Science, 1977. Member: Amer. Acad. Arts and Scis, 1987; Nat. Acad. of Scis, 1991. Sir Francis Simon Meml Prize, British Inst. of Physics, 1976; Oliver Buckley Prize, APS, 1981; (jtly) Nobel Prize for Physics, 1996. *Publications:* articles in learned jls. *Recreations:* hiking in the mountains, fishing, boating, running. *Address:* Department of Physics and Astronomy, Texas A&M University, 4242 TAMU, College Station, TX 77843–4242, USA.

LEE, Derek William, FCIB; Chairman, Friendly Societies Commission, 1992–98; *b* 11 April 1935; *s* of Richard William Lee and Ivy Elizabeth Lee; *m* 1960, Dorothy Joan Preece; one *d*. *Educ:* St Dunstan's Coll.; London Univ. (LLB Hons external). FCIB 1973. Nat. Service, REME, Malaya, 1953–55. Lloyds Bank, 1955–73, Manager, Threadneedle St Br., 1970–73; Asst Gen. Manager, 1973–77, Gen. Manager, 1977–87, Mercantile Credit Co. Ltd; Man. Dir, H & H Factors, 1988–89; Registrar, Friendly Societies, 1989–95. Gov., Guy's and St Thomas' Hosp. Foundn Trust, 2004–07; Mem. Cttee, Samaritan Fund, Hosp. Authy Charitable Foundn, 2007–08. Freeman, City of London, 1999. *Recreations:* art, golf, bowls. *Clubs:* Bromley Town Bowling; Duke of Kent Bowls.

LEE, Dame Hermione, DBE 2013 (CBE 2003); FRSL; FBA 2001; President, Wolfson College, Oxford, since 2008; Pro-Vice-Chancellor, University of Oxford, since 2014; *b* 29 Feb. 1948; *d* of Dr Benjamin Lee and Josephine Lee (*née* Anderson); *m* 1991, Prof. John Michael Barnard, *qv*. *Educ:* St Hilda's Coll., Oxford (MA; Hon. Fellow, 1998); St Cross Coll., Oxford (MPhil; Hon. Fellow, 1998). Instructor, Coll. of William and Mary, Williamsburg, Va, 1970–71; Lectr, Dept of English, Univ. of Liverpool, 1971–77; Department of English and Related Literature, University of York: Lectr, 1977–87; Sen. Lectr, 1987–90; Reader, 1990–93; Prof., 1993–98; Goldsmiths' Prof. of English Literature, Univ. of Oxford, 1998–2008; Fellow, New Coll., Oxford, 1998–2008 (Hon. Fellow, 2009). Presenter, Book Four, Channel 4, 1982–86. Chair of Judges, Man Booker Prize, 2006. FRSL 1992. For. Hon. Mem., Amer. Acad. of Arts and Scis, 2003. Hon. DLitt: Liverpool; York; KCL. *Publications:* The Novels of Virginia Woolf, 1977; Elizabeth Bowen, 1981, 2nd edn 1999; Philip Roth, 1982; (ed) The Mulberry Tree: writings of Elizabeth Bowen, 1986; Willa Cather: a life saved up, 1989, US edn as Willa Cather: double lives, 1991; (ed) The Selected Stories of Willa Cather, 1989; Virginia Woolf, 1996; Body Parts: essays on life-writing, 2005; Edith Wharton, 2007; Biography: a very short introduction, 2009; Penelope Fitzgerald: a life, 2013. *Recreations:* reading, music, countryside. *Address:* Wolfson College, Oxford OX2 6UD. *Club:* Athenæum.

LEE, James Giles; Principal, Lee & Company, since 1992; *b* 23 Dec. 1942; *s* of John Lee, CBE and Muriel Giles; *m* 1966, Linn Macdonald; one *s* two *d*. *Educ:* Trinity Coll., Glenalmond; Glasgow Univ.; Harvard Univ., USA. Consultant, McKinsey & Co., 1969–80; Mem., Central Policy Review Staff, 1972. Dep. Chm. and Chief Exec., Pearson Longman, 1980–83; Chairman: Penguin Publishing Co., 1980–84; Direct Broadcasting by Satellite Consortium, 1986–87; Deputy Chairman: Westminster Press, 1980–84; Financial Times, 1980–84; Yorkshire TV, 1982–85; Dir, S. Pearson & Son, 1981–84; Chm., 1981–85, Chief Exec., 1983–85, Goldcrest Films and Television; Dir, Boston Consulting Gp, 1987–92. Non-executive Director: Pearson Television, 1993–2001; Phoenix Pictures Inc., 1996–2004; Nation Media Gp, Kenya, 2001–10. Chairman: Performing Arts Labs Trust, 1989–99; Scottish Screen, 1998–2002; Bureau of Investigative Journalism, 2010–; Dir, Film Council, 1999–2004. Chm., Maidstone and Tunbridge Wells NHS Trust, 2003–07. *Publications:* Planning for the Social Services, 1978; The Investment Challenge, 1979. *Recreations:* photography, travelling, sailing. *Address:* Meadow Wood, Penshurst, Kent TN11 8AD. *T:* (01892) 870309. *Clubs:* Reform; Harvard (New York).

LEE, Hon. James Matthew; PC (Can.) 1982; Chairman, PEI Workers Compensation Board, 1998–2007; Leader, Progressive Conservative Party, Prince Edward Island, 1981–96; *b* Charlottetown, 26 March 1937; *s* of late James Matthew Lee and of Catherine Blanchard Lee; *m* 1960, Patricia, *d* of late Ivan Laurie; one *s* two *d*. *Educ:* Queen's Square Sch.; St Dunstan's Univ. Architectural draftsman. Elected MLA (PC) for 5th Queens Riding, by-election, 1975; former Minister: of Health and Social Services; of Tourism, Parks and Conservation; Premier and Pres. Exec. Council, PEI, 1981–86. Comr, Canadian Pension Commn, 1986–97. Jaycee Internat. Senator, 1983. Hon. LLD, 2005. *Address:* 2906 Bayshore Road, Stanhope, PE C0A 1P0, Canada. *T:* (902) 6722870.

LEE, Maj.-Gen. (James) Stuart, CB 1990; MBE 1970; Director of Army Education, 1987–90; *b* 26 Dec. 1934; *s* of George Lee and Elizabeth (*née* Hawkins); *m* 1960, Alice Lorna (*d* 2007); one *s*. *Educ:* Normanton Grammar Sch.; Leeds Univ. (BA Hons); King's Coll., London (MA War Studies, 1976). Pres., Leeds Univ. Union, 1958–59. Educn Officer in UK Trng Units, Catterick, Taunton, Bovington, 1959–64; Mil. Trng Officer, Beaconsfield, 1964; RMCS and Staff Coll., 1964–65; DAQMG HQ Cyprus Dist, 1966 and HQ NEARELF, 1967; SO2 MoD (Army Educn 1), 1968–70; DAA&QMG HQ FARELF, 1970 and GSO2 HQ FARELF, 1970–71; OC Officer Wing, Beaconsfield, 1971–74; Gp Educn Officer, 34 AEC, Rheindahlen, 1974–75; Chief Educn Officer, HQ NE Dist, 1976–78; Hd, Officer Educn Br., 1978–79; SO1 Trng HQ UKLF, 1979; Chief Inspector of Army Educn and Col Res., 1980–82; Res. Associate, IISS, 1982–83; Comdr Educn, HQ BAOR, 1983–87. Dep. Col Comdt, AGC, 1993–97. Pres., RAEC Assoc., 1993–97. Dep. Comr, British Scouts Western Europe, 1983–87; Mem., Management Bd, NFER, 1987–90. Non-exec. Dir, Exhibition Consultants Ltd, 1990–99. Dir and Trustee, Assessment and Qualifications Alliance, 1998–2002; Member: Nat Adv. Bd, Duke of Edinburgh Award Scheme, 1987–90; Council, Scout Assoc., 1988–98. City and Guilds of London Institute: Mem. Council, 1989–2007; Jt Hon. Sec., 1993–2004; Chm., Sen. Awards Cttee, 1990–99; Chm., Inst. Affairs and Awards Cttee, 1999–2002; Chm., Strategy and Advancement Cttee, 2002–04. Trustee and Sec., Gallipoli Meml Lecture Trust, 1987–90. Gov., 1991–99, Mem. Court, 1999, Imperial Coll.; Mem. Court, Univ. of Leeds, 1994–2004. FRSA 1987; FIPD (FITD 1991); Hon. FCGI 1996. *Publications:* contrib. Arms Transfers in Third World Development, 1984; Old Wine in a New Bottle, 2010; Magic Aces, 2011; Out Of The Box, 2012; All Together Now, 2012. *Recreations:* theatre, boats, card magic.

LEE, Jessica Katherine; *b* Nottingham, 7 April 1976; *d* of John Anthony and Rosemary Lee. *Educ:* Loughborough High Sch.; Royal Holloway, Univ. of London (BA Hons); Coll. of Law, London (CPE, BVC). Called to the Bar, Middle Temple, 2000; in practice as barrister, London, 2001–08, 2010–, Nottingham, 2008–. MP (C) Erewash, 2010–15. PPS to Attorney-General, 2010–15. Mem., Justice Select Cttee, 2010–15. *Recreations:* food and drink, theatre, parties, learning to fly. *Club:* Carlton.

LEE, John Michael Hubert; Barrister-at-Law; *b* 13 Aug. 1927; *s* of late Victor Lee, Wentworth, Surrey, and late Renee Lee; *m* 1960, Margaret Ann, *d* of late James Russell, ICS, retired, and late Kathleen Russell; one *s* one *d*. *Educ:* Reading Sch.; Christ's Coll., Cambridge (Open Exhibnr Modern Hist.; 2nd Cl. Hons Pts I and II of Hist. Tripos; MA). Colonial Service: Administrative Officer, Ghana, 1951–58; Principal Assistant Secretary, Min. of Communications, Ghana, 1958. On staff of BBC, 1959–65. Called to the Bar, Middle Temple, 1960; practising, Midland and Oxford Circuit, 1966–; Dep. Circuit Judge, 1978–81; Assistant Recorder, 1981–87. MP (Lab) Reading, 1966–70; MP (Lab) Birmingham, Handsworth, Feb. 1974–1979; Chm., W Midland Gp of Labour MPs, 1974–75. *Recreations:* watching tennis, watching cricket, walking, studying philosophy, studying green issues. *Club:* Royal Over-Seas League.

LEE, Linda Karen Hadfield; Solicitor, specialising in regulatory law, Radcliffes Le Brasseur, London, since 2012; President, Law Society of England and Wales, 2010–11; *b* Sheffield, 28 Nov. 1962; *d* of George Alan Hadfield and late Barbara June Hadfield; *m* Michael Alfred Lee (separated); three *d*. *Educ:* Univ. of Sheffield (BA Law). Admitted as solicitor, 1994; with Hopkins, Solicitors, Mansfield, 1992–99; Shoosmiths, Northampton, 1999–2006. Law Society of England and Wales: Mem. Council, 2003–; Chair: Legal Affairs Policy Bd, 2008–11; Regulatory Affairs Bd, 2013–; Dep. Vice Pres., 2008–09; Vice Pres., 2009–10. Mem., Queen's Counsel Selection Panel, 2011–. Asst Comr, Boundary Commn for England, 2011–13; Legal Chairman: Code Compliance Panel, PhonePay Plus, 2013–; Taxation Disciplinary Bd, 2014–; Legal Chair, Family Health Services Appeal Unit, 2014–; Chair: Voice (Victims and Witness Service, Northants), 2014–; Solicitors' Assistance Scheme, 2015–. Consultant to Action Against Medical Accidents, 2006–10, 2013–. President: Medico-Legal Soc., 2014–; Northants Law Soc., 2013–15. *Publications:* (contrib. ed.) Cordery on Legal Services. *Address:* 91 Buttmead, Blisworth NN7 3DQ. *T:* (01604) 949223. *E:* lindakhlee@aol.com.

LEE, Martin; *see* Lee Chu-Ming, M.

LEE, Dr Melanie Georgina, CBE 2009; FMedSci; Chief Scientific Officer, BTG plc, since 2015 (non-executive Director, 2010–14); *d* of William and Pamela Brown; *m* 1981; two *s*. *Educ:* York Univ. (BSc Hons 1979); NIMR (PhD 1982). Postdoctoral Research Fellow: CRC, London, at Imperial Coll., 1982–85; ICRF, London, at Lincoln's Inn Fields, 1985–88; R&D, Glaxo Gp Res. and Glaxo Wellcome, 1988–98; Bd Dir, Celltech Gp plc, 1998–2004; Exec. Vice-Pres., R&D, 2004–09, Mem. Scientific Adv. Bd, 2009–10, UCB Gp; Chief Executive Officer: Syntaxin Ltd, 2010–13; NightstaRx Ltd, 2014. Non-exec. Dir, H. Lundbeck, 2012–15. Chairman: Applied Genomics Link Scheme, 2000–; Cancer Res.

Technol., 2003–10. Trustee, CRUK, 2004–10 (Dep. Chm., Council, 2007–10). FMedSci 2003. *Recreations:* gym, keeping fit, gardening in containers, flowers. *Address:* BTG plc, c/o 5 Fleet Place, EC4M 7RD.

LEE, Michael Charles M.; *see* Malone-Lee.

LEE, Maj.-Gen. Patrick Herbert, CB 1982; MBE 1964; CEng, FIMechE; Director: Road Haulage Association, 1988–98 (Chairman, 1994–96; Vice-Chairman, 1990–94); Wincanton Ltd (formerly Wincanton Transport, subseq. Wincanton Distribution Services, Ltd), 1983–98; *b* 15 March 1929; *s* of Percy Herbert and Mary Dorothea Lee; *m* 1952, Peggy Eveline Chapman; one *s* one *d. Educ:* King's Sch., Canterbury; London Univ. (BSc (Gen.), BSc (Special Physics)). Commnd RMA Sandhurst, 1948; Staff Coll., 1960; WO Staff Duties, 1961–63; CO, Parachute Workshop, 1964–65; JSSC, 1966; Military Asst to Master General of Ordnance, 1966–67; Directing Staff, Staff Coll., 1968–69; Commander, REME 2nd Div., 1970–71; Col AQ 1 British Corps, 1972–75; Dep. Comdt, Sch. of Electrical and Mechanical Engrg, 1975–77; Comdt, REME Trng Centre, 1977–79; Dir Gen., Electrical and Mechanical Engrg (Army), 1979–83. Col Comdt, REME, 1983–89. Mem., Wessex Water Authy, 1983–88. Confederation of British Industry: Mem. Council, 1991–98; Vice-Chm., 1992–94, Chm., 1994–96, SW Region. Gov., Wellington Sch., Som, 1992–2002 (Chm., 2000–02). FCMI; MIEMA. *Recreations:* gardening, railways, Roman history, industrial archaeology. *Club:* Army and Navy.

LEE, Sir Paul (Joseph) S.; *see* Scott-Lee.

LEE, Paul Winston Michael B.; *see* Boyd-Lee.

LEE, Peter Gavin; DL; Senior Partner, Strutt & Parker, 1979–96; *b* 4 July 1934; *s* of late Mr and Mrs J. G. Lee; *m* 1963, Caroline Green; two *s* one *d. Educ:* Midhurst Grammar School; College of Estate Management; Wye College. FRICS 1966. Joined Strutt & Parker, 1957. Chm., Prince's Trust for Essex, 1998–2005. Gov., Felsted Sch., 1986–. High Sheriff, 1990, DL 1991, Essex. *Recreations:* the restoration and enjoyment of vintage cars, country pursuits. *Address:* Fanners, Great Waltham, Chelmsford, Essex CM3 1EA. *T:* (01245) 360470.

LEE, Peter Wilton, CBE 1994; Vice Lord-Lieutenant of South Yorkshire, 1997–2010; Director, 1987–2009, Chairman, 1994–2005, Edward Pryor & Son Ltd; *b* 15 May 1935; *s* of Sir (George) Wilton Lee, TD and late Bettina Stanley Lee (*née* Haywood); *m* 1962, Gillian Wendy Oates; three *s* one *d. Educ:* Uppingham Sch.; Queens' Coll., Cambridge (MA). Lieut, RE, 1956. Grad. Engr, Davy & United Engrg Co. Ltd, 1958–62; Arthur Lee & Sons plc: Engr, Works Manager, 1962–67; Works Dir, 1967–70; Jt Man. Dir, 1970–72; Man. Dir, 1972–79; Chm. and Man. Dir, 1979–92; Chm., 1992–93; Dep. Chm., 1993–95, Dir, 1995–2003, Carclo Engrg Gp PLC. Dir, Sanderson Gp (formerly Sanderson Electronics) PLC, 1994–2000. Dir, Sheffield Enterprise Agency Ltd, 1987–2002. President: Brit. Independent Steel Producers' Assoc., 1981–83; Engrg Employers' Sheffield Assoc., 1994–96. Confederation of British Industry: Member: Nat. Council, 1992–95; Nat. Mfg Council, 1992–94; Chm., Yorks and Humberside Regl Council, 1993–95. University of Sheffield: Mem. Council, 1965–2005 (Chm., 1996–2005); Pro Chancellor, 1987–2005. Trustee: Sheffield Church Burgesses Trust, 1977–; S Yorks Community Foundn, 1986–99 (Vice-Pres., 1999–); Dir, Sheffield Royal Soc. for Blind, 1997– (Chm., 1998–). Chm. Council, Sheffield & Dist YMCA, 1972–81 (Pres., 2009–11); Pres., YMCA White Rose, 2011–. CCMI (CIMgt 1976). Chm. Govs, Monkton Combe Sch., 1996–2001 (Gov., 1982–2001). Master, Co. of Cutlers in Hallamshire, 1985–86. DL 1978, High Sheriff, 1995–96, S Yorks. Hon. DEng Sheffield, 2005. *Recreations:* family, music and the arts, walking. *Address:* Willow Cottage, Old Fulwood Road, Sheffield S10 3TG. *T:* (0114) 230 5555.

LEE, Philippa Jane; *see* Cross, P. J.

LEE, Phillip James; MP (C) Bracknell, since 2010; *b* Taplow, Bucks, 28 Sept. 1970; *s* of Antony and Marilyn Lee. *Educ:* Sir William Borlase Sch., Marlow, Bucks; King's Coll. London (BSc Hons Human Biol. 1993); Keble Coll., Oxford (MSc Human Biol. 1994); St Mary's Hosp. Med. Sch., London (MB BS 1999). House Officer: Wexham Park Hosp., Slough, 1999–2000; St Mary's Hosp., London, 2000; Sen. House Officer, Stoke Mandeville Hosp., Aylesbury, 2000–02; GP, Thames Valley, 2002–. Mem., Energy and Climate Change Select Cttee, 2010–15; Vice Chm., Parly Space Cttee, 2010–; Vice Chm., Cons. Middle East Council, 2010–. *Recreations:* cricket, water ski-ing, football, ski-ing. *Address:* House of Commons, SW1A 0AA. *T:* (020) 7219 1270. *E:* phillip@phillip-lee.com.

LEE, Prof. Robert Gregory, LLD; Professor of Environmental Law, University of Birmingham, since 2014; *b* Preston, Lancs, 27 Nov. 1952; *s* of Bernard and Violet Lee; *m* 1976, Anne Claire Birkett; one *s* one *d. Educ:* Preston Catholic Coll.; Brunel Univ. (LLB 1977); Cardiff Univ. (LLD 2009). Lectr, 1977–79, Sen. Lectr, 1979, Lancashire Poly.; Lectr and Sen. Tutor, Lancaster Univ., 1979–88; Dir of Res., Denton Wilde Sapte, 1988–94; Develt Dir, Hammonds, 1994–95; Prof. of Law, Cardiff Law Sch., 1995–2013, Co-Dir, ESRC Res. Centre for Business Relationships, Accountability, Sustainability and Society, 2001–12, Cardiff Univ.; Prof. of Law, Univ. of Exeter, 2013–14. FRSocMed 2008. Life Mem., UK Envmtl Law Assoc., 2009. *Publications:* (with C. Douglas) The Estate Agents Act 1979, 1979; Constitutional and Administrative Law, 1985, 4th edn 1995; Statutes on Public Law and Human Rights, 1988, 20th edn 2009; (with G. Bennett) A Practical Guide to Private Residential Lettings, 1989; (with D. Morgan) Guide to the Human Fertilisation and Embryology Act 1990, 1991; (with D. Morgan) Human Fertilisation and Embryology: regulating the reproductive revolution, 2001; (with B. Filgueira) Environmental Law, Vol. 14 of Encyclopaedia of Forms and Precedents, 2008; (jtly) The New Regulation and Governance of Food, 2009; edited collections and res. reports; contrib. papers to jls. *Recreations:* theatre, walking, running, church music group, Preston North End. *Address:* Centre for Professional Legal Education and Research, University of Birmingham, Edgbaston, Birmingham B15 2TT. *E:* r.g.lee@bham.ac.uk.

LEE, Robert William; Co-Founder and Senior Partner, Lee & Thompson, since 1983; *b* Bromley, 18 Oct. 1945; *s* of Jack William Lee; *m* 1976, Caroline Boucher; one *s* one *d. Educ:* King's Sch., Rochester; Bristol Univ. (LLB). Admitted as solicitor, 1970; Solicitor and Partner, Harbottle & Lewis, 1971–83. Trustee, Noel Coward Foundn, 2000–. *Recreations:* theatre, music, reading, sailing, cricket. *Address:* 20 Rossetti Garden Mansions, Flood Street, SW3 5QY. *E:* robertlee@leeandthompson.com. *Clubs:* Groucho, Little Ship; MCC.

LEE, Seng Tee; Director: Singapore Investments (Pte) Ltd, since 1951; Lee Rubber Co. (Pte) Ltd, since 1951; Lee Pineapple Co. (Pte) Ltd, since 1951; Lee Foundation, since 1952; *b* April 1923; *s* of Lee Kong Chian and Alice Lee; *m* 1950, Betty Wu; two *s* one *d. Educ:* Anglo-Chinese Sch., Singapore; Wharton Business Sch., Univ. of Pennsylvania. Member: Singapore Preservation of Monuments Bd, 1971–88; Bd, Singapore Art Mus., 1995– (Mem., Adv. Cttee, 1992–94). Member Council: Univ. of Malaya in Singapore, 1959–61; Univ. of Singapore, 1962–63; Hon. Advr, Xiamen Univ., China, 1993–; Member: Bd of Advrs, Nat. Univ. of Singapore Endowment Fund, 1997–; Adv. Cttee, E Asia Inst., Cambridge Univ., 1998–. Mem., Chancellor's Court of Benefactors, Oxford, 1996–. Hon. Trustee, Royal Botanic Gardens, Kew, 1996. Hon. Foreign Mem., American Acad. of Arts and Scis, 2001. Hon. FBA 1998; Hon. Fellow: Wolfson Coll., Cambridge, 1986; Needham Res. Inst., Cambridge, 1992; Oriel Coll., Oxford, 1992; SOAS, London Univ., 2001. Hon. DTech Asian Inst. of Technol., Thailand, 1998; Hon. LitD Victoria Univ. of Wellington, NZ, 2006. Distinguished Service Award, Wharton Sch., Univ. of Penn., 1995. *Recreations:* reading, natural history. *Address:* Robinson Road PO Box 1892, Singapore 903742, Republic of Singapore. *Club:* Executive (Singapore).

LEE, Prof. Simon Francis; Chairman, Level Partnerships Ltd, since 2009; *b* 29 March 1957; *s* of Norman John Lee and Mary Teresa Lee (*née* Moran); *m* 1982, Patricia Mary, *d* of Bernard Anthony McNulty and Maud Catherine McNulty (*née* Kenny); one *s* two *d. Educ:* Balliol Coll., Oxford (Scholar, BA 1st Cl. Jurisp); Yale Law Sch. (Harkness Fellow, LLM). Lecturer in Law: Trinity Coll., Oxford, 1981–82; KCL, 1982–88; Queen's University, Belfast: Prof. of Jurisprudence, 1989–95; Dean, Faculty of Law, 1992–94; Prof. Emeritus, 1995; Rector and Chief Exec., Liverpool Hope UC, 1995–2003; Vice-Chancellor, Leeds Metropolitan Univ., 2003–09. Gresham Prof. of Law, 1995–98; Hon. Prof., Univ. of Liverpool, 1995–2003. Mem., Standing Adv. Commn on Human Rights, 1992–96. Mem., Nat. Standards Task Force, DFEE, 1997–2001. Non-exec. Dir, S & E Belfast Health and Social Services NHS Trust, 1994–95. Chairman: Merseyside Rapid Transit Project Bd, 1997–99; Netherley-Valley Partnership, 1998–2002; Liverpool & Merseyside Theatres Trust (Everyman & Playhouse), 1998–2002; Ind. Monitoring Bd, Liverpool Educn Authy, 1999–2001; Leeds Carnegie Rugby Union FC, 2007–09; John Paul II Foundn for Sport, 2010–. Co-founder, Initiative '92, 1992. Mem. Bd, The Tablet, 2002–. *Publications:* Law and Morals, 1986; Judging Judges, 1988; (with Peter Stanford) Believing Bishops, 1990; The Cost of Free Speech, 1990; (with Marie Fox) Learning Legal Skills, 1991; (ed) Freedom from Fear, 1992; Uneasy Ethics, 2003. *Recreations:* family, sport. *Address:* Level Partnerships Ltd, 78 Pall Mall, SW1Y 5ES. *E:* simonlee@levelpartnerships.com.

LEE, Simon Philip Guy; International Advisor: Fairfax Financial, since 2014; Global Advisor, SatMap Inc., since 2014; Senior Consultant, GLG Consulting, since 2014; *b* Reading, 4 March 1961; *s* of late Philip Michael Lee, CBE and of Janet Betty Lee; *m* 1987, Fiona Jean Andrews; three *d. Educ:* Tonbridge Sch.; Univ. of Leeds (BA Jt Hons English and French). National Westminster Bank Group, 1983–2002, various posts including: CEO, Mortgage Corp., US, 1992–93; Man. Dir, US Retail Banking, 1993–96; CEO, NatWest Offshore, 1996–98; Dir, Wholesale Mkts, 1998–2002; Royal & Sun Alliance, later RSA Group: CEO, Internat. Business, 2003–11; Dir, 2007–13; Gp CEO, RSA Insurance, 2011–13. Non-exec. Dir, TIA Technology, 2014–. Chm., Hospice in the Weald, 2014–. *Recreations:* cricket, golf, travel, ski-ing. *Club:* Royal Ashdown Forest Golf.

LEE, Prof. Stephen; Chief Executive, CentreForum, since 2012; Professor of Management, Cass Business School, since 2010; *b* London, 26 Dec. 1957; *s* of Robert Lee and Elizabeth Lee; *m* 2003, Vivienne Hibbitt; one *d. Educ:* Huddersfield Poly. (BA (Hons) Pols and Geog. 1979); London Sch. of Econs and Political Sci. (MSc (Econ) Internat. Relns 1980). Tutor in Politics, Lancaster Univ., 1980–83; Dep. Dir, Charities Adv. Trust, 1983–85; Man. Dir, Family Welfare Assoc. Ltd, 1985–89; Chief Exec., Inst. of Fundraising, 1989–2000; Consultant, Kingston Smith, 2000–03; Henley Management College, subseq. Henley Management School: Lectr, 2003–08; Coll. Sec., 2008–09; Faculty Dir, Strategy, 2009–10. Vis. Prof. of Mgt, Bath Spa Univ., 2010–12. FRSA 1987. *Recreations:* Chippenham Town FC, poor golf, wet camping, cooking, family. *Address:* CentreForum, 27 Queen Anne's Gate, SW1H 9BU. *T:* (020) 7340 1166, *Fax:* (020) 7222 3316. *E:* stephen.lee@centreforum.org.

LEE, Maj.-Gen. Stuart; *see* Lee, Maj.-Gen. J. S.

LEE, Prof. Tak Hong, CBE 2012; MD, ScD; FRCP, FRCPath, FMedSci; Director, Allergy Centre and Specialist in Immunology and Allergy, Hong Kong Sanatorium and Hospital, since 2012; *b* 26 Jan. 1951; *s* of Ming and Maria Lee; *m* (marr. diss.); one *s* one *d. Educ:* Clare Coll., Cambridge (BA 1972; MB BChir 1976; MD 1985; ScD 1996). FHKCP 1987; FRCP 1989; FRCPath 1997. House Physician, House Surgeon, then Jun. Registrar, Guy's Hosp., 1975–77; SHO, Brompton Hosp., 1977–78, Nat. Hosp., Queen Square, 1978; Registrar, Guy's Hosp., 1978–89; Clin. Lectr, Cardiothoracic Inst., Brompton Hosp., 1980–82; Res., Fellow, Harvard Univ., USA, 1982–84; Lectr, 1984–85, Sen. Lectr, 1985–88, Guy's Hosp.; Asthma UK Prof. of Allergy and Respiratory Medicine, KCL, 1988–2011; Dir, MRC and Asthma UK Centre in Allergic Mechanisms of Asthma at KCL and Imperial Coll. London, 2005–11. Pres., Hong Kong Inst. of Allergy, 2014–. Hon. Consultant Physician, Guy's and St Thomas' NHS Foundn Trust, 1988–2011. Fellow, Amer. Acad. of Allergy, Asthma and Immunology, 1989; FMedSci 2000; FKC 2007; FAAAAI. *Recreations:* golf, wining and dining, travelling to exotic places. *Address:* Hong Kong Sanatorium and Hospital, Allergy Centre, 9th Floor, Li Shu Pui Building, 2 Village Road, Happy Valley, Hong Kong. *E:* thlee@hksh.com. *Clubs:* Royal Automobile; Wentworth Golf; Hong Kong Jockey, Shek O Golf and Country (Hong Kong).

LEE, Taryn Jane; QC 2012; a Recorder, since 2008; *b* Cleethorpes, 4 March 1968; *d* of Thomas Edwin Lee, BEM, and Joan Gylettie Lee (*née* Meadows); *m* 1994, Andrew Skudder; one *s* one *d. Educ:* Bursar Street Primary Sch., Cleethorpes; Lindsey Comp. Sch., Cleethorpes; Huddersfield Poly. (LLB Hons Business Law); Inns of Court Sch. of Law (BVC). Called to the Bar, Inner Temple, 1992, Bencher, 2012; Jt Hd of Chambers, 37 Park Square, Leeds, 2011–; Public Access trained, 2011–; Mediator, 2012–. Bar Council: Mem., 2004–; Chairman: Annual Bar Conf., 2011; Social Mobility Cttee, 2012–. *Recreations:* family, music, theatre, fitness, literature, good food, wine and company; and I love shoes. *Address:* 37 Park Square Chambers, Leeds LS1 2NY. *T:* (0113) 243 9422, *Fax:* (0113) 242 4229. *E:* tl@no37.co.uk.

LEE, Sir Timothy John B.; *see* Berners-Lee.

LEE, Tsung-Dao; Enrico Fermi Professor of Physics, 1964–2012, and University Professor, 1984–2012, now Emeritus, Columbia University, USA; *b* 25 Nov. 1926; 3rd *s* of C. K. and M. C. Lee; *m* 1950, Jeannette H. C. Chin; two *s. Educ:* National Chekiang Univ., Kweichow, China; National Southwest Associated Univ., Kunming, China; University of Chicago, USA. Research Associate: University of Chicago, 1950; University of California, 1950–51; Member, Inst. for Advanced Study, Princeton, 1951–53. Columbia University: Asst Professor, 1953–55; Associate Professor, 1955–56; Professor, 1956–60; Member, Institute for Advanced Study, Princeton, 1960–63; Columbia University: Adjunct Professor, 1960–62; Visiting Professor, 1962–63; Professor, 1963–. Hon. Professor: Univ. of Sci and Technol. of China, 1981; Jinan Univ., China, 1982; Fudan Univ., China, 1982; Qinghua Univ., 1984; Peking Univ., 1985; Nanjing Univ., 1985; Nankai Univ., 1986; Shanghai Jiao Tong and Suzhou Univs, 1987; Zhejiang Univ., 1988; Northwest Univ., Xian, 1993. Member: Acad. Sinica, 1957; Amer. Acad. of Arts and Scis, 1959; Nat. Acad. of Scis, 1964; Amer. Philosophical Soc., 1972; Acad. Nazionale dei Lincei, Rome, 1982; Chinese Acad. of Scis, Beijing, 1994. Hon. DSc: Princeton, 1958; City Coll., City Univ. of NY, 1978; Bard Coll., 1984; Peking, 1985; Bologna, 1988; Columbia, 1990; Adelphi, 1991; Tsukuba, 1992; Rockefeller, 1994; Hon. LLD Chinese Univ. of Hong Kong, 1969; Hon. LittD Drexel Univ., 1986; Dip. di Perfezionamento in Physics, Scuola Normale Superiore, Pisa, 1982. Nobel Prize for the non-conservation of parity (with C. N. Yang), 1957; Albert Einstein Award in Science, 1957; Ettore Majorana-Erice Sci. for Peace Prize, 1990. Grand'Ufficiale, Order of Merit (Italy), 1986. *Publications:* Particle Physics: an introduction to field theory, 1981; papers mostly in Physical Review, and Nuclear Physics. *Address:* Department of Physics, Columbia University, New York, NY 10027, USA.

LEE, Most Rev. William, DCL; Bishop of Waterford and Lismore, (RC), 1993–2013, now Bishop Emeritus; *b* 2 Dec. 1941; *s* of John Lee and Bridget Ryan. *Educ:* Newport Boys' Nat. Sch.; Rockwell Coll.; Maynooth Coll. (BA, BD, LPh, DCL); Gregorian Univ., Rome.

Ordained priest, 1966; Catholic Curate, Finglas, West Dublin, 1969–71; Bursar, 1971–87, President, 1987–93, St Patrick's Coll., Thurles. Sec., Irish Episcopal Conf., 1998–. *Recreations:* reading, walking, golf.

LEE, Prof. William Edward, DPhil; FREng, FIMMM; Professor of Ceramic Engineering, since 2006 and Director, Centre for Nuclear Engineering, since 2013 (Co-Director, 2011–12), Imperial College London; *b* Gosport, Hants, England, 7 Feb. 1958; *s* of Arthur Edward Lee and Sylvia Lee (*née* Male); *m* 1987, Jacqueline Tonie Tregellis; one *d*. *Educ:* Price's Sch., Fareham; Aston Univ. (BSc Hons 1980); Linacre Coll., Oxford (DPhil 1983). Case Western Reserve Univ., 1983–86; Asst Prof., Ohio State Univ., 1986–89; Lectr, 1989–94, Sen. Lectr, 1994–96, Reader, 1996–98, Prof., 1998–2005, Univ. of Sheffield; Hd, Dept of Materials, Imperial Coll. London, 2006–10. William Penney Fellow, Atomic Weapons Establishment, Aldermarston, 2013–. Dep. Chm., Cttee on Radioactive Waste Mgt, 2007–13. Member: Scientific and Envmtl Adv. Bd, Tokamak Energy plc, 2009–; Nuclear Innovation and Res. Adv. Bd, 2014–; Nat. Nuclear Lab. Technical Adv. Panel, 2014–; Fellow, Amer. Ceramic Soc., 1999 (Pres., Oct. 2016–). FIMMM 1989; FCGI 2009; FREng 2012. *Publications:* (with W. M. Rainforth) Ceramic Microstructures: property control by processing, 1994; (with M. I. Ojovan) An Introduction to Nuclear Waste Immobilisation, 2005, 2nd edn 2014; (jtly) Ceramics for Actinide Immobilisation, 2011; (ed jtly) Radioactive Waste Management and Contaminated Site Clean-up, 2014. *Recreations:* watching Pompey, running, swimming, building walls, walking, family tree. *Address:* Centre for Nuclear Engineering, Department of Materials, Imperial College London, South Kensington Campus, SW7 2AZ. *E:* w.e.lee@imperial.ac.uk.

LEE YONG LENG, Dr; Professor of Geography, National University of Singapore, 1977–90, retired; *b* 26 March 1930; *m* Wong Loon Meng; one *d*. *Educ:* Univs of Oxford, Malaya and Singapore. BLitt (Oxon), MA (Malaya), PhD (Singapore). Research Asst, Univ. of Malaya, 1954–56; University Lectr/Sen. Lectr, Univ. of Singapore, 1956–70; Associate Prof., Univ. of Singapore, 1970–71; High Comr for Singapore in London, 1971–75; Ambassador to Denmark, 1974–75, and Ireland, 1975; Min. of Foreign Affairs, Singapore, 1975–76. Mem., Govt Parly Cttee on Defence and For. Affairs, 1987–90. Chm., Singapore Nat. Library Bd, 1978–80. Dir, Centre for Advanced Studies, National Univ. of Singapore, 1983–85. *Publications:* North Borneo, 1965; Sarawak, 1970; Southeast Asia and the Law of the Sea, 1978; The Razor's Edge: boundaries and boundary disputes in Southeast Asia, 1980; Southeast Asia: essays in political geography, 1982; articles in: Population Studies; Geog. Jl; Erdkunde; Jl Trop. Geog., etc. *Recreations:* swimming, tennis, travelling, reading.

LEE, Prof. Yuan Tseh; President, Academia Sinica, Taiwan, 1994–2006; Distinguished Research Fellow, Institute of Atomic and Molecular Sciences, Taiwan, since 1994; *b* 29 Nov. 1936; *s* of Tse Fan Lee and Pei Tsai; *m* 1963, Bernice Chinli Wu; two *s* one *d*. *Educ:* Nat. Taiwan Univ. (BSc 1959); Nat. Tsinghua Univ., Taiwan (MSc 1961); Univ. of California (PhD 1965). Military service, 1961–62. University of California, Berkeley: Postdoctoral Fellow, 1965–67; Research Fellow, 1967–68; James Franck Inst. and Dept of Chemistry, Univ. of Chicago: Asst Prof. of Chemistry, 1968–71; Associate Prof. of Chemistry, 1971–72; Prof. of Chemistry, 1973–74; University of California, Berkeley: Prof. of Chemistry, 1974–91; Univ. Prof. of Chemistry, 1991–94; Principal Investigator, Materials and Molecular Research Div., Lawrence Berkeley Lab., 1974–94. Vis. Lectr, US and overseas univs. Mem., editl boards, chem. and sci. jls. Mem., Nat. Acad. of Sciences, 1979, and other learned bodies. Nobel Prize in Chemistry (jtly), 1986; numerous awards from US and foreign instns. *Publications:* papers on molecular chemistry and related subjects. *Recreations:* sports (baseball, ping pong, tennis), classical music. *Address:* Academia Sinica, Nankang, Taipei 11529, Taiwan.

LEE CHU-MING, Martin, (Martin Lee); QC (Hong Kong) 1979; JP; Chairman, Democratic Party, Hong Kong, 1994–2002; Member, Hong Kong Legislative Council, 1985–97 and 1998–2008; *b* 8 June 1938; *m* 1969, Amelia Lee; one *s*. *Educ:* Wah Yan College, Kowloon; Univ. of Hong Kong (BA 1960). Called to the Bar, Lincoln's Inn, 1966. Member: Hong Kong Law Reform Commn, 1985–91; Hong Kong Fight Crime Cttee, 1986–92; Basic Law Drafting Cttee, 1985–89; numerous groups and cttees advising on Govt, law, nationality and community matters. Chm., United Democrats of Hong Kong, 1990–94. JP Hong Kong, 1980. *Publications:* The Basic Law: some basic flaws (with Szeto Wah), 1988. *Address:* Admiralty Centre, Room 704A, Tower I, 18 Harcourt Road, Hong Kong. *T:* 25290864. *Clubs:* Hong Kong; Hong Kong Golf, Hong Kong Jockey.

LEE-EMERY, Louise Wendy; *see* Tulett, L. W.

LEE-JONES, Christine; JP; DL; MA; Head Mistress, Manchester High School for Girls, 1998–2008; non-executive Director, Walton Centre NHS Foundation Trust Liverpool, since 2008; *b* 13 June 1948; *d* of George and Marion Pickup; *m* 1972, Denys Lee-Jones; one *d*. *Educ:* Lawnswood High Sch. for Girls, Leeds; St Mary's Coll., Bangor; University Coll. of N Wales (BEd Biblical Studies and Far Eastern Religions); Univ. of London Inst. of Educn (MA 1982); Open Univ. (Advanced Dip. Educnl Mgt 1990). Primary teacher, Bethnal Green, 1970–71; Head, Religious Education: Archbp Temple Sch., London, 1971–74; Archbp Michael Ramsey Sch., London, 1974–82; Sen. Lectr, Woolwich Coll. of Further Educn, 1983–86; Vice-Principal, Leyton Sixth Form Coll., 1986–91; Principal, Eccles Sixth Form Coll., Salford, 1991–98. Teacher/Tutor, Univ. of London Inst. of Educn, 1978–79. University of Manchester: Member: Gen. Assembly, 2005–; Gov. Body, 2010–; Audit Cttee, 2010–; Nominations and Awards Cttee, 2012–. Jt Chair, Professional Develt Cttee, HMC/GSA, 2005–. Trustee: Greater Manchester Police High Sheriff Trust, 2011–; Genesis Breast Cancer Prevention Charity, 2012–; Henshaw Soc. for Blind People, 2013–14; volunteer, Breast Cancer Care, 2013–. Mem., Network Club, 1998–. Mem., RSC, 2003–. FRSA 1999. DL 2007, High Sheriff, 2011–12, Greater Manchester; JP Trafford, 2008. *Recreations:* literature, theatre, the arts, travel, tennis, fine wines. *E:* cleejones@tiscali.co.uk. *Club:* St James's (Manchester).

LEE PENG-FEI, Allen, (Allen Lee), CBE 1988 (OBE 1982); JP; Chairman: Jada Electronics Ltd; Pacific Dimensions Consultants Ltd, since 1998; *b* 24 April 1940; *m* Maria Lee; two *s* one *d*. *Educ:* Univ. of Michigan (BSc Engineering Maths). Test Engineer Supervisor, Lockheed Aircraft International, 1966–67; Engineering Ops Manager, Fabri-teck, 1967; Test Engineer Manager, Lockheed Aircraft International, 1968–70; Test Manager, Ampex Ferrotec, 1970–72; Gen. Manager, Dataproducts HK, 1972–74; Managing Dir, Ampex Ferrotec, 1974–79; Gen. Manager, Ampex World Operations, 1979–83; Managing Dir, Ampex Far East Operations, 1983–84; Pres., Meadville, 1984–95. Appointed Mem., Hong Kong Legislative Council, 1978–98; MEC, Hong Kong, 1985–92; Dep. for HKSAR, 9th Nat. People's Congress, China, 1997–2004; Chm., HK Liberal Party, 1993. Mem., Commn on Strategic Develt, HKSAR, 1998. Chm., Bd of Overseers, Hong Kong Inst. of Biotechnol., 1990–. JP Hong Kong, 1980. FHKIE, 1985. Hon. DEng Hong Kong Poly., 1990; Hon. LLD Chinese Univ. of Hong Kong, 1990. Nat. Award, Asian Productivity Organization, 1986; Outstanding Young Persons Award, Hong Kong, 1977. *Recreations:* swimming, tennis. *Clubs:* Hong Kong Jockey, Hong Kong Country, Dynasty (Hong Kong).

LEE-POTTER, Jeremy Patrick, FRCPath; Consultant Haematologist, Poole General Hospital, 1969–95; *b* 30 Aug. 1934; *s* of Air Marshal Sir Patrick Lee Potter, KBE, MD, QHS and Audrey Mary (*née* Pollock); *m* 1957, Lynda Higginson (OBE 1998) (*d* 2004); one *s* two *d*. *Educ:* Epsom Coll.; Guy's Hosp. Med. Sch. (MB BS 1958). MRCS, LRCP 1958; DTM&H 1963; DCP 1965; FRCPath 1979. Specialist in Pathology, 1960, Sen. Specialist, 1965, RAF (Sqn Ldr); in charge of Haematology Dept, RAF Inst. of Pathology and Tropical Medicine; Lectr in Haematology, St George's Hosp. Med. Sch., 1968–69. British Medical Association: Chm. Council, 1990–93 (Mem. Council, 1988–95); Dep. Chm., Central Consultants and Specialists Cttee, 1988–90 (Chm., Negotiating Cttee); Vice Pres., 1998–; Chm., Audit Cttee, 1999–2002. Member: Standing Med. Adv. Cttee, 1990–93; GMC, 1994–99 (Dep. Chm., Professional Conduct Cttee, 1996–99); Clinical Disputes Forum, 1999. Consultant Surveyor, King's Fund Orgnl Audit, 1993–95. Engineering Council: Mem. Senate, 2000–02; Mem., Bd for Engrs' Regulation, 2001–02. Pres., Old Epsomian Club, 2004–05. *Publications:* A Damn Bad Business: the NHS deformed, 1997. *Recreations:* art, birdwatching, natural history, photography. *Address:* Icen House, Stoborough, Wareham, Dorset BH20 5AN. *T:* (01929) 556307. *Clubs:* Athenæum; Parkstone Golf.

LEE-STEERE, Gordon Ernest; Vice Lord-Lieutenant of Surrey, 1996–2014; *b* 26 Dec. 1939; *s* of Charles Augustus Lee-Steere and Patience Hargreaves Lee-Steere; *m* 1966, Mary Katharine Stuart; one *s* three *d*. *Educ:* Eton; Trinity Coll., Cambridge (MA). Computer consultant, 1966–74; self-employed farmer, 1960–. Pres., CLA, 1987–89. *Recreations:* shooting, walking. *Address:* Hale House, Oakwoodhill, Surrey RH5 5NA. *T:* (01306) 627112. *Club:* Boodle's.

LEECH, John; *b* 11 April 1971; *s* of Rev. John Leech and Jean Leech; partner, Catherine Kilday. *Educ:* Manchester Grammar Sch.; Loreto Coll.; Brunel Univ. (BA Hons Pols and Hist.). Mem. (Lib Dem), Manchester CC, 1998–2008 (Dep. Leader, Lib Dem Gp, 2003–05). MP (Lib Dem) Manchester Withington, 2005–15; contested (Lib Dem) same seat, 2015. Member: Transport Select Cttee, 2005–12; Culture, Media and Sport Cttee, 2012–15. *Recreations:* sport, amateur dramatics, season ticket holder Manchester City. *Address:* 53b Manley Road, Whalley Range, Manchester M16 8HP.

LEECH, John, (Hans-Joachim Freiherr von Reitzenstein), MBE 2014; Head of External Relations and Member of Management Board, Commonwealth Development Corporation, 1981–85; Chairman, Farm Services Co. BV, 1988–2000; Deputy Chairman, Rural Investment Overseas Ltd, 1990–2000 (Chairman, 1985–90); *b* 21 April 1925; *s* of Hans-Joachim and Josefine von Reitzenstein; *m* 1st, 1949, Mair Eiluned Davies (marr. diss. 1958); one *d*; 2nd, 1963, Noretta Conci (MBE 2014), concert pianist. *Educ:* Bismarck Gymnasium, Berlin; Whitgift, Croydon. L. G. Mouchel & Partners, Consulting Civil Engineers, 1942–52; Bird & Co. Ltd, Calcutta, 1953–57; Dir, Europe House, London, and Exec. Mem. Council, Britain in Europe Ltd, 1958–63; Pres., Internat. Fedn of Europe Houses, 1961–65; Dir, Joint Industrial Exports Ltd, 1963–65; with Commonwealth Develt Corp., London and overseas, 1965–85; Co-ordinator, Interact Gp of European develt finance instns, 1973–85; Eur. Co-ordinator, West-West Agenda, 1987–2010. Asst Dir, NATO Parliamentarians' Conf., 1959–60. Vice-Chm., Indian Concrete Soc., 1953–57; Member: Council, Federal Trust for Educn and Research, 1985–; Adv. Council (formerly Exec. Cttee), London Symphony Orch., 1979–96; Council, Royal Commonwealth Soc. for the Blind, 1983–99; Internat. Council, Duke of Edinburgh's Award Internat. Assoc., 1993–98. Chm., Keyboard Charitable Trust for Young Professional Performers, 1991–2013. Liveryman, Worshipful Co. of Paviors, 1968– (Mem. Court of Assts, 1992–2002, now Emeritus). FRSA. *Publications:* The NATO Parliamentarians' Conference 1955–59, 1960; Europe and the Commonwealth, 1961; Aid and the Community, 1972; Halt! Who Goes Where?: the future of NATO in the new Europe, 1991; Asymmetries of Conflict: war without death, 2002; (ed) Whole and Free: EU enlargement and transatlantic relations, 2002; contrib. to jls on aspects of overseas develt, European matters and arts subjects. *Recreations:* music, travel, Italy. *Address:* 8 Chester Square Mews, SW1W 9DS. *T:* (020) 7730 2307. *Club:* Travellers.

LEECH, Kevin Ronald; Founder and Chairman, ML Laboratories plc, 1987–2000; Chairman, Accura Animal Health, 2007–08; *b* 18 Aug. 1943; two *s* one *d* from former marriage. *Educ:* St Bede's Coll., Manchester. Accountancy, until 1964; built up family business, R. T. Leech & Sons Ltd, into UK's largest private funeral dir, 1964–82; entrepreneur, business manager, and venture capitalist, 1982–; non-executive Chairman: Queensborough Holdings plc, 1994–2000; Top Jobs on the Net, 1999; CI4Net.Com Ltd, 1999; non-exec. Dir, Devilfish Gaming plc, 2007–10. FCMI (FIMgt 1983); FInstD 1984; FRSA 1997. Hon. LLD Manchester, 1998. *Recreations:* Manchester United, football generally, ski-ing, sailing, fishing. *Address:* La Vignette, Rue de la Vignette, St Saviour, Jersey JE2 7HY.

LEECH, Melanie Jane, CBE 2015; Chief Executive, British Property Federation, since 2015; *b* 28 May 1962; *d* of Michael and Margaret Leech; two *s*. *Educ:* Brighton and Hove High Sch. for Girls GDST; St Hugh's Coll., Oxford (BA Hons Maths). Principal Private Sec. to Cabinet Sec. and Hd of Home Civil Service, 1992–95; Hd of Arts Policy, 1995–98, Hd of Broadcasting Policy, 1998–99, DCMS; Dir, Office of the Rail Regulator, 1999–2001; Exec. Dir, Assoc. of Police Authorities, 2001–04; Dir of Communications, Cabinet Office, 2004–05; Dir Gen., FDF, 2005–15. Trustee, Carnegie UK Trust, 2005–. MInstD. FRSA. *Address:* British Property Federation, St Albans House, 57–59 Haymarket, SW1Y 4QX.

LEECH, Prof. Rachel Mary, DPhil; Professor of Biology, University of York, 1978–99, now Emeritus; *b* 3 June 1936; *d* of Alfred Jack Leech and Frances Mary Ruth Leech (*née* Cowley). *Educ:* Prince Henry's Grammar Sch., Otley, W Yorks; St Hilda's Coll., Oxford (MA, DPhil 1961; Christopher Welch Scholar). Naples Biol Scholar, Stazione Zoologica, Naples, 1957–60; Professorial Res. Fellow, 1960–63, Lectr in Analytical Cytology, 1963–66, Imperial Coll., London; University of York: Lectr in Biology, 1966–69; Sen. Lectr, 1969–75; Reader, 1975–78. Leverhulme Emeritus Fellow, 2001–02. Mem., BBSRC, 1994–96. *Publications:* (with R. A. Reid) The Biochemistry and Structure of Subcellular Organelles, 1980; articles in Plant Physiology, Nature, The Biochemical Jl, The Plant Jl, Proc. of NAS, NY. *Recreations:* gardening, walking, enjoying the company of friends. *Address:* Department of Biology, University of York, Heslington, York YO10 5DD. *T:* (01904) 430000.

LEECH, Stewart; QC 2011; *b* Willenhall, 23 May 1963; *s* of late William Brian Leech and of Barbara Leech; civil partnership 2006, Olivier Riche. *Educ:* Wolverhampton Grammar Sch.; Christ Church, Oxford (Open Exhibnr; BA Hons; MA); City Univ.; Inns of Court Sch. of Law. Called to the Bar, Lincoln's Inn, 1992; in practice as barrister, 1992–. *Recreations:* reading, painting, gardening. *Address:* 3rd Floor, Queen Elizabeth Building, Temple, EC4Y 9BS.

LEECH, Thomas Alexander Crispin; QC 2010; *b* London, 16 Feb. 1964; *s* of Prof. Geoffrey Neil Leech, FBA; *m* 1990, Jane Elizabeth McKendrick; four *d*. *Educ:* Lancaster Royal Grammar Sch.; Wadham Coll., Oxford (Major Schol.; BA 1st Cl. Juris.; BCL). Called to the Bar, Middle Temple, 1988; in practice as barrister, 1989–. *Publications:* (ed jtly) Spencer Bower: Estoppel by Representation, 4th edn 2004; (ed jtly) Snell's Equity, 30th edn 2005; Flenley and Leech on Solicitors' Negligence and Liability, 1999, 2nd edn 2008. *Recreations:* walking (especially in the Lake District), sport (especially Rugby and cricket). *Address:* Herbert Smith Freehills LLP, Exchange House, Primrose Street, EC2A 2EG.

LEEDER, Prof. Michael Robert, PhD; Professor of Environmental Sciences, University of East Anglia, 1999, then Hon. Research Professor, now Professor Emeritus; *b* 22 Nov. 1947; *s* of Norman George Leeder and Evelyn (*née* Patterson). *Educ:* Univ. of Durham (BSc 1st Cl. Hons Geology); Univ. of Reading (PhD 1972). University of Leeds: Lectr in Earth Scis, 1972–85; Reader, 1985–91; Prof., 1991–99. Lyell Medal, Geol Soc., 1992; Phillips Medal, Geol Soc. of Yorks, 1990. *Publications:* Dynamic Stratigraphy of the British Isles, 1979; Sedimentology, 1982; Sedimentology and Sedimentary Basins, 1999, 2nd edn 2011; Fire Over East Anglia, 1999; Physical Processes in the Earth and Environmental Sciences, 2006; contrib. various scientific papers. *Recreation:* living generally. *Address:* School of Environmental Sciences, University of East Anglia, Norwich NR4 7TJ.

LEEDHAM, Carol Jean; *see* Mountford, C. J.

LEEDS, Bishop of, since 2014; **Rt Rev. Nicholas Baines;** *b* 13 Nov. 1957; *s* of Frank Baines and Beryl Amy Baines; *m* 1980, Linda Margaret Higgins; two *s* one *d*. *Educ:* Holt Comprehensive Sch., Liverpool; Univ. of Bradford (BA (Hons) Mod. Langs); Trinity Coll., Bristol (BA (Hons) Theol Studies). Linguist specialist, GCHQ, Cheltenham, 1980–84; ordained deacon, 1987, priest, 1988; Asst Curate, St Thomas, Kendal, 1987–91; Asst Priest, Holy Trinity with St John, Leicester, 1991–92; Vicar, St Mary and St John, Rothley, Leicester, 1992–2000; Archdeacon of Lambeth, 2000–03; Area Bishop of Croydon, 2003–11 Bishop of Bradford, 2011–14. Non-exec. Dir, Ecclesiastical Insce Gp, 2002–10. English Co-Chair, Meissen Commn, 2007–. Mem., Gen. Synod of C of E, 1995–2005. Took seat in H of L, 2014. Chair, Sandford St Martin Trust, 2008–. Regular broadcaster, BBC Radio. Blog: nickbaines.wordpress.com. Hon. Fellow, Bradford Coll. Hon. Dr Bradford; Hon. Dr Friedrich-Schiller-Univ., Jena. *Publications:* Hungry for Hope, 1991, reissued as Hungry for Hope?, 2007; Speedbumps and Potholes, 2003; Jesus and People Like Us, 2004, reissued as Scandal of Grace: the danger of following Jesus, 2008; Marking Time: 47 reflections on Mark's Gospel for Lent, Holy Week and Easter, 2005; Finding Faith: stories of music and life, 2008; Why Wish You a Merry Christmas?: what matters (and what doesn't) in the festive season, 2009. *Recreations:* music, reading, sport, travelling. *Address:* Hollin House, Weetwood Avenue, Leeds LS16 5NG. *T:* (0113) 284 4300. *E:* bishop.nick@westyorkshiredales.anglican.org. *W:* nickbaines.wordpress.com.

LEEDS, Bishop of, (RC), since 2014; **Rt Rev. Marcus Nigel Ralph Peter Stock;** *b* London, 27 Aug. 1961. *Educ:* Highdown Sch., Caversham; Keble Coll., Oxford (MA Theol.); Pontifical Gregorian Univ. (STL Dogmatic Theol.). Ordained priest, 1988; Asst Priest, Our Lady and St Brigid's Parish, Northfield, 1988–91; Parish Priest: St Birinus, Dorchester-on-Thames, 1991–94; St Peter's, Bloxwich, Walsall, 1994–99; Sacred Heart and St Theresa, Coleshill, 1999–2009; Asst Dir of Schs, 1995–99, Dir of Schs, 1999–2009, Archdiocese of Birmingham; Gen. Sec., Catholic Bishops' Conf. of Eng. and Wales, 2009–14. Apptd Prelate of Honour by Pope Benedict XVI, 2012. *Publications:* Christ at the Centre, 2005, 2nd edn 2013. *Address:* Bishop's House, 13 North Grange Road, Leeds LS6 2BR. *T:* (0113) 230 4533, *Fax:* (0113) 278 9890. *E:* bishop@dioceseofleeds.org.uk.

LEEDS, Archdeacon of; *see* Hooper, Ven. P. D. G.

LEEDS, Sir John (Charles Hildyard), 9th Bt *cr* 1812, of Croxton Park, Cambridgeshire; *b* 25 Dec. 1941; *e s* of late Charles Hildyard Denham Leeds and Merran Elizabeth, *d* of John Hilary Drew; *S* cousin, 2009; *m* 1965, Eileen Rose, *d* of Joseph Francis Shalka; one *s* two *d*. *Educ:* Univ. of Alberta (BSc Civil Engrg 1965). Mem., Assoc. of Professional Engrs and Geoscientists of Alberta (formerly Assoc. of Professional Engrs, Geologists and Geophysicists of Alberta). *Heir: s* Michael John Hildyard Leeds, *b* 16 May 1975.

LEEMING, Cheryl Elise Kendall; *see* Gillan, Rt Hon. C. E. K.

LEEMING, Geraldine Margaret; *see* Coleridge, G. M.

LEEMING, Ian; QC 1988; **His Honour Judge Leeming;** a Circuit Judge, since 2006; *b* Preston, Lancs, 10 April 1948; *s* of late Thomas Leeming (Bombing Leader, RAF), and of Lilian (*née* Male); *m* 1973, Linda Barbara Cook; one *s* two *d*. *Educ:* The Catholic Coll., Preston; Manchester Univ. (LLB 1970). Called to the Bar: Gray's Inn, 1970; Lincoln's Inn (*ad eundem*), 1981; in practice at Chancery and Commercial Bars, 1971–2006; a Recorder, 1989–2006. Dep. Deemster, Manx High Court, 1998; Mem., Court of Appeal, IOM, 1998. Legal Assessor: GMC, 2002–06; GDC, 2003–06. Lectr in Law (part-time), Manchester Univ., 1971–75. Formerly Counsel to Attorneys, Malcolm A. Hoffmann & Co., NY. Dir of limited cos. Vice-Chm., Northern Soc. of Cons. Lawyers, 1985–88. Fellow, Soc. for Advanced Legal Studies, 1998. Member: Chancery Bar Assoc.; Professional Negligence Bar Assoc.; Technol. and Construction Court Bar Assoc. FCIArb, Chartered Arbitrator, 2005–. *Publications:* (with James Bonney) Observations upon the Insolvency Bill, 1985; (ed) Equity and Trusts sect., Butterworth's Law of Limitation, 2000; articles, notes and reviews in legal jls and specialist periodicals. *Recreations:* the family, reading, walking, wine. *Address:* Preston Crown Court, Openshaw Place, Ringway, Preston, Lancs PR1 2LL.

LEEMING, John Coates; retired space consultant; Director General, British National Space Centre, 1987–88 (Director, Policy and Programmes, 1985–87); *b* 3 May 1927; *s* of late James Arthur Leeming and Harriet Leeming; *m* 1st, 1949 (marr. diss. 1974); two *s*; 2nd, 1985, Rt Hon. Cheryl Elise Kendall Gillan, *qv*. *Educ:* Chadderton Grammar Sch., Lancs; St John's Coll., Cambridge (Schol.). Teaching, Hyde Grammar Sch., Cheshire, 1948. Asst Principal, HM Customs and Excise, 1950 (Private Sec. to Chm.); Principal: HM Customs and Excise, 1954; HM Treasury, 1956; HM Customs and Excise, 1958; Asst Sec., HM Customs and Excise, 1965; IBRD (World Bank), Washington, DC, 1967; Asst Sec., 1970, Under Sec., 1972, CSD; a Comr of Customs and Excise, 1975–79; Dept of Industry (later DTI), 1979–85. *Recreation:* golf. *Club:* Royal Automobile.

LEEMING, Michael Peter George; His Honour Judge Michael Leeming; a Circuit Judge, since 2012; *b* Salford, 16 April 1961; *s* of George Leeming and Eileen Leeming (*née* Stanford); *m* 1995, Clare Rees; one *s* one *d*. *Educ:* Thornleigh Salesian Coll., Bolton; Leeds Univ. (LLB Hons). Called to the Bar, Inner Temple, 1983; in practice as barrister, Manchester, 1983–2012; Asst Recorder, 1999–2000; Recorder, 2000–12. *Recreations:* family, ski-ing, football (Manchester City FC). *Address:* Manchester Crown Court, Courts of Justice, Crown Square, Manchester M3 3FL. *T:* (0161) 954 1800. *E:* HHJudgeMichael.Leeming@judiciary.gsi.gov.uk.

LEES, Andrew James; His Honour Judge Andrew Lees; a Circuit Judge, since 2010; *b* Chester, 15 April 1961; *s* of Alan James Lees and Violet Mary Lees (*née* Buckingham); *m* 1986, Clare Milne; two *s* two *d*. *Educ:* Rydal Sch., Colwyn Bay; Queen's Park High Sch., Chester; Liverpool Univ. (LLB Hons). Called to the Bar, Gray's Inn, 1984; a Recorder, 2001–10. *Recreations:* horn playing, walking, wildlife, food and wine, cooking, arts, vintage shops. *Address:* Woolwich Crown Court, 2 Belmarsh Road, SE28 0EY.

LEES, Prof. Andrew John, MD; FRCP, FMedSci; Professor of Neurology, Institute of Neurology, since 1998 and Director, Reta Lila Weston Institute of Neurological Studies, 1998–2012, University College London; Consultant Neurologist, National Hospital for Neurology and Neurosurgery (now part of University College London Hospitals NHS Trust), since 1982; *b* 27 Sept. 1947; *s* of Lewis Lees and Muriel Lees (*née* Wadsworth); *m* 1973, Juana Luisa Pulin Perez Lopez; one *s* one *d*. *Educ:* Roundhay Sch., Leeds; Royal London Hosp. Med. Sch., Univ. of London (MD 1978). FRCP 1982. Co-Ed.-in-Chief, Movement Disorders Jl, 1994–2004. Dir, Sara Koe PSP Res. Centre, Inst. of Neurol., 2002–12. Chm., Med. Adv. Panel, Progressive Supranuclear Palsy (PSP Europe) Assoc., 1995–. Pres., Movt Disorder Soc., 2005–06 (Pres., Eur. Sect., 1998–2000). Appeal Steward, BBB of C, 1998–. Visiting Professor: Univ. of Liverpool, 2002–; São Rafael Hosp., Salvador, Brazil, 2000–; Univ. Fed. de Minas Gerais, Belo Horizonte, Brazil, 2007–. Mem. Council, Acad. of Med. Scis, 2012–. FMedSci 2009. Corresp. Mem., Academia Nacional de Medicina, Brazil. Mem., London Liby. *Publications:* Parkinson's Disease, The Facts, 1980; Tics and Related Disorders, 1984; Ray of Hope: authorised biography of Ray Kennedy, 1992; The Hurricane Port: a social history of Liverpool, 2010; Exploring the Victorian Brain: a biography of Sir William Gowers, 2012; Alzheimer's: the silent plague, 2012. *Recreations:* writer, Brazilian studies, Liverpool FC supporter, St Helens Rugby League supporter. *Address:* Reta Lila Weston Institute for Neurological Studies, Institute of Neurology, 1 Wakefield Street, WC1N 1PG. *T:* (020) 7837 3611. *E:* andrew.lees@ucl.ac.uk. *Club:* Groucho.

LEES, Sir Antony; *see* Lees, Sir W. A. C.

LEES, Sir David (Bryan), Kt 1991; DL; FCA; Chairman, Court of Directors, Bank of England, 2009–14 (a Director, 1991–99); *b* 23 Nov. 1936; *s* of late Rear-Adm. D. M. Lees, CB, DSO, and C. D. M. Lees; *m* 1961, Edith Mary Bernard; two *s* one *d*. *Educ:* Charterhouse. 2nd Lieut, RA, 1955–57. Qualified as a chartered accountant, 1962. Chief Accountant, Handley Page Ltd, 1964–68; GKN Sankey Ltd: Chief Accountant, 1970–72; Dep. Controller, 1972–73; Director, Secretary and Controller, 1973–76; Guest Keen and Nettlefolds, later GKN plc: Group Finance Executive, 1976–77; General Manager Finance, 1977–82; Dir, 1982–2004; Finance Dir, 1982–87; Man. Dir, 1987–88; Chief Exec., 1988–96; Chm., 1988–2004. Chairman: Courtaulds plc, 1996–98 (Dir, 1991–98); Tate & Lyle plc, 1998–2009; Deputy Chairman: Brambles Industries Ltd, and Brambles Industries plc, 2001–06; QinetiQ Gp plc, 2005–12. Mem. Council, CBI, 1988–96 (Chm., Economic Affairs (formerly Economic and Financial Policy) Cttee, 1988–94); Pres., EEF, 1990–92; Member: Audit Commission, 1983–90; Listed Cos Adv. Cttee, 1990–97; European Round Table, 1995–2001; Nat. Defence Industries Council, 1995–2004; Panel on Takeovers and Mergers, 2001–. Dir, Inst. for Manufacturing, 1998–2001. Pres., Soc. of Business Economists, 1994–99. Director: Royal Opera House, 1998–2008; Royal Opera House Enterprises (formerly Opus Arte) Ltd, 2007–; Trustee, Royal Opera House Endowment Fund, 2001–. Mem. Governing Body, Shrewsbury Sch., 1986–2007 (Chm., 2004–07); Governor: Suttons Hosp., Charterhouse, 1995–2005; Shrewsbury Internat. Sch., Bangkok, 2005–; Royal Ballet Sch., 2008–13. Hon. Patron, Shrewsbury Town FC, 2010–. DL Shropshire, 2007. Hon. Fellow, Wolverhampton Poly., 1990. ICAEW Award for outstanding achievement, 1999. Officer's Cross, Order of Merit (Germany), 1996. *Recreations:* walking, golf, opera, music. *Clubs:* Carlton, MCC.

See also Rear-Adm. R. B. Lees.

LEES, Diane Elizabeth, CBE 2015; Director-General, Imperial War Museum, since 2008; *b* 28 March 1964; *d* of late William Lees and of Brenda Lees (*née* Gilman); *m* 2007, Michael Hague. *Educ:* Oriel Bank High Sch.; Stockport Coll. of Technol.; Open Univ. Exhibns Asst, Mary Rose Project, 1982–84; Registrar: Royal Naval Mus., 1984–89; Nottingham City Museums, 1989–91; Nat. Outreach Manager, Museums Documentation Assoc., 1991–94; Chief Exec., Galls of Justice, 1994–2000; Dir, Mus. of Childhood, 2000–08. Vice Chair, Assoc. of Ind. Museums, 2005–08 (Sec., 1998–2002); Instnl Vice Pres., Museums Assoc., 2002–04; Chm., Nat. Mus. Dirs Council, 2013–. Mem., Adv. Bd, Nat. World War One Mus., Kansas City, 2014–. Gov., Univ. of Lincoln, 2014–. FMA 1996; FRSA 2004; CCMI 2011. *Publications:* (ed) Museums and Interactive Multimedia, 1993; Computers in Museums, 1994, 3rd edn 1996; contribs to Museums Jl, IBBY Procs, Library and Inf. Scis. *Recreations:* walking, tennis, cooking, collecting ceramics. *Address:* Imperial War Museum, Lambeth Road, SE1 6HZ. *T:* (020) 7416 5207, *Fax:* (020) 7416 5374. *E:* dlees@iwm.org.uk.

LEES, Michael Anthony M.; *see* Mather-Lees, M. A.

LEES, Captain Nicholas Ernest Samuel; Chairman, Leicester Racecourse, since 2006 (Assistant Manager, 1970–71; Clerk of the Course, 1972–2004; Managing Director, 1972–2005); Chairman, Stratford-on-Avon Racecourse Co. Ltd, since 2001 (Director, since 1990); *b* 3 May 1939; *s* of Ernest William Lees and Marjorie May Lees; *m* 1st, 1969, Elizabeth Helen Spink (marr. diss. 1985); one *d*; 2nd, 1985, Jocelyn Kosina; one *d*. *Educ:* Abbotsholme Sch., Rocester, Staffs. Shell Oil, 1956–59; commnd 17/21 Lancers, 1959; retd from Army, 1967; studied for Chartered Surveyors exams, 1967–69 (passed final exams but never practised); auctioneer, Warner, Sheppard & Wade Ltd, Leicester, 1969–73; Clerk of the Course: Teesside Park, 1972–73; Great Yarmouth, 1977–91; Chief Exec., 1974–97, Clerk of the Course, 1974–2000, and Dir of Racing, 1998–2000, Newmarket. Director: Racecourse Assoc. Ltd, 1988–93, 2004–05; Independent Racecourses Ltd, 2013–. *Recreations:* horse racing, antique furniture, silver, sporting art. *Address:* Capers End, Bradfield St George, Bury St Edmunds, Suffolk IP30 0AY. *T:* (01284) 386651.

LEES, Peter Derick, FRCP, FRCS; Chief Executive and Medical Director, Faculty of Medical Leadership and Management, since 2011; *b* Newcastle under Lyme, 19 April 1953; *s* of George Lees and Doreen Lees; *m* 1987, Ha Yen Chan; one *d*. *Educ:* Manchester Univ. (MB ChB 1975); Univ. of Southampton (MS 1990). FRCS 1981; FRCP 2012. Sen. Lectr in Neurosurgery, Univ. of Southampton, 1989–2012; Dir, R&D, 1995–99, Med. Dir, 1999–2002, University Hosp. Southampton; Med. Dir, NHS Leadership Centre, 2002–05; NHS South Central Strategic Health Authority: Med. Dir, 2009–12; Dir, Leadership, 2009–12; Dir, Workforce and Educn, 2011–12. Mem. Bd, West Hants CCG, 2012–. Mem., Gen. Adv. Council, King's Fund, 2013–. *Publications:* Navigating the NHS, 1996; res. papers on pituitary blood flow and pituitary tumours; articles on leadership (medical). *Address:* Faculty of Medical Leadership and Management, 6 St Andrew's Place, NW1 4LB. *T:* (020) 3075 1471. *E:* peter.lees@fmlm.ac.uk.

LEES, Robert Ferguson, CBE 1999; Regional Procurator Fiscal for Lothian and Borders, 1991–98; *b* 15 Sept. 1938; *s* of William Lees and Martha Lees (*née* McAlpine); *m* 1966, Elizabeth (Elsie) Loughridge. *Educ:* Bellshill Acad.; Strathclyde Univ. (LLB). Joined Procurator Fiscal Service, 1972; Legal Asst, Paisley, 1972–75; Legal Asst, 1975–76, Sen. Legal Asst, 1976–78, and Sen. Depute Fiscal, 1978–81, Glasgow; Asst Procurator Fiscal, Dundee, 1982–88; Regl Procurator Fiscal for N Strathclyde, 1989–91. Vis. Scholar, Valdosta State Univ., Ga, 1999–2000. *Publications:* (jtly) Criminal Procedure, 1990. *Recreations:* music, travel, languages, photography.

LEES, Air Vice-Marshal Robin Lowther, CB 1985; MBE 1962; Air Officer in charge of Administration, RAF Support Command, 1982–85, and Head of Administration Branch, RAF, 1983–85, retired; *b* 27 Feb. 1931; *e s* of late Air Marshal Sir Alan Lees, KCB, CBE, DSO, AFC, and Norah Elizabeth (*née* Thompson); *m* 1966, Alison Mary Benson, *o d* of late Col C. B. Carrick, MC, TD, JP; three *s*. *Educ:* Wellington Coll.; RAF Coll., Cranwell. Commissioned RAF, 1952; served AAFCE Fontainebleau, 1953–56; Waterbeach, 1956–58; UKSLS Ottawa, 1958–61; DGPS(RAF) Staff MoD, 1962–66; Wyton, 1966–68; HQ Far East Comd, 1968–70; Directing Staff RAF Staff Coll., 1971–74; RAF PMC, 1974–76; Dir of Personnel (Ground) MoD, 1976; Dir of Personal Services (2) (RAF) MoD, 1976–80; RCDS 1980; Dir of Personnel Management (Policy and Plans) (RAF) MoD, 1981–82. Chief Exec., BHA, 1986–96. Mem. Council, CBI, 1990–93. Vice-Pres., HOTREC, 1991–93; Mem. Bd, Internat. Hotel and Restaurant Assoc., 1994–95. Gov., Wellington Coll., 1990–2001. Protocol Dir, Wentworth Golf Club, 1996–2006. FBIM, 1974–94; FIPM, 1976–94. *Recreations:* real tennis, lawn tennis, golf. *Address:* c/o Barclays Bank, 6 Market Place, Newbury, Berks RG14 5AY. *Clubs:* Royal Air Force (Chairman, 1977–82); Jesters', All England Lawn Tennis and Croquet.

LEES, Rear-Adm. Rodney Burnett, CVO 2001; Defence Services Secretary to the Queen, and Director General of Reserve Forces and Cadets, 1998–2001; Chief Naval Supply Officer, 1998–2000; *b* 31 Dec. 1944; *s* of Rear-Adm. Dennis Maresceaux Lees, CB, DSO and Daphne Lees; *m* 1st, 1969, Rosemary Elizabeth Blake (marr. diss. 1978); two *s*; 2nd, 1982, Molly McEwen. *Educ:* Charterhouse. Called to Bar, Gray's Inn, 1976. Joined RN 1962; HMS Devonshire, 1966–68; Captain SM10, 1968–70; HMS Apollo, 1972–74; legal training, 1974–77; Staff Legal Adviser to FO Portsmouth and Command Legal Adviser to C-in-C

Naval Home Comd, 1977–79; Dep. Supply Officer, HM Yacht Britannia, 1980; DCSO (Pay), MoD 1980–82; Supply Officer, HMS Illustrious, 1982–83; Fleet Legal and Admin. Officer, 1984–86; Sec. to Chief of Fleet Support, 1986–88; Dep. Comd Sec. to C-in-C Fleet, 1988–90; Sec. to First Sea Lord, 1990–92; Dir, Defence Personnel, 1992–95; Dir Gen., Naval Personnel Strategy and Plans, COS to Second Sea Lord and C-in-C Naval Home Comd, 1995–98. *Recreations:* horse racing, soccer, country and folk music. *Address:* Langham House, Langham, Norfolk NR25 7BX. *Club:* Victory Services.

See also Sir D. B. Lees.

LEES, Sir Thomas (Edward), 4th Bt *cr* 1897; landowner; *b* 31 Jan. 1925; 2nd *s* of Sir John Victor Elliott Lees, 3rd Bt, DSO, MC, and Madeline A. P. (*d* 1967), *d* of Sir Harold Pelly, 4th Bt; *S* father, 1955; *m* 1st, 1949, Faith Justin (*d* 1996), *d* of G. G. Jessiman, OBE, Great Durnford, Wilts; one *s* three *d*; 2nd, 1998, Ann Christine, *d* of Major Cyril Thomas Kelleway, Auckland, NZ. *Educ:* Eton; Magdalene Coll., Cambridge. Served War in RAF; discharged 1945, after losing eye. Magdalene, Cambridge, 1945–47; BA Cantab 1947 (Agriculture). Since then has farmed at and managed South Lytchett estate. Chm., Post Green Community Trust Ltd. Mem., General Synod of C of E, 1970–90. JP 1951, CC 1952–74, High Sheriff 1960, Dorset. Hon. DLitt Bournemouth, 1992. *Recreation:* sailing. *Heir: s* Christopher James Lees [*b* 4 Nov. 1952; *m* 1st, 1977, Jennifer (marr. diss. 1987), *d* of John Wyllie; 2nd, 1989, Clare, *d* of Austen Young, FRCS, Aberystwyth; two *s* three *d*]. *Address:* Little Chimney, Post Green Road, Lytchett Minster, Poole, Dorset BH16 6AP. *T:* (01202) 622048. *Club:* Royal Cruising.

LEES, Sir Thomas Harcourt Ivor, 8th Bt *cr* 1804 (UK), of Black Rock, County Dublin; *b* 6 Nov. 1941; *s* of Sir Charles Archibald Edward Ivor Lees, 7th Bt, and Lily, *d* of Arthur Williams, Manchester; *S* father, 1963. *Heir: (presumptive) kinsman* Trevor John Cathcart d'Olier-Lees [*b* 7 Jan. 1961; *m* 1990, Susan Ciambriello; two *d*].

LEES, Sir (William) Antony Clare, 3rd Bt *cr* 1937; *b* 14 June 1935; *s* of Sir (William) Hereward Clare Lees, 2nd Bt, and of Lady (Dorothy Gertrude) Lees, *d* of F. A. Lauder; *S* father, 1976; *m* 1986, Joanna Olive Crane. *Educ:* Eton; Magdalene Coll., Cambridge (MA). *Heir:* none.

LEESE, Sir Richard Charles, Kt 2006; CBE 2001; Member (Lab), since 1984, and Leader, since 1996, Manchester City Council; *b* 21 April 1951; *s* of Samuel and Hilda Leese; *m* 1st, 1982, Michal Evans (marr. diss. 2000); one *s* one *d*; 2nd, 2003, Joanne Green (marr. diss. 2013). *Educ:* Warwick Univ. (BSc Maths). Teacher of Maths, Sidney Stringer Sch. and Community Coll., Coventry, 1974–78, with one year at Washington Jun. High School, Duluth, Minn; youth worker, 1979–82; researcher, 1983–84; community worker, 1984–88. Manchester City Council: Chair: Educn Cttee, 1986–90; Finance Cttee, 1990–95; Dep. Leader, 1990–96. *Recreations:* running, football (Manchester City), cricket, political campaigning, the Labour Party, travel, friends, family, music. *Address:* Manchester City Council, Town Hall, Albert Square, Manchester M60 2LA. *T:* (0161) 234 3004.

LEESE, Dr Robert Anthony; Chief Executive (formerly Director), Smith Institute for Industrial Mathematics and System Engineering, Guildford, since 1999; Fellow, St Catherine's College, Oxford, since 1993; *b* Warrington, 3 July 1965; *s* of John Malcolm and Alison Marjorie Leese; *m* 1991, Kathleen Erin Patrick; two *s* two *d*. *Educ:* Manchester Grammar Sch.; St John's Coll., Cambridge (BA 1986; Cert. Advanced Study 1987; MA 1990; MMath 2011); Durham Univ. (PhD 1990). Jun. Res. Fellow, St John's Coll., Cambridge, 1990–93. Vis. researcher, Brown Univ., 1990–91. FIMA 2003. *Publications:* (ed jtly) Methods and Algorithms for Radio Channel Assignment, 2002; contrib. articles on maths and physics to learned jls. *Recreations:* family, fell-walking, competitive swimming. *Address:* St Catherine's College, Oxford OX1 3UJ. *T:* (01865) 271700. *E:* robert.leese@smithinst.co.uk.

LEESON, Sir Kevin (James), KCB 2012; CBE 2003; FREng; CEng, FIET; aerospace consultant, since 2012; Senior Advisor, Atkins Defence Ltd, since 2013; Member, Safety Review Committee, British Airways, since 2013; *b* 11 June 1956; *s* of Albert V. Leeson and Joan Leeson (*née* Teale). *Educ:* Univ. of Manchester Inst. of Sci. and Technol. (BSc). CEng 1983; FIET (FIEE 1997); FREng 2012. MoD PE, 1988–93; OC Engrg and Supply Wing, RAF Marham, 1994–96; Gp Capt. Logistics 3, HQ Strike Comd, 1996–99; rcds 1999; Dir, Air Resources and Plans, MoD, 2000–04; ACDS (Logistics Ops), 2005–07; ACDS (Resources and Plans), 2007–09; Chief of Materiel (Air), Defence Equipment and Support and RAF Chief Engr, 2009–12; retired in rank of Air Marshal, 2012. Vice Pres., Royal Internat. Air Tattoo, 2005–11. Mem. Council, IET, 2011–13. Pres., Combined Services Winter Sports Assoc., 2006–12 (Vice Patron, 2012–); Chm., RAF Charitable Trust, 2013– (Vice Patron, 2011–13). *Recreations:* snow ski-ing, water ski-ing, squash, tennis. *Club:* Royal Air Force.

LE FANU, Mark, OBE 1994; General Secretary, The Society of Authors, 1982–2011; *b* 14 Nov. 1946; *s* of Admiral of the Fleet Sir Michael Le Fanu, GCB, DSC and Prudence, *d* of Admiral Sir Vaughan Morgan, KBE, CB, MVO, DSC; *m* 1976, Lucy Cowen; three *s* one *d*. *Educ:* Winchester; Univ. of Sussex. Admitted Solicitor, 1976. Served RN, 1964–73; McKenna & Co., 1973–78; The Society of Authors, 1979–2011. Vice Chm., British Copyright Council, 1992–98. Chm., W11 Opera, 1997–2000. Trustee: Royal Literary Fund, 2011–; Authors' Foundn, 2011–; Harrison Housing, 2012–. *Recreations:* sailing, golf, singing. *Address:* 25 St James's Gardens, W11 4RE. *T:* (020) 7603 4119. *E:* marklefanu@gmail.com. *Club:* Chelsea Arts.

LeFANU, Prof. Nicola Frances; composer; Professor of Music, University of York, 1994–2008, now Emeritus (Head of Department of Music, 1994–2001); *b* 28 April 1947; *d* of late William Richard LeFanu and Dame Elizabeth Violet Maconchy, DBE; *m* 1979, David Newton Lumsdaine; one *s*. *Educ:* St Mary's Sch., Calne; St Hilda's Coll., Oxford (BA Hons 1968, MA 1972; Hon. Fellow, 1993); Royal Coll. of Music; DMus London, 1988. Cobbett Prize for chamber music, 1968; BBC Composers' Competition, 1st Prize, 1971; Mendelssohn Scholarship, 1972; Harkness Fellowship for composition study, Harvard, 1973–74. Dir of Music, St Paul's Girls' Sch., 1975–77; Composer in Residence (jtly with David Lumsdaine), NSW Conservatorium of Music, Sydney, 1979; Sen Lectr in Music, 1977–93, Prof. of Musical Composition, KCL, 1993–94. Deleg. to Moscow Internat. New Music Festival, 1984. Leverhulme Res. Award, 1989; Elgar Bursary, 2014. FRCM 1995. FTCL 2002. Hon. DMus Durham, 1995; DUniv: Open, 2004; Aberdeen, 2006. *Publications:* numerous compositions, incl. opera, orchestral works, chamber music with and without voice, choral music and solo pieces; *major works include:* The Same Day Dawns (for soprano and ensemble), 1974; Columbia Falls (for symphony orch.), 1975; Dawnpath (chamber opera), 1977; The Old Woman of Beare (for soprano and ensemble), 1981; The Story of Mary O'Neill (radio opera), 1986; The Green Children (children's opera), 1990; Blood Wedding (opera), 1992; The Wildman (opera), 1995; Duo Concertante (for violin, viola and orch.), 1999; Amores (for solo horn and strings), 2004; Light Passing (chamber opera), 2004; Dream Hunter (chamber opera), 2010; String Quartet No 3, 2011; Harlequin Memories (quintet), 2012; Tokaido Road, a Journey after Hiroshige (chamber opera), 2014; Threnody (for orchestra), 2015. *Recreations:* natural history, and therefore conservation; peace movement, women's movement. *Address:* 5 Holly Terrace, York YO10 4DS. *T:* (01904) 651759. *W:* www.nicolalefanu.com. *Club:* Athenæum.

LEFF, Prof. Gordon; Professor of History, University of York, 1969–88, now Emeritus; *b* 9 May 1926; *m* 1953, Rosemary Kathleen (*née* Fox) (marr. diss 1980); one *s*. *Educ:* Summerhill Sch.; King's Coll., Cambridge. BA 1st Cl. Hons, PhD, LittD. Fellow, King's Coll., Cambridge, 1955–59; Asst Lectr, Lectr, Sen. Lectr, in History, Manchester Univ., 1956–65; Reader in History, Univ. of York, 1965–69. Carlyle Vis. Lectr, Univ. of Oxford, 1983. *Publications:* Bradwardine and the Pelagians, 1957; Medieval Thought, 1958; Gregory of Rimini, 1961; The Tyranny of Concepts, 1961; Richard Fitzralph, 1963; Heresy in the Later Middle Ages, 2 vols, 1967; Paris and Oxford Universities in 13th and 14th Centuries, 1968; History and Social Theory, 1969; William of Ockham: the metamorphosis of scholastic discourse, 1975; The Dissolution of the Medieval Outlook, 1976; Heresy, Philosophy and Religion in the Medieval West, 2002; Plato: the supremacy of reason, 2012; St Augustine: fallen man, 2012; Man and the Universe: from Plotinus to Cusa, 2012. *Recreations:* walking, gardening, watching cricket, listening to music. *Address:* The Sycamores, 12 The Village, Strensall, York YO32 5XS. *T:* (01904) 490358.

LEFF, Prof. Julian Paul, MD; FRCPsych; Director, Team for Assessment of Psychiatric Services, 1985–2005; *b* 4 July 1938; *s* of Samuel Leff and Vera Miriam (*née* Levy); *m* 1975, Joan Lilian Raphael; three *s* one *d*. *Educ:* University Coll. London (BSc, MB BS); MD London 1972. FRCPsych 1979; MRCP. House Officer: University Coll. Hosp., 1961–62; Whittington Hosp., 1962–63; career scientist, MRC, 1972–2002; Prof. of Social and Cultural Psychiatry, Inst. of Psychiatry, Univ. of London, 1987–2002, now Emeritus; Dir, MRC Social and Community Psychiatry Unit, 1989–95. Hon. Prof., Univ. of Cape Town, 2009–. FMedSci 2000. Starkey Prize, Royal Coll. of Health, 1976; Burghölzli Award, Univ. of Zürich, 1999; Marsh Award for Mental Health Work, Marsh Christian Trust, 2010. *Publications:* Psychiatric Examination in Clinical Practice, 1978, 3rd edn 1990; Expressed Emotion in Families, 1985; Psychiatry around the Globe, 1981, 2nd edn 1988; Family Work for Schizophrenia, 1992, 2nd edn 2002; Principles of Social Psychiatry, 1993; Care in the Community: illusion or reality?, 1997; The Unbalanced Mind, 2001, 2nd edn 2012; Advanced Family Work for Schizophrenia, 2005; Social Inclusion of People with Mental Illness, 2006. *Recreations:* piano, swimming, silversmithing.

LEFKOWITZ, Prof. Robert Joseph, MD; James B. Duke Professor of Medicine and of Biochemistry, Duke University Medical Center, since 1982; Investigator, Howard Hughes Medical Institute, since 1976; *b* New York, 15 April 1943; *s* of Max and Rose Lefkowitz; *m* 1963, Arna Gornstein; three *s* two *d*; *m* 1991, Lynn Tilley. *Educ:* Bronx High Sch. of Science; Columbia Univ. (BA 1962; MD 1966). Hse staff trng in internal medicine, Columbia Presbyterian Med. Center, 1966–68; Clin. and Res. Associate, NIH, Bethesda, Maryland, 1968–70; Sen. Resident and Cardiol. Fellow, Massachusetts Gen. Hosp., Boston, 1970–73; Associate Prof. of Medicine, and Asst Prof. of Biochem., 1973–77, Prof. of Medicine, 1977–82, Duke Univ. Estabd Investigator, Amer. Heart Assoc., 1973–76. Gairdner Foundn Internat. Award, 1988; Bristol-Myers Squibb Award for Dist. Achievement in Cardiovascular Res., 1992; Fred Conrad Koch Award, Endocrine Soc., 2001; Jessie Stevenson Kovalenko Medal, NAS, USA, 2001; Grand Prix for Sci., Inst. de France, Fondn Lefoulon-Delalande, 2003; Nat. Medal of Sci., USA, 2007; Shaw Prize in Life Sci. and Medicine, 2007; Albany Med. Center Prize in Medicine and Biomed. Res., 2007; Res. Achievement Award, Amer. Heart Assoc., 2009; BBVA Foundn Frontiers of Knowledge Award, 2010; (jtly) Nobel Prize in Chemistry, 2012. *Publications:* contrib. papers to Jl Biol Chem., Proc. NAS, Molecular Pharmacol., Nature, Science. *Address:* Duke University Medical Center, PO Box 3821, Durham, NC 27710, USA.

le FLEMING, Sir David (Kelland), 13th Bt *cr* 1705, of Rydal, Westmorland; freelance designer-artist; *b* 12 Jan. 1976; *s* of Sir Quentin John le Fleming, 12th Bt and of Judith Ann le Fleming (*née* Peck); *S* father, 1995. *Educ:* Queen Elizabeth Coll., Palmerston North; Wairarapa Polytech. Coll.; Wellington Polytech. Coll. (BA Visual Communications Design 1997). *Heir: b* Andrew John le Fleming, *b* 4 Oct. 1979. *Address:* 250 Colyton Road, RD5, Feilding, Manawatu, New Zealand. *T:* (6) 3287719.

le FLEMING, Morris John; DL; Chief Executive, Hertfordshire County Council, and Clerk to the Lieutenancy, Hertfordshire, 1979–90; *b* 19 Aug. 1932; *s* of late Morris Ralph le Fleming and Mabel le Fleming; *m* 1960, Jenny Rose Weeks (*d* 2013); one *s* three *d*. *Educ:* Tonbridge Sch.; Magdalene Coll., Cambridge (BA). Admitted Solicitor, 1958. Junior Solicitor, Worcester CC, 1958–59; Asst Solicitor: Middlesex CC, 1959; Nottinghamshire CC, 1959–63; Asst Clerk, Lindsey (Lincolnshire) CC, 1963–69; Hertfordshire CC: Second Dep. Clerk, 1969–74; County Secretary, 1974–79; Clerk, Magistrates' Courts Cttee, 1979–90; Sec., Probation Care Cttee, 1979–90. Dir, Herts TEC, 1989–90. Chm., Stansted Airport Consultative Cttee, 1991–2007; Mem., N Wales Child Abuse Tribunal of Enquiry, 1996–99. Dir, Herts Groundwork Trust, 1990–98; Trustee, Herts Community Trust, 1991–96. Pres., Herts Scouts, 1997–2002 (Chm., 1991–97). DL Herts, 1991. Hon. LLD Hertfordshire, 1994. *Address:* Holt, Wilts BA14 6TB. *T:* and *Fax:* (01225) 783514. *Club:* Royal Over-Seas League.

LEFROY, Jeremy John Elton; MP (C) Stafford, since 2010; *b* London, 30 May 1959; *s* of Rev. Christopher John Elton Lefroy and Sarah Ursula Lefroy (*née* Blacking); *m* 1985, Dr Janet Elizabeth MacKay; one *s* one *d*. *Educ:* Highgate Sch.; King's Coll., Cambridge (BA 1980; MA 1984). ACA 1985. Gen. Manager, 1989–91, Man. Dir, 1991–2000, African Coffee Co. Ltd, Moshi, Tanzania; Dir, African Speciality Products Ltd, Keele, 2000–. Dir, Tanzania Coffee Bd, 1997–99. Mem. (C) Newcastle-under-Lyme BC, 2003–07. *Recreations:* music (playing, singing, listening), walking, cricket, tennis, badminton. *Address:* House of Commons, SW1A 0AA. *T:* (020) 7219 7154. *E:* jeremy.lefroy.mp@parliament.uk.

LEFROY, Timothy Patterson; Chief Executive, Advertising Association, since 2009; *b* Bristol, 3 March 1948; *s* of C. B. H., (Ben), Lefroy and Leonora Lefroy (*née* Vicary); *m* 1978, Susan Russell-Jones; three *d*. *Educ:* All Saints Clifton; Colston's Sch. Marketing: Cadbury, 1966–77; Gillette (Paper:Mate), 1977–78; Dir, McCann Erickson, 1978–85; Dep. Chm., Young & Rubicam, 1985–88; CEO, Yellowhammer, 1988–90; CEO, Young & Rubicam, 1990–91; Chm. and CEO, Alliance Advertising, 1991–94; Founder, Radical, 1994–2009. Mem., Pensions Reform Gp, 2005–. Director: Assoc. for Television on Demand, 2006–10; Advertising Standards Bd of Finance, 2009–; Broadcast Advertising Standards Bd of Finance, 2009–; Cttee of Advertising Practice, 2009–; Broadcast Cttee of Advertising Practice, 2009–. Trustee, Riverside Studios, 2013–. *Recreations:* ski-ing, sailing, golf, opera. *Address:* Advertising Association, 7th Floor North, Artillery House, 11–19 Artillery Row, SW1P 1RT. *T:* (020) 7340 1100. *E:* aa@adassoc.org.uk. *Clubs:* Royal Automobile, Roehampton, Marketing Group of GB, Solus, Thirty Club of London (Sec., 2009–12).

LEGARD, Sir Charles Thomas, 15th Bt *cr* 1660; *S* father, 1984. *Heir: s* Christopher John Charles Legard [*b* 19 April 1964; *m* 1986, Miranda, *d* of Maj. Fane Gaffney; one *s* one *d*].

LÉGER, Most Rev. Ernest Raymond; Archbishop of Moncton, (RC), 1996–2002, now Emeritus; *b* 27 Feb. 1944; *s* of Sifroid Léger and Imelda Johnson. *Educ:* Univ. du Sacré Coeur, Bathurst, NB (BA); Univ. de Moncton (BEd); Univ. Laval, Quebec (MTh); Univ. St Paul, Ottawa (LCL). Ordained, 1968; Parish priest, 1968–96: Moncton, 1968–70, 1972–73; St Louis de Kent, 1970–72, 1974–75; St Charles de Kent, 1975–80; Rogersville, 1980–83; Irishtown, 1985–87; St Paul de Kent, 1988–92, 1995–96; Sackville and Dorchester, 1993–95; Judicial Vicar of Marriage Tribunal, Halifax Region, 1985–96; Vicar General, 1992–94, Administrator, 1995–96, Archdio. of Moncton. *Address:* c/o Paroisse Saint-Paul, CP 160, 425 rue Water, Plantagenet, ON K0B 1L0, Canada.

LEGG, Barry Charles, FCCA; investor and company director; *b* 30 May 1949; *s* of Henry and Elfreda Legg; *m* 1974, Margaret Rose; one *s* two *d*. *Educ:* Sir Thomas Rich's Grammar Sch., Gloucester; Manchester Univ. (BA Hons Hist.). ATII. Courtaulds Ltd, 1971–76; Coopers & Lybrand, 1976–78; Hillsdown Holdings plc, 1978–92. MP (C) Milton Keynes

South West, 1992–97; contested (C) same seat, 1997. Member: Treasury and Civil Service Select Cttee, 1992–96; Treasury Select Cttee, 1996–97 (Chm.). Chief Exec., Conservative Party, 2003. Co-Chm., Bruges Gp, 2005–. *Publications:* Maintaining Momentum: a radical tax agenda for the 1990s, 1992; Who Benefits?—Reinventing Social Security, 1993; Civil Service Reform, a Case for More Radicalism, 1994. *Recreation:* watching cricket. *Club:* Gloucestershire CC.

LEGG, Prof. Brian James, FRSB; FREng; Director, NIAB (formerly National Institute of Agricultural Botany), 1999–2005; *b* 20 July 1945; *s* of Walter and Mary Legg; *m* 1972, Philippa Whitehead; one *s* one *d*. *Educ:* Balliol Coll., Oxford (BA Physics 1966); Imperial Coll. London (PhD 1972). FRSB (FIBiol 1994); FREng (FEng 1994). Voluntary Service Overseas, The Gambia, 1966–67; Res. Scientist, Rothamsted Exptl Station, 1967–83; Head, Res. Divs, Silsoe Res. Inst., 1983–90; Dir, Silsoe Res. Inst., BBSRC (formerly AFRC), 1990–99. Vis. Scientist, CSIRO Div. of Envmtl Mechanics, Canberra, 1980–82; Vis. Prof., Silsoe Coll., Cranfield Univ. (formerly Inst. of Technology), 1990–. *Publications:* contribs to learned jls. *Recreations:* supporting African farmers through 'Send a Cow', volunteering for Woodland Trust, sailing, playing bassoon, golf.

LEGG, Cyrus Julian Edmund; Blue Arrow Personnel Services, 1997–2001; *b* 5 Sept. 1946; *s* of Cyrus and Eileen Legg; *m* 1967, Maureen Jean (*née* Lodge); two *s*. *Educ:* Tiffin School. Agricultural and Food Research Council, 1967–83; HM Treasury, 1983–87; Sec., BM (Natural Hist.) subseq. Natural History Mus., 1987–97. *Recreation:* gardening. *Address:* 34 Colchester Way, Bedford MK41 8BG. *T:* (01234) 364198.

LEGG, Sir Thomas (Stuart), KCB 1993 (CB 1985); QC 1990; Permanent Secretary, Lord Chancellor's Department, and Clerk of the Crown in Chancery, 1989–98; *b* 13 Aug. 1935; *e s* of late Stuart Legg and Margaret Legg (*née* Amos); *m* 2009, Mrs Margaret Wakelin-Saint (*d* 2013); two *d* by a previous marriage. *Educ:* Horace Mann-Lincoln Sch., New York; Frensham Heights Sch., Surrey; St John's Coll., Cambridge (MA, LLM). 2nd Lieut, Royal Marines (45 Commando), 1953–55. Called to the Bar, Inner Temple, 1960, Bencher, 1984; joined Lord Chancellor's Dept, 1962; Private Secretary to Lord Chancellor, 1965–68; Asst Solicitor, 1975; Under Sec., 1977–82; SE Circuit Administrator, 1980–82; Dep. Sec., 1982–89; Dep. Clerk of the Crown in Chancery, 1986–89; Sec. of Commns, 1989–98. Conducted Sierra Leone Arms Investigation, 1998. Consultant, Clifford Chance, 1998–2010. Ext. Mem., Audit Cttee, H of C, 2000–09; Mem., Audit Commn, 2005–11. Conducted Additional Costs Allowance Rev. of MPs' Expenses, 2009–10. Chm., Hammersmith Hosps NHS Trust, 2000–07; Dir, Imperial Coll. Healthcare Trust, 2007–14. Trustee, Civil Service Benevolent Fund, 1998–2000 (Chm., 1993–98). Chm., London Library, 2004–09 (Trustee, 2001–09). Visitor, Brunel Univ., 2001–06 (Mem. Council, 1993–2000). Hon. FRCP 2010; FRSocMed 2014. Hon. LLD Brunel, 2006. *Address:* Flat 54 Greenhill, Prince Arthur Road, Hampstead, NW3 5UA. *Club:* Garrick.

LEGGATT, Rt Hon. Sir Andrew (Peter), Kt 1982; PC 1990; Chief Surveillance Commissioner, 1998–2006; a Lord Justice of Appeal, 1990–97; *b* 8 Nov. 1930; *er s* of late Captain William Ronald Christopher Leggatt, DSO, RN and Dorothea Joy Leggatt (*née* Dreyer); *m* 1953, Gillian Barbara Newton; one *s* one *d*. *Educ:* Eton; King's Coll., Cambridge (Exhibnr). MA 1957. Commn in Rifle Bde, 1949–50; TA, 1950–59. Called to the Bar, Inner Temple, 1954, Bencher, 1976. QC 1972; a Recorder of the Crown Court, 1974–82; Judge, High Court of Justice, QBD, 1982–90. Mem., Top Salaries Review Body, 1979–82; conducted review, Tribunals for Users, 2000–01; Chm. Appeals Cttee, Takeover Panel, 2001–06. Mem., Judges' Council, 1988–97. Pres., Council of Inns of Court, 1995–97; Member: Bar Council, 1971–82; Senate, 1974–83; Chm. of the Bar, 1981–82. Hon. Member: American Bar Assoc.; Canadian Bar Assoc.; non-resident mem., American Law Inst.; Hon. Fellow, Amer. Coll. of Trial Lawyers, 1996. *Recreations:* listening to music, personal computers. *Club:* MCC.

See also Hon. Sir G. A. M. Leggatt.

LEGGATT, Hon. Sir George Andrew Midsomer, Kt 2012; **Hon. Mr Justice Leggatt;** a Judge of the High Court of Justice, Queen's Bench Division, since 2012; *b* 12 Nov. 1957; *s* of Rt Hon. Sir Andrew Peter Leggatt, *qv* and Gillian Barbara Leggatt (*née* Newton); *m* 1987, Dr Stavia Brigitte Blunt; one *s* one *d*. *Educ:* Eton (King's Schol.); King's Coll., Cambridge (MA); Harvard (Harkness Fellow); City Univ. (Dip. Law). Bigelow Teaching Fellow, Univ. of Chicago Law Sch., 1982–83; called to the Bar, Middle Temple, 1983, Bencher, 2004; Associate, Sullivan & Cromwell, New York, 1983–84; QC 1997; a Recorder, 2002–12; a Dep. High Court Judge, 2008–12. Sec., Commercial Bar Assoc., 2004–07. Vice-Chm., Bar Standards Bd, 2006–08. *Recreations:* visiting Greece, cooking, philosophy. *Address:* Royal Courts of Justice, Strand, WC2A 2LL.

LEGGE, family name of **Earl of Dartmouth**.

LEGGE, Anthony; Sir Arthur Sullivan Professor of Opera, Royal Academy of Music, since 2009 (Director of Opera, 2003–08); Associate Music Director, Opera Australia, since 2009; *b* 12 March 1948; *s* of Harry and Nancy, (Judy), Legge; *m* 1980, Christine Elizabeth Anderson Tyrer; one *d*. *Educ:* Dean Close Sch., Cheltenham; Queen's Coll., Oxford (MA). Member, Music Staff: London Opera Centre, 1971–72; Scottish Opera, 1972–77; Visiting Guest Coach: Australian Opera, 1978–88; Bayreuth, 1988–93; Nederlandsche Oper, 1995–; Opera Australia, 2005–; Hd of Music, ENO, 1989–2003; Music Dir, Clonter Opera, 2004–09; Music Advr, Grange Park Opera, 2006–. Chm., The Rehearsal Orch., 2004–09. Reader for the Queen's Anniversary Prize, 1999–. Judge, Operatunity, Channel 4, 2003. Has made numerous recordings. Hon. RAM 2007. *Publications:* The Art of Auditioning, 1988, 2nd edn 1993, updated and re-issued 2001; The Singer's Handbook, 2007. *Recreation:* walking the dog. *Club:* Garrick.

LEGGE, Hon. Henry; QC 2012; *b* London, 28 Dec. 1968; *y s* of 9th Earl of Dartmouth and of Raine, Countess Spencer, *qv*; *m* 1995, Cressida Mary (CBE 2014), *d* of Sir Christopher Anthony Hogg, *qv*; three *d*. *Educ:* Eton Coll.; Worcester Coll., Oxford (BA); City Univ. (Dip. Law). Called to the Bar, Middle Temple, 1993; in practice as a barrister, specialising in trusts, pensions and art law, 1993–. *Publications:* (contrib.) Subrogation, 2007; (contrib.) Company Directors, 2009. *Recreations:* riding, fencing, fishing. *Address:* 5 Stone Buildings, Lincoln's Inn, WC2A 3XT. *T:* (020) 7242 6201.

LEGGE, (John) Michael, CB 2001; CMG 1994; Chairman, Civil Service Healthcare, 2001–11; *b* 14 March 1944; *s* of late Alfred John Legge and Marion Frances Legge (*née* James); *m* 1971, Linda (*née* Bagley); two *s*. *Educ:* Royal Grammar Sch., Guildford; Christ Church Oxford (BA, MA). Ministry of Defence: Asst Principal, 1966; Asst Private Sec. to Sec. of State for Defence, 1970; Principal, 1971; 1st Sec., UK Delegn to NATO, 1974–77; Asst Sec., MoD, 1979–87; Rand Corp., Santa Monica, California, 1982; Asst Under Sec. of State (Policy), MoD, 1987–88; Asst Sec. Gen. for Defence Planning and Policy, NATO, 1988–93; Deputy Under-Secretary of State: NI Office, 1993–96; MoD, 1996–2001. Sec. and Dir of Admin, Royal Hosp. Chelsea, 2001–07. *Publications:* Theatre Nuclear Weapons and the NATO Strategy of Flexible Response, 1983. *Recreations:* golf, gardening, travel. *Address:* 53 St Mary's Road, Leatherhead, Surrey KT22 8HB.

LEGGE-BOURKE, Hon. Dame (Elizabeth) Shân (Josephine), DCVO 2015 (LVO 1988); Lord-Lieutenant of Powys, since 1998; *b* 10 Sept. 1943; *o c* of 3rd Baron Glanusk, DSO and Margaret (*née* Shoubridge, later Dowager Viscountess De L'Isle); *m* 1964, William Legge-Bourke, DL (*d* 2009); one *s* two *d*. Lady-in-waiting to HRH Princess Anne, now HRH Princess Royal, 1978–. President: Royal Welsh Agricl Soc., 1997; Nat. Fedn of Young Farmers Clubs of England and Wales, 1998–2000; Save the Children Fund (Wales), 1989–. High Sheriff of Powys, 1991–92. *Address:* Gliffaes-Fach, Crickhowell, Powys NP8 1RL.

LEGGETT, Sir Anthony (James), KBE 2004; DPhil; FRS 1980; John D. and Catherine T. MacArthur Professor of Physics, and Center for Advanced Study Professor of Physics, University of Illinois, since 1983; Mike and Ophelia Lazaridis Distinguished Research Professor, Institute for Quantum Computing, University of Waterloo, since 2007; *b* 26 March 1938. *Educ:* Balliol Coll., Oxford (BA 1959; Hon. Fellow 1994); Merton Coll., Oxford (BA 1961; Hon. Fellow 2004); Magdalen Coll., Oxford (DPhil 1964). Res. Associate, Univ. of Illinois, 1964–65; Fellow, Magdalen Coll., Oxford, 1963–67; Lectr, 1967–71, Reader, 1971–78, Prof. of Physics, 1978–83, Univ. of Sussex. Hon. FInstP 1999. (Jtly) Nobel Prize for Physics, 2003. *Publications:* The Problems of Physics, 1987; (jtly) Quantum Tunnelling in Condensed Media, 1992; (jtly) Quantum Computing and Quantum Bits in Mesoscopic Systems, 2003; articles in learned jls. *Address:* Department of Physics, University of Illinois at Urbana-Champaign, 1110 West Green Street, Urbana, IL 61801–3080, USA; 607 West Pennsylvania Avenue, Urbana, IL 61801–4818, USA.

LEGGETT, Dr Jeremy Kendal; Founder and Chairman, Solarcentury, 1997–2015; Founder and Chairman, SolarAid, since 2006; Chairman, Carbon Tracker Initiative, since 2011; *b* 16 March 1954; *s* of Dennis and Audrey Leggett; *m* 1st (marr. diss.); one *d*; 2nd (marr. diss); 3rd, Aki Maruyama. *Educ:* Univ. of Wales, Aberystwyth (BSc Hons 1975); Wolfson Coll., Oxford (DPhil (Earth Scis) 1978). Lectr in Earth Scis, 1978–87, Reader, 1987–89, Royal Sch. of Mines, ICSTM; Founder and Dir, Verification Technol. Inf. Centre (VERTIC), 1985–89; Scientific Dir, Climate Campaign, Greenpeace Internat., 1989–96. Vis. Fellow, Centre for Envmtl Policy and Understanding, Oxford Univ., 1996. Blog columnist, Guardian website, 2007–. Award for advancing understanding, US Climate Inst., 1996; Sustainable Leadership Award, Sustainable Asset Mgt, 2006; CNN Principal Voice, 2007; Entrepreneur of Year Award, New Energy Awards, 2009; Hillary Laureate, Hillary Inst. for Internat. Leadership, NZ, 2009. *Publications:* Global Warming: the Greenpeace report, 1990 (ed and contrib.); The Carbon War, 1999; Half Gone, 2005; The Solar Century, 2009; The Energy of Nations: risk blindness and the road to renaissance, 2013. *Recreations:* salsa dancing, golf. *Address:* Solarcentury, 50 Great Sutton Street, EC1V 0DF. *E:* jeremy.leggett@solarcentury.com. *W:* www.jeremyleggett.net.

LEGH; *see* Cornwall-Legh, family name of Baron Grey of Codnor.

LEGH, family name of **Baron Newton**.

LEGH-JONES, (Piers) Nicholas; QC 1987; *b* 2 Feb. 1943; *s* of late John Herbert Legh-Jones and Elizabeth Anne (*née* Halford). *Educ:* Winchester College; New College, Oxford (MA Hist. 1964, Jurisp. 1966). Legal Instructor, Univ. of Pennsylvania, 1966–67; Lectr in Law, New College, Oxford, 1967–71; Eldon Law Scholar, Univ. of Oxford, 1968. Called to the Bar, Lincoln's Inn, 1968; in practice as a barrister, until 2012. Vis. Prof., King's Coll., London, 1998–2005. *Publications:* (ed) MacGillivray and Parkington on Insurance Law, 6th edn, to 8th edn 1988; (gen. ed.) MacGillivray on Insurance Law, 9th edn 1997 to 11th edn 2008; contribs to Modern Law Review and Cambridge Law Jl. *Recreations:* vintage motorcars, modern history.

LEGON, Prof. Anthony Charles, PhD, DSc; FRS 2000; Professor of Physical Chemistry, 2005–08, now Emeritus, and University Senior Research Fellow, since 2008, University of Bristol; *b* 28 Sept. 1941; *s* of late George Charles Legon and Emily Louisa Florence Legon (*née* Conner); *m* 1963, Deirdre Anne Rivers; two *s* one *d*. *Educ:* Coopers' Co. Sch., London (Gibson Exhibnr); UCL (BSc 1963; PhD 1967; DSc 1981). FRSC 1978. Turner & Newall Fellow, Univ. of London, 1968–70; University College London: Lectr, 1970–83, Reader, 1983–84, in Chemistry; Thomas Graham Prof. of Chemistry, 1989–90; Prof. of Physical Chemistry, 1984–89 and 1990–2005, and EPSRC Sen. Fellow, 1997–2002, Univ. of Exeter. Vis. Res. Associate Prof., Univ. of Illinois, 1980; Visiting Professor: Chem. Dept, Texas A&M Univ., 2010–; Univ. of Newcastle, 2013–. Leverhulme Emeritus Fellow, 2009–10. Hassel Lectr, Univ. of Oslo, 1997; Moscowitz Lectr, Dept of Chemistry, Univ. of Minnesota, 2012–13. Mem., Physical Chemistry Sub Cttee, 1984–87, NATO Postdoctoral Fellowships (Chemistry) Cttee, 1987, 1988, 1991–93, Advanced Fellowships (Chemistry) Cttee, 1991–92 (Chm., 1991), SERC; Royal Society of Chemistry: Chairman: Peninsula Section, 1988–89, 2002–03; High Resolution Spectroscopy Gp, 1998–2000; Tilden Lectr and Medallist, 1990; Mem. Council, 1996–99, Vice-Pres., 2001–04, Faraday Div.; Associate Ed., Chem. Communications, 1996–98; Spectroscopy Award, 1999; Liversidge Award, 2012. Springer Award for Outstanding Achievements in Halogen Bonding, Springer-Verlag, 2009. Member Editorial Board: Chemical Physics Letters, 1988–2008; Spectrochimica Acta, 1989–97; Jl of Molecular Structure, 1990–2005; Jl Chem. Soc. Faraday Trans, 1994–98. *Publications:* Principles of Molecular Recognition, 1993; numerous res. papers in learned jls. *Recreations:* watching soccer (Exeter City AFC), reading. *Address:* School of Chemistry, University of Bristol, Bristol BS8 1TS. *E:* A.C.Legon@bristol.ac.uk.

LEGRAND, Janet, (Mrs Neil Tidmarsh); Senior Elected Member of Board, DLA Piper International LLP, since 2012 (Chairman of Board and Senior Partner, 2009–12); *b* London, 2 Oct. 1958; *d* of Charles and Gladys Legrand; *m* 1989, Neil Tidmarsh; one *s* one *d*. *Educ:* Green Sch. for Girls; Trinity Hall, Cambridge (BA Law 1980; MA 1983); Coll. of Law. Trainee and Solicitor, Lovell, White & King, 1981–91; admitted Solicitor, 1983; Partner: Alsop Wilkinson, 1991–96; Dibb Lupton Alsop, 1996–99; DLA Piper International LLP: Mem. Bd, 1999–; Chm., Remuneration Cttee, 1999–2009; Hd, Specialist Litigation, 2008–09. Mem., Adv. Bd, New Perimeter (DLA Piper's internat. pro bono affiliate), 2009–. Chm., Western Riverside Envmtl Fund, 1999–; Mem., Develt Bd, Trinity Hall, Cambridge, 2005–10; a Comr, Marshall Aid Commemoration Commn, 2013–. Director and Trustee: PRIME, 2012–; Leadership Foundn for Higher Educn, 2013–. Vice Chm., Trustee Bd, Children's Soc., 2013–. Member: Audit Cttee, Univ. of Cambridge, 2013–; Council, City Univ., 2015–. *Recreations:* family, walking, reading, cinema. *Address:* DLA Piper UK LLP, 3 Noble Street, EC2V 7EE. *T:* (020) 7796 6827. *E:* janet.legrand@dlapiper.com.

LE GRAND, Sir Julian (Ernest Michael), Kt 2015; PhD; FBA 2012; FAcSS; Richard Titmuss Professor of Social Policy, London School of Economics, since 1993 (on secondment as Senior Policy Adviser, Prime Minister's Office, 2003–05); *b* 29 May 1945; *s* of late Roland John Le Grand and Eileen Joan Le Grand; *m* 1971, Damaris May Robertson-Glasgow; two *d*. *Educ:* Eton; Univ. of Sussex (BA); Univ. of Pennsylvania (PhD 1972). Lectr in Econs, Univ. of Sussex, 1971–78; Lectr in Econs, 1978–85, Sen. Res. Fellow, 1985–87, LSE; Prof. of Public Policy, Univ. of Bristol, 1987–93. Mem., ESRC Bds, 1982–86 and 1988–92. Mem., Commn for Health Improvement, 1999–2003; Chairman: Social Care Practices Wkg Gp, DFES, 2006–07; Health England, DoH, 2007–10; Mutuals Taskforce, Cabinet Office, 2011–13; Panels on Doncaster's and Birmingham's Children's Services, DfE, 2013–14. Sen. Associate, 2005–07, Trustee, 2007–, King's Fund. Non-executive Director: Avon FHSA, 1990–94; Avon HA, 1994–95; Vice-Chm., Frenchay NHS Trust, 1996–99. Gov., LSE, 1999–2003. FAcSS (Founding AcSS 1999). Hon. FPH (Hon. FPHM 1997). Hon. DLitt Sussex, 2006. Eupolis Prize, Eupolis Inst., Milan, 2012. *Publications:* (with R. Robinson) The Economics of Social Problems, 1976, 4th edn 2008; The Strategy of Equality, 1982; (ed with R. Robinson) Privatisation and the Welfare State, 1984; (with R. Goodin) Not Only the Poor, 1987; (ed with S. Estrin) Market Socialism, 1989; Equity and Choice, 1991; (ed with W. Bartlett) Quasi-markets and Social Policy, 1993; (ed with R. Robinson) Evaluating the NHS Reforms, 1994; (with B. New) Rationing in the NHS, 1996; (ed jtly) A Revolution in Social Policy,

1998; (ed jtly) Learning from the NHS Internal Market, 1998; (ed with E. Mossialos) Health Care and Cost Containment in the European Union, 1999; (ed jtly) Understanding Social Exclusion, 2002; Motivation, Agency and Public Policy: of knights and knaves, pawns and queens, 2004, 2nd edn 2006; The Other Invisible Hand, 2007; Government Paternalism, 2015; contrib. articles to Econ. Jl, Jl Public Econs, Economica, Jl Social Policy, Jl Human Resources, Eur. Econ. Review, British Jl Pol Sci., Jl Health Econs, BMJ, Health Affairs, Social Sci. and Medicine, The Lancet, Jl Royal Statistical Soc. *Recreations:* reading, drawing. *Address:* 7 Victoria Square, Bristol BS8 4EU. *T:* (0117) 973 0975, 07771 985294. *E:* J.Legrand@lse.ac.uk.

LE GREW, Daryl John; Vice Chancellor Fellow: Monash University, since 2011; University of Melbourne, since 2011; *b* Melbourne, 17 Sept. 1945; *s* of A. J. and N. M. R. Le Grew; *m* 1971, Josephine de Tarczynska; one *s* two *d. Educ:* Trinity Grammar Sch., Kew; Univ. of Melbourne (BArch, MArch). University of Melbourne: Lectr, Dept of Town and Regl Planning, 1969–73; Lectr, then Sen. Lectr, Dept of Architecture and Bldg, 1973–85; Deakin University: Prof. of Architecture, 1986–98; Dean, Faculty of Design and Technol., 1992–93; Chm., Academic Bd, 1992–98; Pro-Vice-Chancellor (Academic), 1993–94; Dep. Vice-Chancellor and Vice-Pres. (Academic), 1994–98; Vice-Chancellor, Univ. of Canterbury, NZ, 1998–2002; Vice-Chancellor and Pres., Univ. of Tasmania, 2003–10. Sen. Consultant, Gehl Architects, Copenhagen, 2010–. Pres. of Senate, Australian Acad. of Design, 2011–. Life Fellow, Mus. of Victoria, 1997. FAIM. Hon. DLitt Tasmania, 2010. *Recreations:* swimming, music, poetry, philosophy.

LE GRICE, (Andrew) Valentine; QC 2002; barrister; *b* 26 June 1953; *s* of late Charles Le Grice and Wilmay Le Grice (*née* Ward); *m* 1st, 1977, Anne Elizabeth Moss (marr. diss. 2001); two *s* one *d*; 2nd, 2001, Jayne Elizabeth Sandford-Hill; one *d. Educ:* Shrewsbury Sch.; Univ. of Durham (BA Hons). Called to the Bar, Middle Temple, 1977. MCIArb 2011. *Recreations:* watching sport (particularly football), throwing things away. *Address:* 1 Hare Court, Temple, EC4Y 7BE. *Club:* Travellers.

LE GUIN, Ursula Kroeber; writer; *b* Berkeley, California, 21 Oct. 1929; *d* of Alfred L. Kroeber and Theodora Kroeber; *m* 1953, Charles A. Le Guin; one *s* two *d. Educ:* Radcliffe Coll. (BA 1951); Columbia Univ. (MA 1952; Fellow, 1953). Instructor in French, Mercer Coll. and Univ. of Idaho, 1956–57; Lectr, Guest Lectr or Writer in Residence, 1971–, at univs, colls, confs and workshops in USA, Australia and UK, incl. Portland State Univ., Indiana Univ., Kenyon Coll., Stanford Univ., Clarion West, Revelle Coll. of UCSD, Tulane, Bennington, Beloit, Haystack, Flight of the Mind. Arbuthnot Lectr, Amer. Lib. Assoc., 2004. Grand Master, Sci. Fiction and Fantasy Writers of America, 2003. Holds hon. degrees from 9 US univs. Gandalf Award, 1979; Harold Vursell Award, AAIL, 1991; Bumbershoot Arts Award, Seattle, 1998; Robert Kirsch Lifetime Achievement Award, LA Times, 2000; Lifetime Achievement Award, Pacific NW Booksellers' Assoc., 2001; PEN/Malamud Award, World Fantasy Award, 2002; Margaret A. Edwards Award for lifetime achievement, Young Adult Liby Services Assoc., 2004; Maxine Cushing Gray Award for literary achievement, 2006. *Publications: novels:* Planet of Exile, 1966; Rocannon's World, 1966; City of Illusion, 1967; A Wizard of Earthsea, 1968 (Boston Globe – Horn Bk Award, 1968; Lewis Carroll Shelf Award, 1979); The Left Hand of Darkness, 1969 (Nebula and Hugo Awards, 1969; Tiptree Retrospective Award, 1996); The Tombs of Atuan, 1970 (Newbery Silver Medal, 1972); The Lathe of Heaven, 1971 (Locus Readers Award, 1972; filmed 1979); The Farthest Shore, 1972 (Nat. Book Award for Children's Books); The Dispossessed: an ambiguous Utopia, 1974 (Hugo and Nebula Awards, 1975); The Word for World is Forest, 1976 (Hugo Award); Very Far Away From Anywhere Else, 1976 (Prix Lectures-Jeunesse, 1987); Malafrena, 1979; The Beginning Place, 1980; The Eye of the Heron, 1983; Always Coming Home, 1985 (Janet Heidinger Kafka Prize for Fiction, 1986); Tehanu (Nebula Award), 1990; The Telling, 2000 (Locus Readers Award, Endeavour Award, 2001); Tales from Earthsea, 2001 (Locus Readers Award, 2002, Endeavour Award, 2003); The Other Wind, 2001; Gifts, 2004 (Literary Award, PEN Center USA); Voices, 2006; Powers, 2008 (Nebula Award, Science Fiction and Fantasy Writers of America); Lavinia, 2008; *short story collections:* The Wind's Twelve Quarters, 1975; Orsinian Tales, 1976; The Compass Rose, 1982 (Locus Award, 1984); Buffalo Gals, 1987 (Internat. Fantasy Award, Hugo Award, 1988); Searoad, 1991 (H. L. Davis Fiction Award, 1992); A Fisherman of the Inland Sea, 1994; Four Ways to Forgiveness, 1995 (Locus Readers Award, 1996); Unlocking the Air, 1996; The Birthday of the World, 2002; Changing Planes, 2003; The Wild Girls, 2011; The Unreal and the Real, 2012 (Oregon Book Award, 2014); *poetry:* Wild Angels, 1974; Walking in Cornwall, 1976; (with T. Kroeber) Tillai and Tylissos, 1979; Hard Words, 1981; (with H. Pander) In the Red Zone, 1983; Wild Oats and Fireweed, 1988; No Boats, 1992; (with R. Dorband) Blue Moon over Thurman Street, 1993; Going out with Peacocks, 1994; Sixty Odd, 1999; Incredible Good Fortune, 2006; Finding My Elegy, 2012; *translations:* Lao Tzu: Tao Te Ching: a book about the way and the power of the way, 1997; (with D. Bellessi) The Twins, The Dream/Las Gemelas, El Sueño, 1997; Kalpa Imperial, stories by Angelica Gorodischer, 2003; Selected Poems of Gabriela Mistral, 2003; *criticism:* The Language of the Night, 1979, rev. edn 1992; Dancing at the Edge of the World, 1989; Steering the Craft, 1998; The Wave in the Mind, 2004; Cheek by Jowl, 2009; *for children:* Leese Webster, 1979; Cobbler's Rune, 1983; Solomon Leviathan, 1988; A Visit from Dr Katz, 1988; Fire and Stone, 1989; Fish Soup, 1992; A Ride on the Red Mare's Back, 1992; Tom Mouse, 2002; Cat Dreams, 2010; *Catwings books:* Catwings, 1988; Catwings Return, 1989; Wonderful Alexander and the Catwings, 1994; Jane on her Own, 1999; *screenplay:* King Dog, 1985. *Address:* c/o Curtis Brown Ltd, 10 Astor Place, New York, NY 10003, USA.

LEHEC, Stephen Robert; Head, Kingston Grammar School, since 2014; *b* Fulham, 17 Oct. 1970; *s* of Stephen Joseph Lehec and Valerie Frances Seaton Lehec (*née* Reid); *m* 1999, Penelope Anne Vaughn; two *d. Educ:* Archbishop Tenison's C of E Sch.; King Alfred's Coll., Winchester (BA Hons Hist. and English 1993); St Anne's Coll., Oxford (PGCE Hist. 1994); NPQH 2006. Maidstone GS (Boys), 1994–2006 (Asst Headteacher, 2001–06); Dep. Headmaster, 2006–08, Headmaster, 2008–14, Aylesbury GS. *Address:* Kingston Grammar School, 70 London Road, Kingston upon Thames, Surrey KT2 6PY. *Club:* Lansdowne.

LEHMANN, Prof. Alan Robert, PhD; FRS 2010; FMedSci; Professor of Molecular Genetics, University of Sussex, 2001–11, Research Professor of Molecular Genetics, since 2011; *b* Rochdale, Lancs, 30 Aug. 1946; *s* of late Henry Louis Lehmann and Lore Ruth Lehmann; *m* 1967, Judith Selbourne; one *s* one *d. Educ:* Littleborough Central Primary Sch.; Manchester Grammar Sch. (Foundn Schol.); Pembroke Coll., Cambridge (Open Schol. Natural Scis; BA 1st Cl. Biochem. 1967); Inst. of Cancer Res., Univ. of London (PhD 1970). Postdoctoral Investigator, Oak Ridge Nat. Labs, Tenn, 1970–71; University of Sussex: Beit Meml Fellow, Dept of Biochem., 1971–73; Scientific Staff, MRC Cell Mutation Unit, 1973–2001; Professorial Fellow, 1987–2001; Chm., Genome Damage and Stability Centre, 2001–11. FMedSci 2004. *Publications:* contribs to scientific jls and books. *Recreations:* walking, travel, opera, birdwatching. *Address:* 25 Montacute Road, Lewes, E Sussex BN7 1EW.

LEHN, Prof. Jean-Marie, Chevalier, Ordre des Palmes Académiques, 1989; Officier, Ordre National du Mérite, 1993 (Chevalier, 1976); Grand Officier, Légion d'Honneur, 2014 (Chevalier, 1983; Officier, 1988; Commandeur, 1996); Professor of Chemistry, Collège de France, Paris, 1979–2010, now Honorary Professor; Emeritus Professor, University of Strasbourg, since 2010; *b* Rosheim, Bas-Rhin, 30 Sept. 1939; *s* of Pierre Lehn and Marie Lehn (*née* Salomon); *m* 1965, Sylvie Lederer; two *s. Educ:* Univ. of Strasbourg (PhD); Research Fellow, Harvard, 1964. Mem., CNRS, 1960–66; Asst Prof., Univ. of Strasbourg, 1966–69; University Louis Pasteur, Strasbourg: Associate Prof., 1970; Prof. of Chemistry, 1970–79. Visiting Professor: Harvard Univ., 1972, 1974, 1980; ETH, Zürich, 1977; Univ. of Barcelona, 1985; Alexander Todd Vis. Prof. of Chem., Univ. of Cambridge, 1984; Rolf-Sammet Vis. Prof., Univ. of Frankfurt, 1985–86; Heinrich-Hertz Vis. Prof., Univ. of Karlsruhe, 1989; Robert Burns Woodward Vis. Prof., Harvard Univ., 1997, 2000; Newton Abraham Prof., Lincoln Coll., Oxford, 1999–2000; Adjunct Prof., Asian Inst. of Technol., Bangkok, 2005; Prof.-at-Large, City Univ. of Hong Kong, 2008. Hon. Dir, Lehn Inst. of Functional Materials, Guangzhou. Mem. or Associate, and hon. degrees from professional bodies in Europe, Asia and USA; Hon. FRSC 1987; For. Mem., Royal Soc., 1993. Nobel Prize for Chemistry (jtly), 1987, and numerous awards from sci. instns. Orden pour le mérite für Wissenschaften und Künste (FRG), 1990; Österreichisches Ehrenkreuz für Wissenschaft und Kunst, 1st cl. (Austria), 2001; Grand Officer, Order of Cultural Merit (Romania), 2004; Grosses Verdienstkreuz mit Stern (Germany), 2009. *Publications:* three books; 965 chapters in books and contribs to learned jls on supramolecular chemistry, physical organic chemistry and photochemistry. *Recreation:* music. *Address:* Institut de Science d'Ingénierie Supramoléculaires, Université de Strasbourg, 8 Allée Gaspard Monge, 67000 Strasbourg, France. *T:* (3) 68855145, *Fax:* (3) 68855140. *E:* lehn@unistra.fr.

LEHRER, Thomas Andrew; writer of songs since 1943; *b* 9 April 1928; *s* of James Lehrer and Anna Lehrer (*née* Waller). *Educ:* Harvard Univ. (AB 1946, MA 1947); Columbia Univ.; Harvard Univ. Student (mathematics, especially probability and statistics) till 1953. Part-time teaching at Harvard, 1946–53. Theoretical physicist at Baird-Atomic, Inc., Cambridge, Massachusetts, 1953–54. Entertainer, 1953–55, 1957–60. US Army, 1955–57. Lecturer in Business Administration, Harvard Business Sch., 1961; Lecturer: in Education, Harvard Univ., 1963–66; in Psychology, Wellesley Coll., 1966; in Political Science, MIT, 1962–71; Lectr, Univ. of Calif, Santa Cruz, 1972–2008. *Publications:* Tom Lehrer Song Book, 1954; Tom Lehrer's Second Song Book, 1968; Too Many Songs by Tom Lehrer, 1981; contrib. to Annals of Mathematical Statistics, Journal of Soc. of Industrial and Applied Maths. *Recreation:* piano. *Address:* 11 Sparks Street, Cambridge, MA 02138–4711, USA. *T:* (617) 3547708.

LEICESTER, 8th Earl of, *cr* 1837; **Thomas Edward Coke;** Viscount Coke 1837; *b* 6 July 1965; *er s* of 7th Earl of Leicester, CBE and Valeria Phyllis Coke (*née* Potter); *S* father, 2015; *m* 1996, Polly, *y d* of David Whately; one *s* three *d. Educ:* Eton; Univ. of Manchester (BA). Scots Guards, 1987–93. Pres., Caravan Club, 2006–. *Heir: s* Viscount Coke, *qv. Address:* Holkham, Wells-next-the-Sea, Norfolk NR23 1AB. *Clubs:* White's; Norfolk (Norwich).

LEICESTER, Bishop of; *no new appointment at time of going to press.*

LEICESTER, Assistant Bishop of; *see* Boyle, Rt Rev. C. J.

LEICESTER, Dean of; *see* Monteith, Very Rev. D. R. M.

LEICESTER, Archdeacon of; *see* Stratford, Ven. T. R.

LEIFLAND, Leif, Hon. GCVO 1983; Ambassador of Sweden to the Court of St James's, 1982–91; *b* 30 Dec. 1925; *s* of Sigfrid and Elna Leifland; *m* 1954, Karin Abard; one *s* two *d. Educ:* Univ. of Lund (LLB 1950). Joined Ministry of Foreign Affairs, 1952; served: Athens, 1953; Bonn, 1955; Stockholm, 1958; Washington, 1961; Stockholm, 1964; Washington, 1970; Stockholm, 1975. Secretary, Foreign Relations Cttee, Swedish Parliament, 1966–70; Under Secretary for Political Affairs, 1975–77; Permanent Under-Secretary of State for Foreign Affairs, 1977–82; Chm. Bd, Swedish Inst. of Internat. Affairs, 1991–2002. *Publications:* books and articles on foreign policy and national security questions. *Address:* Nybrogatan 77, 11440 Stockholm, Sweden.

LEIGH, family name of **Barons Leigh** and **Leigh of Hurley**.

LEIGH, 6th Baron *cr* 1839, of Stoneleigh, co. Warwick; **Christopher Dudley Piers Leigh;** *b* 20 Oct. 1960; *s* of 5th Baron Leigh and his 1st wife, Cecilia Poppy, *y d* of Robert Cecil Jackson; *S* father, 2003; *m* 1990, Sophy-Ann (marr. diss. 2008), *d* of Richard Burrows, MBE; one *s* one *d. Educ:* Eton; RAC Cirencester. *Heir: s* Hon. Rupert Dudley Leigh, *b* 21 Feb. 1994.

LEIGH OF HURLEY, Baron *cr* 2013 (Life Peer), of Hurley in the Royal County of Berkshire; **Howard Darryl Leigh;** Founder, 1988, and Senior Partner, since 2010, Cavendish Corporate Finance LLP; *b* London, 3 April 1959; *s* of late Philip Mark Leigh and of Jacqueline Leigh (*née* Freeman); *m* 1998, Jennifer Peach; two *d. Educ:* Clifton Coll., Bristol; Univ. of Southampton (BSc (SocSci) Econs). FCA; Mem., Chartered Inst. of Taxation. With Deloitte Haskin & Sells, 1980–88. Mem. Bd, Bolton Building Soc., 1986–92. Mem., DTI Deregulation Task Force Tax Cttee, 1994–97. Sen. Treasurer, Cons. Party, 2005– (Treas., 2000–); Pres., Westminster N Cons. Assoc., 2010–. Mem. Council, ICAEW, 1998–2004 (Chm., Corporate Finance Faculty, 1998–2004; Alt. to Pres. on Takeover Panel Appeal Cttee, 1998–2004). Pres., Westminster Synagogue, 2010– (Chm., 2002–10). Chm., Jewish Care Business Gp, 2000–; Mem. Exec. Bd, Cons. Friends of Israel, 2008–; Vice Pres., Jewish Leadership Council, 2010–. Trustee: The Jerusalem Foundn, 1992–; Jewish Care, 2009–12. *Recreations:* running, The Thames. *Address:* Cavendish Corporate Finance LLP, 40 Portland Place, W1B 1NB. *T:* (020) 7908 6000, *Fax:* (020) 7908 6006. *E:* hleigh@cavendish.com. *Club:* Carlton.

LEIGH, Bertie; *see* Leigh, M. A. M. S.

LEIGH, His Honour Christopher Humphrey de Verd; QC 1989; a Circuit Judge, 2001–08; *b* 12 July 1943; *s* of late Wing Commander Humphrey de Verd Leigh and of Johanna Leigh; *m* 1970, Frances Powell. *Educ:* Harrow. Called to the Bar, Lincoln's Inn, 1967, Bencher, 1999. A Recorder, 1985–2001. *Recreations:* ski-ing, photography. *Address:* Drystone Chambers, 35 Bedford Row, WC1R 4JH.

LEIGH, David, PhD; Secretary-General, International Institute for Conservation, 2006–10; *b* 11 Jan. 1943; *s* of Jacques Leigh and Gwendoline (*née* Bright); *m* 1969, Judith Mary Latham; one *s* two *d. Educ:* Univ. of Durham (BSc Physics 1966); Inst. of Archaeology, Univ. of London (Dip. Archaeol Conservation 1968); UC, Cardiff (PhD 1980). Experimental Officer (Conservation), Dept of Archaeology, Univ. of Southampton, 1968–74; Lectr in Archaeol Conservation, UC, Cardiff, 1975–87; Head of Conservation Unit, Museums and Galls Commn, 1987–93; Dir, Mus. Training Inst., 1993–95; Principal, West Dean Coll., 1995–2000; Exec. Dir, 2001–05, Sen. Policy Advr and Communications Manager, 2005–07, UK Inst. for Conservation, subseq. Inst. of Conservation. Member: Internat. Inst. for Conservation, 1970– (Fellow, 1975; Mem. Council, 1990–94; Treas., 2001–06); Sci. and Conservation Panel, 1984–94, Ancient Monuments Adv. Cttee, 1988–90, English Heritage; Arts Panel, 2004–, Council, 2007–, NT; Cttee B/560: Conservation of Tangible Cultural Heritage, BSI, 2008– (Chm., 2008–11); Bd, Inst. of Conservation, 2011–14; Rescue, 1972– (Trustee, 1972–78). Trustee: Conf. on Trng in Architectural Conservation, 2000–08; Anna Plowden Trust, 2007–. FSA; ACR. Plowden Medal, Royal Warrant Holders' Assoc., 2002. *Publications:* (contrib.) Marine Archaeology, 1973; (contrib.) Rescue Archaeology, 1974; (ed) First Aid for Finds, 1976; articles on Anglo-Saxon artefacts, especially early Anglo-Saxon jewellery, conservation and restoration, training and educn. *Recreations:* family, music, walking, gardening, amateur dramatics.

LEIGH, Prof. David Alan, PhD; FRS 2009; Sir Samuel Hall Professor of Chemistry, University of Manchester, since 2014; *b* Birmingham, 31 May 1963; *s* of Peter Leigh and Hylda Leigh; *m* 1998, Sau Yin Sek; one *d. Educ:* Codsall High Sch.; Sheffield Univ. (BSc Hons Chem. 1984; MSc Organic Chem. 1985; PhD Organic Chem. 1987). Res. Associate, Nat. Res. Council of Canada, Ottawa, 1987–89; Lectr, then Reader, UMIST, 1989–98; Prof. of Synthetic Chem., Univ. of Warwick, 1998–2001; Forbes Prof. of Organic Chem., Univ. of

Edinburgh, 2001–12; Prof. of Organic Chem., Univ. of Manchester, 2012–13. EPSRC Sen. Res. Fellow, 2005–10. FRSC 2005; FRSE 2005. *Recreations:* contract bridge, magic, popular music. *Address:* Meadow Barn, Sugar Lane, Adlington, Cheshire SK10 5SN. *T:* (0161) 275 1926; School of Chemistry, University of Manchester, Oxford Road, Manchester M13 9PL. *E:* David.Leigh@manchester.ac.uk.

LEIGH, Sir Edward (Julian Egerton), Kt 2013; MP (C) Gainsborough, since 1997 (Gainsborough and Horncastle, 1983–97); *b* 20 July 1950; *s* of Sir Neville Egerton Leigh, KCVO; *m* 1984, Mary Goodman; three *s* three *d. Educ:* St Philip's Sch., Kensington; Oratory Sch., Berks; French Lycée, London; UC, Durham Univ. (BA Hons). Called to the Bar, Inner Temple, 1977. Mem., Cons. Res. Dept, seconded to office of Leader of Opposition, GLC, 1973–75; Prin. Correspondence Sec. to Rt Hon. Margaret Thatcher, MP, 1975–76. Member (C): Richmond Borough Council, 1974–78; GLC, 1977–81. Contested (C) Teesside, Middlesbrough, Oct. 1974. PPS to Minister of State, Home Office, 1990; Parly Under-Sec. of State, DTI, 1990–93. Chairman: Public Accounts Cttee, H of C, 2001–10; Public Accounts Commn, H of C, 2011–; Backbench Cttee on Foreign Affairs, Defence, Internat. Develt, 2011–; All-Party Parly Gp on France, 2010– (Mem., 1983–); All-Party Parly Gp on Italy, 2015–; Secretary: Conservative backbench Cttees on agric., defence and employment, 1983–90; All-Party Parly Gp on Insurance, 2010– (Mem., 1993–); Vice Chm., Conservative Back bench Cttees on foreign affairs and social security, 1997–2001; Financial Advr to HM Treasury, 2010–11. Delegate, Parly Assembly, Council of Europe, 2011–. Chm., Nat. Council for Civil Defence, 1980–82; Dir, Coalition for Peace Through Security, 1982–83. Kt of Honour and Devotion, SMO Malta, 1994. *Publications:* Right Thinking, 1979; Responsible Individualism, 1994; Monastery of the Mind, 2012. *Recreations:* walking, reading. *Address:* House of Commons, SW1A 0AA.

LEIGH, Sir Geoffrey (Norman), Kt 1990; Chairman, Leigh Academies Trust, since 2009; Chairman, Allied London Properties, 1987–98 (Managing Director, 1970–87); Director, Arrow Property Investments Ltd, 2000–06; *b* 23 March 1933; *s* of Rose Leigh and Morris Leigh; *m* 1st, 1955, Valerie Lennard (marr. diss. 1975; she *d* 1976); one *s* two *d*; 2nd, 1976, Sylvia Pell; one *s* one *d. Educ:* Haberdashers' Aske's Hampstead Sch.; Univ. of Michigan. Man. Dir, 1965, Chm., 1980–98, Sterling Homes. Founder and First Pres., Westminster Junior Chamber of Commerce, 1959–63; Underwriting Mem., Lloyd's, 1973–97. Special Advisor, Land Agency Bd, Commn for the New Towns, 1994–96; Member: Cttee, Good Design in Housing for Disabled, 1977; Cttee, Good Design in Housing, 1978–79; British ORT Council, 1979–80; Internat. Adv. Bd, American Univ., Washington, 1983–97; Adv. Council, Prince's Youth Business Trust, 1985–2005; Main Finance Bd, NSPCC, 1985–2003 (Hon. Mem. Council, 1995–); Governing Council, Business in the Community, 1987–; Somerville Coll. Appeal, 1987–2010; Royal Fine Art Commn Art and Arch. Educn Trust, 1988–99; Per Cent Club, 1988–2000; Council, City Technology Colls Trust, 1988–2005; City Appeal Cttee, Royal Marsden Hosp., 1990–93; Review Body on Doctors' and Dentists' Remuneration, 1990–93; Wellbeing Council, 1994–2009; Chancellor's Ct of Benefactors, Oxford Univ., 1991–; Emmanuel Coll., Cambridge, Develt Campaign, 1994–96; Chm., St Mary's Hosp. 150th Anniversary Appeal, 1995–2009. Comr and Trustee, Fulbright Commn, 1991–99 (Chm., Fulbright US-UK. Adv. Bd, 1995–2009); Mem., Duke of Edinburgh's Award World Fellowship, 1992–; Sponsor, Leigh City Technology Coll., subseq. Leigh Technology Acad., Dartford (Chm. of Govs, 1988–2006; Chm. of Trustees, 2006–); Founder/Sponsor, Friends of British Liby, 1987– (Vice-Pres., 2000–); Founder, Margaret Thatcher Centre, Somerville Coll., Oxford, 1991; Treasurer: Commonwealth Jewish Council, 1983–89; Commonwealth Jewish Trust, 1983–89; a Treas., Cons. Party, 1995–97; Vice President: Hampstead and Highgate Cons. Assoc., 1997–2005 (Patron, 1991–94; Pres., 1994–97); Conservatives Abroad, 1995–; Republicans Abroad, 1995–2005; Treas. and Trustee, Action on Addiction, 1991–2003; Trustee: Margaret Thatcher Foundn, 1991–; Industry in Educn, 1993–98; Philharmonia, 1992–99. Governor: Royal Sch., Hampstead, 1991–2003; City Lit. Inst., 1991–98. Hon. Mem., Emmanuel Coll., Cambridge, 1995; Foundn Fellow, Somerville Coll., Oxford, 1998; Univ. of Greenwich Assembly, 2003. Hon. Life Mem., Cons. Med. Soc., 1998. Freeman, City of London, 1976; Liveryman: Haberdashers' Co., 1992–; Furniture Makers' Co., 1987– (Chm., Premises Cttee, 2003–06; Asst *hc*, 2006). Mem., Soc. of the Four Arts, 2007–; Dir, Palm Beach Civic Assoc., 2013–; Trustee, Palm Beach United Way, 2014–. FRSA. Hon. FICPD. Presidential Citation, The American Univ., 1987. *Recreations:* photography, reading, golf. *Address:* 42 Berkeley Square, W1J 5AW. *T:* (020) 7409 5054. *Clubs:* Carlton (Hon. Mem., Political Cttee, 2004–), United and Cecil, Pilgrims, Royal Automobile; Pilgrims of the US; St George's Society of New York; Wentworth; Palm Beach Country, Palm Beach Yacht, Palm Beach Ocean, Bikers of Palm Beach.

LEIGH, Prof. Irene May, CBE 2012 (OBE 2006); MD; DSc; FRCP, FMedSci; FRSE; Professor of Cellular and Molecular Medicine, College of Medicine, Dentistry and Nursing, University of Dundee, since 2006 (Vice Principal and Head, 2006–11); Director, CR-UK Skin Tumour Laboratory, since 1989; *b* 25 April 1947; *d* of Archibald and May Lilian Allen; *m* 1st, 1969, (Peter) Nigel Leigh, *qv* (marr. diss. 1999); one *s* three *d*; 2nd, 2000, John E. Kernthaler. *Educ:* London Hosp. Med. Coll. (BSc 1968; MB BS 1971; MD 1992; DSc 1999). FRCP 1987. Consultant Dermatologist and Sen. Lectr, 1983–92, Prof. of Dermatol., 1992–97, Royal London Hosp. and London Hosp. Med. Coll.; St Bartholomew's and Royal London School of Medicine and Dentistry, QMW, then Barts and the London, Queen Mary's School of Medicine and Dentistry, London University: Prof. of Cellular and Molecular Medicine, 1999–2006; Research Dean, 1997–2002; Jt Res. Dir, 2002–05. FMedSci 1999; FRSE 2009. *Publications:* contrib. numerous articles on keratinocyte biol., genodermatoses and skin carcinogenesis to peer-reviewed jls. *Recreations:* music, film, opera, theatre. *Address:* College of Medicine, Dentistry and Nursing, University of Dundee, Level 10, Ninewells Hospital and Medical School, Dundee DD1 9SY.

LEIGH, Jonathan; Master, Marlborough College, since 2012; *b* 17 June 1952; *s* of Rupert M. Leigh and Isabel A. Leigh (*née* Villiers); *m* 1976, Emma Mary, *d* of Rear-Adm. Michael Donald Kyrle Pope, CB, MBE; one *s* one *d. Educ:* Eton Coll.; Corpus Christi Coll., Cambridge (MA History). Cranleigh School: Asst Master, 1976–82; Housemaster, 1982–88; Head of History, 1987; Second Master, 1988–92; Head Master, Blundell's Sch., 1992–2004; Headmaster, Ridley Coll., Ontario, 2005–12. Mem., Devon County Residential Care Standards Adv. Cttee, 1993–2002 (Chm., 1994–98); Vice Pres., Devon Playing Fields Assoc., 1998–2004. Member: Council, ISIS South-West, 1995–2001; Cttee, Belgian Sect., Assoc. Européene des Enseignants, 1994–2004; Admiralty Interview Bd, 1994–2004; Interviewing Panel, ESU, 1996–; Sec., SW Div., HMC, 2000 (Chm., 2001). Member: Adv. Bd, Vimy Foundn, 2005–; Bd, Canadian Accredited Ind. Schs (formerly Canadian Educnl Standards Inst.), 2009– (Mem. Evaluation Gp, 2008–12); Internat. Confedn of Principals, 2009–. Trustee: Tiverton Adventure Playground Assoc., 1992–2004; Inner Cities Young People's Project, 1996–2004. FRSA 1994. Governor: St Petroc's Sch., Bude, 1993–2004; Wolborough Hill Sch., Newton Abbot, 1998–2000; Abbey Sch., Tewkesbury, 2000–03 (Chm., 2002); Director: Highfield Sch., Liphook, 2000–; Cheam Sch., 2013–; Educnl Advr to Pembroke House Sch., Kenya, 2014–. Dir, 2000–, Vice Chm., 2002–04, Devon and Exeter Steeplechases. *Recreations:* singing, horse racing, opera, labradors, late 19th century African history, the Charente. *Address:* Marlborough College, Bath Road, Marlborough, Wilts SN8 1PA. *Club:* East India.

LEIGH, Prof. Leonard Herschel; freelance author and lecturer; Professor of Criminal Law in the University of London, at the London School of Economics and Political Science, 1982–97; *b* 19 Sept. 1935; *s* of Leonard William and Lillian Mavis Leigh; *m* 1960, Jill Diane Gale (*d* 2015); one *s* one *d. Educ:* Univ. of Alberta (BA, LLB); Univ. of London (PhD 1966). Admitted to Bar: Alberta, 1959; NW Territories, 1961; Inner Temple, 1993. Private practice, Province of Alberta, 1958–60; Dept of Justice, Canada, 1960–62; London School of Economics: Asst Lectr in Law, 1964–65; Lectr, 1965–71; Reader, 1971–82. Vis. Prof., Queen's Univ., Kingston, Ont, 1973–74; Bowker Vis. Prof., Univ. of Alberta, 1999. British Council Lecturer: Univ. of Strasbourg, 1978; National Univ. of Mexico, 1980; UN Asia and Far East Inst., Tokyo, 1986; South India, 1989, 1991. Mem., Canadian Govt Securities Regulation Task Force, 1974–78. Bd Mem., Criminal Cases Review Commn, 1997–2005. UK Convenor, Université de l'Europe Steering Cttee, 1987–90; Chm., English Nat. Section, 1988–, Mem., Conseil de Direction, 1989–, Internat. Assoc. of Penal Law. Mem., Exec. Cttee, Canada-UK Colloquia, 1993–. Member, Council of Europe Training Missions: Hungary, 1990; Poland, 1991; Albania, 1992; Mem., Council of Europe Wkg Party on Reform of Russian Penal Law, 1994–95. UK Rep., Internat. Penal and Penitentiary Foundn, 1994–2005. Chm., Awards Cttee, Canada Meml Fellowships, 2002–14. Hon. Fellow, Faculty of Law, Birmingham Univ., 1997–2010. *Publications:* The Criminal Liability of Corporations in English Law, 1969; (jtly) Northey and Leigh's Introduction to Company Law, 1970, 4th edn 1987; Police Powers in England and Wales, 1975, 2nd edn 1986; Economic Crime in Europe, 1980; (jtly) The Companies Act 1981, 1981; (jtly) The Management of the Prosecution Process in Denmark, Sweden and the Netherlands, 1981; The Control of Commercial Fraud, 1982; Strict and Vicarious Liability, 1982; (jtly) A Guide to the Financial Services Act, 1986; (contrib.) Blackstone's Criminal Practice, 1991–2007; (ed) Criminal Procedure in English Public Law, 2005, 2nd edn 2009; articles in British, European, Amer., S Amer. and Canadian jls. *Recreations:* music, walking.

LEIGH, Lucy Claire; *see* Frazer, L. C.

LEIGH, Mark Andrew Michael Stephen, (Bertie); Partner, since 1977, and Senior Partner, since 1998, Hempsons; Solicitor Advocate of the Supreme Court, since 2005; *b* Cheshire, 30 Aug. 1946; *s* of Robert Arthur Leigh and Shelagh Elizabeth Leigh (*née* Ruddin); *m* 1976, Helen Mary; one *s* one *d. Educ:* St Christopher Sch., Letchworth; Univ. of E Anglia (BA 1969). Joined Hempsons, 1973; admitted as solicitor, 1976. Chair: Clin. Disputes Forum, 2009–; Nat. Confidential Enquiry into Patient Outcome and Death, 2009– (Trustee). President: Medico-Legal Soc., 2006–08; Soc. for Ethics in Law and Medicine, 2014–. Trustee: CORE (Gastroenterol.), 2007–11; Charm UK, 2008–. Chair of Govs, St Christopher Sch., 2014–; Gov., City Lit Adult Educn Coll., 2004–12. Hon. FRCPCH 1997; FRCOG *ad eundem* 2003. *Recreations:* theatre, opera, concerts, reading. *Address:* 51 Larkhall Rise, SW4 6HT. *T:* (020) 7622 4243, 07725 938510. *E:* b.leigh@hempsons.co.uk. *Clubs:* Reform, Royal Society of Medicine.

LEIGH, Sir Michael, KCMG 2012; PhD; Senior Adviser, German Marshall Fund of the United States, since 2011; *b* London, 25 Feb. 1948; *s* of Victor Leigh and Esther Leigh; *m* 2010, Ventura Mancilla; two *s* by a previous marriage. *Educ:* Orange Hill County Grammar Sch.; St Catherine's Coll., Oxford (BA PPE); Massachusetts Inst. of Technol. (PhD Pol Sci. 1974). Asst Prof. in Pol Sci., Wellesley Coll., Mass, 1973–74; Lectr in Internat. Relns, Univ. of Sussex, 1974–76; Asst Prof. in Internat. Relns, Johns Hopkins Univ., Sch. for Advanced Internat. Studies, Bologna, 1976–77; Official, Secretariat-Gen., Council of Eur. Communities, 1977–80; European Commission: Directorate-General: for Fisheries, 1980–82; for Information, Press and Information, 1982–85; for External Relns, 1985–88; Member of Cabinet: of Lord Cockfield, Vice-Pres., 1988–89; of Frans Andriessen, Vice-Pres., 1989–92; of Comr Hans van den Broek, 1993–98; Dir, 1998–2000; Dir, Directorate-Gen. Enlargement, Turkey, Cyprus, Bulgaria, Malta, Romania, 2000–03; Dep. Dir-Gen., Directorate-Gen. External Relns, 2003–05; Dir-Gen. for Enlargement, 2006–11. Member, Advisory Board: Salzburg Global Seminar, 2010–12; Wilton Park, 2012–; Foundn for Effective Governance, Kiev, 2012–13. *Publications:* Mobilizing Consent: public opinion and American foreign policy, 1937–1947, 1976; European Integration and the Common Fisheries Policy, 1983; articles on foreign policy. *Recreations:* tango, pilates, travel. *E:* leigh.michael@gmail.com.

LEIGH, Mike, OBE 1993; dramatist; theatre and film director; *b* 20 Feb. 1943; *s* of late Alfred Abraham Leigh, MRCS, LRCP and Phyllis Pauline Leigh (*née* Cousin); *m* 1973, Alison Steadman, *qv* (marr. diss. 2001); two *s. Educ:* North Grecian Street County Primary Sch.; Salford Grammar Sch.; RADA; Camberwell Sch. of Arts and Crafts; Central Sch. of Art and Design (Theatre Design Dept); London Film Sch. Assoc. Dir, Midlands Arts Centre for Young People, 1965–66; Asst Dir, RSC, 1967–68; Drama Lectr, Sedgley Park and De La Salle Colls, Manchester, 1968–69; Lectr, London Film Sch., 1968–74. Arts Council of GB: Member: Drama Panel, 1975–77; Dirs' Working Party and Specialist Allocations Bd, 1976–84; Member: Accreditation Panel, Nat. Council for Drama Trng, 1978–91; Gen. Adv. Council, IBA, 1980–82; Council, RADA, 2009–. Chm., Bd of Govs, London Film Sch., 2001–. NFT Retrospective, 1979, 2005; BBC TV Retrospective (incl. Arena: Mike Leigh Making Plays), 1982. Fellow, BFI, 2005; BAFTA Fellowship, 2015. Hon. Fellow, Univ. of the Arts, 2006. Hon. MA: Salford, 1991; Northampton, 2000; Hon. DLitt Staffordshire, 2000; DU Essex, 2002; Hon. Dr London Metropolitan, 2005; Hon. DA Manchester Metropolitan, 2012. George Devine Award, 1973; Michael Balcon Award, 1995; Alexander Korda Award, 1996. Ordre des Arts et des Lettres (France), 1998. Productions of own plays and films; *stage plays:* The Box Play, 1965, My Parents Have Gone To Carlisle, The Last Crusade Of The Five Little Nuns, 1966, Midlands Arts Centre; Nenaa, RSC Studio, Stratford-upon-Avon, 1967; Individual Fruit Pies, E15 Acting Sch., 1968; Down Here And Up There, Royal Ct Th. Upstairs, 1968; Big Basil, 1968, Glum Victoria And The Lad With Specs, Manchester Youth Theatre, 1969; Epilogue, Manchester, 1969; Bleak Moments, Open Space, 1970; A Rancid Pong, Basement, 1971; Wholesome Glory, Dick Whittington and his Cat, Royal Ct Th. Upstairs, 1973; The Jaws of Death, Traverse, Edinburgh Fest., 1973; Babies Grow Old, Other Place, 1974, ICA, 1975; The Silent Majority, Bush, 1974; Abigail's Party, Hampstead, 1977; Ecstasy, Hampstead, 1979, 2011; Goose-Pimples, Hampstead, Garrick, 1981 (Standard Best Comedy Award); Smelling a Rat, Hampstead, 1988; Greek Tragedy, Sydney, 1989, Edinburgh Fest. and Theatre Royal, Stratford East, 1990; It's A Great Big Shame!, Theatre Royal, Stratford East, 1993; Two Thousand Years, NT, 2005; Grief, NT, 2011 (Critics' Circle and Evening Standard Awards for Best Dir); *opera:* The Pirates of Penzance, ENO, 2015. *BBC radio play:* Too Much Of A Good Thing, 1979; *feature films:* Bleak Moments, 1971 (Golden Hugo, Chicago Film Fest., 1972; Golden Leopard, Locarno Film Fest., 1972); High Hopes, 1989 (Critics' Award, Venice Film Fest., 1988; Evening Standard Peter Sellers Comedy Award, 1989); Life is Sweet, 1991; Naked, 1993 (Best Dir, Cannes Film Fest., 1993); Secrets and Lies, 1996 (Palme d'Or, Cannes Film Fest., 1996; BAFTA Award for Orig. Screenplay, 1997); Career Girls, 1997; Topsy-Turvy, 1999 (Evening Standard Best Film Award, 2001); All or Nothing, 2002; Vera Drake, 2004 (Golden Lion, Venice Film Fest., 2004; BAFTA Award for Best Dir, 2005); Happy-Go-Lucky, 2008; Another Year, 2010; A Running Jump, 2012; Mr Turner, 2014; *BBC TV plays and films:* A Mug's Game, 1972; Hard Labour, 1973; The Permissive Society, Afternoon, A Light Snack, Probation, Old Chums, The Birth Of The 2001 FA Cup Final Goalie, 1975; Nuts in May, Knock For Knock, 1976; The Kiss Of Death, Abigail's Party, 1977; Who's Who, 1978; Grown-Ups, 1980; Home Sweet Home, 1982; Four Days In July, 1984; *Channel Four films:* Meantime, 1983 (People's Prize, Berlin Film Fest., 1984); The Short and Curlies, 1987. *Relevant publications:* The Improvised Play: the work of Mike Leigh, by Paul Clements, 1983; Mike Leigh, by Gilles

Laprevotte, 1991; The World According to Mike Leigh, by Michael Coveney, 1996; The Films of Mike Leigh: embracing the world, by Ray Carney and Leonard Quart, 2000; All or Nothing: the cinema of Mike Leigh, by Edward Trostle-Jones, 2004; The Cinema of Mike Leigh: a sense of the real, by Garry Watson, 2004; Mike Leigh, by Tony Whitehead, 2007; Mike Leigh on Mike Leigh, ed by Amy Raphael, 2008; Mike Leigh, by Stefano Boni and Massimo Quaglia, 2009; Mike Leigh, by Sean O'Sullivan, 2011. *Address:* c/o United Agents, 12–26 Lexington Street, W1F 0LE.

LEIGH, Prof. (Peter) Nigel, PhD; FRCP, FMedSci; Professor of Neurology, Brighton and Sussex Medical School, since 2011; Hon. Consultant Neurologist, Brighton and Sussex University Hospitals NHS Trust, since 2011; Emeritus Professor of Neurology, King's College London, 2010; Hon. Consultant Neurologist, King's College Hospital, since 1989; *b* 26 Sept. 1946; *s* of Dr A. Denis Leigh and Pamela Leigh (*née* Parish); *m* 1st, 1969, Irene May Allen (*see* Irene May Leigh) (marr. diss. 1999); one *s* three *d*; 2nd, 2000, Catherine Margaret Lloyd; one *d*. *Educ:* Sevenoaks Sch., Kent; London Hosp. Med. Sch., Univ. of London (BSc 1st Cl. Hons; MB BS Dist.); PhD London 1986. FRCP 1988. House Physician and House Surgeon, 1970–71, SHO, 1971–72, The London Hosp.; SHO, Hammersmith Hosp., 1972–73; Registrar, UCH, 1974, Hammersmith Hosp., 1974–75; Specialist in Neurology, Muhimbili Hosp., and Lectr in Neurology, Univ. of Dar es Salaam, 1975–77; Sen. Registrar, St George's Hosp., 1977–82; Wellcome Trust Res. Fellow, Inst. of Psychiatry, 1980–81; Consultant Neurologist, Wessex Neurol Centre, Southampton, 1982–86, and Sen. Lectr in Neurology, Southampton Univ., 1984–86; Sen. Lectr in Neurology and Hon. Cons. Neurologist, St George's Hosp. Med. Sch., 1986–89; Prof. of Clinical Neurology, Inst. of Psychiatry and KCL Sch. of Medicine, 1989–2010, Hd, Dept of Clinical Neurosci., 1989–2007, King's Coll. London. FMedSci 2003; FAAN. Forbes Norris Award, Internat. Alliance of ALS/MND Assocs, 1997; Erb-Duchenne Prize, German Neuro-Muscular Soc., 2003; Sheila Essey Prize, Amer. Acad. of Neurology, 2004. *Publications:* (ed with M. Swash) Motor Neurone Disease: biology and management, 1995; articles on motor neurone disease, Parkinson's disease and related disorders and other medical topics. *Recreations:* neurological research, fly-fishing, birdwatching, walking, reading. *Address:* Brighton and Sussex Medical School, Trafford Centre for Biomedical Research, University of Sussex, Falmer, East Sussex BN1 9RY. *T:* (01273) 877357, *Fax:* (01273) 872941. *E:* P.Leigh@bsms.ac.uk.

LEIGH, Sir Richard (Henry), 3rd Bt *cr* 1918, of Altrincham, Cheshire; *b* 11 Nov. 1936; *s* of Eric Leigh (*d* 1982), 2nd *s* of Sir John Leigh, 1st Bt, and his 1st wife, Joan Lane Fitzgerald (*d* 1973), *e d* of M. C. L. Freer, South Africa; *S* uncle, 1992; *m* 1st, 1962, Barbro Anna Elizabeth (marr. diss. 1977), *e d* of late Stig Carl Sebastian Tham, Sweden; 2nd, 1977, Cherie Rosalind, *e d* D. D. Dale, Cherval, France and *widow* of Alan Reece, RMS. *Educ:* England and Switzerland. *Recreations:* fishing, gardening. *Heir:* half *b* Christopher John Leigh [*b* 6 April 1941; *m* 1963, Gillian Ismay, *o d* of W. K. Lowe; one *s* one *d*]. *Address:* PO Box 984, Canterbury CT1 9EB.

LEIGH, Richard Rowland, (Rowley); Chef Proprietor, Le Café Anglais, 2007–14; Chef-Consultant, The Continental, Hong Kong; *b* Manchester, 23 April 1950; *s* of Robert Leigh and Shelagh Ruddin; *m* 1st, 1982, Sara George; two *d*; 2nd, 2001, Katharine Chancellor; one *s*. *Educ:* Clifton Coll.; Christ's Coll., Cambridge. Chef, Roux Restaurants, 1978–87; Chef and Partner, Kensington Place, 1987–2006. Cookery Corresp., Financial Times. *Publications:* No Place Like Home, 2000. *Recreations:* golf, epicureanism. *Club:* Groucho.

LEIGH, Prof. Roger Allen, PhD; Professor, School of Agriculture, Food and Wine, University of Adelaide, 2006–14, now Emeritus (Head, School of Agriculture, Food and Wine, 2006–11); *b* 7 Feb. 1949; *s* of Harry Leigh and Catherine Leigh (*née* O'Neill); *m* 1st, 1974, Beatrice Katherine Halton (marr. diss. 1999); 2nd, 2008, Janet Ann Dibb-Smith. *Educ:* Ellesmere Port Boys' GS; UCNW, Bangor (BSc 1970; PhD 1974). FIBiol 1991. Maria Moors Cabot Fellow in Botanical Res., Harvard Univ., 1974–76; Royal Society Pickering Res. Fellow, Botany Sch., Univ. of Cambridge, 1976–79; Scientist, Rothamsted Experimental Station, Harpenden, 1979–98; Head of Crop Production Dept, 1987–89; Head of Biochemistry and Physiology Dept, 1989–98; Head of Soils and Crop Scis Div., 1989–94; Dep. Dir, 1994–98; Prof. of Botany, Univ. of Cambridge, 1998–2006; Professorial Fellow, Girton Coll., Cambridge, 1998–2006; Dir, Waite Res. Inst., Univ. of Adelaide, 2010–12. President: Soc. for Experimental Biology, 2005–07 (Vice-Pres., 2003–05); Australian Council, Deans of Agriculture, 2008–10. *Publications:* (jtly) Long-Term Experiments in Agricultural and Ecological Sciences, 1994; (jtly) Membrane Transport in Plants and Fungi: molecular mechanisms and control, 1994; scientific papers in learned jls, incl. Plant Physiology, Planta, Jl of Exptl Botany. *Recreations:* sports of all kinds, bird watching, photography. *Address:* School of Agriculture, Food and Wine, University of Adelaide, PMB 1, Glen Osmond, SA 5064, Australia. *T:* (8) 83137136. *E:* roger.leigh@adelaide.edu.au.

LEIGH, Rowley; *see* Leigh, R. R.

LEIGH, Samantha Ceri; Her Honour Judge Leigh; a Circuit Judge, since 2015; *b* Essex, 1970; *d* of Michael Leigh and Maureen Leigh; *m* 2004, Alan Pearce. *Educ:* Univ. of Essex (BA Hons Public Policy and Admin); Guildford Coll. of Law (CPE). Called to the Bar, Inner Temple, 1995; in practice as a barrister specialising in criminal law; a Dep. District Judge (Magistrates' Courts), 2005–15; a Recorder, 2009–15. *Recreations:* scuba diving, travel. *Address:* Basildon Crown Court, The Gore, Basildon, Essex SS14 2BU. *T:* (01268) 458000.

LEIGH-HUNT, Barbara; actress; *b* 14 Dec. 1935; *d* of Chandos A. Leigh-Hunt and Elizabeth Leigh-Hunt; *m* 1967, Richard Edward Pasco, CBE (*d* 2014). *Educ:* Bath, Som; Kensington High Sch.; Bristol Old Vic Theatre Sch. (Most Promising Student, Bristol Evening Post Award, 1953). Began broadcasting for BBC at age 12 in Children's Hour, and has continued to do so regularly on Radios 3 and 4. *Theatre:* début in Midsummer Night's Dream, London Old Vic tour to USA and Canada, 1954–55; subseq. also Twelfth Night and Merchant of Venice, Old Vic and tours, 1957–60; seasons at Nottingham and Guildford, 1960–62; Bristol Old Vic and tours to Europe, Middle East, US and Canada, 1961–68; The Seagull, Hedda Gabler, She Stoops to Conquer, Much Ado About Nothing, Blithe Spirit, Love's Labour's Lost, Hamlet, and Macbeth; A Severed Head, Criterion, 1963; Mrs Mouse, are you within?, Duke of York's, 1968; Venice Preserv'd, Prospect Th. Co. tour, 1970; Royal Shakespeare Company: Sherlock Holmes, Travesties, 1974; A Winter's Tale, Richard III, 1975; King Lear, Troilus and Cressida, 1976; That Good Between Us, Every Good Boy Deserves Favour, 1977; Richard III, Hamlet, 1980; The Forest, La Ronde, 1981; Pack of Lies, Lyric 1983; Barnaby and the Old Boys, Theatr Clwyd, 1987; Royal National Theatre: Cat on a Hot Tin Roof, 1988; Bartholomew Fair, The Voysey Inheritance, 1989; Racing Demon, 1990 and Los Angeles, 1995; An Inspector Calls, 1992 (Best Supporting Actress, Olivier Award, 1993); Absence of War, 1993; A Woman of No Importance, RSC, and Haymarket, 1992; The Importance of Being Earnest, Old Vic, 1995; frequent appearances in poetry and prose anthology progs in UK and abroad; works as speaker with Medici String Quartet. *Films:* Frenzy, 1972, Henry VIII and his Six Wives, 1972; A Bequest to the Nation, 1973; Oh, Heavenly Dog, 1978; Paper Mask, 1990; Keep the Aspidistra Flying, 1997; Billy Elliott, 2000; The Martins, 2000; Iris, 2001; Vanity Fair, 2003. *Television* includes: Search for the Nile, 1971; Loves Lies Bleeding; The Voysey Inheritance; Macbeth; Wagner, 1984; The Siegfried Idyll; All for Love; Tumbledown, 1988; A Perfect Hero; Cold Feet; Pride and Prejudice, 1995; The Echo, 1998; Sunburn, Wives and Daughters, 1999; Longitude, 2000; Kavanagh QC, 1998, 2000; Midsummer Murders, 2001; George Eliot, 2002. Gov. and Associate Actor, RSC; Pres., Friends of the Other Place, 1993–97; Vice-President: Theatrical Guild of Charity (formerly Theatrical Ladies Guild of Charity), 1983–; Royal Theatrical Fund, 1995; J. B. Priestley Soc., 1997–; Patron: Soc. of Teachers of Speech and Drama, 1995; Orch. of The Swan, 1997. Tutor, Samling Foundn, 2002–. *Recreation:* book collecting. *Address:* c/o Conway Van Gelder Grant Ltd, 8–12 Broadwick Street, W1F 8HW. *T:* (020) 7287 0077, *Fax:* (020) 7287 1940.

LEIGH-PEMBERTON, Kathryn Felice; *see* Lampard, K. F.

LEIGH-SMITH, Alfred Nicholas Hardstaff; a District Judge (Magistrates' Courts), since 2004; *b* 21 Dec. 1953; *s* of late Dr Alfred Leigh Hardstaff Leigh-Smith, TD, DL and Marguerite Calvert Leigh-Smith; *m* 1996, Samantha Sian Morgan; two *s*. *Educ:* Epsom Coll.; Leeds Univ. (LLB 1975). Called to the Bar, Lincoln's Inn, 1976; in practice as barrister, Lincoln's Inn, 1976–80; Court Clerk, then Sen. Court Clerk, then Princ. Asst, Willesden Magistrates' Court, 1980–85; Deputy Clerk: to Bromley Justices, 1985–89; to Brent Justices, 1989–94; Clerk to Justices, Cambridge and E Cambs, 1995–2001; in practice as barrister, Leicester, 2001–04. Asst Stipendiary Magistrate, then Dep. Dist Judge (Magistrates' Courts), 1999–2004. *Recreations:* walking, clay-pigeon shooting, church bell ringing, Rugby Union (watching now), reading history and biographies, vegetable gardening. *Address:* Luton Magistrates' Court, Stuart Street, Luton LU1 5BL. *T:* (01582) 524232, *Fax:* (01582) 524259. *E:* a.leighsmith@btinternet.com.

LEIGHFIELD, John Percival, CBE 1998; FBCS; Chairman, RM plc, 1993–2011; *b* 5 April 1938; *s* of Henry Tom Dainton Leighfield and Patricia Zilpha Maud Leighfield (*née* Baker); *m* 1963, Margaret Ann Mealin; one *s* one *d*. *Educ:* Magdalen Coll. Sch., Oxford (State Scholarship); Exeter Coll., Oxford (MA Lit.Hum.). FIDPM 1990; FBCS 1991. Mgt trainee, Ford Motor Co., 1962–65; Systems Manager, EDP Exec., Plessey Telecomms, 1965–69; Systems Planning, EDP Exec., Plessey Co. Ltd, 1969–72; British Leyland: Systems Planning Manager, 1972–75; Systems Dir, 1975–79; Man. Dir, BL Systems Ltd, 1979–84; Man. Dir and Chm. ISTEL Ltd, 1984–89; AT&T ISTEL: Chm., 1989–93; Dir, 1993–97; Officer and Sen. Vice-Pres., AT&T, 1989–93; Chairman: Infinity SDC, 2005–11; Synstar plc, 1998–2004; Minerva Computer Systems, 2001–03; Director: Birmingham Midshires Bldg Soc., 1993–99 (Chm., 1996–99); RM Ltd, 1993–94; ICom Solutions Ltd, 1997–98; Halifax plc, 1999–2001; KnowledgePool Ltd, 2000–01; Getmapping, 2005–. Dir, Central England TEC, 1991–97. Mem., Alvey Prog. Steering Cttee, 1983–87. President: BCS, 1993–94; Computing Services and Software Assoc., 1995–96; Inst. Data Processing Mgt, 2000–06. Hon. Prof., 1992, Chm., Adv. Bd, 1997–2002, Warwick Business Sch.; Vis. Prof., Warwick Manufg Gp, 2011–; Mem. Council, Warwick Univ., 1991–96, 1997– (Pro-Chancellor and Chm., 2002–11); Governor: Magdalen Coll. Sch., Oxford, 1993–2001 (Chm. 1996–2001); WMG Acad. for Young Engrs, 2014– (Chm., 2014–). Mem., Bodleian Library Develt Bd, 2008–. Liveryman: Co. of Information Technologists, 1992– (Master, 2005–06); Educators' Co., 2015– (Master, 2015–June 2016). FInstD 1989; FRSA 1996; FRGS 2012. DUniv Central England, 1993; Hon. DTech: De Montfort, 1994; Wolverhampton, 2001; Hon. DLaws Warwick, 2011. *Publications:* various papers on information technology. *Recreations:* historical cartography, music, walking, computing. *Address:* 91 Victoria Road, Oxford OX2 7QG. *T:* (01865) 559055. *Clubs:* Royal Automobile; Royal Fowey Yacht.

LEIGHTON OF ST MELLONS, 3rd Baron *cr* 1962, of St Mellons, co. Monmouth; **Robert William Henry Leighton Seager;** Bt 1952; *b* 28 Sept. 1955; *er s* of 2nd Baron Leighton of St Mellons and Elizabeth Rosita (*née* Hopgood; *d* 1979); *S* father, 1998; *m* 1978, Wendy Elizabeth Hopwood; one *d*. *Heir:* *b* Hon. Simon John Leighton Seager [*b* 25 Jan. 1957; *m* 1982, Gillian Rawlinson; three *d*].

LEIGHTON, Prof. Angela, FBA 2000; Senior Research Fellow, Trinity College, Cambridge, since 2006; *b* 23 Feb. 1954; *d* of Kenneth Leighton and Lydia Leighton (*née* Vignapiano). *Educ:* St Hugh's Coll., Oxford (BA Hons 1976; MLitt 1981). University of Hull: Lectr in English, 1979–93; Sen. Lectr, 1993–95; Reader, 1995–97; Prof. of English, 1997–2006. *Publications:* Shelley and the Sublime, 1984; Elizabeth Barrett Browning, 1986; Victorian Women Poets: writing against the heart, 1992; Victorian Women Poets: a critical anthology, 1995; A Cold Spell, 2000; On Form: poetry, aestheticism and the legacy of a word, 2007; Sea Level, 2007; (ed) Voyages over Voices: critical essays on Anne Stevenson, 2010; The Messages, 2012. *Address:* Trinity College, Cambridge CB2 1TQ.

LEIGHTON, Sir John (Mark Nicholas), Kt 2013; FRSE; Director-General, National Galleries of Scotland, since 2006; *b* Belfast, 22 Feb. 1959; *s* of Edwin Leighton and Norah Leighton (*née* Winternheim, later Schwab); *m* 1987, Gillian Helen Keay; one *s* one *d*. *Educ:* Portora Royal Sch., Enniskillen; Univ. of Edinburgh (MA Fine Art); Courtauld Inst. of Art, Univ. of London (MA Hist. of Art). Curator, 19th-Century Paintings, Nat. Gall., London, 1986–97; Dir, Van Gogh Mus., Amsterdam, 1997–2006. FRSE 2008. Dr *hc* Edinburgh, 2009. *Publications:* The Van Gogh Museum: a portrait, 2003; exhibn catalogues. *Recreations:* oil painting, hill walking. *Address:* National Galleries of Scotland, 73 Belford Road, Edinburgh EH4 3DS. *E:* jleighton@nationalgalleries.org.

LEIGHTON, Leonard Horace; Under Secretary, Department of Energy, 1974–80; *b* 7 Oct. 1920; *e s* of Leonard and Pearl Leighton, Bermuda; *m* 1945, Mary Burrowes; two *s*. *Educ:* Rossall Sch.; Magdalen Coll., Oxford (MA). FInstF. Royal Engrs, 1940–46; Nat. Coal Bd, 1950–62; Min. of Power, 1962–67; Min. of Technology, 1967–70; Dept of Trade and Industry, 1970–74. *Publications:* papers in various technical jls. *Address:* 18 River Park Drive, Marlborough, Wilts SN8 1NH.

LEIGHTON, Sir Michael (John Bryan), 11th Bt *cr* 1693; *b* 8 March 1935; *o s* of Colonel Sir Richard Tihel Leighton, 10th Bt, and Kathleen Irene Linda (*d* 1993), *o d* of Major A. E. Lees, Rowton Castle, Shrewsbury; *S* father, 1957; *m* 1st, 1974 (marr. diss. 1980); 2nd, 1988 (marr. diss. 1990); 3rd, 1991, Diana Mary Gamble (marr. diss. 1998; remarried 2009); one *d*. *Educ:* Stowe; Tabley House Agricultural Sch.; Cirencester Coll. *Address:* Loton Park, Shrewsbury, Salop SY5 9AJ.

LEIGHTON, Prof. Timothy Grant, PhD; FRS 2014; FREng; CPhys, CEng; FInstP, FIOA; Professor of Ultrasonics and Underwater Acoustics, Institute of Sound and Vibration Research, Faculty of Engineering and the Environment, University of Southampton, since 1999; Founding Chairman: Network for Anti-Microbial Resistance and Infection Prevention, since 2014; Health Effects of Ultrasound in Air, since 2014; *b* Blackburn, Lancs, 16 Oct. 1963; *s* of John Owen Leighton and Christine Leighton (*née* Coulthwaite); *m* 1995, Sian Lloyd Jones; one *s* one *d*. *Educ:* Heversham Grammar Sch., Cumbria; Magdalene Coll., Cambridge (BA Hons Nat. Scis Double 1st Cl. Hons Phys and Theoretical Phys 1985); Cavendish Lab., Univ. of Cambridge (PhD 1989). FIOA 1999; CPhys 2000; FInstP 2000; CEng 2004; FREng 2012. Sen. and Advanced Res. Fellow, Magdalene Coll., Cambridge and EPSRC, 1988–92; University of Southampton: Lectr in Underwater Acoustics, 1992–97; Reader, 1997–99; Associate Dean (Res.), Faculty of Engrg and the Envmt, 2011–15; Founder, Centre for Ultrasonics and Underwater Acoustics, 1992; Chm., Fluid Dynamics and Acoustics Res. Gp, Inst. of Sound and Vibration Res., 2010–. Fellow, Acoustical Soc. of Amer., 1998. A. B. Wood Medal, 1994, Tyndall Medal, 2002, R. W. B. Stephens Medal, 2009, Rayleigh Medal, 2014, Inst. of Acoustics; Internat. Medwin Prize for Acoustical Oceanog., 2001, Helmholtz-Rayleigh Interdisciplinary Silver Medal, 2013, Acoustical Soc. of Amer.; Early Career Medal and Award, Internat. Commn of Acoustics, 2004; Paterson Medal and Prize, Inst. of Physics, 2006; Brian Mercer Award for Innovation, Royal Soc., 2011; Water Management and Supply Award, Inst. of Chem. Engrg, 2012. *Publications:* The Acoustic Bubble, 1994; over 400 articles incl. res. in Procs of Royal Soc. A, Nature Climate Change, Jl Fluid Mechanics, Jl Acoustical Soc. of Amer., Earth Moon and Planets, Icarus, Bulletin of Amer. Meteorol Soc., Physics Letters A, Ultrasound in Medicine and Biol. *Recreations:* lives in New Forest where enjoys activities with family including walking, spotting wildlife, painting and stargazing, sailing yacht moored nearby, plays oboe and cor anglais with Marchwood Orchestra (Chm., 2011–). *Address:* Institute of Sound and Vibration Research, Faculty of Engineering and the Environment, University of Southampton, Highfield, Southampton SO17 1BJ.

LEIGHTON, Trevor; photographer and director; *b* Carlisle, 20 June 1957; *s* of Ronald and Isabella Leighton; *m* 2007, Suzanna; two *s* two *d* and one step *s* one step *d*. *Educ:* Carlisle Coll. of Art and Design. Fashion and portrait photographer; has photographed many of world's most interesting and influential personalities, incl. Sean Connery, Kate Bush, Norman Parkinson, Quentin Crisp, Katherine Jenkins, Tom Jones, Helen Mirren, John Cleese; editorial credits include portraits for Vogue, Elle, Marie Claire, Tatler, Arena, Sunday Times, Daily Telegraph, Observer and Evening Standard and many internat. pubns. One of the largest collections of archive photographs at NPG. *Publications:* The Jokers, 2000. *Recreations:* private pilot, fanatical Liverpool supporter. *E:* trevor@trevorleighton.com. *W:* www.trevorleighton.com. *Club:* Groucho.

LEIGHTON WILLIAMS, John; *see* Williams, John Leighton.

LEINSTER, 9th Duke of, *cr* 1766; **Maurice FitzGerald;** Baron of Offaly, 1205; Earl of Kildare, 1316; Viscount Leinster (GB), 1747; Marquess of Kildare, 1761; Earl of Offaly, 1761; Baron Kildare, 1870; Premier Duke, Marquess, and Earl, of Ireland; landscape and contract gardener; *b* 7 April 1948; *s* of 8th Duke of Leinster, and Anne, *d* of Lt-Col Philip Eustace Smith, MC; *S* father, 2004; *m* 1972, Fiona Mary Francesca, *d* of Harry Hollick; two *d* (only *s* Thomas FitzGerald (Earl of Offaly) *d* 1997). *Educ:* Millfield School. Pres., Oxfordshire Dyslexia Assoc., 1978–2014. Chm., Thomas Offaly Meml Fund. *Address:* Courtyard House, Oakley Park, Frilford Heath, Oxon OX13 6QW.

LEINSTER, Dr Paul, CBE 2008; Chief Executive, Environment Agency, 2008–15; *b* 20 Feb. 1953; *s* of Victor and Eva Leinster; *m* 1976, Felicity Lawrence; two *s* one *d*. *Educ:* Imperial Coll., London (BSc Chemistry 1974; PhD Envmtl Engrg 1977); Cranfield Sch. of Management (MBA 1991). CChem, FRSC 1998; FIEMA 2004; CEnv 2005. BP International plc: Analytical Support and Res. Div., Res. Centre, 1977–79; Health, Safety and Envmt Directorate, 1979–85; Schering Agrochemicals, 1985–88; Thomson-MTS Ltd: Head of Res. and Consultancy, 1988–90; Man. Dir, 1990–94; Dir, Envmtl Services, SmithKline Beecham, 1994–98; Dir of Envmtl Protection, 1998–2004, Dir of Ops, 2004–08, Envmt Agency. Hon. DSc: Cranfield, 2012; UWE, 2012. *Recreations:* golf, local church, reading, walking.
See also S. J. Leinster.

LEINSTER, Prof. Samuel John, MD; FRCS, FRCSE, SFHEA, FAcadMed; Professor of Medical Education, University of East Anglia, 2001–11, now Emeritus (Inaugural Dean, School of Medicine, Health Policy and Practice, 2001–10); *b* 29 Oct. 1946; *s* of Victor and Eva Leinster; *m* 1971, Jennifer Woodward; three *s* one *d*. *Educ:* Univ. of Edinburgh (BSc 1968; MB ChB 1971); Univ. of Liverpool (MD 1990). FRCSE 1976; FRCS 1998. MO, RAF, 1971–77; Lectr in Surgery, Welsh Nat. Sch. of Medicine, 1978–81; University of Liverpool: Sen. Lectr in Surgery, 1982–92; Reader in Surgery, 1992–95; Prof. of Surgery, 1995–2000. FHEA 2007, SFHEA 2008; FAcadMed 2009. *Publications:* Systemic Diseases for Dental Students, 1984; Shared Care in Breast Cancer, 1999; The Changing Face of Medical Education, 2011; The Changing Role of Doctors, 2013; articles on breast cancer care, psychological impact of cancer and med. educn in learned jls. *Recreations:* family, gardening, DIY, wood turning, active committed Christian. *Address:* Vassars, Common Road, East Tuddenham, Dereham, Norfolk NR20 3AH. *E:* s.leinster@uea.ac.uk. *Clubs:* Royal Air Force; Royal Society of Medicine.
See also P. Leinster.

LEIPER, Quentin John, CBE 2009; FREng; FICE; civil engineer, geotechnical engineer and sustainability expert; Group Chief Engineer, Carillion plc, 2006–14; President, Institution of Civil Engineers, 2006–07; *b* 7 Oct. 1951; *s* of John W. G. Leiper and Betty Leiper; *m* 1980, Dorothy Ellen East; two *s* one *d*. *Educ:* King's Sch., Ely; Univ. of Glasgow (BSc 1975); Univ. of Surrey (MSc 1984). CCE 1985; CEng 1985; MICE 1985, FICE 1994; CEnv 2005; FREng 2011. Nuttall Geotechnical Services, 1975–77; Geotechnical Engr, Soil Mechanics, 1977–78; Manager: Nuttall Geotechnical Services, 1978–80; Terresearch, 1982–86; Contracts Manager, GKN Keller Foundns, 1986–89; Chief Engr, Westpile, 1989–91; Piling Ops Manager, Lilley Construction, 1990–91; Chief Geotech. Engr, Tarmac plc, 1991–96; Co. Chief Engr, 1996–2000, Dir for Engrg and the Envmt, 2000–06, Carillion plc. Initiated and developed the Carillion sustainability strategy model and "sun" impacts diagram, 2001. Vis. Prof., Sch. of Civil Engrg, Univ. of Edinburgh, 1998–. Mem., Vice-Chm., 1997–99, Chm., 1999–2001, British Geotechnical Assoc. (formerly British Geotechnical Soc.); Institution of Civil Engineers: Founding Chm. and Hon. Ed., Engineering Sustainability, 2002–04; Vice Pres., 2003–06; Chm., Queen's Jubilee Scholarship Trust, 2007–. Trustee, BRE Trust, 2013–. *Publications:* over 50 jl articles and conf. papers. *Recreations:* hockey, kites (including fighting and traction), sailing, saxophone and clarinet. *Address:* Institution of Civil Engineers, One Great George Street, SW1P 3AA. *E:* qleiper@gmail.com. *Club:* Bridgnorth Cricket and Hockey.

LEISER, Helen; JP; Policy Director, Generation IV International Forum (inter-governmental nuclear energy research collaboration), 2005–07; *b* 3 July 1947; *d* of George and Audrey Leiser. *Educ:* Twickenham County Grammar Sch.; LSE (BScEcon 1968); Birkbeck, Univ. of London (MA Eur. Hist. 2012). Economic Dept, TUC, 1968–73; CAP Br., HM Customs and Excise, 1973–74; Employment Dept, 1974–83; Cabinet Office, Machinery of Govt Div., 1983–85; Asst Sec., gen. policy, then resources and planning, later offshore safety reforms, HSE, 1986–93; Dir of Business Develt, Employment Service, 1993; Head, Industrial Relations Div., Dept of Employment, 1994; Dir, Employment Relns Policy, DTI, 1995–98; Dir, Nuclear Industries, DTI, and non-exec. Dir, UKAEA, 1998–2003; seconded to US Dept of Energy, 2003–05; consultant for Nuclear Decommissioning Authy on Nat. Nuclear Archive, 2005–06. Ind. Mem., DWP Data Access Ethics Cttee, 2008–. Mem., Estates Cttee, Hampstead Garden Suburb Trust, 2010–. JP NW London (formerly Barnet and Hendon), 2006. *Recreations:* travel, music, theatre, time with friends and relatives. *Address:* 11 Asmuns Place, NW11 7XE. *E:* helen.leiser@btinternet.com. *Club:* Lansdowne.

LEITCH, family name of **Baron Leitch**.

LEITCH, Baron *cr* 2004 (Life Peer), of Oakley in Fife; **Alexander Park Leitch;** Chairman: Intrinsic Financial Services Ltd, since 2005; BUPA, since 2005; Chief Executive, Zurich Financial Services (UKISA Asia Pacific) Ltd, 1998–2004; *b* 20 Oct. 1947; *s* of late Donald Leitch, Blairhall, Dunfermline, and Agnes Smith (*née* Park); *m* 1st (marr. diss.); three *d*; 2nd, 2003, Noelle Dowd, Dallas, Texas; one *d*. *Educ:* Dunfermline High Sch. MBCS 1966. Chief Systems Designer, Nat. Mutual Life, then Hambro Life, 1969–88; Allied Dunbar Plc, 1988–96 (Dep. Chm., 1990; Chief Exec., 1993–96); Chm., Allied Dunbar Assce Plc, 1996–2001; Chief Exec., British American Financial Services (UK and Internat.) Ltd, 1996–98; Chairman: Dunbar Bank, 1994–2001; Eagle Star Hldgs Plc, 1996–2004; Threadneedle Asset Mgt, 1996–2004; Dir, BAT Industries Plc, 1997–98; non-executive Director: United Business Media plc, 2005–08; Lloyds Banking (formerly Lloyds TSB) Gp plc, 2005–12 (Dep. Chm., 2009–12); Paternoster, 2006–10; Scottish Widows, 2007–12 (Chm., 2007–12). Chairman: Pensions Protection and Investment Accreditation Bd, 2001–02; Balance Charitable Foundn for Unclaimed Assets, 2004–05; Leitch Rev. of UK Skills, 2005. Mem. Bd, 1996–98, Dep. Chm., 1997–98, Chm., 1998–2000, ABI. Dep. Chm., BITC, 1996–2004; Chm., Nat. Employment Panel, 2001–07; Dep. Chair, Commonwealth Educn Fund, 2003–. Chm., SANE, 1999–2000; Vice-Pres., UK Cares, 2004. Trustee: Nat. Galls Scotland, 1999–2003; Philharmonia Orch., 2000–04. Freeman, City of London, 2002; Mem., Co. of Insurers, 2002. Prince of Wales Ambassador's Award for charitable work, 2001. *Recreations:* football, antiques, poetry, antiquarian books. *Address:* House of Lords, SW1A 0PW.

LEITCH, David Alexander; Under Secretary, Social Work Services Group, Scottish Education Department, 1983–89; *b* 4 April 1931; *s* of Alexander and Eileen Leitch; *m* 1954, Marie (*née* Tain); two *s* one *d*. *Educ:* St Mungo's Acad., Glasgow. Min. of Supply, 1948–58; Dept of Agriculture and Fisheries for Scotland: Asst Principal, 1959; Principal, 1963; Asst Sec., 1971; Asst Sec., Local Govt Finance, Scottish Office (Central Services), 1976–81, Under Sec., 1981–83. Part-time Mem., Scottish Legal Aid Bd, 1989–97. *Recreation:* hill-walking.

LEITCH, Dr John Gaston, FREng; Engineering Authority for BP Global Projects, since 2013; *b* Coleraine, NI, 9 April 1959; *s* of Cecil and Mildred Leitch; *m* 1993, Cornelia Aletta Geldenhuys; one *s* one *d*. *Educ:* Coleraine Academical Instn; Queen's Univ., Belfast (BSc 1st Cl. Civil Engrg 1980; PhD Civil Engrg 1986); Manchester Univ. (Cert. Engrg Mgt 2009). CEng 1989; Eur Ing 1989; MRINA 1991; FICE 2012; FREng 2014. Industrial Associate, Harland & Wolff, 1986–88; Naval Architect and Project Engr, John Brown E & C Ltd, 1988–89; Brown and Root Vickers, then Brown and Root, later Halliburton Brown and Root, subseq. Brown and Root Energy Services, then Kellogg Brown and Root: Naval Architect, North Sea platforms, 1989–93, Qatar Gas develt, 1993; Lead Naval Architect, Lufeng field develt, Ampolex (on secondment), 1993–95; Structural Engr, BHP Liverpool Bay Field, 1996; Project Engr, then Engrg Manager, Terra Nova Floating Prodn Storage and Offloading, S Korea, 1996–2000; short-term projects, incl. assignments in Houston and Bohai Bay, 2000–03; Deptl Manager, Marine, Subsea and Pipelines, 2003–05; Prodn and Engrg Manager, Carrier Vessel Future Project, 2005–06; BP: Team Manager, Subsea and Floating Systems, 2006–09; Dir of Engrg, BP Upstream Engrg Centre, 2009–13. *Recreation:* family. *Address:* BP International Ltd, Chertsey Road, Sunbury on Thames, Middx TW16 7LN. *T:* 07810 056606. *E:* John.leitch@uk.bp.com.

LEITH, family name of **Baron Burgh**.

LEITH, Sir George Ian David F.; *see* Forbes-Leith.

LEITH, Prudence Margaret, (Mrs Rayne Kruger), CBE 2010 (OBE 1989); DL; Chairman, Leith's Ltd, 1992–96; Deputy Chairman, Royal Society of Arts, since 1998 (Council Member, since 1992; Chairman, 1995–97); *b* 18 Feb. 1940; *d* of late Sam Leith and of Margaret Inglis; *m* Rayne Kruger (*d* 2002); one *s* one *d*. *Educ:* Cape Town Univ.; Sorbonne, Paris; Cordon Bleu, London. French studies at Sorbonne, and preliminary cooking apprenticeship with French families; Cordon Bleu sch. course; small outside catering service from bedsitter in London, 1960–65; started Leith's Good Food (commercial catering co.), 1965, and Leith's (restaurant), 1969 (Michelin star, 1994); Man. Dir, Prudence Leith Ltd, 1972; Cookery Corresp., Daily Mail, 1969–73; opened Leith's Sch. of Food and Wine, 1975; added Leith's Farm, 1976; Cookery Corresp., Sunday Express, 1976–80; Cookery Editor, 1980–85, Columnist, 1986–90, The Guardian. Board Member: British Transport Hotels, 1977–83; Halifax plc (formerly Leeds Permanent, then Halifax, Bldg Soc.), 1992–99; Whitbread plc, 1995–2005; Triven VCT, 1999–2003; Woolworths plc, 2002–06; Omega Internat. plc, 2004–09; Nations Healthcare, 2006–07; Belmond (formerly Orient Express Hotels) Ltd, 2006–; pt-time Mem., BRB, 1980–85. Member: Food from Britain Council, 1983–86; Leisure Industries EDC, NEDO, 1986–90; Nat. Trng Task Force, 1989–90; NCVQ, 1992–96; Chm., 3E's Enterprises, 1997–2007. Chm., Restaurateurs' Assoc. of GB, 1990–94; Mem. Council, Museum of Modern Art, Oxford, 1984–90. Governor, City Technology Coll., 1994–2007; Chairman of Governors: King's Coll., Guildford, 1999–2007; Ashridge Mgt Coll., 2002–07 (Gov., 1992–2007). Chairman: British Food Trust, 1997–2006; Forum for the Future, 2000–03; School Food Trust, 2007–10. FRSA 1984–90; FCGI 1992. DL Greater London, 1998. Business Woman of the Year, 1990. *Publications:* Leith's All-Party Cook Book, 1969; Parkinson's Pie (in aid of World Wild Life Fund), 1972; Cooking For Friends, 1978; The Best of Prue Leith, 1979; (with J. B. Reynaud) Leith's Cookery Course (3-part paperback), 1979–80, (comp. hardback with C. Waldegrave), 1980; The Cook's Handbook, 1981; Prue Leith's Pocket Book of Dinner Parties, 1983; Dinner Parties, 1984; (with Polly Tyrer) Entertaining with Style, 1986; Confident Cooking (52 issue part-work), 1989–90; (with Caroline Waldegrave): Leith's Cookery School, 1985; Leith's Cookery Bible, 1991; Leith's Complete Christmas, 1992; Leith's Book of Baking, 1993; Leith's Vegetarian Cookery, 1993; Relish: my life on a plate (autobiog.), 2012; The Food of Love, 2015; *novels:* Leaving Patrick, 1999; Sisters, 2001; A Lovesome Thing, 2004; The Gardener, 2007; Choral Society, 2009; A Serving of Scandal, 2010. *Recreations:* tennis, walking. *Address:* (office) Chastleton Glebe, Chastleton, Moreton-in-Marsh, Glos GL56 0SZ. *T:* (01608) 674908. *E:* pmleith@prue-leith.com.

LEITH-BUCHANAN, Sir Gordon Kelly McNicol, 8th Bt *cr* 1775, of Burgh St Peter, Norfolk; *b* 18 Oct. 1974; *s* of Sir Charles Alexander James Leith-Buchanan, 7th Bt and of Marianne (*née* Kelly); *S* father, 1998, but his name does not appear on the Official Roll of the Baronetage.

le JEUNE d'ALLEGEERSHECQUE, Susan Jane, CMG 2010; HM Diplomatic Service; Ambassador to Austria, and UK Permanent Representative to the United Nations, Vienna, since 2012; *b* 29 April 1963; *d* of Gerald Miller, FCA, and Judith Anne Miller (*née* Rolfe); *m* 1991, Stéphane Hervé Marie le Jeune d'Allegeershecque; two *s*. *Educ:* Ipswich High Sch. for Girls, GPDST; Univ. of Bristol (BA Hons 1985); London Sch. of Econs and Pol Sci. (MSc 2012). Licentiate, CIPD 1999. Joined HM Diplomatic Service, 1985: FCO, 1985–87; Third, later Second Sec., UK Perm. Representation to EC, 1987–90; FCO, 1990–92; Second Sec. (Press/Econ.), Singapore, 1992–95; FCO, 1995–99; Dep. Hd of Mission, Caracas, 1999–2002; Dep. Hd of Mission, Colombia, 2002–05; Consul Gen. and Counsellor (Change Mgt), Washington, 2005–07; Dir, HR, FCO, 2007–12. *Recreations:* art, music, France. *Address:* c/o Foreign and Commonwealth Office, King Charles Street, SW1A 2AH.

LE MARCHANT, Sir Francis (Arthur), 6th Bt *cr* 1841, of Chobham Place, Surrey; artist and farmer; *b* 6 Oct. 1939; *s* of Sir Denis Le Marchant, 5th Bt and of Elizabeth Rowena, *y d* of late Arthur Hovenden Worth; *S* father, 1987. *Educ:* Gordonstoun; Royal Academy Schools. Principal one-man shows include: Agnews; Sally Hunter Fine Art; Roy Miles; Mus. of Arts and Sci., Evansville, USA; ING Bank, sponsored by Barings; group shows include: Leicester Galls; RA Summer Exhibns; Spink; work in public collections includes: Govt Art Collection; FT; Mus. of Arts and Sci., Evansville, USA; Univ. of Evansville, In, collection of late Mrs Anne Kessler. *Recreations:* landscape conservation, garden design, music. *Heir: cousin* Michael Le Marchant [*b* 28 July 1937; *m* 1st, 1963, Philippa Nancy (marr. diss.), *er d* of late R. B. Denby; two *s* two *d*; 2nd, 1981, Sandra Elisabeth Champion (*née* Kirby) (marr. diss.)]. *Address:* c/o HSBC, 88 Westgate, Grantham, Lincs NG31 6LF. *Club:* Savile.

LE MARECHAL, Robert Norford, CB 1994; Deputy Comptroller and Auditor General, National Audit Office, 1989–2000; *b* 29 May 1939; *s* of late Reginald Le Marechal and of Margaret Le Marechal; *m* 1963, Linda Mary (*née* Williams); two *d*. *Educ:* Taunton's School, Southampton. CIPFA 1983. Joined Exchequer and Audit Dept, 1957; Nat. Service, RAEC, 1958–60; Senior Auditor, Exchequer and Audit Dept, 1971; Chief Auditor, 1976; Dep. Dir of Audit, 1980; Dir of Audit, 1983; Dir of Policy and Planning, 1984–86, Asst Auditor General, 1986–89, Nat. Audit Office. FRSA 1997. *Recreations:* reading, gardening. *Address:* 62 Woodcote Hurst, Epsom, Surrey KT18 7DT. *T:* (01372) 721291.

LEMLEY, Jack Kenneth, Hon. CBE 1996; Principal, Lemley International, Inc. (formerly Lemley & Associates), Boise, Idaho, 1988; *b* 2 Jan. 1935; *s* of Kenneth Clyde Lemley and Dorothy Whitsitte; *m* 1st, 1961, Georgia Marshall (marr. diss. 1978); two *s* one *d*; 2nd, 1983, Pamela (*née* Hroza). *Educ:* Coeur d'Alene High Sch., Idaho; Univ. of Idaho (BA Architecture 1960). Asst Project Engineer, Guy F. Atkinson Co., 1960–69; Pres., Healthcare, 1969–70; Manager, Indust. and Power Construction Div., Guy F. Atkinson Co., 1971–77; Sen. Vice-Pres., Constr. Div., Morrison-Knusden Co., 1977–87; Pres. and Chief Exec., Blount Construction Gp, 1987–88; Management Consultant, Lemley & Associates, 1988–89; Chief Exec. Officer, Transmanche-Link, Channel tunnel contractors, 1989–93; Chm. and CEO, American Ecology Corp., 1995–2001. Chm., Olympic Delivery Authy, London, 2006. *Publications:* numerous papers on underground construction projects and international tunnelling. *Recreations:* snow ski-ing, sailing, white water rafting, reading. *Address:* 2045 Table Rock Road, Boise, ID 83712–6664, USA. *T:* (208) 3839253. *Club:* Arid (Boise, Idaho).

LE MOIGNAN, Rev. Christina; Chair, Birmingham Methodist District, 1996–2004; President, Methodist Conference, 2001–02; *b* 12 Oct. 1942; *d* of Edward Frank Le Moignan and (Winifred) Muriel Le Moignan. *Educ:* Somerville Coll., Oxford (MA; Dip. Public and Social Admin); Univ. of Ibadan, Nigeria (PhD 1970); Wesley House, Cambridge (MA). Ordained, 1976; Methodist minister, Huntingdon, Southampton, Portchester, 1976–89; Tutor, Queen's Coll., Birmingham, 1989–94; Principal, W Midlands Ministerial Trng Course (Queen's Coll., Birmingham), 1994–96. Hon. DD Birmingham, 2002. *Publications:* Following the Lamb: a reading of Revelation for the new millennium, 2000. *Recreation:* music. *Address:* 29 Hound Street, Sherborne, Dorset DT9 3AB.

LEMOINE, Prof. Nicholas Robert, MD, PhD; FRCPath, FMedSci; Professor of Molecular Oncology, and Director, Barts Cancer Institute (formerly Institute of Cancer), Queen Mary University of London, since 2003; Director, Cancer Research UK Centre, Barts Health NHS Trust (formerly Barts and the London NHS Trust), since 2003; National Medical Director, National Institute of Health Research Clinical Research Network, since 2014; *b* 11 Dec. 1957; *s* of Robert and Janet Lemoine; *m* 1st, 1980, Louise Nunley (marr. diss. 2008); one *s* one *d*; 2nd, 2010, Christine Rajah. *Educ:* Abingdon Sch.; St Bartholomew's Med. Coll., Univ. of London (BSc 1980; MB BS 1983; MD 1992); PhD Wales 1989. FRCPath 1992. Lectr, University Hosp. of Wales, 1985–88; Lectr, 1989–92, Sen. Lectr, 1992–96, Prof., 1996–2003, RPMS, London; Dir, Cancer Res. Molecular Oncol. Unit, Imperial Coll., London, 1997–2003. FMedSci 2006. Ed. in Chief, Gene Therapy (Nature Specialist Jls), 1997–; Commissioning Ed., British Medical Bulletin, 2008–. *Publications:* Understanding Gene Therapy, 1999; Progress in Pathology, 2001; numerous scientific articles on molecular pathology of cancer and gene therapy. *Recreations:* motorcycles, Rugby football, family and the fruit of serendipity. *Address:* Barts Cancer Institute, Queen Mary University of London, Ground Floor, Old Anatomy Building, Charterhouse Square, EC1M 6BQ. *T:* (020) 7882 3503, *Fax:* (020) 7882 3888.

LEMON, Jane Katherine; QC 2015; *b* Clatterbridge, 19 Sept. 1969; *d* of John Lemon and Margaret Lemon; *m* 2006, Mark Hepburn; two *s* one *d*. *Educ:* King Edward VI High Sch. for Girls; Jesus Coll., Oxford (BA); Coll. of Law, London (CPE 1992). Called to the Bar, Inner Temple, 1993. *Publications:* (contrib.) Professional Negligence and Liability, 2000; (contrib.) Keating on Construction Contracts, 8th edn 2006 to 9th edn 2012. *Recreations:* running, ski-ing. *Address:* Keating Chambers, 15 Essex Street, WC2R 3AA. *T:* (020) 7544 2600. *E:* jlemon@keatingchambers.com.

LEMON, Prof. Roger Nicholas, PhD; FMedSci; Sobell Professor of Neurophysiology, Institute of Neurology, University College London, since 1994 (Director, 2002–08); *b* 6 March 1946; *s* of late Charles Lemon, MBE and Rosaleen Lemon (*née* Morrissey); *m* 1971, Judith Christine (*née* Kirby); two *s* one *d*. *Educ:* Sheffield Univ. (BSc, PhD 1971); MA Cantab. Lectr, Dept of Physiol., Univ. of Sheffield, 1971–77; Res. Fellow, Dept of Physiol., Monash Univ., Australia, 1974–75; Sen. Lectr, Dept of Anatomy, 1977–84, Reader, 1984–85, Erasmus Univ., Rotterdam; Lectr, Dept of Anatomy, 1985–94, and Fellow, New Hall, 1987–94, Univ. of Cambridge; Hd, Sobell Dept, Inst. of Neurol., UCL, 1994–2002 and 2010–11. Guarantor, Brain, 2007–. Mem. Council, Understanding Animal Res., 2009–12. FMedSci 2002 (Mem. Council, 2012–). *Publications:* (with R. Porter) Corticospinal Function and Voluntary Movement, 1993; contrib. papers and articles in general area of motor neurosci. *Recreations:* walking, naval history, Samuel Pepys. *Address:* Institute of Neurology, University College London, Sobell Department of Motor Neurosciences and Movement Disorders (Box 28), Queen Square, WC1N 3BG.

LEMOS, Gerard Anthony, CMG 2001; writer, social researcher; Partner, Lemos & Crane, since 1990; *b* 26 Feb. 1958; *s* of late Ronald Lemos and Cynthia (*née* Mitchell). *Educ:* Dulwich Coll.; Univ. of York. Dir, ASRA Housing Assoc., 1982–85; Area Manager and Dir of Devel t, Circle 33 Housing Trust, 1985–90; Dir of Studies, Sch. for Social Entrepreneurs, 1997–99. Director: Mortgage Code Compliance Bd, 2000–01; Banking Code Standards Bd, 2000–10 (Dep. Chm., 2001–05, Chm., 2005–10); Chairman: Notting Hill Housing Gp, 2004–06; Money Advice Service, 2010–13. Mem., Audit Commn, 2000–04; Civil Service Comr, 2001–06. Non-exec. Dir, CPS, 2006–10; Ind. Dir, Payments Council, 2012– (Chm., 2014–). Vis. Prof., Chongqing Business and Technology Univ., 2006–10. Vice-Pres., BBFC, 2008–. Member of Board: London Internat. Fest. of Theatre, 1993–2001; British Council, 1999–2010 (Dep. Chm., 2003–09; Acting Chm., 2008–10); The Place Theatre, 2002–03; Chm., Bd of Dirs, Akram Khan Dance Co., 2003–08; Trustee, Dartington Hall Trust, 2008–09. *Publications:* Interviewing Perpetrators of Racial Harassment, 1994; Fair Recruitment and Selection, 1995; Safe as Houses: supporting people experiencing racial harassment, 1996; (jtly) The Communities We Have Lost and Can Regain, 1997; Urban Village, Global City: the regeneration of Colville, 1998; Steadying the Ladder: social and emotional aspirations of homeless and vulnerable people, 2006; reports: A Future Foretold: new approaches to meeting the long-term needs of single homeless people, 1999; Racial Harassment: action on the ground, 2000; (jtly) Dreams Deferred: the families and friends of homeless and vulnerable people, 2002; The Search for Tolerance: challenging and changing racist attitudes and behaviour among young people, 2005; Military History: the experiences of people who become homeless after military service, 2005; (jtly) Different World: how young people can work together on human rights and citizenship, 2007; Freedom's Consequences: reducing teenage pregnancies and their negative effects in the UK, 2009; The Meaning of Money: why homeless and vulnerable people see money as a route to security, respect and freedom, 2010; The End of the Chinese Dream: why Chinese people fear the future, 2012; The Good Prison: conscience, crime and punishment, 2015. *Recreations:* literature, cricket. *Address:* (office) 64 Highgate High Street, N6 5HX. *T:* (020) 8348 8263.

LENDRUM, Christopher John, CBE 2005; Group Vice Chairman, 2004, and Executive Director, 1998–2004, Barclays plc; *b* 15 Jan. 1947; *s* of late Herbert Colin Lendrum and of Anne Margaret (*née* Macdonell); *m* 1970, Margaret Patricia Parker; one *s* one *d*. *Educ:* Felsted Sch., Essex; Durham Univ. (BA Econs 1968). FCIB 1992. Joined Barclays Bank plc, 1969: Regl Dir, 1991–93; Dep. Man. Dir of Banking Div., 1993–95; Man. Dir of UK Business Banking, 1995–98; Chief Exec., Corporate Banking, 1998–2003. Chm., Barclays Pension Fund Trustees Ltd, 2005–11. Non-executive Director: Co. Durham Community Foundn, 2008–14; North East Finance Ltd, 2009–; Motability Ops plc, 2009–. Trustee, CAB, 2005–06 (Mem. Adv. Bd, 2001–04); Gov., Motability, 2005–09. Freeman, City of London, 1999; Liveryman, Woolmen's Co., 1999–. CCMI 2002. Gov., Kent Coll., Pembury, 2000–08. Chm., Aston Martin Heritage Trust, 2006–09 (Trustee, 2003–10); Trustee: City of London Trust for St Paul's Cathedral, 2007–; Alnwick Garden, 2012–. Hon. DLitt Durham, 2008. *Recreations:* gardening, travel, restoring neglected motor cars. *Address:* Hazon House, Guyzance, Northumberland NE65 9AT. *E:* lendrumsofhazon@btinternet.com. *Club:* Royal Automobile.

LENG, Gillian Catherine, CBE 2011; MD; Deputy Chief Executive, National Institute for Health and Care Excellence (formerly for Health and Clinical Excellence), since 2007 (Executive Director, since 2004); *b* Newport, 16 Sept. 1960; *d* of Mark Sanderson and Mary Sanderson; *m* 2006, Paul Anthony Cosford, *qv*; two *d* by a previous marriage. *Educ:* Harrogate Grammar Sch.; Univ. of Leeds (BSc Hons 1st Cl. 1982; MB ChB 1987; MD 1994). FFPH 2006; FRCP 2007; FRCPE 2012. HO, St James' Univ. Hosp., Leeds, 1987–88; SHO, Western Gen. Hosp., Edinburgh, 1988–89; Trainee in Gen. Practice, 1989–90; Clin. Res. Fellow, Univ. of Edinburgh, 1990–97; Registrar in Public Health Medicine, W of Scotland and N Thames, 1997–2000; Consultant in Public Health, Beds, 2000–01; Guidelines Prog. Dir, NICE, 2001–04. Hon. Sen. Lectr, LSHTM, 2007–12; Vis. Prof., KCL, 2012–. Trustee: RSM, 2013–; Centre for Ageing Better, 2014–. Assoc. Mem., BUPA, 2014–. FRSocMed 2002. FRSA 2008. *Publications:* Achieving High Quality Care: practical advice from NICE, 2014; contrib. articles to jls relating to evidence-based care, epidemiology and guideline methodology. *Recreations:* walking, painting, keeping the garden free of ubiquitous sycamore saplings. *Address:* National Institute for Health and Care Excellence, 10 Spring Gardens, SW1A 2BU. *T:* 07811 209586. *E:* gcleng@doctors.org.uk.

LENG, James William; European Chairman, AEA Investors (UK) LLP, since 2007; *b* 19 Nov. 1945; *m* 1974, Carole Ann Guyll. John Waddington, 1967–84; Low & Bonar: Man. Dir, Bonar & Flotex, 1984–86; Chief Exec., Plastics Div., 1986–88; Chief Exec., European Ops, 1988–92; Dir, 1989–95; Group Chief Exec., 1992–95; Chief Exec., Laporte plc, 1995–2001; Dep. Chm., 2001–03, Chm., 2003–09, Corus Gp plc, later Corus Gp Ltd (non-exec. Dir, 2001–07); Dep. Chm., Tata Steel of India, 2007–09; Chairman: Doncasters Gp Ltd, 2001–03 and 2006–09; HSBC Bank plc, 2012–13. Lead non-exec. Dir, Ministry of Justice, 2010–12. Sen. non-exec. Dir, Genel Energy (formerly Vallares), 2011–; non-executive Director: Pilkington plc, 1998–2006; IMI plc, 2002–05; Alstom SA, 2003–; Hanson plc, 2004–07; HSBC Bank plc, 2010–12; J O Hambro Investment Mgt Ltd, 2010–12; Aon Corp., 2014–; Ind. Dir, TNK-BP, 2009–11. Vice-Pres., CIA, 1999–2001. Governor: NIESR, 1999–; Univ. of Newcastle-upon-Tyne, 2005–09; Ashridge Coll., 2008–11. FRSA 2005. *Recreations:* sport, music. *Club:* Royal Automobile.

LENG, Virginia Helen Antoinette; *see* Elliot, V. H. A.

LENNAN, David John; Chief Executive, Timber Trades Federation, since 2014; *b* 15 Dec. 1948; *s* of John D. Lennan and Mair E. Lennan; *m* 1975, Diane Griffiths (marr. diss.). *Educ:* Northampton Town and Co. Grammar Sch. ACIB 1971. Joined District Bank, 1966; NatWest Group PLC: Dep. Regl Dir, SE Reg., 1992–93; Dep. Dir, Human Resources, and Hd, UK Develt, 1993–95; Dir, Retail Insce Services, 1995–98; Dir, Corporate Develt, Surrey CC, 1998–2001; Dir Gen., British Chambers of Commerce, 2001–02; Chief Executive: Agricultural Industries Confedn, 2003–04; Business HR Solutions Ltd, 2004–10. Non-executive Chairman: Workwise UK, 2006–; Pilotlight, 2006–; non-exec. Dir, IT Forum Foundn, 2004–; Chm., Eco Answers, 2010–. Tuck Exec. Prog., Dartmouth Univ., USA, 1996. *Recreations:* sailing, theatre, flying. *Address:* 17 Millers Wharf House, 78 St Katharine's Way, E1W 1UE.

LENNARD, Sir Peter John B.; *see* Barrett-Lennard.

LENNIE, family name of **Baron Lennie**.

LENNIE, Baron *cr* 2014 (Life Peer), of Longsands Tynemouth in the County of Tyne and Wear; **Christopher John Lennie;** *b* Perth, Australia, 1953; *s* of Magnus and Elizabeth Lennie; *m* 1978, Anne Doffegnies; one *s* one *d*. *Educ:* Newcastle Poly. (BA Hist. and Eng. Lit. 1976). Unison official, until 2000; Lab Party official, 2000, Dep. Sec. Gen., 2001–12. *Recreations:* Newcastle Utd supporter, running, cycling, golf. *Address:* c/o House of Lords, SW1A 0PW. *Club:* Tynemouth Social Club Institute and Union.

LENNON, Francis Patrick, OBE 2002; Head Teacher, Dunblane High School, since 2011; *b* Glasgow, 18 June 1952; *s* of William and Margaret Lennon; *m* 1974, Marie Connolly; one *s* four *d*. *Educ:* Salesian Coll., Shrigley, Cheshire; Holy Cross High Sch., Hamilton; Univ. of Glasgow (MA Hons English and Hist.); Open Univ. (MPhil). Teacher of English, St Gerard's Secondary Sch., Glasgow, 1975–78; Asst Principal Teacher of English, St Columba of Iona Secondary Sch., Glasgow, 1978–81; Asst Principal Teacher of English, Holyrood Secondary Sch., Glasgow, 1981–84; Principal teacher of English, Holy Cross High Sch., 1984–90; Asst Head Teacher, St Patrick's High Sch., 1990–93; Depute Head Teacher, St Andrew's Secondary Sch., Glasgow, 1993–96; Head Teacher, St Modan's High Sch., Stirling, 1996–2011. *Recreations:* football, American football, music, opera, theatre. *Address:* 6 Richmond Grove, Rutherglen, Glasgow G73 3LD. *T:* (0141) 647 3754. *E:* fpl@sky.com.

LENNON, Prof. (Justin) John, PhD; Director, Moffat Centre, since 1998, Moffat Professor of Travel and Tourism Business Development, since 1999, and Vice Dean, since 2012, Glasgow Caledonian University; *b* Birmingham, 19 June 1961; *s* of John and Mary Lennon; *m* 1985, Joanne Wolstenholme; two *s* one *d*. *Educ:* Oxford Poly. (BSc Hons Hotel and Tourism Mgt); Strathclyde Univ. (MPhil Mgt 1990); Glasgow Caledonian Univ. (PhD Mgt 2010). Mgt trainee, Penta Hotels, Germany, 1980–81; Asst Food and Beverage Manager, Poste Hotels Ltd, 1983–85; Personnel and Trng Manager, Food and Beverage Manager, and Dep. Gen. Manager, Midland Hotels, 1985–88; Gen. Manager, Midland Hotel, Sheffield, 1988–90; Consultant, Hospitality Consultants Ltd, 1990–95; Lectr and Industrial Liaison Tutor, Strathclyde Univ., 1993–95; Sen. Lectr, then Reader in Mgt, 1996–99, Glasgow Caledonian Univ. Principal Advr, All Party Tourism Inquiry, Scottish Govt, 2007–09; Specialist Policy Advr, VisitScotland, 2004–09. Director: Scottish Tourism Forum, 2004–08; Canadian Tourism Commn (Eur. Mktg Bd), 2005–08; non-exec. Dir, Historic Scotland, 2006–. *Publications:* (with M. Peet) Hospitality Management: a case study approach, 1990, instructor's manual, 1990; Guide to Catering Practice, 1996; (with V. Russell) Guide to Events Management, 1997; (ed jtly) Hospitality, Tourism and Leisure Management: issues in strategy and culture, 1997; (with M. Foley) Dark Tourism: the attraction of death and disaster, 2000, 4th edn 2009; (ed) Tourism Statistics: international perspectives and current issues, 2001; (jtly) Benchmarking National Tourism Organisation: lessons from best practice internationally, 2006; contrib. chapters in textbooks; contrib. articles in jls incl. Internat. Jl Hospitality Mgt, Internat. Jl Contemporary Hospitality Mgt, Internat. Jl heritage Studies, Tourism Mgt. *Address:* Shirgarton House, Kippen, Stirlingshire FK8 3EA.

LENNON, Linda Susan, CBE 2009; Chief Executive Officer, London Stadium 185, since 2015; *b* Sutton, Surrey, 13 March 1963; *d* of Anthony Harry Smith and Rita Joan Smith. *Educ:* Wallington High Sch. for Girls; Civil Service Coll. (IPD Trng and Develt). Appts with LCD, MoJ and HM Courts, 1981–2009, incl. Area Dir for London, Civil and Family Courts, until 2009; Chief Executive Officer: Parole Bd (England and Wales), 2009–12; Royal Parks, 2012–15. *Recreations:* swimming, walking my dog, bird watching, reading, theatre and musical performances. *Address:* London Stadium 185, Queen Elizabeth Olympic Park, Stratford, E20 2ST.

LENNON, Hon. Paul Anthony; Chairman: Common Ground Tasmania, since 2012; Australian Bauxite Ltd, since 2014; Premier of Tasmania, Australia, 2004–08; *b* 8 Oct. 1955; *s* of Charles and Marg Lennon; *m* 1978, Margaret Gaff; two *d*. Storeman/clerk, 1974–78; Tasmanian Branch, Storemen and Packers Union: Organiser, 1978–80; Sec., 1980–84; Sen.

Vice-Pres., Federated Storemen and Packers Union of Australia, 1982–84; Sec., Tasmanian Trades and Labor Council, 1984–89; Asst Gen. Manager, Develt, Tasmanian Develt Authy, 1989–90. MHA (ALP) Franklin, Tasmania, 1990–2008; Opposition Whip and Shadow Minister for Police and Emergency Services, 1992; Shadow Minister for: Racing and Gaming, 1992–98; Industrial Relns, 1993–98; Employment and Trng, 1993–95; Forestry, 1995–96; Opposition Leader of Business in the House, 1995–96; Dep. Leader of Opposition, 1996–98; Minister for Workplace Standards and Workers' Compensation, Forests and Mines, 1997–98; Dep. Premier, 1998–2004; Minister for Infrastructure, Energy and Resources and for Racing and Gaming, 1998–2002; Minister for Econ. Develt, Energy and Resources, and for Racing and Sport and Recreation, 2002–04; Treas., 2004–06; Minister for Local Govt, 2004–08, for Econ. Develt and Resources, 2006–08. Mem., Parly Public Accounts Cttee, 1990–96.

LENNOX; *see* Gordon Lennox.

LENNOX, Annie, OBE 2011; singer and songwriter; humanitarian aid campaigner; *b* 25 Dec. 1954; *d* of late Thomas A. Lennox and Dorothy Lennox (*née* Ferguson); *m* 1st, 1984, Radha Raman (marr. diss.); 2nd, 1988, Uri Fruchtmann; two *d* (and one *s* decd) (marr. diss.); 3rd, 2012, Dr Mitch Besser. *Educ:* Aberdeen High Sch. for Girls; Royal Acad. of Music. Singer with: The Catch, subseq. The Tourists, 1977–81; Eurythmics, 1981–89, 1999; solo singer, 1988–. *Albums include:* with The Tourists: The Tourists, 1979; Reality Affect, 1980; Luminous Basement, 1980; with Eurythmics: In the Garden, 1981; Sweet Dreams (Are Made of This), 1983; Touch, 1984; 1984 (For the Love of Big Brother), 1984; Be Yourself Tonight, 1985; Revenge, 1986; Savage, 1987; We Too Are One, 1989; Peace, 1999; solo: Diva, 1992; Medusa, 1995; Train in Vain, 1995; Bare, 2003; Songs of Mass Destruction, 2007; The Annie Lennox Collection, 2009; A Christmas Cornucopia, 2010; Nostalgia, 2014. Mayor of London's HIV Ambassador, 2011–. *Address:* c/o XIX Entertainment Ltd, 33 Ransomes Dock, 35–37 Parkgate Road, SW11 4NP.

LENNOX, Lionel Patrick Madill; Registrar: of the Convocation of York, since 1987; of Tribunals, Province of York, since 2006; of the Diocese of Sodor and Man, since 2014; Deputy Registrar of the Diocese of York, since 2014; Director, Lupton Fawcett Denison Till, since 2013 (Partner, Denison Till, Solicitors, York, 1987–2013); *b* 5 April 1949; *s* of late Rev. James Lennox and May Lennox; *m* 1979, Barbara Helen Firth; two *s* one *d*. *Educ:* St John's Sch., Leatherhead; Univ. of Birmingham (LLB). Admitted Solicitor, 1973; Ecclesiastical Notary, 1987; Notary Public, 1992. Solicitor in private practice, 1973–81; Asst Legal Advr to Gen. Synod, 1981–87. Secretary: Archbishop of Canterbury's Gp on Affinity, 1982–84; Legal Adv. Commn, Gen. Synod of C of E, 1986–; Registrar of Province and Dio. of York, and Legal Sec. to Archbp of York, 1987–2014. Pres., Yorks Law Soc., 2007–08. Sec., Yorks Mus. of Farming, 1991–94. Trustee: Yorks Historic Churches Trust, 1988–2010; St Leonard's Hospice, York, 2000–09; York Centre for Voluntary Service, 2012–. Under Sheriff, City of York, 2006–07. *Address:* Stamford House, Piccadilly, York YO1 9PP. *T:* (01904) 623487.

LENNOX-BOYD, family name of **Viscount Boyd of Merton**.

LENNOX-BOYD, Arabella, (Lady Lennox-Boyd); landscape designer; Principal, Arabella Lennox-Boyd Landscape Design, since 1984; *b* 15 Jan. 1938; *d* of Piero Parisi and Irene Diaz della Vittoria; *m* 1974, Hon. Sir Mark Alexander Lennox-Boyd, *qv*; one *d*, and one *d* from former marriage. *Educ:* privately in Italy. Commissioned designs in UK, Europe and worldwide incl. Russia, USA and Caribbean, range from small town gdns to country landscapes; major projects incl. roof gdn at No 1 Poultry, gdns at Ascott House and Eaton Hall. Trustee: Kew Gdns, 1989–98; Castle Howard Arboretum Trust, 1997–; Chelsea Physic Gdn, 2014–; former Mem., Historic Parks and Gdns Cttee, English Heritage. Hon. DDes Greenwich, 2003. Gold Medals, RHS Chelsea Flower Show, 1990, 1993, 1995, 1998, 2000, 2008. Premio Firenze Donna, 2005; Veitch Meml Medal, RHS, 2008. *Publications:* Traditional English Gardens, 1987; Private Gardens of London, 1990; (jtly) Designing Gardens, 2002. *Recreations:* collecting rare trees and propagating, gardening, listening to music. *Address:* 1–5 Dells Mews, Churton Place, SW1V 2LW. *T:* (020) 7931 9995, *Fax:* (020) 7821 6585. *E:* office@arabellalennoxboyd.com.

LENNOX-BOYD, Hon. Sir Mark (Alexander), Kt 1994; *b* 4 May 1943; 3rd *s* of 1st Viscount Boyd of Merton, CH, PC and of Lady Patricia Guinness, 2nd *d* of 2nd Earl of Iveagh, KG, CB, CMG, FRS; *m* 1974, Arabella Lacloche (*see* A. Lennox-Boyd); one *d*. *Educ:* Eton Coll.; Christ Church, Oxford. Called to the Bar, Inner Temple, 1968. MP (C) Morecambe and Lonsdale, 1979–83, Morecambe and Lunesdale, 1983–97; contested (C) Morecambe and Lunesdale, 1997. Parliamentary Private Secretary: to Sec. of State for Energy, 1981–83; to the Chancellor of the Exchequer, 1983–84; Asst Govt Whip, 1984–86; a Lord Comr of HM Treasury (Govt Whip), 1986–88; PPS to Prime Minister, 1988–90; Parly Under-Sec. of State, FCO, 1990–94. Chm., Georgian Gp, 2014–. *Recreation:* travel. *Address:* Gresgarth Hall, Caton, Lancashire LA2 9NB. *Clubs:* Brooks's, Pratt's, Beefsteak.

LENON, Andrew Ralph Fitzmaurice; QC 2006; *b* 7 April 1957; *s* of late Rev. Philip John Fitzmaurice Lenon and of Jane Alethea Lenon (*née* Brooke); *m* 1987, Sheila Cook; one *s* three *d*. *Educ:* St John's Sch., Leatherhead; Lincoln Coll., Oxford (BA); City Univ. (Dip. Law). Called to the Bar, Lincoln's Inn, 1981; in practice specialising in commercial law; a Chm., Competition Appeal Tribunal, 2012–. *Publications:* contribs to legal jls. *Recreations:* music, languages. *Address:* Chambers of Lord Grabiner, QC, One Essex Court, Temple, EC4Y 9AR. *T:* (020) 7583 2000.

See also B. J. Lenon.

LENON, Barnaby John, MA; Chairman, Independent Schools' Council, since 2011; *b* 10 May 1954; *s* of late Rev. Philip John Fitzmaurice Lenon and of Jane Alethea Lenon (*née* Brooke); *m* 1983, Penelope Anne Thain, BA; two *d*. *Educ:* Eltham Coll.; Keble Coll., Oxford (schol.; BA 1st Cl. Hons 1976; MA); St John's, Cambridge (PGCE; Univ. Prize for Educn 1978). Assistant Master: Eton Coll., 1977; Sherborne Sch., 1978–79; Eton Coll., 1979–90; Teacher, Holland Park Sch., 1988; Dep. Head Master, Highgate Sch., 1990–95; Headmaster: Trinity Sch. of John Whitgift, 1995–99; Harrow School, 1999–2011. Mem. Bd, Ofqual, 2012–. Governor: John Lyon Sch., 1999–2011; Swanbourne Sch., 1999–2005; Orley Farm Sch., 1999–2011; Wellesley House Sch., 1999–2011; Beacon Sch., 2000–05; Papplewick Sch., 2001–11; Francis Holland Schs, 2002–; Aysgarth Sch., 2006–11; Chelsea Acad., 2009–; London Acad. of Excellence, 2011– (Chm., 2012–). Trustee: Vocal Futures, 2011–; Yellow Submarine Charity, Oxford, 2012–; Dir, New Schs Network, 2014–. FRGS 1987 (Mem. Council, 1987–90 and 1998–2000; Chm., Educn Sub-Cttee, 1996–99; Vice-Pres., 2009–12). CGeog 2000. *Publications:* Techniques and Fieldwork in Geography, 1983; London, 1988; London in the 1990s, 1993; Fieldwork Techniques and Projects in Geography, 1994; The United Kingdom: geographical case studies, 1995; (ed jtly) Directory of University Geography Courses, 1995, 2nd edn 1997; Fieldwork and Skills, 2015; contribs to geographical jls. *Recreations:* oil painting, athletics, deserts. *Address:* 55 St John Street, Oxford OX1 2LQ.

See also A. R. F. Lenon.

LEON, Sir John (Ronald), 4th Bt *cr* 1911; actor (stage name, **John Standing**); *b* 16 Aug. 1934; *er s* of 3rd Bt and late (Dorothy) Katharine (stage name Kay Hammond), *d* of Sir Guy Standing, KBE; *S* father, 1964; *m* 1961, Jill (marr. diss. 1972), *d* of Jack Melford; one *s*; *m* 1984, Sarah, *d* of Bryan Forbes, CBE; one *s* two *d*. *Educ:* Eton. Late 2nd Lt, KRRC. *Plays include:* Darling Buds of May, Saville, 1959; leading man, season, Bristol Old Vic, 1960; The Irregular Verb to Love, Criterion, 1961; Norman, Duchess, 1963; So Much to Remember, Vaudeville, 1963; The Three Sisters, Oxford Playhouse, 1964; See How They Run, Vaudeville, 1964; Seasons at Chichester Theatre, 1966, 1967; The Importance of Being Earnest, Ring Round the Moon, Haymarket, 1968; The Alchemist, and Arms and the Man, Chichester, 1970; Popkiss, Globe, 1972; A Sense of Detachment, Royal Court, 1972; Private Lives, Queen's and Globe, 1973, NY and tour of USA, 1974; Jingo, RSC, 1975; Plunder, The Philanderer, NT, 1978; Close of Play, NT, 1979; Tonight at 8.30, Lyric, 1981; The Biko Inquest, Riverside, 1984; Rough Crossing, National, 1984; Hay Fever, Albery, 1992; A Month in the Country, Albery, 1994; Son of Man, RSC, 1995; A Delicate Balance, Haymarket, 1997; Shadowlands, Wyndham's, 2007. *Films:* The Wild and the Willing, 1962; Iron Maiden, 1962; King Rat, 1964; Walk, Don't Run, 1965; Zee and Co., 1973; The Eagle has Landed, 1976; The Class of Miss MacMichael, 1977; The Legacy, 1977; The Elephant Man, 1979; The Sea Wolves, 1980; (TV film) The Young Visiters, 1984; Nightflyers; 8½ Women, Rogue Trader, 1999; The Good Woman, 2003; V for Vendetta, 2005; I Want Candy, Shooter, Before the Rains, 2007. *Television* appearances incl.: for British TV: Arms and the Man; The First Churchills; Charley's Aunt; Rogue Male; The Sinking of HMS Victoria; Home and Beauty; Tinker, Tailor, Soldier, Spy; The Other 'Arf; Old Boy Network; Tonight at 8.30; Count of Solar; Gulliver's Travels; Shadow in the North; for American TV: Lime Street; Hotel; Flap Jack Floozie; Visitors; Murphy's Law; The Endless Game; Murder She Wrote; LA Law; Windmills of the Gods; Drovers' Gold; A Dance to The Music of Time; Longitude; King Solomon's Mines. *Cabaret:* John Standing Sings Coward, 2009; John Standing Swings Cole Porter, 2011. *Recreation:* painting. *Heir: s* Alexander John Leon [*b* 3 May 1965; *m* 1996, Susan Janice Paul; two *s*]. *Address:* c/o United Agents, 12–26 Lexington Street, W1F 0LE.

LEONARD, Anthony James; QC 1999; **His Honour Judge Leonard;** a Circuit Judge, since 2009; *b* 21 April 1956; *s* of late Sir (Hamilton) John Leonard and Doreen Enid Leonard (*née* Parker); *m* 1983, Shara Jane Cormack; two *d*. *Educ:* Hurstpierpoint Coll., Sussex; Council of Legal Educn. Short Service Limited Commn, Queen's Regt, 1975–76; Major, 6/7 Queen's (TA), 1976–85. Called to the Bar, Inner Temple, 1978, Bencher, 2002; Standing Counsel to Inland Revenue, S Eastern Circuit, 1993–99; Recorder, 2000–09. Vice-Chm., Professional Conduct Cttee, 2001–04, 2006–08. Dep. Chancellor, Dio. of St Edmundsbury and Ipswich, 2009–; Chancellor, Dio. of Ely, 2012–; Commissary to the Archbishop of Canterbury, 2012–. Liveryman, Plaisterers' Co. *Recreations:* opera, wine, reading. *Club:* Garrick.

LEONARD, Brian Henry, CBE 2008; Chief Executive, Sporta Ltd, since 2010; Chairman, Push Once Ltd, since 2008; *b* 6 Jan. 1948; *s* of William Henry Leonard and Bertha Florence Leonard (*née* Thomas); *m* 1975, Margaret Meade-King; two *s*. *Educ:* Dr Challoner's Grammar Sch., Amersham; LSE (BSc Econ 1969). Heal & Son, 1969–73; Price Commn, 1973–74; joined DoE, 1974; Circle 33 Housing Trust, 1982–83; Fellow, Hubert H. Humphrey Inst., Minneapolis, 1987–88; Regl Dir, N Reg., DoE and Dept of Transport, 1993–94; Regl Dir, Govt Office for SW, 1994–97; Dir, Envmt Protection Strategy, DETR, 1997–98; Dir, Regions, Tourism, Millennium and Internat., then Tourism, Lottery and Regions, subseq. Tourism, Libraries and Communities, DCMS, 1998–2005; Dir, Industry, DCMS, 2005–08. Chm., Storylines Ltd, 2008–14; Director: Business in Sport and Leisure, 2008–12; South West Screen, 2008–12. Chm., video games wkg gp, UK Council for Child Internet Safety, 2009–10. *Recreations:* friends, games, pottering about. *Address:* 46 Defoe House, Barbican, EC2Y 8DN. *Club:* MCC.

LEONARD, Colum Charles; a Master of the Senior Courts Taxing Office, since 2010; *b* Belfast, 23 Nov. 1956; *s* of Philip and Rose Leonard; *m* 1990, Carole Collins; one *d*. *Educ:* Abbey Primary and Grammar Schs, Newry, Co. Down; Univ. of Southampton (LLB Hons 1979); Guildford Coll. of Law. Admitted Solicitor, 1984; Articled Clerk, 1982–84, Solicitor, 1984–86, Wilde Sapte; Solicitor, Clarke Willmott and Clarke, 1986–89; Partner, Stewarts Law LLP, 1990–2010; a Dep. Dist Judge, 2002–; a Tribunal Judge, First-tier (Property Chamber), 2006–; Dep. Costs Judge, 2006–10. *Recreations:* running slowly, swimming badly, occasional sub-aqua, grandchildren wrangling, theatre and cinema. *Address:* Senior Courts Costs Office, Royal Courts of Justice, Thomas More Building, Strand, WC2A 2LL.

LEONARD, David Charles; Chairman, Kingfieldheath Ltd, 2001–04; Group Chief Executive, BPB plc, 1999–2000; *b* 26 June 1938; *s* of Charles and Audrey Leonard; *m* 1961, Jennifer Capes; two *s* one *d*. *Educ:* Hellesdon Secondary Sch., Norwich. FCMA, ACIS. Managing Dir, food and other manufacturing industries; BPB plc: Man. Dir, British Gypsum, 1990–94; Dir, New Business Develt, 1993–97; Mem. Main Bd, 1995; Dep. Chm., Gypsum, 1996; Chm., British Gypsum, 1996; Chief Operating Officer, all building products, 1997; Dir, BMP, 1999. Dir, Lincoln City FC Ltd, 2010–11. FRSA. *Recreations:* reading, music, opera, an interest in most sports, tennis, walking, golf.

LEONARD, David John, TD 1974; arbitrator, mediator; Judge, Court of Appeal, Brunei Darussalam, since 2010; *b* 18 Sept. 1937; *s* of Jeremiah Leonard and Rosaleen Oonagh Leonard (*née* Mellett); *m* 1966, Frances Helen Good; two *s*. *Educ:* Hendon Grammar Sch.; Magdalene Coll., Cambridge (MA); Bath Spa Univ. Coll. (MA 2005). Admitted solicitor, 1967; admitted solicitor and barrister, Victoria, Australia, 1982. Solicitors' Dept, New Scotland Yard, 1966–71; Batten & Co., Solicitors, Yeovil, 1971–77; Hong Kong: Permanent Magistrate, 1977–81; Dist Judge, 1981–91; Judge, Supreme Ct, 1991–97; Judicial Comr, High Court, Brunei Darussalam, 2001–07. Chm., Judicial Studies Bd, Hong Kong, 1994–97. Served in TA: HAC, RA, Intelligence Corps, 1960–77, Maj. (retd) Intelligence Corps; Royal Hong Kong Regt (Volunteers), 1977–91, Maj. (retd). Part-time Immigration and Asylum Adjudicator, 1997–98. Member: Acad. of Experts, 1995– (Vice-Chm., 1997–98); Arbitration Panel: Hong Kong Internat. Arbitration Centre, 1996–; China Internat. Economic and Trade Arbitration Commn, 1997–; Professional Conduct Cttee, Chartered Inst. of Arbitrators, 2000–06; Qingdao Arbitration Commn, 2001–; Internat. Commn for Holocaust Era Insce Claims, 2002–06; Beijing Arbitration Commn, 2003–. Chm., Bath Br., ESU, 2010–13; Mem. Cttee, Britain Australia Soc., W Country Br., 2009–. Mem. Cttee, Wilts RFCA (formerly TAVRA), 1997–2007. FCIArb 1995–2009. Fellow, Hong Kong Inst. of Arbitrators, 1997–2007. Freeman and Liveryman, Painter-Stainers' Co., 1996–. Member: Devonshire Soc.; RBL. *Recreations:* travel, reading, walking. *E:* dleo1937@aol.com. *Clubs:* Victory Services, HAC Mess; Bath & County (Bath); Hong Kong (Hong Kong).

LEONARD, Dick; *see* Leonard, Richard L.

LEONARD, (Fergus) Miles; Chairman (formerly President), Parlophone Records, since 2008 (Managing Director, 2003–08); Chairman, Warner Bros Records, since 2014 (Co-Chairman, 2013–14); *b* 17 June 1967; *s* of Eric and Yvonne Leonard; *m* 2005, Luca Smit; two *s* one *d*. *Educ:* Great Marlow Sch. A&R Scout, Virgin Records, 1991–93; A&R Manager, Roadrunner Records, 1993–95; Parlophone Records: A&R Manager, 1995–96; Sen. A&R Manager, 1996–99; Dir of A&R, 1999–2003; Pres., Virgin A&R, 2011–13. *Recreations:* Glastonbury, Secrets, Ring O' Bells public house (owner), Christmas. *Address:* Warner Music Group, 27 Wrights Lane, W8 5SW. *T:* (020) 7795 5000. *Clubs:* Soho House; Mendip Shooting Ground; Bowls (Marrakech); DC10 (Ibiza).

LEONARD, Prof. James Vivian, PhD; FRCP, FRCPCH; Professor of Paediatric Metabolic Disease, Institute of Child Health, University of London, 1992–2004; *b* 21 Dec. 1944; *s* of Rt Rev. Mgr and Rt Hon. Graham Douglas Leonard, KCVO, PC; *m* 1966, Dr Halcyon Sheila Deriba (*née* Disney); one *s* one *d*. *Educ:* Pembroke Coll., Cambridge (MB BChir 1970); St Thomas's Hosp. Med. Sch.; Inst. of Child Health, London (PhD 1979). FRCP 1983; FRCPCH 1997. Sen. Lectr, 1979–85, Reader, 1985–92, Inst. of Child Health; Consultant Paediatrician, Gt Ormond St Children's Hosp., 1979–2004. *Publications:* contribs on paediatric metabolic medicine. *Recreations:* gardening, travel, woodturning. *Address:* 40A Bagley Wood Road, Kennington, Oxford OX1 5LY.

LEONARD, Miles; *see* Leonard, F. M.

LEONARD, Richard Lawrence, (Dick Leonard); writer and journalist; *b* 12 Dec. 1930; *s* of late Cyril Leonard, and Kate Leonard (*née* Whyte), Pinner, Middx; *m* 1963, Irène, *d* of late Dr Ernst Heidelberger and Dr Gertrud Heidelberger, Bad Godesberg, Germany; one *s* one *d*. *Educ:* Ealing Grammar Sch.; Inst. of Education, London Univ.; Essex Univ. (MA). School teacher, 1953–55; Dep. Gen. Sec., Fabian Society, 1955–60; journalist and broadcaster, 1960–68; Sen. Research Fellow (Social Science Research Council), Essex Univ., 1968–70. Mem., Exec. Cttee, Fabian Soc., 1972–80 (Chm., 1977–78); Chm., Library Adv. Council, 1978–81. Trustee, Assoc. of London Housing Estates, 1973–78. Vis. Prof., Free Univ. of Brussels, 1988–96. European Advr, Publishers Assoc., 1987–94; Sen. Advr, Centre for European Policy Studies, 1994–99; Sen. Res. Associate, Foreign Policy Centre, London, 2003–. Contested (Lab) Harrow W, 1955; MP (Lab) Romford, 1970–Feb. 1974; PPS to Rt Hon. Anthony Crosland, 1970–74; Mem., Speaker's Conf. on Electoral Law, 1972–74. Introduced Council Housing Bill, 1971; Life Peers Bill, 1973. Asst Editor, The Economist, 1974–85; Brussels and EU correspondent, The Observer, 1989–97; Brussels correspondent, Europe magazine, 1992–2003. *Publications:* Guide to the General Election, 1964; Elections in Britain, 1968, 5th edn 2005; (ed jtly) The Backbencher and Parliament, 1972; Paying for Party Politics, 1975; BBC Guide to Parliament, 1979; (ed jtly) The Socialist Agenda, 1981; (jtly) World Atlas of Elections, 1986; Pocket Guide to the EEC, 1988; Elections in Britain Today, 1991; The Economist Guide to the European Community, 1992, 4th edn as The Economist Guide to the European Union, 1997, 10th edn 2010 (French, German, Polish, Bulgarian, Georgian, Hungarian, Romanian, Serbian, Spanish, Portuguese, Russian and Korean edns); Replacing the Lords, 1995; (jtly) Eminent Europeans, 1996; (ed) Crosland and New Labour, 1999; (ed jtly) The Pro-European Reader, 2001; A Century of Premiers: Salisbury to Blair, 2004; (ed) The Future of Socialism by Anthony Crosland, 50th anniv. edn, 2006; 19th Century Premiers: Pitt to Rosebery, 2008; 18th Century Premiers: Walpole to the Younger Pitt, 2010; The Great Rivalry: Gladstone and Disraeli - a dual biography, 2013; A History of British Prime Ministers: Walpole to Cameron, 2014; contribs to Guardian, Financial Times, TLS, European Voice, The Bulletin, Prospect, and leading newspapers in USA, Canada, Japan, India, Australia and New Zealand. *Recreations:* walking, book-reviewing, family pursuits. *Address:* 16 Albert Street, NW1 7NZ. *Clubs:* Reform; Hampstead Heath Croquet.

LÉOTARD, François Gérard Marie; European Union Special Envoy to Macedonia, 2001; *b* Cannes, 26 March 1942; *s* of André Léotard and Antoinette (*née* Tomasi); *m* 1992, Ysabel Duret; one *s* one *d*. *Educ:* Paris Law Univ.; Institut d'Etudes Politiques de Paris; Ecole Nationale d'Administration. Various appts in French admin, 1968–76; Mem., Nat. Assembly, 1978–86, 1988–92, 1995–2002; Minister of Culture and Communication, 1986–88; Minister of Defence, 1993–95. Mayor of Fréjus, 1977–92, 1993–97; Member: General Council, Var, 1980–88; Regl Council, Provence. Republican Party (Parti Républicain): Gen. Sec., 1982–88; Pres., 1988–90 and 1995–97; Hon. Pres., 1990–95; Pres., UDF, 1996–98. *Publications:* A Mots Découverts, 1987; Culture: les chemins de printemps, 1988; La Ville Aimée: mes chemins de Fréjus, 1989; Pendant la Crise, le Spectacle Continue, 1989; Adresse au Président des Républiques Françaises, 1991; Place de la République, 1992; Ma Liberté, 1995; Pour l'honneur, 1997; Je vous hais tous avec douceur, 2000; Paroles d'immortels, 2001; La Couleur des femmes, 2002; A mon frère qui n'est pas mort, 2003; Ça va mal finir, 2008; Habitare Secum, 2011.

LEPAGE, Robert, CC 2009 (OC 1995); OQ 1999; Director and President, RLI, since 1988; Founder, President and Artistic Director, Ex Machina Theatre Company, since 1994; *b* 12 Dec. 1957; *s* of Fernand and Germaine Lepage. *Educ:* Ecole Joseph-François Perreault, Quebec City; Conservatoire d'Art Dramatique de Québec. Joined Théâtre Repère, as actor, 1980, also Jt Artistic Dir and writer, 1986–89; Artistic Dir, Théâtre Français, Ottawa Nat. Arts Theatre, 1989–93; Artistic Dir, La Caserne, 1997–. *Stage* includes: *joint writer, director and actor:* Théâtre Repère: Circulations, 1984; The Dragons' Trilogy, 1985; Vinci (one-man show), 1986; Polygraph, 1987; Tectonic Plates, 1988; Needles and Opium (one-man show), 1991; The Far Side of the Moon (one-man show), 2000; The Andersen Project (one-man show), 2006; 887 (one-man show), 2015; *director:* Carmen, Théâtre d'Bon'Humeur, 1983; Le songe d'une nuit d'été, Théâtre du Nouveau Monde, Montreal, 1988; A Midsummer Night's Dream, RNT, London, 1992; Le Cycle William Shakespeare, Quebec City, Maubeuge, Frankfurt and Paris, 1992; Macbeth and The Tempest, Tokyo Globe Theatre, Tokyo, 1993; Secret World Tour (Peter Gabriel), 1993; Les Sept branches de la rivière Ota (also jt writer), 1994; Elseneur (one-man show, also adapter and actor), 1995; La géométrie des miracles (world tour; also jt writer), 1998; Zulu Time, 1999; La Damnation de Faust, 1999; Growing Up Tour (Peter Gabriel), 2002; KÀ (Cirque du Soleil show), LA, 2004; 1984, Royal Opera, Covent Garden, 2005; The Rake's Progress, 2007; Lipsynch, 2007; The Blue Dragon, 2008; Eonnagata, Sadler's Wells, 2009; The Nightingale and Other Short Fables, COC Toronto, 2009; Totem (Cirque du Soleil show), 2010; Shakespeare's La Tempête, Quebec City, 2011; Wagner's Ring Cycle, NY Met. Opera; Das Rheingold, 2010; Die Walküre, Siegfried, 2011; Götterdämmerung, 2012; Thomas Adès' The Tempest, Quebec City and NY Met. Opera, 2012; Playing Cards 1: SPADES, Roundhouse, 2013; TV advertisements; *films include: writer and director:* Le Confessionnal, 1995; Le Polygraphe, 1996; Nô, 1997; Possible Worlds, 2000. Chevalier de l'Ordre des Arts et des Lettres (France), 1990. Europe Th. Prize, EC, 2007; Governor General's Performing Arts Award, 2009; Eugene McDermott Award in the Arts, MIT, 2012; Glenn Gould Prize, 2013. *Address:* c/o Lynda Beaulieu, 103 Dalhousie Street, Quebec City, QC G1K 4B9, Canada.

LEPINE, Very Rev. Jeremy John; Dean of Bradford, since 2013; *b* 24 April 1956; *s* of John and Patricia Lepine; *m* 1980, Christine Harvey; one *s* one *d*. *Educ:* Council for Nat. Academic Awards (BA Business); St John's Coll., Nottingham. Ordained deacon, 1984, priest, 1985; Curate, Trinity St Michael, Harrow, 1984–88; Team Vicar, Horley, 1988–95; Evangelism Advr, Croydon Area Mission Team, 1995–2002; Evangelism Advr, Dio. of Southwark, and Hon. Chaplain, Southwark Cath., 1997–2002; Rector, St Leonard, Wollaton, 2002–13; Area Dean, Nottingham N, 2008–13. Hon. Canon, Southwell Minster, 2009–13. *Recreations:* film, theatre, gardening, music. *Address:* The Deanery, 1 Cathedral Close, Bradford BD1 4EG. *T:* (01274) 777722, *Fax:* (01274) 777730.

LE POER TRENCH, family name of **Earl of Clancarty**.

LE POIDEVIN, Nicholas Peter; QC 2010; a Recorder, since 2009; a Deputy High Court Judge, since 2013; *b* Ashbourne, Derbys, 12 Oct. 1950; *s* of Roy Le Poidevin and Barbara Le Poidevin; *m* 1979, Saundra Susan Hicks (*d* 1988); one *d*; partner, Janet Mary Atkinson. *Educ:* Repton Sch.; Trinity Hall, Cambridge (BA 1972; LLB 1973; MA 1975). Called to the Bar, Middle Temple, 1975; Bencher, Lincoln's Inn, 2005. Commons Comr, 2000–10. *Publications:* (ed) Lewin on Trusts, 18th edn 2008 to 19th edn 2015; (contrib.) A Portrait of Lincoln's Inn, 2007; (contrib.) Sham Transactions, 2013. *Recreations:* legal history, concert-going, things other people find boring. *Address:* 12 New Square, Lincoln's Inn, WC2A 3SW. *T:* (020) 7419 8000, *Fax:* (020) 7419 8050. *E:* nicholas.lepoidevin@newsquarechambers.co.uk.

LEPPARD, Adrian Allen, QPM 2012; Commissioner, City of London Police, since 2011; *b* Redhill, Surrey, 11 Feb. 1962; *s* of Norman and Constance Leppard. *Educ:* City Univ. London (MBA 1998). Joined Surrey Police, 1984; various posts up to Divl Comr, 1984–2005; Asst Chief Constable, then Dep. Chief Constable, Kent Police, 2005–10. *Recreations:* paragliding, sailing. *Address:* City of London Police Headquarters, 37 Wood Street, EC2P 2NQ. *T:* (020) 7601 2222. *E:* adrianleppard@cityoflondon.police.uk.

LEPPARD, Captain Keith André, CBE 1977; RN; Secretary, Institute of Brewing, 1977–90; Director Public Relations (Royal Navy), 1974–77; *b* 29 July 1924; *s* of Wilfred Ernest Leppard and Dora Gilmore Keith; *m* 1954, Betty Rachel Smith; one *s* one *d*. *Educ:* Purley Grammar Sch. MRAeS 1973; FCMI (FBIM 1973); FSAE 1985. Entered RN, FAA pilot duties, 1943; Opnl Wartime Service, Fighter Pilot, N Atlantic/Indian Oceans, 1944–45; Fighter Pilot/Flying Instr, Aircraft Carriers and Air Stns, 1946–57; CO 807 Naval Air Sqdn (Aerobatic Display Team, Farnborough), 1958–59; Air Org./Flying Trng Staff appts, 1959–63; Comdr (Air), HMS Victorious, 1963–64; Jt Services Staff Coll., 1964–65; Dir, Naval Officer Appts (Air), 1965–67; Chief Staff Officer (Air), Flag Officer Naval Air Comd, 1967–69; Chief Staff Officer (Ops/Trng), Far East Fleet, 1969–71; CO, Royal Naval Air Stn, Yeovilton, and Flag Captain to Flag Officer Naval Air Comd, 1972–74. Naval ADC to the Queen, 1976–77. *Recreations:* country life, tennis, golf. *Address:* Little Holt, Kingsley Green, Haslemere, Surrey GU27 3LW. *T:* (01428) 642797.

LEPPARD, Raymond John, CBE 1983; conductor, harpsichordist, composer; Music Director, Indianapolis Symphony Orchestra, 1987–2001; *b* 11 Aug. 1927; *s* of A. V. Leppard. *Educ:* Trinity Coll., Cambridge. Fellow of Trinity Coll., Cambridge, and Univ. Lecturer in Music, 1958–68. Hon. Keeper of the Music, Fitzwilliam Museum, 1963–82. Conductor: Covent Garden, Sadler's Wells, Glyndebourne, and abroad; Principal Conductor, BBC Northern Symphony Orchestra, 1972–80; Prin. Guest Conductor, St Louis SO, 1984–93. Hon. RAM 1972; Hon. GSM 1983; Hon. FRCM 1984. Hon. DLitt Univ. of Bath, 1972. Commendatore al Merito della Repubblica Italiana, 1974. *Publications:* realisations of Monteverdi: Il Ballo delle Ingrate, 1958; L'Incoronazione di Poppea, 1962; L'Orfeo, 1965; Il Ritorno d'Ulisse, 1972; realisations of Francesco Cavalli: Messa Concertata, 1966; L'Ormindo, 1967; La Calisto, 1969; Magnificat, 1970; L'Egisto, 1974; L'Orione, 1983; realisation of Rameau's Dardanus, 1980; Authenticity in Music, 1988; Raymond Leppard on Music, 1993; Music Made Me (memoir), 2011; British Academy Italian Lecture, 1969, Procs Royal Musical Assoc. *Recreations:* music, theatre, books, friends. *Address:* 5040 Buttonwood Crescent, Indianapolis, IN 46228–2323, USA. *T:* (317) 259 9020, *Fax:* (317) 259 0916.

LEPPER, David; *b* 15 Sept. 1945; *s* of late Henry George Lepper and Maggie Lepper (*née* Osborne); *m* 1966, Jeane Stroud; one *s* one *d*. *Educ:* St John's C of E Primary Sch., Richmond; Gainsborough Secondary Sch., Richmond; Wimbledon Co. Secondary Sch.; Univ. of Kent (BA Hons); Univ. of Sussex (PGCE); PCL (Dip. Film); Univ. of Sussex (Dip. Media). Teacher: Westlain GS, Brighton, 1968–73; Falmer Sch., Brighton, 1973–96. Mem. (Lab), Brighton BC, 1980–97 (Leader, 1986–87; Mayor, 1993–94). MP (Lab and Co-op) Brighton Pavilion, 1997–2010. Trustee: ARDIS (Alzheimer's and Related Diseases), 1993–; Sussex Beacon, 2010–13; Brighton and Hove Carers' Centre, 2010– (Chm., 2012–). *Publications:* John Wayne, 1986; various articles in film and media jls. *Recreations:* cinema, music, books, watching professional cycling. *Club:* Brighton Trades and Labour.

LEPSCHY, Prof. Giulio Ciro, FBA 1987; Emeritus Professor of Italian, University of Reading, since 2000 (Professor, 1975–97; part-time Professor, 1997–2000); Visiting Professor, University of Cambridge, since 2000; *b* 14 Jan. 1935; *s* of Emilio Lepschy and Sara Castelfranchi; *m* 1962, Anna Laura Momigliano. *Educ:* Univ. of Pisa (Dott. Lett.); Scuola Normale Superiore, Pisa (Dip. Lic. and Perf.). Lib. Doc., Italy. Research, 1957–64, at Univs of Zurich, Oxford, Paris, London, Reading; Lectr 1964, Reader 1967, Univ. of Reading. Mem. Council, Philological Soc., 1984–89, 1992–96; Pres., MHRA, 2001. Corresp. Mem., 1991, Mem., 2011, Accademia della Crusca. Hon. Prof., UCL, 1998; Goggio Vis. Prof., 2000, Adjunct Prof., 2010–, Univ. of Toronto. Hon. Dr, Univ. of Turin, 1998. Serena Medal, British Acad., 2000. Commendatore of the Italian Republic, 2003. *Publications:* A Survey of Structural Linguistics, 1970, new edn 1982; (jtly) The Italian Language Today, 1977, 2nd edn 1988; Saggi di linguistica italiana, 1978; Intorno a Saussure, 1979; Mutamenti di prospettiva nella linguistica, 1981; Nuovi saggi di linguistica italiana, 1989; Sulla linguistica moderna, 1989; Storia della linguistica, 1990; La linguistica del Novecento, 1992; History of Linguistics, 1994; (jtly) L'amanuense analfabeta e altri saggi, 1999; Mother Tongues and Other Reflections on the Italian Language, 2002; Parole, parole, parole e altri saggi di linguistica, 2007; Tradurre e traducibilità, 2009; contribs to learned jls. *Address:* 335 Latymer Court, Hammersmith Road, W6 7LH. *T:* and *Fax:* (020) 8748 7780.

LE QUESNE, Caroline; *see* Lucas, Caroline.

LERCHE-THOMSEN, Kim Stuart, FIA; Founder and Chief Executive, Primetime Retirement (formerly Living Time), since 2004; *b* 2 Sept. 1952; *s* of Paul Lerche-Thomsen and Patricia Lerche-Thomsen (*née* Williams); *m* 1991, Emma Jane Grace Brook; one *s* one *d*. *Educ:* Sevenoaks; Brunel Univ. (BTech). FIA 1984. Dir, Pensions, Prudential, 1991–96; Man. Dir, Prudential Annuities, 1997–2001; Dir, Prudential Assurance Co. Ltd, 1999–2002; Chief Exec., Scottish Amicable, 2001–02; Chm., AssetCo (formerly Asset Investment Gp), 2003–04. FRMetS 1975. *Recreations:* ski-ing, tennis, meteorology. *Address:* Primetime Retirement, Baines House, 4 Midgery Court, Fulwood, Preston PR2 9ZH. *E:* kim.lt@primetimeretirement.co.uk. *Clubs:* Leander, Phyllis Court (Henley-on-Thames).

LEREGO, Prof. Michael John; QC 1995; a Recorder, since 2002; *b* 6 May 1949; *s* of late Leslie Ivor Lerego and Gwendolen Frances Lerego; *m* 1972, Susan Northover; three *d* (one *s* decd). *Educ:* Manchester Grammar Sch.; Haberdashers' Aske's Sch., Elstree; Keble Coll., Oxford (Open Schol.; Dist. Law Mods 1968; Gibbs Prize in Law 1969; BA Jurisp. 1st Cl. 1970; BCL 1st Cl. 1971; MA Oxon 1978). Called to the Bar, Inner Temple, 1972, Bencher, 2006; in practice, 1972–2012; Jt Hd of Chambers, Fountain Ct, 2003–07. Weekender, Queen's Coll., Oxford, 1972–78. Member: Jt Working Party of Law Soc. and Bar on Banking Law, 1987–91; Law Soc.'s Sub-Cttee on Banking Law, 1991–96; an Arbitrator: Lloyd's Modified Arbitration Scheme, 1988–92; Lloyd's Arbitration Scheme, 1993–. Vis. Lectr, 2006–07, Lectr, 2007–08, Sen. Lectr, 2008–09, Prof., 2009–13, Univ. of Law (formerly Coll. of Law). Governor: Wroxham Sch., Potters Bar, 1995–2004. FCIArb 1997; FHEA 2009. *Publications:* (ed jtly) Commercial Court Procedure, 2000; (contrib.) The Law of Bank Payments, 3rd edn 2004, 4th edn 2010; (regulatory editor) Encyclopaedia of Insurance Law, 2007–09; (contrib.) Blackstone's Criminal Practice, 2008–. *Recreation:* watching sport.

LERENIUS, Bo Åke, Hon. CBE 2005; non-executive Chairman: Koole Group, since 2011; Hector Rail, since 2014; Board Director: Westway Group, since 2012; ARR, since 2013; *b* 11 Dec. 1946; *s* of Åke Lerenius and Elisabeth Lerenius; *m* 1st (marr. diss.); one *s* one *d*; 2nd, 2002, Gunilla Jöhncke. *Educ:* St Petri, Malmö, Sweden; Westchester High Sch., LA; Univ. of Lund, Sweden (BA Business Admin). Div. Dir, Tarkett (part of Swedish Match Gp), 1983–85; Gp Pres. and CEO, Ernstromgruppen, 1985–92; Gp Chief Exec., Stena Line, 1992–98; Vice Chm., Stena Line and Dir, New Business Investments, Stena AB, 1998–99; Gp Chief Exec., ABP Hldgs plc, 1999–2007 (non-exec. Dir, 2007). Non-executive Director: G4S plc (formerly Securicor plc, then Group 4 Securicor), 2004–13; Land Securities Gp plc, 2004–12; Thomas Cook Gp plc, 2007–13; non-executive Chairman: Mouchel plc, 2009–11; Brunswick Rail, 2011. Hon. Vice Pres., Swedish Chamber of Commerce for the UK, 2010 (Chm., 2007–10). Hon. DBA London Metropolitan, 2006. *Recreations:* golf, shooting. *Address:* Strandvägen 7B, 11456 Stockholm, Sweden. *Clubs:* Royal Automobile; Royal Bachelors (Gothenburg); Sällskapet (Stockholm); Falsterbo Golf, Halmstad Golf (Sweden).

LE ROY LADURIE, Prof. Emmanuel Bernard; Commandeur de la Légion d'Honneur, 1996; Commandeur de l'Ordre des Arts et des Lettres; Professor of History of Modern Civilisation, Collège de France, 1973–99, now Honorary Professor; *b* 19 July 1929; *s* of Jacques Le Roy Ladurie and Léontine (*née* Dauger); *m* 1955, Madeleine Pupponi; one *s* one *d*. *Educ:* Univ. of Sorbonne (agrégé d'histoire); DèsL 1952. Teacher, Lycée de Montpellier,

1955–57; Res. Assistant, CNRS, 1957–60; Assistant, Faculté des Lettres de Montpellier, 1960–63; Asst Lectr, 1963, Dir of Studies, 1965–, Ecole Pratique des Hautes Etudes; Lectr, Faculté des Lettres de Paris, 1969; Prof., Sorbonne, 1970; UER Prof. of Geography and Social Sci., Univ. de Paris VII, 1971–. General Administrator, Bibliothèque Nationale, 1987–94 (Pres., Conseil scientifique, 1994–99). Mem. de l'Institut, Acad. des Scis morales et politiques, 1993–. Internat. Mem. (formerly Foreign Mem.), Amer. Philosophical Soc., 2000; Foreign Mem., Polish Acad. of Scis, 2000; For. Hon. Mem., American Acad. of Scis, 1984; Hon. FBA 1985. Hon. doctorates incl. Geneva, 1978; Michigan, 1981; Leeds, 1982; East Anglia, 1985; Leicester, York, 1986; Carnegie Mellon, Pittsburgh, 1987; Durham, 1987; Hull, 1990; Dublin, 1992; Albany, Haifa, Montréal, Oxford, 1993; Pennsylvania, 1995; HEC, Paris, 1999. *Publications:* Histoire du Languedoc, 1963; Les Paysans du Languedoc, 1966; Histoire du climat depuis l'an mil, 1967, 2nd edn 1983; Le Territoire de l'historien, vol. 1 1973, vol. 2 1978; Montaillou: village occitan 1294–1324, 1975; (jtly) Histoire économique et sociale de la France, vol. 1 1450–1660, vol. 2 Histoire de la France rurale, 1976; (with B. Bray) Montaillou: Cathars and Catholics in a French village 1294–1324, 1978; (with B. Bray) Montaillou: the promised land of error, 1978, 2008; Le Carnaval de Romans 1579–1580 (Prix Pierre Lafue), 1980; L'Argent, l'Amour et la Mort en pays d'Oc, 1980; (jtly) Inventaire des campagnes, 1980; (jtly) L'Histoire urbaine de la France, vol. 3, 1981; (with J. Goy) Tithe and Agrarian History from the Fourteenth to the Nineteenth Century, 1982, repr. 2008; Paris—Montpellier, 1982; La Sorcière de Jasmin, 1982; Parmi les historiens, 1983; Pierre Prion: scribe, 1987; L'Histoire de France: l'état royal 1460–1610, 1987; (ed) Monarchies, 1987; L'Ancien Régime, 1991; Le siècle des Platter 1499–1628, vol. 1 Le mendiant et le professeur, 1995, vol. 2 Le voyage de Thomas Platter 1595–1599, 2000; vol. 3 L'Europe de Thomas Platter, 2006; (ed jtly) Mémoires de Jacques Le Roy Ladurie, 1997; Saint-Simon et le système de la cour, 1997; L'Historien, le chiffre et le texte, 1997; Histoire de la France des Régions, 2001; Histoire des paysans français de la peste noire à la Révolution, 2002; Histoire humaine et comparée du climat, vol. 1, 2004, vol. 2, 2006, vol. 3, 2009; Personnages et caractères, 2005; Ouverture, société, pouvoir, 2005; Trente-trois questions sur l'histoire du climat: du Moyen Age à nos jours, 2010; Naissance de l'histoire du climat, 2012; Une vie avec l'Histoire, 2014; Les paysans français d'Ancien Régime du 14e au 18e siècle, 2015. *Address:* Collège de France, 11 place Marcelin Berthelot, 75231 Paris cedex 05, France; (home) 88 rue d'Alleray, 75015 Paris, France.

LERWILL, Robert Earl, FCA; Chairman, Synergy Health (formerly Healthcare) plc, 2010–12 (non-executive Director, 2005–12); *b* 21 Jan. 1952; *s* of Colin and Patricia Lerwill; *m* 1994, Nicola Keddie; two *s* three *d*. *Educ:* Nottingham Univ. (BA Hons Industrial Econs 1973); Harvard Univ. (AMP 1996). FCA 1977. Articled clerk to Sen. Manager, Arthur Andersen & Co., 1973–86; Gp Finance Dir, WPP Gp plc, 1986–96; Cable & Wireless plc: Exec. Dir, Finance, 1997–2002; CEO, Cable & Wireless Regl, 2000–03; Dep. Gp CEO, 2002–03; Chief Exec., Aegis Gp plc, 2005–08 (non-exec. Dir, 2000–05). Non-executive Director: British American Tobacco plc, 2005–13; Transcom Worldwide SA, 2010–12; ITC Ltd (India), 2013–; DJI Hldgs plc, 2014–; Spire Healthcare plc, 2014–. Ind. Dir, Payments Council, 2014–. Dir/Trustee, Anthony Nolan Trust, 2002–07. *Recreations:* travel, motoring, motor cruising, shooting. *Clubs:* Old Blues Rugby (Motspur Park); Twickenham Yacht, Royal Burnham Yacht, Crouch Yacht.

LESCHLY, Jan; founding Chairman and Partner, Care Capital LLC, since 2000; *b* 11 Sept. 1940; *m* 1963, Dr Lotte Engelbredt; four *s*. *Educ:* Copenhagen Coll. of Pharmacy (MSc Pharmacy); Copenhagen Sch. of Econs and Business Admin (BS Business Admin). Pharmaceutical industry, 1972–2000: Exec. Vice Pres. and Pres., Pharmaceutical Div., Novo Industries A/S, Denmark, 1972–79; Squibb Corporation: joined 1979; Vice-Pres., Commercial Develt, 1979–81; US Pres., 1981–84; Gp Vice-Pres. and Dir, 1984–86; Exec. Vice-Pres., 1986–88; Pres. and Chief Operating Officer, 1988–90; Chm., SmithKline Beecham Pharmaceuticals, 1990–94; Chief Exec., SmithKline Beecham, 1994–2000. Member, Board of Directors: Amer. Express Co.; Viacom Corp.; Ventro Corp.; APM-Maersk Gp; Mem. Internat. Adv. Bd, DaimlerChrysler. Member: British Pharma Group; Bd of Dirs, Pharmaceutical Res. and Manufrs of America; Pharmaceutical Res. and Manufrs Foundn; Bd of Trustees, Nat. Foundn for Infectious Diseases; Dean's Adv. Council, Emory Univ. Business Sch. *Address:* Care Capital LLC, 47 Hulfish Street, Suite 310, Princeton, NJ 08542, USA.

LESCOEUR, Bruno Jean; Chief Executive Officer, Edison Spa, Italy, since 2012; Member, Executive Committee, Electricité de France, since 2004; *b* 19 Nov. 1953; *m* 1976, Janick Dreyer; two *s* one *d*. *Educ:* Ecole Polytechnique, Paris. Electricité de France (EDF): responsible for pricing, 1978–87, for distribn of gas and electricity, Mulhouse, France, 1987–89; Rep., as Founder Mem., Electricity Pool in London, 1990; Head, Distribution Unit, EDF and GDF, South of France, 1991–93; Dep. Chief Financial Officer, 1994–98; Chm. and Chief Exec., London Electricity Gp plc, 1999–2002; Exec. Vice-Pres., Head of Generation and Trading, 2002–04; Sen. Exec. Vice-Pres., 2004–; Head of Internat. and Gas, 2005–09. Chevalier: Ordre National du Mérite (France), 2001; Légion d'honneur (France), 2012. *Recreation:* sailing. *Address:* (office) Foro Buonaparte 31, 20121 Milan, Italy; (office) 22–30 Avenue de Wagram, 75008 Paris, France.

LESIRGE, Ruth; Head of Governance Practice, 2006–12, and Senior Visiting Fellow, since 2010, Cass Business School, City University (Visiting Fellow, 2006–10); Director, RLP Ltd, and independent consultant, not-for-profit organisations, since 2003; Chief Executive, Mental Health Foundation, 2000–02; *b* 9 Aug. 1945; *d* of Alfred Brandler and Mirjam Brandler; *m* 1969, John Lesirge; two *s*. *Educ:* Manchester Univ. (Cert Ed 1967; Cert Children with Learning Difficulties 1972); Univ. of London Inst. of Educn (Dip. Adult and Contg Educn, 1984); Office of Public Management/Sheffield Hallam Univ. (Post-grad. Cert. in Mgt 2000). Secondary sch. teacher of Eng. and literacy, Haringey, 1967–72; Adult Literacy Develt Worker, Islington and Haringey, 1973–83; Islington Adult Education Institute: Hd, Women's Educn, 1983–85; Hd, Soc. and Cultural Studies Dept, 1985–87; Hd of Area, Camden Adult Educn Inst., 1987–89; Principal, Adult Educn Service, London Bor. Waltham Forest, 1989–92; Chief Exec., Retail Trust charity, 1992–99. Member: Appraisal Cttee, NHS NICE, 2001–04; Private Inquiry, DoH, 2002–05. Vice-Chm., ACENVO, subseq. ACEVO, 1998–2002 (Trustee, 1995–2002); Trustee: Centre for Policy on Ageing, 1997–2002; Nat. Foundn for Entrepreneurship, 2000–; Founding Trustee and Dir, Assoc. of Chairs, 2013– (Chair, 2015–). Hon. Lectr Medical Educn, Univ. of London, 1996. Churchill Fellow, 1981–82; Commonwealth Trust Bursary, 1988. *Publications:* (jtly) On Site, 1976; (jtly) Working Together: an approach to functional literacy, 1977; (jtly) Write Away, 1979; Images and Understandings: sequences for writing and discussion, 1984; (jtly) Appraising the Chief Executive, 2002; (jtly) Tools for Success, 2004, 2nd edn 2009; (jtly) Trustee Recruitment Toolkit, 2006; (jtly) Getting Ready for Enterprise, 2007; (ed jtly) Guide for Chairs, 2014; articles on not-for-profit boards and governance for third sector pubns, 2012–14. *Recreations:* theatre, gardening. *Address:* 100 Holden Road, N12 7DY. *T:* (020) 8445 1864, 07971 109248.

LESITER, Ven. Malcolm Leslie; Archdeacon of Bedford, 1993–2003, now Emeritus; *b* 31 Jan. 1937; *m*; four *d*. *Educ:* Cranleigh Sch.; Selwyn Coll., Cambridge (BA 1961; MA 1965); Cuddesdon Coll., Oxford. Ordained deacon, 1963, priest, 1964; Curate, Eastney, 1963–66; Curate, 1966–71, Team Vicar, 1971–73, St Paul, Hemel Hempstead; Vicar: All Saints, Leavesden, 1973–88; Radlett, 1988–93. RD, Watford, 1981–88. Mem., Gen. Synod, 1985–2000. Chm., St Albans Ministerial Trng Scheme, 1980–82. *Address:* 349 Ipswich Road, Colchester, Essex CO4 0HN.

LESLIE, family name of **Earl of Rothes**.

LESLIE, Dame (Alison) Mariot, DCMG 2012 (CMG 2005); HM Diplomatic Service, retired; UK Permanent Representative, UK Delegation to NATO, 2010–14; *b* Edinburgh, 25 June 1954; *d* of Stewart Forson Sanderson and Alison Mary Sanderson; *m* 1978, Andrew David Leslie; two *d*. *Educ:* George Watson's Ladies' Coll., Edinburgh; Leeds Girls' High Sch.; St Hilda's Coll., Oxford (BA 1975). Scottish Office, 1975; joined HM Diplomatic Service, 1977: Singapore, 1978–81; Bonn, 1982–86; Paris (on secondment to Quai d'Orsay), 1990–92; Head, Envmt, Sci. and Energy Dept, FCO, 1992–93; Scottish Office Industry Dept, 1993–95; Head, Policy Planning Staff, FCO, 1996–98; Minister and Dep. Head of Mission, Rome, 1998–2001; Ambassador to Norway, 2002–06; Dir, Defence and Strategic Threats, 2006–07, Dir Gen., Defence and Intelligence, 2007–10, FCO; Mem., Jt Intelligence Cttee, 2007–10. Mem. Exec. Council, RUSI, 2006–10. DUniv Heriot-Watt, 2013. *Recreations:* food, travel, argument.

LESLIE, Dr Andrew Greig William, FRS 2001; Senior Staff Scientist, MRC Laboratory of Molecular Biology, Cambridge, since 1991 (Staff Scientist, 1988–91); *b* 26 Oct. 1949; *s* of John and Margaret Leslie; *m* 1977, Catherine Alice Fuchs; two *s* one *d* (and one *d* decd). *Educ:* Jesus Coll., Cambridge (BA, MA); Univ. of Manchester (PhD 1974). Res. Asst, Purdue Univ., Indiana, 1974–79; Res. Asst, 1979–83, MRC Sen. Fellow, 1983–88, ICSTM. *Publications:* numerous contribs to scientific jls incl. Nature, Science, Cell, Molecular Cell. *Recreations:* walking, cycling, swimming, films, music. *Address:* MRC Laboratory of Molecular Biology, Francis Crick Avenue, Cambridge CB2 0QH. *T:* (01223) 267072.

LESLIE, Dame Ann (Elizabeth Mary), DBE 2007; journalist and broadcaster; *b* Pakistan, 28 Jan. 1941; *d* of Norman Leslie and Theodora (*née* McDonald); *m* 1969, Michael Fletcher; one *d*. *Educ:* Presentation Convent, Matlock, Derbyshire; Convent of the Holy Child, Mayfield, Sussex; Lady Margaret Hall, Oxford (BA). Daily Express, 1962–67; freelance, 1967–: regular contributor to Daily Mail. Variety Club Women of the Year Award for journalism and broadcasting, 1981; British Press Awards Feature Writer of the Year, 1981, 1989; British Press Awards Commendation, 1980, 1983, 1985, 1987, 1991, 1996, 1999; Feature Writer of the Year Award, What the Papers Say, Granada Television, 1991; Lifetime Achievement Award, Media Soc., 1997; James Cameron Meml Award for internat. reporting, James Cameron Meml Trust, 1999; Gerald Barry Lifetime Achievement Award, BBC2/Granada/What the Papers Say, 2001; Edgar Wallace Award for outstanding reporting, London Press Club, 2002; Foreign Corresp. of the Year, BBC/Granada/What the Papers Say, 2004; Outstanding Contribution to Journalism Award, Next Century Foundn, 2012. *Publications:* Killing My Own Snakes (memoir), 2008. *Recreation:* family life. *Address:* c/o Daily Mail, Northcliffe House, 2 Derry Street, Kensington, W8 5TT. *T:* (020) 7938 6120, *Fax:* (020) 7267 9914. *E:* aemleslie@aol.com.

LESLIE, Charlotte Ann; MP (C) Bristol North West, since 2010; *b* Liverpool, Aug. 1978; *d* of Ian and Jane Leslie. *Educ:* Badminton Sch.; Millfield Sch.; Balliol Coll., Oxford (BA Lit. Hum.). Special Advr to Shadow Sec. of State for Educn and Skills, 2006; Educn Associate, Young Foundn, 2008. Member: Educn Select Cttee, 2010–13; Health Select Cttee, 2013–15. Back Bencher of the Year, Spectator, 2013. *Address:* House of Commons, SW1A 0AA. *T:* (020) 7219 7026, *Fax:* (020) 7219 0921. *E:* charlotte.leslie.mp@parliament.uk.

LESLIE, Christopher Michael; MP (Lab) Nottingham East, since 2010; *b* 28 June 1972; *s* of Michael N. Leslie and Dania K. Leslie; *m* Nicola Murphy; one *d*. *Educ:* Bingley Grammar Sch.; Univ. of Leeds (BA Hons Pol. and Parly Studies 1994; MA Indust. and Labour Studies 1996). Research Assistant: Rep. Bernie Sanders, US Congress, 1992; Gordon Brown, MP, 1993; Adminr, Bradford Labour Party, 1995–97; Researcher, Barry Seal, MEP, 1997. Dir, New Local Govt Network, 2005–10. MP (Lab) Shipley, 1997–2005; contested (Lab) same seat, 2005. PPS to Minister of State, Cabinet Office, 1998–2001; Parly Sec., Cabinet Office, 2001–02; Parly Under-Sec., ODPM, 2002–03; Parly Under-Sec. of State, DCA, 2003–05; Shadow Financial Sec. to HM Treasury, 2010–13; Shadow Chief Sec. to HM Treasury, 2013–15; Shadow Chancellor of the Exchequer, 2015. Mem. (Lab), Bradford MDC, 1994–98. *Recreations:* music, tennis, travel. *Address:* House of Commons, SW1A 0AA.

LESLIE, (Harman) John; Master, Queen's Bench Division, High Court of Justice, since 1996 (Deputy Senior Master, then Acting Senior Master and Queen's Remembrancer, 2013–14); *b* 8 April 1946; *s* of Percy Leslie and Sheila Mary Leslie (*née* Harris); *m* 1st, 1971, Alix Helen Cohen (marr. diss. 1980); two *s*; 2nd, 1986, Valerie Gibson. *Educ:* Dover Coll.; Clare Coll., Cambridge (BA 1968). Called to the Bar, Middle Temple, 1969, Bencher, 2001; in practice at the Bar, 1969–96. Member: Civil Procedure Rule Cttee, 1997–2002; Vice-Chancellor's Wkg Party on Civil Procedure Practice Directions, 1997–2000. Gov., Dover Coll., 1974– (Mem. Council, 1975–84). *Publications:* (contrib.) Halsbury's Laws of England, 4th edn, 1999, reissued 2001; (ed jtly) Civil Court Practice, 1999–; Civil Court Manual, 1999; (contrib.) Atkin's Court Forms, 2001–. *Recreations:* France, bridge, woodworking. *Address:* Royal Courts of Justice, Strand, WC2A 2LL. *Clubs:* Royal Automobile; Slinfold Cricket (Hon. Life Mem.).

LESLIE, Prof. Ian Malcolm, PhD; FREng 2010; Robert Sansom Professor of Computer Science, since 1998 and Head of Department, 1999–2004, University of Cambridge Computer Laboratory; Pro-Vice-Chancellor, University of Cambridge, 2004–09; Fellow of Christ's College, Cambridge, since 1985; *b* 11 Feb. 1955; *s* of Douglas Alexander Leslie and Phyllis Margaret Leslie; *m* 1st, 1986, Patricia Valerie Vyoral (marr. diss. 2000); one *s* one *d*; 2nd, 2001, Celia Mary Denton (marr. diss. 2004); one *d*; 3rd, 2013, Anne Elizabeth Willenbrock. *Educ:* Univ. of Toronto (BASc 1977; MASc 1979); Darwin Coll., Cambridge (PhD 1983). Asst Lectr, 1983–86, Lectr, 1986–98, Univ. of Cambridge Computer Lab. Dir, Cambridge Innovation Capital, 2013–. FREng 2010. *Publications:* guest ed. and contrib. on selected areas in communication to IEEE Jl. *Address:* Christ's College, Cambridge CB2 3BU.

LESLIE, John; *see* Leslie, H. J.

LESLIE, Sir John (Norman Ide), 4th Bt *cr* 1876; *b* 6 Dec. 1916; *s* of Sir (John Randolph) Shane Leslie, 3rd Bt and Marjorie (*d* 1951), *y d* of Henry C. Ide, Vermont, USA; *S* father, 1971. *Educ:* Downside; Magdalene College, Cambridge (BA 1938). Captain, Irish Guards; served War of 1939–45 (prisoner-of-war). Kt of Honour and Devotion, SMO Malta, 1947; KCSG 1958. *Publications:* Never a Dull Moment (memoirs), 2006. *Recreations:* ornithology, ecology. *Heir: nephew* Shaun Rudolph Christopher Leslie [*b* 4 June 1947; *m* 1987, Charlotte Byng (marr. diss. 1989)]. *Address:* Castle Leslie, Glaslough, Co. Monaghan, Ireland. *Clubs:* Travellers; Circolo della Caccia (Rome).

LESLIE, Dame Mariot; *see* Leslie, Dame A. M.

LESLIE, Stephen Windsor; QC 1993; Leader, South Eastern Circuit, 2009–10; Advocate, Public Defender Service, since 2014; *b* 21 April 1947; *s* of Leslie Leonard, (Lou), Leslie and Celia Leslie (*née* Schulsinger); partner, 2006, Melissa Loiuse Barbara Coutinho; one *s* two *d* by previous marriages. *Educ:* Brighton Coll.; King's Coll. London (LLB). Called to the Bar, Lincoln's Inn, 1971, Bencher, 2001. Chm., Commonwealth in England Barristers' Assoc., 2011–14. Liveryman, Feltmakers' Co., 1998–. *Publications:* articles in The Times and New Law Jl. *Recreation:* globe trotting with Melissa. *Address:* 102 Petty France, SW1H 9AJ. *Clubs:* Carlton; Thunderers'.

LESLIE MELVILLE, family name of **Earl of Leven and Melville**.

LESOURNE, Jacques François; Commandeur de la Légion d'Honneur, 2010; Commandeur de l'ordre National du Mérite, 1981; Officier des Palmes Académiques, 1995; Directeur-gérant, Le Monde, 1991–94; Professor of Economics, Conservatoire National des Arts et Métiers, since 1974; *b* 26 Dec. 1928; *s* of André Lesourne and Simone Guille; *m* 1961, Odile Melin; one *s* two *d* (and one *s* decd). *Educ:* Ecole Polytechnique; Ecole Nationale Supérieure des Mines, Paris. Head, Econ. Dept, French Coal Mines, 1954–57; Directeur général, later Pres., SEMA, 1958–75; Dir, Interfutures Project, OECD, 1976–79. Pres., Internat. Fedn of OR Socs, 1986–88; Vice-President: Internat. Inst. for Applied Systems Analysis, 1973–79; Centre for European Policy Studies, 1987–93; Member Council: Inst. of Mgt Science, 1976–79; Eur. Econ. Assoc., 1984–89. Pres., Futuribles International, 1993–. Mem., Acad. des Technologies, 2000–. Harold Lander Prize, Canadian OR Soc., 1991. *Publications:* Technique économique et gestion industrielle, 1958 (Economic Technique and Industrial Management, 1962); Le Calcul économique, 1964; Du bon usage de l'étude économique dans l'entreprise, 1966; (jtly) Matière grise année O, 1970 (The Management Revolution, 1971); Le Calcul économique, théorie et applications, 1972 (Cost-Benefit Analysis and Economic Theory, 1975); Modèles économiques de croissance de l'entreprise, 1972; (jtly) Une Nouvelle industrie: la matière grise, 1973; Les Systèmes de destin, 1976; A Theory of the Individual for Economic Analysis, 1977; (jtly) L'Analyse des décisions d'aménagement regional, 1979; Demain la France dans le monde, 1980; Les Mille Sentiers de l'avenir, 1982 (World Perspectives—a European Assessment, 1982); (jtly) Facilitating Development in a Changing Third World, 1983; Soirs et lendemains de fête: journal d'un homme tranquille, 1981–84 (autobiog.), 1984; (jtly) La gestion des villes, analyse des décisions d'économie urbaine, 1985; (jtly) La Fin des habitudes, 1985; L'Entreprise et ses futurs, 1985; L'après-Communisme, de l'Atlantique à l'Oural, 1990 (After-communism, from the Atlantic to the Urals, 1991); L'economie de l'ordre et du désordre, 1991 (The Economics of Order and Disorder, 1992); Vérités et mensonges sur le chômage, 1995; Le modèle français, grandeur et décadence, 1998; Un homme de notre siècle, 2000; (jtly) Leçons de microéconomie evolutionniste, 2003; Démocratie, marché et gouvernance, 2004; (jtly) Evolutionary Microeconomics, 2006; (jtly) FutuRIS, la recherche et l'innovation en France (annually), 2006–; Les crises et le vingt et unième siècle, 2009; Les temps de la prospective, 2012; L'Europe à l'heure de son crépuscule?, 2014. *Recreation:* piano. *Address:* 52 rue de Vaugirard, 75006 Paris, France.

LESSELS, Norman, CBE 1993; Chairman, Cairn Energy PLC, 1991–2002 (Director, 1988–2002); *b* 2 Sept. 1938; *s* of John Clark Lessels and Gertrude Margaret Ellen Lessels (*née* Jack); *m* 1st, 1960, Gillian Durward Lessels (*née* Clark) (*d* 1979); one *s* (and one *s* one *d* decd); 2nd, 1981, Christine Stevenson Lessels (*née* Hitchman). *Educ:* Melville Coll.; Edinburgh Acad. CA (Scotland) 1961. CA apprentice with Graham Smart & Annan, Edinburgh, 1955–60; with Thomson McLintock & Co., London, 1960–61; Partner, Wallace & Somerville, Edinburgh, merged with Whinney Murray & Co., 1969, latterly Ernst & Whinney, 1962–80; Partner, 1980–93, Sen. Partner, 1993–98, Chiene & Tait, CA. Director: Standard Life Assurance Co., 1978–2002 (Dep. Chm., 1982–88; Chm., 1988–98); Scottish Eastern Investment Trust, 1980–99; Bank of Scotland, 1988–97; Havelock Europa, 1989–98 (Chm., 1993–98); Robert Wiseman Dairies, 1994–2003; Martin Currie Portfolio Investment Trust, 1999–2001. Pres., Inst. of Chartered Accountants of Scotland, 1987–88. *Recreations:* golf, bridge, music. *Address:* 15 India Street, Edinburgh EH3 6HA. *T:* (0131) 225 5596. *Clubs:* New (Edinburgh); Hon. Company of Edinburgh Golfers, Royal & Ancient Golf.

LESSING, Charlotte; Editor of Good Housekeeping, 1973–87; freelance writer; *b* 14 May; *m* 1948, Walter B. Lessing (*d* 1989); three *d*. *Educ:* Henrietta Barnett Sch.; evening classes. Univ. of London Dipl. Eng. Lit. Journalism and public relations: New Statesman and Nation; Royal Society of Medicine; Lilliput (Hulton Press); Notley Public Relations; Good Housekeeping: Dep. Editor, 1964–73; Editor, 1973–87; Founder Editor, Country Living, 1985–86. PPA Editor of the Year (for Good Housekeeping), 1982; Wine Writer of the Year, Wine Guild/Taittinger, 1995. Ordre du Mérite Agricole (France), 1996. *Publications:* short stories, travel and feature articles; monthly wine page in The Lady, 1991.

LESSOF, Leila, OBE 2000; FRCP, FFPH; Chairman, Moorfields Eye Hospital NHS Trust, 1998–2001; *b* 4 June 1932; *d* of Lionel Liebster and Renée (*née* Segalov); *m* 1960, Maurice Hart Lessof, *qv*; one *s* two *d*. *Educ:* Queen's Coll., Harley St; Royal Free Hosp. Sch. of Medicine (MB BS; DMRD). FFPH (FFPHM 1986); FRCP 2000. Jun. posts, Royal Free Hosp., London Hosp. and UCH; Consultant Radiologist and Clinical Tutor, Hackney Hosp., 1964–78; Registrar in Public Health Medicine, KCH and Guy's Hosp., 1978–82; Director of Public Health: Islington HA, 1982–90; Kensington, Chelsea and Westminster HA, 1990–95; Chm., Westminster Assoc. for Mental Health, 1995–98. *Recreations:* opera, theatre, travel. *Address:* 8 John Spencer Square, N1 2LZ. *T:* (020) 7226 0919.

LESSOF, Prof. Maurice Hart, FRCP; Professor of Medicine, University of London at United Medical and Dental Schools (Guy's Hospital), 1971–89, now Emeritus; *b* 4 June 1924; *s* of Noah and Fanny Lessof; *m* 1960, Leila Liebster (*see* L. Lessof); one *s* two *d*. *Educ:* City of London Sch.; King's Coll., Cambridge (MA 1945; MD 1956). Appts on junior staff of Guy's Hosp., Canadian Red Cross Memorial Hosp., Johns Hopkins Hosp., etc; Clinical Immunologist and Physician, Guy's Hosp., 1967. Chairman: SE Thames Regl Med. Audit Cttee, 1990–91; Lewisham NHS Trust, 1993–97 (Dep. Chm., Guy's and Lewisham NHS Trust, 1991–93); Royal Hospitals NHS Trust, 1998–99. Adviser on Allergy, DHSS, 1982–91. Vice-Pres. and Sen. Censor, RCP, 1987–88; Past Pres., British Soc. for Allergy. Mem. Senate, London Univ., 1981–85. Mem., Johns Hopkins Soc. of Scholars, 1991. FKC 2005. *Publications:* (ed) Immunological Aspects of Cardiovascular Diseases, 1981; (ed) Immunological and Clinical Aspects of Allergy, 1984 (Spanish and Portuguese edns, 1987); (ed) Clinical Reactions to Food, 1983; (ed) Allergy: an international textbook, 1987; Food Intolerance, 1992 (Spanish edn 1996); Food Allergy: issues for the food industry, 1997. *Recreations:* sculpting, painting. *Address:* 8 John Spencer Square, Canonbury, N1 2LZ. *T:* (020) 7226 0919. *Club:* Athenæum.

LESSORE, John Viviand; artist; *b* 16 June 1939; *s* of Frederick and Helen Lessore; *m* 1962, Paule Marie Reveille; four *s*. *Educ:* Merchant Taylors' Sch.; Slade Sch. of Fine Art. *Principal exhibitions:* London: Beaux Arts Gall., 1965; New Art Centre, 1971; Theo Waddington, 1981; Stoppenbach & Delestre, 1983, 1985; Nigel Greenwood, 1990; Theo Waddington and Robert Stoppenbach, 1994; Theo Waddington Fine Art, 1997; Berkeley Sq. Gall., 2002; Annely Juda Fine Art, 2004; Kings Place, Thomas Williams Fine Art, 2013; Solomon Gall., Dublin, 1995; Miriam Shiell Fine Art, Toronto, 1997; Wolsey Art Gall., Christchurch Mansion, Ipswich, 1999; Ranger's House, Blackheath, 2000; Annandale Gall., Sydney, 2005; Univ. Gall., Newcastle, 2013; Norwich Castle, Norwich Univ. of the Arts, 2014; *works in public collections* include: Leicester Educn Cttee; Arts Council; Royal Acad.; Tate Gall.; Contemporary Arts Soc.; Norwich Castle; British Council; Accenture; NPG; BM. Co-founder, Prince's Drawing Sch., 2000. Trustee, Nat. Gall., 2003–11. 1st Prize, Korn/Ferry Internat. Public Award, 1991; Lynn Painter-Stainers' 1st Prize and Gold Medal, 2006. *Address:* c/o Thomas Williams Fine Art, 22 Old Bond Street, W1S 4PY. *T:* (020) 7491 1485, *Fax:* (020) 7408 0197. *E:* john.lessore@gmail.com.

LESTER, family name of **Baron Lester of Herne Hill**.

LESTER OF HERNE HILL, Baron *cr* 1993 (Life Peer), of Herne Hill in the London Borough of Southwark; **Anthony Paul Lester;** QC 1975; QC (NI); a Recorder, 1987–93; *b* 3 July 1936; *e s* of Harry and Kate Lester; *m* 1971, Catherine Elizabeth Debora Wassey; one *s* one *d*. *Educ:* City of London Sch.; Trinity Coll., Cambridge (Exhibnr) (BA); Harvard Law Sch. (Harkness Commonwealth Fund Fellowship) (LLM). Served RA, 1955–57, 2nd Lieut. Called to Bar, Lincoln's Inn, 1963 (Mansfield scholar), Bencher, 1985; called to Bar of N Ireland, 1984; Irish Bar, 1983. Special Adviser to: Home Secretary, 1974–76; Standing Adv. Commn on Human Rights, 1975–77; UK Legal Expert, Network Cttee on Equal Pay and Sex Discrimination, EEC, 1983–93. Member: H of L Sub-Cttee, on European Law and Institutions, Inter-Govtl Conf., 1996; Mem., Parly Jt Human Rights Commn, 2001–04, 2005–10; Mem., Commn on Bill of Rights, 2011–12. Ind. Advr to Sec. of State for Justice on aspects of constitutional reform, 2007–08. Hon. Vis. Prof., UCL, 1983–; Hon. Adjunct Prof. of Law, Univ. Coll. Cork, 2007–. Lectures: Owen J. Roberts, Univ. of Pennsylvania Law Sch., 1976; F. A. Mann, London, 1983; Rubin, Columbia Law Sch., 1988; Street, Manchester, 1993; Lionel Cohen, Hebrew Univ. of Jerusalem, 1994; Stephen Lawrence, London, 2000; Thomas More, and Denning Soc., Lincoln's Inn, 2000. Mem., Bd of Overseers, Univ. of Pennsylvania Law Sch., 1978–89. Pres., Interights, 1991–2014; Chm., Runnymede Trust, 1991–93; Member: Council, Justice, 1977–; Amer. Law Inst., 1985–; Bd of Dirs, Salzburg Seminar, 1996–2000; Internat. Adv. Bd, Open Soc. Inst., 2000–; Co-Chm., Exec. Bd, European Roma Rights Center, Budapest, 1999–2001. Gov., British Inst. of Human Rights. Member: Adv. Bd, Inst. of European Public Law, Hull Univ. Adv. Cttee, Centre for Public Law, Univ. of Cambridge, 1999–. Mem., Amer. Philos. Soc., 2003; Hon. Mem., Amer. Acad. of Arts and Scis, 2002. Mem., Bd of Govs, James Allen's Girls' Sch., 1984–94 (Chm., 1987–91); Gov., Westminster Sch., 1998–2001. Mem. Editl Bd, Public Law. Chevalier de la Légion d'Honneur (France), 2009. *Publications:* Justice in the American South, 1964 (Amnesty Internat.); (co-ed.) Shawcross and Beaumont on Air Law, 3rd edn, 1964; (co-author) Race and Law, 1972; (ed) Constitutional Law and Human Rights, 1996; (co-ed) Human Rights Law and Practice, 1999, 3rd edn, 2009; contributor to: British Nationality, Immigration and Race Relations, in Halsbury's Laws of England, 4th edn, 1973, repr. 1992; The Changing Constitution (ed Jowell and Oliver), 1985, 6th edn 2007; (contrib.) Freedom of Expression: essays in honour of Nicolas Bratza, 2012. *Address:* Blackstone Chambers, Blackstone House, Temple, EC4Y 9BW. *T:* (020) 7583 1770.

LESTER, Guy Anthony, TD 2000; Finance Director, Cabinet Office, since 2015; *b* London, 10 July 1963; *s* of Albert Lester and Dr Barbara Lester; *m* 2006, Victoria Bain; one *s*. *Educ:* Dulwich Coll.; Sidney Sussex Coll., Cambridge (BA Chemical Engrg 1984; Dip. Advanced Study 1985; MEng 1993). ACA 1989. KPMG, 1985–88; Ministry of Defence, 1989–2015: Asst Private Sec. to Defence Sec., 1992–93; Defence and Overseas Secretariat, Cabinet Office (on secondment), 1998; PS/Permanent Sec., 1999–2001; Director: Defence Resources and Plans, 2001–04; Capability Resources and Scrutiny, 2004–08; Dir Gen. Equipment, subseq. Dir, Equipment Resources, 2008–11; Comd Sec., subseq. Dir, Resources, Air Comd, 2011–15. Officer, Royal Signals, TA, 1986–97. *Address:* Cabinet Office, 70 Whitehall, SW1A 2AS.

LESTER, Sir James Theodore, (Sir Jim), Kt 1996; adviser on parliamentary and government affairs; *b* 23 May 1932; *s* of Arthur Ernest and Marjorie Lester; *m* (marr. diss. 1989); two *s*; *m* 1989. *Educ:* Nottingham High School. Mem. Notts CC, 1967–74. MP (C) Beeston, Feb. 1974–1983, Broxtowe, 1983–97; contested (C) Broxtowe, 1997. An Opposition Whip, 1976–79; Parly Under-Sec. of State, Dept of Employment, 1979–81. Mem., Select Cttee on Foreign affairs, 1982–97; Vice-Chm., All Party Gp on overseas develt, 1983–97. Deleg. to Council of Europe and WEU, 1975–76. *Recreations:* reading, music, motor racing, travelling. *Address:* 47 St John Drive, Westham, E Sussex BN24 5HX.

LESTER, Nicholas; Corporate Director, Services, London Councils, since 2008; *b* 20 March 1953; *s* of Frank and Eve Lester; partner, Tom Davis. *Educ:* Manchester Grammar Sch.; University Coll. London (BSc 1976; DipArch 1978). FCILT 1986. Architectl Asst, Sutton LBC, 1977–78; Asst Dir, 1978–80, Dir, 1980–84, Transport 2000; Greater London Council: Industry and Employment Officer, 1984–85; Public Transport Officer, 1985–86; Planning and Transport Officer, ALA, 1986–91; London Parking Dir, 1992–98; Chief Exec., Transport Cttee for London, 1998–2001; Dir, Transport, Envmt and Planning, Assoc. of London Govt, subseq. London Councils, 2001–08. Founder and Chm., London Cycling Campaign, 1978–80. Dir, Friends of the Earth Ltd, 1986–88. Chairman: London Transport Passengers' Cttee, 1983–85; Nat. Consumer Congress, 1985; President: British Parking Assoc., 1997–2000; European Parking Assoc., 2009– (Vice Pres., 2004–07); Vice Chm., Eur. Road Traffic Res. Adv. Council, 2014–. *Publications:* (contrib.) Travel Sickness, 1992. *Recreations:* food and drink, travel (especially by train and bicycle), dogs and cats (especially otterhounds), entertaining and being entertained. *Address:* London Councils, 59½ Southwark Street, SE1 0AL. *T:* (020) 7934 9905, *Fax:* (020) 7934 9920. *E:* nick.lester@londoncouncils.gov.uk.

LESTER, Paul John, CBE 2007; non-executive Chairman, Greenergy, since 2010; *b* 20 Sept. 1949; *s* of late John Trevor Lester and Joyce Ethel Lester; *m* 1st, 1973, Valerie Osbourn (marr. diss.); one *s* one *d*; 2nd, Karen White; one *d*. *Educ:* Trent Poly. (BSc (Hons) Mech. Engrg; Dip Mgt Studies (Distinction)). Sen. Management, Dowty Group, 1968–80; Gen. Management, Schlumberger, UK, France, USA, 1980–87; Man. Dir, Defense & Air Systems, Dowty Gp, 1987–90; Chief Exec., Graseby plc, 1990–97; Gp Man. Dir, Balfour Beatty plc, 1997–2002; Chief Exec., VT Gp plc (formerly Vosper Thornycroft Hldgs), 2002–10; Chm., Marine Current Turbines Ltd, 2010–12. Dir, Vosper Thornycroft Hldgs plc, 1998–2002. Chairman: A & P Gp, 1993–99; High Integrity Solutions Ltd, 2003–08; Solent Synergy Ltd, 2006–; John Laing Infrastructure Fund, 2010–; Norland Managed Services, 2011–14; Survitec, 2011–15; Peverel, 2012–; Parabis, 2012–; Signia, 2014–; non-executive Director: Civica plc, 2004–08; Chloride plc, 2007–13; Invensys plc, 2010–14. Mem., Adv. Bd, Alchemy Partners Ltd, 1997–2008. Pres., EEF, 2000–03 (Sen. Dep. Pres., 1999–2000; Chm., Economic Policy Cttee, 1993–2000). Vis. Prof., Nottingham Trent Univ., 2003–11. Member: SE England Sci., Engrg and Technol. Adv. Council, 2003–07; Govt Manufg Forum, 2004–07; Major Projects Rev. Gp, HM Treasury, 2009–; Chairman: SE Regl Adv. Gp, Nat. Skills Acad. for Manufg, 2007–09; SkillENG, 2007–11; Chm., Solent Leadership Team, 2007–11, Mem., SE Leadership Team, 2007–, BITC. President: Business Services Assoc., 2004–07; Soc. of Maritime Industries, 2005–10. Gov., Barnet Coll. of Further Educn, 1993–2002; Mem. Council, Southampton Univ., 2007–11. Hon. LLD Portsmouth, 2008. *Recreations:* tennis, weight training, running, football; life-long West Bromwich Albion supporter. *E:* paul.lester@greenergy.com.

LESTER, Richard; film director; *b* 19 Jan. 1932; *s* of Elliott and Ella Young Lester; *m* 1956, Deirdre Vivian Smith; one *s* one *d*. *Educ:* Wm Penn Charter Sch.; University of Pennsylvania (BSc). Television Director: CBS (USA), 1951–54; AR (Dir TV Goon Shows), 1956. Directed The Running, Jumping and Standing Still Film (Acad. Award nomination; 1st prize San Francisco Festival, 1960). *Feature Films directed:* It's Trad, Dad, 1962; Mouse on the Moon, 1963; A Hard Day's Night, 1964; The Knack, 1964 (Grand Prix, Cannes Film Festival); Help, 1965 (Best Film Award and Best Dir Award, Rio de Janeiro Festival); A Funny Thing Happened on the Way to the Forum, 1966; How I won the War, 1967; Petulia, 1968; The Bed Sitting Room, 1969 (Gandhi Peace Prize, Berlin Film Festival); The Three Musketeers, 1973; Juggernaut, 1974 (Best Dir award, Teheran Film Fest.); The Four Musketeers, 1974; Royal Flash, 1975; Robin and Marian, 1976; The Ritz, 1976; Butch and Sundance: the early days, 1979; Cuba, 1979; Superman II, 1981; Superman III, 1983; Finders Keepers, 1984; The Return of the Musketeers, 1989; Get Back, 1991. *Recreations:* music, tennis.

LESTER, Sheila Mary; *see* Corrall, S. M.

L'ESTRANGE, Michael Gerard, AO 2007; Professor of National Security, Australian National University, since 2015 (founding Executive Director, National Security College, 2009–15); *b* 12 Oct. 1952; *m* 1983, Jane Allen; five *s*. *Educ:* St Aloysius Coll., Sydney; Univ. of Sydney (BA Hons); Oxford Univ. (NSW Rhodes Schol., 1976–79; BA 1st Cl. Hons, MA). Dept of Prime Minister and Cabinet, Canberra, 1981–89; Harkness Fellow, Georgetown Univ. and Univ. of Calif, Berkeley, 1987–89; Sen. Advr, Office of Leader of Opposition, 1989–95; Exec. Dir, Menzies Res. Centre, Canberra, 1995–96; Sec. to Cabinet, and Hd, Cabinet Policy Unit, 1996–2000; High Comr for Australia in UK, 2000–05; Sec., Dept of Foreign Affairs and Trade, 2005–09. Non-exec. Dir, Rio Tinto, 2014–. *Recreations:* cricket, Rugby, golf. *Address:* National Security College, Building 132A, 1 Lennox Crossing, Australian National University, Acton, ACT 0200, Australia.

LE SUEUR, Prof. Andrew Philip; Professor of Constitutional Justice, University of Essex, since 2013; Law Commissioner, Jersey, since 2013; *b* 7 April 1964; *s* of George and Elaine Le Sueur. *Educ:* Hautlieu Sch., Jersey; London Sch. of Econs (LLB 1986). Called to the Bar, Middle Temple, 1987, Bencher, 2010; University College London: Lectr in Laws, 1988–98, Reader in Laws, 1998–2000, Faculty of Laws; Hon. Sen. Res. Fellow, Constitution Unit, 2001–05; Barber Prof. of Jurisprudence, Univ. of Birmingham, 2001–06; Prof. of Public Law, QMUL, 2006–13; Dir of Studies, Inst. of Law, Jersey, 2009–11. Specialist Adviser: H of C Constitutional Affairs Cttee, 2003–05; H of L Select Cttee on Constitutional Reform Bill, 2005; H of C Justice Cttee, 2010; H of L Constitution Cttee, 2011–12 (Legal Advr, 2006–09). Co-Convenor, UK Constitutional Law Gp, 2010–13; Pres., UK Constitutional Assoc., 2013–15; Mem., Exec. Cttee, Internat. Assoc. of Constitutional Law, 2010–. Editor, Public Law, 2002–11. *Publications:* (with M. Sunkin) Public Law, 1997; (ed) Building the UK's New Supreme Court: national and comparative perspectives, 2004; (with Lord Woolf and J. Jowell) de Smith's Judicial Review, 5th edn 1995 to 7th edn 2013; (with M. Sunkin and J. Murkens) Public Law: text, cases, and materials, 2010, 2nd edn 2013; articles on constitutional and administrative law. *Recreation:* pottering about. *Address:* School of Law, University of Essex, Wivenhoe Park, Colchester CO4 3SQ. *E:* alesueur@essex.ac.uk. *Club:* Athenæum.

LETH, Air Vice-Marshal David Richard H.; *see* Hawkins-Leth.

LETHBRIDGE, Prof. Robert David, PhD; Master of Fitzwilliam College, Cambridge, 2005–13; Hon. Professor of Nineteenth-Century French Literature, University of Cambridge, 2006–14, now Emeritus Hon. Professor; *b* 24 Feb. 1947; *s* of Albert Lethbridge and Muriel Alice (*née* de Saram); *m* 1970, Vera Lenore Laycock; one *s* one *d*. *Educ:* Mill Hill Sch.; Univ. of Kent at Canterbury (BA 1st cl. Hons 1969); McMaster Univ. (MA 1970); St John's Coll., Cambridge (MA 1973; PhD 1975). Fitzwilliam College, Cambridge: Fellow, 1973–94 (Life Fellow, 1994; Hon. Fellow, 2013); Leathersellers' Fellow, 1973–78; Tutor, 1975–92, Sen. Tutor, 1982–92; Coll. Lectr (jtly with Trinity Hall), 1978–80; Asst Lectr in French, 1980–85, Lectr, 1985–94, Univ. of Cambridge; University of London: Prof. of French Lang. and Lit., 1994–2005, now Emeritus; Hd, Dept of French, 1995–97, Dean, Grad. Sch., 1997–98, Vice-Principal (Acad.), 1997–2002, Vis. Prof., 2003–05, Royal Holloway; Dir, British Inst. in Paris, later Univ. of London Inst. in Paris, 2003–05. Provost, Gates Cambridge Trust, 2010–13. Visiting Professor: UCSB, 1986; Univ. of Melbourne, 2003; Hon. Prof., Queen Mary, Univ. of London, 2003–05. Commandeur des Palmes Académiques (France), 2012. *Publications:* Maupassant: Pierre et Jean, 1984; (ed with T. Keefe) Zola and the Craft of Fiction, 1990; (ed) Germinal, 1993; (ed with P. Collier) Artistic Relations, Literature and the Visual Arts in Nineteenth-Century France, 1994; (ed with C. Lloyd) Maupassant: conteur et romancier, 1994; (ed) L'Assommoir, 1995; (ed) Pot-Bouille, 2000; (ed) La Débâcle, 2000; (ed) Bel-Ami, 2001; (ed) Pierre et Jean, 2001; contribs to learned jls and collective works. *Recreations:* watching Rugby, contemplating the sea. *Address:* The Old Manse, Kirk Wynd, Markinch, Fife KY7 6DT. *Club:* Oxford and Cambridge.

LETHBRIDGE, Sir Thomas (Periam Hector Noel), 7th Bt *cr* 1804; *b* 17 July 1950; *s* of Sir Hector Wroth Lethbridge, 6th Bt, and of Evelyn Diana, *d* of late Lt-Col Francis Arthur Gerard Noel, OBE; *S* father, 1978; *m* 1st, 1976, Susan Elizabeth Rocke (marr. diss. 1998); four *s* two *d*; 2nd, 2007, Mrs Ann-Marie Fenwick, *d* of Thomas Mott, Ely. *Educ:* Milton Abbey. Studied farming, Cirencester Agricultural Coll., 1969–70; Man. Dir, Art Gallery, Dorset and London, 1972–77; also fine art specialist in sporting paintings and engravings. *Recreations:* riding, shooting, swimming, bicycling. *Heir: s* John Francis Buckler Noel Lethbridge [*b* 10 March 1977; *m* 2006, Nicola Elizabeth, *e d* of Lt Col Anthony Barkas]. *Address:* c/o Drummonds, 49 Charing Cross, SW1A 2DX.

LETT, Hugh Brian Gordon; QC 2008; a Recorder of the Crown Court, since 1993; author of military history; *b* Belfast, 9 Aug. 1949; *s* of Maj. Gordon Lett, DSO and Sheila Buckston Lett; *m* 1979, Angela Susan Jaques; three *s* one *d*. *Educ:* Marlborough Coll.; Council of Legal Educn. Called to the Bar, Inner Temple, 1971; in practice as barrister specialising in fraud, money laundering and serious crime. Asst Recorder, 1990–93; Hd of Chambers, South Western Chambers, Taunton, 1993–2002. Chm., Monte San Martino Trust, 1997–2005. Commendatore, Ordine al Merito della Repubblica Italiana, 2007. *Publications:* SAS in Tuscany, 2011; Ian Fleming and SOE's Operation Postmaster, 2012; The Small Scale Raiding Force, 2013; An Extraordinary Italian Imprisonment, 2014. *Recreations:* mountain walking in Italy, re-creating POW escape routes, history of Italian War of Liberation, watching cricket and Rugby. *Address:* 4 King's Bench Walk, 2nd Floor, Temple, EC4Y 7DL. *T:* (020) 7822 7000, *Fax:* (020) 7822 7022. *E:* bl@4kbw.co.uk, brian@brianlettauthor.com. *Club:* MCC.

LETTE, Kathryn Marie; author; *b* Sydney, 11 Nov. 1958; *d* of Mervyn and Val Lette; *m* 1990, Geoffrey Ronald Robertson, *qv*; one *s* one *d*. Author, playwright, satirical columnist; Writer-in-Residence, Savoy Hotel, London, 2003–04. Ambassador: Plan International; Nat. Autistic Soc. Hon. DA Southampton Solent, 2009. *Publications: novels:* Puberty Blues, 1979 (jtly); Hits and Ms, 1984; Girls' Night Out, 1988; The Llama Parlour, 1991; Foetal Attraction, 1993; Mad Cows, 1996; Altar Ego, 1998; Nip 'n' Tuck, 2000; Dead Sexy, 2002; How to Kill your Husband (and other handy household hints), 2006; To Love, Honour and Betray—Till Divorce Us Do Part, 2008; Men: a user's guide, 2010; The Boy Who Fell to Earth, 2012; Love is Blind, 2013; Courting Trouble, 2014; *plays:* Wet Dreams, 1985; Perfect Mismatch, 1985; Grommitts, 1986; I'm So Happy for You, I Really Am, 1991. *Address:* c/o Ed Victor, 6 Bayley Street, Bedford Square, WC1B 3HB. *T:* (020) 7304 4100.

LETTS, Anthony Ashworth; President, Charles Letts Group, 1994–96 (Chairman, Charles Letts Holdings Ltd, 1977–94); *b* 3 July 1935; *s* of Leslie Charles Letts and Elizabeth Mary (*née* Gibson); *m* 1962, Rosa Maria Ciarrapico; one *s* one *d*. *Educ:* Marlborough Coll.; Cambridge Univ. (MAEcon); Yale Univ. (Industrial Admin). National Service, RE, 2 Lieut, 1954–56. Joined Charles Letts & Co. Ltd, 1960; Man. Dir, 1965 (Charles Letts family business founded by John Letts (g g g grandfather), 1796). Director: Cambridge Market Intelligence, 1994–2002; Accademia Club Ltd, 1996–2002; Gov., Westminster Kingsway (formerly Westminster) Coll., London, 1993–2002. *Recreations:* tennis, sailing, hill walking, theatre. *Address:* The Dell, Pound Lane, Wood Street Village, Guildford GU3 3DT. *T:* 07720 812183. *Club:* Hurlingham.

LETTS, Melinda Jane Frances, OBE 2003; Lecturer, Latin and Greek Languages, Jesus College, Oxford, since 2013; *b* 6 April 1956; *d* of late Richard Letts and of Jocelyn (*née* Adami); *m* 1991, Neil Scott Wishart McIntosh, *qv*; one *s* one *d*. *Educ:* Wycombe Abbey; Cheltenham Coll.; St Anne's Coll., Oxford (BA Hons, Lit Hum Cl. I); Christ Church, Oxford (MSt Classical Langs and Lit.). Theatre Jobs, 1978–80; Res. Asst, Brunel Univ., 1980–81; Head of Admin, CND, 1982–84, VSO, 1985–87; Prog. Funding Manager, 1987, Regl Prog. Manager, ME and S Asia, 1987–89, VSO; Staffing Manager, McKinsey & Co., 1989–91; Dep. Dir, 1991–92, Dir, later Chief Exec., 1992–98, Nat. Asthma Campaign. Chm., Long Term Medical Conditions Alliance, 1998–2004 (Trustee, 1996–2004); Member: Commn for Health Improvement, 1999–2004; NHS Modernisation Bd, 2000–03; Commn for Healthcare Audit and Inspection, 2003–04; Chair, Cttee on Safety of Medicines Working Gp on Patient Information, 2003–05; Dir, Ask About Medicines, 2003–09. Chair, Nat. Strategic Partnership Forum, 2005–07. Sen. Associate, Compass Partnership, 2004–; executive coach and mentor, 2004–. Trustee: NCVO, 1997–2002; Comic Relief, 1998–2002; General Practice Airways Gp, 2001–08; Parkinson's UK (formerly Parkinson's Disease Soc.), 2007– (Vice-Chm., 2008–09; Chair, 2009–11); Patron, Men's Health Forum, 2004; Member: Exec. Cttee, Tobacco Control Alliance, 1997–98; Bd, New Opportunities Fund, 1998–2001. Mem. Council, Cheltenham Coll., 1990–93; Governor, Oakley Hall Sch., Cirencester, 1993–94. Mem., ACENVO, 1992–98. MCMI (MIMgt 1992). FRSA 1996. *Recreations:* reading, swimming, gardening, crosswords. *E:* melindajletts@gmail.com.

See also Q. R. S. Letts.

LETTS, Quentin Richard Stephen; freelance journalist; Parliamentary Sketchwriter, since 2000, and theatre critic, since 2004, Daily Mail; *b* 6 Feb. 1963; *s* of late Richard Francis Bonner Letts, schoolmaster, and of Jocelyn Elizabeth Letts (*née* Adami); *m* 1996, Lois Henrietta, *d* of Patrick and Marion Rathbone; one *s* two *d*. *Educ:* Haileybury; Bellarmine Coll., Kentucky; Trinity Coll., Dublin (BA); Jesus Coll., Cambridge (Dip. Classical Archaeol.). Writer, specialist pubns, Cardiff, 1987; Daily Telegraph, 1988–95: City Diarist, 1989–90; NY Corresp., 1991; Ed., Peterborough Column, 1991–95; NY Bureau Chief, The Times, 1995–97; Parly Sketchwriter, Daily Telegraph, 1997–2000. Creator, 'Clement Crabbe', Daily Mail, 2006–09. Presenter, What's the Point of…?, BBC Radio 4, 2008–; contrib., This Morning, ITV, 2013–. Judge: Stagestruck, 2012; Nation's Best Am-Dram, 2012, Sky Arts. Gov., Hereford Cathedral Perpetual Trust; Dep. Churchwarden, How Caple Ch. Edgar Wallace Award, London Press Club, 2003; Feature Writer of Year, What the Papers Say Awards, 2007; Political Journalist of the Year, 2009, Critic of the Year, 2010, British Press Awards; Westminster Villager, Comment Awards, 2010. *Publications:* 50 People Who Buggered Up Britain, 2008; Bog Standard Britain, 2009; Letts Rip!, 2010. *Recreations:* watching cricket, singing hymns. *Address:* The Old Mill, How Caple, Herefordshire HR1 4SR. *T:* (01989) 740688. *Clubs:* Savile, MCC.

See also M. J. F. Letts.

LETWIN, Isabel Grace, CBE 2013; Director of Legal Services, Department of Health, since 2011; *b* 7 Aug. 1956; *d* of Prof. John Frank Davidson, *qv*; *m* 1984, Oliver Letwin, *qv*; one *s* one *d* (twins). *Educ:* Perse Sch. for Girls; Girton Coll., Cambridge (BA Law Tripos, MA). Admitted solicitor, 1981; Asst Solicitor, Private Client Dept, Macfarlanes, 1981–84; Treasury Solicitor's Department: Litigation Div., 1984–88; on secondment to HSE, 1988–91; Treasury Div., 1991–93; Central Adv. Div., 1994–99; Legal Advr to DCMS, 1999–2006; on secondment to FCO, 2006–09; Dir of Legal Services, DWP, 2009–11. Lector (pt-time) in Family Law, Trinity Coll., Cambridge, 1981–86. *Recreations:* gardening, tennis, alpine walking, cooking.

LETWIN, Rt Hon. Oliver; PC 2002; PhD; MP (C) West Dorset, since 1997; Minister for Government Policy, Cabinet Office, since 2010; Chancellor of the Duchy of Lancaster, since 2014; *b* 19 May 1956; *s* of late Prof. William Letwin; *m* 1984, Isabel Grace Davidson (*see* I. G. Letwin); one *s* one *d* (twins). *Educ:* Eton Coll.; Trinity Coll., Cambridge (BA, MA, PhD 1982). Vis. Fellow, Princeton Univ., 1981; Research Fellow, Darwin Coll., Cambridge, 1982–83; Special Advr, DES, 1982–83; Mem., Prime Minister's Policy Unit, 1983–86; with N. M. Rothschild & Sons Ltd, 1986–2003 (Dir, 1991–2003; non-exec. Dir, 2005–09). Opposition front-bench spokesman on constitutional affairs, 1998–99, on Treasury affairs, 1999–2000; Shadow Chief Sec. to HM Treasury, 2000–01; Shadow Home Sec., 2001–03; Shadow Chancellor, 2003–05; Shadow Sec. of State for Envmt, Food and Rural Affairs, 2005; Chairman: Conservative Policy Review, 2005–10; Conservative Res. Dept, 2005–10; Conservative Policy Forum, 2010–. FRSA 1991. *Publications:* Ethics, Emotion and the Unity of the Self, 1984; Aims of Schooling, 1985; Privatising the World, 1987; Drift to Union, 1990; The Purpose of Politics, 1999; numerous articles in learned and popular jls. *Recreations:* ski-ing, tennis, walking. *Address:* House of Commons, SW1A 0AA. *T:* (020) 7219 3000.

LEUNG Chun-Ying; Chief Executive, Hong Kong Special Administrative Region, since 2012. *Educ:* King's Coll., Hong Kong; Hong Kong Poly.; Bristol Poly. Land and housing reforms, China; preparatory work for estabt of HKSAR, 1984–97; Mem., Exec. Council, 1997–2011; Convenor, non-official mems, 1999–2011. Formerly Asia Pacific Chm., DTZ. Formerly: Chm., RICS Hong Kong; Pres., Inst. of Surveyors in Hong Kong. *Address:* Office of the Chief Executive, Central Government Offices, Lower Albert Road, Hong Kong.

LEUNG Kin Pong, Andrew, SBS 2005; Founder, Andrew Leung International Consultants Ltd, Hong Kong, since 2010 (UK, 2005–10); Director-General, Government Office of Hong Kong Special Administrative Region in United Kingdom, 2000–04; *b* 13 Nov. 1945; *m* 1974, Peggy Fung Lin Tong; one *s* one *d*. *Educ:* BA (ext.) London; Wolfson Coll., Cambridge (postgrad. Dip. in Develt Studies); Harvard Univ. (PMD); Solicitor's qualifying certs, England and Hong Kong. Hong Kong Civil Service: Exec. Officer, then Sen. Exec. Officer, 1967–73; Asst Sec. for Security, 1973–75; Council Office, 1976–77; Asst Financial Sec., 1979–82; on secondment to Standard Chartered Bank, 1982–83; Counsellor (Hong Kong Affairs), Brussels, 1983–87; Dep. Dir-Gen. of Industry, 1987–91; Dep. Sec. for Transport, 1991–92; Police Admin Officer, 1994–96; Dir-Gen. of Social Welfare, 1996–2000. Sen. Consultant, MEC Internat., 2005–. Distinguished Contrib., Asymmetric Threats Contingency Alliance, 2005–; Founding Chm., China Interest Gp, Inst. of Dirs City Br., 2005–10; Global Commercial Agent, Changsha City, China, 2006–; Mem. Cttee, London Reg., RSA, 2007–10; Member: Royal Soc. for Asian Affairs, 2007–; Brain Trust, Evian Gp, Lausanne, 2007–; Expert, Community of Experts, Reuters Insight, 2007–; Council, Gerson Lehrman Gp, 2008–; Harvard Business Sch. Assoc. of Hong Kong, 2010–13; China Features Fellow, Berkshire Publishing Gp LLC, MA, 2011–13; Member, Board of Advisers: Executive Global Network, Hong Kong, 2011–; The Global Analyst, India, 2012–; Sen. Analyst, Wikistrat, 2013–; Mem., Adv. Bd, Eur. Centre for e-Commerce and Internet Law, 2014–. Member: Governing Council, KCL, 2004–10; Adv. Bd, China Policy Inst., Nottingham Univ., 2005–10. Visiting Professor: Internat. MBA Prog., Sun Yat-sen Univ., China, 2005–10; Internat. MBA Prog., Lingnan Univ., China, 2006–07; NIMBAS Graduate Sch. of Mgt, Netherlands, 2006–07; London Metropolitan Univ. Business Sch., 2009–. Mem., Exec. Cttee, 48 Gp Club, 2004–10 (Vice Chm., 2008–10); Network Member: Cambridge Soc., 1978–; Harvard Club UK, 2000–10; Mem., China-Britain Business Council, 2005–10. Mem. Bd, Multitude Foundn, 2012–14. FRSA 2002. JP Hong Kong, 1989. SBS (Hong Kong), 2005. *Recreations:* tennis, swimming, jogging, travelling, singing, reading, Chinese calligraphy, art appreciation. *Address:* 1E Block A, The Beachside, 82 Repulse Bay Road, Hong Kong. *E:* andrewkpleung@hotmail.com. *Club:* Hong Kong Jockey.

LEUNIG, Dr Timothy, FRHistS, FSS; Associate Professor (formerly Reader) in Economic History, London School of Economics and Political Science, since 2008; Chief Analyst and Chief Scientific Adviser, Department for Education, since 2014; *b* London, 1971; *s* of (Patrick) Ray and Judith Leunig; *m* 1996, Julia Cerutti; one *d*. *Educ:* Sir Joseph Williamson's Math. Sch., Rochester; Queen's Coll., Oxford (BA 1st Cl. Modern Hist. and Econs 1992); St Antony's Coll. and Nuffield Coll., Oxford (MPhil Econs 1994; DPhil Econs 1996). FRHistS 2007. Prize Fellow, Nuffield Coll., Oxford, 1995–97; Lectr in Econs, Royal Holloway, Univ. of London, 1997–98; Lectr in Econ. Hist., LSE, 1998–2008; Ed., Explorations in Econ. Hist., 2009–12; Chief Economist, CentreForum think tank, 2011–12; Sen. Ministerial Policy Advr,

DFE, 2012–14. Gov., NIESR, 2015–. Vis. Internat. Fellow, Univ. of Lund, 2010–12. FRSA 2013. *Publications:* In My Back Yard: unlocking the planning system, 2007; Cities Unlimited, 2008; Mastering Postgraduate Funding, 2011; Bigger and Quieter, 2012; contribs to jls incl. Econ. Hist. Rev., Explorations in Econ. Hist., Jl Econ. Hist. *Recreations:* thinking, cycling, gardening. *Address:* London School of Economics and Political Science, Houghton Street, WC2A 2AE. *E:* t.leunig@lse.ac.uk. *W:* www.twitter.com/timleunig.

LEVEN, 15th Earl of, *cr* 1641, **AND MELVILLE**, 14th Earl of, *cr* 1690; **Alexander Ian Leslie Melville;** Baron Melville 1616; Baron Balgonie 1641; Viscount Kirkcaldie 1690; *b* London, 29 Nov. 1984; *s* of Lord Balgonie (*d* 2007) and of Lady Balgonie, Julia Clare, *yr d* of Col Ian Ranald Critchley, OBE; *S* grandfather, 2012. *Educ:* Gordonstoun Sch. *Recreations:* photography, extensive overland travel in Europe, Asia, Middle East, Caucasus, Balkans, Pacific Is, Australia and Africa. *Heir: uncle* Hon. Archibald Ronald Melville [*b* 15 Sept. 1957; *m* 1987, Julia Mary Greville Fox; three *d*]. *Address:* Glenferness House, Nairn IV12 5UP. *T:* (01309) 651202.

LEVENE, family name of **Baron Levene of Portsoken**.

LEVENE OF PORTSOKEN, Baron *cr* 1997 (Life Peer), of Portsoken, in the City of London; **Peter Keith Levene,** KBE 1989; JP; Chairman: Lloyd's, 2002–11; Starr Underwriting Agents Ltd, since 2012; *b* 8 Dec. 1941; *s* of late Maurice Levene and Rose Levene; *m* 1966, Wendy Ann (*née* Fraiman); two *s* one *d*. *Educ:* City of London School; Univ. of Manchester (BA Econ). Joined United Scientific Holdings, 1963; Man. Dir, 1968–85; Chm., 1982–85; Chief of Defence Procurement, MoD, 1985–91; UK Nat. Armaments Dir, 1988–91; Chm., European Nat. Armaments Dirs, 1989–90. Member: SE Asia Trade Adv. Group, 1979–83; Council, Defence Manufacturers' Assoc., 1982–85 (Vice-Chm., 1983–84; Chm., 1984–85; Pres., 2006–); Citizen's Charter Adv. Panel, 1992–93; Personal Adviser to: Sec. of State for Defence, 1984; Sec. of State for the Envmt, 1991–92; Chancellor of the Exchequer on Competition and Purchasing, 1992; Pres. of BoT, 1992–95; Prime Minister on Efficiency and Effectiveness, 1992–97. Mem., Select Cttee on Econ. Affairs, H of L, 2009–. Chm., Defence Reform Gp, MoD, 2010–11. Chairman: Docklands Light Railway Ltd, 1991–94; Bankers Trust Internat. plc, 1998–99; IFSL (formerly British Invisibles), 2000–10; General Dynamics UK Ltd, 2001–; NBNK Investments plc, 2011–12; Tikehau Investment Ltd, 2014–; Chm., Investment Banking Europe, 1999–2001, Vice-Chm., 2001–02, Deutsche Bank; Dep. Chm., Wasserstein Perella & Co. Ltd, 1991–94; Chm. and Chief Exec., Canary Wharf Ltd, 1993–96; Director: Haymarket Gp Ltd, 1997–; J. Sainsbury plc, 2001–04; China Construction Bank, 2005–12; Eurotunnel SA, 2012–. Sen. Advr, Morgan Stanley & Co. Ltd, 1996–98; Member: Supervisory Bd, Deutsche Börse, 2004–05; Bd, Total SA, 2005–11. Chm., World Trade Centre Disaster Fund (UK), 2001–06. Member: Bd of Management, London Homes for the Elderly, 1984–93 (Chm., 1990–93); Internat. Adv. Bd, Singapore Govt Nat. Labs, 1998–99; Chairman's Council, Alcatel, 2000–03. Governor: City of London Sch. for Girls, 1984–85; City of London Sch., 1986–; Sir John Cass Primary Sch., 1985–93 (Dep. Chm., 1990–93). Mem. Court, HAC, 1984–2012; Mem., Court of Common Council, City of London, 1983–84 (Ward of Candlewick); Alderman, Ward of Portsoken, 1984–2005, Ward of Aldgate, 2005–12; Sheriff, City of London, 1995–96; Lord Mayor of London, 1998–99; Liveryman: Carmen's Co., 1984– (Master, 1992–93); Information Technologists' Co., 1993–; Hon. Liveryman, Mgt Consultants' Co. Hon. Col Comdt, RCT, 1991–93, RLC, 1993–2006. JP City of London, 1984. Fellow, QMW, 1995. CCMI; FCIPS. Hon. FCII. Hon. DSc: City, 1998; London, 2005. Insurance Leader of the Year Award, St John's Univ. Sch. of Risk Mgt, USA, 2010. KStJ 1998. Commandeur, Ordre National du Mérite (France), 1996; Kt Comdr, Order of Merit (Germany), 1998; Middle Cross, Order of Merit (Hungary), 1999. *Recreations:* ski-ing, watching association football, travel. *Address:* House of Lords, SW1A 0PW. *Clubs:* Guildhall, Walbrook, Royal Automobile.

LEVENE, Jacqueline Anne; *see* Perry, J. A.

LEVENE, Prof. Malcolm Irvin, MD; FRCP; FRCPCH, FMedSci; Professor of Paediatrics and Child Health, 1989–2010, now Emeritus, Chairman, Division of Paediatrics, 1992–98, University of Leeds; *b* 2 Jan. 1951; *s* of Maurice Levene and Helen Levene (*née* Kutner); *m* 1st, 1972, Miriam Bentley (marr. diss. 1990); three *d*; 2nd, 1991, Susan Anne Cave; one *s* one *d*. *Educ:* Varndean Grammar Sch., Brighton; Guy's Hosp. Med. Sch., London Univ. (MB BS 1972); MD 1981. MRCS, LRCP, 1972; MRCP 1978, FRCP 1988; FRCPCH 1996. Junior posts at Royal Sussex, Northampton General and Charing Cross Hosps, 1974–77; Registrar, Derby Children's and Charing Cross Hosps, 1977–79; Res. Lectr, RPMS, Hammersmith Hosp., 1979–82; Sen. Lectr and Reader, Dept of Paediatrics, Univ. of Leicester, 1982–88; Med. Dir, Women's and Children's Subsidiary, 1998–, Chm., Child Health Cttee, 2005–, Leeds Teaching Hosp. NHS Trust. Mem., DoH Nat. Adv. Body, Confidential Enquiry into Stillbirths and Deaths in Infancy, 1991. Chm., Scientific Adv. Cttee, Action Res., 1994–97. Ed.-in-Chief, MRCPCH Master Course, 2007–10. FMedSci 1999; Fellow, Acad. Perinatal Medicine, 2005. Hancock Prize, RCS, 1974; British Paediatric Association: Donald Paterson Prize, 1982; Michael Blecklow Meml Prize, 1982; Guthrie Medal, 1987; Ronnie MacKeith Prize, British Paed. Neurology Assoc., 1984; BUPA Res. Prize, 1988; William Liley Medal, Internat. Soc. of Fetus as a Patient, 2009; Sir James Spence Medal, RCPCH, 2010. *Publications:* (with H. Nutbeam) A Handbook for Examinations in Paediatrics, 1981; (jtly) Ultrasound of the Infant Brain, 1985; (jtly) Essentials of Neonatal Medicine, 1987, 3rd edn 2000; (ed jtly) Fetal and Neonatal Neurology and Neurosurgery, 1988, 4th edn 2009; Diseases of Children, 6th edn, 1990; Paediatrics and Child Health, 1999, 2nd edn 2006; chapters in books and articles in learned jls on paed. topics, esp. neurology of new-born. *Recreations:* music, occasional gentle golf and gardening. *Address:* Acacia House, Acacia Park Drive, Apperley Bridge, W Yorks BD10 0PH. *T:* (0113) 250 9959.

LEVENSON, Howard; an Upper Tribunal Judge, Administrative Appeals Chamber, since 2009 (Social Security Commissioner and Child Support Commissioner, 1997–2009, and Pensions Appeal Commissioner, 2005–09); *b* 4 Dec. 1949; *s* of Albert and Marlene Levenson; *m* 1971, Ros Botsman; one *s* one *d*. *Educ:* Tottenham Grammar Sch.; Univ. of Sheffield (BJur Hons 1970; LLM 1972); Coll. of Law, London; Birkbeck, Univ. of London (MA 2007); London Sch. of Econs and Pol Sci. (Cert. in Internat. Human Rights Law 2009). Admitted solicitor, 1974; Legal Officer, NCCL, 1974–77; Law Lectr, Poly., then Univ., of E London, 1977–92; Consultant, Nash and Dowell (Solicitors), 1981–91; part-time Chm., Tribunals, 1986–92; Chm., Independent Tribunal Service, 1993–97. Mem., Internat. Adv. Gp, Centre on Human Rights in Conflict, 2010–. Chm., Haldane Soc., 1980–83. Hon. LLD UEL, 2009. *Publications:* The Price of Justice, 1981; (jtly) Social Welfare Law: Legal Aid and Advice, 1985; (jtly) Police Powers, 1985, 3rd edn 1996; (contrib. ed.) Jowitt's Dictionary of English Law, 3rd edn 2010; contrib. vols of Atkin's Court Forms on Child Support, Judicial Review, Personal Rights, Social Security, Tribunals, War Pensions; contrib. to Modern Law Rev., Criminal Law Rev., New Law Jl, etc. *Address:* Upper Tribunal, Administrative Appeals Chamber, 5th Floor, Rolls Building, 7 Rolls Buildings, Fetter Lane, EC4A 1NL. *Club:* Leyton Orient Football.

LEVENTHAL, Colin David; Director, HAL Films Ltd, 2000–12; Partner, HAL Film Services; *b* 2 Nov. 1946; *s* of Morris and Olga Leventhal; *m* 1995, Petrea, *d* of late Thomas Hoving; three *d*. *Educ:* Carmel Coll., Wallingford, Berks; King's Coll., Univ. of London (BA Philosophy). Solicitor of Supreme Court of England and Wales. Admitted Solicitor, 1971; BBC, 1974–81, Head of Copyright, 1978; Head of Prog. Acquisition, Channel Four TV, 1981–87; Dir of Acquisition and Sales, Channel Four TV Co., 1987–92 (Dir, 1988–92); Dir of Acquisition, Channel Four TV Corp., 1993–97; Man. Dir, Channel Four Internat. Ltd, 1993–97; Jt Chief Exec., Miramax HAL Films Ltd, 1998–2000. Mem., Film Council, 1999–2002. *Recreations:* theatre, film. *Address:* 10 Well Walk, Hampstead, NW3 1LD. *T:* (020) 7435 3038.

LEVER, Hon. Bernard Lewis; His Honour Judge Lever; a Circuit Judge, since 2001; *b* 1 Feb. 1951; *s* of Baron Lever and of Ray Rosalia, Lady Lever; *m* 1985, Anne Helen Ballingall, only *d* of Patrick Chandler Gordon Ballingall, MBE; two *d*. *Educ:* Clifton; Queen's Coll., Oxford (Neale Exhibnr; MA). Called to the Bar, Middle Temple, 1975; in practice, Northern Circuit, 1975–2001; Standing Counsel to Inland Revenue, 1997–2001. Co-founder, SDP in NW, 1981. Contested (SDP) Manchester Withington, 1983. *Recreations:* walking, music, picking up litter. *Address:* Manchester Crown Court, Minshull Street, Manchester M1 3FS. *T:* (0161) 954 7500. *Club:* Vincent's (Oxford).

LEVER, Sir Christopher; *see* Lever, Sir T. C. A. L.

LEVER, Sir Jeremy (Frederick), KCMG 2002; QC 1972; QC (NI) 1988; *b* 23 June 1933; *s* of late A. Lever; civil partnership 2006, Brian Collie. *Educ:* Bradfield Coll.; University Coll., Oxford; Nuffield Coll., Oxford. Served RA, 1951–53. 1st cl. Jurisprudence, 1956, MA Oxon; Pres., Oxford Union Soc., 1957, Trustee, 1972–77 and 1988–2014. Fellow, All Souls Coll., Oxford, 1957– (Sub-Warden, 1982–84; Sen. Dean, 1988–2011). Called to Bar, Gray's Inn, 1957, Bencher, 1985. Chairman: Oftel Adv. Body on Fair Trading in Telecommunications, 1996–2000; Appeals Panel, PRS, 1997–2002. Mem. Council, British Inst. of Internat. and Comparative Law, 1987–2004. Director (non-exec.): Dunlop Holdings Ltd, 1973–80; Wellcome plc, 1983–94. Mem., Arbitral Tribunal, US/UK Arbitration concerning Heathrow Airport User Charges, 1989–94. Vis. Prof., Wissenschaftszentrum, Berlin, für Sozialforschung, 1999. Lectures: Hamlyn, Hamlyn Trust, 1991; Lord Fletcher Meml, Law Soc., 1997; Grotius, British Inst. of Internat. and Comparative Law, 1998. Governor, Berkhamsted Schs, 1985–95. FRSA. *Publications:* The Law of Restrictive Practices, 1964; other legal works. *Recreations:* ceramics, music. *Address:* Monckton Chambers, 1 Raymond Buildings, Gray's Inn, WC1R 5NR. *T:* (020) 7405 7211, *Fax:* (020) 7405 2084; All Souls College, Oxford OX1 4AL. *T:* (01865) 279379, *Fax:* (01865) 279299, (01304) 750015. *E:* chambers@monckton.com. *Clubs:* Athenæum, Garrick.

LEVER, John Darcy, MA; Headmaster, Canford School, 1992–2013; *b* 14 Jan. 1952; *s* of late Prof. Jeffrey Darcy Lever; *m* 1981, Alisoun Margaret Yule; one *s* two *d*. *Educ:* Westminster Sch.; Trinity Coll., Cambridge (MA); Christ Church, Oxford (Cert Ed). St Edward's Sch., Oxford, 1974–76; Winchester Coll., 1976–92. *Recreations:* walking, clocks, maps. *Address:* Shores Farm, Lopen, South Petherton, Somerset TA13 5JR.

LEVER, (Keith) Mark; Chief Executive, National Autistic Society, since 2008; *b* 20 Sept. 1960; *s* of Keith Lever and Rosemary Anne Lever (*née* Wakeley); *m* 1989, Amanda Jane Sackville Davison; four *s*. *Educ:* Wakeman Grammar Sch., Shrewsbury; Royal Holloway Coll., London (BSc Hons Physics and Mgt Sci. 1982); Cranfield Univ. Sch. of Mgt (MBA 1999). DipChA; DipM. FCA 2009 (ACA 1986). Partner and Nat. Dir, Mkt Res. and Trng, Kidsons Impey, 1994; Women's Royal Voluntary Service: Dir, Trng, 1995–99; Dir, Strategic Develt, 1999–2002; Chief Exec. Officer, 2002–07. MCIPD 1992; ACIM 2000. *Recreations:* drinking wine with my wife, negotiating peace settlements and behaviour related pay with my four sons, regularly losing at tennis and golf, long distance cycling. *E:* marklever@aol.com. *Clubs:* Harrow Golf Society, Wanborough Amateur Golf Society.

LEVER, Sir Paul, KCMG 1998 (CMG 1991); HM Diplomatic Service, retired; Chairman, Royal United Services Institute, 2004–09; *b* 31 March 1944; *s* of John Morrison Lever and Doris Grace (*née* Battey); *m* 1990, Patricia Anne, *d* of John and Anne Ramsey. *Educ:* St Paul's Sch.; The Queen's Coll., Oxford (MA; Hon. Fellow, 2006). 3rd Secretary, Foreign and Commonwealth Office, 1966–67; 3rd, later 2nd Secretary, Helsinki, 1967–71; 2nd, later 1st Secretary, UK Delegn to NATO, 1971–73; FCO, 1973–81; Asst Private Sec. to Sec. of State for Foreign and Commonwealth Affairs, 1978–81; Chef de Cabinet to Christopher Tugendhat, Vice-Pres. of EEC, 1981–85; Head of UN Dept, FCO, 1985–86; Head of Defence Dept, 1986–87; Head of Security Policy Dept, FCO, 1987–90; Ambassador and Hd, UK Delegn to Conventional Arms Control Negotiations, Vienna, 1990–92; Asst Under-Sec. of State, FCO, 1992–94; Dep. Sec., Cabinet Office, and Chm., Jt Intelligence Cttee, 1994–96; Dep. Under-Sec. of State (Dir for EU and Economic Affairs), FCO, 1996–97; Ambassador to Germany, 1997–2003. Global Develt Dir, RWE Thames Water, 2003–06; non-exec. Dir, Sellafield Ltd, 2007–11. Hon. LLD Birmingham, 2001. *Recreations:* walking, art deco pottery. *Address:* c/o Royal United Services Institute, Whitehall, SW1A 2ET.

LEVER, Sir (Tresham) Christopher (Arthur Lindsay), 3rd Bt *cr* 1911; PhD; *b* 9 Jan. 1932; *s* of Sir Tresham Joseph Philip Lever, FRSL, 2nd Bt, and Frances Yowart (*d* 1959), *d* of Lindsay Hamilton Goodwin; step *s* of Pamela Lady Lever (*d* 2003), *d* of late Lt-Col Hon. Malcolm Bowes Lyon; *S* father, 1975; *m* 1st, 1970; 2nd, 1975, Linda Weightman McDowell, *d* of late James Jepson Goulden, Tennessee, USA. *Educ:* Eton; Trinity Coll., Cambridge (BA Hist. and English 1954; MA 1957; PhD Biol. 2011). FLS; FRGS. Commissioned, 17th/21st Lancers, 1950. Peat, Marwick, Mitchell & Co., 1954–55; Kitcat & Aitken, 1955–56; Dir, John Barran & Sons Ltd, 1956–64. Consultant: Zoo Check Charitable Trust, 1984–91; Born Free Foundn, 1991–2003; Chairman: African Fund for Endangered Wildlife (UK), 1987–90; UK Elephant Gp, 1991–92; UK Rhino Gp, 1992–93; Member: IUCN Species Survival Commn, 1988–; IUCN UK Cttee, 1989–2011; Scientific Advr, Galapagos Conservation Trust, 2012–; Trustee: Internat. Trust for Nature Conservation, 1980–92 (Vice-Pres. 1986–91; Pres., 1991–92); Rhino Rescue Trust, 1986–91 (Patron 1985–2003); Chm., 1990–2004, Hon. Life Pres., 2004, Tusk Trust; Chm., Ruaha Trust, 1990–95; Member Council: Soc. for Protection of Animals in N Africa, 1986–88; British Trust for Ornithology, 1988–91 (Chm., Nat. Centre Appeal, 1987–92); SOS Sahel Internat. (UK), 1995–2010; Director: WSPA, 1998–2003; Earthwatch Inst., Europe, 2003–04; Mem., Council of Ambassadors, WWF-UK, 1999–2005 (Fellow, 2005); Patron: Lynx Educnl Trust for Animal Welfare, 1991–2010; Respect for Animals, 1995–2011; Vice-Patron, Conservation Foundn, 2005–06. MBOU. Hon. Life Member: Brontë Soc., 1988; Butterfly Conservation, 2014. Mem., Editl Bd, Jl of Applied Herpetology, 2005–09. H. H. Bloomer Award, Linnean Soc., 2014. *Publications:* Goldsmiths and Silversmiths of England, 1975; The Naturalized Animals of the British Isles, 1977; (contrib.) Wildlife '80: the world conservation yearbook, 1980; (contrib.) Evolution of Domesticated Animals, 1984; Naturalized Mammals of the World, 1985; Naturalized Birds of the World, 1987; (contrib.) Beyond the Bars: the zoo dilemma, 1987; The Mandarin Duck, 1990; They Dined on Eland: the story of the acclimatisation societies, 1992; (contrib.) The New Atlas of Breeding Birds in Britain and Ireland: 1988–1991, 1993; Naturalized Animals: the ecology of successfully introduced species, 1994; (contrib.) The Introduction and Naturalisation of Birds, 1996; Naturalized Fishes of the World, 1996; (contrib.) Stocking & Introduction of Fish, 1997; (contrib.) The EBCC Atlas of European Breeding Birds: their distribution and abundance, 1997; The Cane Toad: the history and ecology of a successful colonist, 2001; (contrib.) The Migration Atlas: movements of the birds of Britain and Ireland, 2002; Naturalized Reptiles and Amphibians of the World, 2003; (contrib.) Biological Invasions: from ecology to control, 2005; Naturalised Birds of the World, 2005; The Naturalized Animals of Britain and Ireland, 2009; (contrib.) Silent Summer: the state of wildlife in Britain and Ireland, 2010; (contrib.) Encyclopedia of Biological Invasions, 2011; The Mandarin Duck, 2013. *Heir:* none. *Address:* Newell House, Winkfield, Berks SL4 4SE. *T:* (01344) 882604, *Fax:* (01344) 891744. *Clubs:* Boodle's; Swinley Forest Golf.

LEVERTON, Colin Allen H.; *see* Hart-Leverton.

LEVERTON, Roger Frank, FCA; Chairman, Renold plc, 1998–2006; *b* 22 April 1939; *s* of Frank Arthur Leverton and Lucia Jean Leverton (*née* Harden); *m* 1st, 1962, Patricia Jones (marr. diss.); one *s* one *d* (and one *d* decd); 2nd, 1992, Marilyn Williams. *Educ:* Haberdashers' Aske's Sch. FCA 1962. Black & Decker Manufacturing Co., 1968–84: European Dir and Gen. Manager, France, 1978–81; Gp Vice-Pres., Southern Europe, 1981–84; Chief Exec., MK Electric Gp, subseq. Pillar Electrical plc, 1984–89; Pres. and Chief Exec., Indal Ltd (RTZ Corp. plc), 1989–92; Chief Exec., Pilkington plc, 1992–97. Chairman: Infast Gp plc, 1997–2002; Betts Gp Hldgs Ltd, 1998–2005. *Recreations:* tennis, golf, theatre.

LEVESON, Lord; George James Leveson Gower; *b* 22 July 1999; *s* and *heir* of Earl Granville, *qv.*

LEVESON, Rt Hon. Sir Brian (Henry), Kt 2000; PC 2006; President, Queen's Bench Division, since 2013; *b* 22 June 1949; *er s* of late Dr Ivan Leveson and Elaine Leveson, Liverpool; *m* 1981, Lynne Rose (*née* Fishel); two *s* one *d. Educ:* Liverpool College, Liverpool; Merton College, Oxford (MA; Hon. Fellow, 2001). Called to the Bar, Middle Temple, 1970, Bencher, 1995; Harmsworth Scholar, 1970; practised Northern Circuit, 1971; University of Liverpool: Lectr in Law, 1971–81; Mem. Council, 1983–92; Asst Recorder, 1984–88; QC 1986; a Recorder, 1988–2000; a Dep. High Court Judge, 1998–2000; a Judge of the High Court, QBD, 2000–06; a Lord Justice of Appeal, 2006–13; Presiding Judge, Northern Circuit, 2002–05; Sen. Presiding Judge for England and Wales, 2007–09 (Dep. Sen. Presiding Judge, 2006). Chm., Inquiry into Culture, Practices and Ethics of the Press, 2011–12. Mem., Parole Bd, 1992–95. Chairman: Criminal Justice Council, 2008–11; Sentencing Council for England and Wales, 2010–13. Mem. Council, UCS, Hampstead, 1998– (Chm., 2009–); Foundn Mem., Liverpool Coll., 2001–; Chancellor, Liverpool John Moores Univ., 2013–. Pres., Merton Soc., 2010–. Hon. Fellow, Liverpool John Moores Univ., 2012. Hon. LLD Liverpool, 2007. *Recreations:* walking, travel. *Address:* Royal Courts of Justice, Strand, WC2A 2LL.

LEVESON GOWER, family name of **Earl Granville**.

LEVETE, Amanda, RIBA 1984; Principal, Amanda Levete Architects, since 2009; *b* Bridgend, Wales, 1955; one *s*; *m* 2008, Ben Evans. *Educ:* Architectural Assoc. In practice as architect: Alsop & Lyall, 1980–81; YRM Architects, 1982–84; Richard Rogers & Partners, 1984–89; Principal Partner, Powis & Levete, 1983–86; (with Jan Kaplicky) Future Systems, 1989–2009: projects include: Stonehenge Visitor Centre, 1993 (Bovis Royal Acad. Award); Hauer/King House, 1994; West India Quay Bridge, 1998 (British Construction Ind. Award, Civic Trust Award, RIBA Award); Natwest Media Centre at Lord's cricket ground, 1999 (British Construction Ind. Award, Stirling Prize, RIBA, Civic Trust Award, World Architectural Award); Selfridges dept store in Birmingham, 2004 (Civic Trust Award; RIBA Award for Architecture); 10 Hills Place, 2009; Spencer Dock Bridge, 2009; individual furniture pieces for Established & Sons. Vis. Lectr, 1995–, Ext. Assessor, 2004–06, Vis. Prof., 2008–, RCA. Trustee: Architecture Foundn, 1997–2008; Artangel, 2000–; Young Foundn, 2009–. *Recreation:* running. *Address:* 14a Brewery Gardens, N7 9NH. *T:* (020) 7243 7670, *Fax:* (020) 7243 7690. *E:* info@ala.uk.com.

LEVEY, Andrew David; His Honour Judge Levey; a Circuit Judge, since 2011; *b* Nottingham, 15 April 1958; *s* of David Levey and Janet Levey; *m* 1987, Eleanor; two *c. Educ:* West Bridgford Comp. Sch.; Univ. of Wales Inst. of Sci. and Technol., Cardiff (LLB Hons). Solicitor, 1983–2003; a District Judge, 2003–11. *Recreations:* playing guitar, music, family (not really a recreation!), reading, cinema, baking bread. *Address:* Bromley County Court, College Road, Bromley, Kent BR1 3PX. *T:* (020) 8290 9620. *E:* HHJudge.levey@judiciary.gsi.gov.uk.

LEVI, Andrew Peter Robert; HM Diplomatic Service; Vice President, Europe, Middle East, Africa and Russia, Cisco Systems, 2012–14; *b* 4 March 1963; *s* of Paul George Carl Levi and Paula Levi; *m* 2002, Dr Roswitha Elisabeth von Studnitz. *Educ:* Reading Blue Coat Sch. (Aldworth's Hosp.); Univ. of Manchester (BSc Hons 1985); Univ. of Freiburg im Breisgau. Entered FCO, 1987; Bonn, 1990–93; First Secretary: FCO, 1993–96; on secondment to EC (EU enlargement), 1996–98, and to OECD Secretariat, 1998; Bonn, 1998–99; on secondment to: German FO, Bonn, 1999; DCS, Stability Pact for S Eastern Europe, 1999–2001; Dep. Hd, Eastern Adriatic Dept, FCO, 2001–03; Hd, Aviation, Maritime and Energy Dept, FCO, 2003–04; Asst Dir (EU), FCO, 2004–05; Counsellor (Econ.), Moscow, 2005–07; Border Review Team, Cabinet Office, 2007; Dir for Investment, 2008–10, Man. Dir, Business Gp, 2010–12, UK Trade & Investment.

LEVI, Malcolm Sydney; Group Chief Executive, Home Group, 1998–2008; housing adviser and non-executive director; *b* 3 March 1948; *s* of David and Fanny Levi; *m* 1972, Joy Poloway; two *s. Educ:* King Edward's Five Ways Grammar Sch., Birmingham; Mansfield Coll., Oxford (MA (Modern Hist.)). FCA 1978; MCIH 2001. Dir of Finance, Merseyside Improved Houses, 1977–82; Asst Dir of Housing, London Borough of Hammersmith and Fulham, 1983–85; Chief Executive: Paddington Churches Housing Assoc., 1985–94; Warden Housing Assoc., 1994–97; Gp Dep. Chief Exec., Home Gp, 1997–98. Member: Bd, Newcastle Gateshead Housing Mkt Renewal Pathfinder, 2003–08; Bd, Richmond Housing Partnership, 2010–; Adv. Panel, Homes and Communities Agency (formerly Tenant Services Authy), 2009–; Adviser: Savills, 2009–; Coactiva Aspiren, 2011–13; Statutory appointee, Novas Scarman Gp, 2009–10; Chm., Fit for Living, 2010–12. Mem. Bd, Richmond Synagogue, 2002–10, 2013–. Gov. (non-exec. Dir), Peabody, 2009– (Vice Chair, 2014; Actg Chair, 2015). *Recreations:* family and friends, films, theatre, travel, walking in Northumberland. *Address:* 23 Martingales Close, Richmond upon Thames, Surrey TW10 7JJ. *T:* (020) 8948 1683.

LEVI, Renato, (Sonny), RDI 1987; freelance powerboat designer; *b* 3 Sept. 1926; *s* of Mario Levi and Eleonora Ciravegna; *m* 1954, Ann Watson; two *s* one *d. Educ:* Collège de Cannes; St Paul's, Darjeeling. Over 50 years contributing to development of fast planing craft. *Publications:* Dhows to Deltas, 1971; Milestones in my Designs, 1992. *Recreation:* the Far East. *Address:* Sandhills, Porchfield, Isle of Wight PO30 4LH.

LEVICK, William Russell, FRS 1982; FAA; Professor, John Curtin School of Medical Research, Australian National University, 1983–96, now Emeritus Professor; *b* 5 Dec. 1931; *s* of Russell L. S. Levick and Elsie E. I. (*née* Nance); *m* 1961, Patricia Jane Lathwell; two *s* one *d. Educ:* Univ. of Sydney (BSc 1st Cl. Hons, MSc, MB, BS 1st Cl. Hons). Registered Medical Practitioner, State of ACT. RMO, Royal Prince Alfred Hosp., Sydney, 1957–58; National Health and Med. Res. Council Fellow, Univ. of Sydney, 1959–62; C. J. Martin Travelling Fellow, Cambridge Univ. and Univ. of Calif, Berkeley, 1963–64; Associate Res. Physiologist, Univ. of Calif, Berkeley, 1965–66; Sen. Lectr in Physiol., Univ. of Sydney, 1967; Professorial Fellow of Physiology, John Curtin Sch. of Medicine, ANU, 1967–83. FAA 1973; Fellow, Optical Soc. of America, 1977. *Publications:* articles on neurophysiology of the visual system in internat. scientific jls. *Address:* John Curtin School of Medical Research, Australian National University, Canberra, ACT 0200, Australia. *T:* (2) 62950336.

LEVIEN, Robin Hugh, RDI 1995; owner, since 1999, Partner, since 2006, Studio Levien; *b* 5 May 1952; *s* of John Blomefield Levien and Louis Beryl Levien; *m* 1978, Patricia Anne Stainton. *Educ:* Bearwood Coll., Wokingham; Central Sch. of Art and Design (BA Hons 1973); Royal Coll. of Art (MA 1976). MCSD. Joined Queensberry Hunt, 1977; Partner, Queensberry Hunt, later Queensberry Hunt Levien, 1982–99. Designer of mass market products for manufrs and retailers, incl. Thomas China, Wedgwood, Ideal Standard, American Standard, Habitat, Dartington Crystal; *major products designed:* Trend (for Thomas China), 1981 (Die Gute Industrieform, Hanover, 1982; Golden Flame Award, Valencia, 1983); Studio bathroom range (for Ideal Standard), 1986; Domi bathroom taps, 1989; Symphony range of bathtubs (for American Standard), 1990 (Winner, Interior Design Product Award, Amer. Soc. of Interior Designers, 1991); Kyomi bathroom range (for Ideal Standard), 1996 (Winner, Design Week Awards, 1997); Space bathroom range (for Ideal Standard) (D&AD Silver Award; Winner, FX Internat. Interior Design Award), 1999; Home Elements range (for Villeroy & Boch), 2002; Concept bathroom range (for Ideal Standard), 2008; New Cottage tableware (for Villeroy & Boch), 2009. Vis. Prof., London Inst., 1997–. Mem. Council, RCA, 2001–12 (Sen. Fellow, 2013). Master, Faculty of RDI, 2009–11. FRSA 1991 (Chm., Product Design, Student Design Awards, 1991–98; Paul Reilly Meml Lectr, 1998). DUniv Staffs, 2006. *Publications:* articles in Design mag. *Recreations:* Fulham farmer on 1952 Ferguson tractor, films, cooking. *Address:* Cooks Farm, North Brewham, Som BA10 0JQ. *T:* (01749) 850610.

LEVIN, David Roger; Managing Director, Independent Schools, United Learning, since 2014; *b* 2 Oct. 1949; *s* of Jack Levin, Cape Town and Isobel Elizabeth Levin (*née* Robinson), Norfolk, England; *m* 1977, Jean Isobel, *d* of Major J. A. P. Hall. *Educ:* Kearsney Coll., Natal; Univ. of Natal (BEcon); Univ. of Sussex (MA). Gen. Manager, Cutty Sark Hotel, Scottburgh, S Africa (family business), 1972–73; Asst Master, Whitgift Sch., Croydon, 1974–75; Articled Clerk, Radcliffes & Co., Solicitors, 1976–78; Asst Master, Portsmouth Grammar Sch., 1978–80; Head of Economics, 1980–93 and Second Master, 1987–93, Cheltenham Coll.; Headmaster: Royal Grammar Sch., High Wycombe, 1993–99; City of London Sch., 1999–2013. Advr to Minister for London Challenge, 2002–05. Chm., HMC, 2010–11. FRSA. Gov., Canford Sch., 1995–. *Recreations:* long distance swimming, theatre, hill walking, opera, military history. *Address:* United Learning, Fairline House, Nene Valley Business Park, Oundle PE8 4HN. *T:* (01832) 864444; Malden Court, Cheltenham, Glos GL52 2BL. *T:* (01242) 521692.

LEVIN, David Saul; Chief Executive, McGraw-Hill Education, New York, since 2014; *b* 28 Jan. 1962; *s* of late Archie Z. Levin and of Leah S. Levin, OBE; *m* 1992, Lindsay Caroline White; three *s. Educ:* Wadham Coll., Oxford (MA 1983); Stanford Grad. Sch. of Business (MBA 1987). Served Army, SSLC, 2nd Lieut, 1st Bn RRF, 1980. Manager, Bain & Co., 1983–89; Associate Dir, Apax Partners & Co., 1990–94; Man. Dir, Unicorn Abrasives Ltd, 1992–94; Chief Operating Officer, Euromoney Pubns plc, 1994–99; CEO, Psion plc, 1999–2002; CEO, Symbian, 2002–05; Chief Exec., United Business Media plc, 2005–14. *Address:* McGraw-Hill Education, 2 Penn Plaza, New York, NY 10121, USA.

LEVIN, Gerald Manuel; Chief Executive Officer, AOL Time Warner Inc., 2001–02; Presiding Director, Moonview Sanctuary, Santa Monica; *b* 6 May 1939; *m* Barbara J. Riley (marr. diss.); *m* Laurie Ann Perlman. *Educ:* Haverford Coll. (BA 1960); Univ. of Pennsylvania Law Sch. (LLB 1963). Attorney, Simpson Thacher & Bartlett, NYC, 1963–67; Develt and Resources Corp., 1967–71 (Gen. Manager and Chief Operating Officer, 1969–71); Rep., Internat. Basic Economy Corp., Tehran, 1971–72; joined Time Inc., 1972: Vice-Pres., Programming, 1972–73, Pres. and CEO, 1973–76, Chm., 1976–79, Home Box Office; Gp Vice-Pres., Video, 1979–84; Exec. Vice-Pres., 1984–88; Vice-Chm. and Dir, 1988–90; merger with Warner Communications Inc. to form Time Warner, 1990: Chief Operating Officer, Vice-Chm. and Dir, 1991–92; Pres. and Co-CEO, Feb.–Dec. 1992; CEO, 1992–2001; Chm., 1993–2001; merger with AOL to form AOL Time Warner, 2001. Dir, NY Stock Exchange Inc. Member: Council on Foreign Relns; Trilateral Commn. Member, Board: NY City Partnership; Nat. Cable TV Center and Mus., now Hon. Dir; Aspen Inst.; Mus. of Jewish Heritage. Dir and Treas., NY Philharmonic. Hon. LLD: Texas Coll., 1985; Middlebury Coll., 1994; Haverford Coll.; Hon. LHD Denver, 1995. *Address:* Moonview Sanctuary, PO Box 1518, Santa Monica, CA 90406, USA.

LEVIN, Prof. Richard Charles, PhD; Frederick William Beinecke Professor of Economics, Yale University, 1992, now Emeritus (President, 1993–2013); *b* San Francisco, 7 April 1947; *s* of D. Derek Levin and Phylys (*née* Goldstein); *m* 1968, Jane Ellen Aries; two *s* two *d. Educ:* Stanford Univ. (BA 1968); Merton Coll., Oxford (LittB 1971; Hon. Fellow, 1996); Yale Univ. (PhD 1974). Yale University, 1974–: Chm., Econs Dept, 1987–92; Dean, Grad. Sch., 1992–93; Res. Associate, Nat. Bureau of Econ. Res., Cambridge, Mass, 1985–90; Program Dir, Internat. Inst. Applied System Analysis, Vienna, 1990–92. Dir, Yale-New Haven Health Services Corp. Inc., 1993–. Consultant, numerous law and business firms. Trustee: Yale-New Haven Hosp., 1993–; Tanner Lectures on Human Values, 1993–. Member: Univs Res. Assoc., 1994–; Nat. Res. Council Bd on Sci., Technol. and Econ. Policy, 1998–. Member: Amer. Econ. Assoc.; Econometric Soc. Hon. LLD: Princeton, 1993; Harvard, 1994; Hon. DCL Oxford, 1998. *Publications:* The Work of the University, 2003; The Worth of the University, 2013. *Recreations:* hiking, basket-ball. *Address:* Department of Economics, Yale University, PO Box 208268, New Haven, CT 06520-8268, USA.

LEVINE, Gemma; *see* Levine, J. A.

LEVINE, James; American conductor and pianist; Music Director: Metropolitan Opera, New York, since 1976 (Principal Conductor, 1973–2011; Artistic Director, 1986–2004); Boston Symphony Orchestra, 2004–11; *b* 23 June 1943; *s* of Lawrence Levine and Helen Levine (*née* Goldstein). *Educ:* Walnut Hills High Sch.; Juilliard Sch. of Music. Asst Conductor, Cleveland Orch., 1964–70; Music Director: Ravinia Fest., 1973–93; Cincinnati May Fest., 1974–78; UBS Verbier Fest. Youth Orch., 2000–04; Conductor: Salzburg Fest., 1975–93; Bayreuth Fest., 1982–98; Chief Conductor, Munich Philharmonic, 1999–2004. Piano début with Cincinnati SO, 1953; conducting début, Aspen Music Fest., 1961; has conducted many major orchestras throughout US and Europe, incl. Vienna Philharmonic, Berlin Philharmonic, Chicago Symphony, NY Philharmonic, Dresden Staatskapelle, Israel Philharmonic, Philharmonia, London Symphony, Boston Symphony, Philadelphia, etc. Has made numerous recordings. Smetana Medal (Czechoslovakia), 1987; nine Grammy awards; Nat. Medal of Arts, 1997; Kennedy Center Honors, 2002. *Address:* Metropolitan Opera Association Inc., Metropolitan Opera House, Lincoln Center, New York, NY 10023, USA.

LEVINE, Jennifer Ann, (Gemma); photographer; *b* 10 Jan. 1939; *d* of Ellis and Mae Mathilda Josephs; *m* 1961, Eric A. Levine (marr. diss. 1986); two *s. Educ:* Hasmonean Grammar Sch., London. Antique print business, 1961; interior designer, 1970–75; professional photographer, 1975–; author, 1978–. FRSA 1990. *Exhibitions:* Personalities, 1977; Four Seasons, 1977; With Henry Moore, 1978, 1984; My Jerusalem (photographs, poetry and watercolours), 1982; Jerusalem, 1983; Henry Moore, 1982; Henry Moore, Wood Sculpture, 1983, 1984, 1985; My Jerusalem (photographs and poetry), 1983; Tel-Aviv Faces and Places, 1984; Ethiopian Jews, 1985; Faces of the 80's, 1987; Faces of British Theatre, 1990–91; Gemma Levine: 20 Years of Photography, 1995; People of the 90s, 1995, 1996; Henry Moore, 1995; Memories, 1998; Retrospective to celebrate 25 years of photography, NPG, 2001; Claridge's—Within the Image, 2004; Israel Retrospective, 2005; Mayfair, Sotheby's, 2008; Henry Moore (photographic archive), Tate Gall., 2010; Go with the Flow, 2012. *Publications:* Israel: faces and places, 1978; Living with the Bible (painter in watercolour and photographer), 1978; With Henry Moore (author and photographer), 1978; We Live in Israel, 1981; Living in Jerusalem, 1982; The Young Inheritors, 1982; Henry Moore, Wood Sculpture (author and photographer), 1983; Henry Moore: an illustrated biography, 1985; Faces of the 80's, 1987; Faces of British Theatre, 1990; People of the 90's, 1995; Memories, 1998; My Favourite Hymn, 1999; Claridge's Within the Image, 2004; Mayfair, 2008; Go with the Flow, 2012; Just One More: a photographer's memoir, 2014. *Recreations:* swimming, music, interior design. *Address:* 35–37 Grosvenor Square, W1K 2HN. *T:* (020) 7491 4494. *E:* gemmalevine@aol.com.

LEVINE, Simon Robert; Global Co-Chief Executive Officer and Managing Partner, DLA Piper UK LLP, since 2015; *b* Hull, 2 Dec. 1965; *s* of Mark and Patricia Levine; *m* 1992, Jane Golding; one *s* two *d*. *Educ:* Hymers Coll., Hull; Emmanuel Coll., Cambridge (BA 1987; MA 1990; Sen. Exhibnr). Admitted Solicitor, 1990; Solicitor and Partner, Frere Cholmeley, 1990–98; Partner, Denton Wilde Sapte, 1998–2005; DLA Piper UK LLP: Partner and Hd, IP and Technol. Gp, 2005–12; Mem., Exec. and Global Bd, 2012–14. Vis. Lectr, Imperial Coll. Business Sch., Imperial Coll. London, 2013–. Mem., Editl Bd, PLC Mag., 2005–. *Recreations:* music, cinema, travel, sport, family. *Address:* DLA Piper UK LLP, 3 Noble Street, EC2V 7EE. *T:* (020) 7796 6020, *Fax:* (020) 7796 6586. *E:* simon.levine@dlapiper.com.

LEVINE, Sydney; a Recorder, North-Eastern Circuit, 1975–95; *b* 4 Sept. 1923; *s* of Rev. Isaac Levine and Mrs Miriam Levine; *m* 1959, Cécile Rona Rubinstein; three *s* one *d*. *Educ:* Bradford Grammar Sch.; Univ. of Leeds (LLB). Called to the Bar, Inner Temple, 1952; Chambers in Bradford, 1953–98. *Recreations:* music, gardening, painting, learning to use a computer. *Address:* 82A Walsingham Road, Hove, E Sussex BN3 4FF. *T:* (01273) 323590.

LEVINGE, Sir Richard (George Robin), 12th Bt *cr* 1704; farming since 1968; *b* 18 Dec. 1946; *s* of Sir Richard Vere Henry Levinge, 11th Bt, MBE, TD, and Barbara Mary (*d* 1997), *d* of late George Jardine Kidston, CMG; *S* father, 1984; *m* 1st, 1969, Hilary (marr. diss. 1978), *d* of Dr Derek Mark; one *s*; 2nd, 1978, Donna Maria d'Ardia Caracciolo; one *s* one *d*. *Educ:* Brook House, Bray, Co. Wicklow; Hawkhurst Court, West Sussex; Mahwah High School, New York; Craibstone Agricultural Coll. *Heir: s* Richard Mark Levinge, *b* 15 May 1970.

LEVINSON, Prof. Stephen Curtis, PhD; FBA 1988; Director, Max Planck Institute for Psycholinguistics, since 1994 (Managing Director, 1998–2001, 2007–08); Professor, Radboud University (formerly Catholic University), Nijmegen, since 1995; *b* 6 Dec. 1947; *s* of Dr Gordon A. Levinson and Dr Mary C. Levinson; *m* 1976, Dr Penelope Brown; one *s*. *Educ:* Bedales Sch.; King's Coll., Cambridge (Sen. Schol.; 1st Cl. Hons. Archaeology and Anthropology Tripos 1970); PhD Linguistics Anthropology, Calif., 1977. Asst Lectr, 1975–78, Lectr, 1978–91, Reader, 1991–94, Linguistics Dept, Cambridge; Hd, Res. Gp for Cognitive Anthropol., Max Planck Inst. for Psycholinguistics, 1991–97. Vis. Res. Fellow, ANU, 1980–82; Vis. Associate Prof., Stanford Univ., 1987–88. MAE, 2003–. *Publications:* Pragmatics, 1983; (with Dr P. Brown) Politeness, 1987; (with J. Gumperz) Rethinking Linguistic Relativity, 1996; Presumptive Meanings: the theory of generalized conversational implicature, 2000; (ed with M. Bowerman) Language Acquisition and Conceptual Development, 2001; (ed with P. Jaisson) Evolution and Culture, 2006; (ed with D. Wilkins) Grammars of Space, 2006; (ed with N. Enfield) Roots of Human Sociality, 2006; articles in books and jls. *Recreations:* Sunday painting, hiking. *Address:* Payensweg 7, 6523 MB Nijmegen, The Netherlands; Max Planck Institute for Psycholinguistics, PB 310, 6500 AH Nijmegen, The Netherlands.

LEVITT, Alison Frances Josephine, (Lady Carlile of Berriew); QC 2008; a Recorder, since 2007; Partner and Head of Business Crime, Mishcon de Reya, since 2014; *b* London, 27 May 1963; *d* of Frederick David Andrew Levitt, OBE and Her Honour Christian Veronica Bevington, *qv*; *m* 1st, 1993, Matthew Miller (marr. diss.); two *d*; 2nd, 2007, Baron Carlile of Berriew, *qv*. *Educ:* City of London Sch. for Girls; Univ. of St Andrews (MA Hons 1986). Called to the Bar, Inner Temple, 1988, Bencher, 2009. Chm., Young Barristers Cttee, Bar Council, 1995; Sec., Criminal Bar Assoc., 2006–07; Principal Legal Advr to Dir of Public Prosecutions, 2009–14. *Recreations:* crime fiction, film. *Address:* Mishcon de Reya, Summit House, 12 Red Lion Square, WC1R 4QD. *T:* (020) 7440 7450. *E:* alison.levitt@mishcon.com.

LEVITT, Prof. Malcolm Harris, DPhil; FRS 2007; Professor of Physical Chemistry, University of Southampton, since 2001; *b* 10 Jan. 1957; *s* of Max and Stella Levitt; *m* 1990, Latha Kadalayil; one *d*. *Educ:* Keble Coll., Oxford (BA; DPhil 1981). Res. Scientist, MIT, 1986–92; Lectr, 1992–97, Prof. of Chemical Spectroscopy, 1997–2001, Stockholm Univ. *Publications:* Spin Dynamics: basics of nuclear magnetic resonance, 2001, 2nd edn 2007; contribs to jls. *Recreations:* electric guitar, classical guitar, politics, jazz, sketching, walking, gardening. *Address:* School of Chemistry, University of Southampton, Southampton SO17 1BJ. *T:* (023) 8059 6753, *Fax:* (023) 8059 3781. *E:* mhl@soton.ac.uk.

LEVITT, Prof. Michael, PhD; FRS 2001; Robert W. and Vivian K. Cahill Professor of Cancer Research, School of Medicine, Stanford University, California, since 2010 (Professor of Structural Biology, 1987–2010); *b* 9 May 1947; *s* of Nathan and Gertrude Levitt; *m* 1968, Rina Harel; three *s*. *Educ:* King's Coll., London (BSc Physics 1967); Gonville and Caius Coll., Cambridge (PhD Computational Biol. 1972). Royal Soc. Exchange Fellow, Weizmann Inst., Israel, 1967–68; Staff Scientist, MRC Lab. of Molecular Biol., Cambridge, 1973–80; Prof. of Chemical Physics, Weizmann Inst., 1980–87; Chair, 1993–2003, Associate Chair, 2005–10, Dept of Structural Biol., Stanford Univ. Mem., American Acad. of Arts and Scis, 2010. (Jtly) Nobel Prize in Chemistry, 2013. *Publications:* contrib. articles on computational biol. with an emphasis on structure, particularly of protein molecules. *Recreations:* cycling, ski-ing, travel. *Address:* Stanford School of Medicine, Stanford, CA 94305, USA. *T:* (650) 2760500, *Fax:* (650) 7238464. *E:* michael.levitt@stanford.edu.

LEVITT, Tom; freelance writer and consultant on third sector partnerships, since 2010; *b* 10 April 1954; *s* of John and Joan Levitt; *m* 1983, Teresa Sledziewska; one *d*. *Educ:* Lancaster Univ. (BSc Hons 1975); New Coll., Oxford (PGCE 1976). Biology teacher: Wootton Bassett Sch., 1976–79; Cirencester Sch., 1980–81; Brockworth Sch., Glos, 1981–91; supply Teacher, Staffs, 1991–95; freelance res. consultant, 1993–97. Member (Lab): Cirencester Town Council, 1983–87; Stroud DC, 1990–92; Derbys CC, 1993–97. Contested (Lab): Stroud, 1987; Cotswold, EP elecn, 1989; High Peak, 1992. MP (Lab) High Peak, 1997–2010. PPS to Minister of State, Home Office, 1999–2001, Cabinet Office, 2001, ODPM, 2001–03; PPS to Sec. of State for Internat. Develt, 2003–07; Asst Regl Minister, E Midlands, 2008–10. Member: Standards and Privileges Select Cttee, 1997–2003; Jt Cttee on Draft Disability Bill, 2004; DWP Select Cttee, 2007–10. Chm., Community Develt Foundn, 2004–10. Trustee: RNID, 1998–2003; Coalition for Efficiency, 2011–; Work Foundn Alliance, 2012–; Chm., Trustees, Concern Worldwide (UK), 2011–14. Patron, READ Internat., 2007–. DUniv Derby 2011. *Publications:* Sound Practice, 1995; Clear Access, 1997; Partners for Good: business, government and the third sector, 2012; Welcome to GoodCo: using the tools of business to create public benefit, 2014. *Recreations:* cricket, theatre, walking, travel.

LEVVY, (Clinton) George; management consultant, since 2004; *b* 30 Nov. 1953; *s* of late Guildford Albert Levvy and Averil Clinton Levvy (*née* Chance); *m* 1st, 1984, Irené M. Young (marr. diss. 1989); 2nd, 1991, Bethe R. Alpert; one *s* one *d*. *Educ:* Robert Gordon's Coll., Aberdeen; Univ. of Edinburgh (MB ChB). Jun. hosp. doctor, 1977–84; Med. Dir and Consultant, Excerpta Medica, Tokyo, 1984–88; Commercial Manager, Countrywide Communications Gp Ltd, 1988–91; Hd, Mktg and Communications, BRCS, 1991–94; Chief Exec., Motor Neurone Disease Assoc., 1995–2004. Member: Appraisal Cttee, NICE, 2000–06; Adv. Cttee, New and Emerging Applications of Technol., DoH, 2000–03. Trustee: Haemophilia Soc., 1999–2002; Self Help Africa, 2008–13. *Publications:* contribs to jls and ed vols. *Recreations:* walking, singing gospel, tennis, travel. *Address:* GLCE Ltd, North House, Farmoor Court, Cumnor Road, Oxford OX2 9LU. *T:* (01865) 525848.

LEVY, family name of **Baron Levy.**

LEVY, Baron *cr* 1997 (Life Peer), of Mill Hill in the London Borough of Barnet; **Michael Abraham Levy;** International Consultant, Global Consultancy Services, since 2008; *b* 11 July 1944; *s* of Samuel and Annie Levy; *m* 1967, Gilda (*née* Altbach); one *s* one *d*. *Educ:* Fleetwood Primary Sch. (Head Boy); Hackney Downs Grammar Sch. FCA 1966. Lubbock Fine (Chartered Accountants), 1961–66; Principal, M. Levy & Co., 1966–69; Partner, Wagner Prager Levy & Partners, 1969–73; Chairman: Magnet Group of Cos, 1973–88; D & J Securities Ltd, 1988–92; M & G Records, 1992–97; Wireart Ltd, 1992–2002; Chase Music (formerly M & G Music) Ltd, 1992–2002; Internat. Standard Asset Mgt, 2008–11; Vice Chairman: Phonographic Performance Ltd, 1979–84; British Phonographic Industry Ltd, 1984–87. Mem., Develt Bd, BL, 2008–11. Nat. Campaign Chm., United Jt Israel Appeal, 1982–85 (Hon. Vice Pres., 1994–2000; Hon. Pres., 2000–); Chairman: Jewish Care, 1992–97 (Pres., 1998–); Jewish Care Community Foundn, 1995–2010; Vice Chm., Central Council for Jewish Community Services (formerly Central Council for Jewish Social Services), 1994–99. Chairman: Chief Rabbinate Awards for Excellence, 1992–2007; Foundn for Educn, 1993–2006; Member: Jewish Agency World Bd of Governors, 1990–95 (World Chm., Youth Aliyah Cttee, 1991–95); Keren Hayesod World Bd of Governors, 1991–95; World Commn on Israel-Diaspora Relns, 1995–; Internat. Bd of Governors, Peres Center for Peace, 1997–2009; Adv. Council, Foreign Policy Centre, 1997–2006; NCVO Adv. Cttee, 1998–2011; Community Legal Service Champions Panel, 1999–2005; Hon. Cttee, Israel, Britain and the Commonwealth Assoc., 2000–11. Personal Envoy for Prime Minister to Middle East, 1999–2007. Pres., Community Service Volunteers, 1998–; Trustee: Holocaust Educnl Trust, 1998–2007; Policy Network Foundn, subseq. New Policy Network Foundn, 2000–07; Jewish Leadership Council, 2006–10; Mem. Exec. Cttee, Chai-Lifeline, 2001–02; Pres., Specialist Schs and Acads Trust, 2005–08; Patron: British Music Industry Awards, 1995– (Chm., Awards Cttee, 1992–95); Prostate Cancer Charitable Trust, 1997–2011; Friends of Israel Educnl Trust, 1998–2011; Save a Child's Heart Foundn, 2000–; Simon Marks Jewish Primary Sch. Trust, 2002–. Governor, Jews' Free Sch., subseq. JFS, 1990–95 (Hon. Pres., 1995–2001; Pres., 2001–). Hon. Patron, Cambridge Univ. Jewish Soc., 2002–; Pres., Jewish Lads' and Girls' Brigade, 2006–. Hon. Dr Middlesex Univ., 1999. B'nai B'rith First Lodge Award, 1994; Scopus Award, Hebrew Univ. of Jerusalem, 1998; Special Recognition Award, Israel Policy Forum (USA), 2003. *Publications:* A Question of Honour (memoirs), 2008. *Recreations:* tennis, swimming. *Address:* House of Lords, SW1A 0PW.

LEVY, Rabbi Dr Abraham, OBE 2004; Spiritual Head, Spanish and Portuguese Jews' Congregation in UK, 1983–2012, now Emeritus Spiritual Head; *b* 16 July 1939; *s* of Isaac Levy and Rachel (*née* Hassan); *m* 1963, Estelle Nahum; one *s*. *Educ:* Carmel Coll.; Jews' Coll.; UCL (PhD 1978). Minister, Spanish and Portuguese Jews' Congregation, 1962–80; Communal Rabbi and Spiritual Head, 1980–2012. Chaplain to Lord Mayor of London, 1998–99 and 2010–11. (With Chief Rabbi) Ecclesiastical Authy, Bd of Deputies of British Jews, 1980–2012. Founder and Dir, Young Jewish Leadership Inst., 1970–86; Founder and Principal, Naima Jewish Prep. Sch., 1983–; Dep. Pres., London Sch. of Jewish Studies (formerly Jews' Coll.), 1985–2012; Founder, Sephardi Centre, 1993; Hon. Principal, Montefiore Coll., 2005–. Mem., Standing Cttee, Conf. of Eur. Rabbis. Rabbinical Authy, London Bd of Shechitah, 2006–13; Vice Chm., Commn for the Licensing of Shochtim, 2006–13. Jewish Faith Advr, MoD, 2010–. President: Union Anglo-Jewish Preachers, 1973–75; Council of Christians and Jews, 2009–13; Vice President: Anglo-Jewish Assoc., 1984–; Jewish Historical Soc. of England, 2006–; British Friends of Hebrew Univ. Patron: Centre for Jewish-Christian Relations, Cambridge, 2001–; Jewish Med. Assoc. (UK), 2007–13; Hon. Patron, Cambridge Univ. Jewish Soc. Hon. Fellow, QMUL, 2012. Kt Comdr (Encomienda), Order of Merit (Spain), 1993. *Publications:* The Sephardim: a problem of survival, 1972; (jtly) Ages of Man, 1985; (jtly) The Sephardim, 1992. *Recreation:* collecting antique Judaica. *Address:* 2 Ashworth Road, W9 1JY. *T:* (020) 7432 1314.

LEVY, Andrea Doreen; novelist; *b* 7 March 1956; *d* of Winston and Amy Levy; *m* William Mayblin; two step *d*. *Educ:* Middlesex Polytech. (BA Hons (Textiles) 1978). Hon. Fellow, QMUL, 2011. Hon. Dr: Middlesex, 2006; Open, 2014. *Publications:* Every Light in the House Burnin', 1994; Never Far From Nowhere, 1996; Fruit of the Lemon, 1999; Small Island, 2004 (Orange Prize for Fiction, Whitbread Book of the Year, 2004; Commonwealth Writer's Prize, Orange Prize for Best of the Best, 2005); The Long Song, 2010 (Walter Scott Prize for Historical Fiction, 2011); Six Stories and an Essay, 2014. *Recreation:* curiosity and learning things. *Address:* c/o David Grossman, Literary Agency, 118B Holland Park Avenue, W11 4UA. *T:* (020) 7221 2770, *Fax:* (020) 7221 1445.

LEVY, David Anthony Lipton, DPhil; Director, Reuters Institute for the Study of Journalism, Department of Politics and International Relations, University of Oxford, since 2008; Fellow of Green Templeton College, Oxford, since 2008; *b* London, 12 Aug. 1953; *s* of Robert Levy and Rita Levy; *m* 1990, Joanna Moffett; one *s* one *d*. *Educ:* Haberdashers' Aske's Sch., Elstree; Univ. of York (BA Hons Mod. Hist. 1976); London Sch. of Econs and Pol Sci. (MA Area Studies Europe 1977); Nuffield Coll., Oxford (DPhil Mod. Hist. 1982). BBC: talks writer and producer, World Service and Radio 4, 1982–85; News and Current Affairs, 1985–94, Reporter: File on 4, Newsnight, Editor, Analysis; Public Policy, 1995–2007, Controller Public Policy, 2000–07. Lectr in French Politics and Contemp. Hist., Univ. of Salford, 1985–87; Associate Mem., Nuffield Coll., Oxford, 2009–. Vis. Prof., Sciences Po, Paris, 2012. Member: Content Bd, Ofcom, 2011–; Bd, UK Statistics Authy, 2012–. Member: Commn pour une nouvelle télévision publique, France, 2008; Bd, France 24, 2009–12. *Publications:* Europe's Digital Revolution: broadcasting regulation, the EU and the nation state, 1999; (ed with Tim Gardam) The Price of Plurality: choice, diversity and broadcasting institutions in the digital age, 2008; (ed with R. K. Nielsen) The Changing Business of Journalism and its Implications for Democracy, 2010; (ed with Robert G. Picard) Is There a Better Structure for News Providers?: the potential for charitable and trust ownership, 2011; (jtly) The Public Appetite for Foreign News on TV and Online, 2013; (ed jtly) Transparency and Accountability in Media and Government, 2013. *Recreations:* reading politics and history, rural France. *Address:* Reuters Institute for the Study of Journalism, Department of Politics and International Relations, University of Oxford, 13 Norham Gardens, Oxford OX2 6PS. *T:* (01865) 611080, *Fax:* (01865) 611094. *E:* reuters.institute@politics.ox.ac.uk. *Club:* Frontline.

LEVY, Deborah; novelist, playwright and poet; *b* Johannesburg, SA, 1959; *d* of Norman Levy and Philippa Beatrice Levy (*née* Murrell); *m* 1997, David Gale (marr. diss.); two *d*. *Educ:* St Saviour's and St Olave's Sch., London; Hampstead Sch., London; Dartington Coll. of Arts (BA Hons Theatre Lang. 1981). Playwright, incl. for RSC, 1981–. Fellow Commoner, Creative Arts, Trinity Coll., Cambridge, 1989–91; Lannan Lit. Fellow for Fiction, 2001; AHRB Fellow in Creative and Performing Arts, RCA, 2006–09; Vis. Prof., Falmouth Sch. of Art, Falmouth Univ., 2013–15. *Plays:* Pax, 1984; Heresies, 1985; Clam, 1985; The B-File; Call Blue Jane, 1993; Honey Baby, 1995; Macbeth - False Memories, 2000; The Inner Voice - I am Big, 2005. *Libretti include:* Blood Wedding (with composer Nicola LeFanu; adapted from Lorca), 1993; Shiny Nylon, 1994 and Walk Into Me, 2010 (with composer Billy Cowie). *Radio:* dramatisations incl. In a German Pension (Katherine Mansfield short stories), 2006; Freud: The Case Histories (2 episodes), 2012; The Glass Piano - Tormented Objects (drama documentary), 2010. Joseph Beuys Lect., Ruskin Sch. of Art, 2001. Co-Judge, Folio Prize, 2015. *Publications: short stories:* Ophelia and The Great Idea, 1985; Black Vodka, 2013; *novels:* Beautiful Mutants, 1987; Swallowing Geography, 1991; The Unloved, 1994; Billy and Girl, 1996; Swimming Home, 2011 (UK Author of Year, Specsavers Nat. Book Awards, 2012; Wingate Prize, Jewish Qly, 2013); Hot Milk, 2016; *other works:* An Amorous Discourse in the Suburbs of Hell (poetry), 1990; Diary of a Steak, 1997; Levy: Plays 1, 2000; Things I Don't Want to Know: a response to Orwell's essay 'Why I Write' (writing memoir), 2013; introductory essays to books. *Recreations:* wild swimming in rivers, lakes and oceans. *Address:* c/o A. M. Heath, 6 Warwick Court, WC1R 5DJ. *T:* (020) 7242 2811. *E:* victoria.hobbs@amheath.com. *Club:* Blacks.

LEVY, His Honour Dennis Martyn; QC 1982; a Circuit Judge, 1991–2007; a Deputy Circuit Judge, 2007–11; *b* 20 Feb. 1936; *s* of late Conrad Levy and Tillie (*née* Swift); *m* 1967, Rachel Jonah; one *s* one *d. Educ:* Clifton Coll.; Gonville and Caius Coll., Cambridge (MA). Called to the Bar, Gray's Inn, 1960, Hong Kong, 1985, Turks and Caicos Is, 1987. Granada Group Ltd, 1960–63; Time Products Ltd, 1963–67; in practice at the Bar, 1967–91; a Recorder, 1989–91. Member: Employment Appeal Tribunal, 1994–2006; Lands Tribunal, 1998. Vice Pres., UK Assoc. of Jewish Lawyers and Jurists, 2011–. Trustee, Fair Trials Internat. (formerly Fair Trials Abroad), 2002–. *Recreation:* living in London and travelling abroad. *Address:* 25 Harley House, Marylebone Road, NW1 5HE. *T:* 07773 429372, *Fax:* (020) 7487 3231. *E:* dennis.levy.uk@gmail.com.

LEVY, Jacob; QC 2014; *b* Bombay, 1962; *s* of Japheth and Iris Levy; *m* 1989, Sarah Jane; one *s* one *d. Educ:* Beal Grammar Sch. for Boys; London Sch. of Econs and Pol Sci. (LLB Hons). Called to the Bar, Inner Temple, 1986; in practice as barrister, specialising in personal injury and clinical negligence. *Recreations:* film, music, writing unproduced screenplays, watching rock bands. *Address:* 9 Gough Square, EC4A 3DG. *T:* (020) 7832 0538. *E:* jlevy@9goughsq.co.uk.

LEVY, Prof. John Court, (Jack), OBE 1984; FREng; FIMechE, FRAeS, FIEI; FCGI; Managing Director, Levytator Ltd, since 2001; *b* London, 16 Feb. 1926; *s* of Alfred and Lily Levy; *m* 1952, Sheila Frances Krisman; two *s* one *d. Educ:* Owen's Sch., London; Imperial Coll., Univ. of London (BScEng, ACGI, PhD); Univ. of Illinois, USA (MS). Stressman, Boulton-Paul Aircraft, 1945–47; Asst to Chief Engr, Fullers Ltd, 1947–51. Asst Lectr, Northampton Polytechnic, London, 1951–53; Fulbright Award to Univ. of Illinois, for research into metal fatigue, 1953–54; Lectr, Sen. Lectr, Reader, Northampton Polytechnic (later City Univ.), 1954–66; also a Recognised Teacher of the Univ. of London, 1958–66; Head of Department of Mechanical Engineering, 1966–83 (now Prof. Emeritus), and Pro-Vice-Chancellor, 1975–81, City Univ.; Dir, Engrg Profession, Engrg Council, 1983–90, 1997. Consultant to Shell International Marine, 1963–85; Chairman: 1st Panel on Marine Technology, SRC, 1971–73; Chartered Engr Section, Engineers Registration Bd, CEI, 1978–82; non-exec. Dir, City Technology Ltd, 1980–91. Vice Chm., Bd of Govs, Middlesex Univ., 1997–2000; Chm., Mus. of Domestic Design and Architecture, 1999–2002. Freeman, City of London, 1991; Liveryman, Co. of Engineers, 1991. FREng (FEng 1988); FIEI 2002. Hon. DTech CNAA, 1990; DUniv: Leeds Metropolitan, 1992; Middlesex, 2005; Hon DSc City, 1994. Internat. Gold Medal for contribs to engrg educn, WFEO, 1999. *Publications:* The Engineering Dimension in Europe, 1991; papers on metal fatigue, marine technology, engrg educn, in jls of IMechE, RAeS, IEE, etc. *Recreations:* theatre, chess, exploring cities. *Address:* 18 Woodberry Way, Finchley, N12 0HG. *T:* (020) 8445 5227. *Club:* Island Sailing (Cowes).

LEVY, Paul, PhD; FRSL; author and broadcaster; Senior Contributor, Europe Leisure and Arts, Wall Street Journal, since 1993; *b* 26 Feb. 1941; *er s* of late H. S. Levy and Mrs Shirley Meyers, Lexington, Ky, USA; *m* 1977, Penelope, *oc* of late Clifford and Ruby Marcus; two *d. Educ:* Univ. of Chicago (AB); University Coll. London; Harvard Univ. (PhD 1979); Nuffield Coll., Oxford. FRSL 1980. Teaching Fellow, Harvard, 1966–68; lapsed academic, 1971–; freelance journalist, 1974–80; Food Correspondent, 1980–82, Food and Wine Ed., 1982–92, The Observer; Wine and Food Writer, You Mag., Mail on Sunday, 1993–2013; frequent radio and television broadcasting. Dir, Isishome Ltd, 1980–. Member: Soc. of Authors; PEN; Critics' Circle (Music, Drama and Art and Arch. Sections); Mem. Court, Oxford Brookes Univ., 2003–10. Trustee: Strachey Trust, 1972–; Jane Grigson Trust, 1990–2014; Oxford Symposium on Food and Cooking, 2002–09, 2010– (co-Chair, 2005–15; Chair of Trustees, 2011–15). Blog: Plain English, www.artsjournal.com, 2008–. Susan Potter Prize for Comparative Lit., Harvard, 1968; Corning Award for food writing, 1980, 1981; Glenfiddich Food Writer of the Year, 1980, 1983; Glenfiddich Restaurant Critic of the Year, 1983; Specialist Writer Commendation, British Press Awards, 1985, 1987; Wine Journalist of the Year, Wine Guild of the UK, 1986. Confrérie des Mousquetaires, 1981; Chevalier du Tastevin, 1987; Chevalier de l'Ordre des Dames du Vin et de la Table, 1989; Chevalier de l'Ordre de la Dinde de Licques, 1991. *Publications:* (ed) Lytton Strachey: the really interesting question, 1972; The Bloomsbury Group, in Essays on John Maynard Keynes, ed Milo Keynes, 1975; G. E. Moore and the Cambridge Apostles, 1979, 3rd edn 1989; (ed with Michael Holroyd) The Shorter Strachey, 1980, 2nd edn 1989; (with Ann Barr) The Official Foodie Handbook, 1984; Out to Lunch, 1986 (Seagrams/Internat. Assoc. of Cookery Professionals Award, USA, 1988), 2nd edn 2003; Finger-Lickin' Good: a Kentucky childhood (autobiog.), 1990; The Feast of Christmas, 1992 (also TV series); (ed) The Penguin Book of Food and Drink, 1996; (ed) Eminent Victorians: the definitive edition, 2002; Frances Partridge: a memoir, 2004; (ed) The Letters of Lytton Strachey, 2005; Bloomsbury Reassessed, in Irrepressible Adventures with Britannia, ed Wm Roger Louis, 2013; contribs (as obituarist) to Independent, 1990–, Daily and Sunday Telegraph, 2012–; contrib. Oxford DNB, 2000–. *Recreations:* being cooked for, drinking better wine, trying hard to remember, codgering. *Address:* Millwood Farmhouse, Millwood End, Long Hanborough, Witney, Oxon OX29 8BP. *T:* (01993) 881312. *Clubs:* Groucho, Quo Vadis.

LEVY, Prof. Raymond, FRCPE, FRCPsych; Professor of Old Age Psychiatry, University of London at Institute of Psychiatry, 1984–96, now Emeritus Professor, King's College London; Hon. Consultant, Bethlem Royal and Maudsley Hospitals, since 1984; *b* 23 June 1933; *o s* of late Gaston Levy and Esther Levy (*née* Bigio); *m* 1st, 1956, Katherine Margaret Logie (marr. diss. 1982); two *d*; 2nd, 2012, Aykan Pulularş. *Educ:* Victoria Coll., Cairo; Edinburgh Univ. (MB, ChB 1957; PhD 1961); Univ. of London (DPM 1964). Jun. hosp. appts, Royal Infirmary, Northern Gen., Leith, Bethlem Royal and Maudsley Hosps, to 1966; Sen. Lectr and Hon. Consultant Psychiatrist, Middx Hosp. Med. Sch., 1966–71; Consultant Psychiatrist, Bethlem Royal and Maudsley Hosps, 1971–84. Mem., Med. Adv. Commn on Res. into Ageing. Pres., Internat. Psychogeriatric Assoc., 1995–98 (Mem., Bd of Dirs, 1998–2000); Vice-Pres., Eur. Assoc. Geriatric Psych.; Foundn Mem., RCPsych, 1971. Asst Editor, Internat. Jl Geriatric Psych. *Publications:* (all jtly) The Psychiatry of Late Life, 1982; Diagnostic and Therapeutic Assessment in Alzheimer's Disease, 1991; Delusions and Hallucinations in Old Age, 1992; Clinical diversity in late onset of Alzheimer's Disease, 1992; Treatment and Care in Old Age Psychiatry, 1993; Dementia, 1993; The Complex of Beyazid II in Edirne, 2008; The Strange Life and Death of Dr de Clérambault, 2009; Mamnou': a return to Cairo, 2012; contribs to learned jls. *Recreations:* looking at pictures, drinking good wine, travelling, playing tennis. *Address:* Institute of Psychiatry, Psychology and Neuroscience, King's College London, 16 De Crespigny Park, SE5 8AF. *T:* (020) 7467 0512; 4 Hillsleigh Road, W8 7LE. *Clubs:* Campden Hill Lawn Tennis, Holland Park Lawn Tennis.

LEVY, Robert Stuart; QC 2010; *b* London, 18 Jan. 1964; *s* of Dr Ralph Levy and Elizabeth Levy; *m* 1990, Karen Frances Prooth; one *s* two *d. Educ:* City of London Sch.; NE London Poly.; Magdalene Coll., Cambridge (LLB; LLM 1987). Called to the Bar, Middle Temple, 1988; in practice as barrister, specialising in commercial law. *Recreations:* ukelele, piano, banjo, accordion, ski-ing. *Address:* XXIV Old Buildings, Lincoln's Inn, WC2A 3UP. *T:* (020) 7691 2323. *E:* robert.levy@xxiv.co.uk.

LEVY-LANG, André; Légion d'Honneur; Chairman: Compagnie Financière de Paribas, 1990–99; Banque Paribas, 1991–99; *b* 26 Nov. 1937. *Educ:* Ecole Polytechnique; Stanford Univ. (PhD Business Admin; Harkness Fellow, 1963–65). Res. physicist, French Atomic Energy Commn, 1960–62; Schlumberger Gp, 1962–74; Compagnie Bancaire: joined 1974; Mem. Bd, 1979; Chm., 1982; Chm., Adv. Bd, 1993. Director: Schlumberger, 1993–; AGF, 1994; Dexia, 2000; Mem. Exec. Cttee, Pargesa Holding; Chm., Supervisory Bd, Les Echos. Bd mem., banking and employers' assocs. Associate Prof. of Finance, Univ. Paris-Dauphine, 2001, now Emeritus. *Publications:* L'Argent, la Finance et le Risque, 2006. *Address:* 48 boulevard Emile Augier, 75116 Paris, France.

LEW, Julian David Mathew; QC 2002; barrister and international arbitrator; *b* 3 Feb. 1948; *s* of Rabbi Maurice Abram Lew and Rachel Lew (*née* Segalov); *m* 1978, Margot (*née* Perk); two *d. Educ:* Carmel Coll.; Univ. of London (LLB Hons ext. 1969); Catholic Univ. of Louvain (PhD 1977). Barrister at Law, 1970; Solicitor, 1981; Attorney-at-Law, NY, 1981; Partner: S. J. Berwin & Co., 1986–92; Coudert Brothers, 1992–95; Herbert Smith, 1995–2005. Dir, 1983–88, Mem. Court, 2002–07, London Court of Internat. Arbitration; UK Mem., Internat. Court of Arbitration, ICC, 2005–; Mem. Court, Singapore Internat. Arbitration Centre, 2013–15. Mem. Council, ICC Inst. of World Business Law, 2000–; Co-Chm., Taskforce on Costs in Internat. Arbitration, ICC Commn on Internat. Arbitration, 2011–; Mem., Adv. Council, Hong Kong Internat. Arbitration Centre, 2014–. Prof. and Head, Sch. of Internat. Arbitration, Centre for Commercial Law Studies, QMUL (formerly QMC, then QMW), 1986–; Visiting Professor: Faculty of Law, Tel Aviv Univ., 2002; Bar Ilan Univ., Israel, 2005; Hebrew Univ., Jerusalem, 2010. Hon. Fellow, QMUL, 2009. *Publications:* Applicable Law on International Commercial Arbitration, 1978; (ed jtly) International Trade: law and practice, 1983, 2nd edn 1990; (ed) Contemporary Problems in International Commercial Arbitration, 1986; (ed) Immunity of Arbitrators, 1990; (ed jtly) Recognition of Foreign Judgments, 1994–; (jtly) Comparative International Commercial Arbitration, 2003; (jtly) Parallel State and Arbitral Procedures in International Arbitration, 2005; (ed jtly) Pervasive Problems in International Arbitration, 2006; (ed jtly) Arbitration Insights: twenty years of the annual lecture of the School of International Arbitration, 2007; (ed jtly) Arbitration in England (with chapters on Scotland and Ireland), 2013. *Address:* (chambers) 20 Essex Street, WC2R 3AL. *T:* (020) 7842 1200, *Fax:* (020) 7842 1270. *E:* jlew@20essexst.com.

LEWELL-BUCK, Emma Louise; MP (Lab) South Shields, since May 2013; *b* South Shields, 8 Nov. 1978; *d* of David and Linda Lewell; *m* 2010, Simon John Paul Buck. *Educ:* Northumbria Univ. (BA Hons Politics and Media Studies 2002); Durham Univ. (MSW 2008). Sales asst, Fenwick Ltd, 1998–2002; sessional playworker, N Tyneside Council, 2001–02; customer services, Traidcraft plc, 2002–05; Child Protection Social Worker: Sunderland CC, 2007–10; Newcastle CC, 2010–13. Mem. (Lab) S Tyneside Council, 2004–13 (Lead Mem., Adult Social Care and Support Services, 2009–13). PPS to Shadow Sec. of State for NI, 2013–15. *Recreations:* walking, spending time with friends and family, travelling, foreign languages, reading. *Address:* House of Commons, SW1A 0AA. *T:* (020) 7219 4468, *Fax:* (020) 7219 0264; (office) Ede House, 143 Westoe Road, South Shields, Tyne and Wear NE33 3PD. *T:* (0191) 427 1240, *Fax:* (0191) 427 6418. *E:* emma.lewell-buck.mp@parliament.uk.

LEWER, Andrew Iain, MBE 2014; Member (C) East Midlands Region, European Parliament, since 2014; *b* Burnley, Lancs, 18 July 1971; *s* of Clifford and Sandra Lewer; *m* 2005, Maria Gabriela Ciacia Lobo; one *s. Educ:* Queen Elizabeth Grammar Sch., Ashbourne, Derbys; Univ. of Newcastle upon Tyne (BA Hist. 1992). Former Sales and Mktg Manager, Landmark Publishing Ltd. Member (C): Derbys Dales DC, 2003–15; Derbys CC, 2005–15 (Leader, 2009–13). Dep. Chm., 2011–14, Vice-Pres., 2014–, LGA. Dir, Derbys Historic Bldgs Trust, 2003–. Gov., Univ. of Derby, 2009–. *Publications:* (contrib.) The Oxford Companion to British History, 1997. *Recreations:* collecting books, history and conservation, swimming, family, cinema, opera. *Address:* European Parliament, Rue Wiertz 60, 1047 Brussels, Belgium. *T:* 22845598. *E:* andrew.lewer@europarl.europa.eu.

LEWER, Michael Edward, CBE 2002; QC 1983; a Recorder of the Crown Court, 1983–98; a Deputy High Court Judge, 1989–98; *b* 1 Dec. 1933; *s* of late Stanley Gordon Lewer and Jeanie Mary Lewer; *m* 1965, Bridget Mary Gill; two *s* two *d. Educ:* Tonbridge Sch.; Oriel Coll., Oxford (MA). Called to Bar, Gray's Inn, 1958, Bencher, 1992. Territorial Army: Captain, 300 LAA Regt, RA, 1955–64; APIS, Intelligence Corps, 1964–67. Chm., Home Secretary's Adv. Cttee on Local Govt Electoral Arrangements for England, 1971–73; Comr, Parly Boundary Commn for England, 1997–2008 (Asst Comr, 1965–69, 1976–88, 1992–96). Member: Criminal Injuries Compensation Appeals Panel, 1994–2008 (Chm., 1994–2002); Criminal Injuries Compensation Bd, 1986–2000; Consultant, Criminal Injuries Compensation Authy, 2008–09. Mem., European Parly Constituency Cttee for England, 1993–94. Member: Bar Council, 1978–81; Bar Council Professional Conduct Cttee, 1993–95 (Vice Chm., 1995).

LEWERS, Rt Rev. Richard Alexander; *see* Armidale, Bishop of.

LEWES, Bishop Suffragan of, since 2014; **Rt Rev. Richard Charles Jackson;** *b* Hillingdon, 22 Jan. 1961; *s* of Donald and Mary Jackson; *m* 1985, Deborah Lee; two *s* one *d. Educ:* Latymer Upper Sch.; Christ Church, Oxford (MA); Cranfield Univ. (MSc 1985); Trinity Coll., Bristol (DipHE). Sen. Agronomist, Cleanacres Ltd, 1985–92; ordained deacon, 1994, priest, 1995; Curate, Lindfield, 1994–98; Vicar, Rudgwick, 1998–2009; Rural Dean of Horsham, 2005–09; Diocesan Mission and Renewal Advr, 2009–14. *Recreations:* walking, woodwork, motorcycling. *Address:* Church House, 211 New Church Road, Hove BN3 4ED. *T:* (01273) 421021. *E:* bishop.lewes@chichester.anglican.org.

LEWIN SMITH, Jane; Vice Lord-Lieutenant for Cambridgeshire, since 2006; *b* 18 Feb. 1950; *d* of late Brian Frederick Bartholomew and of Thelma Evelyn Bartholomew; *m* 1972, John Mann Lewin Smith; one *s* one *d. Educ:* Perse Sch. for Girls, Cambridge; Univ. of Bristol (BSc Soc. Sci.); Homerton Coll., Cambridge (Cert Ed). Chm., W Suffolk Co. Riding for the Disabled Assoc., 1988–96. Chm., British American Community Relns Cttee, RAF Mildenhall, 2003–09. Patron, Isle of Ely Arts Fest., 2014; Trustee, Ely Cathedral, 2014. JP E Cambs, 1994–2008; High Sheriff, 2002–03, DL 2003, Cambs. *Recreations:* horseracing, fishing, gardening. *Club:* Royal Worlington and Newmarket Golf.

LEWINGTON, Charles; *see* Lewington, T. C.

LEWINGTON, Richard George; HM Diplomatic Service, retired; Chief Technical Adviser, EU Border Management in Central Asia Programme, Dushanbe, Tajikistan, 2007–09; *b* 13 April 1948; *s* of late Jack and Ann Lewington; *m* 1972, Sylviane Paulette Marie Cholet; one *s* one *d. Educ:* Orchard Secondary Modern Sch., Slough; Slough Grammar Sch.; Bristol Coll. of Commerce. Joined HM Diplomatic Service, 1967; full-time Russian lang. trng, RAEC Beaconsfield, 1971–72; Ulaan Baatar, 1972–75; Lima, 1976–80; FCO, 1980–82; Moscow, 1982–83; First Sec. (Commercial), Tel Aviv, 1986–90; FCO, 1991–95; Dep. High Comr, Malta, 1995–99; Ambassador: to Kazakhstan and Kyrgyzstan, 1999–2002; to Ecuador, 2003–06. EU Monitoring Mission, Georgia, 2011–12. Mem. Council, Royal Soc. for Asian Affairs, 2007–. Trustee, Dorset Expeditionary Soc., 2007–; Mem., Soc. of Dorset Men, 2006–. *Recreations:* collecting old books and maps on Dorset, iPodding, country walks.

LEWINGTON, (Thomas) Charles, OBE 1997; Managing Director, Hanover Communications International (formerly Media Strategy Ltd), since 1998; *b* 6 April 1959; *s* of late Maurice Lewington and Sheila Lewington; *m* 1995, Philippa Jane Kelly; one *d*. *Educ:* Sherborne Sch., Dorset; Univ. of Bath (BSc Econs). Reporter, Bath Evening Chronicle, 1981–86; Western Daily Press: Asst News Editor, 1986–88; Political Corresp., 1988–90; Political Corresp., Daily Express, 1990–92; Political Editor, Sunday Express, 1992–95; Dir of Communications, Cons. Party, 1995–97. Non-exec. Dir, Cobra Beers Ltd, 2008–09. Comr, Royal Hosp. Chelsea, 2014–. *Recreations:* reading, playing the piano. *Address:* (office) 70 Gray's Inn Road, WC1X 8BT. *T:* (020) 7400 4480; 62 Wandle Road, SW17 7DW. *T:* (020) 8672 3944. *Clubs:* Garrick, Soho House, Ivy.

LEWINTON, Sir Christopher, Kt 1993; CEng; FIMechE, FREng; FRAeS; Chairman: CL Partners, since 2000; Camper & Nicholsons Marina Investments Ltd, since 2008; *b* 6 Jan. 1932; *s* of Joseph and Elizabeth Lewinton; *m* 1st, Jennifer Alcock (marr. diss.); two *s*; 2nd, 1979, Louise Head; two step *s*. *Educ:* Acton Technical College. CEng 1965; FIMechE 1992. Army Service, Lieut REME. Pres., Wilkinson Sword, N America, 1960–71; Chief Exec., Wilkinson Sword Group, 1970–85; Pres., Internat. Gp, Allegheny International, 1978–85 (Mem. Board, 1976–85); TI Gp plc: Chief Exec., 1986–99; Chm., 1989–2000; Chm., Dowty Gp PLC, 1992–2000. Mem., Exec. Bd, J. F. Lehman & Co., 2000–; non-executive Director: Reed Elsevier, 1993–99; Mannesmann AG, 1995–99; Messier-Dowty, 1994–98; Young & Rubicam, NY, 1996–2001; WPP, 2001–03; Advr, Booz Allen Hamilton, 2001–07; Mem. Adv. Bd, Morgan Stanley/Metalmark Capital, 2001–. FRAeS 1993; FREng (FEng 1994). Hon. DTech Brunel, 1997. *Recreations:* golf, tennis, shooting, reading. *Address:* CL Partners, Fifth Floor, Cording House, 34–35 St James's Street, SW1A 1HD. *T:* (020) 7201 5490. *Clubs:* Boodle's; Royal Thames Yacht; Sunningdale Golf; University (New York); Everglades, Four Arts (Palm Beach).

LEWIS; *see* Day-Lewis.

LEWIS, family name of **Baron Merthyr**.

LEWIS, Adam Anthony Murless, CVO 2006; FRCS, FRCSE; Serjeant Surgeon to the Queen, 2001–06; Consultant Surgeon, Royal Free Hospital, 1975–2006; Surgeon: St John and Elizabeth Hospital, London, 1975–2006; King Edward VII Hospital for Officers, London, 1991–2006; *s* of late Bernard S. Lewis, CBE, DSC and Mary Lewis (*née* Murless); *m* 1964, Margaret Catherine Ann Surgey; two *s* two *d*. *Educ:* St Bartholomew's Hosp. Med. Coll. (MB, BS London 1963); FRCSE 1968; FRCS 1969. Formerly: Sen. Registrar (Surg.), Royal Free Hosp.; Post Doctoral Fellow, Stanford Univ.; Sen. Lectr (Surg.), Univ. of Benin. Surgeon to Royal Household, 1991–2001. *Publications:* papers on general and gastro-intestinal surgery.

LEWIS, Adam Valentine Shervey; QC 2009; *b* Oxford, 20 Feb. 1963; *s* of Peter and Gillian Lewis; *m* 1996, Beate Mjaaland; one *s* one *d*. *Educ:* Trinity Hall, Cambridge (BA 1984). Called to the Bar, Gray's Inn, 1985; in practice as barrister, specialising in public law, EU and competition law, sport. *Publications:* Sport: law and practice, 2003, 3rd edn 2014. *Recreations:* cycling, cross country ski-ing, open water swimming, mountaineering. *Address:* Blackstone Chambers, Blackstone House, Temple, EC4Y 9BW.

LEWIS, Prof. Alastair Charles, PhD; Professor of Atmospheric Chemistry, University of York, since 2006; Research Director, National Centre for Atmospheric Science, since 2006; *b* Chatham, 6 Aug. 1971; *s* of Raymond Ernest Lewis and Dulcie Margaret Lewis (*née* Woods); *m* 1999, Prof. Lucy Jane Carpenter; one *s* one *d*. *Educ:* Sir Joseph Williamson's Mathematical Sch., Rochester; Univ. of Leeds (BSc Hons Chem. 1992; PhD Chem. 1995). Lectr, Univ. of Leeds, 1997–2003; Reader, Univ. of York, 2003–06. Lectr, RMIT Univ., Melbourne, 1999. Advr (pt-time), NERC, 2007–13; Member: Air Quality Expert Gp, DEFRA, 2011–; Sci. Adv. Panel, UNEP, 2015–. FRSC 2012. Desty Meml Prize for Innovation in Separation Sci., 2001; Philip Leverhulme Award, 2004; SAC Silver Medal, 2006, John Jeyes Award, 2012, RSC. *Publications:* Multidimensional Chromatography, 2002; over 200 articles in jls on atmospheric sci. and analytical chemistry. *Recreations:* distance running, cycling, mountain biking. *Address:* Wolfson Atmospheric Chemistry Laboratories, Innovation Way, University of York, Heslington, York YO10 5DD. *T:* (01904) 322522, *Fax:* (01904) 322516. *E:* ally.lewis@york.ac.uk, ally.lewis@ncas.ac.uk.

LEWIS, Andrew William; QC 2009; a Recorder, since 2001; a Deputy High Court Judge, since 2010; *b* London, 23 Oct. 1962; *s* of Norman John Lewis and Sylvia Lillian Lewis (*née* Allen); *m* 1990, Ruth Alison Hobson; four *s*. *Educ:* Beechen Cliff Comprehensive Sch., Bath; Coventry Poly. (BA Hons Business Law). Called to the Bar, Lincoln's Inn, 1985; in practice as barrister, specialising in personal injury and clinical negligence; Hd, Park Square Barristers. Co-Ed., Butterworths Personal Injury Litigation Service, 2012–. *Recreations:* watching four sons play sport, veterans football with HOTH FC, ski-ing, photography. *Address:* Park Square Barristers, 6 Park Square, Leeds LS1 2LW. *E:* lewisqc@psqb.co.uk.

LEWIS, Ann Walford, CMG 2000; HM Diplomatic Service, retired; *b* 2 May 1940; *d* of Dr Gwyn Walford Lewis and Winifred Marguerite Emma Lewis; one *s*. *Educ:* Allerton High Sch., Leeds; Leeds Univ. (BA). Teacher, translator and journalist, Finland, 1962–66; HM Diplomatic Service, 1966–2000: Research Dept, FCO, 1966–70; Second Secretary: Moscow, 1970–71; Res. Dept, FCO, 1971–72; Helsinki, 1972–74; Res. Dept, FCO, 1974–79; on secondment as Mem., Assessments Staff, Cabinet Office, 1979–82; Head of Chancery, E Berlin, 1982–85; Eastern Eur. Dept, FCO, 1985–91 (Dep. Head, 1988–91); Dep. Head, 1991–96, Head, 1996–2000, Cultural Relns Dept, FCO. Founder Dir, 1992, Dep. Chm., 1998–, English Coll. Foundn; Governor: English Coll., Prague, 1995– (Dep. Chm. of Govs, 2009–); St Clare's, Oxford, 2000– (Dep. Chm., 2006–). Trustee, BEARR Trust, 1999–. *Publications:* (ed) The EU and Ukraine: neighbours, friends, partners?, 2002; (ed) The EU and Belarus: between Moscow and Brussels, 2002; (ed) The EU and Moldova: on a fault-line of Europe, 2003; (ed) Old Roots, New Shoots: the story of the English College in Prague, 2004; (ed) Leaves and Branches: the first 20 years of the English College in Prague, 2014. *Recreations:* theatre, gardening, travel. *Address:* 16 Townley Road, SE22 8SR. *T:* (020) 8693 6418.

LEWIS, Anthony Meredith; Senior Partner, 1986–89, Joint Senior Partner, 1989–94, Taylor Joynson Garrett; *b* 15 Nov. 1940; *s* of Col Glyndwr Vivian Lancelot Lewis and Gillian Lewis (*née* Fraser); *m* 1970, Mrs Ewa Maria Anna Strawinska, former Social Editor of Tatler; one *s* one *d*. *Educ:* Rugby School; St Edmund Hall, Oxford (MA Law). Freshfields, 1964–70; Partner, Joynson-Hicks, 1970–86. Chief Exec., City & Thames Gp, 1994–. Panel Mem., The Prince's Trust, 1996–2005. *Recreations:* opera, tennis, ski-ing, golf, piano.

LEWIS, Anthony Robert, (Tony Lewis), CBE 2002; writer; columnist, Western Mail newspaper and Wales Online, since 2015; *b* 6 July 1938; *s* of Wilfrid Llewellyn Lewis and Florence Marjorie Lewis (*née* Flower); *m* 1962, Joan (*née* Pritchard); two *d*. *Educ:* Neath Grammar Sch.; Christ's Coll., Cambridge (MA). Double Blue, Rugby football, 1959, cricket, 1960–62, Captain of cricket, 1962, Cambridge Univ. Glamorgan CCC: cricketer, 1955–74; Captain, 1967–72; Chm., 1988–93; Trustee, 1992–; Pres., 1999–2005; 9 Tests for England, 1972–73 (Captain of 8); Captained MCC to India, Ceylon and Pakistan, 1972–73. MCC: Mem. sub-cttees, 1967–, incl. five years framing 1980 Code of Cricket Laws; Trustee, 2002–03; Chm. of Cricket, 2003–07; Chm., World Cricket Cttee, 2006–. Presenter: sports and arts magazine programmes, HTV, 1971–82; Sport on Four, BBC Radio, 1977–86; BBC TV presenter of cricket and commentator, 1974–98; Cricket Correspondent, Sunday Telegraph, 1974–93; freelance sports contributor, Sunday Telegraph, 1993–99. Chm., World Snooker Ltd, 2003. Dir, Bulldog Publications, 2000–; Marketing Consultant, Long Reach Internat. Insurance, 2003–11. Consultant, Univ. of Wales, Newport, 2004–07. Chm. Cttee, Assoc. of Business Sponsorship of the Arts (Wales), 1988–90; Member: Bd, Sports Council for Wales, 1967–69; Welsh Economic Council, 1994–96; Tourism Action Gp, CBI, 1994–2000; Bd, BTA, 1992–2000; Chm., Wales Tourist Bd, 1992–2000. Chm., Wales Ryder Cup bid, 2000–01. Chm., Bd, WNO, 2003–06. Trustee, Wales Millennium Centre, 2003–07. Pres., Lord's Taverners Wales, 2012–. DL, 1994, High Sheriff, 1998–99, Mid Glam. Hon. Fellow: St David's Univ. Coll., Lampeter, 1993; Univ. of S Wales (formerly Glamorgan Univ.), 1995; Univ. of Wales, Swansea, 1996; Cardiff Univ., 1999; Univ. of Wales, Newport, 2008. *Publications:* A Summer of Cricket, 1976; Playing Days, 1985; Double Century, 1987; Cricket in Many Lands, 1991; MCC Masterclass, 1994; Taking Fresh Guard, 2003. *Recreations:* classical music, golf. *Clubs:* East India (Hon. Mem., 2013), MCC (Pres., 1998–2000; Hon. Life Vice Pres., 2011); Royal Porthcawl Golf (Capt., 2012–13), Royal & Ancient Golf.

LEWIS, Prof. Barry, MD, PhD; FRCP; FRCPath; Professor Emeritus, University of London; *b* 16 March 1929; *s* of George Lewis and Pearl Lewis; *m* 1972, Eve Simone Rothschild; two *s* one *d*, and one *s* two *d* by a previous marriage. *Educ:* Rondebosch School, Cape Town; University of Cape Town (MB ChB 1952; PhD 1956; MD 1958). MRCPE 1959; MRCP 1964, FRCP 1975; FRCPath 1980. Training posts, Groote Schuur Hosp., Cape Town, 1953; lectureship and fellowships, St George's Hosp., 1959; Consultant Pathologist, St Mark's Hosp., 1967; opened lipid clinic, 1968, Sen. Lectr in Chemical Pathology, and Hon. Consultant Physician, 1969–76, Hammersmith Hosp.; Chm., Dept of Chem. Path. and Metabolic Disorders, Hon. Consultant Physician, and Dir of Lipid Clinic, St Thomas' Hosp., 1976–88; Consultant Physician, specialising in lipid disorders: St Thomas' Hosp., 1989–95; 14 Wimpole St, 1995–2002; London Medical, 2002–06. Principal Investigator, St Thomas' Atherosclerosis Regression Trial, 1984–92. Recent research and clinical interests: hyperlipidaemia, causes, prevention and regression of atherosclerosis, prevention of cardiovascular disease. Founder Chm., Internat. Taskforce for Prevention of Coronary Heart Disease, 1987–94. Life FRSocMed, 1989. Heinrich Wieland Prize, 1980. *Publications:* The Hyperlipidaemias: clinical and laboratory practice, 1976; (with Eve Lewis) The Heart Book, 1980; (with N. Miller) Lipoproteins, Atherosclerosis and Coronary Heart Disease, 1981; (jtly) Metabolic and Molecular Bases of Acquired Disease, 1990; Handbook on Prevention of Coronary Heart Disease, 1990; (with G. Assmann) Social and Economic Contexts of Coronary Disease Prevention, 1990; (jtly) Prevention of Coronary Heart Disease in the Elderly, 1991; (jtly) Prevention of Coronary Heart Disease: scientific background and clinical guidelines, 1993; (jtly) Low Blood Cholesterol: health implications, 1993; Paradise Regained: insights into coronary heart disease prevention, 1997; (contrib.) Nutrition, Metabolism and Cardiovascular Disease, 2009; (jtly) On reducing cardiovascular disease to a rarity, 2010; (jtly) The Classification of Dyslipidaemia and its implications for Clinical Management, 2011; (contrib.) Evolution of the Lipid Clinic 1968–2008, 2014; Thought for food: clinical evidence for the dietary prevention strategy in cardiovascular disease, 2013; (contrib.) Lipoproteins in Diabetes Mellitus, 2014; 300 papers on heart disease, nutrition and lipoproteins in med. and sci. jls. *Recreations:* music, travel, reading, French language. *Address:* 48 Landing Drive, Dobbs Ferry, NY 10522, USA.

LEWIS, Bernard, BA, PhD; FBA 1963; FRHistS; Cleveland E. Dodge Professor of Near Eastern Studies, Princeton University, 1974–86, now Emeritus; Director of Annenberg Research Institute, Philadelphia, 1986–90; *b* London, 31 May 1916; *s* of H. Lewis, London; *m* 1947, Ruth Hélène (marr. diss. 1974), *d* of late Overretsagfórer M. Oppenhejm, Copenhagen; one *s* one *d*. *Educ:* Wilson Coll.; The Polytechnic; Universities of London and Paris (Fellow UCL 1976). Derby Student, 1936. Asst Lecturer in Islamic History, Sch. of Oriental Studies, University of London, 1938; Prof. of History of Near and Middle East, SOAS, London Univ., 1949–74 (Hon. Fellow, 1986). Served RAC and Intelligence Corps, 1940–41; attached to a dept of Foreign Office, 1941–45. Visiting Professor: UCLA, 1955–56; Columbia Univ., 1960; Indiana Univ., 1963; Collège de France, 1980; Ecole des Hautes Etudes, Paris 1983, 1988; A. D. White Prof.-at-Large, Cornell Univ., 1984–90; Hon. Incumbent, Kemal Atatürk Chair in Ottoman and Turkish Studies, Princeton Univ., 1992–93. Vis. Mem., 1969, Long-term Mem., 1974–86, Inst. for Advanced Study, Princeton, New Jersey; Lectures: Class of 1932, Princeton Univ., 1964; Gottesman, Yeshiva Univ., 1974; Exxon Foundn, Chicago, 1986; Tanner, Brasenose Coll., Oxford, 1990; Jefferson, NEH, 1990; Il Mulino, Bologna, 1991; Weizman, Rehovot, Israel, 1991; Henry M. Jackson Meml, Seattle, 1992; Merle Curti, Wisconsin, 1993. Mem., Amer. Acad. of Arts and Scis, 1983; Membre Associé, Institut d'Egypte, Cairo, 1969; Mem., Amer. Philosophical Soc., 1973; Corresp. Mem., Institut de France, Académie des Inscriptions et Belles-Lettres, 1994; Hon. Mem., Turkish Acad. of Scis, 1997. Hon. Fellow, Turkish Historical Soc., Ankara, 1972; holds 15 hon. doctorates. Certificate of Merit for services to Turkish Culture, Turkish Govt, 1973. Harvey Prizewinner, 1978; Atatürk Peace Prize, 1998; Award for Peace and Democracy, Atatürk Soc. of America, 2002; Golden Plate Award, Acad. of Achievement, Washington, DC, 2004; Irving Kristol Award, Amer. Enterprise Inst. for Public Policy Res., 2007. *Publications:* The Origins of Ismā'īlism, 1940; Turkey Today, 1940; British contributions to Arabic Studies, 1941; Handbook of Diplomatic and Political Arabic, 1947, 1956; (ed) Land of Enchanters, 1948, 2nd edn (with S. Burstein) 2001; The Arabs in History, 1950, 6th rev. edn 1993; Notes and Documents from the Turkish Archives, 1952; The Emergence of Modern Turkey, 1961, rev. edn 1968; The Kingly Crown (translated from Ibn Gabirol), 1961, 2nd edn (with A. L. Gluck) 2003; co-ed. with P. M. Holt, Historians of the Middle East, 1962; Istanbul and the Civilization of the Ottoman Empire, 1963; The Middle East and the West, 1964; The Assassins, 1968; Race and Color in Islam, 1971; Islam in History, 1973, 2nd edn 2001; Islam from the Prophet Muhammad to the Capture of Constantinople, 2 vols, 1974; History, Remembered, Recovered, Invented, 1975; (ed) The World of Islam: Faith, People, Culture, 1976; Studies in Classical and Ottoman Islam, 7th-16th centuries, 1976; (with Amnon Cohen) Population and Revenue in the Towns of Palestine in the Sixteenth Century, 1978; The Muslim Discovery of Europe, 1982, 2nd edn 2001; The Jews of Islam, 1984, 2nd edn 1987; Le Retour de l'Islam, 1985; (ed, with others) As Others See Us: mutual perceptions East and West, 1985; Semites and Anti-Semites, 1986, rev. edn 1999; The Political Language of Islam, 1988; Race and Slavery in the Middle East, 1990; (ed jtly) Muslims in Europe, 1992; (ed jtly) Religionsgespräche im Mittelalter, 1992; Islam and the West, 1993; The Shaping of the Modern Middle East, 1994; Cultures in Conflict: Christians, Muslims and Jews in the Age of Discovery, 1994; The Middle East: two thousand years of history from the rise of Christianity to the present day, 1995; The Future of the Middle East, 1997; The Multiple Identities of the Middle East, 1998; A Middle East Mosaic: fragments of life, letters and history, 2000; Music of a Distant Drum, 2001; What Went Wrong?: Western Impact and Middle Eastern Response, 2002; The Crisis of Islam: holy war and unholy terror, 2003; From Babel to Dragomans: interpreting the Middle East, 2004; Political Words and Ideas in Islam, 2008; (with B. E. Churchill) Islam: the religion and the people, 2008; Faith and Power: religion and politics in the Middle East, 2010; co-ed, Encyclopaedia of Islam, 1956–87; (ed, with others) The Cambridge History of Islam, vols 1a and 1b, 1970; articles in learned journals. *Address:* Near Eastern Studies Department, Jones Hall, Princeton University, Princeton, NJ 08544–1008, USA. *Clubs:* Athenæum; Princeton (New York).

LEWIS, Brandon; MP (C) Great Yarmouth, since 2010; Minister of State, Department for Communities and Local Government, since 2014; *b* 20 June 1971; *m* 1999, Justine Yolande Rappolt; one *s* one *d*. *Educ:* Forest Sch.; Univ. of Buckingham (BSc Hons Econs; LLB); King's Coll. London (LLM Commercial Law). Called to the Bar, Inner Temple. Dir, Woodlands Schs Ltd, 2001–12. Mem. (C) Brentwood BC, 1998–2009 (Leader, 2004–09). Parly Under-

Sec. of State, DCLG, 2012–14. Mem. Council, Univ. of Buckingham, 2014–. *Recreations:* running, cycling, cinema, triathlon. *Address:* House of Commons, SW1A 0AA. *T:* (020) 7219 7231, *Fax:* (020) 7219 6558. *E:* brandon.lewis.mp@parliament.uk. *Club:* Carlton.

LEWIS, His Honour Brian William; a Circuit Judge, 1997–2015; *b* 23 July 1949; *o s* of Gilbert Pryce Lewis and Mary Williamson Lewis; *m* 1981, Maureen O'Hare; one *s. Educ:* Sale Co. GS for Boys; Univ. of Hull (LLB Hons). Called to the Bar, Inner Temple, 1973; Lectr, Barnet Coll., 1973–74; in practice at the Bar, Cardiff, 1974–75, Liverpool, 1976–97; Asst Recorder, 1989–93; a Recorder, 1993–97. *Recreations:* family life, sport, reading, military history.

LEWIS, Byron; *see* Lewis, D. B.

LEWIS, Carl; *see* Lewis, F. C.

LEWIS, Very Rev. Christopher Andrew, PhD; Dean of Christ Church, Oxford, 2003–14; Pro-Vice-Chancellor, University of Oxford, 2010–14; *b* 4 Feb. 1944; *s* of Adm. Sir Andrew Lewis, KCB and late Rachel Elizabeth (*née* Leatham); *m* 1970, Rhona Jane Martindale; two *s* one *d. Educ:* Marlborough Coll.; Bristol Univ. (BA 1969); Corpus Christi Coll., Cambridge (PhD 1974); Westcott House, Cambridge. Served RN, 1961–66; ordained deacon, 1973, priest, 1974; Asst Curate, Barnard Castle, 1973–76; Tutor, Ripon Coll., Cuddesdon, 1976–81; Dir, Oxford Inst. for Church and Soc., 1976–79; Priest-in-charge, Aston Rowant and Crowell, 1978–81; Vice Principal, Ripon Coll., Cuddesdon, 1981–82; Vicar of Spalding, 1982–87; Canon Residentiary, Canterbury Cathedral, 1987–94; Dir of Ministerial Trng, dio. of Canterbury, 1989–94; Dean of St Albans, 1994–2003. Chm., Assoc. of English Cathedrals, 2000–09. *Recreations:* guinea fowl, bicycles. *Address:* The Old Brewery, 16 Victoria Road, Aldeburgh, Suffolk IP15 5ED. *E:* christopher.lewis@chch.ox.ac.uk.

LEWIS, Clive Anthony; MP (Lab) Norwich South, since 2015; *b* London, 11 Sept. 1971. *Educ:* Univ. of Bradford (Econs). Pres., Univ. of Bradford Students' Union; Vice Pres., NUS. News reporter, BBC TV, incl. Chief Political Reporter, Eastern Reg.; technician, BBC. Served TA (Infantry Officer) (in Afghanistan, 2009). Mem., Public Accounts Select Cttee, 2015–. *Address:* House of Commons, SW1A 0AA.

LEWIS, Hon. Sir Clive (Buckland), Kt 2013; **Hon. Mr Justice Lewis;** a Judge of the High Court, Queen's Bench Division, since 2013; Presiding Judge of the Welsh Circuit, from Jan. 2016; *b* 13 June 1960; *s* of John Buckland Lewis and late Vera May Lewis (*née* Prosser). *Educ:* Cwmtawe Comp. Sch.; Churchill Coll., Cambridge (BA 1981); Dalhousie Univ. (LLM 1983). Lectr, UEA, 1983–86; Fellow, Selwyn Coll., Cambridge, 1986–93; Univ. Lectr, Univ. of Cambridge, 1989–93. Called to the Bar, Middle Temple, 1987, Bencher, 2011; in practice at the Bar, 1992–2013; QC 2006; a Recorder, 2003–13; a Dep. High Court Judge, 2010–13. First Counsel to Nat. Assembly for Wales, later Welsh Assembly Govt, then Welsh Govt, 2000–13. Asst Boundary Comr for England, 2011–13; Asst Boundary Comr for Wales, 2011–. Mem. Editl Bd, Public Law, 2006–. *Publications:* Judicial Remedies in Public Law, 1992, 5th edn 2014; (ed) Civil Procedure (annually); Remedies and the Enforcement of European Community Law, 1996; (gen. ed.) Halsbury's Laws of England, Judicial Rev. *Recreations:* travel, walking, reading, golf, bridge. *Address:* Royal Courts of Justice, Strand, WC2A 2LL. *Clubs:* Athenæum, Royal Automobile.

LEWIS, Clive Hewitt, FRICS; President, Royal Institution of Chartered Surveyors, 1993–94; *b* 29 March 1936; *s* of Thomas Jonathan Lewis, OBE and Marguerite Eileen Lewis; *m* 1961, Jane Penelope White; two *s* one *d. Educ:* St Peter's Sch., York. FRICS 1963; FSVA 1979. With Goddard & Smith, 1957–62; Founder and Sen. Partner, Clive Lewis & Partners, 1963–92, when merged with Edward Erdman; Jt Chm., Colliers Erdman Lewis, 1993–95. Non-executive Director: St Modwen Properties, 1983–2002; Town Centre Securities, 1994–2009; Freeport Leisure, 1997–2004. Dep. Chm., Merseyside Develt Corp., 1989–98. Chm., Bank of England Property Forum, 1994–2002. Mem. Council, Internat. Year of Shelter for the Homeless, 1985–88. Mem., Gen. Council, RICS, 1987–95 (Pres., Gen. Practice Div., 1989–90); President: Eur. Council of Real Estate Professionals, 1990; UK, 1976–77, World, 1984–85, Internat. Real Estate Fedn (Mem. Exec. Cttee, 1977–92). Pres., Land Aid Charitable Trust, 1986–2003. Freeman, City of London, 1983; Liveryman, Chartered Surveyors' Co., 1983–2002. Hon. DLitt S Bank, 1993. *Recreations:* bridge, dogs, golf, cricket. *Address:* 8 The Pastures, Totteridge, N20 8AN. *T:* (020) 8445 5109. *Clubs:* MCC; S Herts Golf; Totteridge Cricket (Pres., 2005–07).

LEWIS, Damian Watcyn, OBE 2014; actor; *b* 11 Feb. 1971; *s* of Watcyn Lewis and Charlotte Lewis; *m* 2007, Helen McCrory; one *s* one *d. Educ:* Ashdown House Prep. Sch.; Eton Coll.; Guildhall Sch. of Music and Drama (Fellow 2006). Actor: *theatre* includes: Hamlet, Open Air Th., Regent's Park, 1994; School for Wives, Almeida, 1994; on Broadway, 1995; RSC, 1996–98; Into the Woods, Donmar, 1999; Pillars of the Community, NT, 2005; The Misanthrope, Comedy, 2009; American Buffalo, Wyndham's Th., 2015; *television* includes: Warriors, 1999; Band of Brothers, 2000; Soames Forsyte in The Forsyte Saga, 2001; Life, 2007; Stolen, 2011; Homeland (3 series), 2012, 2013 (Emmy Award, Best Actor, 2012; Golden Globe Award, Best Actor in TV Drama, 2012); Romeo and Juliet, 2013; Wolf Hall, 2015; *films* include: Dreamcatcher, 2002; An Unfinished Life, 2003; Keane, 2004; The Baker (also producer), 2008; The Silent Storm, 2014; Queen of the Desert, Bill, 2015. Partner, Picture Farm Ltd, prodn co., 2004–. Ambassador for: Prince's Trust, 2002–; Christian Aid, 2005– (made report on privatization in Bolivia, 2005); Patron, Scene and Heard, 2004–. Mem., Stage Golfing Soc. *Recreations:* football, tennis, golf, gardening, bicycling, watching film, theatre, reading, travelling, day dreaming, playing piano badly. *Address:* c/o Markham, Froggatt & Irwin, 4 Windmill Street, W1T 2HZ. *Clubs:* Groucho, Queen's.

LEWIS, (David) Byron, FCA; Lord-Lieutenant of West Glamorgan, since 2008; *b* Swansea, 14 Feb. 1945; *s* of late William Edward Lewis and Eiddwen Lewis; *m* 1969, Hilary Ann Morgan; two *d. Educ:* Gowerton Grammar Sch., Swansea. FCA 1968. Dir, various private companies, 1969–75; Dir. Man. Dir, 1975–85, Asst Gp Man. Dir, 1985–91, Christie-Tyler Gp plc; Man. Dir, subsidiaries of Hillsdown Hldgs plc, 1991–93; non-exec. Chm., Blackwood Ltd, Birdel Ltd and various private companies, 1993–2008. Chairman: W Glam Magistrates' Adv. Cttee; W Glam Jt Archives Service. President: W Glam Council of St John; W Glam SSAFA; W Glam Area Scouts; W Glam ABF; Vice Pres., RFCA Wales. Co. Patron, RBL. Freeman, City of London, 1989. High Sheriff, W Glamorgan, 2004–05. CStJ 2008. *Recreations:* sport, music, gardening. *Address:* Bryn Newydd House, 1 Derwen Fawr Road, Sketty Green, Swansea SA2 8AA. *T:* (01792) 203012. *E:* byron.lewis@btinternet.com. *Clubs:* Army and Navy; Langland Bay Golf.

LEWIS, David John; Chairman, Molyneux Management Services Ltd, since 1974; *b* London, 17 May 1939; *s* of Reuben Lewis and Jean Lewis; *m* 1961, Hannah Schorr; one *s* two *d* (and one *d* decd). *Educ:* Hackney Downs Grammar Sch.; Coll. of Estate Mgt, Univ. of London (BSc 1959). FRICS 1969. Sen. Partner, David Lewis & Partners, 1964–94; Chief Executive Officer: Cavendish Land Co., 1972–73; Hampton Trust plc, 1983–87; Chm., Molyneux Estates plc, 1989–95. Non-executive Director: Mount Martin Gold Mines, 1983–94; TBI plc, 1995–2001. Chairman: Jewish Blind Soc., 1979–90; Jewish Care, 1991–92. Pres., Eur. Council of Jewish Communities, 1992–99; Co-Founder and Co-Chairman, Commn for Looted Art in Europe, 1998–. Chm., Oxford Centre Muller Liby, 1974–2011; Founder Gov., Harris City Technol. Coll., 1990–2009; Gov., Oxford Centre for Hebrew and Jewish Studies, 1992–; Trustee: Inst. for Jewish Studies, 1995–; Leuka, 1998–; Weiner Liby, 2012–; Birmingham Mus Trust, 2012–; Dep. Chm., London Jewish Cultural Centre, 2006–15. *Recreations:* art, music, grandchildren. *Address:* Catherine House, 76 Gloucester Place, W1U 6HJ. *T:* (020) 7487 3401. *E:* david.lewis@catherinehouse.com. *Club:* Savile.

LEWIS, David Patrick; QC 2014; *b* Salisbury, 23 April 1977; *s* of Roger and Deirdre Lewis; *m* 2009, Patricia O'Driscoll; one *s* one *d* (twins). *Educ:* Warwick Sch., Warwick; St Edmund Hall, Oxford (BA 1st Cl. Juris. 1998). Called to the Bar, Middle Temple, 1999; in practice as barrister, specialising in commercial law, 2000–. CEDR Accredited Mediator, 2005. *Recreations:* sport, music, tickling the twins. *Address:* 20 Essex Street, WC2R 3AL. *T:* (020) 7842 1200. *E:* dlewis@20essexst.com.

LEWIS, David Robert; Secretary, Royal Commission on Environmental Pollution, 1992–2002; *b* 27 Nov. 1940; *oc* of William Lewis, Pembroke Dock and Kate Lewis (*née* Sperring); *m* 1965, Christine, *o d* of Leslie and Maud Tye; three *s. Educ:* Tiffin Sch.; New Coll., Oxford (Classical Exhibn; MA; DPhil 1970). Joined Min. of Housing and Local Govt, 1965; Sec., Central Adv. Water Cttee, 1969–73; HM Treasury, 1973–75; Asst Sec., Central Unit on Envmtl Pollution, DoE, 1975–77; Dir, Public Admin and Social Policy, CS Coll., 1978–80; Asst Sec., DoE, 1981–89; Hd, Water Services Div., DoE, 1990–92. Chm., Cymdeithas Eryri—Snowdonia Soc., 2008–12 (Chm., Policy Sub-Cttee, 2003–12); Mem., Exec. Cttee, London Forum of Amenity and Civic Socs, 2003–08 (Vice Pres., 2008–). Chm. Govs, Ernest Bevin Sch., later Coll., 1988–99; Chm., Sir Walter St John's Educnl Charity, 1997–2006. *Publications:* The Electrical Trades Union and the Growth of the Electrical Industry, 1970; (ed jtly) Policies into Practice, 1984. *Recreations:* discovering buildings, 17th and 18th century literature. *Address:* Dolafon, Llanbedr, Gwynedd LL45 2DJ.

LEWIS, Sir David (Thomas Rowell), Kt 2009; JP; DL; Senior Partner, Norton Rose, 1997–2003 (Consultant, 2003–13); Lord Mayor of London, 2007–08; *b* 1 Nov. 1947; *s* of Thomas Price Merfyn Lewis; *m* 1970, Theresa Susan Poole; one *s* one *d. Educ:* Dragon Sch., Oxford; St Edward's Sch., Oxford; Jesus Coll., Oxford (MA 1969; Hon. Fellow 1998; Queen Elizabeth I Fellow 2012). Admitted solicitor, 1972, Hong Kong, 1977; joined Norton Rose, 1969: articled, 1969–72; Asst Solicitor, 1972–76; Partner, 1977; Managing Partner, Hong Kong Office, 1979–82; Head: Corporate Finance, 1989–94; Professional Resources, 1994–99. Non-exec. Dir, Standard Life Assurance Co., 2003–04. Comr, I of M Financial Supervision Commn, 2012–. Trustee: Oxford Univ. Law Foundn, 1997–2007; Oxford Inst. of Legal Practice, 2001–03; Member: Oxford Univ. Law Develt Council, 1997–2006 (Chm., 2003–06); Oxford Univ. Chancellor's Ct of Benefactors, 1997–2009. Member: Royal Soc. of St George, 2004–13; City Pickwick Club, 2007–13. Governor: Dragon Sch., Oxford, 1987– (Chm., 2003–08); Oxford Brookes Univ., 1995–2003; Blackbird Acad., 2013–14; Swansea Univ., 2014–; Gov. and Almoner, Christ's Hosp., 2004–10; Chancellor, City Univ., 2007–08. Mem., Law Soc. Legal Practice Course Bd, 1995–2000. President: St Edward's Sch. Soc., 1995–96; Broad Street Ward Club, 2001–13; City of London Law Soc., 2009–10. Gov., Hon. Irish Soc., 2009–12. Trustee: Wellbeing of Women, 2009–12; Awen Cymru, 2010–12; ORBIS UK, 2011–12. An Ambassador for Wales, 2008–. Churchwarden, St Margaret Lothbury, 2001–13. Alderman, Broad Street Ward, 2001–13; Sheriff, City of London, 2006–07; Liveryman: Solicitors' Co. (Master, 2009–10); Fletchers' Co.; Livery Co. of Wales (formerly Welsh Livery Guild); Hon. Liveryman, Security Professionals Co. JP: City of London, 2002–09; Dinefwr, 2009–; DL Dyfed, 2009. Hon. Fellow: Hunan, 2008; Xiamen, 2008; GSMD, 2008; Cardiff, 2009; Trinity Coll., Carmarthen, 2009. Hon. DCL: City, 2007; Wales, 2008. KStJ 2008. *Publications:* Cynwyl Gaeo The Land of My Fathers, 2009; Family Histories and Community Life in North Carmarthenshire, 2012; contrib. articles in jls. *Recreations:* charity, spoiling my dogs, collecting maps, travel, supporting Welsh Rugby. *Address:* Erwhen, Cwrt-y-Cadno, Pumsaint, Cynwyl Gaeo, Carms SA19 8YP. *E:* lewis.erwhen@btinternet.com. *Clubs:* Achilles, Pilgrims; Hong Kong (Hong Kong).

LEWIS, David Whitfield, RDI 1995; freelance design consultant, since 1967; *b* 19 Feb. 1939; *s* of John Whitfield Lewis and Joan Lewis; *m* 1964, Marianne Mygind; one *s* one *d. Educ:* Central Sch. of Design, London. Employed by Danish design consultancy, working on radio and television equipment designs, incl. designs for Beolab 5000 Series Hi-Fi music systems for Bang & Olufsen, and invented slide rule motif, 1960–68; collaborated with Henning Moldenhawer on television equipment for Bang & Olufsen, and industrial processing machinery and marine products, 1968–80; work included in Design Collection, Mus. of Modern Art, NY. Hon. FRIBA, 2007. ID Prize, Danish Design Centre, 1976 (marine folding propeller), 1982 (dental tools), 1986 (television set), 1990 (push button system), 1994 (audio system); Design Prize, EC, 1988; MITI, G-Mark Grand Prix, 1991 (audio hi-fi system); Internat. Design Prize, Baden-Württemberg, 1993 (audio hi-fi system); Annual Prize, Danish Design Council, 2003. Knight of the Order of Dannebrog (Denmark), 2003. *Address:* David Lewis Designers Aps, Blegdamsvej 28F, 2200 Copenhagen N, Denmark. *T:* 33139635; Piniehøj 2, 2960 Rungsted Kyst, Denmark.

LEWIS, Denise, OBE 2001 (MBE 1999); athlete; *b* 27 Aug. 1972; *d* of Joan Lewis; one *d* by Patrick Stevens; *m* 2006, Stephen Joseph Finan; two *s.* Mem., Birchfield Harriers. Heptathlon wins include: Commonwealth Games: Gold Medal, 1994, 1998; European Cup: Gold Medal, 1995, Silver Medal, 2003; Olympic Games: Bronze Medal, 1996, Gold Medal, 2000; World Championships: Silver Medal, 1997, 1999; European Championships: Gold Medal, 1998. *Publications:* Personal Best (autobiog.), 2001; The Flat Tummy Book, 2008.

LEWIS, Denise, (Mrs Mark Poulton); a Trustee, Wallace Collection, since 2009; *b* Adpar, Newcastle Emlyn, Cardiganshire; *d* of William David Lewis and Valmai Jones; *m* 1998, Mark Poulton; one *s* one *d. Educ:* Llandysul Grammar Sch.; King's Coll., London (BD 1987; AKC). Dir, Corporate Communications, Encom, later Bell Cablemedia, 1993–97; Gp Vice Pres., Corporate Affairs, Orange plc, 1997–2003; Co-Founder, www.Blodwen.com, 2010–. Vice Pres., Hay Literary Fest., 1998–; Trustee: Wessex Youth Trust, 1999–; Cadwgan Building Preservation Trust, 2010–; non-exec. Dir, WNO, 2003–. FRSA. Hon. Mem., BAFTA, 2002. *Recreation:* Welsh affairs. *E:* Denise@Blodwen.com.

LEWIS, Dr Dennis Aubrey, MBE 2014; Director, Aslib, the Association for Information Management, 1981–89; *b* 1 Oct. 1928; *s* of Joseph and Minnie Lewis; *m* 1956, Gillian Mary Bratby; two *s. Educ:* Latymer Upper Sch.; Univ. of London (BSc 1st Cl. Hons Chemistry, 1953; PhD 1956). FCLIP (FIInfSc 1984). Res. Chemist, 1956–68, Intelligence Manager, 1968–81, ICI Plastics Div. Member: Adv. Council, British Library, 1976–81; Library Adv. Cttee, British Council, 1981–. Member: Welwyn Garden UDC, 1968–74; Welwyn Hatfield DC, 1974–2007 (Chm., 1976–77); Chm., Welwyn Hatfield Alliance, 2004–08. Hon. LLM Herts, 2005. Welwyn Hatfield Civic Award, 2013. *Publications:* Index of Reviews in Organic Chemistry, annually 1963–; (ed jtly) Great Information Disasters, 1991; pubns on information management in Aslib Procs and other journals. *Recreations:* music, old churches, 'futurology'.

LEWIS, Derek (Compton); Director, Protocol Associates, since 2002 (Chairman, 2002–09); *b* 9 July 1946; *s* of late Kenneth Compton Lewis and Marjorie Lewis; *m* 1969, Louise (*née* Wharton); two *d. Educ:* Wrekin Coll., Telford; Queens' Coll., Cambridge (MA); London Business Sch. (MSc). Ford Motor Co., 1968–82, Dir of Finance, Ford of Europe, 1978–82; Dir of Corporate Develt and Gp Planning Man., Imperial Gp, 1982–84; Granada Group: Finance Dir, 1984–87; Man. Dir, 1988–89; Gp Chief Exec., 1990–91; Dir, Courtaulds Textiles, 1990–93; Chief Exec. and Dir Gen., HM Prison Service, 1993–95. Chairman: UK Gold Television Ltd, 1992–97; Sunsail International, 1997–99; Patientline plc, 1998–2006 (Chief Exec., 1998–2001; Pres., 2006–07); Director: JHP Gp Ltd, 2008–12 (Chm., 2010–12); learndirect, 2012–14. Chm., Drinkaware Trust, 2008–14; Chm. Trustees, Royal Mencap

Soc., 2014–; Trustee: Patients Assoc., 1999–2002; RVS (formerly WRVS), 2007–13. Mem. Council, Univ. of Essex, 1999–2009 (Treas., 2001–07; Pro-Chancellor, 2007–09). *Publications:* Hidden Agendas, 1997. *Club:* Caledonian.

LEWIS, (Derek) Trevor; Chairman, Bradford & Bingley Pensions Ltd, 1995–2012; Vice-Chairman, Bradford & Bingley plc (formerly Bradford & Bingley Building Society), 1995–2003 (Director, 1990–2003); *b* 21 Oct. 1936; *s* of Lionel Lewis and Mabel (*née* Clare); *m* 1961, Pamela Jean Ratcliffe; one *s* one *d*. *Educ:* Bradford Grammar Sch.; Leeds Univ. (LLB); 2nd Cl. Hons Solicitors' Final Exam., 1960. With A. V. Hammond & Co., subseq. Hammond Suddards: articled to Sir Richard Denby, 1955–60; Asst Solicitor, 1960–63; Partner 1964–87; Jt Sen. Partner, 1987–95. Dir, W Yorks Independent Hosp., 1979–85 (Chm., 1985–88); Chairman: Little Germany Urban Village Co. Ltd, 1999–2003; Arts and Business Yorkshire Ltd, 2000–10; Bradford Breakthrough Ltd, 2005–10; Dep. Chm., Bradford City Centre Urban Regeneration Co. Ltd, 2003–10. *Address:* 5 Royal Gardens, Harrogate, N Yorks HG2 0NR. *T:* (01423) 523996.

LEWIS, Dr Dewi Meirion, FInstP; Head of Physics, GE Healthcare (formerly Nycomed Amersham, then Amersham plc), 1999–2010; *b* Chester, 4 Sept. 1948; *s* of Hugh and Mair Lewis; *m* 1972, Elizabeth Mary Williams; two *s* one *d*. *Educ:* Ysgol Ardudwy Harlech, Gwynedd; UCW, Swansea (BSc 1969; PhD 1972). FInstP 1995; FRAS 2004. Res. Fellow, CERN, Geneva, 1973–74; Engr i/c, CERN ISR collider, 1974–79; Cyclotron Ops Manager, TRC Ltd, 1979–83; Amersham International plc: Hd, Cyclotron Dept, 1983–88; Business Manager, Cyclotron and Reactor Pharmaceuticals, 1988–91; Mfg Strategy Manager, 1991–94; R&D Strategy Manager, 1994–99. Visiting Professor of Physics: Liverpool Univ., 1997–2001; Cockcroft Inst., 2008–10 (Mem., Industrial Adv. Bd, 2009–10); Vis. Lectr of Physics, Oxford Univ., 2008–10. Non-exec. Dir, Reviss Services Ltd, 1992–95. Member: OECD/NEA Expert Panel on Isotopes, 1997–99; PPARC, 2000–06 (Mem., 2000–07, Chm., 2001–04, Audit Cttee); EPSRC Coll., 2000–10; CCLRC, 2006–07; Adv. Bd, All-Wales PET Imaging Centre, 2008–10; CLASP grant panel, STFC, 2008–10; Case Studentship Panel, MRC, 2009. Vice-Pres., Assoc. of Imaging Producers and Equipment Suppliers (Chm., Cttee on Isotopes and Reactors, 1992–2007); Scientific Advr, EC DG XII, 1994–97; Mem., EMIR Network, Brussels, 2001– (Chm., Isotopes Cttee, 2001–). Member: British Astronomical Soc., 2001; UK Res. Council. Member: Amer. Assoc. Physicists in Medicine, 2001; Eur. Assoc. Nuclear Medicine, 2001–10; Soc. of Nuclear Medicine, 2003–10. Mem., Mgt Cttee, Amersham Pension Scheme, 2005–07; Dir and Trustee, Bd, GE Pension Plan, 2010. *Publications:* contrib. articles to res. jls. *Recreations:* ski-ing, Alpine walking, golf, choral music, astronomy. *Club:* Harewood Downs (Bucks).

LEWIS, Rev. Edward John; JP; Vicar, St Mary the Virgin, Kenton, since 2011; Chaplain to the Queen, since 2008; *b* Swansea, 4 Aug. 1958; *s* of Donald Lewis and Adeline Lewis; *m* 2000, Katherine; two *s*. *Educ:* Univ. of Wales (BEd 1980; BA Theol. 1982); Theol Coll., Chichester (DipTh 1983); Univ. of Surrey (MA Bioethics 2007). Ordained deacon, 1983, priest, 1984; Curate, Parish of Llangiwg, Pontardawe, 1983–85; Sen. Curate, Parish of Morriston, and Asst Chaplain, Morriston Hosp., Swansea, 1985–87; Vicar Tregaron, Strata Florida, Ystrad Meurig, and Chaplain, Tregaron Hosp., 1987–89; Sen. Chaplain, Walsall Hosps NHS Trust, 1989–2000; Asst, later Acting Rural Dean, Walsall, 1995–2000; CEO, Hosp. Chaplaincies Council, C of E, 2000–10; Priest-in-charge, St John's, Watford, 2010–11. Priest Associate, Shrine of our Lady of Walsingham, 2000; Priest Vicar, Westminster Abbey, 2006–10. Chaplain: RBL, 1987–89; Nat. Band of Church Lads & Church Girls, 1995–2000. Trustee: St Luke's Hospice, Kenton Grange, 2011–; Harrow Bereavement Gp, 2011–. JP Walsall, 1993–2000, City of Westminster, 2000. Freedom, City of London, 2006. MInstD 2000. FRSA 1997. *Recreations:* entertaining friends, theatres, travel in Italy. *Address:* St Mary's Vicarage, 3 St Leonard's Avenue, Kenton, Middx HA3 8EJ. *T:* 07500 557953. *E:* fr@fredward.org.uk.

LEWIS, Frederick Carlton, (Carl); athlete; *b* 1 July 1961; *s* of Bill and Evelyn Lewis. *Educ:* Univ. of Houston. Winner, 100m, 200m, and long jump, US National Athletics Championships, 1983; *Olympic Games:* Gold medals, 100m and 200m, long jump and 4×100m, 1984; Gold medals, 100m and long jump, Silver medal, 200m, 1988; Gold medals, long jump and 4×100m, 1992; Gold medal, long jump, 1996; *World Championships:* Gold medals, 100m, long jump, 4×100m, 1983; Gold medals, long jump, 4×100m, 1987; Gold medals, 100m, 4×100m, 1991. World Record: long jump (8.79m), 1983; 100m (9.86 seconds), 1991. James E. Sullivan Meml Award, Amateur Athletic Union of US, 1981; Athlete of the Century, IAAF, 1999. UN Goodwill Ambassador, FAO, 2009.

LEWIS, Gillian Marjorie, FMA, FIIC; heritage consultant, since 1994; *b* 10 Oct. 1945; *d* of late William Lewis and of Marjorie Lewis (*née* Pargeter). *Educ:* Tiffin Sch., Kingston upon Thames; Univ. of Newcastle upon Tyne (BA 1967); DCP, Gateshead Tech. Coll., 1969; Birkbeck Coll., London (Cert. Ecology, 1991). FIIC 1977; FMA 1988. Shipley Art Gallery, Co. Durham, 1967–69; free-lance conservator, 1969–73; Nat. Maritime Mus., 1973–94; Keeper of Conservation, 1978; Hd, Div. of Conservation and Technical Services, 1978–88; Asst Dep. Dir, 1982–86; Hd of Conservation and Registration, 1988–91; Head of Collection Projects, 1991–92; Head of External Affairs, 1992–94. Vice-Chm., UK Inst. for Conservation, 1983–84 (Mem. Cttee, 1978–80). Member: Technical Cttee, City and Guilds of London Sch. of Art, 1981–2012; Cttee, Dulwich Picture Gall., 1983–92; Wallpaintings Conservation Panel, Council for Care of Churches, 1985–88; Volunteer Steering Cttee, Office of Arts and Libraries, 1988–90; Adv. Cttee, Museums and Galleries Commn, 1988–96; Trng Standards Panel, Museums Trng Inst., 1990–93; Council, Leather Conservation Centre, 1991–92; Fabric Adv. Cttee, Southwark Cathedral, 1997–; Preservation Advr to Dean and Chapter, Peterborough Cathedral, 1994–2013; Adviser: Heather Trust for the Arts, 1997–2000; Royal Warrant Holders' Assoc., 1999–2003. Examiner, London Inst., Camberwell Sch. of Art, 1991–93; Assessor: Clore Small Grants Prog., 1998–2003; Attingham Trust, 2002. Trustee: Whatmore Trust, 1988–; Southwark Cathedral Millennium Trust, 1998–2011; Cathedral Camps, 1998–2001; Edward James Foundn, 1999–2013. UN50 UK Ambassador, 1995. FRSA 1987.

LEWIS, Prof. Glyn Hywel, PhD; FRCPsych; Professor of Psychiatric Epidemiology, University College London, since 2013; *b* 6 Dec. 1956; *s* of Jeffrey and Marion Lewis; *m* 1982, Priscilla Hall; one *s*. *Educ:* University Coll., Oxford (MSc 1980; MA 1983); University Coll. London (MB BS 1982); London Sch. of Hygiene and Tropical Medicine (MSc 1989); Inst. of Psychiatry, London Univ. (PhD 1991). FRCPsych 1998. Registrar, Bethlem and Maudsley Hosp., 1983–86; Res. Fellow, 1986–91, Sen. Lectr, 1991–95, Inst. of Psychiatry, London Univ.; on secondment to DoH, 1991–94; Res. Fellow, LSHTM, 1993–95; Prof. of Community and Epidemiological Psychiatry, Univ. of Wales Coll. of Medicine, 1996–2001; Prof. of Psychiatric Epidemiology, Univ. of Bristol, 2001–13. *Address:* UCL Division of Psychiatry, University College London, Charles Bell House, 67–73 Riding House Street, W1W 7EJ.

LEWIS, Dr Gwyneth; writer; *b* Cardiff, 4 Nov. 1959; *d* of Gwilym and Eryl Lewis; *m* 1993, Leighton Denver Davies. *Educ:* Ysgol Gyfun Rhydfelen; Girton Coll., Cambridge (MA 1982); Harvard Univ.; Columbia Univ., NY; Balliol Coll., Oxford (DPhil 1991). Researcher, Agenda Television, 1989–92; Asst Producer, 1992–93, Producer, 1993–98, BBC; Chief Asst to Controller, BBC Wales, 1998–2000. Nat. Poet of Wales, 2005–06. Mildred Londa Weisman Fellow, Radcliffe Inst. of Advanced Study, Harvard Univ., 2008–09; SiCa Fellow, Stanford Humanities Center, Stanford Univ., 2009–10; Mary Amelia Cummins Vis. Commoner, Girton Coll., Cambridge, 2010–11; Bain-Swigget Vis. Lectr in English and Poetry, Princeton Univ., 2014. *Publications:* Sonedau Redsa, 1990; Parables and Faxes, 1995; Cyfrif Un ac Un yn Dri, 1996; Zero Gravity, 1998; Y Llofrudd Iaith, 1999; Sunbathing in the Rain: a cheerful book on depression, 2002; Tair mewn Un, 2005; Two in a Boat: a marital voyage, 2005; Chaotic Angels, 2005; A Hospital Odyssey, 2010; The Meat Tree, 2010; Arthur's Talk with the Eagle, 2011; Sparrow Tree, 2011; Clytemnestra, 2012; Y Storm, 2012; Advantages of the Older Man, 2014; Quantum Poetics, 2015. *E:* gl@gwynethlewis.com.

LEWIS, Sir Harcourt; *see* Lewis, Sir L. V. H.

LEWIS, Helen Alexandra; Deputy Editor, New Statesman, since 2012; *b* Worcester, 1983; *d* of Reginald Lewis and Jillian Lewis; partner, Jonathan Paul Haynes. *Educ:* St Mary's Convent Sch., Worcester; St Peter's Coll., Oxford (BA 1st Cl. Hons Eng. Lang. and Lit. 2004; MA); City Univ., London (Postgrad. Dip. Newspaper Journalism 2005); Open Univ. (MA (Dist.) Eng. Lit. 2011). Graduate trainee, 2005, a sub-editor, 2006–10, a jun. commng editor, Features Desk, 2009–10, Daily Mail; Asst Editor, New Statesman, 2010–12. Dep. Chair, Women in Journalism. Chair, Nia—Ending Violence Against Women, 2014–. *Recreations:* videogames, travel, Twitter. *Address:* New Statesman, 20 Farringdon Road, EC1M 3HE. *E:* helen@newstatesman.co.uk.

LEWIS, Rt Rev. (Hurtle) John, AM 1989; SSM; Bishop of North Queensland, 1971–96; *b* 2 Jan. 1926; *s* of late Hurtle John Lewis and Hilda Aiston Lewis; *m* 2008, Joyce Bleby. *Educ:* Prince Alfred Coll., Adelaide; London Univ. (BD 1972); ThL of ACT; Flinders Univ. (MTh 2006). Royal Australian Navy, 1943–47; Student and Novice SSM, St Michael's House, S Aust., 1947–51; Member, SSM, 1951–; Deacon, 1951, Priest, 1951; Asst Tutor, 1951–58, Sub Prior, 1952–58, Warden, 1962–69, Aust. Coll. of SSM; Prior, St Barnabas Sch., Ravenshoe, 1958–60; Provincial Australia, SSM, 1962–69; Prior, Kobe Priory, Japan, 1969–71. Mem. Council, 1971–98, Acting Warden, St Mark's Coll., 1996–97, James Cook Univ., Qld; Licensed to assist, St James' Cathedral Parish, 1996–2002; permission to officiate, St John's Parish, Adelaide, 2002–. Mem. Council, Good Shepherd Nursing Home, 1973–97 (Chm., 1996–97). Comr, Qld Corrective Service Commn, 1989–92. Chairman: Townsville Dist. Health Service Cttee, 1990–2002; Toc H, Townsville, 1996–2000; Bible Soc., Townsville, 1996–99. Warden, Order of St Luke the Physician, 1996–2006. *Publications:* Finding Them Where They Are, 2009. *Recreations:* rowing, music, horse riding. *Address:* 22 Dunn Street, Bridgewater, SA 5155, Australia. *Clubs:* Royal Australian Naval Association, Royal Australian Navy Corvette Association, Returned Services League of Australia, Legacy (Adelaide).

LEWIS, Huw George; Member (Lab) Merthyr Tydfil and Rhymney, National Assembly for Wales, since 1999; Minister for Education and Skills, since 2013; *b* 17 Jan. 1964; *m* 1996, Lynne Neagle, *qv*; two *s*. *Educ:* Edinburgh Univ. (BSc Hons Chemistry). Teacher, N Berwick High Sch., and Bathgate Acad., 1987–90; House of Commons Researcher, 1990–91; Teacher, Afon Taf High Sch., 1991–94; Asst Gen. Sec., Wales Labour Party, 1994–99. National Assembly for Wales: Dep. Minister for Social Justice and Regeneration, 2003–07, for Regeneration, 2007, for Children, 2009–11; Minister for Housing, Regeneration and Heritage, 2011–13, for Communities and Tackling Poverty, 2013. *Address:* National Assembly for Wales, Cardiff Bay, Cardiff CF99 1NA.

LEWIS, Ivan; MP (Lab) Bury South, since 1997; *b* 4 March 1967; *s* of Joel and Gloria Lewis; *m* 1990, Juliette (marr. diss.), *d* of Leslie and Joyce Fox; two *s*. *Educ:* William Hulme's Grammar Sch.; Stand Coll.; Bury Coll. of FE. Co-ordinator, Contact Community Care Gp, 1986–89; Jewish Social Services: Community Worker, 1989–91; Community Care Manager, 1991–92; Chief Exec., 1992–97. Mem., Bury MBC, 1990–98. PPS to Sec. of State for Trade and Industry, 1999–2001; Parly Under-Sec. of State, DfES, 2001–05; Econ. Sec., HM Treasury, 2005–06; Parliamentary Under-Secretary of State: for Care Services, DoH, 2006–08; DFID, 2008–09; Minister of State, FCO, 2009–10; Shadow Sec. of State for Culture, Media and Sport, 2010–11, for Internat. Develt, 2011–13, for NI, 2013–15. Member: H of C Deregulation Select Cttee, 1997–99; Health Select Cttee, 1999; Sec., All Party Parly Gp on Parenting, 1998–2001; Dep. Chm., Labour Friends of Israel, 1997–2001; Vice Chm., Inter-Parly Council Against Anti-Semitism, 1998–2001. Trustee, Holocaust Educnl Trust. *Recreation:* supporter of Manchester City FC. *Address:* House of Commons, SW1A 0AA; 381 Bury New Road, Prestwich, Manchester M25 1AW. *T:* (0161) 773 5500. *E:* ivanlewis@burysouth.fsnet.co.uk. *W:* www.ivanlewis.org.uk.

LEWIS, James Thomas; QC 2002; a Recorder, since 2000; a Deputy High Court Judge, since 2013; *b* 8 Feb. 1958; *s* of Benjamin Ivor and Kathleen Lewis; *m* 1985, Kathleen Mary Gallacher; one *s* two *d*. *Educ:* St John Fisher Sch., Purley; Kingston Poly. (BSc Hons); City Univ., London (DipLaw). Univ. of London OTC, 1977–80; Commnd 2nd Lieut, 1979; Royal Yeo., 1980–82; RARO, 1982–86, 1993–; HAC, 1986–93. Called to the Bar, Gray's Inn, 1987, Bencher, 2007; Attorney General's List, 2000. Mem., Criminal Cttee, Judicial Studies Bd, 2008–12. *Recreations:* ski-ing, clay pigeon shooting, tennis. *Address:* 3 Raymond Buildings, Gray's Inn, WC1R 5BH. *T:* (020) 7400 6400. *Clubs:* Honourable Artillery Company, Garrick.

LEWIS, Prof. Jane Elizabeth, PhD; FBA 2004; FRSC; Professor of Social Policy, London School of Economics, since 2004; *b* 14 April 1950; *d* of Hedley Lewis and Dorothy Lewis (*née* Beck); *m* 1971, Mark Shrimpton. *Educ:* Reading Univ. (BA Hons 1971); Univ. of Western Ontario (PhD 1979). Department of Social Policy and Administration, London School of Economics: Lectr, 1979–87; Reader, 1987–91; Prof., 1991–96; Fellow of All Souls Coll., and Dir, Wellcome Unit for the Hist. of Medicine, Oxford, 1996–98; Prof. of Social Policy, Nottingham Univ., 1998–2000; Barnett Prof. of Social Policy and Fellow, St Cross Coll., Oxford, 2000–04. FRSC 1995. *Publications:* The Politics of Motherhood: child and maternal welfare in England 1900–1939, 1980; (ed) Women's Welfare/Women's Rights, 1983; Women in England, 1870–1950: sexual divisions and social change, 1984; (ed) Labour and Love: women's experience of home and family 1850–1950, 1986; (ed jtly) Women and Offshore Oil in Britain, Canada and Norway, 1987; (ed) Before the Vote was Won, 1987; (jtly) Daughters Who Care: daughters looking after mothers at home, 1988; (ed jtly) The Goals of Social Policy, 1989; Women and Social Action in Victorian and Edwardian England, 1991; Women in Britain since 1945: women, family and work in the post-war years, 1992; (jtly) Whom God Hath Joined: marriage and the marital agencies 1930–1990, 1992; (ed) Women and Social Policies in Europe, 1993; The Voluntary Sector, the State and Social Work in Britain, 1995; (ed jtly) Comparing Social Welfare Systems in Europe, vol. I, 1995; (ed jtly) Protecting Women: labor legislation in Europe, the United States and Australia 1880–1920, 1995; (jtly) Implementing the New Community Care, 1996; (ed) Lone Mothers in European Welfare Regimes, 1998; (jtly) Lone Motherhood in Twentieth-Century Britain, 1998; The End of Marriage?, 2001; Work-family Balance, Gender and Policy, 2009; articles in jls. *Address:* Department of Social Policy, London School of Economics, Houghton Street, WC2A 2AE.

LEWIS, Jeffrey Allan; His Honour Judge Jeffrey Lewis; a Circuit Judge, since 2002; *b* 25 May 1949; *s* of late David Meyer Lewis and Esther (*née* Kirson); *m* 1985, Elizabeth Ann Swarbrick; one *s* one *d*. *Educ:* Univ. of the Witwatersrand (BA); Univ. of Leeds (LLB). Teacher, 1973–75; called to the Bar, Middle Temple, 1978; in practice, N Eastern Circuit, 1978–2002; Asst Recorder, 1993–97; Recorder, 1997–2002. Chm. (pt-time), Industrial Tribunals, Leeds Reg., 1991–95. *Recreations:* music, reading, ski-ing, gardening. *Address:* Manchester Crown Court, Minshull Street, Manchester M1 3FS. *T:* (0161) 954 7500.

LEWIS, Jeremy Morley, FRSL; freelance writer, since 1989; Commissioning Editor, The Oldie, since 1997; Editor-at-Large, Literary Review, since 2004; *b* Salisbury, 15 March 1942; *s* of George Morley Lewis, FRCS and Janet Lewis (*née* Iles); *m* 1968, Jane Petra Freston; two *d*. *Educ:* Malvern Coll.; Trinity Coll., Dublin (BA 1965); Sussex Univ. (MA 1967). Advertising trainee, Foote, Cone & Belding, 1960–61; taught English in France, 1966; publicity asst, William Collins, 1967–68; Publicity Dir, Geoffrey Bles, 1968; editor, André Deutsch, 1968–70; Literary Agent, A. P. Watt, 1970–76; editor, OUP, 1977–79; Editl Dir, Chatto & Windus, 1979–89; Dep. Ed., London Mag., 1990–94; reader, Peters, Fraser & Dunlop Ltd, 1991–2000. Mem. Cttee, Royal Literary Fund, 2007–. Sec., R. S. Surtees Soc., 2000–. FRSL 1992. *Publications:* Playing for Time, 1987; The Chatto Book of Office Life, 1992; Kindred Spirits, 1995; Cyril Connolly: a life, 1997; Tobias Smollett, 2003; Penguin Special: the life and times of Allen Lane, 2005; Grub Street Irregular, 2008; Shades of Greene: one generation of an English family, 2010; (ed jtly) The Best of the Oldie 1992–2012, 2012; David Astor: a life, 2016. *Recreations:* walking in Richmond Park, re-reading Trollope, talking to the cat. *Address:* 3 Percival Road, SW14 7QE. *T:* (020) 8876 2807. *E:* jeremy.lewis5@me.com. *Club:* Academy.

LEWIS, Rt Rev. John; *see* Lewis, Rt Rev. H. J.

LEWIS, Sir John (Anthony), Kt 2004; OBE 1996; Principal, 1989–2006, Academy Adviser and School Improvement Partner, 2006–11, Dixons City Academy (formerly Technology College), Bradford; *b* 9 May 1946; *s* of John D. C. Lewis and Dorothy Lewis (*née* Roberts); *m* 1969, Penny Ward; three *s*. *Educ:* Queens' Coll., Cambridge (BA (Hist.) 1968; MA 1971); CNAA (MSc Educnl Mgt 1982). History Teacher: Northgate GS, Ipswich, 1969–73; Appleton Hall GS, Warrington, 1973–75; Culcheth High Sch., Warrington, 1975–79; Dep. Hd, Bishop Heber High Sch., Malpas, 1979–84; Head Teacher, Birchwood Community High Sch., Warrington, 1984–89. Hon. DEd Bradford, 2009. *Recreations:* sport (Cambridge soccer Blue, 1968), cricket, tennis. *E:* ja.lewis@dsl.pipex.com.

LEWIS, Ven. John Arthur; Archdeacon of Cheltenham, 1988–98, now Archdeacon Emeritus; *b* 4 Oct. 1934; *s* of Lt-Col Harry Arthur Lewis and Evaline Helen Ross Lewis; *m* 1959, Hazel Helen Jane Morris; one *s* one *d*. *Educ:* Jesus College, Oxford (MA); Cuddesdon College. Assistant Curate: St Mary, Prestbury, Glos, 1960–63; Wimborne Minster, 1963–66; Rector, Eastington with Frocester, 1966–70; Vicar of Nailsworth, 1970–78; Vicar of Cirencester, 1978–88; RD of Cirencester, 1984–88. Hon. Canon, 1985–88, Canon, 1988–98, Canon Emeritus, 1998–, Gloucester Cathedral. Hon. Chaplain, Glos Constabulary, 1988–98. Chairman: Diocesan Stewardship Cttee, 1988–96; Diocesan Redundant Church Uses Cttee, 1988–98; Diocesan Bd of Educn, 1990–98. Mem. Council, Cheltenham Ladies' Coll., 1992–97. *Recreations:* travel, music, walking, gardening. *Address:* 5 Vilverie Mead, Bishops Cleeve, Cheltenham, Glos GL52 7YY. *T:* (01242) 678425.

LEWIS, John Elliott, MA; Head Master, Eton College, 1994–2002; *b* 23 Feb. 1942; *s* of John Derek Lewis and Margaret Helen (*née* Shaw); *m* 1968, Vibeke Lewis (*née* Johansson). *Educ:* King's College, Auckland, NZ; Corpus Christi Coll., Cambridge (Girdlers' Company Schol.; MA Classics). Assistant Master, King's Coll., Auckland, 1964, 1966–70; Jun. Lecturer in Classics, Auckland Univ., 1965; Asst Master, 1971–80, Master in College, 1975–80, Eton College; Head Master, Geelong Grammar Sch., Australia, 1980–94.

LEWIS, Rt Rev. (John Hubert) Richard; Bishop of St Edmundsbury and Ipswich, 1997–2007; *b* 10 Dec. 1943; *s* of John Wilfred and Winifred Mary Lewis; *m* 1968, Sara Patricia Hamilton; two *s* (and one *s* decd). *Educ:* Radley; King's Coll., London (AKC). Curate of Hexham, 1967–70; Industrial Chaplain, Diocese of Newcastle, 1970–77; Communications Officer, Diocese of Durham, 1977–82; Agricultural Chaplain, Diocese of Hereford, 1982–87; Archdeacon of Ludlow, 1987–92; Bishop Suffragan of Taunton, 1992–97. Prebendary, Wells Cathedral, 1992–97. Nat. Chm., Small Farmers' Assoc., 1984–88. Mem., Gen. Synod of C of E, 1987–92. *Publications:* (ed jtly) The People, the Land and the Church, 1987; Sampans and Saffron Cake, 2012. *Recreations:* bricklaying, bumble bees, kit car building.

LEWIS, John Simon Carl, FSA; General Secretary and Chief Executive, Society of Antiquaries of London, since 2010; *b* Three Crosses, Swansea, 19 March 1962; *s* of late Ivor Lewis and of Mary Lewis (*née* Grinter); *m* 1991, Catherine Rogers; two *s* one *d*. *Educ:* Gowerton Comprehensive Sch.; Univ. of London Inst. of Archaeol. (BSc Hons). FSA 2005. Museum of London: Sites and Monuments Record Officer, 1984–86; Sen. Archaeologist, 1986–96; Project Manager, 1996; Wessex Archaeology: Project Manager, 1996–2000; Hd, Framework Archaeol. Jt Venture, 2000–10. *Publications:* contrib. articles to learned jls and monographs. *Recreations:* playing hockey, watching Association Football (Swansea and Arsenal), reading, walking, cooking. *Address:* Society of Antiquaries of London, Burlington House, Piccadilly, W1J 0BE. *T:* (020) 7479 7093, *Fax:* (020) 7287 6967. *E:* jlewis@sal.org.uk. *Clubs:* Salisbury Hockey, Ashford (Middx) Hockey.

LEWIS, Very Rev. John Thomas; Dean of Llandaff, 2000–12; *b* 14 June 1947; *s* of Rev. David Islwyn Lewis and Eleanor Tranter Lewis; *m* 1976, Dr Cynthia Sheelagh McFetridge; two *s*. *Educ:* Dyffryn Grammar Sch., Port Talbot; Jesus Coll., Oxford (scholar; BA (Maths) 1969; Dip. Applied Stats 1970; MA 1973); St John's Coll., Cambridge (BA (Theol.) 1972; MA 1992); Westcott House, Cambridge. Ordained deacon, 1973, priest, 1974. Assistant Curate: Whitchurch, 1973–77; Lisvane, 1977–80; Chaplain, Cardiff Univ., 1980–85; Warden of Ordinands, Llandaff, 1981–85; Vicar, Brecon St David with Llanspyddid and Llanilltyd, 1985–91; Vicar, then Rector, Bassaleg, 1991–2000. Sec., Provincial Selection Panel, Church in Wales, 1987–94; Bishop of Monmouth's Chaplain for Continuing Ministerial Educn, 1998–2000. *Recreations:* hill walking, music, sport, family life. *Address:* 8 Daniell Close, Sully, Vale of Glamorgan CF64 5JY. *T:* (029) 2053 1315.

LEWIS, Rt Hon. Dr Julian Murray; PC 2015; MP (C) New Forest East, since 1997; *b* 26 Sept. 1951; *s* of late Samuel Lewis, tailor and designer, and Hilda Lewis. *Educ:* Dynevor Grammar Sch., Swansea; Balliol Coll., Oxford (MA 1977); St Antony's Coll., Oxford (DPhil 1981). Sec., Oxford Union, 1972. Seaman, RNR, 1979–82. Res. in defence studies, 1975–77, 1978–81; Sec., Campaign for Representative Democracy, 1977–78; Res. Dir and Dir, Coalition for Peace Through Security, 1981–85; Dir, Policy Res. Associates, 1985–; Dep. Dir, Cons. Res. Dept, 1990–96. Contested (C) Swansea W, 1983. Opposition Whip, 2001–02; Shadow Defence Minister, 2002–04, 2005–10; Shadow Minister for the Cabinet Office, 2004–05. Member: Select Cttee on Welsh Affairs, 1998–2001; Select Cttee on Defence, 2000–01 and 2015– (Chm., 2015–); Exec., 1922 Cttee, 2001; Intelligence and Security Cttee, 2010–15; Sec., Cons. Parly Defence Cttee, 1997–2001; Vice-Chairman: Cons. Parly Foreign Affairs Cttee, 2000–01; Cons. Parly European Affairs Cttee, 2000–01. Parly Chm., First Defence, 2004–09. Mem., Armed Forces Parly Scheme (RAF), 1998, 2000, (RN), 2004, (RCDS), 2006, (Jt Services), 2008. Vis. Sen. Res. Fellow, Centre for Defence Studies, Dept of War Studies, KCL, 2010–. Trustee, 1998–2001, Vice-Pres., 2001–07, Pres., 2007–09, British Military Powerboat Trust. Trench Gascoigne Essay Prize, RUSI, 2005 and 2007; Dissertation Prize, RCDS, 2006. *Publications:* Changing Direction: British military planning for post-war strategic defence 1942–47, 1988, 2nd edn 2003; Who's Left?: an index of Labour MPs and left-wing causes 1985–1992, 1992; Labour's CND Cover-up, 1992; Racing Ace: the fights and flights of 'Kink' Kinkead, DSO, DSC★, DFC★, 2011; political pamphlets. *Recreations:* history, fiction, films, music, photography. *Address:* House of Commons, SW1A 0AA. *T:* (020) 7219 4179. *Clubs:* Athenæum; Totton Conservative.

LEWIS, Keith William, AO 1994; CB 1981; Director General and Engineer in Chief, Engineering and Water Supply Department, South Australia, 1974–87; *b* 10 Nov. 1927; *s* of Ernest John and Alinda Myrtle Lewis; *m* 1958, Alison Bothwell Fleming; two *d*. *Educ:* Adelaide High Sch.; Univ. of Adelaide (BE Civil); Imperial Coll., Univ. of London (DIC). FTS. Engineer for Water and Sewage Treatment, Engrg and Water Supply Dept, SA, 1968–74. Chm., Pipelines Authy of SA, 1987–94; Dep. Chm., Electricity Trust of SA, 1994–95. Chairman: S Australian Water Resources Council, 1976–87; Australian Water Res. Adv. Council, 1985–90; Murray-Darling Basin Freshwater Res. Centre, 1986–91; Energy Planning Exec., 1987–93; SA Urban Land Trust, 1990–94; Member: Standing Cttee, Australian Water Resources Council, 1974–87; Electricity Trust of S Australia, 1974–84; State Planning Authority, 1974–82; Golden Grove Jt Venture Cttee, 1984–97; Bd, Amdel Ltd, 1987–94. River Murray Commissioner, representing SA, 1982–87. Hon. FIEAust 1993. Silver Jubilee Medal, 1977. *Recreations:* reading, ornithology, golf, lawn bowls. *Address:* 93 Coopers Avenue, Leabrook, SA 5068, Australia. *T:* (8) 84318860, *Fax:* (8) 83382431. *Clubs:* Adelaide, Kooyonga Golf, Adelaide Oval Bowling (South Australia).

LEWIS, Sir (Lawrence Vernon) Harcourt, KCMG 2010; GCM 1982; Chairman, National Petroleum Corporation, Barbados, since 2008; *b* St Michael, Barbados, 13 March 1932; *s* of Lawrence Lewis and Marie A. Lewis (*née* Ince); *m* 1961, Jocelyn Arlene Claudette Kirton; two *s*. *Educ:* Combermere Sch.; Univ. of W Indies (DPA 1964). Dir, Data Processing, 1970; Accountant Gen., 1971–73; Dep. Financial Sec., 1973; Perm. Sec., Finance, 1973–78; Pres., Barbados Nat. Bank, 1978–81; Chm., Insce Corp. of Barbados, 1978–81; Exec. Dir, Nat. Petroleum Corp., Barbados, 1982–84; Minister of State, CS, 1986–91; Minister: of Agriculture, 1991–93; of Envmt, 1993–94. *Recreations:* football (soccer), lawn tennis. *Address:* #11 West Ridge, Dalkeith Hill, St Michael 14000, Barbados. *T:* 4261319, *Fax:* 4260836; National Petroleum Corporation, PO Box 175, Bridgetown, Barbados. *Club:* Rotary (Barbados) (Paul Harris Fellow).

LEWIS, Sir Leigh (Warren), KCB 2007 (CB 2000); Permanent Secretary, Department for Work and Pensions, 2005–10; *b* 17 March 1951; *s* of Harold and Ray Rene Lewis; *m* 1973, Susan Evelyn Gold; two *s*. *Educ:* Harrow County Grammar Sch. for Boys; Liverpool Univ. (BA Hons 1973). MIPD. Dept of Employment, 1973; Private Sec. to Parly Under Sec. of State, 1975–76; Incomes and Indust. Relations Divs, 1978–84; Principal Private Sec. to Minister without Portfolio and Sec. of State for Employment, 1984–86; Asst Sec., EC Br., 1986–87; Dir of Ops, Unemployment Benefit Service, 1987–88; Group Dir of Personnel, Cable and Wireless plc, 1988–91 (on secondment); Dir, Internat. Div., 1991–94; Dir, Finance and Resource Mgt Div., 1994–95; Dir, Finance, DfEE, 1995–96; Chief Executive: Employment Service, DfEE, then DWP, 1997–2002; Jobcentre Plus, DWP, 2002–03; Perm. Sec., Crime, Policing, Counter-Terrorism and Delivery, Home Office, 2003–05. Chm., UK Bill of Rights Commn, 2011–12. Chairman, Board of Trustees: Broadway, 2011–14; DrinkAware, 2014–; Vice Chm., Bd of Trustees, St Mungo's Broadway, 2014–. Vis. Fellow, Univ. of Greenwich, 2012–. *Publications:* (with John Hutton) How to be a Minister: a 21st-century guide, 2014. *Recreation:* Watford Football Club. *E:* leighwlewis@yahoo.com.

LEWIS, Lennox Claudius, CM 1988; CBE 2002 (MBE 1998); professional boxer, 1989–2004; *b* 2 Sept. 1965; *s* of Violet Blake; *m* 2005, Violet Chang; one *s* two *d*. World jun. heavyweight champion, 1983; Olympic heavyweight champion (rep. Canada), 1988; European heavyweight champion, 1990; British heavyweight champion, 1991; WBC world heavyweight champion, 1993, 1997, 2002–04; undisputed world heavyweight champion, 1999, 2001–02; world heavyweight champion, 2000. Boxing commentator, HBO, 2006–10. Founder: Lennox Lewis Coll., Hackney, London, 1994; Lennox Lewis Family Foundn. DUniv N London, 1999. Inducted into Internat. Boxing Hall of Fame, NY, 2009. *Publications:* Lennox Lewis (autobiog.), 1993, 2nd edn 1997; (jtly) Lennox (autobiog.), 2002. *Recreations:* chess, golf, reading, listening to music.

LEWIS, Marilyn; Director, Cadw, 2005–14; *b* 29 Aug. 1954; *d* of Thomas and Jacqueline Clements; *m* 1979, David Lewis. *Educ:* Univ. of Manchester (BA Hons Medieval Studies 1975); Univ. of Bangor (DAA 1976); Liverpool John Moores Univ. (MBA 1995). Asst Archivist, Suffolk CC, 1976–78; Bor. Archivist, Walsall, 1978–87; City Archivist, Chester CC, 1987–97; Shropshire County Council: Hd, Heritage, 1997–2000; Asst Dir, Cultural Services, 2000–05. *Publications:* The Book of Walsall, 1986. *Recreations:* castles, wildlife, Aston Villa Football Club, Madagascar.

LEWIS, Mark; Partner, Seddons Solicitors, since 2015; *b* Radcliffe, 10 Dec. 1964; *s* of Brian Ellis Aaron Lewis and Elaine Lewis. *Educ:* William Hulme Grammar Sch.; Middlesex Poly. (LLB Hons Law); Chester Law Sch.; Manchester Metropolitan Univ. (Dip. Commercial Litigation). Admitted as solicitor, 1990; Partner: George Davies, 2001–09; Stripes Solicitors, 2009–10; Consultant, 2010–11, Partner, 2011–15, Taylor Hampton. Dir, UK Lawyers For Israel. Member: Lawyers for Media Standards, 2010–; Law Soc., 1990–. *Recreations:* veteran and vintage cars, fashion, music, theatre, Middle Eastern politics. *Address:* Seddons Solicitors, 5 Portman Square, W1H 6NT.

LEWIS, Martin John; Director of Library Services and University Librarian, University of Sheffield, 2003–15; *b* Cardiff, 9 April 1955; *s* of John and Betty Lewis; *m* 1986, Susan Elizabeth Smith; one *d*. *Educ:* Duffryn High Sch., Newport, Wales; Fitzwilliam Coll., Cambridge (BA Natural Scis 1976); Univ. of Wales, Aberystwyth (Postgrad. DipLib). MCLIP 1981. Asst Librarian, Univ. of Leeds, 1978–86; Health Scis Librarian, 1986–94, Dep. Librarian, 1994–2002, Univ. of Sheffield. Vis. Librarian, MIT, 1984–85. Member: Bd, Res. Libraries UK, 2004–10; Adv. Council, BL, 2005–12. Mem. Council, Univ. of Sheffield, 2008–14. *Publications:* contrib. papers to librarianship and information sci. jls, and conf. proceedings. *Recreations:* hill walking, travel, modern architecture.

LEWIS, Martin Steven, OBE 2014; broadcaster and newspaper columnist, since 2000; Money Saving Expert, MoneySavingExpert.com, since 2003; *b* Manchester, 9 May 1972; *s* of Stuart Lewis and late Susan Lewis; *m* 2009, Lara Lewington; one *d*. *Educ:* London Sch. of Econs (BSc Econ 1994); Cardiff Sch. of Journalism (Postgrad. Dip. Broadcast Journalism 1998). Gen. Sec., LSE Students' Union, 1994–95; Account Exec., Brunswick PR, 1995–97; Reporter/Producer, BBC Business Unit, 1998–99; Business Corresp., then Money Saving Expert, Simply Money TV, 2000–01; columnist: Sunday Express, 2001–05; Guardian, 2005–06; Sunday Times, 2006–07; Sunday Post, 2007–; News of the World, 2008–11; Daily Telegraph, 2009–; television: Money Saving Expert: This Morning, 2003–05, 2012–; GMTV, 2006–10; Daybreak, 2010–14; Good Morning Britain, 2014–; presenter: Make Me Rich, 2005; It Pays to Watch, 2008; The Martin Lewis Money Show, 2012–; reporter, Tonight, 2006; contributor: Jeremy Vine Show, BBC Radio 2, 2005–; Radio 5 Consumer Panel, 2010–. Chm., Ind. Taskforce on Student Finance Communication, 2011–13. Chm., MSE charity, 2008–. Gov., LSE, 2009–. *Publications:* The Money Diet, 2004, 2nd edn 2005; Thrifty Ways for Modern Days, 2006; The Three Most Important Lessons, 2008. *Recreations:* trying to get my average Scrabble score above 410 (currently 403) and my 10K time under 50 minutes, reading historic novels, very poor golf, anything with lists, jive, watching athletics, supporting Manchester City. *W:* www.moneysavingexpert.com.

LEWIS, Martyn John Dudley, CBE 1997; journalist, broadcaster and businessman; Chairman, National Council for Voluntary Organisations, since 2010; Director, TS Elite Group, since 2013; *b* 7 April 1945; *s* of late Thomas John Dudley Lewis and Doris (*née* Jones); *m* 1st, 1970, Elizabeth Anne Carse (*d* 2012); two *d*; 2nd, 2012, Patsy St Clair Baker. *Educ:* Dalriada High Sch., Ballymoney, NI; Trinity Coll., Dublin (BA 1967). Reporter: BBC, Belfast, 1967–68; HTV, Cardiff, 1968–70; Independent Television News: reporter, 1970–86;

Head, Northern Bureau, 1971–78; presenter, News at Ten, 1981–86; Presenter: BBC One O'Clock News, 1986–87; BBC Nine O'Clock News, 1987–94; BBC TV Six O'Clock News, 1994–99; Today's the Day, BBC2, 1993–99; Crimebeat, 1996–98; Agenda, The Wireless (Age UK radio), 2012–. Documentaries include: Battle for the Falklands; The Secret Hunters; Fight Cancer; Living with Dying; Great Ormond Street—a Fighting Chance; Health UK; A Century to Remember; series for ITV: Bethlehem—Year Zero, 1999; Dateline Jerusalem, 2000; News 40, 2000; Ultimate Questions, 2000–02. Mem. Bd, IPSO, 2014–. Dir, Drive for Youth, 1986–99 (Chm., 1990–99); Chm. and Founder, YouthNet UK, 1995–2014, Founder at Large, 2014–; Co-Founder and Chairman: Global Intercasting Ltd, 1999–2007; Teliris Ltd, 2001–12; Chm., NICE TV Ltd, 2005–12; EU Chm., Teliris Inc., 2007–12. Chm., Beacon Fellowship, 2005–07. Advr, Ogden Educnl Trust, 2000–11. Member: Policy Adv. Cttee, Tidy Britain Gp, 1988–98; Volunteer Partnership (govt cttee), 1995–97; Internat. Adv. Cttee, RADA, 2007–11; Ext. Adv. Bd, Long Room Hub, TCD, 2009–11; Team London Adv. Bd, 2013–. Director: Hospice Arts, 1989–97; CLIC UK, 1990–96; Adopt-A-Student, 1988–96; Inst. for Citizenship Studies, 1993–97; Friends of Nelson Mandela Children's Fund, 1997–2002; President: United Response, 1989–; George Thomas Centre for Hospice Care, 1996–2005; Vice-President: Macmillan Cancer Support (formerly Cancer Relief Macmillan Fund, then Macmillan Cancer Relief), 1988– (Dir, 1990–96); Marie Curie Cancer Care, 1990–; Help the Hospices, 1990–; British Soviet Hospice Soc., 1990–96; Demelza House Children's Hospice, 1996–; Voices for Hospices, 1996–2011; East Anglia Children's Hospices, 1999–; Barrett's Oesophagus Foundn, 2000–; Chm., Families of the Fallen, 2010–15; Trustee: Windsor Leadership Trust, 2001–10; Edutrust, 2008–10; Patron: London Lighthouse, 1990–99; SW Children's Hospice, 1991–2007; Internat. Sch. for Cancer Care, 1991–99; Hope House Children's Hospice, 1992–2007; Cities in Schools, 1995–97 (Dir, 1989–95); Tomorrow Project, 1996–2007; Dementia UK (formerly Dementia Relief Trust, then For Dementia), 1998–; James Powell (UK) Trust, 1998–2007; Mildmay Mission Hosp., 1998–; Volunteering England (formerly Nat. Centre for Volunteering), 1998–2012; Patchwork Foundn, 2013–; Positive News, 2013–. Chair, Award Cttee, Queen's Award for Voluntary Service, 2009–; Dep. Chair, Lord Mayor of London's Dragon Awards, 2010–. Mem., BAFTA, 1980–. Freeman, City of London, 1989; Liveryman, Pattenmakers' Co., 1989–. FRSA 1990. Hon. DLitt Ulster, 1994. *Publications:* And Finally, 1983; Tears and Smiles—the Hospice Handbook, 1989; Cats in the News, 1991 (trans. Japanese 1994); Dogs in the News, 1992 (trans. Japanese 1996); Go For It: Martyn Lewis's essential guide to opportunities for young people (annual), 1993–97, as Book of the Site, 1998–99; Reflections on Success, 1997; Seasons of our Lives, 1999. *Recreations:* photography, piano, good food, keeping fit. *Address:* c/o Anita Land Ltd, 10 Wyndham Place, W1H 2PU. *T:* 07836 764139. *E:* martyn@martynlewis.tv. *Club:* Garrick.

LEWIS, Mary Elizabeth, (Mrs N. Woolley); Director General, International Federation of Purchasing and Supply Management, 2012–13; *b* 29 Dec. 1952; *d* of Kenneth Richard Lewis and Joan Lewis; *m* 1988, Nicholas Woolley. *Educ:* St Angela's Convent, Harringay; University Coll. of Wales, Aberystwyth (BA Hons English 1975). CDipAF 1991. FCIHT (FIHT 2006). Asst Sec., 1987–94, Dir, Finance and Personnel, 1994–98, CIB; Exec. Sec., Physiol Soc., 1999–2001; Chief Exec., Chartered Instn of Highways and Transportation (formerly Instn of Highways and Transportation), 2001–11. Trustee, Rees Jeffreys Road Fund. *Recreations:* embroidery, gardening, music, travel. *Address:* Manor Farm, East Ilkerton, Barbrook, Lynton, Devon EX35 6PH.

LEWIS, Rt Rev. Michael Augustine Owen; *see* Cyprus and the Gulf, Bishop in.

LEWIS, Michael David; Director, Avenue53 Consulting (communications, broadcasting and media rights consultancy), since 2009; *b* 5 June 1947; *s* of late David Lloyd Lewis and Gwendoline Lewis; *m* 1992, Hilary Anne East; two *d.* *Educ:* Erith Grammar Sch., Kent. Dartford Reporter newspaper, 1966–70; Brighton Evening Argus, 1970–73; LBC/Independent Radio News, 1973–82; BBC Radio Sport: Duty Editor, 1982–83; Dep. Editor, 1983–84; Editor, 1984–91; Head of Sport and Outside Broadcasts, 1991–93; Dep. Controller, BBC Radio 5 Live, 1994–2000; Controller, Radio Sports Rights, BBC Sport, 1996–2007; broadcasting consultant, 2007–14; Dep. Broadcast Manager, All-England Tennis Club, 2010–15. *Recreations:* watching Arsenal through gritted teeth, helping two daughters make their way in the world, enjoying live theatre and dance. *Address:* 53 Wallingford Avenue, W10 6PZ. *T:* 07850 762259.

LEWIS, Pamela; *see* Cameron, Pamela.

LEWIS, Paul Arthur; freelance financial journalist, broadcaster, author and speaker; *b* 22 April 1948; *s* of late William Denis Lewis and Betty Blanche Lewis; *m* 1969, Eileen Margaret Tame (marr. diss. 2002); two *s* one *d*; *m* 2015, Emma Sheila Lynch. *Educ:* Univ. of Stirling (BA Psychology, MSc Res. Psychology 1972). Dep. Dir, Nat. Council for One Parent Families, 1976–83; Dir, Youthaid, 1983–86; Money Corresp., Saga Magazine, 1984–; Presenter, BBC: Wake Up To Money, Radio Five Live, 1998–2000; Money Box, Radio 4, 2000–; contrib., BBC Breakfast, 2008–. Chm., Nat. Right to Fuel Campaign, 1975–81; Gov., Pensions Policy Inst., 2002–. Sec., Wilkie Collins Soc., 1996–. Mem., Maidstone BC, 1974–84. DUniv Essex, 2013. *Publications:* Saga Rights Guide, 1988; Saga Money Guide, 1988; Your Taxes and Savings, 2002, 4th edn 2005; The Complete Money Plan, 2004; Money Magic, 2005; (ed jtly) The Public Face of Wilkie Collins, 2005; Live Long and Prosper, 2006; Understanding Taxes and Savings, 2006; Pay Less Tax (annually), 2007–09; Beat the Banks, 2008; Making Your Money Work, 2008; Can You Claim It? (annually), 2010–; contrib. to The Dickensian, Reader's Digest, Daily Telegraph, Radio Times, TES, Community Care, Good Homes, PensionDCisions, The Oldie, Heathrow Express, Money Marketing. *Recreations:* annoying financial companies, making bad jokes, Wilkie Collins. *E:* paul@paullewis.co.uk. *T:* 07836 217311. *W:* www.paullewis.co.uk, www.paullewismoney.blogspot.com, www.twitter.com/paullewismoney.

LEWIS, Paul Keith; QC 2001; a Recorder, since 2000; *b* 26 May 1957; *s* of late John Keith Lewis and of Susan Patricia Lewis (*née* Cronin); *m* 1983, Siân Price; one *s* one *d.* *Educ:* Pontypridd Grammar Sch. for Boys; Univ. of Leicester (LLB Hons); Inns of Court Sch. of Law. Called to the Bar, Gray's Inn, 1981, Bencher, 2014; in practice, Cardiff and London, 1981–; an Asst Recorder, 1998–2000; Leader, Wales and Chester Circuit, 2014–. *Recreations:* sport, travel, music. *Address:* Farrar's Building, Temple, EC4Y 7BD. *T:* (020) 7583 9241, *Fax:* (020) 7583 0090. *E:* chambers@farrarsbuilding.co.uk. *Club:* Monmouthshire Golf (Abergavenny).

LEWIS, Prof. Penney Jaye, JD; Professor of Law, since 2007, and Co-Director, Centre of Medical Law and Ethics, since 2013, King's College London; *b* London, 3 Nov. 1967; *d* of Alan Michael Lewis and Frumie Lewis (*née* Davson). *Educ:* Havergal Coll., Toronto; Massachusetts Inst. of Technol. (SB Maths 1989); Univ. of Toronto (JD 1992); King's Coll. London (MA Med. Ethics and Law 1994); Columbia Univ. (LLM 1995). Law Clerk, Supreme Court of Canada, 1992–93; Lectr, 1995–2005, Reader, 2005–07, in Law, KCL. Barrister and solicitor, Law Soc. of Upper Canada, 2000–. Mem., UK Donation Ethics Cttee, 2010–. *Publications:* Delayed Prosecution for Childhood Sexual Abuse, 2006; Assisted Dying and Legal Change, 2007. *Recreations:* travel, languages, theatre, art, music. *Address:* Dickson Poon School of Law, King's College London, Strand, WC2R 2LS. *T:* (020) 7848 1103, *Fax:* (020) 7848 2465. *E:* penney.lewis@kcl.ac.uk.

LEWIS, Peter; Director, Policy Co-ordination Unit, 1994–96, and the Tax Simplification Project, 1995–96, Inland Revenue; *b* 24 June 1937; *s* of Reginald George and Edith Lewis; *m* 1962, Ursula Brigitte Kilian; one *s* one *d.* *Educ:* Ealing Grammar School; St Peter's Hall, Oxford. Royal Navy, 1955–57. Inland Revenue Inspector of Taxes, 1960–69; Inland Revenue Policy and Central Divs, 1969–85; Director: Personal Tax Div., 1986–91; Company Tax Div., 1991–95. *Address:* Glyndavas, 9 Waterloo Close, St Mawes, Cornwall TR2 5BD.

LEWIS, Peter Adrian; Interim Director, Children's Services, StubbsStorey Ltd, since 2013; *b* 9 Feb. 1954; *s* of Mrs Beryl Williams; *m* 1976, Lynn Cook. *Educ:* Madeley Coll., Keele (Cert Ed); Bristol Poly. (BEd). Teacher, Eastwood Middle Sch., Stoke on Trent, 1975–77; social worker, Staffs, Avon and Hants, 1977–88; Educn Officer, Hants CC, 1988–96; Asst Dir, Educn and Leisure Services, Southampton CC, 1996–2004; Dir, Educn, Children's Services and Leisure, 2004–09, Dep. Chief Exec., 2008–09, Enfield LBC; Dir, Children's Services, Haringey LBC, 2009–11. *Recreations:* opera, reading, walking, travel.

LEWIS, Peter Ronald; Director General, Bibliographic Services, British Library, 1980–89; *b* 28 Sept. 1926; *s* of Charles Lewis and Florence Mary (*née* Kirk); *m* 1952, June Ashley; one *s* one *d.* *Educ:* Royal Masonic Sch.; Belfast Univ. (MA). FLA; Hon. FCLIP (Hon. FLA 1989). Brighton, Plymouth, Chester public libraries, 1948–55; Head, Bibliographic Services, BoT Library, 1955–65; Lectr in Library Studies, QUB, 1965–69; Librarian: City Univ., 1969–72; Univ. of Sussex, 1972–80. Vice-Pres., 1979–85 and Hon. Treasurer, 1980–82, Library Assoc. Chm., LA Publishing Co., 1983–85. *Publications:* The Literature of the Social Sciences, 1960; The Fall and Rise of National Bibliography (Bangalore), 1982. *Recreations:* acting, editor-publisher. *Address:* Wyvern, Blackheath Road, Wenhaston, Suffolk IP19 9HD.

LEWIS, Peter Tyndale; Chairman, John Lewis Partnership, 1972–93; *b* 26 Sept. 1929; *s* of Oswald Lewis and Frances Merriman Lewis (*née* Cooper); *m* 1961, Deborah Anne (*d* 2014), *d* of late Sir William (Alexander Roy) Collins, CBE and Priscilla Marian, *d* of late S. J. Lloyd; one *s* one *d.* *Educ:* Eton; Christ Church, Oxford (MA 1953). National service, Coldstream Guards, 1948–49; called to Bar (Middle Temple) 1956; joined John Lewis Partnership, 1959. Member: Council, Industrial Soc., 1968–79; Design Council, 1971–74; Chm., Retail Distributors' Assoc., 1972. Member: Southampton Univ. Develt Trust, 1994–2003; Council, Queen's Coll., Harley St, 1994–99. Trustee, Jt Educnl Trust, 1985–87. Governor: NIESR, 1983; Windlesham Hse Sch., 1979–95; The Bell Educnl Trust, 1987–97. *Address:* 145 Rivermead Court, SW6 3SE.

LEWIS, Rhodri Price; QC 2001; a Recorder, since 1998; a Deputy High Court Judge, since 2013; *b* 7 June 1952; *s* of George Lewis and Nansi Lewis (*née* Price); *m* 1983, Barbara Sinden; two *d.* *Educ:* Ysgol Gymraeg Ynyswen; Cowbridge Grammar Sch.; Pembroke Coll., Oxford (MA); Sidney Sussex Coll., Cambridge (Dip. Criminol.). Called to the Bar, Middle Temple, 1975. An Asst Parly Boundary Comr, 2003–. *Publications:* Environmental Law, 2000; contrib. to Jl Planning and Envmt Law. *Recreations:* Rugby, playing the guitar, enjoying the company, coast and country of Pembrokeshire. *Address:* Landmark Chambers, 180 Fleet Street, EC4A 2HG. *Clubs:* Garrick, London Welsh Rugby Football; St David's Rugby Football.

LEWIS, Rt Rev. Richard; *see* Lewis, Rt Rev. J. H. R.

LEWIS, Very Rev. Richard; Dean of Wells, 1990–2003, now Emeritus; *b* 24 Dec. 1935; *m* 1959, Jill Diane Wilford; two *s.* *Educ:* Royal Masonic Sch.; Fitzwilliam House, Cambridge (BA 1958; MA 1961); Ripon Hall, Oxford. Asst Curate, Hinckley, Leicester, 1960–63; Priest-in-Charge, St Edmund, Riddlesdown, 1963–66; Vicar: All Saints, South Merstham, 1966–72; Holy Trinity and St Peter, Wimbledon, 1972–79; St Barnabas, Dulwich and Foundation Chaplain of Alleyn's College of God's Gift at Dulwich, 1979–90. *Publications:* (contrib.) Cathedrals Now, 1996; (contrib.) Wells Cathedral, 2005. *Recreations:* music of all sorts, gardening, reading, tapestry. *Address:* 1 Monmouth Court, Union Street, Wells, Som BA5 2PX. *T:* (01749) 672677. *E:* Dean.Richard@wellshouse.co.uk.

LEWIS, Richard Alan, CBE 2013; Chief Executive, All England Lawn Tennis Club (Championships) Ltd (formerly All England Lawn Tennis and Croquet Club), since 2012; *b* Winchmore Hill, London, 6 Dec. 1954; *s* of Wilfred and Marian Lewis; *m* 2005, Jan; two *s.* *Educ:* Goffs Grammar Sch. Professional tennis player and coach, 1969–87. Dir, Nat. Trng, 1987–96, Dir of Tennis, 1997–2000, LTA; Merryck & Co., 2000–02; Chm., Rugby Football League, 2002–12. Chm., Sport England, 2009–13. Chm., Major Spectator Sports Div., CCPR, 2007–09. Chm., Rugby League Eur. Fedn, 2003–12; Dep. Chm., Rugby League Internat. Fedn, 2003–12. Chm., Rev. of Young Player Develt in Professional Football, 2006–07. *Recreations:* cycling, walking, tennis, gardening. *Address:* Shepley, W Yorks. *Club:* All England Lawn Tennis.

LEWIS, Hon. Robin William, CVO 2015; OBE 1988; Lord-Lieutenant of Dyfed, since 2006; *b* 7 Feb. 1941; *s* of 3rd Baron Merthyr, KBE, TD, PC, and Violet (*née* Meyrick); *m* 1967, Judith Ann Giardelli. *Educ:* Eton; Magdalen Coll., Oxford (MA; Dip. Econ. Develt). Commonwealth Develt Corp., 1964–66; Alcan Aluminium Ltd, 1967–68; Westminster Bank Ltd, 1968–72; Develt Corp. for Wales, 1972–83; Man. Dir, Novametrix Med. Systems Ltd, 1983–90; Chairman: The Magstim Co. Ltd, 1990–2013; J. P. Morgan US Discovery Investment Trust, 2003–08. Chm., Gen. Adv. Council, IBA, 1988–90. Chairman: NT Cttee for Wales, 1994–97; Trustees, Nat. Botanic Garden of Wales, 2006–08. High Sheriff, 1987–88, DL 2002, Dyfed. CStJ 2008. *Address:* The Cottage, Cresswell Quay, Kilgetty, Pembs SA68 0TE. *Club:* Leander (Henley-on-Thames).

LEWIS, Roger Charles; Chairman, Cardiff International Airport Ltd, since 2015; Group Chief Executive, Welsh Rugby Union, 2006–15; *b* 24 Aug. 1954; *s* of late Griffith Charles Job Lewis and Dorothy Lewis (*née* Russ); *m* 1980, Dr Christine Trollope; two *s.* *Educ:* Cynffig Comprehensive Sch., Bridgend; Univ. of Nottingham (BMus Hons 1976). Musician, 1976–80: Avon Touring Th. Co., 1977–79; Birmingham Rep. Th. Studio, 1978; Ludus Dance in Educn Co., 1979; Scottish Ballet Workshop Co., 1979; Music Officer, Darlington Arts Centre, 1980–82; Presenter, Radio Tees, 1981–84; Producer: Capital Radio, 1984–85; BBC Radio 1, 1985–87; Hd of Music, Radio 1, 1987–90; Dir, 1990–95, Man. Dir, 1995, Classical Div., EMI Records; Man. Dir, EMI Premier, 1995–97; Pres., Decca Record Co., 1997–98; Man. Dir and Prog. Controller, Classic FM, 1998–2004; Man. Dir, ITV Wales, 2004–06. Director: GWR plc, 1998–2004; European Rugby Cup Ltd, 2007–14; Celtic Rugby Ltd, 2007–15; Racehorse Media Gp, 2012–; British and Irish Lions, 2014–15; non-exec. Dep. Chm., Boosey & Hawkes, 2004–06; non-exec. Dir, Barchester Gp, 2001–06. Chairman: Classical Cttee, British Phonographic Industry Ltd, 1996–98 (Mem., 1990–96); Music and Dance Scheme Adv. Gp, DFES (formerly DFEE), 2000–04; Arts and Business Wales, 2006; Internat. Adv. Bd, Cardiff Univ. Business Sch., 2008–; Yes for Wales, Referendum Campaign, 2010–11; Cardiff Capital Region, 2013–. Member: Bd, Liverpool European Capital of Culture, 2003–06; Bd, Wales Millennium Centre, 2004–06; Welsh Arts Review Panel, 2006; Adv. Bd, D Gp, 2011–; Six Nations Rugby Council, 2012–15. Chm., Royal Liverpool Philharmonic, 2003–06; Vice-President: London Welsh Male Voice Choir, 2004–; Welsh Music Guild, 2005–. Trustee: Masterprize (Internat. Composers' Competition), 1995–2010; Masterclass Charitable Trust, 2000–04; Chairman: Trustees, Ogmore Centre, 1996–2008; Classic FM Charitable Trust, 2000–04; Trustee, Inst. of Welsh Affairs, 2014–. President: Bromley Youth Music Trust, 2000–06 (Vice-Pres., 2006–); Cefn Cribwr RFC, 2007–; Mem., Founder Partners Bd, Beacon Fellowship Awards, 2003–06. FRSA 2000. Hon. FRWCMD 2004; Hon. RCM 2005; Hon. Fellow, Cardiff Univ., 2007. Hon. DLitt Nottingham, 2010; Hon. Dr Glamorgan, 2011. Sony Radio Award, 1987, 1988, 1989; Grand Award Winner and Gold Medal, NY Radio Fest., 1987; One World Broadcasting Trust Award, 1989; NTL Commercial Radio Programmer of the Year, 2002; Alumni Laureate Lifetime Achievement Award, Univ. of Nottingham, 2009. SBStJ 2015. *Recreations:* music, Rugby, ski-ing, country pursuits, member of Wine Soc. *Club:* Cardiff and County.

LEWIS, Dr Roger Clifford; writer; *b* 26 Feb. 1960; *e s* of late Wyndham Gardner Lewis, Bedwas, Monmouthshire; *m* 1982, Anna Margaret Jane Dickens, educational psychologist, *d* of Eric John Dickens and Iris Grace (*née* Taylor); three *s*. *Educ:* Bassaleg Comp. Sch., Newport; Univ. of St Andrews (Lawson Meml Prize, Gray Prize, Coll. Bursary, Walker Trust Award; MA 1st cl. Hons 1982); Magdalen Coll., Oxford (Charles Oldham Shakespeare Prize, Matthew Arnold Meml Prize, Chancellor's English Essay Prize; MA status 1985); Univ. of Hertfordshire (PhD 2009). University of Oxford: Jun. Res. Fellow, Wolfson Coll., 1985–89, Mem. Common Room, 1989–; Tutor, Univ. of Massachusetts Summer Sch., Trinity Coll., 1985; Lecturer and Tutor: Boston Univ. Mod. British Studies prog., St Catherine's Coll., 1986–90; Stanford Univ. and Smithsonian Instn English Lit. courses, Oxford, 1987; Lectr, Magdalen Coll., 1988. Vis. Prof., Faculty of Law, Humanities, Develt and Society, Birmingham City Univ. (formerly UCE, Birmingham), 2006–09. Arts journalism: American Scholar, American Spectator, Areté: the arts; Encounter, Erotic Review, Financial Times, GQ Magazine, Independent, The Lady, Listener, Mail on Sunday, New Statesman, Observer, Oldie (TV critic), Opera Now, Punch, Spectator, Sunday Times, Telegraph Mag., *etc*; lead book reviewer: Express Newspapers, 2001–09; Daily Mail, 2009–. Frequent interviewee on nat. and local radio and television arts and culture progs; consultant on documentaries: Larry and Viv: the Oliviers in love, C4, 2001; The Paranormal Peter Sellers, C4, 2002; Profondo Rosa: la vera storia della Pantera Rosa, Sky Italia, 2004; Les Couples Mythiques du Cinéma, Adamis Prodns Paris, 2014. Mem., Welsh Acad., 2010–. FRAS; FRGS; FZS; FRSA. Hon. DLitt Herts, 2010. Commnd Col by Gov. of Kentucky, 2007 (Medal of Dist., 2007–09); Admiral, Gt Navy of State of Nebraska, 2007 (Scholarship Donor Medal, 2009). Observer/Anthony Burgess Prize for Arts Journalism, 2013. *Publications:* (contrib.) The New Compleat Imbiber, 1986; (ed) Rewards and Fairies, by Rudyard Kipling (Penguin Classics), 1987; Stage People, 1989; (ed) The Memoirs and Confessions of a Justified Sinner, by James Hogg (Everyman's Liby), 1992; The Life and Death of Peter Sellers, 1994, reissued 2004 (filmed 2004 (Primetime Emmy Award 2005)); The Real Life of Laurence Olivier, 1996, reissued 2007; The Man Who Was Private Widdle: Charles Hawtrey, 2001; Anthony Burgess, 2002; Seasonal Suicide Notes: my life as it is lived, 2009; What am I Still Doing Here?, 2011. *Recreation:* fulminating. *E:* annajlewis@aol.com. *Clubs:* Groucho, English-Speaking Union; Players (NY).

LEWIS, Roger St John Hulton; Chairman, Berkeley Group plc, 1999–2007; *b* 26 June 1947; *m* 1973, Vanessa England; three *s*. *Educ:* Eton Coll. ACA 1969. KPMG, 1966–72; Finance Dir, 1972–75, Man. Dir, 1975–83, Crest Homes; Gp Chief Exec., Crest Nicholson, 1983–91; Finance Dir, 1992–98, Exec. Dir, 1998–99, Berkeley Gp. Ind. Dir, Camper & Nicholsons Marinas International Ltd, 2007–; Independent Director: Picton Property Income Ltd, 2010–; States of Jersey Develt Co. Ltd, 2011–. *Recreations:* cricket, travel, ski-ing, food.

LEWIS, Sean Michael, PhD; Director, British Council, Canada, 1997–2000, retired; *b* 23 Oct. 1943; *s* of Leonard Leon Lewis and Margaret Lewis (*née* Moore); *m* 1971, Jennifer M. Williams; one *s*. *Educ:* Univ. of Liverpool (BSc 1967; PhD 1971). British Council: London, 1970, 1973–75, 1978–89, 1992–97; Nigeria, 1971–73; Sri Lanka, 1975–78; Sweden, 1989–92. *Documentary films:* (co-prod.) There We Are John, 1993; (prod.) Lucky Man, 1995. *Recreations:* minimal effort downhill ski-ing, pyrotechnics, films, landscape gardening, real ale, country pubs. *Address:* 38 Ninehams Road, Caterham on the Hill, Surrey CR3 5LD. *T:* (020) 8763 1644.

LEWIS, Prof. Shôn William, MD; Professor of Adult Psychiatry, since 1994 and Director, Institute of Brain, Behaviour and Mental Health, since 2012, University of Manchester; *b* Stafford, 21 Sept. 1954; *s* of Evelyn Lewis and Gwyn Lewis; *m* 1987, Amanda Poynton; two *d*. *Educ:* Dulwich Coll.; Guy's Hosp. Med. Sch., Univ. of London (BSc 1st Cl. Hons Psychol. 1976; MB BS 1980; MPhil 1986; MD 1993). Registrar and Res. Fellow, Maudsley Hosp. and Inst. of Psychiatry, 1981–89; Sen. Lectr in Psychiatry, Charing Cross and Westminster Med. Sch., 1989–94; Hon. Consultant Psychiatrist, Manchester Mental Health and Social Care Trust, 1994–; Hd, Sch. of Community Based Medicine, Univ. of Manchester, 2008–12. Vis. Prof., Univ. of Melbourne, 2001. Associate Dir, NIHR Mental Health Res. Network, 2004–; NIHR Sen. Investigator, 2008–. Trustee, Rethink, charity, 2009–12. FMedSci 2007. *Publications:* (with J. N. Higgins) Brain Imaging in Psychiatry, 1996; (with R. W. Buchanan) Schizophrenia, 1998, 3rd edn 2007; (with E. Guthrie) Psychiatry: a core clinical text, 2002; 200 articles in learned jls on psychosis and schizophrenia. *Recreations:* theatre, cinema, visual arts, hill walking, ski-ing, family, 1970s jazz fusion, good food and wine. *Address:* Institute of Brain, Behaviour and Mental Health, University Place, University of Manchester, Oxford Road, Manchester M13 9PL. *T:* (0161) 306 7944, *Fax:* (0161) 306 7945. *E:* shon.lewis@manchester.ac.uk.

LEWIS, Simon David, OBE 2014; Chief Executive, Association for Financial Markets in Europe, since 2010; *b* 8 May 1959; *s* of David Lewis and Sally Lewis (*née* Valentine); *m* 1985, Claire Elizabeth Anne Pendry; two *s* one *d*. *Educ:* Whitefield Comprehensive, London; Brasenose Coll., Oxford (MA); Univ. of Calif, Berkeley (Fulbright Scholar; MA). FCIPR (FIPR 1998). PR Consultant, Shandwick Consultants, 1983–86; Head of Communications, SDP, 1986–87; of PR, S. G. Warburg Gp plc, 1987–92; Director, Corporate Affairs: NatWest Gp, 1992–96; Centrica plc, 1996–98; on secondment as first Communications Sec., Buckingham Palace, 1998–2000; Man. Dir, Europe, Centrica plc, 2000–04; Gp Dir, Corporate Affairs, Vodafone plc, 2004–09; Dir of Communications and Prime Minister's Official Spokesman, Prime Minister's Office, 2009–10; Strategic Commns Advr, UK Trade & Investment, 2010. Vis. Fellow, Centre for Corporate Reputation, Oxford Univ., 2007–. Chm., Fulbright Commn, 2008–13 (Patron, 2013–). Member: Governing Council, UCS, 2005– (Chm., 2015–); N American Adv. Council, 2013–, Academic Adv. Bd, Chatham House, 2013–. Pres., IPR, 1997. Hon. Prof., Cardiff Sch. of Journalism, 2000–. *Recreations:* family, sport, current affairs, cinema. *Address:* Association for Financial Markets in Europe, Level 39, 25 Canada Square, E14 5LB. *Club:* Reform.

LEWIS, Simon Jeremy Quentin W.; *see* Wren-Lewis.

LEWIS, Stephen John B.; *see* Brimson-Lewis.

LEWIS, Stephen Michael; a Law Commissioner, since 2015; *b* London, 23 Aug. 1949; *s* of Harry Lewis and Celia Lewis; *m* 1974, Erica Pesate; one *s* two *d*. *Educ:* Orange Hill Co. Grammar Sch. for Boys; St Catherine's Coll., Oxford (BA PPE 1970); Univ. of London ext. (LLB). Admitted solicitor, 1974; Solicitor; Partner, Clifford Chance, 1985–2004; Consultant, Clyde & Co. LLP, 2004–14. *Publications:* articles on English insurance law. *Recreations:* history, opera, travel. *Address:* 37A Stormont Road, N6 4NR. *T:* (020) 8348 4139, 07739 696798. *E:* stephenmichaellewis@gmail.com, stephen.lewis@lawcommission.gsi.gov.uk.

LEWIS, Susan, CBE 2008; HM Chief Inspector of Education and Training in Wales (formerly Chief Inspector of Schools in Wales), 1997–2008; *b* 7 Nov. 1947; *d* of late Kenneth A. L. Lewis and Elsie Stonehouse (*née* Woods). *Educ:* Billingham South Infants' and Jun. Sch.; Lakefield Rd Primary Sch., Llanelli; Henry Smith Sch., Hartlepool; Univ. of Newcastle upon Tyne (BSc Hons); Univ. of Sheffield (DipEd); Sch. of Psychotherapy and Counselling, Regent's Coll., London (certified mediator, 2005, coach, 2006). Asst teacher, Bradfield Sch., WR Yorks, 1970–74; Hd of Dept and Asst Hd of Sixth Form, Shelley High Sch., Kirklees, 1974–80; Dep. Head, later Actg Head, Wisewood Sch., Sheffield, 1980–86; HM Inspector of Schools, 1986–95; Staff Inspector, Office of HM Chief Inspector, 1995–97. Life FRSA. *Publications:* Home on the Range: growing up on Teeside in the 50s and 60s, 2011; Diagonal Ties: a family history in Wales and the North East of England, 2013. *Recreations:* gardening, writing, walking, genealogy, drawing, painting. *E:* hoosehoo08@tiscali.co.uk.

LEWIS, Terence; *b* 29 Dec. 1935; *s* of Andrew Lewis; *m* 1958, Audrey, *d* of William Clarke; one *s* (and one *s* decd). *Educ:* Mt Carmel Sch., Salford. Nat. service, RAMC, 1954–56. Personnel Officer. Member: Kearsley UDC, 1971–74; Bolton BC, 1976–84 (Chm., Educn Cttee, 1982–83). MP (Lab) Worsley, 1983–2005; Mem., Standards and Privileges Select Cttee, 1997–2001. *Address:* 54 Greenmount Park, Kearsley, Bolton, Lancs BL4 8NS.

LEWIS, Tony; *see* Lewis, A. R.

LEWIS, Trevor; *see* Lewis, D. T.

LEWIS, Dr Trevor, CBE 1992; Director, AFRC Institute of Arable Crops Research, 1989–93; Head, 1987–93, Lawes Trust Senior Fellow, 1993–2003, Rothamsted Experimental Station; Visiting Professor in Invertebrate Zoology, University of Nottingham, 1977–98; *b* 8 July 1933; *s* of Harold and Maggie Lewis; *m* 1959, Margaret Edith Wells; one *s* one *d*. *Educ:* Univ. of Nottingham (DSc 1986); Imperial Coll. of Science and Technol., Univ. of London (PhD, DIC 1958); MA Cambridge, 1960. University Demonstr in Agricl Zoology, Sch. of Agriculture, Cambridge, 1958–61; scientific staff, Rothamsted Experimental Station, 1961–2003; seconded to ODA as Sen. Res. Fellow, Univ. of WI, Trinidad, 1970–73; Head, Entomology Dept, 1976–83; Dep. Dir, 1983–87; Hd of Crop and Envmt Protection Div., 1983–89. Special Lectr in Invertebrate Zool., Univ. of Nottingham, 1968–69 and 1973–75. AFRC Assessor to MAFF Adv. Cttee on Pesticides, 1984–89; Member: Management Bd, British Crop Protection Council, 1985–94; Bd, British Crop Protection Enterprises, 1994–2008; R&D Cttee, Potato Marketing Bd, 1985–89. Mem. Council, British Ecological Soc., 1982–84; Pres., Royal Entomol Soc. of London, 1985–87; Pres., Agric. and Forestry Sect., BAAS, 1997. Huxley Gold Medal, Imperial Coll. of Science and Technol., Univ. of London, 1977; British Crop Protection Council Medal, 2002. *Publications:* (with L. R. Taylor) Introduction to Experimental Ecology, 1967; Thrips—their biology, ecology and economic importance, 1973; (ed) Insect Communication, 1984; Thrips as Crop Pests, 1997; contribs to scientific jls on topics in entomology. *Recreations:* music, gardening.

LEWIS, Dame Vera Margaret; *see* Lynn, Dame Vera.

LEWIS-BOWEN, Thomas Edward Ifor; a Circuit Judge, 1980–98; *b* 20 June 1933; *s* of late Lt-Col J. W. Lewis-Bowen and K. M. Lewis-Bowen (*née* Rice); *m* 1965, Gillian, *d* of late Reginald Brett, Puckington, Som; one *s* two *d*. *Educ:* Ampleforth; St Edmund Hall, Oxford. Called to Bar, Middle Temple, 1958. A Recorder of the Crown Court, 1974–80.

LEWIS-JONES, Janet Ann; Vice President, British Board of Film Classification, 1998–2008; Trustee (for Wales), BBC Trust, 2006–10; *b* 12 May 1950; *d* of John Gwilym Jones and Elizabeth Eirliw, (Bethan), Louis Jones. *Educ:* Univ. of Liverpool (LLB 1973); Birkbeck, Univ. of London (MA 2012). VSO, PNG, 1968–69. Called to the Bar, Gray's Inn, 1974. Joined Civil Service as admin trainee, 1974; Home Office, 1974–82; Cabinet Secretariat, Cabinet Office, 1982–83; Prin. Pvte Sec. to Viscount Whitelaw, Lord Pres. of Council, Privy Council Office, 1983–85; Home Office, 1985–86; Welsh Water, 1986–90. Chm., Membership Selection Panel, Welsh Water, 2001–11; Member: S4C, 1992–2003; British Waterways Bd, 1994–2004; Postal Services Commn, 2000–06; Strategic Rail Authy, 2002–05; British Transport Police Authy, 2004–05; Member, Wales Committee: UFC, 1990–92; EOC, 1994–99. Public Affairs Advr to Archbishops of Canterbury, 1991–95, 2005–06, 2011; Specialist Advr, H of L Select Cttee on the Public Service, 1996–98. Trustee: Refugee Legal Centre, 1991–92; Barnardo's, 1992–99; Community Develt Foundn, 1996–99; Baring Foundn, 1996–2009; Police Foundn, 1998–2004; Carnegie UK Trust, 1998–2004; Inst. of Rural Health, 2002–05; Maytree Sanctuary for the Suicidal, 2008–; Refugee and Migrant Justice, 2009–10; Mid Wales Music Trust (formerly Mid Wales Chamber Orchestra), 2010–; Chair, Community Foundn in Wales, 2012–. Vice Pres., Univ. of Wales, Lampeter, 1999–2001. Hon. Fellow, Aberystwyth Univ., 2008. *Recreations:* lettercutting in stone, film, walking. *Address:* 3 Camden Road, Brecon, Powys LD3 7BU. *Club:* Reform.

LEWISHAM AND GREENWICH, Archdeacon of; *see* Cutting, Ven. A. M.

LEWISOHN, His Honour Anthony Clive Leopold; a Circuit Judge, 1974–90; *b* 1 Aug. 1925; *s* of John Lewisohn and Gladys (*née* Solomon); *m* 1957, Lone Ruthwen Jurgensen; two *s*. *Educ:* Stowe; Trinity Coll., Oxford (MA). Royal Marines, 1944–45; Lieut, Oxf. and Bucks LI, 1946–47. Called to Bar, Middle Temple, 1951; S Eastern Circuit.

LEWISON, Jeremy Rodney Pines; freelance curator and art consultant; Director of Collections, Tate Gallery, 1998–2002; *b* 13 Jan. 1955; *s* of late Anthony Frederick Lewison and Dinora Pines; *m* 1993, Caroline Maria Aviva Schuck; one step *s* one step *d*. *Educ:* Westminster Sch.; Magdalen Coll., Oxford (MA; Dip Hist. of Art). Curator, Kettle's Yard, Univ. of Cambridge, 1977–83; Tate Gallery: Asst Keeper, Print Collection, 1983–86; Asst Keeper, 1986–90, Dep. Keeper, 1990–97, Modern Collection. Associate Mem., British Psychoanalytical Soc. Trustee: Arnolfini Gall., Bristol; Tricycle Th., London. *Publications:* Anish Kapoor Drawings, 1990; Ben Nicholson, 1991; David Smith Medals for Dishonour, 1991; Brice Marden Prints 1961–91, 1992; Ben Nicholson, 1993; Shirazeh Houshiary, 1995; Karl Weschke, 1998; Interpreting Pollock, 1999; Looking at Barnett Newman, 2002; Ben Nicholson, 2002; Alice Neel, 2004; Anish Kapoor Drawings, 2005; Ra'anan Levy, 2006; Henry Moore, 2007; Ben Nicholson Prints 1928–1968: the Rentsch collection, 2007; Brice Marden: a retrospective of prints, 2008; Alice Neel: painted truths, 2010; Lundquist and the Post-War Figure, 2010; Turner, Monet, Twombly: later paintings, 2011; Looking at Pistoletto: looking at myself, 2011; The 'Grim' and 'Tragic' Art of Henry Moore, 2012. *Recreations:* tennis, ski-ing, mountain walking, running, cycling. *Address:* 2 Fellows Road, NW3 3LP.

See also Rt Hon. Sir K. M. J. Lewison.

LEWISON, Rt Hon. Sir Kim (Martin Jordan), Kt 2003; PC 2011; **Rt Hon. Lord Justice Lewison;** a Lord Justice of Appeal, since 2011; *b* 1 May 1952; *s* of late Anthony Frederick Lewison and Dinora Lewison (*née* Pines); *m* 1979, Helen Mary Janecek (marr. diss. 1998); one *s* one *d*; *m* 2002, Sharon Moross. *Educ:* St Paul's Sch., London; Downing Coll., Cambridge (MA 1973); Council of Legal Education. Called to the Bar, Lincoln's Inn, 1975, Bencher, 1998; QC 1991. Asst Recorder, 1994–97, Recorder, 1997–2003; a Dep. High Ct Judge, 2000–03; a Judge of the High Court of Justice, Chancery Div., 2003–11. Mem. Council, Liberal Jewish Synagogue, 1990–96. Mem. Council, Leo Baeck Coll., 1997–2002; Gov., Anglo-American Real Property Inst., 1996–2000 (Chm., 2002). *Publications:* Development Land Tax, 1978; Drafting Business Leases, 1979, 6th edn 2000; Lease or Licence, 1985; The Interpretation of Contracts, 1989, 5th edn 2011; (Gen. Editor) Woodfall on Landlord and Tenant, 1990–. *Recreations:* visiting France, avoiding tsores. *Address:* Royal Courts of Justice, Strand, WC2A 2LL.

See also J. R. P. Lewison.

LEWITH, Prof. George Thomas, DM; FRCP; Professor of Health Research, since 2008, and Hon. Consultant Physician, since 1995, Southampton Medical School, University of Southampton; Partner, Centre for Study of Complementary Medicine, Southampton, since 1982; *b* 12 Jan. 1950; *s* of Frank and Alice Lewith; *m* 1977, Nicola Rosemary Bazeley; two *s* one *d*. *Educ:* Queen's Coll., Taunton; Trinity Coll., Cambridge (MA); Westminster Hosp. Med. Sch. (MB BChir); DM Soton 1994. MRCGP 1980; FRCP 1999. Southampton University: Lectr in Primary Med. Care, 1979–82; Sen. Res. Fellow in Univ. Medicine, 1995–2004, Reader in Univ. Medicine, 2005–08, Southampton Med. Sch. Vis. Prof., Univ. of Westminster, 2003–. *Publications:* contribs to numerous academic books and papers in field of complementary medicine. *Recreations:* the theatre, ski-ing, sport, sailing, gardening. *Address:* Sway Wood House, Mead End Road, Sway, Lymington, Hants SO41 6EE. *T:* (01590) 682129.

LEWSLEY-MOONEY, Patricia, CBE 2015; Northern Ireland Commissioner for Children and Young People, since 2007; *b* 3 March 1957; *d* of Patrick and Mary Killen; *m* 1st, 1976, Hugh Lewsley (marr. diss. 1998); three *s* two *d*; 2nd, 2011, William Mooney. *Educ:* St Dominic's High Sch.; Univ. of Ulster. Mem. (SDLP) Lagan Valley, NI Assembly, 1998–2007. Contested (SDLP) Lagan Valley, 2001, 2005. *Recreations:* reading, travel. *Address:* Northern Ireland Commissioner for Children and Young People, Equality House, 7–9 Shaftesbury Square, Belfast BT2 7DP.

LEWTY, (David) Ian; HM Diplomatic Service, retired; *b* 27 July 1943; *s* of late Harry Lewty and Ruby Lewty (*née* Buck); *m* 1968, Mary Law; two *d*. *Educ:* Lancing Coll.; Magdalen Coll., Oxford (MA). Third Sec., FO, 1965; MECAS, Lebanon, 1966; Third, later Second Sec., Ottawa, 1967–71; Hd, British Interests Section, Baghdad, 1971–72; First Sec., FCO, 1972–76; Hd of Chancery, Jedda, 1976–79; (on secondment) L'Ecole Nationale d'Administration, Paris, 1979–81; UK Delegn to OECD, Paris, 1981–84; FCO, 1984–87; Counsellor and Dep. Hd of Mission, Khartoum, 1987–89; Diplomatic Service Inspector, 1989–92; Hd, Migration and Visa Dept, FCO, 1992–95; Ambassador to Bahrain, 1996–99. *Address:* 38 Burlington Avenue, Richmond, Surrey TW9 4DH.

LEXDEN, Baron *cr* 2010 (Life Peer), of Lexden in the County of Essex and of Strangford in the County of Down; **Alistair Basil Cooke,** OBE 1988; PhD; Consultant and Editor in Chief, Conservative Research Department, 2004–10; official historian, Conservative Party, since 2009; official historian and archivist, Carlton Club, since 2007; *b* 20 April 1945; 2nd *s* of Dr Basil Cooke and Nancy Irene Cooke (*née* Neal). *Educ:* Framlingham Coll., Suffolk; Peterhouse, Cambridge (MA 1970); Queen's Univ., Belfast (PhD 1979). Lectr and Tutor in Modern History, Queen's Univ., Belfast, 1971–77; Conservative Research Department: Desk Officer, 1977–83; Political Advr to Shadow Minister for NI, 1977–79; Asst Dir, 1983–85; Dep. Dir, 1985–97. Dir, Conservative Political Centre, 1988–97. Gen. Sec., ISC, 1997–2004. Chm. of Trustees, Friends of the Union, 1995–2003; Founder, 1997, Mem., 2005–, Chm., 2014–, Cons. Party Archive Trust; Sen. Trustee, T. E. Utley Meml Fund, 2000–12; Trustee, Hansard Soc., 2013–. Chm., Conservative History Gp, 2012–. Mem., H of L Select Cttee on the Constitution, 2012–15. Gov., John Lyon Sch., Harrow, 1999–2005. Patron, NI Schs Debating Comp., 2001–. Vice Pres., Council of British Internat. Schs, 2011–; President: Ind. Schs Assoc., 2013–; Council for Ind. Educn, 2013–. *Publications:* (ed jtly) Lord Carlingford's Journal, 1971; (jtly) The Governing Passion; cabinet government and party politics in Britain 1885–86, 1974; (ed) The Ashbourne Papers 1869–1913, 1974; (ed) The Conservative Party's Campaign Guides, 7 vols, 1987–2005; (ed) The Conservative Party: seven historical studies, 1997; (ed) The Conservative Research Department 1929–2004, 2004; (jtly) The Carlton Club 1832–2007, 2007; Tory Heroine: Dorothy Brant and the rise of Conservative women, 2008; A Party of Change: a brief history of the Conservatives, 2008, 3rd edn 2014; (contrib.) Between the Thin Blue Lines, 2008; (jtly) Tory Policy-Making: the Conservative Research Department 1929–2009, 2009; A Gift from the Churchills: the Primrose League 1883–2004, 2010; (contrib.) Enoch at 100: a re-evaluation of the life, politics and philosophy of Enoch Powell, 2012; contrib. DNB; pamphlets on Northern Ireland and constitutional issues; articles in historical jls and educnl pubns. *Recreations:* writing letters to the press (and getting them published), collecting royal and political memorabilia, music, walking as briskly as age allows, book reviewing, adding to my website. *Address:* Flat 1, 68 St George's Square, SW1V 3QT. *T:* (020) 7821 9520. *W:* www.alistairlexden.org.uk. *Club:* Carlton.

LEY, Sir Ian (Francis), 5th Bt *cr* 1905, of Epperstone, Nottingham; *b* 12 June 1934; *o s* of Sir Francis Douglas Ley, 4th Bt, MBE and Violet Geraldine Ley (*née* Johnson) (*d* 1991); *S* father, 1995; *m* 1957, Caroline Margaret (*née* Errington); one *s* one *d*. *Educ:* Eton Coll. Dep. Chm., 1972–80, Chm., 1981–82, Ley's Foundries and Engineering plc. High Sheriff, Derbyshire, 1985. *Recreation:* shooting. *Heir: s* Christopher Ian Ley [*b* 2 Dec. 1962; *m* 1999, Henrietta, *yr d* of David Nicholls]. *Club:* White's.

LEY, Prof. Steven Victor, CBE 2002; FRS 1990; BP (1702) Professor of Organic Chemistry, University of Cambridge, 1992–2013; Fellow of Trinity College, Cambridge, since 1993. *Educ:* Loughborough Univ. of Technology (BSc 1st cl. Hons 1969; DIS 1969; PhD 1972); DSc London 1983; MA 1997, ScD 1999, Cantab. CChem, FRSC 1980; FIC 2000; CBiol, FRSB (FIBiol 2003). Res. Fellow, Ohio State Univ., 1972–74; Imperial College, London: Res. Asst, 1974–75; Lectr, 1975–83; Prof. of Organic Chemistry, 1983–92; Head of Chemistry Dept, 1989–92. Royal Soc. Bakerian Lectr, 1997. Chm. Exec. Cttee, Novartis (formerly Ciba) Foundn, 1993–. Pres., Royal Soc. of Chem., 2000–02. Hon. Fellow, Cardiff Univ., 2005. Hon. DSc: Loughborough, 1994; Salamanca, 2000; Huddersfield, 2003. Royal Society of Chemistry: Hickinbottom Res. Fellow, 1981–83 (1st recipient); Corday Morgan Medal and Prize, 1980; Tilden Lectr and Medal, 1988; Award for Synthetic Chem., 1989; Pedlar Lectr and Medal, 1992; Simonsen Lectr and Medal, 1993; Award for Natural Products Chemistry, 1994; Flintoff Medal, 1996; Rhône-Poulenc Lectureship Medal and Prize, 1998; Haworth Meml Lectr, Medal and Prize, 2001; Award in Carbohydrate Chemistry, 2003; Robert Robinson Award and Medal, 2006; High Throughput Drug Discovery Methodologies Award, 2008; Perkin Prize for Organic Chemistry, 2009; German Chemical Society: Adolf Windaus Medal, 1994; August Wilhelm von Hofmann Medal, 2001; Dr Paul Janssen Prize for Creativity in Organic Synthesis, European Chem. Soc., 1996; Davy Medal, 2000, Royal Medal, 2011, Royal Soc.; Pfizer Central Research: Pfizer Res. Award, 1983 (1st recipient); Pfizer Award for Innovative Science, 2001; Ernst Guenther Award, ACS, 2003; Innovation of the Year Award, CIA, 2003; iAc Award (for Innovation in Applied Catalysis), IChemE, 2004; Alexander von Humboldt Award, 2005; Yamada-Koga Prize, Japan Res. Foundn for Optically Active Compounds, 2005; Nagoya Gold Medal, Banyu Life Sci. Foundn Internat., 2006; Award for Creative Work in Synthetic Organic Chem., ACS, 2007; Paul Karrer Medal, Univ. of Zurich, 2007; Innovation Award, Soc. of Chem. Ind. (1st recipient), 2007; Inhoffen Medal, Helmholtz Zentrum für Infektionsforschung, 2008; Paracelsus Prize, Swiss Chem. Soc., 2010. *Publications:* over 700 papers in internat. jls of chemistry. *Address:* Department of Chemistry, Lensfield Road, Cambridge CB2 1EW. *W:* http://leygroup.ch.cam.ac.uk.

LEYDECKER, (Veronica) Sonya; Joint Chief Executive Officer, Herbert Smith Freehills LLP, since 2014; *b* Scarborough, 18 July 1954; *d* of George Michael Leydecker and Sabina Leydecker (*née* Murtagh); *m* 1997, Steven Roderick Larcombe. *Educ:* Convent of the Ladies of Mary, Scarborough; Univ. of Manchester (BA Hons Hist.); Coll. of Law. Admitted solicitor, 1984; Herbert Smith, later Herbert Smith Freehills: Partner, 1991–, specialising in dispute resolution; Global Head of Dispute Resolution, 2005–14. FRSA. *Recreations:* the arts (especially music and theatre), reading, cycling. *Address:* Herbert Smith Freehills LLP, Exchange House, Primrose Street, EC2A 2EG. *T:* (020) 7466 2337, *Fax:* (direct) (020) 7098 5337, (020) 7374 0888.

LEYLAND, Sir Philip Vyvian N.; *see* Naylor-Leyland.

LEYLAND, Ronald Arthur; Chief Executive, North Yorkshire County Council, 1990–94; *b* 23 Aug. 1940; *s* of Arthur and Lucy Leyland; *m* 1962, Joan Virginia Sinclair; three *s*. *Educ:* Merchant Taylors' Sch., Crosby; Liverpool Univ. (LLB Hons 1961). Solicitor (Hons 1964). Assistant Solicitor: Bootle CBC, 1964–65; Nottingham City Council, 1965–68; Sen. Asst Solicitor, then Dir of Admin, Leeds MDC, 1968–75; County Sec., Hampshire CC, 1975–90. Dir, N Yorks TEC, 1990–94. Chm., Soc. of County Secretaries, 1986–87. *Recreation:* family history. *Address:* 11 Tamarind Way, Earley, Reading RG6 5GR. *Club:* Rotary.

LEYSER, Prof. (Henrietta Miriam) Ottoline, CBE 2009; PhD; FRS 2007; Professor of Plant Development, since 2011, and Director, since 2013, Sainsbury Laboratory, University of Cambridge; *b* 7 March 1965; *d* of Prof. Karl Joseph Leyser, TD, FBA and Henrietta Louise Valerie Leyser (*née* Bateman); *m* 1986, Stephen John Day; one *s* one *d*. *Educ:* Newnham Coll., Cambridge (BA Genetics 1986; PhD Genetics 1990). Post-doctoral Research Fellow: Indiana Univ., Bloomington, 1990–93; Cambridge Univ., 1993–94; Lectr, 1994–99, Reader, 1999–2002, Prof. of Plant Develtl Genetics, 2002–10, Univ. of York. Editor: The Plant Jl, 2001–08; Current Opinion in Plant Biol., 2009–; Development, 2011–; Member, Advisory Editorial Board: Trends in Plant Sci., 1999–; Bioessays, 2001–08; Current Biol., 2003–; Annual Rev. of Plant Biol., 2004–08; Plant Cell Physiol., 2004–08. Gatsby Plant Sci. Advr, 2008–. Biotechnology and Biological Sciences Research Council: Chm., Biosci. Skills and Careers Strategy Panel, 2008–12; Member: Strategy Bd, 2003–04 and 2007–11; Data Policy wkg gp, 2005–06; Bioinformatics and Biol Resources Initiative Panel, 2007. Member: MRC/BBSRC/Wellcome Trust Eur. Bioinformatics Inst. Rev. Panel, 2004; Life Sci. Interface Doctoral Trng Centres Rev. Panel, EPSRC, 2007; Nuffield Council on Bioethics, 2009–12 (Dep. Chair, 2012–). Pres., British Soc. for Develtl Biol., 2014– (Treas., 1999–2004); Mem. Council, Internat. Plant Molecular Biol. (formerly Internat. Soc. for Plant Molecular Biol.), 2003– (Pres., 2011–15). For. Associate, US Nat. Acad. of Sci., 2012–. K. M. Stott Res. Fellow Prize, Newnham Coll., Cambridge, 1993; President's Medal, Soc. for Exptl Biol., 2000; Rosalind Franklin Award, Royal Soc., 2007; Silver Medal, Internat. Plant Growth Substance Assoc., 2010. *Publications:* (with S. Day) Mechanisms in Plant Development, 2002; chapters in: Plant Gene Isolation, 1996; Plant Cell Proliferation and its Regulation in Growth and Development, 1997; Plant Hormone Protocols, 2000; Grafting, 2005; contribs to learned jls incl. Nature, Cell, Current Biol., Development, Plant Physiol., Plant Jl. *Recreations:* singing, walking, swimming. *Address:* Sainsbury Laboratory, Bateman Street, University of Cambridge, Cambridge CB2 1LR. *T:* (01223) 761103. *E:* ol235@cam.ac.uk.

LEZALA, Andrew Peter, CEng, FIMechE; Chief Executive, Metro Trains Melbourne, since 2009; *b* 8 Dec. 1955; *s* of Jozef and Constance Lezala; *m* 1980, Helen Addison; one *s* two *d*. *Educ:* Derby Grammar Sch.; Univ. of Leicester (BSc Hons Eng). CEng, FIMechE 1989. British Rail: Engrg Grad. Trainee, 1977–79; bogie and suspension design engr, 1979–81; Asst Brakes Engr, 1981–84; Project Engr, 1984–86, Chief Engr, New Vehicles, 1986–87, BREL Ltd; Gp Operating and Engrg Dir, RFS Hldgs Ltd, 1987–93; Vice Pres., Business Area Metro's and Multiple Units, ABB Transportation Ltd, 1993–94; Hd of Metro's, ABB China Ltd, 1994–98; Man. Dir, Australia Ltd, 1998–99, Pres., Worldwide Metro Div., 1999–2001, Daimler Chrysler Rail Systems; Pres., Worldwide Services Div., Bombardier, 2001–04; Chief Operating Officer, Jarvis plc, 2004–05; CEO, Metronet Rail BCV Hldgs Ltd and Metronet Rail SSL Hldgs Ltd, 2005–07; Man. Dir, Air Rail Transit Ltd, 2008. Institution of Mechanical Engineers: Mem. Bd, 2000–08, Chm., 2006–07, Railway Div.; Mem., Trustee Bd, 2008–10. Mem. Council, Railway Ind. Assoc., 2004–07. FIEAust 2012. FRSA. *Recreations:* family gatherings, motor sport, swimming, cycling, playing guitar.

LI, Sir David Kwok Po, GBM 2007 (GBS 2001); Kt 2005; OBE 1991; FCIB; FCA; Chairman, since 1997, and Chief Executive, since 1981, Bank of East Asia Ltd; *b* 13 March 1939; *s* of Li Fook Shu and Woo Tze Ha; *m* 1971, Penny Poon; two *s*. *Educ:* Selwyn Coll., Cambridge (BA 1964; MA; LLD 1993). FCPA 1973; FCA 1977; FCIB 1988. Bank of East Asia Ltd: Chief Accountant, 1969–72; Asst Chief Manager, 1973–76; Dep. Chief Manager, 1977–81; Dir, 1977–; Dep. Chm., 1995–97. Hon. Fellow: Robinson Coll., Cambridge, 1989; Selwyn Coll., Cambridge, 1992. Hon. LLD: Warwick, 1994; Hong Kong, 1996; Hon. DSc Imperial Coll. London, 2007; Hon. DLitt Macquarie, 2011. Commandeur de la Légion d'Honneur (France), 2012. *Recreations:* tennis, art, antiques, reading. *Address:* Bank of East Asia Ltd, 21st Floor, 10 Des Voeux Road Central, Hong Kong. *T:* 36080808. *Clubs:* Hong Kong Country, Hong Kong Golf, Hong Kong Yacht (Hong Kong).

LI Ka-shing, Sir, KBE 2000 (CBE 1989); Chairman: CK Hutchison Holdings Ltd; Hutchison Whampoa Ltd; *b* Chaozhou, 1928; *m* Chong Yuet-Ming (decd); two *s*. Moved from mainland China to Hong Kong, 1940; took first job, 1942; promoted to gen. manager, 1947; founded Cheung Kong Plastics Factory (later Cheung Kong (Holdings) Ltd), 1950, listed 1972; acquired Hutchison Whampoa Ltd, 1979; acquired Hongkong Electric Hldgs Ltd, 1985; founded: Cheung Kong Infrastructure Hldgs Ltd, listed 1996; Tom.com (later TOM Group), listed 2000; CK Life Sciences Internat. (Hldgs) Inc., listed 2002; business interests in 52 countries incl. China, UK, Canada, Hong Kong and many other parts of the world. HK Affairs Adviser, 1992–97; Member: Drafting Cttee for Basic Law, HKSAR, 1985–90; Preparatory Cttee for the HKSAR, 1995–97; Selection Cttee for the govt of the HKSAR, 1996. Mem., Internat. Business Adv. Council for the UK, 2006. Established Li Ka Shing Foundn Ltd, 1980; founded Shantou Univ., 1981. Hon. Citizen: Shantou, Guangzhou, Shenzhen, Nanhai, Foshan, Zhuhai, Chaozhou, Beijing (China) and Winnipeg (Canada). JP 1981. Hon. LLD: Hong Kong, 1986; Calgary, 1989; Chinese Univ. of Hong Kong, 1997; Cambridge, 1999; Hon. Dr Beijing, 1992; Hon. DSocSc: Hong Kong Univ. of Sci. and Technology, 1995; City Univ. of Hong Kong, 1998; Open Univ. of Hong Kong, 1999. Entrepreneur of the Millennium Award, Times/Ernst & Young, 1999; Internat. Dist. Entrepreneur Award, Univ. of Manitoba, 2000; Malcolm S. Forbes Lifetime Achievement Award, Forbes, 2006; Lifetime Award for Philanthropy, Chinese Min. of Civil Affairs, 2007; Presidential Award, TESOL, 2007; Robert H. Alway Lifetime Achievement Award, Stanford Univ., 2010; Special Hon. Award for Econ. Contribn, China Central TV, 2007; Lifetime Achievement Award, Hong Kong Business Awards, DHL/South China Morning Post, 2010; Carnegie Medal of Philanthropy, Carnegie Corp., 2011; Berkeley Medal, Univ. of Calif, Berkeley, 2011. Grand Bauhinia Medal, HKSAR, 2001. Grand Officer, Order Vasco Núñez de Balboa (Panama), 1982; Commander: Order of the Crown (Belgium), 1986; Order of Leopold (Belgium), 2000; Commandeur de la Légion d'honneur (France), 2005. *Recreations:* golf, boating. *Address:* CK Hutchison Holdings Ltd, 7–12/F Cheung Kong Center, 2 Queen's Road Central, Hong Kong. *Club:* Hong Kong Golf.

LI Kwok Nang, Andrew, GBM 2008; CBE 1993; JP; Chief Justice, and President of the Court of Final Appeal, Hong Kong, 1997–2010; *b* 12 Dec. 1948; *s* of Li Fook Kow, CMG; *m* 1973, Judy M. Y. Woo; two *d*. *Educ:* St Paul's Primary Sch., Hong Kong; St Paul's Co-Educnl Coll., Hong Kong; Repton Sch.; Fitzwilliam Coll., Cambridge (MA, LLM; Hon. Fellow, 1999). Called to the Bar: Middle Temple, 1970 (Hon. Bencher, 1997); Hong Kong, 1973; QC (Hong Kong) 1988. Guest Prof., Tsinghua Univ., Beijing, 1997–; Hon. Professor of Law: Univ. of Hong Kong, 2010–; Chinese Univ. of Hong Kong, 2010–; City Univ. of Hong Kong, 2010–; Shue Yan Univ., Hong Kong, 2010–. JP Hong Kong, 1985. Hon. Life Member: Hong Kong Bar Assoc., 2011; Law Soc. of Hong Kong, 2011. Hon. DLitt Hong Kong Univ. of Sci. and Technol., 1993; Hon. LLD: Baptist Univ., Hong Kong, 1994; Open Univ., Hong Kong, 1997; Univ. of Hong Kong, 2001; Griffith, 2001; NSW, 2002; Univ. of Technol., Sydney, 2005; Chinese Univ. of Hong Kong, 2006; Shue Yan Univ., Hong Kong, 2009; Lingnan Univ., Hong Kong, 2010; City Univ. of Hong Kong, 2010; Tsinghua, 2013; Oxford, 2013. Woodrow Wilson Award for Public Service, Woodrow Wilson Internat. Centre for Scholars, 2010; Sing Tao Leader of the Year Award, 2010. *Recreations:* hiking, reading, tennis, the turf. *Address:* 2213 Bank of America Tower, 12 Harcourt Road, Hong Kong. *T:* 25213018. *Clubs:* Athenæum; Hong Kong Jockey (Hon. Steward), Hong Kong, Hong Kong Country, Shek O Country (Hong Kong).

LI, Prof. Lin, PhD; CEng, FREng, FIET; Professor of Laser Engineering and Director, Laser Processing Research Centre, since 2000, and Head, Manufacturing Research Group, since 2006, University of Manchester (formerly University of Manchester Institute of Science and Technology); *b* Shenyang, China, 24 June 1959; *s* of Dr Honglian Li and Dr Shuchun Guo; *m* 1986, Dr Zhu Liu; one *d*. *Educ:* Dalian Univ. of Technol. (BSc 1982); Imperial Coll. London (PhD 1989). CEng 2005; FIET 2005; FREng 2013. Res. Associate, Res. Fellow, Laser Gp, Dept of Mech. Engrg, Univ. of Liverpool, 1988–94; University of Manchester Institute of Science and Technology, subseq. University of Manchester: Lectr, then Reader, Dept of Mech. Engrg, 1994–2000; Dir of Res., Dep. Hd, Sch. of Mech., Aerospace and Civil Engrg, 2009–13. Chm., Process and Product Innovation Gp, Assoc. of Laser Users, 2008–14; Pres., Internat. Acad. of Photonics and Laser Engrg, 2013–14. Fellow: Laser Inst. of America, 2007 (a Dir, 2009–14); Internat. Acad. of Prodn Engrg, 2008. Sir Frank Whittle Award, RAEng, 2013; Wolfson Res. Merit Award, Royal Soc., 2014; Researcher of the Yr, Univ. of Manchester, 2014. *Publications:* over 550 articles and 47 patents in lasers, photonics and manufg. *Recreation:* member of Oriental Breeze (Chinese music performance group, Manchester). *Address:* School of Mechanical, Aerospace and Civil Engineering, University of Manchester, Manchester M13 9PL. *T:* (0161) 306 3816, *Fax:* (0161) 306 3803. *E:* lin.li@manchester.ac.uk.

LIANG, Prof. Wei Yao, PhD; Professor of Superconductivity, University of Cambridge, 1994–2007, now Emeritus; Fellow and Lecturer, Gonville and Caius College, Cambridge, since 1971 (President, 2005–13; Life Fellow, 2007); *b* 23 Sept. 1940; *s* of late Tien Fu Liang and of Po Seng Nio Lie; *m* 1968, Lian Choo (*née* Choong) (decd); three *d*. *Educ:* Pah Chung Chinese High Sch., Jakarta; Portsmouth Coll. of Technology; Imperial Coll., London (BSc, ARCS 1st Class Hons Theoretical Physics); Univ. of Cambridge (PhD). Gonville and Caius College, Cambridge: Comyns Berkeley Unofficial Fellow, 1969–71; Dir of Studies in Natural Scis, 1975–89; University of Cambridge: Demonstrator, 1971–75; Lectr in Physics, 1975–92; Reader in high temperature superconductivity, 1992–93; Co-Dir, 1988–89, Dir, 1989–98, Interdisciplinary Res. Centre in Superconductivity. Vis. Scientist, Xerox Palo Alto Res. Centre, 1975, 1976; Visiting Professor: EPF Lausanne, 1978; Inst. of Semiconductors, Beijing, 1983; Sci. Univ. of Tokyo, 2000; Univ. of Tokyo, 2001; Xiamen Univ., 2002; Hon. Fellow and Vis. Prof. of Materials Sci., St John's Coll., Univ. of Hong Kong, 2009–. *Publications:* (ed with A. S. Alexandrov and E. K. H. Salje) Polarons and Bipolarons in High Tc Superconductors and Related Materials, 1995; (ed with W. Zong) Fundamental Research in High Tc Superconductivity, 1999; (ed with D. Shi and W. Zong) Research in HIgh Temperature Superconductivity Applications, 2008. *Recreations:* music, photography. *Address:* Gonville and Caius College, Cambridge CB2 1TA. *T:* (01223) 332425.

LIANOS, Prof. Ioannis, PhD; Professor of Global Competition Law and Public Policy, University College London, since 2014; *b* Athens, 9 March 1975; *s* of Kostantinos Lianos and Pigie Lianou. *Educ:* Univ. of Strasbourg (LLB 1996; LLM Eur. Law 1997; PhD Law 2004); New York Univ. Sch. of Law (LLM Trade Regulation 2003); Ecole Nat. du Barreau. Lecturer: Univ. of Strasbourg, 1997–2002, 2003–04; Univ. of Southampton, 2004–05; Mem., Paris Bar Assoc., 2004; admitted as solicitor, Athens Bar Assoc., 2005; Lectr, then Reader, Faculty of Laws, UCL, 2005–14; Chief Researcher, Higher Sch. of Econs, Nat. Res. Univ., Moscow, 2014–. Visiting Professor: Centre d'Etudes Internat. de la Propriété Intellectuelle, Univ. of Strasbourg, 2004–; Univ. of Chile, Santiago, 2011–; Univ. of Hong Kong Law Sch., 2014; Emile Noel Fellow, NY Univ. Law Sch., 2008–09; Gutenberg Res. Chair, Ecole Nat. d'Admin, 2012–14; Alexander von Humboldt Fellow, 2014–15. Emile Girardeau Prize, Acad. des Scis Morales et Politiques, 2005; Philip Leverhulme Prize, 2012. *Publications:* La Transformation du droit de la concurrence par le recours á l'analyse économique, 2007; The Reform of EC Competition Law, 2010; The EU after the Treaty of Lisbon, 2012; The Global Limits of Competition Law, 2012; Regulating Trade in Services in the EU and the WTO: trust, distrust and economic integration, 2012; Handbook in EU Competition Law: enforcement and procedure, 2013; Handbook in EU Competition Law: substantive aspects, 2013; Competition Law and Development, 2013; Competition and the State, 2014; Damages Claims for the Infringement of Competition Law, 2015; contribs to Common Market Law Rev., Eur. Law Rev., Jl Competition Law and Econs, Antitrust Law Jl, Columbia Business Law Rev., Cambridge Jl Eur. Legal Studies, Eur. Business Law Rev., Revue Française d'Admin Publique, Foreign Affairs, Rev. Trimestrielle de Droit européen, Tulane Jl Internat. and Comparative Law, Current Legal Problems. *Recreations:* sailing, theatre, opera, cinema, archaeology, modern art, politics. *Address:* UCL Laws, Bidborough House, 38–50 Bidborough Street, WC1H 9BT. *T:* (020) 7679 1028, (020) 7679 1407. *E:* i.lianos@ucl.ac.uk.

LIAO Poon-Huai, Donald, CBE 1983 (OBE 1972); company director; *b* 29 Oct. 1929; *s* of late Liao Huk-Koon and Yeo Tsai-Hoon; *m* 1963, Christine Yuen Ching-Me; two *s* one *d*. *Educ:* Univ. of Hong Kong (BArch Hons); Univ. of Durham (Dip. Landscape Design). Architect, Hong Kong Housing Authority, 1960, Housing Architect, 1966; Commissioner for Housing and Member, Town Planning Board, 1968; Director of Housing and Vice-Chm., Hong Kong Housing Authority, 1973; Sec. for Housing and Chm., Hong Kong Housing Authority, 1980; Sec. for Dist Admin, Hong Kong, 1985. Chm., HSBC China Fund, 1992–2004; Dir, TCC Hong Kong Cement Hldgs Co., subseq. TCC Internat. Hldgs Ltd, 1997–. MLC, Hong Kong, 1980; MEC, 1985. Mem., Sino-British Jt Liaison Gp, 1987–89. Fellow, Hong Kong Inst. of Architects. Hon. FIH. Hon. DSc Durham, 2011. *Recreations:* golf, ski-ing, riding. *Address:* (residence) 55 Kadoorie Avenue, Kowloon, Hong Kong. *T:* 27155822. *Clubs:* Athenæum; Hong Kong Golf, Hong Kong Jockey (Hong Kong).

LIARDET, Rear-Adm. Guy Francis, CB 1990; CBE 1985; *b* 6 Dec. 1934; *s* of Maj.-Gen. Henry Maughan Liardet, CB, CBE, DSO; *m* 1962, Jennifer Anne O'Hagan; one *s* two *d*. *Educ:* Royal Naval Coll., Dartmouth; Southampton Univ. (BA Hons 1999). Trng Comdr, BRNC, Dartmouth, 1969–70; comd HMS Aurora, 1970–72; Exec. Officer, HMS Bristol, 1974–76; Defence Policy Staff, MoD, 1978–79; RCDS, 1980; CSO (Trng), C-in-C Naval Home Comd, 1981–82; comd HMS Cleopatra and Seventh Frigate Sqn, 1983–84; Dir of Public Relations (Navy), MoD, 1984–86; Flag Officer Second Flotilla, 1986–88; Comdt, JSDC, 1988–90, retd. Dir of Public Affairs, CIA, 1990–93. Mem., RNSA, 1970–. *Publications:* contrib. Naval Review. *Recreation:* sailing. *Address:* The Downs Cottage, New Road, Meonstoke, Southampton SO32 3NN.

LIBBY, Donald Gerald, PhD; Under Secretary, Office of Science and Technology, Cabinet Office, and Secretary, Advisory Board for the Research Councils, 1991–94; *b* 2 July 1934; *s* of late Herbert Lionel Libby and Minnie Libby; *m* 1st, 1961, Margaret Elizabeth Dunlop McLatchie (*d* 1979); one *d*; 2nd, 1982, June Belcher. *Educ:* RMA, Sandhurst; London Univ. (BSc, PhD Physics). CEng, FIET (FIEE 1993). Department of Education and Science: Principal Scientific Officer, 1967–72; Principal, 1972–74; Asst Sec., 1974–80; Under Sec., 1980–91 (Planning and Internat. Relations Br., 1980–82, Architects, Bldg and Schs Br., 1982–86, Further and Higher Educn Br. 2, 1986–91). Adviser, Logica UK Ltd, 1995–96. *Recreations:* music, rowing, golf. *Address:* 7 Coach House Mews, Whiteley Village, Walton-on-Thames KT12 4BT.

LIBESKIND, Daniel, Hon. RA 2003; Architect, Studio Daniel Libeskind, New York (formerly Architectural Studio Libeskind, Berlin), since 1989; *b* Łódź, Poland, 12 May 1946; *s* of Nachman Libeskind and Dora Libeskind (*née* Blaustein); *m* 1969, Nina Lewis; two *s* one *d*. *Educ:* in Poland and Israel; Bronx High Sch. of Sci., NYC; Cooper Union Sch. of Architecture, NYC (BArch 1970); Sch. of Comparative Studies, Univ. of Essex (MA Hist. and Theory of Architecture 1971). Architectural trng in The Hague, NYC and Helsinki; Inst. for Architecture and Urban Studies, NY, 1971–72; Irving Grossman Associates, Toronto, 1972–73; Project Planners Associates, Toronto, 1973; Asst Prof. of Architecture, Univ. of Kentucky, 1973–75; Unit Master, AA, London, 1975–77; Sen. Lectr, Poly. of Central London, and Critic in Architecture, Centre of Advanced Studies in Architecture, 1975–77; Associate Prof. of Architecture, Univ. of Toronto, 1977–78; Hd, Sch. of Architecture, and Architect-in-Residence, Cranbrook Acad. of Art, Bloomfield Hills, Mich, 1978–85; Founder and Dir, *Architecture Intermundium*, Milan, 1986–89; Architect, Berlin, 1989–94, LA, 1994–95. Vis. Critic in Architecture, Houston, Lund, London, Harvard and Helsinki, 1981–84; Visiting Professor, Europe, US and Canada, 1985–, including: Bannister Fletcher Architecture Prof., Univ. of London, 1990–91; Hochschule Weissensee, Berlin, 1993–95; Sch. of Architecture and Urban Planning, UCLA, 1994–98; Hochschule für Gestaltung, Karlsruhe; First Louis Kahn Prof., Yale Univ. Sch. of Architecture; Univ. of Pennsylvania. Ext. Examr, Bartlett Sch. of Architecture, Univ. of London, 1993. Major works include: Uozu Mt Pavilion, Japan, 1997; Polderland Gdn, Netherlands, 1997; Felix Nussbaum Haus, Osnabrück, 1998, extension, 2011; Jewish Mus., Berlin, 1999 (German Architecture Award, 1999); Imperial War Mus. North, Manchester, 2002 (RIBA Award, 2004); London Metropolitan Univ. Graduate Centre (RIBA Award, 2004); Denver Art Mus., 2006; Grand Canal Th., Dublin, 2010; Creative Media Center, Hong Kong, 2011; Mil. History Mus., Dresden, 2011; Haeundae Udong Hyundai I'Park, Busan, 2012; Reflections at Keppel Bay, Singapore, 2012; Acad. of Jewish Mus., Berlin, 2012. Ongoing projects include: Zlota 44, Warsaw; L Tower, Toronto; Centre des Congrès, Mons; Kö-Bogen, Dusseldorf; Zhang Zhidong and Mod. Industrial Mus., Wuhan; Vitra Tower, Sao Paulo; FieraMilano, Milan; World Trade Centre master plan, NY City; Archipelago 21, Seoul; Harmony Tower, Seoul; Dancing Towers; New York Tower, NY City. Mem., European Acad. of Arts and Letters, 1990. Hon. Dr: Humboldt Univ., 1997; Coll. of Arts and Humanities, Essex Univ.; Edinburgh, 2002; DePaul, Chicago, 2002; Toronto, 2004. Academician, IAA, 2012. Numerous awards, including: 1st prize, Biennale de Vinezia, 1985; Award for Architecture, AAAL, 1996; Berlin Cultural Prize, 1996; Goethe Medallion, 2000; Hiroshima Art Prize, 2001; Lifetime Achievement Award, Emirates Glass LEAF Awards, 2012; AIA Nat. Service Medal, 2012. *Publications:* Breaking Ground: adventures in life and architecture (memoir), 2004; numerous monographs. *Address:* Studio Daniel Libeskind, 2 Rector Street, New York, NY 10006, USA.

LICHFIELD, 6th Earl of, *cr* 1831; **Thomas William Robert Hugh Anson;** Viscount Anson and Baron Soberton, 1806; *b* 19 July 1978; *s* of 5th Earl of Lichfield and of Lady Leonora Grosvenor (LVO 1997), *d* of 5th Duke of Westminster, TD; *S* father, 2005; *m* 2009, Lady Henrietta Conyngham, *er d* of Marquess of Conyngham, *qv*; two *s*. *Heir: s* Viscount Anson, *qv*.

LICHFIELD, Bishop of; *no new appointment at time of going to press.*

LICHFIELD, Dean of; *see* Dorber, Very Rev. A. J.

LICHFIELD, Archdeacon of; *see* Baker, Ven. S. N. H.

LICKISS, Sir Michael (Gillam), Kt 1993; DL; Chairman: VisitBritain (formerly British Tourist Authority), 2003–05; Theatre Royal Plymouth Group, since 2008; *b* 18 Feb. 1934; *s* of Frank Gillam and Elaine Rheta Lickiss; *m* 1st, 1959, Anita (marr. diss. 1979); two *s* two *d*; 2nd, 1987, Anne; one *s*. *Educ:* Bournemouth Grammar Sch.; London Sch. of Economics (BSc Econ 1955; Hon. Fellow 2006). FCA. Articled, Bournemouth, 1955–58; commissioned, Army, 1959–62; practised Bournemouth, 1962–68; Partner, Thornton Baker, Bournemouth, 1968–73, London, 1973–94: Exec. Partner, 1975; Managing Partner, 1985–89; firm's name changed to Grant Thornton, 1986; Sen. Partner, 1989–94. Chm., BTEC, subseq. Edexcel Foundn, 1994–2000 (former Mem., Council; Chm., Finance Cttee, 1985–93). DTI Inspector, jtly with Hugh Carlisle, QC, 1986–88; Lectr, UK and overseas. Chairman: Accountancy Television Ltd, 1992–94; Somerset Economic Partnership, 1994–99; West of England Develt Agency, 1994–97; South West of England RDA, 1998–2002; Director: MAI plc, 1994–96; United News and Media plc, 1996–97, and other cos. Institute of Chartered Accountants: Mem. Council, 1971–81, 1983–95; Vice-Pres., 1988–89; Dep. Pres., 1989–90; Pres., 1990–91; Past Chairman: Educn and Training, Tech. Cttee and Ethics Cttee; Professional Conduct Directorate; Chm., Somerset Rural Youth Project, 1997–99; Dir, British Trng Internat., 1998–2000. Chm., CCAB, 1990–91; Dep. Chm., Financial Reporting Council, 1990–91; Member: FEFCE, 1992–96; Copyright Tribunal, 1994–99; Senate, Engrg Council, 1996–99; Learning and Skills Nat. Council, 2000–02; Industrial Develt Adv. Bd, DTI, 2000–03. Founder President, Assoc. of Accounting Technicians, 1980–82. Chm., Genesis Project, Somerset, 2004–07. Trustee: Parnham Trust, 1992–96; RNAS Mus., 2001–03; World Heritage Coast, 2004–. Mem., Court of Govs, LSE, 1992–2009 (Gov. Emeritus, 2009–); Vice Chm., Court of Govs, Plymouth Univ., 1995–98; Mem. Council, London Univ., 1997–2003. Pres., Royal Cornwall Polytechnic Soc., 2006–08. DL Somerset, 2003. Hon. DBA: Bournemouth, 1994; UWE, 2002; Hon. DEd Plymouth, 2005. *Publications:* articles in learned jls. *Recreations:* walking, gardening. *E:* Lickissm@aol.com. *Club:* Royal Automobile.

LICKLEY, Gavin Alexander Fraser, CA; *b* 14 Aug. 1946; *s* of Alexander Thompson Lickley and Gladys Ann Fraser (*née* Smith); *m* 1973, Anne Muir Forrester; two *d*. *Educ:* Univ. of Edinburgh (LLB Hons 1967). CA 1970. Corporate Finance Exec., GKN plc, 1971–72; with Morgan Grenfell & Co. Ltd, 1972–95: Head of Banking, 1991–95; Chm., 1996–98; Bd Mem., Global Corporates and Instns Div., Deutsche Morgan Grenfell, then Deutsche Bank AG, 1995–99. Non-exec. Dir, Paragon Gp of Cos plc, 2003. *Recreations:* golf, ski-ing. *Address:* 6 Westmoreland Road, SW13 9RY. *T:* (020) 8748 7618. *Clubs:* City of London, Roehampton; Royal Wimbledon Golf.

LICKLEY, Nigel James Dominic; QC 2006; a Recorder, since 2000; *b* 27 Aug. 1960; *s* of James Edwin and Veronica Mabel Lickley; *m* 2000, Melanie De Freitas; two *d*. *Educ:* Queen Mary's Coll., Basingstoke; University Coll. London (LLB 1982). Called to the Bar, Gray's Inn, 1983, Bencher, 2011; Asst Recorder, 1998–2000. Leader, Western Circuit, 2010–13. Mem. (Lab) Winchester CC, 1994–98. Contested (Lab): Christchurch, July 1993; Basingstoke, 1997. *Recreations:* fly fishing, beekeeping. *Address:* 3 Paper Buildings, Temple, EC4Y 7EU. *T:* (020) 7583 8055. *E:* Nigel.Lickley@3paper.co.uk. *Clubs:* Athenæum; Queen's Park Cricket (Trinidad).

LICKORISH, Prof. William Bernard Raymond, ScD; Professor of Geometric Topology, University of Cambridge, 1996–2004, now Emeritus; Fellow, Pembroke College, Cambridge, 1964–2004, now Emeritus; *b* 19 Feb. 1938; *s* of William Percy Lickorish and Florence Lickorish; *m* 1962, Margaret Ann Russell; one *s* two *d*. *Educ:* Merchant Taylors' Sch.; Pembroke Coll., Cambridge (ScD 1991). Asst Lectr in Maths, Univ. of Sussex, 1963–64; University of Cambridge: Asst Lectr, 1964–69; Lectr, 1969–90; Reader, 1990–96; Hd, Dept of Pure Maths and Mathematical Stats, 1997–2002; Asst Dir, then Dir of Studies in Maths, Pembroke Coll., 1964–91. Visiting Professor: Univ. of Wisconsin, 1967–68; Univ. of Calif, Berkeley, 1974, Santa Barbara, 1979–80 and 1996–97; Univ. of Texas, 1989; UCLA, 1990; Univ. of Melbourne, 2002–03. Sen. Whitehead Prize, London Mathematical Soc., 1991. *Publications:* An Introduction to Knot Theory, 1997; contrib. many articles on topology. *Recreations:* gardening, to walk, to bathe. *Address:* Pembroke College, Cambridge CB2 1RF.

LIDDELL, family name of **Baroness Liddell of Coatdyke** and **Baron Ravensworth**.

LIDDELL OF COATDYKE, Baroness *cr* 2010 (Life Peer), of Airdrie in Lanarkshire; **Helen Lawrie Liddell;** PC 1998; High Commissioner to Australia, 2005–09; Chairman, G3 Group, since 2014 (Senior Adviser, 2012–14); *b* 6 Dec. 1950; *d* of late Hugh Reilly and Bridget

Lawrie Reilly; *m* 1972, Dr Alistair Henderson Liddell; one *s* one *d*. *Educ:* St Patrick's High Sch., Coatbridge; Strathclyde Univ. Head, Econ. Dept, 1971–75, and Asst Sec., 1975–76, Scottish TUC; Econ. Correspondent, BBC Scotland, 1976–77; Scottish Sec., Labour Party, 1977–88; Dir, Personnel and Public Affairs, Scottish Daily Record and Sunday Mail (1986) Ltd, 1988–92; Chief Exec., Business Venture Prog., 1993–94. Contested (Lab) Fife E, Oct. 1974; MP (Lab): Monklands E, July 1994–1997; Airdrie and Shotts, 1997–2005. Opposition spokeswoman on Scotland, 1995–97; Economic Sec., HM Treasury, 1997–98; Minister of State, Scottish Office, 1998–99; Minister of Transport, 1999; Minister of State for energy and competitiveness in Europe, DTI, 1999–2001; Sec. of State for Scotland, 2001–03. Non-exec. Dir, Visit Britain, 2010–14. Trustee: Britain Australia Soc. Educn Trust, 2010–; Northcote Educnl Trust, 2011–. *Publications:* Elite, 1990. *Recreations:* cooking, hill-walking, music, writing.

LIDDELL, Dame Jennifer Gita; *see* Abramsky, Dame J. G.

LIDDELL, Air Vice-Marshal Peter, CB 2002; CEng, FIET, FRAeS; Managing Director, Select Solutions Ltd, since 2003; *b* 9 Oct. 1948; *s* of late Stanley Liddell and of Mary Elizabeth Liddell (*née* Underwood); *m* 1979, Jennifer Marion, *d* of late Lt-Col Jack Prichard, DSO, MC and Eilleen Patricia Prichard; two *s* one *d*. *Educ:* Keswick Sch.; Manchester Univ. (BSc). FIET (FIEE 1996); FRAeS 1996. Commnd (Univ. Cadet), 1966; served No 20 Sqn, Wildenrath, 1970–73; St Mawgan, 1973–75; Swanton Morley, 1975–77; MoD, 1978–80; Marham, 1981–82; sc 1983; OC Engrg Wing, Brize Norton, 1984–85; Cranwell, 1986–88; HQ Support Comd, 1989–90; Stn Comdr, Sealand, 1991–92; rcds 1993; HQ Logistics Comd, 1994–96; HQ Strike Comd, 1997–98; AO Communications Inf. Systems and Support Services, 1999–2000; Dir Gen., Equipment Support (Air), Defence Logistics Orgn, 2000–03. *Recreations:* golf, hill walking, theatre. *Club:* Royal Air Force.

LIDDELL-GRAINGER, Ian Richard Peregrine; MP (C) Bridgwater and West Somerset, since 2010 (Bridgwater, 2001–10); *b* 23 Feb. 1959; *s* of late David Ian Liddell-Grainger of Ayton and of Anne Mary Sibylla Liddell-Grainger (*née* Smith); *m* Jill Nesbit; one *s* two *d*. *Educ:* Wellesley House Sch., Kent; Millfield Sch., Somerset; S of Scotland Agricl Coll., Edinburgh (NCA). Farmer, Berwicks, 1980–85; Man. Dir, property mgt and devolt co., 1985–. Mem., Tynedale DC, 1989–95. Contested (C) Torridge and Devon West, 1997. Major, Queen's Div., TA (formerly with 6th (Vol.) Bn), RRF. *Address:* (office) 16 Northgate, Bridgwater, Somerset TA6 3EU; c/o House of Commons, SW1A 0AA.

LIDDIMENT, David; media consultant, since 2015. *Educ:* Liverpool Univ. Benton and Bowles, Advertising Agency, 1974–75; Granada TV: Promotions Scriptwriter, 1975; researcher, dir, prod. and journalist; Exec. Prod., Children's Progs, 1986–88; Head of Entertainment, 1988–92; Dir of Progs, 1992–93; Head of Entertainment Gp, BBC TV, 1993–95; Dep. Man. Dir and Dir of Progs, 1995–96, Dep. Chm., 1997, LWT; Man. Dir, Granada UK Broadcasting, 1996–97; Dir of Progs, ITV Network Ltd, 1997–2002; Producer, The Old Vic Th. Co., 2003–07; Creative Dir, All3Media, 2003–14. Trustee, BBC Trust, 2007–14. Chm., The Hepworth Wakefield Trust, 2010–.

LIDDINGTON, Sir Bruce, Kt 2000; freelance consultant; Managing Director, Transtatus Associates Ltd, since 2013; *b* 4 Sept. 1949; *s* of Gordon Philip Liddington and Joan Liddington; *m* 1978, Carol Jane Tuttle; two *s* one *d*. *Educ:* Queen Mary Coll., London Univ. (BA 1st Cl. Eng. Lit. 1971); King's Coll., Cambridge (PGCE 1972); Washington State Univ., USA (MA Eng. Lit. 1977). Teacher: Northcliffe Sch., Conisbrough, 1972–75; Westfield Sch., Wellingborough, 1975–76; Head of English, Westwood High Sch., Leek, 1977–81; Dep. Head, Ousedale Sch., Newport Pagnell, 1981–86; Headteacher, Northampton Sch. for Boys, 1986–2000. Advr, Quality Assce Unit, DfEE, 1999–2001; Professional Advr, Academies Div., DfES, 2000–06; Schs Comr for England, DfES, later DCSF, 2006–09; Dir Gen., E-ACT, 2009–13. FRSA. *Recreations:* opera, reading, music, films, travel, food, four grandchildren.

LIDDLE, family name of **Baron Liddle**.

LIDDLE, Baron *cr* 2010 (Life Peer), of Carlisle in the County of Cumbria; **Roger John Liddle;** Chairman, Policy Network, since 2009 (Vice-Chairman, 2007–09); Pro-Chancellor, Lancaster University, since 2013; *b* 14 June 1947; *s* of John Thwaites Liddle and Elizabeth Liddle; *m* 1983, Caroline Thomson, *qv*; one *s*. *Educ:* Robert Ferguson Primary Sch., Carlisle; Denton Holme Jun. Sch., Carlisle; Carlisle Grammar Sch.; Queen's Coll., Oxford (BA (Modern Hist.) 1968; MPhil (Mgt Studies) 1970). Oxford Sch. of Social and Administrative Studies, 1970–74; Ind. Relns Officer, Electricity Council, 1974–76; Special Advr to Rt Hon. William Rodgers, MP, 1976–81; Dir, Public Policy Centre, 1982–87; Man. Dir, Prima Europe Ltd, 1987–97; Special Advr on European Affairs to Prime Minister, 1997–2004; Mem., cabinet of Peter Mandelson, EC, 2004–06; Principal Advr to the Pres. of the EC, 2006–07. Chm., Adv. Panel on New Industry, New Jobs to Sec. of State for Business, Innovation and Skills, 2009–10. Opposition front bench spokesman on Europe, H of L, 2011–14. Member: Oxford CC, 1971–76; Lambeth BC, 1982–86, 1994–95; Cumbria CC, 2013–. Chm., Cumbria Vision, 2007–10. *Publications:* (with Peter Mandelson) The Blair Revolution, 1996; The New Case for Europe, 2005; (ed jtly) Global Europe, Social Europe, 2006; (with P. Diamond) Beyond New Labour, 2007; The Europe Dilemma: Britain and the drama of EU integration, 2014. *Recreations:* history, politics, entertaining, holidays in Italy. *Address:* Policy Network, 11 Tufton Street, SW1P 3QB. *Club:* Reform.

LIDDLE, Caroline; *see* Thomson, C.

LIDINGTON, Rt Hon. David (Roy), PhD; PC 2010; MP (C) Aylesbury, since 1992; Minister of State, Foreign and Commonwealth Office, since 2010; *b* 30 June 1956; *s* of Roy N. and Rosa Lidington; *m* 1989, Helen Mary Farquhar Parry; four *s* (incl. twins). *Educ:* Haberdashers' Aske's Sch., Elstree; Sidney Sussex Coll., Cambridge (MA, PhD). British Petroleum plc, 1983–86; RTZ plc, 1986–87; Special Adviser to: Home Sec., 1987–89; Foreign Sec., 1989–90; Consultant, PPU Ltd, 1991–92. PPS to Leader of the Opposition, 1997–99; Opposition front-bench spokesman on: home affairs, 1999–2001; HM Treasury affairs, 2001–02; environment, food and rural affairs, 2002–03; NI, 2003–07; foreign affairs, 2007–10. *Publications:* articles on Tudor history. *Recreations:* history, choral singing. *Address:* House of Commons, SW1A 0AA. *T:* (020) 7219 3000; 100 Walton Street, Aylesbury, Bucks HP21 7QP. *T:* (01296) 482102.

LIDSTONE, Russ; Chief Executive Officer, Havas Worldwide London (formerly Euro RSCG London), since 2009; *b* Brixham, S Devon, 16 March 1970; *s* of Derek Lidstone and Rita Lidstone; *m* 1999, Amanda Rees; one *s* one *d*. *Educ:* Churston Grammar Sch.; Univ. of Keele (BA Jt Hons Hist. and Sociol.). Ethnographic Researcher, Coca-Cola, 1992–93; Planner, McCann Erickson Advertising, 1993–96; Senior Planner: Butterfield Day Devito Hockney, 1996–99; HHCL & Partners, 1999–2001; Head of Planning: Lowe, 2001–05; JWT, 2005–06; Chief Strategy Officer, Euro RSCG London, 2006–09. *Recreations:* gym, spinning, music, basketball, family, eating. *Address:* Havas Worldwide London, Cupola House, 15 Alfred Place, WC1E 7EB. *T:* (020) 7240 4111. *E:* russ.lidstone@havasww.com.

LIEBERMAN, Joseph I.; Member for Connecticut, US Senate, 1989–2012 (Democrat 1989–2006, Ind Democrat, 2006–12); *b* 24 Feb. 1942; *s* of Henry Lieberman and Marcia Lieberman; *m* 1983, Hadassah Freilich; one *d*; one step *s*, and one *s* one *d* from a previous marriage. *Educ:* Yale Univ. (BA 1964; JD 1967). Called to the Bar, Conn, 1967; Partner, Lieberman, Segaloff & Wolfson, New Haven, 1972–83. Mem. (Democrat), State Senate of Connecticut, 1971–81 (Majority Leader, 1975–81); Attorney-Gen., Conn, 1983–89. Democratic candidate for US Vice-President, 2000. *Publications:* The Power Broker, 1966; The Scorpion and the Tarantula, 1970; The Legacy, 1981; Child Support in America, 1986; In Praise of Public Life, 2000.

LIEBESCHUETZ, Prof. (John Hugo) Wolfgang (Gideon), PhD; FSA; FBA 1991; Professor of Classical and Archaeological Studies, Nottingham University, 1979–92, now Professor Emeritus; *b* Hamburg, 22 June 1927; *s* of Prof. H. Liebeschuetz and Dr E. A. R. Liebeschuetz (*née* Plaut); *m* 1955, Margaret Rosa Taylor; one *s* three *d*. *Educ:* UCL (BA 1951; Fellow 1997); PhD London 1957. Schoolteacher, 1957–63; Leicester University: Lectr in Classics, 1963–74; Sen. Lectr, 1974–78; Reader, 1978–79. FSA 1999. Mem., Princeton Inst. for Advanced Study, 1993. Corresp. Mem., German Archaeol Inst., 1994. *Publications:* Antioch: city and imperial administration in the later Roman Empire, 1972; Continuity and Change in Roman Religion, 1979; Barbarians and Bishops: army, church and state in the age of Arcadius and Chrysostom, 1990; From Diocletian to the Arab Conquest: change in the late Roman Empire, 1990; The Decline and Fall of the Roman City, 2001; Ambrose of Milan: political letters and speeches, 2005; Decline and Change in Late Antiquity: religion, barbarians and their historiography, 2006; Ambrose and John Chrysostom: clerics between desert and empire, 2011; contribs to learned jls. *Address:* 1 Clare Valley, The Park, Nottingham NG7 1BU.

LIESNER, Hans Hubertus, CB 1980; Member, 1989–97, Deputy Chairman, 1989–95, Monopolies and Mergers Commission; *b* 30 March 1929; *e s* of Curt Liesner, lawyer, and Edith L. (*née* Neumann); *m* 1st, 1957, Jane Boland (marr. diss. 1964); one *s* one *d*; 2nd, 1968, Thelma Seward. *Educ:* German grammar schs; Bristol Univ. (BA); Nuffield Coll., Oxford; MA Cantab. Asst Lectr, later Lectr, in Economics, London Sch. of Economics, 1955–59; Lectr in Economics, Univ. of Cambridge; Fellow, Dir of Studies in Economics and some time Asst Bursar, Emmanuel Coll., Cambridge, 1959–70; Under-Sec. (Economics), HM Treasury, 1970–76; Dep. Sec., and Chief Econ. Advr, DTI (formerly Industry, Trade and Prices and Consumer Protection), 1976–89. Standing Mem., Adv. Bd on Fair Trading in Telecoms, 1997–2000; Gov., 1989–, Mem. Council of Mgt, 1989–2011, NIESR; Chm. Adv. Gp, ESRC Centre for Economic Learning and Social Evolution, 1996–2010. *Publications:* The Import Dependence of Britain and Western Germany, 1957; Case Studies in European Economic Union: the mechanics of integration (with J. E. Meade and S. J. Wells), 1962; Atlantic Harmonisation: making free trade work, 1968; Britain and the Common Market: the effect of entry on the pattern of manufacturing production (with S. S. Han), 1971; articles in jls, etc. *Recreations:* walking, gardening. *Address:* 32 The Grove, Brookmans Park, Herts AL9 7RN. *T:* (01707) 653269. *Club:* Reform.

LIEU, Prof. Judith Margaret, PhD; FBA 2014; Lady Margaret's Professor of Divinity, University of Cambridge, since 2007 (Chair, Faculty Board of Divinity, 2010–14); Fellow, Robinson College, Cambridge, since 2008; *b* 25 May 1951; *d* of John and Zoe Bending; *m* 1976, Samuel N. C. Lieu; one *d*. *Educ:* Bromley High Sch. for Girls; Univ. of Durham (BA Hons Theol. 1972, MA Theol. 1973); Univ. of Oxford (PGCE 1974); Univ. of Birmingham (PhD 1980). Hd of RE, Abbey Sch., Reading, 1974–76; Lectr in Biblical Studies, Queen's Coll., Birmingham, 1981–84; Lectr in Christian Origins and Early Judaism, 1985–95, Reader in New Testament, 1995, KCL; Sen. Lectr in Hist., 1996–98, Associate Prof., 1998, Macquarie Univ., Sydney; Prof. of New Testament Studies, KCL, 1999–2007. Pres., Studiorum Novi Testamenti Societas, 2015–July 2016. Editor, New Testament Studies, 2003–09. *Publications:* The Second and Third Epistles of John: history and background, 1986; The Theology of the Johannine Epistles, 1991; (ed jtly) The Jews between Pagans and Greeks, 1994; Image and Reality: the Jews in the world of the Christians in the second century, 1996; The Gospel According to Luke, 1997; Neither Jew nor Greek: constructing early Christianity, 2002; Christian Identity in the Jewish and Graeco-Roman World, 2004; (ed jtly) The Oxford Handbook of Biblical Studies, 2006; (ed jtly) Biblical Traditions in Transmission, 2006; I, II, III John, 2008; Marcion and the Making of a Heretic, 2015. *Recreations:* reading, walking, theatre. *Address:* Faculty of Divinity, West Road, Cambridge CB3 9BS.

LIEVEN, Prof. Dominic Christophe Bogdan, PhD; FBA 2001; Senior Research Fellow, Trinity College, Cambridge, since 2011; *b* 19 Jan. 1952; *s* of Prince Alexander Lieven and Veronica Lieven (*née* Monahan); *m* 1985, Mikiko Fujiwara; one *s* one *d*. *Educ:* Downside Sch.; Christ's Coll., Cambridge (BA); SSEES, London Univ. (PhD 1978). Kennedy Schol., Harvard Univ., 1973–74; FCO, 1974–75; London School of Economics and Political Science: Lectr, 1978–93; Prof. of Russian Govt and History, 1993–2011; Hd, Dept of Govt, 2001–04; Hd, Dept of Internat. Hist., 2009–11; Mem., Govg Council, 2005–10. Humboldt Fellow, 1986; Visiting Professor: Univ. of Tokyo, 1992–94; Harvard Univ., 1993. Member, Editorial Board: Jl Contemporary Hist., 1994–2004; Slavonic Rev., 2000–. Order of Friendship (Russia), 2014. *Publications:* Russia and the Origins of the First World War, 1983; Russia's Rulers under the Old Regime, 1989; The Aristocracy in Europe 1815–1914, 1992; Nicholas II, 1993; Empire: the Russian Empire and its rivals, 2000; Russia against Napoleon: the struggle for Europe, 1807–1814, 2009 (Wolfson History Prize, 2009); Towards the Flame: empire, war and the end of Tsarist Russia, 2015; books trans. German, Japanese, Italian, Dutch, Russian, French, Spanish, Portuguese and Chinese. *Recreation:* collecting Russian regimental models. *Address:* Trinity College, Cambridge CB2 1TQ. *E:* dl449@cam.ac.uk. *Club:* Travellers.

LIEVEN, Nathalie Marie Daniella; QC 2006; barrister; *b* 20 May 1964; *d* of Alexander Lieven and Veronica Lieven; *m* 1995, Stewart Wright; one *s* two *d*. *Educ:* Godolphin and Latymer Sch.; Poly. of Central London (Dip. Law); Trinity Hall, Cambridge (BA 1986). Called to the Bar, Gray's Inn, 1989, Hon. Bencher, 2010. *Recreation:* books. *Address:* Landmark Chambers, 180 Fleet Street, EC4A 2HG. *E:* clerks@landmarkchambers.co.uk.

LIEW Foo Yew, PhD, DSc; FRCPath; FRS 2012; FRSE; Gardiner Professor and Head of Department of Immunology, University of Glasgow, since 1991; *b* 22 May 1943; *s* of Liew Soon and Chai Man Ngon; *m* 1973, Dr Woon Ling Chan; one *s*. *Educ:* Monash Univ., Australia (BSc 1st cl. Hons); ANU (PhD; DSc). MRCPath 1990, FRCPath 1996. FRSE 1995. Lectr, Univ. of Malaya, 1972–77; Sen. Scientist, 1977–84, Head, Dept of Immunology, 1984–91, Wellcome Res. Lab., Beckenham. Life Mem., Nat. Biol Standards Bd, 1996. FMedSci 1999. *Publications:* Vaccination Strategies of Tropical Diseases, 1989; Immunology of intracellular parasitism, 1998; more than 250 papers in learned jls. *Recreations:* reading classical Chinese, gardening. *Address:* Department of Immunology, University of Glasgow, Glasgow G11 6NT; 37 Elwill Way, Beckenham, Kent BR3 3AB; 556 Crow Road, Glasgow G13 1NP. *T:* (0141) 211 2695.

LIFE, Vivien Frances; HM Diplomatic Service; Ambassador to Denmark, 2012–Aug. 2016; *b* 30 May 1957; *m* 1989, Timothy Michael Dowse, CMG; two *d*. *Educ:* Univ. of Oxford (BA). Civil Service Fast Stream, 1979–81; HM Treasury, 1981–88; entered FCO, 1988; EU Ext. Dept, FCO, 1988–91; First Sec., Washington, 1992–96; Deputy Head: EU Dept Ext., FCO, 1996–97; Latin America and Caribbean Dept, FCO, 1997–99; Head: Consultancy Gp, FCO Services, 1999–2003; Strategy Gp, FCO, 2003–06; Ext. Relns Gp, Europe Directorate, FCO, 2006–08; Enlargement SE and Wider Europe Gp, FCO, 2008–10; Climate Change and Energy Dept, FCO, 2010–12. *Address:* c/o Foreign and Commonwealth Office, King Charles Street, SW1A 2AH.

LIFFORD, 9th Viscount *cr* 1781 (Ire.); **Edward James Wingfield Hewitt;** DL; Chairman, Rathbone Investment Management International, since 2006; *b* 27 Jan. 1949; *s* of 8th Viscount Lifford and Alison Mary Patricia, *d* of T. W. Ashton; *S* father, 1987; *m* 1976, Alison Mary, *d* of Robert Law; one *s* two *d*. *Educ:* The Old Malthouse, Dorset; Aiglon College, Switzerland. Non-exec. Dir, McKay Securities plc, 2006–. DL Hants, 2004. *Recreation:*

country sports. *Heir: s* Hon. James Thomas Wingfield Hewitt [*b* 29 Sept. 1979; *m* 2008, Lady Iona Douglas-Home, *er d* of Earl of Home, *qv*; one *s*]. *Address:* Field House, Hursley, Hants SO21 2LE. *T:* (01962) 775203. *Clubs:* Boodle's, Pratt's.

LIFSCHUTZ, Alexander Joseph; Director, Lifschutz Davidson Sandilands (formerly Lifschutz Davidson), architects, since 1986; *b* 11 Feb. 1952; *s* of late Simon Lifschutz and of Hanna Lifschutz; *m* 1978, Monique Charlesworth; one *s* one *d*. *Educ:* St Paul's Sch.; Univ. of Bristol (BSc Jt Hons Sociology and Psychology 1974); Architectural Assoc. Foster Associates, 1981–86. *Projects* include: Broadwall Community Housing, 1994 (Royal Fine Arts Commn/ Sunday Times Building of the Year, 1995; RIBA Award, 1995; Nat. Housing Design Award, DoE, 1996; Civic Trust Housing Award, 1996); mixed use develt, Oxo Tower Wharf, 1996 (Urban Regeneration Award, Royal Fine Art Commn, 1997; RIBA Award, 1997; Civic Trust Award, 1997); Oxo 8th Floor Restaurant, 1997 (RIBA Award, 1998); Royal Victoria Dock Bridge, 1999 (AJ/Bovis/Royal Acad. Award, 1997; ICE Merit Award, 1998; RIBA Award, 1999; Civic Trust Award, 2000); Hungerford Bridge, 2002 (Royal Fine Art Commn Award, 2003; Civic Trust Award, 2003); Davidson Bldg, 2003 (RIBA Award, 2004; BCO Award, 2005); Bonhams Auction House, 2013 (AIA Award 2014); JW3, 2013 (RIBA Award, 2014); *current projects* include: Doon St Leisure Centre, London's South Bank. Mem. Council, Architectural Assoc., 2002– (Pres., 2009–11). Chm., Trustees, Body and Soul, 2008–. *Recreation:* family. *Address:* Lifschutz Davidson Sandilands Ltd, Island Studios, 22 St Peter's Square, W6 9NW.

LIGHT, Johanne Erica; *see* Delahunty, J. E.

LIGHT, Prof. Paul Henry, PhD; CPsychol, FBPsS; Vice Chancellor, University of Winchester (formerly Principal and Chief Executive, King Alfred's College, then University College Winchester), 2000–06; *b* 26 Aug. 1947; *s* of Ronald and Gladys Light; *m* 1970, Vivienne Mary Baker; one *s* two *d*. *Educ:* St John's Coll., Cambridge (Schol.; BA 1st cl. Natural Scis 1969; PhD Develtl Psychol. 1975); Univ. of Nottingham (MA Educnl Psychol. 1970). FBPsS 1987; CPsychol 1988. Demonstrator in Exptl Psychol., Univ. of Cambridge, 1972–74; Lectr, then Sen. Lectr, Dept of Psychol., Univ. of Southampton, 1978–87; Prof. of Educn, and Dir, Centre for Human Develt and Learning, Open Univ., 1987–92; Prof. of Psychol., Univ. of Southampton, 1992–97; Pro Vice Chancellor (Acad.), Bournemouth Univ., 1997–2000. Vis. lectureships and professorships at Univ. of NC and Univ. of Provence. FRSA 1995. DUniv Winchester, 2008. *Publications:* The Development of Social Sensitivity, 1979; (with G. Butterworth) Social Cognition, 1982; (with M. Richards) Children of Social Worlds, 1986; (jtly) Learning to Think, 1991; (jtly) Becoming a Person, 1991; (jtly) Growing up in a Changing Society, 1991; (with G. Butterworth) Context and Cognition, 1993; (with K. Littleton) Learning with Computers, 1999; (jtly) Learning Sites, 1999; contrib. numerous articles to ed collections and refereed jls. *Recreations:* gardening, walking, sailing. *Address:* Canterton House, Pitmans Lane, Morcombelake, Bridport DT6 6EB. *T:* (01297) 489760. *E:* paul.light@hotmail.co.uk.

LIGHT, Sally Elizabeth; Chief Executive, Motor Neurone Disease Association, since 2012; *b* Groby, Leics, 9 Dec. 1959; *d* of Herbert Royston Light and Peggy Light. *Educ:* Chelsea Coll., Univ. of London (BSc Nursing Studies 1983); NHS Gen. Mgt Trng Scheme 1995; Univ. of Manchester (MA Health Services Mgt 1998). Acute hospital staff nurse: Salford Royal 1983–84; Manchester Royal Infirmary, 1984–85; health visitor, N Manchester HA, 1985–91; Primary Care Facilitator, Manchester FHSA, 1991–93; Service and Rehab Manager, Central Manchester Healthcare Trust, 1995–98; Associate Dir, Manchester HA, 1998–2000; Service Improvement Mgt, NHS Modernisation Agency, 2000–02; Exec. Dir, Barnsley Hosp. NHS Foundn Trust, 2002–06; Dir, Vancouver HA, Canada, 2006–10; Dir of Rehabilitation, Royal Hosp. for Neuro-Disability, 2010–12. *Recreations:* adventure, travelling, wildlife spotting (home and abroad), cycling, daily yoga and good food (sourcing, cooking and eating). *Address:* Motor Neurone Disease Association, 10–15 Notre Dame Mews, Northampton NN1 2BG. *T:* (01604) 250505, *Fax:* (01604) 611858. *E:* sally.light@mndassociation.org.

LIGHTBOWN, Ronald William, MA; FSA, FRAS; art historian and author; Keeper of the Department of Metalwork, Victoria and Albert Museum, 1985–89; *b* Darwen, Lancs, 2 June 1932; *s* of late Vincent Lightbown and Helen Anderson Lightbown (*née* Burness); *m* 1962, Mary Dorothy Webster; one *s*. *Educ:* St Catharine's Coll., Cambridge (MA). FSA, FRAS. Victoria and Albert Museum: Asst Keeper, Library, 1958–64; Asst Keeper, Dept of Metalwork, 1964–73; Dep. Keeper, 1973–76, Keeper, 1976–85, Library. Fellow, Inst. for Res. in the Humanities, Wisconsin Univ., 1974. Pres., Jewellery History Soc., 1990–93; a Vice-Pres., Soc. of Antiquaries, 1986–90 (Sec., 1979–86); Associate Trustee, Soane Mus., 1981–98. Socio dell' Ateneo Veneto, for contrib. to study of culture of Venice and the Veneto, 1987; Socio dell' Accademia Clementina, Bologna, for contribns to study of Italian art, 1988; Serena Medal for Italian Studies, British Acad., 2005. *Publications:* Secular Goldsmiths' in Medieval France: a history, 1978; Sandro Botticelli, 1978, 2nd edn, 1989 (Prix Vasari, 1990); (with M. Corbett) The Comely Frontispiece, 1978; (ed and trans. with A. Caiger-Smith) Piccolpasso: the art of the potter, 1980, 2nd edn 2007; Donatello and Michelozzo, 1980; Andrea Mantegna, 1986; Piero della Francesca, 1992 (Prix de Mai des Libraires de France, 1992); Viaggio in un capolavoro di Piero della Francesca, 1992; (with J. Delumeau) Histoire de l'art: la Renaissance, 1995; Carlo Crivelli, 2004; An Architect Earl: Edward Augustus Stratford, 2nd Earl of Aldborough (1736–1801), 2008; (ed and introd) History of Art in 18th Century England (series of source-books on 18th century British art), 14 vols, 1970–71; V&A Museum catalogues and publications: (pt author) Italian Sculpture, 1964; Tudor Domestic Silver, 1970; Scandinavian and Baltic Silver, 1975; French Silver, 1979; (with M. Archer) India Observed, 1982; Medieval European Jewellery, 1992; contrib. to books, and many articles in learned jls, incl. Burlington Magazine, Warburg Jl and Art Bulletin. *Recreations:* reading, travel, music, conversation. *Address:* Barrowmount House, Goresbridge, Co. Kilkenny, Ireland.

LIGHTFOOT, His Honour George Michael; a Circuit Judge, 1986–2001; *b* 9 March 1936; *s* of Charles Herbert Lightfoot and Mary Lightfoot (*née* Potter); *m* 1963, Dorothy (*née* Miller); two *s* two *d*. *Educ:* St Michael's Catholic College, Leeds; Exeter College, Oxford (MA). National Service, 1955–57: York and Lancaster Regt; interpreter and interrogator, Intelligence Corps, Cyprus, 1956–57. Schoolmaster, 1962–66. Called to the Bar, Inner Temple, 1966; practised on NE circuit. Recorder, 1985–86; Dep. Circuit Judge, 2001–06. Mem., Home Farm Trust, 1980–; President: Leeds Friends of Home Farm Trust, 1987–; Mencap, Leeds, 1987–2003. Vice-Pres., Hunslet Hawks Rugby League Football Club, 1999–2009. *Recreations:* cricket and sport in general, gardening (labourer), learning to listen to music, reading. *E:* gmlightfoot@hotmail.com. *Clubs:* Catenian Association (City of Leeds Circle); Yorkshire CC; Northern Cricket Society.

LIGHTFOOT, Nigel Francis, CBE 2009; FRCPath, FFPH; Executive Director, Connecting Organizations for Regional Disease Surveillance, since 2012; Managing Director and Head, Chemical, Biological, Radiological and Nuclear strategies and crisis management, Nigel Lightfoot Associates Ltd, since 2010; Chief Advisor, and Head, Pandemic Influenza Programme, Health Protection Agency, 2007–10; *b* 19 March 1945; *s* of Leslie and Joyce Lightfoot; *m* 1967, Antonia Calascione; two *s* one *d*. *Educ:* Brunts Sch.; St Mary's Hospital Med. Sch., London (MB BS 1968); London Sch. of Hygiene and Tropical Medicine (MSc 1976). FRCPath 1979. MO, RN, 1966–82, served in nuclear submarines, Malta and NI, and became consultant med. microbiologist, 1979; Public Health Laboratory Service, 1982–2002: Dir, Taunton Public Health Lab.; Dir, Newcastle Public Health Lab.; Dir, PHLS North; developed chemical, biol, and radionuclear trng and exercises strategy, DoH, 2002; Dir, Emergency Response, HPA, 2003–07. Hon. Consultant to RN, 1982–2010. Mem., Adv. Gp on Medical Countermeasures, MoD, 1995–2010; Special Advr, Global Health Security, DoH, 2002–13. Mem., Kangaroo Gp, EP, 2012–. Visiting Professor: Cranfield Univ., 2007–; Keio Univ., Tokyo, 2008–. FFPH 2010. Associate Fellow, RIIA, 2012–. *Publications:* Microbiological Analysis of Food and Water: guidelines for quality assurance, 1998; over 100 learned papers on microbiology and bioterrorism. *Recreations:* horses, riding to hounds, shooting, photography, cooking. *Address:* 53 Fern Avenue, Jesmond, Newcastle upon Tyne NE2 2QU; 127 rue Vendôme, Lyon 69006, France. *E:* Nigel.Lightfoot@mac.com.

LIGHTING, Jane; non-executive Director: Trinity Mirror plc, since 2008; Countrywide plc, since 2014; *b* 22 Dec. 1956. Founder, and Man. Dir, Minotaur International, 1995–99; Man. Dir, Broadcast and Television, 1999–2002, CEO, 2002–03, Flextech; CEO, Five (formerly Channel Five Broadcasting Ltd), 2003–08. Non-exec. Dir, Paddy Power, 2009–13. Chairman: British Television Distributors Assoc., 1995–96; RTS, 2006– (Trustee, 2008–). Gov., Nat. Film and Television Sch., 2001–07. FRSA 2006. *Recreations:* gardening, escaping to the country. *Club:* Groucho.

LIGHTMAN, Brian Peter Leon; General Secretary, Association of School and College Leaders, since 2010; *b* London, 15 June 1955; *s* of Ivor Harry Lightman, CB; *m* 1981, Eva Maria Ursula; four *d*. *Educ:* Westminster City Sch.; Univ. of Southampton (BA (Hons) German 1978; PGCE Mod. Langs 1979); Open Univ. (MA Educn 1993). Teacher of German and French, Hazelwick Sch., Crawley, 1979–84; Hd, Mod. Langs, 1984–89, Hd, 6th Form, 1986–89, Sondes Place Sch., Dorking; Sen. Teacher and Curriculum Develt Manager, 1989–91, Dep. Hd, 1991–95, St Martin's Sch., Hutton, Brentwood; Headteacher: Llantwit Major Sch., Vale of Glamorgan, 1995–99; St Cyres Sch., Vale of Glamorgan, 1999–2010. O Level Examnr, Oxford Delegacy, 1982–87; ESTYN Ind. Inspector, 1999–2010; Member: Bd of Dirs, Cardiff and the Vale, Careers Wales, 2002–06; 14–19 Specialist Panel, Ministerial Adv. Gp, Welsh Govt, 2006–10. Secondary Heads Association, subseq. Association of School and College Leaders: Welsh rep., Nat. Council, 1998–10; Pres., Wales, 2002–03; Hon. Treas., 2002–05; Pres., 2007–08. Mem. Bd of Dirs, St Donat's Arts Centre, 1996–99; Patron, Nat. Citizen Service, 2014–. FRSA. *Publications:* articles in jls, newspapers, etc. *Recreations:* family, walking, caravanning, music. *Address:* Association of School and College Leaders, 130 Regent Road, Leicester LE1 7PG. *T:* (0116) 299 1122, *Fax:* (0116) 299 1123. *E:* brian.lightman@ascl.org.uk. *Club:* Connections.

LIGHTMAN, Hon. Sir Gavin (Anthony), Kt 1994; a Judge of the High Court of Justice, Chancery Division, 1994–2008; arbitrator, mediator and consultant, since 2008; Consultant with Assersons; *b* 20 Dec. 1939; *s* of Harold Lightman, QC and of Gwendoline Joan (*née* Ostrer); *m* 1965, Naomi Ann Claff; one *s* two *d*. *Educ:* University College London (LLB 1st cl. Hons 1961; Fellow, 2002); Univ. of Michigan (LLM). Called to the Bar, Lincoln's Inn, 1963, Bencher 1987, Treas., 2008–09; QC 1980. Chm., Investment Cttee, Harbour Litigation Funding Ltd, 2010–14. Pres., GEMME (European Assoc. of Judges for Mediation), 2009–12; Chm., UK Assoc. of Jewish Lawyers and Jurists, 2011–. Vice Pres., Anglo Jewish Assoc., 1995– (Dep. Pres., 1986–92); Chairman: Educn Cttee, Anglo Jewish Assoc., 1986–94; Educn Cttee, Hillel House, 1992–96 (Vice-Pres., 1996–); Legal Friends, Haifa Univ., 1990–2001 (Gov., 1994); Leonard Sainer Legal Educn Foundn, 2000–. Patron: Jewish Commonwealth Council, 1994–2000; Hammerson Home, 1996–: British Fulbright Schol. Assoc., 2009–. *Publications:* (with G. Battersby) Cases and Statutes on Real Property, 1965; (with G. Moss) The Law of Administrators and Receivers of Companies, 1986, 5th edn 2011; A Report on the National Union of Miners, 1990. *Recreations:* reading, grandchildren, walking, travel. *Address:* Serle Court, 6 New Square, Lincoln's Inn, WC2A 3QS. *Club:* Royal Automobile.

See also S. L. Lightman.

LIGHTMAN, Lionel; Lay Observer attached to Lord Chancellor's Department, 1986–90; *b* 26 July 1928; *s* of late Abner Lightman and late Gitli Lightman (*née* Szmul); *m* 1952, Helen, *y d* of late Rev. A. Shechter and late Mrs Shechter; two *d*. *Educ:* City of London Sch.; Wadham Coll., Oxford (MA). Nat. Service, RAEC, 1951–53 (Temp. Captain). Asst Principal, BoT, 1953; Private Sec. to Perm. Sec., 1957; Principal 1958; Trade Comr, Ottawa, 1960–64; Asst Sec. 1967; Asst Dir, Office of Fair Trading, 1973–75; Under Sec., Dept of Trade, 1975–78, DoI, 1978–81; Dir of Competition Policy, OFT, 1981–84. *Address:* 73 Greenhill, NW3 5TZ. *T:* (020) 7435 3427.

LIGHTMAN, Prof. Stafford Louis, PhD; FRCP, FMedSci; Professor of Medicine, University of Bristol, since 1993; *b* 7 Sept. 1948; *s* of Harold Lightman, QC and of Gwendoline Joan (*née* Ostrer); *m* 1st, 1977, Susan Louise Stubbs (*see* Susan Lightman) (marr. diss. 1995); three *s* one *d*; 2nd, 2010, Rhona Isabel Macpherson. *Educ:* Repton Sch.; Gonville and Caius Coll., Cambridge (MA, MB BChir, PhD); Middlesex Hosp. Med. Sch. Vis. Sen. Scientist, MRC Neuro. Pharm. Unit, Cambridge, 1980–81; Wellcome Trust Sen. Lectr, St Mary's Hosp. Med. Sch. and Hon. Consultant Physician and Endocrinologist, St Mary's Hosp., 1981–82; Charing Cross and Westminster Medical School: Reader in Medicine, 1982–88; Prof. of Clinical Neuroendocrinology, 1988–92; Consultant Physician and Endocrinologist to Charing Cross and Westminster Hosps, 1988–92; Hon. Sen. Res. Fellow, Inst. of Neurology and Consultant Endocrinologist to Nat. Hosp. for Neurology and Neurosurgery, 1988–. Chm., Pituitary Foundn, 1995–2004. Founder FMedSci 1998. Editor-in-Chief, Jl of Neuroendocrinology, 1989–96. *Publications:* (ed with B. J. Everitt) Neuroendocrinology, 1986; (with Michael Powell) Pituitary Tumours: a handbook on management, 1996, 2nd edn 2003; (ed) Horizons in Medicine Vol. 7, 1996; (with A. Levy) Core Endocrinology, 1997; (with Graham Rook) Steroid Hormones and the T cell Cytokine Profile, 1997. *Recreations:* squash, ski-ing, hill walking, scuba diving, music, theatre, anthropology. *Address:* Henry Wellcome Laboratories, Dorothy Hodgkin Building, Whitson Street, Bristol BS1 3NY. *T:* (0117) 331 3167.

See also Hon. Sir G. A. Lightman.

LIGHTMAN, Prof. Susan Louise, PhD; FRCP, FRCPE, FRCOphth, FMedSci; Professor of Clinical Ophthalmology, Institute of Ophthalmology and Moorfields Eye Hospital, since 1993; *b* 2 Sept. 1952; *d* of John and Valerie Stubbs; *m* 1st, 1977, Prof. Stafford Louis Lightman, FRCP (marr. diss. 1995); three *s* one *d*; 2nd, 1995, Hamish Towler; one *s*. *Educ:* St Paul's Girls' Sch.; Middlesex Hosp., Univ. of London (MB BS Hons 1975); PhD London 1987. MRCP 1978, FRCP 1992; FRCOphth 1988; FRCPE 1998. Wellcome Training Fellowship: in Ophthalmology, Inst. of Ophthalmol. and Moorfields Eye Hosp., 1979–83; in Immunology, NIMR, 1983–85; MRC Travelling Fellowship and Vis. Scientist, NIH, 1985–87; MRC Sen. Clinical Fellow, 1988–90; Duke Elder Prof. of Ophthalmology, BPMF, 1990–93. FMedSci 2000. *Publications:* Immunology of Eye Diseases, 1989; Diagnosis and Management of Uveitis, 1998; HIV and the Eye, 1999; over 200 papers in peer reviewed jls. *Recreations:* walking, music, sewing, reading. *Address:* Institute of Ophthalmology, Moorfields Eye Hospital, City Road, EC1V 2PD. *T:* (020) 7566 2266.

LIGHTON, Sir Thomas (Hamilton), 9th Bt *cr* 1791 (Ire.), of Merville, Dublin; Chairman, Society of London Art Dealers, 1993–95 and 1998–2000; *b* 4 Nov. 1954; *o s* of Sir Christopher Robert Lighton, 8th Bt, MBE and his 2nd wife, Horatia Edith (*d* 1981), *d* of A. T. Powlett; *S* father, 1993; *m* 1990, Belinda, *d* of John Fergusson; twin *s* one *d* (and one *s* decd). *Educ:* Eton. *Heir: s* James Christopher Hamilton Lighton, *b* 20 Oct. 1992.

LIGHTWOOD, Louise Naima Rachell; *see* Kamill, L. N. R.

LIGRANI, Prof. Phillip Meredith, PhD; Eminent Scholar in Propulsion, Professor of Mechanical and Aerospace Engineering, Propulsion Research Center, University of Alabama in Huntsville, since 2014; Distinguished Advisory Professor, Inje University, Gimhae, South Korea, since 2010; *b* 2 Feb. 1952; *s* of Alfred Joseph Ligrani and Marilyn Virginia Ligrani (*née* Whittaker); one *d*. *Educ:* Univ. of Texas at Austin (BS 1974); Stanford Univ. (MS 1975; PhD 1980). Asst Prof., Turbomachinery Dept, von Karman Inst. for Fluid Dynamics, Rhode-St-Genese, Belgium, 1979–82; Vis. Sen. Res. Fellow, Dept of Aeronautics, Imperial Coll., London, 1982–84; Associate Prof., Dept of Mechanical Engrg, US Naval Postgrad. Sch., 1984–92; Prof. and Associate Chm., Dept of Mechanical Engrg, Univ. of Utah, 1992–2006; Donald Schultz Prof. of Turbomachinery, Dir of Rolls-Royce Univ. Technol. Centre in Heat Transfer and Aerodynamics, and Dir of Thermo-Fluids Laboratory, Oxford Univ., 2006–09; Fellow, St Catherine's Coll., Oxford, 2006–09; Oliver L. Parks Endowed Chair and Prof. of Aerospace and Mech. Engrg, Parks Coll. of Engrg, Aviation and Technol., St Louis Univ., 2010–14. Guest Prof., Univ. of Karlsruhe, 2000. Mem., K-14 Gas Turbine Heat Transfer Cttee, ASME, 1986– (Vice Chm., 2014–16); Mem. and Vice Chm., Academic Cttee, Inst. for Turbomachinery, Tsinghua Univ., Beijing, 2012–. Lectures include: 5th Internat. Symposium on Turbulence, Heat and Mass Transfer, Dubrovnik, 2006; Aerospace 2030, Oxford Univ., 2007; 15th Internat. Symposium on Field- and Flow-based Separations, Internat. Separation Sci. Soc., San Francisco, 2011; Turbine Engine Technol. Symposium, Dayton, Ohio, 2012. FASME 2000. Associate Editor: ASME Transactions: Jl Heat Transfer, 2003–07, 2010–13; ASME Transactions: Jl Fluids Engrg, 2005–08; Mem., Editl Rev. Bd, Advances in Transport Phenomena, book series, 2006–. Carl E. and Jessie W. Menneken Faculty Award for Excellence in Scientific Res., 1990; NASA Space Act Tech. Brief Award, 1991; Silver winner, HE Marketing, Educnl Advertising Awards, 2011; Dist. Lecture Award, Coll. of Engrg, Univ. of Wisconsin-Milwaukee, 2011. *Publications:* book chapters and contribs to learned jls incl. Internat. Jl Heat and Mass Transfer, ASME Trans: Jl Turbomachinery, ASME Trans: Jl Heat Transfer, ASME Trans: Jl Fluids Engrg, Jl Fluid Mechanics, AIAA Jl, Expts in Fluids, Physics of Fluids, AIAA Jl Heat Transfer and Thermophysics, Internat. Jl Rotating Machinery, Separation Sci. and Technol., Sensors and Acutors A: Physical, and Jl Microcolumn Separations. *Address:* Propulsion Research Center, Department of Mechanical and Aerospace Engineering, University of Alabama in Huntsville, Huntsville, AL 35811, USA. *T:* (256) 8245173, *Fax:* (256) 8247205. *E:* p_ligrani@msn.com.

LIIKANEN, Erkki Antero; Governor, Bank of Finland, since 2004; *b* 19 Sept. 1950; *m* 1971, Hanna-Liisa Issakainen; two *d*. *Educ:* Helsinki Univ. MP (SDP), Finland 1972–90; Minister of Finance, 1987–90; Ambassador to EU, 1990–95; Mem., EC, 1995–2004. Gen. Sec., SDP, 1981–87. *Address:* Bank of Finland, PO Box 160, 00101 Helsinki, Finland.

LIKIERMAN, Prof. Sir (John) Andrew, Kt 2001; Professor of Management Practice, since 2001 and Dean, since 2009, London Business School; *b* 30 Dec. 1943; *s* of Dolek and Olga Likierman; *m* 1987, Dr Meira, *d* of Joshua and Miriam Gruenspan; one step *s* one step *d*. *Educ:* Stowe Sch.; Univ. of Vienna; Balliol Coll., Oxford (MA). FCMA, FCCA. Divl Management Accountant, Tootal Ltd, 1965–68; Asst Lectr, 1968–69, Lectr, 1972–74, Dept of Management Studies, Leeds Univ.; Qualitex Ltd, 1969–72 (Man. Dir, Overseas Div., 1971–72); Vis. Fellow, Oxford Centre for Management Studies, 1972–74; Chm., Ex Libris Ltd, 1973–74; London Business Sch., 1974–76 and 1979–: Dir, Part-time Masters Programme, 1981–85; Dir, Inst. of Public Sector Management, 1983–88; Prof. of Accounting and Financial Control, 1987–97; Vis. Prof., 1997–2001; Dean of External Affairs, 1989–92; Dep. Principal, 1990–92; Elected Governor, 1986–89, *ex officio* Governor, 1990–93; Acting Dean, 2007. Dir, Bank of England, 2004–08. Asst Sec., Cabinet Office (Mem., Central Policy Review Staff), 1976–79, Advr, 1979–82; Advisor, H of C Select Committees: Treasury and CS, 1981–90; Employment, 1985–89; Transport, 1981, 1987–90; Social Services, 1988; Social Security, 1991; Head, Govt Accountancy Service and Chief Accountancy Advr, HM Treasury, 1993–2003; Principal Finance Officer, 1995–2000, Dir, subseq. Man. Dir, Financial Mgt, Reporting and Audit, 1995–2003, HM Treasury; Chm., Nat. Audit Office, 2009–15; Mem., various govt inquiries including: North Sea Oil Costs, 1975; Power Plant Industry, 1976; Post Office Internat. Comparisons, 1981; Accounting for Econ. Costs (Byatt Cttee), 1986; Professional Liability (Chm.), 1989. Member: Finance Cttee, Oxfam, 1974–84; Audit Commn, 1988–91; Financial Reporting Council, 1990–2003 (Observer, 1993–2003); Cttee on Financial Aspects of Corporate Governance (Cadbury Cttee), 1991–95; Council: RIPA, 1982–88; Consumers' Assoc., 1983–85; Chartered Inst. of Management Accountants, 1985–94 (Pres., 1991–92); Civil Service Coll., 1989–94; Scientific Council, Eur. Inst. of Public Admin, 1990–93; Defence Operational Analysis Centre, 1992–93; Bd, Tavistock and Portman NHS Trust, 2000–08. Non-executive Director: Barclays plc, 2004–13; Market & Opinion Res. Internat. Ltd, 2004–05 (Chm., 2005); Beazley plc, 2015–; non-exec. Chm., Applied Intellectual Capital plc, 2006–08. Non-exec. Dir, Economists' Bookshop, 1981–91 (non-exec. Chm., 1987–91). Mem., Steering Cttee, Governance of the UN, 2006. Trustee, Inst. for Govt, 2008–. Freeman, City of London, 2014. Hon. DBA: Southampton Business Sch., 1997; Oxford Brookes, 2006; Hon. DPhil London Metropolitan, 1999. Gold Medal, CIMA, 2002; Financial Mgt Award, 2004; Public Sector non-exec. Dir of the Year, Sunday Times, 2009. *Publications:* The Reports and Accounts of Nationalised Industries, 1979; Cash Limits and External Financing Limits, 1981; (jtly) Public Sector Accounting and Financial Control, 1983, 4th edn 1992; (with P. Vass) Structure and Form of Government Expenditure Reports, 1984; Public Expenditure, 1988; (jtly) Accounting for Brands, 1989; contribs to academic and professional jls. *Recreations:* cycling, ideas, music, architecture, wine. *Address:* London Business School, Sussex Place, Regents Park, NW1 4SA. *T:* (020) 7000 7012. *Club:* Reform.

LILANI, Nusrat, (Pinky), CBE 2015 (OBE 2007); DL; Chief Executive Officer, Spice Magic Ltd, since 2001; *b* Calcutta, 25 March 1954; *d* of Salim and Sherbanoo Nathani; *m* 1977, Mehboob Lilani; two *s*. *Educ:* Loreto House Sch.; Loreto Coll. (BA Hons); Sophia Coll. (Postgrad. Dip. Media); Croydon Coll. (DMS). Chairman: Asian Women of Achievement Awards, 1999–; Women of the Future Awards, 2006–; Global Empowerment Awards, 2008–. Patron: Asian Women's Resource Centre, 2008–; Westminster Educnl Soc., 2008–. DL Gtr London, 2014. *Publications:* Soul Magic, 1998; Spice Magic, 2001; Coriander Makes the Difference, 2009. *Recreations:* walking, cinema, travelling, cooking, talking to people I don't know, eating out. *Address:* Majon, 1A Furze Lane, Purley, Surrey CR8 3EJ. *T:* (020) 8668 8404, *Fax:* (020) 8668 2558. *E:* pinky@spicemagic.com.

LILEY, Ven. Christopher Frank; Archdeacon of Lichfield, and Treasurer and Canon Residentiary of Lichfield Cathedral, 2001–13; *b* 1947. *Educ:* Nottingham Univ. (BEd 1970); Lincoln Theol Coll. Ordained deacon, 1974, priest, 1975; Curate, Holy Trinity, Kingswinford, 1974–79; Team Vicar, Stafford, 1979–84; Vicar, Norton, 1984–96; RD Hitchin, 1989–94; Vicar, St Chad and St Mary, and Priest i/c St Alkmund, Shrewsbury, 1996–2001. Chm., Lichfield Diocesan Bd of Ministry, 2001–03. *Address:* 15 Holloway Drive, Pershore, Worcs WR10 1JL. *E:* lileyc@aol.com.

LILFORD, 8th Baron *cr* 1797; **Mark Vernon Powys;** *b* 16 Nov. 1975; *s* of 7th Baron Lilford and Margaret, *d* of A. Penman; *S* father, 2005. *Heir: kinsman* Robert Charles Lilford Powys [*b* 15 Aug. 1930; *m* 1st, 1957, Charlotte Webb (marr. diss. 1972); 2nd, 1973, Janet Wightwick; (one *s* decd)].

LILFORD, Prof. Richard James, PhD; FRCP, FRCOG, FFPH; Professor of Public Health, University of Warwick, since 2014; Director: Warwick Centre for Applied Health Research and Delivery, since 2014; NIHR Collaborations for Leadership in Applied Health Research and Care West Midlands, since 2014; *b* Cape Town, 22 April 1950; *m* 1982, Victoria Lomax; one *s* two *d*. *Educ:* St John's Coll., Johannesburg; Univ. of Witwatersrand (MB BCh 1973); PhD London 1984. MRCOG 1979, FRCOG 1996; MRCP 1981, FRCP 1998; MFPHM 1995. House officer in Medicine, Johannesburg Gen. Hosp., 1974; house officer in Surgery, Tygerberg Hosp., Cape Town, 1974–75; GP in S African Army, 1975; Groote Schuur Hospital, Cape Town: SHO in Obstetrics and Gynaecol., 1976; Registrar, 1977–78; Lecturer and Senior Registrar: Royal Free Hosp., London, 1979–80; St Bartholomew's Hosp. and Med. Coll., 1980–83; Sen. Lectr and Consultant in Obstetrics and Gynaecol., Queen Charlotte's Hosp. for Women and Inst. of Obstetrics and Gynaecol., 1983–85; University of Leeds: Prof. of Obstetrics and Gynaecol., 1985–95; Chm., Inst. of Epidemiology and Health Services Res., 1991–95; Dir of Res., United Leeds Teaching Hosps NHS Trust, 1993–95; Dir of R&D, W Midlands Regl Office, NHS Exec., DoH, 1996; Prof. of Health Services Res., 1996, Prof. of Clinical Epidemiology, 2001–14, Univ. of Birmingham; Dir, Birmingham Clinical Res. Acad., 2007. Mem., Internat. Editl Adv. Bd, Jl RSocMed, 1974–. Mem., Leeds E HA, 1989–90. Advr, NHS Nat. Clinical Trials, 1996–2003; Director: NHS Methodology Res. Prog.; NHS Patient Safety Res. Prog. Chm. and Mem., numerous cttees incl. DoH adv. cttees and working parties. Royal College of Obstetricians and Gynaecologists: Mem. Council, 1989–92 and 1992–95; Chm., Audit Cttee, 1992–95; Member: Scientific Adv. Cttee, 1992–95; Educn Bd, 1992–94. *Publications:* (with T. Chard) Basic Sciences for Obstetricians and Gynaecologists, 1983, 4th edn 1995; (with M. Setchell) Multiple Choice Questions in Gynaecology and Obstetrics: with answers and explanatory comments, 1985, 2nd edn 1991; Prenatal Diagnosis and Prognosis, 1990; Computing and Decision Support in Obstetrics and Gynaecology, 1990; (with T. Chard) Multiple Choice Questions in Obstetrics and Gynaecology, 1993; (with M. Levine) Fetal and Neonatal Neurology and Neurosurgery, 1994; contrib. chapters in books and numerous articles to medical and professional jls. *Address:* Warwick Medical School, University of Warwick, Coventry CV4 7AL.

LILL, John Richard, CBE 2005 (OBE 1978); concert pianist; Visiting Professor of Piano, Royal College of Music; *b* 17 March 1944; *s* of George and Margery Lill; *m* Jacqueline Clifton Smith. *Educ:* Leyton County High Sch.; Royal College of Music. FRCM; Hon. FTCL; FLCM; Hon. RAM 1988. Gulbenkian Fellowship, 1967. First concert at age of 9; Royal Festival Hall debut, 1963; Promenade Concert debut, 1969. Numerous broadcasts on radio and TV; has appeared as soloist with all leading British orchestras. Recitals and concertos throughout Great Britain, Europe, USA, Canada, Scandinavia, USSR, Japan and Far East, Australia, New Zealand, etc. Overseas tours as soloist with many orchestras including London Symphony Orchestra and London Philharmonic Orchestra. Complete recordings of Beethoven sonatas and concertos, Prokofiev sonatas, Brahms concertos and Rachmaninov piano music; complete Beethoven cycle, London, 1982, 1986, and Tokyo, 1988. Chappell Gold Medal; Pauer Prize; 1st Prize, Royal Over-Seas League Music Competition, 1963; Dinu Lipatti Medal in Harriet Cohen Internat. Awards; 1st Prize, Internat. Tchaikovsky Competition, Moscow, 1970. Hon. DSc Aston, 1978; Hon. DMus Exeter, 1979. *Recreations:* amateur radio, chess, walking. *Address:* c/o Askonas Holt Ltd, Lincoln House, 300 High Holborn, WC1V 7JH. *T:* (020) 7400 1700.

LILLEY, Anthony William, OBE 2008; Chief Creative Officer and Chief Executive Officer, Magic Lantern Productions Ltd, since 1997; Executive Chairman, Myra Media Ltd, since 2015; *b* Bolton, 8 June 1970; *s* of Bernard Charles Lilley and Brenda Lilley; *m* 2000, Ruth Joanne Harris; one *s* one *d*. *Educ:* Bolton Sch. (Boys' Div.); Magdalen Coll., Oxford (BA Juris. 1991). Member: Content Bd, Ofcom, 2006–13; Gambling Commn, 2012–; AHRC, 2013–. Chm., UK Digital Content Forum, 2002; Vice Chm., Producers Alliance for Cinema and TV Ltd, 2006. News International Vis. Prof. of Broadcast Media, Univ. of Oxford, 2007; Vis. Prof., Centre of Excellence in Media Practice, Bournemouth Univ., 2009; Prof. of Creative Industries, Univ. of Ulster, 2013. Trustee, ENO, 2007–13; Chm., Trustees, Lighthouse Arts and Trng, 2009–15. Mem., BAFTA. FRSA 2004. *Recreations:* theatre and opera, singing, reading, gaming, gardening, football, travel, family, learning new things. *Address:* The Long Barn, Lewes Road, Laughton, E Sussex BN8 6BQ. *E:* anthony.lilley@magiclantern.co.uk. *Club:* Hospital.

LILLEY, Prof. David Malcolm James, PhD; FRS 2002; FRSE; FRSC; Professor of Molecular Biology, since 1989, and Director, Cancer Research UK Nucleic Acid Structure Research Group, since 1993, University of Dundee; *b* 28 May 1948; *s* of Gerald Albert Thomas Lilley and Betty Pamela Lilley; *m* 1981, Patricia Mary Biddle; two *d*. *Educ:* Univ. of Durham (BSc 1st Cl. Hons Chemistry 1969; PhD Physical Chemistry 1973); Imperial Coll., London (MSc Biochem. 1973). FRSC 2002. Lectr, 1981–84, Reader, 1984–89, in Biochem., Univ. of Dundee. Mem., EMBO, 1984. FRSE 1988. Colworth Medal, British Biochemical Soc., 1982; Gold Medal of G. J. Mendel, Czech Acad. Scis, Prague, 1994; Prelog Gold Medal in Stereochemistry, ETH, Zürich, 1996; Award in RNA and Ribozyme Chemistry, 2001, Interdisciplinary Award, 2006, RSC. *Publications:* ed. numerous books, incl. DNA-proteins: structural interactions, 1995; (ed with Dr F. Eckstein, and contrib.) Ribozymes and RNA Catalysis, 2007; (with Dr F. Eckstein) Nucleic Acids and Molecular Biology series, 1987–98; contrib. numerous scientific papers. *Recreations:* foreign languages, running, ski-ing. *Address:* MSI/WTB Complex, University of Dundee, Dundee DD1 5EH. *T:* (01382) 384243. *E:* d.m.j.lilley@dundee.ac.uk.

LILLEY, Prof. Geoffrey Michael, OBE 1981; CEng, FRSA, FRAeS, MIMechE, FIMA; Professor of Aeronautics and Astronautics, University of Southampton, 1964–84, now Emeritus Professor; Vice President, INTECH (formerly Hampshire Technology Centre), since 2007 (Founder Member, 1985; Director, 1985–2007); *b* Isleworth, Middx, 16 Nov. 1919; *m* 1948, Leslie Marion Wheeler (*d* 1996); one *s* two *d*. *Educ:* Isleworth Grammar Sch.; Battersea and Northampton Polytechnics; Imperial Coll. BSc(Eng) 1944, MSc(Eng) 1945, DIC 1945. RAF, 1935–36. Gen. engrg trng, Benham and Kodak, 1936–40; Drawing Office and Wind Tunnel Dept, Vickers Armstrong Ltd, Weybridge, 1940–46; Coll. of Aeronautics: Lectr, 1946–51; Sen. Lectr, 1951–55; Dep. Head of Dept of Aerodynamics, 1955, and Prof. of Experimental Fluid Mechanics, 1962–64. Visiting Professor: Stanford Univ., 1977–78; ME Technical Univ., Ankara, Turkey, 1983–90; Univ. of the Witwatersrand, 1990; Visiting Scientist: Inst. of Computer Applications in Sci. and Engrg, NASA Langley Res. Center, 1992–94, 1997–2006 (Chief Scientist, 1998–2000); Center for Turbulence Res., Stanford Univ., 1995–96. Past Member: Aeronautical Res. Council (past Mem. Council and Chm. Aerodynamics, Applied Aerodynamics, Noise Res., Fluid Motion and Performance Cttees); Noise Advisory Council (Chm., Noise from Air Traffic Working Group); Past Chm., Aerodynamics Cttee, Engrg Sci. Data Unit. Consultant to: Rolls Royce, 1959–61, 1967–84; AGARD, 1959–63 and 1988–89; OECD, 1969–71. FAIAA 2009. Hon. DSc Southampton, 2004. Gold Medal for Aeronautics, RAeS, 1983; Aerodynamic Noise Medal, AIAA, 1985. *Publications:* (jt editor) Proc. Stanford Conf. on Complex Turbulent Flows; articles in reports and memoranda of: Aeronautical Research Council; Royal Aeronautical Soc., and other jls. *Recreations:* music, chess, walking. *Address:* Plovers, Station Road, Sway, Lymington, Hants SO41 6AA. *T:* (01590) 681018. *Club:* Athenæum.

LILLEY, Rt Hon. Peter Bruce; PC 1990; MP (C) Hitchin and Harpenden, since 1997 (St Albans, 1983–97); *b* 23 Aug. 1943; *s* of Arnold Francis Lilley and Lilian (*née* Elliott); *m* 1979, Gail Ansell. *Educ:* Dulwich Coll.; Clare Coll., Cambridge. MA; FInstPet 1978. Economic consultant in underdeveloped countries, 1966–72; investment advisor on energy industries, 1972–84. Chm., London Oil Analysts Gp, 1979–80; Partner, 1980–86, Dir, 1986–87, W. Greenwell & Co., later Greenwell Montagu. Consultant Dir, Cons. Res. Dept, 1979–83. Chm., Bow Group, 1972–75. Contested (C) Tottenham, Oct. 1974. PPS to Ministers for Local Govt, Jan.–Oct. 1984, to Chancellor of the Exchequer, 1984–87; Economic Sec. to

HM Treasury, 1987–89, Financial Sec., 1989–90; Secretary of State: for Trade and Industry, 1990–92; for Social Security, 1992–97; front bench Opposition spokesman on HM Treasury, 1997–98. Co-Chair, All Party Parly Gp, Trade Out of Poverty, 2010–; Chair, Jt Cttee of Financial Services Bill, 2011–12; Member: Energy and Climate Change Select Cttee, 2012–15; Envmtl Audit Cttee, 2015–. Dep. Leader, Cons. Party, 1998–99. *Publications:* (with S. Brittan) Delusion of Incomes Policy, 1977; (contrib.) Skidelsky: End of the Keynesian Era, 1980; various pamphlets. *Address:* House of Commons, SW1A 0AA. *T:* (020) 7219 3000. *Clubs:* Carlton, Beefsteak.

LILLEYMAN, Sir John (Stuart), Kt 2002; DSc; FRCP, FRCPE, FRCPath, FRCPCH, FMedSci; Professor of Paediatric Oncology, St Bartholomew's Hospital Medical College, subseq. Bart's and The London School of Medicine and Dentistry, Queen Mary, University of London, 1995–2006, now Emeritus; *b* 9 July 1945; *s* of Ernest Lilleyman and Frances Lilleyman (*née* Johnson); *m* 1st, 1970, Patricia Ann Traylen (marr. diss. 1996); one *s*; 2nd, 1998, Elizabeth Anne Lawrence. *Educ:* Oundle Sch.; St Bartholomew's Hosp. Med. Coll. (MB BS 1968; DSc Med. 1996). FRCP 1983; FRCPath 1984; FRCPCH 1997; FRCPE 2000. Jun. Posts at St Bartholomew's Hosp. and United Sheffield Hosps, 1968–72; Res. Fellow, Welsh Nat. Sch. of Medicine, 1972–74; Consultant Haematologist, Sheffield Children's Hosp., 1975–95; Prof. of Paediatric Haematology, Univ. of Sheffield Med. Sch., 1993–95. Med. Dir, NHS Nat. Patient Safety Agency, 2004–07; Strategic Advr, Nat. Res. Ethics Service, 2007–09; Dir, Appointing Authy for Phase 1 Ethics cttees, 2007–12. Non-exec. Dir, Medicines and Healthcare Products Regulatory Agency, 2009–12. President: UK Assoc. of Clinical Pathologists, 1998–99; RCPath, 1999–2002; RSocMed, 2004–06. Vice Chairman: Acad. of Med. Royal Colls, 2000–02; Jt Consultants Cttee, 2001–02; Mem., Health Professions Council, 2002–04. FMedSci 2007. Hon. Fellow: Inst. Biomed. Sci., 1996; Faculty of Path., RCPI, 2003; RSocMed, 2007. Hon. MD Sheffield, 2003. *Publications:* (Chief Ed.) Pediatric Hematology, 1992, 2nd edn 2000; Childhood Leukaemia: the facts, 1994, 2nd edn 2000; contrib. articles on childhood leukaemia and blood diseases. *Recreations:* theatre, long distance walking. *Address:* 1 Hetton Hall Cottages, Chatton, Alnwick, Northumberland NE66 5SD. *T:* (01289) 388596.

LILLFORD, Prof. Peter John, CBE 1998; PhD; FRSC; consultant, food science and technology, since 2005; *b* 16 Nov. 1944; *s* of John Leslie Lillford and Ethel Ruth Lillford (*née* Wimlett); *m* 1969, Elisabeth Rosemary Avery; two *s*. *Educ:* King's Coll., London (BSc Hons Chemistry; PhD 1968); Cornell Univ. FRSC 2009. Res. Fellow, Cardio Vascular Res. Inst., San Francisco, 1970–71; Res. Scientist, 1971–87, Principal Scientist, 1987–99, Unilever; Chief Scientist (Foods), Unilever Research, 1999–2001; Pres., Inst. of Food Sci. and Technol., 2001–03; Dir, Nat. Centre for Non Food Crops, 2003–09. Chm., Inst. of Food Res. UK, 2007–13. Special Prof. of Biophysics, Nottingham Univ., 1988–2007; Hon. Prof., Stirling Univ., 1989–2000; Visiting Professor: York Univ., 2000–13; Univ. of Birmingham, 2007–. Chairman: Foresight Food and Drink Panel, OST, 1993–97; Agri-Food Cttee, BBSRC, 1997–2000. Fellow, Internat. Acad. of Food Sci. and Tech., 2003; McMaster Fellow, Food Sci. Australia, 2004–05; Flagship Fellow, CSIRO, 2005–08. FRSA 1996. Hon. DEng Birmingham 1999. Sen. Medal, RSC, 1991; Outstanding Achievement Award, Eur. Fedn of Food Sci. and Technol., 2004. *Publications:* Foods Structure and Behaviour, 1987; Feeding and the Texture of Food, 1991; Glassy States in Foods, 1993; (ed) Technology Foresight, Food and Drink, 1995; Food Materials Science, 2008. *Recreations:* old houses, old cars, old whisky. *Address:* The Firs, 20 Pavenham Road, Carlton, Beds MK43 7LS. *T:* (01234) 720869.

LILLIE, Stephen; HM Diplomatic Service; Director, Asia Pacific, Foreign and Commonwealth Office, since 2013; *b* 4 Feb. 1966; *s* of Christopher Stanley Lillie and Maureen Lillie; *m* 1991, Denise Chit Lo; two *s*. *Educ:* S Wolds Comprehensive Sch., Nottingham; Queen's Coll., Oxford (MA Modern Langs 1988); Sch. of Oriental and African Studies, London and Chinese Univ. of Hong Kong (FCO Chinese lang. trng, 1989–91). HM Diplomatic Service: FCO, 1988–90; Hong Kong, 1990–91; Second, later First Sec., Beijing, 1992–95; First Sec., FCO, 1996–98; Dep. Hd, China Hong Kong Dept, FCO, 1998–99; Consul-Gen., Guangzhou, 1999–2003; Counsellor (Econ. and Commercial), New Delhi, 2003–06; Hd, Far Eastern Dept, FCO, 2006–09; Ambassador to the Philippines, and non-resident Ambassador to Micronesia, the Marshall Is and Palau, 2009–13. *Recreations:* reading, travel, walking. *Address:* c/o Foreign and Commonwealth Office, King Charles Street, SW1A 2AH. *E:* stephen.lillie@fco.gov.uk.

LILLYWHITE, Lt-Gen. Louis Patrick, CB 2009; MBE 1985; FRCPGlas, FRCGP; Chief Medical Officer, St John Ambulance, since 2010; Senior Research Consultant, Centre for Global Health Security, Royal Institute of International Affairs (Chatham House), since 2010; *b* 23 Feb. 1948; *s* of Dr William Henry Lillywhite and Annie Kate (*née* Vesey); *m* 1975, Jean Mary Daly, *d* of Bernard Daly and Margaret Mary (*née* Cooke); one *s* two *d*. *Educ:* King Edward VI Grammar Sch., Lichfield; University Coll. Cardiff and Welsh Nat. Sch. of Medicine (MB BCh 1971); London Sch. of Hygiene and Tropical Medicine (MSc Occupational Medicine 1989, top student prize). MFOM 1990; FRCPGlas 2008; FRCGP 2009. Regtl MO, 3rd Bn Parachute Regt, 1973–77; O i/c Technical Div., RAMC Trng Centre, 1977–81; RMCS and Army Staff Coll. (psc), 1982; SO, Med. Policy, Equipment and Intelligence, 1983–85; CO 23 Parachute Field Ambulance, 1985–89; Comdr Med., HQ 1 UK Armoured Div., incl. Gulf War (despatches 1991), 1990–92; Hd of Personnel, AMS, 1992–93; Mem., MoD Defence Cost Studies, 1993–95; DCS Med., HQ Land Comd, 1995–96; Med. Advr, HQ Allied Forces NW Europe, 1998–99; Dir Med. Personnel, Training and Clinical Policy, MoD, 1999–2001; Dir (CE), BF Germany Health Service, 2001–03; Dir Gen., Army Med. Services, 2003–05; Dir Gen., Med. Operational Capability, 2005–06; Surgeon Gen., MoD, 2006–09. QHS 2002–10. Medical Mem., Tribunal Appeal Service, Social Entitlement Chamber (Wales and S West), 2011–; Mem., Bevan Commn, Welsh Govt, 2012–. Comr, Royal Hosp. Chelsea, 2003–05; Gov., Royal Star and Garter Home, 2003–05; Pres., Bratton Br., RBL, 2011–. Patron: TREAT Wales, 2011–; Orders of St John Care Trust, 2014–. Member: BMA; SOM; Fellow, Medical Soc. of London, 1985 (Pres., 2009–10; Trustee, 2012–); FRSocMed 1999. Mem., Catenian Assoc., 1971–. Member: British Army Orienteering Club; British Army Mountaineering Assoc.; Fell Runners Assoc. Hon. FRCGP 2010. Hon. Member: Assoc. of Military Surgeons of the USA, 2009; Assoc. of Med. Consultants to Armed Forces of the United States, 2009. OStJ 2007. Medal for Exceptional Public Service, Office of Secretary of Defense, USA, 2009. *Publications:* (contrib.) Gulf Logistics: Blackadder's War, 1995; occasional contrib. to prof. jls incl. Philos. Trans. Royal Soc. *Recreations:* cross country, long distance running, genealogy, hashing, computers, mountaineering. *Address:* 4 Cassways Orchard, Bratton, Westbury, Wilts BA13 4TY. *E:* louis@lillywhi.demon.co.uk, louis.lillywhite@nhq.sja.org.uk, llillywhite@chathamhouse.org.

LIM, Prof. C. J.; Founder and Director, Studio 8 Architects, since 1994; Director of International Development, since 2005, and Professor of Architecture and Urbanism, since 2007, The Bartlett, Faculty of the Built Environment, University College London (Vice-Dean, International, 2011–13; Pro-Provost, 2008–11); *b* Malaysia, 1964. *Educ:* Architectural Assoc. (DipArch 1987). Assistant Architect: Eva Jiricna Architects, 1987–88; Rock Townsend Architects, 1988–89; Sidell Gibson Architects, 1989–91; Sen. Lectr, Univ. of East London, 1990–93, Univ. of North London, 1991–99; University College London: Dir, Bartlett Architecture Res. Lab., 1997–2007; Pro-Provost for Canada, Mexico and USA, 2008–11. RIBA External Examiner and Visiting Professor: Curtin Univ., Perth, Australia, 1996; Stadelschule, Frankfurt, 1997, 2000; Mackintosh Sch. of Architecture, Glasgow, 2001–11; Lund Univ., Sweden, 2001, 2003, 2005–12; Aarhus Sch. of Architecture, Denmark, 2002, 2009, 2012–; Waseda Univ., Tokyo, 2002; Chiba Inst. of Technol., Japan, 2004; Oslo Sch. of Architecture, 2005; Royal Danish Acad. Fine Arts, Copenhagen, 2006; Univ. of Girona, Spain, 2008; Seoul Nat. Univ., 2012; RMIT, 2012. Principal investigator for res. projects on eco-cities, sustainable urban planning, landscape and architecture; sustainable masterplanning and infrastructure commns from Chinese and Korean Govts. Solo and group international exhibitions: Chicago, LA, NY, York, Copenhagen, Frankfurt, Lisbon, Istanbul, Beijing, Singapore, Brisbane, Melbourne, Sydney, Orleans; V&A Mus.; Royal Acad. Arts; Dulwich Picture Gall.; RIBA; ICE; Future Cities, Barbican Arts Centre; Venice Architecture Biennale; Hong Kong Shenzhen Urbanism Biennale; Mackintosh Mus., Glasgow; Chicago Architecture Foundn; Storefront Gall., NY; Portland Mus., Oregon; Cincinnati Art Mus.; Acad. de France, Rome; Canadian Inst. Architecture, Montreal; Nara World Architecture Triennale, Union of Internat. Architects 2011; Tokyo Convention, Mori Art Mus., Tokyo; World Art Mus., Beijing; State Liby of Qld, Brisbane; Nat. Gall. Mus., Athens; Museo Nazionale, Rome. Represented UK: Venice Architecture Biennale, 2004; New Trend of Architecture in Europe and Asia Pacific, Japan, 2008–10. FRSA. President's Medal (Internat.), Contribution to Educn Awards, RIBA, 1997, 1998, 1999; Best Work, First-time Exhibitor, 2005, Grand Architecture Prize, 2006, RA Summer Exhibn. *Publications:* 441/10… We'll Reconfigure the Space When You're Ready, 1996; Sins and Other Spatial Relatives, 2000; (ed with Ed Liu) Realms of Impossibility: Vol. 1, Air, Vol. 2, Ground, Vol. 3, Water, 2002; (with Ed Liu) How Green is Your Garden?, 2003; (ed with Ed Liu) Devices, 2005; Neo Architecture, 2005; Virtually Venice, 2006; (with Ed Liu) Smartcities and Eco-warriors, 2010; (with Ed Liu) Short Stories: London in two-and-a-half dimensions, 2011; Food City, 2014; contribs to books, jls and newspapers on cities, urban planning and urbanism. *Address:* The Bartlett, UCL Faculty of the Built Environment, 140 Hampstead Road, NW1 2BX. *T:* (020) 3108 9681. *E:* c.j.lim@ucl.ac.uk.

LIM PIN, Professor, MD; FRCP, FRCPE, FRACP, FACP; University Professor and Professor of Medicine, National University of Singapore, since 2000; Senior Consultant, National University Hospital, since 2000; *b* 12 Jan. 1936; *s* of late Lim Lu Yeh and of Choo Siew Kooi; *m* 1964, Shirley Loo; two *s* one *d*. *Educ:* Queens' Coll., Cambridge (Queen's Schol., 1957; MA; MD 1970). FRCP 1976; FRCPE 1981; FRACP 1978; FACP 1981. MO, Min. of Health, Singapore, 1965–66; Univ. of Singapore: Lectr in Medicine, 1966–70; Sen. Lectr in Medicine, 1971–73; Associate Prof. of Medicine, 1974–77; Prof. and Head, Dept of Medicine, 1978–81; Dep. Vice-Chancellor, 1979–81; Vice-Chancellor, Nat. Univ. of Singapore, 1981–2000. Mem., Lee Kuan Yew Sch. of Public Policy, 2011–. Eisenhower Fellow, USA, 1982. Founder Pres., Endocrine and Metabolic Soc. of Singapore. Chairman: Nat. Wages Council, 2001–; Bio-ethics Adv. Cttee, 2001–; Nat. Longevity Insce Cttee, 2007–08; Co-Chm., Singapore-MIT Alliance for Res. and Technol., 2007–. Chm., Mgt Bd, Tropical Marine Sci. Inst., 2001–. Mem. Bd of Dirs, Raffles Medical Gp, 2001–. Chairman: Special Needs Trust Co., 2008–; Singapore Millennium Foundn Ltd, 2008–; Co-Chairman: ETH Singapore SEC Ltd, 2010–; TUM CREATE Centre, 2011–. Mem., Bd of Govs, Chinese Heritage Centre, 1995–. Dep. Chm., Lee Kuan Yew Water Prize Council, 2009–11. Hon. Fellow: Coll. of Gen. Practitioners of Singapore, 1982; Internat. Coll. of Dentists, USA, 1999; (Dental Surgery), RCSE, 1999; Hon. FRACOG 1992; FRCPSGlas 1997; Hon. FRCSE 1997. Hon. DSc Hull, 1999. Public Administration Medal (Gold), Singapore, 1984; Meritorious Service Medal, Singapore, 1990; Friend of Labour Award, NTUC, 1995; Outstanding Service Award, NUS, 2003. DSO (Singapore), 2000; Officier, Ordre des Palmes Académiques (France), 1988. *Publications:* articles in New England Jl of Medicine, Med. Jl of Australia, BMJ, Qly Jl of Medicine, and Tissue Antigens. *Recreation:* swimming. *Address:* Department of Medicine, National University of Singapore, 5 Lower Kent Ridge Road, Singapore 119074, Republic of Singapore. *Club:* Singapore Island Country.

LIMB, Ann Geraldine, CBE 2015 (OBE 2011); DL; Chair: South East Midlands Local Enterprise Partnership, since 2012; Destination Milton Keynes, since 2009; *b* Moss Side, Manchester, 13 Feb. 1953; *d* of Norman Limb and Elsie Geraldine Limb (*née* Bromley); civil partnership 2006, Margaret Ann Cook, PhD. *Educ:* Marple Hall Girls Grammar Sch.; Univ. of Liverpool (BA Hons French 1975; MA 1976). Lecturer: Univ. de Nancy, 1976–77; St John's Coll., Manchester, 1977–78; Abraham Moss Centre, Manchester, 1978–80; Hd of Langs, High Peak Coll., Buxton, 1980–84; Hd of Business Studies and Mgt, NE Derbyshire Coll., 1984–86; Vice Principal, 1986–87, Principal, 1987–96, Milton Keynes Coll.; Principal, Cambridge Regional Coll., 1996–2001; Gp Chief Exec., Univ. for Industry, 2001–04. Vis. Prof. of Mgt, Univ. of W London (formerly Thames Valley Univ.), 2005–. Chair, Milton Keynes Partnership, 2008–11 (Ind. Mem., 2004–08), Mem. Bd, 2011–, Homes and Communities Agency. Non-executive Director: Electricity Consumer's Council, 1989–92; Trng Standards Council, 1997–2001; Addenbrooke's NHS Trust, 1997–2001 (Chm., Audit Cttee; Vice Chm., Clin. Governance Cttee); DRS plc, 2004–11 (Chm., Remuneration and Ethics Cttees); HM Govt Communications Centre, 2008–; Milton Keynes Hosp. NHS Foundn Trust, 2009–12; Member: Bd, Council for Ind. and Higher Educn, 1996–2004; Bd, Further Educn, NTO, 1996–2001; Bd, Adult Learning Inspectorate, 2001–03; Cambs, Learning and Skills Council, 2001–03; Ministerial Task Force on Feminising IT, 2001–03; Prime Minister's Digital Inclusion Panel, 2001–07; Council, C&G, 2014– (Trustee, 2015–); Chair: Knowledge and Inf. Adv. Bd, British Council, 2002–06; Legal Deposit Adv. Cttee, DCMS, 2005–10; Milton Keynes Higher Educn Bd, 2008–; E-ACT, 2012–15; Women in Labour, 2013–; Adv. Bd, Univ. Campus Milton Keynes, Univ. of Bedfordshire, 2014–; Scout Assoc., 2015–. Mem. Bd, Wavendon All Music Plan, Stables Th., Milton Keynes, 2009– (Chm., Milton Keynes Internat. Fest. 2012). Chair, Board of Trustees: Helena Kennedy Foundn, 1998–; Nat. Extension Coll., 1998–2011; Student Volunteering England, 2005–07; Anne Frank Trust UK, 2006–12; Milton Keynes Arts for Health, 2007–13; Chm., Cambridge Fundraising Bd, Maggie's Cancer Care Centres, 1999–2001; Member, Board of Trustees: Milton Keynes Counselling Foundn, 1992–96; Willen Hospice, Milton Keynes, 1994–96; Trustee and Dir, Centre for Excellence in Leadership, 2006–08; Trustee, Volunteering England, 2006–08; Mem. Bd, ENTRUST, 2012–14 (Chair, 2014–). Member, Council: Open Univ., 2002–08; Univ. of Surrey, 2003–06; Gov., Milton Keynes Acad., 2008–11. Non-exec. Dir, Nat. Council, IoD, 2006–12. First Vis. Scholar, Lucy Cavendish Coll. Centre for Women Leaders, 1997–. FRSA 1997. FCGI 2002. Hon. Fellow, Milton Keynes Coll., 2014. DL Bucks, 2011. Hon. PhD Anglia Ruskin, 2003; Hon. DBA: Manchester Metropolitan, 2011; Bedfordshire, 2014. Mary Lou Carrington Award, Educators' Co., 2012. *Publications:* Introducing PET: the Cambridge Preliminary English Test, 1982; Objectifs: assignments in practical language skills, 1985; Managing Colleges in the 21st Century, 1991; Preparing for Incorporation, 1993; Changing Organisational Cultures, 1994; Further Education Under New Labour, 1999; Taking Education Really Seriously, 2001; Leading, Learning, 2005; Women in Leadership, 2009. *Recreations:* theatre, opera, ski-ing, trekking, bird watching, spending time with my niece, nephew and many godchildren, active member of Quakers. *Address:* Trinity House, 3 Willow Lane, Stony Stratford, Bucks MK11 1FG. *T:* (01908) 307171, 07775 817980. *E:* agl@annlimb.co.uk. *W:* www.annlimb.co.uk. *Club:* Athenæum (Mem., Gen. Cttee, 2014–).

LIMB, Patrick Francis; QC 2006; *b* 23 June 1965; *s* of late Anthony Patrick Limb and of Yvonne Thérèse Léoncie Limb; *m* 1st, 1992, Anne Elizabeth Fentem (marr. diss. 2010); one *s* one *d*; 2nd, 2012, Allison Garner; one step *d*. *Educ:* Edinburgh Acad.; Pembroke Coll., Cambridge (Open Exhibnr; BA Hons 1986). Called to the Bar, Middle Temple, 1987; Jun. Counsel to the Crown, Provincial Panel, 2002–06. *Recreations:* running personal bests, walking through Paris, random acts of dancing. *Address:* c/o Ropewalk Chambers, 24 The Ropewalk, Nottingham NG1 5EF. *T:* (0115) 947 2581, *Fax:* (0115) 947 6532. *E:* patricklimbqc@ropewalk.co.uk.

LIMBU; *see* Rambahadur Limbu.

LIMEBEER, Prof. David John Noel, PhD, DSc; FREng, FIEEE; Professor of Control Engineering, University of Oxford, since 2009; Fellow, New College, Oxford, since 2009; *b* Johannesburg, 31 July 1952; *s* of Gerald J. N. Limebeer and Joan C. Limebeer; partner, Dr Suzanne Margaret Watt, FRCPath. *Educ:* Michaelhouse; Witwatersrand Univ. (BSc Engrg 1974); Natal Univ. (MSc Engrg 1976; PhD 1980); Univ. of London (DSc 1992). Res. Associate, Selwyn Coll., Cambridge, 1980–84; Imperial College London: Lectr, 1984–89; Reader, 1989–93; Prof., 1993–2009; Hd, Dept of Electrical and Electronic Engrg, 1999–2009. FIEEE 1992; FREng 1997. *Publications:* Linear Robust Control (with M. Green), 1995. *Recreations:* cinema, walking, reading, antique lamps and furniture, building restoration. *Address:* Department of Engineering Science, University of Oxford, Parks Road, Oxford OX1 3PJ. *T:* 07894 283013. *E:* david.limebeer@eng.ox.ac.uk.

LIMERICK, 7th Earl of, *cr* 1803 (Ire.); **Edmund Christopher Pery;** Baron Glentworth, 1790 (Ire.); Viscount Limerick, 1800 (Ire.); Viscount Pery, 1800 (Ire.); Baron Foxford, 1815; Partner, Altima Partners LLP, 2005–09; *b* 10 Feb. 1963; *s* of 6th Earl of Limerick, KBE, AM and of Sylvia Rosalind Lush (*see* Sylvia, Countess of Limerick); *S* father, 2003; *m* 1st, 1990, Emily Kate (marr. diss. 2000), *o d* of Michael Thomas; two *s*; 2nd, 2002, Lydia Ann (marr. diss. 2010), 4th *d* of Richard Johnson; 3rd, 2012, Kate Mary, *e d* of Peter Inglis Hall; one *s* one *d*. *Educ:* Eton; New Coll., Oxford (MA); Pushkin Inst., Moscow; City Univ. (Dip. Law). Called to the Bar, Middle Temple, 1987. HM Diplomatic Service, 1987–92: FCO, 1987–88; Ecole Nationale d'Administration, Paris, 1988–89; attachment to Ministère des Affaires Etrangères, Paris, 1990; Second Sec., Senegal, 1990–91, Amman, 1991–92; lawyer: with Clifford Chance, 1992–93; with Freshfields, 1993–94; solicitor with Milbank Tweed, 1994–96; Chief Rep., Morgan Grenfell (Deutsche Bank), Moscow, 1996–98; Dir, Deutsche Bank AG London, 1996–2004; Middle East Regl Manager, Man Gp, Dubai, 2004; Sen. Vice-Pres., Dubai Internat. Capital, 2005. Director: Saddleback Ltd, 2007–; GRDC 1 Ltd, 2007–13; Chagala Gp Ltd, 2009–13; Roxi Petroleum plc, 2010–; Prestige Security Mgt Ltd, 2014–; Chairman: ESL (UK) Ltd, 2010–13; Thermotec South East Ltd, 2012–14. *Recreations:* ski-ing, kitesurfing, tennis. *Heir: s* Viscount Pery, *qv*. *Address:* Chiddinglye, West Hoathly, East Grinstead, W Sussex RH19 4QT. *T:* (01342) 810987. *E:* eclimerick@hotmail.com. *Clubs:* Garrick; Sussex.

LIMERICK, Sylvia Countess of; Sylvia Rosalind Pery, CBE 1991; President, St Catherine's Hospice, 2010–15; Vice-President, Foundation for the Study of Infant Deaths, since 2012 (Vice-Chairman, 1971–2012); Hon. Vice-President, British Red Cross Society, since 1999; *b* 7 Dec. 1935; *e d* of Maurice Stanley Lush, CB, CBE, MC; *m* 1961, Viscount Glentworth (later 6th Earl of Limerick, KBE, AM; *d* 2003); two *s* one *d*. *Educ:* St Swithun's, Winchester; Lady Margaret Hall, Oxford (MA). Research Asst, Foreign Office, 1959–62. British Red Cross Society: Nat. HQ Staff, 1962–66; Pres., Kensington and Chelsea Div., 1966–72; a Vice-Pres., London Br., 1972–85; Vice-Chm., Council, 1984–85; Chm., 1985–95 (Chm. Emeritus, 1995–97); a Vice-Pres., Internat. Fedn of Red Cross Red Crescent Socs, 1993–97. Mem., Bd of Governors, St Bartholomew's Hosp., 1970–74; Vice-Chm., CHC, S District of Kensington, Chelsea, Westminster Area, 1974–77; Chairman: Eastman Dental Inst., 1996–99; Eastman Foundn for Oral Res. and Trng, 1996–2002; Member: Kensington, Chelsea and Westminster AHA, 1977–82; St Mary's Med. Sch. Council and District Ethics Cttee, 1977–83; Eastman Dental Hosp. SHA, 1990–96. Non-exec. Dir, UCL Hosps NHS Trust, 1996–97. A Vice-Pres., 1978–84, Pres., 1984–2002, Health Visitors' Assoc., subseq. Community Practitioners' and Health Visitors' Assoc.; President: UK Cttee for UN Children's Fund, 1972–79 (Vice Pres., 1979–99); Nat. Assoc. for Maternal and Child Welfare, 1973–84 (Vice Pres., 1985–90). Member: Cttee of Management, Inst. of Child Health, 1976–96; Council, King Edward's Hospital Fund, 1977–2008 (Mem., Cttee of Management, 1977–81, 1985–89); Maternity Services Adv. Cttee, DHSS, 1981–84; CS Occupational Health Service Adv. Bd, 1989–92; Vice-Chm., Jt Res. Ethics Cttee, Nat. Hosp. for Neurology and Neurosurgery/Inst. of Neurology, 1993–2004; Chm., CMO's Expert Gp to investigate Cot Death Theories, 1994–98. Trustee: Child Accident Prevention Trust, 1979–87; Voluntary Hosp. of St Bartholomew, 1991–2004; Child Health Res. Appeal Trust, 1996–2006. Patron: Childhealth Advocacy Internat., 1998–2009; Lodge Hill Trust, W Sussex, 2006–. Reviewed National Association of Citizens Advice Bureaux, 1983. FRSocMed 1977. Hon. FRCP 1994 (Hon. MRCP 1990); Hon. FRCPCH 1996 (Hon. Mem., BPA, 1986); Hon. Fellow, Inst. of Child Health, London, 1996. Hon. DLitt CNAA, 1990; Hon. LLD Bristol, 1998. Hon. Freeman: Salters' Co., 1992; World Traders' Co., 2003. Humanitarian Award, European Women of Achievement, 1995. Order of Croatian Star, 2003. *Publications:* (jtly) Sudden Infant Death: patterns, puzzles and problems, 1985. *Recreations:* music, mountaineering, ski-ing. *Address:* Chiddinglye, West Hoathly, East Grinstead, W Sussex RH19 4QT. *T:* (01342) 810214.

LIMERICK AND KILLALOE, Bishop of, since 2015; **Rt Rev. Kenneth Arthur Kearon;** *b* 4 Oct. 1953; *s* of Hubert Kenneth Maurice Kearon and Ethel Maria Kearon (*née* Shattock); *m* 1978, Jennifer Poyntz; three *d*. *Educ:* Trinity Coll., Dublin (BA Mod. 1976, MA 1979); Irish Sch. of Ecumenics (MPhil Ecum. 1991); Jesus Coll., Cambridge. Ordained deacon, 1981, priest, 1982; Curate, All Saints Raheny and St John's Coolock, Dublin, 1981–84; pt-time Lectr, 1981–99, Dean of Residence, 1984–91, Trinity Coll., Dublin; Rector, Tullow Parish, Dublin, 1991–99; Dir, Irish Sch. of Ecumenics, Trinity Coll., Dublin, 1999–2004; Sec. Gen., Anglican Communion, 2005–15. Canon, 1996–2015, Chancellor, 2002–04, Christ Church Cathedral, Dublin. Hon. Canon: St Paul's Cathedral, London, 2005; St George's Cathedral, Jerusalem, 2005; Christ Church Cathedral, Canterbury, 2005–15; Christ Church Cathedral, Cape Coast, W Africa, 2013–. Hon. DD General Theological Seminary, NY, 2006. *Publications:* Medical Ethics: an introduction, 1995, 2nd edn 1999; (ed with F. O'Ferrall) Medical Ethics and the Future of Healthcare, 2000; *contributions to:* A Parish Adult Education Handbook, 1987; Ethics and the Christian, 1991; Family: fading embers, kindling flames, 1994; Minorities—the right to be different, 1995; Relationships and Sexuality Education in Primary Schools, 1996; Bioethics Research: policy methods and strategy, 1997; A Time to Build, 1999; A New Dictionary of Christian Spirituality, 2006; The Irish School of Ecumenics (1970–2007), 2008; jls, inc. Search, Medico-Legal Jl of Ireland. *Club:* Blainroe Golf (Wicklow).

LINACRE, Christina Margaret; *see* McComb, C. M.

LINAKER, Lawrence Edward, (Paddy); Deputy Chairman and Chief Executive, M&G Group, 1987–94; *b* 22 July 1934; *s* of late Lawrence Wignall and Rose Linaker; *m* 1963, Elizabeth Susan Elam; one *s*. *Educ:* Malvern College. FCA. Esso Petroleum, 1957–63; joined M&G Group, 1963; Man. Dir, 1972, Chm., 1987–94, M&G Investment Management. Chairman: Fisons, 1994–95; Marling Industries, 1996–97; Fleming Technol. Investment Trust plc, 1997–2001; Director: Fleming Mercantile Investment Trust, 1994–2005; TSB Gp, 1994–95; Lloyds TSB Gp, 1995–2001; Wolverhampton & Dudley Breweries plc, 1996–2002. Chm., Institutional Fund Managers' Assoc., 1992–94; Dir, Securities Inst., 1992–94. Trustee, Lloyds TSB Foundn for Eng. and Wales, 1995–2001; Life Trustee, Carnegie UK Trust, 1995–2005. Chm., YMCA Nat. Coll., 1992–2000; Treas., Childline, 1994–2000; Member: Council, RPMS, 1977–88; Governing Body, SPCK, 1976–95; Council, Malvern College, 1988–2003 (Treas., 1993–2002); Governing Body, Canterbury Christ Church Coll., 1993–98; Court, ICSTM, 1999–2005. *Recreations:* music, wine, gardening. *Clubs:* Athenæum, Brooks's.

LINCOLN, 19th Earl of, *cr* 1572; **Robert Edward Fiennes-Clinton;** *b* 19 June 1972; *s* of Hon. Edward Gordon Fiennes-Clinton and Julia (*née* Howson); *S* grandfather, 2001. *Educ:* Pinjarra High Sch., WA. FZS 2010. *Heir: b* William James Howson (name assumed in 1996 in lieu of William Roy Fiennes-Clinton) [*b* 6 March 1980; *m* 1999, Rebecca Danielle Hazell; one *s*].

LINCOLN, Bishop of, since 2011; **Rt Rev. Christopher Lowson;** *b* 3 Feb. 1953; *s* of George Frederick Lowson, CEng, FIMarE and Isabella Annie Lowson (*née* Spence); *m* 1976, Susan Mary Osborne, RGN, RSCN, MSc; one *s* one *d*. *Educ:* Newcastle Cathedral Sch.; Consett Grammar Sch.; King's Coll. London (AKC 1975); St Augustine's Coll., Canterbury; Pacific Sch. of Religion, Berkeley, Calif (STM 1978); Heythrop Coll., Univ. of London (MTh 1996); Cardiff Law Sch. (LLM 2003). Deacon 1977, priest 1978; Asst Curate, Richmond, Surrey, 1977–82; Priest in charge, 1982–83, Vicar 1983–91, Holy Trinity, Eltham; Chaplain: Avery Hill Coll., 1982–85; Thames Poly., 1985–91; Vicar of Petersfield and Rector of Buriton, Hants, 1991–99; RD of Petersfield, 1995–99; Archdeacon of Portsmouth, 1999; Archdeacon of Portsdown, 1999–2006, Archdeacon Emeritus, 2006–11; Dir, Ministry Div., Archbishops' Council, 2006–11; Priest Vicar, Westminster Abbey, 2006–11. Chm., Portsmouth Diocesan Bd of Ministry, 1999–2006; Bp of Portsmouth's Liaison Officer for Prisons, 1999–2003; Bp of Portsmouth's Advr to Hosp. Chaplaincy, 2003–06. Vis. Lectr, Portsmouth Univ., 1998–2004; Dir, Portsmouth Educn Business Partnership, 2000–03. Foundn Trustee, Gallipoli Meml Lecture Trust, 1985–91. *Recreations:* watching cricket, the theatre. *Address:* Bishop's Office, The Old Palace, Minster Yard, Lincoln LN2 1PU. *Clubs:* Athenæum, MCC, Royal Automobile; Castle Hill (Lincoln).

LINCOLN, Dean of; *see* Buckler, Very Rev. P. J. W.

LINCOLN, Archdeacon of; *no new appointment at time of going to press.*

LINCOLN, Paul Arthur; Chief Operating and Education Officer, USA, EdisonLearning Inc., 2011–13 (Managing Director UK and Senior Vice President International, 2010); *b* 11 April 1946. *Educ:* Clare Coll., Cambridge (BA (Hons) History; PGCE 1969; MA 1971). Various teaching posts in secondary schools in Sussex and Essex, 1969–82; Sen. Dep. Head, William de Ferrers Sch., Essex, 1982–88; Essex County Council Education Department: Sen. Inspector, 1988–89; Principal Inspector, 1989–91; Head of Strategic Planning, 1991–92; Principal Educn Officer, Quality, 1992–93; Dep. County Educn Officer, 1994–95; Dir of Educn, 1995–97; Dir of Learning Services, Essex CC, 1997–2002; Chief Exec., Eastern Leadership Centre, Cambridge, 2003–04; Dir of Educn, EdisonLearning UK and Internat. (formerly Edison Schs UK Ltd), 2003–10. Chm., Collaborative Academies Trust, 2013–15. *Publications:* The Learning School, 1987; Supporting Improving Primary Schools, 1999. *Recreations:* reading, walking, gardening.

LINDAHL, Göran; company director; *b* Umeå, Sweden, 28 April 1945; *s* of Sven Lindahl and Frida (*née* Johansson); *m* 1971, Kristina Gunnarsdotter; one *s* one *d*. *Educ:* Chalmers Univ. of Technology, Gothenburg (MSc Electrical Eng 1971); Univ. of Gothenburg (Astronomy). ASEA Ludvika, Sweden: various positions in Engrg Res., Mktg and Sales, 1971–83; Pres., ASEA Transformers, 1983–85; Pres., ASEA Transmission, 1985–86, Exec. Vice-Pres. and Mem. ASEA Gp Mgt, ASEA AB, 1986–87, Västerås, Sweden; ABB Ltd, Zurich: Exec. Vice-Pres. and Mem. Gp Mgt Cttee, responsible for Power Transmission and Distribution Segment, 1988–93, responsible for Asia, 1993–96; Pres. and CEO, 1996–2001; Mem. Bd, ABB Ltd, 1999–2001. Chm., Alliance for Global Sustainability, 2001–02; Under-Sec.-Gen. of UN and Special Advr on Global Compact to Kofi Annan, UN Sec.-Gen., 2001–02. Member Board: Saab AB, Sweden, 1991–97; Atlas Copco AB, Sweden, 1994–97; Ericsson AB, Sweden, 1999–2002; DuPont, USA, 1999–2004; INGKA Holding BV (IKEA), Holland, 2001–; Sony Corp., Japan, 2001–07 (Mem. Internat. Adv. Bd, 2007–11); Nanomix Inc., USA, 2001–06; Sony Ericsson AB, Sweden, 2003–07; iGate Corp., 2006–; Patni Computer Systems Ltd, India, 2011–12; Vice-Chm. Bd, Anglo American plc, 2001–05; Chairman, Board: Sony Group Europe, UK, 2003–04; LivSafe Gp, Sweden and USA, 2005–; West Coast Locators Inc., USA, 2005–13; IKEA GreenTech AB, Sweden, 2006–; Cuptronic Technology AB, Sweden, 2008–; Avinode Holding AB, Sweden, 2009–14; Evry ASA, Norway, 2015–; Mem. Internat. Adv. Bd, Citigroup USA, 1999–2006; Chm. Internat. Adv. Bd, IIT, USA, 2003–12. Chm., World Childhood Foundn, USA, 2001–02 (Mem. Bd, World Childhood Foundn, Sweden, USA, Germany, 2001–02); Vice Chairman Board: Prince of Wales Business Leaders Forum, 1998–2001; John F. Kennedy Center Corporate Fund, 1999–2001; Mem. Bd, Schwab Foundn for Social Entrepreneurship, Switzerland, 2001–02. Mem. Bd Trustees, Illinois Inst. of Technol., 2006–12. Chm., EU-Hong Kong Business Co-operation Cttee, 1999–2000; Co-Chm., ASEAN-EU Industrialists Round Table, 1998–2000; Member: EU-Russia Industrialists Round Table, 1999–2000; US-EU-Poland Action Commn, 1999–2000; Member: EU-Japan Industrialists Round Table, 1999–2000; European Round Table of Industrialists, 2000–01. Mem. Royal Swedish Acad. of Engrg Scis, 1999. Hon. DSc Eng Chalmers Univ. of Technol., Gothenburg, 1993; Hon. PhD Umeå, 2001. Paul Harris Fellow, Rotary Club Internat., 1997. *Recreations:* astronomy, golf. *Address:* Ginstvägen 14, 23642 Höllviken, Sweden. *E:* nstargl@aol.com.

LINDAHL, Tomas Robert, MD; FRS 1988; Principal Scientist, Cancer Research UK London Research Institute (formerly Imperial Cancer Research Fund), 1981–2010, now Emeritus; *b* 28 Jan. 1938; *s* of Robert and Ethel Lindahl; *m* 1967, Alice Adams (marr. diss. 1979); one *s* one *d*. *Educ:* Karolinska Inst., Stockholm (MD). Research Fellow, Princeton Univ., 1964–67; Helen Hay Whitney Fellow, 1967–69, Asst Prof., 1968–69, Rockefeller Univ.; Asst Prof., 1969–75, Associate Prof., 1975–77, Karolinska Inst.; Prof. of Medical Biochemistry, Univ. of Gothenburg, 1978–81; Imperial Cancer Research Fund: Staff Scientist, 1981–83; Dir, Clare Hall Labs, 1983–2005; Asst Dir of Research, 1985–89; Associate Dir of Research, 1989–91; Dep. Dir, Res., 1991–96; Dir, Res., 1996–98; Dep. Dir, Res., 1998–2005. Croonian Lecture, Royal Soc., 1996. Member: EMBO; Royal Swedish Acad. of Scis; Norwegian Acad. of Sci. and Letters; Academia Europaea. Founder FMedSci 1998. Royal Medal, 2007, Copley Medal, 2010, Royal Soc.; Prix Étranger, INSERM, France, 2008; (jtly) Nobel Prize in Chemistry, 2015. *Publications:* res. papers in biochem. and molecular biol. *Recreations:* piano, wine, modern art. *Address:* c/o Clare Hall Laboratories, South Mimms, Herts EN6 3LD.

LINDBLOM, Rt Hon. Sir Keith John, Kt 2010; PC 2015; **Rt Hon. Lord Justice Lindblom;** a Lord Justice of Appeal, since 2015; *b* 20 Sept. 1956; *s* of John Eric Lindblom and June Elizabeth Lindblom (*née* Balloch); *m* 1991, Fiona Margaret Jackson; one *s* three *d*. *Educ:* Whitgift Sch.; St John's Coll., Oxford (MA). Called to the Bar: Gray's Inn, 1980, Bencher, 2003; NI, 2002; admitted to: Hong Kong Bar, 2000 and 2008; Bar of Turks and Caicos Is, 2006; in practice as barrister, 1981–2010; QC 1996; Recorder, 2001–10; Deputy High Court Judge, 2009–10; a Judge of the High Court of Justice, QBD, 2010–15; Pres., Upper Tribunal (Lands Chamber), 2013–15; Planning Liaison Judge, 2014–15. An Asst Parly Boundary Comr, 2000. *Recreations:* music, reading, walking. *Address:* Royal Courts of Justice, Strand, WC2A 2LL. *Club:* Caledonian.

LINDEN, Anya, (Lady Sainsbury of Preston Candover), CBE 2003; Ballerina, Royal Ballet, 1958–65, retired; *b* 3 Jan. 1933; English; *d* of George Charles and Ada Dorothea Eltenton; *m* 1963, John Davan Sainsbury (*see* Baron Sainsbury of Preston Candover); two *s* one *d.* *Educ:* Berkeley, Calif; Sadler's Wells Sch., 1947. Entered Royal Ballet (formerly Sadler's Wells) Co. at Covent Garden, 1951; promoted Soloist, 1952; Ballerina, 1958. Principal rôles in the ballets: Coppelia; Sylvia; Prince of Pagodas; Sleeping Beauty; Swan Lake; Giselle; Cinderella; Agon; Solitaire; Noctambules; Fête Etrange; Symphonic Variations; Hamlet; The Invitation; Firebird; Lady and the Fool; Antigone; Ondine; Seven Deadly Sins. Ballet coach: Royal Ballet Sch., 1989–; Rambert Sch., 1989–. Member: Nat. Council for One-Parent Families, 1978–90 (Hon. Vice-Pres., 1985–90; Mem. Appeal Cttee, 1966–87); Adv. Council, British Theatre Museum, 1975–83; Drama and Dance Adv. Cttee, British Council, 1981–83; Theatre Museum Assoc., 1984–86. Dep.-Chm. and Dir, Rambert Dance Co. (formerly Ballet Rambert), 1975–89. Trustee: Royal Opera Hse, 2003–07; Rambert Sch. of Ballet and Contemp. Dance, 2003– (Mem. Adv. Cttee, 1985–2003). Gov., Royal Ballet Sch., 1977–2004; Dep. Chm. and Mem. Council of Management, Benesh Inst. of Choreology (formerly Benesh Inst. of Movement Notation), 1986–97. Founder and Chm., Linbury Prize for Stage Design, 1987–2010. Dir, Anvil Trust, 1992–98; Trustee, Galitzine Library—St Petersburg, 1993–2004. Patron: Landlife, 1993–; Heatherley Sch. of Fine Art, 2007–. FRWCMD 2008. DUniv Brunel, 1995. *Recreations:* gardening, painting, photography.

LINDEN, Ian, CMG 2000; PhD; Associate Professor, Department for the Study of Religion, School of Oriental and African Studies, University of London, since 2002; Executive Director, Catholic Institute for International Relations, 1986–2001; *b* 18 Aug. 1941; *s* of Henry Thomas William Linden and Edna Jessie Linden; *m* 1963, Jane Winder; two *s* two *d.* *Educ:* Southend High Sch. for Boys; St Catharine's Coll., Cambridge (MA 1966); PhD London Univ. (Middx Hosp. Med. Sch., 1966, SOAS 1975). Asst Lectr in Zoology, Nat. Univ. of Ireland, 1965–66; Res. Associate, Rockefeller Univ., NY, 1966–68; Lectr in Biology, Univ. of Malaŵi, 1968–71; Lectr, subseq. Sen. Lectr, in History, Ahmadu Bello Univ., 1973–76; Researcher, Arbeitskreis Entwicklung und Frieden, 1977–79; Prof. of African History, Univ. of Hamburg, 1979–80; Southern Africa Desk Officer and Co-ordinator of Policy Dept, Catholic Inst. for Internat. Relns, 1980–86. Hon. PhD Southampton, 1998. *Publications:* Catholics, Peasants and Chewa Resistance in Nyasaland, 1974; Church and Revolution in Rwanda, 1977; The Catholic Church and the Struggle for Zimbabwe, 1980; (jtly) Islam in Modern Nigeria, 1984; Christianisme et pouvoirs au Rwanda 1900–1990, 1999; A New Map of the World, 2004; Global Catholicism, 2009. *Recreations:* swimming, theology, walking. *Address:* 31 Royal Close, Manor Road, N16 5SE.
See also T. D. Linden.

LINDEN, Prof. Paul Frederick, PhD; FRS 2007; G. I. Taylor Professor of Fluid Mechanics, Department of Applied Mathematics and Theoretical Physics, 2010–14, now Emeritus, and Director of Research, since 2014, University of Cambridge; Fellow, Downing College, Cambridge, 2010–14, now Emeritus; *b* 29 Jan. 1947; *s* of Frederick Henry Victor Linden and Muriel Constance Linden; *m* 1979, Diana Readman; two *d.* *Educ:* Univ. of Adelaide (BSc Hons 1967); Flinders Univ. of South Australia (MSc 1968); Emmanuel Coll., Cambridge (PhD 1972). University of Cambridge: Asst Dir of Res., 1976–91; Reader in Geophysical Fluid Dynamics, 1991–98; Dir, Fluid Dynamics Lab., 1976–98; Fellow, Downing Coll., 1977–98; University of California, San Diego: Blasker Distinguished Prof. of Envmtl Sci. and Engrg, 1998–2010, now Emeritus; Chm., Dept of Mechanical and Aerospace Engrg, 2004–10; Director: Envmt and Sustainability Initiative, 2007–08; Sustainability Solutions Inst., 2009–10. Dep. Ed., Jl Fluid Mechanics, 2010– (Associate Ed., 2005–10); Editor: JFM Rapids, 2013–15; JFM Perspectives, 2015–. *Publications:* over 130 articles in refereed jls. *Recreations:* running, swimming, clarinet. *Address:* Department of Applied Mathematics and Theoretical Physics, Centre for Mathematical Sciences, Wilberforce Road, Cambridge CB3 0WA. *E:* p.f.linden@damtp.cam.ac.uk.

LINDEN, Thomas Dominic; QC 2006; a Recorder, since 2005; *b* London, 26 Nov. 1964; *s* of Ian Linden, *qv*; *m* 1991, Brigit Connolly; four *d.* *Educ:* Beechen Cliff Comp. Sch., Bath; St Brendan's Sixth Form Coll., Bristol; Keble Coll., Oxford (BA Juris. 1st Cl. 1987; BCL 1988). Called to the Bar, Gray's Inn, 1989. *Recreations:* cycling, playing with our children. *Address:* Matrix Chambers, Griffin House, Gray's Inn, WC1R 5LN. *T:* (020) 7404 3447. *E:* tomlinden@matrixlaw.co.uk.

LINDESAY-BETHUNE, family name of **Earl of Lindsay**.

LINDISFARNE, Archdeacon of; *see* Robinson, Ven. P. J. A.

LINDLEY, Bryan Charles, CBE 1982; Chairman and Chief Executive, Lord Lindley Associates, since 1990; Director, J & B Imaging, since 1998; *b* 30 Aug. 1932; *m* 1987; one *s* by former *m.* *Educ:* Reading Sch.; University Coll. London (Fellow 1979). BSc (Eng) 1954; PhD 1960. FIMechE 1968; FIET (FIEE 1968); FInstP 1968; FInstD 1968; FPRI 1984. National Gas Turbine Establishment, Pyestock, 1954–57; Hawker Siddeley Nuclear Power Co. Ltd, 1957–59; C. A. Parsons & Co. Ltd, Nuclear Research Centre, Newcastle upon Tyne, 1959–61; International Research and Development Co. Ltd, Newcastle upon Tyne, 1962–65; Man., R&D Div., C. A. Parsons & Co. Ltd, Newcastle upon Tyne, 1965–68; Electrical Research Assoc.: Dir, 1968–73; Chief Exec. and Man. Dir, ERA Technology Ltd, 1973–79; Dir, ERA Patents Ltd, 1968–79; Chm., ERA Autotrack Systems Ltd, 1971–79. Director: Dunlop Ltd, 1982–85; Soil-Less Cultivation Systems, 1980–85; Chm. and Dir, Thermal Conversions (UK), 1982–85; Dir of Technology, Dunlop Holdings plc, 1979–85; Director: BICC Cables Ltd, 1985–88; BICC Research and Engineering Ltd, 1985–88; Thomas Bolton & Johnson Ltd, 1986–88; Settle-Carlisle Railway Develt Co., 1992–94; Chairman: Optical Fibres, 1985–87; Linktronic Systems Ltd, 1990–92; Wetheriggs Pottery Ltd, 1992–94; SKAND Systems Ltd, 1995–97; Chief Exec., Nat. Advanced Robotics Res. Centre, 1989–90. Chm., N Lakeland Healthcare NHS Trust, 1993–97. Vis. Prof., Univ. of Liverpool, 1989–. Chairman: Materials, Chemicals and Vehicles Requirements Bd, DTI, 1982–85; RAPRA Council, 1984–85; Dir, RAPRA Technology Ltd, 1985–97; Member: Nat. Electronics Council, 1969–79; Res. and Technol. Cttee, CBI, 1974–80; Design Council, 1980–86 (Mem., Design Adv. Cttee, 1980–86); Cttee of Inquiry into Engineering Profession, 1977–80; Adv. Council for Applied Research and Develt, 1980–86; Adv. Cttee for Safety of Nuclear Installations, 1987–90; Chm., Sci. Educn and Management Div., IEE, 1974–75; Dep. Chm., Watt Cttee on Energy Ltd, 1976–80. Mem., SAE, 1984. *Publications:* NOMAD: a life story (autobiog.), 2012; articles on direct generation of electricity, plasma physics, electrical and mechanical engineering, technological innovation, etc, in learned jls. *Recreations:* music, photography, ski-ing, fell-walking, sailing, cycling. *Address:* Lindenthwaite, Beacon Edge, Penrith, Cumbria CA11 8BN.

LINDLEY, Jonathan Mark; Transformation Director, Department for Work and Pensions, since 2011; *b* Huddersfield, 9 July 1962; *s* of late Rev. Harold Lindley and of Betty Lindley; *m* 1987; three *d.* *Educ:* Repton Sch. Civil Servant with DWP, 1981–2003, Legal Services Commn, 2003–07; Strategic Dir, Enforcement, Border and Immigration Agency, 2007–08; Regl Dir, Govt Office for the E Midlands, 2008–09; Integration Dir, Change Prog., DWP, 2009–11. *Recreations:* cycling, ski-ing, walking, reading.

LINDLEY, Simon Geoffrey; Master of the Music, Leeds Minster (formerly Leeds Parish Church), since 1975; Leeds City Organist, since 1976; General Secretary, Guild of Church Musicians, since 2013; *b* 10 Oct. 1948; *s* of Rev. Geoffrey Lindley and Jeanne Lindley (*née* Cammaerts); *m*; three *s* one *d.* *Educ:* Magdalen Coll. Sch., Oxford; Royal Coll. of Music. FRCO(CHM), FTCL, GRSM (Lond), ARCM, LRAM. Studies with Richard Silk, David Carver, Dr Bernard Rose, Vincent Packford, Dr Philip Wilkinson and, principally, Dr John Birch. Dir of Music, St Anne & St Agnes and St Olave, London, 1968–70; Asst Master of Music, St Alban's Abbey, 1970–75; Dir of Music, St Alban's Sch., 1971–75; Sen. Lectr, Leeds Poly., 1976–88. Sen. Asst Music Officer, Leeds City Council, 1988–2011. Chorus Master: Leeds Phil. Soc., 1975–83 (Vice-Pres., 2005–); Halifax Choral Soc., 1975–87 (Vice-Pres., 1988–); Conductor: St Peter's Singers and Chamber Orch., 1977–; Univ. of Huddersfield Chamber Choir, 1997–98; Leeds Coll. of Music Choral Soc., 1999–; Chief Guest Conductor, Yorkshire Evening Post Band, 1998– (Resident Conductor, 1995–98); Music Dir, Overgate Hospice Choir, Halifax, 1997–; Conductor: Sheffield Bach Soc., 2009–; Doncaster Choral Soc., 2010–. Grand Organist, Utd Grand Lodge of England, 2010–12; Provincial Grand Organist, Masonic Province of Yorks West Riding, 2010–. Special Comr, RSCM, 1975–; Centre Chm., ISM, 1976–82; Mem. Council, RCO, 1977–98, 2012– (Pres., 2000–02; Vice-Pres., 2003); Sec., Church Music Soc., 1991–; Pres., IAO, 2003–05. Dir, English Hymnal Co. Ltd, 1996. Advr, Yorks TV Religious and Educnl Progs, 1981; Artistic Advr, Leeds Summer Heritage Festivals, biennially, 1989–97. Hon. Life Patron, Doncaster Choral Soc., 2006. Pres., Campaign for the Traditional Cathedral Choir, 2008–. Chm., Friends of Musicians' Chapel, St Sepulchre-without-Newgate, 2004–; Trustee: Sir George Thalben-Ball Meml Trust, 1989–; Ecclesiastical Music Trust, 1998– (Chm., 2004–); Pilling Trust, 1999–. Governor: Whinmoor St Paul C of E Primary Sch., 2003–10 (Vice Chm., 2005–10); Yorkshire Coll. of Music and Drama, 2005– (Chm., 2006–). Churchwarden, St Sepulchre-without-Newgate, 2006–. Liveryman, Co. of Musicians, 2006. Concert Organist début, Westminster Cathedral, 1969; tours of USA, France, Germany, Far East, Russia. Numerous recordings as organist and as conductor. FRSCM 2002. Hon. FGMS 1996; Hon. FGCM 2000; Hon. Fellow, Leeds Coll. of Music, 2000. DUniv: Leeds Metropolitan, 2001; Huddersfield, 2012. Spirit of Leeds Award, Leeds Civic Trust, 2006. *Compositions:* Anthems for Unison and 2 part singing, vol. 2, 1979; Ave Maria, 1980, 2003; Matthew, Mark, Luke and John, 1986; Lord, I Have Loved the Habitation of Thy House, 2002; Confitemini Domino, 2011; Confortare, 2012; *carols:* Come, sing and dance, 1977; How far is it to Bethlehem?, Jacob's Ladder, Now the Green Blade riseth, On Easter Morn, 1995; The Bellman's Song, Here is joy for every age, 2004. *Publications:* (ed jtly) New English Praise, 2006; contribs to Musical Times, Choir and Organ, Organists' Review, The Dalesman, The Organ. *Recreations:* churches, cathedrals, Victorian architecture, food. *Address:* 17 Fulneck, Pudsey LS28 8NT. *T:* and *Fax:* (0113) 255 6143. *E:* simon@simonlindley.org.uk; Leeds Minster and Parish Church of St Peter, Kirkgate, Leeds LS2 7DJ. *T:* and *Fax:* (0113) 245 4012. *E:* choir@leedsminster.com. *Clubs:* Leeds (Leeds) (Hon. Mem., 2004), Leeds Rotary (Hon. Mem. 2009).

LINDO, Samuel; Winemaker, Camel Valley, since 2002; *b* 12 Sept. 1976; *s* of Robert and Anne Lindo; *m* 2009, Kathryn Richards; one *d.* *Educ:* Univ. of Bath (BSc Mathematical Scis). Lectr in Maths, Ngee Ann Poly., Singapore. Chm., UK Vineyard Assoc., 2015–. UK Winemaker of Year, UK Vineyards Assoc., 2007, 2010, 2011. *Recreations:* cycling, swimming. *E:* info@camelvalley.com.

LINDOP, Prof. Patricia Joyce, (Mrs G. P. R. Esdale); Professor of Radiation Biology, University of London, 1970–84, now Emeritus; Chairman, Thames Liquid Fuels (Holdings) Ltd, since 1992; *b* 21 June 1930; 2nd *c* of Elliot D. Lindop and Dorothy Jones; *m* 1957, Gerald Paton Rivett Esdale (*d* 1992); one *s* one *d.* *Educ:* Malvern Girls' Coll.; St Bartholomew's Hospital Med. Coll.; BSc (1st cl. Hons), MB, BS, PhD; DSc London 1974; MRCP 1956; FRCP 1977. Registered GP, 1954. Research and teaching in physiology and medical radiobiology at Med. Coll. of St Bartholomew's Hosp., 1955–84. UK Mem., Council of Pugwash Confs on Science and World Affairs, 1982–87 (Asst Sec. Gen., 1961–71); Mem., Royal Commn on Environmental Pollution, 1974–79; Chm. and Trustee, Soc. for Education in the Applications of Science, 1968–91; Member: Cttee 10 of ICRU, 1972–79; ESRO-NASA, 1970–74; Soc. for Radiol Protection, 1987–. Member Council: Science and Society, 1975–90; Soc. for Protection of Science and Learning, 1974–86; formerly Mem. Council, British Inst. of Radiology; Chairman: Univ. of London Bd of Studies in Radiation Biology, 1979–81; Interdisciplinary Special Cttee for the Environment, 1979–81. Governor, St Bartholomew's Hosp. Med. Coll., 1984–. Hon. Member: RCR, 1972; ARR, 1984. Ciba Award, 1957; Leverhulme Res. Award, 1984. *Publications:* in field of radiation effects. *Address:* 58 Wildwood Road, NW11 6UP. *T:* (020) 8455 5860. *Club:* Royal Society of Medicine.

LINDSAY, family name of **Earl of Crawford** and **Baron Lindsay of Birker**.

LINDSAY, 16th Earl of, *cr* 1633 (Scot.); **James Randolph Lindesay-Bethune;** DL; Lord Lindsay of The Byres, 1445; Lord Parbroath, 1633; Viscount of Garnock, Lord Kilburnie, Kingsburn and Drumry, 1703; *b* 19 Nov. 1955; *s* of 15th Earl of Lindsay and of Hon. Mary Clare Douglas-Scott-Montagu, *y d* of 2nd Baron Montagu of Beaulieu; *S* father, 1989; *m* 1982, Diana, *er d* of Major Nigel Chamberlayne-Macdonald, Cranbury Park, Winchester; two *s* three *d* (of whom one *s* one *d* are twins). *Educ:* Eton; Univ. of Edinburgh (MA Hons); Univ. of Calif, Davis. A Lord in Waiting (Govt Whip), 1995; Parly Under-Sec. of State, Scottish Office, 1995–97; elected Mem., H of L, 1999. Chairman: Assured British Meat, 1997–2001; Aquaculture Scotland, 1998–2000; Scottish Quality Salmon, 1998–2006; Genesis Quality Assurance Ltd, 2001–02; UK Accreditation Service, 2002–; SRUC (formerly Scottish Agricultural College Ltd), 2007– (Dir, 2005–; Vice-Chm., 2006–07); British Polythene Pension Scheme, 2009–; Greenfield Hldgs, 2009–11; Director: UA Group plc (formerly United Auctions (Scotland) Ltd), 1998–2005; Scottish Resources Gp (formerly Mining (Scotland) Ltd), 2001–13; British Polythene Industries plc, 2006–; Bd Mem., Cairngorms Partnership, 1998–2003. Member: UK Round Table on Sustainable Develt, 1998–2000; Better Regulation Commn, 2006–07 (Vice Chm., 2007); Commn on Scottish Devolution, 2008–09; Risk and Regulation Adv. Council, 2008–10; Better Regulation Strategy Gp, 2013–; Vice Pres., Trading Standards Inst., 2011–. Advr, IndigoVision Ltd, 2006–07. Dir, Leven Valley Develt Trust, 2009–. Trustee, Gardens for the Disabled Trust, 1984–98. Chairman: Landscape Foundn, 1991–95; Moorland Forum, 2007–; President: Internat. Tree Foundn, 1995–2005 (Vice-Pres., 1994–95, 2005–); RHASS, 2005–06; RSGS, 2005–12 (Vice-Pres., 2004–05, 2012–); Nat. Trust for Scotland, 2012–. Mem., Adv. Council, World Resource Foundn, 1994–98. Chm., RSPB Scotland, 1998–2003 (Mem., UK Council, 1998–2003); Vice-Pres., RSPB, 2004–. Chm., Elmwood Coll., 2001–09. Vice-Pres., Royal Smithfield Club, 1999–. ARAgS 2000. DL Fife, 2007. *Publications:* (jtly) Garden Ornament, 1989; Trellis, 1991. *Heir: s* Viscount Garnock, *qv*. *Address:* Lahill, Upper Largo, Fife KY8 6JE.
See also Sir G. R. B. Wrey, Bt.

LINDSAY, Master of; Alexander Thomas Lindsay; *b* 5 Aug. 1991; *s* and *heir* of Lord Balniel, *qv*.

LINDSAY OF BIRKER, 3rd Baron *cr* 1945, of Low Ground, Co. Cumberland; **James Francis Lindsay;** Co-founder and Chief Technical Officer, Sun Fire Cooking, since 2003; *b* 29 Jan. 1945; *s* of 2nd Baron Lindsay of Birker and Li Hsiao-li, *d* of Col Li Wen-chi; *S* father, 1994; *m* 1st, 1969, Mary Rose (marr. diss. 1985), *d* of W. G. Thomas, Cwmbran, Mon; no *c*; 2nd, 2000, Pamela Collett, *d* of late Lon Hutchison, Kansas City, Mo. *Educ:* Univ. of Keele (BSc 1966); Univ. of Liverpool (Post-grad. Dip. in transport design). Lectr in physics, Tunghai Univ., Taichung, Taiwan, 1967–68; exploration geophysicist, Darwin, Australia, 1969–70; Australian Foreign Service, 1972–2000; served in Chile, 1973–76; Laos, 1980–81; Bangladesh, 1982–84; Venezuela, 1987–90; Deputy High Commissioner: Pakistan, 1993–96; Kenya, 1996–2000; Dep. Perm. Rep. for Australia to UN Envmt Prog., 1996–2000. Consultant: Horn Relief (formerly Horn of Africa Relief and Develt), 2000–; Uganda Rural Develt and Trng, 2002–03. *Recreation:* hiking. *Heir: cousin* Alexander Sebastian Lindsay, *b* 27 May 1940. *Address:* 21 Carnegie Crescent, Narrabundah, Canberra, ACT 2604, Australia. *E:* mukindu@yahoo.com.

LINDSAY, His Honour Crawford Callum Douglas; QC 1987; a Circuit Judge, 1998–2008; *b* 5 Feb. 1939; *s* of Douglas Marshall Lindsay, FRCOG and Eileen Mary Lindsay; *m* 1963, Rosemary Gough; one *s* one *d*. *Educ:* Whitgift Sch., Croydon; St John's Coll., Oxford. Called to the Bar, Lincoln's Inn, 1961, Bencher, 1994. A Recorder, 1982–98. Mem., Criminal Injuries Compensation Bd, 1988. *Clubs:* Garrick, MCC.

LINDSAY, David Christopher; Lord-Lieutenant of Co. Down, since 2009; *b* Belfast, 25 Sept. 1946; *s* of Christopher and Lesley Lindsay; *m* 1970, Judy Sinclair; one *s* three *d*. *Educ:* Ludgrove Sch., Wokingham; Eton; Royal Military Acad., Sandhurst. Served Inniskilling Dragoon Guards (Lieut), 1967–69. With Lindsay Cars Ltd, 1969–2008, Man. Dir, 1972–2008; IT Consultant (pt-time), 2008–11. Chm., UK Ford Dealers, 2007–08. *Recreations:* sailing, ski-ing, vintage tractors, bee-keeping. *Address:* Clerk to the Lieutenancy, Crawford & Lockhart, 7/11 Linenhall Street, Belfast BT2 8AH. *Club:* Strangford Lough Yacht.

LINDSAY, Iain Ferrier, OBE 2002; HM Diplomatic Service; Ambassador to Hungary, from Jan. 2016; *b* Falkirk, 9 March 1959; *s* of James and Margaret Lindsay; *m* 1983, Bridget O'Riordan; one *s*. *Educ:* John Lyon Sch.; Edinburgh Acad.; Glasgow Univ. Entered FCO, 1980; Japanese lang. trng, SOAS, 1981–82; Warsaw, 1982–83; Doha, 1983; Asst Mgt Officer, Tokyo, 1983–86; Third, later Second Sec. (Political), Canberra, 1986–89; Australia Desk Officer, FCO, 1989–91; Hd, Baltic Unit, FCO, 1991–94; First Sec. (Political), Tokyo, 1994–99; Dep. Hd, S Asian Dept, FCO, 1999–2002; Romanian lang. trng, 2003; Advr to Romanian Foreign Minister, 2003; Dep. Hd and Political Counsellor, Bucharest, 2003–07; Dep. Hd and Dir, Trade and Investment, Hong Kong, 2007–11; Ambassador to Bahrain, 2011–15. *Recreations:* cinema, history, travel, cricket, golf, ski-ing, scuba diving, watching Rugby and football (Stenhousemuir FC). *Address:* c/o Foreign and Commonwealth Office, King Charles Street, SW1A 2AH.

LINDSAY of Dowhill, Sir James Martin Evelyn, 3rd Bt *cr* 1962, of Dowhill, co. Kinross; 24th Representer of Baronial House of Dowhill; *b* 11 Oct. 1968; *s* of Sir Ronald Alexander Lindsay of Dowhill, 2nd Bt and of Nicoletta Lindsay; *S* father, 2004; *m* 2000, Annabel Julia, *yr d* of Dr Peter Knight; one *s* one *d*. *Educ:* Shiplake Coll.; RMA Sandhurst; UMIST (BSc). Lieut, Grenadier Guards, 1988–93. Cheshire Yeomanry, 1994– (Major). *Heir: s* Archibald Ronald Frederick Lindsay, *b* 26 Oct. 2004.

LINDSAY, Hon. Sir John (Edmund Fredric), Kt 1992; a Judge of the High Court of Justice, Chancery Division, 1992–2008; *b* 16 Oct. 1935; *s* of late George Fredric Lindsay and Constance Mary Lindsay (*née* Wright); *m* 1967, Patricia Anne Bolton; three *d*. *Educ:* Ellesmere Coll.; Sidney Sussex Coll., Cambridge (BA 1959; MA). Fleet Air Arm, 1954–56; Sub-Lt, RNVR. Called to the Bar, Middle Temple, 1961, Bencher, 1987; joined Lincoln's Inn (*ad eundem*); Junior Treasury Counsel, *bona vacantia*, 1979–81; QC 1981; a Judge of the Employment Appeals Tribunal, 1996–99; Pres., Employment Appeal Tribunal, 1999–2002; a Judge of the Administrative Court, 2002–08. Member: Senate of Inns of Court and Bar, 1979–82; Legal Panel, Insolvency Law Review Cttee (Cork Report), 1980–82; Insolvency Rules Adv. Cttee, 1985–92. *Recreations:* works of A. A. Scott, L. van Beethoven, H. R. Godfrey and Henry Royce, as he then was. *Club:* Athenæum.

LINDSAY, Mark Stanley Hunter; QC (Scot.) 2011; *b* Irvine, Ayrshire, 17 May 1969; *s* of Martin and Sandra Lindsay; *m* 1993, Rosemary; two *s* one *d*. *Educ:* Carrick Acad., Maybole, Ayrshire; Univ. of Glasgow (LLB Hons; DipLP). Trainee solicitor, Tods Murray, 1991–93; Solicitor, Scottish Office, 1993–95; admitted to Faculty of Advocates, 1996. *Recreations:* squash, ski-ing, golf, Lotus sports cars. *Address:* Advocates Library, Parliament House, Parliament Square, Edinburgh EH1 1RF. *T:* (0131) 226 5071. *E:* mark.lindsay@axiomadvocates.com.

LINDSAY, Most Rev. and Hon. Orland Ugham, OJ 1997; OD (Antigua) 1996; Archbishop of the West Indies, 1986–98; Bishop of the North-Eastern Caribbean and Aruba (formerly Antigua), 1970–98; *b* 24 March 1928; *s* of Hubert and Ida Lindsay; *m* 1959, Olga Daphne (*née* Wright); three *s*. *Educ:* Culham Coll., Oxon (Teachers' Cert.); St Peter's Coll., Jamaica; McGill Univ. BD (London) 1957. RAF, 1944–47. Teacher, Franklyn Town Govt School, Jamaica, 1949–52; Asst Master, Kingston College, 1952–53. Deacon 1956, priest 1957; Asst Curate, St Peter's Vere, Jamaica, 1956–57; Asst Master, Kingston Coll., 1958–67, Chaplain 1962–63; Priest-in-Charge, Manchioneal Cure, Jamaica, 1960; Chaplain, Jamaica Defence Force, 1963–67; Principal, Church Teachers' Coll., Mandeville, 1967–70. Sec. to Jamaica Synod, 1962–70. Hon. DD: Berkeley Divinity School at Yale, 1978; St Paul's Coll., Va, 1998; Hon. STD, Montreal Diocesan Theol Coll., 1997. *Recreations:* jazz music, photography. *Address:* Flagstaff, Crosbies, PO Box 3456, St John's, Antigua.

LINDSAY, Robert; *see* Stevenson, R. L.

LINDSAY, Shuna Taylor, (Mrs D. R. Waggott), CBE 2001; Deputy Director, Strategy and Projects, Defence Academy College of Management and Technology, Ministry of Defence, 2008–09; *b* 24 Nov. 1954; *d* of late John Lindsay and Jessie Simpson Lindsay (*née* Taylor); *m* 1979, David Reginald Waggott. *Educ:* Greenock Acad.; Univ. of Geneva (Cert. d'Etudes Françaises 1975); Univ. of Aberdeen (MA Hons French Studies 1977). Entered MoD as admin trainee, 1977; policy appts, 1977–81; Private Sec. to Air Mem. for Supply and Orgn, 1981–82; First Sec., Defence Procurement, Paris, 1989–93; Project Dir, Mil. Aircraft Projects, 1998–99; Integrated Project Team Leader for Airlift and Future Tanker Progs, 2000–01; on secondment to Rand, Calif, 2001–02; Minister, Defence Materiel, Washington, 2002–04; Dir Gen., Acquisition People, MoD, 2005–06; Dir, Defence Mgt Consultancy Services, MoD, 2007–08. *Publications:* (jtly) Re-examining Military Acquisition Reform: are we there yet?, 2005. *Recreations:* music, family research, learning Spanish, building wooden replica model warships, collecting dolphins, walking the dog, playing golf badly. *T:* (01454) 618404. *E:* shuna.lindsay@gmail.com.

LINDSAY, Vaughan Emerson; Chief Executive, Alzheimer's Research UK, since 2015; *b* Canterbury, 24 Sept. 1962; *s* of John and Audrey Lindsay; *m* 1994, Rachel Carter; one *d*. *Educ:* Simon Langton Grammar Sch.; Hertford Coll., Oxford (BA); London Sch. of Econs (MSc); London Business Sch. (MBA). Mktg post, Proctor & Gamble, 1986–87; Manager, King's Fund, 1987–89; Dep. Dir, Shelter, 1989–95; Dir, NCVO, 1995–98; Consultant, McKinsey & Co., 1998–2004; CEO, Dartington Hall Trust, 2004–15. *Recreations:* running, triathlons, cycling. *Address:* Alzheimer's Research UK, 3 Riverside, Granta Park, Cambridge CB21 6AD.

LINDSAY-HOGG, Sir Michael Edward, 5th Bt *cr* 1905, of Rotherfield Hall, Rotherfield, Sussex; film and theatre director; *b* 5 May 1940; *o s* of Sir Edward William Lindsay-Hogg, 4th Bt and Geraldine Mary, *d* of E. M. Fitzgerald; *S* father, 1999, but his name does not appear on the Official Roll of the Baronetage; *m* 1st, 1967, Lucy Mary (marr. diss. 1971), *o d* of Donald Davies; 2nd, 2002, Lisa, *e d* of Benjamin Holt Ticknor III. *Films* include: Let It Be, 1970; Nasty Habits, 1977; Dr Fischer of Geneva, 1983; The Object of Beauty, 1992; Frankie Starlight, 1996; Waiting for Godot, 2001; *theatre* includes: Whose Life Is It Anyway?, Mermaid, 1978, transf. NY, 1979; *television* includes: Electra, 1962; Professional Foul, 1977; (co-dir) Brideshead Revisited, 1981. *Publications:* Luck and Circumstance (memoir), 2011. *Heir:* none.

LINDSAY-SMITH, Iain-Mór; Deputy Managing Director, 1987–90, Chief Executive and Managing Director, 1991–97, and Executive Deputy Chairman, 1997–98, Lloyd's of London Press Ltd, later LLP Group Ltd; Chairman, Lloyds List, 1990–98 (Publisher, 1984–98); *b* 18 Sept. 1934; *s* of Edward Duncanson Lindsay-Smith and Margaret Wilson Anderson; *m* 1st, 1960, Carol Sara Paxman (marr. diss. 1997); one *s*; 2nd, 2014, Jane Elizabeth Cramp. *Educ:* High Sch. of Glasgow; London Univ. (diploma course on Internat. Affairs). Scottish Daily Record, 1951–57; Commissioned 1st Bn Cameronians (Scottish Rifles), 1953–55; Daily Mirror, 1957–60; Foreign Editor, subseq. Features Editor, Daily Mail, 1960–71; Dep. Editor, Yorkshire Post, 1971–74; Editor, Glasgow Herald, 1974–77; Exec. Editor, The Observer, 1977–84. Lloyd's of London Press, subseq. LLP Ltd: Exec. Dir, 1984–87; Chm. and Chief Exec., Lloyd's, then LLP, Information Services Ltd, 1990–98; Chm., LLP Business Publishing Ltd, 1990–98; Director: LLP Incorporated, USA, 1985–97 (Chm., 1992–97); LLP Asia, 1989–98; LLP GmbH, Germany, 1989–96; Lloyd's Maritime Information Services Ltd, 1990–97 (Chm., 1993–97); Lloyd's Maritime Information Services Inc., USA, 1990–97 (Chm., 1992–97); Lutine Publications Ltd, 1984–97 (Chm., 1992–97); Internat. Art & Antique Loss Register Ltd, 1990–97; PPA, 1992–98; DYP Gp Ltd, 1995–98; IBJ Associates Ltd, 1995–98; Cotton Investments Ltd, 1995–98. Dir, Mercury Th., Colchester, 1990–95. Member: Little Horkesley Parish Council, 1987–91; PCC, 1985–92. Chm., Glasgow Newspaper Press Fund, 1974–77. Founding Fellow, Inst. of Contemp. Scotland, 2001–. FRSA 1992. *Publications:* article in Electronics and Power. *Recreations:* shooting (game and clay), playing Highland bagpipes, the outdoors.

LINDSELL, David Clive, FCA; Partner, Ernst & Young, 1978–2007; Independent non-executive Director: Drax Group plc, since 2008; Premier Oil plc, since 2008; HellermannTyton Group plc, since 2013; *b* 9 May 1947; *s* of late Alfred and Florence Lindsell; *m* 2008, Felicity Daphne Hother; two *d*. *Educ:* Haberdashers' Aske's, Hampstead; Elstree Sch.; Christ's Coll., Cambridge (BA 1968). FCA 1972. Joined Ernst & Young, 1969; Ernst & Young International: Dir, Planning and Mktg, 1985–88; Chm., Accounting and Auditing Standards Cttee, 1989–95; Chm., Multinat. Client Gp, 1995–99; Global Dir, Internat. Financial Reporting Standards, 2003–07; Mem. Council, Ernst & Young UK, 1991–2007. Mem. Adv. Bd, Gartmore Investment Ltd, 2007–09; non-exec. Dir, Gartmore Gp Ltd, 2009–11. Institute of Chartered Accountants in England and Wales: Member: Business Law Cttee, 1989–94; Turnbull Cttee, 1999; Chm., Co. Law Sub-Cttee, 1989–94. Dep. Chm., Financial Reporting Review Panel, 2008–12; Member: Oil Industry Accounting Cttee, 1982–85; Auditing Practices Bd for UK and Ireland, 1994–2002 (Mem., Ethics Gp, 2003–04); Bd, Eur. Financial Reporting Adv. Gp, 2004–09; Standards Adv. Council, Internat. Accounting Standards Bd, 2005–08. Trustee, 1999–2008, Mem., Audit Cttee, 2006–14, BM; Dir, British Mus. Co. Ltd, 2005–12; Trustee, Cancer Res. UK, 2014– (Chm., Audit Cttee, 2014–). University of the Arts London: Mem., Audit Cttee, 2009– (Chm., 2011–15); Gov., 2011– (Dep. Chm. Govs, 2015–). Governor: Cranleigh Sch., 1979–85; St Albans Sch., 1995–2010. *Recreations:* playing and listening to jazz, museums and galleries, theatre, opera. *Club:* Oxford and Cambridge.

LINDSEY, 14th Earl of, *cr* 1626, **AND ABINGDON,** 9th Earl of, *cr* 1682; **Richard Henry Rupert Bertie;** Baron Norreys, of Rycote, 1572; *b* 28 June 1931; *o s* of Lt-Col Hon. Arthur Michael Bertie, DSO, MC (*d* 1957) and Aline Rose (*d* 1948), *er d* of George Arbuthnot-Leslie, Warthill, Co. Aberdeen, and *widow* of Hon. Charles Fox Maule Ramsay, MC; *S* cousin, 1963; *m* 1957, Norah Elizabeth Farquhar-Oliver, *yr d* of late Mark Oliver, OBE; two *s* one *d*. *Educ:* Ampleforth. Late Lieut, Royal Norfolk Regt. Insurance broker and underwriting agent at Lloyd's, 1958–92. Chm., Dawes and Henderson (Agencies) Ltd, 1988–92. Chm., Anglo-Ivory-Coast Soc., 1974–77. High Steward of Abingdon, 1963–. *Heir: s* Lord Norreys, *qv*. *Address:* The Old Farmhouse, Blairston Mains, Ayr KA7 4EF. *Club:* Turf.

LINDSEY, Prof. Keith, PhD; FRSB, FLS; Professor of Plant Molecular Biology, since 1996, and Head, School of Biological and Biomedical Sciences, 1997–2000 and since 2013, Durham University; *b* London, 22 Aug. 1957; *s* of Brian and Sylvia Lindsey; *m* 1989, Jennifer Topping; one *s* one *d*. *Educ:* Skinners' Sch., Tunbridge Wells; St Catherine's Coll., Oxford (BA 1978); Edinburgh Univ. (PhD 1982). FRSB (FIBiol) 2004. Res. Fellow, Edinburgh Univ., 1981–86; Higher Scientific Officer, Rothamsted Exptl Station, 1986–88; Lectr, 1989–95, Sen. Lectr, 1995, Leicester Univ. Member: Adv. Cttee on Releases to the Envmt, 2003–13; BBSRC, 2010–14. Pres., Soc. for Exptl Biol., 2011–13. Chm., New Phytologist Trust, 2012–. FLS 2014. *Publications:* Plant Biotechnology in Agriculture, 1989, 2nd edn 1992; Plant Tissue Culture Manual, 1991, 9th edn 1997; Transgenic Plant Research, 1998; Polarity in Plants, 2004. *Recreations:* playing guitar, photography, cinema, art history, the gym. *Address:* School of Biological and Biomedical Sciences, Durham University, South Road, Durham DH1 3LE. *T:* (0191) 334 1309, *Fax:* (0191) 334 1202. *E:* keith.lindsey@durham.ac.uk.

LINE, Frances Mary, (Mrs James Lloyd), OBE 1996; Controller, BBC Radio 2, 1990–96; *b* 22 Feb. 1940; *d* of Charles Edward Line and Leoni Lucy Line (*née* Hendriks); *m* 1972, James Richard Beilby Lloyd. *Educ:* James Allen's Girls' Sch., Dulwich. Joined BBC as clerk/typist, 1957; Sec. in TV and Radio, 1959–67; Radio 2 producer, 1967–73; senior producer, 1973–79; Chief Assistant: Radio 2, 1979–83; Radio 4, 1983–85; Head, Radio 2 Music Dept, 1985–89. Vice-Pres., Eastbourne Soc., 1998–. Hon. Fellow, Radio Acad., 1996. *Recreations:* visual arts, theatre. *Address:* 24 Marlborough Court, Eastbourne, E Sussex BN21 1BT.

LINE, Matthew John Bardsley; Director, Rivington Bye Ltd (formerly Craft London Ltd), since 2010; *b* 22 April 1958; *s* of John Line and Jill Line (*née* Rowland); *m* 1987, Elinor Jane Fairhurst; two *d*. *Educ:* Chiswick Sch.; Exeter Univ. (BA Hons Drama). Actor, 1982; Asst Publisher, Shepheard-Walwyn Publishers, 1984–87; Production Dir, Concertina Publications, 1988; freelance journalist, 1987–92; Editor: Up Country, 1992–93; Dialogue, 1993–95; Launch Editor, Colour, 1995; Gp Editor, home interest titles, Redwood Publishing, 1996–97; Ed., Homes & Gardens, 1997–2002; Chief Exec., The Prince's Foundn, 2002–04; Ed. in Chief, relaunched She, 2004–06; Editl Consultant, Rich, 2006; Editl Dir, Craft Publishing, 2007–10. Launched annual Homes & Gardens V&A Mus. Classic Design Awards, 1999–. *Publications:* Homes & Gardens Book of Design, 2000. *Recreations:* family, gardening, philosophy. *Address:* Rivington Bye Ltd, 3 Albemarle Way, EC1V 4JB.

LINEHAN, Anthony John; President, Construction Health & Safety Group, 1993–2003; *b* 27 June 1931; *s* of Daniel and Ada Linehan; *m* 1955, Oonagh Patricia FitzPatrick; two *s* two *d*. *Educ:* Bristol Univ. (BA Hons 1952). Short Service Commission, RN, 1953–57. HM Factory Inspectorate: joined 1958; HM District Inspector, 1969; Labour Adviser, Hong Kong Govt, 1973–76; Health and Safety Executive: HQ, 1976–79; Area Dir, Wales, 1979–84; HM Dep. Chief Inspector of Factories, 1984–88; Chief Inspector of Factories, 1988–92; Dir of Field Ops, 1990–92. *Recreations:* walking, reading, watching Rugby. *Address:* 2 Brookside Manor, Leigh Road, Wimborne, Dorset BH21 2BZ. *T:* (01202) 848597.

LINEHAN, Fergus; Festival Director, Edinburgh International Festival, since 2014; *b* Dublin, 14 May 1969; *s* of Fergus and Rosaleen Linehan; *m* 2014, Sophie Hodges; two *s* one *d*. *Educ:* Gormonston Coll., Co. Meath, Ireland; University Coll. Dublin (BA English and Greek and Roman Civilization). Dir and Founder, Pigsback Th. Co., Dublin, 1991; Gen. Manager, Tivoli Th., Dublin, 1992; Dublin Theatre Festival: Gen. Manager, 1993–96; Dep. Dir, 1996–99; Fest. Dir, 2000–04; Fest. Dir, Sydney Fest., 2005–09; Dir, Warehouse Arts Ltd, 2010–14; Hd of Contemp. Music, Sydney Opera Hse, 2011–13. *Address:* Edinburgh International Festival, The Hub, Castlehill, Edinburgh EH1 2NE. *T:* (0131) 473 2099. *E:* director@eif.co.uk.

LINEHAN, Dr Peter Anthony, FBA 2002; FRHistS; Fellow, St John's College, Cambridge, since 1966; *b* 11 July 1943; *er s* of John James Linehan and Kathleen Margaret Linehan (*née* Farrell); *m* 1971, Christine Ann Callaghan; one *s* two *d*. *Educ:* St Benedict's Sch., Ealing; St John's Coll., Cambridge (Mullinger Schol.; BA 1st Cl. 1964, MA 1968 (Thirlwall Prizeman and Seeley Medallist), PhD 1968). FRHistS 1971. St John's College, Cambridge: Res. Fellow, 1966–69; Lectr, 1969–2010; Tutor, 1977–97; Tutor for Grad. Affairs, 1983–97; Dean, 1999–2010; University of Cambridge: Sen. Proctor, 1976–77; affiliated lectr, Faculty of Hist., 1976–92. Woodward Lectr, Yale Univ., 1999; Birkbeck Lectr in Ecclesiastical Hist., Trinity Coll., Cambridge, 1999. Co-Ed., Jl Ecclesiastical Hist., 1979–91. Member: Accad. Senese degli Intronati, 1988; IAS, Princeton, NJ, 1988; Séminaire Interdisciplinaire de Recherches sur l'Espagne Médiévale, CNRS, Univ. of Paris 13, 2000. Corresp. Mem., Real Acad. de la Historia, Madrid, 1996. Gov., Giggleswick Sch., 1983–96. Antiquary Prizeman, Univ. of Edinburgh, 1985. *Publications:* The Spanish Church and the Papacy in the Thirteenth Century, 1971 (trans. Spanish 1975); (ed with B. Tierney) Authority and Power, 1980; Spanish Church and Society 1150–1300, 1983; (ed) Proceedings of the Seventh International Congress of Medieval Canon Law 1984, 1988; Past and Present in Medieval Spain, 1992; History and the Historians of Medieval Spain, 1993 (trans. Spanish 2012); The Ladies of Zamora, 1997 (trans. French 1998, Spanish 2000, Portuguese 2008); (ed) Life, Law and Letters, 1998; (ed with J. L. Nelson) The Medieval World, 2001; The Processes of Politics and the Rule of Law, 2002; (with J. C. de Lera Maíllo) Las postrimerías de un obispo alfonsino, 2003; (with F. J. Hernández) The Mozarabic Cardinal, 2004; Spain, 1157–1300: a partible inheritance, 2008 (trans. Spanish 2009); (ed with S. Barton) Cross, Crescent and Conversion, 2008; (ed) St John's College Cambridge: a history, 2011; Historical Memory and Clerical Activity in Medieval Spain and Portugal, 2012; Portugalia Pontificia, 2013; contribs to learned jls. *Recreation:* reading obituaries. *Address:* Brookside, 20 Glebe Way, Impington, Cambs CB24 9HJ. *T:* (01223) 233934; St John's College, Cambridge CB2 1TP. *T:* (01223) 338720. *E:* pal35@cam.ac.uk. *Club:* Hawks (Cambridge).

LINEHAN, Stephen; QC 1993; a Recorder, since 1990; *b* 12 March 1947; *s* of Maurice Gerald Linehan and Mary Joyce (*née* Norrish); *m* 1976, Victoria Maria Rössler; one *s*. *Educ:* Mount St Mary's Coll., Spinkhill, Derbys; King's Coll., London (LLB Hons). Called to the Bar, Lincoln's Inn, 1970, Bencher, 1999. *Address:* St Philips Chambers, 55 Temple Row, Birmingham B2 5LS. *T:* (0121) 246 7000.

LINEKER, Gary Winston, OBE 1992; journalist and broadcaster; professional footballer, 1976–94; *b* 30 Nov. 1960; *s* of Barry and Margaret Lineker; *m* 1st, 1986, Michelle Cockayne (marr. diss. 2006); four *s*; 2nd, 2009, Danielle Bux. Football Clubs played for: Leicester City, 1976–85; Everton, 1985–86; Barcelona, 1986–89; Tottenham Hotspur, 1989–92; Nagoya Grampus 8, 1993–94; England team, 1984–92: Captain, 1990–92; 80 appearances, 48 goals. Presenter, Match of the Day, BBC TV, 1995–. Freeman, City of Leicester, 1995. Hon. MA: Loughborough, 1992; Leicester, 1992. *Recreations:* golf, cricket, snooker, theatre. *Address:* c/o Jon Holmes Media Ltd, 3 Wine Office Court, EC4A 3BY. *T:* 07802 461706. *Clubs:* Groucho, MCC.

LING, Jeffrey, CMG 1991; HM Diplomatic Service, retired; Chairman and Chief Executive, Dean & Drysdale Ltd, 1999–2007; *b* 9 Sept. 1939; *s* of Frank Cecil Ling and Mary Irene Nixon; *m* 1967, Margaret Anne Tatton; one *s*. *Educ:* Bristol Univ. BSc (Hons); FInstP; FIMgt; FBCS. FCO, 1966–69; Private Sec. to HM Ambassador, Washington, 1969–71; First Sec., Washington, 1971–73; Perm. Delegn to OECD, Paris, 1973–77; FCO, 1977–79; on secondment as Special Adviser to HM the Sultan of Brunei, 1979–82; Counsellor (Technology), Paris, 1982–86; Dir of Res., FCO, 1986–89; Asst Under-Sec. of State and Dir of Communications, subseq. of Information Systems, FCO, 1989–96; Dir Gen., Trade and Inward Investment in US, and Consul-Gen., NY, 1996–99. Dir (non-exec.), RTZ Borax and Minerals, 1991–96; Mem., Internat. Adv. Bd, Buchanan Ingersoll, 2000–02; Chairman: Soho 4 Associates, 2000–03; Casmir Ltd, 2001–02; Special Advr to Chm. and CEO, Maxim Pharmaceuticals, 2000–05; Advisor: to CEO of Basepoint plc, 2000–03; Cedar Gp plc, 2000–01; Bd, E-Lynxx Corp., 2000–04; to Man. Dir of Dorsey and Whitney, 2002–04; to Chm. of London First, 2002–04. Chm., London New York City Alliance, 2000–01. *Recreation:* walking.

LING, Norman Arthur; HM Diplomatic Service, retired; Ambassador to the Federal Democratic Republic of Ethiopia, Djibouti and the African Union, 2008–11; *b* 12 Aug. 1952; *s* of late William Arthur Ling and of Helma Ling (*née* Blum); *m* 1979, Selma Osman. *Educ:* Sheffield Univ. (BA Hons German and Econ. Hist.). British Commercial Transport, 1975–76; Ocean Transport and Trading, 1976–78; joined Diplomatic Service, 1978; FCO, 1978–80; Second Sec., Tripoli, 1980–81; Second, later First, Sec., British Interests Section, Tehran, 1981–84; FCO, 1984–88; Dep. Consul Gen., Johannesburg, 1988–92; Dep. Head of Mission, Ankara, 1993–97; Head, Aviation, Maritime, Sci. and Energy Dept, FCO, 1997–2001; High Comr, Malaŵi, 2001–04; Change Dir, FCO, 2005–07. Non-executive Director: Nyota Minerals, 2012–14; Kefi Minerals, 2014–. *Recreations:* travel, walking, gardening. *Address:* Little Newbold, Long Bredy, Dorchester, Dorset DT2 9HW.

LING, Prof. Roger John, PhD; FSA; Professor of Classical Art and Archaeology, University of Manchester, 1992–2010, now Emeritus; *b* 13 Nov. 1942; *s* of Leslie James Ling and Kathleen Clara Ling (*née* Childs); *m* 1967, Lesley Ann Steer. *Educ:* Watford Grammar Sch.; St John's Coll., Cambridge (BA 1964; MA 1969; PhD 1970). FSA 1979. Lectr in Classics, UC of Swansea, 1967–71; University of Manchester: Lectr in History of Art, 1971–75; Sen. Lectr, 1975–83; Reader, 1983–92; Head of Dept of Hist. of Art, 1988–91. British Acad. Res. Reader, 1991–93; Balsdon Sen. Res. Fellow, British Sch. at Rome, 1994–95. *Publications:* The Greek World, 1976, 2nd edn as Classical Greece, 1988; (jtly) Wall Painting in Roman Britain, 1982; (ed) Cambridge Ancient History, Plates to vol. VII.1, 1984; Romano-British Wall Painting, 1985; Roman Painting, 1991; The Insula of the Menander at Pompeii I: the structures, 1997; Ancient Mosaics, 1998; Stuccowork and Painting in Roman Italy, 1999; (ed) Making Classical Art: process and practice, 2000; (with L. A. Ling) The Insula of the Menander at Pompeii II: the decorations, 2005; Pompeii: history, life and afterlife, 2005; numerous articles in learned jls. *Recreations:* fresh air and exercise, watching football. *Address:* School of Arts, Histories and Cultures, University of Manchester, Manchester M13 9PL. *T:* (0161) 275 3020.

LINGARD, Joan Amelia, MBE 1998; author, since 1963; *b* 1932; *d* of Henry James Lingard and Elizabeth Lingard; *m* Martin Birkhans; three *d*. *Educ:* Bloomfield Collegiate Sch., Belfast; Moray House Coll. of Educn. Mem. Bd and Mem., Literature Cttee, Scottish Arts Council, 1980–84. Chair, Soc. of Authors in Scotland, 1980–84. Hon. Pres., Scottish Pen, 2013. Hon. Fellow, Assoc. for Scottish Literary Studies, 2013. *Publications: novels:* Liam's Daughter, 1963; The Prevailing Wind, 1964; The Tide Comes In, 1966; The Headmaster, 1967; A Sort of Freedom, 1968; The Lord on Our Side, 1970; The Second Flowering of Emily Mountjoy; Greenyards; Reasonable Doubts, 1979; The Women's House, 1981; Sisters by Rite, 1984; After Colette, 1993 (Scottish Arts Council Award); Dreams of Love and Modest Glory, 1995; The Kiss, 2002; Encarnita's Journey, 2005; After You've Gone, 2007; *children's novels:* The Twelfth Day of July, 1970; Frying as Usual, 1971; Across the Barricades, 1972 (Buxtehude Bülle, 1986); Into Exile, 1973; The Clearance, 1973; A Proper Place; The Resettling; Hostages to Fortune; The Pilgrimage, 1975; The Reunion, 1977; Snake among the Sunflowers, 1977; The Gooseberry, 1978; The File on Fraulein Berg, 1980; Strangers in the House, 1981; The Winter Visitor, 1983; The Freedom Machine, 1986; The Guilty Party, 1987; Rags and Riches, 1988; Tug of War, 1989; Glad Rags, 1990; Between Two Worlds, 1991; Secrets and Surprises, 1991; Hands off Our School, 1992; Night Fires, 1993; Clever Clive and Loopy Lucy, 1993; Slo Flo and Boomerang Bill, 1994; Sulky Suzy and Jittery Jack, 1995; Lizzie's Leaving, 1996; Morag and the Lamb, 1996; Dark Shadows, 1998; A Secret Place, 1998; Tom and the Tree House, 1998 (Scottish Arts Council Award); Can You Find Sammy the Hamster?, 1998; The Egg Thieves, 1999; River Eyes, 2000; Natasha's Will, 2000; The Same Only Different, 2000; Me and My Shadow, 2001; Tortoise Trouble, 2002; Tell the Moon to Come Out, 2003; Tilly and the Wild Goats, 2005; The Sign of the Black Dagger, 2005; The Eleventh Orphan, 2008; What to do about Holly, 2009; The Chancery Lane Conspiracy, 2010; The Stolen Sister, 2011; What Holly Did, 2012; What To Do About Holly, 2013. *Recreations:* reading, walking, travelling. *Address:* c/o David Higham Associates, 7th Floor, Waverley House, 7–12 Noel Street, W1F 8GQ. *Club:* Lansdowne.

LINGARD, Robin Anthony; owner/manager, Kinnairdie Consulting, 1997–2009; *b* 19 July 1941; *s* of late Cecil Lingard and Lucy Lingard; *m* 1968, Margaret Lucy Virginia Elsden; two *d*. *Educ:* Felsted School; Emmanuel College, Cambridge (Exhibnr, MA). Min. of Aviation, 1963–66; Min. of Technology, 1966–70 (Private Sec. to Jt Parly Sec., 1966–68); DTI, 1971–74; DoI, 1974–83, Asst Sec., 1976; Under Sec., DTI, 1984, Cabinet Office (Enterprise Unit), 1984–85; Hd, Small Firms and Tourism Div., Dept of Employment, 1985–87; Mem. Bd, Highlands and Islands Develt Bd, 1988–91; Dir of Trng and Social Develt, 1991–93, Dir of Highlands and Is Univ. Project, 1993–97, Highlands and Islands Enterprise. Member: NEDC Sector Gp for Tourism and Leisure Industries, 1987–92; Scottish Tourist Bd, 1988–92; Management Bd, Prince's Trust and Royal Jubilee Trusts, 1989–95; Chairman: Highlands, Orkney and Western Isles Cttee, Prince's Trust, 1992–98; YouthLink Scotland, 1997–2000; BBC Scotland Appeals Adv. Cttee, 1998–2004; Fusion Scotland, 2002–05; Sustainable Develt Res. Centre, 2005–09; Highland Community Care Forum, 2007–09. FTS 1988. *Recreations:* reading, walking, watching birds, aviation history. *Address:* Kinnairdie House, Dingwall, Ross-shire IV15 9LL. *T:* (01349) 861044.

LINGFIELD, Baron *cr* 2010 (Life Peer), of Lingfield in the County of Surrey; **Robert George Alexander Balchin,** Kt 1993; DL; Knight President, Imperial Society of Knights Bachelor, since 2012; *b* 31 July 1942; *s* of late Leonard George Balchin and Elizabeth Balchin (*née* Skelton); *m* 1970, Jennifer, OStJ, *d* of late Bernard Kevin Kinlay, Cape Town; twin *s* (of whom one decd). *Educ:* Bec Sch.; Univ. of London; Univ. of Hull. Teacher, 1964–69; Res., Univ. of Hull Inst. of Educn, 1969–71; Chairman: HSW Ltd, 1972–2000; Pardoe-Blacker (Publishing) Ltd, 1989–99; Blacker Publishing Ltd, 2003–09; Grant-Maintained Schs Foundn and Centre, 1989–99; Centre for Educn Mgt, 1994–2002; CEFM (formerly Centre for Education Finance) Ltd, 2002–; Cadet Vocational Qualification Orgn, 2012–. Chairman: Educn Commn, 2003–10; Commn on Special Educn Needs, 2006–10; Govt Review of Professionalism in Further Educn, 2012–13; Chartered Instn for Further Educn, 2013–. St John Ambulance: Asst Dir-Gen., 1982–84; Dir-Gen., 1984–90; Mem. Chapter-Gen., Order of St John, 1984–99. Imperial Society of Knights Bachelor: Mem. Council, 1995–; Registrar, 1998–2006; Knight Principal, 2006–12. Mem., FAS, 1994–97 (Chairman: New Schs Cttee, 1994–97; Schs Improvement Cttee, 1996–97); President: English Schs Orch., 1998–; League of Mercy, 1999–; Chm., ARNI Trust, 2008–. Chairman: Balchin Family Soc., 1993–; Maritime Heritage Foundn, 2011–. Mem., Surrey CC, 1981–85. Member: Court, Univ. of Leeds, 1995–2000; Council, Goldsmiths' Coll., London, 1997–2005 (Dep. Chm. Council, 1999–2005); Pro-Chancellor, Brunel Univ., 2006–13. Freeman, 1980, Liveryman, 1987, Goldsmiths' Co.; Soc. of Apothecaries of London, 2013. Hon. Col, Humberside & S Yorks ACF, 2004–12. DL Greater London, 2001. FCP 1971 (Hon. FCP 1987); Hon. FHS 1987; Hon. FCGI 1998. Hon. DLitt Hull, 2006; Hon. EdD Brunel, 2013. KStJ 1984. Cross of Merit (Comdr 1st Cl.), SMO Malta, 1987; Grand Cross, Order of the Eagle of Georgia, 2014. *Publications:* Emergency Aid in Schools, 1984; New Money, 1985, 2nd edn 1989; (jtly) Choosing a State School, 1989; numerous articles on educn/politics. *Address:* New Place, Lingfield, Surrey RH7 6EF; House of Lords, SW1A 0PW. *T:* (020) 7219 3000. *Club:* Athenæum.

LINGWOOD, James, MBE 2012; Co-Director: Artangel, since 1991; Artangel Media Ltd, since 2000; *b* 28 May 1959; *s* of Robert Lingwood and Patricia Brown; partner, Jane Sarah Hamlyn, *qv*; one *s* two *d*. *Educ:* Corpus Christi Coll., Oxford (BA Hons Mod. Hist. 1979; MPhil dist. Art Hist. 1980). Curator: Inst. of Contemporary Arts, 1986–90; TSWA Sculpture Projects, 1987–90; independent curator, internat. museums, 1992–. Trustee: Paul Hamlyn Foundn, 2003–; Art Fund, 2008–. Hon. Fellow, Goldsmiths, Univ. of London, 2012. *Publications:* (jtly) Une Autre Objective, 1989; (ed) Rachel Whiteread, House, 1993; Robert Smithson: the entropic landscape, 1993; The Epic and the Everyday: contemporary photographic art, 1994; Juan Muñoz: monologues and dialogues, 1996; (ed) Vija Celmins: works 1963–1996, 1997; Juan Muñoz: Double Bind, 2001; (ed) Field Trips: Robert Smithson, Bernd and Hilla Becher, 2002; (jtly) Off Limits: 40 Artangel projects, 2002; Susan Hiller: Recall, 2004; (ed and contrib.) Francis Alÿs: Seven Walks, 2005; (ed) Gregor Schneider: Die Familie Schneider, 2006; (contrib.) Thomas Schütte: Political Work, 2007; (ed jtly) Thomas Struth Photographs 1978–2010, 2010; (ed jtly) Yael Bartana, And Europe will be Stunned, 2012; (ed and contrib.) Julião Sarmento, White Nights, 2012; (ed) Susan Philipsz, You Are Not Alone, 2014; (ed and contrib.) Cristina Iglesias, Tres Aguas, 2015. *Address:* Artangel, 31 Eyre Street Hill, EC1R 5EW. *T:* (020) 7713 1400, *Fax:* (020) 7713 1401. *E:* jl@artangel.org.uk. *Club:* MCC.

LINK, Joan Irene, LVO 1992; HM Diplomatic Service, retired; independent consultant in human resources and business coaching, since 2007; *b* 3 March 1953; *d* of William and Kathleen Mary Wilmot; *m* (marr. diss.); two *s*. *Educ:* Pear Tree Infant and Jun. Schs, Derby; Homelands Grammar Sch. for Girls, Derby; Lady Margaret Hall, Oxford (BA Mod. Langs); Open Univ. (Dip. Internat. Relns). FCIPD. Entered FCO, 1974; UK Delegn to the Cttee on Disarmament, 1980–83; Hd, Press and Inf., British Embassy, FRG, 1990–94; Hd, Resource Mgt Gp, 1996–2001, Hd, Conflict Prevention Unit, 2002–04, Hd, Conflict Issues Gp, 2004–07, FCO. Trustee: Gender Action for Peace and Security, 2008–; Peace Direct, 2008–. HR Advr and Tour Guide (volunteer), Arkwright Mills, Cromford, 2010–. *Recreations:* talking and walking, crafts and sewing, singing, writing. *Address:* c/o FCO Association, Foreign and Commonwealth Office, King Charles Street, SW1A 2AH.

LINKLATER, family name of **Baroness Linklater of Butterstone**.

LINKLATER OF BUTTERSTONE, Baroness *cr* 1997 (Life Peer), of Riemore in Perth and Kinross; **Veronica Linklater;** Founder, 1991, Executive Chairman, 1991–2004, President, since 2004, The New School, Butterstone; *b* 15 April 1943; *d* of late Lt-Col A. M. Lyle, OBE, and Hon. Elizabeth Lyle, *y d* of 1st Viscount Thurso, KT, CMG, PC; *m* 1967, Magnus Duncan Linklater, *qv*; two *s* one *d*. *Educ:* Cranborne Chase Sch.; Univ. of Sussex; Univ. of London (DipSoc Admin). Child Care Officer, 1967–68; Co-Founder, Visitors' Centre, Pentonville Prison, 1971–77; Winchester prison project, Prison Reform Trust, 1981–82; Founder, Administrator, then Consultant, The Butler Trust, 1983–87 (Trustee, 1987–2001; Vice Pres., 2001–); Trustee, Esmée Fairbairn Foundn, 1991–; Dir, Maggie Keswick Jencks Cancer Caring Centres Trust, 1997–2004. Chm., H of L All-Party Gp on Offender Learning and Skills, 2005–06. Chm., Rethinking Crime and Punishment, 2001–08; Pres., Crime Reduction Initiative, 2007–11; Member: Children's Panel, Edinburgh S, 1989–97; Scottish Assoc. for the Study of Offending, 2005–. Member: Scottish Cttee, Barnardo's, 2001–04; Adv. Bd, Beacon Fellowship Charitable Trust, 2003–; Council, Winston Churchill Meml Trust, 2005–. Co-ordinator, Trustee and Vice Chm., Pushkin Prizes (Scotland), 1989–; Trustee: Lyle Charitable Trust, 2001–; Riemore Trust, 2007–; Adviser, Koestler Award Trust, 2004–. President: Soc. of Friends of Dunkeld Cathedral, 1989–; SOVA, 2009–. Patron: Airborne Initiative, 1998–2004; Nat. Schizophrenia Fellowship Scotland, 2000–; Nat. Family & Parenting Inst., 2002–; Research Autism (formerly Autism Intervention Res. Trust), 2004–; The Calyx—Scotland's Garden Trust, 2004–08; Probation Bds Assoc., 2005–; Action for Prisoners' Families, 2005–; Univ. of St Andrews Medical Campaign Cttee, 2007–; PUSH, 2007–; Home Start, 2007–; Epilepsy Scotland, 2009–; TACADE, 2009–; Contact a Family,

2011–. Foundn Patron, Queen Margaret Univ. Coll., Edinburgh, 1998–. Contested (Lib Dem) Perth and Kinross, May 1995. JP Inner London, 1985–88. *Recreations:* music, theatre, gardening. *Address:* Flat 1f2, 71 Cumberland Street, Edinburgh EH3 6RD. *T:* (0131) 558 9616. *E:* veronica.linklater@gmail.com.

LINKLATER, Prof. Andrew, PhD; FBA 2005; FLSW; Woodrow Wilson Professor of International Politics, Aberystwyth University (formerly University of Wales, Aberystwyth), since 2000; *b* 3 Aug. 1949; *s* of Andrew Linklater and Isabella (*née* Forsyth); *m* 1971, Jane Adam. *Educ:* Univ. of Aberdeen (MA 1971); Balliol Coll., Oxford (BPhil 1973); London Sch. of Econs (PhD 1978). Lectr, Univ. of Tasmania, 1976–81; Lectr, 1982–84, Sen. Lectr, 1985–91, Associate Prof., 1992, Monash Univ.; Prof., Keele Univ., 1993–99. Founding FLSW 2010. *Publications:* Men and Citizens in the Theory of International Relations, 1982, 2nd edn 1990; Beyond Realism and Marxism, 1990; The Transformation of Political Community, 1998; (with H. Suganami) The English School of International Relations, 2006; Critical Theory and World Politics: citizenship, sovereignty and humanity, 2007; The Problem of Harm in World Politics: theoretical investigations, 2011. *Recreations:* the Turf, Australian aboriginal art, woodland work, ECM recordings, classical guitar practice, perfume. *Address:* Department of International Politics, Aberystwyth University, Aberystwyth SY23 3FE. *T:* (01970) 621596. *E:* adl@aber.ac.uk.

LINKLATER, Magnus Duncan, CBE 2013; FRSE; Scotland Editor, The Times, 2007–12; *b* 21 Feb. 1942; *s* of late Eric Robert Linklater, CBE, TD, and Marjorie MacIntyre; *m* 1967, Veronica Lyle (*see* Baroness Linklater of Butterstone); two *s* one *d*. *Educ:* Eton Coll.; Freiburg Univ.; Sorbonne; Trinity Hall, Cambridge (BA 2nd Cl. Hons (Mod. Lang.)). Reporter, Daily Express, Manchester, 1965–66; Diary Reporter, London Evening Standard, 1966–67; Editor: Londoner's Diary, Evening Standard, 1967–69; 'Spectrum', Sunday Times, 1969–72; Sunday Times Colour Magazine, 1972–75; Assistant Editor: News, Sunday Times, 1975–79; Features, Sunday Times, 1979–81; Exec. Editor (Features), Sunday Times, 1981–83; Man. Editor (News), The Observer, 1983–86; Editor: London Daily News, 1987; The Scotsman, 1988–94; columnist: The Times, 1994–; Scotland on Sunday, 1998–2007; broadcaster, Radio Scotland, 1994–97. Chairman: Edinburgh Book Fest., 1995–96; Scottish Arts Council, 1996–2001; Horsecross Arts (Perth Concert Hall and Th.), 2013–. Mem. judging panel, 2008 City of Culture, 2002–03. Chm., Little Sparta Trust, 2001–. Pres., Saltire Soc., 2011–. FRSE 2002. Hon. DArts Napier, 1994; Hon. LLD Aberdeen, 1997; Hon. DLitt: Glasgow, 2001; Queen Margaret Univ., 2007. Lifetime Achievement Award, Scottish Daily Newspaper Soc., 2005. *Publications:* (with Stephen Fay and Lewis Chester) Hoax—The Inside Story of the Howard Hughes/Clifford Irving Affair, 1972; (with Lewis Chester and David May) Jeremy Thorpe: a secret life, 1979; Massacre: the story of Glencoe, 1982; (with the Sunday Times Insight Team) The Falklands War, 1982; (with Isabel Hilton and Neal Ascherson) The Fourth Reich—Klaus Barbie and the Neo-Fascist Connection, 1984; (with Douglas Corrance) Scotland, 1984; (contrib.) A Scottish Childhood, 1985; (with David Leigh) Not With Honour: inside story of the Westland Scandal, 1986; (with Christian Hesketh) For King and Conscience: the life of John Graham of Claverhouse, Viscount Dundee, 1989; (ed jtly) Anatomy of Scotland, 1992; (with Colin Prior) Highland Wilderness, 1993; People in a Landscape, 1997. *Recreations:* fishing, book-collecting. *Address:* Flat 1f2, 71 Cumberland Street, Edinburgh EH3 6RD. *T:* (0131) 558 9616. *E:* magnus.linklater1@gmail.com. *Club:* MCC.

LINLEY, Viscount; David Albert Charles Armstrong-Jones; *b* 3 Nov. 1961; *s* and *heir* of 1st Earl of Snowdon, *qv*, and *s* of HRH the Princess Margaret, CI, GCVO (*d* 2002); *m* 1993, Hon. Serena Alleyne Stanhope, *o d* of Earl of Harrington, *qv*; one *s* one *d*. *Educ:* Bedales; Parnham School for Craftsmen in Wood. Designer and Cabinet maker; Chairman: David Linley Furniture Ltd, 1985–; David Linley & Company Ltd, 1998–; Christie's UK, 2006– (Dir, Christie's International, 2005–). *Publications:* Classical Furniture, 1993, 2nd edn 1998; Extraordinary Furniture, 1996; Design and Detail in the Home, 2000; Star Pieces, 2010. *Heir:* *s* Hon. Charles Patrick Inigo Armstrong-Jones, *b* 1 July 1999. *Address:* Linley, 60 Pimlico Road, SW1W 8LP.

See under Royal Family.

LINLITHGOW, 4th Marquess of, *cr* 1902; **Adrian John Charles Hope;** Bt (NS) 1698; Baron Hope, Viscount Aithrie, Earl of Hopetoun 1703 (Scot.); Baron Hopetoun 1809 (UK); Baron Niddry 1814 (UK); Stockbroker; *b* 1 July 1946; *s* of 3rd Marquess of Linlithgow, MC, TD, and Vivienne (*d* 1963), *d* of Capt. R. O. R. Kenyon-Slaney and of Lady Mary Gilmour; *S* father, 1987; *m* 1st, 1968, Anne (marr. diss. 1978), *e d* of A. Leveson, Hall Place, Hants; two *s*; 2nd, 1980, Peta C. Binding (marr. diss. 1997; she *d* 2009); one *s* one *d*; 3rd, 1997, Auriol Mackeson-Sandbach (marr. diss. 2007), former wife of Sir John Ropner, *qv*. *Educ:* Eton. Joined HM Navy, 1965. *Heir:* *s* Earl of Hopetoun, *qv*. *Address:* Philpstoun House, Linlithgow, West Lothian EH49 7NB. *T:* (01506) 834685.

LINNANE, Prof. Anthony William, AM 1995; FRS 1980; FAA; FTSE; Director, Centre for Molecular Biology and Medicine, since 1983; Professor of Biochemistry, Monash University, Australia, 1965–94, Emeritus Professor, since 1996; *b* 17 July 1930; *s* of late W. Linnane, Sydney; *m* 1956, Judith Neil (marr. diss. 1980); one *s* one *d*; *m* 1980, Daryl, *d* of A. Skurrie. *Educ:* Sydney Boys' High School; Sydney Univ. (PhD, DSc); Univ. of Wisconsin, USA. FAA 1972; FTSE 1999. Lecturer, then Senior Lectr, Sydney Univ., 1958–62; Reader, Monash Univ., Aust., 1962–65. Visiting Prof., Univ. of Wisconsin, 1976; Prof. (part-time), Centre for Clinical and Molecular Medicine, Faculty of Medicine, Univ. of Queensland, 2007–11; Adjunct Prof., Sch. of Medicine, Univ. of Sydney, 2014–. President: Aust. Biochemical Soc., 1974–76; Fedn of Asian and Oceanic Biochemical Socs, 1975–77; 12th Internat. Congress of Biochemistry, 1982; Treasurer, Internat. Union of Biochemistry and Molecular Biol., 1988–97; Founder and Dir, 2000, Pres., 2001–06, Australian Soc. for Cellular and Molecular Gerontology. Work concerned especially with the biogenesis and genetics of mitochondria, mucinous cancers and the human ageing process. Distinguished Service Award, 2000, Centenary Medal, 2003, Internat. Union of Biochem. and Molecular Biol. Editor-in-Chief, Biochemistry and Molecular Biol. Internat., 1988–97. *Publications:* Autonomy and Biogenesis of Mitochondria and Chloroplasts, 1971; over 300 contributions to learned journals. *Address:* 24 Myrtle Road, Canterbury, Vic 3126, Australia. *Clubs:* Athenæum; VRC; Anglesea Golf.

LINNARD, Robert Wynne; Director of Rail Strategy, Department for Transport, 2007–10; Specialist Adviser, House of Commons Transport Committee, since 2011; *b* 18 June 1953; *s* of late John Adrian Linnard and Gwenita Linnard (*née* Johns); *m* 1974, Sally Judith Gadsden; three *s* three *d*. *Educ:* Dulwich Coll. Entered Civil Service, DoE, 1973; Principal, Dept of Transport, 1984–91; Asst Sec., 1991–99; Dir of Railways, DETR, subseq. DTLR, 1999–2002; Dir, Local Govt Finance, DTLR, then ODPM, 2002–04; Dir of Integrated and Local Transport, subseq. Regl and Local Transport Policy, DfT, 2004–07. Mem. Bd, Passenger Focus, 2013–. *Recreations:* family, labradors, walking. *Address:* Field House, Downe Road, Keston, Kent BR2 6AD. *T:* (01689) 852367. *E:* rlinnard@hotmail.co.uk.

LINNELL, Andrew John, CGeog, FRGS; Head of Geography, Prospect School, since 2012; *b* 28 June 1956; *s* of late Cyril Barrie Linnell and of Maureen (*née* Goodyear); *m* 1989, Juliet, *d* of late Prof. Oswald Hanfling and of Helga Hanfling; one *s* one *d*. *Educ:* Wolstanton Grammar Sch., Staffs; Univ. of Salford (BSc); Univ. of Keele (PGCE). FRGS 1983, CGeog 2002; ACP 1988, MCollP 1988, FCollP 2005. Teacher, Howard Sch., Gillingham, Kent, 1979–86; Educn Officer, Kent CC, 1986–92; Dep. Headteacher, Sir Joseph Williamson's Mathematical Sch., Rochester, 1992–97; Head Master, Reading Sch., 1997–2005; Head Teacher, Desborough Sch., 2005–12. Mem. Council, RGS, 2005–09, 2013–15 (Vice-Pres., 2006–09, 2013–15). *Recreations:* jogging, swimming, cycling, travelling. *Address:* Prospect School, Cockney Hill, Tilehurst, Reading RG30 4EX. *T:* (0118) 959 0466.

LINNETT, Simon John Lawrence; Executive Vice Chairman, N. M. Rothschild & Sons Ltd, since 2004; *b* Oxford, 14 Feb. 1954; *s* of John Wilfrid Linnett and Rae Ellen Fanny Linnett; *m* 1987, Penelope Jane, *d* of Sir Charles Willink, 2nd Bt; two *s*. *Educ:* Leys Sch.; Balliol Coll., Oxford (MA Maths 1975). With N. M. Rothschild & Sons Ltd, 1975–; Banking Div., 1975–78; Dir, 1987–98, Man. Dir, 1998–2004, Corporate Finance, then Investment Banking, later Global Financial Advisory. Chm., Ind. Transport Commn, 2010– (Mem., 2000–). Mem., Adv. Bd, Nat. Railway Mus., 1997– (Dep. Chair, 2013–). Chm., Luton and Dunstable Univ. Hosp. NHS Foundn Trust, 2014–. Treasurer: QMUL, 2010–; NESTA, 2014–. Trustee: Queen's Nursing Inst., 2000–10; Science Mus. Gp (formerly Nat. Mus. of Sci. and Industry), 2011–; Exbury Gardens Trust, 2012–. *Recreations:* walking, heavy gardening, reading, community action. *Address:* N. M. Rothschild & Sons Ltd, New Court, St Swithin's Lane, EC4N 8AL. *E:* simon.linnett@rothschild.com. *Clubs:* Athenæum; Bosham Sailing.

See also Sir E. D. Willink, Bt.

LINNEY, (Jonathan) Piers (Daniel); Co-Founder and Joint Chief Executive Officer, Outsourcery plc, since 2011; Founder and Trustee, workinsight.org, since 2014; *b* Stoke-on-Trent, 15 Feb. 1971; *s* of Derek and Norma Linney; *m* 2003, Tara Bishop; two *d*. *Educ:* Univ. of Manchester (BA Jt Hons Accounting and Law). Trainee solicitor, SJ Berwin, 1995–97; admitted solicitor, 1997; Exec., Investment Banking, Barclays de Zoete Wedd, 1997; Sen. Associate, M&A, Credit Suisse, 1997–2000; investor, 2000–; corporate finance and fund mgt, 2003–08; Jt Chief Exec., Genesis Communications td, 2008–11. Trustee: Powerlist Foundn, 2010–; Nesta, 2014–; Plotr, 2014–. Appeared as investor, Dragons' Den, BBC TV series, 2013–15. *Recreations:* family, downhill mountain biking and cycling, personal fitness, motor boating, field target shooting, cinema. *Address:* Outsourcery plc, 10 Whitfield Street, W1T 2RE. *T:* 0330 313 0077. *W:* www.pierslinney.com.

LINSTEAD, Stephen Guy; Director, Department of Trade and Industry, West Midlands Region, 1990–94; *b* 23 June 1941; *s* of late George Frederick Linstead and May Dorothy Linstead (*née* Griffiths); *m* 1st, 1971 (marr. diss.); two *s*; 2nd, 1982, Rachael Marian Feldman; two *d*. *Educ:* King Edward VII Sch., Sheffield; Corpus Christi Coll., Oxford (MA Mod. Hist.; Dip. Public and Social Admin.); Carleton Univ., Ottawa (MA Political Sci.); Huddersfield Univ. (Dip. Law). Board of Trade, 1964–76 (Private Sec. to Minister of State, 1967–69); Principal, 1969; Asst Sec., Dept of Prices and Consumer Protection, 1976–79; Dept of Trade, 1979–82; Office of Fair Trading, 1982–90; Under-Sec., DTI, 1990–94. Mem. Steering Gp, Industry '96, 1994–96. Vice-Chm., Assoc. of First Div. Civil Servants, 1982–84. Member: Exec. Cttee, Solihull Chamber of Commerce and Industry, 1996–2002 (Vice-Pres., 2000–02); Oversight Cttee, United Coll. of the Ascension, Selly Oak, 1996–2002. Reader, dio. of Birmingham, 1991–. Sec., St Alphege Millennium Co-ordinating Cttee, 2010–12. Chair, English Spelling Soc., 2013–. *Publications:* Hymns of Hope for a New Millennium, 2008; contrib. Ottawa Law Review. *Recreations:* hymn writing (various hymns in Worship Live), swimming, travel, entertainment. *Address:* 20 Silhill Hall Road, Solihull B91 1JU. *T:* and *Fax:* (0121) 705 1376. *Club:* Royal Over-Seas League.

LINTON, Martin; Director, Travel2Palestine, since 2011; Chairman, Make Votes Count, since 2011; *b* 11 Aug. 1944; *s* of Sydney and Karin Linton; *m* 1st, 1975, Kathleen Stanley (*d* 1995); two *d*; 2nd, 2008, Sara Apps. *Educ:* Christ's Hosp.; Pembroke Coll., Oxford (MA). Journalist: Daily Mail, 1966–71; Labour Weekly, 1971–79; Daily Star, 1979–81; The Guardian, 1981–97. Mem. (Lab), Wandsworth LBC, 1971–82. MP (Lab) Battersea, 1997–2010; contested (Lab) same seat, 2010. PPS to Minister for the Arts, 2001–03, to Leader of Commons, 2003–05, to Lord Chancellor, 2005–07. Member: Home Affairs Select Cttee, 1997–2001; Admin Cttee, 2001–05; Modernisation Cttee, 2003–05. Dir, Labour Friends of Palestine and the Middle East, 2010–12 (Chm., 2009–10). *Publications:* The Swedish Road to Socialism, 1974; Guardian Guide to the House of Commons, 1992; Money and Votes, 1994; Was It the Sun Wot Won It?, 1995; Guardian Election Guide, 1997; Making Votes Count, 1998; Beyond 2002: long-term policies for Labour, 1999. *Recreations:* playing music, watching football. *T:* (020) 7228 4897. *E:* martin@martinlinton.org.

LINTON, Prof. Oliver Bruce, PhD; FBA 2008; Professor of Political Economy, University of Cambridge, since 2011; Fellow of Trinity College, Cambridge, since 2011; *b* Gloucester, 20 Dec. 1960; *s* of Geoffrey and Margaret Linton; *m* 1st, 1990, Elisabetta Zancan (marr. diss. 2010); one *s* one *d*; 2nd, 2011, Jianghong Song; one *s*. *Educ:* Hereford Cathedral Sch.; London Sch. of Econs (BSc 1st cl. Hons Maths 1983; MSc Econometrics and Math. Econs 1986; Univ. of Calif, Berkeley (PhD Econs 1991). Jun. Res. Fellow, Nuffield Coll., Oxford, 1991–93; Yale University: Asst Prof., 1993–97; Associate Prof., 1997–98; Prof. of Economics, 1998–2000; Prof. of Econometrics, LSE, 1998–2011. Fellow, Econometric Soc., 2007; FIMS 2007. *Address:* Department of Economics, University of Cambridge, Austin Robinson Building, Sidgwick Avenue, Cambridge CB3 9DD. *T:* (01223) 335299. *E:* obl20@cam.ac.uk.

LINTOTT, Robert Edward; Chief Executive, Coverdale Organisation, 1987–91; *b* 14 Jan. 1932; *s* of Charles Edward and Doris Mary Lintott; *m* 1958, Mary Alice Scott; three *s*. *Educ:* Cambridgeshire High School; Trinity College, Cambridge. BA Nat. Scis 1955, MA. Served RAF, 1950–52 (Flying Officer); joined Esso Petroleum Co. Ltd, 1955; Corporate Planning Dept, Exxon Corp., 1975–78; Exec. Asst to Chm., Exxon Corp., 1978–79; Director: Esso Petroleum Co. Ltd, 1979–84; Esso Pension Trust, 1979–87; Esso Exploration & Production UK, 1984–87; Esso UK plc, Esso Petroleum, 1984–87 (Man. Dir, 1984–86); Matthew Hall Engineering Holdings Ltd, 1987–89; CSM Parly Consultants Ltd, 1995–2012; MLD (Hong Kong) Ltd, 1995–; Chairman: Irish Refining Co., 1979–82; Esso Teoranta, 1982–84. Vice-Pres., UK Petroleum Industry Assoc., 1985–86; Pres., Oil Industries Club, 1986–88. Mem., Standards Bd, BSI, 1991–2000. Council Mem., 1979–2011, and Chm. Exec. Cttee, 1987–2008, Foundn for Management Educn; Member: Council for Management Educn and Develt, 1989–2000; Steering Cttee, Oxford Summer Business Sch., 1979–94 (Chm., 1987–91); Council, Manchester Business Sch., 1985–92; Finance Cttee, Methodist Ind. Schs, 2008–12. Councillor, Royal Bor. of Windsor and Maidenhead, 1987–91. Chm. of Govs, Queen's Coll. Taunton, 1994–2007. Chm., ESU, Taunton, 2007–, Gov., ESU, 2012–15. *Recreations:* cricket, vintage and modern motoring. *Address:* Huish Barton, Watchet, Somerset TA23 0LU. *T:* (01984) 640208. *Clubs:* Royal Air Force, MCC.

LIPMAN, Maureen Diane, (Mrs J. M. Rosenthal), CBE 1999; actress; *b* 10 May 1946; *d* of late Maurice and Zelma Lipman; *m* 1973, Jack Morris Rosenthal, CBE (*d* 2004); one *s* one *d*. *Educ:* Newland High Sch. for Girls, Hull; London Acad. of Music and Dramatic Art. Professional début in The Knack, Watford, 1969; Stables Theatre, Manchester, 1970; National Theatre (Old Vic), 1971–73: The Front Page; Long Day's Journey into Night; The Good Natur'd Man; *West End:* Candida, 1976; Outside Edge, 1978; Meg and Mog, 1982; Messiah, 1983; Miss Skillen, in See How They Run, 1984 (Laurence Olivier Award; Variety Club of GB Award); Wonderful Town, Queen's, 1986; Re: Joyce!, Fortune, 1988, Vaudeville, 1989 and 1991, Long Wharf, Conn, USA, 1990; The Cabinet Minister, Albery, 1991; Lost in Yonkers, Strand, 1992 (Variety Club Best Stage Actress, 1993); The Sisters Rosenweig, Old Vic, 1994; Live and Kidding, Duchess, 1997; Oklahoma!, RNT, 1998, transf. Lyceum, 1999; Peggy For You, Comedy, 2000; Thoroughly Modern Millie, Shaftesbury, 2003; Aladdin, Old Vic, 2004; Glorious!, Duchess, 2005–06; When We Are

Married, Garrick, 2010; other plays include: Celia, in As You Like It, RSC, 1974; Jenny, in Chapter Two, Hammersmith, 1981; Kitty McShane, in On Your Way, Riley, Stratford East, 1983; The Rivals, Manchester Royal Exchange, 1996; Sitting Pretty, Th. Royal, Bath, 2001; Martha Josie & the Chinese Elvis, touring, 2007; The Cherry Orchard, Chichester, 2008; A Little Night Music, Menier Chocolate Factory, 2008, transf. Garrick, 2009; Barefoot in the Park (also co-dir), touring, 2012; Old Money, Hampstead Th., 2012; Daytona, Park Th., London, 2013, Th. Royal, 2014; Harvey, Birmingham Repertory Th., transf. Th. Royal, 2015; Dir, The Sunshine Boys, Royal Lyceum, Edinburgh, 1993; *television:* plays, series and serials include: The Evacuees; Smiley's People; The Knowledge; Rolling Home; Outside Edge; Princess of France, in Love's Labour's Lost; Absurd Person Singular; Shift Work; Absent Friends; Jane Lucas, in 4 series of Agony; All at No 20 (TV Times Award, 1989); About Face, 1989 and 1990; Re: Joyce; Enid Blyton, in Sunny Stories, 1992; Eskimo Day, 1996; Cold Enough for Snow, 1997; The Fugitives, 2004; In Search of Style, 2005; Sensitive Skin, Dr Who, Casualty, 2007; He Kills Coppers, 2008; Minder, Ladies of Letters (2 series), 2009–10; Midsomer Murders, 2013; presenter, If Memory Serves Me Right (documentary), 2013; *films include:* Up the Junction, 1969; Educating Rita, 1983; Captain Jack, 1998; Solomon and Gaenor, 1999; Oklahoma! (video), 1999; Discovery of Heaven, 2001; The Pianist, 2002; Caught in the Act, 2008; *radio:* The Lipman Test (2 series), 1996, 1997; Choice Grenfell, 1998; dir, Jack Rosenthal's Last Act, 2006. BAFTA Award, for BT Commercials, 1992. Magazine columnist: Options, 1983–88; She, 1988–91 (PPA Columnist of the Year, 1991); Good Housekeeping, 1993–2003. Hon. DLitt: Hull, 1994; Sheffield, 1999; Hon. MA Salford, 1995; Hon. PhD Tel Aviv, 2012. *Publications:* How Was it for You?, 1985; Something to Fall Back On, 1987; You Got an 'Ology?, 1989; Thank You for Having Me, 1990; When's It Coming Out?, 1992; You Can Read Me Like a Book, 1995; Lip Reading, 1999; The Gibbon's in Decline, but the Horse is Stable, 2006; Past-it Notes, 2008; I Must Collect Myself, 2011.

LIPNER, Prof. Julius Joseph, PhD; FBA 2008; Professor of Hinduism and the Comparative Study of Religion, University of Cambridge, 2003–13, now Emeritus; Fellow, Clare Hall, Cambridge, 1990–2013, now Emeritus (Vice-President, 2007–09); *b* Patna, India, 11 Aug. 1946; *s* of Vojtech Lipner and Sylvia Teresa Lipner (*née* Coutts); *m* 1971, Anindita Neogy; one *s* one *d*. *Educ:* Pontifical Athenæum (Jnana Deepa Vidyapeeth), Pune, India (Licentiate in Philosophy *summa cum laude* 1969); King's Coll., London (PhD 1974); MA Cantab 1975. Lectr in Indian Religions, Dept of Theol., Univ. of Birmingham, 1973–74; University of Cambridge: Lectr in Indian Religion and Comparative Study of Religion, 1975–99, Reader in Hinduism and Comparative Study of Religion, 1999–2003, Dir of Research, 2013, Divinity Faculty; Fellow, St Edmund's Coll., 1976–89; Chm., Faculty Bd of Divinity, 2003–06. Visiting Professor: Univ. of Calgary, 1987, 1989, 1996; Vanderbilt Univ., Nashville, 1992; Liverpool Hope Univ., 2003–04; Hon. Prof., Kurukshetra Univ., India, 1995–97; Vis. Fellow, Vishwabharati Univ., India, 1984; Sen. Fellow, Oxford Centre for Hindu Studies, 2014–; Dist. Vis. Fellow, S. Rajaratnam Sch. of Internat. Studies, Nanyang Technol Univ., Singapore, 2015. Named Lectures. Member, Editorial Advisory Board: Jl Hindu-Christian Studies; Internat. Jl Hindu Studies; (Jl) Religions of S Asia; Jl of Hindu Studies, 2008–; (Jl) Relegere: Studies in Religion and Reception, 2009–. Trustee: Spalding Trusts, 1992–; Woolf Inst. (formerly Centre for Study of Jewish Christian Relations), 2001–; Teape Trust, 2008–; Ancient India and Iran Trust, 2012–. *Publications:* The Face of Truth: a study of meaning and metaphysics in the Vedantic theology of Ramanuja, 1986; (ed jtly) A Net Cast Wide: investigations into Indian thought in memory of David Friedman, 1986; (jtly) Hindu Ethics: purity, abortion and euthanasia, 1989; (ed jtly) The Writings of Brahmabandhab Upadhyay, vol 1, 1991, vol 2, 2002; Hindus: their religious beliefs and practices, 1994, 2nd edn 2010; (ed) The Fruits of our Desiring: an enquiry into the ethics of the Bhagavadgita, 1997; Brahmabandhab Upadhyay: the life and thought of a revolutionary, 1999; Bankimchandra Chatterji's Anandamath or the Sacred Brotherhood (introd., trans. and critical apparatus), 2005 (A. K. Ramanujan Prize for trans., Assoc. for Asian Studies, 2008); (ed) Truth, Religious Dialogue and Dynamic Orthodoxy: essays in honour of Brian Hebblethwaite, 2005; Bankimchandra Chatterji's Debi Chaudhurani or The Wife Who Came Home (introd., trans. and critical apparatus), 2009; contrib. articles to learned jls and edited collections. *Recreations:* following Test Cricket (especially England and India), enjoying good food, listening to Indian and Western music, reading, travel, enjoying my six grandchildren growing up. *Address:* Divinity Faculty, University of Cambridge, West Road, Cambridge CB3 9BS.

LIPPIETT, Rear-Adm. Richard John, CB 2004; CBE 2014 (MBE 1979); DL; Chief Executive Officer, Mary Rose Trust, since 2003; *b* 7 July 1949; *s* of late Rev. Canon Vernon Kingsbury Lippiett and Katharine F. I. S. Lippiett (*née* Langston-Jones); *m* 1976, Jennifer Rosemary Wratislaw Walker; two *s* one *d*. *Educ:* Brighton, Hove and Sussex Grammar Sch.; BRNC, Dartmouth. Joined RN 1967; served HM Ships Appleton, Eagle, Yarmouth, Achilles, Fife, Ambuscade and ashore at HMS Raleigh and Fleet HQ; Flag Lieut to C-in-C Fleet, 1973–74; Comd, HMS Shavington, 1975–77 and HMS Amazon, 1986–87; jsdc 1987; Naval Asst to First Sea Lord, 1988–90; Comd, HMS Norfolk and 9th Frigate Sqdn, 1991–92; rcds, 1993; COS Surface Flotilla, 1993–95; Comd, HMS Dryad and Sch. of Maritime Ops, 1995–97; Flag Officer Sea Trng, 1997–99; COS to Comdr Allied Naval Forces Southern Europe, and Sen. British Officer Southern Region, 1999–2002; Comdt, JSCSC, 2002–03. Trustee: Naval Review, 2001–14; Royal Mint Mus., 2011–. Naval Vice Pres., CCF, 2004–; Pres., Ton Class Assoc., 2007–. Patron, Nautical Trng Corps, 2007–. Gov., Bedales Sch., 2011–. Younger Brother of Trinity House, 1993. DL W Sussex, 2014. Hon. Dr Maritime Southampton Solent, 2011; Hon. DLaws Portsmouth, 2012. *Publications:* The Type 21 Frigate, 1990; War and Peas: intimate letters from the Falklands War 1982, 2007. *Recreations:* family, classical music, gardening, sailing, maritime history. *Address:* Mary Rose Trust, College Road, HM Naval Base, Portsmouth PO1 3LX.

LIPPINCOTT, Dr Kristen Clarke; Director, The Exhibitions Team, since 2007; *b* 18 Nov. 1954; *d* of Lt-Col Clifford Ellwood Lippincott and Maureen Virginia Lippincott (*née* O'Brien); *m* 1992, Gordon Stephen Barrass, *qv*. *Educ:* Bennington Coll., Vermont, USA (BA); Univ. of Chicago (MA, PhD). Fellowships in Italy and at Warburg Inst., 1982–90; National Maritime Museum: Curator of Astronomy, 1990 and Head of Navigational Scis, 1991–94, Old Royal Observatory; Mus. Planner and Strategist, 1994–95; Director: Display Div., 1995–96; Millennium Project, Old Royal Observatory, Greenwich, 1996–2000; Royal Observatory Greenwich, 1998–2001; Dep. Dir, Nat. Maritime Mus., 2000–06. Vis. Prof., Harvard Univ., Villa I Tatti, Florence, 2004. Council Mem., Scientific Instruments Soc., 1994–96; Trustee: Bennington Coll., Vt, 1976–81; Cubitt Gall., 1996–2003. Freeman, Clockmakers' Co., 2000. FRAS 2004; FRSA 1997. *Publications:* Eyewitness Science: Astronomy, 1994; The Story of Time, 1999; (ed) Symbols of Time in the History of Art, 2002; A Guide to the Royal Observatory, Greenwich, 2007; The Stained Glass Windows of King's College Chapel, 2012; An Introduction to King's College Chapel, 2013; numerous articles on Italian Renaissance and on history of art, of science, of scientific instruments, in learned jls. *Recreations:* travelling, photography. *E:* kl@theexhibitionsteam.com.

LIPPONEN, Paavo Tapio; MP (SDP) Helsinki, Finland, 1983–87 and 1991–2006; Speaker of Parliament, 1995 and 2003–07; Proprietor, Cosmopolis Oy, since 2007; *b* 23 April 1941; *s* of Orvo and Hilkka Lipponen; *m* 1998, Paivi Hertzberg; two *d*, and one *d* from former marriage. *Educ:* Kuopio; Univ. of Helsinki (MScSoc 1971); Dartmouth Coll., USA. Journalist, 1963–67; SDP Res. and Internat. Affairs Sec. and Head, political section, 1967–79; Prime Minister's Sec. (Special Political Advr), 1979–92; Head, Finnish Inst. Internat. Affairs, 1989–91; Mem., Helsinki City Council, 1985–95; Prime Minister of Finland, 1995–2003. Social Democratic Party: Chm., Helsinki Dist, 1985–92; Member: Exec. Cttee, 1987–90; Party Council, 1990–93; Chm., 1993–2005. Man. Dir, Viestinta Teema Oy, 1988–95; Chm., Supervisory Bd, Outokumpu Oy, 1989–90. Member: Exec. Cttee, Internat. Commn on Employment, 1987–89; Adv. Bd, Notre Europe Jacques Delors Inst., 2005–; Adv. Bd, Oslo Center, 2010–. Hon. LLD: Dartmouth Coll., USA, 1997; Finlandia Univ., USA, 2000; Hon. Dr: Tampere Univ. of Tech., Finland, 2002; Åbo Akademi Univ., Finland, 2002; Univ. of Art and Design, Finland, 2007; Univ. of Joensuu. Grand Cross, Order of White Rose (Finland). Holds several foreign decorations. *Publications:* Muutoksen Suunta, 1986; Kohti Eurooppaa, 2001; articles in Finnish, Swedish, English and German in domestic and foreign books, newspapers and periodicals. *Recreations:* swimming, architecture. *Address:* Dagmarinkatu 5B8, 00100 Helsinki, Finland. *Club:* Finnish (Helsinki).

LIPSCOMB, Rachel Elizabeth, OBE 2006; JP; a Vice President, Magistrates' Association, since 2005 (Deputy Chairman, 1999–2002, Chairman, 2002–05, of Council); *b* 24 Aug. 1948; *d* of George Edwards and Joan (*née* Button); *m* 1969, Peter W. Lipscomb, OBE; two *s* one *d*. *Educ:* St Felix Sch., Southwold; Middlesex Hosp., London (SRN). Magistrates' Association: Mem. Council, 1994–; Chm., Sentencing Guidelines Working Party, 2002–05; Chm., Criminal Justice Cttee, 2000–02; Mem., Street Crime Action Gp, 2002–05. Member: Adv. Gp on Prison Popn, 2002–04; Audit Commn Victims and Witnesses Adv. Gp, 2002–04. Member: Unified Admin Judicial Cttee, 2002–04; Judges Council, 2003–05. Chm., Local Crime Community Sentence, 2008–13; Mem. Adv. Bd, Rethinking Crime and Punishment - Implementing the Findings, Esmée Fairbairn Foundn, 2005–08. Chm., Mediation, Support and Counselling for Separating Partners and Families, 2009–. Governor, Kingston Grammar Sch., 1996–2002. JP Kingston upon Thames, 1981. *Publications:* articles for The Magistrate and other criminal and civil justice pubns. *Recreations:* gardening, outdoor sports, family life. *Address:* c/o Magistrates' Association, 28 Fitzroy Square, W1T 6DD. *T:* (020) 7387 2353, *Fax:* (020) 7383 4020.

LIPSEY, family name of **Baron Lipsey**.

LIPSEY, Baron *cr* 1999 (Life Peer), of Tooting Bec in the London Borough of Wandsworth; **David Lawrence Lipsey;** *b* 21 April 1948; *s* of Lawrence and Penelope Lipsey; *m* 1982, Margaret Robson; one *d*, and two step *s*. *Educ:* Bryanston Sch.; Magdalen Coll., Oxford (1st Cl. Hons PPE). Research Asst, General and Municipal Workers' Union, 1970–72; Special Adviser to Anthony Crosland, MP, 1972–77 (Dept of the Environment, 1974–76; FCO, 1976–77); Prime Minister's Staff, 10 Downing Street, 1977–79; Journalist, New Society, 1979–80; Sunday Times: Political Staff, 1980–82; Economics Editor, 1982–86; Editor, New Society, 1986–88; Co-founder and Dep. Editor, The Sunday Correspondent, 1988–90; Associate Ed., The Times, 1990–92; journalist, The Economist, 1992–99 (Political Ed., 1994–98); Chm., Impower plc, 2001–03. Vis. Prof. in Public Policy, Univ. of Ulster, 1993–98; Vis. Fellow, Health and Social Care, LSE, 2002–04; Vis. Prof., Salford Univ., 2008–12. Member: Royal Commn on Long Term Care of the Elderly, 1997–99; Ind. Commn on the Voting System, 1997–98; Licence Fee Rev. Panel (Davies Inquiry), 1999; Council, ASA, 1999–2005; Bd, Starting Price Regulatory Commn; Chairman: Make Votes Count, 1999–2008; Social Market Foundn, 2001–10; Shadow Racing Trust, 2002–07; British Greyhound Racing Bd, 2004–08; Financial Services Consumer Panel, 2008; Campaign for Straight Statistics, 2009–12. Chairman: All Party Statistics Gp; All Party Classical Music Gp; Vice-Chairman: All Party Media Gp; All Party Betting and Gaming Gp, 2009–14; All Party Channel 4 Gp; Council, Constitution Unit; Editl Bd, Study on Decumulation, Assoc. of Ind. Financial Advrs, 2009. Secretary, Streatham Labour Party, 1970–72; Chm., Fabian Soc., 1981–82; Mem., Exec. Cttee, Charter for Jobs, 1984–86. A public interest Dir, PIA, 1994–2000; non-executive Director: Horserace Totalisator Bd, 1998–2002; LWT, 2002–03; London ITV, 2003–05; Consultant, Greyhound Bd of Great Britain, 2009–. Trustee: Retired Greyhound Trust, 2003–11; Cambrian Music Trust, 2009–; Sidney Nolan Trust (Chm., 2013–); President: British Harness Racing Club, 2004–; Soc. of Later Life Advisers, 2009–; Patron, Glasbury Festival; Chm., Trinity Laban Conservatoire of Music and Dance, 2012–. *Publications:* Labour and Land, 1972; (ed, with Dick Leonard) The Socialist Agenda: Crosland's Legacy, 1981; Making Government Work, 1982; The Name of the Rose, 1992; The Secret Treasury: how Britain's economy is really run, 2000; In the Corridors of Power (autobiog.), 2012; Counter Coup, 2014. *Recreations:* golf, greyhound racing, harness racing, horse racing, music, opera. *Address:* House of Lords, SW1A 0PW. *T:* (020) 7219 8509.

LIPSEY, Prof. Richard George, OC 1991; FRSC; Professor of Economics, Simon Fraser University, Burnaby, BC, 1989–97, now Emeritus; Fellow, Canadian Institute for Advanced Research, 1989–2002; *b* 28 Aug. 1928; *s* of R. A. Lipsey and F. T. Lipsey (*née* Ledingham); *m* 1960, Diana Louise Smart; one *s* two *d*. *Educ:* Univ. of British Columbia (BA 1st Cl. Hons 1950); Univ. of Toronto (MA 1953); LSE (PhD 1957). Dept of Trade and Industry, British Columbia Provincial Govt, 1950–53; LSE: Asst Lectr, 1955–58; Lectr, 1958–60; Reader, 1960–61; Prof. 1961–63; Univ. of Essex: Prof. of Economics, 1963–70; Dean of School of Social Studies, 1963–67; Sir Edward Peacock Prof. of Econs, Queen's Univ., Kingston, Ont, 1970–87. Vis. Prof., Univ. of California at Berkeley, 1963–64; Simeon Vis. Prof., Univ. of Manchester, 1973; Irving Fisher Vis. Prof., Yale Univ., 1979–80. Economic Consultant, NEDC, 1961–63; Sen. Econ. Advr, C. D. Howe Inst., Toronto, 1984–89. Member of Council: SSRC, 1966–69; Royal Economic Soc., 1968–71. President: Canadian Economics Assoc., 1980–81 (Life Fellow, 2010); Atlantic Economic Assoc., 1986–87. Editor, Review of Economic Studies, 1960–64. Fellow, Econometric Soc., 1972. FRSC 1980. Hon. LLD: McMaster, 1984; Victoria, 1985; Carleton, 1987; Queen's Univ. at Kingston, 1990; Guelph, 1993; Western Ontario, 1994; Essex, 1996; British Columbia, 1999; Simon Fraser Univ., 2007; Hon. DSc Toronto, 1992. Gold Medal, Social Scis and Humanities Res. Council, 2005. *Publications:* An Introduction to Positive Economics, 1963, 13th edn (with A. Chrystal) as Economics, 2014; (with P. O. Steiner) Economics, 1966, 12th edn 1999; (with G. C. Archibald) An Introduction to a Mathematical Treatment of Economics, 1967, 3rd edn 1977; The Theory of Customs Unions: a general equilibrium analysis, 1971; (with G. C. Archibald) An Introduction to Mathematical Economics, 1975; (with C. Harbury) An Introduction to the UK Economy, 1983, 5th edn 1993; (with F. Flatters) Common Ground for the Canadian Common Market, 1984; (with M. Smith): Canada's Trade Options in a Turbulent World, 1985; Global Imbalance and US Policy Response, 1987; (with R. York) A Guided Tour through the Canada-US Free Trade Agreement, 1988; (with C. Harbury) First Principles of Economics, 1988, 2nd edn 1992; (jtly) The NAFTA: what's in, what's out, what's next, 1994; (with K. Carlaw) A Structuralist Assessment of Innovation Policies, 1998; (jtly) Economic Transformations: general purpose technologies and long-term economic growth, 2005 (Schumpeter Prize for best writing in evolutionary econs (jtly), 2006); articles in learned jls on many branches of theoretical and applied economics. *Recreations:* travel, sailing, rambling. *Address:* 1125 West 26th Street, North Vancouver, BC V7R 1A4, Canada. *E:* rlipsey@sfu.ca.

LIPSON, Julian David; Partner, since 2003, and Head of Family Law, since 2008, Withers LLP; *b* Liverpool, 5 July 1969; *s* of Gerald Lipson and Marion Lipson (*née* Elman). *Educ:* King David High Sch., Liverpool; St Edmund Hall, Oxford (MA Juris. 1990). Admitted Solicitor, 1996; trainee solicitor, then Solicitor, Macfarlanes, 1994–97; Solicitor, Withers LLP, 1997–. Fellow, Internat. Acad. of Matrimonial Lawyers, 2009. *Recreations:* travel, cinema, theatre. *Address:* Withers LLP, 16 Old Bailey, EC4M 7EG. *T:* (020) 7597 6098, *Fax:* (020) 7597 6543. *E:* julian.lipson@withersworldwide.com.

LIPTON, Elliot; Managing Director, First Base Ltd, since 2002; *b* London, 17 March 1969; *s* of Sir Stuart (Anthony) Lipton, *qv*; *m* 1999, Alex Miller; one *s* two *d*. *Educ:* Mill Hill Sch.; Imperial Coll. London (BSc Hons Estate Mgt; MBA). FRICS 2014. Chm., Winnicott Foundn. Dir, Inst. for Sustainability. Gov., Mill Hill Sch. FRSA. *Recreation:* ski-ing. *Address:* First Base Ltd, 33 Cavendish Square, W1G 0DT. *T:* (020) 7851 5555. *E:* info@firstbase.com.

LIPTON, Prof. Michael, CMG 2003; DLitt; FBA 2006; Research Professor, Poverty Research Unit, Sussex University, since 1997; *b* 13 Feb. 1937; *s* of Leslie and Helen Lipton; *m* 1966, Merle Babrow; one *s*. *Educ:* Haberdashers' Aske's Sch., London; Balliol Coll., Oxford (BA 1st Cl. Hons PPE 1960, MA 1963); Massachusetts Inst. of Technol.; DLitt Sussex 1982. Fellow, All Souls Coll., Oxford, 1961–68 and 1983–84; University of Sussex: Fellow, Inst. of Develt Studies, and Professorial Fellow, 1970–94; Founding Dir, Poverty Res. Unit, 1994–97; 50th Anniversary Fellow, 2012–; Emeritus Fellow, Inst. of Develt Studies, 2014–. Dir, Consumption and Nutrition Prog., Internat. Food Policy Res. Inst., 1987–89. Employment Advr, Govt of Botswana, 1977–79; Sen. Advr, World Bank, 1981–82. Sen. Advr and topic leader, Quality of Life, ADB study of Emerging Asia, 1995–97; Lead Schol., Rural Poverty Report, IFAD, 1994–2001. Member: Wkg Party on GM crops, Bioethics Council, Nuffield Foundn, 1998–99 and 2002–03; Prog. Adv. Cttee, HarvestPlus (Biofortification) Prog. (formerly Biofortification Challenge Grant), Consultative Gp for Internat. Agricl Res., 2002–; UK and Internat. Bds, Internat. Develt Enterprises, 2004–; Bd, Centre for Chinese Agricl Policy, Chinese Acad. Scis, 2005–. Mem., Council, 2000–05, Bd, 2005–, ODI. Fellow, Stellenbosch Inst. for Advanced Studies, 2011. Leontief Prize for Advancing Frontiers of Econ. Thought, Global Develt and Envmt Inst., Tufts Univ., 2012. *Publications:* Chess Problems: introduction to an art, 1963; (jtly) The Two-move Chess Problem: tradition and development, 1966; Assessing Economic Performance, 1968; Why Poor People Stay Poor: urban bias and world development, 1977, 2nd edn 1988; (with R. Longhurst) New Seeds and Poor People, 1989; (with J. Toye) Does Aid Work in India?, 1991; (ed jtly and contrib.) Including the Poor, 1993; Successes in Anti-poverty, 1998, 2nd edn 2002; Land Reform in Developing Countries: property rights and property wrongs, 2009; Malthus in Africa, 2016; contrib. learned jls. *Recreations:* chess problems (Pres., British Chess Problem Soc., 1999–2001; Internat. Master of Chess Problem Composition, 1975–), classical music, poetry, theatre. *Address:* 15 Eaton Place, Brighton, Sussex BN2 1EH. *Club:* Lansdowne.

LIPTON, Sir Stuart (Anthony), Kt 2000; Deputy Chairman, Chelsfield LLP, since 2006; Director, Lipton Rogers Developments LLP, since 2013; *b* 9 Nov. 1942; *s* of late Bertram Green and Jeanette Lipton; *m* 1966, Ruth Kathryn Marks; two *s* one *d*. *Educ:* Berkhamsted Sch. Director: Sterling Land Co., 1971–73; First Palace Securities Ltd, 1973–76; Man. Dir, Greycoat PLC, 1976–83; Chief Exec., Stanhope Properties PLC, 1983–95; Chief Exec., 1995–2003, Chm., 2003–06, Stanhope PLC. Advr to Hampton Site Co. for Sainsbury Bldg, Nat. Gall., 1985–91; Advr, new Glyndebourne Opera House, 1988–94; Member: Adv. Bd, Dept of Construction Management, Reading Univ., 1983–91; Property Adv. Gp, DoE, 1986–96; Mil. Bldgs Cttee, MoD, 1987–98; Barbican Centre Adv. Council, 1997–2007. Mem. Council, British Property Fedn, 1987–99. Mem., Royal Fine Art Commn, 1988–99; Chm., CABE, 1999–2004. Dir, Nat. Gall. Trust Foundn, 1998–. Trustee: Whitechapel Art Gall., 1987–94; Architecture Foundn, 1992–99 (Dep. Chm., 1992–99); Urban Land Inst., Washington, 1996–; Millennium Bridge Trust, 1998–2002; King Edward VII Hosp., 2014–; Member: English Partnerships Millennium Housing Trust Jury, 1998–99; Jury, RIBA Gold Medal Award, 1998–99. Member of Board: Royal Nat. Theatre, 1988–98; Royal Opera House, 1998–2006. Edward Bass Vis. Architectural Fellow, Yale Sch. of Architecture, 2006. Member, Governing Body: Imperial Coll., 1987–2002 (FIC 1998); LSE, 2000–06. Liveryman, Goldsmiths' Co., 1997–. Hon. Bencher, Inner Temple, 2002. Hon. RIBA 1986. Hon. LLD Bath, 2005; Hon. DSc(Eng) UCL, 2009. Bicentenary Medal, RSA, 1999. *Recreations:* architecture, art and technology, opera. *Address:* (office) 33 Cavendish Square, W1G 0DT.

See also E. Lipton.

LIPWORTH, Sir (Maurice) Sydney, Kt 1991; Trustee, International Accounting Standards Committee Foundation, 2000–06; Chairman, Financial Reporting Council, 1993–2001; *b* 13 May 1931; *s* of Isidore and Rae Lipworth; *m* 1957, Rosa Liwarek (CBE 2010); two *s*. *Educ:* King Edward VII Sch., Johannesburg; Univ. of the Witwatersrand, Johannesburg (BCom, LLB). Admitted Solicitor, Johannesburg, 1955; called to the South African Bar, 1956; called to Bar, Inner Temple, 1991; in practice at the Bar, 2002–. Barrister, Johannesburg, 1956–64; non-exec. Dir, Liberty Life Assoc. of Africa Ltd, 1956–64; Director: private trading/financial gps, 1965–67; Abbey Life Assurance Gp, 1968–70; Allied Dunbar Assurance plc (formerly Hambro Life Assurance), 1971–88 (Jt Man. Dir, 1980–84; Dep. Chm., 1984–87); Chairman: Dunbar Bank, 1983–88; Allied Dunbar Unit Trusts, 1985–88 (Man. Dir, 1983–85); ZENECA Group, 1995–99 (Dir, 1994–99); Dep. Chm., Nat. Westminster Bank, 1993–2000; Director: J. Rothschild Holdings plc, 1984–87; BAT Industries plc, 1985–88; Carlton Communications plc, 1993–2004; Centrica plc, 1999–2002; Goldfish Bank Ltd, 2001–04; Cazenove Gp Ltd, 2005–. Mem., 1981–93, Chm., 1988–93, Monopolies and Mergers Commn; Member: Sen. Salaries Review Body, 1994–2002; Cttee on Financial Aspects of Corporate Governance, 1994–95. Mem. Adv. Panel, BreakThrough Breast Cancer Res. Trust, 1990; Trustee: Allied Dunbar Charitable Trust, 1971–94; Philharmonia Orchestra, 1982– (Dep. Chm., 1986–93, Chm., 1993–, of Trustees); Royal Acad. Trust, 1988–2003; South Bank Foundn Ltd, 1996–2003; Chairman: NatWest Gp Charitable Trust, 1994–2001; Marie Curie Cancer Care 50th Anniversary Appeal, 1997–2002; Governor: Contemp. Dance Trust, 1981–87; Sadler's Wells Foundn, 1987–90. Chm., Bar Assoc. for Commerce, Finance and Industry, 1991–92. Mem., Gen. Council of the Bar, 1992–94. Hon. Bencher, Inner Temple, 1989; Hon. QC 1993. Hon. LLD Witwatersrand, 2003. *Publications:* chapters and articles on investment, life insurance, pensions and competition law. *Recreations:* tennis, music, theatre. *Address:* International Accounting Standards Board, 30 Cannon Street, EC4M 6XH. *Clubs:* Reform, Queen's.

LISBURNE, 9th Earl of, *cr* 1776 (Ire.); **David John Francis Malet Vaughan;** Baron Fethard, 1695; Viscount Lisburne and Lord Vaughan, 1695; artist; *b* 15 June 1945; *e s* of 8th Earl of Lisburne and Shelagh Vaughan (*née* Macauley); *S* father 2014; *m* 1973, Jennifer Jane Sheila Fraser Campbell, artist, *d* of James and Dorothy Campbell, Invergarry; one *s* one *d*. *Educ:* Ampleforth Coll. *Heir:* *b* Hon. Michael John Wilmot Malet Vaughan [*b* 26 June 1948; *m* 1978, Hon. Lucinda Mary Louis Baring, *d* of 7th Baron Ashburton, *qv*; one *s* two *d*].

LISHMAN, (Arthur) Gordon, CBE 2006 (OBE 1993); Director General, Age Concern, and Chief Executive, Age Concern Group, 2000–09; *b* 29 Nov. 1947; *s* of Dr Arthur Birkett Lishman and Florence May Lishman; *m* 1st, 1968, Beverley Ann Witham (marr. diss. 1972); 2nd, 1973, Stephanie Margaret Allison-Beer (marr. diss. 1984); one *s* one *d*; 3rd, 1988, Margaret Ann Brodie-Browne (*née* Long); one step *d*. *Educ:* Univ. of Manchester (BA Econ 1968). Age Concern England, 1974–2009: Field Officer, 1974–77; Head of Fieldwork, 1977–87; Ops Dir, 1987–2000; Dir, Age Concern Hldgs Ltd, 1995–2009. Member: Steering Gp for Commn on Equalities and Human Rights, 2004–06; Nat. Stakeholder Forum, DoH, 2006–09; Chairman: Nutrition Action Plan Delivery Bd, DoH, 2008–10; Audit Cttee, Older People's Comr in Wales, 2009–14. Vice-Pres., Internat. Fedn on Ageing, 2004–12 (Dir, 2001–12); Sec.-Gen., Eurolink Age, 2001–; Sec., AGE—the Eur. Older People's Platform, 2001–07 (Council Mem., 2001–08). Campaigner on age equality, 1971–; involvement in Campaign for Homosexual Law Reform/Campaign for Homosexual Equality and Stop the Seventy Tour; former Mem., Race Equality Councils in Manchester, Northants and E Lancs; Member: Liberty; Fawcett Soc.; British Humanist Assoc.; Friends of Ruskin's Brantwood. Gov., Pensions Policy Inst., 2002–. Mem., Liberal, later Liberal Democrat, Party, 1963– (Mem., Federal Exec., 1969–; Mem., Internat. Relns Cttee, 1990–); Mem. Council, Eur. Liberal Democrat and Reform Party, 1977–; Chm., Human Rights Cttee, Liberal Internat., 2009–11; Pres., NW Liberal Democrats, 2010–14; Chm., Burnley Liberal Democrats, 2011–13. Founder, Africa Liberal Network, 2001–. Chair: Burnley and Pendle CAB, 2011–; Gas Safe Charity, 2012–. Hon. Fellow, Univ. of Central Lancs, 2002. MCMI. FRSA. MMLJ 2006. *Address:* 42 Halifax Road, Briercliffe, Burnley BB10 3QN. *T:* (01282) 421865. *E:* gordon@lishman.co.uk. *Club:* National Liberal.

LISHMAN, Suzannah Claire, FRCPath; Consultant Histopathologist, Peterborough and Stamford Hospitals NHS Foundation Trust, since 2006; President, Royal College of Pathologists, since 2014; *b* Beverley, 16 Dec. 1967; *d* of Dr John Derek Lishman and Bridgette Lishman (*née* McLaughlin); *m* 2011, Douglas Mackay Pattisson. *Educ:* Neale Wade Community Coll., March; Girton Coll., Cambridge (BA 1989; BChir 1992, MB 1993); London Hosp. Med. Sch. MRCPath 1999, FRCPath 2007. Hse Surgeon, Harold Wood Hosp., 1992–93; Hse Physician, Newham Gen. Hosp., 1993; Histopathol. Trainee, UCH, 1993–99; Consultant Histopathologist, Hinchingbrooke Healthcare NHS Trust, 1999–2006. Royal College of Pathologists: Asst Registrar, 2005–09; Registrar, 2009–11; Vice-Pres., 2011–14. *Publications:* A History of Pathology in 50 Objects, 2012. *Recreations:* scuba diving, Italian Renaissance art. *E:* suzylishman@doctors.org.uk.

LISHMAN, Prof. William Alwyn, MD, DSc; FRCP, FRCPsych; Professor of Neuropsychiatry, Institute of Psychiatry, University of London, 1979–93, now Professor Emeritus; Consultant Psychiatrist, Bethlem Royal and Maudsley Hospitals, 1967–93; *b* 16 May 1931; *s* of George Hackworth Lishman and Madge Scott (*née* Young); *m* 1966, Marjorie Loud (*d* 2000); one *s* one *d*. *Educ:* Houghton-le-Spring Grammar Sch.; Univ. of Birmingham (BSc Hons Anatomy and Physiology, 1953; MB, ChB Hons 1956; MD 1965). DPM London, 1963; DSc London, 1985. MRCP 1958, FRCP 1972; FRCPsych 1972. House Phys. and House Surg., Queen Elizabeth Hosp., Birmingham, 1956–57; MO Wheatley Mil. Hosp., 1957–59 (Major, RAMC); Registrar, United Oxford Hosps, 1959–60; Registrar, later Sen. Registrar, Maudsley Hosp., London, 1960–66; Consultant in Psychol Medicine, Nat. Hosp. and Maida Vale Hosp., London, 1966–67; Sen. Lectr in Psychol Medicine, Hammersmith Hosp. and RPMS, 1967–69; Consultant Psychiatrist, Bethlem Royal and Maudsley Hosps, 1967–74; Reader in Neuropsychiatry, Inst. of Psychiatry, 1974–79. Vis. Fellow, Green Coll., Oxford, 1983. Advisor to Bermuda Hosps Bd, 1971; Scientific Advisor, DHSS, 1979–82; Civilian Consultant, RAF, 1987–93. Member: Neurosciences Bd, MRC, 1976–78 (Dep. Chm., 1976–77); Scientific Adv. Panel, Brain Res. Trust, 1986–93; Adv. Cttee, Mason Med. Res. Trust, 1986–93. Examiner: Univ. of Oxford (also Mem. Bd of Examrs), 1975–79; Univ. of Birmingham, 1984–87; Nat. Univ. of Malaysia, 1989. Chm., British Neuropsychiatry Assoc., 1987–93; (Hon. Life Pres., 1993); Member: Experimental Psychology Soc., 1975–95; Assoc. of British Neurologists, 1979–95; Court of Electors, and Exams Subcttee, RCPsych, 1991–96. Trustee, Psychiatry Res. Trust, 1999–2007. Gaskell Gold Medal, Royal Medico-Psychol Assoc., 1965. Member, Editorial Boards: Psychological Medicine, 1970–93; Neuropsychiatry, Neuropsychology and Behavioral Neurology, 1988–95; Cognitive Neuropsychiatry, 1996–. Guarantor of Brain, 1984–99. *Publications:* Organic Psychiatry: the psychological consequences of cerebral disorder, 1978, 3rd edn 1998; physiol and psychol papers on brain maturation, cerebral dominance, organisation of memory; clinical papers on head injury, dementia, epilepsy, neuroimaging, and alcoholic brain damage. *Recreations:* organ, piano, harpsichord, travelling.

LISLE, 9th Baron *cr* 1758 (Ire.), of Mount North, co. Cork; **John Nicholas Geoffrey Lysaght;** *b* 20 May 1960; *s* of 8th Baron Lisle and Mary Louise Lysaght (*née* Shaw, now Blackwell); *S* father, 2003. *Educ:* Lingfield. Gardener, specialising in exotic climbers; bee-keeper; charity shop volunteer. *Recreations:* collecting early 20th-century Christmas tree decorations, gardening, writing rhymes and poems. *Heir:* *b* Hon. David James Lysaght [*b* 10 Aug. 1963; *m* 1989, Rebecca Tamsin, *d* of Russell Charles Abbott; one *s* two *d*]. *Address:* 50 The Fairstead, Scottow, Norwich, Norfolk NR10 5AQ.

LISLE, Paul David O.; *see* Orchard-Lisle.

LISS, Prof. Peter Simon, CBE 2008; PhD; FRS 2008; Professor, School of Environmental Sciences, University of East Anglia, 1985–2008, now Professorial Fellow; *b* 27 Oct. 1942; *s* of Michael and Gertrude Liss; *m* 1967, Ruth Adler; three *s*. *Educ:* University College, Durham (BSc); Marine Science Labs, Univ. of Wales (PhD). NERC Post-doctoral Res. Fellow, Dept of Oceanography, Southampton Univ., 1967–69; Lectr, 1969–77, Reader, 1977–85, Sch. of Envmtl Scis, UEA. Vis. Prof., Univ. of Washington, Seattle, 1977; Visiting Scientist: Ocean Chem. Lab., Canada, 1975; Grad. Sch. of Oceanography, Univ. of Rhode Island, 1989, 1990; Guest Prof., Ocean Univ., Qingdao, China, 1997–. Envmtl Chemistry Dist. Lectr, 2002, John Jeyes Lect. Award, 2003, RSC; Eminent Schol., Texas Inst. for Advanced Study, Texas A&M Univ., 2013–14. Scientific Advisor, CEGB, London, 1979–82. Exec. Dir, ICSU, 2014–15 (Mem., Task Team for Future Earth, 2011–12). Member: NERC, 1990–95; Royal Commn on Envmtl Pollution, 2005–11; Science Adv. Council, DEFRA, 2011–; Cttee for Life, Envmt and Geo-Scis, Science Europe, 2012–. Treasurer, 1990–93, Chm., 1993–97, Sci. Cttee for Internat. Geosphere-Biosphere Prog.; Chairman: Scientific Steering Cttee, Surface Ocean - Lower Atmosphere Study (SOLAS), 2001–07; Global Envmtl Res. Cttee, Royal Soc., 2007–09 (Vice-Chm., 1998–2007); Associates Bd, Nat. Oceanography Centre, 2011–; Adv. Bd, Marine Alliance for Sci. and Technol. Scotland, 2011–; Ind. Mem., Inter-Agency Cttee for Marine Sci. and Technol., 2000–08. Chm., Earth System Sci. Advanced Grants Panel, 2008–12, Mem., Consolidator Grants Panel, 2014–, European Res. Council. President: Challenger Soc. for Marine Sci., 2006–08 (Challenger Medal, 2000); Sir Alister Hardy Foundn for Ocean Sci., 2011–. MAE 2012. *Publications:* Estuarine Chemistry, 1976; Environmental Chemistry, 1980; Man-Made Carbon Dioxide and Climatic Change, 1983; Quimica Ambiental, 1983; Air-Sea Exchange of Gases and Particles, 1983; Power Generation and the Environment, 1990; An Introduction to Environmental Chemistry, 1996, 2nd edn 2004; The Sea Surface and Global Change, 1997; Ocean-Atmosphere Interactions of Gases and Particles, 2014. *Recreations:* reading, music, house renovation. *Address:* 5 Chester Place, Norwich, Norfolk NR2 3DG. *T:* (01603) 623815. *E:* p.liss@uea.ac.uk.

LISSACK, Richard Antony; QC 1994; a Recorder, since 1999; a Deputy High Court Judge, since 2010; *b* 7 June 1956; *s* of late Victor Jack Lissack and Antoinette Rosalind Lissack; *m* 1986, Carolyn Dare Arscott (marr. diss. 2014); three *d* (incl. twins); *m* 2014, Susan Jane Stille (*née* Stone). *Educ:* UCS, Hampstead. Called to the Bar, Inner Temple, 1978, Bencher, 2007; an Asst Recorder, 1993–99; QC: Eastern Caribbean, 2002; New York, 2007; NI, 2007; admitted DIFC, Dubai, 2008; Head of Strategic Develt, Outer Temple Chambers, 2008–11; Head of Internat. Law, Riverview Law, 2012–. Chairman: S & W Wilts Hunt, 1996–2002 (Pres., 2002–); Disciplinary Cttee, British Horse Trials, 2000–05. Ambassador for ActionAid, 2008–. Mem., Develt Bd, RADA, 2009–. *Recreations:* sailing, climbing, theatre, occasionally falling off thoroughbred horses. *Address:* The Outer Temple, 222 Strand, WC2R 1BA. *T:* (020) 7353 6381. *Clubs:* Soho House; Rock Sailing.

LISTER; *see* Cunliffe-Lister, family name of Earl of Swinton.

LISTER OF BURTERSETT, Baroness *cr* 2011 (Life Peer), of Nottingham in the County of Nottinghamshire; **(Margot) Ruth (Aline) Lister,** CBE 1999; FBA 2009; Professor of Social Policy, Loughborough University, 1994–2010, now Emeritus; *b* 3 May 1949; *d* of Dr Werner Bernard Lister and Daphne (*née* Carter). *Educ:* Univ. of Essex (BA Hons Sociology); Univ. of

Sussex (MA Multi-Racial Studies). Child Poverty Action Group: Legal Res. Officer, 1971–75; Asst Dir, 1975–77; Dep. Dir, 1977–79; Dir, 1979–87; Prof. of Applied Social Studies, Univ. of Bradford, 1987–93. Donald Dewar Vis. Prof. of Social Justice, Univ. of Glasgow, 2005–06. Vice-Chair, NCVO, 1991–93. Member: Opsahl Commn, 1992–93; Commn for Social Justice, 1992–94; Commn on Poverty, Participation and Power, 1999–2000; Fabian Commn on Life Chances and Child Poverty, 2004–06; Nat. Equality Panel, 2008–10; Jt Cttee on Human Rights, 2012–15; Bishop of Leicester Commn on Poverty, 2014. Hon. Pres., CPAG, 2011–. Eleanor Rathbone Meml Lect., Univ. of Leeds, 1989; British Acad. Annual Lect., 2015. Founding Academician, Acad. of Social Scis, 1999. Hon. LLD: Manchester, 1987; Brighton, 2012; Hon. DLitt Glasgow Caledonian, 2011; DUniv Essex, 2012; Hon. DSc Lincoln, 2013; Hon. LLD Bath, 2014. Lifetime Achievement Award, Social Policy Assoc., 2010. *Publications:* Supplementary Benefit Rights, 1974; Welfare Benefits, 1981; The Exclusive Society, 1990; Women's Economic Dependency and Social Security, 1992; Citizenship: feminist perspectives, 1997, 2nd edn 2003; Poverty, 2004; (jtly) Gendering Citizenship in Western Europe, 2007; (co-ed) Why Money Matters, 2008; Understanding Theories and Concepts in Social Policy, 2010; pamphlets, articles, and contrib. to many books on poverty, social security and women's citizenship. *Recreations:* walking, music, films, Tai Chi, watching tennis, meditation, pilates. *Address:* House of Lords, SW1A 0PW; 45 Quayside Close, Nottingham NG2 3BP.

LISTER, Andrew; *see* Lister, T. A.

LISTER, Sir Edward Julian Udny-, Kt 2011; Chief of Staff and Deputy Mayor Policy and Planning, Greater London Authority, since 2011; *b* London, 25 Oct. 1949; *s* of George and Margot Udny-Lister; *m* 1979, Eileen Elizabeth McHugh; one *s* one *d* (and one *s* decd). *Educ:* London Nautical Sch. Trainee, Mather and Platt Ltd, Manchester, 1969–79; Commercial Dir, Mather and Platt Alarms, London, 1979–87; Sales Manager, Britannia Security plc, 1987–90; Major Projects Dir, ADT Security Ltd, 1990–98; Gen. Manager, London ADT Fire and Security plc, 1998–2007; Director: Govt Relns, Tyco Fire and Security, 2007–11; Localis, 2010–; GLA Hldgs Ltd, 2011–; GLA Property, 2011–; London Legacy Develt Corp., 2012–15; London and Partners Ltd, 2015– (Chm., 2015–); Dep. Chm., Old Oak and Park Royal Develt Corp., 2015–. Mem. Bd, Euralarm, 2009–12. Mem. (C) Wandsworth LBC, 1976–2011 (Leader, 1992–2011). *Publications:* Local Limits, 1995; LEA's Old and New, 1997. *Recreations:* gardening, walking, travel. *Address:* Greater London Authority, City Hall, The Queen's Walk, SE1 2AA. *T:* (020) 7983 4538. *E:* Edward.lister@london.gov.uk; 51 Seymour Road, SW18 5JB. *E:* edwardlister@btconnect.com.

LISTER, Geoffrey Richard, CBE 1994; FCA; FCIB; Joint Vice Chairman, 1996–97, Director, 1988–97, Bradford & Bingley Building Society; *b* 14 May 1937; *s* of Walter and Margaret Lister; *m* 1962, Myrtle Margaret (*née* Cooper); one *s* two *d*. *Educ:* St Bede's Grammar Sch., Bradford. Articled clerk, J. Pearson & Son, 1955–60, qual. chartered accountant, 1960; Computer and Systems Sales, Burroughs Machines Ltd, 1961–63; Audit Man., Thos Gardner & Co., 1963–65; Bradford & Bingley Building Society: Asst Accountant, 1965–67; Computer Man., 1967–70; Chief Accountant, 1970–73; Asst Gen. Man., 1973–75; Dep. Gen. Man., 1975–80; Gen. Man., 1980–84; Dep. Chief Exec., 1984–85; Chief Exec., 1985–95. Director: NHBC, 1992–97; PIA, 1994–95; Anchor Trust, 1997–99. Building Societies' Association: Mem. Council, 1984–97; Dep. Chm., 1992–93; Chm., 1993–94. CCMI. *Recreations:* walking, gardening. *Address:* Harbeck House, Harbeck Drive, Harden, Bingley, W Yorks BD16 1JG. *T:* (01535) 272350. *Clubs:* Carlton; Bradford and Bingley Sports (Bingley, W Yorks).

LISTER, Jane Sara Anne; Senior Partner, Foot Anstey Solicitors, 2008–12; *b* Plymouth; *d* of Roger and Maureen Morris; *m* 1982, Paul Lister; two *d*. *Educ:* Bath High Sch.; Plymouth High Sch.; Coll. of Law. Solicitor and NP, 1976–2012; Man. Partner, Foot Anstey Solicitors, 1997–2008. Mem., S Western RHA, 1986–90; Vice-Chm., Plymouth Hosps Trust, 1990–92. Dir, Theatre Royal (Plymouth) Ltd, 1995–2003. Pres., Plymouth Law Soc., 1993–94. Gov., Univ. of Plymouth, 1992–94. *Recreation:* my family. *Address:* Foot Anstey Solicitors, Salt Quay House, 4 North East Quay, Sutton Harbour, Plymouth PL4 0BN. *T:* (01752) 675000, *Fax:* (01752) 675500.

LISTER, Monica; *see* Burch, M.

LISTER, (Robert) Patrick, CBE 1993; retired; *b* 6 Jan. 1922; *s* of Robert B. Lister; *m* 1942, Daphne Rosamund, *d* of Prof. C. J. Sisson; three *s* one *d* (and one *s* decd). *Educ:* Marlborough College; Cambridge University (MA); Harvard Business School (MBA). Captain Royal Engineers, 1942–46; Massey Harris, Toronto, 1949–51; joined Coventry Climax Ltd, 1951, Managing Director, 1971–80, Deputy Chairman, 1980–81; Dir, Climax Fork Trucks, 1981–83; Dir and Chief Exec., Engrg Employers W Midlands Assoc., 1983–84. President: Fedn Européenne de la Manutention, 1978–80; Coventry and Dist Engineering Employers' Assoc., 1979–80 and 1983; British Indust. Truck Assoc., 1980–81; Vice-Pres., Inst. of Materials Handling, later Inst. of Materials Management, 1982–93 (FILog Emeritus, 1993). Mem., 1984–97, Chm., 1986–97, Bd of Govs, and Pro-Chancellor, 1997–2005, Coventry Univ.; Gov., Coventry Technical Coll., 1984–2002. Hon. DBA Coventry, 1997. KSS 1992. *Recreations:* pastoral work, gardening, DIY.

LISTER, Prof. (Thomas) Andrew, MD; FRCP, FRCPath, FMedSci, FRCR; Professor of Medical Oncology, 1995–2010, now Emeritus, and Director of Cancer Research UK (formerly Imperial Cancer Research Fund) Medical Oncology Unit, since 1995, Barts and The London School of Medicine and Dentistry, Queen Mary (formerly St Bartholomew's and the Royal London School of Medicine and Dentistry, Queen Mary and Westfield College), University of London, at St Bartholomew's Hospital; *b* 15 Dec. 1944; *s* of late John and Eileen Lister; *m* 1969, Sarah Leigh Martin; two *s*. *Educ:* Shrewsbury; St John's Coll., Cambridge (BA Hons 1966; MB BChir 1969); St Bartholomew's Hosp. Med. Sch. FRCP 1982; FRCPath 1994; FRCR 2001. St Bartholomew's Hospital Medical Coll., later St Bartholomew's and the Royal London Sch. of Med. and Dentistry, QMW Coll., Univ. of London: Sen. Lectr and Hon. Consultant Physician, Dept of Med. Oncology, 1977–83; Reader in Clinical Oncology, 1983–87; Prof. of Clinical Oncology, 1987–95; Postgrad. Asst Dean, and Clinical Tutor, Med. Coll. of St Bartholomew's, 1987–93; Dir of Cancer Services and Clinical Haematol., St Bartholomew's Hosp. and Bart's and the London NHS Trust, 1994–2004. Hon. Consultant Physician, Broomfield Hosp., Chelmsford, 1979–. FMedSci 2002. Associate Ed., Jl of Clinical Oncology, 2008–. *Publications:* (ed jtly) Leukemia, 6th edn 1996, 7th edn 2002; (ed jtly) The Lymphomas, 1997, 2nd edn 2006; contrib. Jl of Clinical Oncology, Blood, British Jl of Cancer, British Jl of Haematology, Annals of Oncology. *Recreations:* golf, bird watching. *Address:* Director's Office, Old Anatomy Building, Charterhouse Square, EC1M 6BQ. *T:* (020) 7882 3503. *E:* a.lister@qmul.ac.uk. *Clubs:* New (Edinburgh); Honourable Company of Edinburgh Golfers.

LISTER-KAYE, Sir John (Phillip Lister), 8th Bt *cr* 1812, of Grange, Yorks; OBE 2003; Director of the Aigas Trust, since 1979; *b* 8 May 1946; *s* of Sir John Christopher Lister Lister-Kaye, 7th Bt and Audrey Helen (*d* 1979), *d* of E. J. Carter; *S* father, 1982; direct linear descendant of Kaye Btcy *cr* 1641, of Woodsome (ext 1809); *m* 1st, 1972, Lady Sorrel Deirdre Bentinck (marr. diss. 1987), *d* of 11th Earl of Portland; one *s* two *d*; 2nd, 1989, Lucinda Anne (formerly Hon. Mrs Evan Baillie), *d* of Robin Law, Withersfield; one *d*. *Educ:* Allhallows School. Naturalist, author, lecturer. Created first field studies centre in Highlands of Scotland, 1970; Founder Director of Scottish conservation charity, the Aigas Trust, 1979; Dir, Aigas Quest Ltd, 1997–. Mem., Internat. Cttee, World Wilderness Foundn, 1983–; Chairman: Scottish Adv. Cttee, RSPB, 1986–92; Cttee for Scotland, NCC, 1989–91; NW Region, NCC for Scotland, 1991–92; NW Region, Scottish Natural Heritage, 1992–96. Pres., Scottish Wildlife Trust, 1996–2001 (Hon. Mem., 2003); Vice-Pres., Council for Protection of Rural Scotland, 1998–; Hon. Vice-Pres., RSPB, 2006–. DUniv Stirling, 1995; Hon. LLD St Andrews, 2005. *Publications:* The White Island, 1972; Seal Cull, 1979; The Seeing Eye, 1980; One for Sorrow, 1994; Ill Fares The Land, 1995; Song of the Rolling Earth, 2003; Nature's Child, 2004; At the Water's Edge: a personal quest for wildness, 2010; Gods of the Morning, 2014. *Recreations:* beach-combing, driving hydraulic diggers. *Heir:* *s* John Warwick Noel Lister-Kaye, *b* 10 Dec. 1974. *Address:* House of Aigas, Beauly, Inverness-shire IV4 7AD. *T:* (01463) 782729, *Fax:* (01463) 782097. *Club:* Caledonian.

LISTON, Gerald John, CMG 2002; Regional Director, Central and South Asia, British Council, 2008–10; *b* 21 April 1949; *s* of Sidney George Liston and Ivy Mary Liston (*née* Matthews). *Educ:* Cheltenham Grammar Sch.; St Catherine's Coll., Oxford (BA Physics, MA); London Sch. of Econs (MSc Econs). Volunteer, VSO, Malaysia, 1970–71; joined British Council, 1972: Secretariat, 1972–73; Asst Regl Dir, Kumasi, Ghana, 1973–75; Asst Rep., Malaysia, 1975–80; Staff Insp., Mgt Services, 1980–84; Director: Office Systems, 1985–88; Corporate IT, 1988–96; UK Ops, 1996–98; Resources, 1999–2003; Dir, Malaysia, 2003–08. *Recreations:* music, reading, walking, travel, modern prints, growing tropical palms in Malaysia. *Address:* 19 The Hall, Foxes Dale, SE3 9BE. *E:* gerry_liston@yahoo.co.uk.

LISTON, Stephanie Way; Senior Counsel, Charles Russell LLP, since 2011; *b* Galesburg, Ill, USA, 15 March 1958; *d* of Thomas S. Liston and Susan Liston (*née* Way); partner, Genevieve Liston-Oakden; one *d*. *Educ:* Colorado Coll. (BA 1980); Univ. of San Diego (JD 1983); Trinity Hall, Cambridge (LLM 1984). Mem., Corp., Banking and Business and Internat. Law Sections, 1984–89, Participating Associate, 1989, Fulbright and Jaworski, London, Houston and Washington; admitted: to State Bar of Texas, 1985; to DC Bar, 1988; Sen. Attorney, MCI Communications Corp., 1990–92; Manager, Freshfields, London, 1992–95; admitted as solicitor, England and Wales, 1994; Partner: Baker & McKenzie, London, 1995–99; McDermott, Will & Emery, London, 1999–2003; Partner, 2003–05, Sen. Counsel, 2005–06, WilmerHale LLP, London. Non-exec. Dir, Ofcom, 2005–08. Mem., Adv. Bd, Orga Systems GmbH, 2010–. Mem., Equality of Access Bd, BT, 2013–. Co-founder and Dir, Women in Telecoms and Technol. Member: Law Soc.; Internat. Bar Assoc. (Co-Chair, Communications Cttee, 2004–06). MInstD. Freeman, Information Technologists' Co. *Publications:* Planning your Information Super Highway: Telecommunications Users' Association official reference book, 1995; contribs to jls incl. Global Telecoms Business, IoD Mag., Global Counsel Jl, Legal Week, Computer and Telecommunications Law Rev., The Voice. *Address:* The Hall, Peasenhall, Suffolk IP17 2HL. *T:* 07713 786666. *E:* stephanie.liston@pvl.uk.com.

LISTOWEL, 6th Earl of, *cr* 1822 (Ire.); **Francis Michael Hare;** Baron Ennismore (Ire.), 1800; Viscount Ennismore and Listowel (Ire.), 1816; Baron Hare (UK), 1869; *b* 28 June 1964; *s* of 5th Earl of Listowel, GCMG, PC and of his 3rd wife, Pamela Reid (*née* Day); *S* father, 1997. *Educ:* Westminster Sch.; Queen Mary and Westfield Coll., London Univ. (BA 1992). Elected Mem., H of L, 1999; Mem., Sub-Cttee F (Home Affairs), Select Cttee on EU, H of L, 2003–07; Treas., All-Party Parly Gp for Children; Vice-Chm., Associate Parly Gp for Children in Care. Trustee, Michael Sieff Foundn. *Heir:* *b* Hon. Timothy Patrick Hare, *b* 23 Feb. 1966.

LISVANE, Baron *cr* 2014 (Life Peer), of Blakemere in the County of Herefordshire and of Lisvane in the City and County of Cardiff; **Robert James Rogers,** KCB 2013; DL; Clerk of the House of Commons, and Chief Executive of the House of Commons Service, 2011–14; *b* 5 Feb. 1950; *o s* of late Francis Barry Day Rogers and Jeanne Turner Prichard Rogers (*née* Prichard-Williams); *m* 1st, 1973, Sarah Elizabeth Anne Howard (marr. diss. 1978); 2nd, 1981, Rev. Constance Jane Perkins; two *d*. *Educ:* Tonbridge Sch. (Scholar); Lincoln Coll., Oxford (Scholar and Judd Exhibitioner; BA Hons 1971; Rhodes Res. Scholar 1971; MA 1978; Hon. Fellow 2012). MoD, 1971–72; House of Commons: an Asst Clerk, 1972; a Sen. Clerk, 1977; a Dep. Principal Clerk, 1985; Clerk: of Select Cttee on Defence, 1983–89; of Private Members' Bills, 1989–92; of Select Cttee on European Legislation, 1993–98; Parly Counsellor to the Pres., Parly Assembly of Council of Europe, 1992–95; Principal Clerk: of Delegated Legislation, 1998–99; of Select Cttees, 1999–2001; of Domestic Cttees, and Sec., H of C Commn, 2001–04; Clerk of the Journals, 2004–05; Principal Clerk of the Table Office, 2005–06; Clerk of Legislation, 2006–09; Clerk Asst and Dir Gen., Chamber and Cttee Services, 2009–11. Mem., Select Cttee on Delegated Powers and Regulatory Reform, H of L, 2015–. Ind. Chm., Standards Cttee, Herefords CC, 2002–11; Ind. Chm., 2002–06, Mem., 2006–12, Standards Cttee, Herefords and Worcs Fire Authy; Ind. Mem., 2002–04, Chm., 2004–08, Selection Panel, Ind. Mem., Standards Cttee, 2007–11, W Mercia Police Authy. Gov., Skinners' Co. Sch. for Girls, 2005–10. Chm., Hereford Cathedral Perpetual Trust, 2007–09. Fellow, Industry and Parliament Trust, 1981 (Trustee, 2009–11). Trustee, History of Parliament, 2009–11. Associate, Nat. Sch. of Govt, 2007–12. Hon. Bencher, Middle Temple, 2013. Liveryman, Skinners' Co., 2004 (Mem. Court, 2005–07). DL Herts, 2015. Churchwarden, St Leonard's, Blakemere. Patron, Herefordshire Headway. Parliamentarian of Year, Spectator, 2014. *Publications:* How Parliament Works (with Rhodri Walters), 5th edn 2004 to 7th edn 2015; Order! Order!: a parliamentary miscellany, 2009; Who Goes Home?: a parliamentary miscellany, 2012; contribs to various books and jls on European and Parly affairs. *Recreations:* music (church organist), cricket, Real tennis, sailing, shooting, the natural world. *Address:* Blakemere House, Blakemere, Herefordshire HR2 9JZ. *E:* lisvane@parliament.uk. *Club:* Travellers.

LIT, Avtar; Chairman and Chief Executive: Litt Corporation, 1989–2014; London Media Company, 2003–14; *b* 7 April 1950; *s* of Gurbax Kaur Lit and late Sarwan Singh Lit; *m* 1995, Anita Loomba; three *s* two *d*. *Educ:* Temple Secondary Sch., Rochester; Collingwood Naval Coll., Chatham. Man. Dir, Cable Vision, 1982–; Chairman and Chief Executive: Sunrise Radio Ltd, 1989–2014; Kismat Radio; Punjabi Radio; Sunrise TV; Time 106.6 FM; Time 107.5 FM; Palm FM; Exeter FM. Former Dir, West London TEC. Hon. PhD Thames Valley, 2003. *Recreations:* new projects, travelling, fundraising, para-sailing, ski-ing. *Club:* Reform.

LITHERLAND, Prof. Albert Edward, (Ted), FRS 1974; FRSC 1968; University Professor, 1979–93, now Emeritus, and Professor of Physics, 1966–93, University of Toronto; *b* 12 March 1928; *e s* of Albert Litherland and Ethel Clement; *m* 1956, (Elizabeth) Anne Allen; two *d*. *Educ:* Wallasey Grammar Sch.; Univ. of Liverpool (BSc, PhD). State Scholar to Liverpool Univ., 1946; Rutherford Memorial Scholar to Atomic Energy of Canada, Chalk River, Canada, 1953; Scientific Officer at Atomic Energy of Canada, 1955–66. Dir, Isotrace Lab., 1982–2009, Guggenheim Fellow, 1986–87, Univ. of Toronto. Hon. DSc Toronto, 1998. Canadian Assoc. of Physicists Gold Medal for Achievement in Physics, 1971; Rutherford Medal and Prize of Inst. of Physics (London), 1974; JARI Silver Medal, Pergamon Press, 1981; Henry Marshall Tory Medal, RSC, 1993. Izaac Walton Killam Memorial Scholarship, 1980. *Publications:* numerous, in scientific jls. *Address:* Apt #801, 120 Rosedale Valley Road, Toronto, ON M4W 1P8, Canada. *T:* (416) 9235616. *E:* ted.litherland@utoronto.ca.

LITHGOW, Sir William (James), 2nd Bt *cr* 1925, of Ormsary; DL; CEng; industrialist and farmer; General Partner, Ormsary Farmers and Inver Farmers, since 1995; Director, Lithgows Ltd, 1956–2006 (Chairman, 1959–84 and 1988–99); *b* 10 May 1934; *o s* of Colonel Sir James Lithgow, 1st Bt of Ormsary, GBE, CB, MC, TD, DL, JP, LLD, and Gwendolyn Amy, *d* of late John Robinson Harrison of Scalesceugh, Cumberland; *S* father, 1952; *m* 1964, Valerie Helen (*d* 1964), 2nd *d* of late Denis Scott, CBE and Mrs Laura Scott; *m* 1967, Mary Claire,

(DL Argyll and Bute), *d* of Colonel F. M. Hill, CBE and Mrs Hill; two *s* one *d*. *Educ:* Winchester Coll. CEng; FRINA; CCMI (FBIM 1969; CBIM 1980). Chm., Scott Lithgow Drydocks Ltd, 1967–78; Vice-Chm., Scott Lithgow Ltd, 1968–78; Chairman: Western Ferries (Argyll) Ltd, 1972–85; Hunterston Develt Co. Ltd, 1987–2008 (Dir, 1971–2008); Director: Bank of Scotland, 1962–86; Campbeltown Shipyard Ltd, 1970–96; Lithgows Pty Ltd, 1972–2008; Landcatch, 1981–96. Member: Council, Shipbuilding Employers Fedn, 1961–62; British Cttee, Det Norske Veritas, 1966–92; Exec. Cttee, Scottish Council Develt and Industry, 1969–85; Scottish Regional Council of CBI, 1969–76; Clyde Port Authority, 1969–71; Bd, National Ports Council, 1971–78; West Central Scotland Plan Steering Cttee, 1970–74; General Board (Royal Soc. nominee), Nat. Physical Lab., 1963–66; Greenock Dist Hosp. Bd, 1961–66; Scottish Milk Marketing Bd, 1979–83. Chm., Iona Cathedral Trustees Management Bd, 1979–83; Mem. Council, Winston Churchill Meml Trust, 1979–83. Hon. President: Mid Argyll Agricl Soc., 1976–99; Inverclyde and Dist Bn, Boys' Brigade, 1998–2000 (Vice Hon. Pres., 2000–); former Hon. Pres., W Renfrewshire Bn Boys' Brigade. Hon. Pres., Students Assoc., and Mem. Court, Univ. of Strathclyde, 1964–69. Petitioner in case of Lithgow and others *v* UK, at Eur. Court of Human Rights, 1986. Member, Queen's Body Guard for Scotland (Royal Company of Archers), 1964. Fellow: Scottish Council, 1988; Bishop Mus., Hawaii, 1969. FRSA 1990. DL Renfrewshire, 1970. Hon. LLD Strathclyde, 1979. *Publications:* lectures and papers. *Recreations:* rural life, invention, photography. *Heir: s* James Frank Lithgow [*b* 13 June 1970; *m* 1997, Claire, *yr d* of Nicholas du Cane Wilkinson; two *s* one *d*]. *Address:* Ormsary House, by Lochgilphead, Argyllshire PA31 8PE. *T:* (01880) 770252; Drums, Langbank, Renfrewshire PA14 6YH. *T:* (01475) 540606; (office) Ormsary Estate Office, Ormsary, Lochgilphead, Argyllshire PA31 8PE. *T:* (01880) 770715. *E:* wjlithgow@ormsary.demon.co.uk. *Clubs:* Oriental; Western (Glasgow).

LITHMAN, Nigel Mordecai Lloyd; QC 1997; a Recorder, since 2000; *b* 9 March 1952; *s* of Dr Leslie Henry Lithman, FFARCS, and Ethel Imber Lithman; *m* Debbie; three step *s*. *Educ:* Bancroft's Sch., Woodford Green; Mid Essex Coll., Chelmsford (LLB Hons). Called to the Bar, Inner Temple, 1976, Bencher, 2009; in practice at the Bar, 1976–; Asst Recorder, 1996–2000. Chm., Criminal Bar Assoc., 2013–14 (Vice Chm., 2012–13). Chm., Essex Bar Mess. Chm., Highgate Synagogue, 2008–. *Recreations:* fresh air, the arts. *Club:* Garrick.

LITTLE, Alastair; *see* Little, R. A.

LITTLE, Allan; *see* Little, J. A. S.

LITTLE, Anthony Richard Morrell; Chief Education Officer, GEMS Education, since 2015; *b* 7 April 1954; *s* of Edward Little and Rosemary Margaret Little (*née* Morrell); *m* 1978, Jennifer Anne Greenwood; one *d*. *Educ:* Eton Coll.; Corpus Christi Coll., Cambridge (MA English); Homerton Coll., Cambridge (PGCE). FCollP 1990. Asst Master, Tonbridge Sch., 1977–82; Hd of English and Boarding Housemaster, Brentwood Sch., 1982–89; Headmaster: Chigwell Sch., 1989–96; Oakham Sch., 1996–2002; Eton Coll., 2002–15. Mem. Council, Brunel Univ., 2013–. President: Internat. Boys' Schs Coalition, 2012–15 (Vice Pres., 2010–12); Boarding Schs Assoc., 2015–. Governor: Northwood Coll., 1990–98; St Albans Sch., 1994–2014; Windsor Boys' Sch., 2002–15; Oakham Sch., 2009–; Sevenoaks Sch., 2011–; London Acad. of Excellence, 2012–15; Holyport Coll., 2013–15. Chairman: Mvumi Sch. Trust, 2008–15; World Leading Schs Assoc., 2009–. FRSA 1991. *Publications:* An Intelligent Person's Guide to Education, 2015. *Recreations:* films, theatre, music, Norfolk. *Address:* GEMS Education, 2nd Floor, 57–59 Haymarket, St Albans House, SW1Y 4QX.

LITTLE, Ian; *see* Little, J. MacC.

LITTLE, (James) Allan (Stuart); Chairman, Edinburgh International Book Festival, since 2015; *b* Dunragit, Wigtownshire, 11 Oct. 1959; *s* of Francis Robert Little and Elizabeth Margaret Little (*née* Clive); *m* 2006, Sheena Elizabeth McDonald. *Educ:* Univ. of Edinburgh (MA 1982). BBC: researcher, BBC Scotland, 1983; reporter: BBC Radio, 1984; Today prog., Radio Four, 1988; reporter and correspondent, BBC Foreign News, 1990–95, Iraq, 1990–91, former Yugoslavia, 1991–95; BBC Africa Corresp., Johannesburg, 1995–97 and 2000–01; Moscow Corresp., 1997–99; Presenter, Today prog., Radio Four, 1999–2003; Paris Corresp., 2003–05; World Affairs Corresp., 2005–08, Special Correspondent, 2008–14, BBC News. Mem., Scotch Malt Whisky Soc., Edinburgh. Hon. Fellow in History, Univ. of Edinburgh. *Publications:* (with Laura Silber) Death of Yugoslavia, 1995. *Recreations:* books, countryside, walking. *Club:* Frontline.

LITTLE, John MacCalman, (Ian), CMG 2003; CBE 1983; Deputy Chairman and Chief Executive, Anderson Strathclyde plc, 1980–88; *b* 23 Feb. 1936; *s* of John Little and Margaret Haddow Little (*née* King); *m* 1962, Irene Pirrie Frame; one *s* one *d*. *Educ:* Marr Coll., Troon. CA 1958; ACMA 1962. Financial positions: Stewarts & Lloyds Ltd, 1961–63; Pressed Steel Fisher Ltd, 1963–69; Anderson Strathclyde plc: Gp Accountant, 1969–70; Divl Financial Dir, 1971–73; Financial Dir, 1973–77; Asst Man. Dir, 1977–80. Dir, Scottish Exhibition Centre Ltd, 1989–96. Member: Council, CBI Scotland, 1980–89 (Chm., 1985–87); Scottish Industrial Adv. Bd, 1981–93; Accounts Commn for Scotland, 1989–97; Eur. Econ. and Social Gp, 1990–2002 (Chm., Employers' Gp, 2000–02). Treas., Strathaven Rankin Parish Church, 1974–2007. *Recreations:* golf, gardening, bridge. *Address:* 8 Wateryett Loan, Strathaven, Lanarkshire ML10 6EJ. *T:* (01357) 520762. *E:* jmlittle@btinternet.com. *Clubs:* Strathaven Golf (Chm., 2000–04); Strathaven Bridge (Capt., 2013–).

LITTLE, Maria Milagros; *see* Delgado, M. M.

LITTLE, Prof. Richard, PhD; FBA 2010; Professor of International Politics, Bristol University, 1993–2009, now Emeritus; *b* Shotley Bridge, 26 Oct. 1944; *s* of late Thomas Lowden Little and Marjorie Annie Little; *m* 1981, Christine Stratford. *Educ:* Dame Allan's Boys' Sch., Newcastle upon Tyne; University Coll. London (BSc (Econ)); Lehigh Univ., Penn (MA); Lancaster Univ. (PhD 1973). Lecturer: Lancaster Univ., 1969–76; Open Univ., 1976–80; Lectr, 1980–82, Sen. Lectr, 1982–93, Lancaster Univ. *Publications:* Intervention: external involvement in civil wars, 1975; (ed with M. Smith) Perspectives on World Politics, 1981; (with R. D. McKinlay) Global Problems and World Order, 1986; (jtly) The Logic of Anarchy, 1991; (with B. Buzan) International Systems in World History, 2000; The Balance of Power, 2007. *Address:* 11 Canynge Square, Bristol BS8 3LA. *E:* r.little@bris.ac.uk.
See also T. W. A. Little.

LITTLE, (Robert) Alastair; chef and delicatessen proprietor; *b* 25 June 1950; *s* of Robert Geoffrey Little and Marion Irving Little; one *s* one *d*; *m* 2000, Sharon Jacob; one *s*. *Educ:* Kirkham Grammar Sch., Lancs; Downing Coll., Cambridge (MA). Chef proprietor: Le Routier, Suffolk, 1976; Simpson's, Putney, 1979; L'Escargot, Soho, 1981; 192, London, 1983; Alastair Little, Soho, 1985–2002; Alastair Little, Lancaster Road, 1995–2002; proprietor: La Cacciata, Orvieto, Italy, 1994; Tavola delicatessen, Westbourne Grove, 2003–. *Publications:* (with Richard Whittington) Keep it Simple, 1993; (with Richard Whittington) Food of the Sun, 1995; Alastair Little's Italian Kitchen, 1996; Soho Cooking, 1999. *Recreations:* reading, mycology. *Address:* Tavola, 155 Westbourne Grove, Notting Hill, W11 2RS. *Club:* Groucho.

LITTLE, Tasmin, OBE 2012; violinist; *b* 13 May 1965; *d* of George Villiers Little and Gillian (*née* Morris); one *s* one *d*. *Educ:* Yehudi Menuhin Sch.; Guildhall Sch. of Music (DipGSM 1986). ARCM 1984. Has performed as soloist in UK, Europe, USA, Scandinavia, S America, Hong Kong, Oman, Zimbabwe and SA. Concerto performances with leading orchestras including: Leipzig Gewandhaus; Berlin Symphony; LSO; Philharmonia; Royal Philharmonic; Hallé; Bournemouth; Royal Liverpool Philharmonic; EC Chamber Orch.; Royal Danish; Stavanger Symphony; NY Philharmonic; Cleveland; Sir Simon Rattle and Berlin Philharmonic; acknowledged interpreter of music of Delius. TV appearances, radio broadcasts; 27 commercial recordings released (incl. Classic BRIT Award for Elgar violin concerto, 2011). Ambassador: Prince's Foundn for Children and the Arts; for Youth Music. Pres., Yehudi Menuhin Sch. 50th Anniv. Appeal, 2013–16. Former Pres., Eur. String Teachers' Assoc. FGS. Hon. DLitt Bradford, 1996; Hon. DMus Leicester, 2002; Hon. Dr: Herts; City London. Gold Badge Award for services to music, BASCA, 2009. *Publications:* contrib. Delius Soc. Jl. *Recreations:* theatre, cinema, swimming, cooking, languages. *Address:* c/o Kantor Concert Management & PR, 67 Teignmouth Road, NW2 4EA. *T:* (020) 8208 2480. *W:* www.tasminlittle.org.uk.

LITTLE, Dr Thomas William Anthony, CBE 2001; FRSB; Director and Chief Executive, Veterinary Laboratories Agency (formerly Central Veterinary Laboratory), Ministry of Agriculture, Fisheries and Food, 1990–2000; *b* 27 June 1940; *s* of late Thomas Lowden Little and Marjorie Annie Little; *m* 1st, 1963 (marr. diss.); one *s* one *d*; 2nd, 1985, Sally Anne Headlam; two *s*. *Educ:* Dame Allan's Sch., Newcastle upon Tyne; Edinburgh Univ. (BVMS); London Univ. (Dip. Bact., PhD). MRCVS 1963. General veterinary practice, March, Cambs, 1963–66; joined MAFF, 1966; Central Vet. Lab., Weybridge, 1966–82, Sen. Res. Officer 1973–82; Dep. Regl Vet. Officer, 1982–85, Vet. Head of Section, 1985–86, Tolworth; Dep. Dir, Central Vet. Lab., 1986–90. Vice-Pres., BVA, 2000–02. Chair of Govs, Fullbrook Sch., 2006–. FRSA. *Publications:* contribs to veterinary jls and text books. *Recreation:* outdoor activities. *Address:* 10 Fox Close, Pyrford, Woking, Surrey GU22 8LP.
See also R. Little.

LITTLECHILD, Prof. Stephen Charles; international consultant on privatisation, competition and regulation, since 1999; Fellow (formerly Senior Research Associate), Judge Business School (formerly Judge Institute of Management Studies), University of Cambridge, since 2004 (Principal Research Fellow, 2000–04); *b* 27 Aug. 1943; *s* of Sidney F. Littlechild and Joyce M. Littlechild (*née* Sharpe); *m* 1974, Kate Crombie (*d* 1982); two *s* one *d*. *Educ:* Wisbech Grammar Sch.; Univ. of Birmingham (BCom); Univ. of Texas (PhD). Temp. Asst Lectr in Ind. Econs, Univ. of Birmingham, 1964–65; Harkness Fellow, Stanford Univ., 1965–66; Northwestern Univ., 1966–68; Univ. of Texas at Austin, 1968–69; ATT Post-doctoral Fellow, UCLA and Northwestern Univ., 1969; Sen. Res. Lectr in Econs, Graduate Centre for Management Studies, Birmingham, 1970–72; Prof. of Applied Econs and Head of Econs, Econometrics, Statistics and Marketing Subject Gp, Aston Management Centre, 1972–75; Prof. of Commerce and Hd of Dept of Industrial Econs and Business Studies, Univ. of Birmingham, 1975–89; Dir Gen., Electricity Supply, 1989–98. Vis. Scholar, Dept of Econs, UCLA, 1975; Vis. Prof., New York, Stanford and Chicago Univs, and Virginia Polytechnic, 1979–80; Hon. Prof., Sch. of Business, Univ. of Birmingham, 1994–2004, now Emeritus Prof. Member: Monopolies and Mergers Commn, 1983–89; Sec. of State for Energy's Adv. Council on R&D, 1987–89; Postal Services Commn, 2006–11. Dist. Fellow, Regulatory Policy Inst., Univ. of Oxford, 2009. Hon. DSc Birmingham, 2001; Hon. DCL UEA, 2004. Zale Award, Stanford Univ., 1999; Pace Catalyst Award, UMS Gp, 2000. *Publications:* Operational Research for Managers, 1977, 2nd edn (with M. F. Shutler) as Operations Research in Management, 1991; The Fallacy of the Mixed Economy, 1978, 2nd edn 1986; Elements of Telecommunications Economics, 1979; Energy Strategies for the UK, 1982; Regulation of British Telecommunications' Profitability, 1983; Economic Regulation of Privatised Water Authorities, 1986; Privatization, Competition and Regulation in the British Electricity Industry, with Implications for Developing Countries, 2000; 200 articles in books and jls. *Recreations:* football, genealogy. *Address:* White House, The Green, Tanworth-in-Arden B94 5AL. *E:* sclittlechild@tanworth.mercianet.co.uk.

LITTLEJOHN, Bel; *see* Brown, C. E. M.

LITTLEJOHN, Doris, CBE 1998; President, Industrial Tribunals (Scotland), 1991–2000; *b* 19 March 1935; *m* 1958, Robert White Littlejohn (decd); three *d*. *Educ:* Univ. of Glasgow (BL). Chm., Forth Valley Primary Care NHS Trust, until 2004. Mem., Govt Human Genetics Adv. Commn, until 1999. Non-executive Director: Law at Work (Holdings) Ltd, 2002–14; Saga Radio (Glasgow) Ltd, 2004–06. Chm. Ct, Univ. of Stirling, 1999–2007. JP Stirlingshire, 1970–2010. DUniv Stirling, 1993. *Address:* 125 Henderson Street, Bridge of Allan, Stirlingshire FK9 4RQ. *T:* (01786) 832032.

LITTLER, Rosalyn Elaine; *see* Moore, R. E.

LITTLETON, family name of **Baron Hatherton**.

LITTLEWOOD, Mark James; Director General, and Ralph Harris Fellow, Institute of Economic Affairs, since 2009; *b* Reading, 28 April 1972; *s* of Kenneth Littlewood and Elizabeth Sheila Littlewood; partner, Angela Harbutt. *Educ:* Forest Sch., Winnersh; Henley Coll., Henley-upon-Thames; Balliol Coll., Oxford (BA Hons 1993); City Univ., London. Hd, Regl Campaigning, European Movement, 1996–99; Campaign Director: Pro-Euro Conservative Party, 1999–2001; Liberty, 2001–04; Hd of Media, Liberal Democrats, 2004–07; Communications Dir, Progressive Vision, 2007–09. Chm., NO2ID, 2005–09. MInstD 2010. *Recreations:* long suffering season ticket holder of Southampton Football Club, enthusiastic - and acceptably competent - player of Texas hold'em poker, British cult television - especially Doctor Who. *Address:* 2 Lord North Street, SW1P 3LB. *T:* (office) (020) 7799 8900. *E:* mlittlewood@iea.org.uk. *Club:* Reform.

LITTLEWOOD, Prof. Peter Brent, PhD; FRS 2007; FInstP; Director, Argonne National Laboratory, since 2014 (Associate Laboratory Director for Physical Sciences and Engineering, 2011–14); Professor of Physics, James Franck Institute, University of Chicago, since 2011; *b* 18 May 1955; *s* of Horace Victor Littlewood and Edna May Littlewood; *m* 1978, Elizabeth Lamb; one *s* one *d*. *Educ:* St Olave's Sch., Orpington; Trinity Coll., Cambridge (BA 1976); Massachusetts Inst. of Technol. (Kennedy Schol.); Clare Coll., Cambridge (Denman Baynes Student; PhD 1980). FInstP 2007. Bell Laboratories, Murray Hill, New Jersey: Mem., Technical Staff, 1980–97; Hd, Theoretical Physics Res. Dept, 1992–97; Prof. of Physics, 1997–2012, Hd, Dept of Physics, 2005–11, Cavendish Lab., Univ. of Cambridge; Fellow, Trinity Coll., Cambridge, 1997–2012. Mem., TWAS, 2009. Fellow, APS, 1988. *Publications:* numerous contribs to learned jls on theoretical condensed matter physics. *Recreations:* squash, music. *Address:* Argonne National Laboratory, 9700 S Cass Avenue, Argonne, IL 60439, USA; Cavendish Laboratory, Cambridge University, J. J. Thomson Avenue, Cambridge CB3 0HE.

LITTON, Andrew; conductor and pianist; Music Director, Colorado Symphony Orchestra, since 2013; *b* New York, 16 May 1959; *m*; one *c*. *Educ:* Fieldston Sch., NYC; Juilliard Sch. of Music, NYC (piano with Nadia Reisenberg; Bruno Walter Meml Conducting Scholar). Rehearsal pianist, La Scala, Milan, 1980–81; Staff Conductor, 1983–85, Associate Conductor, 1985–86, National SO, Washington; sometime Principal Conductor, Virginia Chamber Orch.; Principal Guest Conductor, 1986–88, Principal Conductor and Artistic Advr, 1988–94, Bournemouth SO, now Conductor Laureate; Music Director: Dallas SO, 1994–2006, now Music Dir Emeritus; Bergen Philharmonic Orch., 2005–15, now Music Dir Laureate. Début piano recital, Carnegie Hall, NY, 1979; conducting débuts include: Henry Wood Promenade Concert, 1983; RPO, 1983; Royal Opera House, Covent Garden, 1992. Winner: William Kapell Piano Comp., 1978; BBC/Rupert Foundn Internat. Conductors Comp., 1982. *Address:* c/o MusicVine, 2576 Broadway #239, New York, NY 10025, USA.

LITTON, John Letablere; QC 2010; *b* Hong Kong, 20 May 1966; *s* of Henry and Jennifer Litton; *m* 1997, Christine Lowthian; two *s* one *d*. *Educ:* Sedbergh Sch.; Southampton Univ. (LLB). Called to the Bar, Middle Temple, 1989; in practice as barrister, specialising in town and country planning and envmtl and public law; Treasury Counsel, A Panel, 2004–09. *Recreations:* ski-ing, running, food and wine. *Address:* Landmark Chambers, 180 Fleet Street, EC4A 2HG. *T:* (020) 7430 1221, *Fax:* (020) 7421 6060. *E:* Jlitton@landmarkchambers.co.uk.

LIU XIAOBO, PhD; literary critic, writer, independent intellectual and political activist; *b* Changchun, Jilin, China, 28 Dec. 1955; *m* Liu Xia. *Educ:* Jilin Univ. (BA Literature); Beijing Normal Univ. (MA; PhD). Former Prof., Beijing Normal Univ.; former Vis. Scholar: Univ. of Oslo; Univ. of Hawaii; Columbia Univ., until 1989. Returned to Beijing to participate in Democracy Movement, April 1989; held in Qincheng Prison, Beijing, 1989–91; found guilty of 'counter-revolutionary propaganda and incitement' but exempted from punishment, 1991; kept under residential surveillance, 1995–96; sentenced to Reeducation-Through-Labour, 1996–99; co-author, Charter 08 manifesto, 2008; detained, Dec. 2008; found guilty of 'inciting subversion of state power' and sentenced to 11 years imprisonment, Dec. 2009. Pres., Independent Chinese PEN Center, 2003–07. Nobel Peace Prize, 2010. *Publications:* No Enemies, No Hatred: selected essays and poems, 2012; numerous essays.

LIVELY, Dame Penelope (Margaret), DBE 2012 (CBE 2002; OBE 1989); writer; *b* 17 March 1933; *d* of Roger Low and Vera Greer; *m* 1957, Jack Lively (*d* 1998); one *s* one *d*. *Educ:* St Anne's Coll., Oxford (BA Mod. History; Hon. Fellow, 2007). Member: Soc. of Authors, 1973–; PEN, 1985–; British Library Bd, 1993–99; Bd, British Council, 1998–2002. FRSL 1985. Hon. Fellow, Swansea Univ., 2002. Hon. DLitt: Tufts, 1992; Warwick, 1998. *Publications: children's books:* Astercote, 1970; The Whispering Knights, 1971; The Wild Hunt of Hagworthy, 1971; The Driftway, 1972; The Ghost of Thomas Kempe, 1973 (Carnegie Medal); The House in Norham Gardens, 1974; Going Back, 1975; Boy Without a Name, 1975; A Stitch in Time, 1976 (Whitbread Award); The Stained Glass Window, 1976; Fanny's Sister, 1976; The Voyage of QV66, 1978; Fanny and the Monsters, 1979; Fanny and the Battle of Potter's Piece, 1980; The Revenge of Samuel Stokes, 1981; Fanny and the Monsters (three stories), 1983; Uninvited Ghosts and other stories, 1984; Dragon Trouble, 1984; Debbie and the Little Devil, 1987; A House Inside Out, 1987; The Cat, the Crow and the Banyan Tree, 1994; Staying with Grandpa, 1997; In Search of a Homeland: the story of the Aeneid, 2001; *non-fiction:* The Presence of the Past: an introduction to landscape history, 1976; Oleander, Jacaranda: a childhood perceived, 1994; A House Unlocked (memoir), 2001; Ammonites & Leaping Fish: a life in time, 2013; *fiction:* The Road to Lichfield, 1976; Nothing Missing but the Samovar and other stories, 1978 (Southern Arts Literature Prize); Treasures of Time, 1979 (National Book Award); Judgement Day, 1980; Next to Nature, Art, 1982; Perfect Happiness, 1983; Corruption and other stories, 1984; According to Mark, 1984; Pack of Cards, collected short stories 1978–86, 1986; Moon Tiger, 1987 (Booker Prize); Passing On, 1989; City of the Mind, 1991; Cleopatra's Sister, 1993; Heat Wave, 1996; Beyond the Blue Mountains, 1997; Spiderweb, 1998; (ed with George Szirtes) New Writing 10, 2001; The Photograph, 2003; Making It Up, 2005; Consequences, 2007; Family Album, 2009; How It All Began, 2011; television and radio scripts. *Recreations:* gardening, landscape history, talking and listening. *Address:* c/o David Higham Associates, 7th Floor, Waverley House, 7–12 Noel Street, W1F 8GQ. *T:* (020) 7434 5900.

LIVERMAN, Prof. Diana Margaret, PhD; Regents Professor, School of Geography and Development, and Co-Director, Institute of the Environment, University of Arizona, since 2009; *b* 15 May 1954; *d* of late John Gordon Liverman, CB, OBE, and Peggy Liverman. *Educ:* University Coll. London (BA Geog. 1976); Univ. of Toronto (MA Geog. 1980); Univ. of Calif, LA (PhD Geog. 1984). Asst Prof. of Geog., Univ. of Wisconsin, Madison, 1984–89; Associate Prof. of Geog. and Associate Dir, Earth System Science Center, Penn State Univ., 1990–96; University of Arizona: Prof. of Geog. and Dir, Center for Latin American Studies, 1997–2003; Dean, Coll. of Social and Behavioral Science, 2002; University of Oxford: Prof. of Envmtl Science, 2003–09; Dir, Envmtl Change Inst., 2003–09 (Sen. Res. Fellow, 2009–); Vis. Prof. of Envmtl Policy and Develt, 2009–. Founder's Gold Medal, RGS, 2010; Dist. Scholarship Hons, Assoc. American Geographers, 2011. *Publications:* People and Pixels: linking remote sensing and social science, 1988; (jtly) World Regions in Global Context, 2002, 5th edn 2013; (ed jtly) A Companion to Environmental Geography, 2009; (ed jtly) Global Environmental Change and Food Security, 2010; (jtly) Climate Change: global risks, challenges and decisions, 2011. *Address:* Institute of the Environment, University of Arizona, PO Box 210158b, Tucson, AZ 85721, USA.

LIVERPOOL, 5th Earl of, *cr* 1905 (2nd creation); **Edward Peter Bertram Savile Foljambe;** Baron Hawkesbury, 1893; Viscount Hawkesbury, 1905; Joint Chairman, Melbourns Brewery Ltd, since 1975 (Managing Director, 1970–87); Chairman and Managing Director, Rutland Properties Ltd, since 1987 (Director, since 1986); Chairman, Rutland Group, since 1996; *b* (posthumously) 14 Nov. 1944; *s* of Captain Peter George William Savile Foljambe (killed in action, 1944) and of Elizabeth Joan (who *m* 1947, Major Andrew Antony Gibbs, MBE, TD), *d* of late Major Eric Charles Montagu Flint, DSO; *S* great uncle, 1969; *m* 1st, 1970, Lady Juliana Noel (marr. diss. 1994), *e d* of 5th Earl of Gainsborough; two *s*; 2nd, 1995, Marie-Ange (marr. diss. 2001), *e d* of Comte Géraud Michel de Pierredon; 3rd, 2002, Georgina, *yr d* of late Stanley and of Hilda Rubin. *Educ:* Shrewsbury School; Univ. for Foreigners, Perugia. Director: Rutland Properties Ltd, 1985–; Hart Hambleton Plc, 1986–92; J. W. Cameron & Co., 1987–90; Hilstone Developments Ltd, 1987–91; Rutland Management Ltd, 1989–. Elected Mem., H of L, 1999. *Heir: s* Viscount Hawkesbury, *qv*. *Address:* House of Lords, SW1A 0PW. *Clubs:* Turf, Pratt's, Air Squadron.

LIVERPOOL, Archbishop of, (RC), and Metropolitan of the Northern Province with Suffragan Sees, Hallam, Hexham, Lancaster, Leeds, Middlesbrough and Salford; since 2014; **Most Rev. Malcolm Patrick McMahon,** OP; *b* 14 June 1949; *s* of Patrick McMahon and Sarah McMahon (*née* Watson). *Educ:* St Aloysius Coll., Highgate; Univ. of Manchester Inst. of Sci. and Technol. (BSc); Blackfriars, Oxford; Heythrop Coll., London Univ. (BD; MTh). Pres., Students' Union, UMIST, 1970–71; contracts engr, London Transport, 1971–76; joined Dominican Order, 1976; ordained priest, 1982; Student Chaplain, Leicester Univ., 1984–85; Asst Priest, 1985–89, Prior and Parish Priest, 1989–92, St Dominic's Priory, NW5; Prior Provincial, English Province of Order of Preachers (Dominican Order), 1992–2000; Prior of Blackfriars, Oxford, 2000; Bishop of Nottingham, (RC), 2000–14. John Hopton Fellow, Blackfriars Hall, Oxford, 2001. Chairman: Catholic Educn Service of England and Wales, 2010–; Bishop's Dept of Educn and Formation, 2010–; Catholic Trust for England and Wales, 2010–. *Publications:* contrib. articles and reviews in New Blackfriars, Dominican Ashram and Signum. *Recreations:* walking, golf, reading thrillers. *Address:* Lowood, Carnatic Road, Liverpool L18 8BY.

LIVERPOOL, Bishop of, since 2014; **Rt Rev. Paul Bayes;** *b* Bradford, 2 Nov. 1953; *m* 1976, Katharine Soley; one *s* two *d*. *Educ:* Birmingham Univ. (BA 1975); Queen's Coll., Birmingham. Ordained deacon, 1979, priest, 1980; Asst Curate, St Paul, Cullercoats, 1979–82; Chaplain: Queen Elizabeth Coll., 1982–87; Chelsea Coll. of Art and Design, 1985–87; Team Vicar, High Wycombe Team Ministry, 1987–90; Team Rector, All Saints, High Wycombe, 1990–94; Team Rector, Totton, 1995–2004; Area Dean, Lyndhurst, 2000–04; Nat. Mission and Evangelism Advr, Archbishop's Council, 2004–10; Bishop Suffragan of Hertford, 2010–14. Hon. Canon, Worcester Cathedral, 2007–10. *Recreations:* walking, reading, conversation and laughter. *Address:* Bishop's Lodge, Woolton Park, Woolton, Liverpool L25 6DT. *T:* (0151) 421 0831.

LIVERPOOL, Auxiliary Bishop of, (RC); *see* Williams, Rt Rev. T. A.

LIVERPOOL, Dean of; *see* Wilcox, Very Rev. P. J.

LIVERPOOL, Archdeacon of; *see* Panter, Ven. R. J. G.

LIVERSIDGE, Pamela Edwards, OBE 1999; DL; DSc; FREng, FIMechE; Managing Director, Quest Investments Ltd, since 1997; President, Institution of Mechanical Engineers, 1997–98; *b* 23 Dec. 1949; *d* of William H. Humphries and Dorothy Humphries; *m* 1st, 1971, Dr Dale S. Edwards (marr. diss. 1980); 2nd, 1991, Douglas B. Liversidge; two step *s* one step *d*. *Educ:* Aston Univ. (BSc Hons 1971; DSc 1998). CEng 1980; FIMechE 1988; FCGI 1997; FREng 1999. Graduate trainee and project engr, GKN plc, 1971–73; Thornton Precision Forgings: Asst Technical Manager, 1973–78; Prodn Control Manager, 1978–81; Aerofoils Product Manager, 1981–86; Sales and Mkting Dir, 1986–89; Strategic Planning Manager, E Midlands Electricity plc, 1989–93; Man. Dir, Scientific Metal Powders Ltd, 1993–97. Dir, Tool and Steel Products Ltd, 1993; non-executive Director: Rainbow Seed Fund, Spectrum Ltd, 2006–13; Source BioScience plc. Dir, Sheffield TEC, 1997–98; Chm., Sheffield Business Link, 1998–2001; non-exec. Dir, Chesterfield Royal Foundn Trust Hosp., 2006–12. Vis. Prof., Sheffield Univ., 1996–99. Gov., Sheffield Hallam Univ., 1994–2006. Mem. Chapter, Sheffield Cath., 2013–. Trustee and Mem., Exec. Cttee and Council, City and Guilds of London Inst., 2006–11. FRSA 1996. DL, 1999, High Sheriff, 2004–05, S Yorks. Liveryman, Engineers' Co., 1997– (Mem., Ct of Assts, 2000–06); Master, Co. of Cutlers in Hallamshire, 2011–12. A Guardian, Sheffield Assay Office, 2005–. DUniv: UCE, 1998; Sheffield Hallam, 2006; Hon. DEng: Bradford, 2000; Sheffield, 2005; Hon. DSc: Aston, 1998; Huddersfield, 2001. *Recreations:* golf, public speaking at specialist events. *Address:* Nicholas Hall, Thornhill, Bamford, Hope Valley S33 0BR. *T:* (01433) 651475. *E:* liversidge1@btconnect.com.

LIVESEY, Bernard Joseph Edward; QC 1990; *b* 21 Feb. 1944; *s* of late Joseph Augustine Livesey and Marie Gabrielle Livesey (*née* Caulfield); *m* 1971, Penelope Jean Harper; two *d*. *Educ:* Cardinal Vaughan Sch., London; Peterhouse, Cambridge (MA, LLB). Called to the Bar, Lincoln's Inn, 1969, Bencher, 1999; a Recorder, 1987–2011; a Dep. High Court Judge, 1998–2012. Fellow, Internat. Acad. of Trial Lawyers, 1993. Mem. Adv. Bd, City Univ., 2001–08. Chm. Council, Friends of Peterhouse, 2002–10. *Address:* Hailsham Chambers, 4 Paper Buildings, Temple, EC4Y 7EX. *T:* (020) 7643 5000.

LIVESEY, David Anthony, PhD; Secretary-General, League of European Research Universities, 2005–09; Fellow, Emmanuel College, Cambridge, since 1974; *b* 30 May 1944; *s* of Vincent Livesey and Marie Livesey (*née* Parr); *m* 1967, Sally Anne Vanston; one *s* two *d*. *Educ:* Derby Sch.; Imperial Coll., Univ. of London (ACGI; BSc Eng); Christ's Coll., Cambridge (PhD 1971). University of Cambridge: Res. Officer in Applied Econs, 1969–75; Lectr in Engrg, 1975–91; Sec. Gen. of Faculties, 1992–2003; Cambridge Dir, Cambridge-MIT Inst., 1999–2000; Res. Fellow, Peterhouse, 1971–74; Tutor, 1975–83, Bursar, 1983–91, Vice-Master, 2006–11, Emmanuel Coll. Mem., HM Treasury Cttee on Policy Optimisation, 1976–78. Dir, Cambridge Econometrics Ltd, 1981–84 (Chm., 1982–84). Non-exec. Dir, Addenbrooke's NHS Trust, 1993–99. Trustee: Bedford Charity (Harpur Trust), 2004–09; Citizens Advice, 2005–11; Cambridge and Dist CAB, 2004– (Chm. Trustees, 2004–10); Cambridge City Foodbank, 2011–. Chm., Vital Spark Forum, 2005–11. Chm., Friends of Fulbourn Hosp. and the Community, 2009–. Governor: St Albans RC Primary Sch., 1977–92, 2001–05 (Chm., 1984–92, 2001–05); Henley Mgt Coll., 2005–07; St Mary's Univ. (formerly St Mary's Coll.), Twickenham, 2013–. DUniv Derby, 2011. *Recreations:* books, swimming, trying to learn Welsh. *Address:* Emmanuel College, Cambridge CB2 3AP. *T:* (01223) 334243.

LIVESEY, Timothy Peter Nicholas; Chief of Staff to Leader of the Opposition, since 2011; *b* 29 June 1959; *s* of Kevin and Mary Livesey; *m* 1986, Catherine Joan Eaglestone; two *s* three *d*. *Educ:* Stonyhurst Coll.; New Coll., Oxford (BA Modern Hist. 1981). 2nd Lieut, Royal Irish Rangers, 1977–78. Asst Registrar and Dep. Sec., UMDS, Guy's and St Thomas' Hosps, 1984–87; Foreign and Commonwealth Office, 1987–2006: First Sec. (Aid), Lagos, 1989–93; Hd, Press and Public Affairs, Paris, 1996–2000; Asst Press Sec., 10 Downing St, 2000–02; on secondment as Principal Advr for Public Affairs to Cardinal Archbp of Westminster, 2002–04; Asst Dir, Information and Strategy, FCO, 2004–06; Archbishop of Canterbury's Sec. for Public Affairs, 2006–10, for Internat. Affairs, 2010–11. *Recreations:* family, reading, writing, running. *Address:* Office of the Leader of the Opposition, House of Commons, SW1A 0AA.

LIVESLEY, Prof. Brian, MD; FRCP; medical historian, since 1973; Professor in the Care of the Elderly, University of London at Imperial College School of Medicine (formerly Charing Cross and Westminster Medical School), 1988–2001, Emeritus Professor, 2003; Consultant Forensic Physician, 2001–11; Senior Member, Harris Manchester College, Oxford, since 2012; *b* 31 Aug. 1936; *s* of late Thomas Clement Livesley and Stella Livesley; *m* 1st, 1963, Beryl Hulme (*d* 1966); one *s*; 2nd, 1969, Valerie Anne Nuttall; two *d*. *Educ:* King George V Grammar Sch., Southport; Leeds Univ. Med. Sch. (MB, ChB 1960); Univ. of London (MD 1979). MRCP 1971, FRCP 1989. DHMSA 1973. Hospital appointments: Leeds Gen. Infirmary, 1961–62; Dist and Univ. Hosps, Leeds, Manchester and Liverpool, 1963–68; Harvey Res. Fellow, KCH, 1969–72; Cons. Physician in Geriatric Medicine, Lambeth, Southwark and Lewisham HA, 1973–87. Asst Dir-Gen., 1993–94, Dir-Gen., 1994–96, St John Ambulance. Clinical Examr in Medicine, Univ. of London, 1980–94 (Sen. Examr, 1990–94); External Examr, Royal Free and UC Med. Sch., 1998–2001; Examiner: for Dip. in Geriatric Medicine, RCP, 1987–93; in Medicine, Soc. of Apothecaries, 1987–93; Mem., United Examng Bd for England and Scotland, 1993–96. NW Thames Regl Advr on Medicine for the Elderly, 1990–2001; Chm., N Thames Regl Trng Commn, 1993–96. Mem., Med. Commn on Accident Prevention, 1984–89 (Chm., Home and Family Safety Commn, 1988–89). NHS Exec. Assessor for NHS R&D Nat. Primary Care Awards, 2002–03. Member: British Acad. Forensic Sci., 2002–08; Assoc. of Forensic Physicians, 2004–06. Lectures: Osler, 1975, Gideon de Laune, 2001, Faculty of Hist. of Medicine and Pharmacy, Soc. of Apothecaries; Hunterian, 2003; Med. Soc. of London and Osler Club (jt meeting), 2006; John Keats, Guy's Hosp., 2009. Liveryman, Soc. of Apothecaries, 1980– (Yeoman, 1975; Mem. Ct of Assts, 1990–; Master, 2005–06; Immediate Past Master, 2006–07; Chm., Futures Cttee, 1999–2004; Chm., Acad. Cttee, 2000–03). JP SE London, 1983–96. KStJ 1994. *Publications:* The Dying Keats: a case for euthanasia?, 2009; monographs and investigations on scientific, historical, educnl and forensic problems of medicine in our ageing soc. *Recreations:* family, Christian culture study at the time of St Paul, encouraging people to think. *Address:* Wolfson House, Yarnells Hill, Oxford OX2 9BG.

LIVINGSTON, family name of **Baron Livingston of Parkhead**.

LIVINGSTON OF PARKHEAD, Baron *cr* 2013 (Life Peer), of Parkhead in the City of Glasgow; **Ian Paul Livingston;** *b* Glasgow, 1964; *m* Debbie; one *s* one *d*. *Educ:* Univ. of Manchester (BA Econ). ACA 1987. With Arthur Andersen, 1984–87; with Bank of America, 1987–88; with 3i Gp plc, 1988–91; sen. mgt roles, 1991–96, Chief Finance Officer, 1996–2002, Dixons Gp plc; Chief Finance Officer, BT Gp plc, 2002–05; CEO, BT Retail, 2005–08; Chief Exec., BT Gp plc, 2008–13. Non-executive Director: Freeserve plc, 1999–2001; Hilton Gp plc, 2003–06; Celtic plc, 2007–. Minister of State (Minister for Trade and Investment), BIS and FCO, 2013–15. *Recreation:* football. *Address:* Department for Business, Innovation and Skills, 1 Victoria Street, SW1H 0ET. *E:* mpst.livingston@bis.gsi.gov.uk.

LIVINGSTON, Prof. Andrew Guy, PhD; FREng; Professor of Chemical Engineering, since 1999, and Head, Department of Chemical Engineering, since 2008, Imperial College London; *b* 4 Nov. 1962; *s* of Derek Heathcoat Livingston and Muriel Livingston; *m* 1996, Luisa Freitas dos Santos; one *s* one *d. Educ:* Univ. of Canterbury, NZ (BEng Hons Chem. 1984); PhD Cantab 1990; London Sch. of Econs (MSc Econs 1994). Company Chem. Engr, Canterbury Frozen Meat Co., NZ, 1984–86; Cambridge Commonwealth Trust Scholar, Trinity Coll., Cambridge, 1986–89; Lectr, 1990–96, Reader, 1996–99, Imperial College, London. Founder, and Man. Dir, Membrane Extraction Technology Ltd, 1996–. FREng 2006. Cremer and Warner Medal, IChemE, 1997. *Publications:* over 150 articles in learned jls and monographs. *Recreations:* fruit trees, windsurfing. *Address:* c/o Department of Chemical Engineering, Imperial College London, SW7 2AZ. *T:* (020) 7594 5382, *Fax:* (020) 7584 5629. *E:* a.livingston@imperial.ac.uk.

LIVINGSTON, Dorothy Kirby; Consultant, Herbert Smith Freehills LLP (formerly Herbert Smith LLP), since 2008; *b* Gosforth, Northumberland, 6 Jan. 1948; *d* of Albert Paulus Livingston and Margaret Alice Livingston (*née* Kirby); *m* 1971, Julian Millar (marr. diss. 2001); two *d. Educ:* Central Newcastle High Sch. GDST; St Hugh's Coll., Oxford (BA Juris. 1969; MA); Coll. of Law. Admitted Solicitor, 1982; solicitor advocate, higher courts civil, 2002; Herbert Smith LLP: trainee, 1970; Asst Solicitor, 1972–80; Partner, 1980–2008. Chm., Financial Law Cttee, 1997–; Member: Competition Law Cttee, City of London Law Soc., 2001–; Financial Mkts Law Cttee, 2002–05; Banking Liaison Panel, 2009–. Chm., Cttee on Banking Reforms, Law Soc. of Eng. and Wales, 2011–. City of London Law Soc. Lifetime Achievement Award, British Legal Awards, 2013. *Publications:* Competition Law and Practice, 1995; The Competition Act 1998: a practical guide, 2001; *contributor:* Leasing and Asset Finance, 3rd edn 1997, 4th edn 2003; Business Innovation and the Law: perspectives from intellectual property, labour, competition and corporate law, 2013. *Recreations:* photography, history, art, gardening in Cornwall, family and friends. *Address:* Herbert Smith Freehills LLP, Exchange House, Primrose Street, EC2A 2EG. *T:* (020) 7374 8000, *Fax:* (020) 7374 0888. *E:* dorothy.livingston@hsf.com.

LIVINGSTONE, Prof. David Noel, OBE 2002; PhD; FBA 1995; MRIA; Professor of Geography and Intellectual History, Queen's University of Belfast, since 1997 (Professor of Geography, 1993–97); *b* 15 March 1953; *s* of Robert Livingstone and Winifred (*née* Turkington); *m* 1977, Frances Allyson Haugh; one *s* one *d. Educ:* Queen's Univ. of Belfast (BA; PhD; DipEd). Queen's University, Belfast: Curator of Maps, 1984–89; Lectr, 1989–91; Reader, 1991–93; British Acad. Res. Reader, 1999–2001. Visiting Professor: Calvin Coll., Michigan, 1989–90; Univ. of Notre Dame, Indiana, 1995; Regent Coll., Vancouver, 1997, 2000, 2003; Dist. Vis. Prof., Baylor Univ., Texas, 2004–05; Vis. Noted Scholar, Univ. of BC, 1999; Leverhulme Maj. Res. Fellow, 2011–12 and 2013–15. Lectures: Charles Lyell, BAAS, 1994–95; Hettner, Univ. of Heidelberg, 2001; Murrin, Univ. of BC, 2002; Progress in Human Geography, RGS, 2005; Appleton, Univ. of Hull, 2007; Humboldt, UCLA, 2007; Manley, Royal Holloway, Univ. of London, 2007; Gunning, Univ. of Edinburgh, 2009; Gregory, Univ. of Southampton, 2010; Gifford, Univ. of Aberdeen, 2014; Dudleian, Harvard Univ., 2015; Walton, Christians in Science Ireland, 2015. Mem., RAE 2001 Geog. Panel, RAE 2008 Geog. and Envmtl Studies sub-panel, HEFCE. Mem. Ct, Univ. of Ulster, 1996–2000, 2001–04. Pres., Geog. Sect., BAAS, 2005; Vice-Pres., Research, RGS, 2007–10; Mem. Council, British Soc. for History of Sci., 2009–11. MRIA 1998 (Mem., Nat. Cttee for Hist. and Philosophy of Sci., 1988–96, for Geography, 1996–2000; Mem. Council, 2001–02); FRSA 2001; MAE 2002; FAcSS (AcSS 2002). Corresp. Mem., Internat. Acad. of Hist. of Sci., 2011. Hon. DLitt Aberdeen, 2013. Adm. Back Award, RGS, 1997; Centenary Medal, RSGS, 1998; Templeton Foundn Lect. Award, 1999; Gold Medal in Soc. Scis, RIA, 2008; Founder's Medal, RGS, 2011. *Publications:* Nathaniel Southgate Shaler and the Culture of American Science, 1987; Darwin's Forgotten Defenders, 1987; The Preadamite Theory, 1992; The Geographical Tradition, 1992; (ed jtly) The Behavioural Environment, 1989; (ed jtly) Charles Hodge, What is Darwinism, 1994; (ed jtly) Human Geography: an essential anthology, 1996; (jtly) Them and Us, 1997; (jtly) Ulster-American Religion, 1999; (ed jtly) Evangelicals and Science in Historical Perspective, 1999; (ed jtly) Geography and Enlightenment, 1999; Science, Space and Hermeneutics, 2002; Putting Science in its Place, 2003; (ed jtly) Geography and Revolution, 2005; Adam's Ancestors: race, religion and the politics of human origins, 2008; (ed jtly) Geographies of Nineteenth Century Science, 2011; (ed jtly) The Sage Handbook of Geographical Knowledge, 2011; (ed jtly) Geographies of Science, 2010; Dealing with Darwin: place, politics and rhetoric in religious encounters with evolution, 2014; articles in learned jls. *Recreations:* music, photography. *Address:* School of Geography, Archaeology and Palaeoecology, Queen's University of Belfast, Belfast BT7 1NN. *T:* (028) 9097 5145.

LIVINGSTONE, Dawn Lesley; *see* Warwick, D. L.

LIVINGSTONE, Ian, CBE 2013 (OBE 2006); Co-founder, The Livingstone Foundation, 2013; Co-founder and Chairman, The Livingstone Foundation Academies Trust, since 2013; *b* 29 Dec. 1949; *s* of Neville and Anna Livingstone; *m* 1997, Frances Patricia Fletcher; two *s* two *d. Educ:* Stockport Coll. of Technology (HND 1970); Roehampton Inst. of Higher Educn (BEd 1976). MCIM 1970. Co-founder and Jt Man. Dir, 1975–85, non-exec. Dir, 1985–91, Games Workshop Ltd (launched Dungeons and Dragons game in Europe); writing children's books and designing board games, 1982–93; Dep. Chm., Domark Ltd, 1993–95; Eidos plc, later Eidos Interactive Ltd: Exec. Chm., 1995–2002; Creative Dir, 2002–06; Product Acquisition Dir, 2006–09; Pres., 2009–13. Non-executive Chair: Bright Things plc, 2004–10; Playdemic Ltd, 2012–; Playmob Ltd, 2012–; Midoki Ltd, 2013–; non-executive Director: SocialGO plc, 2010–13; Mediatonic Ltd, 2012–14; Creative England, 2014–; Young Rewired State, 2014–. Creative Industries advr, British Council, 2003–; Chair: Skillset Computer Games Skills Council, 2005–12; Video Games Skills Council, 2012–14; Co-Chair, Next Gen Skills Cttee, 2011–; Mem., Creative Industries Council, 2012–. Non-executive Director: Entertainment and Leisure Software Publishers Assoc., 2009–10; UK Interactive Entertainment Assoc., 2012–. Creative Industries Champion, BIS, 2014–. Mem., BAFTA, 2005–. Trustee, GamesAid, 2010–. Patron, Creative Skillset, 2014. Hon. DTech: Abertay Dundee, 2000; Greenwich, 2014; Hon. DArt Bournemouth, 2011. Special Award, BAFTA, 2002. *Publications:* Warlock of Firetop Mountain (with Steve Jackson), 1982; Dicing with Dragons, 1982; The Forest of Doom, 1983; City of Thieves, 1983; Deathtrap Dungeon, 1984; Island of the Lizard King, 1984; Caverns of the Snow Witch, 1984; Freeway Fighter, 1985; Temple of Terror, 1985; Trial of Champions, 1986; Crypt of the Sorcerer, 1987; Casket of Souls, 1987; Armies of Death, 1988; Return to Firetop Mountain, 1992; Legend of Zagor, 1993; Darkmoon's Curse, 1995; The Demon Spider, 1995; Mudworm Swamp, 1995; Ghost Road, 1995; Eye of the Dragon, 2005; (with Jamie Thomson) How Big is Your Brain?, 2007; Blood of the Zombies, 2012. *Recreations:* golf, photography, games design, writing. *E:* ian.livingstone@gmail.com. *W:* www.twitter.com/ian_livingstone. *Clubs:* Roehampton; Wimbledon Park Golf.

LIVINGSTONE, Ian Lang, CBE 1998 (OBE 1993); Chairman: Lanarkshire Health Board, 1993–2002 (Member, 1989–2002); Scottish Enterprise Lanarkshire (formerly Lanarkshire Development Agency), 1991–2000; *b* 23 Feb. 1938; *s* of John Lang Livingstone and Margaret Steele Livingstone (*née* Barbour); *m* 1967, Diane Hales; two *s. Educ:* Hamilton Acad.; Glasgow Univ. (BL). NP 1960. Qualified as solicitor, 1960; apprentice, Alex L. Wright & Co., Solicitors, 1957–60, legal asst, 1960–62; Ballantyne & Copland, Solicitors: Partner, 1962–70; Sen. Partner, 1970–86; Consultant, 1986–2013; Chm. and Dir, Bowmere Properties Ltd, 1967–; Chairman: House Sales (Motherwell) Ltd, 1978–; New Lanarkshire Ltd, 1993–2014; Kingdom FM Radio Ltd, 2008–; David Livingstone Centre, Blantyre, 2008–14; NL2017 Ltd. Chm., Scottish Local Authorities Remuneration Cttee, 2005–13; Hon. Pres., Lanarkshire Chamber of Commerce, 2006–13. Chm., Motherwell Coll. Bd, 1991–98. Chm., Motherwell FC, 1975–88. DL Lanarkshire, 2008. Hon. Dr West of Scotland, 2008. *Recreations:* football, walking, travelling, music. *Address:* Roath Park, 223 Manse Road, Motherwell, Strathclyde ML1 2PY. *T:* (01698) 253750.

LIVINGSTONE, Kenneth Robert, (Ken); radio presenter; Mayor of London, 2000–08 (Ind 2000–04, Lab 2004–08); *b* 17 June 1945; *s* of late Robert Moffat Livingstone and Ethel Ada Livingstone. *Educ:* Tulse Hill Comprehensive Sch.; Philippa Fawcett Coll. of Educn (Teacher's Cert.). Technician, Chester Beatty Cancer Res. Inst., 1962–70. Joined Labour Party, 1969; Reg. Exec., Greater London Lab. Party, 1974–86; Lambeth Borough Council: Councillor, 1971–78; Vice-Chm., Housing Cttee, 1971–73; Camden Borough Council: Councillor, 1978–82; Chm., Housing Cttee, 1978–80; Greater London Council: Mem. for Norwood, 1973–77, for Hackney N, 1977–81, for Paddington, 1981–86; Lab. Transport spokesman, 1980–81; Leader of Council and of Lab. Gp, 1981–86. Mem., NEC, Labour Party, 1987–89, 1997–98, 2010–. Contested (Lab) Hampstead, 1979. MP (Lab) Brent East, 1987–2001. Mem., NI Select Cttee, 1997–99. London Mayoral Candidate, 2012. Mem. Council, Zoological Soc. of London, 1994–2000 (Vice-Pres., 1996–98). FZS. *Publications:* If voting changed anything they'd abolish it, 1987; Livingstone's Labour, 1989; You Can't Say That, 2011. *Recreations:* cinema, science fiction, thinking while gardening, natural history. *E:* emmabeal@btinternet.com.

LIVINGSTONE, Marilyn; Member (Lab Co-op) Kirkcaldy, Scottish Parliament, 1999–2011; *b* 30 Sept. 1952; *m* Peter W. Livingstone; two *d. Educ:* Viewforth Secondary Sch.; Fife Coll. Fife College of Further and Higher Education: Youth Trng Manager; Hd, Admin and Consumer Studies; Hd, Business Sch., until 1999. Former Member: Kirkcaldy DC; Fife Council. Chm., Scottish PLP, 1999–2003; Ministerial Parly Aid to the First Minister, 2003–07. Contested (Lab) Kirkcaldy, Scottish Parlt, 2011.

LIVINGSTONE, Michael William; Strategic Director of Children's Services, Manchester City Council, 2011–14; *b* Hazel Grove, Stockport, 23 Oct. 1961; *s* of Richard and Mary Livingstone; *m* 1996, Linda Ann Smith. *Educ:* Hazel Grove High Sch.; Manchester Univ. (BA Dist.); Manchester Metropolitan Univ. (CQSW 1985; Postgrad. DipSW; MA Dist.). Social Worker: Sefton MBC, 1985–86; Trafford MBC, 1986–91; Principal Manager, Social Services, Oldham MBC, 1991–99; Asst Dir, Children's Services, Wirral MBC, 1999–2001; Social Services Inspectorate, 2001–07; Asst Dir, Children's Services, 2007–10, Dep. Dir, Children's Services, 2010–11, Manchester CC. *Recreations:* philately, very keen Manchester United fan.

LIVINGSTONE, Prof. Sonia Mary, OBE 2014; DPhil; Professor of Social Psychology, Department of Media and Communications, London School of Economics and Political Science, since 2003; *b* Adelaide, Australia, 30 April 1960; *d* of Prof. Rodney Simon Livingstone and Prof. Angela Mary Livingstone; partner, Prof. Peter Lunt; one *s* one *d. Educ:* University Coll. London (BSc Hons Psychol.); Wolfson Coll., Oxford (DPhil 1987). Lectr, Dept of Human Scis, Brunel Univ., 1987–88; Open Prize Res. Fellow, Nuffield Coll., Oxford, 1988–89; Lectr, Inst. of Social and Applied Psychol., Univ. of Kent, 1990; Lectr, 1990–97, Sen. Lectr, 1997–99, Prof., 1999–2003, Dept of Social Psychol., LSE. Guest Prof., Media, Film and Television, Copenhagen Univ., 1996; Bonnier Prof. of Journalism, Media and Communication, Stockholm Univ., 1998; Visiting Professor: Speech Communication/Inst. of Communication Res., Univ. of Illinois-Urbana-Champaign, 2000; Dept of Communication, Univ. of Bergen, 2002; Libera Univ. di Lingue e Communicazione, Milan, 2004; Univ. Panthéon Assas, Paris II, 2009; Guest Prof., InterMedia, Univ. of Oslo, 2008; Vis. Researcher, Microsoft Res. New England, Cambridge, Mass, 2013; Faculty Fellow, Berkman Center for Internet and Society, Harvard Univ., 2013–14. Member: Res. Priorities Bd, ESRC, 1996–98; Bd, Internet Watch Foundn, 2001–07 (Vice Chm., 2004–06); Bd of Dirs, Voice of the Listener and Viewer, 2006–09; Exec. Bd, UK Council for Child Internet Safety, 2008–. Hon. Dr: Erasmus, Rotterdam, 2008; Montreal, 2014. FRSA. *Publications:* Making Sense of Television: the psychology of audience interpretation, 1990, 2nd edn 1998 (trans. Chinese 2006); (with P. Lunt) Mass Consumption and Personal Identity: everyday economic experience, 1992; (with P. Lunt) Talk on Television: audience participation and public debate, 1994; (ed with M. Bovill) Children and their Changing Media Environment: a European comparative study, 2001; Young People and New Media: childhood and the changing media environment, 2002; (ed with L. Lievrouw) Handbook of New Media: social shaping and social consequences, 2002, rev. and updated student edn 2006 (trans. Italian 2007, Chinese 2008); (ed) Audiences and Publics: when cultural engagement matters for the public sphere, 2005; (jtly) Harm and Offence in Media Content: a review of the empirical literature, 2006, 2nd edn 2009; Lo Spettatore Intraprendente: analisi del pubblico televisivo, trans. D. Cardini, 2006; (jtly) Media Consumption and Public Engagement: beyond the presumption of attention, 2007, 2nd edn 2010; (with K. Drotner) The International Handbook of Children, Media and Culture, 2008; Children and the Internet: great expectations, challenging realities, 2009 (trans. Italian 2010, Chinese 2013); (ed with L. Lievrouw) New Media: Sage benchmarks in communication, vols 1–4, 2009; (ed with L. Haddon) Kids Online: opportunities and risks for children, 2009; (with P. Lunt) Media Regulation: governance and the interests of citizens and consumers, 2012; (ed jtly) Children, Risk and Safety Online: research and policy challenges in comparative perspective, 2012; (ed with R. Butsch) Meanings of Audiences: comparative discourses, 2013; (ed jtly) Digital Technologies in the Lives of Young People, 2014; contrib. articles to peer-reviewed acad. jls. *Recreations:* walking, baking, gardening, listening to music, yoga. *Address:* London School of Economics and Political Science, Houghton Street, WC2A 2AE. *E:* s.livingstone@lse.ac.uk.

LIZIERI, Prof. Colin Martyn, PhD; Grosvenor Professor of Real Estate Finance, University of Cambridge, since 2009; Fellow of Pembroke College, Cambridge, since 2009; *b* Beverley, Yorks, 27 July 1955; *s* of Ronald Lizieri and Marjorie Lizieri (*née* Maher); one *s. Educ:* Magdalen College Sch., Oxford; St Edmund Hall, Oxford (BA Hons Geog. 1976); London Sch. of Econs (PhD 1982). Res./Proj. Officer, London Bor. of Hammersmith and Fulham, 1979–82; Computer Liaison Officer, Royal Bor. of Kensington and Chelsea, 1982–85; Lectr, Sch. of Built Envmt, South Bank Poly., 1985–88; Reader in Internat. Real Estate Mkts, City Univ. Business Sch., 1988–95; Sen. Lectr, 1996–99, Prof. of Real Estate Finance, 1999–2009, Univ. of Reading. Vis. Prof., Univ. of Toronto, 1995. Weimer Fellow, Homer Hoyt Inst., 2012. Chm., Industry Council on Future of Real Estate and Urbanisation, WEF. Consultant, GHK Internat., 1996–; Mem., Academic Adv. Panel, Acadametrics, 2009–; non-exec. Dir, Howard Day Associates, 2007–13. FRGS 1995. Hon. FRICS 2004. David Ricardo Medal, American Real Estate Soc., 2014. *Publications:* The Economics of Commercial Property Markets, 1998; Towers of Capital, 2009; over 50 articles in leading academic jls. *Recreations:* cycling, music, football, hurricanes. *Address:* c/o Pembroke College, Cambridge CB2 1RF.

LLANDAFF, Bishop of; *see* Wales, Archbishop of.

LLANDAFF, Assistant Bishop of; *see* Wilbourne, Rt Rev. D. J.

LLANDAFF, Dean of; *see* Capon, Very Rev. G. H.

LLANDAFF, Archdeacon of; *see* Jackson, Ven. F. A.

LLANWARNE, Trevor John, CB 2013; FIA; Government Actuary, 2008–14; consultant on strategic risk, since 2014; *b* Farnborough, Hants, 31 Dec. 1952; *s* of Douglas and Margaret Llanwarne; *m* 1984, Margaret Kirstine Hansen; two *s* one *d. Educ:* Forest Fields Grammar Sch.,

Nottingham; Christ Church, Oxford (MA). FIA 1979. Actuarial trainee and actuary, Sun Life, 1974–84; Hd, SSAS, Pointon York Ltd, 1984–88; with Price Waterhouse, later PricewaterhouseCoopers, 1988–2008: Partner, 1992–2008, latterly Chief Actuary, Pensions and Leader, Pensions Practice. Mem., Govt steering gps on heads of analysis, 2011–14, on demography, 2013–14, on quality assurance on modelling, 2013. Mem. Council, Inst. of Actuaries, subseq. Inst. and Faculty of Actuaries, 2009–13. Gov., PPI, 2009–. Trustee, Internat. Longevity Centre UK, 2015. *Publications:* 2005 Quinquennial Review of the National Insurance Fund, 2010; 2010 Quinquennial Review of the National Insurance Fund, 2014. *Recreations:* family history, bridge. *Address:* 19 Kippington Road, Sevenoaks, Kent TN13 2LJ. *T:* (01732) 460709. *E:* trevor@llanwarne.com.

LLEWELLIN, Rt Rev. (John) Richard (Allan); Head of the Archbishop of Canterbury's staff (with title of Bishop at Lambeth), 1999–2003; an Hon. Assistant Bishop, Diocese of Canterbury, since 2008; *b* 30 Sept. 1938; *s* of John Clarence Llewellin and Margaret Gwenllian Llewellin; *m* 1965, Jennifer Sally (*née* House); one *s* two *d*. *Educ:* Clifton College, Bristol; Westcott House and Fitzwilliam Coll., Cambridge (MA). Solicitor, 1960. Ordained deacon, 1964; priest, 1965; Curate at Radlett, Herts, 1964–68; Curate at Johannesburg Cathedral, 1968–71; Vicar of Waltham Cross, 1971–79; Rector of Harpenden, 1979–85; Suffragan Bishop: of St Germans, 1985–92; of Dover, 1992–99. Chm., USPG, 1994–97. *Recreations:* sailing, DIY. *Address:* 15a The Precincts, Canterbury, Kent CT1 2EL. *T:* (01227) 764645. *E:* rllewellin@clara.co.uk.

LLEWELLIN, Magnus Clenyg Crush; Editor, The Herald, since 2012; *b* Oswestry, Shropshire, 6 Aug. 1965; *s* of Phil Llewellin and Beth Llewellin; *m* 2004, Katie; two *d*. *Educ:* Oswestry Boys' High Sch.; St David's University Coll., Lampeter, Univ. of Wales (BA Hons Hist. 1986); Watford Coll. (Post Grad. Dip. Advertising 1987). Newsdesk, Edinburgh Evening News, 1990–95; Asst News Editor, Daily Record, 1995–98; News Editor, The Scotsman, 1998–2000; Asst Editor, Business AM, 2000–02; The Herald: News Editor, 2002–06; Sen. Asst Editor, 2006–11; Dep. Editor, Glasgow, 2011–12. *Recreations:* family, friends, travel, cinema, walking. *Address:* c/o The Herald, 200 Renfield Street, Glasgow G2 3QB.

LLEWELLYN, Anthony John S.; *see* Seys Llewellyn.

LLEWELLYN, Bryan Henry; Director, Granada Travel PLC, 1989–92; *s* of Nora and Charles Llewellyn; *m* 1983, Joanna (*née* Campbell) (marr. diss. 2012); two *s*. *Educ:* Charterhouse; Clare Coll., Cambridge (BA). Commissioned, The Queen's, 1946. Research Asst, Dept of Estate Management, Cambridge, 1954; joined Fisons Ltd, 1955; Marketing Manager, Greaves & Thomas Ltd, 1960; Regional Marketing Controller, Thomson Regional Newspapers Ltd, 1962; Marketing Dir, TRN Ltd, 1966; Managing Director: Thomson Holidays Ltd, 1969; Thomson Travel Ltd, 1972 (Chm., 1977–78); Exec. Dir, Thomson Organisation Ltd, 1972–80; Man. Dir and Chief Exec., Thomson Publications Ltd, 1977–80; Dir, Burlington Magazine, 1983–2013; Man. Dir, The Kitchenware Merchants Ltd, 1985–88. Non-exec. Dir, Orion Insurance Ltd, 1976–92.

LLEWELLYN, Dr David George, FIAgrE; Vice-Chancellor, Harper Adams University (formerly Principal, Harper Adams University College), since 2009; *b* Cardiff, 14 Dec. 1960; *s* of George Llewellyn and Heather Llewellyn (now Fountain); *m* 1984, Noelle Winterburn; one *d*. *Educ:* University Coll. London (BSc); Birkbeck Coll., Univ. of London (MSc); Univ. of Bath (DBA). FIAgrE 2009; ARAgS 2013. Admin. Asst and Asst Sec., 1983–88, Asst Registrar, 1988–90, Queen Mary Coll., Univ. of London; Sch. Admin. Officer, KCL, 1990–94; Sec., Inst. of Psychiatry, 1994–98; Dir, Corporate Affairs, Harper Adams Agricl Coll., later UC, 1998–2009. Chm. Govs, Newport Girls High Sch., 2008–. *Recreations:* Antarctic book collecting, family, music, coastal and mountain walking. *Address:* Harper Adams University, Newport, Shropshire TF10 8NB. *T:* (01952) 815240, *Fax:* (01952) 814783. *E:* dllewellyn@harper-adams.ac.uk. *Club:* Farmers'.

LLEWELLYN, Prof. David Thomas; Professor of Money and Banking, Loughborough University, since 1976; *b* 3 March 1943; *s* of Alfred George Llewellyn and Elsie Alexandria Frith; *m* 1970, Wendy Elizabeth James; two *s*. *Educ:* William Ellis Grammar Sch., London; London Sch. of Econs and Pol Science (BSc Econ). FCIB. Economist: Unilever NV, Rotterdam, 1964; HM Treasury, London, 1965–67; Lectr in Econs, Nottingham Univ., 1967–73; Economist, IMF, Washington, 1973–76; Chm., Banking Centre, Loughborough Univ., 1976–2004. Public Interest Dir, PIA, 1994–2001; Dir, PIA Ombudsman Bureau Ltd, 1994–2001. Visiting Professor: City Univ. Business Sch., 2001–; Cass Business Sch., London, 2003–; Swiss Finance Inst. (formerly Swiss Banking Sch.), Zurich, 2003, 2006–09; IESE Business Sch., Madrid, 2006–07; Vienna Univ. of Econs and Admin, 2007–; Res. Assoc., Centre for European Policy Studies, Brussels, 2009–; Associate Mem., Kellogg Coll., Oxford, 2010–. Consultant Economist to: Harlow Butler Ueda, 1981–99; Garban Intercapital plc; ICAP plc, 2004–; Member: London Bd of Dirs, Halifax Building Soc., 1988–93; Expert Panel on Banking, Bank Indonesia, 2004–; Credit Risk Consortium, Harland Financial Solutions, 2009–; at various times Consultant to World Bank, Building Societies Assoc., bldg socs, banks, central banks and regulatory authorities in UK and overseas. Member: Bank of England Panel of Academic Consultants; Banking Competition Task Gp, S Africa, 2003–04; Internat. Adv. Bd, Italian Bankers' Assoc., 1994–; Exec. Bd, European Financial Management Assoc., 1994–; Internat. Adv. Bd, NCR Financial Solutions (formerly NCR Financial Systems) Gp, 1997–2001; Financial Services Panel, DTI Technology Foresight Prog., 1997–2000; Consultative Gp, IMF, 2004–; Academic Bd, Internat. Centre for Financial Regulation, 2010–12; Banking Stakeholder Gp, Eur. Banking Authy, 2011– (Vice Chm., 2011–13; Chm., 2013–). Special Advr, H of C and H of L Jt Cttee on Financial Services and Markets, 1999–. Pres., Société Universitaire Européenne Recherches Financières, 2000–08 (Mem., Council of Mgt, 1998–). TV and radio broadcasts on financial issues. Member of Editorial Board: Jl of Financial Regulation and Compliance, 2002–; Bombay Technology, 2004–; Jl of Bank Regulating, 2005–. FRSA. *Publications:* International Financial Integration, 1980; Framework of UK Monetary Policy, 1984; The Evolution of the British Financial System, 1985; Prudential Regulation and Supervision of Financial Institutions, 1986; Reflections on Money, 1989; (ed) Recent Developments in International Monetary Economics, 1991; (ed) Surveys in Monetary Economics, vols 1 and 2, 1991; Competition or Credit Controls?, 1991; (jtly) Financial Regulations: why, how and where now?, 1998; Economic Rationale of Financial Regulation, 1998; The New Economics of Banking, 1999; Competitive Strategy in the New Economics of Retail Financial Services, 2002; (ed jtly) Financial Innovation in Retail and Corporate Banking, 2009; (jtly) Investigating Diversity in the Banking Sector in Europe, 2010; The Global Banking Crisis and the Post-Crisis Banking and Regulatory Scenario, 2011; New Paradigms in Banking, Financial Markets and Regulation, 2012; (contrib.) Stability of the Financial System, 2013; Fifty Years of Bank Business Models, 2013; articles in academic and professional jls and books on monetary policy and instns, and on internat. finance. *Recreations:* DIY, culinary arts, travel, boating. *Address:* 8 Landmere Lane, Ruddington, Notts NG11 6ND. *T:* (0115) 921 6071; School of Business and Economics, Loughborough University, Loughborough, Leics LE11 3TU. *T:* (01509) 222700. *E:* D.T.Llewellyn@lboro.ac.uk; Hameau des Pins, Les Hauts du Golf, Villa 10, 8760 chemin de la Tire, 06250 Mougins, France.

LLEWELLYN, David Walter, CBE 1983; Director, Walter Llewellyn & Sons Ltd, and other companies in the Llewellyn Group, 1953–2002; *b* 13 Jan. 1930; *s* of late Eric Gilbert and Florence May Llewellyn; *m* 1st, 1955, Josephine Margaret Buxton (marr. diss. 1985); three *s*; 2nd, 1985, Tessa Caroline Sandwith. *Educ:* Radley College. FCIOB. Commissioned Royal Engineers, 1952. Industrial Adviser to Minister of Housing and Local Govt, 1967–68; Mem., Housing Corp., 1975–77; Pres., Joinery and Timber Contractors' Assoc., 1976–77; Chm., Nat. Contractors' Gp of Nat. Fedn of Building Trades Employers (now Building Employers Confedn), 1977; Chm., Building Regulations Adv. Cttee, 1977–85 (Mem., 1966–74); Dep. Chm., Nat. Building Agency, 1977–82 (Dir, 1968–82). Pres., CIOB, 1986–87. Master, Worshipful Co. of Tin Plate Workers alias Wireworkers, 1985. Governor, St Andrew's Sch., Eastbourne, 1966–78; Trustee, Queen Alexandra Cottage Homes, Eastbourne, 1973–94. Provincial Grand Master, Sussex, United Grand Lodge of Freemasons of England, 1989–97. *Recreations:* the use, restoration and preservation of historic vehicles. *Address:* Cooper's Cottage, Chiddingly, near Lewes, East Sussex BN8 6HD. *Clubs:* Reform; Devonshire (Eastbourne).

LLEWELLYN, Rt Hon. Edward David Gerard, OBE 2006 (MBE 1997); PC 2015; Chief of Staff to the Prime Minister, since 2010; *b* 23 Sept. 1965; *s* of Comdr David Llewellyn, RN (Retd) and Margaret Llewellyn (*née* Chapman); *m* 2010, Dr Anne Charbord; one *d*. *Educ:* Eton Coll.; New Coll., Oxford (BA Hons Modern Langs). Cons. Res. Dept, 1988–92 (on secondment as Private Sec. to Margaret Thatcher, 1990–91); Personal Advr to Gov. of Hong Kong, 1992–97; Office of High Rep. for Bosnia and Herzegovina, 1997–99; Cabinet of Eur. Comr for Ext. Relns, 1999–2002; Chief of Staff: to High Rep. for Bosnia and Herzegovina, 2002–05; to Leader of Opposition, 2005–10. *Recreation:* ski-ing. *Address:* 10 Downing Street, SW1A 2AA. *T:* (020) 7930 4433.

LLEWELLYN, Rear-Adm. Jack Rowbottom, CB 1974; Assistant Controller of the Navy, 1972–74; retired; *b* 14 Nov. 1919; *s* of Ernest and Harriet Llewellyn, Ashton under Lyne, Lancs; *m* 1944, Joan Isabel, *d* of Charles and Hilda Phillips, Yelverton, Devon; one *s*. *Educ:* Purley County Sch. Entered RN, 1938; RNEC, Keyham, 1939. Served War of 1939–45: HMS Bermuda, 1942; RNC, Greenwich, 1943; HMS Illustrious, 1945. Engr in Chief's Dept, Admty, 1947; HMS Sluys, 1949; HMS Thunderer, 1951; HMS Diamond, 1953; Comdr, 1953; Asst Engr in Chief, on loan to Royal Canadian Navy, 1954; in charge Admty Fuel Experimental Station, Haslar, 1958; HMS Victorious, 1960; Asst Dir, Marine Engrg, MoD (N), 1963; Captain, 1963; in command, HMS Fisgard, 1966; Dep. Dir, Warship Design, MoD (N), 1969; Rear-Adm., 1972. *Recreations:* travel, gardening. *Address:* 3 Jubilee Terrace, Chichester, W Sussex PO19 7XT. *T:* (01243) 780180.

LLEWELLYN, John, DPhil; Partner, Llewellyn Consulting, since 2009; *b* 13 Sept. 1944; *s* of Sir (Frederick) John Llewellyn and Joyce Llewellyn; *m* 1990, Ruth Mariette; three *s* two *d*. *Educ:* Christchurch Boys' High Sch.; Scots Coll., Wellington; Victoria Univ. of Wellington (BA Hons 1st Cl. Econs 1966); Trinity Coll., Oxford (DPhil Econs 1970). Res. Officer, Dept of Applied Econs, 1970–74, Asst Dir of Res., Fac. of Econs, 1974–77, Univ. of Cambridge; Fellow, St John's Coll., Cambridge, 1972–77; OECD: Hd, Econ. Prospects Div., 1978–86; Dep. Dir for Social Affairs, Manpower and Educn, 1986–89; Hd, Private Office of Sec.-Gen., 1989–94; Lehman Brothers: Chief Economist Europe, 1995–96; Global Chief Economist, 1996–2006; Sen. Economic Policy Advr, Lehman Brothers, 2006–08. Dir, Genesis Emerging Markets Fund, 2009–; Member, Advisory Board: Ondra Partners LLP, 2009–; Osmosis Hldgs Ltd, 2013–. Mem., President of EC's Gp of Econ. Analysis, 2000–04; Advr, HM Treasury, 2009–12; Mem., Adv. Panel, Office for Budget Responsibility, 2011–. Member of Council: Chatham House, 2007–13; UK Soc. of Business Economists, 2006–09; Nat. Inst. of Economic and Social Res., 2010–. Member, Editorial Board: OECD Economic Studies, 1983–89; Economic Modelling, 1983–93. *Publications:* (jtly) Economic Forecasting and Policy: the international dimension, 1985; (ed jtly) Economic Policies for the 1990s, 1991; reports, and articles in learned jls. *Recreations:* motorsport, writing, photography, music. *E:* john.llewellyn@llewellyn-consulting.com. *Clubs:* Athenæum, Royal Automobile.

LLEWELLYN, Rev. Richard Morgan, CB 1992; OBE 1979 (MBE 1976); DL; Director, Christ College, Brecon Foundation, 2001–05; *b* 22 Aug. 1937; *s* of Griffith Robert Poyntz Llewellyn and Bridget Margaret Lester Llewellyn (*née* Karslake); *m* 1964, Elizabeth Lamond (Polly) Sobey; three *s* one *d* (and one *d* decd). *Educ:* Haileybury; Imperial Service College; rcds, psc; Salisbury and Wells Theol Coll. (Dip. Theol. and Christian Ministry); Open Univ. (BA 2012). Enlisted Royal Welch Fusiliers (Nat. Service), 1956; active service, Malaya and Cyprus, 1957–59; Instructor, Army Outward Bound Sch., 1962–63; Staff Coll., 1970; MA to CGS, 1971–72; Brigade Major, 1974–76; CO, 1st Bn RWF, 1976–79; Directing Staff, RCDS, 1979–81; Comdr, Gurkha Field Force, 1981–84; Dir, Army Staff Duties, 1985–87; GOC Wales, 1987–90; C of S, HQ UKLF, 1990–91; retired in rank of Maj.-Gen. Ordained deacon, 1993, priest, 1994; Minor Canon, Brecon Cathedral and Asst Curate, Brecon with Battle and Llanddew, 1993–95; Chaplain, Christ Coll., Brecon, 1995–2001. Regtl Col, Gurkha Transport Regt, subseq. Queen's Own Gurkha Transport Regt, 1984–94; Col, RWF, 1990–97. Chairman: Army Mountaineering Assoc., 1988–91; Gurkha Welfare Trust in Wales, 1995–2010; Powys Br., Army Benevolent Fund, 2001–12; Armed Forces Art Soc., 2007–11; Vice-Pres., Soldiers' and Airmen's Scripture Readers Assoc., 1996–. Hon. Chaplain, Univ. of Wales OTC, 2002. Welsh Vice-Patron, War Memls Trust (formerly Friends of War Memls), 1999–. DL Powys, 2006. FCMI. OStJ 2011. *Recreations:* most outdoor pursuits, gardening, painting, reading. *Address:* Field House, The Legar, Llangattock, Crickhowell, Powys NP8 1HL. *Club:* Army and Navy.

LLEWELLYN, Sir Roderic Victor, 5th Bt *cr* 1922, of Bwllfa, Aberdare, co. Glamorgan; landscape architect, author, lecturer and presenter; *b* Crickhowell, 9 Oct. 1947; *yr s* of Sir Harry Llewellyn, 3rd Bt, CBE and Hon. Christine Saumarez, 2nd *d* of 5th Baron de Saumarez; *S* brother, 2009; *m* 1981, Tatiana Manora Caroline, *d* of late Paul Soskin; three *d*. *Educ:* Shrewsbury; Aix-en-Provence. Designed gardens worldwide, 1977–. Consultant Gardens Director, Sudeley Castle gardens, 2010–. Gardening Presenter: TV AM, 1983–84; The Home Show, 1990; The Gardening Roadshow, 1992–93; Grass Roots, 1993–2003 (guest presenter); This Morning, 1996–2000; Roddy Llewellyn's Garden Guide, 1997–99; Grand Gardens, 2001–02; Turf Wars, 2003; Best of Britain, 2003; Gardeners' World, 2008. Gardening corresp., The Star, 1981–85; Garden writer, Oracle, 1982–83; Gardening corresp., Mail on Sunday, 1987–99. Regular contribs to magazines incl. Country Life, Cotswold Life, Country Illustrated and Saga Mag. Lectr in UK, USA and Australia; lecture series, Sotheby's Inst. of Art, 2001–02. Patron: Southport Flower Show, 1996–; Gardening Disabled Trust, 2011–. Silver Gilt Medal, Chelsea Flower Show and Hampton Court Palace Flower Show, 1998. *Publications:* Town Gardens, 1981; Beautiful Backyards, 1985; Water Gardens: the connoisseur's choice, 1987; Elegance & Eccentricity, 1989; Growing Gifts, 1992; Grow It Yourself: gardening with a physical disability, 1993; Roddy Llewellyn's Gardening Year, 1997. *Recreations:* walking, talking, philately. *Heir: cousin* Robert Crofts Williams Llewellyn [*b* 19 Nov. 1952; *m* 1st, 1975, Susan Constance Miller-Stirling (*d* 1980); 2nd, 1981, Lucinda Roberte (marr. diss. 1989), *o d* of late Alexander Clement Gilmour, CVO; one *s* one *d*; 3rd, 1989, Sarah Dominica, *d* of Maj. Gavin Anderson]. *E:* roddy.llewellyn@virgin.net. *Club:* Chelsea Arts.

LLEWELLYN, Susan Pauline; *see* Holdham, S. P.

LLEWELLYN, Timothy David, OBE 2007; Chairman, The Burlington Magazine Publications Ltd and supporting foundations, since 2008 (Director, since 2006); *b* 30 May 1947; *s* of late Graham David Llewellyn and Dorothy Mary Driver; *m* 1st, 1970, Irene Sigrid Mercy Henriksen (marr. diss.); one *s*; 2nd, 1978, Elizabeth Hammond. *Educ:* St Dunstan's College; Magdalene College, Cambridge. Sotheby's: Old Master Painting Dept, 1969; Director, 1974; Man. Dir, 1984–91; Chief Exec., 1991–92; Dep. Chm., Europe, 1992–94. Chm., Friends of the Courtauld Inst. of Art, 1986–2002. Mem. Council, Harvard Univ.

Center for Italian Renaissance Studies, Villa I Tatti, 1996–2005 (Mem., Internat. Council, 1990–96). Co-Chm., Elgar Birthplace Appeal, 1992–99; Trustee: Elgar Foundn, 1992–99; Bd, Courtauld Inst. of Art, 1992–2001; Gilbert Collection Trust, 1998–2001; Kettles Yard, Univ. of Cambridge, 2000–; Metropole Arts Trust, 2004–, and Creative Foundn, 2008–; Samuel Courtauld Trust, 2007–; Chm., Henry Moore Sculpture Trust, 1994–99; Dir, 1994–2007, Mem. of Adv. Bd, 2007–, Henry Moore Foundn; Member: Council, Walpole Soc., 1994–99; Visual Arts Adv. Cttee, British Council, 1995–2007; Council, British Sch. at Rome, 2000– (Chm., 2013–). Fellow, Ateneo Veneto, 1992. Hon. DLitt Southampton Inst., 1998. Order of Cultural Merit, Min. of Culture and Fine Arts, Poland, 1986. *Publications:* Owen McSwiny's Letters, 1720–1744, 2010. *Recreations:* music, travel. *Address:* 3 Cranley Mansion, 160 Gloucester Road, SW7 4QF. *T:* (020) 7373 2333, *Fax:* (020) 7244 0126. *E:* tdllewellyn@btinternet.com. *Club:* Brooks's.

LLEWELLYN-JONES, Benedict, OBE 2009; HM Diplomatic Service; Head of Chancery, Abuja, since 2014; *b* Cardiff, 29 Nov. 1976; *s* of Christopher and Christine Llewellyn-Jones; *m* 2007, Laura Harries; one *d. Educ:* Jesus Coll., Oxford (BA). Joined CS, 2000; Desk Officer, EU and Internat. Affairs, 2000–01, Press Officer for Internat. Affairs, 2002, Home Office; Second Sec., Policing and Drugs, 2002–04, First Sec., Policing and Organised Crime, 2005–06, UK Perm. Repn to EU, Brussels; Head: Third Country Relns Team, Home Office, 2006; Zimbabwe Team, FCO, 2007–08; Dep. Hd, Climate Change and Energy Gp, FCO, 2009–11; High Comr to Rwanda and non-resident Ambassador to Burundi, 2011–14. *Address:* British High Commission, 19 Torrens Close, Mississippi, Maitama, Abuja, Nigeria.

LLEWELLYN SMITH, Prof. Sir Christopher Hubert, (Sir Chris), Kt 2001; FRS 1984; Director of Energy Research, since 2010 and Visiting Professor, Department of Physics, since 2004, University of Oxford; Director, Culham Division, United Kingdom Atomic Energy Authority, and Head of Euratom/UKAEA Fusion Association, 2003–08; *b* 19 Nov. 1942; *s* of late J. C. and M. E. F. Llewellyn Smith; *m* 1966, Virginia Grey; one *s* one *d. Educ:* Wellington College; New College, Oxford (Scholar; BA 1964; DPhil 1967; Hon. Fellow, 2002; full Blue for cross-country running, 1961–63, Captain 1963; full Blue for Athletics, 1963). Royal Society Exchange Fellow, Lebedev Inst., Moscow, 1967; Fellow, CERN, Geneva, 1968; Research Associate, SLAC, Stanford, Calif, 1970; Staff Mem., CERN, 1972; Oxford University: Lectr, 1974; Reader in Theoretical Physics, 1980; Prof. of Theoretical Physics, 1987–98 (on leave of absence, 1994–98); Chm. of Physics, 1987–92; Fellow, St John's Coll., 1974–98 (Hon. Fellow, 2000); Dir-Gen., CERN, 1994–98; Provost and Pres., UCL, 1999–2002. Chm., Adv. Cttee on Maths Educn, 2002–04. Mem. of various policy and programme cttees for CERN (Chm., Scientific Policy Cttee, 1990–92), SLAC, Deutsches Elektronen-Synchrotron Hamburg and SERC, 1972–92; Mem., ACOST, 1989–92; Chairman: Consultative Cttee on Fusion, Euratom, 2004–09; Council, Internat. Tokamak Experimental Reactor, 2007–09; Pres., Council, Synchrotron Light for Experimental Sci. and Applications in the ME, 2007–. Vice-Pres., Royal Society, 2008–10. MAE 1989; Fellow, APS, 1994; For. Fellow, INSA, 1998. Hon. Fellow, Cardiff Univ., 1998. Hon. FIMA 2003. Hon. DSc: Bristol, 1997; Shandong, 1997; York, 2014; Hon. DCien Granada, 1997. Maxwell Prize and Medal, Inst. of Physics, 1979; Medal, Japanese Assoc. of Med. Scis, 1997; Gold Medal, Slovak Acad. of Scis, 1997; Glazebrook Medal, Inst. of Physics, 1999; Distinguished Associate Award, US Dept of Energy, 1998; Distinguished Service Award, US Nat. Sci. Foundn, 1998. *Publications:* numerous articles in Nuclear Physics, Physics Letters, Phys. Rev., etc. *Recreations:* books, travel, opera. *Address:* Theoretical Physics, 1 Keble Road, Oxford OX1 3NP. *E:* c.llewellyn-smith@physics.ox.ac.uk.

See also E. M. Llewellyn-Smith, Sir M. J. Llewellyn-Smith.

LLEWELLYN-SMITH, Elizabeth Marion, CB 1985; Principal, St Hilda's College Oxford, 1990–2001; *b* 17 Aug. 1934; *d* of late John Clare Llewellyn Smith and Margaret Emily Frances (*née* Crawford). *Educ:* Christ's Hospital, Hertford; Girton Coll., Cambridge (MA; Hon. Fellow, 1992). Joined Board of Trade, 1956; various appointments in Board of Trade, Cabinet Office, Dept of Trade and Industry, Dept of Prices and Consumer Protection, 1956–76; Royal Coll. of Defence Studies, 1977; Under Sec., Companies Div., Dept of Trade, later DTI, 1978–82; Dep. Dir Gen., OFT, 1982–87; Dep. Sec., DTI, 1987–90. UK Dir, EIB, 1987–90. Member: Hebdomadal Council, Oxford Univ., 1993–2000; Res. Ethics Cttee, HSE, 1993–2004; Business Appointments Panel, DTI, 1996–2002; Investigation and Discipline Bd, Accountancy Foundn, later Accountancy Investigation and Discipline Bd, then Accountancy and Actuarial Investigation and Discipline Bd, Financial Reporting Council, 2001–09; Council, Consumers' Assoc., 2002–08. Ind. Public Appts Assessor, 2008–12. Trustee: Jacqueline du Pré Meml Fund, 1991–2001; Auditory Verbal UK Ltd, 2004–11. Mem., Governing Body, Rugby Sch., 1991–2004. Chm., Charlotte M. Yonge Fellowship, 1995–2011. Hon. Fellow: St Mary's Coll., Univ. of Durham, 1999; St Hilda's Coll., Oxford, 2001. *Recreations:* travel, books, especially Trollope and C. M. Yonge, entertaining, Burmese cats. *Address:* Brook Cottage, Taston, near Charlbury, Oxon OX7 3JL. *T:* (01608) 811874. *Club:* University Women's.

See also Sir C. H. Llewellyn Smith, Sir M. J. Llewellyn-Smith.

LLEWELLYN-SMITH, Sir Michael (John), KCVO 1996; CMG 1989; HM Diplomatic Service, retired; Ambassador to Greece, 1996–99; *b* 25 April 1939; *s* of late J. C. Llewellyn Smith and M. E. F. Crawford; *m* 1967, Colette Gaulier; one *s* one *d. Educ:* Wellington Coll.; New Coll., Oxford; St Antony's Coll., Oxford (MA, DPhil; Hon. Fellow, 2007). FCO, 1970; Cultural Attaché, Moscow, 1973; Paris, 1976; Royal Coll. of Defence Studies, 1979; Counsellor and Consul Gen., Athens, 1980–83; Hd of Western European Dept, FCO, 1984–85; Hd of Soviet Dept, FCO, 1985–87; Minister, Paris, 1988–91; Ambassador to Poland, 1991–96. Non-exec. Dir, Coca-Cola HBC SA, 2000–. Vice-Chm., Cathedrals Fabric Commn for England, 1999–2006. Vice-Pres., British Sch. at Athens, 2000–. *Publications:* The Great Island: a study of Crete, 1965, 2nd edn 1973; Ionian Vision: Greece in Asia Minor 1919–22, 1973, 2nd edn 1998; The British Embassy Athens, 1998; Olympics in Athens 1896: the invention of the modern Olympic Games, 2004; Athens: a cultural and literary history, 2004. *Recreations:* music, walking. *Address:* 4 Frouds Close, Childrey, Wantage OX12 9NT. *Club:* Oxford and Cambridge.

See also Sir C. H. Llewellyn Smith, E. M. Llewellyn-Smith.

LLEWELYN, Sir John Michael Dillwyn-V.; *see* Venables-Llewelyn.

LLOWARCH, Martin Edge, FCA; Chairman (part-time): Transport Development Group plc, 1992–2000; Firth Rixson (formerly Johnson & Firth Brown) plc, 1993–2001; *b* 28 Dec. 1935; *s* of Wilfred and Olga Llowarch; *m* 1965, Ann Marion Buchanan; one *s* two *d. Educ:* Stowe Sch., Buckingham. FCA 1973. Coopers & Lybrand, 1962–68; British Steel Corporation, subseq. British Steel plc: Hd of Special Projects, 1968; Man. Dir (S Africa), 1971; Dir, Finance and Admin (Internat.), 1973; Finance Dir, Tubes Div., 1975; Finance Controller, Strip Products Gp, 1980; Man. Dir, Finance, 1983; Mem., Main Bd, 1984–91; Dep. Chief Exec., 1986; Chief Exec., 1986–91. Dep. Chm., Abbey National plc, 1994–99; non-exec. Dir, Hickson Internat., 1992–99. Mem., Accounting Standards Cttee, 1985–87. CCMI (CBIM 1985). Chairman: Govs, Stamford Endowed Schs, 1998–2004; Stamford Endowed Schs Foundn, 2005–14. *Recreations:* most forms of sport, music, gardening, reading.

LLOYD OF BERWICK, Baron *cr* 1993 (Life Peer), of Ludlay in the County of East Sussex; **Anthony John Leslie Lloyd,** Kt 1978; PC 1984; DL; a Lord of Appeal in Ordinary, 1993–99; Chairman, Security Commission, 1992–99 (Vice-Chairman, 1985–92); *b* 9 May 1929; *o s* of late Edward John Boydell Lloyd and Leslie Johnston Fleming; *m* 1960, Jane Helen Violet, MBE, DL, *er d* of C. W. Shelford, Chailey Place, Lewes, Sussex. *Educ:* Eton (Schol.); Trinity Coll., Cambridge (Maj. Schol.). 1st cl. Classical Tripos Pt I; 1st cl. with distinction Law Tripos Pt II. National Service, 1st Bn Coldstream Guards, 1948. Montague Butler Prize, 1950; Sir William Browne Medal, 1951. Choate Fellow, Harvard, 1952; Fellow of Peterhouse, 1953 (Hon. Fellow, 1981); Fellow of Eton, 1974–86. Called to Bar, Inner Temple, 1955 (Bencher, 1976; Treasurer, 1999); QC 1967; Attorney-General to HRH The Prince of Wales, 1969–77; Judge of the High Court of Justice, Queen's Bench Div., 1978–84; a Lord Justice of Appeal, 1984–93; Mem., H of L, 1993–2015. Vice-Chm., Parole Bd, 1984–85; Mem., Criminal Law Revision Cttee, 1981. Chairman: Inquiry into Legislation against Terrorism (reported 1996); Inquiry into Gulf War Illnesses (reported 2004). Chm., Sussex Assoc. for Rehabilitation of Offenders, 1985–91; Pres., Sussex Downsmen, 1995–2004; Vice-Pres., British Maritime Law Assoc., 1983–. Mem., Top Salaries Review Body, 1971–77. Chm., H of L Select Cttee on the Speakership, 2003–05. Chm., Jt Ecclesiastical Cttee, 2003–. Trustee: Smiths Charity, 1971–94; Glyndebourne Arts Trust, 1973–94 (Chm., 1975–94); Dir, RAM, 1979– (Hon. FRAM 1985). Chm., Chichester Diocesan Bd of Finance, and Mem., Bishop's Council, 1972–76; Vice-Pres., Corp. of the Sons of the Clergy, 1997–2004. Hon. Mem., Salters' Co., 1988 (Master, 2000–01). DL E Sussex, 1983. Hon. LLD: QUB, 2005; Sussex, 2006. *Recreations:* music, carpentry; formerly running (ran for Cambridge in Mile, White City, 1950). *Address:* 2 Mitre Court, Temple, EC4Y 7BX. *T:* (020) 7583 9335; Ludlay, Berwick, East Sussex BN26 6TE. *T:* (01323) 870204. *Club:* Brooks's.

LLOYD, Andrew, CMG 2011; MBE 1995; Vice President, Communication, Global Strategy and Business Development, since 2012, and Global Politics and Public Affairs, since 2014, Statoil (UK) Ltd; *b* 22 Oct. 1964; *s* of Roderick Allen Lloyd and Jacqueline Lloyd (*née* Quinn); *m* 1997, Tania Mechlenborg; one *s* one *d*, and one *s* from previous marriage. *Educ:* Birkbeck Coll., London (BSc Hons Financial Econs); London Business Sch. (MBA); Columbia Univ., NY (MBA). Joined HM Diplomatic Service, 1982; FCO, 1982–84; Washington, 1984–87; Nigeria, 1987–90; FCO, 1990–92; Second Sec. (Econ.), Korea, 1992–95; Spokesman, UK Mission to UN, NY, 1995–2000; Hd of Post, Kosovo, 2000–02; rcds 2003; Hd, Africa Dept (Southern), 2003–06, Dir (Africa), 2006–08, Dir, Corporate Services, 2008–10, FCO; High Comr to Nigeria, 2011–12. *Recreations:* fly-fishing, long distance running, travel, design, cooking.

LLOYD, Ann Judith, CBE 2008; independent advisor and coach, since 2012; *b* 22 April 1948; *d* of Joseph Barnard and Beryl Greer; *m* 1998, Dr Geert Jan Koning. *Educ:* St Asaph Grammar Sch.; University Coll. of Wales, Aberystwyth (BSc (Hons)); University Coll. of Wales, Cardiff, (MSc Econ); Bristol Poly. (DMS); Univ. of Aberdeen (DipHEcon); Univ. of Strathclyde (Dip. Mentoring). Area Planning Dir, Dyfed HA, 1974–82; Unit Gen. Manager, Llanelli-Dinefwr, 1982–88; Dist Gen. Manager, Frenchay HA, 1988–92; Chief Executive: Frenchay Healthcare NHS Trust, 1992–99; N Bristol NHS Trust, 1999–2001; Dir Gen. Health and Social Services, Welsh Assembly Govt and Chief Exec., NHS Wales, 2001–09; Health and Social Care Comr for London, Appts Commn, 2009–11. Chm., Welsh Health Services Specialist Commn, 2015–; Mem., Bevan Commn, 2014–. Associate Fellow, Office of Public Mgt, 2012–. Sen. Associate, Good Governance Inst., 2012–. Chair, Caxton Foundn, 2013–15. Trustee: Shaw Trust, 2009–; Patients' Assoc., 2009–12. *Publications: contributions to:* Managing Service Quality, 1992; The Health Care Management Handbook, 2nd edn 1997; NHS Handbook: 1996–1997, 1997–1998, 1998–1999; Clinical Governance: the sequel, 2000; contrib. articles in Health Service Jl, BMJ, Health Services Mgt, Croner's Health Service Manager, Health Mgt. *Recreations:* horse riding, dancing, playing the piano. *Address:* Fairview, 4 Woodcroft Close, Woodcroft, Glos NP16 7HX. *T:* (01291) 627008. *E:* ann.lloyd.koning@gmail.com.

LLOYD, Anthony Joseph; Police and Crime Commissioner (Lab) for Greater Manchester, since 2012; interim Mayor of Greater Manchester, since 2015; *b* 25 Feb. 1950; *s* of late Sydney and Ciceley Beaumont Lloyd; *m* 1974, Judith Ann Tear; one *s* three *d. Educ:* Stretford Grammar Sch.; Nottingham Univ. (BSc Hons); Manchester Business Sch. (DipBA). Lectr, Dept of Business and Administration, Salford Univ., 1979–83. MP (Lab): Stretford, 1983–97; Manchester Central, 1997–Oct. 2012. Opposition spokesman: on transport, 1988–89; on employment, 1988–92, 1993–94; on education, 1992–94; on the environment, 1994–95; on foreign and commonwealth affairs, 1995–97; Minister of State, FCO, 1997–99. Chm., PLP, 2006–12. Leader, British delegn to parly assembly of Council of Europe and of WEU, 2002–07, and of OSCE, 2005–12. *Address:* Office of the Police and Crime Commissioner for Greater Manchester, Civic Centre Complex, Chorley Road, Salford M27 5DA.

LLOYD, Ven. (Bertram) Trevor; Archdeacon of Barnstaple, 1989–2002; *b* 15 Feb. 1938; *s* of Bertram and Gladys Lloyd; *m* 1962, Margaret Eldey; two *s* one *d* (and one *s* decd). *Educ:* Highgate School; Hertford Coll., Oxford (schol.; BA History 1960, Theology 1962; MA 1962); Clifton Theol Coll., Bristol. Curate, Christ Church, Barnet, 1964–69; Vicar, Holy Trinity, Wealdstone, 1970–84; Priest-in-charge, St Michael and All Angels, Harrow Weald, 1980–84; Vicar, Trinity St Michael, Harrow, 1984–89; Area Dean of Harrow, 1977–82; Prebendary of Exeter Cathedral, 1991–2002. Member: C of E Liturgical Commn, 1981–2002; Gen. Synod of C of E, 1990–2002 (Mem., Standing Cttee, 1996–98); Central Bd of Finance, C of E, 1990–98; Council for the Care of Churches, 1992–2001; Churches' Main Cttee, 1996–2001. Chairman: Children's Hospice South West, 1991–; Living Stones Trust, 2002–08. *Publications:* Informal Liturgy, 1972; Institutions and Inductions, 1973; The Agape, 1973; Liturgy and Death, 1974; Ministry and Death, 1974; Lay Presidency at the Eucharist?, 1977; Evangelicals, Obedience and Change, 1977; (ed) Anglican Worship Today, 1980; Ceremonial in Worship, 1981; Introducing Liturgical Change, 1984; Celebrating Lent, Holy Week and Easter, 1985; Celebrating the Agape today, 1986; The Future of Anglican Worship, 1987; A Service of the Word, 1999; Dying and Death Step by Step, 2000; (consultant ed.) Common Worship Today, 2001; Thanksgiving for the Gift of a Child, 2001; Celebrating Forgiveness, 2004; Pocket Prayers for Healing and Wholeness, 2004; Introducing Times and Seasons 1, 2006; (ed) Connecting with Baptism, 2007; How to Share the Leadership of Worship, 2009; How to Plan Seasonal Events, 2010; Children at Communion, 2010; (with J. Steven and P. Tovey) Social Science Research Methods in Contemporary Liturgical Research: an introduction, 2010; Rites Surrounding Death, 2012; How to Distribute Communion, 2014. *Recreations:* hill and beach walking, photography, swimming, making things from wood. *Address:* 8 Pebbleridge Road, Westward Ho!, Bideford, N Devon EX39 1HN. *T:* (01237) 424701.

LLOYD, Christopher Hamilton, CVO 2002 (LVO 1996); Surveyor of The Queen's Pictures, 1988–2005; *b* 30 June 1945; *s* of Rev. Hamilton Lloyd and Suzanne Lloyd (*née* Moon); *m* 1967, Christine Joan Frances Newth; four *s. Educ:* Marlborough Coll.; Christ Church, Oxford (BA 1967; MA 1971; MLitt 1972). Asst Curator of Pictures, Christ Church, Oxford, 1967–68; Dept of Western Art, Ashmolean Museum, 1968–88. Fellow of Villa I Tatti, Florence (Harvard Univ.), 1972–73; Vis. Res. Curator of Early Italian Painting, Art Inst., Chicago, 1980–81. Mem., Exhibitions Cttee, RA, 2008–. Pres., NADFAS, 2007–14. Trustee, Art Fund, 2005–15; Patron, Living Paintings Trust, 2009– (Trustee, 2005–09). Gov., Gainsborough's House, 2005–13. *Publications:* (ed) Studies on Camille Pissarro, 1986; The Royal Collection: a thematic exploration of the paintings in the collection of HM the Queen, 1992; (with John Berger and Michael Hofmann) Arturo di Stefano, 2001; Philip Morsberger: a passion for painting, 2007; In Search of a Masterpiece: an art lover's guide to Great Britain and Ireland, 2011; Edgar Degas Drawings and Pastels, 2014; Cezanne: drawings and watercolours, 2015; *catalogues of permanent collections:* Catalogue of Earlier Italian Paintings in the Ashmolean Museum, 1977; (with Richard Brettell) Catalogue of Drawings by Camille

Pissarro in the Ashmolean Museum, 1980; (introd. and ed) Catalogue of Old Master Drawings at Holkham Hall, by A. E. Popham, 1986; Early Italian paintings in the Art Institute of Chicago, 1993; *exhibition catalogues:* Art and its Images, 1975; Camille Pissarro, 1980; (with Richard Thomson) Impressionist Drawings from British Collections, 1986; (with Simon Thurley) Henry VIII—images of a Tudor King, 1990; The Queen's Pictures: Royal collectors through the centuries, 1991; (contrib.) Alfred Sisley, ed M. A. Stevens, 1992; Gainsborough and Reynolds: contrasts in Royal patronage, 1994; (with Vanessa Remington) Masterpieces in Little: portrait miniatures from the collection of Her Majesty Queen Elizabeth II, 1996; The Quest for Albion: monarchy and the patronage of British painting, 1998; (contrib.) Royal Treasures: a Golden Jubilee celebration, 2002; Ceremony & Celebration: Coronation Day 1953, 2003; (contrib.) George III and Queen Charlotte: patronage, collecting and Court taste, 2004; Enchanting the Eye: Dutch paintings of the Golden Age, 2004; Impressionism: pastel, watercolour, drawings, 2011; (with Daniel Charles and Phillip Dennis Cate) Impressionists on the Water, 2013; (contrib.) American Adversaries: West and Copley in a Transatlantic World, 2013; (contrib.) Toulouse-Lautrec and La Vie Moderne: Paris 1880–1910, 2013; reviews and contribs to learned jls. *Recreations:* books, theatre, cinema, music, Real tennis. *Address:* Apartment 4, Benacre Hall, Benacre, Beccles, Suffolk NR34 7LJ.

LLOYD, Clive Hubert, AO 1985; CBE 1992; OJ 1985; OB 1986; International Match Referee, 2002–06, Chairman, Cricket Committee, 2008–12, International Cricket Council; *b* Georgetown, Guyana, 31 Aug. 1944; *er s* of late Arthur Christopher Lloyd and of Sylvia Thelma Lloyd; *m* 1971, Waveney Benjamin; one *s* two *d. Educ:* Chatham High Sch., Georgetown (schol.). Clerk, Georgetown Hosp., 1960–66. Began cricket career, Demerara CC, Georgetown, 1959; début for Guyana, 1963; first Test Match, 1966; played for Haslingden, Lancs League, 1967; Lancashire County Cricket Club: Mem., 1968–86, capped 1969; Captain, 1981–84 and 1986; Captain, W1 cricket team, 1974–78 and 1979–85; World Series Cricket in Australia, 1977–79. Made first 1st class century, 1966; passed total of 25,000 runs (incl. 69 centuries), 1981; captained WI teams which won World Cup, 1975, 1979; Manager, WI cricket tour in Australia, 1988–89; WI Team Manager, 1996–99, 2007–08. First Pres., WI Players' Assoc., 1973. West Indies Cricket Board: Mem., Bd of Dirs; Chm., Cricket Cttee. Exec. Promotion Officer, Project Fullemploy, 1987. Former Dir, Red Rose Radio. Mem. (part-time), Commn for Racial Equality, 1987–90. Hon. Fellow: Manchester Polytechnic, 1986; Lancashire Polytechnic, 1986. Hon. MA: Manchester; Hull; Hon. Dr of Letters, Univ. of West Indies, Mona. Golden Arrow of Achievement (Guyana), 1975; Cacique Crown of Honours, Order of Rorima (Guyana), 1985. *Publications:* (with Tony Cozier) Living for Cricket, 1980; *relevant publications:* Clive Lloyd, by Trevor McDonald, 1985; Supercat: the authorised biography of Clive Lloyd, by Simon Lister, 2007.

LLOYD, David Alan; Chairman, David Lloyd Associates, since 1980; *b* 3 Jan. 1948; *s* of Dennis and Doris Lloyd; *m* 1972, Veronica Jardine; one *s* two *d. Educ:* Southend High Sch. Tennis player; mem., British Davis Cup team, 1973–82; ranked in Britain's top ten, 1970–81; semi-finalist, Wimbledon Championship doubles, 1973; British Wightman Cup coach, 1981; non-playing Captain, British Davis Cup team, 1995–2000. Chm., David Lloyd Leisure, 1981–96; Chm. and owner, Hull City AFC, 1997–2002; Man. Dir, Next Generation Clubs, 1998–2006; Chm., David Lloyd Signature Homes, 2007–13. Freeman, City of London, 1985. Entrepreneur of the Year, PLC Awards, 1994. *Publications:* Improve Your Tennis Skills, 1989; Successful Tennis, 1989; Winning Tennis Fitness, 1991; How to Succeed in Business by Really Trying, 1995. *Recreations:* golf, swimming, tennis, football. *Clubs:* All England Lawn Tennis; Queenwood and Loch Lomond Cricket.

LLOYD, David Andrew, OBE 1993; HM Diplomatic Service, retired; Senior Consultant, Middle East Association, since 2007 (Director of Information Services, 2001–06); *b* 24 Dec. 1940; *s* of John Owen Lloyd and Ellen Marjorie Howard Lloyd; *m* 1st, 1965, Janet Elizabeth Rawcliffe (*d* 2011); one *s* one *d*; 2nd, 1979, Patricia Villa (marr. diss.); 3rd, 1987, Katharine Jane Smith; three *d. Educ:* Lancing Coll.; Clare Coll., Cambridge (BA Hons Arabic). Entered Foreign Office, 1964; served Kuwait, Bogotá, FCO and Madrid; First Sec., FCO, 1983–88; Head, British Trade Office, Al Khobar, Saudi Arabia, 1988–93; FCO, 1994–96; Ambassador to Slovenia, 1997–2000. Trustee and Patron, British-Slovene Soc., 2003– (Chm., 2013–). *Recreations:* indoor rowing, tennis, theatre, concerts. *Address:* 19 Brewhouse Lane, Hertford SG14 1TZ. *T:* (01992) 583795. *E:* davidalloyd@btinternet.com.

LLOYD, David Bernard; Secretary, Royal College of Physicians, 1986–98; *b* 14 Jan. 1938; *s* of George Edwards and Lilian Catherine Lloyd; *m* 1968, Christine Vass; three *d. Educ:* Presteigne Grammar Sch.; Hereford High Sch. FCCA. Early posts in local govt, UCL, UCH Med. Sch.; Royal College of Obstetricians and Gynaecologists: Accountant, 1971–76; Secretary, 1976–82; Secretary, Nat. Inst. of Agricultural Engineering, 1982–86. Chm., Management Cttee, St Albans CAB, 1990–94 (Mem., 1985–94); Dir, Harpenden Day Centre Assoc., 2000–14 (Co. Sec., 2000–11). Member (C): Harpenden Town Council, 1992–99, 2001–03; Herts CC, 1997–2013 (Chm., Protection Cttee, 1999–2000; Cabinet, 2001–03; Chm., Health Scrutiny Cttee, 2006–09; Chm., 2009–11). Hon. Vice Pres., Hitchin and Harpenden Cons. Assoc., 2014–. Trustee and Dir, Herts Healthwatch, 2013–15. Chm., Harpenden Trust, 1995–96. Governor: Sir John Lawes Sen. Sch., 1986–87 (also Chm.); Roundwood Jun. Sch., 1980–89 (Chm., 1985–88). Hon. FRCP 1998; Hon. FFPM 1998. *Recreations:* local charity, walking. *Address:* 8 Graces Maltings, Tring, Herts HP23 6DL. *T:* (01442) 890822.

LLOYD, David Mark; Head of News, Current Affairs and Business, Channel Four Television, 1997–2004; *b* 3 Feb. 1945; *s* of late Maurice Edward and Roma Doreen Lloyd; *m* 1982, Jana Tomas; one *s* one *d*, and one step *s. Educ:* Felsted Sch.; Brentwood Sch.; Brasenose Coll., Oxford (MA 1967). Joined BBC as Gen. Trainee, 1967: Dep. Ed., Nationwide, 1978; Editor: Money Prog., 1980; Newsnight, 1982; Sixty Minutes, 1983; Breakfast Time, 1984; Sen. Commng Editor, News and Current Affairs, Channel 4, 1988–97. Vis. Prof. of TV Journalism, City Univ., 2005–. Shell Film and TV Award, 1982; Judges Award, RTS, 2003. *Recreations:* cricket, golf, music, travel. *Address:* 9 Richmond Crescent, Islington, N1 0LZ.

LLOYD, David Rees, FRCGP; General Practitioner, Swansea, since 2011; *b* 2 Dec. 1956; *s* of Aneurin Rees Lloyd and Dorothy Grace Lloyd; *m* 1982, Dr Catherine Jones; two *s* one *d. Educ:* Lampeter Comprehensive Sch.; Welsh Nat. Sch. of Medicine, Cardiff (MB BCh 1980; Dip. in Therapeutics, 1995). MRCGP 1989, FRCGP 2001. Jun. hosp. med. posts, 1980–84; GP, 1984–99. Mem. (Plaid Cymru) S Wales W, Nat. Assembly for Wales, 1999–2011; contested same seat, 2011; Shadow Health Sec., 1999–2003; Shadow Finance Minister, 2003–07. *Recreation:* lay preacher. *E:* dailloydplaid@gmail.com.

LLOYD, Rev. David Richard, (Rev. Denys Lloyd); Parish Priest, Our Lady and St Joseph, Sheringham and Cromer, since 2008; *b* 28 June 1939; *s* of Richard Norman Lloyd and Grace Enid Lloyd. *Educ:* Brighton College (George Long Scholar); Trinity Hall, Cambridge (Exhibitioner; BA 1961, MA 1965); Leeds Univ. (MA 1969). Asst Curate, St Martin's, Rough Hills, Wolverhampton, 1963–67; professed as Mem. of Community of Resurrection, 1969 (taking name Denys); Tutor, Coll. of Resurrection, 1970–75, Vice-Principal, 1975–84; Principal, 1984–90; Associate Lecturer, Dept of Theology and Religious Studies, Univ. of Leeds, 1972–90. Received into Roman Catholic Church at Quarr Abbey, 1990; Missionary Inst., London, 1993–94; ordained priest, 1994; Asst Priest, St Mark's, Ipswich, and RC Chaplain, Ipswich Hosp., 1994–96; Parish Priest, Our Lady's, Stowmarket, 1996–2008. Rural Dean: Bury St Edmunds, 2001–08; Norfolk Deanery, 2014–. *Publications:* The Sheringham Stations of the Cross, 2010; contribs to theol. jls. *Address:* The Presbytery, 58 Cromer Road, Sheringham, Norfolk NR26 8RT. *T:* (01263) 822036.

LLOYD, Eve, (Lady Lloyd); *see* Pollard, E.

LLOYD, Frances Mary, (Mrs James Lloyd); *see* Line, F. M.

LLOYD, Sir Geoffrey (Ernest Richard), Kt 1997; PhD; FBA 1983; Professor of Ancient Philosophy and Science, University of Cambridge, 1983–2000, now Emeritus; Master of Darwin College, Cambridge, 1989–2000 (Hon. Fellow, 2000); *b* 25 Jan. 1933; *s* of William Ernest Lloyd and Olive Irene Neville Lloyd; *m* 1956, Janet Elizabeth Lloyd; three *s. Educ:* Charterhouse; King's Coll., Cambridge (BA 1954; MA 1958; PhD 1958). Cambridge University: Asst Lectr in Classics, 1965–67; Lectr, 1967–74; Reader in Ancient Philosophy and Science, 1974–83; Fellow, 1957–89 (Hon. Fellow, 1990), and Sen. Tutor, 1969–73, King's Coll. Bonsall Prof., Stanford Univ., 1981; Sather Prof., Berkeley, 1983–84; A. D. White Prof.-at-large, Cornell Univ., 1990–97. Chm., E Asian Hist. of Sci. Trust, 1992–2002. Fellow, Japan Soc. for the Promotion of Science, 1981. Hon. For. Mem., Amer. Acad. of Arts and Scis, 1995. Hon. LittD: Athens, 2003; Oxford, 2012. Sarton Medal, History of Science Soc., USA, 1987; Kenyon Medal, British Acad., 2007; Dan David Prize, Dan David Foundn, 2013; Internat. Prize, Fyssen Foundn, 2014. *Publications:* Polarity and Analogy, 1966; Aristotle: the growth and structure of his thought, 1968; Early Greek Science: Thales to Aristotle, 1970; Greek Science after Aristotle, 1973; (ed) Hippocratic Writings, 1978; (ed) Aristotle on Mind and the Senses, 1978; Magic, Reason and Experience, 1979; Science, Folklore and Ideology, 1983; Science and Morality in Greco-Roman Antiquity, 1985; The Revolutions of Wisdom, 1987; Demystifying Mentalities, 1990; Methods and Problems in Greek Science, 1991; Adversaries and Authorities, 1996; Aristotelian Explorations, 1996; (ed) Le Savoir grec, 1996 (English edn, Greek Thought, 2000); (with N. Sivin) The Way and the Word, 2002; The Ambitions of Curiosity, 2002; In the Grip of Disease: studies in the Greek imagination, 2003; Ancient Worlds, Modern Reflections: philosophical perspectives on Greek and Chinese science and culture, 2004; The Delusions of Invulnerability: wisdom and morality in ancient Greece, China and today, 2005; Principles and Practices in Ancient Greek and Chinese Science, 2006; Cognitive Variations: reflections on the unity and diversity of the human mind, 2007; Disciplines in the Making, 2009; Being, Humanity and Understanding: studies in ancient and modern societies, 2012; The Ideals of Inquiry, 2014; contribs to classical and philosophical jls. *Recreation:* travel. *Address:* 2 Prospect Row, Cambridge CB1 1DU; Needham Research Institute, Sylvester Road, Cambridge CB3 9AF.

LLOYD, Graham; *see* Lloyd, J. G.

LLOYD, Heather Claire, (Mrs P. N. D. Kennedy); Her Honour Judge Heather Lloyd; a Circuit Judge, since 2007; *b* Bebington, Wirral, 16 May 1957; *d* of John Howson Lloyd and late Nancy Beatrice Lloyd (*née* Barlow); *m* 1982, (Peter) Nicholas (Dodgson) Kennedy, barrister; two *s. Educ:* St Edmund's Coll., Liverpool; Univ. of Liverpool (LLB Hons 1978). Called to the Bar, Gray's Inn, 1979; in practice at Peel House Chambers, Liverpool, 1979–99, Chavasse Court Chambers, Liverpool, 1999–2007; Asst Recorder, 1998–2000; Recorder, 2000–07. *Address:* Preston Combined Court Centre, The Law Courts, Ringway, Preston PR1 2LL.

See also W. J. Lloyd.

LLOYD, His Honour Humphrey John; QC 1979; arbitrator; a Judge of the Technology and Construction Court (formerly an Official Referee) of the High Court, 1993–2005; *b* 16 Nov. 1939; *s* of Rees Lewis Lloyd of the Inner Temple, barrister-at-law, and Dorothy Margaret Ferry (*née* Gibson); *m* 1969, Ann Findlay; one *s* one *d. Educ:* Westminster; Trinity Coll., Dublin (BA (Mod), LLB; MA). Called to the Bar, Inner Temple, 1963, Bencher, 1985. A Recorder, 1990–93. Chm., Architects' Registration Bd, 2002–07. Pres., Soc. of Construction Law, 1985–88. Vis. Prof., Leeds Beckett (formerly Leeds Metropolitan) Univ., 2002–. Hon. Sen. Vis. Fellow, QMC, 1987; Professorial Fellow, 2005–11, Hon. Prof., 2011–, Queen Mary, London Univ. Pres., Electricity Arbitration Assoc., 2009–. Hon. Fellow: Amer. Coll. of Construction Law, 1997; Canadian Coll. of Construction Lawyers, 2002. Editor-in-chief: Building Law Reports, 1977–93 (Consultant Editor, 1993–98); The Internat. Construction Law Rev., 1983–2015; Consultant Editor: Emden's Construction Law, 1993–; Technology and Construction Law Reports, 1999–. Hon LLD Leeds Metropolitan, 2009. *Publications:* (ed) The Liability of Contractors, 1986; (contrib.) Halsbury's Laws of England, 4th edn, 1992. *Address:* Atkin Chambers, 1 Atkin Building, Gray's Inn, WC1R 5AT. *Club:* Reform.

LLOYD, Illtyd Rhys; HM Chief Inspector of Schools (Wales), 1982–90, retired; *b* 13 Aug. 1929; *s* of John and Melvina Lloyd; *m* 1955, Julia Lewis; one *s* one *d. Educ:* Port Talbot (Glan-Afan) County Grammar Sch.; Swansea UC (Hon. Fellow, Univ. of Wales, 1987). BSc, MSc; DipStat, DipEd. Commnd Educn Br., RAF, 1951–54 (Flt Lieut). Second Maths Master, Howardian High Sch. for Boys, Cardiff, 1954–57; Hd of Maths Dept, Pembroke Grammar Sch., 1957–59; Dep. Headmaster, Howardian High Sch., 1959–63; Welsh Office: HM Inspector of Schs, 1964–70; Staff Inspector (Secondary Educn), 1971–82. Chm., Educn Resources Centre, Aberystwyth Univ., 1991–2001; Vice-Chm., S Glam FHSA, 1993–96 (Mem., 1990–96); Member: Ind. Schs Tribunal Educn Panel, 1990–2004; Exec. Cttee, Council for Educn in World Citizenship-Cymru, 1990–2003 (Treas., 1962–63; Chm., 1997–2003). Churches Together in Wales: Mem. Council, 1991–2003; Treas., 1999–2003; Mem., Finance Cttee, 1990–2003 (Vice Chm., 1995–98; Chm., 1999–2003); Baptist Union of Wales: Mem. Council, 1990–; Treas., 1992–2003; Vice-Pres., 1995–96; Pres., 1996–97; Member: Educn Cttee, Free Churches Council, 1993–2001; Finance Cttee, CTBI, 1994–2003. Cardiff Theological College: Trustee, 1973–2010; Mem. Council, 1990–2003 (Chm., 1995–2003); Univ. of Wales, Lampeter, 1999–2004; Gov., Swansea Inst. of Higher Educn, 1990–95. Chairman: Mgt Cttee, Glyn Nest Christian Home, 1992–2003; Bryn Llifon Baptist Home, 1999–2003; Sec., Capel Gomer Church, Swansea, 1969–83; Treas., Tabernacl Welsh Baptist Church, Cardiff, 1992–2012. Trustee: Churches Counselling Service, 1994–2000; Churches Tourism Network Wales, 2001–05. Hon. Mem., Gorsedd of Bards, 1990. *Publications:* Geirfa Mathemateg, 1956; Secondary Education in Wales 1965–85, 1991; Gwyr y Gair, 1993; Yr Hyn a Ymddiriedwyd i'n Gofal, 1996. *Recreation:* walking. *Address:* 134 Lake Road East, Roath Park, Cardiff CF23 5NQ. *T:* (029) 2075 5296.

LLOYD, Janet Frances; *see* Gough, J. F.

LLOYD, (John) Graham; consultant, 1994–96; Director of Property Services, Commission for the New Towns, 1992–94; *b* Watford, 18 Feb. 1938; *s* of late Richard and Edith Lloyd; *m* 1st, 1960, Ann (*née* Plater) (marr. diss. 1989); three *s*; 2nd, 1989, Monica (*née* Barlow). *Educ:* City of London Sch.; College of Estate Management, London Univ. (BSc Estate Management). FRICS. In private practice, London and Leamington Spa, 1959–75. Commission for the New Towns: Commercial and Industrial Manager, 1975–78, Manager, 1978–81, Hemel Hempstead; Exec. Officer/Commercial Surveyor, Corby, 1981–91; Head of Estate Management Services, 1991–92. *Recreations:* soccer, motor racing, jazz and popular music, gardening. *Address:* 4 Fairway, Kibworth Beauchamp, Leics LE8 0LB.

LLOYD, John Nicol Fortune; journalist; Contributing Editor, Financial Times, since 2006; Director of Journalism, Reuters Institute for the Study of Journalism, University of Oxford, since 2006; Associate Fellow, Nuffield College, Oxford; *b* 15 April 1946; *s* of Joan Adam Fortune and Christopher Lloyd; *m* 1983, Marcia Levy (marr. diss. 1997); one *s*; *m* 2000, Ilaria Poggiolini. *Educ:* Waid Comprehensive School; Edinburgh Univ. (MA Hons). Editor, Time Out, 1972–73; Reporter, London Programme, 1974–76; Producer, Weekend World, 1976–77; industrial reporter, labour corresp., industrial and labour editor, Financial Times, 1977–86; Editor, New Statesman, 1986–87; re-joined Financial Times, 1987; E European

Editor, 1987–90; Moscow Correspondent, 1991–95; Associate Ed., New Statesman & Soc., subseq. New Statesman, 1996–2003; columnist, The Times, 1997–98; founding Editor, FT Magazine, 2003–05. Director: East-West Inst., NY, 1997–2004; Foreign Policy Centre, 1999–2004. Sen. Associate Fellow, Kennedy Sch., Harvard Univ., 1995; Sen. Associate Mem., St Antony's Coll., Oxford, 1996–99. Journalist of the Year, Granada Awards, 1984; Specialist Writer of the Year, IPC Awards, 1985; Rio Tinto David Watt Meml Prize, 1997; Biagio Agnes Premio Internazionale, 2013. *Publications:* (with Ian Benson) The Politics of Industrial Change, 1982; (with Martin Adeney) The Miners' Strike: loss without limit, 1986; (with Charles Leadbeater) In Search of Work, 1987; (contrib.) Counterblasts, 1989; Rebirth of a Nation: an anatomy of Russia, 1998; Re-engaging Russia, 2000; The Protest Ethic, 2001; What the Media have done to our Politics, 2004; (with F. Giugliano) Eserciti di Carta, 2013; (with C. Marconi) Reporting the EU, 2014; (with L. Toogood) Journalism and PR, 2015. *Recreations:* opera, hill walking. *Address:* c/o Reuters Institute, University of Oxford, 13 Norham Gardens, Oxford OX2 6PS.

LLOYD, Prof. John Raymond; *see* Lloyd, M. R.

LLOYD, John Wilson, CB 1992; JP; Clerk and Head of the Office of the Presiding Officer, National Assembly for Wales, 1999–2001; *b* 24 Dec. 1940; *s* of late Dr Ellis Lloyd and Mrs Dorothy Lloyd; *m* 1967, Buddug Roberts (*d* 1996); two *s* one *d*. *Educ:* Swansea Grammar Sch.; Clifton Coll., Bristol; Christ's Coll., Cambridge (MA). Asst Principal, HM Treasury, 1962–67 (Private Sec. to Financial Sec., 1965–67); Principal, successively HM Treasury, CSD and Welsh Office, 1967–75 (Private Sec. to Sec. of State for Wales, 1974–75); Welsh Office: Asst Sec., 1975–82; Under Sec., 1982–88; Principal Establishment Officer, 1982–86; Hd, Housing, Health and Social Servs Policy Gp, 1986–88; Dep. Sec., 1988; Dir, Social Policy and Local Govt Affairs, 1988–98. Mem., Royal Commn on Ancient and Historical Monuments of Wales, 2002–11. JP Cardiff, 2001–10. *Recreations:* walking, swimming. *Address:* c/o National Assembly for Wales, Cardiff Bay, Cardiff CF99 1NA. *T:* (029) 2082 5111. *Club:* Oxford and Cambridge.

LLOYD, Jonathan Bruce; composer; writer; *b* 30 Sept. 1948; *s* of Geoffrey and Nancy Lloyd; *m* 1st, 1970, Poppy Holden (marr. diss. 1975); one *s*; 2nd, 1981, Katherine Bones; two *s*. *Educ:* Royal Coll. of Music. Mendelssohn Scholar, 1969; Fellow, Berkshire Music Centre, Tanglewood, USA, 1973 (Koussevitzky Composition Prize); Composer-in-residence, Dartington Coll., 1978–79. Paul Hamlyn Foundn Composers' Award, 2007; Elgar Bursary Award, Royal Philharmonic Soc., 2011. *Principal works:* Cantique, 1968; Till the Wind Blows, 1969; Scattered Ruins, 1973; Everything Returns, 1977; Viola Concerto, 1979; Toward the Whitening Dawn, 1980; Waiting for Gozo, 1981; Three Dances, 1982; Mass, 1983; 5 Symphonies, 1983–89; The Shorelines of Certainty, 1984; The Adjudicator, 1985; Almeida Dances, 1986; Revelation, 1990; Wa Wa Mozart, 1991; Ballad for the Evening of a Man, 1992; Blackmail, 1993; Tolerance, 1994; Violin Concerto, 1995; And Beyond, 1996; A Dream of a Pass, 1997; Shadows of our Future Selves, 1998; The Beggar's Opera (musical adaptation), 1999; Inventing Bach, Summon the Spirit, 2000; Music to Maze, Songs, 2001; Between us a River before us the Sea, 2002; What 'ave we got 'ere? (music'all opera in 3 acts), 2008–10; There's Only You (play in 3 acts), 2009; Old Racket, 2012; New Balls, 2013. *Recreations:* tennis, walking, cycling. *Address:* 18 Emmanuel Court, Guthrie Road, Bristol BS8 3EP.

LLOYD, Jonathan Salusbury; Chairman, Curtis Brown Group Ltd, since 2012 (Director, 1994–2012; Group Managing Director, 1995–2012); *b* 1 Dec. 1946; *s* of late Reginald Lloyd and Maureen Lloyd; *m* 1977, Marion Dickens; two *s* one *d*. *Educ:* Shrewsbury Sch.; Alliance Française, Paris. Joined Collins publishers as mgt trainee, 1967; export sales in Europe and Middle E, incl. Afghanistan; UK Sales Manager, 1976; Sales and Mktg Dir, 1980; Gp Rights and Contracts Dir, 1983; Managing Director: Grafton Books, 1986–91; HarperCollins, 1991–94. Vice-Pres., 1997–2000, Pres., 2000–02, Assoc. of Authors' Agents. Chm., Soc. of Bookmen, 2011–12 (Dep. Chm., 2010–11). *Recreations:* reading, sailing, theatre, opera, film, squash, running for one hour (except in the 2006 London Marathon which took longer). *Address:* c/o Curtis Brown, Haymarket House, 28–29 Haymarket, SW1Y 4SP. *T:* (020) 7393 4408, *Fax:* (020) 7393 4399. *E:* jlloyd@curtisbrown.co.uk. *Clubs:* Garrick, Royal Automobile, MCC.

LLOYD, Marie-Pierre; High Commissioner for the Republic of the Seychelles in the United Kingdom, since 2012; *b* Victoria, Seychelles, 15 June 1952; *d* of François Sinon and Monique Woodcock; *m* 1978, Alan Lloyd (marr. diss.); two *d*. *Educ:* St Teresa Primary Sch.; Regina Mundi Convent Grammar Sch.; Seychelles Coll.; Liverpool Univ. (BA Hons Sociol. 1976); Loughborough Univ. of Technol. (MSc Negotiating Studies 1991). Special Advr to Minister for Social Affairs, 2000–03; owner/Manager: Holistic Living, 2003–12; MPower (Seychelles), 2003–12; CEO, MP Consulting Services, 2011–. Minister for Health and Social Develt, 2007–10; Ambassador for Women and Children, 2010–12. *Recreations:* reading, dancing, listening to music. *Address:* Republic of the Seychelles High Commission, 4th Floor, 111 Baker Street, W1U 6RR. *T:* (020) 7602 5595. *E:* lloydmpe@gmail.com. *Club:* Rotary (Victoria, Seychelles) (Pres., 2004–05).

LLOYD, Mark; Chief Executive, Cambridgeshire County Council, since 2008; *b* 4 July 1967; *s* of David Lloyd and late Joan Lloyd (*née* Bowyer); *m* 2007, Shân Warren; one *s* one *d*. *Educ:* Rhyn Park Comp. Sch., St Martins, Shropshire; Oswestry Coll.; Durham Univ. (MBA Distn 2002). Civil Service, 1985–93: actg Chief Exec., Powys TEC, 1992–93; served on Lord Justice Scott's Inquiry into defence related exports to Iraq, 1993; Dir, Educn and Trng, Central England TEC, 1994–96; Dep. Chief Exec., Bolton and Bury Chamber of Commerce, Trng and Enterprise, 1996–99; Chief Exec., Co. Durham TEC and Business Link, 1999–2000; Durham County Council: Dir, Econ. Develt and Planning, 2000–03; Man. Dir, Co. Durham Develt Company, 2000–05; Dep. Chief Exec. (Policy and Strategy), 2003–05; Chief Exec., 2005–08. *Recreations:* travel, running, gadgets, Rugby. *Address:* c/o Cambridgeshire County Council, Shire Hall, Castle Hill, Cambridge CB3 0AP. *T:* (01223) 699188. *E:* mark.lloyd@cambridgeshire.gov.uk.

LLOYD, Rev. Dr Michael Francis; Principal, Wycliffe Hall, Oxford, since 2013; *b* Bishop's Waltham, Hants, 1 Nov. 1957; *s* of Major David P. J. Lloyd and Beryl M. D. Lloyd; *m* 2008, Abigail. *Educ:* Highfield Sch., Liphook; Radley Coll., Abingdon; Downing Coll., Cambridge (BA 1979); St John's Coll., Durham (BA Theol. 1983); Worcester Coll., Oxford (DPhil Theol. 1997). Ordained deacon, 1984, priest, 1985; Asst Curate, St John's, Locks Heath, 1984–87; Chaplain: Christ's Coll., Cambridge, 1990–94; Fitzwilliam Coll., Cambridge, 1995–96; Hon. Curate, St James the Less, Pimlico, 1996–2003; Tutor in Doctrine, St Stephen's House, Oxford, 2003–05; Tutor, St Mellitus' Coll., London, 2006–13; Associate Vicar, St Andrew, Holborn, 2006–10; Chaplain, Queen's Coll., Oxford, 2010–13. *Publications:* Café Theology: exploring love, the universe and everything, 2005, 3rd edn 2012; academic articles, chapters and reviews on theol. *Recreations:* walking, theatre (especially puppetry), music (especially Handel). *Address:* Wycliffe Hall, 54 Banbury Road, Oxford OX2 6PW. *T:* (01865) 274209. *E:* principal@wycliffe.ox.ac.uk.

LLOYD, Air Vice-Marshal Michael Guy, CB 2013; International Programme Director and General Manager in Abu Dhabi; *b* Shifnal, Shropshire, 7 Dec. 1959; *s* of Air Vice-Marshal Darrell Clive Arthur Lloyd, CB and of Pamela Lloyd (*née* Woodside); one *s* one *d*; *m* 2014, Ghislaine Fluck. *Educ:* Kent Coll., Canterbury; qualified as helicopter and tactics instructor and display pilot, 1989; RAF Staff Coll. Commnd RAF, 1979; operational helicopter pilot, 1981–92; Personnel Desk Officer, RAF Innsworth, 1992–93; Advanced Staff Coll., Bracknell, 1994; Operational Requirements (RAF), MoD, 1995–97; in command: No 72 Sqdn, RAF Aldergrove, 1997–99; RAF Benson, 2001–02; rcds 2003; HCSC 2004; Director: PR, 2004–06; Reserve Forces and Cadets, 2007–09; COS Personnel and Air Sec., 2009–11; AOC No 22 Gp and COS Trng, HQ Air Comd, 2011–14. *Recreations:* golf, ski-ing, walking, Rugby Union, history of the First World War. *Club:* Royal Air Force.

LLOYD, Prof. Michael Raymond; Professor, Oslo School of Architecture, 1993–96; Executive Architect/Planner, Norconsult International, Oslo, 1981–93; *b* 20 Aug. 1927; *s* of W. R. Lloyd; *m* 1957, Berit Hansen; one *s* two *d*. *Educ:* Wellington Sch., Somerset; AA School of Architecture. AA Dip. 1953; ARIBA 1954; MNAL 1960. Private practice and Teacher, State School of Arts and Crafts, Oslo, 1955–60 and 1962–63; First Year Master, AA School of Architecture, 1960–62; Dean, Faculty of Arch., and Prof. of Arch., Kumasi Univ. of Science and Technology, 1963–66; Principal, AA Sch. of Architecture, 1966–71; Consultant, Land Use Consultants, 1971–72; Senior Partner, Sinar Associates, Tunbridge Wells, 1973–78; Consultant Head, Hull Sch. of Architecture, 1974–77; Technical Officer, ODA, Central America, 1979–81. Prof., Bergen Sch. of Architecture, 1986–92. Leverhulme Sen. Res. Fellow, UCL, 1976–78. *Publications:* (as J. R. Lloyd) Tegning og Skissing; ed World Architecture, Vol. I Norway, Vol. III Ghana; Norwegian Laftehus; Environmental Impact of Development Activities. *Recreations:* sailing, ski-ing.

LLOYD, Sir Nicholas (Markley), Kt 1990; MA; Chairman, BLJ London (formerly Brown Lloyd James), since 1997; *b* 9 June 1942; *s* of Walter and Sybil Lloyd; *m* 1st, 1968, Patricia Sholliker (marr. diss. 1978); two *s* one *d*; 2nd, 1979, Eve Pollard, *qv*; one *s*. *Educ:* Bedford Modern Sch.; St Edmund Hall, Oxford (MA Hons History); Harvard Univ., USA. Reporter, Daily Mail, 1964; Educn Correspondent, Sunday Times, 1966; Dep. News Editor, Sunday Times, 1968; News Editor, The Sun, 1970; Asst Editor, News of the World, 1972; Asst Editor, The Sun, 1976; Dep. Editor, Sunday Mirror, 1980; Editor: Sunday People, 1982–83; News of the World, 1984–85; Daily Express, 1986–95. Presenter, LBC, 1997–99. *Recreations:* Arsenal, golf, books, theatre. *Address:* 15 and 17 Grosvenor Gardens, SW1W 0BD.

LLOYD, Prof. Noel Glynne, CBE 2010; PhD; FLSW; Vice-Chancellor and Principal, 2004–11, and Professor of Mathematics, 1988–2011, now Distinguished Research Professor, Aberystwyth University (formerly University of Wales, Aberystwyth); *b* 26 Dec. 1946; *s* of Joseph John Lloyd and Gwenllian Lloyd; *m* 1970, Dilys June Edwards; one *s* one *d*. *Educ:* Llanelli Grammar Sch.; Queens' Coll., Cambridge (BA 1968, MA 1972; PhD 1972). FTCL 1965. Res. Fellow, St John's Coll., Cambridge, 1972–74; University College of Wales, then University of Wales, Aberystwyth: Lectr, 1974–77; Sen. Lectr, 1977–81; Reader, 1981–88; Hd, Mathematics Dept, 1991–97; Dean of Sci., 1994–97; Pro Vice-Chancellor, 1997–99; Registrar and Sec., 1999–2004. Chairman: Higher Educn Wales, 2008–11; High Performance Computing Wales, 2011–13; Fair Trade Wales, 2011–. Mem., Maths Cttee, 1989–93, Educn and Trng Cttee, 1993–95, SERC/EPSRC. Member: Selection Cttee, Royal Soc. Exchange Fellowship Prog., 1991–94; Bd, Mid-Wales TEC, 1999–2001; Mid-Wales Regl Cttee, Educn and Learning Wales, 2001–04; Bd, Inst. of Grassland and Envmtl Res., 2004–08; Bd, UCEA, 2005–11 (Chm., Health and Safety Cttee, 2007–11); Bd, QAA, 2005–11 (Chm., Access Regulation and Licensing Cttee, 2006–11); Shadow Bd, 2011–12, Bd, 2012–14, JISC; Commn on Devolution in Wales, 2011–14; Judicial Appts Commn, 2012–. Vice-Pres., UUK, 2008–11. Sec., Capel y Morfa, Aberystwyth, 1989–2004; Chm., Ch and Soc. Bd, Presbyterian Ch of Wales. Mem. Bd, Aberystwyth Challenge Fund, 1999–2011. Ed., Jl of London Math. Soc., 1983–88. Hon. Mem., Gorsedd of Bards, 2012. FLSW 2012. *Publications:* Degree Theory, 1978; numerous jl articles on Nonlinear Differential Equations. *Recreation:* music (piano, organ). *Address:* 44 Erw Goch, Waunfawr, Aberystwyth, Ceredigion SY23 3AZ. *E:* ngl@aber.ac.uk. *Club:* Oxford and Cambridge.

LLOYD, Rt Hon. Sir Peter (Robert Cable), Kt 1995; PC 1994; President, National Council of Independent Monitoring Boards for Prisons, 2003–07; *b* 12 Nov. 1937; *s* of late David and Stella Lloyd; *m* 1967, Hilary Creighton (*d* 2008); one *s* one *d*. *Educ:* Tonbridge Sch.; Pembroke Coll., Cambridge (MA). Formerly Marketing Manager, United Biscuits plc; Chm., London English Sch. Ltd, 2007–13. MP (C) Fareham, 1979–2001. Sec., Cons. Party Employment Cttee, 1979–81; Vice-Chm., Cons. European Affairs Cttee, 1980–81; PPS to Minister of State, NI Office, 1981–82, to Sec. of State for Educn and Sci., Sir Keith Joseph, 1983–84; Asst Govt Whip, 1984–86; a Lord Comr of HM Treasury (Govt Whip), 1986–88; Parly Under-Sec. of State, Dept of Social Security, 1988–89, Home Office, 1989–92; Minister of State, Home Office, 1992–94. Member: Select Cttee on Public Affairs, 1996–97; Treasury Select Cttee, 1997–99; Chm., All Party Penal Affairs Cttee, 1997–2001; Vice-Chm., All Party Human Rights Gp, 1997–2001; Mem., H of C Commn, 1998–2000; Chm., Home Office Prisons Bds of Visitors Review Cttee, 2000–01. Vice-Chm., British Section, IPU, 1994–99; Parly Advr, Police Fedn, 1997–2001. Chairman, Bow Group, 1972–73; Editor of Crossbow, 1974–76. Jt Chm., CAABU, 1997–2001; Chm., Arab British Centre, 2001–03. Chm., New Bridge, 1994–2008. *Recreations:* theatre, gardening. *Address:* 32 Burgh Street, N1 8HG. *T:* (020) 7359 2871. *Club:* Players' Theatre.

LLOYD, Philip Michael; Director, Adults, Community, Health and Wellbeing, Cheshire East Council, 2010–11; *b* Stockport, 3 Nov. 1952; *s* of James and Dorothy Lloyd; *m* 2010, Ceri Harrison; four *d* from previous marriages. *Educ:* Moseley Hall Grammar Sch.; Univ. of York (BA Hons Hist. and Politics 1974); Univ. of Manchester (MA (Econ) Social Admin 1978). Probation Officer, Gtr Manchester, 1978–98; Principal Social Care Manager, Manchester CC, 1998–99; Youth Offending Team Manager, Manchester and Cheshire, 1999–2006; County Manager, Cheshire CC, 2006–09; Hd, Adult Services, Cheshire E Council, 2009–10. Mem., Neston Town Council, 2014–. History PhD student, Univ. of York, 2013–. *Recreations:* walking the Welsh mountains, reading, military history and walking battlefields, supporting Stockport County.

LLOYD, Phyllida Christian, CBE 2010; freelance theatre director; *b* 17 June 1957; *d* of late Patrick Lloyd and Margaret (*née* Douglas-Pennant). *Educ:* Birmingham Univ. (BA English and Drama 1979). Arts Council trainee dir, Wolsey Theatre, Ipswich, 1985. Cameron Mackintosh Vis. Prof. of Contemporary Th., Oxford Univ., 2006; Fellow Emeritus, St Catherine's Coll., Oxford, 2007. Productions include: The Comedy of Errors, A Streetcar Named Desire, Dona Rosita the Spinster, Oliver Twist, Bristol Old Vic, 1989; The Winter's Tale, The School for Scandal, Death and the King's Horseman, Medea, Manchester Royal Exchange, 1990–91; The Virtuoso, Artists and Admirers, RSC, 1991–92; L'Etoile, La Bohème, Gloriana, Medea, Opera North, 1991–96; Six Degrees of Separation, Hysteria, Royal Court, 1992, 1993; Pericles, What the Butler Saw, The Way of the World, RNT, 1994–95; Threepenny Opera, Donmar Warehouse, 1994; Doña Rosita, Almeida, 1997; The Prime of Miss Jean Brodie, RNT, 1998; Carmen, Opera North, 1998; Macbeth, Paris Opera, 1999, Royal Opera, 2002; The Carmelites, 1999, Verdi's Requiem, 2000, ENO; Mamma Mia!, Prince Edward, 1999, and worldwide; The Handmaid's Tale, Royal Danish Opera, 2000, ENO, 2003; Gloriana (BBC TV film), 2000 (Internat. Emmy, Royal Philharmonic Soc. award, FIPA d'or); Boston Marriage, Donmar Warehouse, transf. New Ambassadors, 2001; Albert Herring, Opera North, 2002; The Duchess of Malfi, NT, The Taming of the Shrew, Globe, 2003; The Ring Cycle, ENO, and Macbeth, Liceu Th., Barcelona, 2004; Wild East, Royal Court, 2005; Mary Stuart, Donmar Warehouse, transf. Apollo, 2005 (South Bank Award, 2005); Twilight of the Gods, ENO, 2005; The Fall of the House of Usher, Bregenz, Peter Grimes (South Bank Award, 2006), Opera North, 2006, 2013; Mamma Mia! (film), 2008; The Iron Lady (film), 2012; Julius Caesar, Donmar, 2012, trans. NY, 2013; Josephine and I, Bush Th., 2013; Henry IV, Donmar, 2014. Hon. DLitt: Bristol, 2006; Birmingham, 2009. *Address:* c/o Annette Stone, Arthouse, B7–3, 1 York Way, N1C 1AT. *T:* (020) 3725 6893.

LLOYD, Sir Richard (Ernest Butler), 2nd Bt *cr* 1960, of Rhu, Co. Dunbarton; Chairman: Vickers plc, 1992–97 (Director, 1978–97; Deputy Chairman, 1989–92); Argos plc, 1995–98; *b* 6 Dec. 1928; *s* of Major Sir (Ernest) Guy Richard Lloyd, 1st Bt, DSO, and Helen Kynaston (*d* 1984), *yr d* of Col E. W. Greg, CB; *S* father, 1987; *m* 1955, Jennifer Susan Margaret, *e d* of Brigadier Ereld Cardiff, CB, CBE; three *s*. *Educ:* Wellington Coll.; Hertford Coll., Oxford (MA). Nat. Service (Captain, Black Watch), 1947–49. Joined Glyn, Mills & Co., 1952; Exec. Dir, 1964–70; Chief Executive, Williams & Glyn's Bank Ltd, 1970–78; Hill Samuel & Co. Ltd: Dep. Chm., 1978–87, 1991–95; Chief Exec., 1980–87; Chm., 1987–91. Member: CBI Council, 1978–96; Industrial Develt Adv. Bd, 1972–77; Nat. Econ. Develt Council, 1973–77; Cttee to Review the Functioning of Financial Institutions, 1977–80; Overseas Projects Bd, 1981–85; Advisory Bd, Royal Coll. of Defence Studies, 1987–95; Chm., Business and Industry Adv. Cttee, OECD, Paris, 1998–99. Hon. Treas., 1989–94, Pres., 1995–2004, British Heart Foundn; Gov., Ditchley Foundn, 1975–2004 (Chm., Finance Cttee, 1985–93). *Recreations:* walking, fly-fishing, gardening. *Heir: s* Richard Timothy Butler Lloyd [*b* 12 April 1956; *m* 1989, Wilhelmina, *d* of Henri Schut]. *Address:* Easton Court, Little Hereford, Ludlow SY8 4LN. *T:* (01584) 810475. *Club:* Boodle's.

LLOYD, Richard Hey; *b* 25 June 1933; *s* of Charles Yates Lloyd and Ann Lloyd (*née* Hey); *m* 1962, Teresa Morwenna Willmott; four *d*. *Educ:* Lichfield Cathedral Choir Sch.; Rugby Sch. (Music Scholar); Jesus Coll., Cambridge (Organ Scholar). MA, FRCO, ARCM. Asst Organist, Salisbury Cath., 1957–66; Organist and Master of the Choristers, Hereford Cath., 1966–74; Conductor, Three Choirs Festival, 1966–74 (Chief Conductor 1967, 1970, 1973); Organist and Master of the Choristers, Durham Cathedral, 1974–85; Dep. Headmaster, Salisbury Cathedral Choir Sch., 1985–88. Examiner, Associated Bd of Royal Schs of Music, 1967–2011. Mem. Council, RCO, 1974–93. *Publications:* church music. *Recreations:* cricket, theatre, travel, reading. *Address:* Duneaves, Lucton, Herefordshire HR6 9PH. *T:* (01568) 780735.

LLOYD, Robert Andrew, CBE 1991; freelance opera singer, broadcaster, writer and teacher; *b* 2 March 1940; *s* of William Edward Lloyd and May (*née* Waples); *m* 1st, 1964, Sandra Dorothy Watkins (marr. diss. 1990); one *s* three *d*; 2nd, 1992, Lynda Anne Hazell (*née* Powell). *Educ:* Southend-on-Sea High Sch.; Keble Coll., Oxford (MA Hons Mod. History; Hon. Fellow, 1990). Instructor Lieut RN (HMS Collingwood), 1963–66; Civilian Tutor, Police Staff Coll., Bramshill, 1966–68; studied at London Opera Centre, 1968–69; début in Leonore, Collegiate Theatre, 1969; Principal Bass, Sadler's Wells Opera, Coliseum, 1969–72; Principal Bass, 1972–82, Sen. Artist, 2004–10, Royal Opera House; Parsifal, Covent Garden, 1988; Flying Dutchman, La Scala, 1988; début at Metropolitan Opera, NY, in Barber of Seville, 1988; début at Vienna State Opera in La Forza del Destino. Guest appearances in Amsterdam, Berlin, Hamburg, Aix-en-Provence, Milan (La Scala), San Francisco, Florence, Paris, Munich, Nice, Boston, Toronto, Salzburg, Tokyo; soloist with major orchestras; over 90 recordings; associated with rôles of King Philip, Boris Godunov (first British bass to sing this rôle at Kirov Opera), Gurnemanz (opened 1991 season, La Scala), Fiesco, Banquo, King Henry; created rôle of Tyrone in Tower (opera by Hoddinott), 1999; film, Parsifal; TV productions: Six Foot Cinderella, 1988; Bluebeard's Castle (opera), 1988; Bob the Bass, 2002; 20 progs for BBC Radio 3, incl. presenter, Opera in Action, 2000–01. Vis. Prof., RCM, 1996. President: British Youth Opera, 1989–94; Southend Choral Soc., 1996–; ISM, 2005–06; Member: Exec. Cttee, Musicians Benevolent Fund, 1988–94; Conservatoires Adv. Gp, HEFCE, 1993–97; Patron, Carl Rosa Trust, 1993–. Hon. RAM 1999. FRWCMD 2005. Sir Charles Santley Award, Musicians' Co., 1997; Foreign Artist of the Year Medal, Buenos Aires, 1997; Chaliapin Commem. Medal, St Petersburg, 1998. *Publications:* contrib. miscellaneous jls. *Recreations:* sailing, straight theatre. *Address:* c/o Askonas Holt Ltd, Lincoln House, 300 High Holborn, WC1V 7JH.

LLOYD, Prof. Robert Glanville, DPhil; FRS 2000; Professor of Genetics, University of Nottingham, since 1990; *b* 25 June 1946; *m* Priscilla Barbara Vaughton; two *d*. *Educ:* Univ. of Bristol (BSc); Univ. of Sussex (DPhil). University of Nottingham: Lectr, 1974–85; Reader in Genetics, 1985–90; Head of Dept of Genetics, 1993–96. *Address:* Centre for Genetics and Genomics, School of Life Science, University of Nottingham, Queen's Medical Centre, Nottingham NG7 2UH; 199 Attenborough Lane, Attenborough, Nottingham NG9 6AB.

LLOYD, Stephen; *b* Mombasa, Kenya, 15 June 1957; *s* of John Lloyd and Nuala Lloyd. *Educ:* St George's Coll., Weybridge. Commodity broker, Cominco (UK) Ltd, 1977–80; actor, 1980–82; proprietor, Tamarind Sound, radio prodn co., 1982–88; charity consultant, 1988–98; Business Develt Dir, Grass Roots Gp plc, 1998–2005; consultant, 2005–06; Business Develt Consultant, FSB, 2006–10. Contested (Lib Dem): Beaconsfield, 2001; Eastbourne, 2005. MP (Lib Dem) Eastbourne, 2010–15; contested (Lib Dem) same seat, 2015. FRSA. *Recreations:* film, current affairs, motor racing, theatre, history. *Club:* National Liberal.

LLOYD, His Honour Stephen Harris; a Circuit Judge, 1995–2007; a Deputy Circuit Judge, since 2007; *b* 16 Sept. 1938; *s* of Thomas Richard Lloyd and Amy Irene Lloyd; *m* 1972, Joyce Eileen Baxter; two step *d*. *Educ:* Ashville Coll., Harrogate; Leeds Univ. (LLB). Dale & Newbery, solicitors: articled, 1961; admitted solicitor, 1965; Partner, 1968–85; Sen. Partner, 1985–95; Asst Recorder, 1989–93; Recorder, 1993–95. Chairman: Nat. Council for One Parent Families, 1975–83; Mediation in Divorce, 1986–90. Vice-Chm., St Peter's NHS Trust, Chertsey, 1991–95. Chm., Bd of Govs, Manor House Sch., 1987–95. Member: Morris Register, 1985–2001; Post Vintage Humber Club, 1992–2001; Alvis Owners Club, 2001–. *Recreations:* two 1936 motor cars, a 1966 Alvis TF 21 saloon, charity and committee work, walking, arts. *Address:* Brighton County Court, Family Centre, 1 Edward Street, Brighton BN2 0JD. *T:* (01273) 811333, *Fax:* (01273) 607638.

LLOYD, Thomas Owen Saunders, OBE 2004; DL; FSA; heritage consultant; Wales Herald of Arms Extraordinary (Herodr Arbennig Cymru), since 2010; *b* 26 Feb. 1955; *s* of John Audley Lloyd, MC and Mary Ivy Anna Lloyd (*née* Owen); *m* 1987, Christabel Juliet Anne Harrison-Allen (*d* 1996). *Educ:* Radley; Downing Coll., Cambridge (MA Law). FSA 1992. Solicitor, in private practice, London, 1978–87; Dir and Co. Sec., Golden Grove Book Co., Carmarthen, 1987–89; non-executive Director: Dyfed FHSA, 1990–95 (also Chm., Patients' Complaints Cttees); Wales Tourist Bd, 1995–99. Consultant (Wales), Sotheby's, 1999–2012. Chairman: Historic Buildings Council for Wales, 1992–2004; Cathedrals and Churches Commn (Ch in Wales), 2012–; Mem., Royal Commn on the Ancient and Historical Monuments of Wales, 2010–. Chairman: Pembrokeshire Historical Soc., 1991–94; Buildings at Risk Trust, 1992–; Carmarthenshire Antiquarian Soc., 1999–2002 and 2009–; Picton Castle Trust, 2006–; Pres., Cambrian Archaeological Assoc., 2007–08. Trustee, Architectural Heritage Fund, 2006–; Vice Patron for Wales, War Memls Trust, 2014–. DL 2001, High Sheriff, 2011–12, Dyfed. Hon. Fellow: Soc. of Architects in Wales, 1993; Univ. of Wales Trinity St David, 2011. *Publications:* The Lost Houses of Wales, 1986, 2nd edn 1989; Pevsner Buildings of Wales series: (jtly) Pembrokeshire, 2004, 2nd edn 2010; (jtly) Carmarthenshire & Ceredigion, 2006; contribs to jls of various Welsh historical socs. *Recreation:* old books and bookplates. *Address:* Freestone Hall, Cresselly, Kilgetty, Pembrokeshire SA68 0SY. *T:* (01646) 651493.

LLOYD, Rt Hon. Sir Timothy (Andrew Wigram), Kt 1996; PC 2005; a Lord Justice of Appeal, 2005–13; *b* 30 Nov. 1946; *s* of late Thomas Wigram Lloyd and Margo Adela Lloyd (*née* Beasley); *m* 1978, Theresa Sybil Margaret Holloway. *Educ:* Winchester College; Lincoln College, Oxford (Hon. Fellow, 2006). MA. Called to the Bar, Middle Temple, 1970, Bencher, 1994; QC 1986; Mem., Middle Temple and Lincoln's Inn; a Judge of the High Ct of Justice, Chancery Div., 1996–2005. Attorney Gen., Duchy of Lancaster, 1993–96; Vice-Chancellor, County Palatine of Lancaster, 2002–05. *Publications:* (ed) Wurtzburg & Mills, Building Society Law, 15th edn 1989. *Recreations:* music, travel.

LLOYD, Tom, RDI 2008; Founding Partner and Director, PearsonLloyd, since 1997; *b* London, 18 Sept. 1966; *s* of Sam and Jane Lloyd; *m* 1998, Polly Richards; two *d*. *Educ:* Trent Poly. (BA 1st Cl. Hons 1991); Royal Coll. of Art (MA Dist. 1993). Sen. Designer, Pentagram, 1993–97. *Recreations:* family, food, Cornwall. *Address:* PearsonLloyd, 117 Drysdale Street, N1 6ND. *T:* (020) 7033 4440, *Fax:* (020) 7033 4441. *E:* tom.lloyd@pearsonlloyd.com.

LLOYD, Ven. Trevor; *see* Lloyd, Ven. B. T.

LLOYD, Valerie; Member (Lab) Swansea East, National Assembly for Wales, Sept. 2001–2011; *b* 16 Nov. 1943; *m* 1964, Robert John Lloyd; two *d*. *Educ:* Llwyn-y-Bryn High Sch. for Girls; Univ. of Wales, Swansea (BEd 1986; MEd 1992). SRN 1966; RNT 1980. Staff nurse, Swansea, 1966–69, 1971–73; nursing sister, Zambia, 1969–71; teacher: Cwmrhydyceirw Primary Sch., Swansea, 1976–77; St Christopher's Sch., Bahrain, 1977–80; Nurse Tutor, 1980–86, Sen. Nurse Tutor, 1986–92, W Glamorgan Sch. of Nursing; Sen. Lectr in Nursing, Sch. of Health Sci., Univ. of Wales, Swansea, 1992–2001. Mem. (Lab) Swansea City and County Councils, 1999–2003.

LLOYD, Vanessa; a District Judge (Magistrates' Courts), since 2013; *b* Hammersmith, 17 Feb. 1966; *d* of Alan Lloyd and late Leonora Lloyd; *m* 2003, Mark Martynski; one *s* two *d*. *Educ:* Lady Margaret Sch., London; Trent Poly. (LLB Hons); Coll. of Law. Admitted as solicitor, 1991; Hudson Freeman Berg, 1990–2000; Lewis Nedas & Co., 2000–13. Dep. District Judge, Magistrates' Cts, 2005–13. Mental Health Tribunal Judge, 2002–. *Recreations:* reading, walking, knitting, badminton, theatre. *Address:* Bromley Magistrates' Court, 1 London Road, Bromley, Kent BR1 1RA. *T:* (020) 8437 3585. *E:* DistrictJudgeVanessaLloyd@judiciary.gsi.gov.uk.

LLOYD, Wendy Jane, (Mrs M. Sellars); a District Judge (Magistrates' Courts), Merseyside; *b* 31 Oct. 1960; *d* of John and Nancy Lloyd; *m* 1987, Michael Sellars; one *s* two *d*. *Educ:* Liverpool Univ. (LLB Hons). Called to the Bar, Middle Temple, 1983; in practice as barrister, Liverpool, 1984–2005; Dep. Dist Judge (Crime), 2003–05; a Dist Judge (Magistrates' Courts), Gtr Manchester, 2005. *Recreation:* amateur operatics and theatre (mainly Gilbert and Sullivan).
See also H. C. Lloyd.

LLOYD-DAVIES, Andrew; an Upper Tribunal Judge (Administrative Appeals Chamber) (formerly Social Security and Child Support Commissioner), since 1998; Deputy Social Security and Child Support Commissioner for Northern Ireland, since 2011; *b* 18 June 1948; *s* of late Martyn Howard Lloyd-Davies and Penelope Catherine (*née* Vevers); *m* 1989, Lucy Laetitia Anne, *d* of late Christopher William Trelawny Morshead, MC, and Hope (*née* Rodd); one *s* one *d*. *Educ:* Haileybury; St John's Coll., Oxford (BA Lit. Hum.). Called to the Bar, Lincoln's Inn, 1973; in practice at Chancery Bar, 1975–98; Dep. Social Security Comr, 1996–98. *Address:* Upper Tribunal, Administrative Appeals Chamber, 5th Floor, Rolls Building, 7 Rolls Buildings, Fetter Lane, EC4A 1NL. *Club:* MCC.

LLOYD-EDWARDS, Captain Sir Norman, KCVO 2008; RD 1971 and Bar 1980, RNR; JP; Lord-Lieutenant of South Glamorgan, 1990–2008 (Vice Lord-Lieutenant, 1986–90); *b* 13 June 1933; *s* of Evan Stanley Edwards and Mary Leah Edwards. *Educ:* Monmouth School for Boys; Quaker's Yard Grammar School; Univ. of Bristol (LLB). Joined RNVR 1952, RN 1958–60; RNR 1960–86; CO S Wales Div., RNR, 1981–84; Naval ADC to the Queen, 1984. Partner, Cartwrights, later Cartwrights, Adams & Black, Solicitors, Cardiff, 1960–93, Consultant, 1993–98. Cardiff City Councillor, 1963–87; Dep. Lord Mayor, 1973–74; Lord Mayor, 1985–86. Member: Welsh Arts Council, 1983–89; BBC Adv. Council (Wales), 1987–90. Chapter Clerk, Llandaff Cathedral, 1975–90. Chm. of Wales, 1981–96, Pres., 1996–, Duke of Edinburgh's Award; Nat. Rescue Training Council, 1983–95. Chm., Glamorgan TAVRA, 1987–90; President: Utd Services Mess, Cardiff, 1986–; S Glam Scouts, 1989–2008; Cardiff Assoc., National Trust, 1990–2013; Seafarers UK (formerly King George's Fund for Sailors), 1990–; Friends of Llandaff Cath., 1990–; Friends of St John's Ch, Cardiff, 1990–; Christian Aid (Cardiff and Dist), 1992–2003; Wales Community Foundn (formerly SE Wales Community Foundn), 1993–; Masonic Samaritan Fund, 1998–2007; RFCA Wales, 1999–2005; Cowbridge Charter Trust, 2004–; George Thomas Hospice, 2006–; Cardiff and Vale of Glamorgan Br., SSAFA, 2011– (Patron, 1997–2012). Vice-Pres., RWCMD (formerly WCMD), 1995–; Chm., NYO of Wales, 2009–. Chm., Insole Court Trust, 2011–. Founder Master, Welsh Livery Guild, 1992–95. Patron: British Red Cross (S Glam), 1991–2008; Welsh Music Guild, 2008–. Hon. Colonel: 2 Bn (TA), Royal Regt of Wales, 1996–99; Royal Welsh Regt, 1999–2003; 160 (Wales) Bde, 2007–11. DL S Glamorgan 1978; JP 1990. Provincial Grand Master, S Wales Freemasons, 2008–13. Hon. LLD Wales, 2008; Hon. Dr Glamorgan, 2008. Paul Harris Fellow, Rotary, 2009. GCStJ 1996 (KStJ 1988, Prior of Wales, 1989–2005; Dep. Lord Prior, 2005–11). Gold Medal, RNLI, 2015. *Recreations:* music, gardening, table talk. *Address:* Hafan Wen, Llantrisant Road, Llandaff CF5 2PU. *Clubs:* Army and Navy; Cardiff and County, United Services Mess (Cardiff).

LLOYD GEORGE, family name of **Earl Lloyd-George of Dwyfor**.

LLOYD-GEORGE, family name of **Viscount Tenby**.

LLOYD-GEORGE OF DWYFOR, 4th Earl *cr* 1945; **David Richard Owen Lloyd George;** Viscount Gwynedd, 1945; *b* 22 Jan. 1951; *er s* of 3rd Earl Lloyd George of Dwyfor and Ruth Margaret (*née* Coit); *S* father, 2010; *m* 1985, Pamela, *o d* of late Alexander Kleyff; two *s*. *Educ:* Eton. *Heir: s* Viscount Gwynedd, *qv*.
See also S. E. Prior-Palmer.

LLOYD-JONES, David Mathias; freelance conductor; *b* 19 Nov. 1934; *s* of late Sir Vincent Lloyd-Jones, and Margaret Alwena, *d* of late G. H. Mathias; *m* 1964, Anne Carolyn Whitehead; two *s* one *d*. *Educ:* Westminster Sch.; Magdalen Coll., Oxford (BA). Repetiteur, Royal Opera House, Covent Garden, 1959–60; Chorus Master, New Opera Co., 1961–64; conducted at: Bath Fest., 1966; City of London Fest., 1966; Wexford Fest., 1967–70; Scottish Opera, 1968; WNO, 1968; Royal Opera House, 1971; ENO (formerly Sadler's Wells Opera), 1969 (Asst Music Dir, 1972–78); Artistic Dir, Opera North, 1978–90; Cheltenham, Leeds and Edinburgh Fests; also conductor of BBC broadcasts, TV operas (Eugene Onegin, The Flying Dutchman, Hansel and Gretel), and operas and concerts in France, Holland, Russia, Germany, Italy, Switzerland, Bulgaria, Poland, Chile, America, Canada, Argentina, Ireland, Norway, Sweden, Japan and Australia; has appeared with most British symph. orchs. Numerous recordings with LPO, RSNO, Bournemouth SO and Sinfonietta, BBC SO, Royal Liverpool Philharmonic Orch., Nash Ensemble and English Northern Philharmonia (Founder Conductor). Chm., Delius Trust, 1997–. Gen. Ed., William Walton Edition, 1996–2014. Hon. Mem., Royal Philharmonic Soc., 2007. FGS (FGSM 1992). Hon. DMus Leeds, 1986. *Publications:* (trans.) Boris Godunov (vocal score), 1968; (trans.) Eugene Onegin (vocal score), 1971; Boris Godunov (critical edn of original full score), 1975; The Gondoliers, 1986; contrib. 6th edn Grove's Dictionary of Music and Musicians, 1981; contrib. Musik in Geschichte und Gegenwart, Music and Letters, and The Listener. *Recreations:* theatre, old shrub roses, travel. *Address:* 94 Whitelands House, Cheltenham Terrace, SW3 4RA. *T:* (020) 7730 8695.

LLOYD-JONES, Prof. Guy Charles, DPhil; FRS 2013; FRSC; FRSE; Forbes Chair of Organic Chemistry, University of Edinburgh, since 2013; *b* London, 17 May 1966; *s* of Peter George and Jennifer Mary Lloyd-Jones; *m* 2004, Kathryn Anne Stockley. *Educ:* Huddersfield

Poly. (BSc Chem. 1989); Linacre Coll., Oxford (DPhil Chem. 1992). FRSC 2003. Res. Associate, Basel Univ., 1993–95; University of Bristol: Lectr, 1996–2000; Reader, 2000–03; Prof., 2003–13. FRSE 2015. DUniv. Huddersfield, 2014. *Recreations:* fly fishing, salmon and trout. *Address:* School of Chemistry, University of Edinburgh, Joseph Black Building, West Mains Road, Edinburgh EH9 3JJ. *T:* (0131) 650 4795. *E:* guy.lloyd-jones@ed.ac.uk.

LLOYD JONES, John; *see* Jones, John Lloyd.

LLOYD-JONES, John Benedict; QC 2013; *b* Liverpool, 4 June 1965; *s* of Elwyn and Anne Lloyd-Jones; *m* 1997, Gaile; one *s* one *d. Educ:* Eton Coll.; Univ. of Durham (BA Hons Anthropol.); Poly. of Central London (CPE); Inns of Court Sch. of Law. Served as Officer, Coldstream Guards, 1988–91. Called to the Bar, Inner Temple, 1993; Hd, Criminal Team, 36 Bedford Row, 2011–. *Recreation:* collecting 2000 AD and Judge Dredd comics. *Address:* 36 Bedford Row, WC1R 4JH. *T:* (020) 7421 8000. *E:* jlloyd-jones@36bedfordrow.co.uk.

LLOYD JONES, Sir Richard (Anthony), KCB 1988 (CB 1981); Permanent Secretary, Welsh Office, 1985–93; Chairman, Arts Council of Wales, 1994–99; *b* 1 Aug. 1933; *s* of Robert and Anne Lloyd Jones; *m* 1st, 1955, Patricia Avril Mary Richmond (*d* 2002); two *d*; 2nd, 2005, Helen Margaret Yewlett (*née* Lewis). *Educ:* Long Dene Sch., Edenbridge; Nottingham High Sch.; Balliol Coll., Oxford (MA). Entered Admiralty, 1957; Asst Private Sec. to First Lord of the Admiralty, 1959–62; Private Sec. to Secretary of the Cabinet, 1969–70; Asst Sec., Min. of Defence, 1970–74; Under Sec., 1974–78, Dep. Sec. 1978–85, Welsh Office. Chairman: Civil Service Benevolent Fund, 1987–93 (Trustee, 1993–2000); Adv. Cttee on local govt staff transfers (Wales), 1993–94; Local Govt Staff Commn for Wales, 1994–97. Member: BBC Gen. Adv. Council, 1994–96; Commn for Local Democracy, 1994–95. President: Welsh Council, Ramblers' Assoc., 1993–2011; Groundwork Merthyr and Rhondda Cynon Taff, 1996–2013; Chm., Age Concern Cymru, 1999–2005 (Pres., 1996–99); Vice-Chairman: Prince of Wales' Cttee, 1993–96; Prince's Trust Bro, 1996–99; Age Concern England, 2005–09. Vice Pres., Univ. of Wales, Cardiff, 1993–2004; Member: Ct, Univ. of Wales, 1995–2000; Ct, Nat. Mus. of Wales, 1996–99; Ct and Council, Cardiff Univ., 2004–10. Chm., Fishguard Internat. Music Fest., 1999–2005. Hon. Fellow: UCW Aberystwyth, 1990; Trinity Coll., Carmarthen, 1996. Hon. Dr Glamorgan, 1996; Hon. LLD Wales, 2004. *Recreations:* music, railways. *Address:* Radyr, Cardiff. *Clubs:* Oxford and Cambridge; Cardiff and County.

LLOYD MOSTYN, family name of **Baron Mostyn**.

LLOYD WEBBER, family name of **Baron Lloyd-Webber**.

LLOYD-WEBBER, Baron *cr* 1997 (Life Peer), of Sydmonton in the co. of Hampshire; **Andrew Lloyd Webber,** Kt 1992; composer; *b* 22 March 1948; *s* of late William Southcombe Lloyd Webber, CBE, DMus, FRCM, FRCO, and Jean Hermione Johnstone; *m* 1st, 1971, Sarah Jane Tudor (*née* Hugill) (marr. diss. 1983); one *s* one *d*; 2nd, 1984, Sarah Brightman (marr. diss. 1990); 3rd, 1991, Madeleine Astrid Gurdon; two *s* one *d. Educ:* Westminster Sch.; Magdalen Coll., Oxford; Royal Coll. of Music (FRCM 1988). Composer: (with lyrics by Timothy Rice): The Likes of Us, 1965; Joseph and the Amazing Technicolor Dreamcoat, 1968, rev. 1973, 1991, 2003 and 2007; Jesus Christ Superstar, 1970, rev. 1996; Evita, 1976 (stage version, 1978, rev. 2006); (with lyrics by Alan Ayckbourn) Jeeves, 1975, revived as By Jeeves, 1996; (with lyrics by Don Black) Tell Me on a Sunday, 1980, rev. 2003; Cats, 1981, rev. 2014 (based on poems by T. S. Eliot); (with lyrics by Don Black) Song & Dance, 1982; (with lyrics by Richard Stilgoe) Starlight Express, 1984; (with lyrics by Richard Stilgoe and Charles Hart) The Phantom of the Opera, 1986; (with lyrics by Don Black and Charles Hart) Aspects of Love, 1989; (with lyrics by Christopher Hampton and Don Black) Sunset Boulevard, 1993; (with lyrics by Jim Steinman) Whistle Down the Wind, 1996; (with lyrics by Ben Elton) The Beautiful Game, 2000; (with lyrics by David Zippel) The Woman in White, 2004; (with lyrics by Glenn Slater) Love Never Dies, 2010; Stephen Ward (with lyrics by Christopher Hampton and Don Black), 2013. Producer: *theatre:* Joseph and the Amazing Technicolor Dreamcoat, 1973, 1974, 1978, 1980, 1991; Jeeves Takes Charge, 1975; Cats, 1981; Song and Dance, 1982; Daisy Pulls It Off, 1983; The Hired Man, 1984; Starlight Express, 1984; On Your Toes, 1984; The Phantom of the Opera, 1986; Café Puccini, 1986; The Resistible Rise of Arturo Ui, 1987; Lend Me a Tenor, 1988; Aspects of Love, 1989; Shirley Valentine, 1989 (Broadway); La Bête, 1992; Sunset Boulevard, 1993; By Jeeves, 1996; Jesus Christ Superstar, 1996, 1998; Whistle Down the Wind, 1996, 1998; Bombay Dreams, 2002; The Sound of Music, 2006; The Wizard of Oz, 2011, and others; *film:* Phantom of the Opera, 2004. Film scores: Gumshoe, 1971; The Odessa File, 1974. Composed "Variations" (based on A minor Caprice No 24 by Paganini), 1977, symphonic version, 1986; Requiem Mass, 1985. Awards include Acad. Award (Oscar), Golden Globe, Tony, Drama Desk, Grammy, and Kennedy Center Honor. *Publications:* (with Timothy Rice) Evita, 1978; Cats: the book of the musical, 1981; (with Timothy Rice) Joseph and the Amazing Technicolor Dreamcoat, 1982; The Complete Phantom of the Opera, 1987; The Complete Aspects of Love, 1989; Sunset Boulevard: from movie to musical, 1993. *Recreations:* architecture, art. *Address:* 17 Slingsby Place, WC2E 9AB.

See also J. Lloyd Webber.

LLOYD WEBBER, Prof. Julian, FRCM; 'cellist; Founder, In Harmony, 2008; Chairman, Sistema England, since 2012; Principal, Birmingham Conservatoire, since 2015; *b* 14 April 1951; *s* of late William Southcombe Lloyd Webber, CBE, DMus, FRCM, FRCO, and Jean Hermione Johnstone; *m* 1st, 1974, Celia Mary Ballantyne (marr. diss. 1989); 2nd, 1989, Princess Zohra Mahmoud Ghazi (marr. diss. 1999); one *s*; 3rd, 2001, Kheira Bourahla (marr. diss. 2007); 4th, 2009, Jiaxin Cheng; one *d. Educ:* University College Sch., London; Royal College of Music. ARCM 1967, FRCM 1994. Studied 'cello with: Douglas Cameron, 1965–68; Pierre Fournier, Geneva, 1972. Début, Queen Elizabeth Hall, 1972; USA début, Lincoln Center, NY, 1980. Has performed with the world's major orchestras; toured: USA, Germany, Holland, Africa, Bulgaria, S America, Spain, Belgium, France, Scandinavia, Portugal, Denmark, Australasia, Singapore, Japan, Korea, Czechoslovakia, Austria, Canada, Hong Kong, Taiwan, Vietnam, Turkey, Lebanon and China. Has made first recordings of works by Benjamin Britten, Frank Bridge, Gavin Bryars, Michael Nyman, Delius, Rodrigo, Holst, Vaughan Williams, Haydn, Philip Glass, Sullivan, John McCabe, Malcolm Arnold, John Ireland, Eric Whitacre; recorded: Elgar Cello Concerto (cond. Menuhin), 1985 (British Phonographic Industry Award for Best Classical Recording, 1986); Dvořák Cello Concerto with Czech Philharmonic Orchestra, 1988; Evening Songs; also concertos by Britten, Delius, Glass, Haydn, Honegger, Lalo, Miaskovsky, Rodrigo, Saint-Saëns, Walton, Vivaldi and Tchaikovsky Rococo Variations; Unexpected Songs. Pres., Elgar Soc., 2009–. Crystal Award, World Economic Forum, Switzerland, 1998; Classic FM Red Award, 2004; Dist. Musician Award, ISM, 2014. *Publications:* Travels with My Cello, 1984; Song of the Birds, 1985; *edited:* series, The Romantic 'Cello, 1978, The Classical 'Cello, 1980, The French 'Cello, 1981; Frank Bridge 'Cello Music, 1981; Young Cellist's Repertoire, Books 1, 2, 3, 1984; Holst, Invocation, 1984; Vaughan Williams, Fantasia on Sussex Folk Tunes, 1984; Recital Repertoire for Cellists, 1987; Short, Sharp Shocks, 1990; The Great 'Cello Solos, 1992; Cello Moods, 1999; Made in England, 2004; A Tale of Two 'Cellos, 2014; contribs to music jls and national Press in UK, US, Canada and Australia. *Recreations:* countryside (especially British), Leyton Orient FC. *E:* julian@julianlloydwebber.com.

See also Baron Lloyd-Webber.

LLOYD WILLIAMS, Ven. Martin Clifford; Archdeacon of Brighton and Lewes, since 2015; *b* Watford, 12 May 1965; *s* of Peter and Angela Lloyd Williams; *m* 1989, Jacqueline; one *s* two *d. Educ:* Westminster Coll. (BEd 1987); Trinity Coll., Bristol (BA 1993). Ordained deacon, 1993, priest, 1994; Curate, St Swithun's, Walcot, 1993–97; Rector, St Michael's Without, Bath, 1997–2014; Rural Dean, Bath, 2010–15. *Publications:* Beauty and Brokenness, 2007. *Recreations:* supporting Bath RFC, working with people with learning disabilities, walking, cooking and eating. *Address:* 12 Walsingham Road, Hove, E Sussex BN3 4FF. *T:* (01273) 725479. *E:* archbandl@chichester.anglican.org.

LLWYD, Rt Hon. Elfyn; PC 2011; *b* 26 Sept. 1951; *s* of late Huw Meirion Hughes and Hefina (*née* Roberts); surname Hughes abandoned by deed poll, 1970; *m* 1974, Eleri Llwyd; one *s* one *d. Educ:* Ysgol Dyffryn Conwy Llanrwst; Univ. of Wales, Aberystwyth (LLB Hons); Coll. of Law, Chester. Admitted solicitor, 1977; called to the Bar, 1997. MP (Plaid Cymru) Meirionnydd Nant Conwy, 1992–2010, Dwyfor Meirionnydd, 2010–15. Plaid Cymru Parly Whip, 1995–2002; Plaid Cymru Parly Leader, 1998–2015. Parly Ambassador to NSPCC. Pres., Gwynedd Law Soc., 1990–91. Member, Court: Univ. of Wales, Aberystwyth, 1993–; of Govs, Nat. Liby of Wales, 1994–2001; of Govs, Nat. Eisteddfod, 1995–; Vice-Pres., Llangollen Internat. Eisteddfod, 2000–. President: Clwb Rygbi y Bala, 1985–; Betws-y-Coed FC, 1998–; Clwb Peldroed Llanuwchllyn, 2005–; Three Peaks Yacht Race, Barmouth, 2013–; Vice-Pres., Dolgellau Rugby Club. Pres., Estimaner Angling Soc., 1989–. Fellow, Inst. of Welsh Affairs. Mem., Gorsedd of Bards. *Recreations:* pigeon breeding, Rugby, choral singing, fishing. *Address:* Glandwr, Llanuwchllyn, Y Bala, Gwynedd LL23 7TW.

LLWYD MORGAN, Derec; *see* Morgan, Derec L.

LO, Anna Manwah, MBE 2000; Member (Alliance) Belfast South, Northern Ireland Assembly, since 2007; *b* 17 June 1950; *m* (marr. diss.); two *s. Educ:* Univ. of Ulster (Dip. Soc. Work; MSc). Social Worker: N Down and Ards HSS Trust, 1993; Barnardo's, 1995; Chief Exec., Chinese Welfare Assoc., 1997–2007. Vice Chair (first), NI Council for Ethnic Minorities, 1995; founding Mem., Equality Commn for NI, 1999. Chair (first), S Belfast Partnership Bd, 1997–. Contested (Alliance) Belfast S, 2010. Chair, Cttee for Envmt, NI Assembly, 2011–. *Address:* Northern Ireland Assembly, Parliament Buildings, Stormont, Belfast BT4 3XX. *T:* (028) 9052 1560, *Fax:* (028) 9052 0304. *E:* anna.lo@mla.niassembly.gov.uk.

LO, Prof. Yuk Ming Dennis, SBS 2011; DM, DPhil; FRCP, FRCPE, FRCPath; FRS 2011; Professor of Chemical Pathology, since 2003, Li Ka Shing Professor of Medicine, since 2005 and Director, Li Ka Shing Institute of Health Sciences, since 2007, Chinese University of Hong Kong; *b* Hong Kong, 1963; *s* of Wai Hoi Lo and Chiu Man Ku; *m* 1994, Siu Ling Alice Wong. *Educ:* St Joseph's Coll., Hong Kong; Emmanuel Coll., Cambridge (BA 1986); Christ Church, Oxford (BM BCh 1989); Hertford Coll., Oxford (DPhil 1994). MRCP 1995; DM 2001; FRCPE 2004; FRCPath 2005; FRCP 2006. University of Oxford: Wellcome Med. Graduate Fellow, 1990–93; Wellcome Career Develt Fellow, 1993–94; Lectr in Clin. Biol., 1994–97; Fellow, Green Coll., Oxford, 1994–97; Chinese University of Hong Kong: Sen. Lectr, 1997–2000; Reader, 2000–03. Foreign Associate, US NAS, 2013; King Faisal Prize for Medicine, 2014. Hon. FHKCPath 2010. *Publications:* over 300 articles in learned jls incl. Lancet, BMJ and Science Translational Medicine. *Recreations:* cinema, travel, photography, golf. *Address:* Department of Chemical Pathology, Prince of Wales Hospital, Shatin, New Territories, Hong Kong. *T:* 37636001, *Fax:* 26365090. *E:* loym@cuhk.edu.hk. *Clubs:* Hong Kong Jockey; Kowloon Cricket; Mission Hills Golf (China).

LOACH, Kenneth; television and film director; *b* 17 June 1936; *s* of late John Loach and of Vivien Loach (*née* Hamlin); *m* 1962, Lesley Ashton; two *s* two *d* (and one *s* decd). *Educ:* King Edward VI School, Nuneaton; St Peter's Hall, Oxford (Hon. Fellow, St Peter's Coll., 1993). BBC Trainee, Drama Dept, 1963. *Television:* Diary of a Young Man, 1964; 3 Clear Sundays, 1965; The End of Arthur's Marriage, 1965; Up The Junction, 1965; Coming Out Party, 1965; Cathy Come Home, 1966; In Two Minds, 1966; The Golden Vision, 1969; The Big Flame, 1969; After A Lifetime, 1971; The Rank and File, 1972; Days of Hope, 1975; The Price of Coal, 1977; The Gamekeeper, 1979; Auditions, 1980; A Question of Leadership, 1981; Questions of Leadership, 1983 (banned from TV); The Red and the Blue, 1983; Which Side Are You On?, 1985; The View from the Woodpile, 1988; Dispatches, 1991; Flickering Flame, 1996; Another City, 1998; The Navigators, 2001. *Films:* Poor Cow, 1968; Kes, 1970; In Black and White, 1970; Family Life, 1972; Black Jack, 1979; Looks and Smiles, 1981; Fatherland, 1987; Hidden Agenda, 1990; Riff-Raff, 1991; Raining Stones, 1993; Ladybird, Ladybird, 1994; Land and Freedom, 1995; Carla's Song, 1996; My Name is Joe, 1998; Bread and Roses, 2000; Sweet Sixteen, 2002; Ae Fond Kiss, 2004; Tickets, 2005; The Wind that Shakes the Barley, 2006 (Palme d'Or, Cannes Film Fest.); It's a Free World, 2007; Looking for Eric, 2009; Route Irish, 2010; The Angels' Share, 2012 (Jury Prize, Cannes Film Fest.); The Spirit of '45, 2013; Jimmy's Hall, 2014. BAFTA Fellow, 2006. *Address:* Sixteen Films, 2nd Floor, 187 Wardour Street, W1F 8ZB.

LOACH, Phil; Chief Fire Officer, West Midlands Fire Service, since 2013; *b* 1 Dec. 1966; *m* Samantha; one *s* one *d. Educ:* Univ. of Worcester (Dip. Mgt Studies 2005); Univ. of Coventry (Leadership capability prog. 2010; Postgrad. Cert. Mgt and Leadership 2011; MA Leadership 2014); Fire Service Coll. (Gold Comdr 2011). West Midlands Fire Service: fire fighter, 1994–97; Leading Fire Fighter, 1997–99; Sub Officer, 1999–2001; Sub Officer, Trng Centre, 2001–03; Stn Officer Project Manager, 2003–05; Stn Comdr, B Sutton, 2005–07; Group Commander: A Sheldon, 2007; B Birmingham Central, 2007–09; B Birmingham N, 2009–10; Area Comdr, B Hd of Emergency Response, 2010–11; Asst Chief Fire Officer, Dir of Ops, 2011–13; Actg Dep. Chief Fire Officer, 2013. Gov., W Midland Ambulance. Patron, Burn Aid. *Recreation:* fishing. *Address:* West Midlands Fire Service, 99 Vauxhall Road, Birmingham B7 4HW. *T:* (0121) 380 6909. *E:* phil.loach@wmfs.net.

LOADER, Air Chief Marshal Sir Clive (Robert), KCB 2006; OBE 1996; FRAeS; Police and Crime Commissioner (C) for Leicestershire, since 2012; *b* 24 Sept. 1953; *s* of Ralph George Loader and Vera May Harrington; *m* 1976, Alison Anna Louise Leith. *Educ:* Judd Sch., Tonbridge; Southampton Univ. Officer/Flying Trng, 1973–76; Harrier Pilot and Weapons Instructor, 1977–87; RAF Staff Coll., 1988; Sqn Ldr, Air Offensive, MoD, 1989; Wing Comdr, Air Offensive, HQ RAF Germany, 1990–91; PSO to C-in-C Strike Command, 1991–93; Comdg Harrier Sqn and Stn, 1993–99; Air Cdre, Harrier, HQ 3 Gp (Strike Comd), 1999–2001; ACDS (Ops), MoD, 2002–04; Dep. C-in-C, RAF Strike Comd, 2004–07; C-in-C, HQ Air Comd, 2007–09; Air ADC to the Queen, 2007–09. FRAeS 2004. *Recreations:* golf, cricket, military history, rowing. *Club:* Royal Air Force.

LOADER, Prof. Ian Spencer, PhD; Professor of Criminology, University of Oxford, since 2005 (Director, Centre for Criminology, 2005–12); Fellow, All Souls College, Oxford, since 2005; *b* Harrow, 2 April 1965; *s* of Tony and Pamela Loader; partner, Penelope Fraser; three *d. Educ:* Park High Sch., Harrow; Lowlands Sixth Form Coll., Harrow; Univ. of Sheffield (LLB 1986); Univ. of Edinburgh (MSc 1988; PhD 1993). Lectr in Law, Liverpool Poly., 1986–87; Lectr in Criminol. and Jurisprudence, Univ. of Edinburgh, 1990–92; Keele University: Lectr, 1992–99, Sen. Lectr, 1999–2002, Reader, 2002–04, in Criminol.; Prof. of Criminol., 2004–05. Jean Monnet Fellow, European University Inst., Florence, 2004. Res. Associate, IPPR, 2009–. Trustee, Police Foundn, 2007–11; Member: Commn on English Prisons Today, 2007–09; Ind. Commn on Future of Police in England and Wales, 2011–13. Mem. Council, Liberty, 2008–12. FRSA. *Publications:* (jtly) Cautionary Tales, 1994; Youth, Policing and Democracy, 1996; (jtly) Crime and Social Change in Middle England, 2000; (with Aogan Mulcahy) Policing and the Condition of England, 2003; (with Neil Walker) Civilizing Security, 2007; (with Richard Sparks) Public Criminology?, 2010; (ed jtly) Emotions, Crime and Justice, 2011; (ed with A. Dockley) The Penal Landscape, 2013.

Recreations: road cycling, Arsenal FC. *Address:* Centre for Criminology, Manor Road Building, Manor Road, Oxford OX1 3UQ. *T:* (01985) 279288. *E:* ian.loader@crim.ox.ac.uk.

LOADES, Prof. Ann Lomas, CBE 2001; PhD; Professor of Divinity, Durham University, 1995–2003, now Emeritus; *b* 21 Sept. 1938; *d* of Gerard Joseph Glover and Amy Lomas. *Educ:* Durham Univ. (BA Theol. 1960; PhD 1975); McMaster Univ. (MA 1965). Durham University: Lectr in Theology, 1975–81; Sen. Lectr, 1981–90; Reader, 1990–95; Chm., Bd of Studies in Theol., 1989–91. Arts and Humanities Research Board: Convenor, assessment panel for postgrad. awards in philosophy, law and religious studies, 1999–2003; Mem., Postgrad. Cttee, 1999–2003; Mem., Res. Centres Scheme Cttee, 1999–2003. Pres., Soc. for the Study of Theol., 2005 and 2006. Scholar Consultant, Christian-Muslim Forum, 2005–; Mem., Council of Archbishop's Examination in Theology, 2006–. Res. Assessor for Res. Council for Culture and Soc., Acad. of Finland, 2007, 2010, 2011, 2013. Lay Mem., Chapter, 2001–07, Lay Canon Emeritus, 2008, Chm., Choir Assoc., 2003–11, Durham Cathedral. Hon. Prof., Sch. of Divinity, Univ. of St Andrews, 2009–. Editor, Theology, 1991–97. *Publications:* (ed) W. A. Whitehouse, The Authority of Grace, 1981; (ed with J. C. Eaton) For God and Clarity, 1983; Kant and Job's Comforters, 1985; Searching for Lost Coins (Scott Holland Lectures), 1987; (ed) Feminist Theology: a reader, 1990; (ed with M. McLain) Hermeneutics, the Bible and Literary Criticism, 1992; (ed with L. Rue) Contemporary Classics in Philosophy of Religion, 1991; (ed) Dorothy L. Sayers, Spiritual Writings, 1993; (ed with D. W. Brown) The Sense of the Sacramental, 1995; (ed) Spiritual Classics from the late Twentieth Century, 1995; (ed with D. W. Brown) Christ: the sacramental word, 1996; Evelyn Underhill, 1997; Feminist Theology: voices from the past, 2001; (ed with J. Astley and D. W. Brown) Problems in Theology series: Creation, 2003; Evil, 2003; War and Peace, 2003; Science and Religion, 2004; God in Action, 2004; (ed with R. C. MacSwain) The Truth-Seeking Heart: Austin Farrer and his writings, 2006; Christology, 2009; (contrib.) From the Margins 2, 2009; (contrib.) New Perspectives on the Nativity, 2009; (contrib.) The Cambridge Companion to C. S. Lewis, 2010; (contrib.) C. S. Lewis and Friends: faith and the power of imagination, 2011; (contrib.) The Oxford Handbook of the Reception History of the Bible, 2011; (contrib.) The Sacred Plays of Dorothy Sayers, 2011; (contrib.) Theology, Aesthetics and Culture, 2012; (contrib.) The Routledge Companion to Modern Christian Thought, 2013; (contrib.) Exploring Lost Dimensions of Christian Mysticism, 2013. *Recreations:* going to the theatre, cooking, coaching Cecchetti Method classical ballet.

LOADES, David Henry, CB 1996; FIA; Directing Actuary, Government Actuary's Department, 1983–97; *b* 16 Oct. 1937; *s* of John Henry Loades and Evelyn Clara Ralph; *m* 1962, Jennifer Glenys Stevens (*d* 2008); one *s* two *d. Educ:* Beckenham and Penge County Grammar Sch. for Boys. BA. FIA 1961. Govt Actuary's Dept, 1956–97. Medal of Merit for services to the Scout Assoc., 1986. *Publications:* papers in actuarial jls. *Recreations:* painting, visiting art galleries.

LOASBY, Prof. Brian John, FBA 1994; FRSE; Professor of Management Economics, University of Stirling, 1971–84, Emeritus and Hon. Professor of Economics, since 1984; *b* 2 Aug. 1930; *s* of Frederick Thomas Loasby and Mabel Phyllis Loasby; *m* 1957, Judith Ann Robinson; two *d. Educ:* Kettering GS; Emmanuel Coll., Cambridge (BA 1952; MLitt 1958; MA 1998). Assistant in Pol Economy, Aberdeen Univ., 1955–58; Bournville Res. Fellow, Birmingham Univ., 1958–61; Tutor in Management Studies, Bristol Univ., 1961–67; Stirling University: Lectr in Econs, 1967–68; Sen. Lectr, 1968–71. Management Fellow, Arthur D. Little Inc., Cambridge, Mass, 1965–66; Vis. Fellow, Oxford Centre for Management Studies, 1974. Shackle Meml Lect., Univ. of Cambridge, 2010. Pres., Scottish Economic Soc., 1987–90; Vice-Pres., Internat. Schumpeter Soc., 2000–04. FRSE 2007. DUniv Stirling, 1998. (Jtly) Schumpeter Prize, 2000. *Publications:* The Swindon Project, 1973; Choice, Complexity and Ignorance, 1976; The Mind and Method of the Economist, 1989; Equilibrium and Evolution, 1991; (ed with N. J. Foss) Economic Organization, Capabilities and Co-ordination: essays in honour of G. B. Richardson, 1998; Knowledge, Institutions and Evolution in Economics, 1999; contrib. books, and econs and management jls. *Recreation:* gardening. *Address:* Division of Economics, University of Stirling, Stirling FK9 4LA. *T:* (01786) 467470; 8 Melfort Drive, Stirling FK7 0BD. *T:* (01786) 472124.

LOBBAN, Sir Iain (Robert), KCMG 2013; CB 2006; Director, Government Communications Headquarters, 2008–14; *b* 1960; *s* of late Tony and Judy Lobban; *m* 1993, Jane Elizabeth Gully; one *d. Educ:* Merchant Taylors' Sch., Crosby; Univ. of Leeds (BA Hons French with German). Joined GCHQ, 1983; Dir Gen. Ops, 2004–08; HCSC (Jt) 2001. Sen. Advr, Standard Chartered, 2015–. *Recreations:* travel, photography, cricket, football (Everton FC), birdwatching.

LOBBAN, Prof. Michael John Warrender, PhD; FBA 2015; Professor of Legal History, London School of Economics and Political Science, since 2013; *b* Cape Town, 22 Oct. 1962; *s* of John Lobban and Faith Lobban (*née* Cassy, later McDonald). *Educ:* Dulwich Coll.; Corpus Christi Coll., Cambridge (BA 1984; MA 1987; PhD 1988). Jun. Lectr, Dept of Hist., Univ. of Witwatersrand, Johannesburg, 1988; Jun. Res. Fellow, St John's Coll., Oxford, 1988–91; Lectr, 1991–95, Reader in Law, 1995–97, Univ. of Durham; Reader in Law, Brunel Univ., 1997–2000; Reader, 2001–03, Prof. of Legal Hist., 2003–13, Queen Mary, Univ. of London. *Publications:* The Common Law and English Jurisprudence, 1760–1850, 1991; White Man's Justice: South African political trials in the black consciousness era, 1996; A History of the Philosophy of Law in the Common Law World, 1600–1900, 2007; (jtly) The Oxford History of the Laws of England, vols XI–XIII, 2010. *Recreations:* art, travel, music. *Address:* Department of Law, London School of Economics and Political Science, Houghton Street, WC2A 2AE. *E:* m.j.lobban@lse.ac.uk.

LOBBENBERG, Nicholas; QC 2014; *b* Shrewsbury, 19 April 1964; *s* of George and Margaret Lobbenberg; *m* 2001, Anna; two *s* one *d. Educ:* Shrewsbury Sch.; Magdalen Coll., Oxford (BA Law); Inns of Court Sch. of Law. Called to the Bar, Gray's Inn, 1987; in practice as barrister, specialising in crime, 1987–. *Recreations:* Rugby, fine wine, travel, toy soldiers, jazz, obscure history. *Address:* 4 Breams Buildings, Chancery Lane, EC4A 1HP. *T:* (020) 7092 1900. *E:* niclobb@aol.com.

LOBO, António C.; *see* Costa-Lobo.

LOCATELLI, Giorgio; Chef Proprietor, Locanda Locatelli, London, since 2002; Consultant, Ronda Locatelli, Atlantis Hotel, Dubai, since 2008; *b* 7 April 1973; *s* of Ferrucio Locatelli and Giuseppina Caletti; *m* 1995, Plaxy Exton; one *s* one *d.* Worked in local restaurants, N Italy and Switzerland; came to England and joined kitchens of Anton Edelmann at The Savoy, London, 1986; worked at Restaurant Laurent and La Tour D'Argent, Paris, 1990; returned to London as Hd Chef, Olivo, 1991; opened restaurants: Zafferano, 1995 (Michelin Star, 1999); Spighetta, 1997; Spiga, 1999; Locanda Locatelli, 2002 (Michelin Star, 2003–14). Television series: (with Tony Allan) Tony and Giorgio, 2000; Pure Italian, 2002; (with Andrew Graham-Dixon): Sicily Unpacked, 2012; Italy Unpacked, 2013–15. *Publications:* Tony & Giorgio (with Tony Allan), 2003; Made in Italy, 2006; Made in Sicily, 2011. *Recreations:* motorbikes, swimming. *Address:* Locanda Locatelli, 8 Seymour Street, W1H 7JZ. *T:* (020) 7486 9271, *Fax:* (020) 7486 9628. *E:* info@locandalocatelli.com. *Clubs:* Home House, Soho House, Shoreditch House.

LOCH, Prof. Christoph Hubert, PhD; Director, Cambridge Judge Business School, University of Cambridge, since 2011; *b* Saarbrücken, Germany, 20 June 1960; *s* of August Loch and Irmgard Loch; *m* 1991, Ingela Björk; one *s. Educ:* Technical Univ. of Darmstadt (Diplom-Wirtschafts-Ingenieur 1985); Univ. of Tennessee, Knoxville (MBA 1986); Stanford Graduate Sch. of Business (PhD 1991); INSEAD (Dip. Clin. Organizational Psychol. 2009). Strategic analyst, Siemens AG, 1986–89; Associate, McKinsey & Co., 1991–93; INSEAD, Fontainebleau: Asst Prof., 1994–97, Associate Prof., 1997–2001, of Technol. Mgt; Prof. of Technol. and Operations Mgt, 2001–11; GlaxoSmithKline Prof. of Corporate Innovation, 2006–11; Dean, PhD prog., 2006–09. Visiting Professor: Information Dynamics Lab., Hewlett Packard Labs, Palo Alto, 2002–03; Stockholm Sch. of Econs, 2009. *Publications:* Industrial Excellence, 2003; Managing the Unknown, 2006; Handbook of New Product Development Management, 2007; Management Quality and Competitiveness, 2008. *Recreations:* soccer, family, golf, caricatures. *Address:* Cambridge Judge Business School, Trumpington Street, Cambridge CB2 1AG. *T:* (01223) 339592, *Fax:* (01223) 339701. *E:* c.loch@jbs.cam.ac.uk.

LOCHHEAD, Richard Neilson; Member (SNP) Moray, Scottish Parliament, since April 2006; Cabinet Secretary for Rural Affairs, Food and the Environment, since 2014; *b* 24 May 1969; *s* of Robert William Lochhead and Agnes Robertson Cloughley; *m;* two *s. Educ:* Williamwood High Sch., Clarkston, Glasgow; Central Coll. of Commerce; Univ. of Stirling (BA Hons Political Studies, 1994). SSEB, 1987–89; Office Manager for Alex Salmond, MP, 1994–98; Develt Officer, Dundee CC, 1998–99. Contested (SNP) Gordon, 1997; MSP (SNP) NE Scotland, 1999–2006; Cabinet Sec. for Rural Affairs and the Envmt, Scottish Parlt, 2007–14. *Recreations:* travel, reading novels and history books, cinema, cycling, listening to mainly pop and rock music, attending gigs, Aberdeen Football Club and occasionally Elgin City Football Club, learning to play the drums and golf! *Address:* (office) 9 Wards Road, Elgin, Moray IV30 1NL. *W:* www.twitter.com/RichardLochhead.

LOCHORE, Sir Brian (James), ONZ 2007; KNZM 1999; OBE 1970; farmer; Chairman, Queen Elizabeth II Trust, since 2003; *b* 3 Sept. 1940; *s* of James Denniston Lochore and Alma Joyce Lochore (*née* Wyeth); *m* 1963, Pamela Lucy, *d* of David and Nancy Young; one *s* twin *d. Educ:* Opaki Primary Sch.; Wairarapa Coll. Farmer of own property, 1961–. Tennis Rep., 1957–65 and 1973–84, Rugby Rep., 1959–71, Wairarapa; Mem., NZ All Black Rugby Team, 1963–71 (Capt., 1966–70); Rugby Coach: Wairarapa Bush team, 1980–82 (Life Mem., 1988); NZ team, 1985–87 (incl. inaugural World Cup); World XV, IRB Centennial, 1986; NZ Rugby Selector, 1983–87, 2003–; Manager and Selector, World XV, 1992; Campaigns Manager, All Blacks World Cup, 1995. Mem., 1995–2002, Chm., 1998–2002, Hillary Commn. Member: Electoral Coll., Meat & Wool Bd, 1972–73; Romney Breeders' Council, 1993–97; Dir, Wool Grower Hldgs, 2008–. Bd Mem., Sports Foundn, 1996–98 (Chm., High Perf. Funding Cttee, 1997–98); Mem., NZRU Selection Panel, 2004–07. Trustee: Masterton Charitable Trust, 1989–90; Halberg Trust, 1992–. Member: Mauriceville Sch. Cttee, 1973–79 (Chm., 1975–79); Masterton Secondary Schs Bd, 1980–86 (Chm., 1987–88); Comr, Kuranui Coll., 1994–95. *Recreations:* golf, tennis, thoroughbred horse breeding. *Address:* Riverlands, Paierau Road, Masterton, New Zealand. *T:* (6) 3770195.

LOCHRANE, Damien Horatio Ross; His Honour Judge Lochrane; a Circuit Judge, since 2009; *b* London, 6 Feb. 1958; *s* of Charles Leo Horatio Ross Lochrane and Emmeline Jeanne Effie Lochrane (*née* Lomont); civil partnership 2006, Steven William Mertz. *Educ:* Ampleforth Coll., Yorks; Royal Grammar Sch., Worcester; Christ Church, Oxford (BA Hist. 1980; MA); City Univ., London (DipLaw). Called to the Bar, Gray's Inn, 1983; a Recorder, 2002–09. Treasurer: Bar Lesbian and Gay Gp, 1998–2009; Wessex Family Law Bar Assoc., 2000–09. *Recreations:* cooking, the Vienne (France). *Address:* Chelmsford County Court, Priory Place, New London Road, Chelmsford CM2 0PP. *T:* (01245) 264670, *Fax:* (01245) 295395. *Club:* Boodle's.

LOCK, Prof. Andrew Raymond, PhD; CITP, FSS, FCIM; Professor of Marketing and Business Administration, 2000–08, now Emeritus, and Dean, 2000–08, now Emeritus, Leeds University Business School; *b* 23 Sept. 1947; partner, Sally Cooper; one *s* one *d. Educ:* Manchester Grammar Sch.; Solihull Sch.; Univ. of Leeds (BA French 1970); London Business Sch. (MSc Econ 1972; PhD 1979). Kingston Polytechnic: Lectr, then Sen. Lectr, 1972–85; Principal Lectr, 1978; Hd, Sch. of Mktg and Corp. Strategy, 1985–87; Manchester Polytechnic, subseq. Manchester Metropolitan University: Dean, Faculty of Mgt and Business, and Asst Dir, 1988–92; Dean and Pro-Vice-Chancellor, 1993–2000. Vis. Asst Prof. in Mktg, Univ. of British Columbia, 1979–80. Chm., Assoc. of Business Schs, 1998–2000; Assessor, Business Sch. Accreditation Scheme, Eur. Quality Improvement System, 1998–; Mem., 2002–, Chm., 2014–, Internat. Academic Adv. Bd, Assoc. of MBAs. Liveryman, Co. of Marketors, 1999–. CCMI; Companion, Assoc. of Business Schs; FRSA. Hon. FIDM. *Publications:* contrib. Jl of Mktg Mgt, European Jl of Mktg, Jl of Advertising Research, Jl of OR Soc. and Mgt Learning. *Recreations:* ski-ing, classic motorcycles, watching Rugby and cricket. *Address:* Biscay House, 153 Craig Walk, Bowness on Windermere, Cumbria LA23 3AX. *E:* arl@lubs.leeds.ac.uk.

LOCK, David; *see* Lock, G. D.

LOCK, David Anthony; QC 2011; barrister; with Landmark Chambers, since 2014; *b* 2 May 1960; *s* of late John Kirby Lock and of Jeannette Mary Lock (*née* Bridgewater); *m* 1985, Dr Bernadette Clare Gregory; one *s* two *d. Educ:* Jesus Coll., Cambridge (MA 1982); Central London Poly. (Dip. Law 1984). Mgt Trainee, GEC Telecommunications, 1982–83; called to the Bar, Gray's Inn, 1985 (Wilson Schol.); started practice at the Bar, 1987; Head of Healthcare Law, Mills & Reeve, 2003–07; with No5 Chambers, Birmingham, London and Bristol, 2008–14. Mem. (Lab), Wychavon DC, 1995–97 (Chairman: Amenities and Economic Develt Cttee, 1995; Community and Leisure Cttee, 1995–97). MP (Lab) Wyre Forest, 1997–2001; contested (Lab) same seat, 2001. PPS, Lord Chancellor's Dept, 1997–98, to Lord Chancellor and Minister of State, Lord Chancellor's Dept, 1998–99; Parly Sec., Lord Chancellor's Dept, 1999–2001. Secretary: All-Party Occupational Pensions Gp, 1997–99; All Party Cycling Gp, 1998–99; Vice Chm., Textiles, Carpets and Footwear Industry Gp, 1998–99. Chm., Labour W Mids Finance & Industry Gp, 2006–. Chm., Service Authorities, Nat. Crime Squad and Nat. Criminal Intelligence Service, 2002–03. Director: Conveyancing Channel Ltd, 2002–06; Insolvency Management Ltd, later IM Litigation Funding Ltd, 2002–07; Lawbook Consulting Ltd, 2002–; MDA Searchflow, 2006–. Non-exec. Dir, Heart of England NHS Foundn Trust, 2013–. Chm., Child Advocacy Internat., 2003–07. *Recreations:* cycling, family, wine and friends, paragliding.

LOCK, David Peter, CBE 2007; Chief Planning Adviser, Department of the Environment, 1994–97; Strategic Planning Adviser, David Lock Associates Ltd, since 2013 (Chairman, 1988–2013); *b* 12 March 1948; *s* of Arthur Lovering Lock and late Kathleen Barbara (*née* Nash); *m* 1970, Jeanette Anita Jones; three *d. Educ:* Sir Roger Manwood's Grammar Sch., Sandwich, Kent; Nottingham Coll. of Art and Design/Trent Poly. (DipT&CP). MRTPI 1975. Area Planning Officer, Leicester CC, 1970–73; Planning Aid Officer, TCPA, 1973–78; Planning Manager, Milton Keynes Develt Corp., 1978–81; Associate Dir, Conran Roche Ltd, 1981–88. Chairman: DLA Architects Ltd, 1998–; David Lock Associates (Australia) Pty Ltd, 1999–; DLA Architects Practice Ltd, 2001–; Director: City Discovery Centre Ltd, 1987–2010; City Discovery Centre (Trading) Ltd, 1997–; non-exec. Dir, Rapid Transport Technol. Ltd (formerly Rapid Transport Internat. plc), 1997–2004; Dir, Integrated Transport Planning Ltd, 2000–09; Mem. Bd, Ebbsfleet UDC, 2015–. Visiting Professor: Univ. of Central England in Birmingham, 1988–98; Univ. of Reading, 2002–10. Chm., 2001–08, Vice Pres., 2008–, TCPA. *Publications:* (contrib.) People and their Settlements, 1976; (contrib.) Growth and Change in the Future City Region, 1976; (contrib.) New Towns in National Development, 1980; Riding the Tiger: planning the South of England, 1989; (jtly)

Alternative Development Patterns: new settlements, 1993; (contrib.) Best Practice in Urban Extensions and New Settlements, 2007. *Recreations:* history, geography, reading, research. *Address:* David Lock Associates Ltd, 50 North Thirteenth Street, Central Milton Keynes, Bucks MK9 3BP. *T:* (01908) 666276.

LOCK, (George) David; Managing Director, Private Patients Plan Ltd, 1975–85; *b* 24 Sept. 1929; *s* of George Wilfred Lock and Phyllis Nita (*née* Hollingworth); *m* 1965, Ann Elizabeth Biggs; four *s* one *d*. *Educ:* Haileybury and ISC; Queens' Coll., Cambridge (MA). British Tabulating Machine Co. Ltd (now ICL), 1954–59; Save & Prosper Group Ltd, 1959–69; American Express, 1969–74; Dir, Plan for Active Retirement, Frizzell Insce and Financial Services Ltd (formerly New Business Ventures, Frizzell Consumer Services Ltd), 1986–89. Director: Priplan Investments Ltd, 1979–85; Priplan Services Ltd, 1979–85; PPP Medical Centre Ltd (incorp. Cavendish Medical Centre), 1981–85. Director: Home Concern for the Elderly, 1985–87, 1989–96; The Hosp. Management Trust, 1985–92; Bd of Management, St Anthony's Hosp., Cheam, 1986–2009; HMT Hospitals Ltd, 1993–2005 (Vice-Pres., 2006–); Gainsborough Clinic Ltd, 2000–03; Sec., Frizzell Foundn, 1989–93. Sec., Friends of Children of Great Ormond Street, 1986. Trustee, Eynsham Trust, 1975–83; Gov., PPP Medical Trust Ltd (Dir, 1983–89). Member: Nuffield Nursing Homes Trust, 1979–; Exec. Cttee, Assoc. of Independent Hosps, 1981–87. Mem., RSocMed, 1979–92. Freeman, Barbers' Co., 1982–. *Recreations:* bridge, golf, music, family activities, entertaining. *Address:* Bell House, Bonfire Lane, Horsted Keynes, Sussex RH17 7AJ. *T:* (01825) 790599.

LOCK, Graham; *see* Lock, T. G.

LOCK, Ven. Peter Harcourt D'Arcy; Archdeacon of Rochester and Residentiary Canon of Rochester Cathedral, 2000–09; *b* 2 Aug. 1944; *s* of Edward and Ruth Lock; *m* 1968, Susan Reed; one *s* one *d*. *Educ:* King's College, London (AKC 1967). Ordained deacon, 1968, priest, 1969; Curate: Meopham, 1968–72; Wigmore with Hempstead, 1972; S Gillingham, 1972–77; Rector: Hartley, 1977–83; Fawkham and Hartley, 1983–84; Vicar: Holy Trinity, Dartford, 1984–93; St Peter and St Paul, Bromley, 1993–2000; RD Bromley, 1996–2000. Mem., Gen. Synod, 1980–2000. *Recreations:* cricket, football, calligraphy, walking. *E:* peter.lock123@btinternet.com.

LOCK, Air Vice-Marshal Raymond, CBE 2004 (OBE 2002); FRAeS; Chief Executive, Forces in Mind Trust, since 2012; *b* Worcester Park, Surrey, 2 Nov. 1958; *s* of Frank Deccan Lock and Margaret Lock (*née* Youdale); *m* 1988, Sarah Elizabeth Jones; two *s* one *d*. *Educ:* Glyn Grammar Sch., Ewell; Bristol Univ. (BSc Hons Mech. Engrg). FRAeS 2010. Flying trng completed 1983; qualified Flying Instructor, RAF Cranwell, 1983–84; served 16 Sqdn, RAF Laarbruch, Germany, 1987–90; Sqdn Ldr, 1990; Flt Comdr, IX Sqdn, RAF Bruggen, 1990–93; Fast Jet Staff Officer, HQ Strike Comd, 1993–95; acsc 1995; OC, Flying Wing, RAF Valley, 1996–99; Directing Staff, JSCSC, 1999–2000; OC, RAF Lyneham, 2002–03; ADC to the Queen, 2002–03; DACOS J3 Perm. Jt HQ, 2004–05; Director: Advanced Comd and Staff Course, JSCSC, 2007–09; Doctrine Air and Space, Develt Concepts and Doctrine Centre, 2009–10; Comdt, JSCSC, 2010–12. FCMI 2012. *Recreations:* cycling and camping, and sometimes the two combined, refereeing, for the Gloucester and District Referees Society, teams well versed in the art of coarse Rugby. *Club:* Royal Air Force.

LOCK, Sheila Mary; Managing Director, LMC Ltd, since 2012; *b* 7 Dec. 1959; *d* of Thomas and Kate Donaghy. *Educ:* Our Lady's Grammar Sch., Newry; Manchester Univ. (BSc Hons; DipSW 1989; CQSW 1989); London Sch. of Econs and Pol Sci. (MBA 1984). Social worker, 1987–89, Prin. Social Worker, Child Protection, 1989–91, Tameside; Prin. Officer, 1992–96, Asst Dir, 1996–98, Children's Services, Barnsley; Hd, Children's Services, Sheffield CC, 1998–2002; Hd of Student and Community Services, Calderdale MBC, 2002–06; Corporate Dir, Children & Young People's Services, 2006–08, Interim Chief Exec., 2008, Chief Exec., 2008–11, Leicester CC. Dir, Nat. Space Centre, Sch. Standards and Develt Agency, 2006. Mem., Nat. Migration Impact Forum, 2010–. Trustee, Sports Partnership Trust. *Recreations:* walking, sport, music, cooking.

LOCK, Stephen Penford, CBE 1991; MA, MD; FRCP; Research Associate in History, Wellcome Trust (formerly Wellcome Institute for the History of Medicine), 1992–2000; Editor, British Medical Journal, 1975–91; Volunteer assistant, Britten-Pears Library, Aldeburgh, since 2006; *b* 8 April 1929; *er s* of Wallace Henry Lock, Romford, Essex; *m* 1955, Shirley Gillian Walker, *d* of E. W. Walker, Bridlington, Yorks; one *d* (one *s* decd). *Educ:* City of London Sch.; Queens' Coll., Cambridge; St Bartholomew's Hosp., London. MA 1953; MB 1954; MD 1987; MRCP 1963; FRCP 1974; FACP 1989; FRCPE 1989. Jun. hosp. appts, 1954–63; Asst Editor, British Med. Jl, 1964–69, Sen. Asst Editor, 1969–74, Dep. Editor, 1974–75. Consulting Editor: Encyclopaedia Britannica Year Book of Medicine, 1992–99; Med. Jl of Australia, 1994–96; an Associate Ed., DNB, 1995–. Organiser and/or participant in numerous Postgrad. Courses in Med. Writing and confs in scientific editing worldwide, 1971–2010. Mem., Res. Ethics Cttee, KCH Medical Sch., 1992–96. Mem. Council, Harveian Soc., 1992–96 (Pres., 1994); Founder Pres., 1982–85, Mem. Council, 1985–91, European Assoc. of Sci. Editors. Vis. Prof. in Medicine, McGill Univ., 1978; Visitor, Acad. Dept of Medicine, Monash Univ., 1982; Rockefeller Scholar, Villa Serbelloni, Bellagio, 1985; Foundn Vis. Prof. in Medicine, RCSI, 1986; Vis. Prof. in Epidemiology and Biostatistics, McGill Univ., 1992; Vis. Lectr, Erasmus Summer Sch., Rotterdam, 1993–2006; Vis. Prof., Norwegian Tech. Univ., Trondheim, 2003–10. Lectures: Wade, Keele Univ., 1980; Morgan, Royal Cornwall Hosp., 1984; Rock Carling, Nuffield Provincial Hosps Trust, 1985; Maurice Bloch, Glasgow Univ., 1986; Wolfson, Wolfson Coll., Oxford, 1986; Estelle Brodman, Washington Univ., St Louis, 1989; Sarah Davies, TCD, 1990; William Hey, Leeds Univ., 1990; George McGovern, Med. Library Assoc. of America, San Francisco, 1991; College, RCP, 1996; Carmichael, RCSI, 1999. Chairman: Friends of Dulwich Picture Gall., 1993–96; Aldeburgh Soc., 1998–2001 (Mem., Cttee, 1997–; Acting Sec., 2001–02; Vice-Pres., 2002–05; Pres., 2005–08); Aldeburgh Fest. Club, 2003–05 (Vice-Chm., 2001–03; Pres., 2008–12). Hon. FRCPI 1987; Hon. Fellow, Amer. Med. Writers Assoc., 1994; Hon. Founder Fellow, RCPCH, 1997 (Hon. Mem., BPA, 1991). Hon. MSc Manchester, 1985. Donders Medal, Ned. Tijdsch. Geneesk, 1981; Internat. Medal, Finnish Med. Soc. Duodecim, 1981; Medal of Honour, Finnish Med. Jl, 1987; Fothergillian Medal, Med. Soc., London, 1992; Meritorious Award, Council of Biol. Eds, 1993. Officer, first cl., White Rose of Finland, 1982. *Publications:* An Introduction to Clinical Pathology, 1965; Health Centres and Group Practices, 1966; The Enemies of Man, 1968; Better Medical Writing, 1970; Family Health Guide, 1972; (ed) Personal View, 1975; Medical Risks of Life, 1976; Thorne's Better Medical Writing, 2nd edn 1977; (ed) Adverse Drug Reactions, 1977; (ed) Remembering Henry, 1977; (contrib.) Oxford Companion to Medicine, 1983; (ed) As You Were, 1984; A Difficult Balance: editorial peer review in medicine, 1985; (ed) The Future of Medical Journals, 1991; Medical Journals and Medical Progress, 1992; (ed) Fraud and Misconduct in Medical Research, 1993, 3rd edn 2001; (ed) Eighty-five Not Out: essays to honour Sir George Godber, 1993; (ed jtly) The Oxford Medical Companion, 1995; (contrib.) Oxford Illustrated History of Medicine, 1996; (ed) Ashes to Ashes, 1998; (contrib.) Our NHS, 1998; (ed) Oxford Illustrated Companion to Medicine, 2001; (contrib.) Leoš Janáček: years of a life, vol. 1, 2006, vol. 2, 2008; (contrib.) World Dictionary of Medical Biography, 2007; (contrib.) Medisinsk publisering og fagformidling, 2008; (contrib.) Great Discoveries in Medicine, 2011; contrib. DNB and Oxford DNB. *Recreations:* reading reviews of operas I can't afford to see, avoiding operas whose producers know better than the composer. *Address:* 3 Alde House, Alde House Drive, Aldeburgh, Suffolk IP15 5EE. *T:* (01728) 452411. *E:* splock@globalnet.co.uk.

LOCK, (Thomas) Graham; Chief Executive, Amalgamated Metal Corporation plc, 1983–91; *b* 19 Oct. 1931; *s* of Robert Henry Lock and Morfydd Lock (*née* Thomas); *m* 1st, 1954, Janice Olive Baker Lock (*née* Jones) (marr. diss. 1992; she *d* 1995); two *d*; 2nd, 2005, Judith Elizabeth Lucy (*née* Butterworth) (marr. diss. 2010). *Educ:* Whitchurch Grammar School; University College of South Wales and Monmouthshire (BSc Metall); College of Advanced Technology, Aston; Harvard Business School. CEng, FIMMM. Instructor Lieut, RN, 1953–56; Lucas Industries and Lucas Electrical, 1956–61; Dir, Girling Bremsen GmbH, 1961–66; Gen. Man. and Overseas Ops Dir, Girling Ltd, 1966–73; Gen. Man. and Dir, Lucas Service Overseas Ltd, 1973–79; Man. Dir, Industrial Div., Amalgamated Metal Corp., 1979–83; non-exec. Director: Marshall's Universal plc, 1983–86; Evode Gp plc, 1985–91. CCMI. Liveryman, Co. of Gold and Silver Wyre Drawers, 1988–. Freeman, City of London, 1987. *Recreations:* sailing, music, ski-ing. *Address:* Parolas Villa, 4520 Parekklisia, near Limassol, Cyprus. *Clubs:* Army and Navy; Royal Naval Sailing Association (Portsmouth).

LOCKE, John Christopher, FRICS; Chief Executive, Property Advisers to the Civil Estate, 1997–2000; *b* 4 March 1947; *s* of late Comdr Cyril Frederick Locke, RN, CEng, FIEE and Marjorie Alice Batt Locke (*née* Collins); *m* 1st, 1969 (marr. diss. 1989); two *s*; 2nd, 1990, Maria Patricia, *d* of late Eileen Rogers (*née* Mahony). *Educ:* Pangbourne Coll.; Regent Street Poly.; Brixton Sch. of Building; Northern Poly. ARICS 1971 (Wainwright Prizewinner), FRICS 1981. Prudential Assurance Co. Ltd, 1964–88 (Dir, Estate Management, 1987–88); Divl Dir, Estate Management, Prudential Portfolio Managers Ltd, 1989–91; Director: Southbank Technopark Ltd, 1985–91 (Chm., 1989–90); City Aviation Insurance Tenancies Ltd, 1989–90; Chm., Briggait Co. Ltd, 1987–90; Surveyor, Watling Street Properties, 1989–90; Chief Exec., NHS Estate Mgt and Health Bldg Agency, 1991–97. Member: Commercial Property Cttee, RICS, 1983–89; Central Govt Support Panel, RICS, 1997–2000 (Chm., 1999–2000); Mgt Consultancy Practice Panel, RICS, 1997–2000; Govt Construction Client Panel, HM Treasury, 1997–2000 (Chm. of Strategy, Dialogue with Industry Gp, 1998–2000); Bd of Mgt, British Council for Offices, 1997–2000 (Mgt Exec., 1999–2000). Mem. Editl Adv. Bd, Property Week, 2000. Hon. FIHEEM (Hon. FIHospE 1992). *Recreations:* opera, theatre, music, film, reading, travel, family, home. *Address:* 11 Shrewsbury Road, Beckenham, Kent BR3 4DB.

LOCKERBIE, Catherine; Director, Edinburgh International Book Festival, 2000–09; *b* 4 Sept. 1958; *d* of Prof. Samuel Ian Johnstone Lockerbie and Rowena May Lockerbie (*née* Berry); one *s*. *Educ:* Univ. of Edinburgh (MA 1st Cl. double Hons French and Philosophy). Literary Ed., 1990–2000, Chief Leader Writer, 1995–97, The Scotsman. Founding Trustee, Edinburgh UNESCO City of Literature, 2004. Hon. LLD Dundee, 2005; Hon. DLitt: Queen Margaret UC, 2006; Edinburgh, 2007; Napier Univ., 2008; DUniv Open, 2007. *Publications:* (ed) Looking for the Spark: Scottish short stories, 1994. *Recreations:* reading, reading, and learning to understand my fellow humans (through reading).

LOCKETT, Sir Michael (Vernon), KCVO 2012 (CVO 2002); Chief Executive, Thames Diamond Jubilee Foundation, since 2011; *b* Bury St Edmunds, Suffolk, 8 April 1948; *s* of Francis and Vera Lockett; *m* 1975, Margaret Dietzold; one *s* two *d*. *Educ:* Woolverstone Hall, Suffolk. Account Dir, Grey Advertising, 1970–75; Chairman: WCT Live, 1975–97; CCO Conferences, 1993–2009; Booth, Lockett Makin, 1993–94; Carabiner, 1998–99; Live Communication, 2000–08; Aura Events, 2005–; Strategic Communications Alliance, 2008–; Unspun, 2009–; Leadership Agency, 2009–; non-executive Director: Populus, 2001–; Grace Blue, 2009–; CTN, 2010–; Grace Blue USA, 2012–. Dir, Oracle Cancer Trust, 2010–. FRSA. *Recreations:* sport (past player at Leicester Tigers), travel. *Address:* Audley House, 13 Palace Street, SW1E 5HX. *T:* (020) 7592 0898, *Fax:* (020) 7963 0989. *E:* mlockett@sca.uk.com. *Clubs:* Arts, Royal Automobile, 5 Hertford Street, Ivy, Annabel's; Guards Polo; Thorpeness Golf.

LOCKETT, Rev. Preb. Paul; Chaplain to the Queen, since 2011; Priest-in-charge, Hempton with Pudding Norton, since 2012; Chantry Priest, Guild of All Souls and Pastoral Assistant, Shrine of Our Lady of Walsingham, since 2012; *b* Wolverhampton, 13 Feb. 1948; *s* of Peter and Freda Joyce Lockett. *Educ:* Regis Comp. Sch., Tettenhall; Wulfrun Coll. of Further Educn (HNC Business Studies); Salisbury and Wells Theol Coll.; Southampton Univ. (CTh). Ordained deacon, 1976, priest, 1977; Curate: Horninglow, Burton-on-Trent, 1976–78; Tewkesbury Abbey, 1978–81; Priest-in-charge, St Peter, W Bromwich, 1981–90; Rector, Norton Canes, 1990–95; Vicar, St Mary and Chad, Longton, 1995–2012. Dean's Vicar, 1991–2012, Preb., 2004–12, Lichfield Cath. Chaplain, Heath Lane Hosp., W Bromwich, 1985–90; Staffs Wing Chaplain, ATC, 1985–2000. Mem., British Pottery Manufacturers Fedn, 1996–2012. *Recreations:* France, music, antiques. *Address:* 20 Cleaves Drive, Walsingham, Norfolk NR22 6EQ. *T:* (01325) 820030. *Club:* Royal Over-Seas League.

LOCKEY, John Charlton Gerard; QC 2006; barrister; *b* 8 April 1963; *s* of Bryan Lockey and Anne Lockey (*née* Conroy, now Day); *m* 1992, Louise O'Sullivan; two *d*. *Educ:* Haberdashers' Aske's Sch., Elstree; Downing Coll., Cambridge (BA 1985); Harvard Law Sch. (LLM 1986). Called to the Bar, Middle Temple, 1987; in practice, specialising in insurance and commercial law, 1988–. Chm., British Insce Law Assoc., 2004–06. *Address:* Essex Court Chambers, 24 Lincoln's Inn Fields, WC2A 3EG. *T:* (020) 7813 8000, *Fax:* (020) 7813 8080.

LOCKHART, Andrew William Jardine; QC 2010; **His Honour Judge Lockhart;** a Circuit Judge, since 2014; *b* Northampton, 15 March 1963; *s* of Alec Lockhart and Jean Lockhart; *m* 1990, Joanna Freeman; two *s* one *d*. *Educ:* Rugby Sch.; King's Coll., London (LLB Hons 1985). Army Officer, 7th Parachute Regt RHA, 1985–90. Called to the Bar, Lincoln's Inn, 1991; in practice as a barrister, St Philips Chambers, 1991–2014; a Recorder, 2005–14. Mem., RFU Disciplinary Panel, 2007–. *Recreations:* family, sailing, military history, watching children play sport. *Address:* Wolverhampton Combined Court, Pipers Row, Wolverhampton WV1 3LQ.

LOCKHART, Brian Alexander; Sheriff Principal of South Strathclyde, Dumfries and Galloway, 2005–14; Temporary High Court Judge, since 2008; *b* 1 Oct. 1942; *s* of John Arthur Hay Lockhart and Norah Lockhart; *m* 1967, Christine Ross Clark; two *s* two *d*. *Educ:* Glasgow Academy; Glasgow Univ. (BL). Qualified as solicitor, 1964; Partner in Robertson Chalmers & Auld, Solicitors, Glasgow, 1966–79; Sheriff in North Strathclyde, 1979–81, in Glasgow and Strathkelvin, 1981–2005. Mem., Parole Bd for Scotland, 1997–2003. Pres., Sheriffs' Assoc., 2004–05 (Sec., 1997–2002; Vice-Pres., 2002–04). Comr, Northern Lighthouse Bd, 2005–14. *Recreations:* fishing, golf, family. *Address:* 18 Hamilton Avenue, Glasgow G41 4JF. *T:* (0141) 427 1921.

LOCKHART, Brian Robert Watson; Headmaster, Robert Gordon's College, Aberdeen, 1996–2004; *b* 19 July 1944; *s* of late George Watson Lockhart and Helen Lockhart (*née* Rattray); *m* 1970, Fiona Anne Sheddon, MA; one *s* two *d*. *Educ:* Leith Acad.; George Heriot's Sch.; Aberdeen Univ. (MA); Edinburgh Univ. (DipEd); Moray House Coll. (Cert Ed). History Teacher, 1968–72, Principal History Teacher, 1972–81, George Heriot's Sch.; Dep. Rector, High Sch. of Glasgow, 1981–96. Council Mem., 1988–2004, Asst Sec. and Exec. Mem., 1989–94, Headteachers' Assoc. of Scotland; Mem., Higher Still Implementation Gp, 1997–2000; Chm., UCAS Scottish Standing Cttee, 2001–02 (Mem., 1994–2003; Co-Chm., 1998–99); Mem., HMC Univs Working Party, 1999–2003; Sec., 2003, Chm., 2004, Scottish Div., HMC. University of Aberdeen: Member: Business Cttee, 2001–12 (Vice Convener, 2006–10); Audit Cttee, 2007–13; Teaching and Learning Cttee, 2009–12; Remuneration Cttee, 2010–12; Staff Promotion Cttee, 2012; Gen. Council Assessor to Court, 2008–12; Chm., Student Affairs Cttee, 2010–12. Mem. Bd, Voluntary Service Aberdeen, 2004–11.

Member: Council, St Margaret's Sch. for Girls, Aberdeen, 2004–13; Bd, Hutchesons' GS, Glasgow, 2005–12 (Educn Cttee Convener, 2011–12); Bd, Lathallan Sch., 2013–; Friends of Aberdeen Univ. Liby Exec., 2013–. Trustee, Robert Nicol Trust, 2006–14 (Convener, 2015–). *Publications:* History of the Architecture of George Heriot's Hospital and School 1628–1978, 1978; Jinglin' Geordie's Legacy, 2003, 350th anniv. edn 2009; Robert Gordon's Legacy, 2007; The Town School: a history of the High School of Glasgow, 2010; Bon Record: a history of Aberdeen Grammar School, 2012; A Great Educational Tradition: a history of Hutchesons' Grammar School, 2015. *Recreations:* architecture, reading biographies, sport, films, politics, educational history research. *Address:* 80 Gray Street, Aberdeen AB10 6JE. *T:* (01224) 315776.

LOCKHART, Harry Eugene, (Gene), CPA; Chairman, Financial Institutions, Diamond Castle Holdings LLC, since 2005; *b* 4 Nov. 1949; *s* of Harry Eugene Lockhart, Sen., Austin, Texas, and Gladys Cummings Lockhart; *m* 1974, Terry Lockhart; one *s* three *d*. *Educ:* Univ. of Virginia (MechEng degree); Darden Graduate Bus. Sch. (MBA). CPA 1976. Sen. Cons., Arthur Anderson & Co., 1974–77; Man. Principal, Europe, Nolan Norton & Co., 1977–82; Gp Dir, Management Services, C. T. Bowring & Co., 1982–85; Vice Pres., First Manhattan Consulting Gp, 1985–87; Chief Exec., IT, 1987–88, Gp Ops, 1988–92, UK Banking, 1990–92, Midland Bank; Pres., First Manhattan Consulting Internat., 1992–94; Pres. and CEO, Mastercard International, 1994–97; Pres. and CEO, The New Power Co., 2000–03. Dir, Qsent Inc., 2003. *Recreations:* tennis, golf, running, ski-ing, photography, riding, classical music, ballet. *Address:* Diamond Castle Holdings LLC, 280 Park Avenue, 25th Floor, East Tower, New York, NY 10017, USA. *Clubs:* Blind Brook; Indian Harbor Yacht; Mill Reef.

LOCKHART, James Lawrence, FRCM, FRCO(CHM); Director of Opera, London Royal Schools' Vocal Faculty, 1992–96 (Opera Consultant, 1996–98); *b* 16 Oct. 1930; *s* of Archibald Campbell Lockhart and Mary Black Lawrence; *m* 1954, Sheila Margaret Grogan; two *s* one *d*. *Educ:* George Watson's Boys' College; Edinburgh Univ. (BMus); Royal College of Music (ARCM, FRCM). Yorkshire Symphony Orchestra, 1954–55; Münster City Opera, 1955–56; Bavarian State Opera, 1956–57; Glyndebourne Festival Opera, 1957, 1958, 1959; Opera Workshop, Univ. of Texas, 1957–59; Royal Opera House, Covent Garden, 1959–60; BBC Scottish Orchestra, 1960–61; Scottish Opera, 1960–61; Conductor, Sadler's Wells Opera, 1961–62; Conductor and Repetiteur, Royal Opera House, Covent Garden, 1962–68; Music Dir, Welsh National Opera, 1968–73; Generalmusikdirektor: Staatstheater, Kassel, 1972–80; Koblenz Opera, 1981–88; Rheinische Philharmonie, 1981–91 (Ehrendirigent, 1991); Dir of Opera, RCM, 1986–96. Guest Conductor, Sydney Conservatorium of Music, 2005. Guest Prof. of Conducting, Tokyo Nat. Univ. of Fine Arts and Music (Tokyo Geidai), 1998–2001, now Prof. Emeritus. Hon. RAM 1993. *Recreations:* swimming, hill-walking, travel, languages. *Address:* 5 The Coach House, Mill Street, Fontmell Magna, Shaftesbury, Dorset SP7 0NU. *T:* and *Fax:* (01747) 811980.

LOCKHART, Logie B.; *see* Bruce Lockhart.

LOCKHART, Sir Simon John Edward Francis S.; *see* Sinclair-Lockhart.

LOCKHART-MUMMERY, Christopher John; QC 1986; a Recorder, 1994–2004; a Deputy High Court Judge, 1995–2004; *b* 7 Aug. 1947; *s* of Sir Hugh Lockhart-Mummery, KCVO, MD, MChir, FRCS and late Elizabeth Jean Crerar, *d* of Sir James Crerar, KCSI, CIE; *m* 1st, 1971, Elizabeth Rosamund (marr. diss. 1992), *d* of late N. P. M. Elles and Baroness Elles; one *s* two *d*; 2nd, 1993, Mary Lou Putley (MBE 2015). *Educ:* Stowe; Trinity College, Cambridge (BA). Called to the Bar, Inner Temple, 1971 (Bencher, 1991). Specialist Editor, Hill and Redman's Law of Landlord and Tenant, 1974–89. *Recreations:* fishing, listening to music, opera, walking the dog. *Address:* Landmark Chambers, 180 Fleet Street, EC4A 2HG. *T:* (020) 7430 1221; 83 Abbotsbury Road, W14 8EP. *T:* (020) 7603 7200; Hookeswood House, Farnham, Blandford Forum, Dorset DT11 8DQ. *T:* (01725) 516259. *Club:* Garrick.

LOCKHEAD, Sir Moir, Kt 2008; OBE 1996; Chairman: Scottish Rugby Union, since 2011; National Trust for Scotland, since 2015; Deputy Chairman and Chief Executive, FirstGroup plc, 1995–2010; *b* 25 April 1945; *s* of Len and Ethel Lockhead; *m* 1966, Audrey Johnson; three *s* one *d*. Chief Engr, Strathclyde Passenger Transport Exec., 1979–85; Gen. Manager, Grampian Transport, 1985–89; led employee/mgt buyout, 1989; Exec. Chm., Grampian Transport, subseq. GRT Bus plc, FirstBus plc, then FirstGroup plc, 1989–94. Sen. Gov., Univ. of Aberdeen, 2009–. Patron, Soc. of Ops Engrs, 2013–. *Recreations:* amateur farming, breeding Highland cattle. *Address:* c/o Scottish Rugby Union, Murrayfield Stadium, Edinburgh EH12 5PJ. *Club:* Royal Northern University (Aberdeen).

LOCKLEY, Andrew John Harold; Judge of the Health, Education and Social Care Chamber, First-tier Tribunal (formerly Chairman, Special Educational Needs Tribunal, later Special Educational Needs and Disability Tribunal), since 1996; Judge of the Social Entitlement Chamber, First-tier Tribunal, since 2010; *b* 10 May 1951; *s* of late Ven. Harold Lockley and Ursula Margarethe Lockley, JP; *m* 1st, 1974, Ruth Mary Vigor (marr. diss.); two *s* one *d*; 2nd, 2005, Caryl Jane Berry (*née* Seymour). *Educ:* Marlborough Coll.; Oriel Coll., Oxford (BA Lit. Hum. 1973; MA 1982). Admitted a Solicitor, 1979. Res. Fellow, World Council of Churches, 1973–75; Solicitor in private practice, 1979–82; Law Society: Asst Sec., 1982–85, Sec., 1985–87, Contentious Business Dept; Dir, Legal Practice, 1987–95; Dir, Corporate and Regl Affairs, 1995–96; Hd of Public Law (formerly Professional Services and Public Law), Irwin Mitchell, Solicitors, 1996–2013. Legal Assessor, Medical Practitioners Tribunal Service (formerly Fitness to Practise Panels), GMC, 2007–; Legal Advr, Professional Conduct Cttees, Gen. Teaching Council, 2009–12, Teaching Agency, 2012–13. Chm., Ind. Policing Ethics Panel for S Yorks, 2014–. Mem., Editl Adv. Bd, Educn, Public Law and the Individual, 2005–12. Non-exec. Chm., Solicitors Property Centres Ltd, 1998–2000 (Dir, 1997–98); non-exec. Dir, Legal Aid Agency, 2013–. Member: Commn on Efficiency in the Criminal Courts, 1986–93; Working Party, Delivering Justice in an Age of Austerity, Justice, 2014–. Mem., IT and Courts Cttee, 1990–95. Gov., William Austin Sch., Luton, 1992–96. Hon. Fellow, Univ. of Sheffield, 1999. *Publications:* Christian Communes, 1976; (ed) The Pursuit of Quality: a guide for lawyers, 1993; contribs to legal periodicals. *Recreations:* growing fruit and vegetables, choral singing, swimming, walking, cooking. *E:* alockley1@yahoo.co.uk.

LOCKLEY, Stephen Randolph, FCILT; transport consultant; *b* 19 June 1943; *s* of Randolph and Edith Lockley; *m* 1968, Angela; two *d*. *Educ:* Manchester Univ. (BScCivEng, 1st Cl. Hons). MICE; MCIHT; FCILT (FCIT 1987, FILT). Lancashire County Council: North West Road Construction Unit, Highway Engrg and Planning, 1964–72; Highway/Transportation Planning, 1972–75; Lanarkshire CC, Strathclyde Regional Council: Prin. Engr (Transportation), 1975–77; Depute Dir of Policy Planning, 1977–80; Prin. Exec. Officer, 1980–86; Dir Gen., Strathclyde PTE, 1986–97. *Address:* 64 Townhead Street, Strathaven ML10 6DJ. *T:* (01357) 521774.

LOCKWOOD, Baroness *cr* 1978 (Life Peer), of Dewsbury, W Yorks; **Betty Lockwood;** DL; President, Birkbeck College, London, 1983–89; a Deputy Speaker, House of Lords, 1989–2007; *b* 22 Jan. 1924; *d* of Arthur Lockwood and Edith Alice Lockwood; *m* 1978, Lt-Col Cedric Hall (*d* 1988). *Educ:* Eastborough Girls' Sch., Dewsbury; Ruskin Coll., Oxford. Chief Woman Officer and Asst Nat. Agent of Labour Party, 1967–75; Ed., Labour Woman, 1967–71; Chm., Equal Opportunities Commn, 1975–83. Vice-Chm., Internat. Council of Social Democratic Women, 1969–75; Chm., Adv. Cttee to European Commn on Equal Opportunities for Women and Men, 1982–83. Chm., Mary Macarthur Educnl Trust, 1971–94; Pres., Mary Macarthur Holiday Trust, 1990–2002 (Chm., 1971–90). Member: Dept of Employment Adv. Cttee on Women's Employment, 1969–83; Adv. Council on Energy Conservation, 1977–80; Council, Advertising Standards Authority, 1983–93; Leeds Urban Develt Corp., 1988–95. Pres., Hillcroft Coll., 1987–95. Chancellor, Bradford Univ., 1997–2005 (Mem. Council, 1983–2005; a Pro-Chancellor, 1988–97); Leeds Univ., 1985–91; Vice Pres., UMIST, 1992–95. Pres., Nat. Coal Mining Mus., 2007– (Chm. Bd of Trustees, 1995–2007). DL W Yorks, 1987. Hon. Fellow: UMIST, 1986; Birkbeck Coll., 1987. Hon. DLitt Bradford, 1981; Hon. LLD Strathclyde, 1985; DUniv Leeds Metropolitan, 1999; Dr *hc* Edinburgh, 2004. *Recreations:* country pursuits, music. *Address:* 6 Sycamore Drive, Addingham, Ilkley LS29 0NY. *Club:* Soroptomist.

LOCKWOOD, David Charles, OBE 2011; FCA; Chief Executive, Laird plc, since 2012; *b* Ilford, 23 March 1962; *s* of Kenneth Lockwood and Irene Lockwood; *m* 1987, Sarah Willis; one *s* two *d*. *Educ:* Saffron Walden County High Sch.; Univ. of York (BA Maths). ACA 1988, FCA 2014. Various roles, GPT Ltd, 1989–95; Managing Director: Defence Control Systems, Marconi, 1995–97; Sensor Systems, BAE Systems, 1998–2000; CEO, Intense Ltd, 2001–06; Thales UK: Man. Dir, Thales Optronics Ltd, 2007–10; Vice Pres., Defence and Security C4I Systems and Air Ops, 2010–11; Vice Pres., Global Defence and Security, BT Global Services, BT plc, 2011–12. Non-exec. Chm., Knowledge Transfer Network Ltd, 2014–; non-exec. Dir, Samsung Thales Corp. (Korea), 2008–11. Chm., Technol. Adv. Gp, Scottish Govt, 2006–11. Vis. Prof., Univ. of Glasgow, 2005–11. FRSA. *Recreations:* sailing, running, bridge. *Address:* Laird plc, 100 Pall Mall, SW1Y 5NQ. *T:* (020) 7468 4040, *Fax:* (020) 7839 2921. *E:* d.lockwood@laird-plc.com. *Club:* Royal Air Force.

LOCKWOOD, Prof. Michael, PhD; FRS 2006; Professor of Space Environment Physics, and Director of Research, School of Mathematical and Physical Sciences, Reading University, since 2009; *b* 29 April 1954; *s* of Fred T. Lockwood, CBE and Stephanie Lockwood; *m* 1976, Celia; one *s* one *d*. *Educ:* Skinners' Sch., Tunbridge Wells; Univ. of Exeter (BSc 1st Cl. Hons Physics 1975; PhD Physics 1978). FRAS 1985; CPhys, FInstP 2003. Res. Fellow, Auckland Univ., 1978–79; Higher SO, RAE, Farnborough, 1979–80; Prof. of Physics and Astronomy, Southampton Univ., 2000–09. Scientist, Space Sci. and Technol. Dept, Rutherford Appleton Lab., 1980 (Chief Scientist, 2001). Res. Associate, NASA/Marshall Space Flight Center, Huntsville, 1984–85. Vis. Hon. Lectr, 1987–2004, Vis. Hon. Prof., 2004–, Imperial Coll., London; Guest Lectr, Univ. Centre in Svalbard, Longyearbyen, Svalbard, 1994–. Mem., NERC, 2007–. Vice Pres. (Geophysics), RAS, 1995–97; President: Div. III, Internat. Assoc. of Geomagnetism and Aeronomy, 1999–2003; Solar-Terrestrial Physics Sect., Eur. Geophysical Soc., 2000–03; Chm. Council, Internat. EISCAT Scientific Assoc., 2001–03; Mem., Astronomy Cttee, 1997–2000, Sci. Cttee, 2002–05, PPARC. Mem., American Geophysical Union, 1981. Issac Koga Gold Medal, URSI, 1990; Zel'dovich Award for Commn C (Ionospheric Phys), COSPAR, 1990; Chapman Medal, RAS, 1998; Charles Chree Medal and Prize, Inst. of Physics, 2003. *Publications:* (jtly) The Sun, Solar Analogs and the Climate, 2004; over 260 articles in jls on solar influences on the Earth. *Recreations:* playing music, watching cricket, Rugby and soccer. *Address:* Department of Meteorology, University of Reading, Earley Gate, PO Box 243, Reading RG6 6BB.

LOCKWOOD, Robert; General Director, Overseas Planning and Project Development, General Motors Corporation, 1982–85, retired; *b* 14 April 1920; *s* of Joseph A. Lockwood and Sylvia Lockwood; *m* 1947, Phyllis M. Laing; one *s* one *d*. *Educ:* Columbia Univ. (AB); Columbia Law Sch. (LLB). Attorney, Bar of New York, 1941; US Dist of New York and US Supreme Court, 1952. Pilot, USAAF (8th Air Force), 1944–45. Attorney: Ehrich, Royall, Wheeler & Holland, New York, 1941 and 1946–47; Sullivan & Cromwell, New York, 1947–54; Sec. and Counsel, Cluett, Peabody & Co., Inc., New York, 1955–57; Man. Dir, Cluett, Peabody & Co., Ltd, London, 1957–59; General Motors: Overseas Ops, Planning and Develt, 1960–61; Asst to Man. Dir, GM Argentina, Buenos Aires, 1962; Asst to Man. Dir, and Manager, Parts, Power and Appliances, GM Continental, Antwerp, 1964–66; Branch Man., Netherlands Br., GM Continental, Rotterdam, 1967–68; Man., Planning and Develt, GM Overseas Ops, New York, 1969–73; Vice Pres., GM Overseas Corp., and Gen. Man., Japan Br., 1974–76; Exec. Vice Pres., Isuzu Motors Ltd, Tokyo, 1976; Chm., GM European Adv. Council, 1977–82. Mem., Panel of Arbitrators, Amer. Arbitration Assoc., 1989–. *Recreations:* tennis, bridge, reading. *Club:* Marines' Memorial (San Francisco).

LOCKWOOD, Rear Adm. Roger Graham, CB 2005; Chief Executive, Northern Lighthouse Board, 2006–14; *b* 26 June 1950; *s* of Eric Garnett Lockwood and Nunda Lockwood (*née* Doak); *m* 1984, Susan Jane Cant; three *s* two *d*. *Educ:* Kimbolton Sch., Cambs; Univ. of Warwick (BA Maths). BRNC Dartmouth, 1971; Sub Lieut, HMS Fearless, 1972; Lieut, HMS Soberton, 1973; Supply Officer (Cash), HMS Tiger, 1974–76; Captain's Sec., 2nd Submarine Sqn, 1976–78; Supply Officer, HMS Naiad, 1979–81; Lt Comdr, 1980; Flag Lieut to CDS, 1981–82; Captain's Sec., RNAS Culdrose, 1982–84; jsdc 1985; Comdr, 1985; Base Supply Officer, HMS Dolphin, 1985–87; Comdr, RN Supply Sch., 1987–89; Supply Officer, HMS Ark Royal, 1989–91; Captain, 1991; Dep. Dir, Naval Service Conditions (Pay), 1991–93; rcds 1994; Secretary to: Second Sea Lord, 1995–96; First Sea Lord, 1996–98; Cdre, 1998; Cdre, HMS Raleigh, 1998–2000; Rear Adm., 2000; COS to Second Sea Lord, and C-in-C Naval Home Comd, 2000–02; Sen. Naval Directing Staff, RCDS, and Chief Naval Supply, subseq. Chief Naval Logistics, Officer, 2002–05. Chairman: Forth Pilots Disciplinary Cttee, 2006–; Perth Sea Cadet Unit, 2006–10. Mem. Council, RNLI, 2015. Mem., Hon. Co. of Master Mariners, 2007–15. Co. Sec., Dunblane Develt Trust, 2005–07; Dir, Scottish Shipping Benevolent Assoc., 2009–12 (Pres., 2011–12). Area Vice Patron (Scotland), War Memorials Trust, 2007–; Trustee: Merchant Navy Memorial Trust (Scotland), 2009–; Bell's Nautical Trust, 2015. Gov., Kimbolton Sch., 2001–05; Comr, Queen Victoria Sch., Dunblane, 2006–. High Constable of Port of Leith, 2008–. *Recreations:* family, studying the history of the SOE in France, reading the complete works of Charles Dickens, European history. *Address:* Springbank, 2 Bellenden Grove, Dunblane, Perthshire FK15 0FD. *Club:* New (Edinburgh).

LOCKYER, Rear-Adm. (Alfred) Austin, LVO 1973; Chief Staff Officer (Engineering) to Commander-in-Chief Fleet, 1982–84, retired; Director General, Timber Trade Federation, 1985–92; *b* 4 March 1929; *s* of late Austin Edmund Lockyer and Jane Russell (*née* Goldman); *m* 1965, Jennifer Ann Simmons; one *s*. *Educ:* Frome County School; Taunton School; Royal Naval Engineering College. Entered RN 1947; Comdr 1965; Staff of Commander Far East Fleet, 1965–67; jssc, 1968–69; Ship Dept, 1969–71; HMY Britannia, 1971–73; Captain 1973; sowc, 1973–74; Naval Ship Production Overseer, Scotland and NI, 1974–76; Dep. Dir, Fleet Maintenance, 1976–78; Dir, Naval Officers Appointments (Engrg), 1978–80; HMS Sultan in Comd, 1980–82; ADC to the Queen, 1981; Rear-Adm. 1982. Governor: Forres Sch., Swanage, 1980–92 (Chm., 1983–92); Sherborne Sch., 1981–97. *Recreations:* gardening, golf, listening to good music. *Address:* The Old Malt House, 3 Widcombe Hill, Bath BA2 6AD. *Club:* Army and Navy.

LOCKYER, Lynda Dorothy; on secondment to Civil Contingencies Secretariat, Cabinet Office, 2002; *b* 17 Aug. 1946; *d* of Donald Lockyer and Gwendoline Lockyer (*née* Fulcher); *m* 1984, John Anthony Thompson; one *s*. *Educ:* Bromley High Sch.; Newnham Coll., Cambridge (MA Classics); Warburg Inst., Univ. of London (MA 2005; PhD 2013); University Coll. London (MA 2008). Press Officer: Shell-Mex, BP Ltd, 1968–73; Sperry Univac, 1974; DHSS, later DoH, 1974–96; Home Office, 1996–2002; Head of Police Resources Unit, 1996–99; Dir, Corporate Resources, 1999–2000; Dir, Corporate Develt and Services, 2000–02. *Recreations:* films, theatre, opera, Europe.

LOCKYER, Roger Walter, FRHistS, FSA; Reader in History, Royal Holloway College, University of London, 1983–84, now Emeritus; *b* 26 Nov. 1927; *s* of Walter Lockyer and May Florence (*née* Cook); partner, Percy Steven. *Educ:* King's College Sch., Wimbledon; Pembroke Coll., Cambridge (Foundn Schol.; 1st cl. Hons BA 1950; Hadley Prize for Hist. 1951; MA 1955). FRHistS 1977; FSA 1981. Instructor-Lieut, RN, 1946–48; Asst d'Anglais, Lycée Louis-le-Grand, Paris, 1951–52; Hd of Hist., Haileybury and Imperial Service Coll., 1952–53; Editor, Blue Guides, Ernest Benn Ltd, 1953–54; Hd of Hist., Lancing Coll., 1954–61; Lectr, then Sen. Lectr, Royal Holloway Coll., Univ. of London, 1961–83. Vis. Prof., Univ. of Maryland, 1991. *Publications:* (jtly) A History of England, 1961; Tudor and Stuart Britain 1471–1714, 1964, 3rd edn 2005; Henry VII, 1968, 2nd edn 1997; Habsburg and Bourbon Europe 1470–1720, 1974; Buckingham: the life and political career of George Villiers, first Duke of Buckingham 1592–1628, 1981; (contrib.) For Veronica Wedgwood These: studies in Seventeenth-century history, 1986; The Early Stuarts: a political history of England 1603–1642, 1989, 2nd edn 1999; (ed jtly) Shakespeare's World: background readings in the English Renaissance, 1989; James VI & I, 1998. *Recreations:* reading, theatre, architecture, living in France. *Address:* 63 Balcombe Street, NW1 6HD. *T:* (020) 7706 1258. *E:* airlock63@btinternet.com.

LODDER, Peter Norman; QC 2001; **His Honour Judge Lodder;** a Senior Circuit Judge and Resident Judge, Kingston-upon-Thames Crown Court, since 2015; *b* 3 Feb. 1958; *s* of Lt Comdr Norman George Lodder, RN and Ann Lodder; *m* 1992, Elizabeth Gummer (marr. diss. 2007); two *c*. *Educ:* King's Sch., Gloucester; Portsmouth Grammar Sch.; Univ. of Birmingham (LLB). Called to the Bar, Middle Temple, 1981 (Jules Thorn Major Schol. 1982), Bencher, 2010; specialist in fraud and criminal law; Asst Recorder, 1998–2000; Recorder, 2000–15. Mem., Gen. Council of the Bar, 1994– (Vice Chm., 2010; Chm., 2011); Chm., Criminal Bar Assoc., 2008–09. *Address:* Kingston-upon-Thames Crown Court, 6–8 Penrhyn Road, Kingston-upon-Thames, Surrey KT1 2BB.

LODER, family name of **Baron Wakehurst**.

LODER, Sir Edmund Jeune, 4th Bt *cr* 1887, of Whittlebury, Northamptonshire, and of High Beeches, Slaugham, Sussex; *b* 26 June 1941; *er s* of Sir Giles Rolls Loder, 3rd Bt and Marie Violet Pamela Loder (*née* Symons-Jeune); *S* father, 1999; *m* 1st, 1966, Penelope Jane Forde (marr. diss. 1971); one *d*; 2nd, 1992, Susan Warren Pearl. *Address:* Eyrefield Lodge, The Curragh, Co. Kildare, Ireland.

LODGE, Anton James Corduff; QC 1989; a Recorder, since 1985; *b* 17 April 1944; *s* of Sir Thomas Lodge and Aileen (*née* Corduff). *Educ:* Ampleforth College; Gonville and Caius College, Cambridge (MA). Called to the Bar, Gray's Inn, 1966, Bencher, 1998. *Recreations:* cricket, tennis, ski-ing, music, theatre. *Address:* New Park Court Chambers, 16 Park Place, Leeds LS1 2SJ. *T:* (0113) 243 3277. *Club:* Yorkshire (York).

LODGE, Prof. David John, CBE 1998; MA, PhD; FRSL; writer; Emeritus Professor of English Literature, University of Birmingham, since 2001 (Professor of Modern English Literature, 1976–87, Hon. Professor, 1987–2000); *b* 28 Jan. 1935; *s* of William Frederick Lodge and Rosalie Marie Lodge (*née* Murphy); *m* 1959, Mary Frances Jacob; two *s* one *d*. *Educ:* St Joseph's Acad., Blackheath; University College, London (Hon. Fellow, 1982). BA hons, MA (London); PhD (Birm). FRSL 1976. National Service, RAC, 1955–57. British Council, London, 1959–60. Univ. of Birmingham: Asst Lectr in English, 1960–62; Lectr, 1963–71; Sen. Lectr, 1971–73; Reader in English, 1973–76. Harkness Commonwealth Fellow, 1964–65; Visiting Associate Prof., Univ. of California, Berkeley, 1969; Henfield Writing Fellow, Univ. of E Anglia, 1977. Hon. Fellow, Goldsmiths' Coll., London, 1992. Hon. DLitt: Warwick, 1997; Birmingham, 2001. Yorkshire Post Fiction Prize, 1975; Hawthornden Prize, 1976; Whitbread Book of the Year Award, 1980; Sunday Express Book of the Year Award, 1988. Chevalier, l'Ordre des Arts et des Lettres (France), 1997. Stage plays: The Writing Game, Birmingham Rep., 1990 (adapted for television, 1996); Home Truths, Birmingham Rep., 1998; Secret Thoughts, Bolton Octagon Th., 2011 (Best New Play, Manchester Th. Awards, 2011). Adaptation of Dickens, Martin Chuzzlewit, for television, 1994. *Publications: novels:* The Picturegoers, 1960; Ginger, You're Barmy, 1962; The British Museum is Falling Down, 1965; Out of the Shelter, 1970, rev. edn 1985; Changing Places, 1975; How Far Can You Go?, 1980; Small World, 1984 (televised 1988); Nice Work, 1988 (adapted for television, 1989); Paradise News, 1991; Therapy, 1995; Home Truths: a novella, 1999; Thinks..., 2001; Author, Author, 2004; Deaf Sentence, 2008; A Man of Parts, 2011; *plays:* The Writing Game, 1991; Home Truths, 1998; Secret Thoughts, 2011; *criticism:* Language of Fiction, 1966; The Novelist at the Crossroads, 1971; The Modes of Modern Writing, 1977; Working with Structuralism, 1981; Write On, 1986; After Bakhtin (essays), 1990; The Art of Fiction, 1992; The Practice of Writing, 1996; Consciousness and the Novel (essays), 2002; The Year of Henry James (essays), 2006; Lives in Writing (essays), 2014; *edited:* Jane Austen's Emma: a casebook, 1968; Twentieth Century Literary Criticism, 1972; Modern Criticism and Theory, 1988, 3rd edn 2008; *non-fiction:* Quite a Good Time to be Born: a memoir 1935–1975, 2015. *Recreations:* television, cinema, theatre. *Address:* c/o Curtis Brown, 28–29 Haymarket, SW1Y 4SP.

LODGE, Dr Denise Valerie; Headmistress, Putney High School, GDST, since 2002; *m*; one *s* one *d*. *Educ:* Bury Grammar Sch. (Girls); Royal Holloway Coll., London Univ. (BSc Botany and Zool.; PhD Zool. 1979); Chelsea Coll., London Univ. (MSc Applied Hydrobiol.); Reading Univ. (PGCE). Teacher, later Hd of Chem., Hd of Sixth Form, and Sen. Teacher, Curriculum, Sir Roger Manwood's Sch., Sandwich, 1987–96; Dep. Hd, Sheffield High Sch., GDST, 1996–99; Headmistress, Sydenham High Sch., GDST, 1999–2002. Treas., GSA, 2004–07. Mem. Ct, Imperial Coll. London, 2007–. *Recreations:* jazz, cooking, the gym, theatre, art. *Address:* Putney High School, 35 Putney Hill, SW15 6BH. *Club:* Lansdowne.

LODGE, Prof. Geoffrey Arthur, BSc, PhD; FRSB; FRSE 1986; Professor of Animal Science, Sultan Qaboos University, Muscat, 1986–90, retired; *b* 18 Feb. 1930; *m* 1956, Thelma (*née* Calder); one *s* two *d*. *Educ:* Durham University (BSc). PhD Aberdeen. Formerly Reader in Animal Production, Univ. of Nottingham School of Agriculture, and Principal Research Scientist, Animal Research Inst., Ottawa; Strathcona-Fordyce Prof. of Agriculture, Univ. of Aberdeen, and Principal, North of Scotland Coll. of Agriculture, 1978–86. *Publications:* (ed jointly) Growth and Development of Mammals, 1968; contribs to journals and books. *Recreations:* food, malt whisky, travelling. *Address:* 18 Queen Victoria Park, Inchmarlo, Banchory, Kincardineshire AB31 4AL.

LODGE, John Robert; His Honour Judge Lodge; a Circuit Judge, since 2008; Resident Judge, Basildon Combined Court Centre, since 2011; *b* Alvanley, Cheshire, 6 Oct. 1958; *s* of Anthony William Rayner Lodge and Monica Lodge (*née* Beddow); *m* 1986, Sally Nicole Cummings, (Rev. Sally Lodge); two *s* one *d*. *Educ:* Ripon Grammar Sch.; Wadham Coll., Oxford (BA Juris. 1979). Called to the Bar, Middle Temple, 1980; in practice as barrister, Leeds, 1982–2008. *Recreations:* running, ski-ing, watching Rugby Union, modern military history. *Address:* c/o Basildon Combined Court Centre, The Gore, Basildon, Essex SS14 2EW. *T:* (01268) 458000, *Fax:* (01268) 458100. *E:* hhjudge.lodge@judiciary.gsi.gov.uk.

LODGE, Prof. Juliet, DLitt; PhD; Professor of European Integration and Politics and Director, Jean Monnet Centre of Excellence, University of Leeds, since 1996; *b* London; *d* of Arthur and Lenore; two *s* one *d*. *Educ:* Univ. of Reading (MA; DLitt); Univ. of Hull (PhD). Fellow in Internat. Relns, LSE, 1977; Lectr in Euro Politics, Univ. of Auckland, 1978; Prof. of EU Politics, Univ. of Hull, 1978–95; Prof. of Internat. Politics, Vrije Universiteit Brussel, 1994; Prof. of EU Politics, Institut für Höhere Studien, Vienna, 1995. Vis. Prof. of EU Politics, Université Libre de Bruxelles, 1993; Vis. Lectr and Hon. Cormorant, JSDC. Expert Mem., Privacy Cttee, Biometrics Inst., 2011–; Mem., Patients Reference Gp, Coll. of Optometrists, 2011–. Sen. Analyst, Aimtech, Leeds, 2010–. Freelance broadcaster and journalist on EU policies and instns; res. evaluator for EU. Convenor, UK Ethics Cttee on judicial co-operation in EU, 2004. Carer Ambassador, Carers UK, 2010–. Woman of Europe Award, 1992. *Publications:* The European Policy of the SPD, 1977; (jtly) European Parliament and the European Community, 1978; (ed) Terrorism: a challenge to the state, 1981; (jtly) Direct Elections to the European Parliament: community perspective, 1982; The European Community and New Zealand, 1982; Direct Elections to the European Parliament 1984, 1986; (ed) European Union: the European Community in search of a future, 1986; Threat of Terrorism, 1987; The 1989 Election of the European Parliament, 1990; (ed) The European Community and the Challenge of the Future, 1993; (ed) The 1994 Elections to the European Parliament, 1995; (ed) The 1999 Elections to the European Parliament, 2001; The European Union, 2003; The 2004 Elections to the European Parliament, 2005; (ed) Are You Who You Say You Are: the EU and biometric borders, 2007; The 2009 Elections to the European Parliament, 2010; Communication, Mediation and Culture in the Making of Europe, 2013; chapters on EU, borders, biometrics, transparency and democratic accountability, constitutional reform, e-citizenship, proportionality in data, ethics and e-governance in smart environments; reports on biometrics, interoperability, ICT ethics and liberty for the EP and nat. parlts, research on e-security, e-identity, interoperability, robotics and ICTs, biometrics and border controls, cybercrime and disappearing interfaces, e-gov and e-society. *Recreations:* art, laughing, ceramics. *T:* (0113) 343 4443. *E:* j.e.lodge@leeds.ac.uk. *Club:* Women of Europe.

LODGE, Matthew James; HM Diplomatic Service; Ambassador to Kuwait, since 2014; *b* Crosby, Lancs, 3 June 1968; *s* of David James Lodge and Helen Mary Lodge; *m* 2001, Alexia Ipirotis; two *s*. *Educ:* Abingdon Sch.; Birmingham Univ. (BA Hons French and Russian). Officer, RM, 1986–96; joined FCO, 1996; Desk Officer, Bosnia Sect., E Adriatic Dept, FCO, 1996–97; Entry Clearance Officer, Tbilisi and Yerevan, 1997; Second Sec. (Pol/EU/Press and Public Affairs), Athens, 1998–2000; Desk Officer, Czech Republic and Slovakia, Central NW Europe Dept, FCO, 2000; Second Secretary: (Press and Public Affairs), Paris, 2001; (Pol/Mil.), UKREP, Brussels, 2001–03; Hd, Cyprus and Greece Sect., Europe Directorate, 2003–04, Private Sec., Perm. Under Sec.'s Office, 2004–07, FCO; Dep. Hd of Mission, Baghdad, 2007; HCSC, UK Defence Acad., 2008; Hd, Afghanistan Gp, S Asia and Afghanistan Directorate, FCO, 2008–10; Ambassador to Finland, 2010–13; FCO, 2014. *Recreations:* family, swimming, music, outdoors. *Address:* c/o Foreign and Commonwealth Office, King Charles Street, SW1A 2AH. *E:* matthew.lodge@fco.gov.uk.

LODGE, Nicholas John; Director General, Benefits and Credits, and a Commissioner, HM Revenue and Customs, since 2012; *b* Ipswich, 7 Oct. 1961; *s* of John and Pauline Lodge; *m* 1988, Angela Garnham; one *s* one *d*. *Educ:* Northgate Grammar Sch., Ipswich. With Inland Revenue, 1990–93, then HM Treasury and Cabinet Office, 1993–95; Inland Revenue, later HM Revenue and Customs: Ops Manager, 1995–98; Prog. Dir for tax credits and child benefit, 1998–2005; Dir, Customer Contact, 2005–07; work on data security, 2007–08; Dir for Debt Mgt and Banking, 2008–11; Personal Tax Change Dir and Dir, Customer Contact, 2011–12; Change Dir for Personal Tax, 2012. *Address:* HM Revenue and Customs, 100 Parliament Street, SW1A 2BQ.

LOEHNIS, Anthony David, CMG 1988; Chairman, Alpha Bank London, 2005–15 (Director, since 1994); *b* 12 March 1936; *s* of Sir Clive Loehnis, KCMG; *m* 1965, Jennifer Forsyth Anderson; three *s*. *Educ:* Eton; New Coll., Oxford (MA); Harvard Sch. of Public Administration. HM Diplomatic Service, 1960–66; J. Henry Schroder Wagg & Co. Ltd, 1967–80 (on secondment to Bank of England, 1977–79); Bank of England: Associate Dir (Overseas), 1980–81; Exec. Dir, 1981–89; Dir, S. G. Warburg Group plc, 1989–92; a Vice-Chm., S. G. Warburg & Co., 1989–92. Director: St James's Place Capital plc, 1993–2005; Mitsubishi UFJ Securities Internat., 1996–2007 (formerly Tokyo-Mitsubishi Internat., then Mitsubishi Securities Internat.); AGCO Corp. (US), 1997–2005; VTB Capital (formerly VTB Bank Europe) plc, 2007–13. A Public Works Loan Comr, 1994–2005 (Chm., 1997–2005). Exec. Dir, UK-Japan 21st Century (formerly UK-Japan 2000) Gp, 1999–2002 (Dir, 1990–2005). Member: Council: Ditchley Foundn, 1992–2012 (Chm., F & G P Cttee, 1993–2009); Baring Foundn, 1994–2005; Japan Soc., 1998–2005. Chm., Villiers Park Educnl Trust, 2000–09. Gov., British Assoc. for Central and Eastern Europe, 1994–2003. *Address:* 55 Bainton Road, Oxford OX2 7AG. *Clubs:* Garrick, Beefsteak.

LOEWE, Very Rev. Andreas, FRHistS; Dean of Melbourne, since 2012; *b* Munich; *m* Dr Katherine Firth. *Educ:* St Peter's Coll., Oxford (BA Hons 1st cl. Theol. 1995; MPhil Ecclesiastical Hist. 1997; MA 1999); Selwyn Coll., Cambridge (PhD 2001). FRHistS 2011. Ordained deacon, 2001, priest, 2002; Asst Curate, Upton-cum-Chalvey Team, Dio. of Oxford, 2001–04; Sen. Mem., Faculty of Divinity, Cambridge Univ., 2004–09; Assoc. Vicar, Gt St Mary's, Cambridge, 2004–09; Chaplain of Michaelhouse, Dio. of Ely, 2004–09; University of Melbourne: Coll. Chaplain, Trinity Coll., 2009–12; Anglican Chaplain, 2010–12; Gavan Sen. Lectr in Theology, Trinity Coll. Theol Sch., MCD Univ. of Divinity, 2010–12. Rex J. Lipman Fellow, St Peter's Coll., Adelaide, 2012–; Fellow and Lectr in Music, Melbourne Conservatorium of Music, 2012–. Member: Council, Dio. of Melbourne, 2012–; Chapter, St Paul's Cathedral, Melbourne, 2012–; Trustee, Melbourne Anglican Trust Corp., 2012–. Member, Synod: Dio. of Ely, 2006–09; Dio. of Melbourne, 2009–. Theol Sec., Ecumenical Forum for Young Theologians, 2001–09; Comr, Nat. Council of Churches in Australia Faith and Unity Commn, 2010–12. Member, Council: Trinity Coll., Melbourne, 2009–12; MCD Univ. of Divinity, Melbourne, 2010–; Melbourne Girls' Grammar Sch., 2012–. Chair, Art Beyond Belief, 2004–09; Mem. Bd, Michaelhouse Centre, Cambridge, 2004–09. OStJ. *Publications:* (contrib.) Die Zürcher Reformation, 2000; (contrib.) Peter Martyr Vermigli: humanism, republicanism, reformation, 2002; Richard Smyth and the Language of Orthodoxy: re-imagining Tudor Catholic polemicism, 2003; Johann Sebastian Bach's St John Passion: a theological commentary, 2013. *Recreations:* classical music, jazz, opera, gardening. *Address:* St Paul's Cathedral, 209 Flinders Lane, Melbourne, Vic 3000, Australia. *E:* dean@stpaulscathedral.org.au.

LOFTHOUSE, Simon Timothy; QC 2006; a Recorder, since 2003; *b* 25 Aug. 1966; *s* of Adam Robert Lofthouse and Angela Anne Lofthouse (*née* Manning); *m* 1994, Sophia Ann Gawlik. *Educ:* Fernwood Comp. Sch., Nottingham; Becket Upper Sch., Nottingham; University Coll. London (LLB Hons 1987). Called to the Bar, Gray's Inn, 1988, Bencher, 2009; in practice specialising in international arbitration, construction, energy and professional negligence. Mem., Professional Conduct Cttee, Bar Council, 2001–04. Bar Standards Board: Prosecutor, 2005–07; Vice-Chm., 2008–11, Chm., 2011–, Complaints Cttee; Mem. Bd, 2011–. *Recreations:* opera, sculpture, travel. *Address:* Atkin Chambers, 1 Atkin Building, Gray's Inn, WC1R 5AT. *T:* (020) 7404 0102, *Fax:* (020) 7405 7456. *E:* slofthouse@atkinchambers.com. *Club:* Reform.

LOFTUS, Simon Pierse Dominic, OBE 2007; Chairman, 1996–2006, non-executive Director, 2006–14, Adnams plc; *b* 5 Aug. 1946; *s* of late Nicholas Alastair Ayton Loftus and Prudence Loftus (*née* Wootten); *m* 1980, Irène Yamato; one *d*. *Educ:* Ampleforth; Trinity Coll., Cambridge (MA). Joined Adnams, 1968, Dir, 1973. Dir, Aldeburgh Music (formerly Aldeburgh Productions), 1998–2010; non-executive Director: 1st East, 2005–10; Norwich & Peterborough Bldg Soc., 2007–11; St George's Theatre Trust Ltd, 2010–13. Pres., Southwold Mus. and Archaeol Soc., 2011–. Chm., Suffolk Foundn, 2003–06; Trustee, Adnams Charity, 1990– (Chm., 1992–2006). Hon. DCL Suffolk Coll., UEA, 2010. *Publications:* Anatomy of the Wine Trade, 1985; A Pike in the Basement, 1987; Puligny Montrachet, 1992; (ed) Guides to the Wines of France series, 1988–90; An Illustrated History of Southwold, 2012; The Invention of Memory, 2013; numerous articles in jls. *Recreations:* cooking, Anglo-Irish history, writing, being a grandfather. *Address:* Bulcamp House, Halesworth, Suffolk IP19 9LG. *T:* (01502) 478409. *Club:* Groucho.

LOGAN, Andrew David; sculptor, since 1968; *b* 11 Oct. 1945; *s* of William Harold Logan and Irene May Logan. *Educ:* Oxford Sch. of Architecture (DipArch Oxon 1970). Founded Alternative Miss World (performance event), London, 1972; opened Andrew Logan Mus. of Sculpture, Berriew, Wales, 1991. Work in public collections: Australian Gall. of Nat. Art; NPG; Arts Council of GB; Warner Bros, UK; Costume Inst., Metropolitan Mus., NY; Curzon Tussaud, London; Cleveland Jewellery Collection, Middlesbrough; Nat. Museums and Galls on Merseyside. Member: Contemporary Glass Soc.; RSA. *Recreations:* yoga, travel, theatre. *E:* andrewdl@andrewlogan.com.

LOGAN, Sir David (Brian Carleton), KCMG 2000 (CMG 1991); HM Diplomatic Service, retired; Director, Centre for Studies in Security and Diplomacy, and Hon. Professor, School of Social Sciences, University of Birmingham, 2002–06; *b* 11 Aug. 1943; *s* of late Captain Brian Ewen Weldon Logan, RN (Retd) and Mary Logan (*née* Fass); *m* 1967, Judith Margaret Walton Cole; one *s* one *d* (and one *s* decd). *Educ:* Charterhouse; University College, Oxford (MA). Foreign Office, 1965; served Istanbul, Ankara and FCO, 1965–70; Private Sec. to Parly Under Sec. of State for Foreign and Commonwealth Affairs, 1970–73; First Sec., 1972; UK Mission to UN, 1973–77; FCO, 1977–82; Counsellor, Hd of Chancery and Consul-Gen., Oslo, 1982–86; Hd of Personnel Ops Dept, FCO, 1986–88; Sen. Associate Mem., St Antony's Coll., Oxford, 1988–89; Minister and Dep. Head of Mission, Moscow, 1989–92; Asst Under Sec. of State (Central and Eastern Europe), 1992–94, (Defence Policy), 1994–95, FCO; Minister, Washington, 1995–97; Ambassador to Turkey, 1997–2001. Chairman: GAP Activity Projects, 2002–07; British Inst. of Archaeology, Ankara, 2006–; Member: Internat. Advisory Bd, Thames Water, 2002–07; Supervisory Bd, Efes Pilsen Internat., 2004–10; Director: European Nickel plc, 2004–10; Magnitogorsk Iron and Steel Co., 2007–14. Sen. Fellow, Inst. for Strategic Dialogue, 2013–. Trustee, St Andrew's Ecumenical Trust, 2006–13. DUniv Birmingham, 2014. *Recreations:* music, reading, sailing. *Club:* Royal Ocean Racing.

LOGAN, Prof. David Edwin, PhD; Coulson Professor of Theoretical Chemistry, University of Oxford, and Fellow, University College, Oxford, since 2005; *b* 27 Aug. 1956; *s* of late James Henry Logan and Mona Elizabeth Logan; *m* 1981, Philippa Mary Walmsley; two *s* two *d*. *Educ:* Gilnahirk Primary Sch., E Belfast; Sullivan Upper Sch., Holywood; Trinity Coll., Cambridge (BA 1978; PhD Theoretical Chem. 1982). Jun. Res. Fellow, Christ's Coll., Cambridge, 1982–86; Postdoctoral Res. Associate, Univ. of Illinois, Urbana-Champaign, 1982–83; University of Oxford: Univ. Lectr in Phys. Chem., 1986–96; Prof. of Chem., 1996–2005; Official Fellow, Waters Fellow and Tutor in Phys. and Theoretical Chem., Balliol Coll., 1986–2005, Emeritus Fellow, 2005. Staff Mem., Theory Div., Institut Laue-Langevin, Grenoble, 1996. Foreign Fellow, NAS, India, 2012. Royal Society of Chemistry: Marlow Medal and Prize, Faraday Div., 1990; Corday-Morgan Medal and Prize, 1994; Tilden Lecture and Medal, 2007. *Publications:* numerous res. articles on theoretical condensed matter chem. and phys. *Recreations:* music, poetry, weeding, liberal baiting. *Address:* Physical and Theoretical Chemistry Laboratory, South Parks Road, Oxford OX1 3QZ. *T:* (01865) 275418. *E:* david.logan@chem.ox.ac.uk.

LOGAN, Fergus; *see* Logan, J. F. G.

LOGAN, Gabrielle Nicole; broadcaster, presenter and journalist; *b* Leeds, 24 Jan. 1973; *d* of Terry and Christine Yorath; *m* 2001, Kenny Logan; one *s* one *d* (twins). *Educ:* Notre Dame Sixth Form Coll., Leeds; Durham Univ. (BA Law 1995). Gymnast; represented Wales in rhythmic gymnastics, Commonwealth Games, Auckland, 1990. Radio broadcaster, Metro FM, 1992–96; football presenter, Sky Sports, 1996–98; with ITV, 1998–2007: presenter, On the Ball, World Cup, Champions League and Premiership football, Boat Race; with BBC, 2007–: Radio 5 Live: Sunday morning show, 2008–09; Gabby Logan Show, 2010–11; BBC One: presenter, Final Score, Inside Sport, Six Nations, Autumn Rugby Internats, Match of the Day, Olympic Games, Beijing, 2008 and London, 2012, FIFA 2010 World Cup, Eur. Football Championships, 2012; FIFA 2011 Women's World Cup, BBC Three; Live with Gabby Logan, Channel 5, 2011–12; Sports Personality of the Year, 2014; columnist, The Times, 2002–. Chancellor, Leeds Trinity Univ., 2013–. Patron: Disabilities Trust, 2002–; Prince's Trust, 2002–; Gt Ormond St Hosp., 2002–; Vice Pres., Sparks, 2002–. Hon. DSc Leeds Metropolitan, 2009. *Address:* c/o James Grant Management, 94 Strand on the Green, Chiswick, W4 3NN.

LOGAN, (James) Fergus (Graeme); Chief Executive, PSP Association, since 2011; *b* 20 June 1950; *s* of late James John Forbes Moffat, (Hamish), Logan and Lorna Jane Logan; *m* 1977, Wendy Elizabeth Plaskett, *d* of Maj.-Gen. F. J. Plaskett, *qv*; three *s* one *d*. *Educ:* Monmouth Sch. Gen. Sec., Nat. Youth Theatre, 1969–80; Head of Appeals, MENCAP, 1981–86; Head of Ops, UNICEF UK, 1986–88; Develt Dir, Bath Internat. Fest. of the Arts, 1988–90; Dir, Meml Fund for Disaster Relief, 1990; Exec. Dir, Muscular Dystrophy Gp, 1990–97; Chief Exec., Arthritis Res. Campaign, 1998–2009. Founder and Chm., "Batteries not included" (250 charity consortium), 1992–96; Chairman: Exec. Cttee, European Neuromuscular Centre, Baarn, Netherlands, 1992–98; AMRC, 1995–99 (Mem. Exec. Council, 1992–95); Res. for Health Charities Gp, 1996–98. Trustee, Neuromuscular Centre, Winsford, Ches., 1991–97. *Recreations:* family, sport, books, beer. *Address:* 1 Queen's Lane, Eynsham, Oxon OX29 4HL. *T:* (01865) 883732.

LOGAN, Joseph Andrew; Chairman, Hay & Kilner, Solicitors, Newcastle, Wallsend and Gosforth, 1998–2001; *b* 5 Nov. 1942; *s* of late Joseph Baird Logan and Hellen Dawson Logan (*née* Wink); *m* 1964, Heather Robertson; one *s* one *d*. *Educ:* Hilton Acad., Aberdeen. Sales Manager: Aberdeen Journals, 1958–69; Newcastle Evening Chronicle, 1969–77; Newcastle Chronicle and Journal: Exec. Asst, 1976–77; Asst Man. Dir, 1979–82; Dir, 1984–89; Man. Dir, 1985–89; Asst Man. Dir, Evening Post, Luton and Evening Echo, Watford, 1977–79; Man. Dir, Peter Reed and Co., 1982; Dep. Man. Dir, Aberdeen Journals, 1982–83 (Dir, 1984); Man. Dir, Scotsman Publications, 1989–94; Pres. and Chief Exec., Thomson Newspaper Corp., Western USA, 1994–97. Director: Weekly Courier Ltd, 1971–89; Thomson Regional Newspapers, 1984–94; Thomson Scottish Organisation Ltd, 1989–94; Northern Rock Building Soc. Scotland, 1989–94 (Dep. Chm., Northern Rock Foundn, 1989–2000). Pres., Scottish Daily Newspaper Soc., 1990–92 (Vice Pres., 1989–90); Trustee, NE Civic Trust, 1984–89; Member: British Airways Consumer Council, 1986–89; Bd, BITC, 1985–89; ScotBIC, 1989–94; Dir, Prince's Scottish Youth Business Trust, 1989–94. Mem. Council, Univ. of Newcastle upon Tyne, 1985–89. *Address:* 5 Burnside, Ponteland, Newcastle upon Tyne NE20 9AQ. *T:* (01661) 822280. *E:* jalogan@onetel.com.

LOGAN, Prof. Malcolm Ian, AC 1996; PhD; Chairman, Education Gateway Holdings Ltd, since 1998; *b* 3 June 1931; *m* 1954, Antoinette, *d* of F. Lalich; one *d*. *Educ:* Univ. of Sydney (BA Hons 1951, DipEd 1952, PhD 1965). Lectr in Geography, Sydney Teachers Coll., 1956–58; Lectr in Geog., 1959–64, Sen. Lectr, 1965–67, Univ. of Sydney; Prof. of Geog. and of Urban and Regional Planning, Univ. of Wisconsin, Madison, USA, 1967–71; Monash University: Prof. of Geog., 1971–81; Pro Vice-Chancellor, 1982–85; Dep. Vice-Chancellor, 1986; Vice-Chancellor, 1987–96. Visiting Professor: Univ. of Ibadan, Nigeria, 1970–71; LSE, 1973; Nanyang Univ., Singapore, 1979. Chm., Open Learning Agency, Australia Pty Ltd, 1993–96. Australian Newspaper Australian of the Year, 1996. *Publications:* (jtly) New Viewpoints in Economic Geography, 1966; Studies in Australian Geography, 1968; New Viewpoints in Urban and Industrial Geography, 1971; Urban and Regional Australia, 1975; Urbanisation, the Australian Experience, 1980; (jtly) The Brittle Rim, 1989; contribs to Aust. Geographical Studies, Regional Studies, Land Econs, and Econ. Geography. *Address:* 1/50 Bourke Street, Melbourne, Vic 3000, Australia. *Clubs:* Athenæum, Melbourne (Melbourne).

LOGAN, Rt Rev. Vincent; Bishop of Dunkeld, (RC), 1981–2012, now Bishop Emeritus; *b* 30 June 1941; *s* of Joseph Logan and Elizabeth Flannigan. *Educ:* Blairs College, Aberdeen; St Andrew's Coll., Drygrange, Melrose. Ordained priest, Edinburgh, 1964; Asst Priest, St Margaret's, Davidson's Mains, Edinburgh, 1964–66; Corpus Christi Coll., London, 1966–67 (DipRE); Chaplain, St Joseph's Hospital, Rosewell, Midlothian, 1967–77; Adviser in Religious Education, Archdiocese of St Andrews and Edinburgh, 1967; Parish Priest, St Mary's, Ratho, 1977–81; Episcopal Vicar for Education, Archdiocese of St Andrews and Edinburgh, 1978. *Address:* Croghmore, 10 Arnhall Drive, Dundee DD2 1LU.

LOGIE, John Robert Cunningham, PhD; FRCS, FRCSEd, FRCPSGlas; JP; Consultant General Surgeon, Raigmore Hospital, Inverness, 1981–2011; Hon. Senior Lecturer in Surgery, Aberdeen University, 1981–2011; *b* 9 Sept. 1946; *s* of Norman John Logie and Kathleen Margaret Cameron Logie (*née* Neill); *m* 1st, 1981, Sheila Catherine Will (*d* 2001); one *s* one *d*; 2nd, 2004, Carol Joan MacDonald. *Educ:* Robert Gordon's Coll., Aberdeen; Trinity Coll., Glenalmond; Aberdeen Univ. (MB ChB 1970; PhD 1978). FRCSEd 1974; FRCS 1975; FRCPSGlas 1993. Various jun. surg. hosp. posts, Aberdeen Royal Infirmary, 1970–75; Lectr in Surgery, Aberdeen Univ., 1975–81. Vice Pres., RCSE, 2006–09 (Mem. Council, 1991–2002; Treas., 2002–06). Med. Mem., First-tier Tribunal (Social Entitlement Chamber), 2013–Sept. 2016. JP Grampian, Highlands and Islands, 2010–16. *Recreations:* breeding waterfowl, railways in Britain, opera (especially Wagner). *Address:* The Darroch, Little Cantray, Culloden Moor, Inverness IV2 5EY. *T:* (01463) 792090. *E:* john.r.c.logie@lineone.net.

LOGSDAIL, (Christopher) Nicholas (Roald); owner and Director, Lisson Gallery, since 1967; *b* 21 June 1945; *s* of late John Logsdail and Else Logsdail (*née* Dahl); *m* 1st, 1968, Fiona McLean (*d* 2011); one *s*; 2nd, 1985, Caroline Mockett; two *s* one *d*. *Educ:* Bryanston Sch.; Slade Sch., University College London. Opened Lisson Gallery, 1967; represents internationally acclaimed artists: minimal and conceptual artists, incl. Donald Judd, Sol LeWitt and Dan Graham; British sculptors, incl. Richard Deacon, Tony Cragg, Anish Kapoor; new generation of award-winning artists, incl. Santiago Sierra, Tim Lee, Ceal Floyer, Julian Opie, Allora and Calzadilla, Ryan Gander, Haroon Mirza. Mem., Soc. of London Art Dealers. *Publications:* over 50 monographs and artists' books, 1970–. *Recreations:* collecting 20th century art and furniture, paleoanthropology, African studies. *Address:* Lisson Gallery, 52–54 Bell Street, NW1 5DA. *T:* (020) 7724 2739. *E:* nicholas@lissongallery.com.

LOHN, Matthew Simon; Senior Partner, Field Fisher Waterhouse, since 2013; *b* Brentwood, 19 Nov. 1965; *s* of Carl William Lohn and Ann Isobel Lohn; *m* 1992, Johanna Gabriella Miranda Cornwell; one *d*. *Educ:* Brentwood Sch.; London Hosp. Med. Coll. (BSc Hons Cl. I Physiol.; MB BS); Coll. of Law (DipLaw Distinction); Harvard Business Sch. House Officer, Epsom Hosp., 1991–92; Field Fisher Waterhouse, 1994–: Partner, 1998–; Mem., Main Bd, 2004–11; Managing Partner, 2011–13. Member: Determinations Panel, Pensions Regulator, 2013–; Complaints Panel, IPSO, 2014–. Chm., Appeal Panel, RFU, 2006–12; Legal Chairman: Disciplinary Panel, British Horseracing Authy, 2008–; Nat. Anti Doping Panel, 2009–. Mem., Licensing Appeals Bd, Dubai Healthcare City Authy, 2014–. *Recreations:* gardening, racing, shooting. *Address:* Oak Farm, Scaldwell, Northants NN6 9JY. *T:* (01604) 889140. *Club:* Royal Society of Medicine.

LOISELLE, Hon. Gilles; PC (Can.) 1990; Advisor to the Chairman, Executive Committee, Power Corporation of Canada, since 1993; *b* 20 May 1929; *s* of Arthur Loiselle and Antoinette Lethiecq; *m* 1962, Lorraine Benoît; one *s* one *d*. *Educ:* Sacred-Heart Coll., Sudbury, Ont; BA Laval. Teacher, Tafari Makonnen Sch., Addis Ababa, 1951–53; Journalist, Le Droit, Ottawa, 1953–56; Haile Selassie First Day Sch., Addis Ababa, 1956–62; Dir, Behrane Zarie Néo Inst., Addis Ababa, 1958–62; Canadian Broadcasting Corporation: Editor, TV French Network, 1962–63; Quebec and Paris correspondent, French Radio and TV Network, 1963–67; Counsellor, Quebec House, Paris, 1967–72; Dir Gen. of Quebec Govt Communications, 1972–76; Pres., Intergovtl Deptl Cttee for Olympic Year, 1976; Dir, Interparly Relations, Quebec Nat. Assembly, 1977; Agent General for Quebec in London, with responsibility for Scandinavian countries, Iceland, and Ireland, 1977–83; Dep. Minister for federal provincial relations, 1983–84, for Cultural Affairs, Quebec, 1984–85; Agent Gen. for Quebec in Rome, 1985–88. MP (PC) Langelier, 1988–93; Minister of State for Finance, 1989–93; Pres., Treasury Bd of Canada, 1990–93; Minister of Finance, 1993. Dir, Mines Richmont Inc. Founder Mem., Assoc. France-Québec, 1969–72. Hon. Col, 55th Bde. *Recreation:* reading. *Address:* Power Corporation of Canada, 751 Victoria Square, Montreal, QC H2Y 2J3, Canada.

LOLE, Simon Richard Anthony; freelance musician, composer, arranger and broadcaster; Director of Music and Master of the Choristers, Salisbury Cathedral, 1997–2005; *b* 23 Dec. 1957; *s* of Margaret and Dennis Lole; *m* 2010, Gwen Carvill; one *s* two *d*. *Educ:* St Paul's Cathedral Choir Sch.; King's Coll., London (BMus 1978); Guildhall Sch. of Music. ARCO(CHM). Organist and Choirmaster: Barking Parish Church, 1978–80; Croydon Parish Church, 1980–85; Dir of Music, St Mary's Collegiate Church, Warwick, 1985–94; Master of the Music, Sheffield Cathedral, 1994–97; Actg Dir of Music, Jesus Coll., Cambridge, 2005 and 2009. Mem. Council, Incorp. Guild of Church Musicians, 2008–. Hon. FGCM 2005. *Publications:* many church compositions. *Recreations:* walking, reading, sport. *Address:* Cockhill Farm, Haddon, Sturminster Newton, Dorset DT10 2LB. *E:* simon@simonlole.com. *W:* www.simonlole.com.

LOMAS, Alfred; *b* 30 April 1928; *s* of Alfred and Florence Lomas; one *s* one *d*. *Educ:* St Paul's Elem. Sch., Stockport; various further educnl estabs. Solicitor's clerk, 1942–46; Radio Telephony Operator, RAF, 1946–49; various jobs, 1949–51; railway signalman, 1951–59; Labour Party Sec./Agent, 1959–65; Pol Sec., London Co-op., 1965–79. MEP (Lab) London NE, 1979–99; Leader, British Lab Gp, EP, 1985–87. *Publications:* The Common Market—why we should keep out, 1970. *Recreations:* chess, arts, sport. *Address:* 28 Brookway, SE3 9BJ. *T:* (020) 8852 6689. *Club:* Hackney Labour.

LOMAS, Anthony Victor, FCA; Chairman, Business Recovery Services, PricewaterhouseCoopers, since 2006; *b* London, 26 Nov. 1956; *s* of Victor and Patricia Lomas; *m* 1989, Kerry; two *s*. *Educ:* University Coll. London (BA Geog.). FCA 1982. Joined Price Waterhouse, later PricewaterhouseCoopers, 1978; Lead Administrator: Enron Europe, 2001–; MG Rover, 2005–; Lehman UK, 2008–. Chm., Insolvency Cttee, ICAEW, 2004–. *Recreations:* family, travel. *Address:* PricewaterhouseCoopers, 7 More London Riverside, SE1 2RT. *T:* (020) 7583 5000.

LOMAS, Prof. David Arthur, ScD, PhD; FRCP, FMedSci, FHEA; Professor of Medicine, since 2013, Head of Medical School, since 2014, and Vice Provost Health, since 2015, University College London (Dean, Faculty of Medical Sciences, 2013–15); *b* 19 Feb. 1962; *s* of Peter Harry Lomas and Margaret Lomas (*née* Halsall); *m* 1987, Judith Amanda Glasbey; three *s*. *Educ:* Univ. of Nottingham (BMedSci 1983; BM BS Hons 1985); Trinity Coll., Cambridge (PhD 1993); ScD Cambridge 2004. MRCP 1988, FRCP 1997; ILTM 2000. SHO, Central Birmingham HA, 1986–88; Registrar, Gen. Hosp., Birmingham, 1988–90; MRC Trng Fellow, and Mem., Trinity Coll., Cambridge, 1990–93; MRC Clinician Scientist Fellow, Cambridge, 1993–95; Lectr in Medicine, 1995–98, Prof. of Respiratory Biol.,

1998–2012, Univ. of Cambridge; Dep. Dir, Cambridge Inst. for Medical Res., 2002–12; Hon. Consultant Physician, Addenbrooke's and Papworth Hosps, 1995–2012; Fellow, St John's Coll., Cambridge, 2008–12. Sen. Investigator, NIHR, 2014–. Chairman: Grants Cttee, Asthma UK, 2006–10; Grants Cttee, British Lung Foundn, 2010–13; Respiratory Therapy Area Bd, GlaxoSmithKline, 2012–15; MRC Population and Systems Medicine Bd, 2012–March 2016. Croonian Lectr, RCP, 2005; Gordon Cummings Lect., Med. Res. Soc., 2008. FMedSci 2001; FHEA 2007. Res. Award, BUPA Foundn, 1996; Oon Internat. Prize in Preventative Medicine, Downing Coll., Cambridge, 1996; Biochem. Soc. GSK Prize, 2004. *Publications:* res. on α:-antitrypsin deficiency, conformational diseases and chronic obstructive pulmonary disease in med. jls. *Recreations:* family life, cricket, hill walking, modern literature. *Address:* Vice Provost Health, University College London, 1st Floor, Maple House, 149 Tottenham Court Road, W1T 7NF. *T:* (020) 3108 2105.

LOMAS, Prof. David John, FRCP, FRCR; Professor (formerly Amersham Professor) of Clinical Magnetic Resonance Imaging, University of Cambridge, since 2001; *b* 21 March 1957; *s* of Geoffrey and Sheila Lomas; *m* 1986, Rebecca Steward; two *d*. *Educ:* Emmanuel Coll., Cambridge (MA Engrg; MB BChir). MRCP 1985, FRCP 1998; FRCR 1989. Medical Registrar, Princess Margaret Hosp., Swindon, 1985–87; Radiology Registrar, 1987–93, Hon. Consultant Radiologist and Univ. Lectr, 1993–2001, Addenbrooke's Hosp., Cambridge. Vis. Scientist, Mayo Clinic, USA, 1993. *Publications:* contrib. papers to Clinical Radiol., Radiol., Science, Jl Magnetic Resonance Imaging, British Jl Radiol. *Recreations:* industrial archaeology, photography, plumbing. *Address:* Department of Radiology, University of Cambridge School of Clinical Medicine, Box 218, Cambridge Biomedical Campus, Cambridge CB2 0QQ. *T:* (01223) 336890, *Fax:* (01223) 330915.

LOMAS, Eric George; Managing Director, Gatwick Airport, 1994–97; *b* 26 June 1938; *s* of Arthur Edward Lomas and Florence Lomas; *m* 1959, Carol Letitia Davies; two *d*. *Educ:* Willesden County Grammar School; Templeton Coll., Oxford (Sen. Exec. Leadership Prog.); Cranfield Inst. (Computer Prog.); London Business Sch. (Aviation Prog.). FCIT. PLA, 1954–69; served with RE, 1957–59; Associated Container Transportation, 1969–70; BAA, 1970–86, BAA plc, 1986–97; Man. Dir, Stansted Airport, 1989–94. Trustee Dir, BAA Pension Fund Co. Ltd, 2003–06. Dir, Sussex TEC, 1995–97. Mem., SE Reg., CBI, 1995–97. Chm., Lapwing Flying Club Ltd, 1979–82; Vice Cdre, British Motor Yacht Club Ltd, 1994–96. Member: Petersham Book Club; Square Rigger Club. *Recreations:* reading, classic car rallies, boating, travel, house parties in France.

LOMAS, Joanne; HM Diplomatic Service; High Commissioner to Namibia, since 2015; *b* High Wycombe, 7 Sept. 1970; *d* of Geoffrey Lomas and Judith Lomas; *m* 2008, Christopher Finucane; one *d*. *Educ:* Univ. of Bristol (BSc Politics). Joined FCO, 1993; Third Sec., Damascus, 1997–2000; Second Sec., UK Mission to the UN, Geneva, 2001–06; Hd, Global Response Centre, FCO, 2009; Dep. Hd of Mission, Sarajevo, 2011–15. *Recreations:* hiking, ski-ing, the great outdoors. *Address:* British Residence, 15 Conrad Rust Street, Windhoek, Namibia.

LOMAS, Ven. John Derrick Percy; Archdeacon of St Asaph, since 2014; Rector, St Michael's, Caerwys and St Stephens, Bodfari, since 2015; *b* 19 Aug. 1958. *Educ:* St Michael's Coll., Llandaff. Ordained deacon, 1994, priest, 1995; Curate, Parish of Rhyl, 1994–2000; RN Chaplain, 2000–01; Vicar, St James, Holywell, 2001–11; Area Dean, Holywell, 2001–11; Transition Missioner: St Mael and St Sulien, Corwen, 2011–13; St Dunawd, Bangor Monachorum and Benefice of Wrexham, 2013–14. Canon Cursal, St Asaph Cathedral, 2008–14. *Address:* 14 Lon yr Ysgol, Caerwyd, Mold CH7 5PZ.

LOMAS, Julia Carole; Partner, since 2002, and National Head, Court of Protection Department, since 2008, Irwin Mitchell, Solicitors (Consultant, 2000–02); *b* 9 Dec. 1954; *d* of Charles James Lomas and Sadie Lomas; *m* (marr. diss.); one *s*; *m* 2014, William Frederick Hill. *Educ:* Lanchester Poly. (BA Business Law). Admitted solicitor, 1980. Articled clerk, London Borough of Islington, 1977–80; Dep. Borough Solicitor, London Borough of Waltham Forest, 1980–89; Borough Solicitor, London Borough of Haringey, 1989–94; Public Trustee, and Chief Exec., Public Trust Office, 1994–99. FCMI (FIMgt 1994). *Recreations:* theatre, crosswords, dining out. *Address:* Irwin Mitchell, 40 Holborn Viaduct, EC1N 2PZ.

LOMAS, Mark Henry; QC 2003; *b* 17 Nov. 1948; *s* of Keith and Margaret Lomas; *m* 1st, 1980, Caroline Margaret Mary Agnew (marr. diss. 2005); three *d*; 2nd, 2010, Joanna Jane Allen (*née* Wigglesworth) (*d* 2012). *Educ:* Oundle Sch.; Trinity Hall, Cambridge (BA Hons, MA). Called to the Bar, Middle Temple, 1977; in practice as barrister, specialising in professional negligence, 1977–2009; Accredited Mediator, 2001; Mem., London Court of Internat. Arbitration, 2008–; in practice as Commercial Mediator and sitting as Commercial Arbitrator, 2009–. *Recreations:* hunting, shooting, salmon fishing. *Address:* Littleton Chambers, 3 King's Bench Walk North, Temple, EC4Y 7HR. *Club:* Boodle's.

LOMAX, (Janis) Rachel; Deputy Governor, Bank of England, 2003–08; *b* 15 July 1945; *d* of William and Dilys Salmon; *m* 1967, Michael Acworth Lomax (marr. diss. 1990); two *s*. *Educ:* Cheltenham Ladies' Coll.; Girton Coll., Cambridge (MA); LSE (MSc). HM Treasury: Econ. Assistant, 1968; Econ. Advr, 1972; Sen. Econ. Advr, 1978; Principal Pvte Sec. to Chancellor of the Exchequer, 1985–86; Under-Sec., 1986–90; Dep. Chief Econ. Advr, 1990–92; Dep. Sec. (Financial Instns and Markets), 1992–94; Dep. Sec., Cabinet Office, 1994–95; Vice Pres. and Chief of Staff, World Bank, 1995–96; Permanent Secretary: Welsh Office, 1996–99; DSS, then DWP, 1999–2002; DTLR, then DfT, 2002–03. Non-executive Director: HSBC Hldgs, 2008– (Sen. Ind. Dir, 2015–); Heathrow (SP) Ltd (formerly BAA), 2010–; CityUK, 2013–; Serco, 2014–; Breugel, 2014–; Ditchley Park, 2014–. Pres., IFS, 2007–. Mem. Bd, RNT, 2002–11. Mem. Council, Imperial Coll. London, 2010–. *Address:* 25 Henning Street, SW11 3DR.

LOMAX, Kevin John; Founder, Misys plc, 1979 (Chairman, 1985–2005; Chief Executive Officer, 2005–06); *b* 8 Dec. 1948; *s* of late Brig. Kenneth John Lomax and of Mary Lomax (*née* Foley); *m* 1975, Penelope Frances Flynn; one *s* two *d*. *Educ:* Ampleforth Coll.; Manchester Univ. (BSc Hons 1970). Advanced Project Manager, J & S Pumps Ltd, 1970–73; Asst to Divl Chm., Allied Polymer Gp, 1973–75; Managing Director: British Furnaces Ltd, 1975–77; Wellman Incandescent Ltd, 1977–80; Dir and Divl Chm., Caparo Industries (CMT) Ltd, 1980–83; Dir and Divl CEO, Electronic Components Div., STC plc, 1983–85. Non-exec. Dir, Marks & Spencer, 2000–06. Trustee/Dir, Royal Opera House, 2000–05. Hon. DSc Birmingham, 2003. *Recreations:* golf, shooting, fishing, horse-racing, military history, music. *Address:* Clarence House, The Vineyard, Richmond, Surrey TW10 6AQ.

LOMAX, Rachel; *see* Lomax, J. R.

LOMBARD, Rt Rev. Charles F.; *see* Fitzgerald-Lombard.

LOMBE, Hon. Sir Edward Christopher E.; *see* Evans-Lombe.

LOMER, Geoffrey John, CBE 1985; MA; FREng; FIET; Chairman, Satellite Information Services Ltd, 1993–96; Director (non-executive), Vodafone Group plc, 1992–97; *b* 5 Jan. 1932; *s* of Frederick John Lomer and Dorothy Lomer; *m* 1st, 1955, Pauline Helena May (*d* 1974); one *s* one *d*; 2nd, 1977, Antoinette Ryall (*d* 2003); one step *s* one step *d*. *Educ:* St Austell Grammar School; Queens' College, Cambridge (MA). FREng (FEng 1984). Research Engineer, EMI Research Laboratories, 1953–57; Head of Radio Frequency Div., Broadcast Equipment Dept, EMI Electronics, 1957–63; Head of Transmitter Lab., Racal Communications, 1963–68; Technical Dir, Racal Mobilcal, 1968–70; Dir in Charge, Racal Communications Equipment, 1970–76; Dep. Man. Dir, Racal Tacticom, 1976–77; Technical Dir, Racal Electronics plc, 1977–92. Vice Pres., IEE, 1991–94; Hon. FIET (Hon. FIEE 1998). *Recreations:* music, theatre. *Address:* Ventana, The Devil's Highway, Crowthorne, Berks RG45 6BJ.

LONDESBOROUGH, 9th Baron *cr* 1850; **Richard John Denison;** *b* 2 July 1959; *s* of John Albert Lister, 8th Baron Londesborough, TD, AMICE, and Elizabeth Ann (*d* 1994), *d* of late Edward Little Sale, ICS; *S* father, 1968; *m* 1987, Rikki Morris, *d* of J. E. Morris, Bayswater; one *s* one *d*. *Educ:* Wellington College; Exeter Univ. *Heir: s* Hon. James Frederick Denison, *b* 4 June 1990. *Address:* Edw Cottage, Aberedw, Builth Wells, Powys LD2 3UR.

LONDON, Bishop of, since 1995; **Rt Rev. and Rt Hon. Richard John Carew Chartres,** KCVO 2009; PC 1995; Prelate of the Order of the British Empire, since 1995; Dean of the Chapels Royal, since 1995; *b* 11 July 1947; *s* of Richard and Charlotte Chartres; *m* 1982, Caroline Mary, *d* of Sir (Charles) Alan McLintock; two *s* two *d*. *Educ:* Hertford Grammar Sch.; Trinity Coll., Cambridge (BA 1968; MA 1973); Cuddesdon Theol Coll., Oxford; Lincoln Theol Coll. Ordained: deacon, 1973; priest, 1974; Asst Curate, St Andrew's, Bedford, Dio. of St Albans, 1973–75; Bishop's Domestic Chaplain, St Albans, 1975–80; Archbishop of Canterbury's Chaplain, 1980–84; Vicar, St Stephen with St John, Westminster, 1984–92; Area Bishop of Stepney, 1992–95. Chairman: C of E Church Bldgs Div. (formerly C of E Heritage Forum), 1998–; C of E Shrink the Footprint Envmtl Campaign, 2006–14; Actg Chm., Bd of Govs, Church Comrs, 2005–. Mem., Central Cttee, Conf. of European Chs. Gresham Prof. of Divinity, 1986–92. Six Preacher, Canterbury Cathedral, 1991–96. Founder and Chm. of Trustees, 1997–2011, St Ethelburga's Centre for Reconciliation and Peace (Life Pres., 2011); Co-Chm., Partner and Trustee, St Mellitus Coll., 2007–. Hon. Bencher, Middle Temple, 1998. Liveryman: Merchant Taylors' Co., 1997; Drapers' Co., 2000; Hon. Freeman: Weavers' Co., 1998; Leathersellers' Co., 1999; Woolmen's Co., 2000; Vintners' Co., 2001; Grocers' Co., 2008; Water Conservators' Co., 2009. FSA 1999. Ehrendomprediger, Berliner Dom, 2001. BD Lambeth, 1983. Hon. DLitt London Guildhall, 1998; Hon. DD: London, 1999; City, 1999; Brunel, 1999; KCL, 2010. *Publications:* The History of Gresham College 1597–1997, 1998; Tree of Knowledge, Tree of Life, 2005. *Address:* The Old Deanery, Dean's Court, EC4V 5AA. *T:* (020) 7248 6233.

LONDON, Archdeacon of; *see* Miller, Ven. L. J.

LONDONDERRY, 10th Marquess of, *cr* 1816; **Frederick Aubrey Vane-Tempest-Stewart;** Baron Londonderry 1789; Viscount Castlereagh 1795; Earl of Londonderry 1796; Baron Stewart 1814; Earl Vane, Viscount Seaham 1823; *b* 6 Sept. 1972; *s* of 9th Marquess of Londonderry and of Doreen Patricia Wells, *qv*; *S* father, 2012. *Heir: b* Lord Reginald Alexander Vane-Tempest-Stewart [*b* 30 May 1977; *m* 2004, Chloe Belinda Guinness; one *s* two *d*].

LONDONDERRY, Doreen, Marchioness of; *see* Wells, D. P.

LONG, family name of **Viscount Long.**

LONG, 4th Viscount *cr* 1921, of Wraxall; **Richard Gerard Long,** CBE 1993; *b* 30 Jan. 1929; *s* of 3rd Viscount and Gwendolyn (*d* 1959), *d* of Thomas Reginald Hague Cook; *S* father, 1967; *m* 1957, Margaret Frances (marr. diss. 1984), *d* of late Ninian B. Frazer; one *s* one *d* (and one *d* decd); *m* 1984, Catherine Patricia Elizabeth Mier-Woolf (marr. diss. 1990); *m* 1990, Helen Fleming-Gibbons. *Educ:* Harrow. Wilts Regt, 1947–49. Opposition Whip, 1974–79; a Lord in Waiting (Govt Whip), 1979–97. Vice-Pres. and formerly Vice-Chm., Wilts Royal British Legion. Freeman, City of London, 1991. *Heir: s* Hon. James Richard Long, *b* 31 Dec. 1960. *Address:* Bonjedward Hill, Sharplaw Road, Jedburgh, Roxburghshire TD8 6SF. *Club:* Pratt's.

LONG, Prof. Adrian Ernest, OBE 2006; PhD, DSc; FREng, FIAE; Professor of Civil Engineering, Queen's University, Belfast, 1976–2006, now Professor Emeritus; Leverhulme Emeritus Research Fellow, 2009–11; *b* 15 April 1941; *s* of Charles Long and Sylvia Long; *m* 1967, Elaine Thompson; one *s* one *d*. *Educ:* Royal Sch., Dungannon; QUB (BSc 1st cl. Hons (Civil Engrg) 1963; PhD (Structural Engrg) 1967; DSc (Civil Engrg) 1984). Bridge design engr, Foundn Engrg Co. of Canada, Toronto, 1967–68; Asst Prof., Dept of Civil Engrg, Queen's Univ., Kingston, Ont, 1968–71; Queen's University, Belfast: Lectr, 1971–76, Hd, 1977–89, Dept of Civil Engrg; Dean, Fac. of Engrg, 1988–91, 1998–2002; Dir, Sch. of Built Envmt, 1989–98. Pres., ICE, 2002–03. Hon. UK Rep., Tech. Cttee, EU Co-operation Sci. and Technol. Urban Civil Engrg, 1991–2006; Chm., Civil Engrg Sub-Panel, Res. Assessment Exercise for UK, 2008. Ed., Jl of Engrg Structures, 1986–94. FREng 1989; FIAE, 1998. Hon. DSc City, 2007. (Jtly) Esso Energy Gold Medal, Royal Soc., 1994; Ewing Medal, ICE and Royal Soc., 2009; ICE Gold Medal, 2010. *Publications:* patent for FlexiArch for construction of short-span bridges, 2004; over 350 tech. papers in jls and procs of confs. *Recreations:* walking, travel, gardening, occasional golf, Elder in a Presbyterian Church in Belfast. *Address:* School of Civil Engineering, Queen's University, Belfast, Belfast BT7 1NN. *T:* (028) 9097 6950, *Fax:* (028) 9097 4278. *E:* a.long@qub.ac.uk.

LONG, Amanda; Director General, Consumers International, since 2014; *b* Herts, 25 March 1969; *m* 1996, Mark Long; one *s* one *d*. *Educ:* De Montfort Univ. (BA Jt Hons English Lit. and Hist.). Internat. Projects Manager, Birds Eye Wall's Ltd, Unilever plc, 1996–99; Dir and Nat. Rep., Plant Publicity Holland UK and Ireland Bureau, 2000–10; Hd, Corporate Responsibility, Anglian Water Services, 2010–11; CEO, Corporate Culture, 2011–12; Dir, Membership, Mktg and Media, E of England Co-operative Soc., 2012–14. FCIM; FRSA. Responsible Business Game Changer Award, Business in the Community, 2013. *Publications:* (contrib.) Addressing Tipping Points for a Precarious Future, 2013. *Recreations:* sailing, tennis. *Address:* Consumers International, 24 Highbury Crescent, N5 1RX. *E:* along@consint.org.

LONG, Athelstan Charles Ethelwulf, CMG 1968; CBE 1964 (MBE 1959); Chairman, International Management Group, 1988–92; Chairman, Public Service Commission, 1987–98; Deputy Chairman, Public Service Pensions Board, 1992–96; *b* 2 Jan. 1919; *s* of Arthur Leonard Long and Gabrielle Margaret Campbell (historical writer and novelist, Marjorie Bowen); *m* 1948, Edit Mäjken Zadie Harriet Krantz, *d* of late Erik Krantz, Stockholm; two *s*. *Educ:* Westminster Sch.; Brasenose Coll., Oxford. Served War of 1939–45: commnd into RA, 1940; seconded 7th (Bengal) Battery, 22nd Mountain Regt, IA, 1940; served Malaya; POW as Capt., 1942–45; appointed to Indian Political Service, 1946. Cadet, Burma Civil Service, 1947–48; Colonial Admin. Service (N Nigeria), 1948; Sen. District Officer, 1958; Resident, Zaria Province, 1959; Perm. Sec., Min. of Animal Health and Forestry, 1959; started new Min. of Information as Perm. Sec., 1960; Swaziland: appointed Govt Sec., 1961; Chief Sec., 1964; Leader of Govt business in Legislative Council and MEC, 1964–67; HM Dep. Comr, 1967–68; Administrator, later Governor, of the Cayman Is, 1968–71; Comr of Anguilla, March–July 1972; Admin. Sec., Inter-University Council, 1972–73. Man. Dir, Anegada Corp. Ltd, 1973–74; Pres., United Bank Internat., Cayman Is, 1976–96; Dir and Chm., Cayman Airways, 1977–81. Chairman: Planning Appeals Tribunal, 1982–84; Coastal Works Adv. Cttee, 1986–91. Chm. Governing Council, Waterford Sch., Swaziland, 1963–68. FRAS; FRGS. *Recreations:* travel, tropical farming, reading. *Address:* Box 131, Savannah, Grand Cayman, Cayman Islands, West Indies.

LONG, Christopher William, CMG 1986; HM Diplomatic Service, retired; non-executive Director, Gedeon Richter plc, Budapest, since 1998; *b* 9 April 1938; *s* of late Eric and May Long; *m* 1972, Patricia, *d* of late Dennis and May Stanbridge; two *s* one *d*. *Educ:* King Edward's

Sch., Birmingham; Balliol Coll., Oxford (Deakin Scholar); Univ. of Münster, W Germany. Served RN, 1956–58. HM Diplomatic Service, 1963–98: FO, 1963–64; Jedda, 1965–67; Caracas, 1967–69; FCO, 1969–74; Budapest, 1974–77; Belgrade (CSCE), 1977; Counsellor, Damascus, 1978–80; Counsellor and Dep. Perm. Rep., UKMIS, Geneva, 1980–83; Head, Near East and N Africa Dept, FCO, 1983–85; Asst Under-Sec. of State (Dep. Chief Clerk and Chief Inspector), FCO, 1985–88; Ambassador: to Switzerland, 1988–92 and also to Liechtenstein, 1992; to Egypt, 1992–95; to Hungary, 1995–98. Dir, Foreign Service Prog., Oxford Univ., 1999–2003. Non-exec. Dir, KFKI Computer Systems Corp., Budapest, 2001–04. Dir, World Faiths Develt Dialogue, 2004–05. Trustee, Orders of St John Care Trust, 2003–10. Gov., Prior Park Coll., Bath, 2000–09. *Recreations:* family, notably grandchildren, Middle East, Hungary and Switzerland, geriatric tennis, growing vegetables and fruit for home consumption. *Club:* Athenæum.

LONG, Dr Ian Edward, FRGS; Headmaster, Albyn School, Aberdeen, since 2008; *b* Sutton, Surrey, 26 Aug. 1959; *s* of late Gerald and Mimi Long; *m* 1998, Gwyneth Rogers. *Educ:* King's Coll., Sch., Wimbledon; King's Coll. London (BA Hons Geog., AKC, PGCE, PhD); Birkbeck Coll., London (MA N American Geog. Studies). Work for Shell and in a home for children in care; teacher: Royal Grammar Sch., High Wycombe, 1993–96 (Hd of Dept); Brentwood Sch., Essex, 1996–99 (Hd of Sixth Form); Dep. Hd, City of London Freemen's Sch., 1999–2008. Freeman: City of London; Co. of Educators. FRSA. *Publications:* contrib. Jl Rural Studies. *Recreations:* former oarsman at Molesey, Kingston, Globe Rowing Club, former researcher at King's College London, reading, theatre, keeping warm in the Granite City. *Address:* Albyn School, 17–23 Queen's Road, Aberdeen AB15 4PB. *T:* (01224) 322408. *E:* i.long@albynschool.co.uk. *Club:* Royal Over-Seas League.

LONG, John Richard, CBE 1987; *b* 9 March 1931; *s* of late Thomas Kendall Long and Jane Long; *m* 1952, Margaret (*née* Thistlethwaite); one *s* two *d.* *Educ:* Kirkham Grammar School; Dip. in EU Law, KCL, 1993. Clerical Officer, Customs and Excise, 1947; Exec. Officer, Min. of Pensions, subseq. DHSS, 1949; various posts on health functions; Asst Sec., 1978 (posts on regulation and pricing of medicines, maternity and child health, and communicable diseases); Under Sec., 1987 (NHS Personnel Div.), resigned 1988. *Publications:* co-author, articles on regulation of medicines. *Recreations:* family, vegetable growing, wild life. *Address:* 77 Prospect Road, Farnborough, Hants GU14 8NT. *T:* (01252) 548525.

LONG, Kieran William John; Senior Curator, Contemporary Architecture, Design and Digital, Victoria and Albert Museum, since 2013; *b* Lyndhurst, 19 Aug. 1977; *s* of Colin Long and Margaret Long; *m* 2012, Sofia Lagerkvist. *Educ:* King Edward VI Sch., Southampton; Cardiff Univ. (BA Eng. Lit. 1998). Deputy Editor: Building Design Mag., 1998–2001; Icon Mag., 2003–07; Editor-in-Chief, Architects' Jl and Architectural Rev., 2007–10; Architecture Critic, Evening Standard, 2010–13. Television presenter: Restoration Home, 2010–13; The House that £100K Built, 2013–15. Tutor, RCA, 2011–12; Asst Dir, Venice Architectural Biennale, 2012. *Publications:* (ed jtly) Common Ground: a critical reader, 2012. *Recreations:* playing guitar, folk music, American fiction, tennis, cricket, golf. *Address:* Victoria and Albert Museum, Cromwell Road, SW7 2RL. *E:* k.long@vam.ac.uk.

LONG, Martin Paul; Chairman: Churchill Properties (Southern) Ltd, since 2003; M4 Underwriting Ltd, since 2006; Co-Chairman, Crystal Palace Football Club, since 2010; *b* 27 Aug. 1950; *s* of Robert and Alice Long; five *s* one *d.* *Educ:* St Joseph's Coll., SE19. FCII 1981. Prudential Assce Co., 1968–69; Guardian Royal Exchange Assce Co., 1970–74; Sphere Drake Insce Co., 1975–78; Northern Star Insce Co., 1979–83; Man. Dir, Halifax Insce Co., 1983–84; Dir and Gen. Manager, Direct Line Insce, 1984–87; setting up Churchill Insce Gp, 1987–89; Founder Chm. and CEO, Churchill Insurance Gp plc, 1989–2003; Dep. Chm., Royal Bank of Scotland Insurance, 2003–04; Chairman, Ashworth Mairs Gp, 2005–08; AMG (Chartered Loss Adjusters), 2005–08. Owner of Sweetwoods Park Golf Course, 2008–. *Recreations:* sports (watching and playing), socialising, spending time with my children. *Address:* Churchill Properties (Southern) Ltd, c/o K. A. Jeffries & Co., 18 Melbourne Grove, SE22 8RA. *T:* 07982 273327. *E:* martin@martinlong.co.uk.

LONG, Naomi Rachel; *b* 13 Dec. 1971; *d* of James Dobbin Johnston and Olive Emily Johnston; *m* 1995, Michael Andrew Long. *Educ:* Mersey Street Primary Sch.; Bloomfield Collegiate Grammar Sch.; Queen's Univ., Belfast (MEng Dist. Civil Engrg 1994). Asst Engr, Parkman Consulting Engrs, 1994–96; Res. Asst, QUB, 1996–99; Graduate Civil and Envmtl Engr, Mulholland & Doherty, 1999–2003. Mem. (Alliance), Belfast CC, 2001–10 (Lord Mayor of Belfast, 2009–10). Mem. (Alliance) Belfast E, NI Assembly, 2003–10. Vice Chm., Cttee for Office of First and Dep. First Minister, NI Assembly, 2007–10. MP (Alliance) Belfast E, 2010–15; contested (Alliance) same seat, 2015. Dep. Leader, Alliance Party of NI, 2006–. *Recreations:* Guide leader, reading, travel, choral singing.

LONG, Richard Julian, CBE 2013; RA 2001; artist; *b* 2 June 1945; *s* of Maurice Long and Frances Carpenter; *m* 1969, Denise Johnston (marr. diss. 1999); two *d.* *Educ:* West of England Coll. of Art, Bristol; St Martin's Sch. of Art, London. *Exhibitions include:* Mus. of Modern Art, NYC, 1972; Scottish Nat. Gall. of Modern Art, Edinburgh, 1974; Venice Biennale, 1976; Nat. Gall. of Victoria, Melbourne, 1977; Fogg Art Mus., Harvard Univ., 1980; Nat. Gall. of Canada, Ottawa, 1982; Century Cultural Centre, Tokyo, 1983; Guggenheim, NYC (retrospective), 1986; Tate Gall., 1990; Hayward Gall. (retrospective), 1991; ARC, Paris, 1993; Kunstsammlung Nordrhein-Westfalen, Düsseldorf, 1994; Palazzo Dell Esposizioni, Rome, 1994; Guggenheim, Bilbao, 2000; Royal Acad. (one-man), 2004; Scottish Nat. Gall. of Modern Art, 2007; Tate Britain, 2009; Lisson Gall. (solo), 2014; Faena, Buenos Aires, 2014; Alan Cristea Gall. (solo), Arnolfini, Bristol (solo), 2015. Hon. DLitt: Bristol, 1995; St Andrews, 2011. Kunstpreis, Aachen, 1988; Turner Prize, 1989. Chevalier de l'Ordre des Arts et des Lettres (France), 1990; Praemium Imperiale (Japan), 2010. *Publications include:* South America, 1972; Twelve Works, 1981; Countless Stones, 1983; Stone Water Miles, 1987; (with Anne Seymour) Old World New World, 1988; Nile, 1990; Walking in Circles, 1991; Mountains and Waters, 1992; River to River, 1993; Mirage, 1997; A Walk Across England, 1997; Every Grain of Sand, 1999; Midday, 2001; Walking the Line, 2003; Walking and Sleeping, 2005; Dartmoor, 2006; Heaven and Earth, 2009; Karoo Highveld, 2011. *Address:* c/o Lisson Gallery, 52–54 Bell Street, NW1 5DA.

LONG, Prof. Stephen Patrick, PhD; FRS 2013; Edward William and Jane Marr Gutgsell Endowed University Professor of Plant Biology and of Crop Sciences, University of Illinois, Urbana-Champaign, since 2008; *b* Camden, London, 13 Aug. 1950; *s* of Frederick George Long and Amy Edith Helen Long; *m* 1972, Ann Denise Baron; two *s.* *Educ:* Pinner Grammar Sch.; Univ. of Reading (BSc 1st Cl. Hons 1972); Univ. of Leeds (PhD 1976). University of Essex: Lectr, 1975–87; Sen. Lectr, 1987–88; Reader, 1988–90; Prof. of Envmtl Physiol., 1990–98; University of Illinois, Urbana-Champaign: Robert Emerson Prof. of Plant Biol. and Crop Scis, 1999–2008; Center for Advanced Studies Prof., 2013–. Vis. Prof., Chinese Acad. of Scis, Jt Max-Planck Inst. of Computational Biol., Shanghai, 2013. Chief and Founding Editor, Global Change Biology, 1994–. Lectures: Riley Meml, World Food Prize/AAAS, Washington, DC, 2013; CeBiTec Annual Dist., Univ. Bielefeld, 2013. Hon. DSc Lancaster, 2007. Marsh Award for Climate Change Res., British Ecol Soc., 2012; Innovation Award, Internat. Soc. for Photosynthesis Res., 2013. *Publications:* over 300 articles in jls incl. Sci., Nature, Plant Physiol., Plant Cell and Envmt, Ecol., Jl of Experimental Botany. *Recreations:* distance running, triathlons, classical music. *Address:* University of Illinois, 1206 W Gregory Drive, 134 IGB, Urbana, IL 61801, USA. *T:* (217) 2440881, *Fax:* (217) 2442496. *E:* slong@illinois.edu. *Club:* Royal Over-Seas League.

LONG BAILEY, Rebecca; MP (Lab) Salford and Eccles, since 2015; *b* 22 Sept. 1979; *m;* one *c.* *Educ:* Catholic High Sch., Chester; Manchester Metropolitan Univ. (BA Politics and Sociol.). Landlord and Tenant Solicitor, Halliwells, 2003–07; Solicitor (Healthcare), Hill Dickinson LLP, 2007–. *Address:* House of Commons, SW1A 0AA.

LONGAIR, Deborah Janet; *see* Howard, D. J.

LONGAIR, Prof. Malcolm Sim, CBE 2000; PhD; FRS 2004; FRSE 1981; Jacksonian Professor of Natural Philosophy, 1991–2008, Head of Department of Physics, 1998–2005, and Director of Research, since 2008, Cavendish Laboratory, University of Cambridge; Professorial Fellow, Clare Hall, Cambridge, 1991–2008, now Emeritus; *b* 18 May 1941; *s* of James Sim Longair and Lily Malcolm; *m* 1975, Prof. Deborah Janet Howard, *qv;* one *s* one *d.* *Educ:* Morgan Acad., Dundee; Queen's Coll., Dundee, Univ. of St Andrews (BSc Electronic Physics, 1963); Cavendish Lab., Univ. of Cambridge (MA, PhD 1967). Res. Fellow, Royal Commn for Exhibn of 1851, 1966–68; Royal Soc. Exchange Fellow to USSR, 1968–69; University of Cambridge: Res. Fellow, 1967–71, and Official Fellow, 1971–80, Clare Hall; Univ. Demonstrator in Phys., 1970–75; Univ. Lectr in Phys., 1975–80; Astronomer Royal for Scotland, Regius Prof. of Astronomy, Univ. of Edinburgh, and Dir, Royal Observatory, Edinburgh, 1980–90. Visiting Professor: of Radio Astronomy, Calif Inst. of Technol., 1972; of Astronomy, Inst. for Advanced Study, Princeton, 1978; Space Telescope Sci. Inst., 1997; Regents' Fellow, Carnegie Inst., Harvard Univ., 1990. Pres., RAS, 1996–98 (Editor, Monthly Notices, 1974–78). Foreign Member: Accad. Nazionale dei Lincei, 2000; Istituto Veneto di Scienze, Lettere ed Arte, 2007. Hon. LLD Dundee, 1982; Hon. DSc Edinburgh, 2013. Britannica Award, 1986. *Publications:* (ed) Confrontation of Cosmological Theories with Observational Data, 1974; (ed with J. Einasto) The Large-Scale Structure of the Universe, 1978; (with J. E. Gunn and M. J. Rees) Observational Cosmology, 1978; (ed with J. Warner) The Scientific Uses of the Space Telescope, 1980; High Energy Astrophysics: an informal introduction, 1980, 3rd edn 2011; (ed with H. A. Brück and G. Coyne) Astrophysical Cosmology, 1982; Theoretical Concepts in Physics, 1984, 2nd edn 2003; Alice and the Space Telescope, 1989; The Origins of Our Universe, 1991; (with A. R. Sandage and R. G. Kron) The Deep Universe, 1995; Our Evolving Universe, 1996; Galaxy Formation, 1998, 2nd edn 2008; The Cosmic Century: a history of astrophysics and cosmology, 2006; Quantum Concepts in Physics, 2013; over 200 papers, mostly in Monthly Notices of RAS. *Recreations:* music, art, architecture, mountain walking. *Address:* c/o Cavendish Laboratory, J. J. Thomson Avenue, Cambridge CB3 0HE. *T:* (01223) 765777.

LONGBOTHAM, His Honour Tom; a Circuit Judge, 1999–2010; *b* 9 Aug. 1942; *s* of George Ferrand Longbotham and Elizabeth Ann Longbotham; *m* 1964, Eirlys Thomas; one *s* (and one *s* decd). *Educ:* Rossall Sch.; Bristol Univ. (LLB). Admitted Solicitor, 1966; Sen. Litigation Partner, Bishop Longbotham & Bagnall, Solicitors, until 1999; Asst Recorder, 1990–95; a Recorder, 1995–99. *Recreations:* golf, gardening, hill walking, theatre. *Club:* West Wiltshire Golf.

LONGDEN, Wilson; JP; industrial relations consultant, 1987–2005; *b* 26 May 1936; *s* of late Harold and Doris Longden; *m* 1st, 1966 (marr. diss. 1982); two *s;* 2nd, 1985 (marr. diss. 1993). *Educ:* Chesterfield Grammar Sch.; Univ. of Hull (BA Hons, Dip Ed); Univ. of Bradford (MSc). National service, RAF, 1955–57; Teacher, Northmount High Sch., Canada, 1961–62; Lecturer: Matthew Boulton Tech. Coll., Birmingham, 1962–66; Bingley Coll. of Educn, 1966–67; Margaret McMillan Coll. of Educn, 1967–68; Hatfield Polytechnic, 1968–69; Coventry (Lanchester) Polytechnic, 1969–73; Vice-Principal, Barnfield College, Luton, 1973–87. Sec., Assoc. of Vice-Principals of Colleges, 1986–87 (Pres., 1982–84). Comr, MSC, 1983–85. JP Luton, 1980; Mem., Beds Magistrates' Courts Cttee, 1998–2000. *Publications:* The School Manager's and the School Governor's Handbook, 1977; Meetings, 1977, 2nd edn 1997; Making Secondments Work, 1990. *Recreations:* travel, music, playing the piano, family history (www.4chesterfieldfamilies.org.uk). *Address:* 311 Turnpike Drive, Luton LU3 3RE. *T:* (01582) 658695. *E:* wilsonlongden@hotmail.com.

LONGDON, Patricia Joyce; Director, Trish Longdon Associates, since 2008; *b* 19 Jan. 1952; *d* of Fred and Nell Morgan; *m* 1st (marr. diss. 1987); 2nd, 1995, Mick Penny; one step *s* two step *d.* *Educ:* Brighton and Hove High Sch.; UCL (BSc 1st cl. Hons 1973); Sch. of Envmtl Studies, London (MPhil 1977). DoE, 1973–80; London Rape Crisis Centre, 1980–83; Asst Dir, Local Govt Ombudsman, 1983–89; Dir, People Develt, Audit Commn, 1989–2003; Dep. Parly and Health Service Ombudsman, 2003–08. Independent Complaints Monitor: Criminal Records Bureau, 2009–12; Disclosure and Barring Service, 2012–14. Non-exec. Dir, Hammersmith and Fulham NHS, 2009–12; Mem., Appts Cttee, GDC, 2010–12 (Chair, 2012–14); Vice Chair, NW London NHS Cluster Bd, 2012–13; Lay Mem., Hammersmith and Fulham CCG, 2013–. *Recreations:* family and friends, reading, listening to classical music, climbing mountains, exploring the world. *E:* trish@trishlongdon.co.uk.

LONGFIELD, Anne Elizabeth, OBE 2000; Children's Commissioner for England, since 2015; *b* 5 July 1960; *d* of James Vincent Longfield and Jean Elizabeth Longfield; *m* 2003, Richard Reeve; one *s.* *Educ:* Prince Henry's Grammar Sch., Otley; Univ. of Newcastle upon Tyne (BA Hons History). Researcher, Save the Children Fund, 1982–83; community develt in London, 1983–87; Develt, Kids' Clubs Network, 1987–93; Dir, then Chief Exec., Kids' Clubs Network, later 4Children, 1994–2015. Performance and Innovation Unit, Cabinet Office, 2001–02. Non-exec. Dir, Social Investment Business, 2009–11. Trustee, Early Intervention Foundn, 2012–15. FRSA 1998. *Publications:* campaign and policy reports, articles on children, families, communities and inequalities. *Recreations:* family, gardening, cycling, heritage. *Address:* Office of the Children's Commissioner, Sanctuary Buildings, Great Smith Street, SW1P 3BT.

LONGFORD, Earldom of; *cr* 1785; title not used by 8th Earl (*see* Pakenham, T. F. D.).

LONGHURST, Andrew Henry, FCIB; FBCS; Deputy Chairman, Royal London Assurance Society Ltd, 2000–02; *b* 23 Aug. 1939; *s* of Henry and Connie Longhurst; *m* 1962, Margaret; one *s* two *d.* *Educ:* Nottingham University (BSc Hons). FBCS 1968; FCIB (FCBSI 1990). Computer systems consultancy, 1961; Cheltenham & Gloucester Building Society: Data Processing Manager, 1967; Asst Gen. Manager (Admin), 1970; Dep. Gen. Manager, 1977; Chief Exec. and Dir, 1982–95; Cheltenham & Gloucester plc: Chief Exec., 1995–96; Dir, 1995–98; Chm., 1997–98; Gp Dir Customer Finance, and Dir, Lloyds TSB Group plc, 1997–98; Chm., United Assurance Gp plc, 1998–2000. Director: Lloyds Bank plc, 1995–98; TSB Bank plc, 1995–98; Chairman, 1997–98: Lloyds UDT Ltd; Lloyds Bowmaker Ltd; United Dominions Trust Ltd; Dir, Cardnet Merchant Services Ltd, 1997–98. Non-executive Director: Hermes Focus (formerly Hermes Lens) Asset Management, 1998–2009 (Chm., 2008–09); Thames Water Plc, 1998–2000; Abbey National plc, 2005–08. Mem. Council, Univ. of Glos, 2004–12. CCMI (CBIM 1989); FRSA. Chm., Council of Mortgage Lenders, 1994. *Recreation:* golf. *Address:* Riverhaven, Riverside Road East, Newton Ferrers, Plymouth PL8 1AE.

LONGHURST, Prof. James William Stuart, PhD; CSci, CEnv, FIEnvSc; Professor of Environmental Science, since 1996, Associate Dean (Learning, Teaching and the Student Experience), Faculty of Environment and Technology, since 2010, and Assistant Vice Chancellor, Environment and Sustainability, since 2011, University of the West of England; *b* 25 Feb. 1958; *s* of late Leonard Longhurst, DFC and bar, and Isabella (*née* Laing); *m* 1984, Denise Barlow; two *d.* *Educ:* Univ. of Plymouth (BSc Hons Envmtl Sci. 1980); Univ. of Aston (MSc Resource Utilisation and Envmtl Sci. 1981); Univ. of Birmingham (PhD 1983). Envmtl Officer, Gtr Manchester Council, 1984–86; Dir, Atmospheric Res. and Inf. Centre, Dept of

Envmtl and Geographical Scis, Manchester Poly., later Manchester Metropolitan Univ., 1986–96; University of the West of England: Associate Dean and Hd, Dept of Envmtl Scis, 1996–2001; Associate Dean: Res. and Ext. Affairs, 2001–03; (Academic), Faculty of Applied Scis, 2003–07; (Envmt and Ext. Affairs), Faculty of Envmt and Technol., 2007–10; Co-Dir, Inst. for Sustainability, Health and Envmt, 2008–14. Visiting posts: Swedish Envmtl Protection Agency, 1988; Academia Istropolitana, Bratislava, 1994; Univ. Poly. Catalonia, Barcelona, 1996. Series Ed., Advances in Air Pollution, 1997–2007; Mem., Scientific Adv. Cttee, Advances in Transport, 2000–03; Mem., Editl Adv. Bd, The Environmentalist, 1995–. Mem., 1999–2000, Chm., 2006–, QAA Benchmarking Rev. Panel for Earth Scis, Envmtl Scis and Envmtl Studies. Higher Education Academy: Co-Chair, Adv. Bd for Geog., Earth and Envmtl Scis Subject Centre, 2008–09; Mem., 2012–, Chair, 2013–14, Educn for Sustainable Develt Adv. Gp. Member: Gt Western Res. Sustainability Panel, 2005–11 (Chm., 2008–11); Low Carbon South West (formerly Bristol Envmtl Technology Partnership Bd), 2007–; Low Carbon Consensus Panel, Acad. of Sci. of S Africa, 2009–11. Mem. Bd, Science Council, 2001–03. Chair, Envmt and Global Changes Panel, Portuguese Foundn for Sci. and Technol., 2012–13. Mem., 1982–, Fellow, 1994, Chm. Council, 2000–06, Vice Pres., 2006–, Instn of Envmtl Scis; Co. Sec., Instn of Envmtl Scis Ltd, 2009–; Mem., Environmental Protection, UK (formerly Nat. Soc. for Clean Air and Envmtl Protection), 1986–; Founder Mem., Inst. Air Quality Mgt, 2002–. Vice Chm., 2002–04, Chm., 2004–06, 2007–09, Cttee of Heads of Envmtl Scis. Mem., Bd of Dirs, Soc. of the Envmt, 2004–06. MIEnvSc 1982, FIEnvSc 1994; FHEA (ILTM 2001); CEnv 2004; CSci 2011; Fellow, Wessex Inst. of GB, 2004. *Publications:* editor: Acid Deposition: sources, effects and controls, 1989; Acid Deposition: origins, impacts and abatement strategies, 1991; Air Pollution VIII, 2000; Air Quality Management, 2000; Local and Regional Aspects of Air Quality Management, 2004; (with C. A. Brebbia) Air Pollution VIII, 2000, XIV, 2006, XVI, 2008, XVIII, 2010, XIX, 2011, XX, 2012, XXI, 2013, XXII, 2014; Urban Transport and the Environment, 2012; contrib. numerous refereed scientific papers to learned jls incl. Atmospheric Envmt, Envmtl Pollution, Jl Envmtl Mgt, Urban Studies, Water, Air and Soil Pollution, Local Envmt, Jl of Envmtl Planning and Mgt. *Recreations:* reading, walking in the Alps, football (sadly now only watching West Ham United). *Address:* University of the West of England, Frenchay Campus, Coldharbour Lane, Bristol BS16 1QY; 8 Kent Road, Bishopston, Bristol BS7 9DN.

LONGHURST, William Jesse; HM Diplomatic Service; Ambassador to Cambodia, since 2014; *b* Chelmsford, 7 Feb. 1967; *s* of William Peter Longhurst and Gillian Carey Longhurst (*née* Hardwick); *m* 2006, Kathryn Scheding; one *s* three *d*. *Educ:* King Edward VI Grammar Sch., Chelmsford; Univ. of Sheffield (BA Hons Japanese and Business Studies). Joined Diplomatic Service, 1990; Third Sec., 1992–93, Second Sec., 1993–95, Seoul; First Sec., Tokyo, 1995–98; Hd, Exports to Japan Unit, DTI, London (on secondment), 1998–2001; First Sec., UK Mission to the UN, NY, 2001–06; Dep. Hd of Mission and HM Consul-Gen., Belgrade, 2007–11; Dep. Hd, ASEAN Dept, FCO, 2011–13. *Recreations:* cello, piano, tennis, squash, badminton, golf (badly). *Address:* British Embassy Phnom Penh, c/o BFPO 5455, HA4 6EP. *T:* (23) 427124, *Fax:* (23) 427125. *E:* bill.longhurst@fco.gov.uk.

LONGLEY, Mrs Ann Rosamund; Head Mistress, Roedean School, 1984–97; *b* 5 March 1942; *d* of late Jack Gilroy Dearlove and of Rhoda E. M. Dearlove (*née* Billing); *m* 1964, Stephen Roger Longley (*d* 1979); one *s* two *d*. *Educ:* Walthamstow Hall School, Sevenoaks; Edinburgh University (MA 1964); PGCE Bristol University, 1984. Wife and mother, 1964–; Teacher, Toorak Coll., Victoria, Australia, 1964–65; Asst Housemistress, Peninsula C of E Sch., Victoria, 1966–67; Residential Teacher, Choate School, Conn, USA, 1968–73; Teacher, Webb School, Calif, 1975–78; Headmistress, Vivian Webb School, Calif, 1981–84. FRSA 1987. DUniv Sussex, 1991. *Recreations:* film, theatre, fishing, walking.

LONGLEY, Most Rev. Bernard; *see* Birmingham, Archbishop of, (RC).

LONGLEY, Clifford Edmund; journalist, author, novelist, broadcaster, lecturer and consultant; *b* 6 Jan. 1940; *s* of Harold Anson Longley and Gladys Vera (*née* Gibbs); *m* 1st, 1962, Anne Patricia Clough; 2nd, 1980, Elizabeth Anne Holzer; one *s* two *d*. *Educ:* Trinity Sch., Croydon; Univ. of Southampton (BSc Eng.). Reporter: Essex and Thurrock Gazette, 1961–64; Portsmouth Evening News, 1964–67; The Times, 1967–92 (Religious Affairs Ed., 1972–92; Asst Ed. (Leaders), 1990–92); leader writer and columnist, Daily Telegraph, 1992–95; editorial consultant and columnist, The Tablet, 1996– (Actg Ed., 1996); columnist, Daily Telegraph, 1995–2000; freelance broadcaster and author; regular contributor, BBC Radio 4: Thought for the Day, 2002–; The Moral Maze, 2005–12. Chm., Portsmouth Br., NUJ, 1966–67; Father of The Times NUJ Chapel, 1972–74 and 1986–89; Chm., Docklands Br., NUJ, 1988–89. Consultant, RC Bishops' Conf. of England and Wales, 1996–. Mem. Adv. Council, Three Faiths Forum, 1995–. Select Preacher, Oxford Univ., 1988. Principal author of reports: The Common Good, for Catholic Bishops' Conf. of England and Wales, 1996; Prosperity with a Purpose, for CTBI, 2005; Choosing the Common Good, for Catholic Bishops' Conf. of England and Wales, 2010. Member, Steering Committee: True Wealth of Nations Project, Inst. for Advanced Catholic Studies, Univ. of S California, 2006–10; Centre for Catholic Social Thought and Teaching, 2013–; Blueprint for Better Business, 2011–14. Pres., Bromley Neighbourhood Watch Assoc., 2010–. Hon. Fellow, St Mary's UC Strawberry Hill, Surrey Univ., 1999. MLitt Lambeth, 2012. Specialist Writer of the Year, British Press Awards, 1986; Gold Medallist, Peace Through Dialogue, Internat. CCJ, 2006. JP Bromley, 1999, transf. Supplementary list, 2010. *Publications:* The Times Book of Clifford Longley, 1991; The Worlock Archive, 1999; Chosen People, 2002; The Babylon Contingency (novel), 2013; Just Money: how Catholic social teaching can redeem capitalism, 2014; numerous articles and book chapters. *Recreations:* classical music (piano), grandchildren, reading, theology, musicology, pilot, Biggin Hill (general aviation). *Address:* 24 Broughton Road, Orpington, Kent BR6 8EQ. *T:* (01689) 853189. *E:* clifford.longley@ntlworld.com.

LONGLEY, Prof. Edna Mary, FBA 2006; Professor of English Literature, Queen's University Belfast, until 2002, now Emerita; *b* 24 Dec. 1940; *d* of Timothy Stanislaus Broderick and Agnes Watson McDiarmid; *m* 1964, Michael George Longley, *qv*; one *s* two *d*. *Educ:* Trinity Coll. Dublin (BA). Lectr, Sch. of English, QUB, 1963, then Reader. MRIA 2000. *Publications:* Poetry in the Wars, 1986; Louis MacNeice: a study, 1988; The Living Stream: literature and revisionism in Ireland, 1994; Poetry and Posterity, 2000; (ed) The Bloodaxe Book of 20th Century Verse, 2000; (with Declan Kiberd) Multiculturalism: the view from the two Irelands, 2001; (contrib.) Cambridge Companion to the Literature of the First World War, 2005; Yeats and Modern Poetry, 2013; *edited:* Edward Thomas: first and last poems, 1972; Selected James Simmons, 1978; Selected Paul Durcan, 1982; A Language Not to be Betrayed: selected prose of Edward Thomas, 1985; (jtly) Across a Roaring Hill: the Protestant imagination in modern Ireland, 1985; Marin Sorescu: the biggest egg in the world, 1987; Dorothy Hewett: Alice in wormland: selected poems, 1990; Culture in Ireland: division or diversity?, 1991; (jtly) Yeats Annual No 12: that accusing eye - Yeats and his Irish Readers, 1996; (jtly) Ireland (Ulster) Scotland: concepts, contexts, comparisons, 2003; Edward Thomas: the annotated collected poems, 2008; (jtly) Modern Irish and Scottish Poetry, 2011; (jtly) Incorrigibly Plural: Louis MacNeice and his legacy, 2012. *Address:* Seamus Heaney Centre for Poetry, School of English, Queen's University Belfast, Belfast BT7 1NN.

LONGLEY, Michael George, CBE 2010; freelance writer, since 1991; *b* 27 July 1939; *s* of Richard Cyril Longley and Constance Evelyn (*née* Longworth); *m* 1964, Edna Mary Broderick (*see* E. M. Longley); one *s* two *d*. *Educ:* Royal Belfast Academical Instn; Trinity Coll., Dublin (BA). Teacher, secondary schs in Dublin, Belfast and London, 1963–69; Combined Arts Dir, Arts Council of NI, 1970–91. Ireland Prof. of Poetry, 2007–10. Hon. LLD: QUB, 1995; TCD, 1999; Open, 2004. Literary prizes include: Eric Gregory Award, 1966; Cholmondeley Award, 1991; Queen's Gold Medal for Poetry, 2001. *Publications:* Poems 1963–1983, 1985; Gorse Fires (Whitbread Prize), 1991; The Ghost Orchid, 1995; Louis MacNeice: selected poems, 1998; The Weather in Japan (Hawthornden Prize, T. S. Eliot Prize), 2000; Snow Water (Librex Montale Prize), 2004; Collected Poems, 2006; (jtly) John Hewitt: selected poems, 2007; A Hundred Doors, 2011; (ed) Robert Graves: selected poems, 2013; The Stairwell, 2014. *Recreations:* jazz, classical music, ornithology, botany, cooking. *Address:* c/o Lucas Alexander Whitley, 14 Vernon Street, W14 0RJ. *T:* (020) 7471 7900.

LONGLEY-COOK, Robert Edward; Chief Executive, Hft (formerly Home Farm Trust), since 2010; *b* Midhurst, Sussex, 7 Dec. 1958; *s* of Hilary Longley-Cook and Virginia Longley-Cook (*née* Firth); *m* 1984, Sarah Waters; one *s* two *d*. *Educ:* Wellington Coll.; Bristol Univ. (BSc Hons Chem. 1980). With BP, 1980–2006; Exec. Dir, Fundraising, Mktg and Communication, WRVS, 2007–10. *Recreations:* running, fishing, theatre, golf. *Address:* Hft, 5/6 Brook Office Park, Folly Brook Road, Emersons Green, Bristol BS16 7FL. *T:* (0117) 906 1728. *E:* robert.longley-cook@hft.org.uk.

LONGMAN, Gary Leslie; Headteacher, King's (The Cathedral) School (formerly King's Cathedral School), Peterborough, 1994–2014; *b* 14 April 1954; *s* of late Bernard Longman and of Betty Longman; *m* 1977, Alison Mary Shepherd; one *s* one *d*. *Educ:* Univ. of Nottingham (BSc Hons Botany). FCollP 1994. Assistant science teacher: Dayncourt Sch., Nottingham, 1977–79; Queen Elizabeth's Sch., Mansfield, 1979–82; Hd of Biology, 1982–85, Hd of Sci., 1985–88, Toot Hill Sch., Bingham, Notts; Dep. Head Teacher, Heysham High Sch., Morecambe, Lancs, 1988–94. *Recreations:* my family, travel, walking, gardening, cooking, wine-tasting, DIY. *Address:* The Ridings, Station Road, Barnack, Stamford, Lincs PE9 3DW.

LONGMAN, Michael James; His Honour Judge Longman; a Circuit Judge, since 2006; *b* 5 July 1955; *s* of late Geoffrey James Longman and Beatrice Isobel Longman (*née* Dixon); *m* 1989, Gillian Sheila Nicholas; two *s* one *d*. *Educ:* Highgate Sch.; St John's Coll., Cambridge (Open Exhibn; BA 1977; MA). Called to the Bar, Middle Temple, 1978; in practice, S Eastern Circuit, 1978–90, Western Circuit, 1991–2006; Recorder, 2000–06. *Recreations:* family, music, walking, sailing. *Address:* The Law Courts, Small Street, Bristol BS1 1DA. *T:* (0117) 976 3030. *E:* HHJudge.Longman@judiciary.gsi.gov.uk.

LONGMAN, Peter Martin; Consultant, The Theatres Trust, 2006–08 (Trustee, 1991–95; Director, 1995–2006); *b* 2 March 1946; *s* of Denis Martin Longman and Mary Joy Longman; *m* 1976, Sylvia June Prentice; two *d*. *Educ:* Huish's School, Taunton; University College, Cardiff; Univ. of Manchester. Finance Dept and Housing the Arts Officer, Arts Council, 1968–78; Dep. Dir, Crafts Council, 1978–83; Dep. Sec., 1983–84, Dir, 1984–95, Museums and Galleries Commn. Director: Caryl Jenner Productions Ltd, 1983–87; Scottish Museums Council, 1986–95; Walpole Foundn, 1997–2005; Orange Tree Theatre Ltd, 2004–10 (Chm., 2008–10); Scarborough Th. Trust, 2005–11; Charcoalblue LLP (formerly Ltd), 2006–; Member: Council, Textile Conservation Centre Foundn (formerly Ltd), 1983–2011 (Chm., 1998–2000; Dep. Chm., 2000–11; Mem., Exec. Cttee, 1983–85, 1996–99); BTA Heritage Cttee, 1991–95; Exec., Council for Dance Educn and Trng, 1996–97; Adv. Council, Art in Churches, 1996–98; Chichester Fest. Theatre Trust, 1998–2003; Develt Cttee, ENO, 1999–2004; Covent Garden Area Trust, 2001–03; Theatre Planning and Historical Res. Cttee, Assoc. of British Theatre Technicians, 2006–. FRSA 1989. Hon. FMA 1995. *Publications:* Working Party Reports: Training Arts Administrators, Arts Council, 1971; Area Museum Councils and Services, HMSO, 1984; Museums in Scotland, HMSO, 1986; Act Now!, Theatres Trust, 2003; (contrib.) Theatre Buildings: a design guide, 2010; articles on theatre, the arts, museums. *Recreations:* discovering Britain, listening to music, studio ceramics, avoiding having to mow the lawn. *Address:* 37 Castle Road, Walton St Mary, Clevedon BS21 7DA. *T:* (01275) 544039.

LONGMORE, Rt Hon. Sir Andrew (Centlivres), Kt 1993; PC 2001; **Rt Hon. Lord Justice Longmore;** a Lord Justice of Appeal, since 2001; *b* 25 Aug. 1944; *s* of John Bell Longmore and Virginia Longmore (*née* Centlivres); *m* 1979, Margaret Murray McNair; one *s*. *Educ:* Winchester College; Lincoln College, Oxford (MA; Hon. Fellow, 2001). Called to the Bar, Middle Temple, 1966, Bencher, 1990. QC 1983; a Recorder, 1992–93; a Judge of the High Court, QBD, 1993–2001. Chm., Law Reform Cttee, Bar Council, 1987–90. Pat Saxton Meml Lectr, British Insce Law Assoc., 2001. *Publications:* (co-editor) MacGillivray and Parkington, Law of Insurance, 6th edn 1975, 9th edn 1997. *Recreation:* fell-walking. *Address:* Royal Courts of Justice, Strand, WC2A 2LL.

LONGRIGG, Anthony James, CMG 1992; HM Diplomatic Service, retired; Governor, Montserrat, 2001–04; *b* 21 April 1944; *m* 1967, Jane Rosa Cowlin; three *d*. Joined FCO, 1972; Second, later First, Sec., Moscow, 1975; FCO 1978; Brasilia, 1981; First Sec., FCO, 1985; Counsellor, Moscow, 1987; Counsellor, Madrid, 1991; Head, S Atlantic and Antarctic Dept, FCO, 1995–97; Minister, Moscow, 1997–2000.

LONGSDON, Col (Robert) Shaun, LVO 2006; Lieutenant, Queen's Body Guard of the Yeomen of the Guard, 2002–06; *b* 5 Dec. 1936; *s* of Wing Comdr Cyril Longsdon, Foxcote, Warwicks, and Evadne (*née* Flower); *m* 1968, Caroline Susan, *d* of late Col Michael Colvin Watson, OBE, MC, TD; three *s* one *d*. *Educ:* Eton. Regular Army Officer, 17th/21st Lancers, 1955–81: ADC to CIGS, 1961–62; Sen. Mil. Asst to CGS, 1975–77; CO, 17th/21st Lancers, 1977–79; GSO1 DS, NDC, 1979–81. Dir of Mktg, Knight Frank & Rutley, 1981–95; Man. Dir, Visual Insurance Protection Ltd, 1995–97. Queen's Body Guard of Yeomen of the Guard, 1985–2006: Ensign, 1987; Clerk of the Cheque and Adjutant, 1993. Col of Regt, 17th/21st Lancers, 1988–93. Gov., 1982–99, Mem. Council, 1988–99, RSC; Chm., Leonard Cheshire Home, Glos, 1995–99; Trustee, 2000–07, Chm., Central Region, 2000–07, Leonard Cheshire. Chm., Glos Br., SSAFA Forces Help, 2004–08. *Recreation:* country sports. *Address:* The Old Bakehouse, Eastleach, Cirencester, Glos GL7 3NQ. *T:* (01367) 850284. *E:* longsdon_shaun@hotmail.com. *Clubs:* White's, Pratt's, Cavalry and Guards.

LONGSTONE, Lesley, CB 2010; Chief Executive, Independent Police Complaints Commission, since 2014; *b* 9 Dec. 1964; *d* of John and June Broomhead; *m* 1985, Paul Longstone; two *s* one *d*. *Educ:* Univ. of Sheffield (BSc Hons Probability and Stats 1986). Civil Service: Manpower Services Commn, then Employment Service, later DfEE, 1985–2001; on secondment to Australian Dept of Employment, 2000–01; Department for Education and Skills, later Department for Children, Schools and Families, then Department for Education: Divl Manager, Sch. Diversity, 2001–03; Actg Dir, Secondary Educn, 2003–04; Higher Educn Bill Manager and Dir, Internat. Strategy, 2004–05; Dir, Schs White Paper Implementation, subseq. Sch. Formation, 2006–07; Director General: Young People, 2007–10; Infrastructure and Funding, 2010–11; Chief Exec. and Sec. for Educn, Ministry of Educn, NZ, 2011–13; Lead Investigator, MoD, 2013–14. *Recreations:* Church, family. *Address:* Independent Police Complaints Commission, 90 High Holborn, WC1V 6BH.

LONGSTRETH THOMPSON, Francis Michael; *see* Thompson, Francis M. L.

LONGUET-HIGGINS, Michael Selwyn, FRS 1963; Senior Research Physicist, University of California at San Diego, 1989–2001, now Research Physicist Emeritus; Adjunct Professor, Scripps Institution of Oceanography, La Jolla, California, since 1989; Fellow, Trinity College, Cambridge, since 1969; *b* 8 Dec. 1925; *s* of late Henry Hugh Longuet and Albinia Cecil Longuet-Higgins; *m* 1958, Joan Redmayne Tattersall; two *s* two *d*. *Educ:* Winchester Coll. (Schol.); Trinity Coll., Cambridge (schol.; BA); Rayleigh Prize, 1951; PhD Cantab 1951. Admiralty Research Lab., Teddington, 1945–48; Res. Student, Cambridge, 1948–51;

Commonwealth Fund Fellowship, 1951–52; Res. Fellow, Trinity Coll., Cambridge, 1951–55; Nat. Inst. of Oceanography, 1954–69; Royal Soc. Res. Prof., Univ. of Cambridge, 1969–89. Visiting Professor: MIT, 1958; Institute of Geophysics, University of California, 1961–62; Univ. of Adelaide, 1964; Prof. of Oceanography, Oregon State Univ., 1967–69. Foreign Associate, US Nat. Acad. of Sci., 1979. Hon. DTech Tech. Univ. of Denmark, 1979; Hon. LLD Glasgow, 1979. Sverdrup Gold Medal, Amer. Meteorol Soc., 1983; Internat. Coastal Engrg Award, Amer. Soc. of Civil Engineers, 1984; Oceanography Award, Soc. for Underwater Technol., 1990. *Publications:* papers in applied mathematics, esp. physical oceanography, dynamics of sea waves and currents. *Recreations:* music, mathematical toys. *Address:* Gage Farm, Comberton, Cambridge CB23 7DH.

LONGWORTH, Ian Heaps, CBE 1994; PhD; FSA, FSAScot; Keeper of Prehistoric and Romano-British Antiquities, British Museum, 1973–95; *b* 29 Sept. 1935; *yr s* of late Joseph Longworth and Alice (*née* Heaps); *m* 1967, Clare Marian Titford; one *s* one *d. Educ:* King Edward VII, Lytham; Peterhouse, Cambridge. Open and Sen. Scholar, Matthew Wren Student, 1957, MA, PhD, Cantab. Temp. Asst Keeper, Nat. Museum of Antiquities of Scotland, 1962–63; Asst Keeper, Dept of British and Medieval Antiquities, Brit. Mus., 1963–69; Asst Keeper, Dept of Prehistoric and Romano-British Antiquities, Brit. Mus., 1969–73. Member: Ancient Monuments Bd for England, 1977–84; Ancient Monuments Adv. Cttee, Historic Buildings and Monuments Commn, 1991–94. Chairman: Area Archaeol. Adv. Cttee for NW England, 1978–79; Standing Conf. of London Archaeol., 2003–05. Hon. Sec., 1966–74, Vice-Pres., 1976–80, Hon. Life Mem., 2002, Prehistoric Soc.; Sec., 1974–79, Vice-Pres., 1985–89, Soc. of Antiquaries of London. Chm. Adv. Bd, Alexander Keiller Mus., Avebury, 1994–2005. *Publications:* Yorkshire (Regional Archaeologies Series), 1965; (with G. J. Wainwright) Durrington Walls—excavations 1966–68, 1971; Collared Urns of the Bronze Age in Great Britain and Ireland, 1984; Prehistoric Britain, 1985; (with I. A. Kinnes) Catalogue of the Excavated Prehistoric and Romano-British Material in the Greenwell Collection, 1985; (ed with J. Cherry) Archaeology in Britain since 1945, 1986; (with A. Ellison and V. Rigby) Excavations at Grimes Graves, Norfolk, 1972–76, Fasc. 2, 1988, (*et al.*) Fasc. 3, 1991, Fasc. 4, 1992, Fasc. 5, 1996, Fasc. 6, 2012; articles in various learned jls on topics of prehistory. *Address:* 2 Hurst View Road, South Croydon, Surrey CR2 7AG. *T:* (020) 8688 4960.

LONGWORTH, John; Chairman, SVA Ltd, since 2008; Director General, British Chambers of Commerce, since 2011; *b* Bolton, 14 May 1958; *s* of Norman and Edith Longworth; *m* 1983, Sheila McGivern; one *s* one *d. Educ:* Smithills Moor Grammar Sch.; Univ. of Salford (BSc Hons; MSc; Postgrad. Cert. Microbiol.); Univ. of London (Chartered Co. Sec., Law and Accountancy, 1987). ACIS 1987. Asst Sec. and Dir, Trade Liaison, CWS Ltd, 1983–90; Dir, Tesco Stores Ltd, 1991–2003; Executive Director: Asda Stores, 2003–08; Asda Financial Services Ltd, 2004–08. Dir, Barts and the London NHS Hosp. Trust, 2008–10. Non-executive Director: Cooperative Food Ltd, 2009–14; Nichols plc, 2010–. Hon. PhD BPP, 2013. *Publications:* Due Diligence in Relation to Consumer Products, 2000. *Recreations:* opera, arts, theatre, cycling, running, travel. *Address:* British Chambers of Commerce, 65 Petty France, SW1H 9EU. *T:* (020) 7654 5800. *E:* j.longworth@britishchambers.org.uk. *Club:* Reform.

LONGWORTH, Peter, CMG 2001; HM Diplomatic Service, retired; independent government affairs consultant, since 2012; *b* 26 May 1942; *y s* of late Frank Longworth and of Edith E. (*née* Robinson); *m* 1975, Christina Margareta, *d* of late Folke Wallin and Gun Wallin, Växjö. *Educ:* Chislehurst and Sidcup Grammar Sch.; Univ. of Sheffield (BA). Journalist, 1963–74: Labour and Ind. Corresp., Bristol Evening Post, 1964–66; Lobby Corresp., Western Daily Press., 1966–68; Diplomatic Corresp., Westminster Press., 1968–74; joined FCO, 1974; First Secretary: FCO, 1974–77; (Econ.), Bonn, 1977–81; Head of Chancery and HM Consul, Sofia, 1981–84; FCO, 1984–87; Counsellor (Econ. and Commercial), Copenhagen, 1987–91; Dep. Hd of Mission, Counsellor (Econ. and Commercial) and Consul Gen., Seoul, 1991–94; Consul-Gen., Johannesburg, and Dir of UK Trade Promotion and Investment, S Africa, 1994–98; High Comr, Zimbabwe, 1998–2001. Dir, Corporate and Govt Affairs, 2002–12, Interim Dir-Gen. and CEO, 2012–13, Commonwealth Business Council. Govt and Strategy Advr, Oval Observer Foundn, 2014–. Mem., Adv. Bd, Nollywood Business Frontiers, Lagos, 2008–. Editl Advr, OMFIF, 2015–. Mem., Royal African Soc. *Club:* Reform.

LONGWORTH, Wilfred Roy, AM 1986; MSc, PhD; FRSC, FRACI; Principal Director (formerly Director), Swinburne Institute of Technology and College of Technical and Further Education, 1970–86, retired; *b* 13 Dec. 1923; *s* of Wilfred Arnold Longworth and Jessie Longworth; *m* 1951, Constance Elizabeth Dean; two *d. Educ:* Bolton Sch.; Manchester Univ. (BSc, MSc, PhD). FRIC 1963; FRACI 1970. Commnd Royal Signals, 1944–46. Works Manager and Chief Chemist, Blackburn & Oliver, 1948–56; postgrad. res., Univ. of Keele, 1956–59; Lectr in Physical Chemistry, Huddersfield Coll. of Technol., 1959–60; Sen. Lectr in Phys. Chem., Sunderland Technical Coll., 1960–64; Head, Dept of Chem. and Biol., Manchester Polytechnic, 1964–70. Pres., World Council on Co-op. Educn, 1983–85. *Publications:* articles on cationic polymerisation in learned jls. *Recreations:* lawn bowls, gardening. *Address:* The Heights, 39–41 Mitcham Road, Donvale, Vic 3111, Australia. *T:* (3) 88418251.

LÖNNGREN, Thomas; Strategic Adviser, NDA Advisory Services Ltd, since 2011; *b* Sweden, 16 Dec. 1950; *m* 1988, Ann-Charlotte Fondelius; one *s* one *d. Educ:* Univ. of Uppsala (MSc Social Pharmacy 1976); Stockholm Sch. of Econs (Advanced Course in Health Econ. 1999). Pharmacist, 1976; Lectr, Pharmaceutical Faculty, Uppsala Univ., 1976–78; Sen. Pharmaceutical Officer, Dept of Drugs, Nat. Bd of Health and Welfare, Sweden, 1978–90; Sen. Pharmaceutical Consultant for Swedish health co-operation prog. in Vietnam, 1982–94; Dir of Ops, 1990–98, Dep. Dir Gen., 1998–2000, Med. Products Agency, Sweden; Exec. Dir, EMEA, 2001–11.

LONSDALE, 8th Earl of, *cr* 1807 (UK); **Hugh Clayton Lowther;** Baron and Viscount Lowther, 1797; Bt 1764; *b* 27 May 1949; *s* of 7th Earl of Lonsdale and Tuppina Cecily, *d* of late Captain G. H. Bennet; *S* father, 2006; *m* 1971, Pamela Middleton; *m* 1986, Angela M., *d* of Captain Peter J. Wyatt, RN and Mrs Christine Wyatt; *m* 1999, Elizabeth Margaret, *d* of Stanley Frazer Arnison. *Heir: half-b* Hon. William James Lowther [*b* 9 July 1957; *m* 1999, Angela Ann Tinker].

LONSDALE, Anne Mary, CBE 2004; President, New Hall, Cambridge, 1996–2008; Deputy High Steward, Cambridge University, since 2009 (Pro-Vice-Chancellor, 1998–2003; Deputy Vice-Chancellor, 2003–08); Provost, Nazarbayev University, Astana, Kazakhstan, 2010–12 (Trustee, since 2013); *b* 16 Feb. 1941; *d* of Dr Alexander Menzies and Mabel Menzies; *m* 1st, 1962, Geoffrey Griffin (*d* 1962); 2nd, 1964, Roger Harrison Lonsdale, *qv* (marr. diss. 1994); one *s* one *d. Educ:* St Anne's Coll., Oxford (BA Hons Lit. Hum. 1962; BA Hons Chinese (Oriental Studies) 1965; MA 1965; Hon. Fellow, 1996). Oxford University: Davis Sen. Schol. and Lectr in Chinese, St Anne's Coll., 1965–74; Univ. Adminr, 1974–90; Dir, External Relations, 1990–93; Sen. Associate Mem., St Antony's Coll., 1991–2011; Sec.-Gen., Central European Univ., Budapest, Prague, and Warsaw, 1993–96. Chairman: Conf. of Univ. Admin, UK and Ireland, 1991–93; Interdisciplinary Envmtl Studies Cttee, 1996–2001; Jt Chm., Assoc. of Univ. Admin, 1993–94; Member: Commonwealth Scholarships Commn, 1996–2002; Council of Senate, Cambridge Univ., 1997–2004; Council for At-Risk (formerly Assisting Refugee) Academics, 2006– (Hon. Sec., 2008; Chm., 2009–). Trustee: Open Society (formerly Inter-Univ.) Foundn, 1988–2014; Cambridge Commonwealth Trust, 1995–2005; Cambridge Overseas Trust, 1996–2005; Cambridge European Trust, 1998–2007; Newton Trust, 1999–2008; Moscow Sch. of Social and Econ. Scis, 1999–2008; British Assoc. for Central and Eastern Europe, 2000–08; Camfed Internat., 2006–10 (Chm., 2008–10); European Humanities Univ., Vilnius, 2007–. Chm., Syndics, Fitzwilliam Mus., 2002–08; Syndic, CUP, 2006–08; Chm., Mgt Cttee, Kettle's Yard, 2012–. Hon. Dr Tashkent State Univ. for Oriental Studies, 2001; Liverpool Hope, 2014. Cavaliere, Order of Merit (Italy), 1988; Officier, Ordre des Palmes Académiques (France), 2002. *Recreation:* travelling. *Address:* 74 French's Road, Cambridge CB4 3LA. *T:* (01223) 362131.

See also C. J. Lonsdale.

LONSDALE, Charles John; HM Diplomatic Service; Deputy Head of Mission, UK Delegation, Organisation for Security and Co-operation in Europe, since 2012; *b* Oxford, 5 July 1965; *s* of Prof. Roger Harrison Lonsdale, *qv* and Anne Mary Lonsdale, *qv*; *m* 2011, Maria Sadoyan. *Educ:* Merton Coll., Oxford (BA Mod. Hist. 1987). Joined FCO, 1987; Vienna, 1988–89; FCO, 1989; Third, later Second Sec., Budapest, 1990–93; FCO, 1995; First Sec., Moscow, 1998–2003; Dep. Hd, Afghanistan Gp, 2003–05, Dep. Hd, Human Rights, Democracy and Governance Gp, 2005–08, FCO; Ambassador to Armenia, 2008–11. *Recreations:* music, walking, cats. *Address:* c/o Foreign and Commonwealth Office, King Charles Street, SW1A 2AH.

LONSDALE, Prof. Roger Harrison, DPhil; FBA 1991; Fellow and Tutor in English, Balliol College, Oxford, 1963–2000, now Fellow Emeritus; Professor of English Literature, University of Oxford, 1992–2000; *b* 6 Aug. 1934; *s* of Arthur John Lonsdale and Phebe (*née* Harrison); *m* 1st, 1964, Anne Mary Menzies (*see* A. M. Lonsdale) (marr. diss. 1994); one *s* one *d*; 2nd, 1999, Nicoletta Momigliano. *Educ:* Hymers Coll., Hull; Lincoln Coll., Oxford (BA 1st class Hons 1957); DPhil (Oxon) 1962. National Service, RAF, commnd as Navigator, 1952–54. English Dept, Yale Univ., 1958–60; Oxford University: Bradley Jun. Res. Fellow, Balliol Coll., 1960–63; Reader in English Literature, 1990–92. *Publications:* Dr Charles Burney: a literary biography, 1965; *edited:* The Poems of Gray, Collins and Goldsmith, 1969; Vathek, by William Beckford, 1970; Dryden to Johnson, 1971; The New Oxford Book of Eighteenth-century Verse, 1984; The Poems of John Bampfylde, 1988; Eighteenth-century Women Poets: an Oxford anthology, 1989; The Lives of the English Poets, by Samuel Johnson, 2006. *Recreations:* music, book-collecting. *Address:* c/o Balliol College, Oxford OX1 3BJ.

See also C. J. Lonsdale.

LONZARICH, Prof. Gilbert George, PhD; FRS 1989; Professor of Condensed Matter Physics, since 1997, Director of Research, since 2012, and Fellow of Trinity College, since 1977, University of Cambridge. *Educ:* Univ. of California (BA 1967); Univ. of Minnesota (MS 1970); PhD British Columbia 1973; MA Cantab 1977. University of Cambridge: Demonstrator, Physics Dept, 1978–81; Lectr in Physics, 1981–90; Reader in Physics, 1990–97. *Address:* Department of Physics, Cavendish Laboratory, J. J. Thomson Avenue, Cambridge CB3 0HE. *T:* (01223) 764454; Trinity College, Cambridge CB2 1TQ; 6 Hicks Lane, Girton, Cambridge CB3 0JS. *T:* (01223) 742056.

LOOMBA, family name of **Baron Loomba**.

LOOMBA, Baron *cr* 2011 (Life Peer), of Moor Park in the County of Hertfordshire; **Rajinder Paul Loomba, (Raj),** CBE 2008; Founder and Executive Chairman, Rinku Group, since 1981; *b* Dhilwan, Punjab, India, 13 Nov. 1943; *s* of late Shri Jagiri Lal Loomba and Shrimati Pushpa Wati Loomba; *m* 1966, Veena; one *s* two *d. Educ:* DAV Coll., Jalandhar, Punjab, India; State Univ. of Iowa, USA. Founder and Chairman of Trustees: Shrimati Pushpa Wati Loomba Meml Foundn, 1997–; British Indian Golden Jubilee Banquet Fund, 1999–2014; India First plc, 1999–. Mem. Council, RIIA, 2002–09. Member: Bd, 2000–04, Pres.'s Council, 2004–06, London First; Bd of Develt, Oxfam, 2008–11; Vice President: Barnardo's, 2005–; Safer London Foundn, 2006–12; Chm., Friends of Three Faiths Forum, 2007–. Mem., All Party Parly Gp on India, on UN Women. Founding Patron, World Punjabi Orgn, 2002–; Patron, Patrons Council, Youth Business Internat., 2007–; Vice Pres. for Europe, Global Orgn for People of Indian Origin, 2008–11. Chm., Lib Dem Friends of India, 2014–. Mem., CPA. Mem., Bd of Govs, UEL, 2008–12. Freeman, City of London, 2000. FRSA 2004; MInstD. Paul Harris Fellow, Rotary Internat., 2001. Hind Rattan Award, India, 1991; Priyadarshni Acad. Global Award, 2006; Philanthropy Award, Forbes India, 2012; Lifetime Achievement Award, UN Assoc. of NY, 2014; Parman Patra Award, Punjab State, 2015. Pravasi Award (India), 2015. *Recreations:* travelling, reading, cooking. *Address:* Loomba House, 622 Western Avenue, W3 0TF. *T:* (020) 8102 0351, *Fax:* (020) 8993 2736. *E:* raj@loomba.com, loombar@parliament.uk. *Club:* Royal Automobile.

LOOMES, Prof. Graham, FBA 2010; Professor of Economics and Behavioural Science, University of Warwick, since 2009; *b* London, 5 Aug. 1950; *s* of Frederick and Gladys Loomes; one *s* two *d. Educ:* Christ's Hosp., Horsham; Westminster City Sch.; Essex Univ. (BA (Econ) 1970); Birkbeck Coll., Univ. of London (MSc (Econ) 1978). School teacher, 1970–77; Res. Officer, Dept of Econs, then Lectr, Health Care Res. Unit, Univ. of Newcastle upon Tyne, 1978–84; University of York: Sen. Lectr and Dir of Graduate Prog. in Health Econs, Dept of Econs and Related Studies, 1984–88; Sen. Lectr, 1988–91; Prof. of Econs, 1991; Co-Dir, Centre for Experimental Econs, 1988–95, (part-time) 1996, 1999–2000; Prof. of Econs and Co-Dir, Centre for the Analysis of Safety Policy and Attitudes to Risk, Univ. of Newcastle upon Tyne, (part-time) 1996, 1999–2000; Prof. of Econ. Behaviour and Decision Theory, UEA, 2001–09. *E:* g.loomes@warwick.ac.uk.

LOOSEMORE, Thomas; Deputy Director, Government Digital Service, Cabinet Office, since 2011; *b* Solihull, 22 May 1971; *s* of Geoff and Jean Loosemore; *m* 2003, Jo Angell; one *s* one *d. Educ:* Bristol Univ. (MEng Civil Engrg). Internet ed., Wired UK mag., 1995–97; web ed., Capital Radio, 1997–98; Sen. Producer, BBC News Online, 1998–99; Dir of Applications, Chello Broadband, 1999–2001; Hd of Broadband, BBC New Media, 2001–07; Digital Media Strategist, Ofcom, 2007–08; Hd of 4IP, Channel 4, 2008–10. *Recreation:* dinghy sailing. *Address:* Government Digital Service, Aviation House, 125 Kingsway, WC2B 6NH.

LOOSLEY, Brian; a District Judge (Magistrates' Courts) (formerly Metropolitan Stipendiary Magistrate), 1989–2010; *b* 20 Dec. 1948; *s* of late Bernard Allan Loosley and Barbara Clara Randle; *m* 1971, Christine Mary Batt; one *s* one *d. Educ:* Sir William Borlase Grammar Sch., Marlow; Leeds Univ. (LLB 1971). Admitted Solicitor 1974; Prosecuting Solicitor, Thames Valley Police, 1975–78; practised privately, 1978–89. *Recreations:* history, foreign travel.

LOPES, family name of **Baron Roborough**.

LOPES CARDOZO KINDERSLEY, Lydia Helena, (Lida), MBE 2015; owner, Cardozo Kindersley Workshop, since 1981 (co-owner, 1981–95 and since 1998); *b* 22 July 1954; *d* of late Prof. Dr Paul Lopes Cardozo and of Ottoline Baronesse van Hemert tot Dingshof; *m* 1st, 1986, David Kindersley, MBE (*d* 1995); three *s*; 2nd, 1998, Graham F. Beck. *Educ:* Royal Acad. of Fine Arts, Den Haag, Netherlands. David Kindersley's Workshop: Lettercutter, 1976; Partner, 1981; Founder Editor, Cardozo Kindersley Editions, 1989. Associate Mem., 1999–2003, Life Mem., 2003, Clare Hall, Cambridge. Member: Assoc. Typographique Internationale, 1974–; Wynkyn de Worde Soc., 1978– (Chm., 1988; Hon. Fellow, 2001); Double Crown Club, 1996–; Cttee, Hazlitt Soc., 2005–06. Patron, Michaelhouse Project, Cambridge, 1999–2013. Gov., Impington Village Coll., 1997–2000. Brother, Art Workers Guild, 2000–. Fellow, 1994, Honoured Fellow, 2007, Calligraphy and Lettering Arts Soc. Hon. Fellow, Magdalene Coll., Cambridge, 2014. *Publications:* Glass & Engraver, 1983; (with

David Kindersley) Letters Slate Cut, 1981, 3rd edn 2004; (with R. McKitterick) Lasting Letters, 1992; Oxford Handwriting Practice, 1993, 2nd edn 2006; The Cardozo Kindersley Workshop: a guide to commissioning work, 1996, 3rd edn 2004; (with Emma Lloyd-Jones) Letters for the Millennium, 1999; (with W. Graham Cannon) Kindersley at Addenbrooke's Hospital, 2000; (jtly) Optical Letter Spacing, 2001; (jtly) Apprenticeship, 2003; (with Michael Wheeler) The kindest cut of all, 2005; The Annotated Capital, 2009; with Tom Sherwood: Cutting through the Colleges, 2010; Cutting across Cambridge, 2011; Cutting around Cambridgeshire, 2012; (with Lottie Hoare and Tom Sherwood) Cutting into the Workshop, 2013; (with David Meara) Remembered Lives, Personal Memorials in Churches, 2013; (ed) Mr Eric Gill, 2014; (with Fiona Boyd and Tom Sherwood) David Kindersley, vol. I, The Boy, 2015. *Recreations:* letter writing, religion. *Address:* Cardozo Kindersley Workshop, 152 Victoria Road, Cambridge CB4 3DZ. *T:* (01223) 362170. *Club:* Athenæum.

LOPEZ, Paul Anthony; His Honour Judge Lopez; a Circuit Judge, since 2014; a Deputy High Court Judge (Family and Queen's Bench Divisions), since 2014; *b* Wolverhampton, 22 Oct. 1959; *s* of Anthony William Lopez and late Lilian Lopez (*née* Rowley); *m* 1984, Diana Douglas Black; two *d. Educ:* Pendeford High Sch., Wolverhampton; Univ. of Birmingham (LLB Hons). Called to the Bar, Middle Temple, 1982; in practice as a barrister, St Ives Chambers, Birmingham, 1983–2014; a Recorder, 2001–14; a Dep. High Court Judge (Family), 2013. Member: Nelson Soc.; 1805 Club. *Recreations:* history, working, collecting Nelson memorabilia, my family. *Address:* Wolverhampton Combined Courts Centre, Pipers Row, Wolverhampton WV1 3LQ. *T:* (01902) 481000; Birmingham Civil and Family Justice Centre, Bull Street, Birmingham B4 6DS. *T:* (0121) 681 4441.

LOPEZ CABALLERO, Alfonso; Ambassador of Colombia to the Court of St James's, 2002–06; *b* 17 Aug. 1944; *s* of Alfonso Lopez Michelsen and Cecilia Caballero de Lopez; *m* 1969, Josefina Andreu de Lopez; one *d. Educ:* Sch. of Foreign Service, Georgetown Univ., Washington (BSFS Internat. Affairs); INSEAD, Fontainebleau (MBA); Columbia Univ., NY (MA, MPhil Econs). Asst Manager, First Nat. City Bank of NY; Business Consultant, Arthur Young & Co.; Congressman, Colombia, 1986–90; Senator, 1990–94; Ambassador of Columbia to France, 1990–91; Minister of Agriculture, 1991–92; Ambassador to Canada, 1994–97; Minister: of the Interior, 1997–98; i/c Presidential functions (during several Presidential trips abroad). Govt negotiator with FARC guerrillas during peace process, 2000–01. *Publications:* Un nuevo modelo de desarrollo para el campo, 1988. *Club:* Jockey (Bogota).

LOPEZ-FABREGAT, Fernando; Ambassador of Uruguay to the Court of St James's and to Republic of Ireland and Iceland, since 2014; *b* Montevideo, Uruguay; *m* 1987, Maria Carolina Silveira; one *s* one *d. Educ:* Catholic Univ. of Uruguay (Master in Human Resources Mgt); Univ. of Republic of Uruguay (law degree). First Secretary: Pretoria, SA, 1991–93; Quito, 1993–97; Counsellor, Ottawa, 1999–2004; Dir, HR, Min. of Foreign Affairs, Uruguay, 2004–06; Consul Gen., Toronto, 2006–12; Dir Gen. for Internat. Econ. Affairs, Ministry of Foreign Affairs, 2012–14. *Address:* Embassy of Uruguay, 150 Brompton Road, SW3 1HX. *T:* (020) 7584 4200. *E:* urureinounido@mrree.gub.uy.

LOPPERT, Max Jeremy; writer on music, musicologist; *b* Johannesburg, 24 Aug. 1946; *m* 1972, Delayne Aarons. *Educ:* Univ. of Witwatersrand, Johannesburg (BA 1966); Univ. of York (BA Music 1971). Chief Music Critic, FT, 1980–96; Associate Editor, Opera, 1986–97. Vis. Music Schol., Univ. of Natal, 1998–99; residency: Rockefeller Foundn Study Center, Bellagio, Italy, 2004; Centro Studi Ligure, Bogliasco, Italy, 2005. Founder, Opera Sch. and Voice Acad., Music Sch., Univ. of Natal, 1999 (opened 2002). Hon. Res. Fellow, Univ. of Kwa Zulu Natal, 2007–. *Publications:* contrib. to: Opera on Record (ed Alan Blyth), 3 vols, 1979, 1983, 1984; The New Grove Dictionary of Music and Musicians, 1980; The New Grove Dictionary of Opera, 1992; Who's Who in Hollywood, 1993; (ed) Words and Music, 2003. *Recreations:* cinema, cooking, pottery. *Address:* Via Buonabitacolo 15/6, 31053 Pieve di Soligo, Italy.

LOPRESTI, Jack; MP (C) Filton and Bradley Stoke, since 2010; *b* Bristol, 23 Aug. 1969; *s* of Domenico and Grace Lopresti; *m* 1992, Lucinda Catherine Lovell Cope; two *s* one *d. Educ:* Brislington Comprehensive Sch. Worked for family catering and ice cream business, 1985–97; consultant and manager, financial services and residential property, 1997–2007. Mem. (C) Bristol CC, 1999–2007. Contested: (C) Bristol E, 2001; SW, Eur. Parlt, 2004. Territorial Army, 2006–12: gunner, 266 Battery, RA (Glos Vol. Artillery); served with 29 Commando RA in Afghanistan. Mem., RUSI. Member: Gen. George Patton Histl Soc.; Internat. Churchill Centre. *Recreations:* running, hill-walking, military and political history. *Address:* House of Commons, SW1A 0AA. *T:* (020) 7219 7070. *E:* jack.lopresti.mp@parliament.uk. *Club:* Military and Naval.

LORAINE-SMITH, Nicholas George Edward; His Honour Judge Loraine-Smith; a Circuit Judge, since 2002; *b* 24 Jan. 1953; *s* of Maj. Bernard Lawson Loraine-Smith, MC, and Rachel Anne Loraine-Smith; *m* 1980, Annabelle Catherine Schicht; two *d. Educ:* Eton Coll.; Oriel Coll., Oxford (BA English). Called to the Bar, Inner Temple, 1977; Jun. Treasury Counsel, 1994–99, Sen. Treasury Counsel, 1999–2002, Central Criminal Court; Asst Recorder, 1997–2000; a Recorder, 2000–02.

LORD, family name of **Baron Framlingham**.

LORD, Alan, CB 1972; Deputy Chairman and Chief Executive, Lloyd's of London, 1986–92; *b* 12 April 1929; *er s* of Frederick Lord and Anne Lord (*née* Whitworth), Rochdale; *m* 1953, Joan Ogden; two *d. Educ:* Rochdale; St John's Coll., Cambridge (BA 1950 (1st Cl. Hons); MA 1987). Entered Inland Revenue, 1950; Private Sec. to Dep. Chm. and to Chm. of the Board, 1952–54; HM Treasury, 1959–62; Principal Private Sec. to First Secretary of State (then Rt Hon. R. A Butler), 1962–63; Comr of Inland Revenue, 1969–73, Dep. Chm. Bd, 1971–73; Principal Finance Officer to DTI, subseq. to Depts of Industry, Trade, and Prices and Consumer Protection, 1973–75; Second Permanent Sec. (Domestic Econ.), HM Treasury, 1975–77. Man. Dir, 1980, Chief Exec., 1982–84, Dunlop Hldgs plc; formerly: Exec. Dir, Dunlop Hldgs; Man. Dir, Dunlop Internat. AG, 1978. Director: Allied-Lyons plc, 1979–86; Bank of England, 1983–86; Johnson Matthey Bankers, 1985–86. Chm., CBI Taxation Cttee, 1979–81. Mem. Council of Management, Henley Centre for Forecasting, 1977–82. Gov., NIESR, 1975–2013. Pres., Johnian Soc., 1985–86. *Publications:* A Strategy for Industry (Sir Ellis Hunter Meml Lecture, Univ. of York), 1976; Earning an Industrial Living (1985 Johnian Society Lecture). *Recreations:* reading, music, gardening. *Address:* Mardens, Hildenborough, Tonbridge, Kent TN11 8PA. *Club:* Reform.

LORD, Hon. Bernard, ONB 2007; President and Chief Executive, Canadian Wireless Telecommunications Association, since 2008; Chairman, Ontario Power Generation, since 2014; *b* 27 Sept. 1965; *s* of Ralph and Marie-Émilie Lord; *m* 1990, Diane Haché; one *s* one *d. Educ:* Mathieu-Martin High Sch., Dieppe; Univ. of Moncton, Canada (BScSoc Econs 1988; LLB 1992). Called to the Bar, New Brunswick, 1993; in private law practice, Founding Partner, LeBlanc, Desjardins, Lord, Moncton, 1995–99; Counsel, McCarthy Tétrault, 2007. MLA (Progressive C) Moncton E, NB, 1998–2007; Leader of Opposition, 1998–99; Premier of NB, 1999–2006; Pres., Exec. Council and Minister, 1999–2006: Intergovtl Affairs; resp. for NB Adv. Council on Youth; resp. for council on status of disabled persons. Leader, Progressive Cons. Party of NB, 1997–2006. Hon. LLD New Brunswick, 2001; St Thomas Univ.; Mt Allison Univ.; Hon. Dr Pol Sci. Moncton, 2002. Grand Officier, Ordre de la Pléiade, Internat. Assoc. of Francophone Parliamentarians, 2001. *Recreations:* golf, chess. *Address:* Canadian Wireless Telecommunications Association, 80 Elgin Street, Suite 300, Ottawa, ON K1P 6R2, Canada.

LORD, (Charles) Edward, OBE 2011; JP; Managing Director, Edward Lord Ltd, since 2015 (Principal, Edward Lord Consultants, 2002–15); *b* Littleborough, Lancs, 13 Jan. 1972; *s* of Charles Andrew Lord and Vivienne Marie Lord (*née* Fairbank, now Brittain); partner, Dr Meg John Barker. *Educ:* Bury Grammar Sch.; Univ. of Essex (BA Public Policy and Public Mgt 1994); BPP Law Sch. Mem., Nat. Exec., NUS, 1994–96. Dir, John Moores Univ. Trust, 1998–2000; Develt Dir, City Univ., 2000–02. Chairman: Public Private Partnerships Prog., 2005–09; Local Partnerships LLP, 2009–12 (non-exec. Dir, 2012–); Dep. Chm., Whittington Hosp. NHS Trust, 2008–10. Chm., Capital Ambition, 2011–; non-executive Director: London Strategic Housing Ltd, 2006–09; Parkwood Hldgs plc, 2011–12; Social Investment Business Ltd, 2013–. Mem. Bd, and Lead Mem. for Equality, LGA, 2004–13. Chm., Gp Bd, Amateur Swimming Assoc., 2013–15; Chm., Inclusion Adv. Gp, London FA, 2013–; Mem., Inclusion Adv. Bd, FA, 2013–14. Member: Council, Coll. of Optometrists, 2000–03; Council for Registration of Forensic Practitioners, 2006–09. Mem. Court, Univ. of Essex, 2011–. Chm., Sir John Cass's Foundn Sch., 2001–03; Governor: GSMD, 2002–09; City of London Sch., 2009–. Trustee: British Youth Council, 1995–97; Trust for London, 2001–05 and 2015–; Anne Frank Trust, 2006–09; Nat. Campaign for the Arts, 2012–; BiCon Continuity Ltd, 2014–. JP Central London, 2002. Mem., Court of Common Council, City of London, 2001– (Chairman: Licensing Cttee, 2010–13; Standards Cttee, 2013–). Freeman: City of London, 2000; Fletchers' Co., 2001; Leathersellers' Co., 2002; Liveryman, Broderers' Co., 2012–. *Publications:* (ed) Civic Ceremonial: advice on protocol to the Mayors of the London Boroughs, 2009. *Recreations:* contemporary and classical music, theatre, watching sport, urban and country walking, swimming, reading, good food, travel. *Address:* Nicholas House, 3 Laurence Pountney Hill, EC4R 0EU. *T:* (020) 7448 8014. *E:* contact@edwardlord.org. *Clubs:* Guildhall, MCC, Soho House; Middlesex County Cricket, Rochdale Amateur Football.

LORD, David William; QC 2009; *b* Farnborough, Kent, 28 Sept. 1964; *s* of John and Pat Lord; *m* 2004, Julia Fitzpatrick; two *s* one *d* and one step *d. Educ:* King's Sch., Rochester; Bristol Univ. (LLB Hons). Called to the Bar: Middle Temple, 1987; BVI, 2000. *Recreations:* ski-ing, golf. *Address:* 3 Stone Buildings, Lincoln's Inn, WC2A 3XL. *T:* (020) 2242 4937, *Fax:* (020) 3405 3896. *E:* dlord@3sb.law.co.uk.

LORD, Edward; *see* Lord, C. E.

LORD, Geoffrey, OBE 1989; Founder Trustee, 1989–2008, and Vice President, 2000–08, Adapt Trust (Founder Director, 1989–96); *b* 24 Feb. 1928; *s* of Frank Lord and Edith Lord; *m* 1955, Jean; one *s* one *d. Educ:* Rochdale Grammar Sch.; Univ. of Bradford (MA Applied Social Studies). AIB. Midland Bank Ltd, 1946–58; Probation and After-Care Service, 1958–76: Dep. Chief Probation Officer, Greater Manchester, 1974–76; Sec. and Treas., Carnegie UK Trust, 1977–93. Chairman: Unemployed Voluntary Action Fund (Scotland), 1990–95; Pollock Meml Missionary Trust, 1985–2004; Pres., Centre for Envmtl Interpretation, 1984–97. Member, Scottish Arts Lottery Bd, 1994–98; Council, NYO of Scotland, 1998–2013. Trustee: Home-Start (formerly Home-Start Consultancy) UK, 1993–98; Faith in Older People Trust, 2007–13; Murrayfield Dementia Project, 2008–13; BSS Ltd, 2009–15; Sec. and Trustee, Edin. Vol. Orgns' Trusts, 1996–2015. FRSA 1985. Hon. Fellow, Manchester Metropolitan Univ. (formerly, Manchester Poly.), 1987. *Publications:* The Arts and Disabilities, 1981; Access for Disabled People to Arts Premises: the journey sequence, 2003; Cathedrals for the Curious, 2011. *Recreations:* Church of the Good Shepherd Edinburgh, philately, walking, appreciation of the arts. *Address:* 9 Craigleith View, Ravelston, Edinburgh EH4 3JZ. *T:* (0131) 337 7623. *Club:* New (Edinburgh).

LORD, Jonathan George Caladine; MP (C) Woking, since 2010; *b* Oldham, 17 Sept. 1962; *s* of His Honour John Herent Lord and of (June) Ann Lord (*née* Caladine); *m* 2000, Caroline Commander; one *s* one *d. Educ:* Shrewsbury Sch.; Kent Sch., Connecticut (Schol.); Merton Coll., Oxford (BA Hist. 1985). Dir, Saatchi & Saatchi, 1998–2000; campaign manager, Anne Milton, MP, gen. election, 2005. Member (C): Westminster CC, 1994–2002 (Dep. Leader, 1998–2000); Surrey CC, 2009–11. Contested (C) Oldham W and Royton, 1997. Chm., Guildford Cons. Assoc., 2006–10; Dep. Chm., Surrey Area Conservatives, 2007–09. *Recreations:* cricket, theatre, walking in the Surrey Hills. *Address:* House of Commons, SW1A 0AA. *T:* (020) 7219 6913. *E:* jonathan.lord.mp@parliament.uk.

LORD, Peter Duncan Fraser, CBE 2006; Co-founder (with D. Sproxton), owner and Creative Director, Aardman Animations, since 1972; *b* 4 Nov. 1953; *s* of Peter and Margaret Lord; *m* 1976, Karen Jane Bradshaw; two *s* one *d. Educ:* Univ. of York (BA 1976). Films directed include: The Amazing Adventures of Morph, 1981–83; Conversation Pieces, 1982–83; Wat's Pig, 1996; Chicken Run, 2000; The Pirates!, 2012. Hon. Fellow, BKSTS, 2000. Hon. Dr Design UWE, 1995; DUniv York, 2003; Hon. LLD Exeter, 2007. Chevalier, Ordre des Arts et des Lettres (France), 2001. *Publications:* Cracking Animation, 1999, 3rd edn 2010. *Recreations:* cricket, comic books, walking. *Address:* Aardman Animations, Gas Ferry Road, Bristol BS1 6UN. *T:* (0117) 9848485. *Club:* MCC.

LORD, Peter Herent, OBE 1991; FRCS; Consultant Surgeon, Wycombe General Hospital, High Wycombe, 1964–90; *b* 23 Nov. 1925; *s* of Sir Frank Lord, KBE, JP, DL and Rosalie Jeanette Herent; *m* 1952, Florence Shirley Hirst; two *s* two *d. Educ:* Manchester Grammar Sch.; St John's Coll., Cambridge (MA, MChir). St George's Hosp., Salford Royal Hosp., Christie Hosp., Manchester, St Margaret's, Epping, St George's Hosp., 1949–63 (Captain, RAMC, 1952–53). Royal College of Surgeons: H. N. Smith Research Fellow, 1964; Penrose May Teacher, 1970; Mem. Council, 1978–90; Vice-Pres., 1986–88. *Publications:* Cardiac Pacemakers, 1964; Pilonidal Sinus, 1964; Wound Healing, 1966; Haemorrhoids, 1969; Hydrocoele, 1972, Surgery in Old Age, 1980. *Recreations:* sailing, fishing. *Address:* Sunrise Senior Living, 30–34 Station Road, Beaconsfield, Bucks HP9 1AB. *T:* (01494) 739600.

LORD, Richard Denyer; QC 2002; *b* 2 Jan. 1959; *s* of Arthur James Lord and Daphne Anne Lord (now Beaumont); *m* 1992, Alexandra Barnes; one *s* two *d. Educ:* Stowe Sch.; Sidney Sussex Coll., Cambridge (MA). Called to the Bar, Inner Temple, 1981. Exec. Dir, Union Foundn, 2002–; Trustee, Web of Hope, 2003–. *Publications:* Controlled Drugs: law and practice, 1984; (with Simon Salzedo) Guide to the Arbitration Act 1996, 1996; (with R. Aikens and M. Bools) Bills of Lading, 2006; (ed jtly) Climate Change Liability, 2011. *Recreations:* cricket, reggae music, planting trees. *Address:* Brick Court Chambers, 7–8 Essex Street, WC2R 3LD. *T:* (020) 7379 3550, *Fax:* (020) 7379 3558. *E:* richard.lord@brickcourt.co.uk. *Club:* MCC.

LORD, Stuart; Lay Member, Fitness to Practise Panel, General Medical Council, 2006–14; *b* 10 Feb. 1951; *yr s* of William Ughtred Lord and Sybil Lord (*née* Greenhalgh); *m* 1970, Dwynwen Williams; one *s* one *d. Educ:* Manchester Grammar Sch.; University Coll. of Swansea (BScEcon Hons). DHSS, later DSS, then Department for Work and Pensions, 1972–2002; Principal Private Sec. to Sec. of State, 1988–91; Asst Sec. seconded to DoE, 1991; seconded to Prudential Life and Pensions, 1993; Head of Security, Benefits Agency, 1993–94; Head of Planning and Finance Divisions, and Prin. Finance Officer, 1994–98; Head of Transport and Corporate Directorate, Govt Office for London (on secondment), 1998–2000; Dir, Modernisation Strategy, Service Strategy and Commercial Partnerships, 2000–02. Non-exec. Dir, Richmond and Twickenham PCT, 2003–07. *Publications:* (contrib.) Economics of Unemployment, 1981. *Recreations:* travel, photography, consumer electronics. *Address:* 49 Ditton Reach, Thames Ditton, Surrey KT7 0XB.

LORD, Hon. Timothy Michael; QC 2008; *b* Cambridge, 10 Feb. 1966; *s* of Baron Framlingham, *qv*; *m* 2001, Amanda Jane Green; two *s*. *Educ:* Bedford Modern Sch.; Christ's Coll., Cambridge (BA 1st Cl. Hons Law 1987; MA). Admitted solicitor, 1991; Slaughter & May, 1989–92. Called to the Bar, Inner Temple, 1992; in practice at the Bar, 1993–. Sec., London Common Law and Commercial Bar Assoc., 2000–06. *Recreations:* Rugby (Cambridge blue 1986), cricket (playing Mem., MCC), sailing, ski-ing, golf. *Address:* Brick Court Chambers, 7–8 Essex Street, WC2R 3LD. *T:* (020) 7379 3550, *Fax:* (020) 7379 3558. *Club:* MCC.

LOREN, Sophia; film actress; *b* 20 Sept. 1934; *d* of Ricardo Scicolone and Romilda Villani; *m* 1957, Carlo Ponti (*d* 2007), film producer (marriage annulled in Juarez, Mexico, Sept. 1962; marriage in Paris, France, April 1966); two *s*. *Educ:* parochial sch. and Teachers' Institute, Naples. First leading role in, Africa sotto i Mari, 1952; acted in many Italian films, 1952–55; subsequent films include: The Pride and the Passion, Boy on a Dolphin, Legend of the Lost, 1957; The Key, Desire under the Elms, Houseboat, 1958; The Black Orchid (Venice Film Festival Award, 1958), That Kind of Woman, 1959; It Started in Naples, Heller in Pink Tights, A Breath of Scandal, 1960; The Millionairess, Two Women (Cannes Film Festival Award, 1961), Madame sans Gêne, El Cid, 1961; Boccaccio 70, 1962; Five Miles to Midnight, 1963; Yesterday, Today and Tomorrow, The Fall of the Roman Empire, Marriage, Italian Style, 1964; Operation Crossbow, Lady L, 1965; Judith, Arabesque, 1996; A Countess from Hong Kong, 1967; Sunflower, 1970; The Priest's Wife, 1971; Man of La Mancha, 1972; The Voyage, 1973; The Verdict, 1974; A Special Day, The Cassandra Crossing, 1977; Firepower, 1979; Blood Feud, 1980; Running Away, 1989; Saturday, Sunday and Monday, 1990; Prêt-à-Porter, 1994; Between Strangers, 2003; Nine, 2009. Chevalier, Legion of Honour (France), 1991. *Publications:* Eat with Me, 1972; Sophia Loren on Woman and Beauty, 1984; Yesterday, Today, Tomorrow: my life, 2014; *relevant publication:* Sophia: living and loving, by A. E. Hotchner, 1979. *Address:* Case Postale 430, 1211 Geneva 12, Switzerland.

LORENZ, Andrew Peter Morrice; Chairman, Financial Communications Group, FTI Consulting (formerly Financial Dynamics), since 2006 (Managing Director and Head of Industrials Group, 2001–06); *b* 22 June 1955; *s* of Hans Viktor Lorenz and Catherine Jesse Cairns Lorenz (*née* James); *m* 1988, Helen Marianne Alway; two *s*. *Educ:* Stamford Sch., Lincs; Worcester Coll., Oxford (MA Mod. Hist.). The Journal, Newcastle: News Reporter, 1978–80; Educn Correspondent, 1980–81; Industrial Correspondent, 1981–82; Business Correspondent, The Scotsman, 1982–86; City Correspondent, 1986–88, Dep. City Editor, 1988–89, Sunday Telegraph; Industrial Editor, 1989–95, Business Editor, 1995, Sunday Times; joined FTI Strategic Communications, London, 2000. Business Journalist of the Year, UK Press Awards, 1999; Business Journalist of the Year, Corp. of London, 2000. *Publications:* A Fighting Chance: British manufacturing industry in the 1980s, 1989; BZW: the first ten years, 1996; Lurssen: the story of a shipbuilder, 1997; Rover Reborn: the road to BMW, 1999; (jtly) End of the Road: BMW and Rover - a brand too far, 2000, 2nd edn as End of the Road: the true story of the downfall of Rover, 2005; Kumar Bhattacharyya: the unsung guru, 2002; GKN: the making of a business, 1759–2009, 2009. *Recreations:* film, music, sport. *Address:* Brook House, Monkey Island Lane, Bray, Maidenhead, Berks SL6 2ED.

LORIMER, Prof. (Andrew) Ross, CBE 2004; MD; FRCP, FRCPE, FRCPGlas, FMedSci; President, Royal College of Physicians and Surgeons of Glasgow, 2000–03; *b* 5 May 1937; *s* of James Lorimer and Katherine Lorimer (*née* Ross); *m* 1963, Fiona Marshall; three *s*. *Educ:* Uddingston Grammar Sch.; High Sch. of Glasgow; Univ. of Glasgow (MD Hons 1976). FRCPGlas 1972; FRCP 1978; FRCPE 1981. Res. Fellow in Medicine, Vanderbilt Univ., Nashville, 1961–63; Registrar in Medicine, Royal Infirmary, Glasgow, 1963–66; Lectr in Cardiol., Glasgow Univ., 1966–71; Consultant Cardiologist, Royal Infirmary, Glasgow, 1971–91; Hon. Prof. of Medicine, Glasgow Univ., 1991–2001. FMedSci 1998; FACP 2001; FFPH (FFPHM 2001); FRCPI 2002; Fellow, Bangladesh Coll. of Physicians and Surgeons, 2002; FRCS, FRCSE, 2003; FRACP 2004; FRCSI 2004; FCP(SoAf) 2004. DUniv Glasgow, 2001. *Publications:* Preventive Cardiology, 1988. *Recreations:* golf, cricket, hill-walking. *Address:* Woodlands Cottage, 12 Uddingston Road, Bothwell, Glasgow G71 8PH.

LORIMER, Sir Desmond; *see* Lorimer, Sir T. D.

LORIMER, Prof. George Huntly, FRS 1986; Professor, Department of Chemistry and Biochemistry, University of Maryland, since 1998; *b* 14 Oct. 1942; *s* of late Gordon and Ellen Lorimer; *m* 1970, Freia (*née* Schulz-Baldes); one *s* one *d*. *Educ:* George Watson's College, Edinburgh; Univ. of St Andrews (BSc); Univ. of Illinois (MS); Michigan State Univ. (PhD). Scientist, Max-Planck Society, Berlin, 1972–74; Research Fellow, Inst. for Advanced Studies, ANU, Canberra, 1974–77; Scientist, Society for Radiation and Environmental Research, Munich, 1977; Prin. Investigator, then Res. Leader, E. I. Du Pont de Nemours & Co., 1978–91; Dupont Fellow, Central Res. Dept, Dupont Co., Delaware, 1991–97. Adjunct Prof., Dept of Biochemistry, Univ. of Pennsylvania, 1992. Member: Amer. Soc. of Biochemistry and Molecular Biology; NAS, USA, 1997. Editor, Biochimica et Biophysica Acta, 1995; Mem Editl Bd, Jl of Biol Chem., 1998. Res. Award, Alexander von Humboldt Foundn, 1997. *Publications:* contribs to Biochemistry, Jl of Biological Chemistry, Nature, Science. *Recreations:* music, political history. *Address:* 7705 Lake Glen Drive, Glenn Dale, MD 20769–2028, USA. *T:* (home) (301) 3523679, (office) (301) 4051828. *E:* glorimer@umd.edu.

LORIMER, Ross; *see* Lorimer, A. R.

LORIMER, Sir (Thomas) Desmond, Kt 1976; Chairman, Northern Bank Ltd, 1986–97 (Director, 1983–97; Deputy Chairman, 1985); *b* 20 Oct. 1925; *s* of Thomas Berry Lorimer and Sarah Ann Lorimer; *m* 1957, Patricia Doris Samways; two *d*. *Educ:* Belfast Technical High Sch. Chartered Accountant, 1948; Fellow, Inst. of Chartered Accountants in Ireland, 1957. Practised as chartered accountant, 1952–74; Sen. Partner, Harmood, Banner, Smylie & Co., Belfast, Chartered Accountants, 1960–74; Chairman: Lamont Holdings PLC, 1973–96; Northern Ireland Electricity, 1991–94; Dir, Irish Distillers PLC, 1986–98. Chm., Industrial Develt Bd for NI, 1982–85; Pres., Inst. of Chartered Accountants in Ireland, 1968–69; Chairman: Ulster Soc. of Chartered Accountants, 1960; NI Housing Exec., 1971–75; Mem., Rev. Body on Local Govt in NI, 1970. *Recreations:* gardening, golf. *Address:* Windwhistle Cottage, 6A Circular Road West, Cultra, Holywood, Co. Down BT18 0AT. *T:* (028) 9042 3323. *Clubs:* Royal Belfast Golf, Royal Co. Down Golf (Co. Down).

LORNE, Marquess of; Archie Frederick Campbell; *b* 9 March 2004; *s* and *heir* of Duke of Argyll, *qv*. A Page of Honour to the Queen, 2015–.

LOSOWSKY, Prof. Monty Seymour, FRCP; Professor of Medicine and Head of University of Leeds Department of Medicine, St James's University Hospital, Leeds, 1969–96, now Emeritus Professor; *b* 1 Aug. 1931; *s* of Dora and Myer Losowsky; *m* 1971, Barbara Malkin; one *s* one *d*. *Educ:* Coopers' Company's Sch., London; Univ. of Leeds (Hons MB, ChB; MD). House appts, Leeds Gen. Infirmary, 1955–56; Registrar in Medicine, Epping, 1957–59; Asst, Externe Hôpital St Antoine, Paris, 1960; Research Fellow, Harvard Med. Unit, 1961–62; Lectr, Sen. Lectr, Reader in Medicine, 1962–69, Dean, Faculty of Medicine, 1989–94, Univ. of Leeds. Member: Leeds Eastern Health Authy, 1981–89; Specialist Adv. Cttee on General (Internal) Medicine, 1984–88; Systems Bd Grants Cttee B, MRC, 1984–88; Panel of Studies Allied to Medicine, UGC, 1982–89; British Digestive Foundn Sci. and Res. Awards Cttee, 1987–90; Yorks RHA, 1989–90; Working Gp, France Steering Gp on Undergrad. Medical and Dental Educn, DoH, 1990–94; Council, British Nutrition Foundn, 1991–2014 (Mem. Scientific Adv. Cttee, 1987–91; Scientific Governor, 1991–2014); GMC, 1991–96; CVCP Rep., Acad. and Res. Staff Cttee of DoH Jt Planning and Adv. Cttee, 1990–94 (Mem., General Purposes Working Gp, 1989–94); Chm., Other Studies and Professions Allied to Medicine Panel, HEFCE, 1995–97. Lectures: Watson Smith, RCPE, 1995; Simms, RCP, 1996. Pres., British Soc. of Gastroenterol., 1993–94. Chm., Coeliac Trust, 1983–95; Governor: Coeliac Soc., 1975–2005 (Chm., Med. Adv. Council, 1995–2003); British Liver Trust, 1999–2001 (Chm., Med. Adv. Cttee, 1999–2001). Examr for Membership, RCP, 1982–96; Academic Observer and Ext. Examr, Utd Examining Bd, 1994–96. Trustee, 1995–2012, Exec. Chm., 1997–2012, Life Pres., 2012–, Thackray Med. Mus. Gov., Leeds GS, 1988–2005. *Publications:* (jtly) Malabsorption in Clinical Practice, 1974; (ed) The Gut and Systemic Disease, 1983; (ed jtly) Advanced Medicine, 1983; (jtly) The Liver and Biliary System, 1984; (jtly) Clinical Nutrition in Gastroenterology, 1986; (jtly) Gut Defences in Clinical Practice, 1986; (jtly) Gastroenterology, 1988; Consensus in Clinical Nutrition, 1994; Getting Better: stories from the history of medicine, 2007; chapters and papers relating to haematology, hepatology, gastroenterology and history of medicine. *Recreations:* golf, medical history, walking, DIY, medical biography. *Club:* Royal Society of Medicine.

LOTEN, Alexander William, CB 1984; FCIBSE; Under Secretary, Department of the Environment, and Director, Mechanical and Electrical Engineering Services, Property Services Agency, 1981–85, retired; *b* 11 Dec. 1925; *s* of late Alec Oliver Loten and Alice Maud Loten; *m* 1954, Mary Diana Flint; one *s* one *d*. *Educ:* Churcher's Coll., Petersfield; Corpus Christi Coll., Cambridge Univ. (BA). CEng, FIMechE 1980; FCIBSE 1970. Served War, RNVR, 1943–46 (Air Engr Officer). Engineer: Rolls-Royce Ltd, Derby, 1950–54; Benham & Sons, London, 1954–58; Air Min. Work Directorate, 1958–64; Sen. Engr, 1964–70, Superintending Engr (Mechanical Design), 1970–75, MPBW; Dir of Works, Civil Accommodation, PSA, 1975–81. Pres., CIBS, 1976–77. Lt-Col, Engr and Railway Staff Corps RE, T&AVR, 1979–97. *Recreations:* walking, gardening, bridge. *Address:* Hockridge House, London Road, Maresfield, E Sussex TN22 2EH.

LOTEN, Graeme Neil; Executive Director, Imbabazi NGO, Rubavu, Rwanda, since 2013; *b* 10 March 1959; *s* of Richard Maurice Loten and Brenda Ivy Elizabeth Loten. *Educ:* Portsmouth Grammar Sch.; Liverpool Univ. (BA). Entered Diplomatic Service, 1981; Private Sec. to Ambassador to NATO, 1983–86; Third Sec., Khartoum, 1986–87; Second Sec., The Hague, 1988–92; Dep. Head of Mission, Almaty, 1993–97; Ambassador: to Rwanda and (non-resident) to Burundi, 1998–2001; to Mali, 2001–03; on temp. attachment to Dio. of Cyangugu, Rwanda, 2003–04; Ambassador to Tajikistan, 2004–09; Country Representative: Fondation Hirondelle, Sierra Leone, 2009–11; Fondation Hirondelle, Democratic Republic of Congo, 2011–12. *Recreations:* travel, tennis, Portsmouth FC. *Address:* c/o 12 Brunswick Gardens, Havant, Hants PO9 3HZ.

LOTERY, Prof. Andrew John, MD; FRCOphth; Professor of Ophthalmology, University of Southampton, since 2002; *b* 6 Dec. 1965; *s* of John Samuel Lotery and Caroline Lotery; *m* 1993, Helen Elizabeth Gore; two *s* one *d*. *Educ:* Queen's Univ., Belfast (MD 1997). FRCOphth 1994. Jun. hosp. appts, Belfast, 1989–91; trng in ophthalmology, Belfast, 1991–98; Molecular Ophthalmology Fellowship, 1998–2000, Asst Prof. of Ophthalmology, 2000–02, Univ. of Iowa. Current research developing novel treatments for age related macular degeneration. *Publications:* res. articles in jls incl. New England Jl of Medicine, Nature Genetics. *Recreations:* time with family, reading, running, travel. *Address:* Southampton Eye Unit, Southampton General Hospital, Tremona Road, Southampton SO16 6YD. *T:* (023) 8179 4590, *Fax:* (023) 8179 4120.

LOTHIAN, 13th Marquess of, *cr* 1701; **Michael Andrew Foster Jude Kerr, (Rt Hon. Michael Ancram);** PC 1996; DL; QC (Scot.) 1996; Lord Newbottle, 1591; Earl of Lothian, 1606; Lord Jedburgh, 1622; Earl of Ancram, Baron Kerr of Nisbet, Longnewton and Dolphinstoun, 1633; Viscount of Briene, Baron Ker of Newbattle, 1701; Baron Ker (UK), 1821; Baron Kerr of Monteviot (Life Peer), 2010; *b* 7 July 1945; *s* of 12th Marquess of Lothian, KCVO and Antonella (OBE 1997), *d* of Maj.-Gen. Sir Foster Newland, KCMG, CB; *S* father, 2004; *m* 1975, Lady Jane Fitzalan-Howard, *y d* of 16th Duke of Norfolk, KG, PC, GCVO, GBE, TD, and Lavinia Duchess of Norfolk, LG, CBE; *heir presumptive* to Lordship of Herries of Terregles; two *d*. *Educ:* Ampleforth; Christ Church, Oxford (BA); Edinburgh Univ. (LLB). Advocate, Scottish Bar, 1970. Contested (C): W Lothian, 1970; Edinburgh S, 1987. MP (C): Berwickshire and East Lothian, Feb.–Sept. 1974; Edinburgh S, 1979–87; Devizes, 1992–2010. Parly Under-Sec. of State, Scottish Office, 1983–87, NI Office, 1993–94; Minister of State, NI Office, 1994–97; Opposition front bench spokesman on constitutional affairs, 1997–98; Dep. Leader of the Opposition and Shadow Foreign Sec., 2001–05; Shadow Sec. of State for Internat. Affairs, 2003–05, for Defence, 2005. Member: Select Cttee on Energy, 1979–83; Intelligence and Security Cttee, 2006–10, 2011–. Chairman: Cons. Party in Scotland, 1980–83 (Vice-Chm., 1975–80); Cons. Party, 1998–2001. Chm., Northern Corporate Communications, 1989–91; Dir, CSM Parly Consultants, 1988–92; Mem. Bd, Scottish Homes, 1988–90. Chairman: Global Strategy Forum, 2006–; Gulf Policy Forum, 2007–. Grand Prior (England and Wales), Order of St Lazarus of Jerusalem, 2013–. DL Roxburgh, Ettrick and Lauderdale, 1990. Freeman: Devizes, 2010; City of Gibraltar, 2010. GCLJ 2013. *Recreations:* ski-ing, photography, folksinging. *Heir: b* Lord Ralph William Francis Joseph Kerr [*b* 7 Nov. 1957; *m* 1st, 1980, Lady Virginia FitzRoy (marr. diss. 1987); 2nd, 1988, Marie-Claire Black; four *s* two *d*]. *Address:* Monteviot, Jedburgh TD8 6UQ. *Clubs:* Beefsteak, Pratt's, White's.

See also N. R. Hurd.

LOTHIAN, Prof. Niall, OBE 2012; Professor, Graduate Business School, Heriot-Watt University, 1996–2011; President, Institute of Chartered Accountants of Scotland, 1995–96; *b* 27 Feb. 1948; *s* of Rev. Thomas Lothian and Jean Morgan Lothian (*née* Henderson); *m* 1971, Carol Miller; one *s* one *d*. *Educ:* Daniel Stewart's Coll.; Heriot-Watt Univ. (BA 1971). CA 1972. Lectr, Sen. Lectr, 1973–88, Prof. of Accounting, 1988–96, Director, 1991–93, Business School, Heriot-Watt Univ. Visiting Professor: IMEDE, Lausanne, 1979–80; Univ. of Witwatersrand, 1984; Mem., internat. vis. faculty, INSEAD, Fontainebleau, 1984–; Consultant: UNIDO, China, 1980; NZ Soc. of Accountants, 1992. Mem., Internat. Exec. Adv. Bd, Coll. of Finance and Accountancy, Budapest. Chm., Chiene + Tait, CA, 2005–08; non-exec. Dir, Stoddard Internat. plc, 1998–2002. Chm., Adv. Audit Bd, Scottish Parly Corp. Body, 2002–09. Chm., Inspiring Scotland, 2009–. Mem. Council, Edinburgh Internat. Fest., 2011– (Dep. Chm., 2014–). Trustee, Lloyds TSB Charitable Foundn for Scotland, 1997–99. Governor: George Watson's Coll., 1991–2004 (Chm., 1999–2004); RSAMD, later Royal Conservatoire of Scotland, 2007–11. *Publications:* How Companies Manage R&D, 1984; Measuring Corporate Performance, 1987; (jtly) Accounting, 1991; (contrib.) Ernst and Young Manager's Handbook, 2nd edn 1992; articles in professional jls. *Recreations:* graveyards, golf. *Address:* 30 Granby Road, Edinburgh EH16 5NL. *T:* (0131) 667 4429. *Clubs:* New (Edinburgh); Royal & Ancient Golf; Luffness New Golf.

LOTON, Brian Thorley, AC 1989; FTS; Chairman: Broken Hill Proprietary Co. Ltd, 1992–97; Atlas Copco Australia Pty Ltd, 1996–2001; Director, Australian Foundation Investment Co. Ltd, 1993–2001; *b* Perth, WA, 17 May 1929; *s* of Sir (Ernest) Thorley Loton and Grace (*née* Smith); *m* 1956, Joan Kemelfield; two *s* two *d*. *Educ:* Hale Sch., Perth; Trinity Coll., Melbourne Univ. (BMetEng 1953). Joined BHP as Cadet 1954; Technical Asst, 1959; Asst Chief Engr, 1961; Gen. Manager Planning and Develt, 1969, Gen. Manager Newcastle

Steel Works, 1970; Exec. Gen. Manager Steel Div., 1973; Dir, 1976; Chief Gen. Manager, 1977; Man. Dir, 1982; Chief Exec. Officer, 1984, Dep. Chm., 1991. Director: Nat. Australia Bank, 1988–99; Amcor Ltd, 1992–99. President: Aust. Inst. of Mining and Metallurgy, 1982; Australian Mining Industry Council, 1983–84; Business Council of Aust., 1990–92; Vice-Chairman: Internat. Iron and Steel Inst., 1988, 1992–94 (Chm., 1991–92); Defence Industry Cttee, 1976–88; Member: Aust. Sci. and Technol. Council, 1977–80; Aust. Manufg Council, 1977–81; Vict. Govt Long Range Policy Planning Cttee, 1980–82; Aust. Council on Population and Ethnic Affairs, 1980–82. Internat. Counsellor, The Conf. Bd, 1984–97. Pres., Vic. Br., Scout Assoc. of Australia, 1997–2002. Mem. Faculty Engrg, Melbourne Univ., 1980–83. FIE (Aust) 1984 (Hon. Fellow); FAIM 1973; FIDA 1980. *Address:* c/o GPO Box 86, Melbourne, Vic 3001, Australia. *Clubs:* Melbourne, Australian (Melbourne).

LOTT, Dame Felicity (Ann Emwhyla), DBE 1996 (CBE 1990); FRCM; soprano; *b* 8 May 1947; *d* of John Albert Lott and Whyla (*née* Williams); *m* 1st, 1973, Robin Mavesyn Golding (marr. diss. 1982); 2nd, 1984, Gabriel Woolf; one *d*. *Educ:* Pate's Grammar Sch. for Girls, Cheltenham; Royal Holloway Coll., Univ. of London (BA Hons French; Hon. Fellow, 1995); Royal Acad. of Music (LRAM; ARAM 1976; FRAM 1986). FRCM 2006. Début: ENO, 1975; Covent Garden, 1976; Glyndebourne, 1977. Particularly associated with Mozart and Richard Strauss, whose operas she has sung in Glyndebourne, Covent Garden, Cologne, Hamburg, Brussels, Paris, Vienna, Munich, Dresden, Milan, NY, Chicago and Japan; gives recitals worldwide; many recordings. Pres., British Youth Opera. Founder Mem., The Songmakers' Almanac. Hon. FGS 2014. Dr *hc*: Sussex, 1989; Sorbonne, 2010; Hon. DLitt Loughborough, 1996; Hon. DMus: London, 1997; RSAMD 1998; Leicester, 2000; Oxford, 2001. Wigmore Hall Medal, 2010. Bayerische Kammersängerin, 2003; Distinguished Musician Award, ISM, 2014. Officier, Ordre des Arts et des Lettres (France), 2000 (Chevalier, 1993); Chevalier de la Légion d'Honneur (France), 2001. *Recreations:* reading, gentle gardening. *Address:* c/o Askonas Holt Ltd, Lincoln House, 300 High Holborn, WC1V 7JH. *T:* (020) 7400 1700.

LOTT, Timothy; novelist and journalist; teacher of Creative Writing, Guardian Master Classes, since 2011; *b* Southall, Middx, 23 Jan. 1956; *s* of Jack and Jean Lott; *m* 1st, 1991, Sarigna Lavigna (*d* 2000); 2nd, 2007, Rachael Newberry. *Educ:* Greenford Co. Grammar Sch.; London Sch. of Econs and Pol Sci. (BA Govt and Hist. 1986). Reporter, Uxbridge Gazette, 1976–77; feature writer: Sounds, 1977–78; Record Mirror, 1978–79; Founder and publisher, Flexipop, 1980–83; researcher and producer, Mentorn Films, 1988–89; feature writer, Sunday Corresp. mag., 1989–90; teacher of creative writing, Brunel Univ., 2011. *Publications:* The Scent of Dried Roses (memoir), 1996 (PEN/J. R. Ackerley Prize for Autobiog.); *novels:* White City Blue, 1999 (Whitbread First Novel Award); Rumours of Hurricane, 2002; The Love Secrets of Don Juan, 2003; The Seymour Tapes, 2005; Under the Same Stars, 2012; The Last Summer of the Water Strider, 2015; for young adults: Fearless, 2007; How to be Invisible, 2013. *Recreations:* navel gazing, fence sitting, eating, tweeting, shopping, talking, dozing, observing, some racquet sports, occasional cigarette, cheese, theatre, Zen. *Address:* 51 Burrows Road, NW10 5SJ. *T:* 07812 043453. *E:* timlott@me.com.

LOUDON, Deborah Jane, (Mrs H. R. Woudhuysen); Partner, Saxton Bampfylde (formerly Saxton Bampfylde Hever), since 2010; Director General, Civilian Personnel, Ministry of Defence, 2005–07; *b* 4 June 1955; *d* of Joseph Buist Loudon and Joan Katherine Loudon (*née* Ede); *m* 1987, Prof. Henry Ruxton Woudhuysen, *qv*; two *s*. *Educ:* Malvern Girls' Coll.; Somerville Coll., Oxford (MA PPE). Home Office, 1977–2003: Private Sec. to Minister of State, 1983–84; Principal, Prison Service, 1984; Grade 5, Police Dept, 1993–99; HR Dir, 2000–03; Dir Gen., Security and Safety, MoD, 2003–05. Trustee, Crime Reduction Initiatives, 2011–. FCIPD 2002. *T:* (020) 7227 0820. *E:* deborah.loudon@saxbam.com.

LOUDON, Maj. Gen. Euan; *see* Loudon, Maj. Gen. W. E. B.

LOUDON, George Ernest; Chairman: Altius Holdings Ltd, 1999–2014; Pall Mall Capital Ltd, 2001–14; GAM Diversity Inc., since 2014; *b* 19 Nov. 1942; *m* 1968, Angela Mary Goldsbrough; one *s* one *d*. *Educ:* Christelijk Lyceum, Zeist; Balliol Coll., Oxford (BA); Johns Hopkins Univ., Washington (MA). Lazard Frères & Cie, Paris, 1967–68; Ford Foundn, New York and Jakarta, 1968–71; McKinsey & Co., Amsterdam, 1971–76; Amro Bank, Amsterdam: Gen. Man., 1976–83; Mem., Bd of Man. Dirs, 1983–88; Dir, Midland Group, 1988–92; Chief Exec., 1988–92, Chm., 1991–92, Midland Montagu; Chm., Helix Associates Ltd, 1993–2005. Non-executive Director: M&G Gp, 1993–94; Arjo-Wiggins Appleton, 1993–2000; Harrison/Parrott Ltd, 1993–; Global Asset Management, 1994–99; Logica CMG (formerly CMG) plc, 1998–2007; Evolution (formerly Beeson Gregory) Gp plc, 2001–04. Mem. Bd, Multiple Sclerosis Internat. Fedn, 1999–2007. Trustee and Chm., Finance Cttee, Royal Botanic Gardens, Kew, 2007–. *Address:* PO Box 34865, W8 7WL.

LOUDON, James Rushworth Hope; DL; Chairman, Caledonia Investments plc, 2008–12 (non-executive Director, 1995–2012); *b* Newbury, Berks, 19 March 1943; *s* of late Francis William Hope Loudon and Lady Prudence Katharine Patton Loudon (*née* Jellicoe); *m* 1975, Jane Gavina Fryett; two *s* one *d*. *Educ:* Eton Coll.; Magdalene Coll., Cambridge (BA Hons 1965); Stanford Business Sch., Calif (MBA 1971). RTZ Corp. Ltd, 1966–69; Samuel Montagu & Co. Ltd, 1971–72; Cons. Central Office, 1972–75; Overseas Containers Ltd, 1975–77; Blue Circle Industries plc, 1977–2001, Gp Finance Dir, 1987–2001. Non-executive Director: Lafarge Malayan Cement, 1989–2004; James Hardie Industries NV, 2002–08. Mem., Kent CC, 1977–81. Ind. Mem., Selection Panel, Kent Police Authy, 1994–98. Mem., Ind. Monitoring Bd, HMP Swaleside, 2013–. Mem., Fundraising Adv. Council, VSO, 1994–99. Governor: Univ. of Greenwich, 2001–10 (Dep. Chm., 2008–10); Royal Sch. for Deaf Children, 2002–05; Caldecott Foundn, 2002–12. Trustee: Kent, Surrey and Sussex Air Ambulance Trust, 2005–; Canterbury Cathedral Trust, 2005– (Dep. Chm., 2008–). High Sheriff, 2004–05, DL, 2011, Kent. DUniv Greenwich, 2011. *Recreations:* golf, cricket, ski-ing, opera, cabinet making. *Address:* Olantigh, Wye, Kent TN25 5EW. *T:* (01233) 812294, *Fax:* (01233) 813833. *E:* JLoudon@olantigh.fsnet.co.uk. *Clubs:* MCC; Rye Golf, Royal St George's Golf.

LOUDON, John Duncan Ott, OBE 1988; FRCSE, FRCOG, FFSRH; retired; Consultant Obstetrician and Gynaecologist, Eastern General Hospital, Edinburgh, 1960–87; Senior Lecturer, University of Edinburgh, 1962–87; *b* 22 Aug. 1924; *s* of late James Alexander Law Loudon and Ursula (*née* Ott); *m* 1953, Nancy Beaton (*née* Mann) (OBE 1992) (*d* 2009); two *s*. *Educ:* John Watson's Sch., Edinburgh; Wyggeston Sch., Leicester; Univ. of Edinburgh (MB, ChB 1947). FRCSE 1954; FRCOG 1973 (MRCOG 1956). National Service, RAF, 1948–50. House appts, Edinburgh and Cambridge, 1948–52; Registrar, Sen. Registrar and Consultant Obstetrician and Gynaecologist, Simpson Maternity Pavilion and Royal Infirm., Edinburgh, 1954–66. Formerly Examiner in Obstetrics and Gynaecology: Univs of Cardiff, Manchester, Leeds, Dundee, Glasgow, Aberdeen, Newcastle upon Tyne, Cape Town, RCSI, RCSE, RCOG and RACOG. Adviser in Family Welfare to Govt of Malta, 1976–81. Vice Pres., RCOG, 1981–84 (Mem. Council, 1966–72 and 1976–81). Member: Interim Licensing Authority for IVF, 1985–91; GMC, 1986–92. *Publications:* papers to obstetric and gynaecol jls. *Recreations:* bridge, reading. *Address:* 13/10 Ravelston Terrace, Edinburgh EH4 3TP. *T:* (0131) 332 4288. *Club:* Bruntsfield Links Golfing Society (Edinburgh).

LOUDON, Prof. Rodney, FRS 1987; Professor of Physics, Essex University, 1967–2008, now Emeritus; *b* 25 July 1934; *s* of Albert Loudon and Doris Helen (*née* Blane); *m* 1960, Mary Anne Philips; one *s* one *d*. *Educ:* Bury Grammar Sch.; Brasenose Coll., Oxford (MA, DPhil). Postdoctoral Fellow, Univ. of California, Berkeley, 1959–60; Scientific Civil Servant, RRE Malvern, 1960–65; Member, Technical Staff: Bell Labs, Murray Hill, NJ, 1965–66, 1970; RCA Labs, Zurich, 1975; Essex University: Reader in Physics, 1966–67; Dean of Sch. of Physical Scis, 1972–74; Chm. of Physics Dept, 1976–79 and 1988–89. Visiting Professor: Yale Univ., 1975; Univ. of California, Irvine, 1980; Ecole Polytechnique, Lausanne, 1985; Univ. of Rome, 1988 and 1996; Univ. of Strathclyde, 1998–2012. Chm., Bd of Editors of Optica Acta, 1984–87. Fellow, Optical Soc. of America, 1994. Thomas Young Medal and Prize, Inst. of Physics, 1987; Max Born Award, Optical Soc. of Amer., 1992; Alexander von Humboldt Prize, 1998. *Publications:* The Quantum Theory of Light, 1973, 3rd edn 2000; (with W. Hayes) Scattering of Light by Crystals, 1978; (ed with V. M. Agranovich) Surface Excitations, 1984; (with D. J. Barber) An Introduction to the Properties of Condensed Matter, 1989; papers in Nature, Phys. Rev., JL Mod. Opt., Jl Phys., etc. *Recreations:* music, gardening. *Address:* 3 Gaston Street, East Bergholt, Colchester, Essex CO7 6SD. *T:* (01206) 298550.

LOUDON, Maj. Gen. (William) Euan (Buchanan), CBE 2004 (OBE 1991); Chief Executive, St Andrews Links Trust, since 2011; *b* 12 March 1956; *s* of David Christie Buchanan Loudon and Doreen Mary Loudon; *m* 1981, Penelope Jane Head. *Educ:* Uddingston Grammar Sch.; Royal Military Acad., Sandhurst. Commnd Royal Highland Fusiliers, 1975; Adjt 1st Bn, 1980–83; Exchange Officer, CTC RM, 1983–85; Army Staff Coll., 1988; Bde Maj. 7th Armoured Bde, 1989–91; UN Monitoring Orgn, Zagreb, 1995; CO 1RHF, 1995–97; Mil. Sec. (A), 1997–99; HCSC, 1999; Comdr 39th Inf. Bde, 1999–2001; COS and Comdr Force Troops HQ NI, 2001–03; GOC 2nd Div., and Gov., Edinburgh Castle, 2004–07; Chief Exec., Edinburgh Military Tattoo, later Royal Edinburgh Military Tattoo, 2007–11. Chairman: St Andrews Links Ltd, 2012–; Tom Morris Internat., 2012–. FCMI 2003. QCVS 2002. *Recreations:* field sports, fishing, golf, music, farming. *Clubs:* Caledonian; New (Edinburgh).

LOUDOUN, 15th Earl of, *cr* 1633; **Simon Michael Abney-Hastings;** Lord Campbell of Loudoun, 1601; Lord Mauchline, 1633; *b* 29 Oct. 1974; *s* of 14th Earl of Loudoun and Noelene Margaret (*née* McCormick) (*d* 2002); *S* father, 2012; *co-heir* to Baronies of Botreaux 1368, Stanley 1456 and Hastings 1461. *Heir: b* Hon. Marcus William Abney-Hastings, *b* 1 Sept. 1981. *Address:* Wangaratta, Vic 3677, Australia.

LOUGH, Paula Jane; *see* Radcliffe, P. J.

LOUGHBOROUGH, Lord; Jamie William St Clair-Erskine; *b* 28 May 1986; *s* and *heir* of Earl of Rosslyn, *qv*. *Educ:* Eton Coll.; Bristol Univ.

LOUGHBOROUGH, Archdeacon of; *see* Newman, Ven. D. M. F.

LOUGHHEAD, John Neil, OBE 2011; FREng, FIMechE, FIET; Chief Scientific Adviser, Department of Energy and Climate Change, since 2014; *b* Derby, 24 Sept. 1948; *s* of Neil Loughhead and late Mary Charlotte Loughhead; *m* 2007, Ellen Tingle. *Educ:* Bemrose Sch., Derby; Imperial Coll., London (BSc (Eng), MSc; DIC). CEng 1984; FIMechE 1988; FIET 1995; FREng 2008. Res. technologist, GEC Mech. Engrg Lab., 1975–83; Manager, Thermofluids Div., 1983–87, Man. Dir, 1987–92, GEC Engrg Res. Centre; R&D Dir, GEC Alsthom, 1992–98; Vice-Pres., Alstom Gp, 1998–2004; Exec. Dir, UK Energy Res. Centre, 2004–15. Non-executive Director: R&D Bd, MoD, 2008–; Carbon Mgt Canada Ltd, 2011–; Samad Power Ltd, 2014–. Focal Point UK-China energy collaboration, BIS, 2013–14. Member: EPSRC, 2003–05 (Chm., User Panel, 2004–05); Eur. Adv. Gp for Energy, 2008–; Comité Energie, Agence Nat. de Recherche, France, 2011–. Co-Chair, Internat. Partnership for Hydrogen Econ., 2007–10; Founding Mem., Eur. Energy Res. Alliance, 2008–15. Mem., Univ. Industrial Adv. Bds at Cardiff Univ., Loughborough Univ., QMUL, Sheffield Univ., Leeds Univ. and Durham Univ. Hon. Prof., Cardiff Univ., 2009–. Mem. Council, 2012–14, Trustee Bd, 2014–15, RAEng. President: IET, 2007–08; City & Guilds Coll. Assoc., 2009–10. FCGI 2007; FRSA; Foreign FTSE 2011. Freeman, City of London, 2009; Liveryman, Engineers' Co., 2009. Hon. Fellow, QMUL, 2009. Hon. DSc Keele, 2013. *Recreations:* travel, gardening, cooking, cherishing an MGB. *Address:* Department of Energy and Climate Change, 3 Whitehall Place, SW1A 2AW. *T:* (0300) 068 5758.

LOUGHLIN, Prof. John Patrick, PhD; FRHistS, FAcSS, FLSW; Director, Von Hügel Institute, and Fellow, St Edmund's College, Cambridge, 2010–15, now Emeritus Fellow; Fellow, Blackfriars, Oxford, since 2015; *b* Belfast, 9 Sept. 1948; *s* of John Patrick Loughlin and Margaret Loughlin; one *d*. *Educ:* St Malachy's Coll., Belfast; Our Lady of Bethlehem Abbey, NI; Ulster Poly. (BA Hons 1982); European University Inst., Florence (PhD 1987). Army, 1964–68; Cistercian monk, 1968–74; religious orgns, 1974–78; Lectr, Univ. of Ulster, 1985–91; Associate Prof., Erasmus Univ., Rotterdam, 1991–95; Prof. of Politics, Cardiff Univ., 1995–2010. Visiting Professor: Eur. Univ. Inst., Florence, 1994; Inst. d'Etudes Politiques, Paris, 1999–2002; Univ. of Umeå, 2003–07; Univ. of Santiago da Compostela, 2005; Inst. d'Etudes Politiques, Aix-en-Provence, 2005–12; Univ. Libre de Bruxelles, 2012–13 (Chaire Ganshof van der Meersch, 2013–14); Visiting Fellow: Eur. Univ. Inst., Florence, 2001–02; Eur. Studies, St Antony's Coll., Oxford, 2006–07; St Edmund's Coll., Cambridge, 2009; Dist. Vis. Res. Fellow, QMUL, 2009; Vis. Res. Fellow, Merton Coll., Oxford, 2004; Sen. Vis. Res. Scholar, Centre for Contemp. Hist., Univ. of Oxford, 2005–06; Vis. Scholar, Nuffield Coll., Oxford, 2009–10; Mem., Residential Colloquium, Centre of Theol Inquiry, Princeton, 2010. FRHistS 2007; FAcSS (AcSS 2008); FRSA 2008; Fellow, Eur. Acad. of Scis and Arts, 2013; FLSW 2014. Hon. PhD Umeå, 2009. Officier, Ordre des Palmes Academiques (France), 2010. *Publications:* Public Policy in Northern Ireland, 1995; The Political Economy of Regionalism, 1997; Regional and Local Democracy in the EU, 1999; Subnational Democracy in the EU, 2001; Albania and the EU, 2007; Subnational Government: the French experience, 2007; numerous articles and book chapters. *Recreations:* travel, music, choral singing, reading. *Address:* St Edmund's College, Cambridge CB3 0BN. *T:* (01223) 746866. *E:* jl602@cam.ac.uk. *Clubs:* Oxford and Cambridge, Victory Services.

LOUGHLIN, Prof. Martin, FBA 2011; Professor of Public Law, London School of Economics and Political Science, since 2000 (Head, Department of Law, 2009–12); *b* Birtley, Co. Durham, 16 July 1954; *s* of Martin Loughlin and Ann Loughlin (*née* Casey); *m* 1982, Christine Foley; two *d*. *Educ:* St Bede's Sch., Lanchester; London Sch. of Econs and Pol Sci. (LLB 1975); Univ. of Warwick (LLM 1977); Law Sch., Harvard Univ. (LLM 1977). Lecturer: Osgoode Hall Law Sch., York Univ., Toronto, 1977–78; in Law, Univ. of Warwick, 1978–84; in Law, LSE, 1984–88; John Millar Prof. of Public Law, Univ. of Glasgow, 1988–91; Prof. of Law, Univ. of Manchester, 1991–2000 (Dean of Faculty, 1998–2000). Leverhulme Trust Maj. Res. Fellow, 2000–02; Fellow, Wissenschaftskolleg zu Berlin, 2007–08; Law and Public Affairs Fellow, Princeton Univ., 2012–13. Hon. LLD Edinburgh, 2015. *Publications:* Local Government in the Modern State, 1986; Public Law and Political Theory, 1992; Administrative Accountability in Local Government, 1992; Legality and Locality: the role of law in central-local government relations, 1996; Sword and Scales: an examination of the relationship between law and politics, 2000; The Idea of Public Law, 2003; Foundations of Public Law, 2010; The British Constitution: a very short introduction, 2013. *Address:* Law Department, London School of Economics and Political Science, Houghton Street, WC2A 2AE. *T:* (020) 7849 4642. *E:* m.loughlin@lse.ac.uk.

LOUGHRAN, Sir Gerald (Finbar), KCB 2002; Head, Northern Ireland Civil Service, 2000–02; *b* 22 Feb. 1942; *m* Gemma, (Her Honour Judge Gemma Loughran); one *s* one *d* (and one *s* decd). *Educ:* St Malachy's Coll., Belfast; QUB (BSc (Econ)). Northern Ireland Civil Service: posts in Dept of Econ. Develt and Dept of Envmt; Perm. Sec., Dept of Econ. Develt, 1991–2000. Chairman: Phoenix Natural Gas, 2003–; Lionrai Gp, 2013–; Director: W. G. Baird Gp, 2003–; Irish Inst., Louvain, 2003–; Forward Emphasis Internat., 2009–. Hon. Prof., QUB. Hon. DLitt Ulster, 2004.

LOUGHRAN, James, CBE 2010; conductor; *b* 30 June 1931; *s* of James and Agnes Loughran; *m* 1st, 1961, Nancy Coggon (marr. diss. 1983; she *d* 1996); one *s* (and one *s* decd); 2nd, 1985, Ludmila (*née* Navratil). *Educ:* St Aloysius' Coll., Glasgow; Bonn, Amsterdam and Milan. FRNCM 1976; FRSAMD 1983. 1st Prize, Philharmonia Orchestra's Conducting Competition, 1961. Associate Conductor, Bournemouth SO, 1962–65; Principal Conductor: BBC Scottish SO, 1965–71; Bamberg SO, 1979–83; Prin. Conductor and Musical Advr, 1971–83, Conductor Laureate, 1983–91, Hallé Orchestra; Musical Dir, English Opera Gp, 1966 (Festivals of Drottningholm, Versailles and Aldeburgh); Chief Conductor, 1996–2003, Principal Guest Conductor, 2003–11, Aarhus SO, Denmark. Guest conductor of principal orchestras of Europe, America, Australasia and Japan; conducted opera at Sadler's Wells, Royal Opera House, Scottish Opera, Netherlands Opera and Montpellier Opera; Guest Conductor, Stockholm Philharmonic, 1977–92; Guest Conductor, 1980–, Permanent Guest Conductor, 1993–, Hon. Conductor, 2006, Japan Philharmonic SO; Chief Guest Conductor, BBC Welsh SO, 1987–90. Internat. festivals and tours with Bamberg and Hallé orchestras, as well as Munich Philharmonic, BBC Symphony, Stockholm Philharmonic, London Philharmonic and Scottish Chamber orchestras; conductor, BBC Proms, 1965–89, incl. 5 last nights. Many recordings, including complete Beethoven, Brahms and Elgar symphonies. Gold Disc, EMI, 1983. Freeman, City of London, 1991; Liveryman, Musicians' Co., 1992. Hon. DMus: Sheffield, 1983; RSAMD, 2005. *Address:* 18 Hatfield Drive, Glasgow G12 0YA.

LOUGHRAN, Rear-Adm. Terence William, CB 1997; Chief Executive, Sabrage Enterprises, since 1998; *b* Newcastle-upon-Tyne, 27 March 1943; parents decd; *m* (marr. diss. 1988); one *s* two *d*; *m* 1995, Philippa Mary Vernon. *Educ:* Devonport High Sch.; Britannia Royal Naval Coll. FRAeS 1997. Qualified as: rotary wing pilot, 1967; flying instructor, 1971; graduated Canadian Forces Comd and Staff Coll., 1976; i/c 706 Naval Air Sqdn, 1976–77; Comdr 1979; i/c HMS Phoebe, 1980–81; Executive Officer: HMS Bristol, 1983–84; HMS Intrepid, 1984–85; Captain 1986; i/c HMS Gloucester and Comdr Armilla Patrol, Arabian Gulf Task Unit, 1986–88; Dep. Dir, Internat. Affairs in Naval Staff Duties, 1988–90; Dir, Naval Manpower Planning, 1990–92; i/c HMS Ark Royal and Comdr, Grapple Adriatic Task Gp, 1993–94; Rear-Adm., 1995; Flag Officer, Naval Aviation, 1995–98. Mem., Rona Trust, 1991– (Skipper Emeritus, 2004); Chairman of Trustees: FAA Mus., 2005–15; Fly Navy Heritage Trust, 2005–15 (Hon. Life Vice Pres., 2015); Founder Mem. and Trustee, Nat. Mus. of the RN, 2008–15. Gov., Countess Gytha Sch., 1996–2005. *Publications:* (contrib.) Royal United Services Inst. Jl, Defence Mgt Jl. *Recreations:* sailing, motor cycling, spinning yarns. *Address:* Court Lodge, St Margarets Road, Tintinhull, Somerset BA22 8PL. *T:* and *Fax:* (01935) 824298. *E:* twl@sabrage.com. *Clubs:* Royal Navy; Travellers (Newcastle); Yeovil Beefsteak and Kidney Pudding.

LOUGHREY, (Stephen Victor) Patrick; Warden, Goldsmiths, University of London, since 2010; *b* 29 Dec. 1955; *s* of Eddie Loughrey and Mary Loughrey (*née* Griffin); *m* 1978, Patricia Kelly; one *s* two *d*. *Educ:* Loreto Coll., Milford; Univ. of Ulster (BA); Queen's Univ. (MA). Res. student, Trent Univ., Canada, 1977; teacher, St Colm's Draperstown, 1978–84; BBC: Producer, Educn, 1984–88; Hd, Educnl Broadcasting, 1988–91; Hd of Progs, NI, 1991–94; Controller, NI, 1994–2000; Dir, Nations and Regions, 2000–09. Fellow, Radio Acad., 2004–. Trustee, Teaching Awards Trust, 2008–12. Jt Editor, Ulster Local Studies, 1988–91. FRSA. *Publications:* People of Ireland, 1988. *Recreations:* walking, talking. *Address:* Goldsmiths, University of London, New Cross, SE14 6NW. *Clubs:* Athenæum, Century.

LOUGHTON, David Clifford, CBE 2010; Chief Executive: The Royal Wolverhampton Hospitals NHS Trust, since 2004; National Institute for Health Research (West Midlands), since 2014; *b* 28 Jan. 1954; *s* of late Clifford Loughton and of Hazel Loughton; *m* 1986, Deborah Wellington; one *s* one *d*. *Educ:* Roxet Manor Sch., Harrow; tech. colls in Harrow, Watford and Southall. MIHospE 1974; MIPlantE 1976; TEng (CEI) 1978; MHSM 1993. Asst hosp. engr, Hillingdon AHA, 1974–76; hosp. engr, Herts AHA, 1976–78; Dir and Gen. Manager, Ducost Ltd, 1978–83; Divl Manager, GEC Electrical Projects, 1984–86; Chief Exec., Walsgrave Hosps, subseq. Univ. Hosps Coventry and Warwicks, NHS Trust, 1986–2002; Develt Dir, InHealth Gp, 2002–04. Chm., Coventry and Warwicks Educn and Trng Consortium, 1996–2001; Member: NHS Confedn Nat. Council, 2007–; Adv. Bd, NHS Nat. Inst. for Health Res., 2007–. *Recreations:* home improvements, walking, sport. *Address:* The Royal Wolverhampton Hospitals NHS Trust, Hollybush House, New Cross Hospital, Wolverhampton WV10 0QP. *T:* (01902) 695951.

LOUGHTON, Timothy Paul; MP (C) East Worthing and Shoreham, since 1997; *b* 30 May 1962; *s* of Rev. Michael Loughton and Pamela Dorothy Loughton (*née* Brandon); *m* 1992, Elizabeth Juliet MacLauchlan; one *s* two *d*. *Educ:* Priory Sch., Lewes; Univ. of Warwick (BA 1st cl. Hons); Clare Coll., Cambridge. Joined Montagu Loebl Stanley, then Fleming Private Asset Mgt, 1984, Dir 1992–2000. Formerly: Member: Wandsworth CHC; Substance Misuse Cttee, Wandsworth HA; Battersea Sector Policing Gp; Vice-Chm., Wandsworth Alcohol Gp. Joined Conservative Party, 1977; various posts in local assocs in Lewes, Warwick Univ., Cambridge Univ. and Battersea, 1978–91; Dep. Chm., Battersea Cons. Assoc., 1994–96. Contested (C) Sheffield Brightside, 1992. Opposition spokesman: for envmt, transport and the regions, 2000–01; for health, 2001–07; for children, 2003–10; Parly Under-Sec. of State for Children and Families, DFE, 2010–12. Member: Finance Bill Standing Cttee, 1997–98; Envmtl Audit Select Cttee, 1997–2001; Jt House Cttee on Financial Services and Markets Bill, 1999; Home Affairs Select Cttee, 2014–15; Treasurer: Parly Maritime Gp, 1997–2008; Parly Animal Welfare Gp, 2001–07; Parly Archaeology Gp, 2002–10; Vice Chairman: All Party Autism Gp; All Party Cardiac Risk in the Young Gp, 2005–09; Parly Gp for Children, 2005–10, 2014–; All Party Parly Child Protection Gp, 2013–; Chairman: All Party Gp for Wholesale Financial Mkts, 2005–10; Cons. Disability Gp, 1998–2006; All Party Parliamentary Group: on British Mus.; on 1001 Critical Days; on Wine and Spirits; Jt Chm., Parly Mental Health Gp, 2005–10; Mem., Exec. Cttee, Inter Parly Union (UK), 2006–10 and 2013–. Captain, Commons and Lords Hockey Team, 2003–. Member: Sussex Archaeol Soc.; BM Soc. *Recreations:* archaeology, classics, wine, ski-ing, tennis, hockey. *Address:* House of Commons, SW1A 0AA.

LOUIS, Prof. (William) Roger, Hon. CBE 1999; DLitt; FBA; Kerr Professor of English History and Culture, since 1985, Distinguished Teaching Professor, since 1998, University of Texas at Austin; Supernumerary Fellow, St Antony's College, Oxford, 1986–96 (Hon. Fellow, since 1996); *b* 8 May 1936; *s* of Henry Edward and Bena May Louis; *m* 1st, 1960, Patricia Ann Leonard; one *s* one *d*; 2nd, 1983, Dagmar Cecilia Friedrich. *Educ:* Univ. of Oklahoma (Phi Beta Kappa, BA 1959; Dist. Alumnus, 2013); Harvard (Woodrow Wilson Fellow; MA 1960); St Antony's Coll., Oxford (Marshall Scholar; DPhil 1962); DLitt Oxon 1979. FRHistS 1984; Corresp. FBA 1993. Asst and Associate Prof., Yale, 1962–70; Humanities Research Center, University of Texas: Prof. of History and Curator, Historical Collections, 1970–85; Dir, British Studies, 1975–; Teaching Awards, 1984, 1992, 1993, 1998; National Endowment Humanities: Sen. Fellow, 1974–75; Dir, Seminars, 1985–2000. Guggenheim Fellow, 1979–80; Vis. Fellow, 1979–80, 2004, Chichele Lectr, 1990, 2002, 2003, 2006, 2010, All Souls Coll., Oxford; Vis. Fellow, Balliol Coll., Oxford, 2005; Fellow/Lecturer: Churchill Coll., Cambridge, 1985; Brookings Instn, 1989; LSE, 1992; Woodrow Wilson Internat. Center for Scholars, 1994–95, 2000 (Sen. Scholar, 2012–); lectures: Cust, Univ. of Nottingham, 1995; British Acad. Inaugural Elie Kedourie Meml, 1996; Churchill Meml, Westminster Coll., Fulton, Mo, 1998; Antonius, Oxford Univ., 2002; Leonard Stein, Oxford, 2005; Strelitz, Tel Aviv, 2008. Dist. Visitor, Dept of Hist., Univ. of Peking, 1998; Dist. Vis. Prof., Amer. Univ. in Cairo, 2001. Founding Dir, Nat. History Center, 2001–13. Chm., US Dept of State Histl Adv. Cttee, 2001–08; Member: Scholars' Council, 2006–, Kluge Chair, 2010, Liby of Congress; Amer. Acad. of Arts and Scis, 2011. Pres., Amer. Historical Assoc., 2001–02. Trustee, British Empire Mus., Bristol, 2005–13. Editor, British Documents on the End of Empire, 1988–; Editor-in-Chief, Oxford History of the British Empire, 1992–. Hon. DPhil Westminster Coll., 1998. Prof. of the Year, Univ. of Texas, 2009; Benson Medal, Royal Soc. of Literature, 2013. *Publications:* Ruanda-Urundi, 1963; Germany's Lost Colonies, 1967; (ed with P. Gifford) Britain and Germany in Africa, 1967; (with J. Stengers) Congo Reform Movement, 1968; British Strategy in the Far East, 1971; (ed with P. Gifford) France and Britain in Africa, 1971; (ed) Nationalism Security and International Trusteeship in the Pacific, 1972; (ed) A. J. P. Taylor and his Critics, 1972; (ed) Imperialism: the Robinson and Gallagher controversy, 1976; Imperialism at Bay, 1977; (ed with W. S. Livingston) Australia, New Zealand and the Pacific Islands, 1979; (ed with P. Gifford) The Transfer of Power in Africa, 1982; The British Empire in the Middle East 1945–51, 1984 (Amer. Hist. Assoc. Prize); (ed with R. Stookey) The End of the Palestine Mandate, 1986; (ed with H. Bull) The Special Relationship, 1986; (ed with P. Gifford) Decolonization in Africa, 1988; (ed with J. A. Bill) Musaddiq, Nationalism and Oil, 1988; (ed with R. Owen) Suez 1956, 1989; (ed with R. Fernea) The Iraqi Revolution, 1991; In the Name of God Go! Leo Amery and the British Empire, 1992; (ed with R. Blake) Churchill, 1993; (ed) Adventures with Britannia: personalities, politics and culture in Britain, 1995; (ed) More Adventures with Britannia, 1998; (ed with Michael Howard) The Oxford History of the Twentieth Century, 1998; (ed with J. M. Brown) The Oxford History of the British Empire, vol. IV: the twentieth century, 1999; (ed with Roger Owen) A Revolutionary Year: the Middle East in 1958, 2002; (ed) Still More Adventures with Britannia, 2003; (ed) Yet More Adventures with Britannia, 2005; (ed) Burnt Orange Britannia, 2005; Ends of British Imperialism, 2006; (ed) Penultimate Adventures with Britannia, 2007; Ultimate Adventures with Britannia, 2009; Resurgent Adventures with Britannia, 2011; (ed with Avi Shlaim) The 1967 Arab-Israeli War: origins and consequences, 2012; (ed) History of Oxford University Press, 1896–1970, 2013; (ed) Irrepressible Adventures with Britannia, 2013; *festschrift:* (ed Robert King and Robin Kilson) The Statecraft of British Imperialism: essays in honor of Wm Roger Louis, 1999. *Recreation:* a German wife. *Address:* Humanities Research Center, University of Texas, Austin, TX 78712, USA. *Clubs:* Reform; Century (NY), Metropolitan (Washington).

LOUISY, Dame (Calliopa) Pearlette, Grand Cross, Order of St Lucia, 1997; GCMG 1999; Governor General, St Lucia, since 1997; *b* 8 June 1946; *d* of Rita Louisy. *Educ:* St Joseph's Convent; Univ. of West Indies (BA); Université Laval, Quebec (MA); Univ. of Bristol (PhD 1994). Principal, St Lucia A-Level Coll., 1981–86; Sir Arthur Lewis Community College: Dean, 1986–94; Vice Principal, 1994–95; Principal, 1996–97. Paul Harris Fellow, 2001. FRSA 1999. Hon. LLD: Bristol, 1999; Sheffield, 2003; Univ. of W Indies, 2011. DStJ 2001; DSG 2002. Internat. Woman of the Year, 1998, 2001; Woman of Great Esteem, QKingdom Ministries, 2003; Caribbean Luminary Award, 2007. *Recreations:* horticulture, performing arts, reading. *Address:* Government House, Morne Fortune, Castries, St Lucia. *T:* 4522481.

LOUSTAU-LALANNE, Bernard Michel; barrister; international copyright consultant; *b* 20 June 1938; *s* of Michel Loustau-Lalanne, OBE, and Madeleine (*née* Boullé); *m* 1974, Debbie Elizabeth Grieve (*née* Temple-Brown) (marr. diss. 1982); one *d*. *Educ:* Seychelles Coll.; St Mary's Coll., Southampton; Imperial Coll., London. Called to the Bar, Middle Temple, London, 1969. Assistant Inspector, Northern Rhodesia Police, 1962–64; Crown Counsel, Seychelles, 1970–72; Sen. State Counsel and Official Notary, 1972–76; Attorney-General, Seychelles, 1976–78; High Comr for Seychelles, in London, 1978–80; concurrently Seychelles Ambassador to USA, and Seychelles Perm. Rep. to UN; Internat. Rep., PRS, 1980–90; Sec.-Gen., Eur. Fedn of Mgt Consulting Assocs, 1991–92. *Recreations:* international affairs, French literature, theatre, tennis. *Address:* 2 Albert Mansions, Luxborough Street, W1U 5BQ.

LOUTH, 17th Baron *cr* 1541 (Ire.); **Jonathan Oliver Plunkett;** *b* 4 Nov. 1952; *s* of 16th Baron Louth and Angela Patricia Plunkett (*née* Cullinane); *S* father, 2013; *m* 1981, Jennifer Hodgetts (separated 2000; marr. diss. 2015); one *s* one *d*. *Educ:* De La Salle Coll., Jersey; Hautlieu Sch., Jersey; Univ. of Hull (BSc 1975). MIET. Diamond Jubilee Medal, 2012. *Heir:* *s* Hon. Matthew Oliver Plunkett [*b* 22 Dec. 1982; *m* 2008, Jenna Maree Baker; two *s*]. *Club:* St Helier Yacht (Jersey).

LOUTH, Rev. Prof. Andrew, DD; FBA 2010; FSA; Professor of Patristic and Byzantine Studies, Durham University, 1998–2010, now Emeritus; *b* Louth, Lincs, 11 Nov. 1944; *s* of Cecil George Louth and Mary Louth; *m* 1st, 1966, Janet Sisson (marr. diss. 1990); one *s* two *d*; 2nd, 1991, Carol Harrison (marr. diss. 2010); one *s*. *Educ:* Queen Elizabeth Grammar Sch., Wakefield; Waterloo Grammar Sch., Liverpool; St Catharine's Coll., Cambridge (BA 1965); Univ. of Edinburgh (MTh 1968); Univ. of Oxford (DD 1991). Fellow and Chaplain, Worcester Coll., Oxford, 1970–85; Goldsmiths College, London: Sen. Lectr, 1985–89, Reader, 1989–91, in Religious Studies; Prof., 1992–96; Reader in Greek Patristics, Durham Univ., 1996–98. Vis. Prof. of Eastern Orthodox Theol., Free Univ., Amsterdam, 2010–14. Ordained priest, Russian Orthodox Ch, Moscow Patriarchate, 2003; archpriest, 2014. Pres., Ecclesiastical Hist. Soc., 2009–10. FSA 2001. *Publications:* The Origins of the Christian Mystical Tradition: from Plato to Denys, 1981, 2nd edn 2007; Discerning the Mystery: an essay on the nature of theology, 1983; Denys the Areopagite, 1989, 2nd edn 2001; The Wilderness of God, 1991, 2nd edn 2003; Maximus the Confessor, 1996; St John Damascene: tradition and originality in Byzantine theology, 2002; Greek East and Latin West: the Church AD 681–1071, 2007; Introducing Eastern Orthodox Theology, 2013. *Recreations:* reading, playing and listening to music, walking. *Address:* 13 Uplands Road, Darlington DL3 7SZ. *T:* (01325) 481080. *E:* louth.andrew@gmail.com.

LOVAT, 18th Lord (S) *cr* 1458–1464 (*de facto* 16th Lord, 18th but for the attainder); **Simon Fraser;** Baron (UK) 1837; *b* 13 Feb. 1977; *er s* of Hon. Simon Augustine Fraser, Master of Lovat (*d* 1994) and of Virginia Fraser (who *m* 1998, Frank Robert Johnson, journalist (*d* 2006)), *d* of David Grose; *S* grandfather, 1995. *Educ:* Harrow; Edinburgh Univ. *Heir:* *b* Jack Fraser, Master of Lovat, *b* 22 Aug. 1984.

LOVE, Andrew; *b* 21 March 1949; *s* of late James Love and Olive Love (*née* Mills); *m* 1983, Ruth, *d* of late Jack and Esther Rosenthal. *Educ:* Strathclyde Univ. (BSc Hons). FCIS. Parly Officer, Co-operative Party, 1993–97. Mem. (Lab), Haringey LBC, 1980–86 (Chairman: Finance, 1984–85; Housing, 1985–86). Mem., NE Thames RHA, 1988–90. Contested (Lab and Co-op) Edmonton, 1992. MP (Lab and Co-op) Edmonton, 1997–2015. PPS to Minister of State: DoH, 2001–03; for Industry and the Regions, DTI, 2003–05; for Local Govt, 2008–10. Member: Public Accounts Cttee, H of C, 1997–2001; Deregulation Select Cttee, 1999–2001; Regulatory Reform Select Cttee, 2001–05; Treasury Select Cttee, 2005–15. Chairman: All Party Bldg Socs and Financial Mutuals Gp (formerly All Party Building Socs Gp), 1997–2002; All Party Lebanon Gp, 2005–15; PLP Backbench Treasury Cttee, 2010–15; Co-Chairman: All Party Homelessness and Housing Needs Gp, 2000–08; All Party Sri Lanka Gp, 2004–15 (Sec., 1999–2004); Vice Chm., All Party Small Businesses Gp, 2010–15 (Sec., 2000–05; Chm., 2005–10); Sec., All Party Opera Gp, 2010–15 (Vice Chm., 2005–10). Trustee, Industrial Common Ownership Finance, 1991–. Chairman: Citizens Advice Haringey, 2015–; Peter Bedford Housing Assoc., 2015–. FRSA. *Publications:* (contrib.) Parliament in the 21st Century, 2004; (contrib.) More Homes for Rent: stimulating supply to match growing demand, 2006. *Recreations:* golf, opera, reading, history. *Address:* 3 Queen Anne's Gardens, Bush Hill Park, Enfield, Middx EN1 2JN. *E:* andylove1949@gmail.com.

LOVE, Graham Carvell, FCA; Principal, Chertoff Group, since 2010; *b* 18 March 1954; *s* of Peter and Nancy Love; *m* (marr. diss.); one *s* one *d*. *Educ:* Fitzwilliam Coll., Cambridge (BA Hons Eng. 1975; MA). FCA 1979; CCIM 2007; FRAeS 2008. Gp Financial Controller, Shandwick plc, 1988–92; Finance Dir, Defence Res. Agency, 1992–96; Chief Exec., Comax Secure Business Services, 1996–99; Chief Financial Officer, 2001–05, Chief Exec., 2005–09, QinetiQ. Chairman: Racing Green Cars, 1999–; LGC Science Gp, 2010–; Eversholt Rail Gp, 2011–14; 2e2 Gp, 2011–13; SLR Consulting, 2012–. *Recreations:* historic motor racing, shooting, ski-ing, sailing. *Address:* 39 Smith Street, SW3 4EP. *E:* graham@grahamlove.com.

LOVE, Prof. Philip Noel, CBE 1983; DL; Vice Chancellor, University of Liverpool, 1992–2002; *b* 25 Dec. 1939; *o s* of Thomas Isaac and Ethel Violet Love; *m* 1st, 1963, Isabel Leah (*d* 1993), *yr d* of Innes Taylor and Leah Wallace Mearns; three *s*; 2nd, 1995, Isobel, *widow* of David Pardey. *Educ:* Aberdeen Grammar Sch.; Aberdeen Univ. (MA 1961, LLB 1963). Admitted Solicitor in Scotland, 1963; Advocate in Aberdeen, 1963–; Partner, Campbell Connon, Solicitors, Aberdeen, 1963–74, Consultant, 1974–2004. University of Aberdeen: Prof. of Conveyancing and Professional Practice of Law, 1974–92; Dean, Faculty of Law, 1979–82, 1991–92; Vice Principal, 1986–90. Law Society of Scotland: Mem. Council, 1975–86; Examr, 1975–83 (Chm. Examrs, 1977–80); Vice-Pres., 1980–81; Pres., 1981–82. Local Chm., Rent Assessment Panel for Scotland, 1972–92; Chairman: Sec. of State for Scotland's Expert Cttee on house purchase and sale, 1982–84; Scottish Conveyancing and Executry Services Bd, 1991–96; Vice-Pres., Scottish Law Agents Soc., 1970; Member: Jt Standing Cttee on Legal Educn in Scotland, 1976–85 (Chm., 1976–80); Rules Council, Court of Session, 1968–92; Council, Internat. Bar Assoc., 1983–87 (Vice-Chm., Legal Educn Div., 1983–87); Jt Ethical Cttee, Grampian Health Bd, 1984–92 (Vice-Chm., 1985; Chm., 1986–92); Scottish Law Commn, 1986–95; Council, CVCP, then UUK, 1996–2002. Chairman: Univs and Colls Employers Assoc., 1995–2002; NW Univs Assoc., 2001–02. Chm., Aberdeen Home for Widowers' Children, 1971–92. Pres., Aberdeen Grammar Sch. Former Pupils' Club, 1987–88. Hon. Sheriff of Grampian, Highland and Islands, 1978–. Chm., Registers of Scotland Customer Adv. Gp, 1990–92. Trustee: Grampian and Islands Family Trust, 1988–92; St George's Hall Trust, 1996–2013; Merseyside Police and High Sheriff's Charitable Trust, 1998–2009; Liverpool Charity and Voluntary Services (formerly Council of Social Service), 2003–11; Liverpool Philharmonic Foundn, 2005–11. Chairman: Mersey Partnership, 1995–98; NW Regl Assembly, Knowledge Economy Gp, 2000–02; Mem., NW Sci. Council, 2001–02. Gov., Inst. of Occupational Medicine Ltd, 1990–2013; Gov., 2003–10, Trustee, 2014–, Liverpool Coll. Dir, Rising Stars Growth Fund Ltd, 2001–05. Mem., Editl Consultative Bd for Scotland, Butterworth & Co. (Publishers) Ltd, 1990–95. DL 1997, High Sheriff, 2007–08, Merseyside. FAcSS (AcSS 2002). Hon. Fellow, Liverpool John Moores Univ., 2002. Hon. LLD: Abertay Dundee, 1996; Aberdeen, 1997; Liverpool, 2002; Hon. DLitt Chester, 2013. *Address:* 1 Mayfield Court, Victoria Road, Formby, Merseyside L37 7JL. *T:* (01704) 832427. *Clubs:* Artists (Liverpool); New (Edinburgh); Aberdeen Grammar School Former Pupils' Club Centre (Aberdeen); Formby Golf.

LOVE, Rear Adm. Robert Thomas, CB 2011; OBE 2004; FREng; Chief Naval Engineer Officer, 2008–11; Deputy Chief Executive Officer, Babcock Pty Ltd (Australia), since 2011; *b* 21 July 1955; *s* of late Bill and Ellen Love; *m* 1983, Jean Francis; two *s* one *d*. *Educ:* Ashton-in-Makerfield Grammar Sch.; RNEC (BSc 1978). CEng 1984; FIMarEST 1987; CMarEng 2006; FREng 2011; FAPM 2007; FIET 2011. HM Yacht Britannia, 1982–84; Comdr E HMS Ark Royal, 1992–94; Desk Officer, DN Plans, MoD, 1994–96; SMEO to Flag Officer Sea Trng, 1997–98; Captain 1998; Team Leader Major Warships, 2001; recovered HMS Nottingham from grounding off coast of Australia, 2003; Cdre 2003; Defence Advr to Australia, 2003–06; Team Leader, Carrier Vessel Future and Maritime Airborne Surveillance and Control, later Capital Ships Dir, incl. Future Carriers, 2007–08, Dir Ships, 2008–11, Defence Equipment and Support, MoD. Pres., RN Golf Assoc., 2009–11. Mem., MENSA. *Publications:* papers at various confs. *Recreations:* cricket, golf, Rugby, fitness, food, wine, music. *Address:* 102 Seaview Road, Tennyson, Adelaide, SA 5022, Australia. *Club:* MCC.

LOVE, Prof. Seth, PhD; FRCP, FRCPath; Professor of Neuropathology, University of Bristol, since 2001; *b* Johannesburg, SA; *s* of Frank and Dora Love; *m* 1978, Lynn Hirschowitz; one *s* one *d*. *Educ:* Univ. of Witwatersrand (MB BCh *cum laude* 1978); Inst. of Neurol., Univ. of London (PhD 1984). MRCP 1980, FRCP 1996; MRCPath 1985, FRCPath 1996. Internships, Johannesburg Gen. Hosp., 1979; Lectr, Inst. of Neurol., 1980–83, Sen. Registrar, 1983–85, Nat. Hosp. for Nervous Diseases, London; Fogarty Fellow, Univ. of Calif, San Diego, 1985–87; Consultant in Neuropathol., 1987–2001, Hon. Consultant in Neuropathol., 2001–, Frenchay Hosp., N Bristol NHS Trust; Hon. Prof. of Neuropathol., Univ. of Bristol, 1995–2001. Dir, MRC Brain Banks UK Network, 2013–. Ed.-in-Chief, Brain Pathol., 2014–. *Publications:* (ed with D. Ellison) Neuropathology, 1998, 3rd edn 2013; (ed) Current Topics in Pathology: neuropathology, 2001; (contrib.) Greenfield's Neuropathology, 7th edn 2002, 9th edn (ed jtly) 2015. *Recreations:* music, walking, cycling, ski-ing. *Address:* School of Clinical Sciences, University of Bristol, Learning and Research Level 2, Southmead Hospital, Bristol BS10 5NB. *T:* (0117) 414 2402. *E:* seth.love@bris.ac.uk.

LOVEDAY, Alan (Raymond); solo violinist; *b* 29 Feb. 1928; *s* of Leslie and Margaret Loveday; *m* 1952, Ruth Stanfield; one *s* one *d*. *Educ:* privately; Royal College of Music (prizewinner). Made debut at age of 4; debut in England, 1946; has given many concerts, broadcasts, and made TV appearances, in this country and abroad, playing with all leading conductors and orchestras; repertoire ranges from Bach (which he likes to play on an un-modernised violin), to contemporary music. Prof., RCM, 1955–72. Formerly full-time Mem. and Soloist, Acad. of St Martin-in-the-Fields. *Recreations:* chess, bridge.

LOVEDAY, Mark Antony; Senior Partner, Cazenove & Co., 1994–2001; *b* 22 Sept. 1943; *s* of George Arthur Loveday and Sylvia Mary Loveday; *m* 1981, Mary Elizabeth Tolmie; one *s* one *d*. *Educ:* Winchester Coll.; Magdalen Coll., Oxford (MA). Cazenove & Co., 1966–2001; Partner, 1974–2001. Chm., Foreign & Colonial Investment Trust PLC, 2002–10 (Dir, 2001–10). Chm., Grosvenor Pension Plan, 2008–. Trustee: Magdalen Coll. Develt Trust, 1982– (Chm., 2006–); Grosvenor Estate, 1999–2008; Westminster Foundn, 2008–. Liveryman, Skinners' Co., 1972 (Mem. Court, 2014–). Fellow, Winchester Coll., 2008–14. *Recreations:* golf, trekking. *Address:* 42 Royal Avenue, SW3 4QF. *T:* (office) (020) 7730 6335. *Clubs:* Boodle's, City University, Hurlingham, MCC; Royal St George's Golf.

LOVEGROVE, Ross Nigel, RDI 2003; FCSD; Principal, Lovegrove Design Studio, London, since 1990; *b* 16 Aug. 1958; *s* of Herbert William John Lovegrove, OBE and Mary Eileen Lovegrove; *m* 1997, Maria (*née* Miller); one *s*. *Educ:* Manchester Polytech. (BA 1st cl. Industrial Design 1980); Royal Coll. of Art (MDes 1983). FCSD 1990. Designer, Frog Design, W Germany, working on projects, e.g. Walkmans for Sony, computers for Apple Computers, 1980s; Consultant, Knoll Internat., Paris, 1984–87; with Atelier de Nimes, consultants to Cacharel, Louis Vuitton, Hermes and Dupont, *etc*, 1984–86; London, 1986–: projects for clients including Airbus Industries, Driade, Peugeot, Apple Computers, Issey Miyake, Olympus Cameras, Yamagiwa Corp., Tag Heuer, Hackman, Herman Miller, Japan Airlines, Toyo Ito Architects, Japan, Lasvit, Vondom, and Renault. Has exhibited in MOMA, NY, Guggenheim Mus., NY, Axis Centre, Japan, Pompidou Centre, Paris and Design Mus., London; *work in permanent collections* including: MOMA, NY; Design Mus., London; Vitra Design Mus., Weil Am Rhein, Basel; *solo exhibitions* include: Danish Mus. of Decorative Art, Copenhagen; Stockholm; Idee, Tokyo; Yamagiwa Corp., Tokyo; Rheinauen Space, Cologne, 2001; Designosaurs, Segheria, Milan, 2004; Superliquidity, Le Bain Gall., Tokyo, 2005; Endurance, Phillips de Pury New York Chelsea Galls, 2007; Solar Tree, Vienna, 2007; Cellular Automation, Tokyo 2008; Liquid Space, Miami, 2008; Primordial, Istanbul, 2009; Endless, Milan, 2011; UFO, Lille, 2012; Future Primitives, Kortrijk, 2012. Hon. Fellow, UWIC, 2002. Numerous internat. awards, including: D&AD Silver Medal, 1997; Médaille de la Ville de Paris, 1998; George Nelson Award, 1998; iF Industrie Forum Design Award, Hanover, 1999; Good Design Award, ID mag., 2000; G Mark Federal Design Prize, Japan, 2001; Janus, Paris, 2004; World Technol. Prize, San Francisco, World Technol. Network, 2005; Condé Nast Traveller Ecology Prize, 2007; Product Designer of the Year, FX, 2012. *Publications:* Designing the 21st Century, 1998; (ed) International Design Yearbook, 2002, 2003; Supernatural: the work of Ross Lovegrove, 2004; (contrib.) Designers on Design, 2005. *Recreations:* evolution, biomimicry, paleontology, materials technology, digital architecture, form related sculpture, travel. *Address:* Lovegrove Design Studio, 21 Powis Mews, W11 1JN. *T:* (020) 7229 7104, *Fax:* (020) 7229 7032. *E:* general@rosslovegrove.com. *Club:* Groucho.

LOVEGROVE, Stephen Augustus, CB 2013; Permanent Secretary, Department of Energy and Climate Change, since 2013; *b* Solihull, 30 Nov. 1966; *s* of John Lovegrove and Zenia Stewart Lovegrove; *m* 1997, Kate Constantia Brooke; two *d*. *Educ:* Warwick Sch.; Corpus Christi Coll., Oxford (BA 1989). Consultant, Hydra Associates, 1990–94; Man. Dir, Morgan Grenfell, Deutsche Bank, 1995–2004; Dir, Shareholder Exec., DTI, subseq. BERR, 2004–07; Chief Exec., Shareholder Exec., BERR, later BIS, 2007–13. Mem. Bd, LOCOG, 2007–13. Trustee, CAF, 2010–13. *Recreations:* bricolage, reading detective stories. *Address:* Department of Energy and Climate Change, 3 Whitehall Place, SW1A 2AW. *Clubs:* Brooks's, Tapper's Cricket.

LOVEJOY, Joseph Reginald; freelance football writer and author; *b* 23 June 1951; *s* of Reginald Henry Lovejoy and Ivy May Lovejoy; *m* 1st, 1973, Cynthia Turner (marr. diss. 1990); one *s* one *d*; 2nd, 1995, Lesley Griffiths. *Educ:* Bancroft's Sch., Woodford Green; Portsmouth Tech. Coll. (NCTJ Proficiency). Reporter: Kentish Observer, 1969–73; Doncaster Evening Post, 1973; Derby Evening Telegraph, 1973–77; South Wales Echo, 1977–83; Mail on Sunday, 1983–86; Independent, 1986–94; Football Correspondent, Sunday Times, 1994–2009. *Publications:* Bestie: portrait of a legend, 1998; Sven Goran Eriksson, 2002; (jtly) Giggs: the autobiography, 2005; Glory, Goals, and Greed: 20 years of the Premier League, 2011; The Auschwitz Goalkeeper, 2013. *Recreations:* reading, watching Rugby. *Address:* 30 Twmpath Road, Pontypool, Gwent NP4 6AQ. *Clubs:* Pontypool Rugby Football, Pontypool Working Men's.

LOVELACE, 5th Earl of, *cr* 1838; **Peter Axel William Locke King;** Baron King and Ockham, 1725; Viscount Ockham, 1838; *b* 26 Nov. 1951; *s* of 4th Earl of Lovelace and Manon Lis (*d* 1990), *d* of Axel Sigurd Transo, Copenhagen, Denmark; *S* father, 1964; *m* 1994, Kathleen Anne Smolders, Melbourne, Aust. *Address:* Torridon House, Torridon, Ross-shire IV22 2HA.

LOVELL, Alan Charles; DL; FCA; FSA; Chairman: Tidal Stream, since 2009; Consumer Council for Water, since 2015; *b* Winchester, 19 Nov. 1953; *s* of William George Lovell and Mary Kerr Lovell (*née* Briant); *m* 1982, Hon. Virginia, *d* of Baron Weatherill, PC; two *d*. *Educ:* Winchester Coll.; Jesus Coll., Oxford (MA Lit. Hum. 1976). FCA 1999. Price Waterhouse, 1976–80; Plessey, 1980–89; Finance Dir, 1989–91, Chief Exec., 1991–92, Conder; Finance Dir, 1992–95, Chief Exec., 1995–97, Costain; Finance Dir, 1997–2004, Chief Exec., 2004, Dunlop Slazenger; Chief Executive: Jarvis, 2004–06; Infinis, 2006–09; Chm., 2011–15, Chief Exec., 2012–13, Tamar Energy. Chief Advr to PricewaterhouseCoopers, 2009–. Non-executive Member: Council, Lloyd's, 2007–; Assoc. of Lloyd's Members, 2006– (Chm., 2012–). Gov., Univ. of Winchester, 2009–. Chairman: Blue Lamp Trust, 2010–; Hants Cultural Trust, 2014–; Trustee: Mary Rose Trust, 2006– (Vice Chm., 2013–); Winchester Cathedral, 2010– (Mem. Council, 2008–). FSA 2009. High Sheriff, 2010–11, DL 2012, Hants. *Recreations:* sport, especially Real tennis, opera and theatre, forestry and gardening. *Address:* The Palace House, Bishop's Lane, Bishop's Waltham, Hants SO32 1DP. *T:* (01489) 892838, 07767 874052. *E:* alan.lovell@philtd.com. *Clubs:* All England Lawn Tennis, MCC, Queen's.

LOVELL, Dr (Julian Patrick) Bryan, OBE 1989; CGeol; Senior Research Fellow in Earth Sciences, University of Cambridge, since 1996; President, Geological Society of London, 2010–12; *b* Bath, 10 Feb. 1942; *s* of Sir (Alfred Charles) Bernard Lovell, OBE, FRS and Mary Joyce Lovell; *m* 1964, Caroline Stansfield; two *s* one *d*. *Educ:* King's Sch., Macclesfield; New Coll., Oxford (BA Geol. 1963; MSc Geol. 1964); Harvard Univ. (PhD Geol. 1968). CGeol 1991. Teaching Fellow, Harvard Univ., 1965–68; Lectr in Geol., Univ. of Edinburgh, 1969–81; BP Exploration: Chief Sedimentologist, 1981–84; Exploration Manager, Ireland, 1984–87; Gen. Manager, Ireland, 1987–89; Internat. Exploration Manager, with responsibility for ME and N Africa, 1989–92; Manager, Petrotechnical Resource Develt, 1992–94; Hd, Recruitment, BP Gp, 1994–96. Chm., Petrological Services Edinburgh Ltd, 1980–81; Dir, Lovell Consultants Hertford Ltd, 2002–. Mem. Bd, British Geol Survey, 1996–2000. Energy spokesman, Scottish Liberal Party, 1978–79. Contested (L) Edinburgh S, 1979. *Publications:* The British Isles Through Geological Time: a northward drift, 1977; Challenged by Carbon: the oil industry and climate change, 2009; contrib. articles to learned jls. *Recreations:* cricket, gardening, racing, beer, poetry, Hertfordshire Puddingstone. *Address:* 7 The Avenue, Hertford SG14 3DQ. *T:* and *Fax:* (01992) 551737. *E:* lovell@esc.cam.ac.uk.

LOVELL-BADGE, Dr Robin Howard, FRS 2001; Group Leader, Stem Cell Biology and Developmental Genetics, Francis Crick Institute, since 2015; *b* 14 June 1953; *s* of Don Lovell-Badge and Eileen Betty Cator (*née* Daniels). *Educ:* Norwich Sch. (King Edward VI); University Coll. London (BSc Hons Zool. 1975; PhD Embryol. 1978). Postdoctoral research: Dept of Genetics, Univ. of Cambridge, 1978–81; EMBO Long Term Fellow, Institut Jacques Monod, Univ. Paris VII, 1981–82; Member: Scientific Staff, MRC Mammalian Develt Unit, UCL, 1982–88; MRC Scientific Staff, NIMR, 1988–2015; Hd, Div. of Develtl Genetics, then Div. of Stem Cell Biol. and Develtl Genetics, MRC NIMR, 1993–2015. Hon. Sen. Res. Fellow, subseq. Hon. Prof., Dept of Biomedical Scis (formerly Dept of Anatomy and Develtl Biol.), UCL, 1994–; Vis. Prof., Dept Biochem., Univ. of Hong Kong, 1996–. Pres., Inst. of Animal Tech., 2006–. Mem., EMBO, 1993. FMedSci 1999. Louis Jeantet Prize for Medicine, 1995; Amory Prize, Amer. Acad. Arts and Scis, 1996; Wilhelm Feldberg Prize, Feldberg Foundn, 2008; Waddington Medal, British Soc. for Develtl Biol., 2010. *Publications:* contribs to learned jls. *Recreations:* drawing, painting, sculpture, cooking, good food and wine. *Address:* Francis Crick Institute, The Ridgeway, Mill Hill, NW7 1AA. *T:* (020) 8816 2126. *E:* robin.lovell-badge@crick.ac.uk.

LOVELL-PANK, Dorian Christopher; QC 1993; a Chairman, Police Appeals Tribunals (formerly Police Discipline Appeal Tribunals), since 1991; *b* 15 Feb. 1946; *s* of late Christopher Edwin Lovell-Pank, Madrid and Jean Alston de Oliva-Day (*née* McPherson), Cape Town and Buenos Aires; *m* 1983, Diana, *d* of late Michael Cady Byford and Sonia Byford, Claret Hall, Clare, Suffolk; one *s* one *d*. *Educ:* Downside; Colegio Sarmiento, Buenos Aires; LSE; Inns of Court Sch. of Law. Called to the Bar, Inner Temple, 1971, Bencher, 1998; in practice SE Circuit; Junior, Middlesex Bar Mess, 1977–80; Asst Recorder, 1985–89; Recorder, 1989–2006. Member: Cttee, Criminal Bar Assoc., 1989–2006 (Chm., Internat. Relations Sub-Cttee, 1993–2006); Gen. Council of Bar, 1989–92, 1998–2005 (Chm., Internat. Relations Cttee, 2001–05); Internat. Bar Assoc., 1993– (Mem. Council, 2001–05); Human Rights Inst., 1996– (Mem. Council, 2000–04); British Spanish Law Assoc., 2001–; FCO Pro Bono Lawyers Panel, 2002–. Associate Mem., ABA, 1997–. Chm., Bar Conf.,

1999. *Recreations:* travel, reading, things latin. *Address:* 6 KBW, 21 College Hill, EC4R 2RP. *T:* (020) 3301 0910, *Fax:* (020) 3301 0911. *E:* dorian.lovell-pank@6kbw.com. *Club:* RNVR Yacht.

LOVELOCK, Derek John; Executive Chairman, Mamas & Papas, since 2015; *b* Sutton, Surrey, 1 Jan. 1950; *m* 1976, Deborah Susan; one *s* one *d*. *Educ:* King's Coll. Sch., Wimbledon; Enfield Coll. of Technol. (BA Hons). C&A, 1972–84: Mgt Trainee; Mktg Manager; Buyer, Co-ordinates; Buyer, Clockhouse; Buying Team Leader; Storehouse Gp plc, 1985–92: Buying and Merchandise Controller, then Dir, Richards; Chief Exec., Richards; Chief Exec., Mothercare; Chief Exec., Sears Clothing, Sears plc, 1992–99; Chief Exec., Mosaic Fashions Ltd, 1999–2009; CEO, 2009, Exec. Chm., 2009–14, Aurora Fashions; Exec. Chm., Karen Millen, 2011–12. Ind. Dir, Spartoo.com, 2015–.

LOVELOCK, Prof. James Ephraim, CH 2003; CBE 1990; FRS 1974; independent scientist, since 1964; Senior Research Fellow, Green Templeton College (formerly Green College), Oxford, since 2012 (Hon. Visiting Fellow, 1994–2012); Fellow, Birkbeck, University of London, since 2007; *b* 26 July 1919; *s* of Tom Arthur Lovelock and Nellie Ann Elizabeth (*née* March); *m* 1st, 1942, Helen Mary Hyslop (*d* 1989); two *s* two *d*; 2nd, 1991, Sandra Jean Orchard. *Educ:* Strand Sch., London; Manchester and London Univs. BSc, PhD, DSc, ARIC. Staff Scientist, Nat. Inst. for Med. Research, 1941–61; Rockefeller Fellow, Harvard Univ., 1954–55; Yale Univ., 1958–59; Prof. of Chemistry, Baylor Univ. Coll. of Medicine, Texas, 1961–64. Vis. Prof., Univ. of Reading, 1967–90. Pres., Marine Biol Assoc., 1986–90 (Founding Hon. Fellow, 2014). Mem. Sigma Xi, Yale Chapter, 1959. Hon. ScD East Anglia, 1982; Hon. DSc: Exeter, 1988; Plymouth Poly., 1988; Stockholm, 1991; Edinburgh, 1993; Kent, 1996; E London, 1996; Colorado, 1997; KCL, 2008; Goldsmiths Coll., London, 2011. Amsterdam Prize, Roy. Netherlands Acad. of Arts and Scis, 1990; Prize, Volvo Envmt Prize Foundn, 1996; Nonino Prize, Italy, 1996; Blue Planet Prize, Asahi Glass Foundn, Tokyo, 1997; Wollaston Medal, Geol Soc., 2006; John Collier, IChemE, 2006; Edinburgh Medal, 2006; Basile J. Luyet Medal, Soc. for Cryobiology, 2010; Climate Change Award, Foundn of Prince Albert II of Monaco, 2010; Pioneering Achievement in Exobiology, NASA, 2010; Observer Lifetime Ethical Achievement Award, 2011. *Publications:* Gaia, 1979; (with Michael Allaby) The Great Extinction, 1983; (with Michael Allaby) The Greening of Mars, 1984; The Ages of Gaia, 1988; Gaia: the practical science of planetary medicine, 1991; Homage to Gaia: the life of an independent scientist (autobiog.), 2000; The Revenge of Gaia, 2006; The Vanishing Face of Gaia, 2009; A Rough Ride to the Future, 2014; numerous papers and patents. *Recreations:* walking, digital photography, reading. *Address:* Matthew Cottage, The Old Coastguards, Abbotsbury, Dorset DT3 4LB.

LOVELUCK, Paul Edward, CBE 1993; Parliamentary Boundary Commissioner for Wales, since 2011; *b* 3 Feb. 1942; *s* of Edward Henry Loveluck and Elizabeth Loveluck (*née* Treharne); *m* 1965, Lynne Gronow; one *s* one *d*. *Educ:* Maesteg Grammar Sch.; UCW, Cardiff (BA). Board of Trade, 1963–69; Welsh Office, 1969–84 (Asst Sec., 1975–84); Chief Executive: Wales Tourist Bd, 1984–95; Countryside Council for Wales, 1996–2002. Chm., Wales New Deal Task Force, 1999–2003; Pres., Nat. Mus and Galls of Wales, later Nat. Mus. Wales, 2002–11. President: Maesteg Male Voice Choir, 1990–; Montgomeryshire Ladies Choir, 2007–. Chair: Montgomery Community Bldgs Preservation Trust, 2008–; Alliance for Nat. Parks Cymru, 2014–; Trustee of various mid-Wales charitable orgns. JP Cardiff, 1982–2006, Dyfed-Powys, 2006–12. *Recreations:* music, grandparenting. *Address:* Dôl Awel, 8 Corndon Drive, Montgomery, Powys SY15 6RE.

LOVEMAN, Stephen Charles Gardner; Under Secretary, Department of Employment, then Department for Education and Employment, 1989–96; *b* 26 Dec. 1943; *s* of Charles Edward Loveman and Edith Mary Gardner; *m* 1972, Judith Pamela Roberts; one *s* one *d*. *Educ:* Arnold Sch., Blackpool; Emmanuel College, Cambridge (BA). Dept of Employment, 1967; Private Sec. to Minister of State for Employment, 1972–74; Health and Safety Exec., 1974–77; Dept of Employment, 1977–80; Manpower Services Commn, 1980–87; Dept of Employment, 1987–88; Cabinet Office, 1988–89. *Recreations:* TV, cinema, theatre, opera, reading, walking, French, swimming, voluntary work (witness support).

LOVENDUSKI, Prof. Joni, PhD; FBA 2007; Anniversary Professor of Politics, Birkbeck College, University of London, since 2000; *b* 19 May 1945; *d* of Austin Lovenduski and Teresa Lovenduski (*née* Allan); *m* 1993, Prof. Alan Ware; one *s*, and one step *s*. *Educ:* Manchester Univ. (BSc Hons Econ. 1970; MA Govt 1976); Loughborough Univ. (PhD Politics 1986). Loughborough University: Lectr, then Sen. Lectr, in Politics, 1972–88; Reader in Politics, 1988–92; Prof. of Comparative Politics, 1992–94; Prof. of Politics, Southampton Univ., 1995–2000. Dir, British Candidate Study, 1992, British Representation Study, 1997, 2001, 2005. European Consortium for Political Research: Publications Dir, Exec. Cttee, 1997–2000; Vice-Chair, 2000–03; Founding Mem. and Convener, Standing Gp on Women and Politics, 1985. Mem., Res. Council, Eur. Univ. Inst., 2003–08. Founding Mem. and Convener, Women's Gp, Pol Studies Assoc. UK, 1977–. AcSS 2009. Prize for Special Achievement in Study of Politics, Pol Sci. Assoc., 2008; Gender and Politics Award, Eur. Consortium for Pol Res., 2009; Sir Isaiah Berlin Award for lifetime contribn to Pol Sci., Pol Studies Assoc., 2013. Chm. Editl Bd, Pol Quarterly, 2009–; Member, Editorial Board: British Jl of Pol Sci., 1995–; French Politics, 2003–; British Politics, 2006–; Eur. Pol Sci. Review, 2010–; Former Member, Editorial Board: Pol Studies, Politics and Gender, Social Movt Studies. *Publications:* (ed jtly) The Politics of the Second Electorate, 1981; (ed jtly) The New Politics of Abortion, 1986; Women and European Politics: contemporary feminism and public policy, 1986; (jtly) Politics and Society in Eastern Europe, 1987; (jtly) Contemporary Feminist Politics, 1993; (ed jtly) Gender and Party Politics, 1993; (ed jtly) Different Voices, Different Lives: gender and politics, a reader, 1994; (jtly) Political Recruitment: gender, race and class in the British Parliament, 1995; (ed jtly) Women in Politics in Britain, 1996; (ed) Feminism and Politics, 2 vols, 2000; Feminizing Politics, 2005; (ed) State Feminism and Political Representation, 2005; (jtly) Women in Parliament, 2005; contribs to British Jl Political Sci., Political Studies, Party Politics, Political Qly, Parly Affairs, Govt & Opposition, W Eur. Politics. *Recreations:* Italy, reading, gardening, bridge. *Address:* Department of Politics, Birkbeck College, Malet Street, WC1E 7HX.

LOVERANCE, Rowena Kathryn; writer and consultant; Head of Outreach and Learning Resources, then Head of e-learning, British Museum, 2001–07; *b* 4 Sept. 1952; *d* of Maurice and Wilfreda Loverance. *Educ:* Manchester High Sch. for Girls; Somerville Coll., Oxford (BA Hons Modern History; Dip. Archaeol.). Res. Fellow, Univ. of Birmingham, 1979–80; Lectr, Dept of Ancient History and Classical Archaeology, Univ. of Sheffield, 1980–83; Education Officer, 1985–98, Head of Educnl IT, 1998–2001, BM. Trustee, Culture24 (formerly 24 Hour Museum), 2005–13. Chm., Publications Cttee, Soc. for Promotion of Byzantine Studies, 2008–. Pres., Churches Together in England, 1998–2001. *Publications:* Byzantium, 1988; The British Museum Christ, 2004; Christian Art, 2007. *Recreations:* Byzantine studies, archaeology.

LOVERING, John David; Partner, Montagu Private Equity Advisors, since 2011; *b* 11 Oct. 1949; *s* of John George and Ruby Beatrice Lovering; *m* 1971, Brenda Joan Wotherspoon; two *s* one *d*. *Educ:* Dulwich Coll.; Exeter Univ. (BA Hons); Manchester Business Sch. (MBA). Planning Manager, Spillers Internat. Div., 1975–78; Corporate Strategy Manager, Lex Service plc, 1978–83; Grand Metropolitan plc, Commercial Dir, Express Dairy Ltd, 1983–85; Head of Gp Finance and Planning, Imperial Gp plc, 1985–86; Finance Dir, Sears plc, 1986–93; Chief Operating Officer, Tarmac plc, 1993–95; Chairman: Birthdays Gp Ltd, 1996–2002; Fired Earth Ltd, 1998–2001; Homebase Ltd, 2001–02; Debenhams plc, 2003–10; Somerfield Ltd, 2005–09; Mitchells & Butlers plc, 2010–11. Sen. Partner, Echelon Capital LLP, 2005–12. Non-executive Chairman: Peacock Gp Ltd, 1997–2004; Odeon Cinemas Ltd, 2000–03; Laurel Pub Co., 2002–04; Fitness First, 2003–05; GO Outdoors, 2010–11; Retail Trust, 2011–14; Maplin Electronics, 2011–14; Jamella plc, 2011–13; Host Europe Ltd Gp, 2012–13; EmiTel, Poland, 2012–13; itim, 2013–14; Vice-Chm., Barclays Capital, 2007–08; Director: Aga Foodservice, 2003–06; Meyer Department Stores Pty, Australia, 2006–09; A/S Solstra, Denmark, 2010–13. Trustee and Dir, SCF, 1990–96; Chm., Hastings Pier Charity, 2012–; Committee Member: Mending Broken Hearts Appeal, BHF, 2009–12; Retail Leadership Gp, Prince's Trust, 2009–11; Diamond Woods Adv. Gp, Woodland Trust, 2010– (Ambassador for Woodland Trust, 2013–). Member: Tonbridge Sch. Foundn, 2003–06; Vice-Chancellor's Cttee, Exeter Univ., 2003–; Dir, Dulwich Coll. Enterprises, 2008–; Gov., Dulwich Coll., 2010–. *Recreations:* sport, walking, farming. *Clubs:* Alleyn (Dulwich); Steenberg Golf.

LOVERING, Prof. John Francis, AO 1993; FAA; FTSE; Chairman: WaterEd Australia Pty Ltd, 2003–07; WaterSmart, 2004–06; Uniwater, since 2007; Board Member, Southern Rural Water, 2001–07; *b* 27 March 1930; *s* of George Francis Lovering and Dorothy Irene Mildwater; *m* 1954, Jennifer Kerry FitzGerald; two *s* one *d*. *Educ:* Canterbury High Sch., Sydney; Univ. of Sydney (MSc); Univ. of Melbourne (MSc); California Inst. of Technology (PhD). FAA 1982; FTSE (FTS 1993). Asst Curator of Minerals, Australian Museum, 1951–55; Research Fellow, Fellow and Sen. Fellow, Dept of Geophysics and Geochemistry, ANU, 1956–69; University of Melbourne: Prof. of Geology, 1969–87; Dean of Science, 1983–85; Dep. Vice-Chancellor (Research), 1985–87; Vice-Chancellor and Prof. of Geology, Flinders Univ. of SA, 1987–95. Professorial Fellow, Sch. of Earth Scis, Univ. of Melbourne, 1999–. Presiding Officer, Natural Resources Council of SA, 1992–94; Chairman: Australian Antarctic Sci. Adv. Cttee, 1985–89; Envmt Conservation Council of Victoria, 1998–2002; Australian Nat. Seismic Imaging Resource, 1998–2001; Gippsland Res. Coordination Gp, 1999–2001; Office for Environmental Programs: Chm., Academic Adv. Bd, 1999–2013; Mem., Community and Industry Adv. Bd, 1999–2013. Chairman of Directors: Comlabs Ltd, 1985–93; Geotrack International Pty Ltd, 1987–93; Open Learning Technology Corp., 1992–96. Pres., Murray-Darling Basin Commn, 1994–99. President: Royal Soc. of Victoria, 1977–79 (Mem. Bd, 1969–2014); and Mem. Bd, Internat. Geol Correlation Prog., 1981–87; Vice Pres., Internat. Union of Geol Scis, 1990–96. Hon. DSc: Flinders Univ., 1995; Melbourne Univ., 1999. Chevalier des Palmes Académiques, 1981. *Publications:* Last of Lands: Antarctica (with J. R. V. Prescott), 1979; contribs to learned jls. *Recreations:* music, wine, food. *Address:* 9 Park Square, Port Melbourne, Vic 3207, Australia. *Clubs:* Melbourne, Wallaby (Melbourne).

LOVESEY, Peter Harmer; crime writer, since 1970; *b* 10 Sept. 1936; *s* of Richard Lear Lovesey and Amy Lovesey (*née* Strank); *m* 1959, Jacqueline Ruth Lewis; one *s* one *d*. *Educ:* Hampton Grammar Sch.; Reading Univ. (BA Hons 1958). Flying Officer, RAF, 1958–61; Lectr, Thurrock Technical Coll., 1961–69; Head of Gen. Educn Dept, Hammersmith & West London Coll., 1969–75. Crime Writers' Association: Chm., 1991–92; Cartier Diamond Dagger, 2000. Grand Prix de Littérature Policière (French Crime Writers' Assoc.), 1985; Vikelas Plaque, Internat. Soc. of Olympic Historians, 2008; Grand Master, Swedish Acad. of Detection, 2010. *Publications:* Wobble to Death, 1970 (televised 1980); The Detective Wore Silk Drawers, 1971 (televised 1980); Abracadaver, 1972 (televised 1980); Mad Hatter's Holiday, 1973 (televised 1981); Invitation to a Dynamite Party, 1974 (televised 1981); A Case of Spirits, 1975 (televised 1980); Swing, Swing Together, 1976 (televised 1980); Waxwork (Silver Dagger), 1978 (televised 1979); The False Inspector Dew (Gold Dagger), 1982; Keystone, 1983; Rough Cider, 1986; Bertie and the Tinman, 1987; On the Edge, 1989 (televised as Dead Gorgeous, 2002); Bertie and the Seven Bodies, 1990; The Last Detective, 1991; Diamond Solitaire, 1992; Bertie and the Crime of Passion, 1993; The Summons (Silver Dagger), 1995; Bloodhounds (Silver Dagger), 1996; Upon a Dark Night, 1997; The Vault, 1999; The Reaper, 2000; Diamond Dust, 2002; The House Sitter, 2003; The Circle, 2005; The Secret Hangman, 2007; The Headhunters, 2008; Skeleton Hill, 2009; Stagestruck, 2011; Cop to Corpse, 2012; The Tooth Tattoo, 2013; The Stone Wife, 2014; Down Among the Dead Men, 2015; *short stories:* Butchers and Other Stories of Crime, 1985; The Crime of Miss Oyster Brown and Other Stories, 1994; Do Not Exceed the Stated Dose, 1998; The Sedgemoor Strangler and Other Stories of Crime, 2001; Murder on the Short List, 2008; *non-fiction:* The Kings of Distance, 1968; (jtly) The Guide to British Track and Field Literature, 1969; The Official Centenary History of the Amateur Athletic Association, 1979; (jtly) An Athletics Compendium: an annotated guide to the UK literature of track and field, 2001; *as Peter Lear:* Goldengirl, 1977 (filmed 1979); Spider Girl, 1980; The Secret of Spandau, 1986. *Recreations:* researching athletics history, visiting teashops. *Address:* c/o Vanessa Holt Ltd, 59 Crescent Road, Leigh-on-Sea, Essex SS9 2PF. *Club:* Detection.

LOVESTONE, Prof. Simon Harold; Professor of Translational Neuroscience, University of Oxford, since 2014; *b* 16 Feb. 1961. *Educ:* Univ. of Sheffield (BSc Microbiol. 1982); Univ. of Southampton (BM 1986); PhD London 1998. MRCPsych. Sen. Lectr, 1995–99, Reader, 1999–2000, in Old Age Psychiatry, Prof. of Old Age Psychiatry, 2000–14, Inst. of Psychiatry, London Univ.; Hon. Consultant, Maudsley Hosp., 1995–2014. Dir, NIHR Biomedical Res. Centre for Mental Health, 2007–14; Dir of Res., King's Health Partners, 2010–14. Chm., Sci. Adv. Bd, Alzheimer's Res. Trust, 2004–09. *Publications:* scientific papers on old age psychiatry and neuroscience. *Address:* Department of Psychiatry, University of Oxford Medical Sciences Division, Warneford Hospital, Oxford OX3 7JX.

LOVILL, Sir John (Roger), Kt 1987; CBE 1983; DL; Chairman, Sloane Square Investments, 1980–99 (Director, 1960–99); *b* 26 Sept. 1929; *s* of Walter Thomas Lovill and Elsie Lovill (*née* Page); *m* 1958, Jacqueline (*née* Parker); two *s* (one *d* decd). *Educ:* Brighton Hove and Sussex Grammar School. S. G. Warburg, 1951–55; Dep. Gen. Manager, Securicor Ltd, 1955–60; Dir, Municipal Gen. Insce Co., 1984–95; Managing Trustee, Municipal Mutual Insce, 1988–2013 (Chm., 1993–2013); Chm., Nationwide Small Business Property Trust, 1988–96; Chm., Prime Health Ltd, 1992–94. Contested (C) Ebbw Vale, 1966; Mem., East Sussex CC, 1967–89, Leader, 1973–77; Chairman: Sussex Police Authority, 1976–79; Local Authority Conditions of Service Adv. Bd, 1978–83; ACC, 1983–86; Pres., Sussex Assoc. of Local Councils, 1987–97; Vice Pres., Nat. Assoc. of Local Councils, 1991–93; Leader, Conservative Assoc. of County Councils, 1981–83. DL E Sussex 1983. *Recreations:* opera, politics, marine paintings. *Address:* 34 Sadlers Way, Ringmer, Lewes, Sussex BN8 5HG.

LOW, family name of **Barons Aldington** and **Low of Dalston**.

LOW OF DALSTON, Baron *cr* 2006 (Life Peer), of Dalston in the London Borough of Hackney; **Colin MacKenzie Low,** CBE 2000; Vice-President, Royal National Institute of Blind People (formerly Royal National Institute for the Blind), since 2009 (Chairman, 2000–09); President, International Council for Education of People with Visual Impairment, since 2010 (Member, Executive Committee, 1987–2010); *b* 23 Sept. 1942; *s* of Arthur Eric Low and Catherine Cameron (*née* Anderson); *m* 1969, Jill Irene Coton; one *s* one *d*. *Educ:* Worcester Coll. for the Blind; Queen's Coll., Oxford (BA Juris, MA 1987); Churchill Coll., Cambridge (Dip. Criminol.). Lectr in Law, Univ. of Leeds, 1968–84; Dir, Disability Resource Team, 1984–94; Sen. Res. Fellow, 1994–2000, Vis. Prof., 2000–, City Univ. Member: Special Educnl Needs Tribunal, 1994–2007; Nat. Disability Council, 1996–2000; Disability Rights Task Force, 1997–99; Disability Rights Commn, 2000–02. Chm., Low Commn on Future of Advice and Legal Support, 2012–. President: European Blind Union, 2003–11; Skill, 2008–11 (Mem. Council, 1975–2003; Vice-Pres., 2003–08); Disability Alliance, 2010–11 (Mem. Cttee, 1974–2011; Chm., 1991–97; Vice-Pres., 1997–2010); Visionary (formerly Nat. Assoc. of Local Socs for Visually Impaired People), 2010–; Mem. Council, St

Dunstan's, 2000–10. *Publications:* contrib. articles to learned periodicals. *Recreations:* music, wine appreciation. *Address:* Royal National Institute of Blind People, 105 Judd Street, WC1H 9NE. *T:* (020) 7392 2205. *E:* colin.low@rnib.org.uk.

LOW, Brian Buik, CBE 1994; HM Diplomatic Service, retired; High Commissioner to Papua New Guinea, 1994–97; *b* 15 Nov. 1937; *s* of Robert James Low and Helen Duncan Low; *m* 1960, Anita Joan Allum; three *d. Educ:* Arbroath High Sch. Served RAF, 1956–61. Joined Diplomatic Service, 1962; FO, 1962–65; Sofia, 1965–67; Sydney, 1967–69; Kuala Lumpur, 1969–73; Moscow, 1973–74; FCO, 1974–78; Singapore, 1978–81; Commercial Consul, British Trade Develt Office, NY, 1981–84; First Sec., FCO, 1984–88; Head of Chancery, Lima, 1988–91; Ambassador to Estonia, 1991–94. *Recreations:* music, reading, golf, watching sport. *Clubs:* Carnoustie Golf; Singapore Cricket.

LOW, Prof. Donald Anthony, AO 2005; DPhil, LittD; FRHistS, FAHA, FASSA; President of Clare Hall, 1987–94, Smuts Professor of the History of the British Commonwealth, 1983–87, and Deputy Vice-Chancellor, 1990–94, University of Cambridge; *b* 22 June 1927; *o s* of late Canon Donald Low and Winifred (*née* Edmunds); *m* 1952, Isobel Smails; one *s* two *d. Educ:* Haileybury and ISC; Exeter Coll., Oxford (Open Scholar in Modern History, 1944; Amelia Jackson Sen. Student, 1948; MA, DPhil; Hon. Fellow, 1992); PhD 1983, LittD 1998, Cantab. Lectr, subseq. Sen. Lectr, Makerere Coll., University Coll. of E Africa, 1951–58; Uganda corresp., The Times, 1952–58; Fellow, subseq. Sen. Fellow in History, Res. Sch. of Social Sciences, ANU, 1959–64; Founding Dean of Sch. of African and Asian Studies, and Prof. of Hist., Univ. of Sussex, 1964–72; Australian National University: Prof. of History, 1973–83; Dir, Res. Sch. of Pacific Studies, 1973–75; Vice Chancellor, 1975–82; University Fellow, 1997–2000; University of Cambridge: Fellow, Churchill Coll., 1983–87; Dir, Centre of Internat. Studies, 1985–87; Mem., Council of Senate, 1985–88. Sen. Visitor Nuffield Coll., Oxford, 1956–57; Smuts Fellow and Vis. Fellow, Clare Hall, Cambridge, 1971–72 (Hon. Fellow, 1999). Chm., Educn Adv. Cttee, Aust. Develt Assistance Bureau, 1979–82; Mem. Exec., 1976–82, Dep. Chm., 1980, Aust. Vice-Chancellors' Cttee; Member: Council, Univ. of Papua New Guinea, 1974–82; Standing Cttee, Aust. Univs Internat. Develt Program, 1975–82; Council, ACU, 1980–82; Cttee, Australian Studies Centre, London Univ., 1983–94; Governing Body: Inst. of Develt Studies, Sussex Univ., 1966–72 and 1984–91; SOAS, 1983–94; Haileybury, 1985–94; Chm., Cttee of Management, Inst. of Commonwealth Studies, London Univ., 1984–94. Hon. Fellow: Inst. of Develt Studies, UK, 1972; University House, ANU 1983. President: African Studies Assoc. of Aust. and Pacific, 1979–82; Asian Studies Assoc. of Aust., 1980–82; British Australian Studies Assoc., 1984–86; Chm., Co-ordinating Council, Area Studies Assoc., 1988–91; Vice-Pres., Australian Acad. of Humanities, 1996–98. Chm., Round Table Moot, 1992–94. Commander of the Order of Civil Merit (Spain), 1984. *Publications:* Buganda and British Overrule, 1900–1955 (with R. C. Pratt), 1960; (ed) Soundings in Modern South Asian History, 1968; (with J. C. Iltis and M. D. Wainwright) Government Archives in South Asia, 1969; Buganda in Modern History, 1971; The Mind of Buganda, 1971; Lion Rampant, 1973; (ed) Congress and the Raj 1917–1947, 1977; Oxford History of East Africa: (contrib.) Vol. I, 1963 and Vol. II, 1965; (contrib. and ed jtly) Vol. III, 1976; (ed) Constitutional Heads and Political Crises, 1988; (ed) The Indian National Congress, 1988; (ed jtly) Sovereigns and Surrogates, 1990; Eclipse of Empire, 1991; (ed) Political Inheritance of Pakistan, 1991; The Egalitarian Moment: Asia and Africa 1950–80, 1996; Britain and Indian Nationalism, 1997; (ed) Keith Hancock: legacies of an historian, 2001; Fabrication of Empire, 2009; articles on internat. history in jls. *Address:* H114 Goodwin Village, 35 Bonney Street, Ainslie, ACT 2602, Australia.

LOW, Dr (George) Graeme (Erick), CBE 1989; Member, 1986–91, Managing Director, Site Operations, 1990–91, United Kingdom Atomic Energy Authority; *b* Palmerston North, NZ, 29 Nov. 1928; *s* of George Eric Low and Evelyn Edith Low (*née* Gillman); *m* 1st, 1952, Marion Townsend (marr. diss. 1977); two *d*; 2nd, 1985, Joan Kathleen Swinburne. *Educ:* New Plymouth Boys' High Sch., NZ; Canterbury Coll., Univ. of NZ (BSc, MSc); Univ. of Reading (PhD, DSc). FInstP. Special Branch, RNZN, 1952–58; Research Scientist, 1958–68, Head of Materials Physics Div., 1968–70, AERE Harwell; Special Asst to Dir, UKAEA Research Gp, 1970–73; Programme Dir (Applied Nuclear), 1973–76, Research Dir (Industry), 1976–81, Dir of Environmental Research, 1981–83, AERE Harwell; Dir, AEE, Winfrith, 1983–86; Dir, AERE Harwell, 1986–87; Mem. for Estabts, UKAEA, 1987–90. Dir, UK Nirex Ltd, 1986–91. *Publications:* papers on semi-conductors, neutron beam studies of the solid state, magnetism and management. *Recreations:* reading, walking, family and friends. *Address:* 21 New Road, Reading RG1 5JD.

LOW, Gillian; Head Mistress, The Lady Eleanor Holles School, Hampton, 2004–14; *b* 21 Feb. 1955; *d* of William Edward Coysh and Elizabeth Joyce Coysh (*née* Legge); one *s* two *d. Educ:* North London Collegiate Sch.; Somerville Coll., Oxford (Emma Clarke Beilby Schol.; BA Hons 1977, MA 1982); Trinity Coll., Cambridge (Tripos Prize; PGCE 1981). Mgt trainee, Courtaulds Ltd, 1977–79; teacher of English as foreign lang., British Coll., Reggio di Calabria, Italy, 1979–80; Asst English Teacher, then Dep. Hd of Dept, Claverham Community Coll., Battle, 1981–88; Hd of English, then Dir of Studies, Bishop Ramsey Sch., Ruislip, 1989–94; Dep. Headmistress, Godolphin and Latymer Sch., Hammersmith, 1994–98; Headmistress, Francis Holland Sch., N London, 1998–2004. Mem., Humanities Ext. Adv. Panel, Univ. of Oxford, 2013–14. Member: ASCL (formerly SHA), 1994–2014; GSA, 1998–2014 (Pres., 2010; Vice-Pres., 2011; Hon. Mem., 2014; representative: Council, Internat. Confedn of Principals, 2008–13; Ind. Schs Travel Assoc., 2008–14 (Trustee, 2010–14); Ind. Schs Inspectorate, 2014–); GSA/HMC Educn and Acad. Policy Cttee, 2004–08; GSA/HMC Universities Cttee, 2009–12. Governor: Sarum Hall Sch., Hampstead, 2003–05; Moat Sch., Fulham, 2003–06 (Chm., Educn Cttee, 2004–06); Queen's Coll., London, 2006–14; St Paul's Girls' Sch., 2015–; Warwick Ind. Schs Foundn, 2015–. *Recreations:* travel, reading, art, photography. *Club:* Lansdowne.

LOW, Dr John Menzies, CBE 2008; Chief Executive, Charities Aid Foundation, since 2007; *b* 1 July 1953; *s* of late David Low and Helen Low (*née* Menzies); *m* 1977, Alison Jean Donald; two *d. Educ:* Aberdeen Acad.; Robert Gordon's Inst. of Technol. (BSc); Univ. of Aberdeen (MSc, PhD); Templeton Coll., Oxford. CEng, FIET. John Brown Engrg (UDI), 1979–84; Wm McGeogh, Birmingham, 1984–87; Booker plc (Sortex), 1988–93; Bühler AG (Sortex), 1993–99; with RNID, 1999–2007, Chief Exec., 2002–07. Mem., Assoc. of Offshore Diving Contractors Task Force on safe use of electricity underwater, 1983–84. Ind. Mem., H of L Appts Commn, 2008–13. Chm., Disability Charities Consortium, 2003–07; non-executive Director: Euclid Network of European Third Sector Leaders, 2007–; CAF Bank Ltd, 2007–. Trustee: ACEVO, 2003–09 (Chm., 2005–09); Charity Bank, 2010–. Ind. Mem. Council, City Univ. London, 2011–. Deacon: Gilcomston Park Baptist Ch, 1977–84; Hertford Baptist Ch, 1991–2003 (Treas., 1994–2003). CCMI. FRSA. *Publications:* 6 patents in optics and automated sorting; contrib. articles on speech fluency, auditory feedback, image processing, marketing and voluntary sector; commentator on social investment, philanthropy, economy and civil society. *Address:* Charities Aid Foundation, 10 St Bride Street, EC4A 4AD. *T:* 0300 012 3010. *E:* jlow@cafonline.org.

LOW, Sir Richard Walter Morrison-, 4th Bt *cr* 1908, of Kilmaron, co. Fife; *b* 4 Aug. 1959; *o s* of Sir James Richard Morrison-Low, 3rd Bt and Ann Rawson Morrison-Low (*née* Gordon); *S* father, 2012; *m* 1994, Sandra Scott Newman; one *s* one *d. Heir: s* Rory James Morrison-Low, *b* 1997. *Address:* Kilmaron Farm, Cupar, Fife KY15 4NE.

LOWCOCK, Andrew Charles; His Honour Judge Lowcock; a Circuit Judge, since 2001; *b* 22 Nov. 1949; *s* of Eric and Elizabeth Lowcock; *m* 1st, 1976, Patricia Anne Roberts (marr. diss. 1985); 2nd, 1985, Sarah Elaine Edwards; two *s. Educ:* Malvern Coll.; New Coll., Oxford (MA). Called to the Bar, Middle Temple, 1973; barrister, specialising in criminal and family law, Northern Circuit, 1974–2001; Asst Recorder, 1993–97; Recorder, 1997–2001. Gov., The Ryleys School, 1996–2007. *Recreations:* music, theatre, watching cricket and football. *Address:* The Crown Court, Minshull Street, Manchester M1 3FS. *Clubs:* MCC; Lancashire County Cricket, Nefyn Golf.

LOWCOCK, Mark Andrew, CB 2011; Permanent Secretary, Department for International Development, since 2011; *b* 25 July 1962; *s* of Brian Lowcock and Stella Connolly; *m* 1991, Dr Julia Watson; two *s* one *d. Educ:* Christ Church, Oxford (BA Hons 1985); Birkbeck Coll., Univ. of London (MSc Econs Dist. 1988). Grad. Fellow, Boston Univ., 1989. Mem. CIPFA 2007. Overseas Development Administration, then Department for International Development, 1985: Private Sec. to Minister for Overseas Develt, 1992–94; Dep., then Hd, Central Africa, Harare, 1994–97; Hd, EU Dept, 1997–99; Hd, Eastern Africa, 1999–2001; Dir, Finance and Corporate Performance, 2001–03; Director General: Corporate Performance and Knowledge Sharing, 2003–06; Policy and International, 2006–08; Country Progs, 2008–11. *Recreations:* Manchester United Football Club, Africa, reading. *Address:* Department for International Development, 22 Whitehall, SW1A 2EG. *T:* (020) 7023 0500, *Fax:* (020) 7023 0634. *E:* pspermsec@dfid.gov.uk.

LOWDEN, Prof. John Hopkins, PhD; FBA 2013; Professor of the History of Art, Courtauld Institute of Art, London, since 2002; *b* 1 May 1953; *s* of Eric Walter and Muriel Florence Amelia Lowden; *m* 1980, Joanna Louise Cannon; one *s* one *d. Educ:* Leys Sch., Cambridge (Schol.); Emmanuel Coll., Cambridge (Exhibnr; MA (English) 1974; Hon. Fellow 2011); Courtauld Inst. of Art, London (MA 1977; PhD (Hist. of Art) 1980). Jun. Fellow, Dumbarton Oaks, 1979–80; Temp. Lectr, Univ. of St Andrews, 1981; Lectr, 1982–94, Reader, 1994–2002, Courtauld Inst. of Art, London. Leverhulme Sen. Res. Fellow, 1992–93; Grinfield Lectr, Univ. of Oxford, 1996–98. MAE 2006. Corresp. Fellow, Medieval Acad. of America, 2010. Otto Gründler Prize, Western Michigan Univ., 2002. *Publications:* Illuminated Prophet Books, 1988; The Octateuchs, 1992; Early Christian and Byzantine Art, 1997, 6th edn 2008 (trans. French, Greek, Japanese, Korean); The Making of the 'Bibles Moralisées', vol. I, The Manuscripts, vol. II, The Book of Ruth, 2000; (with Alixe Bovey) Under the Influence, 2007; (with John Cherry) Medieval Ivories and Works of Art, 2008; The Jaharis Gospel Lectionary, 2009; (with Eberhard König) Biblia Moralizada de los Limbourg, 2010; (with Scot McKendrick and Kathleen Doyle) Royal Manuscripts: the genius of illumination, 2011; numerous contribs, primarily on manuscript illumination, to scholarly jls, standard ref. works, conf. procs, exhibn catalogues, etc. *Recreation:* family. *Address:* Courtauld Institute of Art, Somerset House, Strand, WC2R 0RN. *T:* (020) 7848 2668, *Fax:* (020) 7848 2410. *E:* John.Lowden@courtauld.ac.uk.

LOWE, Prof. (Alan) Vaughan; QC 2008; barrister; Chichele Professor of Public International Law, University of Oxford, 1999–2012, now Emeritus; Fellow of All Souls College, Oxford, 1999–2012, now Emeritus; *b* 1952; *m* Sally. *Educ:* UWIST (LLB 1973; LLM 1978; PhD 1980); MA Cantab 1991; MA Oxon 1999. Called to the Bar, Gray's Inn, 1993, Bencher, 2008; in practice at the Bar, Essex Court Chambers, 1993–. Lectr, Cardiff Law Sch., 1973–79; Lectr, 1979–86, Sen. Lectr, 1986–88, Manchester Univ.; Cambridge University: Lectr, 1988–94; Reader in Internat. Law, 1994–99; Fellow of Corpus Christi Coll., 1988–99; Warden of Leckhampton, 1998–99. Visiting Professor: Duke Law Sch., USA, 1990; Tulane Law Sch., USA, 2000. Mem., Institut de droit international (Associé, 2005); Judge, European Nuclear Energy Tribunal, 2006–; *ad hoc* Judge, ECHR, 2009–10. Pres. or Mem., various arbitral tribunals, 2004–. Order of the Rising Sun, Gold Rays with Neck Ribbon (Japan), 2008; Cavaler, Ordinul Nat. Serviciul Credincios, Romania, 2009; Darjah Paduka Seri Laila Jasa Yang Amat Berjasa (Darjah Ke-Dua), Brunei, 2010. *Publications:* Extraterritorial Jurisdiction, 1983; (jtly) The Law of the Sea, 1983, 3rd edn 1999; (jtly) Fifty Years of the International Court of Justice, 1996; (jtly) The Settlement of International Disputes, 1999; International Law, 2007; papers in jls. *Recreations:* ambling, rambling, music. *Address:* Essex Court Chambers, 24 Lincoln's Inn Fields, WC2A 3EG. *T:* (020) 7813 8000.

LOWE, Prof. (Charles) Fergus, PhD; CPsychol, FBPsS; Professor of Psychology, Bangor University (formerly University College of North Wales, then University of Wales, Bangor), 1988–2011, now Emeritus; Chief Executive Officer, Food Dudes Health Ltd, since 2012; *b* 24 April 1946; *s* of Charles Lowe and Bridget Lowe (*née* Harte); *m* 1971, Patricia Mary Sheehy; two *d. Educ:* De La Salle Coll., Waterford; Trinity Coll., Dublin (BA Hons Phil. and Psychol.); UCNW (PhD Psychol. 1973). FBPsS 1986; CPsychol 1989. University College of North Wales, later University of Wales, Bangor: Lectr, then Sen. Lectr in Psychol., 1973–88; Hd, Sch. of Psychol., 1987–2005; Dir, Centre for Child Develt, 1990–2004; Dir, Bangor Food Res. Unit (Food Dude Prog.), 1989–; Pro Vice-Chancellor, 2003–04; Dep. Vice-Chancellor, 2004–11; Acting Vice-Chancellor, 2010. Mem., Vice-Chancellors' Bd, Univ. of Wales, 1994–95. Res. Consultant, 1990–, Sci. Dir for Exploratory Consumer Sci., 1994–2001, Unilever. Healthy Eating Consultant for Irish Govt, 2005–, for various English PCTs, 2010–; Vice Chm., EC Scientific Gp of Experts for Sch. Fruit Scheme, 2011–. Chm., Exptl Analysis of Behaviour Gp, 1977–2005. Pres., Eur. Assoc. for Behaviour Analysis, 2001–02. Caroline Walker Trust Award, 1998; WHO Award for Counteracting Obesity, 2006; Gold Medal, CMO's Public Health Awards, 2010; Scientific Translation Award, Soc. for Advancement of Behaviour Analysis, Seattle, 2012. *Publications:* (ed jtly) Quantification of Steady-State Operant Behaviour, 1981; (ed jtly) Behaviour Analysis and Contemporary Psychology, 1985; (with Dr Brigid Lowe) Teach Yourself Brain Training for Babies, 2011; contrib. numerous papers to scientific jls. *Recreations:* family, art, architecture, literature, classical and world music, film, wildlife, football, food. *Address:* School of Psychology, Brigantia Building, Bangor University, Bangor, Gwynedd LL57 2AS. *T:* (01248) 430410, 07818 412893. *E:* c.f.lowe@bangor.ac.uk.

LOWE, Prof. Christopher Robin, OBE 2011; PhD; FREng; Fellow, Trinity College, Cambridge, since 1984; Director of Biotechnology, since 1984, Director, Institute of Biotechnology, since 1988, and Professor of Biotechnology, since 1999, University of Cambridge; *b* 15 Oct. 1945; *s* of late Thomas Lowe and of Hilda Lowe (*née* Moxham); *m* 1974, Patricia Margaret Reed; one *s* one *d. Educ:* Univ. of Birmingham (BSc 1967; PhD Biochem., 1970). FREng 2005. Postdoctoral Research Associate: Dept of Biochem., Univ. of Liverpool, 1970–73; Pure and Applied Biochem., Univ. of Lund, Sweden, 1973–74; Lectr in Biochem., 1975–82, Sen. Lectr, 1982–84, Univ. of Southampton. Visiting Professor: Univ. of Lund, 1995–; Univ. of Bath, 1996–. *Publications:* Affinity Chromatography, 1974; An Introduction to Affinity Chromatography, 1979; numerous contribs to learned jls; 83 patents. *Recreations:* antiques, travel. *Address:* Institute of Biotechnology, University of Cambridge, Tennis Court Road, Cambridge CB2 1QT. *T:* (01223) 334160; The Limes, Hempstead, Saffron Walden, Essex CB10 2PW. *T:* (01799) 599307.

LOWE, David Alexander; QC 1984; *b* Kilbirnie, Ayrshire, 1 Nov. 1942; *o s* of late David Alexander Lowe and Rea Sadie Aitchison Lowe (*née* Bridges); *m* 1972, Vivian Anne Langley; three *s* two *d. Educ:* Pocklington Sch., York; St John's Coll., Cambridge (schol.; MA; MacMahon Law Student). Called to Bar, Middle Temple, 1965 (Harmsworth Schol.; Bencher, 1992), *ad eundem*; Lincoln's Inn, 1975. In practice at the Chancery Bar, 1966–. *Address:* 13 Old Square Chambers, 13–14 Old Square, Lincoln's Inn, WC2A 3UE.

LOWE, Hon. Douglas Ackley, AM 2000; Chairman: Premier's Physical Activity Council, 2004–07; Board of Governance, GP Assist Tasmania, 2004–11; Executive Officer, Tasmanian Branch, Australian Medical Association, 1992–2004; *b* 15 May 1942; *s* of Ackley Reginald Lowe and Dulcie Mary Lowe (*née* Kean); *m* 1963, Pamela June (*née* Grant); two *s* two *d*. *Educ:* St Virgil College, Hobart. Mem. Tasmanian House of Assembly, for Franklin, 1969–86: ALP, 1969–82; Ind., 1982–86. Minister for Housing, 1972; Chief Secretary, 1974; Deputy Premier, 1975–77; Chief Sec. and Minister for Planning and Reorganisation, 1975; Premier, 1977–81; Treasurer, 1980–81; Minister for: Industrial Relations, Planning and the Environment, 1976; Industrial Relations and Health, Aug. 1976; Industrial Relations and Manpower Planning, 1977–79; Economic Planning and Development, 1979–80; Energy, 1979–81; MLC (Ind.) Buckingham, Tas., 1986–92; Dep. Leader for Govt, Legislative Council, 1989–92. Australian Labor Party: State Sec. 1965–69, State Pres. 1974–75, Tasmanian Section. Tasmanian Deleg. to Aust. Constitutional Convention, 1973–85. Senator, Jaycees Internat. State Pres., Tasmanian Swimming Inc., 1990–98; Mem. Panel, Australian Swimming Disciplinary Tribunal, 1996–98. Treas., 2011–12, Sec., 2012–, Berriedale Bowls Club Inc. Silver Jubilee Medal, 1977; Australian Sports Medal, 2000; Centenary Medal (Tasmania), 2003; President's Award, AMA, 2004. *Publications:* The Price of Power, 1984. *Address:* 1 Michele Court, Berriedale, Tas 7011, Australia.

LOWE, Air Chief Marshal Sir Douglas (Charles), GCB 1977 (KCB 1974; CB 1971); DFC 1943; AFC 1946; *b* 14 March 1922; *s* of John William Lowe; *m* 1944, Doreen Elizabeth (*née* Nichols) (*d* 2008); one *s* one *d*. *Educ:* Reading School. Joined RAF, 1940; No 75 (NZ) Sqdn, 1943; Bomber Comd Instructors' Sch., 1945; RAF Coll., Cranwell, 1947; Exam. Wing CFS, 1950; Air Min. Operational Requirements, 1955; OC No 148 Sqdn, 1959; Exchange Officer, HQ SAC, USAF, 1961; Stn Comdr Cranwell, 1963; idc 1966; DOR 2 (RAF), MoD (Air), 1967; SASO, NEAF, 1969–71; ACAS (Operational Requirements), 1971–73; AOC No 18 Group, RAF, 1973–75; Controller, Aircraft, MoD Procurement Executive, 1975–82; Chief of Defence Procurement, MoD, Sept. 1982–June 1983. Air ADC to the Queen, 1978–83. Chairman: Mercury Communications Ltd, 1984–85; Band III Hldgs, 1986–91; Director: Royal Ordnance plc, 1984–7; Rolls Royce, 1984–92. Mem. Council, St John's Sch., Leatherhead, 1984–94. CRAeS 1982; CCMI (CBIM 1984). *Recreations:* gardening, domestic odd-jobbing, photography, theatre, music. *Club:* Royal Air Force.

See also Baron Glanusk.

LOWE, Fergus; *see* Lowe, C. F.

LOWE, Sir Frank (Budge), Kt 2001; Founder, 1981, and Chairman Emeritus, since 2003, Lowe and Partners Worldwide (formerly Lowe Howard Spink); *b* 23 Aug. 1941; *s* of Stephen and Marion Lowe; two *s* one *d*. *Educ:* Westminster School. Vis. Prof., UCL, 1990–. Founder and Trustee, Capital City Acad., 2003–. FRSA.

LÖWE, Dr Jan, FRS 2008; Joint Head, Structural Studies Division, MRC Laboratory of Molecular Biology, University of Cambridge, since 2010; Fellow, Darwin College, Cambridge, since 2012. *Educ:* Univ. of Hamburg (BSc Chem. 1992); Max-Planck-Inst. for Biochem. (PhD 1996). MRC Laboratory of Molecular Biology, University of Cambridge: Fellow, 1996–98; tenure-track Gp Leader, Bacterial Cytoskeleton Gp, 1998–2002; tenured Gp Leader, 2002–. Mem., EMBO, 2004. Young Investigator Award, 2001, Gold Medal, 2007, EMBO. *Publications:* contribs to jls incl. Cell, Nature, Annual Revs in Biochem. *Address:* MRC Laboratory of Molecular Biology, Francis Crick Avenue, Cambridge CB2 0QH.

LOWE, Janet, CBE 2003; FRSE 2010; Principal, Lauder College, Dunfermline, 1996–2005 (Depute Principal, 1992–95); *b* South Normanton, 27 Sept. 1950; *d* of George Frederick and Sheila Lowe; *m* 1982, Dr Donald Thomas Stewart. *Educ:* Swanwick Hall Grammar Sch.; Univ. of Hull (BA Hons French and Italian 1973); Univ. of Dundee (MBA 1990); Univ. of Stirling (EdD 2005). Immigration Officer, Home Office, 1973–76; Personnel Asst, Univ. of Hull, 1976–80; Adminr, Lothian Regl Council, 1980–82; Personnel Officer, 1982–86, Asst Registrar, 1986–88, Napier Univ.; Sec. and Registrar, Duncan of Jordanstone Coll. of Art, 1988–92. Member: Bd of Mgt, Scottish Further Educn Unit, 1993–2001; Scottish Consultative Council on the Curriculum, 1995–99; Scottish Cttee, Nat. Cttee of Inquiry into Higher Educn, 1996–97; Bd, Scottish Enterprise, 1998–2004; Bd, Assoc. of Scottish Colls, 2002–05; Ind. Rev. of Local Govt Finance, 2004–07; SFC, 2005–13; Bd, Skills Develt Scotland, 2008–13. US/UK Fulbright Comr, 2009–12. Hon. Prof. of Applied Social Scis, Univ. of Stirling, 2010–. Trustee, Carnegie Trust for Univs of Scotland, 2005–. Member of Court: Heriot-Watt Univ., 1999–2005; Univ. of Dundee, 2005–13. FRSE 2010. Hon. DEd Queen Margaret Univ., Edinburgh, 2007. *Recreations:* Rotary (Pres., Rotary Club of Dunfermline Carnegie, 2008–09; Foundn Chm., District 1010, 2012–), gardening, keeping fit, reading novels, visiting Italy. *Address:* 42 Gamekeepers Road, Kinnesswood, Kinross KY13 9JR. *T:* (01592) 840277. *E:* janetlowe@aol.com.

LOWE, Prof. (Joseph) John, PhD; CGeol, FGS, FRGS; Gordon Manley Professor of Geography (formerly Professor of Geography and Quaternary Science), Royal Holloway, University of London, 1992–2013, now Emeritus; Leverhulme Trust Emeritus Fellow, 2014–Sept. 2016; *b* 12 June 1946; *s* of Joseph Lowe and Margaret (*née* Rooney); *m* 1969, Jeanette P. Bell; two *s*. *Educ:* Univ. of St Andrews (MA 1st Cl. Hons Geog. 1970); Univ. of Edinburgh (PhD 1977). City of London Polytechnic: Lectr, 1973–77; Sen. Lectr, 1977–85; Principal Lectr and Reader, 1985–88; Prof. and Hd, Dept of Geog., 1988–89; Royal Holloway and Bedford New College, University of London: Sen. Lectr, 1989–90; Reader, 1990–92; Dean of Science, 1997–2000; Dir, Centre for Quaternary Res., Univ. of London, 1989–97 and 2006. Pres., UK Quaternary Res. Assoc., 2005–08 (Vice-Pres., 1992–97); Sen. Vice-Pres., Internat. Union of Quaternary Assocs, 2011–15 (Vice-Pres., 2007–11). Chm., Earth Scis Cttee, NERC, 1993–96. Univ. of Helsinki Medal, 1996; Coke Medal, Geol Soc. of London, 2003; Victoria Medal, RGS, 2011; Croll Medal, Quaternary Res. Assoc., 2013. *Publications:* Studies in the Scottish Lateglacial Environment, 1977; Studies in the Lateglacial Environment of North-West Europe, 1980; (with M. J. C. Walker) Reconstructing Quaternary Environments, 1984, 3rd edn 2015; contrib. to Nature, Jl Geol Soc., Jl Ecology, Phil. Trans Royal Soc., Quaternary Sci. Rev. and others. *Recreations:* music, hill-walking, soccer (training). *Address:* Department of Geography, Royal Holloway, University of London, Egham, Surrey TW20 0EX. *T:* (01784) 443565. *E:* j.lowe@rhul.ac.uk.

LOWE, (Nicholas) Mark; QC 1996; a Recorder, since 2000; *b* 17 June 1947; *s* of late John Lancelot Lowe, solicitor, and Margaret Janet Lowe (*née* Hucklesby); *m* 1975, Felicity Anne Parry-Williams; two *s* one *d*. *Educ:* Colchester Royal Grammar Sch.; Leicester Univ. (LLB 1969). Called to the Bar, Gray's Inn, 1972, Bencher, 2004; in practice at the Bar, 1973–; Head of Chambers, 2006–11. *Recreations:* fishing (occasional), walking, birdwatching, gardening, allotment bashing, Friary rebuilding. *Address:* Cornerstone Barristers, 2–3 Gray's Inn Square, WC1R 5JH. *T:* (020) 7242 4986.

LOWE, Peter Alexander; Group Applications Director, Department for Work and Pensions, until 2013; *b* 1 March 1955; *s* of James Thomas Lowe and Dorothy Jean Bell Lowe; one *s* one *d*; *m* 2009, Marion Chuter. *Educ:* Wallace Hall Acad.; Heriot-Watt Univ. (BSc Hons Mech. Engrg). ESSO/EXXON, 1977–99: Maintenance Manager, Fawley Refinery, 1996–97; Prog. Manager, EXXON Year 2000, 1998–99; Principal Consultant, Booz Allen Hamilton, 1999–2003; Dir, IT, Home Office, 2003–06; Chief Inf. Officer and Dir, Inf. and Workplace Services, DTI, later BERR, 2006–09; Change and Transformation Dir, Pension, Disability and Carers Service, DWP, 2009. *Recreations:* golf, running. *Club:* Bramley Golf.

LOWE, Prof. Philip David, OBE 2003; Duke of Northumberland Professor of Rural Economy, University of Newcastle upon Tyne, since 1992; Director, UK Research Councils' Rural Economy and Land Use Programme, since 2003; *b* 29 March 1950; *s* of Wilf and Lena Lowe; *m* 1972, Veronica Gibbins; one *s* one *d*. *Educ:* Exeter Coll., Oxford (MA); Manchester Univ. (MSc); Univ. of Sussex (MPhil). Res. Officer, Union of Internat. Assocs, Brussels, 1973; Lectr in Countryside Planning, 1974–89, Reader in Envmtl Planning, 1989–92, UCL; Founder and Dir, Centre for Rural Economy, Univ. of Newcastle upon Tyne, 1992–2004. Vis. Fellow, Science Centre, Berlin, 1983; Res. Fellow, Woodrow Wilson Internat. Center for Scholars, Washington, 1985. Expert Advr, H of C Select Cttee on the Envmt, 1996–99; Member: Minister of Agriculture's Adv. Gp, 1997–98; Science Adv. Council, DEFRA, 2004–09; Chm., Vets' Working Gp, DEFRA, 2007–09. Mem. Bd, Countryside Agency, 1999–2006; Chm., Market Towns Adv. Forum, 2001–06. FAcSS (AcSS 2009). *Publications:* Environmental Groups in Politics, 1983; Locality and Rurality, 1984; Countryside Conflicts, 1986; Deprivation and Welfare in Rural Areas, 1986; Rural Studies in Britain and France, 1990; Constructing the Countryside, 1993; European Integration and Environmental Policy, 1993; Moralising the Environment, 1997; British Environmental Policy and Europe, 1998; CAP Regimes and the European Countryside, 2000; The Differentiated Countryside, 2003; The Ageing Countryside, 2006; Unlocking Potential: veterinary expertise in food animal production, 2009. *Recreations:* cycling, cinema.

LOWE, Sir Philip (Martin), KCMG 2014; Director General for Energy, European Commission, 2010–14; *b* 29 April 1947; *s* of late Leonard Ernest Lowe and Marguerite Helen Lowe (*née* Childs); *m* 1st, 1967, Gillian Baynton Forge (marr. diss. 1980); two *s*; 2nd, 1984, Nora Mai O'Connell. *Educ:* Leeds Grammar Sch.; Reading Sch.; St John's Coll., Oxford (MA in PPE); London Business Sch. (MSc Business Studies). Tube Investments, 1968–73; Commission of the European Communities, later European Commission: Directorate-Gen. for Credit and Investments, Luxembourg, 1973–82; Mem., Cabinet of President Gaston Thorn, 1982–85, of Alois Pfeiffer, 1985–86; Directorate-Gen. for Co-ordination of Structural Instruments, 1986–89; Chef de Cabinet to Rt Hon. Bruce Millan, Comr for regl policy, 1989–91; Dir, Rural Develt, 1991–93; Dir, Merger Task Force, 1993–95; Chef de Cabinet to Rt Hon. Neil Kinnock, Comr for transport, 1995–97, Vice-Pres. for admin. reform, 2000–02; Director-General: Develt, 1997–2000; Competition, 2002–10. Non-exec. Dir, UK Competition and Mkts Authy, 2013–. *Recreations:* music, running, hillwalking. *Address:* 5 Columbus House, Trossachs Drive, Bathampton, Bath BA2 6RP. *T:* (Belgium) (2) 491743341, 07857 221766. *E:* philiplowe7@yahoo.co.uk.

See also Rt Rev. S. R. Lowe.

LOWE, Dr Robert David; Dean, St George's Hospital Medical School, 1971–82; Medical Research Consultant, National Heart Foundation of Australia, 1986–89; *b* 23 Feb. 1930; *s* of John Lowe and Hilda Althea Mead; *m* 1952, Betty Irene Wheeler; one *s* three *d*. *Educ:* Leighton Park Sch.; Emmanuel Coll., Cambridge; UCH Medical School. BCh, MB, MA, MD, PhD Cantab; FRCP, LMSSA. Medical Specialist, RAMC, 1955–59; Research Asst, UCH Med. Sch., 1959–61; St George's Hosp. Med. Sch.: MRC Res. Fellow, 1961–62; Wellcome Sen. Res. Fellow in Clinical Science, 1963–64; Sen. Lectr in Medicine, St Thomas' Hosp. Med. Sch., 1964–70; Hon. Consultant to St Thomas' Hosp., 1966–70. AUCAS: Exec. Mem., 1967; Chm., 1972–78. *Publications:* (with B. F. Robinson) A Physiological Approach to Clinical Methods, 1970; papers on peripheral circulation, hypertension, adrenergic mechanisms, central action of angiotensin, control of cardiovascular system. *Recreations:* bridge, squash, hill-walking, sailing. *Address:* 54 Drovers, Sturminster Newton, Dorset DT10 1QY.

LOWE, Roger Stephen Richard; Executive Director, since 2010, and Director, Portfolio Unit, since 2014, Shareholder Executive, Department for Business, Innovation and Skills; *b* Epsom, Surrey, 12 Sept. 1966; *s* of Stephen and Margaret Lowe; *m* 1998, Sandra Hey; one *s* one *d*. *Educ:* Epsom Coll.; Peterhouse, Cambridge (BA Hons 1987). Asst Dir, Lazard, 1987–98; Gp Dir of Corporate Finance, TI Gp plc, 1998–2001; Dir, Poyry Capital, 2001–10; Dir, Royal Mail and Post Office Unit, Shareholder Exec., BIS, 2012–14. *Recreations:* tennis, reading, ski-ing. *Address:* 33 Tregunter Road, SW10 9LS.

LOWE, Rosalynde Cathryn Anne, CBE 2011; Chair, Queen's Nursing Institute, 2003–12; *b* High Wycombe, 1 Dec. 1948; *d* of Thomas Pearce and Florence Evans Pearce; *m* 1st, 1968, James Lowe (marr. diss. 1980); one *s* one *d*; 2nd, 1993, Peter Farmer (*d* 2012); two step *d*. *Educ:* Didcot Girls' Grammar Sch.; Newcastle upon Tyne Poly. (BA Nursing; RGN 1980); New Coll., Durham (RHV 1981). Health Visitor, Gateshead, 1981–87; Dir, Community Nursing Services, Tower Hamlets, 1987–89; Dep. Gen. Sec., Health Visitors' Assoc., 1989–90 (Chm., 1986–88); Regl Nurse, NW Thames, 1990; Dir, Operational Services and Hd, Nursing, Hillingdon Hosp., 1992–97; Chief Exec., Hounslow and Spelthorne NHS Trust, 1997–2002. Member: UKCC, 1988–93; English Nat. Bd for Nurses, Midwives and Health Visitors, 1988–93; Audit Commn, 1995–2001; Associate Fellow, King's Fund, 2001–06; Chm., Govt Review of Health Visiting (Facing the Future), 2007. Consultant to WHO in Serbia and Moscow, 2000–07. Gov., Univ. of Brighton, 2008–; Mem., Jt Bd, Brighton and Sussex Med. Sch., 2008–14. *Recreations:* grandchild-bothering whenever possible, unofficial theatre critic, travelling, theatre, cinema, art galleries, walking, friends, books. *Address:* Apt 74 New River Head, 173 Rosebery Avenue, EC1R 4UP.

LOWE, Stephen; playwright; Artistic Director, Meeting Ground Theatre, since 1984; *b* 1 Dec. 1947; *s* of Harry Wright and Minnie Wright; *né* Stephen James Wright; changed name to Stephen Lowe; *m* 1st, 1975, Tina Barclay (marr. diss. 1985); one *s*; 2nd, 1999, Tanya Myers; two *d*. *Educ:* Birmingham Univ. (BA English and Theatre Studies; MA). Actor, Scarborough Theatre in the Round, 1974–78; Sen. Lectr, Writing for Performance, Dartington Coll., 1978–82; Resident Playwright, Riverside Studios, London, 1982–84. Chm., Year of Artist Adv. Gp (E Midlands), 2001–02; actg Chm., E Midlands Arts, 2001–02; Mem., Arts Council of England, then Arts Council England, and Chm., E Midlands Regl Arts Council, 2002–06; Chair, Artists taking the Lead, Culture Olympiad/Arts Council England, 2009–. Special Lectr, Nottingham Univ., 2011–. Hon. DLitt Nottingham, 2011. *Publications:* Touched, 1981; Ragged Trousered Philanthropists, 1983; Divine Gossip/Tibetan Inroads, 1984; Moving Pictures and Other Plays, 1985; (ed) Peace Plays, vol. 1, 1985, vol. 2, 1990; Revelations, 2004; Old Big 'Ead in the Spirit of the Man, 2007; The Fox & Empty Bed Blues, 2009. *Recreations:* Buddhism, walking, snooker, history. *Address:* c/o Howard Gooding, Judy Daish Associates, 2 St Charles Place, W10 6EG. *T:* (020) 8964 8811, *Fax:* (020) 8964 8966.

LOWE, Rt Rev. Stephen Richard; Bishop Suffragan of Hulme, 1999–2009; Bishop for Urban Life and Faith, 2006–09; an Honorary Assistant Bishop, Diocese of Liverpool, since 2015; *b* 3 March 1944; *s* of Leonard Ernest Lowe and Marguerite Helen Lowe; *m* 1967, Pauline Amy Richards; one *s* one *d*. *Educ:* Leeds Grammar School; Reading School; Birmingham Poly (BSc London); Ripon Hall, Oxford. Curate, St Michael's Anglican Methodist Church, Gospel Lane, Birmingham, 1968–72; Minister-in-Charge, Woodgate Valley Conventional District, 1972–75; Team Rector of East Ham, 1975–88; Archdeacon of Sheffield, 1988–99; Asst Bp, St Asaph, 2009; Priest-in-Charge, St Mary Towyn, St Asaph, 2011–12. Hon. Canon, Chelmsford Cathedral, 1985–88; Chelmsford Diocesan Urban Officer, 1986–88. A Church Comr, 1992–99, 2001–08 (Member: Bd of Govs, 1994–99, 2001–08; Bishoprics Cttee, 1995–99, Dep. Chm., 2001–08); General Synod: Mem., 1991–99, 2000–09; Member: Exec., Central Bd of Finance, 1993–96; House of Bishops, 2000–09; Urban Bishops' Panel, 2001–09 (Chm., 2006–09); Bd for Social Responsibility, 2000–02. Member: Churches Council for Britain and Ire., 1991–96; Bishoprics and Cathedrals Cttee, 1991–2009 (Dep. Chm., 2002–09); Archbishop's Commn on Orgn of C of

E, 1994–95; Bishops' Adv. Gp on urban priority areas, 1993–97; Archbishops' Commn on Urban Life and Faith, 2004–06; Trustee, Church Urban Fund, 1991–97 (Chm., Grants Cttee, 1993–96). Hon. Asst Bishop, St Asaph, 2009–. Chairman: Sheffield Somalian Refugees Trust, 1990–94; William Temple Foundn, 2006–09. Mem., Standards Cttee, Salford CC, 2010–. Mem., Duke of Edinburgh Commonwealth Study Conf., 1989. Travelling Fellowship, Winston Churchill Meml Trust, 1980; Paul Cadbury Travelling Fellowship on Urban Empowerment, 1996. Regular contributor, Stephen Nolan Show, BBC Radio 5, 2009–; Panellist, The Big Questions, BBC 1, 2009–; paper reviewer, BBC1 Breakfast, 2012–. *Publications:* The Churches' Role in the Care of the Elderly, 1974; What Makes a Good City, 2009. *Recreations:* watching football, cinema, theatre, travel, photography, broadcasting. *Address:* 2 Pen-y-Glyn, Bryn-y-maen, Colwyn Bay LL28 5EW. *T:* (01492) 533510. *E:* lowehulme@btinternet.com.

See also Sir P. M. Lowe.

LOWE, Sir Thomas (William Gordon), 4th Bt *cr* 1918, of Edgbaston, City of Birmingham; QC 2008; *b* 14 Aug. 1963; *s* of Sir Francis Reginald Gordon Lowe, 3rd Bt and of Franziska Cornelia, *d* of Siegfried Steinkopf; *S* father, 1986; *m* 1996, Mozhgan, *d* of Hassan Asilzadeh; one *s*. *Educ:* Stowe School; London School of Economics (LLB 1984); Jesus Coll., Cambridge (LLM 1986). Called to the Bar, Inner Temple, 1985. *Publications:* articles in various legal periodicals. *Heir: s* Theodore Christopher William Lowe, *b* 23 Aug. 2000. *Address:* Wilberforce Chambers, 8 New Square, Lincoln's Inn, WC2A 3QP.

LOWE, Rear Adm. Timothy Miles; National Hydrographer, and Deputy Chief Executive, UK Hydrographic Office, since 2015; *b* Folkestone, 31 July 1963; *s* of Colin Lowe and Gillian Lowe; *m* 1985, Lynda Jane Beard; one *s*. *Educ:* Harvey Grammar Sch., Folkestone; BRNC. Joined Royal Navy, 1981; PWO, 1992; specialist navigator, 1994; in command: HMS Sandpiper, 1989–91; jsdc 1997; i/c HMS Sheffield, 1999–2001; Office of Dep. SACEUR, 2004–06; i/c HMS Albion, 2006–08; UK Maritime Component Comdr Bahrain, 2008–10; i/c Maritime Warfare Sch. and HMS Collingwood, 2010–12; Dep. FOST, 2012; Dep. Comdr Striking Force NATO, 2012–15. Pres., Sutton Sea Cadets, TS Puma, 2008–. Trustee, Bastion Baton Charity, 2012–. QCVS 2010. *Recreations:* family, DIY, classic vehicles, reading, local history. *Address:* c/o Naval Secretary, Navy Command Headquarters, Mail Point 3.1, Leach Building, Whale Island, Portsmouth PO2 8BY. *T:* (023) 9262 5542. *E:* navsec-navsec@mod.uk.

LOWE, Vaughan; *see* Lowe, A. V.

LOWE, Veronica Ann; a Judge of the First-tier Tribunal (Immigration and Asylum Chamber) (formerly Immigration Appeals Adjudicator, later Immigration Judge), since 2001, and a Judge of the First-tier Tribunal (Social Entitlement Chamber), since 2011; *b* 29 June 1951; *d* of late Arthur Ernest Bagley and Agatha (*née* Blackham); *m* 1977, Ian Stanley Lowe; one *d*. *Educ:* King Edward VI Grammar Sch. for Girls, Handsworth, Birmingham; St Hugh's Coll., Oxford (MA); Oxford Polytechnic (MIL Exams); City of Birmingham Polytechnic. Articled Clerk, Ryland, Martineau & Co., Birmingham, 1976–78; Lectr in Labour Law, Univ. of Aston in Birmingham, 1978–80; admitted solicitor, 1979; solicitor in private practice, 1979–86; Asst Area Dir, Legal Aid Area No 8, 1986–88; Area Dir (W Midlands), Legal Aid Area No 6, 1988–89; Gp Manager (Midlands), Legal Aid Bd, 1989–90; Dir, Solicitors' Complaints Bureau, 1990–95; Chief Exec., Valuation Office Agency, 1996–97; mgt consultant and author, 1998–; solicitor, Pinsent Curtis, 1999–2000; Hd of Legal Services, Oxford Brookes Univ., 2000; Sen. Legal Counsel, 2000–03, European Legal Affairs Consultant, 2003–07, Mayne Pharma (formerly Faulding Pharmaceuticals) plc. Mem. Bd, Eur. Generic Medicines Assoc., 2002–07 (Mem., Legal Affairs Cttee, 2002–07). *Publications:* contribs to publications on law for accountants and businessmen; articles on intellectual property law, generic medicines, Eur. legislation and CPD in immigration, asylum and human rights law. *Recreations:* cooking, eating and drinking, reading, writing unfinished novels, listening to music, travel, talking, current affairs, being with my daughter, all historical subjects. *Address:* Phoenix Cottage, 6 Rugby Road, Dunchurch, Warwicks CV22 6PE.

LOWEN, Barry Robert; HM Diplomatic Service; Head, Commercial and Economic Diplomacy Department, Foreign and Commonwealth Office, since 2014; *b* 9 Jan. 1964; *s* of Robert Lowen and Pamela Lowen; *m* 1989, Karin (*née* Blizard); three *s*. *Educ:* Jesus Coll., Oxford (MA PPE); Open Univ. (MBA). Joined HM Diplomatic Service, 1986: Arab-Israeli Desk Officer, FCO, 1986; Arabic trng, 1987–89; Second Sec., Kuwait, 1989–93; Head of Section: Non-Proliferation Dept, FCO, 1993–95; ME Dept, FCO, 1995–97; First Sec., UKMIS, NY, 1997–2001; Dep. Hd, ME Dept, FCO, 2001–03; Dir, Trade and Investment, 2003–04, Dep. Hd of Mission, 2004–06, Riyadh; Hd, Engaging with the Islamic World Gp, FCO, 2006–07; Dir Asia, UK Trade and Investment, 2008–10; Dir, Trade and Investment, New Delhi, 2010–14. *Recreations:* cycling, ski-ing, hang-gliding, family. *Address:* c/o Foreign and Commonwealth Office, King Charles Street, SW1A 2AH. *E:* bklowen@yahoo.com.

LOWEN, David Travers; Director, International TV and Media Consulting, since 1998; *b* London, 20 June 1946; *s* of Norman Frederick Lowen and Beatrice Lowen; *m* 1970, Jennifer Durston; one *s* one *d*. *Educ:* Queen Elizabeth's Sch., Barnet; Emmanuel Coll., Cambridge (BA 1967; Hon. Fellow 2009). Newspaper journalist, Kent Messenger Gp, 1968–71; Southern TV, 1971–74; Hd of News, Westward TV, 1974–77; Yorkshire TV: producer, 1977–92; Dir, Network Prog. Develt, 1992–95; Dir, Corporate Develt, 1995–98; Dir, Millbank TV Studios, 1995–98. Dir Gen., Euronews, 2003. Non-exec. Chm., Sysmedia Gp plc, 2003–; non-executive Director: Palm FM, 2006–13; Radio Plymouth, 2008–13; Green Gaia Films Ltd, 2012–15; Dir, Media Local Solutions Ltd, 2007–14. Chm., Bd of Govs, Leeds Beckett Univ., 2014–. Trustee and Hon. Sec., RTS, 2000– (Fellow, 1995). Chm., Emmanuel Soc. FRSA. *Publications:* Stay Alive with Eddie McGee, 1979; Fighting Back: a woman's guide to self-defence, 1982. *Recreations:* cricket, horse-racing. *E:* d_lowen@btinternet.com. *Club:* Lord's Taverners.

LOWEN, His Honour Jonathan Andrew Michael; a Circuit Judge, 2000–13; *b* 16 Aug. 1943; *s* of George Lowen, QC and Vera Fanny Lowen; *m* 1974, Eve Susan Karpf; two *s*. *Educ:* Witwatersrand Univ., Johannesburg (BA); Christ Church, Oxford (MA). Called to the Bar, Gray's Inn, 1972; a Recorder, 1995–2000.

LOWENSTEIN, Paul David; QC 2009; *b* London, 31 Dec. 1963; *s* of John and Vivien Lowenstein; *m* 1st, 1991, Nadine Shenton (marr. diss. 2010); three *s*; 2nd, 2010, Carolyn Greene; two *s*. *Educ:* Manchester Univ. (LLB Hons 1986); Queens' Coll., Cambridge (LLM 1987). Called to the Bar, Middle Temple, 1988; in practice as barrister, specialising in commercial, financial and business litigation, 1989–; Accredited Mediator, 2000. Chm., Operating Cttee, Internat. Law Book Facility, 2005–. Trustee, Internat. Law Book Facility, 2010–. *Recreations:* sailing, Cornwall. *Address:* 3 Verulam Buildings, Gray's Inn, WC1R 5NT. *T:* (020) 7831 8441, *Fax:* (020) 7831 8479. *E:* pdl@3vb.com. *Clubs:* United and Cecil; St Mawes Sailing.

LOWENTHAL, Prof. David, PhD; FBA 2001; Professor of Geography, University College London, 1972–85, now Professor Emeritus (Hon. Research Fellow, 1986); *b* 26 April 1923; *s* of Max Lowenthal and Eleanor Lowenthal (*née* Mack); *m* 1970, Mary Alice Lamberty; two *d*. *Educ:* Harvard (BS Hist. 1943); Univ. of Calif, Berkeley (MA Geog. 1950); Univ. of Wisconsin (PhD Hist. 1953). Served US Army (infantry, OSS, Europe), 1943–45. US State Dept, 1945–46; Asst Prof. of Hist. and Hd, Dept of Geog., Vassar Coll., 1952–56; Consultant, Inst. of Social and Econ. Studies, Dept of Hist., Univ. of WI, 1956–70; Inst. Race Relns, UK, 1961–72. Regents Prof., UC Davis, Calif, 1973; Katz Dist. Prof. of Humanities, Univ. of Washington, 1988; Visiting Professor: Univs of Calif, Berkeley, Minn, Washington, Clark and Harvard; CUNY; MIT; West Dean Coll.; St Mary's UC, Strawberry Hill; Lectures: Dist., Center of Humanities and Arts, Univ. of Georgia, 1998; A. W. Franks, BM, 1999; H. Harvey Dist., Univ. of Newfoundland, 1999; Dist., Pinchot Conservation Inst., US, 2001. Member, Editorial Boards, including: Envmt and Behaviour, 1969–76; Geog. Rev., 1973–95; London Jl, 1974–86; Progress in Geog., 1976–90; Internat. Jl Cultural Property, 1989–. Member: Council, AAAS, 1964–71; Council, Assoc. Amer. Geographers, 1968–71; US Nat. Res. Council, 1968–71; SSRC Ethnic Relns Cttee, 1972–77; Bd, Insts of Latin American Studies and Commonwealth Studies, Univ. of London, 1972–87; Landscape Res. Gp, 1984–89 (Chair). Advisor to various organisations, including: US Peace Corps on the Caribbean; UNESCO, IGU on envmtl perception; English Heritage, V&A, Sci. Mus., BM, ICOMOS, UNESCO, ICCROM on heritage. Fellowships: Fulbright, 1956–57; Guggenheim, 1965; Res. Inst. for Study of Man, Landes (US), 1992–93; Leverhulme, 1992–94. Hon. DLitt Memorial Univ., Newfoundland, 2008. Victoria Medal, RGS, 1997; Cullum Medal, Amer. Geog. Soc., 1999; RSGS Medal, 2004; Forbes Prize, Internat. Inst. for Conservation, 2010. *Publications:* George Perkins Marsh: versatile Vermonter, 1958 (Assoc. Amer. Geographers Award); West Indies Federation, 1961; West Indian Societies, 1972; (with M. J. Bowden) Geographies of the Mind, 1975; (with M. Binney) Our Past Before Us, 1981; The Past is a Foreign Country, 1985 (Historic Preservation (US) Book Prize); (with E. C. Penning-Rowsell) Landscape Meanings and Values, 1986; (with P. Gathercole) Politics of the Past, 1989; Heritage Crusade and the Spoils of History, 1997; George Perkins Marsh: prophet of conservation, 2000 (J. B. Jackson Book Prize, Assoc. Amer. Geographers); (with K. R. Olwig) The Nature of Cultural Heritage and the Culture of Natural Heritage, 2006; Passage du temps sur le paysage, 2008; (jtly) To Pass on a Good Earth: the life and work of Carl O. Sauer, 2014; The Past is a Foreign Country - Revisited, 2015. *Address:* 22 Heron Place, 9 Thayer Street, W1U 3JL; 1401 Le Roy Avenue, Berkeley, CA 94708–1911, USA.

LOWER, Adrian Christopher; a District Judge (Magistrates' Courts), since 2012; *b* Newton Abbot, 9 May 1970; *s* of Geoffrey McDougall and Georgina Rosemary Lower; two *s*. *Educ:* Colfox Sch., Bridport; Univ. of Southampton (LLB Hons); Coll. of Law, Chester. Higher Rights of Audience (Criminal), 2001. Admitted as solicitor, 1994; Crown Prosecution Service: Crown Prosecutor, 1994–96; Sen. Crown Prosecutor, 1996–2004; District Crown Prosecutor, 2004–10; Hd of Complex Casework Unit, S Yorks and Humberside, 2010–11; Legal Asst to Principal Legal Advr to DPP, CPS HQ, 2011–12; a Dep. Dist Judge (Civil), 2010–12. *Recreations:* cricket, current affairs, encouraging sons to practise music and complete their homework. *Address:* The Court House, Cliff Parade, Wakefield WF1 2TW. *T:* (01924) 231100.

LOWMAN, Ven. David Walter; Archdeacon of Chelmsford, since 2013; *b* 27 Nov. 1948; *s* of Cecil Walter Lowman and Queenie Norah Lowman. *Educ:* Crewkerne Sch., Somerset; City of London Coll. (Dip. in English Civil Law 1970); King's Coll. London (BD 1973; AKC 1973). Estate Duty Office, Inland Revenue, 1966–70. Ordained deacon, 1975, priest, 1976; Curate: Notting Hill Team Ministry, 1975–78; St Augustine, Kilburn, 1978–81; Vocations Adviser and Selection Sec., ACCM, and Chaplain, Church House, Westminster, 1981–86; Team Rector, Wickford and Runwell, Dio. Chelmsford, 1986–93; Diocesan Dir of Ordinands, and Non-residentiary Canon of Chelmsford Cathedral, 1993–2001; Archdeacon of Southend, 2001–13. Mem. Wkg Pty, House of Bishops (reported on marriage in church after divorce), 1999. Chair: Vocations Adv. Panel, Ministry Div., Archbishops' Council, 2001–; N Thames Ministerial Trng Course, 2001–. Trustee: SE Essex Christian Hospice, 2001–06; Corp. of Sons of the Clergy and Friends of the Clergy, 2012–; Vice Chair, Trustees, St Mellitus Coll., 2008–. Gov., Brentwood Sch., 2001–. *Recreations:* cricket, travel (France, Italy, USA, Cyprus), opera, red wine. *Address:* The Archdeacon's Lodge, 136 Broomfield Road, Chelmsford, Essex CM1 1RN. *T:* (01245) 258257.

LOWNIE of Largo, Andrew James Hamilton; literary agent; Proprietor, Andrew Lownie Literary Agency Ltd, since 1988; writer; *b* 11 Nov. 1961; *s* of His Honour Dr Ralph Hamilton Lownie of Largo; *m* 1998, Angela Doyle; one *s* one *d*. *Educ:* Fettes Coll.; Asheville Sch., NC (ESU Schol.); Westminster Sch.; Magdalene Coll., Cambridge (MA); Edinburgh Univ. (MSc); Coll. of Law, London. Pres., Cambridge Union Soc., 1984. Graduate trainee, Hodder & Stoughton Publishers, 1984–85; John Farquharson Literary Agents, 1985–88 (Dir, 1986–88); Director: Denniston & Lownie Ltd, 1991–93; Thistle Publishing, 1996–. Literary Agent to PEN, 2001–04. Contested (C) Monklands West, 1992. Vice-Chm., Cons. Gp for Europe, 1992–95. Mem., Adv. Bd, Biographers' Internat. Orgn, 2012–. Sec., 1998–2008, Pres., 2008–, Biographers' Club. Trustee, Iain MacLeod Award, 1986–. *Publications:* (ed) North American Spies, 1991; The Edinburgh Literary Guide, 1992; John Buchan: the Presbyterian Cavalier, 1995; (ed) John Buchan's Collected Poems, 1996; (ed) John Buchan: the complete short stories, vols 1–3, 1996–97; (ed) John Buchan: shorter Scottish fiction, 1997; The Literary Companion to Edinburgh, 2000; The Edinburgh Literary Companion, 2005; Stalin's Englishman, 2015. *Recreations:* history, music, tennis, travel. *Address:* Andrew Lownie Literary Agency Ltd, 36 Great Smith Street, SW1P 3BU. *T:* (020) 7222 7574, *Fax:* (020) 7222 7576. *E:* Lownie@globalnet.co.uk.

LOWRY, Her Honour Noreen Margaret, (Nina); a Circuit Judge, 1976–95; *b* 6 Sept. 1925; *er d* of late John Collins, MC, and Hilda Collins; *m* 1st, 1950, Edward Lucas Gardner, QC (marr. diss. 1962); one *d* (one *s* decd); 2nd, 1963, His Honour Richard John Lowry, QC (*d* 2001); one *d*. *Educ:* Bedford High Sch.; Birmingham Univ. LLB Birmingham, 1947. Called to the Bar, Gray's Inn, 1948, Bencher, 1995. Criminal practice on S Eastern Circuit, Central Criminal Court, Inner London Sessions, etc., practising as Miss Nina Collins; Metropolitan Stipendiary Magistrate, 1967–76. Member: Criminal Law Revision Cttee, 1975; Criminal Injuries Compensation Bd, 1995–2000. Freeman, City of London, 1985. Hon. LLD Birmingham, 1992. *Recreations:* theatre, travel.

See also S. A. C. Gardner.

LOWRY-CORRY, family name of **Earl of Belmore.**

LOWSON, Rt Rev. Christopher; *see* Lincoln, Bishop of.

LOWSON, Sir Ian (Patrick), 2nd Bt *cr* 1951; *b* 4 Sept. 1944; *s* of Sir Denys Colquhoun Flowerdew Lowson, 1st Bt and Hon. Patricia, OStJ, *yr d* of 1st Baron Strathcarron, PC, KC; *S* father, 1975; *m* 1979, Mrs Tanya Du Boulay, *d* of R. F. A. Judge; one *s* one *d*. *Educ:* Eton; Duke Univ., USA. OStJ. *Heir: s* Henry William Lowson [*b* 10 Nov. 1980; *m* 2009, Rocio R. Acal Mendez; two *s*]. *Address:* 23 Flood Street, SW3 5ST. *Clubs:* Boodle's, Pilgrims; Brook (NY).

LOWSON, Robert Campbell; consultant on space and research questions, since 2011; Director, Regulation, Department for Environment, Food and Rural Affairs, 2007, on secondment to European Environment Agency, 2007–11; *b* 7 March 1949; *s* of late George Campbell Lowson and Betty Lowson (*née* Parry); *m* 1973, Hilary Balsdon; one *s* one *d*. *Educ:* Gravesend Grammar Sch.; Brasenose Coll., Oxford (BA History 1970). Joined Ministry of Agriculture, Fisheries and Food, 1970: UK Mission, Geneva, 1977; Principal Private Sec. to Minister of Agric., Fisheries and Food, 1982; successively Head of Cereals, Milk, Animal Health, and Agric. Resource Policy Divs, 1983–94; Under Sec., 1994; Minister, UK Repn Brussels, on loan to FCO, 1995–99; Dir of Communications, MAFF, subseq. DEFRA, 1999–2001; Dir of Envmt Protection Strategy, later Envmt Strategy, DEFRA, 2001–07. Consultant on space and res. questions, Technol. Strategy Bd, 2011–14. *Recreations:* all the usual things. *Club:* Athenæum.

LOWTHER, family name of **Earl of Lonsdale** and **Viscount Ullswater**.

LOWTHER, Col Sir Charles (Douglas), 6th Bt *cr* 1824; farmer, company director; *b* 22 Jan. 1946; *s* of Lt-Col Sir William Guy Lowther, 5th Bt, OBE, and Grania Suzanne, *d* of late Major A. J. H. Douglas Campbell, OBE; *S* father, 1982; *m* 1975, Florence Rose, *y d* of Colonel Alexander James Henry Cramsie, O'Harabrook, Ballymoney, Co. Antrim; one *s* one *d*. *Educ:* Winchester College. Commissioned, Queen's Royal Irish Hussars, 1966; Regimental Duty UK and BAOR, 1974–76; Army Staff College, Camberley, 1978–79; Staff appointment, 1981; CO, QRIH, 1986–89; Officer i/c, Household Cavalry and RAC Manning and Record Office, 1989–93. Mem., HM Body Guard, Hon. Corps of Gentlemen-at-Arms, 1997–. High Sheriff, Clwyd, 1997. Racing Mem., Jockey Club, 1999. *Recreations:* fieldsports, travel. *Heir: s* Patrick William Lowther [*b* 15 July 1977; *m* 2006, Sarah Jane, *o d* of William Davis; two *s*]. *Club:* Cavalry and Guards.

LOWTHER, James; Founding Partner, M&C Saatchi (UK), 1995 (Chairman, 2000–06); *b* 27 Jan. 1947; *s* of George Hugh Lowther and Sheila Rachel Isabelle Lowther; *m* 1987, Karen Healey Wallace; one *s* three *d*. *Educ:* Eton Coll.; Keble Coll., Oxford (MA Hons Hist.). Saatchi & Saatchi, 1977–95, Creative Dir and Dep. Chm., 1991–95. Dir, British Television Advertising Awards, 1992; Exec. Producer, Britain's Brilliant Prodigies, 2002, 2003. Trustee, Children in Crisis, 2000–10; Develt Cttee, Mayor of London's Fund for Young Musicians, 2012–. *Publications:* (contrib.) The Copy Book, 1995; (contrib.) The 22 Irrefutable Laws of Advertising (and When to Violate Them). *Recreations:* listening to, playing and writing music, restoring beautiful but hungry historic house. *Address:* 4 Fawcett Street, SW10 9HZ. *T:* (020) 7352 2735. *E:* jamesl@mcsaatchi.com; Holdenby House, Northampton NN6 8DJ. *T:* (01604) 770241. *Club:* Bluebird.

LOWTHER, Merlyn Vivienne; a Director, 2011–14, and Chairman of Risk Committee, 2012–13, Co-operative Banking Group; *b* 3 March 1954; *d* of Norman Edward Douglas Humphrey and Joan Margaret Humphrey (*née* Hewitt); *m* 1975, David John Lowther; one *s* one *d*. *Educ:* Manchester High Sch. for Girls; Univ. of Manchester (BSc Hons Maths 1975); London Business Sch. (MSc Econs 1981); Central Sch. of Speech and Drama (MA Actor Trng and Coaching 2007). FCIB 1999. Bank of England, 1975–2004: Sen. Dealer, Gilt Edged Div., 1985–87; Head, Banking Div. and Dep. Chief Cashier, 1991–96; Personnel Dir, 1996–98; Dep. Dir and Chief Cashier, 1999–2004; Schroders plc: a Dir, 2004–13; Chm., Audit and Risk Cttee (formerly Audit Cttee), 2010–13. Trustee: Henry Smith's Charity, 1999–; Winston Churchill Meml Trust, 2003–. Gov., Manchester High Sch. for Girls, 2015–. FRSA 1996. Hon. LLD Manchester, 1999. *Recreations:* theatre, singing, reading, family.

LOWTHER-PINKERTON, (Anthony) James (Moxon), LVO 2013 (MVO 1986); MBE 1990; DL; Extra Equerry to the Duke and Duchess of Cambridge and Prince Henry of Wales, since 2014; *b* 28 Sept. 1960; *s* of Anthony Hull Lowther-Pinkerton and Sue Lowther-Pinkerton (*née* Leslie-Smith); *m* 1995, Susannah Lucy (*née* Richards); one *s* three *d*. *Educ:* Eton Coll.; RMA Sandhurst. Irish Guards, 1979–98; Equerry to HM Queen Elizabeth the Queen Mother, 1984–86; 22 SAS Regt, 1987–94; sc 1995; Balkans desk officer, Directorate of Mil. Ops, MoD, 1996–98. Dir, Objective Team Ltd, 2001–09; Sen. Consultant, Kroll Security Gp, 2004–06. Private Sec. to Prince William of Wales, later as Duke of Cambridge and Prince Henry of Wales, 2005–12, and to Duchess of Cambridge, 2011–12; Principal Private Sec. to Duke and Duchess of Cambridge and Prince Henry of Wales, 2012–14. Consultant, GEMS Educn. Mem., Adv. Council, Cranemere Gp Ltd. Mem., RIIA, 2014–. Trustee: HALO Trust, 2005–; Sentebale - The Princes' Fund for Lesotho, 2006–09, 2010–13; Royal Foundn of Duke and Duchess of Cambridge and Prince Harry (formerly Charitable Foundn of Prince William and Prince Harry), 2009–. Pres., RBL, Suffolk Co., 2015–. Fellow, British American Project. FRGS. Hon. Bencher, Middle Temple, 2012. DL Suffolk, 2013. *Recreations:* Nelson, castles, the Suffolk coast, watercolour painting. *Address:* Methersgate Hall, Sutton, Woodbridge, Suffolk IP12 3JL. *T:* (01394) 385928. *Clubs:* Pratt's, 1805, White's.

LOXDALE, Prof. Hugh David, MBE 2007; DPhil; CBiol; FLS; FRES; FRSB; Editor-in-Chief, Brambleby Books (UK) Ltd, since 2012; Professor of Ecology, Institute of Ecology, Friedrich Schiller University and Max Planck Institute for Chemical Ecology, Jena, Germany, 2009–11 (Senior Research Fellow in Entomology, 2006–09); *b* 9 Sept. 1950; *s* of late John David Loxdale and Phyllis Marjorie Loxdale (*née* Duke); *m* 1993, Nicola von Mende, MSc, PhD. *Educ:* Apsley Grammar Sch., Hemel Hempstead; Univ. of Reading (ARC Bursary; BSc Hons (Zool. with Biochem. and Physiol.) 1974); Linacre Coll., Oxford (DPhil 1980). MIBiol 1974, FRSB (FIBiol 2001); CBiol 1979. Entomologist, Rothamsted Experimental Station, subseq. Rothamsted Research: scientific asst, 1969–71; returned to Rothamsted, 1977; SO, 1977; HSO, 1979; SSO, 1985; Principal Res. Scientist, 1991–2005. Hon. Vis. Prof., Cardiff Sch. of Bioscis, Cardiff Univ., 2015–. Lectr in field; Special Lectr in insect molecular ecol., Sutton Bonington, Univ. of Nottingham, 1993–96. Mem., Co-ordination Cttee, ESF network, PARTNER (Parthenogenesis Network), 2003–05. Royal Entomological Society: Fellow, 1985; Mem. Council and Trustee, 2000–03; Vice Pres., 2003; Pres., 2004–06; Hon. Treas., 2011–. Mem. Council, Systematics Assoc., 1986–89. Beds, Essex and Herts Branch, Institute of Biology: Mem. Cttee, 1998–99; Sec., 1999–2003; Chm., 2003–06. Life Gov., ICRF, 1989–2003; Hon. Fellow, CRUK, 2003–. FLS 2002. Freeman, Shrewsbury, 1993. Ed.-in-Chief, The Entomologist (Jl of Royal Entomol. Soc.), 1987–89; Member, Editorial Board: Molecular Ecol., 2000–05; Molecular Ecol. Resources, 2000–; Subject Ed., 2002–05, Associate Ed., 2010–13, Bulletin Entomol Res.; English Lang. Ed. and Mem., Editl Bd, Eur. Jl Entomol., 2012–. *Publications:* (ed with J. Den Hollander) Electrophoretic Studies on Agricultural Pests, 1989; (ed with G. Lushai) Intraclonal Genetic Variation: ecological and evolutionary aspects, 2003; *natural history poetry:* The Eternal Quest: a celebration of nature in poetry, 1988, 2nd edn 2003; Blue Skies in Tuscany, 2000, 2nd edn 2003; Fascinating Felines: sixty cat poems, 2002; Bird Words: poetic images of wild birds, 2003; The Jena Poems, 2010; Love and the Sea, 2010; Nevisian Days: poetry from a Caribbean Isle, 2011; Bird of Paradise: selected poems, 1968–2011, 2011; Zoooo… Living Poems for Children, 2012; numerous contribs to internat. scientific jls, res. and review papers, book chapters and popular articles, esp. about insect migration using molecular markers, clonality and generalism in nature. *Recreations:* natural history, genealogy, history, writing poetry, walking, debating. *Address:* 15 Lyngford Square, Taunton, Somerset TA2 7ES. *T:* (01823) 259615. *E:* Loxdale@web.de.

LOY, Francis David Lindley, CBE 1997; Stipendiary Magistrate at Leeds, 1974–97; a Recorder of the Crown Court, 1983–96; *b* 7 Oct. 1927; *s* of late Archibald Loy and late Sarah Eleanor Loy; *m* 1954, Brenda Elizabeth Walker; three *d*. *Educ:* Repton Sch.; Corpus Christi Coll., Cambridge. BA Hons (Law) 1950. Royal Navy, 1946–48. Called to the Bar, Middle Temple, 1952; practised North-Eastern Circuit, 1952–72; Recorder (Northern Circuit), 1972; Stipendiary Magistrate of Leeds, 1972–74. Hon. Sec., Soc. of Provincial Stipendiary Magistrates, 1980–89, Chm., 1990–96. *Recreations:* reading, English History, walking, travel. *Address:* 4 Wedgewood Drive, Roundhay, Leeds LS8 1EF; 14 The Avenue, Sheringham, Norfolk NR26 8DG. *T:* (01263) 822697.

LOYD, Sir Julian (St John), KCVO 1991 (CVO 1979); DL; FRICS; Land Agent to HM The Queen, Sandringham Estate, 1964–91; *b* 25 May 1926; *s* of General Sir Charles Loyd, GCVO, KCB, DSO, MC and Lady Moyra Loyd; *m* 1960, Mary Emma, *d* of Sir Christopher Steel, GCMG, MVO and Lady Steel; one *s* two *d* (and one *s* decd). *Educ:* Eton Coll.; Magdalene Coll., Cambridge (MA). FRICS 1955. Coldstream Guards, 1944–45. Partner in Savills, Norwich, 1955–64. Chm., King's Lynn and Wisbech NHS Trust, 1991–94. DL Norfolk, 1983. *Recreation:* fishing. *Address:* Perrystone Cottage, Burnham Market, King's Lynn PE31 8HA. *T:* (01328) 730168. *Club:* Sloane.

LUBA, Jan Michael Andrew; QC 2000; a Recorder, since 2000; a Judge of the Employment Appeal Tribunal (part-time), since 2002; *b* 12 Feb. 1957; *s* of Zenon and Marlene Luba; *m* 1978, Adriana; two *d*. *Educ:* London Sch. of Economics (LLB); Univ. of Leicester (LLM). Called to the Bar, Middle Temple, 1980, Bencher, 2009; Legal Officer, CPAG, 1987–89; Nat. Housing Law Service, 1990–92; private practice at the Bar, England and Wales, 1992–. Patron, Croydon Housing Aid Soc., 2003–10. Chair, Zacchaeus 2000 Trust, 2013–. *Publications:* Repairs: Tenant's Rights, 1986, 4th edn (with Beatrice Prevatt and Deirdre Forster) 2010; Housing and the Human Rights Act, 2000; (jtly) Defending Possession Proceedings, 1987, 7th edn 2010; The Homelessness Act 2002, 2002, 2nd edn (with Liz Davies) 2003; Housing Allocation and Homelessness, 2006, 3rd edn (with Liz Davies) 2012. *Recreations:* spending time with my family, walking. *Address:* Garden Court Chambers, 57–60 Lincoln's Inn Fields, WC2A 3LJ.

LUBBERS, Rudolphus Frans Marie, (Ruud); Chairman, Supervisory Board, Energy research Centre of the Netherlands, 2005–12; *b* Rotterdam, 7 May 1939; *s* of Paulus J. Lubbers and Wilhelmine K. Van Laack; *m* 1962, Maria E. J. Hoogeweegan; two *s* one *d*. *Educ:* Erasmus Univ., Rotterdam. Sec. to Mgt Bd, 1963–65, Co-Dir, 1965–74, Lubbers Hollandia Engrg Works; Minister of Econ. Affairs, Netherlands, 1973–77; Mem., Second Chamber of States-Gen., 1977–82; Sen. Dep. Leader, then Leader, Christian Democratic Alliance, 1977–82; Prime Minister of the Netherlands, 1982–94; Prof. on Globalisation, Faculty of Econs and Business Admin, Tilburg Univ., 1995–2000; UN High Comr for Refugees, 2001–05. Chm., Internat. Adv. Bd Rotterdam, 2006–09. Vis. Prof., John F. Kennedy Sch. of Govt, Harvard Univ. Internat. Pres., WWF, 1999–2000. Kt, Order of the Lion (Netherlands), 1994.

LUBBOCK, family name of **Baron Avebury**.

LUBBOCK, John David Peter, OBE 2015; FRAM; Founder and Musical Director, Orchestra of St John's, since 1967; Founder and Director, Music for Autism, since 2000; *b* 18 March 1945; *s* of Michael Lubbock and Diana (*née* Crawley); *m* 1st, 1977, Eleanor Sloan (marr. diss.); two *s*; 2nd, 1991, Christine Cairns; two *s*. *Educ:* St George's Choir Sch., Windsor Castle (Chorister); Radley Coll.; Royal Acad. of Music (FRAM 1999). Mem., Swingle Singers, 1971–74. Guest conductor, USA, Canada, Europe. Trustee: Music of Life Foundn; Clear Sky Foundn; Thomley Hall Activity Centre. *Recreation:* tennis. *Address:* 7 Warborough Road, Shillingford, Oxon OX10 7SA. *T:* (01865) 858210.

LUCAN, 7th Earl of, *cr* 1795 (Ire.); **Richard John Bingham;** Bt 1632; Baron Lucan, 1776; Baron Bingham (UK), 1934; *b* 18 Dec. 1934; *e s* of 6th Earl of Lucan, MC; *S* father, 1964; *m* 1963, Veronica, *d* of late Major C. M. Duncan, MC, and of Mrs J. D. Margrie; one *s* two *d*. *Educ:* Eton. Lieut (Res. of Officers) Coldstream Guards. *Heir: s* Lord Bingham, *qv*.

See also Lady Camilla Bingham.

[The Earl has been missing since Nov. 1974 and was 'presumed deceased' in Chambers on 11 Dec. 1992. In 1999 the Lord Chancellor ruled against the application by Lord Bingham for a writ of summons to Parliament in the UK Barony of Bingham.]

LUCAS, family name of **Baron Lucas of Chilworth**.

LUCAS OF CHILWORTH, 3rd Baron *cr* 1946, of Chilworth; **Simon William Lucas;** *b* 6 Feb. 1957; *er s* of 2nd Baron Lucas of Chilworth and of Ann-Marie (*née* Buck); *S* father, 2001; *m* 1993, Fiona, *yr d* of Thomas Mackintosh, Vancouver; two *s*. *Educ:* Leicester Univ. (BSc); RMA Sandhurst. Late RE. *Heir: s* Hon. John Ronald Muir Lucas, *b* 21 May 1995.

LUCAS OF CRUDWELL, 11th Baron *cr* 1663, **AND DINGWALL,** 14th Lord *cr* 1609; **Ralph Matthew Palmer;** *b* 7 June 1951; *s* of 10th Baroness Lucas of Crudwell and 13th Lady Dingwall and of Maj. the Hon. Robert Jocelyn Palmer, MC, 3rd *s* of 3rd Earl of Selborne, PC, CH; *S* mother, 1991; *m* 1st, 1978, Clarissa Marie (marr. diss. 1995), *d* of George Vivian Lockett, TD and Alice Jeannine Lockett; one *s* one *d*; 2nd, 1995, Amanda Atha (*d* 2000); 3rd, 2001, Antonia Vera Kennedy, *d* of late Anthony Benno John Stanley Rubinstein and Anne Langford Dent; one *d*. *Educ:* Eton; Balliol Coll., Oxford (BA (Hons) Physics). BDO Binder Hamlyn, 1972–76; S. G. Warburg & Co. Ltd, 1976–88. A Lord in Waiting (Govt Whip), 1994–97; Govt spokesman on educn, 1994–95, social security and Wales, 1994–97, agric. and envmt, 1995–97; Opposition spokesman on internat. develt, 1997–98; elected Mem., H of L, 1999. Ed., Good Schs Guide, 2000–; Chm., Good Careers Guide, 2014–. *Heir: s* Hon. Lewis Edward Palmer, *b* 7 Dec. 1987. *Address:* House of Lords, SW1A 0PW. *T:* (020) 7219 4177. *E:* lucasr@parliament.uk.

LUCAS, Adrian Paul, FRCO(CHM); freelance conductor, organist, animateur, adjudicator and examiner; *b* 14 March 1962; *s* of Kenneth David Lucas and Kathleen Lucas (*née* Mash); *m* 1986, Joanna Louise Harrison; one *s* one *d*. *Educ:* St John's Coll., Cambridge (Organ Schol.; MA). FRCO(CHM) 1990. Actg Asst Organist, Salisbury Cathedral, 1980; Asst Organist, Norwich Cathedral, 1983–90; Tutor, UEA, 1985–90; Organist, Portsmouth Cathedral, 1990–96; Organist and Master of the Choristers, Worcester Cathedral, 1996–2011. Musical Director: Worcester Fest. Choral Soc., 1997–2011; Worcs SO, 2000–02; City of Birmingham Choir, 2002–; Millennium Youth Choir, 2015–. Pres., Cathedral Organists' Assoc., 2003–05. Guest Conductor: Philharmonia Orch., 2000–; Classic FM Live, 2010. Examr, Associated Bd, RSM, 1989–; former Ext. Examr, RAM; Ext. Examr, Birmingham Conservatoire, 2000–. Freelance recitalist, broadcaster and conductor, incl. Three Choirs Fest. Founder, Acclaim Prodns, 2011–. Recordings incl. 4 solo organ discs and choral works with Portsmouth and Worcester Cathedral Choirs, and Choirs of Three Choirs Fest. Responsible for installation of new organ at Worcester Cathedral, 2008. *Publications:* various musical compositions, incl. Noël for boys' voices, harp and organ, 1998 (also recorded), Creation Canticles, 2004; contrib. to musical training books. *Recreations:* flying (NPPL licence for microlight and SEP aircraft), bread making, wine. *Address:* 2 Field Terrace, Worcester WR5 3BN. *T:* (01905) 352136.

LUCAS, Prof. Alan, MD; FRCP, FRCPCH, FMedSci; MRC Clinical Research Professor, MRC Childhood Nutrition Research Centre, since 1996, and concurrently Professor of Paediatric Nutrition, since 2001, Institute of Child Health, University College London; Fellow, Clare College, Cambridge, since 1982; *b* 30 June 1946; *s* of late Dr Saul H. Lucas, Maj., RAMC, and Dr Sophia Lucas; *m* 1st, 1967, Sally Wedeles (marr. diss.); 2nd, 1978, Penny Hodgson; one *s* two *d*. *Educ:* Bedales Sch., Hants; Clare Coll., Cambridge (Foundn Schol.; BA Med. & Natural Sci. Tripos 1st Cl. Hons 1968; BChir 1971, MB 1972; MA 1985); MD Cantab 1991; Oxford Univ. Med. Sch. FRCP 1991; FRCPCH 1997. Jun. posts, Radcliffe Infirmary, Oxford and Addenbrooke's Hosp., Cambridge, 1971–77; Lector, Trinity Coll., Cambridge, 1972–76; University of Oxford: Wellcome Res. Fellow, Dept of Paediatrics, 1977–79; Lectr, St Edmund Hall, 1977–80; University of Cambridge: Clinical Lectr, 1980–82, Hon. Consultant, 1982–96, Dept of Paediatrics; Dir, Med. Studies, Peterhouse, 1980–86; Dir, Studies in Medicine and in Anatomy, Clare Coll., 1982–97; Hd, Infant and Child Nutrition, MRC Dunn Nutrition Unit, Cambridge, 1982–96; Dir, MRC Childhood Nutrition Res. Centre, Inst. of Child Health, UCL, 1996–2011; Hon. Consultant, Gt Ormond St Hosp. for Children, 1996–. Lectures include: McCance, 1995, George Alexander Gibson, Widdowson, 2009, Neonatal Soc., London; Edna Park, Toronto; Telford, Manchester, 2011. Member: Panel on Child Nutrition, DHSS, 1988–96; Wkg Gp on Infant Formula, EEC, 1988; Standing Cttee on Nutrition, BPA, subseq. RCPCH, 1988–2000 (Mem., Acad. Bd, 1989–94); Physiol Medicine and Infections Bd, 1992–96, Wkg Gp on Fluoride and Osteoporosis, 1994 (Chm.) and Health Services Res. Bd, 1995–96, MRC. FMedSci 2000. Hon. Citizen, Georgia, USA (for educnl services), 1994. Guthrie Medal, RCPCH, 1982. *Publications:* over 400 scientific papers and articles, and contrib. to books, on child health, nutrition and metabolism, notably long term health effects of early nutrition. *Recreations:* art, art history, music, sports. *Address:* Institute of Child Health, 30 Guilford Street, WC1N 1EH. *T:* (020) 7905 2389.

LUCAS, Andrew, FRCO; Master of the Music, Cathedral and Abbey Church of St Alban, since 1998; *b* 19 Aug. 1958; *s* of Richard John Lucas and Vera Mary Lucas (*née* Lawrence). *Educ:* Wakeman Sch., Shrewsbury; Royal Coll. of Music (GRSM 1979; BMus (London) 1981); Sweelinck Conservatoire, Amsterdam. FRCO 1979. Dir of Music, St James', Sussex Gardens, London, 1981–85; St Paul's Cathedral: organ student, 1980–84; Asst Sub-Organist, 1985–89; Sub-Organist and Asst Dir of Music, 1990–98; Acting Organist and Master of Choristers, St Andrew's Cathedral, Sydney, Aust., 1997. Conductor, St Albans Bach Choir, 1998–; Artistic Dir, St Albans Internat. Organ Fest., 1999–2007. Pres., Asst Cathedral Organists' Assoc., 2002– (Chm., 1993–98); Mem. Council, RCO, 1997–2006. Liveryman, Co. of Musicians, 1998–. Hon. FGCM 2006. *Recreations:* theatre, travel, architecture, gardens, good food and coffee. *Address:* Cathedral and Abbey Church of St Alban, St Albans, Herts AL1 1BY. *T:* (01727) 568721. *E:* andrewl01@aol.com; 31 Abbey Mill Lane, St Albans, Herts AL3 4HA.

LUCAS, Anne Katharine; *see* Stevenson, A. K.

LUCAS, Prof. Arthur Maurice, AO 2005; CBE 2002; PhD; Professor of Science Curriculum Studies, 1980–2003, now Emeritus, and Principal, 1993–2003, King's College, London; *b* 26 Oct. 1941; *s* of Joseph Alfred Percival Lucas and May Queen Lucas (*née* Griffin); *m* 1970, Paula Jean Williams; one *s* one *d*. *Educ:* Univ. of Melbourne (BSc 1963; BEd 1968); Ohio State Univ. (PhD 1972; Fulbright Award). FRSB (FIBiol 1981); FACE 1995. Appts at Yallourn and Newborough High Schs, 1964–66; Flinders Univ. of SA, 1967–70; Ohio State Univ., 1970–72; Warrnambool Inst. of Advanced Educn, 1973; Flinders University: Lectr in Sci. Educn, 1974–80; Sen. Lectr, 1976; Vice-Chm., 1976, Chm., 1977–79, Sch. of Educn; King's College, London: Asst Principal, 1987–89; Vice-Principal, 1991–93; Actg Principal, 1992; London University: Chm., Bd of Educnl Studies, 1986–88; Mem. Council, 1995–2003; Chm., Mgt Bd, Marine Biol. Stn, Millport, 1995–2002; Dep. Vice Chancellor, 1997–2002. Hon. Vis. Prof., Sch. of Educn, UEA, 2005–12. Mem., Lord Chancellor's Adv. Council on Nat. Records and Archives, 2006–15. Member, Council: Commonwealth Assoc. for Sci., Maths and Technol. Educn, 1981–89; Zoological Soc. of London, 1992–93 (Vice Pres., 1993); Royal Instn, 1998–2004; British Soc. for History of Sci., 1999–2002; Member: Exec. Cttee, Field Studies Council, 1986–92, 1994–2000, 2002–07; COPUS, 1993–95; Bd, Univs and Colls Employers Assoc., 1996–2003; Bd, QAA, 2002–08; Parly and Scientific Cttee, 2002–03. Chm., Medicine and Soc. Panel, Wellcome Trust, 1998–2002. Mem., SE Thames RHA, 1993–94. Pres., 2006–09, Hon. Mem., 2010, Soc. for Hist. of Natural Hist. Trustee, Samuel Courtauld Trust, 1997–2002. Mem. Cttee, Wymondham Arts Forum, 2009–15; Chm., Wymondham Arts Centre, 2009–15. *Publications:* Review of British Science Curriculum Projects (with D. G. Chisman), 1973; Environment and Environmental Education, 1979; (ed jtly) New Trends in Biology Education, 1987; (ed with P. J. Black) Children's Informal Ideas in Science, 1993; (ed jtly) Regardfully Yours: selected correspondence of Ferdinand von Mueller, vol. 1 1840–1859, 1998, vol. 2 1860–1875, 2002, vol. 3 1876–1896, 2006; numerous articles in learned jls. *Recreation:* reading. *Club:* Athenæum.

LUCAS, Ven. Brian Humphrey, CB 1993; author; Chaplain-in-Chief, and Archdeacon of the Royal Air Force, 1991–95, Archdeacon Emeritus, 1996; *b* 20 Jan. 1940; *s* of Frederick George Humphrey Lucas and Edith Mary Lucas; *m* 1966, Joy Penn, BA, MEd, FRGS; two *s* one *d*. *Educ:* St David's Coll., Lampeter (BA); St Stephen's House, Oxford. Ordained deacon 1964, priest 1965; Curate: Llandaff Cathedral, 1964–67; Parish of Neath, 1967–70; Royal Air Force: Chaplain, 1970–87; Asst Chaplain-in-Chief, 1987–91; Canon and Prebendary of Lincoln Cathedral, 1991–95, now Emeritus; Priest-in-charge, St Clement Danes, 1991–95; Priest-in-charge, 1996–2000, Rector, 2000–03, of Caythorpe, Fulbeck, and Carlton Scroop with Normanton, Diocese of Lincoln. QHC, 1989–95. Mem., Gen. Synod of C of E, 1991–95. Hon. Chaplain: Assoc. of London Clubs, 2004–; Bomber Command Assoc., 2004–; Coastal Command Assoc., 2005–; Horners' Co., 2011–; Hon. Pres., No. 3 Welsh Wing, ATC, 2007–; Chaplain to High Sheriff of Lincs, 2005–06. Vice-Pres., Clergy Orphan Corp., 1991–95; Visitor, Soldiers' and Airmen's Scripture Readers Assoc., 1991–95; Mem. Council, Bible Reading Fellowship, 1992–95. Mem. Council, RAF Benevolent Fund, 1991–95. Chm., Governing Body, Sir William Robertson Acad., Welbourn, 2012–. FRSA 1993. *Publications:* Reflections in a Chalice: the memoirs of a practical priest, 2011; A Glimpse of Glory in the Gothic Cathedrals of France, vol. 1, 2014, vol. 2, 2015. *Recreations:* archaeology of the Near East, travel (excluding tourist areas), watching Welsh Rugby football, researching Gothic architecture. *Address:* Pen-y-coed, 6 Arnhem Drive, Caythorpe, Lincs NG32 3DQ. *Clubs:* Savage (Hon. Sec., 1998–2008), Royal Air Force, Civil Service.

LUCAS, Dr Caroline; MP (Green) Brighton Pavilion, since 2010; *b* 9 Dec. 1960; *d* of Peter and Valerie Lucas; *m* 1991, Richard Le Quesne Savage; two *s*. *Educ:* Exeter Univ. (BA English Lit. 1983; PhD 1989). Oxfam: Press Officer, 1989–91; Communications Officer for Asia, 1991–93; Policy Adviser on trade and envmt, 1993–97; on secondment to Trade Team, DFID, 1997–98; Team Leader, Trade and Investment Policy Team, 1998–99. Mem., Oxford CC, 1993–97. European Parliament: Mem. (Green) SE Region, England, 1999–2010; Mem., Cttee on Internat. Trade, 1999–2010, on Transport and Tourism, 1999–2004, on Envmt, Public Health and Food Safety, 2004–10; Mem., Palestine Delegn, 1999–2010. Green Party: Mem., 1986–; Nat. Press Officer, 1987–89; Co-Chair, 1989–90; Leader, 2008–12. *Publications:* (as Caroline Le Quesne): Writing for Women, 1989; Reforming World Trade: the social and environmental priorities, 1996; (as Caroline Lucas): (with Mike Woodin) Green Alternatives to Globalisation, 2004; Honourable Friends?: Parliament and the fight for change, 2015. *Recreations:* gardening, walking, piano playing. *Address:* House of Commons, SW1A 0AA.

LUCAS, Christopher Tullis, CBE 1994; Founder, 2004, and Chairman, since 2010, Eastfeast (Director, 2005–07); *b* 20 Dec. 1937; *s* of late Philip Gaddesden Lucas, GM and Maise Lucas; *m* 1962, Tina Colville; two *d*. *Educ:* Winchester Coll. Apprenticeship with Thomson McLintock & Co.; CA 1965; Chief Exec., ICEM Ltd, 1966–72; Sen. Radio Officer, IBA, 1972–74; first Man. Dir, Radio Forth, Edinburgh, 1974–77; Dir and Sec., RSA, and Sec., Faculty of Royal Designers for Industry, 1977–94. Founder and Dir, Animarts, 2000–03; Chm., Wonderful Beast, 2012. *Recreation:* Suffolk and Saxmundham. *Address:* The Clock House, Church Street, Saxmundham, Suffolk IP17 1ER.

LUCAS, Sir Colin (Renshaw), Kt 2002; DPhil; FRHistS; Chief Executive, Rhodes Trust and Warden of Rhodes House, 2004–09 (Trustee, Rhodes Trust, 1995–2004); Fellow, All Souls College, Oxford, 2001–09; Vice-Chancellor, University of Oxford, 1997–2004; *b* 25 Aug. 1940; *s* of Frank Renshaw Lucas and Janine (*née* Charpentier); *m* 1st, 1964, Christiane Berchon de Fontaine Goubert (marr. diss. 1975); one *s*; 2nd, 1990, Mary Louise Hume. *Educ:* Sherborne Sch.; Lincoln Coll., Oxford (MA, DPhil; Hon. Fellow 1995). FRHistS 1974. Asst Lectr, then Lectr, Sheffield Univ., 1965–69; Vis. Asst Prof., Indiana Univ., 1969–70; Lectr, Manchester Univ., 1970–73; Fellow, Balliol Coll., Oxford, and Lectr in Modern History, Oxford University, 1973–90; Prof., 1990–94, and Dean, Div. of Social Scis, 1993–94, Chicago Univ.; Master of Balliol Coll., Oxford, 1994–2001 (Hon. Fellow, 2001). Chm. Bd, BL, 2006–10 (Mem., 2004–10). Trustee: Andrew W. Mellon Foundn, 2001–13; Eur. Inst. for Innovation and Technol. Foundn, 2010–15. Member: Hong Kong UGC, 2003–14; Academic Adv. Council, Heidelberg Univ., 2006–. Hon. Dr of University: Lyon, 1989; Princeton, 2002; Peking, 2002; Heidelberg, 2013; Hon. DLitt: Sheffield, 2000; Western Australia, 2000; St Francis Xavier, 2003; Oxford Brookes, 2004; Hon. LLD: Glasgow, 2001; Warwick, 2006; Hon. DCL Oxford, 2003. Officier: Ordre des Arts et des Lettres (France), 1989; Légion d'Honneur (France), 2005 (Chevalier, 1998); Chevalier, Ordre du Mérite (France), 1994; Bronze Bauhinia Star (Hong Kong), 2014. *Publications:* The Structure of the Terror, 1973; (with G. Lewis) Beyond the Terror, 1983; (ed) The Political Culture of the French Revolution, 1988; numerous articles.

LUCAS, Cristina; *see* Odone, C.

LUCAS, Geoffrey Haden; Secretary, Headmasters' and Headmistresses' Conference, 2000–11; *b* 1 Sept. 1951; *s* of Alfred Philip Lucas and Joyce Lucas; *m* 1974, Elaine Jean Helsby; two *s* one *d*. *Educ:* Northgate Grammar Sch. for Boys, Ipswich; Univ. of Birmingham (BA Hons); Univ. of Leeds (MEd Dist.); Trinity and All Souls Coll., Leeds (PGCE). Asst teacher, then Hd of Dept, George Dixon Sch., Birmingham, 1974–80; Sen. Lectr, then Principal Lectr and Dir, PGCE Secondary Course, Trinity and All Souls Coll., Leeds, 1980–89; Professional Officer, Modern Langs/Teacher Educn, Nat. Curriculum Council, York, 1989–93; Asst Chief Exec., SCAA, 1993–97; Hd, Corporate Policy and Dir, Special Projects, QCA, 1997–2000. *Recreations:* golf, gardening, cooking, family holidays. *Clubs:* East India, Lansdowne.

LUCAS, George; film director, producer and screenwriter; Chairman: Lucasfilm, 1974–2012 (Creative Consultant, since 2012); George Lucas Educational Foundation; *b* 14 May 1944; *s* of George and Dorothy Lucas; *m* 2013, Mellody Hobson. *Educ:* Univ. of Southern California (Bachelor of Fine Arts, 1966). Asst to Francis Ford Coppola on The Rain People, 1967 (winner, Grand Prize, Nat. Student Film Festival for short film, THX-1138, 1967); director, co-author of screenplays: THX-1138, 1970; American Graffiti, 1973; director, author: Star Wars, 1977; director, author, executive producer: Star Wars, Episode I: The Phantom Menace, 1999; Star Wars, Episode II: Attack of the Clones, 2002; Star Wars, Episode III: The Revenge of the Sith, 2005; executive producer, author: More American Graffiti, 1979; The Empire Strikes Back, 1980; Return of the Jedi, 1983; Indiana Jones and the Temple of Doom, 1984; Willow, 1988; The Young Indiana Jones Chronicles (TV series), 1992–93; Indiana Jones and the Kingdom of the Crystal Skull, 2008; Star Wars: The Clone Wars, 2008; co-executive producer: Raiders of the Lost Ark (and co-author), 1981; Land Before Time, 1988; Indiana Jones and the Last Crusade, 1989; executive producer: Mishima, 1985; Howard the Duck, 1986; Labyrinth, 1986; Tucker, the Man and his Dream, 1988; Radioland Murders, 1994; Red Tails, 2012. Irving G. Thalberg Meml Award, Acad. of Motion Picture Arts and Scis, 1992; Lifetime Achievement Award, Amer. Film Inst. *Publications:* Star Wars, 1976. *Address:* Lucasfilm Ltd, PO Box 29901, San Francisco, CA 94129–0901, USA.

LUCAS, Prof. Ian Albert McKenzie, CBE 1977; Principal, 1977–88, Fellow, since 1992, Wye College, Professor, 1988, University of London, now Professor Emeritus; *b* 10 July 1926; *s* of Percy John Lucas and Janie Inglis (*née* Hamilton); *m* 1950, Helen Louise Langerman; one *s* two *d*. *Educ:* Clayesmore Sch.; Reading Univ.; McGill Univ. BSc, MSc; CBiol, FRSB; FRAgS. Lectr, Harper Adams Agricl Coll., 1949–50; pig nutrition res., Rowett Res. Inst., Aberdeen, 1950–57 and 1958–61; Res. Fellow, Ruakura Res. Station, New Zealand, 1957–58; Prof. of Agriculture, UCNW, Bangor, 1961–77. Chm., Agricl and Vet. Cttee, British Council, 1978–87. Member: Jt Cttee on use of antibiotics in animal husbandry and vet. medicine, 1967–69; MAFF Adv. Council for Agric. and Hort., 1969–79; Agric. and Vet. Sub-Cttee, UGC, 1972–77; CVCP, 1985–88; Cttee, Internat. Co-operation in Higher Educn, British Council, 1986–90. President: Sect. M, BAAS, 1983; Agricl Educn Assoc., 1987; Rural Educn and Develt Assoc., 1994. Member Governing Body: Grassland Res. Inst., 1970–79; Rydal Sch., 1975–77; RVC, 1978–88; E Malling Res. Station, 1978–87; Hadlow Agric. Coll., 1978–88; Inst. for Grassland and Animal Production Research, 1987–89. Hon. Life Mem., British Council, 1987. Hon. DSc McGill, 1996. *Publications:* scientific papers in Jl Agricl Science, Animal Production, Brit. Jl Nutrition and others. *Recreation:* sailing. *Address:* Valley Downs, Brady Road, Lyminge, Folkestone, Kent CT18 8DU. *T:* (01303) 863053.

LUCAS, Ian Colin; MP (Lab) Wrexham, since 2001; *b* 18 Sept. 1960; *s* of Colin and Alice Lucas; *m* 1986, Norah Anne (*née* Sudd); one *s* one *d*. *Educ:* New Coll., Oxford (BA Jurisprudence). Articled Clerk, then Solicitor, Russell-Cooke, Potter and Chapman Solicitors, Putney and Kingston, 1983–85; Solicitor: Percy, Hughes and Roberts, Chester, 1985–86; Lees, Moore and Price, Birkenhead, 1986–87; Kirwan Nicholas Jones, then Roberts Moore Nicholas Jones, Birkenhead and Wrexham, 1987–92; D. R. Crawford, Oswestry, 1992–97; Sole Principal, Crawford Lucas, Oswestry, 1997–2000; Partner, Stevens Lucas, Oswestry and Chirk, 2001. Contested (Lab) N Shropshire, 1997. An Asst Govt Whip, 2008–09; Parly Under-Sec. of State, BIS, 2009–10; Shadow Minister: BIS, 2010–11; FCO, 2011–14; Defence, 2014–15. Non-exec. Dir, Robert Jones and Agnes Hunt Hosp., Gobowen, Shropshire, 1997–2001. *Recreations:* history, sport, art. *Address:* (office) Vernon House, 41 Rhosddu Road, Wrexham LL11 2NS. *T:* (01978) 355743.

LUCAS, Irene, (Mrs John Hays), CBE 2008; private consultant, since 2011; Chair, Hays Travel Group, since 2011; Senior Adviser, Newton Europe, since 2011; *b* Newcastle upon Tyne, 4 Feb. 1954; *d* of Vincent and Isabelle Lucas; *m* 1997, John Hays; one *s* one *d*. *Educ:* Univ. of Sunderland (MBA). Sunderland City Council, 1977–2002: various posts incl. Asst Dir, and Dir, Community and Cultural Services; Asst Chief Exec., 1999–2002; Chief Exec., South Tyneside Metropolitan BC, 2002–09; Dir Gen., Local Govt and Regeneration and Actg Perm. Sec., DCLG, 2009–11. *Recreations:* family, football, travel. *Address:* Whitburn House, 47 Front Street, Whitburn, Sunderland SR6 7JD.

LUCAS, Iris Grace; *see* Burton, I. G.

LUCAS, Hon. Ivor Thomas Mark, CMG 1980; HM Diplomatic Service, retired; Assistant Secretary-General, Arab-British Chamber of Commerce, 1985–87; *b* 25 July 1927; 2nd *s* of George William Lucas, 1st Baron Lucas of Chilworth, and Sonia Lucas; *m* 1954, Christine Mallorie Coleman; three *s*. *Educ:* St Edward's Sch., Oxford; Trinity Coll., Oxford (MA). Served in Royal Artillery, 1945–48 (Captain). BA Oxon 1951. Entered Diplomatic Service, 1951; Middle East Centre for Arab Studies, Lebanon, 1952; 3rd, later 2nd Sec., Bahrain, Sharjah and Dubai, 1952–56; FO, 1956–59; 1st Sec., Karachi, 1959–62; 1st Sec. and Head of Chancery, Tripoli, 1962–66; FO, 1966–68; Counsellor, Aden, 1968–69 (Chargé d'Affaires, Aug. 1968–Feb. 1969); Dep. High Comr, Kaduna, Nigeria, 1969–71; Counsellor, Copenhagen, 1972–75; Head of Middle East Dept, FCO, 1975–79; Ambassador to Oman, 1979–81, to Syria, 1982–84. Fellow in Internat. Politics of ME, Centre of Internat. Studies, Cambridge, 1991–94. Mem., Central Council, Royal Over-Seas League, 1988–94, 1996–2003; Chm., Anglo-Omani Soc., 1990–95 (Vice Pres., 1996–); Mem. Council, RSAA, 1988–94; Chm. Editl Bd, Asian Affairs, 1995–2002. Chm. Adv. Bd, Centre of Near and Middle Eastern Studies, SOAS, 1987–90. Trustee, Commonwealth Linking Trust, 1996–2003. *Publications:* A Road to Damascus: mainly diplomatic memoirs from the Middle East, 1997; 80 @ 80: reviews in 'Asian Affairs' 1989–2007, 2008; chapters in: Politics and the Economy in Syria, 1987; The Middle East: a handbook, 1988; various articles and reviews. *Recreations:* music, crosswords, Scrabble. *Club:* Royal Over-Seas League.

LUCAS, John Randolph, FBA 1988; Fellow and Tutor of Merton College, Oxford, 1960–96; *b* 18 June 1929; *s* of late Rev. E. de G. Lucas, sometime Archdeacon of Durham, and Joan Mary Lucas; *m* 1961, Morar Portal, *er d* of Sir Reginald Portal, KCB, DSC; two *s* two *d*. *Educ:* St Mary's Coll., Winchester; Balliol Coll., Oxford (1st cl. Maths Mods; 1st cl. Lit.Hum. 1951; John Locke Schol., 1952; MA 1954). Jun. Res. Fellow, Merton Coll., Oxford, 1953–56; Fellow and Asst Tutor, Corpus Christi Coll., Cambridge, 1956–59; Reader in Philosophy, Oxford Univ., 1990–96. Jane Eliza Procter Vis. Fellow, Princeton Univ., 1957–58; Leverhulme Res. Fellow, Leeds Univ., 1959–60. Chm., Oxford Consumers' Gp, 1961–63, 1965. Member: Archbishops' Commn on Christian Doctrine, 1967–76; Lichfield Commn on Divorce and Remarriage, 1975–78. Pres., British Soc. for the Philosophy of Sci., 1991–93. Lectures: (jtly) Gifford, Univ. of Edinburgh, 1971–73; Margaret Harris, Univ. of Dundee, 1981; Harry Jelema, Calvin Coll., Grand Rapids, 1987; Darwin, Cambridge Univ., 2000. *Publications:* Principles of Politics, 1966, 2nd edn 1985; The Concept of Probability, 1970; The Freedom of the Will, 1970; (jtly) The Nature of Mind, 1972; (jtly) The Development of Mind, 1973; A Treatise on Time and Space, 1973; Essays on Freedom and Grace, 1976; Democracy and Participation, 1976 (trans. Portuguese 1985); On Justice, 1980; Space, Time and Causality, 1985; The Future, 1989; (jtly) Spacetime and Electromagnetism, 1990; Responsibility, 1993; (jtly) Ethical Economics, 1997; The Conceptual Roots of Mathematics, 1999; (jtly) An Engagement with Plato's Republic, 2003; Reason and Reality, 2006; Economics as a Moral Science, 2012, rev. edn 2014; various articles in learned jls. *Recreations:* walking and talking. *Address:* Lambrook House, East Lambrook, South Petherton, Som TA13 5HW. *T:* (01460) 240413. *E:* john.lucas@merton.ox.ac.uk. *W:* http://users.ox.ac.uk/~jrlucas.

LUCAS, Matt; actor and writer; *b* London, 1974; *s* of John and Diana Lucas. *Educ:* Haberdashers' Aske's Sch. for Boys, Elstree; Univ. of Bristol. Started in stand-up comedy, 1992; *television* includes: as actor and writer: Sir Bernard's Stately Homes, 1999; Rock Profile, 1999–2000; Da Ali G Show, 2000; Little Britain, 2003–06 (Best Comedy Perf., RTS, 2003; Best TV Comedy, British Comedy Awards, 2004; Best Comedy Prog., 2003, 2004, Best Comedy Perf., 2004, BAFTA); Little Britain USA, 2008; Come Fly With Me, 2010; (host) The Matt Lucas Awards, 2012, 2013; as actor: The Smell of Reeves and Mortimer, 1995; Shooting Stars, 1995–2003 and 2009; Catterick, 2004; Casanova, 2005; The Wind in the Willows, 2006; Kröd Mändoon and the Flaming Sword of Fire, 2009; Portlandia (USA), 2012; Super Fun Night (USA), 2013–14; as actor, writer and director: Pompidou, 2015; *theatre* includes: Troilus and Cressida, Oxford Stage Co., 2000; Little Britain Live, UK and Australian tour, 2005–07; Prick Up Your Ears, Comedy, 2009; Les Miserables 25th Anniv. Concert, O2, 2010; Les Miserables, Queen's, 2011; *films* include: Shaun of the Dead, 2004; Alice in Wonderland, Infidel, 2010; Bridesmaids, 2011; Gnomeo and Juliet, 2011; The Look of Love, 2013; The Harry Hill Movie, 2013; In Secret, 2013; Small Apartments, 2013; Paddington, 2014. *Recreations:* eating crisps, watching football, eating chocolate, watching stage musicals, sleeping, eating crumpets. *Address:* c/o Troika Talent, 10a Christina Street, EC2A 4PA. *Club:* Arsenal Football Supporters.

LUCAS, Neil Raymond; author; Director, Knoll Gardens Ltd, since 2013 (Owner, 1994–2012); *b* London, 6 June 1957; *s* of Ian Raymond Edwin Lucas and Janet Elizabeth Lucas; *m* 1985, Susan Deidre Smith (marr. diss. 1995). *Educ:* Bassingbourn Village Coll.; Cambridge Coll. of Arts. MCIHort (MIHort 2004). With MoD, 1975–77; Gardens Manager, S Devon Health Trust, 1977–93. Chm., Knoll Gdns Foundn, 2008–13. Mem. Council, RHS, 2012–. *Publications:* Designing with Grasses, 2011; contribs to horticultural jls and periodicals. *Recreations:* gardening, walking, photography. *Address:* Knoll Gardens, Hampreston, Wimborne, Dorset BH21 7ND. *T:* (01202) 873931, *Fax:* (01202) 870842. *E:* neil@knollgardens.co.uk.

LUCAS, Noel John Mac; QC 2008; **His Honour Judge Lucas;** a Circuit Judge, since 2014; *b* Asansol, India, 5 Dec. 1952; *s* of Armenian parents, John Joseph Lucas and Aroosiak Lucas (*née* Sarkies); *m* 1994, Sylvia Hagopian; two *s*. *Educ:* King's Sch., Ely; Queen Mary Coll., Univ. of London (BSc Biol.). Called to the Bar, Middle Temple, 1979; in practice as a barrister, 187 Fleet St, 1981–2005, Red Lion Chambers, 2005–14. *Recreations:* sailing, ski-ing, walking, reading, classic cars, motorcycling. *Address:* Guildford Crown Court, Bedford Road, Guildford, Surrey GU1 4ST. *T:* (01483) 468500.

LUCAS, Prof. Robert Emerson, PhD; John Dewey Distinguished Service Professor of Economics, University of Chicago, since 1980; *b* 15 Sept. 1937; *s* of Robert Emerson Lucas and Jane Templeton Lucas; *m* 1959, Rita Cohen (marr. diss.); two *s*. *Educ:* Roosevelt High Sch., Seattle; Univ. of Chicago (BA 1959; PhD 1964). Lectr, Dept of Econs, Univ. of Chicago, 1962–63; Asst Prof. of Econs, Carnegie Inst. of Technol., 1963–67; Associate Prof., 1967–70, Prof. of Econs, 1970–74, Carnegie-Mellon Univ.; University of Chicago: Ford Foundn Vis. Res. Prof., 1974–75; Prof. of Econs, 1975–80; Vice-Chm., 1975–83, Chm., 1986–88, Dept of Econs. Fellow, Amer. Acad. of Arts and Scis, 1980; Mem., NAS, USA, 1981. Nobel Prize for Economics, 1995. *Publications:* Studies in Business-cycle Theory, 1981; (with T. J. Sargent) Rational Expectations and Econometric Practice, 1981; Models of Business Cycles, 1987; (with N. L. Skokey) Recursive Methods in Economic Dynamics, 1989; Customer Service: skills and concepts for business, 1996; Lectures on Economic Growth, 2002; papers on growth theory, public finance and monetary theory. *Address:* Department of Economics, University of Chicago, 1126 East 59th Street, Chicago, IL 60637, USA.

LUCAS, Prof. Sebastian Brendan, FRCP, FRCPath; Professor of Clinical Histopathology, King's College London School of Medicine, 1995–2012, now Emeritus; *b* London, 12 Sept. 1947; *s* of Edward and Branwen Lucas; *m* 1970, Susan Jay; one *s* one *d*. *Educ:* King's Coll. Sch., Wimbledon; Magdalen Coll., Oxford (BA); University Coll. Hosp. Med. Sch. (BM BCh). FRCPath 1990; FRCP 1992. Wellcome Trust Res. Fellow, 1979, 1982; Sen. Lectr, Univ. of Nairobi, 1980–82; Sen. Lectr and Consultant Pathologist, UCH and Hosp. for Tropical Diseases, 1983–. Hon. Prof., LSHTM, 2005–. Advr on pathology develt in Africa. Expert witness work to forestall unjust outcomes. *Publications:* contrib. articles to jls and textbook chapters on infectious diseases, HIV pathology, leprosy, maternal mortality, sickle cell disease, autopsy practice and governance, sepsis and the coronial system. *Recreations:* classical music, opera, family, church bell ringing, Gothic cathedrals, challenging political correctness in medicine. *Address:* Department of Histopathology, St Thomas' Hospital, Lambeth Palace Road, SE1 7EH. *E:* sebastian.lucas@kcl.ac.uk.

LUCAS, Stephen Bryan; Partner, Kirkland & Ellis International LLP, since 2014; *b* London, 14 Dec. 1968; *s* of John and Pamela Lucas; *m* 2002, Dina, *d* of Michael Charles Flesch, *qv*; three *s*. *Educ:* University Coll. London (LLB 1st Cl. Hons 1990; LLM Dist. 1991; PhD Soviet Corporate Law 2002); Harvard Univ. Law Sch. (Fulbright Schol.; LLM 1992). Mem., NY State Bar, 1993; admitted Solicitor, England and Wales, 1996. Associate, 1992–2002, Partner, 2002–04, Clifford Chance LLP; Partner: Linklaters LLP, 2004–11; Weil, Gotshal & Manges LLP, 2011–14. Pres., UCL Law Soc., 1990. *Recreations:* Shakespeare, Russia, history, football. *Address:* Kirkland & Ellis International LLP, 30 St Mary Axe, EC3A 8AF. *T:* (020) 7469 2233.

LUCAS, Sir Thomas (Edward), 5th Bt *cr* 1887; MA; research engineer, scientist, author, lecturer, mind-body consultant and chairman; *b* 16 Sept. 1930; *s* of late Ralph John Scott Lucas (killed in action, Libya, 1941), and Dorothy (*d* 1985), *d* of late H. T. Timson, Tatchbury Mount, Hants; *S* cousin, 1980; *m* 1st, 1958, Charmian (*d* 1970), *d* of late Col J. S. Powell; one *s*; 2nd, 1980, Ann Graham Moore. *Educ:* Wellington College; Trinity Hall, Cambridge; Farnborough Sch. of Gas Turbine Technol. Engr, Bristol Cars Ltd; Develt Engr, Rolls-Royce-Bristol Aero Engines Ltd; Tech. Dir, Vacuum Research (Cambridge) Ltd; Founder, Engineering Capacity Exchange (London); Consultant to European Commn DG XIII, INCRA Inc., The Hale Clinic, RTZ plc, and to other orgns; formerly Director: SGF Properties plc; Columbia Industrial Gp; Vacuum Metallizing Processes Inc.; EMDI Ltd; Digital Health Research Ltd, and other cos. Senior Trustee and Chairman: Inlight Trust; Truemark Trust. *Recreations:* motor sport, art, architecture, traditional Eastern medicines. *Heir:* *s* Stephen Ralph James Lucas [*b* 11 Dec. 1963; *m* 1993, Charlotte Johnson; one *s* one *d*]. *Address:* c/o Drummonds Bank, 49 Charing Cross, SW1A 2DX.

LUCAS-TOOTH, Sir (Hugh) John, 2nd Bt *cr* 1920, of Bught; *b* 20 Aug. 1932; *s* of Sir Hugh Vere Huntly Duff Munro-Lucas-Tooth of Teananich, 1st Bt and Laetitia Florence, OBE (*d* 1978), *er d* of Sir John Ritchie Findlay, 1st Bt, KBE; *S* father, 1985; *m* 1955, Hon. Caroline, *e d* of 1st Baron Poole, PC, CBE, TD; three *d*. *Educ:* Eton College; Balliol Coll., Oxford. *Address:* Parsonage Farm, East Hagbourne, Didcot, Oxon OX11 9LN. *Clubs:* Brooks's, Beefsteak.

LUCE, family name of **Baron Luce**.

LUCE, Baron *cr* 2000 (Life Peer), of Adur in the co. of West Sussex; **Richard Napier Luce,** KG 2008; GCVO 2000; Kt 1991; PC 1986; DL; Lord Chamberlain of HM Household, 2000–06; a Permanent Lord in Waiting to the Queen, since 2007; High Steward of Westminster Abbey, since 2011; *b* 14 Oct. 1936; *s* of late Sir William Luce, GBE, KCMG, and Margaret, *d* of late Adm. Sir Trevylyan Napier, KCB; *m* 1961, Rose, *d* of Sir Godfrey Nicholson, 1st Bt; two *s*. *Educ:* Wellington Coll.; Christ's Coll., Cambridge (2nd cl. History; Hon. Fellow, 2005); Wadham Coll., Oxford. Nat. Service officer, 1955–57, served in Cyprus. Overseas Civil Service, served as District Officer, Kenya, 1960–62; Brand Manager, Gallaher Ltd, 1963–65; Marketing Manager, Spirella Co. of GB; Dir, National Innovations Centre, 1968–71; Mem. European Adv. Bd, Corning Glass International, 1975–79; Director: Booker Tate, 1991–96; Meridian Broadcasting, 1991–96. Vice-Chancellor, Univ. of Buckingham, 1992–96. Contested (C) Hitchin, 1970. MP (C) Arundel and Shoreham, April 1971–74, Shoreham, 1974–92. PPS to Minister for Trade and Consumer Affairs, 1972–74; an Opposition Whip, 1974–75; an Opposition spokesman on foreign and commonwealth affairs, 1977–79; Parly Under Sec. of State, 1979–81, Minister of State, 1981–82 and 1983–85, FCO; Minister of State, Privy Council Office (Minister for the Arts), 1985–90. Governor and C-in-C, Gibraltar, 1997–2000. Chm., Crown Nominations Commn for See of Canterbury, 2012. Chairman: Commonwealth Foundn, 1992–96; Atlantic Council of the UK, 1993–96. Mem., Royal Mint Adv. Cttee, 2000–06. President: Voluntary Arts Network, 1993–2013; King George V Fund for Actors and Actresses, 2007–12; Commonwealth Youth Orch., 2010–12, Emeritus President, 2013. Gov., RSC, 1994–2003. Mem., Bd of Trustees, Royal Collection Trust, 2000–06; Trustee, Geographers' A–Z Map Trust, 1993–; Emeritus Trustee, RA, 2001–. Patron, Sir William Luce Meml Trust, 1994–; Founding Patron, Voluntary Arts Network, 2013–. DL W Sussex, 1991. *Publications:* Ringing the Changes: a memoir, 2007. *Recreations:* painting, piano, reading, walking. *Address:* House of Lords, SW1A 0PW. *Clubs:* Royal Automobile, Royal Over-Seas League (Pres., 2002–).

LUCE, Thomas Richard Harman, CB 1996; Member, Regulatory Decisions Committee, Financial Services Authority, 2001–08 (a Deputy Chairman, 2004–08); *b* 11 July 1939; *s* of late Air Cdre Charles Luce, DSO, and Joyce Marjorie Elizabeth Luce (*née* Johnson); *m* 1991, Virginia Manson Hunt; two step *s*. *Educ:* Clifton Coll.; Christ's Coll., Cambridge (BA Hons); Indiana Univ., USA. HM Inspector of Taxes, 1965–67; Asst Principal, Ministries of Aviation and Technology, 1967–69; Principal, CSD, 1969–72; Department of Health and Social Security: Principal, 1972–75; Asst Sec., 1975–84; Under Sec., 1984; seconded to HM Treasury (Head of Management Policy and Running Costs Gp), 1987–90; Dep. Dir, NHS Finance, 1990; Under Sec., Community Services Div., 1990–94, Hd of Social Care Policy, 1995–99, DoH. Chm., Home Office Review of Coroners, 2001–03. Trustee and Council Mem., CSV, 1999–2003; Trustee, Internat. Social Services (UK), 2001–04. Trustee, Hampstead and Highgate Fest., 1997–2001 (Chm. Trustees, 1997–2000). A music critic, Crosscut, Seattle, 2007–12. *Publications:* articles on coroner and death certification reform; music criticism. *Recreations:* music, reading, walking, swimming. *Address:* 6 Morpeth Mansions, Morpeth Terrace, SW1P 1ER. *T:* (020) 7834 6835; 1068 East Newton, Seattle, WA 98102, USA. *E:* tom.luce@btinternet.com. *Clubs:* Athenæum; Seattle Monday.

LUCIE, Gary Allan; a District Judge (Magistrates' Courts), since 2011; *b* 16 Jan. 1966; *s* of late David Lucie and of Patricia Lucie (*née* Jones). *Educ:* Broomfield Secondary Sch.; Havant Coll.; Local Govt Training Bd (Dip. Trading Standards 1988); Manchester Univ. (LLB Hons 1993). Trading Standards Officer, various appts, 1984–95; called to the Bar, Middle Temple, 1994; in practice as a barrister, 1995–2011; a Dep. Dist Judge (Magistrates' Courts), 2009–11. *Recreations:* astronomy, hiking, travel, socialising. *Address:* c/o Barkingside Magistrates' Court, 850 Cranbrook Road, Barkingside, Essex IG6 1HW.

LUCIE-SMITH, (John) Edward (McKenzie); poet, art critic and photographer; *b* Kingston, Jamaica, 27 Feb. 1933; *s* of John Dudley Lucie-Smith and Mary (*née* Lushington); unmarried. *Educ:* King's Sch., Canterbury; Merton Coll., Oxford (MA). Settled in England, 1946. Education Officer, RAF, 1954–56; subseq. worked in advertising and as free-lance journalist and broadcaster. Curator of a number of exhibns, UK and USA, 1977–. Digital projects include: (with Zavier Ellis), 100 London Artists, 2014. FRSL. *Publications:* A Tropical Childhood and other poems, 1961 (jt winner, John Llewellyn Rhys Mem. Prize; winner, Arts Council Triennial Award); (ed, with Philip Hobsbaum) A Group Anthology, 1963; Confessions and Histories, 1964; (with Jack Clemo, George MacBeth) Penguin Modern Poets 6, 1964; (ed) Penguin Book of Elizabethan Verse, 1965; What is a Painting?, 1966; (ed) The Liverpool Scene, 1967; (ed) A Choice of Browning's Verse, 1967; (ed) Penguin Book of Satirical Verse, 1967; Thinking about Art, 1968; Towards Silence, 1968; Movements in Art since 1945, 1969; (ed) British Poetry Since 1945, 1970; (with Patricia White) Art in Britain 69–70, 1970; (ed) A Primer of Experimental Verse, 1971; (ed with S. W. Taylor) French Poetry: the last fifteen years, 1971; A Concise History of French Painting, 1971; Symbolist Art, 1972; Eroticism in Western Art, 1972; The First London Catalogue, 1974; The Well Wishers, 1974; The Burnt Child (autobiog.), 1975; The Invented Eye (early photography), 1975; World of the Makers, 1975; (with Celestine Dars) How the Rich Lived, 1976; Joan of Arc, 1976; (with Celestine Dars) Work and Struggle, 1977; Fantin-Latour, 1977; The Dark Pageant (novel), 1977; Art Today, 1977, revd edn 1999; A Concise History of Furniture, 1979; Super Realism, 1979; Cultural Calendar of the Twentieth Century, 1979; Art in the Seventies, 1980; The Story of Craft, 1981; The Body, 1981; A History of Industrial Design, 1983; Art Terms: an illustrated dictionary, 1984; Art in the Thirties, 1985; American Art Now, 1985; Lives of the Great Twentieth Century Artists, 1986, rev. edn 2009; Sculpture since 1945, 1987; (ed) The Essential Osbert Lancaster, 1988; (with Carolyn Cohen, Judith Higgins) The New British Painting, 1988; Art in the Eighties, 1990; Art Deco Painting, 1990; Fletcher Benton, 1990; Jean Rustin, 1991; Harry Holland, 1992; Art and Civilisation, 1992; (ed) The Faber Book of Art Anecdotes, 1992; Andres Nagel, 1992; Wendy Taylor, 1992; Alexander, 1992; British Art Now, 1993; Race, Sex and Gender: issues in contemporary art, 1994; (with Elisabeth Frink) Elisabeth Frink: a portrait, 1994; American Realism, 1994; Art Today, 1995; Visual Arts in the Twentieth Century, 1996; Ars Erotica: an arousing history of erotic art, 1997; Adam, 1998; Zoo, 1998; (with Judy Chicago) Women and Art: contested territory, 1999; Judy Chicago: an American vision, 2000; Flesh and Stone (photographs), 2000; Flora, 2001; Art Tomorrow, 2002; Changing Shape (poems), 2002; Roberto Marquez, 2002; Carlo Bertocci, 2002; Stefano di Stasio, 2002; Paola Gandolfi, 2003; Ricardo Cinalli, 2004; Philip Pearlstein, 2004; John Kirby, 2004; Elias Rivera, 2006; Harry Holland, 2006; Censoring the Body, 2007; The Glory of Angels, 2009; (with Dominique Nahas) Margaret Evangeline, 2011; The Face of Jesus, 2011; Milos Sobaïc, 2012; Jamil Naqsh: the painted word, 2013; contribs to Times, Sunday Times, Independent, Mail-on-Sunday, Listener,

Spectator, New Statesman, Evening Standard, Encounter, London Magazine, Illustrated London News, etc. *Recreation:* the Internet. *Address:* 104 West Kensington Court, Edith Villas, W14 9AB.

LUCIER, Pierre; President, University of Quebec, 1996–2003; Fernand-Dumont Professor, Institut National de la Recherche Scientifique, Centre Urbanisation, Culture et Société, Quebec, 2006–10, now Associate Professor; *b* 15 Oct. 1941. *Educ:* Univ. of Montreal (BA 1963; LRelSc 1970); Jesuit Coll. Maximum (MA Philosophy 1965; MA Theology 1971); Univ. des Sciences Humaines, Strasbourg (Dr d'Etat (Phil.) 1975). Prof., Faculty of Theology, Univ. of Montreal, 1970–75; Sen. Researcher, Center for Res. in Educn, Montreal, 1975–78; Sen. Counselor, Cultural and Scientific Develt Secretariat, Exec. Council, Quebec, 1978–80; Asst Dep. Minister of Educn, Quebec, 1980–84; President: Superior Council for Educn, Quebec, 1984–89; Council of Univs, Quebec, 1989–90; Dep. Minister of Higher Educn and Sci., Quebec, 1990–93; Dep. Minister of Educn, Quebec, 1993–96. Canadian Member: Centre for Educnl Res. and Innovation, OECD, Paris, 1984–86; Cttee of Educn, OECD, Paris, 1996–97; Chm., Council of Canadian Dep. Ministers of Educn, 1993–95; Member: Sci. and Technology Council of Quebec, 1990–96; Standing Adv. Cttee for Univ. Res., Assoc. of Univs and Colls of Canada, 1998–2003; Vice-Pres., Bd of Dirs and Council of Govs, Agence Universitaire de la Francophonie, 1998–2003; Pres., Conf. of Univ. Rectors and Principals of Quebec, 2001–03 (Vice-Pres., 1997–2001). *Publications:* approx. 150 pubns, incl. a treatise on logical empiricism, and papers and articles on culture, epistemology, educn, educnl systems, instnl evaluation and higher learning. *Recreations:* reading, travelling, cinema. *Address:* INRS Urbanisation, Culture et Société, 490 rue de la Couronne, Quebec, QC G1K 9A9, Canada.

LUCK, Keith Frank; Finance and Commercial Director, Strategic Partnerships Division, Serco plc, since 2014; *b* 18 July 1960; *s* of Jack Luck and Mauree Luck (*née* Campbell); *m* 1987, Michelle Susan Harris; one *s* one *d. Educ:* Sidney Sussex Coll., Cambridge (BA Hons 1981; MA 1985). ACMA 1986, FCMA 1993; Associate Mem., ACT, 1994. Internal audit, then financial accounting, BT, 1981–85 (CIMA Inst. Prize and Harold Wilmot Prize, 1985); BT Schol., RAPC, Worthy Down, 1983–85; Head of Financial Training, BT Mgt Coll., 1986–87; Consultant, Deloitte, Haskins & Sells, 1987–89; Business Systems Manager, 1989–90, Project Dir, 1990–91, Financial Controller, 1991–93, Midland Bank; Head of Corporate Finance, 1993–94, Asst Dir (Corporate Finance and Property) and Chief Internal Auditor, 1994–97, Tower Hamlets LBC; Dir of Finance and Support Services, Lewisham LBC, 1997–99; Dir, Support Services, Accord plc, 1999–2000; Dir of Resources, Metropolitan Police Service, 2000–06; Dir Gen., Finance, FCO, 2007–10; Strategic Advr to Govt of Cayman Islands, 2011; Dir, Strategic Progs, Serco, 2011–14; Chief Operating Officer, MoD's Defence Business Service (on secondment), 2012. Alternate Director: Northern Rail Ltd, 2015– (Dir, 2014); Mersey Rail Ltd, 2015–. Conservator, Wimbledon and Putney Commons, 2015–. Chartered Institute of Management Accountants: Mem., Adv. Panel, 2005–09; Mem., Internat. Develt/Global Markets Cttee, 2006–11; Mem., Exec. Cttee, 2010–; Mem., Members' Services Cttee, 2011–12; Vice Pres., 2012–13; Dep. Pres., 2013–14; Pres., 2014–15. Dep. Chm., JV Bd for Global CGMA Designation with AICPA. Member: IFAC (Bd Observer); Professional Accountants in Business, 2007–12. Pres., Comets (Met. Police Sports and Social Club), 2002–06. Trustee: Civil Staff Welfare Fund, 2001–06; London Gdns Scheme, 2005–06. Mem. Court, City Univ., 2009–14. FCMI (FIMgt 1987); FRSA 2000; FInstD 2010 (MInstD 2006); Fellow, ACT, 2015. Editl Advr, Excellence in Leadership, 2006–11. Business Leader of Year, CIMA, 2004. *Recreations:* family, local history, historical geography, archaeology, distance running, swimming. *Address:* SW20. *E:* keith.luck@yahoo.co.uk. *Club:* Oxford and Cambridge.

LUCKETT, Dr Richard; Fellow, 1978–2012, now Emeritus Fellow, and Pepys Librarian, 1982–2012, Magdalene College, Cambridge; *b* 1 July 1945; *s* of late Rev. Canon Gerald Archer Luckett and of Margaret Mary Luckett (*née* Chittenden). *Educ:* St John's Sch., Leatherhead; St Catharine's Coll., Cambridge (MA, PhD). Lectr, RMA, Sandhurst, 1967–69; Cambridge University: Res. Fellow, 1970–72, Fellow, 1972–78, Dean, 1974–78, St Catharine's Coll.; Univ. Asst Lectr in English, 1973–78; Lectr, 1978–2001; Precentor, Magdalene Coll., 1982–94. *Publications:* The White Generals, 1971, 2nd edn 1988; The Fabric of Dryden's Verse (Chatterton Lect.), 1981; (ed with C. Hogwood) Music in Eighteenth Century England, 1983; (contrib.) The Pepys Companion, 1983; Handel's Messiah: a celebration, 1992; (ed) The Cryes of London, 1994. *Address:* 20 Eagle Road, Rye, E Sussex TN31 7NS.

LUCKHURST, Prof. Timothy Colin Harvey; Professor of Journalism, University of Kent, since 2007; *b* Sheffield, 8 Jan. 1963; *s* of Colin Luckhurst and Barbara Luckhurst (*née* Harvey); *m* 1989, Dorothy Ann Williamson; one *s* three *d. Educ:* Peebles High Sch.; Robinson Coll., Cambridge (BA Hist. 1983). Parly Res. Asst to Rt Hon. Donald Dewar, MP, 1986–89; Broadcast Journalist, Today Prog., BBC Radio 4, 1989–93; Washington Producer, BBC News, 1992; Asst Ed., BBC Radio 5 Live, 1993–95; Ed., News Progs, BBC Scotland, 1995–97; The Scotsman: Asst Ed., News, 1997–98; Dep. Ed., 1998–2000; Ed., 2000; columnist and contrib. to Scottish Daily Mail, Independent, Times, Guardian and New Republic, 2000–07. *Publications:* This is Today: a biography of the Today Programme, 2001; (contrib.) Afghanistan, War and the Media: frontlines and deadlines, 2010; (contrib.) Face the Future: tools for the modern media age, 2011; (contrib.) The Phone Hacking Scandal: journalism on trial, 2012; Responsibility Without Power: Lord Justice Leveson's constitutional dilemma, 2012; (contrib.) Routledge Companion to British Media History, 2014; contribs to jls incl. Ethical Space, British Journalism Rev., THES, Eur. Jl of Communication and Journalism Studies. *Recreations:* walking, playing guitar, motorcycling. *Address:* Centre for Journalism, University of Kent, Gillingham Building, Chatham Maritime ME4 4AG. *T:* (01634) 202913. *E:* Journalism@kent.ac.uk. *Club:* Frontline.

LUCKIN, Prof. Rosemary Helen, PhD; Professor of Learner Centred Design, Institute of Education, University College London (formerly Institute of Education, University of London), since 2006; *b* Leatherhead, 8 June 1958; *d* of Marcel Galster and Gladys Galster; one *s* one *d. Educ:* Rosebery Sch., Epsom; Univ. of Sussex (BA Hons 1st Cl. Computer Sci. and Artificial Intelligence 1993; PhD 1997). ACIB 1982. Midland Bank, 1978–83. University of Sussex: Lectr, 1999–2002, Reader, 2002–04, in Computer Sci. and Artificial Intelligence; Director: Undergraduate Studies, 2002–04; Human Centre Technol. Gp, 2002–04; Pro-Vice-Chancellor, 2004–06. Non-exec. Dir, British Educnl Communications and Technol. Agency, 2006–11. Gov., St Paul's Sch., 2011–. FRSA. *Publications:* Re-Designing Learning Contexts, 2010; articles in learned jls on technol. and learning design and use; learning contexts. *Recreations:* family, the sea, walking, cinema, politics. *Address:* London Knowledge Lab, Culture, Communications and Media, UCL Institute of Education, 23–29 Emerald Street, WC1N 3QS. *T:* (020) 7763 2176, 2164, *Fax:* (020) 7763 2138. *E:* r.luckin@ioe.ac.uk.

LUCKING, Adrienne Simone; QC 2014; a Recorder, since 2009; *b* Leicester, 28 Oct. 1966; *d* of Robert Dorrien Coombe and Patricia Alice Maud Coombe (*née* Pardoe, later Claxton); *m* 1st, Mr Lucking (marr. diss.); 2nd, Andrew Collie. *Educ:* Prince William Sch., Oundle; De Montfort Univ. (LLB Hons). Called to the Bar, Inner Temple, 1989; in practice as barrister, specialising in crime, 1989–. Mem., Ind. Rugby Judiciary Panel, 2013–. *Recreations:* horses, Rugby Union, reading, classical music. *Address:* 36 Bedford Row, WC1R 4JH. *T:* (020) 7421 8000.

LUCRAFT, Mark; QC 2006; **His Honour Judge Lucraft;** a Circuit Judge, since 2012; *b* 28 Dec. 1961; *s* of Rev. Cyril William Lucraft and Ann Elizabeth Lucraft; *m* 1985, Fiona Carmel Ovington; three *s. Educ:* Wood Green Sch.; Univ. of Kent at Canterbury (BA Hons Law 1983). Called to the Bar, Inner Temple, 1984; in practice as a barrister, 1985–2012; Recorder, 2003–12. Mem. Standards Cttee, Bar Standards Bd, 2005–11; Chm., Remuneration Cttee, Bar Council, 2012 (Vice Chm., 2010–12); Legal Assessor: Gen. Optical Council, 2008–12; GMC, 2010–12. *Publications:* (contrib.) Archbold: Criminal Pleading, Evidence and Practice, 1996–; (ed jtly) Encyclopedia of Road Traffic Law and Practice, 2002–; Fraud: criminal law and procedure, 2009; (consultant ed.) Halsbury's Laws of England, Road Traffic, 4th edn 2007, 5th edn 2011; (ed jtly) Crown Court Index, 2015–. *Recreations:* cricket, classical music, gardening, good food and wine. *Address:* Cambridge Crown Court, 83 East Road, Cambridge CB1 1BT. *Club:* MCC.

LUCY, Sir Edmund John William Hugh Cameron-Ramsay F.; *see* Fairfax-Lucy.

LUDEMAN, Keith Lawrence; Chairman: Bristol Water Company plc, since 2012; Eversholt Rail Group, since 2014; *b* 28 Jan. 1950; *s* of Joseph William Lawrence and Joan Violet Ludeman (*née* Dopson); *m* 1974, Diane June Eatock; two *d. Educ:* Newcastle Univ. (BA Hons Geog. 1971); Salford Univ. (MSc Transport Engrg and Planning 1973). Area Traffic Manager, Gtr Manchester Transport, 1974–82; Sen. Transport Officer, Hong Kong Govt, 1982–85; Sen. Consultant, MVA Consultancy, 1985–86; Managing Director: Burnley & Pendle Transport & Viscount Central, 1986–88; London Gen. Transport, 1988–96; London Bus Div., Go-Ahead Gp, 1996–99; Thameslink Rail and Thames Trains, 1999–2000; Chief Exec., Rail, 2000–06, Exec. Dir, 2003–06, Gp Chief Exec., 2006–11, Go-Ahead Gp. Dir, ATOC Ltd, 2003–11; non-executive Director: Interserve plc, 2011–; Network Rail, 2011–14 (Sen. Ind. Dir, 2012–14). Mem. Council, Confedn of Passenger Transport, 1997–2000; Mem., British Transport Police Authy, 2003–05. Chm., Assoc. Train Operating Cos, 2003–05. FRSA; FCILT; Fellow, Inst. of Railway Operators. Hon. DSc Salford, 2010. *Recreations:* sailing, scuba diving, swimming. *E:* ludemankd@aol.com. *Club:* Royal Automobile.

LUDER, (Harold) Owen, CBE 1986; architect and construction industry consultant; Principal, Owen Luder Consultancy, Communication in Construction, since 1987; President, Royal Institute of British Architects, 1981–83 and 1995–97; *b* London, 7 Aug. 1928; *s* of late Edward Charles and Ellen Clara Luder; *m* 1st, 1951, Rose Dorothy (Doris) Broadstock (marr. diss. 1988; she *d* 2010); four *d* (one *s* decd); 2nd, 1989, Jacqueline Ollerton (*d* 2008). *Educ:* Ecclesbourne Rd Sch., Islington; Deptford Park Primary Sch.; Peckham Sch. for Girls; Brixton Sch. of Building; Regent St Evening Sch. of Architecture. ARIBA 1954, FRIBA 1967. Private practice in architecture, 1957–87; Owen Luder Architect, 1957–65; Founder and Sen. Partner, Owen Luder Partnership, 1965–78, when it became one of the first architectural partnerships to convert to an unlimited co., Chm. and Man. Dir, 1978–87; on withdrawal from architectural practice, set up Owen Luder Consultancy (specialising in communication in construction), 1987; Director: Communication in Construction Ltd, 1990–2004; Jarvis PLC, 1995–2003. Non-exec. Dir, The Investment Company PLC, 1975–80. Principal architectural works in commercial and industrial architecture and environmental and urban planning in UK and abroad; consultant: to NCB for Vale of Belvoir coal mining project, 1975–87; to BR for re-use of Engrg Works, Shildon and Swindon, 1985–86; Consultant Architect, RCS, 1974–87; Architect/Planning Consultant, Marine Soc., 1990–99; Architect for: Trinity Square Car Park, Gateshead, 1960; Tricorn Centre, Portsmouth, 1965; Dunston Rocket, Gateshead, 1974; Tiaf City Hall, Saudi Arabia; Nat. Stadium, Abuja, Nigeria. Gave evidence to US Congress Cttee on Urban Develt, 1967; Mem., UK Govt Delegation to the Conference on Cities, Indianapolis, 1971. Royal Institute of British Architects: Mem. Council, 1967–97, 2010–; Hon. Treasurer, 1975–78; Vice-Pres., Membership Communications, 1989–90; Pres., Doric Club, 1994–; Hon. Sec./Treasurer, Commonwealth Assoc. of Architects, 1985–87; Chm. Organising Cttee, IUA Congress 1987; Vice-Chm., 1997–2002, Chm., 2002–03, Architects Registration Bd; Chm., Internat. Bldg Study Gp, 2010–12. Pres., Norwood Soc., 1981–92. Columnist: Building magazine, 1969–78, 1983–90; Building Design magazine, 1978–81, 1994–95; Editor and Presenter, Architectural Practice Video Magazine, 1987–90; Consultant and Presenter: RIBA Technical Seminar Prog., 1985–93; Building Design Update Seminars, 1994–2004. Regular lecturer: UCL Bartlett Sch. of Architecture; Oxford Brookes Univ. Occasional radio and TV broadcaster, UK and USA; featured in documentary film, Get Luder, 2010. British Kart Racer, 1961–63; survivor, Lakonia cruise-liner disaster, 1963. FRSA 1984. Mem., British Acad. of Experts, 1991 (Vice Chm., 1997–99); expert witness; qualified mediator. Trustee, Children Nationwide, 1997–2001. Freeman: City of London, 2010; Architects' Co., 1994 (Liveryman, 2010). RIBA Architecture Bronze Medal (for Eros House, Catford), 1963; various Civic Trust architectural and housing awards and commendations; Silver Jubilee Medal, for Housing Strategy for the 80s, Town Planning Assoc., 1981; Business Columnist of the Year, Publisher magazine, 1985. Arkansas Traveller, USA, 1971; Freedom, State of Arkansas, 1971. *Publications:* Sports Stadia after Hillsborough, 1990; Keeping out of Trouble, 1999, 4th edn 2012; contribs on architectural, planning and building matters to various jls. *Recreations:* enjoying my ever-expanding family, writing prose and poetry, swimming, photography, theatre, used to play golf badly, supporting Arsenal FC avidly. *Address:* (office) 702 Romney House, 47 Marsham Street, Westminster, SW1P 3DS.

LUDER, Ian David, CBE 2010; JP; freelance independent non-executive director and advisor; Chairman, Basildon and Thurrock University Hospitals NHS Foundation Trust, 2012–15; Lord Mayor of London, 2008–09; *b* London, 13 April 1951; *s* of late Mark Luder and of Frances Luder (*née* Stillerman); *m* 1999, Lin Jane Surkitt. *Educ:* Haberdashers' Aske's Sch.; University Coll. London (BSc Econ.; Fellow 2009). FCA 1980; FTII 1983. Tax Partner: Arthur Andersen, 1989–2002; Grant Thornton UK LLP, 2002–09. Mem., Bedford BC, 1976–99. Contested (UK Ind) S Basildon and E Thurrock, 2015. Mem. Council, Chartered Inst. of Taxation, 1983–97 (Pres., 1994–95). City of London: Mem., Court, Common Council, 1998–; Chm., Finance Cttee, 2003–06; Alderman, Castle Baynard Ward, 2005–; Sheriff, City of London, 2007–08; Liveryman: Coopers' Co., 1999–; Tax Advisers' Co., 2005–; Art Scholars' Co., 2014–. JP City of London, 2002. Hon. Fellow, GSMD, 2009. Hon. DSc City, 2008. KStJ 2009. *Recreations:* cricket, Rugby, gardening. *Clubs:* City Livery, MCC, East India.

LUDER, Owen; *see* Luder, H. O.

LUDFORD, Baroness *cr* 1997 (Life Peer), of Clerkenwell in the London Borough of Islington; **Sarah Ann Ludford;** *b* 14 March 1951; *m* 1982, Stephen Hitchins. *Educ:* Portsmouth High Sch.; London Sch. of Economics (BSc Econ; MSc Econ); Inns of Court Sch. of Law. Called to the Bar, Gray's Inn, 1979. With European Commn, 1979–85; European Advr, Lloyd's of London, 1985–87; Vice Pres., Corporate External Affairs, American Express Europe, 1987–90. Mem. (Lib Dem) Islington LBC, 1991–99. Mem., Lib Dem Federal Policy Cttee, 1990– (Vice Chm., 1992–98); Vice Chm., London Lib Dems, 1990–94. Contested: (L) Wight and Hampshire E, 1984, (Lib Dem) London Central, 1989 and 1994, EP elections; (Lib Dem) Islington N, 1992, Islington S and Finsbury, 1997. Mem. (Lib Dem) London Reg., EP, 1999–2014; contested same seat, 2014. *Address:* House of Lords, SW1A 0PW.

LUDLOW, Bishop Suffragan of, since 2009; **Rt Rev. Alistair James Magowan;** Archdeacon of Ludlow, since 2009; *b* 10 Feb. 1955; *s* of Samuel and Marjorie Magowan; *m* 1979, (Margaret) Louise Magowan (*née* Atkin); one *s* two *d. Educ:* King's Sch., Worcester; Leeds Univ. (BSc Hons Animal Physiol. and Nutrition); Trinity Coll., Bristol (DipHE); MTh Oxon 2002. Ordained deacon, 1981, priest, 1982; Curate: St John the Baptist, Owlerton,

Sheffield, 1981–84; St Nicholas, Durham, 1984–89; Chaplain, St Aidan's Coll., Durham Univ., 1984–89; Vicar, St John the Baptist, Egham, 1989–2000; RD, Runnymede, 1993–98; Archdeacon of Dorset, 2000–09. Canon, Salisbury Cathedral, 2000–09; Prebendary, Hereford Cathedral, 2010–. Chairman: Guildford Diocesan Bd of Educn, 1995–2000; Salisbury Diocesan Bd of Educn, 2003–09. *Recreations:* walking, fly fishing, oil painting, stamp collecting. *Address:* The Bishop's House, Corvedale Road, Craven Arms, Shropshire SY7 9BT.

LUDLOW, Archdeacon of; *see* Ludlow, Bishop Suffragan of.

LUDLOW, (Ernest John) Robin, TD 1979; career consultant, since 1996; *b* 2 May 1931; *s* of late Donald Ernest Ludlow, Blandford, Dorset, and Buxted, Sussex; *m* 1st, 1970, Sonia Louise Hatfeild (marr. diss. 1993); one *s* one *d*; 2nd, 1996, Mrs Primrose June King (*née* Palmer). *Educ:* Framlingham Coll., Suffolk. RMA Sandhurst, 1949–52; commissioned RASC, 1952; Staff, RMA Sandhurst, 1954–57; retd 1957. J. Lyons & Co. Ltd, 1957–59; The Economist, 1959–72; Press Sec. to the Queen, 1972–73; Dep. Dir, Aims of Industry, 1973–77; Head of Publicity, Strutt and Parker, 1977; Man. Dir, Kiernan and Co. Ltd (Exec. Search), 1977–79; Partner, Boyden Internat. (Exec. Search), 1979–81; Managing Director: Robin Ludlow & Associates (Exec. Search), 1981–89; Management Search Internat., 1985–89; Managing Consultant, Euro Management Search, 1990–95. Governor: Clergy Orphan Corp. (St Edmund's Sch. Canterbury, St Margaret's Sch. Bushey), 1973–83; Royal Star and Garter Home for Disabled Servicemen, 1987–91; Chairman: The Yeomanry Benevolent Fund, 1981–90 (Mem. Cttee, 1975–2000); Sharpshooters Yeomanry Assoc., 1973–83 (Mem. Cttee, 1972–2000). Kent and Co. of London Yeomanry (Sharpshooters), TA, 1959–69; The Queen's Regt, TA, 1971–78 (Maj.). Vice Chm., SE, TA&VRA, 1988–91 (Mem., F and GP Cttee, 1973–91; Mem., 1973–86, Chm., 1988–91, Kent Cttee). *Recreations:* shooting, gardening, conservation, genealogy. *Address:* 4 Homeminster House, Station Road, Warminster, Wilts BA12 9BP. *T:* (01985) 217917. *E:* robin.ludlow@btinternet.com.

LUDMAN, Harold, FRCS; Consultant Surgeon in Neuro-otology, National Hospital for Neurology and Neurosurgery, 1967–98; Consultant Surgeon to Ear, Nose and Throat Department, King's College Hospital, 1965–94; *b* 23 Feb. 1933; *s* of Nathan Ludman and Fanny Dinah Jerome; *m* 1957, Lorraine Israel; one *s* one *d*. *Educ:* Bradford Grammar Sch.; Sidney Sussex Coll., Cambridge (BA 1954; MB, BChir 1957; MA 1958). FRCS 1961. House Physician, UCH, 1957; House Surgeon: Royal Ear Hosp., UCH, 1957; Edgware Gen. Hosp., 1958; Royal Marsden Hosp., 1958–59; Registrar and Sen. Registrar, Ear, Nose and Throat Dept, KCH, 1960–65. President: British Assoc. Otolaryngology, 1990–93; Section of Otology, RSocMed, 1985; Chm., Soc. Audiology Technicians, 1967–75. Chm., Specialist Adv. Cttee in Otolaryngology, Jt Cttee Higher Surgical Trng, 1988–91; Mem., Intercollegiate Bd in Otolaryngology, RCS (formerly Mem. Court of Examiners); Chm., working party on deafness, MRC, 1973–77; formerly Mem., Hearing Aid Council. W. J. Harrison Prize, RSocMed, 1987; W. Jobson Horne Prize, BMA, 1990. *Publications:* (jtly) Diseases of the Ear, 1963, 6th edn 1997; (contrib.) Scott-Brown's Diseases of the Ear, Nose and Throat, 4th edn 1979 to 6th edn 1996; ABC of Ear, Nose and Throat, 5th edn 2007 to 6th edn 2012; contribs to books on ear diseases; numerous papers to learned jls on diseases of the ear. *Recreations:* photography, computers, reading, theatre, bird watching.

LUDWIG, Christa; singer; *b* Berlin, 16 March; *d* of Anton Ludwig, singer, stage director and opera general manager and Eugenie (*née* Besalla), singer; *m* 1st, 1957, Walter Berry (marr. diss. 1970), baritone; one *s*; 2nd, 1972, Paul-Emile Deiber (*d* 2011), actor and stage-director. *Educ:* Matura. Staedtische Buehnen, Frankfurt; Landestheater Darmstadt; Landestheater, Hannover; Vienna State Opera; guest appearances in New York, Chicago, London, Berlin, Munich, Tokyo, Milan, Rome, Lucerne, Salzburg, Epidauros, Zürich, Holland, Los Angeles, Cleveland, Saratoga, Bayreuth, Copenhagen, Gent, Montreal, Prague, Budapest and others. Hon. Prof., Senat Berlin, Germany, 1995. Dr *hc* Warsaw, 2008. Kammersängerin, Austria, 1962; Grand Prix du Disque, 1966; Grammy Award, 1967; Mozart Medal, Mozartgemeinde, Vienna, 1969; First Class Art and Science, Austria, 1969; Deutscher Schallplattenpreis, 1970; Orphée d'Or, 1970; Prix des Affaires Culturelles, 1972; Vienna Philharmonic Silver Rose, 1980; Hugo Wolf Medal, 1980; Gustav Mahler Medal, 1980; Ehrenring, Staatsoper Vienna, 1980, Hon. Mem., 1981, Fidelio Medal, 1991; Golden Medal, City of Salzburg, 1988, and Vienna, 1988; Echo Prize, Germany, 1994; Musician of the Year, Musical America, 1994; Hugo Wolf Medal, 2010. Grosses Bundesverdienstkreuz (Germany), 2004. Commandeur: des Arts et des Lettres (France), 1988; Ordre pour le Mérite (France), 1997; Légion d'Honneur (France), 2011; Grosses Ehrenzeichen (Austria), 1994; Silver Great Honour (Austria), 2007. *Publications:* Und ich wäre so gern Primadonna gewesen (autobiog.), 1994 (French edn 1996, US edn 1999). *Recreations:* listening to music, theatre, concerts, reading.

LUDWIG, Karen Heather; *see* Vousden, K. H.

LUE, Dr Abraham Sek-Tong, CMG 1998; MBE 1984; *b* 7 Jan. 1939; *s* of Lue Phang and Chin Choy Keow; *m* 1985, Dr Adaline Mang-Yee Ko. *Educ:* King George V Sch., Hong Kong; University Coll. London (BSc); King's Coll. London (PhD 1965; FKC 1993). King's College London: Lectr and Sen. Lectr in Maths, 1962–86; Asst Principal, 1986–92, Asst Principal Emeritus, 2006. Dir, Fleming Chinese Investment Trust PLC, 1993–2004. Dir, Chelsea and Westminster NHS Healthcare Trust, 1994–96. Mem., Home Sec.'s Adv. Cttee on Race Relns, 1979–86; Chm., 1988–92, Hon. Vice Pres., 1992–, Westminster Race Equality Council. Founder and Chm., Chinese Community Centre, London, 1980–96; GB/China Centre: Mem., Exec. Cttee, 1992–2002; Hon. Treas., 1994–95; Vice Chm., 1996–2002. European Rep., K. C. Wong Educn Foundn, Hong Kong, 1987–96; Vice Chm., Lloyd George Asia Foundn, 2007–11. Chm., British Liby Internat. Dunhuang Project, 1994–. *Publications:* Basic Pure Mathematics II, 1974; Little Jade and the Celestial Guards, 2011; mathematical papers on homological algebra in learned jls. *Recreation:* reading. *Address:* 27 Magazine Gap Road, Hong Kong. *T:* 28492880, *Fax:* 28492881; 18 Randolph Road, W9 1AN. *Clubs:* Athenæum, Hurlingham; Hong Kong Jockey (Hong Kong).

LUESLEY, Prof. David Michael, MD; FRCOG; Group (formerly Divisional) Director of Women's and Children's Health, Sandwell and West Birmingham NHS Trust, 2010–14; Director, Pan-Birmingham Gynaecological Cancer Centre, City Hospital, Birmingham, since 2005; consultant gynaecological oncologist; *b* 14 Feb. 1952; *s* of Michael James Joseph and Elizabeth Margaret Luesley; *m* 1996, Gabrielle Patricia Downey; two *d*. *Educ:* Queen Elizabeth Grammar Sch., Wakefield; Downing Coll., Cambridge (BA 1972); Birmingham Univ. (MB ChB 1975; MD 1985). FRCOG 1993. University of Birmingham: Sen. Lectr, 1986–93, Reader, 1993–96, in Obstetrics and Gynaecol.; Prof. of Gynaecol Oncology, 1996–2003; Lawson-Tait Prof. of Gynaecol Oncology, 2003–12, now Emeritus. Hon. Consultant Gynaecol Oncologist, Birmingham Women's Hosp., 2000–05. *Publications:* Intraepithelial Neoplasia of the Lower Genital Tract, 1995; Handbook of Colposcopy, 1996, 2nd edn 2002; Understanding Gynaecology: a problem solving approach, 1997; Cancer and Pre-Cancer of the Cervix, 1998; Cancer and Pre-Cancer of the Vulva, 1999; Handbook of Gynaecological Oncology, 2000. *Recreations:* food, wine, painting, photography. *Address:* 32 Chantry Road, Moseley, Birmingham B13 8DH. *T:* (0121) 249 2279, *Fax:* (0121) 449 7438. *E:* d.luesley@virgin.net.

LUETCHFORD, Teresa Jane; *see* Kingham, T. J.

LUFF, Rev. Canon Alan Harold Frank; Canon Residentiary of Birmingham Cathedral, 1992–96, Canon Emeritus, 1996; *b* 6 Nov. 1928; *s* of late Frank Luff and Elsie Lilian Luff (*née* Down), Bristol; *m* 1956, Enid Meirion, *d* of late Robert Meirion Roberts and Daisy Harker Roberts; three *s* one *d*. *Educ:* Bristol Grammar School; University Coll., Oxford (BA 1951, Dip. Theol. 1952, MA 1954); Westcott House, Cambridge. ARCM 1977. Deacon, 1956; priest, 1957; Assistant Curate: St Matthew, Stretford, Manchester, 1956–59; St Peter, Swinton, Manchester (with charge of All Saints, Wardley), 1959–61; Precentor of Manchester Cathedral, 1961–68; Vicar of Dwygyfylchi (otherwise Penmaenmawr), Gwynedd, dio. Bangor, 1968–79; Precentor, 1979–92, also Sacrist, 1979–86, Westminster Abbey; licensed to officiate, dio. Llandaff, 1996–. Chm., Hymn Soc. of Great Britain and Ireland, 1987–93 (Hon. Sec., 1973–86; Hon. Vice Pres., 2014–); Vice Pres., Internat. Arbeitsgemeinschaft für Hymnologie, 1999–2009. Chm., Pratt Green Trust, 1988–2006. Hon. FGCM 1993 (Warden, 1984–97; Vice Pres., 1997–); ARSCM 2000. Editor, Hymn Quest, 2000–. *Publications:* Hymns and Psalms (composer and author), 1981; Welsh Hymns and their tunes, 1990; (ed) Story Song, 1993; (ed) Sing His Glory, 1997; (ed and trans.) Ann Griffiths, Hymns and Letters, 1999; (ed) Strengthen for Service: 100 years of the English Hymnal, 2005; contribs to New Christian, Musical Times, Choir and Organ, etc. *Recreations:* singing, conducting, cooking. *Address:* 12 Heol Tyn y Cae, Rhiwbina, Cardiff CF14 6DJ.

LUFF, Geoffrey Shadrack, IPFA; County Treasurer, Nottinghamshire County Council, 1984–91; *b* 12 July 1933; *s* of Shadrack Thomas Luff and Rosie Winifred Luff (*née* Lister); *m* 1st, 1956, Gloria Daphne Taylor (*d* 1992); one *s* one *d*; 2nd, 1997, Brenda Wilson. *Educ:* Mundella Grammar Sch., Nottingham; BA Hons Open, 1998. Various posts in City Treasury, Nottingham CC, 1949–67; Sen. Technical Asst and Asst Bor. Treasurer, Derby CBC, 1967–73; Asst County Treasurer, Derbyshire CC, 1973–78; Dep. County Treasurer, Nottinghamshire CC, 1978–84. *Recreations:* bowls, gardening, birdwatching, photography.

LUFF, Sir Peter (James), Kt 2014; Chair, National Heritage Memorial Fund and Heritage Lottery Fund, since 2015; *b* 18 Feb. 1955; *s* of Thomas Luff and Joyce (*née* Mills); *m* 1982, Julia Jenks; one *s* one *d*. *Educ:* Windsor Grammar Sch.; Corpus Christi Coll., Cambridge (MA Econs). Research Asst to Rt Hon. Peter Walker, 1977–80; Head of Private Office to Rt Hon. Edward Heath, 1980–82; Dir, Good Relations Public Affairs, 1982–87; Special Advr to Rt Hon. Lord Young of Graffham, 1987–89; Sen. Consultant, Lowe Bell Communications, 1989–90; Asst Man. Dir, Good Relations Ltd, 1990–92. MP (C) Worcester, 1992–97, Mid Worcestershire, 1997–2015. PPS to Minister for Industry and Energy, 1993–96, to Lord Chancellor, 1996–97, to Minister of State, Home Office, 1996–97; an Opposition Whip, 2000–05; Opposition Asst Chief Whip, 2002–05; Parly Under-Sec. of State, MoD, 2010–12 (Minister for Defence Equipment, Support and Technol.). Chairman: Agriculture Select Cttee, 1997–2000; Trade and Industry Select Cttee, 2005–07; Business and Enterprise Select Cttee, 2007–09; Business, Innovation and Skills Cttee, 2009–10; Mem., Internat. Develt Cttee, 2014–15; Dep. Chm., All-Party India Gp, 2006–15; Chm., Cons. Parly Friends of India, 2001–05. Mem., Exec. Cttee, CPA, 2001–06. Patron, Conservative Students, 1995–98. Vice-Pres., Severn Valley Railway, 1997–. Chm., Worcester Cathedral Council, 2002–08. FCIPR (FIPR 1998; Hon. Fellow, 2008). *Recreations:* performing arts, shooting, photography. *E:* peter@peterluff.com.

LUFF, Peter John Roussel, FRGS; Director, Mass 1 Ltd, since 2012; *b* Brussels, 14 Sept. 1946; *s* of Edward and Yvonne Luff; *m* 1969, Carolyn Watson; three *s* one *d* (and one *d* decd). *Educ:* Eltham Coll.; Swansea Univ. (BA Hons Politics and Internat. Relns); Sch. of African and Oriental Studies, Univ. of London (MA 2013). FRGS 1971. Asst Dir, Amnesty Internat. UK, 1974–78; originated and co-produced first two shows in The Secret Policeman's Ball comedy series, 1976–77; Dir, All-Party Parly Human Rights Gp, 1976–78; Asst Producer, BBC TV, 1978–81; Funding and Mktg Dir, SDP, 1981–86; Dir, Eur. Movement UK, 1986–92; Vice Pres., Internat. Eur. Movement, 1992–95; Partner, Matrix Communications Ltd, 1995–97; Dir Gen., Royal Commonwealth Soc., 1997–2001; Consultant, Umeed health prog., Punjab, 2001–03; Exec. Dir, Action for a Global Climate Community, 2003–12. Chm., Eur. Movement, 2007–12. Member: Internat. Council, World Federalist Movement/Inst. of Global Policy, 2004–; Bd, Coalition for Creation of Internat. Court for Envmt, 2009–; Bd, One World Trust, 2000–06; Dir, Mass1, 2011–. Trustee: Eur. Multicultural Foundn, 2001–; Responding to Conflict, 2002–; Mass Extinction Meml Observatory, 2012–. FRSA. *Publications:* The Simple Guide to Maastricht, 1992; A Brilliant Conspiracy?, 1997. *Recreations:* travel, theatre, cinema, boating, walking. *Address:* PO Box 8, 47–49 Chelsea Manor Street, SW3 5RZ. *E:* peterluff@hotmail.com. *Clubs:* Athenæum, Two Brydges, Royal Over-Seas League.

LUFFINGHAM, Prof. John Kingley, FDSRCSE; Professor of Orthodontics, University of Glasgow, 1976–93, now Emeritus; *b* 14 Aug. 1928; *s* of Alfred Hulbert Carr Luffingham and Frances Tugby; *m* 1968, Elizabeth Margaret Anderson; two *s* one *d*. *Educ:* Haileybury; London Hosp. Med. Coll. (BDS, PhD London); Dip. Orth RCSE. House Surgeon, London Hosp. Med. Coll., 1957–58; Registrar, KCH, 1959–61; Clinical Research Fellow, MRC, 1961–64; Sen. Registrar, Guy's Hosp., 1965–67; Sen. Lectr, Glasgow Univ., 1968–76; Consultant Orthodontist, Greater Glasgow Health Board, 1968–76. *Publications:* articles in dental jls, incl. British Jl of Orthodontics, European Jl of Orthodontics, Archives of Oral Biology. *Recreation:* golf.

LUKE, 3rd Baron *cr* 1929, of Pavenham, Co. Bedford; **Arthur Charles St John Lawson Johnston;** fine art dealer, since 1972; an Opposition Whip, House of Lords, 1997–2010; *b* 13 Jan. 1933; *e s* of 2nd Baron Luke and Barbara, *d* of Sir FitzRoy Hamilton Anstruther-Gough-Calthorpe, 1st Bt; *S* father, 1996; *m* 1st, 1959, Silvia Maria (marr. diss. 1971), *yr d* of Don Honorio Roigt, Argentina; one *s* two *d*; 2nd, 1971, Sarah Louise, *d* of Richard Hearne, OBE; one *s*. *Educ:* Eton; Trinity Coll., Cambridge (BA Hons Hist.). Elected Mem., H of L, 1999–2015; Opposition spokesman on defence, and on culture, media and sport, 2004–10; Chm., Works of Art Cttee, 2010–14. Mem., Beds CC, 1965–70 (Chm., Staffing Cttee, 1967–70). President: Nat. Assoc. of Warehousekeepers, 1962–78; Internat. Assoc. of Book-Keepers, 1997–2001. Comdr, St John Ambulance, Beds, 1985–90 (Comr, 1972–85). Member Court: Corp. of Sons of the Clergy, 1980–2005; Drapers' Co., 1993– (Master, 2001–02). High Sheriff, Beds, 1969–70, DL Beds, 1989–2004. KStJ 1988. *Recreations:* shooting, fishing. *Heir:* *s* Hon. Ian James St John Lawson Johnston [*b* 3 Oct. 1963; *m* 1998, Rowena Jane, *y d* of John Aldington; two *s* one *d*]. *Address:* The Hollies, Gretton, Corby, Northants NN17 3DL.

LUKE, Iain Malone; *b* 8 Oct. 1951; *m* 1987, Marie (*d* 2009). *Educ:* Dundee Coll.; Univ. of Dundee (MA 1980); Univ. of Edinburgh (DipBA 1981); Jordanhill Teacher Trng Coll. (FE Teaching Qualif.). Asst Collector of Taxes, Inland Revenue, 1969–74; Asst Sales Manager, Brown & Tawse Steel Stockholder, 1974–75; Asst Bar Manager, 1981–83; Lectr, then Sen. Lectr, Dundee Coll. of Further Educn, 1983–2001. Member (Lab): Dundee DC, 1984–96; Dundee CC, 1995–2001. MP (Lab) Dundee E, 2001–05; contested (Lab) same seat, 2005. JP Dundee, 1996–2001.

LUKE, Robert Haydon Vernon; HM Diplomatic Service; High Commissioner, Malta, since 2012; *b* 9 Sept. 1974; *m* Louise Elwell; two *s* one *d*. *Educ:* St George's Sch., Harpenden; St Catharine's Coll., Cambridge (BA 1995). Grant Scheme Manager, Millennium Commn, 1997–2000; joined FCO, 2000; Desk Officer, Middle East Peace Process Section, Nr East and N Africa Dept, FCO, 2000–01; on secondment to Brazilian Diplomatic Inst., 2002; Second Sec. (Pol/Press and Public Affairs), Brasilia, 2002–05; Hd, War Crimes Section, Internat. Orgns Dept, FCO, 2005–08; on secondment to French Immigration Ministry, 2008; Counsellor, Justice and Home Affairs, Paris, 2009–12.

LUKES, Prof. Steven Michael, DPhil; FBA 1987; Professor of Sociology, New York University, since 1998; *b* 8 March 1941; *o s* of S. Lukes; *m* 1977, Nina Vera Mary Stanger (*d* 1999); two *s* one *d*; *m* 2006, Katha Pollitt. *Educ:* Royal Grammar School, Newcastle upon Tyne; Balliol Coll., Oxford (MA 1965; DPhil 1968). Student, 1962–64, Res. Fellow, 1964–66, Nuffield Coll., Oxford; Fellow of Balliol Coll., Oxford, 1966–88; Lectr in Politics, Oxford Univ., 1967–88; Prof. of Political and Social Theory, European Univ. Inst., Florence, 1987–95; Prof. of Moral Philosophy, Univ. of Siena, 1995–2000. Vis. Centennial Prof., LSE, 2001–03. *Publications:* (ed jtly) The Good Society, 1972; Emile Durkheim: his life and work, 1972; Individualism, 1973; Power: a radical view, 1974, 2nd enlarged edn 2005; Essays in Social Theory, 1976; (ed) Durkheim: Rules of Sociological Method, 1982; (ed jtly) Rationality and Relativism, 1982; (ed jtly) Durkheim and the Law, 1984; Marxism and Morality, 1985; (jtly) No Laughing Matter: a collection of political jokes, 1985; (ed) Power, 1986; Moral Conflict and Politics, 1991; The Curious Enlightenment of Professor Caritat: a comedy of ideas, 1995; Liberals and Cannibals: the implications of diversity, 2003; Moral Relativism, 2009. *Recreation:* playing jazz piano. *Address:* Department of Sociology, New York University, 295 Lafayette Street, 4th Floor, New York, NY 10012, USA. *E:* steven.lukes@nyu.edu; 175 Riverside Drive, Apartment 13G, New York, NY 10024, USA.

LUKIES, Alastair, CBE 2014; Co-founder and Chief Executive, Monitise, 2003–15; *b* Harlow, 26 Sept. 1973; *s* of Robert Lukies and Melanie Harris (*née* Carver); *m* 2003, Helen Reeves; one *s*. *Educ:* Bishops Stortford Coll. Rugby player for Saracens and London Irish; Dir, Asia Pacific, Internat. Communications Mgt Commonwealth Games Hospitality Div., 1999–2000; Co-founder, ePolitix, 2000–03. Non-exec. Chm., Innovate Finance, 2014–. UK Business Ambassador for Financial Services, 2014–. Member, UK Trade and Investment delegation: to Africa, 2011; to Indonesia, 2012; to China, 2013. Entrepreneur of Year, Growing Business Awards, 2011. *Recreations:* Rugby, swimming, ski-ing, Baptist Church, family roast dinners, long walks with wife Helen and son Jacob.

LUKŠIĆ, Igor, PhD; Deputy Prime Minister and Minister of Foreign Affairs and European Integration, Montenegro, since 2012; *b* Bar, Montenegro, 14 June 1976; *s* of Božidar and Nada Lukšić; *m* 2005, Nataša Bajović; two *d*. *Educ:* Univ. of Montenegro (BA 1998; MA 2002; PhD 2005). Docent and Lectr, Faculty of Internat. Econs, Finance and Business, Univ. of Montenegro; Sec., Min. of Foreign Affairs, 2001. MP (Democratic Party of Socialists) Montenegro, 2001–; Finance Minister, 2004–10; Dep. Prime Minister, 2008–10; Prime Minister, 2010–12. *Publications:* Book of Laughter (poetry and prose), 2001; (jtly) The Quest for Economic Freedoms, 2010; Fear, 2011; Book of Fear, 2013. *Recreations:* occasional basketball and tennis. *Address:* Ministry of Foreign Affairs and European Integration, Stanka Dragojevića 2, Podgorica, Montenegro. *T:* 20246357, 20201530, *Fax:* 20224670. *E:* kabinet@mfa.gov.me.

LUMLEY, family name of **Earl of Scarbrough**.

LUMLEY, Joanna Lamond, OBE 1995; FRGS; actress; *b* Kashmir, India, 1 May 1946; *d* of late Maj. James Rutherford Lumley, 6th Gurkha Rifles and Thyra Beatrice Rose Lumley (*née* Weir); one *s*; *m* 1st, Jeremy Lloyd (marr. diss. 1971; he *d* 2014); 2nd, 1986, Stephen William Barlow, *qv*. *Theatre* includes: Don't Just Lie There, Say Something, Garrick, 1972; Private Lives, tour, 1983; Hedda Gabler, Dundee, 1985; Blithe Spirit, Vaudeville, 1986; An Ideal Husband, Chichester, 1989; The Cherry Orchard, 1989; Vanilla, Brighton, transf. Lyric, 1990; The Revengers' Comedies, Strand, 1991; Who Shall I Be Tomorrow?, Greenwich, 1992; The Letter, Lyric, Hammersmith, 1995; The Cherry Orchard, Crucible, Sheffield, 2007; La Bête, Comedy, transf. NY, 2010; The Lion in Winter, Th. Royal, Haymarket, 2011; *television* includes: General Hospital, 1973; Coronation Street, 1973; Steptoe and Son; The New Avengers, 1976–78 (BAFTA Special Award, 2000); Sapphire and Steel, 1979; The Weather in the Streets, 1983; Mistral's Daughter; Oxbridge Blues, 1984; The Glory Boys; guest presenter, Wogan; A Perfect Hero, 1989; Lovejoy, 1992; Absolutely Fabulous, 1992–96, 2001–03, 2011 (2 BAFTA Awards; British Comedy Award, 1993); Class Act, 1994; Coming Home, A Rather English Marriage, 1998; Nancherrow, Dr Willoughby, MD, 1999; Mirrorball, 2000; (co-prod) The Cazalets, 2001; Up in Town, 2002; Born to be Wild, 2002; Sensitive Skin, 2005, 2007; Last Chance to Save, 2005; Jam and Jerusalem, 2006; Mistresses, 2010; The Making of a Lady, 2012; documentaries: White Rajahs of Sarawak, 1991; Girl Friday, 1994; Joanna Lumley in the Kingdom of the Thunder Dragon, 1997; Joanna Lumley's Nile, 2010; Joanna Lumley on Broadway, 2011; Joanna Lumley's Greek Odyssey, 2011; Joanna Lumley in search of Noah's Ark, 2013; Joanna Lumley meets Will.i.am, 2014; Joanna Lumley's Trans-Siberian Adventure, 2015; *radio* includes: The Psychedelic Spy, 1990; The Fortunes of War, 2008; *films* include: On Her Majesty's Secret Service; The Satanic Rites of Dracula; Trail of the Pink Panther; Curse of the Pink Panther; Shirley Valentine, 1989; Innocent Lies, 1995; James and the Giant Peach, Cold Comfort Farm, 1996; Prince Valiant, 1997; Sweeney Todd, 1998; Parting Shots, Mad Cows, 1999; Maybe Baby, 2000; Ella Enchanted, The Cat's Meow, 2004; The Magic Roundabout, 2005; Corpse Bride, 2005; Boogie Woogie, 2010; The Wolf of Wall Street, 2014; She's Funny That Way, 2015. Hon. Patron, Trinity Coll. Dublin Philosophical Soc., 2007. Hon. DLitt: Kent, 1995; St Andrews, 2006; DUniv Oxford Brookes, 2000. *Publications:* (ed) Peacocks and Commas, 1983; Stare Back and Smile (autobiog.), 1989; Forces Sweethearts, 1993; Girl Friday, 1994; In the Kingdom of the Thunder Dragon, 1997; No Room for Secrets (autobiog.), 2004; Absolutely: a memoir, 2011; articles in jls. *Recreations:* reading, music, travelling, granddaughters, daydreaming. *Address:* c/o Conway Van Gelder Grant Ltd, 8–12 Broadwick Street, W1F 8HW.

LUMLEY, Karen Elizabeth; MP (C) Redditch, since 2010; *b* 28 March 1964; *d* of Derek and Sylvia Allott; *m* 1984, Richard Gareth Lumley; one *s* one *d*. *Educ:* Rugby High Sch. for Girls; E Warwicks Coll., Rugby. Trainee accountant, Ford Motor Co., 1982–84; Co. Sec., RKL Geological Services Ltd, 1985–. Member (C): Wrexham BC (Gp Leader, 1991–96); Clwyd CC, 1993–96; Redditch BC, 2001–03. Contested (C) Delyn, 1997; Redditch, 2001, 2005. *Recreations:* knitting, cooking, reading. *Address:* House of Commons, SW1A 0AA. *T:* (020) 7219 7133. *E:* karen.lumley.mp@parliament.uk.

LUMLEY, Nicholas James Henry; QC 2012; a Recorder, since 2008; *b* Nottingham, 29 March 1969; *s* of Henry Lumley and Christine Lumley (*née* Rodger); *m* 1st, 1997 (marr. diss. 2007); one *d*; 2nd, 2012, Ruth Phillips; one *s* one *d*, and one step *d*. *Educ:* Pocklington Sch.; Newcastle Univ. (LLB Hons); Inns of Court Sch. of Law. Called to the Bar, Lincoln's Inn, 1992; Jun., 1997–98, Sec., 2004–11, N Eastern Circuit. Mem., Merchant Taylors' Co., York, 2013–. Vigneron d'honneur, St Emilion, 2005. *Recreations:* perusing wine lists, cooking for (and slaking the thirst of) friends, ski-ing, becoming an embarrassment to my children, failed Labrador trainer. *Address:* New Park Court Chambers, 16 Park Place, Leeds LS1 2SJ. *T:* (0113) 243 3277, *Fax:* (0113) 242 1285. *E:* nicholas.lumley@npc-l.co.uk. *Clubs:* Northern Counties; Primary Cricket.

LUMLEY-SAVILE, family name of **Baron Savile**.

LUMSDAINE, Nicola Frances; *see* LeFanu, N. F.

LUMSDEN, Prof. Andrew Gino, PhD; FRS 1994; Professor of Developmental Neurobiology, King's College London School of Biomedical and Health Sciences (formerly United Medical and Dental Schools of Guy's and St Thomas' Hospitals, then Guy's, King's and St Thomas' Hospitals' Medical and Dental School, King's College London), London University, since 1989; Director, MRC Centre for Developmental Neurobiology, 2000–14; *b* 22 Jan. 1947; *s* of Dr Edward Gilbert Sita-Lumsden, MD and Stella Pirie Lumsden; *m* 1st, 1970, Anne Farrington Roberg (marr. diss. 1996); two *d*; 2nd, 2002, Kathleen Marie Wets. *Educ:* Kingswood Sch., Bath; St Catharine's Coll., Cambridge (BA 1968; MA 1972; Frank Smart Scholar); Yale Univ.; PhD London 1978. Fulbright Scholar, 1968–70; Lectr in Anatomy, 1973–87, Reader in Craniofacial Biology, 1987–89, Guy's Hosp. Med. Sch. Miller Foundn Vis. Prof., Univ. of California, Berkeley, 1994; Lectr, Coll. de France, Paris, 1991; Yntema Lectr, SUNY, 1993; Howard Hughes Internat. Res. Scholar, 1993–98; Jenkinson Meml Lectr, Univ. of Oxford, 1994; Seymour Kreshover Lectr, NIH, 1996; Brooks Lectr, Harvard Univ., 1996; Ferrier Lectr, Royal Soc., 2001. Mem., EMBO, 2008–. Founder FMedSci 1998; FKC 1999. Freeman, Clockmakers' Co., 2006. W. Maxwell Cowan Prize, Soc. for Neurosci., 2007. Médaille de la Ville de Paris, 1986. *Publications:* (jtly) The Developing Brain, 2001; reports in learned jls. *Recreations:* mechanical engineering, natural history, Lotus Sevens, bridge. *Address:* MRC Centre for Developmental Neurobiology, King's College London, SE1 1UL.

LUMSDEN, Andrew Michael; Organist and Director of Music, Winchester Cathedral, since 2002; *b* 10 Nov. 1962; *s* of Sir David James Lumsden, *qv*. *Educ:* Winchester Coll.; Royal Scottish Acad. of Music and Drama; St John's Coll., Cambridge (MA Hons). ARCO 1979. Asst Organist, Southwark Cathedral, 1985–88; Sub-organist, Westminster Abbey, 1988–91; Organist and Master of the Choristers, Lichfield Cathedral, 1992–2002. Ext. Examr, Birmingham Conservatoire, RNCM, 1995–2005. Hon. FRCO 2004; Hon. FGCM 2008. *Recreations:* travel, flying, wine. *Address:* Cathedral Office, 9 The Close, Winchester SO23 9LS. *T:* (01962) 857200, *Fax:* (01962) 857201. *E:* andrew.lumsden@winchester-cathedral.org.uk.

LUMSDEN, Sir David (James), Kt 1985; Principal, Royal Academy of Music, 1982–93; *b* Newcastle upon Tyne, 19 March 1928; *m* 1951, Sheila Daniels; two *s* two *d*. *Educ:* Dame Allan's Sch., Newcastle upon Tyne; Selwyn Coll., Cambridge (Hon. Fellow, 1986). Organ scholar, Selwyn Coll., Cambridge, 1948–51; BA Class I, 1950; MusB (Barclay Squire Prize) 1951; MA 1955; DPhil 1957. Asst Organist, St John's Coll., Cambridge, 1951–53; Res. Student, 1951–54; Organist and Choirmaster, St Mary's, Nottingham, 1954–56; Founder and Conductor, Nottingham Bach Soc., 1954–59; Rector Chori, Southwell Minster, 1956–59; Dir of Music, Keele, 1958–59; Prof. of Harmony, Royal Academy of Music, 1959–61; Fellow and Organist, New Coll., Oxford (Hon. Fellow, 1996), and Lectr in the Faculty of Music, Oxford Univ., 1959–76; Principal, RSAMD, Glasgow, 1976–82. Conductor: Oxford Harmonic Soc., 1961–63; Oxford Sinfonia, 1967–70; BBC Scottish Singers, 1977–80; Organist, Sheldonian Theatre, 1964–76; Choragus, Oxford Univ., 1968–72. Harpsichordist to London Virtuosi, 1972–75. Member of Board: Scottish Opera, 1977–83; ENO, 1983–88. President: Inc. Assoc. of Organists, 1966–68; ISM, 1984–85; RCO, 1986–88; Chairman: NYO, 1985–94; Early Music Soc., 1985–89. Hugh Porter Lectr, Union Theological Seminary, NY, 1967; Vis. Prof., Yale Univ., 1974–75. Hon. Editor, Church Music Soc., 1970–73. Hon. FRCO 1976; Hon. RAM 1978; FRCM 1980; FRNCM 1981; FRSAMD 1982; Hon. GSM 1984; FLCM 1985; FRSA 1985; FRSCM 1987; Hon. FTCL 1988; FKC 1991. Hon. DLitt Reading, 1990. *Publications:* An Anthology of English Lute Music, 1954; Thomas Robinson's Schoole of Musicke, 1603, 1971; Articles in: The Listener; The Score; Music and Letters: Galpin Soc. Jl; La Luth et sa Musique; La Musique de la Renaissance, etc. *Recreations:* reading, theatre, photography, travel, hill-walking, etc. *Address:* 26 Wyke Mark, Dean Lane, Winchester SO22 5DJ. *E:* lumsdendj@aol.com.

See also A. M. Lumsden.

LUMSDEN, Iain Cobden, FFA; Group Chief Executive, Standard Life Assurance Co., 2002–04; *b* 6 June 1946; *s* of John A. Lumsden and Helen H. Lumsden (*née* Foster); *m* 1970, Rosemary Hoey; one *s* one *d*. *Educ:* Exeter Coll., Oxford (BA 1967; MA). FFA 1971. Standard Life Assurance Co., 1967–2004: Gp Finance Dir, 1990–2001.

LUMSDEN, Prof. Keith Grant, FRSE; Director, Edinburgh Business School, since 1995; *b* 7 Jan. 1935; *s* of Robert Sclater Lumsden and Elizabeth Brow; *m* 1st, 1961, Jean Baillie Macdonald (*d* 2005); one *s*; 2nd, 2009, Ruth Edith Reid. *Educ:* Univ. of Edinburgh (MA Hons Econ 1959); Stanford Univ., California (PhD 1968). FRSE 1992. Stanford University: Instructor, Dept of Econs, 1960–63; Asst Prof., Graduate Sch. of Business, 1964–67; Research Associate, Stanford Res. Inst., 1965–71; Associate Prof., Grad. Sch. of Business, 1968–75; Dir, Esmée Fairbairn Res. Centre, Heriot-Watt Univ., 1975–95. Vis. Prof., Heriot-Watt Univ., 1969–70; Affiliate Prof. of Econs, INSEAD, 1975; Acad. Dir, Sea Transport Exec. Programme, 1979; Prof. of Econs, Advanced Management Coll., Stanford Univ., 1971. Director: Economic Educn Project, 1969–74; Behavioral Res. Labs, 1970–72; Capital Preservation Fund, 1971–75; Nielsen Engineering Research, 1972–75; Hewlett-Packard Ltd, 1981–92. *Publications:* The Free Enterprise System, 1963; The Gross National Product, 1964; International Trade, 1965; (jtly) Macroeconomics, 1966, 4th edn 1981; (ed) New Development in the Teaching of Economics, 1967; Excess Demand and Excess Supply in World Tramp Shipping Markets, 1968; (ed) Recent Research in Economics Education, 1970; (jtly) Basic Economics: theory and cases, 1973, 2nd edn 1977; (ed) Efficiency in Universities: the La Paz papers, 1974; (jtly) Division Management Simulation, 1978; (jtly) Economics Education in the UK, 1980; (jtly) Basic Macroeconomic Models, 1981; (jtly) Running the British Economy, 1981, 6th edn 1990; (jtly) Managing the Australian Economy, 1985; (jtly) Shipping Management Model—Stratship, 1983; (jtly) Macroeconomic Database, 1984; (jtly) Strategies for Life—Stratlife, 1988; Economics, 1991; articles in professional jls. *Recreations:* tennis, deep sea game fishing. *Address:* 40 Lauder Road, Edinburgh EH9 1UE. *Clubs:* New (Edinburgh); Waverley Lawn Tennis & Squash (Edinburgh).

LUMSDEN-COOK, Lucy; Head of Comedy, BSkyB, since 2009; *b* London, 24 Oct. 1968; *d* of Joseph Andrew Christopher Hoare and Lady Christina Alice Hoare; *m* 2002, Mark Lumsden-Cook; one *s* one *d*. *Educ:* King's Sch., Canterbury; Univ. of Edinburgh (MA Hist. of Art). Production roles, Comic Strip Ltd, Red Rooster Films and Big Talk Prodns, 1992–99; Commissioning Exec., 2000–05, Controller of Comedy Commissioning, 2005–09, BBC. *Recreations:* drawing, children's illustration (illustrator for Daunt Books), family history, tennis, writing, theatre, funny people. *Address:* BSkyB, Grant Way, Isleworth, Middx TW7 5QD. *E:* lucy.lumsden@bskyb.com.

LUNA MENDOZA, Ricardo Victor; Ambassador of Peru to the Court of St James's and concurrently Ambassador to Ireland, 2006–10; *b* 19 Nov. 1940; *s* of Ricardo Luna and Victoria Mendoza; *m* 1969, Margarita Proaño; one *d*. *Educ:* Princeton Univ. (BA Hons Politics 1962); Columbia Univ., NY (Master Internat. Affairs 1964); Peruvian Diplomatic Acad. Diplomatic Service of Peru: served in London, Tel-Aviv, Geneva, Washington, Paris, Quito and NY, 1966–86; Ambassador, 1986; Under-Sec., Multi-lateral Affairs, Lima, and Co-ordinator, Contadora-Apoyo and Rio Gps, 1987–89; Ambassador: to UN, NY, 1989–92; to USA, 1992–99; Weinberg Vis. Prof. of Foreign Affairs, Princeton Univ., 2000–01; Tinker Vis. Prof. of Foreign Affairs, Columbia Univ., NY, 2002; Prof. of Internat. Affairs, Govt Inst., San Martín de Porres Univ., Lima, 2003; Advr to Peruvian Finance Minister for Internat. Affairs, 2004; Cogut Vis. Prof. of Internat. Affairs, Brown Univ., 2005; Vis. Prof. of Internat. Affairs and Co-ordinator, Latin-American Area, Fletcher Sch. of Law and Diplomacy, Tufts Univ., 2005–06; Kluge Distinguished Schol., Liby of Congress, Washington DC, 2011–. Fellow, Centre for Internat. Affairs, 1980–81, Inst. of Politics, 2006, Harvard Univ. Pan American Order, Panamerican Foundn, 1990. Commander: Order de Mayo (Argentina); Order Rio Branco (Brazil). *Publications:* Política Exterior del Perú, 1981; Carlos García Bedoya, 1993; Revaluación de la Idea del Hemisferio Occidental, 2002; contribs to jls.

Address: c/o Embassy of Peru, 52 Sloane Street, SW1X 9SP. *Clubs:* Athenæum, Travellers; University, Cosmos (Washington); Harvard (New York); Colonial (Princeton Univ.); Phoenix (Lima).

LUNAN, Very Rev. David Ward; Moderator of the General Assembly of the Church of Scotland, 2008–09; *b* London, 29 Feb. 1944; *s* of Andrew Lunan and Jean Lunan (*née* Orr); *m* 1974, Margaret Ann Fiddes Young; four *s.* *Educ:* Glasgow High Sch.; Univ. of Glasgow (MA 1965; BD 1968). Ordained C of S, 1970; Asst Minister, Calton New Parish, 1969–75; Minister: St Andrews Lhanbryd, Moray, 1975–87; Renfield St Stephens, Glasgow, 1987–2002; Clerk to Presbytery of Glasgow, 2002–08. Moderator: Presbytery of Moray, 1985–86; Presbytery of Glasgow, 2000–01. Hon. DLitt Strathclyde, 2010; Hon. DD Glasgow, 2011. *Recreations:* hill walking, music, reading, travel, family. *Address:* c/o Church of Scotland, 121 George Street, Edinburgh EH2 4YN. *T:* (0131) 225 5722. *E:* amurray@cofscotland.org.uk.

LUND, Helge; Chief Executive, BG Group, since 2015. Dep. CEO and Chief Financial Officer, pharmaceutical div., Hafslund Nycomed; Chief Executive: Aker Kvaerner; Statoil, 2004–14. *Address:* BG Group, 100 Thames Valley Park Drive, Reading, Berks RG6 1PT.

LUND, Mark Joseph; consultant; Chairman, MyCSP Trustee Company Ltd, since 2012; *b* 1 July 1957; *s* of Joseph and Maureen Lund; *m* 1986, Karen Will; two *s* one *d.* *Educ:* Liverpool Polytech. (BA Hons Social Studies); Univ. of Leeds (MA Transport Econs). Transport economist, BR, 1983–84; Management Consultant: Spicer & Oppenheim, 1984–89; Booz Allen Hamilton, 1989–91; Dir, Henderson Investors plc, 1991–2001; Chief Executive: J. P. Morgan Fundshub, 2001–03; St James's Place Capital, later St James's Place plc, 2004–07; Money Portal Ltd, later Honister Capital Ltd, 2008–11. Non-executive Director: MyCSP Ltd, 2012–; Skipton Financial Services Ltd, 2014–; Sen. Ind. Dir, British Ski and Snowboard, 2013–. Chartered FCSI 2011. *Recreations:* family activities, cycling, ski-ing.

LUND, Prof. Raymond Douglas, PhD; FRS 1992; Hatch Professor of Ophthalmology and Research Director, Moran Eye Center, University of Utah, 2000–06, now Professor Emeritus; *b* 10 Feb. 1940; *s* of Henry Douglas Lund and Rose Lund; *m* 1963, Jennifer Sylvia Hawes; two *s.* *Educ:* University College London (BSc 1st cl. Hons, PhD). LRAM. Asst Lectr, then Lectr, Anatomy Dept, UCL, 1963–66; Res. Associate, Univ. of Pennsylvania, 1966–67; Asst Prof., Anatomy Dept, Univ. of Stanford, 1967–68; Asst Prof., then Prof., Depts of Biological Structure and Neurological Surgery, Univ. of Washington, 1968–79; Prof. and Chm., Dept of Anatomy, Univ. of S Carolina, 1979–83; Prof. and Chm., Dept of Neurobiology, Anatomy and Cell Sci., Univ. of Pittsburgh, 1983–91 (Dir, Centre for Neuroscience, 1984–87); Prof. and Head of Dept of Anatomy, and Fellow of Clare College, Cambridge, 1992–95; Duke-Elder Prof. of Ophthalmology, Inst. of Ophthalmol., UCL, 1995–2000. Adjunct Prof. of Ophthalmology, Casey Eye Inst., Oregon Health and Sci. Univ., 2006–11. Chm. Scientific Cttee, Internat. Spinal Res. Trust, 1994–97; Trustee, Corporate Action Trust, 1997–2008. Founder FMedSci 1998. NIH Merit Award, 1988. *Publications:* Development and Plasticity of the Brain, 1978; contribs to learned jls. *Recreation:* music. *Address:* 708 NW Westover Terraces, Portland, OR 97210, USA; 541 Willoughby House, EC2Y 8BN.

LUND, Prof. Valerie Joan, CBE 2008; FRCS, FRCSEd; Professor of Rhinology, University College London, since 1995; *b* Wallasey, Cheshire, 9 May 1953; *d* of George Andrew Lund and Joan Lund (*née* Henry); *m* 2010, David John Howard. *Educ:* Charing Cross Hosp. Med. Sch., Univ. of London (MB BS 1977; MS 1987). Final FRCS Otolaryngol. 1982; FRCS *ad eundem* 1993; FRCSEd *ad eundem.* Trained RNTNEH, 1980–84, Charing Cross Hosp., 1984–86; Lectr, Inst. of Laryngol. and Otol., 1986–87; Sen. Lectr, 1987–93, Reader, 1993–95, UCL. Hon. Consultant: RNTNEH, 1987–; Moorfields Eye Hosp., 1990–; UCH, 2005–; Imperial Coll. NHS Trust, 2009–. Pres., British Assoc. of Otolaryngology-Head Neck Surgery, 2012–15. Mem., German Nat. Acad. of Scis Leopoldina, 2009–. *Publications:* (with A. G. D. Maran) Clinical Rhinology, 1990; (with D. F. N. Harrison) Tumours of the Upper Jaw, 1993; (jtly) Nasal Polyps, 1997; (jtly) Endonasal Sinus Surgery, 1999; (with G. K. Scadding) Investigative Rhinology, 2004; (contrib. and vol. ed.) Rhinology: Scott Brown's Otolaryngology, 2008, 8th edn 2014; (contrib.) Cumming's Otolaryngology Head and Neck Surgery, 2010, (vol. ed.) 6th edn 2014; Tumors of the Nose, Paranasal Sinuses and Nasopharynx, 2014; contrib. 86 chapters in books and over 300 peer-reviewed papers. *Recreations:* cooking and eating. *Address:* Royal National Throat, Nose and Ear Hospital, 330 Gray's Inn Road, WC1X 8DA. *T:* (020) 3456 5197.

LUNGHI, Cherie Mary; actress; *b* 4 April 1952; *d* of late Allessandro Lunghi and Gladys Corbett Lee; one *d* by Roland Joffé. *Educ:* Arts Educnl Trust, London; Central Sch. of Speech and Drama. *Theatre includes:* The Three Sisters, Owners, Newcastle, 1973; She Stoops to Conquer, Nottingham Playhouse, 1974; Teeth 'n' Smiles, Royal Court, 1975; RSC, 1976–80: Much Ado About Nothing; The Winter's Tale; King Lear; Destiny; Bandits; As You Like It; Saratoga; Twelfth Night; Uncle Vanya, RNT, 1982; Holiday, Old Vic, 1987; The Homecoming, Comedy, 1991; Arcadia, RNT, 1993; Passion Play, Donmar, 1999; Afterplay, Pushkin House, 2010; The Syndicate, Chichester, 2011; Steel Magnolias, New Alexandra Th., 2012; The Importance of Being Earnest, Harold Pinter Th., 2014. *Films include:* Excalibur, 1980; King David, 1984; The Mission, 1986; To Kill a Priest, 1987; Jack and Sarah, 1995; Mary Shelley's Frankenstein, 1995. *Television includes: series and serials:* The Praying Mantis, 1982; Master of the Game, 1984; The Monocled Mutineer, 1986; Ellis Island, 1987; The Manageress, 1988, 1989; The Buccaneers, 1995; Little White Lies, 1998; The Knock, 1999; Hornblower, 1999; David Copperfield, 1999; Cutting It, 2003; Casualty 1906, 2006; Casualty 1907, 2007; Secret Diary of a Call Girl, 2007; A Touch of Frost, 2008; Casualty 1909, 2009; Starlings, 2013; Pat and Cabbage, 2013; *plays and films:* The Misanthrope, 1978; Oliver Twist, 1983; Much Ado About Nothing, 1984; Letters to an Unknown Lover, 1986; The Lady's Not for Burning, 1987; The Canterville Ghost, 1995; Le Vipère au Poing, 2004. *Address:* c/o Creative Artists Management, 55–59 Shaftesbury Avenue, W1D 6LD.

LUNN, Rt Rev. David Ramsay; Hon. Assistant Bishop, Diocese of York, since 1998; *b* 17 July 1930. *Educ:* King's College, Cambridge (BA 1953; MA 1957); Cuddesdon College, Oxford. Deacon 1955, priest 1956, Newcastle upon Tyne; Curate of Sugley, 1955–59; N Gosforth, 1959–63; Chaplain, Lincoln Theological College, 1963–66; Sub-Warden, 1966–70; Vicar of St George, Cullercoats, 1970–75, Rector, 1975–80; Rural Dean of Tynemouth, 1975–80; Bishop of Sheffield, 1980–97. *Address:* Rivendell, 28 Southfield Road, Wetwang, Driffield, E Yorks YO25 9XX. *T:* (01377) 236657.

LUNN-ROCKLIFFE, Victor Paul; Director, Business Group, Export Credits Guarantee Department, 2005–06; artist (illustrations, paintings and cartoons), since 2006; *b* 5 Dec. 1948; *s* of Col W. P. Lunn-Rockliffe, DSO, MC and J. Jéquier; *m* 1971, Felicity Ann O'Neill; two *d.* *Educ:* Keele Univ. (Jt Hons French History). Export Credits Guarantee Department: joined, 1973; Head, Project Underwriting Div., ME and N Africa, 1987; Head, Risk Management Div., 1989; Head, Claims Div., 1994; Director: Asset Mgt Gp, subseq. Portfolio and Asset Mgt Gp, 1995–2004; Credit Risk Gp, 2004–05; Business Gp, 2005–06. *Publications:* Drawing ECGD 1973–2006 (also illustrated), 2006; *illustrated:* Living without Asthma, 2004: Blistered Feet—Blissful Mind, 2009; Change, Bring it On!, 2010. *Recreations:* drawing, painting, reading, walking, ballet, cinema.

LUNNY, William Francis; Sheriff of South Strathclyde, Dumfries and Galloway, 1984–98; *b* 10 Dec. 1938; *s* of James F. Lunny and Sarah Ann Crawford or Lunny; *m* 1967, Elizabeth McDermott; two *s* one *d.* *Educ:* Our Lady's High School, Motherwell; Glasgow Univ. (MA, LLB). Solicitor, 1961–67; Depute Procurator Fiscal, 1967–74; Crown Counsel/Legal Draftsman, Antigua, 1974–76; Advocate, 1977. Barrister, Antigua, 1981. KHS 1989. *Recreations:* walking, travelling.

LUNT, Beverly Anne; Her Honour Judge Lunt; a Circuit Judge, since 2004; *b* 8 March 1954; *d* of late Thomas Gordon Lunt and of Mary Lunt. *Educ:* Oxford Poly. (BA). Called to the Bar, Gray's Inn, 1977; in practice as a barrister, 1977–2004, Hd of Chambers, Kingsgate Chambers, Manchester, 1990–2004. *Recreations:* reading, cinema, walking, theatre, supporting animal charities (WSPA, Dogs Trust, RSPCA, IFAW). *Address:* Burnley Crown Court, Hammerton Street, Burnley BB11 1XD. *T:* (01282) 855300.

LUNTS, David; Executive Director, Housing and Land, Greater London Authority, since 2012; *b* 31 Oct. 1957; *s* of Lawrence Henry Lunts and Kvetinka Sonja Lunts; *m*; one *s.* *Educ:* Univ. of Manchester (BA Hons Pols and Mod. Hist.). Chm., Hulme Regeneration Ltd, 1992–95; Chief Executive: Urban Villages Forum, 1995–98; Prince's Foundn, 1998–2002; Dir, Urban Policy Unit, ODPM, 2002–05; Exec. Dir, Policy and Partnerships, GLA, 2005–08; Exec. Dir, London, Homes and Communities Agency, 2008–11. Mem., Urban Task Force, 1997–99. *Recreations:* cinema, cycling, food. *Address:* Greater London Authority, City Hall, The Queen's Walk, SE1 2AA. *E:* David.Lunts@london.gov.uk.

LUPTON, family name of **Baron Lupton**.

LUPTON, Baron *cr* 2015 (Life Peer), of Lovington in the County of Hampshire; **James Roger Crompton Lupton,** CBE 2012; Chairman, Greenhill Europe, since 2011; *b* Whalley, Lancs, 15 June 1955; *s* of Alec William and Margaret Crompton Lupton; *m* 1983, Béatrice Marie-Françoise Delaunay; one *s* three *d.* *Educ:* Sedbergh Sch., Yorks; Lincoln Coll., Oxford (MA Juris.). Admitted as solicitor, 1979; Baring Brothers, 1980–98 (Dep. Chm., 1995–98); Greenhill & Co., 1998–. Mem., Internat. Adv. Bd, Global Leadership Foundn, 2011–. Co-Treas., Cons. Party, 2013–. Trustee: Dulwich Picture Gall., 1997–2011 (Chm., 2006–11); BM, 2012–. Mem., Adv. Bd, Grange Park Opera, 1997–2011. Gov., Downe Hse Sch., 1998–2006. *Recreations:* collecting art, opera, shooting, ski-ing. *Address:* Greenhill & Co., Lansdowne House, 57 Berkeley Square, W1J 6ER. *T:* (020) 7198 7401. *E:* jlupton@greenhill.com. *Clubs:* Brooks's, London Capital.

LUPU, Radu; pianist; *b* 30 Nov. 1945; *s* of late Meyer Lupu, lawyer, and Ana Gabor, teacher of languages. *Educ:* Moscow Conservatoire. Debut at age of twelve with complete programme of own music; studied with Florica Muzicescu, Cella Delavrancea, Heinrich Neuhaus and Stanislav Neuhaus. 1st prize: Van Cliburn Competition, 1966; Enescu Internat. Competition, 1967; Leeds Internat. Pianoforte Competition, 1969; Abbiati Prize, Italian Critics' Assoc., 1989, 2006; Premio Internazionale Arturo Benedetti Michelangeli, 2006. Débuts: London, 1969; Berlin, 1971; NY and Chicago, 1972. Numerous recordings include complete Mozart violin and piano sonatas, complete Beethoven Piano Concertos, 1979. *Recreations:* history, art, sport. *Address:* c/o Barbara Golan, Stettbachstrasse 131H, 8051 Zurich, Switzerland. *T:* 443220704. *E:* golan@bluewin.ch.

LURIE, Prof. Alison; writer; Professor of English, Cornell University, 1976–2006, now Professor Emerita; *b* 3 Sept. 1926; *d* of Harry Lurie and Bernice Stewart; *m* 1st, 1948, Jonathan Bishop (marr. diss. 1985); three *s*; 2nd, 1995, Edward Hower. *Educ:* Radcliffe Coll., Cambridge, Mass (AB). Mem., AAAL 2005. *Publications:* Love and Friendship, 1962; The Nowhere City, 1965; Imaginary Friends, 1967 (televised, 1987); Real People, 1969; The War Between the Tates, 1974; Only Children, 1979; Foreign Affairs, 1984 (Pulitzer Prize, 1985); The Truth About Lorin Jones, 1988; (ed) The Oxford Book of Modern Fairy Tales, 1993; Women and Ghosts (short stories), 1994; The Last Resort, 1998; Truth and Consequences, 2005; *non-fiction:* The Language of Clothes, 1981; Don't Tell the Grown-ups, 1990; Familiar Spirits, 2001; Boys and Girls Forever, 2003; The Language of Houses, 2014; *children's books:* Clever Gretchen, 1980; The Heavenly Zoo, 1980; Fabulous Beasts, 1981. *Address:* c/o English Department, 263 Goldwin Smith Hall, Cornell University, Ithaca, NY 14853–3201, USA.

LUSBY, John Martin; Adjudicator (panel member), Tribunals Service, Criminal Injuries Compensation Appeals Panel, 1997–2008; Tribunal Member, First-tier Tribunal (Social Entitlement Chamber), 2008–09; *b* 27 April 1943; *s* of late William Henry Lusby and Florence Mary (*née* Wharam); *m* 1966, (Mary) Clare, *d* of late John Gargan and Ellen (*née* Myers); one *s* one *d.* *Educ:* Marist Coll., Hull; Ushaw Coll., Durham; Maryvale Inst., Birmingham (DipTh (with commendation) 1997); Open Univ. (MA Theol. (with distinction) 1998). DipHSM 1972; MHSM (AHA 1972). Entered NHS, 1961; junior appointments: De la Pole Hosp., Hull, Hull 'B' Gp HMC, 1961–66; County Hosp., York, York 'A' Gp HMC, 1966–67; Kettering Gen. Hosp., Kettering and District HMC, 1967–68; Admin. Asst, United Sheffield Hosps, 1968–70; Dep. Hosp. Sec., E Birmingham Hosp., E Birmingham HMC, 1970–72; Hosp. Sec., Pontefract Gen. Infirmary and Headlands Hosp., Pontefract, Pontefract, Castleford and Goole HMC/Wakefield AHA, 1972–74; Area Gen. Administrator, Kirklees AHA, 1974–76; Asst Dist Administrator (Patient Services), 1976–79, Dist Administrator, Wandsworth and E Merton Dist, 1979–81, Merton, Sutton and Wandsworth AHA(T); Area Administrator, Doncaster AHA, 1981; Dist Administrator, 1981–84, Dist Gen. Man., 1984–90, Exec. Dir, 1990, Doncaster HA; Mem., 1990–91, Gen. Manager, 1990–95, and Exec. Dir, 1991–95, Lothian Health Bd; Chm., Ind. Review Panel, NHS Complaints Procedure, Northern and Yorks Reg., NHS Exec., 1996–97. Member: Scottish Council for Postgrad. Med. and Dental Educn, 1992–95; Health Services and Public Health Res. Cttee, Chief Scientist Orgn, SHHD, 1993–95; Scottish Implementation Gp, Jun. Doctors and Dentists Hrs of Work, 1993–95; Jt Wkg Gp on Information Services, NHS in Scotland, 1993–95. Trustee: Dementia Services Develt Centre, Univ. of Stirling, 1991–95; Scottish Dementia Appeal Trust, 1994–95. Member: Catholic Theol Assoc. of GB, 1997–2008; Catholic Biblical Assoc. of GB, 1998–; Catholic Inst. for Internat. Relations, 1999–2004; Soc. for the Study of Theology, 2000–08; European Soc. for Catholic Theology, 2004–08; Catholic Union of GB, 2012–15. *Recreations:* study of theology, music, reading, travel. *Address:* Flat A, Copper Beech, 31 North Grove, N6 4SJ. *T:* (020) 8341 3426. *E:* john.lusby@sky.com. *Club:* Middlesex CC.

LUSCOMBE, Christopher David; theatre director; *b* Ashtead, Surrey, 6 Nov. 1963; *s* of David and Jill Luscombe. *Educ:* King's Coll. Sch., Wimbledon; Pembroke Coll., Cambridge (BA 1985; MA 1989). Actor: Cambridge Footlights, 1984–85; repertory th., 1985–90; Kean, Old Vic, 1990; RSC, 1991–98; Half Time, Donmar Warehouse, 1994; Peter Pan, NT, 1998; Chichester Fest. Th., 1999–2000; Art, Whitehall, 2002; The Iron Lady (film), 2011; plays directed include: The Shakespeare Revue, RSC, 1994, Vaudeville, 1995; Star Quality, Apollo, 2001; Home and Beauty, Lyric, 2002; Fascinating Aïda: One Last Flutter, Comedy, 2003; The Rocky Horror Show, Playhouse, 2006, then tour, 2006–15; The Comedy of Errors, 2006, The Merry Wives of Windsor, 2008, 2010, Shakespeare's Globe; A Midsummer Night's Dream, Regent's Park, 2007; Enjoy, Gielgud, 2009; Alphabetical Order, Hampstead, 2009; When We Are Married, Garrick, 2010; The Madness of George III, Apollo, 2011; Travels with my Aunt, Menier Chocolate Factory, 2013; Nell Gwynn, Shakespeare's Globe, 2015; others include: Masterpieces, Birmingham Rep., 2002; Little Shop of Horrors, 2003, The History Boys, 2010, W Yorks Playhouse; Things We Do For Love, Harrogate, 2004; Candida, Oxford Stage Co., 2004; The Likes of Us, Sydmonton, 2005; Arms and the Man, Salisbury, 2006; A Small Family Business, Watford, 2007; Hobson's Choice, Sheffield

Crucible, 2011; Hay Fever, Minneapolis, 2012; Henry V, Chicago, 2014; Love's Labour's Lost, Love's Labour's Won, RSC, 2014; tours of: The Importance of Being Earnest, Tell Me on a Sunday, The Lady in the Van, 2004; Lord Arthur Savile's Crime, 2005, 2010; Single Spies, 2008; Spamalot, 2010–12 (then Harold Pinter Th., 2012, Playhouse, 2012–14, UK tour, 2015); Dandy Dick, Blue/Orange, 2012. Trustee: Actors' Benevolent Fund, 2001–; Noël Coward Foundn, 2002–; Royal Theatrical Support Trust, 2012–. *Publications:* The Shakespeare Revue (with M. McKee), 1994; Star Quality (adapted from play by Noël Coward), 2001; Dandy Dick (adapted from play by Arthur Wing Pinero), 2012. *Recreations:* reading, music, travel. *Address:* c/o Nicki Stoddart, United Agents Ltd, 12–26 Lexington Street, W1F 0LE. *T:* (020) 3214 0800. *E:* nstoddart@unitedagents.co.uk. *Club:* Royal Automobile.

LUSCOMBE, Prof. David Edward, LittD; FSA; FRHistS; FBA 1986; Professor of Medieval History, 1972–95, Leverhulme Personal Research Professor of Medieval History, 1995–2000, Research Professor of Medieval History, 2000–03, now Emeritus, University of Sheffield; *b* 22 July 1938; *s* of Edward Dominic and Nora Luscombe; *m* 1960, Megan Phillips; three *s* one *d. Educ:* St Michael's Sch., North Finchley; Finchley Catholic Grammar Sch.; King's Coll., Cambridge (BA, MA, PhD, LittD). Fellow, King's Coll., Cambridge, 1962–64; Fellow and Dir of Studies in History, Churchill Coll., Cambridge, 1964–72; Sheffield University: Head of Dept of History, 1973–76, 1979–84; Dep. Dean, 1983–85, Dean, 1985–87, Faculty of Arts; Pro-Vice-Chancellor, 1990–94; Chm., Humanities Res. Inst., 1992–2003; Res. Dir for Arts and Humanities, 1994–2003. Vis. Prof., Univ. of Connecticut, 1993; Leverhulme European Fellow, 1973; Vis. Fellow, All Souls Coll., Oxford, 1994; British Acad./RSC Exchange Visitor to Canada, 1991; British Acad./Japan Acad. Exchange Visitor to Japan, 1996. Raleigh Lectr, British Acad., 1988. External examiner for higher degrees in Univs of Cambridge, Oxford, London, Liverpool, Bangor, Lancaster, ANU, Toronto, Groningen, for BA degrees at Bangor, Leicester and Leeds. Dir, Historical Assoc. Summer Vacation Sch., 1976 and 1992. Member: Governing Body, later Assoc. St Edmund's House, Cambridge, 1971–84; Cttee, Ecclesiastical History Soc., 1976–79; Council, RHistS, 1981–85; Council, British Acad., 1989–97 (Publications Sec., 1990–97; Member: Medieval Texts Cttee, 1982– (Chm., 1991–2004); Publications Cttee, 1987–97 (Chm., 1990–97); Postgrad. Studies Cttee, 1988–90; Humanities Res. Bd, 1994–96); Cttee on Acad. Res. Projects, 1990–97; Commonwealth Scholarships Commn in UK, 1994–2000; Auditor, HEQC, 1994–97. Mem. Council, Worksop Coll. and Ranby House, 1996–2008. Fellow, later Hon. Fellow, Woodard Corp. Hon. Pres., Soc. internat. pour l'étude de la philosophie médiévale, 2002– (Vice-Pres., 1987–97; Pres., 1997–2002); Mem. Cttee, Soc. for Study of Medieval Langs and Lit., 1991–96. Trustee, Church Burgesses Educnl Foundn, Sheffield, 2012–. Hon. LittD Sheffield, 2013. Gen. Editor, Cambridge Studies in Medieval Life and Thought, 4th series, 1988–2004 (Adv. Editor, 1983–88); Mem., Jt Supervisory Cttee, British Acad./OUP, for Oxford DNB, 1992–99 (Associate Editor, 1993–2004). British Acad. Medal for Outstanding Academic Achievement, 2014. *Publications:* The School of Peter Abelard, 1969; Peter Abelard's Ethics, 1971 (trans. Italian 1976); (ed jtly) Church and Government in the Middle Ages, 1976; (ed jtly) Petrus Abaelardus 1079–1142: Person, Werk und Wirkung, 1980; (jtly) David Knowles Remembered, 1991; (ed jtly) Anselm: Aosta, Bec and Canterbury, 1996; Medieval Thought, 1997 (trans. Portuguese 2000, Greek 2007); The Twelfth-Century Renaissance: monks, scholars and the shaping of the European mind, (in Japanese) 2000; (ed jtly) Peter Abelard, Expositio in Hexameron, 2004; (ed jtly) The New Cambridge Medieval History, vol. 4, *c* 1024–*c* 1198, parts 1 and 2, 2004; (ed jtly) Peter Abelard, Sententie, 2006; (ed jtly) A Monastic Community in Local Society: the Beauchief Abbey Cartulary, 2011; (ed and rev. trans.) The Letter Collection of Peter Abelard and Heloise, 2013; articles in learned jls and contribs to books. *Recreations:* family and grandchildren, walking, using libraries, cooking for two. *Address:* 28 Endcliffe Hall Avenue, Sheffield S10 3EL. *T:* (0114) 222 2555.

LUSCOMBE, Rt Rev. Lawrence Edward; Bishop of Brechin, 1975–90; Primus of the Episcopal Church in Scotland, 1985–90; *b* 10 Nov. 1924; *s* of Reginald John and Winifred Luscombe; *m* 1946, Doris Carswell Morgan, BSc, MB, ChB (*d* 1992); one *d. Educ:* Torquay Grammar Sch.; Kelham Theological Coll.; King's Coll., London; Univ. of Dundee (MA; MPhil 1991; PhD 1993). CA 1952, ASAA 1957. FSAScot 1980. Served Indian Army, 1942–47, Major. Partner, Galbraith, Dunlop & Co., Chartered Accountants, Glasgow, 1952–63. Ordained deacon, 1963; priest, 1964; Curate, St Margaret's, Glasgow, 1963–66; Rector, St Barnabas', Paisley, 1966–71; Provost of St Paul's Cathedral, Dundee, 1971–75. Hon. Canon, Trinity Cathedral, Davenport, Iowa, 1983. A Trustee, Scottish Episcopal Ch, 1985–. Hon. Res. Fellow, Dundee Univ., 1993–. Chm. of Council, Glenalmond Coll., 1987–94. FRSA 1987. Hon. DLitt Geneva Theological Coll., 1972; Hon. LLD Dundee, 1987. OStJ 1986; ChStJ 1996. *Publications:* Matthew Luscombe, Missionary Bishop, 1992; A Seminary of Learning, 1994; The Scottish Episcopal Church in the 20th Century, 1996; Episcopacy in an Angus Glen, 2003; Steps into Freedom, 2004; Hands Across the Sea, 2006; Episcopacy in the Heart of Dundee, 2009. *Address:* Woodville, Kirkton of Tealing, by Dundee DD4 0RD. *T:* (01382) 380331.

LUSH, Denzil Anton; His Honour Judge Lush; Senior Judge (formerly Master) of the Court of Protection, since 1996; *b* 18 July 1951; *s* of Dennis John Lush, MBE and late Hazel June Lush (*née* Fishenden). *Educ:* Devonport High Sch., Plymouth; University Coll. London (BA, MA); Corpus Christi Coll., Cambridge (LLM); Coll. of Law, Guildford. Admitted Solicitor, England and Wales, 1978; in private practice, 1978–96; admitted Solicitor and Notary Public, Scotland, 1993. Chm., Social Security Appeals Tribunals, 1994–96. Member: Law Soc. Mental Health and Disability Sub-Cttee, 1993–96; BMA Steering Gp on advance statements about medical treatment, 1994; Judicial Mem., Soc. of Trust and Estate Practitioners, 1996– (Geoffrey Shindler Award for Outstanding Contrib. to the Profession, 2009). Hon. Mem., Assoc. of Contentious Trust and Probate Specialists, 1998–. Trustee, Pan-European Org. of Personal Injury Lawyers Foundn, 2003–06; Patron, Solicitors for the Elderly, 2003–. Lay Reader, 1982–98. FRSocMed 2001. *Publications:* Cohabitation and Co-Ownership Precedents, 1993, 5th edn as Cohabitation Law Practice and Precedents, 2012; Elderly Clients: a precedent manual, 1996, 4th edn 2013; (with Stephen Cretney) Enduring Powers of Attorney, 4th edn 1996, 6th edn, as Cretney & Lush on Lasting and Enduring Powers of Attorney, 2009, 7th edn 2013; numerous contribs to legal publications. *Recreations:* supporting Plymouth Argyle FC, collecting commemorative and parliamentary pottery. *Address:* The Court of Protection, First Avenue House, 42–49 High Holborn, WC1V 6NP. *E:* denzil.lush@judiciary.gsi.gov.uk. *Club:* Athenæum.

LUSH, Ian Frank; Chief Executive, Imperial College Healthcare Charity, since 2014; *b* 13 July 1960; *s* of late Cecil Lush and Dolly Lush; *m* 1st, 1985, Margaret Clare Hindle (marr. diss. 2002); one *d*; 2nd, 2005, Ceri-Louise Hunter; one *s* one *d. Educ:* King Alfred Sch., Hampstead; Univ. of York (BA Hons (Music) 1981, MA (Music) 1982); City Univ., London (Dip. Arts Admin 1986). ARCM 1982. Co-Principal Viola, Iceland SO, 1982–83; rank and file Viola, Royal Liverpool Philharmonic Orch., 1983–85; Mktg Manager, Philharmonia Orch., 1986–87; Barbican Centre: Mktg and Promotions Manager, 1987–91; Mktg Dir, 1991–93; Hd of Mktg, LSO, 1993–95; Man. Dir, London Mozart Players, 1995–2003; CEO, Architectural Heritage Fund, 2003–14. Chm., NI Built Heritage Forum, 2006–14; Dep. Chm., Heritage Alliance (formerly Heritage Link), 2006–12; Director: Croydon Marketing and Development Ltd, 1996–2001; Croydon Partnership, 1997–2001; Innovative Enterprise Action, 2006–09. Member: Welsh Assembly Govt Historic Envmt Gp, 2005–14; Prince's Regeneration Trust Adv. Gp, 2005–14; Gt Ormond St Hosp. Foundn Trust Members' Council (formerly Forum), 2008–15 (Lead Councillor, 2012–15). FRSA. *Publications:* more than 120 concert progs and CD sleeve notes; articles for English Heritage Conservation Bulletin, SPAB Cornerstone magazine, Local Government Rev. and others. *Recreations:* sport (especially fanatical devotion to Chelsea Football Club), playing tennis (Stormont Lawn Tennis Club), theatre, cinema and concert going, urban and rural walking, cooking. *Address:* Imperial College Healthcare Charity, Ground Floor, Clarence Memorial Wing, St Mary's Hospital, Praed Street, W2 1NY. *T:* (020) 3312 2037, *Fax:* (020) 3312 2100. *E:* ian.lush@imperial.nhs.uk.

LUSH, Jane Elaine; Joint Managing Director, Kalooki Pictures, since 2013; *b* 10 Aug. 1952; *d* of Sidney and Rebecca Lush; *m* 1974, Peter Tenenbaum, landscape designer; one *s* one *d. Educ:* Camden Sch. for Girls. Joined BBC as trainee, 1970; BBC Television: Exec. Prod., Features Dept, 1989–90; Ed., Holiday, Commissioning Exec., Have I Got News For You, 1990; Dep. Hd, Features, 1995–2000; Controller: Daytime Television, 1998–2001; Entertainment Commissioning, 2002–05; Jt Man. Dir, Splash Media, 2005–13. *Recreations:* my children, family, friends, reading, holidays, Tottenham Hotspur.

LUSHINGTON, Sir John (Richard Castleman), 8th Bt *cr* 1791, of South Hill Park, Berkshire; *b* 28 Aug. 1938; *s* of Sir Henry Edmund Castleman Lushington, 7th Bt and Pamela Elizabeth Daphne, *er d* of Major Archer Richard Hunter; *S* father, 1988; *m* 1966, Bridget Gillian Margaret, *d* of late Colonel John Foster Longfield; three *s. Educ:* Oundle. *Publications:* From Gavelkinders to Gentlemen: a history of the Lushington family in East Kent from 1200–1700, 2012. *Heir: s* Richard Douglas Longfield Lushington, BA, Wing Comdr RAF, retd [*b* 29 March 1968; *m* 1st, 2001, Christianne Jane Tipping, Flight Lieut RAF (marr. diss. 2004); 2nd, 2006, Sarah Alice Butler; one *s* two *d* (of whom one *s* one *d* are twins)]. *Address:* Kent House, Barrington, Ilminster, Somerset TA19 0JP.

LUSK, (Ormond) Felicity (Stewart); Head, Abingdon School, since 2010; *b* 25 Nov. 1955; *d* of late Harold Stewart Lusk, QC (NZ), and of Janet Kiwi Lusk; *m* 1976 (marr. diss. 1996); two *s. Educ:* Marsden Coll., Wellington, NZ; Victoria Univ. (BMus); Massey Univ. (DipEd); Christchurch Teachers' Coll. (Dip Teaching); Univ. of York (Cert. Mus. Educn). Head of Music Department: Wellington E Girls' Coll., NZ, 1980–86; Aotea Coll., NZ, 1986–89; Hasmonean High School, London: Sen. Teacher and Head of Music Dept, 1990–93; Dep. Headteacher, 1993–96; Headmistress, Oxford High Sch., 1997–2010. Woolf Fisher Fellowship, NZ, 1985. Councillor, London Borough of Enfield, 1990–94. Mem., Standards Cttee, City of London Corporation, 2009–. Member: SHA, 1993–99; GSA, 1997–2010; Forum UK, 2009–; HMC, 2010–. Member: Court, Oxford Brookes Univ., 1999–2010; Council, Univ. of Buckingham, 2013–. Gov., GSMD, 1999–2010. Mem., Adv. Council, Oxford Philomusica, 2002–. Freeman, City of London, 2010. *Recreations:* reading, conversation, travel, Lhasa apso Dudley. *Address:* Abingdon School, Park Road, Abingdon, Oxon OX14 1DE.

LÜST, Prof. Reimar; President, Alexander von Humboldt Foundation, Bonn, 1989–99, now Hon. President; Director General, European Space Agency, 1984–90; *b* 23 March 1923; *s* of Hero Lüst and Grete (*née* Strunck); *m* 1986, Nina Grunenberg; two *s* by a previous marriage. *Educ:* Univ. of Frankfurt; Univ. of Göttingen (Dr rer. nat.). Max-Planck-Institut of Physics: Staff Scientist, 1950–60; Head of Astrophysics Dept, 1960–63; Dir, Max-Planck-Institut of Extraterrestrial Physics, 1963–72; Pres., Max-Planck-Gesellschaft zur Förderung der Wissenschaften, 1972–84. Vis. Prof., Univs of Princeton, Chicago, New York, MIT, CIT, 1955–63; Hon. Prof., Technical Univ. of Munich, 1965; Hon. Prof., Univ. of Hamburg, 1992. Chm., German Science Council, 1969–72. Chm., Bd of Govs, Internat. Univ., Bremen, 1999–2004, Hon. Chm., 2005–. Mem. and Hon. Mem. of eight academies. Dr *hc:* Sofia, 1991; Birmingham 1993. Planet No 4386 named Lüst, 1991. Adenauer-de Gaulle Prize, 1994. Grand Cross, Order of Merit (FRG), 1984; Officier, Légion d'Honneur (France), 1984; Grand Cross of Merit with Star and Shoulderblade (FRG), 1990. *Publications:* Hydrodynamik, 1955; articles in scientific jls. *Recreations:* tennis, history, ski-ing. *Address:* Max-Planck-Institute of Meteorology, Bundesstrasse 53, 20146 Hamburg, Germany. *T:* (40) 41173300.

LUSTIG, Robin Francis; journalist and broadcaster; *b* 30 Aug. 1948; *s* of Fritz Lustig and late Susan (*née* Cohn); *m* 1980, Ruth Kelsey; one *s* one *d. Educ:* Univ. of Sussex (BA Politics). With Reuters, 1970–77: Madrid, 1971–72; Paris, 1972–73; Rome, 1973–77; The Observer, 1977–89: reporter, 1977–81; News Ed., 1981–85; ME Corresp., 1985–87; Home Affairs Ed., 1987–88; Asst Ed., 1988–89; BBC, 1989–2012; progs on Radio 4 and World Service; Presenter, The World Tonight, BBC Radio 4, 1989–2012.

LUSZTIG, Prof. George, PhD; FRS 1983; Professor of Mathematics, Massachusetts Institute of Technology, Cambridge, USA, since 1978; *b* 20 May 1946; *s* of Akos and Erzsébet Lusztig; *m* (marr. diss.); two *d*; *m* 2003, Gongqin Li. *Educ:* Univ. of Bucharest, Rumania; Princeton Univ. (MA, PhD). Asst, Univ. of Timisoara, Rumania, 1969; Mem., Inst. for Advanced Study Princeton, 1969–71; Univ. of Warwick: Res. Fellow, 1971–72; Lectr in Maths, 1972–74; Prof. of Maths, 1974–78. Mem., US Nat. Acad. of Scis, 1992. *Publications:* The Discrete Series of GL_n over a Finite Field, 1974; and Characters of Reductive Groups over a Finite Field, 1984; Introduction to Quantum Groups, 1993; Hecke Algebras with Unequal Parameters, 2003. *Address:* 106 Grant Avenue, Newton, MA 02459, USA.

LUTHER, Anne Margaret, (Mrs A. N. Brearley-Smith); Director General, Action Research, 1990–2001; *b* 19 Jan. 1946; *d* of Dermot William Richard O'Leary and Eva Margaret (*née* Christie); *m* 1st, 1969, Philip John Luther (marr. diss. 1988); two *d*; 2nd, 1992, Andrew Neville Brearley-Smith. *Educ:* Ursuline Convent, Ilford; Chelsea Coll., London (BSc 1967). King's Fund Trainee, 1967–69; PA to House Governor, Westminster Hosp., 1969–71; Dir of Res., Action Research, 1982–90. Association of Medical Research Charities: Hon. Sec., 1982–87; Mem., Exec. Council, 1991–95. Mem., Prince of Wales Adv. Gp on Disability, 1990–95. Trustee, Common Investment Funds for Charities, 1991–98. Mem., Ashridge Mgt Coll. Assoc., 1984–2001. MInstD 1994–2001. FRSocMed, 1982–2008. *Recreations:* music, watercolours, theatre, cookery.

LUTON, Jean-Marie; Officier de la Légion d'Honneur; Commandeur de l'Ordre National du Mérite; Chairman, Arianespace, 2002–07 (Chief Executive Officer, 1997–2002); Chief Executive Officer, Starsem, 2002–06, now Hon. President; *b* Chamalières, 4 Aug. 1942; *m* 1967, Cécile Robine; three *s. Educ:* Ecole Polytechnique. Centre National de la Recherche Scientifique: researcher, 1964–71; Chargé de Recherches, 1971–74; Chargé de Mission, Service des Programmes des Organismes de Recherche, Min. for Industrial and Scientific Develt, 1971–73; Centre National d'Etudes Spatiales: Hd, Res. Progs Div., Progs and Indust. Policy Directorate, 1974–75; Hd, Planning and Projs Div., Progs and Indust. Policy Directorate, 1975–78; Dir, Progs and Planning, 1978–84; Dep. Dir Gen., 1984–87; Dir for Space Progs, Space Systems Div., Aérospatiale, 1987–89; Director General: Centre National d'Etudes Spatiales, 1989–90; ESA, 1990–97. Mem., Internat. Acad. of Astronautics, 1986. Astronautics Prize, French Assoc. for Aeronautics and Astronautics, 1985. *Recreations:* tennis, sailing. *Address:* c/o Arianespace, boulevard de l'Europe, 91006 Evry, France.

LUTZ, Marianne Christine, (Mrs C. A. Whittington-Smith); Headmistress, Sheffield High School for Girls (Girls' Public Day School Trust), 1959–83; *b* 9 Dec. 1922; *d* of Dr H. Lutz; *m* 1981, Charles Alexander Whittington-Smith, LLM, FCA (*d* 1997). *Educ:* Wimbledon High Sch., GPDST; Girton Coll., Cambridge (Schol.; MA Historical Tripos); University of London (DipEd, DipTh). Asst Mistress (History) at: Clergy Daughters' Sch., Bristol, 1946–47; South Hampstead High Sch., GPDST, 1947–59. Former Member: History Textbooks Panel for W Germany (under auspices of FO and Unesco); Professional Cttee, Univ. of Sheffield;

Historical Assoc.; Secondary Heads' Assoc. *Publications:* several in connection with Unesco work and Historical Assoc. *Recreations:* crosswords, opera, art, theatre. *Address:* Evona House, Hydro Close, Baslow, Bakewell, Derbyshire DE45 1SH. *T:* (01246) 582152.

LUXMOORE-BALL, Simon Coryndon, FRAeS; Chief Executive, Royal Aeronautical Society, since 2009; *b* Chew Magna, 9 April 1951; *s* of Cecil Michael and Felicity Luxmoore-Ball; *m* 2011, Pauline Sirrell. *Educ:* Millfield Sch., Som; Univ. of Bath (MBA); Univ. of West of England. Dowty Aerospace: Hd, Design Engrg, 1991–94; Mktg, Sales and Product Support Dir, 1995–97; Mktg Dir, 1998, Vice Pres., Business Develt, 1999–2000, Messier-Dowty Europe; Pres., Messier Dowty Ltd and Gp Vice Pres., Boeing and military business, 2001–04; Sen. Vice Pres. and Dep. Chief Exec., Messier Dowty, 2004–08. Non-executive Director: Aero Vodochody, 2009–13; Beagle Aerospace, 2010–. Mem. Council, Air League, 2012–. Trustee, Kennel Club, 2011–. FRAeS 2003. *Publications:* The Complete Siberian Husky, 2002. *Recreations:* Siberian husky sled dogs - all aspects, including judging, general canine interests, sport, in particular Rugby and cricket, walking, countryside activities, reading. *Address:* c/o Royal Aeronautical Society, No 4 Hamilton Place, W1J 7BQ. *T:* (020) 7670 4300. *E:* simon.luxmoore@aerosociety.com. *Clubs:* Royal Air Force; Kennel.

LUXON, Benjamin Matthew, CBE 1986; FGS; narrator and performer; *b* Camborne, Cornwall, 1937; US citizen, 2002; *m* 1969, Sheila Amit; two *s* one *d*; *m* 2002, Susan Crofut. *Educ:* Truro Sch.; Westminster Trng Coll.; Guildhall Sch. of Music. Teacher of Physical Education until becoming professional singer (baritone), 1963; due to severe hearing loss in 1996, eventually finished career as a professional singer. Repertoire included lieder, folk music, Victorian songs and duets, oratorio (Russian, French and English song), and operatic rôles at major opera houses at home and abroad. Major rôles included: Eugene Onegin, Don Giovanni, Wozzeck, Papageno, Julius Caesar, Posa, Gianni Schicchi, Falstaff. Numerous recordings. Appointed Bard of the Cornish Gorsedd, 1974. Third prize, Munich Internat. Festival, 1961; Gold Medal GSM, 1963. FGS (FGSM 1970); Hon. RAM 1980; Hon. DMus: Exeter, 1980; RSAMD, 1996; Canterbury Christ Church Coll., 1997. *Recreations:* collecting English water-colours and drawings; tennis, swimming.

LUZIO, Prof. (John) Paul, PhD; FRCPath; FMedSci; Professor of Molecular Membrane Biology, 2001–14, now Emeritus, and Voluntary Director of Research, since 2014, University of Cambridge; Master, St Edmund's College, Cambridge, 2004–14 (Fellow, 1987–2004; Hon. Fellow 2014); *b* 15 Aug. 1947; *s* of (Fadri Gian) John Luzio and Brenda Luzio (*née* Barnwell); *m* 1st, 1977, Alison Turner (*née* Ford) (marr. diss. 1981); one *s*; 2nd, 1986, Toni Copeland (*née* Stanton) (marr. diss. 1991); 3rd, 1992, Jane Edson (*née* Geering). *Educ:* Shene Grammar Sch., London; Clare Coll., Cambridge (BA 1968; PhD 1974). MRCPath 1991, FRCPath 1998; FRSB (FIBiol 2004). Lectr, Dept of Med. Biochem. (Chem. Pathol.), Welsh Nat. Sch. of Medicine, 1974–77; University of Cambridge: Sen. Res. Associate, Dept of Clin. Biochem., 1977–79; Lectr in Clinical Biochem., 1979–96; Reader in Molecular Membrane Biol., 1996–2001; Dir, Cambridge Inst. for Med. Res., 2002–12; Dep. Head, Sch. of Clinical Medicine, 2012–14; Sen. Tutor, St Edmund's Coll., 1991–96. Chm., MRC Molecular and Cellular Medicine Bd, 2007–12. FMedSci 1999; FHEA (ILTM 2002). Foundn Award, Assoc. of Clinical Biochemists, 2005. *Publications:* contribs to professional jls in biochem. and molecular cell biology. *Recreations:* gardening, fishing. *Address:* Pippin Meadow, 32 Lowfields, Little Eversden, Cambridge CB23 1HJ. *T:* (office) (01223) 336780. *E:* jpl10@cam.ac.uk.

LUZZATTO, Prof. Lucio, MD; FRCP, FRCPath; Scientific Director, Istituto Toscano Tumori, Italy, since 2005; Hon. Professor of Haematology, University of Firenze, since 2011 (Professor of Haematology, 2006–11); *b* 28 Sept. 1936; *s* of Aldo and Anna Luzzatto; *m* 1963, Paola Caboara; one *s* one *d*. *Educ:* Genoa Univ. (MD 1959); Pavia Univ. (Spec. Haematology 1962); Lib. Doc. Italy, 1968. FRCPath 1982; FRCP 1983. Research Fellow in Haematology, Columbia Univ., 1963–64; Lectr, then Prof. of Haematology, Univ. of Ibadan, 1964–74; Dir, Internat. Inst. of Genetics and Biophysics, Naples, 1974–81; Prof. of Haematology, RPMS, 1981–94; Hon. Dir, MRC Leukaemia Res. Fund's Leukaemia Unit, 1987–93; Chm., Dept of Human Genetics, Meml Sloan-Kettering Cancer Center, NY, 1994–2000; Scientific Dir, Nat. Inst. for Cancer Res., Italy, 2000–04; Prof. of Haematology, Univ. of Genoa, 2002–06. Pres., Italian Fedn of Life Scis, 2008–11. Foreign Mem., Amer. Acad. of Arts and Scis, 2004. Hon. DSc Ibadan, 1998; Hon. MD Patras, 2006. Pius XI Medal, 1976; Laurea ad hon., Univ. of Urbino, 1990; Chiron award, Italian Acad. of Medicine, 1995. *Publications:* Understanding Cancer, 2006 (G. M. Pace Prize, 2008); 370 contribs to learned jls. *Address:* c/o Istituto Toscano Tumori, Viale Pieraccini 6, 50139 Firenze, Italy. *T:* (055) 7944575. *E:* lucio.luzzatto@ittumori.it.

LYALL, Andrew Gardiner, CMG 1976; Under Secretary, Department of Transport, 1981–86, retired; *b* 21 Dec. 1929; *s* of late William and Helen Lyall (*née* Gardiner); *m* 1953, Olive Leslie Gennoe White; one *s* one *d*. *Educ:* Kirkcaldy High Sch. Joined MoT, 1951; Asst Shipping Attaché, British Embassy, Washington, DC, 1961–64; Principal, Nationalised Industry Finance and Urban Transport Planning, 1965–70; Asst Sec., Railways Div., 1970–72; seconded to FCO as Counsellor, UK Representation to European Communities, 1972–75; Assistant Secretary: Land Use Planning, DoE, 1975–76; Central Unit on Environmental Pollution, 1976–77; Under Sec., PSA, 1978–81. *Recreations:* reading, mind games. *Address:* Apartment 20, The Hawthorns, 4 Carew Road, Eastbourne, E Sussex BN21 2BF.

LYALL, John Adrian; Director, Lyall Bills & Young Architects, since 2011 (Managing Director, John Lyall Architects Ltd, 1991–2011); *b* 12 Dec. 1949; *s* of Keith Lyall and Phyllis Lyall; *m* 1991, Sallie Jean Davies; one *s* one *d*. *Educ:* Southend High Sch. for Boys; Architectural Association Sch. of Architecture, London. RIBA 1980. Partner, Alsop & Lyall, 1980–91. Major completed projects include: Leeds Corn Exchange, 1990; Cardiff Bay Visitor Centre, 1992; White Cloth Hall, Leeds, 1992; Tottenham Hale Station, 1992; N Greenwich Jubilee Line Station, 1999; Crystal Palace Park, 2000; Hammersmith Pumping Station, 2007; Cranfields Mill Develt, Ipswich, 2009; Jerwood Dance House, Ipswich, 2009; Pudding Mill Pumping Station, 2009; pumping stations, Olympic site, Stratford, 2011; Goldsmiths Centre, Clerkenwell, 2012. Member: Design Panel, Cardiff Bay Develt Corp., 1989–95; Nat. Design Adv. Panel, English Partnerships, 1998–2005; Acad. of Urbanism, 2011– (Vice-Chm.); Quality Rev. Panel, London Legacy Develt Corp., 2012–; Oxford City Design Panel, 2014–; Vice Chm., Nat. Design Adv. Panel, CABE, 2007–11; Built Envmt Expert, Design Council, and Vice Chm., Design Rev. Panel, CABE, 2011–. Sir Bannister Fletcher Vis. Prof., UCL, 1998. Vice Pres., RIBA, 1997, 1999; Vice Chm., RIBA Trust, 2004–08; Council Mem., AA, 2005–10. Founder Mem., Architects 4 Education, 2007. Organiser, Polyark2, 2009–10. External Examiner: Univ. of Greenwich, 2011–; Univ. of Brighton; Tutor, Bartlett Sch. of Architecture, UCL, 2007–. FRSA. *Publications:* (with W. Alsop) Architecture Projects & Drawings, 1984; (jtly) John Lyall: contexts and catalysts, 1999; contrib. Architecture Today, RIBA Jl, Architects Jl and Building Design. *Recreations:* choral singing, cycling, gardening, fruit trees. *Address:* Lyall Bills & Young, 70 Cowcross Street, EC1M 6EJ. *T:* (020) 7253 1630. *E:* john.lyall@lbyarchitects.com. *Club:* Chelsea Arts.

LYALL, Katharine Elizabeth; *see* Whitehorn, K.

LYALL GRANT, Maj.-Gen. Ian Hallam, MC 1944; Director General, Supply Co-ordination, Ministry of Defence, 1970–75; retired; *b* 4 June 1915; *s* of Col H. F. Lyall Grant, DSO and Lucy Ellinor (*née* Hardy); *m* 1951, Mary Jennifer Moore (*d* 2007); one *s* two *d*. *Educ:* Cheltenham Coll.; RMA, Woolwich; Gonville and Caius Coll., Cambridge (MA). CEng, MICE 1968; FGA 1978. Regular Commission, RE, 1935; service in: India, Burma and Japan, 1938–46 (MC; twice mentioned in despatches); Cyprus and Egypt, 1951–52; CO 131 Para Engr Regt (TA), 1954–56; Instructor, JSSC, 1957–58; Imperial Defence Coll., 1961; Aden, 1962–63; Comdt, Royal School of Mil. Engineering, 1965–67; Maj.-Gen. 1966; Dep. QMG, 1967–70, retired 1970. Col Comdt, RE, 1972–77. President: Bengal Sappers Officers' Assoc., 1987–95; Burma Campaign Fellowship Gp, 1996–2002 (Chm., 1991–96). Proprietor, Zampi Press, 1991–2011. *Publications:* Burma: the turning point, 1993; (with Kazuo Tamayama) Burma 1942: the Japanese Invasion, 1999. *Recreations:* travel, writing. *Address:* 6 St Martin's Square, Chichester, W Sussex PO19 1NT. *T:* (01243) 784214. *Club:* Naval and Military.

See also Sir M. J. Lyall Grant.

LYALL GRANT, Sir Mark (Justin), KCMG 2006 (CMG 2003); HM Diplomatic Service; National Security Adviser, since 2015; *b* 29 May 1956; *s* of Maj.-Gen. I. H. Lyall Grant, *qv*; *m* 1986, Sheila Jean Tresise; one *s* one *d*. *Educ:* Eton; Trinity Coll., Cambridge (MA Law). Called to the Bar, Middle Temple, 1980, Bencher, 2011; joined FCO, 1980; Second Sec., Islamabad, 1982–85; FCO, 1985–87; Private Sec. to Minister of State, FCO, 1987–89; First Sec., Paris, 1990–93; FCO 1993; seconded to European Secretariat, Cabinet Office, 1994–96; Dep. High Comr and Consul Gen., S Africa, 1996–98; Hd, EU Dept (Internal), FCO, 1998–2000; Dir, Africa, FCO, 2000–03; High Comr to Pakistan, 2003–06; Political Dir, FCO, 2007–09; Permanent Representative to the UN, 2009–15. *Recreations:* golf, tennis, sailing, bridge. *Address:* Cabinet Office, 70 Whitehall, SW1A 2AS. *Club:* Royal Automobile.

LYDIARD, Andrew John; QC 2003; a Recorder, since 2010; *b* 25 Aug. 1957; *s* of George Frederick Lydiard and Beryl Lydiard (*née* Taylor); *m* 1983, Mary Adair; two *s*. *Educ:* King's Sch., Chester; University Coll., Oxford (BA); Harvard Law Sch. (LLM). Called to the Bar, Inner Temple, 1980; Tutor in Law (pt-time), Pembroke Coll., Oxford, 1982–87. *Address:* Brick Court Chambers, 7–8 Essex Street, WC2R 3LD. *T:* (020) 7379 3550, *Fax:* (020) 7379 3558. *E:* andrew.lydiard@brickcourt.co.uk.

LYDON, Prof. Julie Elspeth, OBE 2014; Vice Chancellor and Chief Executive, University of South Wales (formerly University of Glamorgan), since 2010; *b* Builth Wells, Powys, 14 June 1954; *d* of Dennis and Rosalind Hodges; *m* 1985, Stephen Lydon; two *s*. *Educ:* Wolverhampton Poly. (BA Hons Econs 1975); Part 1, ICMA, 1977; Cert. of Proficiency, Chartered Insce Inst., 1987; Univ. of Wolverhampton (MBA 2000). Graduate mgt trainee, then Computer Systems Analyst/Programmer, TI Gp, 1975–79; Mktg and Sales Rep., 1980–82, Sales and Mktg Manager, 1982–85, TI Accles & Pollock; Regl and Project Manager, MAI plc, 1986–89; Wolverhampton Polytechnic, later University of Wolverhampton: Sen. Lectr, Inf. Mgt, 1989–92; Principal Lectr, Inf. Mgt and Strategic Mgt, and Dep. to Hd of Undergrad. Studies, 1992–97; Associate Dean, Business Sch., 1997–2002; Asst Vice Chancellor, UWE, 2003–06; Dep. Vice Chancellor, Univ. of Glamorgan, 2006–10. Director: RWCMD, 2010–; Merthyr Tydfil Coll., 2010–. FHEA 2007; CCMI 2013; FRSA 2013. *Publications:* (contrib.) The Evolving Academic e-Learning Endeavour: the impact of using technology in learning and teaching, 2008; (contrib.) Collaborative Working in Higher Education: the social academy, 2009; contribs to Jl Applied Res. in Higher Educn. *Recreations:* walking, theatre, travel. *Address:* University of South Wales, Pontypridd CF37 1DL. *T:* (01443) 482001, *Fax:* (01443) 482390. *E:* julie.lydon@southwales.ac.uk.

LYE, David William Frederick; freelance consultant, since 2011; Fellow, since 2011 and Director, since 2014, SAMI Consulting; *b* 13 Jan. 1958; *s* of Frederick Hayle Lye and Barbara Criddle Lye; *m* 2008, Jacqueline Helen Warwick Karas. *Educ:* Radley Coll.; Lincoln Coll., Oxford (BA Hons Modern Hist. 1979). Joined Civil Service, 1985; Hd, NHS Trusts Unit, DoH, 1991–93; Dir, Performance Mgt, NHS W Midlands, 1993–98; Project Dir, Children and Family Court Adv. and Support Service, 1999–2001; Chief Exec., Public Guardianship Office, 2001–04; Department of Health: Project Manager, Social Care, Local Govt and Care Partnerships Directorate, DoH, 2004–07; Hd of Dental and Eye Care Services, 2007–11. Associate Mem., Primary Care Commng, 2011–. *Publications:* contrib. articles to various NHS-related jls. *Recreations:* travel, cookery, armchair sports. *Address:* 6 Clock Tower Mews, N1 7BB. *E:* lye_david@hotmail.com.

LYELL, family name of **Baron Lyell**.

LYELL, 3rd Baron *cr* 1914, of Kinnordy; **Charles Lyell;** DL; Bt 1894; *b* 27 March 1939; *s* of 2nd Baron, VC (killed in action, 1943), and Sophie (*d* 2012), *d* of Major S. W. and Lady Betty Trafford; *S* father, 1943. *Educ:* Eton; Christ Church, Oxford. 2nd Lieut Scots Guards, 1957–59. CA Scotland. An Opposition Whip, 1974–79; a Lord in Waiting (Govt Whip), 1979–84; Parly Under-Sec. of State, NI Office, 1984–89; elected Mem., H of L, 1999. Mem., Queen's Body Guard for Scotland (Royal Company of Archers). DL Angus, 1988. *Heir:* none. *Address:* Kinnordy House, Kirriemuir, Angus DD8 5ER. *T:* (01575) 572848. *Clubs:* Turf, White's.

LYGO, Kevin Antony; Managing Director, ITV Studios, since 2010; *b* 19 Sept. 1957; *s* of Adm. Sir Raymond Derek Lygo, KCB and Pepper Lygo (*née* Van Osten); *m* 1999, Suzy Solomon; one *d*, and one step *s*. *Educ:* Cranbrook Sch.; Durham Univ. (BA Psychol.). BBC TV: comedy scriptwriter, 1981–83; gen. trainee, 1983–85; Producer, Omnibus, Wogan, 1985–96; Head of Ind. Commng Gp, 1996–97; Head of Entertainment, Channel 4, and Controller, E4, 1998–2001; Dir of Progs, Five (formerly Channel Five TV), 2001–03; Dir of TV, 2003–07, Dir of TV and Content, 2007–10, Channel 4. *Recreations:* Islamic art, Tibetan culture, tennis. *Address:* ITV Studios, London Television Centre, Upper Ground, SE1 9LT.

LYKIARDOPOULOS, Andrew Nicolas; QC 2014; *b* Bucks, 27 Jan. 1968; *s* of Nico and Margaret Lykiardopoulos; *m* 1993, Amanda Mary Heaslip; three *s*. *Educ:* Beacon Sch., Chesham Bois; Radley Coll.; Bristol Univ. (BA 1st Cl. Hons Hist. 1990); Coll. of Law, Lancaster Gate. Admitted as solicitor, 1994; Partner, Bristows Solicitors, 2000–04; in practice as solicitor advocate, 2000–04; called to the Bar, Middle Temple, 2004; in practice as barrister, specialising in intellectual property, 2004–. *Recreations:* music, history, travel, family. *Address:* 8 New Square, Lincoln's Inn, WC2A 3QP. *T:* (020) 7405 4321. *E:* andrew.lykiardopoulos@8newsquare.co.uk.

LYLE, Alexander Walter Barr, (Sandy), MBE 1987; professional golfer, since 1977; *b* 9 Feb. 1958; *s* of late Alex and Agnes Lyle; *m* (marr. diss.); two *s*; *m* 1989, Brigitte Jolande Huurman; one *s* one *d*. *Educ:* Shrewsbury local sch. Rookie of the Year, 1978; 1st in European order of merit, 1979, 1980, 1985; Open Champion, Royal St George's, 1985; won US Masters, 1988. *Publications:* Learning Golf the Lyle Way, 1986; To the Fairway Born, 2006. *Recreation:* cars.

LYLE, Sir Gavin Archibald, 3rd Bt *cr* 1929; estate manager, farmer; company director; *b* 14 Oct. 1941; *s* of late Ian Archibald de Hoghton Lyle and Hon. Lydia Yarde-Buller (who *m* 1947, as his 2nd wife, 13th Duke of Bedford; marr. diss. 1960; then Lydia Duchess of Bedford), *d* of 3rd Baron Churston; *S* grandfather, 1946; *m* 1967, Suzy Cooper (marr. diss. 1985); five *s* one *d*. *Heir:* *s* Ian Abram Lyle, *b* 25 Sept. 1968. *Address:* Glendelvine, Caputh, Perthshire PH1 4JN.

LYLE, Jonathan Henry, RCNC; Chief Executive, Defence Science and Technology Laboratory, since 2012 (Director, Programme Office, 2010–12); *b* 25 Feb. 1959; *s* of John Henry Turner Lyle and Gillian Lucy Lyle; *m* 1981, Beverley Nichola Uren; one *s* one *d*. *Educ:* Kingswood Sch., Bath; Royal Naval Engrg Coll., Plymouth (BSc Electrical and Electronic Engrg 1979); University Coll. London (MSc Microwaves and Mod. Optics 1980). FIET 2009 (MIEE 1984); CEng 1984. RCNC 1976; Procurement Exec., MoD, 1982–91; Cabinet Office, 1991–95; DTI, 1995–96; Defence Procurement Agency: Directorate of Mil. Aircraft Projects, 1996–2000; Integrated Project Team Leader, 2000–04; Ops Dir, Air and Weapon Systems, 2004–07; Dir Gen., Helicopters, Defence Equipment and Support, MoD, 2007; Dir,

Defence Acad.—Coll. of Mgt and Technol. (formerly Comdt, Defence Coll. of Mgt and Technol., Defence Acad.), 2007–10; Hd, RCNC, 2007–12. *Recreations:* orienteering, watching Bath Rugby, inland waterways. *Address:* Defence Science and Technology Laboratory, Porton Down, Salisbury, Wilts SP4 0JQ. *Club:* Bristol Orienteering.

LYLE, Richard; Member (SNP) Scotland Central, Scottish Parliament, since 2011; *b* Bothwell, Lanarkshire, 12 June 1950; *s* of Richard and Margaret Lyle; *m* 1973, Marion Smith; one *s* one *d*. *Educ:* Lawmuir Sch.; Bellshill Acad. Grocer, 1965–79; credit advr, 1979–90; Area Manager, Royal Bank of Scotland, 1990–2000; credit advr, 2000–11. Joined SNP, 1966; Member (SNP): Motherwell DC, 1976–96 (Leader, SNP Gp, 1976–96); N Lanarks Council, 1996–2012 (Leader, SNP Gp, 1996–2011). Leader, COSLA SNP Gp, 2007–09. *Recreations:* politics, reading. *Address:* Scottish Parliament, Edinburgh EH99 1SP. *T:* (0131) 348 6394. *E:* richard.lyle.msp@scottish.parliament.uk. *Club:* Orbiston Bowling (Hon. Pres.).

LYLE, Sandy; *see* Lyle, A. W. B.

LYMBERY, Philip John; Chief Executive, Compassion in World Farming, since 2005; *b* Luton, 23 Sept. 1965; *s* of Peter Lymbery and Evelyn Lymbery; *m* 2011, Helen Roberts; one step *s*. *Educ:* Vandyke Upper Sch. and Coll., Leighton Buzzard. Packaging Designer, Bowater, 1987–90; Campaigns Dir, Compassion in World Farming, 1990–2000; freelance strategist, 2000–02; Dir, Communications, WSPA, 2003–05. Wildlife tour leader, Gullivers Natural History Holidays, 1995–2005. FRSA; MInstD. *Publications:* (with Isabel Oakeshott) Farmageddon: the true cost of cheap meat, 2014. *Recreations:* birdwatching, walking, song-writing, guitar, my dog, gardening. *Address:* c/o Compassion in World Farming, River Court, Mill Lane, Godalming, Surrey GU7 1EZ. *T:* 07818 071918. *E:* philip.lymbery@ciwf.org.

LYMINGTON, Viscount; Oliver Henry Rufus Wallop; *b* 22 Dec. 1981; *s* and *heir* of Earl of Portsmouth, *qv*. *Educ:* Eton. *Recreations:* shooting, cars. *Clubs:* Buck's, White's.

LYNAGH, Richard Dudley; QC 1996; a Recorder, 2000–10; *b* 14 Nov. 1952; *s* of Charles Lynagh and Mary Browne; *m* 1979, Regula Wegmann (*d* 2004); two *s* one *d*. *Educ:* Kettering Grammar Sch.; University Coll. London (LLB Hons). Called to the Bar, Gray's Inn, 1975, Bencher, 2004; an Asst Recorder, 1999–2000. *Address:* 2 Crown Office Row, Temple, EC4Y 7HJ.

LYNAM, Desmond Michael, OBE 2008; broadcaster; *b* 17 Sept. 1942; *s* of Edward Lynam and Gertrude Veronica Lynam (*née* Malone); *m* 1965, Susan Eleanor Skinner (marr. diss. 1974); one *s*; *m* 2011, Rosemary Elizabeth Diamond. *Educ:* Varndean Grammar Sch., Brighton; Brighton Business Coll. ACII. Business career in insurance, until 1967; also freelance journalist; reporter for local radio, 1968–69; reporter, presenter and commentator, BBC Radio, 1969–78; presenter and commentator, BBC TV Sport, 1978–99, incl. Grandstand, Sportsnight, Match of the Day, Commonwealth and Olympic Games, and World Cup; presenter: Holiday, BBC TV, 1988–89; How Do They Do That?, BBC TV, 1994–96; The Des Lynam Show, BBC Radio, 1998–99; ITV Sport, 1999–2004; Des Meets…, BBC Radio, 2004–05; We'll Meet Again, BBC TV, 2005; The World's Greatest Sporting Legend, Sky One, 2005; Des At Wimbledon, BBC Radio, 2005; Are You Younger Than You Think?, BBC TV, 2005; Countdown, Channel 4, 2005–06; Sport Mastermind, BBC TV, 2008; Touchline Tales, BBC Radio, 2010, 2011. TV Sports Presenter of the Year, TRIC, 1985, 1987, 1988, 1993, 1997; Radio Times Male TV Personality, 1989; RTS Sports Presenter of the Year, 1994, 1998; Richard Dimbleby Award, BAFTA, 1994; Variety Club of GB Media Award, 1997; RTS Lifetime Achievement Award, 2003. *Publications:* Guide to Commonwealth Games, 1986; The 1988 Olympics, 1988; The 1992 Olympics, 1992; I Should Have Been At Work! (autobiog.), 2005. *Recreations:* golf, tennis, Brighton and Hove Albion, reading, theatre. *Address:* c/o Jane Morgan Management Ltd, Argentum, 2 Queen Caroline Street, W6 9DX. *T:* (020) 3178 8071.

LYNCH, Christopher Charles B.; *see* Balogun-Lynch.

LYNCH, His Honour David; a Circuit Judge, 1990–2005; *b* 23 Aug. 1939; *s* of Henry and Edith Lynch; *m* 1974, Ann Knights; two *s*. *Educ:* Liverpool Collegiate Grammar School. LLB London (ext.); Liverpool John Moores Univ. (MRes.). Served RAF, 1958–61. Sharman & Sons, Solicitors, 1955–57; Bremner Sons & Corlett, Solicitors, 1961–66; Schoolmaster, 1966–68. Called to the Bar, Middle Temple, 1968; Northern Circuit; Asst Recorder, 1983–88; a Recorder, 1988–90; Liaison Judge: St Helens Justices, 1991–2005; Liverpool John Moores Univ., 1994–2005 (Hon. Fellow, 2003). Pres., Mental Health Review Tribunals (restricted patients), 1991–2001. Northern Circuit Remembrancer, 2006–. Hon. Vice Pres., Merseyside Br., Magistrates' Assoc., 1991–2005. *Publications:* (contrib.) A Century of Liverpool Lawyers, 2002; Northern Circuit Directory 1876–2004, 2005. *Recreations:* classical guitar, golf, bookbinding, photography, history of the Northern Circuit. *Address:* c/o The Queen Elizabeth II Law Courts, Derby Square, Liverpool L2 1XA. *T:* (0151) 473 7373. *Club:* Caldy Golf.

LYNCH, David Keith; film director and producer; *b* Missoula, MT, USA, 20 Jan. 1946; *m* 1st, 1967, Peggy Reavey (marr. diss. 1974); one *d*; 2nd, 1977, Mary Fisk (marr. diss. 1987); one *s*; 3rd, 2006, Mary Sweeney (marr. diss.); one *s*; 4th, 2009, Emily Stofle; one *d*. *Educ:* Sch. of Mus. of Fine Arts, Boston; Pennsylvania Acad. of Fine Arts. Fellow, Center for Advanced Film Studies, Amer. Film Inst., 1970. *Films:* writer and director: Eraserhead (also prod.), 1977; The Elephant Man, 1980; Dune, 1984; Blue Velvet, 1986; Wild at Heart, 1990; Twin Peaks: Fire Walk with Me (also prod.), 1992; Lost Highway, 1997; Mulholland Drive, 2002; Inland Empire, 2006 (also prod.); dir, The Straight Story, 1999; prod., Surveillance, 2008; *television series:* writer, director and producer: Twin Peaks, 1990; On the Air, 1992. Recorded albums: Crazy Clown Time, 2011; The Big Dream, 2013. Exhibn, The Factory Photographs, Photographers' Gall., London, 2014. Founder, 2005, and Chm. Bd of Trustees, David Lynch Foundation for Consciousness-Based Education and World Peace. *Publications:* Catching the Big Fish: meditation, consciousness and creativity, 2006; The Factory Photographs, 2014.

LYNCH, Holly Jamie; MP (Lab) Halifax, since 2015; *b* Northowram, 8 Oct. 1986; *m* 2014, Chris Walker. *Educ:* Brighouse High Sch.; Lancaster Univ. With Matrix Technol. Solutions; Communications Officer for Linda McAvan, MEP. Co-Chair, All Party Parly Gp on Population, Develt and Reproductive Health, 2015–; Mem., Envmtl Audit Cttee, 2015–. *Address:* House of Commons, SW1A 0AA.

LYNCH, Prof. James Michael, OBE 2007; PhD, DSc; CSci, CChem, FRSC; CBiol, FRSB, FIBiotech; Distinguished Professor of Life Sciences, University of Surrey, since 2004; *b* 24 Nov. 1945; *s* of James Michael Lynch and Constance Violet Lynch; *m* 1971, Mary Elizabeth Gibbons; two *s* two *d*. *Educ:* Wilson's Grammar Sch., London; Loughborough Univ. (BTech Chem. 1968); King's Coll. London (PhD 1971, DSc 1984, Microbiol.). CChem 1975; FRSC 1984; CBiol 1984; FRSB (FIBiol 1984); FIBiotech 1993; CSci 2005. Microbiologist, Letcombe Lab., 1971–83; Hd, Microbiol. and Crop Protection, Horticultural Res. Internat., 1983–93; Prof. of Biotechnol., and Head, Sch. of Biomed. and Life Scis, Univ. of Surrey, 1993–2003. Vis. Lectr, Univ. of Oxford, 1980–84; Visiting Professor: Washington State Univ., 1981–83; KCL, 1986–93; Oregon State Univ., 1995; Univ. of Reading, 2007–11; Univ. of Helsinki, 2009–12. Mem., editl bds of scientific jls, 1978–. Chm., Internat. Union of Soil Sci., Soil Biol. Commn, 1990–94. Co-ordinator, OECD Prog. on Biol Resource Mgt for Sustainable Agricl Systems, 1989–2006. Dir, Internat. Inst. of Biotechnol., 1998–2008; Bd Mem., Eur. Forestry Inst., 2006–; Chief Exec., Forest Research, 2007–10; Sen. Advr, Thames Gateway Inst. for Sustainability, 2007–10; Dir of Forestry, DMC Internat. Imaging, 2011–13. Mem. Bd, Council for Frontiers of Knowledge, Africa, 2010–. Vice-Chm., Blasker Award Cttee, USA, 1996–2001. Chm. Govs, Univ. of Chichester, 2014–. FRSA 1997; MInstD 2004. Res. Award for Foreign Specialists, Japanese Govt, 1987, 1991; Prize for Microbiol. (Carlos J. Finlay Award), UNESCO, 1993. *Publications:* Soil Biotechnology: microbiological factors in crop productivity, 1983; (ed) The Rhizosphere, 1990; joint editor: Microbial Ecology: a conceptual approach, 1979; Contemporary Microbial Ecology, 1980; Microbial Adhesion to Surfaces, 1980; Microbiological Methods for Environmental Biotechnology, 1984; Micro-organisms in Action: concepts and applications in microbial ecology, 1988; Terrestrial Gene Exchange: mathematical modelling and risk assessment, 1994; Biocontrol Agents: benefits and risks, 1995; Ecotoxicology: responses, biomarkers and risk assessment, 1997; Environmental Biomonitoring: the biotechnology ecotoxicology interface, 1998; Biological Resource Management: connecting science and policy, 2000; Innovative Soil-Plant Systems for Sustainable Agricultural Practices, 2003; Remote Sensing for Agriculture and the Environment, 2004; Forestry and Climate Change, 2007; contrib. numerous review articles and res. papers. *Recreations:* running, cycling, sailing, gardening, walking, music, kayaking. *Address:* Tudor Close, 12 The Drive, Angmering on Sea, W Sussex BN16 1QH. *T:* (01903) 785534. *E:* j.lynch@surrey.ac.uk. *Clubs:* English-Speaking Union, London Athletic.

LYNCH, Jerome Cecil Alfonso; QC 2000; *b* 31 July 1955; *s* of late Clifford James Lynch and Loretta Rosa Lynch; *m* 1983, Jacqueline Theresa O'Sullivan (marr. diss. 2011); two *s*. *Educ:* Lancashire Poly. (BA Hons). Called to the Bar, Lincoln's Inn, 1983, Bencher, 2008; in practice at the Bar, 1983–. Co-Presenter, Nothing But the Truth, Channel 4, 1998, 1999; Presenter, Crime Team, Channel 4, 2001, 2002; Co-Presenter, The People's Court, ITV1, 2005. *Recreations:* ski-ing (well), golf (badly), drinking good wine. *Address:* Charter Chambers, 33 John Street, WC1N 2AT. *T:* (020) 7618 4400. *Club:* Royal Automobile.

LYNCH, Prof. John; Director of Institute of Latin American Studies, 1974–87 and Professor of Latin American History, 1970–87, University of London, now Professor Emeritus; *b* 11 Jan. 1927; *s* of late John P. Lynch and Teresa M. Lynch, Boldon Colliery, Co. Durham; *m* 1960, Wendy Kathleen, *d* of late Frederick and Kathleen Norman; two *s* three *d*. *Educ:* Corby Sch. Sunderland; Univ. of Edinburgh; University College, London. MA Edinburgh 1952; PhD London 1955. FRHistS 1958. Army, 1945–48. Asst Lectr and Lectr in Modern History, Univ. of Liverpool, 1954–61; Lectr in Hispanic and Latin American History, 1961–64, Reader, 1964–70, UCL. Harrison Vis. Prof., Coll. of William and Mary, Williamsburg, 1991–92. Corresp. Member: Academia Nacional de la Historia, Argentina, 1963, Academia Nacional de la Historia, Venezuela, 1980; Academia Panameña de la Historia, 1981; Academia Chilena de la Historia, 1985; Real Academia de la Historia, Spain, 1986; Sociedad Boliviana de Historia, 1987; Academia Colombiana de Historia, 2008. Dr *hc* Seville, 1990. Distinguished Service Award, Conf. on Latin American History, Amer. Histl Assoc., 1997. Comdr, Order of Isabel la Católica (Spain), 1988; Order of Andrés Bello, 1st class (Venezuela), 1995. *Publications:* Spanish Colonial Administration 1782–1810, 1958; Spain under the Habsburgs, vol. 1 1964, vol. 2 1969; (with R. A. Humphreys) The Origins of the Latin American Revolutions, 1808–1826, 1965; The Spanish American Revolutions 1808–1826, 1973; Argentine Dictator: Juan Manuel de Rosas, 1829–52, 1981; (ed) Andrés Bello: the London years, 1982; (ed) Past and Present in the Americas, 1984; Hispanoamérica 1750–1850, 1987; Bourbon Spain 1700–1808, 1989; Caudillos in Spanish America 1800–1850, 1992; Latin American Revolutions 1808–1826: old and new world origins, 1994; Massacre in the Pampas, 1872: Britain and Argentina in the age of migration, 1998; Latin America between Colony and Nation, 2001; Simón Bolívar: a life, 2006; San Martín: Argentine soldier, American hero, 2009; New Worlds: a religious history of Latin America, 2012; (contrib.) Cambridge History of Latin America, vol. III 1985, vol. IV 1986; (contrib.) UNESCO Historia General de América Latina, vol. V, 2003; (contrib.) Cambridge History of Christianity, vol. VIII, 2006. *Address:* 8 Templars Crescent, N3 3QS. *T:* (020) 8346 1089.

LYNCH, Prof. Michael, PhD; FRSE; Sir William Fraser Professor of Scottish History and Palaeography, University of Edinburgh, 1992–2005, then Research Professor, now Hon. Professorial Fellow; *b* 15 June 1946; *s* of Francis J. and Kathleen Lynch. *Educ:* Aberdeen Grammar Sch.; Univ. of Aberdeen (MA Eng. Lit. and Hist. 1st cl. hons 1969); Inst. of Historical Res., Univ. of London (PhD 1977). Lectr in History, UCNW, Bangor, 1971–79; Lectr, 1979–88; Sen. Lectr, 1988–92, Dept of Scottish History, Univ. of Edinburgh. Chm., Ancient Monuments Bd for Scotland, 1996–2003; Publications Sec., Scottish History Soc., 1990–93; President: Historical Assoc. of Scotland, 1992–2002; Soc. of Antiquaries of Scotland, 1996–99. Trustee, Nat. Mus Scotland (formerly Nat. Mus of Scotland), 2002–10. FRHistS 1982; FRSE 1995. Editor, The Innes Review, 1984–92. *Publications:* Edinburgh and the Reformation, 1981; The Early Modern Town in Scotland, 1986; The Scottish Medieval Town, 1987; Mary Stewart: Queen in three kingdoms, 1988; Scotland: a new history, 1991, 2nd edn 1992; (ed with Julian Goodare) The Reign of James VI, 2000; (ed) The Oxford Companion to Scottish History, 2002; Aberdeen before 1800: a new history, 2002. *Address:* School of History, Classics and Archaeology, University of Edinburgh, William Robertson Wing, Old Medical School, Teviot Place, Edinburgh EH8 9AG.

LYNCH, Michael Francis, CBE 2008; AM 2001; Chief Executive Officer, West Kowloon Cultural District Authority, since 2011; *b* 6 Dec. 1950; *s* of Wilfred Brian Lynch and Joan Margaret Lynch; *m* 1976, Jane Scott (marr. diss. 1987); one *d*; *m* 1990, Christine Josephine Sharp; two step *s*. *Educ:* Marcellin Coll., Randwick; Univ. of Sydney. Australia Council for the Arts, 1973; Gen. Manager, King O'Malley Theatre Co., Australian Theatre for Young People; Administrator, Aust. Nat. Playwrights Conf.; Gen. Manager, Nimrod Th., 1976–78; Casting Dir and Man. Partner, Forcast Pty Ltd, 1981–89; General Manager: Sydney Th. Co., 1989–94; Australia Council for the Arts, 1994–98; Chief Executive: Sydney Opera House, 1998–2002; South Bank Centre, London, 2002–09; Dir, Australian Broadcasting Corp., 2009–11. Mem. Bd, Visit London, 2004–09. Prod., film, Raw Nerve, 1988. Garrett Award, Arts & Business, 2008. *Address:* West Kowloon Cultural District Authority, 29/F, Tower 6, The Gateway, 9 Canton Road, Tsim Sha Tsui, Kowloon, Hong Kong.

LYNCH, Michael Richard, OBE 2006; DL; PhD; FRS 2014; FREng; Founder, Invoke Capital, since 2012; *b* 16 June 1965; *s* of Michael and Dolores Lynch. *Educ:* Christ's Coll., Cambridge (BA; PhD 1991; Hon. Fellow). Founder, Cambridge Neurodynamics, 1991; Founder and Gp CEO, Autonomy Corp. plc, 1996–2012; founding investor, Bridges Venturing. Non-executive Director: BBC, 2007–12; Cambridge Enterprise, 2010–. Member, Board: British Library, 2011–14; Create the Change campaign, Francis Crick Inst., 2012–. Member: Council for Sci. and Technol., 2011–; Investment Cttee Adv. Bd, Tech City; Advr, Prince's Trust Technol. Gp. Mem. Council, RAEng. Trustee: NESTA, 2009–12; Foundn for Sci. and Technol. FREng 2008. DL Suffolk 2012. *Recreations:* jazz saxophone, preserving rare breeds.

LYNCH, Niamh; *see* Cusack, N.

LYNCH, Noel; Member (Green) London Assembly, Greater London Authority, May 2003–04; *b* 20 Jan. 1947; *s* of William and Nancy Lynch; *m* 1976, Angela Enright (marr. diss. 1988); one *d*. *Educ:* Kilmallock Nat. Sch.; Charleville Christian Brothers Sch., Co. Cork; University Coll. Cork (night classes) (Dip. Social Studies). Freelance auctioneer, 1986–2004; shopkeeper, E Finchley, 1992–2003. Member: Metropolitan Police Authy, 2003–04; London Fire and Emergency Planning Authy, 2003–04. Chm., Standards, GLA, 2003–04. London Green Party Co-ordinator, 2001–03, 2004–. *Publications:* Setting up Green Secondhand Shops, 1989. *Recreation:* conducting charity auctions. *Address:* c/o Green Party, Development House, 56–64 Leonard Street, EC2A 4LT. *T:* (020) 8340 7759. *E:* noellynch@tiscali.co.uk.

LYNCH, Sir Patrick (Joseph), KNZM 2015; QSO 1991; Chief Executive Officer, New Zealand Catholic Education Office, 1994–2016; *b* Otahuhu, Auckland, NZ, 18 March 1942; *s* of James David Lynch and Mavis Amelia Lynch (*née* Wilson). *Educ:* De La Salle Coll., Mangere, Auckland; Auckland Univ. (BA 1972); Massey Univ. (DipEd 1977). Primary Teacher, St Mary's Boys' Sch., 1963–66; De La Salle College, Auckland: Dean of Form 4, 1976–77; Dep. Principal, 1978; Principal, 1979–93. Mem., NZ Nat. Commn for UNESCO, 1996–2000. Pres., Secondary Principals' Assoc. NZ, 1991–93. Brother, De La Salle Order, 1961–. *Recreations:* walking, music, gardening. *Address:* 81 Gray Avenue, Mangere East, 2158 Auckland, New Zealand. *T:* (9) 0274905396; PO Box 86099, Mangere East, 2158 Auckland, New Zealand.

LYNCH, Roderick Robertson; Chairman and Chief Executive Officer, GSS Ltd, since 2001; *b* 22 May 1949; *s* of Nanson Lynch and Catherine (*née* Robertson); *m* 1972, Christina Williams; two *s*. *Educ:* Perth Acad.; Dundee Univ. (MA 1971). Served RAC, 1966–67. British Airways, 1971–89: Gen. Manager, Southern Europe, 1983–84; Man. Dir, British Airtours, 1984–86; Head, Customer Service, 1986–89; Man. Dir, Air Europe, 1989–91; Dir, Forte Hotels, 1991–93; Man. Dir, then Chief Exec., Resources, BBC, 1993–99; CEO, Olympic Airways, 1999–2000. Bd Mem., CAA, 1993–99; Dir, NATS Ltd, 1996–99. *Recreations:* Rugby football, military history, music, aviation. *Club:* Caledonian.

LYNCH, Sarah Jane; Her Honour Judge Lynch; a Circuit Judge, since 2012. Admitted as solicitor, 1989; solicitor: Edward Fail Bradshaw & Waterson, 1989–90; Wake Smith & Tofields, 1990–2008; Howells, 2008–12; a Recorder, 2008–12. *Address:* Leeds Combined Court Centre, The Court House, 1 Oxford Row, Leeds LS1 3BG. *T:* (0113) 306 2800.

LYNCH-BLOSSE, Sir Richard Hely, 17th Bt *cr* 1622; RAMC, 1975–85, retired; general medical practitioner, since 1985 (senior partner, since 2000); *b* 26 Aug. 1953; *s* of Sir David Edward Lynch-Blosse, 16th Bt, and of Elizabeth, *er d* of Thomas Harold Payne, Welwyn Garden City; *S* father, 1971; *m* 1st, 1976, Cara (marr. diss. 1999), *o d* of late George Sutherland, St Ives, Cambs; two *d*; 2nd, 2000, Jacqueline, *o d* of late Gordon Francis, Yardley Gobion, Northants. *Educ:* Royal Free Hosp. Sch. of Medicine. Commnd RAMC, July 1975; LRCP MRCS 1978; MB BS 1979; DRCOG 1983; MRCGP 1984. Medical Officer: European Sch., Culham, 1987–2012; Oxon ACF, 1993–. Mem., Soc. of Ornamental Turners, 1992–. *Publications:* contrib. to Jl of RAMC. *Heir: cousin* David Ian Lynch-Blosse [*b* 14 Jan. 1950; *m* 1st, 1984, Mrs Barbara Susan McLaughlin (*d* 1985); 2nd, 1989, Nadine, *d* of John Baddeley; one *s* one *d*]. *Address:* The Surgery, Watery Lane, Clifton Hampden, Oxon OX14 3EL.

LYNCH-ROBINSON, Sir Dominick (Christopher), 4th Bt *cr* 1920, of Foxrock, co. Dublin; novelist and creative consultant; Global Creative Director, J. Walter Thompson, 2004–13; *b* 30 July 1948; *o s* of Sir Niall Lynch-Robinson, 3rd Bt, DSC, and Rosemary Seaton; *S* father, 1996; *m* 1973, Victoria, *d* of Kenneth Weir; one *s* one *d*, and one step *d*. *Recreations:* reading, cinema, writing, travel. *Heir: s* Christopher Henry Jake Lynch-Robinson, *b* 1 Oct. 1977.

LYNDEN-BELL, Prof. Donald, CBE 2000; FRS 1978; Professor of Astrophysics, University of Cambridge, 1972–2001, now Emeritus; Director, Institute of Astronomy, Cambridge, 1972–77, 1982–87, and 1992–94; *b* 5 April 1935; *s* of late Lt-Col L. A. Lynden-Bell, MC and M. R. Lynden-Bell (*née* Thring); *m* 1961, Ruth Marion Truscott (*see* R. M. Lynden-Bell); one *s* one *d*. *Educ:* Marlborough; Clare Coll., Cambridge (MA, PhD). Harkness Fellow of the Commonwealth Fund, NY, at the California Inst. of Technology and Hale Observatories, 1960–62; Research Fellow and then Fellow and Dir of studies in mathematics, Clare Coll., Cambridge, 1960–65; Asst Lectr in applied mathematics, Univ. of Cambridge, 1962–65; Principal Scientific officer and later SPSO, Royal Greenwich Observatory, Herstmonceux, 1965–72. Visiting Associate, Calif Inst. of Technology and Hale Observatories, 1969–70; Visiting Professorial Fellow, QUB, 1996–2003; H. N. Russell Lectr, AAS, 2000; Oort Prof., Univ. of Leiden, 1992; Blaauw Prof., Univ. of Groningen, 2007. Pres., RAS, 1985–87. FHMAAAS 1985. Foreign Associate: US NAS, 1990 (J. J. Carty Award, 2000); RSSAf 1994; Foreign Mem., Norwegian Acad. of Sci. and Letters, 2009–. Hon. Fellow, Inter-Univ. Centre for Astronomy and Astrophysics, Pune, India, 2004. Hon. DSc Sussex, 1987; Hon. Dr: Hebrew Univ. of Jerusalem, 2010; Charles Univ., Prague, 2012. Eddington Medal, RAS, 1984; Brouwer Prize, AAS, 1990; Gold Medal, RAS, 1993; Bruce Medal, Astronomical Soc. of the Pacific, 1998; first recipient (jtly), Kavli Prize for Astrophysics, Norwegian Acad. of Sci. and Letters, 2008. *Publications:* contrib. to Monthly Notices of Royal Astronomical Soc. *Recreations:* hill walking, golf. *Address:* Institute of Astronomy, The Observatories, Madingley Road, Cambridge CB3 0HA. *T:* (01223) 337525.

LYNDEN-BELL, Ruth Marion, PhD, ScD; FRS 2006; Professor of Condensed Matter Simulation, Queen's University, Belfast, 1995–2003, now Emeritus; *b* 7 Dec. 1937; *d* of David and Priscilla Truscott; *m* 1961, Donald Lynden-Bell, *qv*; one *s* one *d*. *Educ:* Newnham Coll., Cambridge (BA 1959, MA 1962; PhD 1962; ScD 1989). FRSC; FInstP. Fellow, New Hall, Cambridge, 1962–65; Lectr, Univ. of Sussex, 1965–72; Fellow, New Hall, Cambridge, 1972–95, now Emerita; Coll. Lectr, St John's Coll., Cambridge, 1975–95. Acting Pres., Murray Edwards Coll., Cambridge, 2012–13. Paul Walden Award, German Res. Foundn, 2012. *Publications:* (with R. K. Harris) Nuclear Magnetic Resonance Spectroscopy, 1969; numerous articles in scientific jls. *Recreations:* gardening, walking. *Address:* Department of Chemistry, Lensfield Road, Cambridge CB2 1EW.

LYNDHURST, Nicholas; actor, since 1971; *b* 20 April 1961; *m* 1999, Lucy Smith; one *s*. *Theatre includes:* Harding's Luck, Greenwich; Trial Run, Oxford Playhouse, 1980; Black Comedy (tour); The Private Ear (tour); The Foreigner, Albery, 1987; Straight and Narrow, Wyndham's, 1992; The Dresser, Duke of York's, 2005; The Tempest, Haymarket Th. Royal, 2011. *Television includes:* Going Straight, 1978; Spearhead, 1978; Butterflies, 1978–83; Father's Day, 1979; To Serve Them All My Days, 1980; Fairies; Losing Her; Only Fools and Horses, 1981–91; It'll All Be Over in Half an Hour, 1983; The Two of Us, 1986–90; The Piglet Files, 1990; Goodnight Sweetheart, 1993–99; Gulliver's Travels, 1996; David Copperfield, 1999; Thin Ice, 2000; Murder in Mind, 2003; After You've Gone, 2007; Rock and Chips, 2010–11; New Tricks, 2013–. *Radio includes:* My First Planet, BBC Radio 4, 2012. *Address:* c/o Chatto & Linnit Ltd, Worlds End Studios, 132–134 Lots Road, SW10 0RJ.

LYNE, Prof. Andrew Geoffrey, PhD; FRS 1996; FRAS; Langworthy Professor of Physics, University of Manchester, 2002–08, now Hon. Professor of Physics; *b* 13 July 1942; *s* of Lionel Geoffrey Lyne and Kathleen Elizabeth Lyne; *m* 1st, Jennifer Anne Duckels; two *d*; 2nd, 1994, Diane Elizabeth Stanway; one step *s* one step *d*. *Educ:* Portsmouth GS; St John's Coll., Cambridge (MA); Manchester Univ. (PhD). Manchester University: Lectr in Radio Astronomy, 1969–79; Sen. Lectr, 1979–90; Prof. of Radio Astronomy, 1990–2002. Dir, Nuffield Radio Astronomy Labs, subseq. Jodrell Bank Observatory, 1998–2006. Vis. Scientist, CSIRO Div. of Radiophysics, Sydney, 1975–76; Leverhulme Fellow, Royal Soc., 1994. Mem., PPARC, 1997–. Herschel Medal, RAS, 1992; Sir George Thomson Gold Medal, Inst. of Measurement and Control, 1993. *Publications:* Pulsar Astronomy, 1990, 4th edn 2012; contrib. Nature, Monthly Notes of RAS and other scientific jls. *Recreations:* tennis, golf, walking, sailing. *Address:* Tall Trees, New Road, Moreton, Congleton, Cheshire CW12 4RX.

LYNE, Colin Gwaynten; Commercial Director, Department for Constitutional Affairs, 2003–06; *b* 10 Feb. 1945; *s* of William Henry Lyne and Ada Lilian Lyne (*née* Brownsell); *m* 1978, Hilary Janet Luscombe; two *s* one *d*. *Educ:* Humphry Davy Grammar Sch., Penzance; Bristol Univ. (Open Schol.). Various posts in NHS, 1973–85; Co. Supplies Officer, 1985–88, Dir, Commercial Services, 1988–93, Surrey CC; Director: Commercial Services, Essex CC, 1993–99; Purchasing and Contract Mgt, LCD, 1999–2003. Non-exec. Dir, Investment and Implementation Bd, Office of Govt Commerce, HM Treasury, 2005–07. Chm., 1992–93, Pres., 1994–95, Chartered Inst. Purchasing and Supply. Chm., Eur. Council of Purchasing and Supply, 2000–02. Mem., Bd of Advrs, Southampton Univ. Sch. of Mgt, 2005–07. FCIPS 1990. FRSA 1995. *Recreations:* golf, bridge, genealogy. *Address:* Thornberry, 105 New Forest Drive, Brockenhurst, Hants SO42 7QW. *T:* (01590) 623099. *Club:* Brokenhurst Manor Golf (Brockenhurst).

LYNE, Kevin Douglas; HM Diplomatic Service, retired; consultant, since 2014; *b* 6 Nov. 1961; *s* of Douglas Lyne and Anne Lyne; *m* 1988, Anne Dabbadie; two *d*. *Educ:* Richard Hale Sch., Hertford; Portsmouth Poly. (BA Hons Latin Amer. Studies); Univ. of Essex (MA Govt and Politics). Res. Cadre, FCO, 1988–91; Second Sec., Santiago, 1991–94; Principal Res. Officer, FCO, 1994–96; First Secretary: FCO, 1996–98; UK Mission to UN, Geneva, 1998–2003; Dep. Hd of Mission, Rabat, 2003–07; Ambassador to Montenegro, 2007–09; Conflict Team Leader, Res. Analysts, FCO, 2010–11; UK Stabilisation Planner, ISAF, 2011; FCO, 2012; Stabilisation Advr, Stabilisation Unit, 2013–14. *Recreation:* fishing. *Address:* 64130 Idaux-Mendy, France.

LYNE, Richard John; HM Diplomatic Service, retired; High Commissioner to Solomon Islands, 2004–08; *b* 20 Nov. 1948; *s* of late John Arthur Lyne and Sylvia Mary Raven Lyne (*née* Knott); *m* 1977, Jennifer Anne Whitworth; one *s* one *d*. *Educ:* Kimbolton Sch. RAPC, 1967–70; joined HM Diplomatic Service, 1970; Archivist and Communications Officer, Belgrade, 1972–74; Accountant and Dep. Mgt Officer, Algiers, 1974–76; Third Sec., Damascus, 1977–80; Second Sec., New Delhi, 1984–87; Second, later First Sec., Stockholm, 1987–91; Dep. High Comr, Port of Spain, Trinidad, 1997–2000; Deputy Head: Conf. and Visits Gp, FCO, 2000–02; Personnel Services Dept, FCO, 2002–04. Church Warden, St Peter and St Sigfried Anglican Ch, Stockholm, 1989–91. Chm., St Albans Dio. Property Cttee, 2010–; Mem., St Albans Diocesan Synod, 2013–; Dir, St Albans Dio. Property Co., 2013–. Mem., St John Boxmoor PCC, Hemel Hempstead, 1994–96, 2000–04 and 2009–; Mem. Bd and Trustee, Music at St John's, Boxmoor, Hemel Hempstead, 2009–. *Recreations:* family, reading, genealogy, watching sport. *Address:* 12 Campion Road, Chaulden Vale, Hemel Hempstead HP1 2DN. *Club:* Royal Over-Seas League.

LYNE, Rt Hon. Sir Roderic (Michael John), KBE 1999; CMG 1992; PC 2009; HM Diplomatic Service, retired; consultant and lecturer; non-executive Director, Petropavlovsk plc (formerly Peter Hambro Mining), since 2009; *b* 31 March 1948; *s* of Air Vice-Marshal Michael Dillon Lyne, CB, AFC and Avril Joy, *d* of Lt-Col Albert Buckley, CBE, DSO; *m* 1969, Amanda Mary, *d* of Sir Howard Frank Trayton Smith, GCMG; two *s* one *d*. *Educ:* Legbourne County Primary Sch., Lincs; Highfield Sch., Hants; Eton Coll.; Leeds Univ. (BA Hist. 1970). FCO 1970; Army Sch. of Langs, 1971; Moscow, 1972–74; Dakar, 1974–76; Eastern European and Soviet Dept, FCO, 1976–79; Rhodesia Dept, FCO, 1979; Asst Pvte Sec. to Sec. of State for Foreign and Commonwealth Affairs, 1979–82; UK Mission to UN, NY, 1982–86; Vis. Res. Fellow, RIIA, 1986–87; Counsellor and Hd of Chancery, Moscow, 1987–90; Hd of Soviet Dept, 1990–92, Hd of Eastern Dept, 1992–93, FCO; Pvte Sec. to Prime Minister, 1993–96 (on secondment); Dir for Policy Develt, CIS ME and Africa, British Gas, 1996 (on secondment); UK Perm. Rep. to Office of UN and other internat. orgns, Geneva, 1997–2000; Ambassador to Russia, 2000–04. Hon. Prof., Moscow Sch. of Social and Economic Studies, 2001; Vis. Prof., Faculty of Business and Law, 2005–11, Mem., 2007–13 and Chm., 2011–13, Bd of Govs, Kingston Univ. Non-executive Director: Accor, 2006–09; Aricom, 2006–09; JPMorgan Bank Internat. LLC, 2013–; Mem., Strategic Adv. Gp, QucomHaps Hldgs Ltd, 2005–; Special Adviser: HSBC, 2004–07; BP, 2005–09; Chm., Internat. Adv. Bd, Altimo, 2006–07; Special Rep., ITE Gp plc, 2005–10; Special Advr, JPMorgan Chase Bank, 2007–10. Member: Bd, Russo-British Chamber of Commerce, 2006–09; Exec. Cttee, UK/Russia Round Table, 2005–07; Trilateral Commn's Task Force on Russia, 2005–07; Oxford Univ. Task Force on Energy, the Envmt and Develt, 2006–07; Iraq Inquiry Cttee, 2009–; Dep. Chm., Council, RIIA, 2009– (Mem., 2008–); Chm., Adv. Cttee, Centre for E European Language Based Area Studies, 2007–. Mem. Bd, Internat. Early Music Trust, St Petersburg, 2007–10. Hon. Vice-Pres., GB-Russia Soc., 2005–. Patron, AMUR, 2001–. Trustee, World Race Trust, 2004–07. Gov., Ditchley Foundn, 2005–11. Hon. Dr Rostov State Construction Univ., 2001; Hon. LLD Leeds, 2002; Hon. DBA Kingston, 2004; Hon. DLit Heriot-Watt, 2004; DUniv Birmingham, 2012. *Publications:* (jtly) Engaging with Russia: the next phase, 2006; (contrib.) Russia: the challenges of transformation, 2011. *Recreations:* sport, grandchildren. *Address:* 39 Richmond Park Road, East Sheen, SW14 8JU. *Club:* Travellers.

LYNE, William Macquarie, CBE 2002 (MBE 1986); AM 2002; Director, Wigmore Hall, 1966–2003 (Assistant Manager, 1957–66), Director Emeritus, since 2006; *b* 28 Nov. 1932; *s* of Harold Baden Lyne and Marie Veronica Lyne (*née* Catalano). *Educ:* Canterbury High Sch., Sydney, Australia. Transcription Officer, Australian Broadcasting Commn, 1951–56. Mem. Bd, Henry Wood Hall, 1991–2013; Trustee, Geoffrey Parsons Meml Trust, 1995–2012; Internat. Artistic Advr, Melbourne Internat. Chamber Music Competition, 2007–; Mem. Cttee, Queen's Medal for Music, 2004–. Hon. FTCL 1997; Hon. GSM 1997; Hon. RAM 1999; Hon. RCM 1999. Evening Standard Award for Outstanding Achievement for Classical Music, 1997; Ambassador for London Award for lifetime achievement, 1997; Cobbett Medal for Services to art of chamber music, Musicians' Co., 2001; Internat. Artists' Mgt Assoc. award, 2003. Chevalier, Ordre des Arts et des Lettres (France), 1996; Grand Cross of Honour (First Class) for Sci. and the Arts (Austria), 2001. *Publications:* (contrib.) Wigmore Hall 1901–2001: a celebration, 2001. *Recreations:* collecting gramophone records, incl. vintage; cinema, esp. films from the thirties; reading, visiting art galleries, fell walking, travel, theatre, concerts, opera. *Address:* c/o Wigmore Hall, 36 Wigmore Street, W1U 2BP. *E:* wmlyne@virginmedia.com, wmlyne@outlook.com. *Club:* Reform.

LYNK, Roy, OBE 1990; consultant in human resources, since 1996; National President, Union of Democratic Mineworkers, 1987–93; General Secretary, Nottingham Section, 1985–93; *b* 9 Nov. 1932; *s* of John Thomas Lynk and Ivy Lynk; *m* 1978, Sandra Ann; three *s* three *d*. *Educ:* Station Road Higher Sch. and Healdswood Sch., Sutton-in-Ashfield; Nottingham Univ. Cert. in Industrial Relations. Miner at Teversal Colliery, Nottingham, 1947; RN 1948; Miner at various collieries, Nottingham, 1950–79. National Union of Mineworkers: Branch Sec., Sutton Colliery, 1958–79; full time Area Official, Nottingham, 1979–83; Financial Sec., Nottingham Area, 1983–85, Gen. Sec., 1985; Union of Democratic Mineworkers: formed, Dec. 1985; Nat. Gen. Sec., 1985–86. Member: European Coal and Steel Community's Consultative Cttee, 1988–93; Industrial Appeal Tribunal, Nottingham, 1993–; Board, Coal Authy, 1995–98. *Recreation:* watching football. *Address:* Columbia House, 143 Huthwaite Road, Sutton-in-Ashfield, Notts NG17 2HB.

LYNN, Bishop Suffragan of, since 2011; **Rt Rev. (Cyril) Jonathan Meyrick;** *b* 23 April 1952; *s* of Christopher and Isolde Meyrick; *m* 1984, Rebecca Keatley; one *s* two *d*. *Educ:* Lancing Coll.; St John's Coll., Oxford (BA Hons 1973, MA 1977); Salisbury and Wells Theol Coll. Ordained deacon, 1976, priest, 1977; Curate, Bicester, 1976–78; Domestic Chaplain to Bishop of Oxford, 1978–81; Tutor in Old Testament Studies, Codrington Coll., Barbados, 1981–84; Team Vicar, Taplow, Burnham Team Ministry, 1984–90; Team Rector, Tisbury, 1990–98; RD, Chalke Valley, 1997–98; Canon Residentiary, Rochester Cathedral, 1998–2005; Acting Dean, Rochester, 2003–05; Dean of Exeter, 2005–11. Chairman: Cathedrals Plus (formerly Pilgrims Assoc.), 2008–11; Papua New Guinea Church Partnership,

2013–. Trustee, Emmaus Exeter, 2010–11. Regular columnist, Exeter's Express and Echo, 2008–11. Released charity CD, The Rocking Bishop: everlasting smiles from the 60s, 2013. *Publications:* Old Testament Syllabus for Developing Ministries Programme, Diocese of Rochester, 2001; (contrib.) Cultural Diversity Guide, 2001, rev. edn 2003; Rochester Cathedral Official Guidebook, 2004; A Carol of Hope, 2008; (contrib.) The Church in the City, 2008. *Recreations:* acting, singing, punting, croquet, tennis. *Address:* The Old Vicarage, Priory Road, Castle Acre, Kings Lynn, Norfolk PE32 2AA. *T:* (office) (01760) 755553. *E:* bishop.lynn@dioceseofnorwich.org. *Clubs:* Garrick; Norfolk (Norwich).

LYNN, Archdeacon of; *see* Ashe, Ven. F. J.

LYNN, Inez Therese Philomena Alice; Librarian, The London Library, since 2002; *b* 15 March 1960; *d* of Jack Basil Lynn and Mari Therese Philomena Josephine Patricia Lynn (*née* Prendergast). *Educ:* La Sagesse Convent High Sch., Newcastle upon Tyne; Univ. of Liverpool (BA); Univ. of Toronto; Pembroke Coll., Oxford (MLitt); University Coll. London (DipLib). MCLIP (ALA 1992). SCONUL trainee, Warburg Inst., 1984–86, Inst. of Advanced Legal Studies, 1986–88, Univ. of London; London Library: Cataloguer, 1988–90; Chief Cataloguer, 1990–93; Prin. Asst Librarian, 1993–94; Dep. Librarian, 1994–2001. Trustee: Maitland Trust, 2002–06; R. M. Chambers Settlement Trust, 2002–10; London Library Trust, 2002–12; London Library Staff Superannuation Fund, 2002–. *Publications:* (contrib.) Libraries: case studies in re-planning and refurbishment, 2009. *Recreations:* editing Medieval Latin poetry, dressage. *Address:* The London Library, 14 St James's Square, SW1Y 4LG. *T:* (020) 7766 4712.

LYNN, Jonathan Adam; director, writer and actor; *b* 3 April 1943; *s* of Robin and Ruth Lynn; *m* 1967, Rita Merkelis; one *s*. *Educ:* Kingswood Sch., Bath; Pembroke Coll., Cambridge (MA). Acted in Cambridge Circus, New York, 1964; TV debut, Ed Sullivan Show, 1964; actor in repertory, Leicester, Edinburgh and Bristol Old Vic, and in London; performances include: Green Julia, 1965; Fiddler on the Roof, 1967–68; Blue Comedy, 1968; The Comedy of the Changing Years, 1969; When We Are Married, 1970; Dreyfus, 1982; actor in TV comedy programmes and plays, including: Barmitzvah Boy, 1975; The Knowledge, 1979; Outside Edge, 1982; Diana, 1984; actor in films including: Prudence and the Pill, 1967; Into the Night, 1984; Three Men and a Little Lady, 1990; Greedy (also dir.), 1994; Artistic Dir, Cambridge Theatre Co., 1977–81 (dir. 19 prodns); *director: London:* The Plotters of Cabbage Patch Corner, 1970; The Glass Menagerie, 1977; The Gingerbread Man, 1977 and 1978; The Unvarnished Truth, 1978; The Matchmaker, 1978; Songbook, 1979 (SWET Award, and Evening Standard Award, for Best Musical, 1979); Tonight at 8.30, 1981; Arms and the Man, 1981; Pass the Butler, 1982; Loot, 1984; *National Theatre:* A Little Hotel on the Side, 1984; Jacobowski and the Colonel, 1986; Three Men on a Horse, 1987 (Olivier Award for Best Comedy); *RSC:* Anna Christie, Stratford 1979, London 1980; *Broadway:* The Moony Shapiro Songbook, 1981; Yes, Prime Minister (also co-wrote), Chichester Festival Th., 2010, Gielgud Th., 2010, Apollo Th., 2011, Trafalgar Studios, 2012, LA, 2013 (WhatsOnStage Award for Best Comedy); *films:* Mick's People (also wrote), 1982; Clue (also wrote), 1984; Nuns on the Run (also wrote), 1990; My Cousin Vinny, 1991; The Distinguished Gentleman, 1992 (Envmtl Media Award, 1993); Greedy (also acted), 1994; Sgt Bilko, 1996; Trial and Error, 1997; The Whole Nine Yards, 2000; The Fighting Temptations, 2003 (NAACP Image Award for Best Dir); Wild Target, 2008; *screenplay:* The Internecine Project, 1974; *TV scriptwriter:* situation comedies, including: My Brother's Keeper, 2 series, 1974 and 1975 (also co-starred); Yes, Minister (also radio scripts), 3 series, 1980, 1981 and 1982; Yes, Prime Minister, 1986, 1987, 2013; Life After Life, 1990. Hon. MA Sheffield, 1987; Hon. PsyD Amer. Behavioral Studies Inst., 2000. Writer's Award, BAFTA, 1987; Pye TV Writers Award (for Yes, Minister and Yes, Prime Minister), 1981, 1986; Broadcasting Press Guild Award, 1980, 1986; ACE Award for Amer. Cable TV Best Comedy Writing (for Yes, Prime Minister), 1988; Diamond Jubilee Award for Best Political Satire, Pol Studies Assoc., 2010; Outstanding Career Achievement Award, Anaheim Internat. Film Fest., 2010; Friends of Film Lifetime Achievement Award, 2011. *Publications:* A Proper Man (novel), 1976; Comedy Rules!, 2011; with Antony Jay: Yes, Minister, The Diaries of a Cabinet Minister: Vol. I, 1981; Vol. II, 1982; Vol. III, 1983; The Complete Yes Minister, 1984; Yes, Prime Minister, the Diaries of the Rt Hon. James Hacker: Vol. I, 1986; Vol. II, 1987; The Complete Yes Prime Minister, 1989; Mayday (novel), 1993; Yes, Prime Minister (play), 2010. *Recreation:* changing weight. *Address:* c/o Alan Brodie Representation, Paddock Suite, The Courtyard, 55 Charterhouse Street, EC1M 6HA.

LYNN, Maurice Kenneth, MA; Head of French, Westminster School, 1983–88 and 1999–2008; *b* 3 March 1951. *Educ:* Thornleigh Salesian College, Bolton; Magdalen College, Oxford (Open Scholar; BA Hons 1973; MA 1977). Asst Master, Oratory Sch., 1973–79; Asst Master, Radley Coll., 1979–83; Headmaster, The Oratory Sch., 1989–91; Westminster School: Asst Master, 1992–95; Hd, Mod. Langs, 1995–99. Dir of Eur. interests for The Oratory Sch. Assoc., 1992. *Recreations:* English Catholic poetry, twentieth century French drama, soccer, ski-ing, cricket, acting and producing, cycling, travel. *Address:* 10 impasse Molière, 34300 Agde, France.

LYNN, Michael David; Corporate Development Director, The Stationery Office Ltd, 1996–99; *b* 18 July 1942; *s* of Martin and Dorothy Lynn; *m* 1965, Hilary Smyth; one *s* one *d*. *Educ:* Lincoln Sch. Joined HMSO 1960; Director: Publications Distribution, 1980; Finance, 1983; Print Procurement, 1984; Dir-Gen., Corporate Services, 1987; Dep. Chief Exec., 1989; Controller and Chief Exec., 1995–96. *Recreations:* chess, crosswords.

LYNN, Prof. Richard, PhD; FBPsS; Professor of Psychology, University of Ulster, 1972–95, now Emeritus; *b* 20 Feb. 1930; *s* of Ann Lynn; *m* 1st, 1956, Susan Maher (marr. diss. 1978); one *s* two *d*; 2nd, 1990, Susan Hampson (*d* 1998); 3rd, 2004, Joyce Dora Walters, *qv*. *Educ:* Bristol Grammar Sch.; King's Coll., Cambridge (BA 1953; PhD 1956; Passingham prizeman). FBPsS 1965. Lectr in Psychology, Univ. of Exeter, 1956–67; Prof. of Psychology, Dublin Economic and Social Res. Inst., 1967–72. US Mensa Award for Excellence, for work on intelligence, 1985, 1988, 1993. *Publications:* Attention, Arousal and the Orientation Reaction, 1966; The Irish Braindrain, 1969; The Universities and the Business Community, 1969; Personality and National Character, 1971; An Introduction to the Study of Personality, 1972; The Entrepreneur, 1974; (ed) Dimensions of Personality, 1981; Educational Achievement in Japan, 1987; The Secret of the Miracle Economy, 1991; Dysgenics: genetic deterioration in modern populations, 1996, 2nd rev. edn 2011; Eugenics: a reassessment, 2001; The Science of Human Diversity, 2001; The Chosen People: Jewish IQ and achievement, 2011; with T. Vanhanen: IQ and the Wealth of Nations, 2002; Race Differences in Intelligence, 2005; IQ and Global Inequality, 2006; The Global Bell Curve, 2008; Intelligence: a unifying construct for the social sciences, 2012; articles on personality, intelligence and social psychology. *Recreations:* do-it-yourself house renovation, bridge. *Address:* University of Ulster, Coleraine, Northern Ireland BT52 1SA. *E:* Lynnr540@aol.com. *Club:* Oxford and Cambridge.

LYNN, Dame Vera, (Dame Vera Margaret Lewis), DBE 1975 (OBE 1969); singer; *b* 20 March 1917; *d* of Bertram Samuel Welch and Annie Welch; *m* 1941, Harry Lewis; one *d*. *Educ:* Brampton Rd Sch., East Ham. First public appearance as singer, 1924; joined juvenile troupe, 1928; ran own dancing school, 1932; broadcast with Joe Loss and joined Charlie Kunz, 1935; singer with Ambrose Orch., 1937–40, then went solo; voted most popular singer, Daily Express comp., 1939, and named Forces Sweetheart; own radio show, Sincerely Yours, 1941–47; starred in Applesauce, London Palladium, 1941; sang to troops in Burma, etc, 1944 (Burma Star, 1985); subseq. Big Show (radio), USA; London Laughs, Adelphi; appeared at Flamingo Hotel, Las Vegas, and many TV shows, USA and Britain, including own TV series on Rediffusion, 1955; BBC TV, 1956; BBC 2, 1970; also appearances in Holland, Denmark, Sweden, Norway, Germany, Canada, NZ and Australia; in seven Command Performances, also films and own shows on radio. 14 Gold Records; records include Auf Wiederseh'n (over 12 million copies sold), became first British artiste to top American Hit Parade. Pres., Printers' Charitable Corp., 1980. Internat. Ambassador, Variety Club Internat., 1985. Founder and Pres., Dame Vera Lynn Trust for Children with Cerebral Palsy, 2001–. Hon. Citizen: Winnipeg, 1974; Nashville, Tennessee, 1977. Freedom: City of London, 1978; City of Corner Brook, Newfoundland, 1981. FInstD. Fellow, Univ. (formerly Poly.) of E London, 1990. Hon. LLD Memorial Univ. of Newfoundland, 1977 (founded Lynn Music Scholarship, first award, 1982); Hon. MMus London, 1992. Show Business Personality of the Year, Grand Order of Water Rats, 1973; Music Publishers' Award, 1975; Ivor Novello Award, 1975; Humanitarian Award, Variety Club Internat., 1985; BBC TV Woman of the Year, 1994; Lillian K. Keil Award for outstanding service by a woman during World War II, 2005; Women of the Year Lifetime Achievement Award, 2009; Nordoff Robbins Icon of the Century Award, 2010. Dutch War Veteran Medal, 2010. Comdr, Order of Orange-Nassau, Holland. *Publications:* Vocal Refrain (autobiog.), 1975; (jtly) We'll Meet Again, 1989; Unsung Heroines, 1990; Some Sunny Day: my autobiography, 2009. *Recreations:* gardening, painting, sewing, swimming.

LYNNE, Elizabeth, (Liz); Member (Lib Dem) West Midlands Region, European Parliament, 1999–Feb. 2012; *b* 22 Jan. 1948. *Educ:* Dorking Co. Grammar Sch. Actress, 1966–89; numerous theatre appearances in repertory and West End, and television, film and radio roles. Speech consultant, 1989–92 and 1997–99. Contested (L) Harwich, 1987. MP (Lib Dem) Rochdale, 1992–97; contested (Lib Dem) same seat, 1997. Lib Dem spokesperson: on health and community care, 1992–94; on social security and disability, 1994–97. Vice-Pres., Eur. Employment and Social Affairs Cttee, EP, 2004–12. Mem. Bd, EEF, 2012–. Mem., Lib Dem Federal Conf. Cttee, 2012–; Pres., Mid-Worcs Lib Dems, 2013–; Vice-Pres., Lib Dem Women, 2014–. *Recreations:* tennis, motorcycling.

LYNNE, Dame Gillian, DBE 2014 (CBE 1997); director, choreographer, dancer, actress; *d* of late Leslie Pyrke and Barbara (*née* Hart); *m* 1980, Peter Land, actor. *Educ:* Baston Sch., Bromley, Kent; Arts Educnl Sch. Leading soloist, Sadler's Wells Ballet, 1944–51; star dancer, London Palladium, 1951–53; role in film, Master of Ballantrae, 1952; lead in Can-Can, Coliseum, 1954–55; Becky Sharp in Vanity Fair, Windsor, 1956; guest principal dancer: Samson and Delilah, Sadler's Wells, 1957; Aida, and Tannhauser, Covent Garden, 1957; Puck in A Midsummer Night's Dream, TV, 1958; star dancer in Chelsea at Nine (featured dance segments), TV, 1958; Peter and the Wolf (narrated and mimed all 9 parts), TV, 1958; lead in New Cranks, Lyric, Hammersmith, 1959; roles in Wanda, Rose Marie, Cinderella, Out of My Mind, and lead in revue, 1960–61; leading lady, 5 Past Eight Show, Edinburgh, 1962; conceived, dir., chor. and starred in Collages (mod. dance revue), Edinburgh Fest., 1963, transf. Savoy; *choreographed:* The Owl and the Pussycat (1st ballet), Western Theatre Ballet, 1962; Queen of the Cats, London Palladium, 1962–63; Wonderful Life (1st film), 1963–64; Every Day's a Holiday, and Three Hats for Lisa (musical films), 1964; The Roar of the Greasepaint, and Pickwick, Broadway, 1965; The Flying Dutchman, Covent Garden, 1966; Half a Sixpence (film), 1966–67 (also staged musical nos); How Now Dow Jones, Broadway, 1967; Midsummer Marriage, Covent Garden, 1968; The Trojans, Covent Garden, 1969, 1977; Breakaway (ballet), Scottish Theatre Ballet, 1969; Phil the Fluter, Palace, 1969; Ambassador, Her Majesty's, 1971; Man of La Mancha (film), 1972; The Card, Queen's, 1973; Hans Andersen, London Palladium, 1975; The Way of the World, Aldwych, 1978; My Fair Lady, national tour and Adelphi, 1979; Parsifal, Covent Garden, 1979; (also Associate Dir) Cats, New London, 1981 (Olivier Award, 1981), Broadway 1982, US nat. tour, 1983, Vienna, 1984 (Austrian Silver Order of Merit), Los Angeles, Sydney, 1985, East Berlin, 1987, Canada, Japan, Australia, Holland, Paris, 1989 (Molière Award, Best Musical), UK tour, 2003, Madrid, 2003, Moscow, 2004, German tour, 2010, London revival, 2014; Café Soir (ballet), Houston Ballet Co., 1985; Cabaret, Strand, 1986; The Phantom of the Opera, Her Majesty's, 1986, Broadway, Japan, Vienna, 1989, Stockholm, Chicago, Hamburg, Australia, Canada, 1990, Las Vegas, 2006; A Simple Man (ballet), Sadler's Wells, 1988, revived 2009; The Brontës (ballet), Northern Ballet Theatre, 1995; The Secret Garden, RSC, Stratford and Aldwych, 2000; Chitty Chitty Bang Bang, London Palladium, 2002, NY, 2005; Four Classical Variations, for Royal Acad. of Dance, 2005; On Such a Night, Northern Ballet Th., 2009; Miracle in the Gorbals, 2014; *directed and choreographed:* The Match Girls, Globe, 1966; Bluebeard, Sadler's Wells Opera, 1966, new prodn, Sadler's Wells Opera, Coliseum, 1969; Love on the Dole (musical), Nottingham Playhouse, 1970; Liberty Ranch, Greenwich, 1972; Once Upon a Time, Duke of York's, 1972; Jasperina, Amsterdam, 1978; Cats, Vienna, 1983 (1st proscenium arch prodn; Silver Order of Merit, Austria, 1984), Paris, 1989; Valentine's Day, Chichester, 1991; Dancing in the Dark, 1991; Dance for Life Gala, 1991; Valentine's Day, Globe, 1992; What the World Needs, Old Globe, San Diego, 1997–98; Gigi, Vienna, 1999; Richard Whittington, Sadler's Wells, 1999; Some You Win (dance drama), Sadler's Wells, 2000; Dear World, Charing Cross Th., 2013; *directed:* Round Leicester Square (revue), Prince Charles, 1963; Tonight at Eight, Hampstead, 1970 and Fortune, 1971; Lillywhite Lies, Nottingham, 1971; A Midsummer Night's Dream (co-dir.), Stratford, 1977; Tomfoolery, Criterion, 1980; Jeeves Takes Charge, Fortune, 1980, off-Broadway, 1983, Los Angeles, 1985; To Those Born Later, New End, 1981; That's What Friends Are For!, May Fair, 1996; Avow, USA, 1996; (Additional Dir) La Ronde, RSC, Aldwych, 1982; (also appeared in) Alone Plus One, Newcastle, 1982; The Rehearsal, Yvonne Arnaud, Guildford and tour, 1983; Cabaret, Strand, 1986; I'd Like to Teach the World to Sing (Ian Adam Gala), Her Majesty's, 2008; Waxing Lyrical, New Diorama, 2011; Now or Never, King's Head, 2011, York Th., NY, 2012; *staged:* England Our England (revue), Princes, 1961; 200 Motels (pop-opera film), 1971; musical nos in Quilp (film), 1974; A Comedy of Errors, Stratford, 1976 (TV musical, 1977); musical As You Like It, Stratford, 1977; Songbook, Globe, 1979; Once in a Lifetime, Aldwych, 1979; new stage act for Tommy Steele, 1979; wedding sequence in Yentl (film), 1982; European Vacation II (film); Pirelli Calendar, 1988; Pickwick, Chichester and Sadler's Wells, 1993; Le Malade Imaginaire, Washington, 2008; Phantom of the Opera 25th Anniversary Gala, Royal Albert Hall, 2011; *choreographed for television:* At the Hawk's Well (ballet), 1975; There was a Girl, 1975; The Fool on the Hill (1st Colour Special for ABC), with Australian Ballet and Sydney Symph. Orch., staged Sydney Opera House, 1975; Muppet Show series, 1976–80; (also musical staging) Alice in Wonderland (mini-series), 1985; shows and specials for Val Doonican, Perry Como, Petula Clark, Nana Mouskouri, John Curry, Harry Secombe, Ray Charles, and Mike Burstein; also produced and devised Noel Coward and Cleo Laine specials; *directed for television:* Mrs F's Friends, 1981; Easy Money, 1982; Le Morte d'Arthur (also devised), 1983 (Samuel G. Engel Award, Univ. of Michigan); The Simple Man, 1987 (BAFTA award for direction and choreog.); The Look of Love, 1989; That's What Friends Are For!, 1996. Patron: Develt Appeal, Central Sch. of Ballet, 2003; Gordon Edwards Charitable Trust; Benesh Inst.; Betty Laine Th. Arts; Council for Dance Educn and Trng; Dancers' Career Develt Trust (formerly Independent Dancers' Resettlement Trust), 2005– (Bd Mem., 1993–); Liverpool Inst. for Performing Arts; London Internat. Dance Film Festival; Showbiz Pops Orch.; Lang. of Dance Centre, Holland Pk; Doreen Bird Coll. of Performing Arts; Stella Mann Coll. of Performing Arts; Dance UK (formerly British Assoc. of Choreographers); British Sch. of Osteopathy. Mr Abbott Award, Soc. of Stage Dirs and Choreographers, NY, 1999; Queen Elizabeth II Coronation Award, Royal Acad. of Dance, 2001; Olivier Special Award, 2013. *Publications:* (contrib.) Cats, The Book of the Musical; A Dancer in Wartime: one girl's journey from the Blitz to Sadler's Wells, 2011; articles in Dancing Times.

LYNTON, Michael Mark; Chairman and Chief Executive, Sony Pictures Entertainment, since 2004; *b* London, 1 Jan. 1960; *s* of Mark O. L. Lynton and Marion Lynton; *m* 1994, Elizabeth Jamie Alter; two *d*. *Educ:* Harvard Coll. (BA 1982); Harvard Business Sch. (MBA 1987). Associate, First Boston Corp., 1982–87; Pres., Disney Publg, 1987–92, Hollywood Pictures, 1992–96, Walt Disney Co.; Chm. and CEO, Penguin Gp, 1996–2000; Pres., America Online Internat., 2000–03; CEO, AOL Europe, 2001–02; Pres., Internat., AOL Time Warner, subseq. Time Warner, 2002–03. *Recreations:* tennis, ski-ing. *Address:* Sony Pictures Entertainment Inc., 10202 Washington Boulevard, Culver City, CA 90232, USA.

LYON; *see* Bowes Lyon.

LYON, His Honour Adrian Pirrie; a Circuit Judge, 2000–12; *b* 18 Oct. 1952; *s* of Alexander Ward Lyon and Hilda Lyon; *m* 1976, Christina Margaret Harrison (*see* C. M. Lyon); one *s* one *d*. *Educ:* Leeds Grammar Sch.; Hampton Grammar Sch.; University Coll. London (LLB). Called to the Bar, Gray's Inn, 1975; Head of Chambers, 1997–2000. Mem., Bar Council, 1995–97. *Recreations:* travel, reading, theatre, computers.

LYON, Christina Margaret; Her Honour Judge Lyon; a Circuit Judge, since 2007; *b* 12 Nov. 1952; *d* of Edward Arthur Harrison and Kathleen Joan Harrison; *m* 1976, Adrian Pirrie Lyon, *qv*; one *s* one *d*. *Educ:* Wallasey High Sch. for Girls; University Coll. London. LLB (1st Cl. Hons) 1974; admitted Solicitor, 1977. Tutor and sometime Lectr in Law, University Coll. London, 1974–75; Trainee and Asst Solicitor, Bell & Joynson, 1975–77; Liverpool University: part-time Tutor in Law, 1976–77; Lectr in Law, 1977–80; Manchester University: Lectr in Law and Law and Social Work, 1980–86; Sub-Dean, Law Faculty, 1986; Prof. of Law, Head of Dept and of Sch. of Law, Keele Univ., 1987–93; Liverpool University: Prof. of Common Law, 1993–98; Head, Dept of Law, 1993–97; Dean, Faculty of Law, 1994–97; Dir, Centre for the Study of the Child, the Family and the Law, 1995–2007; Queen Victoria Prof. of Law, 1998–2007, now Emeritus. Asst Recorder, 1998–2000; Recorder, 1999–2007. Member: ESRC Res. Grants Bd, 1988–91; Child Policy Review Gp, Nat. Children's Bureau, 1989–; Chm., Independent Representation for Children in Need, 1991–; Member: Nat. Exec. Cttee and Fundraising Cttee, Relate, 1990–94 (Pres., N Staffs Relate, 1987–93); Merseyside Panels of Guardians *ad Litem*, 1993–2002 (Vice-Chm., 1993–97); Child Protection and Family Justice Cttee, Nuffield Foundn, 1994–. Dr Barnardo's Research Fellow, 1987–92. Advisory Editor, Jl of Social Welfare and Family Law (formerly Jl of Social Welfare Law) (Jt Ed.,1984); Mem. Editl Bd, Representing Children, 1996–. FRSA 1991. *Publications:* Matrimonial Jurisdiction of Magistrates' Courts, 1981; Cohabitation without Marriage, 1983; (ed) Butterworth's Family Law Service Encyclopaedia, 1983, rev. edn 2006; Law of Residential Homes and Day Care Establishments, 1984; (ed) Child Abuse, 1990, 3rd edn 2003; The Law Relating to Children in Principles and Practice of Forensic Psychiatry, 1990; (ed with A. P. Lyon) Butterworth's Family Law Handbook, 1991; Atkins Court Forms on Infants, vols I and II, 1992; The Law Relating to Children, 1993; Legal Issues Arising from the Care and Control of Children with Learning Disabilities who also Present Severely Challenging Behaviour, vol. I, Policy Guidance, vol. II, A Guide for Parents and Carers, 1994; Child Protection and the Civil Legal Framework in The Child Protection Handbook, 1995; Children's Rights and The Children Act 1989 in Children's Rights, 1995; Working Together: an analysis of collaborative inter-agency responses to the problem of domestic violence, 1995; Law and Body Politics, 1995; (jtly) Effective Support Services for Children, 1998; (jtly) A Trajectory of Hope, 2000; Loving Smack, Lawful Assault: a contradiction in human rights and law, 2000. *Recreations:* riding, swimming, foreign travel, reading, theatre, opera.

LYON, Rt Hon. Clare; *see* Short, Rt Hon. C.

LYON, Dr (Colin) Stewart (Sinclair), FIA; FSA, FRNS; General Manager (Finance), Group Actuary and Director, Legal & General Group Plc, 1980–87; *b* 22 Nov. 1926; *s* of late Col Colin Sinclair Lyon, OBE, TD and Mrs Dorothy Winstanley Lyon (*née* Thomason); *m* 1958, Elizabeth Mary Fargus Richards; four *s* one *d*. *Educ:* Liverpool Coll.; Trinity Coll., Cambridge (MA; PhD 2004). FIA 1954; FSA 1972; FRNS 1955. Chief Exec., Victory Insurance Co. Ltd, 1974–76; Chief Actuary, Legal & General Assurance Soc. Ltd, 1976–85. Director: Lautro Ltd, 1987–92; Cologne Reinsurance Co. Ltd, 1987–97; City of Birmingham Touring Opera Ltd, 1987–90; Ætna Internat. (UK) Ltd, 1988–91; Pearl Gp PLC, 1991–97; UK Bd, AMP and London Life, 1991–97. Member: Occupational Pensions Bd, 1979–82; Inquiry into Provision for Retirement, 1983–85; Treasure Trove Reviewing Cttee, 1986–93. President: Inst. of Actuaries, 1982–84 (Gold Medal, 1991); British Numismatic Soc., 1966–70 (Vice-Pres., 1976–2008 and 2010–; Sanford Saltus Gold Medal, 1974). Trustee, Disablement Income Gp Charitable Trust, 1967–84; Dir, Disablement Income Gp, 1984–94 (Vice-Pres., 1995–2002); Trustee, Independent Living Fund, 1988–93. *Publications:* (with C. E. Blunt and B. H. I. H. Stewart) Coinage in Tenth-Century England, 1989; papers on Anglo-Saxon coinage, particularly in British Numismatic Jl; contrib. Jl of Inst. of Actuaries and Trans Internat. Congress of Actuaries. *Recreations:* numismatics, music, amateur radio (call sign GW3EIZ). *Address:* Ardraeth, Malltraeth, Bodorgan, Anglesey LL62 5AW. *T:* (01407) 840273. *Club:* Actuaries'.

LYON, David; *see* Lyon, J. D. R.

LYON, George; Senior Consultant, Hume Brophy, since 2015; *b* 16 July 1956; *s* of Alister and Mary Lyon; *m* (marr. diss.); three *d*. *Educ:* Rothesay Acad. Family business, farming, A. H. Lyon, 1972–94, A. K. Farms, 1994–2010, Isle of Bute. Mem., NFU Scotland, 1990– (Pres., 1997–99). Mem. (Lib Dem) Argyll and Bute, Scottish Parlt, 1999–2007. Dep. Minister for Parly Business and for Finance and Public Services Reform, Scottish Exec., 2005–07. MEP (Lib Dem) Scotland, 2009–14; contested (Lib Dem) same seat, 2014. Dir, Agricl and Horticultural Develt Bd, 2015–. FRAgS 2000. *Recreations:* football, reading, cycling. *Club:* Farmers.

LYON, (John) David (Richard), MBE 2009; Chief Executive, Rexam plc (formerly Bowater Industries, then Bowater plc), 1987–96; *b* 4 June 1936; *s* of John F. A. Lyon and Elizabeth Lyon (*née* Owen); *m* 1st, 1960, Nicola M. E. Bland (marr. diss. 1986); two *s* (and one *s* decd); 2nd, 1987, Lillis Lanphier. *Educ:* Wellington College; Magdalen College, Oxford (BA Modern History 1959); Harvard Business Sch. (Advanced Management Programme, 1973). 1st Bn The Rifle Brigade, Kenya and Malaya, 1954–56 (despatches). Courtaulds, 1959–70; Rank Organisation, 1970–71; Redland, 1971–87 (Dir, 1976; Man. Dir, 1982); Dir, Smiths Industries, 1991–94. Chm., Stocks Austin Sice, 1997–2002. Mem., Adv. Cttee on Business and the Envmt, 1991–93. Col Comdt, SAS Regt, 1994–2000. Non-executive Member: Field Army Command Gp, 2003–11; Land Forces Command Gp, 2011–12. Trustee, Army Museums Ogilby Trust, 1998–2011 (Vice Patron, 2011–). Hon. Treas., 2002–08, Hon. Fellow, 2012, RGS. *Recreations:* trekking, blacksmithing, woodworking. *Address:* Oak Tree House, Church Street, Amberley, W Sussex BN18 9ND.

LYON, John MacDonald, CB 2003; Director, Strategy and Implementation, Woolf Institute, Cambridge, since 2015; Parliamentary Commissioner for Standards, 2008–12; *b* 12 April 1948; *m* Juliet Christine Southall (*see* J. C. Lyon); one *s* one *d*. *Educ:* Selwyn Coll., Cambridge (BA, MA). Home Office, 1969; Principal, 1974; Asst Sec., 1982; Grade 3, 1991; Director General: Police Policy, 1999; Policing and Crime Reduction Gp, 2000–03; Legal and Judicial Services Gp and Sec. of Commns, LCD, later DCA, then MoJ, 2003–07. Lay Mem., Bar Tribunals and Adjudication Service, 2013–. Mem. Council, Nat. Trust, 2013– (Chm. Nominations Cttee for 2014 Elections). Expert advr, parly standards, OSCE, 2013. FRSA 2000.

LYON, Juliet Christine, CBE 2009; Director, Prison Reform Trust, since 2000; *b* 8 April 1950; *d* of Christopher Redhead Southall and Jewel Eugenie Carr; *m* 1986, John MacDonald Lyon, *qv*; one *s* one *d*. *Educ:* Univ. of Exeter (BA Comb. Hons 1971); Univ. of London (MA Rights Dist.); Tavistock Inst. of Human Relns. Head: Adolescent Unit Sch., Exevale Hosp., 1973–76; Community Educn, Court Fields Sch., Somerset, 1976–79; Regl Manager, Richmond Fellowship Therapeutic Communities, 1980–90; Associate Dir, Trust for Study of Adolescence, 1990–99. Hon. Res. Fellow, QUB, 1994–99. Social Exclusion Unit Advr, 2001–02. Professional Advr, Childline, 1993–2003. Trustee: Children's Express, 1997–2000; Hanover Foundns, 2007–10. Sec. Gen., Penal Reform Internat., 2007–; Women's Nat. Comr, 2008–10. Vice-Pres., British Assoc. of Counselling and Psychotherapy, 2009–. Part-time columnist and broadcaster, 2000–. *Publications:* Tell Them So They Listen: messages from young people in custody, 2000; jl articles and chapters. *Recreations:* gardening, theatre, bee-keeping. *Address:* Prison Reform Trust, 15 Northburgh Street, EC1V 0JR. *T:* (020) 7251 5070, *Fax:* (020) 7251 5076. *E:* juliet.lyon@prisonreformtrust.org.uk.

LYON, Maj.-Gen. Robert, CB 1976; OBE 1964 (MBE 1960); Bursar, Loretto School, Musselburgh, 1979–91; *b* Ayr, 24 Oct. 1923; *s* of David Murray Lyon and Bridget Lyon (*née* Smith); *m* 1st, 1951, Constance Margaret Gordon (*d* 1982); one *s* one *d*; 2nd, 1992, Rosemary Jane, *d* of G. H. Allchin, Torquay. *Educ:* Ayr Academy. Commissioned, Aug. 1943, Argyll and Sutherland Highlanders. Served Italy, Germany, Palestine, Greece; transf. to Regular Commn in RA, 1947; Regtl Service, 3 RHA in Libya and 19 Field in BAOR, 1948–56; Instr, Mons Officer Cadet Sch., 1953–55; Staff Coll., 1957; DAQMG, 3 Div., 1958–60; jssc, 1960; BC F (Sphinx) Batt. 7 PARA, RHA, 1961–62 (Bt Lt-Col); GSO1, ASD2, MoD, 1962–65 (Lt-Col); CO 4 Lt Regt, RA, 1965–67, Borneo (despatches), UK and BAOR (Lt-Col); as Brig.: CRA 1 Div., 1967–69, BAOR; IDC, 1970; Dir Operational Requirements, MoD, 1971–73; DRA (Maj.-Gen.), 1973–75; GOC SW District, 1975–78; retired 1979. Pres., Army Hockey Assoc., 1974–76; Chm., Army Golf Assoc., 1977–78. Chm., RA Council of Scotland, 1984–90. Col Comdt RA. Director: Braemar Civic Amenities Trust, 1986–90; Edinburgh Military Tattoo Ltd, 1988–98; Financial Forum, 1996–2000. Regl Dir Scotland, Manufacturing Forum, 1994–2000. HM Comr, Queen Victoria Sch., Dunblane, 1984–95. Pres., La Punta Urbanisation, Los Cristianos, 1995–98. FCMI 1982 (MBIM 1978). *Publications:* Irish Roulette, 1991. *Recreations:* golf, writing, gardening. *Address:* Woodside, Braemar, Aberdeenshire AB35 5YT. *T:* and *Fax:* (013397) 41667. *E:* RandRLyon@btinternet.com.

LYON, Stewart; *see* Lyon, C. S. S.

LYON-DALBERG-ACTON, family name of **Baron Acton**.

LYON-DALBERG-ACTON, Edward David Joseph; *see* Acton, E. D. J. L.-D.

LYONS, Maj.-Gen. Adrian William, CBE 1994; Director General, Railway Forum, 2001–06; *b* 26 Dec. 1946; *s* of late Gp Capt. W. M. Lyons and M. P. Lyons (*née* Willis); *m* 1993, Rosemary Ann Farrer; one *d*. *Educ:* Merchant Taylors' Sch. Commnd RCT, 1966, transf. RAOC, 1972; various logistic mgt and planning appts, largely MoD based, 1977–94; psc 1980, jsdc 1986, rcds 1995; Dep. UK Mil. Rep., Brussels, 1996–98; Dir Gen. Logistic Support (Army), then Defence Logistic Support, MoD, 1998–2000. Col Comdt RLC, 2000–06; Hon. Col 168 Pioneer Regt RLC(V), 2001–07. Member: Railway Safety Adv. Bd, 2001–06; Strategy and Policy Steering Cttee, BSI, 2005–13; Adv. Bd, Railway Heritage Trust, 2011–. Chairman: Hong Kong Locally Enlisted Personnel Trust, 1998–2001; Lady Grover's Fund, 2007–; Drapers' Acad., 2009–13. Librettist for opera, Reluctant Highwayman, music by Sir Nicholas Jackson, Bt, first performed Broomhill Fest., 1995. Master, Drapers' Co., 2010–11; Liveryman, Carmen's Co., 1998–. Chm. of Govs, Bancroft's Sch., 2003–08. Pres., Rail Study Assoc., 2004–05. Trustee, RLC Assoc., 2012–. Pres., RAOC Officers' Club, 2012–. Hon. Fellow, QMUL, 2012. *Recreations:* theatre, travel, collecting (almost) anything that makes the past come alive, esp. coins (FRNS; Council Mem., British Numismatic Soc., 2005–08, 2009–12). *Address:* Stoke Farm, Beechingstoke, Pewsey, Wilts SN9 6HQ. *T:* (01672) 851634. *Club:* Cavalry and Guards.

LYONS, Alastair David, CBE 2001; non-executive Chairman, Admiral Group plc, since 2000; *b* 18 Oct. 1953; *o s* of late Alexander Lyons and of Elizabeth (*née* Eynon); *m* 1980, Judith Shauneen Rhodes; one *s* two *d*. *Educ:* Whitgift Sch.; Trinity Coll., Cambridge (Sen. Schol.; MA 2nd Cl. Hons). With Price Waterhouse & Co., 1974–79; N. M. Rothschild & Sons Ltd, 1979; H. P. Bulmer Holdings PLC, 1979–89: Gp Treas., 1979–82; Gp Financial Controller, 1983–88; Actg Gp Finance Dir, and Finance Dir, H. P. Bulmer Drinks Ltd, 1988–89; Divl Dir, Corporate Finance, Asda Gp PLC, 1989–90; Finance Dir, ASDA Stores Ltd, 1990–91; Finance Dir, 1991–94, Chief Exec., 1994–96, Nat. & Provincial Building Soc.; Man. Dir, Insurance, and Exec. Dir, Abbey National plc, 1996–97; Chief Exec., NPI, 1997–99; Dir of Corporate Projs, Nat. Westminster Gp, 1999–2000. Non-executive Chairman: Legal Mktg Services Ltd, 2002–; In Retirement Services Ltd, 2003–09; Equity Release Services Ltd, 2003–09; Health & Case Mgt Ltd, 2003–08; Buy-as-you-View Ltd, 2004–07; Higham Gp plc, 2005–07; Cardsave Ltd, 2007–10; Serco Gp plc, 2010–15; Towergate Insce Gp, 2011–15; Dep. Chm., Bovis Homes Gp plc, 2008–; Sen. Ind. Dir, Phoenix Gp plc, 2010–13; non-executive Director: Wishstream Ltd, 2001–02; Sesame Group Ltd, 2003–04. Non-executive Director: Benefits Agency, 1994–97; DSS, 1997–2001; DWP, 2001–02; DFT, 2002–05. Mem., Yorks Regl Cttee, NT, 1994–96. Gov., Giggleswick Sch., 1994–97. *Recreations:* cycling, running, riding, hill walking, ski-ing, collecting antiques.

LYONS, Dr Gerard Patrick; Chief Economic Adviser to Mayor of London, since 2013; *b* London, 31 March 1961; *s* of Francis Joseph Lyons and Anne Lyons (*née* Moran); *m* 1990, Annette Lambert; one *s* two *d*. *Educ:* St Mary's Primary Sch., Kilburn; Cardinal Vaughan Sch., Kensington; Univ. of Liverpool (BA Econs 1982); Univ. of Warwick (MA Econs 1983); Univ. of London (PhD Econs 1985). Registered Rep. of Stock Exchange 1986. Economist, Chase Manhattan Bank, 1985–86; Chief UK Economist: Savory Milln Stockbrokers, 1986–87; Swiss Bank Corp., 1987–89; Chief Economist and Exec. Dir, DKB Internat., 1989–99; Chief Economist, Gp Hd of Global Res. and Econ. Advr, Bd of Standard Chartered Bank, 1999–2012. Dir, CityUK, 2015–. Advr, Business Council for Britain, 2007–08. Mem., Commn on £ Sterling, 1999 (Co-author of Report, Britain and the Pound). Member: Global Agenda Council on Banking and Capital Mkts, 2009–14, on Global Investment Flows, 2009–10, on Financing and Capital, 2013–14, WEF; Expert Cttee, Annual Financial Develt Report, WEF, 2010–13; Informal Network of China Experts, EC, 2011–13; Adv. Council, Official Monetary and Financial Instns Forum, 2012–. Co-Chair, UK-Hong Kong Business Partnership, 2006; Vice-Chm., 48 Gp Club, 2009–. Chm., Steering Cttee, Asia Study at RIIA, 2002–05; Member: Council, Warwick Univ., 2006–12; Adv. Bd, Grantham Inst., LSE and Imperial Coll. London, 2008–; Adv. Bd, Warwick Univ. Business Sch., 2014–. Member, Council: REconS, 2010–15; RSAA, 2015–. Mem. Cttee, Hong Kong Assoc., 2007–. Fellow, Soc. of Business Economists, 2010. FRSA. Trustee, Benenden Sch., 2004–15. *Publications:* The Consolations of Economics, 2014; contribs on econ. and financial issues to books, newspapers, etc. *Recreations:* being with the family, watching Fulham FC, theatre, travel, reading, watching stand-up comedy, public speaking, giving talks about economic affairs to students, walking. *Address:* City Hall, The Queen's Walk, More London, SE1 2AA. *E:* drgerardlyons@yahoo.com. *W:* www.twitter.com/DrGerardLyons. *Club:* London Capital.

LYONS, Sir John, Kt 1987; FBA 1973; Master of Trinity Hall, Cambridge, 1984–2000; *b* 23 May 1932; *s* of Michael A. Lyons and Mary B. Lyons (*née* Sullivan); *m* 1959, Danielle J. Simonet; two *d*. *Educ:* St Bede's Coll., Manchester; Christ's Coll., Cambridge. MA; PhD 1961; LittD 1988. Lecturer: in Comparative Linguistics, SOAS, 1957–61; in General

Linguistics, Univ. of Cambridge, 1961–64; Prof. of General Linguistics, Edinburgh Univ., 1964–76; Prof. of Linguistics, 1976–84, Pro-Vice-Chancellor, 1981–84, Sussex Univ. DèsL (*hc*): Univ. Catholique de Louvain, 1980; Toulouse, 2009; Hon. DLitt: Reading, 1986; Edinburgh, 1988; Sussex, 1990; Antwerp, 1992. *Publications:* Structural Semantics, 1964; Introduction to Theoretical Linguistics, 1968; New Horizons in Linguistics, 1970; Chomsky, 1970, 3rd edn 1991; Semantics, vols 1 and 2, 1977; Language and Linguistics, 1981; Language, Meaning and Context, 1981, 2nd edn 1991; Natural Language and Universal Grammar, 1991; Linguistic Semantics, 1995; articles and reviews in learned journals.

LYONS, John, CBE 1986; General Secretary, Engineers' and Managers' Association, 1977–91, and Electrical Power Engineers' Association, 1973–91; *b* 19 May 1926; *s* of Joseph and Hetty Lyons; *m* 1954, Molly McCall; two *s* two *d. Educ:* St Paul's Sch.; Polytechnic, Regent Street; Cambridge Univ. (BA Econ). RN 1944–46. Asst to Manager of Market Research Dept, Vacuum Oil Co., 1950; Research Officer: Bureau of Current Affairs, 1951; Post Office Engineering Union, 1952–57; Asst Sec., Instn of Professional Civil Servants 1957–66, Dep. Gen. Sec. 1966–73. Member: TUC Gen. Council, 1983–91 (Chm., Energy Cttee, 1988–91); Nat. Enterprise Bd, 1975–79; Exec. Cttee PEP, 1975–78; Council, PSI, 1978–80; Adv. Council for Applied R&D, 1978–81; Engrg Council, 1982–86; PO Bd, 1980–81, British Telecommunications Bd, 1981–83; Sec., Electricity Supply Trade Union Council (formerly Employees' Nat. Cttee for Electricity Supply Industry), 1976–91; Chm., NEDO Working Party on Industrial Trucks, 1977–80. Vice-Pres., Industrial Participation Assoc., 1976–90; British rep., Econ. and Social Cttee, EU (formerly EC), 1988–96 (Vice Pres., Energy Section, 1993–96; Pres., 1992–94, Vice Pres., 1994–96, Single Market Observatory). Governor, Kingsbury High School, 1974–86; Member: Court of Governors, LSE, 1978–84; Bd of Governors, London Business Sch., 1987–88. Hitachi Lectr, Sussex Univ., 1983; addresses to: British Assoc., 1973; IEE, 1977; Internat. Monetary Conference, 1984; Newcastle Univ., 1989. FRSA 1979. Hon. Fellow, IIEXE, 1992; Hon. FIET, 2006. *Publications:* various papers and articles. *Recreations:* several.

LYONS, John; *b* 11 July 1949; one *s* one *d. Educ:* Woodside Secondary Sch.; Stirling Univ. (MSc 2000). Mechanical engr, 1971–88; Officer UNISON, 1988–2001. MP (Lab) Strathkelvin and Bearsden, 2001–05. Mem., Forth Valley Health Bd, 1999–2001.

LYONS, Prof. Malcolm Cameron; Sir Thomas Adams's Professor of Arabic, University of Cambridge, 1985–96; Fellow, Pembroke College, Cambridge, since 1957 (President, 1989–93); *b* Indore, India, 11 Feb. 1929; *s* of Harold William Lyons and Florence Katharine (*née* Cameron); *m* 1961, Ursula Schedler. *Educ:* Fettes Coll.; Pembroke Coll., Cambridge (Major Open Classical Schol., 1946; John Stewart of Rannoch Classical Schol. in Latin and Greek, 1948; Browne Medallist, 1948, 1949; 1st cl. hons Pts I and II, Classical Tripos, 1948, 1949; 1st cl. hons Pts I and II, Oriental Studies, Arabic and Persian, 1953; E. G. Browne Prize, 1953; MA 1954; PhD 1957; LittD 1997). RAF, 1949–51, commissioned 1950. University of Cambridge: Asst Lectr in Arabic, 1954–59; Lectr, 1959–84; Reader in Medieval Islamic Studies, 1984–85. Seconded to FO as Principal Instructor, MECAS, Lebanon, 1961–62. Founder Editor: Arabic Technical and Scientific Texts, 1966–78; Jl of Arabic Literature, 1970–. *Publications:* Galen on Anatomical Procedures (with W. Duckworth and B. Towers), 1962; In Hippocratis de Officina Medici, 1963, and De Partibus Artis Medicativae, De Causis Contentivis, De Diaeta in Morbis Acutis (in Corpus Medicorum Graecorum), 1967; An Arabic Translation of Themistius' Commentary on Aristotle's De Anima, 1973; Aristotle's Ars Rhetorica, Arabic version, 1982; (with E. Maalouf) The Poetic Vocabulary of Michel Trad, 1968; (with J. Riley-Smith and U. Lyons) Ayyubids, Mamlukes and Crusaders, 1971; (with D. Jackson) Saladin, The Politics of the Holy War, 1982; (jtly) Meredith Dewey: diaries, letters, writings, 1992; The Arabian Epic, 1995; Identification and Identity in Classical Arabic Poetry, 1999; (with U. Lyons) The Thousand and One Nights: a new translation, 2008; The Man of Wiles in Popular Arabic Literature, 2012; Tales of the Marvellous and News of the Strange: a translation, 2014; articles and reviews in learned jls. *Recreation:* golf. *Address:* Pembroke College, Cambridge CB1 2RF. *Club:* Royal and Ancient Golf (St Andrews).

LYONS, Sir Michael (Thomas), Kt 2000; Chairman: English Cities Fund, since 2002; SQW Ltd, since 2013 (Director, since 2007); *b* West Ham, 15 Sept. 1949; *s* of Thomas Lyons and Lillian Lyons (*née* Stafford); *m* 1976, Gwendolene Jane Calvert; two *s* one *d. Educ:* Stratford Grammar Sch.; Middlesex Polytechnic (BA Soc. Scis Hons); Queen Mary Coll., London (MSc Econ; Hon. Fellow, 2003). Street market trader, 1970–72; Brand Manager, Crookes-Anestan, 1971–72; Lectr and Res. Fellow, Dept of Industrial Econs, Univ. of Nottingham, 1973–75; Sen. Res. Officer, DoE, 1975–78; W Midlands County Council: Principal Economist, 1978–82; Dep. Dir and Dir, Economic Develt, 1982–85; Chief Executive: Wolverhampton MBC, 1985–90; Notts CC, 1990–94; Birmingham CC, 1994–2001. Birmingham University: Dir, Inst. of Local Govt Studies, 2001–04; Prof. of Public Policy, 2001–06; Hon. Prof., 1999–2001 and 2006–. Sec., W Midlands Regl Chamber, 1998–2001. Councillor, Birmingham City Council, 1980–83. Director: Mouchel (formerly Parkman) plc, 2001–12; Wragge & Co., 2001–13; ITV (Central Ind. Television), 2002–06; Redrow, 2015–. Chairman: BBC Trust, 2007–11; Tindal Street Press, 2010–13; Participle Ltd, 2010–13; YourTV Ltd, 2012–14. Mem., Public Services Productivity Panel, HM Treasury, 2000–07; Dep. Chm., 2003–05, Acting Chm., 2005–06, Audit Commn. Strategic Advr, CBRE, 2011–. Mem., Ind. Review of the Fire Service, 2002; conducted: Ind. Review of Public Sector Relocation, 2004 (report, 2004); Ind. Review of Mgt of Public Assets, 2004 (report, 2004); Ind. Review of Council Tax and the Funding of Local Govt, later Lyons Inquiry into Local Govt, 2005–07 (final report, 2007); Lyons Housing Review for Lab. Party, 2013–14 (report, 2014); Chm., Cardiff CC Corporate Governance Commn, 2004. Chm., CBSO, 2001–07; Gov., RSC, 1999–2005, 2006–. FRSA. Hon. Dr: Middlesex, 1997; UCE, 2001; Wolverhampton, 2004; Birmingham, 2009. *Publications:* (ed with A. Johnson) The Winning Bid, 1992; (with Sir Ian Byatt) The Role of External Review in Improving Performance, 2001; contribs to professional jls. *Recreations:* music, theatre, cinema, walking. *Address:* 48 Hartopp Road, Four Oaks, Sutton Coldfield B74 2QR. *E:* m.t.lyons@btconnect.com.

LYONS, Roger Alan; Joint General Secretary, Amicus, 2002–04; consultant on business services and public policy, since 2005; *b* 14 Sept. 1942; *s* of late Morris and Phyllis Lyons; *m* 1971, Kitty Horvath; two *s* two *d. Educ:* Roe Green Junior Sch., Kingsbury; Christ's Coll., Finchley; University Coll. London (BSc Hons Econ.; Fellow, 1996). Voter Organiser, Mississippi Civil Rights Project, 1965. Regional Officer, ASSET, then ASTMS, 1966–70; Nat. Officer 1970–87, Asst Gen. Sec. 1987–89, ASTMS; Asst Gen. Sec., 1989–92, Gen. Sec., 1992–2002, MSF; MSF merged with AEEU to form Amicus, 2002. Exec., European Metalworker Fedn, 1987–2004; Mem., Gen. Council, 1990–2004, Pres., 2003–04, TUC. Member: Central Arbitration Cttee, 2002–13; Employment Appeal Tribunal, 2003–12. Advr, Anti-Apartheid Movt. EU Observer, first free S African elections, 1994. Mem., Design Council, 1998–2004. Mem., Council, UCL, 1997–2005. Patron: Envmtl Industries Commn, 2000–; Burma Campaign, 2003–. Chm., Trade Union Friends of Israel, 2004–14. *Recreations:* family, take-aways, cinema, football (Arsenal in particular). *Address:* 22 Park Crescent, N3 2NJ. *T:* (020) 8346 6843, 07768 737475. *E:* rogerlyons22@hotmail.com.

LYONS, Shaun, CBE 2004; **His Honour Judge Lyons;** a Circuit Judge, since 1992; a Senior Circuit Judge, since 2002; Resident Judge, Wood Green Crown Court, since 1995; *b* 20 Dec. 1942; *s* of late Jeremiah Lyons and of Winifred Ruth Lyons; *m* 1970, Nicola Rosemary, *d* of late Capt. D. F. Chilton, DSO, RN; one *s* one *d. Educ:* Portsmouth Grammar Sch.; Inns of Court Sch. of Law. Joined RN, 1961; Lt 1966; Lt Comdr 1974; called to the Bar, Middle Temple, 1975, Bencher, 2008; Comdr 1981; Captain 1988; Chief Naval Judge Advocate, 1989–92; retd RN, 1992. Asst Recorder and Recorder, 1988–92. Chm., Middx Adv. Cttee for Magistrates, 2004–07 (Dep. Chm., 1996–2004). *Clubs:* Army and Navy; Royal Yacht Squadron.

LYONS, Stuart Randolph, CBE 1993; Chairman: Airsprung Group (formerly Airsprung Furniture Group) plc, since 2005; Beale plc, since 2015 (Director, 2013); *b* 24 Oct. 1943; 3rd *s* of late Bernard Lyons, CBE and Lucy Lyons; *m* 1969, Ellen Harriet Zion; two *s* one *d. Educ:* Rugby; King's Coll., Cambridge (Major Scholar, Classics; Fellow Commoner, 2014); Wharton Sch., Univ. of Pennsylvania (AMP 1991); Open Univ. (LLB Hons 2014). Man. Dir, John Collier Tailoring Ltd, 1969–74 (Chm., 1975–83); Dir, UDS Group plc, 1974–83 (Man. Dir, 1979–83); Chm., Colmore Trust Ltd, 1984–; Chief Exec., Royal Doulton plc, 1985–97 (Chm., 1987–93); Director: British Ceramic Res. Ltd, 1987–94; Hogg Robinson plc, 1998–2000; Aurora Computer Services Ltd, 1999–2003; Chairman: Gartmore Absolute Growth & Income Trust plc, 2004–06 (Dir, 2000–06); The Wensum Co. plc, 2003–09 (Dir, 2001–09). Member: Leeds CC, 1970–74; Yorkshire and Humberside Econ. Planning Council, 1971–75; Clothing EDC, 1976–79; Ordnance Survey Review Cttee, 1978–79; Monopolies and Mergers Commn, 1981–85; Council, CBI, 1991–96; Nat. Manufacturing Council, 1992–95; Dir, Staffs TEC, 1990–93. Pres., BCMF, 1989–90; Chairman: British Ceramic Confedn, 1989–95; Staffs Develt Assoc., 1992–95; DTI Tableware Strategy Group, 1994–96; W Midlands Develt Agency, 1995–99; Vice-Chm., Industry 96 (W Midlands Fest. of Industry and Enterprise), 1994–96. Mem. Council, Keele Univ., 1989–97; Gov., Staffs Univ. (formerly Staffs Poly.), 1991–97; Chm., Develt Bd, King's Coll., Cambridge, 2010–13. Mem., Vice-Chancellor's Circle, Univ. of Cambridge, 2014. Contested (C) Halifax, Feb. and Oct. 1974. Chief Policy Advr to Shadow Sec. of State for Trade and Industry, then Health and Educn, subseq. Transport and the Envmt, 2003–05. Hon. DLitt Keele, 1994. *Publications:* The Fleeting Years: Odes of Horace, 1996; Can Consignia Deliver?, 2001; A Department for Business, 2001; Harnessing our Genius, 2003; Horace's Odes and the Mystery of Do-Re-Mi, 2007; Music in the Odes of Horace, 2010. *Address:* 50 Seymour Walk, SW10 9NF. *T:* (020) 7352 3309. *E:* stuartlyons.cbe@gmail.com. *Club:* Hurlingham.

LYONS, Prof. Terence John, DPhil; FRS 2002; FRSE; FLSW; Wallis Professor of Mathematics, University of Oxford, since 2000; Fellow, St Anne's College, Oxford, since 2000; Director, Oxford-Man Institute of Quantitative Finance, since 2010; *b* 4 May 1953; *s* of late Peter Lyons and Valerie (*née* Hardie); *m* 1975, Barbara, *d* of late Joseph and Barbara Epsom; *m*; one *s* one *d. Educ:* St Joseph's Coll., W Norwood; Trinity Coll., Cambridge (BA Maths 1975 and 1976); Christ Church, Oxford (DPhil 1980). FRSE 1988. Jun. Res. Fellow, Jesus Coll., Oxford, 1979–81; Lectr in Maths, Imperial Coll., London, 1981–85; Colin Maclaurin Prof. of Maths, 1985–93, Hd, Dept of Maths and Stats, 1988–91, Univ. of Edinburgh; Prof. of Maths, Imperial Coll., London, 1993–2000; Dir, Wales Inst. of Mathematical and Computational Scis, 2007–10. Hendrick Vis. Asst Prof., UCLA, 1981–82; Visiting Professor: Univ. of BC, 1990; Univs of Paris VI and XI; Univ. of Toulouse; Inst. des Hautes Etudes Scientifiques. Sen. Fellow, EPSRC, 1993–98. Vice Pres., 2000–02, Pres., 2013–15, LMS. FIMS 2005; FLSW 2011. Hon. Fellow: Aberystwyth Univ., 2010; Cardiff Univ., 2012. Dr *hc* Univ. Paul Sabatier, France, 2007. Rollo Davidson Prize, 1985, Jun. Whitehead Prize, 1986, Polya Prize, 2000, LMS; Humboldt Res. Award, Humboldt Foundn, 2015. *Recreations:* reading, cycling, computer programming, family life. *Address:* Oxford-Man Institute of Quantitative Finance, Eagle House, Walton Well Road, Oxford OX2 6ED. *T:* (01865) 616611/08/00. *E:* director@oxford-man.ox.ac.uk.

LYONS, Dr Timothy John; QC 2003; *b* 27 Dec. 1957; *s* of Kenneth Sidney Lyons and late Margaret Winifred Lyons (*née* Sim); *m* 1993, Patricia Anne Webb. *Educ:* Bristol Univ. (LLB Hons 1979); Queen Mary Coll., Univ. of London (LLM 1981); Queen Mary and Westfield Coll., Univ. of London (PhD 1991). CTA (Fellow) (FTII 1996). Called to the Bar, Inner Temple, 1980; joined Lincoln's Inn, 1994; Mem., Hon. Soc. of King's Inns and called to the Bar, Ireland, 1998; in private practice, specialising in revenue, customs, trade law and EU matters. Mem. and Co-Rapporteur, Expert Gp on Taxation of Individuals. Visiting Professor: Law Dept, LSE, 2008–; Law Faculty, Univ. of Porto, 2010–. Regular lectr, UK and continental Europe. Gen. Ed., European Cross-Border Estate Planning (formerly Capital Taxes and Estate Planning in Europe), 1991–; Asst Ed. (European Law), British Tax Review, 2004–. *Publications:* (ed) Chapman's Inheritance Tax, 7th edn, 1987, 8th edn 1990; Insolvency: law and taxation, 1989; Inheritance Tax Planning through Insurance, 1990; (jtly) Historic Buildings and Maintenance Funds, 1991; (jtly) Capital Gains Tax Roll Over Relief for Business Assets, 1993; (ed jtly) The International Guide to the Taxation of Trusts, 1999; EC Customs Law, 2002, 2nd edn 2008; (contrib.) Value Added Tax: commentary and analysis, 2009; (contrib.) De Voil Indirect Tax Service, 2012; contrib. articles to jls incl. British Tax Rev., EC Tax Jl, European Taxation, Global Trade and Customs Jl. *Recreations:* reading, music, collecting antiquarian maps. *Address:* 39 Essex Street, WC2R 3AT. *T:* (020) 7832 1111.

LYSAGHT, family name of **Baron Lisle**.

LYSCOM, David Edward; HM Diplomatic Service, retired; Policy Director, Chartered Institute of Internal Auditors, since 2012; *b* 8 Aug. 1951; *s* of late William Edward Lyscom and Phyllis Edith May Lyscom (*née* Coyle); *m* 1973, Dr Nicole Ward; one *s* two *d. Educ:* Latymer Upper Sch.; Pembroke Coll., Cambridge (BA 1972). Joined HM Diplomatic Service, 1972; Vienna, 1973–76; Ottawa, 1977–79; FCO, 1979–83; First Secretary: Bonn, 1984–87; Riyadh, 1988–90; Asst Head, Aid Policy Dept, FCO, 1990–91; Counsellor, Science, Technology and Envmt, Bonn, 1991–95; Head of Envmt, Science and Energy Dept, FCO, 1995–98; Ambassador to Slovak Republic, 1998–2001; FCO, 2002–03; UK Perm. Rep. to OECD, Paris, 2004–08; Chief Exec., ISC, 2008–11. *Recreations:* music, theatre, squash, tennis.

LYSTER, Simon; DL; PhD; conservationist; Chief Executive (formerly Executive Director), LEAD International, 2005–11 (Director of Development and Programmes, 2003–05); *b* 29 April 1952; *s* of John Neal Lyster and Marjorie Aird, (Peggy), (*née* Everard); *m* 1990, Sandra Elizabeth (*née* Charity); one *s* one *d. Educ:* Radley Coll.; Magdalene Coll., Cambridge (MA Hons; PhD). Admitted solicitor, 1978; Slaughter and May, 1976–78; Envmtl Defense Fund, NY, 1978–79; admitted to NY Bar, 1979; Defenders of Wildlife, Washington, 1979–81; Dir, Falklands Conservation, 1982–86; Hd, Conservation Policy, WWF UK, and Internat. Treaties Officer, WWF Internat., 1986–95; Dir-Gen., The Wildlife Trusts, 1995–2003. Non-exec. Dir, Northumbrian Water Gp (formerly Ltd), 2006–. Mem., Darwin Adv. Cttee, 1997–2003; Mem. Bd, Natural England, 2014–; Trustee: Kilverstone Wildlife Charitable Trust, 2002–; World Land Trust, 2004– (Chm., 2014–); Conservation Internat. - UK, 2005–; Rural Community Council of Essex, 2013–. DL Essex, 2013. *Publications:* International Wildlife Law, 1985; numerous articles in mags and newspapers and contribs to books. *Recreations:* natural history, tennis, cricket, walking, golf. *Address:* Great Prestons Farm, Stock, Essex CM4 9RN. *Club:* Queen's.

LYSTER-BINNS, Benjamin Edward Noël; HM Diplomatic Service; Ambassador to Uruguay, since 2012; *b* 19 Oct. 1965; *m* 1995, Belinda Hunter Blair; one *s* two *d.* Entered FCO, 1989; Desk Officer, Non-Proliferation Dept, FCO, 1989–91; Third Secretary: (Develt) Lilongwe, 1991–94; (Chancery/Inf.), Muscat, 1994–98; Desk Officer, Human Rights Policy Dept, FCO, 1998–2000; Dep. Eur. Corresp. and Hd, EU Gen. Affairs and Ext. Relns Council/G8 Team, Common Foreign and Security Policy Dept, FCO, 2000–03; Dep. Hd of

Mission, Lisbon, 2003–07; Policy Advr, Counter Terrorism Dept, FCO, 2007–10; Dep. Hd, Internat. Orgns Dept, FCO, 2010–12. *Address:* c/o Foreign and Commonwealth Office, King Charles Street, SW1A 2AH.

LYTHELL, Jane; *see* Clarke, J.

LYTHGO, Adrian; Chief Executive, Kirklees Metropolitan Borough Council, since 2010; Head of Paid Service, West Yorkshire Combined Authority, since 2014; *b* Cyprus, 3 Dec. 1962; *s* of Derek and Beryl Lythgo; *m* 1996, Melanie Pilbrough; one *s* one *d*. *Educ:* Edgbarrow Sch., Crowthorne; Univ. of Loughborough (BSc). CPFA 1990. Audit Commn, 1984–88; Royal Bor. of Windsor and Maidenhead, 1989–90; Audit Commn, 1990–92; KPMG, 1993–95; Dist Auditor, Audit Commn, 1995–99; Associate Partner, KPMG, Leeds, 1999–2009; Dir of Finance, Kirklees MBC, 2009–10. Mem., Audit Cttee, Leeds City Coll., 2010–15. *Recreations:* Rugby nut, sliding down mountains. *Address:* Kirklees Council, Civic Centre III, Market Street, Huddersfield HD1 2TG. *T:* (01484) 226600. *E:* adrian.lythgo@kirklees.gov.uk.

LYTTELTON, family name of **Viscounts Chandos** and **Cobham**.

LYTTELTON, Hon. Richard Cavendish; Chairman: Help Musicians UK (formerly Musicians Benevolent Fund), 2008–14; Artis, since 2010; *b* Pershore, Worcs, 24 July 1949; 3rd *s* of 10th Viscount Cobham, KG, GCMG, GCVO, TD, PC and Elizabeth Alison, *d* of J. R. Makeig-Jones, CBE; *m* 1971, Romilly Sybil Barker; one *s* one *d*. *Educ:* Eton Coll.; Birmingham Sch. of Music. Founder, Richard Lyttelton Hldgs, 1969–74; Manager, New Projects, EMI Leisure Enterprises Ltd, 1974–76; Man. Dir, Oy EMI Finland AB, 1977–80; Dir, Internat. Ops, EMI Records (UK) Ltd, 1980–83; Gp Man. Dir, EMI S Africa, 1984–86; President: Capitol Records, EMI Canada, 1986–88; EMI Classics and Jazz, 1988–2006. Chm., English Touring Opera, 2003–09. Pres., Royal Albert Hall, 2010–11. Mem. Council, RCM, 2009– (Charity Trustee). Trustee: EMI Music Sound Foundn; EMI Archive Trust. *Recreations:* music, shooting, fishing, theatre, opera. *Address:* 5 Queens Gate Place Mews, SW7 5BG. *T:* (020) 7823 8128. *E:* richard.lyttelton@gmail.com.
See also Viscount Cobham.

LYTTLE, Brian; *see* Lyttle, J. B. C.

LYTTLE, Christopher; Member (Alliance) Belfast East, Northern Ireland Assembly, since 2010; *b* Belfast, 19 Jan. 1981; one *c*. *Educ:* Queen's Univ., Belfast (BA Hons 1st Cl. Pols 2003). Frank Knox Fellow in Public Policy, Kennedy Sch. of Govt, Harvard Univ., 2006. Constituency and Res. Asst to Naomi Long, 2007–10. *Recreation:* Amateur Association Football. *Address:* Parliament Buildings, Stormont, Belfast BT4 3XX. *T:* (028) 9047 2004. *E:* chris.lyttle@allianceparty.org.

LYTTLE, (James) Brian (Chambers), OBE 1996; Secretary, Probation Board for Northern Ireland, 1987–97; *b* 22 Aug. 1932; *s* of late James Chambers Lyttle and Margaret Kirkwood Billingsley; *m* 1957, Mary Alma Davidson; four *d*. *Educ:* Bangor Grammar Sch.; Trinity Coll., Dublin (BA 1st Cl. Hons Classics). Entered NI Civil Service as Asst Principal, 1954; Private Sec. to Minister of Commerce, 1960–62; Chief Exec., Enterprise Ulster, 1972–75; Dir, Employment Service, Dept of Manpower Services, 1975–77; Dir, Industrial Develt Orgn, Dept of Commerce, 1977–81; Under Secretary, Dept of Commerce, later Dept of Economic Develt, 1977–84; Under Sec., Dept of Finance and Personnel, 1984–87. Mem., Prison Arts Foundn, 1996–2010. *Recreations:* reading, walking, music, poetry.

LYTTON, family name of **Earl of Lytton**.

LYTTON, 5th Earl of, *cr* 1880; **John Peter Michael Scawen Lytton;** Baron Wentworth, 1529; Bt 1838; Baron Lytton, 1866; Viscount Knebworth, 1880; DL; chartered surveyor, Lawrence Foote & Partners, since 2014; *b* 7 June 1950; *s* of 4th Earl of Lytton, OBE, and Clarissa Mary, *d* of Brig.-Gen. C. E. Palmer, CB, CMG, DSO, RA; *S* father, 1985; *m* 1980, Ursula Alexandra (*née* Komoly); two *s* one *d*. *Educ:* Downside; Reading Univ. (BSc, Estate Management). FRICS 1987 (ARICS 1976); IRRV 1990. Sole practitioner, John Lytton & Co. Ltd, Chartered Surveyors and Valuers, 1988–2015. President: Sussex Assoc. of Local Councils, 1997–2014; Nat. Assoc. of Local Councils, 1999–2014; Chm., Leasehold Adv. Service (formerly Leasehold Enfranchisement Adv. Service), 1994–2000. Member: Council, CLA, 1993–99 (Exec., 1994–99); Bd, Sussex Rural Community Council, 2000–09; Council, S of England Agricl Soc., 2004–; Chm., Rights of Way Rev. Cttee, 2012–. Pres., Newstead Abbey Byron Soc., 1988–. Elected Mem., H of L, 2011. Mem., Information Cttee, H of L, 2012–. DL W Sussex, 2011. Hon. FBEng 1997. *Heir: s* Viscount Knebworth, *qv*. *Address:* (office) Estate Office, Newbuildings Place, Shipley, Horsham, West Sussex RH13 8GQ. *T:* (01403) 741650.

LYTTON COBBOLD, family name of **Baron Cobbold**.

LYVEDEN, 7th Baron *cr* 1859, of Lyveden, co. Northampton; **Jack Leslie Vernon;** self-employed painter and interior decorator, since 1978; *b* 10 Nov. 1938; *e s* of 6th Baron Lyveden and Queenie Constance Vernon (*née* Ardern); *S* father, 1999; *m* 1961, Lynette June Lilley; one *s* two *d*. *Educ:* Te Aroha District High Sch. Apprentice, painting and decorating industry, 1955–60 (NZ Trade Cert.). Life Mem., Te Aroha Fire Brigade (joined Brigade, 1959; Fire Officer, 1975; Dep. Chief Fire Officer, 1981; Chief Fire Officer, 1987–94). *Heir: s* Hon. Colin Ronald Vernon [*b* 3 Feb. 1967; *m* 2009, Rachel Marie Rainey]. *Address:* 17 Carlton Street, Te Aroha 3320, New Zealand. *Clubs:* Te Aroha, Returned Services Association.

M

MA LIN, Hon. CBE 1983; PhD; JP; Emeritus Professor of Biochemistry, 1986, and Chairman of Board of Trustees of Shaw College, 1986–2011, now Senior Adviser, The Chinese University of Hong Kong; *b* 8 Feb. 1925; *s* of late Prof. Ma Kiam and Sing-yu Cheng; *m* 1958, Dr Meng-Hua Chen; three *d*. *Educ:* West China Union Univ., China (BSc); Univ. of Leeds (PhD). Post-doctorate Fellow, University College Hosp. Med. Sch., London, and St James's Hosp., Leeds, 1955–56. Assistant Lectr, 1957–59, and Lectr, 1959–64, in Clinical Chemistry, Dept of Pathology, Univ. of Hong Kong; Chinese University of Hong Kong: part-time Lectr in Chemistry, 1964; Sen. Lectr, 1965–72, Reader, 1972–73, Prof., 1973–78, in Biochemistry; Dean of Faculty of Science, 1973–75; Vice-Chancellor, 1978–87. Visiting Biochemist, Hormone Research Laboratory, Univ. of California, San Francisco, 1969. FRSA 1982. Unofficial JP, 1978. Hon. DSc Sussex, 1984; Hon. DLit East Asia, 1987; Hon. LLD: Chinese Univ. of Hong Kong, 1987; Leeds, 1996; Hon. DHL SUNY, 1989; Hon. PhD Tianjin, 1998. Order of the Rising Sun, Gold Rays, with neck ribbon (Japan), 1986; Commander's Cross, Order of Merit (FRG), 1988. *Publications:* various research papers in academic jls. *Recreations:* swimming, table-tennis. *Address:* Shaw College, The Chinese University of Hong Kong, Hong Kong.

MA Tao Li, Hon. Geoffrey, GBM 2012; Chief Justice, Court of Final Appeal of the Hong Kong Special Administrative Region of the People's Republic of China, since 2010; *b* Hong Kong, 11 Jan. 1956; *s* of late George Ma and Margaret Ma (*née* Wei); *m* 1984, Maria Candace Yuen, (Madam Justice Yuen); one *d*. *Educ:* Altrincham Grammar Sch.; Univ. of Birmingham (LLB 1977). Called to the Bar: Gray's Inn, 1978 (Hon. Bencher 2004); Hong Kong, 1980; State of Vic., Australia, 1983; Singapore, 1990; QC (Hong Kong) 1993. Legal Consultant to Messrs David Chong & Co., Singapore, Advocates and Solicitors, 1995–2001; Hd of Chambers, Temple Chambers, Hong Kong, 1999–2001; High Court of Hong Kong: a Recorder, 2000–01, Judge, 2001–02, Court of First Instance; Justice of Appeal, Court of Appeal, 2002–03; Chief Judge, 2003–10. Adjudicator, Registration of Persons Tribunal, Hong Kong, 1987–96. Hon. Lectr, Dept of Professional Legal Educn, Univ. of Hong Kong, 1987–. Dep. Chm., Bd of Review (Inland Revenue), 1997–2000. Chm., Appeal Tribunal Panel (Bldgs), 1994–2001; Mem., Hong Kong Futures Exchange Disciplinary Appeal Tribunal, 1994–2001. Chm., Judicial Officers Recommendation Commn, 2010–; Member: Criminal and Law Enforcement Injuries Compensation Bd, 1991–2001; Law Reform Commn, 2010–; Dep. Chm., Appeals Panel, 1999–2001, Takeovers Appeals Cttee, 1999–2001, Securities and Futures Commn. Hong Kong International Arbitration Centre: Member: Appt Adv. Bd, 1997–; Arbitration Ordinance Rev. Cttee, 1998–; Internat. Adv. Bd, 2011–. Mem., Wkg Party on Civil Justice Reform, 2000–01; Chairman: Steering Cttee on Civil Justice Reform, 2004–09; Monitoring Cttee on Civil Justice Reform, 2009–10; Rules Cttee, Court of Final Appeal, 2010–; Wkg Gp on Use of Chinese, 2010–; Steering Cttee on Relocation of Court of Final Appeal, 2010–; Chief Justice's Cttee on Community-Related Projects, 2011–; Hong Kong Judicial Inst., 2013–; Mem., Civil Court Users Cttee of Judiciary, 1993–2001; Mem., 1994–97, Vice Chm., 1997–98, Mgt Cttee, Consumer Legal Action Fund. Mem., Bar Council, Hong Kong Bar Assoc., 1982–84 and 1992–96. Patron: Hong Kong Acad. of Law, Law Soc. of Hong Kong, 2010–; Soc. of Rehabilitation and Crime Prevention, Hong Kong, 2010–; Bingham Centre for Rule of Law, 2010–; Hong Kong Inst. of Arbitrators, 2011–; Internat. Advocacy Trng Council, Hong Kong, 2012–. Pres., Scout Assoc. of Hong Kong, 2008–. Hon. Fellow, Harris Manchester Coll., Oxford, 2012. Hon. LLD Birmingham, 2011. *Publications:* (contributing and adv. ed.) Hong Kong Civil Procedure, 2001; (contrib.) Litigation in the Commercial List: 2002 Law Lectures for Practitioners, 2002; (contrib.) The Interpretation of Hong Kong's Constitution: a personal view, 2013; Editor-in-Chief: Arbitration in Hong Kong: a practical guide, 2003, 3rd edn 2014; Professional Conduct and Risk Management in Hong Kong, 2007. *Recreations:* badminton, golf, tennis, films. *Address:* Court of Final Appeal, 1 Battery Path, Central, Hong Kong. *T:* 21230011. *E:* enquiry@judiciary.gov.hk. *Clubs:* Chinese Recreation, Victoria Recreation, Hong Kong; Hong Kong Golf, Shek O Golf and Country, Hong Kong Jockey, Hong Kong Cricket.

MA YING-JEOU; President of Taiwan, since 2008; *b* Hong Kong, 13 July 1950; *s* of late Ma Ho-ling and of Chin Hou-hsiu; *m* Chow Mei-Ching; two *d*. *Educ:* National Taiwan Univ. (LLB 1972); New York Univ. (LLM 1976); Harvard Law Sch. (SJD 1981). Legal Consultant, First Nat. Bank of Boston, 1980–81; Res. Consultant, Sch. of Law, Univ. of Maryland, 1980–81; Associate Lawyer, Cole & Deits, NY, 1981; Government of Taiwan: Dep. Dir-Gen., First Bureau, Office of the Pres., 1981–88; Sen. Sec., Office of the Pres., 1982; Minister, Res., Develt and Evaluation Commn, 1988–91; Sen. Dep. Minister and spokesperson, Mainland Affairs Council, 1991–93; Minister of Justice, 1993–96; Minister without Portfolio, 1996–97; Associate Prof. of Law, Nat. Chengchi Univ., 1997–98; Mayor, Taipei City, 1998–2006. Mem., National Assembly, 1992–96. Kuomintang: Dep. Sec.-Gen., 1984–88, Mem., 1993–97, Central Club Clique; Mem., Central Standing Cttee, 1999–2001; Vice-Chm., 2004–05; Chm., 2005–07, 2009–14. *Publications:* Legal Problems of Seabed Boundary Delimitation in the East China Sea, 1984; Two Major Legal Issues Relating to the International Status of the Republic of China, 1986; Taipei-Beijing Relations and East Asian Stability: implications for Europe, 1993; The Republic of China (Taiwan)'s Entry into the World Trade Organisation: problems and prospects, 1996. *Address:* Office of the President, No 122, Sec. 1, Chongqing S Road, Zhongzheng District, Taipei City 10048, Taiwan. *T:* (2) 23113731, *Fax:* (2) 23311604. *E:* public@mail.oop.gov.tw.

MA, Yo-Yo; 'cellist; *b* Paris, 7 Oct. 1955; of Chinese parentage; *m* 1978, Jill A. Horner; one *s* one *d*. *Educ:* Harvard Univ.; Juilliard Sch. of Music, NY. First public recital at age of 5 years; winner Avery Fisher Prize, 1978; has performed under many distinguished conductors with all major world orchestras including: Berlin Philharmonic; Boston Symphony; Chicago Symphony; Israel Philharmonic; LSO; NY Philharmonic; also appears in chamber music ensembles; regular participant in festivals at Tanglewood, Edinburgh, Salzburg and other major European fests. Founder and Artistic Dir, Silk Road Project, 1998–. Has made numerous recordings. Dr *hc*: Northeastern, USA, 1985; Harvard, 1991. Numerous Grammy Awards. Presidential Medal of Freedom, 2010. *Address:* c/o Opus 3, 470 Park Avenue South, 9th Floor North, New York, NY 10016, USA. *T:* (212) 5847500.

MA Zhengang; President, China Arms Control and Disarmament Association; Chairman, Chinese National Committee, Council for Security Cooperation in the Asia Pacific; *b* 9 Nov. 1940; (to a worker's family); *m* 1972, Chen Xiaodong; one *s*. *Educ:* Beijing Foreign Langs Univ.; post-grad. study at Ealing Tech. Coll. and LSE. Staff Mem., N American and Oceanian Affairs Dept (NAOAD), Min. of Foreign Affairs, China, 1967–70; Staff Mem., then Attaché, Yugoslavia, 1970–74; Attaché, NAOAD, 1974–81; Consul, Vancouver, 1981–85; Dep. Dir, then Dir, NAOAD, 1985–90; Counsellor, Washington, 1990–91; Dep. Dir-Gen., then Dir-Gen., NAOAD, 1991–95; Vice-Minister, Foreign Affairs Office of State Council, 1995–97; Ambassador of China to the Court of St James's, 1997–2002; Ambassador, Min. of Foreign Affairs, 2002–04; Pres., China Inst. of Internat. Studies, 2004–10. *Recreations:* table tennis, bridge, literature. *Address:* China Arms Control and Disarmament Association, 3 Toutiao, Taijichang, Beijing 100005, People's Republic of China.

MAAN, Bashir Ahmed, CBE 2000; JP; DL; Member, Scottish Constitutional Convention, 1988–98; Judge, City of Glasgow District Courts, 1968–97; *b* Maan, Gujranwala, Pakistan, 22 Oct. 1926; *s* of late Choudhry Sardar Khan Maan and Mrs Hayat Begum Maan; *m*; one *s* three *d*. *Educ:* D. B. High Sch., Qila Didar Singh; Panjab Univ.; Strathclyde Univ. (MSc 1994). Involved in struggle for creation of Pakistan, 1943–47; organised rehabilitation of refugees from India in Maan and surrounding areas, 1947–48; emigrated to UK and settled in Glasgow, 1953; Glasgow Founder Sec., Pakistan Social and Cultural Soc., 1955–65, Pres., 1966–69; Pres., Islamic Centre, Glasgow, 2007–10; Vice-Chm., Glasgow Community Relations Council, 1970–75; Pres., Standing Conf. of Pakistani Orgns in UK, 1974–77; a Dep. Chm., Commn for Racial Equality, 1977–80; Founder Chm., Scottish Pakistani Assoc., 1984–98; Pres., Nat. Assoc. of British Pakistanis, 2000–07; Member: Overseas Pakistanis Adv. Council, Govt of Pakistan, 2001–04; President's Task Force on Human Develt of Pakistan, 2001–04; Scottish rep., Muslim Council of Britain, 1998–2008; Convenor, Muslim Council of Scotland, 2007–10; Chairman: Strathclyde CRC, 1987–93 and 1994–96; Strathclyde Interpreting Services Adv. Cttee, 1988–96; Council of Ethnic Minority Orgns Scotland, 2002–11 (Pres., 2012–). Member: Immigrants Prog. Adv. Cttee, BBC, 1972–80; Gen. Adv. Cttee, BBC, 1991–95; Scottish Selecting Panel, BBC, 1992–96. Hon. Res. Fellow, Univ. of Glasgow, 1988–91. Councillor, Glasgow Corp., 1970–75, City of Glasgow Dist, 1974–84 (Bailie, 1980–84); Mem., Glasgow City Council, 1995–2003 (Bailie, 1996–99); Magistrate, City of Glasgow, 1971–74; Vice-Chm. 1971–74, Chm. 1974–75, Police Cttee, Glasgow Corp.; Police Judge, City of Glasgow, 1974–75; Mem., 1995–2003, Convenor, 1999–2003, Strathclyde Jt Police Bd. Mem. Exec. Cttee, Glasgow City Labour Party, 1969–70. Contested (Lab) East Fife, Feb. 1974. Convener, Pakistan Bill Action Cttee, 1973; Member: Nat. Road Safety Cttee, 1971–75; Scottish Accident Prevention Cttee, 1971–75; Scottish Gas Consumers' Council, 1978–81; Greater Glasgow Health Bd, 1981–91; Hon. Pres., SCVO, 2001–06 (Mem., Mgt Bd, 1988–95). Chm., Organising Cttee, Glasgow Internat. Sports Festival Co. Ltd, 1987–89. Mem. Bd of Governors, Jordanhill Coll. of Educn, Glasgow, 1987–91. JP 1968, DL 1982, Glasgow. Hon Fellow, Glasgow Caledonian Univ., 2003–07. Hon. LLD Strathclyde, 1999; DUniv Glasgow, 2001; Hon. DLitt Glasgow Caledonian, 2002. *Publications:* The New Scots, 1992; The Thistle and the Crescent, 2008; articles, contrib. to press. *Recreations:* golf, reading. *Address:* 8 Riverview Gardens, Flat 6, Glasgow G5 8EL. *T:* (0141) 429 7689. *Club:* Douglas Park Golf.

MAAS, Rupert Nicholas; Managing Director, Maas Gallery, since 1993; *b* Chelsea, 23 July 1960; *s* of late Jeremy Maas and of Antonia Maas; *m* 1991, Tamar Seaborn; three *d*. *Educ:* Sherborne Sch.; Essex Univ. (BA Art Hist.). Joined Maas Gall., 1983. Expert in English painting, Antiques Roadshow, BBC, 1996–. Brand Ambassador, Ballantine's Whisky, China, 2009–12. *Recreations:* mending things, sailing, playing the piano in secret, harassing the Council. *Address:* Maas Gallery, 15a Clifford Street, W1S 4JZ. *T:* (020) 7734 2302. *E:* mail@maasgallery.com.

MABB, David Michael; QC 2001; *b* 12 June 1956; *s* of Kenneth George Mabb and Joyce Madeline Mabb. *Educ:* King James' Grammar Sch., Almondbury; St Nicholas Grammar Sch., Northwood; Gonville and Caius Coll., Cambridge (BA 1978; MA 1982). Called to the Bar, Lincoln's Inn, 1979. Mem., Financial Reporting Rev. Panel, 2009–. *Address:* Erskine Chambers, 33 Chancery Lane, WC2A 1EN. *T:* (020) 7242 5532.

MABB, Katherine Anne; *see* Green, K. A.

MABEY, Richard Thomas, FRSL; writer and broadcaster; *b* 20 Feb. 1941; *s* of late Thomas Gustavus Mabey and Edna Nellie (*née* Moore). *Educ:* Berkhamsted Sch.; St Catherine's Coll., Oxford (BA Hons 1964, MA 1971). Lectr in Social Studies, Dacorum Coll. of Further Educn, 1963–65; Sen. Editor, Penguin Books, 1966–73; freelance writer, 1973–; columnist: BBC Wildlife, 1984–; The Times, 2004–06. Mem. Mgt Cttee, Soc. of Authors, 1998–2000. Presenter: Tomorrow's World, BBC TV, 1995; Mabey in the Wild, BBC Radio 4, 2013. Member: Nature Conservancy Council, 1982–86; Council, Botanical Soc. of the British Isles, 1981–83; President: London Wildlife Trust, 1982–92; Richard Jefferies Soc., 1995–98; Norfolk and Norwich Naturalists' Soc., 2005–06; Waveney and Blyth Arts, 2010–; Vice-Pres., Open Spaces Soc., 2003–. Dir, Common Ground, 1988–. Patron: Thomas Bewick Trust, 1986–; John Clare Soc., 2006–; Mem. Adv. Council, Plantlife, 1992–. Leverhulme Trust Res. Award, 1983–84; Leverhulme Res. Fellowship, 1993–94; Writer-in-Residence, New Writing Partnership, UEA, 2008; Burrows Lectr, Univ. of Essex, 2013; Derek Brewer Vis. Fellow, Emmanuel Coll., Cambridge, 2014. FRSL 2012. Hon. DSc St Andrews, 1997; DUniv: Essex, 2007; Open, 2014; Hon. DLitt UEA, 2011. Granted a civil list pension, 2008. Peter Scott Meml Award and Hon. Fellow, British Naturalists' Assoc., 2012. *Publications:* (ed) Class, 1967; The Pop Process, 1969; Food for Free, 1972, 2nd edn 1989; Children in Primary School, 1972; The Unofficial Countryside, 1973; The Pollution Handbook, 1973; The Roadside Wildlife Book, 1974; Street Flowers, 1976 (TES Inf. Book Award); Plants with a Purpose, 1977; The Common Ground, 1980; The Flowering of Britain, 1980; (ed) Landscape with Figures, 1983; Oak and Company, 1983 (NY Acad. of Sci. Children's Book Award, 1984); In a Green Shade, 1983; Back to the Roots, 1983; (ed) Second Nature, 1984; The Frampton Flora, 1985; Gilbert White: a biography, 1986 (Whitbread Biography Award); Gen. Ed., The Journals of Gilbert White, 1986–89; (ed) The Gardener's Labyrinth,

1987; The Flowering of Kew, 1988; Home Country, 1990; (ed) The Flowers of May, 1990; A Nature Journal, 1991; Whistling in the Dark, 1993; Landlocked, 1994; (ed) The Oxford Book of Nature Writing, 1995; Flora Britannica (British Bk Awards Illustrated Book of the Year), 1996; Selected Writings 1974–1999, 1999; Nature Cure, 2005; (with Mark Cocker) Birds Britannica, 2005; Fencing Paradise, 2005; Beechcombings: the narratives of trees, 2007; The Full English Cassoulet, 2008; (with Peter Marren) Bugs Britannica, 2010; A Brush with Nature, 2010; Weeds, 2010; The Barley Bird, 2010 (E Anglian Book Award, 2010); The Perfumier and the Stinkhorn, 2011; A Good Parcel of English Soil, 2013; Turned Out Nice Again: on living with the weather, 2013; The Ash and the Beech: the drama of woodland change, 2013; Dreams of the Good Life: the life of Flora Thompson and the creation of Lark Rise to Candleford, 2014; Moonflowers: plants and the imagination, 2015. *Recreations:* food, meandering, early music. *Address:* c/o Sheil Land Associates, 52 Doughty Street, WC1N 2LS. *W:* www.richardmabey.co.uk.

MABEY, Roger Stanley, CMG 1997; Director, Sweett Group (formerly Cyril Sweett Group) Ltd, since 2003; *b* 11 Aug. 1944; *s* of Stanley Mabey and Edith Mabey (*née* Stride); *m* 1968, Margaret Marian Watkins; one *s* one *d*. *Educ:* Cleeve Sch., Cheltenham; Gloucestershire Coll. of Technology (HND 1964); Lancaster Coll. of Technology, Coventry; Eur. Centre of Continuing Educn, INSEAD. Joined Bovis, 1967; Project Manager, Bristol, 1967–73; Regl Dir, Harrow office, 1973–79; a Divl Dir, 1979–86; Dir, Bovis Construction Ltd, 1986–93; Asst Man. Dir, 1993–94, Man. Dir, 1994–97, Bovis Internat. Ltd; Executive Director: Bovis Construction Gp, 1998–2000; Bovis Lend Lease Ltd, 2000–03. Chm., Housing Solutions Gp, 2011–14 (Vice Chm., 2005–11). Member: DTI Adv. Gps on India, 1994, and S Africa; Market Gp, Cttee for S African Trade, 1996; BOTB, 1998. Vice Chm., Cookham Soc., 1998–2000. FCIOB 1980; FRSA 1998. *Recreations:* travel, gardening, painting, food, music, athletics, family, ski-ing. *Address:* Carrol Lodge, Sutton Road, Cookham, Maidenhead, Berks SL6 9RD.

MABRO, Robert Emile, CBE 1996; Fellow of St Antony's College, Oxford, 1971–2002, now Emeritus, and of St Catherine's College, Oxford, since 2007; President, Oxford Institute for Energy Studies, 2003–06, now Hon. President (Director, 1982–2003); *b* 26 Dec. 1934; *s* of Emile Mabro and Tatiana Mabro (*née* Bittar); *m* 1967, Judith Howey; two *d*. *Educ:* Coll. St Marc, Alexandria, Egypt; Univ. of Alexandria (BSc Engrg); SOAS, London Univ. (MSc Econs). Civil engr, Egypt, 1956–60; Leon Fellow, Univ. of London, 1966–67; Res. Officer, SOAS, 1967–69; Sen. Res. Officer in econs of ME, Univ. of Oxford, 1969–; Director: ME Centre, St Antony's Coll., Oxford, 1976–79; Oxford Energy Seminar, 1978–. Vice Chm. Bd, Econ. Res. Forum for Arab Countries, Iran and Turkey, 1994–97. Hon. Sec., Oxford Energy Policy Club, 1976–. Charles Hedlund Vis. Prof., Amer. Univ. in Cairo, 1997. Award, Internat. Assoc. for Energy Econs, 1990. Medal of the Pres. (Italy), 1985; Order of the Aztec Eagle (Mexico), 1997; Order of Francisco Miranda (Venezuela), 1999; Officier des Palmes Académiques (France), 2001. *Publications:* The Egyptian Economy 1952–1972, 1974; (with S. Radwan) The Industrialization of Egypt 1939–73, 1976; (ed) World Energy: issues and policies, 1980; (ed) OPEC and the World Oil Market, 1986; (jtly) The Market for North Sea Crude Oil, 1986; (with P. Horsnell) Oil Markets and Prices, 1993; (ed) Oil in the 21st Century, 2006; articles in jls. *Recreations:* cooking; collecting books, postcards, etc on Alexandria, Egypt; reading, poetry, philosophy. *Address:* (office) 57 Woodstock Road, Oxford OX2 6FA. *T:* (01865) 311377; 52 Lonsdale Road, Oxford OX2 7EP. *T:* (01865) 557623.

MABUZA, Lindiwe; High Commissioner for the Republic of South Africa to the United Kingdom, 2001–09; *b* Natal, 13 Aug. 1938. *Educ:* Grailville Community Coll., Ohio (Dip. Home Econs 1959); Roma, Lesotho, Univ. of S Africa (BA 1961); Stanford Univ., Calif (MA English 1966); Univ. of Minnesota (MA American Studies 1968); Diplomatic Trng, Kuala Lumpur (Dip. 1993). Teacher, English and Zulu Lit., Manzini Central Sch., Swaziland, 1962–64; Lectr, Dept of Sociol., Univ. of Minnesota, 1968–69; Asst Prof. of Lit. and Hist., Ohio Univ., 1969–77; radio journalist with ANC's Radio Freedom (broadcasting into SA from Zambia), 1977–79; Chief Representative of ANC: to Scandinavia, based in Sweden, 1979–87 (opened ANC offices in Denmark, Norway and Finland); to US, 1989–94; Mem., first democratic Parliament, SA, 1994–95; first Ambassador for S Africa to Germany, 1995–99; High Commissioner: to Malaysia, 1999–2001 (also to Brunei and the Philippines (non-resident)). Ed., Voice of Women, Jl by ANC women, 1977–79. Chm., ANC Cultural Cttee, Lusaka, 1977–79. Hon. PhD Durban-Westville, 1997. Yari Yari Award, New York Univ., 1997. *Publications:* (ed) Malibongwe: poetry by ANC women, 1980 (trans. German and Russian); (ed) One Never Knows: short stories by ANC women in exile, 1989; From ANC to Sweden: Olof Palme poem in English and Swedish 1986 (trans. Norwegian and Finnish); Letter to Letta: selected poetry from 1970–1987, 1993; Africa to Me: poetry from 1976–1996 in English and German, 1998; Voices that Lead: poetry selection from 1976–1996, 1998; contrib. to various poetry and short story anthologies. *Address:* c/o South African High Commission, Trafalgar Square, WC2N 5DP.

MAC; *see* McMurtry, S.

McADAM, Douglas Baxter; HM Diplomatic Service, retired; Consul General, Hamburg, 1999–2004; *b* 25 June 1944; *s* of late John Watson McAdam and Jean Cook McAdam; *m* 1965, Susan Clare Jarvis; one *s* one *d*. *Educ:* Musselburgh Burgh Sch.; Musselburgh Grammar Sch. Entered Foreign Office, 1961; served Ulan Bator, Luanda, New Delhi and FCO, 1966–78; Dep. Hd of Mission, Ulan Bator, 1978; Vice-Consul, Rio de Janeiro, 1979–82; 2nd, later 1st Sec., UK Delegn MBFR, Vienna, 1983–87; FCO, 1987–90; 1st Sec., Lagos, 1990–94; FCO, 1994–95; Ambassador to Kazakhstan and Kyrgyzstan (resident in Almaty), 1996–99. Mem., RSAA, 1997. Pres., Fiscal Council, Assoc. of Foreign Property Owners in Portugal, 2010–. Mem. Bd, Madrugada Assoc., 2015–. Chieftain, St Andrew's Soc. of the Algarve, 2010–. *Recreations:* fly fishing, swimming, eating well. *Address:* Colinas Verdes Lote 105, 8600–074 Bensafrim, Lagos, Portugal.

McADAM, Dr Ellen; Director, Birmingham Museums Trust, since 2013; *b* Dumfries, 23 May 1952; *d* of William McAdam and Helen Robertson McAdam; partner, Mark Richard Roberts; one *s*. *Educ:* Dumfries Acad.; Univ. of Edinburgh (MA); Somerville Coll., Oxford (DPhil 1982); HNC Computer Studies 1987. Katherine and Leonard Woolley Jun. Res. Fellow, Somerville Coll., Oxford, 1977–79; excavations and post-doctoral res., 1982–84; Res. Fellow, British Sch. of Archaeology in Iraq, 1984–86; Gp Manager, Gtr Manchester Archaeol Unit, 1988–89; Post-excavation Manager, Oxford Archaeol Unit, 1990–95; Academic Ed., English Heritage, 1995–98; Hd, Specialist Services, Mus. of London, 1998–2001; Collections Services Manager, 2001–09, Hd of Museums and Collections, 2009–13, Glasgow Museums. Member: Council, British Inst. for Study of Iraq, 2014–; Humanities Ext. Adv. Bd, Univ. of Oxford, 2015–. Mem., Women Leaders in Museums Network, 2008. MCIfA (MIFA 1994). FSAScot 1972. *Publications:* contribs to jls on British and Near East archaeol. *Recreations:* opera, theatre, gardening, cooking, small fat terriers. *Address:* Birmingham Museums, Chamberlain Square, Birmingham B3 3DH. *T:* (0121) 348 8008. *E:* ellen.mcadam@birminghammuseums.org.uk.

McADAM, James, CBE 1995; Chief Executive, 1992–2000, and Chairman, 1992–2006, Signet Group plc; *b* 10 Dec. 1930; *s* of John Robert McAdam and Helen McAdam (*née* Cormack); *m* 1955, Maisie Una Holmes; two *d*. *Educ:* Lenzie Academy. Joined J. & P. Coats Ltd, 1945; Finance Dir, Coats Chile, 1962–66, Coats India, 1966–70, Coats Patons UK, 1972–75; Dir, 1975, Chief Exec., 1985–86, Chm., 1986–91, Coats Patons plc; Dep. Chm. and Chief Operating Officer, Coats Viyella (merged co.), 1986–91. Chm., Bisley Office Equipment Co., 1991–2010. Dir, London Region Post Office, 1985–87. Chm., British Clothing Industry Assoc., 1991–2008; Mem., Exec. Cttee, Scottish Council Develt and Industry, 1988–99. FRSA; CCMI. *Recreations:* theatre, travel. *Address:* 143 Whitehall Court, Westminster, SW1A 2EP. *Clubs:* Royal Automobile, Farmers.

McADAM, John David Gibson; Chairman: United Utilities, since 2008; Rentokil Initial, since 2008; *b* 30 April 1948; *s* of John McAdam and Sarah McAdam (*née* Gibson); *m* 1979, Louise Mary Mann; one *s* one *d*. *Educ:* Kelsick Grammar Sch., Ambleside; Lakes Secondary Sch., Windermere; Manchester Univ. (BSc 1st Cl. Hons Chem. Physics; Dip. Adv. Studies in Science (Physics) 1971; PhD 1973). MRC Fellowship, Manchester and Cambridge Univs; Sen. Vice Pres., Quest Internat., 1987–90; Tech. Dir, Birds Eye Walls Ltd, 1990–93; Chairman and Chief Executive Officer: Unichema Internat., 1993–97; Quest Internat., 1997; Exec. Vice-Pres., ICI plc, 1997–98; Chm. and CEO, ICI Paints, 1998–2003; Dir, 1999–2008, Chief Exec., 2003–08, ICI plc. Non-executive Director: Severn Trent plc, 2000–05; Sara Lee Corp., 2008–12; Rolls Royce, 2008–; Sen. non-exec. Dir, J. Sainsbury plc, 2005–; Sen. Advr, TPG Capital LLP, 2008–. *Publications:* scientific papers in scientific jls on macromolecular motion in solutions. *Recreations:* Rugby, cricket, soccer (now as a spectator), walking, listening to music. *Address:* United Utilities Group plc, 55 Grosvenor Street, W1K 3LJ.

McADAM, Prof. Keith Paul William James; DL; FRCP, FWACP; Special Advisor for East, Central and Southern Africa, Royal College of Physicians, since 2013 (Associate International Director, 2010–13); Wellcome Professor of Tropical Medicine, London School of Hygiene and Tropical Medicine, London University, 1984–2004, now Emeritus (Head of Department of Clinical Sciences, 1988–94); *b* 13 Aug. 1945; *s* of Sir Ian William James McAdam, OBE, and of Mrs L. M. Hrothgaarde Bennett (*née* Gibson); *m* 1968, Penelope Ann (*née* Spencer); three *d*. *Educ:* Prince of Wales School, Nairobi; Millfield School, Som.; Clare Coll., Cambridge (MA, MB BChir); Middlesex Hosp. Med. Sch. FRSTM&H; Dip. Amer. Bd of Internal Medicine, Dip. Amer. Bd of Allergy and Clinical Immunology. Medical posts at Middlesex Hosp., Royal Northern Hosp., Brompton Hosp., Nat. Hosp. for Nervous Diseases, 1969–73; Lectr in Medicine, Inst. of Med. Research, Goroka, Papua New Guinea, 1973–75; MRC Travelling Fellow, 1975–76; Vis. Scientist, Immunology Branch, Nat. Cancer Inst., NIH, Bethesda, 1976–77; Asst Prof., Tufts Univ. Sch. of Medicine, 1977–82; Associate Prof., Divs of Allergy, Exptl Medicine and Geographic Medicine, Tufts Univ., 1982–84; Consultant Physician, Hosp. for Tropical Diseases, NW1, 1984–95; Dir, MRC Labs, The Gambia, 1995–2003 (on secondment); Dir, Infectious Diseases Inst., Mulago Hosp., Makerere Univ. Med. Sch., Kampala, Uganda, 2004–07; Member: Academic Alliance for AIDS Care and Prevention in Africa, 2007–; Internat. Bd of Dirs, African Medical and Res. Foundn, 2011–. Adjunct Professor: Tufts New England Med. Center, Boston, 2004–07; Univ. of Minnesota Med. Sch., 2006–14. Trustee, BBC Media Action, 2013–. DL Herts, 2013. *Publications:* scientific articles on immunology and tropical medicine, esp. on amyloidosis, acute phase proteins, leprosy, tuberculosis, AIDS, malaria, inflammation. *Recreations:* cricket, tennis, golf, gardening. *Address:* Oakmead, 70 Luton Lane, Redbourn, Herts AL3 7PY. *T:* (01582) 792833. *Clubs:* MCC, Jesters.

MACADIE, Jeremy James; HM Diplomatic Service, retired; Chief Executive Officer, Ainsley International (Norway) Ltd; *b* 10 July 1952; *s* of Donald Jaimeson Macadie and Olga May Sheck; *m* 1975, Chantal Andrea Jacqueline Copiatti; one *d*. *Educ:* Yeovil Grammar Sch. Joined FCO, by open competition, 1972; Dakar, 1975; Addis Ababa, 1980; Sana'a, 1984; Dep. Hd of Mission, Antananarivo, 1987; Foreign Office Spokesman, 1990; Asst Private Sec. to Minister for Europe, 1995; Dep. Hd of Mission, Algiers, 1997; on secondment to African Directorate, French Ministry of Foreign Affairs, 2003; Ambassador to Republics of Rwanda and Burundi, 2004–07; Consul General, Erbil, Iraq, 2009–11; FCO, 2011–12. Dir, RTEC Security Ltd. Commnd TAVR (Intelligence and Security Gp), 1983. *Recreations:* country pursuits, turning wine into water.

McAFEE, Raymond Noel, CB 2002; consultant in international trade; Managing Director, UK Division, GlobalLink Trade Consulting, Washington, 2004–07; Associate Director, GlobalLink Border Solutions, 2007–08; *b* 15 Dec. 1943; *s* of late James Hill and Sarah McAfee (*née* O'Kane); *m* 1966, Margot McGowan; one *s* one *d*. *Educ:* Strabane Coll.; Portadown Coll. Joined HM Customs and Excise, 1963: Officer, 1963–74; Surveyor, 1974–79; Asst Collector, 1979–85; Sen. Principal, HQ London, 1985–89; Collector, NI, 1989–93; Asst Sec., HQ London, 1993–96; Dir, Central Ops, 1996–99; Comr, 1996–2003; Dir, Outfield, 1999–2001; Dir, Regl Business Services, 2001–03; Acting Dir Gen., 2003. Mem., Standards Cttee, Tunbridge Wells BC, 2004–. Reviewer of mgt articles for Chartered Mgt Inst., 2012–. FIMMM (FIM 1991). *Recreations:* golf, theatre, music. *E:* ray.mcafee@btinternet.com.

McAFEE, Maj.-Gen. Robert William Montgomery, CB 1999; *b* 8 Nov. 1944; *s* of Andrew Montgomery McAfee and Jane Beryl McAfee; *m* 1967, Erica-May MacLennan; one *s* one *d*. *Educ:* Inverness Royal Academy; Mons Officer Cadet Sch. Commnd, RTR, 1965; served Aden, BAOR, NI (despatches), Cyprus, Gulf, Bosnia; CO 2nd RTR, 1982–84; Instructor, Staff Coll., 1985–86; Col, Higher Command and Staff Course, 1987; Comdr 6 Armd Bde, 1988–89; ACOS (Land), HQ British Forces, ME, 1990; COS HQ 1 (BR) Corps, 1991–92; RCDS 1993; DG, Army Training, 1993–95; Comdr, Multi Nat. Div. (Central), 1996–99, retired. Dir of Admin, Norton Rose, 1999–2004. Rep. Col Comdt, RTR, 1995–99; Hon. Col Westminster Dragoons, 2003–09. Chm., RAC War Meml Benevolent Fund, 2004–11. Comr, Duke of York's Royal Mil. Sch., 2004–10. Chm., British Bobsleigh Assoc., 1998–2000; Dep. Pres., Army Rugby Union, 1994–99. *Recreations:* golf, ski-ing, watching Rugby and motor racing. *Address:* c/o Clydesdale Bank, 15 Academy Street, Inverness IV1 7JN. *Club:* Army and Navy (Chm., 2009–12).

MACAIRE, Robert Nigel Paul, CMG 2009; HM Diplomatic Service; on leave of absence as Director for Political Risk, BG Group, since 2011; *b* 19 Feb. 1966; *s* of James and Tatiana Macaire; *m* 1996, Alice Mackenzie; two *d*. *Educ:* Cranleigh Sch.; St Edmund Hall, Oxford (BA Modern Hist.). Gen. Staff Secretariat and Policy Studies Secretariat, MoD, 1987–90; entered FCO, 1990; Falkland Is Dept, FCO, 1990–91; Bucharest, 1992–95; Near East and N Africa Dept, then Africa Dept Southern, FCO, 1995–98; First Sec., Washington, 1998–2002; Hd, Counter Terrorism Policy Dept, FCO, 2002–04; Counsellor (Political), New Delhi, 2004–06; Dir, Consular Services, FCO, 2006–08; High Comr, Kenya, 2008–11. *Recreations:* sailing, riding, polo. *Address:* c/o Foreign and Commonwealth Office, King Charles Street, SW1A 2AH. *Clubs:* Royal Ocean Racing; Nairobi Polo.

McALEER, Declan Martin; Member (SF) West Tyrone, Northern Ireland Assembly, since July 2012; *b* Omagh, 10 July 1973; *s* of Barney and Kathleen McAleer; *m* 2001, Geraldine Rafferty; two *s* one *d*. *Educ:* Univ. of Ulster (BSc Hons Social Psychol. and Sociol.; PGCFHE; MSc Applied Psychol.). Lectr in Psychol., Omagh Coll., 1999–2012; teacher in Psychol. and Health and Social Care, Dean Maguire Coll., 2003–07. Mem., Western Educn Liby Bd, 2006–12. Chair and Dir, Loughmacrory Community Develt Assoc., 2011–. *Recreations:* community development, Gaelic football. *Address:* 4 James Street, Omagh, Co. Tyrone BT78 1DH. *T:* (028) 8225 3040. *E:* declanmcaleer@ymail.com.

McALEESE, Kevin Stanley, CBE 1998; education consultant; Chairman, NHS North Yorkshire and York, 2009–13; *b* 28 Feb. 1947; *s* of late James McAleese, DFM and of Marjorie N. A. McAleese; (*née* Stromberg); *m* 1st, 1976, Dorothy Anne Nelson (*d* 1998); one *s* one *d*; 2nd, 2000, Jenny Louise Brindle (*née* Grant). *Educ:* London Nautical Sch.; Keele Univ. (BEd 1972); Univ. of Kent (MA 1985). Midshipman, subseq. Navigating Officer, Blue Funnel Line, 1964–68; Asst Teacher, West Hatch Technical High Sch., 1972–75; Head of Dept, Queen's Sch., Jt HQ Rheindahlen, 1975–78; Head of Faculty, Grange County Secondary Sch., 1978–81; Sen. Teacher, Sheppey Sch., 1981–84; Dep. Head Teacher, Geoffrey Chaucer Sch.,

Canterbury, 1984–87; Head Teacher: Alec Hunter High Sch., Braintree, 1987–91; Harrogate Grammar Sch., 1992–2002. Joint Chairman for NHS Employers: NHS Wkg Longer Rev. Steering Gp, 2012–14; NHS Pension Scheme Governance Gp, 2012–14. Ind. Chm., City of York Safeguarding Adults Bd, 2013–. Vice Chm., Northern Education, 2009–11. Chm., York Housing Assoc., 2014–. Chm., Ind. Adv. Panel, Army Foundn Coll., Harrogate, 2012–. Non-exec. Dir, 2002–06, Vice-Chm., 2004–06, Craven, Harrogate and Rural Dist PCT; non-exec. Dir and Vice-Chm., N Yorks and York PCT, 2006–09. Chm., RAF Menwith Hill British-Amer. Cttee, 2003–09. FRSA 1993; FCMI (FIMgt 1995). *Publications:* Managing the Margins, 1996; Balancing the Books, 2000; articles and series in TES and Managing Schools Today. *Recreations:* cinema, photography, music, walking, travelling. *Address:* 11 Hazel Drive, Burn Bridge, Harrogate, N Yorks HG3 1NY. *T:* (01423) 815147.

McALEESE, Mary Patricia, (Mrs Martin McAleese); President of Ireland, 1997–2011; *b* 27 June 1951; *d* of Patrick Leneghan and Claire (*née* McManus); *m* 1976, Martin McAleese; one *s* two *d*. *Educ:* QUB (LLB 1973); TCD (MA 1986); Dip. in Spanish, Inst. of Linguists, 1994; Nat. Univ. of Ireland (MA Theol. 2010); Pontifical Gregorian Univ., Rome (Lic. Canon Law 2012). AIL. Called to the Bar: N Ireland, 1974; King's Inns, Dublin, 1978. Barrister, NI, 1974–75; Reid Prof. of Criminal Law, Criminology and Penology, TCD, 1975–79 and 1981–87; journalist and TV presenter, Radio Telefis Eireann, 1979–81 (part-time presenter, 1981–85); Queen's University, Belfast: Dir, Inst. of Professional Legal Studies, 1987–97; Pro Vice-Chancellor, 1994–97. Burns Schol., Boston Coll., 2013; Vis. Fellow, Univ. of Notre Dame, 2014. Director: Northern Ireland Electricity, 1991–97; Channel 4 Television, 1992–97; Royal Gp of Hospitals HSS Trust, Belfast, 1996–97. *Publications:* (jtly) Reports on Irish Penal System, 1981; Children in Custody (ed Stewart and Tutt), 1987; (jtly) Sectarianism: a discussion document, 1993; Reconciled Being, 1997; Building Bridges, 2011; Quo Vadis? Collegiality in the Code of Canon Law, 2012; contrib. legal and religious jls. *Recreations:* hill-walking, set dancing, reading, theology.

McALISKEY, (Josephine) Bernadette, (Mrs Micheal McAliskey); Co-ordinator, South Tyrone Empowerment Programme; *b* 23 April 1947; *d* of late John James Devlin and Elizabeth Devlin; *m* 1973, Micheal McAliskey; three *c*. *Educ:* St Patrick's Girls' Acad., Dungannon; psychology student at Queen's Univ., Belfast, 1966–69. Youngest MP in House of Commons when elected at age of 21; MP (Ind. Unity) Mid Ulster, April 1969–Feb. 1974. Founder Member and Mem. Exec., Irish Republican Socialist Party, 1975–76. Former Chm., Ind. Socialist Party, Ireland. Contested: (Ind) N Ireland, European Parlt, 1979; (People's Democracy), Dublin N Central, Dáil Eireann, Feb. and Nov. 1982. *Publications:* The Price of my Soul (autobiog.), 1969. *Recreations:* walking, folk music, doing nothing, swimming.

McALISTER, William Harle Nelson; Associate Director, Media Trust, since 2013; independent arts producer; *b* 30 Aug. 1940; *s* of Flying Officer William Nelson, DFC (*d* 1940) and late Marjorie Isobel (*née* McIntyre); adopted by late William Edwyn McAlister (whom she *m* 2nd); *m* 1968 (marr. diss. 1985); two *s* two *d*; one *s*. *Educ:* Sorbonne, Paris; Univ. of Copenhagen; University Coll. London (BA Hons Psychology, 1967). Dir, Almost Free Theatre, 1968–72; Dep. Dir, Inter-Action Trust, 1968–72; Founder Dir, Islington Bus Co., 1972–77; Director: Battersea Arts Centre, 1976–77; ICA, 1977–90; Creative Research Ltd, 1989–91; Beaconsfield Gall., 1999–; Ambient TV Ltd, 2000–; hiddenart.com, 2002–. Dir, Sense of Ireland Fest., 1980; Bd Dir, London International Theatre Fest., 1983; Chm. for the Arts, IT 82 Cttee, 1982. Chm., Recreational Trust, 1972–88; Co-Founder, Fair Play for Children, 1974–75; Advr, Task Force Trust, 1972–74; Cultural Policy Advr, Soros Foundns, 1992–97; Sen. Advr, Tonguesten, 2013–. Trustee: Circle 33 Housing Trust, 1972–75; Moving Picture Mime Trust, 1978–80; Shape (Arts for the Disadvantaged), 1979–81. Trustee: International House, 1989–; Africa Centre, 1990–2000; World Circuit Arts, 1996–2000. Governor: Holloway Adult Educn Inst., 1974–76; Byam Shaw Sch. of Art, 2000–. Patient Gov., UCL Hosp. Foundn Trust, 2011–. Mem. Court, RCA, 1980–90. CSCE British Deleg., Krakow, Poland, 1991. *Publications:* Community Psychology, 1975; EEC and the Arts, 1978; (contrib.) Art and Society, 1999; articles on arts policy. *Recreations:* mycology, angling, tennis, travel. *Address:* 151c Grosvenor Avenue, N5 2NH. *T:* 07956 229796. *E:* bill.mcalister@gmail.com.

McALLION, John; Member (Lab) Dundee East, Scottish Parliament, 1999–2003; *b* 13 Feb. 1948; *s* of Joseph and Norah McAllion; *m* 1971, Susan Jean Godlonton; two *s*. *Educ:* St Augustine's Comprehensive School, Glasgow; St Andrews Univ. (MA Hons 2nd cl. Modern and Medieval Hist. 1972); Dundee Coll. of Education. Civil Servant, Post Office, 1967–68; History Teacher, St Saviour's High Sch., Dundee, 1973–78; Social Studies Teacher, Balgowan Sch., Dundee, 1978–82; Research Asst to Bob McTaggart, 1982–86. Regional Councillor, 1984–87, Convener, 1986–87, Tayside Regional Council. MP (Lab) Dundee East, 1987–2001. Contested (Lab) Dundee E, Scottish Parlt, 2003. *Recreations:* sport, reading, music. *Address:* 3 Haldane Street, Dundee DD3 0HP. *T:* (01382) 826678.

McALLISTER, Adrian; Chief Executive, Office of Police Ombudsman for Northern Ireland, since 2013; *b* Walsall, W Midlands, 20 Sept. 1962; *s* of Peter Ernest McAllister and Patricia Hilda McAllister; *m* 2007, Julie Winfield; one *d*. *Educ:* Streetly Comprehensive Sch.; Univ. of Loughborough (BA Hons Politics with Econs); Univ. of Manchester (MA Police and Public Sector Mgt); Univ. of Cambridge (Dip. Applied Criminol.). With W Midlands Police, 1985–97; Detective Superintendent, Merseyside Police, 1997–2000; Lancashire Police: Detective Chief Superintendent, 2000–02; Asst Chief Constable, 2002–05; Actg Dep. Chief Constable, 2005–07; Chief Exec., Ind. Safeguarding Authy, 2007–12. *Recreations:* sport, football, squash, golf, cycling, contemporary music, cooking, current affairs. *Address:* Police Ombudsman Office, New Cathedral Buildings, 11 Church Street, Belfast BT1 1PG. *T:* (028) 9082 8680, *Fax:* (028) 9082 8615. *E:* adrian.mcallister@policeombudsman.org.

McALLISTER, Sir Ian (Gerald), Kt 2008; CBE 1996; Chairman, Carbon Trust, 2001–11; *b* 17 Aug. 1943; *s* of Ian Thomas McAllister and Margaret Mary McAllister (*née* McNally); *m* 1968, Susan Margaret Frances Mitchell; three *s* one *d*. *Educ:* Thornleigh College, Bolton; University College London (BScEcon; Fellow, 2009). Ford Motor Co.: operations and marketing appts, 1964–79; Director: Parts Sales, 1980; Product and Marketing Parts Ops, 1981; Car Sales Ops, 1983; Marketing Plans and Programmes, 1984; Sales, Ford Germany, 1987; Gen. Marketing Manager, Lincoln Mercury Div., USA, 1989; Man. Dir, 1991–2002, and Chm. and Chief Exec., 1992–2002. Chm., Network Rail, 2002–09. Vice-President: Inst. of the Motor Industry, 1992–2002; SMMT (Pres., 1996–98). Mem. Bd and Council, BITC, 1994–2002. Non-executive Director: Scottish & Newcastle plc, 1996–2008; UCL Business Bd, 2007–. Mem. Adv. Bd, Victim Support, 1994. Member: Adv. Cttee on Business and the Envmt, 1996–2004; Welfare to Work Task Force, 1997–2001; Bd, QCA, 1997–2003 (Dep. Chm., 2000–03); Co-Chm., Cleaner Vehicles Task Force, 1997–2000; Chairman: Greater Essex Prosperity Forum, 2007–09; Essex Economic Bd, 2009–10. Hon. PhD: E London, 1993; Loughborough, 1999; Hon. LLD Nottingham, 1995. *Recreation:* golf.

McALLISTER, John Brian; Chairman, Selbourne Care Ltd, since 2004; *b* 11 June 1941; *s* of late Thomas McAllister and of Jane (*née* McCloughan); *m* 1st, 1966, Margaret Lindsay Walker (*d* 2002); two *d*; 2nd, 2004, Lynne Patricia Oldham. *Educ:* Royal Belfast Academical Instn; Queen's Univ., Belfast (BA Hons). Joined NI Civil Service as Asst Principal, Dept of Educn, 1964; Dep. Principal, Higher Educn Div., 1968; Principal: Secondary Schs Br., 1969; Re-Organisation of Local Govt Br., 1970; Principal, Dept of Finance, 1971, Dept's Central Secretariat, 1972; Asst Sec. 1973, Sen. Asst Sec. 1976, Dep. Sec., 1978–80, Dept of Educn; Dep. Sec., later Under Sec., Dept of Finance, 1980–83; Under Sec., DoE, NI, 1983–84; Dep. Chief Exec., 1984–85, Chief Exec., 1985–88, Industrial Develt Bd for NI; Chief Exec., Crestacare (formerly Cresta Hldgs Ltd), 1990–93 (Gp Man. Dir, 1988–90); consultant, 1993–94; Chief Exec., 1994–96, Chm., 1996–99, Craegmoor Healthcare; Chief Exec., Sapphire House Ltd, 1999–2006. *Recreations:* watching sport of all kinds, reading, travel.

See also Dame J. I. Harbison.

McALLISTER, Prof. Laura, PhD; Professor of Governance, University of Liverpool, since 2004; *b* Bridgend, Wales, 10 Dec. 1964; *d* of William Keith McAllister and Ann Eiluned McAllister; partner, 2002, Llinos Jones. *Educ:* Bryntirion Comprehensive Sch., Bridgend; London Sch. of Econs and Pol Sci. (BSc (Econ) Hons 1988); Cardiff Univ. (PhD 1996; Hon. Fellow, 2013). Chair, Sport Wales, 2010–; Board Member: Welsh Football Trust, 2004–; UK Sport, 2010–. Mem., Welsh Assembly Remuneration Bd, 2014–. Chair, Inst. of Welsh Affairs Women, 2009–; Board Member: Wales Adv. Cttee, British Council, 2011–; Stonewall, 2012–15. Hon. Fellow: Bangor Univ., 2011; Cardiff Metropolitan Univ., 2014. Hon. Dr Glamorgan, 2011. *Publications:* Plaid Cymru: the emergence of a political party, 2001; Women, Politics and Constitutional Change, 2006; contribs to internat. jls. *Recreations:* sport, football, dogs. *Address:* Management School, University of Liverpool, Chatham Building, Chatham Street, Liverpool L69 7ZH. *T:* (0151) 795 3815, *Fax:* (0151) 795 3104. *E:* l.mcallister@liv.ac.uk. *Clubs:* Cardiff City Amateur Football, Cardiff City Ladies Football.

McALPINE, Joan; Member (SNP) Scotland South, Scottish Parliament, since 2011; *b* Gourock, Renfrewshire, 28 Jan.; *d* of James Campbell McAlpine and Mary Esther McAlpine (*née* McCourt); *m* 1987, Patrick Kane (separated 2002); two *d*. *Educ:* St Columba's Comprehensive Sch., Greenock; Univ. of Glasgow (MA Hons Econ. Hist. and Scottish Hist. 1985); City Univ., London (Postgrad. Dip. Newspaper Journalism). Writer: Greenock Telegraph, 1987–89; Scotsman, 1989–95; Daily Record, 1995–96; writer, columnist, then Ed., Sunday Times Scotland, 1996–2001; Dep. Ed., The Herald, 2001–07; columnist and Ed. of Features, Sunday Times Scotland, 2007–10. *Recreations:* family, reading, the arts. *Address:* Scottish Parliament, Edinburgh EH99 1SP. *T:* (0131) 348 6885. *E:* joan.mcalpine.msp@scottish.parliament.uk.

McALPINE, Robert James, FCIOB; Director, Alfred McAlpine plc, 1957–94 (Chairman, 1983–92); *b* 6 May 1932; *s* of late Alfred James McAlpine and of Peggy (*née* Saunders); *m* 1st, Mary Jane Anton; two *s* one *d*; 2nd, Angela Bell (*née* Langford Brooke); one *d*. *Educ:* Harrow Sch. FCIOB. Director: Chester Racecourse Co., 1976–2008 (Chm., 1994–2008; Pres., 2008–); Haynes Hanson & Clark, 1978– (Chm., 1993–); Hall Engrg plc, 1985–99; Aintree Racecourse Co., 1988–2007. Chm., Export Gp for Constructional Industries, 1975–77. Mem., Jockey Club. High Sheriff, Cheshire, 1994–95. *Recreations:* racing, shooting, golf, bridge. *Address:* Tilstone Lodge, Tilstone Fearnall, Tarporley, Cheshire CW6 9HS. *Clubs:* White's, Turf, Portland, MCC.

McALPINE, Hon. Sir William (Hepburn), 6th Bt *cr* 1918, of Knott Park; FRSE; FCILT; company director; *b* 12 Jan. 1936; *s* of Lord McAlpine of Moffat (Life Peer) and Ella Mary Gardner Garnett (*d* 1987); *S* to baronetcy of father, 1990; *m* 1st, 1959, Jill Benton (*d* 2004), *o d* of Lt-Col Sir Peter Fawcett Benton Jones, 3rd Bt, OBE, ACA; one *s* one *d*; 2nd, 2004, Judy, *d* of late William Harry Sanderson and *widow* of Graham Nicholls. *Educ:* Charterhouse. Life Guards, 1954–56. Dir, Sir Robert McAlpine Ltd (formerly Sir Robert McAlpine & Sons Ltd), 1952–2007. FRSA. High Sheriff, Bucks, 1999–2000. *Recreation:* railways. *Heir: s* Andrew William McAlpine [*b* 22 Nov. 1960; *m* 1991, Caroline Claire, *yr d* of Frederick Hodgson; four *s*]. *Address:* Fawley Hill, Fawley Green, Henley-on-Thames, Oxon RG9 6JA. *Clubs:* Garrick, Caledonian.

MACAN, Thomas Townley; HM Diplomatic Service, retired; Governor, British Virgin Islands, 2002–06; *b* 14 Nov. 1946; only *s* of late Dr Thomas Townley Macan and Zaida Bindloss (*née* Boddington); *m* 1976, Janet Ellen Martin, Hollidaysburg, Penn; one *s* one *d*. *Educ:* Shrewsbury Sch.; Univ. of Sussex (BA Hons Econs; Pres., Students' Union, 1967–68). MCIL (MIL 1982). Joined HM Diplomatic Service, 1969; UN Dept, FCO, 1969–71; Bonn, 1971–74; Brasilia, 1974–78; Maritime, Aviation and Envmt Dept, FCO, 1978–81; Press Sec., Bonn, 1981–86; Hd, Commonwealth Co-ordination Dept, FCO, 1986–88; Hd, Trng Dept, FCO, 1988–90; Counsellor, Lisbon, 1990–94; Ambassador to Lithuania, 1995–98; on secondment to BOC Group, 1998–99; Minister and Dep. High Comr, New Delhi, 1999–2002. Mem., Inst. of Tourist Guiding, 2011–; Blue Badge Guide for Cumbria, 2011–. *Recreations:* steam boats, sailing, church architecture, walking. *Address:* Stevney, Outgate, Ambleside, Cumbria LA22 0NH. *Clubs:* Naval; Royal British Virgin Islands Yacht.

McANALLY, Vice-Adm. John Henry Stuart, CB 2000; LVO 1983; Naval Adviser, 2001–05, Senior Military Advisor, 2006–10, to VT Flagship (formerly Flagship Training Ltd); National President, Royal Naval Association, since 2001; *b* 9 April 1945; *s* of late Arthur Patrick McAnally and Mrs Basil Hamilton Stuart McAnally. *Educ:* Willington Prep. Sch., Putney; Westminster Sch. FNI 1999; FRIN 1999. BRNC (RN Scholarship); HM Ships Wizard, Ashanti, Walkerton, Leverton, 1963–67; USS Moale (Exchange), 1967–68; HMS Eskimo, 1968–69; HMA Ships Melbourne and Torrens, 1971–73; CO HMS Iveston, 1973–75; Adv. Navign Course, 1975; HMS Fife, 1976–77; Staff Course, 1978; HMS Birmingham and HMY Britannia, 1979–81; MoD, 1982–83; Comd HM Ships Torquay and Alacrity, 1984–86; Staff of C-in-C Fleet, 1986–87; Captain Sixth Frigate Sqdn and CO HM Ships Ariadne and Hermione, 1987–89; Asst Dir (Warfare), Dir Naval Plans, 1989–91; RCDS 1992; HCSC 1993; Dir, Naval Logistics Staff Duties and Naval Staff Duties, MoD, 1993–95; Flag Officer Trng and Recruiting, and Chief Exec., Naval Recruiting and Trng Agency, 1996–98; Comdt, RCDS, 1998–2001. Ind. Chm., Retired Officer Selection Bds, 2001–03. Pres., Internat. Maritime Confedn, 2009–11. Gov., Corps Security, 2010–; Gov. and Trustee, Corps of Commissionaires Mgt Ltd and Trustees Ltd, 2010–. President: TS Barrosa, 2001–; RN Golf Soc., 2009–14. Mem., Hon. Co. of Master Mariners, 2002. Younger Brother, Trinity House. *Recreation:* golf. *Clubs:* Naval and Military (Vice Chm., 2010–12; Chm., 2012–), National Liberal; Royal Mid-Surrey Golf; Royal Naval and Royal Albert Yacht (Portsmouth); Hayling Golf; Rye Golf; Liphook Golf.

See also M. B. H. McAnally.

McANALLY, Mary Basil Hamilton, (Mrs Hugh Macpherson); media consultant, since 2002; Chairman: That's Media Ltd, since 2012; That's Solent Ltd, since 2012; Director, That's Oxford Ltd, since 2012; *b* 9 April 1945; *d* of late Arthur Patrick McAnally and Basil Hamilton Stuart McAnally; *m* 1979, Hugh Macpherson. *Educ:* Tiffin Girls' Sch.; Wimbledon Art Sch.; London Business Sch. Internat. tennis player, 1963–67; winner, Jun. Indoor Championships of GB, 1963. Researcher, Man Alive, BBC TV, 1969; Prog. Associate, This is Your Life, Thames TV, 1969–71; Series Producer, Thames TV: Money Go Round, 1973–82; Could Do Better, What About the Workers, and The John Smith Show, 1978–80; Series Editor, For What It's Worth, Channel 4, 1982–90 (Winner, Freedom of Information Media Award, 1990); Thames TV: Editor, Daytime, 1984–87; Exec. Prod., The Time the Place, and Anglo-Soviet 'Spacebridges', 1987–91; Head of Features, 1989–92; Meridian Broadcasting Ltd: Controller of Regl Progs and Community Affairs, 1992–94; Dir of Progs, 1994–96; Man. Dir, 1996–2002. Member: Bd, NCC, 1987–97; Adv. Cttee on Advertising, 1999–2002; Ind. Mem., Balancing and Settlement Code Panel, 2002–04; Ind. Dir, Exec. Bd, DTI, 2002–06; Director: Southern Screen Commn, 1997–2000; Screen South, 2002–03; Media Local Solutions Ltd, 2006–14; Chm., Media and Creative Industries Task Force, 1999–2003, and Mem. Bd, 2000–07, SEEDA; Mem. Bd, SE England Cultural Consortium, 2000–03; Mem., SE Regl Assembly, 2007–09. Chm., SE England Regl Sports Bd, 2003–09; SE Regl Rep., 2012 Nations and Regions Gp, 2004–11; non-exec. Dir, Sport England, 2004–06. Pres., Nat. Consumer Fedn, 2009–. FRSA 1990; FRTS 1998. Gov., Portsmouth Univ., 1998–2000.

Publications: (jtly) Buy Right, 1978. *Recreations:* tennis, painting, golf. *Clubs:* Naval and Military, Forum UK; All England Lawn Tennis and Croquet (Mem., Mgt Cttee, 2002–09), Cumberland Lawn Tennis, Highgate Golf, Leckford Golf; Gardeners (Chesham).

See also Vice-Adm. J. H. S. McAnally.

MacANDREW, family name of **Baron MacAndrew**.

MacANDREW, 3rd Baron *cr* 1959, of the Firth of Clyde; **Christopher Anthony Colin MacAndrew;** farmer; *b* 16 Feb. 1945; *s* of 2nd Baron MacAndrew and Ursula Beatrice (*née* Steel) (*d* 1986); *S* father, 1989; *m* 1975, Sarah (marr. diss. 2005), *o d* of Lt-Col P. H. and Mrs Brazier; one *s* two *d*. *Educ:* Malvern. Tax Comr, 1996–2009. *Recreations:* follower of cricket, football, Rugby, golf, tennis and motor racing. *Heir: s* Hon. Oliver Charles Julian MacAndrew, *b* 3 Sept. 1983. *Address:* 54B Sutherland Avenue, W9 2QU.

McANDREW, Daisy Candida Leslie; freelance reporter, presenter and journalist, since 2013; Special Correspondent, ITV News, 2011–13; *b* London, 20 May 1972; *d* of Alistair and Camilla Sampson; *m* 2005, John McAndrew; one *s* one *d*. *Educ:* Wycombe Abbey Sch.; Cambridge Coll. of Sixth Form Studies. Researcher for Sir Patrick Cormack, MP, 1991; political journalist, Press Gall., H of C, 1992–99; Man. Ed., House Mag., 1995–97; Press. Sec. to Charles Kennedy, MP, 1999–2001; Co-presenter, Daily Politics prog. and political corresp., Breakfast News, BBC TV, 2001–05; presenter, Drivetime, LBC Radio, 2005; Chief Political Corresp., 2005–08, Econs Ed., 2008–11, ITV News. *Publications:* (consultant) BBC's A-Z of Politics, 2000; (ed) The Politics Companion, 2004. *Recreations:* entertaining friends and family, playing with my children.

McANDREW, Nicolas; Chairman, Murray Johnstone Ltd, 1992–99; *b* 9 Dec. 1934; *s* of late Robert Louis McAndrew and Anita Marian McAndrew (*née* Huband); *m* 1960, Diana Leonie Wood (*d* 2015); two *s* one *d*. *Educ:* Winchester Coll. CA 1961. Commnd Black Watch, 1953–55. With Peat, Marwick, Mitchell & Co., 1955–61; S. G. Warburg & Co. Ltd, 1962–78: Dir, 1969–78; Chm., Warburg Investment Mgt, 1975–78; Dir, Mercury Securities Ltd, 1975–78; N. M. Rothschild & Sons Ltd, 1979–88 (Man. Dir, 1980–88); Murray Johnstone Ltd, 1988–99 (Man. Dir, 1988–92). Board Member: Highlands & Islands Enterprise, 1993–97; N of Scotland Water Authy, 1995–2002. Deputy Chairman: Burn Stewart Distillers PLC, 1991–99; Liverpool Victoria Friendly Soc., 1995–2005; Chairman: Martin Currie Enhanced Income Trust (formerly Moorgate Investment Trust) PLC, 1996–2005; Guinness Flight Extra Income Trust, 1995–2002; Derby Trust PLC, 1999–2003. Chairman: Highlands and Is Rivers Assoc., 2001–05; Beauly Dist Fishery Bd, 2003–12. Master, Grocers' Co., 1978–79. *Recreations:* shooting, fishing, golf, bridge. *Address:* Ard-na-Coille, Ruisaurie, by Beauly, Inverness-shire IV4 7AJ. *T:* (01463) 782524. *Club:* White's.

MACAPAGAL-ARROYO, Dr Gloria; Member for 2nd District of Pampanga, House of Representatives, Republic of the Philippines, since 2010; *b* 5 April 1947; *d* of Diosdado Macapagal (former Pres. of the Philippines), and Dr Evangelina Macaraeg-Macapagal; *m* Jose Miguel Arroyo; two *s* one *d*. *Educ:* Georgetown Univ. (BA Econs); Assumption Coll. (BSc Commerce *magna cum laude*); Ateneo de Manila Univ. (MA Econs); Univ. of the Philippines (PhD Econs). Chair, Econs Dept, Assumption Coll.; Asst Prof., Ateneo de Manila Univ.; Sen. Lectr, Sch. of Econs, Univ. of the Philippines; Asst Sec., 1986–89, Under-Sec., 1989, DTI, Philippines; Sec., Dept of Social Welfare and Develt, 1998; Vice-Pres., 1998–2001, Pres., 2001–10, Republic of the Philippines. Exec. Dir, Garments and Textiles Bd, 1987. Mem., Senate of the Philippines, 1992–98. Hon. Mem., Philippine Mil. Acad. Cl. of 1978. Hon. Dr: Tsinghua, China, 2001; Chulalongkorn, Thailand, 2002; Hon. LLD Waseda, Japan, 2002. *Publications:* (with V. M. Cunanan) Socio-Economic Impact of Tourism: a measurement and analysis system, 1979; (with M. San Buenaventura) The Economic and Social Impact of Tourism, 1983; The Services Sector in the Philippines, 1984; Getting Our Act Together: a President's campaign against the sexual exploitation of children, 2001; contrib. papers on tourism. *Recreations:* playing golf with the First Gentleman, watching movies with children, reading good books. *Address:* House of Representatives, Constitution Hills, Quezon City 1126, Philippines.

MACARA, (John David) Murray; QC (Scot.) 2008; Partner, Beltrami & Co., since 1975; *b* Glasgow, 22 July 1949; *s* of Alexander Macara and Mary Hamilton Macara (*née* Smillie); *m* 1981, Elaine Graham; one *d*. *Educ:* Loretto Sch., Musselburgh; Univ. of Glasgow (LLB 1970). Admitted solicitor, 1973; Solicitor Advocate, 1993. *Recreations:* golf, travel, the company of friends. *Address:* 10 Rowan Road, Glasgow G41 5BS. *T:* (0141) 427 4060. *E:* macara@btinternet.com. *Club:* Pollok Golf.

McARDLE, Tony, TD 1990; Chief Executive, Lincolnshire County Council, since 2005; *b* 31 Jan. 1958; *s* of William and Olive McArdle; one *s* two *d*. *Educ:* Knockbreda Primary Sch., Belfast; Methodist Coll., Belfast; Univ. of Essex (BA Hons Govt). Free Trade Dept, Adnams plc, 1980–85; East Cambridgeshire District Council: Emergency Planning Officer, 1985–87; Asst to Chief Exec., 1987–89; Corp. Support Manager, 1989–92; Hd, Community Services, 1992–95; Asst Chief Exec., 1995–98; Chief Exec., Wellingborough BC, 1998–2005. Territorial Army, 1977–99: commnd; Royal Anglian Regt, 1979; regtl appts, 1979–95; Second i/c, Cambridge Univ. OTC, 1995–98; CO 49 Bde BSTT, 1998–99. *Address:* c/o Lincolnshire County Council, Newland, Lincoln LN1 1YQ. *T:* (01522) 514985, *Fax:* (01522) 552004. *E:* tony.mcardle@lincolnshire.gov.uk.

McAREAVEY, Most Rev. John; *see* Dromore, Bishop of, (RC).

MacARTHUR, Brian; Associate Editor, The Times, 1995–2006 (Executive Editor (Features), 1991–95); Assistant Editor, Daily Telegraph, 2006–10; *b* 5 Feb. 1940; *o s* of late S. H. MacArthur and Mrs M. MacArthur; *m* 1st, 1966, Peta Deschampsneufs (*d* 1971); 2nd, 1975, Bridget Trahair (marr. diss. 1997); two *d*; 3rd, 2000, Maureen Waller. *Educ:* Brentwood Sch.; Helsby Grammar Sch.; Leeds Univ. (BA). Yorkshire Post, 1962–64; Daily Mail, 1964–66; The Guardian, 1966–67; The Times: Education Correspondent, 1967–70; Founder Editor, The Times Higher Educn Supplement, 1971–76; Home News Editor, 1976–78; Dep. Editor, Evening Standard, 1978–79; Chief Asst to the Editor, The Sunday Times, 1979–81; Exec. Editor (News), The Times, 1981–82; Jt Dep. Editor, The Sunday Times, 1982–84; Editor, Western Morning News, 1984–85; Editor-in-Chief, Today, 1986–87; Exec. Ed., The Sunday Times, 1987–91. Hon. MA Open Univ., 1976; Hon. DArts Plymouth, 2011. *Publications:* Eddy Shah: Today and the Newspaper Revolution, 1988; Deadline Sunday, 1991; (ed) The Penguin Book of Twentieth Century Speeches, 1992; (ed) The Penguin Book of Historic Speeches, 1995; Requiem, 1997; (ed) The Penguin Book of Twentieth Century Protest, 1998; Gulf War Despatches, 2001; Surviving the Sword: prisoners of the Japanese 1942–1945, 2005; For King and Country: voices from the First World War, 2008; (ed) The Penguin Book of Modern Speeches, 2012. *Recreations:* vegetable gardening, cooking. *Address:* Church Farm House, The Street, Little Barningham, Norwich NR11 7AG. *T:* (01263) 577369. *Club:* Garrick.

McARTHUR, Surgeon Rear Adm. Calum James Gibb, FRCGP; Commander Joint Medical Command, and Medical Director General (Naval) and Chief Naval Medical Officer, 2012–14; *b* Glasgow, 10 Nov. 1956; *s* of James McArthur and Joan McArthur; *m* 1989, Barbara Halliday. *Educ:* Glasgow Acad.; Royal Coll. of Surgeons in Ireland (MB BCh 1980; BAO 1980; LRCPI 1980). MRCGP 1986, FRCGP 2005; DRCOG 1990; Dip. Occupational Medicine 1995. PMO HM Naval Base Portsmouth and Advr in Gen. Practice, RN, 2001–04; rcds 2005; Dep. ACOS Med. PJHQ, 2005–07; Standing Jt Comdr Med., 2007–09; Comdr Defence Med. Gp, 2009–11; Hd Med. Operational Capability, 2011–12; QHP 2011–15. Non-exec. Dir, Poole Hosp. NHS Foundn Trust, 2014–. *Recreations:* antiques, paintings, gardening, keeping fit. *Address:* c/o Naval Secretary, Fleet Headquarters, Whale Island, Portsmouth PO2 8BY. *T:* (020) 7807 0471. *E:* cjgmcarthur@gmail.com. *Club:* Army and Navy.

McARTHUR, Douglas Brown, OBE 2001; Chairman, UK Online Measurement Ltd, since 2010; Managing Consultant, Planning for Results, since 2006; *b* Dundee, March 1951; *s* of Ronald McArthur and Edith McArthur; *m* 2006, Miranda Kennett; three *d*. *Educ:* Univ. of Glasgow (BSc Hons 1st Cl.). Marketing Manager: Procter & Gamble, 1973–75; Scottish and Newcastle, 1976–79; Founder, Town Art and Design, 1979–79; Sales and Mktg Dir, Radio Clyde, 1983–85; Dir, Baillie Marshall Advertising, 1986–90; Dir, Mktg, Campbell's Soups, 1990–92; Founder and CEO, Radio Advertising Bureau, 1992–2006. Mem., Marketing Soc. *Recreations:* trekking, theatre, arts. *Clubs:* 30; Marketing Gp of GB; Solus.

MACARTHUR, Dame Ellen (Patricia), DBE 2005 (MBE 2001); professional offshore sailor; *b* 8 July 1976; *d* of Kenneth John Macarthur and Avril Patricia Macarthur. *Educ:* Anthony Gell Sch., Wirksworth. RYA Yachtmaster Commercial; RYA Yachtmaster Instructor. Winner: Class II (Open 50) Route du Rhum solo trans-Atlantic race, 1998, Class I (Open 60), 2002; (Open 60) Europe 1 New Man STAR solo trans-Atlantic race, 2000; EDS Atlantic Challenge, 2001; 2nd overall, Vendée Globe non-stop solo round-the-world race, 2001; fastest solo circumnavigation of the globe (World Record, 71 days, 14 hours, 18 mins and 33 secs), 2005. Founder: Ellen MacArthur Cancer Trust, 2002–; Founder and Chair of Trustees, Ellen Macarthur Foundn, 2009–. Young Sailor of the Year, 1995, Yachtsman of the Year, 1999, Yachting Journalists' Assoc.; FICO World Champion, 2001; ISAF World Champion Woman Sailor, 2001. Freeman, Skye and Lochalsh, 2006. Chevalier, Légion d'Honneur (France), 2008. *Publications:* Taking on the World (autobiog.), 2002; Race Against Time, 2005; Full Circle, 2010.

McARTHUR, Dr John Duncan, FRCPGlas; Consultant Cardiologist, Western Infirmary, Glasgow, 1978–2003; *b* 7 Jan. 1938; *s* of Neil McPhail McArthur and Elizabeth Duncan; *m* 1st, 1963, Elizabeth Agnew Bowie (*d* 2004); two *s* one *d*; 2nd, 2014, Elizabeth, (Betty) Gray King. *Educ:* Univ. of Glasgow (BSc Hons 1960; MB ChB Hons 1963); DM Madras 1970. DObstRCOG 1965; MRCP 1966; MRCPGlas 1966, FRCPGlas 1980; MRCPE 1967, FRCPE 1994. Junior House Officer, Glasgow Royal Infirmary and Ayrshire Hosps, 1963–65; Senior House Officer and Registrar, Glasgow Royal Inf., 1965–67; Lectr, Sen. Lectr, Reader, Christian Med. Coll. Hosp., Vellore, India, as Missionary, Church of Scotland, 1968–73; Sen. Registrar, Medicine/Cardiology, Glasgow Teaching Hosps, 1973–78; Consultant Cardiologist, Nuffield Hosp., Glasgow, 1985–2007. Elder, Ch of Scotland. *Publications:* articles on valvular heart disease and pacemakers. *Recreations:* DIY, gardening. *E:* jd.mcarthur@ntlworld.com.

MacARTHUR, Judy Anne; *see* MacArthur Clark, J. A.

McARTHUR, Liam Scott; Member (Lib Dem) Orkney, Scottish Parliament, since 2007; *b* 8 Aug. 1967; *s* of William Archibald McArthur and Susan Margaret McArthur; *m* 1998, Tamsin Bailey; two *s*. *Educ:* Sanday Jun. High Sch.; Kirkwall Grammar Sch.; Univ. of Edinburgh (MA Pols 1990). Res. Asst to Jim Wallace, MP, 1990–92; Stagiaire, External Affairs, EC, 1992–93; Account Dir, APCO Worldwide, London and Brussels, 1995–2002; Special Advr to Dep. First Minister, Scottish Exec., 2002–05. Scottish Parliament: Lib Dem spokesman on enterprise, energy and tourism, 2007–08, on envmt, rural develt and energy, 2008–11, on educn, skills and energy, later energy, educn and young people, 2011–; Member: Finance Cttee, 2007–08; Rural Affairs and Envmt Cttee, 2008–11; Educn and Culture Cttee, 2011–. Mem., Scottish Lib Dem Policy Cttee, 2007–. *Recreations:* football, music. *Address:* Scottish Parliament, Edinburgh EH99 1SP. *T:* (0131) 348 5815. *E:* liam.mcarthur.msp@scottish.parliament.uk.

McARTHUR, Dr Thomas Burns, (Tom); English teacher, since 1959; feature writer, since 1962; lecturer and writer on yoga and Indian philosophy, since 1962; author and language consultant, since 1970; Editor, English Today, 1984–2007; *b* 23 Aug. 1938; *s* of Archibald McArthur and Margaret Burns; *m* 1st, 1963, Fereshteh Mottahedin (*d* 1993); one *s* two *d*; 2nd, 2001, Jacqueline Lam Kam-mei. *Educ:* Glasgow Univ. (MA 1958); Edinburgh Univ. (MLitt 1970; PhD 1978). Officer-Instr, RAEC, 1959–61; Asst Master, Riland Bedford Sch., Warwicks, 1961–63; Head of English, Cathedral and John Connon Sch., Bombay, India, 1965–67; Vis. Prof. in the English of the Media, Rajendra Prasad College of Mass Communication (Bharatiya Vidya Bhavan), Univ. of Bombay, 1965–67; Dir of Extra-Mural English Language Courses, Univ. of Edinburgh, 1972–79; Associate Prof. of English, Université du Québec à Trois-Rivières, Canada, 1979–83; Recognised Teacher (pt-time), 1986–2001, Res. Fellow, 1992–2001, Exeter Univ. Co-founder (with Reinhard Hartmann), Internat. Lexicography Course, Univ. of Exeter, 1987–2001. Consultant: Min. of Educn, Quebec, 1980–81; Société pour la promotion de l'enseignement de l'anglais (langue seconde) au Québec, 1980–83; Henson International Television (the Muppets), 1985–86; Dictionary Res. Centre, Exeter Univ., 1987–90; BBC Policy Planning Unit, 1992; also on dictionaries, encyclopedias and ELT books published by Century Hutchinson, Chambers, Collins, CUP, Longman, Macmillan, OUP and Time-Life. The Story of English (BBC radio series with D. Crystal), 1987. Member, Editorial Board: Internat. Jl of Lexicography, 1988–98; World Englishes, 1993–; Editl Advr, The Good Book Guide, 1992–; Mem., Internat. Adv. Bd, Logos, 1994–96. Hon. PhD Uppsala, 1999. *Publications:* Patterns of English series, 1972–74; English for Students of Economics, 1973; (with Beryl Atkins) Collins Dictionary of English Phrasal Verbs, 1974; (ed with A. J. Aitken) Languages of Scotland, 1979; Longman Lexicon of Contemporary English, 1981; A Foundation Course for Language Teachers, 1983; The Written Word, Books 1 and 2, 1984; Worlds of Reference, 1986; Yoga and the Bhagavad-Gita, 1986; Understanding Yoga, 1986; Unitive Thinking, 1988 (Beyond Logic and Mysticism, USA, 1990); The English Language as Used in Quebec: a survey, 1989; (ed) The Oxford Companion to the English Language, 1992, concise edn 1998; (ed with Ilan Kernerman) Lexicography in Asia, 1998; Living Words: language, lexicography and the knowledge revolution, 1998; The English Languages, 1998; The Oxford Guide to World English, 2002. *Recreations:* reading, television, walking, cycling, travel. *Address:* 22–23 Ventress Farm Court, Cherry Hinton Road, Cambridge CB1 8HD. *T:* (01223) 245934.

MacARTHUR CLARK, Dr Judy Anne, CBE 2004; FRSB; Principal, JMC Consultancy, since 1991; Head, Animals in Science Regulation Unit, Home Office, since 2011; *b* 18 Nov. 1950; *d* of Archibald Alastair Cameron MacArthur and Elinore Muriel MacArthur (*née* Warde); *m* 1991, David Wayne Clark; two *s* two *d*. *Educ:* Orton Longueville Grammar Sch.; Glasgow Univ. (BVMS 1973); MRCVS 1973; DLAS 1985; DipECLAM 2001; DACLAM 2007. Vet. Officer, UFAW, 1974–76; SSO, MoD, 1976–82; Director: G. D. Searle, 1982–86; Pfizer, UK, 1986–91; Vet. Dir, BioZone Ltd, 1992–2005; Vice-Pres., Worldwide Comparative Medicine, Pfizer, USA, 2005–07; Chief Inspector, Animals Scientific Procedures Inspectorate, 2007–11. Mem., BBSRC, 1996–99; Chair, Farm Animal Welfare Council, 1999–2004. Pres., RCVS, 1992–93. FRSB (FIBiol 1997); FRAgS 2007 (ARAgS 2002). Hon. DVMS Glasgow, 2001. *Publications:* numerous scientific papers. *Recreations:* gardening, exploring remote places, especially with my family. *Address:* Home Office, Peel Building, 2 Marsham Street, SW1P 4DF. *T:* (020) 7035 0751. *E:* judy.macarthurclark@homeoffice.gsi.gov.uk. *Club:* Farmers.

MACARTNEY, Sir John Ralph, 7th Bt *cr* 1799, of Lish, Co. Armagh; *b* 24 July 1945; *o s* of Sir John Barrington Macartney, 6th Bt and Amy Isobel Reinke; *S* father, 1999, but his name does not appear on the Official Roll of the Baronetage; *m* 1966, Suzanne Marie Fowler; four *d*. *Heir: cousin* John Alexander Macartney [*b* 1961; *m* 1986, Robyn Mary Norling (marr. diss. 2003)].

MacASKILL, Ewen; Defence and Security Correspondent, The Guardian, since 2013 (US Bureau Chief, 2007–13); *b* 29 Oct. 1951; *s* of John Angus MacAskill and Catherine Euphemia MacAskill (*née* MacDonald); *m* 1976, Sarah Anne Hutchison; three *s*. *Educ:* Woodside Secondary Sch., Glasgow; Glasgow Univ. (MA Hons Modern History and Politics). Reporter, Glasgow Herald, 1973–77; VSO, working as journalist, Nat. Broadcasting Commn, Papua New Guinea, 1978–79; journalist: Reuters, 1980; Scotsman, 1981–83; China Daily, Beijing, 1984–85; Political Correspondent, 1986–90, Political Editor, 1990–96, Scotsman; Chief Pol Correspondent, 1996–99, Diplomatic Ed., 2000–07, The Guardian. Lawrence Sterne Fellow, Washington Post, 1986. Mem., St Margarets Film Club. Member: Scoop of the Year team, What the Papers Say awards, 1999; Pulitzer Prize team for public service, 2014; Emmy Award team, 2014. Scotland's Young Journalist of Year, 1974; (jtly) George Polk Award for nat. security reporting, Long Island Univ., NY, 2013; (jtly) Investigative Reporters and Editors Award, 2013; (jtly) Walkley Award, Walkley Foundn, 2014. *Recreations:* mountaineering, film, books. *Club:* Junior Mountaineering of Scotland.

MacASKILL, Kenneth Wright; solicitor; Member (SNP) Edinburgh Eastern, Scottish Parliament, since 2011 (Lothians, 1999–2007, Edinburgh East and Musselburgh, 2007–11); *b* 28 April 1958; two *s*. *Educ:* Linlithgow Acad.; Edinburgh Univ. (LLB Hons). Cabinet Secretary for Justice, Scottish Parlt, 2007–14. Mem., SNP, 1981– (Mem., Nat. Exec., 1984–2003; Treas., until 1999). Contested (SNP): Livingston, 1983, 1987; Linlithgow, 1992, 1997; Scotland Mid and Fife, EP elecns, 1989. *Address:* Scottish Parliament, Edinburgh EH99 1SP.

McASLAN, John Renwick, CBE 2012; RSA 2014; RIBA; FRIAS; FRICS; FICE; Executive Chairman, John McAslan + Partners, since 1996; *b* Glasgow, 16 Feb. 1954; *s* of Prof. T. Crawford McAslan and Jean McAslan; *m* 1981, Dava Sagenkahn; one *s* two *d*. *Educ:* Dunoon Grammar Sch.; Dollar Acad.; Edinburgh Univ. (MA; DipArch). RIBA 1982; ARIAS 2005, FRIAS 2012; FRICS 2013; FICE 2013. With Cambridge Seven Associates, Boston, 1978–79; Richard Rogers and Partners, 1980–83; Troughton McAslan, 1984–95. Teaching, throughout UK and worldwide, 1990–; Prof., Welsh Sch. of Architecture, Univ. of Wales, 1998–2001; Architectural Advr to Govs, Dollar Acad., 2006–12; Prof., Sch. of Architecture and Design, Univ. of Ulster, 2009–11. Chm., Architect Adv. Panel, RBK&C, 2008–; Mem. Council, Tate Britain, 2008–14. Hon. Consul for Haiti in London, 2012–13. Numerous exhibns, 1984–. Chm., many cttees and awards gps. Internat. Associate, AIA, 2000; Mem., Japan Inst. of Architects, 1993. Founding Mem., Volubilis Foundn, Morocco, 2001. Foundation Trustee: Whitechapel Art Gall., 1989–96; John McAslan Family Charitable Trust, 1997–; RIBA/ICE McAslan Bursary, 2004–; Trustee, Photographer's Gall., 2005–09; Chm., Dunoon Burgh Hall Trust, 2009–. Mem., Clinton Global Initiative, 2007–11. FRSA 1989. *Completed* works include: *London*: RSA; Christopher Place Sch.; Trinity Coll. of Music; Swiss Cottage Liby; Peter Jones; Roundhouse; Royal Acad. of Music; Harris Acad.; King's Cross Station; Thomas Tallis Sch., Greenwich; London Olympics 2012 Energy Centres; Wellington House; Dulwich Coll.; RMA Woolwich; SOAS; Art Fund HQ; *other*: Southampton Univ.; De La Warr Pavilion, Bexhill-on-Sea; Derngate, Northampton; Kingston Univ.; Postgrad. Centre, Lancaster Univ.; Student Centre and Sch. of Nursing, Manchester Univ.; Oasis Acad., Enfield; RSA Acad., Tipton; Charles Carter Bldg, Univ. of Lancaster; *international*: St Catherine's Coll., Kobe; Yapi Kredi HQ, Istanbul; Florida Southern Coll.; Max Mara HQ, Reggio Emilia; British Embassy, Algiers; Stanislavsky Centre, Moscow; Delhi Metro; Iron Market, Port-au-Prince, Haiti; *ongoing* works include: *London*: Benjamin Franklin House; Cross Rail Bond Street Station; Smithfield Market; Heals; Friends House; St Paul's Girls Sch.; Mus. of London; Courtauld Inst.; Nat. Hist. Mus.; John Roan Sch., Greenwich; Harrow Sch.; *other*: Engrg Bldg, Univ. of Lancaster; *international*: Memorial Centre, Rwanda; Malawi Schs; Cultural Forum; Mosque, Mandarin Oriental Hotel and Heritage Houses, Msheireb, Doha, Qatar; Ciftciler, Istanbul; Kericho Cathedral, Kenya; Bolshevik Factory, Moscow; Royal BC Mus., Vic, Canada; British Sch., Rio de Janeiro. Numerous internat. architectural awards incl. Architectural Practice of the Year, Builder Gp, 1998, 1999, 2002; Civic Trust Award, 1999, 2000, 2008 (2 awards), 2009, 2012 (2 awards); Millennium Award, Design Council, 2000; British Construction Industry Award, 2000, 2007, 2010, 2012; Concrete Soc. Award, 2001, 2002; AIA Merit Award, 2001, 2003; RIBA Award for Architecture, 1996, 2002, 2005 (3 awards), 2007 (3 awards), 2008 (3 awards), 2009, 2011 (3 awards), 2013 (2 awards), 2014 (2 awards); Royal Fine Art Commn Trust Award, 2004; Roses Award, 2004, Roses Gold Award, 2009; EU Cultural Heritage Prize, diploma 2006, medal 2007, award 2013; English Heritage Award, 2006; Camden Design Award, 2006; Architect of the Year, 2006, Masterplanning Architect of the Year, 2006, Retail Architect of the Year, 2007, World Architect of the Year, 2009, Transport Architect of the Year, 2009, Building Design; Internat. Property Award, 2011; Chicago Athenæum Award, 2011; ICE Award, 2012; Elle Decoration Awards, 2012; Nat. Rail Award, 2012; Nat. Transport Award, 2012; IStructE Award (2 awards), 2012; New London Awards, 2012 (3 awards); London Planning Awards, 2013; German Design Council Awards, 2013; AJ 100 Building of the Year, 2013; Building Awards, 2013; AIA UK Design Awards, 2013; MIPIM Awards (2 awards), 2013; European Property Awards, 2013; Queen's Award for Enterprise, 2014. *Publications:* numerous articles and monographs. *Recreation:* spending time with family. *Address:* John McAslan + Partners, 7–9 William Road, NW1 3ER. *T:* (020) 7313 6000. *E:* j.mcaslan@mcaslan.co.uk. *Clubs:* Athenæum; Caledonian; Stoke Park (Stoke Poges); Royal Bombay Yacht.

McATASNEY, Philippa Mary; QC 2006; *b* 29 Sept. 1962; *d* of Patrick Anthony McAtasney and Mary Dianne McAtasney (*née* Swateridge); *m* 2003, Richard George Leach; two *d*. *Educ:* Brookfield Comp. Sch.; Itchen Sixth Form Coll.; London Sch. of Econs and Pol Sci. (LLB Hons 1984). Called to the Bar, Lincoln's Inn, 1985, Bencher, 2012; in practice specialising in law of sexual offences, violent crime, fraud, judicial review and police discipline work; Mem., SE and W Circuits. *Recreations:* theatre, cinema, reading, swimming, socialising with family and friends. *Address:* Furnival Chambers, 30–32 Furnival Street, EC4A 1JQ. *T:* (020) 7405 3232.

McATEER, Rev. Bruce James; General Secretary of the General Synod, Anglican Church of Australia, 2004–08; Rector, St Luke's Anglican Church, Mosman, 2008–14; *b* 21 Dec. 1946; *s* of Alwyn James McAteer and Olive Ellen McAteer (*née* Child); *m* 1970, Margaret Lorraine Pocock; one *s* one *d*. *Educ:* Australian Coll. of Theol. (DipTh); Charles Sturt Univ. (Grad. Dip. Ch Leadership and Mgt). Accountant, 1962–71; CA 1973. Ordained deacon, 1973, priest, 1975; parochial appts, dios Newcastle and Grafton, NSW, 1972–89; Gen. Manager and Bishop's Registrar, Anglican Dio. Grafton, 1989–2004; Canon in Residence, and Hon. Associate Priest, 1991–2004, Hon. Canon, 2004–08, Christ Church Cathedral, Grafton. Hon. Chaplain, TS Shropshire, Grafton, 1991–2004. *Recreations:* reading, listening to music, walking. *Address:* 571/8 Carrak Road, Kincumber, NSW 2251, Australia. *E:* bmcateer@tpg.com.au. *Clubs:* NSW Masonic (Sydney); Davistown RSL.

McATEER, Michael; Founder Director, Financial Inclusion Centre, since 2007; *b* Derry, NI, 19 Nov. 1962; *s* of Patrick McAteer and Margaret McAteer (*née* McLaughlin); *m* 2002, Margaret Donnelly; one *s*. *Educ:* St Columb's Coll., Derry, NI. Henderson Investors, 1986–89; Framlington Investment Mgt, 1989–91; business advr, 1991–93; Principal Policy Advr, Consumers' Assoc., 1994–2006. Founder Dir, Hackney Credit Union, 2005–07. Non-executive Director: Pensions Adv. Service, 2007–10; FSA, 2009–13; Financial Conduct Authy, 2013–. Member: Professional Oversight Bd, Financial Reporting Council, 2009–12; Registry Trust Consumer Panel, 2009–. Mem., Financial Users Expert Panel, EC, 2007–10 (Chair, 2010); Chm., EC Financial Services Users Gp, 2011–. Member, Consultative Panel: Cttee of Eur. Insce and Occupational Pension Supervisors, 2006–10; Cttee of Eur. Banking Supervisors, 2009–10; Cttee of Eur. Securities Regulators, 2010–11; Adv. Bd, CARITAS Westminster, 2012–. Trustee, Share Action. *Recreations:* reading (European history), running, experimental cinema, following Manchester United, Member of Mildmay Club and Institute Union. *Address:* Financial Inclusion Centre, 6th Floor, Lynton House, 7–12 Tavistock Square, WC1H 9LT. *T:* (020) 7391 4594.

McAULAY, Ian James; Chief Executive, Viridor Ltd, since 2013; Executive Director, Pennon Group plc, since 2013; *b* Glasgow, 25 April 1965; *s* of John McAulay and Anne McAulay; *m* 1997, Victoria; two *d*. *Educ:* Univ. of Strathclyde (BEng Civil Engrg 1988); Harvard Business Sch. (AMP 2001). Sen. Engr, Crouch, Hogg, Waterman, 1988–94; Business Dir, 1994–2005, Man. Dir, 2005–07, MWH UK Ltd; Exec. Dir, United Utilities plc, 2007–10; Chief Strategy Officer, MWH Global Inc., 2010–13. *Recreations:* football, golf, Rugby, reading. *Address:* Viridor Ltd, Viridor House, Youngman Place, Priory Bridge Road, Taunton, Somerset TA1 1AP. *T:* (01823) 712515. *E:* imcaulay@viridor.co.uk.

MacAUSLAN, Harry Hume; Vice Chairman, Europe, Middle East and Africa, Leo Burnett, 2004; *b* London, 2 Oct. 1956; *s* of John and Constance MacAuslan; *m* 1981, Fiona Caroline (*née* Boag); two *s* one *d*. *Educ:* Charterhouse; Manchester Univ. (BA Hons Hist.). Mktg Exec., De La Rue, 1979–80; JWT: Advertising Exec., 1980–89; Bd Dir, 1989–96; Dep. Chm., 1996–2004. Non-executive Director: Octopus Investments, 2007–; Perfect Pizza, 2009–. Trustee, Mental Health Foundn, 2009–. Trustee and Gov., Sadler's Wells, 1996– (Vice Chm., 2009–). Chm., Russell Maliphant Dance Co., 2010–12. *Recreation:* portrait painting. *E:* harry@macauslan.co.uk. *T:* 07770 735907.

McAVAN, Linda; Member (Lab) Yorkshire and the Humber Region, European Parliament, since 1999 (Yorkshire South, May 1998–99). *Educ:* St Joseph's RC Coll., Bradford; Heriot-Watt Univ. (BA Hons Interpreting and Translation 1984); Univ. Libre de Bruxelles (MA Internat. Relns 1991). Work in Brussels for various European agencies, 1984–91; European Officer, Coalfield Communities Campaign, Barnsley, 1991–95; Sen. Strategy Officer on European Affairs, Barnsley BC, 1995–98. European Parliament: Lab spokesman on Envmt, Food Safety and Public Health, 2004–14; Socialist and Democrat Gp Spokesperson/Coordinator on Envmt, Food Safety and Public Health, 2009; Mem., Temp. Cttee on Climate Change, 2007–09; Chairman: Fair Trade Wkg Gp, 2004–; Cttee for Internat. Develt, 2014–; Vice Chair, Afro-Caribbean and Pacific Cttee, 2009–12; Dep. Leader, European Parly Lab. Party, 1999–2004; Mem., PES, 2004– (Treas., 2004–06; Vice Pres. (climate change portfolio), 2006–09). Mem., Convention on the Future of Europe, 2002–03. British European Woman of the Year, 2002. *Address:* 79 High Street, Wath-upon-Dearne, Rotherham, S Yorks S63 7QB. *T:* (01709) 875665. *W:* www.lindamcavanmep.org.uk.

McAVEETY, Francis; Member (Lab) Glasgow City Council, since 2012; *b* 27 July 1962; *s* of Philip and Anne Marie McAveety; *m* 1985, Anita Mitchell; one *s* one *d*. *Educ:* Strathclyde Univ. (BA Jt Hons English and History 1983); St Andrew's Coll. of Educn, Glasgow (post grad. teaching qualification, 1984). Teacher: Glasgow, 1984–94; Renfrewshire, 1994–99. Member (Lab): Glasgow DC, 1988–95; Glasgow City Council, 1995–99 (Convener, Arts and Culture, 1995–97; Leader, 1997–99). Mem. (Lab) Glasgow Shettleston, Scottish Parlt, 1999–2011. Scottish Executive: Dep. Minister for Local Govt, 1999–2000, for Health, 2002–03; Minister for Tourism, Culture and Sport, 2003–04; Shadow Minister for Sport, 2007–10; Convenor, Public Petitions Cttee, Scottish Parlt, 2007–10. Contested (Lab) Glasgow Shettleston, Scottish Parlt, 2011. DL Glasgow 1998. *Recreations:* sport, reading, record collecting. *Address:* 156 Glenbuck Avenue, Glasgow G33 1LW.

McAVOY, family name of **Baron McAvoy**.

McAVOY, Baron *cr* 2010 (Life Peer), of Rutherglen in Lanarkshire; **Thomas McLaughlin McAvoy,** PC 2003; *b* 14 Dec. 1943; *m* 1968, Eleanor Kerr; four *s*. Employee, Hoover, Cambuslang; shop steward, AEU. Mem., Strathclyde Regl Council, 1982–87; former Chm., Rutherglen Community Council. MP (Lab and Co-op) Glasgow, Rutherglen, 1987–2005, Rutherglen and Hamilton W, 2005–10. An Opposition Whip, 1990–93; Comptroller of HM Household, 1997–2008; Treasurer of HM Household (Dep. Chief Whip), 2008–10; an Opposition Whip, H of L, 2011–. *Address:* House of Lords, SW1A 0PW; 9 Douglas Avenue, Rutherglen, Lanarkshire G73 4RA.

McAVOY, Prof. Brian Ramsay, MD; FRCP, FRCGP, FRACGP, FRNZCGP, FAChAM; Addiction Medicine Specialist, Capri Hospital Trust, Auckland, since 2012; *b* 2 Jan. 1949; *s* of Thomas Ramsay McAvoy and Christine McMillan McAvoy. *Educ:* Eastwood Sen. Secondary Sch., Glasgow; Univ. of Glasgow (BSc; MB ChB); Leicester Univ. (MD). FRCGP 1988; FRCP 1992; FRNZCGP 1999; FRACGP 2000; FAChAM 2005. Vocational Trainee in Gen. Practice, Southern Gen. Hosp. Scheme, Glasgow, 1973–76; Teaching Fellow, Dept of Family Medicine, McMaster Med. Sch., Hamilton, Ont, 1976–77; Principal in General Practice: Byfield, Northants, 1977–84; Leicester, 1984–89; Guidepost, Northumberland, 1994–2000; Lectr, 1977–84, Sen. Lectr, 1984–89, in General Practice, Univ. of Leicester; Elaine Gurr Foundation Prof. of General Practice, Univ. of Auckland, NZ, 1989–94; William Leech Prof. of Primary Health Care, Univ. of Newcastle upon Tyne, 1994–2000; GP, Melbourne, 2000–06; Dir, Res. and Practice Support, RACGP, 2000–01; Dep. Dir, Nat. Cancer Control Initiative, Melbourne, 2002–06; Specialist Med. Officer, Auckland Community Alcohol and Drug Service, 2006–10; Addiction Medicine Specialist, Alcohol and Drug Service, Tasmanian Dept of Health and Human Services, Hobart, 2010–12. Adjunct Prof. of Gen. Practice, Univs of Melbourne and Queensland, 2000–; Hon. Professor of General Practice: Monash Univ., 2000; Auckland Univ., 2006–. *Publications:* (ed jtly) Asian Health Care, 1990; (contrib.) Clinical Method: a general practice approach, 1988, 2nd edn 1992; (jtly) General Practice Medicine: an illustrated colour text, 2003; articles on addiction, workplace bullying, med. educn, health care delivery, cancer, ethnic minority health, alcohol and health promotion. *Recreations:* cycling, walking, music, reading. *Address:* Capri Hospital, PO Box 62044, Mt Wellington, Auckland, New Zealand.

McBAIN, (David) Malcolm, LVO 1972; HM Diplomatic Service, retired; Founder, British Diplomatic Oral History Programme, at Leicester University, 1995–97, Churchill Archives Centre, Churchill College, Cambridge, since 1997; *b* 19 Jan. 1928; *s* of David Walker McBain and Lilian J. McBain; *m* 1951, Audrey Yvonne Evison; one *s* three *d*. *Educ:* Sutton County School; London School of Economics (evening student). Min. of Civil Aviation appts in Tripoli, Libya, 1949–51, New Delhi, 1953–54; Diplomatic Service: New Delhi, 1958–61; Kenya, 1963–67; Thailand, 1968–75; Brunei, 1978–81; Texas, 1981–84; Ambassador to Madagascar, 1984–87. Order of Crown of Thailand, 1972. *Address:* 7 Charter Court, Gigant Street, Salisbury, Wilts SP1 2LH.

McBARNET, Prof. Doreen Jean, CBE 2006; PhD; Professor of Socio-Legal Studies, University of Oxford, 2004–14, now Emeritus; Fellow, Wolfson College, Oxford, since 1977. *Educ:* Dunoon Grammar Sch., Argyll; Univ. of Glasgow (MA 1st Cl. Hons Hist. and Sociol.; PhD 1980). Lectr in Sociol., Univ. of Glasgow, 1969–77; University of Oxford: Res. Fellow in Socio-Legal Studies, 1977–85; Sen. Res. Fellow, 1985–2000; Reader, 2000–04. Adjunct Prof., Res. Sch. of Social Scis, ANU, 2002–05; Vis. Prof., Sch. of Law, Edinburgh Univ., 2008–14. *Publications:* Conviction: law, the state and the construction of justice, 1981;

(ed jtly) Law, State and Society, 1981; (with C. Whelan) Creative Accounting and the cross-eyed javelin thrower, 1999; Crime, Compliance and Control (collected essays), 2004; (ed jtly) The New Corporate Accountability: corporate social responsibility and the law, 2007; contrib. articles to learned jls incl. Internat. Jl Sociol. of Law, British Jl Criminol., British Jl Sociol., Modern Law Rev., Jl Law and Society, Criminal Law Rev., Accounting Orgns and Society. *Address:* Centre for Socio-Legal Studies, University of Oxford, Manor Road, Oxford OX1 3UQ.

MacBEATH, Prof. John Ernest Carmichael, OBE 1997; Professor of Educational Leadership, 2000, now Emeritus, and Director of Leadership for Learning: the Cambridge Network, and Wallenberg Research Centre, University of Cambridge; Fellow of Hughes Hall, Cambridge, 2000; *b* Bolobo, Congo, 23 May 1940; *m* Sandra; two *d*. *Educ:* Univ. of Glasgow (MA, MEd); Jordanhill Coll. (PGCE). Prof., Dept of Educnl Studies, and Dir, Quality in Educn Centre, Univ. of Strathclyde, until 2000. Mem., Govt Task Force on Standards, 1997–2001. Consultant: OECD; UNESCO; ILO; EC; Scottish Exec.; Educn Dept, HK; Govt of Switzerland; Bertelsmann Foundn; Prince's Trust; Varkey Gp, Dubai. Hon. Dr Edinburgh. *Publications:* (ed) Effective School Leadership: responding to change, 1998; (with K. Myers) Effective School Leaders, 1999; Schools Must Speak for Themselves: arguments for school self-evaluation, 1999; (jtly) Self-evaluation in European Schools: a story of change, 2000; (with P. Mortimore) Improving School Effectiveness, 2001; (with A. McGlynn) Self-evaluation: what's in it for schools?, 2002; (jtly) Self-evaluation in the Global Classroom, 2002; (ed with L. Moos) Democratic Learning, 2003; (jtly) School Inspection and Self-evaluation, 2006; (ed with Neil Dempster) Connecting Leadership and Learning, 2008; Learning In and Out of School: the selected works of John MacBeath, 2012; (ed with Mike Younger) A Common Wealth of Learning, 2013; Education and Schooling: myth, heresy and misconception, 2014. *Address:* Faculty of Education, 184 Hills Road, Cambridge CB2 8PQ; Hughes Hall, Cambridge CB1 2EW.

MacBETH, Elizabeth Browel; *see* Robson, E. B.

McBRATNEY, George, CEng, FIMechE; Principal, College of Technology, Belfast, 1984–89; *b* 5 May 1927; *s* of George McBratney and Sarah Jane McBratney; *m* 1949, Margaret Rose Patricia, (Trissie), *d* of late John Robinson, Melbourne, Australia; one *s*. *Educ:* Coll. of Technology, Belfast (BScEng 1948); Northampton Coll. of Advanced Technol.; QUB (Dip Ed 1976). CEng, FIMechE 1971. Apprentice fitter/draughtsman, Harland and Wolff, Belfast, 1943–47; Teacher, Comber Trades Prep. Sch., 1947–54; College of Technology, Belfast: successively Asst Lectr, Lectr and Sen. Lectr, 1954–67; Asst to Principal, 1967–69; Vice-Principal, 1969–84. Council Member: IMechE, 1984–86 (Chm., NI Br., 1984–86); NI Manpower Council, 1984; Lambeg Industrial Res. Assoc. (formerly Linen Industry Res. Assoc.), 1984–90; BTEC, 1986–89; Chm., Further Educn Adv. Cttee, Faculty of Educn, Univ. of Ulster, 1986–90. *Publications:* Mechanical Engineering Experiments, vols 1 and 2 (with W. R. Mitchell), 1962, vol. 3 (with T. G. J. Moag), 1964; (with T. G. J. Moag) Science for Mechanical Engineering Technicians, vol. 1, 1966. *Recreation:* gardening. *Address:* 16 Glencregagh Drive, Belfast BT6 0NL. *T:* (028) 9079 6123.

McBRATNEY, Samuel; writer, since 1976; *b* Belfast, NI, 1 March 1943; *s* of Samuel and Verina McBratney; *m* 1964, Maralyn Green; two *s* one *d*. *Educ:* Friends' Sch., Lisburn; Trinity Coll., Dublin (BA Modern Hist. and Pol Sci. 1965). Teaching appts at primary, secondary and further educn levels, 1965–93. *Publications:* over 100 books and scripts, mainly children's fiction, including: Mark Time, 1976; The Chieftain's Daughter, 1993; Guess How Much I Love You, 1994; You're All My Favourites, 2004; There, There, 2013; for adults: Lagan Valley Details, 1976; One Grand Sweet Song, 1999. *Recreations:* watching sport, playing chess badly, viniculture (7 vines). *Address:* Shirping World Resources Ltd, 101 Antrim Road, Lisburn, Northern Ireland BT28 8EA. *E:* sam@mcbratney.org.uk.

McBREARTY, Anthony; regeneration consultant, since 2008; Senior Research Fellow, University of East London, since 1997; *b* 26 April 1946; *s* of Patrick and Mary McBrearty; *m* 1969, Heather McGowan (marr. diss. 1994; she *d* 2003), solicitor; one *s*; two *d* by former partner Lesley Seary. Councillor (Lab) London Borough of Haringey, 1975–86 (Chm. of Personnel Cttee, 1976–79; Chm. of Housing Cttee, 1979–82); Mem. (Lab) Enfield N, 1981–86, Chm., Housing Cttee, 1982–86, GLC. Contested (Lab) W Herts, 1987. Mem., Central Technical Unit, 1986–88; Hd of Policy, London Bor. of Newham, 1988–96; Dep. Chief Exec., Thames Gateway London Partnership, 2002–08. Mem., Mgt Cttee, Thames Reach (formerly Thames Reach Bondway) Housing Assoc., 1987–. Special Advr for the Public Sector, London Metropolitan Univ., 2008–. *Recreations:* politics, history. *Address:* 56 First Avenue, Manor Park, E12 6AN. *T:* 07503 246751. *E:* tony.mcbrearty@tiscali.co.uk.

McBRIDE, Brian James; Chairman: ASOS plc, since 2012; Wiggle, since 2015; *b* Glasgow, 15 Oct. 1955; *s* of Alexander and Maire McBride; *m* 1980, Linda Wilson; two *d*. *Educ:* Lourdes Secondary Sch., Glasgow; Univ. of Glasgow (MA Hons). Salesman, Xerox, 1977–81; IBM, 1981–93; Man. Dir, Crosfield Electronics, 1993–95; Pres., Europe, Madge Networks, 1996–98; Vice Pres., Dell Computers, 1998–2002; Man. Dir, T-Mobile UK, 2003–05; Vice-Pres. and Man. Dir, Amazon.co.uk, 2006–11. Sen. Advr, Scottish Equity Partners, 2011–. Non-executive Director: SThree plc, 2001–08; Celtic plc, 2005–09; BBC, 2012–14; Senior Independent non-executive Director: Computacenter plc, 2011–15; AO.com, 2014–. Member, Advisory Board: Huawei UK, 2011–14; Numis plc, 2011–14. Trustee, In Kind Direct, 2009–12. *Recreations:* golf, tennis, watching football, music. *Clubs:* Camberley and District; Camberley Heath Golf.

McBRIDE, Dianne Gwenllian; *see* Nelmes, D. G.

McBRIDE, William Griffith, AO 1977; CBE 1969; Medical Director, Foundation 41 (for the study of congenital abnormalities and mental retardation), 1972–2001; Consultant Obstetrician and Gynaecologist, St George Hospital, Sydney, 1957–93; *b* 25 May 1927; *s* of late John McBride, Sydney; *m* 1957, Patricia Mary, *d* of late Robert Louis Glover; two *s* two *d*. *Educ:* Canterbury High Sch., Sydney; Univ. of Sydney; Univ. of London. MB, BS Sydney 1950; MD Sydney 1962; FRCOG 1968 (MRCOG 1954); FRANZCOG (FRACOG 1979). Resident: St George Hosp., Sydney, 1950; Launceston Hosp., 1951; Med. Supt, Women's Hosp., Sydney, 1955–57; Cons. Gynaecologist, Bankstown Hosp., Sydney, 1957–66; Consultant Obstetrician and Gynaecologist: Women's Hosp., Sydney, 1966–83; Royal Hosp. for Women, 1983–88; Vis. Consultant, L. B. J. Tropical Medical Center, American Samoa, 1998–. Lectr in Obstetrics and Gynaecology, Univ. of Sydney, 1957–83; Examiner in Obstetrics and Gynaecology: Univ. of Sydney, 1960–83; Australian Med. Council, 2000–. Vis. Prof. of Gynaecology, Univ. of Bangkok, 1968. Mem., WHO Sub-Cttee on safety of oral contraceptives, 1971. Pres. Sect. of Obstetrics and Gynæcology, AMA, 1966–73. Fellow, Senate of Univ. of Sydney, 1976–90; FRSocMed 1988; Mem., Amer. Coll. of Toxicology, 1985. Member: Soc. of Reproductive Biology; Endocrine Soc.; Teratology Soc.; Soc. for Risk Analysis; NY Acad. of Scis, 1987; AAAS, 1992. Mem. Council, Royal Agricl Soc. of NSW, 1987–; Delegate, Council meeting of Royal Agricl Socs, Calgary, 1992; breeder and judge of Hereford cattle; judged Shropshire and W Midlands Show, 1989. Member: Bd of Dirs, Australian Opera, 1979–82; Australian Opera Council, 1982–. BP Prize of Institut de la Vie, 1971 (for discovery of the teratogenic effects of the drug Thalidomide; first person to alert the world to the dangers of this drug and possibly other drugs). *Publications:* Drugs, 1960–70; Killing the Messenger, 1994; over 100 pubns in internat. med. or scientific jls including: (on teratogenic effect of the drug Thalidomide), Lancet 1961 (London); (on mutagenic effect of Thalidomide), BMJ 1994; (on Thalidomide and DNA in rats and rabbits), Teratogenesis, Carcinogenesis, Mutagenesis, 1997; (on interaction of Thalidomide with DNA or rabbit embryos), Pharmacology & Toxicology, 1999; Bitter Pills, 2001; Good from Evil, 2012. *Recreations:* tennis, swimming, riding, music, cattle breeding. *Address:* 1101/1 Watson Street, Neutral Bay, NSW 2089, Australia. *Clubs:* Union, Australian Jockey, Palm Beach Surf, Royal Sydney Golf, Palm Beach Golf (Sydney).

McBRIEN, Philippa Jill Olivier; *see* Harris, P. J. O.

McBURNEY, Simon Montagu, OBE 2005; actor, director and writer, since 1980; *s* of late Prof. Charles B. M. McBurney and Anne F. E. McBurney (*née* Charles). *Educ:* Peterhouse, Cambridge (BA 1980); École Lecoq, Paris. Founder and Artistic Director, Theatre de Complicite, 1983–: *performer:* Put it on Your Head; A Minute Too Late, 1987, Dir, revival, NT, 2005; More Bigger Snacks Now; Please, Please, Please; Burning Ambition; The Winter's Tale; *director/adaptation:* The Street of Crocodiles, 1992; Out of a house walked a man…; *director/adaptation/performer:* The Three Lives of Lucie Cabrol, 1994; To the Wedding; The Encounter, 2015; *director/performer:* The Visit (co-dir); The Caucasian Chalk Circle; Mnemonic, 1999; Endgame, 2009; *director:* The Chairs, NY, 1998; Light, 2000; The Noise of Time, 2001; Genoa 01; The Elephant Vanishes, 2003; Measure for Measure, 2004; Strange Poetry (for LA Philharmonic Orch.); A Disappearing Number, 2007, 2008, 2010; Shun-kin, 2008, 2010; A Dog's Heart (opera), 2010; The Master and Margarita, 2011–13; The Magic Flute (opera), 2012–13; *freelance director:* French and Saunders Live, Apollo, Hammersmith, 2000; The Resistible Rise of Arturo Ui, NY, 2002; So Much Things to Say, Wyndhams, 2003; All My Sons, NY; *actor: films* include: Kafka, 1991; Tom and Viv, 1994; Cousin Bette, 1998; Skaggerak, 2003; Bright Young Things, 2003; The Manchurian Candidate, 2004; The Last King of Scotland, 2006; The Golden Compass, 2007; Body of Lies, 2008; The Duchess, 2008; Tinker, Tailor, Soldier, Spy, 2011; Jane Eyre, 2011; Magic in the Moonlight, 2014; *television* includes: The Comic Strip Presents, 1992–93; The Vicar of Dibley, 1994–2004; Rev, 2010–12; *writer and producer:* Mr Bean's Holiday (film), 2007. *Publications:* Who You Hear It From, 2012; contrib. Guardian, Independent, The Times and Telegraph. *Address:* c/o Complicite, 14 Anglers Lane, NW5 3DG.

McBURNIE, Tony; Chairman: The Strategic Index, since 1994; The Strategic Marketing Index, since 1994; *b* 4 Aug. 1929; *s* of William McBurnie and Bessie McKenzie Harvey McBurnie; *m* 1954, René Keating; one *s* one *d*. *Educ:* Lanark Grammar Sch.; Glasgow Univ. (MA). FCIM (FInstM 1984). National Service, RAF (FO), 1951–53. Divisional Manager Mullard Ltd, 1958–65; Group Marketing Dir, United Glass Ltd, 1965–69; Chairman and Managing Director: Ravenhead Co. Ltd, 1970–79; United Glass Containers Ltd, 1979–82; Man. Dir, United Glass PT&D Gp, 1982–84; Dir, United Glass Holdings PLC, 1966–84; Dir Gen., Chartered Inst. of Marketing (formerly Inst. of Marketing), 1984–89; Managing Director: Coll. of Marketing Ltd, 1985–89; Marketing Training Ltd, 1984–89; Marketing House Publishers Ltd, 1985–89. Chairman: Reed QT Search, 1989–90; Marketing Quality Assurance, 1991–95. Director: Reed Executive plc, 1987–90; Beard Dove Ltd, 1988–97; Needles Point Mgt Co. Ltd, 2003–. Pres., Assoc. of Glass Container Manufacturers, 1981–83; Chm., NJIC for Glass Industry, 1982–83; Dir, European Glass Fedn, 1979–83. *Publications:* (with David Clutterbuck) The Marketing Edge, 1987; Marketing Plus, 1989. *Recreations:* golf, swimming, theatre, the arts. *Address:* Craigwood Lodge, Prince Consort Drive, Ascot, Berks SL5 8AW. *Club:* Wentworth.

McCABE, Bernice Alda; Headmistress, North London Collegiate School, since 1997; *b* 7 Oct. 1952; *d* of Alan Collis Wood and Eileen May Wood (*née* Bolton); *m* 1st, 1971, Anthony Hugh Lowther Davis; 2nd, 1988, Thomas Patrick McCabe. *Educ:* Clifton High Sch. for Girls; Bristol Univ. (BA, PGCE); Leeds Metropolitan Univ. (MBA 1995). Asst English Teacher, Filton High Sch., Bristol, 1974–81; Head of English: Cotham Grammar Sch., Bristol, 1981–83; Collingwood Sch., Camberley, 1984–86; Dep. Headteacher, Heathland Sch., Hounslow, 1986–90; Headmistress, Chelmsford County High Sch. for Girls, 1990–97. Expert Advr to Mayor of London's Schs Excellence Fund, 2013–. Member: GSA, 1997– (Mem., Univs Sub-cttee, 2001–08); Adv. Cttee, Nat. Curriculum, 2010–14. Gov., Orley Farm Sch., 1997–2001. Dir, Prince of Wales' Educn Summer Sch., 2002–; Co-Dir, The Prince's Teaching Inst., 2006–. FRSA 1995. *Recreations:* family, homes in Suffolk and S Devon, walking, travel, gym, running, reading, Argentine tango. *Address:* North London Collegiate School, Canons, Canons Drive, Edgware, Middx HA8 7RJ. *T:* (020) 8951 6401.

MACCABE, Christopher George, CB 2004; consultant and lecturer on peace processes and political development; British Joint Secretary, British-Irish Intergovernmental Conference, and Political Director (formerly Associate Political Director), Northern Ireland Office, 2000–08; *b* 17 Dec. 1946; *s* of late Max Maccabe, FRSA, and of Gladys Maccabe (*née* Chalmers), MBE; *m* 1974, Jenny Livingston; one *s* two *d*. *Educ:* Royal Belfast Academical Instn; Univ. of London (LLB); Queen's Univ., Belfast (LLM). Civil Servant, 1968–2008: Researcher: NI Cabinet Office, 1971–72; NI Office, 1972–73; Asst Private Sec. to Chief Minister, NI Power Sharing Exec., 1973–74; Private Sec. to Minister of State, NI Office, 1974–77; NI Office, 1977–80; seconded as Special Asst to Chief Constable, RUC, 1980–84; NI Office, 1984–88; Dir of Regimes, NI Prison Service, 1988–92; Hd, Political Affairs Div., NI Office, 1992–2000. Mem., Assessment Team assessing Minister of Justice's agreement with dissident republican prisoners in Maghaberry Prison, 2010–. Mem., Belfast Conflict Resolution Consortium, 2015–. UK Special Envoy to Sri Lanka peace process, 2006–09; Mem., Internat. Verification Commn to monitor ETA ceasefire, 2011–. Mem. Adv. Bd, Centre for Advancement of Women in Politics, QUB, 2001–06. Gov., Victoria Coll., Belfast, 1989– (Chm., 2002–09). FRSA 2001. Hon. Fellow, Inst. of Irish Studies, Univ. of Liverpool, 2009. *Publications:* (contrib.) The British and Peace in Northern Ireland, ed G. Spencer, 2015. *Recreations:* golf, Rugby Union, reading, Anglo-Zulu War of 1879. *Clubs:* Instonians Rugby, Dunmurry Golf (Belfast).

MacCABE, Prof. Colin Myles Joseph; Distinguished Professor of English and Film, University of Pittsburgh, since 2002 (Professor of English, 1985–2002); Executive Producer, Derek Jarman Lab, Birkbeck, Univ. of London, since 2012; *b* 9 Feb. 1949; *s* of Myles Joseph MacCabe and Ruth Ward MacCabe; *m* 2009, Flavia Mary Lambert; two *s* one *d*. *Educ:* Trinity College, Cambridge (BA English and Moral Scis 1971, MA 1974, PhD 1976); Ecole Normale Supérieure, 1972–73 (pensionnaire anglais). University of Cambridge: Research Fellow, Emmanuel College, 1974–76; Fellow, King's College, 1976–81; Asst Lectr, Faculty of English, 1976–81; Prof. of English Studies, 1981–85, Vis. Prof., 1985–91, Strathclyde Univ.; Head of Production, 1985–89, Head of Res., 1989–98, BFI; Prof. of English, Univ. of Exeter, 1998–2006, Vis. Prof., 2006–; Prof. of English and Humanities, Birkbeck, Univ. of London, 2006–10. Chm., 1995–2005, Associate Dir, 2006–12, London Consortium. Chm., John Logie Baird Centre for Research in Television and Film, 1985–91 (Dir, 1983–85). Vis. Fellow, Sch. of Humanities, Griffith Univ., 1981, 1984; Mellon Vis. Prof., Univ. of Pittsburgh, 1985; Vis. Prof., Birkbeck Coll., Univ. of London, 1992–2006; Vis. Fellow, All Souls Coll., Oxford, 2014. Mem., Editl Bd, Screen, 1973–81; Editor, Critical Qly, 1990– (Critical Editor, 1987–90). *Publications:* James Joyce and the Revolution of the Word, 1979, 2nd edn 2002; Godard: Images, Sounds, Politics, 1980; (ed) The Talking Cure: essays in psychoanalysis and language, 1981; (ed) James Joyce: new perspectives, 1982; Theoretical Essays: film, linguistics, literature, 1985; (ed jtly) The BBC and Public Sector Broadcasting, 1986; (ed) High Theory/Low Culture: analysing popular television and film, 1986; (ed) Futures for English, 1987; (ed jtly) The Linguistics of Writing, 1987; (with Isaac Julien) Diary of a Young Soul Rebel, 1991; (ed jtly) Who is Andy Warhol?, 1996; Performance, 1998; The Eloquence of the Vulgar, 1999; Godard: a portrait of the artist at 70, 2003; T. S. Eliot, 2006;

The Butcher Boy, 2007; (ed jtly) True to the Spirit: adaptation and the question of fidelity, 2011; (ed jtly) Cinema and Empire: film and the end of the empire, 2012; (ed jtly) Godard's Contempt: essays from the London Consortium, 2013. *Recreations:* eating, drinking, talking.

McCABE, Eamonn Patrick; portrait photographer; Picture Editor, The Guardian, 1988–2001; *b* 28 July 1948; *s* of James and Celia McCabe; *m* 1st, 1972, Ruth Calvert (marr. diss. 1993); one *s*; 2nd, 1997, Rebecca Smithers; one *d*. *Educ:* Challoner School, Finchley; San Francisco State Coll. FRPS 1990. Freelance photographer on local papers and with The Guardian for one year; staff photographer, The Observer, 1977–86 and 1987–88; official photographer for the Pope's visit to England, 1982; Picture Editor, Sportsweek, 1986–87. Dir, Newscast, 2001–06. Work in Nat. Portrait Gall. Hon. Prof., Thames Valley Univ., 1994; Sen. Vis. Lectr in Photography, Univ. Campus Suffolk, 2011–. Fellow in Photography, Nat. Mus. of Photography and TV, Bradford, 1988. Hon. DLit UEA, 2007; DUniv Staffordshire, 2010. Sports photographer of the year, RPS and Sports Council, 1978, 1979, 1981, 1984; News photographer of the year, British Press Awards, 1985; Picture Editor of the Year, Nikon Press Awards, 1992, 1993, 1995, 1997, 1998. *Publications:* Sports Photographer, 1981; Eamonn McCabe, Photographer, 1987; The Making of Great Photographs, 2006; Artists and Their Studios, 2008; Decade, 2010. *Recreations:* cycling, cinema, taking photographs. *Address:* c/o The Guardian, Kings Place, 90 York Way, N1 9AG. *Club:* Chelsea Arts.

McCABE, Ven. (John) Trevor, RD 1976; Archdeacon of Cornwall, 1996–99, now Emeritus; *b* 26 Jan. 1933; *s* of John Leslie McCabe and Mary Ena McCabe; *m* 1959, Mary Thomas; three *s* one *d*. *Educ:* Falmouth Grammar Sch.; Nottingham Univ. (BA Hons); St Catherine's Coll., Oxford; Wycliffe Hall, Oxford (DipTh). Ordained, 1959; served Plymouth and Exeter; Vicar of Capel, Surrey, 1966–71; Chaplain, Isles of Scilly, 1971–81; Residentiary Canon, Bristol Cathedral, 1981–83; Vicar, Manaccan St Anthony and St Martin in Meneage, Helston, 1983–96; RD of Kerrier, 1987–90 and 1993–96; Hon. Canon of Truro, 1993–99. Non-exec. Dir, Cornwall Partnership Trust, 1999–2005. Chm., NHS Trust for Learning Disability, 1990–99. Served RNVR/RNR, 1955–57, 1963–83. *Recreations:* shrub gardening, local Cornish history. *Address:* Sunhill, School Lane, Budock, Falmouth TR11 5DG. *T:* (01326) 378095.

McCABE, Prof. Mary Margaret Anne, PhD; Professor of Ancient Philosophy, King's College, London, 1998–2014, now Emerita; Keeling Scholar in Residence and Hon. Fellow, University College London, since 2014; Bye Fellow, Newnham College, Cambridge, since 2014; *b* 18 Dec. 1948; *d* of late Edward McCabe and Sarah Frances McCabe; *m* 1993, Martin William Denton Beddoe, *qv*; two *d*. *Educ:* Oxford High Sch. for Girls; Newnham Coll., Cambridge (BA 1970; MA 1973; PhD 1977). Fellow in Classics, New Hall, Univ. of Cambridge, 1981–90; King's College, London: Lectr in Philosophy, 1990–92; Reader in Philosophy, 1992–98; Leverhulme Trust Major Res. Fellow, 2005–08. Vis. Res. Fellow, Dept of Philosophy, Princeton Univ., 2015. Pres., British Philosophical Assoc., 2009–12; Vice-Pres., 2015–June 2016, Pres., July 2016–, Mind Assoc. *Publications:* (as M. M. Mackenzie) Plato on Punishment, 1981; (ed jtly, as M. M. Mackenzie) Images of Authority, 1989; Plato's Individuals, 1994; (ed jtly) Form and Argument in Late Plato, 1996; Plato and his Predecessors: the dramatisation of reason, 2000; (ed jtly) Perspectives on Perception, 2007; (ed jtly) Aristotle and the Stoics reading Plato, 2010; Platonic Conversations, 2015. *Recreations:* horseracing, orchestral percussion. *Address:* Department of Philosophy, King's College London, Strand, WC2R 2LS. *T:* (020) 7848 2309. *E:* mm.mccabe@kcl.ac.uk.

McCABE, Michael Benedict; Owner, Michael McCabe Productions Ltd, since 2009; Co-Founder, Joe Public Marketing Ltd, since 2009; Co-Founder and co-owner, Andrews McCabe Productions Ltd, since 2015; *b* Brighton, 1 June 1965; *s* of Timothy and Jill McCabe; civil partnership 2011, Anthony J. McNeill. *Educ:* Shoreham Coll. Man. Dir, Michael McCabe Associates, 1998–2003; Internat. Mktg Dir, 1998–2004, Associate Producer, 2003–04, Mamma Mia!; Producer, Spring Awakening, London, 2009; Associate Producer, Promises, Promises, NY, 2010; Producer: Million Dollar Quartet, London, 2011; How to Succeed in Business Without Really Trying, NY, 2011–12; Sweeney Todd, London, 2012; Wicked The Musical, London, 2006–, UK and Ireland tour, 2013–. Mem. Bd, Crystal Ballet, 2014–. Member: SOLT, 2011–; Broadway League, 2014–. Trustee, English Touring Th., 2015–. *Recreations:* theatre, cinema, opera, literature, travel. *Address:* Michael McCabe Productions, c/o Joe Public Ltd, The Dutch House, 307–308 High Holborn, WC1V 7LL. *T:* (020) 7831 7077. *E:* mailbox@michaelmccabe.net. *W:* www.michaelmccabe.net. *Clubs:* Ivy, Hospital.

McCABE, Primrose Smith; *see* Scott, P. S.

McCABE, Prof. Richard Anthony, PhD; FBA 2007; Professor of English Language and Literature, University of Oxford, since 2002; Fellow, Merton College, Oxford, since 1993 (Sub-Warden, 2008–10); *b* 2 Sept. 1954; *s* of Edward McCabe and Jenny (*née* Synnott). *Educ:* Trinity Coll., Dublin (Foundn Schol.; BA 1976 (Gold Medallist)); Pembroke Coll., Cambridge (PhD 1980). Robert Gardiner Meml Schol., Univ. of Cambridge, 1976–78. Drapers' Res. Fellow, Pembroke Coll., Cambridge, 1978–82; Lecturer: UCD, 1982–86; TCD, 1986–93; Reader in English Lang. and Lit., Univ. of Oxford, 1996–2002. Chatterton Lectr in Poetry, 1991, Res. Reader, 1999, British Acad. Major Leverhulme Fellow, 2011–14. Mem. Council, British Acad., 2014–. Chm. Council, Friends of Bodleian Library, 2009–. *Publications:* monographs: Joseph Hall: a study in satire and meditation, 1982; The Pillars of Eternity: time and providence in The Faerie Queene, 1989; Incest, Drama and Nature's Law 1550–1700, 1993; Spenser's Monstrous Regiment: Elizabethan Ireland and the poetics of difference, 2002; editor: (with H. Erskine-Hill) Presenting Poetry: Composition, Publication, Reception: essays in honour of Ian Jack, 1995; Edmund Spenser, The Shorter Poems, 1999; (with D. Womersley) Literary Milieux: essays in text and context presented to Howard Erskine-Hill, 2007; The Oxford Handbook of Edmund Spenser, 2010. *Recreations:* book collecting, theatre going, writing, walking. *Address:* Merton College, Oxford OX1 4JD. *T:* (01865) 276289. *E:* Richard.mccabe@ell.ox.ac.uk.

McCABE, Stephen James; MP (Lab) Birmingham Selly Oak, since 2010 (Birmingham, Hall Green, 1997–2010); *b* 4 Aug. 1955; *s* of late James and Margaret McCabe; *m* 1991; one *s* one *d*. *Educ:* Univ. of Bradford (MA); Moray House Coll., Edinburgh (Dip. and CQSW). Social worker, Generic Team, 1977–79, Intermediate Treatment Worker, 1979–83, Wolverhampton; Manager, The Priory, Newbury, 1983–85; Lectr in Social Services, NE Worcs Coll., 1986–89; social policy researcher, BASW, and part-time child care worker, Solihull, 1989–91; Educn Advr, CCETSW, 1991–97. An Asst Govt Whip, 2006–07; a Lord Comr, HM Treasury (Govt Whip), 2007–10. *Recreations:* cooking, hill-walking, reading, football. *Address:* House of Commons, SW1A 0AA. *T:* (020) 7219 3509.

McCABE, Ven. Trevor; *see* McCabe, Ven. J. T.

McCAFFER, Prof. Ronald, FREng; FRSE; Professor of Construction Management, Loughborough University (formerly Loughborough University of Technology), 1986–2009, now Emeritus; Chairman, European Construction Institute, 2007–10 (Finance Director, 1990–2007); *b* 8 Dec. 1943; *s* of late John Gegg McCaffer and Catherine Turner (*née* Gourlay); *m* 1966, Margaret Elizabeth, *d* of late Cyril Warner and Mary Huntley (*née* Mason); one *s*. *Educ:* Albert Sch., Glasgow; Univ. of Strathclyde (BSc 1965; DSc 1998); PhD Loughborough 1977. FICE 1988; FCIOB 1988; FREng (FEng 1991); Eur Ing 1990; FRSE 2009. Design Engr, Babtie, Shaw & Morton, 1965–67; Site Engineer: Nuclear Power Gp, 1967–69; Taylor Woodrow Construction Ltd, 1969–70; Loughborough University of Technology: Lectr, 1970–78; Sen. Lectr, 1978–83; Reader, 1983–86; Head of Civil Engrg, 1987–93; Dean of Engineering, 1992–97; Loughborough University: Sen. Pro-Vice-Chancellor, then Dep. Vice-Chancellor, 1997–2002; Dir, Strategic Business Partnership Innovation and Knowledge Transfer, 2002–06. Chairman: Loughborough University Utilities Ltd, 1997–02; Loughborough Univ. Enterprises Ltd, 2002–06; Loughborough Univs Innovation Center Ltd, 2002–06; Construction Industry Simulations Ltd, 2006–; Director: Loughborough Consultants Ltd, 1997–2003; Peterborough HE Co. Ltd, 1997–02; Innovative Projects Worldwide Ltd, 1998–2004; Emman Ltd, 2002–06; Imago Ltd, 2003–06. Mem., Programme Cttee, 1992–95, Educn, Trng and Competence to Practise Cttee, 1995–98, Strategy Rev. Gp, 1996, Royal Acad. of Engrg. Member: Engrg Construction Industry Trng Bd, 1994–2003; Technical Opportunities Panel, EPSRC, 2000–04; Civil Engrg Panel, 2001 RAE; Civil Engrg Sub-Panel, 2008 RAE; Associate Parly Gp for Engrg Develt, 1995–2009; Council Mem., E Midlands Innovation, 2005–09; Engrg Sectional Cttee, RSE, 2011–14. Member: BIM, later Chartered Mgt Inst., 1989–2010; ASCE, 1999–2010; Smeatonian Soc. Civil Engrs, 2011–. Visiting Professor: Univ. of Moratuwa, Sri Lanka, 1986–92; Technol Univ. of Malaysia, 1996, 2000, 2007, 2008, 2010; Sch. of Built and Natural Envmt, Glasgow Caledonian Univ., 2007–10. Mem., Bd of Trustees and Advr, British Univ. in Egypt, 2005–10. Moderating Examr, Engrg Council, 1988–92; past and present examr, univs in UK and overseas. Fellow, Instn of Shipbuilders and Engrs in Scotland, 2012–. Mem., Incorporation of Hammermen of Glasgow, 2015–. Editor, Engineering, Construction and Architectural Management, 1994–2014. *Publications:* Modern Construction Management, 1977, 7th edn 2013; Worked Examples in Construction Management, 1978, 2nd edn 1986; Estimating and Tendering for Civil Engineering Works, 1984, 2nd edn 1991; Management of Construction Equipment, 1982, 2nd edn 1991; International Bid Preparation, 1995; International Bidding Case Study, 1995; Management of Off-highway Plant and Equipment, 2002; jl articles and conf. papers. *Recreation:* being patient with administrators. *Address:* Department of Civil Engineering, Loughborough University, Loughborough, Leics LE11 3TU. *T:* (01509) 222600, 07710 975495, *Fax:* (01509) 223980. *E:* ronald@mccaffer.com. *W:* www.mccaffer.com.

McCAFFERTY, Christine; *b* 14 Oct. 1945; *d* of late John and Dorothy Livesley; *m* 1st, Michael McCafferty; one *s*; 2nd, David Tarlo. *Educ:* Whalley Range Grammar Sch. for Girls, Manchester; Footscray High Sch., Melbourne. Welfare Worker (Disabled), CHS Manchester, 1963–70; Educn Welfare Officer, Manchester Educn Cttee, 1970–72; Registrar of Marriages, Bury Registration Dist, 1978–80; Project worker, Calderdale Well Women Centre, 1989–96. Member: Calderdale MBC, 1991–97; W Yorks Police Authy, 1994–97. MP (Lab) Calder Valley, 1997–2010. Mem., Select Cttee on Internat. Develt, 2001–05; Chair, All-Pty Parly Gp on Population, Develt and Reproductive Health, 1999–2010, on Guides, 2000–10, on Compassion in Dying, 2007–10. Mem., Council of Europe/WEU, 1999–2010; Chm., Social Health and Family Affairs Cttee, Council of Europe, 2008–10. Dir, Royd Regeneration Ltd, 1996–2012. Mem. Exec., N Reg. Assoc. for the Blind, 1993–96. Gov., Luddenden Dene Sch.

McCAFFERTY, Ian Alexander; Member, Monetary Policy Committee, Bank of England, since 2012; *b* London, 1 July 1956; *s* of William John Edward McCafferty and Mary McCafferty (*née* Cutts); *m* 1982, Susan Jean Craig; two *s*. *Educ:* Dulwich Coll.; Univ. of Durham (BA Hons Econ 1978); Univ. of Amsterdam (Dip. European Integration 1979). Economist, ICC, 1980–83; Head: Statistics, The Economist, 1983–85; Economic Trends, CBI, 1985–88; Chief Internat. Economist, Baring Securities, 1987–92; Dir, Internat. Econs, NatWest Markets, 1993–97; Hd, Macroeconomics, BP, 1998–2001; Chief Econ. Advr, CBI, 2001–12. FRSA. Hon. DEcon Nottingham Trent, 2012. *Recreations:* golf, Rugby, cooking, music, France. *Address:* 25 Hayne Road, Beckenham, Kent BR3 4JA. *T:* (020) 8650 2442. *E:* ian.mccafferty@bankofengland.co.uk. *Club:* Sundridge Park Golf.

McCAFFERY, Prof. Peter, PhD; Deputy Vice Chancellor and Professor of Educational Leadership, London Metropolitan University, since 2011; *b* Durham, 2 Nov. 1952; *s* of Lawrence McCaffery and Margaret McCaffery (*née* Byrne); *m* 1977, Carol Stapleton; two *s*. *Educ:* St Bede's Grammar Sch., Lanchester; Univ. of Ulster (BA Hons Hist.); Swansea Univ. (MSc (Econ) Modern Social Hist.); Keele Univ. (PGCE); Univ. of Pennsylvania, Philadelphia; London Sch. of Econs and Political Sci. (PhD). QTS 1977. Hist. and politics teacher, Worthing Sixth Form Coll., 1978–84; Lectr, then Sen. Lectr, later Principal Lectr, Hist. and Amer. Studies, Ealing Coll. of HE, 1984–92; Associate Dean, Faculty of Creative, Cultural and Social Studies, 1992–96, Dean, Faculty of Eur., Internat. and Social Studies, 1996–99, Thames Valley Univ.; Vice Principal, Bolton Inst. of HE, 1999–2003; Pro-Vice Chancellor, London South Bank Univ., 2004–09; Vice Chancellor and Chief Exec., Univ. of Cumbria, 2009–10. Assessor, QAA, 1996–98. Mem. Bd, UCAS, 2010–. Idlewild Internat. Teaching Fellow, Univ. of Pennsylvania, Philadelphia, 1981–82; Churchill Fellow, 1997; Fellow, Leadership Foundn for HE, 2005. Gov., Holland Park Acad. Sch., 2013–. FCMI 2000; FRSA 2002; FCIPD 2003. *Publications:* When Bosses Ruled Philadelphia: the emergence of the Republican machine, 1867–1933, 1993; The HE Manager's Handbook: effective leadership and management in universities and colleges, 2004, 2nd edn 2010; 38 articles and reviews in Jl of Interdisciplinary Hist., Urban Hist., etc. *Recreations:* swimming (internat. masters swimmer), literature, music, theatre, Newcastle United Football Club. *Address:* London Metropolitan University, 166–220 Holloway Road, N7 8DB. *T:* (020) 7133 2401, *Fax:* (020) 7133 2476. *E:* peter.mccaffery@londonmet.ac.uk.

McCAFFREY, Sir Thos Daniel, (Sir Tom), Kt 1979; public affairs consultant; *b* 20 Feb. 1922; *s* of William P. and B. McCaffrey; *m* 1949, Agnes Campbell Douglas; two *s* four *d*. *Educ:* Hyndland Secondary Sch. and St Aloysius Coll., Glasgow. Served War, RAF, 1940–46. Scottish Office, 1948–61; Chief Information Officer, Home Office, 1966–71; Press Secretary, 10 Downing Street, 1971–72; Dir of Information Services, Home Office, 1972–74; Head of News Dept, FCO, 1974–76; Chief Press Sec. to Prime Minister, 1976–79; Chief of Staff to Rt Hon. James Callaghan, MP, 1979–80; Chief Asst to Rt Hon. Michael Foot, MP, 1980–83; Hd, Chief Executive's Office, BPCC, 1983–84; Dir, Public Affairs, and Special Advr to the Publisher, Mirror Gp Newspapers, 1984–85. *Address:* Balmaha, 2 The Park, Great Bookham, Surrey KT23 3JL. *T:* (01372) 454171.

McCAHILL, Patrick Gerard; QC 1996; **His Honour Judge McCahill;** a Circuit Judge, since 2001; a Specialist Chancery Circuit Judge, since 2007; *b* 6 May 1952; *s* of John McCahill and Josephine McCahill (*née* Conaghan); *m* 1979, Liselotte Gabrielle Steiner; two *d*. *Educ:* Corby GS; St Catharine's Coll., Cambridge (1st cl. Hons; MA); LLM London ext. 2003; BSc (1st cl. Hons) Open Univ. 2004. FCIArb 1992. Called to the Bar: Gray's Inn, 1975 (Bacon Schol., 1973; Atkin Schol., 1975), Bencher, 2014; King's Inns, Dublin, 1990; Asst Dep. Coroner for Birmingham and Solihull, 1984–99; Asst Recorder, 1993–97; a Recorder, 1997–2001. Member: Mental Health Review Tribunal, 2000–07; Parole Bd, 2004–07. *Recreations:* humour, family history, sport. *Address:* Bristol Civil Justice Centre, 2 Redcliff Street, Bristol BS1 6GR.

McCAIG, Callum; MP (SNP) Aberdeen South, since 2015; *b* 6 Jan. 1985. *Educ:* Cults Acad.; Edinburgh Univ. (MA Politics). Parly Asst to Maureen Watt, MSP, 2006. Mem. (SNP) Aberdeen CC, 2007–15 (Leader of Council, 2011–12; Leader, SNP Gp, 2011–15). *Address:* House of Commons, SW1A 0AA.

McCAIG, Prof. Colin Darnley, PhD; FRSE; Regius Professor of Physiology, since 2002, and Head, School of Medical Sciences, since 2003, University of Aberdeen; *b* 26 June 1953. *Educ:* Univ. of Edinburgh (BSc); Univ. of Glasgow (PhD). Beit Meml Res. Fellow, Univ. of Edinburgh, 1983–86; University of Aberdeen: MRC Sen. Fellow, 1986–88; Wellcome Trust

Univ. Award Lectr, 1988–93; Lectr, 1993–95; Sen. Lectr, 1995–99; Prof., 1999–2002; Hd, Dept of Biomed. Scis, 1998–2003. FRSE 2007. *Address:* School of Medical Sciences, Institute of Medical Sciences, University of Aberdeen, Foresterhill, Aberdeen AB25 2ZD.

McCAIN, John Sidney, III; US Senator from Arizona, since 1987; *b* Canal Zone, Panama, 29 Aug. 1936; *s* of John Sidney McCain and Roberta McCain (*née* Wright); *m* 1st, 1965, Carol Shepp (marr. diss. 1980); one *d*, and two step *s*; 2nd, 1980, Cindy Hensley; two *s* one *d*, and one adopted *d*. *Educ:* US Naval Acad.; Nat. War Coll. Naval aviator, USN, 1958–81; POW, Vietnam, 1967–73; Capt. 1977; Dir, Navy Senate Liaison Office, Washington, 1977–81; retd USN 1981. Vice-Pres., PR, Hensley & Co., 1981–83. Mem., US House of Reps from 1st Arizona Dist, 1983–86; Senate Committees: Member: Armed Services; Sci. and Transport; Chairman: Indian Affairs, 1995–97 and 2005–07; Commerce, 1997–2001 and 2003–05. Mem., Commn on Intelligence Capabilities of US regarding weapons of mass destruction, 2004. Republican Candidate: for Presidential nomination, 2000; for Presidency of USA, 2008. Chm., Internat. Republican Inst., 1993–. Legion of Merit (USA); Silver Star (USA); Purple Heart (USA); DFC (USA); Legion of Honour (Vietnam). *Publications:* (with Mark Salter): Faith of My Fathers, 1999; Worth the Fighting For: a memoir, 2002; Why Courage Matters: the way to a braver life, 2004; Character is Destiny, 2005; Hard Call, 2007.

McCALL, Carolyn, (Mrs P. Frawley), OBE 2008; Chief Executive, easyJet plc, since 2010; *b* 13 Sept. 1961; *d* of late Colleen and of Arthur McCall; *m* 1986, Peter Frawley; two *s* one *d*. *Educ:* Univ. of Kent (BA Hons Hist. and Politics); Inst. of Educn, Univ. of London (PGCE); Univ. of London (MA Politics). Risk Analyst, Costain Gp plc, 1984–86; The Guardian: planner, 1986–88; advertising exec., 1988–89; advertising manager, 1989–91; Product Develt Manager, 1991–92; Display Advertising Manager, 1992; Advertising Dir, Wire UK, 1992–94; Dep. Advertising Dir, 1994–95; Advertising Dir, 1995–97; Commercial Dir, 1997–98; Guardian Newspapers Ltd: Dep. Man. Dir, 1998–2000; Chief Exec., 2000–06; Chief Exec., Guardian Media Gp plc, 2006–10. Non-executive Director: New Look plc, 1999–2005 and 2010; Tesco plc, 2005–08; Lloyds TSB Gp, then Lloyds Banking Gp plc, 2008–09. Chair, Opportunity Now, 2005–09. Member: WACL, 1995–; Mktg Gp of GB. *Address:* easyJet plc, Hangar 89, London Luton Airport, Luton, Beds LU2 9PF.

McCALL, Christopher Hugh; QC 1987; *b* 3 March 1944; *yr s* of late Robin Home McCall, CBE and Joan Elizabeth (*née* Kingdon); *m* 1981, Henrietta Francesca Sharpe. *Educ:* Winchester (Scholar); Magdalen Coll., Oxford (Demy; BA Maths, 1964; Eldon Law Scholar, 1966). Called to the Bar, Lincoln's Inn, 1966, Bencher, 1993. Second Jun. Counsel to the Inland Revenue in chancery matters, 1977–87; Jun. Counsel to Attorney Gen. in charity matters, 1981–87. Mem., Bar Council, 1973–76. Trustee, British Mus., 1999–2004. *Recreations:* music, travel, Egyptomania. *Address:* Maitland Chambers, 7 Stone Buildings, Lincoln's Inn, WC2A 3SZ. *T:* (020) 7406 1200; Sphinx Hill, Ferry Lane, Moulsford on Thames OX10 9JF. *T:* (01491) 652162. *Clubs:* Alpine; Leander (Henley-on-Thames).

McCALL, Rt Rev. David; *see* McCall, Rt Rev. W. D. H.

McCALL, David Slesser, CBE 1988; DL; Chairman, Anglia Television Ltd, 1994–2001 (Director, 1970–2001; Chief Executive, 1976–94); *b* 3 Dec. 1934; *s* of Patrick McCall and Florence Kate Mary Walker; *m* 1968, Lois Patricia Elder. *Educ:* Robert Gordon's Coll., Aberdeen. Mem., Inst. of Chartered Accountants of Scotland, 1958. National Service, 1959–61. Accountant, Grampian Television Ltd, 1961–68; Company Sec., Anglia Television Ltd, 1968–76; Dir, 1970–98, Chief Exec., 1986–94, Chm., 1994–98, Anglia Television Gp. Chairman: Oxford Scientific Films Ltd, 1982–89; Greene King plc, 1995–2005; United Trustees Ltd, 1997–; United Exec. Trustee Ltd, 1998–; 99.9 Radio Norwich Ltd, 2006–; Director: ITN, 1978–86, 1991–96; Ind. Television Publications Ltd, 1971–89; Ind. Television Assoc. Ltd, 1976–96; Sodastream Holdings Ltd, 1976–85; Norwich City Football Club, 1979–85; Channel Four Television Co., 1981–85; Radio Broadland, 1984–91; Super Channel Ltd, 1986–88; British Satellite Broadcasting, 1987–90; Regl Adv. Bd, National Westminster Bank, 1988–92; TSMS Group Ltd, 1989–96; Hodder & Stoughton Holdings Ltd, 1992–93; Cosgrove Hall Films, 1993–96; MAI plc, 1994–96; MAI Media UK Ltd, 1995–96; Meridian Broadcasting Ltd, 1994–96; Satellite Inf. Services, 1994–96; Village Roadshow Ltd, Australia, 1994–96; Bakers Dozen Inns Ltd, 1996–2006; Anglia FM Ltd, 1996–99; Anglo Welsh Group PLC, 1996–2000; Bernard Matthews Gp PLC, 1996–2000; Granada Pension Trust Co. Ltd, 2000–03; Bernard Matthews Hldgs Ltd, 2002–; Bernard Matthews Ltd, 2009–13. Chm., Forum Trust Ltd (formerly Norfolk and Norwich Millennium Bid), 1996–2005; Dep. Chm., United Broadcasting and Entertainment, 1996. Mem., ITCA, subseq. Ind. Television Assoc., 1976–95 (Chm., 1986–88); Pres., Cinema and Television Benevolent Fund, 1998–2001 (Trustee, 1995–). Pres., Norfolk and Norwich Chamber of Commerce, 1988–90 (Dep. Pres., 1986–88); Chm., Norwich Playhouse Theatre, 1992–98. Treas., 1995–97, Chm. Council, 1997–2006, UEA. FRTS 1988; FRSA 1993. CCMI (CBIM 1988). DL Norfolk, 1992. Hon. DCL UEA, 2006. *Recreations:* sport, travel. *Address:* Woodland Hall, Redenhall, Harleston, Norfolk IP20 9QW. *T:* (01379) 854442.

McCALL, Duncan James; QC 2008; *b* 8 May 1965; *s* of John Berry McCall and Stella McCall. *Educ:* Magdalen Coll., Oxford (BA). Called to the Bar, Gray's Inn, 1988; in practice as barrister, 1989–. *Address:* 4 Pump Court, Temple, EC4Y 7AN. *T:* (020) 7842 5555, *Fax:* (020) 7583 2036. *E:* dmccall@4pumpcourt.com.

McCALL, William; General Secretary, Institution of Professional Civil Servants, 1963–89; *b* 6 July 1929; *s* of Alexander McCall and Jean Corbet Cunningham; *m* 1955, Olga Helen Brunton; one *s* one *d*. *Educ:* Dumfries Academy; Ruskin College, Oxford. Civil Service, 1946–52; Social Insurance Dept, TUC, 1954–58; Asst Sec., Instn of Professional Civil Servants, 1958–63; Mem., Civil Service Nat. Whitley Council (Staff Side), 1963–89, Chm. 1969–71, Vice-Chm. 1983. Hon. Treasurer, Parly and Scientific Cttee, 1976–80; Part-time Mem., Eastern Electricity Board, 1977–86; Member: Cttee of Inquiry into Engrg Profession, 1977–79; PO Arbitration Tribunal, 1980–90; TUC Gen. Council, 1984–89; Pay and Employment Policy Cttee, CVCP, 1990–94; Police Complaints Authority, 1991–94. Member Council: Univ. of London, 1994–97 (Mem. Ct, 1984–94); Goldsmiths' Coll., 1989–95 (Hon. Fellow, 1996). *Address:* Foothills, Gravel Path, Berkhamsted, Herts HP4 2PF. *T:* (01442) 864974.

McCALL, Rt Rev. (William) David (Hair); Priest-in-charge, St Cyprian's, North Adelaide, 2010–15; *b* 29 Feb. 1940; *s* of late Rt Rev. Theodore Bruce McCall, ThD, Bishop of Wangaratta, and Helen Christie McCall; *m* 1969, Marion Carmel le Breton; two *s* three *d*. *Educ:* Launceston and Sydney Grammar Schools; Saint Michael's House, Crafers. Deacon 1963, priest 1964, dio. Riverina; Assistant Curate: St Alban's, Griffith, 1963–64; St Peter's, Broken Hill, 1965–67; Priest-in-charge, Barellan-Weethalle, 1967–73; Rector: St John's, Corowa, 1973–78; St George's, Goodwood, 1978–87; Pastoral Chaplain, St Barnabas' Theol Coll., 1980–87; Bishop of Willochra, 1987–2000; Bishop of Bunbury, 2000–10. Bishop assisting Archbishop of Adelaide, 2010–15; permission to officiate, 2015–. *Recreations:* reading, walking, gardening.

McCALL SMITH, Prof. Alexander, CBE 2007; PhD; FRSE, FMedSci; writer; Professor of Medical Law, University of Edinburgh, 1995–2005, now Emeritus; *b* 24 Aug. 1948; *s* of Sandy McCall Smith and Daphne McCall Smith (*née* Woodall); *m* 1982, Dr Elizabeth Parry; two *d*. *Educ:* Christian Brothers Coll., Bulawayo; Univ. of Edinburgh (LLB; PhD). Admitted to Faculty of Advocates, 2010. Lectr in Law, Queen's Univ., Belfast, 1973–74; Lectr in Law, subseq. Reader in Law, Univ. of Edinburgh, 1974–95; Hd, Dept of Law, Univ. of Botswana, 1981 (on secondment). Vis. Prof. of Law, Law Sch., Southern Methodist Univ., Dallas, 1988. Vice-Chm., Human Genetics Commn, 2000–04; Mem., Internat. Bioethics Cttee, UNESCO, 1997–2004. FRSE 2001; FMedSci 2005. Hon. FRCPE 2004. Hon. DIur Parma, 2005; Hon. DLitt: Napier, 2005; Aberdeen, 2006, BC, 2006; Southern Methodist Univ., Dallas, 2009; Leicester, 2008; QUB, 2009; Buckingham, 2010; Hon. LLD Edinburgh, 2007; Queen's Univ., Ont, 2008; Hon. DSc UEA, 2007. Saga Award, 2004; Author of the Year, British Book Awards, 2004; Gold Medal, American Acad. of Achievement, 2009; Burke Medal, Trinity Coll. Dublin Histl Soc., 2012. Presidential Order of Meritorious Service (Botswana), 2010. *Publications:* over 80 books including: (with J. K. Mason) Law and Medical Ethics, 1983, 6th edn 2002; (with K. Frimpong) The Criminal Law of Botswana, 1991; (with C. Shapiro) Forensic Aspects of Sleep, 1997; (with A. Merry) Errors, Medicine and the Law, 2001; *fiction:* Portuguese Irregular Verbs, 1997; The Finer Points of Sausage Dogs, 1998; 2½ Pillars of Wisdom, 2002; At the Villa of Reduced Circumstances, 2003; The Girl Who Married a Lion (short stories), 2004; Dream Angus, 2006; La's Orchestra Saves the World, 2008; Unusual Uses for Olive Oil, 2011; Trains & Lovers, 2012; What W. H. Auden Can Do For You, 2013; The Forever Girl, 2014; Emma: a modern retelling, 2014; *The No 1 Ladies' Detective Agency series:* The No 1 Ladies' Detective Agency, 1998; Tears of the Giraffe, 2000; Morality for Beautiful Girls, 2001; The Kalahari Typing School for Men, 2002; The Full Cupboard of Life, 2003; In the Company of Cheerful Ladies, 2004; Blue Shoes and Happiness, 2006; The Good Husband of Zebra Drive, 2007; The Miracle at Speedy Motors, 2008; Tea Time for the Traditionally Built, 2009; The Double Comfort Safari Club, 2010; The Saturday Big Tent Wedding Party, 2011; The Limpopo Academy of Private Detection, 2012; The Minor Adjustment Beauty Salon, 2013; The Handsome Man's De Luxe Cafe, 2014; *The Sunday Philosophy Club series:* The Sunday Philosophy Club, 2004; Friends, Lovers, Chocolate, 2005; The Right Attitude to Rain, 2006; The Careful Use of Compliments, 2007; The Comfort of Saturdays, 2008; The Lost Art of Gratitude, 2009; The Charming Quirks of Others, 2010; The Forgotten Affairs of Youth, 2011; The Uncommon Appeal of Clouds, 2012; *The 44 Scotland Street series:* 44 Scotland Street, 2005; Espresso Tales, 2005; Love Over Scotland, 2006; The World According to Bertie, 2007; The Unbearable Lightness of Scones, 2008; The Importance of Being Seven, 2010; Bertie Plays the Blues, 2011; Sunshine on Scotland Street, 2012; Bertie's Guide to Life and Mothers, 2013; *Corduroy Mansions series:* Corduroy Mansions, 2009; The Dog Who Came in from the Cold, 2010; A Conspiracy of Friends, 2011; books for children incl. Precious and the Puggies, 2011; Precious and the Monkeys, 2012; Precious and the Mystery of Meerkat Hill, 2012; The Great Cake Mystery, 2012; *librettos:* The Okavango Macbeth, 2011; A Tapestry of Many Threads, 2012. *Recreation:* wind instruments. *Clubs:* New, Scottish Arts (Edinburgh).

McCALLA, Hon. Zaila Rowena, OJ 2007; Chief Justice of Jamaica, since 2007; *b* Westmoreland, Jamaica, 31 Jan. 1948; *d* of Herbert and Beryl Morris; *m* Adolph Holness (marr. diss.); *m* 1981, William McCalla; two *s* one *d*. *Educ:* Univ. of West Indies (LLB Hons); Norman Manley Law Sch. (Cert. Legal Educn). Manager, Montego Bay Co-op. Credit Union, 1971–72; Dep. Clerk of Courts, 1976–77; Clerk of Courts, 1977–80; Crown Counsel, Office of the DPP, 1980–85; Actg Asst DPP, 1985; Resident Magistrate, 1985–96; Sen. Resident Magistrate, 1996; Actg Master in Chambers, 1993–96, Master in Chambers, 1996–97; Judge, Supreme Court of Jamaica, 1997; Actg Judge, Grand Court of Cayman Is, 2006; Actg Judge of Appeal, 2004–06, Judge of Appeal, 2006–07. Chm., Judicial Service Commn. Chairman: Supreme Court Rules Cttee; Queen's Counsel Cttee; Resident Magistrates' Rules Cttee; Archives Adv. Cttee; Co-Chm., Consultative Cttee, Jamaican Bar Assoc. and Bench; Member: Cttee reviewing Legal Aid system; Cttee formulating Code of Conduct for Justice of the Peace, 2006. Former Pres., Resident Magistrates' Assoc. Chm., Justice Trng Inst. Adv. Bd. Mem., Council of Legal Educn. Keeper of Records, Island Record Office. Mem., Editl Bd, Caribbean Civil Court Practice. Mem., St Margaret Anglican Ch. *Recreations:* gardening, cooking, reading. *Address:* Supreme Court, Public Building East, PO Box 491, King Street, Kingston, Jamaica. *T:* 92283006, *Fax:* 9670669.

McCALLUM, His Honour Alastair Grindlay; a Circuit Judge, 1992–2012; *b* 28 Feb. 1947; *s* of William and Catherine McCallum; *m* 1969, Lindsay Sheila Watkins; two *d*. *Educ:* Gilbert Rennie, Northern Rhodesia; Leeds Univ. (LLB, LLM (Com.)). Called to the Bar, Inner Temple, 1970; Asst Recorder, 1984; Recorder, 1989; Head of Chambers, 1990. *Recreations:* golf, travel, reading. *Club:* Bradford.

McCALLUM, Helen Mary; Director General, Consumers International, 2011–13; *b* 23 Dec. 1952; *d* of Edward James Ward and Pauline Ward; *m* 1980, Duncan Peter Finlay McCallum; two *d*. *Educ:* Queen Elizabeth's Girls' Grammar Sch., Barnet; Nottingham Univ. (BA Hons English Lit.). Sabbatical Sec., Students' Union, Univ. of Nottingham, 1973–74; Admin. Asst (PR), Univ. of Sheffield, 1974–78; PRO, Univ. of Salford, 1978–81; freelance publications work, 1981–85; Alumni Officer, Univ. of Sheffield, 1985–88; Sen. PR Manager, 1989–92, Hd of Communications, 1992–94, E Anglian RHA; Hd of Communications, NHS Exec., 1994–98; Dir of Communications, DoH, 1999–2001; Dir of Corporate Affairs, Envmt Agency, 2001–07; Dir, Policy, 2007–08, Dir, Policy, Campaigns and Communications, 2008–11, Which? (Consumers' Assoc.). Mem., Assoc. of Health Care Communicators, 1989. Chm., Cambs and Peterborough Arts and Minds, 2015–. Trustee: Keep Britain Tidy, 2007–12; Diabetes UK, 2014–. *Recreations:* amateur dramatics, keeping moderately fit. *Address:* 79 Gilbert Road, Cambridge CB4 3NZ.

McCALLUM, Ian Stewart; Executive Sales Manager, Save & Prosper Sales Ltd, 1989–95 (Sales Manager, 1985–87, Area Manager, 1987–89); *b* 24 Sept. 1936; *s* of late John Blair McCallum and Margaret Stewart McCallum; *m* 1st, 1957, Pamela Mary (*née* Shave) (marr. diss. 1984); one *s* two *d*; 2nd, 1984, Jean (*née* Lynch); two step *d*. *Educ:* Kingston Grammar Sch. Eagle Star Insurance Co. Ltd, 1953–54; National Service, Highland Light Infantry, 1954–56; Eagle Star Insce Co. Ltd, 1956–58; F. E. Wright and Co., Insurance Brokers, 1958–63; H. Clarkson (Home) Ltd, Insurance Brokers, 1963–68; Save & Prosper Group Ltd, 1968–95. Leader, Woking Borough Council, 1972–76 and 1978–81, Dep. Leader, 1981–82; Mayor of Woking, 1976–77; Chm., Assoc. of Dist Councils, 1979–84 (Leader, 1974–79); Vice-Chairman: Standing Cttee on Local Authorities and Theatre, 1977–81; UK Steering Cttee on Local Authority Superannuation, 1974–84; Member: Local Authorities Conditions of Service Adv. Bd, 1973–84; Consultative Council on Local Govt Finance, 1975–84; Council for Business in the Community, 1981–84; Audit Commn, 1983–86; Health Promotion Res. Trust, 1983–97. Vice-Chm., Sports Council, 1980–86; Pres., European Sports Conf., 1983–85. *Recreations:* swimming, walking, reading, bowls. *Address:* 20 Perch Close, Leybourne Lakes, Larkfield, Kent ME20 6TN. *T:* (01622) 719442.

McCALLUM, Martin; producer; theatre designer and consultant; *b* 6 April 1950; *s* of Raymond and Jessie; *m* 1st, 1971, Lesley Nunnerley (marr. diss.); one *s* one *d*; 2nd, 1986, Julie Edmett (marr. diss.); one *d*; 3rd, 1989, Mary Ann Rolfe (marr. diss.); two *s*. *Educ:* Barfield Sch., Surrey; Frensham Heights Sch., Surrey. Entered theatre as student asst stage manager, Castle Th., Farnham, 1967; worked throughout rep. system; Prodn Manager, NT at Old Vic, 1971–75; prodns incl. Merchant of Venice, Long Day's Journey into Night, Saturday Sunday Monday; moved to S Bank, 1975; founder and Prodn Manager, The Production Office, West End, 1978–84; prodns incl. Filumena, Evita, Sweeney Todd, Cats; Man. Dir, 1981–2000, Vice-Chm., 2000–03, Cameron Mackintosh Ltd; prodns incl. Les Miserables, Phantom of the Opera, Miss Saigon, Oliver!; Director: Donmar Warehouse Th., 1992–2008 (Chm., 1996–2004); Philip Quast: live at the Donmar, 2002; Sydney Theatre Co., 2005–; prod., Edward Scissorhands, London and world tour, 2005, UK tour, 2014–15 (New York Drama Desk Award, 2007); exec. prod., Spider-Man Turn Off the Dark, NY, 2011, The Cripple of Inishmaan, NY, 2014; Dirty Dancing, Australian tour, 2014–15. Consultant: to

Glyndebourne Fest. Opera, 1980–81; to Regl Th. Scheme, Arts Council, 1980. Theatre designer and consultant: Old Fire Station Th., Oxford, 1991; Musical Hall, Stuttgart, 1994; Musical Th., Duisburg, 1996; Schaumburg Village Th., Ill, 2002; restorations: Prince Edward Th., London, 1993; Capital Th., Sydney, 1995; Th. Royal, Sydney, 1998; Auditorium Th., Chicago, 2001; Fine Arts Bldg Theatres, Chicago, 2003; Prince of Wales' Th., London, 2004; Montecasino Th., Johannesburg, 2007. Initiated Wyndham Report (on economic importance of West End theatre), 1998; initiated Theatre 2001 - Future Directions, inaugural jt theatre conference of SOLT/TMA/ITC, 2001. Mem., SOLT, 1999– (Pres. 1999–2002). Member: Drama Panel, 1999–2004, Adv. Task Gp, 2003–05, Arts Council England (formerly Arts Council of England); London's Cultural Strategy Gp, 2000–04; Th. Mus. Cttee, V&A, 2002–06. FRSA 1995. Mem., Broadway League (formerly League of Amer. Theatres and Producers), 1988–2011. *Recreations:* the performing arts, music, art, gardens.

MacCALLUM, Very Rev. Norman Donald; Dean of Argyll and the Isles, 2005–12; Provost of St John's Cathedral, Oban, and Priest-in-charge, St James', Ardbrecknish and Church of the Holy Spirit, Ardchattan, 2000–12; *b* 26 April 1947; *s* of James MacCallum and Euphemia MacCallum (*née* Campbell); *m* 1972, Barbara MacColl Urquhart; one *s* one *d*. *Educ:* St John's Episcopal Sch., Ballachulish; Kinlochleven Jun. Secondary Sch.; Oban High Sch.; Edinburgh Univ. (LTh 1970); Edinburgh Theol Coll. Midlothian, E Lothian and Peebles Social Work Dept, 1970; ordained deacon, 1971, priest, 1972; Livingston Ecumenical Experiment, 1971–82; Rector, St Mary's, Grangemouth, and Priest-in-charge, St Catharine's, Bo'ness, 1982–2000; Synod Clerk, Dio. Edinburgh and Canon of St Mary's Cathedral, Edinburgh, 1996–2000. Adminr, Scottish Episcopal Clergy Appraisal Scheme, 1997–2006; Mem., Scottish Religious Adv. Cttee, BBC Scotland, 1997–2005. *Recreations:* hill-walking, photography, history. *Address:* Kinnoull, 57 Nant Drive, Oban PA34 4NL. *T:* (01631) 569846, 07776 496487.

McCAMLEY, Sir Graham (Edward), KBE 1986 (MBE 1981); owner, cattle properties, since 1954; *b* 24 Aug. 1932; *s* of Edward William George and Ivy McCamley; *m* 1956, Shirley Clarice Tindale (*d* 2010); one *s* two *d*. *Educ:* Rockhampton Grammar Sch. President: Aust. Brahman Breeders, 1971–74; Central Coastal Graziers, 1974–75; Cattlemen's Union of Australia, 1976–78. Mem. Producer of Australian Meat and Livestock Co., 1982–84; Chm., Beeflands Australia Pty Ltd, 1994–97. *Recreations:* tennis, flying helicopter and fixed wing aircraft. *Clubs:* Queensland (Brisbane); Rockhampton and District Masonic.

McCANDLESS, Air Vice-Marshal Brian Campbell, CB 1999; CBE 1990; Director, Government Consultancy Services, since 2002; e-Government Director, Oracle Corporation UK, 1999–2002; *b* 14 May 1944; *s* of Norman Samuel McCandless and Rebecca Campbell; *m* 1969, Yvonne Haywood; one *s*. *Educ:* Methodist Coll., Belfast; RAF Tech. Coll., Henlow (BSc 1967); Birmingham Univ. (MSc 1972); RAF Staff Coll. RAF, 1962–99: posts included: OC 26 Signals Unit, 1985–87; OC RAF Henlow, 1987–89; Dep. Chief, Architecture and Plans Div., NATO CIS Agency, Brussels, 1989–92; Dir, Comd Control and Management Inf. Systems, RAF, 1992–93; Dir, Communications and Inf. Systems, RAF, 1993–95; AO Communications and Inf. Systems, and AOC Signals Units, 1996–99. *Recreations:* bridge, music, sailing, hill walking. *Club:* Royal Air Force.

McCANN, Michael; *b* Glasgow, 2 Jan. 1964; *s* of Charles and Bridget McCann; *m* 1989, Tracy Anne Thomson; one *s* one *d*. *Educ:* St Bride's High Sch.; St Andrew's High Sch. Admin. Officer, ODA, 1982–92; Scottish Officer, CPSA, 1992–98; Dep. Scottish Officer, PCS, 1998–2008. Mem. (Lab) S Lanarks Council, 1999– (Vice-Chair: E Kilbride Area Cttee, 1999–2003; Social Work Resources, 2003–07; Depute Leader, 2007–10). MP (Lab) E Kilbride, Strathaven and Lesmahagow, 2010–15; contested (Lab) same seat, 2015. *Recreations:* golf, football (watching it!).

McCANNY, Prof. John Vincent, CBE 2002; FRS 2002; FREng; Professor of Microelectronics Engineering, since 1988, Director, Institute of Electronics, Communications and Information Technology, since 2001, and Principal Investigator, Centre for Secure Information Technology, since 2009, Queen's University of Belfast; *b* 25 June 1952; *s* of Patrick Joseph McCanny and Kathleen Brigid McCanny (*née* Kerr); *m* 1979, Maureen Bernadette Mellon; one *s* one *d*. *Educ:* Univ. of Manchester (BSc Physics Hons 1973); Univ. of Ulster, Coleraine (PhD Solid State Physics 1978); Queen's Univ., Belfast (DSc Electronics Eng 1998). CPhys, MInstP 1982, FInstP 1992; CEng, MIEE 1985, FIET (FIEE 1992); IEEE Fellow 1999; FREng 1995; MRIA 2000; FIAE 2006; FIEI 2006. Lectr in Physics, Univ. of Ulster, Coleraine, 1977–79; Higher SO, 1979–82, SSO, 1982–84, PSO, 1984, RSRE, Malvern; Queen's University of Belfast: EPSRC IT Res. Lectr, Sch. of Electrical and Electronic Engrg, 1984–87; Reader in VLSI Signal Processing, 1987–88; Hd, Digital Signal Processing and Telecommunications Res. Div., 1988–2004; Hd, Sch. of Electronics, Electrical Engrg and Computer Sci., 2005–10. Guest Prof., Shanghai Univ., 2010–. Founder, 1988, Dir, 1988–96, Audio Processing Technology Ltd; Founder, 1994, pt-time Chief Technology Officer, 1994–2004, Amphion Semiconductor Ltd (formerly Integrated Silicon Systems Ltd). Dir, Inst. of Advanced Microelectronics in Ireland, 1989–91. Mem. Bd, Nat. Tyndall ICT Inst., Ireland, 2004–11; Mem., Sectl Cttee 4, 2004–06 and 2011–14 (Chm., 2005, 2006), Mem., Hook Cttee, 2010–13, Chair, Policy Steering Cttee, 'Cyber Security research: a vision for the UK', 2013–14, Royal Soc.; Member: Sub-Panel 24, Electrical and Electronics Engrg, 2008 RAE, HEFCE, 2005–08; IT Strategic Adv. Team, EPSRC, 2006–11; Emerging Technols and Industries Strategy Gp, UK Technol. Strategy Bd, 2010–; Sub-Panel 13, Electrical and Electronic Engrg, Metallurgy and Materials, HEFCE REF, 2011–14. Mem., Council, 2008–11, Internat. Cttee, 2009–13, RAEng; Mem. Council, Royal Irish Acad., 2012–13. Mem., Internat. Adv. Bd, German Excellence Initiative Centre for Ultra High Speed Mobile Information and Communication, RWTH Aachen Univ., 2007–13. FRSA 1996. Silver Medal, Royal Acad. of Engrg, 1996; Millennium Medal, IEEE, 2000; Boyle Medal, Royal Dublin Soc./Irish Times, 2003; IT Professional of the Year, BCS (Belfast Br.), 2004; Faraday Medal, IET, 2006; Cunningham Medal, RIA, 2011. *Publications:* (ed jtly) VLSI Technology and Design, 1987; (ed jtly) Systolic Array Processors, 1989; (ed jtly) VLSI Systems for DSP and Control, 1991; (ed jtly) Signal Processing Systems: design and implementation, 1997; (with Maire McLoone) System-on-Chip Architectures and Implementation for Private-Key Data Encryption, 2003; 360 scientific papers in major internat. jls and confs; 25 patents. *Recreations:* golf, soccer, Rugby, cricket, guitar, photography, films. *Address:* Institute of Electronics, Communications and Information Technology, Queen's University of Belfast, Northern Ireland Science Park, Queen's Road, Queen's Island, Belfast BT3 9DT. *Club:* Clandeboye Golf.

McCARRY, Frances Jane; *see* McMenamin, F. J.

McCARTAN, Patrick Anthony, CBE 2008; Chairman, Belfast Health and Social Care Trust, 2006–12; *b* Belfast, 28 Dec. 1945; *s* of Henry McCartan and Margaret McCartan (*née* Gillespie); *m* 1972, Margaret Petrea Owens; one *s* one *d*. *Educ:* Queen's Univ. Belfast (Trade Union studies); Henley Mgt Coll.; Univ. of Ulster (MSc Dist. 1988). FCIPD 1991. NI Civil Service, 1962–72; NI Area Sec., APEX, 1972–90; Sen. Lectr and Hd of Dept, Centre for Mgt Educn, Univ. of Ulster, 1990–2002; Chairman: NW Belfast HSS Trust, 2001–06; Labour Relns Agency, 2002–08. Chm., Ind. Financial Rev. Panel, NI Assembly, 2011–. Trustee, NHS Confedn, 2005–11. Consultant, employment relns and mgt devel, 1990–. Chm. and Mem. Bd, Co-operation Ireland, 1991–2004; Member Board: SE Educn and Liby Bd, 1976–83; NI Econ. Council, 1978–82; IDB, 1982–89; Council for Catholic Maintained Schs, 1996–2004, 2014–. Mem. Bd, St Columbanus Coll., Bangor, 1976– (Chm., 2000–08, 2013–). *Recreations:* motorcycling (former road racer), golf, singing, playing guitar badly. *E:* mccartan@btinternet.com. *T:* (028) 9096 0000.

McCARTHY, Anthony David; consultant on leadership, change, productivity and performance; *b* 14 April 1956; *s* of Robert Alan and Ena Mary McCarthy; *m* 1983, Patricia Barbara Blakey; one *s* one *d* (and one *d* decd). *Educ:* Sheffield Poly. (BA Hons (Business Studies) 1978); Salford Univ. (Postgrad. Dip. 1982). MCIPD 1980. British Aerospace, subseq. BAESYSTEMS, 1978–2003: various human resource appts; HR Dir, Royal Ordnance, 1995–97; Chm., Royal Ordnance Pensions Trustees, 1997–98; Gp HR Dir, 2001–03; Gp Dir People, Royal Mail Gp, 2003–07; Dir, People and Orgnl Effectiveness, British Airways, 2007–11. *Recreations:* golf (not very well!), most sports as spectator, keen supporter of Burnley FC. *Club:* Preston Golf.

McCARTHY, Arlene, OBE 2015; Director, AMC Strategy, 2014–15; *b* 10 Oct. 1960; *d* of J. J. McCarthy and F. L. McCarthy. *Educ:* South Bank Poly. (BA Hons). Researcher and Press Officer to Leader of European PLP, 1990–91; Lectr in Politics, Freie Univ., Berlin, 1991–92; Head of European Affairs, Kirklees MBC, W Yorks, 1992–94. MEP (Lab) Peak Dist, 1994–99, NW Reg., 1999–2014. European PLP (formerly Socialist Gp and European PLP) spokesperson on regl affairs, 1994–2004; on internat. mkt and legal affairs, 1999–2004; on internal mkt and consumer protection, 2004–14; on legal affairs, 2004–14. Mem., Internal Mkt and Consumer Protection Cttee, EP, 2004–09 (Chm., 2006–09); Vice Chm., EP Cttee on Econ. and Monetary Affairs, 2009–14; Mem., EP Delegn for Relns with Switzerland, Iceland and Norway and to Eur. Econ. Area Jt Parly Cttee, 2009–14; Substitute Mem., EP Delegn to EU-Turkey Jt Parly Cttee, 2009–14. *Publications:* (ed jtly) Changing States: a Labour agenda for Europe, 1996; EP reports on reform of structural funds and gen. provisions of structural funds and on intellectual property and financial services; articles on European issues for local govt jls. *E:* arlenemccarthyobe@icloud.com.

McCARTHY, Sir Callum, Kt 2005; PhD; Chairman, Financial Services Authority, 2003–08; Member of Court, Bank of England, 2003–08; *b* 29 Feb. 1944; *s* of Ralph and Nan McCarthy; *m* 1966, Penelope Ann Gee; two *s* one *d*. *Educ:* Manchester Grammar Sch.; City of London Sch.; Merton Coll., Oxford (BA 1965); Stirling Univ. (PhD 1971); Grad. Sch. of Business, Stanford Univ. (Sloan Fellow; MS 1982). Operations Res., ICI, 1965–72; various posts from Economic Adv. to Under Sec., DTI, 1972–85; Dir, Kleinwort Benson, 1985–89; Man. Dir, BZW, 1989–93; CEO, Barclays Bank, Japan, 1993–96, Barclays Bank, N America, 1996–98; Dir Gen., subseq. Chief Exec., Ofgem, 1999–2003 (Gas Supply, 1998–2003, Electricity Supply, 1999–2003); Chm., Gas and Electricity Mkts Authy, 2000–03; European Chm., JC Flowers, 2009–12. Freeman, City of London, 2008. *Publications:* (with D. S. Davies) Introduction to Technological Economics, 1967. *Recreations:* walking, cooking, reading, beekeeping.

See also T. P. McCarthy.

MacCARTHY, Fiona, OBE 2009; biographer and cultural historian; *b* 23 Jan. 1940; *m* 1966, David Mellor (*d* 2009), CBE, RDI; one *s* one *d*. *Educ:* Wycombe Abbey Sch.; Lady Margaret Hall, Oxford (MA Hons Eng. Lang. and Lit.; Hon. Fellow, 2007). FRSL 1997. Design Correspondent, Guardian, 1963–69; Women's Editor, Evening Standard, 1969–70; Literary Critic: The Times, 1980–90; Observer, 1990–98; an Associate Editor, Oxford DNB, 1998–2005. Sen. Fellow, RCA, 1997 (Hon. Fellow, 1990). Hon. FRIBA 2012. Hon. DLitt Sheffield, 1996; DUniv Sheffield Hallam, 2001. Bicentenary Medal, RSA, 1986. *Publications:* All Things Bright and Beautiful: British design 1830 to today, 1972; The Simple Life: C. R. Ashbee in the Cotswolds, 1981; The Omega Workshops: decorative arts of Bloomsbury, 1984; Eric Gill, 1989; William Morris: a life for our time, 1994 (Wolfson History Prize; Yorkshire Post Art Book Award; Writer's Guild Non-Fiction Award); Stanley Spencer: an English vision, 1997; Byron: life and legend, 2002; Last Curtsey: the end of the debutantes, 2006; The Last Pre-Raphaelite: Edward Burne-Jones and the Victorian Imagination, 2011 (James Tait Black Prize, 2012); Anarchy and Beauty: William Morris and his legacy, 2014; articles in The Guardian, TLS, New York Review of Books. *Recreations:* museums, theatre, looking at buildings, wasting time. *Address:* The Round Building, Hathersage, Sheffield S32 1BA. *T:* (01433) 650220. *E:* fionamaccarthy@davidmellordesign.co.uk.

McCARTHY, John Patrick, CBE 1992; journalist; *b* 27 Nov. 1956; *yr s* of late Pat and Sheila McCarthy; *m* 1999, Anna Ottewill; one *d*. *Educ:* Haileybury; Hull Univ. (BA 1979). Joined UPITN (later WTN) as journalist, 1982. Kidnapped and held hostage in Beirut, 17 April 1986–8 Aug. 1991. BBC TV series (with Sandi Toksvig), Island Race, 1995; ITV series: It Ain't Necessarily So, 2001; John Meets Paul, 2003; Faultlines, 2003; ITV documentary, Out of the Shadows, 2004; BBC Radio 4 series: John McCarthy's Bible Journey, 1999; A Place Called Home, 2000. Patron, Medical Foundn for the Care of Victims of Torture. Hon. DLitt Hull, 1991. *Publications:* (with Jill Morrell) Some Other Rainbow, 1993; (with Sandi Toksvig) Island Race: improbable voyage around the coast of Britain, 1995; (with Brian Keenan) Between Extremes, 1999; A Ghost Upon your Path, 2002; You Can't Hide the Sun: a journey through Israel and Palestine, 2012. *Address:* c/o LAW, 14 Vernon Street, W14 0RJ.

McCARTHY, John Sidney, MBE 1984; FCIOB; Executive Chairman, 1990–2000, non-executive Chairman, 2001–03, McCarthy & Stone; *b* 31 Dec. 1939; *s* of John James McCarthy and Helen Caroline McCarthy; *m* 1982, Gwendoline Joan Holmes; three *s* one *d*. McCarthy & Stone: Joint Founder, 1963; Chief Exec./Chm., 1963–90. Founder, 1987, and Trustee, 1996–98, McCarthy Foundn. Non-exec. Dir, Churchill Retirement Living plc, 2004–. *Recreations:* ski-ing, golf, shooting, polo, sailing, subaqua diving, furniture making, big game hunting. *Clubs:* Royal Ocean Racing; Royal Guernsey Golf; Salisbury and S Wilts Golf; Rushmore Golf; Remedy Oak Golf.

McCARTHY, Kerry; MP (Lab) Bristol East, since 2005; *b* 26 March 1965; *d* of late Oliver Thomas Haughney and of Sheila Ann Rix (*née* Smith); name changed to McCarthy, 1992. *Educ:* Univ. of Liverpool (BA Hons Russian, Politics and Linguistics); City of London Poly. Legal Asst, S Beds Magistrates' Court, 1986–88; Litigation Asst, Neves (Solicitors), 1988–89; trainee, Wilde Sapte, 1992–94; admitted solicitor, 1994; Lawyer, Abbey National Treasury Services plc, 1994–96; Sen. Counsel, Merrill Lynch Europe plc, 1996–99; Lawyer, Labour Party, 2001; Regl Dir, Britain in Europe, 2002–04; Hd, Public Policy, Waterfront Partnership, 2004–05. Dir, London Luton Airport Ltd, 1999–2003. PPS to Minister of State, Dept of Health, 2007, to Sec. of State for Internat. Develt, 2007–09; an Asst Govt Whip, 2009–10; Shadow Minister for Work and Pensions, 2010; Shadow Econ. Sec. to HM Treasury, 2010–11; Shadow Foreign Office Minister, 2011–15; Shadow Sec. of State for Envmt, Food and Rural Affairs, 2015–. Mem., Treasury Select Cttee, 2005–07. Mem. (Lab) Luton BC, 1995–96 and 1999–2003. *Recreations:* travel, scuba-diving, music. *Address:* House of Commons, SW1A 0AA. *T:* (020) 7219 4510. *E:* mccarthyk@parliament.uk; (constituency) 326a Church Road, Bristol BS5 8AJ. *T:* (0117) 939 9901, *Fax:* (0117) 939 9902. *Club:* St George Labour (Bristol).

McCARTHY, Kieran; JP; Member (Alliance) Strangford, Northern Ireland Assembly, since 1998; *b* 9 Sept. 1942; *s* of James and Elizabeth McCarthy; *m* 1967, Kathleen Doherty; two *s* two *d*. *Educ:* Newtownards Coll. of Technol. Formerly textile worker and sales clerk; joint partner, discount drapery, 1965–87; retailer, 1987–. Councillor, 1985–, Alderman, 1997–, Ards BC. Contested (Alliance) Strangford, 2005. JP Ards, 1990. *Recreations:* gardening, reading, cycling. *Address:* Loughedge, 3 Main Street, Kircubbin, Newtownards, Co. Down BT22 2SS. *T:* (028) 4273 8221.

McCARTHY, Prof. Mark Ian, MD; FRCP, FMedSci; Robert Turner Professor of Diabetic Medicine, University of Oxford, since 2002; Fellow of Green Templeton College (formerly Green College), Oxford, since 2002; *b* 18 July 1960; *s* of Roy Allen McCarthy and Marion Eluned McCarthy. *Educ:* Pembroke Coll., Cambridge (BA 1981; MB BChir 1985; MD 1995); St Thomas's Hosp. Med. Sch. FRCP 1999. MRC Clin. Trng Fellow, London Hosp. Med. Coll., 1991–94; MRC Travelling Fellow, Whitehead Inst., Cambridge, Mass, 1994–95; Sen. Lectr in Molecular Genetics, 1995–98, Reader, 1998–2000, Prof. of Genomic Medicine, 2000–02, Imperial Coll., Univ. of London. Hon. Consultant, Oxford Radcliffe Hosps NHS Trust, 2002–. Mem. Council, Human Genome Orgn, 2008–. FMedSci 2006. *Address:* Diabetes Research Laboratories, Oxford Centre for Diabetes, Endocrinology & Metabolism, Churchill Hospital, Headington, Oxford OX3 7LJ.

McCARTHY, Nicholas Melvyn, OBE 1983; HM Diplomatic Service, retired; High Commissioner to Cameroon, and also Ambassador (non-resident) to Gabon, Chad, Equatorial Guinea and the Central African Republic, 1995–98; *b* 4 April 1938; *s* of Daniel Alfred McCarthy and Florence Alice McCarthy; *m* 1961, Gillian Eileen Hill; three *s* one *d*. *Educ:* Queen Elizabeth's Sch., Faversham; London Univ. (BA Hons). Attaché, Saigon, 1961–64; Language Student, then Second Sec., Tokyo, 1964–69; FCO, 1969–73; First Sec., Brussels, 1973–78; FCO, 1978–80; Head of Chancery, Dakar, 1980–84; FCO, 1984–85; Consul-Gen., Osaka, 1985–90; Dep. Hd of Mission, Consul-Gen. and Counsellor, Brussels, 1990–94. *Recreations:* golf, bridge, opera, tennis, Japanese pottery, writing, cooking. *Address:* The Old Rectory, 34 Cross Street, Moretonhampstead, Devon TQ13 8NL.

McCARTHY, Richard John, CBE 2009; FCIH; FRICS; Executive Director, Capita Local Government, Health and Property Services (formerly Capita Symonds, later Capita Property and Infrastructure), since 2012; Chairman, Smart Meters DCC, since 2013; *b* 28 April 1958; *s* of John Anthony McCarthy and Anna Patricia (*née* Sheehan); *m* 1983, Judith Karen McCann; two *s* one *d*. *Educ:* Richard Challoner Sch., New Malden; Univ. of Southampton (BA Hons Geog.); Hackney Coll. FCIH 1987; FRICS 2013. Housing Officer etc, 1979–87, Ops Dir, 1987–94, Hyde Housing Assoc.; Chief Executive: S London Family Housing Assoc., 1994–99; Peabody Trust, 1999–2003; Director General: Sustainable Communities, ODPM, subseq. Places, Planning and Communities, DCLG, 2003–06; Progs, Policy and Innovation, later Housing and Planning, then Neighbourhoods, DCLG, 2006–11. Chm., Care and Repair, 1986–93. Member: Council, Nat. Housing Fedn, 1998–2003 (Chm., 2000–03); Bd, 1066 Housing Assoc., 2000–03; Housing Panel, Audit Commn, 2003. Columnist, Building mag. *Publications:* articles in various housing jls. *Recreations:* theatre, music, opera, tennis, football, watching Rugby. *Address:* Capita Local Government, Health and Property Services, 65 Gresham Street, EC2V 7NQ. *T:* (020) 7492 0260. *E:* richard.mccarthy@capita.co.uk.

MacCARTHY, Very Rev. Robert Brian, PhD; Dean of St Patrick's Cathedral, Dublin, 1999–2012 (Prebendary, 1994–99); *b* 28 March 1940; *o c* of Richard Edward MacCarthy and Dorothy MacCarthy (*née* Furney), Clonmel. *Educ:* St Columba's Coll., Rathfarnham; Trinity Coll., Dublin (BA, MA; PhD 1983); St John's Coll., Cambridge; Trinity Coll., Oxford (MA); Cuddesdon Theol Coll.; MA NUI 1965. Ordained deacon, 1979, priest, 1980; Curate, Carlow, 1979–81; Librarian, Pusey House, and Fellow, St Cross Coll., Oxford, 1981–82; Curate, 1982–83, Team Vicar, 1983–86, Bracknell; Curate, Kilkenny, 1986–88; Bp's Vicar in Kilkenny Cath., 1986–88; Domestic Chaplain to Bp of Ossory, 1986–89; Rector, Castlecomer, and RD of Carlow, 1988–95; Rector, St Nicholas' Collegiate Church, Galway and Provost of Tuam, 1995–99. *Publications:* The Estates of Trinity College, Dublin, 1992; Ancient and Modern, 1995; How Shall They Hear, 2002. *Recreation:* architectural history. *Address:* Suirmount, Clonmel, Co. Tipperary, Ireland. *T:* (52) 6136395. *Clubs:* Kildare Street and University (Dublin); Royal Irish Yacht (Dun Laoghaire).

McCARTHY, Shaun Patrick, OBE 2013; Owner and Director, Action Sustainability, since 2006; *b* London, 2 Aug. 1957; *s* of Terence McCarthy and Ethel McCarthy; *m* 1983, Kay; one *s* one *d*. *Educ:* Lanchester Poly. (HND Mech. Engrg 1981). MCIPS 1992; MIEMA 2005. Apprentice Mechanical Fitter, Esso Petroleum Co., 1973–77; Applications Engr, Worthington Pumps, 1981–83; Sales Engr, Sulzer UK, 1983–85; Procurement Manager, Shell UK Ltd, 1986–95; BAA plc: Hd, Procurement Develt, 1995–2000; Hd, Utilities, 2000–03; Hd, Utilities and Sustainability, 2003–06. Chm., Commn for a Sustainable London 2012, 2006–13; Mem., London Sustainable Develt Commn, 2004–15. Trustee, Greenshoots Fund, 2011–. MInstD. FRSA. *Publications:* Principles and Practice of Sustainable Procurement, 2011; (with C. Berry) Guide to Sustainable Procurement in Construction, 2011; contribs to reports for Commn for a Sustainable London 2012. *Recreations:* family, music, boating. *E:* shaun.mccarthy@actionsustainability.com.

McCARTHY, Steven Scott; Minister (Defence and Materiel), British Defence Staff, British Embassy, Washington, DC, since 2014; *b* Caterham, Surrey, 29 June 1958; *s* of Leslie McCarthy and Cynthia McCarthy; *m* 1998, Dawn Oliver; two *d*. *Educ:* de Stafford Sch., Caterham. Joined MoD, 1977; Asst Private Sec. to Sec. of State for Defence, 1988–89; Hd, Net Assessment Unit, MoD, 1989–92; Sec., Equipment Approvals Cttee, 1992–96; Private Sec. to Chief of Defence Procurement, 1996–98; Counsellor (Defence Equipment), Washington, DC, 1998–2002; Sec., Defence Procurement Agency, 2002–08; Dir, Change, 2008–10, COS, 2010–11, Defence Equipment and Support; Dir, Internat. Security Policy, MoD, 2011–14. *Publications:* (with M. Gilbert) The Crystal Palace Dinosaurs, 1994. *Recreations:* military history (especially tramping battlefields), gardening, (watching) sport, supporting Liverpool FC, just being with my wife. *Address:* c/o British Embassy, 3100 Massachusetts Avenue NW, Washington, DC 20008, USA.

McCARTHY, Suzanne Joyce; Immigration Services Commissioner, 2005–15; *b* 21 Nov. 1948; *d* of Leo and Lillian Rudnick; *m* 1990, Brendan McCarthy. *Educ:* New York Univ. (BA 1970; Phi Beta Kappa); Wolfson Coll., Cambridge (Dip Social Anthropol. 1971); Lucy Cavendish Coll., Cambridge (LLM 1986); Univ. of E London (MSc 2010). Admitted Solicitor, 1976; Solicitor in private practice, 1977–86; Lectr in Law, Univ. of Manchester, 1986–89; joined Civil Service, 1989; posts with Home Office (incl. Private Sec. to Home Sec.), Treasury, Civil Service Coll. (Dir, Policy, Govt and Europe), 1989–96; Chief Executive: HFEA, 1996–2000; Financial Services Compensation Scheme, 2000–04. Chm., Depaul UK, 2015–; Trustee, Depaul Internat., 2015–. Member: Determinations Panel Pensions Regulator, 2005–13; Conduct Disciplinary Cttee, CIMA, 2006–08; Council, GMC, 2009–12; Disciplinary and Regulatory Cttees, Assoc. of Chartered Certified Accountants, 2011–June 2016; UK and Ireland Regulatory Bd, RICS, 2012–16; Adv. Bd, LSE Centre for Analysis of Risk and Regulation, 2014–; Advertising Standards Authy, 2015–; Independent Appointed Person: GLA, 2012–15; London Emergency and Fire Planning Authy, 2012–14; Lay Reviewer, RCSE, 2009–. Chm., Gen. Chiropractic Council, 2013–. Non-executive Director: Royal Brompton and Harefield NHS Trust, 1998–2006; Candoco Dance Co., 2000–04; RIBA, 2004–14; Public Guardian Bd, 2007–12; Human Tissue Authy, 2010–March 2016. Chm., European Forum of Deposit Insurers, 2002–04 (Hon. Chm. 2008); Mem. Exec. Council, British and Irish Ombudsman Assoc., 2008–12. Mem. Panel (Dance), SOLT (Laurence Olivier) Awards, 2002. Trustee, RNIB, 2002–04. University of London: Mem. Council, 2003–08 (Dep. Chm., 2006–08); Mem., Bd of Trustees, 2008–July 2016. Mem., Internat. Women's Forum UK, 2012–. Freeman, City of London, 2006; Yeoman, 2006–08, Liveryman, 2008–, Co. of Ironmongers. *Recreations:* dance, travel, Italian cookery. *Club:* Athenæum.

McCARTHY, Thomas Patrick; novelist; *b* Stirling, 22 May 1969; *s* of Sir Callum McCarthy, *qv*; *m* 2009, Eva Stenram; two *d*. *Educ:* Dulwich Coll.; New Coll., Oxford (BA Hons 1990). Writer and conceptual artist. *Publications: novels*: Remainder, 2005; Men in Space, 2007; C, 2010, Satin Island, 2015; *non-fiction*: Tintin and the Secret of Literature, 2006. *Recreation:* listening to Test Cricket. *Address:* c/o Jonathan Pegg Literary Agency, 32 Batoum Gardens, W6 7QD.

McCARTHY, William Joseph Anthony; Deputy Vice-Chancellor, Operations, University of Bradford, since 2014; *b* Leeds, 14 June 1963; *s* of Shaun and Patricia McCarthy; *m* 1986, Rose Coady; four *s* one *d*. *Educ:* Prior Park, Bath; Queen Mary Coll., Univ. of London (BSc Econ.); London Sch. of Econs (MSc). Asst Economist, DoH, 1986–88; Analyst, Herts CC and ACC, 1988–91; rejoined Department of Health, 1991: Principal, 1991–94; Asst Sec., Primary Care, 1994–97; Head: of Public Expenditure Survey Br., 1997–99; of Finance and Performance Div. A, NHS Exec., 1999–2000; Dir of Planning and Performance, Leeds Teaching Hosps NHS Trust, 2000–02; Dir, Strategic Develt, W Yorks Strategic HA, 2002–06; Dir, Policy and Strategy, DoH, 2006–07; Chief Executive: York CC, 2007–09; Yorks and the Humber Strategic HA, 2009–11; Man. Dir, NHS Commissioning Bd, 2011–13; Nat. Dir, Policy, NHS England, 2013–14. *Recreations:* playing with the children, eating out, weekends away, watching sport.

McCARTHY-FRY, Sarah; Finance Director, Cowes, Isle of Wight and Western Approach, Bristol, GKN Aerospace Services, since 2012 (Financial Controller, Cowes, Isle of Wight, 2010–12); *b* 4 Feb. 1955; *d* of Sidney and Constance Macaree; *m* 1st, 1973, Roger Fry (marr. diss. 1997); one *s* one *d*; 2nd, 1997, Anthony McCarthy. *Educ:* Portsmouth High Sch.; BPP Coll., Southampton. ACMA 2004. Financial Accountant, FPT Industries, Portsmouth, 1988–2000; GKN Aerospace Services: Financial Analyst, Farnham, 2000–03; Financial Controller, Cowes, IoW, 2003–05. Dep. Leader, Portsmouth CC, 1995–2000. MP (Lab and Co-op) Portsmouth N, 2005–10; contested (Lab and Co-op) same seat, 2010. Parly Under-Sec. of State, DCSF, 2008–09, DCLG, 2009; Exchequer Sec. to HM Treasury, 2009–10. *Recreations:* tap dancing, dog walking.

McCARTIE, Rt Rev. (Patrick) Leo; Bishop of Northampton, (RC), 1990–2001, now Emeritus; *b* 5 Sept. 1925; *s* of Patrick Leo and Hannah McCartie. *Educ:* Cotton College; Oscott College. Priest, 1949; on staff of Cotton College, 1950–55; parish work, 1955–63; Director of Religious Education, 1963–68; Administrator of St Chad's Cathedral, Birmingham, 1968–77; Aux. Bp of Birmingham, and Titular Bp of Elmham, 1977–90. Pres., Catholic Commn for Racial Justice, 1978–83; Chm., Cttee for Community Relations, Dept for Christian Responsibility and Citizenship, Bishops' Conf. on Eng. and Wales, 1983–90; Mem., Churches Main Cttee, 1996–2002. Church Representative: Churches Together in England, 1990; Council of Churches for Britain and Ireland, 1990. *Recreations:* music, walking. *Address:* 71 Queen's Road, Birmingham B32 2LB.

McCARTNEY, Gordon Arthur; consultant; Managing Director, Gordon McCartney Associates, since 1991; *b* 29 April 1937; *s* of Arthur and Hannah McCartney; *m* 1st, 1960, Ceris Ysobel Davies (marr. diss. 1987); two *d*; 2nd, 1988, Wendy Ann Vyvyan Titman. *Educ:* Grove Park Grammar Sch., Wrexham. Articled to Philip J. Walters, MBE (Town Clerk, Wrexham), 1954–59; admitted solicitor, 1959. Asst Solicitor, Birkenhead County Bor. Council, 1959–61; Asst Solicitor, 1961–63, Sen. Asst Solicitor, 1963–65, Bootle County Bor. Council; Dep. Clerk, Wrexham RDC, 1965–73; Clerk, Holywell RDC, 1973–74; Chief Exec., Delyn Bor. Council, 1974–81; Sec., Assoc. of Dist Councils, 1981–91; Associate, Succession Planning Associates, 1991–96. Dir, Nat. Transport Tokens Ltd, 1984–92. Secretary-General, British Section, IULA/CEMR, 1984–88; Chairman: CEMR Individual Members Gp, 1992–97; Local Govt Gp for Europe, 1997–2005 (Hon. Sec., Local Govt Gp for Europe, later Local Govt Section, Eur. Movt, 2006–); Co. Sec., Local Govt Internat. Bureau, 1988–91. Mem., Hansard Soc. Commn on Legislative Process, 1991–93. Director: Leisure England Ltd, 1993–; White Rock Developments Ltd, 1996–97. Organist, Elton Methodist Ch, 1991–2015. *Recreations:* cricket, music. *Address:* 21 Challenger Quay, Falmouth TR11 3YL. *T:* 07951 703992. *Club:* MCC.

McCARTNEY, Rt Hon. Sir Ian; Kt 2010; PC 1999; *b* 25 April 1951; *s* of late Hugh McCartney and Margaret McCartney (*née* McDonald); *m* (marr. diss.); two *d* (one *s* decd); *m* 1988, Ann Parkes (*née* Kevan). *Educ:* State primary, secondary schools; Tech. Colls. Led paper boy strike, 1965; joined Labour Party, 1966; joined trade union, 1966; seaman, local govt manual worker, chef, 1966–71; unemployed, 1971–73; Labour Party Organiser, 1973–87. Councillor, Wigan Borough, 1982–87. MP (Lab) Makerfield, 1987–2010. Hon. Parly Adviser: to Greater Manchester Fire and Civil Defence Authy, 1987–92 (Mem., 1986); to Nat. Assoc. for Safety in the Home, 1989–92. Opposition spokesperson on NHS, 1992–94, on employment, 1994–96, chief spokesperson on employment, 1996–97; Minister of State: DTI, 1997–99; Cabinet Office, 1999–2001; Minister for Pensions, DWP, 2001–03; Minister without Portfolio and Chair, Labour Party, 2003–06; Minister of State, FCO and DTI, 2006–07. Mem., Parly Select Cttee on Health and Social Security, 1991–92; Sec., All Party Parly Gp on Credit Unions, 2007–10. Chm., T&GWU Parly Gp, 1989–91. Sponsored by TGWU. Prime Minister's Rep., Socialist Internat., 2008–10. Mem., Nat. Constitutional Cttee, Lab. Party, 2012–. Hon. Pol Sec. Nat. Union of Labour and Socialist Clubs, 2013–. Pres., 2007–10, Ambassador, 2012–, Money Advice Trust. UK Comr-Gen., Shanghai Expo 2010, 2007–10. Advr, Drop in and Share, 2012–; Chair, Healthwatch Wigan, 2013–. Hon. President: Wigan Wheelchair Fund 1987–; Mencap, Ashton, Lowton and Golborne, 2012–. *Recreations:* Wigan Rugby League fanatic (supports Wigan Warriors); head of McCartney family, a family of proud working class stock. *Club:* Platt Bridge Labour.

McCARTNEY, Sir (James) Paul, Kt 1997; MBE 1965; musician, composer; *b* Allerton, Liverpool, 18 June 1942; *s* of James McCartney and Mary McCartney; *m* 1st, 1969, Linda Eastman (*d* 1998); one *s* two *d*, and one step *d*; 2nd, 2002, Heather Mills (marr. diss. 2008); one *d*; 3rd, 2011, Nancy Shevell. *Educ:* Liverpool Inst. Mem., skiffle group, The Quarry Men, 1957–59; toured Scotland with them and Stuart Sutcliffe as the Silver Beetles, 1960; first of five extended seasons in Hamburg, Aug. 1960; made 1st important appearance as the Beatles at Litherland Town Hall, nr Liverpool, Dec. 1960; appeared as mem. of Beatles: UK, Sweden, and Royal Variety perf., London, 1963; UK, Netherlands, Sweden, France, Denmark, Hong Kong, Australia, NZ, Canada, 1964; TV appearances, USA, and later, coast-to-coast tour, 1964; UK, France, Italy, Spain, USA, Canada, 1965; West Germany, Japan, Philippines, USA, Canada, 1966; Beatles disbanded 1970; formed MPL group of cos, 1970, and own group, Wings, 1971; toured: UK, Europe, 1972–73; UK, Australia, 1975; Europe, USA, Canada, 1976; UK, 1979; Wings disbanded 1981; Europe, UK, Canada, Japan, USA, Brazil, 1989/90; USA, 2002; UK, Europe, 2003; USA, 2005; USA, Europe, UK, 2009; USA, UK, 2010; USA, Europe, UK, 2011; Europe, S America, 2012; Europe, 2015. Wrote (with Carl Davis) Liverpool Oratorio, 1991; *symphony:* Standing Stone, 1997; Ecce Cor Meum (oratorio), 2006; Ocean's Kingdom (ballet), 2011. *Songs* with John Lennon include: Love Me Do; Please Please Me; From Me To You; She Loves You; Can't Buy Me Love; I Want to Hold Your Hand; I Saw Her Standing There; Eight Days a Week; All My Loving; Help!; Ticket to Ride; I Feel Fine; I'm A Loser; A Hard Day's Night; No Reply; I'll Follow The Sun; Yesterday; For No One; Here, There and Everywhere; Eleanor Rigby; Yellow Submarine; Penny Lane; All You Need Is Love; Lady Madonna; Hey Jude; We Can Work It Out; Day Tripper; Paperback Writer; When I'm Sixty-Four; A Day in the Life; Back in the USSR; Hello, Goodbye; Get Back; Let It Be; The Long and Winding Road; subseq. *songs* include: Maybe I'm Amazed; My Love; Band on the Run; Jet; Let 'Em In; Silly Love Songs; Mull of Kintyre; Coming Up; Ebony and Ivory; Tug of War; Pipes of Peace; No More Lonely Nights; My Brave Face.

Albums with the Beatles: Please Please Me, 1963; With The Beatles, 1963; A Hard Day's Night, 1964; Beatles for Sale, 1964; Help!, 1965; Rubber Soul, 1965; Revolver, 1966; Sgt Pepper's Lonely Hearts Club Band, 1967; Magical Mystery Tour, 1967; The Beatles (White Album), 1968; Yellow Submarine, 1969; Abbey Road, 1969; Let it Be, 1970; Anthology I, II and III, 1995–96; other albums: McCartney, 1970; Ram, 1971; Wild Life, 1971; Red Rose Speedway, 1973; Band on the Run, 1973; Venus and Mars, 1975; Wings at the Speed of Sound, 1976; Wings over America, 1976; London Town, 1978; Wings Greatest, 1978; Back to the Egg, 1979; McCartney II, 1980; Tug of War, 1982; Pipes of Peace, 1983; Give My Regards to Broad Street, 1984; Press to Play, 1986; All the Best!, 1987; CHOBA B CCCP, 1988; Flowers in the Dirt, 1989; Tripping the Live Fantastic, 1990; Unplugged: The Official Bootleg, 1991; Paul McCartney's Liverpool Oratorio, 1991; Off The Ground, 1993; Paul Is Live, 1993; Flaming Pie, 1997; Standing Stone, 1999; Run Devil Run, 1999; Wingspan, 2001; Driving Rain, 2001; Chaos and Creation in the Back Yard, 2005; Memory Almost Full, 2007; Electric Arguments, 2008; Kisses on the Bottom, 2012; New, 2013. *Films* (with the Beatles): A Hard Day's Night, 1964; Help!, 1965; Magical Mystery Tour (TV), 1967; Yellow Submarine, 1968; Let It Be, 1970; (with Wings) Rockshow, 1981; (wrote, composed score, and acted in) Give My Regards To Broad Street, 1984; (wrote, composed score and produced) Rupert and the Frog Song, 1984 (BAFTA award, Best Animated Film); Get Back, 1991. *Film scores:* The Family Way, 1966; Live and Let Die, 1973 (title song only); Twice In A Lifetime, 1984 (title song only); Spies Like Us, 1985 (title song only); *TV scores:* Thingumybob (series), 1968; The Zoo Gang (series), 1974. One-man art exhibn, Walker Gall., Liverpool, 2002. Live Russian 'phone link-up, BBC Russian Service, 1989. FRCM 1995. Numerous Grammy Awards, Nat. Acad. of Recording Arts and Scis, USA, incl. Lifetime Achievement Awards, 1990 and (for The Beatles), 2014; Ivor Novello Awards include: for Internat. Achievement, 1980; for Internat. Hit of the Year (Ebony and Ivory), 1982; for Outstanding Contrib. to Music, 1989; PRS special award for unique achievement in popular music, 1990; Kennedy Center Honor, 2010. Officier de la Légion d'honneur (France), 2012. Freeman, City of Liverpool, 1984. Fellow, British Acad. of Composers and Songwriters, 2000. DUniv Sussex, 1988. *Publications:* The Beatles Anthology (with George Harrison and Ringo Starr), 2000; Paintings, 2000; Blackbird Singing: poems and lyrics 1965–1999, 2001; Wingspan: Paul McCartney's band on the run, 2002; *for children:* (jtly) High in the Clouds, 2005.

See also M. A. McCartney, S. McCartney.

McCARTNEY, Jason Alexander; MP (C) Colne Valley, since 2010; *b* Harrogate, 29 Jan. 1968; *s* of Wing Comdr Robert McCartney and Jean McCartney; two *d.* *Educ:* Lancaster Royal Grammar Sch.; RAF Coll., Cranwell; Leeds Trinity University Coll. (Postgrad. Dip. Broadcast Journalism). Officer, RAF, 1988–97; journalist, Radio Cleveland and Leeds, BBC, 1997–98; journalist and presenter, ITV Yorkshire, 1998–2007; Sen. Lectr, Leeds Metropolitan Univ., 2008–10. Member: Transport Select Cttee, 2013–15; Culture, Media and Sport Cttee, 2015–; 1922 Exec. Cttee, 2013–. *Recreations:* Huddersfield Town AFC, Huddersfield Giants RLFC, Yorkshire CCC, tennis, eating Hinchcliffe's Pies. *Address:* Upperbridge House, 24 Huddersfield Road, Holmfirth HD9 2JS. *T:* (01484) 688364, 688378; House of Commons, SW1A 0AA. *E:* jason.mccartney.mp@parliament.uk. *Club:* Royal Air Force.

McCARTNEY, Joanne; Member (Lab) Enfield and Haringey, London Assembly, Greater London Authority, since 2004. *Educ:* Univ. of Warwick (LLB); Univ. of Leicester (LLM). Barrister, specialising in employment law; adjudicator, Housing Ombudsman. Mem. (Lab) Enfield BC, 1998–2006. Mem., Metropolitan Police Authy, 2004–12; Chair, Police and Crime Cttee, GLA, 2012–. *Address:* Greater London Authority, City Hall, Queen's Walk, SE1 2AA.

McCARTNEY, Karl Ian; JP; MP (C) Lincoln, since 2010; *b* St Catherine's, Birkenhead, 25 Oct. 1968; *s* of John McCartney and Brenda McCartney (*née* Weir); *m* 1999, Cordelia Pyne; two *s.* *Educ:* Woodfall Lane Prim. and Jun. Schs; Birkenhead Sch. for Boys; Neston High Sch.; Willink Sch.; St David's University Coll., Wales (BA Hons Geog. 1991; Pres., Student Union, 1991–92); Kingston Business Sch., Kingston Univ. (MBA 1998). Logistics Analyst, Hasbro, 1992–93; Agent and Researcher, Conservative Central Office, 1993–96; Corporate Affairs, Corp. of London, 1996–2001. Dir, MLSystems, mgt consultancy, 1999–. Campaign Dir, 2007–10, Dep. Chm., 2010–12, Sir Keith Park Meml Campaign. Member: Transport Select Cttee, 2012–; 1922 Exec. Cttee, 2012–. Contested (C) Lincoln, 2005. JP Dartford, later Maidstone, then Lincoln, 1999–. *Recreations:* myriad of sports—football, Rugby, cricket, croquet, snowboarding, shooting; classic cars, green laning, trains, gardens, architecture, history, dance music, relaxing with family and friends, cooking. *Address:* Lincoln Conservative Association, 1A Farrier Road, Lincoln LN6 3RU; House of Commons, SW1A 0AA. *T:* (020) 7219 7221. *E:* karl.mccartney.mp@parliament.uk.

McCARTNEY, Mary Anna; freelance photographer; author; *b* London, 1969; *d* of Sir (James) Paul McCartney, *qv*; *m* 2010, Simon Aboud; two *s*, and two *s* by a previous marriage. *Solo exhibitions:* Off Pointe, Royal Opera House, 2004, Dimbola Lodge, I of W, 2005, Crane Kalman Gall., Brighton, 2007; Playing Dress Up, Goss Michael Foundn, Dallas, 2007; Backup, OXO Tower Wharf, London, 2007; British Style Observed, Natural Hist. Mus., 2008; Collective Works, Nunnington Hall, Yorks, 2009; From Where I Stand, NPG and Michael Hoppen Gall., 2010, Staley Wise Gall., NY, 2010, Contributed, Berlin, 2011, Tres Hombres, Sweden, 2012; Developing, Lowry Galls, Manchester, Izzy Gall., Toronto, 2013; *group exhibitions:* NPG, 1995, 2009; Plymouth Arts Centre, 2004; RCA and Waterfront, NY, 2007. Trustee, NPG, 2011–. *Publications:* From Where I Stand, 2010; Food, 2012; Monochrome & Colour, 2014; At My Table, 2015.

See also S. McCartney.

McCARTNEY, Sir Paul; *see* McCartney, Sir J. P.

McCARTNEY, Robert Law; QC (NI) 1975; Member (UKU) North Down, Northern Ireland Assembly, 1998–2007; *b* 24 April 1936; *s* of William Martin McCartney and Elizabeth Jane (*née* McCartney); *m* 1960, Maureen Ann Bingham; one *s* three *d.* *Educ:* Grosvenor Grammar Sch., Belfast; Queen's Univ., Belfast (LLB Hons 1958). Admitted solicitor of Supreme Court of Judicature, NI, 1962; called to NI Bar, 1968. MP (UKU) N Down, June 1995–2001; contested (UKU) same seat, 2001; contested (UKU) N Down, NI Assembly, 2007. Chm., Nat. Grammar Schs Assoc., 2008–. *Publications:* Liberty and Authority in Ireland, 1985; Liberty, Democracy and the Union, 2001; political reports and pamphlets. *Recreations:* reading (biography and military history), walking. *Address:* St Catherines, 2 Circular Road East, Cultra, Holywood, Co. Down, Northern Ireland BT18 0HA.

McCARTNEY, Stella, OBE 2013; fashion designer; *b* 13 Sept. 1971; *d* of Sir (James) Paul McCartney, *qv*; *m* 2003, Alasdhair Willis; two *s* two *d.* *Educ:* Central St Martin's Coll. of Art and Design. Set up own clothing line, London, 1995; Creative Dir, Chloe, Paris, 1997–2001; estabd own fashion house, in partnership with Gucci Gp, 2001–; opened stores in NY, 2002, London, and Los Angeles, 2003. Creative Dir, Team GB, London Olympics, 2012. British Designer of the Year, 2007, 2012, Red Carpet Award, 2011, Designer Brand of the Year, 2012, British Fashion Awards.

See also M. A. McCartney.

McCARTNEY, Thomas; Sheriff of North Strathclyde at Paisley, since 2012; *b* Glasgow, 9 Aug. 1958; *s* of Thomas McCartney and Theresa McCartney (*née* Logan); *m* 1982, Patricia Frances Potts. *Educ:* St Aloysius Coll., Glasgow; Univ. of Glasgow (LLB 1979). Admitted Solicitor, 1981; Partner, Fitzpatrick & Co., solicitors, Glasgow, 1983–99; sole practitioner, 1999–2009; Sheriff of Tayside Central and Fife at Falkirk, 2009–12. A pt-time Chm., Appeals Service, 2001–09; Mem., Scottish Solicitors' Discipline Tribunal, 2005–09. *Recreations:* golf, running, ski-ing, Scottish art. *Address:* c/o Paisley Sheriff Court, St James Street, Paisley PA3 2AW.

McCARTY, Marie Elizabeth; *see* Mallon, M. E.

McCAUGHRAN, John; QC 2003; *b* 24 April 1958; *s* of Desmond McCaughran and Elizabeth McCaughran (*née* Miller); *m* 1985, Catherine Françoise Marie Mondange; one *s.* *Educ:* Methodist Coll., Belfast; Trinity Hall, Cambridge (MA 1980). Called to the Bar, Gray's Inn, 1982, Bencher, 2009. *Recreations:* reading, weeding, la vie française. *Address:* One Essex Court, Temple, EC4Y 9AR. *T:* (020) 7583 2000, *Fax:* (020) 7583 0118. *E:* jmccaughran@oeclaw.co.uk.

McCAUGHREAN, Geraldine Margaret, FRSL, FEA; author; *b* 6 June 1951; *d* of Lesley Arthur Jones and Ethel Jones (*née* Thomas); *m* 1988, John McCaughrean; one *d.* *Educ:* Enfield County Grammar Sch. for Girls; Southgate Technical Coll.; Christ Church Coll. of Educn, Canterbury (BEd Hons 1977; Hon. Fellow, Canterbury Christ Church Univ., 2006). Sec., Thames TV, 1970–73; Sec. 1977–79, and Sub-Editor, 1983–88, Marshall Cavendish; Editorial Asst, Rothmans Internat., 1980–82; Editor, Focus, 1982. Radio play, Last Call, 1991; stage play, Dazzling Medusa, Polka Children's Theatre, 2005. FRSL 2010; FEA 2010. *Publications:* over 160 titles, various trans. into 42 languages, including: *for children:* A Little Lower than the Angels (Whitbread Children's Book Award), 1987; A Pack of Lies (Guardian Children's Award, Carnegie Medal), 1988; Gold Dust (Whitbread Children's Book Award), 1994; Plundering Paradise (Smarties Bronze Award), 1996; Forever X (UK Reading Assoc. Award), 1997; The Stones are Hatching, 1999; Britannia, 1999; (new version) A Pilgrim's Progress, 1999 (Blue Peter Book of the Year, 2000); The Kite Rider (Smarties Bronze Award), 2001; Stop the Train (Smarties Bronze Award), 2001; Gilgamesh the Hero, 2002 (staged Bristol Old Vic, 2006); Bright Penny, 2003; The Jesse Tree, 2003; Smile! (Smarties Bronze Award), 2004; Questing Knights of the Faerie Queen, 2004; Cyrano, 2005; Peter Pan In Scarlet, 2006 (trans. 42 langs); Tamburlaine's Elephants, 2007; The Death Defying Pepper Roux, 2009; Pull Out All the Stops, 2010; Monacello, 2011; Pittipat's Saucer of Moom, 2012; Monocello - The Wish Bringer, 2012; The Nutcracker Moving Picture Book, 2012; The Positively Last Performance, 2013; Go! Go! Chichico!, 2013; The Middle of Nowhere, 2013; *for teenagers:* Not the End of the World (Whitbread Children's Book Award), 2004 (staged Bristol Old Vic, 2007); The White Darkness, 2005 (Michael L. Printz Award, 2008); *for adults:* The Maypole, 1989; Fire's Astonishment, 1990; Vainglory, 1991; Lovesong, 1996; The Ideal Wife, 1997; contribs to anthologies for children and young people. *Recreation:* theatre. *Address:* c/o David Higham Associates, 7th Floor, Waverley House, 7–12 Noel Street, W1F 8GQ. *W:* www.geraldinemccaughrean.co.uk.

McCAUL, Colin Brownlie; QC 2003; *b* 21 Oct. 1954; *s* of Ian and Elizabeth McCaul; *m* 1988, Claire Louise Carden; two *s* three *d.* *Educ:* Dulwich Coll.; University Coll. London (LLB Hons). Called to the Bar, Gray's Inn, 1978, Bencher, 2006. *Recreations:* horses, surfing, English history. *Address:* 39 Essex Street, WC2R 3AT. *T:* (020) 7832 1111, *Fax:* (020) 7353 3978. *E:* colin.mccaul@39essex.com.

McCAUSLAND, Benedict Maurice Perronet T.; *see* Thompson-McCausland.

McCAUSLAND, Nelson; Member (DemU) Belfast North, Northern Ireland Assembly, since 2003; *b* N Belfast, 1951; *m* Mary. *Educ:* Belfast Royal Acad.; Worcester Coll., Oxford; Queen's Univ., Belfast (DipEd). Teacher of Science, Belfast; NI Sec., Lord's Day Observance Soc., 1983–93; Chm., 1995–97, Dir, 1997–2003, Ulster-Scots Heritage Council. Minister for Culture, Arts and Leisure, 2009–11, for Social Develt, 2011–14, NI. Mem., Belfast CC, 1989–2010 (Ind U, 1989–93; UU, 1993–2001; DemU, 2001–10); High Sheriff of Belfast, 1997–98. *Address:* Northern Ireland Assembly, Parliament Buildings, Stormont, Belfast BT4 3XX.

McCAVE, Prof. (Ian) Nicholas, FGS; Woodwardian Professor of Geology, University of Cambridge, 1985–2008, now Emeritus; Fellow, St John's College, Cambridge, since 1986; *b* 3 Feb. 1941; *s* of Thomas Theasby McCave and Gwendoline Marguerite McCave (*née* Langlois); *m* 1972, Susan Caroline Adams (*née* Bambridge); three *s* one *d.* *Educ:* Elizabeth Coll., Guernsey; Hertford Coll., Oxford (MA, DSc); Brown Univ., USA (PhD). FGS 1963. Fulbright Scholar, 1963–67; Instructor in Geology, Brown Univ., 1967; NATO Research Fellow, Netherlands Inst. for Sea Research, 1967–69; Lectr 1969–76, Reader 1976–84, UEA, Norwich; Hd, Dept of Earth Scis, Univ. of Cambridge, 1988–98. Visiting Professor: Oregon State Univ., 1974; MIT, 1999; Columbia Univ., NY, 2007; Adjunct Scientist, Woods Hole Oceanographic Instn, 1978–87. Chm., Atmospheric and Aquatic Physics Sci. Cttee, NERC, 1982–85; Mem., Scientific Cttee on Oceanic Res., ICSU, 1989–2001 (Pres., 1992–96). Leverhulme Emeritus Res. Fellow, 2008–10. Shepard Medal for Marine Geol., US Soc. for Sedimentary Geol., 1995; Huntsman Medal for Marine Scis, Canada, 1999; Lyell Medal, Geol Soc. of London, 2009. *Publications:* (ed) The Benthic Boundary Layer, 1976; (ed) The Deep Sea Bed, 1990; over 150 papers in jls. *Recreations:* pottering about in the garden, rough carpentry, travel. *Address:* Marlborough House, 23 Victoria Street, Cambridge CB1 1JP.

McCAWLEY, Leon Francis; concert pianist, since 1989; Professor of Piano, Royal College of Music, since 2008; *b* Culcheth, 12 July 1973; *s* of Bernard McCawley and Marian McCawley; *m* 1996, Anna Hyunsook Paik. *Educ:* Chetham's Sch. of Music, Manchester; Curtis Inst. of Music, Philadelphia (BMus 1995). ARCM (Hons) 1991. Royal Festival Hall début with LPO, 1991; performances with leading orchestras worldwide incl. Philadelphia, Vienna Symphony, RPO, LPO, Philharmonia, BBC Philharmonic, Netherlands Philharmonic; notable recitals incl. Wigmore Hall, QEH, Lincoln Center, NY, Rudolfinum, Prague and Philharmonie, Berlin. Numerous recordings. Winner, Piano Section, BBC Young Musician of the Year, 1990; First Prize, Internat. Beethoven Piano Competition, Vienna, 1993. *Recreations:* cooking, travelling, cinema, art. *Address:* c/o Ikon Arts Management Ltd, 114 Business Design Centre, 52 Upper Street, N1 0QH. *T:* (020) 7354 9199, *Fax:* 0870 130 9646. *E:* info@ikonarts.com. *W:* www.leonmccawley.com. *Club:* Garrick.

McCLARAN, Anthony Paul; Chief Executive Officer, Tertiary Education Quality and Standards Agency, since 2015; *b* 5 Nov. 1957; *s* of John Edwin McClaran and Sheila Margaret McClaran (*née* Rayner); *m* 1986, Mary-Ann Helen Smith; two *s* two *d.* *Educ:* The John Lyon Sch., Harrow-on-the-Hill; Univ. of Indiana (scholarship, 1979–80); Univ. of Kent (BA 1st cl. Hons (English and American Lit.) 1981). University of Warwick: Admin. Asst, 1985–89; Asst Registrar, 1989–92; Sen. Asst Registrar, 1992; University of Hull: Acad. Registrar, 1992–95; Actg Registrar and Sec., 1995; Universities and Colleges Admissions Service: Hd, Acad. Services and Develt, 1995–96; Dep. Chief Exec., 1996–2003; Actg Chief Exec., Jan.–Dec. 2003; Chief Exec., 2003–09. Man. Dir, UCAS Media Ltd (formerly UCAS Enterprises), 1996–2009; Chm., SDS Ltd, 2003–09; Chief Exec., QAA, 2009–15; Man. Dir, QAA Enterprises Ltd (formerly Partners in Quality Ltd), 2011–15. Member: Bd of Dirs, Hero UK, 2001–06; Exec. Cttee, AUA, 2003–06; Leadership Council, Nat. Centre for Univs and Business (formerly Council for Industry and Higher Educn), 2009–; UK HE Internat. Unit Strategic Adv. Bd, 2010–; Bd, Eur. Assoc. for Quality Assurance in Higher Educn, 2013–; Internat. Educn Council, 2013–. University of Gloucestershire: Mem. Council, 1997–2005; Chair of Council, 2007–09; Pro-Chancellor, 2007–09. Chm., Employment and Skills Adv. Panel, Gloucestershire First, 2009–11; Mem. Bd, Glos Develt Agency, 2010–11. Trustee: Inspiring Futures Foundn, 2007–13; Summerfield Trust, 2010–15. Governor: St Edward's Sch., Cheltenham, 2003–09; Nat. Star Coll., 2006–09; Cheltenham Kingsmead Sch., 2007–09; John Lyon Sch., 2008–15 (Dep. Chm., 2013–); John Lyon's Foundn (formerly

Harrow Sch. Foundn), 2011–15; All Saints' Acad., Cheltenham, 2011–15 (Chm., 2011–15). FCMI 2007. Mem., 2007–, Trustee, 2012–, Hon. Co. of Glos. Freeman: Co. (formerly Guild) of Educators, 2007; City of London, 2012. *Publications:* articles and chapters on higher educn policy and practice. *Recreations:* reading, polyphony, tennis, walking. *Address:* Tertiary Education Quality and Standards Agency, GPO Box 1672, Melbourne, Vic 3001, Australia. *T:* (3) 83062411. *E:* anthony.mcclaran@teqsa.gov.au. *Club:* Athenæum.

McCLARKIN, Emma; Member (C) East Midlands, European Parliament, since 2009; *b* Stroud, 9 Oct. 1978; *d* of George McClarkin and Maria McClarkin. *Educ:* Stroud Girls High Sch.; Bournemouth Univ. (LLB (Hons) Business Law 2001). Legal clerk, Goldinghams solicitors, Stroud, 2001–02; Press Officer, East Midlands MEPs, 2002–04; Pol Advr to MEP (C) for E Midlands, 2004–08; Govt Relns Exec., Rugby Football Union, 2008–09. *Recreations:* countryside walking, photography, Rugby, kayaking, ski-ing. *Address:* European Parliament, 60 Rue Wiertz, 1047 Brussels, Belgium. *T:* (2) 2845684, *Fax:* (2) 2849684. *E:* emma.mcclarkin@europarl.europa.eu.

McCLEAN, Prof. (John) David, CBE 1994; FBA 2003; Professor of Law, 1973–2004, now Emeritus, Public Orator, 1988–91 and 1994–2007, University of Sheffield; *b* 4 July 1939; *s* of Major Harold McClean and Mrs Mabel McClean; *m* 1966, Pamela Ann Loader; one *s* one *d*. *Educ:* Queen Elizabeth's Grammar Sch., Blackburn; Magdalen Coll., Oxford (DCL, 1984). Called to the Bar, Gray's Inn, 1963, Bencher, 2001. University of Sheffield: Asst Lectr 1961; Lectr 1963; Sen. Lectr 1968; Dean, Faculty of Law, 1978–81, 1998–2002; Pro-Vice-Chancellor, 1991–96. Vis. Lectr in Law, Monash Univ., Melbourne, 1968, Vis. Prof., 1978. Chancellor: dio. of Sheffield, 1992–2014; dio. of Newcastle, 1998–2009. Vice-Chm., C of E Bd for Social Responsibility, 1978–80. Member: Gen. Synod of C of E, 1970–2005 (Vice-Chm., House of Laity, 1979–85, Chm. 1985–95); Crown Appts Commn, 1977–87. Pres., Eur. Consortium for Church and State Res., 1995. Hon. QC 1995. Hon. LittD Sheffield, 2012. *Publications:* Criminal Justice and the Treatment of Offenders (jtly), 1969; (contrib.) Halsbury's Laws of England, Vol. 8, 4th edn 1974, re-issue 1996, Vol. 2 (re-issue), 4th edn 1991; The Legal Context of Social Work, 1975, 2nd edn 1980; (jtly) Defendants in the Criminal Process, 1976; (ed jtly) Shawcross and Beaumont, Air Law, 4th edn 1977, and loose-leaf issues, 1977– (Gen. Ed., 2000–); (jtly) Recognition and Enforcement of Judgments, etc, within the Commonwealth, 1977; (ed jtly) Dicey and Morris, Conflict of Laws, 10th edn 1980 to 15th edn (as Dicey Morris and Collins, Conflict of Laws) 2012; Recognition of Family Judgments in the Commonwealth, 1983; International Judicial Assistance, 1992, 2nd edn 2002 as International Co-operation in Civil and Criminal Matters, 3rd edn 2012; (ed) Morris, The Conflict of Laws, 4th edn 1993 to 8th edn 2012; (contrib.) Chitty, Contracts, 27th edn 1994 to 31st edn 2012; Transnational Organized Crime, 2007. *Recreation:* detective fiction. *Address:* Hall House, Ingrams, Sturminster Newton, Dorset DT10 1FR.

McCLEARY, Ann Heron, (Mrs David McCleary); *see* Gloag, A. H.

McCLEARY, (William) Boyd, CMG 2010; CVO 2004; HM Diplomatic Service, retired; Governor, British Virgin Islands, 2010–14; *b* 30 March 1949; *s* of Robert McCleary and Eleanor Thomasina McCleary (*née* Weir); *m* 2000, Jeannette Ann Collier; three *d*. *Educ:* Queen's Univ., Belfast (BA 1st Cl. Hons German Lang. and Lit. 1972). Asst, then Dep. Principal, Dept of Agric. for NI, 1972–75; First Sec. (Agric., then Chancery), Bonn, 1975–80; Western European Dept, then EC Dept (Ext.), FCO, 1981–85; First Sec., Hd of Chancery and Consul, Seoul, 1985–88; Asst Hd, Far Eastern Dept, FCO, 1988–89; Dep. Hd of Mission and Dir of Trade Promotion, Ankara, 1990–93; Counsellor (Econ. and Trade Policy), Ottawa, 1993–97; Hd, Estate Dept, FCO, 1997–2000; Consul-Gen., Düsseldorf, and Dir-Gen., Trade and Investment in Germany, 2000–05; Dir for Global Rollout of Oracle System, FCO, 2005–06; High Comr to Malaysia, 2006–10. Hon. LLD Nottingham, 2010. *Recreations:* spending time with my family, tennis, walking, reading. *Address:* Sycamore House, Bentworth, Alton, Hants GU34 5RB. *Club:* Royal Over-Seas League.

McCLELLAN, John Forrest; Under Secretary, Industry Department for Scotland (formerly Scottish Economic Planning Department), 1980–85, retired; *b* 15 Aug. 1932; *s* of John McClellan and Hester (*née* Niven); *m* 1956, Eva Maria Pressel; three *s* one *d*. *Educ:* Ferryhill Primary Sch., Aberdeen; Aberdeen Grammar Sch.; Aberdeen Univ. (MA). Served Army, 2nd Lieut, Gordon Highlanders and Nigeria Regt, RWAFF, 1954–56. Entered Civil Service, 1956; Asst Principal, Scottish Educn Dept, 1956–59; Private Sec. to Perm. Under Sec. of State, Scottish Office, 1959–60; Principal, Scottish Educn Dept, 1960–68; Civil Service Fellow, Glasgow Univ., 1968–69; Asst Sec., Scottish Educn Dept, 1969–77; Asst Under Sec. of State, Scottish Office, 1977–80. Dir, 1986–2001, Trustee, 2001–10, Scottish Internat. Educn Trust; Mem., Management Cttee, Hanover (Scotland) Housing Assoc., 1986–2007. Hon. Fellow, Dundee Inst. of Technology, 1988. *Publications:* Then a Soldier, 1991. *Recreation:* vegetable gardening. *Address:* 7 Cumin Place, Edinburgh EH9 2JX. *T:* (0131) 667 8446. *Club:* Royal Scots (Edinburgh).

McCLELLAND, Donovan; Member (SDLP) Antrim South, 1998–2003, and Deputy Speaker, 2000–02, Northern Ireland Assembly; *b* 14 Jan. 1949; *s* of Dan and Virginia McClelland; *m* 1974, Noreen Patricia Young; two *s* one *d*. *Educ:* Queen's Univ., Belfast (BSc Econ). Lectr and researcher in Economics, QUB, 1973–75; Civil Servant, Dept of Agriculture, 1975–78; Lectr in Economics, Univ. of Ulster, 1978–98. Chm., Standards and Privileges Cttee, NI Assembly, 2000–02. *Recreation:* reading. *Address:* 18 Roseville Crescent, Randalstown, Co. Antrim BT41 2LY.

McCLELLAND, Hon. Douglas, AC 1987; Chairman, Australian Political Exchange Council, 1993–95; *s* of Alfred McClelland and Gertrude Amy Cooksley; *m* Lorna Belva McNeill; one *s* two *d*. Mem. NSW ALP Executive, 1956–62; Hon. Dir, St George Hosp., Sydney, 1957–68. Member, Australian Senate for NSW, 1962–87; Senate appointments: Minister for the Media, 1972–75; Manager, Govt Business, 1974–75; Special Minister of State, June–Nov. 1975; Opposition spokesman on Admin. Services, 1976–77; Manager, Opposition Business, 1976–77; Dep. Leader of Opposition, May–Dec. 1977; Dep. Pres. and Chm. of Cttees, 1981–82; Pres. of the Australian Senate, 1983–87; High Commissioner in UK, 1987–91; Comr-Gen., Australian Pavilion, Expo '92, Seville, Spain, 1992. Chm., Old Parliament House Redevelt Cttee, 1993–95. Australian rep., Commonwealth War Graves Commn, 1987–91. Chm., Bobby Limb Foundn, 1999–2002; Member: Bd of Govs, St George Foundn, 1993–2002; Bd of Govs, Mick Young Trust, 1998–2002. Patron: Intellectual Disability Foundn of St George, 1995–; St George Illawarra Rugby League FC, 2002– (Chm., 1998–2000). Queen's Jubilee Medal, 1977; Centenary Medal (Australia), 2001; Citizen of the Year, Kogarah, NSW, 2010. *Recreations:* reading, films, Rugby league, making friends. *Address:* 103/172 Russell Avenue, Dolls Point, NSW 2219, Australia. *Clubs:* City Tattersalls (Life Mem.), St George Leagues (Life Mem.), St George Rugby League Football (Life Mem.); St George Motor Boat (Veteran Mem.), Georges River Sailing (Sydney); Bankstown Sports (Sydney); Cronulla.

McCLEMENT, Vice Adm. Sir Tim(othy Pentreath), KCB 2006; OBE 1990; non-executive Chairman: Marine Rescue Technologies, since 2013 (non-executive Director, since 2012); Mobilarm, since 2013; Executive Chairman, Protection Group International, since 2013; *b* 16 May 1951; *s* of late Capt. Reginald McClement, RN retd, and of Winnifred McClement (*née* Pentreath); *m* 1980, Lynne Laura Gowans; two *s*. *Educ:* Douai Sch., Berks. Joined Royal Navy, 1971: appts in various submarines, 1975–81; passed SMCC 1981; 2nd i/c HMS Conqueror during Falklands Conflict, 1982; in command: HMS Opportune, 1983–84; Staff of Captain Submarine Sea Training as a Command Sea Rider, 1984–87; CO, SMCC, 1987–89 (Comdr); HMS Tireless, 1989–92 (surfaced at North Pole, 8 May 1990, and played cricket); HMS London, 1992–94 (Capt., Wilkinson Sword of Peace, 1993); HMS Cornwall, 1999–2001 (led Task Gp around world, May–Nov. 2000); Rear-Adm. 2001; ACNS, 2001–03; COS (Warfare) and Rear-Adm. Surface Ships, 2003–04; Vice Adm. 2004; Dep. C-in-C Fleet, 2004–06. Man. Dir, Flagship Superyacht Acad., 2007–09. Dir, World Defence Forum, 2010–11. Dir, Pentreath Enterprises Ltd, 2007–. Non-exec. Chm., Protection Vessels Internat., 2011–13. Non-exec. Dir, CWind, 2012–. Mem. Defence Adv. Bd, Babcock Internat., 2010–12. Chm. Trustees, RN Submarine Mus., 2011–. Younger Brother, Trinity House, 2006. Freeman, City of London, 1993. MInstD. *Recreations:* keeping fit, dog walking. *Clubs:* Royal Navy of 1765 and 1785, Special Forces.

MACCLESFIELD, 9th Earl of, *cr* 1721; **Richard Timothy George Mansfield Parker;** Baron Parker, 1716; Viscount Parker, 1721; *b* 31 May 1943; *s* of 8th Earl of Macclesfield and Hon. Valerie Mansfield (*d* 1994), *o d* of 4th Baron Sandhurst, OBE; *S* father, 1992; *m* 1967, Tatiana Cleone, *d* of Major Craig Wheaton-Smith; three *d* (including twins); *m* 1986, Mrs Sandra Hope Mead. *Educ:* Stowe; Worcester Coll., Oxford. *Heir: b* Hon. (Jonathan) David (Geoffrey) Parker [*b* 2 Jan. 1945; *m* 1968, Lynne Valerie Butler; one *s* two *d*]. *Address:* Rectory Farmhouse, Church Lane, North Stoke, Wallingford, Oxon OX10 6BQ.

MACCLESFIELD, Archdeacon of; *see* Bishop, Ven. I. G.

McCLEVERTY, Prof. Jon Armistice; Professor of Inorganic Chemistry, 1990–2003, now Emeritus, and Senior University Research Fellow, 2003–07, University of Bristol; *b* 11 Nov. 1937; *s* of John and Nessie McCleverty; *m* 1963, Dianne Barrack; two *d*. *Educ:* Univ. of Aberdeen (BSc 1960); Imperial College, London (DIC, PhD 1963); Massachusetts Inst. of Technology. Asst Lectr, part-time, Acton Coll. of Technology, 1962–63; Asst Lectr, then Lectr, Sen. Lectr, and Reader, Univ. of Sheffield, 1964–80; Prof. of Inorganic Chem., 1980–90, and Head of Dept of Chem., 1984–90, Univ. of Birmingham. Chairman: Cttee of Heads of Univ. Chem. Depts, 1989–91; Internat. Cttee, RSC, 1994–97; Chemistry Cttee, SERC, 1990–93; Vice-Chm., Chairman of Eur. Res. Council Chemistry Cttees, 1992–93, 1995, 1997–99 (Chm., 1996–97); Member: Science Bd, SERC, 1990–93; Technical Cttee for Chemistry, Co-operation in Sci. and Technol. in Europe, EU, 1990–96; Physical Scis and Technol. Panel, NATO Sci. Affairs Div., 1999–2002 (Chm., 2001). Royal Society of Chemistry: Pres., Dalton Div., 1999–2001; Chm., Sci. and Technol. Bd, 2001–05; Chm., Awards Cttee, 2006–. Tilden Lectr, 1981, Sir Ronald Nyholm Lectr, 2001–02, RSC. RSC Medal, for work on chem. and electrochem. of transition metals, 1985. Golden Order of Merit (Poland), 1990. *Publications:* numerous articles, principally in Jl of Chem. Soc. *Recreations:* gardening, travel, music of the 20s, 30s and 40s. *Address:* School of Chemistry, University of Bristol, Cantock's Close, Bristol BS8 1TS.

McCLINTOCK, Sir Eric (Paul), Kt 1981; investment banker; *b* 13 Sept. 1918; *s* of Robert and Ada McClintock; *m* 1942, Eva Lawrence; two *s* one *d*. *Educ:* De La Salle Coll., Armidale; Sydney Univ. (DPA). Supply Dept, Dept of the Navy, Australia, 1935–47; served successively in Depts of Commerce, Agriculture, and Trade, in Washington, New York, Melbourne and Canberra, 1947–61 (1st Asst Sec. on resignation); investment banking, 1962–. Chairman: McClintock Associates Ltd; Aust. Overseas Projects Corp., 1978–84; Woolworths Ltd, 1982–87; AFT Ltd, 1984–87; Plutonic Resources Ltd, 1990–96; Malaysia Mining Corp. Australia Pty Ltd, 1993–2002; Dep. Chm., Development Finance Corp. Ltd, 1980–87; Director: Philips Industries Holdings Ltd, 1978–85; O'Connell Street Associates Pty Ltd, 1978–2010; Ashton Mining Ltd, 1986–93. Chm., Trade Develt Council, 1970–74. Pres., Royal Life Saving Soc. (NSW), 1987–96. Governor, Sydney Inst., 1990–95. *Recreations:* reading, travel. *Address:* 69 Upper Pitt Street, Kirribilli, NSW 2061, Australia. *T:* (2) 92231822. *Club:* Australian (Sydney).

McCLINTOCK-BUNBURY, family name of **Baron Rathdonnell**.

McCLOSKEY, Dr Brian Gerald, CBE 2013; FFPH; Director, Global Health, Public Health England, since 2013; Adviser to UN Special Envoy on Ebola, since 2014; *b* Derry, NI, 20 Oct. 1952; *né* Bernard Gerald McCloskey, changed name to Brian, 2013; *m* 1976, Oonagh McConaghy. *Educ:* St Columb's Coll., Derry; Trinity Coll., Dublin (MB BCh BAO 1976; MA; MD 1988). FFPH 1995. Dir, Public Health, Worcestershire, 1988–2002; Dep. Regl Dir, Public Health, West Midlands, 2002–04; Health Protection Agency: Dep. Dir, Local and Regl Services, 2004–06; Advr to Chief Exec., 2006–08; Regl Dir, London, 2008–13. *Recreations:* rowing, eating, theatre. *Address:* Public Health England, Wellington House, 133–155 Waterloo Road, SE1 8UG.

McCLOUD, Victoria Helen, DPhil; a Master of the Senior Court, Queen's Bench Division, since 2010; *b* 13 Oct. 1969; *d* of Ronald Henry Williams and Valerie Margaret Josephine Williams; civil partnership 2006, Dr Annie Siobhan McCloud. *Educ:* Christ Church, Oxford (BA Hons Experimental Psychol. 1990; DPhil Experimental Psychol. 1993); City Univ. (DipLaw 1994). Called to the Bar, Lincoln's Inn, 1995; in practice as a barrister, 1995–2010; a Dep. Costs Judge, 2006; Dep. Adjudicator to HM Land Registry, 2007; Qual. Mediator, 2009. Mem., Bar Equality and Diversity Cttee, 2004–10. Mem., Zool Soc. of London. *Publications:* (as Williams until 2009, then McCloud): (ed) The White Book, 2000–; Civil Procedure Handbook (annually), 2004–; The Surveillance and Intelligence Law Handbook, 2006; Personal Injury Pleadings, 2008. *Recreations:* American constitutional history and Revolutionary War history, history of transatlantic cable telecommunications, nature conservation, biotechnology, computing, flying, jazz, hiking, failing at vermiculture. *Address:* Royal Courts of Justice, Strand, WC2A 2LL. *T:* (020) 7947 6000. *Club:* Reform.

McCLOY, Dr Elizabeth Carol, FRCP, FFOM; Chief Medical Officer and Medical Services Director, UNUM Ltd, 1997–98; *b* 25 April 1945; *d* of Edward Bradley and Ada Entwisle; *m* 1969, Rory McCloy (marr. diss. 1989); two *s*. *Educ:* Guildford Grammar Sch.; University Coll. and UCH, London (BSc Hons 1966; MB BS Hons 1969). MFOM 1988, FFOM 1993; FRCP 1995. Clinical Asst, Medicine, W Middlesex Univ. Hosp., 1972–83; Manchester Royal Infirmary: Sen. Clinical MO, Occupational Health, 1984–88; Consultant in Occupational Medicine, 1988–93; Dir of Occupational Health and Safety, Central Manchester Healthcare Trust, 1988–93; Chief Exec. and Dir, CS Occupational Health Service, later CS Occupational Health and Safety Agency, and Med. Advr to CS, 1993–96. Pres., Soc. of Occupational Medicine, 1993–94. *Publications:* (ed jtly) Practical Occupational Medicine, 1994; (contrib.) Hunters Diseases of Occupations, 7th edn 1987, 8th edn 1994; (contrib.) Oxford Textbook of Medicine, 1994; articles on hepatitis. *Recreations:* theatre, gardening, antiques.

McCLURE, Prof. John, OBE 2007; MD; FRCPath; Procter Professor of Pathology, University of Manchester, 1987–2003, now Emeritus; Hon. Professor, University of Ulster, since 2003; *b* 2 May 1947; *s* of Richard Burns McClure and Isabella McClure (*née* Nelson); *m* 1970, Sheena Frances Tucker; three *d*. *Educ:* Queen's Univ. Belfast (BSc Hons, MB, BCh, BAO, MD, DMJPath). Training posts in Pathology, QUB, 1972–78; Clinical Sen. Lectr and Specialist/Sen. Specialist in Pathology, Univ. of Adelaide and Inst. of Med. and Vet. Sci., Adelaide, 1978–83; University of Manchester: Sen. Lectr and Hon. Consultant in Histopathology, 1983–87; Head of Pathological Scis, 1987–95; Associate Dean, Faculty of Medicine, 1995–98. Dir, Laboratory Medicine, Central Manchester Healthcare Trust, 1996–2001. British Red Cross: Chm., Northern Regl Council, 1998–99; Mem., Nat. Bd of Trustees, 1998– (Chm., 2001–07); Pres. and Trustee, Gtr Manchester Br., 1994–99. *Publications:* papers in med. and path. jls. *Recreation:* DIY. *Address:* Rushfield, 8 Drumquin Road, Castlederg, Co. Tyrone BT81 7PX. *T:* (028) 8167 1999.

McCLURE, Dr Judith, CBE 2003; FSAScot; Head of St George's School, Edinburgh, 1994–2009; Convener, Scotland-China Educational Network, since 2006; *b* 22 Dec. 1945; *d* of James McClure and Vera (*née* Knight); *m* 1977, Roger John Howard Collins, DLitt, FRHistS, FSAScot. *Educ:* Newlands GS, Middlesbrough; Coll. of Law, London; Somerville Coll., Oxford (Shaw Lefevre Scholar; BA 1st Cl. Hons 1973; MA 1977; DPhil 1979). Canoness of St Augustine, Les Oiseaux, Westgate, Kent, 1964–70; Sir Maurice Powicke Meml Res. Fellow, LMH, Oxford, 1976–77; Lecturer: in Medieval Latin and Medieval History, Univ. of Liverpool, 1977–79; in History, Jesus, Somerville and Worcester Colls, Univ. of Oxford, 1979–81; School of St Helen and St Katharine, Abingdon: teacher of History and Politics, 1981–83; Head, History and Politics Dept, 1983–84; Asst Head, Kingswood Sch., Bath, 1984–87, Dir of Studies, 1986–87; Head, Royal Sch., Bath, 1987–93. Mem., Sch. Reform Commn, Scotland, 2011–13. Member: Governing Body, 1995–2007, Mgt Cttee, 1998–2007 (Chm., 2001–07), Scottish Council of Ind. Schs; Regl Standing Cttee for Scotland, UCAS, 1997–99; Bd of Mgt, Scottish Qualifications Authy, 1999–2000; Scottish Ministerial Strategy Cttee on Continuing Professional Develt of Teachers, 2000–03 (Chm., Leadership and Mgt Pathways Subgroup, 2001–03); Scottish Adv. Cttee on Continuing Professional Develt of Teachers, 2004–07; Commn for Sch. Reform, 2012–; Chair, Adv. Bd, Scottish Centre for Studies in Sch. Admin, 2012–; Chm., Scottish Region, and Mem. Council, GSA, 1996–99. Member: Judicial Studies Cttee, 2006–13; China Forward Planning Gp, Scottish Exec., 2006–08; Cross-Pty Working Gp on China, Scottish Parlt, 2009– (Sec., 2013–); Scottish Schs Adv. Gp on China, 2010–12; Lay Mem., Judicial Inst. for Scotland Adv. Council, 2013–; Mgt Cttee, Scottish Chs China Gp, 2014–15; Adv. Gp, China-Scotland Business Forum, 2014–. Convener, Scottish Leadership, Mgt and Admin Soc., 2004–10. Mem. Adv. Cttee, Edinburgh Youth Transition and Crime Survey, 2002–08. Mem., Court, Bath Univ., 1989–92; Heriot-Watt University: Mem., Gen. Convocation, 1994–2012; Mem., Court, 2003–13 (Convener, Staffing Strategy Cttee, 2009–13); Member: Adv. Bd, Open Univ. in Scotland, 2000–08; Bd, Inst. of Sci. Educn in Scotland, 2003–08; Bd, Confucius Inst., Univ. of Edinburgh, 2006–; Educn Cttee, RSE, 2010–13; Member, Board of Governors: Selwyn Sch., Gloucester, 1988–90; Clifton Hall Sch., Lothian, 1995–99; Merchiston Castle Sch., 1999–2006; The New Sch., Butterstone, 2004–05. Trustee: Hopetoun House Preservation Trust, 1997–2003; Soc. of Antiquaries Scotland, 2010–; Scottish Internat. Educn Trust, 2013–. Jt Pres., Royal Sch. Association, 1994–. Chm., Women of Lothian Lunch, 1998–2001. FRSA 1997; FSQA 2009. DUniv Heriot-Watt, 2014. Scotland Icebreaker Award and Fellow, 48 Group Club, 2009 (Mem. Cttee, 2014–). *Publications:* Gregory the Great: exegesis and audience, 1979; Introduction and notes to Bede's Ecclesiastical History, 1994; articles in Jl Theol Studies, Peritia, Papers of Liverpool Latin Seminar, Prep. School and in Festschriften. *Recreations:* reading, travel, e-mails. *Address:* 12A Ravelston Park, Edinburgh EH4 3DX. *Club:* New (Edinburgh).

McCLURE, Roger Niall; Chief Executive, Scottish Funding Councils for Further and Higher Education, later Scottish Further and Higher Education Funding Council, 2002–08; Honorary Research Associate, University of Cambridge, since 2010; *b* 28 Dec. 1950; *s* of late Rev. Canon Hugh Norman McClure and Jane Paterson Brown; *m* 1974, Catherine Lynne Thomas; four *d*. *Educ:* King Edward VI Sch., Norwich; Corpus Christi Coll., Cambridge (MA); Corpus Christi Coll., Oxford (Postgrad. Dip); City of London Polytechnic (Dip Public Finance & Accountancy). CPFA 1982. Auditor, Nat. Audit Office, 1978–84; Sen. Consultant, then Manager, Deloitte Haskins & Sells Mgt Consultancy, 1984–88; seconded as Financial Advr to UGC, 1985–87; Dir of Finance, PCFC, 1988–92; Dir of Finance, FEFC, 1992–96; Pro-Rector, London Inst., 1996–2002; Chief Exec., Learning and Skills Improvement Service, 2008–09; Chm., JANET (UK), 2008–12. Harkness Fellow, Center for Higher Educn Studies, Univ. of California, Berkeley, 1990–91; Special Advr, H of C Educn Sub-Cttee, 1997–98; Member, Council: KCL, 1988–97; Business and Technol. Educn Council, 1995–98; City Literary Inst., 1998–2002; Inst. for Employment Studies, 2004–13 (Mem. Bd, 2008–13); Mem. Bd, JISC, 2008–12. CCMI 2003. *Publications:* (contrib.) Further Education Reformed, 2000. *Recreations:* music, sport, current affairs, reading, cinema. *E:* mcclure.roger@gmail.com.

McCLURE, Ven. Timothy Elston; Archdeacon of Bristol, 1999–2012; *b* 20 Oct. 1946; *s* of late Kenneth Elston McClure and Grace Helen McClure (*née* Hoar); *m* 1969, Barbara Mary Marchant; one *s* one *d*. *Educ:* Kingston Grammar Sch.; St John's Coll., Durham (BA); Ridley Hall, Cambridge. Deacon 1970, priest 1971; Curate, Kirkheaton Parish Church, Huddersfield, 1970–73; Marketing Mgr, Agrofax Labour Intensive Products Ltd, Harrow, Middx, 1973–74; Chaplain, Manchester Poly., 1974–82; Curate, St Ambrose, Chorlton-on-Medlock, 1974–79; Team Rector, Parish of Whitworth, Manchester and Presiding Chaplain, Chaplaincies to Higher Educn in Manchester, 1979–82; Gen. Sec., SCM, 1982–92; Dir, Churches' Council for Industry and Social Responsibility, Bristol, 1992–99; Hon. Canon, Bristol Cathedral, 1992–2012; Lord Mayor's Chaplain, Bristol, 1996–99. Chairman: Traidcraft plc, 1990–97; Christian Conference Trust, 1998–2003. *Recreations:* cooking, gardening, sailing, living sustainably. *Address:* Park House, Denton, Gilsland, Brampton, Cumbria CA8 7AG. *T:* (01697) 747415.

McCLUSKEY, family name of **Baron McCluskey**.

McCLUSKEY, Baron *cr* 1976 (Life Peer), of Churchhill in the District of the City of Edinburgh; **John Herbert McCluskey;** a Senator of the College of Justice in Scotland, 1984–2004; *b* 12 June 1929; *s* of Francis John McCluskey, Solicitor, and Margaret McCluskey (*née* Doonan); *m* 1956, Ruth Friedland; two *s* one *d*. *Educ:* St Bede's Grammar Sch., Manchester; Holy Cross Acad., Edinburgh; Edinburgh Univ. Harry Dalgety Bursary, 1948; Vans Dunlop Schol., 1949; Muirhead Prize, 1949; MA 1950; LLB 1952. Sword of Honour, RAF Spitalgate, 1953. Admitted Faculty of Advocates, 1955; Standing Jun. Counsel to Min. of Power (Scotland), 1963; Advocate-Depute, 1964–71; QC (Scot.) 1967; Chm., Medical Appeal Tribunals for Scotland, 1972–74; Sheriff Principal of Dumfries and Galloway, 1973–74; Solicitor General for Scotland, 1974–79. Chm., Scottish Assoc. for Mental Health, 1985–94. Independent Chairman: Scottish Football League's Compensation Tribunal, 1988–2014; Scottish Football Association's Appeals Tribunal, 1990–2014. Chair: Expert Gp on appeals from Scotland to Supreme Ct, 2011–12; Expert Gp on implementation in Scotland of the Leveson Report, 2012–13. Reith Lectr, BBC, 1986. Chm., John Smith Meml Trust, 1997–2004. Editor, Butterworth's Scottish Criminal Law and Practice series, 1988–2005. Hon. LLD Dundee, 1989. *Publications:* Law, Justice and Democracy, 1987; Criminal Appeals, 1992, 2nd edn 2000. *Recreations:* tennis, pianoforte. *Address:* c/o House of Lords, SW1A 0PW. *Club:* Royal Air Force.

McCLUSKEY, Len; General Secretary, Unite, since 2011 (Assistant General Secretary, 2007–10; General Secretary designate, 2010–11); *b* 23 July 1950; *s* of Leonard and Margaret McCluskey. *Educ:* Cardinal Godfrey High Sch., Merseyside. Dockworker, 1968–79; Transport and General Workers' Union: District Official, Merseyside, 1979–89; Political Officer, NW Region, 1985–89; Nat. Sec., 1990–2004; Nat. Organiser, 2004–05; Asst Gen. Sec., 2005–07, when T&GWU merged with Amicus to form Unite. Mem., TUC Gen. Council and Exec., 2007–. Alumnus, Duke of Edinburgh's 8th Commonwealth Study Conf., 1998. FRSA 2013. *Recreations:* football, sport, reading, politics, chess, poetry. *Address:* Unite, 128 Theobalds Road, Holborn, WC1X 8TN.

McCLUSKIE, John Cameron, CB 1999; QC (Scot.) 1989; Consultant Parliamentary Counsel to Irish Government, 2006–08; *b* 1 Feb. 1946; *m* 1970, Janis Mary Helen McArthur; one *s* one *d*. *Educ:* Hyndland Sch., Glasgow; Glasgow Univ. (LLB Hons 1967). Admitted Solicitor, Scotland, 1970; admitted Faculty of Advocates, 1974. Apprentice Solicitor, Boyds, Glasgow, 1967–69; Asst Town Clerk, Burgh of Cumbernauld, 1969–70; Legal Assistant: Macdonald, Jameson and Morris, Glasgow, 1970; SSEB, 1970–72; Asst, then Sen. Asst, Legal Sec. and Parly Draftsman, Lord Advocate's Dept, 1972–89; Legal Sec. to Lord Advocate, 1989–99; First Scottish Parly Counsel, later First Parly Counsel, Scottish Exec., 1989–2006. Trustee and Co. Sec., Leuchie, 2011–. *Recreations:* watching mogs, walking dogs, cutting logs. *Address:* Law View, Redside Farm Steading, North Berwick, East Lothian EH39 5PE.

McCLYMONT, Dr Gregg; Head of Retirement Savings, Aberdeen Asset Management, since 2015; *b* Glasgow, 3 June 1976; *s* of Hugh Forbes McClymont and Sheila McClymont (*née* McGalliard). *Educ:* Cumbernauld High Sch.; Glasgow Univ. (MA Hons); Univ. of Pennsylvania (AM); St John's Coll., Oxford (DPhil 2006; MA 2007). Fellow in History, St Hugh's Coll., Oxford, 2007–10; Vis. Fellow, Nuffield Coll., Oxford, 2014–. MP (Lab) Cumbernauld, Kilsyth and Kirkintilloch E, 2010–15; contested (Lab) same seat, 2015.

McCOLGAN, Elizabeth, MBE 1992; athlete and coach; Owner, Liz McColgan Health Clubs; *b* 24 May 1964; *d* of Martin and Elizabeth Lynch; *m* 1987, Peter McColgan (marr. diss. 2013); three *s* two *d*. *Educ:* St Saviour's High Sch., Dundee; Univ. of Alabama. Athletic achievements include: Commonwealth Games: Gold Medal, 10,000m, Edinburgh, 1986, Auckland, 1991; Bronze Medal, 3,000m, Auckland, 1991; World Cross Country Championships: Silver Medal, Warsaw, 1987; Bronze Medal, Antwerp, 1991; Silver Medal, 10,000m, Olympic Games, Seoul, 1988; Silver Medal, 3,000m, World Indoor Championships, Budapest, 1989; Gold Medal, 10,000m, World Championships, Tokyo, 1991; Gold Medal, World Half-Marathon Championships, 1992; Marathons: winner, NYC, 1991; winner, 1992, 3rd, 1996, Tokyo; 3rd, 1993, 5th, 1995, winner, 1996, 2nd, 1997 and 1998, London; retd 2001. Chair, Scottish Athletics, 2003–05. Patron, Leukaemia and Lymphoma Res. (formerly Leukaemia Res. Fund). BBC Sports Personality of the Year Award, 1991. *Recreations:* reading, movies, eating out, keeping fit. *Address:* c/o Silver Fox Media, 3 Sauncey Wood, Harpenden, Herts AL5 5DP.

McCOLL, family name of **Baron McColl of Dulwich**.

McCOLL OF DULWICH, Baron *cr* 1989 (Life Peer), of Bermondsey in the London Borough of Southwark; **Ian McColl,** CBE 1997; MS, FRCS, FACS, FRCSE; Professor of Surgery, University of London at Guy's, King's and St Thomas' School of Medicine of King's College London (formerly United Medical Schools of Guy's and St Thomas' Hospitals), 1971–98, now Emeritus; Director of Surgery, 1985–98, and Consultant Surgeon, 1971–98, Guy's Hospital; Consultant Surgeon to Mercy Ships, since 2000; *b* 6 Jan. 1933; *s* of late Frederick George McColl and Winifred E. McColl, Dulwich; *m* 1960, Dr Jean Lennox, 2nd *d* of Arthur James McNair, FRCS, FRCOG; one *s* two *d*. *Educ:* Hutchesons' Grammar Sch., Glasgow; St Paul's Sch., London; Guy's Hosp., London. MB, BS 1957; FRCS 1962; FRCSE 1962; MS 1966; FACS 1975. Junior staff appts at St Bartholomew's, Putney, St Mark's, St Peter's, Great Ormond Street, Barnet, St Olave's and Guy's Hosps, 1957–67; Research Fellow, Harvard Med. Sch., and Moynihan Fellowship, Assoc. of Surgeons, 1967; Reader in Surgery, St Bartholomew's Hosp. Med. Coll., 1967 (Sub Dean, 1969–71). Visiting Professor: Univ. of South Carolina, 1974; Johns Hopkins Hosp., 1976. Consultant Surgeon: KCH, 1971–98 (FKC 2001); Edenbridge Dist Meml Hosp., 1978–91; Lewisham Hosp., 1983–90; Hon. Consultant in Surgery to the Army, 1982–98. External examiner in Surgery to Univs of Newcastle upon Tyne and Cardiff, QUB, TCD and NUI. Royal College of Surgeons: Examr in Pathology, 1970–76; Regl Advr, SE Reg., 1975–80; Mem. Council, 1986–94; Arris and Gale Lectr, 1964, 1965; Erasmus Wilson Lectr, 1972; Haig Gudenian Meml Lectr, 1988; Henry Cohen Meml Lectr, 1994; Lettsomian Lectr, Med. Soc. of London, 1993. Medical Advisor, BBC Television, 1976–92. PPS (Lord's) to the Prime Minister, 1994–97; a Dep. Speaker, H of L, 1994–2004; opposition spokesman on health, 1997–2010. Member: Central Health Services Council, 1972–74; Standing Medical Adv. Cttee, 1972–82; Management Cttee, King Edward VII Hospital Fund (Chm., R&D Cttee), 1975–80; Council, Metrop. Hosp. Sunday Fund, 1986–91; Council, Imperial Cancer Res. Fund, 1986–94; Exec. Council, British Limbless Ex-Service Men's Assoc., 1991–; Chairman: King's Fund Centre Cttee, 1976–86; Govt Wkg Pty on Artificial Limb and Appliance Centres in England, 1984–86; Vice Chm., SHA for Disablement Services, 1987–91. Hon. Sec., British Soc. of Gastroenterology, 1970–74. President: Soc. of Minimally Invasive Gen. Surgery, 1991–94; Limbless Assoc. (formerly Nat. Assoc. for Limbless Disabled), 1992– (Patron and Hon. Consultant, 1989–); Internat. Wheelchair Fedn, 1991–; Assoc. of Endoscopic Surgeons of GB and Ireland, 1994–98; The Hospital Saving Assoc., 1994–2001; Leprosy Mission, 1996–; REMEDI, 1996–99; Royal Med. Foundn of Epsom Coll., 2001–; Vice-Pres., Livability (formerly John Grooms Assoc. for Disabled People), 1990–. Governor-at-Large for England, Bd of Governors, Amer. Coll. of Surgeons, 1982–88. Pres., 1985–94, Chm. Bd of Govs, 1994–2002, Mildmay Mission Hosp.; Chm., Mercy Ships UK, 2005–; Vice Chm., Mercy Ships Internat. and Surgeon to Mercy Ships, 2005–. Governor: Dulwich Coll. Prep. Sch., 1978–2002; James Allen's Girls' Sch., 1994–2004 (Chm., 1998–2004); St Paul's Sch., 2001–11 (Pres., Old Pauline Club, 2005–07); Pres., King's Coll. Alumni, 2010–12. Trustee, Wolfson Foundn, Dulwich Estate, 1994–; Chm., Dulwich Estate Trustees, 2007–08 (Chm., Mgt Cttee, 2003–07). Master, Barbers' Co., 1999–2000. FKC 2002. Hon. FDSRCS 2007. Edenbridge Medal for Services to the Community, 1992; George and Thomas Hutcheson's Award, 2000; Great Scot Award, 2002; Dist. Award, Nat. Maritime Assoc., NY, 2003. *Publications:* (ed jtly) Intestinal Absorption in Man, 1975; Talking to Patients, 1982; NHS Data Book, 1984; (contrib.) 60 Years of the NHS, 2008; med. articles, mainly on gastroenterology, rehabilitation and NHS management. *Recreations:* forestry, ornithology. *Address:* House of Lords, SW1A 0PW. *Clubs:* Royal College of Surgeons Council, Royal Society of Medicine.

McCOLL, (Christopher) Miles; a District Judge (Magistrates' Courts) (formerly Provincial Stipendiary Magistrate), Birmingham, 1993–2009; *b* 18 April 1946; *s* of John Parr McColl and Lilian McColl (*née* Oddy); *m* 1971, Susan Margaret Rathbone; three *d*. *Educ:* Liverpool Coll. Admitted solicitor, 1971. Articled clerk in private practice, St Helens, 1965–69; trainee, Court Clerk, then Principal Court Clerk, Manchester City Magistrates' Court, 1969–74; Dep. Clerk to Stockport Justices, 1974–78; Clerk to Leigh Justices, 1978–93. Sec., Gtr Manchester Justices' Clerks and Courts Liaison Cttee, 1984–90; Member: Magistrates' Courts Rev. of Procedure Cttee, 1989–91; Magistrates' Courts Consultative Council, 1992–93; Children Act Procedure Adv. Gp, 1989–90; Pres. of Family Division's Cttee, 1990–92; Legal Aid Steering Cttee, 1992; Pre-trial Issues Steering Gp, 1992–93; Legal Cttee, Dist Judges (Magistrates' Cts) (formerly Jt Council of HM Stipendiary Magistrates), 1997–2009 (Chm., 2000–09); Magistrates' Cts Rule Cttee, 2001–09; Consultee, Sentencing Adv. Panel, 1998–2009. Secretary: S Lancs Br., Magistrates' Assoc., 1979–85; British Juvenile and Family Courts' Soc., 1980–81; Justices' Clerks' Society: Mem. Council, 1988–93; Chm., Parly Cttee, 1989; Chm., Professional Purposes Cttee, 1989–93; Pre-trial Issues Nat. Action Manager, 1991–93; Vice-Pres., Duchy of Lancaster Br., 1993. Ed., 1979–87, Jt Ed., 1987–2004, Family Law. *Publications:* Court Teasers: practical situations arising in magistrates' courts, 1978; contrib. to legal jls. *Recreations:* sport, reading, music, British countryside.

McCOLL, Sir Colin (Hugh Verel), KCMG 1990 (CMG 1983); HM Diplomatic Service, retired; Head of MI6, 1988–94; *b* 6 Sept. 1932; *s* of Dr Robert McColl and Julie McColl; *m* 1st, 1959, Shirley Curtis (*d* 1983); two *s* two *d*; 2nd, 1985, Sally Morgan; one *s*. *Educ:* Shrewsbury School; The Queen's College, Oxford (BA; Hon. Fellow 1996). Foreign Office, 1956; Third Secretary, Bangkok, 1958, Vientiane, 1960; Second Secretary, FO, 1962; First Secretary, Warsaw, 1966; Consul and First Secretary (Disarmament), Geneva, 1973; Counsellor, FCO, 1977. Chm., Pimpernel Trust, 1997–2014. *Recreations:* music, walks, classics.

McCOLL, Isabella Garden; Sheriff of Lothian and Borders at Edinburgh, since 2005; *b* 7 Nov. 1952; *m* Alexander James; one *s* two *d. Educ:* James Gillespie's High Sch.; Edinburgh Univ. Admitted: Solicitor, 1975; Advocate, 1993; Sheriff of Tayside, Central and Fife at Dunfermline, 2000–05. *Address:* Sheriff Court House, 27 Chambers Street, Edinburgh EH1 1LB.

McCOLL, Gen. Sir John Chalmers, KCB 2008; CBE 1997; DSO 2002; Lieutenant-Governor and Commander-in-Chief, Jersey, since 2011; *b* 17 April 1952. Commnd Royal Anglian Regt, 1973; sc, 1984; Staff Officer, Germany; Rifle Co. Comdr, 2nd Bn, 1987; 3rd Royal Tank Regt, 1989; Mem., Directing Staff, Staff Coll., Camberley, 1990; Comdr, 2nd Bn, 1992; COS 1st (UK) Armoured Div., 1995; Comdr, 1st Mechanized Bde, 3rd (UK) Div., 1997–99; ACOS Commitments, HQ Land Comd, 1999–2000; GOC 3rd (UK) Div., 2000–03; Comdr Internat. Security Assistance Force, Afghanistan, 2002; Comdt, JSCSC, 2003–04; Sen. British Mil. Rep., Iraq, subseq. Dep. Comdg Gen. Multinational Corps, Iraq, 2004; Comdr, Regl Forces Land Comd, 2004–07; Prime Minister's Special Envoy to Afghanistan, 2004–05; Dep. Supreme Allied Comdr Europe, 2007–11. Col Comdt, Queen's Div., 2002–10. Gov., Dean Close Sch., Cheltenham, 2006–. Officer, Legion of Merit (USA), 2006.

McCOLL, Miles; *see* McColl, C. M.

McCOLLUM, Prof. Charles Nevin, MD; FRCS, FRCSE; Professor of Surgery, University of Manchester, and Hon. Consultant Surgeon, University Hospital of South Manchester NHS Foundation Trust (formerly South Manchester University Hospitals NHS Trust), since 1989; *b* 17 April 1950; *m*; two *d. Educ:* Tettenhall Coll.; Millfield Sch.; Medical Sch., Univ. of Birmingham (MB ChB 1972; MD 1981); Cert. Higher Surgical Trng 1981. FRCS 1976; FRCSE 1976. Registrar in Surgery, St James's Univ. Hosp., Leeds, 1976–78; Lectr in Surgery, Univ. of Birmingham, 1978–83; Sen. Lectr, 1983–88, Reader in Surgery, 1988–89, Charing Cross and Westminster Hosp. Med. Sch., London; Hon. Consultant Surgeon, Charing Cross Hosp., 1983–89. Director: Manchester Surgical Res. Trust; IVS Ltd; VTE Ltd; Rinicare Ltd. Dir, Gtr Manchester AAA Screening Prog., 2008–. Examiner in Surgery: Univ. of London; Univ. of Manchester; Univ. of Glasgow. NIHR Sen. Investigator, 2012–. Chm., Exec. Cttee on Clinical Governance, NW Vascular Surgeons; Treas. and Cttee Mem., Surg. Res. Soc. of GB and Ire; Scientific Cttee, Internat. Soc. on Thrombosis and Haemostasis. Editl Bd, British Jl of Surgery. Hunterian Prof., RCS, 1985. Moynihan Prize, Assoc. of Surgeons of GB and Ire., 1979; Patey Prize, Surg. Res. Soc. of GB and Ire., 1983, 1995. *Publications:* over 40 chapters; over 300 papers on original res. *Recreations:* tennis, country sports, riding, ski-ing, sailing. *Address:* Academic Surgery Unit, 2nd Floor, Education and Research Centre, University Hospital of South Manchester, Southmoor Road, Manchester M23 9LT. *T:* (0161) 291 5853, *Fax:* (0161) 291 5854. *E:* cnmcc@manchester.ac.uk. *Clubs:* Manchester Tennis and Racquet, Alderley Edge Tennis.

McCOLLUM, Rt Hon. Sir William Paschal, (Rt Hon. Sir Liam McCollum), Kt 1988; PC 1997; a Surveillance Commissioner, 2004–10; *b* 13 Jan. 1933; *s* of Patrick McCollum and Mary Ellen McCollum (*née* Strain); *m* 1958, Anne Bernadette Fitzpatrick (CBE 1995); six *s* two *d. Educ:* Waterside School; St Columb's Coll., Derry; University College Dublin (BA 1953; LLB 1954). Called to the Bar of N Ireland, 1955; called to Irish Bar, 1963; QC 1971; High Court Judge, NI, 1987–97; a Lord Justice of Appeal, Supreme Court of Judicature, NI, 1997–2004.

McCOMB, Christina Margaret; Chief Executive Officer, C5 Capital Ltd, 2011–13; *b* 6 May 1956; *d* of Patrick William John McComb and Margaret McComb; *m* 1980, Peter John Linacre; two *s* one *d. Educ:* London Sch. of Econs (BA French and Russian 1978); London Business Sch. (MBA 1989). FCO, 1978–88; Director: 3i plc, 1989–2003; Shareholder Exec., DTI, 2003–06; Partnerships UK plc, 2004–06. Non-executive Director: Engage Mutual Assce, 2005– (Chm., 2014–); Nexeon Ltd, 2007–; Baronsmead VCT2, 2011–; Senior Independent Director: Standard Life European Private Equity Trust plc, 2013–; British Business Bank, 2013–. Trustee, Land Restoration Trust, 2010–. *Recreations:* running, travel.

McCOMB, Leonard William Joseph, RA 1991 (ARA 1987); RE, RWS, RP; painter, sculptor, printmaker, potter, draughtsman; Keeper of the Royal Academy, 1995–98; *b* 3 Aug. 1930; *s* of Archibald and Delia McComb, Glasgow; *m* 1st, 1955, Elizabeth Henstock (marr. diss. 1963); 2nd, 1966, Joan Allwork (*d* 1967); 3rd, 1973, Barbara Eleonora Gittel (marr. diss. 1999). *Educ:* Manchester Art Sch.; Slade Sch. of Fine Art, Univ. of London (Dip. Fine Art, 1960). RE 1994, Hon. RE 1995; RP 2003; Hon. RWS 1996. Teacher at art schools, Bristol, Oxford, RA schools, Slade, Goldsmiths', Sir John Cass, 1960–. Founder and Patron, Sunningwell Sch. of Art. *One-man exhibitions include:* Blossoms and Flowers, Coracle Press Gall., London, 1979; Drawings, Paintings and Sculpture, Serpentine Gall., London and tour, 1983; Paintings from the South, Gillian Jason Gall., London, 1989; Drawings and Paintings, Darby Gall., London, 1993; Portraits, NY Studio Sch. Gall.; The Upright Figure, Tate Modern, 2002; Leonard McComb: Drawings, Painting and Sculpture, Talbot Rice Gall., Edinburgh, 2004, Wolsey Art Gall., Ipswich, 2005; Leonard McComb RA: A Retrospective, 1976–2006, Agnew's Gall., 2006; exhibits annually, Royal Acad. of Arts; *group exhibitions include:* Arts Council, 1976, 1980, 1982, 1987; RA, 1977, 1989; Venice, 1980; Whitechapel, 1981; Tate, 1984; Hirshorn Gall., Washington, 1986; Raab Gall., Berlin, 1986; Museum of Modern Art, Brussels, 1987; Gillian Jason Gall., London, 1990, 1991; Kettles Yard Gall., 1994, 1995, 1997; Walker Art Gall., Liverpool, 1995; Aspects Gall., Portsmouth, 1997; Mus. of Modern Art, Dublin, 1997; Flowers East Gall., London, 1998; Henry Moore Inst., Leeds, 2011; *work in public collections:* Arts Council; British Council; ICA; Cambridge Univ.; Tate; V&A; BM; Ulster Mus.; Art Galls of Birmingham, Manchester, Swindon, Worcester, Eastbourne, Bedford, Belfast; *commissions* for cos and educnl bodies include paintings, plates, tapestry, plaques; mosaics of St Francis of Assisi and St Anthony of Padua for Westminster Cathedral, 2005–10. DUniv Oxford Brookes, 2004. Prizes include: Jubilee Prize, RA, 1986; Korn Ferry Award, 1990; Times Watercolour Comp. Prize, 1992, 1993; Nordstern Printmaking Prize, RA, 1992; RWS Prize, 1998; Hugh Casson Drawing Prize, 2006, Turner Watercolour Award and Medal, 2007, RA. *Recreations:* travelling, walking in the countryside.

McCOMBE, Rt Hon. Sir Richard (George Bramwell), Kt 2001; PC 2012; **Rt Hon. Lord Justice McCombe;** a Lord Justice of Appeal, since 2012; *b* 23 Sept. 1952; *s* of Barbara Bramwell McCombe, MA, FCA; *m* 1st (marr. diss.); 2nd, 1986, Carolyn Sara Birrell (marr. diss. 2009); one *s* one *d*; 3rd, 2013, Rt Hon. Dame Jill Margaret Black, *qv. Educ:* Sedbergh Sch.; Downing Coll., Cambridge (MA). Called to the Bar, Lincoln's Inn, 1975, Bencher, 1996; admitted (*ad hoc*) to Bars of Singapore, 1992, Cayman Is, 1993. Second Jun. Counsel to Dir-Gen. of Fair Trading, 1982–87, First Jun. Counsel, 1987–89; QC 1989; an Asst Recorder, 1993–96, Recorder, 1996–2001; Attorney Gen., Duchy of Lancaster, 1996–2001; a Dep. High Ct Judge, 1998–2001; a Judge of the High Court of Justice, QBD, 2001–12; Presiding Judge, Northern Circuit, 2004–07. Mem., Senate of Inns of Court and of Bar Council, 1981–86; Chm., Young Barristers' Cttee, Bar Council, 1983–84; Co-opted Mem., Bar Council Cttees, 1986–89; Mem., Gen. Council of the Bar, 1995–97 (Chm., Internat. Relns Cttee, 1997); Chm., Assoc. of High Court Judges, 2008–09. Head of UK Delegn to Council, Bars and Law Socs of EC, 1996–98. Inspector into affairs of Norton Group PLC, 1991–92 (report, with J. K. Heywood, 1993). Mem., Singapore Acad. of Law, 1992. Pres., Assoc. of Lancastrians in London, 2008. Gov., Sedbergh Sch., 2002–13. Chm., Oversight Cttee, RCSE, 2012–. Trustee, Duchy of Lancaster Housing Trust, 2008–14. *Publications:* (ed jtly) Performance Appraisal of the Judiciary and Judicial Independence, 2014. *Recreations:* cricket, Rugby, flying light aircraft. *Address:* Royal Courts of Justice, Strand, WC2A 2LL. *Clubs:* Garrick, Royal Automobile, MCC; London Scottish Football, Lancs CC.

McCOMBIE, John Alexander Fergusson, FRICS; General Manager, Glenrothes Development Corporation, 1993–96; *b* 13 Sept. 1932; *s* of Alexander William McCombie and Charlotte Mary McCombie (*née* Fergusson); *m* 1959, Seana Joy Cameron Scott; two *s* one *d. Educ:* Perth Acad.; Coll. of Estate Management. ARICS 1968, FRICS 1982; IRRV 1969. Nat. service, RAF, 1955–57 (MEAF). E Kilbride Develt Corp., 1959–67; Irvine Develt Corp., 1968–70; Glenrothes Develt Corp., 1970–96: Chief Estates Officer, 1970–74; Commercial Dir, 1975–93. Director: Glenrothes Enterprise Trust, 1983–94; Mid-Fife Business Trust, 1994–2003 (Chm., 1997–2003); Chairman and Director: Age Concern Glenrothes Ltd, 1996–2010; Leven Valley Develt Trust, 1997–; Ecowise Fife Ltd, 1999–2002; GIA Properties Ltd, 1999–; Chm., Wolseley Register, Scottish Gp, 1999–; Dir and Sec., 1996–, Chm., 1997–2011, Fife Historic Bldgs Trust. Mem. Bd of Mgt, Glenrothes Coll., 1999–2003. *Recreations:* gardening, golf, philately, reading, classic cars. *Address:* 13 Carnoustie Gardens, Glenrothes, Fife KY6 2QB. *T:* (01592) 345470. *Club:* Balbirnie Park Golf.

McCONNELL, family name of **Baron McConnell of Glenscorrodale.**

McCONNELL OF GLENSCORRODALE, Baron *cr* 2010 (Life Peer), of the Isle of Arran in Ayrshire and Arran; **Jack Wilson McConnell;** PC 2001; Member (Lab) Motherwell and Wishaw, Scottish Parliament, 1999–2011; Founder and Chairman, McConnell International Foundation; *b* 30 June 1960; *s* of William Wilson McConnell and Elizabeth McEwan McConnell; *m* 1990, Bridget Mary McLuckie (*see* B. M. McConnell); one *s* one *d. Educ:* Arran High Sch., Isle of Arran; Stirling Univ. (BSc 1983; DipEd 1983). Mathematics Teacher, Alloa, 1983–92; Gen. Sec., SLP, 1992–98. Mem. (Lab) Stirling DC, 1984–93 (Treas., 1988–92; Leader, 1990–92). Contested (Lab) Perth and Kinross, 1987. Scottish Executive: Minister for Finance, 1999–2000; Minister for Educn, Europe and External Affairs, 2000–01; First Minister, 2001–07. Special Rep. of the Prime Minister on Peacebuilding, 2008–10. Member: COSLA, 1988–92; Scottish Constitutional Convention, 1990–98; Bd, Inst. for Cultural Diplomacy; Adv. Bd, UK-Japan 21st Century Gp, PwC, 2010–. Pres., Gp of EU Regions with Legislative Powers, 2003–04. Chm., SSE Sustainable Develt Fund. Fellow, UK-China 48 Gp Club. Ambassador, Action for Children UK; Chm., Radio Clyde Cash for Kids; Patron: Positive Women; Diana Awards. DUniv Stirling, 2008. *Publications:* political articles in newspapers, jls and booklets. *Recreations:* music, gardening, golf, other sports. *Address:* House of Lords, SW1A 0PW.

McCONNELL, Prof. Alison Kay, PhD; CSci; Professor of Exercise Science, Bournemouth University, since 2015; *b* Singapore, 17 Oct. 1961; *d* of late Ian Harrison McConnell and of Audrey McConnell; civil partnership 2008, Melanie Varvel. *Educ:* Chase High Sch., Malvern; Univ. of Birmingham (BSc Biol Scis 1983); King's Coll., London (MSc Human and Applied Physiol. 1984; PhD Respiratory Physiol. 1989). CSci 2014. Res. Fellow, Univ. of Birmingham, 1986–89; Lectr, Loughborough Univ., 1989–94; Dir, Centre for Sports Medicine, Univ. of Birmingham, 1994–98; Res. Dir, IMT Technologies Ltd, 1996–2000; Reader, 2000–05, Prof., 2005–15, Brunel Univ. Fellow: Amer. Coll. Sports Medicine, 2006; British Assoc. of Sport and Exercise Scis, 2010. *Publications:* Breathe Strong, Perform Better, 2011; Respiratory Muscle Training: theory and practice, 2013; contrib. articles to learned jls; five patents. *Recreations:* cycling, running, free diving, dog walking, fast cars, inventing useful stuff that improves people's lives (e.g. POWERbreathe®). *E:* hello@breathestrong.com.

McCONNELL, Bridget Mary, (Lady McConnell of Glenscorrodale), CBE 2015; EdD; Chief Executive, Glasgow Life (formerly Culture & Sport Glasgow), since 2007; *b* 28 May 1958; *d* of Robert Rankin McLuckie and Patricia McLuckie (*née* Airlie); *m* 1990, Jack Wilson McConnell (*see* Baron McConnell of Glenscorrodale); one *s* one *d. Educ:* St Patrick's Jun. Secondary Sch., Kilsyth; Our Lady's High Sch., Cumbernauld; St Andrews Univ. (MA Hons 1982); Dundee Coll. of Commerce (DIA 1983); Stirling Univ. (MEd 1992; EdD 2009). Curator, Doorstep Gall., Fife Regl Council, 1983–84; Arts Officer, Stirling DC, 1984–88; Principal Arts Officer, Arts in Fife, Fife Regl Council, 1988–96; Service Manager, Community Services/Arts, Libraries, Museums, Fife Council, 1996–98; Dir, Cultural and Leisure Services, 1998–2005, Exec. Dir (Culture and Sport), 2005–07, Glasgow CC. Chair, Scottish Assoc. of Dirs of Leisure Services, 2001–02. Member: Bd, Workshop and Artists Studio Provision Scotland Ltd, 1985–90; Combined Arts Cttee, Scottish Arts Council, 1988–94; Heritage Lottery Fund Cttee for Scotland, 2004–10; Bd, 2014 Commonwealth Games Organising Cttee, 2008–; Bd, UNESCO City of Music, 2009–. Chair, Scottish Youth Dance Fest., 1993–96 (Founder Mem., 1988); Co-ordinator, Fourth Internat. Conf. in Adult Educn and the Arts, 1995. Chm., Vocal - Voice of Chief Officers of Cultural, Community and Leisure Services in Scotland, 2002–04. Mem. Bd of Govs, 2001–, Vice Chm., 2007–13, RSAMD, later Royal Conservatoire of Scotland. DHC Aberdeen, 2008; Hon. DLitt St Andrews, 2008; Hon. Dr Royal Conservatoire of Scotland, 2013; DUniv Glasgow, 2014. *Publications:* (contrib.) Modernising Britain: creative futures, 1997; internat. conf. papers, ed conf. proceedings. *Recreations:* walking, playing the piano, swimming, reading. *Address:* (office) 220 High Street, Glasgow G4 0QW. *T:* (0141) 287 5058.

McCONNELL, Carmel Bridget; Founder and Chief Executive Officer, Magic Breakfast, since 2001; *b* Romford, Essex, 17 Aug. 1961; *d* of Gerald McConnell and Patricia Donaghey; civil partnership, Catherine Purkiss. *Educ:* Sacred Heart Convent, Dagenham; Cass Business Sch. (MBA). Technologist, BT plc, 1989–94; mgt consultant, Holistic Mgt, 1995–2001. *Publications:* Change Activist, 2001, 2002; Soul Trader, 2002; (jtly) Float You, 2003; Make Money Be Happy, 2004; The Happiness Plan, 2007. *Recreations:* open water swimming, guitar, creating the national will to end child hunger. *Address:* Magic Breakfast, 190 High Holborn, WC1V 7BH. *E:* carmel@magicbreakfast.com.

McCONNELL, Prof. (Francis) Ian, PhD; FRSE; Professor of Veterinary Science and Director of Research, Centre for Veterinary Science, Department of Veterinary Medicine (formerly of Clinical Veterinary Medicine), University of Cambridge, 1994, now Professor Emeritus; Professorial Fellow of Darwin College, Cambridge, 2003, now Emeritus; *b* 6 Nov. 1940; *s* of Edward McConnell and Pearl McConnell (*née* Quigley); *m* 1967, Anna Farren; three *s* two *d. Educ:* St Aloysius' Coll., Glasgow; Univ. of Glasgow (BVMS 1965); St Catharine's Coll., Cambridge (Scholar; BA 1st Cl. Hons 1967; MA 1970; PhD 1970). MRCVS 1965; MRCPath 1981, FRCPath 1992. Fellow, Clare Hall, Cambridge, 1967–72; Wellcome Trust Res. Fellow, Inst. of Animal Physiology, Cambridge, 1970–72; Sen. Lectr in Immunology, RPMS, Hammersmith Hosp., 1972–76; MRC Sen. Scientist, MRC Lab. of Molecular Biology, Cambridge, 1976–83; Hon. Associate Lectr in Pathology, Dept of Pathology, Univ. of Cambridge, 1976–83; Prof. and Hd of Dept of Vet. Pathology, Univ. of Edinburgh, 1983–94. Member: Selbourne Cttee of Enquiry into Vet. Res., 1996–98; Wellcome Trust Vet. Medicine Interest Panel, 1998–; Govt's Spongiform Encephalopathy Adv. Cttee (SEAC), 2000–; HEFCE Panel of Experts for 2001 RAE; Working Gp on TSE, Royal Soc. and Acad. of Med. Scis, 2001–02; Adv. Gp on use of Genetically Modified Animals, Royal Soc., 2001–02; Inquiry into Infectious Diseases in Livestock, Royal Soc., 2001–02; Nuffield Council for Bioethics Wkg Party on the Ethics of Res. Involving Animals, 2004–. Mem., Governing Body, Inst. for Animal Health, 1988–94. FRSE 1987; FMedSci 1998; FRSocMed 2000. Wellcome Trust Medal for Vet. Res., 1997. *Publications:* (with M. J. Hobart) The Immune System: a course on the molecular and cellular basis of immunity, 1976, 2nd edn (with A. J. Munro and H. Waldmann) 1981; res. papers in immunology, pathology and veterinary sci. *Recreations:* ski-ing, mountain walking, family. *Address:* Department of Veterinary Medicine, University of Cambridge, Madingley Road, Cambridge CB3 0ES. *T:* (01223) 337654, *Fax:* (01223) 337671. *E:* im200@cam.ac.uk.

McCONNELL, Prof. James Desmond Caldwell, FRS 1987; Professor of the Physics and Chemistry of Minerals, Department of Earth Sciences, University of Oxford, 1986–95, now Emeritus (Head of Department, 1991–95); Fellow of St Hugh's College, Oxford, 1986–95 (Hon. Fellow, 1995); *b* 3 July 1930; *s* of Samuel D. and Cathleen McConnell; *m* 1956, Jean Elspeth Ironside; one *s* two *d*. *Educ:* Queen's Univ. of Belfast (BSc, MSc 1952); Univ. of Cambridge (MA 1955; PhD 1956); MA Oxon 1986. Univ. of Cambridge: Demonstrator, 1955; Lectr, 1960; Reader, 1972–82; Churchill College: Fellow, 1962–82; Extraordinary Fellow, 1983–88; Head of Dept of Rock Physics, Schlumberger Cambridge Research, 1983–86. Alex von Humboldt Prize, Alexander von Humboldt Stiftung, Germany, 1996. *Publications:* Principles of Mineral Behaviour (with A. Putnis), 1980, Russian edn, 1983; papers in physics jls and mineralogical jls. *Recreations:* local history, singing. *Address:* 19 Gilmerton Court, Cambridge CB2 9HQ. *T:* (01223) 843711.

McCONNELL, John, RDI 1987; FCSD; graphic designer; freelance design practice, McConnell Design, 1963–74 and since 2005; Director, Pentagram Design, 1974–2005; *b* 14 May 1939; *s* of Donald McConnell and Enid McConnell (*née* Dimberline); *m* 1963, Moira Rose Macgregor; one *s* one *d*. *Educ:* Borough Green Secondary Modern School; Maidstone College of Art (NDD). FCSD (FSIAD 1980). Employed in advertising and design, 1959–62; Lectr, Colchester College of Art, 1962–63; co-founder, Face Photosetting, 1968. Design consultant, Boots, 1984–2002; design adviser to John Lewis Partnership, 2001–10, to British Museum, 2010–. Mem., Post Office Stamp Adv. Cttee, 1984–2012; Pres., D&AD, 1986 (President's Award, 1985); served on design competition juries, D&AD. Gold medallist at Biennale, Warsaw; Special Commendation, Prince Phillip Designer's Prize, 2002. *Publications:* (jtly) Living by Design, 1978; (jtly) Ideas on Design, 1986; (jtly) The Compendium, 1993; (ed jtly) Pentagram Book 5, 1999; Editor, Pentagram Papers. *Recreations:* house restoration, cooking. *Address:* (office) 11 Needham Road, W11 2RP. *T:* (020) 7229 3477; (home) 12 Orme Court, W2 4RL.

McCONNELL, Philippa Mary; *see* Harrison, P. M.

McCONNELL, (Sir) Robert Shean, (4th Bt *cr* 1900); *S* father, 1987, but does not use the title. *Educ:* Stowe; Queens' Coll., Cambridge (MA Urban Estate Management); Regent St Polytech. (DipTP); Univ. of BC (MSc Community and Regl Planning). FRTPI; MRICS; MCMI. Worked as a trainee surveyor in Belfast and as a town planner in UK, Canada and USA. Lectured in town planning and principles of management at univs in UK and Australia. Chm., Lambeth Race Scrutiny Commn, 2002–03. Member: London SE Valuation Tribunal, 1995–2002; Community Police Consultative Gp for Lambeth, 1995–2005; Health Scrutiny Cttee for Lambeth and Southwark, 2002–06; Health Watch, Lambeth and Southwark, 2012–; Lambeth Patient Participation Gp Network (formerly Lambeth Link Patient Participation Gp), 2012– (Co-Vice Chm.); Chm., Patient Participation Gp, Stockwell Practice, 2013–. Mem., Bruce House Appeal Cttee, 1994. Governor: South Bank Poly., 1973–75; Tulse Hill Sch., 1976–90; Stockwell Infant Jun. Sch., 1983–88; Norwood Park Primary Sch., 1996–2002; Crown Lane Primary Sch., 2003–12. Councillor (Lib Dem) Lambeth BC, 1996–2006. Voluntary Manager, St Michael's Church Hall, Stockwell, 2012–. Zeta Psi Fraternity (Canada), 1957. *Publications:* Theories for Planning, 1981; (contrib.) Planning Ethics, ed Hendler, 1995; (contrib.) Housing: the essential foundations, ed Balchin and Rhoden, 1998; The Peace Bug, 2010; articles in professional jls on planning matters; unsuccessful playwright and novelist. *Recreation:* gardening. *Heir:* *b* James Angus McConnell [*m* Elizabeth Jillian (*née* Harris); two *s* four *d* (incl. twins)].

McCONNELL, Wendy Jane; *see* Miles, W. J.

McCORD ADAMS, Rev. Marilyn; *see* Adams, Marilyn McC.

McCORKELL, George Alexander, CB 2002; management consultant, G. A. McCorkell Ltd, since 2004; Director, Pensions Change Programme, Department for Work and Pensions, 2001–04; *b* 6 Jan. 1944; *s* of Samuel Robert McCorkell and Sarah McCorkell; *m* 1967, Nuala McCarthy; two *s*. *Educ:* Foyle Coll., Londonderry, NI; BA Math. Open, 1978; MSc Information Systems, LSE, 1982. Computer Programmer, MoD, 1967–69; Systems Analyst: Min. of Finance, 1970–74; DHSS, 1974–76; Liaison Officer, CCTA, 1976–79; Department of Health and Social Security, later Department of Social Security: Operational Systems Team Leader, 1979–83; Principal, 1983–86; Sen. Principal, 1987–88; Director: ITSA, 1988–95; Benefits Agency, 1995–99; Chief Exec., ITSA, 1999–2000; Chief Inf. Officer, 2000–01, Hd of Inf. Systems and Commercial Mgt Div., 2001, DSS. *Recreation:* golf. *Address:* 46 West Drive, Thornton-Cleveleys, Lancs FY5 2BH.

McCORMAC, Prof. Francis Gerard, (Gerry), PhD; FSA; Principal and Vice Chancellor, University of Stirling, since 2010; *b* Belfast, 1 Aug. 1958; *s* of Francis Gerald McCormac and Jane Philomena McCormac; *m* 1982, Catherine Marie Louise Gormley; three *s*. *Educ:* Ulster Poly. (BSc Hons 1980); Univ. of Southampton (PhD Physics 1984); London Business Sch. (Sen. Exec. Prog. 2005). Lectr in Physics, Ulster Poly., 1985–86; Post-doctoral Res. Fellow, Space Physics, 1986–87, Asst Res. Scientist, Space Physics, 1987–90, Univ. of Michigan; Queen's University of Belfast: Lectr in Carbon Dating/Envmtl Monitoring, 1990–94, Sen. Lectr, 1994–99; Dir, Radiocarbon Res. Facility/CHRONO Centre, 1990–2010; Hd, Sch. of Archaeol. and Palaeoecol., 1998–2001; Prof., Science Based Archaeol., 1999–2010; Pro Vice-Chancellor, 2001–10. Dir, NI Sci. Park, 2007–10. Dir and Chm. Mgt Bd, QUBIS Ltd, 2006–10. Member: Inter-agency Strategy Gp, Belfast CC, 2004–10; HE/FE Business Alliance, 2004–10; Bd, Business in the Community, 2005–10; Econ. Develt Forum, 2006–10; MATRIX, NI Sci. and Ind. Panel, 2007–10; Bd, Invest NI, 2008–14. Member: Bd, Universities UK, 2010–; Universities Scotland, 2010–; Scottish Cttee, Univs and Colls Employers' Assoc., 2010–; UCEA, 2015–. Mem., Carnegie Trust for Univs of Scotland, 2010–. FHEA 1998; FSA 2001. FRSA 1999. *Publications:* (contrib.) Advances in the Astronautical Sciences, 1992; (contrib.) Energy and the Environment: geochemistry of fossil, nuclear and renewable resources, 1998; (with B. Maloney) A 30,000-year pollen, radiocarbon and d^{13}C record from Highland North Sumatra and South China Deep Sea Core: 17940 results compared, 2000; (contrib.) Hambledon Hill, Dorset, England: excavation and survey of a Neolithic monument complex and its surrounding landscape, 2008; (contrib.) Radiocarbon Dates, 2008; contribs to learned jls incl. Radiocarbon, Geophysics Res. Letters, Space Sci., Jl Geophysics Res., The Holocene. *Address:* Principal's Office, University of Stirling, Stirling FK9 4LA. *T:* (01786) 467012. *E:* principal@stir.ac.uk. *Club:* Caledonian.

McCORMICK, Dr Andrew Graham, FGS; Permanent Secretary, Department of Enterprise, Trade and Investment, Northern Ireland, since 2014; *b* 26 Aug. 1957; *s* of Jackson and Helen McCormick; *m* 1981, Alison Griffiths; one *s*. *Educ:* University Coll., Oxford (BA 1st Cl. Geol. 1978; MA 1989); Queen's Univ., Belfast (PhD Geochem. 1989). Joined NI Civil Service, 1980; Dept of Finance and Personnel, 1980–93; Sen. Civil Service, Dept of Educn, 1993–98; Dep. Sec., 1998–2002; Second Perm. Sec., Dept of Finance and Personnel, 2002–05; Perm. Sec., Dept of Health, Social Services and Public Safety, 2005–14. FGS 2005. *Publications:* co-author several res. papers in geochemistry. *Recreations:* hill-walking, photography, classical music. *Address:* Department of Enterprise Trade and Investment, Netherleigh, Massey Avenue, Belfast BT4 2JP. *T:* (028) 9052 9441, *Fax:* (028) 9052 9545. *E:* andrew.mccormick@detini.gov.uk.

McCORMICK, Prof. Barry, CBE 2010; PhD; Director, Centre for Health Service Economics and Organisation, Department of Economics, Oxford, since 2010; *b* 3 Aug. 1949; *s* of Leonard McCormick and Lucy Adelaide McCormick; *m* 1975, Doreen Foti; two *s*. *Educ:* Co. High Sch., Arnold, Nottingham; Manchester Univ. (BA, MA); MIT (PhD 1976). Harkness Fellow, 1972–74, Instructor, 1974–75, MIT; Asst Lectr, Univ. of Cambridge, and Fellow, Robinson Coll., Cambridge, 1976–80; Southampton University: Lectr, 1981–87; Sen. Lectr, 1987–89; Reader, 1989–90; Prof. of Econs, 1991–2002; Prof. Emeritus, 2009; Chief Economist and Dir, Econs and Ops Res., DoH, 2002–04; Chief Analyst, DoH, 2004–10. Sir Norman Chester Vis. Fellow, Nuffield Coll., Oxford, 1989. Academic Consultant to HM Treasury, 2001–02. Mem. Council, REconS, 2003–08. *Publications:* (with G. Hughes) Housing Policy and Labour Market Performance, 2000; (jtly) Immigration Policy and the Welfare State, 2002; scientific papers and govt reports on policy in labour markets, develt and health. *Recreations:* music, theatre, art, walking. *Address:* Flat 9A, Vincent House, Vincent Square, SW1P 2NB. *T:* (020) 7821 6433. *E:* barry.mccormick@nuffield.ox.ac.uk.

McCORMICK, Caroline; Founder and Director: Rien Qui Bouge Ltd (cultural project development), since 2013; Achates Philanthropy, since 2014; *b* 14 Oct. 1971; *d* of Anthony and Marie McCormick; *m* 2001, Ian Whitaker (marr. diss. 2008). *Educ:* Astbury Primary Sch.; Heathfield High Sch.; Univ. of Sheffield (BA Hons Eng. Lit. 1993; MA Contemp. Writing 1995). Res. Officer, Rotherham TEC, 1995–96; Trust Fundraising Manager, RNID, 1996–97; Hd, Trust Fundraising, Nat. Th., 1997–99; Dir, Develt, Coin Street Community Builders, 1999–2001; Hd, Develt, Natural Hist. Mus., 2001–05; Dir, Internat. PEN, 2005–10. Established strategy and fundraising consultancy in 2005. Board Member: DanceEast, 2010–12; The Green Belt Movement, 2010–13; Old Vic Th. Develt Council, 2013–. *Recreations:* reading, writing, thinking, talking, swimming, theatre, film. *E:* rienquibouge@gmail.com.

McCORMICK, Prof. Francis Patrick, PhD; FRS 1996; Director, Helen Diller Family Comprehensive Cancer Center, 1997–2014, David A. Wood Distinguished Professor of Tumor Biology and Cancer Research, since 1997, and E. Dixon Heise Distinguished Professor in Oncology, University of California, San Francisco (Director, Cancer Research Institute, 1997–2009); *b* 31 July 1950; *s* of late David and of Jane McCormick; *m* 1979, Judith Anne Demske (marr. diss. 1995). *Educ:* Univ. of Birmingham (BSc 1972); St John's Coll., Cambridge (PhD 1975). Post-doctoral Fellow: SUNY, 1975–78; ICRF, London, 1978–81; Scientist, 1981–89, Vice-Pres., Res., 1989–90, Cetus Corp.; Vice-Pres., Res., Chiron Corp., 1991–92; Founder and Vice-Pres., Res., Onyx Pharmaceuticals, 1992–96. Associate Dean, Sch. of Medicine, UCSF, 1997–. Mem., Inst. of Medicine, 2005. *Publications:* (jointly): Origins of Human Cancer, 1991; The GTPase Superfamily, 1993; The ras Superfamily of GTPases, 1993. *Recreations:* motor racing, African history. *Address:* Helen Diller Family Comprehensive Cancer Center, UCSF School of Medicine, 1450 3rd Street, Room 371, San Francisco, CA 94158, USA.

McCORMICK, John, FRSE; Member for Scotland, UK Electoral Commission, since 2008; *b* 24 June 1944; *s* of Joseph and Roseann McCormick; *m* 1973, Jean Frances Gibbons; one *s* one *d*. *Educ:* St Michael's Acad., Irvine; Univ. of Glasgow (MA Modern History with Econ. History 1967; MEd 1970). Teacher, St Gregory's Secondary Sch., Glasgow, 1968–70; Education Officer, BBC School Broadcasting Council, 1970–75; Senior Education Officer, Scotland, 1975–82; Sec., and Head of Information, BBC Scotland, 1982–87; The Sec. of the BBC, 1987–92; Controller of BBC Scotland, 1992–2004; Chm., Scottish Qualifs Authy, 2004–09. Chm., Edinburgh Internat. Film Fest., 1996–2008; Mem., Edinburgh Fests Forum, 2009–; Mem. Bd, 1997–2003, Vice-Chm., 2003–05, Scottish Screen. Non-exec. Dir, Lloyds TSB Scotland, 2005–09. Mem. Bd, Skillset, 2002–04. Mem., Lay Adv. Cttee, RCPE, 2010–15. Member: Glasgow Sci. Centre Charitable Trust, 1999–2005; Bd, Glasgow Sch. of Art, 2004–07; Bd, Scottish Opera, 2005– (Vice-Chm., 2008–). Director: Irvine Bay Urban Regeneration Co., 2006–13; Glasgow Life, 2013–. Mem. Court, Univ. of Strathclyde, 1996–2002; Gov., RSAMD, 2003–08. FRTS 1998; FRSE 2003. Hon. DLitt Robert Gordon Univ., Aberdeen, 1997; Hon. LLD Strathclyde, 1999; DUniv: Glasgow, 1999; Paisley, 2003. *Recreation:* newspapers. *Address:* Electoral Commission, Scotland Office, Lothian Chambers, 59–63 George IV Bridge, Edinburgh EH1 1RN.

McCORMICK, John St Clair, OBE 2002; FRCSE; Medical Director, Dumfries and Galloway Royal Infirmary, 1994–2001; *b* 20 Sept. 1939; *s* of James McCormick and Claire Anne McCormick (*née* Diskett-Heath); *m* 1964, Fiona Helen McLean; two *s*. *Educ:* St Paul's Cathedral Choir Sch.; Sedbergh Sch.; Univ. of Edinburgh (MB ChB 1964). FRCSE 1967. Consultant Surgeon: Dunfermline, 1974–79; Dumfries and Galloway Royal Infirmary, 1979–99. Royal College of Surgeons of Edinburgh: Mem. Council, 1994–2003; Dir of Standards, 1997–2002; Vice Pres., 2000–03. Mem., Clinical Standards Bd, Scotland, 1999–2002. Liveryman, Co. of Wax Chandlers, 1962. *Address:* Ivy Cottage, Kirkpatrickdurham, Castle Douglas DG7 3HG.

McCORQUODALE, David Alexander; Partner, since 1993, and UK Head of Retail, since 2012, KPMG; *b* Aberdeen, 19 April 1962; *s* of Duncan McCorquodale and Helen Margaret McCorquodale (*née* Macdonald); *m* 1987, Kay Roslyn Mackintosh; three *d*. *Educ:* West End Primary Sch., Elgin; Blairmore Prep. Sch., Huntly; Merchiston Castle Sch., Edinburgh; Univ. of Edinburgh (LLB; DipLP). CA 1987. With Thomson McLintock, subseq. KPMG, 1984–: on secondment to Takeover Panel, 1990–92; UK Hd, Consumer Mkts for Corporate Finance, 2002–12; Mem. Bd, KPMG Corporate Finance in US, 2008–10. University of Edinburgh: Mem., Campaign Bd, 2007–12; Regent, 2012–. Ambassador: Retail Trust, 2014–; Pennies Charity, 2014–. *Recreations:* golf, sport in general, family, travel. *Address:* c/o KPMG, Saltire Court, 20 Castle Terrace, Edinburgh EH1 2EG. *T:* (0131) 527 6718. *E:* david.mccorquodale@kpmg.co.uk.

McCOSKER, Penelope Anne; *see* Wensley, P. A.

McCOURT, Arthur David, CBE 2004; Chief Executive, The Highland Council, 1995–2007; *b* 11 July 1947; *s* of Thomas McCourt and Thomasina (*née* Taylor); *m* 1994, Jan McNaughton Smith; two *d*. *Educ:* Bell Baxter High Sch.; Edinburgh Coll. of Art; Heriot-Watt Univ. (BSc Hons Town and Country Planning, 1971). Planner, Northumberland CC, 1974–76; Team Leader, Central Regl Council, 1976–87; Sen. Policy Advr, Stirling DC, 1987–90; Asst Chief Exec., Tayside Regl Council, 1990–95. *Recreation:* keen mountaineer and walker. *Address:* Westcroft, Newtonhill, Lentran, Inverness IV3 8RN.

McCOURT, Martin; Director, Montagu Private Equity Associates, since 2012; *b* Glasgow, 29 Dec. 1956; *s* of Donald and Roseannne McCourt; *m* 2009, Liane; two *d* and one step *s* one step *d*. Cartographic draughtsman, MoD Mapping and Charting Estabt, 1974–77; Develt Exec., Mars Confectionery, 1977–80; Nat. Sales Manager, Personnel Manager, Sales Ops Manager, Sales Trng Manager, Nat. Accounts Manager, Duracell, 1980–87; Gen. Manager, Audiovisual, Toshiba, 1987–88; Sales and Mktg Dir, Office Internat., 1988–91; Man. Dir, Marcus Bohn Associates, 1991–95; Gen. Manager and Internat Account Dir, Pelikan, 1995–97; Dyson Ltd, 1997–2012: Gp Commercial Dir; Man. Dir, Floorcare; Internat. Man. Dir; Chief Exec., 2001–12. Mem., Charting and Cartographic Inst. 1975. Orange Business Leader of Year, 2010. *Recreation:* tennis.

McCOWAN, Sir David William Cargill, 4th Bt *cr* 1934, of Dalwhat, Dumfries; *b* 28 Feb. 1934; *s* of Sir David James Cargill McCowan, 2nd Bt and of Muriel Emma Annie, *d* of W. C. Willmott; *S* brother, 1998, but his name does not appear on the Official Roll of the

Baronetage; *m* 1995, Jean, *d* of A. R. McGhee; one *s* one *d*. *Heir:* *s* David James Cargill McCowan, *b* 2 June 1975. *Address:* Auchendennan Farm, Alexandria, Dunbartonshire G83 8RB.

McCOWEN, Alexander Duncan, (Alec), CBE 1986 (OBE 1972); actor; *b* 26 May 1925; *s* of late Duncan McCowen and Hon. Mrs McCowen. *Educ:* Skinners' Sch., Tunbridge Wells; RADA, 1941. Repertory: York, Birmingham, etc, 1943–50; Escapade, St James's, 1952; The Matchmaker, Haymarket, 1954; The Count of Clérambard, Garrick, 1955; The Caine Mutiny Court Martial, Hippodrome, 1956; Look Back in Anger, Royal Court, 1956; The Elder Statesman, Cambridge, 1958; Old Vic Seasons, 1959–61: Touchstone, Ford, Richard II, Mercutio, Oberon, Malvolio; Dauphin in St Joan; Algy in The Importance of Being Earnest; Royal Shakespeare Company, 1962–63: Antipholus of Syracuse in The Comedy of Errors; Fool, in King Lear; Father Fontana in The Representative, Aldwych, 1963; Thark, Garrick, 1965; The Cavern, Strand, 1965; After the Rain, Duchess, 1967, Golden Theatre, NY, 1967; Hadrian VII, Birmingham, 1967, Mermaid, 1968, New York, 1969; Hamlet, Birmingham, 1970; The Philanthropist, Royal Court, 1970, NY, 1971; Butley, Criterion, 1972; The Misanthrope, NT, 1973, 1975, NY 1975; Equus, NT, 1973; Pygmalion, Albery, 1974; The Family Dance, Criterion, 1976; Antony and Cleopatra, Prospect Co., 1977; solo performance of St Mark's Gospel, Riverside Studios, Mermaid and Comedy, 1978, Globe, 1981, UK tour, 1985, Half Moon, 1990; Tishoo, Wyndham's, 1979; The Browning Version, and A Harlequinade, NT, 1980; The Portage to San Cristobal of A. H., Mermaid, 1982; Kipling (solo performance), Mermaid, 1984; The Cocktail Party, Phoenix, 1986; Fathers and Sons, Waiting for Godot, NT, 1987; Shakespeare, Cole & Co. (solo performance), UK tour, 1988; The Heiress, Chichester, 1989; Exclusive, Strand, 1989; A Single Man, Greenwich, 1990; Dancing at Lughnasa, NT, 1990, transf. Phoenix, 1991; Preserving Mr Panmure, Chichester, 1991; Caesar and Cleopatra, Greenwich, 1992; Someone Who'll Watch Over Me, Hampstead, 1992, transf. Vaudeville, NY, 1992; The Tempest, Elgar's Rondo, 1993, The Cherry Orchard, 1995, RSC, Stratford; Uncle Vanya, Chichester, 1996; Tom and Clem, Aldwych, 1997; Peter Pan, RNT, 1997; Quartet, Albery, 1999. Dir, Definitely the Bahamas, Orange Tree, Richmond, 1987. Films include: Frenzy, 1971; Travels with My Aunt, 1972; Stevie, 1978; Never Say Never Again, 1983; The Age of Innocence, 1994; Gangs of New York, 2001. TV series, Mr Palfrey of Westminster, 1984. Evening Standard (later Standard) Drama Award, 1968, 1973, 1982; Stage Actor of the Year, Variety Club, 1970. *Publications:* Young Gemini (autobiog.), 1979; Double Bill (autobiog.), 1980; Personal Mark, 1984. *Recreations:* music, gardening.

McCOY, Anthony Peter, OBE 2010 (MBE 2003); National Hunt jockey, retired 2015; *b* 4 May 1974; *m* 2006, Chanelle Burke; one *s* one *d*. Apprentice, Jim Bolgers Stables. Champion Nat. Hunt Jockey, 1995–96, 1996–97, 1997–98, 1998–99, 1999–2000, 2000–01, 2001–02, 2002–03, 2003–04, 2004–05, 2005–06, 2006–07, 2007–08, 2008–09, 2009–10, 2010–11, 2011–12, 2012–13, 2013–14, 2014–15. Winner: Cheltenham Gold Cup on Mr Mulligan, 1997, on Synchronised, 2012; Hennessy Gold Cup on Carlingford Lough, 2015; Champion Hurdle on Make A Stand, 1997, on Brave Inca, 2006, on Binocular, 2010; Scottish Grand National on Belmont King, 1997; Grand Annual Chase on Edredon Bleu, 1998; Champion Chase on Edredon Bleu, 2000; King George VI Chase on Best Mate, 2002; Irish Grand National on Butler's Cabin, 2007; Grand National on Don't Push It, 2010. Record 1700 Nat. Hunt wins, 2002; record 18 championships, 2013; first jockey to ride 2,000 Nat. Hunt winners in UK, 2004 and first to ride 3,000 winners, 2009 and 4,000 winners, 2013. Hon. Dr QUB, 2002; Hon. DSc Ulster, 2014. BBC Sports Personality of the Year, 2010. *Publications:* (with Claude Duval) The Real McCoy: my life so far, 1998; McCoy: the autobiography, 2002; (with Donn McClean) My Autobiography, 2011; Taking the Fall (novel), 2013. *Recreations:* golf, football. *Address:* Lodge Down Stables, Lambourn Woodlands, Hungerford, Berks RG17 7BJ.

McCOY, Hugh O'Neill, FICS; Director, since 1998, and Chairman, since 2012, Hadley Shipping Co. Ltd; Chairman, Baltic Exchange, 1999–2001; *b* 9 Feb. 1939; *s* of Hugh O'Neill McCoy and Nora May (*née* Bradley); *m* 1964, Margaret Daphne Corfield; two *s*. *Educ:* Dudley Grammar Sch.; Sir John Cass Coll., Univ. of London (marine qualifications). Man. Dir, Horace Clarkson plc, 1993–98; Chm., H. Clarkson & Co., 1996–98. Vice Chm., Baltic Exchange, 1993–98. Non-exec. Dir, Gartmore Korea Fund plc, 1993–97; Dir, Benor Tankers Ltd, Hamilton, Bermuda, 1998–2002. Pres., Inst. Chartered Shipbrokers, 1992–94. Mem., Gen. Council, Lloyd's Register of Shipping. Former Mem. Mgt, London Sea Cadets. Hon. Vice-Pres., Maritime Volunteer Service; Chm. CAB Brentwood, 2007–10. Former LEA Gov., Warley Sch. Mem., Lord Mayor of London's Policy Cttee, 1999–2001. Freeman, City of London; Liveryman, Co. of Shipwrights; Associate Master Mariner, Master Mariners' Co. *Recreations:* sailing, long distance walking, French wine, voluntary work, sailing. *Address:* 5 Heronway, Hutton, Brentwood, Essex CM13 2LX. *Clubs:* City; Royal Burnham Yacht.

McCRACKEN, Guy; *see* McCracken, P. G.

McCRACKEN, (James) Justin; Chief Executive, Health Protection Agency, 2008–13; *b* 28 April 1955; *s* of late Dermot and Margaret McCracken; *m* (marr. diss.); two *s* one *d*. *Educ:* Rugby Sch.; Jesus Coll., Oxford (MA Physics). Res. scientist, ICI, 1976–91; Business Manager, ICI Acrylics, 1991–97; Man. Dir, ICI Katalco, 1997–98; Regl Dir, Envmt Agency, 1998–2002; Dep. Dir Gen. (Ops), then Dep. Chief Exec. (Ops), Health and Safety Executive, 2002–08. Non-exec. Ind. Dir, Ombudsman Services, 2013–; non-exec. Dir, Office of Rail and Road (formerly Rail Regulation), 2014–. *Recreation:* sailing. *Club:* Coniston Sailing.
See also R. H. J. McCracken.

McCRACKEN, (Philip) Guy, LVO 2004; Chairman, Branston Ltd, since 2010; *b* 25 Nov. 1948; *m* 1972, Frances Elizabeth Addison; one *s* two *d*. *Educ:* Clee Humberston Foundn Sch., Cleethorpes; Nat. Coll. of Food Technology, Reading Univ. (BSc 1st Class Hons Food Technology). Production Manager, Mars, 1972–73; Product Development Manager, Imperial Foods, 1973–75; Marks & Spencer, 1975–2000: Man. Dir, Food Div., 1993–98; Exec. Dir, Internat. Retail and IT, 1999–2000; Chief Exec., Food Retail, Co-operative Gp, 2005–08. Chm., Duchy Originals, 1997–2004. Mem., Council of Food Policy Advrs, 2008–10. Gov., Nuffield Health, 2010–. *Recreations:* golf, ski-ing, food, travel.

McCRACKEN, Robert Henry Joy; QC 2003; *b* 15 March 1950; *s* of late Dermot McCracken, FRCP and Margaret McCracken, MB BCh. *Educ:* Rugby Sch.; Worcester Coll., Oxford (MA). Called to the Bar, Inner Temple, 1973; barrister practising in public, envmtl and planning law. Mem., Animal Procedures Cttee advising Home Sec., 1999–2003. Chm., UK Envmtl Law Assoc., 1995–97; Sec., Planning and Envmtl Bar Assoc., 1992–94. *Publications:* (jtly) Statutory Nuisance, 2000, 2nd edn 2008; contribs to Judicial Rev., Jl Planning and Envmtl Law. *Recreations:* painting, natural science, fell-walking. *Address:* Francis Taylor Building, Inner Temple, EC4Y 7BY. *Clubs:* Reform; Cyclists' Touring, Coniston Sailing.
See also J. J. McCracken.

McCREA, Ian; Member (DemU) Mid-Ulster, Northern Ireland Assembly, since 2007; *b* 12 June 1976; *s* of Dr (Robert Thomas) William McCrea, *qv*; *m* 1998, Wanita Cardwell; two *s* one *d*. *Educ:* Magherafelt Controlled Primary Sch.; Rainey Endowed Grammar Sch.; NE Inst. for Further and Higher Educn, Magherafelt. Unipork, Cookstown, 1996–97; alarm and security installation engr, 1997–99; PA to Dr William McCrea, MP, 1997–2007. Mem. (DemU) Cookstown DC, 2001– (Vice Chm., 2005–06; Chm., 2007–08). Contested (DemU) Mid-Ulster, 2010, 2015. Dir, Cookstown Local Strategy Partnership, 2001–; Chm., Cookstown Dist Policing Partnership, 2006–07; Mem., Northern Ireland Policing Bd, 2011–13. *Address:* Democratic Unionist Party Office, 29 Rainey Street, Magherafelt, Northern Ireland BT45 5DA. *T:* (028) 7963 2664. *E:* ianmccreamla2@gmail.com; Cookstown Democratic Unionist Party Office, 34 Fairhill Road, Cookstown, Co. Tyrone, Northern Ireland BT80 8AG. *T:* (028) 8676 4952. *E:* ianmccreamla@gmail.com.

McCREA, Rev. Dr (Robert Thomas) William; Minister, Magherafelt Free Presbyterian Church of Ulster, since 1969; *b* 6 Aug. 1948; *s* of Robert T. and Sarah J. McCrea; *m* 1971, Anne Shirley McKnight; two *s* three *d*. *Educ:* Cookstown Grammar Sch.; Theol Coll., Free Presbyterian Church of Ulster. Civil servant, 1966; Free Presbyterian Minister of the Gospel, 1967–. Dist Councillor, Magherafelt, 1973–2011; Mem. (DemU) Mid Ulster, NI Assembly, 1982–86 and 1998–2007, Antrim S, 2007–10. MP (DemU) Mid Ulster, 1983–97 (resigned seat Dec. 1985 in protest against Anglo-Irish Agreement; re-elected Jan. 1986); contested (DemU): Mid Ulster, 1997; Antrim S, 2001; MP (DemU) S Antrim, Sept. 2000–2001 and 2005–15; contested (DemU) same seat, 2015. Dir, Daybreak Recording Co., 1981–. Gospel singer and recording artist; Silver, Gold and Platinum Discs for record sales. Hon. DD Marietta Bible Coll., Ohio, 1989. *Publications:* In His Pathway—the story of the Reverend William McCrea, 1980. *Recreations:* music, horse riding.
See also I. McCrea.

McCREADIE, Robert Anderson; QC (Scot.) 2003; PhD; Sheriff of Tayside Central and Fife at Perth, 2004–13; *b* 17 Aug. 1948; *s* of John Walker McCreadie and Jean J. M. McCreadie (*née* Ramsay). *Educ:* Univ. of Edinburgh (LLB Hons); Christ's Coll., Cambridge (PhD 1981). Lecturer in Law: Univ. of Dundee, 1974–78; Univ. of Edinburgh, 1978–92; called to Scottish Bar, 1992; Standing Junior Counsel: Dept of Transport, 1994–95; SHHD/Justice Dept, 1995–2000; Advocate Depute, 2000–02; Standing Jun. Counsel, Advocate Gen. for Scotland, 2002–03; pt-time Sheriff, 2003–04. *Recreations:* Scottish history, music, walking. *Address:* 40 Marchmont Crescent, Edinburgh EH9 1HG. *T:* (0131) 667 1383.

McCREADY, John Francis; Managing Director, Government Property Unit, Cabinet Office, 2010–12; *b* Southborough, Kent, 21 March 1956; *s* of John Robert McCready and Ann McCready (*née* Baxendale); *m* 1986, Alison Julie Perreau; two *d* (and one *d* decd). *Educ:* Eton Coll.; City of London Poly. (Dip. Accounting); INSEAD (MBA 1986). ACA 1983. Arthur Young McLelland Moores, 1978–83; Securicor plc, 1983–85; Goldman Sachs Internat., 1987–89; Arab Banking Corp. Internat., 1989–91; Man. Dir, Bluewater Park plc, 1994–96; Chief Exec., Whitecliff Properties, 1996–2000; Hd, Mergers and Acquisitions, Blue Circle Industries plc, 2000–01; Partner, Ernst & Young LLP, 2001–09. Chairman: Architecture Centre, 2001–09; London and SE Industrial Develt Bd, 2002–09. *Recreations:* tennis, reading, history, flying, countryside, conservation, Swahili. *Address:* Eastbury House, Eastbury, Hungerford, Berks RG17 7JJ. *Clubs:* Turf; Old Etonian Rifle.

McCREADY, Prof. (Victor) Ralph, DSc; FRCR, FRCP; Hon. Consultant, Royal Sussex County Hospital, since 2007; Emeritus Professor, Institute of Cancer Research, since 2002; *b* 17 Oct. 1935; *s* of Ernest and Mabel McCready; *m* 1964, Susan Margaret Mellor; two *d*. *Educ:* Ballyclare High Sch., NI; Queen's Univ., Belfast (MB BCh, BAO, BSc; DSc 1987); Guy's Hosp., London Univ. (MSc 1964). MRCP 1974, FRCP 1994; FRCR 1975. Mem., Scientific Staff, Inst. of Cancer Res., London, 1964–74, 1998–2002; Consultant, Royal Marsden Hosp., 1974–98; Hon. Consultant, Royal Marsden NHS Trust, 1998–2002; Emeritus Hon. Consultant, Hammersmith Hosp., 2004–11. Civilian Consultant, RN, 1993–2010. Hon. Mem., Japanese Radiological Soc., 2002. Hon. FFR, RCSI, 1992. Barclay Prize, British Inst. of Radiology, 1973. *Publications:* med. articles, books and contribs to books on nuclear medicine, ultrasound and magnetic resonance. *Recreations:* aviation, music. *Address:* Nuclear Medicine Department, Royal Sussex County Hospital, Eastern Road, Brighton BN2 5BE. *Club:* Royal Automobile.

McCREATH, Alistair William; His Honour Judge McCreath; a Circuit Judge, since 1996; a Senior Circuit Judge and Resident Judge, Southwark Crown Court, since 2011; *b* 6 June 1948; *s* of late James McCreath and Ruth Mary McCreath (*née* Kellar); *m* 1976, Julia Faith Clark; one *s* one *d*. *Educ:* St Bees Sch.; Univ. of Keele (BA Hons). Called to the Bar, Inner Temple, 1972, Bencher, 2008; in practice at the Bar, 1973–96; Asst Recorder, 1986–90; Recorder, 1990–96; Resident Judge, Worcester Crown Court, 2006–11. Hon. Recorder: of Worcester, 2007–11; of Westminster, 2012–. Course Dir, Criminal Continuation (Judicial Studies Bd), 2007–10. Judicial Mem., Sentencing Council, 2010–13. *Recreations:* golf, theatre, playing on computers. *Address:* Southwark Crown Court, 1 English Grounds, SE1 2HU. *Clubs:* Athenæum; Royal Troon Golf, Blackwell Golf.

McCREDIE, Fionnuala Mary Constance; QC 2013; *b* London, 15 Jan. 1965; *d* of Peter McCredie and Rosemary McCredie; partner, Michael John Mylonas, *qv*; two *d*. *Educ:* North London Collegiate Sch.; Univ. of Manchester (BSc (Hons) Geog. 1986); Brunel Univ. (MA Public and Social Admin 1990); Middlesex Poly. (CPE 1991). Called to the Bar, Middle Temple, 1992, Bencher, 2010; in practice as barrister, specialising in construction and procurement. Mem. Bd, Coin Street Community Builders, 2012–. *Publications:* (contrib. researcher) Keating on Construction Contracts, 9th edn 2012. *Recreations:* family, ski-ing, horses, rock climbing, theatre, friends. *Address:* Keating Chambers, 15 Essex Street, WC2R 3AA. *T:* (020) 7544 2600. *E:* fmccredie@keatingchambers.com.

McCREDIE, Ian Forbes, CMG 2004; OBE 1984; Chief Executive, Forbes Research Group, since 2010; *b* 28 Dec. 1950; *s* of John and Diana McCredie; *m* 1998, Katherine Heiny; two *s*, and one *s* one *d* from previous marriage. *Educ:* Churchill Coll., Cambridge (BA 1972; MA 1975); Sch. of Oriental and African Studies, Univ. of London. Entered FCO, 1975; Third Sec., 1975; Third, later Second Sec. (Econ.), Lusaka, 1976–79; FCO, 1979–81; First Secretary: (Econ./Commercial), Tehran, 1981–83; FCO, 1983–85; Copenhagen, 1985–89; FCO, 1989–92; Counsellor: UKMIS, NY, 1992–97; FCO, 1997–99; Washington, 1999–2004; Vice Pres., Corporate Security, Royal Dutch Shell, 2004–10. *Recreations:* cycling, military history.

McCREESH, Paul; Founder, Director and Conductor, Gabrieli Consort & Players; Principal Conductor and Artistic Adviser, Gulbenkian Orchestra, Lisbon, since 2013; *b* 24 May 1960; *s* of Patrick Michael McCreesh and Valerie McCreesh (*née* Connors); *m* 1983, Susan Hemington Jones; one *s* one *d*. *Educ:* Manchester Univ. (MusB 1981; Alumnus of Yr, 2012). Freelance conductor; founded Gabrieli Consort & Players, internat. ensemble specialising in choral and orchestral music, 1982; Artistic Dir, Wratislava Cantans Fest., Poland, 2006–12. Dir, Brinkburn Music, 1994–2013; Founder, Winged Lion, record label, 2010. Guest conductor of modern orchs incl. Budapest Fest., Gothenburg Symphony, Orch. Philharmonique de Radio France, Orch. di Santa Cecilia di Roma, Basel Chamber Orch., Zurich Tonhalle, Nederlands Philharmonic Orch., Bergen Philharmonic, Spanish Nat. Orch., Sydney SO, Leipzig Gewandhaus, St Paul Chamber, Hong Kong Philharmonic, Teatro Real Madrid, Royal Danish, Komische Oper Berlin, Vlaams Opera, Verbier Fest., Berlin Konzerthaus. Numerous recordings and internat. recording awards. Hon. LLD Loughborough, 2005. *Recreations:* countryside, walking, children. *Address:* c/o Intermusica Artists' Management Ltd, Crystal Wharf, 36 Graham Street, N1 8GJ. *T:* (020) 7608 9900.

McCREEVY, Charlie; Member, European Commission, 2004–10; *b* 30 Sept. 1949; *s* of Charles McCreevy and Eileen Mills; *m* Noeleen Halligan; three *s*, and one *s* three *d* by a previous marriage. *Educ:* University Coll., Dublin (BComm). FCA 1973. Partner, Tynan, Dillon and Co., Chartered Accountants, 1974–92. Mem., Kildare CC, 1979–85. TD (FF) Kildare, 1977–2004; Minister for: Social Welfare, 1992–93; Tourism and Trade, 1993–94; frontbench spokesperson on Finance, 1995–97; Minister for Finance, Republic of Ireland,

1997–2004. Non-executive Director: Ryanair, 2010–; Sports Direct, 2011–14. *Recreations:* golf, horse-racing, Gaelic Athletic Association. *Address:* Blundell House, Millicent, Sallins, Co. Kildare, Ireland.

McCRICKARD, Donald Cecil, FCIB; Director, American Express International Inc., 1978–83; Chairman, Hill Samuel Bank, 1990–92; *b* 25 Dec. 1936; *s* of late Peter McCrickard and Gladys Mary McCrickard; *m* 1st, 1960, Stella May, JP (marr. diss.), *d* of Walter Edward Buttle, RN retd; two *d*; 2nd, 1991, Angela Victoria Biddulph, JP, *d* of late Robert Biddulph Mitchell and of Mary Buckley Mitchell. *Educ:* Hove Grammar Sch.; LSE; Univ. of Malaya. FCIB 1988. Financial, marketing and gen. management appts to 1975; Chief Exec., American Express Co. UK, 1975, American Express Co. Asia, Pacific, Australia, 1980; Man. Dir, UDT Holdings, later TSB Commercial Holdings, 1983; Chairman: Swan National, 1983; UDT Bank, 1983; Dir, and Dep. Group Man. Dir, 1987, Chief Exec., Banking, 1988, Gp Chief Exec., 1990–92, TSB Group plc; Chief Exec., TSB Bank plc, 1989–92. Non-executive Chairman: London Town plc, 1995–2003; TM Group Holdings Ltd, 1996–98; Verdandi Ltd (formerly SGi Gp), 1998–2006; Digitalbrain plc, 1999–2004; non-executive Director: Carlisle Gp, 1993–96; Nat. Counties Building Soc., 1995–2007 (Vice Chm., 2001–07); Allied London Properties, 1997–2000; Sen. non-exec. Dir, Brit Insurance Hldgs PLC (formerly Benfield & Rea Investment Trust), 1995–2006. Mem., Deposit Protection Bd, Bank of England, 1990–92. Chm., Barnet Enterprise Trust, 1985–88. Mem., Exec. Cttee, British Bankers Assoc., 1989–92. Trustee: Crimestoppers (formerly Community Action) Trust, 1991–2004; Industry in Educn, 1993–2005. *Recreations:* cricket (Vice Pres., Youth Cricket, Sussex CCC), photography, theatre, writing, restaurants, the countryside. *Club:* Royal Automobile.

McCRIRRICK, (Thomas) Bryce, CBE 1987; FREng; FIET; Director of Engineering, BBC, 1978–87; *b* 19 July 1927; *s* of late Alexander McCrirrick and Janet McCrirrick (*née* Tweedie); *m* 1953, Margaret Phyllis Yates; two *s* (and one *s* decd). *Educ:* Galashiels Academy; Heriot-Watt Coll., Edinburgh; Regent Street Polytechnic, London. BBC Radio, Studio Centres in Edinburgh, Glasgow and London, 1943–46; served RAF, 1946–49; BBC Television, 1949; Engineer-in-Charge Television Studios, 1963; Head of Engineering Television Recording, and of Studio Planning and Installation Dept, 1969; Chief Engineer, Radio Broadcasting, 1970; Asst Dir of Engrg, 1971; Dep. Dir of Engrg, 1976. Technical Assessor, Investigation into Clapham Junction Rly Accident, 1989. Pres., Soc. of Electronic and Radio Technicians, 1981–85 (Vice-Pres., 1979–80); Vice-Pres., IERE, 1985–88; Pres., IEE, 1988–89 (Dep. Pres., 1986–88, Vice-Pres., 1982–86; Hon. FIEE 1995); Mem. Council, Fellowship of Engrg, 1989–92. Gov., Imperial Coll., 1985–99; Mem. Court, Heriot-Watt Univ., 1991–94; Mem. Senate, London Univ., 1992–94. FRTS 1980; FREng (FEng 1981); FBKSTS 1982; FSMPTE 1989; Hon. FIET (Hon. FIEE 1995). Hon. DSc Heriot-Watt, 1987. *Recreation:* theatre. *Address:* Surrey Place, Coach House Gardens, Fleet, Hants GU51 4QX. *T:* (01252) 623422.

McCRONE, Prof. David, FBA 2005; FRSE; Professor of Sociology, 1996–2011, now Emeritus, and Co-Director, Institute of Governance, 1997–2011, University of Edinburgh; *b* 8 Oct. 1945; *s* of Alexander McCrone and Mary McCrone; partner, Prof. Janette Webb. *Educ:* Univ. of Edinburgh (MA Hons 1969, MSc 1971). Lectr, 1975–85, Sen. Lectr, 1985–92, Reader, 1992–96, in Sociology, Univ. of Edinburgh. FRSE 2002. *Publications:* (jtly) Property and Power in a City, 1989; Understanding Scotland, 1992, 2nd edn 2001; (jtly) Scotland: the brand, 1995; The Sociology of Nationalism, 1998; (jtly) Living in Scotland: social and economic change since 1980, 2004; (jtly) National Identity, Nationalism and Constitutional Change, 2009; (jtly) National Days: constructing and mobilising national identity, 2009; (jtly) Revolution or Evolution?: the 2007 Scottish elections, 2009; (jtly) The Crisis of Social Democracy, 2013; (jtly) Understanding National Identity, 2015. *Recreations:* walking, reading. *Address:* Institute of Governance, University of Edinburgh, Chisholm House, High School Yards, Edinburgh EH1 1LZ. *T:* (0131) 650 2459. *E:* d.mccrone@ed.ac.uk.

McCRONE, Robert Gavin Loudon, CB 1983; FRSE 1983; General Secretary, Royal Society of Edinburgh, 2005–07 (Vice-President, 2002–05); Hon. Fellow, Europa Institute, University of Edinburgh, since 1992; *b* 2 Feb. 1933; *s* of Robert Osborne Orr McCrone and Laura Margaret McCrone; *m* 1st, 1959, Alexandra Bruce Waddell (*d* 1998); two *s* one *d*; 2nd, 2000, Olive Pettigrew Moon (*née* McNaught); two step *d*. *Educ:* St Catharine's Coll., Cambridge (Economics Tripos; MA); University Coll. of Wales, Aberystwyth (Milk Marketing Bd Research Schol. in agricl economics; MSc 1959); Univ. of Glasgow (PhD 1964). Fisons Ltd, 1959–60; Lectr in Applied Economics, Glasgow Univ., 1960–65; Economic Consultant to UNESCO, 1964; Fellow of Brasenose Coll., Oxford, 1965–72; Mem. NEDC Working Party on Agricl Policy, 1967–68; Economic Adviser to House of Commons Select Cttee on Scottish Affairs, 1969–70; Special Economic Adviser to Sec. of State for Local Govt and Regional Planning, 1970; Head of Economics and Statistics Unit, 1970–72, Under-Sec. for Regional Develt, 1972–80, Chief Econ. Advr, 1972–92, Scottish Office; Secretary: Industry Dept for Scotland, 1980–87; Scottish Office Envmt Dept (formerly Scottish Develt Dept), 1987–92. Prof. of Economics, Centre for Housing Res., Glasgow Univ., 1992–94; Vis. Prof., Dept of Business Studies, later Mgt Sch., Edinburgh Univ., 1994–2005. Member: Adv. Cttee, Constitution Unit (formerly Inquiry into Implementation of Constitutional Reform), 1995–97; Steering Gp for Review of Resource Allocation for NHS in Scotland (Arbuthnott Cttee), 1997–2000. Chm., Cttee of Inquiry into Professional Conditions of Service for Teachers' in Scotland, 1999–2000; Vice Chairman: RSE Inquiry into Foot and Mouth Disease, 2001–02; RSE Inquiry into Future of Scottish Fishing Industry, 2003–04; Chm., RSE Inquiry on the Future of Hills and Island Areas in Scotland, 2007–08. Comr, Parly Boundary Commn for Scotland, 1999–2006. Deputy Chairman: Royal Infirmary of Edinburgh NHS Trust, 1994–99; Lothian Univs Hosps NHS Trust, 1999–2001. Member Council: Royal Economic Soc., 1977–82; Scottish Economic Soc., 1982–91; ESRC, 1986–89. Member, Board: Scottish Opera, 1992–98; Queen's Hall, Edinburgh, 1999–2002; Trustee: Scottish Opera Endowment Trust, 1999–2011; Scottish Housing Assocs Charitable Trust, 1992–98. Hon. FRSGS 1993. Hon. LLD Glasgow 1986. Bicentenary Medal, RSE, 2008. *Publications:* The Economics of Subsidising Agriculture, 1962; Scotland's Economic Progress 1951–60, 1963; Regional Policy in Britain, 1969; Scotland's Future, 1969; (with Mark Stephens) Housing Policy in Britain and Europe, 1995; European Monetary Union and Regional Development, 1997; Scottish Independence: weighing up the economics, 2013, 2nd enlarged edn 2014; contribs to various economic jls. *Recreations:* music, walking. *Address:* 11A Lauder Road, Edinburgh EH9 2EN. *T:* (0131) 667 4766. *Club:* Oxford and Cambridge.

McCRORIE, Linda Esther, (Mrs Peter McCrorie); *see* Gray, L. E.

McCRUDDEN, Prof. (John) Christopher, DPhil; FBA 2008; Professor of Human Rights and Equality Law, Queen's University Belfast, since 2011; *b* 29 Jan. 1952; *s* of Gerard and Theodora McCrudden; *m* 1990, Caroline Mary Pannell; one *s* one *d*. *Educ:* Queen's Univ., Belfast (LLB 1974); Yale Univ. (Harkness Fellow, 1974–76; LLM 1975); MA 1980, DPhil 1981, Oxon. Called to the Bar: Gray's Inn, 1996; NI, 2006; non-resident Tenant, Blackstone Chambers, 2009–. University of Oxford: Lectr in Law, 1976–77, Jun. Res. Fellow, 1976–80, Balliol Coll.; CUF Lectr, 1980–96; Fellow, Lincoln Coll., 1980–2011; Reader in Law, 1996–99; Prof. of Human Rights Law, 1999–2011. Visiting Professor: QUB, 1994–98; Univ. of Texas Sch. of Law, 1996; Univ. of Haifa, 1996; Univ. of Mich Law Sch., 1998–2009; Univ. of Oxford, 2011–14; Vis. Sen. Fellow, PSI, 1987–89; Vis. Fellow and Lectr, Yale Law Sch., 1986; William W. Cook Global Law Prof., Univ. of Michigan Law Sch., 2009–; Leverhulme Maj. Res. Fellow, 2011–14; Jt Straus/Sen. Emile Noël Fellow, Straus Inst. for Advanced Study of Law and Justice, 2013–14, Vis. Fellow, Center for Constitutional Transitions, 2013–14, NYU; Fellow, Wissenschaftskolleg zu Berlin, 2014–15. Member: Sec. of State for NI's Standing Adv. Commn on Human Rights, 1984–88; Expert Network on Application of Equality Directives, EC, 1986–; NI Procurement Bd, 2003–08; Specialist Advr, NI Affairs Select Cttee, H of C, 1999; Mem., Public Procurement Implementation Gp, NI Exec., 2001. Mem., Adv. Cttee, ESRC Res. Unit on Ethnic Relns, 1982–85. Jt Ed., Law in Context series, 1978–; Member, Editorial Board: Oxford Jl Legal Studies, 1983–; Internat. Jl Discrimination and the Law, 1996–; Jl Internat. Econ. Law, 1998–; European Public Law, 2003–. Hon. LLD QUB, 2006. *Publications:* (with R. Baldwin) Regulation and Public Law, 1987; (ed) Women, Employment and European Community Law, 1988; (ed) Fair Employment Handbook, 1990, 3rd edn 1995; (jtly) Racial Justice at Work: the enforcement of the Race Relations Act 1976 in employment, 1991; Equality in Law between Men and Women in the European Community: United Kingdom, 1994; (ed with G. Chambers) Individual Rights and the Law in Britain, 1994; (ed) Equality between Women and Men in Social Security, 1994; (ed) Regulation and Deregulation, 1998; Buying Social Justice, 2007 (Cert. of Merit, Amer. Soc. of Internat. Law, 2008); (with B. O'Leary) Courts and Consociations, 2013; (ed) Understanding Human Dignity, 2013; (ed jtly) Reasoning Rights, 2014; (ed jtly) Law's Ethical, Global and Theoretical Contexts, 2015. *Recreation:* my family. *Address:* School of Law, Queen's University Belfast, 27–30 University Square, Belfast BT7 1NN. *T:* (028) 9097 3597. *Club:* Yale (New York).

McCRUM, (John) Robert; writer; Associate Editor, The Observer, since 2008; *b* 7 July 1953; *s* of late Michael William McCrum, CBE, and of Christine Mary Kathleen (*née* fforde); *m* 1st, 1979, Olivia Timbs (marr. diss. 1984); 2nd, 1995, Sarah Lyall; two *d*. *Educ:* Sherborne Sch.; Corpus Christi Coll., Cambridge (Schol.; BA 1st Cl. Hons Hist.; MA); Univ. of Pennsylvania (Thouron Fellow; MA); PhD Cantab 2012. House Reader, Chatto & Windus, 1977–79; Faber and Faber Ltd: Editl Dir, 1979–89; Editor-in-Chief, 1990–96; Literary Ed., The Observer, 1996–2008. Scriptwriter and co-producer, The Story of English, BBC TV, 1980–86. Patron, Different Strokes, 2000–. Chair, Norwich Writer's Centre, 2009–12. By-Fellow, Churchill Coll., Cambridge, 2001–03. Hon. DLitt Heriot-Watt, 2011. Tony Godwin Prize, 1979; Peabody Award, 1986; Emmy Award, 1987. *Publications:* In the Secret State, 1980; A Loss of Heart, 1982; The Fabulous Englishman, 1984; The Story of English, 1986; The World is a Banana, 1988; Mainland, 1991; The Psychological Moment, 1993; Suspicion, 1996; My Year Off, 1998; Wodehouse: a life, 2004; Globish: how the English language became the world's language, 2010. *Recreation:* music and dance. *Address:* 15 Bracknell Gardens, NW3 7EE. *Club:* Groucho.

McCUBBIN, Henry Bell; Joint Editor, Scottish Left Review, since 2000; *b* 15 July 1942; *s* of Henry McCubbin and Agnes (*née* Rankine); *m* 1967, Katie M. Campbell; three *d*. *Educ:* Allan Glen's Sch., Glasgow; BA Hons Open Univ. Film Cameraman: BBC TV, 1960–77; Grampian TV, 1977–89. MEP (Lab) Scotland NE, 1989–94; contested (Lab) Scotland NE, Eur. Parly elecns, 1994. Head, European Office, Assoc. of Gtr Manchester Authorities, 1996–99. *Recreations:* theatre, hill walking, politics. *E:* editorial@scottishleftreview.org.

McCUE, Jason Daniel; Senior Partner, McCue and Partners LLP, since 2011; *b* Warrington, 4 June 1969; *s* of Terrence McCue and Janet McCue; *m* 2003, Mariella Frostrup, *qv*; one *s* one *d*. *Educ:* Stockton Heath Secondary Sch.; Queen Mary Coll., Univ. of London (LLB 1990); Coll. of Law. Admitted solicitor, 1992; Mishcon de Reya, 1991–96; Goodman Derrick, 1996–97; Co-founder and Sen. Partner, H2O Law LLP, 1997–2011. Advr on law, crisis mgt and private/public affairs to individuals, pol, media and business orgns and to govts and NGOs, 1993–; business, develt and investment interests with focus on Africa and Middle E. Humanitarian campaigner: Chm., Adv. Council, Crisis Action, 2007–; Ambassador for Femmes Africa Solidarité, 2007–; Mandate Darfur, 2008–09; Communications Bd, Oxfam, 2009–10; Dir, The GREAT Initiative (formerly FAST Foundn), 2010–; Hd, non govt Libyan Reconciliation and Co-ordination Team liaising with FCO, 2009–; ad hoc UN facilitator to Sudan Peace Process, 2011–12; Special Envoy to Govt of Somaliland, 2013. Hon. LLD Chester, 2011. UK Solicitor of the Year Private Practice, Law Soc., 2009. *Recreations:* family, travelling, fishing and shooting, fires. *Address:* c/o McCue and Partners LLP, 4th Floor, 158 Buckingham Palace Road, SW1W 9TR. *E:* jason.mccue@mccue-law.com.

McCUE, Mariella; *see* Frostrup, M.

McCULLAGH, Keith Graham, PhD; Executive Chairman, Xention Pharma (formerly Xention) Ltd, since 2010 (non-executive Chairman, 2008–10); non-executive Chairman: Torpedo Factory (formerly Phenomenon) Group Ltd, since 1999; Ario Pharma (formerly Provesica) Ltd, since 2010; *b* 30 Nov. 1943; *s* of John Charles McCullagh and Kathleen Doreen McCullagh (*née* Walton); *m* 1967, Jean Elizabeth Milne; one *s* two *d*. *Educ:* Latymer Upper Sch.; Univ. of Bristol (BVSc 1965); St John's Coll., Cambridge (PhD 1970). MRCVS 1965. Royal Soc. Leverhulme Schol., 1966; Medical Research Council: Mem., External Staff, Uganda, 1967; Mem., Scientific Staff, Dunn Nutrition Lab., Cambridge, 1967–69; Cleveland Clinic Foundation, USA: Res. Fellow, 1970; Mem., Res. Staff, 1971–73; Lectr in Veterinary Pathol., Univ. of Bristol, 1974–80; G. D. Searle & Co. Ltd: Dir of Biol., 1980–84; Dir of Res., 1984–86; Founder and Chief Exec., British Biotech plc, 1986–98; Pres. and Chief Exec., Santaris Pharma A/S, 2004–08. Chm., Action Medical Research, 2007–09; Director: MVM Ltd (formerly Medical Ventures Management Ltd), 1998–2005 (Mem., Investment Cttee, MVM LLC, 2006–10); Isis Innovation Ltd, 1998–99; Pharmacy2U Ltd, 2012– (non-exec. Chm., 2000–12); Taconic Farms Inc., 2013–. Non-executive Chairman: Affitech A/S, 2008–10 (Vice Chm., 2010–); Clavis Pharma ASA, 2009–10. Chm., HM Treasury Wkg Gp on Financing of High Technol. Businesses, 1998; Mem., DTI Adv. Gp on Competitiveness and the Single Mkt, 1997–98. Chm., BioIndustry Assoc., 1993–96. Vice Chm., European Assoc. of BioIndustries, 1996–98. Chm., British Admiral's Cup Sailing Team, 1999. *Publications:* numerous scientific articles and reviews in learned jls. *Recreations:* visiting grandchildren in California, New Zealand and the UK, playing many sports poorly, gardening. *Address:* Cuddington Mill, Cuddington, Bucks HP18 0BP. *E:* keith.mccullagh@btinternet.com. *Clubs:* Royal Automobile; Ellesborough Golf (Aylesbury); Royal Ocean Racing (Cowes and London); Racquets Squash (Thame).

McCULLAGH, Prof. Peter, PhD; FRS 1994; John D. MacArthur Distinguished Service Professor, Department of Statistics, University of Chicago, since 2003; *b* N Ireland, 8 Jan. 1952; *s* of John A. McCullagh and Rita McCullagh (*née* Devlin); *m* 1977, Rosa Bogues; one *s* three *d*. *Educ:* Univ. of Birmingham (BSc 1974); Imperial Coll., London, (PhD 1977). Vis. Asst Prof., Univ. of Chicago, 1977–79; Lectr, Imperial Coll., London Univ., 1979–85; Prof., 1985–, Chm., 1992–98, Dept of Stats, Univ. of Chicago. FIMS, FAAAS. President's Award, Cttee of Presidents of Statistical Socs of N Amer., 1990. *Publications:* Generalized Linear Models (with J. A. Nelder), 1983, 2nd edn 1989; Tensor Methods in Statistics, 1987. *Recreation:* swimming. *Address:* Department of Statistics, University of Chicago, 5734 South University Avenue, Chicago, IL 60637, USA. *T:* (312) 7028340.

McCULLIN, Donald, CBE 1993; freelance photojournalist; *b* 9 Oct. 1935; *m* 1959 (marr. diss. 1987); two *s* one *d*; one *s* by Laraine Ashton; *m* 1995, Marilyn Bridges; *m* 2002, Catherine, *er d* of Sir Patrick Fairweather, *qv*; one *s*. *Educ:* Tollington Park Secondary Sch., Morden; Hammersmith Jun. Art Sch. Started work at 15 yrs of age after death of father; National Service (RAF), 1954–56; first pictures published by The Observer, 1958; thereafter began photographic career; worked for The Sunday Times for 18 yrs, covering wars, revolutions and travel stories. Exhibitions: Shaped by War, Imperial War Mus. North, 2010; Tate Britain, 2011. Hon. Fellow, Hereford Coll. of Arts, 2009. Hon. FRPS 1977. DUniv: Bradford, 1993;

Open, 1994; Hon. DA: Lincoln, 2005; Bath, 2011; Hon. LittD Glos, 2008. *Publications:* Destruction Business, 1971; Is Anyone Taking Any Notice, 1971; The Palestinians, 1979; Homecoming, 1979; Hearts of Darkness, 1980; Battle Beirut, a City in Crisis, 1983; Perspectives, 1987; Skulduggery, 1987; Open Skies, 1989; (with Lewis Chester) Unreasonable Behaviour (autobiog.), 1990; Sleeping with Ghosts, 1995; India, 1999; Don McCullin, 2001; Cold Heaven: Don McCullin on AIDS in Africa, 2001; In England, 2007; Shaped by War, 2010; Southern Frontiers, 2010. *Recreations:* protecting the English countryside, travelling the world, blackberry picking.

McCULLOCH, Andrew Grant; Sheriff of Tayside, Central and Fife at Kirkcaldy, since 2008; President, Law Society of Scotland, 1996–97; *b* 10 Feb. 1952; *s* of late Frederick McCulloch and of Jean McCulloch (later McGregor); *m* 1988, Mave Curran; one *s* one *d*. *Educ:* Glasgow Acad.; Edinburgh Univ. (LLB, BSc SocSci). Joined Drummond & Co., Edinburgh, 1974; Partner, Drummond Miller, WS, 1979–2004; Solicitor-Advocate, 1994. Part-time Sheriff, 2003–04; Sheriff of Tayside, Central and Fife at Dundee, 2004–08. *Recreations:* golf, opera, wine. *Address:* Bracarmi, Cammo Parkway, Edinburgh EH4 8EP.

McCULLOCH, Dr Andrew William; Chief Executive, Picker Institute Europe, since 2013; *b* 21 April 1956; *s* of Ian Robert McCulloch and Marguerite Elizabeth McCulloch; partner, Louise Villeneau; one *s* one *d*. *Educ:* Eltham Coll.; Peterhouse, Cambridge (BA Natural Scis 1978); Univ. of Southampton (PhD Psychol. 1986). Principal, 1987–92, Asst Sec., 1992–96, DoH; Dir of Policy, Sainsbury Centre for Mental Health, 1996–2001; Chief Exec., Mental Health Foundn, 2002–13. Non-exec. Dir, Haringey Healthcare NHS Trust, 1998–2001. Chair: Mental Health Media, 1999–2002; Children and Young People's Mental Health Coalition, 2009–10; Future Visions Alliance, 2009–13; Mem., Public Health Bd, NIHR, 2011–12. Member: Workforce Numbers Adv. Bd, DoH, 2002–04; Ministerial Adv. Gp on Vulnerable Children, 2004–05; Ministerial Adv. Gp on Mental Health, 2007–09 and 2011–13; Expert Advr to Council of Europe, 2007–08. Trustee, UK Council for Psychotherapy, 2009–12. Patron, Healthy Minds: Calderdale Wellbeing, 2013–. President's Medal, RCPsych, 2011. *Publications:* (contrib.) Developing a National Mental Health Policy (Maudsley monograph), 2002; numerous articles on gerontology and on mental health. *Recreations:* birdwatching, reading, wine, cinema, Italy, dining, art. *Address:* Picker Institute Europe, Buxton Court, 3 West Way, Oxford OX2 0JB. *E:* andrew.mcculloch@pickereurope.ac.uk.

MacCULLOCH, Prof. Diarmaid Ninian John, Kt 2012; DD; FBA 2001; FSA, FRHistS; Professor of the History of the Church, University of Oxford, since 1997; Fellow, St Cross College, Oxford, since 1995; *b* 31 Oct. 1951; *s* of Rev. Nigel MacCulloch and Jennie (*née* Chappell). *Educ:* Stowmarket Grammar Sch.; Churchill Coll., Cambridge (MA, PhD 1977); Univ. of Liverpool (Dip. Archive Admin 1973); DipTh Oxon 1987; DD Oxon 2001. FSA 1978; FRHistS 1981. Jun. Res. Fellow, Churchill Coll., Cambridge, 1976–78; Tutor in Hist., Librarian and Archivist, Wesley Coll., Bristol, 1978–90; Lectr, Faculty of Theol., Oxford Univ., 1995–; Sen. Tutor, St Cross Coll., Oxford, 1996–2000. Ordained deacon, 1987. Presenter: TV series: A History of Christianity, 2009; How God Made The English, 2012; Sex and the Church, 2015; TV documentary, Thomas Cromwell, 2013. Pres., C of E Record Soc., 2001–. Co-patron, No Anglican Covenant Coalition, 2012–. Co-Ed., Jl Ecclesiastical Hist., 1995–2014. Histl Project Dir, Bishop Auckland Castle Faith Heritage Exhibn, 2011–. Freeman, Barbers' Co., 2009 (Liveryman, 2012). Hon. LittD UEA, 2003; Hon. DD: Virginia Theol Seminary, 2011; Univ. of South at Sewanee, 2012; St Andrews, 2013. *Publications:* Suffolk and the Tudors: politics and religion in an English county (Whitfield Prize, RHistS), 1986; Groundwork of Christian History, 1987, rev. edn 1994; The Later Reformation in England 1547–1603, 1990, rev. edn 2000; (ed) The Reign of Henry VIII: politics, policy and piety, 1995; Thomas Cranmer: a life (Whitbread Biography Prize, Duff Cooper Prize, James Tait Black Prize), 1996; Tudor Church Militant: Edward VI and the Protestant Reformation, 1999; Reformation: Europe's house divided 1490–1700 (Wolfson History Prize, British Academy Prize, Nat. Book Critics' Circle of US Award for non-fiction), 2003; A History of Christianity: the first three thousand years, 2009 (Hessell-Tiltman Prize, Cundill Prize, 2011); Silence: a Christian history, 2013. *Recreations:* church architecture, music. *Address:* St Cross College, Oxford OX1 3LZ. *T:* (01865) 278458. *Club:* Athenæum.

McCULLOCH, Prof. Gary James, PhD; Brian Simon Professor of the History of Education, since 2003, and Head, Department of Humanities and Social Sciences, since 2012, Institute of Education, University College London (formerly Institute of Education, University of London); *b* 13 March 1956; *s* of late Edward Joseph McCulloch and of Vera Evelyn McCulloch (*née* Saunders); *m* 1984, Sarah Margaret Buyekha; one *s*. *Educ:* Caldecot Primary Sch., London; Wilson's Grammar Sch., London; Christ's Coll., Cambridge (MA, PhD History 1981). Res. Fellow, Sch. of Educn, Univ. of Leeds, 1981–83; Lectr, 1983–88, Sen. Lectr, 1988–91, in Educn, Univ. of Auckland, NZ; Prof. of Educnl Res., Lancaster Univ., 1991–94; Prof. of Educn, Univ. of Sheffield, 1994–2003; Dean of Res. and Consultancy, 2004–07, Asst Dir (Res., Consultancy and Knowledge Transfer), 2007–08, Inst. of Educn, Univ. of London. Member: Council, British Educnl Res. Assoc., 2012–; Exec. Cttee, Internat. Standing Conf. for History of Educn, 2012–; Exec. Cttee, Soc. for Educnl Studies, 2014–. Pres., Hist. of Educn Soc. of GB, 2005–07 (Vice-Pres., 2002–04). Editor: History of Education, 1996–2003; British Jl of Educnl Studies, 2014–; Jt Editor, Secondary Education in a Changing World, 2003–. FRHistS 1995; FRSA 2006; FAcSS (AcSS 2010). *Publications:* (jtly) Technological Revolution?, 1985; The Secondary Technical School, 1989; (jtly) Schooling in New Zealand, 1990; Philosophers and Kings, 1991; (ed) The School Curriculum in New Zealand, 1992; Educational Reconstruction, 1994; (ed jtly) Teachers and the National Curriculum, 1997; Failing the Ordinary Child?, 1998; (jtly) The Politics of Professionalism, 2000; (jtly) Historical Research in Educational Settings, 2000; Documentary Research in Education, History and the Social Sciences, 2004; (ed) The Routledge Falmer Reader in the History of Education, 2005; (jtly) Succeeding with your Doctorate, 2005; Cyril Norwood and the Ideal of Secondary Education, 2007; (ed jtly) Politics and Policy-Making in Education, 2007; (ed jtly) The Death of the Comprehensive High School?, 2007; (ed jtly) Routledge International Encyclopedia of Education, 2008; (ed jtly) Social Change in the History of British Education, 2008; (ed jtly) International Perspectives on Veteran Teachers, 2010; The Struggle for the History of Education, 2011; (jtly) Coming of Age?: secondary education and the school leaving age, 2013. *Recreations:* cinema, reading, travel, walking. *Address:* UCL Institute of Education, University College London, 20 Bedford Way, WC1H 0AL.

McCULLOCH, James Macdonald; Chief Inquiry Reporter, 2002–09, and Director for Planning and Environmental Appeals, 2007–09, Scottish Government (formerly Scottish Executive); Principal, James McCulloch Consulting, 2009–14; *b* Dec. 1948; *s* of Thomas and Jane Ann Reid McCulloch; *m* 1992, Jennifer Anne Hay; three *s*. *Educ:* Hardye's Sch., Dorchester; Lanchester Polytechnic, Coventry (BA Hons Urban & Regl Planning). MRTPI 1973. Planning Asst, Coventry Corp., 1971–73; Sen. Planner, then Prin. Planner, Scottish Develt Dept, 1973–84; Inquiry Reporter, then Prin. Reporter, subseq. Dep. Chief Reporter, Scottish Executive (formerly Scottish Office) Inquiry Reporters' Unit, 1984–2002. Mem., Specialist Accreditation Panel for Planning Practitioners, Law Soc. of Scotland, 2009–14. *Recreations:* walking, travel, eating, the people and landscapes of Spain, motorcycling. *E:* james.mcculloch100@gmail.com.

McCULLOCH, James Rae, OBE 2001; HM Diplomatic Service, retired; Ambassador to Iceland, 1996–2000; *b* 29 Nov. 1940; *s* of William McCulloch and Catherine (*née* Rae); *m* 1965, Margaret Anderson; two *s*. *Educ:* Ardrossan Acad. Joined FO, 1958; Bamako, Mali, 1962; NY, 1964; Lusaka, 1967; FCO, 1969; Algiers, 1972; Kabul, 1973; Second Sec., FCO, 1977; Luanda, 1980; Second, subseq. First Sec. (Commercial), Bangkok, 1982; First Sec., UKMIS to UN, Geneva, 1986; FCO, 1990; Dep. Hd of Mission, Hanoi, 1992–96.

MacCULLOCH, Prof. Malcolm John, MD; FRCPsych; Emeritus Professor, Wales College of Medicine, Biology, Health and Life Sciences, Cardiff University (Professor of Forensic Psychiatry, University of Wales College of Medicine, and Hon. Consultant Forensic Psychiatrist, Caswell Clinic, Bridgend & District NHS Trust, 1997–2001); *b* 10 July 1936; *s* of William MacCulloch and Constance Martha MacCulloch; *m* 1962, Mary Louise Beton (marr. diss. 1975); one *s* one *d*; *m* 1975, Carolyn Mary Reid; two *d*. *Educ:* King Edward VII Sch., Macclesfield, Cheshire; Manchester Univ. (MB, ChB, DPM, MD). Consultant Child Psychiatrist, Cheshire Child Guidance Service, 1966–67; Director Univ. Dept, Child Psychiatry and Subnormality, Birmingham Univ., 1967–70; Sen. Lectr, Adult Psychiatry, Univ. of Liverpool, 1970–75; PMO, DHSS, 1975–78; SPMO, Mental Health Div., DHSS, 1979–80; Dir, Special Hosps Res. Unit, London, 1979–86; Med. Dir, Park Lane Hosp., Liverpool, 1979–89; Res. Psychiatrist, Ashworth Hosp., Merseyside, 1990–93. Advr to Ontario Govt on Forensic Psychiatric Services, 1988–92. Vis. Prof., Clarke Inst. of Psychiatry, Toronto, 1987–88. Ed.-in-Chief, Jl of Forensic Psychiatry and Psychology, 2002–07. *Publications:* Homosexual Behaviour: therapy and assessment, 1971; Human Sexual Behaviour, 1980; numerous med. papers on aspects of psychiatry and forensic psychiatry. *Recreations:* cars, inventing, playing music. *Address:* 14 Tall Trees, Baunton Lane, Cirencester GL7 2AF. *T:* (01285) 642689.

McCULLOCH, Prof. Malcolm Thomas, PhD; FRS 2010; FAA; Professor, School of Earth and Environment, Premier's Research Fellow and Deputy Director, ARC Centre of Excellence for Coral Reef Studies, since 2009, University of Western Australia; *b* Collie, WA, 9 Sept. 1950. *Educ:* Western Australia Inst. of Technol. (BAppSc; MAppSc); Calif Inst. of Technol. (PhD). Trainee teacher, WA, 1968–72; Teacher of Sci., Governor Stirling Sen. High Sch., WA, 1972; Sen. Tutor, Physics Dept, WA Inst. of Technol., 1972–74; Grad. Res. Asst, Div. of Geol. and Planetary Scis, CIT, 1974–80; Research School of Earth Sciences, Australian National University: Res. Fellow, 1980–83; Fellow, 1983–90; Sen. Fellow, 1990–96; Prof. and Hd, Envmt Geochem. and Geochronol. Res., 1996–2009. FAA 2004; Fellow: Amer. Geophysical Union, 2002; Geol Soc. of Australia, 2007; Geochem. Soc., 2008. Jaeger Medal, Australian Acad. Scis, 2009. *Publications:* contribs to scientific jls incl. Science, Nature. *Address:* School of Earth and Environment, University of Western Australia, 35 Stirling Highway, Crawley, WA 6009, Australia.

McCULLOCH, Margaret; Member (Lab) Scotland Central, Scottish Parliament, since 2011; *b* Glasgow, 9 May 1952; *d* of Joseph Gorman and Margaret Gorman; *m* 1994, Ian McCulloch; two *s*. *Educ:* Holyrood Sen. Secondary Sch.; South Lanarkshire Coll. (HNC IT); Glasgow Caledonian Univ. (Post Grad. Cert. Electronic Business). Trng Exec., Univ. of Strathclyde, 1992–2009; owner, ITC, 2009–10; Dir, Independent Training Consultants Ltd, 2010–11. *Recreations:* family, socialising with family and friends, reading, gardening. *Address:* Scottish Parliament, Edinburgh EH99 1SP. *E:* margaret.mcculloch.msp@scottish.parliament.uk.

McCULLOCH, Michael Cutler; Member, Investment Committee, Europolis AG (formerly Europolis Invest), 2002–11; *b* 24 April 1943; *s* of late Ian James McCulloch and Elsie Margaret Chadwick; *m* 1st, 1968, Melody Lawrence (marr. diss. 1975); 2nd, 1975, Robin Lee Sussman; two *d*. *Educ:* Prince of Wales Sch., Nairobi; Clare Coll., Cambridge (BA History 1964; MA 2004); Yale Univ. (Mellon Fellow, 1964–66; MA Internat. Relations 1967). ODM, Asst Principal, 1969; Asst Private Sec. to Minister for Overseas Develt, 1972–73, Principal, 1973, ODA; First Sec. (Aid), Dhaka, FCO, 1976–78; Resident Observer, CSSB, 1978–79; Overseas Development Administration: Rayner Scrutiny and Mgt Review Team, 1979–80; E Africa Dept, 1980–83; EC Dept, 1983–84; Principal Private Sec. to Minister for Overseas Develt, 1984–85; Asst Sec., 1985; Head: Evaluation Dept, 1985–86; British Develt Div. in E Africa, 1986–89; Finance Dept, 1990–92; Know How Fund for former Soviet Union, FCO, 1992–97; UK Exec. Dir, 1997–2001, Advr to the Pres., 2003–04, EBRD. Trustee: BBC World Service Trust, 2001–11; British Consultancy Charitable Trust, 2006–11; BBC Media Action, 2011–; Chairman of Trustees: BEARR Trust, 2003–08 (Trustee, 2001–08); Riders for Health, 2003–10 (Trustee, 2001–13). Pres., Bishopsgate Ward Club, 2012–13. Gov., Bledington Primary Sch., 2008–13. FRSA 1995. *Recreations:* Baroque to Romantic classical music, African wildlife and photography, walking, garden design. *Address:* New Oak Barn, The Green, Bledington, Chipping Norton OX7 6XQ. *T:* (01608) 658941. *E:* mcmcculloch@btinternet.com. *Club:* Lansdowne.

McCULLOCH, Rt Rev. Nigel Simeon, KCVO 2013; Lord High Almoner to the Queen, 1997–2013; Bishop of Manchester, 2002–13; *b* 17 Jan. 1942; *s* of late Pilot Officer Kenneth McCulloch, RAFVR, and of Audrey Muriel McCulloch; *m* 1974, Celia Hume Townshend, *d* of Canon H. L. H. Townshend; two *d*. *Educ:* Liverpool College; Selwyn Coll., Cambridge (Kitchener Schol., BA 1964, MA 1969); Cuddesdon Coll., Oxford. Ordained, 1966; Curate of Ellesmere Port, 1966–70; Chaplain of Christ's Coll., Cambridge, 1970–73; Director of Theological Studies, Christ's Coll., Cambridge, 1970–75; permission to officiate, dio. of Liverpool, 1970–73; Diocesan Missioner for Norwich Diocese, 1973–78; Rector of St Thomas' and St Edmund's, Salisbury, 1978–86; Archdeacon of Sarum, 1979–86; Bishop Suffragan of Taunton, 1986–92; Bishop of Wakefield, 1992–2002. Prebendary of Ogbourne, Salisbury Cathedral, 1979–86, of Wanstrow, Wells Cathedral, 1986–92; Canon Emeritus of Salisbury Cathedral, 1989. Took his seat in H of L, 1997; Mem., H of L Select Cttee, on BBC Charter Review, 2005–06, on Communications, 2007–10. Mem., House of Bishops, Gen. Synod of C of E, 1990–2013. Chairman: Finance Cttee, ACCM, 1988–92; Decade of Evangelism Steering Gp, 1989–96; C of E Communications Unit, 1993–2011; C of E Mission, Evangelism and Renewal Cttee, 1996–99; Gen. Synod Legislation Gp on Women Bishops, 2006–12; CCJ, 2006–. Chaplain to Council of St John: Somerset, 1987–92; SW Yorks, 1992–2002; Greater Manchester, 2009–13; Hon. Nat. Chaplain, RBL, 2001–. Chm., Sandford St Martin Trust, 1999–2008. Pres., Somerset Rural Music Sch., 1986–92; Member, Council: Marlborough Coll., 1984–91; RSCM, 1984–2007. Chm., Somerset County Scout Assoc., 1988–92; Pres., Central Yorks Scouts, 1992–2002. Pres., St Anne's Hospice, Gtr Manchester, 2003–13. Governor: King's Bruton, 1988–91; Bolton Univ., 2008– (Chm., Bd of Govs, 2013–). Hon. DCL Huddersfield, 2003; Hon. DLitt Salford, 2013; Hon. DEd Manchester Metropolitan, 2013. OStJ 2012. *Publications:* A Gospel to Proclaim, 1992; Barriers to Belief, 1994; Broadcasting - a service?, 2007. *Recreations:* music, brass bands, walking in the Lake District. *Address:* Stonelea, 1 Heads Drive, Grange-Over-Sands LA11 7DY. *Club:* Athenæum.

McCULLOUGH, Angus Maxwell Thomas; QC 2010; *b* 14 July 1966; *s* of Sir (Iain) Charles (Robert) McCullough, *qv*; *m* 2002, Sarah Barclay; one *s* one *d*. *Educ:* Pembroke Coll., Oxford (BA Zool. 1987; MA). Pres., Oxford Union, Michaelmas, 1986. Safari guide, Zambia, 1987–88, 1990; called to the Bar, Middle Temple, 1990 (Harmsworth Entrance Exhibnr, 1989; Inns of Ct Studentship, 1989); Treasury Counsel (Civil), 1997–2010; Special Advocate in nat. security cases, 2003–. Trustee: Kasanka Trust, 1999–; Barristers' Benevolent Assoc., 2000–; Internat. Trust for Zool Nomenclature, 2003–14; Buglife, 2010–. FLS 2011. *Publications:* (contrib.) Burnett-Hall on Environmental Law, 2nd edn 2009, 3rd edn 2012; contrib. papers on entomology (hoverflies and butterflies). *Address:* 1 Crown Office Row, Temple, EC4Y 7HH.

McCULLOUGH, Sir (Iain) Charles (Robert), Kt 1981; a Surveillance Commissioner, 1998–2009; *b* 1931; *o s* of Thomas W. McCullough, CB, OBE and Lisette Hunter McCullough; *m* 1965, Margaret Joyce, JP, LLB, BCL, AKC, *o d* of David H. Patey, Middx Hosp.; one *s* one *d*. *Educ:* Dollar Acad.; Taunton Sch. (Exhibnr); Trinity Hall, Cambridge (Dr Cooper's Law Student, 1955; BA 1955; MA 1960). National Service, 1950–52, commnd RA; RA (TA) 1952–54. Called to the Bar, Middle Temple, 1956 (Harmsworth Law Scholar, Blackstone Pupillage Prize, J. J. Powell Prize, 1956); Bencher, 1980; Treas., 2000. Practised Midland Circuit, 1957–71, Midland and Oxford Circuit, 1972–81; a Dep. Chm., Notts QS, 1969–71; QC 1971; a Recorder of the Crown Court, 1972–81; a Judge of the High Court, QBD, 1981–98. Member: Gen. Council of the Bar, 1966–70 (Mem., Exec. Cttee, Professional Conduct Cttee, 1968–80); Criminal Law Revision Cttee, 1973–; Parole Bd, 1984–86. Trustee, Uppingham Sch., 1984–94. Pres., Trinity Hall Assoc., 1986–87. Visitor, Loughborough Univ., 2003–13. *Recreations:* foreign travel, formerly walking, watching birds. *Address:* c/o Middle Temple Treasury, Temple, EC4Y 9AT. *Clubs:* Garrick; Pilgrims.
See also A. M. T. McCullough.

McCULLY, Andrew John, OBE 2001; Director General, Infrastructure and Funding Directorate, Department for Education, since 2013; *b* 14 Nov. 1963; *s* of John McCully and Lilian McCully; partner, Nicholas Howard. *Educ:* Birkenhead Sch.; Worcester Coll., Oxford (BA Hons 1986). Joined Dept of Employment as Admin. Trainee, 1986; Department for Education and Employment: Sec. to New Deal Task Force, 1997–99; Manager, Learning and Skills Bill, 1999–2000; Dep. Dir, Children and Young People's Unit, 2000–02; Divl Manager, Pupil Standards Div., DFES, 2002–04; Dir, Sch. Standards Gp, DFES, subseq. DCSF, 2004–08; Dir, Supporting Children and Young People Gp, DCSF, subseq. DFE, 2008–10; Dir, Academies Delivery Gp, DFE, 2010–11; Acting Dir Gen., Sch. Infrastructure and Funding Directorate, DFE, 2011–13. *Recreations:* listening to music, shopping for, cooking and eating food. *Address:* 26 Carysfort Road, N16 9AL. *T:* (020) 7254 0639. *E:* andrew.mccully@education.gsi.gov.uk.

McCURDY, Ven. Hugh Kyle; Archdeacon of Huntingdon and Wisbech, since 2005; *b* 9 March 1958; *s* of William Eric McCurdy and Elenor Anne McCurdy; *m* 1984, Ruth Searle; one *s* two *d*. *Educ:* Portsmouth Poly. (BA Econs 1980); Trinity Coll., Bristol (DipHE 1983); Univ. of Wales (PGCE 1984). Ordained deacon, 1985, priest, 1986; Curate: St John's, Egham, 1985–88; St John's, Woking, 1988–91; Vicar, St Andrew's, Histon, 1991–2005; Priest-in-charge, St Andrew's, Impington, 1998–2005; RD N Stowe, 1994–2005. Hon. Canon, Ely Cathedral, 2004–. Mem., Gen. Synod of C of E, 2010–. Mem. Council, Ridley Hall Cambridge, 2003–; Gov., Wisbech Grammar Sch., 2006–. Trustee: Cambridgeshire ACRE, 2007–; Beds and Cambs Rural Support Gp, 2012–. Pres., Huntingdon Soc. for the Blind, 2013–. *Recreations:* eating, laughing, Dr Who, cycling, travel, family. *Address:* Whitgift House, The College, Ely, Cambs CB7 4DL. *E:* archdeacon.handw@ely.anglican.org.

McCURLEY, Anna Anderson; freelance communications consultant; Partner, Hamilton Anderson Solutions; *b* 18 Jan. 1943; *d* of George Gemmell and Mary (*née* Anderson); *m* (marr. diss.); one *d*. *Educ:* Glasgow High Sch. for Girls; Glasgow Univ. (MA); Jordanhill Coll. of Educn (Dip. in Secondary Educn); Strathclyde Univ. Secondary history teacher, 1966–72; College Methods Tutor, Jordanhill Coll. of Educn, 1972–74. Strathclyde Regional Councillor, Camphill/Pollokshaws Div., 1978–82. Sen. Exec., Dewe Rogerson, 1987–89; Head of Govt Affairs, Corporate Communications Strategy, 1990–92. Contested: (C) Renfrew W and Inverclyde, 1987; (Scottish Lib Dem) Eastwood, Scottish Parlt, 1999. MP (C) Renfrew W and Inverclyde, 1983–87. Mem., Scottish Select Cttee, 1984–87. Mem., Horserace Betting Levy Bd, 1988–97. Trustee, Nat. Galleries of Scotland, 1996–99. *Recreations:* music, cookery, cats.

McCUSKER, Malcolm James, AC 2012 (AO 2005); CVO 2011; QC 1982; Governor of Western Australia, 2011–14; *b* Perth, WA, 6 Aug. 1938; *s* of Sir James Alexander McCusker and Mary Martindale McCusker; *m* 2006, Tonya Batalin; one *d* and two step *s*; one *s* and two *d* from previous marriage. *Educ:* Perth Modern Sch.; Hobart High Sch.; Univ. of Western Australia (LLB). Admitted to practice, 1961; in practice as barrister, 1961–2011. Chairman: Legal Aid Commn of WA, 1984–2011; Adv. Bd, WA Constitutional Centre, 1997–2011; Parly Inspector, Corruption and Crime Commn of WA, 2004–08. Hon. LLD WA, 2008; DUniv: Edith Cowan, 2009; Curtin, 2015; Hon. LLD Murdoch, 2011. Civil Justice Award, Australian Lawyers' Alliance, 2007; Australian of Year, WA, 2010. *Recreations:* surf ski, farming, reading, family. *Address:* Government House, 3rd Floor, 45 St George's Terrace, Perth, WA 6000, Australia. *T:* (8) 93232222. *E:* mccuskerqc@iinet.net.au. *Clubs:* Weld (Perth); North Cottesloe Surf Lifesaving.

McCUTCHEON, Alison; *see* Allden, A.

McCUTCHEON, Prof. John Joseph, CBE 1994; PhD, DSc; FFA; FRSE; Professor of Actuarial Studies, Heriot-Watt University, 1975–2001; *b* 10 Sept. 1940; *s* of James Thomson McCutcheon and Margaret (*née* Hutchison); *m* 1978, Jean Sylvia Constable. *Educ:* Glasgow Acad.; St John's Coll., Cambridge (schol.; Wright's Prize, 1960, 1962; MA 1966); Univ. of Liverpool (PhD 1969, DSc 1990). FFA 1965. Scottish Amicable Life Assce Soc., 1962–65; Consulting Actuary, Duncan C. Fraser and Co., 1965–66; Demonstrator, then Sen. Demonstrator in Pure Maths, Univ. of Liverpool, 1966–70; Associate Prof., Univ. of Manitoba, 1970–72; Heriot-Watt University: Sen. Lectr, 1972–75; Dean, Faculty of Science, 1995–98. Pres., Faculty of Actuaries in Scotland, 1992–94. FRSE 1993. *Publications:* (with W. F. Scott) An Introduction to the Mathematics of Finance, 1986; various papers on mathematics, actuarial science, mortality studies. *Recreations:* tennis, cycling, opera, reading, travel. *Address:* 14 Oswald Court, Edinburgh EH9 2HY. *T:* (0131) 667 7645. *Clubs:* Woodcutters Cricket, Colinton Lawn Tennis.

McCUTCHEON, Dr William Alan, FSA, MRIA; archaeologist (industrial), historian (industry, technology, engineering, transport), archivist, author; Hon. Senior Research Fellow, School of Geography (formerly of Geosciences), Queen's University, Belfast, 1999–2004; *b* 2 March 1934; *s* of late William John and Margaret Elizabeth McCutcheon; *m* 1956, Margaret Craig; three *s*. *Educ:* Royal Belfast Academical Instn; The Queen's University of Belfast (Hugh Wisnom Scholar, 1960; BA (Hons Geog.) 1955, MA 1958, PhD 1962). FRGS (1958–94); FSA 1970; MRIA 1983. School Teacher (Geography Specialist), Royal Belfast Academical Instn, 1956–62; Director, N Ireland Survey of Industrial Archaeology, 1962–68; Keeper of Technology and Local History, Ulster Museum, Belfast, 1968–77; Dir, Ulster Museum, 1977–82; sch. teacher (geography specialist), Ditcham Park Sch., Petersfield, 1986–93. Vis. Teacher, Glenalmond Coll., 1984, 1986. Chairman: Historic Monuments Council (NI), 1980–85; Jt Cttee on Industrial Archaeology (NI), 1981–85; Member: Malcolm Cttee on Regional Museums in Northern Ireland, 1977–78; Industrial Archaeol. Cttee, Council for British Archaeol., 1981–85. Created major Industrial Heritage Archive, 1982 and 2010, now with NI Envmt Agency, Belfast. *Publications:* The Canals of the North of Ireland, 1965; Railway History in Pictures, Ireland: vol. 1 1969, vol. 2 1970; (contrib.) Travel and Transport in Ireland, 1973; (contrib.) Folk & Farm, 1976; Wheel and Spindle—Aspects of Irish Industrial History, 1977; The Industrial Archaeology of Northern Ireland, 1980 (Library Assoc. high commendation as an outstanding reference book); (contrib.) Some People and Places in Irish Science and Technology, 1985; (contrib.) An Economic and Social History of Ulster 1820–1939, 1985; numerous papers and articles. *Recreations:* reading, Schubert lieder, landscape photography, gardening. *Address:* Ardmilne, 25 Moira Drive, Bangor, Co. Down BT20 4RW. *T:* (028) 9146 5519.

MacDAID, Most Rev. Liam Sean; *see* Clogher, Bishop of, (RC).

McDERMID, Prof. John Alexander, OBE 2010; PhD; FREng; FIET; Professor of Software Engineering, University of York, since 1987 (Head of Department of Computer Science, 2006–12); *b* 5 Oct. 1952; *s* of John Alexander McDermid and Joyce Winifred McDermid (*née* Whiteley); *m* 1980, Heather Mair Denly (marr. diss. 2015); two *d*. *Educ:* Trinity Coll., Cambridge (BA 1975); Univ. of Birmingham (PhD 1981). CEng 1980, FIET (FIEE 1986). MoD student engr, then res. scientist, RSRE, Malvern, 1971–82; Computing Consultant, then Divl Manager, Systems Designers, 1982–87. Non-exec. Dir, High Integrity Solutions, 2002–08; Dir, Origin Consulting (York), 2003–. Mem., DSAC, 2004–10, 2011–. FBCS 1988; FRAeS 1998; FREng 2002; FSaRS 2009. *Publications:* (with K. Ripken) Life Cycle Supporting in the Ada Environment, 1984; (ed) Integrated Project Support Environments, 1985; (ed) The Theory and Practice of Refinement, 1989; (ed and contrib.) Software Engineers Reference Book, 1991; (jtly) Software Engineering Environments, 1992; numerous articles in jls. *Recreations:* reading, music, walking, badminton. *Address:* Department of Computer Science, University of York, Deramore Lane, York YO10 5GH. *T:* (01904) 325400, *Fax:* (01904) 325699. *E:* john.mcdermid@york.ac.uk; Yggdrasil, Scrayingham, York YO41 1JD. *Club:* Athenæum.

MacDERMOT, Prof. John, MD, PhD; FRCP, FWACP, FMedSci; Head of Undergraduate Medicine, Imperial College, London, 2002–06, now Professor Emeritus of Clinical Pharmacology; Hon. Medical Advisor (formerly Undergraduate Medical Academic Links Co-ordinator), Tropical Health and Education Trust, since 2006; International Director, Royal College of Physicians, 2008–12; *b* 24 March 1947; *s* of Niall and Violet MacDermot; *m* 1976, Kay Krnakova; one *d*. *Educ:* Imperial Coll. of Sci. and Technol.; Charing Cross Med. Sch., Univ. of London (MD 1979); PhD Inst. of Neurology, London, 1977. FRCP 1989; FCWAP 2011. Fogarty Internat. Fellow, Lab. of Biochemical Genetics, NIH, 1977–78; Wellcome Sen. Clinical Res. Fellow, RPMS, 1981–87; Professor: of Pharmacology, Univ. of Birmingham, 1987–88; of Clinical Pharmacology, RPMS, later Imperial Coll., Univ. of London, 1989–99; of Medicine and Therapeutics, ICSM, 2000–02. FMedSci 1999. *Publications:* papers on processes involved in signalling from one cell to another. *Recreation:* tour guide at British Museum (Mesopotamia). *Address:* Tropical Health and Education Trust, 1 Wimpole Street, W1G 0AE. *T:* (020) 7290 3892. *E:* john@thet.org.

MacDERMOTT, Alasdair Tormod; HM Diplomatic Service, retired; *b* 17 Sept. 1945; *s* of late Norman MacDermott and Mary MacDermott; *m* 1st, 1966 (marr. diss. 1992); two *d*; 2nd, 1994, Gudrun Geiling. *Educ:* University Coll. Sch., Hampstead; lang. trng, SOAS, Univ. of London; Open Univ. (DipCS 2009). Entered FO, later FCO, 1966; Kabul, 1971–72; FCO, 1973; Accra, 1973–77; FCO, 1977; lang. trng, Tokyo, 1978; Second Secretary: Tokyo, 1979–82; Accra, 1982–83; Political Sec., Colombo, 1983–86; First Secretary: Press Officer, Tokyo, 1986–91; FCO, 1991–95; Turkish lang. trng, 1995; (Commercial), Ankara, 1995–98; Southern African Dept, FCO, 1998–2002; High Comr, Namibia, 2002–07. Internat. Policy Advr, Europe, Leonard Cheshire Internat., 2008–09; Brussels Rep., Electoral Reform Services Internat., Brussels, 2010–11. Member: John Muir Trust, 1990–; Roman Soc., 2008–. Trustee, Community Action, Africa, 2007–. Pres., SOAS Alumni Assoc., Belgium, 2010–12. *Recreations:* wood carving, reading Maigret, researching WWII escape lines from Belgium to Spain. *Address:* Achnacone Farmhouse, Achnacone Estate, Appin, Argyll PA38 4BG. *Clubs:* Royal Over-Seas League; Hill (Nuwara Eliya, Sri Lanka); Ceylon Sea Anglers (Trincomalee, Sri Lanka).

McDERMOTT, Gerard Francis; QC 1999; a Deputy High Court Judge, since 2008; *b* 21 April 1956; *s* of late Joseph Herbert McDermott, BSc, and Winifred Mary McDermott (*née* Limon); *m* 1992, Fiona Johnson. *Educ:* De La Salle Coll., Salford; Manchester Univ. (LLB Hons 1977). Called to the Bar, Middle Temple, 1978, Bencher, 2005; Barrister, Manchester, 1979–; Attorney-at-Law, NY, 1990; a Recorder, 1999–2014. General Council of the Bar: Mem., 1983–88, 1990–96, 1998–99 and 2003–08; Chm., Internat. Relns Cttee, 1999–2000. Dir, Amer. Counsel Assoc., 1997– (Pres., 2003–04); Mem., Internat. Assoc. of Defense Counsel, 2000–; Leader, European Circuit of the Bar, 2006–08. Fellow, Amer. Bar Foundn, 2010. Presidential Citation, ABA, 2015. *Recreations:* travel, music, classic cars. *Address:* Outer Temple Chambers, 222 Strand, WC2R 1BA. *T:* (020) 7353 6381; 9 John Street Chambers, Manchester M4 3DN. *T:* (0161) 955 9000. *Club:* Athenæum.

McDERMOTT, Jennifer; Partner and Head of Media and Public Law, Withers LLP, 2007–13; *b* Sunderland, 1957; *d* of Stanley Keith Harding and Elizabeth Harding; *m* 1983, Thomas Francis McDermott (marr. diss. 2003; he *d* 2015); one *s* one *d*. *Educ:* University Coll. London (LLB Hons 1979). With Lovell, White & King, 1979–2004, Partner, 1989–2004, Hd, Media and Public Law, 1995–2004; Hd, Media and Public Law, Addleshaw Goddard, 2004–07. Exec. Bd, Justice, 2004–. Patron, Tim Bull and Jonathan Parry Peace Foundn, 2009–. *Recreations:* swimming, walking three Cavalier King Charles spaniels. *T:* (01923) 710202, 07715 820398.

MacDERMOTT, Rt Hon. Sir John Clarke, Kt 1987; PC 1987; a Lord Justice of Appeal, Supreme Court of Judicature, Northern Ireland, 1987–98; *b* 1927; *s* of Baron MacDermott, PC, PC (NI), MC, and of Louise Palmer, *o d* of Rev. J. C. Johnston, DD; *m* 1953, Margaret Helen, *d* of late Hugh Dales, Belfast; four *d*. *Educ:* Campbell Coll., Belfast; Trinity Hall, Cambridge (BA); QUB. Called to Bar, Inner Temple and Northern Ireland, 1949; QC (NI) 1964. Judge, High Court of NI, 1973–87. *Address:* 6 Tarawood, Holywood, Co. Down BT18 0HS.

McDERMOTT, Patrick Anthony, MVO 1972; HM Diplomatic Service, retired; Deputy Bursar, Ampleforth Abbey and College, 2002–06; *b* 8 Sept. 1941; *e s* of Patrick McDermott and Eileen (*née* Lyons); *m* 1976, Christa, *d* of Emil and Anne-Marie Herminghaus, Krefeld, W Germany; two *s*, and two *s* by previous *m*. *Educ:* Clapham College, London. FO 1960; Mexico City, 1963; Attaché, UK Delegn to UN, NY, 1966; Vice-Consul, Belgrade, 1971; Second Sec., FCO, 1973; Second Sec., Bonn, 1973; First Sec., Paris, 1976; First Sec., FCO, 1979; Consul-Gen., and Econ. and Financial Advr to British Military Government, W Berlin, 1984; Asst Hd of Dept, FCO, 1988–89; Counsellor, Paris, 1990; Dept Head, FCO, 1995–97; Consul Gen., Moscow, and to Republic of Moldova, 1998–2001 (Chargé d'Affaires, 1998, 1999). Trustee, Helmsley Walled Garden Trust, 2005–08. Freeman, City of London, 1986. *Publications:* short stories published in UK and USA. *E:* patrickmcdermott@hotmail.com.

McDEVITT, Conall; Director, Hume Brophy Dublin, since 2013; *b* Dublin; *s* of late Rory McDevitt and Cathy McDevitt; *m* 1997, Dr Joanne Murphy; two *s* one *d*. *Educ:* Instituto de Bachillerato Mixto, Fuengirola, Malaga. Political Asst to Joan Burton, TD; Dir, Communications, SDLP, 1996–99; Hd, Communications, Viridian Gp, 1999–2000; Special Advr to Minister for Agric. and Rural Develt, NI, 2000–02; Public Relns Consultant, 2002–06, Man. Dir, 2006–09, Weber Shandwick, NI. Mem. (SDLP) S Belfast, NI Assembly, Jan. 2010–Sept. 2013. Chm., CIPR NI, 2007. Nat. Sec., Labour Youth, 1993; Vice Pres., Eur. Young Socialists, 1994. *Recreations:* running, cycling, Gaelic football, soccer. *Address:* Hume Brophy Dublin, 32 Merrion Street Upper, Dublin 2, Ireland.

McDEVITT, Prof. Denis Gordon, MD, DSc; Professor of Clinical Pharmacology, University of Dundee, 1984–2002, now Emeritus; Hon. Consultant Physician, Dundee teaching hospitals, 1984–2002; *b* 17 Nov. 1937; *s* of Harry and Vera McDevitt; *m* 1967, Anne McKee; two *s* one *d*. *Educ:* Queen's Univ., Belfast (MB ChB, BAO Hons 1962; MD 1968; DSc 1978). FRCPI 1977; FRCP 1978; FRCPE 1984. House Physician and Surg., 1962–63, SHO, 1963–64, Royal Victoria Hosp., Belfast; SHO, Registrar, Sen. Registrar, Dept of Therapeutics and Pharmacology, QUB and Belfast teaching hosps, 1964–68; Asst Prof. of Medicine and Cons. Physician, Christian Med. Coll., Ludhiana, India, 1968–71; Cons.

Physician, Belfast teaching hosps, 1971–83; Queen's University, Belfast: Sen. Lectr, 1971–76, Reader, 1976–78, in Clin. Pharmacology and Therapeutics; Prof. of Clin. Pharmacology, 1978–83; Dean, Faculty of Medicine, Dentistry and Nursing, Univ. of Dundee, 1994–97. Merck Internat. Fellow in Clin. Pharmacology, Vanderbilt Univ., 1974–75. Civil Cons. in Exptl Medicine, RAF, 1987–2002. Member: British Pharmacol Soc., 1972– (SKF Medal and Lecture, 1975); Assoc. of Physicians, 1978– (Pres., 1987–88; Hon. Mem., 1988–); Medicines Commn, 1986–95 (Vice-Chm., 1992–95); GMC, 1997–2003 (Treas., 2001–03; Associate, 2003–07 and 2009–15); Council, RCPE, 2003–08; Faculty Bd, FPM, 2003–08; Chm., Specialist Adv. Cttee on Clin. Pharmacol. and Therapeutics, 1980–83; Vice-Chm., Ethics Cttee, Centre for Human Scis, DERA, 1994–2003. FFPM 1990; FRSE 1996; FRSocMed 1996; Founder FMedSci 1998. Man. Editor, European Jl of Clin. Pharmacology, 1998–2002. *Publications:* papers on clin. pharmacology in learned jls. *Recreations:* golf, music, opera. *Address:* Mariners View, 10 Ogilvie Road, Broughty Ferry, Dundee DD5 1LU. *T:* (01382) 739483. *Club:* Royal and Ancient Golf.

MACDIARMID, Hugh Finlay, CB 2003; Solicitor to Advocate General for Scotland, 1999–2005; *b* 1 Aug. 1944; *s* of Finlay Macdiarmid and Winifred Stalker Macdiarmid; *m* 1976, Catherine Rose Smith; two *s*. *Educ:* Morrison's Acad., Crieff; St Andrews Univ. (MA); Edinburgh Univ. (LLB). Admitted as solicitor, 1974; Office of Solicitor to Sec. of State for Scotland, 1974–99, Divl Solicitor, 1986–99. Legal Mem., Mental Health Tribunal for Scotland, 2005–14. *Recreations:* reading, contemplating. *Address:* 27/22 Maxwell Street, Edinburgh EH10 5FT.

McDIARMID, Ian; actor, director; Joint Artistic Director, Almeida Theatre, 1989–2002; *b* 11 Aug. 1944; *s* of Frederick McDiarmid and Hilda (*née* Emslie). *Educ:* Morgan Acad.; St Andrews Univ.; Royal Scottish Acad. of Music and Dramatic Art (Gold Medal, 1968). *Theatre* includes: Mephisto, Round House, 1981; Insignificance, Royal Court, 1982; Tales from Hollywood, NT, 1983; The Black Prince, Aldwych, 1989; Royal Shakespeare Company: joined, 1978; Shylock in Merchant of Venice, Henry V, The Party, 1984; Red, Black and Ignorant, War Plays, The Castle, 1985; The Danton Affair, 1986; A Life of Galileo, 2013, tour, 2014; Royal Exchange, Manchester: The Wild Duck, 1983; Edward II, 1986; Don Carlos, 1987; Associate Dir, 1986–88; Jonah and Otto, 2008; Almeida: Volpone, The Rehearsal (dir), Scenes from an Execution (dir), 1990; Hippolytos, Lulu (dir), 1991; Terrible Mouth (opera), A Hard Heart (dir), 1992; School for Wives, 1993; Siren Song (opera) (dir), 1994; Tartuffe, 1996; The Cenci (opera), The Government Inspector, 1997; The Doctor's Dilemma, 1998; The Jew of Malta, 1999; The Tempest, 2000; Faith Healer, 2001, Dublin and NY, 2006 (Tony Award for best featured actor); The Embalmer, 2002; The Merchant of Venice, 2014; The Soldier's Tale, LSO, 1987; The King Goes Forth to France, Royal Opera House, 1987; Henry IV, Donmar, 2004; Lear, Crucible, Sheffield, 2005; John Gabriel Borkman, Donmar, 2007; Six Characters in Search of an Author, Minerva, Chichester, transf. Gielgud, 2008; Be Near Me, Donmar, transf. Nat. Theatre of Scotland (and adapted), 2009; The Prince of Homburg, Donmar, 2010; Emperor and Galilean, NT, 2011; The Faith Machine, Royal Court, 2011; Timon of Athens, Chicago Shakespeare, 2012; Bakersfield Mist, Duchess Th., 2014; *films* include: The Return of the Jedi, 1983; Restoration, 1996; Star Wars, Episode I: the phantom menace, 1999; Sleepy Hollow, 2000; Star Wars, Episode II: attack of the clones, 2002, Episode III: revenge of the Sith, 2005; *television:* Karaoke, 1996; Hillsborough, 1996; Great Expectations, 1999; All the King's Men, 1999; Crime and Punishment, 2002; Charles II: The Power and the Passion, 2003; Elizabeth I, 2005; Our Hidden Lives, 2005; City of Vice, 2008; Margaret, 2009; 37 Days, 2014; Utopia 2, 2014. *Address:* c/o Troika Talent, 10a Christina Street, EC2A 4PA.

McDONAGH, Baroness *cr* 2004 (Life Peer), of Mitcham and of Morden in the London Borough of Merton; **Margaret Josephine McDonagh;** management consultant; Founder and Chair, The Pipeline, since 2013; *b* 26 June 1961; *d* of Cumin McDonagh and Breda McDonagh (*née* Doogue). *Educ:* Brunel Univ. (BSc); Kingston Business Sch. (MA); Harvard Business Sch. (AMP). Labour Party: Gen. Election Co-ordinator, 1997; Gen. Sec., 1998–2001; Gen. Manager, Express Newspapers, 2001–02. Chm., iPublic, 2004; Director: TBI plc, 2004–14; Standard Life plc, 2007–12; CareCapital plc, 2008–10; Chair, Smart Energy, 2013–15. Chair, Standard Life Charitable Trust, 2009–12; Dir, AFC Wimbledon Foundn; SW London Elective Orthopaedic Centre. *Address:* House of Lords, SW1A 0PW.
See also S. A. McDonagh.

MacDONAGH, Lesley Anne; Managing Partner, Lovells (formerly Lovell White Durrant), Solicitors, 1995–2005; *b* 19 April 1952; *d* of Arthur George Payne and Agnes Dowie Scott; *m* 1st, 1975, John Belton (marr. diss. 1985); one *d*; 2nd, 1987, Simon Michael Peter MacDonagh; three *s*. *Educ:* Queen Elizabeth I Sch., Wimborne; College of Law, Guildford and London. Admitted Solicitor, 1976; Partner, Lovell White Durrant, subseq. Lovells, 1981–2006, Support Dir and Solicitor, 2005–07. Member: Council, Law Society, 1992–2001 (Mem., Planning and Envmtl Cttee, 1988–95); Lands Tribunal Consultative Cttee, 1991–95; Property Adv. Gp, 1993–. Non-executive Director: Bovis Homes plc, 2003; SEGRO (formerly Slough Estates plc), 2007–09; Ogier, 2009–11; BDO (formerly BDO Stoy Hayward), 2009–; Speechly Bircham, 2010–; Univ. of Law, 2013–. Trustee, Citizenship Foundn, 1991–. Vice-Chm., Envmt Cttee, Knightsbridge Assoc., 1991–. Former Gov., LSE. Liveryman, Solicitors' Co., 1982– (Mem. Court, 1997–2006). Hon. Fellow, Soc. for Advanced Legal Studies, 1998. *Recreations:* family life, painting, theatre, dining.

McDONAGH, Robert, (Bobby); Ambassador of Ireland to Italy, since 2013; *b* Washington, DC, 29 June 1954; *s* of Robert and Roisín McDonagh; *m* 1979, Mary Garvey; four *d*. *Educ:* Gonzaga Coll., Dublin; Balliol Coll., Oxford (MA Classics). Pres., Oxford Union. Entered Dept of Foreign Affairs, Ireland, 1977; Third Secretary: Political Div., 1977–80; Luxembourg, 1980–83; Gen. Secretariat of EP, 1983–85 (on special leave); First Secretary: Econ. Div., 1985–87; Perm. Representation of Ireland to EU, Brussels, 1987–90; Mem. Cabinet of Raymond McSharry, 1990–92, Dep. Chef de Cabinet of Padraig Flynn, EC, 1993–94 (on special leave); Counsellor, Econ. Div., 1995–2000; Ambassador to Malaysia, also accredited to Laos, Thailand and Vietnam, 2000–01; Asst Sec., EU Div., 2001–05; Perm. Rep. to EU, Brussels, 2005–09; Ambassador of Ireland to the Court of St James's, 2009–13. *Publications:* Original Sin in a Brave New World: the paradox of Europe, 1998; (contrib.) Genesis and Destiny of the European Constitution, 2007. *Address:* c/o Department of Foreign Affairs, 80 St Stephen's Green, Dublin 2, Ireland.

McDONAGH, Siobhain Ann; MP (Lab) Mitcham and Morden, since 1997; *b* 20 Feb. 1960; *d* of Cumin McDonagh and Breda McDonagh (*née* Doogue). *Educ:* Holy Cross Convent; Essex Univ. (BA Hons 1981). Clerical Officer, DHSS, 1981–82; Wandsworth Council: Admin. Asst, 1982–83; Receptionist, Homeless Persons Unit, 1983–86; Housing Advr, Housing Aid Centre, 1986–88; Devlt Co-ordinator, Battersea Churches Housing Trust, 1988–97. An Asst Govt Whip, 2007–08. Mem., South Mitcham Community Centre, 1988. *Recreations:* shopping, music, women's magazines. *Address:* 1 Crown Road, Morden SM4 5DD. *T:* (020) 8542 4835.
See also Baroness McDonagh.

MACDONALD, family name of **Barons Macdonald, Macdonald of River Glaven** and **Macdonald of Tradeston**.

MACDONALD, 8th Baron *cr* 1776; **Godfrey James Macdonald of Macdonald;** JP; DL; Chief of the Name and Arms of Macdonald; *b* 28 Nov. 1947; *s* of 7th Baron Macdonald, MBE, TD, and Anne (*d* 1988), *o d* of late Alfred Whitaker; *S* father, 1970; *m* 1969, Claire, *e d* of Captain T. N. Catlow, CBE, RN, Gabriel Cottage, Tunstall, Lancs; one *s* three *d*. JP Skye and Lochalsh, 1979; DL Ross and Cromarty, Skye and Lochalsh, 1986. *Heir: s* Hon. Godfrey Evan Hugo Thomas Macdonald of Macdonald, yr, *b* 24 Feb. 1982. *Address:* Kinloch Lodge, Isle of Skye. *Club:* New (Edinburgh).

MACDONALD OF RIVER GLAVEN, Baron *cr* 2010 (Life Peer), of Cley-next-the-Sea in the County of Norfolk; **Kenneth Donald John Macdonald,** Kt 2007; QC 1997; Warden, Wadham College, Oxford, since 2012; *b* 4 Jan. 1953; *s* of late Dr Kenneth Macdonald, scientist, and Maureen Macdonald (*née* Sheridan); *m* 1980, Linda Zuck, television producer; two *s* one *d*. *Educ:* St Edmund Hall, Oxford (BA Hons PPE 1974; Hon. Fellow, 2012). Called to the Bar, Inner Temple, 1978, Bencher, 2004. A Recorder, 2001–03 and 2010–; Dir of Public Prosecutions, 2003–08; Mem., Matrix Chambers, 2000–03, 2008–; a Dep. High Court Judge, 2010–. Mem., Treasury Counsel Selection Cttee, Central Criminal Court, 2001–03. Criminal Bar Association: Mem. Cttee, 1997–2003; Chm., Educn Sub-Cttee, 1999–2001; Vice Chm., 2002–03; Chm., 2003; Member: Bar Council, 2000; Bar Public Affairs Gp, 2001–03 (Vice-Chm., 2001–02); Sentencing Guidelines Council, 2003–08; Criminal Procedure Rules Cttee, 2003–08; Nat. Criminal Justice Bd, 2003–08; Ind. Commn on Youth Crime, 2008–11; H of L Constitution Cttee, 2012–13. Vis. Prof. of Law, LSE, 2009–12; Mem., Adv. Bd, Centre for Criminol., Univ. of Oxford, 2010–. Chair, Reprieve, 2011–. Mem. Council, ICA, 2012–. Trustee, Index on Censorship, 2009–12. *Recreations:* 20th century history, crime fiction, film noir. *Address:* Wadham College, Oxford OX1 3PN.

MACDONALD OF TRADESTON, Baron *cr* 1998 (Life Peer), of Tradeston in the City of Glasgow; **Angus John Macdonald,** CBE 1997; PC 1999; Senior Adviser, Macquarie Group, since 2004; *b* 1940; *s* of Colin and Jean Macdonald; *m* 1963, Theresa McQuaid; two *d*. *Educ:* Allan Glen's Sch., Glasgow. Marine fitter, 1956–63; Circulation Manager, Tribune, 1964–65; journalist, The Scotsman, 1965–67; Granada Television: Editor/Exec. Producer, World in Action, 1969–75; successively Head of Current Affairs, Regl Progs, Features, 1975–82; presenter, variously, Camera, Granada 500, Party conferences, Union World; Presenter, Right to Reply, Channel 4, 1982–88; Dir of Progs, 1985–90, Man. Dir, 1990–96, Chm., 1996–98, Scottish Television, subseq. Scottish Media Gp. Chm., Taylor & Francis Group, 1997–98; Director: GMTV, 1991–97; Bank of Scotland, 1998; Scottish Enterprise, 1998. Parly Under-Sec. of State (Minister for Business and Industry), Scottish Office, 1998–99; Minister of State (Minister for Transport), DETR, 1999–2001; Minister for the Cabinet Office and Chancellor of the Duchy of Lancaster, 2001–03; Mem., Select Cttee on Econ. Affairs, 2004–08, on Communications, 2008–12, on Digital Skills, 2014–15, H of L; Mem., Cabinet Office Adv. Cttee on Business Appts, 2009–13. Chm., All Party Parly Humanist Gp, 2005–10. Member: OECD Futures Project on Global Infrastructure, 2004–07 and 2009–11; Adv. Bd, OECD Internat. Transport Forum, 2009–13. Non-exec. Dir, Scottish Power, 2009–. Chm., Cairngorms Partnership Bd, 1997–98. Founder Chm., Edinburgh Television Festival, 1976; Chairman: Edinburgh Film Fest., 1994–96; ITV Broadcasting Bd, 1992–94. Vice Pres., RTS, 1994–98. Vis. Prof., Film and Media Studies, Stirling Univ., 1985–98. Governor: Nat. Film and Television Sch., 1986–97; BFI, 1997–98. Chancellor, Glasgow Caledonian Univ., 2007–12; Mem. Council, 2006–08, Mem. Ct, 2009–11, Univ. of Sussex. Patron, Dystonia Soc., 2006–. DUniv: Stirling, 1992; Glasgow, 2001; Hon. DLitt: Napier, 1997; Robert Gordon, 1998; Hon. DBA Lincoln, 2007. BAFTA Award, Best Factual Series (World In Action), 1973; Chairman of the Year, and Business Leader of the Year, Scottish Business Elite Awards, 1997; BAFTA Scotland Lifetime Achievement Award, 1997. *Publications:* Camera: Victorian eyewitness, 1979. *Recreations:* music, pictures, sports. *Address:* House of Lords, SW1A 0PW. *Club:* Royal Automobile.

McDONALD, Very Rev. Alan Douglas; Moderator of the General Assembly of the Church of Scotland, 2006–07; Minister, St Leonard's and Cameron, St Andrews, since 1998; *b* 6 March 1951; *s* of Douglas Gordon McDonald and Ray Lindsay Bishop McDonald (*née* Craig); *m* 1975, Dr Judith Margaret McDonald (*née* Allen); one *s* one *d*. *Educ:* Glasgow Acad.; Strathclyde Univ. (LLB 1972); Edinburgh Univ. (BD 1978; MTh 1996). Legal apprentice, Biggart Baillie & Gifford, 1972–74; Solicitor, Farquharson Craig, 1974–75. Community Minister, Pilton, Edinburgh, 1979–83; Minister, Holburn Central, Aberdeen, 1983–98. Convener, Church and Nation Cttee, Gen. Assembly of C of S, 2000–04. Mem. Bd, Christian Aid, 2012–. Hon. DLitt Strathclyde, 2007; Hon. DD St Andrews, 2007. *Recreations:* music, poetry, hillwalking, running, golf. *Address:* 1 Cairnhill Gardens, St Andrews, Fife KY16 8QY. *T:* (01334) 472793. *E:* alan.d.mcdonald@talk21.com.

MACDONALD, Sir Alasdair (Uist), Kt 2008; CBE 2001; Advocate for the Pupil Deprivation Grant (Welsh Government), and Champion for Schools Challenge, Cymru, since 2014; Headteacher, Morpeth School, Tower Hamlets, 1992–2013; *b* Glasgow, 15 July 1949; *s* of William Uist and Patricia Joan Macdonald; *m* 1981, Susan Catherine Roberts; two *s*. *Educ:* Morgan Primary Sch.; Morgan Acad., Dundee; Aberdeen Univ. (MA Hons Geog.); Leeds Univ. (PGCE). Teacher of English, Nkhota Kota Secondary Sch., Malawi, 1971–73; Project Manager, Christian Service Cttee, Blantyre, Malawi, 1973–74; Teacher of Geog., 1975–77, Hd of Geog., 1977–80, Dep. Hd, 1980–82, George Green's Sch., Tower Hamlets; Dep. Principal, 1983–85, Principal, 1986, Passam Nat. High Sch., Wewak, PNG; Dep. Headteacher, Quintin Kynaston Sch., Westminster, 1987–92. Consultant, Nat. Coll. of Sch. Leadership, 2006–12; educational consultant for London Bor. of Tower Hamlets and Inst. of Educn, 2013. Unilever Fellow, London Leadership Centre, 2000. Hon. DEd E London 2008. *Recreations:* travelling with family, hiking, theatre, education, Dundee United FC, East and Central Africa. *Address:* 55 Hervey Road, SE3 8BS. *T:* (020) 8856 5684. *E:* uistmac@aol.com.

MACDONALD, Alastair John Peter, CB 1989; a Civil Service Commissioner, 2001–07; Director General, Industry (formerly Deputy Secretary), Department of Trade and Industry, 1992–2000; *b* 11 Aug. 1940; *s* of late Ewen Macdonald and Hettie Macdonald; *m* 1969, Jane, *d* of late T. R. Morris; one *s* two *d*. *Educ:* Wimbledon Coll.; Trinity Coll., Oxford. Editorial staff of Spectator, 1962; Financial Times, 1963–68: Washington DC, 1965–66; Features Editor, 1966–68; joined Home Civil Service as Asst Principal, DEA, 1968; Principal, DTI, 1971; Sec., Lord Devlin's Commn into Industrial and Commercial Representation, 1971–72; Asst Sec., DoI, 1975; RCDS, 1980; Under Sec., DTI, 1981. Dep. Sec., DTI, 1985–90; Dep. Under Sec. of State, MoD (PE), 1990–92. Non-exec. Dir, Parity Gp plc, 2002–08. Mem., Design Council, 2001–04. Pres., BCS, 2000–01. FBCS 1999. Trustee, Chatham Historic Dockyard Trust, 2001–09. *Address:* 13 Burbage Road, SE24 9HJ.

McDONALD, Very Rev. Alexander; General Secretary, Board of Ministry, Church of Scotland, 1988–2002; Moderator of the General Assembly of the Church of Scotland, 1997–98; *b* 5 Nov. 1937; *s* of Alexander McDonald and Jessie Helen (*née* Low); *m* 1962, Essdale Helen (*née* McLeod) (*d* 2007); two *s* one *d*. *Educ:* Bishopbriggs Higher Grade Sch.; Whitehill Senior Secondary Sch.; Stow Coll.; Scottish Coll. of Commerce; Trinity Coll., Glasgow Univ. (Dip. 1968); BA Open Univ. CMIWSc. Trainee management in timber trade, 1954–56; RAF, 1956–58; timber trade, 1958–62; Minister: St David's Church, Bathgate, 1968–74; St Mark's Church, Paisley, 1974–88. Hon. Pres., Paisley and Dist Bn, Boys' Bde, 2010. Broadcaster on TV and radio, 1969–2002. DUniv Open, 1999. *Publications:* numerous articles in jls and newspapers. *Recreations:* hill walking, swimming, reading, fishing. *Address:* Flat 51, Kelburne Court, 51 Glasgow Road, Paisley PA1 3PD. *T:* (0141) 560 1937.
See also D. J. McDonald.

McDONALD, Prof. Alexander John, MA (Cantab), LLB; WS; Professor of Conveyancing, University of Dundee (formerly Queen's College), 1955–82, now Emeritus (Dean of the Faculty of Law, 1958–62, 1965); Senior Partner, Thornton, Dickie & Brand, WS, Dundee, 1978–84, Consultant to Thorntons, WS, 1984–2000; *b* 15 March 1919; *o s* of late John

McDonald, and Agnes Mary Stewart McDonald; *m* 1951, Doreen Mary, *o d* of late Frank Cook, OBE; two *s* two *d*. *Educ:* Cargilfield Sch.; Fettes Coll. (open scholar); Christ's Coll., Cambridge (Classical Exhibn, BA 1942); Edinburgh Univ. (Thow Schol. and John Robertson Prize in Conveyancing; LLB with dist., 1949). Admitted as solicitor and Writer to the Signet, 1950; Lectr in Conveyancing, Edinburgh Univ., 1952–55. *Publications:* Conveyancing Case Notes, 1981, 2nd edn 1984; Conveyancing Manual, 1982, 7th edn 2004; Registration of Title Manual, 1986. *Address:* 16 Broomwell Gardens, Broughty Ferry, Dundee DD5 3QP. *T:* (01382) 370398.

MacDONALD, Hon. Sir Alistair William Orchard, Kt 2015; **Hon. Mr Justice MacDonald;** a Judge of the High Court of Justice, Family Division, since 2015; *b* Sudbury, Suffolk, 22 Feb. 1970; *s* of Murray and Mary MacDonald; *m* 2000, Penelope Melville. *Educ:* Nottingham Univ. (BA Hons Archaeol. 1991); City Univ. (DipLaw 1994). Field Archaeologist, Trent and Peak Archaeol Trust, 1992–93. Called to the Bar, Inner Temple, 1995; barrister, specialising in family law, 1995–2015; a Recorder, 2009–15; QC 2011. *Publications:* The Rights of the Child: law and practice, 2011, annotated materials, 2014; (gen. ed.) Clarke Hall & Morrison on Children, looseleaf edn 2012, 2015; (contrib.) Family Court Practice, 2012, 2015. *Recreations:* amateur astronomy, ski-ing, biography. *Address:* Royal Courts of Justice, Strand, WC2A 2LL.

MACDONALD, Andrew; producer; Head: DNA Films, since 1997; DNA TV, since 2013; *b* Glasgow, 1 Jan. 1966; *s* of William Macdonald and Angela Pressburger; *m* 1997, Rachael Fleming; four *s* one *d*. Producer: Shallow Grave, 1994; Trainspotting, 1996; A Life Less Ordinary, 1997; The Beach, 2000; The Parole Officer, 2001; Alien Love Triangle, 2002; 28 Days Later, 2002; Sunshine, 2007; 28 Weeks Later, 2007; Never Let Me Go, 2010; Dredd, 2012; Sunshine on Leith, 2013; Ex Machina, 2015; Far From The Madding Crowd, 2015; Executive Producer: Twin Town, 1997; Beautiful Creatures, 2000; Strictly Sinatra, 2001; Heartlands, 2002; The Final Curtain, 2002; The Last King of Scotland, 2006; The History Boys, 2006; Notes on a Scandal, 2006; The Sweeney, 2012. *Recreations:* food, football, film. *Address:* DNA Films, 10 Amwell Street, EC1R 1UQ. *T:* (020) 7843 4410, *Fax:* (020) 7843 4411. *E:* info@dnafilms.com.

McDONALD, Dr Andrew John, CB 2015; Chair, Scope, since 2014; *b* 27 June 1962; *s* of A. J. W. McDonald and Eileen McDonald (*née* Sharkey); *m* 1992, Louise London; one *d*. *Educ:* St John's Coll., Oxford (BA Hons (Modern Hist.) 1983; MA 1989); Bristol Univ. (PhD 1988). PRO, 1986–2000 (Mem., Management Bd, 1997–2000); Client Services Dir/Actg Chief Exec., Public Guardianship Office, 2000–01; Tribunals Prog. Dir, LCD, 2001–02; Constitution Dir, DCA, 2003–05; Chief Exec., Govt Skills, Cabinet Office, then at DIUS, later at BIS, 2006–09; Chief Exec., Ind. Parly Standards Authy, 2009–14. Gwilym Gibbon Fellow, Nuffield Coll., Oxford, 1996–97; Fulbright Fellow, Inst. of Govtl Studies, Univ. of Calif, Berkeley, 2005–06. FRHistS 2000. FRSA 1999–2010. Hon. Fellow, Sch. of Public Policy, UCL, 1998–. Trustee: Action for Children, 2007–14; Cure Parkinson's Trust, 2012–. *Publications:* (ed with G. Terrill) Open Government, 1998; (ed) Reinventing Britain, 2007; articles on modern hist. and public policy. *Recreations:* history, sport, walking, travel, writing, swimming. *Club:* MCC.

McDONALD, Andrew Joseph; MP (Lab) Middlesbrough, since Nov. 2012; *b* Middlesbrough, 8 March 1958; *m* 1987, Sally. *Educ:* Leeds Poly. (BA Hons). Admitted Solicitor, 1990. Wilson-McDonald Solicitors, 1990–94; McDonald Solicitors, 1994–99; Thompson's Solicitors, 1999–2012. PPS to Shadow Attorney Gen., 2013, to Shadow Minister for Business, Innovation and Skills, 2013–15. Mem. (Lab) Middlesbrough Council, 1995–99. Governor: Abingdon Primary Sch., Middlesbrough, 1995–2010; Middlesbrough Coll., 2012–. *Address:* House of Commons, SW1A 0AA; (office) Unit 4 Broadcasting House, Newport Road, Middlesbrough TS1 5JA.

MacDONALD, Angus; Member (SNP) Falkirk East, Scottish Parliament, since 2011; *b* Stornoway, 11 Oct. 1963; *s* of William James MacDonald and Enid MacDonald; *m* Linda Sim; one *s*. *Educ:* Keil Sch.; Grangemouth High Sch.; Coll. of Estate Mgt. Agriculture, until 1992. Member (SNP): Falkirk DC, 1992–96; Falkirk Council, 2004–. Parliamentary Liaison Officer: to Cabinet Sec. for Rural Affairs, Climate Change and Envmt; to Minister for Envmt and Climate Change. Gov., Stirlingshire Educn Trust, 2007–. JP, 1992–96. *Address:* Scottish Parliament, Edinburgh EH99 1SP. *T:* (0131) 348 5489.

MACDONALD, His Honour Angus Cameron; a Circuit Judge, 1979–98; *b* 26 Aug. 1931; *o s* of late Hugh Macdonald, OBE, and Margaret Cameron Macdonald (*née* Westley); *m* 1956, Deborah Anne, *d* of late John Denny Inglis, DSO, MC, JP, and Deborah Margery Meiklem Inglis (*née* Thomson); two *d* (and one *d* decd). *Educ:* Bedford Sch.; Trinity Hall, Cambridge (BA 1954; MA 1960). Nat. service, 1950–51, commissioned, TA, 1951–57. Called to Bar, Gray's Inn, 1955; Resident Magistrate, then Crown Counsel, Nyasaland Govt, 1957–65; Sen. State Counsel, Malawi Govt, 1965–67; practised, NE Circuit, 1967–79; a Recorder of the Crown Court, 1974–79. *Recreations:* singing, fishing, shooting. *Clubs:* Northern Counties (Newcastle upon Tyne); New (Edinburgh).

MACDONALD, Angus David; Headmaster, Lomond School, 1986–2009; *b* Edinburgh, 9 Oct. 1950; *s* of Iain and Molly Macdonald; *m* 1976, Isabelle Marjory; two *d*. *Educ:* Jesus Coll., Cambridge (BA 1972); Edinburgh Univ. (DipEd). Teacher: Alloa Acad., 1972; Edinburgh Acad., 1973–82; Kings Sch., Paramatta, NSW, 1978; Dep. Hd, George Watson's Coll., 1982–86. *Recreations:* outdoor ed., gardening, piping. *Address:* Shenavail, Camserney, Aberfeldy, Perth and Kinross PH15 2JF. *T:* (01887) 820728. *E:* angusmacdonald910@btinternet.com.

McDONALD, Prof. Arthur Bruce, OC 2006; OOnt 2012; PhD; FRSC; FRS 2009; Director, Sudbury Neutrino Observatory, since 1989, and Gordon and Patricia Gray Professor of Particle Astrophysics, 2006–13, now Emeritus, Queen's University, Ontario; *b* 29 Aug. 1943; *m* Janet; four *c*. *Educ:* Dalhousie Univ., Halifax (BSc 1964; MSc 1965; Hon. LLD 1997); Calif Inst. of Technol. (PhD 1969). Chalk River Nuclear Laboratories, Atomic Energy of Canada Ltd: Postdoctoral Fellow, 1969–70; Asst Res. Officer, 1970–75; Associate Res. Officer, 1975–80; Sen. Res. Officer, 1980–82; Prof. of Physics, Princeton Univ. and Co-Principal Investigator, Princeton Cyclotron, 1982–89; Queen's University, Ontario: Prof. of Physics, 1989–2013; Univ. Res. Chair in Physics, 2002–06; Dir, 1991–2003, 2006–09, Associate Dir, 2009–13, Sudbury Neutrino Observatory Inst. Rutherford Meml Fellow, 1969–70; Killam Res. Fellow, 1998–2000. Associate, Cosmology and Gravity Prog., Canadian Inst. for Advanced Res., 2000– (Chair, Adv. Bd, 2000–05). Member: Canadian Assoc. of Physicists, 1964; Professional Engrs of Ontario, 2004. Fellow, APS, 1983; FRSC 1998. Hon. LLD: Cape Breton, 1999; St Francis Xavier, 2009; Hon. DSc: Royal Military Coll., 2001; Chicago, 2006; Alberta, 2011; Waterloo, 2012. Tom W. Bonner Prize in Nuclear Physics, APS, 2003; Medal for Lifetime Achievement in Physics, Canadian Assoc. of Physicists, 2003; Herzberg Medal, NSERC, 2003; Bruno Pontecorvo Prize, Jt Inst. for Nuclear Res. Dubna, 2005; (jtly) J. C. Polanyi Award, NSERC, 2006; (jtly) Benjamin Franklin Medal in Physics, 2007; Killam Prize in Nat. Scis, 2010; Tory Medal, RSC, 2011; Cocconi Prize, Eur. Physical Soc., 2013; (jtly) Nobel Prize in Physics, 2015. *Publications:* more than 140 pubns on nuclear and particle physics in scientific jls. *Address:* Department of Physics, Engineering Physics and Astronomy, Queen's University, Kingston, ON K7L 3N6, Canada.

MACDONALD, Prof. Averil Mary, OBE 2015; PhD; CPhys, FInstP; Professor of Science Communication, University of Reading, 2007–14, now Emeritus; *b* Walsall, 15 Oct. 1957; *d* of late Joseph Henry and Clara Eleanor Frost; *m* 1986, George Macdonald (marr. diss. 1998); two *d*; *m* 2001, Prof. Alun Vaughan. *Educ:* Univ. of York (BSc Physics 1980); Open Univ. (MA Educn Mgt 1996); Southampton Univ. (PhD Chem. 2004). CPhys 1987; FInstP 1999. Teacher of physics, Ingatestone, Essex, 1981–86; Hd of Physics, Kenilworth Sch., 1986–93; Lectr (pt-time), Univ. of Reading, 1996–2007. Educnl Consultancy business, 1996–. Trustee, Science Mus. Gp (formerly NMSI), 2008–. Freeman, Horners' Co. Bragg Medal, Inst. Physics, 1999; Woman of Outstanding Achievement in Sci., UK Res. Council for Women in Sci., 2007; Plastics Industry Award for Personal Contribn to the Plastics Industry 2007. *Publications:* jointly: Reading into Science: physics, 2003; Fantastic Plastic; co-author of school textbooks in series incl. Science Web Readers, GCSE Modular Science, GCSE Gateway Science, Salters A-level Physics, Science Through Hydrogen, Essential Physics Revision. *Recreations:* talking to husband in pubs (when time permits), keeping tropical fish, 2 cats, 2 daughters and 1 husband.

MACDONALD, Dr Calum Alasdair; Executive Director, Point and Sandwick Power, 2010–12; Development Director, An Teallach Energy, since 2010; *b* 7 May 1956; *s* of Malcolm and Donella Macdonald. *Educ:* Bayble Sch.; The Nicolson Inst.; Edinburgh Univ.; Univ. of California at Los Angeles (PhD). MP (Lab) Western Isles, 1987–2005; contested (Lab) Na h-Eileanan An Iar, 2005. Parly Under-Sec. of State, Scottish Office, 1997–99. Chm., Forestry Commn Scotland, 2006–09. Vice-Chm., Point Power & Energy Co. Ltd, 2006. Member: TGWU; Scottish Crofting Foundn (formerly Crofters Union). *Address:* 21 New Garrabost, Isle of Lewis HS2 0PH.

MACDONALD, Charles Adam; QC 1992; **His Honour Judge Macdonald;** a Circuit Judge, since 2005; *b* 31 Aug. 1949; *s* of late Alasdair Cameron Macdonald, VRD, MB ChB, FRCP, FRCPGlas and of Jessie Catherine Macdonald, BA; *m* 1978, Dinah Jane Manns; three *d*. *Educ:* Glasgow Academy; New Coll., Oxford (MA Hons Jurisp.). Called to the Bar, Lincoln's Inn, 1972. An Asst Recorder, 1996–99; a Recorder, 1999–2005. Mem. Panel, Lloyd's Salvage Arbitrators, 2000–05. Tribunal Mem., Mental Health Review Tribunal Restricted Patients Panel, 2009–13; Mem., Parole Bd for England and Wales, 2010–13. *Publications:* Butterworths Commercial Court and Arbitration Pleadings, 2005. *Recreation:* owns sport horses. *Address:* Maidstone Combined Court, Barker Road, Maidstone, Kent ME16 8EQ.

MACDONALD, Clare; *see* Moriarty, C.

MacDONALD, Colin Cameron, CB 1999; Secretary, Sound of Iona Harbours Committee, since 2004; Chairman, South West Mull and Iona Development Company Ltd, since 2014; *b* 13 July 1943; *s* of Captain Colin D. C. MacDonald and Ann MacDonald (*née* Hough); *m* 1969, Kathryn Mary Campbell. *Educ:* Allan Glen's Sch., Glasgow; Univ. of Strathclyde (BA Hons Econ. 1967). Scottish Development Department, 1967–92: Asst Sec., Housing Div., 1988–91, Management Orgn, 1991–92; Under Sec. and Principal Estab. Officer, Scottish Office, then Scottish Exec., 1992–2000; Man. Dir, Colmcille Fisheries (Iona), 2000–03. Non-exec. Dir, TSB Bank Scotland, 1994–98. *Recreations:* tennis, fishing, music. *Address:* Caol Ithe, Iona, Argyll PA76 6SP. *T:* (01681) 700344.

McDONALD, David Arthur; Chairman, Willow Housing and Care Ltd, 2004–05 and 2006–11; *b* 16 Jan. 1940; *s* of late Campbell and Ethel McDonald; *m* 1st, 1963, Barbara MacCallum (marr. diss.); one *d*; 2nd, 1971, Mavis Lowe (*see* Dame Mavis McDonald); one *s*. *Educ:* Campbell College, Belfast; Trinity College, Dublin. BA (Moderatorship) Classics. Asst Master, Classics, Methodist College, Belfast, 1963–66; Press Sec. to Minister of Education, N Ireland, 1967–68; joined Min. of Housing and Local Govt, later DoE, 1970; Asst Private Sec. to Sec. of State for the Envmt, 1974–76; Asst Sec., Local Govt Finance Divs, 1977–82; Dir of Information, 1982–87; Under Sec., Construction Industry, and Sport and Recreation, Directorates, 1987–90; Dir of Information, 1990–92; Under Sec., Urban Develt and Relocation Directorate, 1992–94; Under-Sec., Cities, Countryside and Private Finance Directorate, 1994. Mem., Local Govt Area Cost Adjustment Rev. Panel, 1995–96. Chm., Network Housing Assoc., later Stadium Housing Assoc., 1996–2006; Vice-Chm., London Strategic Housing Ltd, 1999–2002; Mem. Bd, Network Housing Gp, 2003–11 (Chm. Council, 2003–08; Ind. Mem., Investment Cttee, 2011–15). *Recreations:* golf, watching sport. *Clubs:* Middlesex CC; London Scottish Rugby.

MACDONALD, David Cameron; Chairman, National Kidney Foundation of New Zealand, 1998–2003; *b* 5 July 1936; *s* of James Fraser Macdonald, OBE, FRCS and Anne Sylvia Macdonald (*née* Hutcheson); *m* 1st, 1968, Melody Jane Coles (marr. diss. 1980); two *d*; 2nd, 1983, Mrs Sally Robertson; one *s* one *d*. *Educ:* St George's Sch., Harpenden; Newport Grammar Sch. Admitted a solicitor with Slaughter and May, 1962; joined Philip Hill Higginson Erlangers, later Hill Samuel & Co. Ltd, 1964: Dir, 1968; Dep. Chm., 1979–80; Dir, Hill Samuel Gp Ltd, 1979–80; Chief Exec., Antony Gibbs Holdings Ltd and Chm., Antony Gibbs & Sons, 1980–83; Chairman: Bath and Portland Gp, 1982–85; Pittards, 1985–97 (Dir, 1984); Sound Diffusion, 1987–89; Director: Coutts and Co., 1980–95; Sears, 1981–97; Merivale Moore, 1985–98; Cogent Elliott, 1986–97; Foster Yeoman Ltd, 1993–95. Sen. UK Advr, Credit Suisse First Boston, 1983–91. Dir Gen., Panel on Takeovers and Mergers, 1977–79. Adviser to Govt on Upper Clyde Shipbuilders crisis, 1971. Chm., Issuing Houses Assoc., 1975–77. Mem., BTA, 1971–82. Trustee, London City Ballet, 1983–87. *Recreations:* music, fishing. *Address:* Laburnum Cottage, Westcombe, Shepton Mallet, Som BA4 6ER. *T:* (01749) 838724.

McDONALD, David John, (David Tennant); actor; *b* 18 April 1971; *s* of Very Rev. Alexander McDonald, *qv*; *m* 2011, Georgia Moffett; one *d*, and one step *s*. *Educ:* Royal Scottish Acad. of Music and Drama (BA). *Theatre* includes: appearances with 7:84 Theatre Co.; Royal Shakespeare Co.: As You Like It, 1996; Romeo and Juliet, 2000; Comedy of Errors, 2000; Hamlet, 2008; Love's Labour's Lost, 2008; Lobby Hero, Donmar and New Ambassadors, 2002; Much Ado About Nothing, Wyndham's, 2011; Richard II, Stratford, 2013; *films* include: Bright Young Things, 2003; Harry Potter and the Goblet of Fire, 2005; Glorious 39, St Trinian's 2: the Legend of Fritton's Gold, 2009; Fright Night, 2011; What We Did On Our Holiday, 2014; *television* includes: He Knew He Was Right, 2004; Blackpool, 2004; Casanova, 2005; The Doctor in Doctor Who, 2006–10; Recovery, 2007; Hamlet, 2009; Single Father, 2010; United, 2011; This Is Jinsy, 2011; Spies of Warsaw, 2013; Broadchurch, 2013, 2015; The Politician's Husband, 2013; The Escape Artist, 2013; *radio*: The Purple Land, Kafka: The Musical, 2011; Love, Virtually, 2012. *Address:* c/o Independent Talent Group Ltd, 40 Whitfield Street, W1T 2RH.

MACDONALD, Prof. David Whyte, CBE 2010; DPhil, DSc; FRSE; FRGS, FRSB; Founding Director, Wildlife Conservation Research Unit, since 1986, and Professor of Wildlife Conservation, since 2004, University of Oxford; Senior Research Fellow in Wildlife Conservation, Lady Margaret Hall, Oxford, since 1986; *b* Oxford, 30 Sept. 1951; *s* of Dr William Alexander Fraser Macdonald and Williamina Stirrat (*née* Whyte), Glasgow; *m* 1975, Jennifer Mary Wells; one *s* two *d*. *Educ:* St Lawrence Coll., Ramsgate; Wadham Coll., Oxford (Wells Schol.; BA 1972); Balliol Coll., Oxford (DPhil 1977); DSc Oxon 2004. FRGS 1978; FRSB (FIBiol 1990). University of Oxford: Jun. Res. Fellow, Balliol Coll., 1976–79; Ernest Cook Res. Fellow, 1979–84, Nuffield Res. Fellow, 1984–87, Dept of Zool. A. D. White Prof.-at-Large, Cornell Univ., 1997–2003; Vis. Prof., Imperial Coll., London, 2004–. Department for Environment, Food and Rural Affairs: Mem., Adv. Cttee on Pesticides, 2002–05 (Mem., Envmtl Panel, 2003–05); Advr to UK Biodiversity Res. Adv. Gp, 2002–; Mem., 2003–04, Chm., 2004–, Darwin Adv. Cttee. Advr to Burns Inquiry into hunting with hounds, 2000; Comr, Ind. Supervisory Authy for Hunting, 2000–05. Biodiversity Advr to Esmée Fairbairn Foundn, 2002–11. Founding Chm., IUCN/Species Survival Commn Canid

Specialist Gp, 1985–2005. Member: Council, English Nature, 2003–05; Bd, Natural England, 2005–14 (Chm., Sci. Adv. Cttee, 2006–14); Council, Wildfowl and Wetlands Trust, 2005–10; Inter Agency Climate Change Forum, JNCC, 2007–10. Trustee, Macaulay Land Use Res. Inst., 1999–2003; Mem., NERC Peer Rev. Coll., 2006–08. Vice-President: Royal Soc. of Wildlife Trusts, 1999–; RSPCA, 2001–05. Zoological Society of London: Scientific Fellow, 1993; Mem. Council, 2001–06; Vice-Pres., 2003–06. FRSE 2008; Emer. Fellow, IUCN Survival Commn, 2005. Vice Pres., Eur. Soc. of Mammalogists, 1993–2004; Mem. Council, Fauna and Flora Internat., 1995–2002. Trustee: Earthwatch Europe, 2007– (Chm., 2009–); WWF UK, 2008–. Natural history films: The Night of the Fox, BBC TV, 1976; Meerkats United, BBC TV, 1987 (Wildscreen Award, 1988); One for All, All for One, 1988; The Velvet Claw (series), BBC TV, 1992. T. H. Huxley Prize, Zool Soc., 1978; Dawkins Prize for Animal Conservation and Welfare, Balliol Coll., Oxford, 2004; Merriam Prize for res. in mammalogy, Amer. Soc. of Mammalogists, 2006; Medal for outstanding services to mammalogy, Mammal Soc. of GB, 2007; Silver Medal for contribs to understanding and appreciation of zoology, Zool Soc. London, 2010. *Publications:* Rabies and Wildlife: a biologist's perspective, 1980; *joint editor:* A Handbook on Biotelemetry and Radio Tracking, 1979; Social Odours in Mammals, vols 1 and 2, 1985; Carnivore Conservation, 2001; The Biology and Conservation of Wild Canids, 2004; Key Topics in Conservation Biology, 2007; *popular science*: Vulpina: story of a fox, 1977; Expedition to Borneo, 1980; Running with the Fox, 1987 (Natural Hist. Author of Year Award); The Velvet Claw: a natural history of the carnivores, 1992; Field Guide to Mammals of Britain and Europe, 1993; European Mammals: evolution and behaviour, 1995 (Natural Hist. Author of Year Award); Meerkats, 1999; Foxes, 2000; (ed) Encyclopedia of Mammals, 3rd edn 2006; contrib. learned jls incl. Nature and Science. *Recreations:* farming (sheep and sheep dogs), Burns' poetry, photography, rowing, golf, surviving. *Address:* Wildlife Conservation Research Unit, Department of Zoology, University of Oxford, Recanati-Kaplan Centre, Tubney House, Tubney, Oxon OX13 5QL. *T:* (01865) 611100, *Fax:* (01865) 393101. *E:* david.macdonald@zoo.ox.ac.uk, wcru@zoo.ox.ac.uk. *Club:* Athenæum.

MACDONALD, Hon. Donald (Stovel); PC (Canada) 1968; CC 1994; Senior Policy Adviser, McMillan (formerly Lang Michener) LLP, Toronto, 2002–13; *b* 1 March 1932; *s* of Donald Angus Macdonald and Marjorie Stovel Macdonald; *m* 1st, 1961, Ruth Hutchison (*d* 1987), Ottawa; four *d*; 2nd, 1988, Adrian Merchant; three step *s* three step *d* (and one step *d* decd). *Educ:* Univ. of Toronto (BA 1951); Osgoode Hall Law Sch. 1955 (LLB *ex post facto* 1991); Harvard Law Sch. (LLM 1956); Cambridge Univ. (Dip. in Internat. Law, 1957). Called to Ont Bar, 1955; Prize in Insurance Law, Law Soc. of Upper Canada, 1955; Rowell Fellow, Canadian Inst. of Internat. Affairs, 1956; McCarthy & McCarthy, law firm, Toronto, 1957–62, Partner, 1978–88; High Comr for Canada in UK, 1988–91; Counsel, McCarthy Tétrault, 1991–2000. Special Lectr, Univ. of Toronto Law Sch., 1978–83, 1986–88. MP Rosedale, 1962–78; Parly Sec. to Ministers of Justice, Finance, Ext. Affairs, Industry, 1963–68; Minister without Portfolio, 1968; Pres., Queen's Privy Council, and Govt House Leader, 1968–70; Minister of National Defence, 1970–72; Minister of Energy, Mines and Resources, 1972–75; Minister of Finance, 1975–77. Director: McDonnell Douglas Corp., 1978–88; Du Pont Canada Inc., 1978–88; Bank of Nova Scotia, 1980–88; Alberta Energy Co. Ltd, 1981–88; MacMillan-Bloedel Ltd, 1986–88; Celanese Canada, 1991–99 (Chm., 1997–99); Sun Life Assurance Co. of Canada, 1991–2002; TransCanada Pipelines, 1991–2002; Slough Estates Canada Ltd, 1991–2001; Siemens Canada (formerly Siemens Electric) Ltd, 1991–2004 (Chm., 1991–2004); Alberta Energy Co. Ltd, 1992–2002; Hambros Canada Inc., 1994–98; BFC Construction Corp. (formerly Banister Foundn Inc.), 1994–99; Boise Cascade Corp., 1996–2004; AT&T Canada Corp., 1999; Aber Diamond Corp. (formerly Aber Resources Ltd), 1999–2003; Century Mining Corp., 2004–08. Sen. Advr, UBS Bunting Warburg, Toronto, 2000–02. Chairman: Internat. Develt Res. Centre, Canada, 1981–84; Inst. for Res. on Public Policy, Montreal, 1991–97; Design Exchange, 1993–96. Chairman: Royal Commn on Econ. Union and Develt Prospects for Canada, 1982–85; Canadian Council for Public-Private Partnerships, 1993–99; Adv. Cttee on Competition in Ont's Electricity System, 1995–96; Atlantic Council of Canada, 1998–2003. Chm. and Trustee, IPC US Income Commercial Real Estate Investment Trust, 2001–07; Trustee, Clean Power Income Trust, 2001–07. Trustee, Clan Donald Lands Trust, Armadale, Skye, 1991–2007. Chm., Canadian Friends of Cambridge, 1993–97. Freeman, City of London, 1990; Liveryman, Distillers' Co. Hon. Fellow, Trinity Hall, Cambridge, 1994. LLD (*hc*): St Lawrence, 1974; New Brunswick at Saint John, 1990; Toronto, 2000; Carleton, Ottawa, 2003; Hon. DEng Colorado Sch. of Mines, 1976; Hon. DSL Trinity Coll., Toronto, 2009. *Publications:* Thumper: the memoirs of the Honourable Donald S. Macdonald, 2014. *Recreation:* silviculture. *Address:* 98 Pleasant Boulevard, Toronto, ON M4T 1J8, Canada. *T:* (416) 9759119.

McDONALD, Elaine Maria, OBE 1983; ballerina; Director, Creative Dance Artists Trust, 1993–2001 (Chairman, 1997–2001); Ballet Teacher (Faculty), Legat School, 1997–99; *b* 2 May 1943; *d* of Wilfrid Samuel and Ellen McDonald. *Educ:* Convent of the Ladies of Mary Grammar Sch., Scarborough; Royal Ballet Sch., London. Throughout dancing career was coached and trained by Madame Cleo Nordi. Walter Gore's London Ballet, 1962–64; Western Theatre Ballet, 1964–69; Principal Dancer, 1969–89, Artistic Controller, 1988–89, Scottish Ballet; has also danced with London Fest. Ballet, Portuguese Nat. Ballet, Galina Samsova and Andre Prokovsky's New London Ballet, Cuban Nat. Ballet; Associate Artistic Dir, Northern Ballet Th., 1990–92. Mem., Scottish Arts Council, 1986–90 (Mem., Dance and Mime Cttee, 1982–92). Patron, Peter Darrell Trust. Hon. LittD Strathclyde, 1990. *Relevant publication:* Elaine McDonald, ed J. S. Dixon, 1983. *Recreations:* physical therapy, theatre, travel, reading.

MACDONALD, Prof. Ewan Beaton, OBE 2002; FRCP, FRCPE, FRCPGlas, FFOM, FFOMI; Professor and Head, Healthy Working Lives Group, Public Health and Health Policy Section, University of Glasgow, since 2004 (Senior Lecturer, 1990–2004); *b* 11 Jan. 1947; *s* of Dr Duncan Macdonald, MBE and Isabel Dow Macdonald; *m* 1971, Patricia Malloy; three *s* one *d*. *Educ:* Keil Sch.; Univ. of Glasgow (MB ChB). FFOM 1988; FRCPGlas 1992; FRCP 1994; FRCPE 1996; FFOMI 1997. General medicine, Western Infirmary, Glasgow, 1971–75; National Coal Board: MO, 1975–80; PMO, Yorks, 1980–85; Hon. Consultant in Rehabilitation, Firbeck Hosp., 1980–85; IBM UK: SMO, 1986; CMO, 1987–90; Chm., IBM European Occupational Health Bd, 1988–90; Dir, SALUS (Lanarks Occupnl Health and Safety Service), 1990–2011. Dean, Faculty of Occupational Medicine, RCP, 1994–96; Pres., Sect. of Occupnl Medicine, Union of Eur. Med. Specialists, 2001–05 (Sec., 1997–2001). Mem., Bevan Commn, 2012–. Founder and Chm., Kinloch Castle Friends Assoc., 1996–. Hon. Col, 225 Med. Regt (V), 2007–13. *Publications:* numerous articles and chapters on occupational health. *Recreations:* mountaineering, sailing, fishing. *Address:* Public Health and Health Policy Section, 1 Lilybank Gardens, University of Glasgow, Glasgow G12 8RZ. *T:* (0141) 330 3719. *E:* ewan.macdonald@glasgow.ac.uk. *Club:* Loch Lomond Sailing.

MACDONALD, Very Rev. Dr Finlay Angus John; Principal Clerk, 1996–2010, Moderator, 2002–03, General Assembly of the Church of Scotland; an Extra Chaplain to the Queen in Scotland, since 2015 (a Chaplain to the Queen, 2001–15); *b* 1 July 1945; *s* of late Rev. John Macdonald, AEA, MA and Eileen Ivy Sheila (*née* O'Flynn); *m* 1968, Elizabeth Mary Stuart; two *s*. *Educ:* Dundee High Sch.; Univ. of St Andrews (MA 1967; BD 1970; PhD 1983). Pres. Students' Representative Council, St Andrews Univ., 1968–69. Licensed by Presbytery of Dundee, 1970; ordained by Presbytery of Stirling and Dunblane, 1971; Minister: Menstrie Parish Ch, 1971–77; Jordanhill Parish Ch, Glasgow, 1977–96. Convener, Business Cttee, Gen. Assembly, 1988–92. Mem., Scottish Inter-Faith Council, 2005–08. Co-leader, Scottish Inter-Faith Pilgrimage, 2008. Chm., Iona Cathedral Trust, 2005–. Gov., Jordanhill Coll., 1988–93; Lay Mem. Court, Strathclyde Univ., 1993–96 (Fellow, 2002). Hon. DD St Andrews, 2002. *Publications:* Confidence in a Changing Church, 2004; Luke Paul, 2012; Luke Paul and the Mosque, 2013. *Recreations:* music, gardening, hill-walking. *Address:* 8 St Ronan's Way, Innerleithen, Peeblesshire EH44 6RG. *T:* (01896) 831631.

MacDONALD, Gavin; *see* MacDonald, S. G. G.

McDONALD, Gillian Clare; President, North West Division, Europe, McDonald's Restaurants, since 2014; *b* Birmingham, 15 May 1964; *d* of John and Mavis Manaton; *m* 2001, David McDonald; two *s*. *Educ:* Sevenoaks Sch.; Brighton Univ. (BA 1st Cl. Hons Business Studies). Mktg posts with Colgate Palmolive, 1987–90; mktg and gen. mgt rôles with British Airways, 1990–2006; Chief Mktg Officer, UK and Northern Europe, 2006–10, UK CEO and Pres., Northern Europe, 2010–13, McDonald's Restaurants. *Address:* McDonald's Restaurants Ltd, 11–59 High Road, E Finchley, N2 8AW.

MACDONALD, Howard; *see* Macdonald, J. H.

MACDONALD, Prof. (Hugh) Ian, OC 1977; Professor of Economics and Public Policy, Schulich School of Business (formerly Faculty of Administrative Studies), since 1974, Director, Programme in Public Administration, since 1992, York University, Toronto; President Emeritus, York University, since 1984; *b* Toronto, 27 June 1929; *s* of Hugh and Winnifred Macdonald; *m* 1960, Dorothy Marion Vernon; two *s* three *d*. *Educ:* public schs, Toronto; Univ. of Toronto; Oxford Univ. BCom (Toronto), MA (Oxon), BPhil (Oxon). Univ. of Toronto: Lectr in Economics, 1955; Dean of Men, 1956; Asst Prof., Economics, 1962. Govt of Ontario: Chief Economist, 1965; Dep. Provincial Treas., 1967; Dep. Treas. and Dep. Minister of Economics, 1968; Dep. Treas. and Dep. Minister of Economics and Intergovernmental Affairs, 1972. Pres., York Univ., 1974–84; Dir, York Internat., 1984–94. Director: the AGF Cos, 1982–2014; McGraw-Hill Ryerson Ltd, 1984–2014 (Chm., 1996–). Hon. Prof., Hunan Univ., 2009–. Member: Canadian Economics Assoc.; Amer. Economics Assoc.; Canadian Assoc. for Club of Rome; Inst. of Public Admin of Canada; Lambda Alpha Fraternity (Land Economics); Amer. Soc. for Public Admin. President: Empire Club of Canada, 1969–70; Ticker Club, 1971–72; Couchiching Inst. of Public Affairs, 1975–77; Canadian Rhodes Scholars Foundn, 1986–92; World Univ. Service of Canada, 1992–93; Chairman: Toronto Men's Br. of CIIA, 1959–61; Inst. for Political Involvement, 1974–76; Bd, Corp. to Promote Innovation Develt for Employment Advancement (Govt of Ontario), 1984–86; Commn on Financing of Elementary and Secondary Educn in Ontario, 1984–87; Ont. Municipal Trng and Educn Adv. Council, 1984–86; Hockey Canada, 1987–94; Annual Fund Appeal in Canada of Balliol Coll., Oxford Univ., 1992–98; The Commonwealth of Learning, 1994–2003 (Fellow, 2004). Member: Attorney General's Cttee on Securities Legislation, 1963–65; Economic Council of Canada, 1976–79; Bd, Council for Canadian Unity, 1978–99; Admin. Bd, Internat. Assoc. of Univs, 1980–90; Council and Exec. Cttee, Interamerican Orgn for Higher Educn, 1980–88 (Vice-Pres., Canada); Canadian Exec. Service Orgn, 1998–2001. Advr, Commonwealth Assoc. for Public Admin and Mgt, 2004–. Hon. Councillor, Internat. Orgn for Higher Educn, 1992. Hon. Life Mem., Canadian Olympic Assoc., 1997. KLJ 1978; Citation of Merit, Court of Canadian Citizenship, 1980. Hon. LLD Toronto, 1974; DUniv Open, 1998; Hon. DLitt: Sri Lanka Open, 1999; Dr B. R. Ambedkar Open, Hyderabad, 2001; York, 2008. Canada Centennial Medal, 1967; Silver Jubilee Medal, 1977; Commemorative Medal, 125th Anniversary of Confedn of Canada, 1992; Award of Merit, Canadian Bureau for Internat. Educn, 1994; Vanier Medal, for distinction in public service and excellence in public admin, Inst. of Public Admin of Canada, 2000; Senator Peter Boorsma Award, S Eastern Conf. for Public Admin, 2006; President's Award, Lambda Alpha Internat. Land Use Soc., 2010. Golden Jubilee Medal, 2002; Diamond Jubilee Medal, 2012. *Recreations:* hockey, tennis; public service in various organizations. *Address:* 7 Whitney Avenue, Toronto, ON M4W 2A7, Canada. *T:* (416) 9212908; York University, 4700 Keele Street, Toronto, ON M3J 1P3, Canada. *T:* (416) 7365632.

MACDONALD, Prof. Hugh John; Avis Blewett Professor of Music, Washington University, St Louis, 1987–2011, now Emeritus (Chair, Music Department, 1997–99); *b* 31 Jan. 1940; *s* of Stuart and Margaret Macdonald; *m* 1st, 1963, Naomi Butterworth; one *s* three *d*; 2nd, 1979, Elizabeth Babb; one *s*. *Educ:* Winchester College; Pembroke College, Cambridge (MA; PhD). FRCM 1987. Cambridge University: Asst Lectr, 1966–69; Lectr, 1969–71; Fellow, Pembroke Coll., 1963–71; Lectr, Oxford Univ., 1971–80, and Fellow, St John's Coll.; Gardiner Prof. of Music, Glasgow Univ., 1980–87. Vis. Prof., Indiana Univ., 1979. Gen. Editor, New Berlioz Edition, 1966–2006. Szymanowski Medal, Poland, 1983. *Publications:* Berlioz Orchestral Music, 1969; Skryabin, 1978; Berlioz, 1981; (ed) Berlioz Selected Letters, 1995; Berlioz's Orchestration Treatise, 2002; Beethoven's Century, 2008; Music in 1853, 2012; Bizet, 2014; articles in New Grove Dict. of Music and Musicians, Musical Times, Music and Letters, Revue de Musicologie. *Recreation:* bridges. *Address:* 18 Fishergate, Norwich NR3 1SE.

MACDONALD, Iain Smith, CB 1988; MD; FRCPE, FFPH; Chief Medical Officer, Scottish Home and Health Department, 1985–88, retired; *b* 14 July 1927; *s* of Angus Macdonald, MA and Jabina Urie Smith; *m* 1958, Sheila Foster; one *s* one *d*. *Educ:* Univ. of Glasgow (MD, DPH). Lectr, Univ. of Glasgow, 1955; Deputy Medical Officer of Health: Bury, 1957; Bolton, 1959; joined Scottish Home and Health Dept, 1964, Dep. Chief Med. Officer, 1974–85. Mem., MRC, 1985–88. QHP 1984–87. *Publications:* Glencoe and Beyond: the sheep-farming years 1780–1830, 2005. *Address:* 4 Skythorn Way, Falkirk FK1 5NR. *T:* (01324) 625100.

MACDONALD, Ian; *see* Macdonald, H. I.

MACDONALD, Ian Alexander; QC 1988; *b* 12 Jan. 1939; *s* of late Ian Wilson Macdonald and Helen Nicolson, MA; *m* 1st, 1968, Judith Roberts (marr. diss.); two *s*; 2nd, 1978, Jennifer Hall (marr. diss.); one *s*; 3rd, 1991, Yasmin Sharif (marr. diss.); 4th, 2008, Brigid Baillie. *Educ:* Glasgow Acad.; Cargilfield Sch., Edinburgh; Rugby Sch.; Clare Coll., Cambridge (MA, LLB). Called to the Bar, Middle Temple, 1963 (Astbury Scholar, 1962–65; Bencher, 2002); SE Circuit. Lectr in Law, Kingston Polytechnic, 1968–72; Senior Legal Writer and Research Consultant, Incomes Data Services Ltd, 1974–80 (monitoring develts in employment law). Mem., Cttee of Inquiry into disappearance of Gen. Humberto Delgado, 1965; Chm., Ind. Inquiry into Racial Violence in Manchester Schs, 1987–88. Special Advocate, Special Immigration Appeals Commn, 1999–2004. Pres., Immigration Law Practitioners' Assoc., 1984–2014. Mem. Editl Adv. Bd, Immigration and Nationality Law and Practice. Grand Cross, Order of Liberty (Portugal), 1995. *Publications:* Resale Price Maintenance, 1964; (with D. P. Kerrigan) The Land Commission Act 1967, 1967; Race Relations and Immigration Law, 1969; Immigration Appeals Act 1969, 1969; Race Relations: the new law, 1977; (with N. Blake) The New Nationality Law, 1982; Immigration Law and Practice, 1983, 9th edn 2015; Murder in the Playground: report of Macdonald Inquiry into Racial Violence in Manchester Schools, 1990; (contrib.) Family Guide to the Law, 1971, 1972; articles in professional jls. *Recreations:* swimming, watching football, reading. *Address:* Garden Court Chambers, 57–60 Lincoln's Inn Fields, WC2A 3LS. *T:* (020) 7993 7600. *Club:* Cumberland Lawn Tennis.

MACDONALD OF SLEAT, Sir Ian Godfrey B.; *see* Bosville Macdonald of Sleat.

MACDONALD, Prof. Ian Grant, FRS 1979; Professor of Pure Mathematics, Queen Mary College, subsequently Queen Mary and Westfield College, University of London, 1976–87, now Professor Emeritus, Queen Mary, University of London; *b* 11 Oct. 1928; *s* of Douglas Grant Macdonald and Irene Alice Macdonald; *m* 1954, Margaretha Maria Lodewijk Van Goethem; two *s* three *d*. *Educ:* Winchester Coll.; Trinity Coll., Cambridge (MA). Asst Principal and Principal, Min. of Supply, 1952–57; Asst Lectr, Univ. of Manchester, 1957–60; Lectr, Univ. of Exeter, 1960–63; Fellow, Magdalen Coll., Oxford, 1963–72; Fielden Prof. of Pure Maths, Univ. of Manchester, 1972–76. *Publications:* Introduction to Commutative Algebra (with M. F. Atiyah), 1969; Algebraic Geometry, 1969; Symmetric Functions and Hall Polynomials, 1978, 2nd edn 1995; Symmetric Functions and Orthogonal Polynomials, 1998; Affine Hecke Algebras and Orthogonal Polynomials, 2003; articles in math. jls. *Address:* 56 High Street, Steventon, Abingdon, Oxon OX13 6RS.

McDONALD, Iona Sara MacIntyre; DL; Sheriff of North Strathclyde at Kilmarnock, since 2002; *b* 18 Nov. 1954; *d* of Thomas and Isabella MacIntyre; *m* 1978, Colin Neale McDonald (*d* 2001); one *s* one *d*. *Educ:* Glasgow Univ. (MA 1976; LLB 1978). NP 1980. Admitted solicitor, 1980; Partner, Messrs Mathie-Morton Black & Buchanan, Solicitors, Ayr, 1982–2000; Reporter to the Court, Safeguarder and Curator ad Litem, 1985–2000; Temp. Sheriff, 1995, Hon. Sheriff at Ayr, 1995–2000; All Scotland Floating Sheriff, 2000–02. Mem., Scottish Court Service Bd, 2010–. DL Ayrshire and Arran, 2013. *Recreations:* gardening, skiing, walking, travel. *Address:* Kilmarnock Sheriff Court, St Marnock Street, Kilmarnock KA1 1ED. *T:* (01563) 520211.

MACDONALD, Most Rev. James Hector, DD; CSC; Archbishop of St John's (Newfoundland), (RC), 1991–2000, now Emeritus; *b* 28 April 1925; *s* of Alexander and Mary Macdonald. *Educ:* St Joseph's Univ., 1944–45. Ordained priest, 1953. Congregation of the Holy Cross: Mission Bank, 1954–56; Dir, Holy Cross Minor Seminary, St Joseph's, NB, 1956–62; Sec., Provincial Council, 1956–63; Dir of Vocations, 1962–63; Superior, Holy Cross House of Studies, 1964–69; Asst Provincial, 1966–72; Pastor, St Michael's, Waterloo, Ont., 1969–77; Dean, Waterloo County Priests, dio. of Hamilton, 1974–77; Aux. Bishop of Hamilton, 1978–82; Bishop of Charlottetown, 1982–91.

McDONALD, Sir James (Rufus), Kt 2012; PhD; FREng, FIET, FInstP; FRSE; Principal and Vice-Chancellor, University of Strathclyde, since 2009; *b* 1957. *Educ:* Univ. of Strathclyde (BSc, MSc, PhD). Electricity supply industry; University of Strathclyde, 1984–: Sen. Lectr, Dept of Electronic and Electrical Engrg; Rolls Royce Prof. of Electrical Power Systems, 1994–; Chm., Rolls Royce Univ. Technol. Centre, 1997–; Dir, Inst. for Energy and Envmt, 2001–; Dep. Principal, 2006–09. Chm., Scottish Energy Technol. Partnership, 2007–; Co-Chair, Energy Adv. Bd in Scotland; Co-Director: Centre for Sustainable Electricity and Distributed Generation, DTI, later BERR, 2004–; Scottish Res. Partnership in Energy Exec., 2006–. Non-exec. Dir, Weir Gp plc, 2014–. Member: Scottish Enterprise Bd; Scottish Sci. Adv. Cttee, 2008–; Energy Excellence Bd, UK Trade and Investment. Trustee and Vice Pres., IET, 2012–15. FREng 2003; FRSE 2003. *Publications:* three books; contrib. jl and conf. papers. *Address:* University of Strathclyde, 16 Richmond Street, Glasgow G1 1XQ.

McDONALD, Jane Elizabeth; *see* Cross, J. E.

McDONALD, Prof. John Corbett, MD; FRCP, FFCM, FFOM; Professor, Department of Occupational and Environmental Medicine, National Heart and Lung Institute (Royal Brompton Hospital), University of London, 1986, now Emeritus; *b* 20 April 1918; *s* of John Forbes McDonald and Sarah Mary McDonald; *m* 1942, Alison Dunstan Wells; one *s* three *d*. *Educ:* London Univ. (MD); Harvard Univ. (MS). DPH, DIH; FRCP (Canada) 1970; FRCP 1976; FFCM 1976; FFOM 1978. Served War, MO, RAMC, 1942–46. Epidemiologist, Public Health Lab. Service, 1951–64 (Dir, Epidemiol Res. Lab., 1960–64); Prof. and Head, Dept of Epidemiology and Health, McGill Univ., Montreal, 1964–76; Prof. of Occupational Health, LSHTM, London Univ., 1976–81, now Emeritus; Prof. of Epidemiol. and Hd, Sch. of Occupational Health, McGill Univ., 1981–83, Prof. Emeritus, 1988–; Chm., Dept of Clinical Epidemiology, Nat. Heart and Lung (formerly Cardiothoracic) Inst. (Royal Brompton Hosp.), Univ. of London, 1986–90. *Publications:* (ed) Recent Advances in Occupational Health, 1981; Epidemiology of Work-related Diseases, 1995, 2nd edn 2000; papers on epidemiol subjects. *Recreation:* croquet. *Address:* 26 Charlton, Chichester PO18 0HU. *Club:* Athenæum.

MacDONALD, Maj.-Gen. John Donald, CB 1993; CBE 1986 (OBE 1981); DL; Chief Executive (formerly General Secretary): The Earl Haig Fund, 1994–2003; Officers Association Scotland, 1994–2003; *b* 5 April 1938; *s* of Lt-Col John MacDonald, OBE; *m* 1964, Mary, *d* of Dr Graeme M. Warrack, CBE, DSO, TD; one *s* two *d*. *Educ:* George Watson's Coll., Edinburgh; RMA Sandhurst. Commnd, 1958; saw service with KOSB, RASC, RCT and Airborne Forces Berlin, UK, BAOR, N Africa, India (Defence Services Staff Coll.), 1958–71; ndc, 1976; Turkey NATO HQ Izmir, CO 4 Armoured Div., Transport Regt RCT, 1978–80; Instr Australian Comd and Staff Coll., 1980–82; Chief Instr and Comdt, RCT Officers' Sch., 1983; DCS 3 Armoured Div., 1983–86; Col Personnel Br. Sec., MoD, 1987–88; Comdr Transport, 1st BR Corps and Garrison Comdr Bielefeld, 1988–91; DG Transport and Movements, MoD, 1991–93. Col Comdt RLC, 1993–2003. Hon. Col, Scottish Transport Regt plc, 1997–2004. Gen. Sec., RBL, Scotland, 1994–2000. Chm., Sportsmatch, Scotland, 1993–98; Mem., Sports Council, Scotland, 1994–99. Queen's Councillor, Queen Victoria Sch., Dunblane, 1994–2004. Chm., Combined Services Rugby, 1991–93. Freeman, City of London, 1991; Hon. Mem. Ct of Assts, Carmen's Co., 1991. DL City of Edinburgh, 1996. *Recreations:* Rugby (played for Scotland, Barbarians, Combined Services and Army), ski-ing, golf, travel, music, collecting. *Address:* Ormiston Hill, Kirknewton, West Lothian EH27 8DQ. *Clubs:* Army and Navy; London Scottish, Royal & Ancient (St Andrews), Honourable Co. of Edinburgh Golfers (Muirfield), Rugby Internationalists Golfing Society.

MacDONALD, John Grant, CBE 1989 (MBE 1962); HM Diplomatic Service, retired; re-employed at Foreign and Commonwealth Office, since 1993; Special Representative of Secretary of State for Foreign and Commonwealth Affairs, since 2010 (Representative, 1997–2010); *b* 26 Jan. 1932; *er s* of late John Nicol MacDonald and Margaret MacDonald (*née* Vasey); *m* 1955, Jean (*d* 2003), *oc* of late J. K. K. Harrison; one *s* two *d*. *Educ:* George Heriot's School. Entered HM Foreign (later Diplomatic) Service, 1949; FO, 1949; served HM Forces, 1950–52; FO, 1952; Berne, 1954–59; Third Sec. and Vice Consul, Havana, 1960–62; FO, 1962; DSAO, 1965; Second, later First Sec. (Comm.), Lima, 1966–71; Nat. Defence Coll., Latimer, 1971–72; Parly Clerk of FCO, 1972–75; First Sec. (Comm.), Hd of Trade Promotion Sect., Washington, 1975–79; Hd of Chancery, Dhaka, 1980–81; Chargé d'affaires during Falklands War and on various other occasions, 1981–84; Hd of Chancery and HM Consul, Bogotá, 1981–84; Counsellor, FCO, 1985–86; Ambassador to: Paraguay, 1986–89; Panama, 1989–92; Head UK Delegn, and Dep. Head (Political), EC Monitor Mission, 1992; temp. duty as Charter Mark Assessor, Cabinet Office, 1994, 1995; UK Mem., OSCE Observer Gp, elections in Macedonia, 1994. Vis. Lectr, Foreign Services Inst., S Africa, 1997. *Recreations:* travel, photography, swimming. *Address:* c/o Foreign and Commonwealth Office, SW1A 2AH. *Clubs:* Naval and Military, Royal Over-Seas League.

MACDONALD, (John) Howard, CA; FCT; Director: BOC Group plc, 1991–2002; Weir Group plc, 1991–2001; *b* 5 June 1928; *s* of John and Helen Macdonald; *m* 1961, Anne Hunter; three *d*. *Educ:* Hermitage, Helensburgh. CA 1954. Thomson McLintock & Co. (served articles), 1949–55; Walter Mitchell & Sons, 1955–58; Aircraft Marine Products, 1958; Finance Manager, Keir & Cawder Arrow Drilling, 1958–60; Royal Dutch Shell Group, 1960–83, Group Treasurer, 1978–83; Chairman and Chief Executive: Dome Petroleum, 1983–88; NatWest Investment Bank, 1989–91; Director: National Westminster Bank, 1989–91; McDermott Internat. Inc., 1985–97; J. Ray McDermott Inc., 1985–97; Reed Internat., until 1983. Financial Advr to new Hong Kong Airport, 1991–93. Mem., Assoc. of Corporate Treasurers, 1979. *Recreations:* golf, theatre. *Address:* Blackdown Border, Tennysons Lane, Haselmere, Surrey GU27 3AF. *T:* (01428) 654953. *Club:* Caledonian.

MACDONALD, John Reginald; QC 1976; barrister-at-law; Commercial, Chancery and Administrative Lawyer; *b* 26 Sept. 1931; *s* of Ranald Macdonald and Marion Olive (*née* Kirkby); *m* 1958, Erica Stanton; one *s* one *d*. *Educ:* St Edward's Sch., Oxford; Queens' Coll., Cambridge. Called to Bar, Lincoln's Inn, 1955, Bencher, 1985; called to Bar of Eastern Caribbean, 1988. Represented: the people of Ocean Island, 1975; Yuri Orlov, the Soviet dissident, 1977–86; Canadian Indians, 1982; the Ilios, who were removed from Diego Garcia to make way for a US base, 1983; appeared for the people of Barbuda at the Antigua Ind. Conf. at Lancaster House in 1980; represented majority shareholders in battle fought in Nevis and BVI for control of only co. producing oil in Belize, and advised Seigneur of Sark and acted for major shareholder in closing stages of contest for control of three of London's leading hotels, 2010–13; Mem., Internat. Commn of Jurists missions to investigate violence in S Africa, 1990, 1992, 1993. Drafted written constitution for the UK (We the People), proposed by Liberal Democrats, 1990, revised 1993; Mem., Jt Lib Dem Labour Cttee on Constitutional Reform, 1996–97. Contested: Wimbledon (L) 1966 and 1970; Folkestone and Hythe (L) 1983, (L/Alliance) 1987; E Kent (Lib Dem), Eur. election 1994. Chm. Council, New Kent Opera, 1996–2008. *Publications:* (ed with Clive H. Jones) The Law of Freedom of Information, 2003, 3rd edn (ed with Ross Grail) 2016. *Recreation:* the theatre. *Address:* 12 New Square, Lincoln's Inn, WC2A 3SW. *T:* (020) 7419 8000. *Club:* MCC.

MACDONALD, Sir John Ronald M.; *see* Maxwell Macdonald, Sir J. R.

MacDONALD, John William; HM Diplomatic Service, retired; *b* 13 June 1938; *s* of John MacDonald and Anne MacDonald (*née* Richards); *m* 1960, Margaret Millam Burns. *Educ:* Boteler Grammar Sch.; NDC; Manchester Business Sch. Foreign Office, 1955, and 1959–94; Royal Navy, 1957–59; Diplomatic Service appts include Cairo, Tokyo, Dhaka, Dar es Salaam; Consul-Gen., Shanghai, 1991–94. *Recreations:* walking, golf, listening to music. *Address:* 12 Snells Wood Court, Little Chalfont, Bucks HP7 9QT.

MACDONALD, Sir Kenneth (Carmichael), KCB 1990 (CB 1983); Chairman, Raytheon Systems Ltd (formerly Cossor Electronics, later Raytheon Cossor Ltd), 1991–2000; *b* 25 July 1930; *s* of William Thomas and Janet Millar Macdonald; *m* 1960, Ann Elisabeth (*née* Pauer); one *s* two *d*. *Educ:* Hutchesons' Grammar Sch.; Glasgow Univ. MA (Hons Classics). RAF, 1952–54. Asst Principal, Air Ministry, 1954; Asst Private Sec. to Sec. of State, 1956–57; Private Sec. to Permanent Sec., 1958–61; HM Treasury, 1962–65; MoD, 1965; Asst Sec., 1968; Counsellor (Defence), UK Delegn to NATO, 1973–75; Asst Under-Sec. of State, 1975, Dep. Under-Sec. of State, 1980, Second Perm. Under-Sec. of State, 1988–90, MoD. Chairman: Raytheon (Europe) Ltd, 1991–94, 1995–2000; Internat. Military Services Ltd, 1993–2005. Chm., Council of Voluntary Welfare Work, 1993–2005. Trustee, Chatham Historic Dockyard Trust, 1992–2000. *Recreation:* golf. *Address:* c/o Barclays Bank, 27 Regent Street, SW1Y 4UB. *Club:* Royal Air Force.

McDONALD, Most Rev. Kevin John Patrick; Archbishop of Southwark, (RC), 2003–10, now Archbishop Emeritus; *b* 18 Aug. 1947. *Educ:* St Joseph's Coll., Stoke; Birmingham Univ. (BA Latin); Ven. English Coll., Rome; Gregorian Univ. (STL); Angelicum Univ. (STD). Ordained priest, 1974; Asst Priest, All Saints, Stourbridge, 1975–76; Lectr in Moral Theol., St Mary's Coll., Oscott, 1976–85; official with resp. for Anglican and Methodist relns, Pontifical Council for Promoting Christian Unity, Rome, 1985–93; Parish Priest, English Martyrs, Sparkhill, Birmingham, 1993–98; Rector, Oscott Coll., 1998–2001; Bishop of Northampton, 2001–03. Chairman: Ecumenical Commn, Archdio. Birmingham, 1980–85; Archdiocesan Commn for Inter-Religious Dialogue, 1998–2001; Bishops' Conf. Cttee for Catholic-Jewish Relns, 2001–; Bishops' Conf. Cttee for Other Faiths, 2001–; Bishops' Conf. Dept of Dialogue and Unity, 2004–; Consultor to Holy See Commn for Religious Relns with the Jews, 2008–. Canon, St Chad's Cathedral, Birmingham, 1998–2001. Hon. DD Birmingham, 2005. *Recreations:* music, reading, walking.

MACDONALD, Lewis; Member (Lab) Scotland North East, Scottish Parliament, since 2011 (Aberdeen Central, 1999–2011); *b* 1 Jan. 1957; *s* of late Rev. Roderick Macdonald and Margaret Macdonald (*née* Currie); *m* 1997, Sandra Inkster; two *d*. *Educ:* Inverurie Acad.; Univ. of Aberdeen (MA, PhD). Parly Researcher, office of Frank Doran, MP, 1987–92 and 1997–99; Adviser to Tom Clarke, MP, 1993–97. Mem., Exec. Cttee, SLP, 1997–99. Dep. Minister for Transport and Planning, 2001, for Enterprise, Transport and Lifelong Learning, 2001–03, for Enterprise and Lifelong Learning, 2003–04, for Envmt and Rural Develt, 2004–05, for Health and Community Care, 2005–07, Scottish Exec. Convenor, Holyrood Progress Gp, 2000–01. Contested: (Lab) Moray, 1997. *Recreations:* walking, football, history. *Address:* (office) 80 Rosemount Place, Aberdeen AB25 2XN. *T:* (01224) 646333.

MacDONALD, Madeleine Mary; *see* Arnot, M. M.

MACDONALD, Dame Mary (Beaton), DBE 2005; Headteacher, Riverside Primary School, North Shields, 1994–2010; *b* 29 July 1950; *d* of Robert Beaton Skinner and Mary Ann Skinner (*née* Gregory); *m* (marr. diss.); two *s* one *d*. *Educ:* Jordanhill Coll., Glasgow (DipEd (Scotland)). Primary teacher, Isle of Bute, 1970–75; career break (short-term supply work), 1975–87; Sen. Teacher, Hawthorn Primary Sch., Newcastle upon Tyne, 1987–90; Dep. Hd, Montagu Primary Sch., Newcastle upon Tyne, 1990–94. Nat. Leader of Educn, Nat. Coll. for Sch. Leadership, 2008. DUniv Strathclyde, 2006. *Recreations:* reading, gardening.

McDONALD, Dame Mavis, DCB 2004 (CB 1998); Permanent Secretary, Office of the Deputy Prime Minister, 2002–05; Chairman, Catalyst Housing Group Ltd, 2005–11; *b* 23 Oct. 1944; *d* of late Richard Henry and of Elizabeth Lowe; *m* 1971, David Arthur McDonald, *qv*; one *s*. *Educ:* Chadderton Grammar Sch. for Girls; London Sch. of Econs and Pol Science (BSc Econ). Min. of Housing and Local Govt, later DoE, then DETR, 1966–2000: Asst Private Sec. to Minister for Housing and Local Govt, 1969–70, to Sec. of State for the Environment, 1970–71; Private Sec. to Perm. Sec., 1973–75; Asst Sec., Central Policy Planning Unit, 1981–83; Head of Personnel Management (Envmt) Div., 1983–86; Finance, Local Authority Grants, 1986; Dep. Dir, Local Govt Finance, 1987; Under Secretary: Directorate of Admin. Resources, 1988–90; Directorate of Personnel Management, 1990–91; Directorate of Housing Resources and Management, 1990–93; Directorate of Local Govt, 1994–95; Prin. Estab. Officer, 1995; Sen. Dir, Housing, Construction, Planning and Countryside, then Dir Gen., Housing, Construction, Regeneration and Countryside Gp, 1995–2000; Perm. Sec., Cabinet Office, 2000–02. Non-exec. Dir, Tarmac Housing Div., 1988–91. Member: Cttee of Mgt, Broomleigh Housing Assoc., 1995–96; Bd, Ealing Family Housing Assoc., 2001–02. Hon. MCIH 2001. Trustee, Joseph Rowntree Foundn, 2006–. Ext. Mem. Council, Univ. of Cambridge, 2009–14 (Dep. Chm., 2011–14). Lay Gov., Birkbeck Coll., London, 1999–2008 (Fellow, Birkbeck, Univ. of London, 2009).

McDONALD, Prof. Michael, PhD; CEng, FICE, FCILT; Professor of Transportation, 1992–2008, now Emeritus, and Director, Transportation Research Group, 1986–2008, University of Southampton; *b* 10 Dec. 1944; *s* of late Douglas Frederick McDonald and Joyce Mary Kathleen McDonald (*née* Burke); *m* 1970, Millicent Elizabeth Agnew; three *s*. *Educ:* Univ. of Newcastle upon Tyne (BSc); Univ. of Southampton (PhD 1981). MCIHT (MIHT

1973); MICE 1975; CEng 1975; FCILT (FCIT 1998); FICE 2004. University of Southampton: Rees Jeffreys Lectr in Highway and Traffic Engrg, 1971–86; Sen. Lectr, 1986–88; Reader in Transportation, 1988–92; Hd, Dept of Civil and Envmtl Engrg, 1996–99. Consultant, Roughton & Partners, 1985–2005 (Exec. Dir, 1990–95); Chm., ITSUK, 2004–07. Member: European Road Transport Res. Adv. Council (Vice Chm., 2004–09); Strategic Bd, Local Authy and Res. Councils' Initiative, 2009. Hills Rees Award, ITS UK, 2009; CIHT Award, 2010. *Address:* School of Civil Engineering and the Environment, University of Southampton, Highfield, Southampton SO17 1BJ.

MACDONALD, Morag, (Mrs Walter Simpson), CBE 1993; PhD; Secretary of the Post Office, 1985–94; *b* 8 Feb. 1947; *d* of Murdoch Macdonald Macdonald and Isobel Macdonald (*née* Black); *m* 1st, 1970, Adam Somerville; 2nd, 1983, Walter Simpson; one *d. Educ:* Bellahouston Academy, Glasgow; Univ. of Glasgow (LLB Hons 1968; PhD 2002); College of Law, London; King's Coll., London (BA 1997). Called to the Bar, Inner Temple, 1974. Joined Post Office as graduate trainee, 1968; posts in Telecommunications and Corporate HQ, 1969–79; PA to Managing Dir, Girobank, 1980; Dep. Sec., Post Office, 1983–85. Mem. Management Cttee, Industry and Parlt Trust, 1986–94. Council Mem., St George's Hosp. Med. Sch., 1994–97. Chairman: Adamson Trust, 2007–11; Glasgow City Heritage Trust, 2011–14 (Trustee, 2006–14; Vice-Chm., 2009–11); Scottish Consortium for Learning Disability, 2013–. Gen. Council Assessor, 2014–, Mem. Bd, Chancellor's Fund Adv. Bd, 2015–, Univ. of Glasgow. FRSA 1990. *Recreations:* walking, embroidery, very indifferent piano playing. *Address:* Flat 0/2, 15 Falkland Street, Glasgow G12 9PY. *Club:* Western (Glasgow).

MACDONALD, Muir, FREng; Managing Director, BMT Defence Services Ltd, since 2008; *b* Leamington Spa, 6 Jan. 1958; *s* of Keith Macdonald and Cynthia Macdonald; *m* 1988, Siân Davies; two *s. Educ:* University Coll. London (MSc Naval Arch. 1980). RCNC 1980; Ministry of Defence: Asst Constructor, 1981–86; Constructor, 1987–94; Asst Dir Warship Integration, 1994–97; rcds 1998; Dir Procurement Policy, 1999–2002; Dir Attack Submarines Proj., 2002–06; BMT Defence Services Ltd (on secondment), 2006–07; Dir Gen. Air Support, 2007–08. FREng 2014. *Recreation:* the outdoors. *Address:* BMT Defence Services Ltd, Maritime House, 210 Lower Bristol Road, Bath BA2 3DQ. *T:* (01225) 473701. *E:* mmacdonald@bmtdsl.co.uk.

McDONALD, Neil Kevin; independent adviser and commentator on housing and planning issues, since 2011; *b* 1 April 1957; *s* of Eric and Margaret McDonald; *m* 1982, Barbara Moyser; two *s* one *d. Educ:* Kingsbury High Sch.; Newcastle-under-Lyme High Sch.; St John's Coll., Cambridge (BA 1979). Entered Civil Service, 1979; Admin. Trainee, Depts of Trade and Industry, 1979–82; Department of Transport, 1982–97: Principal: civil aviation, 1984–87; Driver Testing Review, 1987; LT, 1987–91; Asst Sec., Railways, 1991–93; on secondment to Office of Passenger Rail Franchising, 1994–97; Department of the Environment, Transport and the Regions: Divl Manager, Roads Policy, 1997–2000; Ed., Urban White Paper, 2000; Divl Manager, Local Authy Housing, 2000–02; Prog. Dir, Communities Plan, ODPM, 2002–03; Dir, Housing, ODPM, later DCLG, 2003–06; Department for Communities and Local Government: Dir, Home Inf. Pack Implementation, 2006–07; Dir, Planning Policy, 2007–08; Dir, Planning for Major Infrastructure, 2008–09; Chief Exec., Nat. Housing and Planning Advice Unit, 2009–10; Dir, Housing Mgt, Homelessness and Support, DCLG, 2010–11. Vis. Fellow, Cambridge Centre for Housing and Planning Res., 2013–. *Publications:* What Homes Where?, 2013; Planning for Housing in England, 2014. *Recreations:* classic car restoration, badminton, cycling. *E:* neilkmcdonald@gmail.com.

MACDONALD, Nigel Colin Lock; Partner, Ernst & Young, 1976–2003; *b* 15 June 1945; *s* of late Trevor William and Barbara Evelyn Macdonald; *m* 1st, 1972, Elizabeth Ruth Leaney (*d* 1981); 2nd, 1983, Jennifer Margaret Webster; one *d. Educ:* Cranleigh Sch.; Inst. of Chartered Accountants of Scotland. Thomson McLintock & Co., 1962–68; Whinney Murray & Co., 1968–70; Whinney Murray Ernst & Ernst, Netherlands, 1970–72; Whinney Murray, later Ernst & Whinney, then Ernst & Young, 1972–2003. Dir, James Lock & Co., 1976– (Chm., 1986–). Bd Mem., Coca-Cola Hellenic (formerly Coca-Cola HBC), 2005–. Accounting Advr, Internat. Oil Pollution Compensation Fund, 2002–11. Mem. Council, 1989–93, Pres., 1993–94, Inst. of Chartered Accountants of Scotland. Member: Cadbury Cttee on corporate governance, 1991; Review Panel, Financial Reporting Council, 1991–2006; Bd, BSI, 1992–2004; Industrial Develt Adv. Bd, 1995–2001; Competition (formerly Monopolies and Mergers) Commn, 1998–2005. Chm., Royal Museums Greenwich Foundn, 2013–; Trustee: Nat. Maritime Mus., 2003–13; Scottish Chartered Accountants' Trust for Educn, 2006–11; Scottish Accountancy Trust for Educn and Res., 2006–11 (Chm., 2006–11). FRSA 1993. Mem., Mission Council, URC, 2005–08; Elder, St Andrew's URC, Cheam, 1978–. *Recreations:* old cars, swimming, topography. *Address:* 10 Lynwood Road, Epsom, Surrey KT17 4LD. *T:* (01372) 720853. *Clubs:* Royal Automobile, City of London.

McDONALD, Dr Oonagh, CBE 1998; international regulatory and public policy consultant, since 1989; Director, Oonagh McDonald Ltd, since 2008; *b* Stockton-on-Tees, Co. Durham; *d* of Dr H. D. McDonald, theologian. *Educ:* Roan Sch. for Girls, Greenwich; East Barnet Grammar Sch.; Univ. of London (BD Hons 1959; MTh 1962, PhD 1974, King's Coll.). Teacher, 1959–64; Lectr in Philosophy, Bristol Univ., 1965–76. Gwilym Gibbon Res. Fellow, Nuffield Coll., Oxford, 1988–89; Sen. Res. Fellow, Univ. of Warwick, 1990. Contested (Lab): S Glos, Feb. and Oct. 1974; Thurrock, 1987. MP (Lab) Thurrock, July 1976–87. PPS to Chief Sec. to Treasury, 1977–79; Opposition front bench spokesman on defence, 1981–83, on Treasury and economic affairs, 1983–87, on Civil Service, 1983–87. Consultant, Unity Trust Bank plc, 1987–88. Non-executive Director: Investors' Compensation Scheme, 1992–2001; SAGA Gp, 1995–98; Gen. Insce Standards Council, 1999–2005; British Portfolio Trust plc, 1999–2008; Gibraltar Financial Services Commn, 1999–; Scottish Provident, 1999–2001; Skandia, 2001–04; Dresdner RCM Global Investors, 2001–09. Director: FSA (formerly SIB), 1993–98 (Chm., Consumer Panel, 1994–95); FSA Ombudsman Scheme, 1998–2001; Bd for Actuarial Standards, 2010–13. Complaints Commissioner: London Metal Exchange, 2001–10; Virt-x, 2001–09; ICE Futures (formerly IPE), 2001–; ICE Clear Europe Ltd, 2008–. Chair: Public Inquiry into Property Valuation, 2013–14 (report, 2014); Fair Banking Panel, 2014–. Editor, Jl of Financial Regulation and Compliance, 1998–2008. *Publications:* (jtly) The Economics of Prosperity, 1980; Own Your Own: social ownership examined, 1989; Parliament at Work, 1989; The Future of Whitehall, 1992; The Future of European Retail Banking: the view from the top, 2002; Fannie Mae and Freddie Mac: turning the American dream into a nightmare, 2012; Lehman Brothers: a crisis of value, 2015. *Address:* Flat 23, Grenville Court, 79 Gloucester Street, SW1V 4EA. *T:* (020) 7931 8278.

McDONALD, Patrick Anthony, CChem, CEng, FRSC, FIChemE; Director, Department for Business, Innovation and Skills, 2011; *b* 22 June 1958; *s* of late Patrick Bernard and Mary Ellen McDonald; *m* 1980, Anne Holtham. *Educ:* Rutherford Comp. Sch.; Kingston Poly. (BSc Hons Applied Chem.). CChem 1983; CEng; FRSC 2005; FIChemE. Forensic Scientist, Lab. of Govt Chemist, 1980–87; Department of Trade and Industry: Administrator, 1987–93; Dep. Dir, 1993–2002; Dir, Key Business Technols, 2002–04; Technology Dir, 2004–06; Chief Scientific Advr, HSE, 2006–11. Dir, Britech Foundn, 2004–06. Lay Mem., Res. Awards Cttee, Stroke Assoc., 2012–. *Publications:* papers in Jl of Forensic Sci. *Recreations:* travel, early music, good food, playing cricket, drinking beer. *T:* 07599 505966. *E:* pmac.holmdene@googlemail.com. *Clubs:* Erith Cricket, Statics Cricket.

MACDONALD, Patrick James; Chairman, Reconomy, since 2011 (Chief Executive, 2009–11); Partner, School for CEOs, since 2011; *b* 14 May 1962; *s* of Charles Patrick Macdonald and Frances Gillian Macdonald; *m* 1987, Jacqueline Ann Willis; one *s* two *d. Educ:* Stowe Sch.; Oriel Coll., Oxford (BA Hons Engrg Sci.); INSEAD, Fontainebleau (MBA with dist.). CEng 1990; MIMechE 1990; MIET (MIEE 1990); Eur Ing 1990. RCNC, 1984–85; Project Manager, Unilever, 1985–91; Manager, Boston Consulting Gp, 1993–97; Vice-Pres., Sourcing, GE Capital, Gen. Electric, 1997–2002; Chief Exec., John Menzies plc, 2003–07; Advr, 2007–09; CEO, Dalestone Energy, 2012–14. Mem., Scottish Adv. Cttee, Duke of Edinburgh's Award, 2005–. Trustee, Woodland Trust, 2012–. FRSA; CCMI 2004. *Recreations:* ski-ing, hill-walking, canoeing, sailing, rowing, extreme gardening. *Address:* Reconomy, 81 Fulham Road, SW3 6RD.

MacDONALD, Philip Geoffrey; Headmaster, City of London Freemen's School, 2007–15; *b* Bath, 30 Jan. 1956; *s* of Philip MacDonald and Margaret MacDonald; *m* 1990, Michelle Spencer; two *s* two *d. Educ:* St Brendan's Coll., Bristol; Hertford Coll., Oxford (BA Classics); Bristol Univ. (PGCE). Teacher of English, Venice, 1978–80; Classics Teacher, Rougemont Sch., 1982–85; Hd of Classics/Dir of Studies, Douai Sch., 1985–92; Dep. Hd, Marist Sch., 1993–98; Headmaster, Mount St Mary's Coll., 1998–2007. Mem., HMC, 1998–2015. *Publications: translations:* Don Luigi Orione, The Restless Apostle, 1981; Cecilia Vianelli, The Way of the Carts, 1982. *Recreations:* music (listening), family, church, woodwork, Italian opera. *Address:* Ferndale House, Church Road, Chavey Down, Ascot, Berks SL5 8RR. *E:* philip.macdonald@tiscali.co.uk.

MACDONALD OF CLANRANALD, Ranald Alexander; 24th Chief and Captain of Clanranald; formerly Chairman and Managing Director, Tektura Ltd; *b* 27 March 1934; *s* of late Captain Kenneth Macdonald of Inchkenneth, DSO, and late Marjory Broad Smith, Basingstoke; *S* kinsman as Chief of Clanranald, 1944; *m* 1961, Jane Campbell-Davys, *d* of late I. E. Campbell-Davys, Llandovey, Carms; two *s* one *d. Educ:* Christ's Hospital. Founded: Fairfix Contracts Ltd, 1963; Tektura Wallcoverings, 1970. Chm., British Contract Furnishing Assoc., 1975–76. Lieut (TA) Cameron Highlanders, 1958–68. Mem., Standing Council of Scottish Chiefs, 1957–; Pres., Highland Soc. of London, 1988–91 (Dir, 1959–80); Chief Exec., Clan Donald Lands Trust, 1978–80; Chm., Museum of the Isles, 1981–90; Founding Trustee, Lord of the Isles Galley Proj., 1989–. Vice Pres., Les Avants Bobsleigh and Toboggan Club, 1987–. *Recreation:* avoidance of boredom. *Heir: s* Ranald Og Angus Macdonald, younger of Clanranald, *b* 14 Sept. 1963. *Address:* 13 Eccleston Street, Belgravia, SW1W 9LX. *Clubs:* Beefsteak, Pratt's; New, Puffin's (Edinburgh); British (Bangkok).

MACDONALD, Richard Auld, CBE 2002; Director General, National Farmers' Union, 1996–2009; *b* 31 Oct. 1954; *s* of Anthony Macdonald and Gillian Macdonald (*née* Matthews); *m* 1980, Susan Jane Reynolds; two *d. Educ:* Bishop's Stortford Coll.; Queen Mary Coll., London Univ. (BSc Hons Biology). National Farmers' Union: Parly Sec., 1978–85; County Sec., Devon, 1985–89; Regl Dir, SW, 1989–92; Dir, 1992–96. Chm., Better Regulation Task Force on food and farming, DEFRA, 2010–13. Chairman: Associa Ltd, 2001–09; SALSA, 2010–; Farm Africa, 2014–; non-executive Director: Moy Park Ltd, 2010–; Dairy Crest plc, 2010–; NIAB Ltd, 2011– (Vice Chm., 2014–). Mem. Bd, Envmt Agency, 2013–. Trustee: Farm Africa, 2009–; Earth (formerly Northmoor) Trust, 2011–. Gov., Royal Agricl Univ. (formerly Coll.), Cirencester, 2010–. FRASE 2005. *Recreations:* golf, cricket, Rugby, travel. *Address:* Woodpeckers, Hithercroft, South Moreton, Oxon OX11 9AL. *E:* richard.macdonald@woodpeckers.biz. *Clubs:* Naval and Military, Farmers; Moreton Cricket; Springs Golf.

MACDONALD, Roderick Francis; *see* Uist, Hon. Lord.

MACDONALD, Dr Rosemary Gillespie, FRCP, FRCA; Dean, Post-graduate Medical Education (Yorkshire), University of Leeds and Northern and Yorkshire NHS Executive, 1992–2001, now Emeritus; *b* 25 March 1944; *d* of John Mackenzie Paterson and Mary McCauley Paterson; *m* 1968, Hamish Neil Macdonald; one *s* one *d* (twins). *Educ:* Univ. of Glasgow (MB ChB); Univ. of Bradford (PhD 1976). FRCA 1971; FRCP 1999. Lectr in Anaesthesia, Univ. of Leeds, 1973–76; Consultant Obstetric Anaesthetist, St James's Univ. Hosp., Leeds, 1976–92. Chair, St Gemma's Hospice, 2010– (Trustee, 2003–). Hon. FRCPsych 2002. *Publications:* contribs to British Jl Anaesthesia, Anaesthesia, BMJ, etc. *Recreations:* cooking, walking, opera, ballet, art, human beings. *Address:* The Hawthorns, Moreton OX9 2HX. *T:* (01844) 761067.

MacDONALD, Sally; Director, Public and Cultural Engagement, University College London, since 2006; *b* Carlisle, 18 June 1959; *d* of Neil MacDonald and Helen MacDonald; *m* 1987, Hilary James Young; two *s. Educ:* Cheadle Hulme Sch.; Univ. of Bristol (BA Jt Hons 1st Cl. Latin, Archaeol. and Ancient Hist. 1980); Study Centre, London (Dip. Hist. of Architecture, Fine and Decorative Arts (Dist.) 1983); Museums Assoc. (Dip. 1987). FMA 1998. Asst Keeper, Decorative Arts, Manchester City Art Galls, 1984–87; Asst Curator, and Actg Dep. Dir, Geffrye Mus., 1987–89; Principal Mus Officer, London Bor. of Croydon, 1989–98; University College London: Manager, Petrie Mus. of Egyptian Archaeol., 1998–2005; Project Manager, Inst. for Cultural Heritage, 2005–06; Member: Bd, UCL-Qatar, 2011–; UK-Qatar Year of Culture 2013 Steering Gp, 2013–. Co-Founder and Co-Dir, Heritage Without Borders, 2011–; Co-Chm., Women Leaders in Mus Network, 2012–. Member, Board: Culture Unlimited, 2003–11; Jewish Mus., 2011–13; Mus Assoc., 2011–13; Bloomsbury Fest., 2012–14; Mem., Our Mus Steering Gp, Paul Hamlyn Foundn, 2011–. FRSA 2008. *Publications:* articles in jls and book chapters on public engagement with univ. and public museums, touch and object handling in museums, and 3D scanning applications in museums; mus. catalogues on design hist. and decorative arts. *Recreations:* visiting places I think I won't like in order to confound my expectations, outdoor swimming. *Address:* Vice-Provost's Office, University College London, Gower Street, WC1E 6BT. *T:* (020) 7697 2825. *E:* sally.macdonald@ucl.ac.uk.

MACDONALD, Sharman; playwright, screenwriter and novelist; *b* 8 Feb. 1951; *d* of Joseph Henry Hosgood Macdonald and Janet Rowatt Williams; *m* 1976, Kevin William Knightley; one *s* one *d. Educ:* Hutchesons' Girls' GS, Glasgow; George Watson's Ladies' Coll., Edinburgh; Univ. of Edinburgh (MA 1972). *Theatre:* When I Was a Girl I Used to Scream and Shout, 1984; The Brave, 1988; When We Were Women, 1988; All Things Nice, 1990; Shades, 1992; The Winter Guest, 1995; Borders of Paradise, 1995; After Juliet, 1999; The Girl With Red Hair, 2005; Broken Hallelujah, 2005; *radio:* Sea Urchins, 1997 (Bronze Sony Drama Award; adapted for stage, 1998); Gladly My Cross-eyed Bear, 2000; Soft Fall the Sounds of Eden, 2004; *opera libretto:* Hey Persephone!, 1998; *films:* Wild Flowers, 1989; The Winter Guest, 1998; The Edge of Love, 2008. Most Promising Playwright Award, Evening Standard Awards, 1984. *Publications: plays:* When I Was a Girl I Used to Scream and Shout, 1984; When We Were Women, 1988; The Brave, 1988; All Things Nice, 1990; Shades, 1992; Sharman Macdonald Plays I, 1995; Sea Urchins, 1998; After Juliet, 1999; The Girl with Red Hair, 2005; *novels:* The Beast, 1986; Night Night, 1988. *Recreation:* body boarding. *Address:* c/o United Agents, 12–26 Lexington Street, W1F 0LE.

MacDONALD, Prof. (Simon) Gavin (George), FRSE; Professor of Physics, University of Dundee, 1973–88, now Emeritus; *b* 5 Sept. 1923; *s* of Simon MacDonald and Jean H. Thomson; *m* 1948, Eva Leonie Austerlitz; one *s* one *d. Educ:* George Heriot's Sch., Edinburgh; Edinburgh Univ. (MA (1st Cl. Hons) Maths and Nat. Phil); PhD (St Andrews). FIP 1958, FRSE 1972. Jun. Scientific Officer, RAE, Farnborough, 1943–46; Lectr, Univ. of St Andrews, 1948–57; Senior Lecturer: University Coll. of the West Indies, 1957–62; Univ. of St Andrews, 1962–67; Visiting Prof., Ohio Univ., 1963; University of Dundee: Sen. Lectr, then Prof., 1967–88; Dean of Science, 1970–73; Vice-Principal, 1974–79. Convener, Scottish Univs Council on Entrance, 1977–83 (Dep. Convener, 1973–77); Chm., Stats Cttee, UCCA, 1989–93 (Mem. Exec. Cttee, 1977–93; Chm., Technical Cttee, 1979–83; Dep. Chm., 1983–89). Chm., Bd of Dirs, Dundee Rep. Th., 1975–89; Chm., Fedn of Scottish Theatres, 1978–80. *Publications:* Problems and Solutions in General Physics, 1967; Physics for Biology and Premedical Students, 1970, 2nd edn 1975; Physics for the Life and Health Sciences, 1975; *novels*: Death is My Mistress, 2007; The Crime Committee, 2007; Publish and Be Dead, 2007; My Frail Blood, 2007; Swallow Them Up, 2008; Dishing the Dirt, 2008; A Family Affair, 2009; Playing Away, 2009; Bloody and Invisible Hand, 2009; The Truth in Masquerade, 2009; I Spy, I Die, 2010; Bow at a Venture, 2010; Passport to perdition, 2010; The Plaintive Numbers, 2010; The Root of All Evil, 2011; Pay the Price, 2011; The Forsyth Saga, 2011; Murder at the Museum, 2012; The Second Forsyth Saga, 2012; Mysteries of Space and Time, 2013; Murder of an Unknown, 2013; The Long Arm, 2014; A Further Forsyth Saga, 2014; Amorphous, 2014; Double Jeopardy, 2014; Rendezvous with Death, 2015; articles in physics jls. *Recreations:* bridge, golf, fiction writing. *Address:* 7A Windmill Road, St Andrews KY16 9JJ. *T:* (01334) 478014.

McDONALD, Sir Simon (Gerard), KCMG 2014 (CMG 2004); KCVO 2015; Permanent Under-Secretary of State, Foreign and Commonwealth Office and Head of the Diplomatic Service, since 2015; *b* 9 March 1961; *s* of James B. McDonald and Angela (*née* McDonald); *m* 1989, Hon. Olivia Mary, *o d* of Baron Wright of Richmond, *qv*; two *s* two *d*. *Educ:* De La Salle Coll. Grammar Sch., Salford; Pembroke Coll., Cambridge (MA). Joined FCO, 1982; Jedda, 1985; Riyadh, 1985–88; Bonn, 1988–90; FCO, 1990; Private Sec. to Perm. Under-Sec. of State, FCO, 1993–95; First Sec., Washington, 1995–98; Counsellor, Dep. Hd of Mission and Consul-Gen., Riyadh, 1998–2001; Principal Private Sec. to Sec. of State for Foreign and Commonwealth Affairs, 2001–03; Ambassador to Israel, 2003–06; Dir, Iraq, FCO, 2006–07; Foreign Policy Advr to Prime Minister and Hd, Overseas and Defence Secretariat, later Foreign and Defence Policy Secretariat, Cabinet Office, 2007–10; Ambassador to Germany, 2010–15. *Address:* c/o Foreign and Commonwealth Office, King Charles Street, SW1A 2AH. *E:* the6mcdonalds@yahoo.co.uk.

McDONALD, Stewart Malcolm; MP (SNP) Glasgow South, since 2015; *b* Glasgow, 24 Aug. 1986. *Educ:* Govan High Sch. Tour guide, Canary Is; work on campaigns and res. for MSPs. Mem., Transport Select Cttee, 2015–. *Address:* House of Commons, SW1A 0AA.

McDONALD, Stuart Campbell; MP (SNP) Cumbernauld, Kilsyth and Kirkintilloch East, since 2015; *b* Glasgow, 2 May 1978. *Educ:* Kilsyth Acad.; Univ. of Edinburgh (LLB Hons; DipLP 2001). Legal trainee, Simpson and Marwick, Solicitors, 2001–03; Solicitor, NHS Central Legal Office, 2003–05; Human Rights Solicitor, Immigration Adv. Service, 2005–09; Researcher, then Sen. Researcher, Scottish Parlt, 2009–13; Sen. Researcher and Hd of Information, Yes Scotland HQ, 2013–14; work for anti-racism charity, 2014–15. SNP spokesperson on immigration, asylum and border control, 2015–. Mem., Home Affairs Select Cttee, 2015–. *Address:* House of Commons, SW1A 0AA.

MACDONALD, Very Rev. Susan Elizabeth; Rector, Christ Church, Morningside, since 2007; Dean of Edinburgh, since 2012; *b* 11 July 1951. *Educ:* Edinburgh Theol Coll. Ordained deacon, 1996, priest, 1997; Asst Curate, St John's, Jedburgh, 1996–98; Priest, St Peter, Galashiels, 1998–2001; Priest-in-charge, Gordon Chapel, Fochabers, 2001–04; Mission 21 Co-ordinator, Dio. of Moray, Ross and Caithness, 2001–04; Mission and Ministry Officer, Dio. of Aberdeen and Orkney, 2005–07. Canon, St Andrew's Cath., Inverness, 2003–04. *Address:* 4 Morningside Road, Edinburgh EH10 4DD. *T:* (0131) 229 0090.

McDONALD, Sir Trevor, Kt 1999; OBE 1992; DL; newscaster, 1990–2005, presenter, News at Ten, ITN, 1992–99, and ITV News at Ten, 2001–05 and 2008; *b* Trinidad, 16 Aug. 1939; *m*; two *s* one *d*. Work on newspapers, radio and television, Trinidad, 1962–69; producer for Caribbean Service and World Service, BBC Radio, London, 1969–73; Independent Television News: reporter, 1973–78; sports corresp., 1978–80; diplomatic corresp., 1980–82; diplomatic corresp. and newscaster, 1982–87, Diplomatic Ed., 1987–89, Channel Four News; newscaster, News at 5.40, 1989–90; presenter: The ITV Evening News, 1999–2001; Tonight with Trevor McDonald, 1999–2007; presenter, TV series: The Secret Caribbean with Trevor McDonald, 2009; The Secret Mediterranean with Trevor McDonald, 2011; The Mighty Mississippi, 2012; The Mafia with Trevor McDonald, 2015. Trustee, Historic Royal Palaces, 2007–. Gov. ESU, 2000–06. DL Greater London, 2006. Chancellor, London South Bank (formerly S Bank) Univ., 1999–2012. Fellow, BAFTA, 2011. Newscaster of the Year, TRIC, 1993, 1997, 1999; Gold Medal, RTS (for outstanding contrib. to television news), 1998. *Publications:* Clive Lloyd: a biography, 1985; Vivian Richards: a biography, 1987; Queen and Commonwealth, 1989; Fortunate Circumstances (autobiog.), 1993; (ed) Trevor McDonald's Favourite Poems, 1997; Trevor McDonald's World of Poetry (anthology), 1999. *Address:* c/o ITN, 200 Gray's Inn Road, WC1X 8XZ.

MACDONALD, Valerie Frances; *see* Gooding, V. F.

McDONALD, Very Rev. William James Gilmour; Moderator of the General Assembly of the Church of Scotland, 1989–90; Parish Minister of Mayfield, Edinburgh, 1959–92; *b* 3 June 1924; *s* of Hugh Gilmour McDonald and Grace Kennedy Hunter; *m* 1952, Margaret Patricia Watson; one *s* two *d*. *Educ:* Daniel Stewart's College, Edinburgh; Univ. of Edinburgh (MA, BD); Univ. of Göttingen. Served Royal Artillery and Indian Artillery, 1943–46. Parish Minister, Limekilns, Fife, 1953–59. Convener, Assembly Council, 1984–87. Chaplain, Edinburgh Merchant Co., 1982–2002. Warrack Lectr, Edinburgh and Aberdeen Univs, 1992, Glasgow and St Andrews Univs, 1995; Turnbull Trust Preacher, Scots Ch, Melbourne, 1993. Hon. DD Edinburgh, 1987. *Publications:* Words Thought and Said: prayers and reflections, 2014. *Address:* 7 Blacket Place, Edinburgh EH9 1RN. *T:* (0131) 667 2100.

MACDONALD-DAVIES, Isobel Mary; Deputy Registrar General for England and Wales, 1994–2005 (Registrar General, April–June 2000); *b* 7 Feb. 1955; *d* of Henry Alexander Macdonald and Freda Matilda Macdonald; *m* 1977, Peter Davies; one *s* two *d*. *Educ:* Bar Convent Grammar Sch., York; St Andrews Univ. (BSc 1977). CStat 1993. Asst Statistician, OPCS, 1977–84; Statistician, Dept of Educn and OPCS, 1984–94. Mem. Mgt Exec. Bd, ONS, 2001–04. *Recreations:* family, music, reading.

McDONNELL, family name of **Earl of Antrim**.

McDONNELL, Dr Alasdair; MP (SDLP) Belfast South, since 2005; Leader, Social Democratic and Labour Party, since 2011; general medical practitioner, since 1979; *b* Cushendall, Co. Antrim, 1 Sept. 1949; *s* of Charles McDonnell and Margaret (*née* McIlhatton); *m* 1998, Olivia Nugent; two *s* two *d*. *Educ:* St MacNissi's Coll., Garron Tower; University Coll., Dublin Med. Sch. (MB, BCh, BAO 1974). Jun. hosp. med. posts, 1975–79. Mem. (SDLP) Belfast CC, 1977–2001; Dep. Mayor, Belfast, 1995–96. Mem. (SDLP) Belfast S, Northern Ireland Assembly, 1998–June 2015. Contested (SDLP) Belfast South, 1979, 1982, 1983, 1987, 1992, 1997, 2001. Dep. Leader, SDLP, 2004–10. *Address:* House of Commons, SW1A 0AA; 22 Derryvolgie Avenue, Belfast BT9 6FN.

McDONNELL, David Croft, CBE 2005; DL; Vice Lord-Lieutenant of Merseyside, since 2010; *b* 9 July 1943; *s* of late Leslie and Catherine McDonnell; *m* 1967, Marieke (*née* Bos); three *d*. *Educ:* Quarry Bank High School, Liverpool. FCA. Qualified Chartered Accountant, 1965; Partner, Thornton Baker, later Grant Thornton, 1972; Nat. Managing Partner, Grant Thornton, 1989–2001; Chief Exec. Worldwide, Grant Thornton, 2001–09. Chm. Bd of Trustees, Nat. Museums Liverpool (formerly Nat. Museums and Galls on Merseyside), 1995–2005; Chm., Arena and Convention Centre, Liverpool, 2010–. Pres., Univ. of Liverpool, 2007–. Deputy Chairman: Community Foundn for Lancashire, 2014–; Community Foundn for Merseyside, 2014– (Trustee, 2011–). DL 2003, High Sheriff, 2009–10, Merseyside. *Recreations:* sailing, motor racing (spectating), mountain walking. *Address:* Burn Lea, 18 The Serpentine, Grassendale, Liverpool L19 9DT. *Clubs:* Athenæum; Artists' (Liverpool).

McDONNELL, John Beresford William; QC 1984; DL; *b* 26 Dec. 1940; *s* of Beresford Conrad McDonnell and Charlotte Mary McDonnell (*née* Caldwell); *m* 1968, Susan Virginia, *d* of late Wing Comdr H. M. Styles, DSO and of Audrey (*née* Jorgensen, who *m* 2nd, 1947, Gen. Sir Charles Richardson, GCB, CBE, DSO); two *s* one *d*. *Educ:* City of London School (Carpenter Scholar); Balliol College, Oxford (Domus Scholar; Hon. Mention, Craven Scholarship, 1958; 1st Cl. Hon. Mods 1960; 2nd LitHum 1962, 2nd Jurisp 1964; MA); Harvard Law Sch. (LLM 1965). Called to the Bar, Inner Temple, 1968; Bencher, Lincoln's Inn, 1993; a Dep. High Ct Judge, 1993–. Pres., Oxford Union Soc. and Amer. Debating Tour, 1962; Harkness Fellowship, 1964–66; Amer. Political Science Assoc. Congressional Fellowship, 1965–66 (attached Rep. Frank Thompson Jr, NJ and Senator George McGovern, SDak); Cons. Research Dept, 1966–69; HM Diplomatic Service, 1969–71, First Sec., Asst Private Sec. to Sec. of State for Foreign and Commonwealth Affairs, 1970–71; practising at Chancery Bar, 1972–. Cllr, Lambeth Borough Council, 1968–69. Cons. Candidate for Grimsby, 1974–75. Trustee: Trireme Trust, 1980–; Bowes Mus., 2000–08; Auckland Castle Trust, 2011–. Gov., Inns of Ct Sch. of Law, 1995–2000. London Rowing Club Grand VIII, Henley, 1958. FRSA 1994. DL Durham, 2012. *Recreation:* sculling. *Address:* Mortham Tower, Rokeby DL12 9RZ. *T:* (01833) 626900; 17 Rutland Street, SW7 1EJ. *T:* (020) 7584 1498; 13 Old Square, Lincoln's Inn, WC2A 3UE. *Club:* Athenæum.

McDONNELL, John Martin; MP (Lab) Hayes and Harlington, since 1997; *b* 8 Sept. 1951; *s* of Robert and Elsie McDonnell; *m* 1st, 1971, Marilyn Jean Cooper (marr. diss. 1987); two *d*; 2nd, 1995, Cynthia Marie Pinto; one *s*. *Educ:* Great Yarmouth Grammar Sch.; Burnley Technical Coll.; Brunel Univ. (BSc); Birkbeck Coll., Univ. of London (MSc Politics and Sociology). Prodn worker, 1968–72; Research Assistant: NUM, 1976–78; TUC, 1978–82; full-time GLC Councillor, Hillingdon, Hayes and Harlington, 1982–86; Dep. Leader, GLC, 1984–85; Chm., GLC F and GP Cttee, 1982–85; Prin. Policy Advr, Camden Bor. Council, 1985–87; Secretary: Assoc. of London Authorities, 1987–95; Assoc. of London Govt, 1995–97. Editor, Labour Herald, 1985–88. Member: Gtr London Lab. Party Regl Exec. Cttee, 1982–87; for Gtr London, Lab. Party Nat. Policy Forum, 1993–; Chairman: Lab. Party Irish Soc.; Labour Repn Cttee. Advr, Guildford Four Relatives Campaign, 1984–; Chair, Britain and Ireland Human Rights Centre, 1992–; Founding Mem., Friends of Ireland, 1998–. Contested (Lab): Hampstead and Highgate, 1983; Hayes and Harlington, 1992. Shadow Chancellor of Exchequer, 2015–. Secretary: All Pty Britain-Kenya Gp of MPs, 1997–; All Pty Kurdish Gp, 1997–; All Pty Irish in Britain Parly Gp, 1999–; All Pty Gp on Endometriosis; Chair, All Party Punjabi Community in Britain Gp of MPs, 1999–; Secretary: Fire Brigades Union Parly Gp; Justice Unions Parly Gp; NUJ Parly Gp; PCS Trade Union Gp; Chair: Socialist Campaign Gp of MPs, 1998–; PCS Parly Gp; Labour Repn Cttee; Left Economists Adv. Panel; Co-ordinator, RMT Parly Gp. Housefather (pt-time) of family unit, children's home, 1972–87. Chairman: Hayes and Harlington Community Develt Forum, 1997–; Barra Hall Regeneration Cttee; Friends of Lake Farm; Friends of Minet Country Park; Mem., Hayes Horticultural Show Assoc.; Hon. Vice Pres., Hayes FC; Patron, Hayes CC. *Publications:* articles and pamphlets incl. contribs to Labour Herald, Briefing, Tribune, Campaign News. *Recreations:* gardening, reading, cycling, music, theatre, cinema, Wayfarer dinghy sailing, supporting Liverpool, Hayes and Yeading Football Clubs, football refereeing; generally fermenting the overthrow of capitalism. *Address:* House of Commons, SW1A 0AA; Beverley, Cedar Avenue, Hayes, Middx UB3 2NE. *Clubs:* London Irish, Blues West 14; Hillingdon Irish Society; St Claret's, Working Men's (Hayes); Hayes and Harlington Community Centre.

McDOUGALL, Hon. Barbara Jean; PC (Can.) 1984; OC 2001; Advisor, Aird & Berlis LLP, 2004; *b* Toronto, 12 Nov. 1937; *m* 2005, Adam Hartley Zimmerman, OC, FCA. *Educ:* Univ. of Toronto (BA Hons Econ. and Pol Sci. 1960). Chartered Financial Analyst, 1973. Worked in financial sector in Vancouver, Edmonton and Toronto; Exec. Dir, Canadian Council Financial Analysts, 1982–84; financial columnist, national magazines and on TV. MP (PC) St Paul's, Toronto, 1984–93; Minister of State: Finance, 1984–86; Privatisation, 1986–88; Minister Responsible for Status of Women, 1986–90 and for Regulatory Affairs, 1986–88; Minister, Employment and Immigration, 1988–91; Sec. of State for External Affairs, 1991–93; Chairperson, Cabinet Cttee on Foreign Affairs and Defence Policy, 1991–93; Member Cabinet Cttees: Planning and Priorities, 1991–93; Canadian Unity and Constitutional Negotiations, 1991–93. Chairperson: Morguard Real Estate Investment Trust, 1997–99; AT&T Canada Corp., 1996–99; Pres. and CEO, Canadian Inst. of Internat. Affairs, 1999–2004. Director: Corel Corp., 1998–2003; Bank of Nova Scotia, 1999–2008; Stelco, Inc., 1999–2006; Sun Media Corp., 1999–2001; Unique Design Solutions, Halifax, 2001–11; Imperial Tobacco Ltd, 2004–10. Dir, Inst. for Res. on Public Policy, 2004; Chm., Internat. Develt Res. Centre, 2008–12; Director: Canadian Opera Co., 1993–2007; Inter-Amer. Dialogue, 1994–2008; Internat. Crisis Gp, 1995–2006; Ind. Order of Foresters, 1998–2009. Mem., Internat. Adv. Bd, Council on Foreign Relns, NY, 1995–2002. Governor, York Univ., 1995–2006. Hon. LLD St Lawrence, 1992.

McDOUGALL, Douglas Christopher Patrick, OBE 2001; Chairman: Law Debenture Corporation plc, 2000–13 (Director, 1998–2000); Independent Investment Trust plc, since 2000; *b* 18 March 1944; *s* of late Patrick McDougall and Helen (*née* Anderson); *m* 1986, Hon. Carolyn Jane Griffiths, *d* of Baron Griffiths, MC, PC; two *d*. *Educ:* Edinburgh Acad.; Christ Church, Oxford (MA; Hon. Student 2008). Partner, 1969–89, Sen. Partner, 1989–99, Baillie Gifford & Co., Investment Managers, Edinburgh. Chairman: Eur. Investment Trust plc (formerly Foreign and Colonial Eurotrust plc), 1999–; 3i Bioscience Investment Trust plc, 2001–06 (Dep. Chm., 2000–01); Scottish Investment Trust plc, 2003– (Dir, 1998–); Dep. Chm., Sand Aire Investments plc, 1999–2003; Director: Provincial Insce plc, 1989–94; Baillie Gifford Japan Trust plc, 1989–99; Pacific Horizon Trust plc, 1993–; Stramongate Assets plc, 2003–11; Monks Investment Trust plc, 1999–; Herald Investment Trust plc, 2002–. Chairman: Institutional Fund Managers Assoc., 1994–96; Assoc. Investment Trust Cos, 1995–97; IMRO, 1997–2000 (Dir, 1988–2000). Mem., Investment Bd, Cambridge Univ., 2005–11. *Address:* Linplum House, Haddington, East Lothian EH41 4PE. *T:* (01620) 810242. *Clubs:* Brooks's; New (Edinburgh); Honourable Company of Edinburgh Golfers.

MacDOUGALL, Hugh; *see* MacDougall, R. H.

MACDOUGALL, Neil; Justice of Appeal, 1989–95, and Vice-President of the Court of Appeal, 1993–95, Supreme Court of Hong Kong; *b* 13 March 1932; *s* of Norman Macdougall and Gladys Clare Kennerly; *m* 1987, Helen Lui. *Educ:* Aquinas Coll., Perth, WA; Univ. of Western Australia (LLB 1954). Admitted Barrister and Solicitor of Supreme Court, WA, 1957, and of High Court of Australia, 1958; Solicitor of Supreme Court of England, 1976, and of Supreme Court of Hong Kong, 1977. Crown Counsel, Hong Kong, 1965; Director of Public Prosecutions, Hong Kong, 1978; a Judge of the High Court, Hong Kong, 1980; Comr, Supreme Court of Brunei, 1987; a Non-Permanent Judge, Court of Final Appeal, Hong Kong, 1997–2003. Chairman: Insider Dealing Tribunal, Hong Kong, 1987–88; Air Transport Licensing Authy, Hong Kong, 1992–95. *Recreations:* classical music, study of natural history, physical training. *Club:* Hong Kong (Hong Kong).

MACDOUGALL, Patrick Lorn, FCA; Chairman: Arlington Securities plc, 1999–2005; West Merchant Bank Ltd (formerly Standard Chartered Merchant Bank, then Chartered WestLB), 1989–98 (Chief Executive, 1985–97); *b* 21 June 1939; *s* of late James Archibald Macdougall, WS, and Valerie Jean Macdougall; *m* 1st, 1967, Alison Noel Offer (marr. diss. 1982); two *s*; 2nd, 1983, Bridget Margaret Young; three *d*. *Educ:* schools in Kenya; Millfield; University Coll., Oxford (MA Jurisprudence). FCA 1976. Called to the Bar, Inner Temple, 1962. Manager, N. M. Rothschild & Sons Ltd, 1967–70; Exec. Dir, Amex Bank (formerly Rothschild Intercontinental Bank Ltd), 1970–77, Chief Exec., 1977–78; Exec. Dir, Jardine Matheson Holdings Ltd, 1978–85; Gp Exec. Dir, Standard Chartered PLC, 1988–89. Member: Internat. Adv. Bd, Creditanstalt-Bankverein, Vienna, 1982–85; Mem., Sen. Adv. Council, Seagull Energy Inc., Houston, 1996–99; Director: Global Natural Resources Inc., USA, 1994–96; Nuclear Electric plc, 1994–96; Panmure Gordon & Co. Ltd, 1996–98 (Dep. Chm., 1997–98); National Provident Instn, 1997–99; Chm., China Private Equity Investment Hldgs Ltd, 2009–13. Dir and Trustee, SANE, 2001– (Chm., 2002–06). FRSA 1988. *Recreations:* opera, bridge, tough crosswords. *Address:* 110 Rivermead Court, SW6 3SB. *T:* (020) 7736 3506. *Clubs:* Athenæum, Hurlingham; Hong Kong, Shek O (Hong Kong).

MacDOUGALL, Prof. (Robert) Hugh, FRCSE, FRCR, FRCPE; Bute Professor of Medicine, Head, School of Medicine (formerly Bute Medical School), and Dean, Faculty of Medicine, University of St Andrews, 2002–14, now Emeritus Professor; Hon. Consultant Clinical Oncologist, Edinburgh Cancer Centre, Lothian University Hospitals, 1986–2014; *b* 9 Aug. 1949; *s* of Dr John David Bathgate MacDougall and Isabella Williamson MacDougall (*née* Craig); *m* 1977, Moira Jean Gray; one *s* two *d*. *Educ:* High Sch. of Dundee; Univ. of St Andrews (MB ChB 1972); Univ. of Edinburgh (DMRT 1979). FRCSE 1977; FRCR 1981; FRCPE 1996. House physician and house surgeon, Dundee Royal Infirmary, 1972–73; Registrar in Surgery, Aberdeen Royal Infirmary, and Hon. Clin. Tutor in Surgery, Univ. of Aberdeen, 1976–77; Lectr in Clin. Oncol., Univ. of Edinburgh, 1979–82; Consultant Radiotherapist and Oncologist, Tayside Health Bd, and Sen. Lectr, Univ. of Dundee, 1982–86; Sen. Lectr in Oncol., Univ. of Edinburgh, 1986–2002. Vis. Prof., Coll. of Medicine, Univ. of Edinburgh, 2014–. HM Inspector of Anatomy for Scotland 2014–. Lay Mem. Bd, Scottish Courts Service, 2014–. Gov., St Columba's Hospice, Edinburgh, 2012–. *Publications:* (jtly) Helpful Essential Links to Palliative Care, 1992, 5th edn 1999; contribs to internat. jls on neutron therapy. *Recreations:* reading, music, project management. *Address:* 21 GF Belgrave Crescent, Edinburgh EH4 3AJ. *Club:* New (Edinburgh).

McDOUGALL, Prof. Trevor John, FRS 2012; FAA; FInstP; Professor of Ocean Physics, School of Mathematics and Statistics, UNSW Australia (formerly University of New South Wales), since 2012; *b* Adelaide, 1 July 1952; *s* of Jack Ronald McDougall and Violet Holly McDougall; *m* 1978, Brita Kathryn Hack; one *s* two *d*. *Educ:* Unley High Sch., Adelaide; Univ. of Adelaide (BE 1st cl. Hons Mech. Engrg 1973); St John's Coll., Cambridge (PhD 1978). Queen's Fellow in Marine Sci., 1978–80, Res. Fellow, 1980–83, Res. Sch. of Earth Scis, ANU; CSIRO: Sen. Res. Scientist, subseq. Sen. Principal Res. Scientist, Div. of Oceanography, Hobart, 1983–96; Chief Res. Scientist, 1996–2006, CSIRO Fellow, 2007–11, Div. of Marine and Atmospheric Res. Chm., Scientific Cttee on Oceanic Res. and Internat. Assoc. of Phys. Scis of Ocean Wkg Gp 127 on Thermodynamics and Equation of State of Seawater, 2005–11. FAA 1997; Fellow, Aust. Meteorol and Oceanographic Soc., 2004; FInstP 2012. Frederick White Prize, Aust. Acad. of Scis, 1988; Centenary Medal (Australia), 2003; A. G. Huntsman Award, Bedford Instn of Oceanography, 2005; Anton Bruun Medal and Meml Lect., IOC, Paris, 2009; Prince Albert I Medal and Meml Lect., Internat. Assoc. for Phys. Scis of Oceans, 2011. *Recreations:* bush walking, cycling, boot camp. *Address:* School of Mathematics and Statistics, UNSW Australia, Sydney, NSW 2052, Australia. *T:* (2) 93853498, *Fax:* (2) 93857123. *E:* Trevor.McDougall@unsw.edu.au.

McDOWALL, Andrew Gordon; His Honour Judge McDowall; a Circuit Judge, since 1998; *b* 2 Sept. 1948; *s* of William Crocket McDowall and Margery Haswell McDowall (*née* Wilson); *m* 1976, Cecilia Clarke; one *s* one *d*. *Educ:* Glasgow Acad.; Queen's Coll., Oxford (Open Hastings Schol.; BCL, MA). Called to the Bar, Gray's Inn, 1972; in practice at the Bar, 1972–98; a Recorder, 1993–98; South Eastern Circuit. *Recreations:* reading, music (London Orpheus Choir), squash, paronomasia. *Address:* c/o 1 King's Bench Walk, Temple, EC4Y 7DB.

McDOWALL, Maj. Gen. David, CBE 2009 (MBE 1993); Chief Executive and Lieutenant Governor, Royal Hospital Chelsea, since 2014; *b* 16 Aug. 1954; *s* of David and Mary McDowall; *m* 1977, Valerie King; two *s* one *d*. *Educ:* Rephad Primary Sch.; Stranraer Acad.; RMA Sandhurst; RMCS. CO 7th Signal Regt, 1993–96; Comdr 1st Signal Bde, 2000–02; Signal Officer in Chief, 2002–04; Dir Comd and Battlespace Mgt (Army), 2004–07; GOC Second Div., 2007–09. FIET 2004; FBCS 2005. Chm., Army Football Assoc. *Recreations:* golf, bagpipes. *Address:* Royal Hospital Chelsea, Royal Hospital Road, SW3 4SR. *Clubs:* Army and Navy, Caledonian; New (Edinburgh).

MacDOWALL, Dr David William, MA, DPhil; FSA, FRAS; Chairman, Society for South Asian Studies (formerly Society for Afghan Studies), 1982–98 (Hon. Secretary, 1972–82; Hon. Fellow, 1999); Hon. Research Fellow, Centre for Research in East Roman Studies, University of Warwick, since 1993; *b* 2 April 1930; *o s* of late William MacDowall and Lilian May MacDowall (*née* Clarkson); *m* 1962, Mione Beryl, *yr d* of late Ernest Harold Lashmar and Dora Lashmar; two *d*. *Educ:* Liverpool Inst.; Corpus Christi Coll., Oxford; British Sch. at Rome. Hugh Oldham Scholar 1947, Pelham Student in Roman History 1951; Barclay Head Prize for Ancient Numismatics, 1953 and 1956. 2nd Lieut Royal Signals, 1952. Asst Principal, Min. of Works, 1955; Asst Keeper, Dept of Coins and Medals, British Museum, 1956; Principal, Min. of Educn, 1960; Principal, Univ. Grants Cttee, 1965; Asst Sec. 1970; Master of Univ. Coll., Durham, 1973; Hon. Lectr in Classics and in Oriental Studies, Univ. of Durham, 1975; Dir, Polytechnic of N London, 1980–85. Hon. Treasurer, Royal Numismatic Soc., 1966–73; Vice-Pres., British Archaeol Assoc., 1993–95 (Hon. Treas., 1989–93); Pres., Royal Asiatic Soc., 1994–97 (Vice-Pres., 1993–94, 1997–2000). Mem. Governing Body, SOAS, 1990–97. Trustee, UK Trust, Indian Nat. Trust for Architectl and Cultural Heritage, 1994–2009. Corresponding Member: Istituto Italiano per il Medio ed Estremo Oriente, 1987; Amer. Numismatic Soc., 1991. Hon. Fellow, Asiatic Soc. of Mumbai, 2004. *Publications:* Coin Collections, their preservation, classification and presentation, 1978; The Western Coinages of Nero, 1979; (contrib.) Mithraic Studies, 1975; (contrib.) The Archaeology of Afghanistan, 1978; (ed jtly) Indian Numismatics: history, art and culture, 1992; (jtly) The Roman Coins, Republic and Empire up to Nerva, in the Provinciaal Museum G. M. Kam at Nijmegen, 1992; (ed jtly) Foreign Coins Found in the Indian Sub-Continent, 2003; (jtly) A Catalogue of Coins from the Excavations at Bir-kot-Ghwandai 1984–1992, 2004; articles in Numismatic Chron., Jl Numismatic Soc. India, Schweizer Münzblätter, Acta Numismatica, S Asian Archaeology, Afghan Studies, S Asian Studies, Numismatic Digest, Res Orientales, etc. *Recreations:* travel, antiquities, photography, natural history, gardening, genealogy. *Address:* High Trees, 106 Whitedown Lane, Alton, Hants GU34 1QR. *Club:* Athenæum.

McDOWALL, Keith Desmond, CBE 1988; Chairman, Keith McDowall Associates, 1988–2001; *b* 3 Oct. 1929; *s* of William Charteris McDowall and Edna Florence McDowall; *m* 1st, 1957, Shirley Margaret Russell Astbury (marr. diss. 1985); two *d*; 2nd, 1988, Brenda Dean (*see* Baroness Dean of Thornton-le-Fylde). *Educ:* Heath Clark Sch., Croydon, Surrey. Served RAF, National Service, 1947–49. South London Press, 1947–55; Daily Mail, 1955–67: Indust. Corresp., 1958; Indust. Editor, 1961–67; Man. Dir, Inca Construction (UK) Co. Ltd, 1967–69; Govt Information Service: successively Chief Inf. Officer, DEA, BoT, Min. of Housing and Local Govt, DoE, and Home Office, 1969–72; Dir of Inf., NI Office, 1972–74; Dir of Inf., Dept of Employment, 1974–78; Man. Dir Public Affairs, British Shipbuilders, 1978–80. Dir, Govan Shipbuilders Ltd, 1978–80. Dir of Information, 1981–86, Dep. Dir Gen., 1986–88, CBI. Chm., Kiss FM Radio, 1990–92 (Chm., steering cttee, 1989–90). Freeman, City of London, 1997; Liveryman, Shipwrights' Co., 1998–. *Publications:* articles in newspapers and various pubns. *Recreations:* classic cars, cricket, jazz, mingling. *Address:* 2 Malvern Terrace, N1 1HR. *Clubs:* Reform, MCC; Royal Cornwall Yacht (Falmouth).

MacDOWALL, Simon Charles, CD 1985; self-employed communications consultant and author, since 2013; *b* 18 July 1956; *s* of Joseph and Oonagh MacDowall; *m* 1981, Gabriele Kuzaj (marr. diss. 2010); one *s* one *d*; partner, Caroline Way. *Educ:* Collège Militaire Royal, St Jean, Quebec (BA 1978). Royal Canadian Dragoons, 1978–87; Canadian Army: Public Affairs Officer, 1987–91; Regl Communications, NW Canada, 1991–93; NATO: Press Officer, SHAPE, Belgium and Bosnia, 1993–94; UN Spokesman, Sarajevo, 1994; Chief of Press and Inf., Allied Forces NW Europe, 1995–99; Communications Director: DSS, 1999–2001; DWP, 2001–06; Dir Gen., Media and Commns, MoD, 2006–07; Director: Communications and Mktg, HMRC, 2007–11; Emic Communications, 2011–13. *Publications:* Late Roman Infantryman, 1994; Late Roman Cavalryman, 1995; Germanic Warrior, 1996; Battle of Adrianople, 2001; Battle of the Catalaunian Fields, 2015. *Recreations:* travel, running, cycling, scuba diving, good food and wine, painting historical figurines. *Clubs:* Reform, Frontline.

McDOWALL, Stuart, CBE 1984; Chairman, Fife Healthcare NHS Trust, 1994–96; economic consultant; Senior Lecturer in Economics, University of St Andrews, 1967–91; *b* 19 April 1926; *s* of Robert McDowall and Gertrude Mary Collister; *m* 1951, Margaret Burnside Woods Gyle; three *s*. *Educ:* Liverpool Institute; St Andrews University (MA Hons 1950). Personnel Manager, Michael Nairn & Co., 1955–61; Lectr in Econs, St Andrews Univ., 1961–67; Master, United Coll. of St Salvator and St Leonard, 1976–80. Dep. Chm., Central Arbitration Cttee, 1976–96; Local Govt Boundary Comr for Scotland, 1983–99; Member: Monopolies and Mergers Commn, 1985–89; Restrictive Practices Court, 1993–96. Econ. Consultant to UN in Saudi Arabia, 1985–89. Sec., Scottish Economic Soc., 1970–76. *Publications:* (with P. R. Draper) Trade Adjustment and the British Jute Industry, 1978; (with H. M. Begg) Industrial Performance and Prospects in Areas Affected by Oil Developments, 1981; articles on industrial economics and regional economics. *Recreations:* golf, hill walking. *Address:* 10 Woodburn Terrace, St Andrews, Fife KY16 8BA. *T:* (01334) 473247. *Club:* Royal and Ancient Golf (St Andrews).

McDOWELL, Alexander Blair, RDI 2006; production designer, since 1980; *b* 11 April 1955; *s* of late (Hamilton) Blair McDowell and Pamela McDowell (*née* Howe); *m* 1995, Kirsten Everberg; one *s* one *d*. *Educ:* Downs Sch., Colwall; Bootham Sch., York; Central Sch. of Art, London. Graphic Designer and owner, Rocking Russian Design, 1977–86; production designer: *films* designed include: The Crow, 1994; Fear and Loathing in Las Vegas, 1998; Fight Club, 1999; Minority Report, 2002; The Terminal, 2004; Charlie and the Chocolate Factory, 2005; Corpse Bride, 2005; Breaking and Entering, 2006; Watchmen, 2009. Adv. Bd, University Art Mus., Long Beach, CA, 2005–. Vis. Artist, MIT Media Lab, 2006. Founder, Matter Art and Science, 2002–. Founder and Co-Dir, 5D Immersive Design Conference, 2008–. *Recreations:* art, reading, food, walking. *Address:* 2288 Earl Street, Los Angeles, CA 90039, USA. *E:* alexmcdowell1@mac.com.

See also J. B. McDowell.

McDOWELL, Sir Eric (Wallace), Kt 1990; CBE 1982; FCA; Partner, Wilson Hennessey & Crawford, later (following merger in 1973) Deloitte, Haskins & Sells, 1952–85 (Senior Partner, Belfast, 1980–85); *b* 7 June 1925; *s* of Martin Wallace McDowell and Edith Florence (*née* Hillock); *m* 1954, Helen Lilian (*née* Montgomery); one *s* two *d*. *Educ:* Royal Belfast Academical Instn. FCA 1957. Served War, 1943–46. Student Chartered Accountant, 1942, qualified 1948. Chm., Capita Mgt Consultants Ltd, 1992–98; Director: NI Transport Holding Co., 1971–74; Spence Bryson Ltd, 1986–89; TSB Northern Ireland, 1986–92; AIB Group Northern Ireland, 1992–97; Shepherd Ltd, 1992–2004. Member: Council, Inst. of Chartered Accountants in Ireland, 1968–77 (Pres., 1974–75); Industries Develt Adv. Cttee, 1971–82 (Chm., 1978–82); Adv. Cttee of NI Central Investment Fund for Charities, 1975–98 (Chm., 1980–98); NI Econ. Council, 1977–83; Industrial Develt Bd for NI, 1982–91 (Chm., 1986–91); Exec. Cttee, Relate: Marriage Guidance, NI, 1981–2002 (Chm., 1992–96); Nat. Exec. Cttee, Relate, 1992–2000; Broadcasting Council for NI, 1983–86; Financial Reporting Review Panel, 1990–94; Senate, QUB, 1993–2001. Trustee, Presbyterian Church in Ireland, 1983–2012. Treas., Abbeyfield Belfast Soc., 1986–99. Governor, Royal Belfast Academical Instn, 1959–2012 (Chm. of Governors, 1977–86); President: Belfast Old Instonians Assoc., 1993–94; Confedn of Ulster Socs, 1989–98. Hon. DSc(Econ) QUB, 1989. *Recreations:* music, drama, foreign travel. *Address:* Apt 7, Newforge Manor, 11 Newforge Lane, Belfast BT9 5NT. *T:* (028) 9066 8771. *Clubs:* Royal Over-Seas League; Ulster Reform (Belfast).

McDOWELL, Rt Rev. (Francis) John; *see* Clogher, Bishop of.

McDOWELL, Prof. Gary Linn, PhD; FRHistS; Tyler Haynes Professor of Leadership Studies, Political Science and Law, University of Richmond, USA, since 2005 (Tyler Haynes Professor of Leadership Studies and Political Science, 2003–05); *b* 4 June 1949; *s* of Samuel Earl McDowell and Violet Marie McDowell (*née* Harris); *m* 1990, Brenda Jo Evans. *Educ:* Univ. of S Florida (BA 1972); Memphis State Univ. (MA 1974); Univ. of Chicago (AM 1978); Univ. of Virginia (PhD 1979). Social Studies Teacher, Dunedin Jun. High Sch., 1972–73; Asst Prof. of Political Sci., Dickinson Coll., 1979–83; Liberal Arts Fellow, Harvard Law Sch., 1981–82; Asst Prof., 1983–85, Associate Prof., 1985–86, of Political Sci., Tulane Univ.; Dir, Office of the Bicentennial of the Constitution, Nat. Endowment for the Humanities, 1984–85; Associate Dir of Public Affairs, US Dept of Justice, 1985–87; Resident Schol., Center for Judicial Studies, 1987–88; Fellow, Woodrow Wilson Internat. Center for Scholars, 1987–88; Vice Pres., Nat. Legal Center for Public Interest, 1988–89; Bradley Vis. Schol., Harvard Law Sch., 1990–92; Lectr, Harvard Univ., 1992; Dir, Inst. of US Studies, 1992–2003, and Prof. of American Studies, 1993–2003, Univ. of London. Fellow, Nat. Endowment for the Humanities, 2007–08. Mem., Fulbright Commn, 1997–2003. Member: Bd, Landmark Legal Foundn, 1992–; Bd of Visitors, Pepperdine Univ. Sch. of Public Policy, 2000–04; Soc. of Scholars, James Madison Prog. in American Ideals and Instns, Princeton Univ., 2002–. FRHistS 1996. FRSA. Dist. Educator Award, Univ. of Richmond, 2005. *Publications:* (ed jtly and contrib.) The American Founding, 1981; (ed jtly and contrib.) Taking the Constitution Seriously, 1981; Equity and the Constitution, 1982; Curbing the Courts, 1988; (jtly) Justice *vs* Law, 1993; (ed jtly and contrib.) Our Peculiar Security, 1993; (ed jtly and contrib.) Reason and Republicanism, 1997; (ed jtly) Juvenile Delinquency in the United States and the United Kingdom, 1999; (ed jtly and contrib.) America and Enlightenment Constitutionalism, 2006; (ed jtly and contrib.) Lincoln's Legacy of Leadership, 2010; The Language of Law and the Foundations of American Constitutionalism, 2010; (ed jtly) Executive Power in Theory and Practice, 2012; numerous contribs to learned jls and other publications. *Recreations:* walking, reading, bluegrass music, martinis, mint juleps and Cuban cigars, playing fetch with incomparable yellow labrador, Travis. *Address:* Jepson School of Leadership Studies, University of Richmond, Richmond, VA 23173, USA. *T:* (804) 2876085. *Club:* Reform.

McDOWELL, Rt Rev. John; *see* McDowell, Rt Rev. F. J.

McDOWELL, Prof. John Henry, FBA 1983; FAAAS; Distinguished University Professor of Philosophy, University of Pittsburgh, since 2009 (Professor of Philosophy, 1986–88; University Professor of Philosophy, 1988–2009); *b* 7 March 1942; *s* of Sir Henry McDowell, KBE and Norah, *d* of Walter Slade Douthwaite; *m* 1977, Andrea Lee Lehrke. *Educ:* St John's College, Johannesburg; University College of Rhodesia and Nyasaland; New College, Oxford (MA); BA London. FAAAS 1993. Fellow and Praelector in Philosophy, UC, Oxford, 1966–86, Emeritus Fellow, 1988, Hon. Fellow, 2007; Univ. Lectr (CUF), Oxford Univ., 1967–86. James C. Loeb Fellow in Classical Philosophy, Harvard Univ., 1969; Visiting Professor: Univ. of Michigan, 1975; Univ. of California, Los Angeles, 1977; Univ. of Minnesota, 1982; Jadavpur Univ., Calcutta, 1983; John Locke Lectr, Oxford Univ., 1991. Sen. Fellow, Council of Humanities, Princeton Univ., 1984. Hon. DHumLit Chicago, 2008; Hon. DLit UCD, 2013. Dist. Achievement Award, Andrew W. Mellon Foundn, 2011. *Publications:* Plato, Theaetetus (trans. with notes), 1973; (ed with Gareth Evans) Truth and Meaning, 1976; (ed) Gareth Evans, The Varieties of Reference, 1982; (ed with Philip Pettit) Subject, Thought, and Context, 1986; Mind and World, 1994; Mind, Value, and Reality (collected articles), 1998; Meaning, Knowledge, and Reality (collected articles), 1998; Having the World in View (collected articles), 2009; The Engaged Intellect (collected articles), 2009; articles in jls and anthologies. *Recreations:* reading, music, gardening. *Address:* c/o Department of Philosophy, University of Pittsburgh, Pittsburgh, PA 15260, USA. *T:* (412) 6245792.

McDOWELL, Jonathan Bruce, RIBA; architect; Partner, McDowell+Benedetti, since 1996; Director, McDowell+Benedetti Ltd, since 1998; *b* 18 March 1957; *s* of late Hamilton Blair McDowell and Pamela (*née* Howe); *m* 2001, Rebecca Wells; two *d*. *Educ:* The Downs Sch.; Bootham Sch.; Downing Coll., Cambridge (MA, DipArch); Graduate Sch. of Design, Harvard Univ. RIBA 1985. Associate, Munkenbeck & Marshall, 1986–90; Principal, Jonathan McDowell Architects, 1991–96; with Renato Benedetti, formed McDowell+Benedetti, 1996; main projects include: Oliver's Wharf Penthouse, Wapping, 1996; Assoc. of Photographers, New Gall. and HQ, London, 1998; Nursing Home for Merchant Taylors' Co., Lewisham, 2002; Suncourt Hse, 2002; Springboard Centre, Stokesley, 2005; Castleford Bridge, 2008; JCB Uttoxeter Masterplan, 2008; Claremont Fan Court Sch., Esher, 2009–; Hull Footbridge, 2011. Member: CABE Enabling Panel, 2001–11; Hackney Design Review Panel, 2007–; Yorks and Humber Reg. Design Review Panel, 2010–. FRSA 1999. *Recreations:* Balinese, Javanese and contemporary gamelan. *Address:* (office) 34–35 Hatton Garden, EC1N 8DX.

See also A. B. McDowell.

McDOWELL, Kathryn Alexandra, CBE 2011; DL; Managing Director, London Symphony Orchestra, since 2005; *b* 19 Dec. 1959; *d* of late John McDowell and (Kathleen) Avril McDowell; *m* 1997, Ian Charles Stewart Ritchie, *qv*. *Educ:* Belfast High Sch.; Univ. of Edinburgh (BMus 1982); Stranmillis Coll. of Education (PGCE 1983). LTCL 1980, Hon. FTCL 1996; ARCM 1981; Hon. RCM 1999. Marketing and Educn Assistant, WNO, 1984–85; Develt Manager, Scottish Chamber Orch., 1985–89; Dep. Gen. Manager, Ulster Orch., 1989–92; Music Officer, Arts Council, 1992–94; Music Dir, Arts Council of England, 1994–99; Chief Exec., Wales Millennium Centre, 1999–2001; Dir, City of London Festival, 2001–05. Member, Council: Royal Philharmonic Soc., 1999–2008; St Paul's Cathedral, 2008–. Governor, GSMD, 2008–. Hon. FGS 2013. DL Greater London, 2009. *Recreations:* tennis, walking, travel. *Address:* London Symphony Orchestra, Barbican Centre, Silk Street, EC2Y 8DS.

McDOWELL, Prof. Linda Margaret, PhD, DLitt; FBA 2008; Professor of Human Geography, University of Oxford, and Professorial Fellow, St John's College, Oxford, since 2004; *b* 1 Jan. 1949; *d* of Frederick Herbert Leigh and Olive Morgan Leigh (*née* Nicholson); *m* 1972, Christopher James McDowell; one *s* one *d*. *Educ:* Newnham Coll., Cambridge (BA Hons 1971); Bartlett Sch., University Coll. London (MPhil 1973; PhD 1986); Univ. of Oxford (DLitt 2011). Res. Fellow, Centre for Res. in Soc. Scis, Univ. of Kent, Canterbury, 1973–76; Res. Officer, Inst. of Community Studies, London, 1976–78; Open University: Lectr, then Sen. Lectr in Geog., 1978–92; Dep. Dean, Soc. Scis Faculty, 1989–92; University of Cambridge: Univ. Lectr in Geog., 1992–99; Fellow and Coll. Lectr, 1992–99, Vice Principal, 1997–99, Newnham Coll.; Prof. of Human Geog., LSE, 1999–2000; Prof. of Econ. Geog., UCL, 2000–04. Visiting Lecturer: Univ. of Southampton, 1976; Univ. of Kent, 1978; UCLA, 1990; UCL, 1991. FAcSS (AcSS 2001). Hon. Fellow, Gender Inst., LSE, 2000–. Back Award, 2001, Victoria Medal, 2008, RGS. *Publications:* (with D. Morgan) Patterns of Residence, 1979; (ed jtly) Urban Change and Conflict, 1981; (ed jtly) City, Economy and Society, 1981; (ed jtly) Geography and Gender, 1984; (ed jtly) Divided Nation: social and cultural change in Britain, 1989; (ed jtly) The Changing Social Structure, 1989; (with J. Allen) Landlords and Property, 1989; (jtly) The Transformation of Britain, 1989; (ed jtly) Defining Women: social institutions and gender divisions, 1992; Capital Culture: gender at work in the City, 1997; Undoing Place?, 1997; (ed jtly) Space, Gender, Knowledge, 1997; (ed jtly) A Feminist Glossary of Human Geography, 1999; Gender, Identity and Place, 1999; Redundant Masculinities?: employment change and white working class youth, 2003; Hard Labour: the forgotten voices of Latvian 'volunteer' workers, 2005; (ed jtly) Gender Divisions and Working Time in the New Economy, 2005; Working Bodies, 2009; (ed jtly) Sage Handbook of Qualitative Research in Human Geography, 2010; (ed jtly) A Companion to Economic Geography, 2011; Working Lives, 2013; Migrant Women's Voices, 2015; contrib. numerous book chapters and to learned jls. *Recreations:* cities, cycling, contemporary fiction, gardening. *Address:* School of Geography and the Environment, University of Oxford, South Parks Road, Oxford OX1 3QY. *T:* (01865) 275843. *E:* linda.mcdowell@geog.ox.ac.uk; St John's College, Oxford OX1 3JP. *T:* (01865) 277300.

McDOWELL, Malcolm, (Malcolm Taylor); actor; *b* 13 June 1943; *m* 1992, Kelley Kuhr; two *s*; one *s* one *d* from former marriage. *Educ:* Leeds. *Stage:* RSC Stratford, 1965–66; Entertaining Mr Sloane, Royal Court, 1975; Look Back in Anger, NY, 1980; In Celebration, NY, 1984; Holiday, Old Vic, 1987; Another Time, NY, 1993; *films:* If, 1969; Figures in a Landscape, 1970; The Raging Moon, 1971; A Clockwork Orange, 1971; O Lucky Man, 1973; Royal Flash, 1975; Aces High, 1976; Voyage of the Damned, 1977; Caligula, 1977; The Passage, 1978; Time After Time, 1979; Cat People, 1981; Blue Thunder, 1983; Get Crazy, 1983; Britannia Hospital, 1984; Gulag, 1985; Cross Creek, 1985; Sunset, 1988; Assassin of the Tsar, 1991; Milk Money, 1993; Star Trek Generations, 1994; Tank Girl, 1995; Exquisite Tenderness, 1995; Mr Magoo, 1998; Gangster No 1, 2000; Just Visiting, 2002; I Spy, 2003; The Company, 2004; Rag Tale, 2005; Never Apologise, 2008; Bolt, 2008; Easy A, 2010; The Artist, 2011; Sanitarium, 2013; *television:* Our Friends in the North, 1996; Entourage (series), 2005–11; Heroes (series), 2007–08; Franklin & Bash (series), 2011–14. *Address:* c/o Markham, Froggatt and Irwin, 4 Windmill Street, W1T 2HZ.

McDOWELL, Michelle Janet, MBE 2010; FREng, FICE; Chair, Civil and Structural Engineering, since 2004 and Chair, London Studio, since 2011, BDP; *b* Coleraine, NI, 6 April 1963; *d* of Ronald McDowell and Doris McDowell; partner, Jason Mark Fox; one *s*. *Educ:* Coleraine High Sch.; Bristol Univ. (BSc Hons Civil Engrg 1984). MICE 1990, FICE 1999. Engineer: W. S. Atkins & Partners, 1984–87; John Laing Construction, 1988; Associate, Whitby, Bird & Partners, 1989–97; BDP: Associate Dir, 1997–2003; Company Dir, 2003–; Exec. Bd, 2005–. Vice Pres., ICE, 2000; Fellow, ACE, 1998 (Chm., 2010); FREng 2011. FRSA 2001. Hon. DEng Bristol, 2012. *Recreations:* travel, cooking, piano playing. *Address:* BDP, 16 Brewhouse Yard, EC1V 4LJ. *T:* (020) 7812 8000. *E:* michellejmcdowell@gmail.com.

McDOWELL, Paul Duncan; criminal justice, public sector and charity consultant, since 2015; *b* Luton, 15 Aug. 1962; *s* of Thomas Morris McDowell and Christine Anne McDowell (*née* Moore, now Burgess); *m* 2001, Janine Marcelle Morris; two *s* one *d*. *Educ:* Queensbury Sch., Dunstable; Univ. of Central England (Dip. Criminal Justice, Policy and Practice 1998); Fitzwilliam Coll., Cambridge (MSt Applied Criminology and Mgt 2003). Served HMP Gartree, Prison Service Coll., HMP Wellingborough, HMP Woodhill, HM YOI Stoke Heath, 1990–2000; Prison Minister's Private Office, Home Office, 2000–01; Dep. Gov., HM YOI Feltham, 2001–03; Governor: HMP Coldingley, 2003–06; HMP Brixton, 2006–09; CEO, Nacro, 2009–14; HM Chief Inspector of Probation, 2014–15. Member: Enquiry Panel, Community or Custody, Make Justice Work Nat. Enquiry, 2009–12; Adv. Gp, Young Offender Acad., 2009–13; Adv. Gp, Impetus Trust, 2010–11. Trustee, Prison Radio Assoc., 2010–; Mem., Bd of Trustees, Eisenhower Foundn, Washington, DC, 2010–. FRSA. DUniv Birmingham City, 2015. *Recreations:* supporting Luton Town Football Club, attending Glastonbury Festival, collecting music, sport, travel, family. *Club:* Burhill Golf.

McDOWELL, Stanley; Town Clerk and Chief Executive, Belfast City Council, 1989–92; *b* 14 June 1941; *s* of William McDowell and Annie Storey; *m* 1966, Charlotte Elizabeth Stockdale; three *d*. *Educ:* Royal Belfast Academical Instn; Queen's Univ. of Belfast (BSc Econ). FCIS. Belfast City and Dist Water Comrs, 1959–70; Asst Sec. (Actg), Antrim County Council, 1971–73; Roads Service Divl Finance Officer, DoE (NI), 1973–79; Belfast City Council, 1979–92; Asst Town Clerk (Admin), 1979–89. Non-exec. Dir, Ulster Community and Hosps Trust, 1998–2002 (Chm., Audit Cttee, 1998–2002); Chm., Belfast Abbeyfield Soc. Ltd, 2011– (Dep. Chm., 2002–11). *Address:* 209 Bangor Road, Holywood, N Ireland BT18 0JG. *T:* (028) 9042 5132.

MACDUFF, Earl of; *see* Earl of Southesk.

MacDUFF, Hon. Sir Alistair (Geoffrey), Kt 2008; a Judge of the High Court of Justice, Queen's Bench Division, 2008–15; *b* 26 May 1945; *s* of late Alexander MacDonald MacDuff and Iris Emma Jarvis (*née* Gardner); *m* 1st, 1969, Susan Christine Kitchener (*d* 1991); two *d*; 2nd, 1993, Katherine Anne Buckley; one *s* one *d*. *Educ:* Ecclesfield Grammar Sch., Sheffield; LSE (LLB 1965); Sheffield Univ. (LLM 1967). Called to the Bar, Lincoln's Inn, 1969, Bencher, 2003. QC 1993; Asst Recorder, 1983–87; Recorder, 1987–97; Circuit Judge, 1997–2008; Sen. Circuit Judge, 2002–08; Designated Civil Judge, Birmingham Gp, 2000–08. *Recreations:* theatre, opera, wine, Rugby football. *Clubs:* East India; Painswick Rugby Football.

McDUFF, Prof. (Margaret) Dusa, PhD; FRS 1994; Helen Lyttle Kimmel '42 Chair of Mathematics, Barnard College, Columbia University, since 2008; *b* 18 Oct. 1945; *d* of Conrad Hal Waddington and Margaret Justin (*née* Blanco White); *m* 1st, 1968, David William McDuff (marr. diss. 1978); one *d*; 2nd, 1984, John Willard Milnor; one *s*. *Educ:* Univ. of Edinburgh (BSc Hons); Girton Coll., Cambridge (PhD 1971). Lecturer: Univ. of York, 1972–76; Univ. of Warwick, 1976–78; Asst Prof., 1978–80, Associate Prof., 1980–84, Prof. of Maths, 1984–98, Dist. Prof. of Maths, 1998–2008, SUNY at Stony Brook. Asst Prof., MIT, 1974–75; Mem., Inst. for Advanced Study, Princeton, 1976 and 1977; Vis. Prof., Univ. of Calif, Berkeley, 1993. Fellow, Amer. Acad. of Arts and Scis, 1995; Mem., NAS, USA, 1999. Hon. Mem., LMS, 2007. Corresp. Mem., RSE, 2008. Hon. DSc: Edinburgh, 1997; York, 2000; Louis Pasteur, Strasbourg, 2008. *Publications:* (with D. Salamon): J-Holomorphic Curves and Quantum Cohomology, 1994; Introduction to Symplectic Topology, 1995; J-Holomorphic Curves and Symplectic Topology, 2004. *Recreations:* chamber music, reading, walking. *Address:* Mathematics Department, Columbia University, 2990 Broadway, New York, NY 10027, USA.

MACE, Dr (Alan) Christopher (Hugh), CBE 1991; Director, Defence Support Review, 2010–11, and Director, Defence Transformation, 2011, Ministry of Defence; Senior Responsible Owner, Defence Training Systems and Infrastructure Change Programme, 2010–11; *b* 17 Sept. 1953; *s* of late Maurice William Mace and of Josephine Mary Mace; *m* 1979, Sian Avery; one *s* one *d*. *Educ:* Weymouth Grammar Sch.; Univ. of Exeter (BSc 1975; PhD 1981). Ministry of Defence, 1979–99: rocketry and combustion res., 1979–86; novel weapon res., 1986–88; Asst Dir, Personnel, 1988–89; Project Manager procuring Army equipt, 1990–91; Director: Res. and Internat. Collaboration, 1991–94; Finance and Secretariat, Weapons and Electronic Systems Procurement, 1994–96; on secondment as Dir, Business Develt, Avery Berkel, 1996–97; Project Dir implementing resource accounting and planning systems, MoD, 1997–99; Dep. Dir Gen. (Ops), Immigration and Nationality Directorate, Home Office, 1999–2003; Chief Inspector, Immigration Service, 2000–03; Dir Gen., Logistics Resources, Defence Logistics Orgn, MoD, 2003–07; COS, Defence Equipment and Support, MoD, 2007; Dir (formerly Dir Gen.) Ops, Sci. and Technol., MoD, 2007–10. FRSA 2000. *Publications:* res. papers on combustion. *Recreations:* music, walking.

MACE, Andrew Stephen; Senior UK Government Relations Officer, Bill & Melinda Gates Foundation, since 2014; *b* Woolwich, 31 Dec. 1973; *s* of Raymond and Pauline Mace. *Educ:* Chislehurst and Sidcup Grammar Sch.; Emmanuel Coll., Cambridge (BA 1995). Entered FCO, 1995; Asst Desk Officer, EU Dept (Internal), FCO, 1995–97; Mem., UK Representation to EU, 1997–99; Pol Sec., Copenhagen, 1999–2003; Hd of Pol Team, UN Dept, 2003–05, Dep. Hd, Conflict Issues Gp, 2005–07, FCO; Pol Counsellor, Monrovia, 2007–08; Ambassador to Cambodia, 2008–11; Hd of Sudan Unit, FCO, 2011–14. *Address:* Bill & Melinda Gates Foundation, 62 Buckingham Gate, SW1E 6AJ.

MACE, Brian Anthony; Director, Revenue Policy: Employment Initiatives, Board of Inland Revenue, 2002–04; *b* 9 Sept. 1948; *s* of late Edward Laurence Mace and Olive (*née* Bennett); *m* 1973, Anne Margaret Cornford. *Educ:* Maidstone Grammar Sch.; Gonville and Caius Coll., Cambridge (MA Mathematics). Admin. trainee, Bd of Inland Revenue, 1971–73; seconded to Secretariat, Inflation Accounting Cttee, 1974–75; Inland Revenue: Principal, 1975–82; Asst Sec., 1982–90; Under Sec., 1990–2004; Dir, Savings and Investment Div., 1990–98, and Capital and Valuation Div., 1995–98; Dir, Personal Tax, 1998–2000; Dir, Study of Personal Tax, 2000–02. Mem., Tax Law Rev. Cttee, 2007–. *Recreations:* opera, chamber music and song, theatre, cricket, historic buildings. *Address:* 406 Faraday Lodge, Renaissance Walk, SE10 0QL. *T:* (020) 8305 0420.

MACE, Christopher; *see* Mace, A. C. H.

MACE, Prof. Georgina Mary, CBE 2007 (OBE 1998); DPhil; FRS 2002; Professor of Biodiversity and Ecosystems, University College London, since 2012; *m* 1985, Roderick O. Evans; one *s* two *d*. *Educ:* Univ. of Liverpool (BSc Hons 1976); Univ. of Sussex (DPhil 1979). Postdoctoral Fellow, Smithsonian Instn, Washington, DC, 1980–81; Sir James Knott Res. Fellow, Dept of Zoology, Univ. of Newcastle upon Tyne, 1981–83; Res. Fellow, Inst. of Zoology, and Hon. Fellow, Dept of Biology, UCL, 1983–89; Institute of Zoology, Zoological Society of London: Pew Scholar in Conservation and the Envmt, 1991–94; NERC Advanced Fellow, 1994–99; Dir of Sci., 2000–06; Prof. of Conservation Sci., 2006–12, Dir, NERC Centre for Population Biology, 2006–10, Imperial Coll. London. Mem., NERC, 2011–. Member Council: Durrell Wildlife Conservation Trust, 1998–2004; RSPB, 2000–04; Royal Soc., 2005–06. Trustee, Nat. Hist. Mus., 2004–12. *Publications:* (jtly) Creative Conservation: interactive management of wild and captive animals, 1993; (ed jtly) Conservation in a Changing World, 1999; (ed jtly) Conservation of Exploited Species, 2001; articles in learned jls. *Address:* Division of Biosciences, Darwin Building, University College London, Gower Street, WC1E 6BT.

MACE, Lt-Gen. Sir John (Airth), KBE 1990 (OBE 1974; MBE 1967); CB 1986; New Zealand Chief of Defence Force, 1987–91; *b* 29 June 1932; *m* 1962, Margaret Theodocia (*née* McCallum); one *s* one *d*. *Educ:* Ashburton High Sch., NZ; Nelson Coll., NZ; RMC Duntroon, Australia. Commissioned NZ Army, 1953; NZ SAS, 1955–57; active service in Malayan Emergency (despatches, 1958); Comd SAS Sqdn, 1960–62 and 1965; Comd Co. of 1 RNZIR 1st Bn, Borneo, 1966; Vietnam, 1967; appts include: Dir of Infantry and NZ SAS; CO, 1st Bn RNZIR, Singapore; Dir, Officer Postings; Comdr, Army Logistics Support Gp; Comdr, 1st Inf. Bde Gp; Army Staff Coll., Camberley; JSSC, Canberra; Comdr, NZ Force SE Asia, 1979–80; RCDS 1981; Dep. Chief of Defence Staff, 1982–84; Chief of General Staff, 1984–87. Hon. Col, First Bn, Royal NZ Inf. Regt, 2005–08. *Recreations:* golf, walking, reading.

MACE, Prof. Ruth, DPhil; FBA 2008; Professor of Evolutionary Anthropology, University College London, since 2004; *b* London, 9 Oct. 1961; *d* of David Mace and Angela Mace; partner, Prof. Mark Pagel, *qv*; two *s*. *Educ:* South Hampstead High Sch. for Girls; Westminster Sch.; Wadham Coll., Oxford (BA Zool. 1983; DPhil Zool. 1987). Res. Fellow, Imperial Coll. London, 1987–89; Lectr, Univ. of East Anglia, 1989–91; Lectr, then Reader in Evolutionary Anthropol., UCL, 1991–2004. Ed.-in-Chief, Evolution and Human Behavior, 2005–10. Vis. Prof., Chinese Acad. of Scis, Beijing, 2014–. *Publications:* The Conservation of Biological Resources, 1998; The Evolution of Cultural Diversity: a phylogenetic approach, 2005; Substitute Parents, 2008; over 100 jl articles and book chapters. *Recreations:* rowing badly, singing badly. *Address:* Department of Anthropology, University College London, 14 Taviton Street, WC1H 0BW. *T:* (020) 7679 8845. *E:* r.mace@ucl.ac.uk.

McEACHRAN, Colin Neil; QC (Scot.) 1982; *b* 14 Jan. 1940; *s* of Eric Robins McEachran and Nora Helen Bushe; *m* 1967, Katherine Charlotte Henderson; two *d*. *Educ:* Trinity Coll., Glenalmond; Merton Coll., Oxford (BA 1961); Univ. of Glasgow (LLB 1963); Univ. of Chicago (Commonwealth Fellow; JD 1965). Admitted Solicitor, 1966; admitted to Faculty of Advocates, 1968. Advocate Depute, 1975–78. Mem., Scottish Legal Aid Bd, 1990–98; Pres., Pension Appeal Tribunals for Scotland, 1995–2013. Chm., Commonwealth Games Council for Scotland, 1995–99. *Recreations:* target rifle shooting (Silver Medal, Commonwealth Games, NZ, 1974), golf. *Address:* 13 Saxe-Coburg Place, Edinburgh EH3 5BR. *T:* (0131) 332 6820.

MACEDO, Prof. Helder Malta, Comendador, Ordem de Santiago da Espada (Portugal), 1993; PhD; Camoens Professor of Portuguese, University of London at King's College, 1982–2004, now Professor Emeritus; *b* 30 Nov. 1935; *s* of Adelino José de Macedo and Aida Malta de Macedo; *m* 1960, Suzette Armanda (*née* de Aguiar). *Educ:* Faculty of Law, Univ. of Lisbon; King's Coll., Univ. of London (BA, PhD); FKC 1991. Lectr in Portuguese and Brazilian Studies, KCL, 1971–82; Sec. of State for Culture, Portuguese Govt, 1979. Visiting Professor: Harvard Univ., 1981; Ecole des Hautes Etudes et Sciences Sociales, Paris, 1992, 1995. President: Internat. Assoc. of Lusitanists, 1994–99 (Hon. Pres., 2002); Modern Humanities Res. Assoc., 2009–10. Fellow, Academia das Ciências de Lisboa, 1987. Editor, Portuguese Studies Jl, 1985–2002. *Publications:* Nós, Uma Leitura de Cesário Verde, 1975, 4th edn 1999; Do Significado Oculto da 'Menina a Moça', 1977, 2nd edn 1999; Poesia 1957–77, 1978; Camões e a Viagem Iniciática, 1980; The Purpose of Praise: Past and Future in The Lusiads of Luís de Camões, 1983; Cesário Verde: O Romântico e o Feroz, 1988; Partes de Africa, 1991; Viagem de Inverno, 1994; Pedro e Paula, 1998, 2nd edn 1998 (Brazilian edn, 1999); Viagens do Olhar, 1998; Vícios e Virtudes, 2000, 2nd edn 2001 (Brazilian edn, 2002); Sem Nome, 2004 (Brazilian edn, 2006); Trinta Leituras, 2007; Natália, 2009 (Brazilian edn, 2010); Poemas Novos e Velhos, 2011; Tão Longo Amor Tão Curta A Vida, 2013. *Address:* Department of Portuguese and Brazilian Studies, King's College London, Strand, WC2R 2LS. *T:* (020) 7873 2507.

McELVOY, Anne; Senior Editor and Director, Economist Audio, The Economist, since 2015; columnist, Evening Standard, since 2002; broadcaster; *b* 25 June 1965; *d* of Alexander and Mary McElvoy; *m* 1994, Martin Paul Ivens, *qv*; two *s* one *d*. *Educ:* St Bede's RC Comprehensive Sch., Lanchester; Wadham Coll., Oxford (MA German and Philosophy); Humboldt Univ., Berlin. Foreign corresp., The Times, 1989–94; Dep. Ed., Spectator, 1995–97; Executive Editor: Independent, 1997–2002; Evening Standard, 2002–09; Public Policy Ed., The Economist, 2011–15. Presenter: Nightwaves, BBC Radio 3, 2009–; Free Thinking, BBC Radio 3, 2009–; Start the Week, BBC Radio 4, 2013–. Mem., Global Adv. Council, WEF, 2014–. Mem., Educn Bd, Royal Opera Hse, 2012–. *Publications:* The Saddled Cow: East Germany's life and legacy, 1991; Man Without a Face: the memoirs of Markus Wolf, 1995. *Recreations:* herding teenagers, theatre. *Address:* The Economist, 25 St James's Street, SW1A 1HG.

McENERY, Judith Mary; *see* Chessells, J. M.

McENERY, Peter; actor; Associate Artist, Royal Shakespeare Co.; *b* 21 Feb. 1940; *s* of Charles and Mary McEnery; *m* 1978; one *d*. *Educ:* various state and private schs. First stage appearance, Brighton, 1956; first London appearance in Flowering Cherry, Haymarket, 1957; *stage:* rôles with RSC include, 1961–: Laertes, Tybalt, Johnny Hobnails in Afore Night Come, Bassanio, Lorenzaccio, Orlando, Sachs in The Jail Diary of Albie Sachs, Pericles, Brutus, Antipholus of Ephesus, Godber in A Dream of People; other rôles include: Rudge in Next Time I'll Sing to You, Criterion, 1963; Konstantin in The Seagull, Queen's, 1964; Harry Winter in The Collaborators, Duchess, 1973; Trigorin in The Seagull, Lyric, 1975; Edward Gover in Made in Bangkok, Aldwych, 1986; Fredrik in A Little Night Music, Chichester, transf. Piccadilly, 1989; Torvald in The Doll's House, Robert in Dangerous Corner, Chichester, 1994; Menelaus in Women of Troy, NT, 1995; Hector Hushabye in Heartbreak House, Almeida, 1997; Claudius in Hamlet, RNT, 2000; directed: Richard III, Nottingham, 1971; The Wound, Young Vic, 1972. *Films* include: Tunes of Glory, 1961; Victim, 1961; The Moonspinners, 1963; Entertaining Mr Sloane, 1970; *television:* Clayhanger, 1976; The Jail Diary of Albie Sachs, 1980; Pictures, 1983; The Collectors, 1986; The Mistress, 1986; Witchcraft, 1992. *Recreations:* steam railway preservation, ski-ing, American football. *Address:* c/o United Agents Ltd, 12-26 Lexington Street, W1F 0LE.

McENROE, John Patrick; tennis player and commentator; *b* Wiesbaden, 16 Feb. 1959; *s* of John Patrick McEnroe and Katherine, (Kay), McEnroe (*née* Tresham); *m* 1st, 1986, Tatum O'Neal (marr. diss. 1994); two *s* one *d*; 2nd, 1997, Patty Smyth; two *d*, and one step *d*. *Educ:* Trinity High Sch., NYC; Stanford Univ., Calif. Amateur tennis player, 1976–78, turned professional, 1978; winner of 77 singles titles and 77 doubles titles, including: US Open (singles) 1979, 1980, 1981, 1984, (doubles) 1979, 1981, 1983, 1989; Wimbledon (singles) 1981, 1983, 1984, (doubles) 1979, 1981, 1983, 1984, 1992; Grand Prix Masters 1979, 1983, 1984. Mem., US Davis Cup team, 1978–84, 1987–89, 1991, 1992, Captain, 1999–2000. Tennis commentator, USA TV, 1992–, BBC TV, 2000–; host, TV quiz show, The Chair, 2002. Owner, John McEnroe Gall., NY. *Publications:* (with James Kaplan) Serious (autobiog.), 2002. *Address:* The John McEnroe Gallery, 41 Greene Street, New York, NY 10013, USA.

MACER, Dr Richard Charles Franklin, MA, PhD; consultant on biotechnology and genetics, 1985–95; *b* 21 Oct. 1928; *s* of Lionel William Macer and Adie Elizabeth Macer; *m* 1952, Vera Gwendoline Jeapes; three *d*. *Educ:* Worthing High Sch.; St John's Coll., Cambridge. Research, St John's Coll., Cambridge, 1949–55, Hutchinson Res. Student, 1952–53; Hd of Plant Pathology Section, Plant Breeding Inst., Cambridge, 1955–66; Dir and Dir of Res., Rothwell Plant Breeders Ltd, Lincs, 1966–72; Prof. of Crop Production, Univ. of Edinburgh, 1972–76; Dir, Scottish Plant Breeding Station, 1976–81; Gen. Manager, Plant Royalty Bureau Ltd, 1981–85. *Publications:* papers on fungal diseases of cereals. *Recreations:* hill walking, archaeology, reading.

McEVOY, His Honour David Dand; QC 1983; a Circuit Judge, 1996–2008; *b* 25 June 1938; *s* of David Dand McEvoy and Ann Elizabeth McEvoy (*née* Breslin); *m* 1974, Belinda Anne Robertson; three *d*. *Educ:* Mount St Mary's Coll.; Lincoln Coll., Oxford. BA (PPE). 2nd Lieut The Black Watch, RHR, 1958–59. Called to the Bar, Inner Temple, 1964; a Recorder, 1979–96. *Recreations:* golf, fishing. *Clubs:* Garrick; Blackwell Golf; Seniors Golfing Society; Highland Brigade.

McEWAN, Hon. Lord; Robin Gilmour McEwan; a Senator of the College of Justice in Scotland, 2000–08; *b* 12 Dec. 1943; *s* of late Ian G. McEwan and Mary McEwan, Paisley, Renfrewshire; *m* 1973, Sheena, *d* of late Stewart F. McIntyre and Lilian McIntyre, Aberdour; two *d*. *Educ:* Paisley Grammar Sch.; Glasgow Univ. (1st Cl. Hons LLB; PhD). Faulds Fellow in Law, Glasgow Univ., 1965–68; admitted to Faculty of Advocates, 1967; QC (Scot.) 1981. Standing Jun. Counsel to Dept of Energy, 1974–76; Advocate Depute, 1976–79; Sheriff of S Strathclyde, Dumfries and Galloway, at Lanark, 1982–88, at Ayr, 1988–2000; Temp. Judge, Court of Session and High Court of Justiciary, 1991–99. Chm., Industrial Tribunals, 1981–82; Mem., Scottish Legal Aid Bd, 1989–96. Dep. Chm., Boundary Commn for Scotland, 2007–08. Mem., Scottish Civil Courts Review, 2007–09. Chancellor, dio. of Glasgow and Galloway, 2005–. *Publications:* Pleading in Court, 1980, 2nd edn 1995; (with Ann Paton) A Casebook on Damages in Scotland, 1983; contrib. Stair Memorial Encyclopaedia of the Laws of Scotland, 1987. *Recreation:* golf. *Clubs:* New (Edinburgh); Prestwick Golf.

McEWAN, Ian Russell, CBE 2000; FRSL; author; *b* 21 June 1948; *s* of late Major (retd) David McEwan and Rose Lilian Violet Moore; *m* 1982, Penny Allen (marr. diss. 1995); two *s* two *d*; *m* 1997, Annalena McAfee. *Educ:* Woolverstone Hall Sch.; Univ. of Sussex (BA Hons Eng. Lit.); Univ. of East Anglia (MA Eng. Lit.). Began writing, 1970. Hon. Member: Amer. Acad. of Arts and Scis, 1996; Amer. Acad. of Arts and Letters, 2006. FRSL 1982; FRSA. Hon. DLitt Sussex, 1989; Hon. DLit London, 1998; Hon. LittD: E Anglia, 1993; UCL, 2008; Hull, 2009. Shakespeare Prize, FVS Foundn, Hamburg, 1999. *Films:* The Ploughman's Lunch, 1983; Last Day of Summer, 1984; Soursweet, 1988; The Innocent, 1993; The Good Son, 1994. *Publications:* First Love, Last Rites, 1975 (filmed, 1997); In Between the Sheets, 1978; The Cement Garden, 1978 (filmed, 1993); The Imitation Game, 1981; The Comfort of Strangers, 1981 (filmed, 1991); Or Shall we Die? (oratorio; score by Michael Berkeley), 1982; The Ploughman's Lunch (film script), 1985; The Child in Time, 1987 (Whitbread Award; Prix Fémina, 1993); Soursweet (film script), 1989; The Innocent, 1990; Black Dogs, 1992; The Daydreamer, 1994; The Short Stories, 1995; Enduring Love, 1997 (filmed, 2004); Amsterdam (novel), 1998 (Booker Prize, 1998); Atonement, 2001 (filmed, 2006); Rose Blanche, 2004; Saturday, 2005 (James Tait Black Meml Prize, 2006); On Chesil Beach, 2007; For You (opera libretto; score by Michael Berkeley), 2008; Solar, 2010; Sweet Tooth, 2012; The Children Act, 2014. *Recreations:* hiking, tennis, cooking. *Address:* c/o Jonathan Cape, Random Century House, 20 Vauxhall Bridge Road, SW1V 2SA.

McEWAN, Leslie James; JP; independent consultant, since 2004; Associate Consultant, Care and Health Ltd, 2004–09; *b* 26 Feb. 1946; *s* of Charles and Ann McEwan; *m* 1966, Catherine Anne Currie; two *s*. *Educ:* Lasswade High Sch.; St Andrews Univ. (MA); Dundee Univ. (Dip Social Admin); Univ. of Edinburgh (Dip Social Work). Midlothian, East Lothian and Peebles: Child Care Officer, Children's Dept, 1967–69; Social Worker, 1969–71; Sen. Social Worker, 1971–74; Social Work Advr, 1974–75; Divisional Director of Social Work: Midlothian-Lothian Reg., 1975–80; West Lothian, 1980–85; Lothian Region: Depute Dir of Social Work, 1985–90; Sen. Depute Dir, 1990–95; Dir, 1995–96; Dir of Social Work, City of Edinburgh Council, 1996–2003. Chm., FAIR charity, Edinburgh, 2007–; Mem. Bd, MYPAS charity, Midlothian, 2007–. Volunteer woodturning instructor, Grassmarket Community Project, Edinburgh, 2011–. Mem., Bonnyrigg and Lasswade Burgh Council, 1969–75 (Baillie, 1972–75). JP Midlothian, 1975–2007, Edinburgh, Lothian and Borders, 2007–. *Recreations:* fly-fishing, golf, woodturning, choral music. *Address:* 1 Eskglades, Dalkeith, Midlothian EH22 1UZ.

McEWAN, Morag Barbara; *see* Wise, M. B.

McEWAN, Robin Gilmour; *see* McEwan, Hon. Lord.

McEWEN, Dame Hilary Mary; *see* Mantel, Dame H. M.

McEWEN, Prof. James, FRCP, FFPH, FFOM, FDSRCS, FMedSci; Professor of Public Health, University of Glasgow, 1989–2002, now Emeritus (Henry Mechan Professor of Public Health, 1989–2000); President, Faculty of Public Health Medicine, Royal Colleges of Physicians of the United Kingdom, 1998–2001; *b* 6 Feb. 1940; *s* of Daniel McEwen and Elizabeth Wells (*née* Dishington); *m* 1964, Elizabeth May Archibald; one *s* one *d*. *Educ:* Dollar Acad.; Univ. of St Andrews (MB ChB 1963). FFPH (FFPHM 1981); FFOM 1990; FRCPGlas 1991; FRCP 1999; FRCPE 1999; FDSRCS 2003. Asst MO of Health, City of Dundee, 1965–66; Lectr, Univ. of Dundee, 1966–74; Sen. Lectr, Univ. of Nottingham, 1975–81; CMO, Health Educn Council, 1981–82; Prof. of Community Medicine, King's Coll. Sch. of Medicine and Dentistry, Univ. of London, 1983–89. Hon. Consultant in Public Health Medicine, Gtr Glasgow Health Bd, 1989–2002; Hon. Civilian Advr in Public Health to the Army, 2001–06; non-exec. Dir, Glasgow Royal Infirmary and Univ. NHS Trust, 1994–99. Chm., Health Protection Adv. Gp, Scotland, 2005–13. Mem., NRPB, 1996–2003. Distinguished Visitor, Univ. of Tucuman, Argentina, 1993. Hon. Chairman: UK Register for Public Health (formerly UK Voluntary Register for Public Health Specialists), 2003–09; Pharmacy Health Link, 2004–07. Chair, Bd of Govs, Dollar Acad., 2014– (Hon. Vice-Chm., 2003–14). FCPS (Pak), 1996; Founder FMedSci 1998. Hon. FFPHMI 1997. Hon. DSc Glasgow Caledonian, 2008. *Publications:* (with A. Finlayson) Coronary Heart Disease and Patterns of Living, 1977; (jtly) Measuring Health Status, 1986; (ed jtly) Oxford Textbook of Public Health, 3rd edn 1997, 4th edn 2002; contrib. articles on public health, health services and quality of life. *Recreations:* Church, gardening, architectural heritage. *Address:* Auchanachie, Ruthven, Huntly AB54 4SS. *T:* (01466) 760742. *Club:* Royal Society of Medicine.

McEWEN, Sir John (Roderick Hugh), 5th Bt *cr* 1953; writer; *b* 4 Nov. 1965; *s* of Sir Robert Lindley McEwen, 3rd Bt, of Marchmont and Bardrochat, and of Brigid Cecilia, *d* of late James Laver, CBE, and Veronica Turleigh; *S* brother, 1983; *m* 2000, Rachel, *er d* of Gerald Soane, Wallington, Surrey; two *s* two *d*. *Educ:* Ampleforth; University Coll. London; Glasgow Univ. (MPhil 1999). Comdr of Clan McEwen. *Heir:* *s* Joseph Mungo James McEwen, *b* 18 Oct. 2008. *Address:* The Steadings, Polwarth, Berwickshire TD10 6YR.

MACEY, Air Vice-Marshal Eric Harold, OBE 1975; Director General of Training (Royal Air Force), 1989–91, retired; *b* 9 April 1936; *s* of Harold Fred and Katrina Emma Mary Macey; *m* 1957, Brenda Ann Bracher; one *s* one *d*. *Educ:* Shaftesbury Grammar School; Southampton Tech. Coll. Asst Sci. Officer, Min. of Supply, 1953–54; RAF, 1954; commissioned, 1955; Pilot's Wings, 1956; RAF Staff Coll., 1966; RCDS 1983; AOC and Comdt, RAF Coll., Cranwell, 1985–87; ACDS (Policy and Nuclear), 1987–89. Pres., RAF Chilmark Assoc., 1994–2013; Vice-President: 214 Sqdn Assoc., 1990–; 101 Sqdn Assoc., 1999–; Bomber Comd Assoc., 1998–. *Recreations:* music, DIY. *Address:* Ebblemead, Homington, Salisbury, Wilts SP5 4NL.

McFADDEN, Rev. Mgr Andrew, QHC 2011; Vicar-General (Bishopric of the Forces) and Principal Roman Catholic Chaplain (Naval), since 2011; Principal, Armed Forces Chaplaincy Centre, since 2014; *b* Glasgow, 26 March 1964; *s* of Samuel Gerard McFadden and Frances Mary McFadden (*née* McAnulty). *Educ:* St Vincent's Coll., Langbank; Blairs Coll., Aberdeen; Pontifical Scots Coll., Rome; Gregorian Univ., Rome (PhB 1984; STL 1989). Ordained priest, Dio. Paisley, 1989; Assistant Priest: St Mary's, Paisley, 1990; St Andrew's, Larkfield, 1990–93; St Mirin's Cathedral, Paisley, 1993–96; St Margaret's, Johnstone, 1996–98. Dio. Scout Chaplain, 1990–93; Hosp. Chaplain and Chaplain, Reid Kerr Coll., 1993–96. Royal Naval Chaplain: Royal Naval Hosp., Haslar, 1998; Fourth Frigate Sqdn, 1999–2000; HMS Sultan, and Parish Priest, St Benedict's Catholic Naval Community, 2000–03; HMS Nelson, 2003–05; HMS Ocean, 2005–07; HMS Raleigh, 2007–09; Cdre Faslane Flotilla, 2009–11. Prelate of Honour to HH Pope Benedict XVI, 2012. *Recreations:* music, art, hill-walking, all things Italian, steamers of the Clyde and the Western Isles. *Address:* Principal Chaplain's Office, Armed Forces Chaplaincy Centre, Amport House, Amport, Andover, Hants SP11 8BG. *E:* andrew.mcfadden375@mod.uk.

McFADDEN, Prof. Daniel L., PhD; E. Morris Cox Professor of Economics, 1991, now Emeritus, and Director, Econometrics Laboratory, 1991–95 and 1996, University of California, Berkeley (Head, Department of Economics, 1995–96); Presidential Professor of Health Economics, University of Southern California, since 2011; *b* Raleigh, NC, 29 July 1937; *s* of Robert Sain McFadden and Alice Little McFadden; *m* 1962, Beverlee Tito Simboli; two *s* one *d*. *Educ:* Univ. of Minnesota (BS 1957; PhD 1962). Asst Prof. of Econs, Univ. of Pittsburgh, 1962–63; Asst Prof., 1963–66, Associate Prof., 1966–68, Prof. 1968–77, of Econs, Univ. of Calif, Berkeley; Prof. of Econs, 1977–84, James R. Killian Prof. of Econs, 1984–91, Dir, Statistics Center, 1986–88, MIT. (Jtly) Nobel Prize for Economics, 2000. *Publications:* (ed jtly) Essays on Economic Behavior Under Uncertainty, 1974; (jtly) Urban Travel Demand: a behavioural analysis, 1975; (ed jtly) Production Economics: a dual approach to theory and applications (2 vols), 1978; (ed jtly) Structural Analysis of Discrete Data with Econometric Applications, 1981; (jtly) Microeconomic Modeling and Policy Analysis: studies in residential energy demand, 1984; (ed jtly) Preferences, Uncertainty and Optimality: essays in honor of Leonid Hurwicz, 1990; (ed jtly) Handbook of Econometrics, vol. IV, 1994; contrib. learned jls. *Address:* Department of Economics, University of California, Berkeley, CA 94720–3880, USA.

McFADDEN, Jean Alexandra, CBE 1992; JP; DL; MA, LLB; Visiting Lecturer in Law, University of Strathclyde, since 2006 (Senior Lecturer, 1992–2006); Vice Lord Lieutenant of City of Glasgow, 1980–92; *b* 26 Nov. 1941; *d* of John and Elma Hogg; *m* 1966, John McFadden (*d* 1991). *Educ:* Univ. of Glasgow (MA 1st Cl. Hons Classics); Univ. of Strathclyde (LLB 1st Cl. Hons). Principal Teacher of Classics, Strathclyde Schools, 1967–86; part-time Lectr in Law, Univ. of Glasgow, 1991–92. Entered Local Govt as Mem. of Glasgow Corp. for Cowcaddens Ward, 1971 then (following boundary changes) Mem., Glasgow DC for Scotstoun Ward, 1984–96; Mem., City of Glasgow Council, 1995–2012 (Convener, 1995–96; Chair: Labour Gp, 1995–2012; Social Strategy Cttee, 1996–99; Exec. Mem. for Corporate Governance, 2007–10, for Educn, 2010–12); Chm., Manpower Cttee, 1974–77; Leader, Labour Gp, 1977–86, 1992–94; Leader, 1980–86, 1992–94, Treas., 1986–92, Glasgow DC. Convener, Scottish Local Govt Information Unit, 1984–2003; Pres., Convention of Scottish Local Auths, 1990–92; Member Board: SDA, 1989–91; Legal Services Agency, 1992– (Convener, 2015–); Glasgow Develt Agency, 1992–2000. Convener, Strathclyde Police Jt Bd, 2003–07. Chm., Scottish Charity Law Commn, 2000–01; Member: Health Appts Adv. Cttee, Scottish Exec. (formerly Scottish Office), 1995–2000; Ancient Monuments Bd for Scotland, 2000–03. Mem. Council, Royal Glasgow Inst. Fine Arts, 2007– (Pres., 2014–). Chm., W of Scotland Jt Archaeol Cttee, 1997–2012. Chm., Mayfest (Glasgow Internat. Arts Fest.), 1983–97. JP Glasgow, 1972; DL 1980. *Recreations:* theatre, walking, golf, West Highland terriers, Italian language and literature, Modern Greek. *Address:* 16 Lansdowne Crescent, Glasgow G20 6NQ. *T:* (0141) 334 3522.

McFADDEN, Rt Hon. Patrick; PC 2008; MP (Lab) Wolverhampton South East, since 2005; *b* 26 March 1965; *s* of James and Annie McFadden; *m* Marianna; one *s* one *d*. *Educ:* Holyrood Sec. Sch., Glasgow; Univ. of Edinburgh (MA Hons Pols 1988). Res. Asst to Rt Hon. Donald Dewar, MP, 1988–93; Advr to Rt Hon. John Smith, MP, 1993–94; Policy Advr to Rt Hon. Tony Blair, MP, 1994–2001; Political Sec. to the Prime Minister, 2002–05. Parly Sec. (Minister for Social Exclusion), Cabinet Office, 2006–07; Minister of State, BERR, later BIS, 2007–10; Shadow Sec. of State for Business, 2010; Shadow Minister of State for Europe, 2014–15. *Recreations:* sport, reading. *Address:* House of Commons, SW1A 0AA. *T:* (020) 7219 4036, *Fax:* (020) 7219 5665.

McFADYEAN, Colin William; teacher, Gloucestershire, since 2003; Deputy Headteacher, Ilminster Avenue Primary School, Knowle West Bristol, 1999–2003; *b* 11 March 1943; *s* of Captain Angus John McFadyean, MC, 1st Bn London Scottish Regt (killed in action, 1944) and late Joan Mary McFadyean (*née* Irish); *m* 1970, Jeanette Carol Payne; one *s*. *Educ:* Plymouth Coll.; Bristol Grammar Sch.; Loughborough Coll. of Education; Keele Univ. (DLC Hons, Adv. DipEd). Phys. Educn teacher, Birmingham, 1965–67; Phys. Educn Lectr, 1967–72, Sen. Lectr, 1972–74, Cheshire; Dep. Dir, Nat. Sports Centre, Lilleshall, 1974–78; Chief Coach, Jubilee Sports Centre, Hong Kong, 1979–82; Sports Master and House Master, Dulwich Coll., 1983–85; Dir Gen., NPFA, 1985–87; with Croydon Educn Authy, 1988–90; teacher, Avon, then Bristol Educn Authy, 1991–98; Dep. Headteacher, Oldbury Court Primary Sch., 1998–99. Dir Coaching, Bristol FC (Rugby Union), 1990–91; Coach: Moseley FC, 1991–93; Cleve RFC, 1992–99. Internat. Rugby career includes: 11 England caps, 1966–68; 4 Tests British Lions *v* NZ, 1966; (captain) *v* Ireland, 1968; (captain) *v* Wales, 1968; scored 5 tries, 1 dropped goal (in 15 Tests); other sport: coach to Hong Kong disabled team to Olympics, Arnhem, 1980; Adviser, Hong Kong table tennis team to World Championships, Yugoslavia, 1981. Mem., Adv. Gp, RCM, 2004–07. Broadcaster with Hong Kong TV and commercial radio. Hon. BA Loughborough, 2009. *Recreations:* golf, music, theatre, gardening; supporter of Plymouth Argyle FC, 1952–. *Clubs:* British Sportsman's; England Rugby International's; Rugby Internationals Golf, Stinchcombe Hill Golf; Moseley Football (Vice-Pres.); Cleve Rugby Football (Vice-Pres.).

MacFADYEN, Alasdair Lorne; Sheriff of South Strathclyde, Dumfries and Galloway at Hamilton, since 2012; *b* 18 Sept. 1955; *s* of Iain Archibald MacFadyen and Anna MacFadyen; *m* 1978, Lynne Ballantyne; two *d*. *Educ:* High Sch., Glasgow; Glasgow Univ. (LLB). Solicitor in private practice, 1978–2001. Temp. Sheriff, 1995–2000; pt-time Sheriff, 2000–01; all Scotland Floating Sheriff, 2001–02; Sheriff of Grampian, Highland and Islands at Dingwall and Inverness, 2002–12. Pt-time Chm., Employment Tribunals, 2000–01. *Recreations:* sailing in tall ships, music. *Address:* Sheriff Court, 4 Beckford Street, Hamilton ML3 0BT.

MACFADYEN, (David) Matthew; actor, since 1995; *b* Great Yarmouth, 17 Oct. 1974; *s* of Martin Macfadyen and Meinir Macfadyen (*née* Owen); *m* 2004, Keeley Hawes; one *s* one *d*, and one step *s*. *Educ:* Oakham Sch.; Royal Acad. of Dramatic Art. *Theatre* includes: The Duchess of Malfi, Cheek by Jowl, 1995; A Midsummer Night's Dream, RSC, 1996; Much Ado About Nothing, Cheek by Jowl, 1998; The School for Scandal, RSC, 1998; Battle Royal, NT, 1999; Henry IV, Parts 1 and 2, NT, 2004; The Pain and the Itch, Royal Court, 2007; Private Lives, Vaudeville, 2009; Perfect Nonsense, Duke of York's, 2013. *Television* includes: Wuthering Heights, 1998; Warriors, 1999; Perfect Strangers, 2001; The Way We Live Now, 2001; Spooks, 2002–04; The Project, 2002; Secret Life (Best Actor, RTS Award, 2008); Little Dorrit, 2008; Enid, 2009; Criminal Justice, 2009 (Best Supporting Actor, BAFTA Award, 2010); The Pillars of the Earth, 2010; Any Human Heart, 2010; Ripper Street (3 series), 2012–13; Ambassadors, 2013; The Enfield Haunting, 2015. *Films* include: Maybe Baby, 2000; Enigma, 2001; The Reckoning, 2003; In My Father's Den, 2004; Pride and Prejudice, 2005; Middletown, 2006; Death at a Funeral, 2007; Incendiary, 2008; Frost/Nixon, 2008; Robin Hood, 2010; The Three Musketeers, 2011; Anna Karenina, 2012. *Address:* c/o Christian Hodell, Hamilton Hodell, 20 Golden Square, W1F 9JL. *T:* (020) 7636 1221. *E:* info@hamiltonhodell.co.uk. *Club:* Garrick.

MACFADYEN, Air Marshal Sir Ian (David), KCVO 2014; CB 1991; OBE 1984; Constable and Governor of Windsor Castle, 2009–14; *b* 19 Feb. 1942; *s* of Air Marshal Sir Douglas Macfadyen, KCB, CBE and of Lady Macfadyen (*née* Dafforn, now Mrs P. A. Rowan); *m* 1967, Sally Harvey; one *s* one *d*. *Educ:* Marlborough; RAF Coll., Cranwell. Joined RAF, 1960; Cranwell cadet, 1960–63 (Sword of Honour); 19 Sqdn, 1965–68; HQ, RAF Strike Command, 1969; Flying Instructor, RAF Coll., Cranwell, 1970–73; RAF Staff Coll., 1973; 111 Sqdn, 1974–75; Flt Comdr, 43 Sqdn, 1975–76; HQ 2 ATAF, RAF Germany, 1976–79; comd 29 Sqdn, 1980–84; comd 23 Sqdn, 1984; MoD, 1984–85; comd RAF Leuchars, Fife, 1985–87; RCDS, 1988; MoD, 1989–90; COS, then Comdr, HQ British Forces ME, Riyadh, 1990–91; ACDS, Op. Requirements (Air Systems), 1991–94; Dir Gen., Saudi Arabia Armed Forces Project, 1994–98; retd, 1999. Lt Gov., IOM, 2000–05; Nat. Pres., RBL, 2006–09. Trustee, RAF Mus., 1998–2003 (Chm. Trustees, 1999–2001). Chm., Geoffrey de Havilland Flying Foundn, 2002–; Trustee, Bentley Priory Battle of Britain Trust, 2006–; Pres., Popular Flying Assoc., 2004–06. Chairman: IOM Bd, Prince's Trust, 2001–05; IOM Golden Jubilee Trust, 2002–05. Mem. Council, St George's House, 2009–. Patron: Guillain-Barré Syndrome Support Gp, 2010–; Alexander Devine Children's Cancer Trust, 2010–; Vice Patron, Gallantry Medallists League, 2010–. Hon. Air Cdre, 606 (Chiltern) Sqdn, RAuxAF, 2007–. Hon. Inspector Gen., RAuxAF, 2009. Liveryman, Hon. Co. of Air Pilots (formerly GAPAN), 1999–; Hon. Liveryman Lightmongers' Co., 2011–. President: Windsor Fest., 2009–14; Lucifer Golfing Soc., 2012–. QCVSA 1974. OStJ 2001. *Recreations:* aviation history, gliding, golf, photography, shooting, watercolour painting. *Address:* Collyns Mead, Hawkesbury Upton, S Glos GL9 1BB. *Clubs:* Royal Air Force; Royal & Ancient (St Andrews).

McFADYEN, Jock, RA 2012; painter; *b* Paisley, 18 Sept. 1950; *s* of James Lachlan McFadyen and Margaret McFadyen (*née* Owen); *m* 1st, 1972, Carol Hambleton (marr. diss. 1987); one *s*; 2nd, 1991, Susie Honeyman; one *s* one *d*. *Educ:* Chelsea Sch. of Art (BA 1976; MA 1977). Artist-in-Residence, Nat. Gall., 1981; Lectr (pt-time), Slade Sch. of Fine Art, 1985–2004; designed sets and costumes for The Judas Tree, Royal Opera Hse, 1992; est. Grey Gall., 2007. *Solo exhibitions* include: Nat. Gall., 1982; Camden Arts Centre, 1988; Imperial War Mus., 1991; Talbot Rice Gall., Univ. of Edinburgh, 1998; Pier Arts Centre, Orkney, 1999; Agnew's Gall., London, 2001; Rude Wercs, London, 2005; Grey Gall., Edinburgh Fest., 2007; Clifford Chance, London, 2010; Bourne Fine Art, Edinburgh, 2011, 2012; Fine Art Soc., 2012; Fleming Collection, London, 2012; *group exhibitions* incl. John Moores Univ., Hayward annual, British Art Show, Five Centuries of Scottish Portraits at Fine Art Soc. and Bourne Fine Art, 2011, Cohen Collection at Chatsworth Hse, 2012; *work in public collections* incl. Tate Gall., Nat. Gall., V&A, BM and private and corporate collections in Britain, Europe and America. *Recreations:* cycling, motorcycling, exploring Scotland, music. *E:* info@jockmcfadyen.com. *Club:* Vintage Motorcycle.

MACFADYEN, Matthew; *see* Macfadyen, D. M.

McFALL OF ALCLUITH, Baron *cr* 2010 (Life Peer), of Dumbarton in Dunbartonshire; **John Francis McFall;** PC 2004. MP (Lab and Co-op) Dumbarton, 1987–2005, W Dunbartonshire, 2005–10. An Opposition Whip, 1989–91; Opposition front bench spokesman: for education and home affairs, 1992; on Scottish Affairs, 1992–97; a Lord Comr of HM Treasury (Govt Whip), 1997–98; Parly Under-Sec. of State, NI Office, 1998–99. Member, Select Committee: on Defence, 1988; on Sittings of the House, 1991; on Information, 1990–97; Chm., HM Treasury Select Cttee, 2001–10; Mem. Exec. Cttee, Parly Gp for Energy Studies, 1988–97; Secretary: Retail Industry Gp, 1992–97; Hon. Sec., Parly and Scientific Cttee, 1989–92. Founder and non-exec. Chm., New City Agenda, 2013–. Mem., Parly Commn on Banking Standards, 2012–13; Dep. Chm., Banking Standards Bd, 2014–. Visiting Professor: Strathclyde Business Sch., Univ. of Strathclyde, 1991–; Glasgow Univ. Business Sch., 2004–. Hon Dr: Strathclyde, 2010; Stirling, 2011; Glasgow, 2011; W of Scotland, 2012; Hon. DBA BPP Business Sch., 2011. *Recreations:* running, golf, reading. *Address:* House of Lords, SW1A 0PW.

McFALL, Richard Graham; Chairman, 1980–86, Director, 1976–86, Fleming Enterprise Investment Trust plc (formerly Crossfriars Trust plc); *b* 31 Jan. 1920; 3rd *s* of Henry Joseph Marshall and Sarah Gertrude McFall; *m* 1945, Clara Louise Debonnaire Mitford; one *s* one *d*. *Educ:* Holmwood Prep. Sch., Lancs; Clifton Coll., Bristol. Joined Pacol Ltd, 1938; Mil. Service, HAC, 1939–40; Colonial Office, 1941–45 (Asst Sec., then Sec., W African Produce Control Bd); Motor & Air Products Ltd, 1946–48; re-joined Pacol Ltd, 1949, Dir 1951; Chm., London Cocoa Terminal Market Assoc., 1954–55; Chm., Cocoa Assoc. of London, 1958–59; Dir 1962–82, Man. Dir 1965–74, Chm., 1970–76, Vice-Chm., 1976–78, Gill & Duffus Group PLC. *Address:* 7 Yew Tree Walk, Effingham, Surrey KT24 5LJ. *T:* (01372) 452727. *Club:* Effingham Golf.

McFARLAND, Alan; *see* McFarland, R. A.

McFARLAND, Prof. David John, DPhil; Professor of Biological Robotics, University of the West of England, 2000–02; Fellow, Balliol College, Oxford, 1966–2000, now Emeritus; *b* 31 Dec. 1938; *s* of John Cyril and Joan Elizabeth McFarland; *m* 1st, 1962, Frances Jill Tomlin; one *s* one *d*; 2nd, 2013, Penelope Jane Farmer. *Educ:* Leighton Park Sch., Reading; Liverpool Univ. (BSc 1st Cl. Hons Zoology, 1961); Oxford Univ. (DPhil Psychology, 1965). Lectr in Psychology, Durham Univ., 1964; Oxford University: Lectr in Psychology, 1966–74; Reader in Animal Behaviour, 1974–2000; Tutor in Psychology, Balliol Coll., 1966–2000. Hofmeyer Fellow, Univ. of the Witwatersrand, 1974; Visiting Professor: Dalhousie Univ., 1968; Rutgers Univ., 1971; Univ. of Penn, 1977; SUNY, Stonybrook, 1978; Univ. of Oregon, 1978; Univ. of Münster, Germany, 1989. Pres., Internat. Ethological Conf., 1981. Pres., Assoc. of Teachers in the Arts and Scis, Lanzarote, 2004–. Editor, Animal Behaviour, 1969–74. *Publications:* (with J. McFarland) An Introduction to the Study of Behaviour, 1969; Feedback Mechanisms in Animal Behaviour, 1971; (ed) Motivational Control Systems Analysis, 1974; (ed) The Oxford Companion to Animal Behaviour, 1981; (with A. Houston) Quantitative Ethology: the state space approach, 1981; (ed) Functional Ontogeny, 1982; Animal Behaviour, 1985, 3rd edn 1999; Problems of Animal Behaviour, 1989; Biologie des Verhaltens, (Germany) 1989, 2nd edn 1999; (with T. Bosser) Intelligent Behavior in Animals and Robots, (USA) 1993; Le Comportement Animal, (France) 2001; (with O. Holland) Artificial Ethology, 2001; The Oxford Dictionary of Animal Behaviour, 2006, 2nd edn 2014; Guilty Robots, Happy Dogs: the question of alien minds, 2008; Death by Eating: the evolution of human food, 2010; God's Own Geneticist: a fable of our times, 2011; The Biology of Time, 2012; articles in scientific learned jls. *Recreations:* writing, potter. *Address:* 7 Drake Court, Scotts Road, W12 8HG; Calle La Escorta, El Golfo, Yaiza 35570, Lanzarote, Spain.

McFARLAND, Prof. Ian Alexander, PhD; Regius Professor of Divinity, University of Cambridge, since 2015; Fellow, Selwyn College, Cambridge, since 2015; *b* Hartford, Conn, 26 July 1963; *s* of Rodney C. and Sandra K. McFarland; *m* 1994, Ann Elizabeth Lillya; two *d*. *Educ:* Trinity Coll., Hartford, Conn (BA Classics 1984); Union Theol Seminary, NY (MDiv 1989); Lutheran Sch. of Theol., Chicago (ThM 1991); Yale Univ. (MPhil 1994; PhD

1995). Clerk, Music Center, Hawaii, 1995–97; Chaplaincy Staff, Queen's Med. Center, Honolulu, 1997–98; Lectr, 1998–2003, Sen. Lectr, 2003–05, in Systematic Theol., Univ. of Aberdeen; Candler School of Theology, Emory University: Associate Prof., 2005–11, Prof., 2011–13, of Systematic Theol.; Bp Mack B. and Rose Stokes Prof. of Theol., 2013–15; Associate Dean, Faculty and Acad. Affairs, 2012–15. Gillespie Vis. Associate Prof. of Religion, Coll. of Wooster, Ohio, 2003–04. *Publications:* Listening to the Least: doing theology from the outside, 1998; Difference and Identity: a theological anthropology, 2001; The Divine Image: envisioning the invisible God, 2005; In Adam's Fall: a meditation on the Christian doctrine of original sin, 2010; From Nothing: a theology of creation, 2014. *Recreations:* hill walking, classical music, opera. *Address:* Faculty of Divinity, University of Cambridge, West Road, Cambridge CB3 9BS. *T:* (01223) 763002. *E:* iam33@cam.ac.uk.

McFARLAND, Sir John (Talbot), 3rd Bt *cr* 1914, of Aberfoyle, Londonderry; TD 1967; Chairman: Malvay Ltd (formerly Lanes (Business Equipment)), 1977–2001; J. T. McFarland Holdings, 1984–2001; Information and Imaging Systems Ltd, 1994–2001; *b* 3 Oct. 1927; *s* of Sir Basil Alexander Talbot McFarland, 2nd Bt, CBE, ERD, and Anne Kathleen (*d* 1952), *d* of late Andrew Henderson; *S* father, 1986; *m* 1957, Mary Scott, *d* of late Dr W. Scott Watson, Londonderry; two *s* two *d*. *Educ:* Marlborough College; Trinity Coll., Oxford. Captain RA (TA), retired 1967. Chm., R. C. Malseed & Co. Ltd, 1957–90; Chairman, 1977–84: Lanes (Derry) Ltd; Lanes (Fuel) Oils Ltd; Lanes Patent Fuels Ltd; Holmes Coal Ltd; Alexander Thompson & Co. Ltd; Nicholl Ballintyne Ltd; J. W. Corbett Ltd; Wattersons Ltd. Chm., Londonderry Lough Swilly Railway Co., 1978–81; Director: Londonderry Gaslight Co., 1958–89; Donegal Holdings Ltd, 1963–85; G. Kinnaird & Son Ltd, 1981–95; Windy Hills Ltd, 1994–95; Wallcoatings Dublin Ltd, 1995–98; Taughboyne Develt Assoc., 1998–2007. Member: Londonderry County Borough Council, 1955–69; NW HMC, 1960–73; Londonderry Port and Harbour Comrs, 1965–73. Jt Chm., Londonderry and Foyle Coll., 1971–76. High Sheriff, Co. Londonderry 1958, City of County of Londonderry 1965–67; DL Londonderry 1962, resigned 1982. *Recreations:* golf, shooting. *Heir: er s* Anthony Basil Scott McFarland [*b* 29 Nov. 1959; *m* 1988, Anne Margaret, BA, ACA, *d* of T. K. Laidlaw, Gernonstown, Slane, Co. Meath. *Educ:* Marlborough Coll.; Trinity College, Dublin (BA). ACA]. *Address:* Dunmore House, Carrigans, Lifford, Co. Donegal, Ireland. *T:* (91) 40120, *Fax:* (91) 40336.

McFARLAND, (Robert) Alan; Member, North Down, Northern Ireland Assembly (UU, 1998–2010, Ind, 2010–11); *b* 9 Aug. 1949; *s* of Dr Albert John Black McFarland and Mary Elizabeth Florence McFarland (*née* Campbell); *m* 1979, Celia Mary Sharp; one *s* two *d*. *Educ:* Rockport Sch., Craigavad, Co. Down; Campbell Coll., Belfast; RMA, Sandhurst. Commnd RTR, 1975; various regtl appts, 1975–81 (despatches, 1981); SO, Orgn and Deployment, HQ 4th Armd Div., 1981–83; Sqn Ldr, Challenger Tank Sqn and HQ Sqn 2nd RTR, 1983–86; SO, Public Relns, HQ SW Dist and UK Mobile Force, 1987–89; Mgt Consultant, MoD, 1989–92; retd in rank of Major, 1992. Parly Asst to Rev. Martin Smyth, MP and Rt Hon. James Molyneaux, MP, H of C, 1992–95; Dir, Somme Heritage Centre, Newtownards, 1996–98. Mem., NI Policing Bd, 2002–06. Contested (Ind) N Down, NI Assembly, 2011. *Recreations:* military history, folk music.

MACFARLANE, family name of **Baron Macfarlane of Bearsden**.

MACFARLANE OF BEARSDEN, Baron *cr* 1991 (Life Peer), of Bearsden in the district of Bearsden and Milngavie; **Norman Somerville Macfarlane,** KT 1996; Kt 1983; DL; FRSE; Hon. Life President: Macfarlane Group PLC, 1999 (Chairman, 1973–98, Managing Director, 1973–90); United Distillers PLC (Chairman, 1987–96); Lord High Commissioner, General Assembly, Church of Scotland, 1992, 1993 and 1997; *b* 5 March 1926; *s* of Daniel Robertson Macfarlane and Jessie Lindsay Somerville; *m* 1953, Marguerite Mary Campbell; one *s* four *d*. *Educ:* High Sch. of Glasgow. Commnd RA, 1945; served Palestine, 1945–47. Founded N. S. Macfarlane & Co. Ltd, 1949; became Macfarlane Group (Clansman) PLC, 1973. Underwriting Mem. of Lloyd's, 1978–97; Chairman: The Fine Art Society PLC, 1976–98 (Hon. Life Pres., 1998); American Trust PLC, 1984–97; Guinness PLC, 1987–89 (Jt Dep. Chm., 1989–92); Director: Clydesdale Bank PLC, 1980–96 (Dep. Chm., 1993–96); General Accident Fire & Life Assce Corp. plc, 1984–96; Edinburgh Fund Managers plc, 1980–98. Dir, Glasgow Chamber of Commerce, 1976–79; Member: Council, CBI Scotland, 1975–81; Bd, Scottish Develt Agency, 1979–87. Chm., Glasgow Develt Agency (formerly Glasgow Action), 1985–92. Scottish Ballet: Dir, 1975–87; Vice Chm., 1983–87; Hon. Pres., 2001–12; Dir, Scottish National Orch., 1977–82; Pres., Royal Glasgow Inst. of the Fine Arts, 1976–87; Mem., Royal Fine Art Commn for Scotland, 1980–82; Scottish Patron, National Art Collection Fund, 1978–; Governor, Glasgow Sch. of Art, 1976–87 (Hon. Fellow, 1993; Hon. Pres., 2001–12); Trustee: Nat. Heritage Meml Fund, 1984–97; Nat. Galls of Scotland, 1986–97; Dir, Culture & Sport Glasgow, 2007–12. Dir, Third Eye Centre, 1978–81. Hon. Pres., Tenovus Scotland, 2006–. Hon. Pres., Charles Rennie Mackintosh Soc., 1988–. Hon. Pres., High Sch. of Glasgow, 1992– (Chm. Govs, 1979–92); Mem. Court, Univ. of Glasgow, 1979–87; Regent, RCSE, 1997–. President: Stationers' Assoc. of GB and Ireland, 1965; Co. of Stationers of Glasgow, 1968–70; Glasgow High Sch. Club, 1970–72. Patron, Scottish Licensed Trade Assoc., 1992–; Hon. Patron, Queen's Park FC. Vice Pres., PGA. Hon. Life Mem., Scottish Football League, 2006. DL Dunbartonshire, 1993. Freeman: Dumfries and Galloway, 2006; City of Glasgow, 2007. FRSE 1991; CCMI (CIMgt 1996). HRSA 1987; HRGI 1987; Hon. FRIAS 1984; Hon. FScotvec 1991; Hon. FRCPSGlas 1992. Hon. LLD: Strathclyde, 1986; Glasgow, 1988; Glasgow Caledonian, 1993; Aberdeen, 1995; DUniv Stirling, 1992; Dr (*hc*) Edinburgh, 1992. St Mungo Prize, City of Glasgow, 2005; Goodman Award, Art & Business, 2007. *Recreations:* golf, cricket, theatre, art. *Address:* Macfarlane Group PLC, Clansman House, 21 Newton Place, Glasgow G3 7PY; 50 Manse Road, Bearsden, Glasgow G61 3PN. *Clubs:* Glasgow Art (Glasgow); Hon. Co. of Edinburgh Golfers, Glasgow Golf.

MACFARLANE, Prof. Alan Donald James, FRAI; FRHistS; FBA 1986; Professor of Anthropological Science, University of Cambridge, 1991–2009, now Emeritus; Fellow, King's College Cambridge, 1981–2008, now Life Fellow; *b* 20 Dec. 1941; *s* of Donald Kennedy Macfarlane and Iris Stirling Macfarlane; *m* 1st, 1966, Gillian Ions; one *d*; 2nd, 1981, Sarah Harrison. *Educ:* Dragon Sch., Oxford; Sedbergh School; Worcester College, Oxford (MA, DPhil); LSE (MPhil); SOAS (PhD). University of Cambridge: Senior Research Fellow in History, King's College, 1971–74; Univ. Lectr in Social Anthropology, 1975–81; Reader in Historical Anthropology, 1981–91. Lectures: Frazer Meml, Liverpool Univ., 1974; Malinowski Meml, LSE, 1978; Radcliffe-Brown Meml, Univ. of Lancaster, 1992; Marett Meml, Univ. of Oxford, 1995; F. W. Maitland Meml, Univ. of Cambridge, 2000; Maruyama, Univ. of Calif, Berkeley, 2006; Sir Li Ka Sheng Dist., China, 2006; Wang Gouwei Meml, Tsinghua Univ., Beijing, 2011. Rivers Meml Medal, 1984, Huxley Meml Medal, 2012, RAI; William J. Goode Award, Amer. Sociol Assoc., 1987. Principal consultant and presenter, The Day the World Took Off (millennium series), C4, 2000. *Publications:* Witchcraft in Tudor and Stuart England, 1970; The Family Life of Ralph Josselin, 1970; Resources and Population, 1976; (ed) The Diary of Ralph Josselin, 1976; Reconstructing Historical Communities, 1977; Origins of English Individualism, 1978; The Justice and the Mare's Ale, 1981; A Guide to English Historical Records, 1983; Marriage and Love in England, 1986; The Culture of Capitalism, 1987; The Cambridge Database System User Manual, 1990; (jtly) The Nagas: hill peoples of North-east India, 1990; (ed and trans. with S. Harrison) Bernard Pignède, The Gurungs of Nepal, 1993; The Savage Wars of Peace, 1997; The Riddle of the Modern World, 2000; The Making of the Modern World, 2001; (with Gerry Martin) The Glass Bathyscaphe, 2002; (with Iris Macfarlane) Green Gold: the empire of tea, 2003; Letters to Lily: on how our world works, 2005; Japan Through the Looking Glass, 2007; Reflections on Cambridge, 2009; The Invention of the Modern World (in Chinese), 2012; (with J. Bruce Lockhart) Dorset Days, 2012; (with J. Bruce Lockhart) Dragon Days, 2012; Individualism, Capitalism and the Modern World (essays), 2013; The Making of the Modern World, 2013; Thomas Matthus and the Making of the Modern World, 2013; The Invention of the Modern World, 2014. *Recreations:* walking, gardening, second-hand book hunting. *Address:* 25 Lode Road, Lode, near Cambridge CB25 9ER. *T:* (01223) 811976. *W:* www.alanamacfarlane.com.

MacFARLANE, Sir Alistair (George James), Kt 2002; CBE 1987; FRS 1984; FREng; FRSE; Principal and Vice-Chancellor of Heriot-Watt University, 1989–96; *b* 9 May 1931; *s* of George R. MacFarlane; *m* 1st, 1954, Nora Williams (*d* 2005); one *s*; 2nd, 2008, Anwen Tudor Davies. *Educ:* Hamilton Academy; Univ. of Glasgow. BSc 1953, DSc 1969, Glasgow; PhD London 1964; MSc Manchester 1973; MA 1974, ScD 1979, Cantab. FIET; FREng (FEng 1981); FRSE 1990. Metropolitan-Vickers, Manchester, 1953–58; Lectr, Queen Mary Coll., Univ. of London, 1959–65, Reader 1965–66; Reader in Control Engrg, Univ. of Manchester Inst. of Sci. and Technology, 1966–69, Prof. 1969–74; Prof. of Engrg and Hd of Information Engrg Div., Univ. of Cambridge, 1974–88; Fellow, 1974–88, Vice-Master, 1980–88, Hon. Fellow, 1989–, Selwyn Coll., Cambridge. Chm., Cambridge Control Ltd, 1985–90; Non-executive Director: Lothian and Edinburgh Enterprise Ltd, 1990–96; British Nuclear Fuels plc, 1995–2000. Member: Council, SERC, 1981–85; Computer Board, 1983–88; Adv. Cttee for Safety of Nuclear Installations, 1987–90; Engrg Tech. Adv. Cttee, DTI, 1991–93; BT Adv. Forum, 1997–98. Chm., Res. Councils' High Performance Computing Strategy Gp, 1995–98. Comr, Nat. Commn on Educn, 1991–93; Academic Advr, 1997–2000, CEO and Dir, 2000–01, Univ. of Highlands and Islands project; Rector, UHI Millennium Inst., 2002–04. Chairman: Scottish Univs Wkg Party on Teaching and Learning in an Expanding Higher Educn System, 1991–92 (MacFarlane Report, 1992); Scottish Council for Res. in Educn, 1992–98; Scottish Library and Information Council, 1994–98. Royal Society: Vice-Pres., 1997–99; Mem. Council, 1997–99; Chm., Educn Cttee, 2000–04. Trustee, Scottish Internat. Educn Trust, 1994–2010. Hon. DEng: UMIST, 1995; Glasgow, 1995; DUniv: Heriot-Watt, 1997; Paisley, 1997; Hon. DSc Abertay Dundee, 1998; Hon. DLitt Lincolnshire and Humberside, 1999. Medals: Centennial, ASME, 1980; Sir Harold Hartley, Inst. of Measurement and Control, 1982; Achievement, IEE, 1992; Faraday, IEE, 1993; Oldenburger, ASME, 2004. *Publications:* Engineering Systems Analysis, 1964; Dynamical System Models, 1970; (with I. Postlethwaite) A Complex Variable Approach to the Analysis of Linear Multivariable Feedback Systems, 1979; (ed) Frequency-Response Methods in Control Systems, 1979; (ed) Complex Variable Methods for Linear Multivariable Feedback Systems, 1980; (with S. Hung) Multivariable Feedback: a quasi-classical approach, 1982; (with G. K. H. Pang) An Expert Systems Approach to Computer-Aided Design of Multivariable Systems, 1987. *Address:* Tregarth, 2 Marine Parade, Barmouth, Gwynedd LL42 1NA. *E:* alistairmacfarlane33@gmail.com.

MACFARLANE, Rev. Alwyn James Cecil; Parish Minister of Newlands (South), Church of Scotland, 1968–85; Extra Chaplain to the Queen in Scotland, since 1992 (Chaplain, 1977–92); *b* 14 June 1922; *s* of James Waddell Macfarlane and Ada Cecilia Rankin; *m* 1953, Joan Cowell Harris; one *s* one *d*. *Educ:* Cargilfield Sch.; Rugby Sch.; Oxford Univ. (MA); Edinburgh Univ. Served War: N Africa, Italy, Greece; Liaison Officer in Black Watch with 12th Bde, 1942–46. Ordained, 1951; served in parishes in Ross-shire, Edinburgh, Glasgow, Australia. *Recreations:* photography, walking. *Address:* Flat 12, Homeburn House, 177 Fenwick Road, Giffnock, Glasgow G46 6JD.

McFARLANE, Rt Hon. Sir Andrew (Ewart), Kt 2005; PC 2011; **Rt Hon. Lord Justice McFarlane;** a Lord Justice of Appeal, since 2011; *b* 20 June 1954; *s* of Gordon McFarlane and Olive McFarlane (*née* Davies); *m* 1981, Susanna Jane Randolph (DL Herefords); four *d*. *Educ:* Shrewsbury Sch.; Durham Univ. (BA Hons Law 1975); Univ. of Wales (LLM Canon Law 1998). Called to the Bar, Gray's Inn, 1977, Bencher, 2003 (Chm., Mgt Cttee, 2014); QC 1998; an Asst Recorder, 1995–99; a Recorder, 1999–2005; a Dep. High Court Judge, 2000–05; a Judge of the High Court of Justice, Family Div., 2005–11; Family Div. Liaison Judge, Midland Circuit, 2006–11. Mem., Family Justice Review Panel, 2010–11. Chm., Tribunal Appts Bd, Council of Inns of Court, 2012–. Chm., Family Law Bar Assoc., 2001–03. Pres., Clergy Discipline Tribunals, 2014–; Chm., Clergy Discipline Commn, 2014–. Mem., Adv. Bd, UCL Judicial Inst., 2011–. Pres., Collingwood Coll., Durham Alumni Assoc., 2009–. Trustee, Young Minds, 2001–08. Patron, HOPE Family Centre, Bromyard, 2010–. Dep. Chancellor, Dio. of Wakefield, 2004–06; Chancellor, Dio. of Exeter, 2006–. *Publications:* (with David Hershman) Children: law and practice, 1991; (contrib.) Family Court Practice, 1993–; (with Madeleine Reardon) Child Care and Adoption Law, 2006, 2nd edn 2010. *Recreations:* family life, theatre, vegetable gardening, beekeeping. *Address:* c/o Royal Courts of Justice, Strand, WC2A 2LL. *Club:* Garrick.

MACFARLANE, Anne Bridget; Master of the Court of Protection, 1982–95; *b* 26 Jan. 1930; *d* of late Dr David Griffith and Dr Grace Griffith; *m* 1957, James Douglas Macfarlane (*d* 1999); two *d*. *Educ:* nine schools; Bristol Univ. (LLB). Admitted Solicitor, 1954. HM Land Registry, 1966–75; Registrar, Bromley County Court, 1975–82. *Publications:* (contrib.) Atkin's Court Forms, 2nd edn 1983; Older Adults' Decision-Making and the Law, 1996. *Recreation:* collecting Victorian tiles. *Club:* Law Society (Hon. Life Mem., 1996).

MACFARLANE, Christine Anne; *see* Salt, C. A.

MACFARLANE, Sir (David) Neil, Kt 1988; Chairman, Associated Nursing Services, 1994–2004; *b* 7 May 1936; *yr s* of late Robert and of Dulcie Macfarlane; *m* 1961, June Osmond King, Somerset; two *s* one *d*. *Educ:* St Aubyn's Prep. Sch.; Bancroft's Sch., Woodford Green. Short Service Commission, Essex Regt, 1955–58; served TA, 265 LAA, RA, 1961–66. Joined Shell Mex and BP, 1959; contested (C): East Ham (North), 1970; Sutton and Cheam, by-election, 1972. Parly Under-Sec. of State (Dep. Minister for the Arts), DES, 1979–81; Parly Under-Sec. of State, DoE, 1981–85 (with spec. responsibility for Sport, 1981–85, for Children's Play, 1983–85). Mem., All Party Select Cttee on Science and Technology, 1974–79; MP (C) Sutton and Cheam, Feb. 1974–1992. Chairman: Rushman Lloyd PLC, 1994–97; Securicor plc, 1995–2003 (Dir, 1992–2003); Director: RMC, 1987–2001; Bradford and Bingley Bldg Soc., 1987–2000. Chairman: Sports Aid Foundn, 1986–87; Golf Fund PLC; Vice-Pres. PGA, 1985–. Trustee, England and Wales Cricket Foundn, 1997–. Mem., National Trust, 1976–. Pres., Reading Cons. Assoc. Freeman, City of London, 2000; Founder Master, 1999–2002, Guild of Security Professionals (now Security Professionals' Co.). *Publications:* Sport and Politics: a world divided, 1986. *Recreations:* golf, cricket-watching. *Address:* Beechwood House, Pangbourne, West Berks RG8 7AT. *Clubs:* MCC, Lord's Taverners; Essex County Cricket; Royal & Ancient Golf, Huntercombe Golf.

McFARLANE, Prof. Duncan Campbell, PhD; Professor of Industrial Informational Engineering, University of Cambridge, since 2010; Fellow, St John's College, Cambridge, since 1996; *b* 3 May 1963; *m* 1993, Meredith Lillian Bhathal (*d* 2008); one *s* one *d*. *Educ:* Trinity Coll., Univ. of Melbourne (BEng Hons 1984); Queens' Coll., Cambridge (PhD 1988). BHP Co. Ltd: Cadet, 1980; Res. Officer, 1985–92; Co-ordinator, 1992–94; University of Cambridge: Lectr, 1995–2000, Sen. Lectr, 2000–03, Reader, 2003–06, in Automation Systems; Prof. of Service and Support Engrg, 2006–11; Mem., Steering Bd, Cambridge Centre for Smart Infrastructure and Construction, 2011–. Vis. Prof., Univ. of Melbourne, 2008, 2010. Dir, Distributed Automation and Inf. Lab., 2000–; Res. Dir, Auto ID Centre, 2000–03; Dir, Cambridge Auto ID Lab., 2003–07. Chm., RedBite Solutions Ltd, 2007–. *Publications:* (with K. Glover) Robust Controller Design Using Normalised Coprime

Factor Plant Descriptions, 1990; (ed jtly) Holonic and Multi-Agent Systems for Manufacturing, 2003; (with N. Chokshi) A Distributed Coordination Approach to Reconfigurable Process Control, 2008; over 100 jl and conf. papers. *Recreations:* walking, swimming, cricket, green Penguins (collecting), bottle-top collecting. *Address:* St John's College, Cambridge CB2 1TP. *Club:* Melbourne Cricket.

MACFARLANE, Ian John, AC 2004; Governor, Reserve Bank of Australia, 1996–2006; *b* 22 June 1946; *s* of Gordon H. and Lilias E. M. Macfarlane; *m* 1970, Heather (*née* Payne); one *s* one *d*. *Educ:* Monash Univ. Inst. of Econs and Stats, Oxford Univ., 1971–72; OECD, Paris, 1973–78; Reserve Bank of Australia, 1979–2006: various posts, 1979–88; Head, Res. Dept, 1988–90; Asst Gov. (Economic), 1990–92; Dep. Gov., 1992–96. Non-executive Director: Australia and NZ Banking Group Ltd, 2007–; Leighton Hldgs, 2007–13. Dir, Woolworths Ltd, 2007–. International Adviser: Goldman Sachs, 2007–; China Banking Regulatory Commn, 2010–. Centenary Medal, 2003.

McFARLANE, Ven. Janet Elizabeth; Director of Communications, Diocese of Norwich, since 1999; Archdeacon of Norwich, since 2009; *b* Stoke-on-Trent, 25 Nov. 1964; *d* of David James McFarlane and Anne McFarlane; *m* 2004, Andrew Ridoutt. *Educ:* Univ. of Sheffield (BMedSci 1987); St John's Coll., Univ. of Durham (BA 1992); Cranmer Hall, Univ. of Durham (DipMin 1993). Speech Therapist, N Staffs HA, 1987–90; ordained deacon, 1993, priest, 1994; Curate, Stafford Team Ministry, 1993–96; Chaplain: Ely Cathedral, 1996–99; to Bishop of Norwich, 2000–09. *Publications:* (compiled) Pocket Prayers for Advent and Christmas, 2009; Reflections for Daily Prayer: Advent 2010 to Christ the King 2011, 2010; Reflections for Daily Prayer: Advent 2011 to Christ the King 2012, 2011; Pocket Prayers of Blessing, 2012. *Address:* 31 Bracondale, Norwich NR1 2AT. *E:* archdeacon.norwich@dioceseofnorwich.org.

McFARLANE, John, OBE 1995; Chairman, Barclays plc, since 2015; *b* Dumfries, 14 June 1947; *s* of John McFarlane and Margaret Campbell; *m* Anne; three *d*. *Educ:* Dumfries Acad.; Univ. of Edinburgh (MA); Cranfield Univ. (MBA). Man. Dir, Citicorp, UK Reg., 1975–93; Exec. Dir, Standard Chartered plc, 1993–97; CEO, ANZ Banking Gp Ltd, 1997–2007. Chairman: Aviva plc, 2012–15; FirstGroup plc, 2014–15; non-executive Director: Capital Radio plc, 1995–98; Royal Bank of Scotland plc, 2008–12; Westfield Corp., 2008–; Old Oak Hldgs Ltd, 2008–. Chm., TheCityUK, 2015–. Ext. Mem., Financial Services Trade and Investment Bd, 2015–. Centenary Medal (Australia), 2003. *Address:* Barclays plc, 1 Churchill Place, Canary Wharf, EC14 5HP. *T:* (020) 7116 6002. *E:* officeofthechairman@barclays.com.

MACFARLANE, Prof. John Thomson, DM; FRCP, FRCPGlas, FRCGP; Professor of Respiratory Medicine, University of Nottingham, 2004–08, Emeritus Professor, 2013; Consultant General and Respiratory Physician, Nottingham University Hospitals, 1982–2008; *b* 21 Nov. 1948; *s* of Sir George Gray Macfarlane, CB and of Barbara Grant Macfarlane; *m* 1971, Rosamund MacInnes, medical researcher and photographer; two *s*. *Educ:* Merton Coll., Oxford (BA Hons 1970); Oxford University Med. Sch. (BM BCh 1973; MA 1983; DM 1983). MRCP 1976, FRCP 1989; MRCGP 1999, FRCGP 2008; FRCPGlas 2009. LRPS 2009; DPAGB 2012; AFIAP 2013; PPSA 2013, EPSA 2015. Med. trng posts in Oxford, Brompton Hosp., London, and Ahmadu Bello Univ. Hosp., Zaria, Nigeria, 1974–82. Vis. Prof., Faculty of Life Scis, Univ. of Manchester, 2010–. Chm., British Thoracic Soc., 2006–08; Trustee and Mem. Council, RCP, 2006–08. UK Representative: on Council, Eur. Respiratory Soc., 2003–06; to Fedn of Eur. Respiratory Socs, 2006–08. *Publications:* (jtly) Legionella Infections, 1986; (jtly) Colour Atlas of Respiratory Infections, 1993; many articles, revs, guidelines and chapters in major jls and internat. textbooks, incl. Oxford Textbook of Medicine, mainly on pneumonia, legionnaires' disease and lung infections. *Recreations:* mountaineering, travel, photography, cooking, medical and military history. *Address:* Watergate Barn, Loweswater, Cumbria CA13 0RU. *T:* (01900) 85289. *E:* jtmacfarlane@gmail.com.

See also R. G. Macfarlane.

MACFARLANE, Sir Neil; *see* Macfarlane, Sir D. N.

MacFARLANE, Neil; *see* MacFarlane, S. N.

MACFARLANE, Patricia Mary, (Trisha); *see* Greenhalgh, P. M.

MACFARLANE, Dr Robert Grant; writer; Senior Lecturer in English, University of Cambridge, since 2011; Fellow, Emmanuel College, Cambridge, since 2003; *b* Oxford, 15 Aug. 1976; *s* of Prof. John Thomson Macfarlane, *qv*; *m* 2000, Julia Lovell; two *s* one *d*. *Educ:* Nottingham High Sch.; Pembroke Coll., Cambridge (BA 1997; PhD); Magdalen Coll., Oxford (MPhil). Lectr in English, Univ. of Cambridge, 2006–11. Hon. DLitt: Gloucestershire, 2013; Aberdeen, 2014. *Publications:* Mountains of the Mind, 2003; Original Copy, 2007; The Wild Places, 2007; The Old Ways, 2012; (jtly) Holloway, 2013; Landmarks, 2015. *Recreations:* mountaineering and hill walking, conservation, chess. *Address:* Emmanuel College, St Andrew's Street, Cambridge CB2 3AP. *T:* (01223) 334200.

MacFARLANE, Prof. (Stephen) Neil, DPhil; Lester B. Pearson Professor of International Relations, since 1996, and Head, Department of Politics and International Relations, 2005–10, University of Oxford; Fellow, St Anne's College, Oxford, since 1996; *b* 7 March 1954; *s* of David Livingstone MacFarlane and Gertrude Cecile (*née* Straight); *m* 1981, Anne Church Bigelow; three *s* one *d*. *Educ:* Dartmouth Coll., NH (AB); Balliol Coll., Oxford (MA, MPhil, DPhil 1982). University of Virginia, USA: Asst Prof., 1984–87; Associate Prof., 1987–91; Dir, Center for Russian and E European Studies, 1990–91; Queen's University, Kingston, Ontario: Prof. of Political Studies, 1991–96; Dir, Centre for Internat. Relns, 1995–96; Dir, Centre for Internat. Studies, Oxford, 1997–2002. *Publications:* Intervention and Regional Security, 1985; The Idea of National Liberation, 1985; Western Engagement in the Caucasus and Central Asia, 1999; Politics and Humanitarian Action, 2000; Intervention in Contemporary World Politics, 2002; The United Nations and Human Security: a critical history, 2006; articles in Internat. Affairs, Internat. Jl, Survival, Post-Soviet Affairs, World Politics, Security Studies, Third World Qly. *Address:* St Anne's College, Oxford OX2 6HS. *T:* (01865) 274800.

MACFARLANE, Maj.-Gen. William Thomson, CB 1981; Consultant/Administrator, Sion College, 1984–93; *b* Bath, 2 Dec. 1925; *s* of late James and Agnes Macfarlane; *m* 1955, Dr Helen D. Meredith; one *d*. Commissioned Royal Signals, 1947. Served Europe, Near East, ME, and Far East. Commanded 16th Parachute Bde Signal Squadron, 1961–63; Military Asst, Commander FARELF, 1964–66; Comd 1st Div. HQ and Signal Regt, BAOR, 1967–70; Services Mem., Cabinet Office Secretariat, 1970–72; Comd, Corps Royal Signals, 1972–73; Dir of Public Relations (Army), MoD, 1973–75; C of S, UKLF, 1976–78; Chief, Jt Services Liaison Organisation, Bonn, 1978–80. Exec. Dir, Hong Kong Resort Co. Ltd, 1981–84; Dir, Compton Manor Estates (formerly Farms) Ltd, 1990–2010. Col Comdt, 1980–85, Rep. Col Comdt, 1985, Royal Corps of Signals. *Club:* Naval and Military.

MacFARQUHAR, Prof. Roderick Lemonde; Leroy B. Williams Professor of History and Political Science, Harvard University, 1990–2012, now Leroy B. Williams Research Professor (Professor of Government, 1984–2012; Chairman, Department of Government, 1998–2004); *b* 2 Dec. 1930; *s* of Sir Alexander MacFarquhar, KBE, CIE, and of Berenice Whitburn; *m* 1st, 1964, Emily Jane Cohen (*d* 2001); one *s* one *d*; 2nd, 2012, Dalena Wright. *Educ:* Fettes Coll.; Oxford Univ. (BA); Harvard Univ. (AM); LSE (PhD). Specialist on China, Daily Telegraph (and later Sunday Telegraph), 1955–61; Founding Editor, China Quarterly, 1959–68; Rockefeller Grantee, 1962; Reporter, BBC TV programme Panorama, 1963–64. Associate Fellow, St Antony's Coll., Oxford, 1965–68. Mem., Editorial Bd, New Statesman, 1965–69; Ford Foundation Grant, 1968; Senior Research Fellow, Columbia Univ., 1969; Senior Research Fellow, RIIA, 1971–74 (Mem. Council, 1978–83); Co-presenter, BBC Gen. Overseas Services 24 Hours prog., 1972–74, 1979–80. Governor, SOAS, 1978–83; Dir, Fairbank Center for E Asian Res., Harvard Univ., 1986–92, 2005–06; Mem. Adv. Bd, Smith Richardson Foundn, 2001–09. Contested: (Lab) Ealing South, 1966; (Lab) Meriden, March 1968; (SDP) Derbys S, 1983. MP (Lab) Belper, Feb. 1974–1979; PPS to Minister of State, FCO, March 1974; resignation accepted, April 1975; reappointed June 1975; PPS to Sec. of State, DHSS, 1976–78. Member: N Atlantic Assembly, 1974–79; Select Cttee for Sci. and Technology, 1976–79; Trilateral Commn, 1976–98 (Mem. Exec. Cttee, 1976–84); Exec. Cttee, Fabian Soc., 1976–80. Leverhulme Res. Fellow, 1980–83; Fellow: Woodrow Wilson Center, Smithsonian Instn, 1980–81; Amer. Acad. of Arts and Scis, 1986–. Vis. Professor: of Govt, Harvard, 1982; Lee Kuan Yew Sch. of Public Policy, NUS, 2005; Guest Prof., Peking Univ., 1997–2000; Hon. Prof., Shandong Univ., 2011–; inaugurated: Inchon Meml Lectureship, Korea Univ., 1987; Merle Goldman History Lectureship, Boston Univ., 1997; Kimsey Lectureship, Central Party Sch., Beijing, 2003; inaugurated Merle Rosenblatt Goldman Chair in Asian Studies, Sarah Lawrence Coll., NY, 2010; Dist. Vis. Fellow, Stanford Center at Peking Univ., 2013; Sin Wai-Kin Dist. Vis. Prof. in Humanities, Hong Kong Univ., 2015. Trustee, Kennedy Meml Trust, 2001–10. *Publications:* The Hundred Flowers, 1960; The Sino-Soviet Dispute, 1961; Chinese Ambitions and British Policy (Fabian Pamphlet), 1966; (ed) China under Mao, 1966; Sino-American Relations, 1949–71, 1972; The Forbidden City, 1972; The Origins of the Cultural Revolution: Vol. 1, Contradictions among the People 1956–1957, 1974; Vol. 2, The Great Leap Forward 1958–1960, 1983; Vol. 3, The Coming of the Cataclysm 1961–1966, 1997 (Levenson 20th Century China Prize, Assoc. for Asian Studies, 1999; trans. Chinese, 2012); (ed jtly) Cambridge History of China, Vol. 14, 1987, Vol. 15, 1991; (ed jtly) The Secret Speeches of Chairman Mao, 1989; (ed) The Politics of China 1949–1989, 1993, 2nd edn, as The Politics of China, the Eras of Mao and Deng, 1997, 3rd edn, as The Politics of China, Sixty Years of the People's Republic of China, 2011; (ed jtly) The Paradox of China's Post-Mao Reforms, 1999; (jtly) Mao's Last Revolution, 2006 (trans. Chinese, French, Spanish, 2009, Japanese, 2010); articles in Foreign Affairs, The World Today, Atlantic Monthly, Pacific Affairs, Commentary, Newsweek, NY Review of Books, etc. *Recreations:* reading, listening to music, travel, grandchildren. *Address:* Fairbank Center, Harvard University, 1730 Cambridge Street #133, Cambridge, MA 02138, USA. *T:* (617) 495 2810.

McFEE, Bruce James; Director, Environmental Services Pest Control Ltd, Paisley, since 2005; *b* 18 May 1961; *s* of James and Ellen Margaret McFee; *m* 1997, Iris Lille; twin *s*. *Educ:* Johnstone High Sch. Formerly Customer Service Manager, Scotland's largest ind. pest control co. Member (SNP): Renfrew DC, 1988–96 (Sec., 1988–92, Leader, 1992–96, SNP Gp); Renfrewshire Council, 1995–2003 and 2007–12 (Leader, SNP Gp, 1995–2003). MSP (SNP) Scotland West, 2003–07. Est. ABR Scotland, 2012; Ed., www.abrscotland.com. *Recreations:* travel, DIY. *Address:* 36 Troubridge Avenue, Kilbarchan, Johnstone PA10 2AU.

McFEELY, Elizabeth Sarah Ann C.; *see* Craig-McFeely.

McFERRAN, Arthur Joseph, CBE 2005; Managing Director, since 1999, and Vice President, since 2013, Allstate Northern Ireland Ltd (formerly Northbrook Technology of NI Ltd); *b* 30 May 1951; *s* of Dr Francis Michael Joseph McFerran and Margaret Mary Ethna McFerran; *m* 1974, Patricia McNally; two *s* one *d*. *Educ:* St Malachy's Coll., Belfast; Queen's Univ., Belfast. Salesperson, Rank Xerox, 1972–79; Man. Dir, Logicom Ltd, 1979–97; Vice-Pres., Sales and Mktg, IMRglobal Inc., 1997–99; Vice Pres., Allstate Corp., 2013–. Non-executive Director: Northern Bank Ltd, 2005–14; Strategic Investment Bd, NI, 2009–. Board Member: Springvale Trng Ltd, 1999–; BITC NI, 2005–; NI Sci. Park Foundn, 2010–. Pres., NI Chamber of Commerce and Industry, 2008–10 (Vice-Pres., 2006–08). Hon. DSc Ulster, 2010. *Recreations:* golf, ski-ing, walking. *Address:* Allstate Northern Ireland Ltd, 9 Lanyon Place, Belfast BT1 3LZ. *T:* (028) 9067 8000, *Fax:* (028) 9034 6550. *E:* amcfe@allstate.com. *Club:* Fortwilliam Golf (Belfast).

McGAHAN, Bernard Joseph, (Barney), CBE 2014; Permanent Secretary, Department for Regional Development, Northern Ireland, 2014; Interim Chief Executive, Northern Ireland Policing Board, since 2015; *b* 19 March 1954; *s* of Patrick and Rita McGahan; *m* 1976, Teresa Corrigan (marr. diss. 2012); three *d*. *Educ:* Queen's Univ., Belfast (BSc Maths and Computer Sci. 1976). FCCA 1986. Dir, Financial Mgt, Dept of Health and Social Services, NI, 1991–98; Dir, Ops, NI Social Security Agency, 1999–2003; Chief Exec., NI Child Support Agency, 2004–06; Dep. Sec., Dept for Social Develt, 2006–11, Dept for Regl Develt, 2011–14, NI. Chm., Armagh Coll. of Further and Higher Educn, 2002–06. Gov., St Mary's UC, Belfast, 2010–15. *Recreations:* chess, gardening, walking. *Address:* Northern Ireland Policing Board, Waterside Tower, 31 Clarendon Road, Clarendon Dock, Belfast BT1 3BG. *T:* (028) 9040 8535. *E:* barney.mcgahan@nipolicingboard.org.uk.

McGANN, Heidi-Louise; *see* Thomas, H.-L.

McGANN, Prof. Jerome John, PhD; John Stewart Bryan University Professor, University of Virginia, since 1997 (John Stewart Bryan Professor of English, 1987–97); *b* 22 July 1937; *s* of John J. McGann and Marie V. McGann (*née* Lecouffe); *m* 1960, Anne Lanni; two *s* one *d*. *Educ:* Le Moyne Coll. (BS); Syracuse Univ. (MA); Yale Univ. (PhD 1966). Asst Prof., then Prof., Univ. of Chicago, 1966–75; Professor: Johns Hopkins Univ., 1975–81; CIT, 1981–87. Fulbright Fellow, 1965–66; Guggenheim Fellow, 1970–71 and 1976–81; NEH Fellow, 1975–76 and 1987–89. Co-founder: Inst. for Advanced Technol. in the Humanities, 1992; Speculative Computing Lab., 2001; Founding Dir, Networked Infrastructure for Nineteenth-century Electronic Scholarship, 2003–08. Lectures: Clark, Trinity Coll., Cambridge, 1988; Carpenter, Univ. of Chicago, 1988; Alexander, Univ. of Toronto, 1986; Beckman, Univ. of Calif (Berkeley), 1992; Lansdowne, Univ. of Victoria, 1994; Patten, Indiana Univ., 1995; Byron, Univ. of Nottingham, 1998; Hulme, Univ. of London, 1998; James Murray Brown, Univ. of Aberdeen, 2007. Fellow, Amer. Acad. of Arts and Scis, 1994. Hon. DHL Chicago, 1997; Hon. DPhil Athens, 2009. Melville Kane Award, Amer. Poetry Soc., 1973; Distinguished Schol. Award, Byron Soc., 1989; Wilbur Cross Medal, Yale Univ., 1994; Richard Lyman Award, Nat. Humanities Center, 2002; James Russell Lowell Award, MLA, 2002; Lifetime Achievement Award, Mellon Foundn, 2003. *Publications:* Fiery Dust: Byron's poetic development, 1969; (ed) Pelham, or The Adventures of a Gentleman, by Edward Bulwer-Lytton, 1972; Swinburne: an experiment in criticism, 1972; Don Juan in Context, 1976; Air Heart Sermons (poems), 1976; (with J. Kauffman) Writing Home (poems), 1978; (with J. Kahn) Nerves in Patterns (poems), 1979; (ed) Byron: the complete poetical works, Vol. I 1980, Vols II and III 1981, Vols IV and V 1986, Vol. VI 1991, Vol. VII 1993; The Romantic Ideology: a critical investigation, 1983; A Critique of Modern Textual Criticism, 1983, 2nd edn 1992; The Beauty of Inflections: literary investigations in historical method and theory, 1985; (ed) Textual Studies and Literary Interpretation, 1985; (ed jtly) The Manuscripts of the Younger Romantics: Byron, Vol. I 1985, Vol. II 1986, Vols III and IV 1988; (ed) Historical Studies and Literary Criticism, 1985; (ed) The Oxford Authors Byron, 1986; Social Values and Poetic Acts, 1987; Towards a Literature of Knowledge, 1989; (ed) Victorian Connections, 1989; (ed) Postmodern Poetries, 1990; The Textual Condition, 1991; (ed) The New Oxford Book of Romantic Period Verse, 1993; Black Riders: the visible language of modernism, 1993; (ed) A Symposium on Russian Postmodernism, 1993; (ed) Byron: the Oxford poetry library, 1994; Four Last Poems (poems), 1996; Poetics of Sensibility: a revolution in literary style, 1997; (ed jtly) Letitia Elizabeth Landon: selected writings, 1997; Complete Writings and Pictures of Dante Gabriel Rossetti: a hypermedia research archive,

1999; D. G. Rossetti and The Game that Must be Lost, 2000; Radiant Textuality: literature since the World Wide Web, 2001; Byron and Romanticism, 2002; The Collected Writings of Dante Gabriel Rossetti, 2003; Algernon Charles Swinburne: major poems and selected prose, 2004; The Scholar's Art: literature and criticism in a managed world, 2006; The Point is to Change It: poetry and criticism in the continuing present, 2007; Are the Humanities Inconsequent?: an interpretation of Marx's Riddle of the Dog, 2009; Byron's Manfred, 2009; (ed) The Black Riders and Other Lines, by Stephen Crane, 2009; (ed) Online Humanities Scholarship: The Shape of Things to Come, 2010 The Invention Tree, 2012; (ed) Poe and the Remapping of Antebellum Print Culture: a new republic of letters, memory and scholarship in the age of digital republication, 2014; The Poet Edgar Allan Poe: alien angel, 2014. *Recreations:* squash, yoga. *Address:* PO Box 529, Ivy, VA 22945–0529, USA.

McGARRY, Ian; General Secretary, British Actors' Equity Association, 1991–2005; *b* 27 Feb. 1941; *s* of John and Jean McGarry; *m* 1964, Christine Smith (marr. diss. 1989); one *s*. *Educ:* Chichester High Sch.; Lewes County Grammar Sch. Labour Party Constituency Agent, Putney, 1964–76; Asst General Sec., Equity, 1976–91. *Recreations:* golf, football (spectator), horse racing. *Address:* The White Cottage, Barrington, Ilminster, Som TA19 0JB. *T:* (01460) 55243.

McGARRY, Natalie; MP (SNP) Glasgow East, since 2015; *b* Fife, 7 Sept. 1981; partner, David Meikle. *Educ:* Univ. of Aberdeen (law degree). Policy advr in voluntary sector. Columnist: Scotsman, Herald. SNP spokesperson on disabilities, 2015–. *Address:* House of Commons, SW1A 0AA.

McGARVA, John, (Jack); a District Judge (Magistrates' Courts), since 2010; *b* Lancaster, 23 Nov. 1961; *s* of John and Dorothy McGarva; *m* 1991, Tracey Worrall; two *s* two *d*. *Educ:* Queen's Park High Sch., Chester; Sheffield Univ. (LLB Hons 1983). Admitted as solicitor, 1987; Asst Solicitor, 1987–91, Partner, 1991–97, Wayman-Hales, Solicitors; Partner, Hill Dickinson, Solicitors, 1997–2009. Independent Chair: Standards Cttee, Chester CC, 2008–09; Standards Cttee, Cheshire West and Chester, 2009–10. *Recreation:* rowing. *Address:* North Staffordshire Justice Centre, Ryecroft, Newcastle-under-Lyme, Staffs ST5 2AA. *Clubs:* Chester City; Royal Chester Rowing.

McGARVEY, Alan; independent specialist in local community economic and industrial development, 1996–2012; *b* 22 June 1942; *s* of William Johnson and Rosina McGarvey; *m* 1st, 1967, Eileen Cook (*d* 1992); 2nd, 1997, Shirlee Ann Gleeson. *Educ:* Wallsend Grammar Sch.; Rutherford Coll. of Further Educn; Univ. of Newcastle (BSc); Cranfield Sch. of Management (MBA). C. A. Parsons, 1958–64 (apprentice); junior management positions: RTZ, 1968–71; Decca Gp, 1972–76; MK Electric, 1976–78; Director, Small Company Div., NEB, 1978–82; Chief Exec., Greater London Enterprise Bd, 1982–86; management consultant, 1986–88; Chief Exec., Greater Manchester Econ. Develt Ltd, 1987–90; ind. regl/local develt specialist, 1990–93; specialist, Regl and Small and Medium Enterprises Develt, EC, 1993–96. Labour Party, 1974–2013; Mem., Wandsworth Borough Council, 1981–86 (Dep. Opposition Leader, 1982–83); Chm., Battersea Constituency Labour Parties, 1978–82. Exec. Mem., Wandsworth CRC, 1973–82; Board Member: Battersea Arts Centre Trust, 1982–88; Northern Chamber Orch., 1988–93; Member: Jt Governing Board, Centre for Development of Industry (EEC-ACP Lomé), 1981–90; Adv. Council, Cttee for Industrial Co-operation (EEC-ACP), 1990–96. Sch. Gov., 1973–91; Gov., Poynton High Sch., 2013–. *Recreations:* gardening, reading (science fiction, history, philosophy), creative writing and painting, Tai Chi. *Address:* Willowbank, 9 Anglesey Drive, Poynton SK12 1BT. *T:* 07544 409725. *E:* alan.mcgarvey4@gmail.com.

McGAUGHRIN, Anne; Legal Director, Government Legal Department (formerly Treasury Solicitor's Department); *b* Glasgow, 25 Jan. 1957. *Educ:* York Univ. (BA Jt Hons English and Hist.). Admitted solicitor, 1986; Adviser: Plumstead Law Centre, 1979–84; Cullen & Co., 1984–88; PR, Canon Inc., Tokyo, 1988–91; Legal Advr, Govt Legal Service, 1992–. *Publications:* (ed and contrib.) Exploring Japan, 1991. *Recreations:* enjoying family, friends, the arts and the great outdoors.

McGEACHY, Alistair Laird, WS; a Judge of the Upper Tribunal (Immigration and Asylum Chamber) (formerly a Vice President, Immigration Appeal Tribunal, later a Senior Immigration Judge, Asylum and Immigration Tribunal), since 2004; *b* 2 April 1949; *s* of William Laird McGeachy and Alice McGeachy (*née* Hill); *m* 1978, Jennifer Heather Macleod; two *s* one *d*. *Educ:* Strathallan Sch.; Univ. of Edinburgh (LLB Jt Hons Law and Hist.). Admitted solicitor: Scotland, 1974; England, 1982; WS 1975; with Fyfe Ireland, 1974–76; Refugee, then Tribunal, Counsellor, UKIAS, 1976–82; with Manches and Co., 1982–84; Partner, Macdonald Stacey, subseq. incorporated in Kidd Rapinet, 1984–97; Adjudicator of Immigration Appeals, 1997–2004; Judge, Special Immigration Appeals Commn, 2013–. Liveryman, Gardeners' Co., 1990 (Clerk, 1985–90). *Recreations:* reading, visiting art galleries, travel. *Address:* Upper Tribunal (Immigration and Asylum Chamber), Field House, 15 Breams Buildings, EC4A 1DZ.

McGEE, Prof. James O'Donnell, FMedSci; Professor of Morbid Anatomy, University of Oxford, 1975–99, now Emeritus; Fellow of Linacre College, Oxford, 1975, now Emeritus; *b* 27 July 1939; *s* of Michael and Bridget McGee; *m* 1961, Anne Lee (*d* 2012); one *s* two *d*. *Educ:* Univ. of Glasgow. MB, ChB, PhD, MD; MA (Oxon). FRCPath 1986; FRCPGlas 1989. Various appts in Univ. Dept of Pathology, Royal Infirmary, Glasgow, 1962–69; Roche Inst. of Molecular Biology, Nutley, NJ: MRC Fellow 1969–70; Vis. Scientist 1970–71; Distinguished Vis. Scientist, 1981 and 1989; Dept of Pathology, Royal Infirmary, Glasgow: Lectr 1971–74; Sen. Lectr, 1974–75. Member: Scientific Cttee, 1978–88, Grants Cttee, 1988–92, Cancer Res. Campaign; Cttee on Safety of Medicines, 1987–89 (Safety and Efficacy Sub Cttee, 1984–87); Kettle Meml Lectr, RCPath, 1980; Annual Guest Lecturer: Royal Coll. of Physicians, Ireland, 1986; Royal Acad. of Medicine (Ireland), 1985. Founder FMedSci 1998. Bellahouston Gold Medal, Glasgow Univ., 1973. *Publications:* Biopsy Pathology of Liver, 1980, 2nd edn 1988; In Situ Hybridisation: principles and practice, 1990; Oxford Textbook of Pathology, 1992: vol. 1, Principles of Pathology, vols 2a, 2b, Pathology of Systems; The Natural Immune System: The Macrophage, 1992; The Natural Killer Cell, 1992; Diagnostic Molecular Pathology, vols 1 and 2, 1992; papers in scientific jls on liver disease, breast and cervical cancers, telematics/telepathology in health care. *Recreations:* talking with my family, swimming. *Address:* Linacre College, Oxford OX1 3JA.

McGEECHAN, Sir Ian (Robert), Kt 2010; OBE 1990; coaching consultant; Chairman: Yorkshire Carnegie (formerly Leeds Carnegie) Rugby, since 2012; Rugby Coaches Association, since 2012; *b* 30 Oct. 1946; *s* of Bob McGeechan and Hilda (*née* Shearer); *m* 1969, Judy Fish; one *s* one *d*. *Educ:* Carnegie Coll. of Physical Educn (DipPE). Teacher: Moor Grange High Sch., 1968–72; and Hd of Humanities, Fir Tree High Sch., 1972–90; Rugby player: Scottish Internat., 1972–79; Barbarians, 1973–78; British Lions, SA, 1974, NZ, 1977; coach: Headingley, 1980–83; Scotland under 21s, 1981–83; Scotland B, 1983 and 1985–88; Northampton, 1994–99; Asst Coach, Scotland, 1985–88; Nat. Coach, Scotland, 1988–93 and 1999–2003 (incl. Scotland Grand Slam, 1990, 4th place, World Cup, 1991); British Lions Coach: Australia, 1989 (won 2–1); NZ, 1993 (lost 2–1); SA, 1997 (won 2–1); SA, 2009 (lost 2–1); Asst Coach (midweek), NZ, 2005; Director of Rugby: London Wasps, 2005–09; Bath Rugby, 2010–12. Mem. Bd, Sports Coach UK, 1996– (Chm., 2005–08). Hon. MA Nottingham, 1998; Hon. DArts Leeds Metropolitan, 2004. Parly Rugby Medal, 2004. *Publications:* Scotland's Grand Slam, 1990; So Close to Glory: Lions New Zealand, 1993; Winning Lions, South Africa, 1997; Lion Man (autobiog.), 2009. *Recreations:* photography, hill-walking with wife and two dogs. *E:* ianmcgeechan@hotmail.com.

McGEEHAN, Prof. Joseph Peter, CBE 2004; PhD; FREng; Professor of Communications Engineering, Department of Electrical and Electronic Engineering, 1985, now Emeritus, and Director, Centre for Communications Research, since 1987, University of Bristol; Managing Director, Telecommunications Research Laboratory, Bristol, 1998–2011, Senior General Adviser, since 2011, Toshiba Research Europe Ltd; *b* 15 Feb. 1946; *s* of Joseph McGeehan and Rhoda Catherine McGeehan; *m* 1970, Jean Lightfoot; two *d*. *Educ:* Univ. of Liverpool (BEng Hons Electrical Engrg and Electronics 1967; PhD 1971; DEng 2003). FREng 1994. Sen. Scientist, Allan Clark Res. Centre, Plessey Co. Ltd, Caswell, 1970–72; Lectr, then Sen. Lectr, in Electrical Engrg, Sch. of Electrical Engrg, Univ. of Bath, 1972–85; University of Bristol: Hd, Dept of Electrical and Electronic Engrg, 1991–98; Dean of Engrg, 1998–2003. Founding Chm. and non-exec. Dir, Wireless Systems International Ltd, 1995–98; non-executive Director: Renishaw plc, 2001–10; 3CR, 2003–. Non-exec. Dir, Technology Foresight Mobile Virtual Centre of Excellence, 1996–98, 2001–07, 2011–12. Chair, W of England Inward Investment Bd, 2012–. Mem., SW Sci. and Industry Council, 2009–11; Industry Mem., Local Enterprise Partnership, 2010–. Ambassador, SW England RDA, 2003–12. Governor: Bristol Grammar Sch., 2003–04; Colston Sch., Bristol, 2007–. *Publications:* more than 350 articles in internat. acad. jls and confs. *Recreations:* keeping fit, cycling, watching sport (particularly cricket, Rugby Union and F1), amateur photography, theatre, concerts.

McGEGAN, (James) Nicholas, OBE 2010; Music Director, Philharmonia Baroque Orchestra, San Francisco, since 1985; Principal Guest Conductor, Pasadena Symphony Orchestra, since 2013; *b* 14 Jan. 1950; *s* of late (James Edward) Peter McGegan and Christine Mary McGegan (*née* Collier); civil partnership 2006, *m* 2013 (Calif), David von Recklinghausen Bowles. *Educ:* Corpus Christi, Cambridge (BA, MA); Magdalen Coll., Oxford. LTCL 1969. Royal College of Music: Prof., 1973–79; Dir, Early Music, 1976–80; Artist-in-Residence, Washington Univ., St Louis, Mo, 1979–85; Principal Conductor, Drottningholm Court Th., Sweden, 1993–96 (Vänners Hederstecken, 1996); Principal Guest Conductor, Scottish Opera, 1993–98. Artistic Dir, Göttingen Handel Fest., Germany, 1991–2011; Baroque series Dir, St Paul Chamber Orch., 1999–2004. Hon. Prof., Georg-August Univ., Göttingen, 2006. Hon. DMus San Francisco Conservatory of Music, 2013. Hon. RCM 1978. Has made numerous recordings, incl. opera and oratorios. Handel Prize, Halle, Germany, 1993. Cross of Order of Merit of Lower Saxony (Germany), 2011. *Publications:* (ed) Philidor, Tom Jones, 1978. *Recreations:* history, cooking, good wine. *Address:* 722 Wildcat Canyon Road, Berkeley, CA 94708, USA. *T:* (510) 5280862; 1 Kew Terrace, Glasgow G12 0TD. *T:* (0141) 339 0786. *Clubs:* East India, Savile.

McGEOCH, Dr Duncan James, FRSE; Director, Medical Research Council Virology Unit, Glasgow, 1995–2009; *b* 13 Sept. 1944; *s* of Peter and Christina McGeoch; *m* 1971, Jennifer A. Wylie; two *s*. *Educ:* Hutchesons' Grammar Sch., Glasgow; Univ. of Glasgow (BSc 1967; PhD 1971). FRSE 1987. Jane Coffin Childs Postdoctoral Fellow, Dept of Microbiology and Molecular Genetics, Harvard Med. Sch., 1971–73; Researcher, Virology Div., Dept of Pathology, Univ. of Cambridge, 1973–76; Mem. of Scientific Staff, MRC Virology Unit, Glasgow, 1976–95. Hon. Prof., Univ. of Glasgow, 1996–2009. Editor-in-Chief, Jl of General Virology, 1988–92. Fleming Award, Soc. for Gen. Microbiology, 1980. *Publications:* scientific papers. *Recreations:* reading, mountains and sea, ski-ing, walking, sailing.

McGEORGE, Alistair Kenneth; Managing Director, BIG W, since 2014; *b* Glasgow, 6 May 1959; *s* of Sam McGeorge and Wendy McGeorge; *m* 1984, Caroline Herbert; one *s* one *d*. *Educ:* Bramhall Grammar Sch.; Manchester Poly. (BA Hons 1980). FCA 1984. Chartered Accountant, Deloitte, Haskins & Sells, 1980–94; Littlewoods Group: various financial roles incl. Home Shopping Finance Dir, 1994–98; Gp Financial Services Dir, 1998–2000; Gp Supply Chain Dir, 2000–01; CEO, 2001–05; CEO, Matalan, 2006–10; Exec. Chm., New Look Retailers Ltd, 2011–14. *Recreations:* golf, keeping fit, family. *Address:* BIG W, 1 Woolworths Way, Bella Vista, NSW 2153, Australia.

McGEOUGH, Prof. Joseph Anthony, CEng, FREng, FIMechE; Regius Professor of Engineering, University of Edinburgh, 1983–2005, now Professor Emeritus (Head, Department of Mechanical Engineering, 1983–91; Senior Honorary Professorial Fellow, 2007–13); *b* 29 May 1940; *s* of late Patrick Joseph McGeough and Gertrude (*née* Darroch); *m* 1972, Brenda Nicholson; two *s* one *d*. *Educ:* St Michael's Coll., Irvine; Glasgow Univ. (BSc, PhD); Aberdeen Univ. (DSc). Research Demonstrator, Leicester Univ., 1966; Sen. Res. Fellow, Queensland Univ., 1967; Res. Metallurgist, International Research & Development Co. Ltd, Newcastle upon Tyne, 1968–69; Sen. Res. Fellow, Strathclyde Univ., 1969–72; Lectr 1972–77, Sen. Lectr 1977–80, Reader 1980–83, Dept of Engineering, Aberdeen Univ. Royal Society/SERC Industrial Fellow, 1987–89; Hon. Prof., Nanjing Univ. of Aeronautics and Astronautics, 1992–; Visiting Professor: Univ. degli Studi di Napoli Federico II, 1994; Glasgow Caledonian Univ., 1997–2003; Tokyo Univ. of Agric. and Technol., 2004; Monash Univ., 2005. Institution of Mechanical Engineers: Chm., Scottish Br., 1993–95; Mem. Council, 2000–03; Mem., Trustee Bd, 2004–10; Vice-Pres., 2006–10. Chm., CIRP UK Bd, 2000–03 (Mem. Council, 2006–08). Editor: Procs of Internat. Confs on Computer-aided Prodn Engrg, 1986–; Processing of Advanced Materials, 1991–94; CIRP Ed., Jl of Materials Processing Technol., 1995–2005. FRSE 1990. FREng 2009. MRI 2010. *Publications:* Principles of Electrochemical Machining, 1974; Advanced Methods of Machining, 1988; (ed) Micromachining of Engineering Materials, 2001; The Engineering of Human Joint Replacements, 2013; papers mainly in Journal of Mech. Engrg Science, Proc. IMechE; contrib. Encyclopaedia Britannica, Encyclopaedia of Electrochemistry, Encyclopaedia of Production Engineering. *Recreations:* golf, hill-walking. *Address:* 39 Dreghorn Loan, Colinton, Edinburgh EH13 0DF. *T:* (0131) 441 1302.

McGHEE, George Arnott; Programming Director, Snap-B TV, 2013; *b* 8 March 1956; *s* of Douglas and Myra McGhee. *Educ:* Ravensbourne Coll. of Art and Design (Dip. Media and Gen. Art Studies). Asst Film Ed., later Broadcast Exec., Scottish TV, 1979–93; Hd of Acquisitions, Channels TV Max and Max 1, Czech Republic, 1993–94; Carlton Cinema: Hd of Acquisitions, 1994–98; Dir, 1998–2003; Controller, BBC Programme Acquisition, 2003–09. *Recreations:* cinema, theatre, music, ski-ing, entertaining, collecting.

McGHEE, John Alexander; QC 2003; barrister; *b* 11 Feb. 1962; *s* of Alastair Orr McGhee and Joyce Alison McEwen McGhee (*née* Gall); *m* Marianne Richards; one *s* one *d* from a previous marriage. *Educ:* University Coll., Oxford (MA). Called to the Bar, Lincoln's Inn, 1984. *Publications:* Snell's Equity, 30th edn (ed.) 1999 to 33rd edn (gen. ed.) 2015. *Recreation:* flute playing. *Address:* Maitland Chambers, 7 Stone Buildings, Lincoln's Inn, WC2A 3SZ.

McGHEE, Prof. Patrick, CPsychol; Assistant Vice-Chancellor, University of Bolton, since 2014; *b* Glasgow, 3 Feb. 1962; *s* of Patrick and Bridgid McGhee; *m* 1992, Marianne Keirle; two *s*. *Educ:* All Saints' Secondary Sch., Glasgow; Univ. of Glasgow (MA 1st Cl. Hons Psychol. 1983); Wolfson Coll., Oxford (DPhil Psychol. 1987); Harvard Business Sch. (Global Leadership Prog. (CPD) 2009); ACCA Cert. in Internat. Accounting 2013. CPsychol 1989. Res. Fellow in Psychol., St George's Hosp. Med. Sch., Univ. of London, 1986–87; Lectr, Edge Hill, 1987–91; Sen. Tutor and Consultant, Open Univ., 1987–2000; Sen. Lectr, Sheffield City Poly., 1991–92; Hd of Psychol., Univ. of Derby, 1992–97; Associate Dean, 1997–2000, Dean of Learning Support and Develt, 2000, Bolton Inst.; Dean, 2000–02, Pro-Vice-Chancellor, 2003–04, Dep. Vice-Chancellor, 2005–10, Univ. of Central Lancs; Vice-Chancellor, Univ. of E London, 2010–13. Non-exec. Dir, Transformation Bd, Northants

Police and Crime Comr, 2013–. Nat. Teaching Fellow. FRSA 1996; FHEA 2002. Columnist: Guardian, 2010–; BBC News, 2015–. *Publications:* (jtly) Accounting for Relationships, 1987; Thinking Psychologically, 2001; The Academic Quality Handbook, 2007. *Recreation:* chess.

McGHIE, Hon. Lord; James Marshall McGhie; Chairman, Scottish Land Court, 1996–2014; President, Lands Tribunal for Scotland, 1996–2014; *b* 15 Oct. 1944; *s* of James Drummond McGhie and Jessie Eadie Bennie; *m* 1968, Ann Manuel Cockburn; one *s* one *d.* *Educ:* Perth Acad.; Edinburgh Univ. (LLB Hons). Called to the Scottish Bar, 1969; QC (Scot.) 1983; Advocate-Depute, 1983–86; Judge, Inner Hse, Ct of Session, 2012–. Pt-time Chm., Medical Appeal Tribunal, 1987–92; Mem., Criminal Injuries Compensation Bd, 1992–96. *Recreation:* various.

McGHIE, Duncan Clark, CA; Chairman: Scottish Ballet, 1999–2004; Scottish Opera, 1999–2004; *b* 6 Dec. 1944; *s* of William and Helen McGhie; *m* 1969, Una Gray Carmichael; one *s* one *d.* *Educ:* George Watson's Coll., Edinburgh. BSC, 1967–78 (Financial Controller, Scottish Div., 1975–78); Gp Finance Dir, Wm Collins Plc, 1978–84; Partner, Mgt Consultancy, Coopers & Lybrand, subseq. PricewaterhouseCoopers, 1984–2000. Mem., Inland Waterways Adv. Council, 2006–11 (Vice Chm., 2009–11). Mem., ICAS, 1967–. Elder, Ch of Scotland. *Recreations:* golf, music. *Address:* 65 Corrour Road, Newlands, Glasgow G43 2ED. *T:* (0141) 632 4502, *Fax:* (0141) 649 9030. *E:* duncan.mcghie@ntlworld.com. *Clubs:* Pollok Golf, Western Gailes Golf.

McGHIE, James Marshall; *see* McGhie, Hon. Lord.

MacGIBBON, Dr Barbara Haig, (Mrs John Roberts), CB 1988; FRCPath; Chairman, Commission on Environmental Health, 1996–97; Assistant Director (Medical), National Radiological Protection Board, 1988–93; *b* 7 Feb. 1928; *d* of Ronald Ross MacGibbon and Margaret Fraser; *m* 1954, John Roberts; one *s* one *d.* *Educ:* Lady Margaret Hall, Oxford; University College Hosp. Registrar, then Res. Assistant, Dept of Haematology, Royal Postgraduate Med. Sch., 1957–64; Sen. Registrar, Sen. Lectr/Hon. Consultant, then Sen. Res. Fellow, Dept of Haematology, St Thomas' Hosp. Med. Sch., 1969–79; SMO, then PMO, Toxicology and Environmental Health, DHSS, 1979; SPMO, DHSS, 1983–88. Chm., Panel on Energy, WHO Commn on Health and Envmt, 1990–92; Consultant, MRC Inst. for Envmt and Health, 1994–97. *Publications:* (ed) Concern for Europe's Tomorrow: health and environment in the WHO European region, 1995; articles in various med. jls.

MacGIBBON, Ross Arthur; freelance television director and producer, since 2009; *b* Bromley, Kent, 29 Jan. 1955; *s* of Prof. Iain Campbell MacGibbon and Dawn Eleanor MacGibbon; *m* 1984, Julie Cooper Kavanagh; two *s.* *Educ:* Daniel Stewart's Coll., Edinburgh; Royal Ballet Sch. Dancer with Royal Ballet, 1973–86; Ed. and Dir, Dancelines Prodns, 1986–91; Dir, Landseer Films, 1991–2002; Exec. Producer, Dance, BBC TV, 2002–07; Exec. Dir, ScreenStage Prodns, 2007–09. Mem., Dance Panel, Arts Council England, 1993–98. Board Member: Royal Opera House, 1999–2002; Rambert Dance Co., 2001–; Birmingham Royal Ballet, 2013–. Gov., Royal Ballet Cos, 2002–08. Trustee, Council for Dance Educn and Trng, 2008–13. *Recreations:* golf, Clarice Cliff, photography. *Address:* Flat 6, 41 St George's Square, SW1V 3QN. *T:* (020) 7821 1117. *E:* rossmacgibbon@btinternet.com.

McGIBBON, Susanna Justine; Director, Litigation Group, Government Legal Department (formerly Treasury Solicitor's Department), since 2012; *b* 11 Nov. 1967; *d* of Ian and Gwen McGibbon; *m* 2004, Patrick Spencer. *Educ:* Bolton Co. Grammar Sch.; Canon Slade Sch., Bolton; Univ. of Sheffield (LLB Hons 1989); Inns of Court Sch. of Law. Called to the Bar, Lincoln's Inn, 1990; in private practice at the Bar, 1990–93; FCO, 1993–98; Treasury Solicitor's Dept, 1998–2006: MoD, 1998–2000; DfES, 2000–02; Cabinet Office, 2002–06; Dir, Legal Services B, DTI, later BERR, 2006–08; Dir, Legal Services A, BERR, later BIS, 2008–09; Legal Dir, DCLG, 2009–12. *Recreations:* being in the mountains, at the opera or in India. *Address:* c/o Government Legal Department, One Kemble Street, WC2B 4TS.

McGILL, Angus, MBE 1990; journalist; *b* 26 Nov. 1927; *s* of Kenneth and Janet McGill; civil partnership 2006, Robert Jennings. *Educ:* Warehousemen, Clerks' and Drapers' Schools, Addington, Surrey. Reporter, Shields Gazette, 1944; Army service; feature writer, Evening Chronicle, Newcastle, 1948; Londoner's Diary, Evening Standard, 1957; columnist, Evening Standard, 1961–92. Chm., Knobs & Knockers, 1964–77. British Press Award, descriptive writer of the Year, 1968. *Publications:* Augusta, comic strip (drawn by Dominic Poelsma), 1968–; Yea Yea Yea (novel), 1969; Pub: an anthology, 1969; (with Kenneth Thomson) Live Wires, 1982; London Pub Guide, annually 1995–97. *Address:* 83 Winchester Court, Vicarage Gate, W8 4AF. *T:* (020) 7937 2166.

MACGILL, His Honour Kerry Michael Peter; a Circuit Judge, 2000–12; *b* 30 April 1950; *s* of Alan and Betty Macgill; *m* 1973, Janet Hazeldine; one *s* one *d.* *Educ:* Holborn Coll. of Law (LLB Hons London, 1971). Asst Solicitor, T. I. Clough & Co., 1975–77; Partner, Lumb & Kenningham, which later became Lumb & Macgill, criminal law practice, 1977–2000. *Recreations:* walking, golf, sailing.

McGILL, Robin William, CEng; Director, Energy Oil and Gas Europe, Exova Group Ltd, since 2012; *b* 19 Aug. 1955; *s* of William Robertson McGill and Catherine Meikle Leitch; *m* 1977, Susan (*née* McMorran); one *s* one *d.* *Educ:* Univ. of Edinburgh (BSc 1st cl. Hons Engrg Sci. 1977). CEng, MIMechE, 1981, FIMechE; FIET. BP Chemicals, Scotland, 1977–88, Engr, then operational roles, subseq. Polythene Ops Manager; Business Manager, Boron Nitride, Carborundum Inc., Buffalo, NY, 1988–92; BP plc, 1992–2006: Strat. and Projs Manager, BP Chemicals; Distribution Sen. Bus. Advr, BP Oil Internat.; Mktg Div. Manager, Pittsburgh Pa, BP America Inc.; Mergers & Acquisitions Proj. Manager, BP Chemicals Ltd; Business Unit Leader: Plastic Fabrications Gp, BP Amoco Ltd; European Polymers, BP Chemicals Ltd; CEO, BP Solvay HDPE, 2001–04; Man. Dir, BP Grangemouth, 2004–06; Chief Exec. and Sec., IET, 2007–09; Man. Dir, Atomic Weapons Establishment, Aldermaston, 2009–10. Mem. Council, CBI Scotland, 1981–.

McGILL, Stephen Phillip, CBE 2014; Chairman and Chief Executive Officer, Aon Risk Solutions, since 2008; Group President, Aon plc, since 2012; *b* 18 Feb. 1958; *s* of late Maj. James Osmond McGill and Joyce Courteney McGill; *m* Elizabeth Mawbey; one *s* two *d.* *Educ:* Gordon's Boys' Sch., West End, Woking. ACII 1980. Sedgwick, 1977–81; Director: Fenchurch Gp Brokers Internat., 1981–86; Willis Internat., 1986–89; Lloyd Thompson Ltd, 1989–97; Dir, 1997–2002, Gp Chief Exec., 2002–04, Jardine Lloyd Thompson Gp plc; CEO, Aon Global, 2005–06, CEO, Aon Risk Services Americas, 2006–08, Aon Corporation. Dir, Internat. Insce Soc. Inc., 2002–05; Pres., Insce Inst. of London, 2005–06. Mem., Internat. Adv. Bd, British American Business, 2010–. Trustee, Find a Better Way, 2011–. *Recreations:* ski-ing, swimming, tennis. *Address:* Aon Risk Solutions, 8 Devonshire Square, EC2M 4PL.

MacGILLIVRAY, Prof. Ian, MD, FRCP, FRCOG; Regius Professor of Obstetrics and Gynæcology, University of Aberdeen, 1965–84 (Dean of Medical Faculty, 1976–79), now Emeritus Professor; *b* 25 Oct. 1920; *yr s* of W. and A. MacGillivray; *m* 1950, Edith Mary Margaret Cook; one *s* twin *d.* *Educ:* Vale of Leven Academy, Alexandria; University of Glasgow (MB, ChB 1944; MD 1953); MRCOG 1949, FRCOG 1959; FRCPGlas 1973. Gardiner Research Schol., 1949–51, Lectr in Midwifery, 1951–53, Univ. of Glasgow; Senior Lecturer: in Obstetrics and Gynæcology, Univ. of Bristol, 1953–55; in Midwifery and Gynæcology, Univ. of Aberdeen, 1955–61; Prof. of Obstetrics and Gynæcology, University of London, at St Mary's Hospital Medical Sch., 1961–65. Mem., GMC, 1979–84. Founder Pres., Internat. Soc. for Study of Hypertension in Pregnancy, 1976–80; Pres., Internat. Soc. for Twin Studies, 1980–83; Mem. Council, RCOG, 1974–80. *Publications:* Outline of Human Reproduction, 1963; Combined Textbook of Obstetrics and Gynaecology, 1976; Human Multiple Reproduction, 1976; Pre-eclampsia: the hypertensive disease of pregnancy, 1983; contrib. to: British Medical Journal, Lancet, Journal of Obstetrics and Gynæcology of the British Empire; Clinical Science. *Address:* 2 White Gables, 53 Carlisle Road, Eastbourne BN21 4JR.

McGILLIVRAY, Laura Susan; Chief Executive, Norwich City Council, since 2006; *b* 29 Dec. 1953; *d* of late William Watson McGillivray and Marjory Joan McGillivray (*née* Cameron); *m* 1999, Paul Robert Golding Chaplin (marr. diss. 2014); two *d.* *Educ:* Liverpool Univ. (BA Sociol. 1975); Birmingham Univ. (MBA Public Service Mgt 1994). Dir and Sen. Consultant, CAG Consultants, 1985–88; Dir, Manor Gdns Health and Community Centre, Islington, 1988–91; Milton Keynes Council: Community Develt Mgr, 1991–94; Asst Dir, Local Govt Reorganisation, 1994–96; Hd of Policy and Communications, 1996–2000; Strategic Dir, Community Services, Dacorum BC, 2000–03; Dep. Chief Exec., City of York Council, 2003–05; Chief Exec., Gt Yarmouth BC, 2014. Chm., Bd of Trustees, Pregnancy Adv. Service, Greater London, 1985–91. Member: Council, UEA, 2006–; Bd, Sainsbury Centre for the Visual Arts, 2006–; Adv. Bd, Inst. of Local Govt, Univ. of Birmingham, 2010–12; Stakeholder Bd, Norwich Res. Park, 2011–; Bd, Norwich Univ. of Arts, 2013–; Chm., Norfolk Community Safety Partnership, 2012–; Trustee, SOLACE Foundn, 2012–15. *Recreations:* networking, spending time with family and friends, supporting Norwich as UNESCO City of Literature. *Address:* Norwich City Council, City Hall, Norwich NR2 1NH. *T:* (01603) 212001, *Fax:* (01603) 213001. *E:* lauramcgillivray@norwich.gov.uk. *Club:* Druidstone (Pembrokeshire).

McGIMPSEY, Michael; Member (UU) Belfast South, Northern Ireland Assembly, since 1998; *b* 1 July 1948; *s* of Henry and Isabel McGimpsey; *m* 1970, Maureen Elisabeth Speers; one *s* one *d.* *Educ:* Regent House Grammar Sch.; Trinity Coll., Dublin (BA 1970). Mem. (UU), Belfast CC, 1993–2011. Minister of Culture, Arts and Leisure, 1999–2002, of Health, Social Services and Public Safety, 2007–11, NI. Contested (UU) Belfast S, 2005. *Recreations:* reading, gardening, walking. *Address:* Northern Ireland Assembly, Parliament Buildings, Stormont, Belfast BT4 3XX. *T:* (028) 9024 5801.

McGINLEY, Aideen, OBE 2000; Trustee for Northern Ireland, BBC Trust, since 2012; *b* 31 May 1954; *d* of Joseph Slevin and Terry Slevin (*née* O'Brien); *m* 1975, James McGinley; two *s* one *d.* *Educ:* Salford Univ. (BSc Hons Envmtl Sci. 1975); Univ. of Ulster (MSc Social Policy, Admin and Planning 1983). Community Services Officer: Fermanagh DC, 1976; Strabane DC, 1976–89; Fermanagh District Council: Principal Officer, Policy and Planning, 1989–92; Dir of Develt, 1992–95; Chief Exec., 1995–2000; Permanent Secretary: Dept of Culture, Arts and Leisure, NI, 1999–2006; Dept for Employment and Learning, NI, 2006–09; Chief Exec., Ilex, 2009–12. Hon. Mem. RSUA, 2004. DUniv Ulster, 1998. *Recreation:* family.

McGINN, Conor Patrick; MP (Lab) St Helens North, since 2015; *b* Co. Armagh, 31 July 1984; *m*; one *s.* Worked in charity sector and managed health projects; Pol Advr to Labour defence team. Mem., Defence Select Cttee, 2015–. *Address:* House of Commons, SW1A 0AA. *Club:* Windle Labour.

McGINN, Gerry; Managing Director, First Trust Bank, since 2011; Chairman, Strategic Investment Board Ltd, since 2013; *b* 4 May 1957. *Educ:* QUB; Columbia Graduate Business Sch., NY. Joined Nat. Westminster Bank, London; Bank of Ireland: Chief Exec., Corporate and Internat. Banking, 1990–94; Chief Exec., NI, 1994–99; Chief Exec., UK, 1999–2001; Permanent Secretary: Dept of Educn, NI, 2001–05; Dept for Regl Develt, NI, 2006–07; Hd, Goodbody Stockbrokers, NI, 2007–09; Chief Exec., Irish Nationwide Building Soc., 2009–11. *Address:* (office) First Trust House, 92 Ann Street Belfast BT1 3HH.

McGINTY, Kevin Charles Patrick, CBE 2012; HM Chief Inspector, Crown Prosecution Service, since 2015; *b* Swansea, 16 June 1957; *s* of Laurence Patrick McGinty and Joan McGinty (*née* Thomas). *Educ:* St Joseph's Comprehensive Sch., Port Talbot; Poly. of N London (BA). Called to the Bar: Gray's Inn, 1982, Bencher, 2013; NI, 1998; in practice, CPS, 1988–92; Attorney Gen.'s Office, 1992–96; Bank of England, 1996–97; Attorney Gen.'s Office, 1997–2015, Dep. Legal Sec., 2011–15. *Address:* HM Crown Prosecution Service Inspectorate, 4th Floor, One Kemble Street, WC2B 4TS. *T:* (020) 7210 1185. *E:* kevin.mcginty@hmcpsi.gsi.gov.uk.

McGINTY, Lawrence Stanley; Health and Science Editor, ITN, 1989–2014 (Science Editor, 1987–89); *b* 2 July 1948; *s* of Lawrence McGinty and Hilda (*née* Hardman); *m* 1st, 1969, Joan Allen (*d* 2008); 2nd, 2011, Kate Evans. *Educ:* Stand Grammar Sch., Whitefield, Bury; Liverpool Univ. (BSc Zoology). Asst Editor, Chemistry in Britain, 1971–72; Technology Editor, then Health and Safety Editor, later News Editor, New Scientist, 1972–82; Science Correspondent, Channel 4 News, 1982–87. Guest Lectr, Ecole Polytechnique, Paris, 1984. Special Advisor: WHO, 2000; IAEA, 2001–03. Chm., Medical Journalists' Assoc., 2014–. Hon. DLitt Liverpool, 2012. Silver Jubilee Medal, 1977; Lifetime Achievement Award, RTS, 2015. *Recreations:* fine wine, books, walking.

McGIVAN, Alec John; Head, BBC Outreach, 2007–13; *b* 8 Sept. 1953; *s* of Ronald McGivan and Nancy McGivan (*née* Richards); *m* 1992, Elizabeth Ann Astill; one *s* one *d.* *Educ:* Bristol Cathedral Sch.; Wadham Coll., Oxford (MA Modern Hist.). Nat. Organiser, SDP, 1981–88; Events Dir, Corp. of London, 1988–90; Chief Exec., Shakespeare Globe Trust, 1990–91; Hd of Communications, Chapter One, 1991–94; Football Association: Media/Events Manager, Euro 96, 1994–96; Campaign Dir, World Cup Bid 2006, 1996–2000; Dir, Internat. Mktg, Interclubnet, 2000–02; Dir of Sport, DCMS, 2002–04; Hd, Charter Review Campaign, BBC, 2004–07. Trustee: Comic Relief, 2007–11; BBC Performing Arts Fund, 2007–13; Elizabeth R Broadcasting Fund, 2007–; Children's Univ., 2012–. *Recreations:* gardening, music, all sport, Bristol City FC, family and friends. *T:* 07970 237083. *E:* alec.mcgivan@gmail.com.

McGIVERN, Eugene, CB 1997; Under Secretary, Board of Inland Revenue, 1986–98; *b* 15 Sept. 1938; *s* of late James and Eileen McGivern; *m* 1960, Teresa Doran; two *s* one *d.* *Educ:* St Mary's Grammar School, Belfast. Joined Inland Revenue, 1955; seconded to Welsh Office as Private Sec. to Minister of State, 1967–69; Inland Revenue, 1969–98. Mem., CSAB, 1998–2004; Tribunal Mem., AIDB, subseq. AADB, 2005–14.

McGLADE, Prof. Jacqueline Myriam, PhD; Chief Scientist, United Nations Environment Programme, since 2014 (Special Adviser to Executive Director, 2013–14); *b* 30 May 1955; *d* of Bryan Maurice Cox and Maria Alphonsonia (*née* LeClair); *m* 1977, James McGlade (marr. diss. 1994); two *d.* *Educ:* UCNW (BSc; Hon. Fellow, Univ. of Wales, 1999); Univ. of Guelph, Canada (PhD 1981). FRICS 1989. Sen. Res. Scientist, Federal Govt of Canada, 1981–87; Adrian Fellow, Darwin Coll., Cambridge, 1987–90; Associate Prof., Cranfield Inst. of Technology, 1987–88; Schol., Internat. Fedn of Insts of Advanced Studies, Maastricht, 1988–93; Dir, and Prof. of Theoretical Ecology, Forschungszentrum Jülich, 1988–92; Prof. of Biol Scis, Univ. of Warwick, 1992–98 (Hon. Prof., 1998–2003); Dir, Centre for Coastal and Marine Scis, NERC, 1998–2000; Prof., Dept of Maths, UCL, 2000. Exec. Dir, EEA, 2003–13. Member: Bd, Envmt Agency, 1998–2003; Marine Foresight Panel, 1999–2002; UK-China Forum, 1999–; UK-Japan 21st Century Gp, 2002–. Trustee: Earth Centre, 1990–2003; Natural Hist. Mus., 2002–11. Hon. Mem., Internat. Inst. for Dynamical Systems, 1991. FRSA 1997; FLS 1998. Hon. DSc Kent, 2004. Jubileum Award, Chalmers Univ., Sweden, 1991; Minerva Prize, FZ Jülich, Germany, 1992; Masaryk Gold Medal, Univ. of Brno, 2005. *Publications:* Advanced Ecological Theory, 1999; Gulf of Guinea Large Marine

Ecosystem, 2002; papers on math. biology, marine sci. informatics and governance. *Recreations:* sailing, diving, ski-ing, climbing. *Address:* 10 The Coach House, Compton Verney, Warwick CV35 9HJ.

MacGLASHAN, Maureen Elizabeth, CMG 1997; HM Diplomatic Service, retired; indexer, since 1987; Ambassador to the Holy See, 1995–98; *b* 7 Jan. 1938; *d* of Kenneth and Elizabeth MacGlashan. *Educ:* Luton High Sch.; Girton Coll., Cambridge (MA, LLM). Joined FO, 1961; 2nd Sec., Tel Aviv, 1964–67; FCO, 1967–72; Head of Chancery, East Berlin, 1973–75; UK Representation to EEC, 1975–77; seconded to Home Civil Service, 1977–82; Counsellor, Bucharest, 1982–86; Asst Dir, Res. Centre for Internat. Law, and bye-Fellow, Girton Coll., Cambridge Univ., 1986–90; Counsellor, Consul-Gen. and Dep. Head of Mission, Belgrade, 1990; Head, Western European Dept, FCO, 1991–92; on secondment to CSSB, 1992–95. Pres., Soc. of Indexers, 2002–05. Ed., The Indexer, 2005–. *Publications:* (trans.) Weil, Maritime Delimitation, 1989; Consolidated Index and Tables to the International Law Reports, vols 1–125, 2004. *Club:* Royal Over-Seas League.

McGLONE, (John) Alistair (Philip), CBE 2007; international law consultant, since 2013; *b* 21 Feb. 1956; *s* of Walter and Marie McGlone; *m* 1997, Rosanna Heralall; two *s*. *Educ:* Queen's Coll., Oxford (MA). Admitted solicitor, 1981; Department for Environment, Food and Rural Affairs: Legal Advr, 2001–02; Head: Internat. and Biotechnol. Legal team, 2002–06; Water, Soil and Ecology Legal team, 2006–09; Legal Dir, 2009–10; Hd, Internat. Law, 2010–13. *Recreations:* cookery, cycling, walking, supporting Arsenal FC. *Address:* 55 Aberdeen Park, N5 2AZ. *T:* (020) 7359 8616, 07545 306789. *E:* alistairmcglone@virginmedia.com.

McGONIGAL, His Honour Christopher Ian; North Eastern Circuit Mercantile Judge, 1997–2003; a Deputy High Court Judge, 2003–05; *b* 10 Nov. 1937; *s* of Harold Alfred Kelly McGonigal and Cora McGonigal (*née* Bentley); *m* 1961, Sara Ann Sander; three *s* one *d*. *Educ:* Ampleforth Coll., York; Corpus Christi Coll., Oxford (MA). Coward Chance: articled clerk, 1963–65; Asst Solicitor, 1965–68; Sen. Litigation Partner, 1969–79, 1983–87; Sen. Resident Partner, Dubai, Sharjah, Bahrain and Jeddah offices, 1979–83; Clifford Chance: Jt Sen. Litigation Partner, 1987–95; Sen. Partner, Contentious Business Area, 1995–97. Asst Recorder, 1990–95; Recorder, 1995–97. *Recreations:* gardening, opera, local history. *Address:* 90 Seabrook Road, Hythe, Kent CT21 5QA.

McGOUGAN, Donald, OBE 2012; Director of Finance, City of Edinburgh Council, 1995–2011; *b* 26 Dec. 1950; *s* of Louis and Sidney McGougan; *m* 1991, Mandy Dodgson; one *s* one *d*. *Educ:* Hermitage Acad., Helensburgh. CPFA 1976. Trainee Accountant, Midlothian CC, 1971–75; Professional Asst, City of Edinburgh DC, 1975–77; Falkirk District Council: Sen. Accountant, 1977–79; Principal Asst, 1979–81; Depute Dir of Finance, 1981–87; City of Edinburgh District Council: Depute Dir of Finance, 1987–95; acting Dir of Finance, 1995–96. *Recreations:* family, golf, Rugby.

McGOUGH, Rt Rev. David; Auxiliary Bishop of Birmingham, (RC), and Titular Bishop of Cunavia, since 2006; *b* 20 Nov. 1944; *s* of Clement and Ethel McGough. *Educ:* Cotton Coll., N Staffs; Oscott Coll., Birmingham; Ven. English Coll., Rome; Gregorian Univ., Rome (STL 1969); Pontifical Biblical Inst., Rome (LSS 1977). Ordained priest, 1970; Lectr in Biblical Studies, Oscott Coll., Birmingham, 1975–90; Parish Priest: Christ the King, Birmingham, 1986–90; Our Lady & All Saints, Stourbridge, 1990–2006; Canon of Chapter, St Chad's Cathedral, Birmingham, 2002–. Vis. Lectr, Maryvale Inst., Birmingham, 1990–2007. *Recreations:* walking, cricket. *Address:* The Rocks, 106 Draycott Road, Tean, Stoke-on-Trent ST10 4JF. *T:* (01538) 722433.

McGOUGH, Roger, CBE 2004 (OBE 1997); FRSL; poet; *b* 9 Nov. 1937; *s* of Roger Francis and Mary Agnes McGough; *m* 1st, 1970 (marr. diss. 1980); two *s*; 2nd, 1986, Hilary Clough; one *s* one *d*. *Educ:* St Mary's Coll., Crosby, Liverpool; Hull Univ. (BA, Grad. Cert. Ed.). Fellow of Poetry, Univ. of Loughborough, 1973–75. Mem. Exec. Council, 1989–, Pres., 2011–, Poetry Soc. Hon. Prof., Thames Valley Univ., 1993; Hon. Fellow, John Moores Univ., 1999. FRSL 2005. Hon. MA Nene Coll., 1998; Hon. DLitt: Hull, 2004; Roehampton, 2006; Liverpool, 2006; DUniv Open, 2009. *Television:* Kurt, Mungo, BP and Me (BAFTA Award), 1984. Presenter, Poetry Please, BBC Radio 4, 2007–. Lyrics for Wind in the Willows, Broadway, 1985–86; The Elements (RTS Award), 1993. *Publications:* Watchwords, 1969; After The Merrymaking, 1971; Out of Sequence, 1972; Gig, 1972; Sporting Relations, 1974; In The Glassroom, 1976; Summer with Monika, 1978; Holiday on Death Row, 1979; Unlucky For Some, 1981; Waving at Trains, 1982; Melting into the Foreground, 1986; Selected Poems 1967–1987, 1989; You at the Back, 1991; Defying Gravity, 1992; The Spotted Unicorn, 1998; The Way Things Are, 1999; Everyday Eclipses, 2002; Collected Poems, 2003; Said and Done (autobiog.), 2005; Selected Poems, 2006; That Awkward Age, 2009; As Far As I Know, 2012; It Never Rains, 2014; *play adaptations:* Molière: Tartuffe, 2008; The Hypochondriac, 2009; The Misanthrope, 2013; *children's books:* Mr Noselighter, 1977; The Great Smile Robbery, 1982; Sky in the Pie, 1983; The Stowaways, 1986; Noah's Ark, 1986; Nailing the Shadow, 1987; An Imaginary Menagerie, 1988; Helen Highwater, 1989; Counting by Numbers, 1989; Pillow Talk, 1990; The Lighthouse That Ran Away, 1991; My Dad's a Fire-eater, 1992; Another Custard Pie, 1993; Lucky, 1993; Stinkers Ahoy!, 1995; The Magic Fountain, 1995; The Kite and Caitlin, 1996; Bad, Bad Cats, 1997; Until I Met Dudley, 1997; Good Enough to Eat, 2002; Moonthief, 2002; What on Earth?; Dotty Inventions, 2002; The Bee's Knees, 2003; All the Best, 2003; (with Brian Patten) The Monsters' Guide to Choosing a Pet, 2004; Slapstick, 2008; Mind the Gap, 2010; contributed to: Penguin Modern Poets, No 10, Mersey Sound, 1967, rev. edn 1983; Oxford Book of 20th Century Verse, 1973; The Norton Anthology of Modern Poetry, 1973; Penguin Modern Poets, No 4 (new series), 1995; edited: Strictly Private, 1981; Kingfisher Book of Comic Verse, 1986; The Kingfisher Book of Poems about Love, 1997; The Ring of Words (anthology), 1998; Wicked Poems, 2002; Sensational, 2004; You Have Been Warned, 2008. *Address:* c/o United Agents, 12–26 Lexington Street, W1F 0LE. *T:* (020) 3214 0800. *Club:* Chelsea Arts (Chm., 1984–86; Trustee, 1992–).

McGOVERN, Alison; MP (Lab) Wirral South, since 2010; *b* 30 Dec. 1980; *d* of Mike and Ann McGovern; *m* 2008, Ashwin Kumar; one *d*. *Educ:* Wirral Grammar Sch. for Girls; University Coll. London (BA Philosophy). Researcher, H of C, 2002–06; Public Affairs Manager: Network Rail, 2006–08; Art Fund, 2008–09; Creativity, Culture and Educn, 2009. Mem. (Lab) Southwark LBC, 2006–10. PPS to Rt Hon. Gordon Brown, MP, 2010. *Address:* House of Commons, SW1A 0AA.

McGOVERN, James; *b* 17 Nov. 1956; *s* of Thomas McGovern and Alice McGovern; *m* 1991, Norma Ward. *Educ:* Lawside RC Acad., Dundee. Apprentice glazier, 1973–77, glazier, 1977–87, Solaglas; glazier, Dundee DC, 1987–97; trade union organiser, GMB, 1997–2005. Mem., Tayside Regl Council, 1994–96. Chm., Dundee E Labour Party, 1999–2001. MP (Lab) Dundee W, 2005–15. *Recreations:* fitness club, watching football (Celtic FC).

McGOVERN, Jimmy; screenwriter; *b* Liverpool, 1949. Writer for television dramas and series: Brookside, 1983–89; Cracker, 1993, 1994, 1995, 2006; Heart and Minds, 1995; Hillsborough, 1996; The Lakes, 1997, 1999; Dockers, 1999; Sunday, 2002; Gunpowder, Treason and Plot, 2004; (also prod.) The Street, 2006, 2007, 2009; Moving On, 2009, 2010, 2011, 2013; Accused, 2010, 2012; Common, 2014; Banished, 2015; films: Priest, 1994; Go Now, 1995; Heart, 1999; Liam, 2001; musical stage show, King Cotton, Lowry, 2007. *Address:* c/o The Agency, 24 Pottery Lane, Holland Park, W11 4LZ.

McGOWAN, family name of **Baron McGowan**.

McGOWAN, 4th Baron *cr* 1937; **Harry John Charles McGowan;** *b* 23 June 1971; *o s* of 3rd Baron McGowan and Lady Gillian Angela Pepys, *d* of 7th Earl of Cottenham; *S* father, 2003; *m* 2001, Emma, *d* of Duncan Hattersley Smith; four *d* (incl. twin *d*). *Educ:* Harrow. *Heir: uncle* Hon. Dominic James Wilson McGowan [*b* 26 Nov. 1951; *m* 1982, Brigitta Papadimitriou (marr. diss.)].

McGOWAN, Alan Patrick, PhD; Archivist, Royal Naval College, Greenwich, 1989–98; Curator Emeritus, National Maritime Museum, since 1989 (Chief Curator, 1986–88; Callender Curator, 1989–91); *b* 16 Nov. 1928; *s* of Hugh McGowan and Alice Chilton; *m* 1958, Betty Eileen, *e d* of Mr and Mrs F. L. MacDougall, Ontario; three *s*. *Educ:* Spring Grove Grammar Sch.; Borough Road Coll.; Univ. of Western Ontario (BA, MA); Univ. of London (PhD). Served RASC (Air Freight), 1947–49. Asst Master (History), 1953–63; Lectr, Univ. of Western Ont Summer Sch., 1964; Canada Council Fellow, 1964–66; Asst Keeper, 1967–71, Keeper, 1980, Head, Dept of Ships, 1971–86, Dep. Dir, 1986–88, National Maritime Museum. Associate Prof. of History, Univ. of Western Ont Summer Sch., 1977. Member: Council, Navy Records Soc., 1968–; Adv. Council on Export of Works of Art, 1972–88; Victory Adv. Technical Cttee, 1974–2005 (Chm., 1983–2005); Mary Rose Adv. Cttee, 1974–78; Ships Cttee, Maritime Trust, 1977–88; Council, Soc. for Nautical Res., 1981–; Cttee, Falkland Islands Foundn, 1981–83. Trustee, HMS Warrior (1860), 2005–14. Associate RINA, 1980–88. Liveryman, Co. of Shipwrights, 1984–2003. FSA 2005. Soc. for Nautical Res. Centenary Medal, 2010. *Publications:* (ed) Jacobean Commissions of Enquiry, 1608 and 1618, vol. 113 of Navy Records Society, 1971; Royal Yachts, 1975; (with J. Fabb) The Victorian and Edwardian Navy in Photographs, 1976; (ed and prefaced) Steel's Naval Architecture, 1976; Sailor: a pictorial history, 1977; (ed and prefaced) Steel's Rigging and Seamanship, 1978; The Century before Steam, 1980; Tiller and Whipstaff, 1981; (with Ron van der Meer) Sailing Ships: three-dimensional illustrations of history's sailing ships, 1984; HMS Victory 1758–1998: the career and restoration of an icon, 1999; articles in jls of history and in encyclopaedia. *Recreations:* golf, reading, music. *Address:* c/o National Maritime Museum, Greenwich, SE10 9NF.

MACGOWAN, Christopher John, OBE 2008; Chief Executive, Society of Motor Manufacturers and Traders, 1999–2007; *b* 26 April 1947; *s* of Rev. John Macgowan and Dorothy Macgowan; *m* 1st, 1968, Victoria Lindey (*d* 1989); two *d*; 2nd, 1995, Amanda Fuller (*d* 2003). *Educ:* Orwell Park; Marlborough Coll. Export Rep. (Canada), British Leyland, 1965–73; PR Manager, Massey-Ferguson, 1973–90; Sales Dir, Ransomes, 1990–94; Chief Exec., Retail Motor Ind. Fedn, 1994–99. Chm., inpixnow, 2013–; Advr, Alcraft Motor Co. Ltd, 2013–. Vis. Prof., Univ. of Buckingham, 2008–14; External Assessor, Loughborough Univ., 2009–12. Member: DfT Motorists' Forum, 2003–; Public Policy Cttee, RAC Foundn, 2008–. Trustee: Nat. Motor Museum, 1999–; BEN Automotive Benevolent Fund, 2000–14; Farleigh Hospice, 2007–09. Hon. Treas., Caravan Club, 2011–. Freeman, City of London, 1997. *Recreations:* social media, information technology, National Hunt racing, travel. *Club:* Royal Automobile.

McGOWAN, Prof. David Alexander, PhD; Professor of Oral Surgery, University of Glasgow, 1977–99, now Emeritus; Hon. Consultant in Oral Surgery, Greater Glasgow Health Board, 1977–99; *b* 18 June 1939; *s* of George McGowan, MBE, and Annie, (Nan), Hall McGowan (*née* Macormac); *m* 1968, Margaret Vera Macauley; one *s* two *d*. *Educ:* Portadown Coll.; QUB (BDS 1961; MDS 1970); London Hosp. Med. Coll., London Univ. (PhD). FDSRCS 1964; FFDRCSI 1966; FDSRCPSGlas 1978; FDSRCSE 1999. Oral Surgery trng, Royal Victoria Hosp., Belfast and Aberdeen Royal Infirmary, 1961–67; Lectr in Dental Surgery, QUB, 1968; Department of Oral and Maxillo-Facial Surgery, London Hospital Medical College: Lectr, 1968–70; Sen. Lectr, 1970–77; Sen. Tutor, 1970–73; Consultant, 1971–77; Dep. Head, 1973–77. Chm., Nat. Dental Adv. Cttee, Scotland, 1995–99. Post-grad. Advr in Dentistry for W Scotland, 1977–90; Dean: Dental Faculty, RCPSG, 1989–92; Glasgow Univ. Dental Sch., 1990–95; Senate Assessor, Court, Univ. of Glasgow, 1995–99; Mem., GDC, 1989–99 (Dep. Chm., Exec., 1995–99). Ed., Dental History Mag., 2007–12. Univ. Fellow, Univ. of Western Australia, 1986; Caldwell Lectr, Univ. of Glasgow, 1993. Gold Medal, Bulgarian Acad. of Medicine, 1992; University Medal: Malta, 1999; Helsinki, 2000. *Publications:* (jtly) Outline of Oral Surgery, part 1, 1985; An Atlas of Minor Oral Surgery, 1989 (trans. Italian 1991, trans. French 1993), 2nd edn 1999; (jtly) The Maxillary Sinus and its Dental Implications, 1993; (jtly) Outline of Oral Surgery, parts 1 and 2, 1998; numerous articles in jls. *Recreations:* painting, photography, dog-walking, reading novels, listening to music. *Address:* Glenderry, 114 West King Street, Helensburgh, Argyll G84 8DQ. *T:* (01436) 676688.

McGOWAN, Ian Duncan; Librarian, National Library of Scotland, 1990–2002; *b* 19 Sept. 1945; *s* of Alexander McGowan and Dora (*née* Sharp); *m* 1971, Elizabeth Ann Weir; two *d*. *Educ:* Liverpool Inst.; Exeter Coll., Oxford (BA 1st Cl. Hons Russian Lang. and Lit., 1967); Sch. of Slavonic and E European Studies, Univ. of London. National Library of Scotland: Asst Keeper, 1971–78; Keeper (Catalogues and Automation), 1978–88; Sec. of the Library, 1988–90. Chm., Nat. Preservation Adv. Cttee, 1994–96; President: Scottish Library Assoc., 1998 (Vice-Pres., 1996–97); Edinburgh Bibliographical Soc., 2010–13 (Vice-Pres., 2004–10). Editor, Alexandria: jl of nat. and internat. liby and inf. issues, 2003–11. Chm., Britain-Russia Centre, Scotland, 1999–2002; Hon. Treas., Scotland-Russia Forum, 2003–13. Chm., 2006–08, Treas., 2008–, Scottish Working People's History Trust. Founding Fellow, Inst. of Contemporary Scotland, 2000. FRSA 1999. IFLA Medal, 2002. *Recreations:* books, gardens. *Address:* 23 Blackford Road, Edinburgh EH9 2DT. *T:* (0131) 667 2432. *Club:* New (Edinburgh).

McGOWAN, John; Sheriff in Ayr, 2000–12; *b* 15 Jan. 1944; *s* of Arthur McGowan and Bridget McCluskey; *m* 1966, Elise Smith; two *s*. *Educ:* St Joseph's Acad., Kilmarnock; Glasgow Univ. (LLB). Admitted Solicitor, 1967; Partner, Black Hay & Co., 1970–93; Temp. Sheriff, 1986–93; Sheriff in Glasgow, 1993–2000. Chm., DHSS Appeal Tribunal, 1980–86. Mem. Council, Law Soc. of Scotland, 1982–85. *Recreations:* golf, reading, choral singing, theatre. *Address:* 20 Auchendoon Crescent, Ayr KA7 4AS. *T:* (01292) 260139.

McGOWAN, Prof. Margaret Mary, (Mrs Sydney Anglo), CBE 1998; PhD; FBA 1993; Professor of French, 1974–97, Senior Pro-Vice-Chancellor, 1992–97, Research Professor, since 1997, and 50th Anniversary Fellow, since 2012, University of Sussex; *b* 21 Dec. 1931; *d* of George McGowan and Elizabeth (*née* McGrail); *m* 1964, Prof. Sydney Anglo, *qv*. *Educ:* Stamford High Sch.; Univ. of Reading (BA, PhD). Lecturer: Univ. of Strasbourg, 1955–57; Univ. of Glasgow, 1957–64; University of Sussex: Lectr, 1964–68; Reader, 1968–74; Dean, Sch. of European Studies, 1977–80; Pro-Vice-Chancellor (Arts and Social Studies), 1981–86. Leopold Delisle Lectr, Bibliothèque nationale de France, 2012. Mem. Bd, European Strategic Mgt Unit, 1995–2003. Vice-President: British Acad., 1996–98; Early Dance Circle, 2012–. Chm., Adv. Council, Warburg Inst., Univ. of London, 2013– (Chm. of Review of Warburg Inst., 2006–07). Vice-Chm. Bd, British Inst. in Paris, 1978–99; Gov., Ardingly Coll., 1994–2004. FRSA 1997. Freeman, City of Tours, 1986. Hon. DLitt Sussex, 1999. *Publications:* L'Art du Ballet de Cour, 1963; Montaigne's Deceits, 1974; Ideal Forms in the Age of Ronsard, 1985; Louis XIII's Court Ballets, 1989; Moy qui me voy: studies of the self, 1990; The Vision of Rome in Late Renaissance France, 2000; Dance in the Renaissance: European fashion, French obsession, 2008 (Wolfson History Prize, 2008); Sources livresques et albums d'images: la danse à la Renaissance, 2012; Dynastic Marriages 1612/1615: a celebration of the Hapsburg and Bourbon unions, 2013. *Recreations:* music, cooking, tennis. *Address:* 59 Green Ridge, Withdean, Brighton BN1 5LU.

McGOWAN, Hon. Dame Maura Patricia, DBE 2014; **Hon. Mrs Justice McGowan;** a Judge of the High Court, Queen's Bench Division, since 2014; Presiding Judge, South Eastern Circuit, from Jan. 2016; *b* 27 Jan. 1957; *d* of Matthew Vincent McGowan and Bridget McGowan (*née* Helebert). *Educ:* Virgo Fidelis Convent, London; St Mary's Coll., Leeds; Manchester Univ. (LLB Hons). Called to the Bar, Middle Temple, 1980, Bencher, 2005; called to the Irish Bar, 1990, to the Bar of NI, 2013; in practice, specialising in criminal law; a Recorder, 1996–2014; QC 2001; a Dep. High Court Judge, 2010–14. Chm., Bar Council, 2013. *Recreations:* cricket, fishing, opera, theatre, reading. *Address:* Royal Courts of Justice, Rolls Building, Fetter Lane, EC4A 1NL.

McGOWAN, Michael; *b* 19 May 1940; *m*; two *s* one *d*. *Educ:* Leicester University. Formerly: lecturer; BBC journalist; co-operative employment development officer, Kirklees Council, to 1984. MEP (Lab) Leeds, 1984–99.

McGOWAN, Neal Lowson; speaker and presenter on school leadership and education; Headteacher, William de Ferrers School, Chelmsford, since 2013; *b* 12 May 1963; *s* of late John McGowan and Elizabeth (*née* Taylor). *Educ:* Moray House Coll. of Educn, Edinburgh (Dip Tech. Ed); Univ. of Edinburgh (MEd). Teacher, Wester Hailes Educn Centre, 1985–88; Asst Principal Teacher, Lasswade High Sch., 1988–90; Principal Teacher, 1990–93, Asst Head Teacher, 1993–96, Musselburgh Grammar Sch.; Depute Rector, Selkirk High Sch., 1996–97; Head Teacher, Gracemount High Sch., Edinburgh, 1997–2002; Rector, Banchory Acad., Aberdeenshire, 2002–04; Rector, Larbert High Sch., Falkirk, 2004–09; Headteacher, Cherwell Sch., Oxford, 2009–10; Headmaster, Dulwich Coll. Beijing, 2011–12. Sec. to Ministerial Discipline Task Gp, 2001. *Publications:* Standard Grade Technological Studies Revision Notes, 1990; Higher Grade Technological Studies Revision Notes, 1991; Practice Questions for Higher Grade Technological Studies, 1993. *Recreations:* golf, travel, eating out, keep fit, everything 'Apple', West End Theatre.

McGRAIL, Prof. Seán Francis, FSA; Professor of Maritime Archæology, University of Oxford, 1989–93, now Emeritus; Visiting Professor of Maritime Archaeology, University of Southampton, since 1991; Chief Archaeologist, National Maritime Museum, 1976–86; *b* 5 May 1928; *m* 1955, Ursula Anne Yates, BA; one *s* three *d*. *Educ:* Royal Navy (Master Mariner); Univ. of Bristol (BA); Univ. of London (PhD); Campion Hall, Oxford (MA 1987); DSc Oxon 1989. FSA 1981; MCIfA (MIFA 1983). Served RN, 1946–68: Seaman Officer; awarded Wings (pilot), 1952; qualified as Air Warfare Instr, 1954, as Instrument Rating Examr, 1958; comd 849 Sqdn, FAA, 1962–63. Undergrad., Univ. of Bristol, 1968–71 (Harry Crook Scholar, 1969–71); Postgrad. Student, Inst. of Archaeology, London, 1972–73; Postgrad. Student (pt-time), UCL, 1973–78; National Maritime Museum, 1972–86, Hd of Archaeol Res. Centre, 1976–86. Leverhulme Res. Fellow, 1991–94; Visiting Professor: of Maritime Archæology, Oxford Univ., 1986–89; Danish Nat. Museum's Centre for Maritime Archaeology, Roskilde, 1994; Univ. of Haifa, 1995. Mem., Adv. Cttee on Historic Wrecks, Dept of Nat. Heritage (formerly DoE), 1974–98. Mem., Wardour Catholic Cemetery Trust, 1976–2014 (Treas., 1999–2014); Vice-Chm., Trust for Preservation of Oxford Coll. Barges, 1987–95. Prehistoric and medieval excavations, Norway, Denmark, Orkney, Ireland and Britain, 1974–93; maritime ethnographic fieldwork, Bangladesh and east coast of India, 1994–2001. Mem. Editl Bd, Mary Rose Trust, 1998–2002, 2004–12. *Publications:* Building and Trials of a Replica of an Ancient Boat, 1974; Logboats of England and Wales, 1978; Rafts, Boats and Ships, 1981; Ancient Boats, 1983; Ancient Boats of North West Europe, 1987, 2nd edn 1998; Medieval Boat and Ship Timbers from Dublin, 1993; Studies in Maritime Archaeology, 1997; Boats of the World, 2001, 2nd edn 2004; Boats of South Asia, 2003; (with N. Nayling) Barland's Farm Romano-Celtic Boat, 2004; Ancient Boats and Ships, 2006; Early Ships and Seafaring: water transport in European waters, 2014; Water Transport beyond Europe, 2015; *edited:* Sources and Techniques in Boat Archaeology, 1977; Medieval Ships and Harbours, 1979; Paul Johnstone, Seacraft of Prehistory, 1980, 2nd edn 1988; Brigg 'raft' and her Prehistoric Environment, 1981; Woodworking Techniques before 1500, 1982; Aspects of Maritime Archaeology and Ethnography, 1984; (with J. Coates) Greek Trireme of 5th Century BC, 1984; (with E. Kentley) Sewn Plank Boats, 1985; Maritime Celts, Saxons and Frisians, 1990; articles in archaeological and maritime jls. *Recreations:* strategic gardening, real ale specialist. *Address:* Institute of Archaeology, 36 Beaumont Street, Oxford OX1 2PG. *T:* (01865) 278240.

McGRATH, Prof. Alister Edgar, DD, DLitt; Andreas Idreos Professor of Science and Religion, University of Oxford, since 2014; Fellow, Harris Manchester College, Oxford, since 2014; *b* 23 Jan. 1953; *s* of Edgar P. McGrath and Annie J. M. McGrath (*née* McBride); *m* 1980, Joanna Ruth Collicutt; one *s* one *d*. *Educ:* Wadham Coll., Oxford (BA 1975); Linacre Coll., Oxford; Merton Coll., Oxford (MA, DPhil 1978; BD 1983; DD 2001; DLitt 2013); St John's Coll., Cambridge. Ordained deacon, 1980, priest, 1981; Curate, St Leonard's Ch, Wollaton, Nottingham, 1980–83; Lectr, 1983–95, Principal, 1995–2004, Wycliffe Hall, Oxford; Titular Prof. of Historical Theology, 1999–2008, Dir, Centre for Evangelism and Apologetics, subseq. Oxford Centre for Christian Apologetics, 2004–06, Univ. of Oxford; Sen. Res. Fellow, Harris Manchester Coll., Oxford, 2006–14; Prof. of Theol., Ministry and Educn, KCL, 2008–14. Gresham Prof. of Divinity, 2015–. FRSA 2005. Hon. DD: Virginia Theol Seminary, 1996; Union Theol Seminary, Belfast, 2005; Wycliffe Coll., Univ. of Toronto, 2007. *Publications:* Explaining Your Faith… Without Losing Your Friends, 1988; Justification by Faith, 1988; Justitia Dei: history of the Christian doctrine of justification, Vol. I 1989, Vol. II 1993; Doubt: handling it honestly, 1990; Luther's Theology of the Cross: Martin Luther's theological breakthrough, 1990; Cloud of Witnesses: ten great Christian thinkers, 1990; Genesis of Doctrine, 1990; Life of John Calvin: a study in the shaping of Western culture, 1990; Affirming Your Faith: exploring the Apostles' Creed, 1991; Bridge Building: creative Christian apologetics, 1992; Intellectual Origins of the European Reformation, 1992; Making Sense of the Cross, 1992; Reformation Thought: an introduction, 1992; Roots that Refresh, 1992; Suffering, 1992; (with J. McGrath) Dilemma of Self Esteem: the Cross and Christian confidence, 1992; (ed) Blackwell Encyclopedia of Modern Christian Thought, 1993; Christian Theology: an introduction, 1993; Making of Modern German Christology: from the Enlightenment to Pannenberg, 1993; Renewal of Anglicanism, 1993; Jesus: who He is and why He matters, 1994; Evangelicalism and the Future of Christianity, 1994; A Passion for Truth, 1996; (ed jtly) Doing Theology for the People of God, 1996; J. I. Packer: a biography, 1997; The Foundations of Dialogue in Science and Religion, 1998; Historical Theology: an introduction to the history of Christian thought, 1998; T. F. Torrance: an intellectual biography, 1999; Theology for Amateurs, 2000; The Unknown God: searching for spiritual fulfilment, 2000; The Journey: a pilgrim in the lands of the spirit, 2000; (ed) Christian Literature: an anthology, 2000; In the Beginning: the story of the King James Bible, 2001; Knowing Christ, 2001; The Future of Christianity, 2001; A Scientific Theology: vol. 1, Nature, 2001, vol. 2, Reality, 2002, vol. 3, Theory, 2003; Glimpsing the Face of God, 2002; A Brief History of Heaven, 2002; The Re-enchantment of Nature, 2002; The Twilight of Atheism, 2004; Dawkins' God, 2004; Theology—The Basics, 2004; Creation, 2005; Incarnation, 2005; The Science of God: an introduction to scientific theology, 2005; The Order of Things: explorations in scientific theology, 2006; (with J. McGrath) The Dawkins' Delusion, 2007; Christianity's Dangerous Idea: the Protestant revolution, a history from the sixteenth century to the twenty-first, 2007; Resurrection, 2008; The Open Secret: a new vision for natural theology, 2008; The Christian Vision of God, 2008; Heresy: a history of defending the truth, 2009; A Fine Tuned Universe: the quest for God in science and theology, 2009; Mere Theology: Christian faith and the discipleship of the mind, 2010; Darwinism and the Divine: evolutionary thought and natural theology, 2011; Why God Won't Go Away: engaging with the new atheism, 2011; Surprised by Meaning: science, faith and and the search for meaning, 2012; C. S. Lewis: a life, 2013; The Intellectual World of C. S. Lewis, 2013; Christian Belief for Everyone: faith and creeds, vol. 1, 2013; The Living God, vol. 2, 2014; Lord and Saviour: Jesus of Nazareth, vol. 3, 2014; Deep Magic, Dragons and Talking Mice: how C. S. Lewis can change your life, 2014; contrib. articles to learned jls. *Recreations:* walking, French. *Address:* Harris Manchester College, Mansfield Road, Oxford OX1 3TD.

McGRATH, Sir Brian (Henry), GCVO 2001 (KCVO 1993; CVO 1988); MW; an Extra Equerry to the Duke of Edinburgh, since 1996 (Assistant Private Secretary, 1982; Private Secretary, 1982–92; Treasurer, 1984–2000); *b* 27 Oct. 1925; *s* of William Henry and Hermione Gioja McGrath; *m* 1959, Elizabeth Joan Bruce (*née* Gregson-Ellis) (*d* 1977); two *s*, and one step *d*. *Educ:* Eton College. Served War of 1939–45, Irish Guards, 1943–46, Lieut. Cannon Brewery Co., 1946–48; Victoria Wine Co.: joined, 1948; Dir, 1949; Chm., 1960–82; Dir, 1960, Chm., 1975–82, Grants of St James's Ltd; Dir, Allied Breweries Ltd (subseq. Allied-Lyons plc), 1970–82; Chm., Broad Street Securities, 1983–92. Younger Brother of Trinity House, 1993. MW 1956. *Recreations:* gardening, reading. *Address:* Flat 3, 9 Cheyne Gardens, SW3 5QU. *Clubs:* Boodle's, White's.

McGRATH, Prof. Elizabeth, FBA 1998; Curator, Photographic Collection, 1991–2010, and Professor of the History of Art, 2000–10, Warburg Institute, University of London, now Professor Emeritus and Hon. Fellow; *b* 20 March 1945; *d* of Thomas McGrath and Emilie McGrath (*née* Melvin). *Educ:* St Joseph's High Sch., Kilmarnock; Glasgow Univ. (MA 1967); PhD London 1971. Photographic Collection, Warburg Inst., London Univ., 1970–2010; Joint Editor: Jl of Warburg and Courtauld Insts, 1977–2010; Corpus Rubenianum (Antwerp), 2010–. Durning Lawrence Lectr, UCL, 1989; Slade Prof. of Fine Art, Oxford Univ., 1990. Mem., Flemish Acad. for Arts and Scis, 2003. Hans Reimer Prize, Hamburg Univ., 1996; Mitchell Prize for the History of Art, 1998; Eugène Baie Prize for Flemish Cultural History, Province of Antwerp. *Publications:* Rubens: Subjects from History, vol. XIII in *Corpus Rubenianum*, 1997; (ed and contrib.) The Slave in European Art: from Renaissance trophy to Abolitionist emblem, 2012; contrib. to Jl of Warburg and Courtauld Insts, Burlington Mag., etc. *Address:* Warburg Institute, University of London, Woburn Square, WC1H 0AB. *T:* (020) 7862 8949.

McGRATH, Harvey Andrew; Chairman, Big Society Capital Ltd, since 2014; Deputy Chair, London Enterprise Panel, since 2012; *b* Belfast, 23 Feb. 1952; *m* 1978, Allison Baird; one *s* one *d*. *Educ:* Methodist Coll., Belfast; St Catharine's Coll., Cambridge (BA Geog. 1974). Asst Treas. and Second Vice Pres., Chase Manhattan Bank, 1974–80; Finance Dir, 1980–86, Pres., 1986–90, Farr Man & Co. Inc.; Gp CEO, 1990–2000, Chm., 2000–07, Man Gp plc. Chairman: E London Business Alliance, 2003–08; London First, 2004–08; London Develt Agency, 2008–12; Prudential plc, 2009–12; Prince's Teaching Inst., 2009–; Funding London, 2014–; Vice Chm., London Skills & Employment Bd, 2005–12. Trustee: New Philanthropy Capital, 2002–; Royal Anniversary Trust, 2003–; Mayor's Fund for London, 2010–; Pres. and Trustee, Children and Families Across Borders (formerly Internat. Social Service UK), 2008–; Chm., icould, 2008–. Chm., Bd of Govs, Birkbeck, Univ. of London, 2010–. *Recreations:* music, theatre, reading, ski-ing.

McGRATH, Ian; *see* McGrath, J. C.

McGRATH, James Aloysius; reporter and presenter, At The Races, since 2006; Hotspur, Racing Correspondent of the Daily Telegraph, 1991–2014; *b* 13 June 1952; *s* of Brian James McGrath and Kathleen May McGrath; *m* 1977, Anita Lee; two *s* two *d*. *Educ:* Xavier Coll., Melbourne. Cadet racing writer, The Australian, 1972–73; Racing Corresp., China Mail (Hong Kong), 1973–74; Chief Racing Writer, South China Morning Post (Hong Kong), 1975–86; writer, Racing Post, 1986–90; Racing Corresp., Sunday Telegraph, 1988–95. Racing Commentator: BBC, 1992–2012 (Sen. Racing Commentator, 1997–2012); Satellite Information Services, 1993–97. Clive Graham Award for Racing Journalist of the Year, Horserace Writers' Assoc., 1992; Sports Commentator of the Year, RTS, 2001. *Publications:* (with Trevor Marmalade) Great Racetracks of the World, 2014. *Recreations:* golf, ski-ing, watching cricket. *Address:* The Travers, Chobham, Woking, Surrey GU24 8SZ. *T:* (01276) 857155. *Clubs:* Carbine (founding Pres., 1997–2000); Hong Kong Jockey, Hong Kong Golf, Hong Kong Football (Hong Kong).

McGRATH, John Brian; Chairman, The Boots Co. plc, 2000–03 (non-executive Director, 1998–2003); *b* 20 June 1938; *m* 1964, Sandy Watson; one *s* one *d*. *Educ:* Brunel Univ. (BSc 1st Cl. Hons Applied Physics). UKAEA, 1962–65; NCB, 1965–67; Ford Motor Co., 1967–71; Jaguar Cars, 1971–75; Stone-Platt, 1976–82; Man. Dir, Construction and Mining Div. and Chief Exec., Compair, 1982–85; joined Grand Metropolitan PLC, 1985: Gp Dir, Watney Mann & Truman Brewers Ltd, 1985; Chm. and Man. Dir, Grand Metropolitan Brewing, 1986–88; Jt Man. Dir, Internat. Distillers & Vintners, 1988–91; IDV Ltd: Man. Dir and Chief Operating Officer, 1991–92; Chief Exec., 1992–93; Chm. and Chief Exec., 1993–96; Group Chief Executive: Grand Metropolitan PLC, 1996–97; Diageo, 1997–2000. Non-executive Director: Carlton Communications plc, 2003–04; ITV plc, 2004–07. Chm., Scotch Whisky Assoc., 1995–2000. Chm., Cicely Saunders International (formerly Foundn), 2001–. Mem. Council, Brunel Univ., 2004–12. Trustee, Tetbury Hosp. Trust, 2013–. *Address:* c/o Cicely Saunders Institute, Bessemer Road, SE5 9PJ.

McGRATH, Prof. John Christie, (Ian); pharmacologist and physiologist; Editor-in-Chief, British Journal of Pharmacology, since 2009 (Senior Editor, 2001–07); *b* 8 March 1949; *s* of John Christie McGrath and Margaret Gilmore Cochrane McGrath (*née* Murray); *m* 1970, Wilma Nicol (*d* 2007); one *s* one *d*; partner, 2008, Elspeth Mary McLachlan. *Educ:* Cross Arthurlie Primary Sch.; John Neilson Instn; Univ. of Glasgow (BSc 1st class Hons 1970; PhD 1974). FRSB (FSB 2013). Wellcome Interdisciplinary Research Fellowship, Dept of Pharmacology and Univ. Dept of Anaesthesia, Glasgow Royal Infirmary, Univ. of Glasgow, 1973–75; Institute of Biomedical and Life Sciences (formerly Institute of Physiology), University of Glasgow: Lectr, 1975; Wellcome Trust Research Leave Fellowship, 1982; Sen. Lectr, Reader, Titular Prof., 1983–91; Regius Prof. of Physiology, 1991–2012; Hd, Dept of Physiol., 1991–94; Co-Dir, Clinical Res. Initiative, 1994–99; Hd, Div. of Neurosci. and Biomed. Systems, 1997–2004; Hd, Div. of Integrated Biol., 2008–10. Chm. Standing Cttee, Heads of UK Physiology Depts, 2000–. Chm., Physiolog. Soc., 2006–08 (Mem., 1978; Mem. Cttee, 1988–94; Mem. Council, 2004–; Vice-Chm., 2004–06; Chm., Publications Cttee, 2007–10); Mem. Council, Bioscis Fedn, 2007–10. Member: British Pharmacol Soc. 1975 (Sandoz Prize, 1980; FBPhS (FBPharmacolS 2007); JR Vane Medal, 2011); Internat. Soc. for Heart Research, 1989; Amer. Soc. for Pharmacology and Experimental Therapeutics, 1991; Amer. Physiol Soc., 1994; British Neurosci. Assoc., 1994. Hon. Sen. Res. Fellow, Neuroscience Australia, Sydney, 2009; Hon. Prof. of Pharmacology, Univ. of Sydney, 2013. Hon. Mem., Australian Soc. for Clinical and Experimental Pharmacology and Toxicology, 2012. Mem., Labour Party, 1983–. Member Editorial Board: British Jl of Pharmacology, 1985–91; Jl of Cardiovascular Pharmacology, 1988–2010; Pharmacological Reviews, 1990–98; Jl of Vascular Res., 1991–; Jl of Hypertension, 2006–10. 1st Pfizer Award for Biology, 1983. *Publications:* contribs to learned jls in fields of pharmacology and physiology. *Recreations:* running, cycling, politics, travel. *Address:* 7 Horselethill Road, Glasgow G12 9LX.

McGRATH, Patrick; novelist, since 1979; *b* 7 Feb. 1950; *s* of Patrick G. McGrath and Helen McGrath (*née* O'Brien); *m* 1991, Maria Penelope Katharine Aitken, *qv*; one step *s*. *Educ:* City of Birmingham Coll. of Commerce; Univ. of London (external BA Hons 1971). Visiting Professor: Univ. of Texas, 2006; New Sch. of Social Research, NY, 2007–14; Hunter Coll., NY, 2010–12; Lectr, Princeton Univ., 2013–16. FRSL 2002. Hon. Fellow, Manchester Metropolitan Univ., 2009. *Publications:* Blood and Water and Other Tales, 1987; The Grotesque, 1988; Spider, 1990; Dr Haggard's Disease, 1993; Asylum, 1996; Martha Peake, 2000; Port Mungo, 2004; Ghost Town: tales of Manhattan then and now, 2005; Trauma, 2008; Constance, 2013. *Address:* 25 Broad Street, 14–S, New York, NY 10004, USA. *T:* (212) 7661690. *E:* pmcg277@gmail.com. *Club:* Groucho.

McGRATH, Stephen John, CPhys; Chief Executive, Soil Association Certification Ltd, 2010–11; *b* 24 Jan. 1954; *s* of late John Patrick McGrath and of Helena Mary McGrath; *m* 1977, Stephanie Doreen (*née* Powell); three *s*. *Educ:* Southampton Univ. (BSc Hons 1976, MSc 1977). CPhys, MInstP 1978. British Gas, 1978–96: Director: Business Gas, 1993–95; Gas Supplies and Transportation, 1995–96; Ops, 1996; Operations Director: AccuRead, 1996–2001; Serviceteam, 2001–02; Chief Operating Officer, Spark Response, 2002–03; Dir, Nat. Insurance Contribns Office, Bd of Inland Revenue, subseq. HMRC, 2003–06; Chief Exec., Meat Hygiene Service, 2007–10; Interim Dir of Ops, Food Standards Agency, 2010. MInstD 1997. *Recreations:* coastal sailing, campanology, motor bike.

MacGREGOR, family name of **Baron MacGregor of Pulham Market**.

MacGREGOR OF PULHAM MARKET, Baron *cr* 2001 (Life Peer), of Pulham Market in the County of Norfolk; **John Roddick Russell MacGregor,** OBE 1971; PC 1985; *b* 14 Feb. 1937; *s* of late Dr. N. S. R. MacGregor; *m* 1962, Jean Mary Elizabeth Dungey; one *s* two *d*. *Educ:* Merchiston Castle Sch., Edinburgh; St Andrews Univ. (MA, 1st cl. Hons); King's Coll., London (LLB; FKC 1988). Univ. Administrator, 1961–62; Editorial Staff, New Society, 1962–63; Special Asst to Prime Minister, Sir Alec Douglas-Home, 1963–64; Conservative Research Dept, 1964–65; Head of Private Office of Rt Hon. Edward Heath, Leader of Opposition, 1965–68. MP (C) S Norfolk, Feb. 1974–2001. An Opposition Whip, 1977–79; a Lord Comr of HM Treasury, 1979–81; Parly Under-Sec. of State, DoI, 1981–83; Minister of State, MAFF, 1983–85; Chief Sec. to HM Treasury, 1985–87; Minister of Agriculture, Fisheries and Food, 1987–89; Sec. of State for Educn and Sci., 1989–90; Lord Pres. of the Council and Leader of H of C, 1990–92; Sec. of State for Transport, 1992–94. Hill Samuel & Co. Ltd, 1968–79 (Dir, 1973–79), Dep. Chm., 1994–96; Director: Associated British Foods, 1994–2007; Slough Estates, 1995–2006; UK Food and Agric. Adv. Bd, Rabobank Gp, 1995–2011 (Jt Chm., 2006–11); Uniq (formerly Unigate), 1996–2005; London & Manchester Gp, 1997–98; Friends Provident, 1998–2007; European Supervisory Bd, DAF Trucks NV, 2000–09. Chm., Pension Fund Trustees of EDF (formerly British Energy), 2007–14, of SEGRO, 2006–10, of Anglian Water Gp, 2009–12, and of Eggborough Power Ltd, 2010–. Chairman: Fedn of University Cons. and Unionist Assocs, 1959; Bow Group, 1963–64; 1st Pres., Conservative and Christian Democratic Youth Community, 1963–65; Vice-President: ACC, 1995–97; LGA, 1997–99. Mem., Cttee on Standards in Public Life, 1997–2003. Chm., Assoc. of Cons. Peers, 2012–. Member, Council: KCL, 1996–2002; IOD, 1996–2006; Mem., 2002–, Chm., 2007–, Cathedral Council, Norwich Cathedral (High Steward, 2007–). Dep. Chm., GBA, then Assoc. of Governing Bodies of Independent Schs, 1998–2006. Trustee, Royal Norfolk Agricl Assoc., 2007–10. Chm., St Andrew's (Ecumenical) Trust, 2005–12. Hon. LLD Westminster, 1995. *Publications:* contrib. The Conservative Opportunity; also pamphlets. *Recreations:* music, reading, travelling, gardening, conjuring (Member: Magic Circle, 1989; Inner Magic Circle, 2000). *Address:* House of Lords, SW1A 0PW.

McGREGOR, Prof. Alan Michael, MD; FRCP, FMedSci; Professor of Medicine, 1986–2013, and Dean of Research, 1996–2000, King's College London School of Medicine (formerly King's College School of Medicine and Dentistry, subseq. Guy's, King's and St Thomas' School of Medicine, King's College London) (Head of Department of Diabetes, Endocrinology and Internal Medicine, 1996); Dean, Denmark Campus, King's College London, 2005–13; *b* 3 Aug. 1948. *Educ:* Selwyn Coll., Cambridge (BA 1971; MB, BChir 1974; MA 1982; MD 1982). DTM&H 2014; MSc Tropical Medicine 2014. MRCP 1977, FRCP 1985. MRC Trng Fellow, Royal Victoria Infirmary, Newcastle upon Tyne, 1977–80; Lectr, 1980, Wellcome Sen. Res. Fellow, 1981–86, Dept of Medicine, Univ. of Wales Coll. of Medicine. Hon. Consultant Physician, KCH NHS Trust, later KCH NHS Foundn Trust (non-exec. Dir, 2005–12). Mem., MRC, 1995–2000 (Chm., Physiological Medicine and Infections Bd). FKC 1997; Founder FMedSci, 1998. *Publications:* (ed) Immunology of Endocrine Diseases, 1986; contrib. learned jls. *Address:* 5 Colebrooke Row, N1 8DB.

MacGREGOR, Alastair Rankin; QC 1994; Biometrics Commissioner, since 2013; *b* 23 Dec. 1951; *s* of Alexander MacGregor and Anna MacGregor (*née* Neil); *m* 1982, Rosemary Kerslake; one *s* one *d*. *Educ:* Glasgow Acad.; Edinburgh Univ.; New Coll., Oxford Univ. (MA). Called to the Bar, Lincoln's Inn, 1974. Comr, Criminal Cases Review Commission, 2004–13 (Dep. Chm., 2006–13). *Address:* Office of the Biometrics Commissioner, PO Box 72256, SW1P 9DU. *T:* (020) 7035 5549. *E:* Enquiries@BiometricsCommissioner.gsi.gov.uk.
See also R. N. MacGregor.

McGREGOR, Rev. Alexander Scott; Deputy Legal Adviser to the Archbishops' Council and the General Synod, since 2009; Chancellor, Diocese of Oxford, since 2013; *b* London, 23 Oct. 1972; *s* of Donald and Irene McGregor. *Educ:* John Lyon Sch., Harrow; Christ Church, Oxford (MA Ancient and Modern History 2000); Coll. of Law, London; Inns of Court Sch. of Law; St Albans and Oxford Ministry Course. Called to the Bar, Lincoln's Inn, 1996; 3 Temple Gardens, 1996–98; Clarendon Chambers, 1998–2005; Legal Advr, Legal Office of Nat. Instns of C of E, 2006–09; Dep. Chancellor, Dio. of Oxford, 2007–13. Ordained deacon, 2006, priest, 2007; Assistant Curate: St Mary, Harrow on the Hill, 2006–09; St Barnabas, Pimlico, 2009–15; Our Most Holy Redeemer, Clerkenwell, 2015–. Mem., Dacorum BC, 1999–2007; Chm. of Dirs, Dacorum Sports Trust, 2003–07. *Publications:* articles in Ecclesiastical Law Jl. *Recreations:* history, music, conversation. *Address:* Legal Office, Church House, Great Smith Street, SW1P 3AZ. *T:* (020) 7898 1748. *E:* alexander.mcgregor@churchofengland.org. *Club:* Travellers.

McGREGOR, Rev. Alistair Gerald Crichton; QC (Scot.) 1982; WS; Minister, North Leith Parish Church, Edinburgh, 1987–2002; *b* 15 Oct. 1937; *s* of late James Reid McGregor, CB, CBE, MC, and Dorothy McGregor; *m* 1965, Margaret Lees or McGregor; two *s* one *d*. *Educ:* Charterhouse; Pembroke Coll., Oxford (BA (Hons) Jurisprudence); Edinburgh Univ. (LLB; BD). Intelligence Corps, 1956–58. Solicitor and WS, 1965–66; Advocate, 1967–82. Clerk to Court of Session Rules Council, 1972–75; Standing Junior Counsel to: SHHD, 1977–79; Scottish Develt Dept, 1979–82. Chm., Family Care (Scotland), 1983–88; Director: Apex (Scotland), 1988–98; Kirk Care Housing Assoc., 1994–97; Palcrafts (UK) Ltd, 2003– (Chm., 2011–). Governor: Dean Orphanage Trust, 1998–; Loretto Sch., 2000–06. Gen. Trustee, Ch of Scotland, 2004–14. Licensed, Church of Scotland, 1986. *Recreations:* squash, tennis. *Address:* 22 Primrose Bank Road, Edinburgh EH5 3JG. *T:* (0131) 551 2802.

McGREGOR, Hon. Alistair John; QC 1997; *b* 11 March 1950; *s* of Baron McGregor of Durris; *m* 1985, Charlotte Ann East; one *s* one *d*. *Educ:* Haberdashers' Aske's Sch., Elstree; Queen Mary Coll., London Univ. (LLB Hons). Called to the Bar, Middle Temple, 1974, Bencher, 2011. *Recreations:* music, sport. *Club:* Garrick.

McGREGOR, Dr Angus; Regional Medical Officer, West Midlands Regional Health Authority, 1979–88; Visiting Professor, University of Keele, 1988–94; *b* 26 Dec. 1926; *s* of Dr William Hector Scott McGregor and Dr Olwen May Richards; *m* 1951, May Burke, BA; one *d*. *Educ:* Solihull Sch.; St John's Coll., Cambridge. MA, MD; FRCP; FFPH; DPH. Junior hospital posts, 1950; Army service, RAMC, 1951–52; general practice, 1953; Asst MOH, Chester, 1954–56; Deputy Medical Officer of Health: Swindon, 1957–58; Hull, 1958–65; MOH and Port MO, Southampton, 1965–74; District Community Physician, East Dorset, 1974–79. Mem. Bd, FCM, RCP, 1982–88. FRSA 1986. *Publications:* (with T. Bunbury) Disciplining and Dismissing Doctors in the NHS, 1988; contrib. papers to medical journals. *Recreation:* piano. *Address:* (home) Withyholt, 26 Lyttelton Road, Droitwich Spa, Worcestershire WR9 7AA. *T:* (01905) 776077.

McGREGOR, Ewan Gordon, OBE 2013; actor; *b* 31 March 1971; *s* of James and Carol McGregor; *m* 1995, Eve Mavrakis; four *d*. *Theatre:* What the Butler Saw, Salisbury Playhouse, 1992; Little Malcolm, Comedy, 1998–99; Guys and Dolls, Piccadilly, 2005; Othello, Donmar Warehouse, 2007; The Real Thing, NY, 2014; *films:* Family Style, Being Human, 1993; Shallow Grave, 1994; Trainspotting, Swimming with the Fishes, Emma, The Pillow Book, Brassed Off, 1996; The Serpent's Kiss, Blue Juice, A Life Less Ordinary, 1997; Nightwatch, Velvet Goldmine, Little Voice, Desserts, Anno Domini, 1998; Star Wars, Episode I: The Phantom Menace, Rogue Trader, Eye of the Beholder, Tube Tales (also dir.), 1999; Nora (co-producer, 2000); Moulin Rouge, 2001; Black Hawk Down, Star Wars, Episode II: Attack of the Clones, 2002; Young Adam, Down with Love, 2003; Big Fish, 2004; Star Wars, Episode III: Revenge of the Sith, The Island, 2005; Stay, Stormbreaker, Scenes of a Sexual Nature, 2006; Miss Potter, 2007; Deception, Cassandra's Dream, Incendiary, 2008; The Men Who Stare At Goats, 2009; I Love You Phillip Morris, The Ghost, 2010; Beginners, Perfect Sense, 2011; Haywire, Salmon Fishing in the Yemen, 2012; The Impossible, Jack the Giant Slayer, 2013; August: Osage County, 2014; Mortdecai, Son of a Gun, 2015; *television* includes: Lipstick on Your Collar, Scarlet and Black, 1993; Doggin' Around, 1994; Karaoke, 1996; Solid Geometry, 2002; Long Way Round (series), 2004; Long Way Down (series), 2007; The Battle of Britain, 2010. Hon. DLitt Ulster, 2001. *Publications:* (with Charley Boorman) Long Way Round, 2004. *Recreation:* motor bikes. *Address:* c/o Lindy King, United Agents, 12–26 Lexington Street, W1F 0LE.

McGREGOR, Prof. Gordon Peter, DPhil; Professor of Education, University of Leeds, 1991–95, now Emeritus; *b* Aldershot, Hants, 13 June 1932; 2nd *s* of William A. K. McGregor and Mary A. McGregor (*née* O'Brien); *m* 1957, Jean Olga Lewis; three *d*. *Educ:* Bishop Road Jun. Sch., Bristol; St Brendan's Coll., Bristol; Univ. of Bristol (Open Schol.; BA Hons); Univ. of East Africa (MEd); Univ. of Sussex (DPhil); Dip. Coll. of Teachers of the Blind. Educn Officer, RAF, 1953–56; Asst Master, Worcester Coll. for the Blind, 1956–59; Asst Master, King's Coll., Budo, Uganda, 1959–62; Lecturer in English Language, Makerere Univ. Coll., Uganda 1963–66; Univ. of Zambia: Sen Lecturer in Educn, 1966–68; Reader and Head of Dept of Education, 1968–70; Prof. of Educn, 1970; Principal, Bishop Otter Coll., Chichester, 1970–80; Principal, Coll., then UC, of Ripon and York St John, Leeds Univ., 1980–95. Chm., Zambia Braille Press, 1967–70. Danforth Fellow, Colorado Coll., USA, 1972; Commonwealth Educn Consultant, Sri Lanka, 1973; British Council ELT Consultant, Iraq, 1975; CUAC Consultant, univ. colls, India and Australia, 1996; Honorary Visiting Professor: Univ. of Fort Hare, 1997; Makerere Univ., 1998–2007; Oxford Brookes Univ., 2001–09. Chairman: York Diocesan Educn Council, 1980–95; Council of Church and Associated Colls, 1990–95; Mem., UK Commn for UNESCO, 1984–86. Chm., Univs Visitation Cttee, Uganda, 2006–07. Vice-Chm. Govs, York Theatre Royal, 1992–95. Hon. Fellow, Coll. of Ripon and York St John, then York St John Univ., 2001. Hon. DLitt: Ripon Coll., Wisconsin, 1986; York Coll., Penn, 1993; Southampton, 1999; Hon. DHumLitt Union Coll., NY, 1996. *Publications:* King's College, Budo, The First Sixty Years, 1967; Educating the Handicapped, 1967; English for Education?, 1968; The Best Words (braille), 1968; Better English (braille), 1969; Teaching English as a Second Language (with J. A. Bright), 1970; English in Africa, (UNESCO), 1971; Bishop Otter College and Policy for Teacher Education 1839–1980, 1981; A Church College for the 21st Century?: 150 years of Ripon and York St John, 1991; Towards True Education, 1994; English for Life?, 2002; King's College, Budo: a centenary history, 2006; Life More Abundant: York St John University: 1841–2008, 2009; numerous articles. *Recreations:* music, literature, theatre, film, travel, swimming, armchair Rugby and cricket, watching my wife bird-watching. *Address:* 4 Grangers Place, Witney, Oxon OX28 4BS. *T:* (01993) 862988.

MacGREGOR, Heather Margaret; District Judge, Central Family Court (formerly Principal Registry, Family Division), since 2004; *b* 14 June 1952; *d* of James Gibson and Annie Gibson (*née* Ferry); *m* 1977, Dr Arthur MacGregor; one step *s*. *Educ:* Birmingham Univ. (BA); City Univ. (Dip. Law). Archaeologist, York Archaeol Trust, 1975–79; called to the Bar, Gray's Inn, 1982; in practice as barrister, London, 1982–2004; Dep. Dist Judge, Principal Registry, Family Div., 1999–2004. *Address:* Central Family Court, First Avenue House, 42–49 High Holborn, WC1V 6NP.

MACGREGOR, Sir Ian Grant, 8th Bt *cr* 1828, of Savile Row, Middlesex; *b* 22 Feb. 1959; *s* of Sir Edwin Robert Macgregor, 7th Bt and (Margaret Alice) Jean Macgregor (*née* Peake); *S* father, 2003, but his name does not appear on the Official Roll of the Baronetage; *m* Cheryl, *d* of Stephen Macdonald. *Heir: uncle* Arthur Joseph Macgregor [*b* 7 Sept. 1933; *m* 1st, 1957, Carole Isabel Valens (*d* 1984); two *d*; 2nd, 1985, Brenda Margaret Hanson].

McGREGOR, James Stalker; Chairman, Honeywell Ltd, 1981–89; *b* 30 Oct. 1927; *s* of John McGregor and Jean McCabe; *m* 1953, Iris Millar Clark; one *s*. *Educ:* Dumfries Acad.; Royal Tech. Coll., Glasgow (ARTC); Glasgow Univ. BSc (Hons); CEng, MIMechE. Production Engr, Rolls Royce Ltd, 1952–56; Sales Engr, Sandvik Swedish Steels, 1956–57; Honeywell Control Systems: Assembly Manager, later Production Control Manager and Admin Manager, 1957–65; Divl Dir, Temperature Controls Gp, 1965–71; Man. Dir, 1971–86. CCMI. Hon. LLD Strathclyde, 1984. *Recreation:* golf.

MacGREGOR, Joanna Clare, OBE 2012; FTCL, FRAM; concert pianist; Head of Keyboard, Royal Academy of Music, since 2011; Artistic Director, Dartington International Summer School, since 2015; *b* 16 July 1959; *d* of Alfred MacGregor and Angela (*née* Hughes); *m* 1986, Richard Williams; (one *d* decd). *Educ:* S Hampstead Sch. for Girls; New Hall, Cambridge (BA Hons; Hon. Fellow); Royal Acad. of Music. Gresham Prof. of Music (jtly), 1997–2000. Has appeared as a soloist with leading orchestras, including: RPO, LSO, English Chamber Orch., BBC SO, City of London Sinfonia, NYO, London Mozart Players; has toured worldwide, incl. Netherlands, Scandinavia, Africa, Australia, NZ, USA and Far East. Classical repertoire, also jazz and new music (has commissioned and premiered over 100 new works); jtly organised Platform Fest. of New Music, ICA, 1991–93; Artistic Dir, SoundCircus, Bridgewater Hall, Manchester, 1996 and creator, SoundCircus recording label, 1998; Guest Artistic Dir, Britten Sinfonia, 2002–04; Artistic Dir, Bath Internat. Fest., 2006–12; has made numerous recordings. Member: Arts Council of England, 1998–2003; Adv. Bd, British Council, 2002–04. Presenter, Strings, Bow and Bellows (series), BBC TV, 1995. Hon. FTCL (FTCL 1995); Hon. FRAM (FRAM 1991). FRSA 2002. Hon. DMus: Open, 2004; Bath, 2008; Hon. DLitt Bath Spa, 2011. European Encouragement Prize for Music, 1995; South Bank Show Award for Classical Music, 2000; Royal Philharmonic Soc. Prize, 2003. *Publications:* Joanna MacGregor's Piano World (5 vols), 1999. *Address:* c/o Ingpen and Williams, 7 St George's Court, 131 Putney Bridge Road, SW15 2PA. *T:* (020) 8874 3222.

MACGREGOR, John Malcolm, CVO 1992; HM Diplomatic Service, retired; Visiting Professor, Canterbury Christchurch University, since 2011; Partner, Ambassador Partnership LLP, since 2010; *b* 3 Oct. 1946; *s* of late Dr D. F. Macgregor and K. A. Macgregor (*née* Adams); *m* 1982, Judith Anne Brown (*see* J. A. Macgregor); three *s* one *d*. *Educ:* Kibworth Beauchamp Grammar Sch., Leics; Balliol Coll., Oxford (BA 1967; MA 2010); Birmingham Univ., (Cert. Ed. 1969). ARCO 1965. Taught at Cranleigh Sch., Surrey, 1969–73; joined HM Diplomatic Service, 1973; 2nd Sec., UN Affairs, 1973–74; 1st Sec. (political), New Delhi, 1975; FCO, 1979; Pvte Sec. to Minister of State, FCO, 1981; speechwriter to Sec. of State, FCO, 1982; Assistant, Soviet Dept, FCO, 1983; Dep. Head of Mission, Prague, 1986; Head of Chancery, Paris, 1990–93; Head of EU Dept (Ext.), 1993–95; Dir Gen. for Trade Promotion in Germany and Consul-Gen., Düsseldorf, 1995–98; Ambassador to Poland, 1998–2000; Dir, Wider Europe, FCO, 2000–02; Ambassador to Austria, 2003–07; UK Perm. Rep. to UN in Vienna and UK Gov. to IAEA, 2006–07. Dean, Univ. of Kent at Brussels, 2007–09. Occasional Lectr, Univ. of Cape Town, 2014–. Trustee: Shannon Trust, 2007–12; I Fagiolini Trust, 2007–. Gov., Chichester Univ., 2008–13. *Recreations:* music, languages, bricolage, travel. *Address:* c/o British High Commission Pretoria, BFPO 5339, Ruislip HA4 6EP. *T:* (27) 732634074.

MACGREGOR, Judith Anne, CMG 2012; LVO 1992; HM Diplomatic Service; High Commissioner to South Africa, since 2013, and (non-resident) to Lesotho and Swaziland, since 2014; *b* 17 June 1952; *d* of John Richard Brown and Beatrice Brown; *m* 1982, John Malcolm Macgregor, *qv*; three *s* one *d*. *Educ:* St Saviour's and St Olave's Grammar Sch.; Lady Margaret Hall, Oxford (BA 1st cl. Hons (Modern Hist.) 1974). Entered FCO, 1976; First Secretary: Belgrade, 1978–81; FCO, 1981–86; Prague, 1989; Paris, 1992–93; Dep. Hd, Western European Dept, FCO, 1993–95; Counsellor and Hd, Security Strategy, FCO, 2001–03; FCO Chair, CSSB, 2003–04; Ambassador to Slovakia, 2004–07; Dir for Migration, FCO, 2007–09; Ambassador to Mexico, 2009–13. *Recreations:* walking, reading. *Address:* c/o Foreign and Commonwealth Office, King Charles Street, SW1A 2AH.

MacGREGOR OF MacGREGOR, Sir Malcolm (Gregor Charles), 7th Bt *cr* 1795, of Lanrick, co. Perth; 24th Chief of Clan Gregor; writer, photographer; *b* 23 March 1959; *er s* of Brig. Sir Gregor MacGregor of MacGregor, 6th Bt, ADC and of Fanny (*née* Butler); *S* father, 2003; *m* 1st, 1988, Cecilia Campbell (marr. diss. 2004); 2nd, 2005, Fiona, *d* of Robert Armstrong, Preston. *Educ:* Eton; Cranfield Univ. (MBA). Major, Scots Guards, retd. Mem., Queen's Body Guard for Scotland (Royal Co. of Archers). FRGS; FRPS; ABIPP. *Publications:* Wilderness Oman, 2002; Rob Roy's Country, 2003; Light over Oman, 2004; The Outer Hebrides, 2007; Oman: eloquence and eternity, 2009; Mull, Iona and Staffa, 2010. *Heir: b* Ninian Hubert Alexander MacGregor [*b* 30 June 1961; *m* 1999, Fiona Graham; one *s* one *d*]. *Address:* Bannatyne, Newtyle, Angus PH12 8TR.

McGREGOR, Menna Lyn; Clerk to Mercers' Company, 2008–15; *d* of late William Beasley, MD, FRCPath and Elizabeth Beasley; *m* 1976, Bruce McGregor; two *d*. *Educ:* Ardwyn Grammar Sch., Aberystwyth; University Coll. of Wales, Aberystwyth (LLB). Called to the Bar, Lincoln's Inn, 1973; Co. Sec. and Dir, private property develt and investment cos, 1986–91; Bd and Co. Sec., RNT, 1993–2007; Sec., Trustees of RNT Foundn, 1994–2007; Co. Sec., Mercers' Co., 2007–08. Mem., Bd Develt team, Clore Leadership Prog., 2007–11. Mem. Council, Gresham Coll., 2009–13. Trustee: Nat. Foundn for Youth Music, 1999–2012; Wales Millennium Centre, 2006–09; Public Catalogue Foundn, 2009–12; Royal Ballet Sch. Endowment Fund, 2014–. Clerk to the Govs and Co. Sec., St Paul's Girls' Sch., 2007–12. Governor: Royal Central Sch. of Speech and Drama, 2012–; Royal Ballet Sch., 2013–. *Recreations:* music, theatre, opera, walking.

MacGREGOR, Neil; *see* MacGregor, R. N.

McGREGOR, Peter, CEng, FIET; writer and consultant; Director General, Export Group for the Constructional Industries, 1984–91 (Consultant, 1991–94); *b* 20 May 1926; *s* of Peter McGregor and Margaret Thomson McGregor (*née* McAuslan); *m* 1st, 1954, Marion (*d* 2001), *d* of H. T. Downer; one *s* (one *d* decd); 2nd, 2006, Sheena Macmillan, *d* of George Lorimer McCubbin. *Educ:* Cardiff High Sch.; Univ. of Birmingham; London Sch. of Economics (BSc (Econs)). National Service, RE, 1946–48. Various appointments, Ferranti Ltd, 1950–74, incl. Works Manager, Distribution Transformer Dept, Sales Manager, Transformer Div., Gen. Manager, Power Div.; Dir, Industrie Elettriche di Legnano (Italy), 1970–74; Associate Dir, Corporate Renewal Associates Ltd, 1988–93. Dir, Oxford Univ. Business Summer Sch., 1972; first Sec. Gen., Anglo-German Foundn for Study of Industrial Soc., 1974–81; Industrial Dir (Dep. Sec.), NEDO, 1981–84. Chm., Textile Machinery EDC, 1982–86; Dir, Templeton Technol. Seminar, 1985. Member: N American Adv. Gp, BOTB, 1968–74; Eur. Trade Cttee, BOTB, 1981–83; Adv. Bd, Public Policy Centre, 1984–88; Cttee on Exchange Rate, Public Policy Centre, 1984–87. Industrial Advr to Liberal Party, 1960–73; an Industrial Advr to Social and Liberal Democrats, 1988–90; Chm., Hazel Grove Liberal Assoc., 1971–74; contested (L) Ilford South, 1964. Mem., Königswinter Conf. steering cttee, 1976–90. Hon. Treasurer, Anglo-German Assoc., 1983–91. Elder and Hon. Treas., St Columba's Ch, Oxford, 1992–97. MCIM; FCMI. *Publications:* The Retreat (novel), 1997; Lessons in Duplicity (novel), 2005; various articles and pamphlets especially on industrial relations, company structure, market economy. *Recreations:* walking, reading, listening to music, writing, conversation, gardening, drawing attention to the Emperor's lack of clothes. *Club:* Caledonian.

MacGREGOR, Robert Murray Robertson; Partner and Head of Real Estate, Berwin Leighton Paisner LLP, since 2004; *b* London, 14 Jan. 1960; *s* of Ian and Pamela MacGregor; *m* 2000, Sally Gladwell; one *s* one *d*. *Educ:* Berkhamsted Sch.; Nottingham Univ. (LLB Hons). With Titmus, Sainer & Webb, 1983–90 (Partner, 1989–90); Clifford Chance, 1990–2004 (Partner, 1992–2004). *Recreations:* sailing, classic cars. *Address:* Berwin Leighton Paisner LLP, Adelaide House, London Bridge, EC4R 9HA. *E:* robert.macgregor@blplaw.com. *Clubs:* Caledonian; Itchenor Sailing (W Sussex); Aston Martin Owners.

MacGREGOR, (Robert) Neil, OM 2010; Chairman, Advisory Board, Humboldt Forum, from 2016; Director, British Museum, 2002–15; *b* 16 June 1946; *s* of Alexander MacGregor and Anna (*née* Neil). *Educ:* Glasgow Acad.; New Coll., Oxford (Hon. Fellow); Ecole Normale Supérieure, Paris; Univ. of Edinburgh; Courtauld Inst. of Art. Mem., Faculty of Advocates, Edinburgh, 1972. Lectr in History of Art and Architecture, Univ. of Reading, 1976; Editor, The Burlington Magazine, 1981–86; Dir, Nat. Gallery, 1987–2002. Trustee: Pilgrim Trust, 1990–2006; Courtauld Inst. of Art, 2002–08. Member: Supervisory Bd, Rijksmuseum, Amsterdam, 1995–2004; Internat. Adv. Bd, Hermitage, St Petersburg, 1997–; Museums, Libraries and Archives Council, 2003–05; Arts and Humanities Res. Council (formerly Bd), 2003–09; Bd, NT. Presenter of TV series: Seeing Salvation, 2000; Making Masterpieces; Painting the World. Hon. Mem., Royal Scottish Acad., 1995; Hon. FBA 2000. DUniv York, 1992; Dr *hc:* Edinburgh, 1994; Reading, Leicester, 1997; Exeter, Strathclyde, Glasgow, 1998; Hon. DLitt: Oxford, 1998; London, 1999. *Publications:* (jtly) Seeing Salvation: images of Christian art, 2000; (jtly) Britain's Paintings: the story of art through masterpieces in British collections, 2003; A History of the World in 100 Objects, 2010; Shakespeare's Restless World, 2012; Germany: memories of a nation, 2014.

See also A. R. MacGregor.

MacGREGOR, Susan Katriona, (Sue), CBE 2002 (OBE 1992); Presenter for BBC Radio Four: Today, 1984–2002; A Good Read, 2003–10; The Reunion, since 2003; *b* 30 Aug. 1941; *d* of late Dr James MacGregor and Margaret MacGregor. *Educ:* Herschel School, Cape, South Africa. Announcer/producer, South African Broadcasting Corp., 1962–67; BBC Radio reporter, World at One, World This Weekend, PM, 1967–72; Presenter: Woman's Hour, BBC Radio 4, 1972–87; Tuesday Call, 1973–86; Conversation Piece, 1978–94; Around Westminster, BBC TV, 1990–92. Vis. Prof. of Journalism, Nottingham Trent Univ., 1995–2003. Mem. Bd, RNT, 1998–2003. Member: RCP Cttee on Ethical Issues in Medicine, 1985–2000; Marshall Aid Commemoration Commn, 1989–98. Chair: Jury, Orange Prize for Fiction, 2002; Jury, BBC4 Samuel Johnson Prize for Non-Fiction, 2005; Jury, Art Fund Museum Prize, 2008; BBC Nat. Short Story Award, 2011; Mem., Jury, Orwell Literary Prize, 2014. Trustee: John Ellerman Foundn, 2002–12; Young Classical Artists Trust (formerly Young Concert Artists' Trust), 2003–13; UNICEF UK, 2004–13 (Vice-Chm., 2011–13). FRSA 1983; Hon. MRCP 1995. Hon. Fellow, Harris Manchester Coll., Oxford, 2002. Hon. DLitt: Nottingham, 1996; Nottingham Trent, 2000; Staffordshire, 2001; London Metropolitan, 2002; Hon. LLD Dundee, 1997. *Publications:* Woman of Today (autobiog.), 2002. *Recreations:* theatre, cinema, ski-ing. *Address:* c/o Knight Ayton Management, 35 Great James Street, WC1N 3HB. *T:* (020) 7831 4400.

McGREGOR, Wayne, CBE 2011; choreographer; Founder and Artistic Director, Studio Wayne McGregor (formerly Wayne McGregor|Random Dance), since 1992 (resident company of Sadler's Wells, since 2001); Resident Choreographer, Royal Ballet, since 2006; *b* 12 March 1970; *s* of Lawrence and Ella McGregor. *Educ:* Bretton Hall Coll., Univ. of Leeds (BA 1st Cl. Hons Dance); José Limon Sch., NY. AHRB/Arts Council England Res. Fellow in Cognition and Choreography, Sch. of Exptl Psychol., Univ. of Cambridge, 2003; Innovator in Residence, UCSD, 2009; Prof. of Choreography, Trinity Laban Conservatoire of Music and Dance, 2014–. Choreographer in Residence, The Place Th., London, 1992; productions for Studio Wayne McGregor (formerly Wayne McGregor|Random Dance Co.) include: The Millennarium, 1997, Sulphur 16, 1998, and Aeon, 2000, commnd RFH; digit01 (commnd The Place), 2001; Nemesis (co-commnd S Hill Park, Swindon Dance, Sadler's Wells, DanceEast), 2002; Alpha, Polar Sequences (co-commnd The Place, PACT Zollverein), 2003; Ataxia (co-commnd Sadler's Wells, PACT Zollverein), 2004; AMU (co-commnd Sadler's Wells, Wellcome Trust), 2005; Entity (co-commnd Sadlers's Wells, Het Muziektheater, Biennale de la Danse, Dance East, Swindon Dance) 2008; Dyad 1909 (In the Spirit of Diaghilev) (commnd Sadler's Wells), 2009; FAR (co-produced by Sadler's Wells and Peak Performances), 2010; Undance (commnd Sadler's Wells), 2011; Big Dance Trafalgar Square (commnd Big Dance), 2012; Atomos, 2013; Tree of Codes (co-commnd Park Ave Armory, Manchester Internat. Fest., Paris Opera Ballet, Sadler's Wells and FAENA ART Milan), 2015; independent commissions include: Telenoia (Canary Wharf), 2000; (with V. Durante) Fleur de Peux, Symbiont(s) (Royal Ballet, Covent Gdn), 2001; Detritus (Rambert Dance Co.), 2001; Brainstate (Royal Ballet/Random Dance), 2001; PreSentient (Rambert Dance Co.), 2002; 2 Human (English Nat. Ballet), Nautilus (Stuttgart Ballet), 2003; Qualia (Royal Ballet), 2004; Eden/Eden (Stuttgart Ballet), Engram (Royal Ballet), 2005; Skindex (NDT1), 2006; Chroma (Royal Ballet), 2006; Genus (Paris Opera Ballet), 2007; Nimbus (Royal Ballet), 2007; Infra (Royal Ballet), 2008; Re:Nature (NDT1), 2008; Limen (Royal Ballet), 2009; Dyad 1929 (Australian Ballet), 2009; Yantra (Stuttgart Ballet), 2010; Outlier (NY City Ballet), 2010; L'Anatomie De La Sensation (Paris Opera Ballet), 2011; Live Fire Exercise (Royal Ballet), 2011; Carbon Life (Royal Ballet), 2012; Machina (co-commnd Royal Ballet and Nat. Gallery), 2012; Raven Girl (Royal Ballet), 2013; Tetractys - The Art of Fugue (Royal Ballet), 2014; Woolf Works (Royal Ballet), 2015; Kairos (Ballett Zürich), 2015; *theatre* includes: A Little Night Music, RNT, 1995; Cleansed, Royal Court, 1998; Antony and Cleopatra, RNT, 1998; Woman in White, Palace and NY, 2004; Cloaca, 2004, Aladdin, 2005, Old Vic; You Never Can Tell, Much Ado About Nothing, Peter Hall Co., 2005; Kirikov et Karaba, 2007; *opera* includes: Orpheus and Eurydice, 1993, Marriage of Figaro, 1995, Scottish Nat. Op.; Rinaldo, The Mikado, Grange Pk Op., 2000; Hansel and Gretel, Scottish Nat. Op., 2000; Manon, English Touring Op., 2001; La Bohème, Scottish Nat. Op., 2004; The Midsummer Marriage, Chicago Lyric Op., 2005; Salome, ENO, 2005; (dir.) Dido and Aeneas, La Scala, 2006; Dido and Aeneas/Acis and Galatea (Royal Opera/Royal Ballet), 2009; (dir) Twice Through the Heart, Sadler's Wells, 2011; SUM (commnd ROH2), 2012; contribs to TV progs and films include: Bent (C4), 1996; Chrysalis, 2002; Dice Life (C4), 2004; Tremor (C4), 2005; Harry Potter and the Goblet of Fire, 2005; La Danse - The Paris Opera Ballet, 2009; Wayne McGregor - A Moment In Time, 2010; Wayne McGregor - Going Somewhere, 2011; Lotus Flower music video (Radiohead), 2011; (dir) Ingenue music video (Atoms for Peace), 2013. Hon. DSc Plymouth, 2012. Outstanding Achievement in Dance Award, 2001, 2003, Outstanding Choreography Award, 2002, Time Out Live Awards; IMZ Dance Screen Award, 2002; Excellence in Internat. Dance, Internat. Theatre Inst., 2009; Choreographer of the Year, Ballet Tanz, 2009; Movimentos Award, 2009; Dance Magazine Award, 2014. *Address:* Studio Wayne McGregor, Sadler's Wells Theatre, Rosebery Avenue, EC1R 4TN. *T:* (020) 7278 6015, *Fax:* (020) 7278 5469.

McGREGOR-JOHNSON, Richard John; His Honour Judge McGregor-Johnson; a Circuit Judge, since 1998; Resident Judge, Isleworth Crown Court, since 2004; a Senior Circuit Judge, since 2010; *b* 11 July 1950; *s* of Maxwell and Pamela McGregor-Johnson; *m* 1974, Elizabeth Weston; one *s* one *d*. *Educ:* Dean Close Sch., Cheltenham; Bristol Univ. (LLB 1972). Called to the Bar, Inner Temple, 1973, Bencher, 2001; an Asst Recorder, 1990–94; a Recorder, 1994–98. Hon. Recorder, RBK&C, 2012–. *Recreations:* choral singing, sailing. *Address:* Crown Court, 36 Ridgeway Road, Isleworth, Middx TW7 5LP.

McGREGOR-SMITH, Ruby, CBE 2012; Chief Executive, MITIE Group PLC, since 2007; *b* Lucknow, India. *Educ:* Kingston Univ. (BA 1990). ACA 1991. Operational and financial roles with Serco, 1991–2002; Financial Dir, 2002–05, Chief Operating Officer, 2005–07, MITIE Gp PLC. *Address:* MITIE Group PLC, Ground Floor East, Cottons Centre, Cottons Lane, 47/49 Tooley Street, SE1 2QG. *T:* (020) 3123 8180, *Fax:* (020) 3123 8781.

[Created a Baroness (Life Peer) 2015 but title not yet gazetted at time of going to press.]

McGRIGOR, Sir James (Angus Rhoderick Neil), 6th Bt *cr* 1831, of Campden Hill, Middlesex; Member (C) Highlands and Islands, Scottish Parliament, since 1999; *b* 19 Oct. 1949; *er s* of Sir Charles Edward McGrigor, 5th Bt, and of Mary Bettine, *e d* of Sir Archibald Edmonstone, 6th Bt; *S* father, 2007; *m* 1st, 1987, Caroline Roboh (marr. diss. 1993); two *d*; 2nd, 1997, Emma Mary Louise Fellowes; one *s* three *d*. *Educ:* Cladich Sch., Argyll; Sunningdale Sch., Berks; Eton College. Shipping, 1969–71; stockbroking, 1971–74; farmer, 1975–. Mem., Queen's Body Guard for Scotland, Royal Co. of Archers, 1990. Kentucky Col, 2010. Contested (C) Argyll and Bute, 2005. *Recreations:* fishing, music, literature. *Heir: s* Alexander James Edward Lyon McGrigor, *b* 5 Aug. 1998. *Address:* Ardchonnel, by Dalmally, Argyll PA33 1BW. *Clubs:* White's, Chelsea Arts; New (Edinburgh).

McGROUTHER, Prof. (Duncan) Angus, MD; FRCS, FRCSGlas, FRCSE; FMedSci; Professor of Plastic and Reconstructive Surgery, University of Manchester, 2001, now Emeritus; Hon. Consultant Surgeon, South Manchester University Hospitals, since 2001; Clinical Director, Manchester Integrating Medicine and Innovative Technology, 2010, now Ambassador; *b* 3 March 1946; *s* of Dr John Ingram McGrouther and Margot Christina Cooke Gray; *m*; one *s* one *d*; *m* 2005, Gillian Fletcher-Williams. *Educ:* Glasgow High Sch.; Univ. of Glasgow (MB ChB 1969; MD Hons 1988); Univ. of Strathclyde (MSc Bioengineering 1975). Glasgow Royal Infirmary, 1969–74; Cruden Med. Res. Fellow, Bioengrg Unit, Univ. of Strathclyde, 1972–73; Registrar and Sen. Registrar in Plastic Surgery, Canniesburn Hosp., Glasgow, 1975–78; Assistentarzt, Klinikum Rechts der Isar, Munich, 1978; Consultant Plastic Surgeon: Shotley Bridge Gen. Hosp. and Sunderland Dist Gen. Hosp., 1979–80; Canniesburn Hosp., 1981–89; Prof. of Plastic and Reconstructive Surgery (first estabd British chair), UCL, 1989–2001. Christine Kleinert Vis. Prof., Univ. of Louisville, 1988. Mem. Council, RCS,

2010–. Pres., British Soc. for Surgery of the Hand, 2010–11. FMedSci 2005. Kay-Kilner Prize, British Assoc. of Plastic Surgeons, 1979; Pulvertaft Prize, British Soc. for Surgery of the Hand, 1981. *Publications:* (jtly) Principles of Hand Surgery, 1990; (ed jtly) Dupuytren's Disease, 1990; contributor to: Current Surgical Practice, vol. 6, 1992; Microvascular Surgery and Free Tissue Transfer, 1993; Gray's Anatomy, 38th edn, 1995; Bailey and Love's Short Practice of Surgery, 22nd edn, 1995; Green's Operative Surgery, 4th edn 1998, 5th edn 2004; papers on anatomy, biomechanics, plastic surgery, hand surgery, microsurgery, and wound healing. *Recreations:* mountains, sea, books. *Address:* University of Manchester, Stopford Building, Oxford Road, Manchester M13 9PT.

McGUCKIAN, John Brendan; Chairman, UTV Media plc (formerly Ulster Television), 1990–2012; *b* 13 Nov. 1939; *s* of late Brian McGuckian and of Pauline (*née* McKenna); *m* 1970, Carmel, *d* of Daniel McGowan; two *s* two *d*. *Educ:* St MacNissi's Coll., Garrontower; Queen's Univ. of Belfast (BSc). Chairman: Cloughmills Mfg Co., 1967–; Tedcastle Hldgs, 1999–2001; Irish Continental Gp (formerly Irish Ferries) plc, 2004– (Dir, 1988–); Cooneen By Design Ltd (formerly Cooneen Textiles); Director: Munster & Leinster Bank, 1972–2007; Allied Irish Bank plc, 1976–2007; Harbour Group Ltd, 1978–; Aer Lingus plc, 1979–84; Unidare plc, 1987–2006; United Dairy Farmers, 2001–08; TVC Hldgs; Derry Development Commn, 1968–71; Dep. Chm., Laganside Corp., 1988–92; and other directorships. Chairman: Internat. Fund for Ireland, 1990–93; IDB for NI, 1991–98. Former Sen. Pro-Chancellor and Chm. of Senate, QUB. Hon. DLaws QUB, 2000. *Address:* Ardverna, Cloughmills, Ballymena, Co. Antrim, Northern Ireland BT44 9NL. *T:* (028) 2763 8121; Lisgoole Abbey, Culkey, Enniskillen BT92 2FP.

McGUCKIN, Stephen Augustine; Global Managing Director (formerly Managing Director), Turner & Townsend plc, since 2009; *b* Eton, 1961; *s* of Augustus McGuckin and Sarah McGuckin; partner, Linda Cartwright; one *s* one *d*. *Educ:* Univ. of Brighton (BA Hons 1982); Univ. of Bradford (MBA 1986); Univ. of Reading (MSc Proj. Mgt 1991); Univ. of Sheffield (MA Arch. 2001). Associate Dir, Fitch & Co. plc, 1986–89; Proj. Dir, Grimshaws, 1989–92; Director: Mace Ltd, 1992–2001; Land Securities plc, 2001–09. Mem., London 2012 Panel, CABE, 2007–11; Trustee, V&A Mus., 2008–. RIBA 1990; RICS 2004. *Recreations:* ski-ing, scuba diving, motorcycles, history of art, architecture. *Address:* Turner & Townsend plc, 7 Savoy Court, WC2R 0EX. *T:* (020) 7544 4554. *E:* steve.mcguckin@turntown.com.

McGUFFIN, Prof. Peter, PhD; FRCP, FRCPsych, FMedSci; Professor of Psychiatric Genetics, Institute of Psychiatry, King's College London, 1998–2013, now Emeritus (Director, MRC Social, Genetic and Developmental Psychiatry Research Centre, 1998–2006 and 2010–12; Dean, Institute of Psychiatry, 2007–10); *b* 4 Feb. 1949; *s* of Captain W. B. McGuffin, RD, RNR and M. M. McGuffin; *m* 1972, Prof. Anne E. Farmer; one *s* two *d*. *Educ:* Univ. of Leeds (MB ChB); Univ. of London (PhD). MRCP 1976, FRCP 1988; MRCPsych 1978, FRCPsych 1990. St James Univ. Hosp., Leeds, 1972–77; Registrar, Sen. Registrar, Maudsley Hosp., 1977–79; MRC Fellow, MRC Sen. Clinical Fellow, Inst. of Psychiatry, 1979–86; Hon. Consultant, Maudsley and King's Coll. Hosps, 1983–86; Prof. of Psychological Medicine, Univ. of Wales Coll. of Medicine, 1987–98. Vis. Fellow, Washington Univ., St Louis, 1981–82. Founder FMedSci 1998. Pres., Internat. Soc. of Psychiatric Genetics, 1996–2000. *Publications:* Scientific Principles of Psychopathology, 1984; A Psychiatric Catechism, 1987; Schizophrenia, the Major Issues, 1988; The New Genetics of Mental Illness, 1991; Seminars in Psychiatric Genetics, 1994; (ed jtly) Essentials of Postgraduate Psychiatry, 1997, 4th edn as Essentials of Psychiatry, 2008; (jtly) Behavioral Genetics, 4th edn 2001, 5th edn 2008; Measuring Psychopathology, 2002; Psychiatric Genetics and Genomics, 2002; Behavioural Genetics in the Postgenomic Era, 2002; articles, research papers on psychiatry and genetics. *Recreations:* classical guitar, music, running, horse riding, farmland maintenance, sailing. *Address:* 20 Langford Green, SE5 8BX. *Club:* Brading Haven Yacht.

McGUGAN, Irene Margaret; Assistant Director, Barnardo's Scotland, 2007–12; *b* 29 Aug. 1952; *d* of late James Millar Duncan and of Phyllis Margaret Duncan (*née* Smith, now Mrs John Nicoll); *m* 1971, James McGugan; one *s* one *d*. *Educ:* Robert Gordon's Inst. of Technol. (CQSW 1982; Dip. Social Work 1982); Dundee Univ. (Advanced Cert. in Child Protection Studies 1991). VSO, India, 1970–71; full-time mother and voluntary worker, 1971–80; Social Work Dept, Tayside Regl Council, 1985–96, Angus Council, 1996–99 (Manager, Community Support, 1998–99); Project Dir, Children's Services, Aberdeen CC, 2003–07. Mem. (SNP) NE Scotland, Scottish Parlt, 1999–2003. Contested (SNP) Dundee W, Scottish Parlt, 2003. Elder, Church of Scotland, 1985; Mem., Church of Scotland Social Care Council, 2012–. *Recreations:* hill walking and keeping fit, visiting Scottish islands, books, music, theatre, cycling, grandchildren. *E:* irene.mcgugan@btinternet.com.

McGUIGAN, Finbar Patrick, (Barry), MBE 1994; journalist and commentator on boxing; *b* 28 Feb. 1961; *s* of late Patrick McGuigan and of Catherine, (Kate), McGuigan; *m* 1981, Sandra Mealiff; three *s* one *d*. *Educ:* St Louis Convent, Clones, Co. Monaghan; Largy Sch., Clones; St Patrick's High Sch., Clones. Started boxing, 1973, Wattle Bridge ABC, then Smithborough ABC; winner: Ulster and Irish title (Juvenile), 1977; Irish Sen. title, 1978; Commonwealth Gold Medal, 1978; represented Ireland at Olympic Games, Moscow, 1980; turned professional, 1981; winner: British and European Featherweight titles, 1983; World WBA Featherweight title, 1985; made two successful defences, then lost title on third defence, 1986; retd 1989. Pres. and Founder, Professional Boxing Assoc. (formerly Professional Boxers' Assoc., subseq. British Boxers' Assoc.), 1993–. *Publications:* (jtly) Leave the Fighting to McGuigan, 1985; (jtly) McGuigan—The Untold Story, 1991. *Recreations:* fitness, reading, etymology, relaxing with my family. *Address:* PO Box 233, Faversham, Kent ME13 9WP.

McGUIGAN, Rupert Iain Sutherland; HM Diplomatic Service, retired; *b* 25 June 1941; *s* of Hugh and Sue McGuigan; *m* 1968, Rosemary Rashleigh Chaytor; two *d*. *Educ:* Marlborough Coll.; Magdalene Coll., Cambridge (MA Law). With BP Ltd, 1964–72; HM Diplomatic Service, 1972–97: First Secretary: New Delhi, 1974–77; Kingston, Jamaica, 1978–81; Permanent Under-Secretaries Dept, FCO, 1981–85; Bridgetown, 1985–88; Counsellor: Lagos, 1989–93; Kingston, Jamaica, 1994–96. Private Sec. to the Princess Royal, 1997–99. Man. Dir, Private Trust Corporation (East Africa) Ltd, 1999–2007. *Recreations:* most ball games, amateur dramatics, philately, singing in the bath, travel to unusual places. *Address:* Goodhope, Halls Lane, Waltham St Lawrence, Berks RG10 0JB. *T:* (0118) 934 0989. *Clubs:* Hawks (Cambridge); Castle Royle Golf; Muthaiga Country (Nairobi).

McGUIGAN BURNS, Rt Hon. Sir Simon (Hugh); *see* Burns, Rt Hon. Sir Simon H. McG.

McGUINESS, Robert Clayton, PhD; Chief Executive, UK Central Government, Serco Group plc, since 2013; *b* 31 Dec. 1951; *s* of Robert McGuiness and Agnes McGuiness; *m* 1982, Beate Winkelmann; two *d*. *Educ:* Univ. of Glasgow (BSc (Hons) 1973; PhD 1976). ICI plc, 1976–2000: ICI Paints, 1976–93; Gen. Manager Marketing and Planning, ICI Autocolor, 1993–96; Vice Pres., Refinish, Glidden Co., N America, 1996–98; Chief Exec., ICI Autocolor, 1999–2000; Man. Dir, NPL Mgt Ltd, 2000–05; Chief Exec., Serco Science, 2005–06; CEO, Serco Defence, Sci. and Technol., 2006–10; Director: Serco Ltd, 2002–09; AWEML, 2003–09; Serco Global Services (India), 2010–13; SRL Ltd, 2011–12; CEO, Serco Africa, Middle E, Asia and Australasia, 2010–13; Hd, Corporate Renewal, Serco, 2013. *Recreations:* golf, ski-ing. *Address:* Oak Lodge, Bray Road, Maidenhead, Berks SL6 1UF. *T:* (01628) 621699; Serco Group plc, Serco House, 16 Bartley Wood Business Park, Bartley Way, Hook, Hants RG27 9UY. *Clubs:* Maidenhead Golf; DLF Golf and Country (Haryana, India).

McGUINNESS, Andrew Peter; Chief Executive Officer, freuds, since 2014; Chairman, Seven Dials PR, since 2013; *b* Southport, 22 April 1970; *s* of Gerald and Zita McGuinness; *m* 2000, Isabella Wesolowska; one *s* two *d*. *Educ:* St Dominic, Harpenden; Nicholas Breakspear RC Comprehensive Sch., St Albans; Univ. of Salford (BA Hons). Graduate Account Dir, J. Walter Thompson, 1993–97; Gp Account Dir, M&C Saatchi, Sydney, 1997–2000; Gp Account Dir, 2000–01, Man. Dir, 2001–02, CEO, 2002–05, TBWA, Omnicom; Founding Partner, Beattie McGuinness Bungay, 2005–14. Non-exec. Dir, Chorion plc, 2005–06. Chairman, Advertising Assoc., 2009–12. Mem., Mktg Gp of GB, 2007. FIPA 2009; Fellow, Mktg Soc., 2008. *Recreations:* photography, politics, football. *Address:* freuds, 1 Stephen Street, W1T 1AL. *T:* (020) 3003 6351. *E:* andrew@freuds.com. *Clubs:* Ivy, Thirty, Marketing Group of GB.

McGUINNESS, Maj.-Gen. Brendan Peter, CB 1986; consultant in education and training, now retired; Adviser on Engineering to Schools and Colleges, University of Birmingham, 1994–96; Director of Education and Training Liaison, Engineering Employers' Federation, West Midlands, 1988–94 (Head of Educational Liaison, 1987–88); *b* 26 June 1931; *s* of Bernard and May McGuinness; *m* 1968, Ethne Patricia (*née* Kelly) (*d* 2013); one *s* one *d*. *Educ:* Mount St Mary's College. psc, rcds. Commissioned Royal Artillery, 1950; regimental duty, 1950–60; Staff, 1960–62; sc 1963; Adjutant, 1964–65; Staff, 1965–68 (despatches, Borneo, 1966); Battery Comdr, 1968–70; Staff Coll. Directing Staff, 1970–72; CO 45 Medium Regt, 1972–75; CRA 1st Armd Div., 1975–77; RCDS 1978; MoD Staff, 1979–81; Dep. Comdr, NE District, 1981–83; GOC W Dist, 1983–86. Hon. Col, Birmingham Univ. OTC, 1987–97; Hon. Regtl Col, 45 Field Regt, 1985–91. Mem. Cttee, Hereford and Worcester Br., STA, 1991–96. Project Dir, 1987–88, Gov., 1988–, CTC Kingshurst Acad. (formerly The City Technol. Coll., Kingshurst); Mem. Court, Birmingham Univ., 1992–94; Governor: King's Coll. for the Arts and Technol., Guildford, 1999–2013; King's Internat. Coll. for Business and the Arts, Camberley, 2000–10; Guest Gov., Cirencester Coll., 1998–2006. Dir, Acafess Community Trust, Birmingham, 1992–94 (Chm., 1992). *Recreations:* Scottish country dancing (reeling), hill walking, beagling. *Address:* 107 Gloucester Street, Cirencester, Glos GL7 2DW. *T:* (01285) 657861. *Club:* Army and Navy.

McGUINNESS, Frank; playwright; Professor of Creative Writing, School of English, University College, Dublin, since 2007 (Writer in Residence, 1997–2007); *b* 29 July 1953; *s* of Patrick McGuinness and Celine O'Donnell-McGuinness. *Educ:* University College, Dublin (BA 1974; MPhil 1976). *Plays:* The Factory Girls, 1982, Observe the Sons of Ulster Marching Towards the Somme, Baglady, 1985, Abbey Th.; Innocence, Gate Th., 1986; Carthaginians, Abbey, 1988; Peer Gynt (version), Gate, 1988; Mary and Lizzie, RSC, 1989; Three Sisters (version), Gate, 1990; Someone Who'll Watch Over Me, Vaudeville, transf. NY, 1992; The Bird Sanctuary, Abbey, 1994; A Doll's House (version), Playhouse, transf. NY, 1996; Mutabilitie, Caucasian Chalk Circle (version), 1997, RNT; Electra (version), Donmar, transf. NY, 1997; The Storm (version), Almeida, 1998; Dolly West's Kitchen, Abbey, transf. Old Vic, 1999; Miss Julie (version), Haymarket, 2000; Gates of Gold, Gate Th., Dublin, 2002; The Wild Duck, Abbey Th., 2003; Hecuba (version), Donmar, 2004; Rebecca (version), Th. Royal, Newcastle upon Tyne, 2005; Speaking Like Magpies, RSC, 2005; Phaedra, Donmar, 2006; Yerma (trans.), Arcola Th., 2006; There Came a Gypsy Riding, Almeida, 2007; The Lady from the Sea (version), Almeida, 2008; Oedipus, RNT, 2008; The Master Builder, New York, 2008; Helen, Globe, 2009; Greta Garbo Came to Donegal, Tricycle Th., 2010; Ghosts, Duchess, 2010; John Gabriel Borkman (version), Abbey Th., Dublin, 2010; The Match Box, Liverpool Playhouse, 2012, transf. Tricycle Th., 2013; Damned By Despair, RNT, 2012; The Dead, 2012, The Hanging Gardens, 2013, Abbey Th., Dublin; libretto for Thebans, London Coliseum, 2014; *television:* Scout, 1987; The Hen House, 1989; A Short Stay in Switzerland, 2009 (Broadcast Award, Best Single Drama, 2010); A Song for Jenny, 2015; *films:* Talk of Angels, 1998; Dancing at Lughnasa, 1998; The Stronger, 2008. HRHA, 2009. Freeman of Buncrana, 2011. Hon. DLitt Ulster, 2000. Evening Standard Award, 1986; Ewart-Biggs Prize, 1987; NY Critics Circle Award, 1992; Writers' Guild Award, 1992; Ireland Fund Literary Award, 1992; Tony Award, 1997; Lifetime Achievement Award for Irish Writing, Sunday Tribune, 2007; British Classical Assoc. Prize, 2011; Irish PEN Award, 2014. Officier de la République française, 1996. *Publications:* The Factory Girls, 1982; Observe the Sons of Ulster Marching Towards the Somme, 1986; Innocence, 1987; Carthaginians, and Baglady, 1988; Mary and Lizzie, 1989; Someone Who'll Watch Over Me, 1992; Booterstown (poems), 1994; Plays, vol. 1, 1996; Mutabilitie, 1997; Dolly West's Kitchen, 1999; The Sea With No Ships (poems), 1999; Plays, vol. 2, 2002; Gates of Gold, 2002; The Stone Jug: poems, 2003; Dulse (poems), 2008; Greta Garbo Came to Donegal, 2010; The Match Box, 2012; The Hanging Gardens, 2013; Arimathea (novel), 2013; Thebans (libretto), 2014; *versions:* Peer Gynt, 1990; Three Sisters, 1990; A Doll's House, 1996; Electra, 1997; The Storm, 1998; Miss Julie, 2000; Speaking Like Magpies, 2005; There Came a Gypsy Riding, 2007; Oedipus, 2008; The Lady from the Sea, 2008; Helen, 2009; Ghosts, 2010; John Gabriel Borkman, 2010; Damned By Despair, 2012; In A Town of Five Thousand People, 2012; The Dead: a version, 2012. *Recreations:* walking, horse-racing, Irish art. *Address:* Department of Anglo-Irish Literature, University College, Dublin, Belfield, Dublin 4, Ireland.

McGUINNESS, Martin; Member (SF) Mid Ulster, since 1998, and Deputy First Minister, since 2007, Northern Ireland Assembly; *b* 23 May 1950. *Educ:* Christian Brothers' Tech. Coll. Mem., NI Assembly, 1982–86. Chief Negotiator, Sinn Féin. MP (SF) Mid Ulster, 1997–Jan. 2013. Contested (SF) Foyle, 1983, 1987, 1992. Minister of Educn, NI, 1999–2002. *Address:* Sinn Féin, 55 Falls Road, Belfast BT12 4PD.

McGUINNESS, Patrick Joseph, CMG 2014; OBE 1997; Deputy National Security Adviser (Intelligence, Security, Resilience), Cabinet Office, since 2014; *b* Oxford, 27 April 1963; *s* of Prof. Bernard Francis McGuinness and Prof. Rosamond Ziegler, (Corky), McGuinness; *m* 1994, Susannah Mills; one *s* two *d*. *Educ:* Ampleforth Coll., York; Balliol Coll., Oxford (BA Mod. Hist.). Foreign and Commonwealth Office, 1985–2013: Second Sec., Sana'a, 1988–91; First Sec., Abu Dhabi, 1994–96; Counsellor: Cairo, 1996–99; Rome, 2003–06. *Recreations:* dogs, Rugby Union, classical music, sybaritism. *Address:* Cabinet Office, 70 Whitehall, SW1A 2AS. *Club:* Athenæum.

McGUINNESS, Prof. Patrick Robert Anthony, DPhil; FLSW; Professor of French and Comparative Literature, University of Oxford, since 2010; Fellow and Tutor in French, St Anne's College, Oxford, since 1998; *b* Tunis, 2 June 1968; *s* of Kevin McGuinness and Monique McGuinness (*née* Lejeune); partner, Angharad Price; one *s* one *d*. *Educ:* Clifton Coll., Bristol; Downing Coll., Cambridge (BA 1990); Univ. of York (MA 1991); Magdalen Coll., Oxford (DPhil 1994). Fellow and Tutor in French, Jesus Coll., Oxford, 1995–98. FLSW 2010. Chevalier: Ordre des Palmes Académiques (France), 2009; Ordre des Arts et des Lettres (France), 2011. *Publications:* (ed) T. E. Hulme: selected writings, 1998; Maurice Maeterlinck and the Making of Modern Theatre, 2000; Symbolism, Decadence and the fin de siècle, 2000; (ed) Lynette Roberts: collected poems, 2006; Other People's Countries: a journey into memory (memoir), 2014 (Duff Cooper Prize, 2014); *poetry:* The Canals of Mars, 2004; 19th Century Blues, 2006; Jilted City, 2010; *fiction:* The Last Hundred Days, 2011 (Wales Book of the Year, Writers' Guild Fiction Prize, 2012). *Address:* St Anne's College, Oxford OX2 6HS. *T:* (01865) 274836. *E:* patrick.mcguinness@st-annes.ox.ac.uk.

McGUIRE, Prof. Alistair James, PhD; Professor of Health Economics, London School of Economics, since 2002; *b* Coventry, 6 Nov. 1956; *s* of Terence McGuire and Charlotte McGuire (*née* Dolan); one *s* one *d*. *Educ:* Royal High Sch., Edinburgh; Heriot-Watt Univ. (BA Hons Econs); Univ. of Aberdeen (MLitt Econs; PhD Econs 1987). Res. Fellow, Univ.

of Aberdeen, 1980–87; Oxford University: Sen. Res. Fellow, Centre for Socio-Legal Studies, Wolfson Coll., 1987–92; Res. Fellow and Teaching Tutor, Pembroke Coll., 1987–92; Reader, 1992–97, Prof. of Econs, 1997–2002, City Univ. *Publications:* (jtly) Economics of Health Care, 1988; (with G. Mooney) Medical Ethics and Economics in Health Care, 1988; (jtly) Providing Health Care, 1991; (with P. Annand) Issues in the Reformed NHS, 1997; (with M. Drummond) Economic Evaluation in Health Care, 2001; (jtly) The Economics of New Health Care Technologies, 2009. *Recreations:* music, sleeping. *Address:* London School of Economics, Houghton Street, WC2A 2AE. *T:* (020) 7955 6375, *Fax:* (020) 7955 6308. *E:* a.j.mcguire@lse.ac.uk.

McGUIRE, Rt Hon. Dame Anne (Catherine), DBE 2015; PC 2008; *b* 26 May 1949; *d* of Albert Long, CBE and Agnes Long (*née* Coney); *m* 1972, Leonard F. McGuire; one *s* one *d*. *Educ:* Our Lady and St Francis Sch., Glasgow; Univ. of Glasgow (MA Hons 1971); Notre Dame Coll. of Educn. Registrar and Sec., Court's Dept, Univ. of Glasgow, 1971–74; teacher, 1983–85; fieldworker, 1985–89, Nat. Officer, Scotland, 1989–93, CSV; Dep. Dir, Scottish Council for Voluntary Orgns, 1993–97. MP (Lab) Stirling, 1997–2015. PPS to Sec. of State for Scotland, 1997–98; an Asst Govt Whip, 1998–2001; a Lord Comr of HM Treasury (Govt Whip), 2001–02; Parly Under-Sec. of State, Scotland Office, 2002–05; Minister for Disabled People, DWP, 2005–08; PPS to Leader of the Opposition, 2010–11; Shadow Minister for Disabled People, 2011–13. *Recreations:* walking, Scottish traditional music, reading.

McGUIRE, Michael Thomas Francis; *b* 3 May 1926; *m* 1954, Marie T. Murphy (*d* 1998); three *s* two *d*. *Educ:* Elementary Schools. Coal miner. Whole-time NUM Branch Secretary, 1957–64. Joined Lab. Party, 1951. MP (Lab): Ince, 1964–83; Makerfield, 1983–87. PPS to Minister of Sport, 1974–77. Member: Council of Europe, 1977–87; WEU, 1977–87. *Recreations:* most out-door sports, especially Rugby League football; traditional music, especially Irish traditional music.

McGUIRE, Prof. William Joseph, PhD; FGS; Professor of Geophysical and Climate Hazards, University College London, 1997–2012, now Emeritus (Co-Director, UCL Environment Institute, 2010–12); *b* 1 Dec. 1954; *s* of late John McMillan McGuire and of Audrey McGuire (*née* Wade Owens); *m* 2000, Anna Taylor; one *s* and one adopted *s*. *Educ:* St Michael's Coll., Hitchin; University Coll. London (BSc Geol 1976); CNAA (PhD 1980). FGS 1977. Lectr in Igneous Petrology and Geochem., W London Inst. of Higher Educn, 1981–90; Lectr, 1990–93, Sen. Lectr, 1993–95, Reader, 1995–97, in Volcanology and Igneous Petrology, Cheltenham and Gloucester Coll. of Higher Educn; Dir, Aon Benfield (formerly Benfield) UCL Hazard Res. Centre, 1997–2010. Dir, DisasterMan Ltd, 2000–; consultant on natural hazards and climate change, HSBC Gp, 2006–; Mem., Adv. Bd, Contraction and Convergence Foundn, 2011–. Member: UK Govt Natural Hazard Working Gp, 2005; UK Govt Scientific Adv. Gp in Emergencies for Icelandic ash crisis, 2010. Chm. Volcanic Studies Gp, 1993–96, Council Mem., 1997–99, Geol Soc. of London; Mem., Sci. Media Panel, Royal Instn, 2002–. UK Nat. Corresp., Internat. Assoc. of Volcanology and Chemistry of the Earth's Interior, 1993–96; UK Rep., Eur. Volcanology Proj. Cttee, ESF, 1994; Mem., 1993–95, Sec., 1996–2000, UK Panel, IUGG. Presenter: radio: Disasters in Waiting (series), 2000, Scientists Under Pressure (series), 2001; television: The End of the World (series), 2006. Sci. Advr, Footprint Friends, 2009–. FRI 2003. Member, Editorial Board: Volcanology and Seismology, 1994–98; Acta Vulcanologica, 1995–2000; Disasters, 2002–; BBC Focus Magazine, 2005–11; Philosophical Transactions A, 2007–13. *Publications:* (ed jtly) Monitoring Active Volcanoes: strategies, procedures and techniques, 1995; Volcanoes of the World, 1997; Apocalypse: a natural history of global disasters, 1999; Italian Volcanoes, 2001; (jtly) Natural Hazards and Environmental Change, 2002; Raging Planet, 2002; A Guide to the End of the World: everything you never wanted to know, 2002; (with Robert Kovach) Guide to Global Hazards, 2003; (jtly) World Atlas of Natural Hazards, 2004; Surviving Armageddon: solutions for a threatened planet, 2005; Global Catastrophes: a very short introduction, 2005, rev. edn 2014; Seven Years to Save the Planet, 2008; Waking the Giant: how a changing climate triggers earthquakes, tsunamis and volcanoes, 2012; Climate Forcing of Geological Hazards, 2013; learned papers in Nature, Phil Trans of Royal Soc., etc. *Recreations:* playing with sons Fraser and Jake, and cats Dave and Toby, growing vegetables, walking and mountain biking in the Peaks, worrying about the future of our planet, our race and my sons, organising 'Warm Wet & Windy'—the Peak District Climate Change and Eco Festival. *Address:* Aon Benfield UCL Hazard Centre, Department of Earth Sciences, University College London, Gower Street, WC1E 6BT. *T:* (020) 7679 3449, *Fax:* (020) 7679 2390. *E:* w.mcguire@ucl.ac.uk.

McGUIRK, Stephen John Paul, CBE 2005; QFSM 2002; DL; County Fire Officer and Chief Executive, Greater Manchester Fire and Rescue Service, since 2009; *b* 16 July 1960; *m* 1983, Julie Bennion; two *d*. *Educ:* Southbank Univ. (BSc, MA); Open Univ. (BA Hons). Served: Gtr Manchester Co. Fire Service, 1976–86; Royal Berks Fire Service, 1986–89; W Midlands Fire Service, 1989–98; Chief Fire Officer, Cheshire Fire Service, 1999–2009. DL Gtr Manchester, 2011. Long Service Medal, 1996. *Recreations:* running, fitness generally, reading. *Address:* Greater Manchester Fire and Rescue Service, 146 Bolton Road, Swinton, Manchester M27 8US. *T:* (0161) 608 4001. *E:* cfo@manchesterfire.gov.uk.

McGURK, John Callender; writer, media consultant, broadcaster; *b* 12 Dec. 1952; *s* of John B. McGurk and Janet McGurk; *m* 1984, Karen Patricia Anne Ramsay (marr. diss. 2005); one *s* one *d*. *Educ:* Tynecastle Sen. Secondary Sch., Edinburgh. Trainee Journalist, Scottish County Press, 1970–74; Reporter: Evening Post, Nottingham, 1974–75; Scottish Daily News, 1975; Reporter and Broadcaster, Radio Clyde, 1975–78; Sunday Mail: Reporter, 1978–84; News Editor, 1984–88; Dep. Editor, 1988–89; Editor, Sunday Sun, Newcastle, 1989–91; Dep. Editor, Daily Record, 1991–94; broadcaster, BBC Radio Scotland, and media consultant, 1994–95; Editor: Evening News, Edinburgh, 1995–97; Scotland on Sunday, 1997–2001; Editl Dir, The Scotsman Pubns Ltd, 2001–04; Ed., The Scotsman, 2004–06; Gp Man. Ed., Daily Telegraph and Sunday Telegraph, 2006. Chm., Editors' Cttee, Scottish Daily Newspaper Soc., 2001. Mem., Press Complaints Commn, 1999–2001. *Recreations:* newspapers, dining out, travel. *E:* jcmcgurk@blueyonder.co.uk.

MACH, David Stefan, RA 1998; sculptor; *b* 18 March 1956; *s* of Joseph Mach and Martha (*née* Cassidy); *m* 1979, Lesley June White (*d* 2014). *Educ:* Buckhaven High Sch.; Duncan of Jordanstone Coll. of Art (Dip. and Post Dip. in Art); Royal Coll. of Art (MA). Full-time sculptor and occasional vis. lectr, 1982–; Associate Prof., Sculpture Dept, Edinburgh Coll. of Art, 1999; Prof. of Sculpture, Royal Acad., 2000–08; Prof. of Inspiration and Discovery, Univ. of Dundee, 2004–. Work includes Train, Darlington, largest contemp. sculpture in the UK, 1998; sculptures exhibited at galleries in England, Scotland, NY, São Paulo Biennale, Venice Biennale, Paris, Hong Kong, Seoul, Dubai. Trustee, NPG, 2006–10. City of Glasgow Lord Provost Prize, 1992. *Recreations:* music, film, ski-ing, tennis. *Address:* 8 Havelock Walk, Forest Hill, SE23 3HG. *T:* (020) 8699 5659. *E:* davidmach@davidmach.com. *Club:* Chelsea Arts.

McHALE, His Honour Keith Michael; a Circuit Judge, 1980–2000; *b* 26 March 1928; *s* of late Cyril Michael McHale, MC and Gladys McHale; *m* 1966, Rosemary Margaret Arthur; one *s* one *d*. Called to the Bar, Gray's Inn, 1951. *Address:* 1 D'Arcy Place, Bromley, Kent BR2 0RY.

McHARG, Anne Carla; *see* Ferguson-Smith, A. C.

MACHELL, John William; QC 2012; *b* Maidstone, 9 Feb. 1970; *s* of Paul and Jill Machell; *m* 1994, Helen Cheetham; one *s* one *d*. *Educ:* St Albans Sch.; Univ. of Southampton (LLB). Called to the Bar, Inner Temple, 1993; in practice as a barrister, specialising in chancery and commercial law, 1993–. *Publications:* The Law of Limited Liability Partnership, 2001, 3rd edn 2009. *Recreations:* golf, tennis. *Address:* Serle Court, 6 New Square, Lincoln's Inn, WC2A 3QS. *T:* (020) 7242 6105. *E:* jmachell@serlecourt.co.uk.

McHENRY, Rev. Brian Edward, CBE 2008; Vicar, All Saints', Orpington, since 2011; *b* 12 Dec. 1950; *s* of late Alexander Edward McHenry and of Winifred Alice McHenry (*née* Wainford); *m* 1979, Elizabeth Anne Lipsey; two *s*. *Educ:* Dulwich Coll.; New Coll., Oxford (MA); SE Inst. for Theol Educn (Dip. in Applied Christian Theol.); Canterbury Christ Church (BA Ministerial Theol.). Called to the Bar, Middle Temple, 1976. Treasury Solicitor's Dept, 1978–92, 2000; legal advr, Monopolies and Mergers Commn, 1992–96; Solicitor: N Wales Tribunal of Inquiry into Child Abuse, 1996–97; BSE Inquiry, 1998–2000; Chief Legal Advr, Competition Commn, 2000–04; Office of Fair Trading: Solicitor, 2004–06; Gen. Counsel, 2006–08. Mem., Crown Appts Commn, 1997–2002. General Synod of Church of England: Mem., 1980–85 and 1987–2005; Vice-Chm., House of Laity, 2000–05; Chm., Standing Orders Cttee, 1991–99; Member: Standing Cttee, 1990–95; Legislative Cttee, 1981–85, 1991–95 and 2001–05 (Dep. Chm., 2001–05); Business Cttee, 1999–2005; Archbishops' Council, 1999–2005; Lay Vice-Pres., Southwark Diocesan Synod, 1988–96 and 1997–99; Hon. Lay Canon, 2004–08, Mem., Chapter, 2010–12, Southwark Cathedral; Rector of Rochester Chapter, Soc. of Catholic Priests, 2012–15. Trustee: Churches Conservation Trust, 2008–13; Orpington Christian Counselling Service, 2012–; Vice Pres., Churches Together in Orpington, 2013–. A Reader, C of E, 1976–2008; ordained deacon, 2008, priest, 2009; Curate, St Paul's, Deptford, 2008–11. Chaplain, Orpington Br., RBL, 2011–. Governor: Burwood Sch., Orpington, 2012–14; St Olave's and St Saviour's Grammar Sch., Orpington, 2013–. *Recreations:* swimming, walking, jogging, travel, history, Arsenal FC, reading classic fiction. *Address:* 1A Keswick Road, Orpington BR6 0EU. *T:* (01689) 824624, 07887 802641.

McHENRY, Donald F.; Distinguished Professor in the Practice of Diplomacy, School of Foreign Service, Georgetown University, since 1998 (University Research Professor of Diplomacy and International Affairs, 1981–98); *b* 13 Oct. 1936; *s* of Limas McHenry and Dora Lee Brooks; *m* Mary Williamson (marr. diss.); one *s* two *d*. *Educ:* Lincoln Senior High Sch., East St Louis, Ill; Illinois State Univ. (BS); Southern Illinois Univ. (MSc); Georgetown Univ. Taught at Howard Univ., Washington, 1959–62; joined Dept of State, 1963; Head of Dependent Areas Section, Office of UN Pol Affairs, 1965–68; Asst to Sec. of State, US, 1969; Special Asst to Counsellor, Dept of State, 1969–71; Lectr, Sch. of Foreign Service, Georgetown Univ.; Guest Scholar, Brookings Inst., and Internat. Affairs Fellow, Council on Foreign Relations (on leave from State Dept), 1971–73; resigned from State Dept, 1973; Project Dir, Humanitarian Policy Studies, Carnegie Endowment for Internat. Peace, Washington, 1973–76; served in transition team of President Carter, 1976–77; Ambassador and Deputy Rep. of US to UN Security Council, 1977–79, Permanent Rep., 1979; US Ambassador to UN, 1979–81. Founder and Co-Pres., IRC Gp, LLC, 1981–; Director: Internat. Paper Co., 1981; Fleet Boston Financial Co.; Bank of Boston Corp., 1981–2004; GlaxoSmithKline (formerly SmithKline Beecham) plc, 1982–2004; Coca-Cola, 1982–2014; American Telephone and Telegraph, 1987–2005; Inst. for Internat. Economics, 1999. Dir, American Ditchley Foundn; Chm., Bd of Dirs, Africare, 1989–2004; Mem. Bd of Govs, UNA of USA. Mem., American Acad. of Arts and Scis, 1992. Hon. degrees: Dennison, Duke, Eastern Illinois, Georgetown, Harvard, Illinois State, Michigan, Princeton, Southern Illinois, Tufts, and Washington Univs; Amherst, Bates, Boston and Williams Colleges. Superior Honor Award, Dept of State, 1966. Mem. Council on Foreign Relations and Editorial Bd, Foreign Policy Magazine. *Publications:* Micronesia: Trust Betrayed, 1975. *Address:* Georgetown University, 37th and O Streets, NW, Washington, DC 20057, USA.

MACHIN, Anthony; *see* Machin, E. A.

MACHIN, David; Under Treasurer, Gray's Inn, 1989–2000; *b* 25 April 1934; *s* of late Noel and Joan Machin; *m* 1963, Sarah Mary, *yr d* of late Col W. A. Chester-Master, DL; two *d*. *Educ:* Eton (Oppidan Scholar); Trinity Coll., Cambridge. National Service, 1952–54 (2nd Lieut Welsh Guards). Editor, William Heinemann Ltd, 1957–66; Literary Agent, Gregson & Wigan Ltd and London International, 1966–68; Partner, A. P. Watt & Son, 1968–70; Director: Jonathan Cape Ltd, 1970–78; Chatto, Bodley Head and Jonathan Cape Ltd, 1977–78, 1981–87; Jt Man. Dir, 1981, Man. Dir, 1982–87, The Bodley Head Ltd; Dir, Triad Paperbacks Ltd, 1983–86; Gen. Sec., The Society of Authors, 1978–81. Chm. of Trustees, Inns of Court Gainsford Trust, 1992–2000. Vice-Chm., Hammersmith Democrats, 1988–89. Chm., Lansdown Crescent Assoc., 2003–06 (Trustee, 2010–13). Hon. Bencher, Gray's Inn, 2000. *Publications:* (contrib.) Outlook, 1963; (ed) Gray's Inn 2000: a millennium record, 2002; (ed) Simon Phipps: a portrait, 2003; contrib. The Oldie. *Address:* 11 Deanery Walk, Avonpark, Limpley Stoke, nr Bath, Wilts BA2 7JQ. *Club:* Garrick.

MACHIN, (Edward) Anthony; QC 1973; a Recorder of the Crown Court, 1976–90; *b* 28 June 1925; *s* of Edward Arthur Machin and Olive Muriel Smith; *m* 1953, Jean Margaret McKanna; two *s* one *d*. *Educ:* Christ's Coll., Finchley; New Coll., Oxford (BA 1st Cl. 1949; MA 1950; BCL 1st. Cl. 1950; Vinerian Law Scholar, 1950; Tancred Student, 1950; Cassel Scholar, 1951). Called to Bar, Lincoln's Inn, 1951, Bencher, 1980; retired from practice, 1996; Dep. High Court Judge, 1985–95; a Judge of the Courts of Appeal of Jersey and Guernsey, 1988–95. Chm., Exeter Flying Club, 1999. *Publications:* Redgrave's Factories Acts, 1962, 1966, 1972; Redgrave's Offices and Shops, 1965 and 1973; Redgrave's Health and Safety in Factories, 1976, 1982; Health and Safety at Work, 1980; Health and Safety, 1990; (contrib.) Medical Negligence, 1990 and 1994. *Recreations:* music, learning the organ, flying, web-surfing, languages. *Address:* Strand End, Strand, Topsham, Exeter EX3 0BB. *T:* (01392) 877992.

MACHIN, His Honour John Vessey; DL; a Circuit Judge, 1997–2009; *b* 4 May 1941; *s* of late William Vessey Machin and Dona Machin (*née* Pryce), Worksop; *m* 1967, Susan Helen, *d* of Edgar Frank Emery; one *s* one *d*. *Educ:* Dragon Sch., Oxford; Westminster Sch. Called to the Bar, Middle Temple, 1965; Midland and Oxford Circuit; Asst Recorder, 1990–94; Recorder, 1994–97. Chm., Agricl Land Tribunal (Eastern Area), 1999–2013 (Dep. Chm., 1986–99); Regl Judge, First-tier Tribunal (Property Chamber), 2013–14. Judicial Mem., Lincs Probation Bd, 2006–08. Governor: Worksop Coll., Notts, 1986–2012; Ranby House Sch., 1986–2012; Fellow and Midland Dir, Woodard Schs, 1988–2012; Foundn Gov., St Matthew's C of E Primary Sch., Normanton-on-Trent, 2005–. DL Notts, 2011. *Recreation:* aquatic and rural pursuits especially canambulation. *Address:* Normanton Hall, Normanton-on-Trent, Newark, Notts NG23 6RQ. *Clubs:* Garrick, Farmers; Newark Rowing.

MACHIN, Kenneth Arthur; QC 1977; **His Honour Judge Machin;** a Judge, International Criminal Tribunal for Rwanda, United Nations, 2003–09; *b* 13 July 1936; *o s* of Thomas Arthur Machin and Edith May Machin; *m* 1983, Amaryllis Francesca (former ballet dancer and Member of Court of Common Council, Cripplegate Ward, City of London), *o d* of Dr Donald and Lucille Bigley. *Educ:* St Albans School. Called to the Bar, 1960; South Eastern Circuit; Central Criminal Court, 1985–90 and 2001; a Recorder of the Crown Court, 1979–83; a Circuit Judge, 1983–90; a Sen. Circuit Judge, 1990–2001; a Dep. Circuit Judge, 2001–. Chief Social Security and Child Support Comr, 1990–2000. Mem., Judicial Studies Bd and Chm., Tribunals Cttee, 1992–99. Freeman, City of London. *Recreations:* painting, Martello Towers. *Address:* c/o Central Criminal Court, Old Bailey, EC4M 7EH.

MACHIN, Prof. Stephen Jonathan, PhD; FBA 2006; Professor of Economics, University College London, since 1996; Research Director, Centre for Economic Performance, London School of Economics, since 2003; *b* 23 Dec. 1962; *s* of Raymond Edward Machin and Betty Patricia Machin; *m* 2001, Kirstine Hansen; one *s*. *Educ:* Wolverhampton Grammar Sch.; Wolverhampton Poly. (BSc 1st cl. (Econs) 1985); Univ. of Warwick (PhD 1988). Lectr, 1988–93, Reader, 1993–96, UCL. Dir, Centre for Econs of Educn, 2000–. Visiting Professor: Harvard Univ., 1993–94; MIT, 2001–02. Ed., Economic Jl, 1998–. *Publications:* papers in leading academic jls, inc. Qly Jl of Econs, Rev. of Econ. Studies, Econ. Jl, Industrial and Labor Relns Rev. and Jl of European Econ. Assoc. *Address:* Department of Economics, University College London, Gower Street, WC1E 6BT. *T:* (020) 7679 5870, *Fax:* (020) 7916 2773. *E:* s.machin@ucl.ac.uk.

MACHIN, Thomas Paul Edwin; Director: MacGregor Associates, since 2000; Fraser Otis Ltd, since 2000; *b* 14 Sept. 1944; *s* of late Thomas Edwin Machin and Elizabeth Pamela Machin (*née* Collett); *m* 1970, Elizabeth-Ann Suttle. *Educ:* St Joseph's Coll., Stoke-on-Trent; London Sch. of Economics (BSc Econ). Plessey Co., 1966–69; Massey Ferguson, 1969–74; joined British Leyland, 1974; Dir, Engrg Services, 1980–82; Personnel Dir, Cowley, 1983–87; Eur. Employee Relns and Mgt Develt Dir, Lawson Mardon Gp (Europe), 1987–91; Human Resources Dir, James Neill Hldgs Ltd, 1991–92; CEO, States of Jersey Estabt Cttee, 1992–95; Chief Executive, BPIF, 1995–2000. Consultant: Negotiating Solutions, 2002–05; First Class Partnerships, 2002–12. Chairman: Indust. Relns Cttee, BPIF, 1989–91; Trade Assoc. Council, CBI, 2000; Pres., Yorks Publicity Assoc., 1998. Chartered FCIPD (FIPD 1986); FRSA 1996. Freeman, City of London, 1998; Liveryman, Co. of Stationers and Newspaper Makers, 1998–2002. *Recreations:* retired Association Football referee, keeping fit, spectator sports (especially horse racing and Association Football), investment - business and sports, sports politics, skidelling, current affairs. *Address:* 24 Rowallan Castle, Kilmaurs, East Ayrshire KA3 2DP. *T:* (01563) 521797.

MACHRAY, Alastair Hulbert; Editor, Liverpool Echo, since 2005; Editor-in-chief, Trinity Mirror, Merseyside, since 2009, and North Wales and Cheshire, since 2012; *b* 19 June 1961; *s* of Douglas Basil Machray and June Hulbert; *m* 1987, Lynne Elizabeth Ward; one *s* one *d*. *Educ:* Glasgow Acad.; Greencroft Comprehensive. Reporter, Sunderland Echo, 1979–82; sports journalist, Journal, Newcastle, 1982–85; editor, Football Pink, Newcastle, 1985–86; sports journalist, Today, 1986–88; Evening Chronicle, Newcastle: Sub Editor, 1988; Asst Chief Sub Editor, 1988–89; Dep. Chief Sub Editor, 1989–90; Design Editor, 1990–93; Asst Editor, Liverpool Echo, 1994–95; Editor: Liverpool Daily Post, 1995–2002; Daily Post in Wales, 2002–05; Ed.-in-Chief, Trinity Mirror North Wales, 2002–05. *Recreations:* golf, cricket, family, cinema, travel. *Address:* PO Box 48, Old Hall Street, Liverpool L69 3EB.

McILVEEN, David; Member (DemU) North Antrim, Northern Ireland Assembly, since 2011; *b* Belfast, 11 Feb. 1981; *s* of David McIlveen and Mary McIlveen. Mem., NI Policing Bd. *Recreations:* golf, music, travelling, motorcycling. *Address:* Northern Ireland Assembly, Parliament Buildings, Stormont, Belfast BT4 3XX.

McILVEEN, Michelle Elizabeth; Member (DemU) Strangford, Northern Ireland Assembly, since 2007; *b* 21 Jan. 1971; *d* of Henry and Elizabeth McIlveen. *Educ:* Queen's Univ., Belfast (BSSc, MSSc; PGCE). Teacher of hist. and politics, 1994–97; business manager, 1997–2007. Mem. (DemU) Ards BC, 2005–. Jun. Minister, Office of First Minister and Dep. First Minister, NI, 2015. *Address:* Constituency Office, 7 The Square, Town Parks, Comber, Co. Down, Northern Ireland BT23 5DX. *T:* (028) 9187 1441, *Fax:* (028) 9187 1494. *E:* michelle.mcilveen@niassembly.gov.uk.

McILVRIDE, Rhoderick Robert; QC (Scot.) 2014; *b* Campbeltown, Argyll, 19 Jan. 1957; *s* of Daniel and Catherine McIlvride; *m* 1978, Miriam Frances Haig; one *s* three *d*. *Educ:* Kelvinside Acad., Glasgow; Univ. of Glasgow (LLB Hons). Admitted Solicitor, 1981; in practice as solicitor, 1981–2004; Licensed Insolvency Practitioner, 1988–2004; Solicitor Advocate, 1997–2004; Advocate, 2005–. *Recreations:* reading, opera, football, dining out. *Address:* Advocates Library, Parliament House, Edinburgh EH1 1RF. *E:* clerks@terrafirmachambers.com.

McILWHAM, Fiona May Joan; HM Diplomatic Service; Senior Adviser to Director General of Enlargement, European Commission, since 2012 (on secondment); *b* Guildford, 31 Dec. 1973; *d* of John McIlwham and Ann McIlwham; partner, Daniel Korski. *Educ:* St John's Coll., Cambridge (BA Pt 1 Philos. Pt 2 Social and Pol Scis 1995); Sch. of Oriental and African Studies, Univ. of London (MSc Develt Econs 1998). NGO field work, Bangladesh, 1995, Sudan, 1997; EC, 1996; joined FCO, 1998; Second Sec. (Pol and Press), Sarajevo, 2000–02; Hd, British Embassy Office, Banja Luka, 2002–03; EU Presidency team, London, 2004–06; First Sec., Baghdad and Basra, 2006; seconded to US Dept of State, Washington, 2006–07; First Sec. (Pol), Washington, 2007; Ambassador to Republic of Albania, 2009–12. *Recreations:* reading, film, theatre, ski-ing, hiking.

McINDOE, Very Rev. John Hedley; Minister of St Columba's Church, Pont Street, London, 1988–2000; Moderator of the General Assembly of The Church of Scotland, 1996–97; *b* 31 Aug. 1934; *s* of William McIndoe and May (*née* Hedley); *m* 1960, Evelyn Kennedy Johnstone (*d* 2006); three *d*. *Educ:* Greenock Acad.; Glasgow Univ. (MA Hons (Classics), 1956; BD (with distinction), 1959); Hartford Seminary, Conn, USA (STM, 1960). Ordained, 1960; Asst Minister, Paisley Abbey, 1960–63; Minister: Park Church, Dundee, 1963–72; St Nicholas Parish Church, Lanark, 1972–88. Hon. DD Glasgow, 2000. *Recreations:* theatre, films. *Address:* 5 Dunlin, Westerlands Park, Glasgow G12 0FE. *T:* (0141) 579 1366.

McINERNEY, Prof. John Peter, OBE 1995; Glanely Professor of Agricultural Policy and Director of Agricultural Economics Unit, University of Exeter, 1984–2002, now Emeritus; *b* 10 Jan. 1939; *s* of Peter McInerney and Eva McInerney; *m* 1961, Audrey M. Perry; one *s* one *d*. *Educ:* Colyton Grammar Sch., Colyford, Devon; Univ. of London (BScAgric Hons); Univ. of Oxford (DipAgricEcons); Iowa State Univ. (PhD). Lectr in Agricl Econs, Wye Coll., Univ. of London, 1964–66; Lectr and Sen. Lectr in Agricl Econs, Univ. of Manchester, 1967–78; Prof. of Agricl Econs and Management, Univ. of Reading, 1978–84. Research Economist and Cons., World Bank, Washington, 1972–97. Visiting Professor: Res. Sch. of Animal Prodn and Health, Royal Vet. and Agricl Univ., Copenhagen, 1999–2005; RAC, 2001–09. President: Agricl Econs Soc., 1996–97; Rural Educn and Develt Assoc., 1996–97; Member: Dunnet Cttee on TB, Cattle and Badgers, MAFF, 1984–86; Mgt Cttee, MAFF/DTI LINK Sustainable Livestock Prog., 1996–2002; Farm Animal Welfare Council, MAFF, 1996–2004; Bd, UK Register of Organic Food Standards, 1996–2003; Independent Scientific Gp on Cattle TB, MAFF, subseq. DEFRA, 1998–2007; Econs Panel, SW RDA, 2001–06; Econs and Social Studies Prog. Adv. Gp, TB res., DEFRA, 2008–10. Trustee, Farm Animal Welfare Trust, 2008–. Governor, Silsoe Res. Inst., 1996–2003. Phi Kappa Phi 1964, Gamma Sigma Delta 1964. FRSA 1995. Hon. FRASE 1999. Massey Ferguson Nat. Agricl Award, 1998; Agricl Econs Soc. Award, 2011. *Publications:* The Food Industry: economics and policy (jtly), 1983; Badgers and Bovine Tuberculosis (jtly), 1986; Disease in Farm Livestock: economics and policy (jtly), 1987; Diversification in the Use of Farm Resources, 1989; Economic Analysis of Milk Quotas, 1992; Agriculture at the Crossroads, 1998; Who Cares?: a study of farmers' involvement in countryside management, 2000; What's the Damage?: costs of countryside management on farms, 2001; Animal Welfare: economics and policy, 2004; chapters in: Current Issues in Economic Policy, 1975, 2nd edn 1980; Resources Policy, 1982; Grassland Production, 1999, etc; articles in Jl of Agricl Econs, Amer. Jl of Agricl Econs, Canadian Jl of Agricl Econs, Outlook on Agric., Jl of RASE, Farm Mgt, Preventive Vet. Medicine, Agricl Progress, Nature, Jl Applied Ecol. *Recreations:* doing it myself, tentative farming, introspection. *Address:* Old Rectory Farm, Templeton, Tiverton, Devon EX16 8BN. *T:* 07764 516964. *E:* J.P.McInerney@exeter.ac.uk. *Club:* Templeton Social.

MacINNES, Dame Barbara Mary; *see* Stocking, Dame B. M.

McINNES, Elizabeth Anne; MP (Lab) Heywood and Middleton, since Oct. 2014; *b* Oldham, Lancs, 30 March 1959; *d* of George Frederick McInnes and Margaret Elizabeth McInnes; partner, Stephen John Duxbury; one *s*. *Educ:* Hathershaw Comp. Sch., Oldham; St Anne's Coll., Oxford (BA Hons Biochem. 1981); Surrey Univ. (MSc Clin. Biochem. 1983). Trainee Clin. Scientist, Greenwich District Hosp., 1981–83; Basic Grade Biochemist, Royal Hallamshire Hosp., Sheffield, 1983–87; Sen. Clin. Scientist, Pennine Acute Hosps NHS Trust, 1987–2014. Chair, Nat. Health Sector Cttee, Unite, 2013–14. Mem., Rossendale BC, 2010–14. *Recreations:* hill-walking, camping, art, music. *Address:* House of Commons, SW1A 0AA. *T:* (020) 7219 0684. *E:* mcinnesl@parliament.uk.

MacINNES, Hamish, OBE 1979; BEM; Founder and Leader, Glencoe Mountain Rescue Team, 1960–94; author and film consultant, major movies; Director, Glencoe Productions Ltd, since 1989; *b* 7 July 1930. Dep. Leader, British Everest Expedition, 1975. Hon. Dir, Leishman Meml Res. Centre, Glencoe, 1975–92; Mountain Rescue Cttee for Scotland (Past Sec.). Founder and Hon. Pres., Search and Rescue Dog Assoc.; Co-founder, Snow and Avalanche Foundn of Scotland, 1988; Past Pres., Alpine Climbing Group; Pres., Guide Dogs for the Blind Adventure Gp, 1986–. Patron, Equal Adventure, 2005–. Designer of climbing equipment, incl. the first all metal ice axe, terrodactyl ice tools, the MacInnes stretchers, etc. Hon. Member: Scottish Mountaineering Club; Alpine Club. Hon. LLD: Glasgow, 1983; Dundee, 2004; Hon. DSc: Aberdeen, 1988; Heriot-Watt, 1992; DU Stirling, 1997. Mem., Scottish Sports Hall of Fame, 2003. *Publications:* Climbing, 1964; Scottish Climbs, 2 vols, 1971, 2nd edn (1 vol.) 1981; International Mountain Rescue Handbook, 1972, 5th edn 2005; Call-Out: mountain rescue, 1973, 4th edn 1986; Climb to the Lost World, 1974; Death Reel (novel), 1976; West Highland Walks, vols 1 and 2, 1979, Vol. 3, 1983, Vol. 4, 1988; Look Behind the Ranges, 1979; Scottish Winter Climbs, 1980; High Drama (stories), 1980; Beyond the Ranges, 1984; Sweep Search, 1985; The Price of Adventure, 1987; My Scotland, 1988; The Way Through the Glens, 1989; Land of Mountain and Mist, 1989; Mammoth Book of Mountain Disaster, 2003; Murder in the Glen (novel), 2008; Errant Nights (novel), 2011; books have been translated into Russian, Japanese, Italian and German. *Address:* Tigh A'Voulin, Glencoe, Argyll PH49 4HX.

McINNES, Prof. Iain Blair, PhD; FRCPE, FRCPGlas, FMedSci; FRSE; Muirhead Professor of Medicine, since 2012, Arthritis Research UK Professor of Rheumatology, since 2014, Director, Institute of Infection, Immunity and Inflammation, since 2010, and Honorary Consultant Rheumatologist, since 2002, University of Glasgow; *b* Glasgow, 19 Oct. 1964; *s* of John McInnes and Janice McInnes; *m* Karin; two *d*. *Educ:* Hutchesons' Grammar Sch.; Univ. of Glasgow (BSc Immunol. 1st Cl. Hons 1986; MB ChB Hons 1989; PhD 1996). MRCP 1992; Accredited Clin. Rheumatol., 1999; FRCPGlas 2003; FRCPE 2010. Residencies in Medicine/Surgery, Glasgow Royal Inf. and Western Inf., Glasgow, 1989–90; SHO Med. Rotation, Western Inf., Glasgow, 1990–92; SHO III Rheumatol. and Gen. Medicine, Centre for Rheumatic Diseases, Univ. Dept of Medicine, Glasgow, 1992–93; Wellcome Clin. Fellow, Univ. of Glasgow, 1993–96; Arthritis Res. Campaign Travelling Fellow to Arthritis and Rheumatism Br., NIH, Bethesda, Md, 1996–98; University of Glasgow: Lectr in Rheumatol., 1998–99; Sen. Lectr in Rheumatol. and Hon. Consultant Rheumatologist, Centre for Rheumatic Diseases, 1999–2002; Hd, Div. of Immunol., Infection and Inflammation, 2008–10. FRSE 2008; FMedSci 2012. *Publications:* (ed) Kelley's Textbook of Rheumatology, 8th edn 2007 to 10th edn; over 200 scientific articles in learned jls. *Recreations:* golf, music. *Address:* Institute of Infection, Immunity and Inflammation, College of Medical, Veterinary and Life Sciences, University of Glasgow, 120 University Place, Glasgow G12 8TA. *T:* (0141) 330 8412, *Fax:* (0141) 330 4297. *E:* iain.mcinnes@glasgow.ac.uk.

MacINNES, Keith Gordon, CMG 1984; HM Diplomatic Service, retired; Ambassador and UK Permanent Representative to OECD, Paris, 1992–95; *b* 17 July 1935; *s* of late Kenneth MacInnes and Helen MacInnes (*née* Gordon); *m* 1st, 1966, Jennifer Anne Fennell (marr. diss. 1980); one *s* one *d*; 2nd, 1985, Hermione Pattinson. *Educ:* Rugby; Trinity Coll., Cambridge (MA); Pres., Cambridge Union Soc., 1957. HM Forces, 1953–55. FO, 1960; Third, later Second Secretary, Buenos Aires, 1961–64; FO, 1964 (First Sec., 1965); Private Sec. to Permanent Under-Sec., Commonwealth Office, 1965–68; First Sec. (Information), Madrid, 1968–70; FCO, 1970–74; Counsellor and Head of Chancery: Prague, 1974–77; Dep. Perm. Rep., UK Mission, Geneva, 1977–80; Head of Information Dept, FCO, 1980–83; Asst Under-Sec. of State and Principal Finance Officer, FCO, 1983–87; Ambassador to the Philippines, 1987–92. *Recreations:* golf, bridge.

McINTOSH, family name of **Baroness McIntosh of Hudnall**.

McINTOSH OF HUDNALL, Baroness *cr* 1999 (Life Peer), of Hampstead in the London Borough of Camden; **Genista Mary McIntosh;** arts consultant; *b* 23 Sept. 1946; *d* of late Geoffrey Tandy and Maire Tandy; *m* 1971, Neil Scott Wishart McIntosh, *qv* (marr. diss.); one *s* one *d*. *Educ:* Univ. of York (BA Philosophy and Sociology). Press Sec., York Festival of Arts, 1968–69; Royal Shakespeare Co.: Casting Dir, 1972–77; Planning Controller, 1977–84; Sen. Administrator, 1986–90; Associate Producer, 1990; Exec. Dir, RNT, 1990–96 and 1997–2002; Chief Exec., Royal Opera House, Covent Gdn, 1997; Principal, Guildhall Sch. of Music and Drama, 2002–03. Dir, Marmont Management Ltd, 1984–86. Board Member: Roundhouse Trust, 1999–; Nat. Opera Studio, 2005–; RSC, 2010–. Trustee, Southbank Sinfonia, 2003–. Hon. Fellow, Goldsmiths Coll., Univ. of London, 2003. DUniv: York, 1998; Middlesex, 2002; City, 2002. *Address:* House of Lords, SW1A 0PW.

McINTOSH OF PICKERING, Baroness *cr* 2015 (Life Peer), of the Vale of York in the County of North Yorkshire; **Anne Caroline Ballingall McIntosh;** *b* 20 Sept. 1954; *d* of late Dr Alastair Ballingall McIntosh and Grete-Lise McIntosh; *m* 1992, John Harvey. *Educ:* Harrogate Coll., Harrogate, Yorks; Univ. of Edinburgh (LLB Hons); Univ. of Aarhus, Denmark. Admitted to Faculty of Advocates, 1982. Stagiaire, EEC, Brussels, 1978; legal advr in private EEC practice, Brussels, 1979–80; Bar apprentice with Simpson and Marwick, WS, and devilling at Scottish Bar, 1980–82; private legal practice, Brussels, specialising in EEC law, 1982–83; Secretariat Mem., responsible for transport, youth, culture, educn and tourism, and relations with Scandinavia, Austria, Switzerland and Yugoslavia, EDG, Eur. Parlt, 1983–89. European Parliament: Mem. (C), NE Essex, 1989–94, Essex N and Suffolk S, 1994–99; a Jun. Whip, EDG, 1989–92; Mem., Transport and Legal Affairs Cttees; EDG Spokesman on Rules Cttee, 1989–95, Transport and Tourism Cttee, 1992–99; Mem., Norway Parly Delegn, 1989–95, Polish Parly Delegn, 1995–97, Czech Parly Delegn, 1997–99. MP (C) Vale of York, 1997–2010, Thirsk and Malton, 2010–15. Shadow Minister: for Culture, Media and Sport, 2001–02; for Transport, 2002–03; for Envmt and Transport, 2003–05; for Foreign Affairs, 2005; for Work and Pensions, 2005–06; for Educn, 2006–07; for Envmt, 2007–10; Opposition frontbench spokesman on envmt, food and rural affairs, 2007–10. Chm., Select Cttee on Envmt, Food and Rural Affairs, 2010–15 (Mem., 2007–10); Member: Select Cttee on Envmt, Transport and the Regions, 1999–2001, on Transport, Local Govt and the Regions, 2001–02, on Transport, 2003–05; Exec., 1922 Cttee, 2000–01; European Scrutiny Cttee, 1999–2003; European Standing Cttee. President: Anglia Enterprise in Europe,

1989–99; Yorkshire First, Enterprise in Yorks, 1995–99. Mem., Governing Council, Anglia Poly. Univ.; former Mem., Senate, Univ. of Essex; Gov., Writtle Coll. Hon. LLD Anglia Poly. Univ., 1997. *Recreations:* swimming, cinema, walking.

McINTOSH, Alisdair Douglas; Policy and External Relations Director, Chartered Institute of Internal Audit, since 2015; *b* Addlestone, 19 July 1963; *s* of Alexander and Doreen McIntosh; *m* 1998, Sarah Mary Burnett; one *s* one *d. Educ:* Strode's Sch., Egham; Durham and Paris Univs (BA Hons French 1986); Birkbeck Coll., Univ. of London (MA Romance Langs and Lits 1991); INSEAD, Fontainebleau (AMP 2007). Policy official, HM Treasury, 1987–91; Econ. and Financial Attaché, UK Perm. Repn to EU, Brussels, 1991–96; Sen. Policy Advr, Cabinet of Vice-Pres., Eur. Commn, 1997–99; Hd of Secretariat, Cttee of Enquiry into Teachers' Pay and Conditions, Edinburgh, 1999–2000; Scottish Government: Hd of Access to Justice, 2000–03; Hd of Antisocial Behaviour Unit, 2003–05; Hd of Regeneration, 2005–09; Director: Scotland Office, 2009–12; Public Bodies and Public Service Reform, 2012–13; Housing, Regeneration and Welfare, 2013; Dir, Business for New Europe, 2014–15. Non-executive Director: Scottish Urban Regeneration Forum, 2005–09; Real Life Options, 2008–13. *Recreations:* hills, books, visual arts, my children, walking the dog. *Address:* 81 St John's Road, Edinburgh EH12 6NN.

McINTOSH, David Angus; Senior Partner, Davies Arnold Cooper, Solicitors, 1978–2007; Consultant, Rodney Warren & Co., since 2009; President, Law Society, 2001–02; *b* 10 March 1944; *s* of late Robert Angus McIntosh and of Monica Joan (*née* Hillier, now Sherring); *m* 1968, Jennifer Mary Dixon; two *d. Educ:* Selwood Co. Sch., Frome; Coll. of Law, London. Admitted solicitor, 1969. Joined Davies Arnold Cooper, 1963. Consultant, Fox Solicitors, 2007–09. Mem., Legal Consultative Panel, Dept of Constitutional Affairs, 2003–04. Law Society of England and Wales: Mem. Council, 1996–; Chm., Exec. Cttee, 2000–; Member: Court of Appeal Users' Cttee, 1998–2000; Interim Exec. Cttee, 1999; Vice-Chm., 1997–98, Chm., 1999–2000, Civil Litigation Cttee. Chm., Cttee on Consumer Affairs, Advertising, Unfair Competition and Product Liability, Internat. Bar Assoc., 1995–99; Mem., Exec. Cttee (US), Internat. Assoc. Defense Counsel, 1995–98. Chair, City of London Law Society, 2004–10. Chm., Solicitors Indemnity Fund Ltd, 2006–; Chair, Legal and Professional Claims Ltd, 2008–. Chm., Professional Standards Bd, Chartered Insurance Inst., 2006–. Mem. Council, Sch. of Pharmacy, Univ. of London, 2003–04. Hon. QC 2009; Hon. FCII 2014. *Publications:* Personal Injury Awards in EC Countries, 1990; Civil Procedures in EC Countries, 1993; Personal Injury Awards in EU and EFTA Countries, 1994, 2003; numerous contribs on compensation, insurance and products liability to learned jls. *Recreations:* golf, trying to keep fit, choosing ties! *Address:* c/o Rodney Warren & Co., Berkeley House, 26/28 Gildredge Road, Eastbourne, E Sussex BN21 4RW. *T:* (01323) 430430. *Clubs:* Chigwell Golf; Real Sotogrande Golf (Spain).

McINTOSH, John Charles, CBE 2013 (OBE 1996); Headmaster, The London Oratory School, 1977–2007; *b* 6 Feb. 1946; *s* of Arthur and Betty McIntosh. *Educ:* Ebury Sch.; Shoreditch Coll.; Sussex Univ. (MA). The London Oratory School: Asst Master, 1967–71; Dep. Headmaster, 1971–77. Additional Mem., HMC, 1986–2007; Member: Centre for Policy Studies Educn Gp, 1982–99; Inst. of Econ. Affairs Educn Adv. Council, 1988–91; Health Educn Council, 1985–88; Nat. Curriculum Council, 1990–93; Adv. Cttee, Nat. Curriculum Rev., 2010–13; Teachers' Standards Rev. Cttee, 2010–11; Skills Tests Rev. Panel, 2012–13; Bd, Nat. Coll. for Sch. Leadership, 2012–13; Adv. Cttee, Nat. Coll. for Teaching and Leadership (formerly Teaching Agency), 2012–14; Chm., Commn on Assessment Without Levels, 2015–. Mem. (formerly Consultant Dir), Reform, 2007–. Advr to Leader, Hammersmith and Fulham LBC, 2007–12 (Chm., Bilingual Mgt Cttee, 2009–12); Advr on Free Sch. Applications, DfE, 2011–. Member: Abbot's Adv. Council, Ampleforth Coll., 1997–2010 (Chm., Educn Cttee, 2007–10); Council, Buckingham Univ., 2014– (Vis. Tutor, 2004–10); Educn Cttee, David Ross Educn Trust, 2013–15; Interim Exec. Bd, Hurlingham and Chelsea Sch., 2014–15; Interim Exec. Bd, Langford Sch., 2014–; Chm., Mgt Intervention Bd, St Francis of Assisi Sch., Kensington, 2013–15. Dean, Acad. of St Cecilia, 2005– (Hon. Fellow, 2000); Trustee: The Oratory, Oxford, 2003–; English Schs Orch. and Choir, 2007–; London Oratory Schola Foundn, 2007–13; Trustee/Dir, WLFS Multi Academy Trust, 2013–. Governor and Trustee: St Philip's Prep. Sch., 1985– (Chm., 2007–); More House Sch., 2008–11; Governor: W London Free Sch., 2011–13 (Advr, Steering Cttee, 2010–11); Holy Cross Primary Sch., 2011–13. Hon. Patron, W London Free Sch. Trust, 2014–. Mem., Catholic Union of GB, 1978–. FRSA 1981. Hon. FCP 1998. Knight of Merit, Sacred Military Constantinian Order of St George, 2011. *Recreations:* music, opera, ballet, theatre, playing the organ, architecture and design, photography. *Address:* 75 Alder Lodge, River Gardens, Stevenage Road, SW6 6NR. *E:* cantemus@mac.com. *Clubs:* Athenæum, House of St Barnabus.

MACINTOSH, Kenneth; Member (Lab) Eastwood, Scottish Parliament, since 1999; *b* 15 Jan. 1962; *s* of Dr Farquhar Macintosh, CBE; *m* 1998, Claire, *d* of Douglas and Deirdre Kinloch Anderson; two *s* four *d. Educ:* Royal High Sch., Edinburgh; Edinburgh Univ. (MA Hons History). Sen. Broadcast Journalist in News and Current Affairs, BBC, 1987–99. *Recreations:* sport (including football, tennis and golf), music, reading. *Address:* Suite 415, 1 Spiersbridge Way, Thornliebank, Glasgow G46 8NG. *T:* (0141) 620 6310.

McINTOSH, Lyndsay June; JP; Chairman, Central Scotland Rape Crisis and Sexual Abuse Centre, 2003–08; *b* 12 June 1955; *d* of Lawrence S. and Mary Clark (*née* Calderwood); *m* 1981, Gordon McIntosh; one *s* one *d. Educ:* Duncanrig Sen. Secondary Sch.; Dundee Coll. of Technology (Dip. Mgt Studies). Legal Secretary, 1973–75; Civil Servant, Inland Revenue, 1975–84; business consultant, 1996–99. Lay Inspector of Schools, 1994–99. Mem. (C) Central Scotland, Scottish Parlt, 1999–2003; Cons. spokesman on justice, 1999–2001, on social justice, equal opportunities and women's issues, 2001–03; Dep. Convenor, Justice 2 Cttee, 2001. Sec., Assoc. of former Mems of Scottish Parlt, 2003–. Mem., N Lanarks Justices Cttee, 2004–08. JP: N Lanarks, 1993–2008; S Strathclyde, Dumfries and Galloway, 2008. Sec., Tannochside Action Gp. *Publications:* articles on social affairs in newspapers and magazines. *Recreations:* reading, weeding, feeding, travel, stadium concerts, karaoke, Rock Choir. *Address:* 35 Lynnhurst, Uddingston, Glasgow G71 6SA.

McINTOSH, Melinda Jane Frances; *see* Letts, M. J. F.

McINTOSH, Dr Neil; Edward Clarke Professor of Child Life and Health, University of Edinburgh, 1987–2007, now Emeritus; *b* 21 May 1942; *s* of William and Dorothy McIntosh; *m* 1967, Sheila Ann Clarke; two *s* one *d. Educ:* University College Hosp., London (MB BS; DSc Med 1995); Univ. of Southampton (BSc). Sen. Registrar in Paediatrics, UCH, 1973–78; Res. Fellow in Paediatric Endocrinology, Univ. of Calif, San Francisco, 1975–76; Sen. Lectr and Consultant Paediatrician, St George's Hosp. and Med. Sch., 1978–87; Hon. Consultant Paediatrician, Royal Hosp. for Sick Children, Edinburgh, 1987–2007; Hon. Neonatologist, Royal Infirmary, Edinburgh, 1987–2007. Consultant Advr in Neonatology to British Army, 1984–2007. Pres., European Soc. for Pediatric Res., 1993–94; Trustee, Internat. Pediatric Res. Foundn, 1993–97 (Chm., 1995–96); Scientific Vice-Pres., RCPCH, 2002–07. Editor, Current Topics in Neonatology, 1996–2000. *Publications:* (ed with A. G. M. Campbell) Forfar and Arneil's Textbook of Paediatrics, 4th edn 1993, 7th edn (ed with P. Helms and R. Smyth) 2008. *Recreations:* music, family. *Address:* 33 Thomas More House, Barbican, EC2Y 8BT. *T:* (020) 7374 2771.

McINTOSH, Neil Scott Wishart, CBE 2013; Chief Executive, CfBT Education Trust (formerly Centre for British Teachers), 1990–2012; *b* 24 July 1947; *s* of William Henderson McIntosh and Mary Catherine McIntosh; *m* 1st, 1971, Genista Mary Tandy (*see* Baroness McIntosh of Hudnall) (marr. diss. 1990); one *s* one *d*; 2nd, 1991, Melinda Jane Frances Letts, *qv*; one *s* one *d. Educ:* Merchiston Castle Sch., Edinburgh; Univ. of York (BA Politics); London Sch. of Econs (MSc Industrial Relations). Res. Associate, PEP, 1969–73; Res. Dir, Southwark Community Develt Proj., 1973–76; Dir, Shelter, 1976–84; Dir, VSO, 1985–90. Councillor, London Bor. of Camden, 1971–77; Chm., Housing Cttee, 1974–76. Dir, Stonham Housing Assoc., 1982–98. Vice Pres., BSA, 1985–91. Founder and Chm., Homeless Internat., 1988–91; Chm., Campaign for Freedom of Information, 2008– (Treas., 1984–2008; Co-Chm., 1997–2008); Mem., Independent Broadcasting Telethon Trust, 1987–94. Trustee: HOST, 2004–10; CfBT Advice and Guidance, 2012–; Chair, Trustees, Access Project, 2013–; Pres., CfBT Schs Trust, 2013–. Governor: Langtree Sch., Oxon, 2006–; St Andrews Sch., Pangbourne, 2010–; All Saints Free Sch., Reading, 2013–15; Chair of Govs, Oakfield Sch., Dulwich, 2012. Hon. Fellow, Dept of Educn, Univ. of Oxford, 2010–. *Publications:* The Right to Manage?, 1971, 2nd edn 1976. *Recreations:* golf, sailing, theatre. *E:* nswmcintosh@gmail.com. *Clubs:* Goring and Streatley Golf; Plockton Sailing.

McINTOSH, Sir Neil (William David), Kt 2000; CBE 1990; Civil Service Commissioner, 2009–13; New Zealand Honorary Consul for Scotland, since 2014; *b* 30 Jan. 1940; *s* of Neil and Beatrice McIntosh; *m* 1965, Marie Elizabeth Lindsay; one *s* two *d. Educ:* King's Park Sen. Secondary Sch., Glasgow. ACIS 1967; FCIPD (FIPM 1987). J. & P. Coats, 1957–59; Outward Bound, Moray Sea Sch., 1958 (Gold Award); Honeywell Controls, 1959–62; Berks, Oxford and Reading Jt O&M Unit, 1962–64; Stewarts & Lloyds, 1964–66; Sen. O&M Officer, Lanark CC, 1966–69; Estabt/O&M Officer, Inverness CC, 1969–75; Personnel Officer, 1975–81, Dir of Manpower Services, 1981–85, Highland Regl Council; Chief Executive: Dumfries and Galloway Regl Council, 1985–92; Strathclyde Regl Council, 1992–96; Convener, Scottish Council for Voluntary Orgns, 1996–2001. Chairman: Commn on Local Govt and Scottish Parlt, 1998–99; Judicial Appts Bd for Scotland, 2002–08. Mem. Bd, British Telecom, Scotland, 1998–2003. Chm., Nat. Cos Contact Gp, 1996–98; Hd, COSLA Consultancy, 1996–99. Director: Training 2000 (Scotland) Ltd, 1993; Quality Scotland Foundn, 1993; Sportability Strathclyde, 1994. Scottish Advr, 2000–05, Chm., Governance Cttee, 2005–, Joseph Rowntree Foundn; Expert Advr, NI Review of Public Admin, 2002–05; Ind. Reviewer, Scottish Parlt MSP Expenses Scheme, 2009; Mem., Scottish Parlt Ind. Budget Review Panel, 2010. Chief Counting Officer, Scottish Parlt Referendum, 1997; Mem., UK Electoral Commn, 2001–08. Trustee: Nat. Museums Scotland (formerly Nat. Museums of Scotland), 1999–2008; Dumfries Theatre Royal Trust, 2003–06. Member: Comunn na Gàidhlig Wkg Gp on Status of Gaelic Lang., 2000–03; BBC Audience Council for Scotland, 2008–11; Bd, Nat. Library of Scotland, 2014–; Ind. Mem., Crichton Campus Liaison Gp, 2011–. DL Dumfries, 1998; JP 1999. FRSA 1989. Hon. DHL Syracuse Univ., USA, 1993; Hon. LLD Glasgow Caledonian, 1999. *Recreations:* antique bottle collecting, bowling, local history, hill walking, dry stane dyking, curling.

McINTOSH, Dr Robert, CBE 2013; Director, Forestry Commission Scotland (formerly Director, Scotland, Forestry Commission), 2003–15, and Director, Environment and Forestry, Scottish Government, 2012–15; *b* 6 Oct. 1951; *s* of Robert Hamilton McIntosh and Kathleen McIntosh. *Educ:* Linlithgow Acad.; Edinburgh Univ. (BSc Hons 1973; PhD 1985); MICFor 1974. Dist Officer, 1973–78, Res. Project Leader, 1979–84, Forestry Commn; Forest Dist Manager, Kielder Forest, 1984–94; Forest Enterprise: Dir, Ops, 1994–97; Chief Exec., 1997–2003. *Publications:* papers and articles in forestry jls. *Recreations:* shooting, stalking, farming. *Club:* Farmers.

McINTOSH, Sir Ronald (Robert Duncan), KCB 1975 (CB 1968); Chairman, APV plc, 1982–89; *b* 26 Sept. 1919; *s* of Thomas Steven McIntosh, MD, FRCPE and Christina Jane McIntosh; *m* 1951, Doreen Frances (*d* 2009), *o d* of Commander Andrew MacGinnity, RNR and Margaret MacGinnity, Frinton-on-Sea. *Educ:* Charterhouse (Scholar); Balliol Coll., Oxford. Served in Merchant Navy, 1939–45; Second Mate, 1943–45. Assistant Principal, Board of Trade, 1947; General Manager, Dollar Exports Board, 1949–51; Commercial Counsellor, UK High Commn, New Delhi, 1957–61; Under-Secretary: BoT, 1961–64; DEA, 1964–66; Dep. Under-Sec. of State, Dept of Economic Affairs, 1966–68; Dep. Secretary, Cabinet Office, 1968–70; Dep. Under-Sec. of State, Dept of Employment, 1970–72; Dep. Sec., HM Treasury, 1972–73; Dir-Gen. Nat. Economic Development Office, and Mem. NEDC, 1973–77. Director: S. G. Warburg & Co. Ltd, 1978–90; Foseco plc, 1978–90; London & Manchester Gp plc, 1978–90. Chairman: Danish-UK Chamber of Commerce, 1990–92; British Health Care Consortium (for the former Soviet Union), 1992–97. Mem., Council, CBI, 1980–90; Co-Chm., British-Hungarian Round Table, 1980–84. Chm., Centre for Eur. Agricl Studies, Wye Coll., 1979–83. Trustee, The Tablet, 1997–2006. Mem., Master Mariners' Co., 2013–. Companion, NEAC, 2002–. CCMI. Hon. DSc Aston, 1977. *Publications:* (contrib.) Roy Jenkins, a Retrospective, 2004; Challenge to Democracy, 2006; Turbulent Times (memoir), 2014. *Address:* The Thatched Cottage, Parsonage Farm, Throwley, Faversham, Kent ME13 0PN. *Clubs:* Royal Thames Yacht; Band of Brothers (Kent).

MacINTOSH, Sarah, CMG 2009; HM Diplomatic Service; Director General, Defence and Intelligence, Foreign and Commonwealth Office, since 2014; *b* 7 Aug. 1969. Entered FCO, 1991; Third Sec., UK Mission to UN, Vienna, 1994–95; Second Sec. (Econ./EU), Madrid, 1996–97; First Sec., FCO, 1997–2000, UK Mission to UN, NY, 2000–02; FCO, 2002–04; UN Interim Admin Mission, Kosovo, 2004–05; High Comr in Sierra Leone, 2006–08; Fellow, Weatherhead Center for Internat. Affairs, Harvard Univ., 2008–09; Dir, Defence and Internat. Security, FCO, 2011–14. *Address:* c/o Foreign and Commonwealth Office, King Charles Street, SW1A 2AH.

McINTOSH, Stuart; Senior Telecoms Advisor, KPMG, since 2015; *b* Bellshill, Scotland, 28 Oct. 1951; *s* of Peter and Mary McIntosh; *m* 1996, Helen Jean Brass; one *d. Educ:* London Sch. of Econs (BSc Econs, MSc Econs). Partner, Coopers & Lybrand, then PricewaterhouseCoopers, 1990–2000; Sen. Vice Pres., Adventis, 2000–04; Partner, IBM Global Consulting Services, 2004–08; Partner, Competition, and Bd Mem., Ofcom, 2008–14. *Recreations:* guitar, theatre, reading, running. *T:* 07834 432065.

MacINTYRE, Prof. Alasdair Chalmers; Research Professor of Philosophy, University of Notre Dame, 2000–10, now Emeritus; Senior Fellow, Centre for Contemporary Aristotelian Studies in Ethics and Politics, London Metropolitan University, since 2010; *b* 12 Jan. 1929; *o s* of Eneas John MacIntyre, MD (Glasgow), and Margaret Emily Chalmers, MB, ChB (Glasgow); *m* 1977, Lynn Sumida Joy; one *s* three *d* by previous marriages. *Educ:* Epsom Coll. and privately; Queen Mary Coll., Univ. of London (Fellow, 1984); Manchester Univ. BA (London); MA (Manchester); MA (Oxon). Lectr in Philosophy of Religion, Manchester Univ., 1951–57; Lectr in Philosophy, Leeds Univ., 1957–61; Research Fellow, Nuffield Coll., Oxford, 1961–62; Sen. Fellow, Council of Humanities, Princeton Univ., 1962–63; Fellow and Preceptor in Philosophy, University Coll., Oxford, 1963–66; Prof. of Sociology, Univ. of Essex, 1966–70; Prof. of History of Ideas, Brandeis Univ., 1970–72; Univ. Prof. in Philos. and Political Sci., Boston Univ., 1972–80; Luce Prof., Wellesley Coll., 1980–82; W. Alton Jones Prof. of Philosophy, Vanderbilt Univ., 1982–88; McMahon/Hank Prof. of Philosophy, Univ. of Notre Dame, Indiana, 1988–94; Arts and Scis Prof. of Phil., Duke Univ., 1995–2000. Mem., Amer. Philosophical Soc., 2006; Pres., Eastern Div., Amer. Phil Assoc., 1984. Fellow, Amer. Acad. of Arts and Scis, 1985; Corresp. FBA, 1994. Hon. Mem., Phi Beta Kappa, 1973. Hon. MRIA 2000. Hon. DHL: Swarthmore, 1983; New School, 1996; Duke, 2010; Hon. DLit: QUB, 1988; Williams Coll., Mass, 1993; Marquette, 2000; Aberdeen, 2001; UCD, 2009; DU Essex, 1990; Hon. DPhil Maynooth, 2002. *Publications:* Marxism and Christianity, 1954 (revised, 1968); New Essays in Philosophical Theology (ed, with A. G. N. Flew), 1955; Metaphysical Beliefs (ed), 1956; The Unconscious: a conceptual analysis, 1958; A Short History of Ethics, 1965; Secularisation and Moral Change, 1967; Marcuse: an exposition and a polemic, 1970; Sociological Theory and Philosophical Analysis (ed with D. M. Emmet), 1971; Against the Self-Images of the Age, 1971; After Virtue, 1981; Whose Justice? Which Rationality?, 1988; Three Rival Versions of Moral Enquiry, 1990; Dependent Rational Animals, 1999; Edith Stein: a philosophical prologue, 2005; The Tasks of Philosophy: selected essays vol. 1, 2006; Ethics and Politics: selected essays vol. 2, 2006; God, Philosophy, Universities, 2009. *Address:* Philosophy Department, University of Notre Dame, 100 Malloy Hall, Notre Dame, IN 46556, USA.

McINTYRE, Sir Alister; *see* McIntyre, Sir M. A.

McINTYRE, Anthea Elizabeth Joy, (Mrs Frank Myers); Member (C) West Midlands, European Parliament, since Dec. 2011; *b* London, 29 June 1954; *d* of David Scott McIntyre and Joy Irma Stratford McIntyre; *m* 1999, Frank Myers, MBE. *Educ:* Claremont Sch., Esher; Queens Coll., Harley St, London. Partner, Wythall Estate, 1976–; MCP Systems Consultants (formerly MCP Management Consultants): consultant, 1985–91; Partner, 1991–2011; Dir, 2011–. *Recreations:* gardening, wildlife photography, family, Scottish country dancing, cooking. *Address:* Wythall, Walford, Ross-on-Wye HR9 5SD. *T:* (01989) 769544. *E:* anthea@antheamcintyre.com.

MACINTYRE, Benedict Richard Pierce; writer; Associate Editor, since 1995 and Writer at Large, since 2001, The Times; *b* Oxford, 25 Dec. 1963; *s* of Angus Macintyre and Joanna Macintyre; *m* 1993, Kate Muir; two *s* one *d*. *Educ:* Abingdon Sch.; St John's Coll., Cambridge (BA Hist. 1985); Columbia Univ., NY (MA Internat. Affairs 1990). The Times: New York Corresp., 1991–95; Paris Corresp., 1995–98; Chief, Washington Bureau, 1998–2001. Pres., Johnian Soc., 2011–13. *Publications:* Forgotten Fatherland, 1992; Napoleon of Crime, 1997; A Foreign Field, 2001; Josiah the Great, 2004; Agent Zigzag, 2007; For Your Eyes Only, 2008; The Last Word, 2009; Operation Mincemeat, 2010; Double Cross, 2012; A Spy Among Friends: Kim Philby and the great betrayal, 2014. *Recreations:* cricket, sheep farming. *Address:* The Times, 1 London Bridge Street, SE1 9GF. *T:* (020) 7782 5000. *Club:* MCC.

McINTYRE, Blanche Phoebe Katharine; theatre director; Associate Director, Nuffield Theatre, since 2013; *b* London, 5 Sept. 1980; *d* of Grant James McIntyre and Helen Jean Sutherland Fraser, *qv*. *Educ:* St Paul's Girls' Sch., London; Corpus Christi Coll., Oxford (BA Hons 1st cl. Lit.Hum. 2003). *Productions* include: Accolade, Foxfinder, Finborough, 2011 (Most Promising Newcomer, Critics' Circle Awards, 2011); The Birthday Party, Royal Exchange, Manchester, 2013; Ciphers, Out of Joint, 2013; The Seagull, Headlong, Nuffield, 2013 (Best Dir, UK Theatre Awards, 2013); The Comedy of Errors, Shakespeare's Globe, 2014; Tonight at 8:30, Nuffield, 2014; Accolade, St James, 2014; Arcadia, Theatre Royal, Brighton, 2015; As You Like It, Shakespeare's Globe, 2015; Brave New World, Royal, Northampton, 2015; The Oresteia, Home, Manchester, 2015. Winner, Leverhulme Bursary for Emerging Th. Dirs (inaugural), 2009. *Address:* c/o United Agents, 12–26 Lexington Street, W1F 0LE.

McINTYRE, Derrick William McEwen, TD 1980; Sheriff of Lothian and Borders at Jedburgh and Duns, 2013–14 (at Edinburgh, 2000–13); *b* 16 June 1944; *s* of Lt Col Donald and Rosemary McIntyre; *m* 1973, Janet Anna Fraser; one *d* (and one *s* one *d* decd). *Educ:* Wellington Coll.; St Andrews Univ. (LLB). Lieut, 6th Gurkha Rifles, 1966–68; Major, Black Watch (RHR), 1969–85. Solicitor in private practice, 1973–2000; Temp. Sheriff, 1982–2000. Mem., Queen's Body Guard for Scotland (Royal Co. of Archers), 1994–. *Recreations:* riding, shooting, fishing, golf. *Address:* Mainsfield, Mainsfield Avenue, Morebattle, Kelso, Roxburghshire TD5 8QW. *T:* (01573) 440254.

McINTYRE, Sir Donald (Conroy), Kt 1992; CBE 1985 (OBE 1977); opera singer, freelance; *b* 22 Oct. 1934; *s* of George Douglas McIntyre and Mrs Hermyn McIntyre; *m*; three *d*. *Educ:* Mount Albert Grammar Sch.; Auckland Teachers' Trng Coll.; Guildhall Sch. of Music. Debut in Britain, Welsh National Opera, 1959; Sadler's Wells Opera, many roles, 1960–67; Royal Opera, Covent Garden, from 1967; also Vienna, Bayreuth, La Scala, Milan and Metropolitan, NY. *Principal roles:* Barak, in Die Frau Ohne Schatten, Strauss; Wotan and Wanderer, in The Ring, Wagner; Hollander, Wagner; Hans Sachs, in Die Meistersinger von Nürnberg, Wagner; Heyst, in Victory, Richard Rodney Bennett; Macbeth, Verdi; Scarpia, in Tosca, Puccini; Count, in Figaro, Mozart; Doctor, in Wozzeck, Berg; title role in Cardillac, Hindemith; Rocco, in Fidelio; Prospero, in Un Re in Ascolto, Berio; Balstrode, in Peter Grimes, Britten; Bayreuth: Wotan, Wanderer, Hollander; Telramund, in Lohengrin; Klingsor, Amfortas and Gurnemanz in Parsifal; Bayreuth Centenary Ring, 1976–81. *Video and films include:* Der Fliegende Holländer, 1975; Electra, 1976; Die Meistersinger, 1984; Bayreuth Centenary Ring, 1976–81; recordings include Pelléas et Mélisande, Il Trovatore, The Messiah, Oedipus Rex, The Ring, Beethoven's 9th Symphony, Damnation of Faust, Bayreuth Centenary Ring. Fidelio Award, 1989. *Recreations:* gardening, swimming, tennis, farming.

MACINTYRE, Donald John; Parliamentary Sketchwriter, Independent, since 2012; *b* 27 Jan. 1947; *s* of Kenneth Mackenzie Campbell Macintyre and Margaret Macintyre (*née* Freeman); one *s*. *Educ:* Bradfield Coll.; Christ Church, Oxford (BA Lit.Hum.); UC, Cardiff (Dip. Journalism Studies). Reporter, Sunday Mercury, 1971–75; Industrial Reporter, Daily Express, 1975–77; Labour Corresp., The Times, 1977–83; Labour Editor: Sunday Times, 1983–85; The Times, 1985–86; Independent, 1986–87; Political Editor: Sunday Telegraph, 1987–89; Sunday Correspondent, 1989–90; Independent on Sunday, 1990–93; Pol Ed., 1993–96, Chief Pol Commentator, 1996–2004, Asst Ed., 2003–04, Jerusalem Correspondent, 2004–12, Independent. New Century Foundn Peace Through Media Award, 2011. *Publications:* Talking about Trade Unions, 1979; (jtly) Strike!, 1985; Mandelson and the Making of New Labour, 1999. *Recreations:* cinema, walking, bad chess. *Address:* c/o Independent, Northcliffe House, 2 Derry Street, W8 5HF. *Clubs:* Garrick, Soho House.

McINTYRE, Helen Jean Sutherland; *see* Fraser, H. J. S.

MACINTYRE, Iain Melfort Campbell, MD; FRCSE, FRCPE; FSAScot; Consultant Surgeon, Edinburgh, 1979–2004; Surgeon to the Queen in Scotland, 1997–2004; *b* 23 June 1944; *s* of John Macintyre, MA, BD, FSAScot and Mary (*née* Campbell); *m* 1969, Tessa Lorna Mary Millar; three *d*. *Educ:* Daniel Stewart's Coll., Edinburgh; Edinburgh Univ. (MB ChB 1968; MD 1992). FRCSE 1974; FRCPE 1997. FSAScot 1997. Lectr in Surgery, Edinburgh Univ., 1974–78; Vis. Prof., Univ. of Natal, 1978–79; Consultant Surgeon: Leith Hosp., 1979–85; Western Gen. Hosp., 1985–2002; Royal Infirmary, Edinburgh, 2002–04. Royal College of Surgeons of Edinburgh: Mem. Council, 1991–2000; Dir of Educn and Wade Prof., 1997–2000; Hon. Sec., 2001–04; Vice Pres., 2003–06. Mem., Nat. Med. Adv. Cttee, 1992–95. Treas., Scottish Soc. of the Hist. of Medicine, 2010–15; Pres., British Soc. for the Hist. of Medicine, 2015–.

McINTYRE, Jennifer Louise; *see* Armstrong, J. L.

McINTYRE, (John) Paul; Managing Director, E-Serve, Office of Gas and Electricity Markets, 2010–11; *b* 4 Dec. 1951; *s* of John McIntyre and Julia McIntyre; *m* 1984, Jennifer Eastabrook; two *d*. *Educ:* Austin Friars, Carlisle; Churchill Coll., Cambridge (BA Econs); King's Coll. London (MA Mod. Hist. 2013). Joined HM Treasury, 1974: on secondment to: UK Delegn to IMF/IBRD, Washington, 1977–78; Hambros Bank, City of London, 1983–85; Assistant Secretary: Social Security Policy, 1987–90; Monetary and Debt Mgt Policy, 1990–94; Dir, European Policy, 1995–99; Department of Trade and Industry: Dep. Dir Gen., Enterprise and Innovation, Regions (Business Gp), 2000–03; Hd, British Energy Team, 2003–04; Dir, Energy Strategy Unit (Energy Gp), 2004–05; Hd, Energy Policy Rev. Team, 2005–07; Hd, Energy Strategy and Internat. Unit, then Dir, Energy Security and Mkts, DTI, later BERR, then DECC, 2007–09; Dir, Resilience and Risk, DECC, 2009–10. *Recreations:* family, cricket, reading, history, music. *Clubs:* MCC; Mandarins Cricket.

McINTYRE, Sir (Meredith) Alister, Kt 1992; Chairman, Agency for Reconstruction and Development, Grenada, 2004–05; Chief Technical Advisor, Caribbean Regional Negotiating Machinery, Kingston, Jamaica, 1998–2001; *b* Grenada, 29 March 1932; *s* of Meredith McIntyre and Cynthia Eileen McIntyre; *m* Marjorie Hope; three *s* one *d*. *Educ:* LSE (BSc (Econ) 1st Cl. Hons 1957); Nuffield Coll., Oxford (BLitt 1963). Fulbright-Hays Fellow, Columbia Univ., 1963–64; Asst Prof., Woodrow Wilson Sch. of Public Affairs, Princeton Univ., 1962; University of the West Indies: Lectr in Economics, 1960–64; Sen. Lectr and Chm. of Social Scis, 1964–67; Dir, Inst. of Social and Econ. Res., 1964–74; Sec.-Gen., Caribbean Community Secretariat, 1974–77; Dir, Commodities Div., UNCTAD, 1977–82; Dep. Sec.-Gen., UNCTAD, 1982–87; Asst Sec.-Gen., UN, 1987–88. Vice-Chancellor, Univ. of West Indies, 1988–98. Hon. LLD: West Indies, 1980; Sheffield, 1995; Toronto, 1996. Comdr, Order of Distinction (Jamaica), 1975; Cacique's Crown of Honour (Guyana), 1978; Order of Merit (Jamaica), 1992; Order of the Caribbean Community, 1994. *Recreations:* swimming, sailing, reading.

McINTYRE, Michael; *see* McIntyre, T. M.

McINTYRE, Prof. Michael Edgeworth, PhD; FRS 1990; Professor of Atmospheric Dynamics, Cambridge University, 1993–2008, now Emeritus; Co-director, Cambridge Centre for Atmospheric Science, 1992–2003; *b* 28 July 1941; *s* of Archibald Keverall McIntyre and Anne Hartwell McIntyre; *m* 1968, Ruth Hecht; one step *d* two step *s*. *Educ:* King's High School, Dunedin, NZ; Univ. of Otago, NZ; Trinity Coll., Cambridge. PhD Cantab 1967 (geophysical fluid dynamics); postdoctoral Fellow, Woods Hole Oceanographic Inst., 1967. Research Associate, Dept of Meteorology, MIT, 1967; Cambridge University: Asst Dir of Research, 1969; Res. Fellow, St John's Coll., 1968–71; Univ. Lectr, 1972; Reader in Atmospheric Dynamics, 1987; SERC, then EPSRC, Sen. Res. Fellow, 1992–97. Member: Atmospheric Sci. Cttee, NERC, 1989–94; Sci. Steering Gp, UK Univs Global Atmos. Modelling Prog., NERC, 1990–2002; Workshop on Tropical Cyclone Disasters, IUTAM/IUGG/ICSU, 1990–91; Scientific Steering Cttee, STRATEOLE experiment, 1992–2002; Scientific Adv. Cttee and Organizing Cttee, Prog. on Maths of Atmosphere and Ocean Dynamics, Isaac Newton Inst., 1995–96. Member: Academia Europaea, 1989; Eur. Geophys. Soc., later Eur. Geoscis Union (Julius Bartels Medal, 1999); Amer. Geophys. Union (Fellow, 2011); FRMetS; Fellow, Amer. Met. Soc., 1991 (Carl-Gustaf Rossby Res. Medal, 1987; Haurwitz Meml Lect., 2013); FAAAS 1999. *Publications:* numerous papers in professional jls, incl. papers on lucidity principles. *Recreation:* music. *Address:* Centre for Mathematical Sciences, Wilberforce Road, Cambridge CB3 0WA. *W:* www.atm.damtp.cam.ac.uk/people/mem.

McINTYRE, Prof. Neil, FRCP; Professor of Medicine, Royal Free Hospital School of Medicine, 1978–99; Hon. Consultant Physician, Royal Free Hospital, 1968–99; *b* 1 May 1934; *s* of John William McIntyre and Catherine (*née* Watkins); *m* 1966, Wendy Ann Kelsey; one *s* one *d*. *Educ:* Porth County School for Boys; King's Coll. London (BSc 1st Cl. Hons Physiol); King's Coll. Hosp. (MB BS (Hons), MD). House Officer: KCH, 1959; Hammersmith Hosp., 1960; RAF Med. Br. (Flt Lieut), 1960–63; MRC Res. Fellow, Registrar, Lectr in Medicine, Royal Free Hosp., 1963–66; MRC Travelling Fellowship, Harvard Med. Sch., 1966–68; Royal Free Hospital School of Medicine: Sen. Lectr 1968–73, Reader in Medicine 1973–78; Chm., Dept of Medicine, 1983–94; Vice Dean, 1993–96; Dir of Med. Educn, UCL Med. Sch. and Royal Free Hosp. Sch. of Med., 1993–95. Non-exec. Dir, N Middlesex Hosp. NHS Trust, 1991–96. Pres., Hist. of Medicine Soc. of Wales, 2007. FRSocMed 1968. Liveryman, Soc. of Apothecaries, 1971–. Mem., Bd of Govs, Amer. Osler Soc., 2003–06. Sam E. Roberts Medal, Univ. of Kansas Med. Sch., 1980. *Publications:* Therapeutic Agents and the Liver, 1965; The Problem Orientated Medical Record, 1979; Lipids and Lipoproteins, 1990; Clinical Hepatology, 1991; How British Women became Doctors: the story of the Royal Free Hospital and its medical school, 2014; papers on liver disease, lipoprotein metabolism, med. educn, med. history. *Recreations:* reading, medical history, photographing medical statues, golf. *Address:* 7 Butterworth Gardens, Woodford Green, Essex IG8 0BJ. *Clubs:* Athenæum; Highgate Golf.

McINTYRE, Paul; *see* McIntyre, J. P.

MACINTYRE, Dame Sarah Jane, (Dame Sally), DBE 2011 (CBE 2006; OBE 1998); PhD; FRSE; Professor of Social and Public Health Sciences, 2008–14, now Emeritus, Director, Institute of Health and Wellbeing, 2011–14, and Honorary Senior Research Fellow, since 2014, University of Glasgow; *b* 27 Feb. 1949; *d* of late Rev. Angus Macintyre and Evelyn Macintyre; *m* 1980, Dr Guy Paul Muhlemann. *Educ:* Univ. of Durham (BA 1970); Bedford Coll., London (MSc 1971); Univ. of Aberdeen (PhD 1976). FRSE 1998. Res. Fellow, Aberdeen Univ., 1971–75; non-clinical scientist, 1975–84, Dir, 1984–2014, MRC Social and Public Health Sciences (formerly Med. Sociology) Unit, Glasgow. Honorary Professor: Univ. of Glasgow, 1991–2008; Univ. of Strathclyde, 2007–10. Mem., MRC, 2008–. Founder FMedSci 1998. Hon. Fellow, LSHTM, 2003. Hon. MFPHM 1993. Hon. DSc: Aberdeen, 2005; UCL, 2013; Lancaster, 2013. *Publications:* Single and Pregnant, 1977; (jtly) Antenatal Care Assessed, 1985; contrib. jl articles on sociological and public health topics. *Recreations:* mountaineering, rock-climbing, ski-ing, yoga, running. *Address:* c/o Institute of Health and Wellbeing, University of Glasgow, 1 Lilybank Gardens, Glasgow G12 8RZ. *Club:* Pinnacle.

McINTYRE, (Theodore) Michael; Senior Executive, HSBC Private Banking, 1996–2001; *b* 9 Dec. 1941; *s* of James Penton McIntyre and Susan E. M. McIntyre; *m* 1969, Jill Yvonne Mander; one *s* one *d*. *Educ:* Marlborough Coll. Hongkong and Shanghai Banking Corporation Ltd: E Malaysia, Kowloon, Japan, Hong Kong and Brazil, 1959–91; Dep. CEO, 1991–92; CEO, 1992–96, UK. SBStJ 1989. *Recreations:* reading, fishing, gardening. *Address:* The Old School House, Everleigh, Marlborough, Wilts SN8 3EY. *T:* (01264) 850512.

MACINTYRE, William Ian, CB 1992; Chairman, Council, Froebel Trust, since 2012; *b* 20 July 1943; *s* of late Robert Miller Macintyre, CBE and Florence Mary Macintyre; *m* 1967, Jennifer Mary Pitblado; one *s* two *d*. *Educ:* Merchiston Castle School, Edinburgh; St Andrews University. MA. British Petroleum Co. Ltd, 1965–72; ECGD, 1972–73; DTI, later Dept of Energy, 1973–77; seconded to ICFC, 1977–79; Asst Sec., Dept of Energy, Gas Div., 1979–83; Under-Sec. 1983, Dir-Gen., Energy Efficiency Office, 1983–87; Under Sec., Electricity Div., 1987–88, Electricity Div. B, 1988–91, Dept of Energy; Under Sec., Coal Div., Dept of Energy, then DTI, 1991–94; Head, Telecoms Div., 1994–95, Communications and Inf. Industries Directorate, 1996–2002, DTI. Dir, Templeton Estates, 2002–12. Dep. Chm., Froebel Inst., 2001–03 (Mem. Council, 1999–2012); Chm. Council, Incorporated Froebel Educational Inst., 2003–12. Pro-Chancellor, Univ. of Roehampton (formerly Univ. of Surrey Roehampton), 2006–11 (Mem. Council, 2000–06; Hon. Fellow, 2012); Governor: Froebel Coll., 2001–07; Ibstock Sch., 2001–12 (Chm. of Govs, 2002–03).

McISAAC, Ian, FCA; Finance Director and Registered Treasurer, Conservative Party, 2006–10; *b* Surbiton, 13 July 1945; *s* of Archibald McIsaac and Elsie McIsaac (*née* Sampson); *m* 1985, Debrah Ball; one *s* one *d*, and one *s* one *d* from previous marriage. *Educ:* Charterhouse (Scholar). FCA 1969. Touche Ross & Co., later Deloitte: Partner, 1979–2005; UK Chm., DTT Emerging Markets, 2000–04; Man. Partner, Global Risk Mgt, Deloitte Touche

Tohmatsu, 2003–05. Director: C&UCO Properties Ltd, 2006–11; Jubilee Managing Agency Ltd, 2008–10 (Chm., 2010). Dir, City Disputes Panel, 2004–07. Member: Policy Adv. Gp, DFID, 2004–05; Investment Cttee, NESTA, 2007–09. Founder Chm., Inst. for Turnaround, 2001–04 (Fellow, 2004). UK Chm., Care Internat., 1997–2004. Gov., Sutton's Hosp. in Charterhouse, 2006–13. Trustee, Legacy List, 2012–13. Freeman, City of London, 1993; Liveryman, Chartered Accountants' Co., 1993. *Recreations:* golf, photography, travel, cookery. *Address:* 28 Hereford Square, SW7 4NB. *T:* (020) 7373 8742; Parsonage Farm, Pitton, Wilts SP5 1DT. *E:* imcisaac47@gmail.com. *Clubs:* Carlton, Hurlingham; Royal Mid-Surrey Golf.

McISAAC, Shona; *b* 3 April 1960; *d* of late Angus McIsaac and of Isa McIsaac; *m* 1994, Peter Keith. *Educ:* St Aidan's Coll., Durham (BSc Geography). Formerly: Lifeguard, Tooting Pool; Sub-Editor: Chat; Bella; Woman; food writer, Slimmer. Mem. (Lab) Wandsworth BC, 1990–97. MP (Lab) Cleethorpes, 1997–2010; contested (Lab) same seat, 2010. Parliamentary Private Secretary: NI Office, 2001–05; to Minister of State, Home Office, 2004–05; to Minister of State, DTI, 2005–06; to Minister of State, DoH, 2006–07. Mem., Select Cttee on Standards and Privileges, 1997–2001. *Recreations:* family and local history, food, football, cycling, archaeology.

MacIVER, Matthew Macleod, CBE 2008; Chairman, University Court, University of the Highlands and Islands (formerly Chairman, Board of Governors, University of the Highlands and Islands Millennium Institute), 2009–14; *b* Portnaguran, Isle of Lewis, 5 July 1946; *s* of Donald and Henrietta MacIver; *m* 1972, Katrina Robertson; one *s* one *d*. *Educ:* Aird Primary Sch.; Nicolson Inst., Stornoway; Edinburgh Univ. (MA 1968; DipEd 1969; MEd 1979). Teacher, Kilmarnock Acad., 1969–71; teacher, 1971–72, Principal Teacher, 1972–80, Craigmount High Sch., Edinburgh; Asst Rector, Royal High Sch., Edinburgh, 1980–83; Depute Head Teacher, Balerno High Sch., Edinburgh, 1983–86; Rector: Fortrose Acad., Ross-shire, 1986–89; Royal High Sch., Edinburgh, 1989–98; Depute Registrar (Educn), 1998–2001, Chief Exec. and Registrar, 2001–08, Gen. Teaching Council for Scotland. Winston Churchill Travelling Fellow, 1998. Chairman: Teachers' Action Gp on Gaelic Medium Educn, 2005; Bòrd na Gàidhlig (Gaelic Lang. Bd), 2006–08; UK Ind. Mem., Cttee of Experts, European Charter for Regl or Minority Languages, 2013–. Chm., Gaelic Broadcasting Cttee, 1996–2001; Member: Gaelic Television Cttee, 1991–95; for Scotland, Ofcom Content Bd, 2003–06; BBC Audience Council for Scotland, 2011–. Chm., Highlands and Is Educnl Trust, 1994–. Gov., George Watson's College, 2009–. Mem. Cttee, Scottish Assoc. of Churchill Fellows, 2009–13. Hon. Prof., UHI, 2008 (Hon. Fellow, 2013). Hon. Life Mem., Scottish Secondary Teachers' Assoc., 2008. FEIS 2004. Hon. Dhc Aberdeen, 2008; Hon. DEd Edinburgh, 2008. *Publications:* (with A. Hogg) Industry-Coal and Iron 1700–1900, 1977; (contrib.) Scottish Education, 2nd edn 2003, 3rd edn 2008; (contrib.) Report of the Gaelic Medium Teachers' Action Group, 2005; (ed with M. Nicolson) Policy and Practice in Education: Gaelic Medium Education, Series 10, 2006, trans. as Foghlam tro Mheadhan na Gàidhlig, 2007. *Recreations:* reading, Gaelic culture, writing a monthly article for The Rudhach (community newspaper in Lewis), watching Hibernian FC. *Address:* 21 Durham Road, Edinburgh EH15 1NY. *T:* (0131) 669 5029. *Club:* New (Edinburgh).

McIVOR, (Frances) Jane; District Judge (Magistrates' Courts), London, since 2001; *b* NI, 22 Oct. 1959; *d* of Rt Hon. (William) Basil McIvor, OBE, PC (NI) and (Frances) Jill McIvor, *qv*; *m* 1988, Girish Thanki; one *s* one *d*. *Educ:* sch. in Belfast; Univ. of E Anglia (LLB 1982). Called to the Bar, Inner Temple, 1983; in practice on S Eastern Circuit; Actg Metropolitan Stipendiary Magistrate, 1998–2001. Chm., Connexional Discipline Cttee, Methodist Church, 2005–. *Recreations:* golf, cooking. *Address:* Thames Magistrates' Court, 58 Bow Road, E3 4DJ.

McIVOR, (Frances) Jill, CBE 1994; Northern Ireland Parliamentary Commissioner for Administration and for Complaints, 1991–96; *b* 10 Aug. 1930; *d* of Cecil Reginald Johnston Anderson and Frances Ellen (*née* Henderson); *m* 1953, Rt Hon. (William) Basil McIvor, OBE, PC (NI) (*d* 2004); two *s* one *d*. *Educ:* Methodist Coll.; Lurgan Coll.; Queen's Univ. of Belfast (LLB Hons). Called to Bar of Northern Ireland, 1980. Asst Librarian (Law), QUB, 1954–55; Tutor in Legal Res., Law Faculty, QUB, 1965–74; editorial staff, NI Legal Qly, 1966–76; Librarian, Dept of Dir of Public Prosecutions, 1977–79. NI Mem., IBA, 1980–86; Dep. Chm., Radio Authy, 1990–94. Chm., Lagan Valley Regional Park Cttee, 1984–89 (Mem., 1975); Member: Ulster Countryside Cttee, 1984–89; Fair Employment Agency, 1984–89; Fair Employment Commn, 1990–91; Lay Panel, Juvenile Court, 1976–77; GDC, 1979–91; Exec., Belfast Voluntary Welfare Soc., 1981–88; Adv. Council, 1985–90, Bd, 1987–90, Co-operation North; Adv. Panel on Community Radio, 1985–86; NI Adv. Cttee, British Council, 1986–98. Chairman: Ulster-NZ Trust, 1987–2009; Educnl Guidance Service for Adults, 1988–90. NZ Hon. Consul for NI, 1996–2007. Mem. Bd of Visitors, QUB, 1988–2008. FRSA 1988–2001. DUniv Ulster, 1997. QSM 1993. *Publications:* Irish Consultant (and contrib.), Manual of Law Librarianship, 1976; (ed) Elegantia Juris: selected writings of F. H. Newark, 1973; Chart of the English Reports (new edn), 1982. *Recreations:* New Zealand, gardening.

See also F. J. McIvor.

McIVOR, Sarah Oonagh; *see* Rapson, S. O.

MACK, Prof. (Brian) John, DPhil; FBA 2009; FSA; Professor of World Art Studies, since 2004 and Chairman, Sainsbury Institute for Art, since 2012, University of East Anglia (Head, School of World Art and Museology, 2009–12); *b* 10 July 1949; *s* of late Brian Mack and Joan Alexandra Mack (*née* Kelly); *m* 1975, Caroline Jenkins, *d* of late Rev. Dr D. T. Jenkins; one *s* one *d*. *Educ:* Campbell Coll., Belfast; Univ. of Sussex (MA); Merton Coll., Oxford (DPhil 1975). FSA 1994. Res. Asst, 1976, Asst Keeper, 1977, Keeper, 1991–99 and 2002–04, Sen. Keeper, 1998–2002, Dept of Ethnography, BM. Vis. Prof., UCL, 1996–. Member: Council, British Inst. in Eastern Africa, 1981– (Pres., 2005–11); Council, RAI, 1983–86; Council, African Studies Assoc., 1986–88; British Acad. Bd for Academy-sponsored Insts and Schs, 1996–2003; Conseil d'orientation de l'établissement publique de Musée du Quai Branly, Paris, 1999–2000; Pitt-Rivers Cttee, Univ. of Oxford, 2000–12. Trustee, Horniman Mus. and Public Park, 1998–2010. Mem. Editl Bd, Art History, 1982–91. FRSA 2005. Nat. Art Collections Fund Award for Images of Africa, BM, 1991. *Publications:* (with J. Picton) African Textiles (Craft Adv. Council Book of the Year), 1979, 2nd edn 1989; Zulus, 1980; (with P. T. Robertshaw) Culture History in the Southern Sudan, 1982; (with M. D. McLeod) Ethnic Sculpture, 1984; Madagascar, Island of the Ancestors, 1986; Ethnic Jewellery, 1988; Malagasy Textiles, 1989; Emil Torday and the Art of the Congo 1900–1909, 1990; (with C. Spring) African Textile Design, 1991; Masks, the Art of Expression, 1994; (with K. Yoshida) Images of Other Cultures, 1997; Africa, Arts and Cultures, 2000; Museum of the Mind: art and memory in world cultures, 2003; The Art of Small Things, 2007; (with K. Yoshida) Preserving the Cultural Heritage of Africa: crisis or renaissance, 2008; The Sea: a cultural history, 2011; articles and revs in learned jls. *Address:* School of Art History and World Art Studies, University of East Anglia, Norwich NR4 7TJ. *T:* (01603) 592463.

See also K. M. Jenkins, Sir S. D. Jenkins.

MACK, Prof. Peter, PhD; FBA 2012; Professor of English, University of Warwick, since 2001. *Educ:* St Peter's Coll., Oxford (BA English Lang. and Lit. 1976; MPhil Combined Histl Studies 1978); Warburg Inst. (PhD 1983); Warwick Univ. (DLitt). Leverhulme Eur. Student, Inst. of Philosophy, Univ. of Rome and Vatican Liby, 1978–79; University of Warwick: Lectr in English and Comparative Lit., Sen. Lectr, then Reader, 1979–2001; Chair: Arts Faculty, 1995–98; English Dept, 2001–04; Prof. of History of Classical Tradition, Univ. of London and Dir, Warburg Inst., 2010–14 (on secondment). Ed., Rhetorica, 1998–. *Publications:* (ed with E. Chaney) England and the Continental Renaissance, 1990; Renaissance Argument: Valla and Agricola in the traditions of rhetoric and dialectic, 1993; (ed with C. Walton) The General Prologue to the Canterbury Tales, 1994, 2nd edn 2008; (ed) Renaissance Rhetoric, 1994; (ed with C. Walton) The Miller's Tale, 1995, 2nd edn 2007; (ed with A. Hawkins) The Nun's Priest's Tale, 1996, 2nd edn 2006; Elizabethan Rhetoric: theory and practice, 2002; (contrib.) Medieval Rhetoric, 2004; (contrib.) A Concise Companion to English Renaissance Literature, 2006; (contrib.) The Cambridge Companion to Ancient Rhetoric, 2009; Reading and Rhetoric in Montaigne and Shakespeare, 2010; (contrib.) The Classical Tradition, 2010; A History of Renaissance Rhetoric 1380–1620, 2011; articles in jls. *Address:* Humanities Building, University Road, University of Warwick, Coventry CV4 7AL.

MACK SMITH, Denis, CBE 1990; FBA 1976; FRSL; Extraordinary Fellow, Wolfson College, Oxford, 1987–2000 (Hon. Fellow, 2000); Emeritus Fellow, All Souls Coll., Oxford, 1987; *b* 3 March 1920; *s* of Wilfrid Mack Smith and Altiora Gauntlett; *m* 1963, Catharine Stevenson; two *d*. *Educ:* St Paul's Cathedral Choir Sch.; Haileybury Coll.; Peterhouse, Cambridge Univ. (organ and history schols). MA Cantab, MA Oxon. Asst Master, Clifton Coll., 1941–42; Cabinet Offices, 1942–46; Fellow of Peterhouse, Cambridge, 1947–62 (Hon. Fellow, 1986); Tutor of Peterhouse, 1948–58; Univ. Lectr, Cambridge, 1952–62; Sen. Res. Fellow, 1962–87, Sub-Warden, 1984–86, All Souls Coll., Oxford. Hon. Mem., Assoc. for Study of Modern Italy (Chm., 1987). For. Hon. Mem., Amer. Acad. of Arts and Sciences, 1972. Public Orator of the Repubblica di San Marino, 1982; Hon. Citizen, Santa Margherita Ligure, 1999. Hon. DLitt Cambridge, 2015. Awards: Thirlwall, 1949; Serena, 1960; Elba, 1972, 1994; Villa di Chiesa, 1973; Mondello, 1975; Nove Muse, 1976; Duff Cooper Meml, 1977; Wolfson Literary, 1977; Rhegium Julii, 1983; Presidential Medal, Italy, 1984; Polifemo d'Argento, 1988; Fregene, 1990; Sileno d'Oro, 1996. Grande Ufficiale dell'Ordine al Merito della Repubblica Italiana, 1996 (Commendatore, 1978). *Publications:* Cavour and Garibaldi 1860, 1954, enlarged 2nd edn 1985; Garibaldi, 1957; (jtly) British Interests in the Mediterranean and Middle East, 1958; Italy, a Modern History, 1959; Medieval Sicily, 1968; Modern Sicily, 1968; Da Cavour a Mussolini, 1968; (ed) The Making of Italy 1796–1870, 1968, 2nd edn 1988; (ed) Garibaldi, 1969; (ed) E. Quinet, Le Rivoluzioni d'Italia, 1970; Victor Emanuel, Cavour and the Risorgimento, 1971; (ed) G. La Farina, Scritti Politici, 1972; Vittorio Emanuele II, 1972, 2nd edn 1994; Mussolini's Roman Empire, 1976; (jtly) Un Monumento al Duce, 1976; Cento Anni di Vita Italiana attraverso il Corriere della Sera, 1978; L'Italia del Ventesimo Secolo, 1978; (ed) G. Bandi, I mille: da Genova a Capua, 1981; Mussolini, 1981; (ed) F. De Sanctis, Un Viaggio Elettorale, 1983; Cavour, 1985; (jtly) A History of Sicily, 1986; Italy and its Monarchy, 1989; Mazzini, 1993; Modern Italy: a political history, 1997; La Storia Manipolata, 1998; Jt Editor, Nelson History of England, 1962–. *Address:* White Lodge, Osler Road, Headington, Oxford OX3 9BJ. *T:* (01865) 762878.

MACKAY, family name of **Earl of Inchcape, Lord Reay** and **Barons Mackay of Clashfern, Mackay of Drumadoon** and **Tanlaw**.

MACKAY OF CLASHFERN, Baron *cr* 1979 (Life Peer), of Eddrachillis in the District of Sutherland; **James Peter Hymers Mackay,** KT 1997; PC 1979; FRSE 1984; Editor-in-Chief, Halsbury's Laws of England, 1998–2015; Lord High Commissioner, General Assembly, Church of Scotland, 2005–06 and 2006–07; Lord Clerk Register of Scotland and Keeper of the Signet, since 2007; *b* 2 July 1927; *s* of James Mackay and Janet Hymers; *m* 1958, Elizabeth Gunn Hymers; one *s* two *d*. *Educ:* George Heriot's Sch., Edinburgh; Edinburgh Univ. (MA Hons Maths and Nat. Philosophy 1948). Lectr in Mathematics, Univ. of St Andrews, 1948–50; Major Schol., Trinity Coll., Cambridge, in Mathematics, 1947, taken up 1950; Senior Schol. 1951; BA (Cantab) 1952; LLB Edinburgh (with Distinction) 1955. Admitted to Faculty of Advocates, 1955; QC (Scot.) 1965; Standing Junior Counsel to: Queen's and Lord Treasurer's Remembrancer; Scottish Home and Health Dept; Commissioners of Inland Revenue in Scotland; Sheriff Principal, Renfrew and Argyll, 1972–74; Vice-Dean, Faculty of Advocates, 1973–76; Dean, 1976–79; Lord Advocate of Scotland, 1979–84; a Senator of Coll. of Justice in Scotland, 1984–85; a Lord of Appeal in Ordinary, 1985–87; Lord High Chancellor of GB, 1987–97. Chancellor, Heriot-Watt Univ., 1991–2005. Commissary, Univ. of Cambridge, 2003–. Part-time Mem., Scottish Law Commn, 1976–79. Chairman: Commn for rev. of Law of Mauritius, 1997–98; Commn on Admin of Justice, Trinidad and Tobago, 2000. Mem., Ethics Rev. Cttee, 2006–09, Chm., Wkg Party preparing Guide to Sponsored Res., Internat. Agency for Res. on Cancer, 2006. Hon. Master of the Bench, Inner Temple, 1979. Dir, Stenhouse Holdings Ltd, 1976–77. Mem., Insurance Brokers' Registration Council, 1977–79. A Comr of Northern Lighthouses, 1975–84; Elder Brother of Trinity House, 1990. Fellow: Internat. Acad. of Trial Lawyers, 1979; Amer. Coll. of Trial Lawyers, 1990; Hon. Fellow, Chartered Inst. of Taxation (Fellow, Inst. of Taxation, 1981). Hon. Mem., SPTL, 1986. Hon. Fellow: Trinity Coll., Cambridge, 1989; Girton Coll., Cambridge, 1990; Hon. FRCSE 1989; Hon. FRCPE 1990; Hon. FRCOG 1996; Hon. FICE 1988. Hon. LLD: Edinburgh, 1983; Dundee, 1983; Strathclyde, 1985; Aberdeen, 1987; St Andrews, 1989; Cambridge, 1989; Coll. of William and Mary, Va, 1989; Birmingham, 1990; Nat. Law Sch. of India, 1994; Bath, 1994; Glasgow, 1994; Leicester, 1996; De Montfort, 1999; Hon. DCL: Newcastle, 1990; Oxford, 1998; Hon. Dr jur Robert Gordon, 2000. Royal Medal, RSE, 2003. *Publications:* Armour on Valuation for Rating, 5th edn (Consultant Editor), 1985. *Recreations:* walking, travel. *Address:* House of Lords, SW1A 0PW. *Clubs:* Athenæum, Caledonian; New (Edinburgh).

MACKAY OF DRUMADOON, Baron *cr* 1995 (Life Peer), of Blackwaterfoot in the district of Cunninghame; **Donald Sage Mackay;** PC 1996; a Senator of the College of Justice in Scotland, 2000–13; *b* 30 Jan. 1946; *s* of Rev. Donald George Mackintosh Mackay and Jean Margaret Mackay; *m* 1979, Lesley Ann Waugh; one *s* two *d*. *Educ:* George Watson's Boys' Coll., Edinburgh; Univ. of Edinburgh (LLB 1966; LLM 1968); Univ. of Virginia (LLM 1969). Law apprentice, 1969–71; Solicitor with Allan McDougall & Co., SSC, Edinburgh, 1971–76; called to the Scottish Bar, 1976; Advocate Depute, 1982–85; QC (Scot.) 1987; Solicitor-General for Scotland, 1995; Lord Advocate, 1995–97. Mem., Criminal Injuries Compensation Bd, 1989–95. Opposition spokesman on constitutional and legal affairs, H of L, 1997–2000; crossbencher, 2000–. Mem., Sentencing Commn for Scotland, 2003–06. *Recreations:* golf, gardening, Isle of Arran. *Address:* 39 Hermitage Gardens, Edinburgh EH10 6AZ. *T:* (0131) 447 1412; Seafield, Lamlash, Isle of Arran KA27 8LG. *T:* (01770) 600646.

MACKAY, Prof. Alan Lindsay, FRS 1988; Professor of Crystallography, Birkbeck College, University of London, 1986–91, now Emeritus; *b* 6 Sept. 1926; *s* of Robert Lindsay Mackay, OBE, MC, BSc, MD and Margaret Brown Mackay, OBE, MB ChB, JP; *m* 1951, Sheila Thorne Hague, MA; two *s* one *d*. *Educ:* Wolverhampton Grammar Sch.; Oundle Sch.; Trinity Coll., Cambridge (BA, MA); Univ. of London (BSc, PhD, DSc). Lectr, Reader, Prof., Dept of Crystallography, Birkbeck Coll., 1951–91. Visiting Professor: Univ. of Tokyo, 1969; Univ. of Tsukuba, 1980; Korean Advanced Inst. of Sci. and Tech., 1987; Hon. Professor: Central China Univ.; Sichuan Inst. of Sci. Studies; China Inst. for Sci. Studies. Foreign Member: Academia Mexicana de Ciencias, 1998; Korean Acad. of Sci. and Technol., 1999. Oliver E. Buckley Prize for Condensed Matter Physics, APS, 2010. *Publications:* The Harvest of a Quiet Eye, 1977; (with A. N. Barrett) Spatial Structure and the Microcomputer, 1987; (ed) A Dictionary of Scientific Quotations, 1991; (with E. A. Lord and S. Ranganathan) New Geometries for New Materials, 2006; papers in learned jls. *Recreation:* Asian studies. *Address:* 22 Lanchester Road, N6 4TA. *T:* (020) 8883 4810.

MacKAY, Rt Hon. Andrew (James); PC 1998; *b* 27 Aug. 1949; *s* of Robert James MacKay and Olive Margaret MacKay; *m* 1st 1975, Diana Joy (*née* Kinchin) (marr. diss. 1996); one *s* one *d*; 2nd, 1997, Julie Kirkbride, *qv*; one *s*. *Educ:* Solihull. MP (C) Birmingham, Stechford,

March 1977–1979; contested (C) same seat, 1979; MP (C) Berkshire E, 1983–97, Bracknell, 1997–2010. PPS to Sec. of State for NI, 1986–89, to Sec. of State for Defence, 1989–92; an Asst Govt Whip, 1992–93; a Lord Comr of HM Treasury (Govt Whip), 1993–95; Vice Chamberlain of HM Household, 1995–96; Treasurer of HM Household (Dep. Govt Chief Whip), 1996–97; Opposition front bench spokesman on NI, 1997–2001; Sen. Political and Parly Advr to Leader of Opposition, 2005–09. Member: Environment Select Cttee, 1985–86; Standards and Privileges Cttee, 2002–05; Foreign Affairs Select Cttee, 2004–05; Sec., Cons. Parly For. Affairs Cttee, 1985–86. Dep. Chm., Cons. Party, 2004–05; Mem., Cons. Party Nat. Exec., 1979–82. *Recreations:* golf, tennis, good food. *Clubs:* Berkshire Golf; Aberdovey Golf; Royal & Ancient Golf (St Andrews).

MACKAY, Andrew John, OBE 2006; Director, British Council, Spain, since 2015; *b* 28 July 1960; *s* of John and Margaret Mackay; *m* 1990, Margaret Allport; one *d*. *Educ:* Exeter Univ. (BA Combined Hons 1982); Reading Univ. (MA Dist. 1989); Durham Univ. (MBA 1996). British Council: Asst Dir, Teaching Centre, Cairo, 1983–87; Lang. Advr, London, 1988–89; English Lang. Officer, Peru, 1989–92; Director: Dubai, 1992–96; Barcelona, 1996–2001; USA, 2001–06; Hd of Strategy and Evaluation, Public Diplomacy Gp, FCO, 2006–08 (on secondment); Hd, Corporate Affairs, and Sec. to British Council, 2008–12; Dir Operations, 2013–15. Ind. Mem., Standards Cttee, Portsmouth CC, 2008–. Trustee, Lloyds Trust, 2010–. FRSA 2002. *Recreations:* cinema, literature, Hispanic cultures, walking. *Address:* British Council, Paseo General Martinez Campos 31, 28010 Madrid, Spain. *E:* andrewjmackay@hotmail.com.

MacKAY, Angus; Director, MacKay Hannah Ltd, since 2003; *b* 10 Sept. 1964. *Educ:* St Augustine's High Sch., Edinburgh; Edinburgh Univ. (MA Hons Politics and History, 1986). Formerly Campaign Officer, Shelter (Scotland); Parly Asst to Dr Mo Mowlam, 1990–92. Mem. (Lab) City of Edinburgh Council, 1995–99 (Convener, Finance Cttee, 1997–99). Member (Lab) Edinburgh S, Scottish Parlt, 1999–2003; Dep. Minister for Justice, 1999–2000; Minister for Finance and Local Govt, 2000–01. Contested (Lab) Edinburgh S, Scottish Parlt, 2003. *Address:* MacKay Hannah Ltd, Crichton House, 4 Crichton's Close, Edinburgh EH8 8DT.

MACKAY, Prof. Angus Iain Kenneth, PhD; FBA 1991; Professor of History, University of Edinburgh, 1985–97; *b* 1939; *m* 1962; one *s* one *d*. *Educ:* Edinburgh Univ. (MA 1962; PhD 1969). Lectr, Reading Univ., 1965–69; Lectr, then Sen. Lectr, 1969–82, Reader, 1982–85, Edinburgh Univ. *Publications:* Spain in the Middle Ages, 1977; Money, Prices and Politics in Fifteenth-century Castile, 1981; Society, Economy and Religion in late Mediaeval Castile, 1987; (with R. Bartlett) Mediaeval Frontier Societies, 1989; (with D. Ditchburn) Atlas of Medieval Europe, 1997; contribs to learned jls. *Address:* 43 Liberton Drive, Edinburgh EH16 6NL.

MACKAY, Dr Angus Victor Peck, OBE 1997; PhD; FRCPE, FRCPsych; Chair, Advisory Board on Homeopathic Products, and Member, Expert Advisory Group on Patient and Public Engagement, Medicines and Healthcare Products Regulatory Agency (Board Member, 2003); Member, Mental Health Tribunal for Scotland, since 2005; Director, Mental Health Services, Lomond and Argyll Primary Care NHS Trust, 1999–2005; *b* 4 March 1943; *s* of Victor P. Mackay and Christine Mackay (*née* Peck); *m* 1969, Elspeth Margaret Whitton Norris; two *s* two *d*. *Educ:* George Heriot's Sch., Edinburgh; Univ. of Edinburgh (BSc 1st Cl. Hons Pharmacol.; MB ChB 1969); Churchill Coll., Cambridge (PhD 1973). FRCPsych 1983; FRCPE 1989; TPsych 1994. Jun. Res. Fellow, 1970–73, Clin. Res. Fellow, 1973–76, Sen. Clin. Scientist, then Dep. Dir, 1976–80, MRC Neurochem. Pharmacol. Unit, Cambridge; Lector in Pharmacol., Trinity Coll., Cambridge, 1976–80; Physician Superintendent, Argyll and Bute Hosp., 1980–2005. Hon. Fellow in Neurosci., Univ. of Edinburgh, 1999–; Hon. Prof. (formerly MacIntosh Lectr in Psychol Medicine), Glasgow Univ., 1982–. Member: Res. Cttee, Mental Health Foundn UK, 1981–88; Health Services Res. Cttee, 1981–90 (Vice-Chair); Cttee on Safety of Medicines and associated cttees, 1984–2002; Sec. of State's NHS Policy Bd, 1987; UK Panel of Experts to Eur. Cttee on Proprietary and Medicinal Products, 1990–; Scottish Medicines Consortium, 2001–04; UK Monitoring Gp on Creutzfeldt-Jacob Disease, DoH/MRC, 2002–; Scottish Adv. Cttee on Distinction Awards, 1998–2007; Commn on Human Medicines, 2010–12; Chairman: Wkg Gp on Res. into Care of Dementing Elderly, 1986–87; Scottish Wkg Gp on Mental Illness Services, 1992–96; Wkg Gp on Health Technol. Assessment for Scotland; Health Technol. Bd for Scotland, 2000–03; Sec. of State for Health's Ind. Scrutiny Panel on Health Services along the Clyde, 2007–09. Mem., Nat. Prion Cohort Steering Cttee, 2009–. Chm., Scientific Adv. Cttee, Sackler Inst. of Psychobiology, 2005–. Member: George Heriot's First Four (stroke) (Scottish Schs Rowing Champions), 1959–62 (Capt. of Boats, George Herot's Sch.); Edinburgh Univ. First Eight, 1963–66; First Eight, 1970–73, Coxless Pair, 1976–80, Churchill Coll., Cambridge. Jun. Cdre, Fisherrow Yacht Club, 1960–61. *Publications:* over 90 contribs to text books and articles in learned jls, on various aspects of neurochem. and neuropharmacol. (particularly schizophrenic illness and drug-associated movement disorder), mental health service organisation, health technology assessment, and medicines regulation. *Recreations:* rowing, sailing (International Dragon), rhododendrons (Mem., American Rhododendron Soc.). *Address:* Tigh-an-Rudha, Ardrishaig, Argyll PA30 8ER. *T:* (01546) 603272, *Fax:* (01546) 602332. *E:* angus.mackay@nhs.net. *Club:* Ardrishaig Boat.

MACKAY, Charles Dorsey, CBE 2013; Chairman, Opera Holland Park Trust, since 2015; *b* 14 April 1940; *s* of late Brig. Kenneth Mackay, CBE, DSO and Evelyn Maud (*née* Ingram); *m* 1964, Annmarie Joder-Pfeiffer; one *s* one *d* (and one *s* decd). *Educ:* Cheltenham Coll.; Queens' Coll., Cambridge (MA); INSEAD (MBA). British Petroleum Co., 1957–69; commercial apprentice, 1957–59; univ. apprentice, Cambridge, 1959–62; marketing assistant, London, 1962–63; Regl Sales Manager, Algeria, 1963–65; Commercial Dir, Burundi/Rwanda/Congo, 1965–68; sponsored at INSEAD, France, 1968–69; McKinsey & Co. Inc., 1969–76: Consultant; Sen. Engagement Manager, 1972–76; worked in London, Paris, Amsterdam, Dar es Salaam; Pakhoed Holding NV, Rotterdam, 1976–81: Dir, 1976–77, Chm., 1977–81, Paktrans Div.; Chloride Group plc, 1981–86: Dir, 1981–86; Chm., Overseas Div., 1981–85; Chm., Power Electronics Div., 1985–86; Inchcape plc, 1986–96: Dir, 1986–96; Chief Exec., 1991–96; Dep. Chm., 1995–96; Chm., Inchcape (Hong Kong) Ltd and Dodwell and Co. Ltd, 1986–87; Chm. and Chief Exec., Inchcape Pacific Ltd, 1987–91. Chairman: DSL Gp Ltd, 1996–97; TDG plc, 2000–08; Eurotunnel Gp, 2001–04 (non-exec. Dir, 1997–2004; Dep. Chm., 1999–2001); Production Services Network Ltd, 2009–11; Dep. Chm., Thistle Hotels Plc, 1996–2003; non-executive Director: Union Insurance Soc. of Canton Ltd, 1986–91; Hongkong and Shanghai Banking Corp. Ltd, 1986–92; Midland Bank plc, 1992–93; HSBC Holdings plc, 1992–98; British Airways plc, 1993–96; Johnson Matthey PLC, 1999–2008; Member: Supervisory Bd, Gucci Gp NV, 1997–2001; Business Bd, House of Habib, 2007–; Bd, 2000–11, Adv. Council, 2011–, INSEAD. Chm., 2006–15, Hon. Pres., Campaign Bd, 2015–, Historic Royal Palaces. Trustee, Develt Trust (for the mentally handicapped), 1993–. *Recreations:* restoring old buildings, travel, fly-fishing, tennis, ski-ing, opera, classical music. *Address:* 4 Ormonde Gate, SW3 4EU. *T:* 07803 796295. *E:* charles.mackay@hrp.org.uk. *Clubs:* Brooks's, Piscatorial Society; Hong Kong (Hong Kong).

MacKAY, Colin, CBE 2001; FRCS, FRCSE, FRCSGlas, FRCP, FRCPI, FFPH, FRCPE; Consultant Surgeon, Western Infirmary/Gartnavel General Hospital, Glasgow, 1982–96; *b* 8 Nov. 1936; *s* of Kenneth MacKay and Margaret Blair Dawson MacKay; *m* 1966, Dr Helen Paul Miskimmin; one *s* two *d*. *Educ:* Univ. of Glasgow (BSc Hons; MB ChB (Commendation)). FRCS 1966; FRCSE 1966; FRCSGlas 1966; FRCP 1999; FRCPI 1999; FFPH (FFPHM 1999); FRCPE 2000. Surgical trng, Western Infirmary, Glasgow, 1961–69; MRC Travelling Fellow, Boston Univ., 1969–70; Sen. Lectr in Surgery, Univ. of Glasgow, 1970–82. Royal College of Physicians and Surgeons of Glasgow: Mem. Council, 1972–; Hon. Treas., 1976–86; Vice Pres., Surgical, 1992–94; Visitor, 1996–97; Pres., 1997–2000. Chm., Bd of Govs, UHI Millennium Inst., 2001–09. FACP 1998; FCMSA 1998; Fellow, Acad. of Medicine, Singapore 1998. *Publications:* (with I. McA. Ledingham) Textbook of Surgical Physiology, 1978, 2nd edn 1988; contribs to med. jls in field of surgical gastroenterology, in general, and peptic ulcer and gallstone disease, in particular. *Recreations:* travel, walking. *Address:* 73 Buchanan Drive, Bearsden, Glasgow G61 2EP. *T:* (0141) 942 8759.

MACKAY, Hon. Sir Colin (Crichton), Kt 2001; a Judge of the High Court, Queen's Bench Division, 2001–13; *b* 26 Sept. 1943; *s* of Sir James Mackerron Mackay, KBE, CB, and Katherine Millar Crichton Mackay (*née* Hamilton); *m* 1969, Rosamond Diana Elizabeth Collins; one *d* two *s*. *Educ:* Radley Coll.; Corpus Christi Coll., Oxford (Open Classical Schol.; MA). Harmsworth Entrance Exhibnr, 1965, and Astbury Schol., 1967; called to the Bar, Middle Temple, 1967, Bencher, 1995; QC 1989, a Recorder, 1992–2001. Member: Special Immigration Appeals Commn, 2003–13; Parole Bd for England and Wales, 2005–11. Mem., Lambeth Horticultural Soc., 2002–. *Recreations:* opera, growing vegetables, Scotland. *Club:* Vincent's (Oxford).

McKAY, Colin Graham; Sheriff of North Strathclyde at Kilmarnock, 2001–07; part-time Sheriff, since 2007; *b* 20 Jan. 1942; *s* of Patrick Joseph McKay and Mary Kieran; *m* 1966, Sandra Anne Coli; one *d* one *s*. *Educ:* St Aloysius' Coll., Glasgow; Clongowes Wood Coll., by Dublin; Univ. of Glasgow (MA, LLB). Admitted Solicitor, 1966; in private practice, 1966–90; Temporary Sheriff, 1985–90; Sheriff of N Strathclyde: (floater), 1990–95; at Oban and Fort William, 1995–2001.

McKAY, Daithí Gerard; Member (SF) North Antrim, Northern Ireland Assembly, since 2007; *b* 2 March 1982; *s* of Gerard and Anne McKay. *Educ:* St Patrick's Primary Sch., Rasharkin; St Louis Grammar Sch., Ballymena; N Eastern Inst. of Further and Higher Educn, Ballymena; Open Univ. (Dip Soc Scis). Customer Advr, Ulster Bank, 2001–03; Political Advr to Philip McGuigan, MLA, 2003–05. Mem. (SF) Ballymoney BC, 2005–. Contested (SF) N Antrim, 2010, 2015. Chm., Finance and Personnel Cttee, NI Assembly, 2012–. Mem., Gaelic Athletic Assoc. *Recreations:* Gaelic games and culture, reading, keeping fit, travelling. *Address:* 162 Bóthar na d Tullachain, Dún Lathái, Baile Meanach, Co. Antrim, Northern Ireland BT44 9AF. *T:* (028) 2765 7198. *E:* daithimckay@btinternet.com.

MACKAY, David James, FCILT; Chief Executive, John Menzies plc, 1997–2003; *b* 20 May 1943; *s* of David Mackay and Lena Mackay (*née* Westwater); *m* 1966, Jane Brown Hunter; one *s* one *d*. *Educ:* Kirkcaldy High Sch.; post experience programmes at Edinburgh and Bradford Univs. FCILT (FCIT 1993). Various exec. posts in John Menzies plc, 1964–2003, including: Transport Manager, NI, 1965; Asst Regl Dir, Southern & London, 1973; Ops Dir, Edinburgh, 1978; Man. Dir, Wholesale, 1984. Chairman: Malcolm Gp, 2003–06; Transport Edinburgh Ltd, 2006–09; Lothian Buses plc, 2010. Mem., Nat. Employer Adv. Bd, 2007–. Chm., Adv. Gp, Glasgow's Commonwealth Games Bid, 2004–05. CCMI (CIMgt 1998). Hon. Col, Scottish Transport Regt, 2004–11. Pres., Friends of Scottish Rugby, 2014– (Vice Pres., 2004). Chieftain, Inverkeithing Highland Games, 2003–06. *Recreations:* golf, walking. *Address:* 4 East Harbour Road, Charlestown, Fife KY11 3EA. *Clubs:* Caledonian; Bruntsfield Golf (Edinburgh); Aberdour Golf (Fife).

MacKAY, Prof. David John Cameron, PhD; FRS 2009; FInstP; FICE; Regius Professor of Engineering, University of Cambridge, since 2013; Fellow, Darwin College, Cambridge, since 1992; *b* Stoke-on-Trent, 22 April 1967; *s* of Donald MacCrimmon MacKay and Valerie MacKay (*née* Wood); *m* 2011, Ramesh Ghiassi. *Educ:* Newcastle-under-Lyme Sch.; Trinity Coll., Cambridge (BA Natural Scis 1988); California Inst. of Technol. (PhD Computation and Neural Systems 1992). Royal Soc. Smithson Res. Fellow, Darwin Coll., Cambridge, 1992–95; Lectr, Dept of Physics, 1995–99, Reader in Natural Philosophy, 1999–2003, Prof. of Natural Philosophy, 2003–13, Univ. of Cambridge; Chief Scientific Advr, DECC, 2009–14 (on secondment). FInstP 2009; FICE 2010. *Publications:* Information Theory, Inference, and Learning Algorithms, 2003; Sustainable Energy - without the hot air, 2008. *Recreations:* Ultimate, outdoor pursuits, music. *Address:* Department of Engineering, University of Cambridge, Trumpington Street, Cambridge CB2 1PZ. *E:* djcm1@cam.ac.uk.

See also R. S. MacKay.

MACKAY, Derek; Member (SNP) Renfrewshire North and West, Scottish Parliament, since 2011; Minister for Transport, since 2014; *m*; two *c*. *Educ:* Renfrew High Sch.; Glasgow Univ. Mem. (SNP), Renfrewshire Council, 1999–2011 (Leader, 2007). Researcher for Bruce McFee, MSP, 2003–05. Minister for Local Govt and Planning, Scottish Parlt, 2011–14. Non-exec. Dir, Gtr Glasgow and Clyde Health Bd, 2003–11; Chm., Renfrewshire Community Health Partnership, 2007–11. *Address:* Scottish Parliament, Edinburgh EH99 1SP.

MACKAY, Donald George; Hon. Research Fellow, Aberdeen University, since 1990; *b* 25 Nov. 1929; *s* of William Morton Mackay and Annie Tainsh Higgs; *m* 1st, 1965, Elizabeth Ailsa Barr (*d* 1999); two *s* one *d*; 2nd, 2005, Catherine Anne McDonald (*d* 2011). *Educ:* Morgan Academy, Dundee; St Andrews Univ. (MA); Aberdeen Univ. (PhD). Assistant Principal, Scottish Home Dept, 1953; Principal, SHHD, 1962–66; Sec., Royal Commission on Local Govt in Scotland, 1966–69; Asst Sec., Scottish Develt Dept, 1969–79; Asst Sec., 1980–83, Under Sec., 1983–85, Dept of Agric. and Fisheries for Scotland; Under Sec., Scottish Develt Dept, 1985–88. Mem., Scottish Agricl Wages Bd, 1991–97. *Publications:* (contrib.) Rural Land Use: Scotland and Ireland, 1994; Scotland's Rural Land Use Agencies, 1995. *Recreations:* hill walking, photography, music. *Address:* 25 Melville Street, Perth PH1 5PY. *T:* (01738) 621274. *E:* dgmac29@gmail.com.

MacKAY, Sir Donald (Iain), Kt 1996; FRSE; FRSGS; Director, Edinburgh New Income Trust (formerly Edinburgh Income and Value Trust), 1999–2011; *b* 27 Feb. 1937; *s* of William and Rhona MacKay; *m* 1961, Diana Marjory (*née* Raffan); two *d* (one *s* decd). *Educ:* Dollar Academy; Univ. of Aberdeen (MA). FRSE 1988. English Electric Co., 1959–62; Lectr in Political Economy, Univ. of Aberdeen, 1962–65; Lectr in Applied Economics, Univ. of Glasgow, 1965–68, Sen. Lectr, 1968–71; Prof. of Political Economy, Univ. of Aberdeen, 1971–76; Prof. of Economics, Heriot-Watt Univ., Edinburgh, 1976–82, Professorial Fellow 1982–90; Hon. Prof., 1990–. Chairman: Pieda plc, 1974–97; Scottish Enterprise, 1993–97; Grampian Hldgs, 1998–2002 (Dir, 1987–98); Malcolm Gp, 2002–03; Scottish Mortgage Investment Trust, 2003–09 (Dir, 1999–2009); Dir, DTZ Hldgs, 1999–2003. Mem., Scottish Econ. Council, 1985–99. Consultant to Sec. of State for Scotland, 1971–99. Gov., NIESR, 1981–. FRSGS 1996. Hon. LLD Aberdeen, 1994; DUniv Stirling, 1994. *Publications:* Geographical Mobility and the Brain Drain, 1969; Local Labour Markets and Wage Structures, 1970; Labour Markets under Different Employment Conditions, 1971; The Political Economy of North Sea Oil, 1975; (ed) Scotland 1980: the economics of self-government, 1977; articles in Econ. Jl, Oxford Econ. Papers, Manch. Sch., Scottish Jl Polit. Econ., Jl Royal Stat. Soc. *Recreations:* tennis, golf, bridge. *Address:* 17 Lennel Avenue, Edinburgh EH12 6DW.

MACKAY, Douglas Ian; QC (Scot.) 1993; *b* 10 Aug. 1948; *s* of Walter Douglas Mackay and Karla Marie Anna Fröhlich; *m* 1970, Susan Anne Nicholson; two *s* one *d*. *Educ:* Inverness High Sch.; Aberdeen Univ. (LLB). Admitted advocate, 1980. *Recreations:* Scottish art, travel, mountaineering, shooting, gundogs. *Address:* St Ann's House, Lasswade, Midlothian EH18 1ND. *T:* (0131) 660 2634; Mount Pleasant Farm, Fortrose, Ross-shire IV10 8SH; Plantation Village, St Ann's Bay, St Ann, Jamaica, WI.

MACKAY, Eileen Alison, (Lady Russell), CB 1996; FRSE; non-executive Director, Royal Bank of Scotland Group plc, 1996–2005; *b* 7 July 1943; *d* of Alexander William Mackay and Alison Jack Ross; *m* 1983, (Alastair) Muir Russell (*see* Sir A. M. Russell). *Educ:* Dingwall Acad.; Edinburgh Univ. (MA Hons Geography). FRSE 2002. Dept of Employment, Scottish HQ, 1965–72; Scottish Office, 1972–78; HM Treasury, 1978–80; CPRS, Cabinet Office, 1980–83; Scottish Office, 1983–96: Under Sec., Housing, Envmt Dept, 1988–92; Principal Finance Officer, 1992–96. Chm., Castlemilk Partnership, 1988–92; Director: Moray Firth Maltings, 1988–99; Edinburgh Investment Trust plc, 1996–2005; Scottish TV (Regional) Ltd, 1998–99; Lothian and Edinburgh Enterprise Ltd, subseq. Scottish Enterprise Edinburgh and Lothian, 1998–2002; Scottish Financial Enterprise Ltd, 2000–06. Chm., Standing Adv. Cttee on Trunk Road Assessment, 1996–99. Mem., Commn on Local Govt and the Scottish Parlt, 1998–99. Member: Bd, Scottish Screen, 1997–99; ESRC, 1999–2003; Scottish Business and Biodiversity Gp, 1999–2002; Accountancy Review Bd, 2000–03; Bd, British Library, 2003–11; Bd of Govs, Royal Conservatoire of Scotland (formerly RSAMD), 2007– (Vice-Chair, 2013–); Court, UHI (formerly Bd, UHI Millennium Inst.), 2009–. Mem. Bd, Margaret Blackwood Housing Assoc., 1996–2001; Trustee: David Hume Inst., 1996–2008 (Chm. Trustees, 2002–08); Carnegie Trust for Univs of Scotland, 2000–. Mem. Court, Univ. of Edinburgh, 1997–2003. *Club:* New (Edinburgh).

MACKAY, Sir Francis Henry, Kt 2003; FCCA; Founding Member, Graysons Ltd, since 2007; *b* 24 Oct. 1944; *m* 1963, Christine Leach; one *s* two *d*. FCCA 1967. Compass Group: Finance Dir, 1986–91, Chief Exec. and Dep. Chm., 1991–99; Chm., 1999–2006; Jt Dep. Chm., Granada Compass, 2000–01; Chm., Kingfisher, 2001–06. Chairman: ISS, 2006–08; Carlton Partners, 2006–12; non-exec. Dir, Centrica, 1997–2001.

MACKAY, Air Vice-Marshal (Hector) Gavin, CB 2002; OBE 1987; AFC 1982; FRAeS; Qualified Flying Instructor, No 16(R) Squadron, RAF Cranwell, 2009–12; *b* 3 Oct. 1947; *s* of John MacLean Mackay and Isobel Margaret Mackay (*née* Mackay); *m* 1971, Elizabeth Stark Bolton; one *s* one *d*. *Educ:* Dingwall Acad.; Glasgow Univ. (BSc Civil Engrg 1970); RAF Coll., Cranwell. FRAeS 1997. Qualified Flying Instructor, RAF Linton-on-Ouse, 1973–75; Harrier Pilot: No 20 Sqdn, RAF Wildenrath, 1976–77; No 3 (F) Sqdn, RAF Gutersloh, 1977–79; Flight Comdr, No 1 (F) Sqdn, RAF Wittering, 1979–82; RNSC, 1982; Central Tactics and Trials Orgn, 1983–84; OC Examng Wing, CFS, 1984–87; Concept Studies and Operational Requirements, MoD, 1987–90; Station Comdr, RAF Gutersloh, 1991–93; Dep. Dir Air Offensive, MoD, 1993; rcds 1994; ACOS Ops, HQ AIRCENT, 1995–96; Comdt, CFS, 1996–99; Hd, Jt Force 2000 Implementation Team, 1999–2000; AOC, and Comdt, RAF Coll., Cranwell, 2000–02; Sen. Military Advr (formerly Military Dep.) to Hd of Defence Export Services, 2002–09. Hon. Air Cdre 2503 (Co. of Lincoln) Sqdn, RAuxAF Regt, 2005–. Mem. Council, Bishop Grosseteste Univ., Lincoln, 2014–. Liveryman, Hon. Co. of Air Pilots (formerly GAPAN), 2002–. High Sheriff, Lincs, 2015–April 2016. *Recreations:* flying, golf, walking. *Club:* Royal Air Force.

MACKAY, Ian Stuart, FRCS; Consultant Otorhinolaryngologist, Royal Brompton Hospital and Charing Cross Hospital, London, 1977–2003; Hon. Consultant, King Edward VII Hospital for Officers, since 1995; *b* 16 June 1943; *s* of Rev. Gordon Mackay and Sylvia Mackay (*née* Spencer); *m* 1981, Madeleine Hargreaves (*née* Tull); one *d*, and one *s* one *d* from former marriage. *Educ:* Kearsney Coll., Natal, South Africa; Royal Free Hosp. Sch. of Medicine, London (MB BS 1968). FRCS 1974. Cons. Otorhinolaryngologist, Metropolitan ENT Hosp., 1977–86. Hon. Senior Lecturer: Nat. Heart and Lung Inst., 1985–; Inst. of Laryngology and Otology, Univ. of London, 1985–. Vis. Prof., Mayo Clinic, 1996. Hon. Treas., European Acad. of Facial Surgery, 1978–93; Master, British Academic Conf. in Otolaryngology, 2012–15 (Hon. Treas., 1992–99); Mem. Council, Laryngology and Rhinology Section, RSocMed, 1996– (Pres., 2002–03); Founder Mem., British Allergy Foundn, 1995; Pres., British Assoc. of Otolaryngologists, 1999–2002 (Pres.-elect, 1996–99); Chairman: Fedn of Surgical Specialty Assocs, 2001–03; Ind. Doctors Fedn, 2012–14 (Responsible Officer, 2014–). Mem. Editl Bd, Amer. Jl of Rhinology, 1995–2014. *Publications:* (ed) Scott-Brown's Otolaryngology, Rhinology Vols, 5th edn 1987, 6th edn 1997; (contrib.) Facial Plastic Surgery, 1986; Otolaryngology, 1987, 2nd edn 1997; (ed) Rhinitis: mechanisms and management, 1989; chapters in books and papers, mainly on rhinoplasty and endoscopic sinus surgery. *Recreations:* fell walking, carpentry, house restoration. *Address:* Foxhills Farmhouse, Swerford OX7 4BQ. *T:* 07836 555424. *Clubs:* Sloane, Royal Society of Medicine.

MacKAY, Julie; *see* Kirkbride, J.

McKAY, Sir Neil (Stuart), Kt 2009; CB 2001; independent health care management consultant, since 2013; Chief Executive, NHS Midlands and East (formerly East of England Strategic Health Authority), 2006–13; *b* 19 Feb. 1952; *s* of late Roy McKay and of Alison Maude McKay (*née* Dent); *m* 1978, Deirdre Mary McGinn; two *s*. *Educ:* Dame Allan's Boys' Sch., Newcastle upon Tyne. Trainee Adminr, Newcastle upon Tyne Univ. HMC, 1970–72; Asst Hosp. Sec., Dunston Hill Hosp., Gateshead HMC, 1972–74; Admin. Asst, Gateshead AHA, 1974–75; Unit Adminr, Dryburn Hosp., Durham AHA, 1975–76; Commng Officer, St George's Hosp., Merton, Sutton and Wandsworth AHA, 1976–80; Dist Planning Adminr, 1980–82, Hosp. Adminr, Springfield Hosp., 1982–85, Wandsworth HA; Gen. Manager, Doncaster Royal Infirmary, 1985–88; Gen. Manager, 1988–91, Chief Exec., 1991–96, Northern Gen. Hosp. NHS Trust, Sheffield; Regl Dir, Trent Regl Office, 1996–2000, Dep. Chief Exec., 2000, NHS Exec., DoH; Chief Operating Officer, DoH, 2000–02; Chief Exec., Leeds Teaching Hosps NHS Trust, 2002–06. Hon. LLD Sheffield, 2000. *Recreations:* sport of all kinds (especially following Sunderland AFC), reading, gardening.

MACKAY, Neville Patrick; Vice Convener, Scottish Council for Voluntary Organisations, since 2015; *b* 22 June 1958; *s* of Edward William Charles Mackay and Constance Evelyn Mackay; *m* 1996, Gillian Anne Prole; two *d*. *Educ:* Brentwood Sch.; Lancaster Univ. (BA Hons Geog. 1979); University Coll. London. Researcher, DoE, 1983–90; DFE, 1990–92; Department for National Heritage, later Department for Culture, Media and Sport: 1992–99; Dep. Hd, Heritage Div., 1995–97; Hd, Libraries and Inf. Div., 1997–99; Chief Exec., Resource: Council for Museums, Archives and Libraries, 2000–02; Hd, Voluntary Issues Unit, Scottish Exec., 2002–04; Chief Exec., Scottish Public Pensions Agency, 2004. *Recreations:* motor sports, walking, camping, being with my family. *Address:* Scottish Council for Voluntary Organisations, Mansfield Traquair Centre, 15 Mansfield Place, Edinburgh EH3 6BB.

MacKAY, Prof. Norman, CBE 1997; MD; FRCPGlas, FRCPE, FRCSE, FRCGP, FRCP; Dean of Postgraduate Medicine and Professor of Postgraduate Medical Education, University of Glasgow, 1989–2001; *b* 15 Sept. 1936; *s* of Donald MacKay and Catherine MacLeod; *m* 1961, Grace Violet McCaffer; two *s* two *d*. *Educ:* Glasgow Univ. (MB ChB, MD). FRCPGlas 1973; FRCPE 1975; FRCSE 1993; FRCGP 1993. Junior posts, Glasgow hosps, 1959–66; Lectr in Medicine, Nairobi, 1966–67; Sen. Registrar, Victoria Infirmary, Glasgow, 1967–68; Acting Sen. Lectr, Materia Medica, Univ. of Glasgow, 1968–72; Acting Consultant Physician, Falkirk, 1972–73; Consultant Physician, Victoria Infirmary, 1973–89, Hon. Consultant, 1989–94. Mem., GMC, 1999–2003. Pres., RCPSG, 1994–97 (Hon. Sec., 1973–83; Visitor, 1992–94). Vice-Chm., Copmed, 1999–2001. FCPS (Pak) 1993; FRACP; FAMS; FRCPI; FAMM; Hon. FACP 1995; Hon. FCPS Bangladesh; Hon. FRCS. *Publications:* articles in med. jls. *Recreations:* gardening, golf, soccer. *Address:* 5 Edenhall Grove, Newton Mearns, Glasgow G77 5TS. *T:* (0141) 616 2831.

MACKAY, Peter, CB 1993; Chairman, Local Government Boundary Commission for Scotland, 2007–13; *b* Arbroath, 6 July 1940; *s* of John S. Mackay, FRCS, and Patricia M. Atkinson; *m* 1964, Sarah Holdich; one *s* two *d*. *Educ:* Glasgow High Sch.; St Andrews Univ. (MA 1st Cl. Hons Political Economy). Teacher, Kyogle High Sch., NSW, 1962–63; joined Scottish Office as Asst Principal, 1963; various posts, incl. Private Sec. to successive Ministers of State, 1966–68 and Secs of State, 1973–75; Nuffield Travelling Fellow, Canada, Australia and NZ, 1978–79; seconded: as Dir for Scotland, MSC, 1983–85; as Under Sec., Manpower Policy, Dept of Employment, London, 1985–86; Under Sec., Further and Higher Educn, Scottish Educn Dept, 1987–89; Principal Establishment Officer, Scottish Office, 1989–90; Sec. and Chief Exec., Scottish Office Industry Dept, 1990–95. Director: British Linen Bank, 1996–2000; Business Banking Div., Bank of Scotland, 1999–2001; Pacific Horizon Investment Trust plc, 2001–10 (Chm., 2004–10). Member: Competition (formerly Monopolies and Mergers) Commn, 1996–2002; Bd, Scottish Natural Heritage, 1996–2003; Cairngorms Outdoor Access Forum, 2014–; Comr, Northern Lighthouse Bd, 1999–2008 (Chm., 2005–07); Director: Scottish Forest Alliance, 2000–10; Cairngorm Outdoor Access Trust, 2009–13; Chm., Northern Lighthouse Heritage Trust, 2014–. Mem. Court, Napier Univ., 1996–2004. Hon. LLD Robert Gordon's, 1996. *Recreations:* sea canoeing, sculling, Scottish hills in all seasons. *Address:* Silverwood, Kincraig, by Kingussie, Inverness-shire PH21 1QE. *Club:* Loch Lomond Sailing.

MacKAY, Hon. Peter Gordon; PC (Can.) 2006; QC (Can.) 2006; MP (C) Central Nova, since 2004 ((PC) Pictou-Antigonish-Guysborough, 1997–2004); Minister of Justice, Canada, since 2013; *b* New Glasgow, NS, 27 Sept. 1965; *s* of Hon. Elmer M. MacKay, PC (Can.), QC (Can.) and Macha MacKay. *Educ:* Acadia Univ., NS (BA 1987); Dalhousie Univ., NS (LLB 1990). Called to the Nova Scotia Bar, 1991; in private practice specializing in criminal and family law, New Glasgow, NS, 1991–93; Crown Attorney for Central Reg., NS, 1993–97. House Leader, 1997–2003, Leader, 2003–04, PC Party of Canada; Dep. Leader, Cons. Party of Canada, 2004–06; Minister: of Foreign Affairs, 2006–07; Atlantic Canada Opportunities Agency, 2006–10; for the Atlantic Gateway, 2008–10; of Nat. Defence, 2007–13. Nat. Ambassador for Adopt-a-Liby Literacy Prog., Pictou Co., NS, 2000–. Golden Jubilee Medal, 2002. *Recreations:* silviculture, Rugby, baseball, football, ice hockey. *Address:* House of Commons, Ottawa, ON K1A 0A6, Canada. *T:* (613) 992 6022, *Fax:* (613) 992 2337. *E:* MacKay.P@parl.gc.ca.

McKAY, His Honour Randal Joseph; QC (NI) 1989; a County Court Judge, Armagh and South Down Division, Northern Ireland, 1994–2009; *b* Larne, 16 April 1943; *s* of Hugh and Josephine McKay; *m* 1974, Brenda O'Neill; three *s*. *Educ:* Queen's Univ., Belfast (LLB 1969; BL 1970). In practice as barrister, 1970–94. *Recreations:* boxing, pistol shooting, crosswords, motor racing, deflating egos.

MacKAY, Prof. Robert Sinclair, PhD; FRS 2000; FInstP, FIMA; Professor of Mathematics, University of Warwick, since 2000; President, Institute of Mathematics and its Applications, 2012–13; *b* 4 July 1956; *s* of Donald MacCrimmon MacKay and Valerie MacKay (*née* Wood); *m* 1992, Claude Noëlle Baesens; one *s*. *Educ:* Trinity Coll., Cambridge (BA Math.; MA; MMath); Princeton (PhD Astrophys. Scis 1982). FInstP 2000; FIMA 2003. Res. Asst, QMC, 1982–83; Vis. Researcher, Institut des Hautes Etudes Scientifiques, Bures-sur-Yvette, France, 1983–84; Lectr, 1984–90, Reader, 1990–93, Prof., 1993–95, Mathematics, Univ. of Warwick; Prof. of Nonlinear Dynamics, and Fellow of Trinity Coll., Univ. of Cambridge, 1995–2000. Nuffield Foundn Sci. Res. Fellow, 1992–93; Res. Associate, 1994–95, Vis. Prof., 1995, CNRS, Université de Bourgogne, France; Prof. invité, Institut des Hautes Etudes Scientifiques, Bures-sur-Yvette, 2006; Vis. Prof., Physics, Université Libre de Bruxelles, 2010–11. (First) Stephanos Pnevmatikos Internat. Award for Res. in Nonlinear Phenomena, 1993; Jun. Whitehead Prize, London Math. Soc., 1994. *Publications:* Hamiltonian Dynamical Systems, 1987; Renormalisation in area-preserving maps, 1993; over 125 papers in learned jls. *Address:* Mathematics Institute, University of Warwick, Coventry CV4 7AL.

See also D. J. C. MacKay.

MACKAY, Ronald David; *see* Eassie, Rt Hon. Lord.

MACKAY, Prof. Trudy Frances Charlene, (Mrs R. R. H. Anholt), PhD; FRS 2006; William Neal Reynolds and Distinguished University Professor, Department of Biological Sciences (formerly Department of Genetics), North Carolina State University, since 1996; *b* 10 Sept. 1952; *d* of Charles Edward Mackay and Jean Somerville Mackay; *m* 1990, Robert R. H. Anholt. *Educ:* Dalhousie Univ. (BSc Hons 1974, MSc 1976); Univ. of Edinburgh (PhD 1979). Lectr, Dept of Genetics, Univ. of Edinburgh, 1980–87; Associate Prof., 1987–93, Prof., 1993–96, Dept of Genetics, N Carolina State Univ. FAAAS 2003; Fellow: Amer. Acad. of Arts and Scis, 2005; NAS, USA, 2010. N Carolina Award for Sci., 2011. *Publications:* over 180 peer-reviewed articles in scientific jls. *Recreations:* dressage and carriage driving, listening to opera, reading mystery novels. *Address:* Department of Biological Sciences, Campus Box 7614, North Carolina State University, Raleigh, NC 27695, USA. *T:* (919) 5155810, *Fax:* (919) 5153355. *E:* trudy_mackay@ncsu.edu.

McKAY, Sir William (Robert), KCB 2001 (CB 1996); Clerk of the House of Commons, 1998–2002; *b* 18 April 1939; *s* of late William Wallace McKay and Margaret H. A. Foster; *m* 1962, Rev. Margaret M., *d* of late E. M. Fillmore, OBE; twin *d*. *Educ:* Trinity Academy, Leith; Edinburgh Univ. (MA Hons). Clerk in the House of Commons, 1961; Clerk of Financial Cttees, H of C, 1985–87; Clerk of the Journals, H of C, 1987–91; Clerk of Public Bills, H of C, 1991–94; Clerk Asst, H of C, 1994–97. Secretary: to the House of Commons Commn, 1981–84; to the Public Accounts Commn, 1985–87. Chm., Commn on the Consequences of Devolution for H of C, 2012–13. Lay Observer, Law Soc. of Scotland, 2006–11. Mem., Legal Questions Cttee, Church of Scotland, 2006–11. Hon. Prof., Univ. of Aberdeen, 2003–07. Mem. Council, Scottish History Soc., 2012–. *Publications:* (ed) Erskine May's Private Journal 1883–86, 1984; Secretaries to Mr Speaker, 1986; Clerks in the House of Commons 1363–1989: a biographical list, 1989; (ed) Observations, Rules and Orders of the House of Commons: an early procedural collection, 1989; (ed jtly) Erskine May's Parliamentary Practice, 22nd edn 1997, (sole editor) 23rd edn 2004; (contrib.) Stair Memorial Encyclopaedia of the Laws of Scotland, rev. edn 2002; (with M. M. McKay) A United Parish, 2002; (contrib.) Halsbury's Laws of England, 4th edn; (with C. W. Johnson) Parliament and Congress: representation and scrutiny in the twenty-first century, 2010; contrib. historical jls. *Recreation:* reading Scottish history. *Address:* 19 Richmond Road, Huntly, Aberdeenshire AB54 8BH. *Club:* New (Edinburgh).

MACKAY-DICK, Maj.-Gen. Sir Iain (Charles), KCVO 1997; MBE 1981; DL; Clerk to the Trustees and Chief Executive, Morden College, 1997–2011; *b* 24 Aug. 1945; *s* of John Mackay-Dick and Margaret Edith Mackay-Dick (*née* Forty); *m* 1971, Carolynn Hilary Holmes; three *d*. *Educ:* St Edmund's Sch., Hindhead; Sherborne Sch.; RMAS; Staff Coll., Camberley (psc, hcsc). Commnd, Scots Guards, 1965; served Malaysia, Borneo, Germany, Cyprus and UK to 1986, and Falkland Is, 1982; Comdt, Jun. Div. Staff Coll., Warminster, 1986–88; Comdr, 11 Armoured Bde, 1989–91; Dep. Mil. Sec. (A), 1991–92; GOC 1st Armoured Div., Verden, 1992–93; GOC Lower Saxony Dist, Verden, 1993; Comdr British Forces Falkland Is, 1993–94; GOC London Dist and Maj. Gen. commanding Household Div., 1994–97. Mem., RUSI, 1979–2006. Hon. Col, 256 (City of London) Field Hosp., RAMC(V), 2000–07. Member: Public Schools Old Boys LTA; South Atlantic Medal Assoc. Mem., Gov. Council, Union Jack Club, 2011–. Freeman, City of London, 2000. DL Greater London, 2011. FCMI 1996–2011 (FIMgt 1996). Trustee, Falkland Is Meml Chapel, Pangbourne, 2005–; Chm., Guards Chapel Cttee, 2011–. *Publications:* (contrib.) Central

Region versus Out of Area (essays), 1990. *Recreations:* most sports (represented Army in lawn tennis and squash (Army Squash Champion, 1971)), walking, gardening, military history. *Address:* c/o Lloyds Bank, Cox's and Kings, PO Box 1190, 7 Pall Mall, SW1Y 5NA. *Clubs:* Edinburgh Angus (Edinburgh); Jesters; Third Guards; Guards' Golfing Society, Army Golfing Society.

MacKEAN, His Honour Thomas Neill; a Circuit Judge, 1993–2004; *b* 4 March 1934; *s* of late Andrew Neill MacKean and Mary Dale MacKean (*née* Nichol); *m* 1962, Muriel Hodder; four *d.* *Educ:* Sherborne; Trinity Hall, Cambridge (BA). 2nd Lt, Royal Hampshire Regt, 1952–54. Partner, Hepherd Winstanley & Pugh, solicitors, Southampton, 1960–93; HM Coroner, Southampton and New Forest, 1990–93; a Recorder, 1991–93. *Recreations:* sailing, walking. *Clubs:* Royal Cruising; Royal Southern Yacht (Hamble).

McKEARNEY, Philip, CMG 1983; HM Diplomatic Service, retired; *b* 15 Nov. 1926; *s* of Philip McKearney, OBE; *m* 1950, Jean Pamela Walker; two *s.* *Educ:* City of London Sch.; Hertford Coll., Oxford. 4/7th Dragoon Guards, 1946–53; joined HM Diplomatic Service, 1953; 3rd Sec., British Embassy, Damascus, 1955–56; 1st Sec., British Legation, Bucharest, 1959–62; British Political Agent, Qatar, 1962–65; Counsellor and Consul-Gen., Baghdad, 1968–70; Counsellor, Belgrade, 1970–74; Inspector, FCO, 1975–77; Consul-General: Zagreb, 1977–80; Boston, Mass, 1980–83; Amb. to Romania, 1983–86; Dir, Foreign Service Prog., Oxford Univ., 1987–88.

McKECHIN, Ann; *b* 22 April 1961; *d* of late William Joseph McKechin and of Anne McKechin (*née* Coyle). *Educ:* Strathclyde Univ. (LLB, DLP). Solicitor, 1983–; Partner, Pacitti Jones, Glasgow, 1990–2000. MP (Lab) Glasgow, Maryhill, 2001–05, Glasgow N, 2005–15; contested (Lab) same seat, 2015. Parly Under Sec. of State, Scotland Office, 2008–10; Shadow Sec. of State for Scotland, 2010–11. Mem., Business, Innovation and Skills Select Cttee, 2011–15. Vice Chair, Westminster Foundn for Democracy, 2013–15. *Recreations:* films, dancing, art history.

McKECHNIE, Aileen Mary; Director, Advanced Learning and Science, Scottish Government, since 2015; *b* Paisley, 22 Nov. 1966; *d* of Hugh McHale and Celine McHale; *m* 2002, William McKechnie; two *s.* *Educ:* Holyrood Secondary Sch.; Univ. of Glasgow (MA Hons French and German; MBA). Senior Development Manager: Glasgow CC, 1990–94; Scottish Homes, 1994–96; Thistle Housing Assoc., 1996–98; Scottish Executive, subseq. Scottish Government: Head: Local Econ. Develt, 1998–2002; Higher Educn Strategy and Funding, 2002–04; Further and Adult Educn Div., 2004–09; Innovation, Investment and Industries Div., 2009–12; Director: Culture and External Affairs, 2012–13; Culture and Heritage, 2013–14. Dir (pt-time), Scottish Arbitration Centre, 2011–13. *Recreations:* reading, walking, ballet, art, cinema, theatre, spending quality time with family. *Address:* Scottish Government, 5 Atlantic Quay, Glasgow G2 8LU. *T:* 0300 244 1264. *E:* aileen.mckechnie@scotland.gsi.gov.uk.

MACKECHNIE, Sir Alistair (John), Kt 1993; financial consultant, since 1992; *b* 15 Nov. 1934; *s* of Frank Harper McIvor Mackechnie and Ellen Annie (*née* Brophy); *m* 1961, Countess Alexandra Kinsky, *er d* of Count Frederick-Carl Kinsky; three *d.* *Educ:* St Patrick's Coll., Wellington, NZ; Victoria Univ. of Wellington, NZ. ACA 1957. Nat. Service: commnd NZ Scottish Regt, 1955. Director: Henderson Admin, 1976–88; BSI-Thornhill Investment Mgt, 1989–2000; Hori Construction Ltd, 2000–; Carlton Club (London) Ltd, 2008–; Carlton Trustees (London) Ltd, 2008–. Twickenham Conservative Association: Chm., 1985–88; Pres., 1989–; Greater London Area Conservatives: Dep. Chm., 1988–90; Chm., 1990–93; Mem., Exec. Cttee, Nat. Union of Cons. and Unionist Assocs, 1988–96. Mem. Council, Back Care (formerly Nat. Back Pain Assoc.), 1994–2009. Governor: St Mary's UC, 1997–2006; St Catherine's Sch., Twickenham, 1997–2006. *Recreations:* theatre, travel, bird-watching, hill-walking. *Club:* Carlton.

McKECHNIE, George; Director of Participation and Communications, Education and Learning Wales, 2001–04 (Consultant, 2004–06); *b* 28 July 1946; *m* 1971, Janequin (*née* Morris); two *s.* *Educ:* Portobello Sen. Secondary Sch., Edinburgh; Swansea Univ. (MA 2008; PhD 2012). Reporter: Paisley and Renfrewshire Gazette, 1964–66; Edinburgh Evening News, 1966; Scottish Daily Mail, 1966–68; Daily Record, 1968–73; Dep. News Editor and News Editor, Sunday Mail, 1974–76; Asst Editor, 1976–81, Editor, 1981–94, Evening Times, Glasgow; Editor, The Herald, Glasgow, 1994–97; Dir of Public Affairs, Beattie Media, 1998–99; Dir of Communications, Council of Welsh TECs, 1999–2001. Director: George Outram & Co., 1986–92; Caledonian Newspaper Publishing, 1992–97. Mem., Press Complaints Commn, 1992–94. *Recreations:* reading, walking, cinema, Hearts FC. *Address:* Mumbles Hill House, Mumbles Hill, Mumbles, Swansea SA3 4HZ.

McKEE, (Charles Dean) Grant; television executive producer; Director of Programmes, Yorkshire Television, 1993–95 (non-executive Director, 2002–06); *b* 18 Aug. 1951; *s* of Comdr Eric McKee, RN, OBE and Betty (*née* Dean); *m* 1991, Jill Turton; one *d.* *Educ:* Clifton Coll.; Exeter Coll., Oxford (LLB). Journalist: Goole Times, 1974–76; Yorkshire Post, 1976–78; Yorkshire Television, 1979–95: journalist and documentary producer, 1979–88; Editor, First Tuesday, 1988–93; Controller, Documentaries and Current Affairs, 1988–93. Chm., Staithes Arts and Heritage Fest. *Publications:* (with R. Franey) Time Bomb: Irish bombers, English justice and the Guildford Four, 1988; Stronger than the Storm, 2013. *Recreations:* travel, cricket, countryside. *Address:* 5 Summerhouse Mews, York YO30 7ED.

McKEE, Prof. (Clifford) Martin, CBE 2005; MD, DSc; FRCP, FRCPE, FRCPI, FFPH, FMedSci; Professor of European Public Health, since 1997, and Medical Director, London School of Hygiene and Tropical Medicine, University of London; *b* Belfast, 12 July 1956; *s* of Dr Clifford McKee and Dr Anna McKee (*née* Martin); *m* 1987, Dorothy McCrory; two *d.* *Educ:* Royal Belfast Academical Instn; Queen's Univ., Belfast (MB BCh BAO 1979; MD 1990; DSc 2006); Univ. of London (MSc 1986). MRCP 1982, FRCP 1995; MFCM 1988, FFPH (FFCM 1994); FRCPI 1997; FRCPE 2010. Jun. med. posts, Belfast City Hosp., Royal Victoria Hosp., Islington HA, 1979–89; Lectr, Sen. Lectr, then Reader, LSHTM, Univ. of London, 1987–97. Ed., Eur. Jl of Public Health, 1993–2009. Founding Director: WHO Collaborating Centre on Health of Socs in Transition, 1997–2014; Res. Policy, Eur. Observatory on Health Systems and Policies, 1998–; Chm., WHO Eur. Adv. Cttee on Health Res., 2008–13. Member: Public Health sub-bd, 1998–2004, Global Health Adv. Cttee, 2004– (Chm., 2010–), Open Society Inst.; BUPA Med. Adv. Panel, 1999–2012; Expert Panel on Effective Ways of Investing in Health, EC, 2013–. Mem. Council, UK Public Health Assoc., 2009–10; Chm., Soc. for Social Medicine, 2010; Pres., European Public Health Assoc., 2014–. Visiting Professor: Univs of Belgrade and Zagreb, 2005; LSE, 2009–; Taipei Med. Univ., 2010. Lectures: Ferenc Bojan, EUPHA, 1997; Sir Stanley Davidson, RCPE, 2003; Salvatore Lucia, UCSF, 2004; Milroy, RCP, 2005; DARE, FPH, 2006; Cochrane, Soc. for Social Medicine, 2006; Victor Horsley, BMA, 2010; Thackrah, Leeds Univ., 2011; Hjelt, Helsinki Univ., 2011; Duncan, Liverpool Univ., 2012; Sir Thomas and Lady Edith Dixon, Ulster Med. Soc., 2015; Albert Neuberger, Hebrew Univ., 2015. FMedSci 2000; FRSocMed 1985. Hon. Mem., Romanian Acad. of Med. Scis, 1999; For. Associate Mem., US Inst. of Medicine, 2006. Hon. Dr: Debrecen, 1998; Maastricht, 2006; Karlstad, 2010; Nordic Sch. of Public Health, 2013. Andrija Stampar Medal, Assoc. of Schs of Public Health in the Eur. Region, 2003; Alwyn Smith Prize, FPH, 2014; Donabedian Internat. Award, 2015. *Publications:* (ed jtly) International Co-operation and Health, 2001; (ed with Judith Healy) Hospitals in a Changing Europe, 2002; (with Elias Mossialos) EU Law and the Social Character of Health Care, 2002; (jtly) The Impact of EU Law on Health Care Systems, 2002; (ed with Judith Healy) Accessing Health Care: responding to diversity, 2004; (jtly) Health Policy and European Union Enlargement, 2004; (ed with Joceline Pomerleau) Issues in Public Health, 2005; (jtly) Human Resources for Health in Europe, 2005; (jtly) Health: a vital investment for economic development in eastern Europe and central Asia, 2007; (jtly) Responding to the Challenge of Cancer in Europe, 2008; (jtly) Health Systems and the Challenge of Communicable Disease: experiences from Europe and Latin America, 2008; (with Ellen Nolte) Caring for People with Chronic Conditions: a health system perspective, 2008; (jtly) Investing in Hospitals of the Future, 2009; (with Johan Mackenbach) Successes and Failures of Health Policy in Europe, 2013; (with Ingrid Wolfe) European Child Health: services and systems, 2013; over 820 papers in learned jls, esp. on health and health policy in Europe. *Recreations:* reading, ski-ing, complaining about politicians, running through airports, damage control on daughters' credit cards. *Address:* London School of Hygiene and Tropical Medicine, 15–17 Tavistock Place, WC1H 9SH. *T:* (020) 7927 2229. *E:* martin.mckee@lshtm.ac.uk. *Club:* Athenæum.

McKEE, David John; writer, illustrator, painter and film maker; *b* 2 Jan. 1935; *m* Barbara Ennuss (decd); two *s* one *d.* *Educ:* Tavistock Grammar Sch.; Plympton Grammar Sch.; Plymouth Coll. of Art; Hornsey Coll. of Art. Freelance cartoonist, 1955–; films incl. Mr Benn (14 films), 1970; Founder and Dir, King Rollo Films Ltd, 1979–2004; Dir, Rollo Rights Ltd, 2004–. Hon. Dr Open, 2012; Hon. DArts Plymouth, 2012. *Publications:* include: Bronto's Wings, 1964; Two Can Toucan, 1964; Mr Benn series, 1967–; Elmer series, 1968–; Melric the Magician, 1970; Two Admirals, 1977; Tusk Tusk, 1978; King Rollo, 1979; Adventures of King Rollo, 1982; Not Now Bernard, 1980; I Hate My Teddy Bear, 1982; Further Adventures of King Rollo, 1983; Two Monsters, 1985; King Rollo's Letter and Other Stories, 1986; Sad Story of Veronica Who Played the Violin, 1988; Snow Woman, 1989; Zebra's Hiccups, 1991; Isabel's Noisy Tummy, 1994; Charlotte's Piggy Bank, 1996; Monster and the Teddy Bear, 1997; Prince Peter and the Teddy Bear, 1999; Mary's Secret, 1999; King Rollo's New Stockings, 2001; The Conquerors, 2004; Three Monsters, 2006; Four Red Apples, 2006; Denver, 2010. *Address:* c/o Andersen Press, 20 Vauxhall Bridge Road, SW1V 2SA.

McKEE, Grant; *see* McKee, C. D. G.

McKEE, Dr Ian Hume, MBE 2006; Member (SNP) Lothians, Scottish Parliament, 2007–11; *b* 2 April 1940; *s* of late John and Marjory McKee; *m* 1992, Penelope Ann Watson (*née* Bartlett); one *s* two *d*, and one step *s* one step *d.* *Educ:* Fettes Coll., Edinburgh; Univ. of Edinburgh (MB ChB 1965); DRCOG 1970. House Officer: Ingham Infirmary, South Shields, 1965–66; Royal Infirmary, Edinburgh, 1966; MO, RAF, 1966–71; Gen. Med. Practitioner, Sighthill and Wester Hailes Health Centres, 1971–2006. Man. Dir, Hermiston Publications Ltd, 1979–95; Dir, One City Trust Ltd, 2007–08. Scottish Advr, ABPI, 1985–2002. Medical Columnist: Daily Record, 1990–97; Scotsman, 2003–06. Columnist, Scotsman, 2008–09. Mem., Lord Provost of Edinburgh's Commn on Social Exclusion, 1999–2002. Scottish Parliament: Dep. Convener, Subordinate Legislation Cttee, 2008–11, End of Life Assistance Bill Cttee, 2010–11; Mem., Health-Sport Cttee, 2007–11. Fellow, Soc. of Medical Writers, 2007–. Mem., Medical Journalists' Assoc., 1982–. Dir, St Mary's Music Sch., Edinburgh, 2011–. Mem., Merchants' Co., City of Edinburgh, 1982–; Burgess and Freeman, City of Edinburgh, 2007. Friend of Foreign Service Medal (Taiwan), 2011. *Recreations:* hill walking, boating, supporting unsuccessful football clubs, admiring finer things in life, making marmalade. *Address:* Flat 1, 4 The Cedars, Edinburgh EH13 0PL. *Clubs:* Royal Air Force; Scottish National Party (Edinburgh).

McKEE, Martin; *see* McKee, C. M.

McKEE, Richard Anthony; a Judge of the Upper Tribunal (Immigration and Asylum Chamber) (formerly a Senior Immigration Judge, Asylum and Immigration Tribunal), 2006–14; *b* 28 Sept. 1948; *s* of Ian and Ilse McKee. *Educ:* Campbell Coll., Belfast; Jesus Coll., Cambridge (BA Classics 1971); Sch. of Oriental and African Studies, London (MA Linguistics 1983). Lectr in Linguistics, PCL, Central Sch. of Speech and Drama, and Goldsmiths' Coll., London Univ., 1984–90. Called to the Bar, Inner Temple, 1991; in practice as barrister, 1993–2000; Immigration Adjudicator, 2000–06. Mem., Editl Adv. Bd, Jl of Immigration, Asylum and Nationality Law, 1997–2014; Gen. Ed., Butterworth's Immigration Law Service, 2010–14; Dep. Ed., Immigration Case Rev., 2011–13. *Publications:* (jtly) United Kingdom Asylum Law in its European Context, 1999; (contrib.) Butterworths Immigration Law Service, 1999–; (contrib.) Jackson & Warr's Immigration Law and Practice, 2001– (Co-Ed., 2013–14); compiler, Immigration Law Update, 2002–10; numerous articles on immigration and asylum law in various jls. *Recreations:* assiduous gym membership - in vain attempt to combat the effects of wining, dining and general conviviality. *Address:* 71A Victoria Road, NW6 6TB.

McKEE, William Stewart, CBE 2006; management consultant; Chief Executive, Belfast Health and Social Care Trust, 2007–10; *b* 22 Jan. 1952; *s* of James Gardiner McKee and Margaret Elisabeth McKee; *m* 1983, Ursula Byrne; one *s* one *d.* *Educ:* Queen's Univ., Belfast (BSc Hons); Univ. of Ulster (MBA). NHS Nat. Trng Scheme, 1976–78; various NHS mgt posts, NI, 1978–93; Chief Exec., Royal Hosps, Belfast, 1993–2006. Pres., IHM, 2000–02. *Address:* Cluntagh House, 33 Cluntagh Road, Hillsborough, Co. Down BT26 6BW.

McKEEVER, Prof. Ian, RA 2003; artist; Professor in Painting, University of Brighton, since 2001; Professor of Drawing, Royal Academy School of Arts, London, 2006–11; Member of Council, Royal Academy of Arts, 2013–15 (Chairman, Collections and Library Committee, 2009–15); *b* 30 Nov. 1946; *m* 1991, Gerlinde Gabriel; one *s* one *d.* *Educ:* Withernsea High Sch.; Avery Hill Coll. of Educn, London (DipEd). Exhibitions include: Kunst Forum, Städtische Galerie im Lenbachhaus, Munich, 1989; Whitechapel Art Gall., 1990; Haggerty Mus. of Art, Milwaukee, 1994; Kunsthallen Brandts Klaedefabrik, Odense, 2001, 2007; Horsen Kunstmus., Horsens, 2002, 2014; Kettle's Yard, Cambridge, 2004; China Art Gall., Beijing and Nat. Gall., Shanghai, 2005; Morat Inst. für Kunst und Kunstwissenschaft, Freiburg, 2005, 2007; Ny Carlsberg Glyptotek, Copenhagen, 2006; Kings Place Gallery, London, 2009; Galerie Forsblom, Helsinki, 2009; Galleri Sandström Andersson, Stockholm, 2009, 2013; Galleri Susanne Ottesen, Copenhagen, 2010, 2014; RA, 2010, Mus. Sønderjylland, Tønder, 2011, 2015; Tate Britain, 2011; Seongnam Arts Center, S Korea, 2011; Nat. Mus. of Art, Oslo, 2012; Josef Albers Mus., Quadrat Bottrop, Germany, 2012; Queen's Gall., Buckingham Palace, 2013; HackelBury Fine Art, London, 2014; Kunst-Station Sankt Peter, Cologne, 2014; work in collections, including: Tate Gall., London; BM; Govt Art Collection; British Council; Arts Council of GB; Scottish Nat. Gall. of Modern Art; Metropolitan Mus. of Modern Art, NY; Brooklyn Mus.; Boston Mus. of Fine Arts; Cincinnati Mus. of Modern Art; Louisiana Mus., Denmark; Mus. des 20 Jahrhunderts, Vienna; Ny Carlsberg Glyptotek, Copenhagen; Mus. of Contemp. Art, Helsinki; Yale Center for British Art, Connecticut; Royal Acad. of Arts; Royal Collection Trust, London. *Publications:* In Praise of Painting: three essays, 2005; *relevant publications:* Ian McKeever - Paintings, by M. Allthorpe-Guyton, M. Tucker and C. Lampert, 2009; Artists' Laboratory - Ian McKeever: Hartgrove paintings and photographs, 2010; Black and Black Again… Paintings 1987–2010, 2011; Ian McKeever: Hartgrove, 2012. *Address:* c/o Royal Academy of Arts, Burlington House, Piccadilly, W1J 0BD.

MacKEITH, Prof. Margaret Anne, CBE 1997; PhD; FRTPI; FRGS; town planning consultant; Consultant, MacKeith Dickinson & Partners Ltd, 2000–11; Pro Vice-Chancellor, University of Central Lancashire (formerly Lancashire Polytechnic), 1995–99; *b* 26 June 1939; *d* of James and Gertrude Crane; *m* 1962, Charles Gordon MacKeith; two *s.* *Educ:* Shirebrook Grammar Sch., Derbyshire; Univ. of Manchester (DipTP, MA); Heriot-Watt Univ. (PhD). FRTPI 1980; FRGS 1976; MIEnvSc 1977. Planning Officer, Lancs CC, 1961–63; Consultant to MacKeith Dickinson and Partners, 1963–74; Lancashire Polytechnic: Sen., then Principal, Lectr, 1975–87; Hd, Sch. of Construction and Surveying, 1987–90; Dean, Faculty of Technol., 1987–90, Faculty of Design and Technol., 1990–95. Consultant, TradePoint Systems USA, 1999–2003. Mem., Royal Fine Art Commn, 1993–99. Member: BTEC Cttees, 1988–93; NW Cttee, OFFER, 1990–93; Landscape Adv. Cttee, Dept of Transport, 1991–93; NRA NW Cttee, 1994–97. Trustee, Nat. Museums Liverpool (formerly Nat. Museums and Galls on Merseyside), 2000–09. Hon. Prof., Transylvania Univ., Romania, 1998. FRSA 1990. Dr *hc* Cluj, Romania, 1994. *Publications:* Shopping Arcades 1817–1939, 1985; History and Conservation of Shopping Arcades, 1986; articles and conf. papers on conservation, engrg educn and women in engrg and technol. *Recreations:* travel, architectural history, music, opera. *Address:* 104 Breck Road, Poulton-le-Fylde, Lancs FY6 7HT. *T:* (01253) 884774; 4 Breton House, Barbican, EC2Y 8DG.

McKELLAR, Prof. Quintin Archibald, CBE 2011; PhD, DVM; CBiol, FRSB, FRAgS; FRSE; Vice Chancellor, University of Hertfordshire, since 2011; *b* 24 Dec. 1958; *s* of Quintin and Elizabeth McKellar; *m* 1984, Patricia Law; one *s* three *d.* *Educ:* Glasgow Univ. (BVMS 1981; PhD 1984; DVM 2002); Eur. Coll. Vet. Pharmacol. and Toxicol. (DipECVPT). MRCVS 1981; CBiol, FRSB (FIBiol 2001); FRAgS 2003. University of Glasgow: Lectr, 1984–96; Prof. of Veterinary Pharmacol., 1996–97; Chief Exec. and Scientific Dir, Moredun Res. Inst., 1997–2004; Prof. of Veterinary Pharmacol. and Principal, RVC, Univ. of London, 2004–10. Chm., Regulatory Agencies Strategy Bd, 2005–08; Member: Veterinary Products Cttee, 1993–2001; Council, BBSRC, 2005–11; Science Adv. Council, DEFRA, 2011–14; non-exec. Dir, Animal and Plant Health Agency, 2013–. Gov., Inst. Animal Health, 2003–09 and 2011–13; Chm. of Trustees, Pirbright Inst., 2014–. Gov., Queenswood Sch., 2011–. FRSE 2003. *Publications:* numerous contribs to scientific literature. *Recreation:* rowing. *Address:* University of Hertfordshire, College Lane, Hatfield, Herts AL10 9AB. *Clubs:* Athenæum; Leander (Henley-on-Thames).

McKELLEN, Sir Ian (Murray), CH 2008; Kt 1991; CBE 1979; actor and director, since 1961; *b* 25 May 1939; *s* of late Denis Murray McKellen and Margery (*née* Sutcliffe). *Educ:* Wigan Grammar Sch.; Bolton Sch.; St Catharine's Coll., Cambridge (BA; Hon. Fellow, 1982). Cameron Mackintosh Prof. of Contemporary Theatre, Univ. of Oxford, 1991–92. Pres., Marlowe Soc., 1960–61. Elected to Council of Equity, 1971–72. Hon. DLitt Nottingham, 1989. 1st appearance (stage): Belgrade Theatre, Coventry, in a Man for all Seasons, Sept. 1961; Arts Theatre, Ipswich, 1962–63; Nottingham Playhouse, 1963–64; 1st London stage appearance, Duke of York's in A Scent of Flowers, 1964 (Clarence Derwent Award); Recruiting Officer, Chips with Everything, Cambridge Theatre Co., 1971; Founder Mem., Actors Company: Ruling the Roost, 'Tis Pity She's a Whore, Edin. Fest., 1972; Knots, Wood-Demon, Edin. Fest., 1973, and with King Lear, Brooklyn Acad. of Music, Wimbledon Theatre season, 1974; *London stage appearances:* A Lily in Little India, St Martin's; Man of Destiny/O'Flaherty VC, Mermaid Theatre; Their Very Own and Golden City, Royal Court, 1966; The Promise, Fortune, 1967 (also Broadway); White Lies/Black Comedy, Lyric; Richard II, Prospect Theatre Co., 1968 (revived with Edward II, Edin. Fest., British and European tours); Hamlet, Cambridge, 1971 (British and European tours); Ashes, Young Vic, 1975; Bent, Royal Court, Criterion, 1979 (SWET Award, 1979); Short List, Hampstead, 1983; Cowardice, Ambassadors, 1983; Henceforward, Vaudeville, 1988; Dance of Death, Lyric, 2003; Aladdin, Old Vic, 2004, 2005; The Cut, Donmar Warehouse, 2006; Waiting for Godot, UK tour then Theatre Royal Haymarket, 2009, internat. tour, 2010, NY 2013; No Man's Land, NY, 2013; *with Royal National Theatre:* Much Ado About Nothing, Old Vic, 1965; Armstrong's Last Goodnight, Trelawney of the Wells, Chichester Fest., 1965; Venice Preserv'd, Wild Honey (Laurence Olivier Award, Plays and Players Award; Los Angeles and NY, 1986–87), Coriolanus (London Standard Award), South Bank, 1984–85; as Assoc. Dir, produced and acted in The Duchess of Malfi, The Real Inspector Hound with The Critic, The Cherry Orchard (Paris and Chicago), 1984–85; Bent, 1990 (also Garrick); Kent in King Lear, and title role, Richard III, 1990 (Laurence Olivier Award; Assoc. Prod. for world tour, 1990–91); Napoli Milionaria, 1991; Uncle Vanya, 1992; Richard III, US tour, 1992; An Enemy of the People, Peter Pan, 1997–98; *with Royal Shakespeare Co.:* Dr Faustus, Edin. Fest. and Aldwych, 1974; Marquis of Keith, Aldwych, 1974–75; King John, Aldwych, 1975; Too Good to be True, Aldwych and Globe, 1975; Romeo and Juliet, The Winter's Tale, Macbeth (Plays and Players Award, 1976), Stratford, 1976–77; Every Good Boy Deserves Favour, RFH, 1977, Barbican, 1982; Romeo and Juliet, Macbeth, Pillars of the Community (SWET Award, 1977), Days of the Commune, The Alchemist (SWET Award, 1978), Aldwych and RSC Warehouse, 1977–78; King Lear, The Seagull, Stratford and world tour, 2007; Prod. RSC Tour, 1978: Three Sisters, Twelfth Night, Is There Honey Still for Tea; Iago in Othello, The Other Place, Stratford and Young Vic, 1989, BBC TV (Evening Standard and London Critics' Award); *with W Yorks Playhouse, Leeds:* The Seagull, Present Laughter, 1998; The Tempest, 1999; *Directed:* Liverpool Playhouse, 1969; Watford and Leicester, 1972; A Private Matter, Vaudeville, 1973; The Clandestine Marriage, Savoy, 1975; *other performances include:* Words, Words, Words (solo recital), Edin. Fest. and Belfast Fest., 1976 (with Acting Shakespeare, Edin. and Belfast, 1977); Amadeus, Broadhurst, NY, 1980–81 (Drama Desk, NY Drama League, Outer Critics' Circle and Tony Awards); A Knight Out, NY, S Africa, UK, 1994–95; Dance of Death, NY, 2001; The Syndicate, Chichester Festival Th., 2011; *Acting Shakespeare tours:* Israel, Norway, Denmark, Sweden, 1980; Spain, France, Cyprus, Israel, Poland, Romania, 1982; Los Angeles and Ritz, NYC (Drama Desk Award), 1983; San Francisco, Washington DC, Los Angeles, Olney, Cleveland, San Diego, Boston (Elliot Norton Award), 1987 Playhouse, London, 1987–88. *Films:* A Touch of Love, Alfred the Great, 1968; The Promise, 1969; Priest of Love, 1979; Scarlet Pimpernel, 1982; Plenty, Zina, 1985; Scandal, 1988; The Ballad of Little Jo, 1992; Six Degrees of Separation, Last Action Hero, 1993; The Shadow, Jack and Sarah, 1994; Restoration, 1995; Richard III (European Actor of the Year, Berlin Film Fest.), Swept from the Sea, 1996; Apt Pupil, Bent, 1997; Gods and Monsters, 1998; X-Men, 2000; The Fellowship of the Ring, 2001; The Two Towers, 2002; X-Men 2, Return of the King, 2003; Emile, 2004; Asylum, Sprung!, 2005; The Da Vinci Code, X-Men: The Last Stand, Neverwas, Flushed Away, 2006; Stardust, The Golden Compass, 2007; The Hobbit: An Unexpected Journey, 2012; The Hobbit: The Desolation of Smaug, 2013; X-Men: Days of Future Past, The Hobbit: The Battle of the Five Armies, 2014; Mr Holmes, 2015. Has appeared on television, 1966–, incl. Walter, 1982 (RTS Performance Award for 1982); Walter and June, 1983; Mister Shaw's Missing Millions, 1993; Tales of the City, 1993; Cold Comfort Farm, 1995; Rasputin, 1996 (Golden Globe Award); The Prisoner, 2010; Vicious, 2013, 2015; radio performances include Walter Now, 2009. Hon. DLitt Cambridge, 2014. *Address:* c/o Independent Talent Group Ltd, 40 Whitfield Street, W1T 2RH. *T:* (020) 7636 6565, *Fax:* (020) 7323 0101. *W:* www.mckellen.com.

McKELVEY, Very Rev. Houston; *see* McKelvey, Very Rev. R. S. J. H.

McKELVEY, Rev. Dr Robert John; Principal, Northern College, Manchester, 1979–93; Moderator, General Assembly of the United Reformed Church, 1994–95; *b* 12 Oct. 1929; *s* of Robert John McKelvey and Eleanor McMaster McKelvey (*née* Earls); *m* 1957, Martha Esther Skelly; two *s* one *d.* *Educ:* Paton Congregational Coll.; Nottingham Univ. (BA 1955); Pittsburgh Theol Seminary (MTh 1956); Mansfield Coll., Oxford (DPhil 1959). Tutor, 1959–67, Principal, 1968–74, Adams United Coll., S Africa; Pres., Federal Theol Seminary of S Africa, 1970–71; Dir, Internship Trng, United Congregational Church of S Africa, 1975–78; Pres., Northern Fedn for Trng in Ministry, 1984–86. *Publications:* The New Temple: the Church in the New Testament, 1969; The Millennium and the Book of Revelation, 1999; contributor to: New Bible Dictionary, 1962; The Illustrated Bible Dictionary, 1980; New 20th Century Encyclopedia of Religious Knowledge, 2nd edn 1991; New Dictionary of Biblical Theology, 2000; Studies in the Book of Revelation, 2001; Pioneer and Priest: Jesus Christ in the Epistle to the Hebrews, 2013; learned jls incl. NT Studies, Jl of Theol Studies. *Recreations:* gardening, walking, travel, oddjobbery. *Address:* 64 Brooklawn Drive, Withington, Manchester M20 3GZ. *T:* (0161) 434 4936.

McKELVEY, Very Rev. Dr (Robert Samuel James) Houston, OBE 2010; TD; QVRM 2000; Dean of Belfast, 2001–11; *b* 3 Sept. 1942; *s* of Robert and Annie McKelvey; *m* 1969, Eileen Roberta; one *s.* *Educ:* Queen's Univ., Belfast (BA 1965; MA (Ed) 1988); TCD; Garrett-Evangl Theol Seminary, Evanston, Ill. (DMin 1993; Hon. DHL 2003). Ordained deacon, 1967, priest, 1968; Curate, Dunmurry, 1967–70; Rector, Kilmakee, 1970–82; Sec., Gen. Synod Bd of Educn (NI), 1982–2001. Hon. Chaplain, RN Reserve, 2010–. Ed., Ch of Ire. Gazette, 1975–82. CF (TAVR), 1970–99. *Publications:* Forty Days with Jesus, 1991; The Apostles' Creed, 1992; Children at the Table, 1993; In Touch with God, 1997; God, our Children, and Us, 1999. *Recreations:* sailing, photography, travel. *Address:* 9 College Park, Coleraine BT51 3HE. *T:* (028) 7035 3621. *Club:* Ulster (Belfast).

McKELVEY, William; *b* Dundee, 8 July 1934; *m*; two *s.* *Educ:* Morgan Acad.; Dundee Coll. of Technology. Joined Labour Party, 1961; formerly Sec. Organiser, Lab. Party, and full-time union official. Mem., Dundee City Council. MP (Lab) Kilmarnock, 1979–83, Kilmarnock and Loudoun, 1983–97. Chm., Select Cttee on Scottish Affairs, 1992–97.

McKELVIE, Anne; *see* Neville, A.

McKELVIE, Christina; Member (SNP) Hamilton, Larkhall and Stonehouse, Scottish Parliament, since 2011 (Scotland Central, 2007–11); *b* Glasgow, 4 March 1968; *d* of David and Roseann Curran; two *s.* *Educ:* HNC Social Care. Learning Disability Services, then Learning and Develt Officer, Social Work Services, Glasgow City Council. Convenor, Eur. and External Relations Cttee, Scottish Parlt, 2011–. *Recreations:* painting, hill walking, reading. *Address:* Scottish Parliament, Edinburgh EH99 1SP. *T:* (0131) 348 6681. *E:* Christina.McKelvie.MSP@scottish.parliament.uk.

McKELVIE, Peter, FRCS, FRCSE; Consultant Ear, Nose and Throat Surgeon: London Hospital, 1971–98 (Hon. Consulting Surgeon, Bart's and the London (formerly Royal Hospitals) NHS Trust, since 1998); Royal National Throat, Nose and Ear Hospital, London, 1972–95 (Hon. Consulting Surgeon, since 1995); *b* 21 Dec. 1932; *s* of William Bryce McKelvie, MD, ChM, FRCSE, DLO, and Agnes E. McKelvie (*née* Winstanley), Headmistress; *m* Myra Chadwick, FRCP, Cons. Dermatologist; one *d.* *Educ:* Manchester Grammar Sch.; Rugby Sch.; Univ. of Manchester (MB ChB, MD, ChM). FRCS 1962, FRCSE 1989. House Surgeon: Manchester Royal Inf., 1957; Royal Nat. Throat, Nose and Ear Hosp., London, 1958; Lectr in Anatomy, KCL, 1959; Casualty Surg., St Mary's Hosp., London, 1960; Reader in Laryngology, UCL, 1968–70; Dean, Inst. of Laryngology and Otology, London, 1984–89. Examiner: London Univ.; Royal Colls of Surgeons of England, Edinburgh and Glasgow. MRSM 1966 (Pres., Laryngology Sect., 1992–93). *Publications:* numerous, on head and neck cancer. *Recreations:* mirth, watching young surgeons develop, Mediterranean Basin. *Address:* 9 Drakes Drive, Northwood, Middx HA6 2SL. *T:* (01923) 823544.

McKENDRICK, Emma Elizabeth Ann; Headmistress, Downe House, since 1997; *b* 24 June 1963; *d* of Ian and Ann Black; *m* 1987, Iain Alastair McKendrick; two *s.* *Educ:* Bedford High Sch.; Univ. of Liverpool (BA Hons German with Dutch); Univ. of Birmingham (PGCE). Royal School, Bath: Teacher of German, 1986–88; Head of Sixth Form and Careers, 1988–90; Housemistress for Sixth Form, 1989–90; Dep. Head, 1990–93; Headmistress, 1994–97. Member: Exec., Ind. Schs Exam. Bd, 2008–11; Educn Cttee, GSA, 2011–; HMC, 2015–. Governor: Hatherop Castle Prep. Sch., 1997–2002; Study Sch., Wimbledon, 1998–2006; Manor Prep. Sch., Oxford, 1998–2006; Godstowe Prep. Sch., 2000–11; Cheam Prep. Sch., 2002–13; King's Sch., Canterbury, 2003–; Sandroyd Prep. Sch., 2006–; Radley Coll., 2008–; Lambrook Sch., 2011–. FRSA 2008. *Recreations:* travel, theatre. *Address:* St Peter's House, Downe House, Cold Ash, Thatcham, Berks RG18 9JJ. *T:* (01635) 200286. *Club:* Lansdowne.

McKENDRICK, Prof. Ewan Gordon; Professor of English Private Law, since 2000, and Registrar, since 2011, University of Oxford (Chair of Board, Faculty of Law, 2004–06; Pro-Vice-Chancellor, 2006–10); Fellow, Lady Margaret Hall, Oxford, since 2000; *b* 23 Sept. 1960; *s* of Norman and Muriel McKendrick; *m* 1983, Rosemary Grace Burton-Smith; four *d.* *Educ:* Univ. of Edinburgh (LLB Hons); Pembroke Coll., Oxford (BCL). Lecturer in Law: Central Lancashire Poly., 1984–85; Univ. of Essex, 1985–88; LSE, 1988–91; Fellow, St Anne's Coll., Oxford and Linnells Lectr in Law, Univ. of Oxford, 1991–95; Prof. of English Law, UCL, 1995–2000; called to the Bar, Gray's Inn, 1998, Bencher, 2009; in practice as barrister, 1998–. Mem., AHRC, 2010–14. Hon. QC 2015. Deleg., OUP, 2005–. Gen. Editor, Oxford Jl of Legal Studies, 2006–09. *Publications:* Contract Law, 1990, 11th edn 2015; (with A. Burrows and J. Edelman) Cases and Materials on the Law of Restitution, 1997, 2nd edn 2005; (with N. E. Palmer) Interests in Goods, 1993, 2nd edn 1997; (ed) Chitty on Contracts, 27th edn 1995 to 30th edn 2008; Sale of Goods, 2000; Contract Law: text, cases and materials, 2003, 6th edn 2014. *Recreations:* reading, travel. *Address:* University Offices, Wellington Square, Oxford OX1 2JD. *T:* (01865) 270232; 3 Verulam Buildings, Gray's Inn, WC1R 5NT. *T:* (020) 7831 8441.

McKENDRICK, Prof. Melveena Christine, PhD, LittD; FBA 1999; Professor of Spanish Golden Age Literature, Culture and Society, 1999–2008, and Pro-Vice-Chancellor for Education, 2004–08, University of Cambridge; Fellow of Girton College, Cambridge, since 1967; *b* 23 March 1941; *d* of James Powell Jones and Catherine Letitia Jones (*née* Richards); *m* 1967, Neil McKendrick, *qv*; two *d.* *Educ:* Neath Girls' Grammar Sch.; Dyffryn Grammar Sch., Port Talbot; King's Coll., London (BA 1st cl. Hons Spanish); Girton Coll., Cambridge (PhD 1967); LittD Cantab, 2002. Girton College, Cambridge: Jex-Blake Res. Fellow, 1967–70; Tutor, 1970–83; Sen. Tutor, 1974–81; Dir of Studies in Modern Langs, 1984–95; Lectr in Spanish, 1980–92, Reader in Spanish Lit. and Soc., 1992–99, Univ. of Cambridge; British Acad. Reader, 1992–94. Vis. Prof., Univ. of Victoria, 1997. Member: Gen. Bd, Cambridge Univ., 1993–97 (Chair, Educn Cttee, 1995–97); Humanities Res. Bd, British Acad., 1996–98; Arts and Humanities Res. Bd, 1998–99. Consultant Hispanic Ed., Everyman, 1993–99; Member, Editorial Board: Donaire, 1994–; Revista Canadiense de Estudios Hispánicos, 1995–; Bulletin of Spanish Studies (formerly Hispanic Studies (Glasgow)), 1998–. Hon. DLitt South Wales, 2013. *Publications:* Ferdinand and Isabella, 1968; A Concise History of Spain, 1972; Woman and Society in the Spanish Drama of the Golden Age, 1974; Cervantes, 1980 (trans. Spanish 1986); (ed) Golden-Age Studies in Honour of A. A. Parker, 1984; Theatre in Spain 1490–1700, 1989 (trans. Spanish 1994); (jtly) El Mágico Prodigioso, 1992; The Revealing Image: stage portraits in the theatre of the Golden Age, 1996; Playing the King: Lope de Vega and the limits of conformity, 2000; Identities in Crisis: essays on honour, gender and women in the Comedia, 2002; *contributed to:* Critical Studies of Calderón's Comedias, 1973; Women in Hispanic Literature, 1983; El mundo del teatro en el siglo de oro, 1989; Teatro y prácticas escénicas en los siglos XVI y XVII, 1991; Feminist Readings on Spanish and Spanish-American Literature, 1991; Hacia Calderón, 1991; The Comedia in the Age of Calderón, 1993; Teatro y Poder, 1994; Heavenly Bodies, 1996; Texto e Imagen en Calderón, 1996; Calderón 1600–1681, 2000; Calderón: protagonista eminente del barroco europeo, 2000; Spanish Theatre: studies in honour of Victor F. Dixon, 2001; Never-Ending Adventure: studies in medieval and early modern Spanish literature in honour of Peter N. Dunn, 2002; Approaches to Teaching Early Modern Spanish Drama, 2006; Rhetoric and Reality in Early Modern Spain, 2006; articles on Early Modern Spanish theatre in many jls. *Address:* The Manor House, 3 High Street, Burwell, Cambridge CB25 0HB.

McKENDRICK, Neil, FRHistS; historian; Master, 1996–2005, Fellow, 1958–96 and since 2005, Gonville and Caius College, Cambridge; Reader in Social and Economic History, University of Cambridge, 1995–2002; *b* 28 July 1935; *s* of late Robert Alexander McKendrick and Sarah Elizabeth Irvine; *m* 1967, Melveena Jones (*see* M. McKendrick); two *d*. *Educ:* Alderman Newton's Sch., Leicester; Christ's Coll., Cambridge (Entrance Schol.; BA 1st cl. Hons (with distinction) History, 1956; MA 1960; Hon. Fellow, 1996). FRHistS 1971. Cambridge University: Res. Fellow, Christ's Coll., 1958; Asst Lectr in History, 1961–64; Lectr, 1964–95; Sec. to Faculty Bd of History, 1975–77; Chm., History Faculty, 1985–87; Gonville and Caius College: Lectr in History, 1958–96; Dir of Studies in History, 1959–96; Tutor, 1961–69. Lectures: Earl, Univ. of Keele, 1963; Inaugural, Wallace Gall., Colonial Williamsburg, 1985; Chettyar Meml, Univ. of Madras, 1990. Member: Tancred's Charities, 1996–; Sir John Plumb Charitable Trust, 1999–; Properties Cttee, Nat. Trust, 1999–2005; Dr E. N. Williams' Meml Fund, Dulwich Coll., 2003–; Vice-Pres., Caius Foundn in America, 1998–; Chm., Glenfield Trust, 2002–. *Publications:* (ed) Historical Perspectives: studies in English thought and society, 1974; (jtly) The Birth of a Consumer Society: the commercialization of eighteenth century England, 1982, 2nd edn 1983; (ed jtly) Business Life and Public Policy, 1986; L'Impressa Industria Commercio Banca XIII–XVIII, 1991; The Birth of Foreign & Colonial: the world's first investment trust, 1993; Il Tempo Libero Economia e Societa Secc XIII–XVIII, 1995; (jtly) 'F & C': a history of Foreign & Colonial Investment Trust, 1999; contributed to: Essays in Economic History, ed E. M. Carus Wilson, 1962; Rise of Capitalism, ed D. S. Landes, 1966; Changing Perspectives in the History of Science, ed M. Teich and R. M. Young, 1971; The Historical Development of Accounting, ed B. S. Yamey, 1978; Science and Culture in the Western Tradition, ed J. Burke, 1987; Industry and Modernization, ed Wang Jue-fei, 1989; The Social History of Western Civilization, ed R. Golden, 1992; The Other Side of Western Civilization, ed P. Stearns, 1992; The History of Enterprise, ed S. Jones and J. Inggs, 1993; The Industrial Revolution in Britain, ed J. Hoppit and E. A. Wrigley, 1994; Europäische Konsumgeschichte, ed H. Siegrist, H. Kaelble and J. Kocka, 1997; The Modern Historiography Reader: western sources, ed A. Budd, 2008; Hunting Scraps: the hunting diary of Charles James Cropper, 2013; articles in learned jls, mainly on Josiah Wedgwood and the Industrial Revolution. *Recreations:* gardening, antiques, claret, photography, my wife and daughters. *Address:* Gonville and Caius College, Cambridge CB2 1TA. *T:* (01223) 332404; The Manor House, 3 High Street, Burwell, Cambridge CB25 0HB. *T:* (01638) 742312. *E:* nm10000@cam.ac.uk. *Club:* Athenæum.

McKENNA, Alison Jayne; President, First-tier Tribunal (War Pensions and Armed Forces Compensation Chamber), since 2014; Principal Judge, First-tier Tribunal (Charity) (formerly President, Charity Tribunal), since 2008 and Judge, Upper Tribunal (Tax and Chancery Chamber), since 2009, and Upper Tribunal (Administrative Appeals Chamber), since 2009; *b* Redhill, Surrey, 12 Nov. 1963; *d* of Peter and Evelyn Lee; *m* 1998, Jack McKenna (marr. diss. 2011); one *d*. *Educ:* Our Lady's Abingdon; Poly. of the South Bank (LLB 1987); Inns of Court Sch. of Law (Bar Finals). Called to the Bar, Middle Temple, 1988; in practice as a barrister, 1988–93; Investigator, Commn for Local Admin in England, 1993–96; Legal Adviser: Criminal Appeals Office, 1996–97; Charity Commn, 1997–2002; Hd, Charities Dept, Wilsons LLP, 2002–08; admitted Solicitor-Advocate, 2003. Member: Mental Health Act Commn, 1996–2002; Judicial Appts Commn, 2012–14. *Recreation:* anything involving horses. *Address:* First-tier Tribunal (War Pensions and Armed Forces Compensation Chamber), 5th Floor, Fox Court, 14 Gray's Inn Road, WC1X 8HN. *T:* (020) 3206 0701, *Fax:* 0870 324 0104. *E:* Alison.McKenna@judiciary.gsi.gov.uk.

McKENNA, Hon. Francis Joseph, (Frank); PC (Can.) 1987; OC 2008; Deputy Chairman, TD Bank Financial Group, since 2006; *b* 19 Jan. 1948; *s* of Durward and Olive McKenna; *m* Julie Friel; two *s* one *d*. *Educ:* Sussex High Sch.; St Francis Xavier Univ. (BA); Queen's Univ.; Univ. of New Brunswick (LLB). Lawyer; Mem., NB and Canadian Bar Assocs. MLA (L) Chatham, NB, 1982–97; Leader, NB Liberal Party, 1985–97; Premier of NB, 1987–97. Counsel, McInnes Cooper, 1998; Ambassador of Canada to the USA, 2005–06. Hon. DSP Moncton, 1988; Hon. LLD New Brunswick, 1988. Vanier Award, 1988. *Address:* TD Bank Financial Group, TD Tower, 66 Wellington Street West, Toronto, ON M5K 1A2, Canada.

McKENNA, Geraldine Martina Maria; Partner, Cedar Capital Partners, since 2009; *b* 9 Aug. 1955; *d* of late John and Mary McKenna. *Educ:* Loreto Convent, Omagh, NI. British Airways, NI, 1976–81; Enterprise Travel (Aer Lingus), Florida, 1981–84; Belfast City Airport, 1984–87; Inter-Continental Hotel Corp., 1987–96; Gp Dir, Mktg and Sales, Savoy Gp, 1996–2002; Chief Exec., Maybourne Hotel Gp (formerly Savoy Gp), 2002–06. Non-exec. Dir, GuestInvest, 2006–; Advr, Fraser Giles Partnership, 2008–. Mem., British Airways Internat. Business Adv. Gp, 2013–. FRSA 2002. Hon. DHL Schiller Internat., 2004. *Recreations:* sailing, horse-riding, travel. *E:* Geraldine_McKenna@hotmail.com.

McKENNA, Rev. Lindsay Taylor Francis; Vicar, St Andrew the Apostle, Catford, since 2011 (Priest-in-charge, 2010–11); *b* Glasgow, 7 July 1962; *s* of Francis Christopher McKenna and Elizabeth Colquhoun McKenna (*née* Taylor). *Educ:* Univ. of Glasgow (MA Hons 1983); Univ. of Aberdeen (BD 1986); Edinburgh Theol Coll. Ordained deacon, 1987, priest, 1988; Curate, St Mary's, Broughty Ferry, 1987–90; Senior Curate, Wantage, 1990–93; Vicar, St Mary the Virgin, Illingworth, 1993–99; Pastor-Dir, CARA Trust, 1999–2002; Vicar, All Saints, Hanworth, 2002–08; Rector and Provost, St Paul's Cathedral, Dundee, 2008–09. *Recreations:* gardening, keeping fit, cooking, the company of friends, Modern Spanish history, lunch.

McKENNA, Martin Nicholas; His Honour Judge McKenna; a Circuit Judge, since 2000; a Senior Circuit Judge, since 2008; *b* 19 Nov. 1955; *s* of Bernard Malcolm McKenna and Anne Rose McKenna; *m* 1st, 1979, Deborah Jane Scott (marr. diss. 1995); two *d*; 2nd, 1996, Sarah Louise Malden; two step *d*. *Educ:* Birmingham Univ. (LLB 1st Cl. Hons); Lincoln Coll., Oxford. Admitted Solicitor, 1980. Joined Evershed & Tomkinson, Solicitors, 1978: Associate, 1984–87; Partner, 1987–2000; Head of Litigation Dept, 1994–99. Midland Circuit. *Recreations:* Rugby, cricket, sailing, ski-ing. *Address:* Priory Courts, 33 Bull Street, Birmingham B4 6DW. *Club:* East India.

McKENNA, Maureen, OBE 2015; Executive Director of Education (formerly Service Director Education), Glasgow City Council, since 2007; *b* Edinburgh, 2 July 1960; *d* of Adrian and Sheila Hynes; *m* Jack McKenna; two *s* one *d*. *Educ:* Bearsden Acad.; Univ. of Glasgow (BSc Hons Maths); Jordanhill Coll. (PGCE). Maths teacher, Dyce Acad., 1982–85; Asst Principal Teacher, Ellon Acad., 1985–89; Principal Teacher, Northfield Acad., 1989–91; Principal Teacher, 1991–97, Asst Head Teacher, 1997–2000, Kilsyth Acad.; HM Inspector of Educn, 2000–07. Hon. Vice Pres., Basketball Scotland, 2009. *Recreation:* basketball referee (qualified 1980; international referee, 1990; retired 2009). *E:* maureen.mckenna@education.glasgow.gov.uk.

McKENNA, Prof. Patrick Gerald, (Gerry); DL; PhD; Vice-Chancellor and President, University of Ulster, 1999–2006; geneticist; *b* 10 Dec. 1953; *s* of late Gerald Joseph McKenna and Mary Teresa (*née* Smyth); *m* 1976, Philomena Winifred McArdle; two *s*. *Educ:* Univ. of Ulster (BSc 1st Cl. Hons 1976); PhD Genetics, QUB, 1979. FIBMS 1982; FRSB (FIBiol 1988); MRIA 2001; CSci 2006. Lectr, Human Biology, NUU, 1979–84; University of Ulster: Sen. Lectr, Biology, 1984–88; Dir, Biomedical Scis Res. Centre, 1985–88; Prof. and Head of Dept of Biol and Biomed. Scis, 1988–94; Dean, Faculty of Science, 1994–97; Pro-Vice-Chancellor (Res.), 1997–99. Visiting Professor: Univ. Kebangsaan, Malaysia, 1992; Univ. of Malaya, 1993; Univ. of Calif, Berkeley, 2005. Chairman: NI Foresight, Life and Health Technologies Panel, 1995–99; Heads of Univ. Centres Biomed. Sci., 1995–97 (Pres., Emeritus, 2000–; Hon. Exec. Sec., 2011–); UU-Online.com, 2000–05; Univ. of Ulster Sci. Res. Parks Ltd, 2002–04; Univs Ireland, 2003–05; Founder: UU Step Up Programme, 1999; UU e-learning (Campus One), 2001; Harry Ferguson Engineering Village, Jordanstown, 2004; Co-Founder: Universities Ireland, 1993; NI Centre for Diet and Health, 1995; non-executive Director: NI Med. Physics Agency, 1995–2001; NI Sci. Park Foundn, 1999–2005; UK eUnivs Worldwide, 2000–06; eUniv. Hldg Co., 2001–06; UUTECH Ltd, 1997–2005 (Chair, 2002–05); Bd Mem., ILEX, 2003–05. Advr, Biomedical Scis Dept, Hong Kong Polytechnic Univ., 2011–; REF 2014 advr to UK univs, 2012–. Member: Council, Inst. of Biomed. Sci., 1996–2002; Jt Med. Adv. Cttee, 2003–04; Founding Bd Mem., UK Health Educn Partnership, 2003–05. Mem., Shadow Bd for E-nursing educn, 2001–02. Member: US-Ireland R&D Taskforce, 2002–04; Bd, BITC NI, 2002–03; Sci., Engrg and Envmt Adv. Cttee, British Council, 2003–05; Science All-Party Gp, Stormont, 2012–; Exec. Cttee, Heads of Univ. Biosciences, 2013–; Educn Policy Adv. Cttee, Soc. of Biol., 2014–; QAA Benchmarking Wkg Gp, Bioscis, 2014–, Biomed. Scis, 2014–. Royal Irish Academy: Member: North-South Standing Cttee, 2012–; All-island and Internat. Working Gp, 2013–; Standing Cttee for Council-nominated Members, 2014–; Steering Cttee on Govtl Structure for HE and Res., 2015. Vice-Chm., Ulster Cancer Foundn, 1999–2005; Chm., Servite Priory Liby Project Bd, 2011–. Chm., Review Gp, British Jl of Biomed. Sci., 2013. Mem., Armagh Rotary Club, 2015–. Freedom, Borough of Coleraine, 2001; Keys to City of Portland, Maine, 2003. DL Co. Londonderry, 2002. FRSA 1999. Hon. DSc NUI, 2001; Hon. LLD QUB, 2002. Honoree: Friends of Harvard Celtic Studies, 2002; Flax Trust, New York, 2003. *Publications:* over 200 articles on genetics and research policy. *Recreations:* reading, the turf. *Address:* Lemneigh, 20 Tobermesson Road, Dungannon, Northern Ireland BT71 7QE. *T:* 07766 745511. *E:* mckenna.gerry@rocketmail.com. *Club:* Reform.

McKENNA, Rosemary, CBE 1995; *b* 8 May 1941; *d* of Cornelius Harvey and Mary (*née* Crossan); *m* 1963, James S. McKenna; three *s* one *d*. *Educ:* St Augustine's, Glasgow; Notre Dame Coll. (Dip. Primary Educn). Private sec., 1958–64; teacher, various primary schs, 1974–94. Member (Lab): Cumbernauld and Kilsyth DC, 1984–96 (Leader, 1984–88 and 1992–94; Provost, 1988–92); N Lanarks Council, 1995–97. Pres., COSLA, 1994–96. MP (Lab) Cumbernauld and Kilsyth, 1997–2005, Cumbernauld, Kilsyth and Kirkintilloch E, 2005–10. PPS to Minister of State for Foreign and Commonwealth Affairs, 1998–2001. Member, Select Committee: on culture, media and sport, 2001–10; on procedure, 2001–10; Chm., Cttee of Selection, 2005–10. Mem., Cttee of Regions of EU, 1994–98; Chm., UK and European Standing Cttees, CEMR, 1996–98. Chm., Scottish Libraries and Inf. Council, 1998–2002. Member, Management Board: Cumbernauld Coll., 2011–; New College, Lanarkshire, 2014–. *Recreations:* reading, travelling, family gatherings. *Address:* 7 Scott Drive, Cumbernauld G67 4LB.

MACKENZIE, family name of **Earl of Cromartie** and **Barons MacKenzie of Culkein** and **Mackenzie of Framwellgate**.

MACKENZIE of Gairloch; *see* Inglis of Glencorse.

MacKENZIE OF CULKEIN, Baron *cr* 1999 (Life Peer), of Assynt in Highland; **Hector Uisdean MacKenzie;** Associate General Secretary, UNISON, 1993–2000; *b* 25 Feb. 1940; *s* of George MacKenzie and Williamina Budge Sutherland; *m* 1961, Anna Morrison (marr. diss.); one *s* three *d*. *Educ:* Nicolson Inst., Stornoway, Isle of Lewis; Portree High Sch., Skye; Leverndale School of Nursing, Glasgow; West Cumberland School of Nursing, Whitehaven. RGN, RMN. Student Nurse, Leverndale Hosp., 1958–61; Asst Lighthouse Keeper, Clyde Lighthouses Trust, 1961–64; Student Nurse, 1964–66, Staff Nurse, 1966–69, West Cumberland Hosp.; Confederation of Health Service Employees: Asst Regl Sec., 1969; Regl Sec., Yorks and E Midlands, 1970–74; Nat. Officer, 1974–83; Asst Gen. Sec., 1983–87; Gen. Sec., 1987–93. Co. Sec., UIA Insurance Ltd, 1996–2000. Pres., TUC, 1998–99. *Recreations:* reading, aviation, maritime issues, travel. *Address:* House of Lords, SW1A 0PW. *T:* (020) 7219 8515, *Fax:* (020) 7219 8712.

MACKENZIE OF FRAMWELLGATE, Baron *cr* 1998 (Life Peer), of Durham in the co. of Durham; **Brian Mackenzie,** OBE 1998; *b* 21 March 1943; *s* of Frederick George Mackenzie and Lucy Mackenzie (*née* Ward); *m* 1965, Jean Seed (marr. diss.); two *s*. *Educ:* Eastbourne Sch., Darlington; London Univ. (LLB Hons 1974); FBI Nat. Acad. (graduate 1985). Durham Constabulary, 1963–98: Constable, 1963; Sgt (Trng), 1970; Det. Insp., Hd of Drug Squad, 1976; Chief Insp., Hd of Crime Computer Unit, 1979; Supt (Det.), attached to Home Office, 1980; Territorial Comdr Supt, 1983; Divl Comdr, Chief Supt, 1989–98. Nat. Pres., Police Superintendents' Assoc. of England and Wales, 1995–98 (Vice Pres., 1993–95). Vice Pres., BALPA, 2004–08. Studied and lectured extensively on police methods, visiting Europe, USA and Canada. Regular broadcasts on TV and radio on law and policing issues. *Publications:* Two Lives of Brian (memoir), 2004; articles in legal and policing jls. *Recreations:* after-dinner speaking, swimming, music, travel. *Address:* House of Lords, SW1A 0PW. *W:* www.lordmackenzie.com.

McKENZIE OF LUTON, Baron *cr* 2004 (Life Peer), of Luton in the County of Bedfordshire; **William David McKenzie;** *b* 24 July 1946; *s* of Donald McKenzie and Elsie May McKenzie (*née* Doust); *m* 1972, Diane Joyce (*née* Angliss). *Educ:* Bristol Univ. (BA Hons Econs and Accounting). ACA 1971, FCA 1979. Partner, Price Waterhouse UK, 1980–86, Price Waterhouse, Hong Kong, 1993–98 (Partner-in-charge, Vietnam, 1996–98). Mem. (Lab) Luton BC, 1976–92, 1999–2005 (Leader, 1999–2003). Contested (Lab) Luton S, 1987, 1992. A Lord in Waiting (Govt Whip), 2005–07; Parly Under-Sec. of State, DWP, 2007–10, DCLG, 2009–10. *Recreations:* swimming, reading, music. *Address:* 6 Sunset Drive, Luton, Beds LU2 7TN. *T:* and *Fax:* (01582) 455384. *E:* mckenziew@parliament.uk.

MACKENZIE, Sir Alexander Alwyne Henry Charles Brinton M.; *see* Muir Mackenzie.

McKENZIE, Alistair William, MBE 1980; HM Diplomatic Service, retired; *b* 19 Feb. 1945; *s* of late James McKenzie and Barbara McKenzie (*née* Anderson); *m* 1968, Margaret Emily Young; two *s*. *Educ:* Leith Acad., Edinburgh. Entered FCO, 1965; Budapest, 1967–69; Singapore, 1969–72; Brasilia, 1972–75; FCO, 1975–78; Vice Consul: San Salvador, 1978–80; San Jose, 1980–82; Commercial Attaché, Madrid, 1982–84; W Africa Dept, 1984–86; Dep. High Comr and Hd of Chancery, Banjul, 1986–89; Consul-Gen., Bilbao, 1990–94; First Sec., Lagos, 1994–98; Dir, British Trade Internat., 1998–2001; Counsellor and Dep. Head of Mission, Abu Dhabi, 2001–05. Chief of Protocol, Shaheen Business and Investment Gp, Amman, 2006–07; CEO, Pearl Capital LLC, Abu Dhabi, 2007–09. *Recreations:* golf, photography. *Club:* Royal Over-Seas League.

MACKENZIE, Amanda Felicity, OBE 2014; Chief Marketing Officer, Aviva plc, since 2008; *b* Yorks, 6 Dec. 1963; *d* of Frazer Mackenzie and Rachel Mackenzie. *Educ:* Wakefield Girls' High Sch.; Bedford Coll., Univ. of London (BSc Psychol.); INSEAD (AMP). Graduate trainee, WCRS, 1986–88; Bd Dir, DMBB, 1988–98; Mktg Dir, British Airways Air Miles, 1998–2001; Brand and Mktg Dir, BT, 2001–04; Commercial Dir, British Gas, 2005–08. Non-exec. Dir, Mothercare plc, 2011–. Member: Govt Strategic Mktg Adv. Bd, 2009–11; Steering Gp, Lord Davies of Abersoch's ind. rev. into Women on Bds, 2010–. Pres., Marketing Soc., 2011–13. Mem. Bd, NYO, 2007–. *Address:* Aviva plc, St Helens, 1 Undershaft, EC3P 3DQ. *T:* (020) 7662 9531.

MACKENZIE, Prof Andrew Peter, PhD; FRS 2015; Director, Max Planck Institute for Chemical Physics of Solids, Dresden, since 2012; Professor of Condensed Matter Physics, University of St Andrews, since 2001; *b* Elderslie, 7 March 1964; *s* of Alexander Colin Mackenzie and Bridget Mary Mackenzie (*née* Gordon); *m* 1991, Olga Maria Dunin-Borkowski; one *s* two *d*. *Educ:* Hutchesons' Grammar Sch., Glasgow; Univ. of Edinburgh (BSc Hons Phys 1986); Trinity Coll., Cambridge (PhD Phys 1991). Researcher, CERN, Geneva, 1986–87; Res. Associate, 1991–93, Royal Soc. Univ. Res. Fellow, 1993–97, Univ. of Cambridge; Royal Soc. Univ. Res. Fellow and Univ. Reader, Univ. of Birmingham, 1997–2001. *Publications:* 130 res. and review papers in learned jls. *Recreations:* golf, hiking, skiing, travel. *Address:* Max Planck Institute for Chemical Physics of Solids, Nöthnitzer Strasse 40, 01187 Dresden, Germany. *T:* (351) 46465900, *Fax:* (351) 46465902. *E:* mackenzie@cpfs.mpg.de.

MACKENZIE, Andrew Stewart, PhD; FRS 2014; Chief Executive Officer, BHP Billiton Ltd, since 2013; *b* UK, 20 Dec. 1956; *s* of Hugh Mackenzie and Mary Mackenzie; *m* 1977, Liz Allan; two *d*. *Educ:* St Andrews Univ. (BSc Geol. 1st Cl. 1977); Univ. of Bristol (PhD Organic Chem. 1981). Postdoctoral Fellow, Univ. of Bristol, 1981; Humboldt Fellow, Nuclear Res. Centre, Jülich, 1981–82; British Petroleum, 1983–2004: Chief Reservoir Engr, 1993–95; Hd of Corporate Affairs, 1995–96; Chief Technol. Officer, 1997–2001; Gp Vice Pres., Petrochemicals, 2001–04; Product Gp Hd, Diamonds and Minerals, Rio Tinto, 2004–07; Gp Exec., CEO Non Ferrous, and Hd of London Office, BHP Billiton Ltd, 2008–13. Non-exec. Dir, Centrica, 2005–13. Mem., RAE Panel 2008. Treas., 1994–2004, Chm., Bd of Trustees, 2005–07, Demos. Trustee, Mus. of Sci. and Industry, Chicago, 2002–04. Member: Geol Soc., 1982; Soc. of Petroleum Engrs, 1987. Hon. DSc Bristol, 2011. *Address:* BHP Billiton Ltd, 171 Collins Street, Melbourne, Vic 3000, Australia. *T:* 3 9609 3464; BHP Billiton Ltd, Neathouse Place, SW1V 1LH. *T:* (020) 7802 4000. *E:* andrew.mackenzie@bhpbilliton.com. *Clubs:* Reform; British Sub-Aqua.

MacKENZIE, Prof. Angus Buchanan, PhD; Professor, 2005, and Director, 2007–12, Scottish Universities Environmental Research Centre; *b* Glasgow, 23 Jan. 1950; *s* of Hugh C. MacKenzie and Christina MacKenzie; *m* 1983, Shelagh Stenhouse MacKay; one *s* one *d*. *Educ:* Shawlands Acad., Glasgow; Univ. of Glasgow (BSc 1st Cl. Hons Chem.; PhD Chem. 1977). CChem 1979; MRSC 1979, FRSC 1989. Res. Officer, CEGB, 1976–77; Scottish Universities Research and Reactor Centre, later Scottish Universities Environmental Research Centre: Lectr, 1977–91; Sen. Lectr, 1991–99; Reader, 1999–2005. *Publications:* contribs to jls and conf. procs. *Recreations:* walking, fitness, gardening, reading, travel, DIY. *Address:* 11 Claremount Avenue, Giffnoch, Glasgow G46 6UT. *T:* (0141) 569 9566.

MACKENZIE, Colin Douglas; Chief Executive, Aberdeenshire Council, 2008–15; *b* Tripoli, N Africa, 10 March 1950; *s* of late Major John Mackenzie, MC, RA and of Elsie Mackenzie (*née* Stewart); *m* 1976, Lesley Adam, MA, CQSW; five *s*. *Educ:* Forfar Acad.; Strathclyde Univ. (BA 1973); Glasgow Univ. (DipSW, CQSW 1975). Trainee social worker, Dundee City Corp., 1973–75; Child Care Specialist, 1975–77, Area Team Leader, 1977–82, Tayside Regl Council; Social Work Manager, 1982–85, Divl Officer, 1985–96 (Lead Officer, Piper Alpha Disaster response, 1988–90), Grampian Regl Council; Hd of Service, 1996–2000, Dir of Housing and Social Work, 2000–08, Aberdeenshire Council. Mem., 21st Century Rev. of Social Work, 2004–05. Non-exec. Dir, Scottish Prison Service, 2007–08; Jt Chair, Scottish Govt Delivery Gp, Health and Social Care, 2012–15. Pres., ADSW, 2005–06. Dir, NE Scotland Preservation Trust, 2015–. *Recreations:* Rugby, swimming, gardening, good company, family.

MACKENZIE, Colin Scott; DL; Sheriff of Grampian, Highland and Islands at Lerwick and Kirkwall, 1992–2003; part-time Sheriff, 2004–09; Retired Sheriff, Grampian Highlands and Islands, 2009–13, now Honorary Sheriff; Vice Lord-Lieutenant, Western Isles, 1984–92; *b* 7 July 1938; *s* of late Major Colin Scott Mackenzie, BL and Mrs Margaret S. Mackenzie, MA; *m* 1966, Christeen Elizabeth Drysdale McLauchlan. *Educ:* Nicolson Inst., Stornoway; Fettes Coll., Edinburgh; Edinburgh Univ. (BL 1959). Admitted Solicitor and Notary Public, 1960; Procurator Fiscal, Stornoway, 1969–92; Temporary Sheriff, 1992. Clerk to the Lieutenancy, Stornoway, 1975–92. Dir, Harris Tweed Assoc. Ltd, 1979–95; Trustee, Western Isles Kidney Machine Trust, 1977–. Council Mem for Western Isles, Orkney, Shetland etc, Law Soc. of Scotland, 1985–92. General Assembly, Church of Scotland: Comr, Presbytery of Lewis, 1991–92; Mem., Bd of Social Responsibility, 1991–95; Convenor, Study Gp into Young People and the Media, 1991–93; Mem., Judicial Commn, 2011–. Council Mem., Sheriffs' Assoc., 2002–03. DL Islands Area of Western Isles, 1975. Pres., Probus Club, Isle of Lewis, 2010–11; Hon. Mem., Rotary Club, Stornoway, 1992– (Pres., 1976–77). *Publications:* The Last Warrior Band, 2002; Personal Reflections on Shetland, Orkney and Western Isles, 2010; Eaglais na h-Aoidhe, the Overlooked Jewel in our Crown, 2012; Gaels in Gallipoli, 2015; contrib. Stair Memorial Encyclopaedia of Laws of Scotland, 1987. *Recreations:* amateur radio, boating, fishing, local history, shooting, trying to grow trees, travel. *Address:* Park House, 8 Matheson Road, Stornoway, Western Isles HS1 2NQ. *T:* (01851) 702008. *Club:* New (Edinburgh).

McKENZIE, Dan Peter, CH 2003; PhD; FRS 1976; BP Professor of Earth Sciences, Cambridge University, 2006–12, now Emeritus (Royal Society Professor of Earth Sciences, 1996–2006); Fellow of King's College, Cambridge, 1965–73 and since 1977; *b* 21 Feb. 1942; *s* of William Stewart McKenzie and Nancy Mary McKenzie; *m* 1971, Indira Margaret Misra; one *s*. *Educ:* Westminster Sch.; King's Coll., Cambridge (BA 1963, PhD 1966). Cambridge University: Sen. Asst in Res., 1969–75; Asst Dir of Res., 1975–79; Reader in Tectonics, 1979–84; Prof. of Earth Scis, 1984–96. Hon. Mem., Japan Acad. Hon. MA 1966, Hon. DSc 2014, Cambridge. (Jtly) Geology and Geophysics Prize, Internat. Balzan Foundn of Italy and Switzerland, 1981; (jtly) Japan Prize, Science and Technology Foundn of Japan, 1990; Royal Medal, 1991, Copley Medal, 2011, Royal Soc.; Gold Medal, RAS, 1992; Crafoord Medal, Royal Swedish Acad. of Scis, 2002. *Publications:* papers in learned jls. *Recreation:* gardening. *Address:* Bullard Laboratories, Madingley Road, Cambridge CB3 0EZ. *T:* (01223) 337177.

MACKENZIE, Rear-Adm. David John, CB 1983; FNI; Royal Navy, retired 1983; Director, Atlantic Salmon Trust, 1985–97 (Life Vice-President, 1998); *b* 3 Oct. 1929; *s* of late David Mackenzie and of Alison Walker Lawrie; *m* 1965, Ursula Sybil Balfour; two *s* one *d*. *Educ:* Cargilfield Sch., Barnton, Edinburgh; Royal Naval Coll., Eaton Hall, Cheshire. Cadet to Comdr, 1943–72: served in East Indies, Germany, Far East, Home and Mediterranean Fleets, and commanded: HMML 6011, HM Ships: Brinkley, Barrington, Hardy, Lincoln, Hermione; Captain 1972; Senior Officers War Course, 1972; commanded HMS Phoenix (NBCD School), 1972–74; Captain F8 in HMS Ajax, 1974–76; Director of Naval Equipment, 1976–78; Captain: HMS Blake, 1979; HMS Hermes, 1980; Rear Admiral 1981; Flag Officer and Port Admiral, Gibraltar, Comdr Gibraltar Mediterranean, 1981–83. Younger Brother of Trinity House, 1971–. Member, Queen's Body Guard for Scotland (Royal Company of Archers), 1976–. Vice Pres., Nautical Inst., 1985–93. Vice Pres., Seafarers UK (formerly King George's Fund for Sailors) (Scotland), 2009– (Pres., 1996). *Recreations:* shooting, fishing. *Address:* Easter Meikle Fardle, Meikleour, Perthshire PH2 6EF. *Club:* New (Edinburgh).

MacKENZIE, Prof. Donald Angus, PhD; FBA 2004; FRSE; Professor of Sociology, University of Edinburgh, since 1992; *b* 3 May 1950; *s* of Angus MacKenzie and Anne MacKenzie; *m* 1998, Caroline Bamford; one *s* one *d*. *Educ:* Univ. of Edinburgh (BSc 1972; PhD 1978). Lectr, 1975–88, Reader, 1988–92, in Sociology, Univ. of Edinburgh. Vis. Prof. of Hist. of Sci., Harvard Univ., 1997. FRSE 2002. *Publications:* Statistics in Britain 1865–1930, 1981; Inventing Accuracy, 1990; Knowing Machines, 1995; Mechanizing Proof, 2001; An Engine, not a Camera, 2006; Material Markets, 2009. *Recreations:* cycling, walking, chess. *Address:* School of Social and Political Science, University of Edinburgh, Chrystal Macmillan Building, George Square, Edinburgh EH8 9LD.

MacKENZIE, George Paterson; Keeper of the Records of Scotland, 2001–12; Registrar General for Scotland, 2011–12; Chairman, Scottish Ancestral Tourism Group, since 2013; *b* 22 Sept. 1950; *s* of James Sargent Porteous MacKenzie and Flora Black MacKenzie; *m* 1st, 1972, Elizabeth Hamilton (marr. diss. 1988); 2nd, 1995, Katherine Barratt (marr. diss. 2003); 3rd, 2005, Caroline Morgan. *Educ:* Univ. of Stirling (BA 1972; MLitt 1978). Asst history teacher, Larbert High Sch., 1974–75; Res. Asst, Scottish Record Office, 1975–83; Departmental Records Officer, General Register Office for Scotland, 1984–85; Hd of Records Liaison, then Preservation Services, Scottish Record Office, 1986–94; Dep. Sec. Gen., Internat. Council on Archives, Paris, 1995–96; Dir of External Relns, Nat. Archives of Scotland, 1997–2000. Adviser: on protection of archives in former Yugoslavia for UNESCO, 1995–97; on archives for World Bank, 1998–99; External Examiner in archives and records mgt, Univ. of Liverpool, 1998–2002, Univ. of Dundee, 2014–. Pres., Scottish Record Soc., 2014–. *Publications:* articles and conf. papers on protection of archives in armed conflict, electronic records and archives mgt. *Recreations:* reading, travel, cooking. *Address:* Clachan Seil, Oban.

MacKENZIE, Gillian Rachel, (Mrs N. I. MacKenzie); *see* Ford, G. R.

MACKENZIE, Sir Guy; *see* Mackenzie, Sir J. W. G.

McKENZIE, Iain; *b* Greenock, 4 April 1959; *s* of Adam McKenzie and Isobel McKenzie; *m* 1982, Alison Stewart; two *s*. *Educ:* Greenock High Sch.; James Watt Coll. Apprentice mechanic; manufacturing line technician, debug technician, quality assurance officer and large enterprise procurement officer, IBM; Wise Gp. Mem. (Lab), Inverclyde Council, 2003–11 (Leader, 2011). MP (Lab) Inverclyde, July 2011–2015; contested (Lab) same seat, 2015. Mem., River Clyde Homes, 2008–10.

MacKENZIE, James Alexander Mackintosh, CB 1988; FREng; Chief Road Engineer, Scottish Development Department, 1976–88, retired; *b* Inverness, 6 May 1928; *m* 1970, Pamela Dorothy Nixon; one *s* one *d*. *Educ:* Inverness Royal Acad. FICE, FCIHT; FREng (FEng 1982). Miscellaneous local govt appts, 1950–63; Chief Resident Engr, Durham County Council, 1963–67; Dep. Dir, 1967–71, Dir, 1971–76, North Eastern Road Construction Unit, MoT, later DoE. *Recreations:* golf, fishing. *Address:* Pendor, 2 Dean Park, Longniddry, East Lothian EH32 0QR. *T:* (01875) 852643.

MACKENZIE, Sir James William Guy, 5th Bt *cr* 1890, of Glen Muick, Aberdeenshire; Chairman, Kerrier Direct Services, 1995–98 (Vice-Chairman, 1994–95); *b* 6 Oct. 1946; *s* of Lt-Col Eric Dighton Mackenzie, CMG, CVO, DSO (*d* 1972), 4th *s* of Sir Allan Russell Mackenzie, 2nd Bt, and Elizabeth Kathrine Mary, *d* of Captain James William Guy Innes, CBE; *S* cousin, 1993; *m* 1st, 1972, Paulene Patricia Simpson (marr. diss. 1980); two *d*; 2nd, 1996, Sally Ann (*née* Howard). *Educ:* Stowe. Mem. (Ind) Kerrier DC, 1993–2003. *Recreations:* watching cricket and football, walking, music, collecting popular music memorabilia; historic buildings. *Heir:* *b* Allan Walter Mackenzie, *b* 6 Nov. 1952.

MACKENZIE, Gen. Sir Jeremy (John George), GCB 1998 (KCB 1992); OBE 1982; DL; Executive Chairman, Tan Trax International Ltd, since 2014; *b* 11 Feb. 1941; *s* of late Lt-Col John William Elliot Mackenzie, DSO, QPM and of Valerie (*née* Dawes); *m* 1969, Elizabeth Lyon (*née* Wertenbaker); one *s* one *d*. *Educ:* Duke of York Sch., Nairobi, Kenya. psc, HCSC. Commnd Queen's Own Highlanders, 1961; Canadian Forces Staff Coll., 1974; Bde Major, 24 Airportable Bde, 1975–76; CO 1 Queen's Own Highlanders, NI and Hong Kong, 1979–82; Instructor, Staff Coll., 1982–83; Col Army Staff Duties 2, 1983–84; Comdr 12th Armoured Bde, 1984–86; Service Fellowship, King's Coll., Univ. of London, 1987; Dep. Comdt, 1987–89, Comdt, 1989, Staff Coll.; GOC 4th Armoured Div., BAOR, 1989–91; Comdr 1st (British) Corps, 1991–92; Comdr, Ace Rapid Reaction Corps, 1992–94; Dep. SACEUR, 1994–98; ADC Gen. to the Queen, 1997–98. Gov., Royal Hospital, Chelsea, 1999–2006. Director: SIRVA plc, 2003–07; SELEX Communications Ltd, 2004–13; Main Bd, Blue Hackle Security, 2012– (Mem., 2006, Chm., 2011, Adv. Bd); Secure Accommodation, 2013–; Chm., AC Cars, 2012–. Senior Military Adviser: Beretta, 2007–14; Benteler Automotive, 2011–13. Colonel Commandant: WRAC, 1990–92; AGC, 1992–98; Colonel: Highlanders Regt, 1994–2001; APTC, 1997–2012. Lieut, Queen's Bodyguard for Scotland, Royal Company of Archers, 2013 (Mem., 1986–; Brig., 2001–08; Ensign, 2008–13). Pres., Services Br., British Deer Soc., 1993–2015; Life Vice-Pres., Combined Services Winter Sports Assoc., 2001. DL Greater London, 2006; Citizen and Gunmaker, City of London, 2009–. OStJ 2003. Comdr, US Legion of Merit, 1997, 1999 and 2008; Cross of Merit 1st Class (Czech Republic), 1998; Officers' Cross, Order of Merit (Hungary), 1998; 1st Oak Leaf Cluster, 1999; Order of Madara Horseman, 1st Cl. (Bulgaria), 1999; Officers' Gold Medal of Merit (Slovenia), 2002. *Publications:* The British Army and the Operational Level of War, 1989. *Recreations:* shooting, fishing. *Address:* The Old Bell, 20 Long Street, Cerne Abbas, Dorset DT2 7JF. *Club:* Sloane.

MACKENZIE of Gairloch, John Alexander; landowner, Gairloch and Conon estates, since 1980; Vice Lord-Lieutenant of Ross and Cromarty, since 2013; *b* Muir of Ord, Ross-shire, 27 May 1944; *s* of late Brig. William Alexander Mackenzie of Gairloch, DSO, OBE and Marjory Kythé Mackenzie (*née* Stirling); *m* 1969, Frances Marian Williams; one *s* one *d*. *Educ:* Gordonstoun. 2nd Lt, Queen's Own Highlanders, 1962–65. Export Dir, James Buchanan & Co. Ltd, 1966–80. Chm., Black Isle Grain Ltd, 1987–90. Mem., Red Deer Commn, 1987–98. Chm., Highland Reg., Scottish Landowners Fedn, 1990–95. DL Ross, Cromarty, Skye and Lochalsh, 1984. *Address:* Conan House, Conon Bridge, Ross-shire IV7 8AL. *T:* (01349) 861101.

McKENZIE, Prof. John Crawford; Founding Governor, University of the Arts London (formerly The London Institute), since 1996 (Rector, 1986–96); *b* 12 Nov. 1937; *s* of late Donald Walter McKenzie and Emily Beatrice McKenzie; *m* 1960, Ann McKenzie (*née* Roberts); two *s*. *Educ:* London School of Economics and Political Science (BScEcon); Bedford Coll., London (MPhil). Lecturer, Queen Elizabeth Coll., Univ. of London, 1961; Dep. Director, Office of Health Econs, 1966; Market Inf. Manager, Allied Breweries Ltd, 1968; various posts, Kimpher Ltd, 1969, finally Chief Exec., Kimpher Marketing Services, 1973; Head of Dept, London Coll. of Printing, 1975; Principal: Ilkley Coll., 1978; Bolton Inst. of Higher Educn, 1982; Rector, Liverpool Poly., 1984. Visiting Professor: Queen Elizabeth Coll., 1976–80; Univ. of Newcastle, 1981–87. Director: Antiquarian Pastimes Ltd, 1984–; New Frontiers in Educn Ltd, 1993–; Ringmaster Holdings plc, 2001–. Chm., Leeds Utd plc, 2003. Mem., Adv. Council, Univ. of Sarawak, Malaysia, 1994–; Advr, Japan Coll. of Foreign Langs, Tokyo, 1997–; Mem. Consultative Cttee, Eastern Visual Arts and Design Univ. of China, Shanghai, 2002; Sen. Vice-Pres., Shanghai Univ. of Visual Arts, 2003–. Special Advr, Shanghai Metropolitan Govt, 2002–. Chevalier de l'Ordre des Arts et des Lettres (France), 1992. *Publications:* (ed jtly) Changing Food Habits, 1964; (ed jtly) Our Changing Fare, 1966; (ed jtly) The Food Consumer, 1987; many articles in Proc. Nutrition Soc., British Jl Nutrition, Nutrition Bull., etc. *Recreation:* collecting antiquarian books and works of art. *Address:* c/o TSB Bank plc, PO Box 99 BX4 7SB. *Clubs:* Athenæum, Chelsea Arts.

McKENZIE, Julia Kathleen, (Mrs Jerry Harte); actress, singer and director; *b* 17 Feb. 1941; *d* of Albion McKenzie and Kathleen Rowe; *m* 1972, Jerry Harte. *Educ:* Guildhall School of Music and Drama. Hon. FGSM, 1988. *Stage:* Maggie May, Adelphi, 1966; Mame, Drury Lane, 1969; Promises, Promises, Prince of Wales, 1970; Company, Her Majesty's, 1972; Cowardy Custard, Mermaid, 1972; Cole, Mermaid, 1974; Norman Conquests, Globe, 1975; Side by Side by Sondheim, Wyndhams, 1976, NY 1977; Ten Times Table, Globe, 1978; Outside Edge, Queens, 1979; On the 20th Century, Her Majesty's, 1980; Guys and Dolls, NT, 1982; Schweyk in 2nd World War, NT, 1982; Woman in Mind, Vaudeville, 1986; Follies, Shaftesbury, 1987; Into the Woods, Phoenix, 1990; Sweeney Todd, NT, 1993; Communicating Doors, Gielgud, 1995; Kafka's Dick, Piccadilly, 1998; The Royal Family, Th. Royal, Haymarket, 2001; The Philadelphia Story, Old Vic, 2005; directed: Stepping Out, Duke of York's, 1984; Steel Magnolias, Lyric, 1989; Just So, Watermill, Bagnor, Berks, 1989; Putting it Together, Old Fire Station, Oxford, 1992, NY, 1993; A Little Night Music, Tokyo, 1999; Honk! The Ugly Duckling, NT, 1999; Peter Pan, the Musical, RFH, 2001; Fuddy Meers, Arts Th., 2004; *films:* Ike: the war years, 1978; Shirley Valentine, 1989; The Old Curiosity Shop, 1994; Bright Young Things, 2003; Notes on a Scandal, 2006; *television films:* Those Glory Glory Days, 1980; Hotel Du Lac, 1986; Adam Bede, 1992; Jack and the Beanstalk—the Real Story, 2001; Celebration, 2006; You Can Choose Your Friends, 2007; The Mystery of Edwin Drood, 2012; Gangsta Granny, 2013; *television series:* Maggie and Her, 1977–79; Fame is the Spur, 1982; Blott on the Landscape, 1985; Fresh Fields, 1984–86; French Fields, 1989–91; Death In Holy Orders, 2003; Cranford, 2007; Marple, 2008–13; Cranford II, 2009; The Town, 2012; The Casual Vacancy, 2015; *television plays:* Dear Box No, 1983; Sharing Time, 1984; Absent Friends, 1985; Julia and Company (TV special), 1986; The Shadowy Third, 1995; The Last Detective, 2002; numerous TV musicals; *radio:* Sweeney Todd, 1994; The Country Wife, A Room With a View, 1995; Mame, 1996; Follies, Gigi, 1997; Water Babies, 1998; Two Planks and a Passion, 1999; Woman in Mind, She Stoops to Conquer, 2000; On the Town, Past Forgetting, 2001; Pal Joey, On Your Toes, 2002; The Old Curiosity Shop, 2003; *directed for radio:* Rosalind, 2002; A Well Remembered Voice, Barbara's Wedding, Call Me Madam, 2003. *Recreations:* cooking, gardening. *Address:* c/o The Artists Partnership, 101 Finsbury Pavement, EC2A 1RS. *T:* (020) 7439 1456, *Fax:* (020) 734 6530.

MacKENZIE, Kelvin Calder; *b* 22 Oct. 1946; *m* 1st, 1969, Jacqueline (marr. diss. 2006); two *s* one *d;* 2nd, 2008, Sarah McLean. Editor, The Sun, 1981–94; Man. Dir, British Sky Broadcasting, 1994; Dir, 1994–98, Gp Man. Dir, 1998, Mirror Group plc; Chm. and Chief Exec., Wireless Gp plc, 1998–2005; Chm., Base79.com (formerly MyVideoRights.com), 2008–12.

MacKENZIE, Rev. Kenneth Ian; DL; Minister, Parish of Braemar and Crathie, since 2005; Domestic Chaplain to the Queen in Scotland, since 2007; *b* 7 April 1959; *s* of Ian Kenneth MacKenzie and Margaret Vera Matheson; *m* 1987, Jayne Louise Lovett; one *s* three *d. Educ:* RAC, Cirencester; Christ's Coll., Univ. of Aberdeen (BD Hons). Managing Partner, Moy Estate, Inverness, 1981–83; ordained, 1990; Asst Minister, Dyce Parish Church, Aberdeenshire, 1988–91; Associate Pastor, First Presbyterian Church, Burlingame, Calif, USA, 1991–94; Associate Minister, North Church, Perth, 1994–99; Minister, St Columba's, Budapest, 1999–2005. DL Aberdeenshire, 2013. Knight's Cross, Order of Merit (Hungary), 2013. *Recreations:* leading charitable work teams to projects in Romania, countryside pursuits, cycling. *Address:* The Manse, Crathie, Ballater, Aberdeenshire AB35 5UL.

MacKENZIE, Kenneth John, CB 1996; Chairman: Historic Scotland Foundation, 2001–12; Edinburgh City Centre Churches, 2010–12; Secretary, Scottish Executive (formerly Scottish Office) Development Department, 1998–2001; *b* 1 May 1943; *s* of John Donald MacKenzie and Elizabeth Pennant Johnston Sutherland; *m* 1975, Irene Mary Hogarth; one *s* one *d. Educ:* Woodchurch Road Primary School, Birkenhead; Birkenhead School; Pembroke College, Oxford (Exhibnr; MA Mod. Hist.); Stanford Univ., Calif (AM Hist.). Scottish Home and Health Dept, 1965; Private Sec. to Jt Parly Under Sec. of State, Scottish Office, 1969–70; Scottish Office Regional Develt Div., 1970–73; Scottish Educn Dept, 1973–76; Civil Service Fellow, Glasgow Univ., 1974–75; Principal Private Sec. to Sec. of State for Scotland, 1977–79; Asst Sec., Scottish Economic Planning Dept, 1979–83; Scottish Office: Finance Div., 1983–85; Principal Finance Officer, 1985–88; Under Sec., Home and Health Dept, 1988–91; Under Sec., 1991–92, Sec., 1992–95, Agric. and Fisheries Dept; Cabinet Office (on secondment): Dep. Sec. (Hd of Economic and Domestic Affairs Secretariat), 1995–97; Hd, Constitution Secretariat, 1997–98. Mem., BBSRC (formerly AFRC), 1992–95. Quinquennial Reviewer for the Court Service, LCD, 2001–02. Mem., British Waterways Scotland Gp, 2002–07. Mem., Christian Aid Bd, 2005–08. Hon. Prof., Dept of Politics and Internat. Relations, Univ. of Aberdeen, 2001–04. Associate Consultant, Public Admin Internat., 2002–08. Elder, St Cuthbert's Parish Church, 1971–. *Address:* 23C/1 Ravelston Park, Edinburgh EH4 3DX.

MACKENZIE, Lorimer David Maurice; Director, Development Strategy for Enterprises, European Commission, 1996–2002; *b* 4 Aug. 1940; *s* of William David Beveridge Mackenzie and Elizabeth Reid (*née* Peters); *m* 1959, Penelope Marsh Happer; two *s* two *d. Educ:* Hermitage Park Sch., Leith; Royal High Sch., Edinburgh; Edinburgh Univ. (MA Hons Mental Philosophy). Department of Agriculture and Fisheries, Scottish Office: Asst Principal, 1964–68; Principal, 1968–73; Commission of the European Communities: Head of Division: Agricl Res., 1973–77; Food Aid, 1978–82; Develt of Trade, 1982–92; Dir, Budget and Gen. Affairs, Directorate Gen. of Fisheries, 1992–96. Member: Scottish Council, Eur. Movt, 2003–09; Council, Saltire Soc., 2004–12 (Chm., 2010–12). Mem., Editl Bd, Internat. Jl of Entrepreneurship and Innovation, 2001–. Chevalier de l'Ordre National du Mérite (France), 2002. *Recreation:* Scottish history and literature. *Address:* Achadh Na Sgiath, Duror, Argyll PA38 4DA. *Club:* New (Edinburgh).

MacKENZIE, Madeleine; Scottish Parliamentary Counsel, since 2002; *b* 27 Aug. 1963; *er d* of William Gordon MacKenzie and Veronica Dorothy Rachel MacKenzie. *Educ:* Inverness High Sch.; Univ. of Aberdeen (LLB Hons; DipLP). Solicitor in private practice, 1986–90; Asst Scottish Parly Counsel, then Depute Scottish Parly Counsel, 1990–2002. *Recreations:* bridge, reading, music. *Address:* (office) Victoria Quay, Edinburgh EH6 6QQ. *T:* (0131) 244 1667. *E:* madeleine.mackenzie@scotland.gsi.gov.uk. *Clubs:* Athenæum; New (Edinburgh).

MACKENZIE, Mary Margaret; *see* McCabe, M. M. A.

McKENZIE, Michael, CB 1999; QC 1991; Master of the Crown Office and Queen's Coroner and Attorney, Registrar of Criminal Appeals and of the Courts Martial Appeal Court, and Master of the Queen's Bench Division, High Court of Justice, 1988–2003; *b* Hove, Sussex, 25 May 1943; *s* of Robert John McKenzie and Kitty Elizabeth McKenzie; *m* 1964, Peggy Dorothy, *d* of Thomas Edward William Russell and Dorothy Mabel Russell; three *s. Educ:* Varndean Grammar Sch., Brighton. Town Clerk's Dept, Brighton, 1961–63; Asst to Clerk of the Peace, Brighton Quarter Sessions, 1963–67; Sen. Clerk of the Court, 1967–70, Dep. Clerk of the Peace, 1970–71, Middlesex Quarter Sessions; called to the Bar, Middle Temple, 1970, Bencher, 1993; Deputy to Courts Administrator, Middlesex Crown Court, 1972–73; Courts Administrator (Newcastle), NE Circuit, 1974–79; Courts Administrator, Central Criminal Court, and Coordinator for Taxation of Crown Court Costs, S Eastern Circuit, 1979–84; Dep. Circuit Administrator, SE Circuit, 1984–86; Asst Registrar, Ct of Appeal Criminal Div., 1986–88. Registrar, Internat. Civil and Commercial Court and Regulatory Tribunal, Qatar Financial Centre, 2006–11. Adjunct Lectr, SOAS, 2000–03; Adjunct Prof. of Law, Wake Forest Univ., NC, 2002–05. British representative: Internat. Great Debates on Criminal Law, 1987–2003; at internat. judicial conferences in USA, Canada, Aust. and Tasmania, 1990–2003. Mem., Criminal Cttee, Judicial Studies Bd, 1988–2003. Mem., Ind. Monitoring Bd, Lewes Prison, 2004–06. Life Mem., Litigation Section, State Bar, California, 2002. Freeman, City of London, 1979. FRSA 1990. Hon. Fellow, Kent Sch. of Law, Canterbury Univ., 1991. *Publications:* (ed) Rules of Court: criminal procedure, annually 1994–97; (with Lord Woolf) A Review of the Working Methods of the European Court of Human Rights, 2005. *Recreations:* Northumbrian stick dressing, fell walking. *Address:* Selwyns Wood House, Cross in Hand, East Sussex TN21 0QN.

MACKENZIE, Michael Philip; Director-General, Food and Drink Federation, 1986–2001; *b* 26 June 1937; *s* of Brig. Maurice Mackenzie, DSO, and Mrs Vivienne Mackenzie; *m* 1966, Jill (*née* Beckley); one *s* one *d. Educ:* Downside Sch.; Lincoln Coll., Oxford (BA); Harvard Business Sch., USA. United Biscuits plc, 1966–86: Prodn Dir, various businesses within United Biscuits, 1974–83; Man. Dir, D. S. Crawford Bakeries, 1983–86. *Recreations:* walking, gardening, opera, theatre. *Address:* Ebony Cottage, Reading Street, near Tenterden, Kent TN30 7HT. *Club:* Travellers.

MACKENZIE, Sir Peter Douglas, 13th Bt *cr* 1673 (NS), of Coul, Ross-shire; *b* 23 April 1949; *s* of Henry Douglas Mackenzie (*d* 1965) and Irene Carter Freeman; *S* kinsman, 1990, but his name does not appear on the Official Roll of the Baronetage; *m* 1st, 1982, Jennifer, *d* of Ridley Boyce (marr. diss.); two *d;* 2nd, 2000, Margo Lamond, *d* of Albert Gordon. *Heir: kinsman* Miles Roderick Turing Mackenzie [*b* 18 April 1952; *m* 1983, Hiroko Sato].

MACKENZIE, Richard Hill, CB 2002; Member, Boundary Commission for Northern Ireland, 2002–13; *b* 21 Feb. 1942; *s* of late Richard H. Mackenzie and Mary Mackenzie; *m* 1966, Jane Valerie Holmes; two *s* one *d. Educ:* Grosvenor High Sch., Belfast; Queen's Univ., Belfast (BSc Econs). Dep. Sec., DoE (NI), 1987–2000. Jt Sec., North/South Ministerial Council, NI, 2002–02. Local Govt Boundaries Comr, 2006–09. Vis. Prof. in Planning, Univ. of Ulster, 2002–. Hon. MRTPI 2000. *Recreation:* choral singing. *Clubs:* Ulster Reform (Belfast); Grosvenor Rugby.

MACKENZIE, Sir Roderick McQuhae, 12th Bt *cr* 1703, of Scatwell; FRCP(C); medical practitioner, pediatrician; *b* 17 April 1942; *s* of Captain Sir Roderick Edward François McQuhae Mackenzie, 11th Bt, CBE, DSC, RN and Marie Evelyn Campbell (*d* 1993), *oc* of late William Ernest Parkinson; *S* father, 1986, but his name does not appear on the Official Roll of the Baronetage; *m* 1970, Nadezhda, (Nadine), Baroness von Rorbas, *d* of Georges Frederic Schlatter, Baron von Rorbas; one *s* one *d. Educ:* Sedbergh; King's College London. MB, BS; MRCP; DCH. *Recreations:* classical music (violin, viola), horseback riding (3-Day eventing), windsurfing. *Heir: s* Gregory Roderick McQuhae Mackenzie, *b* 8 May 1971. *Address:* 2431 Udell Road NW, Calgary, AB T2N 4H4, Canada.

MACKENZIE, Ruth, CBE 2013 (OBE 1995); Director, Time/Room Productions, since 2002; Artistic Director, Holland Festival, since 2014; *b* 24 July 1957; *d* of Kenneth Mackenzie and Myrna Blumberg. *Educ:* South Hampstead High Sch.; Sorbonne, Paris; Newnham Coll., Cambridge (MA English 1982). Editor's Asst, Time Out magazine, 1980–81; Co-founder, Dir and writer, Moving Parts Theatre Co., 1980–82; Fellow in Theatre, and Dir, Theatre in the Mill, Bradford Univ., 1982–84; Drama Officer, Arts Council of GB, 1984–86; Head of Strategic Planning, South Bank Centre, 1986–90; Exec. Dir, Nottingham Playhouse, 1990–97; Gen. Dir, Scottish Opera, 1997–99; Special Advr to Sec. of State for Culture, Media and Sport, 1999–2002. Artistic Dir, Bradford Multicultural Fest., 1983–84; Artistic Programmer, Theatr Clwyd, 1995–96; Theatre Programmer, Barbican Centre, 1995–97; Artistic Dir, Chichester Fest. Theatre, 2002–06; Gen. Dir, Manchester Internat. Fest., 2006–07; Consultant Dramaturg, Vienna Fest., 2007–10; Dir, Cultural Olympiad, 2010–12; Interim Launch Dir, The Space, 2013–14. Expert Advr, DCMS, 2007–10. Member: Bd, Women in Entertainment, 1987–89; Bd, Paines Plough Theatre Co., 1990–96; Touring Panel, 1992–, Lottery Panel, 1994–97, Arts Council of GB, later Arts Council of England, subseq. Arts Council England; Dance and Drama Panel, British Council, 1992–97; Bd, London Internat. Fest. of Theatre, 1993–97; Nat. Develt Forum, ABSA, 1994–96; Bd, New Millennium Experience Co., 1997–99; Panel 2000, 1998–99; QCDA (formerly QCA) Cttee on Creativity, 2001–12; Chancellor's Forum, London Inst., 2001–; Adv. Council, Tate Modern, 2014–; Warwick Commn, 2014–15; Nat. Campaign for the Arts, 2014–; Chm., Improbable, 2013–. Vis. Prof., City Univ., 2007–. Trustee, Cass Sculpture Foundn (formerly Sculpture at Goodwood), 2005–07, 2013–. Governor: Trinity Coll. of Music, 2002–05; Royal Northern Coll. of Music, 2007. FRSA. Hon. Fellow: Univ. of Nottingham, 1994; QMUL, 2013. Hon. DLitt: Nottingham Trent, 1994; Nottingham, 1997.

MACKENZIE, Dr Ursula Ann; Chairman, Little, Brown Book Group, 2015–Dec. 2016 (Chief Executive Officer, 2006–15); *b* Burton-on-Trent, 11 Dec. 1951; *d* of late Ian Alexander Ross Mackenzie and Phyllis Mackenzie (*née* Naismith); one *s* by Michael Johnson. *Educ:* Malvern Girls Coll.; Nottingham Univ. (BA Jt Hons English and American Studies; PhD American Lit. 1976). Lectr in English and American Lit., Univ. of Hong Kong, 1976–79; Internat. Scripts (literary agency), 1979–80; Rights Manager, Granada Publishing, 1980–84; Transworld Publishers: Editl and Rights Manager, 1985–86, Editl and Rights Dir, 1986–87, Publishing Dir, 1987–95, Bantam Press; Hardcover Publisher, Bantam Press and Doubleday, 1995–2000; Publisher, Little, Brown Book Gp, 2000–05. Chair, Trade Publishers' Council, 2006–11. Publishers' Association: Officer, 2011–14; Pres., 2012–13; Mem. Council, 2014–. *Recreations:* theatre, travel, swimming, cooking. *Address:* Little, Brown Book Group, Carmelite House, 50 Victoria Embankment, EC4Y 0DZ. *T:* (020) 3122 6000. *E:* ursula.mackenzie@littlebrown.co.uk.

MACKENZIE, Wallace John, OBE 1974; Director, Slough Estates plc, 1972–91 (Group Managing Director, 1975–86); *b* 2 July 1921; *s* of Wallace D. Mackenzie and Ethel F. Williamson; *m* 1951, Barbara D. Hopson; two *s* one *d. Educ:* Harrow Weald County Grammar Sch. Gen. Manager, Slough Estates Canada Ltd, 1952–72; Dep. Man. Dir, Slough Estates Ltd, 1972–75. Dir, Investors in Industry plc, 1982–86; Chm., Trust Parts Ltd, 1986–94 (Dir, 1985). Member: Commn for New Towns, 1978–94; London Residuary Body, 1985–95. Trustee, Lankelly Foundn, 1985–2005. *Recreations:* golf, bridge. *Address:* 1 Brampton Mews, Pound Lane, Marlow, Bucks SL7 2SY. *T:* (01628) 478310.

McKENZIE JOHNSTON, Henry Butler, CB 1981; Vice-Chairman, Commission for Local Administration in England, 1982–84 (Commissioner, 1981–84); *b* 10 July 1921; *er s* of late Colin McKenzie Johnston and late Bernardine (*née* Fawcett Butler); *m* 1949, Marian Allardyce Middleton (*d* 2009), *e d* of late Brig. A. A. Middleton and late Winifred (*née* Salvesen); one *s* two *d. Educ:* Rugby. Served with Black Watch (RHR), 1940–46; Adjt 6th Bn, 1944–45; Temp. Major 1945. Staff of HM Embassy, Athens, 1946–47; entered Foreign (subseq. Diplomatic) Service, 1947; Paris, 1948–51; British High Commn, Germany, 1951–54; FO, 1954–56; 1st Sec. (Commercial), Montevideo, 1956–60; FO, 1960–63; Counsellor (Information), Mexico City, 1963–66; Dep. High Comr, Port of Spain, 1966–67; seconded to Min. of Overseas Develt, 1968–70; Consul-Gen., Munich, 1971–73; seconded to Office of Parly Comr for Admin, 1973–79, transferred permanently, 1979–81; Dep. Parly Comr for Admin, 1974–81. Mem., Broadcasting Complaints Commn, 1986–90. Mem., Social Security Appeal Tribunal, Kensington, subseq. Central London, 1985–88. Chm., British-Mexican Soc., 1977–80. *Publications:* Missions to Mexico: a tale of British diplomacy in the 1820s, 1992; Ottoman and Persian Odysseys: James Morier, creator of Hajji Baba of Ispahan, and his brothers, 1998. *Address:* 6 Pembroke Gardens, W8 6HS. *Clubs:* Athenæum, Hurlingham.

McKENZIE-PRICE, Isobel Clare; Content Strategy Director, Homes Network, TimeInc. UK, since 2015; *b* 11 Jan. 1956; *d* of Edward Charles Price and Patricia Price (*née* Edgeley); *m* 1st, 1977, Andrew James Alistair McKenzie (marr. diss. 1981); 2nd, 1983, William Woods; one *s* three *d*. *Educ:* Horsham Girls High Sch.; Univ. of Leeds (BA Hons). Homes Editor, Over 21, 1979–80; Dep. Editor, Wedding and Home, 1983–85; Mem., Launch Team, Country Living, 1985–86; Dep. Editor, Essentials, 1986–90; Editor: Mother and Baby, 1990–91; Parents, 1991–92; Period Living, 1993–94; Editor in Chief, Elle Decoration, and Period Living, 1994–96; Publishing Consultant, Inspirations, 1997; Exec. Editor, Prima, and Launch Editor, Your Home, 1997–98; Ed.-in-Chief, then Editl Dir, IPC Home Interest Magazines (Ideal Home, Living etc, 25 Beautiful Homes, Homes & Gardens, Country Homes & Interiors), 1998–2004; Ed.-in-Chief, All You mag., Time Inc., NY, 2004–07; Editl Dir, housetohome.co.uk and Ideal Home mag., 2007–15. *Recreations:* family, new media, country walking. *E:* isobel.mckenzie-price@timeinc.com.

McKENZIE SMITH, Ian, CBE 2009 (OBE 1992); PPRSA (RSA 1987; ARSA 1973); PPRSW (RSW 1981); artist (painter); *b* 3 Aug. 1935; *y s* of James McKenzie Smith and Mary Benzie; *m* 1963, Mary Rodger Fotheringham; two *s* one *d*. *Educ:* Robert Gordon's Coll., Aberdeen; Gray's Sch. of Art, Aberdeen; Hospitalfield Coll. of Art, Arbroath; Aberdeen Coll. of Educn. SSA 1960; AAS 1963; FSAScot 1970; ASIAD 1975; FMA 1987. SED Travelling Scholarship to France, Italy, Belgium and Netherlands, Gray's Sch. of Art, 1958–59. Teacher of art, 1960–63; Educn Officer, Council of Industrial Design, Scottish Cttee, 1963–68; Dir, Aberdeen Art Gall. and Museums, 1968–89 (Hon. Mem., Friends of Aberdeen Art Gall., 2000); City Arts and Recreation Officer, City of Aberdeen, 1989–96. Work in permanent collections: Scottish Nat. Gall. of Modern Art; Scottish Arts Council; Arts Council of NI; Contemp. Art Soc.; Aberdeen Art Gall. and Museums; Glasgow Art Gall. and Museums; City Art Centre, Edinburgh; Perth Art Gall.; McManus Gall., Dundee; Abbot Hall Art Gall., Kendal; Hunterian Mus., Glasgow; Nuffield Foundn; Carnegie Trust; Strathclyde Educn Authority; Lothian Educn Authority; RSA; DoE; Robert Fleming Holdings; IBM; Deutsche Morgan Grenfell; Grampian Hosps Art Trust; Lord Chancellor; British Library. Mem., Cttee of Enquiry into Econ. Situation of Visual Artists, Gulbenkian Foundn, 1978. Trustee, Nat. Galls of Scotland, 1999–2007. Member: Scottish Arts Council, 1970–77 (Chm., Art Cttee, 1975–77); Scottish Museums Fedn, 1970–86; Scottish Museums Council, 1980–87 (Chm., Industrial Cttee, 1985–87); Aberdeen Univ. Museums Cttee and Music Cttee, 1970–96; ICOM Internat. Exhibns Cttee, 1986–96; Museums and Galls Commn, 1997–2000; Nat. Heritage, Scottish Gp, 1977–99; Bd of Mgt, Grampian Hosps Art Project, 1987–2000; Adv. Council on Export of Works of Art, 1991–2007; Curatorial Cttee, 1991–2001, Council, 1996–99, Bldgs Cttee, 1998–2001, NT for Scotland; RGI, 1998–. Arts Advr, COSLA, 1976–85. Pres., RSW, 1988–98. Royal Scottish Academy: Dep. Pres. and Treas., 1990–91; Sec., 1991–98; Pres., 1998–2007. Governor: Edinburgh Coll. of Art, 1976–88; The Robert Gordon Univ. (formerly Robert Gordon Inst. of Technology), 1989–95. External Assessor: Glasgow Sch. of Art, 1982–86; Duncan of Jordanstone Coll. of Art, 1982–86; Scottish Arts Council Gifting Scheme, 1997. Board Member: RSA Enterprises, and Friends of RSA, 1972–2007; Scottish Sculpture Workshop, 1979–2000; Aberdeen Maritime Mus. Appeal, 1981–98; Aberdeen Art Gall. Redevelt Project, 2009–. Vice Pres., NADFAS, 2000–04. Trustee: Painters Workshop (Scotland), 1975–89; John Kinross Fund, 1990–2007; Alexander Naysmith Fund, 1990–2007; Spalding Fund, 1990–2007; Sir William Gillies Fund, 1990–2007; Hospitalfield Trust, 1991–2007. Chm., Marguerite McBey Trust, 2000–. FSS 1981; FRSA 1973; FRSE 2003. Hon. RA 1999; Hon. RHA 1999; Hon. RUA 1999; Hon. RWA 2000. Hon. Mem., Peacock Printmakers, 1993. Hon. LLD Aberdeen, 1991; Hon. DArt Robert Gordon, 2000. Inst. of Contemp. Prints Award, 1969; Guthrie Award, 1971, Gillies Award, 1980, RSA; ESU Thyne Scholarship, 1980; Eduardo Paolozzi Medal, Nat. Galls of Scotland, 2007; Sir William Gillies Award, RSW, 2008; Arts and Business Scotland Award, Arts and Business Scotland, 2011. *E:* i.mckenziesmith@btinternet.com. *Clubs:* Royal Over-Seas League, Scottish Arts (Edinburgh); Royal Northern (Aberdeen).

MACKENZIE SMITH, Peter; Chairman, Getenergy Ltd, since 2014; *b* 12 Jan. 1946; *s* of late Antony and of Isobel Mackenzie Smith; *m* 1973, Sandra Gay-French; three *d*. *Educ:* Downside; Jesus Coll., Cambridge (BA Classical Tripos). Teacher: British Inst., Oporto, 1967–68; Internat. House, London, 1969; British Council, 1969–97: Asst Rep., Lagos, 1969–72; Asst Cultural Attaché, Cairo, 1972–77; Regl Dir, Southampton, 1977–80; Educnl Contracts Dept, 1980–83; Dep. Rep., Cairo, 1983–87; Director: Educnl Contracts, 1987–89; Projects Div., 1989–92; Nigeria and W Africa, 1992–94; Export Promotion, 1994–96; Africa and S Asia, 1996–97; Dir of Educn, General Electric Co., subseq. Marconi plc, 1997–2003; Export Promoter for Educn and Training, Trade Partners UK, 2001–03; Man. Dir, Prothero Ltd, 2003–12. Mem., Methodology Soc., 2000–. *Address:* Backfields End, Winchelsea, E Sussex TN36 4AB. *Club:* Athenæum.

McKEON, Andrew John; Senior Policy Fellow, Nuffield Trust, since 2014 (Acting Chief Executive, 2013–14); *b* 22 Sept. 1955; *s* of Kenneth and Maurine McKeon; *m* 1989, Hilary Neville; one *s* one *d*. *Educ:* William Hulme's Grammar Sch., Manchester; St Catharine's Coll., Cambridge. Joined DHSS, 1976; Hd of Medicines, Pharmacy and Industry Div., 2000–02, Dir of Policy and Planning, 2002–03, DoH; Man. Dir (Health), Audit Commn, 2003–12. Non-executive Director, NICE, 2009–; EMIS, 2013–. Trustee, Nuffield Trust, 2008–13. Adjunct Prof., Inst. of Global Health Innovation, Imperial Coll. London, 2011–.

McKEON, Simon Vincent, AO 2012; Chairman, Commonwealth Scientific and Industrial Research Organisation, 2010–15; Chairman, AMP Ltd, since 2014 (Director, since 2013); Consultant, Macquarie Group Ltd, since 2014; *b* Melbourne. *Educ:* Univ. of Melbourne (BCom 1976; LLB 1978). Solicitor, Blake Dawson Waldron, Sydney, 1980–83; with Macquarie Group Ltd, 1983–2014: Exec., 1984; Manager, 1985; Associate Dir, 1987; Divl Dir, Macquarie Corp. Finance Ltd, 1988; Exec. Chm., Melbourne Office, 2004–14. Chairman: MYOB, 2006–09; In2Science, 2013–. Mem., Editl Bd, Companies and Securities Law Jl, 1988–2011. Founding Pres., Australian Takeovers Panel, 1999–2010; Pres., Rev. Panel for Australian banking industry's Banking and Finance Oath, 2013–. Chair, Strategic Rev. of Health and Med. Res., 2011–13. Chairman: Business for Millennium Develt, 2007–; Global Poverty Project Australia, 2012–; Dir, Global Poverty Project Inc., 2009–14. Mem., Adv. Panel on Human Rights Grants Scheme, Australian Govt, 2009–13. Founding Chair, MS Res. Australia, 2004–10; Director: World Vision Australia, 1994–2005; Vision Fund, World Vision Internat., 2003–13; MS Soc. Australia, 2001–05; Red Dust Role Models, 2008–; Member: Adv. Bd, Big Issue, 2008–; Business Engagement Steering Cttee, AusAid, 2011–13. Mem., Strategic Adv. Bd, Univ. of Melbourne Law Grad. Prog., 2001–09. Australia Day Ambassador, Govt of Vic, 2007–. Chm., Point Nepean Community Trust, 2004–09. Patron: Australian Cttee, UN Year of Microcredit, 2005; Australian Olympic Sailing Team, 2006–. FAICD 2005. Australian of Year, 2011. Acad. Medal, Australian Acad. Sci., 2014. *Recreations:* yachting, bushwalking. *Clubs:* MCC; McCrae Yacht.

McKEOWEN, David; *see* Wills, Baron.

McKEOWN, Most Rev. Donal; *see* Derry, Bishop of, (RC).

McKEOWN, Dr John; Chief Executive Officer, United Kingdom Atomic Energy Authority, 1997–2003; Director, Hendred Strategy Ltd, 2003–06; *b* 10 March 1945; *s* of Edward McKeown and Anne McGladrigan; *m* 1967, Maureen Susan Doherty; one *s* one *d*. *Educ:* Univ. of Glasgow (BSc 1966; PhD 1971); Harvard Business Sch. CEGB Res. Fellow, 1971–73; Asst, Forward Planning, 1973–76; South of England Electricity Board: Sen. Engr, 1976–79, Principal Engr, 1979–83, Control and Instrumentation Div.; Manager: Electrical Dept, 1983–88; Nuclear Safety, 1988–90; Scottish Nuclear: Director: Safety, 1990–92; Projects, 1992–95; Safety & Envmt, 1995–96; Principal, John McKeown and Associates, 1996–97. Director: UK Nirex, 1997–2003; British Nuclear Industry Forum, 1998–2003; Oxford Economic Partnership, 1999–2010. *Recreations:* golf, music, travel. *Address:* Croft Orchard, Church Street, East Hendred, Oxon OX12 8LA. *Club:* Frilford Heath Golf.

McKEOWN, Prof. Patrick Arthur, OBE 1991; MSc; FREng, FIMechE; Professor of Precision Engineering, 1974–96, now Emeritus, Director of Cranfield Unit for Precision Engineering, 1969–96, Cranfield University (formerly Institute of Technology); Director, Pat McKeown and Associates, since 1995; *b* 16 Aug. 1930; *s* of Robert Matthew McKeown and Augusta (*née* White); *m* 1954, Mary Patricia Heath; three *s*. *Educ:* Cambridge County High Sch. for Boys; Bristol Grammar Sch.; Cranfield Inst. of Technol. (MSc). CEng, MIMechE 1969; FIET (FIProdE 1971); FREng (FEng 1986). National Service, RE, 1949–51; Suez Campaign, 1956: Captain RE; port maintenance. Student apprentice, Bristol Aircraft Co. Ltd, Bristol, 1951–54 (HNC National State Scholarship); Cranfield Inst. of Technol., 1954–56; Société Genevoise, Newport Pagnell and Geneva, 1956–68 (Technical and Works Dir, 1965); Hd of Dept for Design of Machine Systems. Cranfield Inst. of Technol., 1975–85. Chairman: Cranfield Precision Systems Ltd, 1984–87; Cranfield Moulded Structures Ltd, 1984–91; Cranfield Precision Engrg Ltd, 1987–95 (Chief Exec., 1987–92); non-executive Director: Control Techniques plc, 1990–95; AMTRI, 1990–92; Cranfield Aerospace Ltd, 2001–03. Vice-Pres., Inst. of Quality Assurance, 1976; Pres., CIRP (Internat. Instn for Prodn Engrg Res.), 1988–89 (Fellow, 1975). Member: Evaluation Panel, National Bureau of Standards, Washington, USA; Metrology and Standards Requirements Bd, DTI, 1983–86; Advanced Manufg Technol. Cttee, DTI, 1983–87; Vis. Cttee, RCA, 1984–87; ACARD working gp, 1987–88. Internat. Advr, Gintic Inst. of Manufg Technology, Singapore, 1991–97. Vis. Prof., Univ. of Calif, Berkeley, 1994. Mem., Adv. Bd, Kimberley STEM Coll., 2013–. Clayton Meml Lectr, IMechE, 1986. Pres., Eur. Soc. for Precision Engrg and Nanotechnol., 1998–2000. Charter Fellow, Soc. of Manufacturing Engineers, 1985. FSME, USA; Hon. FIED 1990. Hon. DSc: Connecticut, 1996; Cranfield, 1996. Fulbright Award (Vis. Prof. of Mechanical Engrg, Univ. of Wisconsin-Madison), 1982; F. W. Taylor Award, Soc. of Manufacturing Engrs, 1983; Thomas Hawksley Gold Medal, IMechE, 1987; Mensforth Gold Medal, IProdE, 1988; Life Achievement Award, Amer. Soc. for Precision Engrg, 1998; Faraday Medal, IEE, 1999; Life Achievement Award, European Soc. for Precision Engrg and Nanotechnol., 2002; Internat. Prize, Japan Soc. for Precision Engrg, 2003; Georg Schlesinger Preis, Senate, State of Berlin, 2006; James Clayton Prize, IMechE, 2007; M. Eugene Merchant Manufg Medal, ASME/SME USA, 2009. Freedom, City of London, 2007; Liveryman, Co. of Engrs, 2008–. *Publications:* papers in CIRP Annals; project reports and lectures for Royal Acad. of Engrg. *Recreations:* walking, travel, enjoyment of wine, good food, classical music, theatre. *T:* (01234) 267678. *E:* patmckeown37@gmail.com.

McKERNAN, Prof. James, PhD; FRS 2011; Charles Lee Powell Professor of Mathematics, University of California at San Diego, since 2012; *b* 1964. *Educ:* Trinity Coll., Cambridge (BA 1985); Harvard Univ. (PhD 1991). Instructor: Univ. of Utah; Univ. of Texas; Vis. Asst Prof., Oklahoma State Univ., 1994–95; Prof. of Maths, UCSB, 1995–2007; Prof. of Maths, 2007–09, Norbert Wiener Prof. of Maths, 2009–12, MIT. Clay Res. Award, Clay Maths Inst., 2007; (with C. Hacon) Frank Nelson Cole Prize in Algebra, Amer. Maths Soc., 2009. *Address:* Department of Mathematics, University of California at San Diego, 9500 Gilman Drive, La Jolla, CA 92093–0112, USA.

McKERNAN, Ruth Mitchell, CBE 2013; PhD; Chief Executive, Innovate UK, since 2015; *b* Alyth, Scotland, 19 March 1958; *d* of Dr William Mitchell McKernan and Catherine McKernan; *m* 1996, Dr Gerard Dawson; one *s* one *d*. *Educ:* Prendergast Grammar Sch., London; King's Coll. London (BSc (Hons I) Pharmacol. and Biochem.); Inst. of Psychiatry, Univ. of London (PhD Neurosci. 1984). Post-doctoral Fellow, UCSD, 1985–87; Scientist, Biochemistry Dept, Merck Res. Labs, 1987–2005 (Dept Hd, 1997–2002; Site Hd, 2002–05); Vice Pres., Pfizer, 2005–11; Chief Scientific Officer, Neusentis and Sen. Vice Pres., Pfizer, 2011–15. Member: MRC, 2012–; Bd, Cancer Res. Technol., 2013–. Vis. Prof., KCL, 2003–. Patron, Internat. Spinal Res. Trust, 2013– (Trustee, 2003–13). *Publications:* Billy's Halo, 2006; 120 articles in scientific jls. *Recreation:* walking round the garden with a glass of wine. *Address:* Innovate UK, North Star House, North Star Avenue, Swindon SN2 1UE. *T:* (01793) 442701. *E:* ruth.mckernan@innovateuk.gov.uk. *Club:* Royal Society of Medicine.

MacKERRON, Prof. Gordon Stewart; Professor of Science and Technology Policy, SPRU - Science and Technology Policy Research, University of Sussex, since 2013; *b* 15 Jan. 1947; *s* of James and Jessie MacKerron; *m* 1997, Kara Smith; one *s* one *d*. *Educ:* St John's Coll., Cambridge (BA Econs 1968); Univ. of Sussex (MA Develt Econs). Econ. planner, ODI-Nuffield Fellow, Malaŵi, 1969–71; Fellow, SPRU, Univ. of Sussex, 1974–76; Lectr, Griffith Univ., Brisbane, 1976–78; Sen. Fellow, SPRU, Univ. of Sussex, 1978–2000; Dep. Dir, Energy Rev. Team, Perf. and Innovation Unit, Cabinet Office, 2001; Associate Dir, NERA Econ. Consulting, 2001–05; Dir, Sussex Energy Gp, 2005–08, Dir, 2008–13, SPRU, Univ. of Sussex. Chm., Cttee on Radioactive Waste Mgt, 2003–07; Mem., Royal Commn on Envmtl Pollution, 2010–11. *Publications:* (ed) The UK Energy Experience: a model or warning, 1996; (ed) The International Experience, 2000; contrib. jls incl. Energy Policy, Energy Jl, Revue de l'Energie. *Recreations:* singing, salsa (dance), history. *Address:* Science and Technology Policy Research Unit, Jubilee Building, University of Sussex, Falmer, Brighton BN1 9SL. *T:* (01273) 876584, *Fax:* (01273) 685865. *E:* g.s.mackerron@sussex.ac.uk.

McKERROW, June; charity advisor; Director, Mental Health Foundation, 1992–2000; *b* 17 June 1950; *d* of late Alexander Donald and Lorna McKerrow; one adopted *d*. *Educ:* Brunel Univ. (MPhil 1977). Housing management in local govt and housing assocs, 1967–80; Dir, Stonham Housing Assoc., 1980–92. Mem. Cttee, English Rural Housing Assoc., 1997–99. Trustee and Vice-Chm., Shelter, 1985–93; Trustee: Homeless Internat., 1988–93; Cherwell Housing Trust, 1992–97; Charity Projects, 1993–97; Comic Relief, 1995–97; Donnington Doorstep, 2002–09; Winston's Wish, 2002–04; Change of Scene, 2008–; Dir, Soundabout, 2003–11; Mentor, Prince's Trust, 2011–. Patron, Revolving Doors Agency, 1993–99; Chm., Housing Assocs Charitable Trust, 1998–2002; Mem. Bd, Advance Housing and Support, 2001–03. Mem., British Council, UN Internat. Year of Shelter for the Homeless, 1987. Non-exec. Dir, Oxfordshire and Buckinghamshire Mental Health Trust (formerly Oxfordshire Mental Healthcare NHS Trust), 2000–07. Mem. Court, Oxford Brookes Univ., 1999–2007. *Address:* 6 Fryth Wood, Chepstow, Monmouthshire NP16 6DU.

McKERROW, Neil Alexander Herdman; *b* 17 May 1945; *s* of late Anderson Herdman McKerrow, TD, MB ChB and of Joan Ysobel Cuthbertson (*née* Clark); *m* 1971, Penelope Mackinlay (*née* Chiene); one *s* two *d*. *Educ:* Sedbergh Sch.; Emmanuel Coll., Cambridge (MA). Reckitt & Colman (Overseas) Ltd, 1968–69; commnd 1st Bn Queen's Own Highlanders (Seaforth and Camerons), service in Trucial-Oman States, BAOR, 1969–73 (Capt.); Marketing Manager, Distillers Co., 1973–75; Macdonald Martin Distilleries, later Glenmorangie plc: Export Dir, 1975–81; Sales Marketing Dir, 1981–87; Man. Dir, 1987–94; Chief Exec., Forest Enterprise, Forestry Commn, 1995–96. Bursar and Clerk to the Govs, Sedbergh Sch., 1997–2006. Director: Welsh Whisky Co., 2006–; Royal Lyceum Theatre Co., 2007–10. Dep. Dir, Atlantic Salmon Trust, 2006–10. Member: Royal Scottish Pipers Soc., 1971–; High Constabulary, Port of Leith, 1976– (Moderator, 2007–08); Incorp. of Malt Men, 1990–. Liveryman, Co. of Distillers, 2006–. Gov., Belhaven Hill Sch., Dunbar, 1997–2004. *Recreations:* fishing, outdoor pursuits, most sports, malt whisky, local history, traditional jazz. *Clubs:* London Scottish; New (Edinburgh); Hawks (Cambridge); Royal & Ancient Golf (St Andrews).

MACKESON, Sir Rupert (Henry), 2nd Bt *cr* 1954; *b* 16 Nov. 1941; *s* of Brig. Sir Harry Ripley Mackeson, 1st Bt, and Alethea, Lady Mackeson (*d* 1979), *d* of late Comdr R. Talbot, RN; *S* father, 1964; *m* 1968, Hon. Camilla Keith (marr. diss. 1973), *d* of Baron Keith of Castleacre. *Educ:* Harrow; Trinity Coll., Dublin (MA). Captain, Royal Horse Guards, 1967, retd 1968. *Publications:* (as Rupert Collens): (jtly) 'Snaffles' on Racing and Point-to-Pointing, 1988; (jtly) 'Snaffles' on Hunting, 1989; Look at Cecil Aldin's Dogs and Hounds, 1990; 25 Legal Luminaries from Vanity Fair, 1990; Cecil Aldin's Dog Models, 1994; (as Rupert Mackeson): Bet Like a Man (novel), 2001; Flat Racing Scams and Scandals, 2004. *Recreations:* art, racing. *Heir:* none. *Address:* 25 Thirlmere Road, Weston-super-Mare, Somerset BS23 3UY.

MACKESON-SANDBACH, Antoinette, (Mrs M. R. Sherratt); MP (C) Eddisbury, since 2015; *b* London, 15 Feb. 1969; *d* of Ian and Annie Mackeson-Sandbach; one *d* (one *s* decd); *m* 2012, Matthew Robin Sherratt. *Educ:* West Heath; Haileybury Coll.; Nottingham Univ. (BA Hons Law; LLM Internat. Law). Called to the Bar, Lincoln's Inn, 1993; in practice as barrister, 9 Bedford Row, 1995–2006; farmer, 2006–11. Mem. (C) Wales N, Nat. Assembly for Wales, 2011–15; Shadow Minister: for Rural Affairs, 2011–14; for Envmt and Energy, 2014–15. *Address:* House of Commons, SW1A 0AA. *T:* (020) 7219 3000. *E:* antoinette.sandbach.mp@parliament.uk.

MACKEY, Allan Robert; Project Director, International Association of Refugee Law Judges, since 2011; *b* 24 April 1942; *s* of Albert George Mackey and Eileen Annie Mackey; *m* 1966, Mary Anne Kirkness; two *s* one *d*. *Educ:* Otahuhu Coll., Auckland; Auckland Univ. (LLB 1966); Cranfield Univ. (MBA 1976). Barrister and Solicitor, NZ, 1966; Solicitor, NSW, 1968; Barrister and solicitor, Auckland, 1966–68 and 1970–74; Solicitor, Sydney, Australia, 1968–70; Mktg Manager, Todd Motors Ltd, NZ, 1975–79; Gen. Manager, Mazda Motors, NZ, 1980–86; Solicitor/Consultant, Auckland, Hong Kong, Dubai, 1987–91; Mem., Residence, Removal and Refugee Appeal Authy of NZ, 1991–94; Chm., Refugee and Residence Appeal Authorities of NZ, 1994–2001; Legal Chair, Immigration Appeal Tribunal, UK, 1999–2001; Sen. Immigration Judge (formerly a Vice-Pres., Immigration Appeal Tribunal), UK, 2001–07; Chair, Refugee Status Appeals Authy, NZ, 2007–10; Dep. Chair, Immigration and Protection Tribunal, NZ, 2010–12. Vis. Prof., Univ. of Tokyo, 2006. Pres., Internat. Assoc. of Refugee Law Judges, 2002–05 (Vice Pres., 2000–02). *Recreations:* yachting, walking. *Address:* c/o International Association of Refugee Law Judges, PO Box 1621, 2003 BR Haarlem, Netherlands. *T:* (9) 5287660. *E:* arm.mam@gmail.com. *Club:* Wellington (Wellington, NZ).

MACKEY, Craig, QPM 2009; Deputy Commissioner, Metropolitan Police Service, since 2012; *b* Ibadan Town, Nigeria, 26 Aug. 1962; *m* Debbie; one *d*. *Educ:* Open Univ. (BSc Hons); Postgrad. Dip. Econs; Postgrad. Dip. Criminal Justice. Served Merchant Navy, with BP, 1980–84; joined Police Service, 1984; with Wilts Police, 1984–99; specialist staff inspector, HM Inspector of Constabulary, Home Office, 1999–2001; Asst Chief Constable, 2001–05, Dep. Chief Constable, 2005–07, Glos Constabulary; Chief Constable, Cumbria Constabulary, 2007–12. FCMI. *Recreations:* walking, reading, Rugby, mountain biking. *Address:* New Scotland Yard, Broadway, SW1H 0BG. *T:* (020) 7230 2636.

MACKEY, Prof. James Patrick; Thomas Chalmers Professor of Theology, 1979–99, now Emeritus, and Director of Graduate School and Associate Dean, 1995–99, University of Edinburgh (Hon. Fellow, Faculty of Divinity, 1999–2002); *b* 9 Feb. 1934; *e s* of Peter Mackey and Esther Mackey (*née* Morrissey); *m* 1973, Hanorah Noelle Quinlan; one *s* one *d*. *Educ:* Mount St Joseph Coll., Roscrea; Nat. Univ. of Ireland (BA); Pontifical Univ., Maynooth (LPh, BD, STL, DD); Queen's Univ. Belfast (PhD); postgraduate study at Univs of Oxford, London, Strasbourg. Lectr in Philosophy, QUB, 1960–66; Lectr in Theology, St John's Coll., Waterford, 1966–69; Associate Prof. and Prof. of Systematic and Philosophical Theol., Univ. of San Francisco, 1969–79; Dean, Faculty of Divinity, Edinburgh Univ., 1984–88. Visiting Professor: Univ. of California, Berkeley, 1974; Dartmouth Coll., NH, 1989; TCD, 1999–2010; Curricular Consultant, UC Cork, 1999–2003. Member: Ind. Assessment Panel for NI Policing Bd, 2005; Consultative Gp on the Past (NI), 2007–09. Mem., Centre for Hermeneutical Studies, Univ. of California, Berkeley, 1974–79. Organiser, Internat. Conf. on the Cultures of Europe, Derry, 1992. *Television series:* The Hall of Mirrors, 1984; The Gods of War, 1986; Perspectives, 1986–87; radio programmes. Associate Editor: Herder Correspondence, 1966–69; Concilium (church history section), 1965–70; Horizons, 1973–79; Founding Editor, Studies in World Christianity, 1995–2002. *Publications:* The Modern Theology of Tradition, 1962; Life and Grace, 1966 (trans. Spanish 1969); Tradition and Change in the Church, 1968 (trans. French 1969, Polish 1974); Contemporary Philosophy of Religion, 1968; (ed) Morals, Law and Authority, 1969 (trans. Italian 1973); The Church: its credibility today, 1970; The Problems of Religious Faith, 1972; Jesus: the man and the myth, 1979 (trans. German 1981); The Christian Experience of God as Trinity, 1983; (ed) Religious Imagination, 1986; Modern Theology: a sense of direction, 1987; (with Prof. J. D. G. Dunn) New Testament Theology in Dialogue, 1987; (ed) Introduction to Celtic Christianity, 1989; Power and Christian Ethics, 1993; (ed) The Cultures of Europe, 1994; The Critique of Theological Reason, 2000; (ed) Religion and Politics in Ireland, 2003; Christianity and Creation, 2006; The Scientist and the Theologian, 2007; Jesus of Nazareth, 2008; contribs to theol. and philosoph. jls. *Recreations:* yachting; rediscovery of original Celtic culture of these islands. *Address:* 15 Glenville Park, Dunmore Road, Waterford, Eire.

MACKEY, Air Vice-Marshal Jefferson; Chief Executive, Defence Dental Agency, 1996–97; *b* 24 Oct. 1936; *s* of late James Mackey and of Cicely (*née* Hitchman); *m* 1959, Sheila Mary Taylor; one *s* two *d*. *Educ:* Latymer Upper Sch.; Guy's Hosp. (BDS, LDS RCS). Asst Dir, Defence Dental Services, 1982–86; Officer Comdg RAF Inst. of Dental Health and Trng, 1986–87; Principal Dental Officer, RAF Support Command, 1987–90; Dir, RAF Dental Services, 1990–94; Dir, Defence Dental Services, 1992–96. QHDS 1987–97. FInstLM; FCMI; FRGS. *Address:* Takali, Oxford Road, Stone, Bucks HP17 8PB. *T:* (01296) 748823. *Clubs:* Royal Air Force; Mentmore Golf and Country.

McKIBBIN, (David) Malcolm; Head of the Northern Ireland Civil Service, since 2011; *b* Belfast, 20 Nov. 1956; *s* of Desmond and Iris McKibbin; *m* 1981, Susan Crook; two *d*. *Educ:* Univ. of Southampton (BSc Hons Civil Engrg 1978); Univ. of Ulster (DPhil 1987; MBA 1991). CCE 1982. Various posts, NI Roads Service, 1978–98; Dir, Transport Policy Div., 1998–99, Regl Transport Strategy Div., 1992–2002, Dept for Regl Develt; Chief Exec., NI Roads Service, 2002–07; Perm. Sec., Dept of Agriculture and Rural Develt, 2007–10, Dept for Regl Develt, 2010–11, NI. Mem., Bd of Govs, Royal Belfast Academical Instn, 2004–. *Recreations:* Rugby (played for many years for Instonians Rugby Club and coached Under 21 and First team squads, former Mem. Ulster Rugby Squad), playing tennis (at Belfast Boat Club and for Ulster Veterans). *Address:* Office of the First Minister and Deputy First Minister, Stormont Castle, Belfast BT4 3SR. *Clubs:* Instonians Rugby; Belfast Boat.

McKIBBIN, Dr Ross Ian, FBA 1999; Fellow, St John's College, Oxford, 1972–2005, now Emeritus Research Fellow; *b* 25 Jan. 1942; *s* of Arnold Walter McKibbin and Nance Lilian (*née* Spence). *Educ:* Univ. of Sydney (BA, MA); St Antony's Coll., Oxford (DPhil 1970). Lectr in Hist., Univ. of Sydney, 1968–70; Jun. Res. Fellow, Christ Church, Oxford, 1970–72; CUF Lectr, Univ. of Oxford, 1972–2005; Tutor in Modern Hist., St John's Coll., Oxford, 1972–2005. *Publications:* The Evolution of the Labour Party 1910–1924, 1974, 2nd edn 1991; The Ideologies of Class, 1990; Classes and Cultures: England 1918–1951, 1998; (ed) M. Stopes, Married Love, 2004; Parties and People: England 1914–1951, 2010. *Recreations:* gardening, squash, tennis. *Address:* St John's College, Oxford OX1 3JP. *T:* (01865) 277300.

MACKIE, Air Cdre (Retd) Alastair Cavendish Lindsay, CBE 1966; DFC 1943 and Bar 1944; Director General, Health Education Council, 1972–82; Chairman, Ansador Ltd, 1983–2001; *b* 3 Aug. 1922; *s* of George Mackie, DSO, OBE, MD, Malvern, Worcs and May (*née* Cavendish); *m* 1944, Rachel Goodson (*d* 2011); two *s*. *Educ:* Charterhouse. Royal Air Force, 1940–68; Under Treas., Middle Temple, 1968; Registrar, Architects' Registration Council, 1970; Sec., British Dental Assoc., 1971; Pres., Internat. Union for Health Educn, 1979–82. Life Pres., 3rd Parachute Bde, 6th Airborne Div. Meml Assoc., 2006. Vice-Pres., CND, 1990–. *Publications:* Some of the People All the Time, 2006; Flying Scot, 2012. *Address:* 4 Warwick Drive, SW15 6LB. *T:* (020) 8789 4544.

See also D. L. Mackie.

MACKIE, Prof. Andrew George; Professor of Applied Mathematics, 1968–88, Vice-Principal, 1975–80, University of Edinburgh; *b* 7 March 1927; *s* of late Andrew Mackie and Isobel Sigsworth Mackie (*née* Storey); *m* 1959, Elizabeth Maud Mackie (*née* Hebblethwaite); one *s* one *d*. *Educ:* Tain Royal Acad.; Univ. of Edinburgh (MA); Univ. of Cambridge (BA); Univ. of St Andrews (PhD). Lecturer, Univ. of Dundee, 1948–50; Bateman Res. Fellow and Instructor, CIT, 1953–55; Lecturer: Univ. of Strathclyde, 1955–56; Univ. of St Andrews, 1956–62; Prof. of Applied Maths, Victoria Univ. of Wellington, NZ, 1962–65; Res. Prof., Univ. of Maryland, 1966–68. Visiting Professor: CIT, 1984; Univ. of NSW, 1985. FRSE 1962. *Publications:* Boundary Value Problems, 1965, 2nd edn 1989; numerous contribs to mathematical and scientific jls. *Recreation:* bowls. *Address:* 31/7 Hermitage Drive, Edinburgh EH10 6BY. *T:* (0131) 447 2164.

MACKIE, (Ann) Louise; *see* Heathwaite, A. L.

MACKIE, Anne; Director of Programmes, UK National Screening Committee, since 2007; *b* Yorkshire, 8 Aug. 1962; *d* of William Mackie and Jean Mackie; *m* 2006, Jo Mackie; one *d*. *Educ:* Moor End Comprehensive Sch., Huddersfield; King's Coll., London (MB BS 1985). MFPHM 1995, FFPHM 2001. Registrar, SE London HA, 1986–89; Dep. Dir, E London and the City HA, 1987–93; Director of Public Health: Kent and Medway SHA, 1995–2004; SW London SHA, 2004–07; London SHA, 2007–. *Publications:* contribs to BMJ, Heart, Jl of Public Health and annual reports. *Recreations:* family, cycling, literature, modern art, gastronomy. *Address:* UK National Screening Committee, Public Health England, Skipton House, SE1 6LH. *T:* (020) 3312 6927.

MACKIE, Clive David Andrew, FCA, FSS; Secretary-General, Institute of Actuaries, 1983–92; *b* 29 April 1929; *s* of David and Lilian Mackie; *m* 1953, Averil Ratcliff; one *s* three *d*. *Educ:* Tiffin Sch., Kingston-on-Thames. FCA 1956; FSS 1982. Director: cos in Grundy (Teddington) Group, 1959–67; D. Sebel & Co. Ltd, 1967–70; Asst Sec. and Finance Officer, Poly. of the South Bank, 1970–73; Institute of Actuaries: Dep. Sec., 1973–77; Sec., 1977–83. Mem., Catenian Assoc., 1972– (Sec., Hastings, 2002–). *Recreations:* music (post 1780), cricket, carpentry, roaming in the countryside. *Address:* Ashes Lodge, Netherfield, E Sussex TN33 9PP. *T:* (01424) 774203. *Clubs:* Actuaries; Sussex CC.

MACKIE, His Honour David Lindsay, CBE 2004; QC 1998; a Deputy High Court Judge, since 1998; Senior Circuit Judge, 2004–15, Judge in charge, London Mercantile Court, 2006–15; *b* 15 Feb. 1946; *s* of Air Cdre Alastair Cavendish Lindsay Mackie, *qv*; *m* 1971 (marr. diss.); two *s* one *d*; *m* 2015, Katherine Reece. *Educ:* St Edmund Hall, Oxford. FCIArb 1990. Admitted Solicitor, 1971. Joined Allen & Overy, 1968, Partner, 1975–2004, Hd of Litigation, 1988–2004. A Recorder, 1992–2004. Trustee, Royal Courts of Justice Advice Bureau, 1998–; Chairman: Financial Services and Markets Tribunal, 2001–; Pensions Regulator Tribunal, 2005–. Pres., Financial Markets Tribunal, Dubai Internat. Financial Services Authy, 2014–. *Recreation:* climbing.

MACKIE, Eileen Philomena Carroll; *see* Carroll, E. P.

MACKIE, George, DFC 1944; RSW 1968; RDI 1973; freelance graphic artist and painter; Head of Design, Gray's School of Art, Aberdeen, 1958–80 (retd); *b* 17 July 1920; *s* of late David Mackie and late Kathleen Grantham; *m* 1952, Barbara Balmer, RSA, RSW, RGI; two *d*. Served Royal Air Force, 1940–46. Consultant in book design to Edinburgh University Press, 1960–87. Paintings in various private and public collections incl. HRH the Duke of Edinburgh's and Scottish Nat. Gall. of Modern Art. Major retrospective exhibitions: Books, mostly scholarly, and some Ephemera, Nat. Library of Scotland, 1991; Dartmouth Coll., NH, USA, 1991. *Publications:* Lynton Lamb: Illustrator, 1979. *Address:* 32 Broad Street, Stamford, Lincs PE9 1PJ. *T:* (01780) 753296.

MACKIE, Prof. George Owen, FRS 1991; FRSC; DPhil; Professor of Biology, University of Victoria, 1968–94, Professor Emeritus since 1995; *b* 20 Oct. 1929; *s* of late Col (Frederick) Percival Mackie, CSI, OBE, IMS and Mary E. H. Mackie (*née* Owen); *m* 1956, Gillian V. Faulkner; three *s* two *d*. *Educ:* Oxford (BA 1954; MA 1956; DPhil 1956). FRSC 1982. Univ. of Alberta, 1957–68; Univ. of Victoria, 1968–; Chm., Biol. Dept, 1970–73. Killam Res. Fellow, 1986–88. Editor, Canadian Jl of Zoology, 1980–89. Fry Medal, Canadian Soc. of Zoologists, 1989. *Publications:* (ed) Coelenterate Ecology and Behavior, 1976; numerous research articles in books and jls. *Recreations:* chamber music ('cello), earthenware pottery. *Address:* 2173 Tryon Road, North Saanich, BC V8L 5H6, Canada. *T:* (250) 6564291.

MACKIE, Joyce Grant, MBE 2014; Vice Lord-Lieutenant of Aberdeenshire, since 2009; partner, farming business, since 1963; *b* Forfar, Angus, 7 May 1940; *d* of Jay Grant Clark and Winifred Bertram Clark (*née* Wood); *m* 1963, (Bruce) Stephen Mackie (*d* 2011); two *s* two *d*. *Educ:* Montrose Primary Sch.; St Margaret's Sch. for Girls, Aberdeen; Moray House Coll. of Educn, Edinburgh (Cert Ed 1961); Open Univ. (BA Hons 1992). National Trust for Scotland: Member: Council, 1974–79, 1985–90; Exec. Cttee, 1976–86, 1986–2003; Regl Cttee, 1976– (Chm., 1976–2000); Vice-Pres., 1988–2003; Hon. Founder Pres., Chm. and Mem. Cttee, NE Aberdeenshire Members' Centre, 1976–. Member: Aberdeen Cttee, RSSPCC, 1966–96; Agricl Adv. Cttee, BBC, 1976–84; Trustee, David Gordon Meml Trust, 1977–; Pres., NE Scotland and Northern Isles Br., British Red Cross, 2005–13. Dir, Lathallan Prep. Sch., Montrose, 1979–2001 (Chm., 1990–98); Mem. Council, Glenalmond Coll., 1991–2004 (Mem. Cttee, 2001–04), Fellow, 2006; Mem. Exec. Cttee, Aberdeen Univ. Quincentenary Campaign, 1993–96. Mem., Nomination Cttee, Church of Scotland, 1985–88. DL Aberdeenshire, 1992. *Recreations:* art, art history, gardens, National Trust for Scotland. *Address:* Balquhindachy, Methlick, Ellon, Aberdeenshire AB41 7BY. *T:* (01651) 806373, *Fax:* (01651) 806875. *Clubs:* Farmers; New (Edinburgh).

MACKIE, Karl Joseph, CBE 2010; PhD; Chief Executive, Centre for Effective Dispute Resolution, since 1990; *s* of John Mackie and Ethel Mackie (*née* Freedman); *m* 1st, 1968, Ann Douglas (marr. diss.); one *s* one *d*; 2nd, 2001, Eileen Philomena Carroll, *qv*; one step *d*. *Educ:* Buckhaven High Sch.; Univ. of Edinburgh (MA Hons), DipEd; Univ. of London (LLB ext.); Univ. of Nottingham (PhD 1987); Open Univ. (MBA 1990). CPsychol 1989; FCIArb 1992. Accredited Mediator, CEDR. Called to the Bar, Gray's Inn, 1982; Res. Associate, Univ. of Edinburgh, 1971–72; various posts, 1972–73; Lectr, then Sen. Lectr, Law and Social Psychology, Univ. of Nottingham, 1973–90; Partner, Network Associates Strategy Consultants, 1985–90. Hon. Prof. in Alternative Dispute Resolution, Univ. of Birmingham, 1994–2001; Special Prof. in Law, Univ. of Westminster, 2003–09. Vice-Chm., Civil Mediation Council, 2003–10. Chief Adjudicator, OFSTED Ind. Complaints Service, 2009–. Ombudsman, LIFFE NYSE Euronext, 2011–. Member: Panel of Independent Mediators and Arbitrators, ACAS, 1980–; Singapore Internat. Commercial Mediators Panel, 2001–; Panel of Dist. Neutrals, Internat. Inst. for Conflict Prevention and Resolution, 2007–; Panel of

Internat. Mediators, China Internat. Economic and Trade Arbitration Commn, 2012–; Adv. Council, All Pty Parly Gp on Conflict, 2007–. Member: Educn Cttee, Bar Assoc. for Commerce, Finance and Industry, 1987–90; Law Soc. Specialisation Cttee, 1989–92. Chm., Write Away, 2003–06. FRSA 1993. Mem. editl cttee, various jls. *Publications:* (ed jtly) Learning Lawyers' Skills, 1989; Lawyers in Business and the Law Business, 1989; (ed) A Handbook of Dispute Resolution, 1991; (jtly) Commercial Dispute Resolution, 1995, 3rd edn as The ADR Practice Guide, 2007; (with E. Carroll) International Mediation: the art of business diplomacy, 2000, 2nd edn 2006; (ed jtly) The EU Mediation Atlas, 2004. *Recreations:* film, photography, swimming, ski-ing, writing. *Address:* Centre for Effective Dispute Resolution, 70 Fleet Street, EC4Y 1EU. *T:* (020) 7536 6000.

MACKIE, Lily Edna Minerva, (Mrs John Betts), OBE 1986; Head Mistress, City of London School for Girls, 1972–86; *b* 14 April 1926; *d* of Robert Wood Mackie and Lilian Amelia Mackie (*née* Dennis); *m* 1985, John Betts (*d* 1992). *Educ:* Plaistow Grammar Sch.; University Coll., London (BA); Lycée de Jeunes Filles, Limoges; Université de Poitiers. Asst Mistress: Ilford County High Sch. for Girls, 1950–59; City of London Sch. for Girls, 1960–64; Head Mistress: Wimbledon County Sch., 1964–69; Ricards Lodge High Sch., Wimbledon, 1969–72. *Recreations:* theatre, music, gardening, travel. *Address:* Cotswold, 59–61 Upper Tooting Park, SW17 7SU.

MACKIE, Prof. Neil, CBE 1996; FRSE; international concert tenor; Professor, Fine Arts Faculty, University of Agder, Kristiansand, Norway, 2005–14; Professor of Singing, Royal Academy of Music, since 2009; *b* 11 Dec. 1946; *yr s* of late William Fraser Mackie and Sheila Roberta (*née* Taylor); *m* 1973, Kathleen Mary Livingstone, soprano; two *d. Educ:* Aberdeen Grammar Sch.; Royal Scottish Acad. of Music and Drama (DipMusEd, DipRSAMD; FRSAMD 1992); Royal Coll. of Music (Foundn Scholar 1970; ARCM Hons; FRCM 1996). London recital début, Wigmore Hall, 1972; London concert début with English Chamber Orch., 1973; world premières include works by Peter Maxwell Davies, Britten, Henze and Kenneth Leighton; numerous recordings. Prof. of Singing, 1985–2008, Head of Vocal Studies, 1994–2006, Royal Coll. of Music. Artistic Dir, Mayfield Internat. Fest., E Sussex, 2004–12. Hon. RAM 2011. Hon. Mem., Norwegian Acad. of Sci. and Letters, 2012. Hon. DMus Univ. of Aberdeen, 1993. CStJ 1996. *Recreations:* reading, charity work, occasional gardening. *Address:* 70 Broadwood Avenue, Ruislip, Middx HA4 7XR. *T:* (01895) 632115. *E:* neilmackie@talktalk.net. *Club:* Athenæum.

McKIE, Peter Halliday, CBE 1995; CChem, FRSC, CEng; Chairman: PHM Associates (NI) Ltd, since 1996; *b* 20 March 1935; *s* of Harold and Winifred McKie; *m* 1959, Jennifer Anne Parkes; three *s* one *d. Educ:* Bangor Grammar Sch.; Queen's Univ., Belfast (BSc Chem.; Hon. DSc 1993). CChem, FRSC 1988; FCQI (FIQA 1987); CEng 1993. Shift Supervisor, Courtaulds Ltd, 1956–59; Supervisor, Du Pont Mfg, Londonderry, 1959–77; Manager, Du Pont Waynesbro Orlon Plant, USA, 1977–79; Asst Works Dir, Du Pont, Londonderry, 1979–81; Man. Dir, Du Pont Scandinavia and Du Pont Finland, 1981–84; Prodn Manager, Du Pont Europe, 1984–87; Chm., Du Pont (UK) Ltd, 1987–96; Manager, Du Pont Belle Plant, W Virginia, USA, 1995–96; Chm., QUBIS Ltd, 1998–2005. Chm., Industrial Res. & Technol. Unit, Dept of Econ. Develt, NI, 1994–2001. Chm., HSE, NI, 2005–11. Vis. Prof., Dept of Engrg, QUB, 1991–. FInstD 1987. *Recreations:* photography, sport, classic cars and motor cycles. *Address:* 3 The Rookery, Killinchy, Co. Down BT23 6SY.

McKIE, Robin Lewis; Science Editor, The Observer, since 1982; *b* Glasgow, 25 June 1950; *s* of Thomas McKie and Doreen McKie (*née* Pearson); *m* 1993, Sarah Ann Mitchell; one *s* one *d* (and one *d* decd). *Educ:* High Sch. of Glasgow; Univ. of Glasgow (BSc Hons). Trainee, Scotsman Pubns, 1974–78; Science corresp., THES, 1978–82. *Publications:* Genetic Jigsaw, 1988; (with W. Bodmer) The Book of Man, 1994; (with C. Stringer) African Exodus, 1996; Apeman, 2000; Face of Britain, 2006. *Recreations:* squash, walking, travelling on trains. *Address:* 36 Trinity Gardens, SW9 8DP. *T:* (020) 7733 7386. *E:* robin.mckie@observer.co.uk. *Club:* Grafton Tennis.

MacKIE, Prof. Rona McLeod, (Lady Black), CBE 1999; MD, DSc; FRCP, FRCPath, FMedSci; FRSE; Professor of Dermatology, 1978–2001, Professorial Research Fellow, since 2001, Department of Public Health and Health Policy, University of Glasgow; *b* Dundee, 22 May 1940; *d* of late Prof. (James) Norman Davidson, CBE, FRS and Morag McLeod, PhD; *m* 1st, 1962, Euan Wallace MacKie (marr. diss. 1992); one *s* one *d*; 2nd, 1994, Sir James Whyte Black, OM, FRS (*d* 2010). *Educ:* Channing Sch., London; Laurel Bank Sch., Glasgow; Univ. of Glasgow (MB ChB 1963; MD with commendation 1970; DSc 1994). FRCPath 1984; FRCP 1985. Junior hosp. posts, Glasgow, 1964–70; Lectr in Dermatology, Glasgow Univ., 1971–72; Consultant Dermatologist, Greater Glasgow Health Bd, 1972–78. Pres., British Assoc. of Dermatologists, 1994–95 (Sir Archibald Gray Medal, 1999); FRSE 1983 (Meeting Sec., 1994–97; Internat. Convener, 2002–07); FMedSci 1998. Bicentenary Gold Medal, RSE, 2007; Gold Medal for Dermatological Res., British Soc. for Investigative Dermatology, 2011. *Publications:* textbooks and contribs to learned jls in field of skin cancer, particularly malignant melanoma. *Recreations:* family, opera, golf, gardening. *Address:* c/o University of Glasgow, Glasgow G12 8RZ. *E:* rona.mackie@glasgow.ac.uk. *Club:* Glasgow Art.

MACKILLIGIN, David Patrick Robert, CMG 1994; HM Diplomatic Service, retired; Governor, British Virgin Islands, 1995–98; *b* 29 June 1939; *s* of R. S. Mackilligin, CMG, OBE, MC and Patricia (*née* Waldegrave); *m* 1976, Gillian Margaret Zuill Walker; two *d. Educ:* St Mary's Coll., Winchester; Pembroke Coll., Oxford (2nd Cl. Hons PPE). Asst Principal, CRO, 1961–62; Third, later Second Sec., Pakistan, 1962–66; Asst Private Sec. to Sec. of State for Commonwealth Relations, 1966–68; Private Sec. to Minister Without Portfolio, 1968–69; Dep. Comr, Anguilla, 1969–71 (Actg Comr, July–Aug. 1970); First Sec., Ghana, 1971–73; First Sec., Head of Chancery and Consul, Cambodia, 1973–75 (Chargé d'Affaires at various times); FCO, 1975–80 (Asst Head of W African Dept, 1978–80); Counsellor (Commercial and Aid), Indonesia, 1980–85; NATO Defence Coll., Rome, 1985–86; Counsellor (Economic and Commercial), and Dir of Trade Promotion, Canberra, 1986–90; High Comr, Belize, 1991–95. *Recreations:* walking and swimming in remote places, ruins, second-hand bookshops, theatre, literature. *Address:* c/o Foreign and Commonwealth Office, King Charles Street, SW1A 2AH. *Clubs:* Oxford and Cambridge, Reform.

McKILLOP, Elizabeth Dorothy; Director of Collections, since 2007, and Deputy Director, since 2010, Victoria and Albert Museum; *b* 28 May 1953; *d* of Norman R. and Mary M. McConochie; *m* 1973, Andrew C. McKillop; one *s* one *d. Educ:* Univ. of Glasgow (MA 1972); Churchill Coll., Cambridge (MA 1975); University Coll. London (MSc 2004). Ed., BBC Monitoring Service, 1979–81; Curator: Chinese Collection, BL, 1981–90; Samsung Gall. of Korean Art, V&A, 1990–93; Korean Collection, BL, 1993–2004; Keeper, Dept of Asia, V&A, 2004–10. *Publications:* Korean Art and Design, 1992; North Korean Culture and Society, 2004. *Recreations:* food, travel. *Address:* Victoria and Albert Museum, S Kensington, SW7 2RL. *T:* (020) 7942 2000. *E:* bethmckillop@hotmail.com.

McKILLOP, Prof. James Hugh, FRCP, FRCR, FMedSci; Muirhead Professor of Medicine, University of Glasgow, 1989–2011; *b* 20 June 1948; *s* of Patrick McKillop and Helen Theresa McKillop (*née* Kilpatrick); *m* 1972, Caroline Annis Oakley; two *d. Educ:* St Aloysius' Coll.; Univ. of Glasgow (BSc, MB ChB; PhD 1979). FRCPGlas 1986; FRCPE 1990; FRCP 1992; FRCR 1994. University of Glasgow: Lectr in Medicine, 1975–82; Sen. Lectr in Medicine, 1982–89; Associate Dean for Med. Educn, 2000–03; Hd, Undergraduate Med. Sch., 2003–06; Dep. Exec. Dean of Medicine, 2007–10; Dep. Hd, Sch. of Medicine, 2010–11. Harkness Fellow, Stanford Univ., California, 1979–80. Chairman: Intercollegiate Standing Cttee on Nuclear Medicine, 1995–99; Admin of Radioactive Substances Adv. Cttee, DoH, 1996–2004; Scottish Med. and Scientific Adv. Cttee, 2001–07; NHS Educn Scotland Med. Adv. Gp, 2004–11; Scottish Deans Med. Curriculum Gp, 2005–09; Expert Adv. Panel, British Polio Fellowship, 2008–12. General Medical Council: Team Leader, GMC Quality Assurance of Basic Med. Educn, 2003–08; Mem., 2009–; Chair: Undergrad. Educn Bd, 2009–12; Audit and Risk Cttee, 2014–. Pres., British Nuclear Medicine Soc., 1990–92; Congress Pres., Eur. Assoc. of Nuclear Medicine, 1997; Mem., Exec. Cttee, Assoc. of Physicians of UK and Ire., 2000–03. FMedSci 1998. Hon. FAcadMed 2011. Hon. Dr Örebro. *Publications:* (with D. L. Citrin) Atlas of Technetium Bone Scans, 1978; (with A. G. Chalmers and P. J. Robinson) Imaging in Clinical Practice, 1988; (with I. Fogelman) Clinicians' Guide to Nuclear Medicine: benign and malignant bone disease, 1991; 250 papers mainly on nuclear medicine and cardiology. *Recreations:* opera (esp. Verdi), reading fiction, soccer, digital photography, looking at art. *Address:* Flat 1, 6 Kirklee Gate, Glasgow G12 0SZ.

McKILLOP, Murdoch Lang, CA; Partner, Talbot Hughes McKillop (formerly Talbot Hughes McKillop, then Kroll Talbot Hughes) LLP, 2002–13, now Consultant; *b* 30 Oct. 1947; *s* of Graham Lang McKillop and Margaret Morris (*née* Stark); *m* 1972, Elizabeth Leith; two *d. Educ:* Kelvinside Acad., Glasgow; Univ. of Strathclyde (BA Hons 1971). CA 1975; FSPI 1996. Joined Arthur Andersen, subseq. Andersen, Glasgow, as grad. trainee, 1971; Partner, 1984; Jt Administrator, Maxwell Private Gp, 1991; Joint Administrative Receiver: Leyland Daf Ltd, 1993; Ferranti Internat. plc, 1994, and others; Worldwide Head, Corporate Recovery and Turnaround, Arthur Andersen, 1996–98. Pres., Soc. of Practitioners of Insolvency, 1998–99; Institute of Chartered Accountants of Scotland: Jun. Vice-Pres., 2001–02; Sen. Vice-Pres., 2002–03; Pres., 2003–04; Convenor, Investigation and Professional Conduct Enforcement Cttee, 2004–10. Dir, Celsa UK Holdings, 2013–. *Recreation:* sailing. *Address:* 415 Spice Quay, Butlers Wharf, 32 Shad Thames, SE1 2YL. *Club:* Royal Highland Yacht (Oban).

McKILLOP, Sir Thomas Fulton Wilson, (Sir Tom), Kt 2002; PhD; FRS 2005; FRSE; Chief Executive, AstraZeneca plc, 1999–2006; President, Science Council, 2007–11; *b* 19 March 1943; *s* of Hugh McKillop and Annie (*née* Wilson); *m* 1966, Elizabeth Kettle; one *s* two *d. Educ:* Irvine Royal Acad.; Univ. of Glasgow (BSc 1st Cl. Hons; PhD Chem. 1968); Centre de Mécanique Ondulatoire Appliquée, Paris. Res. scientist, ICI Corporate Lab., 1969–75; ICI Pharmaceuticals: Hd, Natural Products Res., 1975–78; Res. Dir, France, 1978–80; Chemistry Manager, 1980–84; Gen. Manager, Res., 1984–85, Develt, 1985–89; Technical Dir, 1989–94; Zeneca Gp, then AstraZeneca: CEO, Zeneca Pharmaceuticals, 1994–99; Dir, 1996–2006. Dep. Chm., 2005–06, Chm., 2006–09, Royal Bank of Scotland Gp. Non-executive Director: Amersham Internat. PLC, 1992–97; Nycomed Amersham PLC, 1997–2000; Lloyds TSB Gp PLC, 1999–2004; BP PLC, 2004–09; Almirall SA, 2007–; UCB, 2009–; Evolva SA, 2010– (Chm., 2012–); Theravectys SAS, 2011–; Alere Inc., 2013–. Adv. Bd, Alsbridge PLC, 2010–12. Pres., European Fedn of Pharmaceutical Industries and Assocs, 2002–04. Trustee, Council for Industry and Higher Educn, 2002–09. Pro-Chancellor and Mem. Gen. Council, Univ. of Leicester, 1998–2007. MRI; MACS; Mem., Soc. for Drug Res. Trustee, Darwin Trust of Edinburgh, 1995–. FMedSci 2002; FRSE 2003. Hon. Fellow, Univ. of Lancs, 2004; Hon. FIChemE 2006; Hon. FRSC 2002. Hon. LLD: Manchester, 1999; Dundee, 2003; Hon. DSc: Glasgow, Leicester, Huddersfield, 2000; Nottingham, 2001; St Andrews, Salford, 2004; Manchester, 2005; Lancaster, 2007; Hon. Dr: Middx, 2000; Paisley, 2006; Hon. DLitt Heriot-Watt, 2006. Royal Medal, RSE, 2007. *Recreations:* music, sport, reading, walking, carpentry. *Address:* c/o Evolva SA, Duggingerstrasse 23, 4153 Reinach, Switzerland. *Club:* Wilmslow Golf.

MACKINLAY, Andrew Stuart; *b* 24 April 1949; *s* of Danny Mackinlay and late Monica (*née* Beanes); *m* 1972, Ruth Segar; two *s* one *d. Educ:* Salesian Coll., Chertsey. ACIS; DMA. A clerk, Surrey CC, 1965–75; Nalgo official, 1975–92. MP (Lab) Thurrock, 1992–2010. An Opposition Whip, 1992–93; Member: Transport Select Cttee, 1992–97; Foreign Affairs Select Cttee, 1997; Chm., All-Party Poland Gp, 1997. *Recreations:* studying battlefields of World War I in France and Belgium, non-league football, Ireland and Poland. *Club:* Chadwell Working Men's.

MACKINLAY, Craig; JP; MP (C) South Thanet, since 2015; *b* Chatham, 7 Oct. 1966; *s* of Colin Francis Mackinlay and Margaret Elizabeth Mackinlay; *m* 2011, Katalin Madi. *Educ:* Rainham Mark Grammar Sch., Rainham; Univ. of Birmingham (BSc Hons Zool. and Comparative Physiol.). FCA 1992; CTA 1993. Self-employed Partner, Beak Kemmenoe, Chatham. Mem. (C), Medway Council, 2007–15. JP N Kent. *Recreations:* sailing, shooting, travel. *Address:* House of Commons, SW1A 0AA. *T:* (020) 7219 4442. *E:* craig@craigmackinlay.com. *Clubs:* Carlton; Castle (Rochester).

MACKINLAY, (Jack) Lindsay; DL; Canon Treasurer, York Minster, 2000–07, now Canon Emeritus; *b* 24 Jan. 1936; *m* 1961, Catherine Elizabeth Houston; one *s* one *d.* FCA, FCMA. Rowntree plc, 1964–89 (Dir, 1973–89); Dir, 1990–2002, Chm., 1995–2002, Bradford & Bingley Bldg Soc., subseq. Bradford & Bingley plc. Dir, Argos, 1990–97; Chm., RPC Gp, 1992–2000. DL N Yorks, 2005. *Recreations:* golf, music. *Address:* The Cottage, Main Street, Stillington, York YO61 1JU.

McKINLAY, Peter, CBE 1998; Chairman, Wise Group, 1998–2001; *b* 29 Dec. 1939; *s* of late Peter McKinlay and of Mary Clegg (*née* Hamill); *m* 1963, Anne Rogerson Aitken Thomson; two *s* one *d. Educ:* Univ. of Glasgow (MA Hons). GPO HQ, Edinburgh, 1963–67; Scottish Office, 1967–91: Private Sec. to Minister of State, 1974–75; Director, Scottish Prison Service, 1988–91; Chief Executive, Scottish Homes, 1991–99. Nat. Exec., First Div. Assoc., 1977–80. Non-exec. Dir, D. S. Crawford Ltd, 1984–86; Chm., Bute Beyond 2000 (formerly Bute Partnership), 1993–98; Member: Bd, Cairngorms Partnership, 1998–99; Accounts Commn for Scotland, 2003–06. Dir, Common Purpose, 1993–97. FRSA 1998. Hon. DBA Napier, 1999. *Recreations:* family, friends, garden, TV, reading, food, drink. *Club:* Machrihanish Golf.

McKINLAY, Robert Murray, CBE 1993; FREng, FRAeS; President, Bristol Chamber of Commerce and Industry, 1994–97; *b* 12 Jan. 1934; *s* of Robert Graham McKinlay and Mary Murray; *m* 1957, Ellen Aikman Stewart; two *s. Educ:* Vale of Leven Acad.; Royal Tech. Coll., Glasgow (BSc Hons, ARTC). Flight testing and project engineering, Bristol Helicopters and Westlands, 1956–66; British Aircraft Corporation, 1966–79: Systems Develt Manager; Designer in charge; Asst Chief Engr; Asst Dir, Flight Test; Concorde Design Dir; British Aerospace, 1979–94: Dir, Airbus; Gp Dir, Man. Dir, Airbus Div.; Man. Dir, Commercial Aircraft; Chm., Airbus, 1991–94. Non-exec. Dir, B. F. Goodrich, Aerospace, Europe, 1998–2003 (Consultant, 2003–06). FREng (FEng 1992). Hon. DTech Bristol, 1991; Hon. DEng Glasgow, 2001. British Gold Medal, RAeS, 1995. *Recreations:* travelling, golf, piano, woodworking. *Address:* 43 Glenavon Park, Bristol BS9 1RW. *T:* (0117) 968 6253. *Club:* Society of Merchant Venturers (Bristol).

McKINNEL, Rt Rev. Nicholas Howard Paul; *see* Plymouth, Bishop Suffragan of.

McKINNELL, Catherine; MP (Lab) Newcastle upon Tyne North, since 2010; *b* Newcastle upon Tyne, 8 June 1976; *d* of John Grady and Agnes Grady (*née* Miller); *m* 2006, James Rhys McKinnell; one *s* one *d. Educ:* Sacred Heart Comprehensive Sch., Fenham, Newcastle upon Tyne; Univ. of Edinburgh (MA Hons Politics and Hist.); Univ. of Northumbria (Postgrad. DipLaw, CPE and Legal Practise Course). Admitted Solicitor 2004; Dickinson Dees LLP, 2002–09. Shadow Solicitor Gen., 2010–11; Shadow Minister for Children, 2011–15; Shadow Attorney Gen., 2015–. Member: Northumbria Assoc.; Unite the Union. Mem., Tyneside Cinema. *Recreations:* swimming, gardening, travel. *Address:* House of Commons, SW1A 0AA. *T:* (020) 7219 7115. *Club:* Tyneside Irish Centre.

McKINNEY, Rt Rev. Patrick Joseph; *see* Nottingham, Bishop of, (RC).

MacKINNON, Charles Archibald, CB 2005; freelance change management consultant, since 2008; *b* 1 July 1950; *s* of Ian MacDougall MacKinnon and Colina (*née* Beaton); *m* 1972, Jane Halpin; one *s* two *d*. *Educ:* Woodside Sen. Secondary Sch.; Sheffield Hallam Univ. (MBA). Various field operational mgt roles, 1968–84; Hd of Section, Policy and Planning, MSC, 1984–86; Project Manager, then Sen. Manager, various large projects in Employment Service, 1986–98; Benefits Agency: Dir, Field Ops (Scotland and N England), 1998–2000; Dep. Chief Exec., 2000–02; Chief Operating Officer, Pension Service, 2002–04; Transformation Dir, Pension Service, DWP, 2004–08. *Recreations:* squash, racquet ball, badminton, chess, theatre, reading, football spectator.

McKINNON, Rt Hon. Sir Donald (Charles), GCVO 2009; ONZ 2008; PC 1992; Commonwealth Secretary-General, 2000–08; *b* 27 Feb. 1939; *s* of Maj.-Gen. Walter Sneddon McKinnon, CB, CBE and Anna Bloomfield McKinnon (*née* Plimmer); *m* 1st, 1964, Patricia Maude Moore (marr. diss. 1995); three *s* one *d*; 2nd, 1995, Clare de Lore; one *s*. *Educ:* Lincoln Univ., New Zealand. AREINZ. Farm Manager, 1964–72; Farm Management Consultant, 1973–78; Real Estate Agent, 1974–78. MP (Nat. Party) NZ, 1978–99, for Albany, 1978–96; Dep. Leader of the Opposition, 1987–90; Dep. Prime Minister, 1990–96; Leader of the House, 1992–96; Minister: of External Relations, then Foreign Affairs, and Trade, 1990–99; of Pacific Island Affairs, 1991–98; for Disarmament and Arms Control, 1996–99; i/c War Pensions, 1998–99. Chairman: Regl Facilities, Auckland, 2011–; NZ-China Council, 2012–. Member: Asia Foundn; Waitangi Nat. Trust. Interim Dir, Auckland War Meml Mus., 2010–11. *Publications:* Six Months in Wyoming, 2006; In The Ring: a Commonwealth memoir, 2013. *Recreations:* enthusiastic jogger and tennis player, horse riding. *Address:* 49 Dell Road, Waua Pa RD 4, Pukekohe 2679, New Zealand.

McKINNON, Sir James, Kt 1992; FCMA; Director General, Office of Gas Supply, 1986–93; *b* 1929. *Educ:* Camphill School. CA 1952–2002, FCMA 1956. Company Secretary, Macfarlane Lang & Co. Ltd, Glasgow, 1955–65; Business Consultant, McLintock, Moores & Murray, Glasgow, 1965–67; Finance Director, Imperial Group plc, London, 1967–86. Chairman: Scotia Hldgs, 1992–2001; MAI plc, 1992–94; Ionica, 1993–98; Trafficmaster plc, 1994–2004; Arriva plc, 1994–99; Thorn Security Systems Ltd, 1994–96; Tyzack Precision plc, 1994–99; Discovery Trust plc, 1995–2006; Glass's Guide Ltd, 1996–98; Dep. Chm., United News & Media, 1994–2000; Director: Admiral plc, 1994–2000; F&C Private Equity Trust plc, 2005–06. Pres., Inst. of Chartered Accountants of Scotland, 1985–86. *Publications:* papers to learned jls and articles in Accountants' magazine. *Recreation:* ski-ing.

MacKINNON, Kenneth Alasdair, CVO 2011; RD 1971; WS; NP; JP; Lord-Lieutenant of Argyll and Bute, 2002–11 (Clerk of Lieutenancy, 1974–95; Vice Lord-Lieutenant, 2001–02); *b* 8 March 1936; *s* of Neil MacKinnon, WS and Janet Alison Mackenzie; *m* 1963, Anne Clare Valentine; one *s* two *d*. *Educ:* Edinburgh Acad.; Fettes Coll. (Pres., Old Fettesian Assoc., 1989–91); Pembroke Coll., Cambridge (BA 1959); Edinburgh Univ. (LLB 1961). Nat. Service, RN, 1954–56; Midshipman, RNVR, 1955; Lt Comdr, RNR, 1956–86. Apprentice Solicitor, Messrs Dundas & Wilson, CS, 1959–62; WS, 1962; D. M. MacKinnon, Oban: Asst Solicitor, 1962–63; Partner, 1963–96; Sen. Partner, 1989–96. Dean, Oban Faculty of Solicitors, 1995–97. Dir, Glasgow Local Bd, Commercial Union Assce, 1981–83. Hon. Sheriff, N Strathclyde at Oban, 1997. Council Member: WS Soc., 1993–96; Macmillan Cancer Relief, subseq. Macmillan Cancer Support, 2002–05 (Chm., Oban and Dist Br., 1993–2007). Pres., Oban Sea Cadet Unit, 2007–. Elder, C of S, 1975–2007. DL 1996, JP 2002, Argyll and Bute. Sec., 1963–76, Trustee, 2002–12, Argyllshire Gathering; Patron, Oban War and Peace Mus., 2009–. *Recreations:* sailing, game shooting, motoring, watching Rugby. *Address:* Ardcuan, Gallanach Road, Oban, Argyll PA34 4PE. *T:* (01631) 562325. *Club:* Royal Highland Yacht (Cdre, 1988–89, Trustee, 2003–11).

McKINNON, Prof. Kenneth Richard, AO 1995; FACE; Chairman: McKinnon Walker Pty Ltd, since 1995; IMB Pty Ltd, 2000–04; Chairman, Australian Press Council, 2000–09; *b* 23 Feb. 1931; *s* of Charles and Grace McKinnon; *m* 1st, 1956 (marr. diss.); one *s*; 2nd, 1981, Suzanne H., *d* of W. Milligan. *Educ:* Univ. of Adelaide; Univ. of Queensland (BA; BEd); Harvard Univ. (EdD). FACE 1972. Teacher, headmaster and administrator, 1957–65; Dir of Educn, Papua New Guinea, 1966–73; Chm., Australian Schs Commn, 1973–81; Vice-Chancellor, 1981–95, and Prof. Emeritus, Univ. of Wollongong; Vice-Chancellor: James Cook Univ. of N Qld, 1997; Northern Territory Univ., 2002–03. Chairman: Bd of Educn, Vic, 1982–85; Australian Nat. Commn for UNESCO, 1984–88; Illawara Technology Corp., 1983–; Marine Sci. and Technol. Review, 1988; Nuclear Res. Reactor Review, 1993; Reviewer, Marine Scis Orgns, 1993. Pres., AVCC, 1991–92. Member: Australia Council, 1974–77 (Dep. Chm., 1976–77); Primary Industries and Energy Res. Council, 1991–92; Prime Minister's Science Council, 1991–92. Consultant in the Arts, Aust. Govt, 1981. Dir, Coll. of Law, NSW, 1993–. Hon. DLitt: Wollongong, 1994; Deakin, 1994; NSW, 1995; DUniv James Cook, 1998. *Publications:* Realistic Educational Planning, 1973; Oceans of Wealth, 1988; Benchmarking in Universities, 2000; articles in jls and papers. *Recreations:* swimming, theatre, music, reading. *Address:* 14 Norfolk House, 1 Sutherland Crescent, Darling Point, NSW 2027, Australia. *T:* (2) 93623427, *Fax:* (2) 93632551.

McKINNON, Malcolm; *see* McKinnon, W. M.

MACKINNON, Neil Joseph; Sheriff of Glasgow and Strathkelvin at Glasgow, since 2014; *b* 24 Jan. 1956; *s* of late Donald Patrick Mackinnon and Catriona Traese Mackinnon (*née* Sinclair); *m* 1990, Anne Helen Gavagan; one *d*. *Educ:* St Aloysius' Coll., Glasgow; Univ. of Glasgow (LLB Hons 1978). Admitted solicitor, Scotland, 1980; Advocate, Scots Bar, 1984. Floating Sheriff, Edinburgh, 2000–05; Sheriff of Tayside Central and Fife at Falkirk, 2005–09; Sheriff of Lothian and Borders at Edinburgh, 2009–14. Mem., Rules Council, Court of Session, 1997–99. *Recreations:* travel, hill-walking. *Address:* c/o Sheriff Court House, 1 Carlton Place, Glasgow G5 9DA.

MacKINNON, Prof. Roderick, MD; John D. Rockefeller Jr Professor and Head of Laboratory of Molecular Neurobiology and Biophysics, Rockefeller University, since 1996; *b* 19 Feb. 1956; *m* Alice Lee. *Educ:* Brandeis Univ. (BA 1978); Tufts Univ. (MD 1982). Harvard Univ., 1985–86; Brandeis Univ., 1986–89; Asst, later Prof., Dept of Neurobiol., Harvard Med. Sch., 1989–96; Investigator, Howard Hughes Med. Inst., 1997–. (Jtly) Nobel Prize for Chemistry, 2003. *Address:* Laboratory of Molecular Neurobiology and Biophysics, Rockefeller University, 1230 York Avenue, New York, NY 10021, USA.

MacKINNON, Rowan Dorothy; *see* Pelling, R. D.

McKINNON, Sir Stuart (Neil), Kt 1988; a Judge of the High Court of Justice, Queen's Bench Division, 1988–2009; *b* 14 Aug. 1938; *s* of His Honour Neil Nairn McKinnon, QC; *m* 1st, 1966, Rev. Helena Jacoba Sara (*née* van Hoorn) (marr. diss. 1999); two *d*; 2nd, 2001, Michelle Jean Mary Withers. *Educ:* King's Coll. Sch., Wimbledon; Council of Legal Educn; Trinity Hall, Cambridge (BA, LLB 1963; MA 1967). Called to the Bar, Lincoln's Inn, 1960, Bencher, 1987; Junior at the Common Law Bar, 1964–80; QC 1980; a Recorder, 1985–88. Chm., Lord Chancellor's Middx Adv. Cttee on JPs, 1990–97. Pres., Cambridge Univ. Law Soc., 1962–63. *Recreation:* golf.
See also W. N. McKinnon.

McKINNON, Warwick Nairn; His Honour Judge Warwick McKinnon; a Circuit Judge, since 1998; Resident Judge, Croydon Crown Court, since 2006; a Senior Circuit Judge, since 2010; *b* 11 Nov. 1947; *s* of His Honour Neil McKinnon, QC; *m* 1978, Nichola Juliet Lloyd; one *s* one *d*. *Educ:* King's Coll. Sch., Wimbledon; Christ's Coll., Cambridge (MA). Called to the Bar, Lincoln's Inn, 1970, Bencher, 2010; in practice on SE Circuit; Asst Recorder, 1991–95; Recorder, 1995–98. Chm., Essex Criminal Justice Strategy Cttee, 1999–2001; IT Liaison Judge for Kent, 2001–06; Magistrates Liaison Judge and Chm., Area Judicial Forum for SE London, 2006–13. Hon. Recorder, Croydon, 2008–. *Recreations:* music, painting, travel, gardening, golf. *Address:* Croydon Crown Court, The Law Courts, Altyre Road, Croydon, Surrey CR9 5AB. *T:* (020) 8410 4700.
See also Sir S. N. McKinnon.

McKINNON, (William) Malcolm; Chief Executive, SITPRO Ltd, 2005–10; *b* Ilford, Essex, 14 Dec. 1953; *s* of William Malcolm McKinnon and Maureen Helena Margaret McKinnon; *m* 1978, Christine Elizabeth Platt; two *d*. *Educ:* Southend High Sch. for Boys; Inst. of Export (MIEx (Grad.) 1982). DTI, then Dept of Trade, subseq. DTI, 1973–2005; EO, Gen. Export Services, 1973–80; Third Sec., Consulate-Gen., Vancouver, 1977–78; EO, Commercial Relns with Republic of Korea, 1980–82; HEO, Internat. Trade Policy, 1983–86; Private Sec., 1987–88; Head: Trade with Soviet Union, 1988–90; EU Insce Policy, 1990–94; WTO Trade in Services, 1994–2005. Mem., Borough of Southend Swimming and Trng Club (Chm., 1992–2000 and 2003–08). Freeman, City of London, 2007. *Recreations:* travel, photography, hill and coastal walking, music, learning to ski and play golf, swimming.

MACKINTOSH, family name of **Viscount Mackintosh of Halifax**.

MACKINTOSH OF HALIFAX, 3rd Viscount *cr* 1957; **John Clive Mackintosh,** FCA; Bt 1935; Baron 1948; Partner, PricewaterhouseCoopers (formerly Price Waterhouse), since 1992; *b* 9 Sept. 1958; *s* of 2nd Viscount Mackintosh of Halifax, OBE, BEM; *S* father, 1980; *m* 1st, 1982, Elizabeth Lakin (marr. diss. 1993); two *s*; 2nd, 1995, Claire Jane, *y d* of Stanislaw Nowak; one *d*. *Educ:* The Leys School, Cambridge; Oriel College, Oxford (MA in PPE). FCA 1995. President, Oxford Univ. Conservative Assoc., 1979. Chartered accountant. *Recreations:* cricket, bridge, golf. *Heir:* *s* Hon. Thomas Harold George Mackintosh, *b* 8 Feb. 1985. *Address:* (office) 1 Embankment Place, WC2N 6RH. *Clubs:* MCC, Royal Automobile, Beefsteak; Ocean Reef (Key Largo).

MACKINTOSH, Sir Cameron (Anthony), Kt 1996; producer of musicals; Chairman, Cameron Mackintosh Ltd, since 1981; Director, Delfont/Mackintosh, since 1991; *b* 17 Oct. 1946; *s* of late Ian Mackintosh and of Diana Mackintosh. *Educ:* Prior Park Coll., Bath. Hon. Fellow, St Catherine's Coll., Oxford, 1990; Hon. DDra Royal Conservatoire of Scotland, 1998. Decided to be producer of musical stage shows at age 8, after seeing Slade's Salad Days; spent brief period at Central Sch. of Speech and Drama; stage hand at Theatre Royal, Drury Lane; later Asst Stage Manager; worked with Emile Littler, 1966, with Robin Alexander, 1967; produced first musical, 1969. Owner of Prince Edward, Prince of Wales, Novello (formerly Strand), Gielgud, Queen's, Wyndhams, Noël Coward (formerly Albery), Victoria Palace and Ambassadors Theatres. *London productions:* Little Women, 1967; Anything Goes, 1969; Trelawny, 1972; The Card, 1973, 1994; Winnie the Pooh, 1974; Owl and Pussycat Went to See, 1975; Godspell, 1975; Diary of a Madam, 1975; Out on a Limb, 1976; Side by Side by Sondheim, 1976; Oliver!, 1977, 1994, 2008; Gingerbread Man, 1978; My Fair Lady, 1979, 2001; Oklahoma!, 1980, 1999; Tomfoolery, 1980; Jeeves Takes Charge, 1980; Cats, 1981; Song and Dance, 1982; Blondel, 1983; Little Shop of Horrors, 1983; Abbacadabra, 1983; The Boyfriend, 1984; Les Misérables, 1985; Café Puccini, 1985; Phantom of the Opera, 1986; Follies, 1987; Miss Saigon, 1989; Just So, 1990; Five Guys Named Moe, 1991; Moby Dick, 1992; Putting It Together, 1992; Carousel, 1993; Martin Guerre, 1996; The Fix, 1997; The Witches of Eastwick, 2000; Mary Poppins, 2004; Avenue Q, 2006; Hair, 2010; Betty Blue Eyes, 2011. Nat. Enjoy England Award for Excellence for Outstanding Contribution to Tourism, 2006. *Recreations:* taking holidays, cooking. *Address:* Cameron Mackintosh Ltd, 1 Bedford Square, WC1B 3RB. *T:* (020) 7637 8866. *Club:* Groucho.

MACKINTOSH, Catherine Anne, (Mrs C. D. Peel), FRCM, FRSAMD; violinist; teacher; *b* 6 May 1947; *d* of late Duncan Robert Mackintosh and Mary Isa Mackintosh; *m* 1973, Charles David Peel; one *s* one *d*. *Educ:* Cranborne Chase Sch.; Dartington Coll. of Arts; Royal Coll. of Music (ARCM; FRCM 1994). FRSAMD 1998. Prof. of Baroque and Classical Violin and Viola, Royal Coll. of Music, 1977–99. Visiting Professor of Early Music: RSAMD, later Royal Conservatoire of Scotland, 1989–; RCM, 2000–; RAM, 2003–; Zagreb Acad., 2007–; Prof. of Baroque Violin, Koninklijk Conservatorium, 2008–11; Vis. Prof., Sydney Conservatorium of Music, 2013–. Leader, Acad. of Ancient Music, 1973–87; Mem., Julian Bream Consort, 1978–88; Founding Mem., Purcell Quartet, 1984–; Founding Mem., 1986–2013, and Co-Leader, 1987–2007, Orch. of Age of Enlightenment; Artistic Dir, Aestas Musica Internat. Summer Sch. of Music and Dance, Croatia, 1996–2007; violinist of Duo Amadè with Geoffrey Govier, 2003–. *Recreations:* trombone playing, crosswords, theatre, knitting. *Address:* 15 Ranelagh Road, W5 5RJ. *W:* www.catherinemackintosh.com.

MACKINTOSH, David James; MP (C) Northampton South, since 2015; *b* Northampton, 2 April 1979; *s* of James Mackintosh and Dolores Mackintosh. *Educ:* Roade Sch., Northants; Univ. of Durham. Member (C): Northamptonshire CC, 2009–; Northampton BC, 2011–15 (Leader, 2011–15). *Address:* House of Commons, SW1A 0AA. *T:* (020) 7219 5756. *E:* david.mackintosh.mp@parliament.uk.

MACKINTOSH, Ian, FCA, FCPA; Vice Chair, International Accounting Standards Board, since 2011; *b* 18 Feb. 1946; *s* of Angus John Mackintosh and Jean Elizabeth Mackintosh (*née* Sanders); *m* 1970, Patricia Caroline (*née* McMahon) (*d* 2006); two *s*. *Educ:* Auckland Grammar Sch.; Auckland Univ. (BComm). Partner, Coopers & Lybrand, Australia, 1976–96, Consultant, 1996–2000; Chief Accountant, Australian Securities & Investment Commn, 2000–02; Manager, Financial Mgt, World Bank, 2002–04; Chm., Accounting Standards Bd (UK), 2004–11. Adjunct Prof., Univ. of Canberra, 2000–06. Chm., Public Sector Cttee, Internat. Fedn of Accountants, 2000–03. *Recreations:* golf, swimming, music, reading. *Address:* International Accounting Standards Board, 30 Cannon Street, EC4M 6XH. *T:* (020) 7246 6410, *Fax:* (020) 7246 6411. *E:* imackintosh@ifrs.org.

McKINTOSH, His Honour Ian Stanley; a Circuit Judge, 1988–2007; *b* 23 April 1938; *s* of late (Herbert) Stanley and of Gertrude McKintosh; *m* 1967, (Alison) Rosemary, *e d* of Kenneth Blayney Large and Margaret Wharton Large; two *s* one *d*. *Educ:* Leeds Grammar Sch.; Exeter Coll., Oxford (MA). Admitted Solicitor of the Supreme Court, 1966. Served RAF, 1957–59. Articled to Town Clerk, Chester and to Laces & Co., Liverpool, 1962–66; Dept of Solicitor to Metropolitan Police, New Scotland Yard, 1966–69; Partner, Lemon & Co., Swindon, 1969–88; a Dep. Circuit Judge, 1976–81; a Recorder, 1981–88. Mem., Local Gen. and Area Appeals Cttees, SW Legal Aid Area, 1970–89. Mem., Stonham Housing Assoc., 1986–88 (Chm., Swindon Br.). *Recreations:* family, cricket, sailing, rowing, talking. *Clubs:* MCC, XL.

McKINTOSH, Peter Finlay; theatre set and costume designer, since 1993; *b* Liverpool, 22 Jan. 1967; *s* of Peter Ewan McKintosh and Beryl Elizabeth McKintosh. *Educ:* Plymouth Coll.; Univ. of Warwick (BA Hons Theatre Studies 1990); Bristol Old Vic Theatre Sch. *Theatre* includes: National Theatre: Honk!, Widowers' Houses, 2000; The Doctor's Dilemma, 2012; Our Country's Good, 2015; Royal Shakespeare Company: Alice in Wonderland, 2001, Pericles, Brand, The Merry Wives of Windsor, 2002; King John, 2006; Donmar Warehouse: Boston Marriage, 2001; The Cryptogram, 2005; John Gabriel Borkman, 2007, The Chalk Garden, 2008; Be Near Me, 2009; Serenading Louie, 2010; Luise Miller, 2011; My Night With Reg, 2014; Almeida Theatre: Romance, 2005; Cloud Nine, 2007; Waste, 2008; House of Games, 2010; The Knot of the Heart, 2011; The Turn of the Screw, 2013; West End: A Woman of No Importance, 2003; The Birthday Party, The Home Place, 2005; The 39 Steps,

2005, UK tours, NY and worldwide, 2005–; Donkeys' Years, 2006; Fiddler on the Roof, The Dumb Waiter, 2007; Entertaining Mr Sloane, Prick Up Your Ears, 2009; Educating Rita, Shirley Valentine, Love Story, 2010; Butley, Noises Off, 2011; Viva Forever!, 2012; The Winslow Boy (also Broadway), Relatively Speaking, 2012; Dirty Rotten Scoundrels, Another Country, 2014; Hay Fever, Harvey, The Importance of Being Earnest, 2015; Open Air Theatre, Regent's Park: Hello Dolly!, 2009; Crazy for You, 2011, transf. West End (Olivier Best Costume Design Award, 2012); The Sound of Music, 2013; Seven Brides for Seven Brothers, 2015; Royal Court: The Heretic, 2011; Chichester: Guys and Dolls, 2014; *Opera* includes: The Handmaid's Tale (world premiere), Royal Danish Opera, 2000, ENO, 2003, Canadian Opera, 2004; Love Counts, 2006, The Silent Twins, 2007, Almeida; The Marriage of Figaro, ENO, 2011. *E:* petermckintosh@mac.com.

McKITTERICK, Dr David John, FSA, FRHistS; FBA 1995; Fellow, since 1986, and Vice-Master, since 2012, Trinity College, Cambridge (Librarian, 1986–2015); *b* 9 Jan. 1948; *s* of Rev. Canon J. H. B. McKitterick and Marjory McKitterick (*née* Quarterman); *m* 1976, Rosamond Deborah Pierce (*see* R. D. McKitterick); one *d. Educ:* King's Coll. Sch., Wimbledon; St John's Coll., Cambridge (Scholar; BA 1969; MA 1973; LittD 1994); University College London (DipLib 1971). Staff, Cambridge Univ. Library, 1969–70, 1971–86; Fellow, Darwin Coll., Cambridge, 1978–86; Hon. Prof. of Historical Bibliography, Cambridge Univ., 2006–. Lyell Reader in Bibliography, Univ. of Oxford, 2000; Sandars Reader in Bibliography, Univ. of Cambridge, 2001–02. Syndic, CUP, 2000– (Chm., Pubns Cttee, 2011–). Hon. Curator, Early Printed Books, Fitzwilliam Mus. Vice-Pres., 1990–98, Pres., 1998–2000, Bibliog. Soc.; Pres., Cambridge Bibliog. Soc., 1991–; Pubns Sec., British Acad., 2002–09. MAE 2011. Gold Medal, Bibliographical Soc., 2005. *Publications:* The Library of Sir Thomas Knyvett of Ashwellthorpe 1539–1618, 1978; (ed) Stanley Morison and D. B. Updike: Selected Correspondence, 1979; (ed) Stanley Morison: selected essays on the history of letter forms in manuscript and print, 1981; (with John Dreyfus) A History of the Nonesuch Press, 1981; Four Hundred Years of University Printing and Publishing at Cambridge 1584–1984, 1984; Cambridge University Library: a history: the eighteenth and nineteenth centuries, 1986; A New Specimen Book of Curwen Pattern Papers, 1987; (ed jtly) T. F. Dibdin: *Horae Bibliographicae Cantabrigiensis*, 1988; Wallpapers by Edward Bawden, 1989; (ed) Andrew Perne: quatercentenary studies, 1991; Catalogue of the Pepys Library at Magdalene College, Cambridge, VII: facsimile of Pepys's catalogue, 1991; A History of Cambridge University Press, vol. 1: printing and the book trade in Cambridge 1534–1698, 1992, vol 2: scholarship and commerce 1698–1872, 1998, vol. 3: new worlds for learning 1873–1972, 2004; (ed) The Making of the Wren Library, 1995; Print, Manuscript and the Search for Order 1450–1830, 2003; (ed) The Trinity Apocalypse, 2005; (ed) The Cambridge History of the Book in Britain, 1830–1914, 2009; Old Books, New Technologies: the representation, conservation and transformation of books since 1700, 2013; contribs to learned jls. *Address:* Trinity College, Cambridge CB2 1TQ. *T:* (01223) 338513. *Clubs:* Roxburghe, Double Crown (President, 1994–95).

See also W. H. McKitterick.

McKITTERICK, Prof. Rosamond Deborah, FRHistS; Professor of Mediaeval History, University of Cambridge, since 1999; Vice-Master, since 2013, and Fellow, since 2007, Sidney Sussex College, Cambridge; *b* Chesterfield, Derbys, 31 May 1949; *d* of Rev. Canon C. A. Pierce, OBE, MA, BD and Melissa (*née* Heaney); *m* 1976, David John McKitterick, *qv*; one *d. Educ:* Univ. of WA (BA 1st cl. Hons 1970); Univ. of Cambridge (MA 1977; PhD 1976; LittD 1991); Univ. of Munich (Graduate Student). FRHistS 1980; Fellow, European Medieval Acad., 1993. University of Cambridge: Asst Lectr, 1979–85; Lectr, 1985–91; Reader, 1991–97; Prof. of Early Mediaeval European Hist., 1997–99; Newnham College: Fellow, 1974–2006; Dir of Studies in Anglo-Saxon, Norse and Celtic, 1979–93; Vice-Principal, 1996–98. Hugh Balsdon Fellow, British Sch. at Rome, 2001–02; Fellow in Residence, Netherlands Inst. of Advanced Study, 2005–06; Fellow, Scaliger Inst., 2005–06, Scaliger Fellow, 2010, Univ. of Leiden; Scholar in Residence, American Acad. in Rome, 2011; LECTIO Chair, KU Leuven, 2015. Guest Lectr in univs in Germany, Austria, USA, Australia, Denmark, Eire, France, Netherlands, Norway, Belgium, Estonia, Italy and Russia, 1978–; lecture tours: USA, 1982, 1990, 1994; Germany, 1987; UK; speaker, internat. confs on early medieval studies, Belgium, France, Netherlands, Germany, Switzerland, Turkey, Italy, USA, UK, Eire, Austria, Luxembourg and Czech Republic. Corresponding Fellow: Monumenta Germaniae Historica, Germany, 1999; Medieval Acad. of America, 2006; philosophisch-historische Klasse, Austrian Acad. Scis, 2006. MAE 2011. FRSA 2001. Vice-Pres., RHistS, 1994–98, 2000–03. Editor: Cambridge Studies in Medieval Life and Thought; Cambridge Studies in Palaeography and Codicology, 1989–2003; Corresp. Ed., Early Medieval Europe, 1999– (Editor, 1992–99). Dr A. H. Heineken Prize in History, Heineken Foundn and Royal Dutch Acad., 2010. *Publications:* The Frankish Church and the Carolingian Reforms 789–895, 1977; The Frankish Kingdoms under the Carolingians 751–987, 1983; The Carolingians and the Written Word, 1989; The Uses of Literacy in early medieval Europe, 1990; (with Lida Lopes Cardozo) Lasting Letters, 1992; Carolingian Culture: emulation and innovation, 1993; Books, Scribes and Learning in the Frankish Kingdoms, Sixth to Ninth Centuries, 1994 (trans. Polish 2011); (ed and contrib.) The New Cambridge Medieval History II, 700–900, 1995; Frankish Kings and Culture in the Early Middle Ages, 1995; (ed jtly and contrib.) Edward Gibbon and Empire, 1996; (ed and contrib.) The Short Oxford History of Europe: the early middle ages 400–1000, 2001 (trans. Spanish 2001, Polish 2010); (ed and contrib.) The Times Atlas of the Medieval World, 2003; History and Memory in the Carolingian World, 2004 (trans. French 2009); Perceptions of the Past in the Early Middle Ages, 2006; Charlemagne: the formation of a European identity, 2008 (trans. German 2008); (ed jtly and contrib.) La culture des élites au haut moyen âge, 2009; (ed jtly and contrib.) Ego Trouble: authors and their identities in the early middle ages, 2010; (ed with C. Bolgia and J. Osborne) Rome across Time and Space c.500–1400: cultural transmission and exchange of ideas, 2011; (jtly) Turning Over a New Leaf: change and development in the medieval book, 2012; (ed jtly) Old St Peter's, Rome, 2013; (ed jtly and contrib.) The Resources of the Past in Early Medieval Europe, 2015; articles in many collections of essays and conf. proc. and jls, incl. English Hist. Rev., Library, Studies in Church History, Trans of RHistS, Early Medieval Europe, Francia, Scriptorium; reviews for TLS and English and continental learned jls. *Recreations:* music, fresh air. *Address:* Sidney Sussex College, Cambridge CB2 3HU. *T:* (01223) 338800.

McKITTERICK, William Henry; independent social worker and adviser, since 2008; *b* 21 Sept. 1949; *s* of Rev. Canon J. H. B. McKitterick and M. G. McKitterick (*née* Quarterman); *m* 1972, Jennifer M. Fisher; one *s* one *d. Educ:* King's College Sch.; Hatfield Poly. (BA, CQSW); Bradford Univ. (MA 1982); Coventry Univ. (Postgrad. dip. 2010). Social Worker: Leics, 1973–75; Oldham, 1975–78; Social Services Manager: Manchester, 1978–84; Oldham, 1984–89; Wakefield, 1989–93; Head of Service, and Dep. Dir of Social Services, Wakefield, 1993–95; Dir of Social Services and Health, City and Co. of Bristol, 1995–2005; Strategic Partnership Dir, Plymouth Children's Services, 2006–08. Chair, Bristol and Swindon Churches Council of Industrial and Social Responsibility, 2000–04. *Publications:* Supervision, 2012; Self-Leadership in Social Work, 2015. *Recreations:* family, walking, books. *Address:* Holly Bank, Grove Orchard, Blagdon, Bristol BS40 7DR. *T:* (01761) 463407. *E:* wmckitterick@btinternet.com.

See also D. J. McKitterick.

McKITTRICK, Ven. Douglas Henry; Archdeacon of Chichester, since 2002; *b* 18 Feb. 1953; *s* of Joseph Henry McKittrick and Doreen Mary (*née* Davidson). *Educ:* John Marley Sch., Newcastle upon Tyne; St Stephen's House, Oxford (BTh). Ordained deacon, 1977, priest, 1978; Curate: St Paul's, Deptford, 1977–80; St John's, Tuebrook, Liverpool, 1980–81; Team Vicar, St Stephen's, Grove Street, Liverpool, 1981–89; Vicar: St Agnes, Toxteth Park, 1989–97; St Peter's, Brighton with Chapel Royal, Chichester, 1997–2002. RD, Brighton, 1998–2002; Preb., 1998–2002, and Canon, 1998–, Chichester Cathedral. Member: Gen. Synod, 2005–; Council, Additional Curates Soc., 2005–; Nat. Healthcare Chaplaincies Council, 2006–; Ecclesiastical Law Soc., 2003–. *Recreations:* long country/coastal walks, cooking, theatre, wine, Brighton and Hove Albion FC. *Address:* 2 Yorklands, Dyke Road Avenue, Hove, E Sussex BN3 6RW. *T:* (home) (01273) 505330, (office) (01273) 421021, *Fax:* (01273) 421041. *E:* archchichester@chichester.anglican.org.

McKITTRICK, His Honour Neil Alastair; DL; a Circuit Judge, 2001–11; Resident Judge, Peterborough and Huntingdon Crown Court, 2009–11; *b* 1 Jan. 1948; *s* of late Ian James Arthur McKittrick and of Mary Patricia McKittrick (*née* Hobbs); *m* 1975, Jean Armstrong; one *s* one *d. Educ:* King's Sch., Ely; College of Law, Guildford. LLB London. Solicitor, 1972. Articled Clerk and Asst Solicitor, Cecil Godfrey & Son, Nottingham, 1967–73; Prosecuting Solicitor, Notts, 1973–77; Clerk to the Justices, 1977–89 (Darlington 1977, E Herts 1981, N Cambs 1986–89); Stipendiary Magistrate, subseq. Dist Judge (Magistrates' Courts), Middx, 1989–2001; a Recorder, 1996–2001; Resident Judge, Ipswich Crown Court, 2006–09; Magistrates' Liaison Judge, Suffolk, 2007–09. Member: Council, Justices' Clerks' Soc., 1985–89 (Chm., Professional Purposes Cttee, 1987–89); Middlesex Probation Cttee, 1990–2001. DL Cambs, 2011. Editor, Justice of the Peace, 1985–89; Licensing Editor, Justice of the Peace Reports, 1983–2003; Editor, Jl of Criminal Law, 1990–2000 (Mem., Editl Bd, 1985–2000). *Publications:* (ed jtly) Wilkinson's Road Traffic Offences, 14th edn to 18th edn, 1997; (with Pauline Callow) Blackstone's Handbook for Magistrates, 1997, 2nd edn 2000; (contrib.) Confronting Crime, 2003; papers and articles in learned jls. *Recreations:* visiting churches, racecourses. *Address:* c/o Peterborough Combined Courts Centre, Rivergate, Peterborough PE1 1EJ.

MACKLE, Joanna, (Mrs David Utterson); a Deputy Director, British Museum, since 2013; *b* Belfast, 7 April 1958; *d* of Henry Mackle and Rosemary Campbell; *m* 1991, David Utterson; one *s* one *d. Educ:* Ursuline Convent Sch., Wimbledon; Univ. of Manchester (BA Hons French 1981). Faber and Faber: publicity asst, 1982–85; Publicity Manager, 1985–87; Publicity Dir, 1987–93; Publishing Dir, 1993–2002; British Museum: Hd of Communications, 2003–07; Dir of Public Engagement, 2007–13. Mem., Speaker's Adv. Council on Public Engagement, 2012–. Gov., Latymer Upper Sch., 2013–. Trustee, Forward Arts Foundn, 1994–. *Recreations:* walking, reading. *Address:* British Museum, Great Russell Street, WC1B 3DG. *T:* (020) 7323 8345. *E:* jmackle@britishmuseum.org.

MACKLOW-SMITH, Roxanna; *see* Panufnik, R.

MACKNEY, Paul Leon John; General Secretary, National Association of Teachers in Further and Higher Education, 1997–2006; Founder and Joint General Secretary, University and College Union, 2006–07; Member, Trades Union Congress General Council, 2002–07; *b* 25 March 1950; *s* of Rev. L. E. Mackney and Margaret Mackney; *m* 1st, 1969, Rosemary A. Draper (marr. diss. 1974); one *s*; 2nd, 1982, Cherry M. Sewell; one *d. Educ:* Exeter Univ. (BA Hons); Birmingham Poly. (RSA DipTEFL); Wolverhampton Poly. (FE CertEd); Warwick Univ. (MA Industrial Relns 1986). Trainee probation officer, 1971–73; General Studies Lectr, Poole Tech. Coll., 1974–75; Hall Green Technical College: ESOL Organiser, 1975–79; Trade Union Studies Tutor, 1980–85; Head, Birmingham Trade Union Studies Centre, S Birmingham Coll., 1986–92; W Midlands Regl Official, NATFHE, 1992–97; Associate Gen. Sec., Univ. and Coll. Union, 2007; Associate Dir for Further Educn, NIACE, 2008–09. Pres., Birmingham TUC, 1980–84 (Life Mem.). Vice-Chair: Unite Against Fascism, 2004–11; Coalition of Resistance, 2010–; Co-Chair, Greece Solidarity Campaign, 2012–; Co-ordinator, Campaigning Alliance for Lifelong Learning, 2008–11. TUC Gold Badge, 1977. *Publications:* Birmingham and the Miners' Strike, 1986; numerous articles. *Recreations:* music, guitar, singing, spending time with my children, Sean and Ruby, and my granddaughter, Thea, researching family history. *T:* 07974 353709. *E:* paulmackney@btinternet.com.

MACKRELL, Judith Rosalind; Dance Critic, The Guardian, since 1995; *b* 26 Oct. 1954; *d* of Alec Mackrell and Margaret (*née* Atkinson, later Halsey); *m* 1977, Simon Henson; two *s. Educ:* York Univ. (BA 1st Cl. Hons Eng. and Philosophy); Oxford Univ. Part-time Lectr in English and Dance at various estabts incl. Oxford Univ., Oxford Poly. and Roehampton Inst., 1981–86; Dance Critic, Independent, 1986–94. Freelance dance writer and arts broadcaster, 1986–. Hon. Fellow, Laban Centre for Dance, 1996. *Publications:* Out of Line, 1994; Reading Dance, 1997; (with Darcey Bussell) Life in Dance, 1998; (ed with Debra Craine) The Oxford Dictionary of Dance, 2000; Bloomsbury Ballerina: Lydia Lopokova, imperial dancer and Mrs John Maynard Keynes, 2008; Flappers: six women of a dangerous generation, 2013. *Recreations:* travel, food, music, reading, my family. *Address:* 73 Greenwood Road, E8 1NT. *T:* (020) 7249 5553.

MACKRELL, Keith Ashley Victor; Chairman, LSE Enterprise, 1992–2004, now Emeritus President; Vice Chairman, Duke Corporate Education Ltd, since 2004; *b* 20 Oct. 1932; *s* of late Henry George Mackrell and Emily Winifred Mackrell (*née* Elcock); *m* 1960, June Yvonne Mendoza, *qv*; one *s* three *d. Educ:* Peter Symonds Sch.; London School of Economics (Harold Laski Schol.; BSc Econs 1953; Hon. Fellow, 1999). Director: Shell International, 1976–91 (Regl Co-ordinator, East and Australasia, 1979–91); BG plc, 1994–2005 (Dep. Chm., 2000–05). Non-executive Director: Standard Chartered Bank, 1991–2002; Regalian Properties, 1991–2002; Rexam (formerly Bowater) plc, 1991–98; Fairey Gp plc, 1993–99; Dresdner Emerging Markets Investment Trust, 1998–2002; Gartmore Asia Pacific (formerly Govett Asian Recovery Trust), 1998–2006; Aberdeen All Asia Trust, 2006–07. Gov., LSE, 1991–2009, now Emeritus Gov. Gov., ESRC, 2015. FInstD 1976; CCMI (CBIM 1978). Hon. LLD Nat. Univ. of Singapore, 1991. *Recreations:* tennis, theatre, reading. *Clubs:* Hurlingham, Wimbledon.

MACKWORTH, Sir Digby (John), 10th Bt *cr* 1776, of The Gnoll, Glamorganshire; *b* 2 Nov. 1945; *s* of Sir David Arthur Geoffrey Mackworth, 9th Bt and his 1st wife, Mary Alice, (Molly), (*née* Grylles); *S* father, 1998; *m* 1971, Antoinette Francesca McKenna; one *d. Educ:* Wellington Coll. Lieut, Australian Army Aviation Corps, 1966; basic flying trng, 63 course, RAAF, Point Cook; helicopter pilot, 28 Commonwealth Bde, Malaysia; 161 (Ind.) Reconnaissance Flt, Australian Task Force, Viet-Nam. Pilot: Bristow Helicopters, Trinidad, Iran, 1972–77; British Airways Helicopters, Shetland, Aberdeen, China, India, 1977–89; British Airways, Heathrow, 1989–2000; easyJet, 2000–05. *Recreations:* amateur workshop practice, LAA inspector. *Heir: kinsman* Norman Humphrey Mackworth [*b* 1917; *m* 1941, Jane Felicity Thring; two *s* one *d*]. *Address:* Blagrove Cottage, Fox Lane, Boars Hill, Oxford OX1 5DS. *T:* (01865) 735543.

MACKWORTH, Rosalind Jean, CBE 1994; Social Fund Commissioner for Great Britain, 1987–96, and for Northern Ireland, 1987–96; Consultant, Ashley Wilson LLP (formerly Mackworth Rowland), Solicitors; *b* 10 Aug. 1928; *d* of Rev. Albert Walters, FRMetS and Alma Walters, sometime Comptroller to Archbishop of Canterbury; *m* 1960, Richard Charles Audley Mackworth, MA, MSc, DIC, CEng (*d* 2014); two *d. Educ:* twelve small schools, following father's postings; Queen's Univ. Belfast (BA); Girton Coll., Cambridge (MA); Law Soc. professional exams. Joined Gregory Rowcliffe, Solicitors, 1956; set up own practice, 1967; amalgamated practice, Mackworth Rowland, 1982, Ashley Wilson, 2005. Mem., VAT

Tribunals, 1976–. Chm., Judicial Commn, Eur. Union of Women, 1984–87 (Vice-Chm., British Section, 1986–87). *Recreation:* everything except golf. *Address:* Ashley Wilson Solicitors LLP, 57 Buckingham Gate, St James's Park, SW1E 6AJ. *T:* (020) 7802 4802.

McLACHLAN, Dr Andrew David, FRS 1989; Scientific Staff, Medical Research Council Laboratory of Molecular Biology, Cambridge, 1967–2000; Fellow of Trinity College, Cambridge, since 1959; *b* 25 Jan. 1935; *s* of late Donald Harvey McLachlan and Katherine (*née* Harman); *m* 1959, Jennifer Margaret Lief Kerr; three *s.* *Educ:* Winchester Coll. (Schol.); Trinity Coll., Cambridge (BA, MA, PhD, ScD). Res. Fellow, Trinity Coll., 1958; Harkness Fellow, USA, 1959–61; Lectr in Physics, Trinity Coll., 1961–87; Lectr in Chemistry, Cambridge Univ., 1965–67. Visiting Professor: CIT, 1964; Brandeis Univ., 1975; UCLA, 1989. *Publications:* (with A. Carrington) Introduction to Magnetic Resonance, 1967; papers in various jls, including Jl of Molecular Biology, Nature, and Acta Crystallographica. *Recreations:* walking, music, camping. *Address:* Trinity College, Cambridge CB2 1TQ; 12 Dane Drive, Cambridge CB3 9LP. *T:* (01223) 361318. *E:* andrew_mclachlan@fastmail.fm.

McLACHLAN, Edward Rolland; freelance cartoonist, illustrator and designer, since 1966; *b* 22 April 1940; *m* 1964, Shirley Ann Gerrard; one *s* three *d.* *Educ:* Humberstone Village Jun. Sch.; Wyggeston Boys' Grammar Sch.; Leicester CAT. Cartoonist for Punch, Private Eye, Spectator, Saga mag., The Oldie, The Cartoonist, Regenerate (formerly Building), Roof, Property Week, IFG; cartoonist and illustrator for The Salisbury Review; illustrator for Document mag.; illustrator of numerous books for publishers, incl. Methuen, Macmillan Heinemann, Profile, John Wiley & Sons, Pearson, Penguin, OUP, Longmans, Cornelsen, and Sound Foundations educnl books for children; television cartoon series, ITV: Simon and the Land of Chalk Drawings, 1977, and Canada, 2001; Bangers and Mash, 1989; titling design for BBC TV series, Just William, 2010; greetings cards for Cardmix Ltd; work for many advertising agencies. Heneage Cup, Cartoon Art Trust, 2011. *Publications:* McLachlan Book of Cartoons, 2000; illustrator: Sorry I'm British, by B. Crystal and A. Russ, 2010; 117 'For Dummies' books. *Recreations:* cycling, weight-training, gardening, pubs. *Address:* 3 Spinney View, Coverside Road, Great Glen, Leics LE8 9EP. *T:* (0116) 259 2632, *Fax:* (0116) 259 3898; Folio, 10 Gate Street, Lincoln's Inn Fields, WC2A 3HP. *E:* mail@edmclachlan.co.uk. *W:* www.edmclachlan.co.uk.

McLACHLAN, Hon. Ian (Murray), AO 1989; Minister for Defence, Australia, 1996–98; Chairman, Australian Wool Innovation Ltd, 2002–08; *b* 2 Oct. 1936; *s* of I. McLachlan; *m* 1964, Janet Lee; two *s* one *d.* *Educ:* Collegiate Sch. of St Peter, SA; Jesus Coll., Cambridge (cricket blue, 1957–58). Played cricket for SA, 1961–64. Director: SA Brewing, 1978–90 (Dep. Chm., 1983–90); Elders IXL, 1980–90. MP (L) Barker, SA, 1990–98; Shadow Minister: for Industry and Commerce, 1990–93; for Infrastructure and Nat. Develt, 1993–94; for Envmt and Heritage, 1994–95. Pres., Nat. Farmers' Fedn, 1984–88. Dir, Clean Seas Tuna Ltd, 2005–10. Pres., SA Cricket Assoc., 1999–2013; Dir, Cricket Australia, 2004–12. *Address:* 5 Fuller Court, Walkerville, Adelaide, SA 5081, Australia.

McLACHLAN, Malcolm Orde, MBE 2007; HM Diplomatic Service; High Commissioner to Fiji, and concurrently to Tonga, Vanuatu, Tuvalu, Kiribati and Nauru, 2009–11; *b* 10 Sept. 1963; *m* 2005, Dr Mary Oswana; one *s* two *d.* Entered FCO, 1981; Archivist and Entry Clearance Officer, Karachi, 1984–87; Third Sec., Guatemala City, 1988–93; Second Sec., EU Directorate, FCO, 1993–96; First Sec. and Hd, Political Sect., Nairobi, 1996–2001; Press Officer, Harare, 2000; Dep. Hd of Mission, Hanoi, 2001–05; Migration Envoy, Horn of Africa, FCO, 2005–06; Dep. Hd, SE Asia and Pacific Gp, FCO, 2006–08. *Address:* c/o Foreign and Commonwealth Office, King Charles Street, SW1A 2AH.

McLACHLAN, Marjory Jane; JP; Lord-Lieutenant of Stirling and Falkirk, since 2005; *b* 15 Feb. 1942; *d* of Walter and Kate Alexander; *m* 1962, Colin McLachlan; two *d.* *Educ:* St Leonard's Sch., St Andrews. Pres., Ladies' Br., Royal Caledonian Curling Club, 1989–90; Scottish Rep., World Curling Fedn, 1991–99. JP Falkirk, 2006. CStJ 2008. *Recreations:* family, bridge, curling, golf, travel. *Address:* Dromore, 23 Majors Loan, Falkirk FK1 5QG. *T:* (01324) 622633. *E:* marjmcl@sky.com.

McLACHLIN, Rt Hon. Beverley; PC 2000; Chief Justice of Canada, since 2000; *b* Pincher Creek, Alberta, 7 Sept. 1943; *m* 1st, 1967, Roderick McLachlin (*d* 1988); one *s*; 2nd, 1992, Frank E. McArdle. *Educ:* Univ. of Alberta (MA 1968, LLB 1968). Called to the Bar: Alberta, 1969; BC, 1971; practised law: with Wood, Moir, Hyde and Ross, Edmonton, 1969–71; with Thomas, Herdy, Mitchell & Co., Fort St John, BC, 1971–72; with Bull, Housser and Tupper, Vancouver, 1972–75; Lectr, 1974–75, Associate Prof., 1975–78, Prof., 1981, Univ. of BC, 1974–81; Judge: County Court of Vancouver, 1981; Supreme Court of BC, 1981–85; Court of Appeal, BC, 1985–88; Chief Justice, Supreme Court of BC, 1988–89; Judge, Supreme Court of Canada, 1989–2000. Hon. LLD: BC, 1990; Alberta, 1991; Toronto, 1995; York, 1999; Law Soc. of Upper Canada, Ottawa, Calgary, Brock, Simon Fraser, Victoria, Alberta, 2000; Lethbridge, Bridgewater State Coll., 2001; Mt St Vincent, Prince Edward Island, 2002; Montreal, 2003; Manitoba, QUB, Dalhousie, Carleton, 2004; Maine at Fort Kent, 2005; Ateneo de Manila Univ., 2006. *Publications:* contrib. to learned jls. *Address:* Supreme Court of Canada, 301 Wellington Street, Ottawa, ON K1A 0J1, Canada.

McLAGGAN, Murray Adams; JP; Lord Lieutenant of Mid Glamorgan, 1990–2002; *b* 29 Sept. 1929; *s* of Sir John Douglas McLaggan, KCVO, FRCS, FRCSE and Elsa Violet Lady McLaggan (*née* Adams), MD, DPH; *m* 1959, Jennifer Ann Nicholl; two *s* one *d.* *Educ:* Winchester College; New College, Oxford (MA 1st Cl. Hons). Called to the Bar, Lincoln's Inn, 1955; Student and Tutor in Law, Christ Church, Oxford, 1957–66. Member: Parly Boundary Commn for Wales, 1980–97; Regl Adv. Bd, Wales, NRA, 1990–96 (Chm., Regl Flood Defence Cttee, 1990–97); Adv. Cttee for Wales, Environment Agency, 1996–98; former Chm., Forestry Commn Regional Adv. Cttee (Wales). Chm., Nat. Trust Cttee for Wales, 1991–93 (Dep. Chm., 1984–91). High Sheriff Mid Glamorgan, 1978–79, DL 1982; JP Glamorgan, 1968. *Recreations:* bibliophily, dendrology, amateur operatics, litter-picking. *Address:* Home Farm, Merthyr Mawr, Bridgend CF32 0LS. *T:* (01656) 653980.

McLAREN, family name of **Baron Aberconway**.

McLAREN, Clare, (Mrs Andrew McLaren); *see* Tritton, E. C.

McLAREN, David John; Chief Executive, London Oncology Clinic, 2007–11; Chairman: McLaren and Partners Ltd, since 2008; Butler and Parker Ltd, since 2013; *b* 14 April 1944; *s* of late Charles Claude McLaren and Eileen Patricia (*née* Shanley); *m* 2002, Anna Maria Jacobson; one *s* three *d.* *Educ:* Merchant Taylors' Sch., Crosby; QMC, KCL, and Courtauld Inst., Univ. of London (BA 1965). Mather & Crowther, 1965–67; Radio Newsroom, BBC, 1967–68; Ogilvy & Mather, 1968–70; KMP Partnership, 1970–82 (Man. Dir, 1974–82); Man. Dir, Collett Dickenson Pearce, 1982–91; Hill & Knowlton: CEO, 1994–2000; Chm., 2000–04. Global Co-ordinator, WPP, 2000–04. Chairman: Gainmedium Ltd, 1992–2008; Cohn & Wolfe, 2005–07. Non-exec. Dir, Corney and Barrow Ltd, 1991–. Council Member: IPA, 1984–89; Advertising Assoc., 1984–89; Dir, PRCA, 2003–06. Trustee, 2006–11, Strategic Advr, 2011–, Oxford Literary Festival. Member: Thames & Solent Cttee, NT, 1999–2008; Nat. Campaign Bd, Maggie's Centres, 2004–11; Business Adv. Bd, Ashmolean Mus., 2005. Trustee: Photographers' Gall., 1986–90; River & Rowing Mus., 2000–09 (Chm., Develt Bd, 1999–2003). Dir, Orch. of St John's, 2012–. FIPA 1987. FRSA 1997. *Recreations:* motoring, opera, wine, shooting, fishing, photography, books, architecture. *Clubs:* Cavalry and Guards, Groucho.

MacLAREN of MacLaren, Donald; Chief of the Clan MacLaren; HM Diplomatic Service; Ambassador to Georgia, 2004–07; *b* 22 Aug. 1954; *s* of late Donald MacLaren of MacLaren, (The MacLaren of MacLaren) and Margaret Sinclair (*née* Miller); *m* 1978, Maida-Jane Aitchison; three *s* two *d.* Joined FCO, 1978; BMG, Berlin, 1980–83; First Secretary: Moscow, 1984–87; FCO, 1987–91; Dep. Hd of Mission, Cuba, 1991–94; FCO, 1994–97; Dep. Hd of Mission, Venezuela, 1997–2000; Consul-Gen. and Dep. Hd of Mission, Ukraine, 2000–04. Contested (Ind) Kirkcaldy and Cowdenbeath, 2010. *Address:* c/o Foreign and Commonwealth Office, King Charles Street, SW1A 2AH.

McLAREN, Iain Archibald; President, Institute of Chartered Accountants of Scotland, 2011–12; *b* Edinburgh, 21 Feb. 1951; *s* of Hugh McLaren and Margaret McLaren; *m* Fiona Gillian Coulter (*née* Maclachlan); two *s* two *d.* *Educ:* Daniel Stewart's Coll., Edinburgh; Heriot-Watt Univ. (BA). Mem. ICAS 1974. CA, Peat Marwick Mitchell, 1971–78; Hd, Internal Audit, Miller Gp, 1978–80; Peat Marwick Mitchell, then Peat Marwick McLintock, subseq. KPMG: Audit Partner, 1981–97; Sen. Partner, Scotland, 1998–2004; Chm., Infrastructure and Govt, 2005–08. Dir, Cairn Energy plc, 2008– (Chm., Audit Cttee, 2008–); Chm., Investors Capital Trust plc, 2010–. Dir, Scottish Enterprise, 2010–15. *Recreations:* golf, hill walking, arts. *Address:* 9 Ravelston Dykes, Edinburgh EH4 3EA. *T:* (0131) 332 3000. *E:* mclaren.ia@gmail.com.

McLAREN, Ian Alban Bryant; QC 1993; a Recorder, 1996–2010 (an Assistant Recorder, 1992–96); *b* 3 July 1940; *yr s* of Alban McLaren and Doris (*née* Hurst); *m* 1964, Margaret Middleton, BA; two *s* one *d.* *Educ:* Sandbach Sch., Blackpool Grammar Sch.; Univ. of Nottingham (LLB 1961). Called to the Bar, Gray's Inn, 1962 (Macaskie Schol.; Bencher, 2004); in practice at the Bar, 1962–2009; Law Tutor, Univ. of Nottingham, 1962–64; Hd of Ropewalk Chambers, 2000–06. Mem., Standards Cttee, Notts CC, 2009–12. Pres., Notts Medico-Legal Soc., 1997–98. Fellow, Soc. for Advanced Legal Studies, 2000–. Hon. LLD Nottingham Trent, 2005. *Recreations:* gardening, photography. *Address:* c/o Ropewalk Chambers, 24 The Ropewalk, Nottingham NG1 5EF. *T:* (0115) 947 2581.

McLAREN, Melanie Elizabeth; Executive Director, Codes and Standards, Financial Reporting Council, since 2012; *b* 1 April 1963; partner, James Hind; two *s* one *d.* *Educ:* Univ. of St Andrews (MA Arabic Studies and German). ACA 1990. Coopers & Lybrand, later PricewaterhouseCoopers, 1985–2008, Partner, Financial Services Practice, 1999–2008; Friends Provident, then Friends Life Group: interim Chief Risk Officer, 2010; Business Risk Dir, 2010–11; interim Chief Risk Officer, 2011–12. *Address:* Financial Reporting Council, Aldwych House, 71–91 Aldwych, WC2B 4HN. *T:* (020) 7492 2406. *E:* m.mclaren@frc.org.uk.

McLAREN, Hon. Michael Duncan; QC 2002; *b* 29 Nov. 1958; *s* of 3rd Baron Aberconway and Ann Lindsay (*née* Aymer); *m* 1985, Caroline Jane, *d* of Air Chief Marshal Sir (William) John Stacey, KCB, CBE, FRAeS; two *s* one *d.* *Educ:* Eton Coll.; Christ's Coll., Cambridge (MA 1st Cl. Law 1980). Called to the Bar, Middle Temple, 1981; in practice at the Bar, 1981–, specialising in regulatory and commercial law (aviation, insurance, etc.). *Recreations:* horticulture, music, travel. *Address:* Fountain Court Chambers, Temple, EC4Y 9DH. *T:* (020) 7583 3335, *Fax:* (020) 7353 0329. *E:* mmclaren@fountaincourt.co.uk.

MacLAREN, Prof. Robert Edward, DPhil; FRCSE, FRCOphth; Professor of Ophthalmology, University of Oxford, since 2009; Consultant Ophthalmologist, Oxford Eye Hospital, since 2009; Bodley Fellow and Lecturer in Human Anatomy, Merton College, Oxford, since 1992; Civilian Consultant Advisor to the Royal Navy, since 2011; *b* Epsom, Surrey, 14 Nov. 1966; *s* of late Michael Gordon MacLaren and Penelope Gael MacLaren (*née* Newbery); *m* 2002, Lucy Amelia Pester; two *s* one *d.* *Educ:* Angmering Sch.; Chichester Coll.; Univ. of Edinburgh (MB ChB 1990); Merton Coll., Oxford (DPhil 1996). FRCSE 1998; FRCOphth 2005. SHO, Guy's Hosp., London, 1991–92; Demonstrator, Univ. of Oxford, 1992–93; MRC Clin. Trng Fellow, 1993–95; Captain, 16 Armoured Field Ambulance, RAMC, 1995–96, temp. Regtl MO, 1 Worcs and Sherwood Foresters Regt, 26 Regt RA, Queen's Royal Hussars, Bosnia Herzegovina, 1996; SHO in Ophthalmol., Reading and Oxford, 1996–99; Moorfields Eye Hospital: Registrar and Fellow in Vitreoretinal Surgery, 1999–2004; Res. Fellow in Med. Retina, 2004–06; Hon. Consultant Vitreoretinal Surgeon, 2006–. Hon. Prof. of Ophthalmol., Inst. of Ophthalmol., UCL, 2009–. Commnd RAMC (Vol.), 1992; Regtl MO, 5th (Vol.) Royal Green Jackets, 1994–95 and 1996–98; MO, 306 Field Hosp. RAMC (Vol.), 1998–2000; Surgeon Maj., HAC, London, 2000–04; Locum Surgeon Maj., Household Cavalry Mounted Regt, London, 2002–03. Lectures: King James IV Professorship of Surgery and Medal, RCSE, 2007; Percival Hay Medal, Northern England Ophthalmol Soc., 2011; Euretina, 2014. Research Gold Medal, Moorfields Eye Hosp., 2005; ARVO Camras Award, 2013. *Publications:* articles on ophthalmology, gene therapy, stem cell research, electronic retinal implants and cataract surgery. *Recreations:* cross-country running, tennis, military history. *Address:* Merton College, Oxford OX1 4JD. *T:* (01865) 276310, *Fax:* (01865) 276361. *Club:* Honourable Artillery.

MacLAREN, Hon. Roy; PC (Can.) 1983; High Commissioner for Canada in the United Kingdom, 1996–2000; *b* 26 Oct. 1934; *s* of Wilbur MacLaren and Anne (*née* Graham); *m* 1959, Alethea (*née* Mitchell); two *s* one *d.* *Educ:* schs in Vancouver, Canada; Univ. of BC (BA); Univ. of Cambridge (MA); Univ. of Harvard; Univ. of Toronto (MDiv). With Canadian Diplomatic Service, in Saigon, Hanoi, Prague, Geneva, NY (UN) and Ottawa, 1957–69; Dir, Public Affairs, Massey Ferguson Ltd, 1969–73; President: Ogilvy & Mather (Canada) Ltd, 1974–76; Canadian Business Media Ltd, 1977–93; Director: Deutsche Bank (Canada), 1984–93; London Life Assurance, 1984–93; Royal LePage Ltd, 1985–93. MP (L) Etobicoke N, 1979–96; Parly Sec., Energy, 1980–82; Minister of: State Finance, 1983; Nat. Revue, 1984; Internat. Trade, 1993–96. Non-executive Director: Standard Life, 2001–04; Brookfield (formerly Brascan), 2001–09; Canadian Tire, 2001–03; Patheon, 2001–06; Algoma Central, 2001–10; Wilton Petroleums, 2008–. Commissioner: Commonwealth War Graves Commn, 1996–2000; Trilateral Commn, 2001–; Trustee, Imperial War Mus., 1996–2000; Dir, Bletchley Park Trust, 2001–; Mem. Adv. Cttee, Scott Polar Res. Inst., 1998–2000; Gov., Ditchley Foundn, 2004–. Mem. Council, IISS, 2001–08; Chairman: Canadian Inst. of Internat. Affairs, 2001–05; Canada-Europe Round Table, 2001–; Canada-India Business Council, 2001–; Atlantic Council of Canada, 2003–06. Sen. Fellow, Massey Coll., Univ. of Toronto, 2013–. Hon. Col, 7th Toronto Regt, Royal Canadian Artillery, 1995–2005. Hon. DSL Toronto, 1996; Hon. DCL N Alabama, 2000; Hon. DLitt New Brunswick, 2001; Hon. LLD Prince Edward Island, 2003. *Publications:* Canadians in Russia 1918–1919, 1976; Canadians on the Nile 1882–1898, 1978; Canadians Behind Enemy Lines 1939–1945, 1981; Honourable Mentions, 1986; African Exploits: the diaries of William Stairs 1887–1892, 1997; Commissions High, 2006; The Fundamental Things Apply, 2011; Empire and Ireland, 2015. *Recreations:* cross country walking, ski-ing. *Address:* 425 Russell Hill Road, Toronto, ON M5P 2S4, Canada. *Clubs:* White's, Pratt's; Rideau (Ottawa); Toronto; Royal Canadian Yacht.

McLAREN-THROCKMORTON, Clare; *see* Tritton, E. C.

McLATCHIE, Cameron, CBE 1996 (OBE 1988); Chairman, British Polythene Industries plc (formerly Scott & Robertson), since 1988 (Chief Executive, 1988–2003); *b* 18 Feb. 1947; *s* of Cameron McLatchie and Maggie McLatchie (*née* Maxwell Taylor); *m* 1973, Leslie Mackie; two *s* one *d.* *Educ:* Univ. of Glasgow (LLB). Apprentice CA, Whinney, Murray & Co., 1968–70; Admin. Asst, subseq. Prodn Manager, then Prodn Dir, Thos Boag & Co. Ltd, 1971–74; Managing Director: Anaplast Ltd, 1975–83; Scott & Robertson plc, 1983–88. Non-executive Director: Motherwell Bridge Hldgs Ltd, 1993–97; Hiscox Select plc, 1993–98

(Chm.); Royal Bank of Scotland Gp, 1998–2002. Dep. Chm., Scottish Enterprise, 1997–2000 (Mem. Bd, 1990–95). Member: Adv. Cttee on Business and the Envmt, 1991–93; Sec. of State for Scotland's Adv. Gp on Sustainable Develt, 1994–95; Bd, Scottish Envmtl Protection Agency, 1995–97. DUniv Paisley 2000. *Recreations:* golf, bridge, gardening. *Address:* c/o British Polythene Industries plc, 96 Port Glasgow Road, Greenock PA15 2RP. *T:* (01475) 501000.

McLAUCHLAN, Prof. Keith Alan, PhD; FRS 1992; Professor of Chemistry, Oxford University, 1996–2002, now Emeritus; Fellow of Hertford College, Oxford, 1965–2002, now Emeritus; *b* 8 Jan. 1936; *s* of Frederick William McLauchlan and Nellie (*née* Summers); *m* 1958, Joan Sheila Dickenson; one *s* one *d. Educ:* Queen Elizabeth's Hosp., Bristol; Univ. of Bristol (BSc, PhD); Univ. of Oxford (MA). Post-doctoral Fellow, NRCC, Ottawa, 1959–60; Post-doctoral Fellow, then Sen. Scientific Officer, NPL, Teddington, 1960–65. Oxford University: Lectr, 1965–94; Reader in Physical Chemistry, 1994–96; Chairman: Inter-deptl Cttee for Chemistry, 1990–93; Cttee of Heads of Sci. Depts, 1991–93; Member: Gen. Bd, 1993–97; Hebdomadal Council, 1998–2000. Erskine Fellow, Univ. of Christchurch, NZ, 1997; Eminent Scientist, RIKEN, Tokyo, 2000–01. Visiting Professor: Tata Inst., Bombay, 1986; Univ. of Konstanz, Germany, 1990; Univ. of Padua, 1998; Ecole Normale Supérieure, Paris, 1998; George Willard Wheland Vis. Prof., Univ. of Chicago, 1998. Chm., Electron Spin Resonance Discussion Gp, RSC, 1989–92. Pres., Internat. Soc. for Electron Paramagnetic Resonance, 1993–96. Mem., Scientific Adv. Bd, Electro Magnetic Field Biol Res. Trust, 1995–2001. Fellow, IES, 2005. Silver Award for Chemistry, 1993, Gold Award, 2002, IES; Bruker Prize, RSC, 1997; Zavoisky Prize for Electron Spin Resonance, Tatarstan, 2001. Radio and television appearances. *Publications:* Magnetic Resonance, 1972; Molecular Physical Chemistry: a concise introduction, 2004; contrib. chaps in books; papers and review articles in Molecular Physics, Chemical Physics Letters, etc. *Recreations:* gardening, walking, ski-ing, reading. *Address:* 29 Cumnor Hill, Oxford OX2 9EY. *T:* (01865) 862570.

McLAUCHLAN, Dr Sylvia June, FFPH; Director General, The Stroke Association, 1993–97; *b* 8 June 1935; *d* of Sydney George Smith and Muriel May (*née* Treweek); *m* 1960, Derek John Alexander McLauchlan, CBE (*d* 2009); two *d. Educ:* High Sch. for Girls, Chichester; Univ. of Bristol (MB ChB 1959); Univ. of Manchester (MSc 1981). FFPH (FFPHM 1989). GP, Bristol, 1960–66; MO, Dept of Public Health, Portsmouth, 1970–76; Clinical MO, Macclesfield, 1976–77; Community Medicine Dept, NW RHA, 1977–86; Public Health Dept, SW Thames RHA, 1986–91; Dir of Public Health, Ealing HA, 1991–93. Chm., Primary Care Facilitation Trust, 2000–03; Trustee, East Thames Care, 2000–04. Gov., Treloar Sch., 2001–03. *Recreations:* theatre, gardening, cooking. *Address:* 7 Holmwood Close, East Horsley, Surrey KT24 6SS.

McLAUGHLIN, Anne; *see* McLaughlin, E. A.

McLAUGHLIN, Christopher John; Editor, Tribune, since 2004; *b* 11 Oct. 1955; *s* of Patrick Thomas McLaughlin and Norah Mary McLaughlin (*née* Walsh). *Educ:* St Helen's, Plaistow; St Bonaventure's, Forest Gate. Gen. reporter, Barking and Dagenham Advertiser, then Newham Recorder, 1974–78; Foreign Ed., 1978–81, Lobby Corresp., 1981–87, Labour Weekly; Parly Corresp. and Dep. Political Ed., 1987–93, European Ed., 1993–96, Scotsman; Political Corresp., Mail on Sunday, 1996–2000; Parly Columnist, Big Issue, 1999–2005; Political Ed., Sunday Mirror, 2000–04. Mem. (Lab) Newham LBC, 1978–82. *Address:* c/o Tribune, Press Gallery, House of Commons, SW1A 0AA. *T:* (020) 7433 6410, *Fax:* (020) 7433 6419. *Club:* Soho House.

McLAUGHLIN, Eleanor Thomson; JP; DL; Lord Provost and Lord Lieutenant of Edinburgh, 1988–92; *b* 3 March 1938; *d* of Alexander Craig and Helen Thomson; *m* 1959, Hugh McLaughlin; one *s* two *d. Educ:* Broughton School. Mem. (Lab), Edinburgh District Council, 1974–96. Chairman: Edinburgh Festival Soc., 1988–92; Edinburgh Military Tattoo Ltd, 1988–92. JP Edinburgh, 1975; DL Edinburgh, 1993. *Recreations:* Shetland lace knitting, gardening (Alpine plants). *Address:* 28 Oxgangs Green, Edinburgh EH13 9JS. *T:* (0131) 445 4052.

McLAUGHLIN, (Elizabeth) Anne; MP (SNP) Glasgow North East, since 2015; *b* Greenock, 8 March 1966; *d* of John Robert McLaughlin and Elizabeth Fulton McLaughlin (*née* Purdie). *Educ:* Port Glasgow High Sch.; Royal Scottish Acad. of Music and Drama and Univ. of Glasgow (BA Dramatic Studies 1987). Anniversary Co-ordinator, Sense Scotland, 1994–96; Scottish Fundraising Manager, ICRF, 1996–2000; Staff Fundraiser, ScottishPower, 2000–01; Man. Dir, Business for Scotland, 2001–06; Internal Communications Exec., SNP HQ, 2002–06; Political Advr to Aileen Campbell, MSP, 2007–08; Communications Manager, Community Business Technol. Developers, Galle, Sri Lanka, 2008; Campaign Co-ordinator, SNP, Glasgow E by-election, 2008; Political Advr to Robert Doris, MSP, 2008–09. MSP (SNP) Glasgow, Feb. 2009–2011; contested (SNP): Glasgow Provan, Scottish Parlt, 2011; Inverclyde, June 2011. *Publications:* (ed) Tall Tales, Short Stories, 1995. *Recreations:* blogging (http:indygalgoestoholyrood.blogspot.com), travel, languages, creative writing, photography. *Address:* House of Commons, SW1A 0AA.

McLAUGHLIN, Léonie Anne; Parliamentary Counsel, since 2003; *b* 15 Nov. 1963; *d* of Timothy Edward Nodder, *qv*; *m* 1996, Wing Comdr Andrew McLaughlin. *Educ:* Christ's Coll., Cambridge (BA English Lit. and Law 1984). Admitted solicitor, 1988; solicitor's articles with May, May & Merrimans, Gray's Inn, 1986–88; Asst, then Sen. Asst, then Dep., Parly Counsel, Parly Counsel Office, 1988–96, 2000–03; self-employed Parly draftsman, 1996–2000. *Recreations:* books, fine art, gardening. *Address:* Parliamentary Counsel Office, 1 Horse Guards Road, SW1A 2HQ. *Club:* Royal Air Force.

McLAUGHLIN, Dr Mark Hugh; Executive Director of Finance, Environment Agency, since 2009; *b* 20 March 1962; *s* of Raymond and Helen McLaughlin; *m* 1988, Clare Louise Hennessy; three *s. Educ:* Univ. of St Andrews (BSc Hons (Zool.) 1983); Univ. of Nottingham (PhD (Zool.) 1988). Res. Fellow, Inst. of Neurol., 1987; Auditor, Audit Commn, 1987–91; Principal Auditor, City of Westminster, 1991–93; Borough of Broxbourne: Asst Dir of Finance, 1993–95; Dir of Resources, 1995–98; Dir of Finance, London Borough of Hammersmith and Fulham, 1998–2001; Dir of Finance and Corporate Resources, London Borough of Enfield, 2001–07; Exec. Dir, Finance and Performance, Identity and Passport Service, 2007–09. *Address:* Environment Agency, Ergon House, Horseferry Road, SW1P 2AL.

McLAUGHLIN, Prof. Martin Leonard, DPhil; Agnelli Serena (formerly Fiat Serena) Professor of Italian Studies, University of Oxford, and Fellow, Magdalen College, Oxford, since 2001; *b* 4 Dec. 1950; *s* of George Vincent McLaughlin and Ann Josephine McLaughlin; *m* 1974, Catherine Ann Gallagher; one *d. Educ:* St Aloysius' Coll., Glasgow; Glasgow Univ. (MA); Balliol Coll., Oxford (MA; DPhil 1984). Lectr, Italian Dept, Edinburgh Univ., 1977–90; Lectr in Italian, and Student, Christ Church, Oxford, 1990–2001; Dir, Eur. Humanities Res. Centre, 2002–04, 2011–14, Res. Dir, Faculty of Medieval and Mod. Langs, 2014–, Univ. of Oxford. Reviews Ed., Italian Studies, 1989–94; Italian Ed., 1994–2001, Gen. Ed., 2001–03, Modern Lang. Rev.; Chm., Editl Bd, Legenda, 2002–09. Member, Executive Committee: Soc. for Italian Studies, 1987–94 (Chm., 2004–10); MHRA, 1994–2004 (Hon. Life Mem., 2004). John Florio Prize for Translation, 2000. Commendatore dell' Ordine della Stella della Solidarietà Italiana, 2008. *Publications:* (ed jtly) Leopardi: a Scottis Quair, 1987; Literary Imitation in the Italian Renaissance, 1995; Italo Calvino, 1998; (trans.) Italo Calvino, Why Read the Classics?, 1999; (ed) Britain and Italy from Romanticism to Modernism, 2000; (trans.) Italo Calvino, Hermit in Paris, 2003; (trans.) Umberto Eco, On Literature, 2005; (ed jtly) Biographies and Autobiographies in Modern Italy, 2007; (ed jtly) Image, Eye and Art in Calvino: writing visibility, 2007; (ed jtly) Petrarch in Britain: interpreters, imitators and translators over 700 years, 2007; (ed jtly) Sinergie Narrative: cinema e letteratura nell'Italia contemporanea, 2008; (trans.) Italo Calvino, The Complete Cosmicomics, 2009; (ed jtly) Dante the Lyric and Ethical Poet: Dante lirico e etico, 2010; (ed jtly) Dante in Oxford: the Paget Toynbee Lectures, 2011; (trans.) Italo Calvino: Into the War, 2011; Letters 1941–1985, 2013; Collection of Sand, 2013. *Recreations:* football, travel, cinema, walking. *Address:* Magdalen College, Oxford OX1 4AU.

McLAUGHLIN, Mary, CBE 2007; Head Teacher, Notre Dame High School, Glasgow, 1990–2007; Principal, Notre Dame New Learning Community, 2003–07; *b* 18 Aug. 1948; *d* of Philip McGachey and Mary McGachey (*née* Ashe); *m* 1972, William McLaughlin; one *d. Educ:* Our Lady and St Joseph's Primary Sch., Glenboig; St Patrick's High Sch., Coatbridge; Univ. of Glasgow (MA); Notre Dame Coll. (DipEd). Principal Teacher, Modern Langs, St Margaret's High Sch., Airdrie, 1975–84; Asst Head, Taylor High Sch., New Stevenson, 1984–90. Member: Bd, Anniesland Coll., 1993–97; Bd, Curriculum for Excellence Prog., 2005–. Leadership in Learning Award, Becta, 2005; Glasgow Archdio. Medal for Services to Educn, 2007. *Recreations:* reading, walking, travel, theatre. *Address:* Notre Dame High School, 160 Observatory Road, Glasgow G12 9LN. *T:* (0141) 582 0190, *Fax:* (0141) 582 0191.

McLAUGHLIN, Mitchel; Member for South Antrim, since 2007 (Foyle, 1998–2007) (SF, 1998–2015, when elected Speaker), and Speaker, since 2015, Northern Ireland Assembly (Deputy Speaker, 2013–15); *b* 29 Oct. 1945; *m* 1975, Mary-Lou Fleming; three *s.* Mem. (SF) Derry CC, 1985–99. Sinn Féin: Mem., Nat. Exec., 1981–; Nat. Chairperson, 1994–2015; peace negotiator, 1997–. Member: Civil Rights Assoc., 1968–; Nat. H-Blocks/Armagh Cttee, 1980–81. Contested (SF): Foyle, 2005; S Antrim, 2010. *Address:* Northern Ireland Assembly, Parliament Buildings, Belfast BT4 3XX.

McLAUGHLIN, Niall; Principal, Niall McLaughlin Architects, since 1990; *b* Geneva, 17 Feb. 1962; *s* of John McLaughlin and Mairin McLaughlin (*née* Cryan); *m* 2006, Mary Miller; one *s* one *d. Educ:* St Michael's Coll., Dublin; University Coll. Dublin (BArch 1984). Architect, Scott Tallon Walker, 1984–89. Projects include: student residence, Somerville Coll., Oxford, 2011; chapel, Ripon Coll., Cuddesdon, 2013. Visiting Professor: Bartlett Sch. of Architecture, UCL, 2007–; UCLA, 2012–13; Lord Norman Foster Vis. Prof. of Architecture, Yale Univ., 2014–15. *Address:* Niall McLaughlin Architects, 3rd Floor, Bedford House, 125–133 Camden High Street, NW1 7JR.

MacLAURIN, family name of **Baron MacLaurin of Knebworth**.

MacLAURIN OF KNEBWORTH, Baron *cr* 1996 (Life Peer), of Knebworth in the county of Hertfordshire; **Ian Charter MacLaurin,** Kt 1989; DL; Chairman, Chartwell Group, 2004–10; *b* Blackheath, 30 March 1937; *s* of Arthur George and Evelina Florence MacLaurin; *m* 1st, 1961, Ann Margaret (*née* Collar) (*d* 1999); one *s* two *d*; 2nd, 2002, Paula Elizabeth Brooke (*née* Morris). *Educ:* Malvern Coll., Worcs. Served in RAF, 1956–58. Joined Tesco, 1959; Dir, 1970; Man Dir, 1973–85; Dep. Chm., 1983–85; Chm., 1985–97. Vodafone (then Vodafone AirTouch, subseq. reverted to Vodafone): non-exec. Dir, 1997–2006; Chm., 1998–99, 2000–06; Dep. Chm., 1999–2000; Chm., Vodafone Gp Foundn, 2006–09; non-executive Director: Enterprise Oil, 1984–90; Guinness PLC, 1986–95; National Westminster Bank plc, 1990–97; Gleneagles Hotels plc, 1992–97; Whitbread plc, 1997–2001 (Dep. Chm., 1999–2001); Evolution Gp plc, 2004–11; Heineken NV, 2006–11. Chm., TCCB, then ECB, 1996–2002. Chm., Food Policy Gp, Retail Consortium, 1980–84; Pres., Inst. of Grocery Distribution, 1989–92. Trustee, Royal Opera House Trust, 1992. Governor and Mem. Council, Malvern Coll. (Chm. Council, 2003–); Chancellor, Univ. of Hertfordshire, 1996–2005. Mem. Cttee, MCC, 1986–96. FRSA 1986; FIMMM (FIM 1987); Hon. FCGI 1992. Liveryman, Carmen's Co., 1982–. DL Herts, 1992, Wilts, 2007. Hon. Fellow, Univ. of Wales, Cardiff, 1996. DUniv: Stirling, 1987; Bradford, 2001; Hon. LLD Hertfordshire, 1995. *Publications:* Tiger by the Tail (memoirs), 1999. *Recreations:* golf, cricket. *Address:* House of Lords, SW1A 0PW. *Clubs:* MCC, Lord's Taverners, XL, Band of Brothers; Royal & Ancient Golf (St Andrews).

MACLAY, family name of **Baron Maclay**.

MACLAY, 3rd Baron *cr* 1922, of Glasgow; **Joseph Paton Maclay;** Bt 1914; Group Marketing Executive, Acomarit Group, 1993–99; *b* 11 April 1942; *s* of 2nd Baron Maclay, KBE, and Nancy Margaret, *d* of R. C. Greig, Hall of Caldwell, Uplawmoor, Renfrewshire; *S* father, 1969; *m* 1976, Elizabeth Anne, *o d* of G. M. Buchanan, Delamere, Pokataroo, NSW; two *s* one *d. Educ:* Winchester; Sorbonne Univ. Managing Director: Denholm Maclay Co. Ltd, 1970–83; Denholm Maclay (Offshore) Ltd, 1975–83; Triport Ferries (Management) Ltd, 1975–83; Dep. Man. Dir, Denholm Ship Management Ltd, 1982–83; Man. Dir, Milton Timber Services Ltd, 1984–90; Dir, Denholm Ship Management (Holdings) Ltd, 1991–93. Director: Milton Shipping Co. Ltd, 1970–83; Marine Shipping Mutual Insce Co., 1982–83; Altnamara Shipping PLC, 1994–2002; Pres., Hanover Shipping Inc., 1982–83. Director: British Steamship Short Trades Assoc., 1978–83; N of England Protection and Indemnity Assoc., 1976–83. A Comr of Northern Lighthouses, 1996–2003 (Vice Chm., 2001–01, Chm., 2001–03, Bd). Chm., Scottish Br., British Sailors Soc., 1979–81; Vice-Chm., Glasgow Shipowners & Shipbrokers Benevolent Assoc., 1982–83 and 1996–97 (Pres., 1998–99); Chm., Scottish Nautical Welfare Soc., 2002–04. Chm., Scottish Maritime Mus., 1998–2005. Trustee: Cattanach Charitable Trust, 1991– (Chm., 2009–11); Western Isles Fisheries Trust, 2004–06; Western Isles Salmon Fishing Bd, 2004–06. DL Renfrewshire, 1986. *Heir: s* Hon. Joseph Paton Maclay [*b* 6 March 1977; *m* 2008, Kathryn Meyricka Bruton Good]. *Address:* Duchal, Kilmacolm, Renfrewshire PA13 4RS.

McLAY, Hon. Sir James Kenneth, (Sir Jim), KNZM 2015 (CNZM 2003); Permanent Representative of New Zealand to the United Nations, since 2009; Managing Director and Principal, J. K. McLay Ltd (international business consultants), since 1987; *s* of late Robert McLay and Joyce McLay; *m* 1983, Marcy Farden. *Educ:* St Helier's Sch.; King's Sch.; King's Coll.; Auckland Univ. (LLB 1967); Pennsylvania State Univ. (EMP 1987). Solicitor in practice on own account, 1971; barrister 1974. MP (National Party) for Birkenhead, NZ, 1975–87; Attorney-Gen. and Minister of Justice, 1978–84; Government Spokesperson for Women, 1979–84; Dep. Prime Minister, 1984; Leader, National Party and Leader of the Opposition, 1984–86. Mem., Ministerial Wkg Party on Accident Compensation and Incapacity, 1990–91; NZ Comr, Internat. Whaling Commn, 1993–2002. Chairman: Wholesale Electricity Market Study, 1991–92; Wholesale Electricity Market Develt Gp, 1993–94. Chairman: OMNIPORT Napier Ltd, 1988–2001; Roading Adv. Gp, 1997; Project Manukau Audit Gp, 1998–; Pharmacybrands Ltd, 1999–2007; Just Water International Ltd, 2004–; Goodman (NZ) Ltd, 2005–; Metlifecare Ltd, 2006–; Macquarie Gp Hldgs New Zealand Ltd; Director: Evergreen Forests Ltd, 1995–2002; Motor Sport New Zealand Ltd, 1996–99; Mem. Adv. Bd, Westfield NZ Ltd, 1998–2002. Founder Chm., 2004, and Patron, 2005–, NZ Council for Infrastructure Develt. Hon. NZ Chm., Trans-Tasman Business Circle, 2004–08. NZ deleg., Australia/NZ Leadership Forum, 2004–08. Advr, UK Cons. Party Commn on Bank of England, 1999–2000. *Recreation:* trout fishing. *Address:* PO Box 8885, Symonds Street Post Office, Auckland 1150, New Zealand.

MacLEAN, Rt Hon. Lord; Ranald Norman Munro MacLean; PC 2001; a Surveillance Commissioner, since 2010; a Senator of the College of Justice in Scotland, 1990–2005; *b* 18 Dec. 1938; *s* of late John Alexander MacLean, CBE; *m* 1963, Pamela Ross (marr. diss. 1993); two *s* one *d* (and one *s* decd). *Educ:* Inverness Royal Acad.; Fettes Coll.; Clare Coll.,

Cambridge Univ. (BA); Edinburgh Univ. (LLB); Yale Univ., USA (LLM). Called to the Scottish Bar, 1964; QC (Scot.) 1977; Advocate Depute, 1972–75, Home Advocate Depute, 1979–82; Standing Jun. Counsel, Health and Safety Exec. (Scotland), 1975–77; Member: Council on Tribunals, 1985–90 (Chm., Scottish Cttee, 1985–90); Scottish Legal Aid Bd, 1986–90; Scottish Judicial Appts Bd, 2002–05. Member: Stewart Cttee on Alternatives to Prosecution, 1977–82; Parole Bd for Scotland, 1998–2000, 2003; Chairman: Cttee on Serious Violent and Sexual Offenders, 1999–2000; Sentencing Commn for Scotland, 2003–05; Billy Wright Inquiry, Banbridge, NI, 2005–10; Vale of Leven Hosp. Inquiry, Glasgow, 2009–14. Mem., Ind. Rev. Commn on Scottish Football, Scottish Football Assoc., 1995–97. Trustee, Nat. Liby of Scotland, 1967–90. Chm. of Council, Cockburn Assoc., 1988–96. Chm. Govs, Fettes Coll., 1996–2006. FSAScot 1994; FRSE 2000. Hon. LLD Aberdeen, 2003. *Publications:* (ed jtly) Gloag and Henderson, Introduction to the Law of Scotland, 7th edn 1968, 8th edn 1980. *Recreations:* hill walking, swimming. *Address:* 67/3 Grange Loan, Edinburgh EH9 2EG. *Clubs:* New, Scottish Arts (Edinburgh).

MACLEAN, Alan John; QC 2009; *b* Glasgow, 6 Aug. 1969; *s* of Dr John and Jean Maclean; *m* 2001, Sarah Joanne Corkish; two *s*. *Educ:* Lenzie Acad., Glasgow; University Coll., Oxford (BA 1st Cl. PPE); Harvard Univ. (Kennedy Meml Schol.); City Univ. London (CPE with Dist.); Inns of Court Sch. of Law. Called to the Bar, Gray's Inn, 1993; in practice as barrister, 1993–. Mem., Attorney Gen.'s Panel of Counsel, 1999–2009. *Recreations:* theatre, tennis, enjoying the frustrations of devotion to Arsenal FC and Glasgow Tigers. *Address:* Blackstone Chambers, Blackstone House, Temple, EC4Y 9BW. *T:* (020) 7822 7351. *E:* alanmaclean@blackstonechambers.com.

McLEAN, Alan William David; QC (Scot.) 2008; *b* London, 27 Dec. 1963; *s* of David Colin Hugh McLean and Deborah McLean (*née* Packe); *m* 1993, Katharine Jane Colwell; one *s* one *d*. *Educ:* Harrow Sch., Middx; Gonville and Caius Coll., Cambridge (BA 1985; MA 1989); Edinburgh Univ. (LLB 1987; DipLP 1988). Solicitor, 1990–92; Advocate, 1993; Stable Dir, Hastie Stable, Faculty of Advocates, 2010–13. *Publications:* (contrib.) Court of Session Practice, 2005. *Address:* Advocates' Library, Parliament House, Edinburgh EH1 1RF. *T:* (0131) 226 5071.

MACLEAN of Dochgarroch, Very Rev. Canon Allan Murray; historian; Provost of St John's Cathedral, Oban, 1986–99; *b* 22 Oct. 1950; *o s* of late Rev. Donald Maclean of Dochgarroch and Loraine Maclean of Dochgarroch (*née* Calvert); *m* 1990, Anne (*née* Cavin), *widow* of David Lindsay; two *s* one *d*. *Educ:* Dragon School, Oxford; Trinity College, Glenalmond; Univ. of Edinburgh (MA 1st cl. Hons Scottish History); Cuddesdon Coll. and Pusey House, Oxford. Deacon 1976, Priest 1977; Chaplain of St Mary's Cathedral, Edinburgh, 1976–81; Rector of Holy Trinity, Dunoon, 1981–86; Exam. Chaplain to Bishop of Argyll and the Isles, 1983–93. Hon. Canon, St John's Cathedral, Oban, 1999–. Pres., Clan Maclean Assoc., 1994–98, 2009–14 (Vice-Pres., 1982–94); Chm., Clan Maclean Heritage Trust, 2001–07; Chm., Clan Chattan Assoc., 2007–10. Editor: Clan Maclean, 1975–85, 2001–04, 2010–; Argyll and the Isles, 1984–93; Edge, 2006–13. *Publications:* Telford's Highland Churches, 1989. *Recreations:* topography, history, genealogy, architecture. *Address:* 5 North Charlotte Street, Edinburgh EH2 4HR. *T:* (0131) 225 8609; Hazelbrae House, Glen Urquhart, Inverness IV63 6TJ. *T:* (01456) 476267. *Clubs:* New, Puffin's (Edinburgh).

McLEAN, Prof. Angela Ruth, (Mrs David van Oss), PhD; FRS 2009; Professor of Mathematical Biology, University of Oxford, since 2004; Senior Research Fellow in Theoretical Life Sciences, All Souls College, Oxford, since 2008; *b* Kingston, Jamaica, 31 May 1961; *d* of Andre and Elizabeth McLean; *m* 1986, David van Oss; one *s* two *d*. *Educ:* Mary Datchelor Girls' Sch.; Somerville Coll., Oxford (BA Maths 1982); Imperial Coll., London (PhD Biomaths 1986). Royal Soc. Res. Fellow, Zool. Dept, Univ. of Oxford, 1990–98; Hd, Mathematical Biol., Inst. for Animal Health, Compton, 1998–2000; Lectr in Biodiversity, Zool. Dept, Univ. of Oxford and Tutorial Fellow, St Catherine's Coll., Oxford, 2000–08. *Publications:* (jtly) SARS: a case study in emerging infections, 2005; (jtly) Theoretical Ecology, Principals and Applications, 2007; contrib. articles to biol jls on infectious disease dynamics, evolution and immune responses. *Address:* Zoology Department, Oxford University, South Parks Road, Oxford OX1 3PS. *T:* (01865) 271210, *Fax:* (01865) 310447. *E:* angela.mclean@zoo.ox.ac.uk.

MACLEAN of Dunconnel, Sir Charles (Edward), 2nd Bt *cr* 1957, of Dunconnel, co. Argyll; *b* 31 Oct. 1946; *s* of Sir Fitzroy Hew Maclean of Dunconnel, 1st Bt, KT, CBE and Hon. Veronica Fraser, *d* of 16th Lord Lovat, KT, GCVO, KCMG, CB, DSO and *widow* of Lt Alan Phipps, RN; *S* father, 1996; *m* 1986, Deborah, *d* of Lawrence Young; four *d*. *Educ:* Eton; New Coll., Oxford. *Publications:* Island on the Edge of the World: story of St Kilda, 1972; The Wolf Children, 1977; The Watcher, 1983; (with C. S. Sykes) Scottish Country, 1993; Romantic Scotland, 1995; The Silence, 1996; Home Before Dark, 2008. *Heir: b* Alexander James Simon Aeneas Maclean [*b* 9 June 1949; *m* 1st, 1983, Sarah (marr. diss. 1989), *d* of Hugh Janson; 2nd, 1993, Sarah, *d* of Nicolas Thompson; two *s*]. *Address:* Strachur House, Strachur, Cairndow, Argyll PA27 8BX.

See also Maj.-Gen. J. J. J. Phipps.

MacLEAN, Colin Ross; Chairman, Partnership Commission on Childcare Reform (Scotland), 2014–15; *b* 22 May 1951; *s* of Maurice MacLean and Freda MacLean; *m* 1974, Ilse Youngman; two *s* one *d*. *Educ:* Univ. of Edinburgh (BSc Pure Maths 1972; DipEd (Sec. Educn) 1973; MSc Microelectronics 1980). Teacher of Maths, Edinburgh, 1973–79; Lothian Region: Asst Advr in Microelectronic Technology, 1980–82; Advr in Educnl Computing, 1982–85; Scottish Office: HM Inspector of Schs, 1985–96; Chief Statistician, 1996–99; Scottish Executive Education Department: HM Depute Sen. Chief Inspector of Schs, 1999–2000; Depute Hd, Schs Gp, 2000–02; Acting Hd of Dept, 2007; Hd, then Dir, Children, Young People and Social Care, Scottish Exec. Educn Dept, later Scottish Govt, 2002–08; Dir, Schs, then Learning, 2008–11, Dir, Financial Strategy, 2011–13, Scottish Govt. Trustee, Barnardo's, 2014– (Chair, Scotland Cttee, 2014–); Mem. Bd and Trustee, Streetwork UK, 2014–. Mem. Court, Heriot-Watt Univ., 2014– (Mem., Audit and Risk Cttee, 2014–). Volunteer with Edinburgh Cyrenians, 2013–. *Publications:* Computing in Schools, 1985. *Recreations:* gardening, travel, music. *E:* crmacl@btinternet.com.

MACLEAN, Colin William, OBE 2000; FRCVS; Chairman, Royal Berkshire NHS Foundation Trust (formerly Royal Berkshire and Battle Hospitals NHS Trust), 2000–12; *b* 19 June 1938; *s* of late Kenneth Percy Maclean and Elsie Violet (*née* Middleton); *m* 1959, Jacqueline Diana Brindley; two *d*. *Educ:* William Hulme's Grammar Sch., Manchester; Liverpool Univ. Sch. of Vet. Sci. (BVSc; MVSc 1971). MRCVS 1961, FRCVS 1969. Veterinary Surgeon and Partner, veterinary practice, Thornbury, Glos, and Wickham, Hants, 1961–66; Unilever Ltd: Chief Vet. Advr, 1966–72; Manager, Pig Breeding, 1972–74; Man. Dir, Farm Mark Ltd and Masterbreeders Ltd, 1974–76; Area Gen. Manager (S), BOCM Silcock Ltd, 1980–83; Glaxo Group: Dep. Man. Dir, 1983–88; Product Develt Dir, Glaxo Animal Health Ltd, 1983–88; Technical Dir, 1988–92, Dir-Gen., 1992–99, MLC. Non-exec. Dir, Solutions for Public Health, 2009–. Special Trustee, Moorfields Eye Hosp., 2012–; Mem. Council, Assoc. of NHS Charities, 2013– (Vice Chair, 2015–). *Publications:* contrib. to Veterinary Record (William Hunting Silver Medal, BVA, 1965, 1967), Res. Vet. Sci., Jl Comparative Pathology. *Recreations:* squash, Rugby, theatre, travel, private pilot's licence. *Address:* Crackwillow, Cock Lane, Bradfield, Reading RG7 6HW. *Club:* Farmers.

McLEAN, Hector John Finlayson, CBE 1995; Secretary, Crown Appointments Commission, and Archbishops' Appointments Secretary, 1987–95; a Civil Service Commissioner, 1996–2001; *b* 10 Feb. 1934; *s* of late Dr Murdoch McLean, MB ChB and Dr Edith Muriel Finlayson McLean (*née* McGill), MB ChB, DPH, DOMS; *m* 1959, Caroline Elizabeth Lithgow; one *s* two *d*. *Educ:* Dulwich Coll.; Pembroke Coll., Cambridge (BA Hons 1958; MA 1997); Harvard Business Sch., Switzerland (SMP6 1976). Chartered FCIPD (FIPM 1965). 2nd Lieut, KOSB, 1954–55. Imperial Chemical Industries, 1958–87: Central Staff Dept, 1958; various personnel and admin. posts in Dyestuffs and Organics Divs, 1959–72; Personnel Manager, Organics Div., 1972–74; Polyurethanes Business Area Manager, 1974–75; Dir, Agricl Div., 1975–86. Non-exec. Chairman: People & Potential Ltd, 1987–97; Positive People Develt (formerly Teesside Positive People), 1987–94. Mem. Exec. Cttee, N of England Develt Council, 1978–83; Teesside Industrial Mission: Mem., Management Cttee, 1978–85; Chm., 1982–85; Dir, Cleveland Enterprise Agency, 1982–87. Mem., Northern Regl Council, CBI, 1981–85; Trustee: NE Civic Trust, 1976–88; Northern Heritage Trust, 1984–87; mediationplus (formerly Family Mediation Service (N Wilts)), 2000–10 (Chm., 2004–09; Pres., 2010–). Mem., Chemical and Allied Products ITB, 1979–82. Chm., Selection Panel, Wilts Police Authy, 1997–2003. Gov. Teesside Polytechnic, 1978–84; Mem. Council, Newcastle Univ., 1985–87. FRSA 1991–2010. Pres., Alleyn Club, 1997–98 (Vice Pres., 1996–97). Hon. DSc Aston, 2004. *Recreations:* family, music (especially choral music), travel, gardening, walking more gently. *Address:* College Farm House, Purton, near Swindon, Wilts SN5 4AE. *T:* (01793) 770525.

McLEAN, Prof. Iain Sinclair, DPhil; FBA 2008; FRSE; Professor of Politics, University of Oxford, and Fellow, Nuffield College, Oxford, since 1993; *b* 13 Sept. 1946; *s* of John and Louisa McLean; *m* 1984, Dr Jo Poulton; one *s* one *d*. *Educ:* Royal High Sch., Edinburgh; Christ Church, Oxford (MA, MPhil; DPhil 1972). Res. Fellow in Politics, Nuffield Coll., Oxford, 1969–71; Lectr in Politics, Univ. of Newcastle upon Tyne, 1971–78; Fellow and Praelector in Politics, University Coll., Oxford, 1978–91; Prof. of Politics, Univ. of Warwick, 1991–93. Visiting Professor: Stanford Univ., 1990; ANU, 1996, 2002; Yale Univ., 2001; Internat. Center for Jefferson Studies, Monticello, Va, 2010. Vice-Pres. for Public Policy, British Acad., 2012–Aug. 2016. Member: (Lab) Tyne and Wear MCC, 1973–79; (SDP) Oxford CC, 1982–86. Chm., Welshpool and Llanfair Light Railway, 2013–. FRSE 2012. *Publications:* Keir Hardie, 1975; Elections, 1976, 3rd edn 1983; Dealing in Votes, 1982; The Legend of Red Clydeside, 1983, 2nd edn 2000; Public Choice: an introduction, 1987; Democracy and New Technology, 1989; (ed, trans. and introd with F. Hewitt) Condorcet: foundations of social choice and political theory, 1994; (ed, trans. and introd with A. B. Urken) Classics of Social Choice, 1995; (gen. ed and contrib.) Concise Oxford Dictionary of Politics, 1996, 2nd edn 2003; (jtly) A Mathematical Approach to Proportional Representation: Duncan Black on Lewis Carroll, 1996; (ed with D. Butler) Fixing the Boundary: defining and redefining single-member electoral districts, 1996; (ed jtly) The Theory of Committees and Elections by Duncan Black and Committee Decisions with Complementary Valuation by Duncan Black and R. A. Newing, 1998; (with M. Johnes) Aberfan: government and disasters, 2000; Rational Choice and British Politics: an analysis of rhetoric and manipulation from Peel to Blair, 2001; (jtly) International Trade and Political Institutions: instituting trade in the long nineteenth century, 2001; The Fiscal Crisis of the United Kingdom, 2005; Adam Smith, 2006; What's Wrong with the British Constitution?, 2009; numerous articles in learned jls. *Recreations:* steam railway preservation, walking, choral music. *Address:* Nuffield College, Oxford OX1 1NF.

McLEAN, His Honour Ian Graeme; a Circuit Judge, 1980–97; *b* Edinburgh, 7 Sept. 1928; *s* of Lt-Gen. Sir Kenneth McLean, KCB, KBE; *m* 1957, Eleonore Maria Gmeiner, Bregenz, Austria; one *d* (and one *d* decd). *Educ:* Aldenham Sch.; Christ's Coll., Cambridge. BA Hons Law 1950; MA 1955. Intell. Corps, 1946–48. Called to English Bar, Middle Temple, Nov. 1951; admitted Faculty of Advocates, Edinburgh, 1985; practised London and on Western Circuit, 1951–55; Crown Counsel, Northern Nigeria, 1955–59; Sen. Lectr and Head of Legal Dept of Inst. of Administration, Northern Nigeria, 1959–62; Native Courts Adviser, 1959–62; returned to English Bar, 1962; practised London and South Eastern Circuit, 1962–70; Adjudicator under Immigration Acts, 1969–70; Metropolitan Stipendiary Magistrate, 1970–80. *Publications:* Cumulative Index West African Court of Appeal Reports, 1958; (with Abubakar Sadiq) The Maliki Law of Homicide, 1959; (with Sir Lionel Brett) Criminal Law Procedure and Evidence of Lagos, Eastern and Western Nigeria, 1963; (with Cyprian Okonkwo) Cases on the Criminal Law, Procedure and Evidence of Nigeria, 1966; (with Peter Morrish) A Practical Guide to Appeals in Criminal Courts, 1970; (with Peter Morrish) The Crown Court, an index of common penalties, etc, 1972–2000, (with Peter Morrish and D. H. D. Selwood), 2001–04, (with Peter Morrish), 2005, (with Peter Morrish and S. Katkhuda), 2006, (with S. Katkhuda), 2007, 2008, 2009, (with S. Katkhuda and J. Dixon), 2010, (with J. Dixon), 2011, 2012, 2013, 2014, 2015; (ed with Peter Morrish) Harris's Criminal Law, 22nd edn, 1972; (with Peter Morrish) The Magistrates' Court, an index of common penalties, annually 1973–92, (with Peter Morrish and John Greenhill), 1996 and 2003; (with Peter Morrish) The Trial of Breathalyser Offences, 1975, 3rd edn 1990; A Practical Guide to Criminal Appeals, 1980; A Pattern of Sentencing, 1981; (with John Mulhern) The Industrial Tribunal: a practical guide to employment law and tribunal procedure, 1982; (with Sheriff Stone) Fact-Finding for Magistrates, 1990; contrib. Archbold's Criminal Pleadings, 38th edn, and Halsbury's Laws of England, 4th edn, title Criminal Law. *Recreations:* writing, languages. *Address:* c/o HSBC, 58 High Street, Winchester, Hants SO23 9BZ.

MACLEAN, Prof. Ian Walter Fitzroy, DPhil; FRHistS; FBA 1994; Titular Professor of Renaissance Studies, Oxford University, 1996–2014, now Emeritus; Fellow, All Souls College, Oxford, 2012–15, now Emeritus (Senior Research Fellow, 1996–2012); *b* 9 Feb. 1945; *s* of James Walter Maclean and Elsie May Maclean (*née* Davis); *m* 1971, Pauline Jennifer Henderson; one *s* two *d*. *Educ:* Christ's Hosp.; Wadham Coll., Oxford (BA 1st Cl. Hons Mod. Lang. 1966; MA, DPhil 1971). FRHistS 1989. Sen. Scholar, Wadham Coll., Oxford, 1967–69; Lectr in French, Univ. of Leeds, 1969–72; Oxford University: CUF Lectr in French, 1972–93; Reader in French, 1994–96; Fellow, 1972–96, Supernumerary Fellow, 1996–, Queen's Coll.; Dir, European Humanities Res. Centre, 1994–99; Lyell Reader in Bibliography, 2009–10. Vis. Fellow, Humanities Res. Centre, Canberra, 1983; Vis. Scholar, Herzog August Bibliothek, Wolfenbüttel, 1986, 1995, 2008; Visiting Professor: Catholic Univ. of Nijmegen, 1993; Collège de France, 2005; Ecole Pratique des Hautes Etudes, Paris, 2007; Dist. Vis. Schol., Centre for Renaissance and Reformation Studies, Victoria Univ., Univ. of Toronto, 1994. MAE 1998. Officier, Ordre des Arts et des Lettres (France), 2005. *Publications:* Woman Triumphant: feminism in French literature, 1977; The Renaissance Notion of Woman, 1980; (ed and contrib.) Montaigne, 1982; (ed and contrib.) The Political Responsibility of Intellectuals, 1990; Meaning and Interpretation in the Renaissance: the case of law, 1992; (trans.) Potocki, The Manuscript Found in Saragossa, 1995; Montaigne philosophe, 1996; Logic, Signs and Nature in the Renaissance: the case of learned medicine, 2001; (ed and contrib.) *Res et verba* in the Renaissance, 2002; (ed) Cardano, *De Libris Propriis*, 2005; (ed and contrib.) Heterodoxy in Early Modern Science and Religion, 2006; (ed and contrib.) Transmitting Knowledge: words, images and instruments in Early Modern Europe, 2006; Le monde et les hommes selon les médecins de la Renaissance, 2006; (trans.) Descartes, A Discourse on the Method, 2006; Learning and the Market Place: essays in the history of the early modern book, 2009; Scholarship, Commerce, Religion: the learned book in the age of confessions, 1560–1630, 2012; articles and essays in learned jls, collective vols, etc. *Recreations:* music, fishing, wine. *Address:* All Souls College, Oxford OX1 4AL. *T:* (01865) 279379.

McLEAN, Irwin; *see* McLean, W. H. I.

MACLEAN, Kate; Member (Lab) Dundee West, Scottish Parliament, 1999–2007; *b* 16 Feb. 1958; *d* of late Alexander Robertson and Sarah Robertson; *m* 1978 (marr. diss.); one *s* one *d*. *Educ:* Craigie High Sch., Dundee. Mem. (Lab) Dundee City Council, 1988–99 (Leader, 1992–99). Convener, Equal Opportunities Cttee, Scottish Parliament, 1999–2007. Vice-Pres., COSLA, 1996–99. *Address:* c/o Scottish Parliament, Edinburgh EH99 1SP.

McLEAN, Keith Richard, FCCA; Chairman: Harrogate Training and Development, 2004–07; Centre for Performance Measurement and Innovation Ltd, since 2007; *b* 27 Oct. 1947; *s* of Bertie and Elsie McLean; *m* 1973, Patricia Ann Morrell; one *d*. *Educ:* J. Rowntree Sch., York. FCCA 1975; CPFA (IPFA 1989); MHSM 1992. Hospital Management Committees: Clerical Officer, York B, 1964–67; Higher Clerical Officer, Leicester No 4, 1967–68; Internal Auditor, Nottingham No 4, 1968–70; Sen. Accountant, Huddersfield, 1970–74; Dep. Area Treas., Calderdale HA, 1974–79; Dist Finance Officer, Derbys AHA, 1979–82; North Derbyshire Health Authority: Dist Treas., 1982–85; Dist Treas. and Dep. Dist Gen. Manager, 1985–87; Dir of Finance and Corporate Strategist, Leics HA, 1987–89; Yorkshire Regional Health Authority: Regl Dir of Finance, 1990–91; Regl Gen. Manager, 1991–94; Regl Gen. Manager, Trent RHA and Regl Dir, NHS Exec., Trent, 1994–96. Director: Harrogate Mgt Centre Ltd, 1996–2004; Key Health Marketing Ltd, 1998–2004; 22/44 The Shambles Ltd, 2008–12; Vintage York Ltd, 2010–12; Partner: Key Health Consulting, 1998–2005; Birchfield Associates, 2004–08. Principal Res. Fellow, Sheffield Univ., 1996–2000; Fellow, Nottingham Univ., 1995. Nat. Chm., Healthcare Financial Mgt Assoc., 1992–93; Mem., Inst. of Healthcare Mgt, 1995. FRSA 1994. *Recreation:* golf.

MacLEAN, Kenneth Walter; QC 2002; *b* 9 Feb. 1959; *s* of Walter and Mary MacLean; *m* 1994, Jane Elizabeth; three *c*. *Educ:* Rugby Sch.; Trinity Hall, Cambridge (MA); Harvard Law Sch. (LLM). Called to the Bar, Gray's Inn, 1985. *Recreations:* ski-ing, Rugby, piping. *Address:* 1 Essex Court, Temple, EC4Y 9AR. *T:* (020) 7583 2000, *Fax:* (020) 7583 0118. *E:* kmaclean@oeclaw.co.uk. *Club:* Harvard (New York).

MACLEAN, Hon. Sir Lachlan Hector Charles, 12th Bt *cr* 1631 (NS), of Duart and Morvern; CVO 2000; DL; Major, Scots Guards, retired; 28th Chief of Clan Maclean; *b* 25 Aug. 1942; *s* of Baron Maclean, KT, GCVO, KBE, PC and of Elizabeth, *er d* of late Frank Mann; *S* to baronetcy of father, 1990; *m* 1st, 1966, Mary Helen (*d* 2007), *e d* of late W. G. Gordon; two *s* two *d* (and one *d* decd); 2nd, 2010, Rosemary, *widow* of Lt-Col Richard Mayfield, DSO, LVO. *Educ:* Eton. DL Argyll and Bute, 1993. *Heir: s* Malcolm Lachlan Charles Maclean [*b* 20 Oct. 1972; *m* 1998, Anna, *e d* of Giles Sturdy; three *s*]. *Address:* Duart Castle, Isle of Mull, Argyll PA64 6AP.

MACLEAN, Mavis, CBE 2002; Founding Director, Oxford Centre for Family Law and Policy, Department of Social Policy and Intervention (formerly Social Policy and Social Work), University of Oxford, since 2001; Senior Research Fellow of St Hilda's College, Oxford, since 2005; *b* 31 Dec. 1943; *m* 1967, Robert Maclean; two *d*. *Educ:* St Hilda's Coll., Oxford (BA (Hist.) 1965); LSE (MSc (Econs) 1967); Univ. of N London (LLB 1990). Res. Fellow, Centre for Socio-Legal Studies, Univ. of Oxford, 1974–2001. Academic Advr to LCD, later DCA, then MoJ, 1997–; Panel Mem., Bristol Royal Infirmary Inquiry, 1998–2001. Hon. Bencher, Middle Temple, 2014. FAcSS (AcSS 2012). *Publications:* (with J. Eekelaar) The Parental Obligation, 1997; (ed jtly) Cross Currents, 2000; (jtly) Family Lawyers, 2000; Family Law and Family Values, 2005; Parenting after Partnering, 2008; (with J. Eekelaar) Family Law Advocacy, 2009; (with Jacek Kurczewski Hart) Making Family Law, 2011; (with J. Eekelaar) Family Justice, 2013; (ed with J. Eekelaar) Managing Family Law in Diverse Societies, 2013; (with J. Eekelaar and B. Bastard) Delivering Family Justice in the 21st Century, 2015; contribs to Family Law, Internat. Jl Law, Policy and the Family, Law and Soc., Jl of Social Welfare and Family Law. *Recreation:* music. *Address:* Department of Social Policy and Intervention, Oxford Centre for Family Law and Policy, 32 Wellington Square, Oxford OX1 2ER. *E:* mavis.maclean@spi.ox.ac.uk. *Club:* Athenæum.

McLEAN, Miller Roy; Group Secretary, 1994–2010, and Group General Counsel, 2003–10, Royal Bank of Scotland Group; *b* Dumbarton, 4 Dec. 1949; *s* of David Peter Miller McLean and Jane Roy McLean (*née* Stenhouse); *m* 1973, Anne Gourlay; one *s* one *d*. *Educ:* Vale of Leven Acad.; Glasgow Univ. (MA); Edinburgh Univ. (LLB with Dist.). MCIBS 1972, FCIBS 1992; NP 1980; FIBI 2007; WS 2009. Royal Bank of Scotland: grad. trainee, 1970; Sec., 1983–88; Gp Sec., 1988–91; Dir, Legal and Regulatory Affairs, 1991–2000; Gp Dir, Legal and Regulatory Affairs, 2000–03. Trustee, 2000–, Chm., 2003–, Royal Bank of Scotland Gp Pension Fund; Trustee, 2006–, Chm., 2007–, Direct Line Gp (formerly Royal Bank of Scotland Insurance) Pension Fund. Director: Banco Santander Portugal SA, 1991–2003 (Vice Chm., 1993–2003); Adam & Co. Gp plc, 1998– (Chm., 2010–); Newton Mgt Ltd, 1998; Ulster Bank Gp, 2001–10. Member, Supervisory Board: ABN AMRO Holdings NV, 2009–11; ABN AMRO Bank NV, 2009–11. Mem., Financial Issues Adv. Gp, Scottish Parlt, 1998–2000; Dir, 1999–2012, Chm., 2001–12, Whitehall and Industry Gp; Dir, Scottish Parlt and Business Exchange, 2001–08. Industry and Parliament Trust: Corporate Fellow, 1989–; Mem. Council, 1990–99 (Chm. Council, 1996–99); Trustee, 2000–10. Chartered Institute of Bankers in Scotland: Mem. Council, 1997–2013; Vice-Pres., 2002–07; Pres., 2007–09. Mem. Council, Soc. of Writers to Signet, Edinburgh, 2009–12. Trustee, National Museums Scotland, 2010–. Gov., Queen Margaret Univ. Coll., 2000–03; Mem. Court, Queen Margaret Univ., 2011–. *Recreations:* golf, reading, music. *Club:* New (Edinburgh).

MACLEAN, Sir Murdo, Kt 2000; Director, Anuua Ltd, since 2014; *b* 21 Oct. 1943; *s* of late Murdo Maclean and of Johanna (*née* Martin). *Educ:* Glasgow. Min. of Labour Employment Exchange, Govan, Glasgow, 1963–64; BoT, 1964–67; Prime Minister's Office, 1967–72; Dept of Industry, 1972–78; Private Sec. to Govt Chief Whip, 12 Downing St, 1978–2000; Chief Exec., Tridos Solutions Ltd, 2000–02; Chm., SiScape Technology Ltd, 2001–02. Advr, CH2M HILL, 2007–12. Dir, Landau Forte Charitable Trust, 2010–; Vice Patron, Ricci Foundn, 2009–; Trustee, Columba 1400 Foundation, 2003–06. Freeman, City of London, 1994. FRSA 1990. *Clubs:* Garrick; Western (Glasgow).

MACLEAN of Pennycross, Nicolas Wolfers Lorne, CMG 2002; 8th Chieftain of Maclean of Pennycross; Chief Executive, MWM (Asia) and MWM (Strategy), since 1999; *b* 3 Jan. 1946; *s* of late Marcel Wolfers and Audrey Wolfers (*née* Maclean of Pennycross); named Nicolas Lorne Maclean Wolfers; *S* kinsman as Maclean of Pennycross, 1993; *m* 1978, Qamar Aziz; two *s*. *Educ:* Eton; Oriel Coll., Oxford (MA PPE 1967); Univ. of Santander (Cert. Spanish). Grad. Trainee, later Manager, Eur. and Japanese Investment Section, J. Henry Schroder Wagg & Co. Ltd, 1967–71; Manager, P. N. Kemp Gee & Co., 1971–72; Samuel Montagu & Co. Ltd: Manager, London Continental Pension Unit Trust, 1972–74; Asst Dir, Project and Export Finance, 1974–82; Asst Dir, Public Finance Dept, 1982–85; Gp Advr, Midland Bank Gp, 1985–93; Sen. Advr, China, Robert Fleming PLC, 1994–97; Gp Advr, Prudential Corp. PLC and Exec. Dir, Prudential Corp. Asia Ltd, 1997–99. Initiated Wolfers Prog. with Japan (subseq. Japan Exchange and Teaching Prog.), 1976. Chairman: Japan Festival Educn Trust, 2002–03 (Dep. Chm., 1992–2002); Council, Project Trust, 2012–; Co-Chm., Japan400, 2012–. Member: RIIA, 1967–; IISS, 2002– (Sen. Fellow, 2000–07); Bd, Canada-UK Council, 2007–. Fellow Emeritus, British Assoc. of Japanese Studies, 2003. *Publications:* (all jointly): Trading with China: a practical guide, 1979; Journey into Japan 1600–1868, 1981; The Eurobond and Eurocurrency Markets, 1984; Mongolia Today, 1988. *Recreations:* history, etymology, performing and visual arts, rowing, broadcasting, international affairs, Scotland. *Heir: s* Mark Maclean, yr of Pennycross, *b* 19 July 1982. *Address:* 30 Malwood Road, SW12 8EN. *T:* (020) 8675 6725, *Fax:* (020) 8675 6886. *E:* nmatmwm@hotmail.com. *Club:* Beefsteak.

MACLEAN, Prof. Norman; JP; PhD; FRSB, FLS; Professor of Genetics, University of Southampton, 1992–2004, now Emeritus (Head of Department of Biology, 1993–97); *b* 23 Sept. 1932; *s* of late Alexander Maclean and Christine Walker; *m* 1962, Dr Jane Kay Smith; one *s* one *d*. *Educ:* George Heriot's Sch., Edinburgh; Edinburgh Sch. of Agriculture; Edinburgh Univ. (SDA, BSc 1st cl. Hons, PhD 1962). FRSB (FIBiol 1990); FLS 1992. Asst Lectr in Zoology, Edinburgh Univ., 1961–64; Sir Henry Wellcome Travelling Fellow, 1964–65; Res. Associate, Rockefeller Inst., NY, 1964; Lectr in Biology, Sen. Lectr and Reader, Southampton Univ., 1965–92. Molecular Scis Ed., Jl Fish Biol., 2006–. Mem., Scientific Adv. Cttee, Aquagene Inc., Fla, 1999–. Advr, Eur. Food Safety Authy, 2008–. Hon. Scientific Advr, Marwell Preservation Trust (Trustee, 1995–2004). Dir, Test and Itchen Assoc. Ltd, 2006–. Edinburgh University: MacGillivray Prize in Zoology, 1956; Moira Lindsay Stuart Prize in Zoology, 1957; Gunning Victoria Jubilee Prize, 1960. JP Southampton, 1976. *Publications:* Control of Gene Expression, 1976; The Differentiation of Cells, 1977; Haemoglobin, 1978; Trout and Grayling: an angler's natural history, 1980; (jtly) DNA, Chromatin and Chromosomes, 1981; (ed jtly) Eukaryotic Genes: structure, activity and regulation, 1983; (ed) Oxford Surveys on Eukaryotic Genes, vols 1–7, 1984–90; (jtly) Cell Commitment and Differentiation, 1987; Macmillan Dictionary of Genetic and Cell Biology, 1987; Genes and Gene Regulation, 1989, 3rd edn 1992; Animals with Novel Genes, 1994; Silent Summer: the state of wildlife in Britain and Ireland, 2010; A Less Green and Pleasant Land: our threatened wildlife, 2015; (ed jtly) Austral Ark: the state of wildlife in Australia and New Zealand, 2015; articles in learned jls. *Recreations:* gardening, fly fishing, tennis, reading. *Address:* 10 Russell Place, Southampton SO17 1NU. *T:* (023) 8055 7649. *E:* nm4@soton.ac.uk.

McLEAN, Peter Standley, CMG 1985; OBE 1965; Head of East Asia Department, Overseas Development Administration, 1985–87; *b* 18 Jan. 1927; *s* of late William and Alice McLean; *m* 1954, Margaret Ann Minns (*d* 2002); two *s* two *d*. *Educ:* King Edward's Sch., Birmingham; Wadham Coll., Oxford (MA). Served Army, 1944–48; Lieut, 15/19th King's Royal Hussars. Colonial Service, Uganda, 1951–65, retired from HMOCS as Permanent Sec., Min. of Planning and Economic Develt; Ministry of Overseas Development: Principal, 1965; Private Sec. to Minister for Overseas Develt, 1973; Head of Eastern and Southern Africa Dept, 1975; Head of Bilateral Aid and Rural Develt Dept, 1979; Minister and UK Perm. Rep to FAO, 1980. Chm., Africa Grants Cttee, Comic Relief, 1989–92. Chm., Internat. Health Solutions Trust, 1997–. Vice-Chm., Overseas Service Pensioners Benevolent Soc., 2001–14. *Recreations:* watching sport, DIY, painting. *Address:* 1 Claverton, Woodfield Lane, Ashtead, Surrey KT21 2BJ. *T:* (01372) 278146.

McLEAN, Philip Alexander, CMG 1994; HM Diplomatic Service, retired; Director-General, Canning House (Hispanic and Luso-Brazilian Council), 1999–2002; *b* 24 Oct. 1938; *s* of late Wm Alexander McLean and Doris McLean (*née* Campbell); *m* 1960, Dorothy Helen Kirkby; two *s* one *d*. *Educ:* King George V Sch., Southport; Keble Coll., Oxford (MA Hons). National Service, RAF, 1956–58. Industry, 1961–68; entered HM Diplomatic Service by Open Supplementary Competition, 1968; Second, later (1969) First, Secretary, FCO; La Paz, 1970–74: Head of Chancery, 1973; FCO, 1974–76; Dep. Director of British Trade Development Office and Head of Industrial Marketing, New York, 1976–80; Counsellor and Consul-Gen., Algiers, 1981–83; Diplomatic Service Inspector, 1983–85; Hd, S America Dept, FCO, 1985–87; Consul-Gen., Boston, 1988–91; Minister and Dep. Head of Mission, Peking, 1991–94; Ambassador to Cuba, 1994–98. Robin Humphreys Vis. Res. Fellow, 1999–2000, Mem. Adv. Council, 1999–2004, Inst. of Latin American Studies, London Univ. Chm., Anglo-Bolivian Soc., 2002–06. Bd Mem., St Luke's Housing Soc., Oxford, 2003–15 (Chm., 2005–11). Member, Council: St Stephen's House, Oxford, 2004–11 (Vice Chm., 2005–11); St Luke's Hosp., Oxford, 2008–15. Trustee, St Mary Magdalen's Restoration and Develt Trust, Oxford, 2008–10 (Chm., 2009–10). Diplomatic Advr, Jumeirah Carlton Tower and Lowndes Hotels, Knightsbridge, 2004–07. Hon. LLD American Internat. Coll., 1991. *Recreations:* charitable voluntary work, hill walking, food and drink, friends. *Address:* 25 Cumnor Rise Rd, Oxford OX2 9HD. *Club:* Oxford and Cambridge.

MacLEAN, Ranald Norman Munro; *see* MacLean, Rt Hon. Lord.

McLEAN, Prof. Sheila Ann Manson, PhD; FRSE; FRCPE; International Bar Association Professor of Law and Ethics in Medicine, 1990, now Emerita, and Director, Institute of Law and Ethics in Medicine, 1985, Glasgow University; *b* 20 June 1951; *d* of late William Black and of Bethia Black (*née* Manson); *m* 1976, Alan McLean (marr. diss. 1987). *Educ:* Glasgow High Sch. for Girls; Glasgow Univ. (LLB 1972; MLitt 1978; PhD 1987). FRSE 1996; FRCPE 1997. Area Reporter, Children's Panel, 1972–75; Lectr, 1975–85, Sen. Lectr, 1985–90, Sch. of Law, Glasgow Univ. Chm., Scottish Criminal Cases Review Commn, 1999–2002. Chairman: Review of consent provisions of Human Fertilisation and Embryology Act, DoH, 1997–98; Ind. Review Gp on Organ Retention at Post Mortem, 2000–03; Member: UK Xenotransplantation Interim Regulatory Authy, 1997–2002; Wellcome Trust Biomedical Ethics Panel, 2002–06; Internat. Fedn of Obstetrics and Gynaecol. Ethics Cttee, 2003–06; UNESCO Biomed. Ethics Cttee, 2006–; Crown Office Inspectorate Review of Organ Retention Practices, 2005–06; Vice Chair, Multi-Centre Res. Ethics Cttee for Scotland, 1997–98. Member: Ethics Cttee, BMA, 2000–; Ethics and Governance Council, UK Biobank, 2004–06; Adv. Cttee, ESRC Genomics Policy and Res. Forum, 2004–. Member: UKCC, 1993–98; SHEFC, 1996–98; AHRC Peer Review Coll., 2005–. Mem., Broadcasting Council for Scotland, 1991–96. FMedSci 2006. FRSA 1996. Hon. FRCGP 2003. Hon. LLD: Abertay Dundee, 2002; Edinburgh, 2002. *Publications:* (jtly) Medicine, Morals and the Law, 1983; A Patient's Right to Know: information disclosure, the doctor and the law, 1989; (jtly) The Case for Physician Assisted Suicide, 1997; Old Law, New Medicine, 1999; (jtly) Legal and Ethical Aspects of Healthcare, 2003; (jtly) Xenotransplantation: law and ethics, 2005; Modern Dilemmas: choosing children, 2006; (jtly) Disability and Impairment: law and ethics at the beginning and end of life, 2006; Assisted Dying: reflections on the need for law reform, 2007; *edited:* Legal Issues in Medicine, 1981; (jtly) Human Rights: from rhetoric to reality, 1986; (jtly) The Legal Relevance of Gender, 1988; Legal Issues in Human Reproduction, 1989; Law Reform and Human Reproduction, 1992; Compensation for Personal Injury: an international perspective, 1993; Law Reform and Medical Injury Litigation, 1995; Law and Ethics in Intensive Care, 1996; Death, Dying and the Law, 1996; Contemporary Issues in Law, Medicine and Ethics, 1996; Medical Law and Ethics, 2002; Genetics and Gene Therapy, 2005; First Do No Harm, 2006. *Recreations:* playing guitar, singing, reading. *Club:* Lansdowne.

McLEAN, Dr Thomas Pearson, CB 1990; FRSE; CPhys, FInstP; Professor of Electrical Engineering and Science, Royal Military College of Science, Shrivenham, 1992–95; *b* Paisley, 21 Aug. 1930; *s* of Norman Stewart McLean and Margaret Pearson McLean (*née* Ferguson); *m* 1957, Grace Campbell Nokes; two *d*. *Educ:* John Neilson Instn, Paisley; Glasgow Univ. (BSc, PhD); Birmingham Univ. Royal Radar Estabt (becoming Royal Signals and Radar Estabt, 1976), 1955–80: Head of Physics Gp, 1973–77; Dep. Dir, 1977–80; Ministry of Defence: Under Sec., Dir Gen. Air Weapons and Electronic Systems, 1980–83; Dir, RARDE, 1984–86; Dep. Controller, Aircraft, 1987; Dir, Atomic Weapons Estabt, 1987–90. Member: Physics Cttee, SRC, 1968–73; Optoelectronics Cttee, Rank Prize Funds, 1972–81; Council, Inst. of Physics, 1980–84. Hon. Prof. of Physics, Birmingham Univ., 1977–80. Dep. Editor, Jl of Physics C, 1976–77. *Publications:* papers in Physical Rev., Jl of Physics, etc. *Recreations:* music, mathematics, computing.

McLEAN, Prof. (William Henry) Irwin, PhD, DSc; FRS 2014; FRSE, FMedSci; Professor of Human Genetics, since 2002, Head, Division of Molecular Medicine, since 2008, and Scientific Director, Centre for Dermatology and Genetic Medicine, since 2012, University of

Dundee; *b* Ballymoney, Co. Antrim, 9 Jan. 1963; *s* of Henry McLean and Rosetta McLean (*née* McAleese). *Educ:* Queen's University Belfast (BSc Hons Microbiol. 1985; PhD Human Genetics 1988; DSc Human Genetics 1999). Res. Asst, 1985–88, Postdoctoral Res. Asst, 1988–91, Dept of Med. Genetics, QUB; Res. Dir, Ångström Labs, Larne, 1991–92; Postdoctoral Res. Fellow, CRC Cell Structure Res. Gp, Univ. of Dundee, 1992–96; Associate Prof., Dept of Dermatol. and Cutaneous Biol., Jefferson Med. Coll., Philadelphia, 1996–98; Wellcome Trust Sen. Res. Fellow and Sen. Lectr, 1998–2002, Hd, Human Genetics Res., 1998–2008, Human Genetics Unit, Div. of Pathol. and Neurosci., Ninewells Med. Sch., Univ. of Dundee. Hon. NHS Clin. Scientist, 2000–06; Hon. Consultant Clinical Scientist in Dermatol., 2006–, in Human Genetics, 2010–, NHS Tayside. FRSE 2005; FMedSci 2009. Wolfson Merit Award, Royal Soc., 2007; Achievement Award, Amer. Skin Assoc., 2009. *Publications:* book chapters; contrib. res. articles to learned jls, incl. Nature Genetics; eight patents. *Recreations:* electronic music, photography, hill-walking, fishing, astronomy, geology, cinema, science fiction. *Address:* Centre for Dermatology and Genetic Medicine, Colleges of Life Sciences and Medicine, Dentistry and Nursing, Dow Street, Dundee DD1 5EH. *T:* (01382) 381172, *Fax:* (01382) 388535. *E:* w.h.i.mclean@dundee.ac.uk.

MACLEAN, Prof. William James, MBE 2006; RSA 1991; RSW 1997; Professor of Fine Art, 1995–2001, now Emeritus Professor of Visual Art, and Research Professor, Visual Research Centre, since 2001, University of Dundee; *b* 12 Oct. 1941; *s* of Capt. John Maclean and Mary Isabella (*née* Reid); *m* 1968, Marian Leven, RSA; two *s* one *d*. *Educ:* Inverness Royal Acad.; HMS Conway MN Cadet Trng Sch., N Wales; Gray's Sch. of Art, Aberdeen (DA 1966; Post-Grad. Dip. 1967). Midshipman, Blue Funnel Line, 1957–59; school teacher, 1971–81; Lectr in Drawing and Painting, Dundee Coll. of Art, 1981–94. Solo exhibns in GB and abroad; *work in Collections of:* Arts Council of GB; British Mus.; Nat. Art Collection; Fitzwilliam Mus. and Art Gall., Cambridge; Yale Centre for British Art; Scottish Nat. Gall. of Modern Art, etc. FRSE, 2010. Hon. Fellow, UHI, 2008. Hon. DLitt: St Andrews, 2000; Aberdeen, 2009. *Publications:* Will Maclean: sculptures and box constructions, 1987; Will Maclean: different meridians, 2009; Will Maclean Collected Works 1970–2010, 2011; *relevant publication:* Symbols of Survival: the art of Will Maclean, by Prof. Duncan Macmillan, 1992. *Recreations:* reading, walking.

MacLEARY, Alistair Ronald; surveyor, retired; Hon. Professor, Heriot-Watt University, 2004–10; *b* 12 Jan. 1940; *s* of Donald Herbert MacLeary and Jean Spiers (*née* Leslie); *m* 1967, Mary-Claire Cecilia (*née* Leonard); one *s* one *d*. *Educ:* Inverness Royal Acad.; Coll. of Estate Management, London; Edinburgh Coll. of Art, Heriot-Watt Univ.; Strathclyde Univ. MSc, DipTP; FRICS, FRTPI. Gerald Eve & Co., 1963–65; Murrayfield Real Estate Co., 1965–67; Dept of Environment (on secondment), 1971–73; Wright, Partners, 1967–76; MacRobert Prof. of Land Economy, 1976–89, Dean, Faculty of Law, 1982–85, Aberdeen Univ. Univ. of Auckland Foundn Visitor and Fletcher Challenge Vis. Fellow, 1985; Memorialist, Macaulay Inst. for Soil Science, 1986–87. Mem., Cttee of Inquiry into Acquisition and Occupancy of Agricl Land, 1977–79; Chm., Watt Cttee, Energy Working Gp on Land Resources, 1977–79; Mem., Exec. Cttee, Commonwealth Assoc. of Surveying and Land Economy, 1980–85 (Chm., Bd of Surveying Educn, 1981–90); Member: Home Grown Timber Adv. Cttee, Forestry Commn, 1981–87; NERC, 1988–91 (Chm., Terrestrial and Freshwater Sci. Cttee, 1990–91); Lands Tribunal for Scotland, 1989–2005; Administrative Justice & Tribunals Council (formerly Council on Tribunals), 2005–09 (Chm., Scottish Cttee, 2005–09). Mem., Gen. Council, RICS, 1983–87 (Pres., Planning and Develt Divl Council, 1984–85). Mem., MacTaggart Chair Adv. Bd, Glasgow Univ., 1992–2000. FRSA. Hon. Fellow, Commonwealth Assoc. of Surveying and Land Economy, 1992. Founder and Editor, Land Development Studies, subseq. Jl of Property Research, 1983–90. *Publications:* (ed with N. Nanthakumeran) Property Investment Theory, 1988; National Taxation for Property Management and Valuation, 1990. *Recreations:* hill walking, field sports, golf. *Address:* St Helen's, Ceres, Fife KY15 5NQ. *T:* (01334) 828862. *Club:* Royal Northern and University (Aberdeen).

See also D. W. Bentham-MacLeary.

MacLEARY, Donald Whyte; *see* Bentham-MacLeary, D. W.

MacLEAY, Rev. John Henry James; Dean of Argyll and The Isles, 1987–99; Rector of St Andrew's, Fort William, 1978–99; retired; *b* 7 Dec. 1931; *s* of James and Isabella MacLeay; *m* 1970, Jane Speirs Cuthbert; one *s* one *d*. *Educ:* St Edmund Hall, Oxford (MA); College of the Resurrection, Mirfield. Deacon 1957, priest 1958, Southwark; Curate: St John's, East Dulwich, 1957–60; St Michael's, Inverness, 1960–62, Rector 1962–70; Priest-in-charge, St Columba's, Grantown-on-Spey with St John the Baptist's, Rothiemurchus, 1970–78; Canon of St Andrew's Cathedral, Inverness, 1977–78; Canon of St John's Cathedral, Oban and Synod Clerk, Diocese of Argyll and the Isles, 1980–87. Hon. Canon, Oban Cathedral, 1999–2003. Received into RC Church, 2003. *Recreations:* reading, visiting cathedrals and churches. *Address:* 47 Riverside Park, Lochyside, Fort William PH33 7RB. *T:* (01397) 700117.

McLEAY, Hon. Leo Boyce; *b* 4 Oct. 1945; *s* of Ron and Joan McLeay; *m* 1969, Janice Delaney; three *s*. *Educ:* De La Salle Sch., Marrickville; North Sydney Technical Coll. Telephone technician, 1962–76; Asst Gen. Sec., ALP (NSW), 1976–79. MP (Lab) Grayndler, 1979–93, Watson, 1993–2004, NSW; Dep. Speaker, 1986–89, Speaker, 1989–93, House of Representatives; Chief Govt Whip, 1993–96; Chief Opposition Whip and Dep. Manager, Opposition business, 1996–2001. Dir, Enhance Gp, 2005–09. Dir, Mary MacKillop Foundn, 2006–11; Chm., Catholic Cemeteries Bd, 2011–; Trustee, Sydney Harbour Fedn Trust, 2011–. *Recreations:* fishing, reading. *Address:* 702/185 Macquarie Street, Sydney, NSW 2000, Australia. *Club:* Canterbury Rugby League (NSW).

MacLEHOSE, Christopher Colin, CBE 2011; Publisher, MacLehose Press, since 2006; *b* Edinburgh, 12 July 1940; *s* of Alexander MacLehose and Elizabeth Hope MacLehose (*née* Bushell); *m* 1985, Koukla Dorange; two *s*. *Educ:* Shrewsbury Sch.; Worcester Coll., Oxford (MA). Literary Ed., The Scotsman, 1964–67; Editor, Cresset Press, Barrie & Rockliff, Cresset Press, then Barrie & Jenkins, 1967–72; Editl Dir, Chatto & Windus, 1973–79; Ed. and Ed.-in-Chief, William Collins, 1979–83; Publisher, Harvill Press, 1983–2004. *Recreations:* dogs, roses. *Address:* 3 Westbourne Road, N7 8AR; Santa Elena, 3 chemin de la Tour des Sarrazins, 83820 Le Rayol-Canadel, France.

McLEISH, Rt Hon. Henry (Baird); PC 2000; Member (Lab) Fife Central, Scottish Parliament, 1999–2003; *b* 15 June 1948; *s* of Harry McLeish and late Mary McLeish; *m* 1968, Margaret Thomson Drysdale (*d* 1995); one *s* one *d*; *m* 1998, Julie Fulton (marr. diss. 2011); *m* 2012, Caryn Nicolson. *Educ:* Heriot-Watt Univ. (BA Hons planning). Research Officer, Social Work Dept, Edinburgh, 1973–74; Planning Officer, Fife County Council, 1974–75; Planning Officer, Dunfermline DC, 1975–87; part time Lectr/Tutor, Heriot-Watt Univ., 1973–87; part-time employment consultant, 1984–87. Member: Kirkcaldy DC (Chm., Planning Cttee, 1974–77); Fife Regl Council (Chm., Further Educn Cttee, 1978–82; Leader, Council, 1982–87). MP (Lab) Central Fife, 1987–2001. Minister of State, Scottish Office, 1997–99; Scottish Executive: Minister for Enterprise and Lifelong Learning, 1999–2000; First Minister, 2000–01. Commnd by SFA to produce Review of Scottish Football, 2009 (report publd 2010). *Publications:* Scotland First: truth and consequences, 2004; Global Scots: voices from afar, 2005. *Recreations:* reading, malt whisky (history and development of), history, life and works of Robert Burns, Highlands and Islands of Scotland, astronomy, history of great speeches.

McLEISH, Prof. Thomas Charles Buckland, PhD; FRS 2011; CPhys, FInstP; FRSC; Professor of Physics, Durham University, since 2008 (Pro-Vice-Chancellor for Research, 2008–14); *b* Farnborough, Kent, 1 May 1962; *s* of Ian Buckland McLeish and Susan Jane McLeish; *m* 1984, Dr Julie Elizabeth King; two *s* two *d*. *Educ:* Sevenoaks Sch., Kent; Emmanuel Coll., Cambridge (BA 1984; MA 1987; PhD 1987). CPhys 2003; FInstP 2003; FRSC 2008. Lectr in Physics, Univ. of Sheffield, 1989–93; Prof. of Polymer Physics, Univ. of Leeds, 1993–2008. Vis. Prof., Univ. of Calif, Santa Barbara, 2002. *Publications:* (ed) Theoretical Challenges in the Dynamics of Complex Fluids, 1997; (jtly) The Dimensions of Colour: Robert Grosseteste's De Colore, 2013; Faith and Wisdom in Science, 2014; contrib. articles to jls incl. Physics, Nature, Science, Physical Rev. Letters. *Recreations:* music (French horn, singing), walking, sailing, scuba-diving. *Address:* Department of Physics, Durham University, South Road, Durham DH1 3LE. *T:* (0191) 334 3642, *Fax:* (0191) 334 5823. *E:* t.c.b.mcleish@durham.ac.uk.

MacLELLAN, Maj.-Gen. (Andrew) Patrick (Withy), CB 1981; CVO 1989; MBE 1964; Resident Governor and Keeper of the Jewel House, HM Tower of London, 1984–89; *b* 29 Nov. 1925; *y s* of late Kenneth MacLellan and Rachel Madeline MacLellan (*née* Withy); *m* 1954, Kathleen Mary Bagnell; one *s* twin *d*. *Educ:* Uppingham. Commnd Coldstream Guards, 1944; served Palestine 1945–48, N Africa 1950–51, Egypt 1952–53, Germany 1955–56; psc 1957; DAA&QMG 4th Guards Brigade Group, 1958–59; Mil. Asst to Chief of Defence Staff, 1961–64; Instructor, Staff Coll., Camberley, 1964–66; GSO1 (Plans) Far East Comd, 1966–67; CO 1st Bn Coldstream Guards, 1968–70; Col GS Near East Land Forces, 1970–71; Comdr 8th Inf. Brigade, 1971–72; RCDS 1973; Dep. Comdr and COS, London District, 1974–77; Pres., Regular Commns Bd, 1978–80. Vice-Patron (formerly Vice-Pres.), Officers' Assoc., 1993–. Mem. Cttee, Royal Humane Soc., 1980–2010; Vice-Pres., First Aid Nursing Yeomanry (The Princess Royal's Volunteer Corps), 2004– (Mem., 1979–2003, Chm., 1997–2003, Adv. Council). FCMI (FBIM 1970). Mem. (Walbrook Ward), Court of Common Council, City of London, 1989–2000 (Chm., Police Cttee, 1995–97). Freeman: City of London, 1984; Co. of Watermen and Lightermen; Liveryman, Fletchers' Co., 1986– (Master, 1997–98). Chevalier de la Légion d'Honneur, 1960; Order of the Sacred Treasure (Japan), 1998. *Address:* c/o Bank of Scotland, 33 Old Broad Street, EC2N 1NZ. *Clubs:* White's, Pratt's.

McLELLAN, Very Rev. Andrew Rankin Cowie, CBE 2009; HM Chief Inspector of Prisons for Scotland, 2002–09; Moderator of the General Assembly of the Church of Scotland, 2000; *b* 16 June 1944; *s* of Andrew Barclay McLellan and Catherine Hilda McLellan (*née* Cowie); *m* 1975, Irene Lamont Meek; twin *s*. *Educ:* Kilmarnock Acad.; Madras Coll., St Andrews; St Andrews Univ. (MA 1965); Glasgow Univ. (BD 1968); Union Theol Seminary, NY (STM 1969; Unitas Award, 2008). Asst Minister, St George's West, Edinburgh, 1969–71; Minister: Cartsburn Augustine, Greenock, 1971–80; Viewfield, Stirling, 1980–86; Parish Church of St Andrew and St George, Edinburgh, 1986–2002. Tutor, Glasgow Univ., 1978–82; Chaplain, HM Prison, Stirling, 1982–85. Dir, Scottish Television, 2004–07. Chairman: George St Assoc. of Edinburgh, 1990–93; Scottish Religious Adv. Cttee, BBC, 1996–2001; Commn to Investigate Safeguarding in the Catholic Church in Scotland, 2013–. Convener, Church and Nation Cttee, 1992–96, Parish Develt Fund, 2002–06, World Mission Council, 2010–14, Gen. Assembly of the Church of Scotland. Nat. Chaplain, Boys' Bde, 2013–. Warrack Lectr on Preaching, Divinity Faculties of Scotland, 2000. Mem., Inverclyde DC, 1977–80. Hon. DD St Andrews, 2000. *Publications:* Preaching for these People, 1997; Gentle and Passionate, 2001. *Recreations:* sport, travel, books, gardening. *Address:* 4 Liggars Place, Dunfermline, Fife KY12 7XZ. *T:* (01383) 725959. *E:* iamclellan4@gmail.com.

McLELLAN, Prof. David, DPhil; Visiting Professor of Political Theory, Goldsmiths (formerly Goldsmiths College), University of London, since 1999; Professor of Political Theory, University of Kent, 1975–99; *b* 10 Feb. 1940; *s* of Robert Douglas McLellan and Olive May Bush; *m* 1967, Annie Brassart; two *d*. *Educ:* Merchant Taylors' Sch.; St John's Coll., Oxford (MA, DPhil). University of Kent: Lectr in Politics, 1966–71; Sen. Lectr in Politics, 1972–73; Reader in Political Theory, 1973–75. Vis. Prof., State Univ. of New York, 1969; Guest Fellow in Politics, Indian Inst. of Advanced Studies, Simla, 1970. Hon. Fellow, Goldsmiths Coll., Univ. of London, 2004. *Publications:* The Young Hegelians and Karl Marx, 1969 (French, German, Italian, Spanish and Japanese edns); Marx before Marxism, 1970, 2nd edn 1972; Karl Marx: The Early Texts, 1971; Marx's Grundrisse, 1971, 2nd edn 1973; The Thought of Karl Marx, 1971 (Portuguese and Italian edns); Karl Marx: His Life and Thought, 1973, 22nd edn 1976 (German, Italian, Spanish, Japanese, Swedish and Dutch edns); Marx (Fontana Modern Masters), 1975; Engels, 1977; Marxism after Marx, 1979, 4th edn 2007 (rev. Chinese edn 2013); (ed) Marx: the first hundred years, 1983; Karl Marx: the legacy, 1983; Ideology, 1986; Marxism and Religion, 1987; Simone Weil: Utopian pessimist, 1989; Christianity and Politics, 1990; Religion and Public Life, 1992; Unto Caesar: the political relevance of Christianity, 1993; Case Law and Political Theory, 1996; (ed) Political Christianity, 1997; Karl Marx: a biography, 2006. *Recreations:* chess, Raymond Chandler, hill walking. *Address:* c/o Goldsmiths, University of London, Lewisham Way, New Cross, SE14 6NW.

McLELLAN, John Crawford; Director, Scottish Newspaper Society, since 2013; *b* Glasgow, 8 Feb. 1962; *s* of John and Margaret McLellan; *m* 1993, Patricia Vasey; two *s* one *d*. *Educ:* High Sch. of Glasgow; Hutchesons' Grammar Sch., Glasgow; Univ. of Stirling (BA 1983); Preston Poly. Sports Ed., NW Evening Mail, 1988–90; Asst Ed., The Journal, 1991–93; Edinburgh Evening News: Dep. Ed., 1993–97; Ed., 1997–2001 and 2004–09; Ed., Scotland on Sunday, 2002–04; Ed.-in-Chief, Scotsman Pubns, and Ed., The Scotsman, 2009–12; Dir, Communications, Scottish Conservatives, 2012–13. Member: Defence, Press and Broadcasting Cttee, 2000–04, 2006–12; Press Complaints Commn, 2009–12; Chm., Editors' Cttee, Scottish Newspaper Soc. Hon. Prof., Univ. of Stirling, 2010–. Trustee, Radio Forth Cash for Kids appeal, 2005–10. *Recreation:* watching Watsonian Rugby and hockey.

MacLELLAN, Maj.-Gen. Patrick; *see* MacLellan, A. P. W.

MACLEMAN, Hugh; a Judge of the Upper Tribunal, Immigration and Asylum Chamber (formerly a Senior Immigration Judge, Asylum and Immigration Tribunal), since 2009; *b* Elgin, 24 Dec. 1953; *s* of William Patience Macleman and Isabella Margaret Macleman (*née* Macmillan); *m* 1980, Dianne Isobel Duncan; two *d*. *Educ:* Lossiemouth High Sch.; Elgin Acad.; Aberdeen Univ. (MA Hons Hist.); Glasgow Univ. (LLB). Admitted solicitor, 1979; solicitor, Elgin, 1979–82; Procurator Fiscal Depute, Elgin, 1982–86; advocate, 1986; Principal Magistrate and Chm. of Trade Disputes Panel, Solomon Is, 1988–91; Sen. Crown Counsel, Turks and Caicos Is, 1991–92; solicitor, Grantown on Spey, 1992–2002; Immigration Adjudicator, part-time 1999–2002, full-time, 2002–05; Immigration Judge, Asylum and Immigration Tribunal, 2005–09. *Recreations:* golf, scuba diving. *Address:* Upper Tribunal (Immigration and Asylum Chamber), Eagle Building, 215 Bothwell Street, Glasgow G2 7EZ. *Clubs:* Royal Over-Seas League; Grantown on Spey Golf.

MACLENNAN, family name of **Baron Maclennan of Rogart**.

MACLENNAN OF ROGART, Baron *cr* 2001 (Life Peer), of Rogart in Sutherland; **Robert Adam Ross Maclennan;** PC 1997; Barrister-at-Law; *b* 26 June 1936; *e s* of late Sir Hector MacLennan and Isabel Margaret Adam; *m* 1968, Mrs Helen Noyes, *d* of late Judge Ammi Cutter, Cambridge, Mass, and *widow* of Paul H. Noyes; one *s* one *d*, and one step *s*. *Educ:* Glasgow Academy; Balliol Coll., Oxford; Trinity Coll., Cambridge; Columbia Univ., New York City. Called to the Bar, Gray's Inn, 1962. MP Caithness and Sutherland, 1966–97 (Lab, 1966–81, SDP, 1981–88, Lib Dem, 1988–97), (Lib Dem) Caithness, Sutherland and Easter

Ross, 1997–2001. Parliamentary Private Secretary: to Secretary of State for Commonwealth Affairs, 1967–69; to Minister without Portfolio, 1969–70; an Opposition Spokesman: on Scottish Affairs, 1970–71; on Defence, 1971–72; Parly Under-Sec. of State, Dept of Prices and Consumer Protection, 1974–79; opposition spokesman on foreign affairs, 1980–81; SDP spokesman on agriculture, fisheries and food, 1981–87; Leader, SDP, 1987–88; Jt Leader, SLD, 1988; Lib Dem spokesman on home affairs and the arts, 1988–94, on constitutional affairs and culture, 1994–2001; on Cabinet Office, Civil Service and Scotland (formerly Scotland and the Civil Service), H of L, 2005–. Member: H of C Estimates Cttee, 1967–69; Select Cttee on Scottish Affairs, 1969–70; Public Accounts Cttee, 1979–99; EU Select Cttee, H of L, 2005–. Pres., Lib Dems, 1994–98. Alternate Mem., Convention on Future of Europe, 2002–03; UK Chm., European Cultural Foundn, 2001–07. Mem., Latey Cttee on Age of Majority, 1968. *Publications:* libretti: The Lie, 1992; Friend of the People, 1999. *Recreations:* theatre, music, visual arts. *Address:* House of Lords, SW1A 0PW.

MacLENNAN, Dr David Herman, OC 2001; OOnt 2008; PhD; FRS 1994; FRSC 1985; University Professor, University of Toronto, since 1993; *b* 3 July 1937; *s* of Douglas Henry MacLennan and Sigridur MacLennan (*née* Sigurdson); *m* 1965, Linda Carol Vass (*d* 2013); two *s* (one *d* decd). *Educ:* Swan River Collegiate Inst., Canada; Univ. of Manitoba (BSA 1959); Purdue Univ. (MS 1961; PhD 1963). Postdoctoral Fellow, 1963–64, Asst Prof., 1964–68, Inst. for Enzyme Res., Univ. of Wisconsin; Banting and Best Department of Medical Research, University of Toronto: Associate Prof., 1969–74; Prof., 1974–93; Acting Chm., 1978–80; Chm., 1980–90; J. W. Billes Prof. of Med. Res., 1987–2007. Principal Investigator, Canadian Genetic Diseases Network, 1991–2005; Consultant, Merck, Sharp & Dohme, PA, 1992–98. Member: Med. Adv. Bd, Muscular Dystrophy Assoc., Canada, 1976–87; Scientists' Review Panel, MRC Canada, 1988–90; Univ. of Ottawa Heart Inst. Res. Review Panel, 1991–94; Chm., Molecular Biol. and Pathol. Cttee, Heart and Stroke Foundn of Canada, 1995–99; Member: Gairdner Foundn Review Panel, 1999–2001; Gairdner Foundn Med. Adv. Bd, 2001–05. Founding Fellow, Internat. Soc. Heart Res., 2001; For. Associate, NAS, USA, 2001; Hon. Mem., Japanese Biochemical Soc., 2004. Hon. DSc Manitoba, 2001. Awards include: Ayerst Award, Canadian Biochem. Soc., 1974; Nat. Lectr Award, Biophys. Soc., 1990; Gairdner Foundn Internat. Award, 1991; Izaak Walton Killam Meml Prize for Health Scis, Canada Council, 1997; Jonas Salk Award, Ontario March of Dimes, 1998; Royal Soc. Glaxo Wellcome Prize, Medal and Lecture, 2000; Salute to the City Award, Toronto, 2002; Rick Gallop Award, Heart and Stroke Foundn of Ontario, 2002. Golden Jubilee Medal, 2002; Diamond Jubilee Medal, 2012. *Publications:* ed and contrib. to numerous learned jls, esp. on study of calcium regulation by muscle membranes. *Recreations:* collecting and restoring Canadian antique furniture, reading fiction and non-fiction, listening to classical music, gardening, ski-ing. *Address:* Banting and Best Department of Medical Research, University of Toronto, C. H. Best Institute, 112 College Street, Toronto, ON M5G 1L6, Canada. *T:* (416) 9785008; 292 Airdrie Road, Toronto, ON M4G 1N3, Canada. *T:* (416) 6962091.

MacLENNAN, David Ross; HM Diplomatic Service, retired; Ambassador and Consul General, Qatar, 2002–05; *b* 12 Feb. 1945; *s* of David Ross MacLennan and Agnes McConnell; *m* 1964, Margaret Lytollis; two *d*. *Educ:* West Calder High Sch. FO, 1963; ME Centre for Arab Studies, 1966–69; Third, later Second Sec., Aden, 1969–71; Second, later First Sec., FCO, 1972–75; First Sec., UK Delegn to OECD, Paris, 1975–79; First Sec., Hd of Chancery, Abu Dhabi, 1979–82; Asst Hd, N America Dept, FCO, 1982–84; EEC, Brussels, 1984–85; Counsellor, Kuwait, 1985–88; Dep. High Comr, Nicosia, 1989–90; Consul Gen., Jerusalem, 1990–93; Counsellor, Head of Africa Dept (Equatorial), FCO, and Comr, British Indian Ocean Territory, 1994–96; Ambassador to Lebanese Republic, 1996–2000. *Recreations:* conservation, gardening. *Address:* c/o Foreign and Commonwealth Office, SW1A 2AH.

MACLENNAN, Prof. Duncan, CBE 1997; FRSE; FAcSS; Professor of Strategic Urban Finance and Management (part-time), University of St Andrews, since 2014 (Professor of Economic Geography and Director, Centre for Housing Research, 2009–14); *b* 12 March 1949; *s* of James Dempster Maclennan and Mary Mackechnie (*née* Campbell); *m* 2005, Sharon Chisholm; one *s* one *d* by a previous marriage. *Educ:* Allan Glen's Sch., Glasgow; Univ. of Glasgow (MA, MPhil). FRSE 1999. Lectr in Pol Econ., Aberdeen Univ., 1976–79; Glasgow University: Lectr in Applied Econs, 1979–81; Sen. Lectr, 1981–84; Titular Prof., 1984–88; Prof. of Urban Studies, 1988–90; Mactaggart Prof. of Land Economics and Finance, 1990–2004; Chief Economist: Dept of Sustainability and Envmt, Govt of Vic, Australia, 2004–05; Dept for Infrastructure and Communities, Canada, 2005–09. Special Advr to First Minister of Scotland, 1999–2003. Director: Centre for Housing Res. and Urban Studies, 1983–96; Cities Programme, ESRC, 1996–99. Susman Prof. of Real Estate Finance, Wharton Bus. Sch., 1988; Regent's Prof., Univ. of Calif at Berkeley, 1996; Prof. of Housing and Urban Econs, RMIT, 2004; Prof. of Public Policy, Univ. of Glasgow, 2014–. Chm., Care and Repair (Scotland), 1987–94; Dir, Joseph Rowntree Res. Programme, 1988–94; Chairman: Joseph Rowntree Area Regeneration Steering Gp, 1996–2000; Cttee on Easing Shortages of Housing, Joseph Rowntree Foundn, 2007. Mem. Bd, Scottish Homes, 1989–99. Mem., HM Treasury Panel of Advisers, 1995–2002. Trustee, David Hume Inst., 1998–2005. FRSA 1993; FAcSS (AcSS 2010). Hon. MRTPI 2001; Hon. MCIH 2001. *Publications:* Regional Policy in Britain, 1979; Housing Economics, 1982; Paying for Britain's Housing, 1990; The Housing Authority of the Future, 1991; Fairer Subsidies, Faster Growth, 1992; Fixed Commitments, Uncertain Incomes, 1997; Changing Places, Engaging People, 2000; Cities, Competition and Economic Success, 2006; contribs to Urban Studies, Housing Studies, Economic Jl, Applied Econs. *Recreations:* walking, cooking, cycling. *Address:* School of Management, University of St Andrews, The Gateway, North Haugh, St Andrews, Fife KY16 9RJ. *E:* dm103@st-andrews.ac.uk.

MacLENNAN, Graeme Andrew Yule, CA; Director, Phillips & Drew Fund Management, 1990–93; *b* 24 Aug. 1942; *s* of Finlay and Helen MacLennan; *m* 1st, 1973, Diane Marion Gibbon (*née* Fyfe) (marr. diss. 1989); two *s* two *d*; 2nd, 1989, Diana Rosemary Steven (*née* Urie). *Educ:* Kelvinside Academy, Glasgow. Asst Investment Manager, Leopold Joseph & Sons Ltd, London, 1964–68; Investment Man., Murray Johnstone & Co., Glasgow, 1969–70; Edinburgh Fund Managers: Investment Man., 1970; Dir, 1980, Jt Man. Dir, 1983–88; Investment Dir, Ivory & Sime plc, 1988–90; Hd, Investment Trust Business, LGT Asset Management, 1995–98; non-executive Director: HTR Japanese Smaller Cos Trust, 1993–96; Premium Trust, 1993–2006 (Chm., 2001–06); Noble, then Cornelian, Asset Managers, 1998–2005 (Chm., 2000–05); TriVen VCT, 1999–2003; Financial Services Compensation Scheme, 2000–06; TriVest VCT, 2000–03. *Recreations:* golf, travel.

MacLENNAN, Prof. Ian Calman Muir, CBE 2005; PhD; FRCP, FRCPath, FMedSci; FRS 2012; Professor of Immunology, 1979–2004, Professor Emeritus, 2005, and Director, MRC Centre for Immune Regulation, 1999–2004 (Deputy Director, 2005–09), University of Birmingham; *b* Inverness, 30 Dec. 1939; *s* of late Calman MacLennan and Mary Helen MacLennan (*née* Muir, subseq. Roxburgh) and step *s* of William Alexander Roxburgh; *m* 1965, Pamela Bennett; two *s*. *Educ:* Guy's Hosp. Med. Sch., Univ. of London (BSc Anatomy 1962; MB BS 1965; PhD 1970). FRCPath 1985; FRCP 1995. SHO, MRC Rheumatism Res. Unit, Taplow, 1966–69 (ARC Res. Fellow); Lectr, Nuffield Dept of Clin. Medicine, Oxford Univ., 1969–79; Hd, Dept of Immunology, 1979–98, Hd, Div. of Immunity and Infection, 1998–2000, Univ. of Birmingham. Medical Research Council: Co-ordinator, trials in Multiple Myeloma, 1980–98; Chm., Wkg Party on Leukaemia in Adults, 1982–92; Dep. Chm., Cell Biol. and Disorders Bd, 1983–87 (Chm., Grants Cttee A, 1982–84); Mem. Council, and Chm., Molecular and Cellular Medicine Bd, 2000–04. Sec., British Soc. for Immunol., 1973–79. Founder FMedSci, 1998. Mem., Birmingham Med. Res. Expeditionary Soc., 1986–. Hon. Life Mem., Scandinavian Soc. Immunol., 1995. *Publications:* Walking the Alps from Mediterranean to Adriatic; numerous contribs to learned jls, incl. Immunological Reviews, Nature, Annual Rev. of Immunol., Jl Exptl Medicine. *Recreations:* hill walking, observing the natural world, listening to and supporting the City of Birmingham SO. *Address:* School of Immunity and Infection, University of Birmingham, Birmingham B15 2TT.

McLENNAN, William Patrick, CBE 1997; AM 1992; Australian Statistician, Australian Bureau of Statistics, 1995–2000; *b* 26 Jan. 1942; *s* of William Freeman McLennan and Linda Maude Shannon; *m* 1st, 1968, Christine Elizabeth Alexander (marr. diss. 2006); one *s* one *d*; 2nd, 2008, Bronwyn Jayne Driscoll. *Educ:* Australian National University (BEcon Hons). Statistician, Aust. Bureau of Statistics, 1960–92; Dep. Aust. Statistician, 1986–92; Dir, CSO, and Head of Govt Statistical Service, UK, 1992–95. Vis. Fellow, Nuffield Coll., Oxford, 1992–95. Centenary Medal, Aust., 2003. *Recreation:* golf. *Address:* 325 Hindmarsh Drive, Rivett, ACT 2611, Australia. *E:* bill.mclennan@mac.com.

MACLEOD, Alison Margaret; *see* Cornwell, A. M.

McLEOD, Prof. David, FRCS, FRCOphth; Professor of Ophthalmology, 1988–2006, now Emeritus, and Head of Department of Ophthalmology, 1988–98, University of Manchester; Hon. Consultant Ophthalmologist, Manchester Royal Eye Hospital, since 1988; Hon. Civilian Consultant Ophthalmologist, Royal Air Force, since 2003; *b* 16 Jan. 1946; *s* of Norman McLeod and Anne McLeod (*née* Heyworth); *m* 1967, Jeanette Allison Cross; one *s* one *d*. *Educ:* Univ. of Edinburgh (BSc 1st cl. Hons Physiology 1966; MB ChB Hons 1969). FRCS 1974; FRCOphth 1989. House Physician and Surg., Edinburgh Royal Infirmary, 1969–70; Sen. House Officer and Res. Fellow, Princess Alexandra Eye Pavilion, Edinburgh, 1970–72; Moorfields Eye Hospital: RSO, 1972–75; Fellow in Vitreoretinal Surgery and Ultrasound, 1975–78; Consultant Ophthalmic Surg., 1978–88. Civilian Consultant Ophthalmologist, RAF, 1984–2003. Vis. Prof., UMIST, 1996–2006. Vice-Pres., Royal Coll. of Ophthalmologists, 1997–2001. Mem., Club Jules Gonin, Lausanne. *Publications:* over 180 publications on retinal vascular disease, diabetic retinopathy, vitreoretinal surgery, vitreous pathology. *Recreations:* golf, ballroom dancing. *Address:* Langdale, 370 Chester Road, Woodford, Stockport, Cheshire SK7 1QG. *Clubs:* Brookdale, Probus (Bramhall); Bramall Park Golf.

McLEOD, Prof. (David) Hugh, PhD; FBA 2008; Professor of Church History, University of Birmingham, 1994–2010, now Emeritus. *Educ:* Trinity Hall, Cambridge (BA Hist. 1966; PhD 1971). Res. Fellow in Modern Hist., Birmingham Univ., 1970; Lectr in History, Univ. of Warwick, 1972–73; University of Birmingham: Lectr in Church History, 1973–86; Sen. Lectr, 1986–94; Hd, Dept of Theol., 1995–97. Vis. posts at Univs of Amsterdam and Uppsala; Fellow, Swedish Collegium for Advanced Studies, Uppsala, 2010. Vonhoff Lectr, Univ. of Gröningen, 2004; Hulsean Lectr, Univ. of Cambridge, 2008. Ed., Christianity and Society in the Modern World series, 1983–. President: Ecclesiastical Hist. Soc., 2002–03; Commn Internat. d'Histoire et d'Etudes du Christianisme, 2005–10. *Publications:* Class and Religion in the late Victorian City, 1974; Religion and the People of Western Europe 1789–1970, 1981, rev. edn as Religion and the People of Western Europe 1789–1989, 1997; Religion and Society in England 1850–1914, 1996; Piety and Poverty: working class religion in Berlin, London and New York 1870–1914, 1996; Secularisation in Western Europe 1848–1914, 2000; (ed with W. Ustorf) The Decline of Christendom, 2003; (ed and contrib.) The Cambridge History of Christianity, vol. 9, 2006; The Religious Crisis of the 1960s, 2007. *Address:* Department of History, Arts Building, University of Birmingham, Edgbaston, Birmingham B15 2TT. *E:* d.h.mcleod@bham.ac.uk.

MacLEOD, David Scott G.; *see* Gordon-MacLeod.

MacLEOD, Donald Alexander; HM Diplomatic Service, retired; *b* 23 Jan. 1938; *er s* of late Col Colin S. MacLeod of Glendale, OBE, TD, and of Margaret Drysdale Robertson MacLeod; *m* 1963, Rosemary Lilian Abel (*née* Randle); two *s* two *d*. *Educ:* Edinburgh Academy; Pembroke Coll., Cambridge, 1958–61 (BA). National Service, Queen's Own Cameron Highlanders, 1956–58. HM Foreign Service, 1961; School of Oriental and African Studies, London, 1961–62; British Embassy, Rangoon, 1962–66; Private Sec. to Minister of State, Commonwealth Office, 1966–69; First Secretary, Ottawa, 1969–73; FCO, 1973–78; First Sec./Head of Chancery, Bucharest, 1978–80; Counsellor (Econ. and Commercial), Singapore, 1981–84. Dep. High Comr, Bridgetown, 1984–87; Hd of Protocol Dept, FCO, 1987–89. *Address:* The Steading, Dunvegan, Isle of Skye IV55 8WQ.

MacLEOD, Donald Roderick; QC (Scot.) 2005; *b* 24 Sept. 1948; *s* of Ian MacCrimmon MacLeod, MB, ChB and Mairi M. E. MacLeod, MA Hons; *m* 1978, Susan Mary Fulton, LLB, solicitor; two *d*. *Educ:* High Sch. of Stirling; Univ. of Glasgow (LLB); Dip. FMS. Solicitor, 1973–77; called to Scottish Bar, 1978; in practice as counsel, 1978–. Temp. Sheriff, 1998–2000. Mem. Bd, Scottish Medico-Legal Soc.; Sec., Faculty of Advocates Criminal Bar Assoc. Contested (Lab) Kinross and W Perthshire, 1979. Founder Mem., Circle of Willis. *Publications:* The Law of Firearms and Related Legislation, 2007; contrib. occasional articles to professional jls. *Recreations:* opera, music, angling (Mem., Cobbinshaw Angling Assoc.), tying classic salmon flies, book-collecting, especially first editions of Neil M. Gunn, studying the natural history of the Highlands and Islands of Scotland and their Gaelic culture, place-names and language, hill-walking, golf, wildfowling, supporting Labour's serious and purposeful politicians, visiting historic buildings and enjoying the landscape of Scotland, savouring malt whisky. *T:* (0131) 260 5607. *E:* donald.macleod@advocates.org.uk.

McLEOD, Fiona Grace; Member (SNP) Strathkelvin and Bearsden, Scottish Parliament, since 2011; Acting Minister for Children and Young People, since 2014; carer; *b* 3 Dec. 1957; *d* of John McLeod and Irene McLeod (*née* Robertson); *m* 1979, Dr Andrew David Rankine; one *s*. *Educ:* Glasgow Univ. (MA Hons Medieval and Modern Hist.); Strathclyde Univ. (Postgrad. DipLib). MCLIP. Librarian: Balfron High Sch., 1983–87; Glasgow North Coll. of Nursing, 1987–90; Marie Curie Centre Huntershill Liby, 1995–98; British Homeopathic Library, 2004–08. Partnership Officer, E Dunbartonshire CVS, 2004. MSP (SNP), West of Scotland, 1999–2003. Contested (SNP) Strathkelvin and Bearsden, 2003, Paisley S, 2007, Scottish Parlt. Chm., E Dunbartonshire Children's Panel Adv. Cttee, 2004–08; Mem., Adv. Cttee for Scotland, Ofcom, 2004–06. Peer Support Worker, Carers Link E Dunbartonshire, 2009–10. Chair, Scottish Liby and Information Council, 2011–14. *Recreations:* Scottish castles, walking. *Address:* (office) Suite 13, Enterprise House, Strathkelvin Business Park, Kirkintilloch G66 1XQ.

MACLEOD, Sir Hamish; *see* Macleod, Sir N. W. H.

McLEOD, Hugh; *see* McLeod, D. H.

MACLEOD, Iain; HM Diplomatic Service; Legal Adviser, Foreign and Commonwealth Office, since 2011; *b* 15 March 1962; *s* of Rev. Allan Macleod and Peggy Macleod (*née* Mackay); *m* 1988, Dr Alison M. Murchison; two *s* two *d*. *Educ:* Portree High Sch., Isle of Skye; Glasgow Univ. (LLB Hons 1983; Dip. Prof. Legal Practice 1985); University Coll. London (LLM 1984). Trainee solicitor, Dundas & Wilson CS, Edinburgh, 1985–87; admitted solicitor, Scotland, 1987, England & Wales, 2007; joined HM Diplomatic Service, 1987; Asst Legal Advr, FCO, 1987–91; First Sec. (Legal), UK Repn to EC, Brussels, 1991–95; Asst Legal Advr, FCO, 1995–96; Legal Counsellor: FCO, 1996–97; on loan to Law Officers' Dept, 1997–2000; FCO, 2000–01; UK Mission to UN, NY, 2001–04; FCO, 2004–05; on loan as Dep. Legal Advr, Home Office and NI Office, 2005–09; on loan as Dir, Central Adv. Div.,

Treasury Solicitors, 2009–11. *Publications:* (jtly) The External Relation of the European Communities, 1995. *Address:* Foreign and Commonwealth Office, King Charles Street, SW1A 2AH.

MacLEOD, Prof. Iain Alasdair, PhD; CEng, FICE, FIStructE, FIES; Professor of Structural Engineering, University of Strathclyde, 1981–2004, now Emeritus Professor; *b* 4 May 1939; *s* of Donald and Barbara MacLeod; *m* 1967, Barbara Jean Booth; one *s* one *d*. *Educ:* Lenzie Acad.; Univ. of Glasgow (BSc 1960, PhD 1966). CEng 1968; FIStructE 1982; FICE 1984. Asst Engr, Crouch & Hogg, Glasgow, 1960–62; Asst Lectr in Civil Engrg, Univ. of Glasgow, 1962–66; Structural Engineer: H. A. Simons Internat., Vancouver, Canada, 1966–67; Portland Cement Assoc., Skokie, USA, 1968–69; Lectr in Civil Engrg, Univ. of Glasgow, 1969–73; Prof. and Head of Dept of Civil Engrg, Paisley Coll. of Technol., 1973–81. Vice-Pres., IStructE, 1989–90; Mem., Standing Cttee on Structural Safety, IStructE and ICE, 1990–97; Pres., IES, 2012–14 (Vice Pres. and Sec., 2010–12). FIES 2006. Lewis Kent Award, IStructE, 1998. *Publications:* Analytical Modelling of Structural Systems, 1990; Modern Structural Analysis, 2005; over 100 published papers. *Recreations:* sailing, hill walking. *Address:* c/o Department of Civil Engineering, University of Strathclyde, Glasgow G1 1XJ.

McLEOD, Brig. Ian, CMG 1999; OBE 1983; MC 1965; Division for Relations with Armed and Security Forces, International Committee of the Red Cross, since 1999; *b* 19 June 1941; *s* of David Drummond McLeod and Eleanor McLeod (*née* Williams); *m* 1966, Janet Edith Prosser Angus (*d* 2004); one *s* two *d*. *Educ:* Rhondda Co. Grammar Sch.; RMA Sandhurst; sc 1973; ndc 1991; Open Univ. (BA 1990); Univ. of Buckingham (MA 2012). Commnd Parachute Regt, 1961; service in 3 Para, UK, Gulf and Aden, 1961–67; Jungle Warfare Sch., Malaya, 1967–69; 2 Para, 1969–71; SC, 1971–73; HQ 44 Para Bde (V), 1974–75; 82 AB Div., US Army, 1976–77; Co. Comd, 3 Para, BAOR, 1977–79; GSO2, Defence Ops Analysis Estabt, 1979–81; CO 1 Para, 1981–84; SO1, SC, 1984–86; Col Operational Requirements, MoD, 1986–87; UK Liaison Officer, US Army, 1987–89; Comd, 42 Inf. Bde, 1989–91; Defence Advr, British High Commn, Islamabad, 1992–94; retd 1995; Mem., EC Monitor Mission to former Yugoslavia, 1995–97; Dep. Hd, Regl Office in Brcko of High Rep. for Bosnia, 1997–98; Mem., Kosovo Verification Mission, OSCE, 1998–99. Mem., Pakistan Soc., 2003–. Freeman, City of London, 1992. *Recreations:* travel, military history. *Address:* c/o HSBC, 33 The Borough, Farnham, Surrey GU9 7NJ.

McLEOD, Sir James (Roderick Charles), 4th Bt *cr* 1925, of The Fairfields, Cobham, Surrey; Certified Master Coach, CONCHIUS, Shanghai, since 2009; *b* Haslemere, 26 Sept. 1960; *o s* of Sir Charles Henry McLeod, 3rd Bt and Ann Gillian McLeod (*née* Bowlby); *S* father, 2012, but his name does not appear on the Official Roll of the Baronetage; *m* 1990, Helen M. Cooper; one *s* one *d*. *Educ:* Eton Coll. Certified Master Coach, Internat. Coaching Council; Certified Exec. Coach, Internat. Coaching Fedn. Man. Dir, Internat. Herald Tribune, 1989–98; Pres., Redwood Publishing International, 1998–2005; Assoc. Publisher, World's Best Hotels, 2005–09. *Recreations:* marathon running (64 completed), cricket. *Heir: s* Rory Andrew McLeod, *b* 7 July 1994. *Address:* 27 F-G, Liang Feng Building, 8 Dong Fang Road, Shanghai 200120, China. *T:* (86) 2158872901. *E:* james@conchius.com. *Club:* MCC.

MACLEOD, Jean Grant; *see* Scott, Jean G.

McLEOD, Rev. John; Minister of Resolis and Urquhart, 1986–93; Chaplain to the Queen in Scotland, 1978–96, an Extra Chaplain, since 1996; *b* 8 April 1926; *s* of Angus McLeod and Catherine McDougall; *m* 1958, Sheila McLeod; three *s* two *d*. *Educ:* Inverness Royal Academy; Edinburgh Univ. (MA); New Coll., Edinburgh. Farming until 1952; at university, 1952–58; ordained, Inverness, 1958. Missionary in India: Jalna, 1959–68; Poona, 1969–74; involved in rural development with special emphasis on development and conservation of water resource; also responsible for pastoral work in Church of N India, St Mary's, Poona, 1970–74; Church of Scotland Minister, Livingston Ecumenical Team Ministry, 1974–86. *Recreation:* gardening. *Address:* Benview, 19 Balvaird, Muir of Ord, Ross-shire IV6 7RQ. *T:* (01463) 871286.

MacLEOD, Hon. Sir (John) Maxwell (Norman), 5th Bt *cr* 1924, of Fuinary, Morven, Co. Argyll; Chief Executive Officer: Edinburgh Energy Consultants, since 2014; Fair Winds for Scotland; *b* 23 Feb. 1952; *s* of Baron MacLeod of Fuinary (Life Peer), MC and Lorna Helen Janet (*d* 1984), *er d* of late Rev. Donald Macleod; *S* to baronetcy of father, 1991. *Educ:* Gordonstoun; Bede Coll., Durham; Lady Spencer Churchill Coll., Oxford. Teacher of the deaf, journalist, cartoonist for The Herald, and property developer. A Founder and Chm., Hebridean Whale and Dolphin Trust, 2010–. Mem., Speculative Soc. *Heir: b* Hon. Neil David MacLeod, *b* 25 Dec. 1959. *Address:* Dowies Mill House, Dowies Mill Lane, Cramond, Edinburgh EH4 6DW; Fuinary, Morven, Argyll. *Club:* New (Edinburgh).

McLEOD, Kirsty, (Mrs Christopher Hudson); author and journalist; *b* 23 Dec. 1947; *d* of late Alexander McLeod and Elizabeth Davidson McLeod; *m* 1978, Christopher Hudson; one *s*. *Educ:* St Leonard's Sch., St Andrews; St Anne's Coll., Oxford (MA). Editorial staff, IPC Magazines, 1970–73; Editor, Fontana Books, 1974–76; Columnist, Daily Telegraph, 1991–93. English Heritage: Comr, 1995–2001; Chm., Historic Parks and Gardens Adv. Cttee, 1998–2001 (Mem., 1995–2001). Trustee, Kent Gardens Trust, 2002–03. *Publications:* The Wives of Downing Street, 1976; Drums and Trumpets: the House of Stuart, 1977; The Last Summer: May to September 1914, 1983; A Passion for Friendship: Sibyl Colefax and her circle, 1991; Battle Royal: Edward VIII and George VI, 1999; The Best Gardens in Italy: a traveller's guide, 2011; numerous newspaper articles. *Recreations:* architecture, visiting Italian gardens, armchair mountaineering. *Address:* Domons, Higham Lane, Northiam, E Sussex TN31 6JT. *T:* (01797) 252007.

MACLEOD, Dr Malcolm David, FIET, FREng; Chief Scientist, CIT Division, QinetiQ Ltd, since 2013; *b* Cathcart, 26 Sept. 1953; *s* of Angus and Mary Macleod; partner, Rita Vehbi; two *d*. *Educ:* Hampton Grammar Sch.; Peterhouse, Cambridge (BA 1974; MA 1978; PhD 1979). FIET 2002; CEng 2004; FREng 2014. Cambridge Consultants: Engr, 1978–82; Gp Leader, 1982–85; Consultant, 1985–88; Fellow, Queens' Coll., Cambridge, 1984–2002; Lectr, 1988–95, Dir of Res., 1995–2002, Engrg Dept, Univ. of Cambridge; Principal Scientist, QinetiQ, 2002–13. Vis. Prof., Univ. of Strathclyde, 2013–. Sen. Mem., IEEE, 2013. FIMA 2014. *Publications:* contrib. jl papers, book chapters and conf. papers. *Recreations:* choral director, singer, organist, accompanist. *Address:* QinetiQ Ltd, St Andrews Road, Malvern, Worcs WR14 3PS. *T:* (01684) 543796. *E:* mmacleod@qinetiq.com.

McLEOD, Prof. Malcolm Donald, CBE 2006; FRSE; FSAScot; Professor of African Studies, 1994–2006, Vice-Principal, 1999–2005 and Pro Vice-Principal, 2005–06, Glasgow University; Director, Hunterian Museum and Art Gallery, Glasgow, 1990–99; *b* 19 May 1941; *s* of Donald McLeod and Ellen (*née* Fairclough); *m*; two *s* one *d*. *Educ:* Birkenhead Sch.; Hertford and Exeter Colls, Oxford (MA, BLitt). FRSE 1995; FSAScot 2012. Lectr, Dept of Sociology, Univ. of Ghana, 1967–69; Asst Curator, Museum of Archaeology and Ethnology, Cambridge, 1969–74; Lectr, Girton Coll., Cambridge, 1969–74; Fellow, Magdalene Coll., Cambridge, 1972–74; Keeper of Ethnography, British Museum, 1974–90. Member: Hist. and Current Affairs Selection Cttee, Nat. Film Archive, 1978–84; Council, Museums Assoc., 1983–86; UK Unesco Cultural Adv. Cttee, 1980–85; Unesco Scotland Cttee, 2008–; Chairman: Scottish Mus Council, 1996–2001; Caledonian Foundn, USA, 2003–08; Trustee: Nat. Mus Scotland (formerly Nat. Mus of Scotland), 2005–13; Borders Sculpture Park, 2013–. Consultant, Manhyia Palace Mus., Kumasi, Ghana, 1994–99; Curator, RSE, 1999–2002; Museum Consultant to Opuku Ware II, King of Asante. Hon. Lecturer: Anthropology Dept, UCL, 1976–81; Archæology Dept, Glasgow Univ., 1991–2006. Lectures: Marett, Exeter Coll., Oxford, 1982; Sydney Jones, Liverpool Univ., 1984; Arthur Batchelor, UEA, 1987; Rivers, Cambridge, 1993. Trustee: Sainsbury Unit, UEA, 1991–2000; Oriental Mus., Univ. of Durham, 1994–2000; Hunterian Collection, London, 1998–; Scottish Mus. of the Year Awards, 1999–2002; Opoku Ware Foundn Award, Ghana, 2005. *Publications:* The Asante, 1980; Treasures of African Art, 1980; (with J. Mack) Ethnic Art, 1984; (with E. Bassani) Jacob Epstein: collector, 1987; An English-Kriolu, Kriolu-English Dictionary, 1990; Collecting for the British Museum, 1994; (with Hector MacLeod) Peter Manuel, Serial Killer, 2009; articles and reviews in learned jls. *Address:* The Schoolhouse, Oxnam, Jedburgh TD8 6NB. *Club:* Athenæum.

McLEOD, (Margaret) Kirsty; *see* McLeod, K.

MacLEOD, Mary; Special Adviser to Secretary of State for Scotland, since 2015; *b* London. *Educ:* Glasgow Univ. (MA Hons). Mgt Consultant, Andersen Consulting, 1990–2002; Man. Dir, MCG, 2002–10, appts incl. Chief Operating Officer for Gp Ops, ABN AMRO, 2003–07, Gp Communications Hd of Transition, RBS, 2007–10. Policy Advr to the Queen's Private Office, Buckingham Palace, 1998–99. Contested (C) Ross, Skye and Inverness W, 1997. MP (C) Brentford and Isleworth, 2010–15; contested (C) same seat, 2015. Parliamentary Private Secretary: to Minister for Policing and Justice, 2010–12; to Sec. of State for Culture, Media and Sport, 2012–14; to Minister for Women and Equalities, 2012–14; to Sec. of State for Northern Ireland, 2014–15. Mem., Home Affairs Select Cttee, 2010; Chm., All-Party Parly Gp for Women in Parlt, 2010–15; Vice Chm., All Party Parly Gp for Microfinance, 2012–15. Prime Minister's Small Business Ambassador for London, 2012–15; Mem., No 10 Policy Bd with resp. for Home and Constitutional Affairs, Justice, Culture, Media and Sport, 2014–15. Non-exec. Dir, Lewis PR, 2014–. Member, Advisory Board: Learning for Life, 2010–; Career Acads UK, 2012–; Mem., Social Integration Commn, 2014–. Pres., Chiswick, RBL, 2010–. Fellow, Sporting Equals, 2011–14; Community Champion for Brentford FC Community Sports Trust, 2011–15. Trustee: Holland Park Sch. Trust, 2009–; Industry Parlt Trust, 2012–15; Hounslow Shelter Project, 2014–. Patron, London's Women Forum, 2014–. FRSA 2007. *Address:* Scotland Office, Dover House, Whitehall, SW1A 2AU.

MacLEOD, Hon. Sir Maxwell; *see* MacLeod, Hon. Sir J. M. N.

MacLEOD, Murdo Angus; QC (Scot.) 2008; *b* 21 Oct. 1967; *s* of Murdo Alexander MacLeod, DA and Dolina MacLeod (*née* Macdonald); *m* 2010, Laura-Anne van der Westhuizen. *Educ:* Nicolson Inst., Stornoway; Univ. of Aberdeen (LLB Hons 1989; DipLP 1990). Admitted to Faculty of Advocates, 1994; Crown Counsel, 2001–03; Sen. Crown Counsel, 2004–05; Counsel to Billy Wright Inquiry, 2005–10; called to the Bar, Middle Temple, 2011; Sheriff (part-time), 2011–. UK delegate to Criminal Law Cttee, Council of Bars and Law Socs of Europe, 2012–. Mem. Bd, Glasgow Print Studio, 2007–13. *Recreations:* art, golf, music. *Address:* Compass Chambers, Parliament House, Edinburgh EH1 1RF. *T:* (0131) 260 5648. *E:* murdo.macleod@advocates.org.uk; Temple Garden Chambers, 1 Harcourt Buildings, Temple, EC4Y 9DA. *T:* (020) 7583 1315. *Clubs:* Scottish Arts (Edinburgh); Bruntsfield Links Golfing Soc.

MACLEOD, Sir (Nathaniel William) Hamish, KBE 1994 (CBE 1992); Financial Secretary, Hong Kong, 1991–95; *b* 6 Jan. 1940; *s* of George Henry Torquil Macleod and Ruth Natalie Wade; *m* 1970, Fionna Mary Campbell; one *s* one *d*. *Educ:* Univ. of St Andrews (MA Soc. Sci. Hons); Univ. of Bristol (Dip. Soc. Sci. Sociology); Birmingham Coll. of Commerce. FCIS 1995. Commercial trainee, Stewarts & Lloyds, Birmingham, 1958–62; Hong Kong Government: Admin. Officer, 1966; Dir of Trade and Chief Trade Negotiator, 1983–87; Secretary for Trade and Industry, 1987–89; Sec. for the Treasury, 1989–91. Director: Scottish Community (formerly Caledonian) Foundation, 1995–2002; Highland Distilleries, 1995–99; Scottish Oriental Smaller Cos Trust, 1995–2011; Chm., JP Morgan Fleming Asian Investment Trust (formerly Fleming Asian Investment Trust), 1997–2003. *Recreations:* golf, walking. *Address:* 20 York Road, Trinity, Edinburgh EH5 3EH. *T:* (0131) 552 5058. *Clubs:* Bruntsfield Links Golf; Hong Kong, Royal Hong Kong Yacht.

MacLEOD, Dr Norman, FGS, FLS; Dean, Post-graduate Education and Training, Department of Earth Sciences, Natural History Museum, London, since 2012; *b* 23 Feb. 1953; *s* of Archibald Alexander MacLeod and Helen Chester MacLeod; *m* 1988, Dr Cecilia McDonald; one *d*. *Educ:* Univ. of Missouri, Columbia (BSc Geol. 1976); Southern Methodist Univ., Dallas (MSc Palaeontol. 1980); Univ. of Texas at Dallas (PhD Palaeontol. 1986). FGS 2002; FLS 2003. Sci. teacher (physics, geol., astronomy, ecol.), H. Grady Spruce High Sch., Segoville, Texas, 1976–78; owner, Boreas Technical Photographers, Dallas, 1982–86; Consultant, Atlantic Richfield (ARCO) Oil and Gas, Richardson, Texas, 1984–86; Michigan Soc. Fellow and Vis. Asst Prof., Dept of Geol Scis, Univ. of Michigan, Ann Arbor, 1986–89; Researcher, Dept of Geol and Geophysical Scis, Princeton Univ., 1989–93; Natural History Museum, London, 1993–: Scientific Officer, 1993–94; SSO, 1994–96; Stratigraphy and Correlation Prog. Leader, 1995–2001; Researcher, 1996–99; Petroleum Sector Leader, 1997–2001; Associate Keeper of Palaeontol., 2000–01; Actg Keeper of Palaeontol., 2001; Keeper of Palaeontol., 2001–12. Hon. Professor: UCL, 2004–; Nanjing Inst. of Geol. and Palaeontol., Chinese Acad. of Sci., 2011–; Vis. Prof., Univ. of Chicago, 2011. Member: Soc. Systematic Biol., 1981; Centre for Evolution and Ecol., 1998; Systematics Assoc., 2001; Palaeontol Assoc., 2003 (Trustee, 2005–09; Vice Pres., 2007–09); Geol Soc. London, 2002. Trustee, Scarborough Mus Trust, 2004–13. *Publications:* The Cretaceous-Tertiary Mass Extinction: biotic and environmental changes, 1996; Morphometrics, Shape and Phylogenetics, 2002; Automated Taxon Identification in Systematics: theory, approaches and applications, 2007; The Great Extinctions: what causes them and how they shape life, 2012; (Ed.-in-Chief) Grzimek's Animal Life Encyclopedia: extinctions (2 vols), 2012; contrib. numerous peer reviewed technical articles, technical reports and reviews. *Recreations:* music, cooking, theatre, wine, dining. *Address:* Department of Earth Sciences, Natural History Museum, Cromwell Road, South Kensington, SW7 5BD. *T:* (020) 7942 5204, *Fax:* (020) 7942 5546.

MacLEOD, Norman Donald; QC (Scot.) 1986; MA, LLB; Advocate; Sheriff Principal of Glasgow and Strathkelvin, 1986–97; *b* 6 March 1932; *s* of late Rev. John MacLeod, Edinburgh and Catherine MacRitchie; *m* 1957, Ursula Jane, *y d* of late George H. Bromley, Inveresk; two *s* two *d*. *Educ:* Mill Hill Sch.; George Watson's Boys' Coll., Edinburgh; Edinburgh Univ.; Hertford Coll., Oxford. Passed Advocate, 1956. Colonial Administrative Service, Tanganyika: Dist Officer, 1957–59; Crown Counsel, 1959–64; practised at Scots Bar, 1964–67; Sheriff of Glasgow and Strathkelvin (formerly Lanarkshire at Glasgow), 1967–86; Hon. Sheriff N Strathclyde, 1986. Vis. Prof., Law Sch., Univ. of Strathclyde, 1988–98. Comr, Northern Lighthouse Bd, 1986–97 (Chm., 1990–91). Hon. Mem., Royal Faculty of Procurators in Glasgow, 1996. *Recreations:* sailing, gardening. *Address:* 23 Lochead Avenue, Lochwinnoch, Renfrewshire PA12 4AW. *T:* (01505) 843340.

MACLEOD, (Roderick) James (Andrew) R.; *see* Robertson-Macleod.

MacLEOD, Roderick John; *see* Minginish, Hon. Lord.

MacLEOD, Sian Christina, OBE 2002; HM Diplomatic Service; Head of UK Delegation to Organisation for Security and Co-operation in Europe, Vienna, since 2015; *b* 31 May 1962; *m* Richard Anthony Robinson. *Educ:* Royal Acad. of Music (BMus 1983). Joined FCO, 1986; Desk Officer, S African Dept, 1986–87; Third, then Second Sec., Moscow, 1988–92; Dep. Hd of Mission, Vilnius, 1992; Foreign and Commonwealth Office: Hd, Russia Section, Jt

Assistance Unit, 1992; Hd of Section, Arms Control and Disarmament Dept, 1993–94; Personnel Mgt Dept, 1995–96; First Sec., The Hague, 1996–2000; Dep. Hd, Counter Terrorism Policy Dept, FCO, 2000–01; on loan to Cabinet Office, 2002–04; Political Counsellor, 2004–05, Minister and Dep. Hd of Mission, 2005–07, Moscow; Hd, Whitehall Liaison Dept, FCO, 2007–08; Ambassador to the Czech Republic, 2009–13; Acting Dir, Eastern Europe and Central Asia, FCO, 2013–15. *Recreations:* music, gardening, cross-country ski-ing. *Address:* c/o Foreign and Commonwealth Office, King Charles Street, SW1A 2AH.

MacLEOD, Tracey Ann; Restaurant Critic, The Independent, since 1997; Director, KBJ Management, since 2007; *b* Ipswich, 30 Oct. 1960; *d* of Donald MacLeod and Colleen MacLeod; partner, Harry Ritchie; two *s*. *Educ:* Ipswich High Sch.; Durham Univ. (BA Eng. Lang. and Lit.). Writer, The Stage, 1984–85; researcher, BBC TV, 1985–87; reporter and producer, Network 7, Channel 4, 1987–88; producer and presenter, The Late Show, BBC, 1989–95; Dir, Planet 24 Prodns, 1997–99. *Recreations:* cooking, eating out, dieting. *Address:* c/o KBJ Management, 22 Rathbone Street, W1T 1LA. *E:* tracey@kbjmanagement.co.uk.

MACLEOD CLARK, Prof. Dame Jill, DBE 2000; PhD; Professor of Nursing, University of Southampton, 1999–2009, now Emeritus Professor in Health Sciences (Dean of Nursing and Health Sciences, until 2012); *b* 11 June 1944; *d* of late George William Charles Tearle Gibbs and Edith Vera Macleod Gibbs; *m* 1st, 1967, Andrew William Clark (marr. diss. 1983); two *s*; 2nd, 1989, William Arthur Bridge. *Educ:* UCH (RGN 1965); LSE (BSc Hons 1972); KCL (PhD 1982). FRCN 1997. Various clin. posts, London, Birmingham and Bedford, 1965–76; Nursing Officer, DoH, 1976–78; Res. Fellow, 1978–81, Lectr in Nursing, 1981–86, Chelsea Coll., London Univ.; King's College London: Sen. Lectr in Nursing, 1986–90; Prof. of Nursing, 1990–93; Dir, Nightingale Inst., 1993–99; University of Southampton: Hd, Sch. of Nursing and Midwifery, 1999–2009; Dep. Dean, Faculty of Medicine, Health and Life Scis (formerly Faculty of Medicine and Health), 1999–2011. Adjunct Prof., Univ. of Toronto, 2015–. FQNI 2004. Hon. DSc: Brighton, 2004; UEA, 2005; QUB, 2010; Robert Gordon, 2013; City, 2014. *Publications:* Research for Nursing, 1979; Communication in Nursing Care, 1981; Further Research for Nursing, 1989; Adult Nursing Care: putting evidence into practice, 2012; numerous res. based papers in learned jls on health promotion, smoking cessation, health prof. educn and communication in health care. *Recreations:* sailing, singing. *Address:* 31 Pacific Close, Ocean Village, Southampton SO14 3TX. *Club:* Royal Southampton Yacht.

McLERNAN, Kieran Anthony; Sheriff of Grampian, Highland and Islands at Aberdeen, 2000–11; *b* 29 April 1941; *s* of James John McLernan and Delia (*née* McEvaddy); *m* 1979, Joan Doherty Larkins; one *s* three *d*. *Educ:* St Aloysius' Coll., Glasgow; Glasgow Univ. (MA 1961; LLB 1965). Admitted solicitor, 1965; Tutor, Glasgow Univ., 1985–91. Temp. Sheriff, 1986–91; Sheriff of Grampian, Highland and Islands at Banff and Peterhead, 1991. KCHS 1998 (KHS 1990). *Recreations:* golf, hockey, ski-ing, etc.

McLINTOCK, Michael George Alexander; Chief Executive, M&G Group Limited (formerly Prudential M&G Asset Management), since 1999; *b* 24 March 1961; *s* of Sir (Charles) Alan McLintock and of Sylvia Mary McLintock; *m* 1996, Nicola Fairles Ogilvy Watson; one *s* two *d*. *Educ:* Malvern Coll.; St John's Coll., Oxford (scholar; BA 1st cl. hons Mod. History and Econs). Morgan Grenfell & Co. Ltd, 1983; Baring Brothers & Co. Ltd, 1987; M&G Group plc, 1992, Chief Exec., 1997–99. Director: Prudential plc, 2000–; Close Brothers Gp plc, 2001–08; Grosvenor Gp Ltd, 2012–. Trustee, Grosvenor Estate, 2008–. *Recreations:* family, friends, good wine. *Address:* (office) Laurence Pountney Hill, EC4R 0HH. *T:* (020) 7626 4588. *Clubs:* Army and Navy, Boodle's, MCC (Member: Finance Cttee, 2005–; Develt Cttee, 2009–11).

McLINTOCK, Sir Michael (William), 4th Bt *cr* 1934, of Sanquhar, Co. Dumfries; *b* 13 Aug. 1958; *s* of Sir William Traven McLintock, 3rd Bt and Andrée, *d* of Richard Lonsdale-Hands; *S* father, 1987; *m* 1991, Jill Andrews; one *s* one *d*. *Heir: s* James Kieron McLintock, *b* 14 Feb. 1995.

McLOUGHLIN, Catherine Mary Anne, CBE 1998; Vice-President, Age UK, since 2009 (Chair, Age Concern England, 2005–09); *b* 26 July 1943; *d* of Peter Patrick McLoughlin and Catherine (*née* McHugh). *Educ:* Ravenswell Convent, Bray, Co. Wicklow. Gen. nurse trng, N Middx Hosp., 1961–64; post-registration psychiatric trng, 1965–66, then specialist posts, 1966–73, Bethlem Royal and Maudsley Hosp.; Principal Nursing Officer, Bexley Hosp., 1973–77; Dep. Area Nursing Officer, Oxon, 1977–79; Chief Nursing Officer, Paddington and N Kensington HA, 1979–85; Dist Gen. Manager, Haringey HA, 1985–89; Dir of Nursing and Dep. Chief Nursing Officer, DoH, 1989–90, retd. Chair: Bromley FHSA, 1992–94; Bromley HA, 1994–99; NHS Confedn, 1997–2000; St George's Healthcare NHS Trust, 1999–2003. Chair: Nat. Network Art in Health, 2000–06; Age Concern Bromley, 2002–05. Dr *hc* Middx 1995. *Recreations:* reading, art, walking, swimming. *Address:* 53 South Croxted Road, West Dulwich, SE21 8BA. *T:* 07768 252300.

McLOUGHLIN, Elizabeth Mary, CBE 1997; Command Secretary, HQ Land Command, Ministry of Defence, 2003–06; *b* 10 April 1947; *d* of Donald Norwood Menzies and late Doreen Mary Menzies (*née* Collinson); *m* 1976, John McLoughlin; three *s*. *Educ:* South Hampstead High Sch.; University College London (BA Hons History). Res., 1969–72; joined MoD, 1972; various posts, 1972–88; Sen. Civil Service, 1988; Comd Sec., Adjutant Gen., 1997–2002; Dir Gen., Service Personnel Policy, 2002–03. Non-executive Director: Great Western Ambulance NHS Trust, 2006–13 (Dep. Chm., 2006–13); Bd, Nat. Offenders Mgt Service, MoJ, 2010–; Bd, Valuation Office Agency, HMRC, 2011–14; Cabinet Office proj. and prog. assurance reviewer, 2009–. Gov., King's Sch., Bruton, and Hazlegrove Prep. Sch., 2006–14 (Sen. Warden, 2012–14). *Recreations:* gardening, reading, walking the dog, music. *E:* emmcloughlin@btinternet.com.

McLOUGHLIN, Sir Frank, Kt 2015; CBE 2009; Principal, City and Islington College, since 2002; *b* London, 30 May 1956; *s* of Patrick McLoughlin and Mary McLoughlin; *m* 1997, Fiona Wallace; one *s* one *d*. *Educ:* Leeds Univ. (BA Hons Pol Studies); London Univ. (PGCE). Range of unskilled jobs before univ.; part-time lectr, Hammersmith and West London Coll., 1979–81; Lectr, then Sen. Lectr, North London Coll., 1981–93; Curriculum Manager, then Dep. Principal, City and Islington Coll., 1993–2002. Chm., Commn on Adult Vocational Learning, 2012–13. Fellow, City Univ. *Recreations:* Irish music and culture, reading, travel, London. *Address:* City and Islington College, Marlborough Building, 383 Holloway Road, N7 0RN. *T:* (020) 7700 9210. *E:* frank.mcloughlin@candi.ac.uk.

McLOUGHLIN, Rt Hon. Patrick (Allen); PC 2005; MP (C) Derbyshire Dales, since 2010 (West Derbyshire, May 1986–2010); Secretary of State for Transport, since 2012; *b* 30 Nov. 1957; *s* of Patrick and Gladys Victoria McLoughlin; *m* 1984, Lynne Newman; one *s* one *d*. *Educ:* Cardinal Griffin Roman Catholic Sch., Cannock. Mineworker, Littleton Colliery, 1979–85; Marketing Official, NCB, 1985–86. PPS to Sec. of State for Trade and Industry, 1988–89; Parly Under-Sec. of State, Dept of Transport, 1989–92, Dept of Employment, 1992–93, DTI, 1993–94; an Asst Govt Whip, 1995–96; a Lord Comr of HM Treasury (Govt Whip), 1996–97; Opposition Pairing Whip, 1997–98; Dep. Opposition Chief Whip, 1998–2005; Opposition Chief Whip, 2005–10; Parly Sec. to HM Treasury (Govt Chief Whip), 2010–12. *Address:* House of Commons, SW1A 0AA.

McLURE, Donald Keith; Corporate Director of Resources, Durham County Council, since 2010; *b* Gateshead, 23 Dec. 1955; *s* of Donald Hall McLure and Florence McLure; *m* 1977, Jacqueline; two *d*. *Educ:* Blaydon Comp. Sch. IRRV; CIPFA. Asst Dir of Finance, Gateshead Council, 1991–2002; Asst Dir of Resources, 2002–07, Strategic Dir of Resources, 2007–10, Derby CC. *Recreations:* keen golfer for nearly 50 years, football fan of Newcastle United and Derby, walking, family including two young grandsons. *Address:* 6 Barnsett Grange, Sunderland Bridge, Durham DH6 5BX. *T:* (0191) 378 1359. *E:* don.mclure@durham.gov.uk. *Clubs:* Brancepeth Castle Golf, Kedleston Park Golf.

MACLURE, Sir John (Robert Spencer), 4th Bt *cr* 1898; Headmaster, Croftinloan School, Pitlochry, Perthshire, 1978–92 and 1997–98; *b* 25 March 1934; *s* of Sir John William Spencer Maclure, 3rd Bt, OBE, and Elspeth (*d* 1991), *er d* of late Alexander King Clark; *S* father, 1980; *m* 1964, Jane Monica, *d* of late Rt Rev. T. J. Savage, Bishop of Zululand and Swaziland; four *s*. *Educ:* Winchester College. DipEd. 2nd Lt, 2nd Bn KRRC, 1953–55, BAOR; Lt, Royal Hampshire Airborne Regt, TA. Assistant Master: Horris Hill, 1955–66 and 1974–78; St George's, Wanganui, NZ, 1967–68; Sacred Heart Coll., Auckland, NZ, 1969–70; St Edmund's, Hindhead, Surrey, 1971–74. *Heir: s* John Mark Maclure [*b* 27 Aug. 1965; *m* 1996, Emily, *d* of Peter Frean; two *s* one *d*]. *Address:* Seaward, Crescent Close, Widemouth Bay, Bude, Cornwall EX23 0AE. *Clubs:* MCC; Royal Green Jackets.

McMAHON, Prof. Andrew Paul, PhD; FRS 2007; W. M. Keck Professor and Chair, Department of Stem Cell Biology and Regenerative Medicine, and Director, Edythe and Eli Broad Center for Regenerative Medicine and Stem Cell Research, University of Southern California, since 2012. *Educ:* St Peter's Coll., Oxford (BA Zool. 1978); University Coll. London (PhD 1981). Postdoctoral Fellow, Div. of Biol., CIT; Staff Scientist, NIMR, London; Adjunct Prof., Dept of Genetics and Biol Scis, Columbia Univ.; Mem., Dept of Cell and Develtl Biol., Roche Inst. of Molecular Biol.; Prof. of Molecular and Cellular Biol., 1993, Frank B. Baird, Jr Prof. of Sci., 2001–12, Chm., Dept of Molecular and Cellular Biol., 2001–04, Harvard Univ. Associate Mem., EMBO. Fellow, Amer. Acad. Arts and Scis, 2003. *Publications:* contribs to jls incl. Science, Develt, Develtl Cell, Cell, Genes & Develt. *Address:* Edythe and Eli Broad Center for Regenerative Medicine and Stem Cell Research, Keck School of Medicine, University of Southern California, 1425 San Pablo Street, Los Angeles, CA 90089, USA.

McMAHON, Prof. April Mary Scott, PhD; FBA 2005; FRSE, FLSW; Vice-Chancellor, Aberystwyth University, since 2011; *b* 30 April 1964; *d* of Irene Dugan (*née* Grant); *m* 1984, Robert McMahon; two *s* one *d*. *Educ:* Univ. of Edinburgh (MA 1986; PhD 1990). Lectr in Linguistics, and Fellow, Selwyn Coll., Cambridge, 1988–2000; Prof. of English Lang. and Linguistics, Univ. of Sheffield, 2000–04; Forbes Prof. of English Lang., 2005–11, Vice-Principal, Planning and Res. Planning, 2009–11, Univ. of Edinburgh. Member, Council: AHRC, 2005–10; British Acad., 2008–11. Pres., Linguistics Assoc. of GB, 2000–05. FRSE 2003; FLSW 2012. *Publications:* Understanding Language Change, 1994; Lexical Phonology and the History of English, 2000; Change, Chance and Optimality, 2000; (ed jtly) Time-depth in Historical Linguistics, 2 vols, 2000; An Introduction to English Phonology, 2001; (with R. McMahon) Language Classification by Numbers, 2005; (ed jtly) The Handbook of English Linguistics, 2006; (with R. McMahon) Evolutionary Linguistics, 2012. *Recreations:* walking, cooking, Scottish country dancing. *Address:* Aberystwyth University, Visualisation Centre, Penglais Campus, Aberystwyth SY23 3BF. *T:* (01970) 622002. *E:* April.McMahon@aber.ac.uk.

McMAHON, Sir Brian (Patrick), 8th Bt *cr* 1817; engineer; *b* 9 June 1942; *s* of Sir (William) Patrick McMahon, 7th Bt, and Ruth Stella (*d* 1982), *yr d* of late Percy Robert Kenyon-Slaney; *S* father, 1977; *m* 1981, Kathleen Joan (marr. diss. 1991), *d* of late William Hopwood. *Educ:* Wellington. BSc, AIM. Assoc. Mem., Inst. of Welding. *Heir: nephew* Patrick John Westropp McMahon, *b* 7 Feb. 1988.

McMAHON, Sir Christopher William, (Sir Kit), Kt 1986; Director, Angela Flowers, 1992–2006; *b* Melbourne, 10 July 1927; *s* of late Dr John Joseph McMahon and late Margaret Kate (*née* Brown); *m* 1st, 1956, Marion Kelso; two *s*; 2nd, 1982, Alison Barbara Braimbridge, *d* of late Dr J. G. Cormie and late Mrs B. E. Cormie. *Educ:* Melbourne Grammar Sch.; Univ. of Melbourne (BA Hons Hist. and English, 1949); Magdalen Coll., Oxford. 1st cl. hons PPE, 1953. Tutor in English Lit., Univ. of Melbourne, 1950; Econ. Asst, HM Treasury, 1953–57; Econ. Adviser, British Embassy, Washington, 1957–60; Fellow and Tutor in Econs, Magdalen Coll., Oxford, 1960–64 (Hon. Fellow, 1986); Tutor in Econs, Treasury Centre for Admin. Studies, 1963–64; Mem., Plowden Cttee on Aircraft Industry, 1964–65; entered Bank of England as Adviser, 1964; Adviser to the Governors, 1966–70; Exec. Dir, 1970–80; Dep. Governor, 1980–85; Chief Exec. and Dep. Chm., 1986–87, Chm. and Chief Exec., 1987–91, Midland Bank. Director: Eurotunnel, 1987–91; Hongkong and Shanghai Banking Corp., 1987–91; Royal Opera House, 1989–97; Taylor Woodrow, 1991–2000 (Dep. Chm., 1997–2000); Newspaper Publishing, 1993–94; Aegis, 1993–99; FI Gp, 1994–2001; HistoryWorld, 2001–; Chairman: Coutts Consulting Gp, 1992–96; Pentos, 1993–95; Arc Dance Co., 2000–03. Mem., Gp of Thirty, 1978–84; Chairman: Working Party 3, OECD, 1980–85; Young Enterprise, 1989–92; Centre for Study of Financial Innovation, 1993–95. Mem. Court, Univ. of London, 1984–86; Gov., Birkbeck Coll., 1991–2003. Trustee: Whitechapel Art Gall., 1984–92; Royal Opera House Trust, 1984–86. Hon. Fellow, UCNW, 1988. Hon. Mem., Antiquarian Booksellers' Assoc., 2000. Chevalier, Légion d'Honneur (France), 1990. *Publications:* Sterling in the Sixties, 1964; (ed) Techniques of Economic Forecasting, 1965. *Recreations:* looking at pictures, buying books, going to the movies. *Address:* 134 Cranmer Court, Whiteheads Grove, SW3 3HE. *Club:* Garrick.

McMAHON, Harvey Thomas, PhD; FRS 2008; Programme Leader, MRC Laboratory of Molecular Biology, Cambridge, since 1995; *b* Belfast, 31 Aug. 1965; *s* of William McMahon and Sarah Jean McMahon (*née* McCrea); *m* 1995, Kelly Lynn Hammonds; two *s*. *Educ:* Trinity College, Dublin (BA Mod. Biochem. 1987); Dundee Univ. (PhD 1990). Res. Asst, Dundee Univ., 1990–91; Postdoctoral Fellow, Howard Hughes Med. Inst., Dallas, 1991–95. *Publications:* regular contribs of papers, reviews and book chapters in scientific literature. *Recreations:* hill walking, travelling, ornithology, gardening (mostly growing weeds), community work. *Address:* MRC Laboratory of Molecular Biology, Neurobiology Division, Francis Crick Avenue, Cambridge CB2 0QH. *T:* (01223) 402311, *Fax:* (01223) 402310. *E:* hmm@mrc-lmb.cam.ac.uk.

McMAHON, Hugh Robertson; UK Political Editor, World Parliamentarian magazine, since 1999; Lecturer in Social Sciences, James Watt College, 1999–2011; Lecturer in Politics, University of Edinburgh, 2002–10; *b* 17 June 1938; *s* of Hugh McMahon and Margaret Fulton Robertson; *m* 1986, Helen Grant; one *s* one *d*. *Educ:* Glasgow University (MA Hons); Jordanhill College. Assistant Teacher: Largs High School, 1962–63; Stevenston High School, 1963–64; Irvine Royal Academy, 1964–68; Principal Teacher of History, Mainholm Academy, Ayr, 1968–71; Principal Teacher of History and Modern Studies, 1971–72, Asst Head Teacher, 1972–84, Ravenspark Academy, Irvine. MEP (Lab) Strathclyde W, 1984–99; contested (Lab) Scotland, 1999. European Parliament: Mem., Budgetary Control Cttee, 1987–92; Social Affairs, Employment and Working Envmt Cttee, 1984–99 (Vice Chm., 1992–94); Fisheries Cttee, 1994–99; Mem., Interparly Delegn with Czech Republic, 1997–99. Formerly Rep. of Scottish MEPs, Scottish Exec. Cttee, Labour Party. Chm., Paisley Bids Gp, 2011–. Mem. Bd, Centre for Russian, Central and Eastern European Studies, 2007–; Member: European Movement; Scotland Russia Forum. *Recreations:* golf, reading, walking, languages, foreign travel. *Address:* 9 Low Road, Castlehead, Paisley PA2 6AQ. *T:* (0141) 889 0885, *Fax:* (0141) 889 4790. *E:* breakplough@btinternet.com. *Clubs:* Saltcoats & Kilbirnie Labour; Irvine Bogside Golf.

McMAHON, Sir Kit; *see* McMahon, Sir C. W.

McMAHON, Most Rev. Malcolm Patrick; *see* Liverpool, Archbishop of, (RC).

McMAHON, Michael Joseph; Member (Lab) Uddingston and Bellshill, Scottish Parliament, since 2011 (Hamilton North and Bellshill, 1999–2011); *b* 18 Sept. 1961; *s* of Patrick McMahon and Bridget Clarke; *m* 1983, Margaret Mary McKeown; one *s* two *d*. *Educ:* Glasgow Caledonian Univ. (BA Hons Social Scis (Politics and Sociology) 1996). Welder, Terex Equipment Ltd, 1977–92; freelance socio-political researcher, 1996–99. *Recreations:* swimming, hill walking, supporting Celtic FC. *Address:* 7 Forres Crescent, Bellshill, Lanarkshire ML4 1HL. *T:* (01698) 306112.
See also S. M. McMahon.

McMAHON, Richard James; QC (Guernsey) 2009; Deputy Bailiff of Guernsey, since 2012; *b* Farnborough, Kent, 1 May 1962; *s* of James Ronald McMahon and Alice Rose McMahon (*née* Skipp); *m* 1998, Sue-Yin Elizabeth Chan; one *s* one *d*. *Educ:* Abingdon Sch.; Univ. of Liverpool (LLB 1984); Emmanuel Coll., Cambridge (LLM 1985); Univ. of Caen (Certificat d'Etudes Juridiques Françaises et Normandes). Called to the Bar: Middle Temple, 1986; Guernsey, 1998; Lectr, Univ. of Reading, 1987–95; Legislative Draftsman, Guernsey, 1995–99; Crown Advocate, Guernsey, 2000–09; HM Comptroller, Guernsey, 2009–12. *Publications:* (contrib.) Blackstone's Criminal Practice, 1995–. *Recreations:* music, reading, Ireland. *Address:* Bailiff's Chambers, Royal Court House, St Peter Port, Guernsey GY1 2PB. *T:* (01481) 726161, *Fax:* (01481) 713861. *E:* Deputy.Bailiff@gov.gg.

McMAHON, Siobhan Marie; Member (Lab) Scotland Central, Scottish Parliament, since 2011; *b* Bellshill, North Lanarks; *d* of Michael Joseph McMahon, *qv*. *Educ:* Glasgow Caledonian Univ. (BA Social Scis Pols with Hist. 2006). Researcher to Rt Hon. James Murphy, MP and Kenneth Macintosh, MSP, 2007–11; Office Manager, Labour Support Unit, Scottish Parlt, 2010–11. *Recreation:* Celtic supporter and season ticket holder. *Address:* Scottish Parliament, Edinburgh EH99 1SP. *T:* (0131) 348 6389. *E:* siobhan.mcmahon.msp@scottish.parliament.uk.

McMAHON, Rt Rev. Thomas; Parish Priest, Stock, since 1969; Bishop of Brentwood, (RC), 1980–2014; *b* 17 June 1936. *Educ:* St Bede's GS, Manchester; St Sulpice, Paris; Wonersh. Ordained priest, 1959; Asst Priest, Colchester, 1959–64; Priest, Westcliff-on-Sea, 1964–69; Chaplain, Univ. of Essex, 1972–80. Hon. Ecumenical Canon, Chelmsford Cathedral, 2005–. Former Member: Nat. Ecumenical Commn; Internat. Commn on English in the Liturgy, 1983–2001; Mem., Churches Together in Essex & E London, 1991– (Chm., 1984–93); Chairman: Brentwood Ecumenical Commn, 1979; Cttee for Pastoral Liturgy, 1983–97; Essex Churches Consultative Council, 1984–; Cttee for Church Music, 1985–2001; Bishop's Patrimony Cttee, 2001–12; Mem., London Church Leaders Gp, 1980–; Rep. of Bps' Conf. on Council of St George's House, Windsor, 2005–. Founder Mem., Movt for Christian Democracy, 1999–. President: Essex Show, 1992; Essex Club, 2009. Vice-President: Pax Christi, 1987–; Friends of Cathedral Music, 2005–; Historic Churches Preservation Trust, 2007–. Hon. Fellow, Hertford Coll., Oxford, 2004. DU: Essex, 1991; Anglia, 2001. Freeman, City of London, 2013. *Address:* Bishop's House, Stock, Ingatestone, Essex CM4 9BU. *T:* (01277) 840268.

McMANNERS, (Joseph) Hugh; author, since 1984; Director, Scars of War Foundation, Queen's College, Oxford, since 2011; *b* Oxford, 9 Dec. 1952; *s* of Rev. Prof. John McManners, CBE, FBA and of Sarah McManners; *m* 1989; two *s*; partner, Margarita Suharchuk. *Educ:* RMA Sandhurst; St Edmund Hall, Oxford (BA Geog. 1975; MA 1980). Commnd RA 1972; served 148 Cdo Forward Observation Battery with Special Boat Sqdn, Falklands War, 1982 (mentioned in despatches); sc Camberley 1984; resigned Commn, 1989. Independent television producer, 1991–96; Defence Corresp., Sunday Times, 1995–2000. Vis. Res. Fellow, Changing Character of War Prog., Univ. of Oxford, 2013. *Television:* co-productions include: Thinking of the Soldier, 1991, P Company, 1992, Inside the Glasshouse, 1994, Cutting Edge Films; series: Battle Cries, 1992; Commando; Top Guns; The Cinderellas; co-presenter, Bare Necessities, 1999–2001. Writer and presenter, BBC Radio 4 series: Taking the Crown, 1990; The Psychology of War, 1994. Band leader and guitarist, 1992–; songwriter, 2010; solo singer-songwriter, 2014. *Publications:* Falklands Commando, 1984; Crowning the Dragon, 1986; The Scars of War, 1993; Commando Survival Manual, 1994; Commando, 1995; The Backpacker's Handbook, 1995; The Children's Outdoor Training Book, 1996; Top Guns, 1996; Outdoor Survival Guide, 1999; Forgotten Voices of the Falklands War, 2002; Gulf War One, 2011. *Recreations:* trips off-grid, dreaming of Norton cafe racers. *E:* hugh@hughmcmanners.com. *W:* www.hughmcmanners.com, music.hughmcmanners.com. *Clubs:* Victory Services, Special Forces.

McMANUS, Christopher; *see* McManus, I. C.

McMANUS, Declan Patrick Aloysius, (Elvis Costello); musician and composer; *b* 25 Aug. 1954; *s* of late Ross McManus and of Lillian McManus (*née* Costello); *m* 1974, Mary; one *s*; *m* 1986, Cait O'Riordan; *m* 2003, Diana Krall; two *s* (twins). Formed Elvis Costello and the Attractions, 1977; has collaborated with, amongst others, Brodsky Quartet, Swedish Radio Symphony Orchestra and Burt Bacharach. Dir, S Bank Centre Meltdown, 1995. Presenter, TV series, Spectacle, 2008–. Recordings include: *albums:* My Aim is True, 1977; This Year's Model, 1978; Armed Forces, 1979; Trust, 1981; Almost Blue, 1981; Imperial Bedroom, 1982; Punch the Clock, 1983; Blood and Chocolate, 1986; Spike, 1989; Mighty Like the Rose, 1991; (with Brodsky Quartet) The Juliet Letters, 1993; Brutal Youth, 1994; Extreme Honey, 1997; Painted from Memory, 1998; (with Anne Sofie von Otter) For the Stars, 2001; When I Was Cruel, 2002; North, 2003; The Delivery Man, 2004; Il Sogno, 2004; Momofuku, 2008; Secret, Profane and Sugarcane, 2009; National Ransom, 2010; The Return of the Spectacular Spinning Songbook, 2011; (with The Roots) Wise Up Ghost, 2013; *singles:* Alison, 1977; Watching the Detectives, 1977; (I Don't Want to Go to) Chelsea, 1978; Oliver's Army, 1979; Accidents Will Happen, 1979; Good Year for the Roses, 1981; Everyday I Write the Book, 1983; Pills and Soap, 1983; The People's Limousine, 1985; Little Atoms, 1996; She, 1999.

McMANUS, Francis Joseph; solicitor; *b* 16 Aug. 1942; *s* of Patrick and Celia McManus; *m* 1971, Carmel V. Doherty, Lisnaskea, Co. Fermanagh; two *s* one *d*. *Educ:* St Michael's, Enniskillen; Queen's University, Belfast. BA 1965; Diploma in Education, 1966. Subsequently a Teacher. MP (Unity) Fermanagh and S Tyrone, 1970–Feb. 1974. Founder Mem. and Co-Chm., Irish Independence Party, 1977. *Address:* Lissadell, 40 Drumlin Heights, Enniskillen, Co. Fermanagh, N Ireland BT74 7NR. *T:* (028) 6632 3401.

McMANUS, Prof. (Ian) Christopher, PhD, MD; FRCP, FRCPEd, FMedSci; Professor of Psychology and Medical Education, University College London, since 1997; *b* 1 March 1951; *s* of Robert Victor McManus and June McManus; *m* 2007, Christine Pleines; one *s* two *d*. *Educ:* Harrow Co. Grammar Sch.; Christ's Coll., Cambridge (BA 1972, MA 1977; PhD 1979); Univ. of Birmingham (MB ChB 1975); Univ. of London (MD 1985). FRCP 1998; FRCPEd 2007. University of London: Lectr in Psychol. as Applied to Medicine, Dept of Psychol., Bedford Coll., then UCL, and Dept of Psychiatry, St Mary's Hosp. Med. Sch., 1979–88; Sen. Lectr in Psychol. as Applied to Medicine, Dept of Psychol., UCL, and Dept of Psychiatry, St Mary's Hosp. Med. Sch., ICSTM, 1988–93; Prof. of Psychol., Dept of Psychol., UCL, and Dept of Psychiatry, ICSM at St Mary's, 1993–97. Examr and Educnl Advr, MRCP(UK), 1999–. Vis. Prof., Univ. of Vienna, 2012. Lectures: C. S. Myers, BPsS, 2005; G. J. Burton, Applied Vision Assoc., 2009; Lord Cohen, ASME, 2011. Pres., Psychol. Section, British Assoc., 2002. Fellow, Internat. Assoc. Empirical Aesthetics, 2000. Ed., Laterality, 1996–. FMedSci 2007. Hon. Fellow, Acad. of Medical Educators, 2014. Ig Nobel Prize, 2002. *Publications:* Psychology in Medicine, 1992; (ed jtly) Cambridge Handbook of Psychology, Health and Medicine, 1997, 2nd edn 2007; Right Hand, Left Hand, 2002 (Wellcome Trust Prize, 1999; Aventis Prize, 2003); The Right Hand and the Left Hand of History, 2010. *Recreations:* all things aesthetic, all things Italian. *Address:* Department of Psychology, University College London, Gower Street, WC1E 6BT. *T:* (020) 7679 5390, *Fax:* (020) 7436 4276. *E:* i.mcmanus@ucl.ac.uk.

McMANUS, Dr James John; human rights consultant, since 1988; Professor of Criminal Justice, Glasgow Caledonian University, 2004–09; *b* 23 June 1950; *s* of David McManus and Alice McManus (*née* Vallely); *m* 1974, Catherine MacKellaig; one *s* four *d*. *Educ:* Our Lady's High Sch., Motherwell; Univ. of Edinburgh (LLB); Univ. of Dundee (PhD 1985). Lectr, UC, Cardiff, 1972–74; Lectr, 1974–76, Sen. Lectr, 1976–2004, Univ. of Dundee. Comr, Scottish Prisons Complaints Commn, 1994–99; Chm., Parole Bd for Scotland, 2000–06; Vice Convenor, Risk Mgt Authy, 2005–13. Expert Advr, 1992–2009, Mem., 2009–, European Cttee for Prevention of Torture. *Publications:* Lay Justice, 1992; Prisons, Prisoners and the Law, 1994. *Recreation:* golf. *Address:* Heathbank, Coupar Angus Road, Blairgowrie PH10 6JY.

McMANUS, John Andrew; HM Diplomatic Service; Administrator, British Indian Ocean Territory, 2011–13; *b* 20 May 1955; *s* of Andrew McManus and Winifred (*née* Hazzard). *Educ:* Univ. of Sussex (BA Econs and Europ. Studies 1977). Joined FCO, 1977; Vice-Consul, Algiers, 1984–85; Commercial Attaché, Moscow, 1988–91; Presidency Co-ordinator, UK Perm. Repn to EU, Brussels, 1992; First Sec., Press and Public Affairs, Berne, 1993–97; Hd of Political Section, Brussels, 2000–04; Ambassador to Guinea, 2004–08; Dep. Dir, 2009–10, Acting Dir, 2010–11, Shanghai Expo 2010. *Recreations:* athletics, food, languages. *Address:* c/o Foreign and Commonwealth Office, King Charles Street, SW1A 2AH. *E:* john_mcmanus1066@hotmail.com.

McMANUS, Jonathan Richard; QC 1999; *b* 15 Sept. 1958; *s* of Frank Rostron McManus and Benita Ann McManus. *Educ:* Neale Wade Comprehensive, March; Downing Coll., Cambridge (MA). Called to the Bar, Middle Temple, 1982; in practice as barrister, 4–5 Gray's Inn, 1983–2013. *Publications:* Education and the Courts, 1998, 3rd edn 2012; contrib. Economic, Social and Cultural Rights: their implementation, in United Kingdom Law, ed Burchill, Harris and Owers, 1999; (consultant ed) Judicial Review: principles and procedures, 2013. *Recreations:* music, travel, photography. *Address:* 262 Liverpool Road, Islington, N1 1LG.

McMANUS, Prof. Richard James, PhD; FRCGP; Professor of Primary Care Research, University of Oxford, since 2012; Fellow, Green Templeton College, Oxford, since 2012; *b* London, 17 April 1967; *s* of Peter and Margaret S. S. McManus; *m* 1993, Dr Lucy P. Caswell; two *d*. *Educ:* St Mary's Coll., Southampton; Peter Symonds Coll., Winchester; St Mary's Hosp. Med. Sch., Univ. of London (BSc Hons Biol and Clin. Scis 1990; MB BS 1991); Univ. of Birmingham (MSc 2000; PhD 2004). MRCGP 1997, FRCGP 2006. Jun. med. posts, St Mary's Hosp., London, 1991–94, Glos, 1994–97; jun. res. posts, 1997–2009, Prof. of Primary Care, 2009–11, Univ. of Birmingham; General Practitioner (part-time): Greenridge Surgery, Birmingham, 1999–2012; The Surgery, Beaumont St, Oxford, 2013–. *Publications:* contribs to jls incl. Lancet, Jl Amer. Med. Assoc., BMJ, British Jl Gen. Practice. *Recreations:* music, both playing (trombone and guitar) and listening, cycling. *Address:* Nuffield Department of Primary Care Health Sciences, University of Oxford, Radcliffe Observatory Quarter, Woodstock Road, Oxford OX2 6GG.

McMASTER, Sir Brian (John), Kt 2003; CBE 1987; Director, Edinburgh International Festival, 1991–2006. International Artists' Dept, EMI Ltd, 1968–73; Controller of Opera Planning, ENO, 1973–76; Gen. Administrator, subseq. Man. Dir, WNO, 1976–91; Artistic Dir, Vancouver Opera, 1984–89. *Address:* 13/5 James Court, Lawnmarket, Edinburgh EH1 2PB.

McMASTER, Hughan James Michael; Chief Architect and Director of Works, Home Office, 1980–87, retired; *b* 27 July 1927; *s* of William James Michael and Emly McMaster; *m* 1950; one *s* two *d*. *Educ:* Christ's Coll., Finchley; Regent Street Polytechnic (DipArch). ARIBA 1951. Served RAF, India and Far East, 1946–48. Joined Civil Service, 1961; Navy Works, 1961–69; Whitehall Development Gp, Directorate of Home Estate Management and Directorate of Civil Accommodation, 1969–76; Defence Works (PE and Overseas), 1976–80. *Recreations:* gardening, reading, theatre, music.

McMASTER, Prof. Paul; Professor of Hepatobiliary Surgery and Transplantation, and Consultant Surgeon, Queen Elizabeth Hospital, University of Birmingham, 1980–2005; *b* 4 Jan. 1943; *s* of Dr James McMaster and Sarah Jane McMaster (*née* Lynn); *m* 1969, Helen Ruth Bryce; two *s* one *d*. *Educ:* Liverpool Coll.; Univ. of Liverpool (MB ChB 1966; ChM 1979); MA Cantab 1978. FRCS 1971. House Surgeon, subseq. House Physician, Liverpool Royal Infirmary, Univ. of Liverpool, 1966–67; SHO in Urology and Transplantation, RPMS, Hammersmith Hosp., 1967–68; Registrar in Surgery, Addenbrooke's Hosp., 1969–72; Sen. Registrar and Res. Fellow, 1972–76, Sen. Lectr in Surgery, 1976–80, Univ. Dept of Surgery, Addenbrooke's Hosp., Cambridge Univ. Visiting Professor: Univs of Rome, Genoa, Cairo, Concepción; RACS Foundn, 1998. FICS. *Publications:* numerous articles on immuno suppression, liver transplantation, develt of laparoscopic and hepatobiliary surgery, advances in major hepatic and biliary surgery. *Recreations:* gardening, sailing, reading. *Address:* c/o Liver Unit, Queen Elizabeth Hospital, Edgbaston, Birmingham B15 2TH.

McMASTER, Peter, CB 1991; Member, Lord Chancellor's Panel of Independent Inspectors, 1991–2001; *b* 22 Nov. 1931; *s* of Peter McMaster and Ada Nellie (*née* Williams); *m* 1955, Catherine Ann Rosborough; one *s* one *d*. *Educ:* Kelvinside Academy, Glasgow; RMA Sandhurst; RMCS Shrivenham. BScEng London. Called to the Bar, Middle Temple, 1969. Commissioned into Royal Engineers, 1952; served Middle and Far East; retired (major), 1970; joined Civil Service, 1970; W Midland Region, Ordnance Survey, 1970–72; Caribbean Region, Directorate of Overseas Survey, 1972–74; Headquarters, 1974–91, Dir Gen., 1985–91, Ordnance Survey. Vis. Prof., Kingston Polytechnic, subseq. Kingston Univ., 1991–93. Member Council: BCS, 1983–92; RGS, 1990–93. FIIM 1990. *Recreations:* travel, walking, chess. *Address:* Hillhead, Stratton Road, Winchester, Hampshire SO23 0JQ. *T:* (01962) 862684.
See also Peter McMaster.

McMASTER, Peter; QC 2008; *b* Dhekelia, Cyprus, 10 Jan. 1959; *s* of Peter McMaster, *qv*; *m* 1992, Natalie Ann Adams; three *s*. *Educ:* North Bromsgrove High Sch.; Winchester Coll.; King's Coll. London (LLB 1980). Called to the Bar, Middle Temple, 1981. *Recreations:* reading, walking, shooting, cooking.

McMEIKAN, Kennedy; Chief Executive, Brakes Group, since 2013; *b* Dumfries, 13 May 1965; *s* of Robert Allan Henry McMeikan and Jessie Ann McMeikan; three *s* two *d*; *m* 2012, Melanie Burton. *Educ:* Stranraer Acad. Joined RN, 1981, Electronic Warfare Operator, 1981–86; Retail Manager, Sears plc, 1986–90; Tesco plc, 1990–2004: Store Manager, then Stores Dir, later CEO, Europa Foods; CEO, Tesco Japan; Retail Dir, J Sainsbury plc, 2004–08; Chief Exec., Greggs plc, 2008–13. Prince of Wales' Ambassador for the NE, 2010–12; Chm., NE, CBI, 2010–12. Mem., Policy Cttee, Inst. of Grocery Distribution, 2013–. *Recreations:* family life, ski-ing, golf, music, EGLST open water swimming. *Address:* Brakes Group, Tower House, 10 Southampton Street, WC2E 7HA.

McMENAMIN, Frances Jane, (Mrs Ian McCarry); QC (Scot.) 1998; *b* 21 May 1951; *d* of Francis and Agnes McMenamin; *m* 1991, Ian McCarry. *Educ:* Our Lady of Lourdes Primary Sch., Glasgow; Notre Dame High Sch., Glasgow; Strathclyde Univ. (BA 1971; LLB 1974).

Mgt trainee, GKN Ltd, 1971–72. Admitted Solicitor, 1976; admitted to Faculty of Advocates, 1985. Legal Apprentice, Hughes, Dowdall & Co., Solicitors, 1974–76; Procurator Fiscal Depute, 1976–84; advocate specialising in criminal law, 1985–; Temp. Sheriff, 1991–97; Advocate Depute, 1997–2000. Member: Adv. Gp on rape and other sexual offences, Scottish Law Commn, 2005–06; Scottish Criminal Cases Review Commn, 2009–; Lord Justice Gen.'s Criminal Courts Rules Council, 2011–14, 2015–; Rt Hon. Lord Bonomy's post-corroboration rev. gp, 2014–; Direct Access Gp, 2015–, Professional Standards Cttee, 2015–, Faculty of Advocates. Vis. Lectr, Scottish Police Coll., Tulliallan Castle, 1991–. Mem., Law Sch. Adv. Panel, 2002–, Mem. of Ct, 2005–09, Univ. of Strathclyde. Dir, Faculty Services Ltd, 2003–07. Mem., Merchants' House of Glasgow, 2015–. DUniv Strathclyde, 2009. *Recreations:* spending time with husband, family and friends, golf, exercise classes, reading, travelling. *Address:* (home) 59 Hamilton Drive, Glasgow G12 8DP. *T:* (0141) 339 0519; Advocates' Library, Parliament House, Parliament Square, Edinburgh EH1 1RF. *T:* (0131) 226 5071. *Club:* Hole in the Head (Edinburgh).

McMICHAEL, Sir Andrew (James), Kt 2008; FRS 1992; Director, 1998–2000, Hon. Director, 2000–10, Medical Research Council Human Immunology Unit, John Radcliffe Hospital, Oxford; Professor of Molecular Medicine and Director, Weatherall Institute of Molecular Medicine, Oxford University, 2000–12; Fellow of Corpus Christi College, Oxford, 2000–12; *b* 8 Nov. 1943; *s* of Sir John McMichael, FRS and late Sybil McMichael; *m* 1968, Kathryn Elizabeth Cross; two *s* one *d*. *Educ:* St Paul's Sch., London; Gonville and Caius Coll., Cambridge (MA; BChir 1968; MB 1969); St Mary's Hosp. Med. Sch., London. PhD 1974; MRCP 1971; FRCP 1985. House Physician, St Mary's Hosp., Royal Northern Hosp., Hammersmith Hosp. and Brompton Hosp., 1968–71; MRC Jun. Res. Fellow, National Inst. for Med. Res., 1971–74; MRC Travelling Fellow, Stanford Univ. Med. Sch., 1974–76; Oxford University: Wellcome Sen. Clin. Fellow, Nuffield Depts of Medicine and Surgery, 1977–79; University Lectr in Medicine and Hon. Consultant Physician, 1979–82; MRC Clinical Res. Prof. of Immunology, 1982–98; Prof. of Immunology, 1999–2000; Fellow, Trinity Coll., 1983–2000. Member: Adv. Bd, Beit Meml Trust, 1984–; MRC AIDS Steering Cttee, 1988–94; Res. Grants Council, Hong Kong, 1990–99; Council, Royal Soc., 1998–99. Founder FMedSci 1998. *Publications:* (ed with J. W. Fabre) Monoclonal Antibodies in Clinical Medicine, 1982; articles on genetic control of human immune response, antiviral immunity and AIDS. *Recreation:* walking and ski-ing in France.

MACMILLAN, family name of **Earl of Stockton**.

MACMILLAN OF OVENDEN, Viscount; Daniel Maurice Alan Macmillan; *b* 9 Oct. 1974; *s* and *heir* of Earl of Stockton, *qv*. Dir, Project Zoltar Ltd, 2002–. *Publications:* (with Kieron Livingstone) Zoltan the Magnificent: 33, 2013.

McMILLAN, Alan Austen, CB 1986; Solicitor to the Secretary of State for Scotland, 1984–87; *b* 19 Jan. 1926; *s* of Allan McMillan and Mabel (*née* Austin); *m* 1949, Margaret Moncur; two *s* two *d*. *Educ:* Ayr Acad.; Glasgow Univ. Served in Army, 1944–47. Qualified Solicitor in Scotland, 1949; Legal Assistant, Ayr Town Council, 1949–55; Scottish Office: Legal Assistant, 1955–62; Sen. Legal Assistant, 1962–68; Asst Solicitor, 1968–82, seconded to Cabinet Office Constitution Unit, 1977–78; Dep. Solicitor, 1982–84. *Recreations:* reading, music, theatre.

McMILLAN, David Loch, FRAeS, FCILT; Director General, European Organisation for the Safety of Air Navigation (EUROCONTROL), 2008–12; *b* 16 Sept. 1954; *s* of David and May McMillan; *m* 1977, Frances Beedham; one *s* two *d*. *Educ:* Royal High Sch., Edinburgh; Univ. of Edinburgh (MA French and Spanish). FCO, 1976; Rabat, 1978; Harare, 1980; Principal, Dept of Transport, 1984–87; First Sec. (Transport), Washington, 1987–92; Hd, Information, Dept of Transport, 1993–97; Hd, Air Traffic Div., DETR, 1997–2001; Dir, Rail Restructuring, DETR, 2001–02; Dir, Strategy and Delivery, 2002–04, Dir Gen., Civil Aviation, 2004–07, DfT. Non-exec. Dir, Gatwick Airport Ltd, 2013–. Mem., Bd of Govs, Flight Safety Foundn, 2008– (Chm., 2012–); Trustee: Bd of Govs, British Sch. of Brussels, 2009–12; BAA Communities Trust, 2008–13 (Chm., 2012–13). FRAeS 2008; FCILT 2010. Médaille de l'Aéronautique (France), 2010. *Recreations:* travel, reading, cricket.

MacMILLAN, Prof. David W. C., PhD; FRS 2012; James S. McDonnell Distinguished University Professor of Chemistry, since 2011, Director, Merck Center for Catalysis, since 2006, and Chair, Department of Chemistry, since 2010, Princeton University; *b* Bellshill, Scotland, 1968. *Educ:* Univ. of Glasgow (BSc Chem. 1991); Univ. of Calif, Irvine (PhD 1996). Postdoctoral Res. Fellow, Harvard Univ., 1996–98; res. at Univ. of Calif, Berkeley, 1998–2000; Dept of Chem., CIT, 2000–06, Earle C. Anthony Prof. of Chem., 2004–06; A. Barton Hepburn Prof. of Chem., Princeton Univ., 2006. Sloan Fellow, 2002. Scientific Consultant: Abbott Res. Labs, 2000–; Johnson & Johnson, 2000–; Bayer Pharmaceuticals, 2001–; Merck Res. Labs, 2001–; Amgen Pharmaceuticals, 2002–; Gilead Pharmaceuticals, 2003–; Constellation Pharmaceuticals, 2009–. Ed.-in-Chief and Mem., Editl Adv. Bd, Chem. Sci. jl, 2010–; Member, Editorial Advisory Board: Tetrahedron & Tetrahedron Letters, 2001–; Chem. Communications, 2004–; Chem., an Asian jl, 2005–; Advanced Synthesis & Catalysis, 2009–. Mem., Amer. Acad. Arts and Scis, 2012. Corday-Morgan Medal, RSC, 2005; Thieme-IUPAC Prize in Organic Synthesis, 2006; Mukaiyama Award, Soc. of Synthetic Organic Chem., Japan, 2007; Harrison Howe Award, Amer. Chem. Soc., 2014. *Publications:* contribs to Jl Amer. Chem. Soc. *Address:* Princeton University, Frick Laboratory, Washington Road, Princeton, NJ 08544, USA.

MACMILLAN, Deborah Millicent, (Lady Macmillan); artist; *b* Boonah, Qld, 1 July 1944; *d* of Dr Dudley Williams and Nina Deborah (*née* Darvall); *m* 1st, 1966, Denis Allard (marr. diss. 1973); 2nd, 1974, Sir Kenneth Macmillan (*d* 1992); one *d*. *Educ:* Wenona, N Sydney; Nat. Art Sch., E Sydney (Painting and Sculpture). Member: Bd, Royal Opera House, 1993–96; Exec. Cttee, Royal Acad. Dancing, 1994–; Council, Arts Council of England, 1996–98 (Chm., Dance Panel, 1996–98); Chm., Friends of Covent Gdn, 1995–96. Mem., Nat. Cttee, Houston Ballet, 1993–; Hon. Mem. Bd, American Ballet Theatre, 1993–. Gov., Nat. Youth Dance Trust, 1999–2004; Trustee, Wimbledon Coll. (formerly Sch.) of Art, 2000–08. Custodian, Sir Kenneth Macmillan's choreography, 1992–. Man. Dir, KM Ballet Prodns. Partner, Avlaki, organic olive oils. *Exhibitions: solo shows:* Charlotte Lampard Gall., 1984; Turtle Key Arts Centre, 1992, 1995; Chelsea Arts Club, 1999; Gall. 27 Cork St, 2005; Water and Light Gall., 2005; oils and watercolours, Gall. 27 Cork St, 2011; *group shows:* Camden Arts Centre, 1990; Royal Acad. Summer Exhibn, 1990; Accrochage, Fischer Fine Art, 1990; Contemporary Art Soc. Mkt, 1990; Drawing Show, Thumb Gall., 1990; Art for Equality, ICA, 1991; Leicestershire Collection, 1992; Gillian Jason Contemporary Portraits Real and Imagined, 1993; Jason Rhodes Gp Show, 1995; Glyndebourne Fest. Opera, 1997–2003; Glyndebourne Ten for Ten Anniv. exhibn, 2004. *Recreations:* gardening, any displacement activity. *Address:* c/o Simpson Fox, 52 Shaftesbury Avenue, W1D 6LP. *Club:* Chelsea Arts.

MACMILLAN, Duncan; *see* Macmillan, J. D.

MACMILLAN, Very Rev. Gilleasbuig Iain, KCVO 2014 (CVO 1999); FRSE; Minister of St Giles', The High Kirk of Edinburgh, 1973–2013; Chaplain to the Queen in Scotland, 1979–2014; Dean of the Order of the Thistle, 1989–2014; an Extra Chaplain to the Queen in Scotland, since 2014; *b* 21 Dec. 1942; *s* of Rev. Kenneth M. Macmillan and Mrs Mary Macmillan; *m* 1965, Maureen Stewart Thomson; one *d*. *Educ:* Oban High School; Univ. of Edinburgh. MA, BD. Asst Minister, St Michael's Parish, Linlithgow, 1967–69; Minister of Portree Parish, Isle of Skye, 1969–73. Extra Chaplain to the Queen in Scotland, 1978–79. Hon. Chaplain: Royal Scottish Academy, 1973–; Royal Coll. of Surgeons of Edinburgh, 1973–2014; Soc. of High Constables of City of Edinburgh, 1973–2014. FRSE 2005. Hon. FRCSE 1998. Hon. DD: Alma Coll., 1997; St Andrews, 2003; Dr *hc* Edinburgh, 1998. *Publications:* A Workable Belief, 1993; Understanding Christianity, 2004. *Address:* 207 Dalkeith Road, Edinburgh EH16 5DS. *T:* (0131) 667 5732. *Club:* New (Edinburgh).

McMILLAN, Hamilton; *see* McMillan, N. H.

MACMILLAN, Iain Alexander, CBE 1978; LLD; Sheriff of South Strathclyde, Dumfries and Galloway at Hamilton, 1981–92; Temporary Sheriff, 1992–94; *b* 14 Nov. 1923; *s* of John and Eva Macmillan; *m* 1954, Edith Janet (*née* MacAulay); two *s* one *d*. *Educ:* Oban High Sch.; Glasgow Univ. (BL). Served war, RAF, France, Germany, India, 1944–47. Glasgow Univ., 1947–50. Subseq. law practice; Sen. Partner, J. & J. Sturrock & Co., Kilmarnock, 1952–81. Law Society of Scotland: Mem. Council, 1964–79; Pres., 1976–77. Pres., Temp. Sheriffs' Assoc., 1993–94. Chairman: Lanarkshire Br., Scottish Assoc. for Study of Delinquency, 1986–92; Victim Support, E Ayrshire, 1998–2001. Trustee, Glasgow Art Club, 2003–. Hon. LLD Aberdeen, 1975. *Publications:* I Had It From My Father, 2011. *Recreation:* music (listening to). *Address:* 2 Castle Drive, Kilmarnock KA3 1TN. *T:* (01563) 525864.

McMILLAN, Sir Iain (Macleod), Kt 2015; CBE 2003; Director, CBI Scotland, 1995–2014 (Assistant Director, 1993–95); *b* 25 April 1951; *s* of late William Catterall McMillan and Helen Macleod McMillan (*née* Paterson); *m* 1975, Giuseppina Silvana Pellegrini; three *s*. *Educ:* Bearsden Acad., Glasgow. AIB 1976, FCIB 1991; AIB (Scot) 1981, FCIBS 1997; FAIA 2004. Bank officer and various mgt and sen. mgt posts, TSB Gp plc, 1970–93; Liaison Officer for Scotland and Northern England, Royal Jubilee and Prince's Trusts, 1984–85 (on secondment). Board Member: Scottish Qualifications Authy, 1997–2006 (Vice Chm., 2004–06); Young Enterprise Scotland, 1999–2003; Scottish N Amer. Business Council, 1999– (Chm., 2009–); British Amer. Business Council, 2010– (Mem., Exec. Cttee, 2010–); Chm., Scottish Business Educn Coalition, 2001–07; Member: Scottish Adv. Bd, Equal Opportunities Commn, 1995–2001; Cttee of Review into Careers Service, Scottish Exec., 1999–2000; Adv. Bd, Scottish Co-investment Fund, 2003–08; Adv. Bd, Scottish Enterprise Investments, 2008–10; Commn on Scottish Devolution, 2008–09; Literacy Commn, 2008–10; Standing Literacy Commn, 2011–15; Chm., Ind. Commn for Competitive and Fair Taxation in Scotland, 2015–. Non-exec. Dir, Special Health Bd, Scottish Ambulance Service, 2000–08. Chm., Adv. Bd, Business Sch. (formerly Grad. Sch. of Business), Univ. of Strathclyde, 2005–. Trustee: Industrial Mission Trust, 2000–13 (Chm., 2008–13); Teaching Awards Trust, 2007–13; Carnegie Trust for Univs of Scotland, 2010–; Grangemouth Spitfire Meml Trust, 2012–15; Chm., Work Place Chaplaincy Scotland, 2014–. Mem., Skillforce Scottish Adv. Cttee, 2015–; mem. or former mem., various adv. bodies and public policy cttees and working gps in Scotland. FRSA 1994; CCMI 2002; FSQA 2007. Hon. Air Cdre, 602 (City of Glasgow) Sqdn, RAuxAF, 2009–; Selected Air Mem., Lowland Reserve Forces' and Cadets' Assoc., 2010–. Freeman, City of Glasgow, 2011. *Recreations:* walking, reading. *Club:* Royal Air Force.

MacMILLAN, Sir James (Loy), Kt 2015: CBE 2004; PhD; composer and conductor; Professor of Theology, Imagination and the Arts, University of St Andrews, since 2015; Professor, Royal Conservatoire of Scotland, since 2014; *b* 16 July 1959; *s* of James MacMillan and Ellen MacMillan (*née* Loy); *m* 1983, Lynne Frew; one *s* two *d*. *Educ:* Edinburgh Univ. (BMus); Durham Univ. (PhD 1987). Lectr, Univ. of Manchester, 1986–88; Featured Composer: Musica Nova, Glasgow, 1990; Huddersfield Contemp. Music Fest., 1991; Edinburgh Fest., 1993; Raising Sparks Fest., S Bank and Barbican, 1997; Artistic Dir, Philharmonia, Music of Today, 1992–2002; composer/conductor, BBC Philharmonic, 2000–09; Principal Guest Conductor, Netherlands Radio Kamer Filharmonie, 2010–13. Founder and Artistic Dir, Cumnock Tryst, music festival, 2014–. FRSAMD 1996; FRNCM 2001; FRSCM 2001; FRSE 2007. Hon. FRIAS 1997. DUniv: Paisley, 1995; Open, 2001; Hon. DLitt: Strathclyde, 1996; UMIST, 2001; Hon. DMus: St Andrews, 2001; Glasgow, 2001; Abertay Dundee, 2004; Edinburgh, 2005; RSAMD, 2005; Newman Coll., Leicester, 2006; Durham, 2007; RCM, 2011. Gramophone Award, 1993; Classic CD Award, 1994; British Classical Music Award, 2006; British Composer Award, 2008; Ivor Novello Classical Music Award, 2009; Royal Medal, RSE, 2010; Assoc. of British Orchestras' Award, 2011. *Compositions* include: Busquéda (music theatre), 1988; Tryst (for orch.), 1989; The Berserking (piano concerto no 1), 1990; Confession of Isobel Gowdie (for orch.), 1990; Veni, Veni Emmanuel (percussion concerto), 1992; Visitatio Sepulchri (one-act opera), 1993; Seven Last Words (chorus and strings), 1994; Ines de Castro (opera), 1996; The World's Ransoming (concerto for cor anglais), 1996; 'Cello Concerto, 1996; Ninian (clarinet concerto), 1997; 14 Little Pictures (for piano trio), 1997; Vigil (symphony), 1997; Raising Sparks (for mezzo-sop. and ensemble), 1997; Quickening (for chorus, orch., boys' choir and four soloists), 1999; Symphony no 2, 1999; Mass (chorus and organ), 2000; Parthenogenesis (for soprano, baritone, actress and small ensemble), 2000; A Deep but Dazzling Darkness (for solo violin, ensemble and tape), 2002; O Bone Jesu (a cappella chorus), 2002; Symphony no 3, 2003; Piano Concerto No. 2, 2004; A Scotch Bestiary (for organ and orch.), 2004; Tenebrae Responsaries (a cappella chorus), 2006; Stomp (with Fate and Elvira) (concert overture for orch.), 2006; From Ayrshire (for violin and orch.), 2006; The Sacrifice (opera), 2007 (Royal Philharmonic Soc. Award, 2008); St John Passion (for baritone, chorus and orch.), 2008; Violin Concerto, 2009; Oboe Concerto, 2010; Clemency (chamber opera), 2011; Woman of the Apocalypse (full orch.), 2011–12; Gloria, 2012; Canite Tuba (brass band), 2012; Since it was the day of preparation… (bass solo, choir and 5 piece ensemble), 2012; Cecilia Virgo (a cappella chorus), 2012; He Rose (solo cello), 2012; St Luke Passion (two choirs, orch. and organ), 2013; Death of Oscar (orch.), 2013; Viola Concerto, 2014; Percussion Concerto No 2, 2014; A Rumoured Seed (a cappella chorus); Seven Angels (chorus and ensemble), 2014; Symphony No. 4 (for orch.), 2014–15. *Address:* c/o Boosey & Hawkes Music Publishers Ltd, Aldwych House, 71–91 Aldwych, WC2B 4HN. *T:* (020) 7054 7200.

MACMILLAN, Prof. (John) Duncan, PhD; FRSE; Curator, Talbot Rice Gallery, 1979–2004, and Professor of History of Scottish Art, 1994–2001, now Emeritus, University of Edinburgh; *b* 7 March 1939; *s* of late William Miller Macmillan and Mona Constance Mary Tweedie; *m* 1971, Vivien Rosemary Hinkley; two *d*. *Educ:* Gordonstoun Sch.; St Andrews Univ. (MA Hons 1961); Courtauld Inst., London (Dip. Hist. of Art 1964); Edinburgh Univ. (PhD 1974). Lectr, 1964–81, Curator of Univ. Collections, 1987–2002, Edinburgh Univ. Curator, RSE, 2008–12. Art critic: The Scotsman, 1994–2000, 2002–; Business am, 2000–02. Visiting Fellow: Yale Centre for British Art, 1991; Japan Soc. for Promotion of Science, 1995. Convener, Scottish Univ. Museums Gp, 1992–99; Chm., Edinburgh Galls Assoc., 1995–98; Vice-Chm., European Union Cultural Forum; Chm., Torvean Project Steering Gp, 1997–2000; Member: Council, Edinburgh Fest. Soc., 1991–97; Cttee, Univ. Museums Gp, 1992–99; Heritage Unit Adv. Bd, Robert Gordon Univ.; comité consultatif, French Inst., Edinburgh, 1997–. Member Editorial Board: Scotlands, 1994–98; British Art Jl, 1999–; Dundee Univ. Press, 2005–08. Hon. Keeper of Portraits, RCSE. Hon. RSA; FRSA; FRSE 2005 (Henry Duncan Prize, 2004). Hon. LLD Dundee, 2004. Andrew Fletcher of Saltoun Prize, Saltire Soc., 2005. *Publications:* (jtly) Miró in America, 1983; Painting in Scotland: the Golden Age 1707–1843, 1986; Scottish Art 1460–1990, 1990 (Scottish Book of the Year, Saltire Soc., 1992), 2nd edn, Scottish Art 1460–2000, 2000; Symbols of Survival: the art of Will Maclean, 1992 (Scottish Arts Council Book Award, 1993), 2nd edn 2002; The Paintings of Steven Campbell: the story so far, 1993; Scottish Art in the Twentieth Century, 1994 (Scottish Arts Council Book Award, 1995), 2nd edn as Scottish Art in the Twentieth Century: 1890–2001, 2001; (jtly) Peter Brandes: stained glass, 1994; (jtly) Eugenio Carmi, 1996;

Elizabeth Blackadder, 1999; (with Tom Hewlett) F. C. B. Cadell, 2011; Victoria Crowe, 2012; Scotland's Shrine: the Scottish National War Memorial, 2014; numerous exhibn catalogues, articles, etc. *Recreations:* walking, landscape photography. *Address:* 20 Nelson Street, Edinburgh EH3 6LJ. *T:* (0131) 556 7100; Wester Balnagrantach, Glen Urquhart, Inverness-shire. *T:* (01456) 450727.

MACMILLAN, John Kenneth; Regional Employment Judge (formerly Regional Chairman, Industrial, later Employment Tribunals), Nottingham, 1997–2012; fee-paid Employment Judge, East Midlands Region, since 2012; *b* 8 July 1946; *s* of late Kenneth Lionel Macmillan, OBE and Marjorie Ethel Macmillan; *m* 1st, 1972, Mary Lister (marr. diss.); 2nd, 1977, Dawn Nelson (marr. diss.); one *d*; 3rd, 1995, Pauline Anne Swain; two step *d*. *Educ:* Carlton le Willows Grammar Sch., Nottingham. Admitted Solicitor, 1970; Asst Solicitor, 1970, Litigation Partner, 1971–84, Haden and Stretton, Solicitors. Pt-time Chm., 1981–87, full-time Chm., 1987–97, Industrial Tribunals, Birmingham; Mem., President's Trng Panel, 1992–2000. Ed., Employment Tribunals Members Handbook, 1999–2006; Principal Consulting Ed., Blackstone's Employment Law Practice, 2007– (a Consulting Ed., 2006–07). Co. Sec., Stafford Rangers FC Ltd, 2014–. Hon. Sec., RSNC, 1992–2003. Trustee, Staffs Wildlife Trust, 1982–99, 2005–09; Chm., Colton Local Nature Reserve, 2014–. *Publications:* (contrib.) Sweet & Maxwell's Employment Court Practice, 2007; Blackstone's Guide to the Employment Tribunals Rules 2013 and the Fees Order, 2013. *Recreations:* bird watching, theatre, gardening, fly fishing, philosophy, non-league football. *Address:* Employment Tribunals, Nottingham Justice Centre, Carrington Street, Nottingham NG2 1EE.

MacMILLAN, Lt-Gen. Sir John Richard Alexander, KCB 1988; CBE 1978 (OBE 1973); fruit farmer; General Officer Commanding Scotland and Governor of Edinburgh Castle, 1988–91; *b* 8 Feb. 1932; *m* 1964, Belinda Lumley Webb; one *s* two *d*. *Educ:* Trinity Coll., Cambridge (BA 1953; MA 1958); rcds, psc. Commnd Argyll and Sutherland Highlanders, 2nd Lieut, 1952; GSO2 (Ops Int. Trng), Trucial Oman Scouts, 1963–64; BM, HQ 24 Inf. Bde, 1967–69; Chief Recruiting and Liaison Staff, Scotland, 1970; CO, 1st Bn The Gordon Highlanders, 1971–73; GSO1 (DS), Staff Coll., 1973–75; Col GS, Mil. Ops 4, 1975–76; Brig., 1976; Bde Comd, 39 Inf. Bde, 1977–78; RCDS 1979; COS, 1 (Br.) Corps, 1980–82; Maj.-Gen., 1982; GOC Eastern Dist, 1982–84; ACGS, MoD, 1984–87; Lt-Gen., 1988. Col, The Gordon Highlanders, 1978–86; Col Comdt, Scottish Div., 1986–91; Hon. Col, Aberdeen Univ. OTC, 1987–97. Chm. Exec Cttee, Scottish Conservation Projects Trust, 1992–98; Chairman: Erskine Hosp. (formerly Princess Louise Scottish Hosp.), 1995–2000; HM Comrs for Queen Victoria Sch., Dunblane, 2000–03. DL Stirling and Falkirk, 1998–2007. *Address:* Boghall Farm, Thornhill, Stirling FK8 3QD.

MacMILLAN, Prof. Margaret Olwen, OC 2005; DPhil; Warden, St Antony's College, Oxford, since 2007; Professor of International History, University of Oxford, since 2007; *b* 23 Dec. 1943; *d* of Robert and Eluned MacMillan. *Educ:* Univ. of Toronto (BA Hons Mod. Hist. 1966); St Hilda's Coll., Oxford (BPhil Pols 1968; Hon. Fellow, 2007); St Antony's Coll., Oxford (DPhil 1974; Hon. Fellow, 2003). Prof. of Hist., 1975–2002, Chair, Hist. Dept, 1987–92, Ryerson Univ.; University of Toronto: Fellow, 1999–, Provost, 2002–07, Trinity Coll.; Prof. of Hist., 2003–07; Sen. Fellow, Massey Coll., 2003; Hon. Fellow, Trinity Coll., 2009. Co-Editor (pt-time), Internat. Jl, 1995–2003. FRSL 2003. Hon. DCL: King's Coll., Halifax, 2004; Royal Mil. Coll., Kingston, 2004; Hon. LLD Ryerson, 2005. *Publications:* Women of the Raj, 1988; (ed jtly) Canada and NATO: uneasy past, uncertain future, 1990; (ed jtly) The Uneasy Century: international relations 1900–1990, 1996; Peacemakers: the Paris Conference of 1919 and its attempt to end war, 2001, revised as Paris, 1919: six months that changed the world (Samuel Johnson Prize), 2002; (ed jtly and contrib.) Parties Long Estranged: Canadian-Australian relations, 2003; (jtly) Canada's House: Rideau Hall and the invention of a Canadian home, 2004; Seize the Hour: when Nixon met Mao, 2006; The Uses and Abuses of History, 2008; Stephen Leacock, 2009; The War that Ended Peace, 2013. *Recreations:* opera, films, tennis, ski-ing, hiking. *Address:* St Antony's College, Oxford OX2 6JF. *Clubs:* Oxford and Cambridge; Toronto Lawn Tennis.

MACMILLAN, Maureen; Member (Lab) Highlands and Islands, Scottish Parliament, 1999–2007; *b* 9 Feb. 1943; *m* 1965, Michael Muirdon Macmillan, LLB; two *s* two *d*. *Educ:* Oban High Sch.; Edinburgh Univ. (MA Hons); Moray House. English Teacher, 1983–99. Co-founder, Ross-shire Women's Aid, 1980–. Mem., EIS, 1980–.

McMILLAN, Neil Macleod, CMG 1997; Director of Advocacy and Political Affairs, EuroCommerce, since 2015; *b* 21 Oct. 1953; *s* of John Howard McMillan, CBE and Ruby Hassell McMillan (*née* Meggs); *m* 1st, 1978, Karin Lauritzen (marr. diss. 1985); 2nd, 1994, Lena Madvig Madsen; one *s*. *Educ:* Westminster City Sch.; Univ. of Regensburg; Univ. of Kiel, Germany; Exeter Univ. (BA Hons Mod. Langs 1977). Admin. Trainee, Dept of Prices and Consumer Protection, 1978–79; Dept of Industry, 1980–81; HEO (Develt), Dept of Trade, 1981–82; Private Sec. to Minister for Industry and IT, 1982–84; seconded to Govt Commn on Telecommunications Reform, Federal Min. of Research, Bonn, 1985; Principal, DTI, 1986–87; First Sec., UK Representation to EU, Brussels, 1987–91; Department of Trade and Industry: Dir, Internat. Communications Policy, 1991–98; Dir, EU Internal Trade Policy, 1998–2000; Dep. Perm. Rep., UK Mission to UN, Geneva, 2001–05; Dir, Europe, DTI, 2005–06; Dir and Dep. Hd, European Secretariat, Cabinet Office, 2006–08; Head, Nabucco Political Strategy, RWE Supply and Trading GmbH, 2008–11; Partner, Brunswick Gp LLP, 2011–14. Mem. Bd, Amer. Chamber of Commerce to EU, Brussels, 2013–. Chairman: European Telecommunications Regulatory Cttee, 1992–96; WTO Negotiating Gp on Basic Telecommunications Services, 1994–97; World Telecommunications Policy Forum, 1998; WTO Budget Cttee, 2002–03. *Recreations:* reading, church architecture. *Club:* Athenæum.

McMILLAN, (Norman) Hamilton, CMG 1997; OBE 1984; Managing Director, Zwischenzug Ltd, since 2006; *b* 28 Oct. 1946; *s* of Neil McMillan and Alma McMillan (*née* Hall); *m* 1969, Dr Carolyn Vivienne Barltrop; one *s* one *d*. *Educ:* Brentwood Sch.; Balliol Coll., Oxford. Joined HM Diplomatic Service, 1968; Third Sec., FCO, 1968–70; Third, later Second Sec., Vienna, 1970–72; Second, later First Sec., FCO, 1972–77; First Secretary: Rome, 1977–81; Dhaka, 1981–84; Cairo, 1984–86; Counsellor: (Chancery), Vienna, 1989–93; FCO, 1993–97. Dir of Ops, CIEX Ltd, subseq. Penumbra, 1997–2003; Gp Security Advr, ABN-AMRO Bank, Amsterdam, 2003–06. *Recreations:* board games, music with bite, cosmology, ceramics. *Club:* Oriental.

McMILLAN, Stuart; Member (SNP) Scotland West, Scottish Parliament, since 2007; *b* 6 May 1972; *s* of Henry McMillan and Janet McMillan; *m* 2003, Alexandra; two *d*. *Educ:* Univ. of Abertay Dundee (BA Hons Europ. Business Mgt and Langs; MBA Europ. 1997). Supply Analyst, IBM UK Ltd, 1998–2000; Parly Researcher, SNP Westminster Gp, 2000–03; Office Manager to Bruce McFee, MSP, 2003–07. *Recreations:* play bagpipes, football, music, travel, reading. *Address:* Scottish Parliament, Edinburgh EH99 1SP. *T:* (0131) 348 6807, *Fax:* (0131) 348 6809. *E:* stuart.mcmillan.msp@scottish.parliament.uk.

McMILLAN-SCOTT, Edward; Member, Yorkshire and the Humber Region, 1999–2014 (C, 1999–2009, Ind C, 2009–10, Lib Dem, 2010–14), and Vice-President, 2004–14, European Parliament (York, 1984–94; North Yorkshire, 1994–99); *b* 15 Aug. 1949; *s* of late Walter Theodore Robin McMillan-Scott, ARIBA and Elizabeth Maud Derrington Hudson; *m* 1972, Henrietta Elizabeth Rumney Hudson, solicitor; two *d*. *Educ:* Blackfriars School, Llanarth; Blackfriars School, Laxton; Exeter Technical College. Tour director in Europe, Scandinavia, Africa and USSR, 1968–75; PR exec., then parly consultant, 1976–84; political adviser to Falkland Islands Govt, London office 1983–84. European Parliament: Member: For. Affairs and Security Cttee, 1989–2004; Transport Cttee, 1989–92; Chm., 1979 Cttee (Cons. back-bench cttee), 1994–95; Leader, Conservatives in EP, 1997–2001 (Treas., 1995); Founder, 1992, and Rapporteur, EU Initiative for Democracy and Human Rights; Chm., Election Observer Missions, Palestine 2005 and 2006, Egypt 2005. Contested (Lib Dem): Yorks and the Humber Reg., EP, 2014; Normanton, Pontefract and Castleford, 2015. Mem. Bd, Cons. Party, 1998–2001. Trustee, BBC World Service Trust, 1999–2009. *Recreations:* music, reading. *Address:* Wick House Farm, Wick, Pershore, Worcestershire WR10 3NU.

McMULLAN, Rt Rev. Gordon; Bishop of Down and Dromore, 1986–97; *b* 1934; *m* 1957, Kathleen Davidson; two *s*. *Educ:* Queen's Univ., Belfast (BSc Econ 1961, PhD 1971); Ridley Hall, Cambridge; Dipl. in Religious Studies (Cantab) 1978; ThD Geneva Theol Coll., 1988; MPhil TCD, 1990; DMin Univ. of the South, USA, 1995; DPhil Ulster, 2004. Deacon 1962, priest 1963, dio. Down; Curate of Ballymacarrett, 1962–67; Central Adviser on Christian Stewardship to Church of Ireland, 1967–70; Curate of St Columba, Knock, Belfast, 1970–71; Bishop's Curate, St Brendan's, East Belfast, 1971–76; Rector of St Columba, Knock, Belfast, 1976–80; Archdeacon of Down, 1979–80; Bishop of Clogher, 1980–86. Merrill Fellow/Resident Fellow, Harvard Divinity Sch., 1997–98. Hon. DCL Univ. of the South, USA, 2001. *Publications:* A Cross and Beyond, 1976; We are called …, 1977; Everyday Discipleship, 1979; Reflections on St Mark's Gospel, 1984; Growing Together in Prayer, 1990; Reflections on St Luke's Gospel, 1994; Opposing Violence/Building Bridges, 1996; The Story of Saint Martin's Church and the Southern Church Mission to Ballymacarrett, 2008. *Address:* 26 Wellington Park, Bangor, Co. Down, N Ireland BT20 4PJ.

McMULLAN, Lynda; Director of Commercial and Finance, Metropolitan Police, since 2014; *b* Belfast, 1966; *d* of Noel McMullan and Pamela McMullan; *m* 1998, Phillip Drysdale; one *d*. *Educ:* Simon Langton Girls' Grammar Sch.; Newcastle Univ. (BA Hons Finance and Accounting). Mem. CIPFA 1992. Gp Accountant, Nottingham CC, 1989–96; Hd, Corporate Finance, Southwark LBC, 1996–2000; Actg Dir of Finance, Hammersmith and Fulham LBC, 2000–02; Co. Finance Manager, 2002–06, Dir of Finance and Procurement, 2006–11, Kent CC; Asst Auditor Gen., Nat. Audit Office, 2011–13; Dir of Public Resources and Perf., Mayor of London's Office for Policing and Crime, 2013–14. *Recreations:* reading, enjoying friends and family. *Address:* Metropolitan Police, New Scotland Yard, The Broadway, SW1H 0BG. *T:* (020) 7230 4321. *E:* Lynda.McMullan@met.police.uk.

McMULLEN, Prof. David Lawrence, FBA 1994; Professor of Chinese, University of Cambridge, 1989–2006, now Professor Emeritus; Fellow of St John's College, Cambridge, since 1967; *b* 10 Aug. 1939; twin *s* of late Alexander Lawrence McMullen and Muriel Felicité McMullen (*née* Sikes); *m* 1983, Sarah Jane Clarice Croft; two *d*. *Educ:* Monkton Combe Sch., Bath; St John's Coll., Cambridge (BA, MA, PhD). National Service, RAF, 1957–59. Taiwan Min. of Educn Schol., 1963–64; Harkness Commonwealth Fellowship, 1965–67; Asst Lectr 1967, Lectr 1972, in Chinese Studies, Cambridge Univ. Pres., British Assoc. for Chinese Studies, 1985–87. *Publications:* Concordances and Indexes to Chinese Texts, 1975; State and Scholars in T'ang China, 1988; contribs to jls of E Asian studies. *Recreation:* gardening. *Address:* Grove Cottage, 35 High Street, Grantchester, Cambridge CB3 9NF. *T:* (01223) 840206.

See also I. J. McMullen.

McMULLEN, Dr Ian James, FBA 2001; Lecturer in Japanese, University of Oxford, 1972–2006 (Pro-Proctor, 1986–87); Fellow, Pembroke College, Oxford, 1989–2006 (Vicegerent, 2003–04), Fellow Emeritus, since 2006; Fellow Emeritus, St Antony's College, Oxford, since 2009; *b* 10 Aug. 1939; twin *s* of late Alexander Lawrence McMullen and Muriel Felicité McMullen (*née* Sikes); *m* 1970, Bonnie Shannon; one *s*. *Educ:* Monkton Combe Sch., Bath; St John's Coll., Cambridge (BA, MA; PhD 1969). Nat. Service, RAF, 1957–59. Schol., Min. of Educn, Japan, 1963–64; Lectr, 1965, Asst Prof., 1966–70, Associate Prof., 1970–72, Univ. of Toronto; Fellow, St Antony's Coll., Oxford, 1972–89. Pres., British Assoc. Japanese Studies, 1997–98. *Publications:* Genji Gaiden: the origins of Kumazawa Banzan's commentary on the Tale of Genji, 1991; Idealism, Protest and the Tale of Genji, 1999; contribs to jls of E Asian studies. *Recreation:* gardening. *Address:* Wilton Lodge, 44 Osberton Road, Oxford OX2 7NU. *T:* (01865) 559859.

See also D. L. McMullen.

McMULLIN, Rt Hon. Sir Duncan (Wallace), Kt 1987; PC 1980; Judge of Court of Appeal, New Zealand, 1979–89; commercial arbitrator, 1990–2004; *b* 1 May 1927; *s* of Charles James McMullin and Kathleen Annie Shout; *m* 1955, Isobel Margaret, *d* of Robert Ronald Atkinson, ED; two *s* two *d*. *Educ:* Auckland Grammar Sch.; Univ. of Auckland (LLB). Judge of Supreme Court, 1970–79. Chm., Royal Commn on Contraception, Sterilisation and Abortion in NZ, 1975–77. Chairman: Wanganui Computer Centre Policy Cttee, 1989–93; Market Surveillance Panel, Electricity Marketing Corp., 1994–2004. Chm., NZ Conservation Authority, 1996–2000. FIArb of NZ, 1990. Augusta Award, Auckland Grammar Sch., 2009. *Publications:* A Lawyer's Tale, 2009. *Recreations:* forestry, farming, conservation, reading. *Address:* 4/456 Remuera Road, Auckland, New Zealand. *T:* (9) 5246583.

McMURRAY, Dr Cecil Hugh, CBE 2002; FRSC, FIFST; Managing Director, Sci-Tec Consultancy, since 2003; *b* 19 Feb. 1942; *s* of late Edwin McMurray and Margaret McMurray (*née* Smyth); *m* 1967, Ann Stuart; two *s* one *d*. *Educ:* Royal Belfast Academical Instn; Queen's University, Belfast (BSc 1965; BAgr 1966); PhD Bristol, 1970. FRSC 1981; FIFST 1987. Res. Fellow, Dept of Chem., Harvard Univ., 1970–72; Head of Biochem. Dept, Vet. Res. Lab., Dept of Agric. for NI, 1972–84; Prof. of Food and Agricl Chem., QUB, and concurrently DCSO, Dept of Agric. for NI, 1984–88; CSO, Dept of Agric. and Rural Develt for NI, 1988–2002. Hon. Prof., QUB, 1998–. Expert Advr, WHO, 1983, 1986; Assessor to: AFRC, 1988–94; Priorities Bd for R&D in Agric. and Food, 1988–93; Technology Bd for NI, 1988–92; NERC, 1992–93; Adv. Cttee on microbiol safety of food, 1992–2002; Dir, NI Public Sector Overseas, 1994–2002. Delivered overseas projects on behalf of Word Bank and EU in Azerbaijan, Uzbekistan, Tajikistan, Kazakhstan (also for Min. of Agriculture in Kazakhstan), Serbia, Montenegro, Philippines, Jamaica and Cambodia. Mem., Steering Gp on chem. aspects of food surveillance, 1992–95. Pres., Agricl Gp, BAAS, 1986–87. Non-exec. Dir, Agri-Food and Biosciences Institute, 2012–; TB Strategic Partnership Gp, 2014–. Mem. Cttee, Coronary Prevention Gp, 1985–89. Trustee, Agricl Inst. for NI, 1985–2002; Mem. Governing Body, Rowett Res. Inst., Aberdeen, 1986–89, 1993–2003. Mem. Editl Bd, Fertiliser Res., 1985–92. *Publications:* (ed jtly) Detection Methods for Irradiated Foods: current status, 1996; over 100 scientific publications in various jls incl. Biochemical Jl, Jl of Amer. Chemical Soc., Clin. Chem., CIBA Foundn Symposia, Jl of Chromatography, British Vet. Jl, Vet. Record, Jl Assoc. of Analytical Chem., Trace Metals in Man and Domestic Animals, Biology of Total Envmt. *Recreations:* reading, photography, walking. *Address:* 25 Sheridan Drive, Helens Bay, Bangor, Co. Down BT19 1LB.

McMURTRY, Sir David (Roberts), Kt 2001; CBE 1994; RDI 1989; FRS 2011; CEng, FREng, FIMechE; Co-founder, Chairman and Chief Executive, Renishaw plc (formerly Renishaw Electrical Ltd), since 1973; *b* Dublin, 5 March 1940. FREng 2001. Formerly with Rolls Royce plc. *Address:* Renishaw plc, New Mills, Wotton-under-Edge, Glos GL12 8JR.

McMURTRY, Hon. (Roland) Roy, OC 2009; OOnt 2007; Counsel, Gowling Lafleur Henderson LLP; Chief Justice of Ontario, 1996–2007 (Associate Chief Justice, 1991–94, Chief Justice, 1994–96, Ontario Court of Justice (General Division)); *b* 31 May 1932; *s* of Roland Roy McMurtry and Doris Elizabeth Belcher; *m* 1957, Ria Jean Macrae; three *s* three *d*. *Educ:* St Andrew's Coll., Aurora, Ont; Trinity Coll., Univ. of Toronto (BA Hons); Osgoode Hall Law Sch., Toronto (LLB). Called to the Bar of Ontario, 1958; QC 1970.

Partner: Benson, McMurtry, Percival & Brown, Toronto, 1958–75; Blaney, McMurtry, Stapells, 1988–91. Elected to Ontario Legislature, 1975; re-elected, 1977 and 1981; Attorney General for Ontario, 1975–85; Solicitor General for Ontario, 1978–82. High Comr in UK, 1985–88. Chancellor, York Univ., Canada, 2008–. Freeman, City of London, 1986. Hon. LLD: Ottawa, 1983; Law Soc. of Upper Canada, 1984; Leeds, 1988; York, 1991; Toronto, 1998. *Recreations:* painting, ski-ing, tennis. *Address:* Gowling Lafleur Henderson LLP, Suite 1600, 1 First Canadian Place, 100 King Street West, Toronto, ON M5X 1G5, Canada. *Clubs:* Albany, York (Toronto).

McMURTRY, Stanley, (Mac), MBE 2004; social and political cartoonist, Daily Mail, since 1970; *b* 4 May 1936; *s* of Stanley Harrison McMurtry and Janet Lind McMurtry; *m* 1st, 1958, Maureen Flaye (marr. diss. 1980); one *s* one *d*; 2nd, 1981, Janet Elizabeth Rattle (marr. diss. 2002); 3rd, 2003, Elizabeth Mary Vaughan. *Educ:* Sharmans Cross Secondary Sch., Birmingham; Birmingham Coll. of Art. Cartoon film animator, 1956–65; social and political cartoonist, Daily Sketch, 1968–70; freelance cartoonist, for Punch and other magazines, 1960–; TV scriptwriter with Bernard Cookson, for Tommy Cooper and Dave Allen, 1973–76. Social and Political Cartoonist of the Year, 1983, Master Cartoonist, 2000, Cartoonist Club of GB; Cartoonist of Year Award, 1982, 1984 and 1999, UK Press Gazette; Cartoonist of the Year, What the Papers Say Awards, 2003, 2007; Political Cartoonist of the Year, 2007, Lifetime Achievement Award, 2010, Cartoon Art Trust. *Publications:* The Bunjee Venture (for children), 1977 (cartoon film, 1979); Mac's Year Books, annually, 1980–; contrib. short story to Knights of Madness, ed Peter Haining, 1998. *Recreations:* golf, writing. *Address:* Daily Mail, Northcliffe House, 2 Derry Street, W8 5TT. *T:* (020) 7938 6369. *Clubs:* Chelsea Arts, Saints and Sinners (Chm., 2015–April 2016).

McNAB, Angela; Chief Executive, Kent and Medway NHS and Social Care Partnership Trust, since 2012; *b* London, 1 April 1957; *d* of Bernard and Doris Hammond; *m* 1st; two *s* one *d*; 2nd, 2005, Carl Powell. *Educ:* Open Univ. (BA Hons); South Bank Univ. (MSc). Nat. Hosps Coll. of Speech Scis (LCST). Speech and language therapist, 1978–92; gen. manager posts, Mid Essex Community and Mental Health Trust, 1992–99; Sen. Policy Manager, Nat. Sexual Health and HIV Strategy, DoH, 1999–2001; Chief Executive: Chingford, Wanstead and Woodford PCT, 2001–02; HFEA, 2002–08; on secondment as Dir of Public Health Delivery, DoH, 2007–08; Chief Exec., NHS Luton, and NHS Bedfordshire, 2008–12. Mem. Bd, Council for Registration of Forensic Practitioners, 2006–10. Mem. Council, Univ. of Kent, 2014–. *Publications:* contrib. health and scientific jls, incl. Cell Stem Cell. *Recreations:* running, theatre, family. *T:* 07860 114553. *E:* angela.mcnab@me.com.

MACNAB of Macnab, James William Archibald; The Macnab; 24th Chief of Clan Macnab; Director, Country House Sales, Savills, since 1999; *b* Edinburgh, 22 March 1963; *er s* of James Charles Macnab of Macnab and Hon. Diana Mary Macnab of Macnab, *er d* of Baron Kilmany (Life Peer), 1st Bt, MC, PC; *S* father, 2013; *m* 1994, Dr Jane Louise Mackintosh; one *s* one *d*. *Educ:* Glenalmond Coll.; RAC Cirencester. MRICS. With Savills, 1987–. Mem., Royal Co. of Archers, Queen's Bodyguard in Scotland. Mem. Exec., Standing Council of Scottish Clan Chiefs. *Recreations:* golf, walking, cycling, shooting, Rugby. *Heir: s* James David Macnab, younger of Macnab, *b* 27 Dec. 2000. *Address:* 22 Royal Crescent, Edinburgh EH3 6QA. *T:* (0131) 247 3711. *E:* jmacnab@savills.com. *Clubs:* Royal & Ancient Golf (St Andrews); Craigielaw Golf (East Lothian).

McNAB, John Stanley; Chief Executive, Port of Tilbury London Ltd (formerly Port of Tilbury (Port of London Authority)), 1987–96; *b* 23 Sept. 1937; *s* of Robert Stanley McNab and Alice Mary McNab; *m* 1st, 1961, Carol Field (marr. diss. 1978); two *d*; 2nd, 1980, Jacqueline Scammell (marr. diss. 1997); 3rd, 2001, Susan Cole. *Educ:* Gravesend Grammar Sch. FCCA 1976; FCIT 1992. Nat. Service, Royal Engineers, Libya, 1956–58. Port of London Authority: joined 1954; Accountant, India and Millwall Docks, 1965, Upper Docks, 1970; Man. Dir, PLA (Thames) Stevedoring, 1973; Dir, Upper Docks, 1974; Exec. Dir (Manpower) and Group Board Mem., 1978; Dir, Tilbury, 1983. Director: Internat. Transport Ltd, 1992–96; Airflights Direct Ltd, 2000–08. FRSA 1991; MCMI (MBIM 1970). Freeman: City of London, 1988; Co. of Watermen and Lightermen of River Thames, 1988. *Recreations:* golf, swimming, DIY, learning Spanish and Portuguese. *Address:* 48 Daines Way, Thorpe Bay, Essex SS1 3PQ. *T:* (01702) 587060.

MACNAGHTEN, Sir Malcolm Francis, 12th Bt *cr* 1836, of Bushmills House, co. Antrim; *b* 21 Sept. 1956; *s* of Sir Patrick Alexander Macnaghten, 11th Bt and of Marianne (*née* Schaefer); *S* father, 2007; *m* 1991, Yvonne Sonia-Louise Greenfield; three *d*. *Heir: b* Edward Alexander Macnaghten [*b* 24 July 1958; *m* 1992, Kon Foong, *d* of Fook Pang; one *s* one *d*].

MACNAGHTEN, Prof. Philip Martin, PhD; Professor of Technology and International Development, Knowledge, Technology and Innovation Group, Wageningen University, Netherlands, since 2015; *b* 6 Aug. 1965; *s* of Antony Martin Macnaghten and Catherine Frances Macnaghten (*née* Young); *m* 2005, Simone Clementino Soares; two *d*, and one step *s*. *Educ:* Univ. of Southampton (BA Psychol. 1987); Univ. of Exeter (PhD Psychol. 1991). University of Lancaster: Res. Associate, Centre for Study of Envmtl Change, 1992–94; British Acad. Postdoctoral Fellow, 1995–97; Lectr, 1998–2002; Sen. Lectr, 2003–06; University of Durham: Dir, Inst. of Hazard and Risk Res., 2006–08; Prof. of Geography, 2006–15. Vis. Prof., Dept of Sci. and Technol. Policy, Univ. of Campinas, 2012–15. Coordinator, Deepening Ethical Engagement and Participation in Emerging Nanotechnologies proj., 2006–09; GM Futuros proj., 2012–14. Mem., Strategic Adv. Panel, EPSRC, 2011–14. FRSA. *Publications:* (jtly) Uncertain World: GMOs, food and public attitudes in Britain, 1997; (with J. Urry) Contested Natures, 1998; (jtly) Wising Up: the public and new technologies, 2000; (ed with J. Urry) Bodies of Nature, 2001; Embodying the Environment in Everyday Life Practices, 2003; Nanotechnology, Governance and Public Deliberation: what role for the social sciences; (jtly) Reconfiguring Responsibility: deepening debate on nanotechnology, 2009; (jtly) Developing a framework for responsible innovation, 2013; (ed with S. Carro-Ripalda) Governing agricultural sustainability: global lessons from GM crops. *Recreations:* reading, travel, film, cooking, hiking, dog walking. *Address:* Knowledge, Technology and Innovation Group, Leeuwenborch, Hollandseweg 1, 6706 KN Wageningen, Netherlands. *E:* philip.macnaghten@wur.nl.

McNAIR, family name of **Baron McNair**.

McNAIR, 3rd Baron *cr* 1955, of Gleniffer; **Duncan James McNair;** Chairman and Managing Director, Applied Learning Techniques International Ltd, since 2004; *b* 26 June 1947; *s* of 2nd Baron McNair and Vera, *d* of Theodore James Faithfull; *S* father, 1989. *Educ:* Bryanston. Former Mem., Parly Gps on Drug Misuse, Alcohol Misuse, Population Develt and Reproductive Health; Vice Chm., Parly Waterways Gp, 1995–99. Mem., Sub-Cttee E (Envmt), EC Select Cttee, H of L, 1990–92. Dir, British Anti-Trafficking Orgn Ltd, 2000–. Member: Resource Use Institute Ltd, 1994–; Adv. Bd, Effective Educn Assoc., 1996–; Council for Human Rights and Religious Freedom, 1996–; Exec. Cttee, Health Freedom Movt UK, 2002–; Exec. Cttee, Commonwealth Forum for Project Mgt, 2002–. Dir, Chelkin Ltd, 2001. Chm., Unitax Assoc., 1994–. Co-Vice-Patron, Nat. Police Community Trust, 2001–. *Heir: b* Hon. William Samuel Angus McNair [*b* 19 May 1958; *m* 1981, Emma Procter (marr. diss. 1990); one *s* one *d*].

MACNAIR, Charles Neville; QC (Scot.) 2002; Sheriff of Tayside, Central and Fife at Dunfermline, since 2014 (at Cupar, 2009–14, at Dundee, 2014); *b* 18 March 1955; *s* of late James T. H. Macnair, MC, and of Dr Margaret E. Macnair (*née* Cameron); *m* 1987, Patricia Anne Dinning; two *d*. *Educ:* Bryanston Sch.; Aberdeen Univ. (LLB). Commnd Queen's Own Highlanders, 1977–80. Apprentice solicitor, Simpson & Marwick WS, Edinburgh, 1980–82; Solicitor: Brodies WS, Edinburgh, 1982–85; Peterkin's, Aberdeen, 1985–87; Advocate, 1988–; Sheriff (pt-time), 2005–06; Floating Sheriff of Tayside, Central and Fife, 2006–09. Mem., Youth Court Feasibility Project Gp, Scottish Exec., 2002. Chm., Child and Family Law Gp, Faculty of Advocates, 2002–06. Served TA, 1980–87 and 1990–92. *Recreations:* reading, walking, sailing. *Address:* Sheriff Court House, 1/6 Carnegie Drive, Dunfermline, Fife KY12 7HJ.

McNAIR-WILSON, Sir Patrick (Michael Ernest David), Kt 1989; consultant; *b* 28 May 1929; *s* of Dr Robert McNair-Wilson; *m* 1953, Diana Evelyn Kitty Campbell Methuen-Campbell (*d* 2015), *d* of Hon. Laurence Methuen-Campbell; one *s* four *d*. *Educ:* Eton. Exec. in French Shipping Co., 1951–53; various appointments at Conservative Central Office, 1954–58; Staff of Conservative Political Centre, 1958–61; Director, London Municipal Society, 1961–63; Executive with The British Iron and Steel Federation, 1963–64. Partner, Ferret PR and Public Affairs, 1995–2000. Dir, Photo-Me International Plc, 1996–2005. MP (C): Lewisham W, 1964–66; New Forest, Nov. 1968–1997. Opposition Front Bench Spokesman on fuel and power, 1965–66; Vice-Chm., Conservative Parly Power Cttee, 1969–70; PPS to Minister for Transport Industries, DoE, 1970–74; Opposition Front Bench Spokesman on Energy, 1974–76; Chm., Jt Lords and Commons Select Cttee on Private Bill Procedure, 1987–88; Mem., Select Cttee on Members Interests, 1985–86. Editor of The Londoner, 1961–63. *Recreations:* sailing, pottery, flying. *Address:* Godfrey's Farm, Beaulieu, Hants SO42 7YP.

McNAIRNEY, John Walter; Chief Planner, Scottish Government, since 2012; *b* East Calder, West Lothian, 12 Sept. 1957; *s* of John McNairney and Grace McNairney; *m* 1989, Ellen Parr; one *s* one *d*. *Educ:* St Mary's Acad., Bathgate; Dundee Univ. (BSc Town and Regl Planning); Edinburgh Napier Univ. (MBA). Consultant, Montgomery Forgan Associates, 1984–87; Town Planner, Fife Council, 1987–99; Policy Manager, Transport Gp, Scottish Office, 1999–2002; Hd, Freedom of Information Br., 2002–05, Asst Chief Planner, 2005–12, Scottish Exec., subseq. Scottish Govt. *Recreations:* walking, reading, football. *Address:* 2–H–73, Scottish Government, Victoria Quay, Edinburgh EH6 6QQ. *T:* (0131) 244 7528, 07795 618393. *E:* john.mcnairney@scotland.gsi.gov.uk.

McNALLY, family name of **Baron McNally**.

McNALLY, Baron *cr* 1995 (Life Peer), of Blackpool in the county of Lancashire; **Tom McNally;** PC 2005; Chairman, Youth Justice Board, since 2014; *b* 20 Feb. 1943; *s* of John P. McNally and Elizabeth May (*née* McCarthy); *m* 1st, 1970, Eileen Powell (marr. diss. 1990); 2nd, 1990, Juliet Lamy Hutchinson; two *s* one *d*. *Educ:* College of St Joseph, Blackpool; University Coll., London (BScEcon; Fellow 1995). President of Students' Union, UCL, 1965–66; Vice-Pres., Nat. Union of Students, 1966–67; Asst Gen. Sec. of Fabian Society, 1966–67; Labour Party researcher, 1967–68; Internat. Sec. of Labour Party, 1969–74; Political Adviser to: Foreign and Commonwealth Sec., 1974–76; Prime Minister, 1976–79. Public Affairs Adviser, GEC, 1983–84; Dir-Gen., Retail Consortium, and Dir, British Retailers Association, 1985–87; Head of Public Affairs, Hill & Knowlton, 1987–93; Head of Public Affairs, 1993–96, Vice-Chm., 1996–2004, Shandwick Consultants, then Weber Shandwick Worldwide, subseq. Weber Shandwick. MP (Lab 1979–81, SDP 1981–83) Stockport S; contested (SDP) Stockport, 1983. SDP Parly spokesman on educn and sport, 1981–83. Mem., Select Cttee on Industry and Trade, 1979–83. House of Lords: Dep. Leader, 2001–04, Leader, 2004–13, Lib Dems; Dep. Leader, 2010–13; Minister of State, MoJ, 2010–13. Trustee, Nat. Liberal Club. Mem. of Court, Univ. of Hertfordshire, 2006–. FRSA; FCIPR. Hon. LLD Hertfordshire, 2010. *Recreations:* watching sport, reading political biographies. *Address:* House of Lords, SW1A 0PW. *E:* mcnallyt@parliament.uk.

McNALLY, Eryl Margaret; Chairman, National Energy Foundation, 2004–07; *b* 11 April 1942; *d* of late Llywelyn Williams, MP and Elsie Williams; *m* 1964, James Frederick McNally; one *s* one *d*. *Educ:* Newbridge Grammar Sch.; Bristol Univ. (BA Langs); University Coll., Swansea (PGCE); Open Univ. (BSc 2006; BSc Hons Psychol. 2013). Modern langs teacher, 1964–84; advisory work, Bucks CC, 1985–93; freelance schools inspector, OFSTED, 1993–94; MEP (Lab) Beds and Milton Keynes, 1994–99, Eastern Region, England, 1999–2004. Councillor: Abbots Langley Parish Council, 1970–73; Watford RDC, 1972–74; Three Rivers DC, 1973–77; Herts CC, 1986–95. Hon. LLD Herts, 2000; Hon. DSc Cranfield, 2003. Chevalier, Légion d'Honneur (France), 2002. *Publications:* articles on language teaching and teacher training in professional jls. *Recreations:* learning languages, reading, world music, films. *Address:* 30 Follet Drive, Abbots Langley, Herts WD5 0LP. *T:* (01923) 662711.

McNALLY, John; MP (SNP) Falkirk, since 2015; *b* Denny, 1 Feb. 1951; *s* of John and Rose McNally; *m* 1980, Sandra Chalmers; one *s* one *d*. *Educ:* St Patrick's Primary Sch., Denny; St Modan's High Sch., Stirling. Hairdresser, 1965–; salon owner, 1970–. Mem. (SNP), Falkirk Council, 2005–15. *Recreations:* cycling, golf. *Address:* House of Commons, SW1A 0AA. *T:* (020) 7219 6525.

McNAMARA, Prof. John Michael, PhD; FRS 2012; Professor of Mathematics and Biology, since 1995, and Director, Research Centre in Behavioural Biology, University of Bristol. *Educ:* Univ. of Oxford (BA Maths 1971; PhD 1977); Sussex Univ. (MSc Astronomy 1972). Postdoctoral Fellow, Univ. of Sussex; Lectr, Univ. of Bristol. Hon. Vis. Prof., Univ. of Exeter. Hon. DSc Sussex, 2012. Hamilton Award (jtly), Internat. Soc. Behavioural Ecol., 2008; Weldon Meml Prize, Univ. of Oxford, 2014. *Publications:* (contrib.) Social Information Transmission and Human Biology, 2006; (contrib.) Conceptual Ecology and Invasion Biology, 2006; articles in jls. *Address:* Department of Mathematics, University of Bristol, University Walk, Clifton, Bristol BS8 1TW.

McNAMARA, (Joseph) Kevin, PhD; *b* 5 Sept. 1934; *s* of late Patrick and Agnes McNamara; *m* 1960, Nora (*née* Jones), Warrington; four *s* one *d*. *Educ:* various primary schools; St Mary's Coll., Crosby; Hull Univ. (LLB); Univ. of Liverpool (PhD 2007). Head of Dept of History, St Mary's Grammar Sch., Hull, 1958–64; Lecturer in Law, Hull Coll. of Commerce, 1964–66. MP (Lab): Kingston-upon-Hull N, Jan. 1966–1974 and 1997–2005; Kingston-upon-Hull Central, 1974–83; Hull N, 1983–97. Opposition spokesman on defence, 1982–83, on defence and disarmament, 1983–85, dep. opposition spokesman on defence, 1985–87, opposition spokesman on Northern Ireland, 1987–94, on Civil Service, 1994–95. Member: Select Cttee on For. Affairs, 1977–82 (former Chm., Overseas Develt Sub-Cttee); Parly Assembly, NATO, 1984–88; Vice-Chm., Economic Cttee, NATO, 1985–87; former Chairman: Select Cttee on Overseas Develt; PLP NI Gp; Sec., Parly Gp, TGWU. Chm., All Party Irish In Britain Gp; Vice-Chm., British-Irish Inter-Parly Body; Founder Mem., Friends of the Good Friday Agreement. Mem., UK Delegn to Council of Europe, 1976–80, 1996–2005. Founder Mem. and Chm., Agreed Ireland Forum, 1995–2005. Hon. Freeman, City of Kingston upon Hull, 1997. Hon. LLD Hull, 2006. KCSG 2006 (KSG 2005). Commendatore, Order Al Merito della Repubblica Italiana, 1977. *Recreations:* family, outdoor activities.

McNANEY, Peter Francis, CBE 2013; Chairman, Belfast Health and Social Care Trust, since 2014; *b* 8 Feb. 1959; *m* 1987, Karen McMillen; two *s* two *d*. *Educ:* Manchester Univ. (LLB Hons); Univ. of Ulster (DMS); Queen's Univ., Belfast (Cert Prof. Legal Studies; Cert Adv. Advocacy for Solicitors). Belfast City Council: Asst Solicitor, 1983–85; Sen. Solicitor, 1985–91; Asst Town Solicitor, 1991–94; Dir, Legal Services, 1994–2002; Chief Executive, Belfast City Council, 2002–14. Member: Bd, Chief Execs' Forum, 2003–; NI Econ. Develt

Forum, 2005–; NI Local Govt Taskforce, 2006–; Bd, Invest NI. Mem. Editl Bd, Local Authorities Chief Execs Imprint Foundn, 2004–. *Address:* Belfast Health and Social Care Trust, Trust Headquarters, A Floor, Belfast City Hospital, Lisburn Road, Belfast BT9 7AB. *T:* (028) 9504 0101. *E:* peter.mcnaney@belfasttrust.hscni.net.

McNAUGHT, Captain Ian; Deputy Master, Corporation of Trinity House, since 2011; *b* Sunderland, 27 Aug. 1954; *s* of Andrew McNaught and Kathleen Olive McNaught; *m* 1980, Susan Sproxton; one *s*. *Educ:* Monkwearmouth Grammar Sch.; Fleetwood Nautical Coll. Pre-Sea Boys; South Tyneside Nautical Coll. (professional certs of competency leading to Master Mariner). Cadet, BP Tanker Co., 1972–76; Third Officer, Bibby Line, 1976–79; Second Officer, then Chief Officer, Hullgates Shipping, 1979–87; Cunard Line: joined as Second Officer, 1987; Master: Sea Goddess I, 2001; QE2, 2003–08; Queen Victoria, 2009; Seabourn Spirit, 2010; Seabourn Odyssey, 2010; Seabourn Cruises, 2010, 2011; Seabourn Pride, 2011. Younger Brother, Trinity House, Newcastle upon Tyne, 2003–. Merchant Navy Medal, 2013. *Recreations:* maritime history, fell walking in the Lake District. *Address:* Corporation of Trinity House, Trinity House, Tower Hill, EC3N 4DH.

McNAUGHT, His Honour John Graeme; DL; a Circuit Judge, 1987–2006; *b* 21 Feb. 1941; *s* of Charles William McNaught and Isabella Mary McNaught; *m* 1966, Barbara Mary Smith; two *s* one *d*. *Educ:* King Edward VII Sch., Sheffield; The Queen's Coll., Oxford (BA Jurisprudence, 1962). Bacon Scholar, Gray's Inn, 1962; called to the Bar, Gray's Inn, 1963; a Recorder, 1981–87; Hon. Recorder, Devizes, 1996–. Judge, High Court of St Helena, 1998–2006. Mem., Parole Bd for England and Wales, 1998–2004; Pres., Mental Health Review Tribunal, 2001–05. Chm., Wilts Criminal Justice Strategy Cttee, 2000–02. UK Council Mem., Commonwealth Magistrates' and Judges' Assoc., 1997–2000. DL Wilts, 2006. *Address:* c/o Swindon Combined Court, Islington Street, Swindon SN1 2HG.

McNAUGHTON, Andrew George, FREng; Technical Director (formerly Chief Engineer), High Speed Two Ltd, since 2009 (Member of Board, 2013–14); *b* 26 July 1956; *s* of late Arthur Alfred George, (Ian), McNaughton and Betty McNaughton; *m* 1984, Jane Evelyn Merriott; two *s*. *Educ:* Univ. of Leeds (BSc Civil Engrg 1978). CEng 1981; FICE 2001; FREng 2007; FCILT 2010; FRGS 2012. Civil Engr, SE British Rail, 1991–94; Railtrack plc: Manager, E Anglia, 1994–96; Hd, Prodn, 1997–99; Dir, Great Western, 1999–2001; Chief Engr, Network Rail, 2001–09. Chm. Adv. Bd, Rail Research UK, 2004–09; non-exec. Dir, Great Central Railway Develt Ltd, 2011–13; Dir, Rail2050 Ltd, 2011–13. Mem., Eur. Rail Res. Council, 2004–12 (Chm., 2008–12); Mem., Railway Heritage Cttee, 2006–12; Chm., Infrastructure Commn, Internat. Railway Union, 2006–10; Vice Chm., EU Transport Adv. Gp, 2006–12. Pres., Railway Study Assoc., 2010–11. Hon. Prof. (formerly Special Prof.), Rail Engrg, Univ. of Nottingham, 2006–; Visiting Professor: Imperial Coll. London, 2010–; Southampton Univ., 2011–. Asst, Engineers' Co., 2009–. FPWI 1975. Mem., Smeatonian Soc., 2013. *Recreations:* mountain walking, road cycling, growing tomatoes. *Address:* High Speed Two Ltd, 20 Great Smith Street, SW1P 3BT. *T:* (020) 7944 0773. *E:* andrew.g.mcnaughton@gmail.com.

MacNAUGHTON, Joan, CB 2005; adviser globally on energy and environmental policies; Executive Chair, Energy and Policy Assessment (Trilemma), World Energy Council, since 2011; *b* 12 Sept. 1950; *d* of Duncan McNaughton and Marion McNaughton (*née* Caldwell); *m* 1979, William Alexander Jeffrey (*see* Sir W. A. Jeffrey). *Educ:* Notre Dame Coll. Sch., Liverpool; Warwick Univ. (BSc Hons Physics). Home Office: Admin. Trainee, 1972–74; HEO (Develt), 1974–76; Asst Sec. to Royal Commn on Criminal Procedure, 1976–80; Criminal Policy Dept, 1981–85; Prin. Private Sec. to Dep. Prime Minister and Lord Pres. of the Council, 1985–87; Head, Women and Young Offenders Div., Prison Service, 1987–89; Dir, Prison Service Industries and Farms, 1989–91; Head, Criminal Policy Div., 1991–92; Prin. Private Sec. to Home Secretary, 1992–95; Chief Exec., Police IT Orgn, 1996–99; Director General: Policy, LCD, 1999–2002; Energy, DTI, 2002–06; Internat. Energy Security, DTI, 2006–07; Sen. Vice Pres., Power and Envmtl Policies, Alstom Power (formerly Alstom Power Systems), 2007–11. Chm., Governing Bd, Internat. Energy Agency, 2004–05. Non-exec. Dir, Quintain Estates and Development plc, 2004–10. Sen. Vis. Res. Fellow, Oxford Inst. for Energy Studies, Oxford Univ., 2006–13. Member, Council: Energy Inst., 2008–14 (Vice Pres., 2009–10; Pres. elect, 2010–11; Pres., 2011–13); Warwick Univ., 2014–; Member, Board: Internat. Emissions Trading Assoc., 2010–12; Carbon Capture and Storage Assoc., 2010–13; James Hutton Inst., 2015–. Chairman: Policy Assessment Study Gp, World Energy Council, 2011–; Internat. Adv. Bd, Energy Acad. of Europe, 2013–; Vice Chm., UN High Level Panel on Policy Dialogue on the Clean Develt Mechanism, 2012; Member: Adv. Council, Jt Inst. for Strategic Energy Analysis, Colo, 2014–; UK Energy Res. Centre, 2015–. Mem., Bd of Govs, Argonne Nat. Lab., Univ. of Chicago, 2007–13 (Chm., Admin and Budget Cttee, 2010–13; Co-Chm., Strategic Rev. of Lab. Operations, 2010–13). Trustee, Climate Gp, 2014–. Hon. FEI 2006; Hon. Fellow, Nat. Emissions Trading Assoc., 2014. *Publications:* (contrib.) The New Economic Diplomacy, 2nd edn 2007, 3rd edn 2011; articles on energy and climate change. *Recreations:* reading, hill walking, watching football, crosswords. *Address:* c/o World Energy Council, 62–64 Cornhill, EC3V 3NH. *Club:* Reform.

MACNAUGHTON, Prof. Sir Malcolm (Campbell), Kt 1986; MD; FRCPG, FRCOG, FFSRH; FRSE; Muirhead Professor of Obstetrics and Gynaecology, University of Glasgow, 1970–90, now Emeritus; *b* 4 April 1925; *s* of James Hay and Mary Robieson Macnaughton; *m* 1955, Margaret-Ann Galt; two *s* three *d*. *Educ:* Glasgow Academy; Glasgow Univ. (MD 1970). FRCOG 1966; FRCPG 1972; FFSRH (FFFP 1994); FRSE 1983. Lectr, Univ. of Aberdeen, 1957–61; Sen. Lectr, Univ. of St Andrews, 1961–66; Hon. Sen. Lectr, Univ. of Dundee, 1966–70. Pres., RCOG, 1984–87; Vice-Pres., Royal Coll. of Midwives, 1992–. Pres., British Fertility Soc., 1992–95. Hon. FACOG; Hon. FSLCOG; Hon. FRCAnaes; Hon. FRACOG. Hon. LLD Dundee, 1988. *Publications:* (ed jtly) Combined Textbook of Obstetrics and Gynaecology, 9th edn 1976; (ed and contrib.) Handbook of Medical Gynaecology, 1985; numerous papers in obstetric, gynaecological, endocrine and general medical jls. *Recreations:* fishing, walking, curling. *Address:* 9 Glenburn Road, Bearsden, Glasgow G61 4PJ. *T:* (0141) 942 1909. *Club:* Glasgow Academical (Glasgow).

McNAUGHTON, Prof. Peter Anthony, DPhil; FMedSci; Professor of Pharmacology, King's College London, since 2013; *b* 17 Aug. 1949; *s* of Anthony Henry McNaughton and Dulcie Helen McNaughton; *m* 1985, Linda Ariza; two *s* two *d*. *Educ:* Univ. of Auckland, NZ (BSc 1970); Balliol Coll., Oxford (DPhil 1974); MA Cantab 1976. University of Cambridge: Res. Fellow, Clare Coll., 1974–78; Physiological Laboratory: Elmore Med. Res. Student, 1977–78; Univ. Demonstrator, 1978–83; Univ. Lectr, 1983–91; Fellow, Christ's Coll., 1983–91; Nuffield Sci. Res. Fellow, 1988–89; King's College London: Halliburton Prof. of Physiology, and Head of Physiology, 1991–99; Dean of Basic Med. Scis, 1993–96. Hon. Prof., Dept of Optometry and Vision Scis, Univ. of Wales, Cardiff, 1998–2002; Sheild Prof. and Hd, Dept of Pharmacol., Univ. of Cambridge, 1999–2013; Fellow, Christ's Coll., Cambridge, 1999–2013. Biotechnology and Biological Sciences Research Council: Member: Biochem. and Cell Biology Panel, 1996–2000; Neurone Initiative Panel, 2001–04; Inst. Assessment Panel, 2001; Chm., Bio-imaging Initiative Panel, 1998–2002; Member: Neurosci. Panel, Wellcome Trust, 1998–2001; Adv. Bd, MRC, 2001–; Performance Based Res. Fund Panel, NZ, 2003. Member: Physiological Soc., 1979– (Mem. Cttee, 1988–92); British Pharmacological Soc., 1999–. FMedSci 2013. *Publications:* articles in fields of physiology, pharmacology and neuroscience in learned jls. *Address:* Wolfson Centre for Age-related Diseases, King's College London, Guy's Campus, SE1 1UL.

McNEE, Sir David (Blackstock), Kt 1978; QPM 1975; Commissioner, Metropolitan Police, 1977–82; non-executive director and adviser to a number of public limited companies; *b* 23 March 1925; *s* of John McNee, Glasgow, Lanarkshire; *m* 1st, 1952, Isabella Clayton Hopkins (*d* 1997); one *d*; 2nd, 2002, Lilian Bissland Campbell (*née* Bogie). *Educ:* Woodside Senior Secondary Sch., Glasgow. Joined City of Glasgow Police, 1946. Apptd Dep. Chief Constable, Dunbartonshire Constabulary, 1968; Chief Constable: City of Glasgow Police, 1971–75; Strathclyde Police, 1975–77. Lectures: Basil Henriques, Bristol Univ., 1978; London, in Contemporary Christianity, 1979; Dallas, Glasgow, 1980; Peter le Neve Foster Meml, RSA, 1981. President: Royal Life Saving Soc., 1982–90; National Bible Soc. of Scotland, 1983–96; Glasgow City Cttee, Cancer Relief, 1987–93; Glasgow Battalion, Boys' Brigade, 1984–87; Hon. Vice-Pres., Boys' Bde, 1980–; Vice-Pres., London Fedn of Boys Clubs, 1982–. Patron, Scottish Motor Neurone Assoc., 1982–97. Hon. Col, 32 (Scottish) Signal Regt (V), TA, 1988–92. Freeman of the City of London, 1977. FCMI (FBIM 1977); FRSA 1981. KStJ 1991. *Publications:* McNee's Law, 1983. *Recreations:* fishing, golf, music. *Clubs:* Caledonian, Naval (Life Mem.).

MacNEE, Prof. William, MD; FRCPE; Professor of Respiratory and Environmental Medicine, University of Edinburgh, since 1997; Hon. Consultant Physician, NHS Lothian, since 1987; *b* Glasgow, 18 Dec. 1950; *s* of James and Elsie MacNee; *m* 1976, Edna Marina Kingsley; one *s* one *d*. *Educ:* Coatbridge High Sch.; Univ. of Glasgow (MB ChB 1975; MD Hons 1985). MRCPGlas 1978; FRCPE 1990. Hse Physician and Hse Surgeon, Glasgow and Paisley, 1975–76; SHO/Registrar in Medicine, Western Infirmary and Gartnavel Hosps, Glasgow, 1976–79; Registrar in Respiratory Medicine, City Hosp., Edinburgh, 1979–80; MRC Res. Fellow and Hon. Registrar, Dept of Respiratory Medicine, Royal Infirmary, Edinburgh, 1980–82; Lectr, Dept of Respiratory Medicine, City Hosp., Edinburgh, 1982–83; Sen. Registrar, Respiratory Medicine and Medicine, Lothian Health Bd, 1983–87; Sen. Lectr in Respiratory Medicine, 1987–93, Reader in Medicine, 1993–97, Univ. of Edinburgh; Hd, Cardiovascular/Thoracic Service, Royal Infirmary of Edinburgh, 1998–99. Clinical Director, Respiratory Medicine: Lothian Univ. Hosps NHS Trust, 1992–97; Lothian Hosps NHS Trust, 1992–2002. MRC Res. Fellow, Univ. of BC, Vancouver, 1985–86; Vis. Prof., Sch. of Life Scis, Napier Univ., Edinburgh. Mem. Council, Scottish Thoracic Soc., 1990–93; Vice Pres., British Lung Foundn, 2007– (Hon. Sec., Scotland, 1993–2004; Chm., Scientific Cttee, 1997–2000). European Respiratory Society: Chm., Scientific Prog. Cttee, 1990–2003; Congress Chair, 2003–04; Pres., 2006–07. *Publications:* Chronic Obstructive Lung Disease, 2002, 2nd edn 2008; The Year in Respiratory Medicine, 2003; Chronic Obstructive Pulmonary Disease, 2nd edn 2003; Fast Facts Chronic Obstructive Pulmonary Disease, 2004; Clinical Management of Chronic Obstructive Pulmonary Disease, 2004; contrib. scientific papers and rev. articles on respiratory medicine topics. *Recreations:* music, walking, reading. *Address:* ELEGI Colt Research Laboratories, MRC Centre for Inflammation Research, Queen's Medical Research Institute, Level 2, Room C2.29, 47 Little France Crescent, Edinburgh EH16 6LF.

MacNEIL, Angus Brendan; MP (SNP) Na h-Eileanan An Iar, since 2005; *b* 21 July 1970; *m* 1998, Jane Douglas. *Educ:* Castlebay Secondary Sch., Isle of Barra; Nicolson Inst., Stornoway; Strathclyde Univ. (BEng 1992); Jordanhill Coll. (PGCE 1996). Civil Engr, Lilley Construction Ltd, 1992–93; reporter, BBC Radio, Inverness, 1993–95; teacher, Salen Primary Sch., Mull, 1996–98; Gaelic Develt Officer, Lochaber, 1998–99; Lectr in Educn (part-time), Inverness Coll., 1999–2000; teacher, various schs incl. Lochaber and Fort William, 2000–03; teacher and crofter, Isle of Barra, 2003–05. Contested (SNP) Inverness E, Nairn and Lochaber, 2001. *Address:* (office) 31 Bayhead Street, Stornoway, Isle of Lewis, Outer Hebrides HS1 2DU; House of Commons, SW1A 0AA.

McNEIL, Duncan; Member (Lab) Greenock and Inverclyde, Scottish Parliament, since 1999; *b* 7 Sept. 1950; *m* Margaret; one *s* one *d*. Apprentice, Cartsdyke Shipyard; shipbuilder; Officer, GMB. Mem., Labour Party Scottish Exec.; Chm., Local Govt Cttee. Mem., Health Cttee, 2003–07, Scottish Parly Corporate Body, 2003–07, Scottish Parlt. *Address:* Scottish Parliament, Edinburgh EH99 1SP.

MacNEIL, Most Rev. Joseph Neil; Archbishop of Edmonton (Alberta), (RC), 1973–99, now Emeritus; *b* 15 April 1924; *s* of John Martin MacNeil and Kate MacNeil (*née* MacLean). *Educ:* St Francis Xavier Univ., Antigonish, NS (BA 1944); Holy Heart Seminary, Halifax, NS; Univs of Perugia, Chicago and St Thomas Aquinas, Rome (JCD 1958). Priest, 1948; pastor, parishes in NS, 1948–55; Chancery Office, Antigonish, 1958–59; admin, dio. Antigonish, 1959–60; Rector, Antigonish Cathedral, 1961; Dir of Extension Dept, St Francis Xavier Univ., Antigonish, 1961–69; Vice-Pres., 1962–69; Bishop of St John, NB, 1969–73. Pres., Canadian Conf. of Catholic Bishops, 1979–81 (Vice-Pres., 1977–79); Member: Commn on Ecumenism, 1985–91; Perm. Council, 1993–95; Commn on Mission, 1991–96); Chm., Alberta Bishops' Conf., 1973–99. Chancellor, Univ. of St Thomas, Fredericton, NB, 1969. Founding Mem., Inst. for Res. on Public Policy, 1968–80; Mem., Bd of Directors: The Futures Secretariat, 1981–85; Centre for Human Develt, Toronto, 1985–90. Chairman: Bd, Newman Theol Coll., Edmonton, 1973–99; Bd, St Joseph's Coll., Alberta Univ., 1973–99. Member, Bd of Management: Edmonton Gen. Hosp., 1983–92; Edmonton Caritas Health Gp, 1992–99. *Address:* (office) 8421–101 Avenue, Edmonton, Alberta T6A 0L1, Canada. *E:* chancery@caedm.ca.

McNEIL, Keith, FRACP; Chief Executive, Cambridge University Hospitals NHS Foundation Trust, 2013–15; *b* London, 28 July 1957; *s* of David Loudon and Pauline Ann McNeil; *m* 1984, Sharyn Lee; one *s* two *d*. *Educ:* Caringbah High Sch.; Cairns State High Sch.; Univ. of Queensland (MB, BS 1981). FRACP 1991. Intern/Jun. Hse Officer, Mater Misericordiae Hosp., Brisbane, 1982–83; Bn MO, 2/4 RAR Australian Infantry, 1984–85, MO, Field Ambulance, 1986–87. Specialist Trng Registrar, 1987–93; Sen. Transplant Fellow, Papworth Hosp., 1993–95; Consultant Transplant Physician: Prince Charles Hosp., Brisbane, 1995–96; Papworth Hosp., 1996–2002; Hd, Heart and Lung Transplantation, Prince Charles Hosp., Brisbane, 2002–07; Chief Executive Officer: Royal Brisbane & Women's Hosp., Brisbane, 2007–08; Metro Health Service, Brisbane, 2008–13. *Publications:* contribs to text books; scientific articles. *Recreations:* running, classical guitar. *Clubs:* Royal Society of Medicine; University of Queensland Cricket.

McNEIL, Paul; Partner, Fieldfisher (formerly Field Fisher Waterhouse), since 1995; *b* Irvine, Scotland, 26 July 1958; *s* of Hugh and Margaret McNeil; *m* 1990, Elizabeth; one *s* two *d*. *Educ:* All Saints' Comprehensive Sch., Huddersfield; Sheffield Univ. (LLB). Admitted Solicitor; personal injury and clin. negligence solicitor, Taylor Joynson Garrett, 1987–92; Field Fisher Waterhouse, subseq. Fieldfisher: Mem., Mgt Bd, 2005–; Hd, Personal Injury and Med. Negligence, 2008–. *Publications:* (contrib.) International Product Liability; (ed) Handbook on Medical Negligence; (contrib.) Expert Witness. *Recreations:* cycling, ski-ing, cooking. *Address:* 103 Deodar Road, SW15 2NU. *T:* (020) 7861 4019, *Fax:* (020) 7488 0084. *E:* paul.mcneil@fieldfisher.com.

MacNEILL, Calum Hector Sinclair; QC (Scot.) 2007; *b* Elgin, 19 May 1964; *s* of late Malcolm Torquil MacNeill and of Morag MacNeill (*née* McKinnon). *Educ:* Robert Gordon's Coll., Aberdeen; Univ. of Aberdeen (LLB Hons 1985; DipLP 1986). Called to the Scottish Bar, 1992; Advocate Depute, 1998–2001; Standing Jun. Counsel to Scottish Exec., 2003–06. Accredited Mediator, CEDR, 2005. Mem. Panel, Police Appeals Tribunal, 2013–. MCIArb 2014. *Address:* Advocates Library, Parliament House, Parliament Square, Edinburgh EH1 1RF. *T:* (0131) 226 5071. *E:* calum.macneill@westwateradvocates.com. *Club:* New (Edinburgh).

McNEILL, (Elizabeth) Jane; QC 2002; a Recorder, since 2005; *b* 18 March 1957; *d* of David McNeill and Margaret McNeill (*née* Lewis); *m* 1990, David Adams; two *s*. *Educ:* St Hilda's Coll., Oxford (BA Hons Mod. Langs); City Univ., London (Dip Law). Called to the Bar, Lincoln's Inn, 1982, Bencher, 2007. Fee-paid Employment Judge. Mem. Council, ACAS, 2014–. *Recreations:* reading, cooking, bridge, walking, cinema. *Address:* Old Square Chambers, 10–11 Bedford Row, WC1R 4BU. *T:* (020) 7269 0300.

McNEILL, James Walker; QC (Scot.) 1991; Judge of the Courts of Appeal of Jersey and Guernsey, since 2006; *b* 16 Feb. 1952; *s* of late James McNeill and Edith Anna Howie Wardlaw; *m* 1986, Katherine Lawrence McDowall; two *s* one *d*. *Educ:* Dunoon Grammar Sch.; Cambridge Univ. (MA); Edinburgh Univ. (LLB). Advocate 1978; Standing Junior Counsel: to Dept of Transport in Scotland, 1984–88; to Inland Revenue in Scotland, 1988–91. Chm., Disciplinary Appts Cttee, Inst. and Faculty of Actuaries, 2013–. Mem., Judicial Appts Bd for Scotland, 2012–. Mem. Council, Commonwealth Lawyers' Assoc., 2005–11. Session Clerk, St Andrew's and St George's Parish Ch, Edinburgh, 1999–2003; Mem. Bd and Chm., Music Cttee, Scottish Internat. Piano Competition, 2004–10; Sec., Edinburgh City Centre Churches Together, 2012–. *Recreations:* music, hill-walking, cycle touring, travel. *Address:* 28 Kingsburgh Road, Edinburgh EH12 6DZ. *Clubs:* New (Edinburgh); Hon. Company of Edinburgh Golfers.

McNEILL, Jane; *see* McNeill, E. J.

McNEILL, Prof. John, PhD; Director Emeritus, Royal Ontario Museum, Toronto, since 1997 (Director, 1991–97; President, 1995–97); Hon. Associate, Royal Botanic Garden, Edinburgh, since 1998 (Regius Keeper, 1987–89); *b* 15 Sept. 1933; *s* of Thomas McNeill and Helen Lawrie Eagle; *m* 1st, 1961, Bridget Mariel Winterton (marr. diss. 1990); two *s*; 2nd, 1990, Marilyn Lois James. *Educ:* George Heriot's, Edinburgh; Univ. of Edinburgh (BSc Hons, PhD 1960). Asst Lectr and Lectr, Dept of Agricl Botany, Univ. of Reading, 1957–61; Lectr, Dept of Botany, Univ. of Liverpool, 1961–69; Plant (later Biosystematics) Research Institute, Agriculture Canada, Ottawa: Res. Scientist, 1969–77, Chief, Vascular Plant Taxonomy Sect., 1969–72; Sen. Res. Scientist, 1977–81; Prof. and Chm., Dept of Biology, Univ. of Ottawa, 1981–87; Associate Dir Curatorial, Royal Ontario Mus., Toronto, 1989–90, Acting Dir, 1990–91; Dir, George R. Gardiner Mus. of Ceramic Art, Toronto, 1991–96. Hon. Prof., Univ. of Edinburgh, 1989; Prof., Dept of Botany, Univ. of Toronto, 1990–2006; Adjunct Prof., Univ. of Ottawa, 1987–91. Mem. Editl Cttee, 1985–2003, Chm. Mgt Cttee, 1998–2001, Mem. Bd of Dirs, 2003–06, Emeritus Mem., 2006–, Flora North America Association; Rapporteur-général, Nomenclature section, Internat. Botanical Congresses, 1997–2012 (Vice-rapporteur, 1982–94); Ed., Nomenclature section, 2000–11, Technical Nomenclature sections, 2011–, Taxon (jl of Internat. Assoc. for Plant Taxonomy). *Publications* include: Phenetic and phylogenetic classification (jt ed), 1964; (jtly) Grasses of Ontario, 1977; (jt ed) International Code of Botanical Nomenclature, 1983, 1988, 1994, 2000, 2006; (jtly) Preliminary Inventory of Canadian Weeds, 1988; (jt ed) Flora of North America north of Mexico, vols 1 and 2, 1993, vol. 3, 1997, vol. 22, 2000, vol. 26, 2002, vol. 23, 2003; (jt ed) International Code of Nomenclature for Cultivated Plants, 1995, 7th edn 2004; (jt ed) International Code of Nomenclature for algae, fungi, and plants, 2012; over 20 chapters or sections of sci. books and over 90 contribs to sci. res. jls. *Recreation:* botanical nomenclature. *Address:* Royal Botanic Garden, 20A Inverleith Row, Edinburgh EH3 5LR.

McNEILL, Johnston David John; Chief Executive, Rural Payments Agency, 2001–06; *b* 15 Aug. 1956; *s* of David McNeill and Mary McNeill (*née* Kane); *m* 1983, Jennifer Fowler (marr. diss. 1997); one *s* two *d*. *Educ:* Lurgan Coll.; Southampton Coll. of Technology (HND Mech. Engrg); Univ. of Ulster (BA); Univ. of Central Lancashire (MBA); Portsmouth Univ. (PGDipPM, MA); PGDipM. Marine engr, 1974–79; mgt posts, private sector cos, 1979–88; Dep. Gen. Manager, Lancs CC, 1988–90; Asst Dir, Southampton CC, 1990–92; Dir of Contract Services, Belfast CC, 1992–94; Chief Executive: Meat Hygiene Service, MAFF, 1994–2000; Food Standards Agency, 2000–01. FIPD. Freeman, City of London; Liveryman, Butchers' Co. *Recreations:* ski-ing, rowing, yacht sailing, guitar, socialising with friends and family. *Club:* Farmers.

McNEILL, Pauline Mary; Co-founder and Partner, McNeill & Stone, since 2015; *b* 12 Sept. 1962; *d* of John Patrick McNeill and Teresa Ward or McNeill; *m* 1999, William Joseph Cahill; two step *s*. *Educ:* Glasgow Coll. of Building and Printing (Dip. 1986); Strathclyde Univ. (LLB 1999). Pres., NUS, 1986–88; Regl Orgnr, GMB Scotland, 1988–99. MSP (Lab) Glasgow Kelvin, 1999–2011; contested same seat (Lab), 2011. Dir of Legal and Public Affairs, Nationwide Milk Services Ltd, 2014–. *Recreations:* guitar, singing, rock music, keep fit.

McNEISH, Prof. Alexander Stewart, PhD; FRCP, FMedSci; Emeritus Professor of Clinical Science, London University, since 2001; Hon. Professor, School of Medicine, Birmingham University, since 2003; *b* 13 April 1938; *s* of Angus Stewart McNeish and Minnie Howieson (*née* Dickson); *m* 1963, Joan Ralston (*née* Hamilton); two *s* (one *d* decd). *Educ:* Glasgow Acad.; Univ. of Glasgow (MB; MPhil 2005); Univ. of Birmingham (MSc); Queen Mary, Univ. of London (PhD 2011). FRCP 1977; FRCPGlas 1985; FRCPCH 1996. Sen. Lectr in Paediatrics and Child Health, Univ. of Birmingham, 1970–76; Foundn Prof. of Child Health, Univ. of Leicester, 1976–80; University of Birmingham: Leonard Parsons Prof. of Paediatrics and Child Health, 1980–95; Dir, Inst. of Child Health, 1980–93; Dean, Faculty of Medicine and Dentistry, 1987–92; Dir of R&D, W Midlands RHA, 1992–95; Dir, MRC Clinical Scis Centre, Hammersmith Hosp., 1995–97; London University: Warden, St Bart's and Royal London Sch. of Medicine and Dentistry, 1997–2001; Vice Principal, 1997–99, Dep. Principal, 1999–2001, QMW. Mem., GMC, 1984–95. Founder FMedSci 1998. Hon. Fellow, QMUL, 2007. *Publications:* papers on paediatric gastroenterology in Lancet, BMJ and in Archives of Disease in Childhood. *Recreations:* golf, music. *Address:* 128 Westfield Road, Edgbaston, Birmingham B15 3JQ. *T:* (0121) 454 6081. *Clubs:* Athenæum; Blackwell Golf, Rye Golf.

McNEISH, Sir James, KNZM 2011; writer; *b* Auckland, NZ, 23 Oct. 1931; *s* of Arthur McNeish and Ina McNeish (*née* Bosworth); *m* 1st, 1960, Felicity Wily (marr. diss. 1964; she *d* 2008); one *d*; 2nd, 1968, Helen Schnitzer; one step *s*. *Educ:* Auckland Grammar Sch.; Univ. of Auckland (BA Langs). Journalist, NZ Herald, Auckland, 1953–57; Theatre Workshop, Stratford, E London, and teaching, 1958–59; recording folk music in 21 countries for BBC Sound Archives, 1960; work with Danilo Dolci, social reformer, Sicily, 1961–63; writer and documentary maker, Home Service and Third Prog., BBC Radio, 1963–67; contrib. articles to Observer, Guardian and various jls, 1961–67; Co-Founder and Dir, Bridge in NZ, educnl trust, 1974–82. Author, report on penal reform, NZ Justice Dept, 1976. Vis. Writer, Berlin Kuenstlerprogramm, 1983; Creative NZ Residency, Berlin, 2009. Katherine Mansfield Fellow, Menton, France, 1973; Res. Fellow, Nat. Liby of NZ, 1999. Hon. Pres., NZ Soc. of Authors, 2012. Prime Minister's Award for Literary Achievement, NZ, 2010. *Publications:* Tavern in the Town, 1957; Fire Under the Ashes: a life of Danilo Dolci, 1965; (with M. Friedlander) Larks in a Paradise, 1974; As for the Godwits, 1977; (with B. Brake) Art of the Pacific, 1980; Belonging: conversations in Israel, 1980; (with H. McNeish) Walking on my Feet: portrait of A. R. D. Fairburn, 1983; Ahnungslos in Berlin: a Berlin diary, 1985; The Man from Nowhere and Other Prose, 1991; The Mask of Sanity: the Bain murders, 1997; An Albatross Too Many, 1998; Dance of the Peacocks: New Zealanders in exile in the time of Hitler and Mao Tse-tung, 2003; The Sixth Man: the extraordinary life of Paddy Costello, 2007; Touchstones: memories of people and place, 2012; *novels:* Mackenzie, 1970; The Mackenzie Affair, 1972 (televised, 1974); The Glass Zoo, 1976; Joy, 1982; Lovelock, 1986, enlarged edn 2009; Penelope's Island, 1990; My Name is Paradiso, 1995; Mr Halliday and the Circus Master, 1996; The Crime of Huey Dunstan, 2010; Spellbinder, 2015; *plays:* The Rocking Cave, 1973; The Mouse Man, 1975; Eighteen-Ninety-Five, 1975; Thursday Bloody Thursday, 1998. *Recreations:* tennis, being wife-beaten at crosswords. *Address:* PO Box 10628, Wellington 6143, New Zealand. *Fax:* (4) 4997837. *E:* godwits@xtra.co.nz; c/o Andrew Hewson, Johnson & Alcock Ltd, EC1R 0HT. *T:* (020) 7251 0125. *E:* andrew@johnsonandalcock.co.uk.

McNELLY, Very Rev. Nicola; Provost, St John the Divine Cathedral, Oban, since 2012; Rector, St James', Arkbrecknish, since 2012; *b* Tredegar, 1 May 1962; *d* of Eric Calder and Beryl Calder (*née* Stock); *m* 1984, Iain McNelly; two *d*. *Educ:* Ebbw Vale Grammar Sch.; Cranmer Hall, St John's Coll., Durham (DipTh and Ministry 2009). Intelligence Corps, WRAC, 1980–84; Sch. Sec., Mountbatten Sch., Celle, W Germany, 1986–89; PA to Customer Services Dir, Magnet Kitchens, 1990–93; SSAFA Forces Help: Admin. positions in Cyprus and NI, 2001–04; Volunteer Develt Manager, NI, 2004–07; Chair, In-Service Cttee, Edinburgh, 2009–11; ordained deacon, 2009, priest, 2010; Chaplain, St Mary's Cath., Edinburgh, 2009–12; Canon, Cathedral of the Isles and Collegiate Ch of the Holy Spirit, Isle of Cumbrae, 2013–. *Recreations:* trekking in Nepal, raising money for AGE/Nepal (A Genuine Effort Nepal, sch. for children with neurological disorders). *Address:* The Rectory, Ardconnel Terrace, Oban PA34 5DJ. *T:* 07825 440580. *E:* nicki.mcnelly@gmail.com.

McNICOL, Prof. Donald; Vice-Chancellor and Principal, University of Tasmania, 1996–2002; *b* 18 April 1939; *s* of Ian Robertson McNicol and Sadie Isabelle Williams; *m* 1963, Kathleen Margaret Wells; one *s* two *d*. *Educ:* Unley High Sch.; Univ. of Adelaide (BA 1964); St John's Coll., Cambridge (PhD 1967). Fellow, Aust. Psych. Soc. Lectr in Psychology, Univ. of Adelaide, 1967–71; Research Fellow, St John's Coll., Cambridge, 1968–69; Sen. Lectr in Psych., Univ. of NSW, 1971–74; Associate Prof. in Psych., Univ. of NSW, 1975–81; Prof. of Psych., Univ. of Tasmania, 1981–86, now Emeritus Prof.; Comr for Univs and Chm., Univs Adv. Council, Commonwealth Tertiary Educn, 1986–88; Vice-Chancellor, Univ. of New England, NSW, 1988–90; Vice-Chancellor and Principal, Univ. of Sydney, 1990–96. President: AVCC, 1994–95; Assoc. of Univs of Asia Pacific, 1998–99; AHEIA, 2000–01. *Publications:* A Primer of Signal Detection Theory, 1972, repr. 2005. *Recreations:* walking, jazz, reading. *Address:* PO Box 1155, Sandy Bay, Tas 7006, Australia.

McNICOL, Iain MacKenzie; General Secretary, Labour Party, since 2011; *b* Kilwinning, 17 Aug. 1969; *s* of Iain and Zoe McNicol; *m* 1995, Shelley; one *s* one *d*. *Educ:* Dundee Inst. of Technol. (HND Bldg Mgt 1991). Pres., Dundee Inst. of Technol. Students' Union (on sabbatical), 1991–93; Campaigns and Membership Officer, Labour Students (on sabbatical), 1993–94; Organiser and Agent, Labour Party, 1994–97; Organiser, 1997–2004, Nat. Political Officer, 2004–11, GMB Union. *Recreations:* karate, playing the bagpipes, golf, cooking. *Address:* Labour Party, One Brewer's Green, SW1H 0RH. *E:* iain_mcnicol@labour.org.uk.

MACNICOL, Malcolm Fraser, FRCS, FRCP, FRCSE(Orth); Consultant Orthopaedic Surgeon: Royal Hospital for Sick Children and Royal Infirmary, Edinburgh, 1979–2007; Spire Murrayfield Hospital, Edinburgh, since 1984; *b* 18 March 1943; *s* of Roy Simson Macnicol and Eona Kathleen Macnicol (*née* Fraser); *m* 1972, Anne Morag Docherty; two *s* one *d*. *Educ:* Royal High Sch., Edinburgh (Capt. of Sch., Dux in English and Biol.); Edinburgh Univ. (BSc Hons 1966, MB ChB 1969); MChOrth Liverpool 1979. FRCS 1973; FRCSE(Orth) 1979; Dip. Sports Med., RCSE, 1998; FRCP 2000. Research Fellow: Stanford Univ., 1966; Harvard Univ., 1970–71; Lectr in Orthopaedics, Edinburgh Univ., 1976–78; Sen. Orthopaedic Lectr, Univ. of W Australia, 1978–79; Sen. Orthopaedic Lectr (pt-time), Univ. of Edinburgh, 1982–. Treas., RCSE, 1987–90. Pres., British Orthopaedic Assoc., 2001–02 (Chm., Medico-legal Sub Cttee, 1998–2003; Mem., Robert Jones Orthopaedic Club); Member: Medico-Chirurgical Soc., 1984–; British Soc. for Children's Orthopaedic Surgery, 1985–; British Assoc. for Surgery of the Knee, 1985–; British Orthopaedic Res. Soc., 1985–; Scottish Soc. of Hist. of Medicine, 2010–. Patron, Scottish Post-Polio Network, 2006–. Hon. Med. Advr, Scottish RU, 2004–08. Mem., Malt Whisky Tasting Soc., 2000–. *Publications:* Princess Margaret Rose Orthopaedic Hospital 1932–1982, 1982, 2nd edn 2002; Aids to Orthopaedics, 1984; Basic Care of the Injured Hand, 1984 (Italian edn 1986); Problem Knee, 1986, 3rd edn 2011; Color Atlas and Text of Osteomy of the Hip, 1995 (Portuguese edn 1997); Children's Orthopaedics and Fractures, 1994, 3rd edn 2010; The Red Sandstone Buildings of Edinburgh, 2009; contrib. numerous peer-reviewed papers and book chapters. *Recreations:* tennis, walking, water-colour painting, theatre, architecture. *Address:* Red House, 1 South Gillsland Road, Edinburgh EH10 5DE. *Clubs:* Robert Jones; Harveian Soc. (Edinburgh); Harvard Research.

McNICOLL, Iain Walter, CB 2006; CBE 2000; defence consultant, since 2011; *b* 3 May 1953; *s* of Walter McNicoll and Maida Cameron McNicoll (*née* Readdie); *m* 1980, Wendelien Henriëtte Maria van den Biggelaar; one *s* two *d*. *Educ:* Dundee High Sch.; Univ. of Edinburgh (BSc 1975). Commnd RAFVR, 1973, RAF, 1975; XV Sqn, 1978–81; qwi 1979; Tornado Weapons Conversion Unit 45 (Reserve) Sqn, 1982–85; 17 (Fighter) Sqn, 1985–86; 16 Sqn, 1986–89; RAF Staff Coll., 1990; PSO to Dep. C-in-C, Strike Command, 1991–92; OC 17 (Fighter) Sqn, 1992–95; MoD, 1995–98; Station Comdr, Brüggen, 1998–2000; Dir, Force Development, MoD, 2000–02; DG, Jt Doctrine and Concepts, MoD, 2002–05; AOC No 2 Gp, 2005–07; Dep. C-in-C Ops Air Comd, 2007–10; retd as Air Marshal, 2010. Associate Partner, Defence Strategy & Solutions LLP, 2010–11. Non-executive Director: Jee Ltd, 2009–; NATS, 2013–. FRAeS 2001. MInstD 2008, CDir 2010. QCVSA 1989. *E:* iain_mcnicoll@hotmail.com. *Club:* Royal Air Force.

MacNISH, Alastair Jesse Head, OBE 2008; FCCA; Chairman, Accounts Commission for Scotland, 2001–07; Chairman of Board, Audit Scotland, 2001–07; *b* 4 Feb. 1947; *m* 1970, Jean Ferguson Bell; one *s* two *d*. *Educ:* Gourock High Sch. FCCA 1972. Chief Auditor, Renfrew CC, 1973–75; Strathclyde Regional Council: Principal Accountant, 1975–77; Asst Dir of Educn, 1977–87; Depute Dir of Social Work, 1987–95; Chief Exec., S Lanarks Council, 1995–99; Chm., Leadership Adv. Panel, Scottish Exec., 1999–2000. Clerk: Strathclyde Jt Fire Bd, 1995–99; Lanarkshire Jt Valuation Bd, 1995–99. Member: Scotland Adv. Cttee, EOC, 1996–2000; Scottish Govt's Ministerial Panel on Fire & Rescue Services, 2007–. Member, Board: Glasgow Housing Assoc., 2009–11; Wheatley Housing Gp, 2012– (Chm., 2015–); Chm., Greenock Med. Aid Soc., 2013–. Chm., Bd of Dirs, Royal Caledonian Curling Club, 1999–2002, 2014–. MCIPD (MIPD 1994). *Recreations:* golf, curling, bridge. *Club:* Gourock Golf (Capt. 1998–99).

McNISH, Althea Marjorie, (Althea McNish Weiss), CMT 1976; freelance textile designer, since 1957; *b* Trinidad; *d* of late J. Claude McNish, educnl reformer, and late Margaret (*née* Bourne); *m* 1969, John Weiss. *Educ:* Port-of-Spain, by her father and others; London Coll. of Printing; Central School of Arts and Crafts; Royal Coll. of Art. NDD, DesRCA; FCSD (FSIA 1968, MSIA 1960). Painted throughout childhood; after design educn in London, freelance practice in textile and other design; commns from Ascher and Liberty's, 1957; new techniques for laminate murals, for SS Oriana and hosp. and coll. in Trinidad; Govt of Trinidad and Tobago travelling schol., 1962; interior design (for Govt of Trinidad and Tobago) in NY, Washington and London, 1962; Cotton Bd trav. schol. to report on export potential for British printed cotton goods in Europe, 1963; collection of dress fabric designs for ICI and Tootal Thomson for promotion of Terylene Toile, 1966; special features for Daily Mail Ideal Home Exhibn, 1966–78; (with John Weiss) etched silver dishes, 1973–; interior design for Sec.-Gen. of Commonwealth, 1975; bedlinen collection for Courtaulds, 1978; (with John Weiss) textile design develt for BRB, 1978–81; textile hangings for BRB Euston offices, 1979; banners for Design Centre, 1981; (with John Weiss) improvements to London office of High Comr for Trinidad and Tobago, 1981; advr on exhibn design for Govt of Trinidad and

Tobago, Commonwealth Inst., 1982–84; fashion textile designs for Slovene textile printers, 1985–91; furnishing textile designs for Fede Cheti, Milan, 1986–91; murals and hangings for Royal Caribbean Cruise Line: MS Nordic Empress, 1990; MS Monarch of the Seas, 1991. Paintings and various work in exhibitions include: individual and gp exhibns, London, 1954–; with Caribbean Artists Movt, Th. Royal, Stratford, 1967, Digby Stuart Coll., LSE and H of C, 1968; Caribbean Artists in England, Commonwealth Inst., 1971; Island Pulse: five Caribbean-born artists, Islington Arts Factory, 1996; solo exhibn, RCA Hockney Gall., 1997; Trinidad & Tobago Through the Eye of the Artist, Commonwealth Inst., 1997; Fine Arts Soc., 198 Gall. and Six into One: Artists from the Caribbean, Morley Gall., 1998; Glebe Place, 2000; paintings, Jamaica, 1975; hangings, Kilkenny, 1981; hangings, individual exhibn, Peoples Gall., 1982; hangings, Magazine Workspace, Leicester, 1983; textile designs in exhibitions: Inprint, Manchester and London, 1964–71; Design Council/BoT, USA and Sweden, 1969, London, 1970, London and USA, 1972; Design-In, Amsterdam, 1972–74; Design Council, 1975–80; The Way We Live Now, V&A Mus., 1978; Indigo, Lille, 1981–82; Commonwealth Fest. Art Exhibn, Brisbane, 1982; Designs for British Dress and Furnishing Fabrics, V&A Mus., 1986; Make or Break, Henry Moore Gall., 1986; Surtex, New York, 1987; Ascher, V&A Mus., 1987; Transforming the Crown: African, Asian and Caribbean Artists in Britain 1966–96, NY, 1996; Trade and Empire: Remembering Slavery, Whitworth Art Gall., Manchester, 2008; Shirley Craven and Hull Traders: Revolutionary Post-War Fabrics and Furniture, Ferens Art Gall., Hull, 2009, Bankfield Mus., Halifax, Arts Centre, King's Lynn, 2010, Harris Mus. and Art Gall., Preston, 2011; RCA Black: Past, Present and Future, RCA, 2011; work represented in permanent collections of V&A Mus. and Whitworth Art Gall., Univ. of Manchester. Vis. Lecturer: Central Sch. of Art and Crafts and other colls and polytechnics, 1960–; USA, 1972; Italy, W Germany and Slovenia, 1985–; Advisory Tutor in Furnishing and Surface Design, London Coll. of Furniture, 1972–90. External assessor for educnl and professional bodies, incl. CSD and NCDAD/CNAA, 1966–; Mem. jury for Leverhulme schols, 1968; Judge: Portuguese textile design comp., Lisbon, 1973; 'Living' Design Awards, 1974; Carnival selection panels, Arts Council, 1982 and 1983. Vice-Pres., SIAD, 1977–78; Design Council: Mem., selection panels for Design Awards and Design Index, 1968–80; Mem. Bd, 1974–81; Mem., Jubilee Souvenir Selection Panel, 1976; Mem., Royal Wedding Souvenir Selection Panel, 1981. Member: Fashion and Textiles Design Bd, CNAA, 1975–78; London Local Adv. Cttee, IBA, 1981–; Formation Cttee, London Inst., ILEA, 1985. Mem. Governing Body, Portsmouth Coll. of Art, 1972–81. *BBC-TV:* studio setting for Caribbean edn of Full House, 1973. Has appeared, with work, in films for COI and Gas Council. Hon. Dr Fine Arts, Trinidad and Tobago, 2006. Chaconia Medal (Gold) (Trinidad and Tobago), 1976, for service to art and design; Scarlet Ibis Award (Trinidad and Tobago), 1993; Award for Achievement in the Arts (Trinidad and Tobago), 2012. *Publications:* textile designs produced in many countries, 1957–; designs and paintings illustrated in: J. Laver, The Liberty Story, 1959; Costumes, Masks and Jewellery of the Commonwealth, ed J. Debayo, 1982; Young Blood, Britain's Design Schools Today and Tomorrow, ed K. Baynes, 1983; V. D. Mendes and F. M. Hinchcliffe, Ascher, 1987; Did Britain Make It?, ed P. Sparke, 1986; M. Schoeser, Fabrics and Wallpapers, 1986; M. Schoeser and C. Rufey, English and American Textiles from 1790 to the Present, 1989; B. Philips, Fabrics and Wallpapers, 1991; S. Calloway, The House of Liberty, 1992; A. Walmsley, The Caribbean Artists Movement 1966–1972, 1992; L. Jackson, 20th Century Pattern Design: textile and wallpaper pioneers, 2002; M. Schoeser, Silk, 2007; E Baxter Wright and Z. Rhodes, Vintage Fashion, 1900–1990, 2007; The Oxford Companion to Black History, 2007; Neo-classicism to Pop, vol. 2, 2008; Africa and the Americas: culture, politics and history: a multi-disciplinary encyclopedia, 2008; L. Jackson, Shirley Craven and Hull Traders: Revolutionary Fabrics and Furniture 1957–1980, 2009; Building Britannia: life experience with Britain, 2009; A. Buruma, Liberty and Co. in the Fifties and Sixties: a taste for design, 2009; A. Rice, Creating Memorials, Building Identities: the politics of memory in the black Atlantic, 2010; Denis Williams: a life in works: new and collected essays, 2010; A. Rice et al., Trade and Empire: remembering slavery, 2011; N. Albrechtsen and F. Solanke, Scarves, 2011; V&A Pattern: Modern British Designers, ed S Safer, 2012; V&A Pattern: Sanderson 1954–74, ed M. Schoeser, 2012; Artists' Textiles, 1940–1976, 2012; L. Jackson, Alastair Morton and Edinburgh Weavers: Visionary Textiles in Modern Art, 2012; published in Decorative Art, Designers in Britain and design jls. *Recreations:* ski-ing, travelling, music, gardening. *E:* althea.mcnish@virgin.net. *Club:* Soroptimist.

MACNIVEN, Duncan, CBE 2012; TD 1985; Registrar General for Scotland, 2003–11; *b* 1 Dec. 1950; *s* of late John and Jenny Macniven; *m* 1976, Valerie Margaret Clark; two *d. Educ:* Melville Coll., Edinburgh; Aberdeen Univ. (MA 1973; MLitt 1978). Joined Scottish Office, 1973; Principal, 1978–85; Asst Sec., 1986–90; Dep. Dir, Historic Scotland, 1990–95; Head of Police Div., 1995–97; Head of Police, Fire and Emergencies Gp, 1997–99; Comr and Hd of Corporate Services, Forestry Commn, 1999–2003. RE, TA, 1969–85 (Major, 1983–85). Hon. LLD: Robert Gordon, 2008; Aberdeen, 2012. *Recreations:* active church membership, being outdoors, walking, ski-ing, Scottish history, family history. *Address:* Ashestiel, Kenmore Street, Aberfeldy, Perthshire PH15 2BL.

McNULTY, Rt Hon. Anthony James; PC 2007; *b* 3 Nov. 1958; *s* of James Anthony McNulty and Eileen Anne McNulty; *m* 2002, Christine Gilbert. *Educ:* Univ. of Liverpool (BA Hons); Virginia Poly. Inst. and State Univ. (MA). Business School, Polytechnic of North London: Research Asst, 1983–85; Res. Fellow and part-time Lectr, 1985–86; part-time Lectr, PCL and Kingston Poly., 1984–86; Sen. Lectr, then Principal Lectr, Business Sch., Poly. of N London, later Univ. of N London, 1986–97. MP (Lab) Harrow E, 1997–2010; contested (Lab) same seat, 2010. Mem. (Lab), Harrow LBC, 1986–97 (Dep. Leader, 1990–96, Leader, 1996–97, Labour Gp). Mem., Regl Exec., Gtr London Labour Party, 1985–87. Mem., NI Grand Cttee. PPS to Min. of State, DfEE, 1997–99; an Asst Govt Whip, 1999–2001; a Lord Comr of HM Treasury (Govt Whip), 2001–02; Parliamentary Under-Secretary of State: ODPM, 2002–03; DfT, 2003–04; Minister of State: DfT, 2004–05; Home Office, 2005–08; DWP, 2008–09; Minister for London, 2008–09. *Publications:* various academic works on local govt, public sector mgt, trng and small firms. *Recreations:* eating out, theatre, films, Rugby, current affairs.

McNULTY, Des(mond); Public Policy Knowledge Exchange Officer, University of Glasgow, since 2012; *b* Stockport, 28 July 1952; *m*; two *s. Educ:* St Bede's Coll., Manchester; York Univ.; Glasgow Univ. Subject Leader in Sociology, 1990–97, Head of Strategic Planning, 1997–99, Glasgow Caledonian Univ. Non-exec. Dir, Gtr Glasgow Health Bd, 1998–99. Member (Lab): Strathclyde Regl Council, 1990–96; Glasgow City Council, 1995–99. Mem. (Lab) Clydebank and Milngavie, Scottish Parlt, 1999–2011; contested (Lab) same seat, 2011. Dep. Minister for Communities, Scottish Exec., 2002–03, 2006–07. Scottish Parliament: shadow spokesman on transport, 2007–09; Shadow Cabinet Sec. for Educn and Lifelong Learning, 2009–11; Member: Transport and Envmt Cttee, 1999–2003; Corporate Body, 1999–2001; Enterprise and Lifelong Learning Cttee, 2000–01; Rural and Environment Cttee, 2007–08; Transport Infrastructure and Climate Change Cttee, 2008–11; Convenor, Finance Cttee, 2001–02, 2003–06. Chairman: Glasgow Healthy City Partnership, 1996–99; Glasgow 1999 Fest. of Architecture and Design. Board Member: Wise Gp, 1995–; Tron Theatre Ltd, 2005–12. Mem., Kemp Commn on Future of Vol. Sector in Scotland, 1995–97. Mem. Ct, Glasgow Univ., 1994–99. *Address:* Adam Smith Building, University of Glasgow G12 8QQ.

McNULTY, Sir (Robert William) Roy, Kt 1998; CBE 1992; Chairman, Gatwick Airport Ltd, since 2013 (non-executive Director, since 2011); *b* 7 Nov. 1937; *s* of Jack and Nancy McNulty; *m* 1963, Ismay Ratcliffe Rome; one *s* two *d. Educ:* Portora Royal School, Enniskillen; Trinity College, Dublin (BA, BComm). Audit Manager, Peat Marwick Mitchell & Co., Glasgow, 1963–66; Accounting Methods Manager, Chrysler UK, Linwood, 1966–68; Harland & Wolff, Belfast: Management Accountant, 1968–72; Computer Services Manager, 1972–74; Management Services Manager, 1975–76; Sen. Management Consultant, Peat Marwick Mitchell & Co., Belfast, 1977–78; Short Brothers plc: Exec. Dir, Finance and Admin, 1978–85; Dep. Managing Dir, 1986–88; Man. Dir and Chief Exec., 1988–92; Pres., Shorts Gp, Bombardier Aerospace, 1992–96; Chm., 1996–99. Chairman: The Odyssey Trust Co. Ltd, 1997–99; NATS Ltd, 1999–2001; CAA, 2001–09 (Mem. Bd, 1999–2000); Ilex URC, 2007–12; Advantage West Midlands, 2009–12; Dep. Chm., Olympic Delivery Authy, 2007–14 (Acting Chm., 2006–07); non-executive Director: Norbrook Laboratories Ltd, 1990– (Chm., 2014–); Ulster Bank Ltd, 1996–2000; Monarch Hldgs Ltd, 2012– (Chm., 2014). Mem., Council, SBAC, 1988–99 (Pres., 1993–94; Treas., 1995–99). Member: IDB for NI, 1992–98; Steering Gp for UK Foresight Programme, 1997–2000; Chairman: NI Growth Challenge, 1993–98; Technology Foresight Defence and Aerospace Panel, 1994–95; DTI Aviation Cttee, 1995–98; Rail Value for Money Study, 2010–11. Industrial Prof., Dept of Engineering, Univ. of Warwick. Vice Pres., EEF, 1997–. CCMI; FIMI. Hon. FRAeS 1995; Hon. DSc QUB, 1999; Hon. DTech Glamorgan, 2011. *Recreations:* walking, golf, reading. *Address:* Gatwick Airport Ltd, Destinations Place, Gatwick Airport, W Sussex RH6 0NP.

McPARTLAND, Stephen; MP (C) Stevenage, since 2010; *b* 9 Aug. 1976; *m* Emma. *Educ:* Liverpool Coll.; Liverpool Univ. (BA Hist. 1997); Liverpool John Moores Univ. (MSc Technol. Mgt 1998). Agent, NE Herts Cons. Assoc., 2001–08; Membership Dir, British Amer. Business, 2008–10. *Address:* House of Commons, SW1A 0AA.

McPARTLIN, Anthony; actor and presenter; *b* Newcastle upon Tyne, 18 Nov. 1975; *m* 2006, Lisa Armstrong. Music career, 1993–97 (14 Top 20 hits; UK, European and world tours); *television:* actor: Byker Grove, 1989–93; A Tribute to the Likely Lads, 2002; presenter of series with Declan Donnelly, *qv* as Ant and Dec: The Ant and Dec Show, 1995; Ant and Dec Unzipped, 1997; SM:TV Live, 1998–2001 (British Comedy Award, 2000; RTS Award, 2001); CD:UK, 1998–2001; Ant and Dec's Secret Camera Show, 2000; Friends Like These, 2000; Slap Bang with Ant and Dec, 2001; Pop Idol, 2001–03; Ant and Dec's Saturday Night Takeaway, 2002– (British Comedy Awards, 2003, 2004, 2005; Nat. TV Awards, 2007, 2010; British Acad. TV Award, 2014); I'm a Celebrity... Get Me Out of Here!, 2002– (British Comedy Award, 2004; Best Entertainment Perf., BAFTA, 2010; Nat. TV Awards, 2011–15; TRIC Special Award, 2013; RTS Award, 2013); Gameshow Marathon, 2005; Pokerface, 2006–07; Britain's Got Talent, 2007–; Wanna Bet? (USA), 2008; Push the Button, 2010–11; Red or Black?, 2011–12; host (with Declan Donnelly) Brit Awards, 2015; *film:* Alien Autopsy, 2006. Awards with Declan Donnelly include: Most Popular Entertainment Presenter of Year, annually, 2001–08 and 2010–15, Landmark Award, 2014, Nat. TV Awards; Best Entertainment Personality, British Comedy Awards, 2003, 2004; Best Entertainment Performers, RTS Awards, 2011; Personality of the Year, Freesat Free TV Awards, 2014; TV Personality of the Year, TRIC Awards, 2013, 2014. *Publications:* (with D. Donnelly) Ooh! What a Lovely Pair: our story, 2009. *Address:* c/o James Grant Media Ltd, 94 Strand on the Green, Chiswick, W4 3NN. *T:* (020) 8742 4950.

McPARTLIN, Noel; Advocate, since 1976; Sheriff of Grampian, Highland and Islands at Elgin, 2008–11; *b* 25 Dec. 1939; *s* of Michael Joseph McPartlin and Ann Dunn or McPartlin; *m* 1965, June Anderson Whitehead; three *s* three *d. Educ:* Galashiels Acad.; Edinburgh Univ. (MA, LLB). Solicitor in Glasgow, Linlithgow and Stirling, 1964–76. Sheriff of Grampian, Highland and Islands at Peterhead and Banff, 1983–85, at Elgin, 1985–2001; Sheriff of Lothian and Borders at Edinburgh, 2001–08. *Recreation:* urban and country life.

McPHAIL, Dr Alastair David, CMG 2014; OBE 2005; HM Diplomatic Service; Consul-General, Jerusalem, since 2014; *b* 2 March 1961; *m* 1989, (Pamela) Joanne Davies; two *s. Educ:* Univ. of Otago (Modern Langs); Univ. of Edinburgh (PhD Russian). Lectr in Russian, Nottingham Univ.; work in publishing; entered FCO, 1994; Nuclear Weapons Desk Officer, Security Policy Dept, FCO, 1994–95; Arabic lang. trng, 1995–96; First Sec. (Pol/Mil), Ankara, 1996–2000; Hd, Egypt, Libya and Sudan Section, Near East and N Africa Dept, 2000–02, Hd, Sudan Unit, 2002–04, FCO; UK Special Rep. for Sudan, 2004–05; Italian lang. trng, 2005; Minister and Dep. Hd of Mission, Rome, 2006–09; UK Special Envoy to Mali and Hd, Crisis Mgt Team, Bamako, 2009; Consul Gen., S Sudan, 2011; Ambassador to S Sudan, 2011–13. *Address:* c/o Foreign and Commonwealth Office, King Charles Street, SW1A 2AH.

McPHAIL, Angus William, MA; Warden, Radley College, 2000–14; *b* 25 May 1956; *s* of Peter Bigham McPhail and Sylvia Bridget McPhail (*née* Campbell); *m* 1980, Elizabeth Hirsch; two *s* one *d. Educ:* Abingdon Sch.; University Coll., Oxford (BA Hons 1978; MA 1982). Overseas Dept, Bank of England, 1978–82; Asst Master, Glenalmond Coll., 1982–85; Head of Econs and Housemaster, Sedbergh Sch., 1985–93; Headmaster, Strathallan Sch., 1993–2000. *Recreations:* cricket, golf, music, walking. *Clubs:* Vincent's (Oxford); Blairgowrie Golf; Cryptics Cricket.

MacPHAIL, Sir Bruce (Dugald), Kt 1992; FCA; Managing Director, Peninsular and Oriental Steam Navigation Co., 1985–2003; *b* 1 May 1939; *s* of late Dugald Ronald MacPhail and Winifred Marjorie MacPhail; *m* 1st, 1963, Susan Mary Gregory (*d* 1975); three *s*; 2nd, 1983, Caroline Ruth Grimston Curtis-Bennett (*née* Hubbard). *Educ:* Haileybury Coll.; Balliol Coll., Oxford (MA); Harvard Business Sch., Mass, USA (MBA 1967). FCA 1976. Articled, Price Waterhouse, 1961–65; Hill Samuel & Co. Ltd, 1967–69; Finance Director: Sterling Guarantee Trust Ltd, 1969–74; Town & City Properties Ltd, 1974–76; Man. Dir, Sterling Guarantee Trust, 1976–85. Non-executive Director: Chelsfield Plc, 1999–2004; Chelsfield Partners, 2006–; Intelligent Engrg Ltd, 2005–; Scarborough Minerals, 2006–08. Gov., Royal Ballet Sch., 1982–99; Life Gov., 1992, and Mem. Council, 1992–2004, Haileybury Coll.; Chairman: Council, Templeton Coll., Oxford, 1993–95; Council for Sch. of Management Studies, Univ. of Oxford, 1995–2001; Business Adv. Forum, Saïd Business Sch., Univ. of Oxford, 2001–08. Barclay Fellow, Green Templeton Coll. (formerly Templeton Coll.), Oxford, 1995–2012 (Hon. Fellow, 2012). Trustee, Sir Jules Thorn Charitable Trust, 1994–. *Recreations:* reading, wine, scuba diving. *Address:* Thorpe Lubenham Hall, Lubenham, Market Harborough, Leics LE16 9TR.

McPHATE, Very Rev. Gordon Ferguson, MD, FRCPE; Dean of Chester, since 2002; *b* 1 June 1950; *s* of David and Grace McPhate; one adopted *s. Educ:* Aberdeen Univ. (MB, ChB 1974); Fitzwilliam Coll., Cambridge (BA 1977, MA 1981, MD 1988); Surrey Univ. (MSc 1986); Edinburgh Univ. (MTh 1994); Westcott House Theol Coll., Cambridge. FRCPE 1998. Ordained deacon, 1978, priest, 1979. Tutor in Physiol., Clare Coll., Cambridge, 1975–77; Lectr in Physiol., Guy's Hosp. Med. Sch., London Univ., 1978–84; Registrar in Pathol., Guildford Hosps, 1984–86; Lectr in Pathol., 1986–93, Sen. Lectr, 1993–2002, St Andrews Univ.; Fife Hospitals: Hon. Sen. Registrar in Pathol., 1988–96; Hon. Consultant Chem. Pathologist, 1996–2002; Consultant Chem. Pathologist, 2001–02. External Mem., GMC, 2000–15. Hon. Curate, Sanderstead, 1978–80; Hon. Minor Canon, Southwark Cathedral, 1980–86; Hon. Chaplain, St Andrews Univ., 1986–2002. Vis. Prof. of Theol. and Medicine, Univ. of Chester (formerly UC Chester), 2003–; Hon. Reader in Medicine, Univ. of Liverpool, 2005–08. FHEA 2007. *Publications:* articles in learned jls. *Recreations:* classical and choral music, 18th and 19th century Western art, cinema, reading history and biography. *Address:* The Deanery, 7 Abbey Street, Chester CH1 2JF. *T:* (office) (01244) 500952, (home) (01244) 500971. *E:* dean@chestercathedral.com.

McPHEE, Robin Alasdair; a District Judge (Magistrates' Courts), since 2002; *b* 3 Sept. 1958; *s* of Kenneth Alfred McPhee and Margaret Thorpe McPhee; *m* 1982, Beverley Jayne Leggatt; one *s* one *d*. *Educ:* Goffs Sch., Cheshunt. Admitted as solicitor, 1983; Clerk: Tottenham Magistrates' Court, 1977–83; Harlow, Epping and Ongar Magistrates' Court, 1983–88; Partner, Attwater & Liell, Solicitors, Harlow, Essex, 1988–2002. *Recreations:* reading, ski-ing, hill walking. *Address:* Highbury Corner Magistrates' Court, 51 Holloway Road, N7 8JA.

MACPHERSON, family name of **Barons Macpherson of Drumochter** and **Strathcarron**.

MACPHERSON OF DRUMOCHTER, 3rd Baron *cr* 1951; **James Anthony Macpherson;** *b* London, 27 Feb. 1979; *o s* of 2nd Baron Macpherson of Drumochter and of Catherine Bridget Macpherson (*née* MacCarthy); *S* father, 2008; *m* 2009, Kitty, *y d* of Mrs Katalin Zetenyi Budai, Budapest; two *s* one *d*. *Educ:* Napier Univ., Edinburgh (BA Hons Business Studies 2002); Aberdeen Univ. (Master of Land Econ. 2010). Dir, Games and Movies, 2003–07; Property Co-ordinator, Alba Residential, 2007–08; Dir, Tomatin Firewood, 2011–. *Recreations:* tennis, field sports, travel, restaurants, films, photography. *Heir:* *s* Hon. Daniel Thomas Macpherson, *b* 23 Jan. 2013. *Address:* Dell Farm House, Tomatin, Inverness-shire IV13 7YA. *T:* 07527 883606. *E:* j-mac@sky.com.

MACPHERSON, (Agnes Lawrie Addie) Shonaig, (Mrs S. Cairns), CBE 2006; FRSE; Chairman, Royal Lyceum Theatre Company, since 2012; *b* 29 Sept. 1958; *d* of Harry Dempster Baird Macpherson and Margaret Douglas McClure; *m* 2002, Scott Cairns; two *s* by Roger Brown. *Educ:* Univ. of Sheffield (LLB Hons); Coll. of Law, Chester. Admitted solicitor: England and Wales (Dist.), 1984; Scotland, 1992; Solicitor: Norton Rose, 1982–85; Corporate Dept, Knapp Fisher, 1985–87; Asst Co. Sec., Storehouse plc, 1987; Hd, Legal Dept, Harrods Ltd, 1987–89; Partner, Calow Easton, 1989–91; McGrigor Donald, later McGrigors, Solicitors: Hd, IP/Technol. Team, 1991–2004; Man. Partner, Edinburgh, 1996–2001; Sen. Partner, 2001–04. Co. Sec., Macpherson Coaches Ltd, 2012–. Chairman: SCDI, 2004–09 (Mem. Bd, 2000–09); Nat. Trust for Scotland, 2005–10. Director: ITI Scotland Ltd, 2003–09 (Chm., 2005–09); Edinburgh Internat. Conf. Centre Ltd, 2005–14; Braveheart Ventures, 2005–08; Braveheart Investment Gp, 2005–08; Edinburgh Military Tattoo Ltd, later Royal Edinburgh Military Tattoo, 2008– (Dep. Chm., 2010–); Euan's Guide Ltd, 2015–. Mem., Scottish Adv. Bd, BT plc, 2002– (Chm., 2008–). Mem., Calman Commn on Scottish Devolution, 2009–10. Scottish Executive: non-exec. Mem., Mgt Gp, 2001–07; Culture Comr, 2004–05. Chm., Scottish Council Foundn, 2000–09. Pres., Edinburgh Chamber of Commerce, 2002–04; Dep. Pres., British Chambers of Commerce, 2004–06. Mem. Bd, Edinburgh Internat. Film Fest., 2000–09. Mem. Ct, Univ. of Edinburgh, 2001–07; Governor: Edinburgh Coll. of Art, 2000–11; Heriot-Watt Univ., 2009–; Mem. Council, Open Univ., 2009–. Chm., Prince's Scottish YBT, 2007–12; Trustee: Robertson Trust, 2005– (Dep. Chm., 2014–); Prince's Trust Scotland, 2005–10 (Chm., 2007–10); Prince's Trust, 2007–10; Dunedin Consort, 2012–; Scottish Chamber Orch. Trust. CCMI 2009. FRSE 2004; FRSA 2000. DUniv Glasgow, 2007. *Recreations:* theatre, golf, film, walking, 20th century literature. *Address:* Lochcote, Linlithgow, W Lothian EH49 6QE. *Fax:* (01506) 655231. *E:* shonaigm@btconnect.com.

McPHERSON, Prof. Andrew Francis; Professor of Sociology, 1989–96, now Emeritus, and Director, Centre for Educational Sociology, 1972–96, University of Edinburgh; *b* 6 July 1942; *m* 1st, 1965, Eldwyth Mary Boyle (*d* 2000); one *s* one *d*; 2nd, 1989, Alison Jean Elphinstone Edward or Arnott (*d* 2002). *Educ:* Ripon Grammar Sch.; The Queen's Coll., Oxford (BA Hist.). DPSA; FEIS; FSCRE; FRSE. Lectr in Sociology, Univ. of Glasgow, 1965; University of Edinburgh: Res. Fellow in Education, 1968; Lectr in Sociology, 1973; Sen. Lectr, 1978; Reader, 1983. FBA 1993–2003. *Publications:* (with G. Neave) The Scottish Sixth, 1976; (with L. Gow) Tell Them from Me, 1980; (jtly) Reconstructions of Secondary Education, 1983; (with C. Raab) Governing Education, 1988; academic articles on history and sociology of education. *Recreations:* music, sport, art history.

MACPHERSON, Ewen Cameron Stewart; Chief Executive, 3i Group plc, 1992–97 (Director, 1989–97); *b* 19 Jan. 1942; *s* of late G. P. S. Macpherson and Elizabeth Margaret Cameron (*née* Smail); *m* 1982, Hon. Laura Anne Baring, *d* of 5th Baron Northbrook; two *s*. *Educ:* Fettes Coll., Edinburgh; Queens' Coll., Cambridge (MA; Hon. Fellow, 1996); London Business Sch. (MSc; Alumni Achievement Award, 1997). Rep., Massey-Ferguson (Export) Ltd, 1964–68; various appointments, ICFC, 1970–82; 3i Group plc and subsidiaries: Dir, City Office, 1982–90; Mem., Exec. Cttee, 1985–97; Man. Dir, Finance & Planning, 1990–92. Non-executive Director: M&G Group, 1996–99; Scottish Power, 1996–2003; Foreign & Colonial Investment Trust, 1997–2008; Booker, 1998–2000; Law Debenture Corp., 1998–2001; Glynwed Internat., 1998–2000 (Chm., 1998–2000); Pantheon Internat. Participations, 1998–2004; Sussex Place Investment Mgt, 1999–2002; Wm Grant & Sons Ltd, 2005–08 (Chm. Audit Cttee); Chm., Black Rock New Energy Investment Trust (formerly Merrill Lynch New Energy Technology) plc, 2000–11. Ind. Trustee, Glaxo-Wellcome Pension Fund, 1997–2005 (Chm., 2000–05). Governor, NIESR, 1993–. Trustee, Develt Trust, Nat. Hist. Mus., 1998–2000. *Recreations:* gardening, sailing, classic cars, former registered crofter. *Address:* Aston Sandford, Bucks HP17 8LP. *Clubs:* Caledonian, City of London; Royal Lymington Yacht.

MACPHERSON, Prof. Fiona Elizabeth, PhD; Director, Centre for Study of Perceptual Experience, since 2004, Professor of Philosophy, since 2011 and Head of Philosophy, since 2014, University of Glasgow; *b* Irvine, Scotland, 19 Oct. 1971; *d* of Matthew Macpherson and Margaret Hyndman Macpherson (*née* Taylor, now Arthur). *Educ:* Ardrossan Acad.; Univ. of Glasgow (MA 1st Cl. Hons 1993); Univ. of St Andrews (MLitt 1995); Univ. of Stirling (PhD 2000). ALCM 1988. Vis. Fellow, Harvard Univ., 1998–99; Teaching Fellow, Univ. of St Andrews, 2000–02; Rosamund Chambers Res. Fellow in Philosophy, Girton Coll., Cambridge, 2002–04; Lectr, 2004–08, Sen. Lectr, 2008–11, Univ. of Glasgow; Res. Fellow, ANU, 2005–06, 2008, 2009; Co-Dir, CenSes: Centre for Study of the Senses, Inst. of Philosophy, Sch. of Advanced Study, Univ. of London, 2009–. Visiting Professor: Umeå Univ., 2011; Univ. of London, 2013. Mem., AHRC, 2014–. Trustee, Kennedy Meml Trust, 2014–. *Publications:* (ed with A. Haddock) Disjunctivism: perception, action, knowledge, 2008; (ed with K. Hawley) The Admissible Contents of Experience, 2011; (ed) The Senses: classical and contemporary philosophical perspectives, 2011; (ed with D. Platchias) Hallucination: philosophy and psychology, 2013; contrib. papers to philosophy and psychol. jls. *Recreations:* blethering and getting stocious with friends, vegan gastronomy, science, walking, travel, music, art, film, Partick Thistle Football Club. *Address:* Department of Philosophy, 67–69 Oakfield Avenue, University of Glasgow, Glasgow G12 8QQ. *E:* fiona.macpherson@glasgow.ac.uk.

McPHERSON, Graeme Paul; QC 2008; barrister; licensed racehorse trainer; *b* Dartford, Kent, 23 Sept. 1970; *s* of Ian Bernard McPherson and Maureen Ethel McPherson (*née* Larkins); *m* 2002, Mary Seanin Gilmore; one *s* two *d*. *Educ:* Canford Sch.; Emmanuel Coll., Cambridge (BA Hons 1992; MA 1995). Called to the Bar, Gray's Inn, 1993; in practice as barrister specialising in professional indemnity and sports law. Holder of public licence to train racehorses, 2006. *Publications:* (ed) Jackson and Powell on Professional Indemnity, 5th edn 2002, 6th edn 2007. *Recreations:* training racehorses, dreaming of winners. *Address:* 4 New Square, Lincoln's Inn, WC2A 3RJ. *T:* (020) 7822 2000, *Fax:* (020) 7822 2001. *E:* g.mcpherson@4newsquare.com.

McPHERSON, Ian Andrew, QPM 2009; Partner, Justice and Security, KPMG Canada, since 2012; *b* Lancs, 25 March 1961; *s* of Ian Douglas McPherson and Mary Elizabeth McPherson (*née* Simpson); *m* 1984, Wendy Spence; one *s* one *d*. *Educ:* Univ. of Central Lancashire (MBA 1999); Cambridge Univ. (Dip. Applied Criminol. 2000). Various ranks, Lancs Constabulary, 1979–2001 (Divl Comdr, Burnley, Pendle and Rossendale, 1999–2001); Asst Chief Constable, Merseyside Police, 2001–05; Dep. Chief Constable, N Yorks Police, 2005–06; Chief Constable, Norfolk Constabulary, 2006–10; Asst Comr of Territorial Policing, Metropolitan Police Service, 2010–11. National Lead: Business Area for Children and Young People, ACPO, 2008–; Police Support Help for Heroes, 2011–. Hon. Fellow, Univ. of Central Lancs, 2008. *Recreations:* running, walking, ski-ing, keen follower of Rugby and supporter of Preston North End FC. *Address:* KPMG LLP, Bay Adelaide Centre, 333 Bay Street, Suite 4600, Toronto, ON M5H 2S5, Canada.

McPHERSON, Katherine; Marketing Director, Field Fisher Waterhouse, since 2013; *b* 23 May 1964; *d* of Ezra Balaraj and Rebecca Balaraj (*née* Jacobs); *m* 1997, Alasdair McPherson; twin *d*. *Educ:* Nat. Univ. of Singapore (BA); Univ. of Kent, Canterbury (MBA). Ernst & Young: Project Manager, 1987–88, Mktg Manager, 1988–90, Exec. Consultant, 1990–92, Mgt Consultants, Singapore; Sen. Manager, Nat. Sales and Mktg, UK, 1992–95; Hd of Sales and Mktg, Media and Resources Office, 1996–98; Nat. Hd of Sales and Mktg, Technol., Communications and Entertainment, 1998–99; Project Dir, BBC, 1999 (on secondment); Mgt Consultant, Cap Gemini Ernst & Young, 1999–2001; Business Develt Manager, 2001–02, Ops Dir, 2002, Lambeth, Lewisham and Southwark YMCA; Dir of Business Develt and Marketing, Europe, Middle East and Africa, White & Case, 2002–04; Head of Business Develt, Corporate, 2004–05, Europe, 2005–07, Herbert Smith; Head of Winning Business, 2007–10, Dir, Global Mkts, 2010–13, KPMG. Mediator, 2013. Mem., S London Bd, Prince's Youth Business Trust, 2000–02. Church of England: Member: Archbishops' Council, 2003–09 (Mem., HR Panel, 2003–09); Dir, Central Bd of Finance, 2003–09; Mem., Gen. Synod, 2003–09. Mem., PCC, St John's Ch, Blackheath, 2006–09. *Recreations:* reading, cooking, walking, music. *E:* mcpherson.katherine@gmail.com.

MACPHERSON, Mary Basil Hamilton; *see* McAnally, M. B. H.

MACPHERSON, Sir Nicholas (Ian), GCB 2015 (KCB 2009); Permanent Secretary, HM Treasury, since 2005; *b* 14 July 1959; *s* of Ewen Macpherson and Nicolette Macpherson (*née* Van der Bijl); *m* 1983, Suky Jane Appleby; two *s*. *Educ:* Eton Coll.; Balliol Coll., Oxford; University Coll. London. Economist: CBI, 1982–83; Peat Marwick and Mitchell, 1983–85; joined HM Treasury, 1985; Principal Private Sec. to Chancellor of the Exchequer, 1993–97; Head of Work Incentives Policy, 1997–98; Dep. Dir, then Dir, (Welfare Reform), Budget and Public Finances, 1998–2001; Man. Dir, Public Services, 2001–04, Budget and Public Finances, 2004–05. Non-exec. Dir, HM Revenue and Customs, 2005–07. Vis. Fellow, Nuffield Coll., Oxford, 2007–; Vis. Prof., QMUL, 2012–. *Address:* HM Treasury, 1 Horse Guards Road, SW1A 2HQ. *T:* (020) 7270 4360. *Clubs:* Athenæum, MCC.

M'PHERSON, Prof. Philip Keith, CEng, FIET; Professor of Systems Science, later Systems Engineering and Management, 1967–87, City University, Professor Emeritus of Systems Engineering, 1988; *b* 10 March 1927; *s* of Ven. Kenneth M'Pherson and Dulce M'Pherson. *Educ:* Winchester Cathedral Sch.; Marlborough Coll.; Royal Naval Engineering Coll.; Royal Naval Coll., Greenwich; Massachusetts Inst. of Technology (SM 1955); MA Oxon 1965. Entered Royal Navy, 1944; Lieut 1948; Engineer Officer, 1948–59: HMS Vanguard; HMS Cleopatra; Naval Ordnance Dept, Bath; Lt-Comdr 1955; research in Admiralty Gunnery Estabt, 1955–59, retired. Head, Dynamics Gp, Atomic Energy Estabt, UKAEA, 1959–65; Fellow of St John's Coll., Oxford, 1965–67; Pro-Vice-Chancellor, City Univ., 1981–87. Vis. Scholar, Internat. Inst. of Applied Systems Analysis, Austria, 1976–77; Adjunct Prof., Xian Jiaotong Univ., China, 1980–84. Man. Dir, MacPherson Systems Ltd, 1984–92; Principal, Value Measurement Practice Ltd, 1992–2004. Member: Executive Cttee, UK Automation Council, 1964–68; SRC Control Engrg Cttee, 1970–75; Chairman: IMechE Automatic Control Gp, 1967–69; IEE Systems Engrg Gp Cttee, 1966–69; IEE Control and Automation Div., 1967–69; IEE Systems Engrg Cttee, 1984–90; Soc. for General Systems Research (UK), 1973–76. Archbishops' Commn on Rural Areas, 1988–89. Freeman, City of London, 1985. Associate, SOSc, 2002. Hon. DSc City, 2008. Pioneer of Systems Engrg Award, Internat. Council on Systems Engrg, 2006. *Publications:* many papers in the scientific literature. *Recreations:* research on measurement of intangible value, gothic cathedrals, Anglican liturgy. *Address:* 5 Cardinal's Way, Ely, Cambs CB7 4GF. *Club:* Royal Over-Seas League.

MACPHERSON, (Philip) Strone (Stewart); Chairman, Close Brothers Group plc, since 2008 (non-executive Director, 2003–08); *b* Edinburgh, 21 July 1948; *s* of Brig. George Philip Stewart Macpherson and Elizabeth Margaret Cameron Smail; *m* 1981, Hon. Alexandra Grace Baring; one *s* two *d*. *Educ:* Summer Fields, Oxford; Fettes Coll., Edinburgh; Oriel Coll., Oxford (MA Juris. 1970); INSEAD (MBA 1975). Chairman: JP Morgan Smaller Companies Investment Trust plc, 1990–2013; Tribal Gp, 2004–10; British Empire Securities and General Trust, 2007–; Estover Energy Ltd, 2010–; Exec. Dep. Chm., Misys, 1991–2002; former Dir, Flemings; non-executive Director: Axa plc; Kleinwort Benson Private Bank, 2003–10. Trustee Mem., Audit Cttee and Chm., Investment Cttee, 2009–, King's Fund. Chm., Audit Cttee and Mem., Develt Trust, Oriel Coll., Oxford. Mem., Highland Soc. *Recreations:* restoring listed buildings, early motor cars, Scottish pictures, travel, active country pursuits. *Address:* Close Brothers Group plc, 10 Crown Place, EC2A 4FT. *T:* (020) 7655 3100. *E:* strone.macpherson@closebrothers.com. *Clubs:* Caledonian; 20 Ghost.

MACPHERSON, Shonaig; *see* Macpherson, A. L. A. S.

MACPHERSON, Strone; *see* Macpherson, P. S. S.

MACPHERSON, Prof. Stuart Gowans, OBE 2007; FRCSGlas, FRCSE, FRCS, FRCP, FRCGP; Professor of Postgraduate Medical Education, University of Edinburgh, 1999–2010, now Emeritus; *b* 11 July 1945; *s* of John Buchanan Macpherson and Elizabeth Doris Macpherson (*née* Gowans); *m* 1970, Norma Elizabeth Carslaw; two *s* one *d*. *Educ:* Allan Glen's Sch., Glasgow; Univ. of Glasgow (MB ChB with Commendation 1968). FRCSGlas 1972; FRCPE 2000; FRCSE 2001; FRCS 2002; FRCGP 2005. Res. Fellow, Harvard Med. Sch., 1973–74; University of Glasgow: Sen. Lectr in Surgery, 1977–99; Associate Undergrad. Dean (Admissions), 1991–99; Associate Postgrad. Dean, 1994–99; Postgrad. Dean, SE Scotland, 1999–2009; Hon. Consultant Surgeon, Western Infirmary, Glasgow, 1977–99. Mem. Bd, 2003–08, Chm., 2008–10, Postgraduate Med. Educn and Trng Bd; Mem., Postgraduate Bd, GMC, 2010–11. Hon. FAcadMed 2009. *Publications:* articles on surgery, transplantation and med. educn in med. jls. *Recreations:* family, golf, travel, Isle of Arran. *Address:* 33/4 Blackford Road, Edinburgh EH9 2DT. *T:* (0131) 668 4574. *Clubs:* New (Edinburgh); Shiskine Golf and Tennis, Bruntsfield Links Golfing Society.

MACPHERSON OF CLUNY (and Blairgowrie), Sir William (Alan), Kt 1983; TD 1966; Cluny Macpherson; 27th Chief of Clan Macpherson; Judge of the High Court of Justice, Queen's Bench Division, 1983–96; *b* 1 April 1926; *s* of Brig. Alan David Macpherson, DSO, MC, RA (*d* 1969) and late Catharine Richardson Macpherson; *m* 1962, Sheila McDonald Brodie (*d* 2003); one *s* one *d* (and one *s* decd). *Educ:* Wellington Coll., Berkshire; Trinity Coll., Oxford (MA; Hon. Fellow, 1991). Called to Bar, Inner Temple, 1952; Bencher, 1978; QC 1971; a Recorder of the Crown Court, 1972–83; Presiding Judge, Northern Circuit, 1985–88; Pres., Interception of Communications Tribunal, 1990–2000; Chm., Stephen Lawrence Inquiry, 1997–99. Mem., Bar Council and Senate, 1981–83; Hon. Mem., Northern Circuit, 1987. Served, 1944–47, in Scots Guards (Capt.). Commanded (Lt-Col) 21st Special Air Service Regt (TA), 1962–65, Hon. Col, 1983–91; Mem., Queen's Body Guard for Scotland, Royal Co. of Archers, 1977–2006, Lieut 2004. Gov., Royal Scottish Corporation, 1972–96 (Vice-Pres., 1989–2005). Mem., Tay Dist Salmon Fisheries Bd,

1996–99. *Recreations:* golf, fishing, archery; Past Pres., London Scottish FC. *Heir:* s James Brodie Macpherson yr of Cluny and Blairgowrie. *Address:* Newton Castle, Blairgowrie, Perthshire PH10 6SU. *Clubs:* Caledonian, Highland Society of London (Pres., 1991–94); New (Edinburgh); Blairgowrie Golf.

MACPHIE, Maj.-Gen. Duncan Love; Executive Director, St John Ambulance, 1994–95 (Medical Director, 1993–94); *b* 15 Dec. 1930; *s* of Donald Macphie and Elizabeth Adam (*née* Gibson); *m* 1957, Isobel Mary Jenkins (*d* 2010); one *s* two *d*. *Educ:* Hutchesons' Grammar Sch.; Glasgow Univ. MB ChB. Stonehouse and Hairmyres Hosps, 1957–58; commnd RAMC, 1958; RMO, 1st Bn The Royal Scots, 1958–61; GP, Glasgow, 1961–63; RMO, 3 RHA, 1963–67; CO, BMH Dharan, Nepal, 1970–72; CO, 24 Field Ambulance, 1972–75; CO, BMH Munster, 1976–78; ADMS, 4 Armd Div., 1978–80; Asst DGAMS, MoD, 1980–83; CO, Queen Elizabeth Mil. Hosp., Woolwich, 1983–85; Chief, Med. Plans Branch, SHAPE, 1985–87; Comdr Med., BAOR, 1987–90, retd. QHS 1985–90. Col Comdt, RAMC, 1990–95. Warden, St John Ophthalmic Hosp., Jerusalem, 1999. *Recreations:* gardening, Rugby, cricket, classical music, reading.

McQUAID, James, CB 1997; PhD; FREng, FIMMM; Director, Science and Technology, and Chief Scientist, Health and Safety Executive, 1996–99; *b* 5 Nov. 1939; *s* of late James and Brigid McQuaid; *m* 1968, Catherine Anne, *d* of late Dr James John Hargan and Dr Mary Helen Hargan; two *s* one *d*. *Educ:* Christian Brothers' Sch., Dundalk; University Coll., Dublin (BEng); Jesus Coll., Cambridge (PhD); DSc NUI 1978. MIMechE 1972; FIMMM (FIMinE 1986); FREng (FEng 1991). Graduate engrg apprentice, British Nylon Spinners, 1961–63; Sen. Res. Fellow 1966–68, Sen. Scientific Officer 1968–72, PSO 1972–78, Safety in Mines Res. Estabt; seconded as Safety Advr, Petrochemicals Div., ICI, 1976–77; Health and Safety Executive: Dep. Dir, Safety Engrg Lab., 1978–80, Dir, 1980–85; Res. Dir, 1985–92; Dir, Strategy and Gen. Div. and Chief Scientist, 1992–96. Mem., Envmtl Security Panel, NATO Sci. Cttee, 2005–08 (Chm., 2007–08). Chm., Electrical Equipment Certification Management Bd, 1985–92; Member: Safety in Mines Res. Adv. Bd, 1985–92; Council, Midland Inst. of Mining Engrs, 1987–98 (Vice-Pres., 1991–93, Pres., 1993–94); Council, IMinE, 1991–95; Council, Royal Acad. Engrg, 1995–98; Adv. Bd for Mech. Engrg, Univ. of Liverpool, 1987–92; Exec. Cttee, RoSPA, 1992–94; Standing Cttee on Scientific Aspects of Internat. Security, Royal Soc., 2006–08; Health Protection Adv. Gp, HPA, 2006–09. Mem. Court, 1985–2003, Mem. Council, 1993–2003, Vis. Prof. of Mechanical Engrg, 1996–, Univ. of Sheffield; Visiting Professor: of Sustainable Develt, Ulster Univ., 1999–2002; of Civil Engrg, QUB, 2002–05. Pres., Sheffield Trades Hist. Soc., 1989–91. Mem., Council, S Yorks Trades Hist. Trust, 1989– (Chm., 1999–). Mem., Bd of Govs, EC Jt Res. Centre, 2001–07. FRSA 2000; FIAE 2001. Hon. DEng Sheffield, 2000. *Publications:* numerous papers in technical jls. *Recreations:* ornamental turning, model engineering, industrial archaeology. *Address:* 61 Pingle Road, Sheffield S7 2LL. *T:* (0114) 236 5349.

McQUAIL, Paul Christopher; Hon. Senior Research Fellow, Constitution Unit, University College London, 1999–2005; consultant, various public bodies, 1994–2005; *b* 22 April 1934; *s* of Christopher McQuail and Anne (*née* Mullan); *m* 1964, Susan Adler; one *s* one *d*. *Educ:* St Anselm's, Birkenhead; Sidney Sussex Coll., Cambridge. Min. of Housing and Local Govt, 1957; Principal, 1962; Asst Sec., 1969; DoE, 1970; Special Asst to Permanent Sec. and Sec. of State, 1972–73; Sec., Royal Commn on the Press, 1974–77; Under Sec., DoE, 1977–88; Chief Exec., Hounslow Bor. Council, 1983–85 (on secondment); Dep. Sec., DoE, 1988–94. Member: Environment and Planning Cttee, ESRC, 1983–87; Policy Cttee, CPRE, 1995–2001; Better Govt Initiative, 2008–12; Chairman: Nat. Urban Forestry Unit, 1995–2002; Nat. Retail Planning Forum, 1995–2005; Alcohol Concern, 1996–2002. Vis. Prof., Bartlett Sch. of Architecture, 1992–2000. Trustee, Sustrans, 2002–10. *Publications:* Origins of DoE, 1994; Cycling to Santiago, 1995; A View from the Bridge, 1995; (with Katy Donnelly) English Regional Government, 1996; Soviet Children's Books of the Twenties and Thirties: the Adler Collection, 2000; Unexplored Territory: elected regional assemblies in England, 2001; Cycling in Good Company, 2014. *Recreations:* books, hill-walking, cycling and other harmless pleasures. *Address:* 158 Peckham Rye, SE22 9QH.

McQUARRIE, Sir Albert, Kt 1987; Chairman: A. McQuarrie & Son (Great Britain) Ltd, 1946–88; Sir Albert McQuarrie & Associates Ltd, since 1988; *b* 1 Jan. 1918; *s* of Algernon Stewart McQuarrie and Alice Maud Sharman; *m* 1st, 1945, Roseleen McCaffery (*d* 1986); one *s*; 2nd, 1989, Rhoda Annie Gall. *Educ:* Highlanders Acad., Greenock; Greenock High Sch.; Royal Coll. of Science and Technology, Univ. of Strathclyde. ARCST 1939; MSE, PEng 1945. Served in HM Forces, 1939–45 (Officer in RE). Dir, Hunterston Develt Co., 1989–. Former Dean of Guild, Gourock Town Council; Chm., Fyvie/Rothienorman/Monquhitter Community Council, 1975–79. Contested (C): Kilmarnock, 1966; Caithness and Sutherland, Oct. 1974; Banff and Buchan, 1987; Highlands and Islands, European Parly elecn, 1989. MP (C): Aberdeenshire E, 1979–83; Banff and Buchan, 1983–87. Chm., British/Gibraltar All Party Gp, 1979–87; Vice Chm., Conservative Fisheries Sub Cttee, 1979–87; Secretary: Scotch Whisky All Party Gp, 1979–87; Scottish Cons. Backbench Cttee, 1985–87; Member: Select Cttees on Scottish Affairs, 1979–83, on Agriculture, 1983–85, on Private Bill Procedure, 1987; Speaker's Panel of Chairmen, 1986–87. Mem. Council, Soc. of Engineers, 1978–87. Chm., St Georges Ltd, 2006–; Consultant, LaKOTA (EU) Internat., 2006–. Dep. Chm., Ayr Cons. Assoc., 1992–94; Hon. Pres., Banff and Buchan Cons. and Unionist Assoc., 1989–. Vice Chm., Mintlaw Community Council, 1999–2002. Pres., Gourock Horticultural Soc., 1993– (Hon. Vice-Pres., 1954–93). Vice-Pres., Gibraltar Assoc. of Europe, 1996–. Mem., Former MPs Assoc., 2005–. FRSPH (FRSH 1952). Freeman, City of Gibraltar, 1982. KSJ 1991; GCSJ 1999 (Grand Prior: of UK and Eire, 1999–2000; of Europe, 2000–06; Grand Councillor, 2002–06; Cross of Merit, 2000); KMLJ 2007. Granted armorial bearings, 1991. *Publications:* A Lifetime of Memories, 2013. *Recreations:* golf, bridge, music, soccer, swimming, horticulture. *Address:* Kintara House, Newton Road, Mintlaw, Aberdeenshire AB42 5EF. *T:* (01771) 623955. *Clubs:* Lansdowne; Queens (San Francisco).

MacQUARRIE, (John) Kenneth; Director (formerly Controller), BBC Scotland, since 2004; *b* 5 June 1952; *s* of Duncan and Peggy MacQuarrie; *m* 1977, Angela Sparks; one *s* two *d*. *Educ:* Oban High Sch.; Univ. of Edinburgh (MA Eng. and Hist. 1973); Moray House Coll. of Educn, Edinburgh (DipEd 1974). BBC Scotland: joined as researcher, 1975; radio producer, BBC Highland, 1976–79; producer, TV, 1979–88; Head: of Gaelic, 1988–92; of Gaelic and Features, 1992–97; of Broadcast, 1997–2000; of Progs, 2000–04. Board Member: Scottish Film Council, 1990–97; Gaelic Media Service, 2004–08; Vice Chm., Celtic Film and TV Assoc., 1986–93; Founder Mem., Scottish Screen Forum, 1986. Chm., Nat. Bd, Skillset Scotland, 2009–. *Recreations:* sailing, reading, walking. *Address:* BBC Scotland, 40 Pacific Quay, Glasgow G51 1DA. *T:* (0141) 422 6000, *Fax:* (0141) 422 7900. *E:* ken.macquarrie@bbc.co.uk.

McQUATER, Ewan Alan; QC 2003; *b* 30 Oct. 1962; *s* of Angus and Doreen McQuater; *m* 1999, Caroline Hudson; two *s*. *Educ:* Robinson Coll., Cambridge (MA 1st cl. Hons Law 1984). Called to the Bar, Middle Temple, 1985; barrister practising in commercial law, 1986–. Asst Ed., Encyclopaedia of Banking Law, 1985–2005. *Recreations:* Rugby, blues piano. *Address:* 3 Verulam Buildings, Gray's Inn, WC1R 5NT. *T:* (020) 7831 8441, *Fax:* (020) 7831 8479. *E:* emcquater@3vb.com. *Club:* Belsize Park Rugby Football.

McQUAY, Prof. Henry John, DM; FRCA, FRCPE; Nuffield Professor of Clinical Anaesthetics, University of Oxford, 2007–10, now Emeritus; Fellow, Balliol College, Oxford, 1987–2010, now Emeritus; *b* 16 Sept. 1948; *s* of T. A. I. and M. D. McQuay; *m* 1st, 1971, Meryl Rhys Jones (marr. diss. 2001); two *d*; 2nd, 2002, Maureen Richfield. *Educ:* Sedbergh Sch.; Balliol Coll., Oxford (MA, BM BCL 1974; DM 1985). FRCA 1979; FRCPE 2002. Clin. Reader in Pain Relief, 1985–98, Prof. of Pain Relief, 1998–2007, Oxford Pain Relief Unit, Nuffield Dept of Anaesthetics, Univ. of Oxford. Consultant, Churchill Hosp., Oxford. Dir, R&D, Oxford Regl HA, 1992–94. Praefectus, Holywell Manor, 1997–2000. *Publications:* An Evidence-based Resource for Pain Relief, 1998; Bandolier's Little Book of Pain, 2003; Bandolier's Little Book of Making Sense of The Medical Evidence, 2006; scientific papers. *Address:* Nuffield Department of Anaesthetics, John Radcliffe Hospital, Headley Way, Oxford OX3 9DU.

MACQUEEN, Angus Donald; Director, Ronachan Films, 2005–06 and since 2008; *b* 20 Oct. 1958; *s* of Angus and Elizabeth Macqueen; *m* 2004, Fiona Marie Currie; one *s*. *Educ:* Lincoln Coll., Oxford (BA English 1980). Lectr, Univ. of Wrocław, Poland, 1981–84; British Council Lectr, Univ. of Novosibirsk, USSR, 1984–85; Dir, October Films, 2000–05; Hd of Documentaries, Channel 4 TV, 2006–08. Documentary Director: The Hand of Stalin, 1990; The Second Russian Revolution, 1991; The Death of Yugoslavia, 1995; The People's Century, 1997; Dancing for Dollars, 1998; Gulag, 1999; Vodka, 2000; The Last Peasants, 2003; Cocaine, 2005; (also presenter) Our Drugs War (series), 2010; 2320 Days in the Jungle, 2010; 17 Days Buried Alive, 2011; Aung San Suu Kyi: the choice, 2012; The Legend of Shorty, 2014. *Recreation:* being in Kintyre, Scotland.

MacQUEEN, Prof. Hector Lewis, PhD; FBA 2006; FRSE; Professor of Private Law, University of Edinburgh, since 1994; Commissioner, Scottish Law Commission, since 2009; *b* 13 June 1956; *s* of Prof. John MacQueen, *qv*; *m* 1979, Frances Mary Young; two *s* one *d*. *Educ:* George Heriot's Sch., Edinburgh; Univ. of Edinburgh (LLB Hons; PhD). Lectr, 1979–91, Sen. Lectr, 1991–94, Reader, 1994, Univ. of Edinburgh. Visiting Professor: Cornell Univ., 1991; Utrecht Univ., 1997; Stetson UC of Law, Florida, 2007–Feb. 2009. Mem., Adv. Panel on Public Sector Information, Cabinet Office, later MoJ, 2004–11. Mem., Co-ordinating Cttee, Eur. Civil Code Study Gp, 1999–2008. Chairman: Scottish Records Adv. Council, 2001–08; Scottish Medievalists, 2007–11; David Hume Inst., 2012–15. Literary Dir, Stair Soc., 1999–. Pres., Soc. of Legal Scholars, 2012–13; Vice-Pres. (Humanities), RSE, 2008–11. FRSE 1995. *Publications:* Common Law and Feudal Society in Medieval Scotland, 1993, repr. 2015; Atlas of Scottish History to 1707, 1996; Copyright, Competition and Industrial Design, 1989, 2nd edn 1995; Studying Scots Law, 1993, 4th edn 2012; (with J. Thomson) Contract Law in Scotland, 2000, 3rd edn 2012; Unjustified Enrichment, 2004, 3rd edn 2013; (jtly) Contemporary Intellectual Property: law and policy, 2007, 2nd edn 2010; (ed with J. N. Adams) Atiyah's Sale of Goods, 12th edn 2010; (ed with Rt Hon. Lord Eassie) Gloag & Henderson, The Law of Scotland, 13th edn 2012; (ed) White & Willock, The Scottish Legal System, 5th edn 2013. *Recreations:* walking, sometimes with golf clubs, more often with the wife and a camera, cricket, Scotland, conviviality. *Address:* Scottish Law Commission, 140 Causewayside, Edinburgh EH9 1PR. *T:* (0131) 622 5222. *E:* hector.macqueen@scotlawcom.gsi.gov.uk. *Club:* Heriot's Former Pupils Cricket.

MacQUEEN, Prof. John; Professor of Scottish Literature and Oral Tradition, University of Edinburgh, 1972–88, now Professor Emeritus, and Hon. Fellow, Faculty of Arts, 1993; *b* 13 Feb. 1929; *s* of William L. and Grace P. MacQueen; *m* 1953, Winifred W. McWalter; three *s*. *Educ:* Hutchesons' Boys' Grammar Sch.; Glasgow Univ.; Cambridge Univ. MA English Lang. and Lit., Greek, Glasgow; BA, MA Archaeology and Anthropology, Section B, Cambridge. RAF, 1954–56 (Flying Officer). Asst Prof. of English, Washington Univ., Missouri, 1956–59; University of Edinburgh: Lectr in Medieval English and Scottish Literature, 1959–63; Masson Prof. of Medieval and Renaissance Literature, 1963–72; Dir, Sch. of Scottish Studies, 1969–88; Endowment Fellow, 1988–92. Barclay Acheson Vis. Prof. of Internat. Relations, Macalester Coll., Minnesota, 1967; Vis. Prof. in Medieval Studies, Australian Nat. Univ., 1971; Winegard Vis. Prof., Univ. of Guelph, Ont, 1981. Chairman: British Branch, Internat. Assoc. of Sound Archives, 1978–80; Exec. Cttee, Scottish Nat. Dictionary Assoc., 1978–87; Scottish Dictionary Jt Council, 1988–92; Pres., Scottish Text Soc., 1989–92; Mem., Scottish Film Council, 1981–92 (Chm., Archive Cttee, 1980–92). FRSE 1992; FRAS 2004. Hon. Fellow, Assoc. for Scottish Literary Studies, 2010. Hon. DLitt NUI, 1985. Fletcher of Saltoun Award, 1990. *Publications:* St Nynia, 1961, 3rd edn 2005; (with T. Scott) The Oxford Book of Scottish Verse, 1966; Robert Henryson, 1967; Ballattis of Luve, 1970; Allegory, 1970; (ed with Winifred MacQueen) A Choice of Scottish Verse, 1470–1570, 1972; Progress and Poetry, 1982; Numerology, 1985; The Rise of the Historical Novel, 1989; (ed with Winifred MacQueen) Scotichronicon, Bks III and IV, 1989, Bks I and II, 1993, Bk V, 1995; (ed) Humanism in Renaissance Scotland, 1990; Place names of the Rhinns of Galloway and Luce Valley, 2002; Complete and Full with Numbers, 2006; (ed with Winifred MacQueen) Latin Poems of Archibald Pitcairne, 2009; Placenames of the Moors and Machars, 2008; (ed) Archibald Pitcairne: the Phanaticks, 2012; articles and reviews in learned jls. *Recreations:* music, walking, astronomy, archaeology. *Address:* Slewdonan, Damnaglaur, Drummore, Stranraer DG9 9QN. *T:* (01776) 840637.

See also Prof. H. L. MacQueen.

McQUEEN, Steve Rodney, CBE 2011 (OBE 2002); artist; *b* 1969. *Educ:* Chelsea Sch. of Art; Goldsmiths' Coll.; Tish Sch. of Arts, NY Univ. Works incorporate film, photography and sculpture. Exhibitions in Europe and USA; solo exhibitions: ICA, 1999; Thomas Dane Gall., 2004, 2007, 2014; represented GB, Venice Biennale, 2009. Works include: Bear, 1993; Five Easy Pieces, 1995; Stage, 1996; Just Above My Head, 1996; Deadpan, 1997; Drumroll, 1998; Cold Breath, 2000; Queen and Country, 2007. Films: Hunger, 2008 (Carl Foreman Award, BAFTA, 2009); Shame, 2012; 12 Years a Slave, 2013 (Best Film, BAFTA, 2014). Turner Prize, 1999. *Address:* c/o Tate Gallery, Millbank, SW1P 4RG.

McQUEEN, William Robert James, CBE 2008; Deputy Chief Executive, Crown Office and Procurator Fiscal Service, Scottish Government (formerly Executive) Justice Department, 2005–08; *b* 19 April 1951; *s* of William Robert McQueen and Mary Jane McQueen (*née* Gregson); *m* 1989, Maureen Frances Hall; two *d*. *Educ:* Queen Mary Coll., London Univ. (BSc Hons Geog.); Univ. of Calif, Los Angeles (MA); Univ. of Strathclyde (MBA). Res. Officer, Local Govt Boundary Commn for Scotland, 1974–78; Scottish Office: Sen. Res. Officer, Central Res. Unit, 1979–85; Principal: Develt Dept, 1985–88; Agric. and Fisheries Dept, 1988–91; Industry Dept, 1991; Central Services, 1991–92; Hd of Mgt and Orgn Div., 1992–95; Head, Transport Div., Scottish Exec. Develt Dept, 1995–2001; Dir, Corporate Services, Crown Office and Procurator Fiscal Service, 2001–05. Member: Accounts Commn for Scotland, 2008–; Scottish Legal Aid Bd, 2010–; non-exec. Dir, Disclosure Scotland Agency, 2010–. *Recreations:* tennis, ski-ing, cooking. *Address:* 91 Trinity Road, Edinburgh EH5 3JX. *T:* (0131) 552 0876.

MACQUIBAN, Rev. Timothy Stuart Alexander, PhD; Director, Methodist Ecumenical Office Rome, and Minister, Pont Sant'Angelo Methodist Church, since 2014; *b* 11 Jan. 1952; *s* of late Gordon and Beryl Macquiban; *m* 1975, Angela (*née* Spencer). *Educ:* King's Sch., Chester; Jesus Coll., Cambridge (MA); Univ. of Liverpool (DipSRAA 1974); Univ. of Bristol (MA 1986); Univ. of Birmingham (PhD 2000). Asst Archivist, Wigan MBC, 1974–77; Borough Archivist, Doncaster MBC, 1977–84; Minister, Halifax Methodist Circuit, 1987–90; Tutor in Hist., Wesley Coll., Bristol, 1990–93; Dir, Wesley and Methodist Studies Centre, Westminster Coll., Oxford, 1993–2002; Principal, Sarum Coll., Salisbury, 2002–08; Sarum Canon, 2004–08; Minister, Wesley Methodist Church, Cambridge, 2008–14; Chaplain, Wesley House, Cambridge, 2008–11; Hon. Chaplain and Sen. Mem., Wolfson Coll., Cambridge, 2009–14; Mem., Select Preacher's Syndicate, Univ. of Cambridge, 2011–14; Superintendent, Cambridge Methodist Circuit, 2012–14. Dep. Chm., E Anglia Dist, Methodist Ch, 2013–. Chm., English Cttee, Waldensian Church Missions, 2011 (Dep. Chm.

1999–2006). British Sec., subseq. Co-Chm., Oxford Inst. for Methodist Theol Studies, 1993–2013; Co-Chm., Internat. Dialogue of Baptists and Methodists, 2014–; Vice President: World Methodist Historical Soc., 1996–2006; Charles Wesley Soc., 2004–11; Mem., Methodist Church Heritage Cttee, 2009–12. Gov., Ley's Foundn, Cambridge, 2009–14. Vis. Prof., Pontifical Univ. of St Thomas Aquinas, Rome. Hon. Fellow, Westminster Inst. of Educn, Oxford Brookes Univ., 2008–14. *Publications:* Methodist Prison Chaplains, 1994; Pure Universal Love, 1995; Methodism and Education, 2000; contributions to: Historical Dictionary of Methodism, 1996; A Dictionary of British and Irish Methodism, 2000; Studies in Church History, 2002, 2004; An Encyclopedia of Protestantism, 2004; Oxford DNB, 2004; Our Calling to Fulfill, 2009. *Recreations:* choral singing, collecting Wesleyana. *Address:* Via del Banco Di Santo Spirito 3, Rome 00186, Italy. *E:* tmacquiban@live.co.uk, macquiban.rome@methodistchurch.org.uk.

McQUIGGAN, John, MBE 1955; Executive Director, United Kingdom-South Africa Trade Association Ltd, 1978–86; retired at own request from HM Diplomatic Service, 1977; *b* 24 Nov. 1922; *s* of John and Sarah Elizabeth McQuiggan; *m* 1950, Doris Elsie Hadler; three *s* one *d*. *Educ:* St Edward's Coll., Liverpool. Served War, in RAF, 1942–47 (W Africa, Europe and Malta). Joined Dominions Office, 1940; Administration Officer, British High Commission, Canberra, Australia, 1950–54; Second Sec., Pakistan, Lahore and Dacca, 1954–57; First Sec. (Inf.), Lahore, 1957–58; Dep. Dir, UK Inf. Services, Australia (Canberra and Sydney), 1958–61; Dir, Brit. Inf. Services, Eastern Nigeria (Enugu), 1961–64; Dir, Brit. Inf. Services in Uganda, and concurrently First Sec., HM Embassy, Kigali, Rwanda, 1964–69; W African Dept, FCO, 1969–73; HM Consul, Chad, 1970–73 (first London based Consul); Dep. High Comr and Counsellor (Econ. and Commercial), Lusaka, Zambia, and sometime Actg High Comr, 1973–76. Dir-Gen., Brit. Industry Cttee on South Africa, 1986. Mem., Royal African Soc. FInstD. Benemerenti Medal awarded by Pope Benedict XVI, 2012. *Publications:* A Time to Heal (for use at Eucharist services), 2001; Prayers for the Sick (USA), 2003; booklets and contribs to trade and economic, technical woodworking, and religious jls. *Recreations:* tennis, carpentry, craftwork, research (current affairs). *Address:* 7 Meadowcroft, Bickley, Kent BR1 2JD. *T:* (020) 8467 0075. *Club:* Royal Over-Seas League.

McQUILLAN, Stephen; Chief Executive, Avingtrans plc, since 2008; *b* Glasgow, 6 Aug. 1961; *s* of Joseph McQuillan and Helen McQuillan (*née* Curran); *m* 1988, Sheena Lang; one *s*. *Educ:* Univ. of Glasgow (BSc Hons Electronics and Electrical Engrg). MIET 1998; FInstP 2006. Engr, Conoco Inc., 1982–85; Mars, Inc.: Proj. Engr, 1985–88; Sen. Mgt Scientist, 1988–90; Internat. Distributor Manager, 1990–91; European Sales Develt Manager, 1992–94; Sales Dir, W Eur., 1994–97; Business Unit Dir, Sodeco Cash Mgt Systems, 1995–97; Global Sales Dir, Marconi Instruments, 1997–98; Man. Dir, Oxford Instruments Superconductivity Ltd, 1998–2004; Chief Exec., NPL, 2005–08. Member Board: Serco Science, 2005–06; Serco Defence Ops, 2007–08; (non-exec.) UKAEA, 2010–15. Mem. Bd, Assoc. of Ind. Res. and Technol. Orgns, 2007–08. FCMI 2008; FInstD 2009. *Recreations:* running, cycling, ski-ing, cinema, theatre, biographies, travel, learning, Celtic FC, Robert Burns poetry. *Address:* Avingtrans plc, Precision House, Derby Road, Sandiacre, Nottingham NG10 5HU. *T:* (0115) 949 9020, *Fax:* (0115) 949 9024. *E:* smcquillan@avingtrans.plc.uk.

MacQUITTY, (Joanna) Jane; freelance wine writer and broadcaster, since 1982; Wine and Drink Correspondent, The Times, since 1982; *b* 14 Oct. 1953; *d* of late William Baird MacQuitty and Betty (*née* Bastin); *m* 1988, Philip Killingworth Hedges; one *s* two *d*. *Educ:* Benenden Sch. Wine and food writer, House & Garden, 1975–82; Editor, Which Wine Guide, and Which Wine Monthly, 1982–84; Wine Editor, Good Housekeeping, 1984–2000. Wine Lectr and Judge, 1982–. Member: Circle of Wine Writers, 1977–; Soc. of Authors, 1982–. Patron, Urology Foundn, 2014–. Glenfiddich Awards: Wine Writer of the Year, 1981; Whisky Writer of the Year, 1981; Special Award (for Which Wine Guide), 1983; Portuguese Wine Journalist of the Year, 2014. *Publications:* Which Wine Guide, 1983, rev. edn 1984; Jane MacQuitty's Guide to Champagne and Sparkling Wines, 1986, 3rd edn 1993; Jane MacQuitty's Guide to Australian and New Zealand Wines, 1988. *Recreations:* my family, eating, drinking, talking, sleep. *Address:* c/o The Times Weekend, The Times, 1 London Bridge Street, SE1 9GF.

McQUOID, Judith Mary; *see* Eve, J. M.

MacRAE, Sir (Alastair) Christopher (Donald Summerhayes), KCMG 1993 (CMG 1987); HM Diplomatic Service, retired; *b* 3 May 1937; *s* of Dr Alexander Murray MacRae and Dr Grace Maria Lynton Summerhayes MacRae; *m* 1963, Mette Willert; two *d*. *Educ:* Rugby; Lincoln Coll., Oxford (BA Hons English); Harvard (Henry Fellow in Internat. Relations). RN, 1956–58. CRO, 1962; 3rd, later 2nd Sec., Dar es Salaam, 1963–65; ME Centre for Arab Studies, Lebanon, 1965–67; 2nd Sec., Beirut, 1967–68; FCO, 1968–70; 1st Sec. and Head of Chancery: Baghdad, 1970–71; Brussels, 1972–76; attached Directorate-Gen. VIII, European Commn, Brussels, on secondment from FCO, 1976–78; Ambassador to Gabon, 1978–80, and to São Tomé and Príncipe (non-resident), 1979–80; Head of W Africa Dept, FCO, 1980–83, and Ambassador (non-resident) to Chad, 1982–83; Political Counsellor and Head of Chancery, Paris, 1983–87; Minister and Head of British Interests Section, Tehran, 1987; Vis. Fellow, IISS, 1987–88; Support Services Scrutiny, FCO, 1988; Under Sec. (on secondment), Cabinet Office, 1988–91; High Comr to Nigeria, and concurrently Ambassador (non-resident) to Benin, 1991–94; High Comr to Pakistan, 1994–97; Sec. Gen., Order of St John, 1997–2000. Asst Prof., Amer. Grad. Sch. of Internat. Relns and Diplomacy, Paris, 2005–08. KStJ 1997. *Address:* 23 Chemin Carboussan, Mormoiron 84570, France.

MACRAE, Prof. (Colin) Neil, PhD, DSc; FBA 2011; FRSE; Professor of Social Cognition, and Head, School of Psychology, University of Aberdeen. *Educ:* Univ. of Aberdeen (BSc 1987; PhD 1990; DSc 2006). Prof. of Psychol. and Brain Scis, Dartmouth Coll., NH, USA; Reader in Psychol., Univ. of St Andrews, 2005. Wolfson Fellow, Royal Soc. FRSE 2008; FAcSS. Spearman Medal, BPsS. *Publications:* (jtly) Stereotypes and Stereotyping, 1996; (ed with S. T. Fiske) The SAGE Handbook of Social Cognition, 2012; contribs to scientific jls. *Address:* School of Psychology, University of Aberdeen, William Guild Building, Room F6, King's College, Old Aberdeen AB24 3FX.

McRAE, Dame Frances Anne; *see* Cairncross, Dame F. A.

McRAE, Hamish Malcolm Donald; Associate Editor, The Independent, since 1991; *b* 20 Oct. 1943; *s* of Donald and Barbara McRae (*née* Budd); *m* 1971, Frances Anne Cairncross (*see* Dame F. A. Cairncross); two *d*. *Educ:* Fettes College; Trinity College, Dublin (BA Hons Economics and Political Science, MA). Liverpool Post, 1966–67; The Banker, 1967–72 (Asst Editor, 1969, Dep. Editor, 1971); Editor, Euromoney, 1972–74; Financial Editor, The Guardian, 1975–89; Business and City Editor, The Independent, 1989–91. Visiting Professor: UMIST, 1999–2004; Univ. of Lancaster, 2005–10; Adjunct Prof., TCD, 2012–. Mem. Council, REconS, 2005–10. Wincott Foundn financial journalist of the year, 1979; David Watt Prize, RTZ awards, 2005; Business and Finance Journalist of the Year, British Press Awards, 2006. *Publications:* (with Frances Cairncross) Capital City: London as a financial centre, 1973, 5th edn 1991; (with Frances Cairncross) The Second Great Crash, 1975; Japan's role in the emerging global securities market, 1985; The World in 2020, 1994; (with Tadashi Nakamae) Wake-up, Japan, 1999; What Works: the secrets of the world's best organisations and communities, 2010. *Recreations:* walking, ski-ing, cooking. *Address:* The Independent, Northcliffe House, 2 Derry Street, W8 5HF.

MACRAE, John Esmond Campbell, CMG 1986; DPhil; HM Diplomatic Service, retired; *b* 8 Dec. 1932; *s* of Col Archibald Campbell Macrae, IMS, and Euretta Margaret Skelton; *m* 1962, Anne Catherine Sarah Strain; four *s*. *Educ:* Sheikh Bagh Sch., Kashmir; Fettes Coll., Edinburgh; Christ Church Oxford (Open Scholar; MA; DPhil Radiation Chem. 1960); Princeton, USA. Atomic Energy and Disarmament Dept, Foreign Office, 1959–60; 2nd Sec., British Embassy, Tel Aviv, 1961–64; 1st Secretary: Djakarta, 1964; Vientiane, 1964–66; FO, NE African Dept, 1966; Central Dept, 1967–69; Southern African Dept, 1970–72; UK Mission to the UN, New York (dealing with social affairs, population and outer space), 1972–75; Counsellor, Science and Technology, Paris, 1975–80; Head of Cultural Relns Dept, FCO, 1980–85; RCDS, 1985; Ambassador: to Senegal, and (non-resident) to Mali, Cape Verde, Guinea and Guinea-Bissau, 1985–90; to Mauritania (non-resident), 1986–92 and to Morocco, 1990–92. *Recreations:* music, hill walking, picnics in unusual places.

MacRAE, His Honour Kenneth Charles; a Circuit Judge, 1990–2009; *b* 14 March 1944; *s* of William and Ann MacRae; *m* 1981, Hilary Vivien Williams; one *d*. *Educ:* Redruth County Grammar School; Cornwall Tech. Coll.; Fitzwilliam Coll., Cambridge (BA Hons). Called to the Bar, Lincoln's Inn, 1969; a Recorder of the Crown Court, 1985. *Recreations:* gardening, walking, music.

McRAE, Lindsay Vere; *see* Duncan, L. V.

MACRAE, Neil; *see* Macrae, C. N.

McRAE, Steven; Principal Dancer, Royal Ballet, since 2009; *b* Sydney; *s* of Phillip McRae and Dianne McRae; *m* 2011, Elizabeth Harrod. *Educ:* Royal Ballet Sch.; Royal Acad. of Dance (Solo Seal); Open Univ. (BA Hons Business Mgt and Leadership). Dip. in Dance. Joined Royal Ballet Co., 2004. Prix de Lausanne, 2003; Best Male Dancer, Critics' Circle UK Awards, 2012; Young Australian of the Yr, Australia Day Foundn, 2014. *Relevant publication:* Steven McRae: dancer in the fast lane, photographs by Andrej Uspenski, 2014. *Address:* Royal Ballet, Royal Opera House, Covent Garden, WC2E 9DD. *E:* tappuppy@hotmail.com. *W:* www.twitter.com/stevenmcrae.

MACREADY, Sir Charles Nevil, 4th Bt *cr* 1923, of Cheltenham, co. Gloucester; vineyard consultant and contract manager, since 2012; *b* Ripley, Surrey, 19 May 1955; *s* of Sir Nevil John Wilfrid Macready, 3rd Bt, CBE and Emma Macready, *d* of Sir (John) Donald (Balfour) Fergusson, GCB; *S* father, 2014; *m* 2001, Jillian Simms; one *s* one *d* from previous marriage. *Educ:* Downside Sch., Somerset. Area supervisor, Augustus Barnett, wine merchants, 1985–87; owner/manager, The Brasserie Restaurant and Wine Cellars, Bury St Edmunds, 1987–92; manager, Wyken Vineyard and Wyken's Leaping Hare Restaurant, 1992–2001; owner/manager, Ickworth Vineyard, 1995–2012. *Recreations:* classical piano music, motorcycling. *Heir:* *s* James Nevil Macready, *b* 26 Nov. 1982. *Address:* Fortlands, Sicklesmere Road, Bury St Edmunds, Suffolk IP33 2BN. *T:* (01284) 723399, 07974 054602. *E:* macready@ickworthvineyard.co.uk.

MacROBBIE, Prof. Enid Anne Campbell, FRS 1991; FRSE; Professor of Plant Biophysics, University of Cambridge, 1987–99, now Emeritus Professor; Fellow of Girton College, since 1958; *b* 5 Dec. 1931; *d* of late George MacRobbie and Agnes Kerr MacRobbie (*née* Campbell). *Educ:* Mary Erskine Sch., Edinburgh; Univ. of Edinburgh (BSc, PhD); MA, ScD Cantab. FRSE 1998. Res. Fellow, Univ. of Copenhagen, 1957–58; Cambridge University: Res. Fellow, Botany Sch., 1958–62; Demonstrator in Botany, 1962–66; Lectr in Botany, 1966–73; Reader in Plant Biophysics, 1973–87. Mem., BBSRC, 1996–99. Foreign Associate, Nat. Acad. of Scis, USA, 1999. *Publications:* papers in sci jls. *Address:* Girton College, Cambridge CB3 0JG. *T:* (01223) 338999.

McROBERT, Rosemary Dawn Teresa, OBE 1985; Deputy Director, Consumers' Association, 1980–88; *b* Maymyo, Burma, 29 Aug. 1927; *e d* of late Lt-Col Ronald McRobert, MB, ChB, FRCOG, IMS, and Julie Rees. *Educ:* privately and at Gloucestershire College of Educn. Journalist and broadcaster on consumer subjects, 1957–63; Founder editor, Home Economics, 1954–63; Chief Information Officer, Consumer Council, 1965–70; Consumer Representation Officer, Consumers' Assoc., 1971–73; Adviser on consumer affairs in DTI and Dept of Prices and Consumer Protection, 1973–74; Dir, Retail Trading Standards Assoc., 1974–80. Member Council: Inst. of Consumer Ergonomics, 1974–81; Consumers' Assoc., 1974–79; Advertising Standards Authority, 1974–80; Member: Adv. Council on Energy Conservation, 1974–82; Design Council, 1975–84; Post Office Review Cttee, 1976; Policyholders' Protection Bd, 1976–92; Nuffield Enquiry into Pharmacy Services, 1984–86; Council for Licensed Conveyancers, 1989–94; British Hallmarking Council, 1989–97. Chm., Management Cttee, Camden Consumer Aid Centres, 1977–80. Vice-Pres., Patients Assoc., 1988–95. Director: Investors Compensation Scheme, 1988–96; CSM Parliamentary Consultants, 1988–2012. Liveryman, Glovers' Co., 1979. *Address:* Well House, Bolton Street, Lavenham, Suffolk CO10 9RG. *Club:* Reform.

MacRORY, Avril; Chief Executive Officer, Silverapples Media, since 2001; *b* 5 April 1956; *d* of Patrick Simon MacRory and Elizabeth (*née* Flynn); *m* 1983, Val Griffin; one *s*. *Educ:* University College, Dublin (BA Hons 1978). Producer and Director, RTE, 1979; Head of Variety, RTE, 1986; Commissioning Editor, Music, Channel 4, 1988; Head of Music Progs, 1993–98, of Millennium Event Progs, 1998–2000, BBC TV. Advr, Programming, Hello! TV. Mem., Exec. Cttee, Women's Irish Network. Pres., Internat. Music Zentrum, Vienna, 1992–. *Recreations:* sailing, music, reading.

MACRORY, Prof. Richard Brabazon, CBE 2000; Professor of Environmental Law, University College, London, since 1999; Barrister-at-law; *b* 30 March 1950; *s* of Sir Patrick Macrory and Lady Marjorie Elizabeth Macrory; *m* 1979, Sarah Margaret Briant; two *s*. *Educ:* Westminster Sch.; Christ Church, Oxford (BA 1972; MA 1976). Called to the Bar, Gray's Inn, 1974, Bencher, 2010; Legal Advr, Friends of the Earth Ltd, 1975–78; Imperial College, London: Lectr, 1980–89; Reader in Envmtl Law, 1989–91; Denton Hall Prof. of Envmtl Law, 1991–94; Dir, Envmtl Change Unit, Univ. of Oxford, 1994–95; Prof. of Envmtl Law, Imperial Coll., London, 1995–99. Leader, Review of Regulatory Sanctions, Cabinet Office, 2005–06. Chairman: UK Envmtl Law Assoc., 1986–88 (Patron, 2007–); Steering Cttee, European Envmtl Adv. Councils, 2001–02; Hon. Standing Counsel, CPRE, 1981–92; Member: Envmtl Adv. Bd, Shanks and McKewan plc, 1989–91; UK Nat. Adv. Cttee on Eco-labelling, 1990–91; Royal Commn on Envmtl Pollution, 1991–2003; Expert Strategy Panel, Inter-Agency Cttee for Global Envmtl Change, 1995–96; Bd, Envmt Agency, 1999–2004; Gen. Electric Ecomagination Bd, 2006–10; Sullivan Working Gp on Access to Envmtl Justice, 2007–08. Specialist Adviser: H of L Select Cttee on EC, 1991–92, and 1996–97; H of C Select Cttee on Envmt, 1989–92, 1993–99. Hon. Chm., Merchant Ivory Prodns Ltd, 1992–2005; Chm., Lady Sale Prodns LLP, 2009–. Hon. Pres., Nat. Soc. for Clean Air, 2004–05. Rapporteur, UK Nat. Biotechnology Conf., 1996; UK nominated expert arbitrator, Law of the Sea Convention, 1998–2003. Fernand Braudel Sen. Fellow, Eur. Univ. Inst., Florence, 2009; Sen. Global Res. Fellow, NYU Sch. of Law, 2010. Hon. QC 2008. Editor, Jl of Envmtl Law, 1988–2006; Legal Corresp., Ends Report, 1982–. Elizabeth Haub Prize for Envmtl Law, 2014. *Publications:* Nuisance, 1982; Water Law: principles and practice, 1985; Water Act 1989, 1989; (with D. Gilbert) Pesticide Related Law, 1989; (with S. Hollins) Bibliography of Community Environmental Law, 1995; (ed) Principles of European Environmental Law, 2004; (ed) Reflections on 30 years of EU Environmental Law, 2005; Regulation, Enforcement, and Governance of Environmental Law, 2008, 2nd edn, 2014; (ed with R. Stewart and I. Havercroft) Legal Aspects of Carbon Capture and Storage, 2011; (ed jtly) National Courts and EU Environmental Law, 2013; articles and reviews in legal and tech. jls.

Recreations: cinema, board-games, cycling. *Address:* Crossing Farmhouse, Tackley, Oxford OX5 3AT. *T:* (01869) 331151; Brick Court Chambers, 7–8 Essex Street, WC2R 3LD. *T:* (020) 7379 3550, *Fax:* (020) 7379 3558; Faculty of Laws, University College, Bentham House, Endsleigh Gardens, WC1H 0EG. *T:* (020) 7679 1543. *E:* r.macrory@ucl.ac.uk. *Clubs:* Athenæum, Polish Hearth.

MacROW-WOOD, Ven. Antony Charles; Archdeacon of Dorset, since 2015; *s* of David and Mary Wood; *m* 1987, Dawn MacRow-Hill; one *s* two *d*. *Educ:* Bishop Wordsworth's Grammar Sch., Salisbury; Univ. of York (BA Hons 1982); Jesus Coll., Cambridge (BA 1991). ACA 1985. Articled Clerk, Deloitte Haskins and Sells, 1982–87; Finance Manager, Rolls Royce plc, 1987–89; ordained deacon, 1992, priest, 1993; Curate, Parks and Walcot, Swindon, 1992–96; Team Vicar, Weymouth, 1996–2004; Team Rector, North Poole Ecumenical Team, 2004–15. President: Assoc. of British Credit Unions Ltd, 2009–12; Churches' Mutual Credit Union, 2015–. *Recreations:* golf, gardening, walking the dog. *T:* 07775 574971. *E:* amacrowwood@mac.com.

MacSHANE, Denis; PhD; *b* 21 May 1948; *e s* of late Jan Matyjaszek and of Isobel MacShane; *m* 1987, Nathalie Pham Minh Duong (marr. diss. 2003); one *s* three *d* (and one *d* decd). *Educ:* Merton Coll., Oxford (MA); Birkbeck Coll., London. (PhD; Hon. Fellow, 2005). BBC reporter, 1969–77; Pres., NUJ, 1978–79; Policy Dir, Internat. Metalworkers Fedn, 1980–92; Dir, European Policy Inst., 1992–. MP (Lab) Rotherham, May 1994–Nov. 2012. PPS, 1997–2001, Parly Under-Sec. of State, 2001–02, Minister of State, 2002–05, FCO. UK Delegate: Council of Europe, 2005–10; NATO Parly Assembly, 2005–10. Vis. Parly Fellow, St Antony's Coll., Oxford, 1998–99. Mem. Council, RIIA, 1998, 2001, 2005–11; Chm., Fabian Soc., 2001–02. *Publications:* Solidarity: Poland's Independent Trade Union, 1981; François Mitterand: a political Odyssey, 1982; Black Workers, Unions and the Struggle for Democracy in South Africa, 1984; International Labour and the Origins of the Cold War, 1992; Britain's Steel Industry in the 21st Century, 1996; Edward Heath, 2006; Globalising Hatred: the new antisemitism, 2008; Why Kosovo Still Matters, 2011; Prison Diaries, 2014; Brexit: how Britain will leave Europe, 2015. *Recreations:* family, the Alps, poetry, friends.

McSHANE, Martin David, FRCS; Director, Domain 2 (Enhancing quality of life for people with long term conditions), NHS England, since 2012; *b* 27 Jan. 1957; *s* of late Jan Matyjaszek and of Isobel Matyjaszek (*née* McShane); *m* 1989, Dr Linda Jewes; one *s* one *d*. *Educ:* St Benedict's Sch., Ealing; University Coll. London and University Coll. Hosp. Med. Sch. (BSc Anatomy 1978; MB BS 1981); Univ. of London (MS 1989); Sheffield Hallam Univ. (MA Writing 1998); Teesside Univ. (Postgrad. Performance Develt Coaching 2013). Gen. and vascular surgical trng and res., 1981–89 (Musgrove Park Hosp., Taunton, Edgware Gen. Hosp., London, Leicester Royal Infirmary, Southampton Gen. Hosp., Sheffield Gen. Hosp., Rotherham Dist Gen. Hosp.); trainee, 1990–92, Partner, 1992–2014, Moss Valley Med. Practice, Eckington; Chair, NE Derbys PCG, 1999–2001; Professional Exec. Chair, 2001–04, Chief Exec., 2004–06, N Eastern Derbys PCT; Dir of Strategy and Health Outcomes, and Dep. Chief Exec., Lincs Teaching PCT, 2006–12. Vice Chair, E Midlands Specialised Commng Gp, 2006–12. Mem., Nat. Patient Safety Forum, 2007–10. *Publications:* papers on Duplex Ultrasound of femorodistal bypass grafts. *Recreations:* cycling, dog walking. *Address:* NHS England, Medical Directorate (4N22), Quarry House, Quarry Hill, Leeds LS2 7UE. *T:* (0113) 825 0633. *E:* m.mcshane@nhs.net.

McSHARRY, Deirdre; Editor-in-Chief and Launch Editor, Country Living, 1986–89; *b* 4 April 1932; *d* of late Dr John McSharry and Mrs Mary McSharry. *Educ:* Dominican Convent, Wicklow; Trinity Coll., Dublin. Woman's Editor, Daily Express, 1962–66; Fashion Editor, The Sun, 1966–72; Editor, Cosmopolitan, 1973–86; Consultant, Nat. Magazine Co., and Magazine Div., The Hearst Corp., 1990–95; Ed., Countryside mag., NY, 1991–92. Curated exhibitions: American Museum in Britain, Bath: Inspirations: the textile tradition, 2001; Quilt Bonanza, 2003; Victoria Art Gallery, Bath: Blue and White Show, 2008; Newark Park, Ozleworth: Bringing Home the East, 2010. Mem. Council and Chm., Bath Friends of American Museum in Britain, 1995–2004; Trustee, 2003–05. Patron, Holburne Mus., Bath, 2007–08. Contrib., Edwardian Revival, BBC2, 2007. Magazine Editor of the Year, PPA, 1981, 1987; Mark Boxer Award, British Soc. of Magazine Editors, 1992. *Publications:* contrib. Selvedge, You mag., Bath Life mag., Bath Mag., America in Britain. *Recreations:* the arts, textiles, costume and fashion. *Address:* 5 Sion Hill Place, Sion Hill, Bath BA1 5SJ.

MacSHARRY, Raymond; Chairman, London City Airport, 1996–2006; Director, Ryanair, 1993–2006 (Chairman, 1993–96); *b* Sligo, April 1938; *m* Elaine Neilan; three *s* three *d*. *Educ:* St Vincent's Nat. Sch., Sligo; Ballincutranta Nat. Sch., Beltra, Co. Sligo; Marist Brothers Nat. Sch., Sligo; Summerhill Coll., Sligo. TD (FF) for Sligo Leitrim, 1969–89; opposition front bench spokesman on Office of Public Works, 1973–75; Mem., Cttee of Public Accts, 1969–77; Minister of State, Dept of Finance and the Public Service, 1977–79; Minister of Agriculture, 1979–81; opposition spokesman on Agric., 1981–82; Tánaiste and Minister for Finance, 1982; Minister for Finance and the Public Service, 1987–88. Mem., Commn of EC, 1989–92. Formerly Member: New Ireland Forum; Nat. Exec., Fianna Fáil Party (later, also an Hon. Treas.). Mem. for Connaught/Ulster, Eur. Parlt, 1984–87; Mem., Council of Ministers, 1984–87. Governor, Eur. Investment Bank, 1982. Director: Jefferson Smurfit Gp, 1993–2002; Bank of Ireland, 1993–2005; Chairman: Telecom Éireann, 1999–2001; Irish Forestry Board, 1999–2002. Councillor, Sligo CC, 1967–78; Chairman: Bd of Management, Sligo Reg. Tech. Coll., 1970–78; Sligo Hosp. Exec. Cttee, 1972–78; NW Health Bd, 1974–75 (Mem., 1971–78); Member: Sligo Corp., 1967–78 (Alderman, 1974–78); Town of Sligo Vocational Educn Cttee, 1967–78; Bd of Management, Sligo-Leitrim Reg. Develt Org., 1973–78; Sligo Jun. Chamber, 1965– (PP). Freeman, Borough of Sligo, 1993. Hon. Dr NUI, 1994; Hon. DEconSc Limerick, 1994. Grand Cross, Order of Leopold II (Belgium), 1993. *Address:* Alcantara, Pearse Road, Sligo, Eire.

McSHERRY, (John) Craig (Cunningham); Sheriff at Dunfermline, since 2006; *b* 21 Oct. 1949; *s* of John and Janet McSherry; *m* 1972, Elaine Beattie; two *s*. *Educ:* Ardrossan Acad.; Univ. of Glasgow (LLB Hons 1972). Lead singer, The Wilderness, 1967–68. Solicitor, 1972–92; Sen. Partner, McSherry Halliday, Solicitors, 1983–92; Advocate, 1993; Temp. Sheriff, 1997–99; Pt-time Sheriff, 2000–03; Immigration Appeals Adjudicator (pt-time), 2001–03; All Scotland Floating Sheriff, Edinburgh, 2003–05. Mem. Council, Law Soc. of Scotland, 1982–85. *Recreations:* country pursuits, ski-ing, music (classical, rock, folk), bridge, golf. *Address:* 2 Heriot Row, Edinburgh EH3 6HU. *T:* (0131) 556 8289. *E:* jccmcs@hotmail.com. *Club:* New (Edinburgh).

MacSWEEN, Sir Roderick (Norman McIver), Kt 2000; MD; FRCPE, FRCPGlas, FRCPath, FMedSci; FRSB; FRSE; Professor of Pathology, University of Glasgow, 1984–99, now Emeritus; President, Royal College of Pathologists, 1996–99; *b* 2 Feb. 1935; *s* of Murdo MacLeod MacSween and Christina (*née* McIver); *m* 1961, Dr Marjory Pentland Brown; one *s* one *d*. *Educ:* Inverness Royal Acad.; Glasgow Univ. (BSc Hons 1956; MD 1973). FRCPGlas 1972; FRCPE 1974; FRCPath 1976; FRSB (FIBiol 1987); FRSE 1985. University of Glasgow: Lectr, then Sen. Lectr in Pathology, 1965–78; Titular Prof. in Pathology, 1978–84. Instructor in Pathology, Univ. of Colo, Denver, 1968–69; Otago Savings Bank Vis. Prof., Univ. of Otago, NZ, 1983. Ed., Histopathology, 1984–95. Mem., GMC, 2000–04. Chm., Unrelated Live Transplant Regulatory Authy, 2000–06. President: Royal Medico-Chirurgical Soc. of Glasgow, 1978–79; British Div., Internat. Acad. of Pathology, 1989–91; Chm., Acad. of Med. Royal Colls, 1998–2000. Hon. Librarian, RCPSG, 1985–95. Chm., Tenovus Scotland, 2006–11. Pres., Royal Philosophical Soc. of Glasgow, 2009–12. Chm., Sen. Fellows' Club, RCPSG, 2011–. Founder FMedSci 1998. Hon. Fellow, Coll. of Pathologists of S Africa, 1998; Hon. FRCP 1999; Hon. FRCS 2013; Hon. FRCSE 2000. Hon. DSc Glasgow, 2007. *Publications:* (ed jtly) Pathology of the Liver, 1979, 5th edn 2007 as MacSween's Pathology of the Liver; (ed with P. P. Anthony) Recent Advances in Histopathology Nos 11–16, 1992–94; (ed with K. Whaley) Muir's Textbook of Pathology, 13th edn 1992. *Recreations:* golf, gardening, hill-walking… and more golf! *Address:* 23 Lochbroom Drive, Newton Mearns, Glasgow G77 5PF. *Clubs:* Athenæum; Glasgow Golf, Dunaverty Golf (Past Capt.), Machrihanish Golf (Past Capt.).

MACTAGGART, Rt Hon. Fiona; PC 2015; MP (Lab) Slough, since 1997; *b* 12 Sept. 1953; *d* of Sir Ian Auld Mactaggart, 3rd Bt and Rosemary, *d* of Sir Herbert Williams, 1st Bt, MP. *Educ:* Cheltenham Ladies' Coll.; King's Coll., London (BA Hons); Inst. of Educn, London (MA). Gen. Sec., London Students' Organisation, 1977–78; Vice-Pres., 1978–80, Nat. Sec., 1980–81, NUS; Gen. Sec., Jt Council for Welfare of Immigrants, 1982–86. Mem. (Lab) Wandsworth BC, 1986–90 (Leader of the Opposition, 1988–90). Teacher, Lyndhurst Sch., Camberwell, 1988–92; Lectr, Inst. of Educn, 1992–97. PPS to Sec. of State for Culture, Media and Sport, 1997–2001; Parly Under-Sec. of State, Home Office, 2003–06. Member: Public Admin Cttee, 1997–98; Educn and Skills, then Children, Schs and Families Cttee, 2006–10; Jt Cttee on Human Rights, 2009–10; Health Cttee, 2010; Public Accounts Cttee, 2011–14; Intelligence and Security Cttee, 2014–. Chm., PLP Women's Cttee, 2001–03, 2008–10, 2011–. Chm., Liberty (NCCL), 1994–96. *Address:* House of Commons, SW1A 0AA.

MACTAGGART, Sir John (Auld), 4th Bt *cr* 1938, of King's Park, City of Glasgow; *b* 21 Jan. 1951; *s* of Sir Ian Auld Mactaggart, 3rd Bt and of Rosemary, *d* of Sir Herbert Williams, 1st Bt, MP; *S* father, 1987; *m* 1st, 1977, Patricia (marr. diss. 1990), *y d* of late Major Harry Alastair Gordon, MC; 2nd, 1991, Caroline (marr. diss. 2014), *y d* of Eric Williams; two *s* two *d*. *Educ:* Shrewsbury; Trinity Coll., Cambridge (MA). Chm., Western Heritable Investment Company, 1987–. *Heir:* *s* Jack Auld Mactaggart, *b* 11 Sept. 1993. *Address:* 2 Babmaes Street, SW1Y 6HD.

See also Rt Hon. F. Mactaggart.

MacTAGGART, Air Vice-Marshal William Keith, CBE 1976 (MBE 1956); CEng, FIMechE; FRAeS; Consultant: MPE Ltd, 1989–91 (Managing Director, 1984–89); Adwest plc, 1989–91; *b* 15 Jan. 1929; *s* of Duncan MacTaggart and Marion (*née* Keith); *m* 1st, 1949 Christina Carnegie Geddes (marr. diss. 1977); one *s* two *d*; 2nd, 1977, Barbara Smith Brown (marr. diss. 1994), *d* of Adm. Stirling P. Smith, late USN, and Mrs Smith; one step *d*; 3rd, 1995, Kathleen Mary Wilkie, *d* of William and Beatrice Booth. *Educ:* Aberdeen Grammar Sch.; Aberdeen Univ. (BScEng 1948). FIMechE 1973; FRAeS 1974. Commnd RAF, 1949; 1949–67: Engr Officer; Pilot; AWRE, Aldermaston (Montebello and Maralinga atomic trials); attended RAF Staff Coll., and Jt Services Staff Coll.; Def. Intell.; Systems Analyst, DOAE, West Byfleet, and MoD (Air); Head of Systems MDC, RAF Swanton Morley, 1968; OC RAF Newton, 1971 (Gp Captain); Dep. Comd Mech. Engr, HQ Strike Comd, 1973; Dir of Air Armament, MoD (PE), 1973 (Air Cdre); RCDS, 1977; Vice-Pres. (Air), Ordnance Bd, 1978 (Air Vice-Marshal), Pres., 1978–80. Dep. Chm., Tomash Holdings Ltd, 1980–84. FCMI (FBIM 1978). *Recreations:* music, travel. *Address:* Croft Stones, Lothmore, Helmsdale, Sutherland KW8 6HP. *T:* (01431) 821439.

MacTHOMAS OF FINEGAND, Andrew Patrick Clayhills; 19th Chief of Clan MacThomas (Mac Thomaidh Mhor); *b* 28 Aug. 1942; *o s* of late Captain Patrick Watt MacThomas of Finegand and Elizabeth Cadogan Fenwick MacThomas (*née* Clayhills-Henderson); *S* father, 1970; *m* 1985, Anneke Cornelia Susanna, *o d* of late Albert and Susanna Kruyning-Van Hout; one *s* one *d*. *Educ:* St Edward's, Oxford. FSA (Scot.) 1973. Hd, Barclaycard/Visa (Scotland), 1975–82; Dir, Scotworld, 1982–85; Public Relations, S Africa, 1985–90; Hd of Govt Relns, Barclays Bank, 1990–97; Public Affairs Dir, Barclays PLC, 1997–2005; Develt Dir, Industry and Parliament Trust, 2005–07. Mem., Exec. Cttee, Standing Council of Scottish Chiefs, 2010–; Pres., Clan MacThomas Soc., 1970–; Hon. Vice-Pres., Clan Chattan Assoc., 1970–. *Publications:* History of the Clan MacThomas, 2009. *Recreations:* Clan, politics, wine and wit. *Heir:* *s* Thomas David Alexander MacThomas, Yr of Finegand, *b* 1 Jan. 1987. *Address:* c/o Barclays Bank, 22 Hide Hill, Berwick-upon-Tweed, Northumberland TD15 1AF. *Club:* Hurlingham.

McTIER, Duncan Paul; international double bass soloist and chamber musician; Member: Nash Ensemble, since 1994; Fibonacci Sequence, since 1995; *b* Stourbridge, 21 Nov. 1954; *s* of John and May McTier; *m* 1984, Yuko Inoue (marr. diss. 2010); one *s* one *d*. *Educ:* King Edward VI Grammar Sch., Stourbridge; Bristol Univ. (BSc Math. Scis 1975). ARCM Hons 1974. With BBC SO, 1975–77; Principal Double Bass, Netherlands Chamber Orch., 1977–84; Sen. Tutor of Double Bass, RNCM, 1984–96; Lectr in Double Bass, RAM, 1996–2014; Professor of Double Bass: Univ. of Limerick, 2000–02; Zürcher Hochschule der Künste, Winterthur, 2002–; Escuela Superior de Música Reina Sofia, Madrid, 2007–. Guest Prof., Utrecht Conservatorium, 1994–96. Double Bass Tutor, NYO of GB, 1983–2002 and 2007–09; Double Bass Consultant, RSAMD, 1991–2000. Vis. Master, Double Bass, Codarts, Hogeschool voor de Kunsten, Rotterdam, 2007–10. FRNCM 1994. Hon. RAM 1998. First Prize, IOM Internat. Double Bass Competition, 1982. Recognition Award for Solo Perf., Internat. Soc. of Bassists, 2005. *Publications:* Daily Exercises for Double Bass, 1994; Tips & Tricks, Vol. 1, Preparation and Practice, Vol. 2, The Koussevitsky Concerto, 1999. *Recreations:* golf, cycling, other sports, walking, theatre, good food and wine.

McTIGHE, (Robert) Michael; Member, Office of Communications, since 2007; *b* Stourbridge, 17 Oct. 1953; *s* of Glenville McTighe and Mary McTighe; partner Terry Vega; two *s* one *d* from previous marriages. *Educ:* University Coll. London (BSc Hons Electrical Engrg 1975). GEC Machines Ltd, 1975–76; Thorn EMI plc, 1976–80; GE Medical Systems, 1980–90; Motorola Inc.: Gen. Manager, UK Manuf. Ops, 1990–91, Dir, Eur. Manuf. Ops, 1991–92, Gen. Manager, Original Equipment Manufacturer Mkts, 1992–93, Gen. Manager, Area III, 1993–94, Eur. Cellular Subscriber Div.; Dir, Ops, Asia/Pacific Cellular Subscriber Div., 1994–95; Philips Electronics NV: Man. Dir, Philips Consumer Communications, Le Mans, 1995–97; Pres. and CEO, Philips Consumer Communications LP, NJ, 1997–98; consultant, 1998–99; Cable & Wireless plc: Exec. Dir and CEO, Global Ops, 1999–2001; Exec. Dir, Strategy and Business Develt, 2001; Chm. and CEO, Carrier1 International SA, 2001–02. Chairman: Pace plc, 2001–11; Red M Gp Ltd, 2001–05; Enition SA, 2002–03; Via Networks, Inc., 2002–05; Radiant Networks plc, 2003–04; Alphamosaic Ltd, 2003–04; Corvil Ltd, 2003–08; Am Beo Ltd, 2004–05; Phyworks Ltd, 2004–10; Frontier Silicon Hldgs Ltd, 2004–11; Nujira Ltd, 2005–; Cambridge Semiconductors Ltd, 2006–10; Perpetuum Ltd, 2006–09; Volex Gp plc, 2008–13; WYG plc, 2009–; Jerrold Hldgs Ltd, 2010–; JJB Sports plc, 2010–12; Quinn Gp Holdco Ltd, 2012–; non-executive Director: European Telecom plc, 1998–2002; Alliance & Leicester plc, 2000–08; Arran Isle Ltd, 2009– (Chm., 2013–); Dir, London Metal Exchange Hldgs Ltd, 2002–08; Sen. Ind. Dir, Betfair Ltd, 2008–14. *Recreations:* gardening, ski-ing, scuba diving. *Address:* Flat 1, 3 Eaton Place, SW1X 8BN. *T:* (020) 7823 1124, 07957 806158. *E:* mike@mctighe.net.

MACUR, Rt Hon. Dame Julia, DBE 2005; PC 2013; **Rt Hon. Lady Justice Macur;** a Lady Justice of Appeal, since 2013; Deputy Senior Presiding Judge of England and Wales, from Jan. 2016; *b* 17 April 1957; *d* of Boleslaw Macur and Betsy Macur; *m* 1981; two *s*. *Educ:* Sheffield Univ. (LLB 1978). Called to the Bar, Lincoln's Inn, 1979 (Bencher, 2005); Midland and Oxford Circuit; QC 1998; a Recorder, 1999–2005; a Judge of the High Ct of Justice, Family Div., 2005–13; Presiding Judge, Midland Circuit, 2008–11. Sen. Judicial Comr, Judicial Appts Commn, 2013–. *Address:* Royal Courts of Justice, Strand, WC2A 2LL.

McVAY, Leslie Elizabeth; *see* Evans, L. E.

McVEIGH, Charles Senff, III; Chairman, Corporate and Investment Banking-Global Wealth Management Partnership, Citigroup (formerly Chairman, Salomon Brothers International Ltd, subseq. Salomon Smith Barney, and then Co-Chairman Schroder Salomon Smith Barney, subseq. European Investment Bank, Citigroup), 1987–2013; Senior Advisor, Citigroup Private Bank, since 2013; *b* New York, 4 July 1942; *s* of Charles S. McVeigh, Jr and Evelyn B. McVeigh; *m* 1st, 1964, Pamela Osborn (marr. diss. 1991); one *s* three *d*; 2nd, 1993, Jennifer Champneys; two *s* one *d*. *Educ:* Univ. of Virginia (BA); Long Island Univ. (MBA). Officer, Morgan Guaranty Trust Co., 1965–71; joined Salomon Brothers, 1971: Vice-Pres. and Manager, NY Internat. Dept, 1974–75; Hd, Salomon Bros Internat., London, 1975–87; General Partner, 1977–81; Mem., European Mgt Cttee, 1981. Chm., Rubicon Fund Mgt LLP, 2015–; non-executive Director: Witan Investment Trust, 1998–2006; Savills plc, 2000–; Petropavlovsk (formerly Peter Hambro Mining) PLC, 2009–. Mem., Fulbright Commn, 1993–2005. Member Board: LIFFE, 1983–89; London Stock Exchange, 1986–92; Clearstream (formerly CEDEL), 1994–2005; Member: City Capital Mkts Cttee, 1989–94; Legal Risk Rev. Cttee, 1990–92. Trustee, Landmark Trust, 2010–. *Recreations:* field sports, gardening. *Address:* Rubicon Fund Management LLP, 103 Mount Street, Mayfair, W1K 2TJ. *Clubs:* White's, Beefsteak, Pratt's; The Brook, Anglers' (NYC).

McVEIGH, (Robert) Desmond; Chairman: Westwind Partners, 2004–08; N. T. Energy Inc., 2005–07; Advisory Board, Oriental Minerals Inc., 2007–10; *b* 10 Jan. 1939; *s* of late Rev. Robert Walker McVeigh and Evelyn Mary (*née* McCoubrey); *m* 1966, Gillian Ann Nash; two *s* one *d*. *Educ:* Methodist Coll., Belfast; QUB (LLB Hons); Univ. of Michigan (LLM). Citibank, London, 1967–71; GATX, London, 1971–72; Citibank, 1972–74; First Nat. Bank, Dallas, 1974–77; Saudi Internat. Bank, London, 1977–85; Lloyds Merchant Bank, 1985–87; independent consultant, 1987–92; Chief Exec., IDB for NI, 1993–95; Man. Dir, Longdown Financial Services Ltd, 1995–2002; Exec. Chm., Asia Broadbent Inc., 2001–03; Dep. Chm., Richard Kleinwort Consultancy Group, 2002–07; non-exec. Dir, Viking Internat. Petroleum plc, 2003–05. Vis. Prof. of Finance and Industrial Relations, Warsaw Univ., 1994–97. CCMI (CIMgt 1994). *Recreations:* golf, tennis, music. *T:* 07710 305380. *E:* dmlfcl@gmail.com. *Clubs:* Royal Over-Seas League; Automobile de Monaco.

McVEY, Rt Hon. Esther (Louise); PC 2014; *b* Liverpool, 24 Oct. 1967; *d* of James and Barbara McVey. *Educ:* Belvedere Acad., Liverpool; Queen Mary and Westfield Coll., Univ. of London (LLB Hons 1990); City Univ., London (postgrad. course in radio journalism 1991); John Moores Univ. (MSc Corporate Governance (Dist.; N of England Excellence Award 2009)). CBBC, BBC 1, 1991; BBC Radio 5, 1992; Reportage, BBC2, 1993; Live TV and Meridian TV, 1994; Living TV, 1995; How Do They Do That?, BBC1, 1996; Nothing but the Truth, Channel 4, 1997; 5's Company, Channel 5, 1998; GMTV, 1999; BBC 1, 2000; Dir, JG McVey & Co. Ltd, 2000–06; Man. Dir, Making It (UK) Ltd, 2002–10. Founder, Winning Women (women's business network), 2003–10. Contested (C) Wirral W, 2005. MP (C) Wirral W, 2010–15; contested (C) same seat, 2015. Parly Under-Sec. of State, 2012–13, Minister of State, 2013–15, DWP. *Publications:* If Chloe Can series, 2010. *Recreations:* charity work, gardening, theatre, walking, cinema. *Club:* West Kirby Sailing.

McVICAR, Sir David, Kt 2012; freelance opera director; *b* Glasgow, 1 June 1966; *s* of John and Morag McVicar; partner, Andrew George. *Educ:* Royal Scottish Acad. of Music and Drama (Acting Dip. 1998; Fellow 2003). Full-time specialist in opera direction, 1993–; prodns at houses incl. Royal Opera Hse, Metropolitan Opera, NY and Glyndebourne. *Recreations:* cookery, reading, music. *Address:* c/o Judy Daish Associates, 2 St Charles Place, W10 6EG. *T:* (020) 8964 8811. *E:* tracey@judydaish.com.

McVICAR, Jessica Francis, (Jekka); organic herb farmer, since 1985; author, since 1993; *b* Bristol, 21 Feb. 1951; *d* of John Oliver Stanley-Clarke and Clare Stanley-Clarke (*née* Lowinsky); *m* 1976, Ian McVicar; one *s* one *d*. *Educ:* Cranborne Chase; Somerset Coll. of Art. Flautist and clarinettist with Marsupilami, heavy progressive pop gp, 1969–71; Prodn Office, Drama Serials, BBC TV, 1971–74; Dir and Prod., Community TV, 1974–79; Dir, Prod. and Unit Manager, Avon and Somerset Constabulary Video Unit, 1979–81. Presenter: Herbs Pure and Simple (2 series), BBC Radio 4, 1999, 2000; Sunday Gardening, BBC Radio Bristol, 2005–. Lecture and book tours: South Africa, 2007; Australia, 2008. Royal Horticultural Society: Mem. Council, 2005–15; Member: Fruit, Veg. and Herb Cttee, 1998–2014; Conservation and Envmt Adv. Cttee, 2003–11; RHS Three Counties Agricl Soc. Jt Cttee, 2007– (Jt Chm., 2011–14); Nominations and Appts Cttee, 2009–14; Judge, Floral Exhibits, 1998; Chm., RHS Moderation of floral judging for Chelsea Flower Show, 2011, 2012, 2013, 2014, 2015. Mem., Horticulture Standards Cttee, Soil Assoc., 2011–. President: W of England Herb Gp, 2006–; Herb Soc., 2013–14; Friends of Univ. of Bristol Botanic Garden, 2014–. Contrib., BBC Gardeners' World Mag., 2002–. 62 Gold Medals, RHS, 1993–2009, incl. 14 Gold Medals, Chelsea Flower Show, 1995–2009; Tudor Rose Award, Hampton Court Palace Flower Show, 2007, 2008; Colin Spires Herb Trophy, RHS, 2004–09; Lawrence Medal, RHS, 2009; Lifetime Achievement Award, Garden Media Guild, 2012. *Publications:* Jekka's Complete Herb Book, 1994, 9th edn 2009; Good Enough to Eat, 1997, 2nd edn as Cooking with Flowers, 2003; Seeds: the ultimate guide to growing successfully from seed, 2001, 3rd edn 2008; The New Book of Herbs, 2002, 2nd edn as Grow Herbs, 2010; The Complete Book of Vegetables, Herbs and Fruit, 2002, 5th edn 2009; Jekka's Herb Cookbook, 2010. *Recreations:* music (classical and modern), cooking, gardening, plant photography. *Address:* Rose Cottage, Shellards Lane, Alveston, Bristol BS35 3SY. *T:* (01454) 418878. *E:* Sales@jekkasherbfarm.com.

MacVICAR, Rev. Kenneth, MBE (mil.) 1968; DFC 1944; Extra Chaplain to the Queen in Scotland, since 1991 (Chaplain in Ordinary, 1974–91); Minister of Kenmore and Lawers, Perthshire, 1950–90; *b* 25 Aug. 1921; *s* of Rev. Angus John MacVicar, Southend, Kintyre; *m* 1946, Isobel Guild McKay; three *s* one *d*. *Educ:* Campbeltown Grammar Sch.; Edinburgh Univ.; St Andrews Univ. (MA); St Mary's Coll., St Andrews. Mem., Edinburgh Univ. Air Squadron, 1941; joined RAF, 1941: Pilot, 28 Sqdn, RAF, 1942–45, Flt Comdr, 1944–45 (despatches, 1945). Chaplain, Scottish Horse and Fife and Forfar Yeomanry/Scottish Horse, TA, 1953–65. Convener, Church of Scotland Cttee on Chaplains to HM Forces, 1968–73. Clerk to Presbytery of Dunkeld, 1955. District Councillor, 1951–74. *Recreation:* golf. *Address:* Illeray, Kenmore, Aberfeldy, Perthshire PH15 2HE. *T:* (01887) 830514.

McVICAR, Dr Malcolm Thomas; DL; Group Chief Executive, University of Central Lancashire, 2013–14 (Vice-Chancellor, 1998–2013); *b* 16 June 1946; *s* of Thomas Frederick McVicar and Rose Edith McVicar; two *s*; *m* 2002, Alison Smith; two step *s*. *Educ:* Univ. of Exeter (BA, MA); Univ. of London (PGCE 1975; DPA 1978; PhD 1989). Portsmouth Polytechnic: Prin. Lectr, then Hd of Dept; Dean, 1989–92; Pro-Vice-Chancellor, Univ. of Portsmouth, 1993–98. DL Lancs, 2011. *Recreations:* ski-ing, sailing.

McVIE, Prof. (John) Gordon, MD; Chairman, Cancer Intelligence Ltd, since 2011 (Director, 2003–11); Senior Consultant, European Institute of Oncology, Milan, since 2003; *b* 13 Jan. 1945; *s* of John McVie and Lindsaye Woodburn McVie (*née* Mair); *m* 1998, Claudia Joan Burke; three *s* by previous marriage. *Educ:* Royal High Sch., Edinburgh; Univ. of Edinburgh (BSc Hons; MB, ChB; MD 1978) MRCP 1971. Edinburgh University: MRC Fellow, 1970–71; Lectr in Therapeutics, 1971–76; CRC Sen. Lectr in Oncology, Glasgow Univ., 1976–80; Netherlands Cancer Institute, Amsterdam: Hd, Clinical Res. Unit, 1980–84; Clinical Res. Dir, 1984–89; Scientific Dir, CRC, 1989–96; Dir Gen., CRC, 1996–2002, Jt Dir Gen., Cancer Res. UK, 2002. Consultant to Dir, Internat. Agency for Res. on Cancer, WHO, Lyon, 2006–08. Chm., Oncology Research Internat. Ltd, Aust., 2009–. Visiting Professor: BPMF, London Univ., 1990–96; Univ. of Glasgow, 1996–; Univ. of Wales, Cardiff, 2003–; Univ. of Milan, 2011–; Sch. of Medicine, KCL, 2014–. Member: Council, Scottish Action for Smoking and Health, 1975–80; Royal College of Physicians: Collegiate Mems Cttee, 1975–80; Standing Cttee on Smoking, 1976–80; MRC Cancer Therapy Cttee UK, 1984–92; Bd of Dirs, Netherlands Cancer Inst., 1984–89; Permanent Cttee on Oncology, Min. of Health, Netherlands, 1986–89; European Organisation for Research and Treatment of Cancer: Chairman: Lung Cancer Co-operation Gp, 1981–88; Pharmacokinetics and Metabolism Gp, 1984–87 (Mem., 1981–87); Protocol Rev. Cttee, 1984–91 (Pres., 1994). Examiner: RCPE, 1976–94; RCPSG, 1978–84. Chm., UICC Fellowships Prog., 1990–98. Member: Nat. Review of Resource Allocation, Scottish Office, 1998–99; Internat. Scientific Cttee, Italian Govt, 1998; Steering Cttee, Alliance of World Cancer Res. Orgns. Sec., Eur. Alliance on Personalised Medicine, 2012–. Mem., editl bds of numerous jls related to cancer; Editor-in-Chief, European Cancer News, 1987–97; European Ed., Jl Nat. Cancer Inst., 1994–2003; Founding Editor, ecancermedicalscience, 2007–. FRCPE 1981; FRCPSGlas 1987; FRCP 1997; FMedSci 1999. Hon. FRCSE 2001. Hon. DSc: Abertay Dundee, 1996; Nottingham, 1997; Portsmouth, 1999; Napier Edinburgh, 2002; Ghent, 2005; Bath, 2014. *Publications:* Cancer Assessment and Monitoring, 1979; Autologous Bone Marrow Transplantation and Solid Tumours, 1984; Microspheres and Drug Therapy, 1984; Clinical and Experimental Pathology and Biology of Lung Cancer, 1985; contrib. chapters in books and articles to jls. *Recreations:* opera, theatre, wine, grandchildren.

McVITTIE, Dame Joan (Christine), DBE 2013; Head Teacher, Woodside High School, Haringey, since 2006; *b* Lanark, Scotland, 15 Sept. 1952; *d* of James Smith Docherty and Anne Frances Docherty; *m* 1977, David McVittie (marr. diss. 2000); two *d*. *Educ:* Hollies Convent Grammar Sch.; Birmingham Univ. (BSc Hons); Open Univ. (MA). Teacher of Biology: Burnage High Sch., Manchester, 1974–77; Loreto Sixth Form Coll., Manchester, 1977–82; Newham FE Coll. and Waltham Forest Coll., 1988–90; Hd of Biology, Ilford Ursuline Sch., 1990–94; Sen. Teacher, St Bonaventure's Sch., 1994–96; Deputy Head Teacher: Langdon Sch., 1996–98; Eastlea Sch., 1998–99; Head Teacher, Leytonstone Sch., 2000–06. Pres., ASCL, 2011–12. Trustee, Youth Sports Trust, 2012–. Gov., Nat. Coll. of Sch. Leadership, 2006–12. *Publications:* contrib. Jl Anatomy. *Recreations:* family, reading, cinema, theatre, gym. *Address:* Woodside High School, White Hart Lane, Wood Green, N22 5QJ. *T:* (020) 8889 6761. *E:* mail@woodsidehighschool.co.uk.

McWALTER, Tony; Teacher of Economics and Mathematics, Barclay School, Stevenage; *b* 20 March 1945; *s* of late Joe McWalter and Anne Murray; *m* 1991, Karry Omer; one *s* two *d*. *Educ:* UC Wales, Aberystwyth (BSc 1968); McMaster Univ., Canada (MA 1969); University Coll., Oxford (BPhil 1971; MLitt 1983); Inst. of Educn, London Univ. (QTS 2010). School teacher, Cardinal Wiseman Sch., Greenford, 1963–64; lorry driver, E. H. Patterson Transport, 1964; Lecturer in Philosophy: Thames Poly., 1972–74; Hatfield Poly., then Univ. of Hertfordshire, 1974–97 (Dir of Computing, 1989–92); Associate Lectr in Maths, Open Univ., 2007–10; Teacher of Maths and Physics, Thomas Alleyne Sch., Stevenage, 2008. MP (Lab and Co-op) Hemel Hempstead, 1997–2005; contested same seat, 2005. Member, Select Committee: NI, 1997–2000; Sci. & Technol., 2001–05; Procedure, 2003–05. Treas., Nat. Cttee for Philosophy, 1984–97. Mem., External Adv. Bd, Faculty of Lit. Hum., Oxford Univ., 2000–; Board Member: Council for Economic and Social Aspects of Genomics, 2003–05; British Philosophical Assoc., 2004–05 (Exec. Mem., 2003–06). Hon. Vice-Pres., Herts Conservation Soc., 1997–2006. Educn consultant, 2005–. *Publications:* (ed jtly) Kant and His Influence, 1990. *Recreations:* tennis, bridge, croquet, theatre. *Address:* 56 St Giles Road, Codicote, Hitchin, Herts SG4 8XW.

McWEENY, Prof. Roy; Professor of Theoretical Chemistry, University of Pisa, 1982–97, Professor Emeritus, since 1998; *b* 19 May 1924; *o s* of late Maurice and Vera McWeeny; *m* 1947, Patricia M. Healey (marr. diss. 1979); one *s* one *d*; *m* 1982, Virginia Del Re. *Educ:* Univ. of Leeds; University Coll., Oxford. BSc (Physics) Leeds 1945; DPhil Oxon 1949. Lectr in Physical Chemistry, King's Coll., Univ. of Durham, 1948–57; Vis. Scientist, Physics Dept, MIT, USA, 1953–54; Lectr in Theoretical Chemistry, Univ. Coll. of N Staffs, 1957–62; Associate Dir, Quantum Chemistry Gp, Uppsala Univ., Sweden, 1960–61; Reader in Quantum Theory, 1962–64, Prof. of Theoretical Chemistry, 1964–66, Univ. of Keele; Prof. of Theoretical Chem., 1966–82, and Hd of Chemistry Dept, 1976–79, Sheffield Univ. Vis. Prof., America, Japan, Europe. Mem., Acad. Européenne des Scis, des Arts et des Lettres, 1988. Spiers Meml Medal, RSC, 2006. *Publications:* Symmetry, an Introduction to Group Theory and its Applications, 1963, repr. 2002; (with B. T. Sutcliffe) Methods of Molecular Quantum Mechanics, 1969, 2nd edn as sole author, 1989; Spins in Chemistry, 1970, repr. 2004; Quantum Mechanics: principles and formalism, 1972, repr. 2003; Quantum Mechanics: methods and basic applications, 1973; Coulson's Valence, 3rd rev. edn 1979; (contrib. and Associate Ed.) Handbook of Molecular Physics and Quantum Chemistry, 3 vols, 2002; (Series Ed. and author) Basic Books in Science, 2005–13; contrib. sections in other books and encyclopædias; many research papers on quantum theory of atomic and molecular structure in Proc. Royal Soc., Proc. Phys. Soc., Phys. Rev., Revs. Mod. Phys., Jl Chem. Phys., etc. *Recreations:* drawing, sculpture, travel. *Address:* Via Consoli del Mare 3, 56126 Pisa, Italy.

McWHA, Prof. James Alexander, AO 2011; Vice-Chancellor and President, University of Rwanda, since 2013; *b* 28 May 1947; *s* of David McWha and Sarah Isabel McWha (*née* Caughey); *m* 1970, Jean Lindsay Farries; one *s* two *d*. *Educ:* Queen's Univ., Belfast (BSc, BAgr Hons); Glasgow Univ. (PhD Plant Physiol. 1973); PhD *aeg* Adelaide, 2002. Lectr in Plant Physiol., 1973–79, Hd, Dept of Plant and Microbial Scis, 1980–85, Univ. of Canterbury; Prof. of Agricl Botany, QUB and Dep. CSO, Dept of Agriculture for NI, 1985–89; Dir, DSIR Fruit and Trees (NZ), 1989–92; CEO, Horticulture and Food Res. Inst., NZ, 1992–95; Vice-Chancellor and President: Massey Univ., NZ, 1996–2002; Univ. of Adelaide, 2002–12. Member: Council, NIAB, Cambridge, 1986–89; Bd, NZ Foundn for Res. Sci. and Technol., 1992–95; Bd, NZ Dairy Res. Inst., 1995–98; Gen. Bd, Amer. Chamber of Commerce in NZ, 2000–02. Association of Commonwealth Universities: Mem. Council, 2000–02 (NZ Rep.), 2006–07, 2011–12 (Aust. Rep.); Hon. Treas., 2007–; Exec. Cttee, 2007–; Convenor, SA Vice-Chancellors' Cttee, 2002, 2007–08; Sec. Gen., Internat. Assoc. of Univ. Presidents, 2002–05, Sec. Gen. Emeritus, 2005; Mem., Universities Australia (formerly Australian Vice-Chancellors' Cttee), 2002–12; Dir, Aust. Univs Quality Agency, 2003–09; Mem., Exec. Cttee, Inter-Univ. Council for East Africa, 2014–. Director: Industrial Res. Ltd, 1996–2001; Gp of Eight Ltd (Aust.), 2002–12; Martindale Hldgs Pty Ltd, 2008–12. Hon. DSc Massey, 2004; DUniv Adelaide, 2012. Centenary Medal (Aust.), 2003. *Publications:* numerous scientific and educnl articles. *Recreations:* classic cars, rallying, motor sport, Rugby Union. *Address:* Kigali, Rwanda. *Clubs:* Wellington (Wellington); Adelaide.

McWHINNEY, Jeffrey Harold; Chairman: Significan't (UK) Ltd, since 2013; Vortex Consulting Ltd, since 2014; *b* 9 May 1960; *s* of late Harold George McWhinney and of Mabel Joan McWhinney (*née* Carlisle); *m* 1989, Brigitte François; three *s* one *d*. *Educ:* Jordanstown Schs, Belfast; Mary Hare Grammar Sch., Newbury; Kingston Univ. (Cert. Mgt 1992; Dip. Mgt 1993). Develt Officer, Breakthrough Trust, 1984–87; Head of Community Services, Disability Resources Team, 1987–91; Sen. Economic Develt Officer, Economic Develt Office, Wandsworth BC, 1991–94; Dir, Greenwich Assoc. of Disabled People, 1994–95; Chief Exec., British Deaf Assoc., 1995–2004; Man. Dir, Significan't (UK) Ltd, 2004–13. Dir, Sign Campaign, 1993–2003; Chief Exec., Big D Trading Co., 1996–2002; Chm., Greater London Initiatives for Disabled Entrepreneurs, 2003–05. Specialist Mem., Special Educnl Needs and Disability Tribunal, 2002–05; Member: Adv. Cttee, Deafness Cognition and Language Res. Centre, UCL, 2011–; Deaf Access to Communication, UK Council on

Deafness (formerly Telecom Action Gp), 2007–. Trustee: UK Council on Deafness, 2001–03; RNID, 2006–09. Chm., Technol. Expert Cttee, 2006–10, Mem., ICT Experts Wkg Gp, 2011–, Eur. Union of the Deaf; Mem., Experts in Design for All, World Fedn of the Deaf, 2008–12. Mem., ACEVO (formerly ACENVO), 1995–2005. Dir, British Sign Lang. Broadcasting Trust, 2012–. MInstD 1996. Deaf Acad. Award, 1996. *Publications:* Deaf Consciousness, 1992; numerous articles in various professional and specialist jls. *Recreations:* golf, reading, family activities, travel, sailing, Charlton Athletic FC. *Address:* Significan't (UK) Ltd, St Agnes House, 6 Cresswell Park, SE3 9RD. *Club:* Greenwich Yacht.

MACWHIRTER, Iain; political commentator and broadcaster; *b* 24 Sept. 1952; *s* of Robert Archibald Macwhirter and Christina Ann Macwhirter (*née* McKean); *m* 1991, Christina Harley (marr. diss. 2006); one *s* two *d*. *Educ:* George Heriot's Sch., Edinburgh; Univ. of Edinburgh (MA Hons Pols). Postgrad. Res. in politics, Univ. of Edinburgh, 1976–78; BBC: Researcher, 1979; TV current affairs reporter, 1980–87; Scottish Political Corresp., 1987–89; Westminster Corresp., 1989–90; presenter, political television: Westminster, 1990–99; Holyrood, 1999–2006; presenter, The Road to Referendum (series), 2013. Columnist: Scotland on Sunday, 1990–94; Observer, 1995–96; Scotsman, 1995–99; political commentator, Sunday Herald, 1999–. Rector, Univ. of Edinburgh, 2009–12. Blog, www.iainmacwhirter2.blogspot.com, 2006–. *Publications:* Road to Referendum, 2013; Disunited Kingdom: how Westminster won a referendum but lost Scotland, 2015; contribs to numerous books and other publications incl. Guardian, New Statesman and Public Finance. *Recreations:* hill walking, yoga, children, travel. *Address:* 19 Lilyhill Terrace, Edinburgh EH8 7DR. *T:* (0131) 667 0845, 07714 667871. *E:* iainmacwhirter@mac.com.

McWHIRTER, Prof. John Graham, PhD; FRS 1999; FREng; Distinguished Research Professor in Engineering, Cardiff University, since 2007; *b* 28 March 1949; *s* of late Francis David McWhirter and Elizabeth McWhirter (*née* Martin); *m* 1973, Avesia Vivianne Wolfe; one *s* one *d*. *Educ:* Newry High Sch.; Queen's Univ., Belfast (BSc 1st Cl. Hons Maths 1970; PhD 1973). CMath, FIMA 1988; FIET (FIEE 1994); FREng (FEng 1996); FInstP 1999. Royal Signals and Radar Establishment: Higher Scientific Officer, 1973–77; SSO, 1977–80; PSO, 1980–86; SPSO, 1986–96; Sen. Fellow, Signal Processing Gp, DERA, later QinetiQ Ltd, 1996–2007. Visiting Professor: Electrical Engrg Dept, Queen's Univ., Belfast, 1986–; Sch. of Engrg, UC, Cardiff, 1997–. Pres., IMA, 2002–03 (Vice Pres., 1998–99; Chm. and Proceedings Ed., IMA Internat. Conf. on Maths in Signal Processing, 1988, 1992, 1996, 2000 and 2004); Mem. Council, Royal Soc., 2011–12. Hon. DSc: QUB, 2000; Edinburgh, 2002. J. J. Thomson Medal, IEE, 1994. *Publications:* over 200 res. papers; inventor or jt inventor of 30 UK, European, US and Canadian patents. *Recreations:* swimming for exercise, building and flying radio-controlled model gliders. *Address:* School of Engineering, Cardiff University, Queen's Buildings, Cardiff CF24 3AA. *E:* mcwhirterjg@cardiff.ac.uk. *Club:* Malvern Soaring Association.

McWIGGAN, Thomas Johnstone, CBE 1976; aviation electronics consultant; Secretary General, European Organisation for Civil Aviation Electronics, 1979–87; *b* 26 May 1918; *s* of late Thomas and Esther McWiggan; *m* 1947, Eileen Joyce Moughton; two *d*. *Educ:* UC Nottingham. Pharmaceutical Chemist. FIET, FRAeS, SMIEEE. Signals Officer (Radar), RAFVR, 1941–46 (despatches, 1945). Civil Air Attaché (Telecommunications) Washington, 1962–65; Dir of Telecommunications (Plans), Min. of Aviation, 1965; Dir of Telecommunications (Air Traffic Services), BoT, 1967; Dir Gen. Telecommunications, Nat. Air Traffic Services, 1969–79 (CAA, 1972–79). *Publications:* various technical papers. *Recreations:* photography, cabinet-making, gardening. *Address:* The Squirrels, Liberty Rise, Addlestone, Weybridge, Surrey KT15 1NU. *T:* (01932) 843068.

McWILLIAM, Sir Michael (Douglas), KCMG 1996; Director, School of Oriental and African Studies, University of London, 1989–96 (Hon. Fellow, 1997); *b* 21 June 1933; *s* of Douglas and Margaret McWilliam; *m* 1st, 1960, Ruth Arnstein (*d* 2009); two *s*; 2nd, 2010, Thalia Sybil Stone. *Educ:* Cheltenham Coll.; Oriel Coll., Oxford (MA; Hon. Fellow 2012); Nuffield Coll., Oxford (BLitt). Kenya Treasury, 1958; Samuel Montagu & Co., 1962; joined Standard Bank, subseq. Standard Chartered Bank, 1966; Gen. Manager, 1973; Gp Man. Dir, 1983–88. Member: Bd, Commonwealth Development Corp., 1990–96; Council, ODI, 1991–94. Chm., Superannuation Fund, London Univ., 1990–97. Hon. Vice Pres., Royal African Soc., 2004– (Mem. Council, 1979–91; Chm., 1996–2004); Vice-Pres., Royal Commonwealth Soc., 2002 (Dep. Chm., 1982–91; Chm., 1996–2002, 2009); Chm., Centre for the Study of African Economies, Oxford, 1998–2012. Trustee, British Empire and Commonwealth Mus., Bristol, 2003–12 (Dep. Chm., 2003–06; Chm., 2006–08); Chm., Bryanston Sq. Trust, 2012–. Dep. Chm., 2006, Chm., 2007–11, Cheltenham Festivals. Pres. Council, Cheltenham Coll., 1988–92 (Mem., 1977–92). Mem., Hon. Co. of Gloucestershire, 2010– (Mem. Court, 2013–). *Publications:* The Development Business: a history of the Commonwealth Development Corporation, 2001. *Address:* Yew Tree Farm, Brimpsfield, Glos GL4 8LD. *Club:* New (Cheltenham).

McWILLIAMS, Douglas Francis; Executive Chairman and Chief Economist, Centre for Economics and Business Research, 2013–15 (Chief Executive, 1993–2013); *b* Leigh, Lancs, 24 Nov. 1951; *s* of Sir Francis McWilliams, *qv*; *m* 1979, Ianthe Wright. *Educ:* Stonyhurst Coll.; Lincoln Coll., Oxford (MA; MPhil Econs). Economist, CBI, 1974–85; Chief Economist, IBM UK, 1985–88; Chief Econ. Advr, CBI, 1988–92. Gresham Prof. of Commerce, Gresham Coll., 2012–14. *Publications:* Basic Economics (with T. Congdon), 1975; The Flat White Economy, 2015. *Recreations:* classic cars, cricket. *Address:* 18 Kent Terrace, NW1 4RP. *T:* (020) 7724 7951. *Clubs:* MCC; Aston Martin Owners.

McWILLIAMS, Sir Francis, GBE 1992; FREng; conciliator and arbitrator, since 1978; Chairman, Centre for Economics and Business Research, 1992–2002; Lord Mayor of London, 1992–93; *b* 8 Feb. 1926; *s* of John J. and Mary Anne McWilliams; *m* 1950, Winifred (*née* Segger); two *s*. *Educ:* Holy Cross Acad., Edinburgh; Edinburgh Univ. (BSc Eng 1945); Inns of Court Sch. of Law. Engineer in local govt, 1945–54; Town Engineer, Petaling Jaya New Town, Malaysia, 1954–64; Consulting Civil and Struct. Engineer, Kuala Lumpur, 1964–76. Bar student, 1976–78; called to the Bar, Lincoln's Inn, 1978, Bencher, 1993. Dir, Hong Kong & Shanghai Bank (Malaysia), 1993–99. Chm., British/Malaysian Soc., 1994–2001. Mem., Common Council, City of London, 1978–80; Alderman, Ward of Aldersgate, 1980–96; Sheriff, City of London, 1988–89. Master: Arbitrators' Co., 1985–86; Engineers' Co., 1990–91; Loriners' Co., 1995–96; Pres., Aldersgate Ward Club, 1980–96. Chm., St John's Ambulance City Br., 1992–96. Pres., Instn of Incorp. Exec. Engrs, 1994–97. Vice Chm. Trustees, Foundn for Manufg and Industry, 1994–2000. FCGI; FREng (FEng 1991). Hon. FICE. Hon. DCL City; Hon. DEng Kingston, 1994; Dr *hc* Edinburgh, 1994. KStJ 1992; KSG 1993. PJK, Selangor, Malaysia, 1963; Dato Seri Selera, Selangor, 1973. Order of Merit (Senegal), 1989; Order of Independence (Cl. III) (UAE), 1989; Grande Official da Ordem do Infante Dom Henrique (Portugal), 1993. *Publications:* Pray Silence for "Jock" Whittington (autobiog.), 2002. *Recreations:* golf, ski-ing. *Address:* Flat 7, Whittingehame House, Whittinghame, E Lothian EH41 4QA. *T:* and *Fax:* (01368) 850619. *Clubs:* Hon. Company of Edinburgh Golfers, Muirfield; Royal Selangor Golf (Kuala Lumpur).

See also D. F. McWilliams.

MADDEN, Sir Charles (Jonathan), 4th Bt *cr* 1919, of Kells, co. Kilkenny; Technical Director, Wind-Ways Pty Ltd, since 2007; *b* 11 Aug. 1949; *yr s* of Lt-Col John Wilmot Madden, MC, RA, *yr s* of 1st Bt, and Beatrice Catherine (*née* Sievwright); *S* brother, 2006; *m* 1st, 1980, Kirsteen Victoria Ronald Noble (marr. diss. 2003); one *s* one *d*; 2nd, 2006, Dr Margaret Elaine Taylor. *Educ:* Blundell's; Portsmouth Poly. (BSc Engrg 1974); Loughborough Univ. (MTech Design 1975); San Diego Univ. (MBA Marketing 1984). *Recreations:* playing the 'cello (Unley SO, Adelaide), sailing. *Heir: s* Samuel Charles John Madden, *b* 22 Sept. 1984. *Address:* 3 Sea View, Lynton, SA 5062, Australia. *E:* charlie.madden@internode.au.net.

MADDEN, Rt Rev. Cuthbert, OSB; Abbot of Ampleforth, since 2005; *b* 12 Feb. 1955; *s* of late James and Joan Madden. *Educ:* Middlesex Hosp. Med. Sch. (MB BS). MRCP 1982. House Surgeon, W Norwich Hosp., 1978–79; House Physician, 1979, SHO, 1979–80, Middlesex Hosp.; Rotating SHO in Medicine, Bath Utd Hosps, 1980–82; Rotating Registrar in Medicine, Royal Hallamshire Hosp., Sheffield, 1982–84; Ampleforth: entered monastic community, 1984; solemn profession, 1988; ordained priest, 1990; Housemaster, St John's, 1997–2005. Hon. FRCP 2006. *Address:* Ampleforth Abbey, York YO62 4EN. *T:* (01439) 766700/710, *Fax:* (01439) 788132.

MADDEN, Sir David (Christopher Andrew), KCMG 2003 (CMG 1996); HM Diplomatic Service, retired; Consultant to World Animal Protection (formerly World Society for the Protection of Animals), since 2007; Senior Member, St Antony's College, Oxford, since 2012; *b* 25 July 1946; *s* of late Dr (Albert) Frederick (McCulloch) Madden and (Alice) Margaret Madden; *m* 1970, Penelope Anthea Johnston; one *s* two *d*. *Educ:* Magdalen Coll. Sch., Oxford; Merton Coll., Oxford (Postmaster; MA); Courtauld Inst. of Art, London Univ. (MA). FCO, 1970–72; British Mil. Govt, Berlin, 1972–75; Cabinet Office, 1975–77; Moscow, 1978–81; Athens, 1981–84; FCO, 1984–87; Counsellor, 1987; Dep. Hd of Mission, Belgrade, 1987–90; Head, Southern European Dept, FCO, 1990–94; High Comr, Republic of Cyprus, 1994–99; Ambassador to Greece, 1999–2004; Pol Advr to OC EU Force, Bosnia and Hercegovina, 2004–05. Accredited Mediator, ADR Gp, 2009–13. Chm., Develt Cttee, SE Eur. Studies at Oxford, 2012–. Trustee: Brooke Hosp. for Animals, 2008–; Compassion in World Farming, 2010–; Patron, Voice for Ethical Research at Oxford, 2008–. Hon. Dr London Metropolitan, 1999. *Publications:* The Mystery of Edwin Drood, by Charles Dickens (completion of an unfinished book), 2011. *Recreations:* animal welfare, cricket, tennis, reading, writing. *Address:* 5 Rawlinson Road, Oxford OX2 6UE.

MADDEN, Dr (John) Lionel, CBE 1999; Librarian, National Library of Wales, 1994–98; *b* 8 Aug. 1938; *s* of late Cyril Madden and Edith (*née* Mottram); *m* 1965, Georgina Mary Hardwick; one *s* one *d*. *Educ:* King Edward VII Grammar Sch., Sheffield; Lincoln Coll., Oxford (MA 1964); University Coll. London (DipLib 1963); Univ. of Leicester (PhD 1970). ALA 1964. Asst Librarian, Univ. of Hull, 1963–67; Bibliographer, Univ. of Leicester Victorian Studies Centre, 1967–72; Sen. Lectr, Coll. of Librarianship, Wales, 1973–87; Keeper of Printed Books, Nat. Liby of Wales, 1987–94. Mem., Pubns Bd, Leicester Univ. Press, 1968–72; Chm., Pubns Bd, Tennyson Soc., 1973–77. Pres., Welsh Liby Assoc., 1994–98; Chairman: Welsh Books Council, 1996–2005 (Vice-Chm., 1994–96); Liby and Inf. Services Council, Wales, 1998–2001; Capel (Welsh Chapels Heritage Soc.), 1999–2009 (Hon. Pres., 2010–). Trustee, St Deiniol's Liby, Hawarden, 1994–2009. Hon. Fellow, Dept of Inf. and Liby Studies, Univ. of Wales, Aberystwyth, 1989–93, Hon. Prof., 1993–; Hon. Fellow, Univ. of Wales, Lampeter, 1998. Hon. FCLIP (Hon. FLA 1998). Hon. Mem., Gorsedd Beirdd Ynys Prydain, 1995–. *Publications:* Thomas Love Peacock, 1967; How to Find Out about the Victorian Period, 1970; Robert Southey: the critical heritage, 1972; Sir Charles Tennyson: an annotated bibliography, 1973; The Nineteenth Century Periodical Press in Britain, 1976; Primary Sources for Victorian Studies, 1977; (ed jtly) Investigating Victorian Journalism, 1990; Methodism in Wales, 2003; articles in learned jls. *Recreation:* walking. *Address:* Hafren, Cae'r Gog, Aberystwyth SY23 1ET. *T:* (01970) 617771.

MADDEN, John Philip; film director; *b* 8 April 1949; *s* of William John Raleigh Madden and Jean Elizabeth Hunt Mills; *m* 1975, Penelope Jane Abrahams; one *s* one *d*. *Educ:* Clifton Coll., Bristol; Sidney Sussex Coll., Cambridge (MA; Hon. Fellow 2000). Artistic Dir, Oxford and Cambridge Shakespeare Co., 1970–73; Associate Prof., Yale Sch. of Drama, 1977–80. *Stage:* Wings, The Bundle, Measure for Measure, The Suicide, Terry by Terry, Grownups, Beyond Therapy, Salonika, Cinders, Between East and West, An American Comedy, Ivanov, Mrs Warren's Profession, Caritas, Proof; *films:* Ethan Frome, 1992; Golden Gate, 1994; Mrs Brown, 1997; Shakespeare in Love, 1998 (seven Academy Awards, four BAFTA Awards, 1999); Captain Corelli's Mandolin, 2001; Proof, 2005; Killshot, 2008; The Debt, 2011; The Best Exotic Marigold Hotel, 2012; The Second Best Exotic Marigold Hotel, 2015; *television:* Poppyland, A Wreath of Roses, Sherlock Holmes, After the War, Widowmaker, Inspector Morse (four films), Prime Suspect: The Lost Child, Meat, Truth or Dare (BAFTA Scotland Award, Best Single Drama, 1997); Masters of Sex, 2013; *radio:* US National Public Radio: Wings (Prix Italia, 1978), Star Wars, The Empire Strikes Back, Return of the Jedi. Hon. DLitt Portsmouth, 2006. *Recreations:* cooking, walking, sailing. *Address:* c/o Jenne Casarotto, Casarotto Ramsay Ltd, Waverley House, 7–12 Noel Street, W1F 8GQ.

MADDEN, Lionel; *see* Madden, J. L.

MADDEN, Max; *b* 29 Oct. 1941; *s* of late George Francis Leonard Madden and Rene Frances Madden; *m* 1972, Sheelagh Teresa Catherine Howard (*d* 2007). *Educ:* Lascelles Secondary Modern Sch.; Pinner Grammar Sch. Journalist: East Essex Gazette; Tribune (political weekly); Sun, London; Scotsman, London; subseq. Press and Information Officer, British Gas Corp., London; Dir of Publicity, Labour Party, 1979–82. MP (Lab): Sowerby, Feb. 1974–1979; Bradford West, 1983–97.

MADDEN, Michael; Under Secretary, Ministry of Agriculture, Fisheries and Food, 1985–96, retired; *b* 12 Feb. 1936; *s* of late Harold Madden and Alice Elizabeth (*née* Grenville); *m* 1st, 1960, Marion Will (marr. diss. 1977); two *s* one *d*; 2nd, 1994, Angela Grace Abell (*d* 2012). *Educ:* King Edward VII Sch., Sheffield. Exec. Officer, Min. of Transport and Civil Aviation, 1955; Ministry of Agriculture, Fisheries and Food: Asst Principal, 1963–67; Asst Private Sec. to Minister, 1966–67; Principal, 1967; Asst Sec. (as Head, Tropical Foods Div.), 1973; Under Sec., 1985; Head, Management Services Gp, 1985; Flood Defence, Plant Protection and Agricl Resources, 1990; Envmt Policy Gp, 1991–96. *Recreations:* walking, eating and drinking with friends, music, theatre going. *Address:* Manor Barn, 1 Priors Court, Baunton, Cirencester GL7 7BB. *T:* (01242) 641423. *Club:* Farmers.

MADDEN, Prof. Paul Anthony, DPhil; FRS 2001; FRSE; Provost, Queen's College, Oxford, since 2008; Pro-Vice-Chancellor, University of Oxford, since 2011; *m*; five *c*. *Educ:* St Bede's Catholic Grammar Sch., Bradford; Univ. of Sussex (BSc, DPhil). Fellow, Magdalen Coll., Cambridge, 1974–82; Lectr in Chemistry, then Prof. of Chemistry, 1984–2004, Univ. of Oxford; Fellow, Queen's Coll., Oxford, 1984–2004; Prof. of Chemistry, 2005–06, Joseph Black Prof. of Chemistry, 2006–08, and Dir, Centre for Sci. at Extreme Conditions, Univ. of Edinburgh, 2005–08. Chair, Conf. of Colleges. FRSE 2006. Eli Burstein Lect., Univ. of Philadelphia, 2004. Tilden Medal, 1993/94, Medal for Statistical Mechanics and Simulation, 2002, RSC; Robert S. Mulliken Award, Univ. of Chicago, 2002. *Address:* Queen's College, Oxford OX1 4AW.

MADDEN, Paul Damian, CMG 2013; FRGS; HM Diplomatic Service; Foreign and Commonwealth Office, London, since 2015; *b* 25 April 1959; *s* of Antony Angus Thomas Madden and Doris May Madden (*née* Brewer); *m* 1989, Sarah Pauline Thomas; two *s* one *d*. *Educ:* King's School, Ottery St Mary; Gonville and Caius Coll., Cambridge (BA Geog. 1980, MA 1983); Sch. of Oriental and African Studies, Univ. of London; Durham Univ. Business Sch. (MBA 2002). DTI, 1980–87, Private Sec. to Minister, 1984–86; Japanese Lang. Studies, SOAS and Kamakura, 1987–89; entered Diplomatic Service, 1989; First Secretary: Tokyo, 1989–92; FCO, 1992–96; Washington, 1996–2000; Dep. High Comr, Singapore, 2000–03; Hd, Public Diplomacy Dept, FCO, 2003–04; Gp Dir, UK Trade and Investment, 2004–07;

High Comr, Singapore, 2007–11; High Comr, Australia, 2011–15. Member, Court: Imperial Coll. London, 2004–07; Cranfield Univ., 2004–07. *Publications:* Raffles: lessons in business leadership, 2003. *Recreations:* travel, family. *Address:* c/o Foreign and Commonwealth Office, King Charles Street, SW1A 2AH.

MADDERS, Rev. Mgr (Brian) Richard, MBE 1996; Parish Priest (RC), Camberley and Bagshot, since 2007; *b* 12 Aug. 1949; *s* of Mervyn and Eleanor Madders. *Educ:* Mayfield Coll.; St John's Seminary, Wonersh; Heythrop Coll., London. Employee, National Bank, 1969–71; ordained priest, 1978; Assistant Priest: Banstead, 1978–81; Brighton, 1981–84; Worthing, 1984–85; Chaplain, RN, 1985–2007: First Flotilla (Seagoing), 1986–87; HMS Sultan, 1987–90; Third Flotilla (Seagoing), 1990–93; Staff Chaplain, FO Surface Flotilla, 1993–95; HMS Raleigh, 1995–99; Australian Defence Force Acad., 1999; HMS Nelson, 2000–01; HMS Drake, 2001–02; Principal RC Chaplain (Naval), VG for Bishopric of the Forces (RC), and Dir, Naval Chaplaincy Service (Training and Progs), 2002–07. QHC, 2002–07. Pres., RN Motorcycle Club, 1989–2000. Trustee, Apostleship of the Sea, 2014–. Travelled to 95 countries and territories. *E:* cbparishpriest@hotmail.co.uk. *Club:* Army and Navy.

MADDERS, Justin; MP (Lab) Ellesmere Port and Neston, since 2015; *b* Manchester, 22 Nov. 1972; *m* Nicole Meardon; three *s*. *Educ:* Univ. of Sheffield. Solicitor, 1998–2015. Member (Lab): Ellesmere Port and Neston BC, 1998–2009 (Leader, 2007–09); Cheshire W and Chester Council, 2009–15 (Leader of Opposition, 2011–14). *Address:* House of Commons, SW1A 0AA. *T:* (020) 7219 6584. *E:* justin.madders.mp@parliament.uk.

MADDICOTT, David Sydney, (Syd); HM Diplomatic Service, retired; Partner and Director, DORIS Resources LLP, since 2013; Chairman, Co-ordinating Committee on Remuneration, since 2015; *b* 27 March 1953; *s* of Patrick McCagh and Eileen Hannigan, and adopted *s* of Sydney Walter Maddicott and Catherine O'Brien; *m* 1980, Elizabeth Wynne; four *s* one *d*. *Educ:* University Coll. London (BA Hons English 1976). Various sales and mktg appts, Rank Xerox (UK) Ltd, 1976–89; Gen. Sales and Mktg Manager, Pitney Bowes (Ireland) Ltd, 1989–90; postgrad. studies, UC, Dublin, 1990–92; self-employed consultant, 1992–94; joined FCO, 1994; Hd of Section, Econ. Relns Dept/UN Dept, 1994–96; on attachment to Canadian Dept of For. Affairs and Internat. Trade, Ottawa, 1996–97; Hd, Pol, Media and Public Affairs Section, High Commn, Ottawa, 1997–2000; Dep. Hd, Latin America and Caribbean Dept, 2000–03, and Hd, Caribbean Unit, 2001–03, FCO; Sen. Duty Manager, FCO Response Centre, 2003–06; High Comr to Cameroon and Ambassador (non-resident) to Central African Republic, Chad and Gabon, 2006–09. *Recreations:* singing, reading, speedway, cricket. *Clubs:* Deddington Cricket, New Edinburgh Cricket (Ottawa).

MADDICOTT, Dr John Robert Lewendon, FBA 1996; FSA; Fellow and Lecturer in Modern History, Exeter College, Oxford, 1969–2006, now Emeritus; *b* Exeter, 22 July 1943; *e s* of late Robert Maddicott, Ipplepen, Devon, and Barbara (*née* Lewendon); *m* 1965, Hilary, *d* of late Thomas and Violet Owen; two *d*. *Educ:* Cheltenham Grammar Sch.; King Edward's Sch., Bath; Worcester Coll., Oxford (BA 1st cl. 1964; DPhil 1968). FSA 1980. Jun. Lectr, Magdalen Coll., Oxford, 1966–67; Asst Lectr, Univ. of Manchester, 1967–69; Sub-Rector, Exeter Coll., Oxford, 1988–90. Vis. Prof., Univ. of S Carolina, 1983. Raleigh Lectr, British Acad., 2001; Ford's Lectr in British Hist., Oxford, 2004; Selden Soc. Lectr, 2011. Jt Editor, English Hist. Review, 1990–2000. *Publications:* Thomas of Lancaster 1307–22, 1970; The English Peasantry and the Demands of the Crown, 1294–1341, 1975; Law and Lordship: Royal Justices as Retainers in Thirteenth- and Fourteenth-Century England, 1978; Simon de Montfort, 1994; The Origins of the English Parliament, 924–1327, 2010; Founders and Fellowship: the early history of Exeter College, Oxford, 1314–1592, 2014; contribs to learned jls. *Recreations:* hill walking, poetry, book collecting. *Address:* Exeter College, Oxford OX1 3DP.

MADDICOTT, Syd; *see* Maddicott, D. S.

MADDISON, Hon. Sir David (George), Kt 2008; a Judge of the High Court, Queen's Bench Division, 2008–13; *b* 22 Jan. 1947; *s* of Claude and Clarice Maddison; *m* 1976, Indira Mary Antoinette Saverymuttu; three *s*. *Educ:* King's Sch., Chester; Grey Coll., Univ. of Durham (BA 1968). Called to the Bar, Inner Temple, 1970 (Bencher, 2005); practised on Northern Circuit, 1972–92; a Recorder, 1990–92; a Circuit Judge, 1992–2008; a Sen. Circuit Judge and Hon. Recorder of Manchester, 2003–08. Mem., Parole Bd, 1996–2002; Dir, Criminal Trng, Judicial Coll., 2010–13 (Hon. Fellow, 2014). *Publications:* (ed) Bingham's Negligence Cases, 4th edn 1996, 5th edn 2002. *Recreations:* classical music, singing, tennis, golf, watching football. *Address:* c/o Royal Courts of Justice, Strand, WC2A 2LL. *Clubs:* East India; Athenæum (Liverpool).

MADDISON, Jane Hope; *see* Kennedy, J. H.

MADDOCK, family name of **Baroness Maddock**.

MADDOCK, Baroness *cr* 1997 (Life Peer), of Christchurch in the co. of Dorset; **Diana Margaret Maddock;** President, Liberal Democrats, 1998–99; *b* 19 May 1945; *d* of Reginald Derbyshire and Margaret Evans; *m* 1st, 1966, Robert Frank Maddock (marr. diss. 2001); two *d*; 2nd, 2001, Rt Hon. Sir Alan Beith, *qv*. *Educ:* Brockenhurst GS; Shenstone Training Coll.; Portsmouth Polytechnic. Teacher: Weston Park Girls' Sch., Southampton, 1966–69; Extra-Mural Dept, Stockholm Univ., 1969–72; Sholling Girls' Sch., Southampton, 1972–73; Anglo-Continental Sch. of English, Bournemouth, 1973–76; Greylands Sch. of English, Southampton, 1990–91. Member: (L, subseq. Lib Dem), Southampton CC, 1984–93; (Lib Dem), Northumberland CC, 2005–08; (Lib Dem) Berwick-upon-Tweed BC, 2007–09. Contested (Lib Dem) Southampton Test, 1992. MP (Lib Dem) Christchurch, July 1993–1997; contested (Lib Dem) same seat, 1997. Chairman: All-Party Anglo-Swedish Gp, 2010–; H of L Works of Art Cttee, 2014–; Vice Chm., All-Party Univ. Gp, 2010–. Lib Dem spokesman on housing, H of L, 1997–2004. Member: Cttee on Standards in Public Life, 2003–09; H of L Merits of Statutory Instruments Cttee, 2005–09; Finance Sub-Cttee, H of L Europe Select Cttee, 2010–14. A Vice-Pres., Nat. Housing Fedn, 1997–2010; President: Anglo-Swedish Soc., 2000–; Sustainable Energy Assoc. (formerly Micropower Council), 2005–; Vice President: Nat. Energy Action, 2000–; Nat. Home Improvement Council, 2004–; Local Government Association, 2010–. *Recreations:* theatre, music, reading, travel. *Address:* House of Lords, SW1A 0PW.

MADDOCKS, Anne Mary Catherine; *see* Ashworth, A. M. C.

MADDOCKS, Arthur Frederick, CMG 1974; HM Diplomatic Service, retired; Ambassador and UK Permanent Representative to OECD, Paris, 1977–82; *b* 20 May 1922; *s* of late Frederick William Maddocks and Celia Elizabeth Maddocks (*née* Beardwell); *m* 1945, Margaret Jean Crawford Holt; two *s* one *d*. *Educ:* Manchester Grammar Sch.; Corpus Christi Coll., Oxford. Army, 1942–46; Foreign (later Diplomatic) Service, 1946–82: Washington, 1946–48; FO, 1949–51; Bonn, 1951–55; Bangkok, 1955–58; UK Delegn to OEEC, 1958–60; FO, 1960–64; UK Delegn to European Communities, Brussels, 1964–68; Political Adviser, Hong Kong, 1968–72; Dep. High Comr and Minister (Commercial), Ottawa, 1972–76. Mem., OECD Appeals Tribunal, 1984–89. *Address:* Lynton House, 83 High Street, Wheatley, Oxford OX33 1XP. *Club:* Hong Kong (Hong Kong).

MADDOCKS, His Honour Bertram Catterall; a Circuit Judge, 1990–2005; *b* 7 July 1932; *s* of His Honour George Maddocks and of Mary Maddocks (*née* Day); *m* 1964, Angela Vergette Forster; two *s* one *d*. *Educ:* Malsis Hall, near Keighley; Rugby; Trinity Hall, Cambridge (schol.; MA; Law Tripos Part 2 1st Cl. 1955). Nat. Service, 2nd Lieut, RA, 1951; Duke of Lancaster's Own Yeomanry (TA), 1958–67. Called to the Bar, Middle Temple, 1956; Harmsworth Schol.; Mem., Lincoln's Inn; a Recorder, 1983–90. Pt-time Chm., VAT Tribunals, 1977–92. *Recreations:* real tennis, lawn tennis, bridge, croquet. *Address:* Moor Hall Barn, Prescot Road, Aughton, Lancashire L39 6RT. *T:* (01695) 421601. *Clubs:* Cavalry and Guards; Manchester Tennis and Racquet, Southport and Birkdale Croquet.

MADDOCKS, Fiona Hamilton; Chief Music Critic, The Observer, 1997–2002, and since 2008; *m* 1st, R. Cooper (marr. diss.); two *d*; 2nd, 1995, Tom Phillips, *qv*. *Educ:* Blackheath High Sch. (GPDST), London; Royal Coll. of Music; Newnham Coll., Cambridge (MA). Taught English Literature, Istituto Orsoline, Cortina d'Ampezzo, Italy, 1977–78; Medici Soc., London, 1978–79; News trainee, Producer and Sen. Producer, LBC, 1979–82; Founder Editor, Comment, 1982–85, Asst Commng Editor, Music, 1985–86, Channel 4; The Independent: Dep. Arts Editor, 1986–88, and writer; Music Editor and Associate Arts Editor, 1988–91; Founding Editor, BBC Music Magazine, 1992–97; Editor, BBC Proms Guide, 1998–99; Exec. Editor, LSO Living Music Magazine, 1998–2003; Chief Opera Critic, Music Critic and Arts Feature Writer, Evening Standard, 2002–08. Writer in Residence and Fellow, Salzburg Global Seminar, 2011. Board Member: Opera magazine, 1998–; Unknown Public, 2006–10; Advr, Editl Bd, RA mag., 2008–. Member: Exec. Cttee, SPNM, 1990–91; Critics' Circle, 1995 (Mem. Council, 1997–99); Cttee, Kim Scott Walwyn Prize, 2003–13; Pimlico Opera, 2012–. Gov., Sherborne Sch., 2001–11. Dir's Visitor, Inst. for Advanced Study, Princeton, 2008–11. FRSA 2006. BP Arts Journalism Press Award, 1991. *Publications:* Hildegard of Bingen, 2001; Harrison Birtwistle: wild tracks, 2014. *Address:* c/o The Observer, Kings Place, 90 York Way, N1 9GU.

MADDOX, Brenda Power, (Lady Maddox); writer; *b* 24 Feb. 1932; *d* of Dr Brendan W. Murphy and Edith Giamperoli Murphy; *m* 1960, Sir John Royden Maddox (*d* 2009); one *s* one *d*, and one step *s* one step *d*. *Educ:* High Sch., Bridgewater, Mass; Radcliffe Coll. (BA *cum laude* 1953). Press Dir, United Community Service of Boston, 1955–57; reporter and columnist, Quincy Patriot Ledger, Mass, 1957–59; UK Reporter, Reuters, 1959–60; The Economist, 1962–72 and 1975–85, latterly as Britain Ed., then Home Affairs Ed.; Media Columnist: Daily Telegraph, 1987–94; The Times, 1994–97; biographer, writer, critic and broadcaster, 1988–. Non-exec. Dir, London Broadcasting Co., 1973–75. Member: UK Nat. Adv. Cttee for UNESCO, 1983–85; Sci. in Society Cttee, Royal Soc., 2000–04. Vice Pres., Hay Fest., 1995–; Member: British Assoc. for Sci. Writers, 1978– (Chm., 1983–84); Broadcasting Press Guild, 1983– (Chm., 1993–94); Mgt Cttee, Soc. of Authors, 1987–90; Council, RSL, 2004–. Mem., 1999–, Vice Chm., 2001–06, Shakespeare Prize Jury, Toepfer Foundn, Hamburg. FRSL 1994. Hon. FKC 2011. Hon. Phi Beta Kappa, Harvard Univ., 1978. Hon. DHL Finch, 2004; Hon. DLitt Glamorgan, 2005. *Publications:* Beyond Babel: new directions in communications, 1972; The Half-Parent, 1975; The Marrying Kind, 1981; *biographies:* Who's Afraid of Elizabeth Taylor?, 1977; Nora: the life of Mrs James Joyce, 1988 (LA Times Biog. Prize, 1988; Silver PEN Award, 1989; Prix du Meilleur Livre Etranger, 1990) (filmed as Nora, 2000); The Married Man: a life of D. H. Lawrence, 1994 (Whitbread Biog. Award); George's Ghosts: the secret life of W. B. Yeats, 1999; Rosalind Franklin: the dark lady of DNA, 2001 (Marsh Biog. Prize, 2001; LA Times Sci. Prize, 2002); Maggie, the First Lady, 2003; Freud's Wizard: the enigma of Ernest Jones, 2006; George Eliot: novelist, lover, wife, 2009; author of reviews and articles for newspapers and mags in UK and USA. *Recreations:* giving parties, cooking, exploring mid-Wales. *Address:* 9 Pitt Street, W8 4NX. *T:* (020) 7937 9750. *E:* bmaddox@pitt.demon.co.uk. *Club:* Athenæum.
See also B. M. Maddox.

MADDOX, Bronwen Maria; Editor and Chief Executive, Prospect, since 2010; *b* 7 May 1963; *d* of Sir John Royden Maddox and of Brenda Power Maddox, *qv*; one *d*. *Educ:* Westminster Sch.; St Paul's Girls' Sch.; St John's Coll., Oxford (BA PPE 1985). Analyst, Charterhouse Venture Capital, 1985–86; Dir and Hd, Media Investment Team, Kleinwort Benson Securities, 1986–91; investigative reporter, then leader writer, FT, 1991–96; The Times: US Editor and Washington Bureau Chief, 1996–99; Foreign Editor, 1999–2006; Chief Foreign Commentator, 2006–10. Mem. Council, Chatham House, 2010–; Trustee: Imperial War Mus., 2010–14; Ditchley Foundn, 2013–. *Publications:* In Defence of America, 2008. *Recreations:* cooking, hiking. *Address:* Prospect, 3rd Floor, 25 Sackville Street, W1S 3AX.

MADDOX, Air Vice Marshal Nigel David Alan, CBE 1999; Chief of Staff (Operations), Headquarters Air Command, 2007–09; *b* 1 April 1954; *s* of Albert and Beverly Maddox; *m* 1979, Sue Elizabeth Armitage; one *d*. *Educ:* Clark's Grammar Sch.; Westcliff High Sch. for Boys; MBA Open Univ. Flight Comdr, No 12 Sqdn, 1987; RNSC, Greenwich, 1988; PSO, AOC No 18 Gp, 1989; OC Ops Wing, RAF Mount Pleasant, Falkland Is, 1990; OC No 12 Sqdn, RAF Lossiemouth, 1991; Asst Dir W, ACDS(Ops), MoD, 1993–96; Sen. RAF Officer, Germany, and Stn Comdr, RAF Brüggen, 1996–99; Air Cdre Maritime, 1999–2002; AOC No 2 Gp, 2002–05; Comdt, Jt Services Comd and Staff Coll., 2005–07. *Recreations:* squash, golf. *Address:* 33 Kilnwood Avenue, Hockley, Essex SS5 4PR. *T:* (01702) 203294. *E:* comao@aol.com. *Club:* Royal Air Force.

MADDOX, Ronald, PRI 1989, 2004 and 2009, Hon. PRI 2014 (RI 1959); artist, illustrator and designer; *b* 5 Oct. 1930; *s* of Harold George and Winifred Maddox; *m* 1st, 1958, Camilla Farrin (*d* 1995); two *s*; 2nd, 1997, Diana Goodwin. *Educ:* Hertfordshire College of Art and Design, St Albans; London College of Printing and Graphic Art. FCSD, FSAI; Hon. RWS 1990; Hon. RBA 2002. Nat. Service, RAF, 1949–51, Air Min. Design Unit. Designer, illustrator, art director, London advertising agencies, 1951–61; private practice, 1962–; commissioned by nat. and multinat. cos and corps, govt depts, public authorities, TV; designer British postage stamps and philatelic material, 1972– (winner Prix de l'art Philatelique, 1987); exhibns, RA, RI, RWS, RBA, London and provincial galls; paintings in royal, govt and public bodies' collections. Assessor: Royal Acad./British Institution Fund (drawings and watercolours), 1996–2000; Turner Watercolour Award/Medal (formerly Winsor & Newton Turner Watercolour Award), RA Summer Exhibn, 2002–07; Turner Watercolour Award, RI/RWS, 2008–. Mem. Council, Artists' Gen. Benevolent Instn, 2000– (Hon. Sec., 2002–10; Chm., 2010; Pres., 2015). Trustee, Digswell Arts Trust, 2007–. Vice-Pres., RI, 1979; Governor, Fedn of British Artists, 1989–2003 (Chm., 1997); Hon. Member: Soc. of Architect Artists; Fedn of Canadian Artists; United Soc. of Artists; Campine Assoc. of Watercolours, Belgium; PS; Soc. of Graphic Fine Art; Wapping Gp of Artists, 2008–. FRSA. Patron: Danesbury and Queen Victoria Meml Hosp., Welwyn, 1998–; Isabel Hospice, E Herts, 2000–; Trustee and Pres., Welwyn Scouts & Guides Assoc., 2005–. Freeman, City of London, 2000; Hon. Freeman, Co. of Painter-Stainers, 2000. Winsor & Newton/RI Award, 1981, 1991; Rowland Hilder landscape painting Award, RI, 1996, 2000. *Recreations:* compulsive drawing, walking, cycling, gardening. *Address:* Herons, 21 New Road, Digswell, Herts AL6 0AQ. *T:* (01438) 714884. *Club:* Arts (Hon. Mem.).

MADDOX, Stephen, OBE 2008; DL; Chief Executive, Metropolitan Borough of Wirral, 1997–2010; *b* Merseyside. *Educ:* Univ. of Kent (BA 1974). Joined Wirral MBC as articled clerk, 1974; admitted as solicitor, 1977; Dep. Borough Solicitor and Sec., Wirral MBC, 1991–98. Freedom, Bor. of Wirral, 2010. DL Merseyside, 2011. *Address:* 8 Fairfield Road, Hoole, Chester CH2 3RN.

MADDRELL, (Catherine) Siân; Head Teacher, The Grey Coat Hospital, since 2011; *b* St Asaph, 19 Nov. 1966; *d* of Geoffrey Keggen Maddrell, *qv*; *m* 2003, Richard Paul Germond; two *s*. *Educ:* Surbiton High Sch.; Durham Univ. (BA Hons French); Exeter Coll., Oxford (PGCE Modern Langs); Inst. of Educn, Univ. of London (NPQH Nat. Coll. for Teaching and Leadership). Buyer, Fenwick Ltd, 1990–91; The Grey Coat Hospital: Teacher of Modern Foreign Langs, 1992–2000; Hd of Year, 1993–95; Hd of Modern Langs, 1995–2000; Hd of Langs and Lang. Coll. Manager, Elliott Sch., 2000–01; Asst Head Teacher, Acland Burghley Sch., 2001–08; First Vice Principal, Pimlico Acad., 2008–11. *Recreations:* family, travel, languages, reading, theatre, art, ski-ing, snowboarding, swimming, tennis. *Address:* The Grey Coat Hospital, Greycoat Place, SW1P 2DY.

MADDRELL, Geoffrey Keggen, OBE 2015; Chairman, Human Recognition Systems Ltd, since 2009; Founder and Chairman, Research Autism, since 2004; *b* 18 July 1936; *s* of Captain Geoffrey Douglas Maddrell and Barbara Marie Kennaugh; *m* 1964, Winifred Mary Daniel Jones (*d* 2014); two *s* one *d*. *Educ:* King William's Coll., Isle of Man (Major Cain Schol.); Corpus Christi Coll., Cambridge (MA Law and Econs); Columbia Univ., New York (MBA). Lieut, Parachute Regt, 1955–57. Shell Internat. Petroleum Co. Ltd, 1961–69; Boston Consulting Gp, Boston, USA, 1971–72; Bowater Corp., 1972–86, apptd to main bd, 1979; Pres., Bowater Europe, 1975–85; Chm., Rhenania Schiffahrtes-und-Speditions GmbH, 1973–80; joined Tootal Gp as Man. Dir, 1986, Chief Exec., 1987–91; Chief Exec., 1991–94, Chm., 1994–2003, ProShare; Chairman: Westbury plc, 1992–2006; F & C UK Select Trust plc (formerly Ivory and Sime ISIS Trust, later ISIS UK Select Trust plc), 1993–10; Macdonald Martin Distilleries, subseq. Glenmorangie plc, 1994–2002; LDV Ltd, 1995–2004 (Dir, 2004–06); Unite Gp plc, 1999–2009; BuildStore Financial Services Ltd (formerly Buildstore Ltd), 1999–2013; Economic Lifestyle Property Investment Co., 2007–10; Director: Transport Develt Gp plc, 1992–97; Goldcrest Homes plc, 2003–08; Adv. Dir, HSBC Investment Bank, 1995–98. Chm., Manchester TEC, 1988–91; Civil Service Comr, 1992–96, 2000–05. Mem., Trng and Affairs Cttee, CBI, 1989–93. Chairman: Friends of Airborne Forces, 1994–2002; UNIAID, 2001–04; Airborne Forces Charities, 2002–04; Res. Autism, 2003–; Nat. Autistic Soc. Prospects Adv. Gp, 2003–; Trustee, Help the Aged, 1983–86. Gov., UMIST, 1987–92. *Recreations:* club running, golf, travel. *Address:* 28 Sussex Street, SW1V 4RL. *T:* (020) 7834 3874.

See also C. S. Maddrell.

MADDRELL, Siân; *see* Maddrell, C. S.

MADDRELL, Simon Hugh Piper, PhD, ScD; FRS 1981; Fellow of Gonville and Caius College, Cambridge, 1964–2007, now Life Fellow; Hon. Professor of Integrative Physiology, Cambridge University, 2003–08, now Emeritus Hon. Professor; *b* 11 Dec. 1937; *s* of late Hugh Edmund Fisher Maddrell and Barbara Agnes Mary Maddrell; *m* 1st, 1961, Anna Myers (marr. diss. 1985, she *d* 1997); three *s* one *d*; 2nd, 1990, Katherine Mona Mapes. *Educ:* Peter Symonds' Sch., Winchester; St Catharine's Coll., Cambridge. BA, MA, PhD 1964, ScD 1978. Res. Fellow, Dalhousie Univ., Canada, 1962–64; SPSO, AFRC Unit of Invertebrate Chem. and Physiology, subseq. Unit of Insect Neurophysiology and Pharmacology, Cambridge Univ., 1968–90; College Fellow and Lectr, Gonville and Caius Coll., Cambridge, 1968–2007; Hon. Reader, Univ. of Cambridge, 1991–2003. Manager of Finances and Investments (formerly Financial Sec. and Investments Manager), 1965–2010, Dir, 2010–, Co. of Biologists Ltd. Scientific Medal, Zool Soc. of London, 1975. *Publications:* Neurosecretion, 1979; contrib. res. papers. *Recreations:* gardening, planting trees (Chm., I of M Woodland Trust, 2004–), play-reading, cinema, wine-tasting. *Address:* Gonville and Caius College, Cambridge CB2 1TA; Ballamaddrell, Ballabeg, Arbory, Isle of Man IM9 4HD. *T:* (01624) 822787.

MADEJSKI, Sir (Robert) John, Kt 2009; OBE 2000; DL; Co-Chairman, Reading Football Club, since 2014 (Chairman, 1990–2014); *b* 28 April 1941; *s* of Zygmunt Madejski and Joan Edith Madejski; two *d*. *Educ:* Reading Collegiate Sch. Encyclopedia salesman, Caxton Press, 1959; biscuit salesman, Huntley & Palmer, 1959–64; various jobs incl. selling Rolls Royce, Jaguar and Aston Martin cars, Calif, 1964–66; sales exec., British Motor Corp., 1966–67; Sales Dir, Stan Hope Mills, 1967–69; Classified Advertising Sales Exec., Reading Evening Post, 1969–76; founder: Auto Trader, 1976; Jt Founder, Hurst Publishing Ltd, 1977–98 (allied with Guardian/Manchester Evening News, 1982). Chairman of companies, including: Royal Palm Hotel, Galapagos Is, 2002–; Reading Broadcasting (107 Jack FM Berkshire) (formerly Reading 107 (local radio)), 2002–. Chancellor, Univ. of Reading, 2007–. DL Berks 2000. Charitable funding of art galls, theatres, lecture theatres, including: Falklands Meml Chapel, Pangbourne Coll., 2000; John Madejski Fine Rooms, Royal Acad. of Arts, 2004. Hon. Fellow, Henley Mgt Coll., 2007. *Recreations:* fine dining (owner of Rossini at the Leatherne Bottel Restaurant, Goring-on-Thames), art, swimming. *Address:* Reading Football Club, Madejski Stadium, Junction 11, M4, Reading, Berks RG2 0FL. *Club:* Annabel's.

MADEL, Sir (William) David, Kt 1994; *b* 6 Aug. 1938; *s* of late William R. Madel and Eileen Madel (*née* Nicholls); *m* 1971, Susan Catherine (*d* 2009), *d* late Lt-Comdr Hon. Peter Carew; one *s* one *d*. *Educ:* Uppingham Sch.; Keble Coll., Oxford. MA Oxon 1965. Graduate Management Trainee, 1963–64; Advertising Exec., Thomson Organisation, 1964–70. Contested (C) Erith and Crayford Nov. 1965, 1966. MP (C): S Bedfordshire, 1970–83; Bedfordshire SW, 1983–2001. PPS to Parly Under-Sec. of State for Defence, 1973–74, to Minister of State for Defence, 1974, to Rt Hon. Sir Edward Heath, KG, MBE, MP, 1991–97; an Opposition Whip, 1997–99. Chm., Cons. Backbench Educn Cttee, 1983–85; Vice-Chm., Cons. Backbench Employment Cttee, 1974–81; Member: Select Cttee on Educn, Sci. and Arts, 1979–83, on Transport, 1995–97, on Foreign Affairs, 1999–2001; H of C European Legislation Cttee, 1983–97. Mem. Ind. Monitoring Bd, HM Prison Hollesley Bay, Suffolk, 2004–. Lay Rep. for Disciplinary Hearings, Council of the Inns of Court, 2005–; Mem., Arbitration Panel, ACAS, 2009–. Mem. Exec., CCJ, 2002–06. Mem. Court, Univ. of Luton, 1993–. *Recreations:* cricket, tennis, reading, walking, campanology. *Address:* Moor House, Middleton Moor, Saxmundham, Suffolk IP17 3LW. *Club:* Carlton.

MADELEY, Richard Holt; television presenter; *b* 13 May 1956; *s* of Christopher Holt Madeley and Mary Claire McEwan; *m* 1st, 1977, Lynda Hooley; 2nd, 1986, Judith Finnigan, *qv*; one *s* one *d*, and two step *s*. *Educ:* Coopers' Co. Grammar Sch., Bow; Shenfield Sch., Essex. Indentured jun. reporter, Brentwood Argus, 1972–74; Asst, then Dep. Ed., E London Advertiser, 1975–76; reporter, 1976–77, producer, 1977–78, BBC Radio Carlisle; reporter: Border TV, 1978–80; and presenter, Yorkshire TV, 1980–82; presenter: Granada Television, 1982–2001: programmes include: Runway, 1987–89; This Morning, 1988–2001; Eye of the Storm, 1997–2000; British Soap Awards, 1999, 2000 and 2001; Channel 4: Richard and Judy, 2001–08; British Book Awards, 2004–; ITV1: Fortune, 2007; Watch: Richard and Judy's New Position, 2008–09. *Publications:* Richard & Judy: the autobiography (with Judith Finnigan), 2001; Fathers and Sons, 2008; Some Day I'll Find You (novel), 2013; The Way You Look Tonight, 2014. *Recreations:* cliff-walking in Cornwall, cycling, acoustic guitar, reading. *Address:* c/o James Grant Management, 94 Strand on the Green, Chiswick, W4 3NN. *T:* (020) 8742 4950. *Club:* Home House.

MADELIN, Robert; Director General for Communication Networks, Content and Technology (formerly Information Society and Media), European Commission, since 2010; *b* 8 May 1957; *s* of John Madelin and Kathleen Madelin (*née* Webb); *m* 1990, Marie-Christine Jalabert. *Educ:* Royal Grammar Sch., High Wycombe; Magdalen Coll., Oxford (BA (Mod. Hist. and Mod. Langs), MA); Ecole Nationale d'Admin, Paris. Principal, Multilateral Trade Policy, DTI, 1979–88; 1st Sec., UK Perm. Repn, Brussels, 1988–93; Mem., then Dep. Hd, Cabinet of Vice-Pres. of Commn, Sir Leon, later Lord, Brittan, 1993–97; European Commission: Dir, Directorate Gen. of Trade, 1997–2003; Dir Gen. for Health and Consumers (formerly for Health and Consumer Protection), 2004–10. Hon. FRCP 2007. *Recreations:* walking, running, swimming, cooking, singing. *T:* (Belgium) (2) 2963338. *E:* robert.madelin@ec.europa.eu.

MADELUNG, Prof. Wilferd Willy Ferdinand, FBA 1999; Laudian Professor of Arabic, University of Oxford, 1978–98; Senior Research Fellow, Institute of Ismaili Studies, London, since 1998; *b* 26 Dec. 1930; *s* of Georg Madelung and Elisabeth (*née* Messerschmitt); *m* 1963, A. Margaret (*née* Arent); one *s*. *Educ:* Eberhard Ludwig Gymnasium, Stuttgart; Univs of Georgetown, Cairo, Hamburg. PhD (Hamburg). Cultural Attaché, W German Embassy, Baghdad, 1958–60. Vis. Professor, Univ. of Texas, Austin, 1963; Privatdozent, Univ. of Hamburg, 1963–64; University of Chicago: Asst Prof., 1964; Associate Prof., 1966; Prof. of Islamic History, 1969. Guggenheim Fellowship, 1972–73; Fellow: Inst. of Advanced Studies, Hebrew Univ. of Jerusalem, 2002–; Inst. of Advanced Studies, Princeton Univ., 2011; Academia Ambrosiana, Milan, 2013. Decoration of Republic of Sudan (4th cl.), 1962. *Publications:* Der Imam al-Qāsim ibn Ibrāhīm und die Glaubenslehre der Zaiditen, 1965; Religious Schools and Sects in Medieval Islam, 1985; Religious Trends in Early Islamic Iran, 1988; Religious and Ethnic Movements in Medieval Islam, 1992; The Succession to Muhammad, 1996; Studies in Medieval Shi'ism, 2012; Studies in Medieval Muslim Thought and History, 2013. *Address:* 21 Belsyre Court, Oxford OX2 6HU.

MADEN, Prof. Margaret; Professor of Education, Keele University, 1995–2001; *b* 16 April 1940; *d* of Clifford and Frances Maden. *Educ:* Arnold High Sch. for Girls, Blackpool; Leeds Univ. (BA Hons); Univ. of London Inst. of Educn (PGCE). Asst Teacher of Geography, Stockwell Manor Comprehensive Sch., SW9, 1962–66; Lectr, Sidney Webb Coll. of Educn, 1966–71; Dep. Head, Bicester Comprehensive Sch., Oxon, 1971–75; Headmistress, Islington Green Comprehensive Sch., 1975–82; Dir, Islington Sixth Form Centre, 1983–86; Principal Advr, Tertiary Develt, ILEA, 1986–87; Dep. County Educn Officer, 1987–88, County Educn Officer, 1989–95, Warwickshire CC. Mem., Nat. Commn on Educn, 1991–93. Member: Basic Skills Agency, 1998–2007; Prince's Trust Adv. Gp, 2001–02; Bd, Royal Opera House, 2002–11; Chm., BBC Regl Adv. Council (South), 2002–05. Governor: Peers Sch., Oxford, 2006–08; Royal Ballet Sch., 2007–; St Christopher's C of E Sch., Oxford, 2012–. Norham Fellow, Dept of Educn, Univ. of Oxford, 2011–. Hon. Pres., BEMAS, 1995–99. Hon. FCP 1994. *Publications:* (ed jtly) Success Against the Odds, 1995; Shifting Gear: changing patterns of educational governance in Europe, 2000; (ed) Success Against the Odds—5 Years On, 2001; contributions to: Dear Lord James, 1971; Teachers for Tomorrow (ed Calthrop and Owens), 1971; Education 2000 (ed Wilby and Pluckrose), 1979; The School and the University, an International Perspective (ed Burton R. Clark), 1984; Education Answers Back (ed Brian Simon and Clyde Chitty), 1993; School Co-operation: new forms of Governance (ed Ransom and Tomlinson), 1994; Living Education (ed John Tomlinson), 1997; Developing Education: fifteen years on (ed Philip Hunter), 1998; Children and the State: whose problem? (ed Jane Tunstill), 1999; Letters to the Prime Minister (ed Ted Wragg), 2005. *Recreations:* European painting, writing and films; politics, opera. *Address:* 12 Dale Close, Oxford OX1 1TU. *T:* (01865) 721372.

MADGE, Nicolas John; His Honour Judge Madge; a Circuit Judge, since 2004; *b* 1953; *s* of John Kenneth Lewis Madge and Lucy Mildred Madge; *m* 2014, Amanda Jane Sigrist West; two *s* by a previous marriage. *Educ:* Cannock Grammar Sch.; St Catharine's Coll., Cambridge (BA 1974). Admitted solicitor, 1978. Solicitor: Camden Community Law Centre, 1978–83; Nash and Dowell, 1984–85; Partner, Bindman and Partners, 1985–95; Dep. Dist Judge (pt-time), 1989–95; Dist Judge, W London Co. Court, 1995–2004; Resident Judge, Peterborough and Huntingdon Crown Courts, 2011–14. Photographic exhibitions: One World, One View, Harrow Crown Court, 2005, Friends Meeting House, London, 2008–09, Jam Factory, Oxford, 2009; Faces of Bangladesh, BM, 2011, Swiss Cottage Gall., 2012. *Publications:* Troubled by the Law?, 1978; Out of School: legal responsibility for children, 1981; (contrib.) Tribunals Practice and Procedure, 1985; (jtly) Defending Possession Proceedings, 1987, 7th edn 2010; (with D. Forbes) Debt and Housing: emergency procedures, 1993; English Roots: a family history, 1995; Housing Law Casebook, 1996, 6th edn 2015; (contrib.) Supreme Court Practice, 1999; (contrib.) Civil Procedure (The White Book), 1999– (Mem., Sen. Editl Bd, 2004–); Annotated Housing Statutes, 2003, 2nd edn 2005; one world one view (photographs), 2007; contribs to Law Soc. Gazette, New Law Jl, Solicitors' Jl, Legal Action, Justice of the Peace, Jl Housing Law, Civil Justice Qly, Criminal Law Rev., Landlord and Tenant Rev., Jl Commonwealth Magistrates and Judges Assoc. *Recreations:* travel and travel writing, walking, photography, bridge, family history. *Address:* Inner London Crown Court, Newington Causeway, SE1 6AZ. *W:* www.nicmadge.co.uk.

MADONNA; *see* Ciccone, M. L. V.

MADRIGAL FERNÁNDEZ, Prof. (José) Alejandro, MD, PhD, DSc; FRCP, FRCPath, FMedSci; Scientific Director, Anthony Nolan Research Institute, since 1995; Professor of Haematology, Royal Free Hospital and University College London, since 1997; Hon. Consultant Haematologist, Royal Free Hospital, since 2001; *b* Mexico City, 4 Nov. 1953; *s* of Luis Madrigal and Aurora Fernandez; *m* 1977, Maria Elena Macarty. *Educ:* Univ. de Valle de Mexico (BS 1973); Univ. Nacional Autonoma de Mexico (MD 1978); Imperial Cancer Res. Fund, London (PhD 1989); Univ. of London (DSc 2001). FRCP 1998; FRCPath 2002. WHO Fellow, Dana Farber Cancer Inst., Harvard Univ., 1983–85; Postdoctoral Res. Fellow, Stanford Univ., 1989–93; Hd of Res., Anthony Nolan Res. Inst., 1993–95; Hon. Lectr in Haematol., Royal Free Hosp., 1993–95; Hon. Lectr, RPMS, 1993–95; Hon. Sen. Lectr in Haematol., Imperial Coll. London, 1995–97; Pro-Provost for the Americas, 2011–14, Pro-Vice Provost for the Americas, 2014–, UCL. Pres., Eur. Gp for Blood and Marrow Transplantation, 2010–14. FMedSci 2013. Hon. DSc Nottingham Trent, 2008. *Publications:* (ed jtly) Cord Blood Characteristics: rôle in stem cell transplantation, 2000; contribs to scientific peer-reviewed jls. *Recreations:* fiction writing, painting, tennis. *Address:* Anthony Nolan Research Institute, Royal Free Hospital, Pond Street, NW3 2QG. *T:* (020) 7284 8315, *Fax:* (020) 7284 8331. *E:* a.madrigal@ucl.ac.uk.

MAEHLER, Prof. Herwig Gustav Theodor, FBA 1986; Professor of Papyrology, University College London, 1981–2000, now Emeritus; *b* 29 April 1935; *s* of Ludwig and Lisa Maehler; *m* 1963, Margaret Anderson; two *d*. *Educ:* Katharineum Lübeck (Grammar Sch.); Univs of Hamburg (PhD Classics and Classical Archaeol.), Tübingen and Basel. British Council Schol., Oxford, 1961–62; Res. Assistant, Hamburg Univ., 1962–63, Hamburg Univ. Liby, 1963–64; Keeper of Greek Papyri, Egyptian Mus., W Berlin, 1964–79; Habilitation for Classics, 1975, Lectr in Classics, 1975–79, Free Univ. of W Berlin; Reader in Papyrology, UCL, 1979–81. Corresp. Mem., German Archaeol Inst., 1979; Mem., Accad. Nazionale dei Lincei, Rome, 2000. Hon. Mem., Hungarian Acad. of Scis, Budapest, 2007. Hon. Fellow UCL, 2000. Hon. PhD: Helsinki, 2000; Budapest, 2001; Rome II (Tor Vergata), 2003. *Publications:* Die Auffassung des Dichterberufs im frühen Griechentum bis zur Zeit Pindars, 1963; Die Handschriften des S Jacobi-Kirche Hamburg, 1967; Urkunden römischer Zeit, (BGU XI), 1968; Papyri aus Hermupolis (BGU XII), 1974; Die Lieder des Bakchylides, Part 1, 2 vols, 1982, Part 2, 1997; (with G. Cavallo) Greek Bookhands of the Early Byzantine Period, 1987; Bacchylides: a selection, 2004; editions of Bacchylides and Pindar, 1970, 1987, 1989, 1992, 2003; Urkunden aus Hermupolis (BGU XIX), 2005; Schrift, Text und Bild (selected essays), 2006; (with G. Cavallo) Hellenistic Bookhands, 2008; articles in learned jls. *Address:* Zeltgasse 6/12, 1080 Wien, Austria.

MAFFEY, family name of **Baron Rugby**.

MAGAN, family name of **Baron Magan of Castletown**.

MAGAN OF CASTLETOWN, Baron *cr* 2011 (Life Peer), of Kensington in the Royal Borough of Kensington and Chelsea; **George Morgan Magan;** Director, Conservative Party Foundation, 2003–13 (Deputy Chairman, 2009–13); *b* 14 Nov. 1945; *s* of late Brig. William Morgan Tilson Magan, CBE and Maxine, *d* of Sir Kenneth Mitchell, KCIE; *m* 1972, Wendy Anne, *d* of Maj. Patrick Chilton, MC; two *s* one *d*. *Educ:* Winchester Coll. FCA. Peat Marwick Mitchell, 1964–70; Kleinwort Benson Ltd, 1971–74; Dir, Morgan Grenfell & Co. Ltd, 1974–88; Co-Founder and Chm., J. O. Hambro Magan, 1988–96; Chairman: Hawkpoint Partners, 1997–2001; emuse (Dublin), 2001–; Lion Capital Partners, 2001–08; Mallett plc, 2001–08; Morgan Shipley Ltd (Dubai), 2001–; Director: Asprey plc, 1980–96; Edmiston & Co., 2001–13; Allied Investment Partners (Abu Dhabi), 2007–12. Dir, Bank of Ireland, 2003–09 (Dep. Gov., 2006–09). Dep. Treas., 2002–03, Treas. and Mem. Bd, 2003, Conservative Pty. Trustee: LPO, 1992–2006 (Chm., 1997–2006); Royal Opera House, Covent Garden, 1995–2001; BM Develt Trust, 1999–2003; Foundn of Coll. of St George, Windsor Castle, 2008–15. Chairman: St George's Chapel, Windsor Castle, Develt Appeal, 2007–13; Develt Bd, Royal Albert Hall, 2014–. Gov., Stowe Sch., 2001–. *Address:* House of Lords, SW1A 0PW. *Club:* Royal Yacht Squadron.

MAGARIAN, Michael; QC 2011; *b* London, 17 June 1964; *s* of Boghos and Ayko Magarian; *m* (marr. diss. 1989); one *d*. *Educ:* City of London Sch.; Trinity Coll., Cambridge (Schol.; BA 1987). Called to the Bar, Gray's Inn, 1988. *Recreation:* épater le bourgeois. *Address:* Drystone Chambers, 35 Bedford Row, WC1R 4JH. *Club:* Blacks.

MAGDALENA RODRIGUEZ, (Jose) Carlos; Senior Tropical Botanical Horticulturist, Royal Botanic Gardens, Kew, since 2006; *b* Gijon, Asturias, Spain, 18 Sept. 1972; *s* of Rafael Magdalena and Edilia Rodriguez; partner, Genieve Gravel. *Educ:* Royal Botanic Gardens, Kew (Kew Dip. Botanical Horticulture 2006). Self-employed in design, construction and maintenance of aquariums, ponds and gardens, Asturias, Spain, 1991–95; Envmtl Technician, Ayuntamiento de Gijon, 1999; Hd Sommelier, Le Meridien Hotels, 1999–2003; propagator, Tropical, Temperate and Arboretum Nurseries, Royal Botanic Gardens, Kew, 2003. Horticl writer for Water Gardeners Internat., Horticultural Week, Garden. *Publications:* contrib. to acad. papers in Annals of Botany, Conservation Biol., Curtis's Botanical Mag., etc. *Recreations:* nature, wildlife, travelling, swimming, music. *Address:* Flat 2, 64 Boileau Road, Barnes, Richmond, Surrey, SW13 9BL. *T:* 07818 496471. *E:* c.magdalena@kew.org, licantropop@hotmail.com. *W:* www.twitter.com/plantmessiah.

MAGDALINO, Prof. Paul, DPhil; FBA 2002; Professor of Byzantine History, Koç University, Istanbul, since 2010 (Professor of History, 2006–08); *b* 10 May 1948; *s* of Andrea and Audrey Magdalino; *m* 1973, Ruth Macrides; one *d*; *m* 2011, Krassimira Tzankova. *Educ:* Oriel Coll., Oxford (BA; DPhil Modern Hist. 1976). Jun. Fellow, Dumbarton Oaks Center for Byzantine Studies, Washington, 1974–75; Andrew J. Mellon Fellow in Early Christian Humanism, Catholic Univ. of America, 1976–77; University of St Andrews: Lectr, 1977–94; Reader, 1994–99; Prof. of Byzantine Hist., 1999–2002; Bishop Wardlaw Prof. of Byzantine Hist., 2002–09. Res. Fellow, Alexander von Humboldt Stiftung, at Inst. für Rechtsgeschichte, Frankfurt, 1980–81, and Inst. für Byzantinistik, Munich, 1983; Vis. Fellow, Humanities Res. Centre, Canberra, 1985; Vis. Prof. of Hist., Harvard Univ., 1995–96; Sen. Fellow, Dumbarton Oaks Center for Byzantine Studies, 2001–07. *Publications:* (jtly) Rome and Byzantium, 1977; (ed) The Perception of the Past in Twelfth Century Europe, 1992; The Empire of Manuel I Komnenos, 1143–1180, 1993; (ed) New Constantines, 1994; Constantinople médiévale, 1996; L'Orthodoxie des Astrologues, 2006; Studies in the History and Topography of Medieval Constantinople, 2007; numerous contribs to ed vols and articles to learned jls. *Recreations:* walking, swimming. *Address:* Department of Archaeology and Art History, Koç University, 34450 Sarıyer, Istanbul, Turkey. *T:* (212) 3381755. *E:* pmagdalino@ku.edu.tr.

MAGEE, Anna; *see* Gregor, A.

MAGEE, Bryan; author; Visiting Professor, King's College, London, 1994–2000 (Hon. Senior Research Fellow in History of Ideas, 1984–94); *b* 12 April 1930; *s* of Frederick Magee and Sheila (*née* Lynch); *m* 1954, Ingrid Söderlund (marr. diss.); one *d*. *Educ:* Christ's Hospital; Lycée Hoche, Versailles; Keble Coll., Oxford (Open Scholar; BA Modern Hist. 1952, PPE 1953; MA 1956; Hon. Fellow, 1994). Nat. Service, Intelligence Corps, Austria, 1948–49. Pres., Oxford Union, 1953. Henry Fellow in Philosophy, Yale, 1955–56. Music criticism for many publications, 1959–; Theatre Critic, The Listener, 1966–67; regular columnist, The Times, 1974–76. Mem., Arts Council, 1993–94 (Chm., Music Panel, 1993–94). Current Affairs Reporter on TV; Critic of the Arts on BBC Radio 3; own broadcast series include: Conversations with Philosophers, BBC Radio 3, 1970–71; Something to Say, Thames TV, 1972–73; Argument, LWT, 1973; Don't Quote Me, BBC TV 2, 1974; Men of Ideas, BBC TV 2, 1978; The Great Philosophers, BBC TV 2, 1987; What's the Big Idea?, BBC Radio 3, 1991–92. Silver Medal, RTS, 1978. Contested (Lab): Mid-Bedfordshire, Gen. Elecn, 1959; By-Elecn, 1960; MP (Lab 1974–82, SDP 1982–83) Leyton, Feb. 1974–1983; contested (SDP) Leyton, 1983. Elected to Critics' Circle, 1970, Pres., 1983–84, Hon. Mem., 2012–. Judge: for Evening Standard annual Opera Award, 1973–84; for Laurence Olivier Annual Opera Awards, 1990–91, 1993–95; Chm. of Judges, Royal Philharmonic Soc. opera awards, 1991–2000. Lectr in Philosophy, Balliol Coll., Oxford, 1970–71; Visiting Fellow: All Souls Coll., Oxford, 1973–74; New Coll., Oxford, 1995; Merton Coll., Oxford, 1998; St Catherine's Coll., Oxford, 2000; Peterhouse, Cambridge, 2001; Clare Hall, Cambridge, 2004 (Life Mem.); Vis. Schol., 1991–93, Vis. Fellow, 1993–94, Wolfson Coll., Oxford (Life Mem.); Vis. Schol. in Philos., Harvard, 1979, Sydney Univ., 1982, Univ. of California, Santa Barbara, 1989 (Girvetz Meml Lectr); German Marshall Fund Fellow to USA, 1989; Visiting Professor: Trinity Univ., San Antonio, Texas, 1997; Univ. of Otago, NZ, 2006, 2009, 2012. Charles Carter Lectr, Univ. of Lancaster, 1985; Bithell Meml Lectr, Univ. of London, 1989. Lecturer: Seattle Opera, 1989, 1991, 1995; Royal Opera House, 1990; San Francisco Opera, 1990; Belgian Nat. Opera, 1991; Bayreuth Festspielhaus, 1994; Los Angeles Opera, 1995 and 1997; Hawaii Opera, 2000; Glyndebourne, 2003; Royal Inst. of Philosophy, 1992, 1994, 2007. Hon. Pres., Edinburgh Univ. Philosophy Soc., 1987–88. Governor, 1979–2008, Mem. Council, 1982–2001, Ditchley Foundn; Acad. Visitor, LSE, 1994–96. Mem., Sen. Common Room, St Antony's Coll., Oxford, 2009–. Hon. Fellow, QMC, 1988; Fellow: QMW, 1989; Royal Philharmonic Soc., 1990. Hon. DLitt Leicester, 2005. *Publications:* Crucifixion and Other Poems, 1951; Go West Young Man, 1958; To Live in Danger, 1960; The New Radicalism, 1962; The Democratic Revolution, 1964; Towards 2000, 1965; One in Twenty, 1966; The Television Interviewer, 1966; Aspects of Wagner, 1968, rev. edn 1988; Modern British Philosophy, 1971; Popper, 1973; Facing Death, 1977; Men of Ideas, 1978, 2nd edn as Talking Philosophy, 2001; The Philosophy of Schopenhauer, 1983, rev. edn 1997; The Great Philosophers, 1987; Misunderstanding Schopenhauer, 1990; (with M. Milligan) On Blindness, 1995, 2nd edn, as Sight Unseen, 1998; Confessions of a Philosopher, 1997; The Story of Philosophy, 1998; Wagner and Philosophy, 2000; Clouds of Glory: a Hoxton childhood, 2003 (J. R. Ackerley Prize for Autobiog., 2004); Growing Up in a War, 2007; Our Predicament: ultimate questions, 2016. *Recreations:* music, theatre. *Address:* Flat 16, Ritchie Court, 380 Banbury Road, Oxford OX2 7PW. *T:* (01865) 512504. *Clubs:* Garrick, Savile.

MAGEE, Sir Ian (Bernard Vaughan), Kt 2006; CB 2002; Senior Fellow, Institute for Government, since 2009; Chairman, Geographic Information Group, since 2011; *b* 9 July 1946. *Educ:* Leeds Univ. (BA Hist.). Joined DHSS, 1969; Private Sec. to Minister for Social Security, 1976–78; seconded to Cabinet Office Enterprise Unit, 1984–86; Department of Social Security, 1986–98: Dep. to Dir of Personnel, 1986–89; Territorial Dir, Benefits Agency, 1990–93; Chief Exec., IT Services Agency, 1993–98; Chief Exec., Ct Service, LCD, 1998–2003; Second Permanent Sec. and Chief Exec., Ops, LCD, then DCA, 2003–05; Hd, Profession for Operational Delivery across Civil Service, 2004–05. Member, Advisory Board: Liaison plc, 2008–; Just Accounts plc, 2010–. *Recreations:* sport, reading. *Clubs:* MCC, Royal Automobile; Verulam Golf.

MAGEE, Prof. Jeffrey Norman, PhD; FREng; FBCS; FCGI; Professor of Computing, since 1999, Head, Department of Computing, since 2004, and Dean, Faculty of Engineering, since 2011, Imperial College London; *b* Londonderry, 12 Feb. 1952; *s* of Norman and Athalie Magee; *m* 1991, Judith O'Brien; two *s* one *d*. *Educ:* Foyle Coll., Londonderry; Queen's Univ., Belfast (BSc Hons 1973); Imperial Coll. London (MSc 1978; PhD 1984). FREng 2013. Exec. Engr, Post Office (Telecomms), 1973–79; Lectr, Imperial Coll. London, 1984–99. Vice Pres. and Trustee, BCS, 2014–March 2016. FBCS 2005; FCGI 2010. *Publications:* Concurrency: state models and Java program, 1999, 2nd edn 2006. *Recreations:* sailing, fishing, dog walking, photography. *Address:* Faculty of Engineering, Faculty Building, Level 2, South Kensington Campus, Imperial College London, SW7 2AZ. *E:* j.magee@imperial.ac.uk.

MAGERS, Philomene Korinna Kornelia; Co-owner, Sprüth Magers, contemporary art gallery, since 1998; *b* Bonn, Germany, 18 March 1965; *d* of Wolfgang and Philomene Magers; *m* 1996, Jan Schmidt-Garré; two *s*. *Educ:* studies of art hist., philosophy, Christian archaeol. and German philology, Rheinische Friedrich-Wilhelms Univ. Bonn and Ludwig-Maximilians Univ. Munich, 1984–90. Direction and dramaturgy trainee and asst in opera and theatre, Städtische Bühnen, Bonn, 1984–86; curatorial assistant: German Pavilion, 43rd Venice Biennale, 1988; Städtische Galerie, Lehnbachhaus, Munich, 1988; Siemens Arts Program, Munich, 1988–90; Gall. Founder, Philomene Magers, Bonn, 1990, relocated Cologne, 1992; merged with Galerie Monika Sprüth, as Sprüth Magers, Cologne, 1998; Sprüth Magers, Munich, opened 2001, addnl project space for young and emerging art, opened 2002; Sprüth Magers, London, opened 2003, Berlin, 2008, LA, 2016. *Address:* Sprüth Magers, Oranienburger Strasse 18, 10178 Berlin, Germany. *E:* info@spruethmagers.com.

MAGINNESS, Alban Alphonsus; barrister; Member (SDLP) Belfast North, Northern Ireland Assembly, since 1998; *b* 9 July 1950; *s* of Alphonsus and Patricia Maginness; *m* 1978, Carmel McWilliams; three *s* five *d*. *Educ:* St Malachy's Coll., Belfast; Univ. of Ulster (BA Hons Mod. Hist. 1973); Queen's Univ., Belfast (LLM Human Rights 2007). Called to the Bar: NI, 1976; Ireland, 1984; in practice at NI Bar, specialising in civil litigation. Chm., SDLP, 1985–91. Mem. (SDLP) Belfast CC, 1985–; Lord Mayor of Belfast, 1997–98 (first SDLP Lord Mayor). Contested (SDLP) Belfast North, 1997, 2001, 2005, 2010. Northern Ireland Assembly: Chairman: Enterprise, Trade and Investment Cttee, 2009–12; Cross-Party Human Trafficking Gp, 2014–; Member: Cross-Party Pro-Life Gp, 2007–; Justice Cttee, 2010–; Envmt Cttee, 2012–; Procedures Cttee, 2013–. Member: NI Forum, 1996–98; Forum for Peace and Reconciliation, Dublin, 1994–96; Cttee of the Regions of the EU, 2002–06; NI Assembly Commn, 2007–09; Mem. and Dir, NI Assembly Business Trust, 2012–. Mem. Bd, Belfast Harbour Comrs, 2006–08. *Recreations:* theatre, history, reading, walking, music. *Address:* 96 Somerton Road, Belfast BT15 4DE. *T:* (028) 9077 0558; (office) 228 Antrim Road, Belfast BT15 2AN. *T:* (028) 9022 0520. *E:* a.maginness@sdlp.ie.

MAGINNIS, family name of **Baron Maginnis of Drumglass**.

MAGINNIS OF DRUMGLASS, Baron *cr* 2001 (Life Peer), of Carnteel in the County of Tyrone; **Kenneth Wiggins Maginnis;** *b* 21 Jan. 1938; *m* 1961, Joy Stewart; two *s* two *d*. *Educ:* Royal Sch., Dungannon; Stranmillis Coll., Belfast. Served UDR, 1970–81, commissioned 1972, Major. Party spokesman on internal security and defence. Mem., Dungannon District Council, 1981–93 and 2001–05; Mem. (UU) Fermanagh and S Tyrone, NI Assembly, 1982–86 and 1994–98. Contested (UU) Fermanagh and S Tyrone, Aug. 1981. MP (UU) Fermanagh and S Tyrone, 1983–2001 (resigned seat Dec. 1985 in protest against Anglo-Irish Agreement; re-elected Jan. 1986). Mem., H of C Select Cttee on Defence, 1984–86, on NI, 1994–97. Vice Pres., UU Council, 1990–2005; Hon. Treas., UU Party, 2005–08. Chm., Moygashel Community Develt Assoc., 1992–. Chairman: Ind. Review Autism Services (NI), 2007–08; NI Regl Reference Gp on Autism, 2008–11. *Address:* House of Lords, SW1A 0PW; 1 Park Lane, Dungannon BT71 6JL.

MAGNUS, Sir Laurence (Henry Philip), 3rd Bt *cr* 1917, of Tangley Hill, Wonersh; Deputy Chairman, Evercore Partners (Europe), since 2011; Chairman, Historic Buildings and Monuments Commission for England (Historic England, formerly English Heritage), since 2013; *b* 24 Sept. 1955; *s* of Hilary Barrow Magnus, QC (*d* 1987), and of Rosemary Vera Anne Magnus (*née* Masefield); *S* uncle, Sir Philip Magnus-Allcroft, 2nd Bt, CBE, 1988; *m* 1983, Jocelyn Mary, *d* of R. H. F. Stanton; two *s* one *d*. *Educ:* Eton College; Christ Church, Oxford (MA). Corporate Finance Executive, 1977–84, Head of Corporate Finance, Singapore Branch, 1984–87, Samuel Montagu & Co. Ltd; Group Country Manager, Singapore Region, Midland Bank plc (Singapore), 1987–88; Exec. Dir, 1988–95 and Dep. Head, UK Corporate Finance Div., 1994–95, Samuel Montagu & Co. Ltd; Dir, Phoenix Securities Ltd, 1995–97 (acquired by Donaldson, Lufkin & Jenrette, 1997); Managing Director: Donaldson, Lufkin & Jenrette Internat., 1997–2000 (acquired by Credit Suisse First Boston, 2000); Credit Suisse First Boston, 2000–01; Vice Chm., 2001–10, Chm., 2010–11, Lexicon Partners Ltd (acquired by Evercore Partners, 2011). Non-exec. Chm., Xchanging ins-sure Services Ltd (formerly Ins-Sure Services Ltd), 2001–09; Chm., JP Morgan Income & Capital Trust plc, 2008–; non-executive Director: Forestry Investment Mgt Ltd, 1997–; TT Electronics plc, 2001–07; J. P. Morgan (formerly J. P. Morgan Fleming) Income & Capital Investment Trust plc, 2001–08; Climate Exchange plc, 2006–10; Cayenne Trust plc, 2006–; Fidelity Japanese Values plc, 2010–; Pantheon International Participations plc, 2011–; Aggregated Micro Power plc, 2011–. National Trust: Dep. Chm., 2005–13; Mem., Finance Cttee, 1997–2005 (Chm., 2002–05); Mem., Bd of Trustees, 2005–13. Trustee: Eating Disorders Assoc. ('B-eat'), 2005–13 (Chm., 2005–11); Windsor Leadership Trust, 2006– (Chm., 2015–); Landmark Trust, 2011–; English Heritage Trust, 2014–. *Recreations:* reading, fishing, walking. *Heir:* *s* Thomas Henry Philip Magnus, *b* 30 Sept. 1985. *Address:* c/o Evercore Partners Ltd, 15 Stanhope Gate, W1K 1LN. *T:* (020) 7653 6030, *Fax:* (020) 7653 6001. *E:* laurie.magnus@evercore.com. *Clubs:* Brooks's, Beefsteak, City of London; Millennium.

MAGNUS, Prof. Philip Douglas, FRS 1985; R. P. Doherty, Jr-Welch Regents Professor of Chemistry, University of Texas at Austin, 1989–2014, now Emeritus; *b* 15 April 1943; *s* of Arthur Edwin and Lillian Edith Magnus; *m* 1963, Andrea Claire (*née* Parkinson); two *s*. *Educ:* Imperial College, Univ. of London (BSc, ARCS, PhD, DSc). Asst Lectr, 1967–70, Lectr, 1970–75, Imperial College; Associate Prof., Ohio State Univ., 1975–81; Prof. of Chemistry, 1981–87, Distinguished Prof., 1987–88, Indiana Univ. Corday Morgan Medal, RSC, 1978; Janssen Prize, Belgian Chemical Soc. and Janssen Foundn, 1992; Robert Robinson Medal, RSC, 1996. *Publications:* papers in leading chemistry jls. *Recreations:* golf, chess. *Address:* 3111D Windsor Road, Austin, TX 78703, USA. *T:* (512) 4713966.

MAGONET, Rabbi Prof. Jonathan David; Editor, European Judaism, since 2005 (Member, Editorial Board, since 1978; Co-Editor, 1992–2005); *b* 2 Aug. 1942; *s* of Alexander Philip and Esther Magonet; *m* 1974, Dorothea (*née* Foth); one *s* one *d*. *Educ:* Westminster Sch.; Middlesex Hosp. Med. Sch. (MB BS). Leo Baeck Coll.; Univ. of Heidelberg (PhD). Junior hosp. doctor, 1966–67; Leo Baeck College, subseq. Leo Baeck College—Centre for Jewish Education: Rabbinic studies, 1967–71; Head of Dept of Bible Studies, 1974–85; Principal, 1985–2005; Prof., 1996–2005, now Emeritus. Vis. Fellow, Tel Aviv Univ., 1990–91; Guest Professor: Kirchliche Hochschule, Wuppertal, Germany, 1992–93, 1995, 2004, 2010; Carl von Ossietzky Univ., Oldenburg, 1999, 2004; Univ. of Luzern, 2004;

Seinan Gakuin Univ., Fukuoka, 2010–; Doshisha Univ., Kyoto, 2012; Vis. Prof., Univs of Würzburg and Augsburg, 2008. Co-organiser: Annual Internat. Jewish-Christian Bible Week, Bendorf/Osnabrueck, 1968–; Annual Jewish-Christian-Muslim Student Conf., Bendorf/Wuppertal, 1972–2014. Vice-President: World Union for Progressive Judaism, 1988–2005; Movt for Reform Judaism, 2007–. Member, Editorial Board: Christian-Jewish Relations, 1987–91; Jl of Progressive Judaism, 1993–99. FRSA. Hon. DTheol: Kirchliche Hochschule Wuppertal, 2005; Seinan Gakuin, Fukuoka, 2014; DUniv Open, 2006; Hon. DHL Hebrew Union Coll., 2007. Verdienstkreuz (Germany), 1999. *Publications:* Form and Meaning: studies in literary techniques in the Book of Jonah, 1976; Forms of Prayer, (ed jtly) vol. I, Daily and Sabbath Prayerbook, 1977, (ed) 8th edn 2008, (ed jtly) vol. III, Days of Awe Prayerbook, 1985, (ed jtly) vol. II, Pilgrim Festival Prayerbook, 1995, (ed) vol. IV, Evening Prayers, 2009, (ed) vol. V, Funeral Service, 2009; (ed jtly) The Guide to the Here and Hereafter, 1988; A Rabbi's Bible, 1991, 2nd edn as A Rabbi Reads the Bible, 2004; Bible Lives, 1992; (jtly) How to Get Up When Life Gets You Down, 1992; (ed jtly) The Little Blue Book of Prayer, 1993; A Rabbi Reads the Psalms, 1994, 2nd edn, 2004; (jtly) Kindred Spirits, 1995; (ed) Jewish Explorations of Sexuality, 1995; The Subversive Bible, 1997; (ed) Das Jüdische Gebetbuch, 2 vols, 1997; Mit der Bibel durch das Jüdische Jahr, 1998; The Explorer's Guide to Judaism, 1998; (jtly) Sun, Sand and Soul, 1999; Abraham-Jesus-Mohammed: interreligiöser Dialog aus jüdischer Perspektive, 2000; From Autumn to Summer: a Biblical journey through the Jewish year, 2000; Talking to the Other: Jewish interfaith dialogue with Christians and Muslims, 2003; Einführung ins Judentum, 2004; Schabbat Schalom: Juedische Theologie - in Predigten entfaltet, 2011; Rabbino Seishokaishak: Yudaiyakuo to Kiristokuo no Taiwa (Japanese), 2012; Netsuke Nation: tales from another Japan, 2013; A Rabbi Reads the Torah, 2013; *festschrift:* Welcome to the Cavalcade, ed by E. Cooper and S. Tikvah, 2013. *W:* www.jonathanmagonet.co.uk.

MAGOS, Adam László, MD; Consultant Obstetrician and Gynaecologist, and Hon. Senior Lecturer, Royal Free Hospital, London, since 1991; *b* 26 Sept. 1953; *s* of László Pál Aurel Magos and Eva Mária Magos (*née* Benjamin); *m* 1991, Anne Cyprienne Coburn; three *s*. *Educ:* Whitgift Sch., Croydon; KCL (BSc 1975); King's Coll. Hosp. Sch. of Medicine (MB BS 1978; MD 1986). MRCOG 1986, FRCOG 1998. House Officer, KCH, 1980–82; Res. Fellow in Obstetrics and Gynaecol., Dulwich Hosp., 1982–84; Registrar, KCH and Dulwich Hosp., 1984–86; Lectr, Nuffield Dept of Obstetrics and Gynaecology, John Radcliffe Hosp., Univ. of Oxford, 1986–90; Sen. Lectr and Hon. Consultant, Academic Dept of Obstetrics and Gynaecology, Royal Free Hosp., Univ. of London, 1990–91; Consultant Gynaecologist, King Edward VII Hosp. for Officers, later King Edward VII Hosp. Sister Agnes, 1992–2013. Treas., British Soc. for Gynaecol Endoscopy, 1989–92; Member: Wkg Gp on New Technol. in Endoscopic Gynaecol Surgery, RCOG, 1993–94; MAS Trng Sub-Cttee, RCOG, 1998–2001. Hon. Member: Aust. Gynaecol Endoscopy Soc., 1994; Egyptian Soc. for Gynaecol Endoscopy, 1996. Ed., Gynaecological Endoscopy, 1990–93. Syntex Award, Internat. Soc. of Reproductive Medicine, 1988; Veress Meml Medal, Hungarian Soc. for Gynaecol Endoscopy, 1997. *Publications:* (ed jtly) Endometrial Ablation, 1993; contribs to books on premenstrual syndrome, hysteroscopic, laparoscopic and vaginal surgery, and to professional jls. *Recreations:* music, IT. *Address:* Royal Free Hospital, Pond Street, NW3 2QG. *T:* (020) 7794 0500.

MAGOWAN, Rt Rev. Alistair James; *see* Ludlow, Bishop Suffragan of.

MAGUIRE, Adrian Edward; National Hunt jockey, retired 2002; trainer, since 2005; *b* 29 April 1971; *s* of Joseph Maguire and of late Phyllis Maguire; *m* 1995, Sabrina; one *s* one *d*. *Educ:* Kilmessan Nat. Sch.; Trim Vocational Sch. Winner: Irish Grand National, on Omerta, 1991; Hennessy Gold Cup, on Sibton Abbey, 1992; Cheltenham Gold Cup, on Cool Ground, 1992; King George VI Chase, on Barton Bank, 1993, on Florida Pearl, 2001; Queen Mother Champion Chase, on Viking Flagship, 1994; Scottish National, on Baronet, 1998, on Paris Pike, 2000; Whitbread Gold Cup, on Call It A Day, 1998; rode 1,000th winner in British racing, 2001. *Address:* Laharn Cross, Lombardstown, Mallow, Co. Cork, Ireland.

MAGUIRE, Prof. David John, PhD; Vice-Chancellor, University of Greenwich, since 2011; *b* Lancaster, 22 Aug. 1958; *s* of Alfred Maguire and Anne Maguire; *m* 1983, Heather Knubley; one *d*. *Educ:* Lancaster Royal Grammar Sch.; Univ. of Exeter (BSc 1979); Univ. of Bristol (PhD 1982). Lecturer: Univ. of Plymouth, 1984–86; Univ. of Leicester, 1987–91; Chief Scientist and Dir of Products, ESRI, 1990–2008; Pro-Vice-Chancellor, Birmingham City Univ., 2008–11. *Publications:* Computers in Geography, 1989; (jtly) Geographical Information Systems: principles, techniques, management and applications, 1991, 2nd edn 2005; (jtly) Geographic Information Systems and Science, 2001, 3rd edn 2010; (jtly) Proving the Business Benefits of GIS: an ROI approach, 2008. *Recreations:* guitar music, wine, walking, squash. *Address:* University of Greenwich, Old Royal Naval College, Park Row, Greenwich, SE10 9LS. *E:* d.maguire@gre.ac.uk.

MAGUIRE, Prof. Eleanor Anne, PhD; CPsychol; FMedSci; Professor of Cognitive Neuroscience, since 2007 and Deputy Director, Wellcome Trust Centre for Neuroimaging, since 2010, University College London; Hon. Neuropsychologist, Department of Neuropsychology, National Hospital for Neurology and Neurosurgery, since 1999; *b* Dublin, 27 March 1970; *d* of Patrick Maguire and Anne Maguire. *Educ:* University College Dublin (BA Hons Psychol. 1990; PhD 1995); Univ. of Wales, Swansea (MSc Clinical and Experimental Neuropsychol. 1991). CPsychol 2002. Richmond Institute for Neurology and Neurosurgery, Beaumont Hospital, Dublin: Clin. Neuropsychologist, 1991–93; Clin. Neuropsychologist, Epilepsy Surgery Prog., 1993–94; Institute of Neurology, University College London: Postdoctoral Res. Fellow and Neuropsychologist, 1995–97, Sen. Res. Fellow and Neuropsychologist, 1997–99, Wellcome Dept of Cognitive Neurol.; Lectr, 1999–2003, Sen. Lectr, 2003–07, Wellcome Dept of Imaging Neurosci.; Wellcome Trust Centre for Neuroimaging: Wellcome Trust Sen. Res. Fellow in Basic Biomed. Sci., 2003–13; Wellcome Trust Principal Res. Fellow, 2013–. FMedSci 2011. Ig Nobel Prize for Medicine, 2003; Young Investigator Award, Cognitive Neurosci. Soc., 2004; Rosalind Franklin Award, Royal Soc., 2008; Feldberg Foundn Prize, 2011; Kemali Prize, 2012; Joan Mott Prize in Physiol., Physiol Soc., 2013. *Publications:* over 100 articles in jls and book chapters on the cognitive neuroscience of memory and navigation. *Recreations:* comedy lover, long-suffering supporter of Crystal Palace Football Club, getting lost. *Address:* Wellcome Trust Centre for Neuroimaging, Institute of Neurology, University College London, 12 Queen Square, WC1N 3BG. *E:* e.maguire@ucl.ac.uk.

MAGUIRE, Kevin John; Associate Editor, Daily Mirror, since 2005; *b* South Shields, 20 Sept. 1960; *s* of John Maguire and Jennie Maguire; *m* 1986, Emma Burstall; two *s* one *d*. *Educ:* Harton, South Shields; Univ. of York (BA Politics 1982); Cardiff Univ. (Dip. Journalism 1984). Western Morning News, 1984–87; New Civil Engineer, 1987; Press Assoc., 1988–89; Daily Telegraph, 1990–94; Daily Mirror, 1994–99; The Guardian, 1999–2005. *Publications:* (with Matthew Parris) Great Parliamentary Scandals, 2004. *Recreations:* beer, history, sport, the outdoors. *Address:* Daily Mirror, Press Gallery, House of Commons, SW1A 0AA. *T:* (020) 7293 3000. *E:* kevin.maguire@mirror.co.uk. *Club:* Sunderland Association Football.

MAGUIRE, Mairead C.; *see* Corrigan-Maguire.

MAGUIRE, Maria Bernadette, (Mrs G. R. Nicholson); QC (Scot.) 2002; *b* 19 Sept. 1961; *d* of late Robert Miller Maguire, Police Inspector, and of Mary Maguire (*née* Tanham); *m* 1991, Gavin Robert Nicholson; one *s* one *d*. *Educ:* Aberdeen Univ. (LLB; DLP). Admitted to Faculty of Advocates, 1987. Standing JC to Home Office, 1999–2002. *Address:* Advocates' Library, Parliament House, Parliament Square, Edinburgh EH1 1RF. *T:* (0131) 226 5071. *E:* maria.maguire@advocates.org.uk.

MAGUIRE, Hon. Sir Paul (Richard), Kt 2012; **Hon. Mr Justice Maguire;** a Judge of the High Court, Northern Ireland, since 2012; *b* Belfast, 10 Nov. 1952; *s* of Patrick and Lucy Maguire; *m* 1994, Patricia Mary Coburn; one *s* one *d*. *Educ:* London Sch. of Econs and Pol Sci. (LLB). Called to the Bar, NI, 1978; Lectr in Public Law, QUB, 1976–82; Jun. Crown Counsel for NI, 2000–04; QC (NI) 2006; Sen. Crown Counsel for NI, 2009–12. Mem. (APNI) N Belfast, NI Assembly, 1982–86. *Publications:* contribs to books and jls in the field of public law. *Recreations:* golf, reading. *Address:* Royal Courts of Justice, Chichester Street, Belfast BT1 3JT.

MAHAREY, Hon. Steven, CNZM 2009; Vice-Chancellor, Massey University, since 2008; *b* Palmerston North, NZ, 3 Feb. 1953; *s* of William Wood Maharey and Irene Maharey; partner, Bette Flagler. *Educ:* Massey Univ. (BA Sociol. 1974; MA Hons Sociol. 1976). Jun. Lectr in Business Admin, 1976–78, Lectr, then Sen. Lectr in Sociol., 1979–90, Massey Univ. Mem. (Ind) Palmerston N CC, 1986–90. MP (Lab) Palmerston N, 1990–2008; Minister: of Social Services and Employment, 1999–2002; for Community and Voluntary Sector, 1999–2002; for Social Develt and Employment, and Associate Minister of Educn, 2002–04; of Broadcasting, 2002–07; of Housing, 2003–05; for Res., Sci. and Technol., 2004–07; for Educn, 2005–07. *Publications:* contrib. articles and chapters on media studies, cultural studies and politics. *Recreations:* mountain and road biking, walking, dog (Hazel), reading, film, cooking, music, travel. *Address:* Massey University, Private Bag 11222, Palmerston North, New Zealand. *T:* 63505096. *E:* s.maharey@massey.ac.nz.

MAHATHIR bin MOHAMAD, Tun Dr; MHR for Kubang Pasu, 1974–2003; Prime Minister of Malaysia, 1981–2003; *b* 20 Dec. 1925; *m* Tun Dr Siti Hasmah bt Mohamad Ali; seven *c*. *Educ:* Sultan Abdul Hamid Coll.; College of Medicine, Singapore (MB BS). Medical Officer, Kedah and Perlis, 1953–57; in private practice, 1957–64. MHR for Kota Star Selatan, 1964–69; Mem., Senate, 1972–74; Minister of: Education, 1974–77; Trade and Industry, 1977–81; Home Affairs, 1986–99; Dep. Prime Minister, 1976–81. President, United Malays Nat. Orgn, 1981–2003 (Mem., Supreme Council, 1972–2003). *Publications:* The Malay Dilemma, 1969; The Way Forward (essays), 1998.

MAHER, Christina Rose, OBE 1994; Co-founder and Director, Plain English Campaign, since 1979; *b* 21 April 1938; *d* of late Fred Lewington and Maureen (*née* Cullen); *m* 1959, George Bernard Maher; three *s* one *d*. *Educ:* St Cecilia's Sch., Liverpool. Community worker, 1969–98. Founder: Tuebrook Bugle (first community newspaper), 1971; Liverpool News (first newspaper for people with learning difficulties), 1974. Chm., Impact Printers Foundn, 1974–98; Founder, Salford Form Market (for NCC), 1975. Hon. Fellow, Liverpool John Moores Univ., 2010. Hon. MA Manchester, 1995; DUniv Open, 1997. Public Affairs Achiever of the Year, and Outstanding Achiever, Women in Public Life Awards, 2010. *Publications:* (jtly) Plain English Story, 1980; How to Write Letters/Reports in Plain English, 1995; Decade of Drivel, 1996; Language on Trial, 1996; A to Z for Lawyers, 1996. *Recreations:* swimming, dance, theatre, keep fit. *Address:* Hillside Farm, Combs, High Peak, Derbys SK23 9UT. *T:* (01298) 815979.

MAHER, Prof. Eamonn Richard, MD; FRCP, FRSB, FMedSci; Professor of Medical Genetics and Genomic Medicine, and Head, Department of Medical Genetics, University of Cambridge, since 2013; Consultant in Clinical Genetics, Addenbrooke's Hospital, Cambridge, since 2013; *b* 20 July 1956; *s* of Richard and Edna Maher; *m* 1980, Helen Marie (*neé* Jackson); two *s* three *d*. *Educ:* Salesian High Sch., Bootle; Univ. of Manchester (BSc 1st Cl. Hons Physiol. 1977; MB ChB Hons 1980; MD 1988); Univ. of Cambridge (MA 1996). MRCP 1983, FRCP 1996. Clinical Lectr, 1988–91, Univ. Lectr, 1991–96, in Med. Genetics, Univ. of Cambridge; Consultant in Med. Genetics, Addenbrooke's Hosp., Cambridge, 1991–96; Prof. of Med. Genetics, and Hd, Dept of Med. and Molecular Genetics, 1996–2013, Dir, Centre for Rare Diseases and Personalised Medicine, 2010–13, Univ. of Birmingham; Consultant in Clin. Genetics, W Midlands Regl Genetics Service, Birmingham Women's Health Care NHS Trust, 1996–2013. Ed., Jl of Med. Genetics, 1998–2009. FMedSci 2006; FRSB (FSB 2012). *Publications:* A Practical Guide to Human Cancer Genetics (with S. V. Hodgson), 1994, 4th edn (with S. V. Hodgson, W. D. Foulkes and C. Eng) 2013; over 400 scientific articles and book chapters on clinical and molecular aspects of cancer and med. genetics. *Recreations:* Everton Football Club, taxi driver for children. *Address:* Department of Medical Genetics, University of Cambridge, Addenbrooke's Treatment Centre, Addenbrooke's Hospital, Cambridge CB2 0QQ. *T:* (01223) 746714, *Fax:* (01223) 746777. *E:* erm1000@medschl.cam.ac.uk, E.R.Maher@bham.ac.uk.

MAHER, (Elizabeth) Jane, (Mrs Peter Krook), FRCP, FRCPE, FRCR; Consultant Clinical Oncologist, Mount Vernon Cancer Centre and Hillingdon Hospital, since 1986; Chief Medical Officer, Macmillan Cancer Support (formerly Macmillan Cancer Relief), since 1999; *b* 31 March 1953; *d* of Matthew Gerard Maher and Stella Marie Maher (*née* Griffiths); *m* 1987, Peter Arthur Larson Krook (*d* 2011); one *d*. *Educ:* Edgbaston C of E Coll. for Girls; King's Coll., London; Westminster Med. Sch. (MB BS 1976); Westminster Hosp.; Middlesex Hosp.; Harvard Univ.; Massachusetts Gen. Hosp. MRCP 1979, FRCP 1997; FRCR 1982; FRCPE 1998. Sen. Clinical Lectr, UCL, 1990–; Med. Dir, Lynda Jackson Macmillan Centre, and Dir, Psychosocial Res., 1998–. Chairman: Nat. Cancer Inst. Consensus Meeting, palliative radiotherapy, 1992; Maher Cttee, mgt of adverse effects of radiotherapy, 1995; London Cancer Task Force, 2000–04; Lead Clinician, Cancer Services Improvement, 2000–. Vis. Prof. of Cancer and Supportive Care, Complexity Management Centre, Hertfordshire Univ., 2005–. *Publications:* articles on breast cancer and psychosocial oncology. *Recreations:* detective fiction, medieval churches. *Address:* Lynda Jackson Macmillan Centre, Mount Vernon Hospital, Rickmansworth Road, Northwood, Middx HA6 2RN. *T:* (01923) 844681, *Fax:* (01923) 844172. *Club:* Blacks.

MAHER, His Honour Terence; a Circuit Judge, 1995–2006; *b* 20 Dec. 1941; *s* of late John Maher and of Bessie Maher; *m* 1965 (marr. diss. 1983); two *d*. *Educ:* Burnley Grammar Sch.; Univ. of Manchester (LLB Hons). Admitted Solicitor, 1966; articled to Town Clerk, Burnley; Asst Solicitor, City of Bradford, 1966–68; Prosecuting Solicitor, Birmingham Corp., 1968–70; Dep. Pros. Solicitor, Thames Valley Police, 1970–73; Asst Solicitor and partner, Cole & Cole, Oxford, 1973–83; Metropolitan Stipendiary Magistrate, 1983–95; a Chm., Inner London Juvenile, subseq. Youth, Courts and Family Proceedings Court, 1985–95; a Recorder, 1989–95. Gen. Sec., Univ. of Manchester Students' Union, 1962–63; Chm., Chipping Norton Round Table, 1975–76; Treas./Vice-Chm. and Chm., Oxford and District Solicitors' Assoc., 1980–83; Mem., Law Society Standing Cttee on Criminal Law, 1980–85. Mem. Editl Bd, Jl of Criminal Law, 1982–95. *Recreations:* walking, reading, anything to do with France and the French. *Address:* c/o Luton Crown Court, 7 George Street, Luton LU1 2AA. *Club:* Frewen (Oxford).

MAHER, Terence Anthony, FCCA; author; *b* 5 Dec. 1935; *s* of late Herbert and Lillian Maher; *m* 1960, Barbara (*née* Grunbaum); three *s*. *Educ:* Xaverian Coll., Manchester. ACCA 1960, FCCA 1970. Carborundum Co. Ltd, 1961–69; First National Finance Corp., 1969–72; Founder, Chm. and Chief Exec., Pentos plc, 1972–93; Chairman: Dillons Bookstores, 1977–93; Athena Internat., 1980–93; Ryman, 1987–93; Tempus Publishing (formerly Chalford Publishing) Co. Ltd, 1994–98; Maher Booksellers Ltd, 1995–2008; Race Dynamics Ltd, 1998–2008. Mem., Adv. Council on Libraries, 1997–98. Contested (L): Accrington, 1964; Runcorn, 1966. Founder Trustee, Lib Dem, 1988–2001. Trustee, Photographers' Gall.,

1994–97. FRSA 1988. Led successful campaign to abolish price control on books. *Publications:* (jtly) Counterblast, 1965; (jtly) Effective Politics, 1966; Against My Better Judgement (business memoir), 1994; Unfinished Business (novel), 2003; Grumpy Old Liberal: a political rant, 2005; What Would a Liberal Do?: a polemic, 2010; One of Lowry's Children (personal memoir), 2015. *Recreations:* reading, ski-ing, tennis, walking, music, bridge. *Address:* 33 Montagu Square, W1H 2LJ. *T:* (020) 7723 4254; The Old House, Whichford, near Shipston-on-Stour, Warwickshire CV36 5PG. *T:* (01608) 684614. *Clubs:* Savile, Portland.

MAHLER, Dr Halfdan Theodor; Director-General, World Health Organization, 1973–88, now Emeritus; Secretary-General, International Planned Parenthood Federation, 1989–95; consultant, international health, since 1996; *b* 21 April 1923; *m* 1957, Dr Ebba Fischer-Simonsen; two *s*. *Educ:* Univ. of Copenhagen (MD, EOPH). Planning Officer, Internat. Tuberculosis Campaign, Ecuador, 1950–51; Sen. WHO Med. Officer, Nat. TB Programme, India, 1951–61; Chief MO, Tuberculosis Unit, WHO/HQ, Geneva, 1961–69; Dir, Project Systems Analysis, WHO/HQ, Geneva, 1969–70; Asst Dir-Gen., WHO, 1970–73. Hon. FFPHM 1975; Hon. FRSocMed 1976; Hon. FRCGP 1986; Hon. FRSTM&H, 1993; Hon. Fellow: Indian Soc. for Malaria and other Communicable Diseases, Delhi; Faculty of Community Med., RCP, 1975; Hon. Professor: Univ. Nacional Mayor de San Marcos, Lima, Peru, 1980; Fac. of Medicine, Univ. of Chile, 1982; Beijing Med. Coll., China, 1983; Shanghai Med. Univ., 1986; Bartel World Affairs Fellow, Cornell, 1988; Peking Univ., 1994; Hon. Advr, China FPA, 1994. Hon. Fellow: LSHTM, 1979; Coll. of Physicians and Surgeons, Dacca, Bangladesh, 1980; Hon. Member: Soc. médicale de Genève; Union internat. contre la Tuberculose; Société Française d'Hygiène, de Médecine Sociale et Génie Sanitaire, 1977; Med. Assoc. of Argentina, 1985; Latin American Med. Assoc., 1985; Italian Soc. of Tropical Medicine, 1986; APHA, 1988; Swedish Soc. of Medicine, 1988; Hon. Foreign Corresponding Member: Inst. of Medicine, NAS, 1989; BMA, 1990; Hon. Life Mem., Uganda Medical Assoc., 1976; Assoc. Mem., Belgian Soc. of Trop. Medicine; Mem., Inst. of Medicine, USA, 1989; List of Honour, Internat. Dental Fedn, 1984; Hon. Academician: Nat. Acad. of Medicine, Mexico, 1988; Nat. Acad. of Medicine, Buenos Aires, 1988; Acad. of Health, Peru, 2001. FRCP 1981. Hon. LLD: Nottingham, 1975; McMaster, 1989; Exeter, 1990; Toronto, 1990; Hon. MD: Karolinska Inst., 1977; Charles Univ., Prague, and Mahidol Univ., Bangkok, 1982; Aarhus, 1988; Copenhagen, 1988; Aga Khan, Pakistan, 1989; Newcastle upon Tyne, 1990; Hon. Dr de l'Univ. Toulouse (Sciences Sociales), 1977; Hon. Dr Public Health, Seoul Nat. Univ., 1979; Hon DSc: Lagos, 1979; Emory, Atlanta, 1989; SUNY, 1990; Hon. Dr Med. Warsaw Med. Acad., 1980; Hon. Dr Faculty of Medicine, Univ. of Ghent, Belgium, and Universidad Nacional Autónoma de Nicaragua, Managua, 1983; Hon. DHL CUNY, 1989; Dr *hc* Universidad Nacional 'Federico Villarreal', Lima, Peru, 1980; Semmelweis Univ. of Medicine, Budapest, 1987. Jane Evangelisty Purkyne Medal, Prague, 1974; Comenius Univ. Gold Medal, Bratislava, 1974; Carlo Forlanini Gold Medal, 1975; Ernst Carlsens Foundn Prize, Copenhagen, 1980; Georg Barfred-Pedersen Prize, Copenhagen, 1982; Hagedorn Medal and Prize, Denmark, 1986; Freedom from Want Medal, Roosevelt Inst., 1988; Bourgeoisie d'Honneur, Geneva, 1989; UK-US Hewitt Award, RSM, 1992; Dr Ved Vias Puri Meml Award, FPA of India, 1994; UN Population Award, 1995; Andrija Stampar Award, Assoc. of Schs of Public Health in European Region, 1995. Grand Officier: l'Ordre Nat. du Bénin, 1975; l'Ordre Nat. Voltaïque, 1978; l'Ordre du Mérite, République du Sénégal, 1982; Ordre National Malgache (Madagascar), 1987; Comdr (1st cl.), White Rose Order of Finland, 1983; Commandeur, l'Ordre National du Mali, 1982; Grand Cordon, Order of the Sacred Treasure (Japan), 1988; Storkors Af Dannebrogordenen (Denmark), 1988; Grand Cross: Order of the Falcon (Iceland), 1988; Order of Merit (Luxembourg), 1990; Ordem do Merito Medico (Brazil), 2003. *Publications:* papers etc on the epidemiology and control of tuberculosis, the political, social, economic and technological priority setting in the health sector, and the application of systems analysis to health care problems. *Recreations:* sailing, ski-ing. *Address:* 12 chemin du Pont-Céard, 1290 Versoix, Switzerland. *E:* halfdan.mahler@bluewin.ch.

MAHMOOD, Khalid; MP (Lab) Birmingham Perry Barr, since 2001; *b* 13 July 1961. Formerly: engr, advr, Danish Internat. Trade Union. Mem., Birmingham CC, 1990–93. *Address:* c/o House of Commons, SW1A 0AA.

MAHMOOD, Shabana; MP (Lab) Birmingham Ladywood, since 2010; *b* Small Heath, Birmingham, 17 Sept. 1980; *d* of Mahmood Ahmed. *Educ:* Lincoln Coll., Oxford (LLB). Called to the Bar, Gray's Inn, 2004; employed as barrister, Berrymans Lace Mawer, 2004–07. Mem., Work and Pensions Select Cttee, 2010; Shadow Home Office Minister, 2010–11; Shadow Minister: for Higher Educn, BIS, 2011–13; for Univs and Sci., BIS, 2013; for the Treasury, 2013–15; Shadow Chief Sec. to the Treasury, 2015. *Address:* House of Commons, SW1A 0AA.

MAHON, Alice; *b* 28 Sept. 1937; *m*; two *s*. *Educ:* Bradford Univ. (BA Hons). Lectr, Bradford and Ilkley Community Coll. Member: Calderdale Bor. Council, 1982–87; Calderdale DHA. MP (Lab) Halifax, 1987–2005. PPS to Sec. of State for Culture, Media and Sport, 1997. Mem., Select Cttee on Health, 1991–97. Mem., Nato Parly (formerly N Atlantic) Assembly, 1992–2005. *Address:* 125 The Hough, Northowram, Halifax, W Yorks HX3 7DE.

MAHON, His Honour Charles Joseph; a Circuit Judge, 1989–2005; *b* 16 Aug. 1939; *s* of late Frank and Amy Agnes Mahon; *m* 1974, Lavinia Gough (*née* Breaks); one *d*, and one step *s* two step *d*. *Educ:* Chetham's Hosp.; Gonville and Caius Coll., Cambridge (BA, LLB). Called to the Bar, Gray's Inn, 1962. Parachute Regt, TA, 1964–72. *Recreations:* music, books, walking.

MAHON, Seán Patrick Lauritson; Director, International Board and Global Board, DLA Piper, since 2007; Chairman, Scottish Coal Group, 2009–12; *b* 16 April 1946; *s* of John Patrick Mahon and Peggy Lauritson Mahon; *m* 1968, Pauline Kathleen Starling; one *s* two *d* (and one *d* decd). *Educ:* Ratcliffe Coll. FCA 1969. Partner, Coopers & Lybrand, subseq. PricewaterhouseCoopers, 1969–2000; Member: UK Bd, Coopers & Lybrand, 1992–98; UK Supervisory Bd, PricewaterhouseCoopers, 1998–2000; Chief Exec., Cattles plc, 2001–07. Chairman: Jerrold Hldgs, 2007–09; Scottish Resources Gp, 2008–10. Accreditation Bd, ICAEW, 1982–88; Pres., Sheffield Soc. of Chartered Accountants, 1990–91. Careers Adv. Bd, Univ. of Sheffield, 1982–88. Dir, S Yorks Ambulance Trust, 1991–97; Chairman: Leeds Cares, 1998–2004; National Cares, 2004–07; HRH Prince of Wales's Ambassador for Yorks Businesses, 2004–07; Vice-Chm., St Luke's Hospice Capital Appeal, 2012–. Hon. Treas., Clubs for Young People, 1984– (Vice Pres., 2007–). Pres., Sheffield Irish Soc., 1990–91. DUniv Sheffield Hallam, 2005. *Recreations:* golf, fishing, shooting. *Address:* Wyngrove, 41 Stumperlowe Crescent Road, Sheffield S10 3PR. *T:* 07802 470100. *Clubs:* Royal Automobile; Woolley Park Golf; Wykeham Shoot Syndicate.

MAHON, Colonel Sir William (Walter), 7th Bt *cr* 1819 (UK), of Castlegar, Co. Galway; LVO 2011; *b* 4 Dec. 1940; *s* of Sir George Edward John Mahon, 6th Bt and Audrey Evelyn (*née* Jagger) (*d* 1957); *S* father, 1987; *m* 1968, Rosemary Jane, *yr d* of late Lt-Col M. E. Melvill, OBE, Symington, Lanarks; one *s* two *d*. *Educ:* Eton. Commnd Irish Guards, 1960; served UK, Germany, Malaysia, Aden, Hong Kong, Pakistan, Spain. HM Body Guard, Hon. Corps of Gentlemen at Arms: Mem., 1993; Clerk of the Cheque and Adjutant, 2006–08; Standard Bearer, 2008–10. Fundraising, Macmillan Cancer Relief, 1993–2002. Chm., Nat. Army Museum Develt Trust, 2003. *Recreations:* shooting, collecting, military history. *Heir: s* James William Mahon [*b* 29 Oct. 1976; *m* 2004, Antonia Williams; one *s* one *d*].

MAHONEY, Dennis Leonard; Chairman, Aon Global, 2007–09; *b* 20 Sept. 1950; *s* of late Frederick Mahoney; *m* 1st, Julia McLaughlin (marr. diss.); one *s* one *d*; 2nd, 1988, Jacqueline Fox; one *s* two *d*. *Educ:* West Hatch Technical High School; Harvard Business Sch. (PMD 1983). Chm. and CEO, Aon Group Ltd, subseq. Aon Ltd, 1997–2007. Dir, Ironshore Inc., 2012–.

MAHONEY, Rev. Prof. John Aloysius, (Jack), SJ; Emeritus Professor of Moral and Social Theology, University of London, since 1999; Emeritus Professor, Gresham College, London, since 2007; *b* Coatbridge, 14 Jan. 1931; *s* of Patrick Mahoney and Margaret Cecilia Mahoney (*née* Doris). *Educ:* Our Lady's High Sch., Motherwell; St Aloysius' Coll., Glasgow; Univ. of Glasgow (MA 1951). LicPhil 1956; LicTheol 1963; DTheol *summa cum laude*, Pontifical Gregorian Univ., Rome, 1967. Entered Society of Jesus, 1951; ordained priest, 1962; Jesuit Tertianship, NY, 1963–64. Lectr in Moral and Pastoral Theology, Heythrop Coll., Oxon, 1967–70, and Heythrop Coll., London, 1970–86; Principal, Heythrop Coll., London, 1976–81 (Fellow, 2000); F. D. Maurice Prof. of Moral and Social Theology, KCL, 1986–93; Founding Dir, KCL Business Ethics Res. Centre, 1987–93; Dean, Faculty of Theol., London Univ., and Faculty of Theol. and Religious Studies, KCL, 1990–92; Dixons Prof. of Business Ethics and Social Responsibility, London Business Sch., 1993–98; Founding Dir, Lauriston Centre for Contemporary Belief and Action, Edinburgh, and Hon. Fellow, Faculty of Divinity, Edinburgh Univ., 1998–2005; Sen. Res. Associate Dir, Heythrop Inst. for Religion, Ethics and Public Life, Heythrop Coll., Univ. of London, 2005–06; Mount Street Jesuit Centre, London, 2006–08. Mercers' Sch. Meml Prof. of Commerce, Gresham Coll., London, 1987–93; Dist. Prof. of Theol., Georgetown Univ., Washington, DC, 2008; Martin D'Arcy Meml Lectr, Campion Hall, Oxford, 1981–82. Vis. Scholar, Boston Coll., Mass, 2005. Mem., Internat. Theol. Commn, Rome, 1974–80; Sector Pres., Nat. Pastoral Congress, 1980; Mem., Internat. Study Gp on Bioethics, Internat. Fedn of Catholic Univs, 1984–93. Pres., Catholic Theolog. Assoc., 1984–86. Chaplain to Tablet Table, 1983–98; Domestic Chaplain to Lord Mayor of London, 1989–90. CCMI (CIMgt 1993). Hon. Fellow: Gresham Coll., City of London, 1999–2000; St Mary's UC, Strawberry Hill, 1999; Campion Hall, Oxford, 2014. Governor, St Aloysius' Coll., Glasgow, 1999–2005 (Chm., 2000–05). Founding Editor, Business Ethics, A European Review, 1992–98. Hon. DD London, 2004. President's Medal, Georgetown Univ., Washington, DC, 2003. *Publications:* Seeking the Spirit, 1981; Bioethics and Belief, 1984; The Making of Moral Theology, 1987; The Ways of Wisdom, 1987; Teaching Business Ethics in the UK, Europe and USA, 1990, 2nd edn 2013; (ed) Business Ethics in a New Europe, 1992; The Challenge of Human Rights: origin, development and significance, 2006; Christianity in Evolution: an exploration, 2011. *Address:* Campion Hall, Brewer Street, Oxford OX1 1QS. *T:* (01865) 286010. *E:* jmlaur@aol.com.

MAHY, Brian Wilfred John, PhD, ScD; Senior Scientific Adviser, Coordinatin (formerly National) Center for Infectious Diseases, Centers for Disease Control and Prevention, Atlanta, Georgia, 2000–10; Adjunct Professor, Emory University, 1993–2010; *b* 7 May 1937; *s* of Wilfred Mahy and Norah Dillingham; *m* 1st, 1959, Valerie Pouteaux (marr. diss. 1986); two *s* one *d*; 2nd, 1988, Penny Scott (*née* Cunningham). *Educ:* Elizabeth Coll., Guernsey; Univ. of Southampton (BSc, PhD); Univ. of Cambridge (MA, ScD 1982). Res. Biologist, Dept of Cancer Res., London Hosp. Med. Coll., Univ. of London, 1962–65; Asst Dir, Res. Virology, Dept of Pathology, Cambridge Univ., 1965–79; Fellow and Tutor, University (Wolfson) Coll., 1967–84; Librarian, Wolfson Coll., 1975–80; Huddersfield Lectr in Special Path. (Virology), 1979–84; Head, Div. of Virology, Cambridge, 1979–84; Head, Pirbright Lab., AFRC Inst. for Animal Health (formerly Animal Virus Res. Inst. and AFRC Inst. for Animal Disease Res.), 1984–89; Dir, Div. of Viral and Rickettsial Diseases, Centers for Disease Control and Prevention, Atlanta, GA, 1989–2000. Vis. Prof., Univ. of Minnesota, 1968; Eleanor Roosevelt Internat. Cancer Fellow, Dept of Microbiol., Univ. of California, San Francisco, 1973–74; Vis. Prof., Inst. für Virologie, Univ. of Würzburg, 1980–81. Convener, Virus Group, 1980–84, Mem. Council, 1983–87, Soc. for General Microbiology; Vice-Chm., 1987–90, Chm., 1990–93, Past Chm., 1994–96, Virology Div., Vice Pres., 1995–99, Pres., 1999–2002, Past Pres., 2002–05, Internat. Union of Microbiol Socs. FRSocMed 1985; Fellow: Infectious Diseases Soc. of America, 1992; Amer. Acad. of Microbiol., 1998–2010. Hon. DSc Southampton, 2001. Editor-in-Chief, Virus Research, 1983–2011; US Editor: Jl of Med. Virology, 1994–2010; Reviews in Med. Virology, 2000–10; Sen. Associate Ed., Emerging Infectious Diseases, 2008–; Virology Ed., Reference Module in Biomed. Scis, 2013–. *Publications:* (jtly) The Biology of Large RNA Viruses, 1970; Negative Strand Viruses, 1975; Negative Strand Virus and the Host Cell, 1978; Lactic Dehydrogenase Virus, 1975; A Dictionary of Virology, 1981, 4th edn 2009; Virus Persistence, 1982; The Microbe 1984: pt 1, Viruses, 1984; Virology: a practical approach, 1985; The Biology of Negative Strand Viruses, 1987; Genetics and Pathogenicity of Negative Strand Viruses, 1989; Concepts in Virology: from Ivanovsky to the present, 1993; Virology Methods Manual, 1996; Immunobiology and Pathogenesis of Persistent Virus Infections, 1996; (ed jtly) Topley & Wilson's Microbiology and Microbial Infections, 9th edn, Vol. 1, 1998, 10th edn, Vol. 1 and Vol. 2, 2005; Encyclopedia of Virology, 3rd edn 2008; (ed jtly) Desk Encyclopedias of General Virology, Plant and Fungal Virology, Human and Medical Virology, and Animal and Bacterial Virology, 2010; over 200 articles on virology in learned jls. *Recreations:* music, reading. *Address:* Herringbone Cottage, Rede Road, Whepstead, Bury St Edmunds IP29 4ST. *E:* bwjmahy@gmail.com.

MAI, Prof. Yiu-Wing, AM 2010; PhD, DSc, DEng; FRS 2008; FREng, FAA, FTSE; University Chair, since 2004, Professor of Mechanical Engineering, since 2007, and Director, Centre for Advanced Materials Technology, 1988–2011, University of Sydney; *b* Hong Kong, 5 Jan. 1946; *s* of Lam Mai and Yuet-Yau Tsui; *m* 1980, Louisa Kit-Ling. *Educ:* Univ. of Hong Kong (BSc Engrg 1969; PhD 1972; DSc 1999); Univ. of Sydney (DEng 1999). FTSE 1992; FHKIE 1994. Mgt and Technol. Trainer, Hong Kong Productivity Council, 1973; Postdoctoral Research Assistant: Univ. of Michigan, 1974–75; Imperial Coll., London, 1975–76; University of Sydney: Lectr, 1976–78; Sen. Lectr, 1978–82; Associate Prof., 1983–87; Prof. of Mechanical Engrg, 1987–2002; Associate Dean, R&D, 1990–93; Dir, Graduate Sch. of Engrg, 1995–98; Dir, Defence Sci. and Technol. Orgn—Airframes and Engines Div. Centre for Expertise in Damage Mechanics, 1997–2003; Pro-Dean, 1998–2004; ARC Federation Fellow, 2002–07. Prof., HKUST, 1993–95; Chair, City Univ. of Hong Kong, 2000–02; Dist. Vis. Prof., Univ. of Hong Kong, 2003–04. Pres., Australian Fracture Gp Inc., 1997. Mem. Council, Asian-Australian Assoc. for Composite Materials, 1999– (Founder Pres., 1997–98); Pres., Internat. Congress on Fracture, 2002–05 (Vice-Pres., 1997–2001). FAA 2001; FHKAES 2003. Mem., Eur. Acad. of Scis, 2008. FASME 1999; Internat. FREng 2011. Hon. DSc Hong Kong, 2013. *Publications:* (with A. G. Atkins) Elastic and Plastic Fracture, 1985; (with B. Cotterell) Fracture Mechanics of Cementitious Materials, 1996; (with J. K. Kim) Engineered Interfaces in Fibre-Reinforced Composites, 1998; (with S.-Y. Fu and B. Lauke) Science and Engineering of Short Fibre Reinforced Polymers, 2009; (with X.-H. Chen) Fracture Mechanics of Electromagnetic Materials, 2013; over 700 articles in scientific jls. *Recreations:* reading mainly Chinese literature, practising Chinese calligraphy, walking. *Address:* School of Aerospace, Mechanical and Mechatronic Engineering, Mechanical Engineering Building J07, University of Sydney, Sydney, NSW 2006, Australia. *T:* (2) 93512290, *Fax:* (2) 93513760. *E:* yiu-wing.mai@sydney.edu.au.

MAIANI, Prof. Luciano; President, Consiglio Nazionale delle Ricerche, Rome, 2008–11; Professor of Theoretical Physics, University of Rome, 1984, now Emeritus; Director General, Organisation Européenne pour la Recherche Nucléaire (CERN), 1999–2003 (President of Council, 1997); *b* 16 July 1941. *Educ:* Univ. of Rome (degree in Physics 1964). Research Associate: Istituto Superiore di Sanità, 1964; Univ. of Florence, 1964; Fellow, Lyman Lab. of

Physics, Univ. of Harvard, 1969; Prof., Inst. of Theoretical Physics, Univ. of Rome, 1976; Vis. Prof., Ecole Normale Supérieure, Paris, 1977; Vis. Prof., 1979–80, 1985–86, Mem. Council, 1993–97, CERN. Pres., Istituto Naz. di Fisica Nucleare, Italy, 1993–98. Fellow, APS, 1991 (J. Sakurai Prize, 1987; E. Fermi Prize, 2003).

MAIBAUM, Prof. Thomas Stephen Edward, PhD; PEng (Ont), CEng, FIET; Professor, Foundations of Software Engineering, and Canada Research Chair, Department of Computing and Software, McMaster University, Canada, since 2004; *b* 18 Aug. 1947; *s* of Leslie Maibaum and Olga Maibaum (*née* Klein); *m* 1971, Janet Hilless; one *s* one *d*. *Educ:* Toronto Univ. (BSc); PhD London Univ. Postdoctoral Fellow, 1973, Asst Prof., 1974–81, Univ. of Waterloo; Imperial College, University of London: Lectr, Dept of Computing, 1981–86; Reader in Computing Science, 1986–90; Hd, Dept of Computing, 1989–97; Prof., Foundns of Software Engrg, 1990–99; King's College London: Prof., Foundns of Software Engrg, 1999–2004; Hd, Dept of Computer Sci., 2001–03. Vis. Prof., Pontificia Universidade Católica de Rio do Janeiro, 1977, 1981 (Hon. Prof., 1992); Royal Soc./SERC Industrial Fellow, 1984; Marie Curie Fellowship (EU), Univ. of Lisbon, 1997–98. MIEEE; MCIPS; FRSA. Engrg Foresight Award, Royal Acad. Engrg, 1998. *Publications:* (jtly) The Specification of Computer Programs, 1987; (ed jtly) Handbook of Logic in Computer Science, vol. I, 1992, vol. II, 1992, vol. III, 1995, vol. IV, 1995, vol. V, 2000. *Recreations:* memorising the films of Mel Brooks, music, opera, travel, literature. *Address:* Department of Computing and Software, McMaster University, 1280 Main Street West, Hamilton, ON L8S 4K1, Canada; 1265 Ontario Street #1510, Burlington, ON L7S 1X8, Canada. *T:* (905) 5259140 ext. 26627.

MAIDEN, Sir Colin (James), Kt 1992; ME, DPhil; Chairman, Tower Insurance Ltd (formerly National Insurance Company of New Zealand Ltd), 1988–2002; Vice-Chancellor, University of Auckland, New Zealand, 1971–94; *b* 5 May 1933; *s* of Henry A. Maiden; *m* 1957, Jenefor Mary Rowe; one *s* three *d*. *Educ:* Auckland Grammar Sch.; Univ. of New Zealand (ME); Rhodes Scholar (NZ) 1955; Exeter Coll., Oxford (DPhil; Hon. Fellow, 1994). Post-doctorate research, Oxford Univ. (supported by AERE, Harwell), 1957–58; Head of Hypersonic Physics Section, Canadian Armament Research and Develt Estabt, Quebec City, Canada, 1958–60; Sen. Lectr in Mechanical Engrg, Univ. of Auckland, 1960–61; Head of Material Sciences Laboratory, Gen. Motors Corp., Defense Research Laboratories, Santa Barbara, Calif, USA, 1961–66; Manager of Process Engineering, Gen. Motors Corp., Tech. Centre, Warren, Michigan, USA, 1966–70. Chairman: NZ Synthetic Fuels Corp. Ltd, 1980–90; Fisher & Paykel Industries Ltd, 1989–2001 (Dir, 1978); Sedgwick Gp (NZ) Ltd, 1996–98 (Dir, 1994–98); Transpower NZ Ltd, 1997–2004 (Dir, 1994–2004); DB Gp Ltd, 2003–08 (Dir, 1994–2008); Director: Mason Industries Ltd, 1971–78; Farmers Trading Co. Ltd, 1973–86; Winstone Ltd, 1978–88; Wilkins & Davies Co. Ltd, 1986–89; NZ Steel Ltd, 1988–92; Independent Newspapers Ltd, 1989–2004 (Chm., 1994–2001); ANZ Banking Gp (NZ) Ltd, 1990–93; NZ Refining Co. Ltd, 1991–2007; Progressive Enterprises Ltd, 1992–2000; Tower Ltd, 1995–2003; Foodland Associated Ltd (WA), 2000–05; Fisher & Paykel Healthcare Corp. Ltd, 2001–11. Chairman: NZ Energy R&D Cttee, 1974–81; Liquid Fuels Trust Bd, 1978–86. Chm., NZ Vice-Chancellors' Cttee, 1977–78, and 1991; Hon. Treasurer, ACU, 1988–98. Member: Spirit of Adventure Trust Bd, 1972–80; NZ Metric Adv. Bd, 1973–77. NZ Agent for Joint NZ/US Sci. and Technol Agreement, 1974–81. Hon. FIPENZ 1999. Hon. LLD Auckland, 1994. Thomson Medal, Royal Soc. NZ, 1986; Medal, Univ. of Bonn, 1983; Symons Award, ACU, 1999. Silver Jubilee Medal, 1977. *Publications:* An Energetic Life (autobiog.), 2008; numerous scientific and technical papers. *Recreation:* tennis. *Address:* Apt 503, 10 Middleton Road, Remuera, Auckland, New Zealand. *T:* (9) 5247412. *Clubs:* Vincent's (Oxford); Northern (Auckland); Remuera Racquets, International Lawn Tennis of NZ, Auckland Golf.

MAIDEN, (James) Dennis, CEng; Director General, Federation of Master Builders, 1991–97; *b* 28 June 1932; *s* of James William Maiden and Elsie (*née* Brotherton); *m* 1953, Irene Harris; one *s* one *d*. *Educ:* Wath-upon-Dearne Grammar Sch. CEng 1966; MIMechE 1966; FFB 1987–2003. Engrg Consultant, Husband & Co., 1958–63; Chief Engr, British Shoe Corp., 1963–67; Construction Industry Training Board: Develt Manager, 1967–73; Gen. Manager, 1973–76; Dir of Trng, 1976–85; Chief Exec., 1985–90; Dir-Gen. designate, Fedn of Master Builders, 1990–91. Chief Exec., Construction Ind. Services Ltd, 1991–97; Managing Director: Nat. Register of Warranted Builders Ltd, 1991–97; Trade Debt Recovery Service Ltd, 1991–97. Pres., Kings Lynn Inst. of Mgt, 1988. Chm., Park House Hotel for Disabled People, 1983–88 and 1995–99. Trustee, Leonard Cheshire Foundn, 1987–92; Pres., Norfolk Outward Bound Assoc., 1988. Hon. Mem., C & G, 1981; CCMI (CIMgt 1986); MIPM 1971; FRSA 1987. Freeman, City of London, 1988; Liveryman, Co. of: Constructors, 1988; Plumbers, 1989. *Recreations:* art, gardening, theatre. *Address:* Micklebring, Church Lane, Bircham, Kings Lynn, Norfolk PE31 6XS. *T:* (01485) 578336.

MAIDEN, Prof. Martin David, PhD; FBA 2003; Professor of the Romance Languages, since 1996, and Director, Oxford Research Centre for Romance Linguistics, since 2007, University of Oxford; Fellow of Trinity College, Oxford, since 1996; *b* 20 May 1957; *s* of Kenneth Henry Maiden and Betty Maiden (*née* Liddiard); *m* 2005, Liliana Buruiana; one step *d*. *Educ:* King Edward VI Sch., Southampton; Trinity Hall, Cambridge (MA, MPhil, PhD). Lectr in Italian, Univ. of Bath, 1982–89; Univ. Lectr in Romance Philology, and Fellow of Downing Coll., Cambridge, 1989–96. Delegate, OUP, 2004–. Pres., Società Internazionale di Linguistica e Filologia Italiana, 1989–91; Mem. Council, Philological Soc., 1996–2000, 2003–10. Associate Member: Centre for Res. on Lang. Contact, York Univ., Toronto, 2005; Associazione Italiana di Romenistica, 2006; Hon. Member: Asociația culturală Alexandru Philippide (Iași, Romania), 2005–; Dacoromania, 2006–. Hon. Dip., Linguistics Inst., Romanian Acad., 2009. Consultant Editor: Revue romanes, 2001–; Diachronica, 2002–; Bollettino linguistico campano, 2002–; Legenda Publications, 2002–; Troubadour Publications, 2002–; L'Italia dialettale, 2006–; Rivista italiana di linguistica, 2006–; Current Issues in Linguistic Theory (Benjamins), 2006; Linguistica, 2007. *Publications:* Interactive Morphonology: metaphony in Italy, 1991; (ed with J. C. Smith) Linguistic Theory and the Romance Languages, 1995; A Linguistic History of Italian, 1995; (ed with M. Parry) The Dialects of Italy, 1997; Storia linguistica dell' italiano, 1998; (with C. Robustelli) A Reference Grammar of Modern Italian, 2000, 2nd edn 2007; (ed with J. C. Smith and A. Ledgeway) Cambridge History of the Romance Languages, Vol. 1, 2011; articles in various jls, incl. Romance Philology, Zeitschrift für romanische Philologie, Jl of Linguistics. *Recreation:* travel. *Address:* 62 Cunliffe Close, Oxford OX2 7BL. *T:* (01865) 511753.

MAIDEN, Robert Mitchell, FCIBS; Managing Director, Royal Bank of Scotland plc, and Executive Director, Royal Bank of Scotland Group plc, 1986–91; *b* 15 Sept. 1933; *s* of Harry and Georgina Maiden; *m* 1958, Margaret Mercer (*née* Nicolson). *Educ:* Montrose Acad., Tayside, Scotland. Royal Bank of Scotland: various appts, 1950–74; Supt of branches, 1974–76; Treasurer, 1976–77; Chief Accountant, 1977–81; Gen. Man. (Finance), 1981–82; Exec. Dir, 1982–86. Vice-Chm., CC-Bank AG, Germany, 1991–93; Chm., Lothian and Edinburgh Enterprise, 1994–96. Member: Accounts Commn for Scotland, 1992–99; Scottish Panel of Adjudicators, Investors in People, Scotland, 1996–2001. Gov., Napier Univ. (formerly Napier Poly.), 1988–98. Trustee, C of S Pension Scheme, 1991–96. FCMI; FRSA. *Recreations:* music, golf, reading. *Address:* Trinafour, 202 Braid Road, Edinburgh EH10 6HS.

MAIDLOW DAVIS, Richard Cuthbert Tolley, (Dom Leo), OSB; monk, since 1975, and Prior Administrator, since 2014, Downside Abbey (Headmaster, Downside School, 2002–14); *b* 22 April 1954; *s* of Michael Maidlow Davis and Yvette Maidlow Davis (*née* Tolley). *Educ:* Downside Sch.; Magdalene Coll., Cambridge (BA 1975); Univ. of London (BD 1982); Gregorianum, Rome (STL 1986). Professed, 1979; ordained priest, 1981; Downside School: Teacher of Classics and Religious Studies, 1982–2014; Novice Master, 1986–91; House Master, Smythe House, 1991–2000; Editor, Raven (Downside Sch. Mag.), 1992–2002; Novice Master, 2000–02. Curate, Midsomer Norton, 1982–84. *Recreations:* carpentry, botany, sundials, riding his racing bike around the local countryside, gardening. *Address:* Downside Abbey, Stratton-on-the-Fosse, Radstock, Bath, Som BA3 4RJ. *T:* (01761) 235107.

MAIDMENT, Francis Edward, (Ted); Headmaster, Shrewsbury School, 1988–2001; *b* 23 Aug. 1942; *s* of late Charles Edward and Olive Mary Maidment. *Educ:* Pocklington Sch., York; Jesus Coll., Cambridge (Scholar). Asst Master, Lancing Coll., 1965–81 (Housemaster, 1975–81); Headmaster, Ellesmere Coll., Shropshire, 1982–88. *Recreations:* lecturing and speaking, singing, medieval history, modest tennis. *Address:* Linden Cottage, Astley, Shrewsbury SY4 4BP. *Clubs:* East India, Devonshire, Sports and Public Schools.

MAIDMENT, Neil, CMG 1996; Executive Director, Glaxo Wellcome plc (formerly Glaxo Holdings plc), 1993–95 (responsible for Asia Pacific, 1993–95, and for Africa, Middle East and Turkey, 1994–95); *b* Oxford, 18 Aug. 1938; *s* of late Kenneth John Maidment, Founding Vice-Chancellor, Univ. of Auckland and Isobel Felicity Maidment (*née* Leitch); *m* 1983, Sandie Shuk-Ling Yuen. *Educ:* Christ Church Cathedral Sch., Oxford; Magdalen Coll. Sch., Oxford; King's Sch., Auckland; King's Coll., Auckland; Univ. of Auckland (Life Mem., Students' Assoc.) (Joynt Scroll Debating Shield, NZ Univs, 1956; Controller, NZ Univs Tournament, 1959). Evacuated to USA with Oxford Univ. children's gp, 1940–45. South British Insurance Co. Ltd, Auckland, Singapore, Calcutta, Bombay, 1958–65; Glaxo Group: Far Eastern Surgical Rep., Singapore, Kuala Lumpur, 1965–68; Manager: Hong Kong, 1968–70; Manila, 1971; Director and General Manager: Glaxo Hong Kong Ltd, 1971–93; Glaxo China Ltd, 1988–93; Area Dir, North Asia, 1990–93. Member: Pharmacy and Poisons Appeal Tribunal, Hong Kong, 1979–88; Sub-Cttee on Biotechnology, Hong Kong, 1988–89; UK/Hong Kong Scholarships Cttee, 1988–94. Pres., Hong Kong Assoc. of Pharmaceutical Industry, 1977–78; Chm., British Chamber of Commerce, Hong Kong, 1989–90. Non-exec. Dir, Hong Kong Inst. of Biotechnol. Ltd, 1996–2002. *Publications:* (with H. Scrimgeour and H. Williams) Arthur Scrimgeour—a life, 1990. *Address:* PO Box 23022, Wanchai, Hong Kong. *Clubs:* Hong Kong, Hong Kong Jockey (Hong Kong); Saturday (Calcutta).

MAIDMENT, Ted; *see* Maidment, F. E.

MAIDSTONE, Viscount; Tobias Joshua Stormont Finch Hatton; *b* 21 June 1998; *s* and *heir* of Earl of Winchilsea and Nottingham, *qv*.

MAIDSTONE, Bishop Suffragan of, since 2015; **Rt Rev. Roderick Charles Howell Thomas;** *b* 7 Aug. 1954; *s* of Alan and Edna Thomas; *m* 1981, Lesley Easton; three *c*. *Educ:* London Sch. of Econs and Pol Sci. (BSc 1975); Wycliffe Hall, Oxford. Dir of Employment and Envmtl Affairs, CBI, 1986–91; ordained deacon, 1993, priest, 1994; Curate, St Andrew, Plymouth with St Paul, Stonehouse, 1993–99; Priest-in-charge, 1999–2005, Vicar, 2005–15, St Matthew, Elburton; Preb., Exeter Cathedral, 2012–15. Chm., Reform, 2007–15. *T:* 07906 331110. *E:* rod.thomas@bishopofmaidstone.org.

MAIDSTONE, Archdeacon of; *see* Taylor, Ven. S. R.

MAIER, Prof. John Paul, DPhil; FRS 1999; Professor of Physical Chemistry, University of Basel, since 1991; *b* 15 Nov. 1947; *s* of Dr H. E. Maier and S. Maier; three *d* (one *s* decd). *Educ:* Univ. of Nottingham (BSc Hons Chemistry 1966); Balliol Coll., Oxford (DPhil Physical Chemistry 1972). University of Basel: Royal Soc. Fellow, 1973–74; Res. Associate, 1975–78; Lectr in Chemistry, 1978–81; Associate Prof. in Physical Chemistry, 1982–90. Werner Prize, Swiss Chem. Soc., 1979; Marlow Medal, RSC, 1980; Chemistry Prize, Göttingen Sci. Acad., 1986; Nat. Latsis Prize, Swiss Nat. Sci Foundn, 1987; ERC Advanced Investigator Grant, 2010; Humbolt Res. Award, 2011; SASP Erwin Schrödinger Medal, 2012. *Recreations:* bridge, golf. *Address:* Department of Chemistry, University of Basel, Klingelbergstrasse 80, 4056 Basel, Switzerland. *T:* (61) 2673826, *Fax:* (61) 2673855. *E:* j.p.maier@unibas.ch.

MAIER, Juergen; Chief Executive, Siemens plc, since 2014; *b* Karlsruhe, Germany, 12 Jan. 1964; *s* of Horst Maier and Sigrun Trotter; civil partnership 2007, Richard Madgin. *Educ:* Allerton Grange High Sch.; Trent Poly. (BSc Hons Prodn Engrg 1986). Siemens: Prodn Engr, 1986–87, Prodn Manager, 1987–94, Prodn Control Manager, 1994–95, Manufg Manager, 1995–96, Automation and Drives Div.; Ops Dir, Birmingham, 1996–97; Gen. Manager, Manchester, 1997–2000; eBusiness Dir, Corporate UK, 2000–01; Man. Dir, Siemens Shared Services, 2001–04; Dir, Sales Europe, 2004–06; Man. Dir, Automation and Drives Div., 2006–08; Man. Dir, Industry Sector, UK, Ire. and Nigeria, 2008–14. Non-exec. Dir, BIS, 2014–. Chm., NW Business Leadership Team, 2009–; non-executive Director: Sci., Engrg, Manufg and Technols Alliance, 2009–15; EEF, 2010–15; High Value Manufg Catapult, 2011–14; Internat. Innovative Technologies, 2011–; Mem., Gtr Manchester Local Enterprise Partnership, 2013–. Hon. Prof., Univ. of Manchester, 2014. FIET 2014. *Recreations:* ski-ing, walking, mountains. *Address:* Siemens plc, Stephenson House, Sir William Siemens Square, Frimley, Camberley, Surrey GU16 8QD.

MAILER, Joanna Mary; *see* Shapland, J. M.

MAIN, Very Rev. Prof. Alan, TD 1982; PhD; Professor of Practical Theology, Aberdeen University, 1980–2001; Master, Christ's College, Aberdeen, 1992–2001; Moderator of the General Assembly of the Church of Scotland, 1998–99; *b* 31 March 1936; *s* of James E. W. Main and Mary A. R. Black; *m* 1960, Anne Louise Swanson; two *d*. *Educ:* Robert Gordon's Coll., Aberdeen; Aberdeen Univ. (MA 1957; BD 1960; PhD 1963); Union Theol Seminary, NY (STM 1961). Minister, Chapel of Garioch Parish, Aberdeenshire, 1963–70; Chaplain to Univ. of Aberdeen, 1970–80. Pres., Boys' Bde, 2005–07. Patron, Seven Incorp. Trades of Aberdeen, 2000–. Hon. DD Aberdeen, 2006. *Publications:* Worship Now, 1989; (ed) But Where Shall Wisdom Be Found?, 1995; (ed) Northern Accents, 2001; articles in jls on pastoral care and counselling, military ethics, medical ethics. *Recreations:* music (piano and organ), golf, bee-keeping. *Address:* Kirkfield, Barthol Chapel, Inverurie AB51 8TD. *Club:* Royal Northern and University (Aberdeen).

MAIN, Anne; MP (C) St Albans, since 2005; *b* 17 May 1957; *d* of late George and of Rita Wiseman; *m* 1st, 1978, Stephen Tonks (*d* 1991); one *s* two *d*; 2nd, 1995, Andrew Jonathan Main; one *s*. *Educ:* Bishop of Llandaff Secondary Sch., Cardiff; Univ. Coll. of Wales, Swansea (BA 1978); Univ. of Sheffield (PGCE 1978). Teacher of English and Drama, Feltham Comp. Sch., 1979–80; supply posts, Bristol, 1991–94. Member (C): Beaconsfield Parish Council, 1999–2002; S Bucks DC, 2001–05. *Address:* (office) 104 High Street, London Colney, St Albans, Herts AL2 1QL; House of Commons, SW1A 0AA.

MAIN, Air Vice-Marshal John Bartram, CB 1996; OBE 1979 (MBE 1977); FREng, FIET; Military Adviser, Matra Marconi Space/Astrium, 1996–2001; *b* 28 Jan. 1941; *s* of late Wing Comdr James Taylor Main, OBE and Nellie Ethel Toleman; *m* 1965, Helen Joyce Lambert; two *d*. *Educ:* Portsmouth Grammar Sch.; Birmingham Univ. (BSc Elect. Eng.); RAF Tech. Coll., Henlow. CEng 1968; MIEE 1968, FIET (FIEE 1983); FRAeS 1984; FREng 2001. Commissioned Engr Branch, RAF, 1960; served Benson, Hiswa (Aden), Thorney Island; mentioned despatches, 1968; Dir of Sci. and Tech. Intell., MoD, 1970–73; OC No 33 Signals Unit, Cyprus, 1974–76; 72 Advanced Staff Course, RAF Staff Coll., 1977; CO RAF Digby, 1977–79; Directing Staff, RAF Staff Coll., 1979–80; RAF Signals Engrg Estabt, 1980–83; Head, Tech. Intell. (Air), 1983–87; RCDS 1986; Dep. Comd Aerosystems Engr, HQ Strike Comd, 1987–88; Comdt, RAF Sigs Engrg Estabt and Air Cdre Sigs, HQ RAF Support

Comd, 1988–89; Dir, Command, Control, Communication and Inf. Systems (Policy and Op. Requirements), 1989–93; DG Support Services (RAF), 1993–94; AO Communications and Inf. Systems, and AOC Signals Units, HQ Logistics Comd, 1994–96. *Recreations:* gardening, cycling, sailing, reading. *Address:* Robin's Mead, 120 Manor Way, Aldwick Bay, West Sussex PO21 4HN. *Club:* Royal Air Force.

MAIN, His Honour John Roy; QC 1974; a Circuit Judge, 1976–95; *b* 21 June 1930; *yr s* of late A. C. Main, MIMechE; *m* 1955, Angela de la Condamine Davies, *er d* of late R. W. H. Davies, ICS; two *s* one *d*. *Educ:* Portsmouth Grammar Sch.; Hotchkiss Sch., USA; Brasenose Coll., Oxford (MA). Called to Bar, Inner Temple, 1954; a Recorder of Crown Court, 1972–76. Mem. Special Panel, Transport Tribunal, 1970–76; Dep. Chm., IoW QS, 1971. Pres., Transport Tribunal, 1996–97 (Chm., 1997–2000). Gov., Portsmouth Grammar Sch., 1988–2000. *Recreations:* walking, gardening, music, local politics. *Address:* 4 Queen Anne Drive, Claygate, Surrey KT10 0PP. *T:* (01372) 466380.

MAIN, Monica Maitland, FRCGP; Lord-Lieutenant of Sutherland, since 2005; *b* 9 Aug. 1952; *d* of Kenneth Morrison and Gwenneth Morrison (*née* Austin); *m* 1975, William George Main; one *s* one *d*. *Educ:* Dingwall Acad.; Univ. of Aberdeen (MB ChB 1975). DRCOG 1978; MRCGP 1979, FRCGP 2011. General Practitioner: Kingsmills Practice, Inverness, 1982–86; Brora Med. Practice, 1992–2011. *Recreations:* gardening, walking. *Address:* Ballamhor, 35 Golf Road, Brora, Sutherland KW9 6QS. *T:* (01408) 621234.

MAIN, Peter Ramsay; QC 2003; **His Honour Judge Main;** a Circuit Judge, since 2008; Designated Civil Judge, Staffordshire and West Mercia, since 2010; a Deputy High Court Judge, since 2008; *b* 17 May 1958; *s* of late Henry James Main and of Rosemary Ina Main (*née* Anderson); *m* 1988, Valerie Marie Ramsden; one *s* one *d*. *Educ:* Repton Sch.; LSE (LLB 1980); Centre for Petroleum and Mineral Law Studies, Univ. of Dundee (Dip Pet. Law 1982). Called to the Bar, Inner Temple, 1981; in practice as a barrister, Manchester, 1983–; Junior, Northern Circuit, 1986; Asst Recorder, 1999–2001; Recorder, 2001–08. *Recreations:* avid sports watcher, golf, Rhodesian ridgebacks.

MAINE, Steven; Deputy Chairman, Six Degrees Group, since 2011; *b* 7 Dec. 1951; s of Gerald Ivor Gordon Maine and Jean Maine; *m* 1990, Sarah Anne Kennard. *Educ:* Oriel Coll., Oxford (MA). BT, 1974–95 (Dir, Visual and Broadcast, 1988–94, India, 1994–95); Chief Executive: Kingston Communications (Hull) plc, 1997–2003; Solaris Mobile, 2008–11; Dep. Chm., Spiritel plc, 2006–10; non-executive Director: SMG plc, 2000–07; Orion Farming Gp, 2013–. Chm., Regl CBI Yorks and Humber, 2000–03. Dir, Urban Regeneration Co., Hull, 2002–03. *Recreations:* golf, cycling, photography.

MAINES, James Dennis, CB 1998; CEng, FIET; Director General, Command Information Systems, Ministry of Defence, 1995–97; *b* 26 July 1937; *s* of Arthur Burtonwood Maines and Lilian Maines (*née* Carter); *m* 1st, 1960, Janet Enid Kemp (marr. diss. 1997); three *s*; 2nd, 1997, Janet Elizabeth Bussey (*née* Franks); two step *d*. *Educ:* Leigh Grammar School; City University (BSc). Joined RSRE (then RRE), Malvern, 1956 (Sandwich course in applied physics, 1956–60); Head of Guided Weapons Optics and Electronics Group, 1981; Head, Microwave and Electro-optics Group, 1983; Head, Sensors, Electronic Warfare and Guided Weapons, ARE, Portsdown, 1984–86; Dep. Dir (Mission Systems), RAE, 1986–88; Dir Gen., Guided Weapons and Electronics Systems, MoD, 1988–95. Wolfe Award for outstanding MoD research (jtly), 1973. *Publications:* (jtly) Surface Wave Filters (ed Matthews), 1977; papers in learned jls. *Recreations:* sailing, cricket, golf, music, painting, non-labour intensive gardening. *Address:* Hollybush Cottage, Folly Hill, Farnham, Surrey GU9 0DR.

MAINI, Prof. Philip Kumar, DPhil; FRS 2015; FRSB; FIMA; Director, Wolfson Centre for Mathematical Biology (formerly Centre for Mathematical Biology), since 1998, and Professor of Mathematical Biology, since 2005, Mathematical Institute, University of Oxford; Fellow, St John's College, Oxford, since 2005; *b* Magherafelt, Co. Londonderry, 16 Oct. 1959; *s* of late Panna Lal Maini and of Satya Wati Maini (*née* Bhandari). *Educ:* Rainey Endowed Sch., Magherafelt; Balliol Coll., Oxford (BA Hons, MA; DPhil 1985). FRSB (FSB 2013). Asst Master, Eton Coll., 1986; Jun. Res. Fellow, Wolfson Coll., Oxford, 1987–88; Asst Prof., Dept of Maths, Univ. of Utah, Salt Lake City, 1988–90; Lectr in Math. Biol., 1990–2005, Titular Prof. of Math. Biol., 1998–2005, Math. Inst., Univ. of Oxford; Tutorial Fellow, Brasenose Coll., Oxford, 1990–2005. Adjunct Professor: Sch. of Math. Scis, Qld Univ. of Technol., 2006–09; Lincoln Univ., Christchurch, NZ, 2010–12. Visiting Professor: Williams Coll., Mass, 1995; Inst. for Maths and its Applications, Univ. of Minn, 1998; Hon. Guest Prof., Univ. of Electronic Sci. and Technol. of China, 2005–; Vis. Fellow, 2001, Vis. Prof., 2004, Qld Univ. of Technol.; Vis. Fellow, Clare Hall, Cambridge, 2001; Tewkesbury Bequest Internat. Visitor, Univ. of Melbourne, 2008; Walker Ames Guest Schol., Univ. of Washington, Seattle, 2011. Royal Soc. Leverhulme Trust Sen. Res. Fellow, 2001–02; Dist. For. Vis. Fellow, Res. Inst. for Electronic Sci., Hokkaido Univ., 2002; Wolfson Res. Merit Award, Royal Soc., 2006–11; Dist. Res. Fellow, African Inst. of Math. Scis, 2010–13; Fellow, SIAM, 2012. Corresp. Mem., Academia Mexicana de Ciencias, 2011. FIMA 2003. (Jtly) Bellman Prize, Math. Bioscis jl, 1997; Naylor Prize and Lectureship, LMS, 2009. *Publications:* (ed jtly and contrib.) Experimental and Theoretical Advances in Biological Pattern Formation, 1993; (ed jtly and contrib.) Mathematical Models for Biological Pattern Formation, 2000; (ed jtly and contrib.) Morphogenesis and Pattern Formation in Biological Systems: experiments and models, 2003; (ed jtly and contrib.) Multiscale Modeling of Developmental Systems, 2008; (ed jtly) Mathematical Biology, 2009. *Recreations:* football, travel, volunteer dog-walking. *Address:* Wolfson Centre for Mathematical Biology, Mathematical Institute, Andrew Wiles Building, Radcliffe Observatory Quarter, Woodstock Road, Oxford OX2 6GG. *T:* (01865) 280497. *E:* maini@maths.ox.ac.uk.

MAINI, Sir Ravinder (Nath), Kt 2003; FRCP, FMedSci; FRS 2007; Professor of Rheumatology, Imperial College School of Medicine at Charing Cross Hospital Campus (formerly Charing Cross and Westminster Medical School), University of London, 1989–2002, now Emeritus Professor; Visiting Professor, University of Oxford, since 2011; *b* 17 Nov. 1937; *s* of Sir Amar (Nath) Maini, CBE and Saheli (*née* Mehra); *m* 1st, 1963, Marianne Gorm (marr. diss. 1986); one *s* one *d* (and one *s* decd); 2nd, 1987, Geraldine Room; two *s*. *Educ:* Sidney Sussex Coll., Cambridge (BA; MB, BChir 1962; Hon. Fellow, 2004). MRCP 1966, FRCP 1977; FRCPE 1994. Jun. med. appts, Guy's, Brompton and Charing Cross Hosps, 1962–70; Consultant Physician: St Stephen's Hosp., London, 1970–79; Rheumatology Dept, Charing Cross Hosp., 1970–81; Hon. Consultant Physician, Charing Cross Hosp., Hammersmith Hosps NHS Trust, 1981–2007; Prof. of Immunology of Rheumatic Diseases, and Hd, Dept of Immunology of Rheumatic Diseases, Charing Cross and Westminster Med. Sch., 1981–89; Dir, Kennedy Inst. of Rheumatology, 1990–2000 then Head, Kennedy Inst. of Rheumatology Div., Imperial Coll. Sch. of Medicine at Charing Cross Hosp. Campus, 2000–02 (Head, Clinical Immunology Div., 1979–2002). President: Brit. Soc. Rheumatology, 1989–90 (Heberden Orator, 1988); Brit. League Against Rheumatism, 1985–89; Chm., Res. Subcttee, 1980–85, and Mem., Scientific Co-ordinating Cttee, 1985–95, Arthritis and Rheumatism Council; Chm., Standing Cttee for Investigative Rheumatology, European League Against Rheumatism, 1992–98; Mem., Exec. Cttee, Assoc. Physicians of GB and Ire., 1988–91; Chm., Rheumatology Cttee, RCP, 1992–96 (Croonian Lectr, 1995; Lumleian Lectr, 1998); Mem., European Union of Medical Specialists, 1991– (Pres., Sect. of Rheumatology, 1994–98; Chm., Eur. Bd of Rheumatology, 1996–99). Samuel Hyde Lectr, 1998, Hon. Fellow, 2004, RSocMed. FMedSci 1999; Fellow British Soc. for Rheumatol., 2003. Member: Slovakian Rheumatol. Soc., 2003–; (Life) Indian Rheumatol. Assoc., 2003; For. Associate, NAS, USA, 2010. Hon. Member: Australian Rheumatism Assoc., 1977; Norwegian Soc. for Rheumatology, 1987; Amer. Coll. of Rheumatology, 1988 (Master, 2004); Hellenic Rheumatology Soc., 1989; Hungarian Rheumatology Soc., 1990; Scandinavian Soc. for Immunology, 1996; Mexican Soc. for Rheumatology, 1996; Eur. League Against Rheumatism, 1997 (jtly, Meritorious Service Award in Rheumatology, 2005); British Soc. for Immunology, 2010; Czech Soc. of Rheumatology, 2012. Trustee: Kennedy Inst. of Rheumatology, 2002–; Sir Jules Thorn Trust, 2004–; Guardian, Wellcome-Beit Fellowship, 2009–. Dr *hc* Univ. René Descartes, Paris, 1994; Hon. DSc Glasgow, 2004. Dist. Investigator Award, Amer. Coll. of Rheumatology, 1999; EULAR Courtin-Clarins Prize (with Prof. M. Feldmann and Prof. J.-M. Dayer), Assoc. de Recherche sur la Polyarthrite, 2000; Outstanding Achievement in Clin. Res. Award, Inst. Clin. Res., 2004; Fothergillian Medal, Med. Soc. of London, 2004; Ambuj Nath Bose Prize, RCP, 2005; Galen Medal, Soc. of Apothecaries, 2006; with Sir Marc Feldmann: Carol Nachman Prize for rheumatology, city of Wiesbaden, 1999; Crafoord Prize, Royal Swedish Acad. of Scis, 2000; Albert Lasker Clin. Med. Res. Award, 2003; Cameron Prize, Edinburgh Univ., 2004; Japan Rheumatism Foundn Internat. Rheumatoid Arthritis Award, 2007; Dr Paul Janssen Award for Biomed. Res., Johnson & Johnson, 2008; Ernst Schering Prize, Ernst Schering Foundn, 2010; Canada Gairdner Internat. Award, 2014. *Publications:* Immunology of Rheumatic Diseases, 1977; (ed) Modulation of Autoimmune Disease, 1981; (contrib.) Textbook of the Rheumatic Diseases, 6th edn 1986; (ed) T cell activation in health and disease, 1989; (ed) Rheumatoid Arthritis, 1992; (contrib.) Oxford Textbook of Rheumatology, 1993; (section ed.) Rheumatology, 1993; (ed jtly) Manual of Biological Markers of Disease, Sect. A, Methods of Autoantibody Detection, 1993, Sect. B, Autoantigens, 1994, Sect. C, Clinical Significance of Autoantibodies, 1996; (contrib.) Oxford Textbook of Medicine, 2001, 4th edn 2003; articles in learned jls. *Recreations:* music appreciation, walking. *Address:* 151 Castlenau, Barnes, SW13 9EW. *Club:* Reform.

MAINLAND, Kathleen Mary, CBE 2014; Chief Executive, Edinburgh Festival Fringe Society, since 2009; *b* Aberdeen, 30 May 1969; *d* of Tommy and Bertha Mainland. *Educ:* Stromness Acad., Orkney; Glasgow Univ. (MA 1990); Strathclyde Univ. (Dip. Accounting 1991). Edinburgh Festival Fringe Soc., 1991–96; Gen. Manager, Assembly Th. Ltd, 1997–2004; Gen. Manager, 2005, Admin. Dir, 2006–09, Edinburgh Internat. Book Fest. Freelance prodn co-ordinator and project manager working on events incl. Edinburgh's Hogmanay, MTV Eur. Music Awards, UEFA Champions League, NVA Virtual World Orch., 1996–2005. *Address:* Edinburgh Festival Fringe Society, 180 High Street, Edinburgh EH1 1QS. *T:* (0131) 226 0026. *E:* admin@edfringe.com.

MAIR, Alexander, MBE 1967; Chief Executive and Director, Grampian Television Ltd, 1970–87, retired; *b* 5 Nov. 1922; *s* of Charles Mair and Helen Dickie; *m* 1953, Margaret Isobel Gowans Rennie. *Educ:* Skene, Aberdeenshire; Webster's Business Coll., Aberdeen; Sch. of Accountancy, Glasgow. Fellow, CIMA, 1992 (Associate, 1953). Chief Accountant, Bydand Holdings Ltd, 1957–60; Company Sec., Grampian Television, 1961–70; apptd Dir, 1967; Director: ITN, 1980–87; Cablevision (Scotland) Ltd, 1983–88; TV Publication Ltd, 1970–87. Chairman: British Regional Television Assoc., 1973–75; ITCA Management Cttee, 1980–87; RGIT Ltd, 1989–98. Pres., Aberdeen Junior Chamber of Commerce, 1960–61; Mem. Council, Aberdeen Chamber of Commerce, 1973–96 (Vice-Pres., 1987–89; Pres., 1989–91). Gov., Robert Gordon's Coll., Aberdeen, 1987–2002. FRSA 1973. FRTS 1987. *Recreations:* golf, ski-ing, gardening. *Address:* Ravenswood, 66 Rubislaw Den South, Aberdeen AB15 4AY. *T:* (01224) 317619. *Club:* Royal Northern (Aberdeen).

MAIR, Alexander Stirling Fraser, (Alistair), MBE 1987; DL; Chairman, 1991–98, and Managing Director, 1977–98, Caithness Glass Ltd; *b* 20 July 1935; *s* of Alexander W. R. Mair and Agnes W. (*née* Stirling); *m* 1st, 1961, Alice Anne Garrow (*d* 1975); four s; 2nd, 1977, Mary Crawford Bolton; one *d*. *Educ:* Robert Gordon's Coll., Aberdeen; Aberdeen Univ. (BSc (Eng)); BA Hist. Open Univ. 2001. SSC, RAF, 1960–62. Rolls-Royce, Glasgow: grad. apprentice, 1957–59; various appts, until Product Centre Manager, 1963–71; Man. Dir, Caithness Glass, Wick, 1971–75; Marketing Dir, Worcester Royal Porcelain Co., 1975–77. Director: Grampian Television, 1986–2001; Crieff Hydro Ltd, 1994–2003 (Chm., 1996–2003); Murray VCT 3 PLC, 1998–2006. Vice Chm., Scottish Cons. and Unionist Party, 1992–93; Chairman: Perth Cons. and Unionist Assoc., 1999–2004; Ochil and S Perthshire Cons. and Unionist Assoc., 2005–09. Mem. Council, CBI, 1985–92 (Chm., Scotland, 1989–91). Pres., British Glass Manufacturers' Confedn, 1997 and 1998; Chm., Crieff and Dist Aux. Assoc. (Richmond House), 1993–99. Hon. Pres., Perth and Kinross Assoc., Duke of Edinburgh's Award Scheme, 1993–. Mem. Court, Aberdeen Univ., 1993–2010 (Convener, Jt Planning, Finance and Estates Cttee, 1998–2004; Chancellor's Assessor and Vice Chm., 2000–10); Chm., Cttee of Chairmen of Scottish Higher Educn Instns, 2001–07. Gov., Morrison's Acad., Crieff, 1985–2006 (Chm., 1996–2006); Comr, Queen Victoria Sch., Dunblane, 1992–97. FCMI; FRSA 1986. DL Perth and Kinross, 1993. Hon. LLD Aberdeen, 2004. *Recreations:* walking, gardening, current affairs, history. *Address:* Woodend, Madderty, by Crieff, Perthshire PH7 3PA. *T:* and *Fax:* (01764) 683210. *Club:* Royal Northern and University (Aberdeen).

MAIR, Colin David Robertson, MA; Rector, High School of Glasgow, 2004–15; *b* 4 Aug. 1953; *s* of late Colin James Robertson Mair and Catherine Barbara Mair (later Welsh). *Educ:* Kelvinside Acad.; St Andrews Univ.; Glasgow Univ. (MA); Jordanhill Coll. (Cert Ed). High School of Glasgow: teacher of Latin, 1976–79; Head: of Rugby, 1977–88; of Latin, 1979–85; Bannerman Housemaster, 1982–85; Asst Rector, 1985–96; Dep. Rector, 1996–2004. Member: Council, Sch. Leaders Scotland (formerly Headmasters' Assoc. of Scotland), 1997–2014; UCAS Standing Gp, Scotland, 2003–; Bd, SCIS, 2013–. Member: Commonweal Cttee, Trades House of Glasgow, 2005–06; Merchants House of Glasgow, 2014–. Mem., Gen. Convocation, Univ. of Strathclyde, 2009–10. Fellowship Award, Scottish Qualifications Authy, 2014. *Recreations:* cricket, golf, Rugby, walking, watching Partick Thistle. *Address:* 17 Ladywood, Milngavie, Glasgow G62 8BE. *T:* (0141) 956 5792. *Clubs:* W of Scotland Cricket, W of Scotland Football (Glasgow); XL.

MAIR, Edward; journalist and broadcaster; *b* 12 Nov. 1965; *s* of Hubert Nicolson Mair and Mary Balneaves Mair (*née* Steele). *Educ:* Whitfield Primary Sch., Dundee; Whitfield High Sch., Dundee. Broadcast Asst, Radio Tay, Dundee, 1983–87 (Host, Tay-Talk-In and Breakfast Show, 1985–87); joined BBC, 1987: sub-ed., News, Glasgow, 1987–89, Presenter, Good Morning Scotland, 1989–93, BBC Radio Scotland; Presenter: Reporting Scotland, BBC TV Scotland, 1989–93; Eddie Mair Live, BBC Radio Scotland, 1993–94; Breakaway, Radio Four, 1993–94; Midday with Mair, Radio Five Live, 1994–98; (jtly) The World, World Service/WGBH Boston, 1996–98; PM, 1998–, Broadcasting House, 1998–2003, iPM, 2007–, Radio Four; Newsnight, BBC2, 2004, 2012, 2013; host, Seven O'Clock News, BBC3, 2004–05. Diarist, The Guardian, 2001–04; columnist, Radio Times, 2010–. Award for Best Breakfast Show, Eddie Mair Live, 1994, Gold Award, News Journalist of Year, 1994, 2005, Gold Award for Speech Broadcaster of the Year, 2006, Interview of the Year, 2012, Gold Award for Speech Radio Broadcaster of the Year, 2013, Sony Radio Awards; Winner, Radio Prog. of Year for Broadcasting House, 2002, Radio Broadcaster of Year, 2009, BPG. *Address:* c/o Anita Land Ltd, 10 Wyndham Place, W1H 2PU. *E:* anita@anitaland.com. *Club:* Soho House.

MAIR, Prof. Robert James, CBE 2010; PhD; FRS 2007; FREng, FICE; Sir Kirby Laing Professor of Civil Engineering (formerly Professor of Geotechnical Engineering) and Head of Civil and Environmental Engineering, University of Cambridge, since 1998; Master of Jesus College, Cambridge, 2001–11; Founding Director, Geotechnical Consulting Group, London, since 1983; *b* 20 April 1950; *s* of late Prof. William Austyn Mair, CBE; *m* 1981, Margaret Mary

Plowden O'Connor; one *s* one *d*. *Educ:* Leys Sch.; Clare Coll., Cambridge (MA 1975; PhD 1979). FICE 1990; FREng (FEng 1992). Scott Wilson Kirkpatrick and Partners, Consulting Engineers: Engr, London and Hong Kong, 1971–76; Sen. Engr, London, 1980–83; Res. Asst, Dept of Engrg, Univ. of Cambridge, 1976–79; Fellow, St John's Coll., Cambridge, 1998–2001. Special Prof., Dept of Civil Engrg, Univ. of Nottingham, 1994–97; Royal Acad. of Engrg Vis. Prof., Univ. of Cambridge, 1997–98. Principal Investigator, Cambridge Centre for Smart Infrastructure and Construction, 2011–; Chief Engrg Advr, Laing O'Rourke Gp, 2012–. Member: Commn of Enquiry into Collapse of Toulon Tunnel, French Govt, 1997; Adv. Bd, Rome Metro, 2008–; Adv. Bd, Barcelona Metro, 2009–; Construction Industrial Strategy Adv. Council, 2013–; Chm., Adv. Bd of Govt of Singapore on Underground Construction Projects, 2004–. Mem. Council, and various cttees, ICE, 1993–95 (Gold Medal, 2004); Sen. Vice-Pres., RAEng, 2008–11; Chm., Royal Soc./RAEng Report to UK Govt on Shale Gas, 2012. Lectures: Rankine, British Geotech. Soc., 2007; Muir Wood, Internat. Tunnelling Assoc., Helsinki, 2011. Hon. Prof., Tongji Univ., Shanghai, 2008–. Hon. DSc Nottingham, 2011. Singapore Public Service Medal, 2011. *Publications:* (with D. M. Wood) Pressuremeter Testing: methods and interpretation, 1987; technical papers, mainly in jls of soil mechanics and geotechnical engrg; conf. proceedings, principally on underground construction and tunnelling. *Recreations:* supporting QPR, sailing, golf, long walks, Asian cities, theatre. *Address:* Department of Engineering, Trumpington Street, Cambridge CB2 1PZ. *T:* (01223) 332631, *Fax:* (01223) 339713. *E:* rjm50@cam.ac.uk.

MAIRS, Christopher John, CBE 2014; FREng; FBCS; Chief Scientist, Metaswitch Networks (formerly Metaswitch), since 2011; *b* 14 Feb. 1957; *s* of late Gordon Mairs and Dinah Mairs (*née* Hipkin); *m* 2012, Shirley Donald. *Educ:* Nottingham High Sch.; Churchill Coll., Cambridge (BA 1st Cl. Hons Computer Sci. 1979). FREng 2006; FBCS 2006. Director, Data Connection Ltd, 1984–2007; Sen. Vice-Pres., Product Mgt, 2004–05, Chief Technical Officer, 2005–11, MetaSwitch; Chief Technol. Officer, Thrutu, 2011. Chairman: a-technic, 2001–; Code Club World Ltd, 2014– (Bd Mem., 2013–14); Spontly Ltd, 2014–; Bd Mem., Elastera Ltd, 2014–; Chief Technical Officer, FDA Ltd, 2013–; Partner (pt-time), Entrepreneur First, 2014–. Chm., UK Forum for Computer Educn, 2013–. Patron, Fight for Sight, 2012–; Trustee, Thomas Pocklington Trust, 2013–. *Publications:* various papers and lectures on telecommunications, digital technology and inclusive design. *Recreations:* water ski-ing (including captaining British Disabled Waterski Team to victory in 3 world championships, 1989, 1997, 2001), walking, good food, tandem cycling (including Land's End to John O'Groats). *Address:* Metaswitch Networks, 100 Church Street, Enfield EN2 6BQ. *T:* (020) 8366 1177, *Fax:* (020) 8363 4478. *E:* chris.mairs@metaswitch.com; 13 Macaulay Buildings, Widcombe, Bath BA2 6AT.

MAIRS, Robin Gordon James; His Honour Judge Mairs; a Circuit Judge, since 2015; *b* Northern Ireland, 10 April 1969; *s* of Gordon Mairs and Elizabeth Mairs (*née* Waugh); *m* 1998, Gaynor Barbara, *d* of late James Crawford and Barbara Crawford; one *s* one *d*. *Educ:* Wallace High Sch., Lisburn; Manchester Univ. (LLB 1991); Hughes Hall, Cambridge (LLM 1993). Called to the Bar, Gray's Inn, 1992 (Sir Raymond Phillips Award); in practice, SE and NE Circuit, 1994–2015; a Recorder, 2009–15; a Judge, First-tier Tribunal, Health, Educn and Social Health Chamber (Mental Health - Restricted Patients' Panel), 2011–. *Recreations:* Rugby, history, food. *Address:* Newcastle upon Tyne Combined Court Centre, The Law Courts, The Quayside, Newcastle upon Tyne NE1 3LA. *T:* (0191) 201 2000. *E:* enquiries@newcastle.crowncourt.gsi.gov.uk. *Club:* West Park Leeds Rugby Union Football.

MAISEY, Prof. Michael Norman, BSc, MD; FRCP; FRCR; FBIR; Professor of Radiological Sciences, Guy's, King's and St Thomas' Hospitals' School of Medicine, King's College London (formerly United Medical and Dental Schools of Guy's and St Thomas's Hospitals), 1984–2002, now Emeritus; *b* 10 June 1939; *s* of Harold Lionel Maisey and Kathleen Christine Maisey; *m* 1965, Irene Charlotte (*née* Askay); two *s*. *Educ:* Caterham Sch.; Guy's Hosp. Med. Sch. (BSc, MD). ABNM 1972; FRCP 1980; FRCR 1989. House appts, 1964–66; Registrar, Guy's Hosp., 1966–69; Fellow, Johns Hopkins Med. Instns, 1970–72; Guy's Hospital: Sen. Registrar, 1972–73; Consultant Physician, Endocrinology and Nuclear Medicine, 1973–; Med. Dir and Chm. of Mgt Bd, 1991–93; Med. Dir, Guy's and St Thomas's Hosp. NHS Trust, 1993–96. Hon. Consultant to the Army in Nuclear Medicine, 1978–. Chairman: ROC and ROCME Ltd, 2004–08; Medical Imaging Gp Ltd, 2006–11; Dir, e-locum Services Ltd, 2003–07. Pres., BIR, 2000–01. FBIR 2008. *Publications:* Nuclear Medicine, 1980; (ed jtly) Clinical Nuclear Medicine, 1983, 3rd edn 1998; (jtly) An Atlas of Normal Skeletal Scintigraphy, 1985; (jtly) An Atlas of Clinical Nuclear Medicine, 1988, 2nd edn 1994; (jtly) New Developments in Myocardial Imaging, 1993; Clinical Positron Emission Tomography, 1999; (jtly) Atlas of Clinical Positron Emission Tomography, 2006; books and papers on thyroid diseases, nuclear medicine and medical imaging. *E:* michael@maisey.org.uk.

MAITLAND, family name of **Earl of Lauderdale**.

MAITLAND, Viscount, Master of Lauderdale; **John Douglas Maitland;** *b* 29 May 1965; *s* and *heir* of Earl of Lauderdale, *qv*; *m* 2001, Rosamund (marr. diss. 2006), *yr d* of Nigel Bennett. *Educ:* Emanuel School; Radley College; Van Mildert College, Durham (BSc). *Recreations:* cycling, camping, sailing. *Address:* 150 Tachbrook Street, SW1V 2NE.

MAITLAND, Charles Alexander, (10th Bt *cr* 1918, of Clifton, Midlothian); *b* 3 June 1986; *s* of Sir Richard John Maitland, 9th Bt (*d* 1994). Has not yet established his claim to the title and his name does not appear on the Official Roll of the Baronetage.

MAITLAND, Prof. Geoffrey Colin, DPhil; CEng, FREng; FIChemE; CChem, FRSC; Professor of Energy Engineering, Imperial College London, since 2005; President, Institution of Chemical Engineers, 2014–15 (Deputy President, 2013–14); *b* Stoke-on-Trent, Staffs, 25 Feb. 1947; *s* of Colin and Betty Maud Maitland; *m* 1969, Margot Yvonne Marks; one *s* two *d*. *Educ:* Hanley High Sch., Stoke-on-Trent; St Catherine's Coll., Oxford (MA; DPhil Chem. 1972). CChem 1987, FRSC 1987; CEng 2004, FREng 2006; FIChemE 2004; CSci 2005. ICI Res. Fellow, Dept of Physical Chem., Univ. of Bristol, 1972–74; Lectr, 1974–83, Sen. Lectr in Chem. Engrg, 1983–86, Imperial Coll. London; Schlumberger Cambridge Research: Sen. Res. Scientist, 1986–87; Dept Hd, 1987–96; Res. Dir, 1999–2005; Chef de Métier, Schlumberger Paris, 1996–98; Sen. Mem., Hughes Hall, Cambridge, 2000–07. Chm., UK Offshore Oil and Gas Regulatory Regime Ind. Rev., 2011. Pres., British Soc. Rheology, 2002–05. Gov., St Paul's Sch., Cambridge, 2001–05. Hutchison Medal, IChemE, 1998; Chem. Engrg Envoy Award, IChemE, 2010; Rideal Lecture Award, RSC/Soc. of Chem. Industry, 2012. *Publications:* (with G. G. Slinn) Ceramicists' Handbook, 1973; (jtly) Intermolecular Forces: their origin and determination, 1981; (jtly) The Forces Between Molecules, 1986; (ed with L. J. Struble) Flow and Microstructure of Dense Suspensions, 1993; contrib. res. papers to scientific jls. *Recreations:* amateur drama, opera and choral singing, football (Stoke City), cricket (England, Middlesex, Somerset), theatre, British coins, grandchildren. *Address:* Department of Chemical Engineering, Imperial College London, SW7 2AZ. *T:* (020) 7594 1830, *Fax:* (020) 7594 5638. *E:* g.maitland@imperial.ac.uk.

MAITLAND, Lady (Helen) Olga, (Lady Olga Hay); journalist, public affairs consultant; Chief Executive Officer, Money Transfer International, 2008–14; *b* 23 May 1944; *er d* of 17th Earl of Lauderdale and Stanka (*née* Lozanitch); *m* 1969, Robin Hay, *qv*; two *s* one *d*. *Educ:* Sch. of St Mary and St Anne, Abbots Bromley; Lycée Français de Londres. Reporter, Fleet St News Agency, Blackheath and Dist Reporter, 1965–67; columnist, Sunday Express, 1967–91, Daily Mail, 1998–2001. CEO, Internat. Assoc. of Money Transfer Networks, 2006–08. Consultant: Kroll Security Internat., 2004–; Sovereign Strategy, 2004–07; Dir, Earthport plc, 2008–12. ILEA Candidate, Holborn and St Pancras, 1986; contested (C) Bethnal Green and Stepney, 1987. MP (C) Sutton and Cheam, 1992–97; contested (C) same seat, 1997, 2001. PPS to Minister of State, NI Office, 1996. Member, Select Committee: on Procedure, 1992–95; on Educn, 1992–96; on Social Security, 1995–96; on Health, 1996–97. Formerly Sec., Cons. back bench Defence Cttee; Sec., Cons. back bench NI Cttee, 1992–97. Founder and Chm., Families for Defence, 1983–; Pres., Defence and Security Forum, 1992–. Chm., Algeria British Business Council, 2005–. Mem. Adv. Bd, Marbella Internat. Univ., 2014–. *Publications:* Margaret Thatcher: the first ten years, 1989; Faith in the Family, 1997; (contrib.) Peace Studies in our Schools, 1984; (contrib.) Political Indoctrination in Schools, 1985. *Recreations:* family, the arts, travel. *Address:* 21 Cloudesley Street, N1 0HX. *T:* (020) 7837 9212.

MAITLAND-CAREW, Captain Hon. Gerald (Edward Ian); Lord-Lieutenant of Roxburgh, Ettrick and Lauderdale, since 2007; *b* 28 Dec. 1941; *s* of 6th Baron Carew, CBE and Lady Sylvia Maitland (*d* 1991), *o d* of 15th Earl of Lauderdale; assumed by Deed Poll, 1971, the surname Maitland-Carew; *m* 1972, Rosalind Averil Speke; two *s* one *d*. *Educ:* Heatherdown Prep. Sch.; Harrow Sch. Served 15th/19th King's Royal Hussars, 1960–72, Captain 1963; ADC to GOC Home Counties, 1964–67. Runs family estate, Thirlestane Castle. Chairman: Lauderdale and Galawater Br., RBL, Scotland, 1974–2004; Gurkha Welfare Trust Scotland, 1996–2004 (Pres., 2004–). Chm. and host, Scottish Horse Trials Championships, Thirlestane Castle, 1982–2009; Chairman: Lauderdale Hunt, 1980–2000; Musselburgh Racecourse, 1988–98; Mem., Jockey Club, 1987–; Vice President: Internat. League for the Protection of Horses, 2006– (Chm., 1999–2006); World Horse Welfare, 2008–. Church of Scotland: an Elder, 1977–; Mem. Architectl and Artistic Cttee, 1986–96. Trustee: Thirlestane Castle Trust, 1982–; Mellerstain House Charitable Trust, 1983–. Brig., Royal Co. of Archers, Queen's Bodyguard for Scotland, 2003–. DL Roxburgh, Ettrick and Lauderdale, 1989. *Recreations:* horses, shooting, racing. *Address:* The Garden House, Thirlestane Castle, Lauder, Berwickshire TD2 6PD. *T:* (01578) 722254. *Clubs:* Cavalry and Guards; Royal Caledonian Hunt, Jed Forest Hunt.

MAITLAND DAVIES, Keith Laurence; a District Judge (Magistrates' Courts) (formerly Metropolitan Stipendiary Magistrate), 1984–2003; *b* 3 Feb. 1938; *s* of Wyndham Matabele Davies, QC and Enid Maud Davies; *m* 1964, Angela Mary (*née* Jenkins); two *d* one *s*. *Educ:* Winchester; Christ Church, Oxford (MA). Called to the Bar, Inner Temple, 1962; private practice, 1962–84. *Address:* c/o Hammersmith Magistrates' Court, 181 Talgarth Road, W6 8DN.

MAITLIS, Emily, (Mrs M. Gwynne); Presenter, Newsnight and News 24, BBC, since 2006; *b* 6 Sept. 1970; *d* of Prof. Peter Michael Maitlis, *qv*; *m* 2000, Mark Gwynne; two *s*. *Educ:* Queens' Coll., Cambridge (BA Hons English Lit. and Medieval Italian 1992). Documentary programme-maker, Radio 1, TVB, 1995–97; Channel 4 producer, Hong Kong handover, 1997; Business corresp., NBC, Hong Kong, 1997–98; presenter and business corresp., Sky News, 1998–2001; presenter, BBC, 2001–. *Address:* c/o Noel Gay, 19 Denmark Street, WC2H 8NA. *E:* emily.maitlis@bbc.co.uk. *Clubs:* Soho House (Mem. Cttee); Foreign Correspondents' (Hong Kong).

MAITLIS, Prof. Peter Michael, FRS 1984; Professor of Inorganic Chemistry, 1972–97, Research Professor, 1997–2002, now Emeritus, Sheffield University; *b* 15 Jan. 1933; *s* of Jacob Maitlis and Judith Maitlis; *m* 1959, Marion (*née* Basco); three *d*. *Educ:* Univ. of Birmingham (BSc 1953); Univ. of London (PhD 1956, DSc 1971). Asst Lectr, London Univ., 1956–60; Fulbright Fellow and Res. Associate, Cornell Univ., 1960–61, Harvard Univ., 1961–62; Asst Prof., 1962–64, Associate Prof., 1964–67, Prof., 1967–72, McMaster Univ., Hamilton, Ont, Canada. Chm., Chemistry Cttee, SERC, 1985–88. Fellow, Alfred P. Sloan Foundn, USA, 1968–70; Tilden Lectr, RSC, 1979–80; Sir Edward Frankland Prize Lectr, RSC, 1985; Ludwig Mond Lectr, RSC, 1996–97; Van der Kerk Lectr, Netherlands, 1999; Paolo Chini Lectr, Italy, 2001; Glenn T. Seaborg Meml Lectr, Univ. of Calif, Berkeley, 2004–05. Vis. Prof., Australia, Belgium, Brazil, Canada, France, Israel and Japan; Assessor for nat. res. assessments, UK, Holland, Italy, Israel and Portugal. Member: Royal Soc. of Chemistry (formerly Chem. Soc.), 1952– (Pres., Dalton Div., 1985–87); Amer. Chemical Soc., 1963–; Council, Royal Soc., 1991–93; BBC Sci. Consultative Gp, 1989–93. Foreign Mem., Accademia Nazionale dei Lincei, Italy, 1999. E. W. R. Steacie Prize (Canada), 1971; Medallist, RSC (Noble Metals and their Compounds), 1981; Kurnakov Medal, Russian Acad. of Scis, 1998. *Publications:* The Organic Chemistry of Palladium, vols 1 and 2, 1971; (jtly) Metal-catalysis in Industrial Organic Processes, 2006; Greener Fischer-Tropsch Processes, 2013; many research papers in learned jls. *Recreations:* travel, music, reading, walking. *Address:* Department of Chemistry, The University, Sheffield S3 7HF. *T:* (0114) 222 9320.

See also E. Maitlis.

MAJOR; *see* Henniker-Major, family name of Baron Henniker.

MAJOR, Rt Hon. Sir John, KG 2005; CH 1999; PC 1987; Prime Minister and First Lord of the Treasury, and Leader of the Conservative Party, 1990–97; *b* 29 March 1943; *s* of late Thomas Major and Gwendolyn Minnie Coates; *m* 1970, Norma Christina Elizabeth Johnson (*see* Dame N. C. E. Major); one *s* one *d*. *Educ:* Rutlish. AIB. Banker, Standard Chartered Bank: various executive posts in UK and overseas, 1965–79. Member, Lambeth Borough Council, 1968–71 (Chm. Housing Cttee, 1970–71). Contested (C) St Pancras North (Camden), Feb. 1974 and Oct. 1974. MP (C) Huntingdonshire, 1979–83, Huntingdon, 1983–2001. PPS to Ministers of State at the Home Office, 1981–83; an Asst Govt Whip, 1983–84; a Lord Comr of HM Treasury (a Govt Whip), 1984–85; Parly Under-Sec. of State for Social Security, DHSS, 1985–86; Minister of State for Social Security, DHSS, 1986–87; Chief Sec. to HM Treasury, 1987–89; Sec. of State for Foreign and Commonwealth Affairs, 1989; Chancellor of the Exchequer, 1989–90. Jt Sec., Cons. Parly Party Environment Cttee, 1979–81. Pres., Eastern Area Young Conservatives, 1983–85. Mem., Cons. Party Adv. Council, 2003–05. Mem., European Adv. Bd, 1998–2005, Chm., European Bd, 2001–05, Carlyle Gp; Chairman: European Adv. Council, Emerson Electric Co., 1999–; Internat. Adv. Bd, Nat. Bank of Kuwait, 2007–14; Adv. Bd, Global Infrastructure Partners, 2007–; Global Adv. Bd, AECOM, 2011–; Sen. Advr, Credit Suisse (formerly Credit Suisse First Boston), 2001–; non-exec. Dir, Mayflower Corporation, 2000–03; Mem. European Bd, Siebel Systems, Inc., 2001–03. Chm., Ditchley Council, 2000–09; Jt Pres., Chatham House, 2009– (Chm., Panel of Sen. Advrs, 2011–); Pres., Bow Gp, 2012–14. Chm., Campaign Bd, KCL, 2010–. Mem., InterAction Council, Tokyo, 1998–2008. President: Asthma UK (formerly Nat. Asthma Campaign), 1998–; British and Commonwealth Cricket Charitable Trust, 2002–; Res. Action Fund, Prostrate Cancer UK, 2009–; Sir Edward Heath Charitable Foundn Centenary Campaign for Arundells, Educn and the Arts, 2014–; Vice-President: Macmillan Cancer Relief, 2001–; Inst. of Sports Sponsorship, 2001–; Gtr London Fund for the Blind; Hon. Pres., Sight Savers Appeal, 2001–; Chm., Queen Elizabeth Diamond Jubilee Trust, 2011–. Patron: Mercy Ships; Support for Africa 2000; Atlantic Partnership, 2001–; FCO Assoc., 2001–; Professional Cricketers' Assoc., 2001–; Deafblind UK, 2002–; Consortium for Street Children, 2002–; 21st Century Trust, 2002–; Goodman Fund, Chicago, 2002–; Norfolk Cricket Umpires and Scorers Assoc., 2002–; Foundation for Peace (formerly Tim Parry Johnathan Ball Trust, then Tim Parry Johnathan Ball Foundn for Peace), 2004–; Dickie Bird Foundn, 2004–; SeeAbility Sight Pioneers, 2006–13 (Vice President, 2013–); Tory Reform Gp, 2009–; Margaret Thatcher Scholarship Trust, 2012–; British Music Hall Soc., 2012–; Hoxton Hall, 2012–; British Gymnastics, 2013–; Ladybird Boat Trust, 2014–; Conservative Alumni, 2014–; Churchill Alliance, 2015–; Vice-Patron, Atlantic Council of UK; Ambassador: Chance to Shine, 2005–; Right to Sight Prog., Vision 2020, 2005–. Mem.

Bd, Warden Housing Assoc., 1975–83. Member: Bd of Advrs, Baker Inst., Houston, 1998–2005; Internat. Bd of Govs, Peres Center for Peace, Israel, 1997–. Pres., Surrey CCC, 2000–02, now Hon. Life Vice-Pres. Hon. Bencher, Middle Temple, 1993. Hon. Freeman, Merchant Taylor's Co., 2002. Hon. Comr, Sir John A Macdonald Bicentennial Commn, 2012–. Hon. FCIB. Freedom, City of Cork, 2008. Elder Brother, Corp. of Trinity House, 2013. Outstanding Contribn to Ireland Award, Business and Finance Irish Business Awards, 2014. Grand Cordon, Order of the Rising Sun (Japan), 2012. *Publications:* The Autobiography, 1999; More Than a Game: the story of cricket's early years, 2007; My Old Man: a personal history of music hall, 2012. *Recreations:* music, theatre, opera, reading, travel, cricket and other sports. *Address:* PO Box 38506, SW1P 1ZW. *Clubs:* Buck's, Carlton, Farmers, Pratt's, MCC (Mem. Cttee, 2001–04, 2005–08, 2009–11), Surrey CC.

MAJOR, John, LVO 1998; consultant surveyor, 2002–07; General Manager, Borde Hill Estate, 2001–06; *b* 16 June 1945; *s* of John Robert Major and Vera Major; *m* 1967, (Mary) Ruth Oddy; one *s* one *d. Educ:* Wellingborough Sch.; RAC, Cirencester. FRICS 1980. Partner, Osmond Tricks, Bristol, 1980–85; Land Agent, Castle Howard, N Yorks, 1986–91; Land Agent to HM the Queen, Sandringham Estate, 1991–98; Chm., Clegg Kennedy Drew, Land Agents and Chartered Surveyors, 1998–99; Dir, F. P. D. Savills, 2000–01. *Recreations:* travelling, gardening, reading, plant collecting. *Address:* Enjoulet, 31230 Coueilles, France.

MAJOR, Lee E.; *see* Elliot Major.

MAJOR, Dame Malvina (Lorraine), ONZ 2012; GNZM 2009 (PCNZM 2008); DBE 1991 (OBE 1985); opera singer; Senior Fellow, University of Waikato, New Zealand, since 2012; *b* 28 Jan. 1943; *d* of Vincent William Major and Eva Gwendolen (*née* McCaw); *m* 1965, Winston William Richard Fleming (*d* 1990); one *s* two *d. Educ:* Hamilton Technical Coll.; London Opera Centre. ATCL, LTCL; LRSM. Studied with Dame Sister Mary Leo, Auckland; winner: NZ Mobil Song Quest, 1963; Melbourne Sun Aria Contest, Australia, 1964; Kathleen Ferrier Award, London, 1966. Camden Fest., London; Salzburg Fest., 1968 (internat. début as Rosina in Barber of Seville), 1969, 1991; returned to NZ, 1970; La Finta Giardiniera, Th. de la Monnaie, Brussels, 1985; Vienna, Amsterdam, New York, Antwerp, Salt Lake City, 1986; Don Giovanni, Drottningholm, Brighton Fest., 1987; Covent Garden début as Rosalinde in Die Fledermaus, 1990; with Australian Opera, and in E Berlin, 30 rôles, including: La Bohème; Madame Butterfly; Faust; Il Seraglio; Rigoletto; Don Pasquale; Lucia di Lammermoor; Magic Flute; Tosca; Merry Widow; La Traviata; Eugene Onegin; Elisabetta Regina d'Inghilterra; Marriage of Figaro; also extensive concert repertoire, TV and recordings. Established Dame Malvina Major Foundn for educn in performing arts, 1992. Prof. of Voice, Univ. of Canterbury, Christchurch, 2003–11. Hon. DLitt Massey, 1993; Hon. Dr Waikato, 1994. Entertainer and Internat. Performer of the Year, NZ, 1992; NZ Classical Disc Award, 1993 and 1994. *Recreations:* golf, sewing, family. *Address:* c/o Dame Malvina Major Foundation, PO Box 9976, Wellington 6141, New Zealand.

MAJOR, Dame Norma (Christina Elizabeth), DBE 1999; *b* 12 Feb. 1942; *d* of late Norman Wagstaff and Edith Johnson; *m* 1970, Rt Hon. Sir John Major, *qv*; one *s* one *d. Educ:* Peckham Sch. for Girls; Battersea Coll. of Domestic Science (Teachers' Cert.). Teacher, Sydenham Sch. and St Michael and All Angels Sch., Camberwell, 1963–70. Campaigned with husband, 7 Gen. Elecns, 1974–97. A Nat. Vice Pres., Mencap, 1995– (Pres., Mencap Challenge Fund, 1992–2002; Pres., Huntingdon, Mencap, 1987–2009 (Hon. Pres., 2013); Patron, Cambs, Mencap, 2009–13); Mem. Bd, WNO, 1999–2003; Mem., League of Mercy, 2004–; Patron: Crossroads Care, 1991–2013; Renton Foundn, 1992–; English Schs Orch., 2005–; Spinal Res. Trust, 1996–2011; Rowan Foundn, 1998–; Mercy Ships; Penfold Trust, 2000–; Shakespeare at The George, Huntingdon, 2006–; Hon. Patron, Joan Sutherland and Richard Bonynge Opera Foundn, 2011–. FRSA 2004. Paul Harris Fellow, Rotary Club, 2007. *Publications:* Joan Sutherland, 1987; Chequers: the Prime Minister's country house and its history, 1996. *Recreations:* opera, theatre, reading. *Address:* PO Box 38506, SW1P 1ZW.

MAJOR, Pamela Ann; HM Diplomatic Service, retired; freelance coach and HR consultant, since 2010; *b* 4 March 1959; *d* of Arthur and Mary Major; *m* 1992, (Robert) Leigh Turner, *qv*; one *s* one *d. Educ:* Hertford Coll., Oxford (BA Russian and French 1981); Bradford Univ. (Post-grad. Dip. Interpreting and Translating 1982); Leicester Univ. (MA Employment Relns and Labour Law 2000). Entered FCO, 1982; Second Sec., Beijing, 1986–88; FCO, 1988–92; First Sec., Moscow, 1992–95; FCO, 1995–2002 (special unpaid leave, 1998–2002); Counsellor (EU and Econ.), Berlin, 2002–06; Equality and Human Rights Commn (on secondment), 2007; Hd of Coaching and Asst Dir, Recruitment and Develt, FCO, 2008–10. Accredited coach, Internat. Coach Fedn, 2009. *Recreations:* theatre, walking, tennis, dance, reading.

MAJOR, Riel Meredith; *see* Karmy-Jones, R. M.

MAK, Alan; MP (C) Havant, since 2015; *b* York, 19 Nov. 1983. *Educ:* St Peter's Sch., York; Peterhouse, Cambridge (BA Hons Law 2005); Oxford Inst. of Legal Practice (DipLP 2006). Parly researcher, Hon. Ed Vaizey, MP, 2006–07; Trainee Solicitor, 2007–09, Solicitor, 2009–14, Clifford Chance LLP; Founder, two small businesses, 2014. Chm., All Party Parly Gp for Entrepreneurship, 2015–. Trustee, Magic Breakfast, 2009–15 (Pres., 2011–15); Founder and Chm., Young Professionals' Br., RBL, 2011–15. FRSA 2008. *Recreations:* watching and playing sport, films, travel. *Address:* House of Commons, SW1A 0AA. *T:* (020) 7219 3000. *E:* alan.mak.mp@parliament.uk.

MAK, Prof. Tak Wah, OC 2000; OOnt 2007; FRS 1994; FRSC 1986; University Professor, University of Toronto, since 1997, Senior Scientist and Director, Advanced Medical Discovery Institute, since 2002, and Director, Campbell Family Institute for Breast Cancer Research, Ontario Cancer Institute, since 2004, University Health Network, Toronto; *b* Canton, China, 4 Oct. 1946; *s* of Kent and Linda Mak; *m* 1969, Shirley Lau; two *d. Educ:* Univ. of Wisconsin (BSc 1967; MSc 1969); Univ. of Alberta (PhD 1972). Research Assistant: Univ. of Wisconsin, Madison, 1967–69; Univ. of Alberta, 1969–72; University of Toronto: Postdoctoral Fellow, 1972–74; Asst Prof., 1974–78; Associate Prof., 1978–84; Prof., 1984–. Founding Dir, Amgen Inst., 1993–2002. Gairdner Internat. Award, Gairdner Foundn, 1989; Novartis Immunol. Prize, Novartis Inc., 1998; Killam Prize, Canada Council, 2003. *Publications:* (ed) Molecular and Cellular Biology of Hemopolitic Stem Cell Differentiation, 1981; (ed) Molecular and Cellular Biology of Neiplasia, 1983; (ed) Cancer: perspective for control, 1986; (ed) The T Receptor, 1987; (ed) AIDS: ten years later, 1991; (with J. L. Simard) Handbook of Immune Response Genes, 1998; (jtly) The Gene Knockout Facts Book, 1998; contrib. Cell, Science, Nature and other learned jls. *Address:* (home) 25 Elgin Avenue, Toronto, ON M5R 1G5, Canada; (office) Princess Margaret Hospital, 620 University Avenue, Room 7–706, Toronto, ON M5G 2C1, Canada.

MAKAROVA, Natalia; dancer and choreographer; *b* Leningrad, 21 Nov. 1940; *m* 1976, Edward Karkar; one *s. Educ:* Vaganova Ballet Sch.; Leningrad Choreographic Sch. Mem., Kirov Ballet, 1959–70; London début, as Giselle, Covent Garden, 1961; joined American Ballet Theatre, 1970; formed dance co., Makarova & Co., 1980; Guest Artist: Royal Ballet, Covent Garden, 1972; London Festival Ballet, 1984. Has danced many classical and contemporary rôles in UK, Europe and USA, 1970–92; appearances include: La Bayadère (which she also staged, and choreographed in part), NY Met, 1980, Manchester, 1985, Royal Opera House, Covent Gdn, 1989; On Your Toes, London and NY, 1984–86; choreographed new productions: Swan Lake, for London Fest. Ballet, London and tour, 1988; Sleeping Beauty, La Bayadère, for Royal Ballet, 2003. Honoured Artist of RSFSR, 1970; Kennedy Center Honors, 2012. *Publications:* A Dance Autobiography, 1979; On Your Toes, 1984. *Address:* 323 Marina Boulevard, San Francisco, CA 94123–1213, USA.

MAKEHAM, Peter Derek James, CB 2003; independent consultant, since 2011; Director General, Strategy (formerly Performance) and International, Home Office, 2006–11; *b* 15 March 1948; *s* of Derrick James Stark Makeham and Margaret Helene Makeham; *m* 1972, Carolyne Rosemary Dawe (marr. diss. 2002); one *s* three *d. Educ:* Chichester High Sch. for Boys; Nottingham Univ. (BA); Leeds Univ. (MA Lab Econs). Economist, Dept of Employment, 1971–82; on secondment to Unilever, 1982–83; HM Treasury, 1983–84; Enterprise Unit, Cabinet Office, 1984–85; Dept of Employment, 1985–87; DTI, 1987–90; Department of Employment, then Department for Education and Employment, subseq. Department for Education and Skills, 1990–2006: Head of Strategy and Employment Policy Div., 1992–95; Director: Employment and Adult Trng, 1995–97; School Orgn and Funding, 1997–99; Teachers Gp, 1999–2000; Dir Gen., Finance and Analytical Services, 2000–06; Dir Gen., Strategy and Reform, 2006–11. *Recreation:* sailing.

MAKEKA, Felleng Mamakeka; High Commissioner of Lesotho in the United Kingdom, also accredited to Spain, Portugal, Malta and Cyprus, since 2013; *b* Thaba Phatsoa, Lesotho, 11 Feb. 1953; *d* of Nchocho Ntšekhe; *m* 1975, Sen. Advocate Thabo Romeo Makeka (*d* 2012); three *s* one *d. Educ:* Univ. of Botswana, Lesotho and Swaziland (Dip. Develt Studies); Univ. of Dist of Columbia (BA Econs); City Univ. of New York (MA Econs). Sen. Economist, Lesotho Nat. Develt Corp., 1988–2003; Economist, Lesotho Investment Promotion Centre, 1996; Dir, Investment Promotion, 2003–05, Actg Chief Exec., 2005–06, Lesotho Tourism Develt Corp.; Vice-Chm., Queen's Nat. Trust Fund, Lesotho, 2006–07; Founder, Owner, Business and Investment Facilitation Services, 2007–08; Owner, Manager, Felleng's Blooming Place (garden centre and events venue), 2006–. Internat. PR Officer, Fedn of Lesotho Women Entrepreneurs, 2011–. *Recreations:* debating international political economy issues, listening to political and parliamentary debates, gardening, entertaining family and friends, reading. *Address:* Lesotho High Commission, 7 Chesham Place, SW1X 8HN. *T:* (020) 7201 8183, *Fax:* (020) 7235 5023. *E:* lesotholondon@gmail.com.

MAKEPEACE, John, OBE 1988; FCSD; FRSA; designer and furniture maker, since 1961; Founder and Director, The Parnham Trust and Parnham College (formerly School for Craftsmen in Wood), 1977–2000; *b* 6 July 1939; *m* 1st, 1964, Ann Sutton (marr. diss. 1979); 2nd, 1983, Jennie Moores (*née* Brinsden). *Educ:* Denstone Coll., Staffs. Study tours: Scandinavia 1957; N America, 1961; Italy, 1968; W Africa, 1972; USA, 1974; Japan, 1994; Yunnan, China, 2005. Fellow: Arts Univ., Bournemouth, 2007; Hereford Coll. of Arts, 2013. Furniture in private and corporate collections in Europe, USA, Asia and S Africa. *Public collections:* Cardiff Museum; Fitzwilliam Museum, Cambridge; Leeds Museum; Court Room, Worshipful Co. of Innholders; Board Room, Grosvenor Estate Holdings; Art Inst., Chicago; Museum für Kunsthandwerk, Frankfurt; Royal Museum of Scotland; V & A Museum; Lewis Collection, Richmond, USA; Banque Générale du Luxembourg; Crab Tree Farm, Chicago. *Exhibitions:* Herbert Art Gall., Coventry, 1963; New Art Centre, London, 1971; Fine Art Soc., London, 1977; Interior, Kortrijk, Belgium, 1978, 1992, 1994; Royal Show, Stoneleigh, 1981–87; Crafts Council Open, 1984; National Theatre, 1980, 1986; Parnham at Smiths Gall., 1988–91; Sotheby's, 1988, 1992, 1993, 1997; New Art Forms, Chicago, 1989–92; Tokyo, 1990; ARCO, Madrid, 1993; Chicago Contemporary Art Fair, 1993–96; Art '93, London; Conservation by Design, Providence, USA, 1993; Creation, Claridge's, 1994; Banque de Luxembourg, 1995; British Embassy, Brussels, 1995; Smithsonian Instn, 1996; Rotunda, Hong Kong, 1996; Chicago Design Show, 1997; Mayor Gall., 1997; Great British Design, Cologne, 1997; Crafts Council, 1999, 2002; Maastricht Fair, 1999–2001; Sotheby's Contemporary Decorative Arts, 2000; Modern Collectibles, London, 2003; Collect, London at Saatchi Gall., 2004, 2007, 2008, 2014, 2015; Grosvenor House Art and Antiques Fair, 2005; Internat. Expo. of Sculpture, Objects and Functional Art, Chicago, 2007; Arts Council Retrospective, John Makepeace: Enriching the Language of Furniture (tour), 2010–11; Somerset House, 2011; The Power of Making, V&A Mus., 2012; British Design 1948–2012, V&A Mus., 2012; Gall. NAGA, Boston, 2012; Pritam and Eames Gall., E Hampton, NY, 2012; Design, Shanghai, 2014. *Consultancies/Lectures:* Crafts Council (and Mem.), 1972–77; India Handicrafts Bd, 1975; Jammu and Kashmir Govt, 1977; Belgrade Univ., 1978; Artist in Context, V&A Mus., 1979; Chm., Wood Programme, World Crafts Conf., Kyoto, Japan, 1979; Australian Crafts Council, 1980; Oxford Farming Conf., 1990; Cheongju Internat. Craft Biennale 2001, Korea. Trustee, V & A Mus., 1987–91. *Films:* Made by Makepeace (filmed by John Read), 1975; History of English Furniture, 1978; Heritage in Danger, 1979; First Edition, 1980; Touch Wood, 1982; Tomorrow's World, 1986; Essays in Wood, 2010; Objects of Desire, 2012. Winner, Observer Kitchen Design, 1971; Hooke Park Winner, UK Conservation Award, 1987; British Construction Industry Award, 1990; Amer. Inst. of Archts Award, 1993; Award of Distinction, 2002, Lifetime Achievement Award, 2004, Furniture Soc. of USA; Claxton Stevens Award, 2009, Lifetime Achievement Award, 2010, Furniture Makers' Co. *Relevant publication:* John Makepeace: a spirit of adventure in craft and design, by Jeremy Myerson, 1995; John Makepeace: enriching the language of furniture, by Jeremy Myerson, 2010; Furniture with Soul, by David Savage, 2011; Handmade in Britain, by Joanna Norman, 2012. *Recreations:* friends, travel, garden design, sylviculture, contemporary art. *Address:* Farrs, Beaminster, Dorset DT8 3NB. *T:* (01308) 862204. *W:* www.johnmakepeacefurniture.com. *Club:* Athenæum.

MAKEPEACE, Richard Edward, CMG 2011; HM Diplomatic Service, retired; Registrar, Oxford Centre for Islamic Studies, since 2011; Fellow, St Cross College, Oxford, since 2011; *b* 24 June 1953; *s* of late Edward Dugard Makepeace and of Patricia Muriel Makepeace; *m* 1980, Rupmani Catherine Pradhan; two *s. Educ:* St Paul's Sch.; Keble Coll., Oxford. Joined FCO, 1976; MECAS, 1977–78; Muscat, 1979–81; Prague, 1981–85; FCO, 1985–86; Private Sec. to Parly Under-Sec. of State, FCO, 1987–88; UK Perm. Repn to EC, 1989–93; Dep. Head, Personnel Mgt Dept, FCO, 1993–95; Counsellor and Dep. Hd of Mission, Cairo, 1995–98; Ambassador to Sudan, 1999–2002; Ambassador to UAE, 2003–06; Consul-Gen., Jerusalem, 2006–10. *Recreations:* travel, reading, scuba diving. *Address:* Oxford Centre for Islamic Studies, George Street, Oxford OX1 2AR.

MAKGILL, family name of **Viscount of Oxfuird**.

MAKGOBA, Most Rev. Thabo Cecil; *see* Cape Town, Archbishop of.

MAKHLOUF, Gabriel; Chief Executive and Secretary, New Zealand Treasury, since 2011 (Deputy Chief Executive, 2010–11); *b* 3 Feb. 1960; *s* of Antoine Makhlouf and Aïda Makhlouf (*née* Lazian); *m* 1984, Sandy Cope; one *s. Educ:* Prior Park Coll., Bath; Univ. of Exeter (BA Hons Econs); Univ. of Bath (MSc Industrial Relns). Board of Inland Revenue: HM Inspector of Taxes, 1984–89; Policy Advr, 1989–92; Head of Secretariat, Change Mgt Gp, 1992–93; Head of Direct Tax Br., Fiscal Policy, HM Treasury, 1993–95; Asst Dir, Personal Tax Div., Bd of Inland Revenue, 1995–97; HM Treasury: Principal Private Sec. to Chancellor of Exchequer, 1997–98; Head, Work Incentives and Poverty Analysis, 1998; Dir, Internat., 1998–2003, Capital and Savings, 2003–05, Bd of Inland Revenue; Dir, Debt Mgt and Banking, HMRC, 2005–08; Dir, Banking Services, HM Revenue and Customs, 2008–10. Chm., Cttee on Fiscal Affairs, OECD, 2000–04. Hon. FICM. *Address:* New Zealand Treasury, 1 The Terrace, Wellington 6011, New Zealand.

MAKHULU, Most Rev. Walter Paul Khotso, CMG 2000; Archbishop of Central Africa, 1980–2000, now Emeritus; Bishop of Botswana, 1979–2000; an Honorary Assistant Bishop, Diocese of London, since 2003; *b* Johannesburg, 1935; *m* 1966, Rosemary Sansom; one *s* one *d. Educ:* St Peter's Theological Coll., Rosettenville; Selly Oak Colls, Birmingham. Deacon 1957, priest 1958, Johannesburg; Curate: Johannesburg, 1957–60; Botswana, 1961–63; St Carantoc's Mission, Francistown, Botswana, 1961–63; St Andrew's Coll., Selly Oak, Birmingham, 1963–64; Curate: All Saints, Poplar, 1964–66; St Silas, Pentonville, with St Clement's, Barnsbury, 1966–68; Vicar of St Philip's, Battersea, 1968–75; Secretary for E Africa, WCC, 1975–79. A President: WCC, 1983–91; All Africa Conf. of Churches, 1981–86. Hon. DD: Kent, 1988; Gen. Theol Seminary, NY, 1990. Officier, Ordre des Palmes Académiques (France), 1981; PH 2000; Order of St Mellitus, 2008.

MAKIN, Claire Margaret, FRICS; business consultant; *b* 21 March 1951; *d* of late James Ernest Makin, CBE and Mary Makin (*née* Morris); *m* 1978, David Anthony Bowman. *Educ:* City Univ. (MBA). FRICS 1988; ACIArb 1985. Partner, Richard Ellis, 1978–90; Consultant, Price Waterhouse, 1990–91; Partner, Bernard Thorpe, 1991–93; Dir, DTZ Debenham Thorpe, 1993–95; Chief Exec., RICS, 1995–97; Chambers Dir, 13 King's Bench Walk, 1998–2001. FRSA 1991. *Recreations:* travelling, food and wine, restoring old houses. *Address:* 66 Alder Lodge, River Gardens, 73 Stevenage Road, SW6 6NR.

MAKINS, family name of **Baron Sherfield**.

MAKINSON, John Crowther, CBE 2001; Chairman, Penguin Random House, since 2013 (Chairman and Chief Executive, Penguin Group, 2002–13); *b* 10 Oct. 1954; *s* of Kenneth Crowther Makinson and Phyllis Georgina Makinson (*née* Miller); *m* 1st, 1985, Virginia Clare Macbeth (marr. diss. 2012); two *d*; 2nd, 2012, Nandana Dev Sen. *Educ:* Repton Sch.; Christ's Coll., Cambridge (BA Hons). Journalist: Reuters, 1976–79; Financial Times, 1979–86; Vice Chm., Saatchi & Saatchi (US), 1986–89; Partner, Makinson Cowell, 1989–94; Man. Dir, Financial Times, 1994–96; Finance Dir, Pearson plc, 1996–2002. Chm. Trustees, IPPR, 2008–10. Chm., Nat. Th., 2010–. *Recreations:* music, cooking. *Address:* 6 York Buildings, WC2N 6JN.

MAKKAWI, Dr Khalil; Chevalier, Order of Cedar, Lebanon; Chairman, Lebanese Palestinian Dialogue Committee, 2005–10; Ambassador and Permanent Representative of Lebanon to the United Nations, New York, 1990–94; *b* 15 Jan. 1930; *s* of Abdel Basset Makkawi and Rosa Makkawi; *m* 1958, Zahira Sibaei; one *s* one *d*. *Educ:* Amer. Univ. of Beirut (BA Polit. Science); Cairo Univ. (MA Polit. Science); Columbia Univ., NY, USA (PhD Internat. Relations). Joined Lebanese Min. of Foreign Affairs, 1957; UN Section at Min., 1957–59; Attaché to Perm. Mission of Lebanon to UN, New York, 1959, Dep. Perm. Rep., 1961–64; First Sec., Washington, 1964–66; Chief of Internat. Relations Dept, Min. of For. Affairs, Beirut, 1967–70; Counsellor, London, 1970–71; Minister Plenipotentiary, London, 1971–73; Ambassador to: German Democratic Republic, 1973–78; Court of St James's, and Republic of Ireland, 1979–83; Dir of Political Dept, Min. of Foreign Affairs, Beirut, 1983–85; Amb. to Italy, and Permanent Rep. to UNFAO, 1985–90. Mem., Lebanese Delegn to UN Gen. Assembly Meetings, 14th–39th Session; Chairman of Lebanese Delegations to: Confs and Councils, FAO, 1985–89; Governing Councils, IFAD, 1985–89; 16th Ministerial Meeting, Islamic conf. in Fès, 1986; 8th Summit Conf. of Non-Aligned Countries, Harare, 1986; Ministerial Meeting, Mediterranean Mems, Non-Aligned Countries, Brioni, Yugoslavia, 1987; IMO Conf., Rome, 1988; Vice-Pres., Lebanese delegn to ME peace negotiations, Washington, 1993–94. A Vice-Chm., Exec. Bd, UNICEF, 1993–95, Pres., 1995–96. Pres., Worldwide Alumni Assoc., Amer. Univ. of Beirut, 2007–11. Grand Cross of Merit (Italian Republic). *Recreations:* sports, music. *Address:* c/o Ministry of Foreign Affairs, Beirut, Lebanon.

MAKLOUF, Raphael David; sculptor; painter; Chairman, Tower Mint, since 1975; *b* Jerusalem, 10 Dec. 1937; *m* 1968, Marillyn Christian Lewis, *d* of Gwilym Hugh Lewis, DFC; two *s* one *d*. *Educ:* studied art at Camberwell School of Art, under Karel Vogel, 1953–58. Official commissions: Tower of London, Carnegie Hall, NY, etc. Portrait effigy of the Queen on all UK and Commonwealth coinage minted 1985–97, on Britannia gold coins minted 1989–97. Bronze portraits of the Queen, 1988, at Royal Nat. Theatre, Richmond Riverside Develt and Westminster Sch. Science Building, unveiled by the Queen. 15 Stations of Cross for new Brentwood Cathedral, 1992. Sitters have included: HM Queen; HRH Prince Philip; Rt Hon. Margaret Thatcher. Designs for National Trust and English Heritage. FRSA 1985. Fellow, Univ. of the Arts London, 2003. *Address:* 3 St Helena Terrace, Richmond, Surrey TW9 1NR. *Clubs:* City Livery, Garrick, Chelsea Arts; Riverside Racquets Centre.

MAKSYMIUK, Jerzy; conductor; Chief Conductor, 1983–93, Conductor Laureate, 1993, BBC Scottish Symphony Orchestra; *b* Grodno, Poland, 9 April 1936. *Educ:* Warsaw Conservatory. First Prize, Paderewski Piano Comp., 1964; worked at Warsaw Grand Theatre, 1970–72; founded Polish Chamber Orchestra, 1972; UK début, 1977; toured all over world incl. European festivals of Aix-en-Provence and Vienna and BBC Promenade concerts; Principal Conductor, Polish Nat. Radio Orch., 1975–77; toured extensively in E Europe and USA; has conducted orchestras in Europe, USA and Japan including: Orch. Nat. de France, Tokyo Metropolitan Symphony, Ensemble Orchestral de Paris, Israel Chamber Orch., Rotterdam Philharmonic and Hong Kong Philharmonic; in UK has conducted BBC Welsh and BBC Philharmonic Orchs, CBSO, LSO, London Philharmonic, ENO, Bournemouth Sinfonietta and Royal Liverpool Phil. Orch.; début for ENO with Don Giovanni, London Coliseum, 1990. Has made numerous recordings. Hon. DLitt Strathclyde, 1990.

MALAHIDE, Patrick; *see* Duggan, P. G.

MALAM, Colin Albert; freelance football writer, Sunday Mirror, 2009–14; *b* 16 Oct. 1938; *s* of Albert and Irene Malam; *m* 1971, Jacqueline Cope; four *s*. *Educ:* Liverpool Inst. High Sch. for Boys; Sidney Sussex Coll., Cambridge (BA Hons History). Trainee, Liverpool Daily Post and Echo, 1961–64; News Reporter, Birmingham Post, 1964–65; Press Officer: Westward TV, 1965–66; GEC (Telecommunications) Ltd, Coventry, 1966; Football Writer, later Football Correspondent, Birmingham Post, 1966–70; Football Writer, The Sun, 1970–73; Football Correspondent, 1973–2003, freelance football writer, 2003–09, Sunday Telegraph. *Publications:* World Cup Argentina, 1978; Gary Lineker: strikingly different, 1993; (with Terry Venables) The Best Game in the World, 1996; The Magnificent Obsession: Keegan, Sir John Hall, Newcastle and sixty million pounds, 1997; (with Malcolm Macdonald) Supermac: my autobiography, 2003; Clown Prince of Soccer?: the Len Shackleton story, 2004; The Boy Wonders: Wayne Rooney, Duncan Edwards and the changing face of football, 2006. *Recreations:* DIY, listening to music, especially jazz, reading anything, watching cricket.

MALAND, David; barrister; *b* 6 Oct. 1929; *s* of Rev. Gordon Albert Maland and Florence Maud Maland (*née* Bosence); *m* 1953, Edna Foulsham; two *s*. *Educ:* Kingswood Sch.; Wadham Coll., Oxford (BA Hons Mod. Hist., 1951; MA 1957; Robert Herbert Meml Prize Essay, 1959); City Univ. (Dip. Law (ext.) 1985). Nat. service commn RAF, 1951–53. Asst Master, Brighton Grammar Sch., 1953–56; Senior History Master, Stamford Sch., 1957–66; Headmaster: Cardiff High Sch., 1966–68; Denstone Coll., 1969–78; High Master, Manchester Grammar Sch., 1978–85. Schoolmaster Commoner, Merton Coll., Oxford, 1975. Chm., Assisted Places Sub-Cttee of Headmasters' Conf., 1982–83. Called to the Bar, Gray's Inn, 1986; in practice, 1987–95. Gen. Gov., British Nutrition Foundn, 1987–95. Governor: Stonyhurst Coll., 1973–80; Abingdon Sch., 1979–91; GPDST, 1984–88. *Publications:* Europe in the Seventeenth Century, 1966; Culture and Society in Seventeenth Century France, 1970; Europe in the Sixteenth Century, 1973; Europe at War, 1600–1650, 1980; (trans.) La Guerre de Trente Ans, by Pagès, 1971; articles and reviews in History. *Address:* Flat 9, Meadsway, Staveley Road, Eastbourne BN20 7LH. *Club:* Athenæum.

MALBON, Vice-Adm. Sir Fabian (Michael), KBE 2001; Lieutenant Governor and Commander-in-Chief of Guernsey, 2005–11; *b* 1 Oct. 1946; *s* of Rupert Charles Malbon and June Marion Downie; *m* 1969, Susan Thomas; three *s*. *Educ:* Brighton, Hove and Sussex Grammar Sch. Joined RN, Dartmouth, 1965; jun. postings, 1969–82; CO, HMS Torquay, 1982–84; MoD, 1984; Comdr Sea Training, 1985–87; CO, HMS Brave, 1987–88; Dir, Naval Service Conditions, MoD, 1988–90; RCDS 1991; CO, HMS Invincible, 1992–93; Naval Sec. and CE Naval Manning Agency, MoD, 1996–98; Dep. C-in-C, Fleet, 1999–2001; Dir, TOPMAST, 2001–02. President: CCF Assoc., 2003–08; Royal Naval Benevolent Trust, 2007–13; Union Jack Club, 2011–. Trustee, Chesil Sailing Trust, 2014–. Mem., RNSA. *Recreations:* sailing, walking.

MALCOLM, Rt Hon. Lord; Colin Malcolm Campbell; PC 2015; a Senator of the College of Justice in Scotland, since 2007; *b* 1 Oct. 1953; *s* of Malcolm Donald Campbell and Annabella Ferguson or Campbell; *m* 1977, Fiona Anderson; one *s* one *d* (and one *d* decd). *Educ:* Grove Acad., Broughty Ferry; Univ. of Dundee (LLB). Passed Advocate, 1977; QC (Scot.) 1990. Lectr, Dept of Scots Law, Univ. of Edinburgh, 1977–79; Standing Junior Counsel: to Scottish Develt Dept (all matters other than Planning), 1984–86; to Scottish Develt Dept (Planning), 1986–90. Vice-Dean, Faculty of Advocates, 1997–2001 (Dean of Faculty, 2001–04). Part-time Mem., Mental Welfare Commn for Scotland, 1997–2001; Mem., Judicial Appts Bd for Scotland, 2002–05. *Address:* Supreme Courts, Parliament House, 11 Parliament Square, Edinburgh EH1 1RQ. *T:* (0131) 225 2595.

MALCOLM, Prof. Alan David Blair, DPhil; CBiol, FRSB, FRSC, FIFST; Chief Executive, Institute of Biology, 1998–2009; *b* 5 Nov. 1944; *s* of late David Malcolm and Helena Malcolm (*née* Blair); *m* 1972, Susan Waller; two *d*. *Educ:* King's Coll. Sch., Wimbledon; Merton Coll., Oxford (MA, DPhil 1970). FIFST 1994; FRSB (FIBiol 1997); FRSC 2004. Demonstrator, Oxford Univ., 1969–72; EMBO Fellow, Max-Planck-Institute, 1971; Lectr, Univ. of Glasgow, 1972–76; St Mary's Hospital Medical School: Lectr, 1976–79; Sen. Lectr, 1979–81; Reader, 1981–84; Prof. of Biochem., Charing Cross and Westminster Med. Sch., 1984–92; Dir Gen., Flour Milling and Baking Res. Assoc., 1992–94; Dir, BBSRC Inst. of Food Res., 1994–98. Vis. Fellow, Yale Univ., 1982; Hon. Res. Fellow, UCL, 1984–89. Vice-Chm., Technol. Foresight Food and Drink Panel, 1995–99; Member: MAFF Food Adv. Cttee, 1995–2001; EU Standing Cttee on Fruit and Vegetables, 1998–; Adv. Cttee on Novel Foods and Processes, 2002–07; UK Deleg. to Eur. Cttee of Biol Assocs, 1998–; Council, Parly and Scientific Cttee, 2000– (Vice-Pres., 2003–12; Exec. Sec., 2012–); Expert Advisor: H of C Select Cttee on Genetically Modified Organisms, 1999; H of L Eur. Affairs Cttee on GM Labelling, 2002. Chm., Res. and Scientific Cttee, Arthritis and Rheumatism Council, 1990–92; Mem., Royal Soc. Cttee on Genetically Modified Organisms, 1998; Scientific Gov., 1995–, Vice-Chm. Council, 1996–98, Chm., 1998–2000, British Nutrition Foundn; Director: Assured Food Standards, 2002–; Sci. Council, 2003–; Chairman: Adv. Bd, ESRC Centre for Econ. and Social Aspects of Genomics, 2008–; Trustees, British Nut Foundn, 2010–12. Dir, Oxford Internat. Biomed. Centre, 2008–12. Chm., Biochemical Soc., 1992–95. Mem. Court, ICSTM, Univ. of London, 1998–2007. Member Editorial Board: Internat. Jl Food Science Nutrition, 1997–; Pesticide Outlook, 1998– (Chm., 2002–03); Outlook on Agriculture, 1999–; Science in Parliament, 2003– (Ed., 2012–). *Publications:* Enzymes, 1971; Molecular Medicine, vol. 1, 1984, vol. 2, 1987; numerous articles, symposia, etc. *Address:* 12 Earl's Court Square, SW5 9DP. *T:* (020) 7373 9505.

MALCOLM, Col Sir Alexander James Elton, 13th Bt *cr* 1665 (NS), of Balbedie and Innertiel, co. Fife; OBE 2000; *b* 30 Aug. 1956; *er s* of Sir James William Thomas Alexander, 12th Bt and Gillian Heather (*née* Humpherus); *S* father, 2012; *m* 1982, Virginia Elizabeth Coxon; two *s* one *d*. *Educ:* Eton; RMA Sandhurst. Col Welsh Guards. *Heir:* *s* Edward Alexander Humpherus Malcolm, *b* 28 Sept. 1984.

MALCOLM, Derek Elliston Michael; Film Critic: The Guardian, 1971–97; London Evening Standard, since 2003; President: International Film Critics, 1990–2001 (Chairman, UK Section, since 1982); British Federation of Film Societies, since 1993; *b* 12 May 1932; *s* of J. Douglas Malcolm and Dorothy Taylor; *m* 1st, 1962, Barbara Ibbott (marr. diss. 1966); one *d*; 2nd, 1994, Sarah Gristwood. *Educ:* Eton; Merton College, Oxford (BA Hons Hist.). Actor, amateur rider (National Hunt), 1953–56; Drama Critic, Gloucestershire Echo, 1956–62; Sub-Editor, The Guardian, 1962–69; Racing correspondent, The Guardian, 1969–71. Dir, London Internat. Film Fest., 1982–84. Gov., BFI, 1989–92. Pres., Critics' Circle of UK, 1980 (Chm., Film Section, 1978–81). Internat. Publishing Cos Critic of the Year, 1972. *Publications:* Robert Mitchum, 1984; A Century of Films, 2001; Family Secrets, 2003. *Recreations:* cricket, tennis, squash, music. *Address:* 28 Avenue Road, Highgate, N6 5DW. *T:* (020) 8348 2013; The Dower House, Hull Place, Sholden, Kent CT14 0AQ. *T:* (01304) 364614. *E:* derekmalcolm@aol.com.

MALCOLM, Helen Katharine Lucy; QC 2006; a Recorder, since 2005; a Deputy High Court Judge, since 2013; *b* 2 Jan. 1962; *d* of Dugald Malcolm and Patricia Malcolm; *m* 1987; one *s* two *d*. *Educ:* New Coll., Oxford (BA 1983). Called to the Bar, Gray's Inn, 1986, Bencher, 2011. *Recreations:* food, horses, ski-ing. *Address:* 3 Raymond Buildings, Gray's Inn, WC1R 5BH. *T:* (020) 7400 6400. *E:* helen.malcolm@3rblaw.com.

MALCOLM, James Ian, OBE 1995; HM Diplomatic Service, retired; travel photographer, including of the Panama Canal; *b* 29 March 1946; *e s* of late William Kenneth Malcolm and Jennie Malcolm (*née* Cooper); *m* 1967, Sheila Nicholson Moore; one *s* one *d*. *Educ:* Royal High Sch., Edinburgh. Joined Foreign Office, 1966; UKDEL NATO, Brussels, 1969–72; Burma, 1972–74; FCO, 1974–77; Commercial Attaché, Kenya, 1977–80; Consul, Syria, 1980–83; Second Sec. (Commercial), Angola, 1983–85; Second, later First, Sec., FCO, 1985–87; First Secretary: (Political/Econ.), Indonesia, 1987–94; FCO, 1994–97; Dep. High Comr, Jamaica, 1997–2001; Ambassador, Panama, 2002–06. Has exhibited as photographer, incl. Edinburgh Fringe Fest. 2010 and contrib. Panama Passages exhibn, Smithsonian Mus., Washington DC, 2009–10; photographer, Panama Maritime Rev., 2007–. Orden de Vasco Nunez de Balboa (Panama), 2007. *Recreations:* riding motorcycles, photography. *Address:* 8/14 Portland Gardens, Britannia Quay, Leith, Edinburgh EH6 6NJ. *Clubs:* Royal Over-Seas League; Rotary (Edinburgh).

MALCOLM, Sir Noel Robert, Kt 2014; PhD; FBA 2001; historian; Fellow of All Souls College, Oxford, since 2002; *b* 26 Dec. 1956. *Educ:* Eton; Peterhouse, Cambridge (BA 1978; Hon. Fellow, 2010); Trinity Coll., Cambridge; Gonville and Caius Coll., Cambridge (MA 1981; PhD 1983). Fellow, Gonville and Caius Coll., Cambridge, 1981–88; political columnist, 1987–91, Foreign Editor, 1991–92, The Spectator; political columnist, Daily Telegraph, 1992–95. Vis. Fellow, St Antony's Coll., Oxford, 1995–96; Vis. Lectr, Harvard, 1999; Carlyle Lectr, Oxford, 2001. Chm., Bosnian Inst., 1997–. FRSL 1997. *Publications:* De Dominis 1560–1624, 1984; George Enescu: his life and music, 1990; Sense on Sovereignty, 1991; Bosnia: a short history, 1994; (ed) The Correspondence of Thomas Hobbes, 2 vols, 1994; The Origins of English Nonsense, 1997; Kosovo: a short history, 1998; (jtly) Books on Bosnia: a critical bibliography, 1999; Aspects of Hobbes, 2002; Agents of Empire: knights, corsairs, jesuits and spies in the sixteenth-century Mediterranean world, 2015. *Address:* All Souls College, Oxford OX1 4AL.

MALCOLM of Poltalloch, Robin Neill Lochnell; Chief of Clan Malcolm; Vice Lord-Lieutenant of Argyll and Bute, 1996–2001; *b* 11 Feb. 1934; *s* of Lt-Col George Ian Malcolm of Poltalloch, A&SH and Enid Gaskell; *m* 1962, Susan Freeman (*d* 2004); two *s* two *d*; *m* 2010, Patricia Currie (*née* Burness). *Educ:* Eton; North of Scotland Coll. of Agriculture. National Service, 1 Argyll and Sutherland Highlanders, 1952–54; TA service, 8 A&SH, 1954–64.

Shipping, and British Iron & Steel Co., 1955–62; farming at Poltalloch, 1963–. Convenor, Highlands and Islands Cttee, NFU, 1972–74; Member: HIDB Consultative Council, 1973–77, 1988–91; Bd, Argyll and Isles Enterprise, 1991–98; Bd, SW Region, Scottish Natural Heritage, 1993–99. Pres., Scottish Agricl Orgn Soc. Ltd, 1983–86. Mem., Argyll and Bute DC, 1976–92. Argyll and Bute: DL, 1974–2004; JP 1976–2004. *Recreations:* shooting, swimming. *Address:* Duntrune Castle, Kilmartin, Argyll PA31 8QQ. *T:* (01546) 510283.

MALCOLM, Dr Wilfred Gordon, CBE 1994; Vice-Chancellor, University of Waikato, New Zealand, 1985–94; *b* 29 Nov. 1933; *s* of Norman and Doris Malcolm; *m* 1959, Edmée Ruth Prebensen; two *s* four *d*. *Educ:* Victoria Univ. of Wellington (MA, PhD); Emmanuel Coll., Cambridge (BA). NZ Teachers Cert. 1954. Victoria University of Wellington: Lectr in Mathematics, 1960–62; Gen. Sec., Inter Varsity Fellowship of Evangelical Unions, 1963–66; Lectr/Reader in Mathematics, 1967–74; Prof. of Pure Mathematics, 1975–84. Vis. Prof., Univ. of Brunei Darussalam, 1997–99. Chairman: Academic Audit Unit, NZ Universities, 2000–03; Ministerial Adv. Cttee on Employment Relations Educn, 2001–06. DUniv Waikato 1995. NZ Commemoration Medal, 1990. *Publications:* Number and Structure 1975; (with Nicholas Tarling) Crisis of Identity?: the mission and management of universities in New Zealand, 2007; Thinking About God and Infinity, 2007. *Recreation:* eighteen grandchildren. *Address:* 18A Raymond Street, Point Chevalier, Auckland 1022, New Zealand.

MALCOMSON, Prof. James Martin, PhD; FBA 2000; Professor of Economics, University of Oxford, 1999–2013, now Emeritus; Fellow, All Souls College, Oxford, 1999–2013, now Emeritus; *b* 23 June 1946; *s* of E. Watlock Malcomson and Madeline Malcomson (*née* Stuart); *m* 1979, Sally Claire Richards; (one *d* decd). *Educ:* Gonville and Caius Coll., Cambridge (BA, MA); Harvard Univ. (MA, PhD 1973). Res. Fellow in Econs, 1971–72, Lectr 1972–83, Sen. Lectr, 1983–85, Univ. of York; Prof. of Econs, Univ. of Southampton, 1985–98. Vis. Fellow, Université Catholique de Louvain, Belgium, 1983–84. Fellow, Econometric Soc., 2005. *Publications:* (contrib.) Efficiency Wage Models of the Labor Market, 1986; (contrib.) Handbook of Labor Economics, 1999; (contrib.) Handbook of Health Economics, 2000; (contrib.) Handbook of Organizational Economics, 2013; numerous articles in learned jls. *Recreations:* walking, music, film, theatre. *Address:* All Souls College, Oxford OX1 4AL. *T:* (01865) 279379.

MALCOMSON, Mark; Principal, City Literary Institute (City Lit), since 2011; *b* Lagos, Nigeria, 29 Nov. 1963; *s* of John and Sandra Malcomson; one *d* with Tony Traxler. *Educ:* Birkenhead Sch.; Univ. of Edinburgh (LLB); Univ. of Strathclyde (DipLP); Univ. of Kent (MA Internat. Relns). Man. Dir, DC Gardner Trng, 1997–2000; Pres., NY Inst. of Finance, 2000–06; Dir, Exec. Educn, London Business Sch., 2007–11. *Recreations:* American political history, cooking, travel. *Address:* City Lit, 1–10 Keeley Street, Covent Garden, WC2B 4BA. *T:* (020) 7492 2590. *E:* mark.malcomson@citylit.ac.uk.

MALCOMSON, Thomas Herbert; HM Diplomatic Service, retired; Vice-President, Board of Directors, British-Peruvian Cultural Association, since 2014 (Executive Director, 2005–14); *b* 9 Oct. 1937; *m* 1st, 1960, Barbara Hetherington (marr. diss. 1985); one *s* two *d*; 2nd, 1986, Blanca Ruiz de Castilla; twin *d*. *Educ:* Univ. of Glasgow. Joined FO, subseq. FCO, 1961; Bangkok, 1963; São Paulo, 1967; FCO, 1971; Colombo, 1972; Consul, Chiang Mai, 1975; FCO, 1978; Dep. High Comr, Brunei, 1981; Acting High Comr, Solomon Is, 1984; Lima, 1985; FCO, 1989; Ambassador to Panama, 1992–96. *Address:* Av. La Floresta 331 apto. 101, Chacarilla, San Borja, Lima 41, Peru.

MALE, Anthony Hubert, (Tony), CMG 1997; National Executive Adviser for Languages, Department for Education and Skills (formerly Department for Education and Employment), 2001–02; Director, Central Bureau for Educational Visits and Exchanges, 1986–99, and Secretary, UK Centre for European Education, 1989–99, British Council; *b* 16 March 1939; *s* of Hubert Edward Male and Louise Irene Lavinia (*née* Thomas); *m* 1960, Françoise Andrée Germaine Pinot, LèsL, PGCE; one *s* one *d*. *Educ:* Yeovil Sch.; Exeter Univ. (BA, PGCE); Sorbonne. FCIL (FIL 1990). Housemaster, 1962–74, Head, Comparative Internat. Studies, 1970–74, Tiverton GS; Central Bureau for Educational Visits and Exchanges: Head, Teacher and Sch. Exchange, Europe, 1974–76; Asst Dir, 1976–78; Dep. Dir, 1978–84; Sec., 1984–86. Expert, Eur. Commn, 1977–99; Consultant, Council of Europe, 1982–99. Chm., Langs Nat. Working Gp, 2001. Pres., Fédn Internat. des Organisations de Correspondances et d'Echanges Scolaires (FIOCES), 1986–94. Member: Adv. Panel, Langs Lead Body, 1991–98; Council, Inst. Linguists, 1997–99. Member: Bd of Dirs, Nat. Youth Jazz Orch., 1975–2004 (Hon. Vice-Pres., 2004–); Jury, Concours Internat. de Guitare, Radio France, 1993–2000; Concours Internat. de Guitare Classique, Barbezieux, France, 2007–09. Trustee, Amer. Field Service, 1981–86; Internat. House, 1989–98; Lefèvre Trust, 1991–93; Technol. Colls Trust, 1996–99. Academic Gov., Richmond Coll., 1990–99. Life FRSA (FRSA 1985). Hon. FCP 1993; Hon. Fellow, Westminster Coll., Oxford, 1999. Hon. Mem., British Council, 1999. Chevalier, 1977, Comdr, 1992, Ordre des Palmes Académiques (France); Chevalier, Ordre National du Mérite (France), 1984; Chevalier, Ordre de Léopold II (Belgium), 1981; Comdr, Orden del Mérito Civil (Spain), 1999. *Publications:* contrib. articles on inter-cultural exchange, modern langs and internat. dimension in education. *Recreations:* music, flamenco and jazz guitar, travel, photography (www.thenomadcamera.com, www.ralphfry.com). *E:* ahmale@aol.com. *Club:* Travellers.

MALE, David Ronald, CBE 1991; FRICS; Consultant, Gardiner & Theobald, Chartered Quantity Surveyors, since 1992 (Senior Partner, 1979–91); a Church Commissioner, 1989–93; *b* 12 Dec. 1929; *s* of Ronald Male and Gertrude Simpson; *m* 1959, Mary Louise Evans; one *s* two *d*. *Educ:* Aldenham Sch., Herts. Served RA, 2nd Lieut, 1948–49. With Gardiner & Theobald, 1950–. Mem., Gen. Council, RICS, 1976–93 (Pres., 1989–90); Pres., Quantity Surveyors Divl Council, 1977–78. Member: Bd of Dirs, Building Centre, 1970–80; Govt Construction Panel, 1973–74; EDC for Building, 1982–86; Chm., NEDC Commercial Bldg Steering Gp, 1984–88; Dir, London and Bristol Developments, 1985–91. Member: Bd of Management, Macmillan Cancer Relief (formerly Cancer Relief Macmillan Fund), 1992–2000; Court of Benefactors, RSocMed, 1986–. Mem. Bd of Govs, Wilson Centre, Cambridge, 1993–97; Governor: Aldenham Sch., 1974–93; Downe House, 2000–07; Pres., Old Aldenhamian Soc., 1986–89. Master, Chartered Surveyors' Co., 1984–85; Liveryman, Painter-Stainers' Co., 1961–93. *Recreation:* opera and ballet. *Address:* Manor Farmhouse, Benham Park, Marsh Benham, Newbury, Berks RG20 8LX. *Clubs:* Boodle's, Garrick, MCC (Mem. Cttee, 1984–96 and 1997–99; Mem., Estates Sub-Cttee, 1984–2000).

MALE, Peter Royston, (Roy), CBE 2003; Chief Executive, Blackpool, Fylde & Wyre Hospitals NHS Trust, 2002–05; *b* 16 March 1948; *s* of Royston Stanley Male and Patricia Male (*née* Kennedy); *m* 1975, Susan Bootle; one *s*. *Educ:* Nottingham High Sch.; King's Coll. Sch., Wimbledon; St John's Coll., Cambridge (BA 2nd Cl. Hons 1970; MA 1974). MHSM 1974; DipHSM 1974; MIPD 1987. Grad. trainee, NHS, Sheffield Reg., 1970–72; Doncaster Royal Infirmary, 1972–73; Fazakerley Hosp., 1973–75; Dist Personnel Officer, S Sefton, 1975–77; Area Personnel Officer, Norfolk HA, 1977–87; Director: of Personnel and Admin, Liverpool HA, 1987–90; of Personnel, Cambridge HA, 1990–92; Dep. Chief Exec., 1992–98, Chief Exec., 1998–2002, Addenbrooke's NHS Trust. Independent Member: Standards Cttee, Lancs Combined Fire and Rescue Authy, 2005–12; Disciplinary Tribunals, Inst. of Legal Execs, 2005–14; Chm., Probation Bd, Lancs Probation Trust (formerly Nat. Probation Service, Lancs), 2007–14; Dir, Cumbria and Lancs Community Rehabilitation Co., 2014–15. Dir, Probation Assoc. Ltd, 2008–11. *Publications:* papers and contribs to jls. *Recreations:* Rotary, keyboard, gardening.

MALEK, Ali; QC 1996; a Deputy High Court Judge, 2008; *b* 19 Jan. 1956; *s* of late Ali Akbar Malek and Irene Elizabeth (*née* Johnson); *m* 1989, Francesca Shoucair; two *d*. *Educ:* Bedford Sch.; Keble Coll., Oxford (MA, BCL). Called to the Bar, Gray's Inn, 1980, Bencher, 2003; in practice at the Bar, 1980–; Asst Recorder, 1998–2000; Recorder, 2000; Hd of Chambers, 2009–. Chm., Commercial Bar Assoc., 2007–09. *Publications:* (jtly) Jack: documentary credits, 4th edn, 2009; various articles on banking law. *Recreations:* running, ski-ing, golf, music. *Address:* 3 Verulam Buildings, Gray's Inn, WC1R 5NT. *T:* (020) 7831 8441. *Club:* Vincent's (Oxford).

See also H. M. Malek.

MALEK, Hodge Mehdi; QC 1999; a Recorder, since 2005; *b* 11 July 1959; *s* of late Ali Akbar Malek and Irene Elizabeth Malek (*née* Johnson); *m* 1st, 1986, Inez Dies Louise Vegelin van Claerbergen (marr. diss. 2010); two *s* one *d*; 2nd, 2010, Azadeh Malek; one *s*. *Educ:* Bedford Sch.; Sorbonne, Univ. of Paris; Keble Coll., Oxford (MA 1981; BCL 1982). Called to the Bar, Gray's Inn, 1983 (Birkenhead Schol.; Atkin Schol.; Band Schol.), Bencher, 2004; in practice at the Bar, 1983–. Chm., Competition Appeal Tribunal, 2013–. Member: Supplementary Treasury Panel (Common Law), 1995–99; Bar Disciplinary Tribunal, 2001–11; Inns of Ct Conduct Cttee, 2010–. *Publications:* Gen. Ed., Phipson on Evidence, 15th edn, 2nd supp., 2002 to 18th edn, 2013; (contrib.) Atkins Court Forms, 2003; (with P. B. Matthews): Discovery, 1992; Disclosure, 2001, 4th edn 2012; (contrib.) Information Rights, 2004; The Dābūyid Ispahbads and Early 'Abbāsid Governors of Tabaristān, 2004; articles on law and history. *Recreations:* swimming, ski-ing, history. *Address:* 39 Essex Street, WC2R 3AT. *T:* (020) 7832 1111.

See also A. Malek.

MALES, Hon. Sir Stephen Martin, Kt 2012; **Hon. Mr Justice Males;** a Judge of the High Court of Justice, Queen's Bench Division, since 2012; *b* 24 Nov. 1955; *s* of Dennis Albert Males and Mary Winifred Males (*née* Bates); *m* 1982, Daphne Clytie Baker; three *s*. *Educ:* Skinners' Sch.; St John's Coll., Cambridge (MA). Called to the Bar, Middle Temple, 1978, Bencher, 2007; QC 1998; Asst Recorder, 1999–2000; Recorder, 2000–12; Deputy High Court Judge, 2008–12. Lay Canon, Rochester Cathedral, 2008–. *Address:* Royal Courts of Justice, Strand, WC2A 2LL.

MALET, Sir Harry (Douglas St Lo), 9th Bt *cr* 1791, of Wilbury, Wiltshire; JP; farmer, Australia and England; *b* 26 Oct. 1936; *o s* of Col Sir Edward William St Lo Malet, 8th Bt, OBE and Baroness Benedicta von Maasburg (*d* 1979); *S* father, 1990; *m* 1967, Julia Gresley, *d* of Charles Harper, Perth, WA; one *s*. *Educ:* Downside; Trinity Coll., Oxford (BA Eng. Lit.). Lt QRIH, 1958–61. JP W Somerset, 1982. *Recreation:* equestrian sports. *Heir:* *s* Charles Edward St Lo Malet [*b* 30 Aug. 1970; *m* 1997, Rachel, *d* of T. P. S. Cane; four *d*]. *Address:* Wrestwood, RMB 184, Boyup Brook, WA 6244, Australia. *Club:* Weld (Perth).

MALHADO, Noël; *see* Harwerth, N.

MALHI, Prof. Yadvinder Singh, PhD; Professor of Ecosystem Science, University of Oxford, since 2008; Jackson Senior Research Fellow, Oriel College, Oxford, since 2005; *b* High Wycombe, 1968; *s* of Jagat Singh Malhi and Gurdeep Kaur Malhi; *m* 2002, Dr Rachel Barbara Hinton; one *s* one *d*. *Educ:* Southend High Sch. for Boys; Queens' Coll., Cambridge (BA Natural Scis 1990); Univ. of Reading (PhD Meteorol. 1993). Envmtl Scis Ed., Nature, 1994; University of Edinburgh: Postdoctoral Res. Associate, 1995–98; Royal Soc. Univ. Res. Fellow, 1998–2005; University of Oxford: Univ. Lectr, 2005–07; Reader in Terrestrial Ecol., 2007–08. Dir, Oxford Centre for Tropical Forests, 2008–. *Publications:* Tropical Forests and Global Atmospheric Change, 2004; numerous articles in jls such as Science, Nature, Philosophical Trans. of Royal Soc. *Recreations:* exploring extraordinary places, finding the extraordinary in the everyday. *Address:* Environmental Change Institute, School of Geography and Environment, University of Oxford, South Parks Road, Oxford OX1 3QY. *T:* (01865) 285188. *E:* yadvinder.malhi@ouce.ox.ac.uk.

MALHOTRA, Seema; MP (Lab and Co-op) Feltham and Heston, since Dec. 2011; *b* Hammersmith, London, 7 Aug. 1972; *d* of late Sushil Kumar Malhotra and of Usha Malhotra; *m* 2005, Sushil Saluja. *Educ:* Green Sch., Isleworth; Univ. of Warwick (BA Hons Politics and Philosophy 1994); Univ. of Massachusetts (Schol.); Aston Univ. (MSc Business IT 1995). Mgt Consultant, Accenture, 1995–2003; Sen. Manager, PricewaterhouseCoopers, 2003–07; Advisor: to Minister for W Midlands, 2007–09; to Chair, Council of Regl Ministers, 2008–09; to video games industry on child safety agenda, 2008; Prog. Leader, cross-govt prog. to increase diversity in public appts, 2009–10; Pol Advr to Actg Leader of Opposition, 2010; Strategic Prog. Advr, UK Interactive Entertainment Assoc., 2011. Shadow Minister for Home Office, 2015; Shadow Chief Sec. to Treasury, 2015–. Mem., Justice Select Cttee, 2012–13. Chair, Young Fabians, 1999–2000; Fabian Society: Exec. Mem., 2000–; Chair, 2005–06; Founder and Dir, Fabian Women's Network, 2005–. Fellow, British American Project, 2007. FRSA. *Publications:* (contrib.) Dictionary of Labour Biography, 2001; (contrib.) From the Workhouse to Welfare, 2009. *Recreations:* running, cinema, music, gardening, playing the guitar. *Address:* House of Commons, SW1A 0AA. *T:* (020) 7219 8957. *E:* seema.malhotra.mp@parliament.uk.

MALIK, Adeeba, CBE 2015 (MBE 2004); Deputy Chief Executive, QED-UK, since 2002; *b* Bradford, 30 Sept. 1966; *d* of Mohammed Sadiq Malik and Fahmeeda Begum Malik. *Educ:* Grange Sch., Bradford; Humberside Poly. (BEd Hons 1990); Open Univ. Joined QED-UK, 1992. Non-executive Director: Yorkshire Forward, 1998–2004; British Waterways, 2001–04; Nat. Clin. Assessment Authy, 2001–05; Mem., 2000–04, Chair, 2005–07, Ethnic Minority Business Forum; Co Chair, Ethnic Minority Business Task Force, 2007–08; Member: Women and Work Commn, 2004–06; Adv. Bd on Naturalisation and Immigration, Home Office, 2004–08; Nat. Women Muslim Adv. Gp, 2007–10. Gov., Sheffield Hallam Univ., 2011–13. *Recreations:* cinema, music, theatre, family and friends. *T:* 07976 658268. *E:* a.malik@qed-uk.org.

MALIK, Rt Rev. Ghais Abdel; President Bishop of the Central Synod of the Episcopal Church in Jerusalem and the Middle East, 1996–2000; Bishop in Egypt, 1984–2000; *b* 21 May 1930; *m* 1956, Fawzia Emsak Gouany; two *s* one *d*. *Educ:* Cairo Univ. (DipEd 1960); St George's Coll., Jerusalem. Ordained deacon 1962, priest 1963, Cairo; Curate, 1963–66, Rector, 1966–84, Jesus Light of the World Ch, Old Cairo; cons. Bishop of Egypt, with N Africa, Ethiopia, Somalia, Eritrea and Djibouti, 1984. Vice-Chm., Council of Anglican Provinces of Africa, 1992–99; Chm., Fellowship of Middle East Evangelical Churches, 1997–2001. *Recreations:* walking, reading, maintenance of harmoniums, fishing. *Address:* c/o Diocesan Office, 5 Michel Lutfallah Street, Zamalek, Cairo 11211, Egypt.

MALIK, Khalid Taj; a District Judge, North Eastern Circuit, since 2013; *b* 29 Dec. 1958; *s* of Taj Ahmed Malik and Anwari Begum Malik; *m* 1986, Ruby Shabnam Khalid Malik; three *s* one *d*. *Educ:* Wyndham Primary Sch.; Kenton Comp. Sch., Newcastle upon Tyne; Univ. of Hull (BSc Hons Econs and Accountancy 1980); Newcastle upon Tyne Poly (Law Soc. finals 1991). Family clothing business, 1980–91; admitted solicitor, 1993; Goldwaters Solicitors, Newcastle upon Tyne, 1991–2006; Dep. Dist Judge, Northern Circuit, 2003–06; District Judge, Principal Registry, Family Div., 2006–13. *Address:* Newcastle upon Tyne Combined Court Centre, The Law Courts, The Quayside, Newcastle upon Tyne NE1 3LA.

MALIK, Moazzam; HM Diplomatic Service; Ambassador to Indonesia (and concurrently to Association of South East Nations and to East Timor), since 2014; *b* London, 29 May 1967; *s* of Mohammed Amin Malik and Shamim Malik; *m* 1993, Rachel Richardson; one *s* two *d*.

Educ: London Sch. of Econs (BSc (Econ) Internat. Trade and Develt); Hertford Coll., Oxford (MSc Develt Econs). Chartered Dip., Accounting and Finance, 1996. Advr, Central Bank of Uganda, 1991–94; Consultant, African Develt Bank and EC, 1994; Consultant Economist, London Economics Ltd, 1994–96; Dir, Global Trade Centre, 1996–97; Team Leader, Internat. Econ. Policy Dept, DFID, 1997–99; Man. Dir, Autum Engrg Ltd, 1999–2001; Department for International Development: Pakistan Prog. Manager, Western Asia Dept, 2001–03; Hd of Dept, Iraq Humanitarian Response, 2003; Principal Private Sec. to Sec. of State, 2003–05; Hd, White Paper Team on Internat. Develt (Eliminating World Poverty), 2005–06; Hd, Dept of Conflict, Humanitarian and Security Affairs, 2006–07; Dir, UN, Conflict and Humanitarian Div., 2007–10; Western Asia and Stabilisation, 2010–13; Acting Dir, Gen. Western Asia, Middle East, Conflict and Humanitarian, 2013–14. *Recreations:* Liverpool FC, cricket (follows Pakistan highs and (many) lows), cooking and eating Asian foods, music, cinema, reading novels and theatre, hacking around municipal golf course, walking around London, holidaying in Scotland. *Address:* c/o Foreign and Commonwealth Office, King Charles Street, SW1A 2AH.

MALIK, Shahid; *b* 24 Nov. 1967; *s* of Rafique Malik. *Educ:* London Poly.; Univ. of Durham (BA 1991). E Lancs TEC; Hd of Policy and Develt, Gtr Nottingham TEC; Chief Exec., PMC Gp; Gen. Manager, KYP Ltd; Chief Executive: Haringey Regeneration Agency, 1997–2001; Inclusive Futures. Vice-Chm., UNESCO UK, 1999–2003. Mem., CRE, 1998–2002; Equality Comr for NI, 1999–2002. MP (Lab) Dewsbury, 2005–10; contested (Lab) same seat, 2010. Parliamentary Under-Secretary of State: DFID, 2007–08; MoJ and Home Office, 2008–09; DCLG, 2009–10. Mem., Lab Party NEC, 2000–05. Chm., World Congress of Muslim Philanthropists, 2011–. Chm. of Govs, Caribbean Develt Bank, 2007–08; Governor: Asian Develt Bank, 2007–08; Inter-American Develt Bank, 2007–08.

MALIM, Prof. Michael Henry, DPhil; FRS 2007; Professor and Head of Department of Infectious Diseases, since 2001, and Head, Division of Immunology, Infection and Inflammatory Disease, since 2013, King's College London; *b* 4 July 1963; *s* of Anthony and Joan Malim; *m* 1990, Prof. Rebecca J. Oakey; one *s* one *d*. *Educ:* Bristol Univ. (BSc Biochem.); Oxford Univ. (DPhil Biochem. 1987). University of Pennsylvania School of Medicine: Asst Prof., Depts of Microbiol. and Medicine, 1992–98, Associate Prof. (with tenure), 1998–2001. Reported discovery of human anti-HIV gene, APOBEC3G, 2002. Mem., EMBO, 2005. FMedSci 2003; Fellow, Amer. Acad. Microbiol., 2005; FKC 2013. Elizabeth Glaser Scientist, Elizabeth Glaser Pediatric AIDS Foundn, 2001; M. Jeang Retrovirology Prize, 2010. *Publications:* articles and reviews on molecular pathogenesis of HIV/AIDS. *Recreations:* parenting, gentle sports, retired varsity golfer, cuisine, achievable DIY, cycling, hiking, bridge. *Address:* c/o Department of Infectious Diseases, King's College London, 2nd Floor, Borough Wing, Guy's Hospital, London Bridge, SE1 9RT. *T:* (020) 7188 0149, *Fax:* (020) 7188 0147. *E:* michael.malim@kcl.ac.uk. *Club:* Oxford and Cambridge Golf Society.

MALIN, Dr Stuart Robert Charles; Professor of Geophysics, Bosphorus University, Istanbul, 1994–2001; *b* 28 Sept. 1936; *s* of late Cecil Henry Malin and Eleanor Mary Malin (*née* Howe); *m* 1st, 1963, Irene Saunders (*d* 1997); two *d*; 2nd, 2001, Lindsey Jean Macfarlane. *Educ:* Royal Grammar Sch., High Wycombe; King's College, London (BSc 1958); PhD 1972, DSc 1981, London. FInstP 1971; CPhys 1985; FRAS 1961 (Mem. Council, 1975–78). Royal Greenwich Observatory, Herstmonceux: Asst Exptl Officer, 1958; Scientific Officer, 1961; Sen. Scientific Officer, 1965; Institute of Geological Sciences, Herstmonceux and Edinburgh: PSO, 1970; SPSO (individual merit), 1976, and Hd of Geomagnetism Unit, 1981; Hd of Astronomy and Navigation, Nat. Maritime Museum, 1982; Maths teacher: Dulwich Coll., 1988–91, 1992–94; Haberdashers' Aske's Hatcham Coll., 1991–92. Cape Observer, Radcliffe Observatory, Pretoria, 1963–65; Vis. Scientist, Nat. Center for Atmospheric Res., Boulder, Colorado, 1969; Green Schol., Scripps Instn of Oceanography, La Jolla, 1981. Visiting Professor: Dept of Physics and Astronomy, UCL, 1983–2001; Univ. of Cairo, 1996–2002. Consultant, Rahmi M. Koç Müzesi, Istanbul, 1995–2001. Pres., Jun. Astronomical Soc., 1989–91. Associate Editor, Qly Jl, RAS, 1987–92; Editor, Geophysical Jl Internat., 1996–2004. Freeman, City of London, 2003; Liveryman, Clockmakers' Co., 2006– (Freeman, 2003). *Publications:* (with Carole Stott) The Greenwich Meridian, 1984; Spaceworks, 1985; The Greenwich Guide to the Planets, 1987; The Greenwich Guide to Stars, Galaxies and Nebulae, 1989; The Story of the Earth, 1991; (with Rahmi M. Koç) Rahmi M. Koç Müzesi Tanıtımı, 1997; The Farnol Companion, 2006; In Remembrance of Me, 2013; over 150 contribs to scientific and horological jls. *Recreations:* Jeffery Farnol novels, clocks. *Address:* 30 Wemyss Road, Blackheath, SE3 0TG. *T:* (020) 8318 3712.

MALINS, Humfrey Jonathan, CBE 1997; lawyer and consultant; a Recorder, since 1996; *b* 31 July 1945; *s* of late Rev. Peter Malins and Lilian Joan Malins; *m* 1979, Lynda Ann; one *s* one *d*. *Educ:* St John's Sch., Leatherhead; Brasenose Coll., Oxford (MA Hons Law). College of Law, Guildford, 1967; joined Tuck and Mann, Solicitors, Dorking, 1967, qual. as solicitor, 1971; Partner, Tuck and Mann, 1973; an Asst Recorder, 1991–96; Actg Dist Judge (formerly Actg Met. Stipendiary Magistrate), 1992–2015. Councillor, Mole Valley DC, Surrey, 1973–83 (Chm., Housing Cttee, 1980–81). Contested (C): Toxteth Division of Liverpool, Feb. and Oct. 1974; E Lewisham, 1979. MP (C) Croydon NW, 1983–92; contested (C) same seat, 1992; MP (C) Woking, 1997–2010. PPS to Minister of State, Home Office, 1987–89, to Minister of State, DoH, 1989–92; Opposition front bench spokesman on home affairs, 2001–05. Chm. of Trustees, Immigration Adv. Service, 1993–96. *Recreations:* Rugby football, golf, gardening, soup making. *Clubs:* Vincent's (Oxford); Richmond Rugby Football; Walton Heath Golf.

See also J. H. Malins.

MALINS, Julian Henry; QC 1991; a Recorder, since 2000; *b* 1 May 1950; *s* of late Rev. Peter Malins and (Lilian) Joan Malins (*née* Dingley); *m* 1972, Joanna Pearce (marr. diss. 2010); three *d*. *Educ:* St John's School, Leatherhead; Brasenose College, Oxford (Boxing Blue; MA). Called to the Bar, Middle Temple, 1972, Bencher, 1996. Mem., Court of Common Council, City of London, 1981–2013 (Alderman, 2013–). Gov., Mus. of London, 1998–. *Recreations:* fishing, walking, conversation. *Address:* 115 Temple Chambers, Temple Avenue, EC4Y 0DA. *T:* (020) 7583 5275. *Club:* Vincent's (Oxford).

See also H. J. Malins.

MALINS, Penelope, (Mrs John Malins); *see* Hobhouse, P.

MALIPHANT, Russell Scott; Artistic Director and Choreographer, Russell Maliphant Company, since 1996; Associate Artist, Sadler's Wells Theatre, since 2005; *b* Ottawa, 18 Nov. 1961; *m* 2001, Diana Fouras; one *s* two *d*. *Educ:* Royal Ballet Sch. (Upper); Rolfing Structural Integration (Bodywork Practice) (Practitioner Cert. 1994). ARAD 1980. Dancer with Sadler's Wells, Royal Ballet and ind. ballet cos. *Works created* include: Torsion, 2003; (jtly) Critics' Choice, 2003; Critical Mass, 2003; Broken Fall, 2003; Push, 2005; Solo, 2005; Two, 2005; Rise and Fall, 2006; Eonnagata, 2009; Afterlight, 2009; The Rodin Project, 2012; Fallen, 2013; Still/Current, 2013; (jtly) Second Breath, 2014; Here and After, 2015; (jtly) Conceal I Reveal, 2015. Arts Council Fellowship, 2000. Hon. DA Plymouth, 2011. Time Out Live Award for Outstanding Collaboration, 2003; South Bank Show Award for Dance, 2003; Nat. Dance Award for Best Choreography (Modern), Critic's Circle, 2006. *E:* info@rmcompany.co.uk.

MALJERS, Floris Anton, Hon. KBE 1992; Chairman, Unilever NV, and Vice Chairman, Unilever PLC, 1984–94; *b* 12 Aug. 1933; *s* of A. C. J. Maljers and L. M. Maljers-Kole; *m* 1958, J. H. Maljers-de Jongh; two *s* (one *d* decd). *Educ:* Univ. of Amsterdam. Joined Unilever, 1959; various jobs in the Netherlands until 1965; Man. Dir, Unilever-Colombia, 1965–67; Man. Dir, Unilever-Turkey, 1967–70; Chairman, Van den Bergh & Jurgens, Netherlands, 1970–74; Co-ordinator of Man. Group, edible fats and dairy, and Dir of Unilever NV and Unilever PLC, 1974–94. Member: Unilever's Special Committee, 1982–94; Supervisory Bd, KLM Royal Dutch Airlines, 1991–2004 (Vice Chm., 1994; Chm., 2000); Supervisory Bd, Philips Electronics NV, 1993–99 (Chm., 1994); Supervisory Bd, Vendex NV, subseq. Vendex-KBB NV, 1996 (Vice Chm., 1998; Chm., 2000–02); Bd, Rand Europe, 1999–2003; Director: Guinness plc, 1994–98; Amoco Petroleum, Chicago, 1994–98; BP (formerly BP Amoco), 1998–2004; Diageo plc, 1998; Air France-KLM, 2004–10. Gov., Eur. Policy Forum, 1993–. Prof. of Mgt, 1994–2004, Chm., Supervisory Bd, Sch. of Mgt, 1999–2010, Erasmus Univ., Rotterdam. Chm., Concertgebouw, 1987–2003; Mem. Bd, Nat. Mus. of Archaeology, 1993–2004. Chairman: Bd of Trustees, Utrecht Univ. Hosp., 1994–2003; Turkije Inst. of the Netherlands, 2008. *Address:* Vleysmanlaan 10, 2242PN Wassenaar, Netherlands.

MÄLK, Raul; Special Diplomatic Representative (formerly Envoy) for the Baltic Sea Region, since 2011; *b* 14 May 1952; *s* of Linda and August Mälk. *Educ:* Tartu State Univ. Res. Fellow, Inst. of Economy, Acad. of Scis, 1975–77; freelance editor, subseq. Editor in Chief, Estonian Radio, 1977–90; Dep. Head and Counsellor, Office of President of Supreme Council, 1990–92; Ministry of Foreign Affairs, Tallinn: Counsellor, 1992–93; Chief of Minister's Office, 1993–94; Dep. Permanent Under Sec. (political affairs, press and inf.), 1994–96; Ambassador to UK, 1996–2001, also (non-resident) to Republic of Ireland, 1996–2003; Minister of Foreign Affairs, Estonia, 1998–99; Ambassador to Portugal (non-resident), 2000–03; Ministry of Foreign Affairs: Dir Gen., Policy Planning Dept, 2001–07; Actg Dep. Perm. Under-Sec. (EU Affairs), 2003–04, 2005–06; Perm. Rep. of Estonia to EU, 2007–11. *Publications:* numerous articles in Estonian and Finnish newspapers; material for Estonian radio and television broadcasts, incl. comment on internat. and home news, and parly reports. *Recreations:* theatre, music, attending sports events (football, basketball, track and field). *Address:* Ministry of Foreign Affairs, Islandi Väljak 1, 15049 Tallinn, Estonia.

MÄLKKI, Susanna Ulla Marjukka; Principal Guest Conductor, Gulbenkian Orchestra, since 2013; *b* Helsinki, 13 March 1969; *d* of Pentti Mälkki and Liisa Mälkki. *Educ:* Edsberg Inst. of Music (Soloist Dip. 1993); Royal Acad. of Music (Dip. RAM 1994); Sibelius Acad., Helsinki (MA Music (Cello and Conducting) 2000). Principal Cellist, Gothenburg Symphony Orch., 1995–98; Artistic Dir, Stavanger Symphony Orch., 2002–05; Music Dir, Ensemble Intercontemporain, 2006–13. Mem., Royal Swedish Acad. of Music, 2008; FRAM 2010. Pro Finlandia Medal, Order of the Lion of Finland, 2011. *Address:* c/o HarrisonParrott Ltd, 5–6 Albion Court, Albion Place, W6 0QT. *T:* (020) 7229 9166. *E:* info@harrisonparrott.co.uk.

MALKOVICH, John Gavin; actor and director; *b* Christopher, Ill, 9 Dec. 1953; *s* of late Dan Malkovich and of Joe Anne Malkovich; *m* 1982, Glenne Headley (marr. diss.); partner, Nicoletta Peyran; one *s* one *d*. *Educ:* Eastern Illinois Univ.; Illinois State Univ. Founding Mem., Steppenwolf Theatre Ensemble, Chicago 1976. *Theatre includes: actor:* True West, 1982; Death of a Salesman, 1984; Burn This, 1987 (transf. London, 1990); Slip of the Tongue, 1992 (transf. London, 1992); Libra, 1994; The Libertine, 1996; The Infernal Comedy, Barbican, 2011; *director:* Balm in Gilead, 1980, 1984; Coyote Ugly, 1985; Arms and the Man, 1985; The Caretaker, 1986; A Celebration of Harold Pinter, 2011. *Films include:* The Killing Fields, Places in the Heart, 1984; Eleni, 1985; Making Mr Right, The Glass Menagerie, 1987; Empire of the Sun, Miles from Home, 1988; Dangerous Liaisons, Jane, La Putaine du Roi, 1989; The Sheltering Sky, 1990; Queen's Logic, The Object of Beauty, 1991; Of Mice and Men, 1992; Shadows and Fog, In the Line of Fire, 1993; Jennifer Eight, Alive, 1994; Beyond the Clouds, The Ogre, 1995; Mary Reilly, Mulholland Falls, 1996; Portrait of a Lady, Con Air, 1997; The Man in the Iron Mask, Rounders, 1998; Time Regained, Ladies Room, Joan of Arc, 1999; Being John Malkovich, 2000; Shadow of the Vampire, Je Rentre à la Maison, 2001; Ripley's Game, 2003; The Hitchhiker's Guide to the Galaxy, The Libertine, 2005; Eragon, 2006; Beowulf, 2007; L'Echange, Burn After Reading, Mutant Chronicles, 2008; Red, Secretariat, 2010; Transformers: Dark of the Moon, 2011; Warm Bodies, Red 2, 2013; *producer:* The Accidental Tourist, 1988; Somewhere Else, Ghost World, 2000; The Gun Seller, Found in the Street, 2001; *director:* The Dancer Upstairs, 2002. *Address:* c/o Finch & Partners, Top Floor, 35 Heddon Street, W1B 4BR.

MALLABER, (Clare) Judith; *b* 10 July 1951; *d* of late Kenneth Mallaber and Margaret Joyce Mallaber. *Educ:* N London Collegiate Sch.; St Anne's Coll., Oxford (BA Hons). Res. Officer, NUPE, 1975–85; Local Govt Information Unit, 1985–96 (Dir, 1987–95). MP (Lab) Amber Valley, 1997–2010; contested (Lab) same seat, 2010. Mem., Select Cttee on Educn and Employment, 1997–2001. Mem. Adv. Council, Northern Coll., Barnsley, 1995–.

MALLABY, Sir Christopher (Leslie George), GCMG 1996 (KCMG 1988; CMG 1982); GCVO 1992; HM Diplomatic Service, retired; *b* 7 July 1936; *s* of late Brig. A. W. S. Mallaby, CIE, OBE, and Margaret Catherine Mallaby (*née* Jones); *m* 1961, Pascale Françoise Thierry-Mieg; one *s* three *d*. *Educ:* Eton; King's Coll., Cambridge. British Delegn to UN Gen. Assembly, 1960; 3rd Sec., British Embassy, Moscow, 1961–63; 2nd Sec., FO, 1963–66; 1st Sec., Berlin, 1966–69; 1st Sec., FCO, 1969–71; Harvard Business Sch., 1971; Dep. Dir, British Trade Develt Office, NY, 1971–74; Counsellor and Head of Chancery, Moscow, 1975–77; Head of Arms Control and Disarmament Dept, FCO, 1977–79, Head of East European and Soviet Dept, 1979–80, Head of Planning Staff, 1980–82, FCO; Minister, Bonn, 1982–85; Dep. Sec., Cabinet Office, 1985–88; Ambassador to Germany, 1988–92; Ambassador to France, 1993–96. Man. Dir, Warburg Dillon Read, subseq. UBS Warburg, then UBS Investment Bank, 2000–06 (Adviser, 1996–2000 and 2006–10); Adviser to: RMC, 1996–2000; Herbert Smith, 1997–2001; Louis Dreyfus Group, 1998–2003; Mem. Supervisory Bd, Vodafone (formerly Mannesmann) AG, 2000–10; non-executive Director: Sun Life and Provincial Hldgs plc, 1996–2000; Charter Pan-European (formerly European) Investment Trust, 1996–2007. Founder, 1995 and Chm., 2001–08, Entente Cordiale Scholarships (Trustee, 1996–2001). Trustee: Tate Gall., 1996–2002; Thomson-Reuters (formerly Reuters), 1998–2013. Chairman: Primary Immunodeficiency Assoc., 1996–2002, and 2005–06; Adv. Bd, GB Centre, Humboldt Univ., Berlin, 1997–2005 (Hon. Fellow, 2005); Adv. Bd, German Studies Inst., Birmingham Univ., 1998–2005; Somerset House Trust, 2002–06; Adv. Bd, 20/21 British Art Fair, 2011–15; Charitable Trust (formerly Foundn) of EORTC, 2001–13 (Hon. Vice Pres., 2013–). Chancellor, Order of St Michael and St George, 2004–11. Hon. LLD Birmingham, 2004. Grand Cross, Order of Merit (Germany), 1992; Grand Officier, Légion d'Honneur (France), 1996; Comdr, Ordre des Palmes Académiques (France), 2004. *Recreation:* grandchildren. *Address:* 112 Ashley Gardens, Thirleby Road, SW1P 1HJ. *E:* christopher.mallaby@tiscali.co.uk. *Clubs:* Brooks's, Beefsteak, Grillions.

MALLALIEU, Baroness *cr* 1991 (Life Peer), of Studdridge in the County of Buckinghamshire; **Ann Mallalieu;** QC 1988; *b* 27 Nov. 1945; *d* of Sir (Joseph Percival) William Mallalieu and Lady Mallalieu; *m* 1979, Timothy Felix Harold Cassel (marr. diss. 2007) (*see* Sir T. F. H. Cassel, Bt); two *d*. *Educ:* Holton Park Girls' Grammar Sch., Wheatley, Oxon; Newnham Coll., Cambridge (MA, LLM; Hon. Fellow, 1992). (First woman) Pres., Cambridge Union Soc., 1967. Called to the Bar, Inner Temple, 1970, Bencher, 1992; a Recorder, 1985–93. Mem., Gen. Council of the Bar, 1973–75. Opposition spokesman on home affairs and on legal affairs, H of L, 1992–97. Chm., Ind. Council of the Ombudsman for Corporate Estate Agents, 1993–2000; Ind. Mem., British Horseracing Bd, 2004–07. Pres., Countryside Alliance,

1998–. Chm., Suzy Lamplugh Trust, 1997–2000. Pres., Horse Trust, 2010–; Trustee: Racing Welfare, 2010–; Nat. Assoc. of Stable Staff, 2010–. *Recreations:* sheep, fishing, hunting, poetry, horseracing. *Address:* House of Lords, SW1A 0PW. *T:* (020) 7219 3000.

MALLALIEU, Angela Maria; *see* Brady, A. M.

MALLET, John Valentine Granville, FSA; FRSA; Keeper, Department of Ceramics, Victoria and Albert Museum, 1976–89; *b* 15 Sept. 1930; *s* of late Sir Victor Mallet, GCMG, CVO, and Lady Mallet (*née* Andreae); *m* 1958, Felicity Ann Basset (*d* 2013); one *s*. *Educ:* Winchester Coll.; Balliol Coll., Oxford (BA Modern History; Hon. Fellow, 1992). Mil. service in Army: commnd; held temp. rank of full Lieut in Intell. Corps, 1949–50. Messrs Sotheby & Co., London, 1955–62; Victoria and Albert Museum: Asst Keeper, Dept of Ceramics, 1962; Sec. to Adv. Council, 1967–73. Ind. Mem., Design Selection Cttee, Design Council, 1981–89; Member: Exec. Cttee, Nat. Art Collections Fund, 1989–2005; Art Adv. Cttee, Nat. Mus. of Wales, Cardiff, 1991–94; Wissenschaftlicher Beirat, Ceramica-Stiftung, Basel, 1990–; Arts Adv. Panel, Nat. Trust, 1996–2005; Pres., English Ceramic Circle, 1999–2009. Mem., Court of Assistants, Fishmongers' Co., 1970– (Prime Warden, 1983–84). *Publications:* (with F. Dreier) The Hockemeyer Collection: maiolica and glass, 1998; Xanto: pottery-painter, poet, man of the Italian Renaissance (catalogue), 2007 (Art Newspaper/AXA Prize, UK and Eire); articles on ceramics in Burlington Magazine, Apollo, Trans English Ceramic Circle, and Faenza; poems in Magma, P. N. Rev. and other literary magazines. *Address:* 11 Pembroke Square, W8 6PA.

MALLICK, Sir Netar (Prakash), Kt 1998; DL; FRCP, FRCPE; Professor of Renal Medicine, University of Manchester, 1994–2000, now Emeritus; Hon. Consultant in Renal Medicine, Manchester Royal Infirmary, 1970–2000; *b* 3 Aug. 1935; *s* of Bhawani Das Mallick and Shanti Devi Mallick; *m* 1960, Mary Wilcockson; three *d*. *Educ:* Queen Elizabeth's Grammar Sch., Blackburn; Manchester Univ. (BSc Hons 1956; MB ChB 1959; Pres., Students' Union, 1958–59). FRCP 1976; FRCPE 1992. Surgical Res. Fellow, Harvard Univ., 1960; Dept of Medicine, Welsh Nat. Sch. of Medicine, 1963–67; Manchester University: Lectr, 1967–72; Sen. Lectr, 1972–92; Hon. Prof. in Renal Medicine, 1992–94; Physician in Charge, Dept of Renal Medicine, Manchester Royal Infirmary, 1973–94. Medical Director: Central Manchester Healthcare NHS Trust, 1997–2000; Adv. Cttee on Distinction Awards, 1999–2003; Adv. Cttee on Clinical Excellence Awards, 2003–07. Vice Chm., Blackburn, Hyndburn and Ribble Valley HA, 1985–90. President: Renal Assoc., 1988–91; Manchester Med. Soc., 2005–06; Chairman: European Dialysis and Transplantation Assoc. Registry, 1991–94; Union Européenne des Médecins Spécialistes, 1993–98 (Pres., Bd of Nephrology, 1993–97). Pres., Manchester Lit. and Phil. Soc., 1986–88. Patron: Nat. Kidney Fedn, 2000–; Indian Assoc., Manchester, 2003–. Hon. FRCPI 1999; Hon. FRCSE 2005. DL, 1999, High Sheriff, 2002, Greater Manchester. Medal of Honour, Univ. of Manchester, 2014. *Publications:* (ed) Glucose Polymers in Health and Disease, 1977; Renal Disease in General Practice, 1979; (ed) Williams, Colour Atlas of Renal Diseases, 2nd edn 1993; Advances in Nephrology, 1994; Atlas of Nephrology, 1994; papers on renal disease and health provision in learned jls. *Recreations:* theatre, literature, wine and food, cricket. *Address:* 812, W3 51 Whitworth Street West, Manchester M1 5ED. *T:* (0161) 237 5323. *Clubs:* Athenæum; St James's (Manchester).

MALLINCKRODT, Georg Wilhelm von; *see* von Mallinckrodt.

MALLINSON, Allan Lawrence; military historian, novelist and defence commentator; *b* Yorks, 6 Feb. 1949; *s* of Alfred Mallinson and Edith Mallinson; *m* 1976, Susan Anne, *yr d* of Major Ronald Routledge; two *d*. *Educ:* various church and state schs; St Chad's Hostel, Hooton Pagnell; St Chad's Coll., Durham; Mons Officer Cadet Sch.; Royal Military Coll. of Sci., Shrivenham; Italian Higher Defence Inst., Rome. Ordinand, 1966. Commnd King's Own Royal Border Regt, 1969, transf. to 13th/18th Royal Hussars (QMO), 1980; Staff Coll., Camberley, 1981; served NI, Far and Near East, Germany, Italy and MoD; Commanded 13th/18th Royal Hussars, 1988–91; retd as Brigadier, 2004. Trustee: Mus. of 13th/18th Royal Hussars, Cannon Hall, Yorks, 2004–; Light Dragoons' Charitable Trust, 2005–; Army Mus Ogilby Trust, 2009– (Chm., Grants Cttee, 2014–). Vice Pres., Victorian Military Soc., 2014–. Kt Comdr, Order of Merit (Italy), 2000. *Publications: non-fiction:* Light Dragoons, 1992, 2nd edn 2006; The Making of the British Army, 2009, 2nd edn 2010; 1914 Fight the Good Fight, 2013; *fiction:* Matthew Hervey series: A Close Run Thing, 1999; The Nizam's Daughters, 2000; A Regimental Affair, 2001; A Call to Arms, 2002; The Sabre's Edge, 2003; Rumours of War, 2004; An Act of Courage, 2005; Company of Spears, 2006; Man of War, 2007; Warrior, 2008; On His Majesty's Service, 2011; Words of Command, 2015. *Recreations:* music, horses, churches. *Address:* c/o Rogers, Coleridge and White, 20 Powis Mews, W11 1JN. *Clubs:* Cavalry and Guards, Beefsteak.

MALLINSON, Sir James; *see* Mallinson, Sir W. J.

MALLINSON, John Russell; Speaker's Counsel, House of Commons, 1996–2000; *b* 29 June 1943; *s* of Wilfred and Joyce Helen Mallinson; *m* 1968, Susan Rebecca Jane Godfree; one *s* one *d*. *Educ:* Giggleswick Sch.; Balliol Coll., Oxford (Keasbey Schol. 1963; BA). Solicitor (Hons), 1972. Asst Solicitor, Coward Chance, 1972–74; Sen. Legal Assistant, DTI, 1974–79; Assistant Solicitor: Law Officers' Dept, 1979–81; DTI, 1982–84; Under Sec. (Legal), DTI, 1985–89; Corporation of Lloyd's: Gen. Manager, 1989–92; Solicitor, 1992–95; Mem., Lloyd's Regulatory Bd, 1993–95. *Recreations:* reading, conversation, music, film, looking at paintings. *Address:* 4 Nunappleton Way, Hurst Green, Surrey RH8 9AW. *T:* (01883) 714775.

MALLINSON, Sir (William) James, 5th Bt *cr* 1935, of Walthamstow; DPhil; Lecturer in Sanskrit and Classical Indian Studies, School of Oriental and Asian Studies, University of London, since 2013; *b* 22 April 1970; *s* of Sir William John Mallinson, 4th Bt and of Rosalind Angela Mallinson (*née* Hoare, now Fishburn); *S* father, 1995; *m* 2002, Claudia Anstice Wright; two *d*. *Educ:* Eton Coll.; St Peter's Coll., Oxford (BA Sanskrit); SOAS, London Univ. (MA); Balliol Coll., Oxford (DPhil). Translator, Clay Sanskrit Liby, 2002–08; teaching Sanskrit, SOAS, 2009–10; Res. Associate, Oriental Inst., Univ. of Oxford, 2012–14. Films: associate prod., Beginners Guide to Yoga, 2007; prod., dir and presenter, Temples in the Clouds, 2009; presenter, West Meets East, 2013. *Publications:* (trans.) Gheranda Samhita, 2004; (trans.) Emperor of the Sorcerers, vols I and II, 2005; (trans.) Shiva Samhita, 2006; Khecarividya, 2006; (trans.) Messenger Poems, 2006; (trans.) The Ocean of the Rivers of Story, vol. I 2007, vol. II 2009. *Recreations:* juggling, yoga, paragliding. *Heir: cousin* Jonathan Justin Stuart Mallinson [*b* 5 Feb. 1971; *m* 1st, 1998, Leann Alyson Llewellyn (marr. diss. 2001); 2nd, 2005, Caroline Hazel Whelham; one *s* one *d*].

MALLOCH BROWN, family name of **Baron Malloch-Brown**.

MALLOCH-BROWN, Baron *cr* 2007 (Life Peer), of St Leonard's Forest in the county of West Sussex; **(George) Mark Malloch Brown,** KCMG 2007; PC 2007; Special Adviser, FTI Consulting (Chairman, Europe, Middle East and Africa, 2010); Chairman, SGO, since 2014; *b* 16 Sept. 1953; *s* of George Malloch Brown and Ursula (*née* Pelly); *m* 1989, Patricia Cronan; one *s* three *d*. *Educ:* Magdalene Coll., Cambridge (BA 1st Cl. Hons Hist.; Hon. Fellow, 2005); Univ. of Michigan (MA Political Sci.). Political corresp., Economist, 1977–79; i/c field ops for Cambodian refugees, Thailand, 1979–81, Dep. Chief, Emergency Unit, Geneva, 1981–83, Office of UNHCR; Founder and Ed., Economist Develt Report, 1983–86; Lead Internat. Partner, Sawyer-Miller Gp, 1986–94; World Bank: Dir, Ext. Affairs, 1994–96; Vice-Pres., Ext. Affairs and for UN Affairs, 1996–99; Administrator, UNDP, 1999–2005; Chef de Cabinet to Sec.-Gen., UN, 2005–06; Dep. Sec.-Gen., UN, 2006; Vice-Chm., Soros Fund Mgt, 2007. Minister of State (Minister for Africa, Asia and UN), FCO, 2007–09; Chief Advr to World Economic Forum, 2009–. Vis. Fellow, Yale Center for the Study of Globalization, 2007. Hon. DLitt: Michigan State, 2002; Catholic Univ. of Peru, 2003; Pace, NY, 2005; Walden Univ., 2008. *Publications:* The Unfinished Global Revolution: the limits of nations and the pursuit of a new politics, 2011. *Address:* House of Lords, SW1A 0PW. *Club:* Beefsteak.

MALLON, Marie Elizabeth; a District Judge (Magistrates' Courts), since 2009; *b* Nuneaton, Warwicks, 13 Nov. 1961; *d* of Matthew Christopher and Mary Geraldine Mallon; *m* 1987, John McCarty; one *d*. *Educ:* University Coll., Cardiff (BSc Econ. Hons); Newcastle Poly. (CPE, LSF). Admitted solicitor, 1992; Partner: Askews, 1992–97; Askews Nixon Mallon, 1997–2004; Brown Beer Nixon Mallon, 2004–09; Dep. Dist Judge (Magistrates' Courts), 2006–09. *Recreations:* family, friends, good food and wine, following Middlesbrough FC, karate. *Address:* Leeds Magistrates' Court, Westgate, Leeds LS1 3JP. *T:* (0113) 9653, *Fax:* (01924) 231146.

MALLON, Seamus; Member (SDLP) Newry and Armagh, Northern Ireland Assembly, 1998–2003; *b* 17 Aug. 1936; *s* of Francis P. Mallon and Jane O'Flaherty; *m* 1966, Gertrude Cush; one *d*. *Educ:* St Joseph's Coll. of Educn. Member: NI Assembly, 1973–74 and 1982; NI Convention, 1975–76; Irish Senate, 1981–82; New Ireland Forum, 1983–84; Armagh Dist Council, 1973–86. Dep. First Minister (designate), 1998–99, Dep. First Minister, 1999–2001, NI Assembly. Dep. Leader, SDLP, 1978–2001. MP (SDLP) Newry and Armagh, Jan. 1986–2005. Member: Select Cttee on Agric., 1987–97; Anglo-Irish Inter-Parly Body, 1990–2005. Author of play, Adam's Children, prod. radio, 1968, and stage, 1969. *Recreations:* angling, gardening. *Address:* 5 Castleview Road, Markethill, Armagh BT60 1QP. *T:* (028) 3755 1411; (office) 2 Bridge Street, Newry, Co. Down BT35 8AE; (office) 8 Cathedral View, Armagh, Co. Armagh BT61 7QX.

MALLUCCI, Prof. Giovanna Rachele, PhD; FRCP; Van Geest Professor of Clinical Neurosciences, University of Cambridge, since 2014; Hon. Consultant Neurologist, Addenbrooke's Hospital, Cambridge, since 2012; *b* London, 29 June 1963; *d* of Livio Mallucci and Una Skelly; partner, Robin Franklin; two *s*. *Educ:* Haberdashers' Aske's Sch. for Girls, Elstree; St Hilda's Coll., Oxford (BA Hons Physiol Scis 1985); University Coll. Hosp. and Middlesex Hosp. Med. Sch., London (MB BS Hons 1988); PhD London 2001. MRCP 1991, FRCP 2012. Clin. trng in gen. medicine and neurol. at London hosps, then Nat. Hosp. for Neurol. and Neurosurgery, Queen Sq., 1989–94; Wellcome Trng Fellow in Neurogenetics, Prion Disease Gp, St Mary's Hosp. Med. Sch., Imperial Coll. London, 1995–2000; MRC Prog. Leader Track, MRC Prion Unit, Inst. of Neurol., Queen Sq., 2003–08; Hon. Consultant Neurologist, Nat. Hosp. for Neurol. and Neurosurgery, 2005–12; MRC Prog. leader and Hd, Neurobiol., MRC Toxicology Unit, Leicester, 2008–; Prof. of Neurosci., Univ. of Leicester, 2008–14. *Publications:* (contrib.) Cognitive Neurology and Dementia, 2009; contrib. original res. to scientific jls, incl. Nature, Science, Translational Medicine, Neuron, EMBO Jl, Proc. NAS, Brain, Nature Reviews Neurosci. *Recreations:* hiking, ski-ing, travel, cooking, music, art. *Address:* Department of Clinical Neurosciences, Clifford Allbutt Building, Cambridge Biomedical Campus, University of Cambridge, Cambridge CB2 0AH. *T:* (01223) 762043. *E:* gm522@cam.ac.uk.

MALLYON, Catherine Rowena; Executive Director, Royal Shakespeare Company, since 2012; *b* Cambridge, 28 Jan. 1962; civil partnership, Susan Foster. *Educ:* Impington Village Coll., Cambs; St John's Coll., Oxford (BA). Administrator and Musician, Big Wheel Th. Co., 1984–85; Arbitrage Trader and Credit Analyst, Charterhouse Bank, 1985–90; trng bursary in arts admin, Arts Council, 1990–91; Gen. Manager, Towngate Th., Basildon, 1991–92; Manager, The Screen at Walton on Thames, 1992–93; General Manager: Oxford Playhouse, 1993–99; Arts and Theatres, Reading BC, 1999–2005; Dep. Chief Exec., Southbank Centre, 2005–12. Mem. Bd, Coventry and Warwickshire LEP, 2014–. *Recreations:* violin playing, walking, surfing, ski-ing. *Address:* c/o Royal Shakespeare Theatre, Stratford-upon-Avon CV37 6BB.

MALMESBURY, 7th Earl of, *cr* 1800; **James Carleton Harris;** DL; Baron 1788; Viscount FitzHarris 1800; *b* 19 June 1946; *o s* of 6th Earl of Malmesbury, TD; *S* father, 2000; *m* 1st, 1969, Sally Ann (marr. diss. 2008), *yr d* of Sir Richard Newton Rycroft, 7th Bt; three *s* two *d*; 2nd, 2013, Sally Ann Clare, *d* of William Bruford. *Educ:* Eton; Queen's Coll., St Andrews (MA). DL Hampshire, 1997. *Heir: s* Viscount FitzHarris, *qv*. *Address:* Greywell Hill, Greywell, Hook, Hants RG29 1DG. *T:* (01256) 703565.

MALMESBURY, Archdeacon of; *see* Froude, Ven. C. A.

MALMSTRÖM, Cecilia; Member, European Commission, since 2010; *b* Sweden; *m*; two *c* (twins). *Educ:* Göteborg Univ. (BA; PhD Pol Sci. 1998). Psychiatric nurse, Lillhagen Hosp., Göteborg; social studies teacher, Lindholmen adult secondary educn service, 1991–92; Res. Asst, 1994–98, Sen. Lectr, 1998–99, Dept of Political Sci., Göteborg Univ.; MEP, 1999–2006; Minister for EU Affairs, Sweden, 2006–10. Mem., Västra Götaland Regl Assembly, 1998–2001. *Address:* European Commission, Rue de la Loi 200, 1049 Brussels, Belgium.

MALONE, Beverly; Chief Executive Officer, National League for Nursing, USA, since 2007; *b* Elizabethtown, Ky, 25 Aug. 1948; *d* of Frank Malone and Dorothy Black. *Educ:* Univ. of Cincinnati (BSN 1970; Dr in clinical psychol., 1981); Rutgers State Univ., NJ (MSN, 1972). Surgical staff nurse; own private practice, Detroit, Mich, 1973–96; clinical nurse specialist, Univ. of Cincinnati, 1973–75; Asst Administrator for nursing, Univ. of Cincinnati Hosp., 1981–86; Prof. and Dean, Sch. of Nursing, N Carolina State Univ., 1986–2000; Dep. Asst Sec. for Health, USA, 2000–01; Gen. Sec., Royal Coll. of Nursing, 2001–06. Mem., NHS Modernisation Bd, 2001–06. Pres., American Nurses Assoc., 1996–2000. *Address:* National League for Nursing, The Watergate, 2600 Virginia Avenue NW, Eighth Floor, Washington, DC 20037, USA.

MALONE, Prof. Caroline Ann Tuke, (Mrs S. K. F. Stoddart), FSA; archaeologist; Professor of Prehistory, Queen's University Belfast, since 2013; *b* 10 Oct. 1957; *d* of Lt Col Henry Charles Malone and Margaret Hope (*née* Kayll); *m* 1983, Dr Simon Kenneth Fladgate Stoddart, *qv*; two *d*. *Educ:* St Mary's Sch., St Leonards on Sea; New Hall, Cambridge (MA Hons Archaeol. and Anthropol. 1984); Trinity Hall, Cambridge (PhD Archaeol. 1986). FSA 1993. Italian Govt Scholarship, Rome Univ., 1980–81; Rome Scholarship in Archaeol., Brit. Sch. in Rome, 1981–82; Curator, Alexander Keiller Mus., Avebury, 1985–87; Inspector of Ancient Monuments, English Heritage, 1987–90; Lectr, then Sen. Lectr, Univ. of Bristol, 1990–97; Cambridge University: Tutor in Archaeol., Continuing Educn, 1997–2000; Affiliated Lectr, Dept of Archaeology, 1998–2000, 2005–; Sen. Proctor, 1998–2001; Fellow, New Hall, 1997–2000; Keeper, Dept of Prehistory and Early Europe, British Mus., 2000–03; Sen. Tutor, Hughes Hall, Cambridge, 2003–07; Queen's University Belfast: Sen. Lectr in Prehistorical Archaeol., 2007–10; Reader, 2010–13; Dir of Educn, Archaeology and Paleoecology, 2009–12. Co-Director: Gubbio Archaeol. Project, 1983–88; Gozo Project, Malta, 1987–98; Troina Project, Sicily, 1997–2001; Lismore, Scotland, 2002–08. Res. Associate Prof. of Archaeol., SUNY, Buffalo, 2004–. Principal investigator, Fragility and Sustainability in Restricted Island Contexts project, 2013–. Mem., BASIS Cttee, British Acad., 2001–09. Ed., 1998–2000, Co-Ed., 2000–02, Antiquity. MCIfA (MIFA 1986). Fellow, McDonald Inst. for Archaeol Res., 1996–2007. *Publications:* (ed with S. Stoddart) Papers in Italian Archaeology, Vols 1–4, 1985; Avebury, 1989; (ed with S. Stoddart) Territory, Time and State, 1994; Neolithic Britain and Ireland, 2001; (with S. Stoddart)

Mortuary Customs in Prehistoric Malta: excavations at the Brochtorff Circle at Xagħra 1987–94, 2009; contrib. numerous academic papers, articles and reviews. *Recreations:* gardening, pottery, good books, ancient monuments, antiques. *Address:* 8 Lansdowne Road, Cambridge CB3 0EU; School of Geography, Archaeology and Palaeoecology, Queen's University Belfast BT7 1NN.

MALONE, (Peter) Gerald; Editor, The Sunday Times Scotland, 1989–90, Editorial Consultant, since 1990; *b* 21 July 1950; *s* of P. A. and J. Malone; *m* 1981, Dr Anne S. Blyth; two *s* one *d*. *Educ:* St Aloysius Coll., Glasgow; Glasgow Univ. (MA, LLB). Admitted solicitor, 1972. MP (C): Aberdeen S, 1983–87; Winchester, 1992–97; contested (C) Winchester, 1997. PPS to Parly Under Secs of State, Dept of Energy, 1985, and to Sec. of State, DTI, 1985–86; an Asst Government Whip, 1986–87; Dep. Chm., Cons. Party, 1992–94; Minister of State, DoH, 1994–97. Company dir, healthcare and financial services sectors, 1997–. Dir of European Affairs, Energy and Envmtl Policy Center, Harvard Univ., 1987–90; Presenter, Talk In Sunday, Radio Clyde, 1988–90. Chm., CGA, 1991. *Recreations:* opera, English church music, history, motoring. *Clubs:* Pratts; Glasgow Arts; Conservative (Winchester); University (New York).

MALONE, Philip, LVO 2006 (MVO 1998); HM Diplomatic Service; Deputy Head, ASEAN Department, Foreign and Commonwealth Office, since 2015; *b* Leeds, 3 Dec. 1961; *s* of James Malone and Sheila Malone; *m* 1999, Yee Whey Sarah Tan; one *s* one *d*. *Educ:* King Edward VII Grammar Sch., King's Lynn; Open Univ. (Professional Cert. Mgt). Joined FCO, 1981; Attaché, Buenos Aires, 1983–86; Third Sec. and Vice Consul, Guatemala City 1986–89; Asst Parly Clerk, FCO, 1989–92; Third Sec., Luxembourg, 1992–95; Second Sec., Bandar Seri Begawan, 1995–99; First Sec., FCO, 1999–2003; Hd, Chancery, Singapore, 2003–08; Dep. Hd of Mission, Helsinki, 2008–12; Ambassador to Laos, 2012–15. Vice-Chm., Bd of Govs, Internat. Sch. of Helsinki, 2009–11. *Recreations:* sports, family, travel, reading. *Address:* ASEAN Department, Foreign and Commonwealth Office, Old Admiralty Building, SW1A 2PA. *E:* Philip.Malone@fco.gov.uk.

MALONE, Rt Rev. Vincent; Auxiliary Bishop of Liverpool, (RC), 1989–2006; a Vicar General of Archdiocese of Liverpool, since 1989; Titular Bishop of Abora, since 1989; *b* 11 Sept. 1931; *s* of Louis Malone and Elizabeth Malone (*née* McGrath). *Educ:* St Francis Xavier's Coll., Liverpool; St Joseph's Coll., Upholland; Liverpool Univ. (BSc 1959); Cambridge Univ. (CertEd 1960; DipEd 1964). FCP 1967. Chaplain to Notre Dame Training Coll., Liverpool, 1955–59; Curate, St Anne's, Liverpool, 1960–61; Asst Master, Cardinal Allen Grammar School, Liverpool, 1961–71; RC Chaplain to Liverpool Univ., 1971–79; Administrator, Liverpool Metropolitan Cathedral, 1979–89. Hon. DD Liverpool Hope, 2012. *Address:* 17 West Oakhill Park, Liverpool L13 4BN. *T:* (0151) 228 7637, *Fax:* (0151) 228 7637. *E:* vmalone@rcaolp.co.uk.

MALONE-LEE, Michael Charles, CB 1995; Vice-Chancellor, Anglia Polytechnic University, 1995–2004; *b* 4 March 1941; *s* of late Dr Gerard Brendan and Teresa Malone-Lee; *m* 1971, Claire Frances Cockin; two *s*. *Educ:* Stonyhurst College; Campion Hall, Oxford (MA); University Coll. Oxford (MSt). Ministry of Health, 1968; Principal Private Sec. to Sec. of State for Social Services, 1976–79; Asst Sec., 1977; Area Administrator, City and East London AHA, 1979–81; District Administrator, Bloomsbury Health Authy, 1982–84; Under Secretary, 1984, Dir, Personnel Management, 1984–87, DHSS; Prin. Fin. Officer, Home Office, 1987–90; Dep. Sec. (Dir of Corporate Affairs, NHS Management Exec.), DoH, 1990–93; Dep. Sec. (Head of Policy Gp), Lord Chancellor's Dept, 1993–95. Non-exec. Dir, ICI (Agrochemicals), 1986–89. Dir, Essex TEC, 1996–2001; Chairman: BBC E Regl Adv. Council, 1997–99; Essex Learning and Skills Council, 2000–03. Mem., Review Body for Nursing Staff, Midwives, Health Visitors and Professions allied to Medicine, 1998–2001; non-exec. Dir, Mid-Essex PCT, 2006–08; Chm., Mid Essex NHS Hosps Trust, 2008–09. Ecumenical Officer, Dio. Brentwood, 2005–09. Chairman Governors: New Hall Sch., 1999–2002; Heythrop Coll., London Univ., 2006–12. DL Essex, 2002. Hon. Fellow, Fachhochschule Für Wirtschaft, Berlin, 2004. Hon. PhD Anglia Poly. Univ., 2005. *Recreations:* natural history, running. *Address:* 22 Henley Street, Oxford OX4 1ER.

MALOUF, David George Joseph, AO 1987; writer; *b* 1934. *Educ:* Brisbane Grammar Sch.; Univ. of Queensland (BA Hons Eng Lang. and Lit.). Teacher, St Anselm's Coll., Birkenhead, 1962–68; Lectr, Dept of English, Univ. of Sydney, 1968–78. Boyer Lectr, ABC, 1998. Hon. DLitt: Macquarie, 1990; Queensland, 1991; Sydney, 1998. *Publications:* Johnno: a novel, 1975; An Imaginary Life, 1978; Child's Play, 1981; Fly Away Peter, 1981; Harland's Half Acre, 1984; Antipodes (stories), 1985; 12 Edmondstone Street, 1986; The Great World, 1990; Remembering Babylon, 1993; The Conversations at Curlow Creek, 1996; A Spirit of Play (Boyer Lectures), 1998; Untold Tales, 1999; Dream Stuff (stories), 2000; Every Move You Make (stories), 2007; The Complete Stories, 2007; Ransom, 2009; The Happy Life: the search for contentment in the modern world, 2011; A First Place (essays), 2014; *poetry:* Bicycle and Other Poems, 1970; Neighbours in a Thicket, 1974; First Things Last, 1981; Selected Poems, 1993; Revolving Days: selected poems, 2008; Typewrite Music, 2008; Earth Hour, 2014; *libretti:* Baa Baa Black Sheep, 1993; Jane Eyre, 2000. *Address:* c/o Rogers, Coleridge & White, 20 Powis Mews, W11 1JN.

MALPAS, Prof. James Spencer, DPhil; FRCP, FRCR, FRCPCH; Master, London Charterhouse, 1996–2001; Consultant Physician, St Bartholomew's Hospital, since 1973; Professor of Medical Oncology, 1979–95, now Professor Emeritus, and Director, Imperial Cancer Research Fund Medical Oncology Unit, 1976–95, St Bartholomew's Hospital; *b* 15 Sept. 1931; *s* of Tom Spencer Malpas, BSc, MICE and Hilda Chalstrey; *m* 1957, Joyce May Cathcart; one *s* (and one *s* decd). *Educ:* Sutton County Grammar Sch.; St Bartholomew's Hosp., London Univ. Schol. in Sci., 1951; BSc Hons, 1952; MB BS, 1955; DPhil, 1965; FRCP 1971; FRCPCH 1978; FRCR 1983; FFPM 1989. Junior appts in medicine, St Bartholomew's Hosp. and Royal Post-Grad. Med. Sch.; Nat. Service in RAF, 1957–60; Aylwen Bursar, St Bartholomew's Hosp., 1961; Lectr in Medicine, Oxford Univ., 1962–65; St Bartholomew's Hospital: Sen. Registrar in Medicine, 1966–68; Sen. Lectr in Medicine, 1968–72; Dean, 1969–72, Gov., 1972–74, Treasurer, 1986–87, and Vice Pres., 1987–93, of Med. Coll.; Dir (Clinical), ICRF, 1986–90. Cooper Res. Schol. in Med., 1966, 1967, 1968. Examiner in Medicine: Univ. of Oxford, 1974; Univ. of London, 1985, 1986. Acad. Registrar, RCP, 1975–80; Treasurer, Postgrad. Med. Fellowship, 1984–87. Pres., Assoc. of Cancer Physicians, 1994–99. Treas., Retired Fellows Soc., RSocMed, 2008–12 (Mem., Academic Bd, 2012–; Trustee and Mem. Council, 2013–). Trustee: St Bartholomew's and Royal London Charitable Foundn (formerly Special Trustees, St Bart's Hosp.), 1997–2007; Med. Coll. of St Bart's Hosp. Trust, 1999–2014; Mason-Le-Page Charitable Trust, 2001–15. Lockyer Lectr, RCP, 1978; Skinner Lectr, RCR, 1986; Subodh Mitra Meml Orator, New Delhi, 1991; Louise Buchanan Lectr, Assoc. of Cancer Physicians, 1993. Editor, British Jl of Cancer, 1992–93. Fellow, Royal Instn, 2002. Freeman, City of London, 1988. Medicus Hippocraticus prize, Internat. Hippocratic Foundn of Kos, 1996. *Publications:* (ed jtly) Multiple Myeloma, 1994, 3rd edn 2003; contrib. many medical textbooks; papers in BMJ, Brit. Jl Haematology, Jl Clinical Oncology, etc. *Recreations:* travel, history, painting, sailing, amateur molecular biologist, avoiding gardening. *Address:* 253 Lauderdale Tower, Barbican, EC2Y 8BY. *T:* (020) 7920 9337. *Club:* Little Ship.

MALPAS, Sir Robert, Kt 1998; CBE 1975; FREng, FIMechE; Chairman, Cookson Group, 1991–98; Co-Chairman, Eurotunnel, 1996–98; *b* 9 Aug. 1927; *s* of late Cheshyre Malpas and Louise Marie Marcelle Malpas; *m* 1st, 1956, Josephine Dickenson (*d* 2004); 2nd, 2005, Joan Holloway. *Educ:* Taunton Sch.; St George's Coll., Buenos Aires; Durham Univ. (BScMechEng (1st Cl. Hons)). Joined ICI Ltd, 1948; moved to Alcudia SA (48.5 per cent ICI), Spain, 1963; ICI Europa Ltd, Brussels, 1965; Chm., ICI Europa Ltd, 1973; ICI Main Board Dir, 1975–78; Pres., Halcon International Inc., 1978–82; a Man. Dir, BP, 1983–89; Chm., PowerGen, 1990. Chm., Ferghana Partners Ltd, 1998–2002; non-executive Director: BOC Group, 1981–96; Eurotunnel, 1987–99; Repsol SA, 1989–2002; Enagas, Spain, 2002–06; Agcert plc, 2005–08. Member: Engineering Council, 1983–88 (Vice-Chm., 1984–88); ACARD, 1983–86; Chairman: LINK Steering Gp, 1987–93; NERC, 1993–96. FREng (FEng 1978; Sen. Vice Pres., 1988–92). Hon. FRSC 1988; Hon. FIMechE 1999. FRSA. Hon. Fellow, Univ. of Westminster, 1992. Hon. DTech Loughborough, 1983; DUniv: Surrey, 1984; Sheffield Hallam, 2001; Hon. DEng Newcastle, 1991; Hon. DSc: Bath, 1991; Durham, 1997. Order of Civil Merit, Spain, 1967. *Recreations:* sport, music, theatre, golf, swimming, walking. *Address:* 2 Spencer Park, SW18 2SX. *Clubs:* Royal Automobile; Mill Reef (Antigua).

MALPASS, Brian William, PhD; CChem; investor and writer; Chief Executive, De La Rue Co. plc, 1987–89; *b* 12 Sept. 1937; *s* of William and Florence Malpass; *m* 1960, Hazel Anne; two *d*. *Educ:* Univ. of Birmingham (Open Schol.; Frankland Prize 1960; BScChem 1st Cl. Hons, PhD). MRSC. Passfield Res. Laboratories, 1963–68; De La Rue Co., 1968–89; Finance Dir, 1980–84; Man. Dir, Thomas De La Rue Currency Div., 1984–87. *Publications:* Bluff Your Way in Science, 1993; Bluff Your Way in Chess, 1993; numerous papers in scientific jls, magazine articles and book reviews. *Recreation:* grandchildren. *Address:* 13 Spinfield Mount, Marlow, Bucks SL7 2JU.

MALTBY, Antony John, MA; JP; Headmaster of Trent College, 1968–88; *b* 15 May 1928; *s* of late G. C. Maltby and Mrs Maltby (*née* Kingsnorth); *m* 1st, 1959, Jillian Winifred (*née* Burt) (*d* 2000); three *d* (and one *d* decd); 2nd, 2001, Mrs Elizabeth Mary Batin (*née* Newman); one step *s* three step *d*. *Educ:* Clayesmore Sch., Dorset; St John's Coll., Cambridge. BA Hons (History) 1950; MA. Schoolmaster: Dover Coll., 1951–58; Pocklington Sch., 1958–68. Mem. (Ind.), Ashford BC, 1991–2007. JP: Ilkeston, 1980; Ashford, 1992; DL Derbyshire, 1984–91. *Recreations:* community matters, travel. *Address:* Little Singleton Farm, Great Chart, Ashford, Kent TN26 1JS. *T:* (01233) 629397. *Club:* Hawks (Cambridge).

MALTBY, Colin Charles; Chairman: Blackrock Absolute Return Strategies Ltd, 2008–14; HarbourVest Senior Loans Europe Ltd, 2010–14; *b* 8 Feb. 1951; *s* of late George Frederick Maltby, MC and Dorothy Maltby; *m* 1983, Victoria Angela Valerie Elton; one *s* two *d*. *Educ:* George Heriot's Sch., Edinburgh; King Edward's Sch., Birmingham; Christ Church, Oxford (MA, MSc); Stanford Business Sch. Pres., Oxford Union, 1973; Chm., Fedn of Cons. Students, 1974–75. With N. M. Rothschild & Sons, 1975–80; Director: Kleinwort Benson Investment Mgt Ltd, 1984–95 (Chief Exec., 1988–95); Banque Kleinwort Benson SA, Geneva, 1985–88; Kleinwort Benson Gp plc, 1989–95; CCLA Investment Mgt Ltd, 1997–2003 (Chm., 1999–2003); Chm., Kleinwort Overseas Investment Trust plc, 1992–96; Chief Investment Officer, Equitas, 1996–2000; Chief Exec., BP Investment Mgt Ltd, 2000–07; Chm., Princess Pte Equity Hldg Ltd, 2007–09. Director: RM plc, 1997–99; H. Young Hldgs plc, 1997–2001; Bilfinger Berger Global Infrastructure SICAV, 2011–; BACIT Ltd, 2012–; Ocean Wilsons Hldgs Ltd, 2013–. Investment Adviser: British Coal Staff Superannuation Scheme, 2001–12; British Airways Pension Schemes, 2003–07. Mem., Finance Cttee, Funding Agency for Schs, 1996–99. Fellow, Wolfson Coll., Oxford, 2002–. FRSA 1993; Fellow, Royal Instn. *Recreations:* music, ski-ing. *Address:* 1224 Chêne-Bougeries, Switzerland.

MALTHOUSE, Christopher Laurie, (Kit); MP (C) Hampshire North West, since 2015; Member (C) West Central, London Assembly, Greater London Authority, since 2008; *b* Liverpool, 27 Oct. 1966; *s* of John Christopher Malthouse and Susan Malthouse; *m* 2007, Juliana Farha; one *s* one *d*; one *s* by a previous marriage. *Educ:* Liverpool Coll.; Newcastle Univ. (BA Jt Hons Pols and Econs). Mem., ICAEW, 1997. Touche Ross & Co., 1992–97; Finance Officer, Cannock Gp, 1997–2001; Chm., County Hldgs, 2001–; Chief Exec., 2005–08, Finance Dir, 2008–, Alpha Strategic plc. Contested (C) Liverpool Wavertree, 1997. Mem., Westminster CC, 1998–2006 (Dep. Leader, 2001–05). Dep. Mayor of London, Policing, 2008–12, Business and Enterprise, 2012–15. Chairman: Hydrogen London, 2008–15; London & Partners, 2014–15; Vice Chair, London Enterprise Panel, 2012–15. *Publications:* (contrib.) A Blue Tomorrow, 2001. *Recreations:* baking bread and policies, writing poetry and prose, watching others dance and play, childcare. *Address:* Greater London Authority, City Hall, The Queen's Walk, SE1 2AA. *T:* (020) 7983 4099. *E:* kit.malthouse@london.gov.uk; House of Commons, SW1A 0AA.

MALTMAN, Christopher John; freelance opera singer (baritone); *b* 7 Feb. 1970; *s* of Robert John Maltman and Christine Maltman; *m* 2000, Leigh Wolf. *Educ:* Warwick Univ. (BSc Hons Biochem.); Royal Acad. of Music (LRAM, Dip. RAM, ARAM; Queen's Commendation for Excellence, 1991). Operatic roles at: Royal Opera House, Covent Gdn; ENO; WNO; Bayerische Staatsoper, Munich; Deutsche Staatsoper, Berlin; La Monnaie, Brussels; Seattle Opera; San Diego Opera; Salzburg Fest.; Glyndebourne; recitals at: Wigmore Hall; Carnegie Hall, Lincoln Centre, NY; Konzerthaus, Vienna; Concertgebouw, Amsterdam; Schwarzenberg Schubertiade; Edinburgh Fest.; Salzburg Fest.; has made numerous recordings. Lieder Prize, Cardiff Singer of the World, 1997; Young Artist of Year, Royal Philharmonic Soc., 1999; Artist of Year, Seattle Opera, 2000–01. *Recreations:* food, wine, physical fitness. *Address:* c/o Askonas Holt Ltd, Lincoln House, 300 High Holborn, WC1V 7JH. *T:* (020) 7400 1700, *Fax:* (020) 7400 1799.

MALVERN, 3rd Viscount *cr* 1955, of Rhodesia and of Bexley, Kent; **Ashley Kevin Godfrey Huggins;** *b* 26 Oct. 1949; *s* of 2nd Viscount Malvern, and of Patricia Marjorie, *d* of Frank Renwick-Bower, Durban, S Africa; *S* father, 1978. *Heir: uncle* Hon. (Martin) James Huggins, *b* 13 Jan. 1928.

MALVERN, John, FRCSE, FRCOG; Consultant Obstetrician and Gynaecologist, Queen Charlotte's and Chelsea Hospital for Women (formerly Queen Charlotte's Hospital and Chelsea Hospital), 1973–2001, now Emeritus; Hon. Consultant Gynaecologist, King Edward VII Hospital for Officers, since 1997; *b* 3 Oct. 1937; *s* of late Harry Ladyman Malvern, CBE, and Doreen Malvern (*née* Peters); *m* 1965, Katharine Mary Monica, *d* of late Hugh Guillebaud; one *s* two *d*. *Educ:* Fettes Coll., Edinburgh; Royal London Hosp. Med. Sch., Univ. of London (BSc 1st Cl. Hons 1959; MB BS 1963). FRCSE 1968; FRCOG 1984. Various jun. posts in surgery and obstetrics and gynaecology at Royal London Hosp., Plymouth Gen. Hosp., Hosp. for Women, Soho Sq., Middx Hosp., Queen Charlotte's and Chelsea Hosp. Hon. Sen. Lectr, RPMS, then ICSTM, 1973–99. Ninian M. Falkiner Lectr, Rotunda Hosp., Dublin, 1980. Chm., Acad. Gp, Inst. Obstetrics and Gynaecol., 1986–88. Royal College of Obstetricians and Gynaecologists: Officer and Hon. Treas., 1991–98; Mem. Council, 1977–83 and 1987–90; Chm., Investment Panel, 2002–06; Hon. Cellarer, 2004–09; Pres., Obstetric and Gynaecol Section, RSocMed, 1989. Former Examiner for RCOG: Central Midwives Bd; Univs of London, Liverpool, Edinburgh, Manchester, Benghazi, Colombo, Khartoum and Hong Kong. Member: Central Manpower Cttee, 1981–84; PPP Healthcare Trust Ltd, 1998–2001. Member: Blair Bell Res. Soc., 1970–; Internat. Continence Soc., 1971–; Fothergill Club, 1977–; Gynaecol Vis. Soc., 1979–; Med. Soc. of London, 2004–; Hon. Mem., New England Obstetrical and Gynecol Soc., 2000. Liveryman, Soc. of Apothecaries, 1978–. FRGS 2001. Advanced Cert. in Wines and Spirits, Wine and Spirit Educn Trust level 3, 2002. *Publications:* (ed jtly) The Unstable Bladder, 1989; (ed jtly) Lecture Notes on Gynaecology, 1996; contributor to: Turnbull's Obstetrics, 1985, 2nd edn 1995; Basic Sciences in Obstetrics and Gynaecology, 1992; Gynaecology by Ten Teachers, 1995;

various contribs on urogynaecology and obstetrics. *Recreations:* wine tasting, history of art, travel, croquet. *Address:* 30 Roedean Crescent, Roehampton, SW15 5JU. *T:* (020) 8876 4943. *Clubs:* Royal Society of Medicine, Hurlingham.

See also Sir H. R. Wilmot.

MALYAN, Hugh David; Member (Lab), Croydon Borough Council, 1994–2006 (Leader, 2000–05; Hon. Alderman, 2006); *b* 7 June 1959; *s* of late Cyril and Brenda Malyan; *m* 1983, Ruth Margaret; one *s* one *d*. *Educ:* Strand Grammar Sch., Brixton. Trustee Savings Bank, 1975–78; fireman, London Fire Bde, 1978–92. Chm., Educn Cttee, Croydon BC, 1997–2000. Vice Chm., Assoc. of London Govt, 2002–05; Chm., Commn for London Governance, 2005–06. *Recreations:* amateur dramatics (former Mem., Downsview Players), singing, football (Crystal Palace supporter!).

MAMET, David Alan; writer; stage and film director; *b* 30 Nov. 1947; *s* of Bernard Morris Mamet and Lenore June Mamet (*née* Silver); *m* 1st, 1977, Lindsay Crouse (marr. diss.); 2nd, 1991, Rebecca Pidgeon. *Educ:* Goddard College, Plainfield, Vt (BA Eng. Lit. 1969); Neighbourhood Playhouse Sch., NY. Founding Mem. and first Artistic Dir, St Nicholas Theater Co., Chicago, 1974. *Plays: written and produced include:* Sexual Perversity in Chicago, 1975; American Buffalo, 1976; A Life in the Theatre, 1976; The Water Engine, 1976; The Woods, 1977; Lakeboat, 1980; Edmond, 1982; Glen Garry Glen Ross, 1984 (Pulitzer Prize for Drama, 1984; filmed, 1992); Speed the Plow, 1987; Bobby Gould in Hell, 1989; The Old Neighborhood (trilogy), 1990, UK 1998; Oleanna, 1992; The Cryptogram, 1994; *written and directed:* Boston Marriage, 1999, UK, 2001; Dr Faustus, 2004; *written:* November, 2008; Speed-the-Plow, 2008; Race, 2009. *Films: written:* The Verdict, 1980; The Untouchables, 1986; Hoffa, 1990; Uncle Vanya on 42nd Street, 1994; The Edge, 1998; Wag the Dog, 1998; (jtly) Hannibal, 2001; *written and directed:* House of Games, 1986; (with Shel Silverstein) Things Change, 1987; Homicide, 1991; State and Main, 2001; Heist, 2001; Spartan, 2004; *directed:* The Winslow Boy, 1999. *Television: written and directed:* The Unit (series), 2006; Phil Spector, 2013. *Publications:* Writing in Restaurants, 1986; Some Freaks, 1989; The Hero Pony, 1990; On Directing Film, 1991; The Cabin, 1992; The Village, 1994; Passover, 1996; True or False—Heresy and Common Sense for the Actor, 1998; The Old Religion, 1998; Wilson: a consideration of the sources, 2000; Three Uses of the Knife, 2002; Bambi vs Godzilla: on the nature, purpose and practice of the movie business, 2007; Theatre, 2010; The Secret Knowledge: on the dismantling of American culture, 2011. *Address:* c/o The Agency (London) Ltd, 24 Pottery Lane, Holland Park, W11 4LZ.

MAN, Archdeacon of; *see* Brown, Ven. A.

MANALO, Enrique Austria; Ambassador of the Philippines to the Court of St James's, since 2011, and to Ireland (non-resident), since 2013; *b* Manila, 21 July 1952; *s* of Armando Manalo and Jimena Austria; *m* 1986, Pamela Louise Hunt; two *s*. *Educ:* Univ. of the Philippines, Manila (BA Econs, MA Econs). Department of Foreign Affairs, Manila: Special Asst, Office of the Dep. Minister, 1979–81; Third Sec. and Vice Consul, 1981–84, Second Sec. and Consul, 1984–86, Philippine Mission to UN, Geneva; First Sec. and Consul, Washington, DC, 1986–89; Special Asst to First Undersec., 1989–92; Minister Counsellor, Philippine Mission to UN, NY, 1992–98; Asst Sec. for Eur. Affairs, 1998–2000; Chargé d'Affaires, Philippine Mission to UN, NY, 2003–07; Ambassador and Perm. Rep., Philippine Mission to UN, Geneva, 2003–07; Undersec. for Policy, 2007–10; Ambassador to Belgium and Luxembourg, and Head, Philippine Mission to EU, 2010–11. Presidential Award, Order of Sikatuna (Philippines), 2010. *Recreations:* reading, walking, listening to classical music. *Address:* Embassy of the Philippines, 6–8 Suffolk Street, SW1Y 4HG. *T:* (020) 7451 1780, *Fax:* (020) 7930 9787. *E:* embassy@philemb.co.uk.

MANASSEH, Leonard Sulla, OBE 1982; RA 1979 (ARA 1976); RWA; FRIBA; FCSD; Partner, Leonard Manasseh Partnership (formerly Leonard Manasseh & Partners), since 1950; *b* 21 May 1916; *s* of late Alan Manasseh and Esther (*née* Elias); *m* 1st, 1947 (marr diss. 1956); one *s* (and one *s* decd); 2nd, 1957, Sarah Delaforce; two *s* (one *d* decd). *Educ:* Cheltenham College; The Architectural Assoc. Sch. of Architecture (AA Dip.). ARIBA 1941, FRIBA 1964; FCSD (FSIAD 1965); RWA 1972 (Pres., 1989–94, PPRWA 1995). Asst Architect, CRE N London and Guy Morgan & Partners; teaching staff, AA and Kingston Sch. of Art, 1941–43; Fleet Air Arm, 1943–46; Asst Architect, Herts CC, 1946–48; Senior Architect, Stevenage New Town Develt Corp., 1948–50; won Festival of Britain restaurant competition, 1950; started private practice, 1950; teaching staff, AA Sch. of Architecture, 1951–59; opened office in Singapore and Malaysia with James Cubitt & Partners (Cubitt Manasseh & Partners), 1953–54. Member: Council, Architectural Assoc., 1959–66 (Pres., 1964–65); Council of Industrial Design, 1965–68; Council, RIBA 1968–70, 1976–82 (Hon. Sec., 1979–81); Council, National Trust, 1977–91; Ancient Monuments Bd, 1978–84; Bd, Chatham Historic Dockyard Trust, 1984. Pres., Franco-British Union of Architects, 1978–79. Governor: Alleyn's Sch., Dulwich, 1987–95; Dulwich Coll., 1987–95; Dulwich Picture Gallery, 1987–94 (Chm., 1988–93). FRSA 1967; Mem., Acad. d'Architecture de France. *Work includes:* houses, housing and schools; industrial work; power stations; conservation plan for Beaulieu Estate; Nat. Motor Museum, Beaulieu; Wellington Country Park, Stratfield Saye; Pumping Station, Weymouth; British Museum refurbishment; (jtly) New Research Centre, Loughborough, British Gas. *Publications:* Office Buildings (with 3rd Baron Cunliffe), 1962, Japanese edn 1964; (jtly) Snowdon Summit Report (Countryside Commission), 1974; Eastbourne Harbour Study (Trustees, Chatsworth Settlement), 1976; New Service Yard, Hampstead Heath (Corp. of London), 1993; (jtly) planning reports and studies; *relevant publication:* Leonard Manasseh & Partners: 20th century architects, by Timothy Brittain-Catlin, 2011. *Recreations:* photography, painting, being optimistic. *Address:* 6 Bacon's Lane, Highgate, N6 6BL. *T:* (020) 8340 5528, *Fax:* (020) 8347 6313. *Clubs:* Athenæum, Arts, Royal Automobile.

MANCE, Baron *cr* 2005 (Life Peer), of Frognal, in the London Borough of Camden; **Jonathan Hugh Mance,** Kt 1993; PC 1999; a Justice of the Supreme Court of the United Kingdom, since 2009 (a Lord of Appeal in Ordinary, 2005–09); *b* 6 June 1943; *e s* of late Sir Henry Stenhouse Mance and Lady (Joan Erica Robertson) Mance; *m* 1973, Mary Howarth Arden (*see* Rt Hon. Dame M. H. Arden); one *s* two *d*. *Educ:* Charterhouse; University Coll., Oxford (MA; Hon. Fellow 2006). Called to the Bar, Middle Temple, 1965, Bencher, 1989. QC 1982; a Recorder, 1990–93; a Judge of the High Court, QBD, Commercial List, 1993–99; a Lord Justice of Appeal, 1999–2005. Worked in Germany, 1965. Chm., Banking Appeal tribunals, 1992–93. Dir, Bar Mutual Indemnity Fund Ltd, 1987–94. Member: Consultative Council of European Judges, 2003–11 (Chm., 2000–03); Judicial Integrity Gp, 2008–; Report for Swedish Foundn for Human Rights and All-Party Parly Gp on Gt Lakes Region on impunity in reln to violence against women in Congo, 2008. Member: H of L Select Cttee on EU, 2007–09 (Chm., Sub-cttee E, Law and Instns, 2007–09); Panel under Article 255 of Treaty on Functioning of EU, 2010–; Chm., Lord Chancellor's Adv. Cttee on Private Internat. Law, 2009–. Chm., Hampstead Counselling Service, 2000–. Pres., British Insurance Law Assoc., 2000–02 (Dep. Pres., 1998–2000); Chm., Internat. Law Assoc., 2009–; Pres., British-German Jurists' Assoc., 2009–. Pres., Bar Lawn Tennis Soc., 2014– (Chm., 2000–14). Trustee, European Law Acad., Trier, 2003–11. University of Oxford: Mem., Ext. Adv. Cttee, History Faculty, 2008–; High Steward, 2012–. Hon. Fellow: Liverpool Moores Univ., 2010; John F. Kennedy Univ., Buenos Aires, 2011; Wolfson Coll., Oxford, 2013. Hon. Dr Canterbury Christ Church, 2013. *Publications:* (asst editor) Chalmer's Sale of Goods, 1981; (ed jtly) Sale of Goods, Halsbury's Laws of England, 4th edn 1983; lectures and articles on various legal subjects. *Recreations:* tennis, languages, music, walking. *Address:* Supreme Court of the United Kingdom, Parliament Square, SW1P 3BD. *Club:* Cumberland Lawn Tennis.

MANCHAM, Sir James Richard Marie, KBE 1976; international statesman for peace; international trade consultant, since 1981; Founding President, Republic of the Seychelles, 1976–77; Chairman: Mahé Publications Ltd, since 1984; International Promotion Marketing and Development Ltd; Publisher, Voice of the Indian Ocean and the Arabian Sea; *b* 11 Aug. 1939; adopted British nationality, 1984; *e s* of late Richard Mancham and Evelyne Mancham, MBE (*née* Tirant); *m* 1963, Heather Jean Evans (marr. diss. 1974); one *s* one *d*; *m* 1985, Catherine Olsen; one *s*. *Educ:* Seychelles Coll.; Wilson Coll., London. Called to Bar, Middle Temple, 1961. Auditeur Libre à la Faculté de Droit ès Sciences Economiques, Univ. of Paris, 1962; Internat. Inst. of Labour Studies Study Course, Geneva, Spring 1968. Legal practice, Supreme Court of Seychelles. Seychelles Democratic Party (SDP), Pres. 1964; Mem. Seychelles Governing Council, 1967; Leader of Majority Party (SDP), 1967; Mem., Seychelles Legislative Assembly, 1970–76; Chief Minister, 1970–75; Prime Minister, 1975–76; Leader of Opposition, 1993–98; led SDP to Seychelles Constitutional Conf., London, 1970 and 1976. Founder, Seychelles Weekly, 1962. Lecturer, 1981, on struggle for power in Indian Ocean, to US and Eur. univs and civic gps; Lectr on geo-politics of Indian Ocean, Internat. Univ. of Japan, 1996. Promoter, Internat. Inst. of Nat. Reconciliation Between Nations, 1997. Delegate: to Conf. on Challenges of Demilitarisation of Africa in Arusha, Tanzania, 1998; to Convocation of Family Fedn for World Peace and Unification Internat., Seoul, 1999; deleg. and keynote speaker, 2000–, many internat. summits, symposia and confs on world peace. Co-Chm., Global Peace Festival Foundn; Vice Pres., Internat. Council of Jurists; Member, Board of Advisors: World Future Council; World Entrepreneurial Forum; Internat. Inst. of Cultural Diplomacy; Member: Academic Council, Eur. Council for Peace Develt; Governing Council, Centrist Asia Pacific Democrats Internat.; Cttee of Elders and Wise, COMESA, 2010; Presidium, Internat. Ecological Congress, 2012; Club de Madrid, 2013; Pioneering Mem., World Entrepreneurship Forum, 2010; Founding Mem., World Energy Parlt. Member: Internat. Palm Soc., 1994; Green Cross Internat. 2013. Hon. Trustee, Cary Ann Lindblad Intrepid Foundn, 1986. Hon. Citizen: Dade County, Florida, 1963; New Orleans, 1965. FRSA 1968. Cert. of Merit for Distinguished Contribn to Poetry, Internat. Who's Who in Poetry, 1974; Ambassador for Peace, Internat. Fedn for World Peace, 2001; Lifetime Achievement Award, Rajiv Gandhi Foundn, 2001. Chevalier, Chaîne des Rôtisseurs, 1993. Officier de la Légion d'Honneur, 1976; Grande Médaille de la Francophonie, 1976; Grande médaille vermeille, Paris, 1976; Quaid-i-Azam Medallion (Pakistan), 1976; Gold Medal, City of Pusan, Repub. of Korea, 1976; Gold Medal for Tourism, Mexico, 1977; Gold Medal of Chamber of Commerce and Industries of France, 1977; Gold Medal des Excellences Européennes, 1977; Plaque of Appreciation, Rotary Club of Manila, Philippines, 1987; Gold Medal, Municipality of Dubai, 1995; Gold Medal, City of Bombay, 1996; Gold Key, Anchorage, Alaska, 2001; Internat. Jurist Award, Internat. Council of Jurists, 2010; Gusi Peace Prize, 2011. *Publications:* Reflections and Echoes from Seychelles, 1972 (poetry); L'Air des Seychelles, 1974; Island Splendour, 1980; Paradise Raped, 1983; Galloo—The undiscovered paradise, 1984; New York's Robin Island, 1985; Peace of Mind, 1989; Adages of an Exile, 1991; Oh, Mighty America, 1998; Who's Who in Seychelles, 1999; Images of Yesterday, 2001; Tel est mon destin, je fais mon chemin, 2001; War on America seen from the Indian Ocean, 2002; (ed jtly) The Future of Peace in the 21st Century, 2002; Personalities of Yesterday, 2005; Seychelles Global Citizen (autobiog.) 2009; Seychelles—The Saga of a Small Nation Navigating Through the Cross-Currents of a Big World, 2014. *Recreations:* travel, fishing, journalism, writing. *Address:* PO Box 29, Mahé, Seychelles. *E:* surmer@seychelles.net. *W:* www.jamesmancham.com. *Clubs:* Royal Automobile, Annabel's, Les Ambassadeurs; Intrepids (NY); Cercle Saint Germain des Prés (Paris).

MANCHESTER, 13th Duke of, *cr* 1719; **Alexander Charles David Drogo Montagu;** Baron Montagu, Viscount Mandeville, 1620; Earl of Manchester, 1626; President, Global Atlantic, since 1983; *b* 11 Dec. 1962; *s* of 12th Duke of Manchester and Mary Eveleen (*née* McClure); *S* father, 2002; *m* 2007, Laura Ann, *d* of Francis Smith, Laguna Beach. *Educ:* Geelong Grammar Sch., Vic; Bancroft Jun. High Sch., Calif.; Kimbolton Grammar Sch., Cambridgeshire. Director: Internal Security, 1991–; Summit Investments, 1994–; Royal Fidelity Trust, 1996–. *Address:* c/o British Consulate-General, 11766 Wilshire Boulevard, Los Angeles, CA 90025–6538, USA; 220 Newport Center Drive, Newport Beach, CA 92660, USA. *E:* globalatlantic@aol.com.

MANCHESTER, Bishop of, since 2013; **Rt Rev. Dr David Stuart Walker;** *b* 30 May 1957; *s* of late Fred Walker and Joyce Walker; *m* 1980, Susan Ann (*née* Pearce); one *s* one *d*. *Educ:* King's Coll., Cambridge (MA 1981); Queen's Coll., Birmingham (DipTh 1982); Warwick Univ. (PhD 2014). Ordained deacon, 1983, priest, 1984; Curate, Handsworth, Sheffield, 1983–86; Team Vicar, Maltby, 1986–91; Industrial Chaplain, 1986–91; Vicar, Bramley and Ravenfield, 1991–95; Team Rector, Bramley and Ravenfield with Hooton Roberts and Braithwell, 1995–2000; Area Bishop of Dudley, 2000–02; Bishop Suffragan of Dudley, 2002–13. A Church Comr, 2014–. Member: Gen. Synod, 2005–; C of E Pensions Bd, 2006–13 (Dep. Vice-Chm., 2010–11; Vice-Chm., 2011–13); Chairman: C of E Remunerations and Conditions of Service Cttee, 2013–; C of E Ministry Council, 2013–; Gtr Manchester Police Ethics Cttee, 2014–. Chairman: Housing Justice, 2003–07; Housing Assocs Charitable Trust, 2004–10; Sandwell Homes Ltd, 2011–12. Member: Council, Nat. Housing Fedn, 1996–2002; Govt Policy Action Team on Housing Mgt, 1998–2001; Member, Lay Advisory Panel: Nat. Police Improvement Agency (formerly Central Police Trng Agency), 2005–13; Homes and Communities Agency, 2009–12. FRSA 2008. *Publications:* (contrib.) Changing Rural Life, 2005; Communion by Extension, 2006; Belonging to Rural Community and Church, 2006; Marks of Mission and Ways of Belonging, 2010; Prayer and Social Capital, 2011; (contrib.) Rural Life and Rural Church: theological and empirical perspectives, 2012; (contrib.) Exploring Ordinary Theology: everyday Christian believing and the Church, 2013; various articles in housing jls. *Recreations:* cricket, hill walking, reading, sudoku puzzles. *Address:* Bishopscourt, Bury New Road, Salford M7 4LE. *E:* bishop.david@manchester.anglican.org.

MANCHESTER, Dean of; *see* Govender, Very Rev. R. M.

MANCHESTER, Archdeacon of; *see* Ashcroft, Ven. M. D.

MANCHIPP, Amelia Anne Doris; *see* Noble, A. A. D.

MANCROFT, family name of **Baron Mancroft**.

MANCROFT, 3rd Baron *cr* 1937, of Mancroft in the City of Norwich; **Benjamin Lloyd Stormont Mancroft;** Bt 1932; *b* 16 May 1957; *s* of 2nd Baron Mancroft, KBE, TD and Diana Elizabeth (*d* 1999), *d* of late Lt-Col Horace Lloyd, DSO; *S* father, 1987; *m* 1990, Emma Louisa, *e d* of Thomas Peart; two *s* one *d*. *Educ:* Eton. MFH, Vale of White Horse Hunt, 1987–89. Chm., Inter Lotto (UK) Ltd, 1995–2007; Dir and Sen. Vice Pres., ROK Entertainment Gp Inc., USA, 2007– (Dep. Chm., ROK Corp. Ltd, 2003–07); Chairman: New Media Lottery Services plc, Ireland, 2006–09; Phoenix Gaming Ltd, 2007–. Dir, St Martin's Magazines plc, 1991–2008. Chairman: Addiction Recovery Foundn, 1989–2007 (Patron, 2008–); Drug and Alcohol Foundn, 1993–2007; Mentor Foundn UK, 2000–07 (Trustee, Mentor Foundn Internat., 1996–2000); Trustee, Hepatitis C Trust, 2000–06 (Patron, 2006–). Deputy Chairman: British Field Sports Soc., 1993–98; Phoenix House Housing Assoc., 1993–96. Dir, Countryside Alliance, 1998– (Dep. Chm., 2005–). Member Executive: Nat. Union of Cons. and Unionist Assocs, 1989–95; Assoc. of Cons. Peers, 1989–95. Elected Mem., H of L, 1999. Pres., Alliance of Ind. Retailers, 1996–2000. Patron: Sick Dentists' Trust, 1991–; Patsy Hardy Trust, 1991–; Osteopathic Centre for Children,

1996–. *Recreations:* field sports, gardening, reading, travelling. *Heir:* s Hon. Arthur Louis Stormont Mancroft, *b* 3 May 1995. *Address:* House of Lords, SW1A 0PW. *Club:* Pratt's.
See also S. C. Dickinson.

MANDELSON, Baron *cr* 2008 (Life Peer), of Foy in the County of Herefordshire and Hartlepool in the County of Durham; **Peter Benjamin Mandelson;** PC 1998; Chairman: Global Counsel LLP, since 2010; Lazard International, since 2012; *b* 21 Oct. 1953; *s* of late George Mandelson and Hon. Mary, *o c* of Baron Morrison of Lambeth, CH, PC. *Educ:* Hendon County Grammar Sch.; St Catherine's Coll., Oxford (Hons degree, PPE). Econ. Dept, TUC, 1977–78; Chm., British Youth Council, 1978–80; producer, LWT, 1982–85; Dir of Campaigns and Communications, Labour Party, 1985–90. MP (Lab) Hartlepool, 1992–Sept. 2004. An Opposition Whip, 1994–95; Opposition spokesman on Civil Service, 1995–97; Minister without Portfolio, Cabinet Office, 1997–98; Sec. of State for Trade and Industry, 1998, for N Ireland, 1999–2001, for Business, Enterprise and Regulatory Reform, later Business, Innovation and Skills, 2008–10; First Sec. of State and Lord Pres. of the Council, 2009–10. Mem., European Commn, 2004–08. Mem. Council, London Bor. of Lambeth, 1979–82. Pres., Policy Network, 2001–. *Publications:* Youth Unemployment: causes and cures, 1977; Broadcasting and Youth, 1980; (jtly) The Blair Revolution, 1996, 2nd edn 2002; The Third Man: life at the heart of New Labour (autobiog.), 2010. *Recreations:* swimming, country walking. *Address:* House of Lords, SW1A 0PW.

MANDELSTAM, Prof. Stanley, FRS 1962; Professor Emeritus of Physics, University of California, 1963–95, now Emeritus. *Educ:* University of the Witwatersrand, Johannesburg, Transvaal, South Africa (BSc); Trinity Coll., Cambridge (BA); PhD Birmingham. Professor of Math. Physics, University of Birmingham, 1960–63; Prof. Associé, Univ. de Paris Sud, 1979–80 and 1984–85. Fellow, Amer. Acad. of Arts and Scis, 1992. Dirac Medal and Prize, Internat. Centre for Theoretical Physics, 1991; Dannie Heineman Prize for Mathematical Physics, APS, 1992. *Publications:* (with W. Yourgrau) Variational Principles in Dynamics and Quantum Theory, 1955 (revised edn, 1956); papers in learned journals. *Address:* Department of Physics, University of California, Berkeley, CA 94720, USA.

MANDER, Sir (Charles) Nicholas, 4th Bt *cr* 1911, of The Mount, Tettenhall, co. Stafford; *b* 23 March 1950; *er s* of Sir Charles Marcus Mander, 3rd Bt and Maria Dolores Beatrice Mander (*née* Brödermann) (*d* 2007); *S* father, 2006; *m* 1972, Karin Margareta, *yr d* of Gustaf Arne Norin; four *s* one *d*. *Educ:* Downside; Trinity Coll., Cambridge (top Scholar; MA). Underwriting Mem. Lloyd's, 1972. Co-founder: Mander Portman Woodward, tutorial coll., London, 1974; Sutton Publishing, Gloucester, 1976; Dir, London & Cambridge Investments, 1985–91; CEO, Flamenco Estates, 1992–2003. Chm., Glos Care Partnership, 2006–14. Chm., Glos County History Trust, 2010–; Trustee: Woodchester Mansion Trust, 1998–; Orders of St John Care Trust, 2006–; Cllr, St John Ambulance for Glos, 2008–12. Mem., Diocesan Adv. Cttee, 1975–92. FSA 2006. Liveryman, Fishmongers' Co. Kt of Grace and Devotion, SMO Malta, 2002; Kt Jure Sanguinis, Sacred Military Constantinian Order of St George, 2008. *Publications:* Varnished Leaves: a biography of the Mander family of Wolverhampton 1750–1950, 2004; Country Houses of the Cotswolds, 2008; Borromean Rings, 2011; The Queen of Severn Swords, 2013. *Recreations:* conversation, conservation, dreaming, arts, travelling, forestry. *Heir: e s* Charles Marcus Septimus Gustav Mander, *b* 26 July 1975. *Address:* Owlpen Manor, Uley, Glos GL11 5BZ. *T:* (01453) 860261. *E:* nicky@owlpen.com. *Club:* Boodle's.

MANDER, Prof. Lewis Norman, FRS 1990; Professor of Chemistry, 1980–2002, Adjunct Professor, 2002–08, now Emeritus Professor, Australian National University; *b* 8 Sept. 1939; *s* of John Eric and Anne Frances Mander; *m* 1965, Stephanie Vautin; one *s* two *d*. *Educ:* Mount Albert Grammar Sch.; Univ. of Sydney (PhD 1965). FRACI 1980; FAA 1983. Postdoctoral Fellow, Univ. of Michigan, 1964–65; Postdoctoral Associate, Caltech, 1965–66; Lectr and Sen. Lectr in Organic Chem., Univ. of Adelaide, 1966–75; Sen. Fellow, 1975–80, Dean, 1981–86 and 1992–95, Res. Sch. of Chem., ANU. Nuffield Commonwealth Fellow, Cambridge, 1972; Fulbright Sen. Schol., Caltech, 1977, Harvard, 1986. H. G. Smith Medal, RACI, 1981; Flintoff Medal and Prize, RSocChem, 1990. *Publications:* numerous articles in learned jls, mainly on synthesis of organic molecules. *Recreations:* bushwalking, speleology. *Address:* Research School of Chemistry, Australian National University, Canberra, ACT 2601, Australia. *T:* (2) 61253761.

MANDER, His Honour Michael Harold; DL; a Circuit Judge, 1985–2001 (Resident Judge, Shrewsbury Crown Court, 1989–2001); *b* 27 Oct. 1936; *e s* of late Harold and Ann Mander; *m* 1960, Jancis Mary Dodd, *er d* of late Revd Charles and Edna Dodd. *Educ:* Workington Grammar School; Queen's College, Oxford (MA, 2nd cl. hons Jurisp.; Rigg Exhibnr). Nat. Service, RA (2nd Lieut) to 1957. Articled clerk; solicitor, 2nd cl. hons, 1963; called to the Bar, Inner Temple, 1972. Asst Recorder, 1982–85. Dep. Chm., Agricultural Lands Tribunal, 1983–85. Freeman, City of London, 1995; Freeman, 1994, Liveryman, 2001–, Information Technologists' Co. DL Shropshire, 2000. *Recreations:* life under the Wrekin, Shropshire life. *Address:* 22 Oakfield Park, Much Wenlock, Shropshire TF13 6HJ. *T:* (01952) 727232. *Club:* Wrekin Rotary (Hon. Mem.).

MANDER, Sir Nicholas; *see* Mander, Sir C. N.

MANDERS, Ann Beasley; *see* Beasley, A.

MANDERSON, Marcus Charles William S.; *see* Scott-Manderson.

MANDLER, Prof. Peter, PhD; FBA 2015; Professor of Modern Cultural History, University of Cambridge, since 2009; Fellow, since 2001 and Bailey Lecturer in History, since 2009, Gonville and Caius College, Cambridge; President, Royal Historical Society, since 2012; *b* Boston, USA, 29 Jan. 1958; *s* of George Mandler and Jean Matter Mandler; *m* 1987, Ruth Ehrlich; one *s* one *d*. *Educ:* Point Loma High Sch.; Magdalen Coll., Oxford (BA 1st Cl. Hons Mod. Hist. 1975); Harvard Univ. (AM Hist. 1980; PhD Hist. 1984). Teaching Fellow in Hist., and in Hist. and Lit., Harvard Univ., 1980–82; Asst Prof. of Hist., Princeton Univ., 1984–91; London Guildhall University: Sen. Lectr, 1991–95, Reader, 1995–97, in Mod. Hist.; Prof. of Mod. Hist., 1997–2001; University of Cambridge: Lectr in Hist., 2001–03; Reader in Mod. Brit. Hist., 2003–09; Lectr, Gonville and Caius Coll., 2001–. Hon. Sec., 1998–2002, Vice Pres., 2009–12, RHistS. Editor, Historical Jl, 2002–06; mem. of various editl bds and adv. bds. *Publications:* (ed) The Uses of Charity: the poor on relief in the nineteenth-century metropolis, 1990; Aristocratic Government in the Age of Reform: Whigs and Liberals, 1830–52, 1990; (ed with Susan Pedersen) After the Victorians: private conscience and public duty in modern Britain, 1994; The Fall and Rise of the Stately Home, 1997; History and National Life, 2002; (ed) Liberty and Authority in Victorian Britain, 2006; The English National Character: the history of an idea from Edmund Burke to Tony Blair, 2006; (ed with Astrid Swenson) From Plunder to Preservation: Britain and the heritage of Empire, *c* 1800–1940, 2013; Return from the Natives: how Margaret Mead won the Second World War and lost the Cold War, 2013. *Recreations:* reading, theatre, politics, argument. *Address:* Gonville and Caius College, Cambridge CB2 1TA. *T:* (01223) 768779, *Fax:* (01223) 332456. *E:* pm297@cam.ac.uk.

MANDUCA, Paul Victor Falzon Sant; Chairman, Prudential plc, since 2012 (Director, 2010; Senior Independent Director, 2011–12); *b* 15 Nov. 1951; *s* of Victor Manduca and Elizabeth Manduca (*née* Johnson); *m* 1982, Ursula Vogt; two *s*. *Educ:* Harrow Sch.; Hertford Coll., Oxford (Hons Mod. Langs). Colegrave & Co., 1973–75; Rowe & Pitman, 1976–79; Hill Samuel Inv. Management, 1979–83; Touche Remnant, 1983–92: Dir 1986; Vice-Chm. 1987; Chm., 1989–92; Dir, Henderson (formerly TR) Smaller Cos Investment Trust (formerly Trustees Corp.), 1986–2006; Man. Dir, TR Industrial & General, 1986–88; Chm., TR High Income, 1989–94; Gp Dep. Man. Dir, Henderson Administration PLC, 1992–94; Chief Executive: Threadneedle Asset Mgt, 1994–99; Rothschild Asset Mgt, 1999–2002; CEO, Deutsche Asset Mgt (Europe), 2002–05. Exec. Chm., Gresham Trust, 1996–99 (Dir, 1994–99); non-executive Chairman: FTSE Trains, 1997–2002; Majid al Futtaim Trust Co., 2005–; Bridgewell Gp, 2006–07; AON UK Ltd, 2008–12 (non-exec. Dir, 2006–08); Microlease plc, 2009–14; Director: Eagle Star Hldgs, 1994–99; Allied Dunbar Assce, 1994–99; non-executive Director: Clydesdale Investment Trust, 1987–88; MEPC plc, 1999–2000; Wolverhampton Wanderers FC, 1999–2006; Development Securities plc, 2001–10 (Sen. Ind. Dir, 2006–10); William Morrison Supermarkets plc, 2005–11 (Sen. Ind. Dir, 2006–); Intrinsic Ltd, 2006–12; KazMunaiGaz Exploration & Production plc, 2006–12; JPM Euro Smaller Companies (formerly JPM Euro Fledgeling) Investment Trust plc, 2006–11 (Chm., 2011–12); Henderson Diversified Income plc, 2007– (Chm., 2007–); Chm., UNIQ Pension Fund Trustees Ltd, 2006–09. Mem., Adv. Bd, Alexandra Proudfoot, 2010–12; Chm., Adv. Council, TheCityUK, 2015–. Chm., Assoc. of Investment Trust Cos, 1991–93 (Dep. Chm., 1989–91); Mem., Takeover Panel, 1991–93. Liveryman, Bakers' Co., 1988–. *Recreations:* golf, squash, shooting. *Address:* 22 Rutland Gate, SW7 1BB. *Clubs:* White's, Lansdowne; Wentworth Golf; St George's Hill Golf; Westhill Golf.

MANDUELL, Sir John, Kt 1989; CBE 1982; FRAM, FRCM, FRNCM, FRSAMD; composer; Principal, Royal Northern College of Music, 1971–96; *b* 1928; *s* of Matthewman Donald Manduell, MC, MA, and Theodora (*née* Tharp); *m* 1955, Renna Kellaway; three *s* one *d*. *Educ:* Haileybury Coll.; Jesus Coll., Cambridge; Univ. of Strasbourg; Royal Acad. of Music. FRAM 1964; FRNCM 1974, CRNCM 1996; FRCM 1980; FRSAMD 1982; FRWCMD (FWCMD 1991); Hon. FTCL 1973; Hon. GSM 1986. BBC: music producer, 1956–61; Head of Music, Midlands and E Anglia, 1961–64; Chief Planner, The Music Programme, 1964–68; University of Lancaster: Dir of Music, 1968–71; Mem. Court and Council, 1972–77, 1979–83. University of Manchester: Hon. Lectr in Music, 1976–96; Mem. Court, 1990–2003. Prog. Dir, Cheltenham Festival, 1969–94; Vice-Pres., Cheltenham (formerly Cheltenham Arts) Festivals Ltd, 1995–. Arts Council: Mem. Council, 1976–78, 1980–84; Mem. Music Panel, 1971–76, Dep. Chm., 1976–78, Chm., 1980–84; Mem. Touring Cttee, 1975–80, Chm., 1976–78; Mem. Trng Cttee, 1973–77. Mem. Music Adv. Cttee, British Council, 1963–72, Chm., 1973–80; Chm. Music Panel, North West Arts, 1973–79; Man., NW Arts Bd, 1991–97. President: British Arts Fests Assoc., 1988–2004 (Vice-Chm., 1977–81, Chm., 1981–88); European Assoc. of Music Academies (now Assoc. of European Conservatoires), 1988–96 (Hon. Pres., 1996); Manchester Olympic Fest., 1990; ISM, 1991–92; Lennox Berkeley Soc., 2001–09; European Music Year (1985): Dep. Chm. UK Cttee, 1982–85; Member: Eur. Organising Cttee, 1982–86; Eur. Exec. Bureau, 1982–86; Internat. Prog. Cttee, 1982–84; Mem. Exec. Cttee, Composers' Guild of GB, 1984–87 (Vice Chm., 1987–89, Chm., 1989–92); Gulbenkian Foundn Enquiry into Trng Musicians, 1978; Mem. Opera Bd, 1988–95, Mem. Bd, 1989–95, Royal Opera House; Chairman: Cttee of Heads of Music Colls, 1986–90; Nat. Curriculum Music Working Gp, 1990–91; European Opera Centre, 1995–2005; Nat. Assoc. of Youth Orchestras, 1996–2005; Governor: Chetham's Sch., 1971–2006; National Youth Orch., 1964–73, 1978–96; President: Lakeland Sinfonia, 1972–89; Jubilate Choir, 1979–91; Director: London Opera Centre, 1971–79; Associated Bd of Royal Schools of Music, 1973–96; Northern Ballet Theatre, 1973–86 (Chm., 1986–89; Vice Pres., 2006–); Manchester Palace Theatre Trust, 1978–84; London Orchestral Concert Bd, 1980–85; Young Concert Artists' Trust, 1983–93; Lake Dist Summer Music Fest., 1984– (Chm., 1996–2005); Chm., Lake Dist Summer Music Trust, 2005–. Mem. Bd, Hallé Concerts Soc. (Dep. Chm., 1997–99). Hon. Member: Roy. Soc. of Musicians, 1972; Chopin Soc. of Warsaw, 1973. Engagements and tours as composer and lectr in Canada, Europe, Hong Kong, S Africa and USA. Chairman: BBC TV Young Musicians of the Year, 1978–84; Munich ARD, 1979–2004; Geneva Internat. Music Comp., 1986–96; Paris Internat. Music Comp., 1992, 1994, 1996, 1998, 2003; Chm. or mem., national and internat. music competition juries. FRSA 1981; Fellow, Manchester Polytechnic, 1983. Hon. DMus: Lancaster, 1990; Manchester, 1992; RSAMD 1996. First Leslie Boosey Award, Royal Phil. Soc. and PRS, 1980. Chevalier de l'Ordre des Arts et des Lettres (France), 1990. *Publications:* (contrib.) The Symphony, ed Simpson, 1966; *compositions include:* Chansons de la Renaissance, 1956; Gradi, 1963; Diversions for Orchestra, 1970; String Quartet, 1976; Prayers from the Ark, 1981; Double Concerto, 1985; Vistas, 1997; Into the Ark, 1997; Flute Concerto, 2002; Nonet, 2005; Quartet, 2007; Calvary Choruses, 2007; Equine Skirmishes, 2009; Double Concerto, 2012; Recit and Aria, 2013. *Recreations:* cricket, travel. *Address:* Chesham, High Bentham, Lancaster LA2 7JY. *T:* (01524) 261702. *Clubs:* Royal Over-Seas League, MCC.

MANGO, Prof. Cyril Alexander, FBA 1976; Bywater and Sotheby Professor of Byzantine and Modern Greek, 1973–95, and Emeritus Fellow of Exeter College, Oxford University; *b* 14 April 1928; *s* of Alexander A. Mango and Adelaide Damonov; *m* 1st, 1953, Mabel Grover; one *d*; 2nd, 1964, Susan A. Gerstel; one *d*; 3rd, 1976, Maria C. Mundell. *Educ:* Univ. of St Andrews (MA); Univ. of Paris (Dr Univ. Paris). From Jun. Fellow to Lectr in Byzantine Archaeology, Dumbarton Oaks Byzantine Center, Harvard Univ., 1951–63; Lectr in Fine Arts, Harvard Univ., 1957–58; Visiting Associate Prof. of Byzantine History, Univ. of California, Berkeley, 1960–61; Koraës Prof. of Modern Greek and of Byzantine History, Language and Literature, King's Coll., Univ. of London, 1963–68; Prof. of Byzantine Archaeology, Dumbarton Oaks Byzantine Center, 1968–73. FSA. *Publications:* The Homilies of Photius, 1958; The Brazen House, 1959; The Mosaics of St Sophia at Istanbul, 1962; The Art of the Byzantine Empire, Sources and Documents, 1972; Architettura bizantina, 1974; Byzantium, 1980; Byzantium and its Image, 1984; Le Développement Urbain de Constantinople, 1985; (ed) The Oxford History of Byzantium, 2002. *Address:* 12 High Street, Brill, Aylesbury, Bucks HP18 9ST.

MANGOLD, Thomas Cornelius; freelance television and radio correspondent and travel writer, since 2003; author; Senior Correspondent, BBC TV Panorama, 1976–2003; *b* 20 Aug. 1934; *s* of Fritz Mangold and Dorothea Mangold; *m* 1st, 1958, Anne (*née* Butler) (marr. diss. 1970); one *d*; 2nd, 1972, Valerie Ann Hare (*née* Dean) (marr. diss. 1991); two *d*; 3rd, 2000, Kathryn Mary Colleton Parkinson-Smith. *Educ:* Dorking Grammar Sch. Reporter, Croydon Advertiser, 1952. Served RA, 1952–54. Reporter: Croydon Advertiser, 1955–59; Sunday Pictorial, 1959–62; Daily Express, 1962–64; BBC TV News, 1964–70; BBC TV Current Affairs (24 Hours, later Midweek), 1970–76. *Publications:* (jtly) The File on the Tsar, 1976; (jtly) The Tunnels of Cu Chi, 1985; Cold Warrior, 1991; Plague Wars, 1999. *Recreations:* writing, playing Blues harp. *Address:* c/o A. M. Heath, 6 Warwick Court, WC1R 5DJ. *T:* (020) 7242 2811. *E:* beebtom@aol.com. *W:* www.tommangold.com.

MANKTELOW, Rt Rev. Michael Richard John; an Hon. Assistant Bishop: of Chichester, since 1994; of Gibraltar in Europe, since 1994; *b* 23 Sept. 1927; *s* of late Sir Richard Manktelow, KBE, CB, and late Helen Manktelow; *m* 1966, Rosamund Mann; three *d*. *Educ:* Whitgift School, Croydon; Christ's Coll., Cambridge (MA 1952); Chichester Theol Coll. Deacon 1953, priest 1954, Lincoln; Asst Curate of Boston, Lincs, 1953–57; Chaplain of Christ's Coll., Cambridge, 1957–61; Chaplain of Lincoln Theological Coll., 1961–64, Sub-Warden, 1964–66; Vicar of Knaresborough, 1966–73; Rural Dean of Harrogate, 1972–77; Vicar of St Wilfrid's, Harrogate, 1973–77; Hon. Canon of Ripon Cathedral, 1975–77; Bishop Suffragan of Basingstoke, 1977–93; Canon Residentiary, 1977–91, Vice-Dean, 1987–91, Hon. Canon, 1991–93, Canon Emeritus, 1993, Winchester Cathedral. Bursalis Prebendary, Chichester Cathedral, 1997–2002, Canon Emeritus, 2002. President: Anglican and Eastern Churches Assoc., 1980–97; Assoc. for Promoting Retreats, 1982–87. *Publications:* Forbes

Robinson: disciple of love, 1961; John Moorman: Anglican, Franciscan, Independent, 1999. *Recreations:* music, walking. *Address:* 14 Little London, Chichester, West Sussex PO19 1NZ. *T:* (01243) 531096.

MANLEY, Andrew Robert, PhD; Chief Executive, Defence Infrastructure Organisation, 2011–14; *b* Wallingford, 17 June 1956; *s* of Anthony John Manley and Gillian Kathleen Manley (*née* West); *m* 1980, Pauline Catterall; one *s* one *d. Educ:* Bradfield Coll.; Univ. of Wales (BSc 1977; PhD 1980); London Business Sch. (MBA 1991). Cert. Co. Directorship 2006. MCIPS 2010; MRICS 2012. Royal Dutch Shell: Mktg Exec., 1980–92; Chief Exec., Shell Cos, Paraguay, 1993–98; Chm., Forestal Yguazu SRL, 1996–98; Commercial Dir, Shell UK Ltd, 1999–2002; Dir, Shell Gas UK Ltd, 1999–2010; Vice Pres., Latin America, 2003–08; Prog. Dir, Shell Canada Ltd, 2008–09; Dir, Downstream Projects, Shell Internat. Ltd, 2009–10; Commercial Dir, MoD, 2010–11; non-executive Director: Defence Equipment and Support, 2010–11; Defence Estates, 2010–11. Non-exec. Dir, Symatrix UK Ltd, 2009–. MInstD 2000. *Recreations:* hiking, sailing, theatre.

MANLEY, David Eric; QC 2003; *b* 30 April 1956; *s* of Eric and May Manley; *m* 1983, Caroline Morgan; one *s* one *d. Educ:* Leeds Univ. (BA Hons). Called to the Bar, Inner Temple, 1981; in practice, specialising in planning and environmental law. *Recreations:* gardening, reading, shooting, fishing. *Address:* King's Chambers, 36 Young Street, Manchester M3 3FT. *T:* (0161) 832 9082, *Fax:* (0161) 835 2139. *E:* clerks@kingschambers.com.

MANLEY, Hilary; Her Honour Judge Manley; a Circuit Judge, since 2014; *b* Sheffield, 17 July 1966; *d* of Peter Scott Manley and Alison Manley (*née* Needham); *m* 1998, Jonathan Gregg; one *d. Educ:* University Coll. London (LLB (Hons)). Called to the Bar, Gray's Inn, 1996; a Recorder, NE Circuit, 2012–14. *Recreations:* music, photography, history, travel. *Address:* Courts of Justice, Crown Square, Manchester M3 3FL.

MANLEY, Ivor Thomas, CB 1984; Deputy Secretary, Department of Employment, 1987–91; *b* 4 March 1931; *s* of Frederick Stone and Louisa Manley; *m* 1952, Joan Waite; one *s* one *d. Educ:* Sutton High Sch., Plymouth. Entered Civil Service, 1951; Principal: Min. of Aviation, 1964–66; Min. of Technology, 1966–68; Private Secretary: to Rt Hon. Anthony Wedgwood Benn, 1968–70; to Rt Hon. Geoffrey Rippon, 1970; Principal Private Sec. to Rt Hon. John Davies, 1970–71; Asst Sec., DTI, 1971–74; Department of Energy: Under-Sec., Principal Estabt Officer, 1974–78, Under Sec., Atomic Energy Div., 1978–81; Dep. Sec., 1981–87. UK Governor, IAEA, 1978–81; Mem., UKAEA, 1981–86. Chm., Task Force on Tourism and the Envmt, 1990–91; Board Member: Business in the Community, 1988–89; BTA, 1991–95 (Chm., Marketing Cttee, 1991–95); Volunteer Centre, UK, 1992–2000; Consortium on Opportunities for Volunteering, 1996–2000; Third Age Trust, 1999–2004 (Vice Chm., 2001–04); Chm., Univ. of Third Age, Farnborough, 2006–11. *Recreations:* walking, reading, travelling, Univ. of the Third Age. *Address:* 28 Highfield Avenue, Aldershot, Hants GU11 3BZ. *T:* (01252) 322707.

MANLEY, Hon. John (Paul); PC (Can.) 1993; OC 2009; President and Chief Executive Officer, Canadian Council of Chief Executives, since 2010; *b* 15 Jan. 1950; *s* of John Joseph and Mildred Charlotte (Scharf) Manley; *m* 1973, Judith Mary Rae; one *s* two *d. Educ:* Carleton Univ. (BA 1971); Univ. of Ottawa (Law 1976). Law clerk for Chief Justice of Canada, 1976–77; Partner, Perley-Robertson, Panet, Hill & McDougall, lawyers, 1977–88; Chm., Ottawa-Carleton BoT, 1985–86. MP (L) Ottawa S, 1988–2004; Minister: of Industry, 1993–2000; of Western Econ. Diversification, Atlantic Canadian Opportunities Agency, 1996; of Econ. Develt for Quebec Regs, 1996–2000; of Foreign Affairs, 2000–02; of Infrastructure and Crown Corporations, and of Finance, 2002–03; Dep. Prime Minister of Canada, 2002–03; Political Minister for Ontario, 2002–03; Sen. Counsel, McCarthy Tétrault LLP, 2004–09. Chairman, Cabinet Committees: on Public Security and Anti-Terrorism, 2001–03; on Econ. Union and Social Union, 2002–03. Chm., Ontario Power Gen. Review Cttee, 2004. Dir, Nortel Networks, 2004–09. Newsmaker of Year, Time Mag. of Canada, 2001. *Recreation:* marathon runner. *Address:* Canadian Council of Chief Executives, 99 Bank Street, Suite 1001, Ottawa, ON K1P 6B9, Canada.

MANLEY, Simon John, CMG 2009; HM Diplomatic Service; Ambassador to Spain and concurrently (non-resident) to Andorra, since 2013; *b* 18 Sept. 1967; *s* of James and Beryl Manley; *m* 1996, Maria Isabel Fernandez Utgès; three *d. Educ:* Montpelier Primary Sch., Ealing; Latymer Upper Sch., Hammersmith; Magdalen Coll., Oxford (BA Hons Modern Hist.); Yale Univ. Grad. Sch. (MA Internat. Relns). Entered HM Diplomatic Service, 1990; UN Dept, FCO, 1990–93; on secondment to DGIV (Competition), EC, 1993; UKMIS to UN, NY, 1993–98; on secondment to EU Council of Ministers, 1998–2002; Dep. Hd, EU (Internal), FCO, 2002–03; Head: Econ. and Central Europe Team, FCO, 2003–06; Counter-Terrorism Policy Dept, FCO, 2006–07; Dir, Defence and Strategic Threats, FCO, 2007–11; Dir, Europe, FCO, 2011–13. Comdr, Order of Merit (Poland), 2004. *Recreations:* theatre, gardens, history. *Address:* c/o Foreign and Commonwealth Office, King Charles Street, SW1A 2AH.

MANLY, Timothy John; Headmaster, Hurstpierpoint College, since 2005; *b* 12 Feb. 1964; *m* 1990, Henrietta Whetstone; two *s* two *d. Educ:* Oriel Coll., Oxford (BA Hons Lit. Hum.); London Sch. of Econs (MSc); Hughes Hall, Cambridge (PGCE). Various appts in commerce, 1987–93; Sevenoaks School: Teacher, 1994–2000; Housemaster, 1996–2000; Hd of Classics Dept, 1996–99; Dep. Headmaster, Oakham Sch., 2000–04. Non-exec. Dir, Harris Fedn of S London Schs, 2007–11. Governor: Hazelwood Prep. Sch., 2009–; Dorset House Prep. Sch., 2010–. Chm., Woodard Heads' Assoc., 2011–13. *Recreations:* family, cross-country and distance running, most racquet sports, bridge, books. *Address:* Hurstpierpoint College, Malthouse Lane, Hurstpierpoint, Hassocks, W Sussex BN6 9JS. *T:* (01273) 833636. *E:* headmaster@hppc.co.uk.

MANN, Hon. Sir Anthony; *see* Mann, Hon. Sir G. A.

MANN, Prof. Anthony Howard, MD; FRCP, FRCPsych; Professor of Epidemiological Psychiatry, Institute of Psychiatry, King's College London, 1989–2013, now Emeritus; *b* 11 Dec. 1940; *s* of Alfred Haward Mann and Marjory Ethel (*née* Weatherly); civil partnership 2006, Pekka Antero Vaalle. *Educ:* Rugby Sch.; Jesus Coll., Cambridge (MD 1982); St Bartholomew's Hosp. FRCPsych 1984; FRCP 1986. Res. worker, and Sen. Lectr, Inst. of Psychiatry, 1972–80; Sen. Lectr, then Prof. of Psychiatry, Royal Free Hosp., 1980–89. Associate Prof., Montpellier Univ., 2002–03. Hon. FRCGP 2001. *Publications:* In Sunshine and Shadow: the family story of Danny Boy, 2013; numerous contribs to scientific jls on psychiatry of old age, general practice and epidemiology. *Recreations:* friends, France, historical research. *Address:* c/o Hoare and Co., 32 Lowndes Street, SW1X 9HZ.

MANN, Prof. (Colin) Nicholas (Jocelyn), CBE 1999; PhD; FBA 1992; Emeritus Professor of Renaissance Studies, since 2007, and Distinguished Senior Fellow, since 2009, School of Advanced Study, University of London; *b* 24 Oct. 1942; *s* of Colin Henry Mann and Marie Elise Mann (*née* Gosling); *m* 1st, 1964, Joëlle Bourcart (marr. diss. 2003); one *s* one *d*; 2nd, 2003, Helen Margaret Stevenson; two *d. Educ:* Eton; King's Coll., Cambridge (MA, PhD). Res. Fellow, Clare Coll., Cambridge, 1965–67; Lectr, Univ. of Warwick, 1967–72; Vis. Fellow, All Souls Coll., Oxford, 1972; Fellow and Tutor, Pembroke Coll., Oxford, 1973–90, Emeritus Fellow, 1991–2006, Hon. Fellow, 2006; University of London: Dir, Warburg Inst., and Prof. of Hist. of Classical Tradition, 1990–2001; Sen. Res. Fellow, Warburg Inst., 2001–07; Dean, Sch. of Advanced Study, 2002–07; Pro-Vice-Chancellor, 2003–07. Visiting Professor: Univ. of Toronto, 1996; Coll. de France, 1998; Univ. of Calabria, 1999–2000. Member Council: Mus. of Modern Art, Oxford, 1984–92 (Chm., 1988–90); Contemporary Applied Arts, 1994–2005 (Chm., 1996–99); British Acad., 1995–98, 1999–2006 (For. Sec., 1999–2006); RHBNC, 1996–98; RCA, 2001–07; Mem., British Library Adv. Council, 1997–2002. Vice-Pres., ALLEA, 2006–11. Trustee: Cubitt Artists, 1996–99; Learning Skills Res., 2010–; Padworth Coll., 2014–. Fellow: European Medieval Acad., 1993; Fondazione Lorenzo Valla, 2007. Romance Editor, Medium Ævum, 1982–90. Hon. DLitt Warwick, 2006. *Publications:* Petrarch Manuscripts in the British Isles, 1975; Petrarch, 1984; A Concordance to Petrarch's Bucolicum Carmen, 1984; (ed jtly) Lorenzo the Magnificent: culture and politics, 1996; (ed jtly) Medieval and Renaissance Scholarship, 1996; (ed jtly) Giordano Bruno 1583–1585: the English experience, 1997; (ed jtly) The Image of the Individual: portraits in the Renaissance, 1998; (ed jtly) Photographs at the Frontier: Aby Warburg in America 1895–1896, 1998; Carnets de voyage, 2003; Pétrarque: les voyages de l'esprit, 2004; (ed jtly) Britannia Latina: Latin in the culture of Great Britain from the Middle Ages to the twentieth century, 2005; articles in learned jls, 1969–2012. *Recreations:* yoga, poetry, sculpture. *Address:* 34 High Street, Axbridge, Som BS26 2AF. *T:* (01934) 732151.

MANN, David William; management consultant, since 2014; *b* 14 June 1944; *s* of William and Mary Mann; *m* 1968, Gillian Mary Edwards; two *s. Educ:* Felixstowe Grammar Sch.; Jesus Coll., Cambridge (MA). CEng; CITP; FBCS. CEIR, 1966–69; Logica: joined 1969; Dir, 1976; Man. Dir, UK Ops, 1979; Dep. Gp Man. Dir, 1982; Gp Man. Dir and Chief Exec., 1987; Dep. Chm., 1993–94. Chairman: Cambridge Display Technol., 1995–97; Flomerics Gp, 1995–2008; Velti plc, 2006–14; Chm., 1996–2007, Dep. Chm., 2007–14, Charteris plc. Director: Industrial Control Services Gp, 1994–2000; Druid Gp, 1996–2000; Room Solutions (formerly Room Underwriting Systems), 1996–2006; Aveva (formerly Cadcentre) Group, 1999–2010; Eurolink Managed Services, 1999–2000; Ansbacher Hldgs, 2000–04. Special Advr, Technical Rev. Cttee of Bd, NATS, 2010–. Mem., Engineering Council, 1993–95. Pres., British Computer Soc., 1994–95. Master, Information Technologists' Co., 1997–98 (Chm., 2002–07, Dir, 2007–11, Charitable Trust). Chm., Livery Past Masters' Assoc. 1997/98, 2006–09. CCMI (CIMgt 1994–2008); FInstD 1994–2006. Chm., Epping Forest Wine Soc., 2005–12. *Recreations:* gardening, walking, ski-ing. *Address:* Theydon Copt, Forest Side, Epping, Essex CM16 4ED. *T:* (01992) 575842, 07956 341105. *Club:* Athenæum (Mem., Wine Cttee).

MANN, Hon. Sir (George) Anthony, Kt 2004; **Hon. Mr Justice Mann;** a Judge of the High Court of Justice, Chancery Division, since 2004; *b* 21 May 1951; *s* of George Edgar and Ilse Beate Mann; *m* 1979, Margaret Ann Sherret; two *d. Educ:* Chesterfield Grammar Sch.; Perse Sch., Cambridge; St Peter's Coll., Oxford (BA 1973; MA 1977; Hon. Fellow 2010). Called to the Bar, Lincoln's Inn, 1974, Bencher, 2002; QC 1992; a Recorder, 2002–04. *Recreations:* French horn playing, music, computers. *Address:* Royal Courts of Justice, 7 Rolls Building, Fetter Lane, EC4A 1NL.

MANN, Prof. Gillian Lesley, (Jill), FBA 1990; Notre Dame Professor of English, University of Notre Dame, Indiana, 1999–2004, now Emeritus Professor; *b* 7 April 1943; *d* of late Edward William Ditchburn and Kathleen Ditchburn (*née* Bellamy); *m* 1st, 1964, Michael Mann (marr. diss. 1976); 2nd, 2003, Michael Lapidge. *Educ:* Bede Grammar Sch., Sunderland; St Anne's Coll., Oxford (BA 1964; Hon. Fellow, 1990); Clare Hall, Cambridge (MA; PhD 1971). Research Fellow, Clare Hall, Cambridge, 1968–71; Lectr, Univ. of Kent at Canterbury, 1971–72; University of Cambridge: Official Fellow, 1972–88, Professorial Fellow, 1988–98, Life Fellow, 1999, Girton Coll.; Asst Lectr, 1974–78; Lectr, 1978–88; Prof. of Medieval and Renaissance English, 1988–98. British Academy Research Reader, 1985–87. *Publications:* Chaucer and Medieval Estates Satire, 1973; Ysengrimus, 1987; (ed with Piero Boitani) The Cambridge Chaucer Companion, 1986, rev. edn 2003; Geoffrey Chaucer, 1991; Feminizing Chaucer, 2002; (ed) Canterbury Tales, 2005; (ed with Maura Nolan) The Text in the Community, 2006; From Aesop to Reynard, 2009; Life in Words: essays on Chaucer, the Gawain-Poet, and Malory, 2014; articles on Middle English, medieval French and medieval Latin. *Recreation:* travel. *Address:* Girton College, Cambridge CB3 0JG.

MANN, Jillian Rose, MBE 2013; FRCP, FRCPCH; Consultant Paediatric Oncologist, Birmingham Children's Hospital, 1979–2002, now Emeritus; *b* 29 April 1939; *d* of William Farmcote Mann and Vera Maud Mann. *Educ:* Pate's Grammar Sch. for Girls, Cheltenham; St Thomas' Hosp. Med. Sch., London (MB BS 1962). LRCP 1962, MRCP 1966, FRCP 1980; MRCS 1962; DCH 1964; FRCPCH 1997, Hon. FRCPCH 2004. Postgrad. trng, St Thomas' and Great Ormond St Children's Hosps, 1963–67, and Birmingham Children's Hosp., 1967–71; Consultant Paediatrician, S Birmingham, and Consultant Associate in Haematological Diseases, Birmingham Children's Hosp., 1972–79. Hon. Prof., Sch. of Medicine, Univ. of Birmingham, 1997–2006. Member: Cttee on Med. Aspects of Radiation in the Envmt, DoH, 1985–89; Standing Med. Adv. Cttee, DoH, 1986–90. Member: Leukaemia in Childhood Wkg party, MRC, 1975–2000; Med. and Scientific Adv. Panel, Leukaemia Res. Fund, 1985–88. Mem. Council, RCP, 1988–91; RCP and RCPCH: Regl Advr, 1994–99; Examr for MRCP/MRCPCH, 1994–2002. Founder Mem., 1977, Sec., 1977–81, Chm., 1983–86, UK Children's Cancer Study Gp; Chm., Educn and Trng Cttee, Soc. Internat. d'Oncologie Pédiatrique Europe and Eur. Soc. of Paediatric Haematol. and Immunol., 2000–03. Trustee, Birmingham Children's Hosp. Charities, 2003–11 (Chm., 2004–09). Mem., Lunar Soc., Birmingham, 1994–2012. Eur. Women of Achievement Award, Humanitarian Section, EUW, 1996; Nye Bevan Lifetime Achievement Award, 2000. *Publications:* numerous book chapters and contribs to learned jls mostly on childhood leukaemia, cancer and blood diseases; numerous abstracts of contribs to nat. and internat. scientific meetings. *Recreations:* music, country pursuits, local history.

MANN, John; MP (Lab) Bassetlaw, since 2001; *b* 10 Jan. 1960; *s* of James Mann and Brenda (*née* Cleavin); *m* 1986, Joanna White; one *s* two *d. Educ:* Manchester Univ. (BA Econ). MIPD. Hd of Res. and Educn, AEU, 1988–90; Nat. Trng Officer, TUC, 1990–95; Liaison Officer, Nat. Trade Union and Lab Party, 1995–2000. Dir, Abraxas Communications Ltd, 1998–2001. Mem. (Lab), Lambeth BC, 1986–90. Mem., Treasury Select Cttee, 2003–05, 2009–. Mem., Editl Adv. Panel, People Management, 2005–. *Publications:* (with Phil Woolas) Labour and Youth: the missing generation, 1985; The Real Deal: drug policy that works, 2006. *Recreations:* football, cricket, hill walking. *Address:* House of Commons, SW1A 0AA. *Clubs:* Manton Miners'; Worksop Town.

MANN, John Frederick; educational consultant; *b* 4 June 1930; *e s* of Frederick Mann and Hilda G. (*née* Johnson); *m* 1966, Margaret (*née* Moore); one *s* one *d. Educ:* Poole and Tavistock Grammar Schs; Trinity Coll., Oxford (MA); Birmingham Univ. Asst Master, Colchester Royal Grammar Sch., 1954–61; Admin. Asst, Leeds County Bor., 1962–65; Asst Educn Officer, Essex CC, 1965–67; Dep. Educn Officer, Sheffield County Bor., 1967–78; Sec., Schools Council for the Curriculum and Exams, 1978–83; Dir of Educn, London Bor. of Harrow, 1983–88. Member: Iron and Steel Industry Trng Bd, 1975–78; Exec., Soc. of Educn Officers, 1976–78; Sch. Broadcasting Council, 1979–83; Council, British Educn Management and Admin Soc., 1979–84; Cttee, Soc. of Educn Consultants, 1990–95 (Sec., 1990–94; Vice Chm., 1994–95). Chm., Standards Cttee, 2002–11, Ind. Person, 2012–, Brent BC. Governor: Welbeck Coll., 1975–84; Hall Sch., 1985–88. Chm., Brent Samaritans, 1995–99. Hon. Fellow, Sheffield Polytechnic, 1980; Hon. FCP, 1986. FRSA. JP Sheffield, 1976–79. *Publications:* Education, 1979; Highbury Fields School, 1994; To Gladly Learn, and Gladly Teach, 2004; contrib. to Victoria County History of Essex, Local Govt Studies, and Educn. *Recreations:* travel, books, theatre, gardening. *Address:* 109 Chatsworth Road, NW2 4BH. *T:* (020) 8459 5419.

MANN, Very Rev. John Owen; Dean of Belfast, since 2011; *b* Blackheath, 20 March 1955; *s* of Dr Edgar Mann and Joan Mann; *m* 1976, Helen Kneale; one *s* one *d. Educ:* Queen's Univ. Belfast (BD 1977; MTh 1986; MPhil 1998); C of I Theol Coll. Ordained deacon, 1979, priest, 1981; Assistant Curate: Cloughfern, 1979–82; St Columba, Knock, 1982–85; Rector: St John the Baptist, Ballyrashane, 1985–89; Parishes of Bentworth, Shalden and Lasham, Dio. of Winchester, 1989–93; Rural Dean, Alton, 1992–93; Rector: Ascension, Cloughfern, 1993–2002; St John, Malone, 2002–11. Preb. of Clonmethan, Nat. Cathedral of St Patrick's, Dublin, 1999–2011. *Address:* The Deanery, 5 Deramore Drive, Belfast BT9 5JQ.

MANN, Jonathan Simon; QC 2015; a Recorder, since 2012; *b* London, 19 June 1966; *s* of Brian Mann and Ruth Mann; *m* 2001, Pamela Reddy; one *s* one *d. Educ:* Atholl Grammar Sch.; Univ. of Essex (LLB Hons 1987). Called to the Bar, Inner Temple, 1989; in practice as barrister, specialising in criminal defence, fraud and regulatory compliance. Mem., Sentencing Adv. Panel, 2010. Mem., Gen. Cttee, 2006–08, Treas., 2008–10, Criminal Bar Assoc. *Recreations:* study of medieval and Tudor history, study and collection of medieval coinage. *Address:* Doughty Street Chambers, 54 Doughty Street, WC1N 2LS. *T:* (020) 7404 1313. *E:* j.mann@doughtystreet.co.uk.

MANN, Martin Edward; QC 1983; a Deputy High Court Judge, Chancery Division, since 1992; *b* 12 Sept. 1943; *s* of late S. E. Mann and M. L. F. Mann; *m* 1966, Jacqueline Harriette (*née* Le Maître); two *d. Educ:* Cranleigh Sch. Called to the Bar, Gray's Inn, 1968 (Lord Justice Holker Sen. Exhibn), Lincoln's Inn, 1973 (*ad eund*); Bencher, Lincoln's Inn, 1991. Mem., Senate of the Inns of Court and the Bar, 1979–82; Chm., Bar Council Fees Collection Cttee, 1993–95; Mem., QC Selection Panel, 2013–. Member of numerous professional assocs including: Chancery Bar Assoc.; Commercial Bar Assoc.; European Circuit; Bar of Eastern Caribbean Supreme Ct; Commercial Fraud Lawyers' Assoc.; Assoc. of Contentious Trust and Probate Specialists; registered practitioner, DIFC (Dubai). Consultant Ed., Palmer's Company Law Manual. *Publications:* (jtly) What Kind of Common Agricultural Policy for Europe, 1975; (contrib.) Tolley's Insolvency Law; (contrib.) Blackstone's Guide to the Companies Act, 2006. *Recreations:* farming, the arts. *Address:* 24 Old Buildings, Lincoln's Inn, WC2A 3UP. *T:* (020) 7404 0946; Kingston St Mary, Somerset. *Club:* Garrick.

MANN, Murray G.; *see* Gell-Mann.

MANN, Nicholas; *see* Mann, C. N. J.

MANN, Paul; QC 2002; a Recorder, since 1999; *b* 4 Feb. 1958; *s* of George Arthur and Elsie May Mann; *m* 1988, Carol Joy Beddows. *Educ:* Trent Coll., Long Eaton, Derbyshire; Manchester Poly. (BA Hons Law). Called to the Bar, Gray's Inn, 1980, Bencher, 2008; in practice as barrister, specialising in crime. Treas., 2002–08, Dep. Leader, Nottingham, 2008–11, Midland Circuit. *Recreations:* travel, cycling, walking, play writing, gardening, local history. *Address:* 1 High Pavement, Nottingham NG1 1HF. *T:* (0115) 941 8218, *Fax:* (0115) 941 8240.

MANN, Sir Rupert (Edward), 3rd Bt *cr* 1905; *b* 11 Nov. 1946; *s* of Major Edward Charles Mann, DSO, MC (*g s* of 1st Bt) (*d* 1959), and Pamela Margaret, *o d* of late Major Frank Haultain Hornsby; *S* great uncle, 1971; *m* 1974, Mary Rose, *d* of Geoffrey Butler, Stetchworth, Newmarket; two *s. Educ:* Malvern. *Heir: s* Alexander Rupert Mann, *b* 6 April 1978. *Address:* Billingford Hall, Diss, Norfolk IP21 4HN. *Clubs:* Boodle's, MCC; Norfolk.

MANN, Scott Leslie; MP (C) North Cornwall, since 2015; *b* 24 June 1977; *s* of Eugene Mann and Peggy Mann; one *d. Educ:* Wadebridge Boys' Sch.; Wadebridge Comp. Sch.; St Austell Coll. (BTEC Business Diploma). Gardener, 1994–97; butcher, 1995–98; postman, 1995–2015; retail worker, 1997–2000. Mem., Cornwall Council, 2009–. Mem., Wadebridge Angling Assoc. *Recreations:* fishing, road cycling, running. *Address:* (office) 10 Market House Arcade, Bodmin Fore Street, Bodmin, Cornwall PL31 2JA. *T:* (01208) 74337. *E:* scott@scottmann.org.uk. *Clubs:* United and Cecil; Wadebridge Cricket (Hon. Vice Pres., 2013–).

MANN, Prof. Stephen, DPhil; FRS 2003; Professor of Chemistry, University of Bristol, since 1998; *b* 1 April 1955; *s* of Harold and Olive Mann; *m* 1977, Jane Lucinda Musgrave; one *s* one *d. Educ:* Univ. of Manchester Inst. of Sci. and Technol. (BSc Hons Chem. 1976); Univ. of Manchester (MSc 1978); DPhil Oxford 1981. University of Bath: Lectr in Chem., 1984–88; Reader, 1988–90; Prof. of Chem., 1990–98. *Publications:* Biomineralization: principles and concepts in bioinorganic materials chemistry, 2001; numerous contribs to learned scientific jls. *Recreations:* running, electric guitar, family life. *Address:* School of Chemistry, University of Bristol, Bristol BS8 1TS. *T:* (0117) 928 9935. *E:* s.mann@bris.ac.uk.

MANNERS, family name of **Duke of Rutland** and **Baron Manners**.

MANNERS, 6th Baron *cr* 1807, of Foston, co. Lincoln; **John Hugh Robert Manners;** Partner, Macfarlanes, 1987–2014 (Head of Litigation, 2000–08); *b* 5 May 1956; *s* of 5th Baron Manners and Jennifer Selena, *d* of Ian Fairbairn; *S* father, 2008; *m* 2007, Juliet Elizabeth Anthea McMyn; one *s* one *d*, and two *d* by former marriage. *Educ:* Eton. Admitted Solicitor, 1980. *Recreations:* shooting, walking, Irish Terriers. *Heir: s* Hon. John Alexander David Manners, *b* 22 Feb. 2011. *Address:* North Ripley House, Avon, Christchurch, Dorset BH23 8EP. *Club:* Pratt's.

MANNERS, Prof. Ian, PhD; FRS 2011; FRS(Can); Professor of Inorganic, Macromolecular and Materials Chemistry, since 2006 and European Union Marie Curie Chair, since 2005, University of Bristol; *b* 1961; *m* 1980, Deborah O'Hanlon; one *s* one *d. Educ:* Univ. of Bristol (BSc 1st Cl. Hons 1982; PhD Chem. 1985). Postdoctoral res., Dept of Inorganic Chem., Univ. of Aachen, 1986–87; Res. Associate, Dept of Chem., Pennsylvania State Univ., 1988–90; Department of Chemistry, University of Toronto: Asst Prof., 1990–94; Associate Prof., 1994–95; Prof., 1995–; Canada Res. Chair, 2001. Tilden Lectr, RSC, 2007. Alfred P. Sloan Fellow, 1994–98. FRS(Can) 2001. Rutherford Meml Medal in Chem., 1996, Peter Days Award, 2012, RSC; Corday-Morgan Medal, 1997, Wolfson Merit Award, 2005, Royal Soc.; Steacie Prize, E. W. R. Steacie Meml Trust, 2000. *Publications:* Synthetic Metal-Containing Polymers; Metal-Containing and Metallosupramolecular Polymers and Materials; Frontiers in Transition Metal-Containing Polymers; Inorganic Rings and Polymers of the P-Block Elements; contrib. papers to scientific jls, incl. Science, Inorganic Chem., Jl Amer. Chem. Soc.; 11 patents. *Address:* School of Chemistry, University of Bristol, Bristol BS8 1TS.

MANNERS, Hon. Thomas (Jasper); Director, Lazard Brothers, 1965–89 (Deputy Chairman, 1986–89); *b* 12 Dec. 1929; *y s* of 4th Baron Manners, MC, and of Mary Edith, *d* of late Rt Rev. Lord William Cecil; *m* 1955, Sarah, *d* of Brig. Roger Peake, DSO; three *s. Educ:* Eton. Lazard Brothers & Co. Ltd, 1955–89; Director: Legal & General Gp, 1972–93; Scapa Gp, 1970–96; Davy Corp., 1985–91. *Recreations:* shooting, fishing. *Address:* Holly House, The Paddock, Newbury Road, Kingsclere, Newbury, Berks RG20 5SP. *Club:* White's.

MANNING, Prof. Aubrey William George, OBE 1998; DPhil; FRSE, FRSB; Professor of Natural History, University of Edinburgh, 1973–97, now Emeritus; *b* 24 April 1930; *s* of William James Manning and Hilda Winifred (*née* Noble); *m* 1st, 1959, Margaret Bastock, DPhil (*d* 1982); two *s*; 2nd, 1985, Joan Herrmann, PhD; one *s. Educ:* Strode's School, Egham, Surrey; University Coll., London (BSc); Merton Coll., Oxford (DPhil). FRSE 1975; FRSB (FIBiol 1980); FRZSScot 1997. Commnd RA, 1954–56. University of Edinburgh: Asst Lectr, 1956–59; Lectr, 1959–68; Reader, 1968–73. Mem., Bd of Trustees, Nat. Museums of Scotland, 1997–2005. Sec. Gen., Internat. Ethological Cttee, 1971–79; Member: Scottish Cttee, NCC, 1982–88; NCC Adv. Cttee on Science, 1984–88; Pop. Studies Panel, Wellcome Trust, 1995–99; President: Assoc. Study Animal Behaviour, 1983–86; Biology Sect., BAAS, 1993; Scottish Earth Sci. Educn Forum, 1999–2005; Royal Soc. of Wildlife Trusts, 2006–10. Chm. Council, Scottish Wildlife Trust, 1990–96. Chm., Edinburgh Brook Adv. Centre, 1975–82. Patron, Population Matters (formerly Optimum Population Trust), 2002–. Advr, Population and Sustainability Network, 2006–. Goodwill Ambassador, UN Internat. Year of Planet Earth, 2009. Presenter: TV series: Earth Story, 1998; Talking Landscapes, 2001; Landscape Mysteries, 2003; radio series: Unearthing Mysteries, 1999–2006; The Sounds of Life, 2004; The Rules of Life, 2005. Hon. Fellow: Geol Soc. of Edinburgh, 2007; Geol Soc., 2010. Dr *hc* Univ. Paul Sabatier, Toulouse, 1981; DUniv Open, 2002; Hon. DSc: St Andrews, 2005; Edinburgh, 2010; Hon. MA Worcester, 2005. Dobzhansky Meml Award, Behavior Genetics Assoc., 1994; Assoc. Study Animal Behaviour Medal, 1998; Silver Medal, Zool Soc., 2003; Beltane Sen. Prize for Public Engagement, Royal Soc. of Edinburgh, 2011; Lifetime Achievement Award, RSPB Nature of Scotland Awards, 2013. *Publications:* An Introduction to Animal Behaviour, 1967, 6th edn (with M. Dawkins) 2012; papers on animal behaviour in learned jls. *Recreations:* woodland regeneration, 19th century novels, theatre. *Address:* The Old Hall, Ormiston, East Lothian EH35 5NJ. *T:* (01875) 340536.

MANNING, Prof. David Andrew Charles, PhD; Professor of Soil Science, Newcastle University, since 2000; President, Geological Society of London, 2014–June 2016; *b* Kilwinning, 27 Aug. 1955; *s* of Leslie Charles Manning and Dorothy Mary Manning; *m* 1978, Lucy Jane Stein; two *s* one *d. Educ:* Nottingham High Sch.; Durham Univ. (BSc Geol. 1976); Univ. of Manchester (PhD 1979). CGeol 1993; CSci 2005; EurGeol 2005. Research Fellow: Univ. of Manchester, 1979–81; Centre de Recherches Pétrographiques et Géochimiques, Nancy, 1981–82; Lectr, Newcastle Univ., 1983–88; University of Manchester: Lectr, 1988–92, Sen. Lectr, 1992–96, Reader, 1996–2000, in Geol.; Prof. of Envmtl Geochem., 2000. Nuffield Fellow, 1988–89; Leverhulme Res. Fellow, 2001–02. Dir, Mineral Solutions Ltd, 1996–2006. Hon. Prof. of Soil Mineral Processes, Univ. of Edinburgh, 2015–. *Publications:* Introduction to Industrial Minerals, 1995; over 200 articles in jls, book chapters and conf. papers. *Recreations:* being outdoors, rowing, walking, gardening (especially exotic fruit and vegetables), reading Zola in French, fiddle and cello music (Scottish repertoire). *Address:* School of Civil Engineering and Geosciences, Drummond Building, Newcastle University, Newcastle upon Tyne NE1 7RU. *T:* (0191) 208 6610, *Fax:* (0191) 208 5322. *E:* david.manning@ncl.ac.uk. *Club:* Cambois Rowing.

MANNING, Sir David (Geoffrey), GCMG 2008 (KCMG 2001; CMG 1992); KCVO 2015 (CVO 2007); HM Diplomatic Service, retired; Ambassador to the United States of America, 2003–07; Registrar, Order of Saint Michael and Saint George, since 2010; *b* 5 Dec. 1949; *s* of John Robert Manning and Joan Barbara Manning; *m* 1973, Catherine Marjory Parkinson. *Educ:* Ardingly Coll.; Oriel Coll., Oxford (Hon. Fellow, 2003); Johns Hopkins Sch. of Advanced Internat. Studies, Bologna (Postgrad. Diploma in Internat. Relations, 1972). FCO, 1972; Warsaw, 1974–76; New Delhi, 1977–80; FCO, 1980–84; First Sec., Paris, 1984–88; Counsellor, seconded to Cabinet Office, 1988–90; Political Counsellor and Head of Political Sect., Moscow, 1990–93; Hd of Eastern Dept, FCO, 1993–94; British Mem., Contact Gp on Bosnia, Internat. Conf. on Former Yugoslavia, April–Nov. 1994; Hd of Policy Planning Staff, FCO, 1994–95; Ambassador to Israel, 1995–98; Dep. Under-Sec. of State, FCO, 1998–2000; Perm. Rep., UK Delegn to NATO, 2000–01; Foreign Policy Advr to Prime Minister, and Hd of Defence and Overseas Secretariat, Cabinet Office, 2001–03. Sen. Advr to Prince William, later to Duke and Duchess of Cambridge, and Prince Harry of Wales, 2009–. Non-executive Director: Lloyds Banking Gp, 2008–09; BG Gp, 2008–; Lockheed Martin UK, 2008–; Dir, Gatehouse Advisory Partners, 2010–. Member: Panel of Sen. Advrs, Chatham House, 2008–; Internat. Adv. Bd, Hakluyt, 2008–11; Council, IISS, 2009–11; Council, Lloyd's of London, 2010–; Adv. Bd, Global Strategy Forum, 2014–; Chm., IDEAS, LSE, 2010–. Trustee: Turner Contemporary, 2008–13; Royal Foundn, 2009–; Fulbright Commn, 2009–. Patron: Afghan Connection, 2008–; World Wide Volunteering, 2009–. Fisher Family Fellow, Harvard Univ., 2012.

MANNING, Dr Geoffrey Lewis, FRCSE; FDSRCS; Chairman, North Staffordshire Hospital NHS Trust, 1993–2000; *b* 21 Sept. 1931; *s* of late Isaac Harold Manning and Florence Hilda Manning; *m* 1978, Patricia Margaret Wilson; one *d. Educ:* Rossall Sch., Fleetwood, Lancs; Univ. of Birmingham (LDS, BDS 1953; MB, ChB 1961). FDSRCS 1964; FRCSE 1986. Nat. service, Capt., RADC, 1954–56. Senior Registrar: Central Middx Hosp., 1964–66; Mt Vernon Hosp., 1966–68; Parkland Meml Hosp., Dallas, 1967; Consultant Oral Surgeon, N Staffs Hosp., 1968–93. Mem., N Staffs DHA, 1986–92. Leader, Health Task Force, Prince of Wales Business Leaders Forum, 1993–2000. Hon. DSc Keele, 2000. *Recreations:* gardening, brick-laying, classic cars. *Address:* The Old Hall, Haughton, Stafford ST18 9HB. *T:* (01785) 780273.

MANNING, Jane Marian, OBE 1990; freelance concert and opera singer (soprano), since 1965; writer and lecturer; *b* 20 Sept. 1938; *d* of Gerald Manville Manning and Lily Manning (*née* Thompson); *m* 1966, Anthony Edward Payne, *qv. Educ:* Norwich High Sch.; Royal Academy of Music (LRAM 1958); Scuola di Canto, Cureglia, Switzerland. GRSM 1960, ARCM 1962. London début (Park Lane Group), 1964; first BBC broadcast, 1965; début Henry Wood Promenade Concerts, 1972; founded own ensemble, Jane's Minstrels, 1988; regular appearances in leading concert halls and festivals in UK and Europe, with leading orchestras and conductors; many broadcasts and gramophone recordings, lectures and master classes. Specialist in contemporary music (over 300 world premières given); Warsaw Autumn Fest., 1975–78, 1987, 1992; Wexford Opera Fest., 1976; Scottish Opera, 1978; Brussels Opera, 1980. Canadian début, 1977; tours: of Australia and New Zealand, 1978, 1980, 1982, 1984, 1986, 1990, 1996, 2000, 2002; of USA, 1981, 1983, 1985, 1986, 1987, 1988, 1989, 1991, 1993, 1996, 1997. Milhaud Vis. Prof., Mills Coll. Oakland, 1983; Lucie Stern Vis. Prof., Mills Coll., Oakland, 1981 and 1986; Vis. Artist, Univ. of Manitoba, Canada, 1992; Vis. Prof., RCM, 1995–; Hon. Prof., Keele Univ., 1996–2002; AHRC (formerly AHRB) Creative Arts Res. Fellow, 2004–07, Vis. Prof., 2007–11, Kingston Univ. Vice Pres., SPNM, 1984–2009; Res. Fellow, GSM, 2013–. Chm., Eye Music (formerly Nettlefold Fest.) Trust, 1990–; Trustee (formerly Mem., Exec. Cttee), Help Musicians UK (formerly Musicians Benevolent Fund), 1989–2014; Mem., Arts Council Music Panel, 1990–95; Internat. Jury, Gaudeamus Young Interpreters Competition, Holland, 1976, 1979, 1987; Jury, Eur. Youth Competition for Composers, Eur. Cultural Foundn, 1985. Hon. ARAM 1972, FRAM 1984; FRCM 1998. DUniv York, 1988; Hon. DMus: Keele, 2004; Durham, 2007; Hon. DArts Kingston, 2012. Special award, Composers Guild of Gt Britain, 1973; Gold Badge, BASCA, 2013. *Publications:* (chapter in) How Music Works, 1981; New Vocal Repertory, vol. I, 1986, vol. II, 1998; (chapter in) A Messiaen Companion, 1996; Voicing Pierrot, 2012; (contrib.) Cambridge History of Musical Performance, 2012; Vocal Repertoire for the 21st Century (2 vols), 2016; articles in Composer, Music and Musicians, and Tempo. *Recreations:* reading, cinema, ornithology, theatre. *Address:* 2 Wilton Square, N1 3DL. *T:* (020) 7359 1593.

MANNING, Jeremy James C.; *see* Carter-Manning.

MANNING, Kingsley; Chairman, Health and Social Care Information Centre, since 2013; *b* Coventry, Feb. 1952; *s* of Alfred Manning and Muriel Manning; *m* 1975, Judy Davies; one *s* one *d. Educ:* King Henry VIII Sch., Coventry; Univ. of Birmingham (BSc Biochem.); London Business Sch. (MBA). Founder and Chief Exec., Newchurch Ltd, 1983–2009; Exec. Chm., Tribal Health Services, 2009–11; Sen. Advr, McKinsey & Co., 2011–13. Trustee, Royal Philharmonic Soc. *Recreations:* opera, chamber music, vegetable growing, learning French. *Address:* Health and Social Care Information Centre, 1 Trevelyan Square, Boar Lane, Leeds LS1 6AE. *T:* (0113) 254 7174. *E:* kingsley.manning@hscic.gov.uk. *Club:* Athenæum.

MANNING, Lee Antony, FCA; Partner in Restructuring Services, Deloitte LLP, since 2004; *b* London, 9 Nov. 1957; *s* of Alan Manning and Judith Manning; *m* 1989, Anne; two *s*. *Educ:* Mill Hill Sch.; Kingston Poly. (BA Hons Accountancy and Finance). FCA 1983; Chartered Accountant; Licensed Insolvency Practitioner. Audit and Insolvency, Touche Ross & Co., 1980–84; Insolvency Gp, Arthur Andersen, 1984–89; Insolvency Partner, Buchler Phillips & Co., 1989–99; Restructuring Partner, Kroll Ltd, 1999–2004. Pres., R3, 2012–12. *Recreations:* cycling, swimming, ski-ing, golf, watching football, live music, travel, photography, world cinema. *Address:* Deloitte LLP, Athene Place, 66 Shoe Lane, EC4A 3BQ. *E:* leemanning@deloitte.co.uk, l_manning@sky.com.

MANNING, Mary Elizabeth; Executive Director, Academy of Medical Sciences, 2000–09; *b* 1 Nov. 1947; *d* of late Charles Frederick Kent and Marie Lucia Kent (*née* Hall); *m* 1972, Keith Quentin Frederick Manning (*d* 2015); two *d*. *Educ:* Stoodley Knowle Sch. for Girls, Torquay; Bedford Coll., Univ. of London (BA Hons Hist. 1968). Royal Insce Co., 1968–69; Desk Officer, 1969–72, Attaché, British High Commn, Singapore, 1972–73, MoD; English lang. teacher, La Petite Ecole Française, Sofia, 1975–78; Royal Society: Meetings Officer, 1987–95; Manager, Scientific Prog., 1995–97; Hd, Sci. Promotion, 1997–2000. Member: Steering Gp for Public Understanding of Sci., Engrg and Technol. EPSRC, 1999–2001; Council for Assisting Refugee Academics, 2009–; Steering Gp, Changing Age, Univ. of Newcastle upon Tyne, 2009–11. Mem., British Sci. Assoc. (formerly BAAS), 1995–2010. Mem., Bd for Social Responsibility, C of E, 2001–03. Chm., Royal Soc. Pensioners' Assoc., 2013–. Trustee and Vice-Chm., Epilepsy Res. UK, 2011–; Trustee, Holy Rood House Centre for Health and Pastoral Care, 2013–. *Recreations:* music, walking, family and friends. *Address:* c/o Academy of Medical Sciences, 41 Portland Place, W1B 1QH.

MANNING, Maurice, DLitt; Chancellor, National University of Ireland, since 2009; Adjunct Professor of Politics, School of Politics and International Relations, University College, Dublin, since 2007; *b* 14 June 1943; *s* of Thomas and Alicia Manning; *m* 1987, Mary Hayes; one *s*. *Educ:* University Coll., Dublin (BA 1964; MA 1966; DLitt 1998). Lectr in Politics, University Coll., Dublin, 1966–2002. TD (FG), 1981–87; Senator, 1987–2002 (Leader of the Opposition, 1987–94, 1997–2002; Leader of Senate, 1994–97). President: Irish Human Rights Commn, 2002–12; European Group of National Human Rights instns, 2006–11. Chair: Irish Govt Adv. Gp on Centenary of Commemorations, 2012–; Irish Govt Wkg Party on Senate Reform, 2014–. MRIA 2009. Hon. DHL Toledo, 2012. *Publications:* The Blueshirts, 1970, 3rd edn 2006; Irish Political Parties, 1972; The Irish Electricity Industry, 1987; Betrayal (novel), 1998; James Dillon: a biography, 1999; (ed jtly) The House of the Oireachtas: Parliament in Ireland, 2010. *Recreations:* tennis, swimming, Gregorian chant, reading. *Address:* 13 Haddington Place, Dublin 4, Ireland. *E:* maurice.a.manning@gmail.com. *Clubs:* Stephen's Green Hibernian, Hypothermia (Dublin).

MANNING, Hon. Patrick Augustus Mervyn; MP (People's National Movement) San Fernando East, since 1971; Prime Minister of Trinidad and Tobago, 1991–95 and 2001–10; *b* 17 Aug. 1946; *s* of late Arnold and Elaine Manning; *m* 1972, Hazel Kinsale; two *s*. *Educ:* Rose Bank Private Sch.; San Fernando Govt Sch.; Presentation Coll.; Univ. of West Indies, Jamaica (BSc Special Hons Geology 1969). Texaco Trinidad Inc.: Refinery Operator, 1965–66; Geologist, 1969–71. Parliamentary Secretary: Min. of Petroleum and Mines, 1971–73; Office of the Prime Minister, 1973–74; Min. of Planning and Develt, 1974–75; Min. of Industry and Commerce, 1975–76; Min. of Works, Transport and Communications, 1976–78; Minister: Min. of Finance (Maintenance and Public Service), 1978–81; Prime Minister's Office (Information), 1979–81; Minister of: Inf. and of Industry and Commerce, 1981; Energy and Natural Resources, 1981–86; Leader of the Opposition, 1986–90 and 1995–2001. Mem., Standing Finance Cttee, House of Representatives, 2010–. Leader, People's National Movement, 1987–2010. *Recreations:* table tennis, chess, reading. *Address:* Port of Spain, Trinidad and Tobago.

MANNING, Paul Andrew, QPM 1996; Assistant Commissioner, Metropolitan Police, 1994–2000; *b* 29 May 1947; *s* of Owen Manning and Joyce Cynthia Manning (*née* Murgatroyd); *m* 1967, Margaret Anne Bucknall; two *s*. *Educ:* Forest of Needwood High Sch., Rolleston-on-Dove; Cranfield Inst. of Technology (MSc). Metropolitan Police Cadet, 1964; Constable, 1966, Chief Supt, 1985, Staffordshire Police; Asst Chief Constable, Avon and Somerset Constabulary, 1988; Dep. Chief Constable, Herts Constabulary, 1992. Chm., ACPO Traffic Cttee, 1997–2000 (Sec., 1996–97); ind. advr, Immigration and Nationality Directorate, Home Office, 2001–06. Director: Educnl Broadcasting Services Trust, 1997–2008; Perseus-Global Security Technols, 2006–. Mem., Amwell Rotary Club. Mem., Guild of Freemen, City of London, 1999–. FCILT (FCIT, FILT 2000). *Recreations:* hill walking, Rotary. *Address:* 6 The Chestnuts, Hertford SG13 8AQ. *T:* (01992) 422106. *E:* paul.manning3@ntlworld.com.

MANNING, Peter; Artistic Director and Conductor, Manning Camerata, since 2005; Concertmaster, Royal Opera House, Covent Garden, since 2000; Professor of New Work, Edinburgh University and Royal Conservatoire of Scotland, since 2013; *b* Manchester, 17 July 1956; *s* of Harry and Breda Manning; *m* 1st, 1980, Elizabeth (marr. diss. 1986); one *s* one *d*; 2nd, 1992, Marion; two *s*. *Educ:* Chetham's Sch., Manchester; Royal Northern Coll. of Music (GRNCM 1978; PPRNCM 1978); Indiana Univ. Prof. of Violin, RNCM, 1981–83; Leader, LPO, 1983–86; Founder and Leader, Britten String Quartet, 1986–96; Leader, RPO, 1997–99; Artistic Dir, Musica Vitae Sweden, 2008–11. Guest Conductor, Dallas Opera, Texas, 2014–. Hon. RCM 1989. FRNCM 1992; Internat. Fellow, Royal Conservatoire of Scotland, 2011–. FRSA. *Recreations:* sailing, fly fishing. *Address:* 52 Stockwell Park Road, SW9 0DA. *E:* peter@manningcamerata.com. *Club:* Garrick.

MANNINGHAM-BULLER, family name of **Viscount Dilhorne**.

MANNINGHAM-BULLER, Baroness *cr* 2008 (Life Peer), of Northampton in the County of Northamptonshire; **Hon. Elizabeth Lydia Manningham-Buller,** LG 2014; DCB 2005; Director General, Security Service, 2002–07; Chair, Wellcome Trust, since 2015 (Governor, since 2008); *b* 14 July 1948; *d* of 1st Viscount Dilhorne, PC, and Lady Mary Lilian Lindsay, 4th *d* of 27th Earl of Crawford, KT, PC. *Educ:* Benenden Sch.; Lady Margaret Hall, Oxford (MA; Hon. Fellow 2004). Entered Security Service, 1974; Dep. Dir Gen., 1997–2002. Mem. Council, Imperial Coll. London, 2008–15 (Chair, 2011–15). BBC Reith Lectr, 2011. Hon. Fellow: Univ. of Northampton, 2007; Cardiff Univ., 2010; Hon. FCGI 2012. DUniv Open, 2005; Hon. DSc Cranfield, 2005; Hon. LLD: St Andrews, 2010; Leeds, 2012; Hon. DCL Oxford, 2012. *Address:* House of Lords, SW1A 0PW.

See also Viscount Dilhorne.

MANNION, Rosa; soprano; Professor of Vocal Studies, Royal College of Music, since 2009; *b* 29 Jan. 1962; *d* of Patrick Anthony Mannion and Maria (*née* MacGregor); *m* 1985, Gerard McQuade; two *s*. *Educ:* Seafield Grammar Sch., Crosby; Royal Scottish Acad. of Music and Drama (BA). Débuts: Scottish Opera, 1984; Edinburgh Fest., 1985; ENO, 1987; Glyndebourne Fest. Opera, 1988; principal soprano: Scottish Opera, 1984–86; ENO, 1989–92; major rôles include: Gilda in Rigoletto; Violetta in La Traviata; Manon (title rôle); Magnolia in Show Boat; Pamina in Die Zauberflöte; Minka in Le Roi malgré lui; Sophie in Werther; Oscar in A Masked Ball; Atalanta in Xerxes; Constanze in Die Entführung aus dem Serail; Countess in Figaro's Wedding; Sophie in Der Rosenkavalier. Has given many concerts and recitals; has a comprehensive discography. Winner, Internat. Singing Competition, Scottish Opera, 1988.

MANOLOPOULOS, Prof. David Eusthatios, PhD; FRS 2011; Professor of Theoretical Chemistry, University of Oxford, since 2005; Fellow, St Edmund Hall, Oxford, since 1995; *b* Gillingham, Kent, 14 Dec. 1961; *s* of Dimitrios Manolopoulos and Anne Margaret Manolopoulos (*née* Langley); *m* 1988, Clare Elizabeth Collinson; one *d*. *Educ:* Howard Sch., Gillingham; Girton Coll., Cambridge (BA 1984); Darwin Coll., Cambridge (PhD 1988). Postdoctoral Res. Fellow, Univ. of Texas at Austin, 1988–90; Lecturer: in Physical Chem., Univ. of Nottingham, 1990–95; in Physical and Theoretical Chem., Univ. of Oxford, 1995–2005. Miller Vis. Prof., Univ. of Calif, Berkeley, 2012. Associate Ed., 2008–, Dep. Ed., 2015–, Jl Chemical Physics. *Publications:* (with P. W. Fowler) An Atlas of Fullerenes, 1995; contrib. papers on theoretical chem. to learned jls. *Recreation:* foreign travel. *Address:* Physical and Theoretical Chemistry Laboratory, South Parks Road, Oxford OX1 3QZ.

MANOR, Prof. James Gilmore, DPhil; Emeka Anyaoku Professor, Institute of Commonwealth Studies, University of London, 2007–12, now Emeritus; *b* 21 April 1945; *s* of James Manor and Ann (*née* Jones); *m* 1974, Brenda Cohen; one *s*. *Educ:* Yale Univ. (BA 1967); Univ. of Sussex (DPhil 1975). Asst Lectr in History, Chinese Univ. of Hong Kong, 1967–69; Tutor, SOAS, 1973–75; Lectr in History, Yale, 1975–76; Lectr in Politics, Univ. of Leicester, 1976–85; Prof. of Govt, Harvard, 1985–87; Professorial Fellow, 1987–2007, Hd of Research, 1988–91, Inst. of Develt Studies, Univ. of Sussex; Dir, and Prof. of Commonwealth Politics, Inst. of Commonwealth Studies, Univ. of London, 1994–97. V. K. R. V. Rao Prof., Inst. for Social and Economic Change, Bangalore, India, 2006–08. Sen. Res. Fellow, US Nat. Endowment for the Humanities, 1980–81; Vis. Fellow, MIT, 1982. Consultant to: Dutch Govt, 1989–90; World Bank, 1994–97; Swedish Govt, 1995, 2013. Editor, Jl of Commonwealth and Comparative Politics, 1980–88. *Publications:* Political Change in an Indian State, 1977; (ed with P. Lyon) Transfer and Transformation, 1983; (ed) Sri Lanka in Change and Crisis, 1984; The Expedient Utopian, 1989; (ed) Rethinking Third World Politics, 1991; (ed with C. Colclough) States or Markets?, 1991; Power, Poverty and Poison, 1993; Nehru to the Nineties, 1994; Aid that Works, 2006; (with E. Raghavan) Broadening and Deepening Democracy, 2009; (with M. Melo and N. Ng'ethe) Against the Odds, 2012; (with R. Jenkins) Politics and the Right to Work, 2015; Politics and State-Society Relations in India: collected writings, 2015. *Recreations:* reading, theatre. *Address:* Institute of Commonwealth Studies, University of London, Senate House, Malet Street, WC1E 7HU. *T:* (020) 7862 8844.

MANS, Keith Douglas Rowland; Member (C), since 2009, and Deputy Leader, since 2013, Hampshire County Council; Chief Executive (formerly Director), Royal Aeronautical Society, 1998–2009 (Member, Council, since 2010); *b* 10 Feb. 1946; *s* of Maj.-Gen. Rowland Spencer Noel Mans, CBE and Veeo Mans; *m* 1972, Rosalie Mary McCann; one *s* two *d*. *Educ:* Berkhamsted School; RAF College Cranwell; Open Univ. (BA). FRAeS. Pilot, RAF, 1964–77 (Flight Lieut); Pilot, RAF Reserve, 1977–2005. Retail Manager, John Lewis Partnership, 1978–87. MP (C) Wyre, 1987–97; contested (C) Lancaster and Wyre, 1997. PPS to Minister of State, Dept of Health, 1990–92, to Sec. of State for Health, 1992–95. Member: H of C Environment Select Cttee, 1987–91; Select Cttee on Defence, 1995–97; Chairman: Parly Envmt Gp, 1993–97; Parly Aerospace Gp, 1994–97; Vice-Chm., Back bench Fisheries Cttee, 1987–96; Secretary: Back bench Aviation Cttee, 1987–90; Back bench Envmt Cttee, 1990–91; All Party Aviation Gp, 1991–94. Public Affairs Advr, Soc. of British Aerospace Cos, 1997–2002. Chm., Air Travel Greener By Design Cttee, 2002–09. Chm., Oakhaven Hospice Charity, 2007–. Chm., 2009–14, Vice Pres., 2014–, Air League. Member, Court: Cranfield Univ., 2002–; Southampton Univ., 2005–15. Liveryman, Guild of Air Pilots and Navigators, 2005–. FRSA 2005. *Recreation:* flying. *Address:* Rowhurst Cottage, De La Warr Road, Milford on Sea, Lymington, Hants SO41 0PS. *Clubs:* Royal Air Force, Carlton.

See also Lt Gen. Sir M. F. N. Mans.

MANS, Lt Gen. Sir Mark (Francis Noel), KCB 2012; CBE 2005; DL; Chief Royal Engineer, since 2013; *b* 7 March 1955; *s* of Maj.-Gen. Rowland Spencer Noel Mans, CBE and Veeo Ellen Mans; *m* 1982, Jane Goode; one *s* one *d*. *Educ:* Berkhamsted Sch. Commnd RE, 1974; CO, 21 Engr Regt, 1993–95; Comdr Engrs, 1999–2001, Asst COS Plans, 2002–04, Land Comd; Dep. Comdg Gen., Multinat. Corps, Iraq, 2005; Dep. Adjt Gen., 2005–08; Military Sec., 2008–09; Comdr Regl Forces, 2009; Adjt Gen., 2009–12. Non-exec. Dir, 2013–. Mem., Scientific Exploration Soc., 1980–. Patron, Defence Med. Welfare Service, 2012–; Vice Patron, Ulysses Trust, 2012–. Col Comdt RE, 2005–. Hon. Vice Pres., Army RU, 2012–. FCMI 1997; FCIPD 2000. DL Hants, 2012. Officer, Legion of Merit (USA), 2006. *Recreation:* sport - sadly increasingly as a spectator.

See also K. D. R. Mans.

MANSEL, Sir Philip, 15th Bt *cr* 1621; Chairman and Managing Director of Eden-Vale Engineering Co. Ltd, 1962–98, retired; *b* 3 March 1943; *s* of Sir John Mansel, 14th Bt and Hannah, *d* of Ben Rees; *S* father, 1947; *m* 1968, Margaret, *o d* of Arthur Docker; two *s* one *d*. *Heir:* *s* John Philip Mansel, *b* 19 April 1982. *Address:* 2 Deyncourt Close, Darras Hall, Ponteland, Northumberland NE20 9JY.

MANSEL, Dr Philip Robert Rhys; historian and author; Editor, The Court Historian, since 1996; *b* London, 19 Oct. 1951; *s* of J. C. Mansel and D. J. Mansel (*née* Hyde-Thomson). *Educ:* Eton Coll. (King's Schol.); Balliol Coll., Oxford (MA); University Coll. London (PhD 1978). Mem., Conseil scientifique, Centre de Recherche, Château de Versailles, 2006–. Fellow, Inst. of Histl Res., 2005. Founding Trustee, Levantine Heritage Foundn, 2011–. Chevalier des Arts et Lettres (France), 2010. *Publications:* Louis XVIII, 1981; Pillars of Monarchy, 1984; The Eagle in Splendour, 1987; Sultans in Splendour, 1988; The Court of France, 1989; Constantinople, 1995; Paris Between Empires, 2001; Prince of Europe, 2003; Dressed to Rule, 2005; Levant, 2010; (with T. Riotte) Monarchy and Exile, 2011. *Recreations:* visiting cities, palaces and museums. *Address:* 13 Prince of Wales Terrace, W8 5PG. *T:* (020) 7937 4734. *E:* philipmansel@compuserve.com. *Club:* Travellers.

MANSEL, Prof. Robert Edward, CBE 2006; FRCS; Professor of Surgery, since 1992, and Chairman, Department of Surgery (formerly Department of Surgery, Anaesthetics, Obstetrics and Gynaecology), since 2008, Cardiff University (formerly University of Wales College of Medicine) (Chairman, Department of Surgery, 2001–08); *b* 1 Feb. 1948; *s* of Regnier Ranulf Dabridgecourt Mansel and Mary Germaine Mansel (*née* Littlewood); *m* 1987, Elizabeth Clare, *d* of John Francis Skone and Daphne Viola (*née* Rees); two *s* four *d*. *Educ:* Llandovery Coll.; Charing Cross Hosp. Med. Sch., Univ. of London (MB BS, MS). LRCP 1971; FRCS 1975. Res. Fellow, 1976–78, Lectr and Sen. Lectr, 1979–89, Univ. of Wales Coll. of Medicine; Prof. of Surgery, Univ. of Manchester, 1989–92. Chm., British Breast Gp, 2010–11. Chm., Breast Speciality Gp, 1997–2002, Pres., 2004–06, British Assoc. of Surgical Oncology; Pres., Eur. Soc. of Mastology, 2014–. Mem., Fitness to Practise Panel, GMC, 2012–. UICC Fellow, Univ. of Texas at San Antonio, 1982–83; Churchill Meml Fellowship, 1982; James IV Fellowship, James IV Assoc., 1989. Hunterian Prof., RCS, 1989. Hon. FRCSE 2003. *Publications:* Fibrocystic Breast Disease, 1986; (with L. E. Hughes and D. J. T. Webster) Benign Breast Disease, 1989, 3rd edn 2009; Atlas of Breast Disease, 1994; contribs to surgical jls. *Recreations:* fishing, Rugby, travel, chess. *Address:* Department of Surgery, Cardiff University, Heath Park, Cardiff CF14 4XN. *T:* (029) 2074 2749, *Fax:* (029) 2076 1623. *E:* manselre@cf.ac.uk.

MANSEL-JONES, David; Chairman, Huntingdon Research Centre plc, 1978–86 (Vice-Chairman, 1974–78); *b* 8 Sept. 1926; *o s* of Rees Thomas Jones and Ceinwen Jones; *m* 1952, Mair Aeronwen Davies; one *s*. *Educ:* St Michael's Sch., Bryn; London Hospital. MB, BS 1950; MRCP 1973; FFPM 1992. Jun. Surgical Specialist, RAMC; Dep. Med. Dir, Wm R. Warner

& Co. Ltd, 1957–59; Med. Dir, Richardson-Merrell Ltd, 1959–65; formerly PMO, SMO and MO, Cttee on Safety of Drugs; formerly Med. Assessor, Cttee on Safety of Medicines; Consultant to WHO, 1970–86; Senior PMO, Medicines Div., DHSS, 1971–74. Vis. Prof., Gulbenkian Science Inst., Portugal, 1981; Examiner, Dip. Pharm. Med., Royal Colls of Physicians, UK, 1980–87. *Publications:* papers related to safety of medicines. *Recreations:* music, painting. *Address:* 39 St John's Court, Princes Road, Felixstowe, Suffolk IP11 7SG. *T:* (01394) 275984.

MANSELL, Ven. Clive Neville Ross; Archdeacon of Tonbridge, since 2002; *b* 20 April 1953; *s* of late (Arthur James) Mervyn Mansell and June Irene Mansell (*née* Duncan); *m* 1980, Jane Margaret (*née* Sellers); one *s* two *d*. *Educ:* City of London Sch.; Leicester Univ. (LLB Hons 1974); Coll. of Law; Trinity Coll., Bristol (DipHE Theol Studies 1981). Solicitor of the Supreme Court, 1977–81. Ordained deacon, 1982, priest, 1983; Curate, Gt Malvern Priory, 1982–85; Minor Canon, Ripon Cathedral, with pastoral care of parishes of Sharow with Copt Hewick and of Marton-le-Moor, 1985–89; Rector, Kirklington with Burneston, Wath and Pickhill, 1989–2002; Area Dean, Wensley, 1998–2002. Mem., Gen. Synod of C of E, 1995–; Dep. Prolocutor, House of Clergy, Northern Convocation, 2001–02. Church Comr, 1997–2008. *Recreations:* cricket, music, reading, history, current affairs, photography, enjoying good meals. *Address:* 3 The Ridings, Blackhurst Lane, Tunbridge Wells, Kent TN2 4RU. *T:* (01892) 520660. *E:* archdeacon.tonbridge@rochester.anglican.org.

MANSELL, Nigel Ernest James, CBE 2012 (OBE 1991); racing driver; *b* 8 Aug. 1953; *s* of Eric and Joyce Mansell; *m* Rosanne Elizabeth Perry; two *s* one *d*. *Educ:* Wellsbourne and Hall Green Bilateral Schools; Matthew Bolton Polytechnic; Solihull Tech. Coll.; N Birmingham Polytechnic (HND). Engineering apprenticeship with Lucas; lab. technician, Lucas Aerospace, later product manager; senior sales engineer, tractor div., Girling. Began racing in karts; won 11 regional championships, 1969–76; Formula Ford and Formula Three, 1976–79; Formula Two, later Formula One, 1980; Lotus team, 1981–84; Williams-Honda team, 1985–87; Williams-Judd team, 1988; Ferrari team, 1989–90; Williams-Renault team, 1991–92 and 1994 (part time); McLaren team, 1995; first competed in a Grand Prix, Austria, 1980; won 31 Grands Prix, 1980–94 (record); Formula One World Drivers Champion, 1992; American Newman-Haas IndyCar Team, 1993; IndyCar Champion, 1993; won Grand Prix Masters, (inaugural race) Kyalomi, 2005, Qatar, 2006. Mem., Commn for Global Road Safety, 2012–. President: Dream-A-Way Charity, 1995–; UK Youth, 2002–; Inst. of Advanced Motorists, 2005–; Vice Pres., British Racing Drivers Club, 2009–. Patron: Driving for Disabled, Jersey, 2007–; St Brelade's Youth Project, 2011–. Grand Fellow, MIRCE Akad. for System Operational Sci., 2000. Hon. DEng Birmingham, 1993. *Publications:* (with Derick Allsop) Driven to Win, 1988; (with Derick Allsop) Mansell and Williams, The Challenge for the Championship 1992; (with Jeremy Shaw) Nigel Mansell's IndyCar Racing, 1993; (with James Allen) Nigel Mansell, My Autobiography, 1995; Staying on Track: the autobiography, 2015. *Recreations:* golf, flying, cycling.

MANSELL, Richard Austin; QC 2009; **His Honour Judge Mansell;** a Circuit Judge, since 2013; *b* Sutton Coldfield, 12 Feb. 1968; *s* of Robert and Lynn Mansell; *m* 2001, Michelle Colborne; one *s* two *d*. *Educ:* Univ. of Leeds (LLB 1st Cl. Hons Law). Called to the Bar, Gray's Inn, 1991; a Recorder, 2005–12. *Recreations:* ski-ing, golf, yoga, cooking, gardening. *Address:* Manchester Crown Court, Crown Square, Manchester M3 3FL. *Club:* Bradford.

MANSELL, Prof. Robin Elizabeth, PhD; Professor (formerly Dixons Professor) of New Media and the Internet, London School of Economics and Political Science, since 2001; *b* Vancouver, 3 Jan. 1952; *d* of Glen Mansell and Esmee Mansell; partner, W. Edward Steinmueller. *Educ:* York House Sch., Vancouver; Univ. of Manitoba (BA Hons Psychol. 1974); London Sch. of Econs and Pol Sci. (MSc Social Psychol. 1976); Simon Fraser Univ. (MA Communication 1980; PhD Communication 1984). Res. Associate, Prog. on Inf. and Communication Technols, ESRC, London, 1985–86; Administrator, Inf., Computers and Communication Policy Div., OECD, Paris, 1986–87; Reader, 1988–94, Prof. in Inf. and Communication Technol. Policy, 1994–2000, Sci. and Technol. Policy Res. Unit, Univ. of Sussex, Hon. Prof., 2001–. Trustee, Inst. of Develt Studies, Sussex, 1999–2009. Hon. Prof., Learning, Inf., Networking Knowledge Centre, Grad. Sch. of Public and Develt Mgt, Univ. of Witwatersrand, 2005–10. *Publications:* The New Telecommunications, 1993; (ed) Communication by Design, 1996; (ed) Knowledge Societies, 1998; Mobilizing the Information Society, 2000; (ed) Trust and Crime in Information Societies, 2005; (ed) The Oxford Handbook of Information and Communication Technologies, 2007; (ed) The Information Society: critical concepts in sociology, 2009; Imagining the Internet: communication, innovation and governance, 2012. *Recreations:* walking, classical music. *Address:* London School of Economics and Political Science, Houghton Street, WC2A 2AE. *T:* (020) 7955 6380. *E:* r.e.mansell@lse.ac.uk. *Club:* Athenæum.

MANSELL-JONES, Richard Mansell; Chairman, Brown, Shipley & Co., 1992–2003; *b* 4 April 1940; *s* of late Arnaud Milward Jones and Winifred Mabel (*née* Foot); *m* 1971, Penelope Marion (*d* 2009), *y d* of Major Sir David Henry Hawley, 7th Bt. *Educ:* Queen Elizabeth's, Carmarthen; Worcester College, Oxford (MA). FCA. Articled to Price, Waterhouse & Co., 1963–68; with N. M. Rothschild & Sons, 1968–72; with Brown, Shipley & Co., 1972–88 (Dir, 1974–84; Dep. Chm., 1984–88); non-exec. Dir, 1982–88, Chm., 1988–2000, Barlow International PLC (formerly J. Bibby & Sons). Director: Brown, Shipley Holdings, 1985–92; Barlow Ltd (formerly Barlow Rand Ltd), 1988–2001; non-executive Director: Barr & Wallace Arnold Trust, 1984–93; Rand Mines Ltd, 1988–93; Barloworld Hldgs, 1990–2003; Standard Bank London, 1992–2005; Standard Internat. Holdings, 2000–05; non-exec. Chm., Amphion Innovations plc, 2005–10. Trustee and Dir, Burlington Magazine Foundn and Burlington Magazine Pubns Ltd, 2009–; Trustee: World Monuments Fund Britain, 2013–; British Sporting Art Trust, 2013–. Mem. Council, CBI, 1999–2000. Mem. Bd, 2003–08, Treas., 2005–08, Royal Hosp. for Neuro-disability. Patron, Shaw Trust, 1996– (Trustee, 1990–96). MCSI (MSI 1992). *Address:* c/o Private Banking, Brown, Shipley & Co. Ltd, Founders Court, Lothbury, EC2R 7HE. *T:* (020) 7606 9833. *Clubs:* Beefsteak, Boodle's, City of London.

MANSER, John; *see* Manser, P. J.

MANSER, Michael John, CBE 1993; RA 1995; architect in private practice, The Manser Practice (formerly Michael Manser Associates, then Manser Associates), since 1961; President, Royal Institute of British Architects, 1983–85; *b* 23 March 1929; *s* of late Edmund George Manser and Augusta Madge Manser; *m* 1953, Dolores Josephine Bernini; one *s* one *d*. *Educ:* Sch. of Architecture, Polytechnic of Central London (DipArch). RIBA 1954; RWA 1994. Intermittent architectural journalist and lectr; News Editor, Architectural Design, 1961–64; Architectural Correspondent, The Observer, 1961–64. TV and radio, 1963–. Councillor: RIBA, 1977–80 and 1982; RSA, 1987–93 (Founder Chm., Art for Architecture Award Scheme, 1990–93); Assessor, Art in the Workplace Awards, 1988–; Chairman: Art and Work Awards, 1996–; Nat. Home Builder Design Awards, 1998–; Stirling Prize Award, RIBA, 2000; Jury, Manser Medal, 2001–; RIBA Rep., Council, Nat. Trust, 1991–93; Member: London Transport Design Policy Cttee, 1991–95; Westminster CC Public Art Adv. Panel, 1999–; Ext. Examiner, Faculty of Architecture, Kingston Univ., 1995–98. Royal Academy: Member: Council, 1998; Architectural Cttee, 1998–; Audit Cttee, 1999–; Works Cttee, 1999–; Remuneration Cttee, 2000–. Mem., Arts Cttee, Chelsea and Westminster Health Charity, 2009–. Chm., British Architectural Liby Trust, 2008–. Hon. Fellow, Royal Architectural Inst. of Canada, 1985. Civic Trust Awards, 1967, 1973 and 1991; Award for Good Design in Housing, DoE, 1975; Eur. Architectural Heritage Year Award, 1975; RIBA Award and Regional Award, 1991, 1995; ICE Merit Award, 1995; Structural Steel Design Award, 1995. *Publications:* (with José Manser) Planning Your Kitchen, 1976; (contrib.) Psychiatry in the Elderly, 1991; (contrib.) Companion to Contemporary Architectural Thought, 1993. *Recreations:* going home, architecture, music, books, boats, sketching, gardening (under supervision). *Address:* 76 Whitehall Court, SW1A 2EL. *Clubs:* Brooks's, Farmers.

MANSER, (Peter) John, CBE 1992; DL; FCA; Chairman, SAB Miller PLC (formerly South African Breweries), 2013–15 (Director, 2001–15; Deputy Chairman, 2012–13); *b* 7 Dec. 1939; *s* of late Peter Robert Courtney Manser and Florence Delaplaine Manser; *m* 1969, Sarah Theresa Stuart (*née* Todd); two *d*. *Educ:* Marlborough Coll. Man. Dir, Jardine Fleming & Co. Ltd, 1975–79; Chief Exec., Save & Prosper Gp Ltd, 1983–88; Chm., Robert Fleming & Co. Ltd, 1990–97. Chairman: Robert Fleming Hldgs, 1997–2000 (Dir, 1972–; Chief Exec., 1990–97); Delancey Estates, 1998–2001; Intermediate Capital Gp, 2001–10; Shaftesbury, 2004–13 (Dir, 1997–2013); London Asia Chinese Private Equity Fund, 2006–07; Dep. Chm., Colliers CRE (formerly Fitzhardinge), 2002–10; Director: Capital Shopping Centres, 1994–2000; Keppel Tatlee Bank, 2000–01. Dep. Chm., FIMBRA, 1984–85; Dir, SIB, 1986–93; Chm., London Investment Banking Assoc., 1994–98; Vice-Pres., BBA, 1994–98. Mem., Finance Cttee, Royal Commn for Exhibn of 1851, 2008–. Dir, Cancer Research Campaign, 1985–2000. Chm., Wilts Community Foundn, 1997–2002. Gov., Marlborough Coll., 2008–; Chm. of Council, Marlborough Coll. Malaysia, 2012–. Pres., Marlburian Club, 1999–2000. DL Wilts, 1999. *Recreations:* gardening, walking, shooting, saving pubs. *Address:* Chisenbury Priory, East Chisenbury, Pewsey, Wilts SN9 6AQ. *Clubs:* Boodle's, MCC.

MANSFIELD, family name of **Baron Sandhurst**.

MANSFIELD AND MANSFIELD, 8th Earl of, *cr* 1776 (and 9th Earl of, *cr* 1792) (GB); **William David Mungo James Murray;** JP, DL; Baron Scone, 1605; Viscount Stormont, 1621; Baron Balvaird, 1641; (Earl of Dunbar, Viscount Drumcairn, and Baron Halldykes in the Jacobite Peerage); Hereditary Keeper of Bruce's Castle of Lochmaben; First Crown Estate Commissioner, 1985–95; *b* 7 July 1930; *o s* of 7th Earl of Mansfield and Mansfield, and of Dorothea Helena (*d* 1985), *y d* of late Rt Hon. Sir Lancelot Carnegie, GCVO, KCMG; *S* father, 1971; *m* 1955, Pamela Joan, *o d* of W. N. Foster, CBE and Millicent Agnes Mary Foster, later Lady Cochrane of Cults; two *s* one *d*. *Educ:* Eton; Christ Church, Oxford. Served as Lieut with Scots Guards, Malayan campaign, 1949–50. Called to Bar, Inner Temple, 1958; Barrister, 1958–71. Mem., British Delegn to European Parlt, 1973–75; an opposition spokesman in the House of Lords, 1975–79; Minister of State: Scottish Office, 1979–83; NI Office, 1983–84. Mem., Tay Salmon Fisheries Bd, 1971–79. Director: General Accident, Fire and Life Assurance Corp. Ltd, 1972–79, 1985–98; American, then US Tracker, Trust, 1985–2002; Pinneys of Scotland, 1985–89; Ross Breeders Ltd, 1989–90. Ordinary Dir, Royal Highland and Agricl Soc., 1976–79. President: Fédn des Assocs de Chasse de l'Europe, 1977–79; Scottish Assoc. for Care and Resettlement of Offenders, 1974–79; Scottish Assoc. of Boys Clubs, 1976–79; Royal Scottish Country Dance Soc., 1977–2007; Chm., Scottish Branch, Historic Houses Assoc., 1976–79. Mem., Perth CC, 1971–75; Hon. Sheriff for Perthshire, 1974–; JP 1975, DL 1980, Perth and Kinross. Hon. Mem., RICS, 1994. *Publications:* articles on agriculture, land management and wine. *Heir:* *s* Viscount Stormont, *qv*. *Address:* Logie House, Logiealmond, Perth PH1 3SD; 16 Thorburn House, Kinnerton Street, SW1X 8EX. *Clubs:* Pratt's, Turf.

MANSFIELD, Prof. Averil (Olive), (Mrs J. W. P. Bradley), CBE 1999; FRCS; FRCP; Professor of Vascular Surgery, Academic Surgical Unit, St Mary's Hospital and Imperial College School of Medicine (formerly St Mary's Hospital Medical School), 1993–2004, now Emeritus (Director, Academic Surgical Unit, 1993–99); Associate Medical Director, St Mary's Hospital, 2002–04 (Consultant Surgeon, 1982–2002); *b* 21 June 1937; *m* 1987, John William Paulton Bradley (*d* 2013). *Educ:* Liverpool Univ. (MB 1960; ChM 1972). FRCS 1966; FRCP 2005. Consultant Surgeon: Royal Liverpool Hosp., 1972–80; Hillingdon Hosp., 1980–82; RPMS, subseq. ICSM, 1980–2002. Royal College of Surgeons: Chm., Court of Examrs, 1990–92; Mem. Council, 1990–2002; Vice-Pres., 1998–2000; President: Assoc. of Surgeons of GB and Ireland, 1992–93; Vascular Surgical Soc. of GB and Ireland, 1996–97; Sect. of Surgery, RSocMed, 1997–98; BMA, 2009–10 (Chm., Bd of Sci., 2010–13). Vice-Chm., 2001–03, Chm., 2004–08, Vice Pres., 2009–, Stroke Assoc. Fellow, Faculty of Medicine, Imperial Coll. London, 2012. Hon. FRACS 1996; Hon. FACS 1998; Hon. FRSocMed 2011; Hon. Fellow, Amer. Surgical Assoc. Hon. MD Liverpool, 1994; Hon. DSc Lancaster, 2010. *Publications:* Clinical Surgery in General, 1993; articles on vascular surgery. *Recreations:* playing the piano and learning to play the cello, walking in the Lake District, restoring old wrecks. *Address:* 31/32 Radnor Mews, W2 2SA.

MANSFIELD, David James; Chairman, Drive Partnership Ltd, since 2011; RAJAR Ltd, since 2008; Visiting Fellow, Oxford University, since 2008; *b* 12 Jan. 1954; *m* 1979, Alison Patricia Pullin; two *s* one *d*. Gen. Sales Manager, Scottish TV, 1977–85; Sales and Marketing Dir, Thames TV, 1985–93; Capital Radio: Gp Commercial Dir, 1993–97; Gp Man. Dir, May–July 1997; Gp Chief Exec., Capital Radio, then Chief Exec., GCap Media plc, 1997–2006. Non-executive Chairman: 1700 Gp plc, 2008–10; 1801 Gp Ltd, 2010–13; LoveLive TV Ltd, 2010–; HelloU Ltd, 2010–; Music Festivals plc, 2011–12; Discover Digital Ltd, 2012–; Field & Flower Ltd, 2013–; Circus Street Ltd, 2014–; non-executive Director: Carphone Warehouse plc, 2005–10; Game Gp plc, 2010–11; Ingenious Media plc, 2006–13.

MANSFIELD, Dr Eric Harold, FRS 1971; FREng, FRAeS, FIMA; Chief Scientific Officer (Individual Merit), Royal Aircraft Establishment, 1980–83; *b* 24 May 1923; *s* of Harold Goldsmith Mansfield and Grace Phundt; *m* 1947; two *s* one *d*; *m* 1974, Eunice Lily Kathleen Shuttleworth-Parker. *Educ:* St Lawrence Coll., Ramsgate; Trinity Hall, Cambridge (MA, ScD). Research in Structures Department, Royal Aircraft Establishment, Farnborough, Hants, 1943–83. Vis. Prof., Dept of Mechanical Engrg, Univ. of Surrey, 1984–90. Member: British Nat. Cttee for Theoretical and Applied Mechanics, 1973–79; Gen. Assembly of IUTAM, 1976–80; Council, Royal Soc., 1977–78. FREng (FEng 1976). James Alfred Ewing Gold Medal for Engrg Res., ICE, 1991; Royal Medal, Royal Soc., 1994. UK winner (with I. T. Minhinnick), World Par Bridge Olympiad, 1951. Member, Editorial Advisory Boards: Internat. Jl of Non-linear Mechanics, 1965–95; Internat. Jl of Mechanical Scis, 1977–84. *Publications:* The Bending and Stretching of Plates, 1964, 2nd edn 1989; Bridge: The Ultimate Limits, 1986; contribs to: Proc. Roy. Soc., Phil. Trans., Quarterly Jl Mech. Applied Math., Aero Quarterly, Aero Res. Council reports and memos, and to technical press. *Recreations:* duplicate bridge, palaeontology, walking the dog. *Address:* Primrose Cottage, Alresford Road, Cheriton, Hants SO24 0QJ. *T:* (01962) 771280.

MANSFIELD, Guy Rhys John; QC 1994; a Recorder, 1993–2012; a Deputy High Court Judge, since 2008; *b* 3 March 1949; *o s* of 5th Baron Sandhurst, DFC and Janet Mary (*née* Lloyd); *S* father, 2002 as 6th Baron Sandhurst, but does not use the title; *m* 1976, Philippa St Clair Verdon-Roe; one *s* one *d*. *Educ:* Harrow Sch.; Oriel Coll., Oxford (MA). Called to the Bar, Middle Temple, 1972 (Harmsworth Exhibnr, Winston Churchill Pupillage award); Bencher, 2000. Chm., Bar Council, 2005 (Member: Gen. Council of the Bar, 1998–2005; Gen. Mgt Cttee, 1998–2005; Chairman: Remuneration and Terms of Work (formerly Legal Aid and Fees) Cttee, 1998–99; Legal Services Cttee, 2000–03); Mem., Queen's Counsel Complaints Cttee, 2006–. Legal Assessor, GMC, 2000–06. Mem. Council, Justice, 2006–. *Publications:* (contrib.) Personal Injury Handbook, 1998, rev. edn 2001; (contrib.) Financial Provision in Family Matters, 1999–2004; (contrib.) An Introduction to Human Rights and the Common Law, 2000. *Recreations:* cricket, opera. *Heir: s* Hon. Edward James Mansfield, *b* 12 April 1982. *Address:* 1 Crown Office Row, Temple, EC4Y 7HH. *T:* (020) 7797 7500. *Clubs:* Reform, MCC; Leander (Henley-on-Thames).

MANSFIELD, Prof. Michael; QC 1989; Professor of Law, City University, since 2007; *b* 12 Oct. 1941; *s* of Frank Le Voir Mansfield and Marjorie Mansfield; *m* 1965, Melian Mansfield (*née* Bordes) (marr. diss. 1992); three *s* one *d* (and one *d* decd); 2nd, 1992, Yvette Vanson; one *s*. *Educ:* Highgate Sch.; Keele Univ. (BA Hons). Called to the Bar, Gray's Inn, 1967, Bencher, 2008. Estabd set of chambers of which head, 1984. Visiting Professor of Law: Westminster Univ., 1997–; Birkbeck, Univ. of London, 2014–. President: Nat. Civil Rights Movt; Haldane Soc.; Amicus. Hon. Fellow, Kent Univ., 1994. Hon. LLD: South Bank, 1995; Keele, 1995; Hertfordshire, 1995; Middx, 1999; Westminster, 2005; Ulster, 2006; Kent, 2007; Wolverhampton, 2010. Legal Aid Lawyer of the Yr Award for Outstanding Achievement, 2010. *Publications:* Presumed Guilty, 1994; The Home Lawyer, 2003; Memoirs of a Radical Lawyer, 2009. *Recreation:* my children's interests. *Address:* Mansfield Chambers, 5 Chancery Lane, WC2A 1LG. *T:* (020) 7406 7550, *Fax:* (020) 7406 7549. *E:* Martin.Parker@mansfieldchambers.co.uk.

MANSFIELD, Penny, CBE 2013; Director, OnePlusOne, since 1997; *b* Surrey, 1951; *d* of Stanley Mansfield and Catherine Corry; *m* 1976, Richard George Dowden, *qv*; two *d*. *Educ:* Ursuline Convent, London; Univ. of Surrey (BSc Hons Human Scis). Res. Officer, Univ. of Surrey; Sen. Res. Officer, Marriage Res. Centre, Central Middx Hosp., London; Hd of Res. and Information, then Dep. Dir, OnePlusOne. *Publications:* (with J. Collard) The Beginning of the Rest of Your Life, 1988; contributor: Couple Therapy: a handbook, 1991; Life Stories, 1994; Partners Become Parents, 1996; No Fault No Flaw, 2000; How Helping Works, 2006. *Recreations:* reading, cinema and theatre, art galleries, spending time with friends and family, gardening and general pottering. *Address:* OnePlusOne, 1 Benjamin Street, EC1M 5QG. *T:* (020) 7553 9530. *E:* penny.mansfield@oneplusone.org.uk.

MANSFIELD, Sir Peter, Kt 1993; FRS 1987; Professor of Physics, University of Nottingham, 1979–94, now Professor Emeritus; *b* 9 Oct. 1933; *s* of late Rose Lilian Mansfield (*née* Turner) and late Sidney George Mansfield; *m* 1962, Jean Margaret Kibble; two *d*. *Educ:* William Penn Sch., Peckham; Queen Mary Coll., London (BSc 1959, PhD 1962; Fellow, 1985). Research Associate, Dept of Physics, Univ. of Illinois, 1962–64; Lectr, Univ. of Nottingham, 1964, Sen. Lectr, 1968, Reader, 1970–79; Sen. Visitor, Max Planck Inst. für Medizinische Forschung, Heidelberg, 1972–73. Society of Magnetic Resonance in Medicine: Gold Medal, 1983; President, 1987–88. Founder FMedSci 1998. Hon. Member: Soc. of Magnetic Resonance Imaging, 1994; British Inst. of Radiology, 1993; Eur. Soc. of Magnetic Resonance in Medicine and Biol., 2002; Mem., Polish Acad. of Medicine, 2007; Hon. FRCR 1992; Hon. FInstP 1996; Hon. FRCP 2004; Hon. Fellow, Hughes Hall, Cambridge, 2004. Hon. MD Strasbourg, 1995; Hon. DSc: Kent, 1996; Nottingham, 2005; Leipzig, 2006; Warsaw, 2007; Cambridge, 2011; Hon. Dr Jagiellonian Univ., Krakow, 2000; DUniv Leicester, 2006. Sylvanus Thompson Lectr and Medal, 1988, Barclay Medal, 1993, British Inst. of Radiology; Gold Medal, Royal Soc. Wellcome Foundn, 1984; Duddell Medal and Prize, Inst. of Physics, 1988; Antoine Béclère Medal, Internat. Radiol Soc. and Antoine Béclère Inst., 1989; Mullard Medal and Award, Royal Soc., 1990; ISMAR Prize, 1992; Gold Medal, Eur. Assoc. of Radiol., 1995; Garmisch-Partenkirchen Prize for Magnetic Resonance Imaging, 1995; Rank Prize, 1997; (jtly) Nobel Prize for Physiology or Medicine, 2003; Nuffield Lectr and Gold Medal, RSocMed, 2006; Euromar Medal, Groupement Ampere, 2006; Galan Medal, Soc. of Apothecaries, 2006; Gold Medal, Medicas Magnus, Warsaw Univ., 2007; Mike Hogg Award, Univ. of Texas, 2007; Millennium Medal, MRC, 2009. *Publications:* NMR Imaging in Biomedicine (with P. G. Morris), 1982; (ed with E. L. Hahn) NMR Imaging, 1991; (ed) MRI in Medicine, 1995; The Long Road to Stockholm: the story of MRI, 2013; papers in learned jls on nuclear magnetic resonance. *Recreations:* languages, reading, travel, flying (Private Pilot's Licence, Private Pilot's Licence for Helicopters). *Address:* Sir Peter Mansfield Magnetic Resonance Centre, Department of Physics, University of Nottingham, Nottingham NG7 2RD. *T:* (0115) 951 4740, *Fax:* (0115) 951 5166.

MANSFIELD, Prof. Terence Arthur, FRS 1987; FRSB; Professor of Plant Physiology, University of Lancaster, 1977–2001, now Emeritus; *b* 18 Jan. 1937; *s* of Sydney Walter Mansfield and Rose (*née* Sinfield); *m* 1963, Margaret Mary James; two *s*. *Educ:* Univ. of Nottingham (BSc); Univ. of Reading (PhD). FRSB (FIBiol 1984). University of Lancaster: Lectr, then Reader, 1965–77; Dir, Inst. of Envmtl and Biol Scis, 1988–94; Provost of Sci. and Engrg, 1993–96. Member: AFRC, 1989–93; Eur. Envmtl Res. Orgn, 1994–. Hon. Fellow, Univ. of Lancaster, 2007. *Publications:* Physiology of Stomata, 1968; Effects of Air Pollutants on Plants, 1976; Stomatal Physiology, 1981; Plant Adaption to Environmental Stress, 1993; many contribs to books and jls in plant physiology. *Recreations:* cricket, classical music. *Address:* 25 Wallace Lane, Forton, Preston, Lancs PR3 0BA. *T:* (01524) 791338. *Club:* Shireshead and Forton Cricket (Pres., 1993–2002).

MANSFIELD, Terence Gordon, CBE 2002; Director, 1993–2004, and a Vice President, 2000–04, Hearst Corporation USA; Consultant, Hearst Corporation UK, since 2003; *b* 3 Nov. 1938; *s* of Archer James Mansfield and Elizabeth Mansfield; *m* 1965, Helen Leonora Russell; two *d*. *Educ:* Maynard Road Jun. Sch., Essex; SW Essex Technical Sch. D. H. Brocklesby, Advertising Agents, 1954; S. H. Benson, Advertising Agents, 1956; served RAF, Christmas Island, 1957–59; Condé Nast Publications, 1960–66; Queen Magazine, 1966; National Magazine Co.: Advertisement Man., Harpers and Queen, 1969; Publisher, Harpers and Queen, 1975; Dep. Man. Dir, 1980, Pres. and CEO, 1982–2003, National Magazine Co.; Chm., COMAG, 1984–2003; Dir, PPA, 1982–. Chm., MOBO Orgn Ltd, 2006–. Chm., Trng Bd, Periodicals Trng Council, 2000–. Member: Marketing Soc., 1975–; British Fashion Council, 1988–; Action Medical Research (formerly Action Res. for the Crippled Child, then Action Res.), 1989–; Campaign Bd, Historic Royal Palaces, 2009–. Chm., Bd of Trustees, Victim Support, 2002–05 (Mem., Adv. Bd, 1996–). Trustee: NewstrAid, 1966–; United World Coll., 1977–; St Bride's Church, 2001–. Chm., Graduate Fashion, 2006– (Vice Chm., 2005–06). Freeman, City of London, 1989; Liveryman, Stationers' & Newspaper Makers' Co., 1997–. MInstM 1969; MInstD 1976. FRSA. *Recreations:* family, running, walking dogs. *Address:* 5 Grosvenor Gardens Mews North, SW1W 0JP. *T:* (020) 7565 6666; Hearst Corporation, 72 Broadwick Street, W1K 9EP. *T:* (020) 7565 6666. *W:* www.terrymansfield.co.uk. *Clubs:* Royal Air Force, Solus; Hanbury Manor.

MANSON, Suzanne Maree; *see* Cotter, S. M.

MANSS, Thomas, FCSD; designer; Founder and Art Director, Thomas Manss & Company, since 1993; *b* Gütersloh, 11 July 1960; *s* of Karlheinz Manss and Ingrid Manss; two *s*. *Educ:* Luise Hensel Schule (primary); Evangelisch Stiftisches Gymnasium, Gütersloh; Fachhochschule Würzburg (Dipl Des). Metadesign, 1984–85; Sedley Place Design, 1985–89; Pentagram, 1989–93, Associate, 1992–93. Vis. Prof., Corporate Identity, Fachhochschule Potsdam, 1994–97. MSTD; FRSA. *Publications:* Ordnung & Eccentricity, 2002; contributed to: Design: wege zum erfolg, 1994; 26 Letters: illuminating the alphabet, 2004; Corporate Identity and Corporate Design, Neues Kompendium, 2007; Thomas Manss & Company: designers, narrators, myth-makers, fabulators and tellers of tales, 2008. *Address:* Thomas Manss & Company, 3 Nile Street, N1 7LX. *W:* www.manss.com.

MANSTEAD, Prof. Antony Stephen Reid, DPhil; FBA 2011; FBPsS; FAcSS; FLSW; Professor of Psychology, Cardiff University, since 2004; *b* 16 May 1950; *s* of Dr Stephen K. Manstead and Katharine E. Manstead; *m* 1997, Prof. Stephanie van Goozen; one *s* one *d*. *Educ:* Univ. of Bristol (BSc Hons); Univ. of Sussex (DPhil). FBPsS 1989. Lectr in Social Psychol., Univ. of Sussex, 1974–76; Lectr, 1976–88, Sen. Lectr, 1988–90, Prof. of Psychol., 1990–92, Univ. of Manchester; Prof. of Social Psychol., Univ. of Amsterdam, 1992–2001; Prof. of Psychol. in the Social Scis, and Fellow of Wolfson Coll., Cambridge Univ., 2002–03. FAcSS (AcSS 2004). Fellow: Soc. for Personality and Social Psychol., 2006; Soc. of Experimental Social Psychol., 2009; Assoc. for Psychological Sci., 2010; FLSW 2012. *Publications:* (jtly) The Accountability of Conduct: a social psychological analysis, 1983; (jtly) Introduction to Psychology: an integrated approach, 1984; (ed jtly) Handbook of Social Psychophysiology, 1989; (ed jtly) Blackwell Encyclopedia of Social Psychology, 1995; (ed jtly) Everyday Conceptions of Emotion, 1995; (ed jtly) Blackwell Reader in Social Psychology, 1997; (ed jtly) Emotions and Beliefs: how feelings influence thoughts, 2000; (ed jtly) Feelings and Emotions: the Amsterdam Symposium, 2004; (jtly) Emotion in Social Relations: cultural, group and interpersonal processes, 2005; (ed) Psychology of Emotions, 5 vols, 2008. *Recreation:* photography. *Address:* School of Psychology, Cardiff University, Tower Building, Park Place, Cardiff CF10 3AT.

MANT, Prof. David Clive Anthony, OBE 2011; FRCP, FRCGP; Professor of General Practice, University of Oxford, 1998–2010, now Emeritus; Fellow, Kellogg College, Oxford, 1998, now Emeritus. *Educ:* Churchill Coll., Cambridge (BA 1972; MA 1976); Birmingham Univ. (MB ChB 1977); London Sch. of Hygiene and Tropical Medicine (MSc (Community Medicine) 1983). MRCGP 1982, FRCGP 1999; MFPHM 1984; FRCP 1999. Trainee in gen. practice, E Oxford Health Centre, 1981–82; Registrar in Community Medicine, Oxford RHA, 1982–84; Clin. Lectr, 1984–93, and Sen. Scientist, Gen. Practice Res. Gp, 1987–93, Oxford Univ.; Prof. of Primary Care Epidemiology, Southampton University, 1993–98; Dir of R&D, S and W Reg., NHS Exec., DoH, 1996–98 (on secondment). Hon. Prof., Bristol Univ., 1996–98. FMedSci 1998.

MANT, Prof. Jonathan William French, MD; FFPH, FRCPE; Professor of Primary Care Research, since 2008, and Head, Primary Care Unit, since 2013, University of Cambridge; Honorary Consultant, Addenbrooke's Hospital, since 2008; *b* London, 16 Nov. 1960; *s* of Prof. Arthur Keith Mant and Heather Mant (*née* Smith); *m* 1983, Frances Joy Randall (*d* 2011); one *s* one *d*. *Educ:* Cranleigh Sch.; Millbrook Sch., NY; Corpus Christi Coll., Cambridge (BA 1982; MD 2004); Guy's Hosp., London (MB BS 1985); London Sch. of Hygiene and Tropical Medicine (MSc 1990). MFPHM 1994, FFPH (FFPHM 2003); FRCPE 2012. House Officer, Buckland Hosp., Dover, 1985–86; SHO, Torbay, and Royal Devon and Exeter Hosps, 1986–89; Registrar, then Sen. Registrar, Public Health Medicine, Oxford, 1989–92; Clin. Lectr in Public Health Medicine, Univ. of Oxford, 1992–97; University of Birmingham: Sen. Lectr, 1997–2006; Reader, 2006–07; Prof., 2007–08. Associate Director (Primary Care), Stroke Res. Network, 2005–15. FESC 2010; Fellow, British Hypertension Soc., 2014. *Publications:* (ed jtly) Evidence Based Practice: a primer for health care professionals, 1999, 2nd edn 2005; (ed jtly) Health Care Needs Assessment: the epidemiologically based needs assessment reviews, 1st series, 2004, 3rd series, 2007; (ed jtly) ABC of Stroke, 2011; contrib. papers on stroke and cardiovascular disease in jls. *Recreations:* amassing unread novels, untidy desks, Tintin memorabilia. *Address:* Primary Care Unit, University of Cambridge, Strangeway's Research Laboratory, Wort's Causeway, Cambridge CB1 8RN. *T:* (01223) 763830. *E:* jm677@medschl.cam.ac.uk.

MANTEL, Dame Hilary (Mary), (Dame Hilary McEwen), DBE 2014 (CBE 2006); author; *b* 6 July 1952; *d* of Henry Thompson and Margaret Mary Thompson (*née* Foster, later Mrs Jack Mantel); *m* 1973, Gerald McEwen. *Educ:* London Sch. of Econs; Sheffield Univ. (BJur). PLR Adv. Cttee, 1997–2003. Vis. Prof., Sheffield Hallam Univ., 2006–09; Hon. Prof., Exeter Univ., 2013. Patron, Endometriosis SHE Trust, 2006–09. FRSL 1990; FEA 2007. Hon. Fellow, RHUL, 2008; Hon. FKC 2011. Hon. LittD Sheffield, 2005; DUniv: Sheffield Hallam, 2009; London, 2013; Hon. DLitt: Exeter, 2011; Kingston, 2011; Cambridge, 2013; QUB, 2013; Bath Spa, 2013; Derby 2014; Open, 2014; Oxford Brookes, 2015; Chester, 2015; Oxford, 2015; Hon. DEcon LSE, 2014. Shiva Naipaul Meml Prize, 1987; Author of the Year, Galaxy Nat. Book Awards, 2010, 2012; David Cohen Award for Lifetime Achievement, 2013; Burke Medal, TCD Historical Soc., 2013; Bodley Medal, 2013. *Publications:* Every Day is Mother's Day, 1985; Vacant Possession, 1986; Eight Months on Ghazzah Street, 1988; Fludd (Winifred Holtby Award, RSL; Southern Arts Lit. Prize; Cheltenham Fest. Prize), 1990; A Place of Greater Safety (Book of Year Award, Sunday Express), 1992; A Change of Climate, 1994; An Experiment in Love, 1995 (Hawthornden Prize for Literature, 1996); The Giant, O'Brien, 1998; Giving Up the Ghost: a memoir, 2003 (Book of the Year Award, MIND, 2005); Learning to Talk (short stories), 2003; Beyond Black, 2005 (Yorkshire Post Fiction Prize, 2006); Wolf Hall, 2009 (Man Booker Prize, US Nat. Book Critics Circle Award for Fiction, 2009; Walter Scott Prize for histl fiction, 2010; Ind. Booksellers' Book of the Yr, 2010); Bring Up the Bodies, 2012 (Man Booker Prize, 2012; Costa Book of the Year, 2013; South Bank Sky Arts Award, 2013); The Assassination of Margaret Thatcher and Other Stories, 2014. *Recreation:* sleeping. *Address:* A. M. Heath & Co., 6 Warwick Court, Holborn, WC1R 5DJ.

MANTELL, Carl Nicholas; counsellor, since 2015; voluntary work, since 2013; Director, College of Management and Technology, Defence Academy of the United Kingdom, 2010–12; *b* 2 Feb. 1954; *s* of Charles Henry Purchase Mantell and Edna Joyce Mantell (*née* Bracey); *m* 1st, 1978, Janet Swinford Martin (marr. diss. 2008); two *s* one *d*; 2nd, 2011, Sarah Elizabeth Mitchell (*née* Sansom). *Educ:* Berkhamsted Sch.; Pembroke Coll., Cambridge (MA); Kendal Coll. (Counselling Skills course); Univ. of Cumbria (Postgrad. Dip. Counselling and Psychotherapy 2015). Joined MoD, 1977; Asst Private Sec. to Minister of State for Armed Forces, 1982–83; Principal (procurement finance, procurement policy, Army equipment planning), 1983–92; Hd of Resources and Progs (Mgt Planning), 1992–94; Sec. to Support Mgt Gp, RAF Logistics Comd, 1994–97; Hd of Resources and Progs (Air), 1997–99; Dir, Capability Resources and Scrutiny, 1999–2002; Dir Gen., Central Budget, 2002–05; Command Secretary: RAF PTC, 2005–06; RAF Strike Comd/PTC, 2006–07; Air Command, MoD, 2007–10. Mem., Audit and Risk Cttee, Kendal Coll., 2014–. *Recreations:* photography, reading, walking, listening to music, military modelling. *E:* carlnicholas@hotmail.co.uk.

MANTHORPE, John Jeremy, CB 1994; Chief Executive, 1985–96, and Chief Land Registrar, 1990–96, HM Land Registry; *b* 16 June 1936; *s* of William Broderick and Margaret Dora Manthorpe; *m* 1967, Kathleen Mary Ryan; three *s* one *d*. *Educ:* Beckenham and Penge Grammar School. HM Land Registry: Plans Branch, 1952; Principal Survey and Plans Officer, 1974; Controller (Registration), 1981–85. Consultant and Advr on Land Registration to HM Land Registry, UNECE, World Bank, and govts in Albania, Bahrain, Bermuda, Macedonia and Romania, 1996–2010. CCMI (CIMgt 1994); Hon. RICS (Hon. ARICS 1992). *Recreation:* walking and watching the Ashdown Forest. *Address:* Beurles, Fairwarp, Uckfield, East Sussex TN22 3BG. *T:* (01825) 712795.

MANTLE, Anthony Dod; director of photography; *b* Witney, 14 April 1955; *s* of Charles Ian Mantle and Dorothy Ruth Mantle; *m* 2000, Susanne; one *s*. *Educ:* London Coll. of Printing (BA Hons); National Film Sch. of Denmark (graduated 1989). Freelance work, 1989–; cinematographer: *films* include: Dogville, 2004; Millions, 2004; Manderlay, 2006; Brothers of the Head, 2006; The Last King of Scotland, 2007; Slumdog Millionaire, 2008 (Academy Award for Best Achievement in Cinematography, BAFTA Award for Best Cinematography, 2009); Antichrist, 2009; *television* includes: Wallander (2 episodes), 2008 (BAFTA Award for Best Photography and Lighting, 2009). Member: British Soc. of Cinematographers; Eur. Film Acad. Hon. Mem., Australian Cinematography Soc., 2009. Eur.

Cinematographer of the Year, Eur. Film Acad., 2003. *Recreations:* tennis, golf, family. *Address:* c/o ICM, 10250 Constellation Boulevard, Los Angeles, CA 90067, USA; c/o Independent Talent Group, 40 Whitfield Street, W1T 2RH.

MANTLE, Richard John, OBE 2013; General Director, Opera North, since 1994; *b* 21 Jan. 1947; *s* of late George William Mantle, OBE and Doris Griffiths; *m* 1970, Carol June Mountain. *Educ:* Tiffin Sch.; Ealing Coll. of Advanced Technology. Personnel Officer, Beecham Group, 1969–72; Associate Dir, J. Walter Thompson Co., 1973–79; Personnel Dir, then Dep. Man. Dir, ENO, 1980–85; Man. Dir, Scottish Opera, 1985–91; Gen. Dir, Edmonton Opera, Canada, 1991–94. Vice-Chm., Walsingham Coll. Trust Assoc. (Yorks Properties), Parcevall Hall, 2003–. Member: Council, Coll. of the Resurrection, Mirfield, 2009–; Gen. Synod of C of E, 2010–; Archbishops' Council (C of E) Finance Cttee, 2010–; Music Adv. Council, Univ. of York, 2012–; Dir, National Opera Studio. A Guardian, Shrine of Our Lady of Walsingham, 1998–. Hon. DMus Leeds, 2009. *Recreations:* music, reading, the country, English churches. *Address:* Cleveland House, Barrowby Lane, Kirkby Overblow, Harrogate, N Yorks HG3 1HQ. *T:* (01423) 815924. *E:* richardmantle@gmail.com. *Club:* Savile.

MANTON, 4th Baron *cr* 1922, of Compton Verney; **Miles Ronald Marcus Watson;** *b* 7 May 1958; *s* of 3rd Baron Manton and of Mary Elizabeth, twin *d* of Major T. D. Hallinan; *S* father, 2003; *m* 1984, Elizabeth, *e d* of J. R. Story; two *s* one *d*. *Educ:* Eton. Major, Life Guards. *Heir:* *s* Hon. Thomas Nigel Charles David Watson, *b* 19 April 1985.

MANTON, Prof. Nicholas Stephen, PhD; FRS 1996; FInstP; Professor of Mathematical Physics, since 1998, and Head of High Energy Physics Group, Department of Applied Mathematics and Theoretical Physics, since 2002, University of Cambridge; Fellow, St John's College, Cambridge, since 1997; *b* 2 Oct. 1952; *s* of Franz Eduard Sigmund Manton and Lily Manton (*née* Goldsmith); *m* 1989, Terttu Anneli Aitta; one *s*. *Educ:* Dulwich Coll.; St John's Coll., Cambridge (BA, MA, PhD 1978). FInstP 1996. Joliot-Curie Fellow, Ecole Normale Supérieure, Paris, 1978–79; Res. Fellow, MIT, 1979–81; Asst Res. Physicist, Inst. for Theoretical Physics, Univ. of Calif, Santa Barbara, 1981–84; Cambridge University: Lectr, 1987–94; Reader in Mathematical Physics, 1994–98; St John's College: Sen. Res. Student, 1985–87; Dir of Studies in Applied Maths, 1997–98; Mem., Coll. Council, 2006–09. Vis. Prof., Inst. for Theoretical Physics, SUNY, Stony Brook, 1988; Scientific Associate, CERN, Geneva, 2001. Emilio Segre Dist. Lectr in Physics, Tel Aviv Univ., 2014. Mem. Prog. Cttee, Internat. Centre for Mathematical Scis, Edinburgh, 2005–08. Chm., Res. Meetings Cttee, London Mathematical Soc., 2008–11; Mem., Mgt Cttee, Isaac Newton Inst. for Mathematical Scis, Cambridge, 2011–. Mem., British Team, Internat. Mathematical Olympiad, 1971. Jun. Whitehead Prize, London Mathematical Soc., 1991; Blaise Pascal Award, Durham Univ., 2010. *Publications:* (with P. M. Sutcliffe) Topological Solitons, 2004; papers in mathematical and theoretical physics in various jls incl. Nuclear Physics, Physics Letters, Physical Rev., Communications in Mathematical Physics, Jl of Mathematical Physics, Jl of Geometry and Physics, arXiv and conf. proceedings. *Recreations:* music, Finland and its culture, binocular astronomy. *Address:* Department of Applied Mathematics and Theoretical Physics, Centre for Mathematical Sciences, University of Cambridge, Wilberforce Road, Cambridge CB3 0WA. *T:* (01223) 765000; St John's College, Cambridge CB2 1TP.

MANUELLA, Sir Tulaga, GCMG 1996; MBE 1981; Governor General, Tuvalu, 1994–98; Chancellor, University of the South Pacific, 1997–2000; *b* 26 Aug. 1936; *s* of Teuhu Manuella and Malesa Moevasa; *m* 1957, Milikini Unifaleti; two *s* three *d*. *Educ:* primary sch., Ocean Is. Gilbert and Ellice Islands Colony: sub-accountant and ledger keeper, 1953–55; clerical officer, 1955–57; Sen. Asst, then Asst Accountant, Treasury, 1957–75; Tuvalu Government: Asst Accountant, Accountant, then Actg Financial Sec., Min. of Finance, 1976–84; Financial Secretary, Financial Division: Church of Tuvalu, 1984–86; Pacific Conf. of Churches, Suva, Fiji, 1987–91; Co-ordinator of Finance and Admin, Ekalesia Kelisiano, Tuvalu, 1992–94. Patron, Pacific Islands Soc. in Britain and Ireland, 1995. *Address:* PO Box 50, Vaiaku, Funafuti, Tuvalu.

MANVILLE, Lesley, OBE 2015; actress, since 1972; *b* Brighton, 12 March 1956; *d* of Ronald Leslie Manville and Nora Elizabeth Manville (*née* Edwards); *m* 1988, Gary Oldman, *qv* (marr. diss. 1990); one *s*. *Educ:* St Andrews C of E Primary Sch., Hove; Nevill Secondary Modern Sch., Hove. *Theatre:* RSC Warehouse: Savage Amusement, 1978; The Sons of Light, 1978; Chorus Girls, Th. Royal, Stratford E, 1981; Royal Court: Borderline, 1981; Rita, Sue and Bob Too, 1981; Top Girls, 1982; Falkland Sound, 1983; The Pope's Wedding, 1984; Saved, 1984; Serious Money, 1989; American Bagpipes, 1989; Three Sisters, 1990; RSC: As You Like It, The Philistines, Les Liaisons Dangereuses, 1985; The Wives' Excuse, 1995; The Cherry Orchard, Aldwych, 1989; Miss Julie, Greenwich, 1990; National Theatre: His Dark Materials, 2005; Pillars of the Community, The Alchemist, 2006; Her Naked Skin, 2008; Grief, 2011; All About My Mother, 2007, Six Degrees of Separation, 2010, Old Vic; Ghosts, Almeida, 2013, transf. Trafalgar Studios, 2014 (Best Actress, Critics' Circle Th. Awards; Olivier Award for Best Actress, 2014); *films* include: Dance with a Stranger, 1985; High Season, 1987; High Hopes, 1988; Secrets and Lies, 1996; Topsy-Turvy, 1999; All or Nothing, 2002 (Critics' Circle Best Actress Award); Vera Drake, 2004; Sparkle, 2007; A Christmas Carol, 2009; Womb, 2010; Another Year, 2010 (Critics' Circle Best Actress Award); Ashes, 2013; Romeo and Juliet, 2013; Spike Island, 2013; Viaggio Sola, 2013; The Christmas Candle, 2013; Maleficent, 2014; Mr Turner, 2014; The Theory of Everything, 2015; *television* includes: Emmerdale Farm, 1974–76; The Emigrants, 1976; Grown-Ups, 1980; The Firm, 1988; Soldier Soldier, 1992; Goggle Eyes, 1993; The Mushroom Picker, 1993; Little Napoleons, 1994; Tears Before Bedtime, 1995; The Bite, 1996; Holding On, 1997; Real Women, 1998, Real Women II, 1999; Other Peoples' Children, 2000; The Cazalets, 2001; Bodily Harm, 2002; North & South, 2004; Cranford, 2007; Mayday, 2013; Fleming: The Man Who Would Be Bond, 2014. *Address:* c/o ARG, 4A Exmoor Street, W10 6BD.

MANZE, Andrew; conductor; Principal Conductor, NDR Radio Philharmonic Orchestra, Hannover, since 2014; *b* 14 Jan. 1965; *s* of Vincent and Ann Manze. *Educ:* Bedford Sch.; Clare Coll., Cambridge (MA Classics). Violinist specialising in repertoire 1610–1830; broadcaster, BBC Radio 3, 1994–; Associate Dir, Acad. of Ancient Music, 1996–2003; Artist in Residence, Swedish Chamber Orch., 2001–; Artistic Dir, The English Concert, 2003–07; Principal Conductor, Helsingborg Symphony Orch., 2006–14. Many recordings incl. Biber Sonatas (Gramophone Award, 1996), Pandolfi Sonatas (Gramophone Award 2000) and music by Bach, Handel, Vivaldi, etc. Rolf Schock Prize, Royal Swedish Acad. of Music, 2004. *Recreations:* music, classics. *Address:* c/o Intermusica Artists' Management, Crystal Wharf, 36 Graham Street, N1 8GJ. *E:* bemmerson@intermusica.co.uk.

MANZIE, Stella Gordon, CBE 2007 (OBE 2001); Managing Director Commissioner, Rotherham Metropolitan Borough Council, since 2015; *b* 13 June 1960; *d* of Sir (Andrew) Gordon Manzie, KCB and Rosalind Manzie (*née* Clay); partner, Trevor McCarthy. *Educ:* Herts and Essex High Sch. for Girls, Bishop's Stortford; Fettes Coll., Edinburgh; Newnham Coll., Cambridge (MA English 1982); Poly. of Central London (Postgrad. DPA); Univ. of Birmingham (MSocSci 1992). Admin. Asst, ACC, 1982–84; Admin. Officer, SOLACE, 1984–86; Team Leader, Mgt Effectiveness Unit, Birmingham CC, 1987–88; Mgt Consultant, Price Waterhouse Mgt Consultants, 1988–92; Borough Dir, Redditch BC, 1992–97; Chief Executive: W Berks Council, 1997–2001; Coventry CC, 2001–08; Scottish Government: Dir Gen., Finance and Corporate Services, 2008–10; Dir Gen., Justice and Communities, 2010–11; Chief Exec., Barking and Dagenham LBC, 2011–12. Kieron Walsh Meml Prize, Birmingham Univ., 1997. *Recreations:* eating, drinking, socialising, travel, watching sport, reading.

MANZONI, Charles Peter; QC 2009; barrister; *b* Birmingham, 17 May 1963; *s* of Michael Manzoni and Julie Manzoni; *m* 1992, Clare Pickering; one *s* three *d*. *Educ:* Uppingham Sch.; Bristol Univ. (BSc Mechanical Engrg); City Univ. (DipLaw). Called to the Bar, Middle Temple, 1988, Hong Kong, 2000; barrister in private practice, 1989–. *Recreations:* sailing, family, ski-ing, music. *Address:* 39 Essex Street, WC2R 3AT. *Clubs:* Royal Ocean Racing; Royal Hong Kong Yacht.

MANZOOR, family name of **Baroness Manzoor**.

MANZOOR, Baroness *cr* 2013 (Life Peer), of Knightsbridge in the Royal Borough of Kensington and Chelsea; **Zahida Parveen Manzoor,** CBE 1998; Managing Director, Property Development and Director, Intellisys Ltd, since 2011; Director, Liberal Democrats Ltd, since 2014; *b* 25 May 1958; *d* of Nazir Ahmed and Mahroof Ahmed; *m* 1984, Dr Madassar Manzoor; two *d*. *Educ:* Leeds Univ. (HVCert 1983); Bradford Univ. (MA Applied Social Studies 1989). Student nurse to Staff Nurse, W Suffolk AHA, 1977–80 (SRN 1980); Staff Nurse, then Staff Midwife, Birmingham AHA, 1980–82 (SCM 1981); Health Visitor, Durham AHA, 1983–84; Lectr, Thomas Danby Coll., 1984–86 and 1987–88; NE Regl Prog. Dir, Common Purpose Charitable Trust, 1990–92; Chm., Bradford HA, 1992–97; Regl Chm., Northern and Yorks Regl Office, NHS, DoH, 1997–2001. Co-founder and Dir, Intellisys Ltd, 1996–2003. Legal Services Ombudsman, 2003–11, and Legal Services Complaints Comr, 2004–10, for England and Wales. Comr and Dep. Chm., CRE, 1993–98. Ind. Assessor, FCO, 1998–. Mem., Race Equality Adv. Panel, Home Office, 2003–. Mem., Bradford Congress, 1992–96; Dir, Bradford City Challenge, 1993–96. Trustee: W Yorks Police Community Trust, 1996–98; Uniting Britain Trust, 1996–2000; NSPCC, 1997; Nat. Media Mus., 2008–. Mem. Ct, Univ. of Bradford, 1992–98; Governor: Sheffield Hallam Univ., 1991–93; Bradford and Airedale Coll. of Health, 1992–93; Keighley Coll., 1994–95. Vice-Patron, Regl Crime Stoppers, 1998. Hon. Fellow, Bolton Inst., 1999. Hon. DSc: Bradford, 1999; Leeds Metropolitan, 2003; Bolton, 2010. *Recreations:* antiques, gardening, painting, historic buildings, photography, travelling, walking. *Address:* House of Lords, SW1A 0PW.

MAPLE, Graham John; District Judge, Principal Registry of Family Division, High Court of Justice, 1991–2005; *b* 18 Dec. 1947; *s* of Sydney George and Thelma Olive Maple; *m* 1974, Heather Anderson; two *s*. *Educ:* Shirley Secondary Modern Sch.; John Ruskin Grammar Sch., Croydon; Bedford Coll., London (LLB 1973). Lord Chancellor's Dept, 1968; Sec., Principal Registry of Family Div., 1989. Member: Outer London, Court Service Cttee, 1991–96; Family Courts Forum, 1996–2005. Chairman: Tenterden Counselling Service, 2007–14; Ind. Monitoring Bd, HM Prison/YOI East Sutton Park, 2010–13 (Mem., 2006–). Church Warden, St Mildred Parish Church, Tenterden, 1992–98. Consulting Editor, Rayden and Jackson on Divorce and Family Matters, 2003–12. *Publications:* (Co-Editor) Rayden and Jackson on Divorce, 12th edn 1974, to 17th edn 2003; (Co-Editor) The Practitioner's Probate Manual, 21st edn 1979; (ed) Holloway's Probate Handbook, 8th edn 1987. *Recreations:* archaeology, Roman Britain, steam and model railways. *Address:* Westbrook, Elmfield, Tenterden, Kent TN30 6RE.

MAPP, Derek; DL; Chairman: Sport England, 2006–07; British Amateur Boxing Association, 2008–13; *b* 17 May 1950; *s* of Thomas Mapp and Edna Mapp; *m* 1971, Karen Edmands; two *s* one *d*. *Educ:* Oakwood Primary Sch.; Boteler Grammar Sch. Dir, Mansfield Brewery, 1981–91; Founder and CEO, Tom Cobleigh plc, 1992–97; Chairman: Leapfrog Day Nurseries, 1998–2004; Imagesound plc, 2005–; Dir, Mapp Devels Ltd, 1996–. Non-executive Chairman: Staffline Recruitment plc, 2005–09; Priority Sites Ltd, 2006–07; Concentia Capital Ltd, 2011–; Huntsworth plc, 2014–; 3aaa Aspire Achieve Advance Ltd, 2014–; Informa (formerly Taylor and Francis) plc: non-exec. Dir, 1998–2009; Sen. Ind. Dir, 2005–08; Chm., 2008–. Chairman: E Midlands Develt Agency, 1998–2004; Mem. Bd, English Partnerships, 1998–2004. DL 2006, High Sheriff, 2013–14, Derbys. Hon. DTech Loughborough, 2004; Hon. Dr Lincoln, 2004. *Recreations:* sport, reading.

MAPP, Hon. Dr Wayne Daniel; Member, Law Commission, New Zealand, since 2012; *b* Te Kopuru, Northland, NZ, 12 March 1952; *s* of Gordon and Heather Mapp; *m* 1981, Denese Letitia Henare. *Educ:* Univ. of Auckland (LLB Hons); Univ. of Toronto (LLM); Christ's Coll., Cambridge (PhD 1988). Legal practitioner, John Collinge, Solicitor, 1979–82; Associate Prof. and Lectr in Commercial Law, Univ. of Auckland, 1984–96. MP (Nat.) N Shore, NZ, 1996–2011; Minister of Defence, Minister of Res., Sci. and Technol., Associate Minister for Econ. Devel and Associate Minister for Tertiary Educn., 2008–11. *Publications:* (with G. H. Harris) Goods and Services Tax: the application of the Act, 1986; The Iran-United States Claims Tribunal: the first ten years, 1993; contribs to internat. law jls. *Recreations:* flying, sailing, diving, tramping, study of history and politics, astronomy. *Address:* Law Commission, PO Box 2590, Wellington 6140, New Zealand.

MAR, Countess of (*suo jure*, 31st in line from Ruadri, 1st Earl of Mar, 1115); Premier Earldom of Scotland by descent; Lady Garioch, *c* 1320; **Margaret of Mar;** *b* 19 Sept. 1940; *er d* of 30th Earl of Mar, and Millicent Mary Salton; *S* father, 1975; recognised in surname "of Mar" by warrant of Court of Lord Lyon, 1967, when she abandoned her second forename; *m* 1st, 1959, Edwin Noel Artiss (marr. diss. 1976); one *d*; 2nd, 1976, (cousin) John Salton (marr. diss. 1981); 3rd, 1982, J. H. Jenkin, MA (Cantab), FRCO, LRAM, ARCM. Lay Mem., Immigration Appeal Tribunal, 1985–2006. Mem., EU Sub-Cttee on environment, health and consumer affairs, H of L, 1995–99, 2001–05; Dep. Speaker, H of L, 1997–2007, 2009–12 and 2014–; elected Mem., H of L, 1999. Mem., Delegated Powers and Regulatory Reform Cttee, H of L, 2014–. Chm., Honest Food, 2000–05. Chm., Environmental Medicine Foundn, 1997–2003. Pres., Guild of Agricl Journalists, 2007–11. Patron: Dispensing Doctors' Assoc., 1985–96; Worcs Mobile Disabled Gp, 1991–2003; Gulf Veterans Assoc., 1995–; Pres., Elderly Accommodation Counsel, 1994–; Chm., Forward-ME, 2008–; patron of several ME/CFS charities; Patron, Global Cabin Air Quality Exec., 2006–. Specialist cheese maker. Governor, King's Sch., Gloucester, 1984–87. Hon. ARCVS 2006; Hon. Associate, BVA, 2007. *Heir:* *d* Mistress of Mar, *qv*. *Address:* St Michael's Farm, Great Witley, Worcester WR6 6JB. *T:* (01299) 896608.

MAR, Mistress of; Lady Susan Helen of Mar; interior designer; *b* 31 May 1963; *d* and *heiress* of Countess of Mar, *qv*; *m* 1989, Bruce Alexander Wyllie; two *d*. *Educ:* King Charles I School, Kidderminster; Christie College, Cheltenham. *Address:* Firethorn Farm Cottage, Plough Lane, Ewhurst Green, Cranleigh, Surrey GU6 7SG.

MAR, 14th Earl of, *cr* 1565, **and KELLIE,** 16th Earl of, *cr* 1619; **James Thorne Erskine;** Baron Erskine, 1429; Viscount Fentoun, 1606; Baron Dirleton, 1603; Baron Erskine of Alloa Tower (Life Peer), 2000; Premier Viscount of Scotland; Hereditary Keeper of Stirling Castle; *b* 10 March 1949; *s* of 13th Earl of Mar and 15th Earl of Kellie, and Pansy Constance Erskine, OBE (*d* 1996); *S* father, 1993; *m* 1974, Mrs Mary Mooney, *yr d* of Dougal McD. Kirk. *Educ:* Eton; Moray Coll. of Education, 1968–71; Inverness Coll. (building course, 1987–88). Thistle Page to the Queen, 1962, 1963. Community Service Volunteer, York, 1967–68; Community Worker, Richmond-Craigmillar Parish Church, Edinburgh, 1971–73; Sen. Social Worker, Family and Community Services, Sheffield District Council, 1973–76; Social Worker: Grampian Regional Council, Elgin, 1976–77, Forres, 1977–78; Highland Regional Council, Aviemore, 1979; HM Prison, Inverness, 1979–81; Inverness W, Aug.–Dec. 1981;

Community Worker, Merkinch Centre, Inverness, Jan.–July 1982; Community Service Supervisor, Inverness, 1983–87; building technician, 1989–91; project worker, SACRO Intensive Probation Project, Falkirk, 1991–93; boatbuilder, 1993. Sits in H of L as Lib Dem; Member: H of L Select Cttee on Constitution, 2001–04, on Religious Offences, 2002–03; Ad Hoc Cttee on Barnett Formula, 2008–09; Jt Cttee on Statutory Instruments, 2008–13. Contested (Lib Dem) Ochil, Scottish Parly elecn, 1999. Chm., Strathclyde Tram Inquiry, 1996; Parly Comr, Burrell Collection (lending) Inquiry, 1997. Pilot Officer, RAuxAF, 1979, attached to 2622 Highland Sqdn, RAuxAF Regt; Flying Officer, RAuxAF, 1982–86; RNXS, 1985–89. DL Clackmannan, 1991–2014. *Recreations:* canoeing, hill walking, railways, gardening, restoration of Alloa Tower. *Heir: b* Hon. Alexander David Erskine [*b* 26 Oct. 1952; *m* 1977, Katherine Shawford, *e d* of Thomas Clark Capel; one *s* one *d*]. *Address:* Hilton Farm, Alloa, Scotland FK10 3PS. *Club:* Farmers.

MARA, Solo Naivakarurubalavu; High Commissioner of Fiji in the United Kingdom, also accredited to Republic of Ireland, Germany, Denmark, Egypt, Israel and the Holy See, since 2012; *b* Suva, Fiji, 14 Sept. 1967; *s* of Kolinio and Litiana Mara; *m* 2001, Kerry; two *s* two *d*. *Educ:* Univ. of S Pacific, Fiji (BA Pol Scis); Internat. Univ. of Japan (MA Internat. Relns). Counsellor, Brussels, until 2008; Perm. Sec., Min. of Foreign Affairs, Fiji, 2008–11. *Address:* High Commission of the Fiji Islands, 34 Hyde Park Gate, SW7 5DN. *T:* (020) 7584 3661. *E:* smara@fijihighcommission.org.uk.

MARAIS, Prof. Richard, PhD; FMedSci; Director, Cancer Research UK Manchester Institute (formerly Paterson Institute for Cancer Research) and Professor of Molecular Oncology, University of Manchester, since 2012; Co-Lead, CRUK Lung Cancer Centre of Excellence, Manchester, since 2014; Scientific Co-Director, Belfast-Manchester Movember Centre of Excellence, since 2014; *b* Witbank, SA, 16 March 1964; *s* of Frans Johannes Marais and Margaret Rose Marais (*née* James); *m* 2000, Katharine Jane Woodward-Nutt. *Educ:* University Coll. London (BSc Genetics and Microbiol. 1985); Ludwig Inst. for Cancer Res. (PhD 1989). Postdoctoral Res. Fellow, ICRF, 1989–92; Institute of Cancer Research: Ind. Postdoctoral Res. Fellow, 1993–98; Team Leader, Signal Transduction Team, 1998–2012; Prof. of Molecular Oncol., 2007–12; Dep. Chair, Section of Cell and Molecular Biol., 2008–11; Hd, Div. of Cancer Biol., 2011–12. Trustee, Melanoma Focus, 2012–. Pres., Eur. Assoc. of Cancer Res., 2014–July 2016; Mem., Bd of Dirs, Amer. Assoc. for Cancer Res., 2015–. *Publications:* contribs to peer-reviewed jls. *Address:* Cancer Research UK Manchester Institute, University of Manchester, Wilmslow Road, Manchester M20 4BX. *T:* (0161) 446 3101. *E:* richard.marais@cruk.manchester.ac.uk.

MARAN, Prof. Arnold George Dominic, MD; FRCS, FRCSE, FRCPE, FACS; Professor of Otolaryngology, University of Edinburgh, 1988–2000, now Emeritus; *b* 16 June 1936; *s* of John and Hilda Maran; *m* 1962, Anna De Marco; one *s* one *d*. *Educ:* Daniel Stewart's Coll., Edinburgh; Univ. of Edinburgh (MB, ChB 1959; MD 1963); Univ. of Iowa. FRCSE 1962; FACS 1974; FRCPE 1989; FRCS 1991. Basic trng in surgery, Edinburgh, followed by specialty head and neck trng, Univ. of Iowa; consultant otolaryngologist, Dundee Royal Infirmary, 1967–73; Prof. of Otolaryngology, W Virginia Univ., 1974–75; consultant otolaryngologist, Royal Infirmary of Edinburgh, 1975–88. Chm., Intercollegiate Bd in Otolaryngology, 1988–91; Sec., Conf. of Royal Colls, Scotland, 1992. Royal College of Surgeons of Edinburgh: Hon. Treasurer, 1976–81; Mem. Council, 1981–86; Hon. Sec., 1988–92; a Vice-Pres., 1995–97; Pres., 1997–2000. President: Scottish Otolaryngol Soc., 1991–92; Laryngology Section, RSM, 1990. Sixteen visiting professorships; sixteen eponymous lectures. Hon. FDSRCS 1995; Hon. FCS(SoAf) 1997; Hon. FCSHK 1997; Hon. Fellow, Acad. of Medicine, Singapore, 1998; Hon. FRSocMed 2002. Hon. Member: S African Otolaryngol Soc., 1986; S African Head and Neck Soc., 1986; Irish Otolaryngol Soc., 1990 (Wilde Medal, 1990); Assoc. of Surgeons of India, 1991. Hon. DSc Hong Kong, 2004. Yearsley Medal, 1985, Semon Medal, 1990, London Univ.; Jobson Horne Prize, BMA, 1985; W. J. Harrison Prize, 1989, Howells Prize, 1991, RSM; Leon Goldman Medal, Univ. of Cape Town, 1994. Order of Gorka Dakshina Bahu (Nepal), 1998. *Publications:* Head and Neck Surgery, 1972, 5th edn 2012; Clinical Otolaryngology, 1979; Clinical Rhinology, 1990; Head and Neck Surgery for the General Surgeon, 1991; (ed) Logan Turner's Diseases of Nose, Throat and Ear, 11th edn, 1992; The Voice Doctor, 2005; Mafia: inside the dark heart, 2008; Golf at the North Pole, 2012; contribs to 14 textbooks; 150 articles. *Recreations:* writing, golf, playing jazz, Member of Magic Circle. *Address:* 2 Orchard Brae, Edinburgh EH4 1NY. *T:* (0131) 332 0055; 2 Double Dykes Road, St Andrews KY16 9DX. *T:* (01334) 472939. *Clubs:* New (Edinburgh); Royal and Ancient Golf (St Andrews); Bruntsfield Golfing Society (Edinburgh).

MARBER, Patrick; writer and director; *b* 19 Sept. 1964; *s* of Brian Marber and Angela (*née* Benjamin). *Educ:* Wadham Coll., Oxford. *Plays:* Dealer's Choice, RNT and Vaudeville, 1995 (Writers' Guild and Evening Standard Awards, 1995); After Miss Julie, BBC, 1995; Closer, RNT, 1997, transf. Lyric, 1998, NY, 1999 (Evening Standard, Time Out, Critic's Circle and Olivier Best Play Awards, 1998), filmed 2005; Howard Katz, 2001, The Musicians, 2004, RNT; Trelawny of the Wells, Donmar, 2013; The Beaux' Stratagem, The Red Lion, Three Days in the Country, RNT, 2015. *Publications:* Dealer's Choice, 1995; After Miss Julie, 1995; Closer, 1997; Howard Katz, 2001.

MARCH AND KINRARA, Earl of; Charles Henry Gordon Lennox; DL; *b* 8 Jan. 1955; *s* and *heir* of Duke of Richmond, Lennox and Gordon, *qv*; *m* 1st, 1976, Sally (marr. diss. 1989), *d* of late Maurice Clayton and of Mrs Denis Irwin; one *d*; 2nd, 1991, Hon. Janet Elizabeth, *d* of 3rd Viscount Astor and of Bronwen, *d* of His Honour Sir (John) Alan Pugh; three *s* one *d* (of whom one *s* one *d* are twins). *Educ:* Eton. Chm., Goodwood Gp of Cos, 1991–. Pres., BARC; Life Vice-Pres., RAC. Patron, TT Riders Assoc. Honorary Member: British Racing Drivers' Club; 500 Owners Club; Guild of Motoring Writers. DL W Sussex, 2006. *Heir: s* Lord Settrington, *qv*. *Address:* Goodwood House, Chichester, West Sussex PO18 0PY.

MARCH, Lionel John, ScD; Professor of Design and Computation, School of the Arts and Architecture, University of California, Los Angeles, 1994–2003, now Emeritus; *b* 26 Jan. 1934; *o s* of late Leonard James March and Rose (*née* Edwards); *m* 1st, 1960, Lindsey Miller (marr. diss. 1984); one *s* two *d*; 2nd, 1984, Maureen Vidler (*d* 2013); one step *s* two step *d*. *Educ:* Hove Grammar Sch. for Boys; Magdalene Coll., Cambridge (MA, ScD). FIMA, FRSA. Nat. Service: Sub-Lt, RNVR, 1953–55. Harkness Fellow, Commonwealth Fund, Harvard Univ. and MIT, 1962–64; Asst to Sir Leslie Martin, 1964–66; Lectr in Architecture, Univ. of Cambridge, 1966–69; Dir, Centre for Land Use and Built Form Studies, Univ. of Cambridge, 1969–73; Prof., Dept of Systems Design, Univ. of Waterloo, Ontario, 1974–76; Prof. of Design, Faculty of Technology, Open Univ., 1976–81; Rector and Vice-Provost, RCA, 1981–84; Prof., Grad. Sch. of Architecture and Urban Planning, 1984–94, Hd of Architecture/Urban Design Prog. 1984–91, UCLA. Chm., Applied Res. of Cambridge Ltd, 1969–73. Mem., Governing Body, Imperial Coll. of Science and Technology, 1981–84. General Editor (with Leslie Martin), Cambridge Urban and Architectural Studies, 1970–; Founding Editor, Environment and Planning B, Planning and Design, 1974–. *Publications:* (with Philip Steadman) The Geometry of Environment, 1971; (ed with Leslie Martin) Urban Space and Structures, 1972; (ed) The Architecture of Form, 1976; (ed with Judith Sheine) R. M. Schindler: composition and construction, 1993; Architectonics of Humanism, 1998; (ed jtly) The Mathematical Works of Leon Battista Alberti, 2010; (ed) Shape and Shape Grammars, 2011. *Address:* Spring Cottage, 20 High Street, Stretham, Ely CB6 3JQ. *T:* (01353) 649891.

MARCH, Prof. Norman Henry; Coulson Professor of Theoretical Chemistry, University of Oxford, 1977–94; Fellow of University College, Oxford, 1977–94, Emeritus since 1994; *b* 9 July 1927; *s* of William and Elsie March; *m* 1949, Margaret Joan Hoyle (*d* 1994); two *s*. *Educ:* King's Coll., London Univ. University of Sheffield: Lecturer in Physics, 1953–57; Reader in Theoretical Physics, 1957–61; Prof. of Physics, 1961–72; Prof. of Theoretical Solid State Physics, Imperial Coll., Univ. of London, 1973–77. Hon. DTech Chalmers, Gothenburg, 1980; Hon. DPhys Catania, Italy, 2003. *Publications:* The Many-Body Problem in Quantum Mechanics (with W. H. Young and S. Sampanthar), 1967; Liquid Metals, 1968; (with W. Jones) Theoretical Solid State Physics, 1973; Self-Consistent Fields in Atoms, 1974; Orbital Theories of Molecules and Solids, 1974; (with M. P. Tosi) Atomic Dynamics in Liquids, 1976; (with M. Parrinello) Collective Effects in Solids and Liquids, 1983; (with S. Lundqvist) The Theory of the Inhomogeneous Electron Gas, 1983; (with M. P. Tosi) Coulomb Liquids, 1984; (with M. P. Tosi) Polymers, Liquid Crystals and Low-Dimensional Solids, 1984; (with R. A. Street and M. P. Tosi) Amorphous Solids and the Liquid State, 1985; Chemical Bonds outside Metal Surfaces, 1986; (with P. N. Butcher and M. P. Tosi) Crystalline Semiconducting Materials and Devices, 1986; (with B. M. Deb) The Single Particle Density in Physics and Chemistry, 1987; (with S. Lundqvist and M. P. Tosi) Order and Chaos in Nonlinear Physical Systems, 1988; (with J. A. Alonso) Electrons in Metals and Alloys, 1989; Liquid Metals, 1990; Chemical Physics of Liquids, 1990; Electron Density Theory of Atoms and Molecules, 1992; (with J. F. Mucci) Chemical Physics of Free Molecules, 1993; Electron Correlation in Molecules and Condensed Phases, 1996; (with L. S. Cederbaum and K. C. Kulander) Atoms and Molecules in Intense External Fields, 1997; Electron Correlation in the Solid State, 1999; (with C. W. Lung) Mechanical Properties of Metals, 1999; (with M. P. Tosi) Introduction to Liquid State Physics, 2002; (with G. G. N. Angilella) Many-Body Theory of Molecules, Clusters and Condensed Phases, 2010; many scientific papers on quantum mechanics and statistical mechanics in Proceedings Royal Society, Phil. Magazine, Phys. Rev., Jl of Chem. Phys, etc. *Recreations:* music, chess, cricket. *Address:* 11 Oxford Court, Lancaster Road, Carnforth, Lancs LA5 9LE.

MARCH, Valerie, (Mrs Andrew March); *see* Masterson, V.

MARCHAMLEY, 4th Baron *cr* 1908; **William Francis Whiteley;** *b* 27 July 1968; *o s* of 3rd Baron Marchamley and of Sonia Kathleen Pedrick; *S* father, 1994; *m* 2000, Amy, *yr d* of Douglas Kyle; one *s* one *d*. *Heir: s* Hon. Leon Whiteley, *b* 2004.

MARCHANT, Clare; Chief Executive, Worcestershire County Council, since 2014; *b* Bournemouth, 16 Aug. 1972; *d* of Philip Mitchell and Elizabeth Mitchell (*née* Kelly, later Styan); *m* 2013, Stephen Marchant; one *s*, and two step *s*. *Educ:* Univ. of Hull (BA Hons Hist. and Politics 1993); Open Univ. (MSc Manufg Mgt and Technol. 1998). Prodn Manager, Rank Hovis McDougall, 1993–97; Manager, Deloitte Consulting, 1997–2003; Chief Deployment Officer, NHS Nat. Prog. for IT, 2003–10; Asst Chief Exec., Worcs CC, 2010–14. *Recreations:* running marathons (eight), baking, volunteering. *Address:* Worcestershire County Council, County Hall, Spetchley Road, Worcester WR5 2NP. *T:* (01905) 766100. *E:* chiefexec@worcestershire.gov.uk.

MARCHANT, Clare Wynne; Director of Social Services and Housing, London Borough of Bromley, 1993–2000; *b* 13 June 1941; *d* of Rev. Glyn Morgan and Elma Morgan; *m* 1980, Harold Marchant. *Educ:* Horley Endowed Sch.; Banbury Grammar Sch.; UC Wales, Aberystwyth (BA Hons Philosophy 1963); UC Wales, Cardiff (DipSocSc 1964); Birmingham Univ. (Dip. Applied Social Sci. 1965). London Borough of Lewisham: Child Care Officer, 1965–67; Team Leader, 1967–71; Social Services Dist Officer, 1971–74; Principal Social Worker, 1974–87; Asst Dir (Social Services), RBK&C, 1987–93. *Recreations:* editorial and design of Greenwich Soc. and Max Wall jls; collecting and editing photographs of a rural community in N Oxfordshire in 20th century, and of the life of farming families in W Breconshire. *Address:* Shaftesbury House, 15 Royal Circus Street, Greenwich, SE10 8SN.

MARCHANT, Graham Leslie, OBE 2011; arts management consultant, since 1989; General Manager, Contemporary Dance Trust, 1994–98; *b* 2 Feb. 1945; *s* of late Leslie and Dorothy Marchant. *Educ:* King's School, Worcester; Selwyn College, Cambridge (MA). Administrator, Actors' Company, 1973–75; General Manager, English Music Theatre, 1975–78; Gen. Administrator, Opera North, 1978–82; Administrator, Tricycle Theatre, 1983–84; Chief Exec., Riverside Studios, 1984; Managing Dir, Playhouse Theatre Co., 1985–86; Dir, Arts Co-ordination, Arts Council, 1986–89; Head of Site Improvement, South Bank Centre, 1989–92. Director: Ballet Rambert Ltd, 1991–93; Lyric Theatre (Hammersmith) Trust, 1993–97; Chairman: London Dance Network, 1998–99; Nat. Dance Co-ordinating Cttee, 2000–03; Director: Shobana Jeyasingh Dance Co., 1999–2001 (Chm., 2011–12). Trustee, Chichester Fest. Th., 2005–06. JP Thames 2003–14. *Recreations:* reading, gardening. *Address:* 43 Canonbury Square, N1 2AW.

MARCHANT, Ian Derek; Independent Chairman, Infinis Energy plc, since 2013; Chairman, John Wood Group PLC, since 2014; *b* 9 Feb. 1961; *s* of Derek William and Rosemary Marchant; *m* 1986, Elizabeth Helen; one *s* one *d*. *Educ:* Trinity Sch., Croydon; Durham Univ. (BA Econs). ACA. Accountant: PricewaterhouseCoopers, 1983–92 (on secondment to Dept of Energy, 1989–90); Southern Electric: Corporate Finance Manager, 1992–96; Finance Dir, 1996–98; Finance Dir, Scottish and Southern Energy plc, 1998–2002; Chief Exec., Scottish and Southern Energy, subseq. SSE plc, 2002–13. Chm., Scotland's 2020 Climate Gp, 2009–15. Pres., Energy Inst., 2013–15. Chm., Maggie's Cancer Caring Centres, 2014–. *Recreations:* Rugby, reading. *Address:* Level 1, 50 Frederick Street, Edinburgh EH2 1EX.

MARCHANT, Ronald John, CB 2007; Chief Executive and Comptroller General, Patent Office, 2004–07; *b* 6 Nov. 1945; *s* of Arthur and Bridget Marchant; *m* 1969, Helen Ruth Walker (*d* 2010); one *s* three *d*. *Educ:* West Ham Coll. of Technol. (BSc Hons (Chem.)). Patent Office: Examr, 1969–90; Principal Examr, 1990–92; Dir, Patents, 1992–2004. Non-exec. Dir, Scottish Intellectual Assets Mgt Ltd, 2007–09. Occasional advr for World Intellectual Property Orgn, 2007–, E Europe, Middle East, the Balkans and Central Asia. Mem., Colchester BC, 1980–86. Chairman of Governors: Abersychan Sch., 2011–; Torfaen Assoc., 2012–. FRSA. *Publications:* contrib. Jl of World Intellectual Property, World Patent Information, Internat. Centre for Trade and Sustainable Develt pubns. *Recreations:* hill walking, reading, conservation, engaging with 9 grandchildren, sailing.

MARCHBANK, Pearce, RDI 2004; graphic designer, since 1969; Principal Partner, design consultancies, Pearce Marchbank Studio and Studio Twenty, London, since 1980; *b* 14 June 1948; *s* of late Harold George Marchbank and of Rachel Pearce Marchbank; *m* 1st, 1975, Sue Miles (marr. diss. 1981); one *s* one *d*; 2nd, 1985, Heather Page (marr. diss. 1996); two *s*; partner, Catherine Cornford. *Educ:* Bedford Sch.; Luton Coll. of Art; Central Sch. of Art and Design (BA 1st Cl. Hons). Art Director: Architectural Design mag., 1969–70; Rolling Stone mag., London, 1970; Friends mag., 1970–71; Co-ed. and designer, OZ mag., 1971 and 1974; design of complete editl set-up, style and logo, 1971–74, cover designer, 1971–80 and 1982–84, Time Out mag. (Publishers Assoc. Cover of the Year Award, 1974); Design Dir, Music Sales music publishers, 1974–93 (incl. design of all music books for The Beatles); Dir, Omnibus Press, 1976–79; Design Consultant, Virgin Records, 1978–80; Dir and Designer, Virgin Books, 1979–81; Co-ed. and Design Dir, Event mag., 1980–81; cover designs for Marxism Today mag. up to final issue, 1990–92; Co-ed. and Designer, Les Routiers (UK), 2000–03; Designer, John Lewis Partnership own-brand packaging designs, 2003–08. Clients include: nat. newspapers (designs for mag. sections of Independent, The Times, Guardian, 1988–89); art galls (Berkeley Sq. Gall., Christie's Fine Art, Yale Center for British Art); music publishers, Chester Music and Novello & Co. (incl. CDs and books for Phillip Glass, Sir John Tavener, Michael Nyman); restaurant designs (Zanzibar, Bank, Corney & Barrow, Opus Birmingham); wine (John Armit, Christian Moueix, Tate Modern, Le Nez Rouge); book design (Yale Centre for British Art, Yale Univ. Press); corporate identities (Eau de Vie Ltd, The Great Tombola nat. lottery); Royal Mail (stamps for Paralympic Games, London, 2012); Compass Pubns (incl. Handbooks for Port of London Authy, for Port of Gibraltar, for Abu Dhabi Port and for Ras Al Khaimah Ports); GroundWork Gall., Kings Lynn; Storyville Records, Copenhagen; Music Sales Creative, London. *Publications:* The Wall Sheet Journal, 1969; The Illustrated Rock Almanac, 1977; (ed) With The Beatles, 1982; Very Flat (monograph), 2014; (ed and designer) The Writing on the Wall, 2015. *Recreations:* landscape photography, Gothic and Modern Movement architecture, driving in continental Europe, slow food, eclectic music, Greece. *Address:* Pearce Marchbank Studio, East End, Newton Road, Castle Acre, Norfolk PE32 2AZ. *T:* (01760) 755886. *E:* mail@pearcemarchbank.com. *W:* www.pearcemarchbank.com.

MARCHWOOD, 3rd Viscount *cr* 1945, of Penang and of Marchwood, Southampton; **David George Staveley Penny;** Bt 1933; Baron 1937; Managing Director, 1987–2004, Chairman, 1997–2004, Moët Hennessy UK Ltd (formerly Moët & Chandon (London) Ltd); *b* 22 May 1936; *s* of 2nd Viscount Marchwood, MBE and Pamela (*d* 1979), *o d* of John Staveley Colton-Fox; *S* father, 1979; *m* 1st, 1964, Tessa Jane (*d* 1997), *d* of W. F. Norris; three *s*; 2nd, 2001, Sylva, *widow* of Peter Willis Fleming. *Educ:* Winchester College. 2nd Lt, Royal Horse Guards (The Blues), 1955–57. Joined Schweppes Ltd, 1958, and held various positions in the Cadbury Schweppes group before joining Moët & Chandon. *Recreations:* Real tennis, golf, shooting, racing. *Heir: s* Hon. Peter George Worsley Penny [*b* 8 Oct. 1965; *m* 1995, Annabel, *d* of Rex Cooper; one *s* one *d*]. *Address:* Woodcock Farm, Chedington, Dorset DT8 3JA. *Club:* MCC.

MARCKUS, Melvyn; communications consultant, associated with Cardew Group (formerly Cardew & Co.), since 1998; *b* 1 Jan. 1944; *s* of late Norman Myer Marckus and Violet Frances Mary Marckus (*née* Hughes); *m* 1st, 1970, Rosemary Virden (marr. diss. 1985); one *s* one *d*; 2nd, 1987, Rachel Mary Frances, *d* of Lord King of Wartnaby. *Educ:* Worthing Grammar Sch. Journalist: Scotsman, 1962–66; Daily Mail, 1966–67; Guardian, 1967; Daily Mail, 1967–70; Daily Express, 1970–72; Sunday Telegraph, 1972–82 (Jt Dep. City Editor, 1979–82); Observer, 1982–93: City Editor, 1982–93; Editor, Observer Business, 1984–93; an Asst Editor, 1987–93; Exec. Dir, 1987–93; City Editor, The Times, 1993–96; Columnist, The Express, 1996–99. Consultant, Luther Pendragon, 1996–98. *Recreations:* fishing, films, literature. *Address:* Cardew Group, Albemarle House, 1 Albemarle Street, W1S 4HA.

MARCUS, Ian; Director, Ian Marcus Consultants Ltd, since 2012; *b* Bournemouth, 16 Jan. 1959; *s* of Monty Marcus and Ruth Marcus; *m* 1984, Beverley Silverman; one *s* one *d*. *Educ:* Westcliff High Sch. for Boys; Fitzwilliam Coll., Cambridge (BA Land Economy 1981). Bank of America, 1981–86; UBS Phillips and Drew, 1986–90; Natwest Markets, 1990–97; Bankers Trust, subseq. Deutsche Bank, 1997–99; Chm., European Real Estate, Credit Suisse, 1999–2012; Chm., Evans Property Gp, 2012; Sen. Ind. non-exec. Dir, Secure Income REIT Plc, 2014–; non-exec. Dir, Town Centre Securities plc, 2015–. Mem., Adv. Bd, Redevco NV, 2013–; Senior Adviser: Eastdil Secured, 2013–; Well Fargo Securities, 2013–. Chm., Commercial Property Forum, Bank of England; a Crown Estate Comr, 2012–. Former Pres., British Property Fedn; Former Chm., Investment Property Forum. Chm., Prince's Regeneration Trust, 2008–. Eminent Fellow, RICS, 2010. Mem., Chartered Surveyors' Co., 2011–. *Recreations:* Rugby (playing and watching), golf, backgammon, Morris Minor driving. *Address:* Ian Marcus Consultants Ltd, Harewood, Priory Drive, Stanmore, Middx HA7 3HJ. *T:* 07747 774290. *E:* imarcus@ianmarcusconsultants.com. *Clubs:* Royal Automobile; Old Merchant Taylors' Rugby, Saracens Rugby.

MARCUS, Prof. Laura, PhD; FBA 2011; Goldsmiths' Professor of English Literature, University of Oxford, since 2010; Fellow of New College, Oxford, since 2010. *Educ:* Univ. of Warwick (BA); Univ. of Kent (MA, PhD). Prof. of English, Univ. of Sussex; Regius Prof. of Rhetoric and English Lit., Univ. of Edinburgh, 2007–09. Jt Editor, Women: a Cultural Review. *Publications:* Auto/biographical Discourses: theory, criticism, practice, 1994; Virginia Woolf: writers and their work, 1997, 2004; The Tenth Muse: writing about cinema in the Modernist Period, 2007 (James Russell Lowell Prize, MLA, 2008); (ed jtly) The Cambridge History of Twentieth-Century English Literature, 2004. *Address:* Faculty of English Language and Literature, University of Oxford, St Cross Building, Manor Road, Oxford OX1 3UL.

MARCUS, Prof. Rudolph Arthur; John G. Kirkwood and Arthur A. Noyes Professor of Chemistry, California Institute of Technology, since 2013 (Arthur Amos Noyes Professor of Chemistry, 1978–2013); *b* Montreal, 21 July 1923; *s* of Meyer Marcus and Esther Marcus (*née* Cohen); *m* 1949, Laura Hearne (*d* 2003); three *s*. *Educ:* McGill Univ. (BSc Chemistry 1943; PhD 1946; Hon. DSc 1988). Postdoctoral research: NRCC, Ottawa, 1946–49; Univ. of N Carolina, 1949–51; Polytechnic Institute, Brooklyn: Asst Prof., 1951–54; Associate Prof., 1954–58; Prof., 1958–64; Acting Head, Div. of Phys. Chem., 1961–62; Prof., 1964–78, Head, Div. of Phys. Chem., 1967–68, Univ. of Illinois. Vis. Prof. of Theoretical Chem., Univ. of Oxford, 1975–76; Linnett Vis. Prof. of Chem., Univ. of Cambridge, 1996; Hon. Professor: Fudan Univ., Shanghai, 1994–; Inst. of Chem., Chinese Acad. of Scis, Beijing, 1995–; Ocean Univ. of China, 2002–; Tianjin Univ., 2002–; Dalian Inst. Chem. Phys., 2005–; Wenzhou Med. Coll., 2005–; Dist. Affiliated Prof., Tech. Univ. of Munich, 2008–; Nanyang Vis. Prof., Nanyang Tech. Univ., Singapore, 2009–14 (Mem., Internat. Panel of Advrs, Inst. of Advanced Studies, 2008–); Hon. Academician, Academia Sinica, Taiwan, 2010–. Mem., Sci. Cttees and Nat. Adv. Cttees, incl. External Adv. Bd, Nat. Sci. Foundn Center for Photoinduced Charge Transfer, 1990–; Internat. Advr in Chem., World Scientific Publishing, 1987; mem., numerous editl bds; Lectr, USA, Asia, Australia, Canada, Europe, Israel, USSR. Mem., Nat. Acad. of Sciences and other learned bodies; Foreign Member: Royal Soc., 1987; RSCan, 1993; Chinese Acad. of Scis, 1998. Hon. MRSC; Hon. Member: Internat. Soc. of Electrochemistry; Korean Chemical Soc., 1996. Hon. Fellow, UC, Oxford, 1995. Hon. DSc Oxford, 1995. Prizes incl. Wolf Prize in Chem., 1985; Nat. Medal of Science, 1989; Nobel Prize in Chem., 1992. *Publications:* contribs to sci jls, incl. articles on electrochemistry, electron transfer, unimolecular reactions, enzymes, quantum dots, mass-independent isotope fractionation and on-water catalysis. *Recreations:* tennis, ski-ing, music. *Address:* Noyes Laboratory of Chemical Physics, Caltech 127–72, Pasadena, CA 91125, USA. *T:* (626) 3956566; 331 S Hill Avenue, Pasadena, CA 91106–3405, USA. *W:* www.cce.caltech.edu/faculty/marcus.

MARDELL, Mark Ian; Presenter, The World This Weekend and The World at One, BBC Radio 4, since 2014; *b* 10 Sept. 1957; *s* of Donald and Maureen Mardell; *m* 1990, Joanne Veale; two *s* one *d*. *Educ:* Priory Sch., Banstead; Epsom Coll.; Univ. of Kent at Canterbury (BA Hons Politics 1979). Journalist: Radio Tees, 1980–82; Radio Aire, 1982; Ind. Radio News, 1983–87; Industrial Ed. and Reporter, Sharp End (C4), 1987–89; Political Corresp., BBC, 1989–93; Political Ed., Newsnight, 1993–2000; Political Corresp., BBC News at Six, 2000–03; Chief Political Corresp., BBC News, 2003–05; European Political Ed., 2005–09, N America Ed., 2009–14, BBC. Writer, Radio 4 short story, Judgement Day, 2004. *Publications:* How to Get On in TV (for children), 2001. *Recreations:* reading, music, swimming, cooking.

MARDEN, Nicholas; Private Secretary to HRH The Duke of Kent, since 2011; *b* Colombo, Ceylon, 2 May 1950; *s* of Thomas, (Bob), Marden and Enid Marden; *m* 1977, Melanie Glover; two *d*. *Educ:* Uppingham Sch.; Southampton Univ. (BSc Politics and Law 1971). 2nd Lieut, Devonshire and Dorset Regt, 1971–74. Entered FCO, 1974; Third Sec., FCO, 1974–77; Second Secretary: Nicosia, 1977–80; FCO, 1980–82; First Secretary: Warsaw, 1982–85; FCO, 1985–88; Paris, 1988–93; Counsellor: FCO, 1993–98; Tel Aviv, 1998–2002; FCO, 2002–11. *Recreations:* sailing, cinema, walking, (watching) Rugby, folk and jazz music. *Address:* Office of the Duke of Kent, St James's Palace, SW1A 1BQ. *E:* nick@marden.name.

MARDER, His Honour Bernard Arthur; QC 1977; a Circuit Judge, 1983–98; President of the Lands Tribunal, 1993–98 (Member, 1989–98); *b* 25 Sept. 1928; *er s* of late Samuel and Marie Marder; *m* 1953, Sylvia Levy (MBE 1988); one *s* one *d*. *Educ:* Bury Grammar Sch.; Manchester Univ. (LLB 1951). Called to the Bar, Gray's Inn, 1952. A Recorder of the Crown Court, 1979–83. Formerly Asst Comr, Local Govt and Parly Boundary Commns; Chairman: Panel of Inquiry into W Yorks Structure Plan, 1979; Mental Health Review Tribunals, 1987–89. Pres., Land Inst., 1997–99. Mem. Bd, Orange Tree Theatre, 1986–2011; Trustee: Richmond Parish Lands Charity, 1987–96 (Chm., 1993–96); Richmond Museum, 1996–2003; Petersham Meadows Trust, 1999–2010. Hon. FSVA 1994; Hon. RICS 1999. *Recreations:* music, theatre, wine.

MAREK, John, PhD; Member for Wrexham, National Assembly for Wales, 1999–2007 (Lab 1999–2003, Ind 2003–07); *b* 24 Dec. 1940; *m* 1964, Anne Pritchard (*d* 2006). *Educ:* King's Coll. London (BSc (Hons), PhD). Lecturer in Applied Mathematics, University College of Wales, Aberystwyth, 1966–83. MP (Lab) Wrexham, 1983–2001. Opposition frontbench spokesman: on health, 1985–87; on treasury and economic affairs, and on the Civil Service, 1987–92. Dep. Presiding Officer, Nat. Assembly for Wales, 2000–07. Treas., CPA, 2000–03. *Publications:* various research papers. *E:* wxm1@fsmail.net.

MARENBON, John Alexander, PhD, LittD; FBA 2009; Senior Research Fellow, Trinity College, Cambridge, since 2005; Honorary Professor of Medieval Philosophy, University of Cambridge, since 2010; *b* London, 26 Aug. 1955; *s* of Arthur Marenbon and Zena Marenbon (*née* Jacobs); *m* 1981, Sheila Lawlor; one *s*. *Educ:* Westminster Sch.; Trinity Coll., Cambridge (BA 1976; PhD 1980; LittD 2001). Trinity College, Cambridge: Res. Fellow, 1978; Fellow and Dir of Studies, 1979–2005. Hon. ThD Helsinki, 2011. *Publications:* From the Circle of Alcuin to the School of Auxerre, 1981; Early Medieval Philosophy, 1983, 2nd edn 1988; Later Medieval Philosophy, 1987; Aristotle in Britain during the Middle Ages, 1996; The Philosophy of Peter Abelard, 1997; (ed) Routledge History of Philosophy III: medieval philosophy, 1998; Aristotelian Logic, Platonism and the Context of Early Medieval Philosophy in the West, 2000; (ed) Poetry and Philosophy in the Middle Ages, 2001; (ed with Giovanni Orlandi) Peter Abelard: Collationes, 2001; Boethius, 2003; Le Temps, la prescience et les futurs contingents, de Boèce à Thomas d'Aquin, 2005; Medieval Philosophy: an historical and philosophical introduction, 2007; (ed) The Many Roots of Medieval Logic: the Aristotelian and non-Aristotelian Traditions, 2008; (ed) The Cambridge Companion to Boethius, 2009; (ed jtly) Aristotelian Logic East and West, 500–1500: on interpretation and prior analytics in two traditions, 2010; (ed jtly) Methods and Methodologies: Aristotelian Logic East and West, 500–1500, 2011; (ed) Oxford Handbook of Medieval Philosophy, 2012; (ed jtly) Paganism in the Middle Ages: threat and fascination, 2012; Abelard in Four Dimension: a twelfth-century philosopher in his context and ours, 2013; (ed jtly) Aristotle's 'Categories' in the Byzantine, Arabic and Latin Traditions, 2013; Pagans and Philosophers: the problem of paganism from Augustine to Leibniz, 2015. *Recreations:* cooking, listening to music. *Address:* Trinity College, Cambridge CB2 1TQ. *T:* (01223) 338524. *E:* jm258@cam.ac.uk.

MARFLEET, Jacqueline Elizabeth; Senate House Librarian, University of London, since 2014; *b* Lincs, 15 Dec. 1962; *d* of Brian Marfleet and Pauline Marfleet. *Educ:* Univ. of Leeds (BA Jt Hons French and German 1985); Loughborough Univ. (MA Liby and Information Studies 1987). Liby Asst, Simmons & Simmons, 1987–89; Information Manager: Braxton Associates, 1989–91; KPMG Peat Marwick, subseq. KPMG, 1992–96; Vice Pres., J. P. Morgan, 1996–2004; Hd, Reference and Res., BL, 2005–07; Knowledge Manager, Ernst & Young, 2007–08; Hd, Advice and Records Knowledge, Nat. Archives, 2009–14. *Publications:* articles for Business Information Rev. and Electronic Liby. *Recreations:* running, cycling, hill walking, travelling. *Address:* University of London, Senate House, Malet Street, WC1E 7HU. *T:* (020) 7862 8412. *E:* jackie.marfleet@london.ac.uk.

MARGADALE, 3rd Baron *cr* 1964, of Islay, co. Argyll; **Alastair John Morrison;** DL; *b* 4 April 1958; *er s* of 2nd Baron Margadale, TD and of Clare (*née* Barclay); *S* father, 2003; *m* 1st, 1988, Lady Sophia Louise Sydney Murphy (marr. diss. 1999), *yr d* of 11th Duke of Devonshire, KG, PC, MC and Dowager Duchess of Devonshire, DCVO; one *s* one *d*; 2nd, 1999, Mrs Amanda Wace, *d* of Michael Fuller. *Educ:* Harrow; RAC Cirencester. DL Wilts 2003. *Heir: s* Hon. Declan James Morrison, *b* 11 July 1993. *Address:* Estate Office, Fonthill Bishop, Salisbury, Wilts SP3 5SH.

See also Viscount Trenchard.

MARGESSON, family name of **Viscount Margesson**.

MARGESSON, 3rd Viscount *cr* 1942, of Rugby; **Richard Francis David Margesson;** *b* 25 Dec. 1960; *o s* of 2nd Viscount Margesson and of Helena Margesson (*née* Backstrom); *S* father, 2014; *m* 1st, 1990, Wendy Maree Hazelton (marr. diss. 2003); one *d*; 2nd, 2003, Rosa Ita Escalona (*née* Rowlands). Major, Coldstream Guards, retd 2001. *Heir:* none.

MARGETSON, Sir John (William Denys), KCMG 1986 (CMG 1979); HM Diplomatic Service, retired; *b* 9 Oct. 1927; *yr s* of Very Rev. W. J. Margetson and Marion Jenoure; *m* 1963, Miranda, *d* of Sir William Menzies Coldstream, CBE and Mrs Nancy Spender; one *s* one *d*. *Educ:* Blundell's; St John's Coll., Cambridge (choral scholar; MA). Lieut, Life Guards, 1947–49. Colonial Service, District Officer, Tanganyika, 1951–60 (Private Sec. to Governor, Sir Edward Twining, subseq. Lord Twining, 1956–57); entered Foreign (subseq. Diplomatic) Service, 1960; The Hague, 1962–64; speech writer to Foreign Sec., Rt Hon. George Brown, MP, 1966–68; Head of Chancery, Saigon, 1968–70; Counsellor 1971, seconded to Cabinet Secretariat, 1971–74; Head of Chancery, UK Delegn to NATO, 1974–78; Ambassador to Vietnam, 1978–80; seconded to MoD as Senior Civilian Instructor, RCDS, 1981–82; Ambassador and Dep. Perm. Rep. to UN, NY, and Pres., UN Trusteeship Council, 1983–84; Ambassador to the Netherlands, 1984–87; Special Rep. of the Sec. of State for For. and Commonwealth Affairs, 1994–98. Gentleman Usher of the Blue Rod, 1992–2002. Dir, John S. Cohen Foundn, 1988–93. Chm., Foster Parents Plan (UK), 1988–90. Patron, Suffolk Internat. Trade Gp, 1988–90; Jt Pres., Suffolk and SE Cambridgeshire 1992 Club, 1988–90. Chairman: RSCM, 1988–94; Jt Cttee, London Royal Schs of Music, 1991–94; Yehudi Menuhin Sch., 1990–94; Trustee: Fitzwilliam Museum Trust, 1990–98; Ouseley Trust, 1991–97; Music in Country Churches, 1993–2000. Hon. RCM 1992; FRSCM 1994. *Recreation:* music. *Address:* 71b Cumberland Street, Woodbridge, Suffolk IP12 4AG. *Club:* Brooks's.

MARGETTS, Prof. Helen Zerlina, PhD; Professor of Society and the Internet, since 2004, and Director, Oxford Internet Institute, since 2011, University of Oxford; Fellow, Mansfield College, Oxford, since 2004; *b* 15 Sept. 1961; *d* of James David Margetts and Helen Jill Scott Margetts (*née* Taylor); partner, Dr Pedro Mascuñán Pérez; one *s*. *Educ:* Univ. of Bristol (BSc Maths 1983); London Sch. of Econs and Pol Sci. (MSc Politics and Public Policy 1990; PhD Govt 1996). Computer programmer/systems analyst, Rank Xerox, 1984–87; Systems Analyst, Amoco Oil Co., 1987–90; Res. Officer, Dept of Govt, LSE, 1991–94; Lectr, then Sen. Lectr in Politics, Dept of Politics and Sociol., Birkbeck Coll., Univ. of London, 1994–99; University College London: Reader, 1999–2001; Prof. of Pol Sci., 2001–04; Dir, Sch. of Public Policy, 2001–04. ESRC Professorial Fellow, 2011–14. *Publications:* (ed jtly) Turning Japanese: Britain with a permanent party of government, 1994; (jtly) Making Votes Count:

replaying the 1990s General Elections under alternative electoral systems, 1997; Information Technology in Government: Britain and America, 1998; (with P. Dunleavy) Government on the Web, 1999; (with P. Dunleavy) Proportional Representation for Local Government: an analysis, 1999; (jtly) Voices of the People, 2001, 2nd edn 2005; (ed jtly) Challenges to Democracy: ideas, involvement and institutions, 2001; (with P. Dunleavy) Government on the Web II, 2002; (with P. Dunleavy) Digital Era Governance: IT corporations, the State, and e-government, 2006; (with C. Hood) The Tools of Government in the Digital Age, 2007; (with P. Dunleavy) Government on the Internet, 2007; (ed jtly) Paradoxes of Modernization: unintended consequences of public policy reform, 2010; (jtly) Political Turbulence: how social media shape collective action, 2015; contrib. articles to learned jls, incl. Public Admin, Public Policy and Admin, British Jl Politics and Internat. Relns, Internat. Review of Pol Sci., Political Studies, Governance, Jl Public Admin Res. and Theory, Parly Affairs, Jl Theoretical Politics, Internat. Review of Admin. Scis, Eur. Pol Sci. Rev., West Eur. Pols, Royal Soc. Philosophical Trans. *Recreations:* art, painting, reading, writing, talking to my son, sailing. *Address:* Oxford Internet Institute, University of Oxford, One St Giles, Oxford OX1 3JS. *T:* (01865) 287210, *Fax:* (01865) 287211. *E:* Helen.Margetts@oii.ox.ac.uk.

MARGETTS, Sir Rob(ert John), Kt 2006; CBE 1996; FREng; FIChemE; Chairman: Ensus Ltd, since 2006; Energy Technologies Institute, since 2007; Ordnance Survey, since 2008; Deputy Chairman, OJSC Uralkali, since 2011; *b* 10 Nov. 1946; *s* of John William and Ellen Mary Margetts; *m* 1969, Joan Sandra Laws; three *s* one *d*. *Educ:* Highgate Sch.; Trinity Hall, Cambridge (BA Natural Scis and Chem. Engrg). FIChemE 1985; FREng (FEng 1988). Joined ICI, 1969: Process Design Engr, Agricl Div., Billingham, 1969; subseq. various managerial posts, including: Director: Agricl Div., 1982–85; Petrochemicals and Plastics Div., 1985; Res. and Ops, ICI Chemicals and Polymers Gp, 1987; ICI PLC: Dir, ICI Engrg, 1987–89; Gen. Manager, Personnel, 1989–90; Chm. and Chief Exec., Tioxide Gp PLC, 1991–92; Exec. Dir, 1992–97; Vice Chm., 1998–2000; Chm., ICI Pension Fund Trustee Ltd, 1994–2000. Vice Chm., 1998–2000, Chm., 2000–10, Legal & Gen. Gp PLC (non-exec. Dir, 1996–2010; Chm., Audit Cttee, 1998–2000); Vice Chm., 2001–02, Chm., 2002–06, BOC Gp PLC; non-executive Director: English China Clays PLC, 1992–99; Anglo American PLC, 1999–2010 (Chm., Remuneration Cttee, 2001–10; Sen. Ind. Dir, 2003–08); Falck Renewables plc, 2007–10; Huntsman Corp. (USA), 2010– (Chm. Europe, 2000–10); Wellstream, 2010–11; Mem., Internat. Adv. Bd, Teijin, Japan, 2004–06; Neochimiki SA, 2008–09. Chm., NERC, 2001–06. Chm., Govt Industry Forum on Non-Food Crops, 2001–04. Dir, Foundn for Sci. and Technol., 2001–. Gov., and Mem. Finance Cttee, ICSTM, 1991–2004; Member: Bd, CEFIC, 1993–95 and 1998–2000; Council, CIA, 1993–96 and 2001–; Council for Sci. and Technol., 1998–2007; Adv. Cttee on Business and the Envmt, 1999–2001; Chm., Action for Engrg, 1995–97; Trustee, Council for Ind. and Higher Educn, 1992–2010. Vice-Pres., Royal Acad. of Engrg, 1994–97. Mem. Ct, Univ. of Surrey, 2002–. Trustee, Brain Res. Trust, 2002–13. Freeman, City of London, 2004; Hon. Freeman, Salters' Co., 2004. FCGI 2001. Hon. FIC 1999; Hon. Fellow: Univ. of Cardiff, 2007; Energy Inst., 2008; Council for Industry and Higher Educn, 2011. Hon. DEng Sheffield, 1997; Hon. DSc Cranfield, 2003. *Recreations:* sailing, ski-ing, tennis, watersports.

MARGOLIN, Daniel George; QC 2015; *b* Dartford, 1972; *m* 2001, Sarah Louise Farmer; one *s* one *d*. *Educ:* Dauntsey's Sch.; Balliol Coll., Oxford (Schol.; Coolidge Pathfinder; BA 1st Cl. Ancient and Modern Hist.); City Univ., London (DipLaw); Inns of Court Sch. of Law (BVC). Called to the Bar, Gray's Inn, 1995; in practice at Chancery Bar, 1996–2015; Jun. Counsel to Crown, 1999–2015. Freeman, City of London, 2012. *Publications:* (Contributing Ed.) Mithani, Directors' Disqualification, 1998–. *Club:* Buck's.

MARGOLYES, Miriam, OBE 2002; actress; *b* 18 May 1941; *d* of late Dr Joseph Margolyes and Ruth (*née* Walters). *Educ:* Oxford High Sch.; Newnham Coll., Cambridge; Guildhall Sch. of Music and Drama (LGSM 1959). *Films* include: A Nice Girl Like Me, 1969; Rime of the Ancient Mariner, 1976; Stand Up, Virgin Soldiers, 1977; Little Shop of Horrors, 1986; The Good Father, 1987; Body Contact, 1987; Little Dorrit, 1988; Pacific Heights, 1990; I Love You to Death, 1990; The Butcher's Wife, 1991; As You Like It, 1992; Ed and His Dead Mother, 1993; The Age of Innocence, 1993; Immortal Beloved, 1994; Babe, 1995; Balto, 1995; James and the Giant Peach, 1996; Romeo and Juliet, 1996; Different for Girls, 1996; The IMAX Nutcracker, 1997; The First Snow of Winter, 1998; Left Luggage, 1998; Sunshine, 1999; Dreaming of Joseph Lees, 1999; End of Days, 1999; House!, 2000; Cats and Dogs, 2001; Harry Potter and the Chamber of Secrets, 2002; Being Julia, 2003; Ladies in Lavender, 2004; Life and Death of Peter Sellers, 2004; Harry Potter and the Deathly Hallows, Pt 2, 2011; The Guilt Trip, 2012; The Wedding Video, 2012; *theatre* includes: Dickens' Women (one-woman show), Duke of York's, 1991, world tour, 2012; She Stoops to Conquer, Queen's, 1993; The Killing of Sister George, Ambassador's, 1995; Wicked, Apollo, 2007, NY, 2008; Endgame, Duchess, 2009; Me and My Girl, Sheffield Crucible, 2010; A Day in the Death of Joe Egg, Glasgow Citizens Th., 2011; Dickens' Women, Artsdepot and UK and US tour, 2012; Neighbourhood Watch, Adelaide, 2014; I'll Eat You Last (one-woman show), Melbourne, 2014; The Importance of Being Miriam, Melbourne, 2015; *television* includes: Take a Letter Mr Jones, A Kick Up the Eighties, The History Man, 1981; Blackadder, 1983, 1986, 1988; Oliver Twist, 1985; Poor Little Rich Girl, 1987; The Life and Loves of a She Devil, 1990; Frannie's Turn, 1992; Cold Comfort Farm, 1995; The Phoenix and the Carpet, 1997; Supply & Demand, 1998; Vanity Fair, 1998; Dickens in America, Wallis and Edward, 2005; Miss Fisher's Murder Mysteries, 2012; Hebburn, 2013; Nina Needs to Go, 2014; Trollied, 2014; *radio performances* include The Queen and I, 1993; Gloomsbury, 2012. Best Supporting Actress, LA Critics Circle, 1989; Best Supporting Actress, BAFTA, 1993. *Publications:* (with Sonia Fraser) Dickens' Women, 2011. *Recreations:* reading, talking, eating, Italy. *Address:* c/o United Agents, 12–26 Lexington Street, W1F 0LE.

MARGRIE, Victor Robert, CBE 1984; FCSD; studio potter, academic, critic; *b* 29 Dec. 1929; *s* of Robert and Emily Miriam Margrie; *m* 1st, 1955, Janet Smithers (marr. diss. 2005); three *d*; 2nd, 2005, Rosemary Ash. *Educ:* Southgate County Grammar Sch.; Hornsey Sch. of Art (NDD, ATD 1952). FCSD (FSIAD 1975). Part-time teaching at various London art colls, 1952–56; own workshop, making stoneware and latterly porcelain, 1954–71; Head of Ceramics Dept, Harrow Sch. of Art, 1956–71 (founded Studio Pottery Course, 1963); Sec., Crafts Adv. Cttee, 1971–77; Dir, Crafts Council, 1977–84; Professorial appt, RCA, 1984–85; own studio, Bristol, 1985. One-man exhibns, British Craft Centre (formerly Crafts Centre of GB), 1964, 1966 and 1969; represented in V&A Mus., Ashmolean Mus. and other collections. Vice-Chm., Crafts Centre of GB, 1965; Member: Cttee for Art and Design, DATEC, 1979–84; Cttee for Art and Design, CNAA, 1981–84; Design Bursaries Bd, RSA, 1980–84; Working Party, Gulbenkian Craft Initiative, 1985–88; Fine Art Adv. Cttee, British Council, 1983–86; UK National Commn for UNESCO, 1984–85 (also Mem., Culture Adv. Cttee); Adv. Council, V&A Mus., 1979–84; Craftsmen Potters Assoc., 1960–89; Internat. Acad. of Ceramics, 1972–; Recording the Crafts (formerly Cttee, Nat. Video and Electronic Archive of the Crafts), 1993–. Ext. Examiner, Royal Coll. of Art: Dept of Ceramics and Glass, 1977; Dept of Silversmithing and Jewellery, 1978–80; Ext. Advisor, Dept of Ceramics, UWE (formerly Bristol Polytechnic), 1987–; Mem., Bd of Studies in Fine Art, Univ. of London, 1989–94; Advr, Faculty of Fine Art, Cardiff Inst. of Higher Educn, 1992–94; Vis. Prof., Univ. of Westminster (formerly Poly. of Central London), 1992–96. Governor: Herts Coll. of Art and Design, 1977–79; Camberwell Sch. of Art and Crafts, 1975–84; W Surrey Coll. of Art and Design, 1978–87; Loughborough Coll. of Art and Design, 1984–89, 1990–93. Associate Editor: Studio Pottery, 1993–2000; Ceramics in Society, 2000–05. *Publications:* contributed to: Oxford Dictionary of Decorative Arts, 1975; Europaische Keramik Seit 1950, 1979; Lucie Rie, 1981; Tradition and Innovation: five decades of Harrow ceramics, 2012; contrib. specialist pubns and museum catalogues. *Address:* 15 Telegraph Street, Shroton (Iwerne Courtney), Blandford Forum, Dorset DT11 8QQ. *T:* (01258) 860944. *E:* margrie@me.com.

MARÍN-GONZALEZ, Manuel; Grand Cross of Isabel la Católica; Chairman, Board of Trustees, Fundación Iberdrola, since 2008; *b* 21 Oct. 1949; *m* 1983; two *d*. *Educ:* Univ. of Madrid; Centre d'études européennes, Univ. of Nancy; Collège d'Europe, Bruges. MP for Ciudad Real, La Mancha, 1977–82 and 2000–07; Sec. of State for relations with EEC, 1982–85; a Vice Pres., CEC, later EC, 1986–99; Pres., Congress of Deputies, 2004–07. Vis. Prof., Univ. of Carlos III, Madrid, 1999. Mem., Spanish Socialist Party, 1974–, Internat. Policy Sec., 2003–04. *Address:* Fundación Iberdrola, Arequipa 1, 4° planta, 28043 Madrid, Spain.

MARINCOWITZ, Dr John; Headmaster, Queen Elizabeth's School, Barnet, 1998–2011; *b* 19 Dec. 1950; s of Nicholas and Diana Marincowitz; *m* 1979, Miriam Salie; one *s* one *d*. *Educ:* St John's Coll., Johannesburg; Witwatersrand Univ. (BA); UCW, Aberystwyth (BA Hons); SOAS, London Univ. (PhD 1985); Inst. of Educn, London Univ. (NPQH). History teacher, Trafalgar High Sch., Cape Town, 1979–82; Queen Elizabeth's School, Barnet: history teacher, 1985–86; Hd of Year, 1986–88; Hd of Sixth Form, Senior Master, 1988–98. Chm. Govs, Little Heath Sch., Herts, 1994–98. Chairman: Mgt Cttee, Northgate Special Sch., Edgware Hosp., 2007–11; Schools' Finance Forum, London Borough of Barnet, 2007–11; Mem., Boys' Academic State Schs, 2005–11. FRSA 1998. Mem., Cruising Assoc., 1999–. Mem., RYA, 1999. *Recreations:* sailing, non-fiction and historical novels, classical music and jazz, Rugby Union (particular interest in English and S African sides), creative writing, abstract art, travel. *E:* jmarincowitz@gmail.com.

MARINKER, Prof. Marshall, OBE 1991; FRCGP; Visiting Professor in General Practice, Guy's, King's and St Thomas' School of Medicine of King's College London (formerly United Medical and Dental Schools of Guy's and St Thomas' Hospitals), 1991–2006; *b* 2 March 1930; *s* of Isidor and Sarah Marinker; *m* 1st, 1955; two *s* one *d*; 2nd, 1978, Jeanette Miller. *Educ:* Haberdashers' Aske's Sch., Hampstead; Middlesex Hosp. Med. Sch., Univ. of London (MB, BS 1956); City Univ. (MA Creative Writing, 2010). FRCGP 1972. Principal in Gen. Practice, Grays, 1959–73; Sen. Lectr, St Mary's Hosp. Med. Sch., 1971–73; Foundation Prof. of Gen. Practice and Head, Dept of Community Health, Univ. of Leicester, 1974–82; Dir, MSD Foundn, 1982–92; Dir of Medical Educn, MSD Ltd, 1992–95. Visiting Professor: Univ. of Iowa, 1973; Univ. of Tampere, 1976; Roche Vis. Prof., NZ Coll. of GPs, 1977; Dozar Prof., Ben Gurion Univ., 1981; Sir James Wattie Meml Vis. Prof., NZ, 1982. Chm., R&D Cttee, High Security Psychiatric Services Bd, NHS, 1996–2000. Royal College of General Practitioners: Res. Registrar, 1967–70; William Pickles Lectr, 1974; Mem. Council, 1974–89; Chm., Educn Div., 1981–84; Chair, Cttee on Med. Ethics, 1987–89; George Abercrombie Prize, 1991. Chm., Council of Europe Wkg Party on the Future of Gen. Practice, 1975–77. Freeman, City of London, 1995. Hon. DM Tampere, 1982. *Publications:* (jtly) Treatment or Diagnosis?, 1970, 2nd edn 1984; (jtly) The Future General Practitioner, 1972; (ed jtly) Practice: a handbook of primary medical care, annually 1978–; (ed jtly) Teaching General Practice, 1981; (ed jtly) Towards Quality in General Practice, 1986; (ed) Medical Audit and General Practice, 1990, 2nd edn 1995; (ed) Controversies in Health Care Policy, 1995; (ed) Sense and Sensibility in Health Care, 1996; (jtly) Clinical Futures, 1998; (ed) Medicine and Humanity, 2001; (ed) Health Targets in Europe, 2002; (ed) Constructive Conversations about Health, 2006; pamphlets, lectures and papers on theory of gen. practice, med. educn, health service policy and med. ethics. *Recreations:* conversation, theatre, cinema, reading, creative writing, classical music, my dog. *Address:* 8 St Peter's Church, 124 Dartmouth Park Hill, N19 5HL. *T:* (020) 7263 1586, *Fax:* (020) 7263 6759.

MARIO, Dr Ernest; Chairman, Capnia, Inc., since 2007 (Chief Executive Officer, 2007–14); *b* 12 June 1938; *s* of Jerry and Edith Mario; *m* 1961, Mildred Martha Daume; three *s*. *Educ:* Rutgers College of Pharmacy, New Brunswick, NJ (BSc Pharmacy); Univ. of Rhode Island (MS; PhD). Vice Pres., Manufacturing Operation, Smith Kline, 1974; E. R. Squibb & Sons: Vice Pres., Manufacturing for US Pharmaceutical Div., 1977; Vice Pres. and Gen. Man., Chemical Div., 1979; Pres., Chemical Engrg Div. and Sen. Vice Pres. of company, 1981; Pres. and Chief Exec. Officer, Squibb Medical Product, 1983; elected to Bd, 1984; joined Glaxo Inc. as Pres. and Chief Exec. Officer, 1986; apptd to Bd of Glaxo Holdings, 1988; Chief Exec., 1989–93; Dep. Chm., 1991–93; Chief Exec., 1993–2001, Co-Chm., 1993–97, Chm., 1997–2001, Alza Corp.; Chm. and CEO, Apothogen Inc., 2002; Chm., IntraBiotics Pharmaceuticals Inc., 2002–03; Chm., 2003–07 and CEO, 2003–06, Reliant Pharmaceuticals Inc. Chairman: Nat. Foundn for Infectious Diseases, Washington, 1989; American Foundn for Pharmaceutical Educn, NY, 1991. *Recreations:* golf, swimming. *Address:* Capnia, Inc., 3 Twin Dolphin Drive, Suite 160, Redwood City, CA 94065, USA.

MARJORIBANKS, John Logan; Chairman, Local Government Boundary Commission for Scotland, 2000–07; *b* 21 Aug. 1944; *s* of William Logan Marjoribanks of that Ilk and Thelma (*née* Williamson); *m* 1976, Andrea Ruth Cox; one *s* two *d*. *Educ:* Merchiston Castle Sch.; St John's Coll., Cambridge (BA 1965, MA 1982). ACCA 1988, FCCA 1993–2010. Scottish Agricl Industries, 1965–73; Dept of Agric., Zambia, 1973–78; Commonwealth Development Corporation: Lectr, then Sen. Lectr, Mananga Agricl Mgt Centre, Swaziland, 1979–85; Ops Exec., London, 1985–87; Country Mgr, Mozambique and Zimbabwe, 1988–93; Dir, Mananga Mgt Centre, Swaziland, 1993–95; Country Mgr, India, 1995–98; Dir, Public Affairs, 1999–2000. On-line Tutor, Imperial Coll. at Wye, 2001–04. Local Govt Political Restrictions Exemptions Adjudicator for Scotland, 2007–15. Member: Cttee of Mgt, Berwickshire Housing Assoc., 2001–07; E Regl Bd, Scottish Envmtl Protection Agency, 2002–05. Chm., Gavinton, Fogo and Polwarth Community Council, 2012–14. Vice-Chm., Berwickshire Civic Soc., 2002–11. Gov., Macaulay Land Use Res. Inst., 2004–07. *Recreations:* Scots heraldry, bridge, curling. *Address:* Eden House, Gavinton, Duns, Scottish Borders TD11 3QS. *T:* (01361) 882692. *Club:* Duns Rotary.

MARK, Sir Alan (Francis), KNZM 2009 (DCNZM 2001); CBE 1989; FRSNZ 1978; Professor of Botany, University of Otago, 1975–98, now Emeritus Professor; *b* 19 June 1932; *s* of Cyril Lionel Mark and Frances Evelyn Mark (*née* Marshall); *m* 1958, Patricia Kaye Davie; two *s* two *d*. *Educ:* Univ. of New Zealand (BSc 1953; MSc 1955); Duke Univ., N Carolina (James B. Duke Fellow, 1957; Phi Beta Kappa, 1958; PhD 1958). Sen. Res. Fellow, 1960–64, Res. Advr, 1965–2000, Chm. Bd of Govs, Hellaby Indigenous Grasslands Res. Trust, 2000–10; University of Otago: Lectr in Botany, 1960–65; Sen. Lectr, 1966–69; Associate Prof., 1969–75. Chm., Guardians of Lakes Manapouri, Monowai and Te Anau, 1973–99; Mem., Fiordland Marine Guardians, 2005–13. Distinguished Life Mem., Royal NZ Forest and Bird Protection Soc., 1998–; Member: NZ Ecol Soc., 1953–2004, now Life Mem.; Ecol Soc. of Amer., 1958–2001, now Emeritus. Hon. DSc Otago, 2014. *Publications:* (with Nancy M. Adams) New Zealand Alpine Plants, 1973, 3rd edn 1995; Above the Treeline: a nature guide to alpine New Zealand, 2013; over 200 scientific papers. *Recreations:* enjoying the outdoors, nature conservation. *Address:* 205 Wakari Road, Helensburgh, Dunedin, New Zealand. *T:* (3) 4763229, (office) (3) 4797573. *E:* alan.mark@otago.ac.nz. *Club:* New Zealand Alpine (Hon. Mem.).

MARK, Rear Adm. Robert Alan, FRIN; Vice President and Partner, Strategy& (formerly Booz & Co.), since 2014 (Vice President, 2011–14); *b* 28 April 1955; *s* of Alexander Mark and Ruby (*née* Oliver); *m* 1978, Wendy Anne Peters; one *s* one *d*. *Educ:* Univ. of Hull (BSc Jt Hons Geol. and Phys. Geog. 1977); London Business Sch., Sloan Prog. (MSc Mgt 2001). Joined RN, 1974; HMS Wolverton, 1976; BRNC 1977; HMS Torquay, 1977–78; HMS

Ajax, 1979–80; HMS Fawn (NO), 1980–82; BRNC staff, 1982–84; HMS Hecla (NO), 1984–85; RN Hydrographic Long Course, 1985 (Internat. Hydrographic Bureau Category A Surveyor, 1985); MV Bon Esprit, UK Civil Hydrographic Prog., 1985; CO, HM Survey Motor Launch Gleaner, 1986–87; Exec. Officer, HMS Fox, 1987–89; MA to Dir, US Hydrographic Dept, US Naval Oceanographic Office, 1989–91; CO, HMS Herald, 1991–93; Comdr (H), FO Surface Flotilla, 1993; SO1 (Policy), Directorate, Naval Surveying, Oceanography and Meteorol., UK, MoD, 1994–96; CO, HMS Scott, 1996–98; Asst Dir (Policy), Directorate, Naval Surveying, Oceanography and Meteorol., UK, MoD, 1998–2000; Dir of Strategy, Defence Logistics, MoD, 2001–04; BAE Systems, 2004; Sen. Directing Staff (Navy), RCDS, 2005–07. Booz Allen Hamilton, later Booz & Co., (UK): Principal, 2007–11; Dir, 2011–14. Mem., SW Regl Adv. Bd (formerly Wessex Regl Cttee), Nat. Trust, 2007–. MInstD 2004, CDir 2006. Freeman, City of London, 2004; Liveryman, Co. of Water Conservators, 2004– (Master, 2009–10). *Recreations:* art, architecture, hill-walking. *E:* bob.mark@strategyand.pwc.com. *Club:* Army and Navy.

MARKESINIS, Sir Basil (Spyridonos), Kt 2005; PhD, LLD, DCL; FBA 1997; Conseiller Scientifique du Premier Président de la Cour de Cassation, France, 2002–07; non-executive Director: Alexander S. Onassis Foundation, 2007–10; Alexander S. Onassis Public Benefit Foundation, 2007–10; *b* 10 July 1944; *s* of Spyros B. Markesinis (former Prime Minister of Greece) and Ieta Markesinis; *m* 1970, Eugenie (*née* Trypanis); one *s* one *d*. *Educ:* Univ. of Athens (LLB, DIur); MA, PhD, LLD Cambridge; DCL Oxford. Asst Prof., Law Faculty, Univ. of Athens, 1965–68; Gulbenkian Res. Fellow, Churchill Coll., Cambridge, 1970–74; called to the Bar, Gray's Inn, 1973, Bencher, 1991; Fellow of Trinity Coll., Cambridge, and Univ. Lectr in Law, 1975–86; Denning Prof. of Comparative Law, Univ. of London, at QMC, subseq. QMW, 1986–93; Dep. Dir, Centre for Commercial Law Studies, Univ. of London, 1986–93; Prof. of Eur. Private Law, UCL, 1993–95; University of Oxford: Fellow: LMH, 1995–99; Brasenose Coll., 1999–2000; Clifford Chance Prof. of European Law, 1995–99, of Comparative Law, 1999–2000; Founder Dir, Centre, then Inst., of Eur. and Comparative Law, 1995–2000; Prof. of Common Law and Civil Law, and Chm., Inst. of Global Law, UCL, 2001–07. Prof. of Anglo-Amer. Private Law, Leiden Univ., 1986–2000, and Founder and Dir, Leiden Inst. of Anglo-American Law, 1987–2000. Advocate to Greek Supreme Court, 1976–86. Sen. Advr on European Affairs, Clifford Chance, 1999–2002. Visiting Professor: Univs of Paris I and II; Siena; Rome; Cornell; Michigan (Ann Arbor); Texas (Austin); Francqui Vis. Prof., Univ. of Gent, 1989–90, 2005–06; Jamail Regents' Prof. of Law, Univ. of Texas, Austin, 1998–2014, now Emer. Prof. of Comparative Law. Lectures: Atkin, Reform Club, 1989; Shimizu, LSE, 1989; Lionel Cohen Meml, Hebrew Univ. of Jerusalem, 1993; Wilberforce, 1998; John Maurice Kelly Meml, 2003; Eason-Weinemann, Tulane, 2005; Peter Taylor Meml, Inner Temple, 2006; Denning, Lincoln's Inn, 2007; Andrew David, Hellenic Soc. Trust, 2010; Key note speaker, Suleimania Forum, Amer. Univ. of Kurdistan, 2013. Mem., Council of Management, British Inst. of Internat. and Comparative Law, 1993–2000. Associate Fellow, Internat. Acad. of Comp. Law, 1987–98; Member: Amer. Law Inst., 1989; Acad. Internat. de Droit Comparé, 2004; Foreign Fellow: Royal Belgian Acad., 1990; Royal Netherlands Acad. of Arts and Scis, 1995; Accademia dei Lincei, Rome, 2005; Corresp. Mem., Acad. of Athens, 1994; Corresp. Fellow, Inst. de France, 2004; Hon. Fellow, Greek Archaeol. Soc., 2004; Corresp. Collaborator, UNIDROIT, 1992. Hon. QC 1998. DIur (*hc*): Ghent, 1992; Paris I (Panthéon-Sorbonne), 1998; Munich, 1999; Athens, 2007. Humboldt Forschungspreise, 1996; Univ. Prize, Leiden, 1996; John Fleming Prize, 2008. Officier, Ordre des Palmes Académiques (France), 1992; Comdr, Légion d'Honneur (France), 2004 (Chevalier, 1995; Officier, 2000); Kt Comdr, Order of Merit (Germany), 2003 (Comdr, 1998; Officer's Cross, 1992); Kt Grand Cross, Order of Merit (Italy), 2002 (Kt Comdr, 1999; Officer, 1995); Comdr, Order of Honour (Greece), 2000; Kt, Grand Cross, Order of Merit (France), 2006. *Publications:* The Mother's right to Guardianship according to the Greek Civil Code, 1968; The Theory and Practice of Dissolution of Parliament, 1972 (Yorke Prize); The English Law of Torts, 1976; (jtly) An Outline of the Law of Agency, 1979, 4th edn 1998; (jtly) Richterliche Rechtspolitik im Haftungsrecht, 1981; (jtly) Tortious Liability for un-intentional harm in the Common Law and the Civil Law, 2 vols, 1982; (jtly) Tort Law, 1984, 7th edn 2013; The German Law of Torts: a comparative introduction, 1986, 5th edn (jtly) as The German Law of Torts: a comparative treatise, 2016; (gen. ed. and contrib.) The Gradual Convergence: foreign ideas, foreign influences and English law on the eve of the 21st century, 1994; (ed and contrib.) Bridging the Channel, 1996; Foreign Law and Comparative Methodology: a subject and a thesis, 1997; (jtly) The German Law of Contract and Restitution, 1998; (gen. ed. and contrib.) Protecting Privacy, 1998; The Impact of the Human Rights Bill on English Law, 1998; (jtly) Tortious Liability of Statutory Bodies, 1999; Always on the Same Path: essays on foreign law and comparative methodology, 2001; (gen. ed. and contrib.) The British Contribution to the Europe of the Twenty-First Century, 2002; Comparative Law in the Courtroom and the Classroom: the story of the last thirty-five years, 2003 (trans. French, German, Italian and Chinese); (jtly) Compensation for Personal Injury in English, German and Italian Law: a comparative overview, 2005; The German Law of Contract: a comparative treatise, 2006; (jtly) Foreign Law in National Courts: a new source of inspiration?, 2006 (trans. Italian); Good and Evil in Art and Law, 2007 (trans. Greek 2009, Chinese 2013); Flawed Grandeur: the secret lives of great adventurers (in Greek), 2008; The Duality of Genius: shades, blemishes and vices of great achievers, 2009; (jtly) Engaging with Foreign Law, 2009; Shadows from America: essays in contemporary geopolitics (in Greek), 2009; A New Foreign Policy for Greece (in Greek), 2010; Writing for Myself: stops in a peripatetic life, 2011; Windows to an Author's Soul: nations, peoples, customs and habits through each other's eyes, 2012; The Legacy of Ancient Greek Drama to European Culture (in Greek), 2014 (Chinese edn 2016); On the Endurance of Ancient Greek Thought Through the Ages, 2015; ed. and contrib. many articles in learned jls in Belgium, Canada, England, France, Germany, Greece, Israel, Italy and USA. *Recreations:* painting, music, fund-raising, archaeological digging, chess. *Address:* Middleton Stoney House, Middleton Stoney, Bicester, Oxfordshire OX25 4TE. *T:* (01869) 343560.

MARKEY, Air Vice-Marshal Peter Desmond, OBE 1986; General Manager, NATO Maintenance and Supply Agency, Luxembourg, 1998–2004; *b* 28 March 1943; *s* of Althorpe Hazel Christopher Markey and Marjorie Joyce Markey (*née* Thomas); *m* 1966, Judith Mary Widdowson; one *s* one *d*. *Educ:* RAF Coll. Cranwell; Open Univ. (BA 1980); Cranfield Univ. (MSc 1994). RAF Supply Officer: commissioned 1964; served Singapore, France and UK to 1981; NDC, 1981–82; HQ Strike Comd, 1982–83; HQ AFCENT, Netherlands, 1983–85; MoD Carlisle, 1986–88; Station Comdr, Carlisle, 1988–89; RCDS 1990; MoD Central Staff, 1991; Dept of AMSO, 1991; HQ Logistics Comd, 1994; Dir Gen., Support Mgt, RAF, 1995–97; Dir of Resources, NATO, Luxembourg, 1997–98. Grand Cross, Order of Merit (Luxembourg), 2004. *Publications:* papers and contribs to learned jls. *Recreations:* cycling, mountain walking, travelling. *E:* Markeypd@aol.com.

MARKHAM, Sir Alexander (Fred), Kt 2008; PhD, DSc; FRCP, FRCPath; West Riding Medical Research Trust Professor of Medicine, University of Leeds, since 1992; Chairman, Lister Institute of Preventive Medicine, since 2011; *b* 30 Nov. 1950; one *s* one *d*. *Educ:* Univ. of Birmingham (BSc 1971; PhD 1974; DSc 1992); Univ. of London (MB BS 1985). FRCPath 1996; FRCP 1998. ICI Pharmaceuticals, 1979–90; Nuffield Dept of Medicine, Univ. of Oxford, 1990–92; Dir, Molecular Medicine Unit, Univ. of Leeds, 1992; Hon. Consultant Physician, Leeds Teaching Hosps NHS Trust; Chief Executive, Cancer Research UK, 2003–07 (on secondment). Chm., NCRI, 2003–06. FMedSci 2004. *Address:* c/o School of Medicine, University of Leeds, Leeds LS2 9JT.

MARKHAM, Sir (Arthur) David, 4th Bt *cr* 1911, of Beachborough Park; *b* 6 Dec. 1950; *er s* of Sir Charles Markham, 3rd Bt and Valerie Markham (*née* Barry-Johnston); *S* father, 2006; *m* 1st, 1977, Carolyn Lorna (*née* Park) (marr. diss. 2007); two *d*; 2nd, 2010, Mrs Sarah Leggett. *Educ:* Milton Abbey Sch. *Recreations:* racing, travel. *Heir:* *b* Richard Barry Markham [*b* 18 April 1954; *m* 1985, Ann Malcolm-Smith; one *s* (and one *s* decd)]. *Address:* PO Box 755, Nanyuki 10400, Kenya. *E:* markham@africaonline.co.ke. *Clubs:* Muthaiga Country, Jockey (Kenya).

MARKLAND, John Anthony, CBE 1999; PhD; Chairman, Scottish Natural Heritage, 1999–2006; *b* 17 May 1948; *s* of late Thomas Henry Markland and Rita Markland (*née* Shippen); *m* 1970, Muriel Harris; four *d*. *Educ:* Bolton Sch., Lancs; Dundee Univ. (MA Geog. 1970; PhD 1975). CDipAF 1979; ACIS 1982. Demographer, Somerset CC, 1974–76; Sen. Professional Asst (Planning Res.), Tayside Regl Council, 1976–79; Fife Regional Council: PA to Chief Exec., 1979–83; Asst Chief Exec., 1983–86; Chief Exec., 1986–95; Chief Exec., Fife Council, 1995–99. Chm., Scottish Br., SOLACE, 1993–95. Chairman: Forward Scotland Ltd, 1996–2000; Scottish Leadership Foundn, 2001–08; Environmental Campaigns, 2003–06. Member: Jt Nature Conservation Cttee, 1999–2006; Scotland Adv. Gp, Woodland Trust, 2011–. Vice Convener, Ct, Edinburgh Univ., 2006–11 (Mem., 2001–11; Convener, Audit Cttee, 2004–06). Dir, Horsecross Arts Ltd, 2007–13. Pres., Old Boltonians' Assoc., 2007. Trustee: Gannochy Trust, 2009–; Kincarrathie Trust, 2012–. Dr *hc* Edinburgh, 2012. *Recreations:* finding the easiest way up Scotland's Munros, attempting to keep fit. *Address:* 3 St Leonard's Bank, Perth PH2 8EB. *T:* (01738) 441798.

MARKOVA, Prof. Ivana, PhD; FBA 1999; FRSE; Professor of Psychology, University of Stirling, 1984–2003, now Emeritus. Formerly Lectr, Sen. Lectr, then Reader, in Psychology, and Head of Dept of Psychology, Univ. of Stirling. FRSE 1997. *Publications:* (ed) Social Context of Language, 1978; Paradigms, Thought and Language, 1982; Human Awareness: its social development, 1987; (with Klaus Foppa) Dynamics of Dialogue, 1990; (ed with Klaus Foppa) Asymmetries and Dialogue, 1991; (ed with R. M. Farr) Representations of Health, Illness and Handicap, 1994; (ed jtly) Mutualities in Dialogue, 1995; Dialogicality and Social Representations, 2003; (with Serge Moscovici) The Making of Modern Social Psychology, 2006. *Address:* Department of Psychology, University of Stirling, Stirling FK9 4LA.

MARKOWICH, Prof. Peter Alexander; Professor of Applied Mathematics, University of Cambridge, since 2007; Fellow, Clare Hall, Cambridge, since 2009; *b* 16 Dec. 1956; *s* of Otto Markowich and Elfriede Markowich; *m*; one *d*. *Educ:* Technical Univ., Vienna (Diploma 1979; Dr Tech. 1980). Res. Asst, Internat. Inst. for Applied Systems Analysis, Austria, 1979–80; Res. Associate, Math. Res. Center, Univ. of Wisconsin-Madison, 1980–81; Asst Prof., Math. and Computer Sci. Depts, Univ. of Texas at Austin, 1981–82; Asst Prof., 1982–84, Associate Prof., 1984–89, Inst. for Applied and Numerical Math., Technical Univ., Vienna; Professor, Department of Mathematics: Technical Univ. of Berlin, 1989–90, 1991–98; Purdue Univ., 1990–91; Prof. of Math. Analysis, Johannes Kepler Univ. Linz, 1998–99; Prof. of Applied Analysis, Faculty of Math., Univ. of Vienna, 1999–. JSPS Fellow, Kyoto Univ., 2005. Corresp. Mem., Austrian Acad. of Scis, 2005. Wittgenstein Award, Austrian Sci. Fund, 2000; Humboldt Res. Award, Alexander von Humboldt Foundn, 2010. *Publications:* The Stationary Semiconductor Device Equations, 1986; (jtly) Semiconductor Equations, 1990; Applied Partial Differential Equations: a visual approach, 2006; articles in learned jls. *Address:* Department of Applied Mathematics and Theoretical Physics, Centre for Mathematical Sciences, University of Cambridge, Wilberforce Road, Cambridge CB3 0WA. *W:* www.peter-markowich.net.

MARKOWITZ, Prof. Harry M., PhD; President, Harry Markowitz Company, since 1984; Adjunct Professor of Finance, Rady School, University of California at San Diego, since 2006; Professor of Finance and Economics, Baruch College, City University of New York, 1982–93; *b* 24 Aug. 1927; *s* of Morris Markowitz and Mildred (*née* Gruber); *m* Barbara Gay. *Educ:* Univ. of Chicago (PhB Liberal Arts 1947; MA 1950, PhD 1954 Econs). Res. Associate, Rand Corp., 1952–60 and 1961–63; Consultant, Gen. Electric Corp., 1960–61; Chm., Bd and Technical Dir, Consolidated Analysis Centres Inc., 1963–68; Prof. of Finance, UCLA, 1968–69; Pres., Arbitrage Management Co., 1969–72, Consultant, 1972–74; Vis. Prof. of Finance, Wharton Bus. Sch., 1972–74; Res. Staff Mem., T. J. Watson Res. Center, IBM, 1974–83; Adj. Prof. of Finance, Rutgers Univ., 1980–82; Consultant, Daiwa Securities, 1990–2000. Director: Amer. Finance Assoc.; TIMS. Fellow: Econometric Soc.; Amer. Acad. Arts and Sciences, 1987. Von Neumann Theory Prize, ORSA/TIMS, 1989; Nobel Prize for Economics, 1990. *Publications:* Portfolio Selection: efficient diversification of investments, 1959, 2nd edn 1991; Simscript: a simulation programming language, 1963; (jtly) Studies in Process Analysis: economy-wide production capabilities, 1963 (trans. Russian 1967); (jtly) The Simscript II Programming Language, 1969; (jtly) The EAS-E Programming Language, 1981; (jtly) Adverse Deviation, 1981; Mean-Variance Analysis in Portfolio Choice and Capital Markets, 1987; Harry Markowitz: selected works (World Scientific-Nobel Laureate Series, Vol. 1), 2008; contrib. chapters to numerous books and papers in professional jls, incl. Jl of Finance, Management Science, Jl of Portfolio Management. *Recreation:* music.

MARKS, family name of **Barons Marks of Broughton** and **Marks of Henley-on-Thames**.

MARKS OF BROUGHTON, 3rd Baron *cr* 1961, of Sunningdale in the Royal Co. of Berks; **Simon Richard Marks;** *b* 3 May 1950; *s* of 2nd Baron Marks of Broughton and his 1st wife, Ann Catherine (*née* Pinto); *S* father, 1998; *m* 1982, Marion, *o d* of Peter F. Norton; one *s* three *d*. *Educ:* Eton; Balliol Coll., Oxford (BA 1971). *Heir:* *s* Hon. Michael Marks, *b* 13 May 1989.

MARKS OF HENLEY-ON-THAMES, Baron *cr* 2011 (Life Peer), of Henley-on-Thames in the County of Oxfordshire; **Jonathan Clive Marks;** QC 1995; *b* 19 Oct. 1952; *s* of late Geoffrey Jack Marks, LDS RCS and Patricia Pauline Marks, LLB; *m* 1st, 1982, Sarah Ann Russell (marr. diss. 1991); one *s* one *d*; 2nd, 1993, (Clementine) Medina Cafopoulos; three *s* two *d*. *Educ:* Harrow; University Coll., Oxford (BA Hons Jurisp.); Inns of Court Sch. of Law. Called to the Bar, Inner Temple, 1975; in practice, Common Law and Commercial Law, Western Circuit. Vis. Lecturer in Advocacy: Univs of Malaya and Mauritius; Sri Lanka Law Coll. Contested (SDP): Weston-Super-Mare, 1983; Falmouth and Camborne, 1987; EP elecn, Cornwall and Plymouth, 1984. Member: Lib Dem Cttee for England, 1988–89; Lib Dem Federal Policy Cttee, 2004–10, 2011–; H of L Delegated Powers and Regulatory Reform Cttee, 2012–15; Co-Chair, Lib Dem Parly Cttee on Home Affairs, Justice and Equalities, 2012–; Lib Dem spokesman on justice, H of L, 2012–. Chm., Lib Dem Lawyers Assoc., 2001–07. Freeman, City of London, 1975; Liveryman, Patternmakers' Co., 1975– (Mem. Ct Assts, 1998–2004). *Recreations:* tennis, ski-ing, theatre, opera, food, wine, travel. *Address:* 4 Pump Court, Temple, EC4Y 7AN. *T:* (020) 7842 5555; House of Lords, SW1A 0PW. *Clubs:* Royal Automobile, Boodle's.

MARKS, Alexandra Louise; a Recorder, since 2002; a Deputy High Court Judge, since 2010; Consultant, Linklaters LLP, since 2011; *b* London, 9 Sept. 1959; *d* of Prof. Vincent Marks and Averil Marks; *m* 1991, Prof. Steven Julius Barnett; two *d*. *Educ:* Guildford Co. Sch. for Girls; Brasenose Coll., Oxford (BA Hons); Coll. of Law, London. Articled clerk, 1981–83; admitted as solicitor, 1983; Assistant Solicitor: Rowe & Maw, 1983–84; Linklaters & Paines, 1984–90; Partner: (equity - full-time), Linklaters, 1990–2003; (salaried - pt-time), Linklaters LLP, 2003–11. Solicitors Regulation Authy Adjudicator, 2008–13. Chm., Professional Conduct Cttee, Architects Registration Bd, 2010–; Legal Assessor, Conduct and Appeals Cttee, RICS, 2011–; Member: Judicial Appts Commn, 2012–; Criminal Cases Review Commn, 2013–. Mem., Adv. Bd, UCL Judicial Inst., 2010–. Law Society: Chair: Internat. Human Rights Wkg Gp, 1986–94; Law Reform Bd, 2004–07; Mem. Council, 2003–07; *ex officio* Mem., Corporate Governance Bd, 2004–07; Pres., City of London Law Soc., 2008–09.

Chair, Bd of Dirs, Amnesty Internat. Charity Ltd, 2000–10; Mem. Exec. Bd, and Trustee, Justice, 1996–2014 (Chm., Exec. Bd, 1999–2004); Member, Board and Trustee: Interights, 2006–; Working Families, 2008–; Prisoners' Educn Trust, 2010– (Chm., 2012–). Mem. Court, Solicitors' Co., 2005– (Master, 2008–09). Sec., Brasenose Soc., 1995– (Pres., 2007–08). *Recreations:* theatre (as audience), walking, weight-training, tidying up (unsuccessfully). *Address:* c/o Linklaters LLP, One Silk Street, EC2Y 8HQ. *T:* (020) 7456 2000, *Fax:* (020) 7456 2222. *E:* alexandra.marks@linklaters.com.

See also L. A. Marks.

MARKS, Christine; *see* Murray, C.

MARKS, David Francis, PhD; CPsychol, FBPsS; publisher and author; *b* 12 Feb. 1945; *s* of Victor William Francis Marks and Mary Dorothy Marks; one *d* by Margaret McGoldrick; one *s* by Elsy Cecilia Clavijo. *Educ:* Southern Grammar Sch. for Boys, Portsmouth; Reading Univ. (BSc); Sheffield Univ. (PhD 1970). FBPsS 1984; CPsychol 1988; Chartered Health Psychologist, 1998. Sen. Demonstrator, Sheffield Univ., 1966–69; Lectr, 1970–74, Sen. Lectr, 1978–86, Univ. of Otago, NZ; Middlesex Polytechnic, subseq. University: Prof. of Psychology, 1986–2000; Head, Sch. of Psychology, 1986–91; Head, Health Research Centre, 1989–2000; Prof. of Psychology, City Univ., London, 2000–10. Visiting Professor: Oregon, 1976; Washington, 1977; Hamamatsu Univ. Sch. of Medicine, Fukuoka Univ., Japan, 1984; Rome, 1997; Hon. Res. Fellow, UCL, 1977. Mem., DoH Scientific Cttee on Tobacco and Health, 1994–98; Convenor, Task Force on Health Psychol., Eur. Fedn of Professional Psychologists' Assocs, 1993–97. Organised internat. confs on mental imagery, 1983, 1985. Consultant to NHS, local govt and EC depts and corps. Sen. Asst Ed., Jl of Mental Imagery, 1987–96; Asst Ed., British Jl of Psychology, 1990–95; Editor: Jl Health Psychol., 1996–; Health Psychol. Open, 2014–. Developer of first smoking cessation prog. on the internet. Vegan. Gold Disk for Music Therapy, NZ Min. of Health, 1979. *Publications:* The Psychology of the Psychic, 1980, 2nd edn 2000; Theories of Image Formation, 1986; Imagery: current developments, 1990; The Quit for Life Programme, 1993; Improving the Health of the Nation, 1996; Health Psychology: theory, research and practice, 2000, 4th edn 2015 (trans. Chinese 2004, Spanish 2008); Dealing with Dementia, 2000; The Health Psychology Reader, 2002; Research Methods for Clinical and Health Psychology, 2004; Overcoming Your Smoking Habit, 2005 (trans. French 2009); Bryan Poole: contemporary botanical aquatint etchings, 2011; (ed) Mark Baker Portraits, 2011; (ed) Ewan McDougall Paintings, 2011; numerous book chapters and contribs to Nature, Science, Brit. Jl of Psych., Jl of Mental Imagery, and many other jls. *Recreations:* photography, painting. *Address:* Apartment 61, 8 Kew Bridge Road, Brentford, Middx TW8 0FD. *E:* editorjhp@gmail.com.

MARKS, David Georges Mainfroy; QC 2009; *b* Manchester, 14 Oct. 1946; *s* of Joseph Marks and Georgette Marks. *Educ:* Manchester Grammar Sch.; Magdalen Coll., Oxford (BA 1968; MA 1972; BCL 1970). Called to the Bar, Gray's Inn, 1974; admitted Illinois State Bar, 1973, US Federal Bar, 1973, Irish Bar, 1998. Dep. Registrar in Bankruptcy, 1985–2013; part-time Tribunal Judge, Administrative Appeals Chamber and Nat. Security Appeals Panel (formerly Dep. Chm., Data Protection and Information Tribunal), 1990–2013. *Publications:* (Gen. Ed) Tolley's Insolvency Law and Practice, 2001–13; (ed jtly) Rowlatt on Principal and Surety, 4th edn 1982 to 6th edn 2011; (contrib. ed.) Lightman and Moss, Law of Administrators and Receivers of Companies, 1986, 5th edn 2011; (contrib. ed.) Moss and Fletcher, The EC Regulation on Insolvency Proceedings, 2002, 2nd edn 2009; (contrib. ed.) Expedited Debt Restructuring, 2007. *Recreations:* theatre, jazz, tennis, wine, music, photography.

MARKS, David Joseph, MBE 2000; RIBA; Co-founder and Director, Marks Barfield Architects, since 1989; *b* 15 Dec. 1952; *s* of late Melville Mark and of Gunilla Marta (*née* Loven); *m* 1981, Julia Barbara Barfield, *qv*; one *s* two *d*. *Educ:* Architectural Assoc. RIBA 1984. Formerly architect, Richard Rogers and Partners; Founder Dir, Tetra Ltd; Co-founder and Man. Dir, London Eye Co., 1994–2006. FRSA 2007. Prince Philip Special Commendation for Outstanding Achievement in Design for Business and Society, 2000; Faculty of Building Trophy, 2001; practice awards: Building Architectural Practice of the Year Award, 2001; Queen's Award for Enterprise (Innovation), 2003. *Recreations:* family, walking, ski-ing. *Address:* Marks Barfield Architects, 50 Bromells Road, Clapham Common, SW4 0BG. *T:* (020) 7501 0180, *Fax:* (020) 7498 7103. *E:* dmarks@marksbarfield.com.

MARKS, Prof. Isaac Meyer, MD; FRCPsych; Professor of Experimental Psychopathology, Institute of Psychiatry, University of London, 1978–2000; Professor Emeritus, King's College London, 2000; Clinical Director, CCBT Ltd, since 2006; *b* 16 Feb. 1935; *s* of Morris Norman and Anna Marks; *m* 1957, Shula Eta Winokur (*see* S. E. Marks); one *s* one *d*. *Educ:* Univ. of Cape Town (MB ChB 1956; MD 1963); Univ. of London (DPM 1963). FRCPsych 1970. Consultant Psychiatrist and research worker, Bethlem-Maudsley Hosp. and Inst. of Psychiatry, 1978–2000. Sen. Res. Investigator, 2000–03, Prof. Emeritus, 2000–03, Vis. Prof., 2003–, Imperial Coll. London; Vis. Prof., Vrije Univ., Amsterdam, 2005–08. Fellow, Center for Advanced Study in Behavioral Scis, Stanford Univ., 1981–82. Coordinator, www.commonlanguagepsychotherapy.org, 2009–. Salmon Medallist, NY Acad. of Medicine, 1978; IT Effectiveness Award, Health Care '98, 1998. *Publications:* Patterns of Meaning in Psychiatric Patients, 1965; Fears & Phobias, 1969; (jtly) Clinical Anxiety, 1971; (jtly) Psychotherapy, 1971; (jtly) Nursing in Behavioural Psychotherapy, 1977; Living with Fear, 1978, 2nd edn 2001; Cure and Care of Neuroses, 1981; Psychiatric Nurse Therapists in Primary Care, 1985; Behavioural Psychotherapy, 1986; (jtly) Anxiety and its Treatment, 1986; Fears, Phobias and Rituals, 1987; (ed jtly) Mental Health Care Delivery, 1990; (jtly) Problem-centred care planning, 1995; (jtly) BT Steps—Behavioural self-assessment and self care for OCD, 1996; (jtly) COPE—online self-help for depression, 1998; FearFighter online self-help for panic/phobia, 1999; (jtly) Hands-on-Help, 2007; (jtly) Classification of Psychotherapy Procedures, 2013; 460 scientific papers. *Recreations:* hiking, gardening, theatre, cinema, socialising. *Address:* 43 Dulwich Common, SE21 7EU. *T:* (020) 8299 4130.

MARKS, John Henry, MD; FRCGP; General Practitioner, Boreham Wood, 1954–90; Medical Director, National Medical Examinations Network Ltd, 1992–2003, later Adviser on Medical Standards; *b* 30 May 1925; *s* of Lewis and Rose Marks; *m* 1954, Shirley Evelyn, *d* of Alic Nathan, OBE; one *s* two *d*. *Educ:* Tottenham County Sch.; Edinburgh Univ. MD; FRCGP; D(Obst)RCOG. Served RAMC, 1949–51. Chairman: Herts LMC, 1966–71; Herts Exec. Council, 1971–74; Member: NHS Management Study Steering Cttee, 1971–72; Standing Med. Adv. Cttee, 1984–90; Council for Postgrad. Med. Educn, 1984–90. British Medical Association: Fellow, 1976; Member: Gen. Med. Services Cttee, 1968–90 (Dep. Chm., 1974–79); Council, 1973–98 (Chm., 1984–90); GMC, 1979–84, 1990–94; Chairman: Representative Body, 1981–84; Foundn for AIDS, 1987–99. Member, Council: ASH, 1991–99; Assurance Medical Soc., 1999–2004. *Publications:* The Conference of Local Medical Committees and its Executive: an historical view, 1979; The NHS, Beginning, Middle and End? (autobiog.), 2008; The NHS: beginning, middle, and end?, 2008; papers on the NHS and general medical practice. *Recreations:* philately, bridge. *Address:* 62 Eyre Court, 3–21 Finchley Road, NW8 9TU. *T:* (020) 7722 5955.

MARKS, Julia Barbara; *see* Barfield, J. B.

MARKS, Laurence; writer and producer; *b* 8 Dec. 1948; *s* of late Bernard and of Lily Marks; *m* 1988, Brigitte Luise Kirchheim; one step *s*. *Educ:* Holloway County Sch., London; Guildhall Sch. of Music, London. Trainee journalist, Thomson Regl Newspapers, 1974; Reporter: N London Weekly Herald, 1975–77; Sunday Times, 1975–76 (freelance) and 1978–79; This Week (TV current affairs prog.), 1977–78; television scriptwriter, 1980–; (with Maurice Gran) creator and writer: Holding the Fort, 1980–82; Roots, 1981; Shine on Harvey Moon, 1982–85, 1995; Roll Over Beethoven, 1985; Relative Strangers, 1985–87; The New Statesman, 1987–91; Birds of a Feather, 1989–98 and 2014–15; Snakes and Ladders, 1989; So You Think You've Got Troubles, 1991; Love Hurts, 1991–93; Get Back, 1992–93; Wall of Silence (film), 1993; Goodnight Sweetheart, 1993–99; Unfinished Business, 1997–98; Mosley (film), 1997; Starting Out, 2000; Dirty Work, 2000; Believe Nothing, 2002; Me, My Dad and Moorgate, 2006; Mumbai Calling, 2007. Stage plays (with Maurice Gran): Playing God, 2005; The New Statesman, 2006; Dreamboats and Petticoats (libretto for musical), 2009; Von Ribbentrop's Watch, 2010; Save the Last Dance for Me (libretto for musical); Birds of a Feather, 2012; Dreamboats and Miniskirts (musical), nat. tour, 2014–15; Love Me Do, Watford Palace, 2014; radio plays (with Maurice Gran): My Blue Heaven, 2006; Dr Freud Will See You Now, Mr Hitler, 2007; My Blue Wedding, 2007; Von Ribbentrop's Watch, 2008; Love Me Do, 2014. Founder (with Maurice Gran and Allan McKeown), Alomo Productions, 1988, subseq. pt of Thames TV. Mem., Television Cttee, BAFTA, 2008–. Vis. Lectr, Univ. of York, 2006–. Pres., Pipesmokers' Council of GB, 2000. Freeman, City of London, 1994; Liveryman, Co. of Tobacco Blenders and Briar Pipe Makers, 1994. Pipesmoker of the Year, 1990. *Publications:* Moorgate: the anatomy of a disaster, 1976; Ruth Ellis: a case of diminished responsibility, 1977; A Fan for All Seasons, 1999; *with Maurice Gran:* Holding the Fort, 1981; The New Statesman Scripts, 1992; Dorien's Diary, 1993; Shine on Harvey Moon, 1995. *Recreations:* music (saxophone player), reading, English churches, tennis, medieval German, the study of Freud, Jung and Breuer, British politics, oriental philology, artificial intelligence, Russian poetry, the work of Leonhard Euler (mathematician), the life and works of Johann Sebastian Bach. *Address:* c/o Laurie Mansfield International Artistes, Suite 17, Adam House, 7–10 John Adam Street, WC2N 6AA. *T:* (020) 7520 9411. *E:* peter@lmassocltd.com. *Clubs:* Reform, Cryptos, Intelligence Squared, PEN.

MARKS, Lewis Adam; QC 2002; *b* 1961; *s* of Prof. Vincent Marks and Averil Marks; *m* 1986, Philippa Johnson; four *s*. *Educ:* City of London Freemen's Sch., Ashtead; Brasenose Coll., Oxford. Called to the Bar, Middle Temple, 1984; in practice, specialising in international divorce and big money financial relief claims. Head of Chambers, 2010–. *Recreations:* walking, family, Country and Western music, watching cricket. *Address:* Hatfield Place, Hatfield Peverel, Essex CM3 2ET; Queen Elizabeth Building, Temple, EC4Y 9BS. *E:* l.marks@qeb.co.uk.

See also A. L. Marks.

MARKS, Michael John Paul, CVO 2014; CBE 1999; Founding Partner, NewSmith Capital Partners LLP, 2003–14; *b* 28 Dec. 1941; *m* 1967, Rosemary Ann Brody; one *s* two *d*. *Educ:* St Paul's Sch. Joined Smith Brothers, subseq. Smith New Court, 1960; Partner, 1969–84; Dir, 1975; Man. Dir, Smith New Court International, 1984–87; Chief Exec., 1987–94, Chm., 1995, Smith New Court PLC; Dep. Chm., Jt Hd of Global Equities, and Mem. Exec. Mgt Cttee, Merrill Lynch Internat., 1995–97; Chief Operating Officer, 1997–98, Exec. Chm., 1998–2003, Merrill Lynch Europe, Middle East and Africa; Exec. Chm., Merrill Lynch Investment Mgrs and Internat. Private Client Gp, 2001–03; Exec. Vice Pres., Merrill Lynch & Co. Inc., 2001–03. Non-exec. Dir, Rothschilds Continuation, 1990–95. Director: Securities Inst., 1992–93; London Stock Exchange, 1994–2004; Trustee, Stock Exchange Benevolent Fund, 1994–97. Trustee: Prince's Trust, 2003–; Queen's Trust, 2009–.

MARKS, Peter Vincent, CBE 2013; Group Chief Executive, Co-operative Group, 2007–13 (Director, 2000–07); *b* Bradford, 27 Oct. 1949; *s* of Vincent Marks and Margaret Marks; *m* 1971, Julia Merry; two *d*. *Educ:* St Bede's Grammar Sch., Bradford; Bradford Coll. (HNC Business Studies). Yorkshire Co-operative Society: mgt trainee, 1967; sen. mgt roles in food and non-food retailing, travel and funeral businesses; Chief Gen. Manager, Retailing, 1996–2000; Chief Exec., 2000–02; Chief Exec., United Co-operatives, 2002–07. Non-exec. Dir, Co-operative Financial Services Ltd, 2009–13. Dir, Greater Manchester Local Enterprise Partnership, 2011–. Member: Policy Issues Council, Inst. of Grocery Distribution, 2008–; Commn on Ownership, 2009–. Vice Pres., RNID, 2010–. *Recreations:* family, golf, football, playing drums in a blues band. *Club:* Lansdowne.

MARKS, Prof. Richard Charles, PhD; FSA; Professor in Medieval Stained Glass, University of York, 1992–2008, now Emeritus Professor in History of Art (Head, Department of History of Art, 2002–04); Honorary Professor of History of Art, University of Cambridge, 2008–12; Bye-Fellow, since 2008, and Keeper of Works of Art, since 2010, Fitzwilliam College, Cambridge; *b* 2 July 1945; *s* of Major William Henry Marks and Jeannie Eileen Marks (*née* Pigott); *m* 1970, Rita Spratley. *Educ:* Berkhamsted Sch.; Queen Mary Coll., Univ. of London (BA (Hons) History); Courtauld Inst. of Art, Univ. of London (MA, PhD, History of European Art). Research Asst for British Acad. *Corpus Vitrearum Medii Aevi* Cttee, 1970–73; Asst Keeper, Dept of Medieval and Later Antiquities, British Mus., 1973–79; Keeper of Burrell Collection and Asst Dir, Glasgow Museums and Art Galls, 1979–85; Dir, Royal Pavilion, Art Gall. and Museums in Brighton, 1985–92. Chm., Group of Directors of Museums, 1989–92; Mem. Cttee, 1985–, Pres. Internat. Bd, 1995–2004, *Corpus Vitrearum Medii Aevi*, British Academy. Mem., York Minster Fabric Adv. Cttee, 2002–; Chairman: York Minster East Window Adv. Gp, 2008–; York Minster Stained Glass Adv. Gp, 2009–. Mem., Adv. Council, Paul Mellon Centre for Studies in British Art, 2012–. FSA 1977 (Mem. Council, 1990–94; Vice-Pres., 1991–94). Trustee: River and Rowing Mus., Henley-on-Thames, 1998–; Stained Glass Mus., Ely, 2010–; Vice-Pres., Beds Historical Record Soc., 2010–. *Publications:* (jtly) British Heraldry from its origins to *c* 1800, 1978; (jtly) The Golden Age of English Manuscript Painting, 1980; Burrell Portrait of a Collector, 1983, 2nd edn 1988; The Glazing of the Collegiate Church of the Holy Trinity, Tattershall, Lincs, 1984; (jtly) Sussex Churches and Chapels, 1989; Stained Glass in England during the Middle Ages, 1993; The Medieval Stained Glass of Northamptonshire, 1998; (jtly) Gothic: art for England 1400–1547, 2003; Image and Devotion in Late Medieval England, 2004; Studies in the Art and Imagery of the Middle Ages, 2012; articles and reviews in learned jls. *Recreations:* opera, cricket, riding, parish churches, travelling in the Levant. *Address:* Hillcroft, 11 Stewkley Road, Soulbury, Bucks LU7 0DH. *Clubs:* Athenæum, MCC; North British Rowing (the Borders).

MARKS, Richard Leon; QC 1999; **His Honour Judge Marks;** a Senior Circuit Judge, Central Criminal Court, since 2012; Common Serjeant, City of London, since 2015; *b* 20 Nov. 1953; *s* of Harry and Denise Marks; *m* 1987, Jane Elizabeth Tordoff; one *s* one *d*. *Educ:* Clifton Coll.; Univ. of Manchester (LLB Hons). Called to the Bar, Gray's Inn, 1975, Bencher 2008; Leader, Northern Circuit, 2008–10; an Asst Recorder, 1991–94; a Recorder, 1994–2012. Pres., Restricted Patients Panel, Mental Health Review Tribunal, 2000–15. Deemster, Isle of Man, 2010–12. Freeman, Cooks' Co., 2013. *Recreations:* travel, cinema, Clarice Cliff, MUFC, cookery, collecting modern art. *Address:* Central Criminal Court, Old Bailey, EC4M 7EH. *E:* r.l.marks7@gmail.com.

MARKS, Sally Hilary; *see* Groves, S. H.

MARKS, Prof. Shula Eta, OBE 1996; PhD; FBA 1995; Professor of Southern African History, School of Oriental and African Studies, University of London, 1993–2001, now Emeritus; *b* Cape Town, S Africa, 14 Oct. 1936; *d* of Chaim and Frieda Winokur; *m* 1957, Isaac Meyer Marks, *qv*; one *s* one *d*. *Educ:* Univ. of Cape Town (Argus Scholar, 1958–59; BA 1959); PhD London, 1967. Came to London, 1960; Lectr in the History of Southern Africa, SOAS and Inst. of Commonwealth Studies, 1963–76, Reader, 1976–83; Dir, 1983–93, Prof. of Commonwealth Hist., 1984–93, Inst. of Commonwealth Studies, London Univ.; Vice-Chancellor's Visitor to NZ, 1978. Dir, Ford Foundn Grant to Univ. of London on S African History, 1975–78; Mem., Commonwealth Scholarships Commn, 1993–. Member: Adv.

Council on Public Records, 1989–94; Humanities Res. Bd, British Acad., 1997–98; AHRB, 1998–2000. Pres., African Studies Assoc. of UK, 1978; Chairman: Internat. Records Mgt Trust, 1989–2004; Council for Assisting Refugee Academics (formerly Soc. for Protection of Sci. and Learning), 1993–2004 (Mem., 1983–2013); Trustee, Canon Collins Educnl Trust for Southern Africa, 2004–14. Editor, Jl of African History, 1971–77; Mem. Council, Jl of Southern African Studies, 1974–2013 (Founding Mem., 1974; Chm. Bd, 1998–2002). Hon. Prof., Univ. of Cape Town, 2006. Dist. Sen. Fellow, Sch. of Advanced Study, 2002, Hon. Fellow, SOAS, 2005, Univ. of London. Hon. DLitt Cape Town, 1994; Hon. DSocSc Natal, 1996; Hon. DLit Johannesburg, 2012. Dist. Africanist Award, African Studies Assoc. of UK, 2002. *Publications:* Reluctant Rebellion: an assessment of the 1906–8 disturbances in Natal, 1970; (ed with A. Atmore) Economy and Society in Pre-industrial South Africa, 1980; (ed with R. Rathbone) Industrialization and Social Change in South Africa, 1870–1930, 1982; (ed with P. Richardson) International Labour Migration: historical perspectives, 1983; The Ambiguities of Dependence in Southern Africa: class, nationalism and the state in twentieth-century Natal, 1986; (ed) Not either an experimental doll: the separate worlds of three South African women, 1987; (ed with Stanley Trapido) The Politics of Race, Class & Nationalism in Twentieth Century South Africa, 1987; Divided Sisterhood: race, class and gender in the South African nursing profession, 1994; (ed jtly) In Defence of Learning: academic refugees—their plight, persecution and placement, 1933–1980s, 2011; chapters in Cambridge Hist. of Africa, vols 3, 4 and 6, and in Cambridge Hist. of South Africa, vol 2, 2011; contrib. Jl of African Hist. and Jl of Southern African Studies. *Address:* Cypress Tree House, Dulwich Common, SE21 7EU.

MARKS, Susan Elizabeth; Headmistress, Withington Girls' School, since 2010; *b* St Asaph, Flintshire, 14 Oct. 1956; *d* of Edward George Howel Jones and Anne Jones; *m* 1980 (marr. diss. 2005); one *s* two *d* (and one *d* decd). *Educ:* Wilmslow Co. Grammar Sch. for Girls; Jesus Coll., Oxford (BA PPE 1978); Univ. of Leicester (Advanced Cert. Educnl Mgt 2000); Univ. of Exeter (Cert. Theol. 2010). Corporate Lending Officer, Chemical Bank, 1978–81; Real Estate Lending Officer, Bank of America, 1981–88; Property Team Manager, Kleinwort Benson, 1988–89; a Vice Pres. and Hd, EMEA Airline Div., Bank of America, 1989–91; career break, 1991–95; Hd, Econs and Politics, St George's Coll., Weybridge, 1995–2000; Hd, Sixth Form, 2000–01, Headmistress, 2001–10, Tormead Sch. Reporting Inspector, ISI, 2013–. Member: GSA, 2001– (Hon. Treas., 2007–12); HMC, 2014–. *Recreations:* reading, painting. *Address:* Withington Girls' School, Wellington Road, Fallowfield, Manchester M14 6BL. *T:* (0161) 249 3451, *Fax:* (0161) 248 5377. *E:* head@wgs.org. *Club:* Lansdowne.

MARKS, Victor James; Cricket Correspondent, The Observer, since 1990; Cricket Writer, The Guardian, since 2006; *b* 25 June 1955; *s* of late Harold George Marks and Phyllis Joan Marks; *m* 1978, Anna Stewart; two *d*. *Educ:* Blundell's Sch.; St John's Coll., Oxford (BA). Professional cricketer, 1975–89: played for: Oxford Univ., 1975–78 (Capt., 1976 and 1977); Somerset, 1975–89; WA, 1986–87; played in 6 Test Matches and 34 One-Day Internationals for England. Summariser, Test Match Special, BBC, 1989–. Cricket Chm., Somerset CCC, 1999–. Mem., Editl Bd, The Cricketer, 1990–2003; Associate Ed., The Wisden Cricketer, 2003–12. *Publications:* Somerset Cricket Scrapbook, 1984; Marks out of XI, 1985; TCCB Guide to Better Cricket, 1987; (with R. Drake) Ultimate One-Day Cricket Match, 1988; Wisden Illustrated History of Cricket, 1989; (with R. Holmes) My Greatest Game, 1994. *Recreation:* golf. *Address:* c/o The Observer, Kings Place, 90 York Way, N1 9GU.

MARKUS, Catherine Mary, (Kate); QC 2014; a Judge of the Upper Tribunal (Administrative Appeals Chamber), since 2014; *b* Billinge, 2 Dec. 1958; *d* of Thomas Markus and Beryl Markus; *m* 1997, Richard Bielby; three *d*. *Educ:* Notre Dame High Sch., Glasgow; Univ. of Manchester (LLB Hons). Called to the Bar, Gray's Inn, 1981; Sen. Legal Advr, Brent Community Law Centre, 1984–94; barrister, Doughty Street Chambers, 1994–2014; a Chm., Employment Tribunals, subseq. an Employment Judge (fee paid), Employment Tribunal, 1998–2014. Member: Exec. Cttee, Law Centres Fedn, 1985–93 (Sec., 1985–88; Chair and Vice-Chair, 1988–93); Legal Aid Bd for England and Wales, 1993–98; Bd, ICSTIS, 1994–2003. Chair, Legal Services Wkg Party, Bar Council, 1998–99. Chair: Public Law Project, 1990–2006; Haldane Soc., 1993–96. Hon. Fellow, Community Law Practice, Univ. of Kent, 1994–98. Co-author, Recent Develts in Public Law, Legal Action, 1996–; Case Law Ed., 2006–14, Mem., Editl Bd, 2014–, Community Care Law Reports. *Publications:* contribs to legal jls. *Recreations:* gardening, painting, drawing. *Address:* Upper Tribunal (Administrative Appeals Chamber), 5th Floor, Rolls Building, 7 Rolls Buildings, Fetter Lane, EC4A 1NL.

MARKWELL, Lisa; Editor, Independent on Sunday, since 2013; *b* Beaconsfield, Bucks, 23 April 1965; *d* of John and Diane Markwell; *m* 1998, John Dempsey; one *s* one *d*. *Educ:* Dr Challoner's High Sch. for Girls; Buckinghamshire Coll. of Higher Educn. Sunday Correspondent, 1989–90; Commissioning Editor: Sunday Times, 1990–92; Mail on Sunday, 1992–95; Ed., Harvey Nichols Mag., 1996–97; Dep. Ed., Frank, 1997–98; Features Ed., Independent, 1998–2004; Features Dir, Condé Nast, 2004–08; Exec. Ed., i newspaper, Independent, 2008–13. *Recreations:* high heels and long journeys, good food and sharp knives, rescuing baby robins, championing my children. *Address:* Independent on Sunday, Northcliffe House, 2 Derry Street, W8 5HF. *T:* (020) 3615 2038. *E:* l.markwell@independent.co.uk. *Club:* Groucho.

MARKWELL, Stephen; Group Chief Executive Officer, National Computing Centre, since 2008; *b* Northwood, Middx, 25 Nov. 1953; *s* of Edwin and Audrey Markwell; *m* 1st, 1984, Linda Smith (marr. diss. 1996); two *s*; 2nd, 1999, Meera Butterworth; one step *s* one step *d*. *Educ:* Brighton Poly. (BA Business Studies); Kingston Poly. (Postgrad. CNAA DipM). Regl Manager, British Olivetti Ltd, 1977–83; Product Manager, Mcdonnel Inf. Systems, 1983–86; Mktg Manager, Prime Computer, 1986–89; Man. Dir and Founder, Prime Mktg Pubns, 1989–2008. Advr, Coopers & Lybrand, 1989–90. Chm., Inst. of IT Trng, 2008–10. Mem., Adv. Cttee, AQA, 2009–. Chair of Judges, BCS Industry Awards, 2008–. *Publications:* (contrib.) Business: the ultimate resource, 2002. *Recreations:* tennis, table tennis, badminton, golf, classical music, opera. *T:* 07880 788530. *E:* steve.markwell@ncc.co.uk. *Club:* Lansdowne.

MARLAND, family name of **Baron Marland**.

MARLAND, Baron *cr* 2006 (Life Peer), of Odstock, in the County of Wiltshire; **Jonathan Peter Marland;** Chairman, J. P. Marland and Sons Ltd, since 2013; *b* 14 Aug. 1956; *s* of late Peter Greaves Marland and of Audrey Joan Marland (*née* Brierley); *m* 1983, Penelope Mary, *d* of late Richard Anthony Lamb; two *s* two *d*. *Educ:* Shrewsbury Sch. Dir, Lloyd Thompson, then Jardine Lloyd Thompson Ltd, 1982–99; Chairman: Herriot Ltd, 1989–; Grainfarmers Pension Fund, 2000–07; Janspeed Performance Ltd, 2001–10; Clareville Capital Partners LLP, 2006–10; Commonwealth Enterprise and Investment Council Ltd, 2014–; Enterprise and Investment Co. Ltd, 2014–; Eco World Mgt and Adv. Services (UK) Ltd, 2015–; Director: Jubilee Hldgs Ltd, 2002–10; Essex Court Mgt Co. Ltd, 2002–12; C&UCO Properties, 2005–10; Hunter Boot Ltd, 2006–10; Insce Capital Partners LLP, 2006–; W. H. Ireland Ltd, 2008–10; Wilton Place Inc., 2013–; Tamara Mellon Inc., 2013–; Test Match Extra.com; AAA Reputation Mgt Ltd, 2015–. Treasurer: Cons Party, 2005–07; Boris Johnson's London Mayoral Campaign, 2007–08. Founder Chm., The Sports Nexus, 2003–13; Dir, CChange, 2001–06; Chairman: Harnham Water Meadows Trust, 1990–2010; Tickets for Troops, 2009–; Trustee: J. P. Marland Charitable Trust, 1995–; Atlantic Partnership, 2001–; Guggenheim UK Charitable Trust, 2002–; Invercauld Estate, 2002–14; Churchill Centre UK (formerly Internat. Churchill Soc.), 2008– (Chm., 2012–); Member: Adv. Cttee, Airey Neave Refugee Trust, 1992–2007; Adv. Bd, Peggy Guggenheim Mus., Venice, 2002–; Develt Cttee, RA, 2008–10; Patron, Wiltshire Churches, 2009–. President: Salisbury FC, 2008–12; Salisbury Cons. Assoc., 2009–; Commonwealth Youth Orch., 2014–; Patron, Salisbury and S Wilts Sports Club, 2010–. Contested (C) Somerton and Frome, 1997. Opposition spokesman in H of L on Energy and Climate Change, 2009–10; Parly Under-Sec. of State, DECC, 2010–12, BIS, 2012; Prime Minister's Trade Envoy, 2012–14; Chm., Prime Minister's Business Ambassadors, 2012–14. FRSA. *Address:* 78 Belgrave Road, SW1V 2BJ. *T:* (020) 7752 0177. *Clubs:* Brooks's, MCC, Garrick.

MARLAND, Paul; farmer, since 1967; *b* 19 March 1940; *s* of Alexander G. Marland and Elsa May Lindsey Marland; *m* 1st, 1965, Penelope Anne Barlow (marr. diss. 1982); one *s* two *d*; 2nd, 1984, Caroline Ann Rushton. *Educ:* Gordonstoun Sch., Elgin; Trinity Coll., Dublin (BA, BComm). Hopes Metal Windows, 1964; London Press Exchange, 1965–66. MP (C) Gloucester West, 1979–97; contested (C) Forest of Dean, 1997; contested (C) South West Region, EP elecns, 1999. Jt PPS to Financial Sec. to the Treasury and Economic Sec., 1981–83, to Minister of Agriculture, Fisheries and Food, 1983–86. Chm., back bench Agric. Cttee, 1989–97. Vice-Pres., 2002–05, Pres., 2005, Nat. Cons. Convention; Mem. Bd, Cons. Party, 2002–05. *Recreations:* ski-ing, shooting, riding, fishing. *Address:* Ford Hill Farm, Temple Guiting, Cheltenham, Glos GL54 5XU.

MARLAR, Robin Geoffrey; former cricket journalist and company director; *b* 2 Jan. 1931; *o s* of late E. A. G. Marlar and Winifred Marlar (*née* Stevens); *m* 1st, 1955, Wendy Ann Dumeresque (*d* 2000); two *s* four *d*; 2nd, 1980, Hon. Gill Taylor, 2nd *d* of Baron Taylor of Hadfield. *Educ:* King Edward Sch., Lichfield; Harrow; Magdalene Coll., Cambridge (BA). Asst Master, Eton Coll., 1953–54; Librarian, Arundel Castle, 1954–59; Captain, Sussex CCC, 1955–59; sportswriter, Daily Telegraph, 1954–60; De La Rue Co., 1960–68; Consultant and Partner, Spencer Stuart and Associates, 1968–71; Cricket Corresp., Sunday Times, 1970–96; Founder, Marlar Group of Consultancies, 1971. Contested (C): Bolsover, 1959; Leicester NE, July 1962; contested (Referendum) Newbury, May 1993. *Publications:* The Story of Cricket, 1978; (ed) The English Cricketers Trip to USA and Canada 1859, 1979; Decision Against England, 1983. *Recreations:* gardening, sport. *Clubs:* Garrick, MCC (Mem. Cttee, 1999–2002; Pres., 2005–06); Sussex CCC (Chm., 1997–98; Pres., 2005–07).

MARLBOROUGH, 12th Duke of, *cr* 1702; **Charles James Spencer-Churchill;** Baron Spencer, 1603; Earl of Sunderland, 1643; Baron Churchill, 1685; Earl of Marlborough, 1689; Marquis of Blandford, 1702; Prince of the Holy Roman Empire; Prince of Mindelheim in Suabia; *b* 24 Nov. 1955; *e s* of 11th Duke of Marlborough and Susan Mary Spencer-Churchill (*née* Hornby, later Heber-Percy); *S* father, 2014; *m* 1st, 1990, Rebecca Mary (marr. diss. 2001), *d* of Peter Few Brown; one *s*; 2nd, 2002, Edla, *o d* of Alun Griffiths, OBE; one *s* one *d*. *Educ:* Pinewood; Harrow; RAC, Cirencester; Royal Berks Coll. of Agric. *Heir: s* Marquess of Blandford, *qv*. *Address:* Blenheim Palace, Woodstock, Oxon OX20 1PP. *E:* blandford@blenheimpalace.com, Lordblandford@aol.com. *Clubs:* White's, 5 Hertford Street, Turf, Tramp's, Annabel's; Racquet and Tennis (New York).

MARLER, David Steele, OBE 1984; Director, Egypt, British Council, 1997–2001; *b* 19 March 1941; *s* of Steele Edward and Dorothy Marler; *m* 1963, Belinda Mary Handisyde; two *s*. *Educ:* Brighton, Hove and Sussex Grammar Sch.; Merton Coll., Oxford (Postmaster; BA, MA). British Council, 1962–2001: seconded SOAS, 1962–63; Asst Rep., Bombay, 1963; Regional Officer, India, 1967; Dep. Rep., Ethiopia, 1970; Rep., Ibadan, Nigeria, 1974; Dir, Policy Res., 1977; Rep., Cyprus, 1980; seconded SOAS, 1984; National Univ., Singapore, 1985; Rep., China, 1987–90; Director: Asia, Pacific and Americas Div., 1990–92; Turkey, Azerbaijan and Uzbekistan, 1993–97. Chm., British Council Assoc., 2005. Mem., Cruising Assoc., 2010–. *Recreations:* sailing, travel, reading, walking, running with the Hash House Harriers. *Address:* 53 The Hall, Foxes Dale, Blackheath, SE3 9BG. *T:* (020) 8318 5874. *Clubs:* Benfleet Yacht; Changi Sailing (Singapore).

MARLESFORD, Baron *cr* 1991 (Life Peer), of Marlesford in the County of Suffolk; **Mark Shuldham Schreiber;** DL; political consultant, farmer and journalist; *b* 11 Sept. 1931; *s* of late John Shuldham Schreiber, AE, DL, Marlesford Hall, Suffolk and Maureen Schreiber (*née* Dent); *m* 1969, Gabriella Federica, *d* of Conte Teodoro Veglio di Castelletto d'Uzzone; two *d*. *Educ:* Eton; Trinity Coll., Cambridge. Nat. Service in Coldstream Guards (2nd Lt), 1950–51. Fisons Ltd, 1957–63; Conservative Research Dept, 1963–67; Dir, Conservative Party Public Sector Research Unit, 1967–70; Special Advr to the Govt, 1970–74; Special Adviser to Leader of the Opposition, 1974–75; Editorial Consultant, 1974–91, lobby correspondent, 1976–91, The Economist. Ind. Nat. Dir, Times Newspaper Holdings, 1991–2014; Director: Royal Ordnance Factories, 1972–74; British Railways (Anglia), 1988–92; Eastern Electricity plc, 1990–95. Adviser: Mitsubishi Corp. Internat. NV, 1990–2003; John Swire & Sons Ltd, 1992–2009. Mem., H of L Select Cttee on EU, 2003–07, 2012–14 (Mem., Econ. and Financial sub-cttee, 2001–05, 2010–14; Mem., Home Affairs sub-cttee, 2005–09). Member: Govt Computer Agency Council, 1973–74; Countryside Commn, 1980–92; Rural Development Commn, 1985–93; Chm., CPRE, 1993–98. Pres., Suffolk Preservation Soc., 1997–. Mem., East Suffolk CC, 1968–70. DL Suffolk, 1991. *Recreation:* gadfly on bureaucracy. *Address:* Marlesford Hall, Woodbridge, Suffolk IP13 0AU; 5 Kersley Street, SW11 4PR. *Club:* Pratt's.

MARLING, Sir Charles (William Somerset), 5th Bt *cr* 1882; *b* 2 June 1951; *s* of Sir John Stanley Vincent Marling, 4th Bt, OBE, and Georgina Brenda (Betty) (*d* 1961), *o d* of late Henry Edward FitzRoy Somerset; *S* father, 1977; *m* 1979, Judi; three *d*.

See also D. C. Greer.

MARLOW, Antony Rivers; *b* 17 June 1940; *s* of late Major Thomas Keith Rivers Marlow, MBE, RE retd, and Beatrice Nora (*née* Hall); *m* 1962, Catherine Louise Howel (*née* Jones) (*d* 1994); three *s* two *d*. *Educ:* Wellington Coll.; RMA Sandhurst; St Catharine's Coll., Cambridge (2nd Cl. Hons (1) Mech Sciences, MA). Served Army, 1958–69; retd, Captain RE; management consultant and industrial/commercial manager, 1969–79. MP (C) Northampton North, 1979–97; contested (C) same seat, 1997. Farming and property design and develt, 1997–. *Recreations:* Rugby spectator, opera, ballet.

MARLOW, David Ellis; Chief Executive, 3i Group, 1988–92; *b* 29 March 1935; *m* 1959, Margaret Anne Smith; one *d* (one *s* decd). Chartered Accountant. Investors in Industry, subseq. 3i, 1960–92. Director: Brixton (formerly Brixton Estate) plc, 1992–2003; Trinity Mirror plc, 1992–2005. *Recreations:* playing tennis, the piano, the organ and the 'cello; ski-ing and scrambling in the Alps. *Address:* The Platt, Elsted, Midhurst, Sussex GU29 0LA. *T:* (01730) 825261. *Club:* Athenæum.

MARLOW, Prof. Neil, DM; FRCP, FRCPCH; FMedSci; Professor of Neonatal Medicine, University College London, since 2008 (Director, Institute of Women's Health, 2009–11); *b* Market Harborough, Leics, 10 Nov. 1951; *s* of Wilfred and Daisy Marlow; *m* 1973, Elaine Susan Floyd; three *s* one *d*. *Educ:* Royal Masonic Sch., Bushey; St John's Coll., Oxford (BA Hons 1973; MB BS 1976; DM 1985). FRCP 1994; FRCPCH 1997. Med. trng, Oxford, Sheffield, Manchester, Liverpool, 1977–89; Sen. Lectr in Child Health, Univ. of Bristol, 1989–96; Prof. of Neonatal Medicine, Univ. of Nottingham, 1997–2008; Hon. Consultant Neonatologist, UCLH, 2008–. President: British Assoc. for Perinatal Medicine, 2004–08; Eur. Soc. for Paediatric Res., 2008–12; Internat. Paediatric Res. Foundn, 2008–10. FMedSci 2007. *Publications:* A Neonatal Vade Mecum, 1992, 3rd edn 1998; A Handbook of Neonatology, 2001; contribs to academic med. and scientific jls, mainly around the sequelae of preterm birth, randomised trials in perinatal medicine and neonatal care. *Recreations:* British music, opera, hill walking, fine dining. *Address:* Institute for Women's Health, 74 Huntley Street, WC1E 6AU. *T:* (020) 7679 0834. *E:* n.marlow@ucl.ac.uk.

MARLOW, Timothy John; art historian, broadcaster and gallery director; Director of Artistic Programmes, Royal Academy of Arts, since 2014; *b* Long Eaton, Derbys, 18 May 1962; *s* of Preb. W. Geoffrey Marlow and Barbara Anne Marlow (*née* Skinner); *m* 2006, Tanya Hudson; one *s*. *Educ:* King's Coll. London (BA Hons 1984); Pembroke Coll., Cambridge (PGCE 1985); Courtauld Inst. of Art (MA 1988). Vis. Lectr, Winchester Sch. of Art, 1990–2003; Hd, Adult Educn, Tate Gall., 1991–92; Ed., Tate mag., 1993–2002; Creative Dir, Sculpture at Goodwood, 2002–03; Dir of Exhibns, White Cube, 2003–14. Dir, Cultureshock Media Ltd, 2002–. Member: Council, ICA London, 2005–14; Faculty of Fine Arts, British Sch. at Rome, 2015. Presenter of radio programmes, including: Kaleidoscope, Radio 4, 1991–98; The Ticket, 2006–08, Culture Shock, 2007–09, BBC World Service; presenter of TV arts documentaries, including: The Impressionists, 1998; The Nude, 2000; Great Artists I and II, 2001–03; Easter in Art, 2003; Tim Marlow on…, 2002–; Judgement Day, 2004; Marlow Meets…, 2009–; guest presenter: Newsnight Rev., 2006–09; The Review Show, 2010–. Bd Mem./Dir, Sadler's Wells Trust, 2014–; Bd Mem./Trustee, Artichoke Trust, 2015–. FRSA. Special Excellence in Broadcasting Award, Voice of Viewer and Listener, 2005. *Publications:* Egon Schiele, 1991; Auguste Rodin, 1994; Anthony Caro, 1997; Great Artists, 2001; David Bailey's Stardust, 2014; catalogue essays. *Recreations:* cycling, surfing badly, Chelsea FC, modern first editions. *Address:* Royal Academy of Arts, Burlington House, Piccadilly, W1J 0BD. *E:* lisa.jones@royalacademy.org.uk. *Clubs:* Groucho, Chelsea Arts, Shoreditch House.

MARLOWE, Hugh; *see* Patterson, Harry.

MARMION, (John) Piers (Tregarthen); Chairman: BPA Group (India), since 2010; Wilton & Bain, since 2011; *b* 7 Feb. 1959; *m* 1986, Roxane; two *s* one *d*. *Educ:* Jesus Coll., Cambridge (BA 1981). Founding Dir, NB Selection, and Selector Europe, 1987–90; Chief Operating Officer and Man. Partner, Europe and Asia, Spencer Stuart, 1990–2000; Heidrick & Struggles Inc.: Pres., Internat., Europe and Asia, and Chief Operating Officer, 2000–01; Chm. and CEO, 2001–03; Man. Partner, Whitehead Mann Partnership, later Chm., EMEA, Korn/Ferry Whitehead Mann, 2006–09. Non-executive Director: Blackwell Ltd, 2003–08; Talent Q, 2005–14; Candex Solutions, 2010–; Chairman: Merryck & Co., 2014–; CompIndex, 2014; Clearwater Solution, 2014. *Recreations:* country pursuits, painting, history, the Mediterranean, classic cars.

MARMOT, Prof. Sir Michael (Gideon), Kt 2000; PhD; FRCP, FFPH, FMedSci; Professor of Epidemiology and Public Health, University College London, since 1985 (MRC Professor, 1995–2013); Director, International Institute for Society and Health (formerly International Centre for Health and Society), since 1994, and Director, Institute of Health Equity, since 2011, University College London; *b* 26 Jan. 1945; *s* of Nathan Marmot and Alice Marmot (*née* Weiner); *m* 1971, Alexandra Naomi Ferster; two *s* one *d*. *Educ:* Univ. of Sydney (BSc Hons, MB BS Hons); Univ. of California, Berkeley (PhD Epidemiology). FFPH (FFCM 1989); FRCP 1996. RMO, Royal Prince Alfred Hosp., 1969–70, Fellowship in Thoracic Medicine, 1970–71, Univ. of Sydney; Res. Fellow and Lectr, Dept of Biomedical and Envmtl Health Scis, Univ. of California, Berkeley, 1971–76 (Fellowships from Berkeley and Amer. Heart Assoc., 1972–76); Lectr and Sen. Lectr in Epidemiology, LSHTM, 1976–85. Adjunct Prof., Dept of Soc., Human Devel and Health, Harvard Univ., 2000–; Associate, Health Policy and Mgt, Johns Hopkins Univ., 2007–08; Vis. Harvard and Lown Prof., Harvard Univ., 2014–. Hon. Consultant, Public Health Medicine: Camden and Islington (formerly Bloomsbury) HA, 1980–2004; N Central London SHA, 2004–06; SHA for London, 2006–. Vis. Prof., RSocMed, 1987. Chm., DoH Scientific Ref. Gp on tackling inequalities, 2003–; Member: Royal Commn on Envmtl Pollution, 1995–2002; Ind. Inquiry into Inequalities in Health, 1997–98. Chairman: Commn on Social Determinants of Health, WHO, 2005–08; Internat. Adv. Bd, Cancer Res. UK/Bupa Foundn Cancer Prevention Initiative, 2014–. President: BMA, 2010–11; British Lung Foundn, 2013–; WMA, 2015–16. Vice-Pres., Academia Europaea, 2003–. Trustee, Early Intervention Foundn, 2012–. Foreign Associate Mem., Inst. of Medicine, NAS, USA, 2002. Founder FMedSci 1998. Hon. FBA 2008; Hon. FRSPH 2008; Hon. FRCPsych 2014; Hon. FRCOG 2015. Jenner Medal, RSocMed, 2010; Manchester Doubleday Award, Manchester Sch. of Medicine, 2010; Ambuj Nath Bose Prize, RCP, 2011; Centennial Winslow Medal, Yale Sch. of Public Health, 2015. *Publications:* (ed jtly and contrib.) Coronary Heart Disease Epidemiology, 1992, 2nd edn 2005; (ed jtly) Social Determinants of Health, 1999, 2nd edn 2006; Status Syndrome, 2004; (contrib.) Food, Nutrition, Physical Activity, and the Prevention of Cancer: a global perspective, 2007; The Health Gap, 2015; contribs to OPCS Medical and Population Studies; numerous papers in learned jls. *Recreations:* tennis, viola. *Address:* Department of Epidemiology and Public Health, University College London, 1–19 Torrington Place, WC1E 6BT.

MARNOCH, Rt Hon. Lord; Michael Stewart Rae Bruce; PC 2001; Senator of the College of Justice in Scotland, 1990–2005; *b* 26 July 1938; *s* of late Alexander Eric Bruce, Advocate in Aberdeen, and late Mary Gordon Bruce (*née* Walker); *m* 1963, Alison Mary Monfries Stewart; two *d*. *Educ:* Loretto Sch.; Aberdeen Univ. (MA, LLB). Admitted Faculty of Advocates, 1963; QC Scot. 1975; Standing Counsel: to Dept of Agriculture and Fisheries for Scotland, 1973; to Highlands and Islands Devel Bd, 1973; Advocate Depute, 1983–86. Mem., Criminal Injuries Compensation Bd, 1986–90. Hon. Vice Pres., Salmon and Trout Assoc., 1994–2008 (Chm., Scotland, 1989–94). Hon. LLD Aberdeen, 1999. *Recreations:* fishing, golf. *Clubs:* New (Edinburgh); Honourable Company of Edinburgh Golfers; Bruntsfield Links Golfing Society (Edinburgh), Rosehall Golf (Turriff), Duff House Royal Golf (Banff), Nairn Golf.

MAROIS, Hon. Pauline; Member (Parti Québécois) Charlevoix-Côte-de-Beaupré, National Assembly of Québec, 2007–14; Premier of Québec, 2012–14; *b* Québec City, 29 March 1949; *d* of Grégoire Marois and Marie-Paule Marois; *m* 1969, Claude Blanchet; three *s* one *d*. *Educ:* Univ. Laval (BA Social Work 1971); HEC Montréal (MBA 1976). Budget consultant and training officer, Co-operative Family Economics Assoc., Outaouais, 1971; resp. for Animation-Participation Service, Conseil régional de développement, Outaouais, 1971–73; Co-ordinator and lectr, social work tech. courses, Cégep de Hull, 1973; CEO, Centre local des services communautaires, l'Île-de-Hull, 1973–74; Hd, Childhood Services Div., Centre des services sociaux, Montréal, 1976–78; Press attaché to Minister of Finance, Québec, 1978–79; COS to Minister of State for Status of Women, 1979. Prof., Univ. of Québec, Hull, 1988. Mem. (Parti Québécois) La Peltrie, 1981–85, Taillon, 1989–2006, Nat. Assembly of Québec. Minister: for Status of Women, 1981–83; of Labor and Income Security, 1983–85; Official Opposition critic: for industry and trade, 1989–91; for public admin and Treasury Bd, 1991–93; Chair, Treasury Bd, 1994–95; Minister: for Admin and Public Service, 1994–95; responsible for Family, 1994–97; of Revenue, and of Finance, 1995–96; of Educn, 1996–98; of Child and Family Welfare, 1997–2001; Minister of State: for Health and Social Services, 1998–2001; for the Economy and Finance, 2001–02; Dep. Premier, 2001–08; Minister: of Res., Sci. and Technol., 2001–02; of Industry and Trade, 2002; of Finance, the Economy and Res., 2002–03; Official opposition critic: for educn, 2003–06; for internat. relns, 2006; Leader: Second Opposition Gp, 2007–08; Official Opposition, 2008–12. *Address:* c/o Conseil exécutif, Édifice Honoré-Mercier, 835 boulevard René-Lévesque Est, 3e étage, Québec, QC G1A 1B4, Canada.

MAROO, Sushil Kumar; Chief Executive Officer and Director, Essar Energy plc, since 2013; *b* Bhilwara, Rajasthan, India, 5 July 1961; *s* of Nand Singh Maroo and Lalita Maroo; *m* 1990, Dr Preeti; one *s* one *d*. *Educ:* Univ. of Rajasthan (BCom). CA Inst. Chartered Accountants of India. Hindustan Lever, 1983–84; Voltas Ltd (Tata Gp), 1984–87; Nippon Dendrolspat Ltd (Mittal Gp), 1987–90; Chambal Fertilizers & Chemicals Ltd (Birla Gp), 1990–97; RPG Dholpur Power Co. Ltd (RP Goenka Gp), 1997–2008; Deputy Managing Director: Jindal Power Ltd, 2008–12; Jindal Steel & Power Ltd, 2012–13. *Recreations:* lawn tennis, chess, badminton. *Address:* Essar House, 11 K. K. Marg, Mahalaxmi, Mumbai 400 034, India. *T:* 2266601100, *Fax:* 2266102868. *E:* sushil.maroo@essar.com. *Clubs:* Vasant Vihar, Delhi Flying (New Delhi); Noida Golf.

MARQUAND, Prof. David (Ian), FBA 1998; FRHistS; FLSW; Principal, Mansfield College, Oxford, 1996–2002, Hon. Fellow, 2002; *b* 20 Sept. 1934; *s* of Rt Hon. Hilary Marquand, PC; *m* 1959, Judith Mary (*née* Reed); one *s* one *d*. *Educ:* Emanuel Sch.; Magdalen Coll., Oxford (BA 1st cl. hons Mod. Hist. 1957); St Antony's Coll., Oxford (Sen. Schol.; Hon. Fellow 2003). FRHistS 1986. Teaching Asst, Univ. of Calif., 1958–59; Leader Writer, The Guardian, 1959–62; Research Fellow, St Antony's Coll., Oxford, 1962–64; Lectr in Politics, Univ. of Sussex, 1964–66. Contested: (Lab) Barry, 1964; (SDP) High Peak, 1983; MP (Lab) Ashfield, 1966–77; PPS to Minister of Overseas Develt, 1967–69; Jun. Opposition Front-Bench Spokesman on econ. affairs, 1971–72; Member: Select Cttee on Estimates, 1966–68; Select Cttee on Procedure, 1968–73; Select Cttee on Corp. Tax, 1971; British Deleg. to Council of Europe, 1970–73. Chief Advr, Secretariat-Gen., European Commission, 1977–78; Prof. of Contemporary History and Politics, Salford Univ., 1978–91; Prof. of Politics, 1991–96 (Hon. Prof., 1997–), and Dir, Political Economy Research Centre, 1993–96, Sheffield Univ. Vis. Scholar, Hoover Instn, Stanford, USA, 1985–86; Vis. Fellow, Dept of Politics and Internat. Relns, Oxford Univ., 2002–. Jt Ed., Political Qly, 1987–97. Member: Nat. Steering Cttee, SDP, 1981–88; Policy Cttee, Soc & Lib Dem, 1988–90. Trustee, Aspen Inst., Berlin, 1982–; Member: Adv. Council, Inst. of Contemporary British History, 1987–; Bd of Trustees, IPPR, 1992–2005; Adv. Council, Demos, 1993–; Social Justice Commn, 1993–94; Commn on Wealth Creation and Social Cohesion, 1994–95. Thomas Jefferson Meml Lectr, Univ. of Calif at Berkeley, 1981. FRSA; FLSW 2013. Hon. DLitt: Salford, 1996; Sheffield, 2002; Hon. Dr rer. pol. Bologna, 2002. George Orwell Meml Prize (jtly), 1980; Sir Isaiah Berlin Prize, Pol Studies Assoc., 2001. *Publications:* Ramsay MacDonald, 1977; Parliament for Europe, 1979; (with David Butler) European Elections and British Politics, 1981; (ed) John Mackintosh on Politics, 1982; The Unprincipled Society, 1988; The Progressive Dilemma, 1991, 2nd edn 1999; (ed with Anthony Seldon) The Ideas That Shaped Post-War Britain, 1996; The New Reckoning, 1997; (ed with R. Nettler) Religion and Democracy, 2000; Decline of the Public, 2004; Britain Since 1918, 2008; The End of the West, 2011; contrib. to: The Age of Austerity, 1964; A Radical Future, 1967; Coalitions in British Politics, 1978; Britain in Europe, 1980; The Political Economy of Tolerable Survival, 1980; The Rebirth of Britain, 1982; European Monetary Union Progress and Prospects, 1982; Social Theory and Political Practice, 1982; The Changing Constitution, 1985; Thatcherism, 1987; The Radical Challenge, 1987; The Ruling Performance, 1987; The Alternative, 1990; Debating the Constitution, 1993; Re-inventing the Left, 1994; The New Social Democracy, 1999; The Market or the Public Domain, 2001; Restating the State, 2004; Building a Citizen Society, 2008; Mammon's Kingdom: an essay on Britain, now, 2014; articles and reviews in The Guardian, The Times, The Sunday Times, New Statesman, Encounter, Commentary, Prospect, and in academic jls. *Recreation:* reading thrillers. *Address:* 37 St Andrew's Road, Oxford OX3 9DL.

MARQUIS, family name of **Earl of Woolton**.

MARR, Andrew William Stevenson; Presenter: Start The Week, Radio 4, since 2002; The Andrew Marr Show (formerly Sunday AM), BBC TV, since 2005; *b* 31 July 1959; *s* of Donald and Valerie Marr; *m* 1987, Jacqueline Ashley, *qv*; one *s* two *d*. *Educ:* Dundee High Sch.; Craigflower, Fife; Loretto School, Musselburgh; Trinity Hall, Cambridge (BA). Trainee and gen. reporter, 1982–85, Parly Corresp., 1985–86, The Scotsman; Political Corresp., The Independent, 1986–88; Political Editor: The Scotsman, 1988; The Economist, 1989–92; political columnist and Associate Editor, 1992–96, Editor, 1996–98, Editor-in-Chief, 1998, The Independent; columnist, The Observer, and The Express, 1998–2000; Political Editor, BBC, 2000–05; columnist, Daily Telegraph, 2000. Presenter: Andrew Marr's History of Modern Britain (series), BBC2, 2007; The Making of Modern Britain (series), BBC2, 2009; Andrew Marr's Megacities (series), BBC1, 2011; The Diamond Queen, BBC1, 2012; Andrew Marr's History of the World (series), BBC1, 2012; The Making of Merkel with Andrew Marr, BBC2, 2013; Andrew Marr's Great Scots, BBC2, 2014; Andrew Marr on Churchill: blood, sweat and oil paint, 2015. Columnist of the Year, What the Papers Say, 1994; Creative Media Journalist of Year, British Press Awards, 2000; Pol Journalist of Year, C4/House Mag., 2001, 2002; Specialist of the Year, RTS Awards, 2001–02; Best Individual TV Performer, Voice of the Listener and Viewer Awards, 2002; Best TV Performer, BPG, 2002; Parly Commentator of the Year, Richard Dimbleby Award, BAFTA, 2004. *Publications:* The Battle for Scotland, 1992; Ruling Britannia, 1995; The Day Britain Died, 2000; My Trade: a short history of British journalism, 2004; A History of Modern Britain, 2007; The Making of Modern Britain, 2009; The Diamond Queen: Elizabeth II and her people, 2011; A History of the World, 2012; A Short Book about Drawing, 2013; Head of State (novel), 2014; Children of the Master (novel), 2015. *Recreations:* reading, painting, talking. *Address:* c/o BBC, Broadcasting House, Portland Place, W1A 1AA.

MARR, Douglas, CBE 2001; HM Inspector of Education, 2004–12; freelance journalist, The Herald and Scottish Review, since 2004; education consultant, since 2004; *b* 7 Feb. 1947; *s* of Douglas N. Marr and Evelyn Marr; *m* 1990, Alison M. Gordon; one *d*. *Educ:* Aberdeen Grammar Sch.; Univ. of Aberdeen (MA Hons 1969, MEd Hons 1982). Teacher of History, Hilton Acad., Aberdeen, 1970–71; Asst Principal Teacher of Hist., Aberdeen GS, 1971–76; Principal Teacher of Hist., Hilton Acad., 1976–81; Asst Rector, Kemnay Acad., 1981–84; Depute Rector, The Gordon Schs, Huntly, 1984–87; Headteacher, Hilton Acad., 1987–88; Rector: St Machar Acad., 1988–95; Banchory Acad., 1995–2002; Schs Mgt and Curriculum Structures Co-ordinator, Aberdeenshire Council, 2002–04; Sen. Teaching Fellow, Sch. of Educn, Univ. of Aberdeen, 2004–06. Sen. Consultant, Acorn Consulting (Scotland), 2004–. Mem., Business Cttee, 2001–06, Ct, 2002–06, Univ. of Aberdeen. *Recreations:* squash, gardening, walking. *Address:* Oak Lodge, Alford, Aberdeenshire AB33 8DH. *T:* (019755) 63062. *E:* douglas.marr@alford.co.uk. *Club:* Leicestershire CC.

MARR, (Sir) Leslie Lynn, (2nd Bt *cr* 1919, but does not use the title); MA Cambridge; painter and draughtsman; late Flight Lieutenant RAF; *b* 14 Aug. 1922; *o s* of late Col John Lynn Marr, OBE, TD, (and *g s* of 1st Bt), and Amelia Rachel, *d* of late Robert Thompson, Overdinsdale Hall, Darlington; *S* grandfather, 1932; *m* 1st, 1948, Dinora Delores Mendelson (marr. diss. 1956); one *d*; 2nd, 1962, Lynn Heneage (marr. diss. 2000); two *d*; 3rd, 2002, Maureen Thelma Monk (*née* Dormer). *Educ:* Shrewsbury; Pembroke Coll., Cambridge. Has exhibited at Ben Uri, Drian, Woodstock, Wildenstein, Whitechapel, Campbell and Franks Galls and Piano Nobile Fine Paintings, London; Art Sch. Gall., Shrewsbury Sch.; Mercer Art Gall., Harrogate; University Gall., Northumbria Univ.; also in Norwich, Belfast, Birmingham, Newcastle upon Tyne, Durham City Art Gall., Bristol and Paris. *Publications:* From My Point of View: personal record of some Norfolk churches, 1979; A Piano Album, 1998; A Second Album for Piano, 1998. *Heir: cousin* James Allan Marr [*b* 17 May 1939; *m* 1965, Jennifer, *yr d* of late J. W. E. Gill; two *s* one *d*]. *Address:* c/o Piano Nobile Fine Paintings, 129 Portland Road, W11 4LW.

MARR-JOHNSON, His Honour Frederick James Maugham; a Circuit Judge, 1991–2006; *b* 17 Sept. 1936; *s* of late Kenneth Marr-Johnson and Hon. Diana Marr-Johnson; *m* 1966, Susan Eyre; one *s* one *d. Educ:* Winchester Coll.; Trinity Hall, Cambridge (MA). Called to the Bar, Lincoln's Inn, 1962, Bencher, 1999; practised on SE Circuit, 1963–91. Judge of Mayor's and City of London Court, 1999–2006. *Recreation:* sailing. *Address:* The South Wing, St Paul's Walden Bury, Hitchin SG4 8BP. *T:* (01438) 871617. *Clubs:* Royal Yacht Squadron (Cowes); Bar Yacht (Rear Cdre, 1999–2000).

MARRA, Jennifer Margaret; Member (Lab) Scotland North East, Scottish Parliament, since 2011; *b* Dundee, 6 Nov. 1977; *d* of Nicholas James Marra and Eileen Margaret Marra. *Educ:* St John's High Sch., Dundee; Univ. of St Andrews (MA Mod. Hist. 1999); Emory Univ., Atlanta (Bobby Jones Schol.); Univ. of Glasgow (LLB 2008); BPP London (Grad. Dip. Law 2009); Univ. of Dundee (DipLP 2010). Hd of Press, Univ. of Dundee, 2000–05; Spokesperson for Labour MEPs, Brussels and Strasbourg, 2005–06; PR consultant, Glasgow, 2006–08. Scottish Parliament: Shadow Minister for Community Safety and Legal Affairs, 2011–13, for Youth Employment, 2013–; Dep. Shadow Finance Minister, 2013–. *Address:* (office) 15/16 Springfield, Dundee DD1 4JE. *T:* (01382) 202584. *E:* jenny.marra.msp@scottish.parliament.uk.

MARRIN, John Wheeler; QC 1990; a Recorder, 1997; a Deputy High Court Judge, 2008; *b* 24 Aug. 1951; *s* of late Dr Charles Ainsworth Marrin and of Cecilia Margaret Marrin (*née* Staveley); *m* 1984, Paquita Carmen Bulan de Zulueta; one *s* three *d. Educ:* Sherborne Sch.; Magdalene Coll., Cambridge (MA). Called to the Bar, Inner Temple, 1974, Bencher, 2002; Head of Chambers, 2005–10. *Recreations:* music, ski-ing, horse-riding, travel. *Address:* Keating Chambers, 15 Essex Street, WC2R 3AA. *T:* (020) 7544 2600.

MARRINER, Andrew Stephen; solo, chamber and orchestral clarinettist; Principal Clarinet, London Symphony Orchestra, since 1985; *b* 25 Feb. 1954; *s* of Sir Neville Marriner, *qv*; *m* 1988, Elisabeth Anne Sparke; one *s. Educ:* King's College Sch., Cambridge (chorister); King's Sch., Canterbury; New Coll., Oxford; Hochschule für Musik, Hannover. Freelance solo, chamber and orchestral clarinettist, 1977–84; Principal Clarinet, Acad. of St Martin-in-the-Fields, 1986–2008; solo and concert appearances at venues incl. RFH and Barbican Hall, and in Paris, Berlin, Vienna, USA, Far East and Australia; concerto work with conductors incl. Sir Neville Marriner, Valery Gergiev, Sir Colin Davis, Leonard Bernstein, Mstislav Rostropovich, Michael Tilson Thomas and Richard Hickox. Numerous recordings. Hon. RAM 1994. *Recreations:* family, cricket. *Address:* 67 Cornwall Gardens, SW7 4BA; c/o Ingpen & Williams Ltd, 7 St George's Court, 131 Putney Bridge Road, SW15 2PA. *T:* (020) 8874 3222, *Fax:* (020) 8877 3113. *Club:* Lord's Taverners.

MARRINER, Sir Neville, CH 2015; Kt 1985; CBE 1979; conductor; Founder and Director, Academy of St Martin in the Fields, 1956–2011, now Life President; *b* 15 April 1924; *s* of Herbert Henry Marriner and Ethel May Roberts; *m* 1955, Elizabeth Mary Sims; one *s* one *d. Educ:* Lincoln Sch.; Royal College of Music (ARCM). Taught music at Eton Coll., 1948; Prof., Royal Coll. of Music, 1950. Martin String Quartet, 1949; Jacobean Ensemble, 1951; London Symphony Orchestra, 1954; Music Director: Los Angeles Chamber Orchestra, 1968–77; Minnesota Orchestra, 1979–86; Stuttgart Radio Symphony Orch., 1984–89. Artistic Director: South Bank Summer Music, 1975–77; Meadow Brook Festival, Detroit Symphony Orchestra, 1979–83; Barbican Summer Festival, 1985–87. President: Oxford and Cambridge Music Soc., 1990–2015; Music Therapy Trust, 2000–14. Chm., Chardstock Cricket Club, 1996–. Hon. ARAM; Hon. FRCM 1983; Hon. Fellow, Hong Kong Acad. Music, 1998. Hon. MusD: RSAMD; Univ. of Hull; Hon. Dr Krakow Acad. of Music, 2015. Kt, Order of the Star of the North (Sweden), 1984; Officer, Ordre des Arts et des Lettres (France), 1995. *Club:* Garrick.

See also A. S. Marriner.

MARRIOTT, Bryant Hayes; Director of Broadcasting, Seychelles Broadcasting Corporation (formerly Radio Television Seychelles), 1991–93; *b* 9 Sept. 1936; *s* of Rev. Horace Marriott and Barbara Marriott; *m* 1963, Alison Mary Eyles; one *s* two *d. Educ:* Tormore Sch., Upper Deal, Kent; Marlborough Coll., Wilts; New Coll., Oxford (MA). Joined BBC, 1961; Studio Manager, 1961; Producer, 1963; Staff Training Attachments Officer, 1973; Chief Asst to Controller Radio 1 and 2, 1976; Head of Recording Services, 1979; Controller, Radio Two, 1983; Controller, Special Duties, Radio BBC, 1990–91. *Recreations:* gardening, sailing, drumming. *Address:* 4 School Pasture, Burnham Deepdale, King's Lynn, Norfolk PE31 8DF. *Club:* Brancaster Staithe Sailing.

MARRIOTT, Jane, OBE 2004; HM Diplomatic Service; Director, Gulf, Arabian Peninsula and North Africa, Foreign and Commonwealth Office, since 2015; *b* Doncaster, 1976; *d* of Derek Marriott and Patricia Marriott; partner, 2012, Paul Lipscombe. *Educ:* Danum Comp. Sch.; Durham Univ. (BA Hons 1st Hist. 1997); Darwin Coll., Cambridge (MPhil Internat. Relns 1998). Diversity Policy, Cabinet Office, 1998; Criminal Justice Bill Team, Home Office, 1999; Foreign Policy Secretariat, Cabinet Office, 2000; Hd, Nuclear Non-Proliferation, FCO, 2001–03; Political Advisor: to Coalition Forces, S Iraq, 2003–04; to US-led Combined Coalition Forces, Afghanistan, 2004; Pol-Mil. Team Leader, Iraq Policy Unit, FCO, 2005; Pol-Mil. Counsellor, Baghdad, 2005–06; Dep. Hd, Afghanistan Gp, FCO and Mem., US CENTCOM Assessment Team, 2007–09; Chief Speechwriter, Sec. of State for Defence, 2009; Sen. Political Advr to US Special Rep. for Afghanistan and Pakistan, 2009; Chargé d'Affaires and Dep. Ambassador, Iran, 2010–11; Dep. Dir, Americas, Middle East and Africa, Nat. Security Council, 2012; Ambassador to Yemen, 2013–15. Chm., British Sch., Tehran, 2010–12. Mil. Campaign Medal, Iraq, 2004, Afghanistan, 2005; Superior Civilian Service Medal (USA), 2005; FCO Civilian Medal, Iraq, 2007. *Recreations:* singing, theatre, scuba-diving, bouldering, playing the cello, hiking. *Address:* Middle East and North Africa Department, Foreign and Commonwealth Office, King Charles Street, SW1A 2AH. *T:* 07932 685433. *E:* janemarriott@hotmail.com.

MARRIOTT, Martin Marriott; Headmaster, Canford School, 1976–92; *b* 28 Feb. 1932; *s* of late Rt Rev. Philip Selwyn Abraham, Bishop of Newfoundland, and Elizabeth Dorothy Cicely, *d* of late Sir John Marriott; *m* 1956, Judith Caroline Guerney Lubbock; one *s* two *d. Educ:* Lancing College; New College, Oxford. MA, DipEd. RAF Educn Branch, 1956–59. Asst Master, Heversham Grammar Sch., 1959–66; Asst Master, Housemaster, Second Master, Acting Master, Haileybury College, 1966–76. Chm., HMC, 1989. *Recreations:* grandchildren, golf, gardening. *Address:* Hillcroft, Meyrick Avenue, Salisbury, Wilts SP2 8ED. *T:* (01722) 330271. *E:* mmarriott32@gmail.com. *Club:* East India.

MARRIOTT, Michael; furniture and product designer; Director, Michael Marriott, since 1994; *b* 7 Jan. 1963; *s* of Michael and Jean Marriott. *Educ:* London Coll. of Furniture (HND); Royal Coll. of Art (MA 1993). Pt-time tutor, RCA, 1998–. Work in exhibitions, including: RFH; Crafts Council; ICA, and countries worldwide, including Italy, Germany, Sweden, Japan and USA; work in public collections: Crafts Council; British Council; Design Mus. Jerwood Prize for Furniture, Jerwood Foundn, 1999. *Recreations:* art, architecture, cycling, cities. *Address:* 11 Ramsgate Street, E8 2FD. *E:* mm@michaelmarriott.com. *W:* www.michaelmarriott.com. *Club:* Hat on Wall.

MARRIOTT, Maj. Gen. Patrick Claude, CB 2012; CBE 2003 (OBE 1999); DL; Commandant, Royal Military Academy, Sandhurst, 2009–12; *b* Oxted, Surrey, 23 Feb. 1958; *s* of Captain P. B. Marriott, DSO, DSC, RN and F. J. Marriott; *m* 1989, Karin Henrietta Warde Ingram; two *s* one *d. Educ:* Gresham's Sch., Holt. Commnd 17th/21st Lancers, 1977–82; Co. Comdr, Multinat. Force and Observers, Sinai, 1982; Adjt, 17th/21st Lancers, 1982–85; Asst Mil. Asst to VCDS (Personnel & Logistics), 1985–87; Sqdn Ldr, 17th/21st Lancers, 1987–90; psc (Can), 1990; SO2 Instructor, Jun. Div., Staff Coll., 1991–93; Sqdn Ldr, Queen's Royal Lancers, 1993–95; SO2 Tactics/Ops, British Army Trng Unit, Suffield, 1995–97; SO1 Jt Ops Centre (Plans), SHAPE, 1998; CO, Queen's Royal Lancers, 1998–2000; COS, HQ 1 (UK) Armd Div., 2000–04; HCSC (J) 2004; Comdr, 7th Armd Bde, 2005–07; ACOS Ops, PJHQ, 2007–09. Army Rep. to House of Laity in Gen. Synod, 2005–12. Dir, British Forces Foundn, 2009–12. Col, Queen's Royal Lancers, 2011–. Chm., Scottish Cttee, Combat Stress. Gov., Loretto Sch., Musselburgh, 2010–. DL Sutherland, 2013. QCVS 2006. *Recreations:* field sports, watercolour painting, natural history, rhetoric, keeping pigs and chickens, writing. *Address:* Fleet Ford, Littleferry, Golspie, Sutherland KW10 6TD. *E:* marriottpckh@hotmail.com.

MARRIOTT, Sir Peter Francis S.; *see* Smith-Marriott.

MARRIOTT, Richard, CVO 2006; TD 1965; Lord-Lieutenant of East Riding of Yorkshire, 1996–2005; *b* 17 Dec. 1930; *s* of late Rowland Arthur Marriott and Evelyn (*née* Caillard), Cotesbach Hall, Leics; *m* 1959, Janet (Sally) Coles; two *s. Educ:* Eton Coll.; Brasenose Coll., Oxford (Schol.). 2nd Lieut, Rifle Bde, 1950–51; Lt-Col comdg 21st SAS Regt (Artists) TA, 1966–69. With Brown Shipley & Co. Ltd, 1954–63; Partner, Mullens & Co. (Govt Brokers), 1964–86; Dir, Mercury Asset Mgt, 1986–96. Mem., Rural Develt Commn, Humberside, 1986–95. Vice-President: Officers' Assoc. (Chm., 1977–86); RUSI, 1993–98; Financial Adviser: Army Benevolent Fund, 1969–97 (Treas., 1997–2000); Airborne Forces Security Fund, 1972–2006; Trustee, Special Air Service Assoc., 1994–2003. Pres., Yorks Agricl Soc., 1995–96. Member Council: Nat. Army Mus., 1991–2005; Hull Univ., 1994–2000. Trustee: Buttle Trust, 1985–98 (Dep. Chm., 1990–96); York Minster Fund, 1987–2000; Nat. Army Mus. Develt Trust, 2006–13; Chm., Burton Constable Foundn, 1992–2008. Mem., Adv. Panel, Greenwich Hosp., 1981–2002. FSA 2013. High Sheriff, Humberside, 1991–92. Hon. Fellow, Sion Coll., 2005–. DUniv Hull, 2003. *Recreations:* books, the arts, travel, field sports. *Address:* Boynton Hall, Bridlington, E Yorks YO16 4XJ. *Clubs:* Beefsteak, Special Forces, White's.

MARRIS, James Hugh Spencer; Director: Newcastle Race Course, 1994–2007; Sedgefield Racecourse, 2002–07; *b* 30 July 1937; *s* of Harry V. Marris and Agnes E. Hutchinson; *m* 1963, Susan Mary Husband; one *s* one *d. Educ:* King William's College, Isle of Man; Royal Technical College, Salford. ARTCS, CEng, FIGEM. Dir of Engineering, E Midlands Gas, 1978–82; Regional Dep. Chm., Eastern Gas, 1982–83; HQ Dir (Ops), British Gas, 1983–87; Regl Chm., British Gas, Northern, 1988–93. *Publications:* contribs to IGasE Jl. *Recreations:* golf, gardening. *Address:* 3 Apple Tree Rise, Corbridge, Northumberland NE45 5HD. *T:* (01434) 633509.

MARRIS, Robert; MP (Lab) Wolverhampton South West, 2001–10 and since 2015; *b* 8 April 1955; *s* of Dr Charles Marris and Margaret Chetwode Marris, JP; partner, Julia Pursehouse. *Educ:* St Edward's Sch., Oxford; Univ. of British Columbia (BA Sociology and Hist. (double 1st) 1976; MA Hist. 1979). Trucker, 1977–79; trolley bus driver, 1979–82; law student, Birmingham Poly., 1982–84; articled clerk, 1985–87; solicitor, 1987. Regl Officer, Stafford, NUT, 2011–13. Contested (Lab) Wolverhampton SW, 2010. *Recreations:* Wolves, Canadiana, bicycling. *Address:* House of Commons, SW1A 0AA.

MARRISON, Rev. Dr Geoffrey Edward; Senior Fellow, South East Asian Studies, University of Hull, 2000–03 (Associate, Centre for South-East Asian Studies, 1989–91; Hon. Fellow, 1992–2003); *b* 11 Jan. 1923; *s* of John and Rose Marrison; *m* 1958, Margaret Marian Millburn; one *s* three *d. Educ:* SOAS, Univ. of London (BA Malay 1948, PhD Linguistics 1967); Bishops' Coll. Cheshunt; Kirchliche Hochschule, Berlin. Indian Army, 1942–46. SOAS, 1941–42 and 1946–49; ordained Priest, Singapore, 1952; in Malaya with USPG, 1952–56; Vicar of St Timothy, Crookes, Sheffield, 1958–61; Linguistics Adviser, British and Foreign Bible Soc., 1962–67, incl. service in Assam, 1962–64; Asst Keeper, British Museum, 1967–71, Dep. Keeper 1971–74; Dir and Keeper, Dept of Oriental Manuscripts and Printed Books, British Library, 1974–83. Permission to officiate, dio. of Carlisle, 1983–; Tutor, Carlisle Diocesan Training Inst., 1984. Res. studies on Indonesian literatures, Leiden and Indonesia, 1990–91. Hon. Canon of All Saints Pro-Cathedral, Shillong, 1963. FRAS. *Publications:* The Christian Approach to the Muslim, 1958; A Catalogue of the South-East Asian Collections of Professor M. A. Jaspan (1926–1975), 1989; A Catalogue of the South-East Asian History Collections of Dr D. K. Bassett (1931–1989), 1992; A Catalogue of the Collections of Rev. Dr Harry Parkin on Asian Religions and Batak Studies (1926–1990), 1993; A Catalogue of the Collections of Dr Roy Bruton on Sarawak, and on the Sociology of Education, 1994; Sasak and Javanese Literature of Lombok, 1999; Catalogue of Javanese and Sasak Texts, 1999; articles in Jl Malayan Branch Royal Asiatic Soc., Bible Translator. *Recreations:* ethno-linguistics of South and South East Asia, Christian and oriental art.

MARS-JONES, Adam; writer; *b* 26 Oct. 1954; *s* of Hon. Sir William Mars-Jones, MBE. *Educ:* Westminster School; Trinity Hall, Cambridge (BA 1976). Film Critic: The Independent, 1986–99; The Times, 1999–2001; book reviewer: The Observer, 2002–13; London Rev. of Bks, 2013–. *Publications:* Lantern Lecture (stories), 1981 (Somerset Maugham Award 1982); (with Edmund White) The Darker Proof (stories), 1987, 2nd edn 1988; Venus Envy (essay), 1990; Monopolies of Loss (stories), 1992; The Waters of Thirst (novel), 1993; Blind Bitter Happiness (essays), 1997; Pilcrow (novel), 2008; Cedilla (novel), 2011; Noriko Smiling (film study), 2011; Kid Gloves (memoir), 2015. *Recreations:* cooking, sight-reading piano music I will never be able to play properly. *Address:* 38 Oakbank Grove, Herne Hill, SE24 0AJ. *T:* (020) 7733 9757.

MARSABIT, Bishop of, since 2011; **Rt Rev. Robert David Markland Martin;** *b* Frimley, 5 May 1949; *s* of Col Alexander Robert Fyers Martin and Alison Mary Martin; *m* 1975, Sue Leney; three *s. Educ:* Woodcote House, Windlesham; Bradfield Coll., Berks; Trinity Coll., Cambridge (BA Hons Modern Langs); Trinity Coll., Bristol (BA Hons Theol.). ACA 1974, FCA 1975. Audit Clerk, 1971–74, Sen. Audit Clerk, 1974–77, Peat Marwick Mitchell; Diocesan Accountant, Dio. of Mt Kenya E, 1978–87; ordained deacon, 1991, priest, 1992; Curate, Kingswood Team Ministry, Bristol, 1991–95; Vicar, Holy Trinity, Frome, 1995–2008; Rural Dean, Frome, 2003–08; Suffragan Bishop, All Saints Cathedral, Nairobi, 2008–11. Chm., Provincial Bd of Finance, Kenya, 2013–. Mission partner, Crosslinks Anglican Mission Agency. Patron, St Philips Community Centre, Mburi, Kenya, 1986–. Gov., Trinity First Sch., Frome, 1995–2008. *Recreations:* languages, travelling, birdwatching, reading, mountain trekking. *Address:* Anglican Church of Kenya Diocese of Marsabit, c/o MAF Kenya, PO Box 21123–00505, Nairobi, Kenya. *T:* (20) 720006693. *E:* ackbishopmarsabit@gmail.com. *Club:* Minoans (Cambridge).

MARSALIS, Wynton; trumpeter; Artistic Director, Jazz at Lincoln Center, New York, since 1987; *b* New Orleans, 18 Oct. 1961; *s* of Ellis and Dolores Marsalis. *Educ:* New Orleans Center for the Creative Arts; Berkshire Music Center (Harvey Shapiro Award); Juilliard Sch., NY (Schol.). Mem., Art Blakey's Jazz Messengers, 1980–81; formed own jazz quintet, 1981; has played with major orchestras worldwide, incl. New Orleans Philharmonic, LSO, English Chamber Orch. Music Dir, Lincoln Center Jazz Orch., 1987–. *Compositions* include: In This House, On This Morning; Blood on the Fields, 1997 (Pulitzer Prize for Music, 1997); Knozz-Moe-King; Jazz (ballet score). Numerous recordings (Grammy Awards for jazz and classical performances). *Publications:* Sweet Swing Blues on the Road, 1994; Marsalis on Music, 1995; (with C. Vigeland) Jazz in the Bittersweet Blues of Life; (with S. Seyfu Hinds) To a Young Musician: letters from the road, 2004; Jazz ABZ, 2005; (with Geoffrey Ward) Moving to Higher Ground: how jazz can change your life, 2009. *Address:* Wynton Marsalis Enterprises, c/o Jazz at Lincoln Center, 3 Columbus Circle, New York, NY 10023, USA; c/o Agency for the Performing Arts, 9200 West Sunset Boulevard, Suite 1200, West 12 Hollywood, CA 90069–5812, USA.

MARSCHALL JONES, Timothy Aidan; HM Diplomatic Service; Team Leader, Economics Trade and Development, Berlin, since 2013; *b* 5 Sept. 1962; *s* of Dr Derek Hugh Powell Jones and Thelma Anne (*née* Gray); *m* 2001, Dr Christin Marschall; one *s* one *d*. *Educ:* Bexhill Co. Grammar Sch.; Christ's Coll., Cambridge (BA Hons 1984). Joined HM Diplomatic Service, 1984: Vienna (CSCE), 1987–88; The Hague, 1988–92; FCO, 1992–94; EU Admin, Mostar, 1994–95; Dep. Head of Mission, Tehran, 1996–99; Ambassador to Armenia, 1999–2002; Hd of Ops, IT Strategy Unit, FCO, 2003–06; HM Consul Gen., Lille, 2006–08; Principal Advr to EU Counter Terrorism Co-ordinator, 2008–12. *Recreations:* swimming, cycling, idle curiosity. *Address:* c/o Foreign and Commonwealth Office, King Charles Street, SW1A 2AH.

MARSDEN, Edmund Murray; Minister (Cultural Affairs)), British High Commission, New Delhi, India, and Regional Director, South Asia, British Council, 2000–05; *b* 22 Sept. 1946; *s* of Christopher Marsden and Ruth Marsden (*née* Kershaw); *m* 1975, Christine Vanner (*d* 1980); *m* 1981, Megan McIntyre; one *s*. *Educ:* Winchester College; Trinity College, Cambridge. Partner, Compton Press, Salisbury, 1968–70; Nuffield Foundn Publications Unit, 1970–71; British Council: Ghana, 1971; Belgium, 1973; Algeria, 1975; Management Accountant, 1977; Syria, 1980; Dir, Educn Contracts, 1982; Turkey, 1987; Dir, Corporate Affairs, 1990–93; Asst Dir-Gen., 1993–99; Chm., Intermediate Technol. Develt Gp, 1995–97 and 1998–2000. *Address:* 21755 Ocean Vista Drive, Laguna Beach, CA 92651, USA. *E:* emarsden01@aol.com.

MARSDEN, Gordon; MP (Lab) Blackpool South, since 1997; *b* 28 Nov. 1953; *s* of late George Henry Marsden and Joyce Marsden. *Educ:* Stockport Grammar Sch.; New Coll., Oxford (BA 1st cl. Hons History; MA); Warburg Inst., London Univ. (postgrad. res.); Harvard Univ. (Kennedy Schol. in Internat. Relations). Tutor and Associate Lectr, Arts Faculty, Open Univ., 1977–97; PR Consultant, 1980–85; Chief Public Affairs Advr, English Heritage, 1984–85; Editor, History Today, 1985–97; Consultant Ed., New Socialist, 1989–90. Chm., Fabian Soc., 2000–01. Contested (Lab) Blackpool S, 1992. PPS, Lord Chancellor's Dept, 2001–03, to Sec. of State for Culture, Media and Sport, 2003–05; Shadow Minister for Skills and FE, 2010–13, for Transport, 2013–15. Mem., Select Cttee on Educn and Employment, 1998–2001, 2005–07, on Innovation, Univs and Skills, 2007–10. Vice-Pres., All Party Arts and Heritage Gp, 2000–; Chair: All Party Skills Gp, 2006–10; All Party Estonia Gp, 2008–; All Party Veterans Gp, 2010–; Co-Chair, All Party Osteoporosis Gp, 2011–; Vice-Pres., PLP Educn and Employment Cttee, 1998–2001; Mem., Ecclesiastical Cttee, 1998–2015. Pres., British Destinations (formerly British Resorts, later British Resorts and Destinations) Assoc., 1998–. Mem. Bd, Inst. of Historical Res., 1995–2001. Trustee, History Today, 2005–14. Vis. Parly Fellow, St Antony's Coll., Oxford, 2003; Centenary Fellow, Historical Assoc., 2006–07. *Publications:* (ed) Victorian Values: personalities and perspectives in Nineteenth Century society, 1990, 2nd edn 1998; (contrib.) The English Question, 2000; (contrib.) The History of Censorship, 2002; contrib. History Today, Independent, Times, Tribune, THES. *Recreations:* world music, travel, medieval culture. *Address:* House of Commons, SW1A 0AA. *T:* (020) 7219 1262.

MARSDEN, Jonathan Mark, CVO 2013 (LVO 2003); FSA; Director, Royal Collection Trust and Surveyor of the Queen's Works of Art, since 2010; *b* 15 Feb. 1960; *s* of Rear-Adm. Peter Nicholas Marsden, *qv*; *m* 2002, Sarah Bernard; two *s*. *Educ:* Sherborne Sch.; Univ. of York (BA Hons Hist.). Asst Curator, The Treasure Houses of Britain exhibn, Nat. Gall. of Art, Washington, 1983–85; Historic Buildings Rep., Nat. Trust N Wales Reg., 1986–92, Thames and Chilterns Reg., 1992–96; Dep. Surveyor of the Queen's Works of Art, 1996–2010. Member: Exec. Cttee, Georgian Gp, 1995–2005; Council, Furniture Hist. Soc., 2002–04 (Hon. Editl Sec., 2005–11); Collections Cttee, RCM, 2003–09; Council, Attingham Trust, 2010–. Trustee: Household Cavalry Mus., 2003–11; Art Fund (formerly NACF), 2005–; Royal Yacht Britannia Trust, 2007–; City & Guilds of London Art Sch., 2008–; Historic Royal Palaces, 2010–. FSA 2006. *Publications:* guidebooks to Penrhyn Castle, Stowe Landscape Garden, Cliveden, Chastleton, Clarence House, Buckingham Palace, Windsor Castle; contribs to exhibn catalogues and learned jls. *Recreations:* gardening, music, cricket, family. *Address:* Buckingham Palace, SW1A 1AA.

MARSDEN, Paul William Barry; international business consultant, since 2010; Head, Building Information Modelling and Business Continuity, Keepmoat Ltd, since 2015 (Group SHEQ Systems Manager, 2014–15); *b* 18 March 1968; *s* of Thomas Darlington Marsden and Audrey Marsden; *m* 1994, Michelle Sarah Bayley (*née* Somerville) (marr. diss. 2005); two *s*; *m* 2009, Elena Sirkina; one step *d*. *Educ:* Open Univ. (Dip. Mgt 1995); Newcastle Coll. (Dip. Business Excellence 2000). Quality Manager: Taylor Woodrow, 1990–94; NatWest Bank, 1994–96; Mitel Telecom, 1996–97. MP (Lab, 1997–2001, Lib Dem, 2001–05, Lab, 2005) Shrewsbury and Atcham. Lib Dem spokesman on health, 2002–03, on transport, 2003–05. Mem., Select Cttee on Agric., 1997–2001, on Transport, 2003–05; Chairman: All Party Gp on Mgt, 1998; Equal Access to Cancer Care Parly Cttee, 2000–01; Jt Chair, All Party Parly Road Safety Gp, 2003–04; Associate Life Mem., Inter-Parly Union All Party Gp, 1997. Business consultant and writer, 2005–07; Dir of Policy, British Union for the Abolition of Vivisection, 2007–08; Chief Exec., Painting and Decorating Assoc., 2008–10; Dir, British Security Ind. Assoc., 2010–12. Vice President: Offa's Dyke Assoc., 1997–2005; Heart of Wales Travellers' Assoc., 1997–2005. Member: Shropshire Chamber of Commerce, Trng & Enterprise, 1997–2005; Agric. & Rural Economy Cttee, CLA, 1997–2001; Assoc. of Former MPs, 2010–. Member: DIAL Shropshire, Telford and Wrekin, 2003–05; Shrewsbury and Newport Canals Trust, 2003–05. Hon. Pres., W Midlands Lib Dem Youth and Students, 2003–05. FCMI (MIMgt 1996); MInstD 2002; Member: Chartered Quality Inst. (CQP), 2014; Eur. Orgn for Quality, 2014; British Standards Soc., 2015. Big Issue Hero of the Year Award, 2001. *Publications:* (contrib.) Voices for Peace, 2001; The Black Friars of Shrewsbury, 2006; Construction Materials Handling and Storage on Site, 2015. *Recreations:* history, social media, marathon running, gardening, politics, family. *E:* paul.marsden1968@gmail.com. *W:* http://paulwbmarsden.blogspot.com.

MARSDEN, Rear-Adm. Peter Nicholas; *b* 29 June 1932; *s* of Dr James Pickford Marsden and Evelyn (*née* Holman); *m* 1956, Jean Elizabeth Mather; two *s* one *d*. *Educ:* Felsted Sch., Essex. Joined RN, 1950; Commander, 1968; Captain, 1976; Commodore, Admiralty Interview Bd, 1983–84; Sen. Naval Mem., DS, RCDS, 1985–88. Exec. Dir, 21st Century Trust, 1989–92. *Recreations:* golf, beagling, gardening. *Address:* c/o National Westminster Bank, Standishgate, Wigan, Lancs WN1 1UE.

See also J. M. Marsden.

MARSDEN, Dame Rosalind (Mary), DCMG 2010 (CMG 2003); DPhil; HM Diplomatic Service, retired; Ambassador to Sudan, 2007–10; European Union Special Representative for Sudan and South Sudan, 2010–13; *b* 1950; *d* of late Major Walter Stancliffe Marsden and Winifred Howells. *Educ:* Woking County Grammar Sch. for Girls; Somerville Coll., Oxford (BA 1st Cl. Hons Mod. Hist.; Hon. Fellow); St Antony's Coll., Oxford (DPhil). Joined FCO, 1974; Tokyo, 1976–80; Policy Planning Staff, 1980–82; EC Dept (Internal), 1983–84; Bonn, 1985–88; Hong Kong Dept, 1989–91; on secondment to National Westminster Bank Gp, 1991–93; Political Counsellor, Tokyo, 1993–96; Hd, UN Dept, 1996–99, Dir, Asia-Pacific, 1999–2003, FCO; Ambassador to Afghanistan, 2003–06; Consul-Gen., Basra, 2006–07. Associate Fellow, RIIA. Fellow, Rift Valley Inst. Mem., Adv. Council, Eur. Inst. Peace. *Recreations:* mountain walking, reading, travel. *E:* rosalindmarsden1@gmail.com.

MARSDEN, Susan; campaigner for legal and consumer rights and for the environment; *b* 6 Dec. 1931; *d* of late John Marsden-Smedley and Agatha (*née* Bethell). *Educ:* Downe House Sch.; Girton Coll., Cambridge (BA). Called to the Bar, Middle Temple, 1957. Worked in consumer organisations in Britain and US, 1957–70; Co-founder, 1972, Exec. Dir, 1972–78, and Course Dir, 1978–81, Legal Action Gp (Editor, LAG Bulletin, 1972–78); Sec., Public Sector Liaison, RIBA, 1981–84; Asst Dir, Nat. Assoc. of CAB, 1985–86; part-time Chairman: Social Security Appeal Tribunals (Leeds), 1987–97; Disability Appeal Tribunals, 1992–97. Chair, Greater London CAB Service, 1979–85; Member: Council, National Assoc. of CAB, 1980–84; Royal Commn on Legal Services, 1976–79; Yorks Regional Rivers Adv. Cttee, Nat. Rivers Authority, 1989–96; Council, Leeds Civic Trust, 1989–92. Chair, 1988–93, Trustee, 1998–2004, EYE on the Aire. Sec., Access Cttee, West Riding Ramblers' Assoc., 2001–11. *Publications:* Justice Out of Reach, a case for Small Claims Courts, 1969. *Recreations:* conservation along the River Aire, tree planting and preservation, gardening, walking, looking at modern buildings. *Address:* 28 Newlay Lane, Horsforth, Leeds LS18 4LE. *T:* (0113) 258 0936.

MARSDEN, Sir Tadgh Orlando Denton, 5th Bt *cr* 1924, of Grimsby, co. Lincoln; *b* 25 Dec. 1990; *s* of Sir Simon Neville Llewelyn Marsden, 4th Bt and of Caroline Marsden (*née* Stanton); *S* father, 2012, but his name does not appear on the Official Roll of the Baronetage.

MARSDEN, Prof. Terry Keith, PhD; Professor of Environmental Policy and Planning, since 1995, Dean of Graduate Studies, since 2008, and Director, Sustainable Places Research Institute, since 2010, Cardiff University; *b* 19 Oct. 1954; *s* of Terence Frederick and Kathleen Marsden; *m* 1982, Mary Anne Speakman; one *s* one *d*. *Educ:* Eccleshall Sec. Mod. Sch., Staffs; Univ. of Hull (BA Hons 1st Cl. Geog. and Sociol. 1976; PhD 1980). MRTPI 1998. Sen. and Principal Lectr in Planning, S Bank Poly., London, 1983–90; Co-Dir, Rural Studies Res. Centre and ESRC Countryside Change Centre, UCL, 1988–93; Reader in Human Geog., Univ. of Hull, 1993–94; Cardiff University: Hd, Sch. of City and Regl Planning, 1999–2009; Dir, Res. and Graduate Sch. in the Social Scis, 2001–02; Mem. Bd, Regeneration Inst., 2000–; Dep. Pro-Vice Chancellor (Res.), 2005–10; Co-Dir, Centre for Business Relationships, Accountability, Sustainability and Society (ESRC Res. Centre), 2002–13. Visiting Professor: Dept of Rural Sociol., Univ. of Wisconsin-Madison, 1990; Econs and Sociol., Univ. of Pernambuco, Brazil, 1993, 1995, 2003; Vis. Internat. Reader in European rural develt, Swedish Sch. of Soc. Scis, Univ. of Helsinki, 2001–03. Special Advisor: Welsh Affairs Select Cttee, 1997–98, 2001; on rural affairs for Nat. Assembly of Wales, 2000–01. Co-Editor, Jl of Environmental Policy and Planning, 1999–. *Publications:* (ed jtly) Critical Perspectives on Rural Change, 6 vols, 1990–94; Constructing the Countryside, 1993; Reconstituting Rurality, 1995; The Condition of Sustainability, 1999; Consuming Interests: the social provision of foods, 2000; (jtly) Worlds of Food, 2006; (ed jtly) The Handbook of Rural Studies, 2006; over 100 refereed jl articles. *Recreations:* running, cycling, squash, gardening, topographical antiquarian books. *Address:* Cardiff School of Planning and Geography, Glamorgan Building, King Edward VII Avenue, Cardiff CF10 3WA. *T:* (029) 2087 5736, *Fax:* (029) 2087 4845. *E:* MarsdenTK@cardiff.ac.uk.

MARSDEN, William, CMG 1991; HM Diplomatic Service, retired; conservationist; *b* 15 Sept. 1940; *s* of Christopher Marsden and Ruth (*née* Kershaw); *m* 1964, Kaia Collingham; one *s* one *d*. *Educ:* Winchester Coll.; Lawrenceville Sch., USA; Trinity Coll., Cambridge (MA); London Univ. (BSc Econs). FO, 1962–64; UK Delegn to NATO, 1964–66; Rome, 1966–69; seconded as Asst to Gen. Manager, Joseph Lucas Ltd, 1970; First Sec., FCO, 1971–76; First Sec. and Cultural Attaché, Moscow, 1976–79; Asst Head, European Community Dept, FCO, 1979–81; Counsellor, UK Representation to EEC, 1981–85; Head, E Africa Dept, FCO, and Comr, British Indian Ocean Territory, 1985–88; Ambassador to Costa Rica, and concurrently Ambassador to Nicaragua, 1989–92; Minister (Trade), Washington, 1992–94; Asst Under-Sec. of State, later Dir, (Americas), FCO, 1994–97; Ambassador to Argentina, 1997–2000. Chairman: Diplomatic Service Assoc., 1987–88; Anglo-Central American Soc., 2003–05. Chm., Chagos Conservation Trust, 2002–11. Internat. Advr, Coiba World Heritage Project, 2003–08. Counsellor, ESU, 2012–. Trustee, World Cancer Res. Fund, 2002–08. *Address:* Highwood, Castlegate, Pulborough, W Sussex RH20 2NJ. *T:* (020) 7233 9538.

MARSH, Andrew David; Chief Constable, Hampshire Constabulary, since 2013 (Deputy Chief Constable, 2010–13); *b* Liverpool, 20 March 1966; *s* of John David Marsh and Carol Marsh (*née* Whipple, now O'Brien); *m* 1990, Nikki Watson; two *d*. *Educ:* Newquay Tretherras Sch., Cornwall; Univ. of Liverpool (BSc Hons Geog. 1987). Joined Avon and Som Constabulary, 1987; Comdr, S Bristol/E Som, 2002–06; Assistant Chief Constable: Wilts Police, 2007–09; Avon and Som Constabulary, 2009–10. *Recreations:* rowing, fly fishing. *Address:* Hampshire Police Headquarters, West Hill, Romsey Road, Winchester, Hants SO22 5DB. *T:* (01962) 871148, *Fax:* (01962) 871189. *E:* andy.marsh@hampshire.pnn.police.uk.

MARSH, Barrie; *see* Marsh, G. B.

MARSH, David Wayne, CBE 2000; Chairman, Official Monetary and Financial Institutions Forum, since 2010; *b* Shoreham, Sussex, 30 July 1952; *s* of Dennis and Marguerite Marsh; *m* 1974, Veronika Dangelmayer; two *d*. *Educ:* Hove Grammar Sch.; Queen's Coll., Oxford (BA). With Reuters, 1973–78; FT, 1978–95 (latterly Eur. Ed.); Dir, Eur. Strategy, Robert Fleming, 1995–99; Vice Chm., Hawkpoint Partners, 1999–2001; Man. Dir, London, Droege Mgt Consultants, 2002–05; Dir, then Chm., London and Oxford Capital Mkts, 2005–09. Member: Bd, German British Forum, 1995–; Adv. Bd, Centre for Eur. Reform, 1998–; Bd, British Chamber of Commerce in Germany, 2010–; Bd, Henderson Eurotrust, 2011–. Hon. Prof., Univ. of Birmingham; Hon. Fellow, S Bank Univ. *Publications:* The Germans: rich, bothered and divided, 1989, 2nd edn 1990; Germany and Europe: the crisis of unity, 1995; The Bundesbank: the Bank that rules Europe, 1992, 2nd edn 1993; The Euro: the politics of the new global currency, 2009, 2nd edn 2011; Europe's Deadlock: how to solve the Euro crisis and why it won't happen, 2013. *Recreations:* tennis, talking and listening, travel. *Address:* Official Monetary and Financial Institutions Forum, One Lyric Square, W6 0NB. *T:* (020) 3008 5262, 07971 614606, *Fax:* (020) 3008 8426. *E:* david.marsh@omfif.org. *Club:* Reform.

MARSH, Derek Richard, CVO 1999; Senior Consultant, IRC Ltd, Seoul, since 2009; Director: Marsh Advisers (Asia) Ltd, since 2010; Marchwood Management (Chichester) Ltd, since 2013; non-executive Chairman, Pressfit Holdings plc, since 2014; *b* 17 Sept. 1946; *s* of Reginald and Minnie Marsh; *m* 1969, Frances Anne Roberts; one *s* one *d*. *Educ:* Queen's Coll., Oxford (Schol.; MA 1973). Ministry of Defence: Asst Principal, 1968–72; Asst Private Sec. to Minister of State for Defence, 1973–74; Principal, 1974–78; ndc, 1975; Admin. Sec., Sovereign Base Areas, Cyprus, 1978–81; Asst Sec., 1982–86; rcds 1987; Department of Trade and Industry: Head of Air 1 and 2, 1988–91; Director: Companies House, 1991–93; Projects Export Promotion, 1994–97; Dep. Hd of Mission and Consul-Gen., Republic of Korea, 1997–2001; Dir Gen., British Trade and Cultural Office, Taipei, 2002–05. Adviser: UK Trade and Investment, 2006; iFafa Tech (Manila), 2006–08. Non-executive Director: Felixstowe Dock and Railway Co., 1990–91; Bovis Homes Ltd, 1992–93; Haike Chemical Gp Ltd, 2007–13; China Food Co. plc, 2007–11; Auhua Clean Energy plc, 2012–14; Pressfit Internat. Enterprise Ltd (Hong Kong), 2014–. Vice Chm., British Korean Soc. *Recreations:* travel, reading, running.

MARSH, Rt Rev. Edward Frank; Bishop of Central Newfoundland, 1990–2000; Diocesan Administrator, Diocese of Central Newfoundland, 2005; *b* 25 Oct. 1935; *m* 1962, Emma Marsh; one *s* two *d. Educ:* Dalhousie Univ., NS (BCom 1956); Univ. of Newfoundland (BA 1960); Queen's Coll., Newfoundland (LTh 1961; BD 1969). Deacon 1959, priest 1960; Curate, Corner Brook, 1959–63; Incumbent, Harbour Breton, 1963–69; Curate, Wickford, 1969–71; Incumbent, Indian Bay, 1971–73; Curate, St John the Baptist Cathedral, St John's, 1973–77; Rector of Cartwright, Dio. of East Newfoundland, 1977–81; Rector, Holy Trinity, Grand Falls, 1981–90.

MARSH, Felicity Margaret Sue; *see* Goodey, F. M. S.

MARSH, Rev. (Francis) John, DPhil; Archdeacon of Blackburn, 1996–2001; Priest in Charge, St Michael the Archangel, Emley and St James the Great, Flockton, and Hon. Diocesan Trng Officer, since 2011; *b* 3 July 1947; *s* of William Frederick and Helena Mary Marsh; *m* 1974, Gillian Popely; two *d. Educ:* York Univ. (BA 1969; DPhil 1976); Cert Theol Cambridge, 1975. ATCL 1965; ARCM 1966; ARCO 1971. Ordained deacon, 1975, priest, 1976; Assistant Curate: St Matthew's, Cambridge, 1975–78; Christ Church, Pitsmoor, Sheffield, 1979–81; Dir of Pastoral Trng, St Thomas', Crookes, Sheffield, 1981–85; Vicar, Christ Church, South Ossett, Wakefield, 1985–96. Rural Dean of Dewsbury, 1993–96. Mem., Gen. Synod of C of E, 1990–96, 1997–2001. Chm. Trustees, Anglican Renewal Ministries, 1989–2001. Mem., Adv. Bd, RSCM, 2000–01. *Address:* The Rectory, 14 Grange Drive, Emley, Huddersfield HD8 9SF. *T:* (01924) 849161.

MARSH, (Graham) Barrie, FCIArb; solicitor; Partner, Mace & Jones, Solicitors, Liverpool and Manchester, 1959–99 (Senior Partner, 1980–97); *b* 18 July 1935; *s* of Ernest Heaps Marsh and Laura Greenhalgh Marsh; *m* 1961, Nancy Smith; one *s* two *d. Educ:* Bury Grammar Sch.; Loughborough Grammar Sch.; Liverpool Univ. (LLB Hons). FCIArb 1982. Admitted as solicitor, 1957. Nat. Chm., Young Solicitors Gp, Law Soc., 1975; President: Liverpool Law Soc., 1978–79; Solicitors' Disciplinary Tribunal, 1988–2001; Liverpool Publicity Assoc., 1980; part-time Chm., Appeals Service, 1989–2008. Chairman: Merseyside Chamber of Commerce and Industry, 1984–86; Radio City PLC, 1988–91. Non-exec. Dir, Liverpool HA, 1996–2000. Trustee, Nat. Museums and Galls on Merseyside, 1998–2006. Hon. Belgian Consul, Liverpool, and for NW, 1987–96. *Publications:* Employer and Employee: a complete and practical guide to the modern law of employment, 1977, 3rd edn 1990; contribs to legal and personnel jls on all aspects of employment law and industrial relations. *Recreations:* Liverpool Football Club, bird-watching, hill-walking. *Address:* Calmer Hey, Benty Heath Lane, Willaston, South Wirral CH64 1SA. *T:* (0151) 327 4863. *E:* g.barrie.marsh@btinternet.com.

MARSH, Henry Thomas, CBE 2010; FRCS; Consultant Neurosurgeon, St George's Hospital (formerly Atkinson Morley Hospital), since 1987; *b* Oxford, 5 March 1950; *s* of Norman Stayner Marsh and Christiane Christinnecke; *m* 2004, Kate Fox; one *s* two *d. Educ:* Westminster Sch.; University Coll., Oxford (BA PPE 1973); Royal Free Hosp. Sch. of Medicine, Univ. of London (MB BS Hons 1979). FRCS 1984. Neurosurgical Registrar, Royal Free Hosp., 1982–84; Sen. Registrar, Nat. Hosp. for Nervous Diseases and Gt Ormond St Hosp., 1984–87. Clin. Prof. of Neurosurgery, Univ. of Washington, Seattle, 1990–; Hon. Consultant Neurosurgeon: Royal Marsden Hosp., 1995–; University Hosp. of Wales, Cardiff, 1996–. Consultant, Internat. Neurosurgical Centre, Kiev, Ukraine, 1992– (featured in documentary The English Surgeon, 2008). *Publications:* Do No Harm: stories of life, death and brain surgery, 2014; contrib. articles on neurosurgical topics to jls incl. British Jl Neurosurgery, Jl Neurol. and Neurosurgery. *Recreations:* furniture making, bee keeping. *Address:* Atkinson Morley Wing, St George's Hospital, SW17 0QT. *T:* (020) 8725 4182.

MARSH, Jean Lyndsey Torren, OBE 2012; actress, writer; Artistic Director, Adelphi University Theatre, Long Island, New York, 1981–83; *b* 1 July 1934; *d* of late Henry Charles and of Emmeline Susannah Marsh; *m* 1955, Jon Devon Roland Pertwee (marr. diss. 1960; he *d* 1996). Began as child actress and dancer; *films:* Return to Oz; Willow; danced in Tales of Hoffmann, Where's Charley?, etc; Fatherland, 1995 (Cable Ace Award for Best Supporting Actress, 1996); acted in repertory companies: Huddersfield, Nottingham, etc; Broadway debut in Much Ado About Nothing, 1959; West End debut, Bird of Time, 1961; *stage:* Habeas Corpus, NY, 1975; The Importance of Being Earnest, 1977; Too True to be Good, 1977; Twelfth Night; Blithe Spirit; Whose Life is it Anyway?, NY, 1979; Uncle Vanya; On the Rocks; Pygmalion; Hamlet; The Chalk Garden; Blow Up does Dallas; The Old Country; Boeing, Boeing, Comedy, 2007; Portrait of a Lady, Th. Royal, Bath, 2008; *television:* series, Nine to Five; co-created and co-starred (Rose) in series Upstairs Downstairs, 1971–75 (Emmy, Best Actress, 1975); co-created series, The House of Eliott; Alexei Sayle Show; The Ghost Hunter (3 series); Bremner, Bird and Fortune; Most Mysterious Murder; Sense and Sensibility; Sensitive Skin; The Crooked House; actress: Upstairs Downstairs, 2010, 2012; *radio* incl. Bleak House, The Pier. Hon. DH Maryland Coll., NY, 1980. *Publications:* The Illuminated Language of Flowers, 1978; The House of Eliott, 1993, repr. 2011; Fiennders Keepers, 1996, repr. as Fiennders Abbey, 2011; Iris, 1999, repr. 2012; articles for Sunday Times, Washington Post, New York Times, Los Angeles Times, Daily Telegraph, Times. *Recreations:* walking, reading, cooking, eating, wine, music. *Address:* c/o Leslie Duff, Diamond Management, 31 Percy Street, W1T 2DD.

MARSH, Dame Jilian Norma; *see* Matheson, Dame J. N.

MARSH, Rev. John; *see* Marsh, Rev. F. J.

MARSH, John Edward; Director, Ernst & Young, since 2008; *b* 18 Dec. 1963; *s* of Keith and Margaret Marsh; *m* 1990, Karen Moors; three *d. Educ:* Ham Dingle Primary Sch., Stourbridge; King Edward VI Coll., Stourbridge; Univ. of Bristol (BA Hons Hist. 1985); Univ. of Warwick (MA Industrial Relns 1986). FCIPD 2006. Home Office, 1986–96, Pvte Sec. to Minister of State, 1994–96; Hd of Voluntary Sector Govt Spending, Dept of Nat. Heritage, 1996–97; Sect. Leader, Public Spending Directorate, HM Treasury, 1997–99; Home Office: Hd of Personnel Mgt, HM Prison Service, 1999–2003; Gp Dir of Human Resources, 2003–07; Dir, Civil Service Capability Gp, Cabinet Office, 2007–08. *Recreations:* football coaching, running, sports, eating out. *Address:* Ernst & Young, 1 More London Place, SE1 2AF.

MARSH, Sir John (Stanley), Kt 1999; CBE 1993; Professor of Agricultural Economics and Management, later of Agricultural and Food Economics, Reading University, 1984–97, now Emeritus; *b* 5 Oct. 1931; *s* of Stanley Albert Marsh and Elsie Gertrude Marsh (*née* Powell); *m* 1958, Kathleen Edith Casey; one *s* one *d. Educ:* St John's Coll., Oxford (BA PPE 1955; MA 1958); Reading Univ. (Dip. Agricl Econs 1956). CIBiol, FRSB (FIBiol 1997). Res. Economist, 1956–63, Lectr, 1963–71, Reader in Agricl Econs, 1971–77, Reading Univ.; Prof. of Agricl Econs, Aberdeen Univ., and Chm. of Econs Gp, N of Scotland Coll. of Agriculture, Aberdeen, 1977–84; Reading University: Dean, Faculty of Agriculture and Food, 1986–89; Dir, Centre for Agricl Strategy, 1990–97. Chairman: Agricl Wages Bd for England and Wales, 1991–99; RURAL, 1997–; Vice-Chm., Sci. Adv. Cttee, DEFRA, 2004–07. Chm., Centre for Dairy Inf. Ltd, 2005–15. Pres., British Inst. of Agricl Consultants, 1998–2009. FRASE 1991; FRAgS 1992. Nat. Agricl Award, RASE, 2011. *Publications:* contribs to books; numerous articles in learned jls. *Recreations:* photography, caravanning, Methodist local preacher. *Address:* 15 Adams Way, Earley, Reading, Berks RG6 5UT. *T:* (0118) 986 8434. *Clubs:* Farmers; Caravan (East Grinstead).

MARSH, Kevin John; Director, OffspinMedia, since 2011; *b* 14 Nov. 1954; *s* of John Marsh and Elizabeth Jill Marsh; *m* 1979, Melissa Sue Fletcher; one *s* one *d. Educ:* Doncaster Grammar Sch.; Christ Church, Oxford (MA). Joined BBC, 1978; Radio 4: Editor: PM, 1989–92; World at One, 1992–96; World at One and PM, 1996–98; launched Broadcasting House, 1998; Editor, Today, 2002–06; Exec. Editor, BBC Coll. of Journalism, 2006–11. Attended Salzburg Seminar, 1984; panelist and moderator, World Econ. Forum, Davos, 2004, 2005, 2006, Warsaw, 2005. Vis. Fellow, 2005–, Practitioner in Residence, 2013–, Bournemouth Univ. Alumnus, Prince of Wales Business and the Envmt Prog., 2005–. Columnist, Press Gazette, 2009–12. Consultant: Birzeit Univ., Palestine, 2013–; Geneva Centre for Security Policy, 2012–; Strategic Asset Recovery Initiative, Washington, 2013; Member, Editorial Board: British Journalism Rev., 2006–; Jl Applied Journalism and Media Studies, 2012–. Mem., RIIA, 2005–. FRSA. Sony Radio Awards, 1991, 1992, 2003, 2004, 2005; Amnesty Internat. Media Award, 2001. *Publications:* (contrib.) Beyond Trust, 2008; Web Journalism: a new form of citizenship?, 2009; (contrib.) Afghanistan, War and the Media, 2010; (contrib.) Future Tools for Journalism, 2011; (contrib.) Investigative Journalism: dead or alive?, 2011; Stumbling Over Truth, 2012; (contrib.) Journalism: new challenges, 2013; Dust, 2015; contrib. various articles to jls incl. Political Qly, British Journalism Rev., Jl Applied Journalism and Media Studies. *Recreations:* Rugby, opera, playing the lute. *E:* kevinjohnmarsh@gmail.com. *Club:* Royal Yachting Association.

MARSH, Prof. Mark Christopher Pakes, PhD; Professor of Molecular Cell Biology, since 2000 and Director, Medical Research Council Laboratory for Molecular Cell Biology, since 2006, University College London; *b* Wokingham, Berks, 4 Aug. 1953; *s* of Justyn Marsh and Patricia Marsh; *m* 2000, Victoria Lewis (separated); three *d. Educ:* Sir Joseph Williamson's Mathematical Sch., Rochester; University Coll. London (BSc Hons 1975; PhD 1979). Royal Soc. Postdoctoral Fellow, EMBL, Heidelberg, 1979–81; EMBO Postdoctoral Fellow, Yale Univ. Med. Sch., New Haven, 1981–85; Group Leader: Inst. of Cancer Res., London, 1985–91; MRC Lab. for Molecular Cell Biol., UCL, 1992–. Mem., EMBO, 2011–. *Publications:* (contrib.) Frontiers in Molecular Biology, 2001; research papers in cell biological and virological jls. *Recreations:* cycling, walking, theatre, opera, cinema, music, daughters and Suryadaya. *Address:* MRC Laboratory for Molecular Cell Biology, University College London, Gower Street, WC1E 6BT. *T:* (020) 7679 7802. *E:* m.marsh@ucl.ac.uk. *Club:* Medical Research.

MARSH, Dame Mary (Elizabeth), DBE 2007; Founding Director, Clore Social Leadership Programme, 2008–14; *b* 17 Aug. 1946; *d* of George Donald Falconer and Lesley Mary (*née* Wilson); *m* 1968, Juan Enrique Marsh (*d* 1999); four *s. Educ:* Birkenhead High Sch., GPDST; Univ. of Nottingham (BSc; Hon. Pres., Students Union, 2005–08); London Business Sch. (MBA). Teacher, Icknield High Sch., 1968; St Christopher School, Letchworth: teacher, 1969–72; Dep. Hd, 1980–90; Head: Queens' Sch., Watford, 1990–95; Holland Park Sch., 1995–2000; Dir and Chief Exec., NSPCC, 2000–08. Mem., Learning and Skills Council, 2005–10. Non-exec. Dir, HSBC Bank plc, 2009–; Mem., Corporate Sustainability Cttee, HSBC Hldgs Bd, 2009–13; Chair and non-exec. Dir, INSSO (UK) Ltd, 2014–. Gov., London Business Sch., 2010– (Chair, Internat. Alumni Council, 2010–13). Dir, Holts Acad. of Jewellery, 2014–. *Recreations:* swimming, reading, music, good company, walking in mountains and by the sea. *Address:* c/o London Business School, Sussex Place, Regent's Park, NW1 4SA. *Club:* Reform.

MARSH, Matthew William Brooker; Master of the High Court, Chancery Division, since 2012; Chief Chancery Master, since 2014; *b* London, 6 June 1953; *s* of Frederick and Elizabeth Marsh; *m* 1981, Andrea Stratford Collins; two *d. Educ:* Sevenoaks Sch.; Kingston Univ. (BA Hons Law). FCIArb 1990. With Sharpe Pritchard, 1975–77; admitted as solicitor, 1977; Stoneham Langton & Passmore, 1977–85; Collyer Bristow, 1985–2012. A Recorder, 2002–12. *Publications:* (ed) Landlord and Tenant Factbook, 2005–11. *Recreations:* tennis, opera, cycling, theatre. *Address:* Royal Courts of Justice, 7 Rolls Building, Fetter Lane, EC4A 1NL. *Clubs:* Clapham Common All Weather Tennis; Waterfront (Bexhill).

MARSH, Paul Henry; Consultant, Downs Solicitors LLP, Dorking, since 2007; President, Law Society of England and Wales, 2008–09 (Vice President, 2007–08); *b* 6 Sept. 1947; *s* of Cyril Samuel Marsh and Ellen Victoria Marsh; *m* 1972, Sheila Slater; one *s* two *d. Educ:* Raynes Park Grammar Sch.; Coventry Univ. (BA Business Law). Partner, Bells Solicitors, Kingston upon Thames, 1976–2007. Law Society: Mem. Council, 1987–2011; Chm., Solicitors Indemnity Fund, 2003–06. Mem. Bd, Solicitors Regulation Authy, 2013–. Chm. of Govs, Kingston Grammar Sch., 2011–. Hon. LLD Kingston, 2008. *Recreations:* gardening, vintage cars, the family. *Address:* Dewlish House, Chinthurst Lane, Shalford, Guildford GU4 8JR. *E:* phmarsh@btinternet.com. *Clubs:* Bentley Drivers, Vintage Sports Car.

MARSH, Prof. Paul Rodney; Professor of Finance, London Business School, 1985–2006, now Emeritus (Professor of Management and Finance, 1985–98, Esmée Fairbairn Professor of Finance, 1998–2002); *b* 19 Aug. 1947; *s* of Harold Marsh and Constance (*née* Miller); *m* 1971, Stephanie (*née* Simonow). *Educ:* Poole Grammar Sch.; London School of Economics (BScEcon, 1st Cl. Hons); London Business Sch. (PhD). Systems Analyst, Esso Petroleum, 1968–69; Scicon, 1970–71; London Business School, 1974–: Bank of England Res. Fellow, 1974–85; Dir, Sloan Fellowship Prog., 1980–83; non-exec. Dir, Centre for Management Develt, 1984–90; Mem. Gov. Body, 1986–90; Faculty Dean, 1987–90; Dep. Principal, 1989–90; Associate Dean, Finance Progs, 1993–2006. Member: CBI Task Force on City-Industry Relationships, 1986–88; Exec. Cttee, British Acad. of Management, 1986–88. Non-executive Director: M&G Investment Management Ltd, 1989–97; M&G Gp, 1998–99; Majedie Investments, 1999–2006; Aberforth Smaller Cos Trust, 2004–14 (Chm., 2010–14); Dir, Hoare Govett Indices Ltd, 1991–2011. Gov. Examng Bd, Securities Inst., 1994–2002. *Publications:* Cases in Corporate Finance, 1988; Managing Strategic Investment Decisions, 1988; Accounting for Brands, 1989; Short-termism on Trial, 1990; The Millennium Book: a century of investment returns, 2000; Triumph of the Optimists, 2002; Numis (formerly HGSC) Smaller Companies Index, annually 1987–; (with E. Dimson) Global Investment Returns Yearbook, annually 2000–; numerous articles in Jl of Financial Econs, Jl of Finance, Jl of Business, Harvard Business Review, Jl of Inst. of Actuaries, Res. in Marketing, Mergers and Acquisitions, Financial Analysts Jl, Jl of Apples Corporate Finance, Long Range Planning, etc. *Recreations:* gardening, investment. *Address:* London Business School, Regent's Park, NW1 4SA. *T:* (020) 7000 7000. *E:* pmarsh@london.edu.

MARSH, Peter Ronald; Deputy Principal, Fareham College, since 2012; *b* Basingstoke, 27 Nov. 1969; *s* of Derek and Christine Marsh; civil partnership 2008, Robert Rees. *Educ:* Univ. of Newcastle upon Tyne (BA Hons Econ. and Geog. 1992); New Coll., Durham. CPFA 1996. Auditor, Dist Audit Durham and NE, 1992–96; Audit Manager, KPMG, 1996–97; Deputy Principal: Gateshead Coll., 1997–99; City & Islington Coll., 2000–05; Dir of Resources, 2005–07, Dep. Chief Exec., 2007–08, Housing Corp.; Chief Exec., Tenant Services Authy, 2008–10. Trustee, Open Coll. Network London, 2001–11 (Chm., 2005–11). Trainee teacher, South Coast School-centred Initial Teacher Trng prog., 2011–12. FRSA 2008. *Recreations:* family, sailing, garden. *Address:* Bramble Cottage, 41 East Stratton, Winchester SO21 3DT. *T:* 07771 521699. *E:* peter.marsh@fareham.ac.uk.

MARSH, Richard St John Jeremy, PhD; Chief Executive, Institute for Food, Brain and Behaviour, since 2010; *b* 23 April 1960; *s* of late Gordon Victor Marsh; *m* 1984, Elizabeth Mary Mullins (marr. diss. 2006); one *s* one *d. Educ:* Trinity Sch. of John Whitgift; Keble Coll., Oxford (BA 1982; MA 1986); Coll. of the Resurrection, Mirfield; Durham Univ. (PhD 1991). Deacon 1985, priest 1986; Curate, Grange St Andrew, Runcorn, 1985–87; Chaplain and Solway Fellow, UC, Durham, 1987–92; Asst Sec. for Ecum. Affairs to Abp of Canterbury, 1992–95, Sec., 1995–2001; Canon Residentiary and Dir, Internat. Study Centre, subseq. Canon Librarian and Dir of Educn, Canterbury Cathedral, 2001–05; Dir, Improving Accountability, Clarity and Transparency (ImpACT) Coalition, 2007–09. Licensed to officiate, Dio. London, 1993–2001; Canon, Dio. Gibraltar in Europe, 1995–2001; Non-Res. Canon, Canterbury Cathedral, 1998–2001. Interim Dir, Intelligent Giving, 2009. Vis. Sen. Lectr, Canterbury Christchurch UC, 2003–. Chm., St Augustine's Foundn, 2003. Trustee, Rye Arts Fest., 2015–. *Publications:* Black Angels, 1998; (contrib.) Ink and Spirit, 2000; (with Katherine Marshall) Millennium Challenges for Development and Faith Institutions, 2003; (ed) Prayers from the East, 2004. *Recreations:* music, cooking. *Address:* 6 Barrack Square, Winchelsea, E Sussex TN36 4EG. *T:* (01797) 225912, 07903 358918. *E:* richard@richardmarsh.org.

MARSH, Roger, OBE 2015; Senior Partner, Leeds Office, and Northern Leader, Government and Public Sector, PricewaterhouseCoopers, 2011–13; *b* 19 Sept. 1953; *s* of late Peter Marsh and of Connie Marsh; *m* 1st, 1981, Susan Smith (marr. diss. 2002); three *d*; 2nd, 2010, Sally Thomson; two *d*. *Educ:* Stockton C of E Grammar Sch.; Univ. of Leeds (BSc Hons Metallurgy 1976). FCA 1990. Price Waterhouse, subseq. PricewaterhouseCoopers: joined, 1976; Partner, 1988; latterly Sen. Business Recovery Partner, Leeds; on secondment as Dir-Gen., Strategic Finance and Ops, Cabinet Office, 2007–09 (Mem. Bd; Chm., Finance Cttee, 2008–09); Sen. Adv. Partner, Govt and Public Sector, 2009–11. Member: Insolvency Licensing Cttee, 1997–2004, Public Sector Adv. Bd, 2009–13, ICAEW; UK Firms Supervisory Bd, 2010–12; HS2 Growth Task Force, 2013–; W Yorks Combined Authy, 2014–. Non-exec. Chm., Leeds City Region Local Enterprise Partnership, 2013–. Mem. Council, Leeds Univ., 2013–. Trustee, Iraq/Afghanistan Meml Project, 2015–. *Recreations:* family, fine wines, fast cars. *Address:* 5 Wedgewood Grove, Roundhay, Leeds LS8 1EG. *E:* r.marsh1953@btinternet.com. *Club:* Reform.

MARSH, Susanna; *see* Nicklin, S.

MARSHALL, Alan Ralph; Managing Director, ARM Educational Consultants Ltd, 1991–94; *b* 27 July 1931; *s* of Ralph Marshall and Mabel Mills; *m* 1958, Caterina Gattico; one *s* one *d*. *Educ:* Shoreditch College (Teacher's Cert. 1953); London Univ. (Dip Ed 1959; MPhil 1965); Eastern Washington State Univ. (MEd 1964); Stanford Univ. (MA 1969). Teacher, schools in UK and USA, 1954–62; Lectr, Shoreditch Coll., 1962–68; Vis. Prof., Eastern Washington State Univ., 1964–65; Field Dir, Project Technology, Schools Council, 1970–72; Editor, Nat. Centre for School Technology, 1972–73; Course Team Chm., Open Univ., 1973–76; HM Inspector, DES, 1976–91, HM Chief Inspector of Schools, 1985–91. Hon. DEd CNAA, 1990. *Publications:* (ed) School Technology in Action, 1974; (with G. T. Page and J. B. Thomas) International Dictionary of Education, 1977; Giving Substance to a Vision, 1990; articles in jls. *Recreations:* painting, reading.

MARSHALL, Alexander John, QPM 2009; Chief Executive, College of Policing, since 2013; *b* Barnet, 7 Dec. 1961; *s* of Clifford and Patricia Marshall; partner, Katherine Pears; two *s* one *d*. *Educ:* Wolfson Coll. and Inst. of Criminol., Univ. of Cambridge (MA Criminol. 2006). Constable to Chief Inspector, Metropolitan Police, 1980–2000; Superintendent to Chief Superintendent, Cambridge Constabulary, 2000–04; Asst Chief Constable, 2004–07, Dep. Chief Constable, 2007–08, Thames Valley Police; Chief Constable, Hants Constabulary, 2008–13. Cropwood Fellow, Univ. of Cambridge, 1999. *Recreations:* old cars, cricket, exercise. *Address:* College of Policing, 10th Floor, Riverside House, 2A Southwark Bridge Road, SE1 9HA.

MARSHALL, Prof. Sir (Arthur) Harold, KNZM 2009 (DCNZM 2008); PhD; FRSNZ 1995; Group Consultant, Marshall Day Acoustics Ltd, since 1991; principal acoustical designer for concert halls; *b* Auckland, NZ, 15 Sept. 1931; *s* of Arthur Cecil Marshall and Flossie May Marshall; *m* 1956, Shirley Anne Lindsey; four *s*. *Educ:* King's Coll., Auckland; Auckland Univ. (BArch Hons; BSc Physics and Maths 1956); Inst. of Sound and Vibration Res., Southampton Univ. (PhD 1967). FNZIA 1973; FRAIA 1973. Sen. Lectr in Architecture, Univ. of Auckland, 1961–67; Sen. Lectr in Building Sci., 1967–70, Associate Prof. in Architecture, 1970–72, Univ. of WA; University of Auckland: Prof. of Architecture, 1973–86; Head, Acoustics Res. Centre, 1983–97; Prof. (Personal Chair), 1986–97. Co-Founder, Marshall Day Associates (Acoustics), 1980; professional work includes: Christchurch Town Hall, NZ, 1972; Michael Fowler Centre, NZ, 1983; Segerstrom Hall, Calif, 1986; Hong Kong Cultural Centre, 1989; Guangzhou Opera House, 2011; La Philharmonie de Paris, 2015. Fellow: Acoustical Soc. of America, 1978; NZ Acoustical Soc., 2013. Sabine Medal, Acoustical Soc. of America, 1994; Pickering Medal, RSNZ, 2013. *Publications:* (contrib.) Encyclopedia of Acoustics, 1997; (contrib.) Encyclopedia of Building Technology, 1988; contribs to Jl Sound and Vibration, Applied Acoustics, Jl Acoustical Soc. America, AA Jl, Acustica, Jl Audio Engrg Soc., Architecture NZ, Arch. Sci. Rev.; contribs to Landfall, Sport (poetry jls). *Recreations:* fly fishing/sea fishing, poetry. *E:* harold.marshall@marshallday.co.nz.

MARSHALL, Arthur Stirling-Maxwell, CBE 1986 (OBE 1979); HM Diplomatic Service, retired; *b* 29 Jan. 1929; *s* of Victor Stirling-Maxwell Marshall and Jeannie Theodora Hunter; *m* 1st, 1955, Eleni Kapralou, Athens (*d* 1969); one *s* two *d*; 2nd, 1985, Cheryl Mary Hookens, Madras; one *d*. *Educ:* Daniel Stewart's Coll., Edinburgh. Served Royal Navy, 1947–59. Foreign Office, 1959; Middle East Centre for Arab Studies, Lebanon, 1959–61; Political Officer, British Political Agency, Bahrain and Registrar of HBM Court for Bahrain, 1961–64; Attaché, Athens, 1964–67; Information Officer, Rabat, Morocco, 1967–69; Commercial Secretary: Nicosia, Cyprus, 1970–75; Kuwait, 1975–79; Deputy High Commissioner, Madras, 1980–83; Counsellor, Kuwait, 1983–85; Ambassador to People's Democratic Republic of Yemen, 1986–89. *Recreations:* music, nature. *Address:* 2 The Larches, Rickmansworth Road, Northwood, Middx HA6 2QY.

MARSHALL, Prof. Barry James, AC 2007; FRS 1999; FRACP; Hon. Clinical Professor of Microbiology, University of Western Australia, since 2000; Director and Chief Executive Officer, Ondek Pty Ltd, since 2005; *b* 30 Sept. 1951; *s* of Robert and Marjorie Marshall; *m* 1972, Adrienne Joyce Feldman; one *s* three *d*. *Educ:* Univ. of Western Australia (MB BS). FRACP 1983. Clinical asst (res.), Gastroenterology Dept, Royal Perth Hosp., 1985–86; University of Virginia: Res. Fellow in Medicine, Div. of Gastroenterology, 1986–87; Asst Prof. of Medicine, 1988–92, Associate Prof., 1992, Prof., 1993; Clinical Prof., 1993–96; Prof. of Res. in Internal Medicine, 1996–2000; Clinical Prof. of Medicine, 1997–2000, NH&MRC Burnet Fellow and Clinical Prof. of Medicine, 1998–2000, Univ. of WA. Hon. Res. Fellow in Gastroenterology, Sir Charles Gairdner Hosp., 1997. (Jtly) Warren Alpert Prize, Harvard Med. Sch., 1995; Albert Lasker Award, NYC, 1995; (jtly) Paul Ehrlich Prize, Frankfurt, 1997; Kilby Prize, Dallas, 1997; Dr A. H. Heineken Prize for Medicine, Amsterdam, 1998; Florey Medal, Aust. Inst. for Pol Sci., Canberra, 1998; Buchanan Medal, Royal Soc., 1998; Benjamin Franklin Medal for Life Sci., Philadelphia, 1999; Prince Mahidol Award, 2001; (jtly) Nobel Prize in Physiology or Medicine, 2005. *Publications:* Campylobacter pylori, 1988; Helicobacter pylori in peptic ulceration and gastritis, 1991; Helicobacter Pylori, 1990 (Proc. 2nd Internat. Symposium), 1991; Gastroenterology Clinics of North America, 2000; contribs to jls incl. The Lancet, Amer. Jl Gastroenterol., Jl Infectious Diseases, Jl Nuclear Medicine, Jl Clinical Pathol., Digestive Diseases and Scis, Gastroenterol., Scandinavian Jl Gastroenterol., Jl Clinical Microbiol., Alimentary Pharmacol. and Therapeutics. *Recreations:* computers, photography, electronics. *Address:* Helicobacter Pylori Research Laboratory, Department of Microbiology, University of Western Australia, QE2 Medical Centre, Nedlands, WA 6009, Australia. *T:* (8) 93464815.

MARSHALL, Catriona Frances; Chief Executive Officer, Hobbycraft, since 2011; *b* Glasgow, 1 March 1967; *d* of Dr David Land and Moira McLean (*née* O'Neill); *m* 2003, Michael Edwin Marshall. *Educ:* Shawlands Acad., Glasgow; Univ. of Dundee (LLB Law). Mktg Manager, Mars Confectionery, 1993–95; Own Brand Dir for UK and Germany, Asda Stores, 1995–2003; Trading and Mktg Dir, Pets at Home, 2003–11. *Recreations:* club runner (Wilmslow Running Club), cycling, support for disadvantaged, founder of Transforming Lives charitable foundation. *Address:* Hobbycraft, 7 Enterprise Way, Aviation Park, Bournemouth Airport, Christchurch, Dorset BH23 6HG. *T:* (01202) 596100. *E:* catriona.marshall@hobbycraft.co.uk.

MARSHALL, Hon. (Cedric) Russell, CNZM 2001; President, New Zealand Institute of International Affairs, 2007–11; High Commissioner for New Zealand in the United Kingdom, also accredited to Nigeria, and as Ambassador of New Zealand to Ireland, 2002–05; *b* 15 Feb. 1936; *s* of Cedric Thomas Marshall and Gladys Margaret Marshall (*née* Hopley); *m* 1961, Barbara May Watson; two *s* one *d* (and one *s* one *d* decd). *Educ:* Nelson Coll.; Christchurch Teachers' Coll.; Auckland Univ. (DipTeaching, 1966); BA Victoria Univ., 1992. Primary teacher, Nelson, 1955–56; Trinity Methodist Theol Coll., 1958–60; Methodist Minister: Christchurch, Spreydon, 1960–66; Masterton, 1967–71; teacher, Wanganui High Sch., 1972. MP (Lab) Wanganui, 1972–90; Opposition education spokesman, 1976–84; Sen. Opposition Whip, 1978–79; Minister of Education, 1984–87, for the Environment, 1984–86, of Conservation, 1986–87, of Disarmament and Arms Control, 1987–89, of Foreign Affairs, 1987–90, for Pacific Island Affairs, 1988–90. Chairman: Commonwealth Observer Mission to Seychelles election, 1993; Commonwealth Observer Mission to South Africa, 1994; Mem., Commonwealth Observer Mission to Lesotho elections, 1993. Chairman: NZ Commn for UNESCO, 1990–99; Polytechnics Internat. New Zealand, 1994–2001; Education New Zealand, 1998–2002; Tertiary Educn Adv. Commn, 2000–02; Tertiary Educn Commn, NZ, 2005–07; Gbool, 2012–; Member: UNESCO Exec. Bd, 1995–99 (Chm., Finance and Admin Commn, 1997–99); Public Adv. Cttee for Disarmament and Arms Control, 1997–2000; Growth and Innovation Adv. Bd, 2005–07; Mem. Council, 1994–2001, Pro-Chancellor, 1999, Chancellor, 2000–01, Hunter Fellow, 2009, Victoria Univ. of Wellington. Mem., 1979–81, Chm., 1981–83, Internat. Affairs Cttee, Christian Conf. of Asia. Chairman: Cambodia Trust (Aotearoa-NZ), 1994–2001; Cambodia Trust (UK), 2002–05 (Trustee, 2000–05); Robson Hanan Trust (Rethinking Crime and Punishment), 2010–11; Gbool Ltd, 2011–; Trustee: Africa Information Centre, 1978–95 (Chm., 1991–95); Mana Educn Centre, 2012–14. Hon. PhD Khon Kaen Univ., 1989. *Recreations:* reading, listening to music, genealogy. *Address:* 5 Whitianga View, Paremata, Porirua 5024, New Zealand. *T:* (4) 2336608, 02115 43753.

MARSHALL, David; former transport worker; *b* 7 May 1941; *m*; two *s* one *d*. *Educ:* Larbert, Denny and Falkirk High Schs; Woodside Sen. Secondary Sch., Glasgow. Joined Labour Party, 1962; former Lab. Party Organiser for Glasgow; Mem., TGWU, 1960–. MP (Lab): Glasgow, Shettleston, 1979–2005; Glasgow East, 2005–June 2008. Chairman, Select Committee: Transport, 1987–92 (Mem., 1985–92); Scottish Affairs, 1997–2001 (Mem., 1981–83, 1994–97); Mem., Chairmen's Panel, 2005–08. Former Chairman: All Party ANZAC Gp; British Canadian Gp; S Pacific Gp; Aviation Gp; Gardening and Horticulture Gp. Hon. Sec. and Hon. Treas., Scottish Gp of Labour MPs, 1981–2001. Private Member's Bill, The Solvent Abuse (Scotland) Act, May 1983. Chairman: British Gp, IPU, 1997–2000; Exec. Cttee, UK Br., CPA, 2003–08. Mem., UK Delegn to Council of Europe and WEU, 2001–08. Member: Glasgow Corp., 1972–75; Strathclyde Reg. Council, 1974–79 (Chm., Manpower Cttee); formerly: Chm., Manpower Cttee, Convention of Scottish Local Authorities; Mem., Local Authorities Conditions of Service Adv. Bd. *Recreations:* gardening, music.

MARSHALL, David Arthur Ambler, CBE 2003; CEng; FRAeS; Director General, Society of British Aerospace Companies, 1997–2003; *b* 4 April 1943; *s* of Henry R. Marshall and Joan E. Marshall; *m* 1968, Karen Elizabeth Marker; two *d*. *Educ:* Brighton Coll.; Churchill Coll., Cambridge (MA). FRAeS 1994; CEng 2005. Joined Rolls Royce Ltd as Apprentice, 1961; Develt Engr, 1970–73; Co. Rep., Airbus, 1973–75; Manager, Eur. Sales, 1975–78; Commercial Manager, 1978–83; Head of Business Planning, 1983–87; Gen. Manager, Mktg, 1987–89; Dir, Business Planning, 1989–90; Commercial Dir, 1990–93; Dir, Business Develt, 1993–96. President: RAeS, 2007–08; Council of Eur. Aerospace Socs, 2013. Mem., L'Academie de l'air et l'espace, 2011. FRSA 1998. Freeman, City of London, 1999. *Recreations:* garden railways, music. *Address:* 8 North Avenue, Ashbourne, Derbys DE6 1EZ. *T:* (01335) 348019.

MARSHALL, Hon. Denis William Anson, QSO 2000; established Hawkshead Vineyard Partnership, Central Otago, 2005; Secretary-General, Commonwealth Parliamentary Association, 2002–06; *b* 23 Sept. 1943; *s* of Lionel Henry Swainson Marshall and Mabel Alice Okeover Marshall; *m* 1965, Annette Kilmister (separated); one *s* two *d*; partner, Ulrike Kurenbach. *Educ:* Christ's Coll., Christchurch, NZ. Nuffield Farming Schol., 1983. MP (Nat. Party) Rangitikei, NZ, 1984–99; Minister: of Conservation, 1990–96; of Sci., 1990–93; of Lands, 1993–96; of Survey and Land Inf., 1993–96; Associate Minister: of Agric., 1990–96; of Employment, 1990–96. Chairman: NZ Rural Communities Trust, 2000–01; NZ Nat. Parks and Conservation Foundn, 2000–02. *Recreations:* hiking, boating, gardening, reading.

MARSHALL, Dr Edmund Ian; Lecturer in Management Science, University of Bradford, 1984–2000; *b* 31 May 1940; *s* of Harry and Koorali Marshall; *m* 1969, Margaret Pamela, *d* of John and Maud Antill, New Southgate, N11; one *d*. *Educ:* Magdalen Coll., Oxford (Mackinnon Schol.; Double 1st cl. hons Maths, and Junior Mathematical Prize, 1961); PhD Liverpool, 1965. Various univ. appts in Pure Maths, 1962–66; mathematician in industry, 1967–71. Mem., Wallasey County Borough Council, 1963–65. Contested (L) Louth Div. of Lincs, 1964 and 1966; joined Labour Party, 1967. MP (Lab) Goole, May 1971–1983; PPS to Sec. of State for NI, 1974–76, to Home Sec., 1976–79; Chm., Trade and Industry sub-cttee of House of Commons Expenditure Cttee, 1976–79; Mem., Chairmen's Panel in House of Commons, 1981–82; Opposition Whip, 1982–83; joined SDP, 1985. Contested (SDP/Alliance) Bridlington, 1987. Chair: Wakefield and Dist Lib Dems, 2005; Herts Co-ordinating Cttee, Lib Dems, 2009–10; Sec., Harpenden Lib Dems, 2008–11. Non-exec. Dir, Wakefield FHSA, 1990–96; Dir, Wakefield Healthcare Commn, 1994–96. Member: British Methodist Conf., 1969–72, 1980, 1985–97 and 2011–12 (Vice-Pres., 1992); World Methodist Conf., 1971; British Council of Churches, 1972–78; Sec., Associate (formerly All-Party) Parly Gp related to Council of Church Colls, 1994–2001; Bishop of Wakefield's Advr for Ecumenical Affairs, 1998–2007. Methodist Local Preacher, 1959–; Reader in C of E, 1994–. Mem., Gen. Synod of C of E, 2000–15. Governor: Woodhouse Grove Sch., Bradford, 1986–94; Wakefield Grammar School Foundn, 1989–97. *Publications:* (jtly) Europe: What Next? (Fabian pamphlet), 1969; Parliament and the Public, 1982; Business and Society, 1993; (jtly) The Times Book of Best Sermons, 1995; various papers in mathematical and other jls. *Recreations:* word games, music, theatre. *Address:* 37 Roundwood Lane, Harpenden, Herts AL5 3BP. *Clubs:* Royal Over-Seas League (Vice-Chm., 2010–12, Chm., 2012–, London Gp); Middlesex CC.

MARSHALL, Dr Frank Graham, FIET; Group Research and Development Director, Colt Group Ltd, 1990–98; technology consultant, 1998–2004; *b* 28 March 1942; *s* of Frank and Vera Marshall; *m* 1965, Patricia Anne (*née* Bestwick); two *s* one *d*. *Educ:* Birmingham Univ. (BSc Physics); Nottingham Univ. (PhD Physics). FIET (FIEE 1984). Joined Royal Signals and Radar Estabt (MoD) (Physics and Electronic Device Res.), 1966; Sen. Principal Scientific Officer, 1975–80; seconded to HM Diplomatic Service as Science and Technology Counsellor, Tokyo, 1980–82. Man. Dir, Plessey Electronic Systems Res., later Plessey Res.

Roke Manor, 1983–87; Technical Dir, Plessey Naval Systems, 1987–90. (Jtly) IEEE Best Paper award, 1973; (jtly) Wolfe Award, 1973. *Publications:* numerous papers on electronic signal processing devices in various jls. *Recreations:* country life, electronics.

MARSHALL, Very Rev. Geoffrey Osborne; Dean of Brecon and Warden of Readers, 2008–14; *b* Rossett, Denbighshire, 5 Jan. 1948; *s* of Dr Harry Marshall and Joan Marshall (*née* Harris); *m* 1972, Hazel Caunce; one *s* two *d*. *Educ:* Repton Sch.; St John's Coll., Univ. of Durham (BA); Coll. of the Resurrection, Mirfield. Ordained deacon, 1973, priest, 1974; Vicar: Christ Church, Belper, 1978–86; Spondon, Derby, 1986–93; Rural Dean, Derby N, 1990–95; Sub-Dean, Derby Cathedral, 1993–2002; Rector, Wrexham, 2002–08; Area Dean, Wrexham, 2002–08. Trustee, Shelter Cymru, 2002–11. Chaplain, Derby High Sch., 1987–2001. *Recreations:* leading pilgrimages to the Middle East, archaeology, walking, cycling, birdwatching. *Address:* 36 Saundersfoot Way, Oakwood, Derby DE21 2RH. *T:* (01332) 280452. *E:* brecondeanery@btinternet.com.

MARSHALL, Prof. Gordon, CBE 2003; DPhil; FBA 2000; FAcSS; Director, Leverhulme Trust, since 2011; *b* 20 June 1952; *s* of Robert Marshall and Ina Marshall; one *s*; partner, Marion Headicar. *Educ:* Falkirk High Sch.; Univ. of Stirling (BA 1st Cl. Hons Sociol. 1974); Nuffield Coll., Oxford (DPhil 1978). Postdoctoral Res. Fellow, Nuffield Coll., Oxford, 1977–78; Lectr and Sen. Lectr, Dept of Sociol., Univ. of Essex, 1978–90; Prof. of Sociol., Univ. of Bath, 1990–93; Official Fellow in Sociol., Nuffield Coll., Oxford, 1993–99; Chief Exec. and Dep. Chm., ESRC, 2000–02; Vice-Chancellor, Univ. of Reading, 2003–11. Chm., Higher Educn Statistics Agency, 2007–11. British Acad./Leverhulme Trust Sen. Res. Fellow, 1992–93. FAcSS (AcSS 2000); Fellow, Royal Norwegian Soc. of Scis and Letters, 2001. DUniv Stirling, 2001; Hon. DLaws Reading, 2012. *Publications:* Presbyteries and Profits, 1980; In Search of the Spirit of Capitalism, 1982; (jtly) Social Class in Modern Britain, 1987; In Praise of Sociology, 1990; (jtly) Oxford Dictionary of Sociology, 1994, 3rd edn 2005; (jtly) Against the Odds?, 1997; (jtly) Repositioning Class, 1997; contrib. numerous articles to jls and symposia. *Recreation:* in my dreams. *Address:* Leverhulme Trust, 1 Pemberton Row, EC4A 3BG. *T:* (020) 7042 9877. *E:* gmarshall@leverhulme.ac.uk.

MARSHALL, Sir Harold; *see* Marshall, Sir Arthur H.

MARSHALL, Her Honour Hazel Eleanor; QC 1988; a Senior Circuit Judge, 2006–13; a Deputy High Court Judge, 1994–2013; *b* 14 Jan. 1947; *d* of late Geoffrey Briddon and Nancy Briddon; *m* 1st, 1969, Robert Hector Williamson (marr. diss. 1980); 2nd, 1983, Harvey Christopher John Marshall; one step *s*. *Educ:* Wimbledon High Sch.; St Hilda's Coll., Oxford (MA Jurisprudence). FCIArb 1992. Atkin Scholar, Gray's Inn. Called to the Bar, Gray's Inn, 1972, Bencher, 1996; Asst Recorder, 1993–96; a Recorder, 1996–2006. Acting Deemster, IOM, 1999–2006. Judicial Mem., Public Guardian Bd, 2007–. Chm., Chancery Bar Assoc., 1994–97. Mem., DfT (formerly DoE, subseq. DETR, then DTLR) Property Adv. Gp, 1994–2003. Hon. Mem., ESU. *Publications:* (with Harvey Marshall) Law and Valuation of Leisure Property, 1994. *Recreations:* gardening, opera, occasional off-shore sailing. *Club:* Royal Over-Seas League (Hon. Mem.).

MARSHALL, Howard; *see* Marshall, I. H.

MARSHALL, Rev. Canon Hugh Phillips; Vicar of Wendover, 1996–2001; *b* 13 July 1934; *s* of Dr Leslie Phillips Marshall and Dr (Catherine) Mary Marshall; *m* 1962, Diana Elizabeth Gosling; one *s* three *d*. *Educ:* Marlborough Coll.; Sidney Sussex Coll., Cambridge (BA, MA); Bishop's Hostel, Lincoln. RN, 1952–54. Ordained deacon 1959, priest 1960, Dio. London; Curate, St Stephen with St John, Westminster, 1959–65; Vicar of St Paul, Tupsley, Hereford, 1965–74; Vicar and Team Rector of Wimbledon, 1974–87; Rural Dean of Merton, 1979–85; Vicar of Mitcham, Surrey, 1987–90; Chief Sec., ABM, 1990–96. Hon. Canon, Southwark Cathedral, 1989, Hon. Canon Emeritus, 1990; Canon, St John's Cathedral, Bulawayo, 1996–. Commissary to Bishop of Matabeleland, 1989–2013. Mem., SE Reg. Awards Cttee, Nat. Lottery Charities Bd, 1998–2002. Chm., Betty Rhodes Fund, 1996–2007 (Mem., 1989–2007). Foundn Gov., Deddington Vol. Aided Sch., 2002–. Hon. Sec., Oxford Diocesan Bd of Patronage, 2001–08. *Recreations:* DIY, cooking, gardening, writing, travel. *Address:* 7 The Daedings, Deddington, Banbury, Oxon OX15 0RT. *T:* (01869) 337761.

MARSHALL, Prof. (Ian) Howard, PhD; Professor of New Testament Exegesis, University of Aberdeen, 1979–99, now Professor Emeritus; *b* 12 Jan. 1934; *s* of Ernest Ewart Marshall and Ethel Marshall (*née* Curran); *m* 1st, 1961, Joyce Elizabeth Proudfoot (*d* 1996); one *s* three *d*; 2nd, 2011, Maureen Wing Sheung Yeung. *Educ:* Univ. of Aberdeen (MA 1955; BD 1959; PhD 1963); Fitzwilliam Coll., Cambridge (BA 1959); Univ. of Göttingen. Asst Tutor, Didsbury Coll., Bristol, 1960–62; pastoral work, Darlington, 1962–64; University of Aberdeen: Lectr, 1964–70; Sen. Lectr, 1970–77; Reader, 1977–79. Hon. DD Asbury, Kentucky, 1996. *Publications:* Eschatology and the Parables, 1963, 2nd edn 1978; Pocket Guide to Christian Beliefs, 1963, 3rd edn 1978, repr. 1989; The Work of Christ, 1969, 2nd edn 1994; Kept by the Power of God, 1969, 3rd edn 1995; Luke: historian and theologian, 1970, 3rd edn 1989; The Origins of New Testament Christology, 1976; (ed) New Testament Interpretation, 1977, 2nd edn 1979; I Believe in the Historical Jesus, 1977; The Gospel of Luke, 1978; The Epistles of John, 1978; Acts, 1980; Last Supper and Lord's Supper, 1980; Biblical Inspiration, 1982, 2nd edn 1995; 1 and 2 Thessalonians, 1983; (ed) Christian Experience in Theology and Life, 1988; Jesus the Saviour: studies in New Testament theology, 1990; 1 Peter, 1991; The Acts of the Apostles, 1992; The Epistle to the Philippians, 1992; (with K. P. Donfried) The Theology of the Shorter Pauline Letters, 1993; (ed with D. Peterson) Witness to the Gospel: the theology of the Book of Acts, 1998; (with P. H. Towner) A Critical and Exegetical Commentary on the Pastoral Epistles, 1999; (contrib.) Exploring the New Testament: Vol. 2: The Letters and Revelation, 2002; (ed) Moulton and Geden: Concordance to the Greek New Testament, 6th edn 2002; New Testament Theology: many witnesses, one Gospel, 2004; (jtly) Beyond the Bible: moving from scripture to theology, 2004; Aspects of the Atonement, 2007; A Concise New Testament Theology, 2008. *Recreations:* hill walking, gardening, music, reading.

MARSHALL, Jeremy Samuel John; Chief Executive, C. Hoare & Co., since 2009; *b* Hemel Hempstead, Herts, 8 May 1963; *s* of John E. Marshall and Susan E. Marshall (*née* Westcott); *m* 1987, Jeanette Bonsels; two *s* one *d*. *Educ:* Hemel Hempstead Sch.; St John's Coll., Cambridge (BA 1984; MA 1987); INSEAD (MBA 1992). Barclays Bank, 1984–86; Bank of Montreal, 1986–88; Crédit Suisse, 1988–2009: Strategic Planning Internat., Zurich, 1993–95; Hd, Planning and Support, Zurich, 1996–97; Hd, New Business Mgt Support, USA, 1997–2002; CEO, UK Private Banking, 2002–08. Non-exec. Dir, Waterlogic plc, 2011–15. Mem. Bd, BBA, 2014–. Chairman: Pastor Training Internat., 2011–; Christian Books Worldwide, 2011–; Christianity Explored, 2013– (Trustee, 2009–13); Trustee: London Theol Seminary, 2003–; Woodland Trust, 2008–; Allied Schs Trust, 2011–. *Recreations:* cricket, reading, golf. *Address:* C. Hoare & Co., 37 Fleet Street, EC4P 4DQ. *T:* (020) 7353 4522. *E:* jeremy.marshall@hoaresbank.co.uk.

MARSHALL, Prof. John, MBE 2013; PhD; FRCPath, FMedSci, FRSB; Frost Professor of Ophthalmology, Institute of Ophthalmology, University College London, since 2011; *b* 21 Dec. 1943; *s* of Henry Thomas George Marshall and Ellen Emily Martha Marshall; *m* 1972, Judith Anne Meadows. *Educ:* Inst. of Ophthalmology, Univ. of London (BSc; PhD 1968). FRCPath 2007; FRSB (FIBiol 2009). Institute of Ophthalmology: Lectr in Anatomy, 1968–73; Sen. Lectr in Visual Sci., 1973–80; Reader in Exptl Pathology, 1981–83; Sembal Prof. of Exptl Ophthalmology, 1983–91; Frost Prof. of Ophthalmology and Chm., Dept of Ophthalmology, United Med. and Dental Schs of Guy's and St Thomas' Hosps, then Guy's, King's and St Thomas' Sch. of Medicine, KCL, later KCL Sch. of Medicine, 1991–2009, now Emeritus; Hon. Consultant in Ophthalmology: St Thomas' Hosp., 1992–2009; Moorfield's Eye Hosp., 2012–. Hon. Dist. Prof., Sch. of Optometry and Visual Sci., Univ. of Cardiff, 2008–; Hon. Professor: UCL, 2009–11; Caledonian Univ., 2011–; Hon. Vis. Prof., City Univ., 2011–. Ed., numerous scientific jls, 1985–. Advr on lasers to WHO, 1974–80, to Internat. Red Cross, 1989–95. Director: DIOMED, 1991–97; Ellex R&D, 2007–11; Ellex Medical Ltd, 2007–11; Laser Inst. of America, 2004–08. Trustee: Brit. Retinitis Pigmentosa Soc., 1978–; Devereux House, 1999–; Co. of Spectacle Makers' Charity, 2004–09; Frost Charitable Trust, 2007–. Ambassador, Fight for Sight, 2008–. Gov., Moorfields Eye Hosp., 1988–90. Mem., Ct of Assts, Spectacle Makers' Co., 2001– (Master, 2011–12). Numerous patents on applications of lasers to eye surgery, 1968–. Fellow: Academia Ophthalmologica Europaea, 2004; Assoc. for Res. in Vision and Ophthalmology, 2009; FMedSci 2009. FRSA 1989. Hon. Fellow: Coll. of Optometrists, 1997; Univ. of Cardiff, 2005; Hon. FRCOphth, 2005. Hon. DSc Glasgow Caledonian, 2013. Nettleship Medal, 1980, Ashton Medal, 1993, RCOphth; Mackenzie Medal, Tennant Inst. of Ophthalmol., Glasgow, 1985; Raynor Medal, Intraocular Implant Soc., UK, 1988; Ridley Medal, Internat. Soc. for Cataract and Refractive Surg., 1990; Wilkening Award, Laser Inst. of Amer., 1999 (Fellow, 2003); Ida Mann Medal, Oxford, 2000; Lord Crook Gold Medal, Spectacle Makers' Co., 2001; Doyne Medal, Oxford Congress of Ophthalmol., 2001; Barraquer Medal, 2001, Lifetime Achievement Award, 2009, Internat. Soc. of Refractive Surg.; Euretina Award, European Soc. of Retinal Specialists, 2003; Innovator Award, Amer. Soc. Cataract & Refractive Surgeons, 2004; Lim Medal, Singapore Nat. Eye Centre, 2004; Sen. Achievement Award, Amer. Acad. of Ophthalmol., 2005; Junius-Kuhnt Award and Medal for work on age-related macular degeneration, 2012; Moorfields' Stars Award for Nat. and Internat. Services to Ophthalmol., Moorfields Eye Hosp., 2012; Bowman Medal and Lect., Royal Coll. of Ophthalmologists, 2014; Zivojnovic Award, European Vitreoretinal Soc., 2014; Lifetime Achievement Award, UK Ireland Cataract and Refractive Surgery Soc., 2014. *Publications:* Hazards of Light, 1986; Laser Technology in Ophthalmology, 1988; Vision and Visual Systems, 1991; Annual of Ophthalmic Laser Surgery, 1992; numerous papers in scientific jls, concerning effect of lasers, light and aging on ocular tissues. *Recreations:* work!, reading, cars. *Address:* Wildacre, 27 Cedar Road, Farnborough, Hants GU14 7AU. *T:* (01252) 543473. *Clubs:* Athenæum, Royal Automobile.

MARSHALL, John; *see* Marshall, R. J.

MARSHALL, Prof. John Charles, PhD; FRS 2008; Professor, since 1993, and Cecil and Ida Green Professor of Oceanography, since 2010, Department of Earth, Atmospheric and Planetary Sciences, Massachusetts Institute of Technology; *b* Nottingham, 12 Oct. 1954. *Educ:* Imperial Coll. London (BSc 1st Cl. Hons Physics 1976; PhD 1980). Postdoctoral Researcher: Imperial Coll. London, 1981; Oxford Univ., 1982–83; Lectr in Physics, 1984–89, Reader, 1989–91, Imperial College London; Associate Prof., Dept of Earth, Atmospheric and Planetary Scis, MIT, 1991–92. L. F. Richardson Prize, 1986, Adrian Gill Prize, 2005, RMetS; Audrey Buyrn and Alan Phillips Ally of Nature Award, 2010. *Publications:* (with A. Plumb) Atmosphere, Ocean and Climate Dynamics, 2007; contribs to jls incl. Ocean Modelling, Jl Physical Oceanography, Qly Jl RMetS, Nature, Jl Atmospheric Scis, Jl Marine Res., Jl Climate. *Address:* Department of Earth, Atmospheric and Planetary Sciences, Massachusetts Institute of Technology, 77 Massachusetts Avenue, Cambridge, MA 02139–4307, USA.

MARSHALL, John Gibb, (John Sessions); actor, writer; *b* 11 Jan. 1953; *s* of John Marshall and Esmé Richardson. *Educ:* Univ. of Wales (MA). Plays and one-man shows, 1982–85; *television:* Spitting Image, 1986; Porterhouse Blue, 1987; A Day in Summer, 1988; Whose Line is it Anyway?, 1988; Single Voices, 1990; Ackroyd's Dickens, 1990; Jute City, 1991; Life with Eliza, 1992; A Tour of the Western Isles, 1993; Citizen Locke, 1994; The Treasure Seekers, 1996; Tom Jones, 1997; My Night with Reg, 1997; Stella Street (4 series), 1997, 1998, 2000, 2001; In the Red, 1998; The Man, 1999; Gormenghast, 2000; Randall & Hopkirk Deceased, 2000; Murder Rooms, 2001; Well-Schooled in Murder, 2002; Judge John Deed, 2002 and 2005; Midsomer Murders, 2002; The Lost Prince, 2002; Dalziel and Pascoe, 2002; The Key, 2003; George Eliot: a life, 2003; QI, 2003, 2004, 2006; Hawking, 2004; The Legend of the Tamworth Two, 2004; Absolute Power, 2005; The English Harem, 2005; The Moving Finger, 2006; Low Winter Sun, 2006; Jackanory, 2006; The Ronni Ancona Show, 2006; Oliver Twist, 2007; Margaret, 2009; Spies and Lies (NZ), 2009; Mr Selfridge, 2013; Outlander, 2014; Jonathan Strange, 2014; one-man shows: New Year Show, 1988; On the Spot, 1989; Tall Tales, 1991; Likely Stories, 1994; *theatre:* The Life of Napoleon, Albery, 1987; The Common Pursuit, Phoenix, 1988; The American Napoleon, Phoenix, 1989; Die Fledermaus, Royal Opera House, 1990; Travelling Tales, Haymarket, 1991; Tartuffe, Playhouse, 1991; The Soldier's Tale, Barbican, 1993, 2003; My Night with Reg, Royal Court, 1994; Paint, said Fred!, Royal Acad., 1996; Mahler and Me, 2010, Gilbert, 2011, Richmond; Longing, Hampstead Th., 2013; *films:* The Bounty, 1984; Whoops Apocalypse, 1986; Castaway, 1987; Henry V, 1989; Sweet Revenge, 1990; The Pope Must Die, 1991; Princess Caraboo, 1994; In the Bleak Midwinter, 1995; The Scarlet Tunic, 1998; Cousin Bette, 1998; A Midsummer Night's Dream, 1999; One of the Hollywood Ten, 2000; High Heels and Low Life, 2001; Gangs of New York, 2002; A Flight of Fancy, 2002; Stella Street: the movie, 2003; Five Children and It, 2003; The Merchant of Venice, 2004; Rag Tale, 2005; The Good Shepherd, 2006; Intervention, 2007; Inconceivable, 2008; Nativity, 2009; The Last Station, 2010; Made in Dagenham, 2010; The Iron Lady, 2011; The Real American - Joe McCarthy, 2011; Filth, 2013; Pudsey The Movie, 2014; Mr Holmes, 2015; Legend, 2015; *radio:* Whose Line is it Anyway?, 1988; Beachcomber, 1989; Mightier than the Sword, 1992; Figaro gets Divorced, 1993; Poonsh, 1993; The Good Doctor, 1994; Private Passions, 1997–2002; The Reith Affair, 1998; Saturday Night Fry, 1998; The Destiny of Nathalie X, 1998; Season's Greetings, 1999; The Man who came to Dinner, 2000; Reconstructing Louis, 2000; Dante's Inferno, 2001; The Haunting, 2002; The Titanic Enquiry, 2002; In the Company of Men, 2003; St Graham and St Evelyn—Pray for Us, 2003; The Possessed, 2006; Eternal Sunshine, 2008; Let Me Entertain You (presenter), 2008; A Dangerous Thing, 2009; The Babylon Hotel, 2009; Myths and Mystery Cycles, 2010; Electric Ink, 2011; Burns and the Bankers, 2012; A Pact of Silence, 2015. *Recreation:* dinner parties. *Address:* c/o Markham, Froggatt & Irwin, 4 Windmill Street, W1T 2HZ. *T:* (020) 7636 4412. *Club:* Groucho.

MARSHALL, John Leslie; Chairman, Beta Global Emerging Markets Investment Trust plc, 2000–01 (Director, 1990–2001); *b* 19 Aug. 1940; *s* of late Prof. William Marshall and Margaret Marshall; *m* 1978, Susan Elizabeth (marr. diss. 2000), *d* of David Mount, Petham, Kent; two *s*. *Educ:* Glasgow Academy; St Andrews Univ. (MA). ACIS. Asst Lecturer in Economics, Glasgow Univ., 1962–66; Lectr in Economics, Aberdeen Univ., 1966–70; Mem., Internat. Stock Exchange; Carr Sebag & Co., 1979–82; Partner, 1983–86, Dir, 1986–90, Analyst, 1990–93, Carr Kitcat & Aitken; Analyst: London Wall Equities, subseq. Mees Pierson Securities (UK) Ltd, 1993–97; New Japan Securities, 1998–99. Sen. Financial Journalist, Shares mag., 1999–2011. Member (C): Aberdeen Town Council, 1968–70; Ealing Borough Council, 1971–86 (Chm., Finance Bd, 1978–82; Chm., Local Services Cttee, 1982–84); Barnet LBC, 1998– (Chm., Cons. Gp, 1998–2000, 2004–05, 2012–; Chm., Council Policy Conference, 2002–03; Dep. Mayor, 2004; Cabinet Mem. for Investment in Educn (formerly Educn and Lifelong Learning), 2004–08; Mayor, 2008–09; Chm., Pension Fund Cttee, 2010–11). Contested (C): Dundee East, 1964 and 1966; Lewisham East, Feb. 1974. MEP (C) London N, 1979–89; Asst Whip, EDG, Eur. Parlt, 1986–89. MP (C) Hendon South, 1987–97; contested (C) Finchley and Golders Green, 1997, 2001. PPS to Minister for the Disabled, Dept of Social Security, 1989–90, to Sec. of State for Social Security, 1990–92, to Leader of H of C, 1992–95. Mem., Select Cttee on health, 1995–97; Vice Chm., All Pty

Mental Health Gp, 1996–97. Chm., British Israel Parly Gp, 1991–97; Vice Pres., Anglo-Israel Assoc., 2001– (Chm., 1994–2000). Consultant, Bus and Coach Council, 1991–97. Chairman: Friends of the Northern Line, 1994–97; Dermatrust Appeal, 1998–2005; Barnet Carers Centre, 2011–15; Barnet Blind and Partially Sighted Bowlers, 2011–. *Publications:* articles on economics in several professional jls; pamphlets on economic questions for Aims. *Recreations:* watching cricket, football and Rugby; gardening, bridge, theatre. *Address:* 3 Westchester Drive, NW4 1RD. *Clubs:* Royal Over-Seas League, MCC; Middlesex County Cricket.

MARSHALL, John Roger; Chairman: Building Software Ltd, since 1997; Supply Chain Partnering, since 1996; *b* 20 April 1944; *s* of late John Henry Marshall and of Betty Alaine Rosetta Marshall; *m* (marr. diss.); one *s* two *d*. *Educ:* Rendcomb College; Bristol Univ. (BSc Hons Civil Eng.). MICE, CEng, FCIHT. Balfour Beatty Consultants, W. C. French and R. McGregor & Sons, 1966–70; Mears Construction, 1970–78; Henry Boot, 1978–83; Man. Dir, Mowlem Management, 1983–87; Dir, 1987–95, Man. Dir, 1989–94, Chief Exec., 1994–95, John Mowlem and Co. PLC. Non-executive Director: St Aldwyns Enterprises (subseq. Resources) Ltd, 1996–2002; BRE Ltd, 1998–2001. *Recreation:* painting and giving unwanted advice. *Address:* 118 Bath Road, Cheltenham, Glos GL53 7JX.

MARSHALL, Katharine Jane, (Mrs H. J. Stevenson); Her Honour Judge Katharine Marshall; a Circuit Judge, since 2008; Designated Family Judge, since 2012; *b* 11 Aug. 1958; *d* of Ian David Gordon Lee and Ivy Margaret Lee (*née* Cox); *m* 1st, 1981, David Forrest Marshall (marr. diss. 1985); one *s*; 2nd, 1996, Huw John Stevenson; one *s* one *d*. *Educ:* Sidney Sussex Coll., Cambridge (Taylor Schol.; MA Natural Scis/Law 1980); Council of Legal Educn; Greenwich Univ. (DMS Dist. 1998). Called to the Bar, Inner Temple, 1983; Dep. Justices Clerk, E Berks, 1997–2001; Actg Stipendiary Magistrate, then Dep. Dist Judge, 1999–2002; District Judge (Magistrates' Courts), 2002–06; Recorder, 2007–08. Member: Family Procedure Rule Cttee, 2004–08; Family Justice Council, 2011–. Mem., Adv. Bd, Cambridge Univ. Alumni, 2010–. *Publications:* Wilkinson's Road Traffic Referencer, 2007, rev. edn 2008. *Recreations:* living a life I love with those I love, 70's rock music, walking in faraway isolated locations; fascinated by life of Napoleon (particularly exile on St Helena). *Address:* Swindon Combined Court Centre, Islington Street, Swindon, Wilts SN1 2HG. *Club:* Oxford and Cambridge.

MARSHALL, Kathleen Anne; child law consultant, since 2009; *b* 4 June 1953; *d* of Matthew Gallagher and Christina McEvoy; *m* 1974, Robert Hunter Marshall; two *s* one *d*. *Educ:* Univ. of Glasgow (LLB 1973); Open Univ. (BA Hons 1979); Maryvale Inst., Birmingham (BA Hons (Divinity) 2003). Legal Apprentice, then Solicitor, Glasgow Corp., subseq. Glasgow DC, 1973–77; full-time mother, 1977–89; Co-Dir, then Dir, Scottish Child Law Centre, 1989–94; child law consultant, 1994–2004; Comr for Children and Young People in Scotland, 2004–09. Visiting Professor: Queen's Coll., Glasgow, subseq. Glasgow Caledonian Univ., 1992–95; Glasgow Centre for the Child and Society, Univ. of Glasgow, 1997–2009. Mem., Law Soc. of Scotland, 1975–. *Publications:* Children's Rights in the Balance: the participation-protection debate, 1997; (with Paul Parvis) Honouring Children: the human rights of the child in Christian perspective, 2004; numerous articles in jls. *Recreation:* dreaming about not being a workaholic. *E:* childlaw@btinternet.com.

MARSHALL, Liza; Head of Film and Television, Scott Free, since 2010; *b* London, 4 March 1972; *d* of Scott and Denise Marshall; *m* Mark Strong; two *s*. *Educ:* St Paul's Girls' Sch.; Wadham Coll., Oxford (BA Modern Hist.). Script ed. for Lynda La Plante, 1995; storyliner and script ed., London Bridge TV prog., 1995–96; Develt Exec., Carlton TV, 1996; BBC: script ed., serials, 1996–98; Producer, progs incl. The Long Firm, The Sins, Fields of Gold, Eroica, Derailed, 1998–2005; Commng Ed., 2005–07, Hd of Drama, 2007–09, Channel 4. *Address:* Scott Free, 42–44 Beak Street, W1F 9RH.

MARSHALL, Margaret Anne, OBE 1999; concert and opera singer; soprano; *b* 4 Jan. 1949; *d* of Robert and Margaret Marshall; *m* 1970, Dr Graeme Griffiths King Davidson; two *d*. *Educ:* High School, Stirling; Royal Scottish Academy of Music and Drama (DRSAMD). Recital début, Wigmore Hall, 1975; performed regularly with all major British orchs, also with ENO and Scottish Opera; opera début as Euridice, in Orfeo, Florence; major rôles include: Countess Almaviva in The Marriage of Figaro; Fiordiligi in Così fan Tutte; Elvira and Donna Anna in Don Giovanni; Violetta in La Traviata; Marschallin in Der Rosenkavalier; Constanze in The Seraglio; many concert and opera performances in Europe and N America; numerous recordings. Hon. MusD St Andrews, 2009. First Prize, Munich International Competition, 1974. Gulliver Award, 1992. *Recreations:* squash, golf. *Address:* Armand, Gensac 82120, Tarn et Garonne, France.

MARSHALL, Mark Anthony, CMG 1991; HM Diplomatic Service, retired; Ambassador to the Republic of Yemen (formerly Yemen Arab Republic) and the Republic of Djibouti, 1987–93; *b* 8 Oct. 1937; *s* of late Thomas Humphrey Marshall, CMG and of Nadine, *d* of late Mark Hambourg; *m* 1970, Penelope Lesley Seymour; two *d*. *Educ:* Westminster Sch.; Trinity Coll., Cambridge (BA). MECAS, 1958; Third Sec., Amman, 1960; FO, 1962; Commercial Officer, Dubai, 1964; FO, 1965; Aden, 1967; First Sec., 1968; Asst Dir of Treasury Centre for Admin. Studies, 1968; UK Delegn to Brussels Conf., 1970; First Sec./Head of Chancery, Rabat, 1972; First Sec., FCO, 1976; Counsellor: Tripoli, 1979–80; Damascus, 1980–83; Head of Finance Dept, FCO, 1984–87. *Recreations:* swimming, fell walking, bridge.

MARSHALL, Prof. Martin Neil, CBE 2005; MD; FRCGP; Professor of Healthcare Improvement, University College London, since 2012; Lead, Improvement Science London, since 2012; *b* 2 Sept. 1961; *s* of Dr Geoffrey Marshall and Mary Marshall; *m* 1988, Susan Miles. *Educ:* University Coll. London (BSc Immunol. 1984); Charing Cross and Westminster Hosp. Med. Sch., Univ. of London (MB BS 1987; MD 1997); Univ. of Exeter (MSc Health Care 1994). DRCOG 1990; DCH 1991; MRCGP 1991, FRCGP 1998. Exeter Vocational Trng Scheme for Gen. Practice, 1988–91; Partner in Gen. Practice, Mt Pleasant Health Centre, Exeter, 1991–99; Lectr in Gen. Practice, Univ. of Exeter, 1994–97; Harkness Fellow in Health Care Policy, Rand Corp., Calif, 1998–99; Hd, Community Health Scis Div., Univ. of Exeter, 1999; University of Manchester: Hon. Res. Fellow, 1998–99, Sen. Clin. Res. Fellow, 2000–01, Nat. Primary Care R&D Centre; Prof. of Gen. Practice, 2001–06; Hd, Div. of Primary Care, 2005–06; Principal in Gen. Practice (pt-time), Robert Darbishire Practice, Manchester, 2000–06; Dep. Chief Med. Officer for England, DoH, 2006–07; Medical Dir, The Health Foundn, 2007–12. Mem., Care Quality Commn, 2009–12. Mem. Council, RCGP, 2005–06, 2007–13. Pres., Eur. Soc. for Quality Improvement in Family Practice, 2005–06. Hon. FRCP 2005; Hon. FFPHM 2005. *Publications:* numerous contribs relating to quality and safety in health care. *Recreation:* being outside.

MARSHALL, Prof. Mary Tara, OBE 1997; Director, Dementia Services Development Centre, University of Stirling, 1989–2005, now Professor Emeritus; Sessional Inspector, Care Inspectorate (formerly Social Work Inspection Agency), since 2007; writer and lecturer in dementia care; *b* 13 June 1945; *d* of Percy Edwin Alan and Phyllis April Trix Johnson-Marshall. *Educ:* Edinburgh Univ. (MA); London School of Economics (DSA); Liverpool Univ. (Dip. in Applied Social Studies). Child Care Officer, Lambeth, 1967–69; Social Worker, Liverpool Personal Service Soc. Project, 1970–74; Organiser, res. project, Age Concern, Liverpool, 1974–75; Lectr in Applied Social Studies, Liverpool Univ. 1975–83; Dir, Age Concern, Scotland, 1983–89. Mem., Royal Commn on Long Term Care for the Elderly, 1998–99. Member: Liverpool Housing Trust, 1976–; Edinvar Housing Assoc., 1988–; Gov., PPP Foundation (formerly Healthcare Med. Trust Ltd), 1998–2003. Member: Centre for Policy on Ageing, 1986– (Gov., 1994–2000); BASW, 1970–; British Soc. of Gerontology, 1977–; 21st Century Social Work Rev. Gp, 2004–05; Ind. Funding Review of Free Personal and Nursing Care. FRSE 2003. FAcSS (AcSS 1999). FRSA 2003. Hon. DEd Queen Margaret Coll., 1998; Hon. DSocSc Edinburgh, 2004; DUniv Stirling, 2006. Medal for Relief of Suffering, British Geriatric Soc., 2008; Lifetime Achievement Award, Faculty of Old Age Psychiatry, RCPsych, 2010. *Publications:* Social Work with Old People, 1983, 4th edn (with J. Phillips and M. Ray), 2006; "I Can't Place This Place At All": working with people with dementia and their carers, 1996, 2nd edn (with M.-A. Tibbs) as Social Work and People with Dementia, 2006; (ed) Food, Glorious Food: perspectives on food and dementia, 2003; (ed) Perspectives on Rehabilitation and Dementia, 2005; (ed with K. Allan) Dementia: walking not wandering, 2006; (ed with J. Gilliard) Time for Dementia, 2010; Designing balconies, roof terraces and roof gardens for people with dementia, 2010; (with J. Gilliard) Transforming the Quality of Life for People with Dementia through Contact with the Natural World, 2011; (with A. Pollock) Designing Outdoor Spaces for People with Dementia, 2012; Designing Mental Health Units for Older People, 2014; (with J. Gilliard) Creating Culturally Appropriate Outside Spaces and Experiences for People with Dementia, 2014; book reviews, papers, reports and articles. *Recreations:* birdwatching, photography. *Address:* 24 Buckingham Terrace, Edinburgh EH4 3AE. *T:* (0131) 343 1732.

MARSHALL, Rt Rev. Michael Eric, MA; an Hon. Assistant Bishop, Diocese of London, since 1984; *b* Lincoln, 14 April 1936. *Educ:* Lincoln Sch.; Christ's Coll., Cambridge (Tancred Scholar, Upper II: Hist. Pt 1 and Theol Pt 1a, MA); Cuddesdon Theological Coll. Deacon, 1960; Curate, St Peter's, Spring Hill, Birmingham, 1960–62; Tutor, Ely Theological Coll. and Minor Canon of Ely Cath., 1962–64; Chaplain in London Univ., 1964–69; Vicar of All Saints', Margaret Street, W1, 1969–75; Bishop Suffragan of Woolwich, 1975–84; Founding Episcopal Dir, Anglican Inst., St Louis, Missouri, 1984–92; Dir of Evangelism, Chichester Theol Coll., 1991–97; Bishop in Residence, 1997–2012, Rector, 2002–12, Holy Trinity, Sloane Street; Interim Rector, Episcopal Ch of the Heavenly Rest, NY, 2012–13; Preb. of Wightring in Chichester Cathedral and Wightring Theol Lectr, 1990–99; an Asst Bp, Dio. Chichester, 1992–2011. Archbishops' Advr on Evangelism, 1992–97; Leader, Springboard, 1992–97. Founder and Director: Inst. of Christian Studies, 1970; Internat. Inst. for Anglican Studies, 1982; Pres., Awareness Foundn, 2009–14 (Dir, Trinity Inst. for Christianity and Culture, 2003–09; Trustee, Trinity Foundn, 2003–09). Exam. Chap. to Bp of London, 1974. Member: Gen. Synod, 1970, also Diocesan and Deanery Synods; Liturgical Commn; Anglican/Methodist Liaison Commn until 1974; SPCK Governing Body; USPG Governing Body. Hon. Chaplain, 2002, Liveryman, 2008, Wheelwrights' Co. Has frequently broadcast on BBC and commercial radio; also lectured, preached and broadcast in Canada and USA. *Publications:* A Pattern of Faith, 1966 (co-author); Glory under Your Feet, 1978; Pilgrimage and Promise, 1981; Renewal in Worship, 1982; The Anglican Church, Today and Tomorrow, 1984; Christian Orthodoxy Revisited, 1985; The Gospel Conspiracy in the Episcopal Church, 1986; The Restless Heart, 1987; The Gospel Connection, 1991; The Freedom of Holiness, 1992; Free to Worship, 1996; Flame in the Mind: a journey of spiritual passion, 2002; The Transforming Power of Prayer: from illusion to reality, 2010; Founder and co-editor, Christian Quarterly. *Recreations:* music, cooking. *Address:* 53 Oakley Gardens, Chelsea, SW3 5QQ. *Club:* Athenæum.

MARSHALL, Sir Michael (John), Kt 2010; CBE 1999; DL; Chairman, since 1989, and Chief Executive, 1989–2010, Marshall of Cambridge (Holdings) Ltd; *b* 27 Jan. 1932; *s* of Sir Arthur Gregory George Marshall, OBE and Rosemary Wynford Marshall; *m* 1st, 1960, Bridget Wykham Pollock (marr. diss. 1977); two *s* two *d*; 2nd, 1979, Sibyl Mary Walkinshaw (*née* Hutton); two step *s*. *Educ:* Eton Coll.; Jesus Coll., Cambridge (MA Hist.; rowing Blue, 1954, rep. GB in Eur. championships, 1955). IEng; FRAeS 1988; FIMI. Nat. Service, Flying Officer, RAF, 1950–52. Joined Marshall of Cambridge (Eng) Ltd, 1955: Dep. Chm. and Man. Dir, Marshall (Cambridge) Ltd, 1964–89. Dir, Eastern Electricity Bd, 1971–77; Chm., BL Cars Distributor Council, 1977, 1983 (Mem., 1975–84); Vice-President: Inst. Motor Ind., 1980–; EEF, 1993–2003; Chm., Cambs Manpower Cttee, 1980–83. Hon. Vis. Prof., Anglia Ruskin Univ., 2009–11. Vice-Chm., Cambs Youth Involvement Cttee, Silver Jubilee Fund, 1977–78; Chm., Cambridge Olympic Appeal, 1984; Mem., Ely Cathedral Restoration Appeal Cttee, 1987–2011 (Vice Patron, 2012–); President: Cambridge Soc. for Blind, 1989–92; Addenbrooke's Charitable Trust, 2000–; Chm., Prince's Trust's Cambs Appeal Cttee, 1991–92; Mem. Council, Prince's Charities, 2009–; Chm., Ct of Benefactors-Council of Reference, E Anglian Air Ambulance, 2006–11. Pres., Cambridge '99 Rowing Club, 1996–2003. Chairman: Civilian Cttee, 104 (City of Cambridge) Sqdn, ATC, 1975–2013; Beds and Cambs Wing, ATC, 1987–2003 (Hon. Pres., 2008–); Member: Air Cadet Council, 1994–2007; Council, Air League, 1995–2009 (Chm., 1998–2003; Pres., 2004–09; Companion, 2012–); Air Squadron, 1998–. Hon. Air Cdre, No 2623 (East Anglian) Sqdn, RAuxAF, 2003–. Hon. Vice Patron, Royal Internat. Air Tattoo, 2003–. Hon. Vice Pres., Cambridge Br., RAeS, 2012–. Ambassador, World Land Trust, 2009–. CCMI (CIMgt 1997); FRSA; Fellow, Order of St Radegund, Jesus Coll., Cambridge, 2007–. Freeman, City of London, 1988; Liveryman, Hon. Co. of Air Pilots (formerly GAPAN), 1989– (Award of Honour, 2014). Cambridgeshire: High Sheriff, 1988–89; DL 1989; Vice Lord-Lieutenant, 1992–2006. DUniv Anglia Poly., 2001; Hon. DSc Kingston, 2014. *Recreations:* flying, reading, lode walking. *Address:* (office) c/o Marshall of Cambridge (Holdings) Ltd, The Airport, Newmarket Road, Cambridge CB5 8RX. *T:* (01223) 373245, *Fax:* (01223) 324224. *E:* mjm@marcamb.co.uk. *Clubs:* Royal Air Force, Air Squadron; Hawks, Cambridge County (Cambridge); Leander (Henley-on-Thames); Eton Vikings.

See also R. D. Marshall.

MARSHALL, Penelope Jane Clucas; Social Affairs Editor, ITV News, 2012–14 and since 2015; *b* Addlestone, 7 Nov. 1962; *d* of Alan Marshall and Mary Marshall; *m* 1992, Timothy Ewart; three *d*. *Educ:* St Helen's, Northwood; London Sch. of Econs and Pol Sci. (BA Hist. 1984). Trainee, Surrey and South London Newspaper Gp, 1984–85; ITN: graduate trainee, 1985; Foreign Corresp., ITV News, 1987–2004; freelance journalist and consultant, 2004–07; Special Corresp., ITV News at Ten, 2007–11. Freelance writer and contrib. to BBC Radio 4, The Times, Guardian, Daily Mail, 2006–. Vis. Prof., City Univ., 2006–. *Recreations:* singing, reading, gardening, bird watching, dog walking, opera. *Address:* ITV News, 200 Gray's Inn Road, WC1X 8XZ.

MARSHALL, Sir Peter (Harold Reginald), KCMG 1983 (CMG 1974); CVO 2003; Chairman, Joint Commonwealth Societies Council, 1993–2003; *b* 30 July 1924; 3rd *s* of late R. H. Marshall; *m* 1st, 1957, Patricia Rendell Stoddart (*d* 1981); one *s* one *d*; 2nd, 1989, Judith (*d* 2013), *widow* of E. W. F. Tomlin. *Educ:* Tonbridge; Corpus Christi Coll., Cambridge (Hon. Fellow 1989). RAFVR, 1943–46. HM Foreign (later Diplomatic) Service, 1949–83: FO, 1949–52; 2nd Sec. and Private Sec. to Ambassador, Washington, 1952–56; FO, 1956–60; on staff of Civil Service Selection Board, 1960; 1st Sec. and Head of Chancery, Baghdad, 1961, and Bangkok, 1962–64; Asst Dir of Treasury Centre for Administrative Studies, 1965–66; Counsellor, UK Mission, Geneva, 1966–69, Counsellor and Head of Chancery, Paris, 1969–71; Head of Financial Policy and Aid Dept, FCO, 1971–73; Asst Under-Sec. of State, FCO, 1973–75; UK Rep. on Econ. and Social Council of UN, 1975–79; Ambassador and UK Perm. Rep. to Office of UN and Other Internat. Organisations at Geneva, 1979–83; Commonwealth Dep. Sec. Gen. (Econ.), 1983–88. Chm., Commonwealth Trust and Royal Commonwealth Soc., 1988–92; Pres., Queen Elizabeth House, Oxford, 1990–94; Vice Pres., Council for Educn in World Citizenship, 1985–98; Member: ICRC Consultative Gp of Internat. Experts, 1984–86; Exec. Cttee, Pilgrims, 1986–2001 and 2004–10; Council, VSO, 1989–95; ODI, 1989–99; Governor, E-SU of the Commonwealth, 1984–90; Trustee: King George VI and Queen Elizabeth Foundn of St Catharine's, 1987–2001; Magna Carta Trust, 1993–2004. Mem., Panel of Judges, WorldAware Business Awards, 1988–2002. Chm.,

Nikaean Club, 1992–2002. Vis. Lectr, Diplomatic Acad. of London, 1989–2001. Hon. Fellow, Univ. of Westminster, 1992. Hon. Vice-Pres., Aircrew Assoc., 2005. *Publications:* The Dynamics of Diplomacy, 1990; (contrib.) The United Kingdom—The United Nations (ed Jensen and Fisher), 1990; (ed) Diplomacy Beyond 2000, 1996; Positive Diplomacy, 1997; (ed) Are Diplomats Really Necessary?, 1998; (ed) The Information Explosion: a challenge for diplomacy, 1998; (ed) Diplomacy and Divinity, 2006; (contrib.) Strategic Public Diplomacy, 2009; Judith: a memoir, 2013; numerous articles on Commonwealth and EU questions. *Recreations:* television, Euro-gazing. *Address:* 34 Stafford Court, 178–188 Kensington High Street, W8 7DL. *Club:* Travellers.

MARSHALL, Prof. Peter James, CBE 2002; DPhil; FBA 1992; Rhodes Professor of Imperial History, King's College, London, 1980–93, now Emeritus; *b* 28 Oct. 1933; *s* of Edward Hannaford Marshall and Madeleine (*née* Shuttleworth). *Educ:* Wellington College; Wadham Coll., Oxford (BA 1957; MA, DPhil 1962; Hon. Fellow, 1997). Military service, King's African Rifles, Kenya, 1953–54. Assistant Lecturer, Lecturer, Reader, Professor, History Dept, King's Coll., London, 1959–80 (FKC 1991). Mem., History Wkg Gp, National Curriculum, 1989–90. Pres., RHistS, 1996–2000 (Vice-Pres., 1987–91; Hon. Vice-Pres., 2000–). Hon. For. Mem., Amer. Historical Assoc., 2003–. Editor, Journal of Imperial and Commonwealth History, 1975–81; Associate Editor, Writings and Speeches of Edmund Burke, 1976–. Hon. DLitt: Bristol, 2008; London, 2008. *Publications:* Impeachment of Warren Hastings, 1965; Problems of Empire: Britain and India 1757–1813, 1968; (ed, with J. A. Woods) Correspondence of Edmund Burke, vol. VII, 1968; The British Discovery of Hinduism, 1972; East India Fortunes, 1976; (ed) Writings and Speeches of Edmund Burke, vol. V, 1981, vol. VI, 1991, vol. VII, 2000, vol. IV (with D. C. Bryant), 2015; (with Glyndwr Williams) The Great Map of Mankind, 1982; Bengal: the British bridgehead (New Cambridge History of India, Vol. II, 2), 1988; Trade and Conquest: studies on the rise of British dominance in India, 1993; (ed) Cambridge Illustrated History of the British Empire, 1996; (ed) Oxford History of the British Empire, Vol. II, The Eighteenth Century, 1998; A Free Though Conquering People: eighteenth-century Britain and its empire, 2003; (ed) The Eighteenth Century in Indian History: evolution or revolution?, 2003; The Making and Unmaking of Empires: Britain, India and America, *c* 1750–1783, 2005; Remaking the British Atlantic: the United States and the British Empire after American independence, 2012; articles in Economic History Rev., History, Modern Asian Studies, etc. *Address:* 7 Malting Lane, Braughing, Ware, Herts SG11 2QZ. *T:* (01920) 822232.

MARSHALL, Peter James, CMG 1996; HM Diplomatic Service, retired; Consul General, Atlanta, USA, 1997–2001; *b* 25 June 1944; *s* of George Aubrey Marshall and Joan Marshall; *m* 1966, Roberta Barlow; one *s* three *d*. *Educ:* Ripon Grammar Sch. Min. of Aviation, 1963–64; CRO, 1964–65; seconded to Commonwealth Secretariat, 1965–67; served Malta, 1967–70; Vice Consul (Commercial), Johannesburg, March–Dec. 1970; 2nd Sec. (Commercial/Information), Kaduna, 1970–74; Vice Consul (Commercial), San Francisco, 1974–79; First Sec., FCO, 1979–83; Dep. High Comr, Malta, 1983–88; First Sec., FCO, 1988–90; Dep. Head, News Dept, FCO, 1990–94; Counsellor, Consul Gen. and Dep. Head of Mission, later Chargé d'Affaires, Algiers, 1994–95; Ambassador to Algeria, 1995–96. *Recreations:* grandchildren, gardening, travel, gliding. *Address:* 2 Hemlock Close, Kingswood, Surrey KT20 6QW.

MARSHALL, Very Rev. Peter Jerome; Dean of Worcester, 1997–2006, now Emeritus; *b* 10 May 1940; *s* of Guy and Dorothy Marshall; *m* 1965, Nancy Jane Elliott; one *s* two *d*. *Educ:* St John's, Leatherhead; Upper Canada Coll., Toronto; McGill Univ.; Westcott House, Cambridge. Ordained deacon, 1963, priest, 1964; Curate, St Mary, E Ham, 1963–66; Curate, St Mary, Woodford, and Curate i/c, St Philip and St James, S Woodford, 1966–71; Vicar, St Peter, Walthamstow, 1971–81; Dep. Dir of Training, dio. of Chelmsford, 1981–84; Canon Residentiary, Chelmsford Cathedral, 1981–85; Dio. Dir of Training, Ripon, and Canon Residentiary, Ripon Cathedral, 1985–97. Chm. Pastoral Cttee, dio. of Worcester, 1997–2006. Chm., Barking and Havering AHA, 1976–82. *Recreations:* swimming, walking, sailing, films, ice-skating, curling. *Address:* 433 Gordon Avenue, Peterborough, ON K9J 6G6, Canada. *T:* (705) 8763381. *E:* petermarshall@bell.net.

MARSHALL, Philip John; QC 2012; *b* Crosby, Liverpool, 12 Oct. 1966; *s* of Robert Marshall and Norma Marshall (*née* Middleton). *Educ:* Merchant Taylors' Sch. for Boys; Liverpool Univ. (LLB). Called to the Bar, Gray's Inn, 1989; in practice as barrister, specialising in matrimonial finance, 1989–. Chm., Family Law Bar Assoc., 2016– (Vice Chm., 2014). Vice Pres., Merchant Taylors' Old Boys' Assoc., 2015–. *Recreations:* music, opera, lapsed golfer. *Address:* 1 King's Bench Walk, Temple, EC4Y 7DB. *T:* (020) 7936 1500. *E:* pmarshall@1kbw.co.uk.

MARSHALL, Philip Scott; QC 2003; a Recorder, since 2008; a Deputy High Court Judge, since 2009; *b* 6 June 1965; *s* of Arthur and Elizabeth Marshall; *m* 1993, Barbara James; two *s* one *d*. *Educ:* Merchiston Castle Sch., Edinburgh; Queens' Coll., Cambridge (MA Hons); Harvard Law Sch. (LLM). Called to the Bar, Lincoln's Inn, 1987, Bencher, 2011; Fellow, Queens' Coll., Cambridge, 1991–94; in practice as barrister, specialising in commercial, company and insolvency law, 1991–. *Publications:* Practice and Procedure of the Companies Court, 1997; (contrib.) Civil Appeals, 2002; contribs to various legal jls. *Recreations:* horse racing, golf. *Address:* (chambers) Serle Court, 6 New Square, Lincoln's Inn, WC2A 3QS. *T:* (020) 7242 6105, *Fax:* (020) 7405 4004.

MARSHALL, Robert David, FRAeS; Chief Executive, Marshall of Cambridge (Holdings) Ltd, since 2011; *b* Cambridge, 21 July 1962; *s* of Sir Michael (John) Marshall, *qv*; *m* 1st, 1992, Julia Kathleen Hamilton Russell (marr. diss. 2011); one *d*; 2nd, 2013, Sheila Anne Kissane; one *d*. *Educ:* Eton Coll.; Pembroke Coll., Cambridge (BA English 1984; MA 1988); Harvard Business Sch. (AMP). FRAeS 2005. Res. Associate, Lockheed Martin, 1984–87; Founder, MBL, 1989–94; joined Marshall of Cambridge Aerospace Ltd as Hd of Projects, 1994; Dir, 1998–; Chief Exec., Marshall SV Ltd, 1999–2006; Develt Dir, Marshall Gp, 2000–07; Exec. Chm., Marshall Motor Gp, 2007–08; Chief Operating Officer, Marshall Gp, 2010–11. Director: e-Go Ltd, 2011–; EEF, 2011–. Mem., Air League, 1999–. Angel Investor, Cambridge Angels, 2010–. Gov., Hills Road Sixth Form Coll., 2007–11. MInstD. *Recreation:* flying (Private Pilot Licence). *Address:* Marshall of Cambridge (Holdings) Ltd, The Airport, Newmarket Road, Cambridge CB5 8RX. *T:* (01223) 373194. *E:* rdm@marcamb.co.uk. *Club:* Royal Automobile.

MARSHALL, (Robert) John; HM Diplomatic Service; Ambassador to Senegal, and concurrently to Guinea-Bissau and Cape Verde, 2011–15; *b* Oxford, 19 June 1965; *s* of Robert Marshall and Rosemary Marshall (*née* Simpkins); *m* 2001, (Helen) Marie Glanfield; one *s* two *d*. *Educ:* St Edward's, Oxford; Bristol Univ. (BA Mod. Langs). Joined FCO, 1988; Japanese lang. trng, 1990–92; Second Sec. (Econ.), Tokyo, 1992–95; Hd, India Sect., S Asian Dept, 1995–97; Hd, Pol Sect., UN Dept, 1997–99; First Sec. (Pol, Econ. and Public Diplomacy), Kuala Lumpur, 2000–03; Hd, Caribbean Team, 2003–04; Dep. Hd, Sustainable Develt and Commonwealth Gp, 2004–06; Dep. Hd of Mission, Addis Ababa, 2007–11. *Recreations:* running, bird watching, travel, diving. *Address:* c/o Foreign and Commonwealth Office, King Charles Street, SW1A 2AH. *E:* john.marshall@fco.gov.uk.

MARSHALL, Prof. Robin, PhD; FRS 1995; Professor of Experimental Physics, 1992–2005, Research Professor of Physics and Life Sciences, since 2005, University of Manchester; *b* 5 Jan. 1940; *s* of Robert Marshall and Grace Eileen Marshall (*née* Ryder); *m* 1963 (marr. diss. 2003); two *s* one *d*; *m* 2005, Jennifer (*née* Dodd). *Educ:* Ermysted's Grammar Sch., Skipton; Univ. of Manchester (BSc 1962; PhD 1965). DSIR Research Fellow, 1965–67; Vis. Scientist, Deutsches Elektronen Synchrotron, Hamburg, 1967–68; Res. Scientist, MIT, 1968–70; Scientist, Daresbury Lab., 1970–78; PSO, 1978–86, Sen. Principal (IM), 1986–92, Rutherford Appleton Lab. Dir and Co. Sec., Frontiers Science and Television Ltd, 1999–2005. Mem., Bd of Govs, Museum of Sci. and Industry, Manchester, 2003–08. Proprietor, Champagne Cat publishers. Mem., Find a Better Way charity, 2011–. Max Born Medal and Prize, German Physical Soc., 1997. *Publications:* High Energy Electron-Positron Physics, 1988; Electron-Positron Annihilation Physics, 1990; numerous scientific papers. *Recreations:* writing and painting in the South of France, running the e-publishing house Champagne Cat. *Address:* 7 impasse des Perrières, 30210 Castillon du Gard, France. *T:* (4) 66209857.

MARSHALL, Rosamund Margaret; Chief Executive Officer, Taaleem, Dubai, since 2013; *b* Cheam, Surrey, 5 July 1959; *d* of Kenneth Wilfrid and Christine Mary Samuda; *m* 1989, Geoffrey James Marshall; three *d*. *Educ:* Wallington High Sch. for Girls; Guildford Coll. (OND Instnl Housekeeping and Catering 1977). Gardner Merchant Ltd: Manager, 1977–86; Area Manager, 1986–88; Business Develt Manager, 1988–94; Dep. Divl Dir, 1994–98; Divl Dir, Sodexo, 1998–2002; Man. Dir, Learning Services, 2002–06, Chief Operating Officer, 2006–08, Nord Anglia Educn plc; CEO, Kidsunlimited, 2010–13. Non-exec. Dir, Knightsbridge Schs Internat., 2009–14. Trustee: Nat. Children's Orchestras of GB, 2009–13; British Council, 2012–. *Recreations:* family, classical music, theatre, opera, ski-ing, walking. *Address:* Springfield House, Chalford, Glos GL6 8NW. *T:* (01453) 887330. *E:* ros.marshall@hotmail.co.uk.

MARSHALL, Roy Thomas, PhD; Director of ICT, Hull University, since 2011; *b* Wolverhampton, 6 Oct. 1955; *s* of Thomas and Brenda Marshall; *m* 1979, Alison Mary Marian Shirley; two *s* one *d*. *Educ:* Univ. of Exeter (BSc 1st cl. Hons Maths and Theoretical Phys 1977; PhD Maths 1980). Geophysicist, BP Exploration, 1980–84; Head, Mapping and Modelling: BP Alaska, 1984–87; BPX London, 1987–92; Head, Systems Integration, Data Services, BPX London, 1992–94; Business Inf. Manager, BP Abu Dhabi, 1994–99; Head, Inf. Systems Gp, National Grid, 1999–2001; Dir, Deanfield Consultancy Ltd, 2003–04; Chief Inf. Officer and Head, ICT, ODPM, subseq. DCLG, 2004–06; Chief Inf. Officer and Dir, Knowledge, Inf. Technol. and Working Envmt, DCLG, 2006–10. Sen. Responsible Officer, Govt Connect, 2006–08. Founder Mem., Govt CIO Council, 2004–. *Recreations:* gardening, DIY. *Address:* Hull University, Hull HU18 1DN.

MARSHALL, Hon. Russell; *see* Marshall, Hon. C. R.

MARSHALL, Steven, FCMA; Chairman, Wincanton plc, since 2011; *b* 11 Feb. 1957; *s* of late Victor Marshall and Kathleen Marshall. *Educ:* Isleworth Grammar Sch. Mgt accountant, BOC Gp, 1977–81; Marketing Analyst, then Systems Accountant, Black & Decker, 1981–84; Treasury Controller, then Sector Financial Controller, Burton Gp, 1984–87; Dep. Gp Finance Dir, and Co. Sec., Parkdale Hldgs plc, 1987–89; Gp Investor Relns Dir, then Eur. Finance Dir, IDV, Grand Metropolitan plc, 1990–95; Gp Finance and Commercial Dir, 1995–98, Gp Chief Exec., 1998–99, Thorn plc; Gp Finance Dir, 1999–2000, Gp Chief Exec., 2000–02, Railtrack Gp plc; Exec. Chm., Queens Moat Houses plc, 2003–04. Chairman: Delta plc, 2005–10 (Sen. Ind. Dir, 2004–05); Torex Retail plc, 2007; Balfour Beatty plc, 2008–15 (Exec. Chm., 2014; non-exec. Dir, 2005–08). Non-executive Director: Southern Water Services, 2005–10; Halma Gp plc, 2010–14. Special Advr to CIMA, 2002–05. Trustee, Chimpanzee Rehabilitation Trust, 2002–. FCMA 1987; CCMI 2012. *Recreations:* wildlife conservation and welfare, natural history, travel.

MARSHALL, Valerie Margaret; Managing Director, Stratagem CFS Ltd, since 2003; *b* 30 March 1945; *d* of Ernest Knagg and Marion Knagg; *m* 1972, Alan Roger Marshall (marr. diss. 1996); two *s* one *d*. *Educ:* Brighton and Hove High Sch.; Girton Coll., Cambridge (MA); London Graduate Sch. of Business Studies (MSc). LRAM. FCSI. Financial Controller, ICFC, 1969–80; Scottish Development Agency: Investment Exec., 1980–84; Investment Man., 1984–88; Head of Business Enterprise, 1988–90; Director: Renfrew Development Co. Ltd, 1988–90; Scottish Food Fund, 1988–90; Grieg, Middleton & Co., 1990–2001; Sitka Capital Partners, 2001–02; Photopharmica Ltd, 2002–03; Fusion Lifestyle (formerly Southwark Community Leisure) Ltd, 2003–. Non-executive Director: Veryan Medical Ltd, 2004–07; Nano Biodesign Ltd, 2006–11. Member: Scottish Cttee, Design Council, 1975–77; Monopolies and Mergers Commn, 1976–81. Chm., Scottish Music Inf. Centre, 1986–90. University of Kent: Mem. Council, 2003–11 (Treas., 2004–05; Chm., 2005–11); Pro-Vice-Chancellor, 2005–11. Governor: Glasgow Sch. of Art, 1989–90; Tonbridge GS for Girls, 1993–97. DCL Kent 2012. *Recreations:* music, ballet, walking, entertaining. *Address:* 6 Egdean Walk, Sevenoaks, Kent TN13 3UQ.

MARSHALL, Wayne; organ recitalist and solo pianist, conductor and composer; Principal Conductor, WDR Funkhausorchester, Cologne, since 2014; *b* 13 Jan. 1961; *s* of Wigley Marshall and Costella (*née* Daniel). *Educ:* Chetham's Sch., Manchester; Royal Coll. of Music; Vienna Hochschule. FRCM 2010. Organ Schol., Manchester Cathedral and St George's Chapel, Windsor. Dir, W11 Opera Gp, 1991; Associate Music Dir and Conductor, Carmen Jones, Old Vic, 1991; Guest Chorus Dir, Royal Opera Hse, 1992; Organist-in-Residence, Bridgewater Hall, Manchester, 1996–; Principal Guest Conductor, Orch. Sinfonica di Milano Giuseppe, 2007–. Organ, solo piano, and duo recitals throughout UK, and overseas incl. US, European and Far East concert series; conductor and soloist with leading orchestras in UK and overseas, incl. CBSO, RPO, Philharmonia, London SO, London Philharmonic, BBCSO, Berlin Philharmonic, LA Philharmonic, Rotterdam Philharmonic and Vienna Symphony. Has made numerous recordings incl. organ music, and works by Hindemith and Gershwin. Artist of Year Award, BBC Music Mag., 1998; ECHO Award, 1998. *Address:* c/o Askonas Holt Ltd, Lincoln House, 300 High Holborn, WC1V 7JH. *T:* (020) 7400 1700, *Fax:* (020) 7400 1799. *E:* info@askonasholt.co.uk.

MARSHALL, Sir Woodville (Kemble), Kt 2011; PhD; Professor of History, Cave Hill Campus, Barbados, 1977–2000, now Emeritus, and Pro-Vice-Chancellor, 1990–2000, University of the West Indies; *b* Ruby Plantation Tenantry, St Philip, Barbados, 27 March 1935; *s* of Colbert and Eileen Marshall; *m* 1961, Dawn Italia Thompson; one *s* one *d*. *Educ:* Harrison Coll., Barbados; University Coll. of W Indies, Mona, Jamaica (BA 1st Cl. Hons Hist. 1958); Cambridge Univ. (PhD Caribbean Hist. 1964). Asst Lectr, Dept of Hist., Univ. of Ibadan, 1962–63; University of the West Indies: Asst Lectr, then Lectr, Dept of Hist., Mona, Jamaica, 1963–70; Sen. Lectr, 1970–77, Hd, 1976–82, Dept of Hist., Cave Hill, Barbados; Dean, Faculty of Arts and Gen. Studies, 1972–74 and 1985–87. Ed., Jl Caribbean Hist., 1981–90. Rapporteur, Editl Cttee, UNESCO Hist. of Caribbean, 1983–2000. Founding Pres., Assoc. of Caribbean Historians, 1974–77. Vice-President: Assoc. of Caribbean Univs and Res. Insts, 1998–2000; Council, Barbados Mus. *Publications:* The Colthurst Journal, 1997; (ed) I Speak for the People: the memoirs of Wynter Crawford, 2003; (ed) Thoughts on the Objectionable System of Labour for Wages and the Necessity of Substituting a System of Tenancy and Allotment of Staple Cultivation, 2005; Freedom is…: the story of the Rock Hall Village, 2006. *Recreations:* reading (light fiction), watching TV sports (mainly cricket), playing card games, especially poker. *Address:* 11 Paradise Heights, Cave Hill, St Michael, Barbados. *T:* 4251485. *E:* wmarsh@caribsurf.com.

MARSHALL-ANDREWS, Robert Graham; QC 1987; a Recorder of the Crown Court, since 1982; *b* 10 April 1944; *s* of late Robin and Eileen Nora Marshall; *m* 1968, Gillian Diana Elliott; one *s* one *d*. *Educ:* Mill Hill Sch.; Univ. of Bristol (LLB; winner, Observer Mace Nat. Debating Competition, 1965). Called to the Bar, Gray's Inn, 1967, Bencher, 1996; Oxford and Midland Circuit. Contested (Lab) Medway, 1992. MP (Lab) Medway, 1997–2010.

Founder Mem., Old Testament Prophets, 1996. Dep. Chm., Theatre Council, 1997–2010. Trustee: George Adamson Wildlife Preservation Trust, 1988–; Geffrye Museum, 1990–2011. Chm. of Govs, Grey Court Sch., 1988–94. *Publications:* The Palace of Wisdom (novel), 1989; A Man without Guilt (novel), 2002; Off Message, 2011; contrib. political articles to nat. periodicals. *Recreations:* theatre, reading, Rugby (watching), travelling about. *Address:* Carmelite Chambers, 9 Carmelite Street, EC4Y 0DR. *T:* (020) 7936 6300. *Clubs:* Garrick; Druidstone (Broadhaven, Pembrokeshire).

MARSHALL EVANS, David; *see* Evans, David M.

MARSHAM, family name of **Earl of Romney**.

MARSHAM, Viscount; David Charles Marsham; *b* 18 April 1977; *s* and *heir* of Earl of Romney, *qv*; *m* 2012, Katherine, *d* of Timothy Phillips; one *s* one *d.* Major, Scots Guards. *Heir: s* Hon. James Julian Marsham, *b* 4 Aug. 2014.

MARSLEN-WILSON, Lorraine Komisarjevsky; *see* Tyler, L. K.

MARSLEN-WILSON, Prof. William David, PhD; FBA 1996; Director of Research, Department of Experimental Psychology, University of Cambridge, since 2011; Fellow, Wolfson College, Cambridge, since 2000; *b* Salisbury, Wilts, 5 June 1945; *s* of David William Marslen-Wilson and Pera (*née* Funk); *m* 1982, Lorraine Komisarjevsky Tyler, *qv*; one *s* one *d*; one *d. Educ:* St John's Coll., Oxford (BA 1st cl. Philosophy and Psychology 1967); PhD MIT 1973. Asst Prof., Cttee on Cognition and Communication, Dept of Behavioral Scis, Chicago Univ., 1973–78; Scientific Associate, Max Planck Inst. for Psycholinguistics, Nijmegen, 1977–82; Lectr, Dept of Exptl Psychol., Cambridge Univ., 1982–84; Co-Dir, Max Planck Inst. for Psycholinguistics, 1985–87; Sen. Scientist, MRC Applied Psychol. Unit, Cambridge, 1987–90; Prof. of Psychology, 1990–97, College Fellow, 2000–, Birkbeck Coll., London Univ.; Dir, MRC Applied Psychol. Unit, subseq. MRC Cognition and Brain Scis Unit, Cambridge, 1997–2010. Hon. Prof. of Language and Cognition, Cambridge Univ., 2002–. MAE 1996. DUniv York, 2012. *Publications:* (ed) Lexical Representation and Process, 1989; over 150 contribs to learned jls incl. Science, Nature, Psychological Rev., Jl of Exptl Psychol., Cognition, Lang. and Cognitive Processes. *Recreations:* photography, cooking, gardening. *Address:* Department of Experimental Psychology, University of Cambridge, Downing Site, Cambridge CB2 3EB. *T:* (01223) 766975.

MARSON, Anthony; Finance Director, C. B. Marketing and Investments Ltd, 1997, retired; *b* 12 Jan. 1938; *m* 1963, Margaret Salmond; three *s. Educ:* Bristol Univ. (BA). Finance Dir, Pharmaceutical Div., Beecham Gp, 1968–90; Gp Finance Dir, PSA Services, DoE, 1990–93. *Address:* Bullbeggars House, Church Hill, Woking, Surrey GU21 4QE.

MARSON, Denise Lynn; Her Honour Judge Marson; a Circuit Judge, since 2015; *b* Manchester, 30 Jan. 1967; *d* of Eric and Joyce Gresty; *m* 1992, Geoffrey Charles Marson, *qv*; two *s. Educ:* Wilmslow Co. High Sch.; Sheffield Univ. (LLB Hons). Called to the Bar, Inner Temple, 1990; pupil and tenant, Sovereign Chambers, Leeds, 1990–2015; a Recorder, 2008–15; Fee-paid Judge of First-tier Tribunal (Health, Educn and Social Care Chamber (Mental Health)), 2011–. *Recreations:* family, dog walking, reading, bee-keeping, cinema. *Address:* Sheffield Family Hearing Centre, The Law Courts, 48 West Bar, Sheffield S3 8PH. *T:* (0114) 201 1140.

MARSON, Geoffrey Charles; QC 1997; **His Honour Judge Marson;** a Circuit Judge, since 2005; *b* 30 March 1952; *s* of Charles Marson and Muriel Annie Marson; *m* 1992, Denise Lynn Gresty (*see* D. L. Marson); two *s. Educ:* Malton Grammar Sch.; King's Coll. London (LLB Hons). Called to the Bar, Gray's Inn, 1975; Asst Recorder, 1991–95; a Recorder, 1995–2005; Head of Chambers, 1997–2005. Pt-time Pres., Mental Health Review Tribunals (Restricted Panel), 2000–07. *Recreations:* family, wine, cooking, travel. *Address:* Leeds Combined Court Centre, 1 Oxford Row, Leeds LS1 3BG.

MARSTON, Nicholas Richard; His Honour Judge Marston; a Circuit Judge, since 2005; a Deputy High Court Judge, since 2007; Regional Judge, Court of Protection, Bristol and Western Circuit, since 2012; *b* 24 March 1952; *s* of late Lt Comdr Max Marston, MBE, DSC, RN retd and Iris May Marston; *m* 1985, Suzanne Amanda Lyons; one *s* one *d. Educ:* UWIST (LLB Hons). Called to the Bar, Middle Temple, 1975; Asst Recorder, 1998–99; a Recorder, 1999–2005; Designated Family Judge, Hants and IoW, 2008–12. *Recreations:* keen historian and traveller, food, wine and friends, cricket, a once misplaced but now largely justified devotion to the Welsh Rugby team. *Address:* The Family Court, Bristol Civil Justice Centre, 2 Redcliff Street, Bristol BS1 6GR.

MARSTON, Stephen Andrew; Vice-Chancellor, University of Gloucestershire, since 2011; *b* Pembury, Kent, 7 June 1961; *s* of Charles and Ann Marston; civil partnership 2011, Anthony Broad. *Educ:* Shrewsbury Sch., Shropshire; Magdalene Coll., Cambridge (BA Hons Classics 1982). DES, 1983–91; Econ. Secretariat, Cabinet Office, 1991–94; Divl Manager, DfEE, 1994–98; Dir for Instns, HEFCE, 1998–2002; Dir for Skills, 2002–05, Dir Gen., Lifelong Learning and Skills, 2005–07, DfES; Director General: Further Educn and Skills, DIUS, 2007–09; Univs and Skills, BIS, 2009–11. *Recreations:* cycling, travel, DIY. *Address:* University of Gloucestershire, The Park, Cheltenham, Glos GL50 2RH. *T:* (01242) 714186. *E:* smarston@glos.ac.uk. *Club:* Naval and Military.

MARTEN, Charlotte Jane; Headteacher, Rugby High School, since 2006; *b* Richmond upon Thames, 2 Aug. 1957; *d* of Lewis Brindley Marten and Audrey Marten; *m* 1st, 1979, Gary Couch (marr. diss. 1991); one *s* two *d*; 2nd, 2008, Nigel Biggs. *Educ:* Mount Sch., York; Univ. of Birmingham (BA Hons Eng. Lang. and Lit. 1978); Inst. of Educn, Univ. of London (PGCE 1982); Univ. of Nottingham (MA Educnl Leadership 2004). Teacher, James Allen's Girls' Sch., 1982–94; Hd of English, Brighton and Hove High Sch., 1995–98; Dep. Hd, Northampton High Sch., 1999–2002; Principal, Jersey Coll. for Girls, 2003–06. Chair, Grammar Sch. Heads' Assoc., 2013–15. Trustee, Kidsaid Foundn, 2008–13. *Publications:* (ed by A. de Waal) The Ins and Outs of Selective Secondary Schools: a debate, 2015. *Recreations:* literature, riding, gardening, theatre. *Address:* Rugby High School, Longrood Road, Rugby, Warwickshire CV22 7RE. *E:* martenc@rugbyhighschool.co.uk.

MARTEN, Jason Nicholas G.; *see* Galbraith-Marten, J. N.

MARTIENSSEN, Prof. Robert Anthony, PhD; FRS 2006; Professor of Plant Genetics, Cold Spring Harbor Laboratory, since 1995; *b* 21 Dec. 1960. *Educ:* Emmanuel Coll., Cambridge (BA 1982; PhD 1986). Univ. of Calif, Berkeley, 1986–88; Cold Spring Harbor Lab., 1989–. Co-founder and Dir, 2000, now Mem., Scientific Adv. Bd, Orion Genomics. *Publications:* articles in learned jls. *Address:* Cold Spring Harbor Laboratory, 1 Bungtown Road, Cold Spring Harbor, NY 11724, USA.

MARTIN, family name of **Baron Martin of Springburn**.

MARTIN OF SPRINGBURN, Baron *cr* 2009 (Life Peer), of Port Dundas in the City of Glasgow; **Michael John Martin;** PC 2000; Speaker of the House of Commons, 2000–June 2009; *b* 3 July 1945; *s* of Michael and Mary Martin; *m* 1966, Mary McLay; one *s* one *d. Educ:* St Patrick's Boys' Sch., Glasgow. Sheet metal worker; AUEW Shop Steward, Rolls Royce, Hillington, 1970–74; Trade Union Organiser, 1976–79; Mem., and sponsored by, AEEU. MP Glasgow, Springburn, 1979–2005, Glasgow NE, 2005–June 2009 (Lab 1979–2000, when elected Speaker). PPS to Rt Hon. Denis Healey, MP, 1981–83; Member: Select Cttee for Trade and Industry, 1983–86; Speaker's Panel of Chairmen, 1987–2000; First Dep. Chm. of Ways and Means, and a Dep. Speaker, H of C, 1997–2000. Chm., Scottish Grand Cttee, 1987–97. Councillor: for Fairfield Ward, Glasgow Corp., 1973–74; for Balornock Ward, Glasgow DC, 1974–79. Mem., Coll. of Piping, 1989–. Mem., Unite Union. DUniv Glasgow, 2003. *Recreations:* hill walking, studying history of Forth and Clyde Canal, local history, piping. *Address:* House of Lords, SW1A 0PW.

See also Hon. P. Martin.

MARTIN, Prof. Alan Douglas, PhD; FRS 2004; Professor of Theoretical Physics, University of Durham, 1978–2003, now Emeritus and Professorial Fellow, Institute for Particle Physics Phenomenology, since 2003; *b* 4 Dec. 1937; *s* of Frederick Charles Martin and Emily May Martin (*née* Berkley); *m* 1st, 1964, Rev. Canon Penelope Johnson (marr. diss. 1999); one *s* two *d*; 2nd, 2000, Robin Louise Thodey. *Educ:* Eltham Coll.; UCL (BSc 1958; PhD 1962). CPhys 1989, FInstP 1989. Res. Associate, Univ. of Illinois, 1962; University of Durham: Lectr, 1964–71; Sen. Lectr, 1971–74; Reader, 1974–78; Hd, Dept of Physics, 1989–93; Derman Christopherson Res. Fellow, 1995–96. Res. Associate, CERN, Geneva, 1971–73. Erskine Fellow, Univ. of Canterbury, NZ, 2003; Leverhulme Emeritus Fellow, 2004–06. Max Born Medal and Prize, Inst. of Physics and German Physical Soc., 2007; Chancellor's Medal, Durham Univ., 2015. *Publications:* (with T. D. Spearman) Elementary Particle Theory, 1969; (with F. Halzen) Quarks and Leptons, 1984; (with P. D. B. Collins) Hadron Interactions, 1984; (jtly) Particle Physics and Cosmology, 1989; more than 300 res. papers in scientific jls. *Recreations:* gardening, ski-ing, tennis, listening to music. *Address:* 8 Quarry Heads Lane, Durham City DH1 3DY. *T:* (office) (0191) 334 3672, *Fax:* (0191) 334 3658. *E:* A.D.Martin@durham.ac.uk.

MARTIN, Alastair Gilbert, FRICS; Secretary and Keeper of the Records, Duchy of Cornwall, since 2013; *b* Reading, 21 Aug. 1960; *s* of Gilbert Martin and Diana Martin (*née* Hartgill); *m* 1988, Esme Marriott; one *s* one *d. Educ:* Royal Agricl Coll., Cirencester. FRICS 1991. Asst, Strutt & Parker, 1982–86; Partner, King Miles, then Mem., Bd of Mgt, Black Horse Agencies Alder King, 1986–91; Dir, Alder King Rural Surveyors, 1991–2001; Partner: Dreweatt Neate, 2001–09; Carter Jonas, 2009–13. Royal Institution of Chartered Surveyors: Pres., Rural Practice Div., 1999–2000; Chairman: Faculties and Forums Bd, 2000–02; Strategy and Resources Bd, 2002–07. *Recreations:* tennis, squash, hunting, shooting. *Address:* Duchy of Cornwall, 10 Buckingham Gate, SW1E 6LA. *T:* (020) 7834 7346. *E:* amartin@duchyofcornwall.org. *Club:* Farmers.

MARTIN, Anna M.; *see* Maxwell Martin.

MARTIN, Barry Robert; educational consultant, since 2013; Headmaster, Hampton School, 1997–2013; *b* 18 July 1950; *s* of late Robert Martin and Peggy Martin; *m* 1983, Fiona MacLeod; one *s* one *d. Educ:* Kingston Grammar Sch.; St Catharine's Coll., Cambridge (MA; Hockey Blue 1973); Inst. of Education, London Univ. (PGCE); Loughborough Univ. (MBA). Cert. Personal Finance Soc. 2009, Dip. Personal Finance Soc. 2013. Asst Master, Kingston GS, 1973–75; Bank of England Overseas Dept, 1975–77; Hd of Econs and Business Studies and Housemaster, Caterham Sch., 1978–83; Hd of Econs, Repton Sch., 1983–85; Housemaster and Dir of Studies, Mill Hill Sch., 1985–92; Principal, Liverpool Coll., 1992–97. Chief Examr, Cambridge A Level Business Studies, 1988–2002. Mem., HMC, 1992–2013 (Hon. Treas., 2007–13); Director: ISC, 2007–08, 2011–13; Ind. Schs Examinations Bd, 2007–13; Forum of Ind. Day Schs, 2011–15. Dir, Courtlands Consulting Ltd, 2013–; Sen. Advr, Wild Search, 2014–. Governor: King's House Sch., 2004–09; Kew Coll., 2008–; Alleyn's Sch., 2010–; Mall Sch., 2010–. FRSA 1994; FCMI (FIMgt 1997). *Publications:* jointly: The Complete A–Z Business Studies Handbook, 1994, 4th edn 2003; The Complete A–Z Economics and Business Studies Handbook, 1996, 3rd edn 2003; Business Studies, 1999, 2nd edn 2003; articles in Business Rev. *Recreation:* Cornwall. *Address:* c/o Hampton School, Hanworth Road, Hampton, Middx TW12 3HD. *T:* (020) 8979 5526. *Clubs:* East India; Hawks (Cambridge).

MARTIN, Prof. Benjamin Raymond; Professor of Science and Technology Policy Studies, University of Sussex, since 1996; Associate Fellow, Centre for Science and Policy, University of Cambridge, since 2010; *b* 9 Aug. 1952; *s* of late Adrian Sidney Martin, MBE and of Joan Dorothy (*née* Mingo); *m* 1973, Valerie Ann Bennett; two *s* one *d. Educ:* Blundell's Sch.; Churchill Coll., Cambridge (Kitchener Schol.; BA, MA); Univ. of Manchester (MSc). VSO sci. teacher, Nigeria, 1973–75; Science Policy Research Unit, University of Sussex: Fellow, 1978–86; Lectr, 1983–90; Sen. Fellow, 1986–96; Sen. Lectr, 1990–96; Dir, Sci. and Technol. Policy Res., Sci. Policy Res. Unit, 1997–2004. Vis. Lectr, Imperial Coll., London, 1983–84; Vis. Fellow, Max-Planck-Inst. für Gesellschaftsforschung, 1987; Vis. Prof., Centre for Advanced Study, Norwegian Acad. Scis and Letters, 2007–08; Vis. Schol., Faculty of Pol Sci., Univ. of Iceland, 2009–11; Sen. Vis. Fellow, Centre for Business Res., Judge Business Sch., Univ. of Cambridge, 2011–. Specialist Advr, H of L Select Cttee on Sci. and Technol., 2009–10. Chm., Internat. Expert Panel on bibliometric indicators for social scis and humanities, ESF, 2008–09; Member: Steering Gp, UK Technol. Foresight Prog., 1993–2000; Technol Opportunities Panel, EPSRC, 2001–04; BMBF Expert Gp on Demands on Res. Landscapes under Changing Framework Conditions, Berlin, 2007–08; Fruits of Curiosity Adv. Gp on econ. and social value of sci., Royal Soc., 2009–10. Mem. Senate, 1997–2004, and Council, 1997–2002, Univ. of Sussex. Ed., Res. Policy, 2004–. Derek de Solla Price Medal for Sci. Studies, Scientometrics jl, 1997. *Publications:* (with J. Irvine) Foresight in Science, 1984; (with J. Irvine) Research Foresight, 1989; (jtly) Investing in the Future, 1990; (jtly) Equipping Science for the 21st Century, 1997; (jtly) Science in Tomorrow's Europe, 1997; (with P. Nightingale) The Political Economy of Science, Technology and Innovation, 2000; (jtly) Creative Knowledge and Environments, 2004; (jtly) Creativity and Leadership in Science, Technology and Innovation, 2013; (jtly) Innovation Studies: evolution and future challenges, 2013; (jtly) The Triple Challenge for Europe: economic development, climate change and governance, 2015; contrib. papers to learned jls and books. *Recreations:* indoor rowing (10th place, World Indoor Rowing Championships, Boston, 1998), ski-ing, reading, DIY, gardening, family, travelling. *Address:* Linden Lea, 4 Foxglove Gardens, Purley, Surrey CR8 3LQ. *T:* (020) 8660 0329. *E:* B.Martin@sussex.ac.uk.

MARTIN, Sir Bruce; *see* Martin, Sir R. B.

MARTIN, Campbell; freelance journalist, since 2007; Member Scotland West, Scottish Parliament, 2003–07 (SNP, 2003–04, Ind, 2004–07); *b* 10 March 1960; *s* of late Campbell Martin and Jeanie, (Bunty), Martin; *m* 1993, Carol Marshall (marr. diss. 2008); one *s* one *d. Educ:* Ardrossan Acad.; James Watt Coll., Greenock (HNC Social Scis). Craft apprenticeship, ICI, Ardeer, Ayrshire, 1976–80; various posts, 1980–93; mature student, 1993–94; Buyer, Prestwick, 1995–97, Purchasing Liaison, Manchester, 1997–99, British Aerospace; Parly Asst, Whip's Administrator and Sec. to Shadow Cabinet, SNP Parly Gp, Scottish Parlt, 1999–2003. *Recreation:* reading.

MARTIN, Charles Edmund, MA; Headmaster, Bristol Grammar School, 1986–99; *b* 19 Sept. 1939; *s* of late Flight Lieut Charles Stuart Martin and of Sheila Martin; *m* 1966, Emily Mary Bozman; one *s* (one *d* decd). *Educ:* Lancing College; Selwyn College, Cambridge (Hons English; MA); Bristol University (PGCE). VSO, Sarawak, 1958–59; Asst Master, Leighton Park School, Reading, 1964–68; Day Housemaster and Hd of Sixth Form, Sevenoaks School, 1968–71; Head of English Dept and Dep. Headmaster, Pocklington School, 1971–80; Headmaster, King Edward VI Camp Hill Boys' School, Birmingham, 1980–86. Sec., 1992–93, Chm., 1993–94, HMC SW Div.; Divl Rep., HMC Cttee, 1992–94; Member: ISC Assisted Places Cttee, 1997–99; HMC Bridges and Partnership Cttee, 1998–99. Chief Examr, A-level English, UCLES, 1978–83. VSO selector, 1999–. Gov., John Cabot Academy (formerly John Cabot City Technol. Coll.), 2000–11 (Vice Chm., 2007–11). Mem., Sarawak Assoc., 2008–. *Recreations:* travel, hill walking, theatre, ornithology. *Address:* Flat 8 Seawalls, Seawalls Road, Bristol BS9 1PG.

MARTIN, Christine Jane; a Judge of the Upper Tribunal (Immigration and Asylum Chamber), and Resident Judge of the First-tier Tribunal (Immigration and Asylum Chamber), Stoke-on-Trent and Nottingham (formerly Resident Senior Immigration Judge, Asylum and Immigration Tribunal, Stoke on Trent and Nottingham), since 2006, and Manchester, since 2011; *b* 20 Jan. 1957; *d* of John Stewart Wreford and Peggy Patricia Wreford (*née* Clark); *m* 1986, Lawford Patrick William Martin; one *s* one *d*. *Educ:* Univ. of Keele (BA Hons 1979); Chester Coll. of Law (Law Soc. Finals 1980). Admitted Solicitor, 1982, then partner in private practice, 1982–2002; Immigration Adjudicator, then Immigration Judge, Manchester, 2003–06. Fee-paid Judge of First-tier Tribunal (Health Educn and Social Care) (formerly Pres. (pt-time), Mental Health Rev. Tribunal), 1996–. *Recreations:* travel, reading, cooking, theatre. *Address:* First-tier Tribunal (Immigration and Asylum Chamber), First Floor, Piccadilly Plaza, Moseley Street, Manchester M1 4AH. *T:* (0161) 234 2073. *Club:* Potters' (Stoke-on-Trent).

MARTIN, Christopher; *see* Martin, K.

MARTIN, Christopher Anthony John; singer and songwriter; *b* Devon, 1977; *m* 2003, Gwyneth Paltrow, *qv*; one *s* one *d*. *Educ:* Sherborne Sch.; University Coll. London. Lead singer, Coldplay, 1997–; albums: Parachutes, 2000 (Grammy Award, 2001; BRIT Award, 2001); A Rush of Blood to the Head, 2002 (Grammy Award, 2002; BRIT Award, 2003); X&Y, 2005; Viva la Vida or Death and All His Friends, 2008 (Grammy Award, 2008); Mylo Xyloto, 2011; Ghost Stories, 2014. BRIT Award for best group (jtly), 2001, 2003, 2012, for best live act (jtly), 2013. *Address:* c/o Parlophone, 5th Floor, EMI House, 43 Brook Green, W6 7EF.

MARTIN, Christopher George; management consultant; Director of Personnel, British Broadcasting Corporation, 1981–89, retired; *b* 29 May 1938; *s* of George and Lizbette Martin; *m* 1st, 1960, Moira Hughes (marr. diss. 1975); one *s* one *d*; 2nd, 1981, Elizabeth Buchanan Keith; one *s* decd. *Educ:* Beckenham Sch., Kent. Royal Marines, 1956–62. Group Personnel Manager: Viyella Internat., 1964–70; Great Universal Stores, 1970–74; Personnel Dir, Reed Paper & Board, 1974–76; UK Personnel Dir, Air Products Ltd, 1976–78; Gp Personnel Controller, Rank Organisation Ltd, 1978–81. CCMI (CBIM 1984); FIPM 1984. *Publications:* contrib. Jl of Textile Inst. *Recreations:* music, sailing. *Address:* Barthefere, 81700 Puylaurens, France. *T:* (5) 63734049.

MARTIN, Christopher Jon, CB 2014; Principal Private Secretary to the Prime Minister and Director General, Prime Minister's Office, since 2012; *b* West Bromwich, 15 May 1973; *s* of Peter and Gwenda Martin. *Educ:* Univ. of Bristol (BSc Hons Pols, BSc Physics 1996). Private Sec. to Financial Sec. to HM Treasury, 1999–2002; Sen. Manager, London Bor. of Hackney, 2002; HM Treasury: Asst Sec., Gen. Expenditure Policy, 2003–04; Hd, Productivity Team, 2004–06; Press Sec. to the Chancellor of the Exchequer and Head of Communications, 2006–07; Dir, Public Services and Envmt, 2007–10; interim Dir, Corporate Services, 2009; Dir, Nat. Security Secretariat, Cabinet Office, 2011. *Recreations:* cooking, running, entertaining. *Address:* 10 Downing Street, SW1A 2AA. *Club:* Arsenal Football.

MARTIN, Christopher Sanford; Headmaster, Millfield School, 1990–98; *b* 23 Aug. 1938; *s* of late Geoffrey Richard Rex Martin and Hazel Matthews; *m* 1st, 1968, Mary Julia Parry-Evans (marr. diss. 2006); one *s* one *d*; 2nd, 2008, Virginia, Lady Acland. *Educ:* St Andrews Univ. (MA Mod. Langs; PGCE). Commissioned 2/10 Gurkha Rifles, 1957. Taught at Westminster Sch., 1963–78, at Philips, Exeter Acad., USA, 1966; Head Master, Bristol Cathedral Sch., 1979–90. Member: Privy Council Educnl Panel, 1986–96; Engrg Council Educn Cttee, 1988–96; Adv. Gp on teaching as a profession, Teacher Trng Agency, 1995–98. Chairman: SW Div., HMC, 1987; Choir Schools' Assoc., 1987–89; HMC/SHA Working Party on teacher shortage, 1987–90; Students Partnership Worldwide, 1998–2005; Nat. Rep., HMC Cttee, 1987–89. Founded Textbooks for Africa scheme (ODA), 1988. Chairman: Mental Health Foundn, 2000–04; Hanover Foundn, 2001–08; Bottletop, 2008–12. Pres., Nat. Assoc. for Gifted Children, 2003–15. Governor: City of London Sch., 1998–; Springfields Acad., Calne, 2011–; Red Maids Sch., 2015–. Gov., Coram Family, 1999–2007; Trustee: Coram, 2008–12; Coram Life Educn, 2010–15; Foundling Mus., 2012–14. *Publications:* Millfield: a school for all seasons, 2007; Head over Heels, 2010. *Recreations:* travel, cycling. *Address:* 28 Caledonia Place, Clifton, Bristol BS8 4DL.

MARTIN, Claire, (Mrs Phillip Jackson), OBE 2011; jazz singer; Presenter, Jazz Line Up, BBC Radio 3, since 2000; Co-curator, South Coast Jazz Festival; *b* 6 Sept. 1967; *d* of David and Carole Godwin; adopted surname Martin as stage name; one *d*; *m* 2008, Phillip Jackson. *Educ:* Carshalton Coll.; Doris Holford Stage Sch. Jazz educator. Has performed with Hallé Orch., Liverpool SO, BBC Big Band, London Jazz Orch., Pete Long Big Band, Laurence Cottle Big Band, HR Big Band (Frankfurt), John Wilson Orch., Rias Big Band (Berlin), Nash Ensemble, Birmingham SO, RTE Orch., Lahti SO (Finland). *Album recordings:* The Waiting Game, 1992; Devil May Care, 1993; Old Boyfriends, 1994; Offbeat, 1995; Make this City Ours, 1997; Take My Heart, 1999; Perfect Alibi, 2000; Every Now and Then, 2001; Too Darn Hot, 2002; Secret Love, 2004; When Lights are Low, 2005; He Never Mentioned Love, 2007; A Modern Art, 2009; (with Sir Richard Rodney Bennett) Witchcraft, 2011; (with Kenny Barron) Too Much in Love to Care, 2012 (Best New Jazz Album, British Jazz Awards, 2013); Time and Place, 2014. Best Vocalist, British Jazz Awards, 1996, 1998, 2000, 2002, 2009, 2010, BBC Jazz Awards, 2003. *Recreations:* yoga, tennis, jazz clubs, basketball (Manager, Brighton Cougars under 14 squad). *Address:* 126 Valley Drive, Brighton, Sussex BN1 5FF. *E:* clairemartinjazz@btopenworld.com.

MARTIN, Dr Claude; Chancellor, International University in Geneva, since 2006; *b* 20 July 1945; *s* of Julien and Anna Martin-Zellweger; *m* 1985, Judith Füglister; two *s* two *d*. *Educ:* Univ. of Zurich (MSc; PhD Wildlife Ecol.). Field project executant, WWF/IUCN, India, 1971–73; Dir, Bia Nat. Park, Ghana, 1975–78; World Wildlife Fund, subseq. World Wide Fund for Nature: Dir, Switzerland, 1980–90; Dep. Dir Gen. (Prog.), Internat., 1990–93; Dir Gen., WWF Internat., 1993–2005, now Hon. Advr. Comdr, Golden Ark (Netherlands), 2003; Officier, Ordre National (Madagascar), 2003. *Publications:* Die Regenwälder Westafrikas, 1989, trans. as The Rainforests of West Africa, 1991. *Recreations:* mountain climbing, restoration of ancient buildings. *Address:* International University in Geneva, ICC 20, route de Pré-Bois, 1215 Geneva 15, Switzerland.

MARTIN, Sir Clive (Haydn), Kt 2001; OBE 1981; TD; DL; Chairman: Europa Publications Ltd, 1978–99; MPG Ltd (formerly Staples Printers Ltd), 1978–2009; Lord Mayor of London, 1999–2000; *b* 20 March 1935; *s* of Thomas Stanley Martin and Dorothy Gladys Martin; *m* 1959, Linda Constance Basil Penn; one *s* three *d*. *Educ:* St Albans Sch.; Haileybury and Imperial Service Coll.; London Sch. of Printing and Graphic Arts. FCIS 1966; FCMA 1971. Nat. Service, Germany, commnd RE (Survey), 1956–58. Man. Dir, Staples Printers Ltd, 1972–85. ADC to The Queen, 1982–86. City of London: Alderman, Aldgate Ward, 1985–2005; Sheriff, 1996–97. Master: Stationers' and Newspaper Makers' Co., 1997–98; Chartered Secs' and Administrators' Co., 2004–05. Hon. Artillery Company: CO, 1978–80; Regtl Col, 1981–83; Master Gunner, Tower of London, 1981–83. Vice-Pres., RFCA for Greater London, 2003–12. Hon. Colonel: 135 Ind. Geographic Sqn, RE, 1999–2004; London Regt, 2001–06. Master, Guild of Freemen of City of London, 1995. Trustee, Morden Coll., 1999–2011; Governor: Haileybury, 2001–; City of London Freemen's Sch., 2008–. Hon. DCL City, 1999; Hon. Dr London Inst., 2001. Comdr 1st Degree, Order of Dannebrog (Denmark). *Recreations:* sailing (British Sardinia Cup Team, 1984), cycling, walking. *Address:* Weathcrbury, 16 Heath Road, Potters Bar, Herts EN6 1LN. *Clubs:* Oriental, Royal Ocean Racing, East India.

MARTIN, Rev. Prof. David Alfred, PhD; FBA 2007; Professor of Sociology, London School of Economics and Political Science, London University, 1971–89, now Emeritus; *b* 30 June 1929; *s* of late Frederick Martin and late Rhoda Miriam Martin; *m* 1st, 1953, Daphne Sylvia Treherne (*d* 1975); one *s*; 2nd, 1962, Bernice Thompson; two *s* one *d*. *Educ:* Richmond and East Sheen Grammar Sch.; Westminster Coll. (DipEd 1952); BSc (ext.) 1st Cl. Hons, London Univ., 1959; PhD 1964; Westcott House, Cambridge. School teaching, 1952–59; postgrad. scholar, LSE, 1959–61; Asst Lectr, Sheffield Univ., 1961–62; Lectr, LSE, 1962–67, Reader, 1967–71. JSPS Scholar, Japan, 1978–79; Scurlock Prof. of Human Values, Southern Methodist Univ., Dallas, Texas, 1986–90; Hon. Prof., Lancaster Univ., 1993–2006; Adjunct Prof., Liverpool Hope Univ., 2006–12. Internat. Fellow, Inst. for Study of Econ. Culture, Boston Univ., 1990–. Lectures: Cadbury, Birmingham Univ., 1973; Ferguson, Manchester Univ., 1977; Gore, Westminster Abbey, 1977; Firth, Nottingham Univ., 1980; Forwood, Liverpool Univ., 1982; Prideaux, Exeter Univ., 1984; F. D. Maurice, KCL, 1991; Sarum, Oxford Univ., 1994–95; Gunning, Edinburgh Univ., 1997; Select Preacher, Cambridge Univ., 1979. Pres., Internat. Conf. of Sociology of Religion, 1975–83. Ordained deacon, 1983, priest 1984; Hon. Asst Priest, Guildford Cathedral, 1983–. Hon. DTheol Helsinki, 2000. *Publications:* Pacifism, 1965; A Sociology of English Religion, 1967; The Religious and the Secular, 1969; Tracts against the Times, 1973; A General Theory of Secularisation, 1978; Dilemmas of Contemporary Religion, 1978; (ed) Crisis for Cranmer and King James, 1979; The Breaking of the Image, 1980; (ed jtly) Theology and Sociology, 1980; (ed jtly) No Alternative, 1981; (ed jtly) Unholy Warfare, 1983; Divinity in a Grain of Bread, 1989; Tongues of Fire, 1990; The Forbidden Revolutions, 1996; Reflections on Sociology and Theology, 1997; Does Christianity Cause War?, 1997; Pentecostalism—The World Their Parish, 2001; Christian Language and its Mutations, 2002; Christian Language in the Secular City, 2002; On Secularization: towards a revised general theory, 2005; Sacred History and Sacred Geography, 2008; The Future of Christianity, 2011; The Education of David Martin, 2013; Religion and Power: no logos without mythos, 2014; contrib. Encounter, TLS, THES, Daedalus, TES. *Recreation:* piano accompaniment. *Address:* Cripplegate Cottage, 174 St John's Road, Woking, Surrey GU21 7PQ. *T:* (01483) 762134.

MARTIN, David Clifford; Head, Schools Programme, British Council, 2012–14; education and management consultant, since 2014; *b* Plymouth, 20 Dec. 1956; *s* of John Bernard Martin and Elizabeth Alma Martin (*née* Jones); *m* 1988, Sally Elizabeth Bennett; two *s* one *d*. *Educ:* Chigwell Sch.; Univ. of Durham (BSc Hons Chem. 1978; PGCE 1980). Teacher, Henry Fanshawe Sch., Dronfield, Derbys, 1980–84; Computer-based Learning Co-ordinator for E Midlands Reg., Microelectronics Educn Prog., 1984–86; British Council: Educn Advr, 1988–94; Dep. Dir, Nigeria, 1994–98; Director: Palestinian Territories, 1998–2002; Central Africa, 2002–06; Hungary, 2006–09; Pakistan, 2009–12. *Recreations:* cycling, walking, gardening, singing. *Address:* Maygrove Consulting Ltd, 31 Oathall Road, Haywards Heath RH16 3EG. *T:* 07769 163353. *E:* davidc_martin@yahoo.co.uk.

MARTIN, David John Pattison; Partner, A., D., P. & E. Farmers, since 1968; *b* 5 Feb. 1945; *s* of late John Besley Martin, CBE and Muriel Martin; *m* 1977, Basia Dowmunt; one *s* three *d* (and one *d* decd). *Educ:* Norwood Sch., Exeter; Kelly College; Fitzwilliam College, Cambridge (BA Hons 1967). Governor, Dummer Academy, USA, 1963–64; called to the Bar, Inner Temple, 1969; practised until 1976; returned to the Bar, 1998–2014; formerly Dir, family caravan and holiday business. Teignbridge District Councillor (C), 1979–83. Contested Yeovil, 1983. MP (C) Portsmouth South, 1987–97; contested (C) same seat, 1997; PPS to Minister of State, Defence Procurement, 1990, to Sec. of State, Foreign and Commonwealth Affairs, 1990–94. Contested (C): South West Region, EP elecns, 1999; Rugby and Kenilworth, 2001; Bristol W, 2005. *Recreations:* music, golf. *Club:* Hawks (Cambridge).

MARTIN, (David) Paul; Chief Executive, Wandsworth Borough Council, since 2010; *b* 10 Aug. 1961; *s* of late Leslie John and of Dora Marguerite Martin; *m* (marr. diss.); two *d*. *Educ:* Ilford Co. High Sch. for Boys; UCW, Aberystwyth (BA Hons); Anglia Business Sch. (MSc). Asst Librarian, Notts CC, 1982–85; Community Services Librarian, Bolton MBC, 1985–87; Area Organiser of Cultural Services, Manchester CC, 1987–91; Hd, Policy and Review, 1991–93, Asst Chief Exec., 1993–97, Cambs CC; Dir, Community Services, 1997–99, Chief Exec., 1999–2002, Peterborough CC; Regl Dir, Govt Office for the SE, 2002–05; Chief Exec., Sutton LBC, 2005–10. *Recreations:* music, theatre, English and American literature, travel, keeping fit. *Address:* The Town Hall, Wandsworth High Street, SW18 2PU. *T:* 07892 401931. *E:* paulmartin_home@msn.com.

MARTIN, David Weir; Member (Lab) Scotland, European Parliament, since 1999 (Lothians, 1984–99); *b* 26 Aug. 1954; *s* of William Martin and Marion Weir. *Educ:* Liberton High School; Heriot-Watt University (BA Hons Econs); Leicester Univ. (MA 1997). Stockbroker's clerk, 1970–74; animal rights campaigner, 1975–78. Lothian Regional Councillor, 1982–84. European Parliament: Leader, British Lab. Gp, 1987–88; a Vice Pres., 1989–2004. Vice-Pres., Internat. Inst. for Democracy; Vice-President: Nat. Playbus Assoc., 1985–; Advocates for Animals (formerly Scottish Soc. for Prevention of Vivisection), 1993–. Dir, St Andrew Animal Fund, 1986–. *Publications:* Europe: an ever closer union, 1991; Fabian pamphlets on the Common Market and on EC enlargement; Wheatley pamphlet on European Union. *Recreations:* soccer, reading. *Address:* (office) Midlothian Innovation Centre, Pentlandfield, Roslin EH25 9RE. *T:* (0131) 440 9040.

MARTIN, Prof. Derek H.; Professor of Physics, Queen Mary and Westfield College (formerly Queen Mary College), University of London, 1967–94, Emeritus Professor since 1995 (Hon. Fellow, 1996); *b* 18 May 1929; *s* of Alec Gooch Martin and Winifred Martin; *m* 1951, Joyce Sheila Leaper; one *s* one *d*. *Educ:* Hitchin Boys' Grammar Sch.; Eastbourne Grammar Sch.; Univ. of Nottingham (BSc; PhD). Queen Mary College, London: Lectr, 1954–58, 1962–63; Reader in Experimental Physics, 1963–67; Dean, Faculty of Science, 1968–70; Head of Dept of Physics, 1970–75. DSIR Res. Fellow, 1959–62; Visiting Professor: Univ. of Calif, Berkeley, 1965–66; Univ. of Essex, 1995–97. Member: Astronomy, Space and Radio Bd, SRC, 1975–78; Bd, Athlone Press, 1973–79; Royal Greenwich Observatory Cttee, 1977–80; Senate, Univ. of London, 1981–86; Court, Univ. of Essex, 1986–98. Fellow, Inst. of Physics (Hon. Sec., 1984–94); Mem., Internat. Astronomical Union. NPL Metrology Award, 1983. Editor, Advances in Physics, 1974–84. *Publications:* Magnetism in Solids, 1967; Spectroscopic Techniques, 1967; numerous articles and papers in Proc. Royal Soc., Jl of Physics, etc. *Address:* 14 Avon Mill Place, Pershore, Worcs WR10 1AZ. *T:* (01386) 555301. *Club:* Athenæum.

MARTIN, Diane Robertson, CBE 2013; Founder and Director, Dovetail Initiative, since 2012; *b* Dundee, 20 March 1964; *d* of Edward Martin and Margaret Rodgers Martin. *Educ:* Canterbury Girls High Sch., Melbourne; Dundee Coll. of Commerce (Cert. Secretarial Studies, Office Skills and Eng. 1982); Sch. for Urban Mission, Washington, DC (Cert. Urban Studies and Soc. Systems 1994); Counselling and Psychotherapy Central Awarding Body (Cert. Integrative Counselling Skills and Theory 1999); Lambeth Coll., London (Dip. Therapeutic Counselling 2008); Middlesex Univ. (Cert. Gender and Sexual Diversity Therapy 2009). Shop Asst, Top Man, Dundee, 1982–83; care asst, Winged Fellowship Trust, 1985–87; nanny, NY, 1987–93; maternity nurse, London, 1994–97; Founder and Dir, Women's Project, 1998–2012. Lead Gp Prog. Facilitator, Living Proj., 2011–; Pan London Strategic Devlt Officer (Prostitution), STRATEtude, 2013–16; Founder and Gp Facilitator,

VOICES, 2013–. Trustee, Beyond the Streets, 2003–07, 2013–. *Recreations:* telly, reading in bed, challenging the sex industry and sexual exploitation, carbohydrates, God, the sea, gospel, soul and hip hop music.

MARTIN, Most Rev. Diarmuid; *see* Dublin, Archbishop of, and Primate of Ireland, (RC).

MARTIN, Dòmhnall, (Donald); Chairman, Acair Ltd, since 2008; Vice Lord-Lieutenant of Western Isles, since 2013; *b* Bunabhainneadarra, Isle of Harris, 21 March 1947; *s* of late Murdo Martin and Mary Martin (*née* Macleod); *m* 1978, Sandra MacLeay; two *s* one *d*. *Educ:* Bunabhainneadarra Primary Sch.; Sir E. Scott Sch., Isle of Harris; Inverness High Sch.; Aberdeen Coll. of Commerce (Dip. Public Admin 1990). Civil Service Administrator, DSS, Dept of Agriculture and Fisheries Scotland, MoD and Highlands and Is Develt Bd, 1965–75; Prin. Admin. Asst, 1975–78, Depute Dir of Admin, 1978–97, Comhairle nan Eilean Siar; Dir, Community Develt, 1997–2001, Chief Exec., 2001–07, Comunn na Gàidhlig; Interim Chief Exec., Bòrd na Gàidhlig, 2009–10. Member: Western Isles Children's Panel, 1976–79; Gaelic Broadcasting Cttee, 1997–2003; Harris Tweed Authy Bd, 1997–2013 (Vice Chair, 2002–07; Chair, 2007–13). Member, Board: Attend (UK), 2007–10 (Chair, Attend (Alba), 2007–10); M G Alba, 2008–14; Lews Castle Coll., 2008–14. Sec., Eur. Bureau for Lesser Used Langs (Scottish and UK), 1984–2003. Trustee: Sabhal Mòr Ostaig, 1992–2004; N of Scotland Hydro Electric Community Trust, 2008–. Clerk, Western Isles Lieutenancy, 1997–. DL Western Isles, 2002. Volunteer, Stornoway League of Friends, 1982– (Chair, 1997–2009). *Recreations:* grandparenting, Gaelic culture and broadcasting, local history, genealogy, gardening, watching Hearts FC. *Address:* Druimard, 4 Airigh Ard, Steòrnabhagh, Eilean Leòdhas HS1 2UN. *T:* (01851) 704890. *E:* domhnallm@aol.com.

MARTIN, Dominic David William, CVO 2007; HM Diplomatic Service; Vice-President, Communications, Global Strategy and Business Development, Statoil, since 2014; *b* 25 Nov. 1964; *s* of Christopher Martin and Felicity Martin (*née* Weston); *m* 1996, Emily Walter; three *d*. *Educ:* Westminster Sch.; Oriel Coll., Oxford (BA Hons). Joined HM Diplomatic Service, 1987; FCO, 1987–89; Third, later Second Sec., New Delhi, 1989–92; FCO, 1992–96; First Secretary: Buenos Aires, 1996–99; FCO, 1999–2001; Political Counsellor, and Hd, Political Dept, New Delhi, 2001–04; Counsellor (Political, Press and Public Affairs), Washington, 2004–08; UK Perm. Rep. to OECD, Paris, 2008–11; Dir, Prosperity, FCO, 2011–12; Dir, G8 Presidency, Cabinet Office, 2012–14. *Address:* Statoil, 1 Kingdom Street, W2 6BD.

MARTIN, Donald; *see* Martin, Dòmhnall.

MARTIN, Most Rev. Eamon; *see* Armagh, Archbishop of, (RC).

MARTIN, Evelyn Fairfax, OBE 1994; Company Secretary, National Council of Women of GB, 1992–2000 (National President, 1986–88); Co-Chair, Women's National Commission, 1991–93; *b* 12 Aug. 1926; *d* of late Kenneth Gordon Robinson and Beatrice Robinson (*née* Munro); *m* 1949, Dennis William Martin; three *d* (and one *d* decd). *Educ:* Belvedere Girls' Sch., Liverpool; Huyton Coll. for Girls, Liverpool; Mrs Hoster's Secretarial Coll. Foster parent, 1960–71. Chairman: Battered Wives Hostel, Calderdale, 1980–82; Calderdale Well Woman Centre, 1982–86; Calderdale CHC, 1982–84; Women's Health and Screening Delegn, 1985–91. FRSA 1991. *Recreations:* gardening, foreign travel, animals. *Address:* 1 Porter Apartments, Haworth Close, Halifax HX1 2NL. *T:* (01422) 360438. *E:* evelynfairfax@tiscali.co.uk. *Club:* University Women's.

MARTIN, Francis James, (Frank); HM Diplomatic Service, retired; High Commissioner to Botswana, 2005–09; *b* 3 May 1949; *s* of Brian and Elizabeth Martin; *m* 1970, Aileen Margaret Shovlin; two *s* two *d*. *Educ:* St Ninian's High Sch., Kirkintilloch; Bourne Sch., Kuala Lumpur; St John's, Singapore. Joined FCO, 1968; Third Sec., Reykjavík, 1971–73; Vice Consul (Commercial), Stuttgart, 1973–76; FCO, 1976–78; Vice-Consul (Political/Inf.), Cape Town, 1979–83; Second, later First, Sec. (Instns), UK Representation to EC, Brussels, 1983–88; FCO, 1988; Dep. High Comr, Freetown, 1988–91; FCO, 1991; on secondment to DTI, 1992–95; lang. student, 1995; Dep. Hd of Mission, Luanda, 1995–98; First Sec., and Hd, Commercial Dept, Copenhagen, 1998–2001; FCO, 2001–02; High Comr to Lesotho, 2002–05. *Recreations:* fishing, walking.

MARTIN, Frank; Change Manager, Tax Policy Project, HM Treasury, 2003–06; *b* 1 April 1946; *s* of Frank and Sylvia Martin; *m* 1975, Jean Richardson; one *s* one *d*. *Educ:* Alsop High Sch. for Boys, Liverpool; Sidney Sussex Coll., Cambridge (MA Hist.); LSE (MSc Internat. Relns). COI, 1969–73; DTI, 1973–76; HM Treasury, 1976–2006: Dep. Dir, Central Unit on Purchasing, 1987–89; on secondment as Principal Establishment and Finance Officer, CSO, 1989–93, and TTA, 1999–2001; Second Treasury Officer of Accounts, 1994–98; Dir, Corporate Services, Commonwealth Secretariat, 2001–03 (on secondment). *Recreations:* walking, reading, gardening, listening to music.

MARTIN, Geoffrey; *see* Martin, T. G.

MARTIN, Prof. Geoffrey Almeric Thorndike, PhD, LittD; FSA; Edwards Professor of Egyptology and Head of Department of Egyptology, University College London, 1988–93, now Emeritus; *b* 28 May 1934; *s* of late Albert Thorndike Martin and Lily Martin (*née* Jackson). *Educ:* Palmer's Sch., Grays Thurrock; University Coll. London (Sir William Meyer Prize, 1961; BA 1963); Corpus Christi Coll., Cambridge; Christ's Coll., Cambridge (MA 1966; PhD 1969; LittD 1994). Chartered Librarian (ALA, 1958–60); FSA 1975. Cataloguer, Brit. Nat. Bibliography, 1957–60; Lady Budge Res. Fellow in Egyptology, Christ's Coll., Cambridge, 1966–70; University College London: Lectr in Egyptology, 1970–78; Reader in Egyptian Archaeology, 1978–87; Prof. (*ad hominem*) of Egyptology, 1987–88. Wilbour Fellow, Brooklyn Museum, 1969; Rundle Fellow, Aust. Centre for Egyptology, Macquarie Univ., 1985, 1995, 2000; Jane and Morgan Whitney Art Hist. Fellow, Met. Mus. of Art, NY, 1999–2001. Vis. Prof., Collège de France, 1986. Glanville Lectr, Cambridge, 1990. Has lectured extensively in UK and abroad. Assisted at excavations of Egypt Exploration Society at: Buhen, Sudan, 1963; Saqqara, Egypt, 1964–68, 1970–71 (Site Dir, 1971–74; Field Dir, 1975–98); Field Director: Epigraphic Mission, Amarna, Egypt, 1969, 1980; Leiden Excavations, Saqqara, 1999–2000 (Hon. Dir, 2001–); Jt Field Dir, 1998–2001, Field Dir, 2002, Amarna Royal Tombs Project, Valley of the Kings, Thebes; Field Dir, Cambridge Expedn to Valley of the Kings, 2005–; Jt Field Dir, Cambridge Expedn to Valley of the Kings and New Kingdom Res. Foundn, 2014–. Mem. Cttee, Egypt Exploration Soc., 1969–97 (Hon. Vice-Pres., 2012); Rep. for GB, Council of Internat. Assoc. Egyptologists, 1976–82; Mem. Cttee, Bd of Management, Gerald Averay Wainwright Near Eastern Archaeol Fund, Oxford Univ., 1985–89; Christ's College, Cambridge: Hon. Keeper of Muniment Room, 1997–2004; Hon. Keeper of the Plate, 2000–13; Hon. Keeper of the Archives, 2004–; Fellow Commoner, 1998–. Patron, Thurrock Local History Soc., 1996–. Corresp. Mem., German Archaeol Inst., 1982. Ed., Egypt in Miniature series (Oxford Expedition to Egypt), 2006–. *Publications:* Egyptian Administrative and Private-Name Seals, 1971; The Royal Tomb at El-Amarna, vol. 1, 1974, vol. 2, 1989; The Tomb of Hetepka, 1979; The Sacred Animal Necropolis at North Saqqara, 1981; (with V. Raisman) Canopic Equipment in the Petrie Collection, 1984; Scarabs, Cylinders and other Ancient Egyptian Seals, 1985; The Tomb Chapels of Paser and Raia, 1985; Corpus of Reliefs of the New Kingdom, vol. 1, 1987; (with A. El-Khouly) Excavations in the Royal Necropolis at El-Amarna, 1987; The Memphite Tomb of Horemheb, 1989; The Hidden Tombs of Memphis, 1991 (German edn 1994); Bibliography of the Amarna Period and its aftermath, 1991; The Tomb of Tia and Tia, 1997; The Tombs of Three Memphite Officials, 2001; Stelae from Egypt and Nubia in the Fitzwilliam Museum, Cambridge, 2005; Private Stelae of the Early Dynastic Period from the Royal Cemetery at Abydos, 2011; The Tomb of Maya and Meryt, I, 2012; Tutankhamun's Regent, 2015; contribs to learned and other jls and to Festschriften. *Recreations:* travel, English and European history, bibliography. *Address:* c/o Christ's College, Cambridge CB2 3BU.

MARTIN, Sir George (Henry), Kt 1996; CBE 1988; Chairman: AIR Group of companies, 1965–2006; Heart of London Radio, 1994–2005; Director, Chrysalis Group, 1978–2006; *b* 3 Jan. 1926; *s* of Henry and Bertha Beatrice Martin; *m* 1st, 1948, Sheena Rose Chisholm; one *s* one *d*; 2nd, 1966, Judy Lockhart Smith; one *s* one *d*. *Educ:* St Ignatius Coll., Stamford Hill, London; Bromley County Sch., Kent; Guildhall Sch. of Music and Drama (Hon. FGSM 1998). Sub-Lieut, FAA, RNVR, 1944–47. BBC, July 1950; EMI Records Ltd, Nov. 1950–1965; formed AIR Gp of cos (originally Associated Independent Recordings Ltd), 1965; built AIR Studios, 1969; built AIR Studios, Montserrat, 1979; completed new AIR Studios, Lyndhurst Hall, Hampstead, 1992; company merged with Chrysalis Gp, 1974; produced innumerable records, including all those featuring The Beatles; scored the music for fifteen films; nominated for Oscar for A Hard Day's Night, 1964; (with G. Martin) produced music for Cirque de Soleil show, Las Vegas, 2006; Grammy Awards, USA, 1964, 1967 (two), 1973, 1993, 1996, 2007 (two); Ivor Novello Awards, 1963, 1979. Hon. RAM 1999. Hon. DMus: Berklee Coll. of Music, Boston, Mass, 1989; Surrey, 1998; Leeds, 2007; Oxford, 2011; RAM, 2011; Hon. MA Salford, 1992; Hon. Dr Lund, Sweden, 2010. Music Industry Trusts' Award, 1998; La Sociedad de Artistas de España Award, 2001; Lifetime Achievement Award, Ghent, 2002. *Publications:* All You Need Is Ears, 1979; Making Music, 1983; Summer of Love, 1994; Playback: an illustrated memoir, 2002. *Recreations:* boats, sculpture, tennis, snooker. *Address:* 55 Lancaster Gate, W2 3NA. *Clubs:* Oriental; Alderney Sailing.

MARTIN, Prof. (George) Steven, PhD; FRS 1998; Research Virologist, Cancer Research Laboratory, since 1983, Professor of Molecular and Cell Biology, since 1989, and Dean, Division of Biological Sciences, since 2012, University of California at Berkeley; *b* 19 Sept. 1943; *s* of Kurt and Hanna Martin; *m* 1969, Gail Zuckman; one *s*. *Educ:* Queens' Coll., Cambridge (MA 1966; PhD 1968). Postdoctoral Fellow, Virus Lab., Univ. of Calif, Berkeley, 1968–71; staff mem., ICRF, London, 1971–75; University of California, Berkeley: Asst Prof., 1975–79, Associate Prof., 1979–83, Prof. of Zoology, 1983–89, Dept of Zool.; Asst Res. Virologist, 1975–79, Associate Res. Virologist, 1979–83, Cancer Res. Lab; Richard and Rhoda Goldman Dist. Prof., Dept of Molecular and Cell Biol., 2002–07; Judy C. Webb Prof. and Chair, Dept of Molecular and Cell Biol., 2007–11. Jane Coffin Childs Meml Fund Fellow, 1968–70; Amer. Cancer Soc. Dernham Fellow, 1970–71; John Simon Guggenheim Meml Foundn Fellow, 1991–92. Scholar Award in Cancer Res., Amer. Cancer Soc., 1991–92. *Publications:* contribs to Nature, Science, Cell and other scientific jls. *Recreations:* hiking, bicycling, reading. *Address:* University of California at Berkeley, Department of Molecular and Cell Biology, Li Ka Shing Center #3370, Berkeley, CA 94720–3370, USA. *T:* (510) 6421508.

MARTIN, Gerard James; QC 2000; a Recorder, since 2000; *b* 27 May 1955; *m* 1980, Deirdre Martin; three *s*. *Educ:* St Joseph's Coll., Blackpool; Trinity Hall, Cambridge (BA Law). Called to the Bar, Middle Temple, 1978; Asst Recorder, 1997–2000. *Recreations:* most sports, good food and wine. *Address:* Exchange Chambers, One Derby Square, Liverpool L2 9XX.

MARTIN, Sir Gregory (Michael Gerard), Kt 2013; Executive Headteacher, Durand Academy, 2010–15; *b* Beverley, E Yorks, 2 July 1952; *s* of George Martin and Thelma Martin; partner, Saffron Elizabeth Rebecca Smith; two *s* two *d*. *Educ:* Norwood Coll., Harrogate; Inst. of Educn, Univ. of London (BEd Hons). Qualified teacher, 1976. Teacher, St Mary's Clapham, 1976–82; Dep. Headteacher, Sudbourne Primary Sch., 1982–86; Headteacher, Durand Jun. Sch., later Durand Primary Sch., 1986–2010, amalgamating Mostyn Gardens Primary Sch., 1999. *Recreations:* talking, sleeping, arguing (but not always in that order). *Club:* Manchester United Football.

MARTIN, Iain James; author; political commentator; Editor, CapX, since 2014; *b* 2 Oct. 1971; *m* Fiona; one *s*. *Educ:* Castlehead High Sch., Paisley; Univ. of Glasgow (MA 1993). Reporter, Sunday Times Scotland, 1993–97; Political Ed., then Asst Ed., Scotland on Sunday, 1997–2000; Asst Ed. and political commentator, The Scotsman, 2000–01; Dep. Ed., Scotland on Sunday, 2001; Ed., The Scotsman, 2001–04; Ed., Scotland on Sunday, 2004–06; Dep. Ed., Sunday Telegraph, 2006; Gp Exec. Ed., 2007, Head of Comment, 2008–09, Telegraph Media Gp; Dep. Ed., Wall Street Journal Europe, 2009–11. *Publications:* Making It Happen: Fred Goodwin, RBS and the men who blew up the British economy, 2013.

MARTIN, Ian; Executive Director, Security Council Report, since 2015; *b* 10 Aug. 1946; *s* of Collin and Betty Martin. *Educ:* Brentwood Sch.; Emmanuel Coll., Cambridge; Harvard Univ. Ford Foundn Representative's Staff, India, 1969–70, Pakistan, 1970–71, Bangladesh, 1972; Community Relations Officer, Redbridge Community Relations Council, 1973–75; Gen. Sec., Jt Council for the Welfare of Immigrants, 1977–82 (Dep. Gen. Sec., 1976–77; Exec. Cttee Mem., 1982–86); Gen. Sec., The Fabian Soc., 1982–85; Sec. Gen., Amnesty Internat., 1986–92 (Hd, Asia Res. Dept, 1985–86). Dir for Human Rights, UN/OAS Internat. Civilian Mission in Haiti, 1993, 1994–95; Chief, UN Human Rights Field Op., Rwanda, 1995–96; Special Advr, UN High Comr for Human Rights, 1998; Dep. High Rep. for Human Rights, Bosnia and Herzegovina, 1998–99; Special Rep. of UN Sec.-Gen., East Timor Popular Consultation, 1999; Dep. Special Rep. of UN Sec.-Gen., UN Mission in Ethiopia and Eritrea, 2000–01; Vice-Pres., Internat. Center for Transitional Justice, NY, 2002–05; Rep. of UN High Comr for Human Rights, Nepal, 2005–06; Special Rep. of UN Sec.-Gen., Nepal, 2007–09; Hd, UN HQ Bd of Inquiry into certain incidents in Gaza Strip, 2009; Special Rep. of UN Sec.-Gen., Libya, 2011–12. Sen. Associate, Carnegie Endowment for Internat. Peace, 1993, 1994; Visiting Fellow: Human Rights Centre, Univ. of Essex, 1996–97; Internat. Peace Acad., NY, 2000. Member: Exec. Cttee, NCCL, 1983–85; Redbridge and Waltham Forest AHA, 1977–82; Redbridge HA, 1982–83. Councillor, London Borough of Redbridge, 1978–82. *Publications:* Immigration Law and Practice (with Larry Grant), 1982; Self-Determination in East Timor, 2001; Nepal's Peace Process at the United Nations, 2010 *contributed to:* Labour and Equality, Fabian Essays, 1980; Civil Liberties, Cobden Trust Essays, 1984; Hard Choices (ed J. Moore), 1998; Honoring Human Rights (ed A. Henkin), 2000; The United Nations and Regional Security (ed M. Pugh and W. P. S. Sidhu), 2003; Humanitarian Intervention and International Relations (ed J. M. Welsh), 2004; The UN Security Council (ed D. Malone), 2004; Nepal in Transition (ed S. Einsiedel, D. Malone and S. Pradhan), 2012; The Libyan Revolution and its Aftermath (ed P. Cole and B. McQuinn), 2015. *Address:* 346 Ben Jonson House, Barbican, EC2Y 8NQ.

MARTIN, Ian Alexander; Chairman, SSL International PLC, 2001–05; Executive Chairman, Heath Lambert Holdings Ltd, 2003–05; *b* 28 Feb. 1935; *s* of Alexander Martin and Eva (*née* Gillman); *m* 1963, Phyllis Mitchell-Bey; one *s* two *d*. *Educ:* Univ. of St Andrews (MA). Mem., Inst. of Chartered Accountants, Scotland. Dir, Mine Safety Appliances Co. Ltd, 1969–72; Div. Dir, ITT Europe, 1977–79; Grand Metropolitan: Dir, 1985–94; Gp Man. Dir, 1991–93; Dep. Chm., 1993–94; Chairman: Intercontinental Hotels, 1986–88; Burger King Corp., 1989–93; Pillsbury Co., 1989–93; Internat. Distillers and Vintners, 1992–93; Chm. and Chief Exec., Glenisla Gp Ltd, 1994–97; Chm., 1995–2001, Chief Exec., 2001, Unigate, then Uniq; Chairman: Baxi Gp (formerly Newmond), 1997–2002; Heath Lambert Fenchurch Hldgs (formerly Erycinus), 1997–2005; William Hill, 1999–; 365 Corporation PLC, 1999–2002; Director: St Paul Companies Inc., 1989–96; Grocery Manufacturers of America, 1989–93; Granada Group, 1992–98; House of Fraser, 1994–2000; Nat. Commn on Children, USA, 1990–93. Chm., Europe Cttee, CBI, 1993–94; Mem. Adv. Cttee, Ian Jones & Partners,

1998–. Trustee, Duke of Edinburgh's Award Scheme, 1991–98; Dir, Friends of the Youth Award Inc., 1991–98. Freeman, City of London, 1982. CCMI (CBIM 1986). *Recreations:* angling, golf, music.

MARTIN, James, FCCA; Chairman: A J Bell Ltd, 2007–13; Christie Hospital NHS Foundation Trust, 2007–11; *b* 9 Dec. 1942; *s* of Warwick Hammond Martin and Elsie Eileen Martin; *m* 1964, Jean Iveson (*d* 2006); two *s.* FCCA 1972. Chief Exec., 1982–2002, Dep. Chm., 2002–05, N Brown Group plc. Non-executive Director: Redrow plc, 1997–2007; Styles & Wood Gp, 2006–14 (Chm., 2009–14); Chairman: Ethel Austin Ltd, 2002–04; Stirling Gp Ltd, 2003–05; Roseby Ltd, 2004–06; Alexon plc, 2005–08. Pres., Eur. Mail Order Traders Assoc., 2002–05. Mem., NW Business Leadership Team, 2000–05; NW Inst. of Direct Marketing, 2002–05. Gov., Manchester Metropolitan Univ., 2002–06. *Recreations:* sport, fishing, shooting, golf. *Address:* The Coach House, Warrington Road, Great Budworth, Northwich, Cheshire CW9 6HB. *T:* (01606) 891436.

MARTIN, James Brown; Scottish Public Services Ombudsman, since 2009; *b* 6 Dec. 1953; *s* of James and Annie Martin; *m* 1st, 1975, Anne McNaughton; one *s* one *d*; 2nd, 2002, Elaine Smith; one *s* one *d. Educ:* Larbert Village and High Schs; Heriot-Watt Univ. (BAEcon); Moray House College of Educn. Teacher, Falkirk High Sch., 1975–79; Field Officer 1979–83, Asst Sec. 1983–88, Gen. Sec., 1988–95, EIS; Dir, Causeway Consulting, 2002–09. Police Complaints Comr for Scotland, 2007–09. Non-exec. Chm., LogicaCMG Scotland, 2002–07. Member: Gen. Council, Scottish TUC, 1987; Exec., ETUCE, 1988; Exec., Education International, 1993; SFC, 2005–09. Mem., Forth Valley Enterprise Bd, 1989. *Recreations:* Hibernian FC, watching football.

MARTIN, Janet, (Mrs K. P. Martin); Relief Warden (Assisted Independence), Test Valley Housing, 1988–91; *b* Dorchester, Dorset, 8 Sept. 1927; *d* of James Wilkinson and Florence Steer; *m* 1951, Peter Martin, sometime of Southampton HA and Senior Consultant AT&T (ISTEL) Ltd (*d* 2004); one *s* one *d. Educ:* Dorchester Co. Sch. for Girls, Dorset; Weymouth Tech. Coll.; occupational training courses. PA to Group Sec., Herrison HMC, 1949; admin./clerical work, NHS and other, 1956; social research fieldwork, mainly NHS (Wessex mental health care evaluation team), and Social Services (Hants CC and Nat. Inst. for Social Work), 1967–76; residential social worker (children with special needs), Southampton, 1976–78; Social Services Officer, Test Valley, 1978–86; Senior Residential Care Officer (Elderly), Test Valley Social Services, 1986–87. Interviewer, MRC 'National' Survey, 1970–85; Psychosexual Counsellor, Aldermoor Clinic, 1981–84. Mem., Press Council, 1973–78. *Recreations:* buildings, books. *Address:* The Old Stables, Linden Avenue, Dorchester, Dorset DT1 1EJ. *T:* (01305) 269839.

MARTIN, Dame Joan Margaret; *see* Higgins, Dame J. M.

MARTIN, John; *see* Martin, L. J.

MARTIN, His Honour John Alfred Holmes; QC (NI) 1989; an Upper Tribunal Judge (Administrative Appeals Chamber), since 2008; *b* 31 May 1946; *s* of Very Rev. Dr Alfred Martin and Doris Muriel Martin; *m* 1983, Barbara Elizabeth Margaret Kyle; one *s* one *d. Educ:* Finaghy Primary Sch.; Royal Belfast Academical Instn; Queen's Univ., Belfast (LLB 1969; Dip. Law 1970). Called to the Bar, NI Inn of Court, 1970, Gray's Inn, 1974, King's Inns, 1975; a Dep. Co. Court Judge, 1983–88; a Co. Court Judge, 1990–2011; Crown Court Judge, 1990–97; Recorder of Londonderry, 1993–94; Additional Judge for Co. Court Belfast, 1994–97. Chief Social Security Comr, and Chief Child Support Comr, NI, 1997–2011; Chief Pensions Appeal Comr, NI, 2005–11; Dep. Social Security Comr, 2005–08. Pt-time Chm., 1981–88, Chm., 1988–89, Vice Pres., 1990, Industrial Tribunals, NI; Vice Pres., Fair Employment Tribunal, NI, 1990; Chm. and Pres., Pensions Appeal Tribunals, NI, 2001–11. Member: NI Bar Council, 1983; Council of HM County Court Judges, 1990–2011 (Hon. Sec., 1995–97); Council of HM Judges of the Upper Tribunal Admin. Appeals Chamber (formerly HM Social Security and Child Support Comrs of the UK), 2004–11. Pres., Irish Legal Hist. Soc., 2004–06. Gov., Presbyterian Orphan Soc., 1991–. Vice Pres., Irish Amateur Rowing Assoc., 1978–79; Mem. Jury and Umpire, rowing events, Olympic Games, 1980 and Commonwealth Games, 1986. *Recreations:* rowing, hill-walking, gardening, reading. *Address:* Royal Courts of Justice, Chichester Street, Belfast BT1 3JE. *T:* (028) 9187 0238. *Clubs:* Ulster Reform; Leander.

MARTIN, Prof. John Francis, MD; FRCP; FMedSci; Professor of Cardiovascular Medicine (formerly British Heart Foundation Professor), since 1996, and Leader, Institute of Cardiovascular Science, 2007–09, University College London; Hon. Consultant Physician, University College Hospitals NHS Trust, since 1996; *b* 8 July 1943; *s* of Francis Martin and Marie-Antoinette Martin (née Bessler); *m* 1979, Íde Leddy (marr. diss. 1987); *m* 1991, Elisabeth Gaillochet (marr. diss. 1995). *Educ:* English Coll., Valladolid, Spain; Univ. of Sheffield (MB ChB 1973; MD 1981). FRCP 1989. Lectr in Medicine, Sheffield Univ., 1975–79; Sen. Lectr, Univ. of Melbourne, 1979–81; Hon. Consultant Physician, St Vincent's Hosp., Melbourne, 1979–81; Sen. Lectr, Sheffield Univ., 1981–86; Hon. Consultant Physician, Hallamshire Hosp., 1981–86; Hd, Cardiovascular Res., Wellcome Foundn Res. Labs, 1986–96; Sen. Lectr, 1986–90, BHF Prof. of Cardiovascular Sci., 1990–96, KCL; Hon. Consultant Physician, KCH, 1986–96. Queen Victoria Eugenia Chair, Complutense Univ., Madrid, 2004–05; Adjunct Prof. of Internal Cardiology, Yale Univ., 2010–. CSO and Dir, Ark Therapeutics (formerly Eurogene), 2000– (Founder, 1997); Chief Scientist and Founder, Magnus Life Science (formerly Magnus), 2009–. Mem., Animal Procedures Cttee, Home Office, 1998–2006. Pres., Eur. Soc. for Clinical Investigation, 1992–95; Vice Pres., Eur. Soc. Cardiology, 2000–02 (FESC 1995; Mem. Bd, 1998–2006; Chm., European Union Relations Cttee (formerly European Affairs Cttee), 2001–06; Gold Medal, 2008); Founder, Eur. Critical Care Foundn, 2008. Captain, RAMC(V), 1977–83, Major, 1983–86; now RARO. FMedSci 2000. Hon. DM Kuopio, 2008. *Publications:* Platelet Heterogeneity, Biology and Pathology, 1990; The Origin of Loneliness: poems and short stories, 2004; The Root of Blue is Yellow: poems, 2010; contrib. articles to learned jls on cardiovascular biol. and medicine, particularly arteriosclerosis, platelets and acute coronary syndromes and gene therapy. *Recreations:* poetry, Mediaeval philosophy, language, music. *Address:* British Heart Foundation Laboratories, Department of Medicine, University College London, 5 University Street, WC1E 6JJ. *T:* (020) 7679 6339; 21 West Square, SE11 4SN. *T:* (020) 7735 2212. *Club:* Athenæum.

MARTIN, John Howard Sherwell, FRICS; Senior Partner, Knight Frank, 1996–2004; *b* 7 Aug. 1945; *s* of John Robert Henry Martin and Lilian Vera Sherwell; *m* 1971, Linda Susan Johnson; one *s* two *d. Educ:* Emanuel Sch. FRICS 1971. Trainee Surveyor, GLC, 1965–71; joined Knight Frank & Rutley, 1971: Partner, 1978–96. Non-exec. Dir, Baltic Exchange, 1993–98. Trustee, St Clement Danes Holborn Estate Charity, 1987–2000. *Recreations:* travel, antiques, gardening. *Address:* Rowlands Court, Newchapel Road, Lingfield, Surrey RH7 6BJ. *Club:* Oriental.

MARTIN, John Neville, FREng, FICE, FIStructE; Chairman, Ove Arup Partnership, 1992–95; *b* 9 April 1932; *s* of Reginald Martin and Dorothy Sylvia Martin (*née* Bray); *m* 1964, Julia Mary Galpin; three *s* one *d. Educ:* Royal Grammar Sch., Guildford. FICE 1957; FIStructE 1957; FREng (FEng 1988). Articled pupil with Engr and Surveyor, Woking UDC, 1949–52; Nat. Service, RE, 1952–54; Asst Engr, Sir William Halcrow & Partners, Consulting Engrs, 1954–57; with Ove Arup Partnership, Consulting Engrs, 1957–95. Chm., Ove Arup Foundn, 1996–2000. Chm., Haslemere Dist Scout Council, 1995–2002. *Publications:* various papers for engrg jls (IStructE). *Recreations:* Scouting, mountain-walking, music, country dancing.

MARTIN, John Paul; Consultant, Bertelsmann Foundation, Germany, since 2013; *b* 6 April 1948; *s* of Denis Martin and Veronica Martin; *m* 1972, Jacqueline Davida Gunn; two *s* one *d. Educ:* University Coll., Dublin (MA Econ); MPhil Oxford. Res. Asst, Econ. and Social Res. Inst., Dublin, 1970–72; Lectr in Econs, Merton Coll., Oxford, 1974–77; Res. Fellow, Nuffield Coll., Oxford, 1975–77; Lectr in Econs, Univ. of Buckingham, 1975–77; Organisation for Economic Co-operation and Development, Paris: Administrator, 1977–80; Principal Administrator, 1980–83; Hd of Div. and Editor of OECD Employment Outlook, 1983–87; Hd of Div., Econs Dept, 1987–93, and Editor, OECD Economic Outlook, 1992–93; Dep. Dir for Employment, Labour and Social Affairs, 1993–2000; Dir for Educn, Employment, Labour and Social Affairs, 2000–02; Dir for Employment, Labour and Social Affairs, OECD, 2002–13. Pt-time Prof., Institut d'Etudes Politiques de Paris, 1993–; Res. Fellow, Inst. for the Study of Labour, Univ. of Bonn, 2005–; Adjunct Res. Fellow, Geary Inst., UCD, 2014–. Mem., Strategic Bd, LIEPP Scis Po, Paris, 2011–. Member: French Prime Minister's Conseil de l'orientation pour l'emploi, 2005–; Expert Gp on Future Skills Needs, Irish Govt, 2007–13; Labour Market Council, Irish Govt, 2013–; Council, Econ. and Social Res. Inst., Dublin, 2015–. Mem., Adv. Bd, World Demographic Assoc., 2006–09. Presidential Dist. Service Award for the Irish Abroad (Ireland), 2013. *Publications:* Trade and Payments Adjustment Under Flexible Exchange Rates, 1977; Youth Unemployment, 1980; The Nature of Youth Unemployment, 1984; many articles in jls such as Economic Jl, Economica, Oxford Economic Papers, Rev. of Econs and Stats, Jl of Internat. Economics, OECD Observer, OECD Economic Studies, Swedish Economic Policy Rev., De Economist, IZA Jl of Labor Policy, Economic and Social Rev. *Recreations:* tennis, golf, reading, wine-tasting.

MARTIN, John Sharp Buchanan, FCIHT; non-executive Director, since 2010, and Senior Independent Director, since 2012, Lothian Buses Ltd (formerly plc); *b* 7 July 1946; *s* of David Buchanan Martin and Agnes Miller Martin (*née* Craig); *m* 1971, Catriona Susan Stewart Meldrum; one *s* one *d. Educ:* Bell Baxter High Sch., Cupar, Fife; Univ. of St Andrews (BSc). FCIHT (FIHT 2003). Asst Principal, Scottish Educn Dept, 1968–71; Private Sec. to Parly Under-Sec. of State for Scotland, 1971–73; Scottish Office: Principal, 1973–80, seconded to Rayner Scrutinies, 1979–80; Asst Sec., 1980–92; Under-Sec., Sch. Educn and Sport, Educn, subseq. Educn and Industry Dept, 1992–98; Hd of Transport and Planning Gp, then Transport Gp, Scottish Office, later Scottish Exec., 1998–2004; concessionary fares appeals adjudicator for DfT, 2006–10. Mem., SE Scotland Transport Partnership, 2006–. Public Mem., Network Rail, 2008–10. Member: Adv. Bd, Transport Res. Inst., Edinburgh Napier Univ. (formerly Napier Univ.), 2005–; Adv. Panel, Rly Heritage Trust, 2010–. *Recreations:* tennis, golf, philately. *Clubs:* Colinton Lawn Tennis, Merchants of Edinburgh Golf.

MARTIN, John Sinclair, CBE 1977; farmer, retired; Chairman, Anglian Flood Defence Committee, Environment Agency (formerly National Rivers Authority), 1989–97; *b* 18 Sept. 1931; *s* of Joseph and Claire Martin, Littleport, Ely; *m* 1960, Katharine Elisabeth Barclay, MB, BS; three *s* one *d. Educ:* The Leys Sch., Cambridge; St John's Coll., Cambridge (MA, Dip. in Agriculture). Chairman: Littleport and Downham IDB, 1971–88; JCO Arable Crops and Forage Bd, 1973–76; Eastern Regional Panel, MAFF, 1981–86 (Mem., 1972–78); Great Ouse Local Land Drainage Cttee, AWA, 1983–88; Anglian Drainage Cttee, 1988–89; Member: Eastern Counties Farmers' Management Cttee, 1960–70; ARC, 1968–78; Great Ouse River Authority, 1970–74; Lawes Agricl Trust Cttee, 1982–84; MAFF Priorities Bd, 1984–88; Anglian Water Authority, 1988–89; Vice-Pres., Assoc. of Drainage Authorities, 1986–2010. Chairman: Ely Br., NFU, 1963; Cambs NFU, 1979. High Sheriff, Cambs, 1985–86. *Address:* Denny Abbey, Waterbeach, Cambridge CB25 9PQ. *T:* (01223) 860282. *Club:* Farmers.

MARTIN, John Vandeleur; QC 1991; a Judge of the Courts of Appeal of Jersey and Guernsey, since 2007; a Justice of the Cayman Islands Court of Appeal, since 2013; *b* 17 Jan. 1948; *s* of Col Graham Vandeleur Martin, MC and Margaret Helen (*née* Sherwood); *m* 1974, Stephanie Johnstone Smith; two *s* one *d. Educ:* Malvern Coll.; Pembroke Coll., Cambridge (MA). Called to the Bar, Lincoln's Inn, 1972, Bencher, 1999; Hd of Wilberforce Chambers, 2010–. Dep. High Court Judge, Chancery Div., 1993. Liveryman, Drapers' Co., 1973. *Recreations:* almost any opera, swimming in warm water. *Address:* Wilberforce Chambers, 8 New Square, Lincoln's Inn, WC2A 3QP. *T:* (020) 7306 0102.

MARTIN, John William Prior; HM Diplomatic Service, retired; Counsellor, Foreign and Commonwealth Office, 1985–89; *b* 23 July 1934; *er s* of late Stanley Gordon Martin and Frances Heather (*née* Moore); *m* 1960, Jean Fleming; three *s* one *d. Educ:* CIM Sch., Chefoo and Kuling; Bristol Grammar Sch.; St John's Coll., Oxford (MA). National Service, 1953–55 (2nd Lieut Royal Signals). Joined Foreign, later Diplomatic, Service, 1959; Beirut, 1960; Saigon, 1963; Language Student, Hong Kong, 1965–67; Dar es Salaam, 1968; FCO, 1971; Singapore, 1974; FCO, 1978; Counsellor, Kuala Lumpur, 1982. *Recreations:* conservation, travel, ornithology.

MARTIN, Jonathan Arthur, OBE 1995; sports broadcasting consultant; Controller, Television Sport, BBC Broadcast, 1996–98; *b* 18 June 1942; *s* of Arthur Martin and Mabel Gladys Martin (*née* Bishop); *m* 1967, Joy Elizabeth Fulker; two *s. Educ:* Gravesend Grammar School; St Edmund Hall, Oxford (BA 1964, English; MA 1992). Joined BBC as general trainee, 1964; producer, Sportsnight, 1969; producer, Match of the Day, 1970; editor, Sportsnight and Match of the Day, 1974; exec. producer, BBC TV Wimbledon tennis coverage, 1979–81; producer, Ski Sunday and Grand Prix, 1978–80; managing editor, Sport, 1980; Head of Sport, 1981–87, Head of Sport and Events, 1987–96, BBC TV. Vice-Pres., EBU Sports Gp, 1984–98; Consultant, Olympic Broadcasting Services, 2000–. *Recreations:* horse-racing, ski-ing, golf, watching sport, especially Watford FC. *Address:* Ty Cerddinen, Penfeidr, Castlemorris, Pembrokeshire SA62 5EN. *Club:* St Davids City Golf.

MARTIN, Prof. Keith Robert Graham, DM; FRCOphth; Professor of Ophthalmology, University of Cambridge, since 2010; Hon. Consultant Ophthalmologist, since 2005, and Clinical Director for Ophthalmology, since 2009, Cambridge University Hospitals NHS Foundation Trust; *b* Portadown, NI, 4 April 1969; *s* of Graham and Mabel Martin; *m* 1996, Susan Harden; two *s* one *d. Educ:* Royal Sch., Armagh; St Catharine's Coll., Cambridge (BA Triple 1st Cl. Hons Med. Scis and Neurosci. 1990); Magdalen Coll., Oxford (BM BCh 1993; DM 1999). MRCP 1996; FRCOphth 1998; ALCM 1986. House Officer: in Gen. Medicine, Nuffield Dept of Medicine, John Radcliffe Hosp., Oxford, 1993; in Gen. Surgery, Royal United Hosp., Bath, 1994; Senior House Officer: in Neurol., Nat. Hosp. for Neurol. and Neurosurgery, London, 1994; in Cardiol. and Clin. Pharmacol., Hammersmith Hosp., London, 1995; in Gen. Medicine, John Radcliffe Hosp., Oxford, 1996; in Ophthalmol., Hillingdon Hosp. and Western Eye Hosp., London, 1996; Specialist Registrar in Ophthalmol., E Anglia Rotation, 1997–2000; Res. Fellow, Wilmer Eye Inst., Johns Hopkins Hosp., Baltimore, 2000–02; Clin. and Res. Fellow, Moorfields Eye Hosp. and Inst. of Ophthalmol., 2003–04; University of Cambridge: GSK Clinician Scientist Fellow, Centre for Brain Repair, 2005–10 (Gp Leader, 2005–); Lectr in Clin. Neuroscis, 2005–10. Faculty Mem., NIHR, 2008–. Section Ed., Jl Glaucoma, 2006–. Treas., World Glaucoma Assoc., 2008–. Carl Camras Translational Res. Award, Assoc. for Res. in Vision and Ophthalmol., 2010; Sen. Clinician Scientist Award, World Glaucoma Assoc., 2011; Bronze Clinical Excellence Award, DoH, 2012. *Publications:* book chapters; contribs to scientific jls and articles on mechanisms of cell death in glaucoma and potential new treatment approaches. *Recreations:* playing the piano, sailing, windsurfing badly, ski-ing, tennis, karate (black belt 2013). *Address:* Eye Department Box 41, Addenbrooke's Hospital, Cambridge CB2 0QQ. *T:* (01223) 216427. *E:* krgm2@cam.ac.uk.

MARTIN, Kevin Joseph; President, Law Society, 2005–06 (Vice-President, 2004–05); *b* 15 June 1947; *s* of James Arthur Martin and Ivy Lilian Martin; *m* 1971, Maureen McCormack; two *s*. *Educ:* Sacred Heart Sch., Coventry; Cotton Coll., N Staffs; Coll. of Law, Guildford. Admitted solicitor, 1970. Articled clerk, Tafft & James, Coventry, 1964–70; Solicitor/Partner, Mackintosh & Co., Birmingham, 1970–79; Partner, K. J. Martin & Co., Balsall Common, Solihull, 1979–2001; Consultant, Lodders, Stratford-upon-Avon, 2001–. Chm., Will Certainty Ltd, 2007–. Council Mem. for Coventry and Warwickshire, Law Soc., 1996–2013. *Recreations:* golf, ski-ing, classical music, cricket, Rugby. *E:* kevinj_martin@me.com. *Clubs:* Royal Automobile; Ladbrook Park Golf; Coventry and N Warwickshire Cricket; Law Society Golf (Captain, 2013–14).

MARTIN, Kit, CBE 2012; Projects Consultant, The Prince's Regeneration Trust, since 2006; *b* 6 May 1947; *s* of Sir (John) Leslie Martin, RA, and Sadie Speight, architect; *m* 1st, 1970, Julia Margaret Mitchell (marr. diss. 1978); 2nd, 1980, Sally Martha, *d* of late Sqdn Ldr Edwin Brookes; one *d*. *Educ:* Eton; Jesus Coll., Cambridge (BA 1969; DipArch 1972; MA 1973). Started Martin & Weighton, architectural practice, 1969–76; partner involved in numerous projects to restore and save listed bldgs in UK, France and Italy; Dir, Kit Martin (Historic Houses Rescue) Ltd, 1974–; initiated rescue and conversion of listed bldgs of outstanding architectural interest, including: Dingley Hall, Northants, 1976–79; Gunton Park, Norfolk, 1980–84; Cullen House, Banffshire, 1982–85; Tyninghame House, E Lothian, 1988–92; Burley on the Hill, Rutland, 1993–97; Formakin, Renfrewshire, 1994–99; Maristow, Devon, 1995–99 (several schemes have won local, nat. or European awards); Dir, Historic Bldgs Rescue Ltd, 1993–2002; initiated rescue and conversion of several listed bldgs, including Royal Naval Hosp., Norfolk to housing, and a chapel. Dir, The Prince of Wales's Phoenix Trust (UK Historic Building Preservation Trust), 1997–2001. Mem., Historic Bldgs Council for Scotland, 1987–99. Trustee, Save Europe Heritage, 1994–. Hon. FRIBA 2000. *Publications:* The Country House: to be or not to be, 1982; Save Jamaica's Heritage (UNESCO Award), 1990; Silesia: the land of dying country houses, 2009. *Recreations:* ski-ing, squash, private flying with wife, landscape gardening, including restoration of Gunton Park according to historic principles. *Address:* (office) Park Farm, Gunton Park, Hanworth, Norfolk NR11 7HL.

MARTIN, Sir Laurence (Woodward), Kt 1994; DL; Senior Adviser, Center for Strategic and International Studies, Washington, 2000–06 (Arleigh Burke Professor of Strategy, 1998–2000); *b* 30 July 1928; *s* of Leonard and Florence Mary Martin; *m* 1951, Betty Parnall (*d* 2005); one *s* (one *d* decd). *Educ:* St Austell Grammar Sch.; Christ's Coll., Cambridge (MA); Yale Univ. (MA, PhD). Flying Officer, RAF, 1948–50; Instr, Yale Univ., 1955–56; Asst Prof., MIT, 1956–61; Rockefeller Fellow for Advanced Study, 1958–59; Associate Prof., Sch. of Advanced Internat. Studies, The Johns Hopkins Univ., 1961–64; Wilson Prof. of Internat. Politics, Univ. of Wales, 1964–68; Prof. of War Studies, King's Coll., Univ. of London, 1968–77, Fellow 1983–; Vice-Chancellor, Univ. of Newcastle upon Tyne, 1978–90, Emeritus Prof., 1991; Dir, RIIA, 1991–96. Research Associate, Washington Center of Foreign Policy Research, 1964–76, 1979–. Barbara Bodichon Fellow, Girton Coll., Cambridge, 2011–. Lees-Knowles Lectr, Cambridge, 1981; BBC Reith Lectr, 1981. Member: SSRC, 1969–76 (Chm. Res. Grants Bd); Internat. Res. Council, Center for Internat. and Strategic Studies (formerly Georgetown Center of Strategic Studies), 1969–77, 1979– (Co-Chm., 1998–); Council, IISS, 1975–83. Consultant, Sandia Labs. DL Tyne and Wear, 1986. Hon. DCL Newcastle, 1991. *Publications:* The Anglo-American Tradition in Foreign Affairs (with Arnold Wolfers), 1956; Peace without Victory, 1958; Neutralism and Non-Alignment, 1962; The Sea in Modern Strategy, 1967; (jtly) America in World Affairs, 1970; Arms and Strategy, 1973; (jtly) Retreat from Empire?, 1973; (jtly) Strategic Thought in the Nuclear Age, 1979; The Two-Edged Sword, 1982; Before the Day After, 1985; The Changing Face of Nuclear Warfare, 1987; (jtly) British Foreign Policy, 1997. *Address:* 35 Witley Court, Coram Street, WC1N 1HD.

MARTIN, (Leonard) John, CBE 1995; Consulting Actuary, R. Watson & Sons, 1954–95; *b* 20 April 1929; *s* of Leonard A. Martin and Anne Elisabeth Martin (*née* Scudamore); *m* 1st, 1956, Elisabeth Veronica Hall Jones (*d* 2006); one *s* one *d*; 2nd, 2007, Jill Corradi. *Educ:* Ardingly Coll.; Open Univ. (BSc Hons 2005). FIA, FSS, FPMI. Joined R. Watson & Sons, 1952, Partner 1954, Sen. Partner 1984–94. Dir, NPI Insurance Co., 1993–99. Pres., Inst. of Actuaries, 1992–94; Chm., Consultative Group of Actuaries in Europe, 1988–91; Rapporteur, Cttee of Actuaries, UN, 1988–2006. FRSA. Liveryman, Hon. Co. of Air Pilots (formerly GAPAN). *Recreations:* flying, sailing, singing. *Address:* Pitt House, Ducie Avenue, Bembridge, Isle of Wight PO35 5NF. *Club:* Naval.

MARTIN, Lewis Vine; Executive Director, 1995–2002, Chief Executive, Priory of England and Islands, 1999–2002, St John Ambulance; *b* 14 Nov. 1939; *s* of Lewis and Else Martin; *m* 1964, Patricia Mary Thorne; two *d*. *Educ:* Clarks Coll., Cardiff. Exec. posts in marketing, investment, admin, major projects and gen. management, UK and Europe, Mobil Oil Co. Ltd, 1955–95. *Recreations:* keep fit, swimming, gardening, Rugby (spectator now).

MARTIN, Louise Livingstone, CBE 2003; nutritionist; Chairman, sportscotland, since 2008 (Board Member, 1997–2005); *b* 2 Sept. 1946; *d* of James Stewart Campbell and Minnie Campbell; *m* 1973, Ian Alexander Martin; one *s* one *d*. *Educ:* Dunfermline High Sch.; Edinburgh Coll. of Domestic Science (Dip. Dom. Sci. Food and Nutrition). Lectr in Nutrition, Edinburgh Coll. of Domestic Science, subseq. Queen Margaret Coll., 1969–72; Head of Department: Glenrothes High Sch., 1972–73; Millburn Acad., Inverness, 1973–75. Tutor, Nat. Coaching Foundn, 1990–2008; Vis. Lectr in Sports Nutrition, Heriot-Watt Univ. and Univ. of Edinburgh, 1994–2001. Board Member: UK Sport, 2002–; Active Stirling, 2006–10; Commonwealth Adv. Bd on Sport, 2009–13 (Chair, 2013–); Chm., Commonwealth Games Council for Scotland, 1999–2008; Vice Chair, Glasgow 2014 Organising Cttee, 2008–14. Hon. Pres., Scottish Gymnastics, 1999 (Pres., 1993–99); Hon. Sec., Commonwealth Games Fedn, 1999–2015. Hon. DArts Abertay, 2007; DUniv: Glasgow Caledonian, 2008; Stirling, 2008; Strathclyde, 2014; Heriot Watt, 2014. *Recreations:* hill-walking, swimming, reading, travel, classical music. *Address:* sportscotland, Doges, Templeton on the Green, 62 Templeton Street, Glasgow G40 1DA. *E:* louise.martin@sportscotland.co.uk.

MARTIN, Michael C.; *see* Craig-Martin.

MARTIN, Micheál; Member of the Dáil (TD) (FF) Cork South Central, since 1989; President, Fianna Fáil, since 2011; *b* Cork, 1 Aug. 1960; *s* of Paddy and Lana Martin; *m* 1990, Mary O'Shea; two *s* two *d*. *Educ:* University Coll., Cork (MA Political Hist.). Secondary sch. teacher, St Kieran's Coll., Cork, 1983–89. Minister: for Educn and Sci., 1997–2000; for Health, 2000–04; for Enterprise, Trade and Employment, 2004–08; for Foreign Affairs, 2008–11. Mem., Cork Corp., 1985–99; Alderman, 1991–99; Lord Mayor of Cork, 1992–93. *Publications:* Freedom to Choose, 2009. *Address:* (office) 137 Evergreen Road, Turner's Cross, Cork, Ireland.

MARTIN, Hon. Paul; Member (Lab) Glasgow Provan, Scottish Parliament, since 2011 (Glasgow Springburn, 1999–2011); *b* 17 March 1967; *s* of Baron Martin of Springburn, *qv*; *m* 1997, Fiona Allen. *Educ:* All Saints Secondary Sch.; Barmulloch Coll., Glasgow. Mem. (Lab) City of Glasgow Council, 1995–99. *Address:* Scottish Parliament, Edinburgh EH99 1SP.

MARTIN, Paul, CBE 2013; PhD; writer, since 2001; Hon. Senior Research Fellow, Institute for Security Science and Technology, Imperial College London, since 2009; Parliamentary Security Director, since 2013; *b* 11 May 1958; *s* of Joseph and Pamela Martin; *m*; two *s* one *d*. *Educ:* Christ's Coll., Cambridge (MA, PhD). Harkness Fellow and Postdoctoral Schol., Stanford Univ., 1982–83; Asst Lectr, Cambridge Univ., 1984–86; Fellow, 1985–86 and 2001–04, Sen. Mem., 2004–09, Wolfson Coll., Cambridge; MoD, 1986–2000; Dir of Communication, Cabinet Office, 2000–01; MoD, 2002–13. *Publications:* (with Patrick Bateson) Measuring Behaviour, 1986, 3rd edn 2007; The Sickening Mind, 1997; (with Patrick Bateson) Design for a Life, 1999; Counting Sheep, 2002; (with Kristina Murrin) What Worries Parents, 2004; Making Happy People, 2005; Sex, Drugs and Chocolate, 2008; (with Patrick Bateson) Play, Playfulness, Creativity and Innovation, 2013; (with Emma Barrett) Extreme, 2014.

MARTIN, Paul; *see* Martin, D. P.

MARTIN, Rt Hon. Paul (Edgar Philippe), CC 2011; PC (Canada) 1993; MP (L) for Lasalle-Emard, Quebec, 1988–2008; Prime Minister of Canada, 2003–06; *b* Windsor, Ont, 28 Aug. 1938; *s* of Paul Joseph James Martin and Eleanor Alice Martin; *m* 1965, Sheila Ann Cowan; three *s*. *Educ:* Univ. of Ottawa; Univ. of Toronto (BA Philos. and Hist. 1962); Univ. of Toronto Law Sch. (LLB 1965). Merchant seaman on salvage ops in Arctic; worked in Legal Dept, ECSC, Luxembourg; with Osler, Hoskin & Harcourt, Toronto; called to the Bar, Ontario, 1966; with Power Corp. of Canada; Chm. and Chief Exec. Officer, Canada Steamship Lines; Corporate Dir for several major cos. Critic for: Treasury Bd and Urban Develt, until 1991; Envmt and Associate Finance Critic, 1991–93; Minister responsible for Federal Office of Regl Develt, 1993–97; Finance Minister, Canada, 1993–2002. First Chm., G-20, 1999–2002. Liberal Party of Canada: Co-Chm., Nat. Platform Cttee, 1993; Leader, 2003–06. Mem. Bd, Coalition for Dialogue on Africa, 2009–. Co-Chm., Congo Basin Forest Fund, 2008–; Chm., Capital for Aboriginal Prosperity and Entrepreneurship Fund, 2009–. Pres., Martin Aboriginal Educn Initiative, 2008–. *Address:* (office) 759 Square Victoria, Suite 300, Montreal, QC H2Y 2J7, Canada.

MARTIN, Paul James, (Paul Merton); comedian, actor, writer; *b* 9 July 1957; *s* of Albert and Mary Martin; *m* 1991, Caroline Quentin, *qv* (marr. diss. 1999); *m* 2000, Sarah Parkinson (*d* 2003); *m* 2009, Suki Webster. *Educ:* Wimbledon Coll. Civil Servant, Dept of Employment. *Stage:* stand-up comic: London Comedy Store, 1981–; London cabaret circuit, 1982–88; toured England, Scotland and Ireland, 1993; London Palladium, 1994; Live Bed Show, Garrick, 1994; presenter, Paul Merton's Silent Clowns, UK tour, 2007; Paul Merton's Impro Chums, UK tour, 2010; Out of My Head, UK tour, 2012; *television* includes: series: Comedy Wavelength, 1987; Whose Line is it Anyway?, 1989–93; Have I Got News For You, 1990–; Paul Merton—the series, 1991, 1993; Paul Merton's Life of Comedy, 1995; Paul Merton's Palladium Story (2 programmes), 1995; Paul Merton in Galton & Simpson, 1996, 1997; The Paul Merton Show, 1996; Room 101, 1999–2007; Paul Merton in China, 2007; Thank God You're Here, 2008; Paul Merton in India, 2008; Paul Merton in Europe, 2010; *films:* An Evening with Gary Lineker, 1994; The Suicidal Dog, 2000 (writer and dir); *radio* series include: Just a Minute, 1988–; I'm Sorry I Haven't a Clue, 1993–; The Masterson Inheritance, 1993–96; Two Priests and a Nun go into a Pub, 2000; Late, 2001. BAFTA Award, Best Entertainer, 2003. *Publications:* (with Julian Clary) My Life with Fanny the Wonderdog, 1988; Paul Merton's History of the 20th Century, 1993; Have I Got News For You, 1994; My Struggle, 1995; Silent Comedy, 2007; Only When I Laugh (autobiog.), 2014. *Recreations:* tropical fish, walking, film comedy. *Address:* c/o Mandy Ward Artist Management, 4th Floor, 74 Berwick Street, W1F 8TE.

MARTIN, Peter; *see* Martin, R. P.

MARTIN, Peter William, CBE 2006; Managing Director, Journeyman Resolutions, 2007–11; *b* 15 May 1947; *s* of Ronald William Martin and Rosemary Joan Damaris Martin; *m* 1981, Rhonda Mary Craker; two *s* one *d*. *Educ:* King's College Sch., Wimbledon; Goldsmiths' Coll., London. Winston Churchill Travelling Fellow, 1986. Regl Dir, Phoenix House, 1978–90; Chief Exec., Addaction, 1990–2005. Non-exec. Dir, Kent and Medway NHS and Social Care Trust, 2007–11. Member: Parole Bd of England and Wales, 1994–2000; Adv. Council for the Misuse of Drugs, 2000–09. Dir and Trustee, Cudham Community Centre Trust, 2009–12. *Recreations:* rambling, field pursuits, Buddhism, organic gardening, reading and writing. *Address:* Forge Cottage, Cudham TN14 7QB. *Club:* Royal Automobile.

MARTIN, Prof. Raymond Leslie, AO 1987; MSc, PhD, ScD, DSc; FRACI, FRSC, FTSE, FAA, FAIM; Professor of Chemistry, Monash University, Melbourne, 1987–92, now Emeritus (Vice-Chancellor, 1977–87); Chairman, Australian Science and Technology Council, 1988–92; *b* 3 Feb. 1926; *s* of Sir Leslie Harold Martin, CBE, FRS, FAA and late Gladys Maude Elaine, *d* of H. J. Bull; *m* 1954, Rena Lillian Laman; three *s* one *d*. *Educ:* Scotch Coll., Melbourne; Univ. of Melbourne (BSc, MSc); Sidney Sussex Coll., Cambridge (PhD, ScD). FRACI 1956; FRSC (FRIC 1974); FTSE (FTS 1989); FAA 1971; FAIM 2003. Resident Tutor in Chemistry, Queen's Coll., Melb., 1947–49 (Fellow, 1979–2004, Sen. Fellow, 2005–); Sidney Sussex Coll., Cambridge: 1851 Exhibn Overseas Scholar, 1949–51; Sen. Scholar, 1952–54; Res. Fellow, 1951–54; Sen. Lectr, Univ. of NSW, 1954–59; Section Leader, 1959–60, and Associate Res. Manager, 1960–62, ICIANZ; Prof. of Inorganic Chem., 1962–72, and Dean of Faculty of Science and Faculty of Music, 1971, Univ. of Melb.; Australian National University, Canberra: Prof. of Inorganic Chem., Inst. of Advanced Studies, 1972–77, Prof. Emeritus 1977; Dean, Res. Sch. of Chem., 1976–77; DSc. Vis. Scientist: Technische Hochschule, Stuttgart, 1953–54; Bell Telephone Labs, NJ, 1967; Vis. Prof., Columbia Univ., NY, 1972. Royal Aust. Chemical Institute: Smith Medal, 1968; Olle Prize, 1974; Inorganic Medal, 1978; Leighton Medal, 1989; Fed. Pres., 1968–69. Chm., Internat. Commn on Atomic Weights and Isotopic Abundances, IUPAC, 1983–87; Mem., Prime Minister's Science Council, 1989–92. Director: Circadian Technologies Ltd, 1986–2002; Heide Park and Art Gall., 1988–92; Winston Churchill Meml Trust, 1983–2006 (Nat. Chm., 1995–2000; Nat. Pres., 2001–06); Chairman: Syngene Ltd, 1996–2008; Optiscan Pty Ltd, 1997–2002; Trustee, Selby Scientific Foundn, 1990–. Council Mem., Victorian Coll. of the Arts, 1984–98 (Dep. Pres., 1991; Pres., 1992–95). Hon. LLD Monash, 1992; Hon. DSc Melbourne, 1996. Queen's Silver Jubilee Medal, 1977; Centenary Medal, Australia, 2003. *Publications:* papers and revs on physical and inorganic chem. mainly in jls of London, Amer. and Aust. Chem. Socs. *Recreations:* ski-ing, golf, lawn tennis (Cambridge Univ. team *v* Oxford, Full Blue; Cambs County Colours). *Address:* PO Box 98, Mount Eliza, Vic 3930, Australia. *Clubs:* Melbourne (Melbourne); Hawks (Cambridge); Frankston Golf (Victoria).

MARTIN, Richard Graham; Vice-Chairman, Allied-Lyons, 1988–92 (Director, 1981–92; Chief Executive, 1989–91); *b* 4 Oct. 1932; *s* of Horace Frederick Martin, MC and Phyllis Jeanette Martin; *m* 1958, Elizabeth Savage; two *s* one *d*. *Educ:* Sherborne School; St Thomas's Hosp. Med. Sch., 1953–54. 2nd Lt, RA, 1951–52. Joined Friary Holroyd & Healy's Brewery, 1955, Dir, 1959; Dir, Friary Meux, 1963–66; Managing Dir, Ind Coope (East Anglia), 1966–69; Director: Joshua Tetley & Son, 1969–72; Allied Breweries, 1972–92; Chief Exec., Joshua Tetley & Son, 1972–78; Vice-Chm., Joshua Tetley & Son and Tetley Walker, 1978–79; Chm., Ind Coope, 1979–85; Man. Dir, 1985–86, Chm. and Chief Exec., 1986–88, Allied Breweries; Chairman: J. Lyons & Co. Ltd, 1989–91; Hiram Walker, 1991 (Dir, 1989–91); Allied-Lyons, later Allied-Domecq, Pensions and Trustee Services, 1992–95; non-exec. Dir, Gibbs Mew plc, 1995–98. Chm., Brewers' Soc., 1991–92 (Vice-Chm., 1989–91). Pres., Shire Horse Soc., 1981–82. *Recreations:* travel, music, food.

MARTIN, Sir (Robert) Bruce, Kt 1992; QC 1977; Chairman, Bob Martin UK Ltd, since 1980; *b* 2 Nov. 1938; *s* of late Robert Martin and Fay Martin; *m* 1st, 1967, Elizabeth Georgina (*née* Kiddie) (marr. diss. 1995); one *s* one *d*; 2nd, 2006, Hester Frieda Beyers. *Educ:* Shrewsbury Sch.; Liverpool Univ. (LLB Hons 1959). Called to the Bar, Middle Temple, 1960; a Recorder of the Crown Court, 1978–86. Vice-Chm., Mersey RHA, 1986–88 (Mem., 1983–88); Chairman: N Western RHA, 1988–94; NHS Litigation Authy, 1996–99. *Address:* 4 Montpelier Terrace, SW7 1JP; Emoyeni, Magaliesburg, South Africa. *Clubs:* Reform; Royal Birkdale Golf; Inanda (Johannesburg).

MARTIN, Rt Rev. Robert David Markland; *see* Marsabit, Bishop of.

MARTIN, Robert George H.; *see* Holland-Martin.

MARTIN, Robert Logan, (Roy); QC (Scot.) 1988; QC 2008; a Judge of the Courts of Appeal of Jersey and Guernsey, since 2013; *b* 31 July 1950; *s* of Robert Martin and Dr Janet Johnstone Logan or Martin; *m* 1984, Fiona Frances Neil; one *s* two *d*. *Educ:* Paisley Grammar Sch.; Univ. of Glasgow (LLB). Solicitor, 1973–76; admitted to Faculty of Advocates, 1976 (Vice Dean, 2001–04; Dean, 2004–07); Mem., Sheriff Court Rules Council, 1981–84; Standing Junior Counsel to Dept of Employment in Scotland, 1983–84; Advocate-Depute, 1984–87; Temporary Sheriff, 1988–90. Admitted to Bar of NSW, 1987; called to the Bar, Lincoln's Inn, 1990; Bencher, Middle Temple, 2011. Chairman: Industrial Tribunals, 1991–96; Police Appeals Tribunal, 1997–. Mem., Judicial Appointments Bd for Scotland, 2007–. Chm., Scottish Planning, Local Govt and Envmtl Bar Gp, 1991–96; Co-Chairman: Forum for Barristers and Advocates, 2002–; Internat. Council of Advocates and Barristers, 2004–. Hon. Prof., Sch. of Law, Univ. of Glasgow, 2006–. Affiliate, RIAS, 1995; Hon. FRIAS 2009. Hon. Mem., Australian Bar Assoc., 2008. Trustee: Nat. Liby of Scotland, 2004–07; Melville Trust for the Care and Cure of Cancer, 2004–07; RCOG, 2013–. Hon. Sec., Wagering Club, 1982–91. Gov., Loretto Sch., 2002–12 (Chm., 2007–12). *Recreations:* shooting, ski-ing, modern architecture, vintage motor cars. *Address:* Kilduff House, Athelstaneford, North Berwick, East Lothian EH39 5BD. *Clubs:* Garrick; New (Edinburgh).

MARTIN, Robin Geoffrey; Director, Hewetson plc, 1980–98 (Chairman, 1980–88); *b* 9 March 1921; *s* of Cecil Martin and Isabel Katherine Martin (*née* Hickman); *m* 1946, Margery Chester Yates; two *s* one *d*. *Educ:* Cheltenham Coll.; Jesus Coll., Cambridge (MA). FIQ. Tarmac Ltd: Dir 1955; Gp Man. Dir 1963; Dep. Chm. 1967; Chm. and Chief Exec., 1971–79; Dir, Serck Ltd, 1971, Dep. Chm., 1974, Chm., 1976–81; Director: Burmah Oil Co., 1975–85; Ductile Steels Ltd, 1977–82. Mem., Midlands Adv. Bd, Legal and General Assurance Soc. Ltd, 1977–84. Chm., Ironbridge Gorge Develt Trust, 1976–78. Life Governor, Birmingham Univ., 1970–85. *Recreations:* gardening, bridge.

MARTIN, Robin Rupert, CB 2004; Director, Tax Law Rewrite Project, HM Revenue and Customs (formerly Board of Inland Revenue), 2003–06; *b* 28 Feb. 1946; *s* of late Rupert Claude Martin and Ellen Martin (*née* Wood); *m* 1972, Jane Elizabeth Mackenzie Smith; three *s*. *Educ:* Harrow Sch.; Worcester Coll., Oxford (MA Hons). VSO: Thailand, 1964–65; India, 1969–70; joined Home Civil Service, 1970: Private Sec. to Chm., Bd of Inland Revenue, 1973–74; Office of Chancellor of Duchy of Lancaster, Cabinet Office, 1976–79; Asst Sec., 1981; Under Sec., 1993; Principal Finance Officer, 1993–2000, Dir, Cross-Cutting Policy, 2000–03, Bd of Inland Revenue. Dir, CS Healthcare, 2003–13. Chm., Shenehom Housing Assoc., 2009–. Member: Methodology Soc., 2007–; Southwold Sailors' Reading Room Assoc. *Recreations:* infrequent leisurely hill-walking, cricket, second-hand books. *Club:* MCC.

MARTIN, Roger John Adam; formerly HM Diplomatic Service; Chairman, Population Matters (formerly Optimum Population Trust), since 2009; *b* 21 Jan. 1941; *s* of late Geoffrey (Richard Rex) Martin and of Hazel (*née* Matthews); *m* 1972, Ann Cornwell (*née* Sharp) (*d* 2009); one *s*. *Educ:* Westminster School; Brasenose College, Oxford (BA). VSO, Northern Rhodesia, 1959–60; Commonwealth Office, 1964–66; Second Sec., Djakarta, 1967, Saigon, 1968–70; First Sec., FCO, 1971–74, Geneva, 1975–79; seconded to Dept of Trade, as Head of Middle East/North Africa Br., 1981–83; Dep. High Comr, Harare, 1983–86; resigned. Vis. Fellow, Univ. of Bath. Mem., Nat. Exec., VSO, 1988–96; Dir, Som Trust for Nature Conservation, subseq. Som Wildlife Trust, 1988–2001 (Vice-Pres., 2001–). Member: Regional Committees: Envmt Agency, 1990–2012; MAFF, 1993–97; Planning Conf., 1996–2000; Heritage Lottery Fund, 2001–06. Founder Mem., SW Regl Assembly, 1998. Mem., Exmoor Nat. Park Authy, 1998–2008; Chm., SW Reg., 2001–06, Trustee, 2003–07, Pres., Som Br., 2006–, CPRE; Pres., Mendip Soc., 2001–09. Hon. DSc UWE, 2001. *Publications:* Southern Africa: the price of apartheid, 1988. *Recreations:* environmental issues, walking, archaeology. *Address:* Barn Cottage, Upper Coxley, near Wells, Somerset BA5 1QS. *T:* (01749) 672180.

MARTIN, Prof. Ronald Leonard, PhD, ScD; FBA 2005; FAcSS; FRGS; Professor of Economic Geography, University of Cambridge, since 2000; President, St Catharine's College, Cambridge, 2010–13 (Professorial Fellow, since 2000); *b* 17 April 1948; *s* of Bertie Leonard Martin and Joan Gladys Martin (*née* Claypole); *m* 1974, Lynda Mary Hunt. *Educ:* Gilberd Sch., Colchester; Trinity Coll., Cambridge (BA 1st Cl. Hons Geog.; MA; PhD Geog. 1978; ScD 2014). University of Cambridge: Asst Lectr in Geog., 1974–79; Lectr in Geog., 1979–98; British Acad. Thank-offering to Britain Fellow, 1997–98; Reader in Econ. Geog., 1998–2000; Leverhulme Major Res. Fellowship, 2007–10. Roepke Lectr in Econ. Geog., Assoc. American Geographers, 2009. Fellow, Cambridge-MIT Inst., 2002–08; Associate, Centre for Business Res., Judge Business Sch., Univ. of Cambridge, 2008–. Mem., Lead Expert Gp, Foresight: Future of Cities, Govt Office for Sci., 2013–. FAcSS (AcSS 2001). FRSA. Hon. Fellow, Regional Studies Assoc., 2005–. *Publications:* Towards the Dynamic Analysis of Spatial Systems, 1978; Regional Wage Inflation and Unemployment, 1981; Recollections of a Revolution: geography as spatial science, 1984; The Geography of Deindustrialisation, 1986; Regional Development in the 1990s, 1992; Human Geography: society, space and the social sciences, 1994; Money, Power and Space, 1994; Union Retreat and the Regions, 1996; Money and the Space Economy, 1999; The Reader in Economic Geography, 1999; Geographies of Labour Market Inequality, 2003; Putting Workforce in Place, 2005; Clusters and Regional Development, 2006; The Competitive Advantage of Regions, 2006; (ed) Critical Concepts in Economic Geography, 5 vols, 2007; Economic Geography, 2008; Handbook of Evolutionary Economic Geography, 2010; Handbook of Regional Growth and Innovation, 2011; contrib. more than 200 articles to various jls, incl. Trans IBG, Envmt and Planning, Jl Econ. Geog., Regl Studies, Econ. Geog., Cambridge Jl Econs, Cambridge Jl of Regions, Economy and Society, Econ. Jl, Jl of Regl Sci. *Recreations:* Italian opera, wine, astronomy, garden design, rabbits, reading everything and anything. *Address:* The Vines, Redgate Road, Girton, Cambridge CB3 0PP. *T:* (01223) 277244; St Catharine's College, Cambridge CB2 1RL. *T:* (01223) 338316. *E:* rlm1@cam.ac.uk.

MARTIN, Ronald Noel, CB 1998; FRCVS; Chief Veterinary Officer, Department of Agriculture for Northern Ireland, 1990–98; *b* 15 Dec. 1938; *s* of Robert John and Margretta Martin; *m* 1962, Alexandrina Margaret McLeod; two *s*. *Educ:* Royal (Dick) Sch. of Veterinary Studies, Univ. of Edinburgh (BVMS). FRCVS 1995 (MRCVS 1961). Private veterinary practice, 1960–64; Ministry of Agriculture, later Department of Agriculture, for Northern Ireland: Vet. Officer, 1964–69; Divl Vet. Officer, 1969–73; Sen. Principal Vet. Officer, 1973–78; Dep. Chief Vet. Officer, 1978–90. Chm., NI Food Chain Certification Cttee, 2001–10. *Recreations:* gardening, walking, cycling. *Address:* 8 Whiteside, Mountain Road, Newtownards, Co. Down BT23 4UP. *T:* (028) 9181 3962.

MARTIN, Rosemary; Headmistress, St Albans High School for Girls, 2009–14; *b* Stourbridge, 29 March 1952; *d* of Leslie and Freda Lay; *m* 1979, Geoffrey Martin; two *s*. *Educ:* Halesowen Grammar Sch.; Liverpool Univ. (BEd); Univ. of E London (MEd); Inst. of Educn, Univ. of London (NPQH 1999). Asst Teacher, then House Mistress, Kirkby Ruffwood Sch., Merseyside, 1974–78; Dep. Hd (Pastoral), Woodside Sch., Newham, 1978–84; Dep. Hd (Curriculum), Loxford Sch., Redbridge, 1984–90; Hd of Girls' Sch., Forest Sch., London, 1990–2000; Headmistress, Combe Bank Sch., Sevenoaks, 2000–09. *Recreations:* reading, keeping fit, ski-ing, travelling, spending time with my family.

MARTIN, Rosemary; General Counsel and Company Secretary, Vodafone Group Plc, since 2010; *b* UK, 12 May 1960; *d* of L. J. and E. V. Martin; *m* 1990, Brian Cooper; two *s* one *d*. *Educ:* Univ. of Sussex (BA Hons 1981); Nottingham Trent Univ. (MBA Legal Practice 1997). Admitted as solicitor, 1985; Solicitor, Rowe & Maw, 1983–97; Gen. Counsel and Co. Sec., Reuters Gp plc, and Dir, Reuters Foundn, 1997–2008; Chief Exec., Practical Law Gp, 2008–09. *Address:* Vodafone Group Plc, One Kingdom Street, Paddington Central, W2 6BY. *E:* rosemary.martin@vodafone.com.

MARTIN, Roy; *see* Martin, Robert L.

MARTIN, (Roy) Peter, MBE 1970; author and critic; *b* 5 Jan. 1931; *s* of Walter Martin and Annie Mabel Martin; *m* 1st, 1951, Marjorie Peacock (marr. diss. 1960); 2nd, Joan Drumwright (marr. diss. 1977); two *s*; 3rd, 1978, Catherine Sydee. *Educ:* Highbury Grammar Sch.; Univ. of London (BA 1953, MA 1956); Univ. of Tübingen. Nat. Service (RAF Educn Branch), 1949–51. Worked as local govt officer, schoolteacher and tutor in adult educn; then as British Council officer, 1960–83; service in Indonesia, Hungary (Cultural Attaché) and Japan (Cultural Counsellor). *Publications:* (with Joan Martin) Japanese Cooking, 1970; The Chrysanthemum Throne, 1997; (as James Melville): The Wages of Zen, 1979; The Chrysanthemum Chain, 1980; A Sort of Samurai, 1981; The Ninth Netsuke, 1982; Sayonara, Sweet Amaryllis, 1983; Death of a Daimyo, 1984; The Death Ceremony, 1985; Go Gently Gaijin, 1986; The Imperial Way, 1986; Kimono For A Corpse, 1987; The Reluctant Ronin, 1988; A Haiku for Hanae, 1989; A Tarnished Phoenix, 1990; The Bogus Buddha, 1990; The Body Wore Brocade, 1992; Diplomatic Baggage, 1994; The Reluctant Spy, 1995; (as Hampton Charles): Miss Seeton At The Helm, 1990; Miss Seeton, By Appointment, 1990; Advantage Miss Seeton, 1990. *Recreations:* music, books. *Address:* c/o Curtis Brown, 28/29 Haymarket, SW1Y 4SP. *Clubs:* Travellers, Detection.

MARTIN, Simon Charles, CMG 2013; HM Diplomatic Service; Ambassador to the Kingdom of Bahrain, since 2015; *b* 15 May 1963; *m* 1988, Sharon Margaret Joel; one *s* one *d*. *Educ:* Nottingham Univ. Entered FCO, 1984; lang. trng, 1986; Third, later Second Sec. and Vice-Consul, Rangoon, 1987–90; Second, later First Sec., FCO, 1990–95; lang. trng, 1995; First Secretary: (Commercial), Budapest, 1996–2001; FCO, 2001–03; on secondment to Unilever plc, 2003–05; Counsellor and Dep. Hd of Mission, Prague, 2005–09; Vice-Marshal of Diplomatic Corps, and Dir of Protocol, FCO, 2009–12; Dep. Private Sec. for Foreign and Commonwealth Affairs to the Prince of Wales (on secondment), 2012–15. *Address:* c/o Foreign and Commonwealth Office, King Charles Street, SW1A 2AH.

MARTIN, Stanley William Frederick, CVO 1992 (LVO 1981); JP; HM Diplomatic Service, retired; Extra Gentleman Usher to the Queen, since 1993; Protocol Consultant, Foreign and Commonwealth Office, since 1993; Chairman, Royal Over-Seas League, 2005–10; *b* 9 Dec. 1934; *s* of Stanley and Winifred Martin; *m* 1960, Hanni Aud Hansen, Copenhagen; one *s* one *d*. *Educ:* Bromley Grammar Sch.; University Coll., Oxford (MA Jurisprudence; Pres., OU Law Soc., 1957); Inner Temple (student Scholar). Nat. Service, 2nd Lieut RASC, 1953–55. Entered CRO, 1958; Asst Private Sec. to Sec. of State, 1959–62; First Secretary: Canberra, 1962–64; Kuala Lumpur, 1964–67; FCO (Planning Staff and Personnel Dept), 1967–70; seconded to CSD (CSSB), 1970–71; HM Asst Marshal of the Diplomatic Corps, 1972–81; First Asst Marshal, 1981–92; Associate Head of Protocol Dept, FCO, 1986–92. Vis. Prof., Diplomatic Acad., Poly. of Central London, subseq. Univ. of Westminster, 1987– (Hon. Fellow, 1998). Diplomatic Consultant: Hyde Park Hotel, then Mandarin Oriental Hyde Park, 1993–99; Grosvenor House, 1999–2002. Member: Cttee, London Diplomatic Assoc., 1972–; Council, Oxford Univ. Soc., 1993–2002; Adv. Council, Spanish Inst. of Protocol Studies, 1997–; Cttee, European-Atlantic Gp, 2003–10. Trustee: Attlee Foundn, 1993–99; Toynbee Hall, 1996–99; Jt Commonwealth Socs Trust, 2005–10; Patron, Apex Trust, 2002– (Vice-Patron, 1995–2002). Adviser: Consular Corps of London, 1993–; London Mayors' Assoc., 2004– (Hon. Mem., 2006). Mem., Commonwealth Observer Gp, Guyana elecns, 1997. Gov., Goodenough Coll. for Overseas Graduates, 2005–10. Freelance lectr, 1993–. Member: Pilgrims; Royal Historical Soc. FRSA 1985. JP Inner London, 1993–2000. Freeman of the City of London, 1988. Companion, Order of Distinguished Service (Brunei), 1992. *Publications:* (jtly) Royal Service: history of the Royal Victorian Order, Medal and Chain, vol. I 1996, vol. II 2001; The Order of Merit: one hundred years of matchless honour, 2006; (contrib.) Diplomatic Handbook, 2nd edn 1977 to 8th edn 2004; (contrib.) Honouring Commonwealth Citizens, 2007; contribs to Jl of Orders and Medals Res. Soc., Jl of Royal Over-Seas League, Bermuda Jl of Maritime History, Diplomat mag. *Recreations:* collecting too many books, manuscripts and obituaries, historical research and writing, travelling by train, walking, siestas, watching old films in the afternoon. *Address:* 14 Great Spilmans, Dulwich, SE22 8SZ. *T:* (020) 8693 8181. *Clubs:* Royal Over-Seas League (Mem., Central Council, 1982–2010, Exec. Cttee, 1993–2010; Vice-Chm., 2002–05; Chm., 2005–10; Vice-Pres., 2009–), Oxford and Cambridge, Danish.

MARTIN, Stephen Harcourt; Chief Executive, Higher Education Funding Council for Wales, 2000–03; *b* 4 Sept. 1952; *s* of Robert Harcourt Martin and Joan Winifred Martin (*née* Carpenter); *m* 1988, Amanda Suna Hodges (marr. diss. 2002); one *s* one *d*. *Educ:* Watford GS for Boys; Haywards Heath GS; Hull Univ. (Pol Studies). Nursing Assistant, De La Pole Psych. Hosp., Willerby, 1973–74; Welsh Office: Exec. Officer, Town and Country Planning Div., 1974–77; Admin. Trainee, Health and Industry Depts, 1977–79; Pvte Sec. to successive Perm. Secs, 1979–81; Principal: Health Dept, 1981–85; Housing Div., 1985–87; Asst Sec., Health and Social Services Divs, 1987–92; Under Sec., later Dir, Educn Dept, 1992–97; Prin. Establishments Officer, 1997–99; Sec. and Dir of Policy, Welsh Fourth Channel Authy, 1999–2000; Chief Executive: Further Educn Funding Council for Wales, 2000–01; Nat. Council for Educn and Trng for Wales, 2000–03. *Recreations:* music, literature.

MARTIN, Prof. Stephen James, PhD; Professor of Public Policy and Management, Cardiff University, since 2000; Director, Public Policy Institute for Wales, since 2013; *b* Chatham, 27 Feb. 1961; *s* of James Martin and Marian Martin; *m* 1988, Harriet Hudson; two *d*. *Educ:* Hertford Coll., Oxford (BA 1st Cl. Hons Geog. 1982); Aston Univ. (PhD 1989); Inst d'admin des entreprises, Univ. of Aix-Marseille (Internat. Teaching Prog. 1992). Lectr, Aston Business Sch., 1988–94; Principal Res. Fellow, 1994–99, Reader, 1999–2000, Warwick Business Sch.; Dir, Centre for Local and Regl Govt Res., Cardiff Univ., 2000–13 Member: Bd of Dirs, Local Govt Improvement and Develt (formerly IDeA), 2002–10; Bd, New Local Govt Network, 2007–; Lead Mem., Expert Panel on Local Govt, DCLG, 2009–10. *Publications:* Public Service Improvement: policies, progress and prospects, 2006; Public Services Inspection in the UK, 2008. *Recreations:* open water diving, watching test cricket, occasional dog breeder. *Address:* Public Policy Institute for Wales, 10 Museum Place, Cardiff CF10 3BG. *T:* 07773 381107. *E:* martinsj@cardiff.ac.uk.

MARTIN, Prof. Hon. Stephen Paul; Chief Executive, Committee for Economic Development of Australia, since 2011; *b* 24 June 1948; *s* of Harold and Vera Martin; *m*; one *s* three *d*. *Educ:* ANU (BA); Univ. of Alberta (MA); Sydney Univ. (MTCP); Univ. of NSW (Dip. Ed); PhD Wollongong. High School teacher, 1970–74; Univ. Lectr, 1975–77; Town Planner, NSW Dept of Planning and Environment, 1977–84. MP (Lab) Cunningham, NSW, 1984–2002; Chm., Banking, Finance and Public Administration Cttee, 1987–91; Parly Sec. to Minister for Foreign Affairs and Trade, 1991–93; Speaker, House of Reps, Aust., 1993–96; Shadow Minister: for Sport and Tourism, and for Veterans' Affairs, 1996–97; for Small

Business, Customs, Sport and Tourism, 1997–98; for Defence, 1998–2001; for Trade and Tourism, 2001–02. Professorial Fellow, Grad. Sch. of Business and Professional Develt, Univ. of Wollongong, 2002–03; CEO, Univ. of Wollongong in Dubai, 2004–05; Pro Vice-Chancellor (Internat.), Victoria Univ., Melbourne, 2005–08; Dep. Vice-Chancellor (Strategy and Planning), Curtin Univ. of Technol., Perth, 2008; Sen. Consultant, Slade Gp, 2009; Prof. of Business Res., Dir of DBA Prog. and Vice Chancellor's Rep., Gold Coast Campus, Southern Cross Univ., 2010. *Recreations:* swimming, Rugby League, movies. *Address:* 1205/39 Caravel Lane, Docklands, Vic 2008, Australia.

MARTIN, Steven; *see* Martin, George S.

MARTIN, (Thomas) Geoffrey, OBE 2002; Adviser, responsible for Strategic Relationships, Office of the Commonwealth Secretary-General, since 2005; *b* 26 July 1940; *s* of Thomas Martin and Saidee Adelaide (*née* Day); *m* 1968, Gay (Madeleine Annesley) Brownrigg; one *s* three *d*. *Educ:* Queen's Univ., Belfast (BSc Hons). President, National Union of Students of England, Wales and Northern Ireland, 1966–68; City of London: Banking, Shipping, 1968–73; Director, Shelter, 1973–74; Diplomatic Staff, Commonwealth Secretariat, 1974–79; Head of EC Office, NI, 1979–85; Head of EC Press and Inf. Services, SE Asia, 1985–87; Hd of External Relations, EC Office, London, 1987–93; Hd of Repn of EC in UK, 1994–2002; Office of Commonwealth Sec.-Gen., 2002–. Vis. Prof., Leeds Univ., 2003–. Hon. DSc Plymouth, 2000. *Address:* Commonwealth Secretariat, Marlborough House, Pall Mall, SW1Y 5HX. *Club:* Travellers.

MARTIN, Prof. Thomas John, AO 1996; MD, DSc; FRACP, FRCPA; FRS 2000; FAA; Director, 1988–2002, and John Holt Fellow, since 2003, St Vincent's Institute of Medical Research, University of Melbourne; *b* 24 Jan. 1937; *s* of Thomas Michael and Ellen Agnes Martin; *m* 1964, Christine Mayo Conroy (*d* 1995); two *s* four *d*. *Educ:* Xavier Coll.; Univ. of Melbourne (MB BS 1960; MD 1969; DSc 1979). FRACP 1969; FRCPA 1985; FAA 1996. Registrar and Res. Fellow, RPMS, London, 1965–66; Sen. Res. Fellow, 1967–68, Sen. Lectr, 1968–73, Dept of Medicine, Univ. of Melbourne; Prof. of Chemical Pathology, Univ. of Sheffield, 1974–77; Prof. of Medicine, Univ. of Melbourne, 1977–98, now Emeritus (Chm., Dept of Medicine, 1985–98). Vis. Prof., RPMS, 1973. Hon. MD Sheffield, 1992; DUniv Australian Catholic, 2010; Hon. LLD Melbourne, 2012. *Publications:* more than 400 scientific papers, reviews and book chapters on endocrinology, bone cell biology, cancer and clinical medicine. *Recreations:* music, golf, fly-fishing, travel. *Address:* #23, 27 Barnsbury Road, Deepdene, Vic 3103, Australia. *T:* (3) 98161123. *Club:* Melbourne.

MARTIN, Timothy Randall; Founder, 1979, and Chairman, since 1983, J. D. Wetherspoon plc; *b* 28 April 1955; *s* of Ray and Olive Martin; *m* Felicity Owen; one *s* three *d*. *Educ:* Nottingham Univ. (LLB). Called to the Bar, 1980. *Address:* J. D. Wetherspoon plc, Wetherspoon House, Central Park, Reeds Crescent, Watford, Herts WD24 4QL. *T:* (01923) 477777. *Club:* Exeter Squash.

MARTIN, Tom, OBE 2015; JP; President, since 2006, and non-executive Director, since 1996, ARCO Ltd; Vice Lord-Lieutenant, East Riding of Yorkshire, 2006–11; *b* 22 March 1936; *s* of Thomas Martin and Marjorie Martin; *m* 1960, Anne, *er d* of Thomas W. Boyd, CBE, DSO and Barbara Boyd; one *s* three *d*. *Educ:* Bramcote Sch., Scarborough; Winchester Coll.; Emmanuel Coll., Cambridge (BA Hons Law 1959; MA 1962). National Service, RNVR (Sub Lt), 1954–56. ARCO Ltd: Dir, 1965–96; Jt Man. Dir, 1969–96; Chm., 1981–2006. Gen. Comr of Income Tax, 1998–2006. Mem. Council, CBI, 1992–99. Mem. (C), Humberside CC, 1977–84. Mem., Magistrates' Adv. Council, 1985–93. Dir, Humber Forum, 2000–10; Founder Chm., E Riding Community Safety Partnership, 1996–2010; Trustee, Humberside Police Tribune Trust, 2001–. Patron, NSPCC, 2004–. Gov., Humberside Univ., 1993–96. JP Hull, 1972; High Sheriff, 1996–97, DL, 1998, ER of Yorks. Hon. Freeman, Beverley, 2015. *Recreations:* a veritable tribe of grandchildren, shooting, travel, antiquarian horology, and in an earlier life rowing, sailing and walking. *Address:* Newbegin House, 14–16 Newbegin, Beverley, E Yorks HU17 8EG. *T:* (01482) 869552, *Fax:* (01482) 887945. *E:* tom.martin@arco.co.uk. *Clubs:* Naval; Leander; Hawks (Cambridge); Royal Yorks Yacht.

MARTIN, Prof. Ursula Hilda Mary, CBE 2012; PhD; Professor of Computer Science, University of Oxford, since 2014; *b* London, 3 Aug. 1953; *d* of late Captain Geoffrey Richard Martin and Anne Louise Martin (*née* Priestman). *Educ:* Abbey Sch., Malvern Wells; Girton Coll., Cambridge (BA 1975); Univ. of Warwick (PhD 1979). Academic roles, univs in London and Manchester, and Univ. of Illinois, Urbana-Champaign, 1979–92; Professor of Computer Science: Royal Holloway, Univ. of London, 1990–92; Univ. of St Andrews, 1992–2002; Prof. of Computer Sci., 2003–14, Vice Principal, Sci. and Engrg, 2005–09, QMUL. *Publications:* articles on maths and computer sci. in learned jls. *Address:* Department of Computer Science, University of Oxford, Oxford OX1 3QD.

MARTINDALE, Anu; *see* Giri, A.

MARTINEAU, His Honour David Nicholas Nettlefold; a Circuit Judge, 1994–2013; *b* 27 March 1941; *s* of Frederick Alan Martineau and Vera Ruth Martineau (*née* Naylor); *m* 1968, Elizabeth Mary Allom; one *s* (one *d* decd). *Educ:* Eton; Trinity Coll., Cambridge (MA, LLM). Called to the Bar, Inner Temple, 1964; Asst Recorder, 1982–86; Recorder, 1986–94. Mem., Exec. Cttee, Cystic Fibrosis Trust, 1990–2004. *Recreations:* ski-ing, water ski-ing, wind-surfing, music, wine and food. *Clubs:* MCC; Hawks (Cambridge).

MARTINEAU, Malcolm John; pianist, accompanist; Professor, Royal Academy of Music, since 1987; *b* 3 Feb. 1960; *s* of George Martineau and Hester Dickson. *Educ:* George Watson's Coll., Edinburgh; St Catharine's Coll., Cambridge (BA 1981); Royal Coll. of Music. Début, Wigmore Hall, 1984; has accompanied many leading singers, incl. Thomas Allen, Dame Janet Baker, Barbara Bonney, Della Jones, Dame Felicity Lott, Ann Murray, Bryn Terfel, Anne Sofie von Otter, Frederica von Stade, and instrumentalists, incl. Emma Johnson; has accompanied master classes, Britten-Pears Sch. Presented song recital series: Debussy and Poulenc, St John's, Smith Square; Britten, Wigmore Hall; Jt Artistic Dir, Liederreise, St John's, Smith Sq., 1998. Recordings incl. complete folk song settings of Beethoven and Britten, instrumental and vocal music incl. Arnold, Brahms, Fauré, Schubert, Schumann, Strauss and song recitals, with various artists. Hon. RAM 1998; Hon. Dr RSAMD, 2004. Accompanist's Prize, Walther Grüner Internat. Lieder Competition, 1983. *Recreations:* theatre-going, cooking. *Address:* c/o Askonas Holt, Lincoln House, 300 High Holborn, WC1V 7JH. *T:* (020) 7400 1700.

MARTINEAU-WALKER, Roger Antony; *see* Walker, Roger A. M.

MARTLEW, Eric Anthony; *b* 3 Jan. 1949; *m* 1970, Elsie Barbara Duggan. *Educ:* Harraby Secondary School, Carlisle; Carlisle Tech. Coll. Nestlé Co. Ltd, 1966–87: joined as lab. technician; later Personnel Manager, Dalston Factory, Carlisle. Member: Carlisle County Borough Council, 1972–74; Cumbria CC, 1973–88 (Chm., 1983–85). Mem., Cumbria Health Authy, later E Cumbria HA, 1977–87 (Chm., 1977–79). MP (Lab) Carlisle, 1987–2010. Opposition spokesman on defence, 1992–95; an Opposition Whip, 1995–97; PPS to Chancellor of Duchy of Lancaster, 1997–98, to Leader of H of L, 1998–2001. Formerly: Chm., All Party Animal Welfare Gp; Joint Chair: W Coast Main Line All Party Gp; All Party Rail Gp; Mem., Chairman's Panel. Patron: Animal Sanctuary, Moorhouse, Carlisle, 2004–; Animal Refuge, 2005; Cerebral Palsy Cumbria, 2005–; Motor Neurone Disease Assoc., 2006–. *Recreations:* photography, fell walking, horse racing.

MARTONMERE, 2nd Baron *cr* 1964; **John Stephen Robinson;** *b* 10 July 1963; *s* of Hon. Richard Anthony Gasque Robinson (*d* 1979) and of Wendy Patricia (who *m* subseq. Ronald De Mara), *d* of late James Cecil Blagden; *S* grandfather, 1989; *m* 2001, Marion Elizabeth Wills, *d* of Ian Wills, Toronto; one *s*. *Educ:* Lakefield College School; Senaca College. *Heir: s* Hon. James Ian Robinson, *b* 26 Feb. 2003. *Address:* 67 Donwoods Drive, Toronto, ON M4N 2G6, Canada.

MARTYN-HEMPHILL, family name of **Baron Hemphill**.

MARTYNSKI, Vanessa; *see* Lloyd, V.

MARTYR, Peter McCallum; Partner, since 1985, and Chief Executive, since 2002, Norton Rose Fulbright (formerly Norton Rose) LLP; *b* 31 March 1954; *s* of John Walton Martyr and Jean Wallace Robertson; *m* 1978, Carol Frances Busby; one *s* one *d*. *Educ:* University Coll., Cardiff (LLB Jt Hons). Admitted solicitor, 1979. With Norton Rose, 1977–: Mem., Exec. Cttee, 1997–. *Recreations:* Rugby (watching), ski-ing, music, classic cars. *Address:* Norton Rose Fulbright LLP, 3 More London Riverside, SE1 2AQ. *T:* (020) 7283 6000, *Fax:* (020) 7283 6500. *E:* peter.martyr@nortonrosefulbright.com.

MARWICK, George Robert, CVO 2007; farmer and company director; Lord-Lieutenant of Orkney, 1997–2007 (Vice Lord-Lieutenant, 1995–97); *b* 27 Feb. 1932; *s* of late Robert William Marwick, BSc Hons, MICE, Civil Engr, and Agnes Kemp Marwick (*née* Robson); *m* 1st, 1958, Hanne Jensen (marr. diss. 1989); three *d*; 2nd, 1990, Norma Gerrard (*née* Helm). *Educ:* Port Regis, Dorset; Bryanston Sch., Dorset; Edinburgh Sch. of Agriculture (SDA 1953). Chm. and Man. Dir, Swannay Farms Ltd, 1972–2009; Chairman: Campbeltown Creamery Ltd, 1974–90; Campbeltown Creamery (Hldgs) Ltd, 1974–90; Director: North Eastern Farmers Ltd, 1968–98; Orkney Islands Shipping Co., 1972–87. Chm., N of Scotland Water Bd, 1970–73; Member: Scottish Agricl Cons. Panel (formerly Winter Keep Panel), 1964–98; Countryside Commn for Scotland, 1978–86; Council, NT for Scotland, 1979–84. Ind. Mem., Orkney CC, then Orkney Is Council, 1968–78 (Vice-Convenor, 1970–74; Convenor, 1974–78). JP, 1970–2008, DL, 1976, Orkney. Hon. Sheriff of Grampian, Highlands and Is, 2000. *Recreations:* shooting, motor sport. *Address:* Whitewisp, Orchil Road, Auchterarder, Perthshire PH3 1NB. *T:* (01764) 662381. *Club:* New (Edinburgh).

MARWICK, Rt Hon. Patricia, (Rt Hon. Tricia); PC 2012; Member for Mid Fife and Glenrothes, Scottish Parliament; Presiding Officer, Scottish Parliament, since 2011; *b* 5 Nov. 1953; *m* 1975, Frank Marwick; one *s* one *d*. *Educ:* Fife. Former public affairs officer, Shelter. Mem., SNP, 1985– (Mem. NEC, 1997–2000). MSP (SNP) Mid Scotland and Fife, 1999–2007, Fife Central, 2007–11, Mid Fife and Glenrothes, 2011, when elected Presiding Officer. Contested (SNP) Fife Central, 1992, 1997. *Address:* Scottish Parliament, Edinburgh EH99 1SP.

MARWOOD, Anthony; violinist; *b* 6 July 1965; *s* of Michael Travers Marwood and Anne (*née* Chevallier). *Educ:* King Edward VI Grammar Sch., Chelmsford; Royal Acad. of Music; Guildhall Sch. of Music and Drama. Internat. engagements as solo violinist; Mem., Florestan Trio, 1995–2012; Artistic Dir, Irish Chamber Orch., 2006–11; Principal Artistic Partner, Les Violons du Roy, chamber orch., Québec, 2015–; collaborator with dancers and actors. Numerous recordings as soloist and chamber musician. FGS 2013. Instrumentalist Award, Royal Philharmonic Soc., 2006. *Recreations:* theatre, finding myself in Cape Town. *Address:* c/o Hazard Chase, 25 City Road, Cambridge CB1 1DP. *W:* www.anthonymarwood.com.

MARX, Clare Lucy, (Mrs A. W. M. Fane), CBE 2007; DL; FRCS; Associate Medical Director, Ipswich Hospital NHS Trust, since 2013 (Consultant Trauma and Orthopaedic Surgeon, 1993–2014); President, Royal College of Surgeons of England, since 2014; *b* Coventry, 15 March 1954; *d* of Francis Marx and Brenda Marx; *m* 1989, Andrew William Mildmay Fane, *qv*. *Educ:* Cheltenham Ladies' Coll.; University Coll. London (MB BS 1977). FRCS 1981. Consultant Orthopaedic Surgeon, St Mary's Hosp. NHS Trust, London, 1990–93; Ipswich Hospital NHS Trust, 1993–: Clin. Dir, Trauma and Orthopaedics, 1994–98; Chm., Med. Staff Cttee, 2003–05. Mem. Council, RCS, 2009– (Chairman: Specialist Adv. Cttee in Orthopaedics, Jt Cttee of Higher Surgical Trng, 2005–07; Invited Rev. Mechanism, 2011–). Mem. Council, 2004–, Pres., 2008–09, British Orthopaedic Assoc. FRCSE *ad hominem* 2009. DL Suffolk, 2008. *Publications:* articles in learned jls on hip and knee arthroplasty and the trauma and orthopaedic curriculum. *Recreations:* walking, gardening, ski-ing. *Address:* Ipswich Hospital NHS Trust, Heath Road, Ipswich, Suffolk IP4 5PD. *T:* (01473) 712233. *E:* clare.marx@ipswichhospital.nhs.uk.

MARYCHURCH, Sir Peter (Harvey), KCMG 1985; Chairman, Associated Board of the Royal Schools of Music, 1994–2000; Director, Government Communications Headquarters, 1983–89; *b* 13 June 1927; *s* of Eric William Alfred and Dorothy Margaret Marychurch; *m* 1965, June Daphne Ottaway (*née* Pareezer). *Educ:* Lower School of John Lyon, Harrow. Served RAF, 1945–48. Joined GCHQ, 1948; Asst Sec. 1975; Under Sec. 1979; Dep. Sec. 1983. Chairman: Cheltenham Arts Festivals, 1994–2000; Cheltenham Internat. Fest. of Music, 1993–97; Cheltenham and Cotswold Relate, 1990–97; Pres., Cheltenham Arts Council, 1998–2007. FRSAMD 1998. Hon. RNCM 2000. Medal for Distinguished Public Service, US Dept of Defense, 1989. *Recreations:* theatre, music (especially opera), gardening. *Address:* HSBC, 2 The Promenade, Cheltenham, Glos GL50 1LS.

MARYON DAVIS, Dr Alan Roger, FRCP; FFPH; FFSEM; Hon. Professor of Public Health, King's College London, since 2007; *b* 21 Jan. 1943; *s* of Cyril Edward Maryon Davis and Hilda May Maryon Davis; *m* 1981, Glynis Anne Davies; two *d*. *Educ:* St Paul's Sch.; St John's Coll., Cambridge (MA 1968; MB BChir 1970); St Thomas's Hosp. Med. Sch. (LRCP, MRCS 1969); London Sch. of Hygiene and Tropical Medicine. MSc (Social Med.) London 1978. MRCP 1972; FFPH (FFCM 1986; MFCM 1978); FRSPH (FRIPHH 1989); FRCP 2005; FFSEM 2007. Early med. career in gen. medicine and rheumatology, later in community medicine; MO, 1977–84, CMO, 1984–87, Health Educn Council; Sen. Med. Adviser, Health Educn Authority, 1987–88; Hon. Consultant, Paddington and N Kensington HA, 1985–88; Hon. Senior Lecturer: in Community Medicine, St Mary's Hosp. Med. Sch., 1985–88; in Public Health, UMDS, then KCL, 1988–2007; Consultant in Public Health Med., W Lambeth, then SE London, subseq. Lambeth, Southwark and Lewisham, HA, 1988–2002; Dir of Public Health, Southwark PCT, 2002–07. Bd Advr, HPA, 2007–10. Vice Chm., Nat. Heart Forum, 2005–; Chair: RIPH, later RSPH, 2006–09 (Vice Chm., 2002–06); NICE Public Health Prog. Develt Gp (Obesity), 2012–; NICE Public Health Adv. Cttee, 2013–; Pres., FPH, 2007–10. Mem., Alcohol and Educn Res. Council, 2010–11; Trustee: Medicinema, 2000–; Drinkaware, 2010–11; Alcohol Res. UK, 2011– (Chm., 2014–); Best Beginnings, 2011– (Chm., 2011–). Vice Chm., MJA, 2010–11. Writer and broadcaster on health matters, 1975–; BBC radio series include Action Makes the Heart Grow Stronger (Med. Journalists' Assoc. Radio Award), 1983; BBC television series include: Body Matters, 1985–89; Health UK, 1990–91. Editor-in-Chief, Health Education Jl, 1984–88; Med. Advice Columnist, Woman magazine, 1988–2005; Editor, Public Health Today, 2010–. Hon. FRCGP 2011; Hon. FCMSA 2010. *Publications:* Family Health and Fitness, 1981; Body Facts, 1984; (with J. Thomas) Diet 2000, 1984; (with J. Rogers) How to Save a Life, 1987; PSSST—a Really Useful Guide to Alcohol, 1989; Cholesterol Check, 1991; The Good Health Guide, 1994; Ruby's Health Quest, 1995; The Body-clock Diet, 1996; Feeling Good, 2007; (jtly) Thinking Ahead: why we need to improve children's mental health and wellbeing, 2011; contrib. academic articles to peer-reviewed jls. *Recreations:* eating well, drinking well, singing (not so well) in the humorous group Instant Sunshine. *Address:* Friary Court, The Friary, Salisbury SP1 2HU. *T:* (01722) 341786.

MASCHLER, Fay, MBE 2004; restaurant critic, Evening Standard, since 1972; *b* 15 July 1945; *d* of Mary and Arthur Frederick Coventry; *m* 1970, Thomas Michael Maschler, *qv* (marr. diss. 1987); one *s* two *d*; *m* 1992, Reginald Bernard John Gadney. *Educ:* Convent of the Sacred Heart, Greenwich, Conn. Copywriter, J. Walter Thompson, 1964; journalist, Radio Times, 1969. *Publications:* Cooking is a Game You Can Eat, 1975; A Child's Book of Manners, 1979; Miserable Aunt Bertha, 1980; Fay Maschler's Guide to Eating Out in London, 1986; Eating In, 1987; Howard & Maschler on Food, 1987; Teach Your Child to Cook, 1988; Evening Standard Restaurant Guides, annually, 1993–. *Address:* 12 Fitzroy Square, W1T 6BU. *Clubs:* Groucho, Car Clamp.

MASCHLER, Thomas Michael; Publisher, Jonathan Cape Children's Books, 1991–97; Director, Jonathan Cape Ltd, 1960–97 (Chairman, 1970–91); Founder, Booker Prize for Fiction, 1969; *b* 16 Aug. 1933; *s* of Kurt Leo Maschler and of Rita Masseron (*née* Lechner); *m* 1970, Fay Coventry (*see* Fay Maschler) (marr. diss. 1987); one *s* two *d*; *m* 1988, Regina Kulinicz. *Educ:* Leighton Park School. Production Asst, Andre Deutsch, 1955; Editor, MacGibbon & Kee, 1956–58; Fiction Editor, Penguin Books, 1958–60; Jonathan Cape: Editorial Dir, 1960; Man. Dir, 1966. Associate Producer, The French Lieutenant's Woman (film), 1981. Founder, Book Bus Foundn, 2007. *Publications:* (ed) Declarations, 1957; (ed) New English Dramatists Series, 1959–63; Tom Maschler Publisher (memoirs), 2005.

MASCIE-TAYLOR, Prof. (Bryan) Hugo, FRCP, FRCPI; Medical Director, Monitor, since 2014; *b* 21 Aug. 1947; *s* of (Henry) Hugo and (Madeline) Eira Mascie-Taylor; *m* 1st, 1972, Heather Chapman (marr. diss. 1994); one *s*; 2nd, 1994, Louise Thomas; two *s*. *Educ:* Sir Thomas Rich's Sch., Gloucester; Univ. of Leeds; Univ. of California, San Francisco; Ashridge Mgt Coll.; Henley Coll. of Mgt (ADipC 1997). FRCPI 1992; FRCP 1994; MIHM (MHSM 1996). Consultant Physician: St James Univ. Hosp., Leeds, 1986–91; (and Clinical Dir), Seacroft Hosp., Leeds, 1991–94; Dir, Strategic Develt, Leeds Community and Mental Health Trust, 1992–94; Med. Dir, 1994–96, Dir, Commng, 1996–98, Leeds HA; Medical Director: Leeds Teaching Hosps NHS Trust, 1998–2009; NHS Confedn, 2009–13; Trust Special Administrator, Mid-Staffs NHS Trust, 2013–14. University of Leeds: Hon. Sen. Clin. Lectr, 1986–2011; Vis. Prof., Sch. of Medicine, 2004–; Vis. Fellow, Univ. of York, 1996–2003. External Examiner: (Masters/Gerontol.), Univ. of Hull, 1996–99; (Masters/Clin. Mgt), Univ. of Durham, 2003–05. Chm., Overseas Partnership and Trng Initiative (OPTIN), 2004–. *Publications:* articles in clinical and mgt jls. *Recreations:* English furniture, ski-ing. *Address:* Monitor, Wellington House, Waterloo Road, SE1 8UG. *T:* 07887 853104. *E:* hugo@mascie-taylor.org.

MASCORD, Dr David John; Headmaster, Bristol Grammar School, 1999–2008; *b* 18 Oct. 1950; *s* of George and Evelyn Mascord; *m* 1974, Veronica Mary Chalton Peers; two *s*. *Educ:* York Univ. (BA 1st Cl. Hons Chemistry 1972); St John's Coll., Cambridge (PhD 1976; PGCE with Dist.). Head of Chemistry, Wellington Coll., 1981–86; Sen. Teacher, Aylesbury GS, 1986–89; Asst Hd, 1989–98, Dep. Hd, 1998–99, Bristol GS. *Publications:* (contrib.) The Head Speaks, 2008; contrib. articles in Faraday Discussions of Chem. Soc., Molecular Physics, Jl Chem. Industry. *Recreations:* walking, swimming, personal computing, cooking, reading, particularly Charles Dickens, sketching, painting.

MASEFIELD, Sir Charles (Beech Gordon), Kt 1997; CEng, FRAeS, FIMechE; President, BAE SYSTEMS, 2003–07 (Group Marketing Director, 1999–2002, Vice-Chairman, 2002–03); *b* 7 Jan. 1940; *s* of Sir Peter (Gordon) Masefield and Patricia Doreen (*née* Rooney); *m* 1970, Fiona Anne Kessler; two *s*. *Educ:* Eastbourne Coll.; Jesus Coll., Cambridge (MA). CEng 1984; FRAeS 1980; FIMechE 1984. Sales Exec. and Test Pilot, Beagle Aircraft, 1964–70; Hawker Siddeley Aviation: Test Pilot, 1970–76; Dep. Chief Test Pilot, Manchester, 1976–78; British Aerospace, Manchester: Chief Test Pilot, 1978–80; Project Dir, 1980–81; Prodn Dir, 1981–84; Gen. Manager, 1984–86; Man. Dir, BAe Hatfield, Manchester, Prestwick, 1986–92; Pres., BAe Commercial Aircraft, 1992–93; Sen. Vice-Pres. and Commercial Dir, Airbus Industrie, Toulouse, 1993–94; Hd, Defence Export Services Orgn, 1994–98; Vice-Chm., GEC, 1998–99. Chairman: Microsulis Ltd, 2003–07; Helvetia Wealth Mgt, Switzerland, 2004–; non-executive Director: Banque Piguet, Switzerland, 2002–04; Qator Foundn, 2003–12; Epicure Berlin, 2012–. Pres., RAeS, 1994–95. FRSA 1999. Hon. FIMechE 2005. *Recreation:* golf. *Address:* Old Hall, Markyate, Herts AL3 8AR. *T:* (01582) 763901.

MASEFIELD, (John) Thorold, CMG 1986; HM Diplomatic Service, retired; Governor and Commander-in-Chief of Bermuda, 1997–2001; *b* 1 Oct. 1939; *e s* of late Dr Geoffrey Bussell Masefield, DSc and Mildred Joy Thorold Masefield (*née* Rogers); *m* 1962, Jennifer Mary, MBE, *d* of late Rev. Dr H. C. Trowell, OBE and late K. M. Trowell, MBE; two *s* one *d* (and one *d* decd). *Educ:* Dragon Sch., Oxford; Repton Sch.; St John's Coll., Cambridge (Scholar) (MA). Joined CRO, 1962; Private Sec. to Permanent Under Sec., 1963–64; Second Secretary: Kuala Lumpur, 1964–65; Warsaw, 1966–67; FCO, 1967–69; First Sec., UK Delegn to Disarmament Conf., 1970–74; Dep. Head, Policy Planning Staff, FCO, 1974–77; Far Eastern Dept, FCO, 1977–79; Counsellor, Head of Chancery and Consul Gen., Islamabad, 1979–82; Head of Personnel Services Dept, FCO, 1982–85; Head, Far Eastern Dept, FCO, 1985–87; Fellow, Center for Internat. Affairs, Harvard Univ., 1987–88; seconded to CSSB, 1988–89; High Comr, Tanzania, 1989–92; Asst Under-Sec. of State, FCO, 1992–94; High Comr, Nigeria, also concurrently Ambassador (non-resident) to the Republics of Benin and of Chad, 1994–97. Dep. Chm., Bermuda Soc., 2006–07. Mem., Brockenhurst Parish Council, 2005–15 (Vice-Chm., 2006–07, 2010–12; Chm., 2007–10). KStJ 1997. *Publications:* article in International Affairs. *Recreation:* fruit and vegetables. *Club:* Brockenhurst Probus.

See also R. C. Masefield, R. F. Masefield.

MASEFIELD, Robin Charles, CBE 2003; Director General, Northern Ireland Prison Service, 2004–10; *b* Oxford, 16 April 1952; *s* of late Dr Geoffrey Bussell Masefield and Mildred Joy Thorold Masefield (*née* Rogers); *m* 1981, Rosemary Elizabeth Drew; one *s* two *d*. *Educ:* Dragon Sch., Oxford; Marlborough Coll.; St John's Coll., Cambridge (Scholar; BA Social Anthropol. 1973). Joined NI Office, 1973; seconded to Hong Kong Govt, 1980–83, to Immigration and Nationality Dept, Home Office, 1983–86, to HM Prison Service, 1991–94; Hd of Efficiency Scrutiny, Cabinet Office, 1994–95; Dir, Change Mgt, NI Office, 1995–96; Sec., Rev. of Parades and Marches, 1996–97; Dir, Finance and Estate Mgt, 1997–2000; Hd, Patten Action Team, 2000–04. *Publications:* Making the Most of Hong Kong (with Robert Phillips), 1983; Oriental and Other Expresses, 1994; (jtly) Limpsfield, Ancient and Modern, 1997; Twixt Bay and Burn, 2011; (with Desmond Rea) Dealing with the Past: a note to Ambassador Haass, 2013; (with Desmond Rea) Policing in Northern Ireland, Delivering the New Beginning?, 2014. *Recreations:* gardening, local history and community activism. *Address:* c/o Department of Justice, Stormont, Belfast BT4 3SU.

See also J. T. Masefield.

MASEFIELD, Roger Francis; QC 2013; *b* Geneva, Switzerland, 24 Dec. 1970; *s* of (John) Thorold Masefield, *qv*; *m* 2001, Catherine Strauss; two *s* one *d*. *Educ:* Dragon Sch., Oxford; Marlborough Coll., Wilts; St John's Coll., Cambridge (Wright Schol.; BA 1st Cl. Law 1993); Magdalene Coll., Cambridge (BCL 1st Cl. 1994; Vinerian Schol.). Called to the Bar, Middle Temple, 1994; pupillage, Brick Court Chambers, 1995–96; in practice as barrister, 1996–. *Publications:* (ed) Butterworth's Banking Law Guide, 2006; (contrib.) Paget's Law of Banking, 13th edn, 2007; Banks and Financial Crime, 2008; Competition Litigation, UK Practice and Procedure, 2009. *Recreations:* croquet, snorkelling. *Address:* Brick Court Chambers, 7–8 Essex Street, WC2R 3LD. *T:* (020) 7379 3550, *Fax:* (020) 7379 3558. *Club:* Royal Automobile.

MASEFIELD, Thorold; *see* Masefield, J. T.

MASERI, Attilio, MD; FRCP; FACC; President, Heart Care Foundation ONLUS, since 2008; *b* 12 Nov. 1935; *s* of Adriano and Antonietta Albini, Italian nobles; *m* 1960, Countess Francesca Maseri Florio di Santo Stefano (*d* 2000); one *s*. *Educ:* Classic Lycée Cividale, Italy; Padua Univ. Med. Sch. Special bds in Cardiology, 1963, in Nuclear Medicine, 1965, Italy. Research fellow: Univ. of Pisa, 1960–65; Columbia Univ., NY, 1965–66; Johns Hopkins Univ., Baltimore, 1966–67; University of Pisa: Asst Prof., 1967–70; Prof. of Internal Medicine, 1970; Prof. of Cardiovascular Pathophysiology, 1972–79; Prof. of Medicine (Locum), 1977–79; Sir John McMichael Prof. of Cardiovascular Medicine, RPMS, Univ. of London, 1979–91; Prof. of Cardiology, and Dir, Inst. of Cardiology, Catholic Univ. of Rome, 1991–2001; Prof. of Cardiology and Dir, Cardiovascular and Thoracic Dept, Vita-Salute San Raffaele Univ., Milan, 2001–08. Lifetime Mem., John Hopkins Soc. of Scholars, 1980. George Von Hevesy Prize for Nuclear Medicine, 1974; King Faisal Prize for Medicine, 1992; Dist. Scientist Award, Amer. Coll. of Cardiology, 1997; Invernizzi Prize for Medicine, Romeo and Enrica Invernizzi Foundn, 1998; Gold Medal Award, Eur. Soc. of Cardiology, 2002; Pres. of Italian Republic's Gold Medal for Culture and Science, 2004; Grand Prix Scientifique, Inst de France, 2004; Gold Medal of Merit, Italian Ministry of Health, 2010. Chevalier d'honneur et devotion, SMO Malta; Knight Grand Cross of Order of Merit (Italy), 2005. *Publications:* Myocardial Blood Flow in Man, 1972; Primary and Secondary Angina, 1977; Perspectives on Coronary Care, 1979; Ischemic Heart Disease: a rational basis for clinical practise and clinical research, 1995; articles in major internat. cardiological and med. jls. *Recreations:* ski-ing, snowboarding, windsurfing, tennis, sailing. *Address:* Heart Care Foundation ONLUS, Via La Marmora 36, 50121 Florence, Italy. *Club:* Queen's.

MASHAM, Lord; Mark William Philip Cunliffe-Lister; *b* 15 Sept. 1970; *s* and *heir* of Earl of Swinton, *qv*; *m* 2000, Felicity Shadbolt.

MASHAM OF ILTON, Baroness *cr* 1970 (Life Peer); **Susan Lilian Primrose Cunliffe-Lister, (Susan, Countess of Swinton);** DL; *b* 14 April 1935; *d* of Sir Ronald Sinclair, 8th Bt and Reba Blair (who *m* 2nd, 1957, Lt-Col H. R. Hildreth, MBE; she *d* 1985), *d* of Anthony Inglis, MD; *m* 1959, Lord Masham (later 2nd Earl of Swinton) (*d* 2006); one *s* one *d* (both adopted). *Educ:* Heathfield School, Ascot; London Polytechnic. Has made career in health and voluntary work. Mem., Peterlee and Newton Aycliffe New Town Corp., 1973–85. Mem., Select Cttee on Sci. and Technol., 1997–. All-Party Parliamentary Groups: Member: British Council Associate Parly Gp, 1999–; Associated Parly Health Gp (formerly Forum), 2001–; Chair: Cancer; Skin; Co-Chair: Antibiotics; Clinical Physiology; Men's Health; Telehealth; HIV/Aids; Autism; Hepatology; Horse; Pro-Life; Tuberculosis; Vice Chairman: Alcohol Misuse; Spinal Cord; Dentistry; Headache Disorders; Heart Disease; Continence Care; Accident Prevention; Animal Welfare; Atrial Fibrillation; Civil Society and Volunteering; First Aid; Muscular Dystrophy; Osteoporosis; Pancreatic Cancer; Stem Cell Transplant; Thrombosis; Vascular Disease; Treasurer: Complex Needs and Dual Diagnosis; Gardening and Horticulture; Primary Care and Public Health; Tranquillizer Addiction; Women's Sport and Fitness; Sec., Malaria and Neglected Tropical Disease. President: N Yorks Red Cross, 1963–88 (Patron, 1989–); Yorks Assoc. for the Disabled, 1963–98; Spinal Injuries Assoc., 1982–; Chartered Soc. of Physiotherapy, 1975–82; Papworth and Enham Village Settlements, 1973–85; Registration Council of Scientists in Health Care, 1991–; Countrywide Workshops Charitable Trust, 1993–97; St Cecilia Orch., Ripon; Vice-President: British Sports Assoc. for the Disabled; Disabled Drivers Assoc.; Assoc. of Occupnl Therapists; Action for Dysphasic Adults; Hosp. Saving Assoc.; Chairman: Bd of Dirs, Phoenix House (Drug Rehabilitation), 1986–92 (Patron, 1992–); Home Office Working Gp on Young People and Alcohol, 1987; Member: Yorks RHA, 1982–90; N Yorks FHSA, 1990–95; Bd of Visitors, Wetherby Young Offenders Instn (formerly Wetherby Youth Custody Centre), 1963–94; Winston Churchill Meml Trust, 1980–2007; Council, London Lighthouse, 1991–98; Trustee, Spinal Res. Trust; Patron many orgns in area of health and disability, including: Disablement Income Gp; Yorks Faculty of GPs; Greenbank Project, Liverpool; Mem. and Governor, Ditchley Foundn, 1980–; former Mem., Volunteer Centre. Freedom, Borough of Harrogate, 1989. DL North Yorks, 1991. Hon. FRCGP 1981; Hon. FCSP 1996; Hon. Fellow, Bradford and Ilkley Community Coll., 1988. Hon. MA Open, 1981; DUniv York, 1985; Hon. LLD: Leeds, 1988; Teesside, 1993; Hon. DSc Ulster, 1990; Hon. DLitt Keele, 1993; Hon. DCL UEA, 2001. *Publications:* The World Walks By, 1986. *Recreations:* breeding highland ponies, swimming, table tennis, fishing, flower decoration, gardening. *Address:* Dykes Hill House, Masham, near Ripon, N Yorks HG4 4NS. *T:* (01765) 689241; 46 Westminster Gardens, Marsham Street, SW1P 4JG. *T:* (020) 7834 0700.

MASHELKAR, Raghunath Anant, PhD; FRS 1998; Council of Scientific & Industrial Research Bhatnagar Fellow, India, since 2007; National Research Professor, India, since 2011; President, Global Research Alliance, since 2007; *b* 1 Jan. 1943; *s* of late Anant Tukaram Mashelkar and Anjani Anant Mashelkar; *m* 1970, Vaishali R. Mashelkar; one *s* two *d*. *Educ:* Univ. of Bombay (BChemEngrg 1966; PhD 1969). Sen. Scientist, 1976–86, Dir, 1989–95, Nat. Chemical Lab., Pune; Dir Gen., Council of Scientific and Industrial Res., and Sec., Dept of Scientific and Industrial Res., India, 1995–2006. Pres., Indian Sci. Congress, 1999–2000. Fellow: Indian Acad. of Scis, 1983 (Vice Pres., 1995–97); Indian Nat. Sci. Acad., 1984 (Viswakarma Medal, 1988); Maharashtra Acad. of Scis, 1985 (Pres., 1991–94); Third World Acad. of Scis, 1994. Hon. DSc: Salford, 1993; Kanpur, 1995; Delhi, 1998; Guwahati Anna (Chennai), Pretoria, 2000; London, 2001; Wisconsin, 2002; Allahabad, 2002; Varanasi, 2002; Baroda, 2003; Kalyani, 2004; Narendra Deva, Faizabad, 2004; Govind Ballabh Pant, Pantnagar, 2004; Maharishi Dayanand, Rohtak, 2005; Guru Nanak Dev, Amritsar, 2005; Mohanlal Sukhadia, Udaipur, 2006; Lucknow, 2006; Hon. DLit Santiniketan, 2006. Herdillia Award, Indian Inst. of Chem. Engrs, 1982; K. G. Naik Gold Medal, 1985; Republic Day Award, NRDC, 1995; Atur Sangtani Award, Atur Foundn, 1998; Lifetime Achievement Award, Indian Analytical Instruments Assoc., 1998; Shanti Sharup Bhatnagar Medal, INSA, 2001; Nat. Award, Lal Bahadur Shastri Inst. of Mgt for Excellence in Public Admin and Mgt Studies, 2002; Medal of Engrg Excellence, WFEO, 2003; New Millennium Innovation Award, Associated Chambers of Commerce and Industry of India, 2003; Lifetime Achievement Award, 2004, Asutosh Mookherjee Meml Award, 2005, Indian Sci. Congress Assoc.; Stars of Asia Award, Business Week, USA, 2005; TWAS Medal, Acad. of Scis for Developing World (TWAS), 2005; Suryadatta Nat. Award, Suryadatta Gp of Insts, 2006. Padmashri, 1991; Padmabhushan, 2000; Padmavibhushan, 2014. *Publications:* (ed jtly) Advances in Transport Processes, vol. 1, 1980, vol. 2, 1982, vol. 3, 1983, vol. 4, 1986, vol. 8, 1992, vol. 9, 1993; (ed jtly and contrib.) Frontiers in Chemical Reaction Engineering, vols 1 and 2, 1984; (ed jtly) Transport Phenomena in Polymeric Systems, vol. 1, 1987, vol. 2, 1989; (ed jtly) Advances in Transport Phenomena in Fluidizing Systems, 1987; (ed jtly) Recent Trends in Chemical Reaction Engineering, vols 1 and 2, 1987; (ed jtly) Reactions and Reaction Engineering, 1987; (ed jtly and contrib.) Heat Transfer Equipment Design, 1988; (ed jtly) Readings in Solid State Chemistry, 1994; (ed jtly and contrib.) Dynamics of Complex Fluids, 1998; (ed jtly and contrib.) Structure and Dynamics in the Mesoscopic Domain, 1999; (jtly) Intellectual Property and Competitive Strategies in the 21st Century, 2004; Timeless Inspirator: reliving Gandhi, 2010; Reinventing India, 2011; numerous articles in jls and contribs to books. *Address:* CSIR-National Chemical Laboratory, Pune 411008, India. *T:* 25902197, 25902605, *Fax:* 25902607.

MASIRE, Quett Ketumile Joni, Hon. GCMG 1991; Naledi Ya Botswana; President of Botswana, 1980–98; Congo Facilitator, Southern African Development Community, since 1999; *b* 23 July 1925; *m* 1957, Gladys Olebile; three *s* three *d*. *Educ:* Kanye; Tiger Kloof. Founded Seepapitso Secondary School, 1950; reporter, later Dir, African Echo, 1958; Mem., Bangwaketse Tribal Council, Legislative Council (former Mem., Exec. Council); founder

Mem., Botswana Democratic Party (Editor, Therisanyo, 1962–67); Member, Legislative Assembly (later National Assembly): Kanye S, 1966–69; Ngwaketse-Kgalagadi, 1974–79; Dep. Prime Minister, 1965–66; Vice-Pres. and Minister of Finance and Development Planning, 1966–80. African Pres. in Residence, Boston Univ., 2006–07. *Publications:* Very Brave or Very Foolish: memoirs of an African diplomat, 2008. *Address:* PO Box 70, Gaborone, Botswana. *T:* 353391.

MASKAWA, Prof. Toshihide, DSc; Special Professor and Director-General, Kobayashi-Maskawa Institute for the Origin of Particles, Nagoya University; *b* 7 Feb. 1940. *Educ:* Nagoya Univ. (DSc 1967). Asst Prof., Faculty of Sci., Kyoto Univ., 1970–76; Prof., Yukawa Inst. for Theoretical Physics, 1980–90; Prof., Faculty and Grad. Sch. of Sci., Kyoto Univ., 1990–97; Dir, Yukawa Inst. for Theoretical Physics, 1997–2003, now Prof. Emeritus. Dir, Maskawa Inst. for Sci. and Culture, Kyoto Sangyo Univ. Sakurai Prize, APS, 1985; Japan Acad. Prize, 1985; Asahi Prize, 1994; (jtly) Nobel Prize for Physics, 2008. *Address:* Kobayashi-Maskawa Institute for the Origin of Particles, Nagoya University, Furo-cho, Chikusa-ku, Nagoya, Aichi 464–8602, Japan.

MASKELL, Prof. Duncan John, MA, PhD; FMedSci; Marks and Spencer Professor of Farm Animal Health, Food Science and Food Safety, since 1996, and Senior Pro-Vice Chancellor, Planning and Resources, since 2015, University of Cambridge; Fellow, Wolfson College, Cambridge, since 1998; *b* 30 May 1961; *s* of Leslie George Maskell and Mary Sheila Horsburgh Maskell; *m* 1992, Dr Sarah Elizabeth Peters; one *s* one *d. Educ:* Gonville and Caius Coll., Cambridge (MA, PhD). Res. Scientist, Wellcome Biotech, 1985–88; Res. Fellow, Inst. of Molecular Medicine, John Radcliffe Hosp., Univ. of Oxford, 1988–92; Lectr, Dept of Biochemistry, Imperial Coll., London Univ., 1992–96; Hd, Dept of Veterinary Medicine, 2004–13, Hd, Sch. of Biol Scis, 2013–15, Univ. of Cambridge. Food Standards Agency: Member: Res. Review Gp, 2000–01; Adv. Cttee on Res., 2002–07; Gen. Adv. Cttee on Sci., 2008–. Member: Agri-Food Cttee, 1997–2003 (Chm., 2000–03), Strategy Bd, 2000–03, BBSRC; Council, RCVS, 2004–13; Scientific Adv. Bd, Pirbright Inst., 2010–; Scientific Adv. Bd, Roslin Inst., 2013–; Internat. Scientific Adv. Bd, Wellcome Trust/Oxford Univ. Clinical Res. Unit, Vietnam, 2012; Internat. Scientific Adv. Bd, WellcomeTrust/Oxford Univ. Clinical Res. Unit, VIZIONS project, 2014; Dist. Vis. Prof. and Mem., 3i Inst. Internat. Scientific Adv. Bd, Univ. of Technol., Sydney, 2011–. Trustee Bd Mem., BBSRC Inst. of Food Res., 2013–. Mem., Global Agenda Council on Pandemics, World Econ. Forum, 2008–09. Co-founder: Arrow Therapeutics Ltd, 1998; Discuva Ltd, 2011; Bactevo Ltd, 2013; non-executive Director: Moredun Res. Inst., 2006–; Genus plc, 2014–. FMedSci 2011. *Publications:* papers in learned jls on molecular microbiol. and bacterial infectious diseases. *Recreations:* watching cricket, Manchester United, cooking, fine wine, music. *Address:* Department of Veterinary Medicine, University of Cambridge, Madingley Road, Cambridge CB3 0ES. *T:* (01223) 339868. *Club:* Athenæum.

MASKELL, Rachael Helen; MP (Lab) York Central, since 2015; *b* 5 July 1972. *Educ:* Univ. of E Anglia (BSc Physiotherapy 1994). Physiotherapist in hosps incl. Barnet Gen. Hosp.; Hd of Health, Unite, until 2015. Mem., Health Select Cttee, 2015–. *Address:* House of Commons, SW1A 0AA.

MASKEY, Alexander; Member (SF) Belfast West, Northern Ireland Assembly, 1998–2003 and since Nov. 2014 (Belfast South, 2003–Nov. 2014); Lord Mayor of Belfast, 2002–03; *b* 8 Jan. 1952; *s* of Alexander and Teresa Maskey; *m* 1976, Elizabeth McKee; two *s. Educ:* Christian Brothers' Primary Sch.; Donegall Street, Belfast; St Malachy's Coll., Belfast. Mem. (SF), Belfast CC, 1983–2010. Member: Nat. Cttee, Ard Chomhairle, 1994–; NI Forum, 1996–98; NI Policing Bd, 2007–11. Contested (SF) Belfast S, 2001, 2005. *Recreations:* photography, reading. *Address:* (office) Connolly House, 147 Andersonstown Road, Belfast BT11 9BW.

MASKEY, Paul; MP (SF) Belfast West, since June 2011; *b* Belfast, 10 June 1967; *s* of Alexander and Teresa Maskey; *m* Patricia; two *c. Educ:* Edmund Rice Coll. Co-ordinator, Fáilte Feirste Thiar; has worked as florist and glass cutter. Mem. (SF) Belfast CC, 2001–09 (Leader, SF Gp, until 2009). Mem. (SF) Belfast W, NI Assembly, 2007–July 2012. *Recreations:* football, walking. *Address:* Sinn Féin, 51–55 Falls Road, Belfast BT12 4PD. *T:* (028) 9034 7350, *Fax:* (028) 9034 7360. *E:* westbelfastmp@sinnfein.ie.

MASKIN, Prof. Eric Stark, PhD; Adams University Professor, Harvard University, since 2012; *b* New York, 12 Dec. 1950; *s* of Meyer and Bernice Rabkin Maskin; *m* 1983, Dr Gayle Sawtelle; one *s* one *d. Educ:* Harvard Univ. (AB Maths 1972; AM Applied Maths 1974; PhD 1976). Res. Fellow, Jesus Coll., Cambridge, 1976–77; Prof., MIT, 1981–84; Prof., 1985–2000, Louis Berkman Prof. of Econs, 1997–2000, Harvard Univ.; Albert O. Hirschman Prof. of Social Sci., Inst. for Advanced Study, Princeton, 2000–11. Guggenheim Fellow, 1980–81; Sloan Res. Fellow, 1983–85. Lectures: Churchill, Cambridge Univ., 1994; Arrow, Stanford Univ., 1998; Schwartz, Northwestern Univ., 2002; Toulouse, Univ. of Toulouse, 2004; Zeuthen, Univ. of Copenhagen, 2004; Marshall, Cambridge Univ., 2007; Klein, Univ. of Penn, 2007. Fellow: Econometric Soc., 1981 (Pres., 2003); Amer. Acad. of Arts and Scis, 1994. Corresp. FBA 2003. Hon. Fellow: St John's Coll., Cambridge, 2004; Jesus Coll., Cambridge, 2009. Mem., NAS, 2008. Hon. MA Cantab, 1977; Hon. DHL Bard Coll., 2008; Dhc Corvinus Univ. of Budapest, 2008. Galbraith Teaching Prize, Harvard Univ., 1990, 1992; (jtly) Nobel Prize in Econs, 2007; Erik Kempe Award, Kempe Foundn, 2007; Centennial Medal, Harvard Univ., 2010. *Publications:* contrib. learned jls incl. Rev. of Econ. Studies, Qly Jl of Econs, Econometrica, Jl of Political Economy. *Recreation:* music. *Address:* Department of Economics, Harvard University, Littauer Center, 1805 Cambridge Street, Cambridge, MA 02138, USA. *T:* (617) 4951746, *Fax:* (617) 4957730. *E:* emaskin@fas.harvard.edu.

MASKREY, Rachel; *see* Langdale, R.

MASLIN, David Michael E.; *see* Eckersley-Maslin.

MASLIN, Prof. Mark Andrew, PhD; FRGS; Professor of Physical Geography, University College London, since 2006 (Director, Environment Institute, 2006–10; Head, Department of Geography, 2007–11); Director, London NERC Doctoral Training Partnership, since 2014; *b* London, 14 March 1968; *s* of Christopher Alan and Catherine Anne Maslin; *m* 1998, Johanna Lucy Andrews; two *d. Educ:* Univ. of Bristol (BSc 1st Cl. Hons); Darwin Coll., Cambridge (PhD 1993). FRGS 2001. Res. Scientist, Kiel Univ., 1993–95; Lectr in Geog., 1995–2002, Reader in Geog., 2002–06, UCL. Associate Ed., Quarternary Sci. Rev., 2005–; Mem., Editl Bd, Geographical Jl, 2010–. Executive Director: Carbon Auditors Ltd, 2007–12; Rezatec Ltd (formerly Carbon Associates Ltd), 2012–; Global Precious Commodities plc, 2012–13. Science Adviser: CarbonSense Ltd, 2007–; Global Cool Foundn, 2009–; Global Precious Commodities plc, 2012–. Royal Soc. Wolfson Res. Merit Award for study of early human evolution in E Africa, 2011–; Royal Soc. Industrial Fellowship, 2012–. Member: UK Global Forest Monitoring Consortium, 2010–; Adv. Bd, Steria Corporate Responsibility, 2011–. Consultant for TV programmes: Supervolcano, Horizon, Superstorm, Around the World in 60 Minutes, Ice Age Giants, Global Warming Special, Dispatches: Greenwash, Green Britain Week, Timeteam, Wild Brazil, Human Universe. Trustee and co-Dir, TippingPoint: Art and Climate Change, 2006–12. Mem., Adv. Cttee, Cheltenham Sci. Fest., 2009–. Pres., Darwin Coll., Cambridge, 1990–91. Gov., St John's C of E Sch., Stanmore, 2010–. FRSA 2009. *Publications:* Restless Planet (series): Floods (with Emma Durham), 1999, Storms, 1999, Earthquakes, 1999; Global Warming, 2002, 2nd edn 2007; The Coming Storm, 2002; Stormy Weather, 2002; Etat d'urgence: Le ciel en colère, 2003; Global Warming: a very short introduction, 2004, 2nd edn 2008; The Complete Ice Age, 2009; (ed with S. Randalls) Future Climate Change (4 vols), 2012; Climate: a very short introduction, 2013; (ed with B. McGuire) Climate Forcing of Geological Hazards, 2013; over 135 articles in jls incl. Science, Nature, Nature Climate Change, Lancet and Geology. *Recreations:* reading, theatre, travel, strategy games. *Address:* Department of Geography, Pearson Building, Gower Street, University College London, WC1E 6BT. *T:* (020) 7679 2000. *E:* m.maslin@ucl.ac.uk. *Club:* Geographical.

MASOJADA, Bronislaw Edmund, (Bronek); Chief Executive Officer, Hiscox Ltd, since 2006; *b* 31 Dec. 1961; *s* of Milek Edmund Masojada and Shirley Mary Masojada (*née* Johnston); *m* 1986, Jane Elizabeth Ann Lamont; three *s* two *d. Educ:* Univ. of Natal, SA (BSc Civil Engrg 1982; MPhil Mgt Studies 1987); Trinity Coll., Oxford (Rhodes Schol. 1985). Nat. Service, Engrg Corps, S African Army, 1983–84. McKinsey & Co., Sydney, London and Tokyo: Jun. Associate, then Associate, 1989–91; Engagement Manager, 1992–93; Managing Director: Hiscox Gp, 1993–95; Hiscox plc, 1996–2006. Dir, Xchanging Insure Services, 2003–06. Chm., Insce Intellectual Capital Initiative, 2008–. Dep. Chm. Council, Lloyd's, 2001–07; Lloyd's Underwriting Agents Association: Mem. Cttee, 1993–98; Chm., 2000–01; Mem., Cttee, Lloyd's Mkt Assoc., 2000–01. Dep. Pres., 2003–04, Pres., 2004–05, Insce Inst. of London. Mem. Bd, Assoc. of British Insurers, 2012–. Trustee, Lloyd's Tercentenary Res. Foundn (formerly Lloyd's Tercentenary Fund), 2007– (Chm., 2008–14). Master, Insurers' Co., 2013–14 (Liveryman, 2006–12). *Recreations:* kite surfing, ski-ing, Caterham racing. *Address:* Hiscox Ltd, 45 Reid Street, Hamilton HM12, Bermuda. *T:* 2788300, *Fax:* 2788301. *E:* bronek.masojada@hiscox.com. *Club:* Goring Water Sports.

MASON, Alastair Michael Stuart, FRCP; Chairman, SSL Ltd, 1996–2003; Partner, Partners in Care, 1996–2003; *b* 4 March 1944; *s* of late Adair Stuart and of Rosemary Mason; *m* 1967 (marr. diss. 2006); two *s* two *d. Educ:* Downside Sch.; London Hosp., London Univ. MB BS. MRCP, FRCP 1993; MRCS; FFPH (FFPHM 1991). Hosp. junior appts, 1967–73; Sen. Medical Officer, Dept of Health, 1974–84; Sen. Manager, Arthur Andersen & Co., 1984–88; RMO, S Western RHA, 1988–94. *Publications:* (ed) Walk don't run, 1985; Information for Action, 1988. *Recreations:* walking, reading, theatre. *Address:* Bridge House, Bowbridge Lane, Prestbury, Cheltenham, Glos GL52 3BL.

MASON, Alison Mary; *see* Etheridge, A. M.

MASON, Hon. Sir Anthony (Frank), AC 1988; KBE 1972 (CBE 1969); Chancellor, University of New South Wales, 1994–99; Chief Justice, High Court of Australia, 1987–95; *b* Sydney, 21 April 1925; *s* of F. M. Mason; *m* 1950, Patricia Mary, *d* of Dr E. N. McQueen; two *s. Educ:* Sydney Grammar Sch.; Univ. of Sydney (BA, LLB). RAAF Flying Officer, 1944–45. Admitted to NSW Bar, 1951; QC 1964. Commonwealth Solicitor-General, 1964–69; Judge, Court of Appeal, Supreme Court of NSW, 1969–72; Justice, High Court of Australia, 1972–87; Judge, Supreme Court of Fiji, 1995–2000; Non-permanent Judge, HK Court of Final Appeal, 1997–; Pres., Solomon Islands Court of Appeal, 1997–99. Mem., Permanent Court of Arbitration, 1987–99. Mem., Panel of Arbitrators and Advrs, INTELSAT, 1965–69; Presiding Arbitrator, Internat. Centre for Settlement of Investment Disputes (dispute under N Amer. Free Trade Agreement), 1999–2001. Nat. Fellow, Res. Sch. of Social Scis, ANU, 1995–99 (Dist. Vis. Fellow, 2000–); Arthur Goodhart Prof. in Legal Sci., and Vis. Fellow, Gonville and Caius Coll., Cambridge, 1996–97. Vice-Chm., UN Commn on Internat. Trade Law, 1968. Chairman: Nat. Liby of Australia, 1995–98; Adv. Bd, Nat. Inst. for Law, Ethics and Public Affairs, Griffith Univ., 1995–99; Member: Council of Management, British Inst. of Internat. and Comparative Law, 1987–98; Council, ANU, 1969–72; Pro-Chancellor, ANU, 1972–75. Mem., Amer. Law Inst., 1995. FASSA 1989. Hon. Bencher, Lincoln's Inn, 1987. Hon. LLD: ANU, 1980; Sydney, 1988; Melbourne, 1992; Monash, 1995; Griffith, 1995; Deakin, 1995; NSW, 2000; Hong Kong 2005; Hon. DCL Oxford, 1993. *Recreations:* gardening, swimming. *Address:* 1 Castlereagh Street, Sydney, NSW 2000, Australia.

MASON, Benedict; composer, sound artist and film maker. *Educ:* King's Coll., Cambridge (schol.; MA); Royal Coll. of Art (MA). Guido d'Arezzo, 1988; John Clementi Collard Fellowship, 1989; Fulbright Fellow, 1990; Deutsche Akademischer Austauschdienst Künstlerprogramm, Berlin, 1994. *Compositions* include: Hinterstoisser Traverse, 1986; 1st String Quartet, 1987; Lighthouses of England and Wales, 1987 (Britten Prize, 1988); Oil and Petrol Marks on a Wet Road are sometimes held to be Spots where a Rainbow Stood, 1987; Horn Trio, 1987; Six Piano Etudes, 1988; Chaplin Operas, 1989; Sapere Aude for Eighteenth Century Period Instrument Orchestra, 1989; Dreams that do what they're told, 1990; Concerto for the Viola Section accompanied by the Rest of the Orchestra, 1990; Nodding Trilliums and Curve-lined Angles, 1990; Self Referential Songs and Realistic Virelais, 1990; Rilke Songs, 1991; Animals and the Origins of the Dance, 1992; Quantized Quantz, 1992; !, 1992; Colour and Information, 1993; 2nd String Quartet, 1993; Playing Away: an opera about Germany, Opera, Pop Music and Football, 1994. *Sound/theatre installations:* Ohne Missbrauch der Aufmerksamkeit, 1993; Second Music for a European Concert Hall: Ensemble Modern/Freiburg Barockorchester/Benoît Régent/Mozartsaal, 1994; third music for a european concert hall (espro: eic: i love my life), 1994; Clarinet Concerto, 1995; ASKO/PARADISO: the Fifth Music. Résumé with C. P. E. Bach, 1995; Schumann-Auftrag: Live Hörspiel ohne Worte, 1996; SEVENTH. (for David Alberman and Rolf Hind) PIANO.WITH.VIOLIN.TO.TOUR.ALL.HALLS.MUSIC, 1996; Carré, Nederlands Kamerkoor, Schoenberg Ensemble, Eighth Music for a European Concert Hall (First Music for a Theatre), 1996; Steep Ascent within and away from a Non European Concert Hall: Six Horns, Three Trombones and a Decorated Shed, 1996; Trumpet Concerto, 1997; The Four Slopes of Twice among Gliders of her Gravity (two Steinway model D pianos, two Ampico player pianos and one human being), 1997; Szene für Jean Nouvel (drei Frauenstimmen, drei Spiegelstimmen, Orch., Sampler und Film), 1998. Solo exhibn, gastronomic amorous gymnastic etc music, Berlin, 1997. *Films:* Horn, 1980; Doppler Between, 1983; Resonating Toner, 1985; all stages, 1987; Leading Articles, 1990; Reassurance, 1991; Disclaimer, 1995. Ernst von Siemens Prize, 1992; Paul Fromm Award, 1995; Britten Award, 1996. *Publications:* outside sight unseen and opened, 2nd edn, 2002. *Recreation:* litigation.

MASON, Colin Rees, OBE 2003; TD 1982; Managing Director: Chiltern Broadcast Management (trading name of Aurora World Ltd), since 1997; Capital Radio (SL) Ltd, Freetown, Sierra Leone, since 2005; Chief Executive Officer, Alderney Broadcasting Company Ltd, since 2014; Vice Lord-Lieutenant for Bedfordshire, since 2005; *b* 19 Aug. 1943; *s* of Clifford Harold Mason and Ann Mason (*née* Jones); *m* 1968, Grace Angela St Helier Tweney; one *s* one *d. Educ:* Gwent Coll., Newport; UCW, Aberystwyth (BA Hons); Magdalene Coll., Cambridge (MPhil); Harvard Grad. Sch. of Business (OPM). Producer, BBC, 1969–74; Prog. Dir, Swansea Sound, 1974–80; Asst Man. Dir, Standard Broadcasting, 1980–82; Man. Dir, Chiltern Radio plc, 1981–95; Dep. Chm., Choice FM, 1995–2004. Dir, Alderney Broadcasting Corp. Ltd, 2003–14. Royal Welsh Regt (formerly Royal Regt of Wales), TA: Lt Col 1984, Col 2000; CO, Pool of Public Information Officers, 1990–93; served Saudi Arabia, Kuwait, 1991, Kosovo, 1999–2000, Sierra Leone, Macedonia, 2001, Afghanistan, 2002, Iraq, 2003; Co. Comdt, 2000–04; Hon. Col, 15 (UK) Psychol Ops Gp, 2004–10; Hon. Col, Beds and Herts ACF, 2008–14. High Sheriff, 2002–03, DL 2002, Beds. *Recreations:* travel, ski-ing. *Clubs:* Army and Navy, Reform.

MASON, David Buchanan; QC 2010; a Recorder, since 2005; *b* Guildford, 16 Jan. 1963; *s* of late Donald Mason and of Lynn Mason; one *d*; partner, Susan Richards. *Educ:* Cranleigh Sch.; Leicester Univ. (LLB). Called to the Bar, Middle Temple, 1986. *Recreations:* golf, skiing, diving, shooting, singing. *Address:* 5 Fountain Court, Steelhouse Lane, Birmingham B4 6DR. *T:* 07831 125522. *E:* dbm@no5.com. *Club:* Blackwell Golf.

MASON, Sir David (Kean), Kt 1992; CBE 1987; BDS, MD; FRCSGlas, FDSRCPS Glas, FDSRCSE, FRCPath; FRSE; Professor of Oral Medicine and Head of the Department of Oral Medicine and Pathology, University of Glasgow Dental School, 1967–92, now Professor Emeritus; Dean of Dental Education, University of Glasgow, 1980–90; *b* 5 Nov. 1928; *s* of George Hunter Mason and Margaret Kean; *m* 1967, Judith Anne Armstrong; two *s* one *d*. *Educ:* Paisley Grammar Sch.; Glasgow Acad.; St Andrews Univ. (LDS 1951, BDS 1952); Glasgow Univ. (MB, ChB 1962, MD (Commendation) 1967). FDSRCSE 1957; FDSRCPS Glas 1967 (Hon. FDSRCPS Glas 1990); FRCSGlas 1973; FRCPath 1976 (MRCPath 1967); FRSE 1999. Served RAF, Dental Br., 1952–54. Registrar in Oral Surgery, Dundee, 1954–56; gen. dental practice, 1956–62; Vis. Dental Surgeon, Glasgow Dental Hosp., 1956–62, Sen. Registrar 1962–64; Sen. Lectr in Dental Surgery and Pathology, Univ. of Glasgow, 1964–67; Hon. Consultant Dental Surgeon, Glasgow, 1964–67. Chm., National Dental Consultative Cttee, 1976–80 and 1983–87; Member: Medicines Commn, 1976–80; Dental Cttee, MRC, 1973–80; Physiol Systems Bd, MRC, 1976–80; Jt MRC/Health Depts/SERC Dental Cttee, 1984–87; GDC, 1976–94 (Mem., Disciplinary Cttee, 1980–85; Health Cttee, 1985–89; Pres., 1989–94); Dental Cttee, UGC, 1977–87 (Chm., 1983–87); Supervised Trng Gp, UGC, 1984–86; Dental Rev. Wkg Party, UGC, 1986–87; Jt Cttee for Higher Trng in Dentistry, 1977–84; Dental Strategy Rev. Gp, 1980–81; Scientific Prog. Cttee, FDI, 1980–87; Consultant to Commn on Dental Res., FDI, 1973–80. President: W of Scotland Br., BDA, 1983–84; British Soc. for Dental Res., 1984–86; British Soc. for Oral Medicine, 1984–86; GDC, 1989–94; Convener, Dental Council, RCPGlas, 1977–80. Lectures: Charles Tomes, RCS, 1975; Holme, UCH, London, 1977; Caldwell Meml, Univ. of Glasgow, 1983; Evelyn Sprawson, London Hosp. Med. Coll., 1984. Hon. Member: BDA, 1993; Amer. Dental Assoc., 1994; Royal Odonto-Chirurgical Soc. of Scotland, 2010. Hon. FFDRCSI 1988; Hon. FRCSE 1995; Hon. FDSRCS 2002. Hon. DDS Wales, 1991; Hon. LLD Dundee, 1993; Hon. DSc Western Ontario, 1997; DUniv Glasgow, 1998. John Tomes Prize, RCS, 1979; Colyer Medal, RCS, 1992. *Publications:* (jtly) Salivary Glands in Health and Disease, 1975; (jtly) Introduction to Oral Medicine, 1978; (jtly) Self Assessment: Manual I, Oral Surgery, 1978; Manual II, Oral Medicine, 1978; (ed jtly) Oral Manifestations of Systemic Disease, 1980, 2nd edn 1990; (jtly) World Workshop on Oral Medicine, 3 vols, 1988, 1993, 1999. *Recreations:* golf, tennis, gardening, enjoying the pleasures of the countryside. *Address:* Cherry Tree Cottage, Houston Road, Kilmacolm, Renfrewshire PA13 4NY. *Clubs:* Royal & Ancient Golf, Elie Golf House, Kilmacolm Golf; Western (Glasgow).

MASON, Frances Jane G.; *see* Gumley-Mason.

MASON, Jane; *see* Mason, T. J.

MASON, Maj. Gen. Jeffrey Sinclair, MBE 2001; Clerk and Chief Executive Officer, Butchers' Company, since 2014; *b* Glasgow, 19 Nov. 1959; *s* of Alexander David Mason and Irene Elizabeth Mason (*née* Keith); *m* 1981, Lucy Mary Evered; one *s* one *d*. *Educ:* Glasgow Acad. Joined RM, 1977; DCS, HQ 3 Commando Bde, 1999–2001; CSO Personnel, HQ RM, 2001–02; CO, Commando Logistic Regt, 2002–04; rcds 2004; ACOS, J1/J4, PJHQ, 2004–06; Dir, Defence Supply Chain Ops and Movements, Defence Equipment and Support, 2006–09; rcds 2009; Asst Chief of Defence Staff (Logistic Ops), 2009–11. Man. Dir, Supreme Gp UK, 2011–13; Commercial Dir, Supreme Gp Europe and Commonwealth, 2013–14. Trustee: Falkland Is Chapel, 2005– (Chm., 2012–); Nat. Mus. of Royal Navy, 2015–; Chm. of Trustees, Royal Marines Mus., 2012–. Chm., E Mersea Parish Council, 2013– (Mem., 2012–). *Recreations:* recent military history, keeping fit (a losing battle), family, renovating house. *Club:* Army and Navy.

MASON, John Fingland; Member (SNP) Glasgow Shettleston, Scottish Parliament, since 2011; *b* 1957. CA 1980. Mem. (SNP), Glasgow CC, 1998–2008 (Leader of the Opposition, 1999–2008). MP (SNP) Glasgow E, July 2008–2010; contested (SNP) same seat, 2010. *Recreations:* Easterhouse Baptist Church, hill-walking, camping. *Address:* Scottish Parliament, Edinburgh EH99 1SP.

MASON, John Kenneth, CBE 2015; Director for Business, Scottish Government, since 2010; *b* 26 June 1956; *s* of Kenneth George Mason and Helen Mary Mason (*née* Green); *m* 1990, Alison Margaret Cruickshanks; one *s* two *d*. *Educ:* Hertford Coll., Oxford (BA Hons Geog. 1978); University Coll. London (MPhil Town Planning 1981). MCIPD 1997. Senior Town Planner: Kent CC, 1980–85; DoE, 1985–87; Principal: DoE, 1988–90; Scottish Office, 1990–94; Dep. Chief Exec., Registers of Scotland, 1994–96; Asst Sec., Enterprise and Industry, Scottish Office, 1996–2000; Scottish Executive: Prin. Private Sec. to First Minister, 2001–02; Under Sec. and Hd, Tourism, Culture and Sport Gp, Educn Dept, 2002–05; Under Sec. and Hd, Envmt Gp, Envmt and Rural Affairs Dept, subseq. Dir, Envmt Gp, 2006–07; Dir for Climate Change, Water Industry and Envmtl Quality, Scottish Exec., later Scottish Govt, 2006–10. Non-exec. Dir, Scottish Swimming, 2006–. *Recreations:* photography, enjoying the best of Scotland. *Address:* Scottish Government, St Andrew's House, Regent Road, Edinburgh EH1 3DG. *E:* u102526@gmail.com.

MASON, Prof. John Kenyon French, CBE 1973; MD; FRSE; Regius Professor of Forensic Medicine, University of Edinburgh, 1973–85, now Emeritus; *b* 19 Dec. 1919; *s* of late Air Cdre J. M. Mason, CBE, DSC, DFC and late Alma French; *m* 1943, Elizabeth Latham (decd); two *s*. *Educ:* Downside Sch.; Cambridge Univ.; St Bartholomew's Hosp. MD, FRCPath, FRCPE 2002, DMJ, DTM&H; LLD Edinburgh 1987. Joined RAF, 1943; Dir of RAF Dept of Aviation and Forensic Pathology, 1956; retd as Group Captain, Consultant in Pathology, 1973. Pres., British Assoc. in Forensic Medicine, 1981–83. FRSE 1995. Hon. Fellow, Edinburgh Law Sch., Univ. of Edinburgh, 1985–2013. Hon. LLD Edinburgh, 2005. L. G. Groves Prize for Aircraft Safety, 1957; R. F. Linton Meml Prize, 1958; James Martin Award for Flight Safety, 1972; Douglas Weightman Safety Award, 1973; Swiney Prize for Jurisprudence, 1978; Lederer Award for Aircraft Safety, 1985. *Publications:* Aviation Accident Pathology, 1962; (ed) Aerospace Pathology, 1973; Forensic Medicine for Lawyers, 1978, 4th edn 2001; (ed) The Pathology of Violent Injury, 1978, 3rd edn as The Pathology of Trauma, 2000; Law and Medical Ethics, 1983, 9th edn 2013; Butterworth's Medico-Legal Encyclopaedia, 1987; Human Life and Medical Practice, 1989; Medico-legal Aspects of Reproduction, 1990, 2nd edn 1998; The Courts and the Doctor, 1990; (ed) Forensic Medicine: an illustrated text, 1993; Legal and Ethical Aspects of Healthcare, 2003; The Troubled Pregnancy, 2007; papers in medical and legal jls. *Address:* 66 Craiglea Drive, Edinburgh EH10 5PF. *Club:* Royal Air Force.

MASON, Rt Rev. Kenneth Bruce, AM 1984; Chairman, Australian Board of Missions, General Synod of the Anglican Church of Australia, 1983–93; *b* 4 Sept. 1928; *s* of Eric Leslie Mason and Gertrude Irene (*née* Pearce); unmarried. *Educ:* Bathurst High Sch.; Sydney Teachers' Coll.; St John's Theological Coll., Morpeth (ThL 1953); Univ. of Queensland (BA DipDiv 1964). Primary Teacher, 1948–51; deacon, 1953; priest, 1954; Member, Brotherhood of the Good Shepherd, 1954; Parish of: Gilgandra, NSW, 1954–58; Darwin, NT, 1959–61; Alice Springs, NT, 1962; student, Univ. of Qld, 1963–64; resigned from Brotherhood, 1965; Trinity Coll., Melbourne Univ.: Asst Chaplain, 1965; Dean, 1966–67; Bishop of the Northern Territory, 1968–83. Member, Oratory of the Good Shepherd, 1962, Superior, 1981–87. Life Gov., YMCA Australia, 1983. *Recreations:* attending opera, listening to music, walking, railways. *Address:* Sirius Cove Nursing Home, 17 Clanalpine Street, Mosman, NSW 2088, Australia. *T:* (2) 99693363. *E:* kmason@ogs.net.

MASON, Rev. Canon Kenneth Staveley; Canon Theologian, Scottish Episcopal Church, 1995–96; Canon of St Mary's Cathedral, Edinburgh, 1989–96, now Canon Emeritus; *b* 1 Nov. 1931; *s* of Rev. William Peter Mason and Anna Hester (*née* Pildrem); *m* 1958, Barbara Thomson; one *s* one *d*. *Educ:* Imperial College of Science, London (BSc, ARCS); BD (ext.) London; Wells Theological Coll. Assistant Curate: St Martin, Kingston upon Hull, 1958; Pocklington, 1961; Vicar of Thornton with Allerthorpe and Melbourne, 1963; Sub-Warden and Librarian, KCL, at St Augustine's Coll., Canterbury, 1969; Dir, Canterbury Sch. of Ministry, 1977, Principal, 1981. Examining Chaplain to Archbp of Canterbury, 1979–91; Six Preacher in Canterbury Cath., 1979–84; Hon. Canon of Canterbury, 1984–89; Principal, Edinburgh Theol Coll., later Dir, Theol Inst., Scottish Episcopal Church, 1989–95. *Publications:* George Herbert, Priest and Poet, 1980; Anglicanism, a Canterbury essay, 1987; Priesthood and Society, 1992; Catholic Tradition and the Ordination of Women, 1993; A Great Joy, 2001. *Address:* 2 Williamson Close, Ripon HG4 1AZ. *T:* (01765) 607041.

MASON, Prof. Malcolm David, MD; FRCP, FRCR; FRSB; oncologist; Professor of Clinical Oncology, Cardiff University (formerly University of Wales College of Medicine), since 1997; *b* 31 May 1956; *s* of Seymour and Marion Mason; *m* 1983, Lee-Anne Isaacs; two *d*. *Educ:* Westminster Sch.; Med. Coll. of St Bartholomew's Hosp. (MB BS 1979; MD 1991). FRCR 1987; FRCP 1997; FRSB (FSB 2011). Lectr in Radiotherapy and Oncol., Inst. of Cancer Res. and Royal Marsden Hosp., 1989–91; Consultant Clinical Oncologist, 1992–96, Hon. Consultant, 1996–, Velindre Hosp., Cardiff. Dir, Wales Cancer Bank, 2004–. Member (pt-time): NRPB, 2000–05; Cttee on Med. Aspects of Radiation in the Envmt, 2003–10. Chm., Prostate Cancer Clin. Studies Gp, NCRI, 2009–15; Chm., UK TNM Evaluation Cttee, UICC, 2009–. Chief Investigator, Intergroup NCIC/MRC study est. role of radiotherapy in locally advanced prostate cancer. *Publications:* (with L. Mofatt) Prostate Cancer: the facts, 2003, 2nd edn 2010; over 300 contribs to learned jls. *Recreation:* playing the piano music of the great classical masters from Bach to Rachmaninov. *Address:* Velindre Hospital, Whitchurch, Cardiff CF14 2TL. *T:* (029) 2031 6964, *Fax:* (029) 2052 9625. *E:* masonmd@cardiff.ac.uk.

MASON, Marion Helen; *see* Smith, M. H.

MASON, Dame Monica, DBE 2008 (OBE 2002); Director, Royal Ballet, 2002–12 (Principal Répétiteur, 1984–91, Assistant Director, 1991–2002); *b* 6 Sept. 1941; *d* of Richard Mason and Mrs E. Fabian; *m* 1968, Austin Bennett. *Educ:* Johannesburg, SA; Royal Ballet Sch., London. Joined Royal Ballet in Corps de Ballet, 1958; Sen. Principal until 1989; created role of Chosen Maiden in Rite of Spring, 1962; also created roles in: Diversions, Elite Syncopations, Electra, Manon, Romeo and Juliet, Rituals, Adieu, Isadora, The Four Seasons, The Ropes of Time. Assistant to the Principal Choreographer, Royal Ballet, 1980–84. Chm., Royal Ballet Benevolent Fund, 2014–. Hon. FKC, 2013; Hon. Fellow, St Hilda's Coll., Oxford, 2013. DUniv Surrey, 1996. Queen Elizabeth II Coronation Award, RAD, 2011; Special Award, Laurence Olivier Awards, 2012.

MASON, Dr Pamela Georgina Walsh, FRCPsych; Vice-Chairman, Taunton and Somerset NHS Trust, 1991–97; Senior Principal Medical Officer (Under Secretary), Department of Health and Social Security, 1979–86, retired; re-employed as Senior Medical Officer, Department of Health, 1986–90; *d* of late Captain George Mason and Marie Louise Walsh; god-daughter and ward of late Captain William Gregory, Hon. Co. of Master Mariners; *m* 1st, 1949, David Paltenghi (*d* 1961); two *s*; 2nd, 1965, Jan Darnley-Smith (*d* 1996). *Educ:* Christ's Hosp. Sch.; Univ. of London, Royal Free Hosp. Sch. of Medicine (MRCS, LRCP, 1949; MB, BS 1950). DPM 1957; MRCPsych 1971. Various appointments at: Royal Free Hosp., 1951–53; Maudsley Hosp. and Bethlem Royal Hosp., 1954–58; Guy's Hosp., 1958–60; Home Office, 1961–71; DHSS, later DoH, 1971–90. Vis. Psychiatrist, Holloway Prison, 1962–67; Adviser: C of E Children's Soc., 1962–; Royal Philanthropic Soc., 1962–; WRAF Health Educn Scheme, 1962–67. Consultant to: Law Commn, 1991–93; Carnegie Inquiry into the Third Age, 1991–92; Nat. Audit Office, 1992–94. Chairman: WHO Working Gp on Youth Advisory Services, 1976; WHO Meeting of Nat. Mental Health Advrs, 1979. Member: Council of Europe Select Cttee of Experts on Alcoholism, 1976–77; Cttee of Experts on Legal Problems in the Medical Field, 1979–80; UK Delegn to UN Commn on Narcotic Drugs, 1980–86; Organising Cttee, World Summit of Ministers of Health on Progs for AIDS Prevention, 1988; Review of Prison Med. Services, 1990. Chm. Appeals Cttee, Somerset Red Cross, 1999–2001. Guide, Bath Abbey Vaults Mus., 2004–07. FRSocMed. QHP 1984–87. *Publications:* contribs to various professional jls and Govt pubns. *Recreations:* antiquities, humanities, ballet, films, tennis, seafaring and expeditions. *Address:* Apartment 8, The Elms, Weston Park West, Bath BA1 4AR.

MASON, Paul; Chairman: Cath Kidston Ltd, since 2010; Mayborn Group Ltd, since 2011; *b* 14 Feb. 1960; *s* of John and Joan Mason; *m* 1984, Juliet Greenway; three *s*. *Educ:* Univ. of Manchester (BA 1st Cl. Hons). Various posts, Mars GB Ltd, 1982–90; Buying and Logistics Dir, B&Q plc, 1990–94; Dir, Mgt Bd, Asda plc, 1994–99; Chief Operating Officer, 1999–2000, Pres. and CEO, 2000–01, Asda Walmart UK; CEO, Matalan plc, 2002–04; Pres., Levi Strauss & Co. Europe, 2004–06; CEO, Somerfield Gp, 2006–09; Chairman: Radley & Co. Ltd, 2008–12; New Look Retailers Ltd, 2014–15.

MASON, Prof. Paul James, CB 2003; PhD; FRS 1995; Professor of Meteorology and Director, NCAS Universities Weather and Environment Research Network, University of Reading, 2003–06, now Professor Emeritus; *b* 16 March 1946; *s* of Charles Ernest Edward Mason and Phyllis Mary Mason (*née* Swan); *m* 1968, Elizabeth Mary Slaney; one *s* one *d*. *Educ:* Univ. of Nottingham (BSc Physics 1967); Univ. of Reading (PhD Geophysics 1972). Meteorological Office: SO, 1967–71; SSO, 1971–74; PSO, 1974–79; Head, Meteorological Res. Unit, Cardington, 1979–85; Asst Dir, Boundary Layer Br., 1985–89; Dep. Dir, Physical Res., 1989–91; Chief Scientist, 1991–2002. Vis. Prof., Univ. of Surrey, 1995–. Chm., Global Climate Observing System Steering Cttee, 2001–04. Member: Editing Cttee, Qly Jl Meteorology, 1983–88; Editl Bd, Boundary Layer Meteorology, 1988–2000. Royal Meteorological Society: Mem. Council, 1989–90; Vice Pres., 1990–92 and 1994–95; Pres., 1992–94. L. G. Groves Prize for Meteorology, MoD, 1980; Buchan Prize, RMetS, 1986. *Publications:* scientific papers in meteorology and fluid dynamics jls. *Recreations:* walking, exploring the countryside. *Address:* Department of Meteorology, University of Reading, PO Box 243, Reading RG6 6BB. *T:* (0118) 931 8954.

MASON, Sir Peter (James), KBE 2002; FREng; non-executive Chairman, Thames Water, since 2006; Chief Executive Officer, AMEC plc, 1996–2006; *b* 9 Sept. 1946; *s* of Harvey John Mason and Jenny Mason (*née* Wilson); *m* 1st, 1969, Elizabeth Ann McLaren (marr. diss. 1992); two *s*; 2nd, 1997, Beverly Ann Hunter. *Educ:* Marr Coll., Troon; Univ. of Glasgow (BSc Hons Engrg 1968). Norwest Holst Group Ltd, 1980–92: Man. Dir, Civil Engrg Div., 1980–85; CEO, 1985–92; BICC plc, 1992–96: Dir, 1992–96; CEO, 1992–96, Chm., 1994–96, Balfour Beatty Ltd. Sen. Ind. Dir, BAE Systems plc, 2003–13; non-exec. Dir, Acergy, 2006–. Board Mem., UK Trade and Investment (formerly British Trade Internat.), 2000–04; Mem., Olympic Delivery Authy, 2006–09. FREng 2009. *Recreations:* opera, sailing, gardening. *Address:* c/o Thames Water, Clearwater Court, Vastern Road, Reading RG1 8DB.

MASON, Rt Rev. Peter Ralph; Development Adviser, Wycliffe College, Toronto (Development Director, 2003); *b* 30 April 1943; *s* of late Ralph Victor Mason and of Dorothy Ida Mullin; *m* 1965, Carmen Ruth Ruddock; one *s* two *d*. *Educ:* McGill Univ., Montreal (BA 1964; BD 1967; MA 1971); Princeton Univ. (DMin 1983). Ordained deacon, 1967, priest, 1968; Asst Curate, St Matthew's, Montreal, 1967–69; Incumbent, parish of Hemmingford, 1969–71; Rector: St Clement's, Montreal, 1971–74; St Peter's, Montreal, 1975–80; St Paul's, Halifax, NS, 1980–85; Principal, Wycliffe Theol Coll., Univ. of Toronto, 1985–92; Bishop of Ontario, 1992–2002. Hon. DD Montreal Diocesan Theol Coll., 1987; Hon. DD: Trinity Coll., Toronto, 1992; Wycliffe Coll., Toronto, 1994. *Recreations:* golf, sailing, ski-ing, opera. *Address:* Wycliffe College, 5 Hoskin Avenue, Toronto, ON M5S 1H7, Canada.

MASON, Philippa; *see* Gregory, Philippa.

MASON, Air Vice-Marshal Richard Anthony, (Tony), CB 1988; CBE 1981; DSc; DL; Hon. Professor, University of Birmingham, 1996–2012; *b* 22 Oct. 1932; *s* of William and Maud Mason; *m* 1956, Margaret Stewart; one *d*. *Educ:* Bradford Grammar Sch.; St Andrews Univ. (MA); London Univ. (MA); DSc Birmingham 1997. Commissioned RAF, 1956; Director of Defence Studies, 1977; Director of Personnel (Ground), 1982; Deputy Air Secretary, 1984; Air Sec., 1985–89; Dir, Centre for Studies in Security and Diplomacy, 1988–2001, Leverhulme Emeritus Fellow, 2002–05, Univ. of Birmingham. Leverhulme Airpower Res. Dir, Foundn for Internat. Security, 1989–94. Advr to H of C Defence Cttee, 2001–06. Hon. Freeman, Bor. of Cheltenham, 2001. DL Glos, 2002. Hon. FRAeS 2006. *Publications:* Air Power in the Next Generation (ed), 1978; Readings in Air Power, 1979; (with M. J. Armitage) Air Power in the Nuclear Age, 1981; The RAF Today and Tomorrow, 1982; British Air Power in the 1980s, 1984; The Soviet Air Forces, 1986; War in the Third Dimension, 1986; Air Power and Technology, 1986; To Inherit the Skies, 1990; Air Power: a centennial appraisal, 1994; Air and Space Power: revised roles and technology, 1998; articles in internat. jls on defence policy and strategy. *Recreations:* Rugby, writing, gardening. *Address:* c/o Lloyds Bank, Montpelier Walk, Cheltenham GL50 1SH. *Club:* Royal Air Force.

MASON, Prof. Sir Ronald, KCB 1980; FRS 1975; Professor of Chemistry, University of Sussex, 1971–86 (Pro-Vice-Chancellor, 1977); Chairman: British Ceramic Research Ltd, 1990–96; University College Hospitals NHS Trust, 1992–2001; *b* 22 July 1930; *o s* of David John Mason and Olwen Mason (*née* James); *m* 1952, E. Pauline Pattinson; three *d*; *m* 1979, Elizabeth Rosemary Grey-Edwards (*d* 2009). *Educ:* Univ. of Wales (Fellow, University College Cardiff, 1981); London Univ. (Fellow, UCL, 1996). CChem, FRSC; FIMMM (FIM 1993). Research Assoc., British Empire Cancer Campaign, 1953–61; Lectr, Imperial Coll., 1961–63; Prof. of Inorganic Chemistry, Univ. of Sheffield, 1963–71; Chief Scientific Advr, MoD, 1977–83. Vis. Prof., Univs in Australia, Canada, France, Israel, NZ and US, inc. A. D. Little Prof., MIT, 1970; Univ. of California, Berkeley, 1975; Ohio State Univ., 1976; North Western Univ., 1977; Prof. associé, Univ. de Strasbourg, 1976; Erskine Vis. Prof., Christchurch, NZ, 1977; Prof., Texas, 1982; Vis. Prof. of Internat. Relns, UCW, 1985–95. Schmidt Meml Lectr, Israel, 1977. SRC: Mem., 1971–75; Chm. Chemistry Cttee, 1969–72; Chm. Science Bd, 1972–75; Consultant and Council Mem., RUSI, 1984–88; UK Mem., UN Commn of Disarmament Studies, 1984–92; Chairman: Council for Arms Control, 1986–90; Engrg Technol. Cttee, DTI, 1991–93. Pres., BHRA, 1986–94 (Chm., BHR Gp, 1990–95); Member: ABRC, 1977–83; BBC Adv. Group, 1975–79. Chairman: Hunting Engineering Ltd, 1987 (Dep. Chm., 1985–87); Science Applications Internat. Corp. (UK) Ltd, 1993–96; Xtreamis plc, 1998–2000; Advanced Messaging Ltd, 2004–06; Zone V, 2012–. Pres., Inst. of Materials, 1995–96. Foundation Chm., Stoke Mandeville Burns and Reconstructive Surgery Res. Trust, 1990–94; Chm., UCL Hosps Charities, 2004–07. Hon. FIMechE 1997. Hon. DSc: Wales, 1986; Keele, 1992. Corday-Morgan Medallist, 1965, and Tilden Lectr, 1970, Chemical Society; Medal and Prize for Structural Chem., Chem. Soc., 1973. *Publications:* (ed) Advances in Radiation Biology, 1964, 3rd edn 1969; (ed) Advances in Structure Analysis by Diffraction Methods, 1968, 6th edn 1978; (ed) Physical Processes in Radiation Biology, 1964; many papers in Jl Chem. Soc., Proc. Royal Soc., etc, and on defence issues.

MASON, Samantha Mary Constance; *see* Beckett, S. M. C.

MASON, Susanna Margaret; Director General, Commercial, Ministry of Defence, since 2012; *b* BMH, Rinteln, W Germany, 12 March 1964; *d* of John Fawkes and Margaret June Fawkes (*née* Desjardins); *m* 1991, Ian Paul Mason; two *d* (one *s* decd). *Educ:* Lilley and Stone High Sch. for Girls, Newark; Sunderland Poly. (BA Hons Business Studies); King's Coll. London (MA Internat. Studies); RCDS. ACMA 1991; MCIPS 2010. Finance Dir and Co. Sec., Hewitt Associates, 1992–94; Exec. Partner, Coopers & Lybrand, later PricewaterhouseCoopers, then IBM, 1994–2004; Associate Partner, Defence Strategy and Solutions, 2004–08; Dir, Exports and Commercial Strategy, MoD, 2008–12. *Recreations:* swimming, camping, knitting, church. *Address:* Ministry of Defence, Main Building, Whitehall, SW1A 2HB. *T:* 07710 041926.

MASON, (Tania) Jane; Regional Chairman of Employment Tribunals, London Central Region, 2000–01; *b* 25 Sept. 1936; *d* of late Edward Warner Moeran, sometime MP, and of Pymonie (*née* Fincham); *m* 1961, (James) Stephen Mason, CB (*d* 2012); one *s* two *d*. *Educ:* Frensham Heights Sch. Called to the Bar, Inner Temple, 1961. Law Reporter, Judicial Cttee of Privy Council, 1976–83; Asst Legal Advr, British Council, 1983–86; full-time Chm. of Industrial Tribunals, 1986–92; Regional Chairman: Industrial Tribunals, London S Reg., 1992–97; Industrial, later Employment, Tribunals, London N Reg., 1997–2000. *Recreations:* country life, English novels, art, architecture. *Address:* Amberley House, Church Street, Amberley, West Sussex BN18 9NF. *Club:* Reform.

MASON, Timothy Ian Godson; arts and heritage consultant; Director, Museums & Galleries Commission, 1995–2000; *b* 11 March 1945; *s* of late Ian Godson Mason and Muriel (*née* Vaile); *m* 1975, Marilyn Ailsa Williams; one *d* one *s*. *Educ:* St Albans Sch., Washington, DC; Bradfield Coll., Berkshire; Christ Church, Oxford (MA). Assistant Manager, Oxford Playhouse, 1966–67; Assistant to Peter Daubeny, World Theatre Season, London, 1967–69; Administrator: Ballet Rambert, 1970–75; Royal Exchange Theatre, Manchester, 1975–77; Director: Western Australian Arts Council, 1977–80; Scottish Arts Council, 1980–90; Consultant on implementation of changes in structure of arts funding, Arts Council of GB, 1990–91; Chief Exec., London Arts Bd, 1991–95. Member: Gen. Adv. Council, BBC, 1990–96; Gen. Council, Commonwealth Assoc. of Museums, 2003–14. Trustee, Civic Trust, 2004–06. Gov., KCH, 2006–11. *Publications:* Care, Diligence & Skill, 1986; Shifting Sands, 2003; Design Reviewed: urban housing, 2004; Designed with Care, 2006. *Recreations:* family, travelling, the arts, museums. *Address:* 15 Towton Road, SE27 9EE. *T:* (020) 8761 1414.

MASON, Air Vice-Marshal Tony; *see* Mason, Air Vice-Marshal R. A.

MASON, William Ernest, CB 1983; Deputy Secretary (Fisheries and Food), Ministry of Agriculture, Fisheries and Food, 1982–89, retired; *b* 12 Jan. 1929; *s* of Ernest George and Agnes Margaret Mason; *m* 1959, Jean (*née* Bossley); one *s* one *d*. *Educ:* Brockley Grammar Sch.; London Sch. of Economics (BScEcon). RAF, 1947–49; Min. of Food, 1949–54; MAFF, 1954; Principal 1963; Asst Sec. 1970; Under Sec., 1975; Fisheries Sec., 1980. Dir, Food and Agric. Div., NATO Central Supplies Agency (West), 1983–93. Dir, Allied-Lyons, then Allied Domecq, PLC, 1989–98; consultant on food and drink industry, 1989–98. Member: EDC for Distribn Trades, 1975–80; EDC for Food and Drink Manufg Inds, 1976–80; Adv. Bd, Inst. of Food Res., 1993–98. Chm. of Govs, Prendergast Sch. for Girls, 1974–86. FRSA 1989; FIGD 1989; Hon. FIFST 1989. Hon. Keeper of the Quaich, 1989–. *Recreations:* music, reading, modern British painting. *Address:* 3 Cranleigh House, 16 Overbury Avenue, Beckenham, Kent BR3 6PY. *T:* (020) 8650 8241.

MASRI, Taher Nashat, Order of the Renaissance (Jewelled), Jordan, 1991; Order of Al-Kawkab, Jordan, 1974; Order of Al-Nahda, Jordan; Hon. GBE 1988; Member of Senate, Jordan, 1998–2001 and since 2005; President of Senate, since 2009 (First Vice President, 2005–09); *b* Nablus, 5 March 1942; *s* of Nashat Masri and Hadiyah Solh; *m* 1968, Samar Bitar; one *s* one *d*. *Educ:* Al-Najah Nat. Coll., Nablus; North Texas State Univ. (BA Business Admin 1965). Central Bank of Jordan, 1965–73; MP Nablus District, Jordan, 1973–74, 1984–88, 1989–97; Minister of State for Occupied Territories Affairs, 1973–74; Ambassador to: Spain, 1975–78; France, 1978–83; Belgium (non-resident), 1979–80; Britain, 1983–84; Perm. Delegate to UNESCO, 1978–83 and to EEC, 1978–80; Foreign Minister, 1984–88 and 1991; Dep. Prime Minister and Minister of State for Economic Affairs, April–Sept. 1989; Chm., Foreign Relations Cttee, 1989–91 and 1992–93; Prime Minister of Jordan and Minister of Defence, June–Nov. 1991; Pres. of Lower House of Parlt, 1993–94. Chm., Foreign Relations Cttee, Jordanian Parlt, 1989–91 and 1992–93. Mem. and Rapporteur, Royal Commn for Drafting of Nat. Charter, 1990; Member and Head of Political Committee: Royal Commn for Drafting Nat. Agenda, 2005–; Cttee of All Jordan (Royal Commn), 2006–; Mem., Royal Commn to Revise Constitution, 2011–. President: Nat. Soc. for Enhancement of Freedom and Democracy, 1993–97; Jordanian Spanish Friends Assoc., 1998–; Nat. Dialogue Cttee, 2011–; Jordan Lebanese Assoc., 2012. Comr for Civil Societies, Arab League, 2002–09; Mem. and Vice Pres., 2006–, Pres., Exec. Cttee, 2009–, Arab Thought Forum. Mem., Adv. Cttee, Anna Lindh Euro-Mediterranean Foundn for Dialogue between Cultures, 2004–06; Chm., 1992–2006, Vice Chm., 2008–, and Vice Pres., Bd of Trustees, 2008–, Princess Haya Cultural Center for Children. Pres., Bd of Trustees, Jordan Univ. for Sci. and Technol., 1998–2010. Pres., Jordan British Soc., 2006–12. Hon. Pres., Arab Student Aid Internat., Jordan, 2012. Grand Cross, Order of Civil Merit, Spain, 1977; Order of Isabel the Catholic, Spain, 1978; Grand Cross, Order of Merit, Germany; Kt Grand Cross, Order of Merit, Italy; Grand Cordon, Ordre Nat. de Cèdre, Lebanon; Grand Decoration with Sash for Services, Austria; Grand Gwanghwa Medal, Order of Diplomatic Service Merit, Rep. of Korea; Grand Officier: Légion d'Honneur, France (Comdr, 1981); Ordre Nat. du Mérite, France. *Address:* PO Box 5550, Amman 11183, Jordan. *T:* (6) 5920600, (office) 4642227, *Fax:* (6) 4642226. *W:* www.tahermasri.com.

MASSENET, Natalie Sara, MBE 2009; Founder and Executive Chairman, Net-A-Porter Group, 2000–15; Chairman, British Fashion Council, since 2013; *b* Los Angeles, 13 May 1965; *d* of Bob Rooney and Barbara Rooney; two *d*. *Educ:* Univ. of Calif, Los Angeles (BA Eng. Lit.). In film business, 1988–90; Moda mag., Italy, 1990–93; W Coast Fashion Ed., WWD and W, 1993–96; Sen. Fashion Ed., Tatler, 1996–99. Entrepreneur of the Year, CNBC Eur. Business Leaders Awards, 2008; Innovator of the Year, Harper's Bazaar Awards, 2010; Award for Excellence, Quintessentially Awards, 2010; Creative Leadership Award, Aenne Burda Awards, 2011; British Inspiration Award, 2012.

MASSER, Prof. David, PhD; FRS 2005; Professor of Mathematics, University of Basel, 1992–2014, now Emeritus; *b* 8 Nov. 1948; *s* of William and Rose Masser; *m* 1988, Hedda Freudenschuss (*d* 2009). *Educ:* Trinity Coll., Cambridge (BA Hons 1970, MA 1974; PhD 1974). University of Nottingham: Lectr, 1973–75 and 1976–79; Reader, 1979–83; Res. Fellow, Trinity Coll., Cambridge, 1975–76; Prof., Univ. of Michigan, Ann Arbor, 1983–92. *Publications:* Elliptic Functions and Transcendence, Lecture Notes in Mathematics, Vol. 437, 1975; over 95 papers in math. jls. *Address:* Nadelberg 17, 4051 Basel, Switzerland.

MASSER, Prof. (Francis) Ian, PhD; LittD; Professor of Urban Planning, International Institute for Aerospace Survey and Earth Sciences, Netherlands, 1998–2002; *b* 14 Sept. 1937; *s* of late Francis Masser and Isabel Masser (*née* Haddaway); *m* 1st, 1962, Alexandra Arnold (*d* 1988); two *d*; 2nd, 1996, Susan Parkin. *Educ:* Malton Grammar Sch.; Univ. of Liverpool (BA, MCD, PhD 1975; LittD 1993). MRTPI 1964. Leverhulme Res. Fellow, UC of Rhodesia and Nyasaland, 1960–61; Associate Planner, Shankland Cox Associates, 1962–64; Lectr, then Sen. Lectr, Univ. of Liverpool, 1964–75; Prof. and Hd of Inst. of Urban and Regional Planning, Univ. of Utrecht, 1975–79; University of Sheffield: Prof. of Town and Regl Planning, 1979–98; Hd, Dept of Town and Regional Planning, 1979–86; Dean, Faculty of Architectural Studies, 1981–84 and 1992–95; Chm., Sheffield Centre for Envmtl Res., 1979–92. Visiting Professor: Hitotsubashi Univ., Tokyo, 1986; Poly. of Turin, 1993–94; Univ. of Utrecht, 1998–2005; UCL, 2003–10; Univ. of Melbourne, 2004–09; Universiti Teknologi Malaysia, 2006. Ed., Papers of Regl Sci. Assoc., 1975–80. Nat. Co-ordinator, ESRC Regl Res. Lab. Initiative, 1986–91; Co-Dir, ESF GISDATA scientific prog., 1991–97. Councillor: Regl Sci. Assoc., 1975–78 (Vice-Pres., 1980–81); Assoc. for Geographic Information, 1991–94, 1999–2003; Chm., Res. Assessment Evaluation Cttee on Geographical and Envmtl Sci., Assoc. of Univs in Netherlands, 1995–96; President: Assoc. of Geographic Information Labs for Europe, 1998–99; European Umbrella Orgn for Geographic Information, 1999–2003; Global Spatial Data Infrastructure Assoc., 2002–04. FRSA 1983. *Publications:* Analytical Models for Urban and Regional Planning, 1972; Inter-regional Migration in Tropical Africa, 1975; (ed) Spatial Representation and Spatial Interaction, 1978; (ed) Evaluating Urban Planning Efforts, 1983; (ed) Learning from Other Countries, 1985; (ed) European Geographic Information Infrastructures, 1998; (ed) Handling Geographic Information, 1991; Geography of Europe's Futures, 1992; (ed) Diffusion and Use of Geographic Information Technologies, 1993; (ed) Planning for Cities and Regions in Japan, 1994; Geographical Information Systems and Organisations, 1995; (ed) GIS Diffusion, 1996; Governments and Geographic Information, 1998; GIS Worlds: creating spatial data infrastructures, 2005; Building European SDIs, 2007, 3rd edn 2015. *Recreations:* walking, travel. *Address:* Town End House, Taddington, Buxton, Derbys SK17 9UF. *T:* (01298) 85232.

MASSEREENE, 14th Viscount *cr* 1660, **AND FERRARD,** 7th Viscount *cr* 1797; **John David Clotworthy Whyte-Melville Foster Skeffington;** Baron Loughneugh (Ire.), 1660; Baron Oriel (Ire.), 1790; Baron Oriel (UK), 1821; stockbroker with M. D. Barnard & Co.; *b* 3 June 1940; *s* of 13th Viscount and Annabelle Kathleen (*d* 2009), *er d* of H. D. Lewis; *S* father, 1992; *m* 1970, Ann Denise, *er d* of late Norman Rowlandson; two *s* one *d*. *Educ:* St Peter's Court, Millfield; Institute Monte Rosa. Grenadier Guards, 1958–61. Stock Exchange, 1961–64; motor trade, 1964–70; Stock Exchange, 1970–; various dirships; landowner. *Recreations:* vintage cars, history, shooting. *Heir:* *s* Hon. Charles John Clotworthy Whyte-Melville Foster Skeffington [*b* 7 Feb. 1973; *m* 2009, Olga, *e d* of Captain Cecil Lewis Dixon-Brown, RM; one *s* one *d*]. *Clubs:* Turf, Pratt's.

MASSEY, family name of **Baroness Massey of Darwen**.

MASSEY OF DARWEN, Baroness *cr* 1999 (Life Peer), of Darwen in the county of Lancashire; **Doreen Elizabeth Massey;** *b* 5 Sept. 1938; *d* of Mary Ann Hall (*née* Sharrock) and Jack Hall; *m* 1966, Dr Leslie Massey; two *s* one *d*. *Educ:* Darwen Grammar Sch., Lancs; Birmingham Univ. (BA Hons French 1961); DipEd 1962; Inst. of Educn, London Univ. (MA 1985). Graduate service overseas, Gabon, 1962–63; teacher: S Hackney Sch., 1964–67; Springside Sch., Philadelphia, 1967–69; Pre-School Play Group Association, 1973–77; teacher, Walsingham Sch., London, 1977–83 (co-ordinator Health Educn, Head of Year, senior teacher); advisory teacher for personal, social and health educn, ILEA, 1983–85; Manager, Young People's Programme, Health Educn Council, 1985–87; Dir of Educn, 1987–89, Dir, 1989–94, FPA. Chm., Nat. Treatment Agency, 2002. Co-Chm., All-Party Parly Gp for Children, 2001–; Member: Information Cttee, H of L, 2012–; Affordable

Childcare Select Cttee, H of L, 2014–15. Pres., Brook Adv. Centres; Mem., Nat. Trust; Patron, FPA, 2009–; Trustee, Unicef England, 2010–; Mem., The Lady Taverners, 2004–. FRSA 1992. Hon. Dr Birmingham, 2014. *Publications:* Sex Education: Why, What and How?, 1988; Sex Education Factpack, 1988; (jtly) Sex Education Training Manual, 1991; (ed) Sex Education Resource Book, 1994; (ed) The Lover's Guide Encyclopedia, 1996; Love on the Road (short stories), 2013; articles on sex educn, family planning, health educn. *Recreations:* reading, cinema, theatre, opera, art and design, yoga, pilates, sports, vegetarian cookery, travel, gardening. *Address:* House of Lords, SW1A 0PW.

MASSEY, Vice Adm. Sir Alan (Michael), KCB 2009; CBE 2003; Chief Executive, Maritime and Coastguard Agency, since 2010; *b* 9 March 1953; *s* of Harry Massey and Astrid Ellen Irene Massey (*née* Lange); *m* 1987, Julie Samantha Smith; two *s* two *d*. *Educ:* Northgate Grammar Sch., Ipswich; Univ. of Liverpool (BA Hons 1975); Keswick Hall Coll. of Educn (PGCE 1976). HMS: Bulwark, 1979; Norfolk, 1980; Leander, 1981; Brazen, 1984; Ark Royal, 1987; RN staff course, 1989; MoD, London, 1990; NATO, Brussels, 1991; CO, HMS Newcastle, 1993; MoD, London, 1995; CO, HMS Campbeltown, 1996; rcds, 1998; MoD, London, 1998; NATO SACLANT, 1999; Commanding Officer: HMS Illustrious, 2001; HMS Ark Royal, 2002; PJHQ Northwood, 2003–05; ACNS, MoD, 2005–08; Second Sea Lord and C-in-C Naval Home Comd, 2008–10; Flag ADC to the Queen, 2008–10. Younger Brother, Trinity House, 2010. Trustee: New Th. Royal, Portsmouth, 2010–; Marine Soc. and Sea Cadets, 2011–. Pres., Victory Services Club, 2014–. Hon. Vice-President: RN and RM Charity; RN Soccer. Cdre, RNSA, 2008–10. Freeman, City of London, 2014; Mem., Shipwrights' Co., 2011–. *Recreations:* sailing, guitar, languages, family. *Address:* Maritime and Coastguard Agency, Spring Place, 105 Commercial Road, Southampton SO15 1EG. *Clubs:* Royal Navy of 1765 and 1785; Fleet Air Arm Officers' Assoc.; Royal Naval and Royal Albert Yacht.

MASSEY, Charles Hamilton; Director General, Strategy and External Relations, Department of Health, since 2012; *b* Southampton, 24 Aug. 1970; *s* of Roger Charles Massey and Catherine Clare Massey (*née* Johnson); *m* 2001, Hilda Anne Hughes; two *s* one *d*. *Educ:* St Catharine's Coll., Cambridge (BA Hist. 1992; MA; MPhil Social Anthropol. and Develt 1993). Policy advr roles, DSS, 1993–2000; Policy Advr, HM Treasury, 2000–01; Deputy Director: Prime Minister's Strategy Unit, 2001–04; Pension Protection, DWP, 2004–05; Exec. Dir for Strategic Develt, Pensions Regulator, 2005–08; Ageing Soc. and State Pensions Dir, DWP, 2008–12. Trustee and Vice Chm., Action on Disability and Develt, 2005–12; Trustee and Chm., Walnut Tree Trust, 2009–. *Address:* Department of Health, Richmond House, 79 Whitehall, SW1A 2NS. *T:* (020) 7210 5368. *E:* charlie.massey@dh.gsi.gov.uk.

MASSEY, Prof. Doreen Barbara, FBA 2002; FAcSS; Professor of Geography, Open University, 1982–2010, now Emerita; *b* Manchester, 3 Jan. 1944; *d* of Jack Massey and Nancy Massey (*née* Turton). *Educ:* St Hugh's Coll., Oxford (BA 1st Cl. Hons Geog. 1966; Hon. Fellow, 2000); Univ. of Pennsylvania (MA Regl Sci. 1972). Centre for Envmtl Studies, 1968–80; SSRC Fellow in Industrial Locn Res., 1980–82. Vis. Researcher, Inst. Nacional de Investigaciones Económicas y Sociales, Managua, 1985–86. Hettner Lectr, Univ. of Heidelberg, 1998. Mem., Editl Bd, Catalyst Trust, 1998–; Co-founder and Ed., Soundings: a jl of politics and culture, 1995–. Member: Bd, Gtr London Enterprise Bd, 1982–87; Adv. Cttee, Centre for Local Econ. Strategies, 1986–88. Mem. Bd, Nat. Inst. for Regl and Spatial Analysis, Ireland, 2001–. Hon. Vice Pres., Geographical Assoc., 1989–93 and 2009–. Trustee, Lipman-Miliband Trust, 1986–. FAcSS (AcSS 1999); FRSA 2000. Hon. DSc: Edinburgh, 2006; QMUL, 2010; Hon. DLitt: NUI, 2006; Glasgow, 2009; Hon. Dr: Harokopio Univ., Athens, 2012; Zurich, 2013. Victoria Medal, RGS, 1994; Prix Vautrin Lud, Fest. Internat. de Géographie, 1998; Anders Retzius Gold Medal, Swedish Soc. for Anthropology and Geography, 2003; Centenary Medal, RSGS, 2003; Residential Achievement Award, Assoc. of American Geographers, 2014. *Publications:* (ed jtly) Alternative Approaches to Analysis, 1975; (with A. Catalano) Capital and Land: landownership by capital in Great Britain, 1978; (with R. Meegan) The Geography of Industrial Reorganisation, 1979; (with R. Meegan) The Anatomy of Job Loss, 1982; Spatial Divisions of Labour: social structures and the geography of production, 1984, 2nd edn 1995; (ed jtly) Geography Matters!, 1984; (ed jtly) Politics and Method: contrasting studies in industrial geography, 1985; Nicaragua: some urban and regional issues in a society in transition, 1987; (ed jtly) The Economy in Question, 1988; (ed jtly) Uneven Re-Development, 1988; (jtly) High-Tech Fantasies, 1992; Space, Place and Gender, 1994; (ed jtly) Geographical Worlds, 1995; (ed jtly) A Place in the World?: places, cultures and globalisation, 1995; (ed jtly) Re-thinking the Region, 1998; (ed jtly) Human Geography Today, 1999; (ed jtly) City Worlds, 1999; (ed jtly) Unsettling Cities, 1999; Power-geometries and the Politics of Space-time, 1999; (jtly) Cities for the Many not the Few, 2000; (jtly) Decentering the nation: a radical approach to regional inequality, 2003; For Space, 2005; (ed jtly) A World in the Making, 2006; World City, 2007, 2010; Samanaikainen Tila, 2008; (jtly) The Kilburn Manifesto, 2013; contrib. articles to learned jls on urban and regl issues, globalisation and the conceptualisation of space and place. *Recreations:* travelling, walking, bird-watching, photography, reading, talking with friends. *Address:* Faculty of Social Sciences, Open University, Walton Hall, Milton Keynes MK7 6AA. *T:* (01908) 654475, *Fax:* (01908) 654488.

MASSEY, Col Hamon Patrick Dunham; Clerk, Ironmongers' Company, since 2005; *b* 18 Aug. 1950; *s* of Lt Col Patrick Massey, MC and Bessie Lee Massey; *m* 1988, Cate Campbell; one *s* three *d*. *Educ:* Harrow; RMA Sandhurst; Army Staff Coll., Camberley. Commnd Blues and Royals, 1970; Adjutant, 1977–79; Army Staff Coll., 1982; CO, Household Cavalry Mounted Regt, 1992–94; Defence Attaché, Buenos Aires, 1997–2000; Comdr, Household Cavalry and Silver Stick in Waiting, 2000–05. *Recreations:* fishing, gardening, dry stone walls. *Address:* Ironmongers' Hall, Shaftesbury Place, EC2Y 8AA. *T:* (020) 7776 2304, *Fax:* (020) 7600 3579. *E:* clerk@ironmongers.org. *Club:* Turf.

See also W. G. S. Massey.

MASSEY, (Robert) Graham; Managing Director, The Science Archive Ltd, 1996–2001; *b* 28 Sept. 1943; *s* of Robert Albert Massey and Violet Edith Massey (*née* Smith); *m* 1965, Allison Ruth Duerden; one *s* one *d*. *Educ:* Manchester Grammar Sch.; Balliol Coll., Oxford (BA 1st Cl. Hons History). Joined BBC 1965 as general trainee; Producer, Science and Features Dept, 1970; Producer, 1972–81, Editor, 1981–85, Horizon; Series Producer, Making of Mankind (with Richard Leakey), 1979–81; Head, Special Features Unit, BBC Drama, 1985–89; Head, Science and Features Dept, BBC, 1989–91; Dir, Co-productions, 1991–92, Dir, Internat., 1992–94, BBC Enterprises. *Recreations:* theatre, cinema, cooking, restoring Gascony farmhouse. *Address:* 76 The Lexington Apartments, 40 City Road, EC1Y 2AN.

MASSEY, Roy Cyril, MBE 1997; Organist and Master of the Choristers, Hereford Cathedral, 1974–2001, Organist Emeritus, 2009; *b* 9 May 1934; *s* of late Cyril Charles Massey and Beatrice May Massey; *m* 1975, Ruth Carol Craddock Grove. *Educ:* Univ. of Birmingham (BMus); privately with David Willcocks. FRCO (CHM); ADCM; ARCM; FRSCM (for distinguished services to church music) 1972. Organist: St Alban's, Conybere Street, Birmingham, 1953–60; St Augustine's, Edgbaston, 1960–65; Croydon Parish Church, 1965–68; Warden, RSCM, 1965–68; Conductor, Croydon Bach Soc., 1966–68; Special Comr of RSCM, 1964–74; Organist to City of Birmingham Choir, 1954–74; Organist and Master of Choristers, Birmingham Cath., 1968–74; Dir of Music, King Edward's Sch., Birmingham, 1968–74. Conductor, Hereford Choral Soc., 1974–2001; Conductor-in-Chief, alternate years Associate Conductor, Three Choirs Festival, 1975–2001; Adviser on organs to dioceses of Birmingham and Hereford, 1974–. Mem. Council and Examiner, RCO, 1970–94 and 1997–2006; Mem., Adv. Council, 1976–78, Council, 1984–98, RSCM; Mem. Council, Friends of Cathedral Music, 1999–2002. President: Birmingham Organists' Assoc., 1970–75; Cathedral Organists' Assoc., 1982–84; IAO, 1991–93; RCO, 2003–05. Fellow, St Michael's Coll., Tenbury, 1976–85. Hon. FGCM 2001. DMus Lambeth, 1990. *Recreations:* motoring, old buildings, walking the dog. *Address:* 2 King John's Court, Tewkesbury, Glos GL20 6EG. *T:* (01684) 290019. *E:* drroymassey@talktalk.net.

MASSEY, William Greville Sale; QC 1996; barrister; *b* 31 Aug. 1953; *s* of late Lt Col Patrick Massey, MC and Bessie Lee Massey (*née* Byrne); *m* 1978, Cecilia D'Oyly Awdry; three *s*. *Educ:* Harrow; Hertford Coll., Oxford (Entrance Schol.; MA). Called to the Bar, Middle Temple, 1977 (Harmsworth Exhibnr), Bencher, 2004. Member: Revenue Bar Assoc., 1978–; Chancery Bar Assoc., 1980–; London Commercial and Common Law Bar Assoc., 1980–. Mem., Tax Cttee, Historic Houses Assoc., 1986–. Governor: Summer Fields Sch., 1996–2013; Harrow Sch., 2000–13. *Recreations:* chess, cricket, opera, gardening, ski-ing. *Address:* Pump Court Tax Chambers, 16 Bedford Row, WC1R 4EF. *T:* (020) 7414 8080, *Fax:* (020) 7414 8099. *E:* clerks@pumptax.com.

See also H. P. D. Massey.

MASSIE, Allan Johnstone, CBE 2013; FRSL; FRSE; author and journalist; *b* 16 Oct. 1938; *s* of late Alexander Johnstone Massie and Evelyn Jane Wilson Massie (*née* Forbes); *m* 1973, Alison Agnes Graham Langlands; two *s* one *d*. *Educ:* Drumtochty Castle Sch.; Trinity College, Glenalmond; Trinity College, Cambridge (BA). Schoolmaster, Drumtochty Castle Sch., 1960–71; TEFL, Rome, 1972–75; fiction reviewer, The Scotsman, 1976–; Creative Writing Fellow: Edinburgh Univ., 1982–84; Glasgow and Strathclyde Univs, 1985–86; columnist: Glasgow Herald, 1985–88; Sunday Times Scotland, 1987–91; Daily Telegraph, 1991–; The Scotsman, 1992–; Daily Mail, 1994–; Sunday Times Scotland, 1996–2007; Spectator. Mem., Scottish Arts Council, 1989–91. Trustee, Nat. Museums of Scotland, 1995–98. Hon. Pres., Classical Assoc. of Scotland, 2003–05. FRSL 1982; FRSE 2011; Hon. FRIAS 1997. Hon. DLitt Strathclyde. Chevalier, Ordre des Arts et des Lettres. *Publications: fiction:* Change and Decay In All Around I See, 1978; The Last Peacock, 1980; The Death of Men, 1981; One Night in Winter, 1984; Augustus, 1986; A Question of Loyalties, 1989; The Hanging Tree, 1990; Tiberius, 1991; The Sins of the Fathers, 1991; Caesar, 1993; These Enchanted Woods, 1993; The Ragged Lion, 1994; King David: a novel, 1995; Shadows of Empire, 1997; Antony, 1997; Nero's Heirs, 1999; The Evening of the World, 2001; Arthur The King, 2003; Caligula, 2003; Charlemagne and Roland, 2007; Surviving, 2009; Klaus and Other Stories, 2010; Death in Bordeaux, 2011; Cold War in Bordeaux, 2014; *non-fiction:* Muriel Spark, 1979; Ill-Met by Gaslight, 1980; The Caesars, 1983; A Portrait of Scottish Rugby, 1984; Colette, 1986; 101 Great Scots, 1987; Byron's Travels, 1988; Glasgow, 1989; The Novel Today, 1990; Edinburgh, 1994; The Thistle and the Rose, 2005; The Royal Stuarts: a history of the family that shaped Britain, 2010; *plays:* Quintet in October; The Minstrel and the Shirra; First-Class Passengers; Changing Lines. *Recreations:* reading, lunching, watching cricket, Rugby, horse-racing, smoking, walking the dogs. *Address:* Thirladean House, Selkirk TD7 5LU. *T:* (01750) 20393. *E:* allan.massie@btinternet.com. *Clubs:* Academy; Selkirk RFC.

MASSIE, Sir Herbert William, (Sir Bert), Kt 2007; CBE 2000 (OBE 1984); DL; Chairman: Bert Massie Ltd, since 2007; Community Equipment Code of Practice Scheme CIC, since 2011; *b* 31 March 1949; *s* of Herbert Douglas and Lucy Joan Massie; *m* 2007, Maureen Lilian Shaw. *Educ:* Portland Trng Coll. for Disabled, Mansfield; Hereward Coll., Coventry; Liverpool Poly. (BA Hons 1977); Manchester Poly. (CQSW). Wm Rainford Ltd, 1967–68; W Cheshire Newspapers Ltd, 1968–70; Liverpool Assoc. for Disabled, 1970–72; Disabled Living Foundn, 1977; RADAR, 1978–99 (Dir, 1990–99). Member: Management Cttee, Disabled Drivers Assoc., 1968–71; Exec. Cttee, Assoc. of Disabled Professionals, 1979 (Trustee, 1979–94; Vice Chm., 1986–94); Careers Service Adv., Council for England, 1979–83; Voluntary Council for Handicapped Children (later Council for Disabled Children), 1980–93 (Vice-Chm., 1985–93); Exec. Cttee, OUTSET, 1983–91; MSC Wkg Party to Review Quota Scheme for Employment of Disabled People, 1984–85; Access Cttee for England, 1984–93; Disabled Persons Tspt Adv. Cttee, 1986–2002; BR Adv. Gp on Disabled People, 1986–94; Tripscope, 1986–2006 (Vice-Chm., 1989–2006); Nat. Adv. Council on Employment of People with Disabilities, 1991–98; Independent Commn on Social Justice, 1993–94; DSS Panel of Experts on Incapacity Benefit, 1993–94; Cabinet Office Adv. Panel on Equal Opportunities in Sen. CS, 1994–2001; Nat. Disability Council, 1996–2000 (Dep. Chm., 1997–2000); Bd, Eur. Disability Forum, 1996–2000; Adv. Cttee, New Deal Task Force, 1997–2000; Disability Rights Task Force, 1997–99; Chm., Disability Rights Commn, 2000–07; Mem., Commn for Equality and Human Rights, 2006–09; Comr for the Compact, 2008–11; Chair, Labour Party Task Force on Disability and Poverty, 2013–14. 1990 BEAMA Foundation for Disabled People: Sec., 1986–90; Trustee, 1990–2000. Vice Pres., Foundn for Assistive Technol., 2000–; UK Nat. Sec., 1993–2000, Dep. Vice-Pres., Europe, 1996–2000, Rehabilitation Internat.; Vice. Pres., Royal Assoc. for Disability and Rights (formerly Rehabilitation), 2009–; Vice President: Muscular Dystrophy UK (formerly Muscular Dystrophy Campaign); Disabled Living Foundn; Phab, 2010–; Pres., Chester, Wirral and N Wales Gp, British Polio Fellowship, 2011–. Patron: Heswall Disabled Children's Holiday Fund, 2003–; Neurosupport (formerly Merseyside Neurological Trust), 2004–; Disability and Deaf Arts, 2009–; Trustee: Independent Living Fund, 1990–93; Habinteg Housing Assoc., 1991–2009; Mobility Choice, 1998–2013; Inst. for Employment Studies, 2000–07; United Trusts, 2006–08; RAISE, Liverpool, 2008–; Local Solutions, Liverpool, 2009–; UK Assoc. of Rights and Humanity, 2010–11 (Chm., 2010–11). Chm., Volunteer Centre, Liverpool, 2012–. Governor: Pensions Policy Inst., 2002–07; Motability, 2002–; Liverpool John Moores Univ., 2008–. Non-exec. Dir, Appleshaw Ltd, 2007–09. FRSA 1988; FCGI 2009. Freeman, City of London, 2008; Mem., Wheelwrights' Co., 2008–. DL Merseyside, 2014. Hon. Fellow, Liverpool John Moores Univ., 2002. Hon. LLD: Bristol, 2005; Liverpool, 2013; DUniv Staffs, 2007. Snowdon Award, 1995; Master Wheelwrights Award, Co. of Wheelwrights, 2002; Duncan Medal, Duncan Soc., Liverpool, 2003; Gold Award for Further Educn Alumni, Assoc. of Colls, 2003; Polio Person of last 70 years, British Polio Fellowship, 2009; Luke Fitzherbert Lifetime Achievement Award, Third Sector mag., 2010. *Publications:* (with M. Greaves) Work and Disability, 1977, 1979; Aspects of the Employment of Disabled People in the Federal Republic of Germany, 1982; (with M. Kettle) Employer's Guide to Disabilities, 1982, 2nd edn 1986; (jtly) Day Centres for Young Disabled People, 1984; Travelling with British Rail, 1985; (with J. Weyers) Wheelchairs and their Use, 1986; (with J. Male) Choosing a Wheelchair, 1990; (with J. Isaacs) Seat Belts and Disabled People, 1990; Social Justice and Disabled People, 1994; Getting Disabled People to Work, 2000; Employmentability, 2010; reports and numerous articles. *Recreation:* reading. *Address:* 2 North Sudley Road, Aigburth, Liverpool L17 0BG. *T:* (0151) 727 3252. *E:* bert@massie.com.

MASSY, family name of **Baron Massy.**

MASSY, 10th Baron *cr* 1776 (Ire.); **David Hamon Somerset Massy;** *b* 4 March 1947; *s* of 9th Baron Massy and Margaret Elizabeth (*née* Flower); *S* father, 1995. *Educ:* St George's Coll., Weybridge. Late Merchant Navy. *Heir:* *b* Hon. John Hugh Somerset Massy [*b* 2 Jan. 1950; *m* 1978, Andrea West; one *s*].

MASTERMAN, His Honour Crispin Grant, FCIArb; a Circuit Judge, 1995–2012; *b* 1 June 1944; *s* of late Osmond Janson Masterman and Anne Masterman (*née* Bouwens); *m* 1976, Clare Fletcher; one *s* two *d*. *Educ:* St Edward's Sch., Oxford; Univ. of Southampton (BA). FCIArb 1991. Called to the Bar, Middle Temple, 1971; a Recorder, 1988–95; Designated Family Judge, Cardiff and Pontypridd, 2006–12; Court of Protection Judge for Cardiff, 2008–12. Legal Mem., Mental Health Review Tribunal for Wales, 2012–. Mem., Council, Cardiff

Univ., 1995–2004 (Vice-Chair, 1998–2004). Commnd RAFVR, 1966 (Actg Pilot Officer); Asst Instructor, British Gliding Assoc., 1977. *Recreations:* family and friends, walking, golf. *Address:* 28 South Rise, Llanishen, Cardiff CF14 0RH. *T:* (029) 2075 4072.

MASTERS, Brian Geoffrey John; author; *b* 25 May 1939; *s* of Geoffrey Howard Masters and Mabel Sophia Charlotte (*née* Ingledew). *Educ:* Wilson's Grammar Sch., London; University Coll., Cardiff (BA 1st cl. Hons 1961); Université de Montpellier. FRSA 1989. *Publications:* Molière, 1969; Sartre, 1969; Saint-Exupéry, 1970; Rabelais, 1971; Camus: a study, 1973; Wynyard Hall and the Londonderry Family, 1974; Dreams about HM The Queen, 1974; The Dukes, 1975; Now Barabbas Was A Rotter: the extraordinary life of Marie Corelli, 1978; The Mistresses of Charles II, 1980; Georgiana, Duchess of Devonshire, 1981; Great Hostesses, 1982; Killing for Company: the case of Dennis Nilsen, 1985 (Gold Dagger Award, CWA); The Swinging Sixties, 1985; The Passion of John Aspinall, 1988; Maharana: the Udaipur Dynasty, 1990; Gary, 1990; The Life of E. F. Benson, 1991; The Shrine of Jeffrey Dahmer, 1993; (ed and trans.) Voltaire's Treatise on Tolerance, 1994; Masters on Murder, 1994; The Evil That Men Do, 1996; She Must Have Known: the trial of Rosemary West, 1996; Thunder in the Air: great actors in great roles, 2000; Getting Personal: a biographer's memoir, 2002; Second Thoughts, 2008; Garrick Collection: the actors, 2010; Six Celebrations on Reaching Seventy, 2013. *Recreations:* etymology, stroking cats. *Address:* 47 Caithness Road, W14 0JD. *T:* (020) 7603 6838; 6 Place E. Granier, 34160 Castries, France. *T:* (4) 67875834. *Clubs:* Garrick (Trustee, 2010–), Beefsteak, Pratt's.

MASTERS, Dr Christopher, CBE 2002; Independent Co-Chair, Scottish Science Advisory Council, since 2011 (Member, since 2010); *b* 2 May 1947; *s* of Wilfred and Mary Ann Masters; *m* 1971, Gillian Mary (*née* Hodson); two *d*. *Educ:* Richmond Sch.; King's Coll. London (BSc, AKC); Leeds Univ. (PhD). Research Chemist, Shell Research, Amsterdam, 1971–77; Corporate Planner, Shell Chemicals UK, 1977–79; Business Develt Manager, Christian Salvesen, 1979–81; Dir of Planning, Merchants Refrigerating Co., NY, 1981–82; Managing Director: Christian Salvesen Seafoods, 1983–86; Christian Salvesen Industrial Services, 1984–89; Chief Exec., Christian Salvesen PLC, 1989–97; Exec. Chm., Aggreko plc, 1997–2002; Chairman: Voxar Ltd, 2002–04; Babtie Gp Ltd, 2002–04; SMG plc, 2004–07; Sagentia Gp plc, 2007–10; Energy Assets Gp plc, 2012–. Director: British Assets Trust plc, 1990–2009; Scottish Widows' Fund or Life Assurance Soc., 1992–2000; Wood Gp, 2002–12; Alliance Trust, 2002–12; Crown Agents, 2005–; Speedy Hire plc, 2011–. Chm., Young Enterprise Scotland, 1993–96; Mem., SHEFC, 1995–2005 (Chm., 1998–2005). Mem. Ct, Edinburgh Univ., 2011–. Chm., Festival City Theatres Trust, 2002–13; Director: Scottish Opera, 1994–99 (Vice Chm., 1996–99); Scottish Chamber Orch., 1995–2012. Master, Merchant Co., City of Edinburgh, 2007–09; Lord Dean, Guild of City of Edinburgh, 2009–11. FRSE 1996. Hon. DBA Strathclyde, 2006; Hon. DLaws St Andrews, 2006; Hon. Dhc Edinburgh 2007; Hon. DEd Abertay Dundee, 2007. *Publications:* Homogeneous Transition—Metal Catalysis, 1981, Russian edn 1983; numerous research papers and patents. *Recreations:* music, wine.

MASTERS, Guy; *see* Masters, T. G.

MASTERS, Robert James; Headmaster, The Judd School, since 2004; *b* 14 July 1964; *s* of Thomas Masters and Judith Lindsey Masters (*née* Boothman); *m* 1988, Rachel Clare Pugh; two *s* one *d*. *Educ:* Univ. of Reading (BSc 1st Cl. Hons Maths); Univ. of Bristol (PGCE Maths with Games). Teacher of maths, Gravesend GS for Boys, 1986–97 (Head: of Middle Sch., 1990–93; of Maths, 1993–97); Dep. Headmaster, Torquay Boys' GS, 1997–2004. Additional Mem., HMC, 2007–. *Recreations:* hockey, cryptic crosswords. *Address:* The Judd School, Brook Street, Tonbridge, Kent TN9 2PN. *T:* (01732) 770880, *Fax:* (01732) 771661. *E:* enquiries@judd.kent.sch.uk.

MASTERS, Sheila Valerie; *see* Baroness Noakes.

MASTERS, Prof. (Thomas) Guy, PhD; FRS 2005; Distinguished Professor, since 2010, and Director, since 2009, Institute of Geophysics and Planetary Physics, University of California, San Diego (Professor of Geophysics, 1985–2010); *b* 5 Oct. 1954; *s* of Thomas James Masters and Joyce Masters; *m* 1982, Virginia Fleming; one *s* one *d*. *Educ:* Victoria Univ. of Manchester (BSc 1st Cl. 1975); King's Coll., Cambridge (PhD 1979). University of California, San Diego: Green Schol., 1979–80, res. geophysicist, 1981–85, IGPP; Dir, Earth Scis, 1999–2002 and 2005–06. Fellow, Amer. Geophysical Union, 1995. Beno Gutenberg Medal, Eur. Geophysical Union, 2011. *Publications:* numerous contribs to leading jls. *Recreations:* horse-riding, ski-ing, gardening. *Address:* Institute of Geophysics and Planetary Physics, Scripps Institution of Oceanography, University of California, San Diego, 9500 Gilman Drive, La Jolla, CA 92093–0225, USA. *T:* (858) 5344122, *Fax:* (858) 5345332. *E:* gmasters@ucsd.edu.

MASTERSON, Valerie, (Mrs Andrew March), CBE 1988; opera and concert singer; *d* of Edward Masterson and Rita McGrath; *m* 1965, Andrew March; one *s* one *d*. *Educ:* Holt Hill Convent; studied in London and Milan on scholarship, and with Eduardo Asquez. Début, Landestheater Salzburg; appearances with: D'Oyly Carte Opera, Glyndebourne Festival Opera, ENO, Royal Opera, Covent Garden, etc; appears in principal opera houses in Paris, Aix-en-Provence, Toulouse, Munich, Geneva, Barcelona, Milan, San Francisco, Chile, etc; leading roles in: La Traviata, Le Nozze di Figaro, Manon, Faust, Alcina, Die Entführung aus dem Serail, Così fan tutte, La Bohème, Semele (SWET award, 1983), Die Zauberflöte, Julius Caesar, Rigoletto, Romeo and Juliet, Carmen, Count Ory, Mireille, Louise, Idomeneo, Les Dialogues des Carmélites, The Merry Widow, Xerxes, Orlando, Lucia di Lammermoor. Recordings include: La Traviata; Elisabetta, Regina d'Inghilterra; Der Ring des Nibelungen; The Merry Widow; Julius Caesar; Scipione; several Gilbert and Sullivan operas. Regular broadcasts on radio and TV. Pres., British Youth Opera, 1995–2001 (Vice-Pres., 2001–). Patron, Mousehole Male Voice Choir, 2002. Hon. Pres., Rossini Soc., Paris. FRCM 1992; Hon. RAM 1993. Hon. DLitt South Bank, 1999.

MASTERTON, Gordon Grier Thomson, OBE 2008; FREng; FRSE; Vice President, Jacobs UK Ltd (formerly Babtie Group Ltd, later Jacobs Babtie), 2004–14; *b* 9 June 1954; *s* of late Alexander Bain Masterton and Mary Masterton (*née* Thomson); *m* 1976, Lynda Christine Jeffries; one *s* one *d*. *Educ:* Dunfermline High Sch.; Univ. of Edinburgh (BSc); Open Univ. (BA); Imperial Coll., London (MSc; DIC 1981). CEng 1980; FREng 2006; FICE; FIStructE; FIES; MCIWEM. Joined Babtie Shaw & Morton, 1976; Babtie Group Ltd: Dir, 1993; Man. Dir of Facilities, 2002–03; Man. Dir, Envmt, 2003–04. Chm., Construction Industry Council, 2010–12 (Chm., Scotland, 2002–04); Mem., Royal Commn on Ancient and Historical Monuments of Scotland, 2003–14 (Vice Chm., 2010–15; Mem., Historic Scotland/RCAHMS Transition Adv. Bd, 2013–15). UK Govt Rep., Crossrail Project, 2009–13; Dir, AWE ML, 2014–. Chm., Standing Cttee on Structural Safety, 2008–. Institution of Civil Engineers: Vice-Pres., 2002–05; Pres., 2005–06; Chm., Asia-Pacific Regl Cttee, 2007–13; Chm., Panel for Histl Engrg Works, 2013–; Vice-Pres., 2008–10, Pres., 2010–12, Instn of Engrs and Shipbuilders in Scotland; Mem. Council, RAEng, 2008–11. Visiting Professor: Univ. of Paisley, 1998–2003; Glasgow Caledonian Univ., 2012–; Univ. of Edinburgh, 2012–. Buchanan Lectr, ICE/Japan Soc. of Civil Engrs, Tokyo, 2012. Chm., Scottish Lime Centre Trust, 2007–09. Chm., Scottish Engrg Hall of Fame, 2011–. Judge, RAEng MacRobert Award, 2013–. Pres., Glasgow Grand Opera Soc., 1991–94. Presenter, TV series, Life After People, 2008–10. FRSE 2007. Liveryman, Engineers' Co., 2010– (Mem., Ct of Assts, 2012–). Hon. DTech Glasgow Caledonian, 2007; Hon. DEng Heriot-Watt, 2012. *Publications:* (ed) Bridges and Retaining Walls—broadening the European horizons, 1994; author of 3 technical design guides on concrete foundations and retaining walls, 1995, 1997, 1999; over 40 technical papers. *Recreations:* music, engineering history, genealogy, webmaster for www.themastertons.org and www.engineeringhalloffame.org. *Address:* Corrievreck, Montrose Terrace, Bridge of Weir, Renfrewshire PA11 3DH. *T:* (01505) 613503. *E:* themastertons@btinternet.com. *Club:* Smeatonians.

MASTERTON-SMITH, Cdre Anthony Philip, RN; CEng; Chairman, Penwood Management Ltd, 2005–13; Chief Executive, Royal College of Physicians, 1998–2005; *b* 2 Aug. 1944; *s* of late Edward Masterton-Smith and Pauline Masterton-Smith (*née* Pilgrim); *m* 1975, Jennifer Sue Sprigings; one *s* one *d*. *Educ:* UCS, Hampstead; BRNC Dartmouth; RNEC Manadon. CEng, MIET (MIEE 1973). Royal Navy, 1962–98: HM Ships Fiskerton, Victorious, Llandaff, Bacchante, Scylla, Southampton; Staff of FO Sea Training, 1978–80; CO, HMS Royal Arthur, 1982–84; jsdc, 1986; Dep. Dir, Naval Recruiting, 1988–91; Defence and Naval Attaché, Tokyo, 1992–95; Cdre, BRNC Dartmouth, 1995–98. Director: RCP Regent's Park Ltd, 2001–05; Vale Health Ltd, 2006–08. FRSA 2002. Hon. FRCP 2006. *Recreations:* opera, gardening, walking, sport. *Address:* Penwood, Whiteleaf, Bucks HP27 0LU. *Clubs:* Monks Risborough Cricket, Whiteleaf Golf.

MASUI, Prof. Yoshio, OC 2003; FRSC 2003; FRS 1998; Professor, University of Toronto, 1978–97, now Emeritus; *b* Kyoto, 6 Oct. 1931; adopted Canadian nationality, 1983; *s* of Fusajiro Masui and Toyoko Masui; *m* 1959, Yuriko Suda; one *s* one *d*. *Educ:* Kyoto Univ. (BSc 1953; MSc 1955; PhD 1961). Lectr, 1958–65, Asst Prof., 1965–68, Prof. Emeritus, 1999, Konan Univ., Japan; Staff Biologist, 1966–68, Lectr, 1969, Yale Univ.; Associate Prof. of Zoology, Univ. of Toronto, 1969–78. Hon. DSc Toronto, 1999. Albert Lasker Basic Medical Res. Award (jtly), for pioneering studies of regulation of cell divisions, 1998. *Address:* Department of Cell and System Biology, University of Toronto, 25 Harbord Street, Toronto, ON M5S 3G5, Canada. *T:* (416) 9783493.

MASUR, Kurt; German conductor; Principal Conductor, London Philharmonic Orchestra, 2000–07; Music Director, Orchestre National de France, 2002–08, now Hon. Music Director; *b* 18 July 1927; *m* 3rd, Tomoko Sakurai, soprano; one *s*; four *c* by previous marriages. *Educ:* Nat. Music Sch., Breslau; Leipzig Conservatory. Orch. Coach, Nat. Theatre of Halle, Saxony, 1948–51; Conductor: Erfurt City Theatre, 1951–53; Leipzig City Theatre, 1953–55; Dresden Philharmonic Orch., 1955–58; Music Director: Mecklenburg State Theatre, Schwerin, 1958–60; Komische Oper, E Berlin, 1960–64; Chief Conductor, Dresden Philharmonic Orch., 1967–72; Artistic Dir, Gewandhaus Orch. of Leipzig, 1970–96 (Hon. Mem., 1981; Conductor Laureate, 1996); Music Dir, NY Philharmonic Orch., 1992–2002, now Emeritus (Guest Conductor, 1982–92); Guest Conductor: Cleveland Orch., 1974; Philadelphia Orch.; Boston SO; Berlin Philharmonic Orch.; Leningrad Philharmonic Orch.; l'Orchestre de Paris; RPO. Prof., Leipzig Acad. of Music, 1975–.

MATANE, Sir Paulias (Nguna), GCL 2005; GCMG 2005 (CMG 1980); Kt 1986; OBE 1975; writer; Governor-General, Papua New Guinea, 2004–11; *b* Papua New Guinea, 21 Sept. 1931; *s* of Ilias Maila Matane and Elsa Toto; *m* 1957, Kaludia Peril Matane; two *s* two *d*. *Educ:* Toma Village Higher Sch.; Keravat High Sch.; Sogeri High Sch.; Teacher's College (Dip. Teaching and Education). Asst Teacher, Tauran Primary Sch., PNG, 1957, Headmaster, 1958–61; School Inspector, 1962–66; Dist Sch. Inspector and Dist Educn Officer, 1967–68; Supt, Teacher Educn, 1969; Foundn Mem., Public Service Bd, 1969–70; Dir, Dept of Lands, Surveys and Mines, 1970; Sec., Dept of Business Develt, 1971–75; Ambassador to USA, Mexico and UN, and High Comr to Canada, 1975–80; Sec., Foreign Affairs, PNG, 1980–85. A Vice-Pres., UN Gen. Assembly, 1979. Dep. Dir Gen., Internat. Biographical Center, 2007. Dir and Dep. Chm., PNG Develt Bank, 1971–75; Dir, Nat. Investment and Develt Authy, 1972–75; Dir, Passenger Transport Control Bd, 1971–75. Chairman: Treid Pacific (PNG) Pty Ltd, 1986–90; Newton Pacific (PNG) Pty Ltd, 1995–. Chairman: Review Cttee on Philosophy of Educn, 1986; Cocoa Industry Investigating Cttee, 1987; Foundn for Peoples of South Pacific, PNG, 1989–94; PNG Censorship Bd, 1989–96; Children, Women and Families in PNG: a situation analysis, 1996; Community Consultative Cttee of E New Britain Provincial Govt of Autonomy, 2002–04 (formerly Dep. Chm.); Asia Pacific Leadership Forum, 2003–04. Producer of regular progs for TV, 1990–2004, and radio, 1998–2002. Director, Board of Trustees: Nat. Mus. and Arts Gall., 1995–99 (Pres., 1999–2004); Nat. Libraries and Archives, 1999–2003. Mem. Council, Univ. of PNG, 1982–92. S Pacific Commn Scholarship, 1963; Winston Churchill Scholarship Award, 1967. Paul Harris Fellow, 2007. Hon. DTech Univ. of Technol., Lae, 1985; Hon. PhD Univ. of PNG, 1986; Hon. DLitt Univ. of PNG, 2008. Forsayth Prize, 1952; UN 40th Anniv. Medal, 1985; Man of the Year Award, American Biographical Inst., 2007. KStJ 2005. Contributor, Radio, Daily and Weekly Newspaper, 1980–2005. *Publications:* Kum Tumun of Minj, 1966; A New Guinean Travels through Africa, 1971; My Childhood in New Guinea, 1972; What Good is Business?, 1972; Bai Bisnis I Helpim Yumi Olsem Wanem?, 1973; Exploring South Asia, vol. 1, Two New Guineans Travel through SE Asia, 1974, 2001, vol. 2, 2001; Aimbe the Challenger, 1974; Aimbe the School Dropout, 1974; Aimbe the Magician, 1976; Aimbe the Pastor, 1979; Two Papua New Guineans Discover the Bible Lands, 1987; To Serve with Love, 1989; Chit Chat, vol. 1, 1991, vol. 2, Let's Do It PNG, 1994, vol. 3, 2000; East to West—the longest train trip in the world, 1991; Trekking Through the New Worlds, 1995; Voyage to Antarctica, 1996; Laughter Made in PNG, 1996; Amazing Discoveries in 40 Years of Marriage, 1997; Laughter: its concept and Papua New Guineans, 1997; The Other Side of Port Moresby—in pictures, 1998; A Trip of a Lifetime, 1998; The Word Power, 1998; Waliling United Church: then and now, 1998; Coach Adventures Down Under, 1999; Management Problems in Papua New Guinea: some solutions, 2000; Further Management Problems in Papua New Guinea: their solutions, 2000; Management for Excellence, 2001; Exploring the Holy Lands, 2001; Humour in Papua New Guinea, 2002; Ripples in the South Pacific Ocean, 2002; India: a splendour in cultural diversity, 2004; Papua New Guinea: land of natural beauty and cultural diversity, 2005; The Time Traveller, 2005; Fifty Golden Years: saga of true love in marital and national life, 2006; Travelling Through Australia by Coach, 2007; Cultural Diversity of India, 2007; Education for Integral Human Development, 2008; Aimbe Braves Through Challenges, 2008; Public Addresses to be Privately Addressed, 2008; Christianity: faith and holy days, 2014. *Recreations:* reading, gardening, squash, fishing, writing. *Address:* PO Box 3405, Kokopo, ENB P, Papua New Guinea. *Clubs:* Tamukavar, Tauran Ex Student and Citizens' (Papua New Guinea).

MATE, Rt Rev. Martin; Bishop of Eastern Newfoundland and Labrador, 1980–92; *b* 12 Nov. 1929; *s* of John Mate and Hilda Mate (*née* Toope); *m* 1962, Florence Hooper, Registered Nurse; two *s* three *d*. *Educ:* Meml Univ. of Newfoundland; Queen's Coll., St John's, Newfoundland (LTh); Bishop's Univ., Lennoxville, PQ. BA (1st Cl. Hons), MA. Deacon 1952, priest 1953; Curate, Cathedral of St John the Baptist, St John's, Newfoundland, 1952–53; Deacon-in-charge and Rector, Parish of Pushthrough, 1953–58; Incumbent, Mission of St Anthony, 1958–64; Rural Dean, St Barbe, 1958–64; Rector of Cookshire, Quebec, 1964–67; Rector of Catalina, Newfoundland, 1967–72; RD of Bonavista Bay, 1970–72; Rector of Pouch Cove/Torbay, 1972–76; Treasurer, Diocesan Synod of E Newfoundland and Labrador, 1976–80. Hon. DD Queen's Coll., St John's, Newfoundland, 2009. *Publications:* Pentateuchal Criticism, 1967. *Recreations:* carpentry, hunting, fishing, camping. *Address:* 417–50 Tiffany Court, St John's, NL A1A 0G1, Canada.

MATEAR, Comr Elizabeth Anne; Commanding Officer, William Booth Memorial Halls, Nottingham, since 2012; *b* 16 Aug. 1952; *d* of Jack and Elizabeth Kowbus; *m* 1978, John Matear; one *s*. *Educ:* Ladybank Primary Sch.; Bell Baxter High Sch.; Jordanhill Coll. (DipSW); Internat. Trng Coll. for Officers, Salvation Army. Social worker: in addiction services, 1973–75, in alcohol assessment, 1977–78; Salvation Army Officer, 1977–; Commanding Officer: Godalming, 1978–80; Reading E, 1980–83; Hove, 1983–85; Chester-le-Street,

1985–87; Divl Youth Work, 1987–90; Church Growth Consultant, 1990–94; CO, Bradford, 1994–95; Dir of Personnel, Yorks Div., 1996–97; Personnel Co-ordinator, UK Territorial HQ, 1997–99; Divl Leader, E Midlands Div., 1999–2001; Caribbean Territorial Leader and Territorial Pres., Women's Ministries, 2001–06; Territorial Leader and Pres., Women's Ministries, UK with Republic of Ireland, 2006–12; Co-Pres., Churches Together in England, 2007–11; Moderator, Free Church Council, 2007–11. *Recreations:* walking, reading, crossword puzzles, people, Rotarian. *Address:* Salvation Army Territorial Headquarters, 101 Newington Causeway, SE1 6BN. *T:* (020) 7367 4603. *E:* elizabeth.matear@salvationarmy.org.uk.

MATERLIK, Prof. Gerhard Theodor, Hon. CBE 2007; FRS 2011; FInstP; Professor of Facilities Science, University College London, since 2013; *b* Marl, Germany, 16 Jan. 1945; *s* of Hans Ptaszynski and Gertrud Marianne Materlik; *m* 1st, 1972, Christa Peters (marr. diss. 2002); two *s*; 2nd, 2008, Sabine Maria Materlik. *Educ:* Univs of Munster and Munich (Dip. Physics 1970); Univ. of Dortmund (Dr rer. nat. 1975). FInstP 2007. Scientific asst, Univ. of Dortmund, 1970–75; Postdoctoral Res. Associate, Cornell Univ., 1975–77; Sen. Res. Associate, Deutsches Elektronen Synchrotron (DESY), 1978–85; Scientific Dir, 1986–93, Associate Dir, and Coordinator for X-ray Free Electron Laser Project, 1994–2001, Hamburg Synchrotron Radiation Lab. at DESY; Scientific Dir, DESY, and Prof. of Physics, Hamburg Univ., 1990–2001; CEO, 2001–13, Principal Diamond Fellow, 2013–14, Diamond Light Source Ltd. Guest Scientist, AT&T Bell Telephone Labs, 1979; Guest Prof. for Academic Industry Cooperation, Stanford Univ. and Stanford Synchrotron Radiation Lab., 1993–94; Visiting Professor: Oxford Univ., 2002–07; Reading Univ., 2003–13; Southampton Univ., 2003–08. Hon. Prof., UCL, 2012–. Hon. DSc Reading, 2004; Hon Dr Nat. Res. Centre Kurchatov Inst., 2012. *Publications:* (ed jtly) Resonant Anomalous X-Ray Scattering, 1994; over 200 articles in learned jls on application of synchrotron x-rays for studying geometric and electronic structure of atoms and solids, dopants and interfaces/surfaces. *Recreations:* reading, walking, music. *Address:* London Centre for Nanotechnology, University College London, 17–19 Gordon Street, WC1H 0AH. *E:* g.materlik@ucl.ac.uk.

MATES, James Michael; Europe Editor, ITN, since 2012; *b* 11 Aug. 1961; *s* of Rt Hon. Michael John Mates, *qv*; *m* 1991, Fiona Margaret Bennett; two *s* one *d*. *Educ:* Marlborough Coll.; Farnham Coll.; Leeds Univ. (BA Hons). Joined Independent Television News, 1983: Tokyo corresp., 1989–91; North of England corresp., 1991–92; Moscow corresp., 1992–94; Diplomatic Ed., 1994–97; Washington corresp., 1997–2002; Sen. Corresp., 2002–11. *Recreations:* bridge, tennis, mountain biking. *Address:* c/o Independent TV News, 200 Gray's Inn Road, WC1X 8XZ. *Club:* Portland.

MATES, Lt-Col Rt Hon. Michael (John); PC 2004; *b* 9 June 1934; *s* of Claude John Mates; *m* 1st, 1959, Mary Rosamund Paton (marr. diss. 1980); two *s* two *d*; 2nd, 1982, Rosellen (marr. diss. 1995); one *d*; 3rd, 1998, Christine, *d* of Count and Countess Moltke, Copenhagen. *Educ:* Salisbury Cathedral Sch.; Blundell's Sch.; King's Coll., Cambridge (choral schol.). Joined Army, 1954; 2nd Lieut, RUR, 1955; Queen's Dragoon Guards, RAC, 1961; Major, 1967; Lt-Col, 1973; resigned commn 1974. MP (C) Petersfield, Oct. 1974–1983, E Hampshire, 1983–2010. Minister of State, NI Office, 1992–93. Vice-Chm., Cons. NI Cttee, 1979–81 (Sec., 1974–79); Chairman: Select Cttee on Defence, 1987–92 (Mem., 1979–92); Select Cttee on NI, 2001–05; Cons. Home Affairs Cttee, 1987–88 (Vice-Chm., 1979–87); All-Party Anglo-Irish Gp, 1979–92; Sec., 1922 Cttee, 1987–88, 1997–2010; Mem., Intell. and Security Cttee, 1994–2010; Mem., Butler Review of Intelligence on Weapons of Mass Destruction, 2004; introduced: Farriers Registration Act, 1975; Rent Amendment Act, 1985. Farriers' Co.: Liveryman, 1975–; Asst, 1981; Master, 1986–87. *E:* matesmichael@gmail.com.
See also J. M. Mates.

MATEV, Dr Lachezar Nikolov; Ambassador at Large for Energy Security, Ministry of Foreign Affairs, Bulgaria, since 2013; *b* 5 Aug. 1951; *s* of Nikola Matev and Roza Mateva; *m* 1977, Bisserka Petrova; one *s* one *d*. *Educ:* Technical Univ., Sofia (MSc Automation and Telemechanics); Sofia Univ. (MSc Applied Maths); Diplomatic Acad., Moscow (MA High Hons Internat. Politics; PhD Internat. Relns 1991). Joined Bulgarian Diplomatic Service, 1982; First Sec., Prague, 1982–89; Diplomatic Acad., Moscow, 1989–91; Internat. Econ. Orgns Directorate, 1991–92; Co-founder and Man. Dir, Internat. Business Develt mag., and Man. Dir, Vecco Ltd, 1992–93; Hd, UN Agencies Sect., Foreign Econ. Policy Dept, 1993–95; Counsellor, Madrid, 1995–98; Mem., Accession Negotiations Team, Eur. Integration Directorate, Foreign Affairs Ministry, 1998–2002; Minister, London, 2002–05; Ambassador to the UK, 2005–09. Perm. Rep. of Bulgaria to IMO, 2007–; Ambassador, Strategic Matters, Ministry of Foreign Affairs, Bulgaria, 2009–13. Patron, Hockerill Anglo-Eur. Coll., 2007–09. Kt Comdr, Royal Order of Francis I, 2006. *Recreations:* art, music (classical, opera), theatre, sport, gardening, business and finance. *Address:* c/o Ministry of Foreign Affairs, 2 Aleksandar Zhendov Str., Sofia 1040, Bulgaria. *Clubs:* Rotary (Sofia-Vitosha); Bulgarian City.

MATHER, Lt-Col Anthony Charles McClure, CVO 1998; OBE 1990 (MBE 1965); Secretary, Central Chancery of the Orders of Knighthood and Assistant Comptroller, Lord Chamberlain's Office, 1991–99; Staff Officer to the Earl Marshal, 1999–2014; *b* 21 April 1942; *s* of late Eric James Mather and Stella Mather (*née* McClure); *m* 1966, Gaye, *d* of late Dr Eric Lindsay Dickson and Mrs Louise Tillett; one *s* two *d*. *Educ:* Eton College. Commissioned, Grenadier Guards, 1962; served UK, British Guyana, Germany and Hong Kong; retired 1991. An Extra Equerry to the Queen, 1992–. Freeman, City of London, 1998. *Recreations:* gardening, fishing, music. *Address:* The Horseshoes, Chirton, near Devizes, Wilts SN10 3QR. *T:* (01380) 840261. *Club:* Army and Navy.

MATHER, Christopher Paul; a Judge of the Upper Tribunal (Immigration and Asylum Chamber) (formerly a Senior Immigration Judge, Asylum and Immigration Tribunal), 2005–13; a Legal Member, Special Immigration Appeals Commission, 2006–13; a Recorder of the Crown Court, 1996–2013 (Assistant Recorder, 1991–96); a Deputy High Court Judge, 2010–13; *b* 20 June 1947; *s* of Bertrand and Jean Barker Mather; *m* 1970, Pauline Mary Man; twin *s* and *d*. *Educ:* Ellesmere Coll., Shropshire. Admitted solicitor, 1973; Partner and Consultant, Penningtons, 1994–2000. Mem., Hants and IoW Valuation Tribunal, 1988–94; Dep. Dist Judge, 1989–91; Immigration Adjudicator, 2000–03; a Vice Pres., Immigration Appeal Tribunal, 2003–05. Mem., Methodology Soc. *Recreation:* managing and improving a 10 acre estate. *Address:* Little Shootash Farm, Romsey, Hants SO51 6FB. *E:* cpm@candpmather.plus.com. *Club:* Goodwood Road Racing.

MATHER, Clive; *see* Mather, H. C.

MATHER, Graham Christopher Spencer; solicitor; President: European Policy Forum, since 1992; European Financial Forum, since 1999; Infrastructure Forum, since 2009; *b* 23 Oct. 1954; *er s* of late Thomas and Doreen Mather; *m* 1st, 1981, Fiona Marion McMillan (marr. diss. 1995), *e d* of Sir Ronald McMillan Bell, QC, MP and of Lady Bell; two *s*; 2nd, 1997, Geneviève, *widow* of James Seton Fairhurst. *Educ:* Hutton Grammar School; New College, Oxford (Burnet Law Scholar); MA Jurisp. Institute of Directors: Asst to Dir Gen., 1980; Head of Policy Unit, 1983; Institute of Economic Affairs: Dep. Dir, 1987; Gen. Dir, 1987–92. MEP (C) Hampshire N and Oxford, 1994–99. Mem., HM Treasury Working Party on Freeports, 1982. Member: Monopolies and Mergers Commission, 1989–94; Competition Appeal Tribunal (formerly Appeal Tribunal, Competition Commn), 2000–11; Ofcom Consumer Panel, 2004–09; non-exec. Dir, Ofcom, 2014–. Vis. Fellow, Nuffield Coll., Oxford, 1992–2000. Mem., Westminster City Council, 1982–86; contested (C) Blackburn, 1983. Radio and television broadcaster. Consultant: Tudor Investment Corp., 1992–2012; Elliott Associates, 2007–; Advr, BIFU, 1997–99; non-exec. Dir, Greenham Common Community Trust, 2000–. Chm., World Free Zone Convention, 2000–. Vice-Pres., Assoc. of Dist Councils, 1994–97. Trustee, Social Market Foundn, 2008–. *Publications:* lectures, papers and contribs to jls; contribs to The Times. *Address:* European Policy Forum, 49 Whitehall, SW1A 2BX. *T:* (020) 7839 7565, *Fax:* (020) 3137 2040. *E:* graham.mather@epfltd.org. *Clubs:* Travellers, Naval.

MATHER, (Harold) Clive; Chairman: Shell Pensions Trust Ltd, since 2008; Tearfund, since 2008; Iogen Corporation, Ottawa, since 2008 (Lead Director, 2007–08); Matthew 25:35 Trust, since 2007; The Garden Tomb (Jerusalem) Association, since 2012 (Trustee, since 2008); UK Shell Pension Plan Trust Ltd, since 2013; *b* 19 Sept. 1947; *m* 1976, Ann (*née* Mason); one *s* two *d*. *Educ:* Warwick Sch.; Lincoln Coll., Oxford (BA 1969; MA). With Shell, 1969–2007: early career in UK, Brunei and Gabon; Retail Regl Manager, Shell UK, 1984–86; Dir of Personnel and Public Affairs, Shell South Africa, 1986–91; Dir of Human Resources and Admin, Shell UK Ltd, and Dir, Shell Res. Ltd, 1991–95; Chief Inf. Officer, Shell Internat., 1995–97; Dir, Internat., Shell, 1997–99; Chief Exec., Shell Services Internat., 1999–2002; Chm., Shell UK Ltd, and Hd of Global Learning, Shell, 2002–04; Pres. and CEO, Shell Canada, 2004–07. Chm., Lensbury Ltd, 1999–2004; Director: Place Dome Inc., 2005–; Badger Explorer ASA, Norway, 2011–13. Mem., Premier of Alberta's Council for Econ. Strategy, 2009–12. Chm., Petroleum Employers' Council, 1994–96. Comr, EOC, 1991–94; Member: Adv. Bd, Relationships Foundn, 1996–; Supervisory Bd, Office of Govt and Commerce, 2002–04; President's Cttee, CBI, 2002–04; British N American Cttee, 2005–; Chairman: Corporate Social Responsibility Acad., 2003–05; IMD Business Council, 2003–04. Chm., Lambeth Educn Action Zone Forum, 1998–2003; Dep. Chm., Windsor Leadership Trust, 1994–2005. Judge, CCEMC Grand Challenge, 2013–. Trustee, Royal Anniversary Trust, 2003–12. MCIPD 2004; CCMI 2004. FRSA 1992. *Recreations:* sport, good food and wine. *Address:* PO Box 1077, Guildford, Surrey GU1 9HQ. *Club:* Lensbury (Teddington).

MATHER, James Stuart, CA; Member (SNP) Argyll and Bute, Scottish Parliament, 2007–11 (Highlands and Islands, 2003–07); Minister for Enterprise, Energy and Tourism, 2007–11; *b* 6 March 1947; *s* of James Stuart Mather and Sarah Morag Mather (*née* MacKenzie); *m* 1980, Maureen Anne (*née* Drysdale); one *s* one *d*. *Educ:* Paisley Grammar Sch.; Greenock High Sch.; Glasgow Univ. Director: Computers for Business (Scotland) Ltd, 1986–96; Business for Scotland, 1997–2004; Scotland in Europe, 2001–03. Opposition spokesman on enterprise and the econ., Scottish Parlt, 2003–07. Nat. Treas., SNP, 2000–04. Visiting Professor: Univ. of Strathclyde, 2011–; Heriot-Watt Univ. Chairman: Gael Ltd, 2011–15; Homes for Scotland. Mem., ICAS, 1971. *Recreations:* cycling, golf, hill-walking, reading. *Address:* 13 Sutherland Avenue, Glasgow G41 4JJ. *Club:* Traigh Golf (Arisaig).

MATHER, Dr John Cromwell; Senior Astrophysicist, since 1993, Goddard Fellow, since 1994, Senior Project Scientist, James Webb Space Telescope, since 2005, Goddard Space Flight Center, NASA; *b* Roanoke, Va, 7 Aug. 1946; *s* of Robert E. Mather and Martha Cromwell Mather; *m* 1980, Jane Hauser. *Educ:* Newton High Sch., NJ; Swarthmore Coll., Penn (BA Physics 1968); Univ. of California, Berkeley (PhD Physics 1974). Postdoctoral Fellow, Goddard Inst. for Space Studies, NASA, 1974–76; Study Scientist, 1976–88, Project Scientist, 1988–98, and Principal Investigator, Far Infrared Absolute Spectrophotometer on Cosmic Background Explorer, Goddard Space Flight Center, NASA. (Jtly) Nobel Prize in Physics, 2006. *Publications:* (with J. Boslough) The Very First Light, 1996; articles in jls. *Address:* Astrophysics Science Division, Goddard Space Flight Center, NASA, Code 443, JWST Project, Greenbelt, MD 20771, USA.

MATHER, John Douglas, FCILT; Chief Executive, National Freight Consortium plc, 1984–93; *b* 27 Jan. 1936; *s* of John Dollandson and Emma May Mather; *m* 1958, Hilda Patricia (*née* Kirkwood); one *s* (one *d* decd). *Educ:* Manchester Univ. (BACom, MAEcon). Personnel Management: Philips Electrical, 1959–66; Convoys Ltd, 1966–67; Personnel Management, Transport Management, National Freight Company, 1967–93. Chairman: Cranfield Ventures, 2000–06; CIT Hldgs, 2000–06 (Dir, 1994–2006); non-executive Director: Charles Sidney plc (formerly Bletchley Motor Gp), 1993–98; Computer Management Gp, 1993–98; Miller Gp, 1993–2003; St Mary's (Paddington) NHS Trust, 1995–97. Chairman: Bedfordshire TEC, 1991–93; Camden Business Partnership, 1991–; London Regeneration Consortium plc, 1993–95. Member: Adv. Bd, Cranfield Sch. of Management, 1992–97; Council, Cranfield Univ., 1993–2006. Trustee, Help The Aged, 1993–2008 (Chm., 1995–2004). Mem., Co. of Carmen. *Recreations:* golf, gardening, travel. *Address:* Roundhale, Love Lane, Kings Langley, Hertfordshire WD4 9HW. *T:* (01923) 263063. *Club:* Woburn Golf and Country.

MATHER-LEES, Michael Anthony; QC 2012; *b* Wales; *m* 2007, Lisa; one *s*. *Educ:* Univ. of London (LLB). Called to the Bar, Inner Temple, 1981. Member: Criminal Bar Assoc.; Eur. Bar Gp. Treas., Wales and Chester Circuit. *Recreations:* fishing, the arts, Sealyham Terriers, horses. *Address:* 30 Park Place, Cardiff CF10 3BS. *T:* (029) 2039 8421. *E:* mml@30parkplace.co.uk; Farrar's Building, Temple, EC4Y 7BD.

MATHERS, Howard Leslie, CBE 2008; FREng, FRINA; Technical Director, Submarines, Babcock International, since 2012; *b* Wellington, Som, 21 Feb. 1956; *s* of Leslie Norman Mathers, OBE and Isabelle Josephine Madge Mathers; *m* 1981, Marianne Lischer; two *s* two *d*. *Educ:* Campbell Coll., Belfast; University Coll. London (MSc Naval Architecture); London Business Sch. (MSc (Sloan) Mgt). RCNC 1973; FRINA 2000; FREng 2013. Ministry of Defence: Naval Architect, Frigates and Destroyers, 1979–81; Manager, Submarines Refitting Trades, 1981–83; Civil Asst to Chief Exec. Dockyards, 1983–85; Prog. Manager, Submarine Refits, 1986–88; Sen. Naval Observer, NI, 1988–91; Hd of Naval Architecture, RN Engrg Coll., 1991–94; Design Authy, Submarines, 1995–2000; Dir, In-service Submarines, 2003–07; Chief Engr, Submarines, 2007–09; Dir, Safety and Engrg, 2009–11, Technical Dir, 2012, Defence Equipt and Support, MoD. Chairman: Ship and Envmt Safety Bd, MoD, 2009–12; Defence Nuclear Envmt and Safety Bd, 2009–11; Defence Fuels and Gases Envmt and Safety Bd, 2011. Founding Trustee, Children's Homes in India Trust, 2005–; Chm., Snowhill Gateway Trust, 2014–. FCMI 2011 (MCMI 1994). *Recreations:* Christian thought, choral singing, golf, scuba diving, DIY. *Address:* Babcock International, PO Box 77, Devonport House, Durley Park, Keynsham BS31 2YH.

MATHERS, Peter James, LVO 1995; HM Diplomatic Service, retired; High Commissioner to Jamaica, 2002–05; *b* 2 April 1946; *s* of Dr James Mathers and Margaret Mathers (*née* Kendrick); *m* 1983, Elisabeth Hoeller; one *s* one *d*. *Educ:* Bradfield Coll., Berks; Open Univ. (BA 1st Cl. Hons). Army SSC, 1968–71. Joined HM Diplomatic Service, 1971: SOAS (Persian), 1972–73; Tehran, 1973–75; Bonn, 1976–78; FCO, 1978–81; Copenhagen, 1981–85; Tehran, 1986–87; FCO, 1987–88; on secondment to UN Office, Vienna, 1988–91; FCO, 1991–95; Dep. High Comr, Barbados and Eastern Caribbean, 1995–98; Counsellor, Commercial and Economic, Stockholm, 1998–2002. *Address:* Doles Ash, Knott Park, Oxshott, Surrey KT22 0HS.

MATHESON, Alexander, OBE 1990; JP; FRPharmS; Lord-Lieutenant of the Western Isles, since 2001 (Vice Lord-Lieutenant, 1994–2001); Chairman: Highlands and Islands Airports Ltd, 2001–07; Harris Tweed Authority, 2001–07; *b* 16 Nov. 1941; *s* of Alex Matheson, MB ChB and Catherine Agnes Matheson (*née* Smith), MA; *m* 1965, Irene Mary Davidson, BSc Hons, MSc; two *s* two *d*. *Educ:* Nicolson Inst., Stornoway; Robert Gordon Inst. of Technol., Aberdeen. MRPharmS 1965, FRPharmS 1993. Pharmacist. Man. Dir, 1966–82 and Chm., 1967–, Roderick Smith Ltd. Member: Stornoway Town Council, 1967–75 (Provost,

1971–75); Ross and Cromarty CC, 1967–75. Member: Stornoway Trust Estate, 1967–2009 (Chm., 1971–81); Stornoway Port Authy (formerly Pier and Harbour Commn), 1968–2010 (Chm., 1971–72 and 1991–2001); Western Isles Island Council, 1974–94 (Convener, 1982–90); Western Isles Health Bd, 1974–2001 (Chm., 1993–2001). Pres., Islands Commn of Peripheral Maritime Regions of Europe, 1988–93. Founding Chm., Hebridean Men's Cancer Support Gp, 2007–12. JP Western Is, 1971; Hon. Sheriff, Stornoway, 1972. *Recreations:* genealogy, research and lecturing on local history. *Address:* 33 Newton Street, Stornoway, Isle of Lewis HS1 2RW. *T:* (01851) 704739, *Fax:* (01851) 700415.

MATHESON of Matheson, yr, Lt Col Alexander Fergus, LVO 2013; Secretary, Central Chancery of the Orders of Knighthood, 2005–14; Gentleman Usher to the Queen, since 2015; *b* 26 Aug. 1954; *o s* and *heir* of Major Sir Fergus John Matheson of Matheson, Bt, *qv*; *m* 1983, Katharine Davina Mary, *d* of Sir (William Richard) Michael Oswald, *qv*; two *s* one *d*. *Educ:* Eton Coll.; Durham Univ.; RMA Sandhurst; Army Staff Coll. Coldstream Guards, 1973–2001; Temp. Equerry to the Queen, 1982–84; COS, British Forces, Belize, 1992–94; Adjt, RMA Sandhurst, 1995–96; Bde Major, Household Div., 1996–98. CO Oxford Univ. OTC, 1998–2000. Exec. Dir, BSES Expeditions, 2001–05. Extra Equerry to the Queen, 2006–. Mem., Royal Co. of Archers (Queen's Body Guard for Scotland), 2009–. *Recreations:* birds, bicycle, bagpipes.

MATHESON, Christian; MP (Lab) City of Chester, since 2015; *b* Cheshire, 2 Jan. 1968; *m* Katherine; two *d*. *Educ:* London Sch. of Econs and Pol Sci. Formerly Manager in electricity industry; roles with Unite Union. Mem., Culture, Media and Sport Select Cttee, 2015–. *Address:* House of Commons, SW1A 0AA.

MATHESON, His Honour Duncan, MA, LLM; QC 1989; a Circuit Judge, 2000–11. *Educ:* Rugby Sch.; Trinity Coll., Cambridge. Bencher, Inner Temple, 1994. Jun. Counsel in Legal Aid Matters, Law Soc., 1981–89; a Recorder, 1985–2000. Chairman, Legal Aid Area Committee: London S, 1989–92; London, 1992–95.

MATHESON of Matheson, Major Sir Fergus (John), 7th Bt *cr* 1882, of Lochalsh, Co. Ross; Chief of Clan Matheson; *b* 22 Feb. 1927; *yr s* of Gen. Sir Torquhil George Matheson, 5th Bt, KCB, CMG and Lady Elizabeth Matheson, ARRC (*d* 1986), *o d* of 8th Earl of Albemarle; *S* brother, 1993; *m* 1952, Hon. Jean Elizabeth Mary Willoughby (*d* 2008), *yr d* of 11th Baron Middleton, KG, MC; one *s* two *d*. *Educ:* Eton. Major, Coldstream Guards, 1944–64. One of HM Body Guard of the Hon. Corps of Gentlemen-at-Arms, 1979–97 (Standard Bearer, 1993–97). Pres., St John Ambulance, Norfolk, 1993–96. CStJ. *Heir:* (to baronetcy and chiefship): *s* Lt-Col Alexander Fergus Matheson of Matheson, yr, *qv*. *Address:* The Old Rectory, Hedenham, Norfolk NR35 2LD.

MATHESON, Jamie Graham; Chairman: Saracen Fund Managers, since 2014; Beatson Cancer Charity, since 2014; *b* Glasgow, 19 May 1954; *s* of James Monteath Matheson and Marjorie Graham Matheson (*née* Todd); *m* 1990, Angela Douglas Thompson. *Educ:* Loretto Sch. FCSI 2010. Stockbroker, Parsons & Co., later Allied Provincial, 1972–96; Divl Dir, Bell Lawrie, Brewin Dolphin Gp, 1996–2002; Dir, 2002–13, Exec. Chm., 2005–13, Brewin Dolphin Hldgs plc. Non-executive Director: Scottish Radio Hldgs plc, 2000–05; Maven Income and Growth VCT 5 plc (formerly Bluehone AIM VCT2 plc), 2000–13; STV Gp plc, 2007–15. OStJ 1998. *Recreations:* sailing, field sports. *Address:* Hallmoss, Dunlop, Ayrshire KA3 4DT. *T:* (01560) 482002, *Fax:* (01560) 483094. *E:* jamie@hallmoss.com. *Clubs:* Royal Yacht Squadron, Royal Thames Yacht; New (Edinburgh); Western Gailes Golf; Coronado Country (Texas).

MATHESON, Dame Jilian Norma, (Dame Jil), DCB 2014; FSS; National Statistician and Chief Executive, Office for National Statistics and UK Statistics Authority, 2009–14; *b* Derby, 27 March 1953; *d* of Norman and Margaret Eileen Chambers; *m* 1983, Alan Marsh; one *s* and one step *d*. *Educ:* Ecclesbourne Sch., Duffield, Derbys; Derby Coll. of Further Educn; Univ. of Sussex (BA Hons). Office of Population Censuses and Surveys, later Office for National Statistics: social survey researcher and statistician, 1975–2014; Dep. Dir, 1998; Dir, Population and Demography, Census, 2004–08; Dir Gen. Stats Delivery, 2008–09. Chair: Cttee on Stats and Statistical Policy, OECD, 2012–14; Statistical Commn, UN, 2014. FAcSS (AcSS 2001). Hon. Dr: Wolverhampton, 2012; Sussex, 2014. *Publications:* (with A. Marsh) Smoking Attitudes and Behaviour, 1983; Voluntary Work, 1990; Participation in Sport, 1991; contrib. articles to learned jls. *Recreations:* cricket, Derby County Football Club, opera, cinema, theatre, novels, walking. *E:* jilmatheson2@gmail.com.

MATHESON, John Alexander, CBE 2015; Director, Health Finance, eHealth and Analytics (formerly Health Finance, later Health Finance, eHealth and Pharmaceuticals), Scottish Government, since 2008; *b* Dingwall, Ross-shire, 23 June 1955; *m* 1979, Sheila Judith Willans; one *s* one *d*. *Educ:* Invergordon Acad.; Heriot Watt Univ. (BA 1976); Univ. of Edinburgh (MBA 1996). Lothian Health Bd, 1979–93; Finance Director: Edinburgh Healthcare NHS Trust, 1994–99; NHS Lothian, 2000–08. Non-exec. Dir, Telford Coll., Edinburgh, 1998–2007. Pres., CIPFA, 2015–16 (Chm., Scottish Br., 1999; Vice Pres., 2014–15). Mem., Scotch Malt Whisky Soc., 1998–. *Recreations:* golf, hill walking, malt whisky. *Address:* Scottish Government Health, St Andrew's House, Regent Road, Edinburgh EH1 3DG. *T:* (0131) 244 3464, *Fax:* (0131) 244 2042. *E:* john.matheson@scotland.gsi.gov.uk. *Clubs:* Blackford Golf; Murrayfield Golf.

MATHESON, Michael; Member (SNP) Falkirk West, Scottish Parliament, since 2007 (Central Scotland, 1999–2007); Cabinet Secretary for Justice, since 2014; *b* 8 Sept. 1970; *s* of Edward and Elizabeth Matheson. *Educ:* Queen Margaret Coll., Edinburgh (BSc Occupational Therapy); Open Univ. (BA; Dip.). Health Profession Council State Registered Occupational Therapist. Community Occupational Therapist: Social Work Dept, Highland Regl Council, 1991–93; Central Regl Council, 1993–97; Social Work Services, Stirling Council, 1997–99. SNP dep. spokesperson on health and social policy, 1997–98; Dep. Opposition spokesman for justice and land reform, 1999–2004, Opposition spokesman for culture and sport, 2004–07, Scottish Parlt; Minister for Public Health, 2011–14. Scottish Parliament: Member: Cross Party Gp on Sport, 2001; Cross Party Gp on Cuba, 2002; Co-Convenor, Cross Party Gp on Malawi, 2006; Member: Health and Sport Cttee, 2007–11; Eur. and Ext. Relns Cttee, 2010–11; End of Life Assistance (Scotland) Bill Cttee, 2010–11. Member: Ochils Mountain Rescue Team; BSES. *Recreations:* mountaineering, travel, supporting Partick Thistle FC. *Address:* Scottish Parliament, Edinburgh EH99 1SP. *T:* (0131) 348 5671, *Fax:* (0131) 348 6474; (constituency office) 15a East Bridge Street, Falkirk FK1 1YD. *T:* (01324) 629271, *Fax:* (01324) 635576.

MATHESON, Stephen Charles Taylor, CB 1993; Deputy Secretary, 1989–2000, and Deputy Chairman, Inland Revenue, 1993–2000; *b* 27 June 1939; *s* of Robert Matheson and Olive Lovick; *m* 1960, Marna Rutherford Burnett; two *s*. *Educ:* Aberdeen Grammar Sch.; Aberdeen Univ. (MA hons English Lang. and Lit., 1961). HM Inspector of Taxes, 1961–70; Principal, Bd of Inland Revenue, 1970–75; Private Sec. to Paymaster General, 1975–76, to Chancellor of the Exchequer, 1976–77; Board of Inland Revenue, 1977–2000; Project Manager, Computerisation of Pay As You Earn Project; Under Sec., 1984; Dir of IT, 1984; Comr, 1989; Dir Gen. (Management), 1989–94, (Policy and Technical), 1994–2000. CITP; FBCS (Pres., 1991–92); FIPPM (FBIPM 1996). Hon. DBA De Montfort Univ., 1994. *Publications:* Maurice Walsh, Storyteller, 1985; (contrib.) The Listowel Literary Phenomenon, 1994. *Recreations:* Scottish and Irish literature, book collecting, cooking, music.

MATHEW, Brian Frederick, MBE 2005; VMH; Editor, Curtis's Botanical Magazine, 1993–2002; *b* 30 Aug. 1936; *s* of Frederick Mathew and Ethel Mathew (*née* Baines); *m* 1966, Helen Margaret Briggs; one *s*. *Educ:* Oxted County Grammar Sch.; RHS Sch. of Horticulture (RHS Dip. in Horticulture (Hons) 1962). Botanist, Royal Botanic Gardens, Kew, 1967–92, Hon. Res. Fellow, 1999. Mem., RHS Horticultural Bd, 2002–04. VMH 1992. *Publications:* Dwarf Bulbs, 1973; The Genus Daphne, 1976; The Larger Bulbs, 1978; A Field Guide to Bulbs of Europe, 1981; The Iris, 1981, 2nd edn 1989; The Crocus, 1982; A Field Guide to the Bulbous Plants of Turkey, 1984; Hellebores, 1989; The Genus Lewisia, 1989; Allium Section Allium, 1996; Growing Bulbs, 1997; Bulbs: the four seasons, 1998; (ed) Genus Cyclamen, 2013. *Recreations:* gardening, photography.

MATHEW, John Charles; QC 1977; *b* 3 May 1927; *s* of late Sir Theobald Mathew, KBE, MC, and Lady Mathew; *m* 1952, Jennifer Jane Mathew (*née* Lagden); two *d*. *Educ:* Beaumont Coll. Served, Royal Navy, 1945–47. Called to Bar, Lincoln's Inn, 1949; apptd Junior Prosecuting Counsel to the Crown, 1959; First Sen. Prosecuting Counsel to the Crown, 1974–77. Elected a Bencher of Lincoln's Inn, 1970. *Recreations:* golf, shooting, cinema. *Address:* 45 Abingdon Court, 17 Abingdon Villas, W8 6BT. *T:* (020) 7937 7535. *Club:* Garrick.

MATHEW, Robert Knox, (Robin); QC 1992; *b* 22 Jan. 1945; *s* of late Robert Mathew, TD, MP and Joan Leslie (*née* Bruce); *m* 1968, Anne Rosella Elliott; one *d*. *Educ:* Eton Coll.; Trinity Coll., Dublin (BA 1967). City and financial journalist, 1968–76. Called to the Bar, Lincoln's Inn, 1974. Asst Parly Boundary Comr, 1992–98. *Recreations:* country pursuits, racing, ski-ing. *Address:* 13–14 Old Square, Lincoln's Inn, WC2A 3UE; Church Farm, Little Barrington, Burford, Oxon OX18 5TE. *T:* (01451) 844311. *Club:* Boodle's.

MATHEWS, Vice Adm. Sir Andrew (David Hugh), KCB 2013 (CB 2008); FREng; non-executive Director, National Nuclear Laboratory, since 2014; *b* Stanford le Hope, Essex, 27 June 1958; *s* of Hugh Leslie Mathews, OBE and Pamela Lorna Mathews (*née* Edwards); *m* 1987, Beverley Yvette Taylor; one *s* one *d*. *Educ:* Newcastle Royal Grammar Sch.; RNEC, Manadon (BSc Hons); RNC, Greenwich (MSc). BRNC, Dartmouth, 1976; nuclear engrg appts at sea and ashore; RN Staff Course, RNC Greenwich, 1989; MEO, HMS Trenchant, 1990–92; MEO, subseq. Captain Sea Trng, 1992–95; Second Sea Lord's Dept, 1995–97; Asst Dir, Nuclear Propulsion Safety, 1997–99; RCDS 2000; Mil. Asst to Chief of Defence Procurement, 2000–02; Naval Base Comdr, Devonport, 2002–05; Dir Gen. Submarines, Defence Equipment and Support, 2005–09; Chief of Materiel (Fleet) and Chief of Fleet Support to Navy Bd, 2009–13. Pres., Navy Rowing, 2006–13. FREng 2009. *Recreations:* dinghy sailing, cycling, gardening, Cornwall. *Club:* Army and Navy.

MATHEWS, Jeremy Fell, CMG 1989; Attorney General of Hong Kong, 1988–97; *b* 14 Dec. 1941; *s* of George James and Ivy Priscilla Mathews; *m* 1st, 1968, Sophie Lee (marr. diss. 1992); two *d*; 2nd, 1992, Halima Guterres. *Educ:* Palmer's Grammar Sch., England. Qualified as solicitor, London, 1963; private practice, London, 1963–65; Dep. Dist Registrar in the High Court of Australia, Sydney, 1966–67; Hong Kong Government: Crown Counsel, 1968; Dep. Law Draftsman, 1978; Dep. Crown Solicitor, 1981; Crown Solicitor, 1982. Dep. Dist Chm., Appeals Service, 1998–2003. Chm. Council, Overseas Service Pensioners' Assoc., 2004–13. *Recreations:* reading, gardening, music. *Club:* Hong Kong.

MATHEWS, Michael Robert; Partner, Clifford Chance, 1971–2000; President, Law Society of England and Wales, 1998–99; *b* 3 Nov. 1941; *s* of late George Walter Mathews and Betty Mathews (*née* Willcox); *m* 1966, Ann Gieve; two *s* one *d*. *Educ:* Uppingham Sch.; King's Coll., Cambridge (MA). Admitted solicitor, 1966; joined Coward Chance (later Clifford Chance), 1963. Vice Pres. and Chm., City of London Law Soc., 1992–95; Law Society of England and Wales: Mem. Council, 1995–2004; Dep. Vice Pres. and Treas., 1996–97; Vice Pres., 1997–98. Master: City of London Solicitors' Co., 1999–2000; Carpenters' Co., 2007–08. Hon. LLD: City, 1999; Westminster, 2009. *Recreations:* walking, watching good cricket. *Address:* 12 Clare Lawn Avenue, East Sheen, SW14 8BG.

MATHEWS, Peter Michael, CMG 2002; Chairman, Black Country Metals Trading Ltd, since 1986; *b* 26 Oct. 1946; *s* of Cyril and Audrey Mathews; *m* 1980, Gillian Anne Hatfield (marr. diss.); one *s* one *d*; *m* 2013, Elizabeth Anne (*née* O'Connell). *Educ:* Ellesmere Coll., Shropshire; Mt Radford Sch., Exeter. UK Trade & Investment (formerly Trade Partners UK): Mem., Bd, 2001–04; Mem., Internat. Trade Develt Adv. Panel, 2001–; Chm., Engrg Sector Adv. Gp, 2006–07; Chm., Advanced Engrg Adv. Bd, 2007–. Pres., Midlands World Trade Forum, 2001–. Mem., Business Forum for Multilingualism, EC, 2007–. Member: Adv. Bd, Bureau of Internat. Recycling, Brussels, 1995–2006; Bd, British Metals Recycling Assoc., 2002–07; Bd, Internat. Reinforcing Bar Assoc., Istanbul; Chm., Convention Cttee, Bureau of Internat. Recycling, 1995–. Nat. Pres., British Metal Fedn, 1997–99. Pres., Dudley Chamber of Commerce, 2002–05; Chm., Black Country Consortium, 2009–; Member: Bd, Black Country Chamber of Commerce, 2002– (Pres., 2007–10); Council, Birmingham Chamber of Commerce, 2002–. Mem., Internat. Adv. Bd, CBI, 2006–10. UKTI Trade Ambassador, West Midlands. Chm., West Midlands Partnership Canal and River Trust, 2012–. Co. Pres., RBL, Staffs, 2013–. MIex 1996; Mem., Inst. of Cast Metal Engrs, 2002; FInstD 1997. FRSA 1990. Hon. Life Mem., Ulster Metals Assoc., 1990. *Recreations:* theatre, golf, snooker, travel. *Address:* Dawlish, Comber Grove, Kinver, W Midlands DY7 6EN. *E:* peter@bcmetals.com.

MATHEWSON, Sir George (Ross), Kt 1999; CBE 1985; BSc, PhD, MBA; FRSE; CEng, MIEE; Chairman: Royal Bank of Scotland Group, 2001–06 (Director, 1987–2006; Deputy Chairman, 2000–01); Royal Bank of Scotland, 2001–06 (Director, 1987–2006); National Westminster Bank, 2001–06; Cheviot Asset Management Ltd, since 2006; Wood Mackenzie Ltd, 2007–09; *b* 14 May 1940; *s* of George Mathewson and Charlotte Gordon (*née* Ross); *m* 1966, Sheila Alexandra Graham (*née* Bennett); two *s*. *Educ:* Perth Academy; St Andrews Univ. (BSc, PhD); Canisius Coll., Buffalo, NY (MBA). Assistant Lecturer, St Andrews Univ., 1964–67; various posts in Research & Development, Avionics Engineering, Bell Aerospace, Buffalo, NY, 1967–72; joined Industrial & Commercial Finance Corp., Edinburgh, 1972; Area Manager, Aberdeen, 1974, and Asst General Manager and Director, 1979; Chief Exec. and Mem., Scottish Develt Agency, 1981–87; Royal Bank of Scotland Group: Dir of Strategic Planning and Develt, 1987–90; Dep. Gp Chief Exec., 1990–92; Gp Chief Exec., 1992–2000. Director: Scottish Investment Trust Ltd, 1981–2009; IIF Inc., 2001–06; Santander Central Hispano, 2001–04; Stagecoach Group plc, 2006–13 (Chm., 2010–13); Chm., Arrow Global Ltd, 2009–15; Shawbrook Bank Ltd, 2010–15. Chm., Council of Econ. Advrs to the Scottish Govt, 2007–10; Mem., Financial Reporting Council, 2004–06. Pres., BBA, 2002–04. Chm., Bd of Trustees, Royal Botanic Garden, Edinburgh, 2007–11. FCIBS 1994; CCMI (CBIM 1985); FRSE 1988. Hon. LLD: Dundee, 1983; St Andrews, 2000; DUniv Glasgow, 2001; Dr *hc* Edinburgh, 2002. *Publications:* various articles on engineering/finance. *Recreations:* Rugby, tennis, business. *Address:* Merklands House, Ballintuim, Blairgowrie, Perthshire PH10 7NN. *Club:* New (Edinburgh).

MATHEWSON, Hew Byrne, CBE 2010; FDSRCSE; Principal Dental Surgeon, Edinburgh, since 1977; President, 2003–09, Chair, 2009, General Dental Council; Chair, Scottish Dental Practice Board, since 2012; *b* 18 Nov. 1949; *s* of late Alexander M. Mathewson and Dorothy W. Mathewson; *m* 1971, Lorna A. M. McConnachie; one *s* one *d*. *Educ:* High Sch. of Glasgow; Glasgow Univ. (BDS 1974); Univ. of Wales, Cardiff (LLM 1990). DGDP 1992; FDSRCSE 1995; FDSRCS 2007. Associate Dental Surgeon, Wishaw and Canterbury, 1974–77. Asst Dir, Dental Studies, Univ. of Edinburgh, 1987–99; Regl Gen. Practice Vocational Trng Advr, SE Scotland, 1988–96. Chm., Scottish Gen. Dental Services Cttee,

1991–97 and 2010–12; Vice-Chm., UK Gen. Dental Services Cttee, 2000–03; Chm. Interim Bd, Mental Health Tribunal for Scotland Admin, 2008–09. Member: GDC, 1996–2009 (Jt Chair, Professional Conduct Cttee, 2001–03); Council for Healthcare Regulatory Excellence (formerly for Regulation of Health Care Professionals), 2003–08 (Vice-Chm., 2005–06); Council for Registration of Forensic Practitioners, 2006–11; Adv. Council on Misuse of Drugs, 2010–13. Pres., Conf. of Orders and Assimilated Bodies of Dental Practitioners in Europe, 2006–08. Special Advr to Med. and Dental Defence Union of Scotland, 2010–13; Mem. Med. and Dental Adv. Bd, Wesleyan Assurance, 2010–. Lay Mem., Appeals Cttee, ICAEW, 2006–12. Chair, Scottish Council, MS Soc., 2012–15. Fellow, British Dental Assoc., 2011–. Mem. Editl Bd, British Dental Jl, 1992–2003. *Recreations:* walking, fishing, travel, carpentry, theatre and cinema, collecting art. *Address:* 176–8 St Johns Road, Edinburgh EH12 8BE.

MATHEWSON, Iain Arthur Gray, CMG 2004; HM Diplomatic Service, retired; independent consultant on international security issues; Associate Fellow, International Security Programme, Chatham House, since 2008; *b* 16 March 1952; *s* of late John Gray Mathewson and of Jane Mathewson (now Murray); *m* 1983, Jennifer Bloch; one *s* one *d. Educ:* Downside Sch.; Corpus Christi Coll., Cambridge. HM Customs and Excise, 1974–77; DHSS, 1977–80; FCO, 1980; First Secretary: UK Mission to UN, NY, 1981–84; Warsaw, 1985–88; FCO, 1989–93; Counsellor: Prague, 1993–96; FCO, 1996–2006. Adviser: Citigroup, 2007–09; Detica plc, 2007–09; Candole Partners, 2007–09; Mem., World Risk Rev. Adv. Bd, Jardine Lloyd Thompson, 2009–. Trustee, Alexandra Rose Charities, 2010–. Mem., British Wireless Dinner Club. *Recreations:* golf, music. *E:* iain@mathewson.co.uk. *Clubs:* Travellers, Beefsteak; Berkshire Golf, St Enodoc Golf.

MATHIAS, Prof. Christopher Joseph, DPhil, DSc; FRCP, FMedSci; Professor of Neurovascular Medicine, University of London, 1991–2013, at Imperial College London (St Mary's Hospital) (formerly Imperial College School of Medicine (St Mary's Hospital), Imperial College of Science, Technology and Medicine), and Institute of Neurology, University College London; Consultant Physician: St Mary's Hospital, since 1982; National Hospital for Neurology and Neurosurgery, since 1985; Hospital of St John and St Elizabeth, since 2012; *b* 16 March 1949; *s* of late Lt Elias Mathias, IN and Hilda Mathias (*née* Pereira); *m* 1977, Rosalind (Lindy) Margaret, *d* of late Ambrose Jolleys, Cons. Paediatric Surgeon and of Betty Jolleys; two *s* one *d. Educ:* St Aloysius Sch., Visakhapatnam; St Joseph's E. H. Sch., Bangalore; St John's Med. Coll., Bangalore Univ. (MB BS 1972); Worcester Coll., Oxford; Wolfson Coll., Oxford (DPhil 1976); Univ. of London (DSc 1995). LRCSE, LRCPSGlas 1974; MRCP 1978, FRCP 1987. Rhodes Schol., 1972–75; Res. Officer and Hon. Registrar, Dept of Neurology, Churchill Hosp., Oxford, 1972–76; Clinical Asst and Res. Fellow, Nat. Spinal Injuries Centre, Stoke Mandeville Hosp., 1973–76; Sen. Hse Officer, Dept of Medicine, RPMS/Hammersmith Hosp., 1976–77; Registrar in Medicine, St Mary's Hosp., Portsmouth and Dept of Renal Medicine, Univ. of Southampton, 1977–79; Wellcome Trust Sen. Res. Fellow in Clinical Sci. at St Mary's Hosp. Med. Sch., 1979–84; Wellcome Trust Sen. Lectr in Med. Sci., St Mary's Hosp. Med. Sch. and Inst. of Neurol., 1984–92. Consultant Physician, Western Eye Hosp., 1982–98. Prof. Ruitinga Foundn Award and Vis. Prof., Acad. Med. Centre, Univ. of Amsterdam, 1988; Nimmo Vis. Prof., Univ. of Adelaide, 1996; Visiting Professor: Univ. of Hawaii, 1999; Univ. of Hong Kong, 2008. Dr J. Thomas Meml Oration, St John's Med. Coll., Bangalore Univ., 1988; Lectures: Lord Florey Meml, and Dorothy Mortlock, Royal Adelaide Hosp., Univ. of Adelaide, 1991; BP Regl, RCP, 1992; Thailand Neurological Soc., 1995; Sir Hugh Cairns Meml, Adelaide, 1996; Allan Birch Meml, London, 1997; Abbie Meml, Univ. of Adelaide, 1999; Coll., RCP, 2001; Sir Robert Menzies Meml Foundn, Sydney, 2001; Wahler Meml, London Jewish Med. Soc., 2002; Inaugural, Portuguese Autonomic Soc., Lisbon, 2002; Prof. Dr R. L. Müller Meml, Univ. of Erlangen, 2002; Prof. Athasit Vejajiva, Bangkok, 2003; Sir Roger Bannister, 2004, Chelsea Therapeutics, 2007, Jt Eur. Fedn of Autonomic Socs and Amer. Autonomic Soc.; Sir Gordon Holmes, London, 2004; Prof. Krishnamoorthy, Srinivas, Chennai, 2005; Keynote, 58th Congress of Japanese Neurovegetative Soc., Chiba, 2005; Valsalva, Bologna, 2006; 20th Shri K. Gopalakrishna, Chennai, 2006; Roche, Internal Medicine Assoc. of Aust. and NZ, 2007; Northern Communities Health Foundn, Adelaide, 2007; Swiss Autonomic Soc., Berne, 2008; G. M. Mascarenhas Oration, St John's Medical Coll. N Atlantic Chapter, Florida, 2008; British Peripheral Nerve Soc., London 2008; 19th World Congress of Neurol., Bangkok, 2009; 12th Eur. Fedn of Autonomic Socs, Taormina, 2010; RSocMed, 2013. Chairman: Clinical Autonomic Res. Soc., 1987–90 (first Sec., 1982–86); Res. Cttee, World Fedn of Neurol., 1993–97 (Mem., 1989–93); Chm., Scientific Panel, 1994–99, Mem., Task Force, 2004–06, Lead, Task Force on Orthostatic Intolerance, 2008–, European Fedn of Neurol Socs; Pres., Eur. Fedn of Autonomic Socs, 1998–2004; Member: Scientific Cttee, Internat. Spinal Res. Trust, 1996–2008; Bd of Dirs, Amer. Autonomic Soc., 1996–2004; Sec. of State's Hon. Med. Adv. Panel on Driving and Disorders of the Nervous System, 2004–09; Task Force, Amer. Spinal Injury Assoc., 2004–07; Mem. and Chm., MSA-Autonomic Gp, Consensus Conference on MSA, Amer. Acad. of Neurology, Boston, 2007. Consultant, ESA, 1997–2000; Mem., Jt ESA/NASA Neuroscience Rev. Panel, 1997. Non-exec. Dir, W London Mental Health Trust, 2008–10. Mem., NW Thames Regl Adv. Cttee for Distinction Awards, 1999–2001; Chm., Dr P. M. Shankland (Pushpa Chopra) Charitable Trust Prize Fund, 1998–2003. Mem., Bd of Govs, Nat. Soc. for Epilepsy, 2004–08. Patron: Autonomic Disorders Assoc. Sarah Matheson Trust, 1997–2010; STARS (Syncope Trust), 2001–; Founder Trustee, Autonomic Charitable Trust, 2012–. FMedSci 2001. Founder Editor-in-Chief, 1991–95, Co-Editor-in-Chief, 1995–2013, Clinical Autonomic Res.; Member, Editorial Board: Hypertension, 1990–93; Jl of Pharmaceutical Medicine, 1991–95; Functional Neurol., 1990–2003; High Blood Pressure and Cardiovascular Prevention, 1992–2005; Jl of Hypertension, 1994–97; Parkinsonism and Related Disorders, 1995–2005, 2008–11; Internat. Jl of Evidence-Based Healthcare, 2007–12. Dr *hc* Lisbon, 2007. *Publications:* (ed jtly) Mild Hypertension: current controversies and new approaches, 1984; (ed jtly) Concepts in Hypertension: a festschrift for Prof. Sir Stanley Peart, 1989; (ed with Sir Roger Bannister) Autonomic Failure: a textbook of clinical disorders of the autonomic nervous system, 3rd edn 1992, 5th edn 2013; chaps in neurol. and cardiovascular textbooks; papers on nervous system and hormonal control of circulation in neurological, cardiovascular and other medical disorders. *Recreations:* gardening, watching cricket and football, observing human (and canine) behaviour. *Address:* Meadowcroft, West End Lane, Stoke Poges, Bucks SL2 4NE. *E:* profmathiasautonomic@gmail.com. *Clubs:* Athenæum, Royal Society of Medicine; Vincent's (Oxford).

MATHIAS, Surg. Rear-Adm. (D) Frank Russell Bentley; retired 1985; Director, Naval Dental Services, 1983–85, and Deputy Director of Defence Dental Services (Organisation), Ministry of Defence, 1985; *b* 27 Dec. 1927; *s* of Thomas Bentley Mathias and Phebe Ann Mathias; *m* 1954, Margaret Joyce (*née* Daniels); one *s* one *d. Educ:* Narberth Grammar Sch.; Guy's Hosp., London. LDSRCS Eng. 1952. House Surgeon, Sussex County Hosp., Brighton, 1952–53; joined RN, 1953; principal appointments: Staff Dental Surgeon, Flag Officer Malta, 1972; Flotilla Dental Surgeon, Flag Officer Submarines, 1972–74; Comd Dental Surgeon, Flag Officer Naval Air Comd, 1974–76; Dep. Dir, Naval Dental Services, 1976–80; Comd Dental Surgeon to C-in-C Naval Home Comd, 1980–83. QHDS 1982–85. OStJ 1981.
See also Rear Adm. P. B. Mathias.

MATHIAS, (Jonathan) Glyn; Member, Content Board, Ofcom, since 2011; *b* 19 Feb. 1945; *s* of late Roland Glyn Mathias and Mary Annie (*née* Hawes); *m* 2000, Ann Bowen (*née* Hughes); one *s* two *d. Educ:* Llandovery Coll., Carmarthenshire; Jesus Coll., Oxford (MA); Univ. of Southampton (MSc). Reporter, South Wales Echo, 1967–70; News Asst, BBC Southampton, 1970–73; ITN: Political Reporter, London, 1973–81; Political Editor, 1981–86; Asst Editor, 1986–91; Controller, Public Affairs, 1991–93; Chief Political Correspondent, 1993–94; BBC Wales: Political Editor, 1994–99; Manager, Public Affairs, 1999–2000. Sen. Lectr, British Politics, UWIC, 2001–03 (Hon. Fellow, 2004). Mem., Electoral Commn, 2001–08. Mem., Adv. Cttee for Wales, Ofcom, 2007–. Chm., Membership Panel, Dwr Cymru/Welsh Water, 2013–. Chm., Govs, Ysgol y Bannau, 2010–12. Chm., Editl Bd, New Welsh Rev., 2011–15. *Publications:* (ed) ITN Election Factbook, 1987; (contrib.) Televising Democracies, 1992; Raising an Echo, 2014. *Recreation:* family life. *Address:* Harddfan, Avenue Court, Brecon, Powys LD3 9BE. *T:* (01874) 623368. *E:* glynmathias@btinternet.com. *Club:* Reform.

MATHIAS, Pauline Mary; Headmistress, More House School, 1974–89; *b* 4 Oct. 1928; *d* of Francis and Hilda Donovan; *m* 1954, Prof. Anthony Peter Mathias; two *s. Educ:* La Retraite High School; Bedford College, London (BA Hons; DipEd). Head of English Dept, London Oratory Sch., 1954–64; Sen. Lectr in English and Admissions Tutor, Coloma Coll. of Education, 1964–74. Mem., ITC, 1991–96. Pres., GSA, 1982–83; Vice-Pres., Women's Careers Foundn, 1985–89; Chairman: ISIS, 1984–86; GBGSA, 1994–98 (Dep. Chm., 1992–94). Governor: Westminster Cathedral Choir Sch., 1978–2003; ESU, 1986–92; St Felix Sch., Southwold, 1986–95 (Chm., 1990–95); London Oratory Sch., 1987–2011 (Dep. Chm., 1994–2000); St Mary's Sch., Ascot, 1995–2002 (Trustee, 2006–); Godolphin and Latymer Sch., 1995–98. *Address:* 18 Lee Road, Aldeburgh, Suffolk IP15 5HG.

MATHIAS, Dr Peter, CBE 1984; MA, DLitt; FBA 1977; Master of Downing College, Cambridge, 1987–95 (Hon. Fellow, 1995); *b* 10 Jan. 1928; *oc* of John Samuel and late Marian Helen Mathias; *m* 1958, Elizabeth Ann (*d* 2013), *d* of Robert Blackmore, JP, Bath; two *s* one *d. Educ:* Colston's Sch., Bristol; Jesus Coll., Cambridge (Schol.; Hon. Fellow, 1987). 1st cl. (dist) Hist. Tripos, 1950, 1951; DLitt: Oxon, 1985; Cantab, 1987. Research Fellow, Jesus Coll., Cambridge, 1952–55; Asst Lectr and Lectr, Faculty of History, Cambridge, 1955–68; Dir of Studies in History and Fellow, Queens' Coll., Cambridge, 1955–68 (Hon. Fellow, 1987); Tutor, 1957–68; Senior Proctor, Cambridge Univ., 1965–66; Chichele Prof. of Economic History, Oxford Univ., and Fellow of All Souls Coll., Oxford, 1969–87; Emeritus Fellow, 1987–. Mem., Council of the Senate, Cambridge Univ., 1991–94. Visiting Professor: Univ. of Toronto, 1961; School of Economics, Delhi, 1967; Univ. of California, Berkeley, 1967; Univ. of Pa, 1972; Virginia Gildersleeve, Barnard Coll., Columbia Univ., 1972; Johns Hopkins Univ., 1979; ANU, Canberra, 1981; Geneva, 1986; Leuven, 1990; San Marino, 1990; Waseda, 1996; Osaka Gakuin, 1998; Free Univ., Bolzano, 1999; Kansai, 2006. Asst Editor, Econ. Hist. Rev., 1955–57; Gen. Editor, Debates in Economic History, 1967–86. Chairman: Business Archives Council, 1968–72 (Vice-Pres., 1980–84 and 1995–; Pres., 1984–95); Econ. and Social History Cttee, SSRC, 1975–77 (Mem., 1970–77); Acad. Adv. Council, University Coll., Buckingham, 1979–84 (Mem., 1984–98); Wellcome Trust Adv. Panel for History of Medicine, 1981–88; Friends of Kettle's Yard, 1989–95; Fitzwilliam Mus. Enterprises Ltd, 1990–99; Syndic of Fitzwilliam Mus., 1987–98; Bd of Continuing Educn, 1991–95; Nat. Adv. Council, British Library, 1994–2000 (Mem., Adv. Cttee (Humanities and Social Scis), 1990–94); Central European Univ. Press, 2000–10; Member: ABRC, 1983–89; Round Table, Council of Industry and Higher Educn, 1989–94; Beirat Wissenschaftskolleg, Berlin, 1992–98; Bd of Patrons, Eur. Banking Hist. Assoc., 1995–. Treasurer, Econ. Hist. Soc., 1968–88 (Pres., 1989–92; Vice Pres., 1992–); Hon. Treasurer, British Acad., 1980–89; International Economic History Association: Sec., 1959–62; Pres., 1974–78; Hon. Pres., 1978–; Vice Pres., Internat. Inst. of Economic History Francesco Datini, Prato, 1987–99 (Mem. Exec. Cttee, 1972–99; Comitato d'Honore, 1999–); Jerusalem Cttee, 1978–93; Mem., Academia Europaea, 1989; Trustee and Mem. Council, GB Sasakawa Foundn, 1994– (Chm., 1997–2005; Pres., 2006–11; Hon. Pres., 2011–); Foreign Member: Royal Danish Acad., 1982; Royal Belgian Acad., 1988. Curator, Bodleian Library, 1972–87. FRHistS 1972 (Vice-Pres., 1976–80; Hon. Vice-Pres., 2001). Hon. DLitt: Buckingham, 1985; Birmingham, 1988; Hull, 1992; Warwick, 1995; De Montfort, 1995; East Anglia, 1999; Hon. DSc Russian Acad. of Scis, 2002; Hon. Dr: Kansai, 2006; Keio, 2008. Order of the Rising Sun with Gold Rays (Japan), 2003. *Publications:* The Brewing Industry in England 1700–1830, 1959, repr. 1993; English Trade Tokens, 1962; Retailing Revolution, 1967; The First Industrial Nation, 1969, rev. edn 1983; (ed) Science and Society 1600–1900, 1972; The Transformation of England, 1979; L'Economia Britannica dal 1815 al 1914, 1994; Cinque Lezioni di Teoria e Storia, 2003; (ed jtly) UNESCO: history of humanity, vol. VI, 2008; General Editor, Cambridge Economic History of Europe, 1968–93. *Recreations:* travel, New Hall china. *Address:* 33 Church Street, Chesterton, Cambridge CB4 1DT. *T:* (01223) 329824.

MATHIAS, Rear Adm. Philip Bentley, MBE 1991; Partner, Ethos; Director, Strategic Defence Review (Nuclear), 2010–12; *b* Plymouth, 21 May 1958; *s* of Surg. Rear-Adm. (D) Frank Russell Bentley Mathias, *qv*; *m* 1985, Jane Amice Cantan; one *s* one *d. Educ:* Churcher's Coll., Petersfield; BRNC Dartmouth. Joined BRNC Dartmouth, 1977; CO, HMS Otus (Gulf War), 1988–91; Sen. Trng Officer, BRNC, 1992; CO, HMS Trenchant (Arctic Ops), 1993–94; Staff of Second Sea Lord, 1995–98; Exec. Officer, HMS Invincible (Balkans conflict), 1998–99; RN HQ, MoD, 2000–03; Pres., Admiralty Interview Bd, 2004; Dir, Nuclear Policy, MoD, 2006–09. Gov., Duke of York Royal Military Sch., Dover. *Recreations:* keeping unusual tropical fish, big game fishing in Kenya. *E:* philipbmathias@gmail.com.

MATHIAS, Sean Gerard; writer and director; *b* 14 March 1956; *s* of John Frederick Mathias and Anne Josephine Patricia Mathias (*née* Harding). *Educ:* Bishop Vaughan Comprehensive Sch., Swansea. Artistic Dir, Haymarket Th., 2009–10. *Writer: plays:* Cowardice, Ambassadors, 1983; A Prayer for Wings, Edinburgh Fest. and Bush Th., 1985; Infidelities, Edinburgh Fest. and Donmar Warehouse, 1985; Poor Nanny, King's Head, Islington, 1989; Swansea Boys, RNT Studio, 1991; *screenplay:* The Lost Language of Cranes, BBC, 1991. *Director: film:* Bent, 1996 (Prix de la Jeunesse, Cannes, 1997); *plays:* Exceptions, New End, 1989; Bent, RNT, transf. Garrick, 1990; Uncle Vanya, RNT, 1992; Ghosts, Sherman Th., Cardiff, 1993; Les Parents Terribles, RNT, 1994; Design for Living, Donmar, transf. Gielgud, 1994; Indiscretions, NY, 1995; A Little Night Music, RNT, 1995; Marlene, Oldham, transf. Lyric, 1996, NY, 1999; Antony and Cleopatra, RNT, 1998; Suddenly Last Summer, Comedy, 1999; Servicemen, NY, 2001; Dance of Death, NY, 2001, Lyric, 2003, Sydney, 2004; The Elephant Man, NY, 2002; Company, Washington, 2002; Antigone, Cape Town, 2004; Aladdin, Old Vic, 2004–05; Shoreditch Madonna, Soho Th., 2005; The Cherry Orchard, LA, 2006; Triptych, Johannesburg, 2007, Southwark Playhouse, 2008; Ring Round the Moon, Playhouse, 2008; Waiting for Godot, UK tour then Th. Royal, Haymarket, 2009–10, Internat. tour, 2010; Breakfast at Tiffany's, Th. Royal, Haymarket, 2009; Heavenly Ivy, The Ivy, 2010; The Syndicate, Chichester Festival Th., UK tour, 2011; Breakfast at Tiffany's, NY, No Man's Land, Berkeley Rep., 2013; Waiting for Godot and No Man's Land as Two Plays in Rep, NY, 2013–14. Dir of the Year, Evening Standard Awards, and Critics' Circle Awards, 1994. *Publications: plays:* A Prayer for Wings, 1985; Infidelities, 1985; *novella:* Manhattan Mourning, 1989. *Address:* c/o St John Donald, United Agents, 12–26 Lexington Street, W1F 0LE. *T:* (020) 3214 0800.

MATHIAS, Tania Wyn; MP (C) Twickenham, since 2015; *d* of Roger Wynn Mathias and Vivienne Desiree Mathias. *Educ:* St Paul's Girls' Sch.; St Catherine's Coll. and Christ Church, Oxford (MB BCh 1988). Refugee Affairs Officer and Health Officer, UNRWA, 1991–93. NHS medical doctor. Mem. (C) Richmond upon Thames LBC, 2010–15. *Recreations:* bird watching, documentary film making. *Address:* House of Commons, SW1A 0AA. *E:* drtania.mathias.mp@parliament.uk.

MATHIES, Monika W.; *see* Wulf-Mathies.

MATHIESON, Rt Hon. Dame Janet Hilary; *see* Smith, Rt Hon. Dame J. H.

MATLHABAPHIRI, Gaotlhaetse Utlwang Sankoloba; MP (Democratic Party), Botswana, since 2004; Assistant Minister, Ministry of Health, Botswana, 2008–09 and since 2010; *b* 6 Nov. 1949; *s* of late Sankoloba and Khumo Matlhabaphiri; four *d. Educ:* Diamond Corporation Training Sch.; London; Friederick Ebert Foundn, Gaborone (Labour Economics). Clerk, Standard Chartered Bank, 1971–72; teacher, also part-time Dep. Head Master, Capital Continuation Classes, Gaborone, 1971–72; diamond sorter valuator, 1973–79. MP, Botswana, 1979–84 and 1989–94; Gen. Sec., Botswana Democratic Party Youth Wing, 1978–85, 1992–96 and 1996–98; Asst Minister of Agriculture, 1979–85; Mem., Central Cttee, Botswana Democratic Party, 1982–85, 1991–95 and 1995–99 (Chm., Labour Cttee, 1991); Ambassador of Botswana to Nordic countries, 1985–86; High Comr for Botswana in UK, 1986–88 (concurrently Ambassador (non-resident) to Romania and Yugoslavia); High Comr of Botswana to Namibia and Ghana, and Ambassador to Angola, 2000–04; Asst Minister of Labour and Home Affairs, 2007–08. Asst Gen. Sec., Bank Employees Union, 1972; Gen. Sec., Botswana Diamond Sorters Valuators Union, 1976–79; Chairman: Botswana Fedn of Trade Unions, 1979; Parly Public Accounts Cttee, 1993–94; Law Reform Cttee, 1993–94; Citizen Cttee of Botswana, 1998–2000. Mem. Bd, Botswana Develt Corp., 1998–2000. Member: CPA; Botswana Br., IPU Cttee, 1993. Sec., Gaborone Union Ch, UCCSA, 1976–77. Conductor/Dir, Botswana Democratic Party Internat. Choir. Governor, IFAD, 1980–84. *Recreations:* footballer, athlete; choral music. *Club:* Gaborone Township Rollers.

MATLOCK, Prof. Jack Foust; American career diplomat; George F. Kennan Professor, Institute for Advanced Study, Princeton, 1996–2001; *b* 1 Oct. 1929; *s* of late Jack F. Matlock and of Nellie Matlock (*née* McSwain); *m* 1949, Rebecca Burrum; four *s* one *d. Educ:* Duke Univ. (BA 1950); Columbia Univ. (MA 1952; PhD 2013). Editor and translator on Current Digest of the Soviet Press, 1952–53; Russian language and literature Instructor, Dartmouth Coll., 1953–56; joined US Foreign Service, 1956; served in Moscow, Austria, Ghana, Zanzibar, Tanzania; Vis. Prof. of Political Science, Vanderbilt Univ., 1978–79; Dep. Dir, Foreign Service Inst., 1979–80; Chargé d'Affaires, Moscow, 1981; Ambassador to Czechoslovakia, 1981; Special Asst to President for Nat. Security Affairs and Sen. Dir, European and Soviet Affairs on Nat. Security Council Staff, 1983–86; Ambassador to Soviet Union, 1987–91. Kathryn and Shelby Cullom Davis Prof., Columbia Univ., 1993–96. Vis. Prof. Princeton Univ., 2001–04; Sol Linowitz Prof. of Internat. Relns, Hamilton Coll., 2006; Cyrus Vance Prof., Mount Holyoke Coll., 2007. Masaryk Award, 1983; Superior Honor Award, Dept of State, 1981; Presidential Meritorious Service Award, 1984, 1987. *Publications:* Handbook to Russian edn of Stalin's Works, 1972; Autopsy on an Empire: the American Ambassador's account of the collapse of the Soviet Union, 1995; Reagan and Gorbachev: how the Cold War ended, 2004; Superpower Illusions: how myths and false ideologies led America astray - and how to return to reality, 2010; articles on US-Soviet relations. *Address:* 32 Wagoner Hill Road, Fayetteville, TN 37334, USA. *W:* www.JackMatlock.com. *Club:* Century Association (NY).

MATOKA, Dr Peter Wilfred, GCCF 2006; Chancellor, Copperstone University, Kitwe, Zambia, since 2010; *b* 8 April 1930; *m* 1957, Grace Joyce; two *s* one *d. Educ:* Mwinilunga Sch.; Munali Secondary Sch.; University Coll. of Fort Hare (BA Rhodes); American Univ., Washington (Dipl. Internat. Relations); Univ. of Zambia (MA); Univ. of Warwick (PhD 1994). MP Mwinilunga, Parlt of Zambia, 1964–78; Minister: of Information and Postal Services, 1964–65; of Health, 1965–66; of Works, 1967; of Power, Transport and Works, 1968; of Luapula Province, 1969; High Comr for Zambia in UK and Ambassador to the Holy See, 1970–71; Minister of Health, 1971–72; Minister of Local Govt and Housing, 1972–77; Minister of Economic and Technical Co-operation and Pres., Africa, Caribbean and Pacific Gp of States, 1977; retd from active politics, 1992; Sen. Regl Advr, Econ. Commn for Africa, UN, Addis Ababa, 1979–83; High Comr in Zimbabwe, 1984–89; Sen. Lectr, Dept of Social Develt Studies, Univ. of Zambia, 1995. Mem. Central Cttee, United National Independence Party, 1971–78 and 1984–91 (Chairman: Social and Cultural Cttee, 1989–90; Sci. and Technol. Cttee, 1990–91). Life Mem., CPA, 1974. Pres., AA of Zambia, 1969–70. Kt of St Gregory the Great, 1964; Mem., Knightly Assoc. of St George the Martyr, 1986–. *Publications:* Child Labour in Zambia, 1999. *Recreations:* reading, walking, watching television. *Address:* Copperstone University, Plot 8122, Copperhouse, Central Street, PO Box 22041, Kitwe, Zambia; (home) 26D Ibex Hill Township, Lusaka, Zambia.

MATOVU, Harold Nsamba; QC 2010; *b* Mengo, Uganda; *s* of Leonard and Ruth Matovu; *m* 1994, Emma Rose Peto; three *s. Educ:* Eton Coll.; Balliol Coll., Oxford (BA Hons Lit.Hum. 1985); Central London Poly. (DipLaw 1986). Called to the Bar, Inner Temple, 1988, Bencher, 2012; in practice as barrister, specialising in commercial law, 1989–; Dep. Counsel to BSE Inquiry, 1998–2000. Member: Professional Conduct Complaints Cttee, 1996–98, Professional Standards Cttee, 2005–06, Bar Council; London Common Law and Commercial Bar Assoc., 1989–; Commercial Bar Assoc., 2000–. *Recreations:* jazz, classical music, theatre, literature, cricket. *Address:* Brick Court Chambers, 7–8 Essex Street, WC2R 3LD. *Club:* Garrick.

MATSUURA, Koïchiro; Director-General of UNESCO, 1999–2009; *b* 29 Sept. 1937; *s* of Seichi and Kiyoko Matsuura; *m* 1967, Takako Kirikae; two *s. Educ:* Univ. of Tokyo; Havenford Coll., USA (MBA). Counsellor, Embassy of Japan, USA, 1977–80; Consul Gen., Hong Kong, 1985–88; Dir-Gen., Econ. Co-operation Bureau, 1988–90, N American Affairs Bureau, 1990–92, Min. of Foreign Affairs; Dep. Minister for Foreign Affairs (Sherpa for Japan at G-7 Summit), 1992–94; Ambassador of Japan to: Djibouti, 1994–99; France, 1994–99; Andorra, 1996–99. Chm., World Heritage Cttee, UNESCO, 1998–99. Bintang Jasa Utama (Indonesia), 1993; Grand Officer, Nat. Order of Merit (France), 1994; Comdr, Nat. Order of 27 June (Djibouti), 1997. *Publications:* In the Forefront of Economic Co-operation Diplomacy, 1990; History of Japan-United States Relations, 1992; Focusing on the Future: Japan's global role in a changing world, 1993; The G-7 Summit: its history and perspectives, 1994; Development and Perspectives of the Relations between Japan and France, 1995; Japanese Diplomacy at the Dawn of the 21st Century, 1998. *Recreations:* Go, tennis, golf, mountain climbing.

MATT; *see* Pritchett, Matthew.

MATTAJ, Iain William, PhD; FRS 1999; FRSE; Director General, European Molecular Biology Laboratory, since 2005; *b* 5 Oct. 1952; *s* of George Eugeniusz Mattaj and Jane Margaret Mattaj; *m* 1974, Ailsa McCrindle. *Educ:* Edinburgh Univ. (BSc); Leeds Univ. (PhD 1980). Postdoctoral research: Friedrich Miescher Inst., Basel, 1979–82; Biocenter, Basel Univ., 1982–85; Gp Leader, 1985–90, Programme Co-ordinator, 1990–99, Scientific Dir, 1999–2005, EMBL, Heidelberg. Exec. Ed., EMBO Jl, 1990–2004. Mem., EMBO, 1989. Pres., Ribonucleic Acid Soc., 1998–2000. FRSE 2000. *Publications:* numerous contribs to scientific jls. *Recreations:* squash, music, literature. *Address:* European Molecular Biology Laboratory, Meyerhofstrasse 1, 69117 Heidelberg, Germany. *T:* (6221) 387393.

MATTHEW, Christopher Charles Forrest; writer and broadcaster; *b* Lewisham, 8 May 1939; *s* of Leonard Douglas and Doris Janet Matthew; *m* 1979, Wendy Mary Mallinson (*née* Whitaker); two *s* and one step *d. Educ:* King's Sch., Canterbury (King's Schol.); St Peter's Coll., Oxford (BA 1963; MA 1989). Copywriter, various London advertising agencies, 1964–70; Ed., The Times Travel Guide, 1972–74; columnist, Punch, Vogue, Daily Telegraph, Observer, Daily Mail, Sunday Times, 1976–2006; presenter, programmes for BBC Radio 4, including: Something to Declare, 1977–82; The Travelling Show, 1982–85; Points of Departure, 1980–82; Invaders, 1982–83; Fourth Column, 1990–93; Plain Tales from the Rhododendrons, 1991; Cold Print, 1992; A Nest of Singing Birds, 1996; (with Alan Coren) Freedom Pass, 2003–05; (with Des Lynam) Touchline Tales, 2010–12; (with Terry Waite) Freedom Pass Special, 2012; (with Martin Jarvis) Grey Shorts and Sandals, 2013; The Sage of Cricklewood, 2014; *radio plays*: A Portrait of Richard Hillary, 1980; Madonna's Plumber, 2003; A Nightingale Sang in Fernhurst Road, 2007; Short Stories for Original Shorts series, BBC Radio 4, 2005–11; *stage play*: Summoned by Betjeman, Yvonne Arnaud Th., Guildford, and tour, 2002; *film*: Three More Men in a Boat, BBC TV, 1983. *Publications:* A Different World: stories of great hotels, 1974; Diary of a Somebody, 1978; Loosely Engaged, 1980; The Long-Haired Boy, 1980 (adapted for TV as A Perfect Hero, 1991); The Crisp Report, 1981; (with Benny Green) Three Men in a Boat (annotated edn), 1982; The Junket Man, 1983; How to Survive Middle Age, 1983; Family Matters, 1987; The Amber Room, 1995; A Nightingale Sang in Fernhurst Road, 1998; Now We Are Sixty, 1999; Knocking On, 2001; Now We Are Sixty (and a Bit), 2003; Summoned by Balls, 2005; When We Were Fifty, 2007; The Man Who Dropped the Le Creuset on his Toe, 2013; Dog Treats, 2014. *Recreations:* golfing, sailing small waters, lunching with friends, walking in the country with a dog. *Address:* Jonathan Pegg Literary Agency, 32 Batoum Gardens, W6 7QD. *Clubs:* Chelsea Arts; Aldeburgh Golf; Slaughden Sailing.

MATTHEWS, Hon. Lord; Hugh Matthews; a Senator of the College of Justice in Scotland, since 2007; *b* 4 Dec. 1953; *s* of Hugh Matthews and Maureen Matthews (*née* Rea); *m* 2000, Lindsay M. A. Wilson. *Educ:* St Columba's Primary Sch., Kilmarnock; St Joseph's Acad., Kilmarnock; Glasgow Univ. (LLB Hons). Admitted to Faculty of Advocates, 1979; QC (Scot.) 1992; Standing Jun. Counsel, Dept of Employment, Office in Scotland, 1984–88; Advocate-Depute, 1988–93; temp. Sheriff, 1993–97; Sheriff of Glasgow and Strathkelvin, 1997–2007; temp. Judge, 2004–07. *Recreations:* ancient history, golf, football, animal husbandry, astronomy, theatre, music. *Clubs:* The Club (Kilmarnock); Scottish Arts (Edinburgh).

MATTHEWS, Prof. Allan, PhD; FREng, CEng, FIMechE, FIET, FIMMM, FIMF; Professor of Surface Engineering, since 2003, and Executive Director, Leonardo Centre for Tribology and Surface Technology, since 2012, University of Sheffield; *b* Wigan, 28 June 1952; *s* of Thomas Matthews and Elizabeth, (Lily), Matthews (*née* Halton); *m* 1975, Helen Irene Gregson; one *s* one *d. Educ:* All Saints Sch., Appley Bridge; Upholland Grammar Sch.; Univ. of Salford (BSc Mech. Engrg 1974; PhD 1980); Manchester Poly. (Dip. Mgt Studies 1976). Technologist apprenticeship, Hawker Siddeley Dynamics, 1970–74; Graduate Technologist, Proj. Mgt Dept, British Aerospace, 1974–76; Res. Asst, 1976–88, Res. Fellow, 1977–82, Univ. of Salford; University of Hull: Lectr, 1982–86; Sen. Lectr, 1986–87; Reader, 1987–89; Prof., 1989–2002; Dir, Res. Centre in Surface Engrg, subseq. at Univ. of Sheffield, 1991–; Hd, Dept of Materials Sci. and Engrg, Univ. of Sheffield, 2007–11. Chm., British Vacuum Council, 2004–05. Dir, Ion Coat Ltd, 1982–. Mem., Exec. Cttee, Advanced Surface Engrg Div., American Vacuum Soc., 2000–04 (Chm., 2003); Mem. Bd, Soc. of Vacuum Coaters, 2008–. FIMechE 1996; FIET (FIEE 1996); FIMMM 1997; FIMF 1997; FREng 2012. Gold Medal, IMMM, 2011. Editor, 1987–2013, Editor-in-Chief, 2013–, Surface and Coatings Technol. *Publications:* (ed jtly) Advanced Surface Coatings: a handbook of surface engineering, 1991; (jtly) The UK Engineering Coatings Industry in 2005, 1992; Coatings Tribology: properties, mechanisms, techniques and applications in surface engineering (with K. Holmberg), 1994, 2nd edn 2009; 2005 Revisited: the UK engineering coatings industry to 2010, 1998; The UK Surface Engineering Industry, 2010; (jtly) Surface Engineering Processes in Design and Manufacture: an introductory guide, 2011; over 350 papers in jls; fifteen patents. *Recreations:* walking, music, football, golf, Rugby. *Address:* Department of Materials Science and Engineering, University of Sheffield, Sir Robert Hadfield Building, Mappin Street, Sheffield S1 3JD. *T:* (0114) 222 5466, *Fax:* (0114) 222 5943. *E:* a.matthews@sheffield.ac.uk.

MATTHEWS, Rt Rev. Anthony Francis Berners H.; *see* Hall-Matthews.

MATTHEWS, Colin, OBE 2011; DPhil; FRNCM, FRCM; composer; Prince Consort Professor of Composition, Royal College of Music, since 2001; *b* 13 Feb. 1946; *s* of Herbert and Elsie Matthews; *m* 1977, Belinda Lloyd; one *s* two *d. Educ:* Univ. of Nottingham (BA Classics, MPhil Composition); Univ. of Sussex (DPhil). Studied composition with Arnold Whittall and Nicholas Maw, 1967–70; collaborated with Deryck Cooke on performing version of Mahler's Tenth Symphony, 1964–74; asst to Benjamin Britten, 1971–76; worked with Imogen Holst, 1972–84; taught at Univ. of Sussex, 1971–72, 1976–77. Associate Composer: LSO, 1990–99; Hallé Orch., 2001–11 (Composer Emeritus, 2011–). Distinguished Vis. Fellow, Univ. of Manchester, 2001–; Special Prof. of Music, Univ. of Nottingham, 2007–. Dir, Holst Estate and Holst Foundn, 1973–; Trustee, Britten-Pears Foundn, 1983– (Music Dir, 2008–); Dir, Britten Estate, 1983– (Chm., 2000–); Mem. Council and Exec. Cttee, SPNM, 1981–93, 1994–99; Exec. Mem. Council, Aldeburgh Foundn, 1984–93; Dir, PRS, 1992–95; Trustee (formerly Mem. Council), RPS, 2005–. Founder, NMC Recordings Ltd, 1988. Gov., RNCM, 2000–08. Patron, Musicians against Nuclear Arms, 1985–. FRNCM 2003; FRCM 2007. Hon. RAM 2010. Hon. DMus Nottingham, 1998. Scottish National Orch. Ian Whyte Award, 1975; Park Lane Group Composer Award, 1983; Royal Philharmonic Soc. Award, 1996; British Composer Award, BASCA, 2012, 2013. *Principal works:* Fourth Sonata, 1974; Night Music, 1976; Sonata no 5 'Landscape', 1977–81; String Quartet no 1, 1979; Oboe Quartet, 1981; The Great Journey, 1981–88; Divertimento for Double String Quartet, 1982; Toccata Meccanica, 1984; Night's Mask, 1984; Cello Concerto, 1984; Suns Dance, 1985; Five Duos, 1985; Three Enigmas, 1985; String Quartet no 2, 1985; Pursuit (ballet), 1986; Monody, 1986–87; Eleven Studies in Velocity, 1987; Two Part Invention, 1987; Cortège, 1988; Hidden Variables, 1989; Quatrain, 1989; Second Oboe Quartet, 1990; Five Concertinos, 1990; Chiaroscuro, 1990; Machines and Dreams, 1990; Broken Symmetry, 1990–91; Renewal, 1990–96; Contraflow, 1992; Memorial, 1992; String Quartet no 3, 1994; …through the glass, 1994; 23 Frames, 1995; Cello Concerto no 2, 1996; Renewal, 1996; My Life So Far (film score), 1998; Two Tributes, 1999; Aftertones, 2000; Pluto, 2000; Continuum, 2000; Horn Concerto, 2001; Debussy Preludes, 2001–07; Reflected Images, 2003; A Voice to Wake, 2005; Berceuse for Dresden, 2005; Turning Point, 2006; Alphabicycle Order, 2007; The Island, 2008; Violin Concerto, 2009; Crossing the Alps, 2010; Night Rides, 2011; No Man's Land, 2011; Grand Barcarolle, 2011; String Quartet no 4, 2012; Nowhere to Hide, 2013; Traces Remain, 2014; The Pied Piper of Hamelin, 2015; String Quartet no 5, 2015. *Publications:* contribs to Musical Times, Tempo, TLS, etc. *Recreations:* wine, very amateur astrophysics. *Address:* c/o Faber Music Ltd, Bloomsbury House, 74–77 Great Russell Street, WC1B 3DA. *T:* (020) 7908 5310, *Fax:* (020) 7908 5339. *E:* information@fabermusic.com. *Club:* Leyton Orient Supporters'.

See also D. J. Matthews.

MATTHEWS, Brother Daniel (Fairbairn), SSF; Minister General, Society of Saint Francis, 1997–2007; *b* 7 Sept. 1936; *s* of Maxwell and Mary Matthews. *Educ:* S Shields Marine Coll. (1st Cl. Marine Engrg); Bishop Patteson Theological Coll., Kohimarama, Solomon Is (DipTh). Chief Engr (Marine), 1957–63; joined Society of St Francis, 1964: Guardian, Solomon Is, 1975–81; Minister Provincial, Australia and NZ, 1981–97. *Recreations:* walking, reading. *Address:* Society of Saint Francis, c/o The Friary, 115 Cornwall Street, Annerley, Qld 4103, Australia.

MATTHEWS, David; *see* Matthews, His Honour William D.

MATTHEWS, David John; composer; *b* 9 March 1943; *s* of Herbert and Elsie Matthews; *m* 1st, 1995, Jean Hasse (marr. diss. 2002); 2nd, 2005, Jenifer Wakelyn. *Educ:* Bancroft's Sch., Woodford; Univ. of Nottingham (BA Classics). Studied composition with Anthony Milner, 1967–69; Asst to Benjamin Britten, 1966–70. Musical Dir, Deal Fest., 1989–2003; Composer in Association, Britten Sinfonia, 1997–2001. Collaborated with Deryck Cooke on performing version of Mahler's Tenth Symphony, 1964–74. Hon. DMus Nottingham, 1997. *Compositions include:* 3 songs for soprano and orchestra, 1968; String Quartet No 1, 1970; Symphony No 1, 1975; String Quartet No 2, 1976; Symphony No 2, 1977; String Quartet No 3, 1977; September Music, for small orch., 1979; Ehmals und Jetzt, 6 songs for soprano and piano, 1979; The Company of Lovers, 5 choral songs, 1980; String Quartet No 4, 1981; Serenade, for chamber orch., 1982; Violin Concerto No 1, 1982; The Golden Kingdom, 9 songs for high voice and piano, 1983; Piano Trio No 1, 1983; Clarinet Quartet, 1984; Symphony No 3, 1985; In the Dark Time, for orch., 1985; Variations for strings, 1986; The Flaying of Marsyas, for oboe and string quartet, 1987; Chaconne, for orch., 1987; Cantiga, for soprano and chamber orch., 1988; The Ship of Death, for chorus, 1989; Piano Sonata, 1989; String Trio, 1989; Romanza, for 'cello and small orch., 1990; The Music of Dawn, for orch., 1990; Symphony No 4, 1990; Capriccio, for 2 horns and strings, 1991; String Quartet No 6, 1991; Oboe Concerto, 1992; The Sleeping Lord, for sop. and ensemble, 1992; A Vision and a Journey, for orch., 1993; Piano Trio No 2, 1993; A Congress of Passions, for voice, oboe and piano, 1994; Vespers, for soli, chorus and orch., 1994; Skies now are Skies, for tenor and string quartet, 1994; A Song and Dance Sketchbook, for piano quartet, 1995; Sinfonia, for orch., 1995; Moments of Vision, for chorus, 1995; Two Pieces for Strings: Little Chaconne, 1996, Fall Dances, 1999; Hurrahing in Harvest, for chorus, 1997; Variations, for piano, 1997; Burnham Wick, for small orch., 1997; Violin Concerto No 2, 1998; String Quartet No 8, 1998; Symphony No 5, 1999; String Quartet No 9, 2000; Aubade, for chamber orch., 2001; String Quartet No 10, 2001; After Sunrise, for chamber orch., 2001; Cello Concerto, 2002; Fifteen Fugues for solo violin, 2002; String Trio No 2, 2003; L'Invitation au voyage, for voice and piano quartet, 2003; Aequam memento, for chorus, 2004; Piano Quintet, 2004; Journeying Songs, for 'cello, 2004; Piano Trio No 3, 2005; Movement of Autumn, for sop. and chamber orch., 2005; Fanfares and Flowers, for symphonic wind band, 2006; Terrible Beauty, for voice and ensemble, 2007; Symphony No 6, 2007; Adonis, for violin and piano, 2007; One Foot in Eden, for tenor and piano quintet, 2008; String Quartet No 11, 2008; Symphony No 7, 2009; Piano Concerto, 2009; Dark Pastoral, for orch., 2009; Actaeon, for narrator and ensemble, 2010; String Quartet No 12, 2010; Horn Quintet, 2010; Toward Sunrise, for orch., 2011; Romanza, for violin and strings, 2012; Fortune's Wheel, for chorus and strings, 2012; A Blackbird Sang, for flute and string trio, 2013; Double Concerto, for violin, viola and strings, 2013; Four Portraits, for piano, 2013; A Vision of the Sea, for orch., 2013; Sonatina, for violin and piano, 2013; Symphony No 8, 2014; To What God shall we chant our songs of battle?, for chorus, 2014; Fifteen Preludes for solo violin, 2014; Nachtgesang, for orch., 2015. *Publications:* Michael Tippett, 1980; Landscape into Sound, 1992; Britten, 2003; David Matthews: essays, tributes and criticism, 2014; contribs to Musical Times, Tempo, TLS. *Recreations:* walking, sketching, birdwatching, wine. *Address:* c/o Faber Music Ltd, Bloomsbury House, 74–77 Great Russell Street, WC1B 3DA.
See also C. Matthews.

MATTHEWS, Prof. David Richard, DPhil; FRCP; Professor of Diabetes Medicine, University of Oxford, since 2002; Fellow and Medical Tutor, Harris Manchester College, Oxford, since 1998; Founder Chairman, Oxford Centre for Diabetes, Endocrinology and Metabolism, 2000–10, now Emeritus; *b* 22 Sept. 1947; *s* of William John Matthews and Ena Matthews (*née* Brading); *m* 1970, Clare Tegla; one *s* two *d*. *Educ:* Chigwell Sch.; Corpus Christi Coll., Oxford (Sen. Schol. 1970; MA, DPhil 1973; BM BCh 1975). FRCP 1994. Oxford University: Nuffield Jun. Res. Fellow, Balliol Coll., 1981–84; Joan and Richard Doll Sen. Res. Fellow, Green Coll., 1984–88; Hon. Consultant Physician, Diabetes Res. Labs, 1988–92; Consultant Physician, Oxford Radcliffe Hosps NHS Trust, 1992–2010; Co-dir, UK Diabetes Res. Network, 2007–14. Sen. Investigator, NIHR, 2009–12. Mem., Assoc. of Physicians. FRSocMed. Methodist lay preacher, 1977–. *Publications:* over 260 peer-reviewed papers in field of diabetes. *Recreations:* science and religion, gardening, playing the piano badly, keeping cheerful. *Address:* Harris Manchester College, Mansfield Road, Oxford OX1 3TD. *E:* david.matthews@ocdem.ox.ac.uk.

MATTHEWS, Douglas, MBE 2013; FRSL; book indexer, since 1957; Librarian, The London Library, 1980–93; *b* 23 Aug. 1927; *s* of Benjamin Matthews and Mary (*née* Pearson); *m* 1968, Sarah Maria Williams (marr. diss. 1991); two *d*. *Educ:* Acklam Hall Sch., Middlesbrough; Durham Univ. (BA). FRSL 1999. Assistant: India Office Library, 1952–62; Kungl. Biblioteket, Stockholm, 1956–57; Librarian, Home Office, 1962–64; Dep. Librarian, London Library, 1965–80. Trustee, Royal Literary Fund, 1993–2014 (Registrar, 2004–14). Mem. Court, Univ. of Sussex, 1983–94. *Address:* 1 Priory Terrace, Mountfield Road, Lewes, Sussex BN7 2UT. *T:* (01273) 475635. *Club:* Garrick.

MATTHEWS, Duncan Henry Rowland; QC 2002; *b* 1 Sept. 1961; *m* 1991, Hon. Emma Elizabeth, *d* of Baron Griffiths, MC, PC; one *s* one *d*. *Educ:* Westminster Sch. (Queen's Schol.); Magdalen Coll., Oxford (MA Modern Hist.); City Univ. (Dip. Law); Inns of Court Sch. of Law. Called to the Bar, Gray's Inn, 1986, Bencher, 2006. Chm., Bar Council Educn and Trng Cttee. *Recreations:* Real tennis, tennis, bridge, theatre, reading, history. *Address:* (chambers) 20 Essex Street, WC2R 3AL. *T:* (020) 7842 1200, *Fax:* (020) 7842 1270. *E:* clerks@20essexst.com. *Clubs:* Garrick, Hurlingham.

MATTHEWS, Elleke Deirdre; *see* Boehmer, E. D.

MATTHEWS, Gillian; QC 2009; **Her Honour Judge Gillian Matthews;** a Circuit Judge, since 2010; Designated Civil Judge for Cleveland and South Durham; *b* Middlesbrough, 22 June 1963; *d* of Ivor Matthews and Jean Matthews (*née* Agar); *m* 1993, John Cowie Elvidge, *qv*; two *d*. *Educ:* Univ. of Hull (LLB). Called to the Bar, Inner Temple, 1985; Recorder, 2005–10. Hon. DLaws Teesside, 2014. *Recreations:* singing in jazz bands, running, tennis, golf. *Address:* Teesside Combined Court Centre, Russell Street, Middlesbrough TS1 2AE.

MATTHEWS, Hugh; *see* Matthews, Hon. Lord.

MATTHEWS, Jeffery Edward, MBE 2004; FCSD; freelance graphic designer and consultant, since 1952; *b* 3 April 1928; *s* of Henry Edward Matthews and Sybil Frances (*née* Cooke); *m* 1953, (Sylvia Lilian) Christine (*née* Hoar) (*d* 1994); one *s* one *d*. *Educ:* Alleyn's; Brixton Sch. of Building (Interior Design; NDD). AIBD 1951; FCSD (FSIAD 1978). Graphic designer with J. Edward Sander, 1949–52; part-time tutor, 1952–55. Lettering and calligraphy assessor for SIAD, 1970–. Designs for Post Office: decimal to pay labels, 1971; fount of numerals for definitive stamps, 1981; stamps: United Nations, 1965; British bridges, 1968; definitives for Scotland, Wales, NI and IOM, 1971; Royal Silver Wedding, 1972; 25th Anniversary of the Coronation, 1978; London, 1980; 80th birthday of the Queen Mother, 1980; Christmas, 1980; Wedding of Prince Charles and Lady Diana Spencer, 1981; Quincentenary of College of Arms, 1984; 60th birthday of the Queen, 1986; Wedding of Prince Andrew and Sarah Ferguson, 1986; Order of the Thistle Tercentenary of Revival, 1987; 150th Anniversary of the Penny Black, 1990; self-adhesive definitives, 1993; The Queen's Beasts, 1998; Jeffery Matthews miniature sheet, 2000; End of War miniature sheet, 2005; Machin definitives 40th Anniversary miniature sheet, 2007; also first-day covers, postmarks, presentation packs, souvenir books and posters; one of three stamp designers featured in PO film, Picture to Post, 1969. Other design work includes: title banner lettering and coat of arms, Sunday Times, 1968; cover design and lettering for official prog., Royal Wedding, 1981; The Royal Mint, commemorative medal, Order of the Thistle, 1987; Millennium commemorative crown piece, 1999; End of War commemorative medal, 2005; stained glass window for Forest Hill Methodist Ch and accompanying film (Light Through Geometry), 2007; official heraldry and symbols, HMSO; hand-drawn lettering, COI; calligraphy, packaging, promotion and bookbinding designs, logotypes, brand images and hand-drawn lettering, for various firms including Unicover Corp., USA, Harrison & Sons Ltd, Metal Box Co., John Dickinson, Reader's Digest Assoc. Ltd, Encyc. Britannica Internat. Ltd, ICI and H. R. Higgins (Coffee-man) Ltd. Work exhibited in A History of Bookplates in Britain, V&A Mus., 1979; contrib. Oral History of the Post Office collection, British Liby, 2001. Citizen and Goldsmith of London (Freedom by Patrimony), 1949. FRSA 1987. Rowland Hill Award for Outstanding Contribution, 2004, Phillips Gold Medal for Stamp Design, 2005, Royal Mail. *Publications:* (contrib.) Designers in Britain, 1964, 1971; (contrib.) 45 Wood-engravers, 1982; (contrib.) Royal Mail Year Book, 1984, 1986, 1987, 1998; (contrib.) Queen Elizabeth II: a Jubilee portrait in stamps, 2002. *Recreations:* furniture restoration, playing the guitar, gardening, DIY.

MATTHEWS, John, CBE 1990; FRAgS; Director, Institute of Engineering Research, Agricultural and Food Research Council (formerly National Institute of Agricultural Engineering), 1984–90; *b* 4 July 1930; *s* of John Frederick Matthews and Catherine Edith Matthews (*née* Terry); *m* 1982 (marr. diss. 1993); two *d*; *m* 2000, June Robinson. *Educ:* Royal Latin School, Buckingham. BSc (Physics) London. CPhys, FInstP; CEng; FIAgrE 1970 (Hon. FIAgrE 1994). Scientist, GEC Res. Labs, 1951–59; National Institute of Agricultural Engineering: joined 1959; Head of Tractor Performance Dept, 1967–73; Head of Tractor and Cultivation Div., 1973–83; Asst Dir, 1983–84; Dir, 1984–90. Vis. Prof., Cranfield Inst. of Technology, 1987. Vice Chm., Ceredigion and Mid-Wales NHS Trust, 2000–03 (Dir, 1992–2003). Mem., Bd of Management, AFRC, 1986–90. Formerly Chm., Technical Cttees, Internat. Standards Orgn and OECD; Pres., Inst. of Agricl Engineers, 1986–88. Pro-Chancellor, Univ. of Luton, 1993–98 (Chm. of Govs, Luton Coll. of Higher Educn, 1989–93). Fellow: Ergonomics Soc.; Academie Georgofili, Italy, 1991. Mem., RAFA; Chm., Teifiside Probus Club, 2002–06. Research Medal, RASE, 1983. Max Eyth Medallion (Germany), 1990; Chevalier de Merite Agricole (France), 1992. *Publications:* (contrib.) Fream's Elements of Agriculture, 1984; (ed) Progress in Agricultural Physics and Engineering, 1991; contribs to other books and jls on agricultural engineering and ergonomics. *Recreations:* gardening, travel. *Address:* Carron, Aberporth, Cardigan, Ceredigion SA43 2DA.

MATTHEWS, Prof. John Burr Lumley, (Jack), FRSE; Director, 1988–96 and Secretary, 1988–99, Scottish Association for Marine Science (formerly Scottish Marine Biological Association) (Hon. Fellow, 1999); *b* 23 April 1935; *s* of Dr John Lumley Matthews and Susan Agnes Matthews; *m* 1962, Jane Rosemary Goldsmith; one *s* two *d*. *Educ:* Warwick Sch.; St John's Coll., Oxford (MA, DPhil). FRSE 1988. Res. Scientist, Oceanographic Lab., Edinburgh, 1961–67; University of Bergen: Lectr, Sen. Lectr, Marine Biology, 1967–78; Prof., Marine Biology, 1978–84; Dep. Dir, Scottish Marine Biol Assoc., 1984–88; Dir, Dunstaffnage Marine Lab., NERC, 1988–94. Vis. Prof., Oceanography, Univ. of British Columbia, 1977–78; Hon. Prof., Biology, Univ. of Stirling, 1984–. Member: Cttee for Scotland, Nature Conservancy Council, 1989–91; SW Regl Bd, Scottish Natural Heritage, 1992–97 (Dep. Chm., 1994–97). Sec., Internat. Assoc. of Biol Oceanography, 1994–2002. Mem., Bd and Acad. Council, Univ. of the Highlands and Islands Ltd, 1993–96. Trustee: Internat. Sch., Bergen, 1980–84; Oban Hospice, 1999–2005; Hebridean Whale & Dolphin Trust, 2000–08 (Chm., 2001–08; Patron, 2009–); Nadair Trust, 2003–07. Founding Fellow, Inst. for Contemp. Scotland, 2000; FRSA 1989. *Publications:* (ed jtly) Freshwater on the Sea, 1976; Aquatic Life Cycle Strategies, 1999; (ed jtly and contrib.) Achievements of the Continuous Plankton Recorder Survey and a Vision for its Future, 2003; contribs to marine sci. jls. *Recreations:* gardening, pethau cymreig. *Address:* The Well, 18 Manse Road, Milnathort, Kinross KY13 9YQ. *T:* (01577) 861066.

MATTHEWS, Prof. John Frederick, DPhil; FRHistS; FSA; FBA 1990; Professor of Roman History, Departments of Classics and History, since 1996, John M. Schiff Professor of Classics and History, 2001, now Emeritus, Yale University (Chair of Classics, 1998–2005 and 2008–09); *b* 15 Feb. 1940; *s* of Jack and Mary Matthews; *m* 1st, 1965, Elaine Jackson (marr. diss. 1995); two *d*; 2nd, 1995, Veronika Grimm. *Educ:* Wyggeston Boys' Sch., Leicester; Queen's Coll., Oxford (MA 1965; DPhil 1970). FRHistS 1986; FSA 1993. Oxford University: Dyson Jun. Res. Fellow in Greek Culture, Balliol Coll., 1965–69; Conington Prize, 1971; Univ. Lectr in Middle and Late Roman Empire, 1969–90; Reader, 1990–92; Prof. of Middle and Later Roman History, 1992–96; Official Fellow, Corpus Christi Coll., 1969–76; Fellow, and Praelector in Ancient History, Queen's College, Oxford, 1976–96. Inst. for Advanced Study, Princeton, 1980–81; British Acad. Reader in Humanities, 1988–90; Fellow, Nat. Humanities Center, N Carolina, 1995–96. Vis. Prof., Sch. of Archaeology and Ancient History, Univ. of Leicester, 2006–. Chm. of Govs, Cheney Sch., Oxford, 1986–91. Hon. DLitt Leicester, 2003. *Publications:* Western Aristocracies and Imperial Court AD 364–425, 1975; (with T. J. Cornell) Atlas of the Roman World, 1982; Political Life and Culture in late Roman Society, 1985; The Roman Empire of Ammianus, 1989; (with Peter Heather) The Goths in the Fourth Century, 1991; Laying Down the Law: a study of the Theodosian Code, 2000; The Journey of Theophanes: travel, business and daily life in the Roman East, 2006 (James Henry Breasted Prize, American Historical Assoc., 2007); Roman Perspectives: studies in the social, political and cultural history of the first to fifth centuries, 2010. *Recreations:* playing the piano, listening to music, suburban gardening. *Address:* 160 McKinley Avenue, New Haven, CT 06515, USA. *T:* (203) 3898137.

MATTHEWS, John Waylett; Chairman, Regus plc, 2002–10; *b* 22 Sept. 1944; *s* of late Percy Victor Matthews and Phyllis Edith Matthews (*née* Waylett); *m* 1972, Lesley Marjorie Halliday; two *s* one *d*. *Educ:* Forest Sch. FCA 1967. Dixon Wilson & Co., 1961–69; N. M. Rothschild & Sons, 1969–71; County Natwest, 1971–88 (Sen. Dir, 1984–88); Dep. Chm./CEO, Beazer plc, 1988–91; CEO, Indosuez Capital, 1991–94; Chm., Crest Nicholson plc, 1996–2007. Non-executive Director: Rotork plc, 1998–2008; SDL plc, 2001–; Diploma plc, 2003–13; Center Parcs plc, 2003–06; Minerva plc, 2007–11; Aurelian Oil and Gas plc, 2010–13. Gov., Forest Sch., 1998– (Chm., 2001–). *Recreations:* golf, shooting, ski-ing. *E:* john.matthews@regus.com. *Clubs:* City of London, Royal Automobile, MCC.

MATTHEWS, Kathryn Ann; Member, Council of Duchy of Lancaster, since 2015; Chairman, Montanaro UK Smaller Companies Investment Trust plc, since 2013 (Director, since 2010); *b* Sheffield, 22 Dec. 1959; *d* of late Gordon Board Matthews and of Ann Clarke Matthews (*née* Micklethwaite, now Graham); *m* 1989, Rupert Wills; two *s* one *d*. *Educ:* Benenden Sch.; Stowe Sch.; Bristol Univ. (BSc Hons Econs). Dir, Baring Asset Mgt, 1995–97; Jt Chief Exec., Santander Global Advrs, 1998–2001; Eur. Partner, Mercer Manager Advrs, 2001–03; Chief Investment Officer, Asia and Japan Equities, Fidelity Internat. (Hong Kong), 2005–09. Non-executive Director: Hermes Fund Managers, 2009–; Rathbone Brothers plc, 2010–; Aperam plc, 2010–. Mem., Bd of Trustees, Nuffield Trust, 2013–. *Recreations:* ski-ing, theatre, opera, family.

MATTHEWS, Lynne Teresa; a District Judge (Magistrates' Courts), since 2011; *b* Stoke-on-Trent, 7 July 1965; *d* of John Sproston and Janet Sproston (now Oakley); *m* 2005, Christopher Austins; two *s* two *d*. *Educ:* Moorside High Sch.; Nottingham Univ. (LLB). Called to the Bar, Inner Temple, 1987; in practice at the Bar, specialising in criminal law, 1987–2011. Gov., Chew Valley Sch., 2007–. *Recreations:* opera, theatre, gardening, hill walking. *Address:* Bristol Magistrates' Court, Marlborough Street, Bristol BS1 3NU.

MATTHEWS, Margaret; *see* Gilmore, M.

MATTHEWS, Paul Bernard, LLD; Consultant Solicitor, Withers LLP, 1996–2015; HM Senior Coroner (formerly HM Coroner), City of London, since 2002; Master of the High Court of Justice, Chancery Division, since 2015 (Deputy Master, 2008–15); a Recorder, since 2010; *b* 21 Aug. 1955; *s* of Leonard William Matthews, KSG and late Noreen Elizabeth Matthews; *m* 1986, Katie Bradford. *Educ:* St Peter's Sch., Bournemouth; UCL (Charlotte Ashby Prize, Andrews Prize, 1976; LLB 1977); St Edmund Hall, Oxford (BCL 1979); Univ. of London (LLD 1995); Inns of Court Sch. of Law (Exam. Prize, Council of Legal Educn, 1981). Called to the Bar, Gray's Inn, 1981; admitted Solicitor: England and Wales, 1987; Ireland, 1997; Solicitor-Advocate (Higher Courts: Civil), 2001. In private practice as barrister, 1982–84; Hopkins & Wood, London: Legal Asst, 1984–87; Partner, 1987–92; Consultant Solicitor, 1992–96; Deputy Coroner: City of London, 1994–2002; Royal Household, 2002–06; (*ad hoc*) N London, 2004–07. Tutor (pt-time), 1978–79, Lectr in Law, 1979–83, UCL; Tutor (pt-time), St Edmund Hall, Oxford, 1979–80. Visiting Lecturer: City Univ., 1981–84; UCL, 1985–86; Inst. de Droit des Affaires, Univ. d'Aix-Marseille, 1991–99; Vis. Sen. Lectr, KCL, 1991–94; Visiting Professor: KCL, 1995–2004 (Hon. Prof., 2004–); Jersey Inst. of Law, 2009–12; Referent, Univ. of Liechtenstein, 2010–15. Mem., Common Core of Eur. Private Law Project, Univ. of Trento, 2001–15. Dep. Chm., Trust Law Cttee, 2005– (Mem., Wkg Parties on Trustees' Exoneration and Trustees' Indemnity, 1997–99); Member: Guernsey Trust Law Review Cttee, 2000–15; Wkg Party on Coroners and Inquests, Law Soc., 2003–15; EC Gp of Experts on property consequences of marriage and on wills and succession in EU, 2005–08; Specialist Advr, H of C Constitutional Affairs Cttee, 2006–08; Coroner Mem., Review Bodies, 2006–. Member: Soc. of Legal Scholars, 1979–; British Inst. of Internat. and Comparative Law, 1989–; Coroners' Soc. of England and Wales, 1994–; Soc. of Trust and Estate Practitioners, 1996–; Internat. Acad. of Estate and Trust Lawyers, 2004–. Member: Selden Soc., 2002–; Stair Soc., 2003–. FRSocMed 2005. FRSA 1994. Liveryman, City of London Solicitors' Co., 1992–. Trustee, David Isaacs Fund, 2002–. Jt Ed., Trust Law Internat., 2005–11 (Asst Ed., 1995–2004); Mem. Editl Bd, Jersey Law Review, 1997–. *Publications:* (ed with K. Bradford) Butterworths Business Landlord and Tenant Handbook, 1996, 6th edn 2012; Jervis on Coroners, 10th edn 1986 to 13th edn 2014 (10th and 11th edns with J. C. Foreman); (with T. Sowden) The Jersey Law of Trusts, 1988, 3rd edn 1994; (with S. C. Nicolle) The Jersey Law of Property, 1991; (with H. M. Malek) Discovery, 1992, 2nd edn as Disclosure, 2000, 4th edn 2012; (with D. Millichap) A Guide to the Leasehold Reform, Housing and Urban Development Act 1993, 1993; (with H. Barraclough) A Practitioner's Guide to the Trusts of Land and Appointment of Trustees Act 1996, 1996; Trusts: migration and change of proper law, 1997; Trust and Estate Disputes, 1999; (ed with D. Hayton and C. Mitchell) Underhill & Hayton's Law of Trusts and Trustees, 17th edn 2006 to 19th edn 2015; Jersey Trusts Law Study Guide, 2009, 4th edn 2012; contrib. Halsbury's Laws of England, 4th edn reissue and 5th edn; articles, notes and reviews in learned jls. *Recreations:* reading, music, local history, cinema, languages. *Address:* Royal Courts of Justice, Rolls Building, 7 Rolls Buildings, Fetter Lane, EC4A 1NL; City of London Coroner's Court, Walbrook Wharf, 78–83 Upper Thames Street, EC4R 3TD. *E:* coroner@cityoflondon.gov.uk; School of Law, King's College, Strand, WC2R 2LS. *E:* paul.matthews@kcl.ac.uk. *Club:* Athenæum.

MATTHEWS, Prof. Paul McMahan, OBE 2008; DPhil, MD; FRCP, FRCPC, FMedSci; Edmond and Lily Safra Professor of Translational Neuroscience and Therapeutics, since 2014, Head, Division of Brain Sciences, since 2012, and Professor of Clinical Neuroscience, since 2006, Imperial College London; *b* Chicago, 30 June 1956; *s* of Charles Vaughn Matthews and Bernice Mary Matthews; *m* 1982, Catherine Comfort; one *s* one *d*. *Educ:* Carbondale Community High Sch., Ill; St Edmund Hall, Oxford (BA Hons 1977; DPhil 1982); Sch. of Medicine, Stanford Univ. (MD 1986). FRCPC 1990; FRCP 2000. Postdoctoral Fellow: Radcliffe Infirmary, Univ. of Oxford, 1982–83; Stanford Univ., 1983–84; intern (Medicine) Stanford Univ. Med. Centre, 1986–87; McGill University, Montreal: Resident in Neurol., 1987–90, Chief Resident, 1989; Clin. Res. Fellow (Neurogenetics), Montreal Neurol Inst., 1989–90; University of Oxford: MRC (Canada) Clinician-Scientist, Genetics Lab., Dept of Biochem., 1990–93; Hon. Sen. Registrar and Actg Clin. Lectr, Dept of Clin. Neurol., 1991–93; Asst Prof. of Neurol., McGill Univ., Montreal, 1993–95; University of Oxford: MRC Clin. Res. Reader, 1995–2000, MRC Clin. Res. Prof., 2000–08, Dept of Neurol.; Dir, Centre for Functional Magnetic Resonance Imaging of the Brain, 1995–2005; Fellow, St Edmund Hall, Oxford, 1997–. GlaxoSmithKline: Vice Pres., Pharmaceuticals, 2005–14; Hd, GSK Clin. Imaging Centre, 2005–11; Hd, Global Imaging Unit, 2011–12. Hon. Prof., Sch. of Med. and Vet. Scis, Univ. of Edinburgh, 2014–; Vis. Prof., Lee Kong Chian Sch. of Medicine, Singapore, 2015–. FMedSci 2014. *Publications:* (ed jtly) Functional Magnetic Resonance Imaging, 2001; (with J. McQuain) The Bard on the Brain, 2003; (ed jtly) The Memory Process, 2010; over 350 academic papers and chapters. *Recreations:* Japanese woodblock print collection, art, reading, walking. *Address:* Imperial College London, Burlington Danes, Hammersmith Hospital, Du Cane Road, W12 0NN. *E:* p.matthews@imperial.ac.uk. *Club:* Athenæum.

MATTHEWS, Prof. Peter Bryan Conrad, FRS 1973; MD, DSc; Professor of Sensorimotor Physiology, 1987–96, now Emeritus and Student of Christ Church, 1958–96, now Emeritus, University of Oxford; *b* 23 Dec. 1928; *s* of Prof. Sir Bryan Matthews, CBE, FRS; *m* 1956, Margaret Rosemary Blears; one *s* one *d*. *Educ:* Marlborough Coll.; King's Coll., Cambridge; Oxford Univ. Clinical School. Oxford University: Univ. Lectr in Physiology, 1961–77; Reader, 1978–86; Tutor, Christ Church, 1958–86. Sir Lionel Whitby Medal, Cambridge Univ., 1959; Robert Bing Prize, Swiss Acad. of Med. Science, 1971. *Publications:* Mammalian Muscle Receptors and their Central Actions, 1972; papers on neurophysiology in various scientific jls. *Address:* The Hurst, 43 Bentley Drive, Oswestry SY11 1TQ. *T:* (01691) 659633.

MATTHEWS, Prof. Peter Hugoe, LittD; FBA 1985; Professor of Linguistics, University of Cambridge, 1980–2001, now Emeritus (Head of Department of Linguistics, 1980–96); Fellow, since 1980, Praelector, 1987–2001, St John's College, Cambridge; *b* 10 March 1934; *s* of John Hugo and Cecily Eileen Emsley Matthews; *m* 1984, Lucienne Marie Jeanne Schleich; one step *s* one step *d*. *Educ:* Montpellier Sch., Paignton; Clifton Coll.; St John's Coll., Cambridge (MA 1960; LittD 1988). Lectr in Linguistics, UCNW, 1961–65 (on leave Indiana Univ., Bloomington, 1963–64); University of Reading: Lectr in Linguistic Science, 1965–69; Reader, 1969–75; Prof., 1975–80 (on leave as Fellow, King's Coll., Cambridge, 1970–71, and as Fellow, Netherlands Inst. of Advanced Study, Wassenaar, 1977–78). Pres., Philological Soc., 1992–96 (Vice-Pres., 1996–). Hon. Mem., Linguistic Soc. of America, 1994–. An Editor, Jl of Linguistics, 1970–79. *Publications:* Inflectional Morphology, 1972; Morphology, 1974, 2nd edn 1991; Generative Grammar and Linguistic Competence, 1979; Syntax, 1981; Grammatical Theory in the United States from Bloomfield to Chomsky, 1993; The Concise Oxford Dictionary of Linguistics, 1997, 3rd edn 2014; A Short History of Structural Linguistics, 2001; Linguistics: a very short introduction, 2003; Syntactic Relations, 2007; The Positions of Adjectives in English, 2014; articles and book chapters. *Recreations:* cycling, gardening. *Address:* 10 Fendon Close, Cambridge CB1 7RU. *T:* (01223) 247553; 22 Rue Nina et Julien Lefevre, 1952 Luxembourg. *T:* 224146.

MATTHEWS, Peter John, OBE 2007; PhD; Chairman, Natural Resources Wales, since 2012; *b* Croydon, 11 Jan. 1943; *s* of Charles George Peter Matthews and Millicent Ethel Matthews; *m* 1965, Elisabeth Mitchell; one *s* one *d*. *Educ:* Harvey Grammar Sch., Folkestone; Medway and Maidstone Coll. of Technol.; Thames Poly.; CNAA (PhD 1973). CChem 1975; MRIC 1967, FRSC 1975; CWEM 1987; CEnv 2006. Anglian Water, 1974–99, latterly Dep. Man. Dir, Anglian Water Internat. Member, Board: EA, 2000–06; Port of London Authy, 2006–12; Mem., Lighthouse Bd, Trinity House, 2012–; Chairman: Sustainable Organic Resources Partnership, 2004–13; NI Utility Regulator, 2006–12; Mem., Royal Commn on Envmtl Pollution, 2008–11. Trustee, 1994–2012, Pres., 1998–99, CIWEM; Mem. Bd, 1982–2011, Pres., 1997–98, Eur. Water Assoc. (Hon. Mem., 2011); Dir, Soc. for Envmt, 2003– (Chm., 2005–06; Hon. Fellow, 2009). Visiting Professor: Imperial Coll. London, 1991–2004; Anglia Ruskin Univ., 2006– (Gov., 1998–2007). William Pitt Fellow, Pembroke Coll., Cambridge, 1999. Freeman, City of London, 1999; Mem., Water Conservators' Co., 1994 (Master, 2012–13). Fellow, Inst. of Water (Fellow, Instn of Water Officers, 1988). Hon. Fellow, Chartered Instn of Wastes Mgt, 2003. Hon. Fellow, Massey Univ., NZ, 1999. Hon. DSc Anglia Ruskin, 1995. William Lockett Award, IWPC, 1967; Res. Prize, Thames Poly., 1973; Carey Premium Award, IWES, 1976; William Hatfield Award, Water Envmt Fedn/CIWEM, 1993; Ehrennadel Award, Abwasser Technische Vereinigung, Germany, 2003; President's Award, CIWEM, 2007; William Dunbar Medal, Eur. Water Assoc., 2010. *Publications:* contribs to books and articles on water sci. and engrg, gen. envmt mgt, innovation, knowledge and wisdom mgt, learning orgns, ethics, gen. orgnl mgt, professional bodies. *Recreations:* sketching and painting, photography, travel, gardening, collecting vintage, antiques (especially model soldiers), writing, publishing. *Address:* Slepey House, 23 Honey Hill, Fenstanton, Cambs PE28 9JP; Natural Resources Wales, Cambria House, 29 Newport Road, Cardiff CF24 0TP. *T:* 0300 065 4333. *E:* peter.matthews@naturalresourceswales.gov.uk.

MATTHEWS, Philip Rodway B.; *see* Bushill-Matthews.

MATTHEWS, Phillip Rowland; His Honour Judge Phillip Matthews; a Circuit Judge, since 2009; *b* Port Talbot, Wales, 18 Nov. 1947; *s* of Abraham and Phyllis Matthews; *m* 1979, Barbara Christine; one *s* two *d*. *Educ:* Marlborough Coll.; St Catharine's Coll., Cambridge (BA 1969). Called to the Bar, Inner Temple, 1974; Asst Recorder, 1990–93, Recorder, 1993–2009; Hd of Chambers, Francis Taylor Bldg, 1991–96. *Recreations:* cricket, hockey, golf, watching Wales Rugby, classical music. *Address:* Isleworth Crown Court, 36 Ridgeway Road, Isleworth, Middx TW7 5LP. *E:* phillipmatthews@blueyonder.co.uk. *Club:* Hawks (Cambridge).

MATTHEWS, Richard Andrew; QC 2010; *b* Maidstone, 5 April 1966; *s* of Stanley Matthews and Shirley Matthews; *m* 1994, Valérie Carnis; one *s* one *d*. *Educ:* Christ's Coll., Finchley; Girton Coll., Cambridge (BA 1987; MA 1991). Called to the Bar, Inner Temple, 1989; in practice as barrister, specialising in criminal and health and safety law. *Publications:* Health and Safety Enforcement: law and practice, 2003, 3rd edn 2010; Blackstone's Guide to the Corporate Manslaughter and Corporate Homicide Act 2007, 2008. *Recreations:* family, reading, opera. *Address:* 2 Bedford Row, WC1R 4BU. *T:* (020) 7440 8888. *E:* rmatthews@2bedfordrow.co.uk.

MATTHEWS, Prof. Roger John, PhD; Professor of Near Eastern Archaeology, University of Reading, since 2011; *b* Cardiff, 21 Aug. 1954; *s* of Bryan and Joyce Matthews; *m* 1988, Dr Wendy Knight. *Educ:* Wilmslow Grammar Sch.; Manchester Univ. (BA 1983); St John's Coll., Cambridge (MPhil 1984; PhD 1990). Director: British Sch. of Archaeol. in Iraq, 1988–95; British Inst. at Ankara, 1995–2001; Lectr, 2001–03, Reader, 2003–07, Prof. of Near Eastern Archaeol., 2007–11, Inst. of Archaeol., UCL. *Publications:* Early Prehistory of Mesopotamia, 2000; Archaeology of Mesopotamia, 2003; At Empires' Edge, 2009; (ed with R. Matthews) Proceedings of the 7th International Congress on the Archaeology of the Ancient Near East, 3 vols, 2012. *Recreations:* gardening, guitar-playing. *Address:* Department of Archaeology, University of Reading, Whiteknights Box 227, Reading, Berks RG6 6AB. *T:* (0118) 378 7564. *E:* r.j.matthews@reading.ac.uk.

MATTHEWS, Her Honour Suzan Patricia, (Mrs A. R. Matthews); QC 1993; a Circuit Judge, 2003–14; *b* 5 Dec. 1947; *y c* of late Sidney Herbert Clark and Susan Hadnett Clark (*née* Mathews); *m* 1970, Anthony Robert Matthews; one *s*. *Educ:* Univ. of Bradford (BSc Hons Business Admin 1972). Called to the Bar, Middle Temple, 1974. Asst Recorder, 1991–95; a Recorder, 1995–2003. Asst Boundary Comr, 1992–2003. Councillor, SE Region, Gas Consumers' Council, 1987–96. Member: Criminal Injuries Compensation Appeals Panel, 1996–2003; Adv. Bd on Family Law, 1997–2002; Criminal Injuries Compensation Bd, 1999–2000; Mental Health Rev. Tribunal (Restricted Patients) Panel, 1999–2003; Dep. Chm., Criminal Injuries Compensation Appeals Panel, 2000–03. Chm., Inquiry into Richard Neale for Sec. of State for Health, 2002–04. Pres., The Valley Trust, 2000–08. *Recreations:* historical research, music, gardening. *Address:* c/o Guildford Crown Court, Bedford Road, Guildford GU1 4ST. *T:* (01483) 468500.

MATTHEWS, Sir Terence (Hedley), Kt 2001; OBE 1994; FREng, FIET; Chairman: Mitel Networks, since 2001; March Networks Corporation, since 2004 (Chief Executive Officer, 2000–04); *b* 6 June 1943. *Educ:* Univ. of Wales, Swansea (BSc). Co-founder, Mitel Corp., 1972–85; Founder, Chm. and CEO, Newbridge Networks Corp., 1986–2000. Founder and Investor, Celtic House Internat., 1994–; founder and Chm., Wesley Clover International Corp.; Chairman: Covendia Corp.; DragonWave; Tundra Semiconductor Corp.; Celtic Manor Resort, Wales. FREng (FEng 1998). *Address:* Mitel Networks, 350 Legget Drive, Kanata, ON K2K 2W7, Canada.

MATTHEWS, Timothy John; Chief Executive, Remploy Ltd, 2008–13; Chair: Coventry University Social Enterprise CIC, since 2013; Pursuing Independent Paths, since 2015; *b* 24 June 1951; *s* of Kenneth James Matthews and Vera Joan Matthews (*née* Fittall); *m* 1984, Sally Vivien Davies; two *s*. *Educ:* Peterhouse, Cambridge (BA Hons History). Admin. Trainee, DHSS, 1974; Private Sec. to Perm. Sec., DHSS, 1978–79; Dist Gen. Administrator, Bloomsbury HA, 1984; Gen. Manager, Middlesex Hosp., 1985; Dist Gen. Manager, Maidstone HA, 1988; Chief Executive: St Thomas' Hosp., 1991; Guy's and St Thomas' Hosp. Trust, 1993–2000; Chief Exec., Highways Agency, 2000–03; Man. Dir, Parsons Brinckerhoff Ltd, 2003–08. Dir, J. Laing plc, 2004–07. Director: S Bank Careers, 1996–2000; Focus Central London TEC, 1997–2001; S Bank Employers' Gp, 1998–2000; Geoffrey Osborne Ltd, 2011–. Trustee, Kent Community Housing Trust, 1991–94. Gov., Univ. of Coventry, 2011–. *Recreations:* opera, long distance walking, watching cricket, collecting wine. *Club:* Surrey CC.

MATTHEWS, Trevor John; Chairman, 1stAvailable Ltd, since 2015; *b* Sydney, 25 March 1952; *s* of Jack and Vinda Latham Matthews; *m* 1999, Michele; two *s*; one *s* from previous marriage. *Educ:* Macquarie Univ., Sydney (MA 1978). FIA 1975. Legal & General Assce Hldgs Australia, 1972–89, Man. Dir, 1989–96; Gen. Manager, Personal Financial Services, National Australia Bank, 1996–98; Exec. Gen. Manager, Canadian Ops, Manulife, 1998–2001; Pres. and CEO, Manulife Japan, 2001–04; Chief Executive: UK Financial Services, Standard Life, 2004–08; Friends Provident, 2008–11; Chief Exec., 2011–12, Chm., 2012–13, Aviva UK; Exec. Dir and Chm., Developed Markets, Aviva plc, 2012–13. Non-executive Director: FNZ Australia Pty Ltd, 2013–; Cover-More Insce, 2013–; Bupa Australia, 2014–; AMP, 2014–. Chm., Financial Skills Partnership (formerly Financial Services Skills Council), 2010–13; Mem., UK Commn for Employment and Skills, 2011–13. *Recreations:* travel, reading, family. *Clubs:* Union, University and Schools of Sydney; Royal Sydney Yacht Squadron.

MATTHEWS, Rt Rev. Victoria; *see* Christchurch, Bishop of.

MATTHEWS, His Honour (William) David; a Circuit Judge, 1992–2008; *b* 19 Nov. 1940; *s* of Edwin Kenneth William Matthews and Bessie Matthews; *m* 1965, Pauline Georgina May Lewis; two *s*. *Educ:* Wycliffe Coll. Admitted Solicitor, 1964; Partner, T. A. Matthews & Co.,

1965–92; a Recorder, 1990–92. Tribunal Judge, First-tier Tribunal (Health, Educn and Social Care Chamber) (formerly Mem., Mental Health Review Tribunal), 2001–11. Chm., W Mercia Criminal Justice Strategy Cttee, 2000–03. Pres., Herefordshire, Breconshire and Radnorshire Incorp. Law Soc., 1988–89. Mem. Council, Three Counties Agricl Soc., 1978–2001. Gov., Wycliffe Coll., 1985–90. *Recreations:* cricket, boats, National Hunt racing.

MATTHIAS, David Huw; QC 2006; FCIArb; *b* Cardiff, 13 Feb. 1954; *s* of David and Joan Matthias; *m* 1981, Sarah Widdows; three *s* one *d.* Lieut, RTR, 1973–76. Called to the Bar, Inner Temple, 1980; in practice as barrister, specialising in commercial litigation and arbitration, judicial review. FCIArb 1999. *Recreations:* supporting Welsh Rugby, sailing, running and walking with my dogs, cooking and eating out, theatre-going. *Address:* Francis Taylor Building, Inner Temple, EC4Y 7BY. *T:* (020) 7353 8415, *Fax:* (020) 7353 7622. *E:* david.matthias@ftb.eu.com.

MATTHIAS, David Richard E.; *see* Everitt-Matthias.

MATTILA, Karita Marjatta; opera singer, soprano; *b* 5 Sept. 1960; *d* of Erkki and Arja Mattila; *m* 1992, Tapio Kuneinen. *Educ:* Sibelius Acad., Helsinki; private studies in London. Début: Finnish Nat. Opera, 1983; Royal Opera House, Covent Garden, 1986; Metropolitan Opera, NY, 1990; has performed in opera houses worldwide; major rôles include: Donna Elvira, Don Giovanni, Vienna State Opera and Metropolitan Opera, 1990; Amelia in Simon Boccanegra, Teatro Colon, 1995, Florence, 2002; title rôle, Manon Lescaut, Tampere Opera, Finland, 1999, Metropolitan Opera, NY, 2008; title rôle, Salome, Paris Opera, 2003, Metropolitan Opera, 2004, 2008; title rôle, Tosca, Metropolitan Opera, 2009, Munich Opera Fest., 2010; created rôle of Emilie in Emilie de Châtelet, Opera Nat. de Lyon, 2010; Marie in Wozzeck, ROH, 2013; title rôle in Ariadne auf Naxos, ROH, 2014; has performed with conductors incl. Abbado, Haitink, Mehta and Solti; has worked with theatre directors incl. Luc Bondy and Lev Dodin; concert and recital performances. Has made numerous recordings. Outstanding Perf. Award, Evening Standard, 1997; François Reichenbech Prize, Académie du Disque Lyrique, 1997; Grammy Awards, 1998, 2004; Musician of Year Award, Musical America, 2005. Hon. RAM 2011. Chevalier des Arts et des Lettres (France), 2003. *Address:* c/o Intermusica Artists' Management Ltd, 36 Graham Street, Crystal Wharf, N1 8GJ.

MATTINGLEY, Brig. Colin Grierson, CBE 1985 (OBE 1980); Clerk to the Grocers' Company, 1988–98; *b* 12 Oct. 1938; *s* of Lt-Col Wallace Grierson Mattingley, KOSB and Jeanette McLaren Mattingley (*née* Service); *m* 1964, Margaretta Eli Kühle; two *d. Educ:* Wellington Coll.; RMA Sandhurst. rcds, ndc, psc. Commnd KOSB, 1958; sc 1971; comd 1st Bn KOSB, 1979–81; Jun. Directing Staff, RCDS, 1981–82; Comdr, 8 Inf. Bde, 1982–84; Dir, Army Service Conditions, 1985–87; retd 1988. Col, KOSB, 1990–95. *Recreations:* sketching, walking, landscape gardening. *Address:* Stockers House, Broad Street, Somerton, Som TA11 7NH. *Clubs:* Army and Navy, St James's.

MATTINGLY, Prof. David John, PhD; FSA; FBA 2003; Professor of Roman Archaeology, University of Leicester, since 1998; *b* 18 May 1958; *s* of Harold B. Mattingly and Erica R. Mattingly (*née* Stuart); *m* 1981, Jennifer Warrell-Bowring; one *s* two *d. Educ:* Univ. of Manchester (BA 1st Cl. Hons History 1980; PhD 1984). British Acad. Postdoctoral Fellow, Inst. of Archaeol., Univ. of Oxford, 1986–89; Asst Prof., Dept of Classical Studies, Univ. of Michigan, 1989–91; University of Leicester: Lectr, 1991–95, Reader, 1995–98, Acting Hd, 1998–99, 2002, 2013–14, Sch. of Archaeol. and Ancient Hist.; Dir of Res., Coll. of Arts, Humanities and Law, 2009–12; Site Dir for Univ. of Leicester, Midlands3Cities PhD consortium, 2013–. British Acad. Res. Reader, 1999–2001. Chm., Soc. for Libyan Studies, 1996–2001. Eur. Res. Council grant assessor, 2009, 2011, 2013; Panel Mem., RAE 2008 (Archaeol. and Classics), REF 2014 (Archaeol.). Lectures: Miriam Balmuth, Tufts Univ., 2006; T. S. Jerome, Rome and Univ. of Michigan, 2013. FSA 1993. MAE 2013. *Publications:* (ed jtly) Town and Country in Roman Tripolitania, 1985; (ed jtly) Libya: research in archaeology, environment, history and society, 1989; (with B. Jones) An Atlas of Roman Britain, 1990, rev. edn 1993; (ed jtly) Leptiminus (Lamta): a Roman port city in Tunisia, Report No 1, 1992; Tripolitania, 1995; (ed jtly) Farming the Desert: the UNESCO Libyan Valleys Archaeological Survey, Vols 1 and 2, 1996 (J. Wiseman Book Award); (ed) Dialogues in Roman Imperialism: power, discourse and discrepant experience in the Roman Empire, 1997; (ed jtly) Life, Death and Entertainment in Ancient Rome, 1999; (ed jtly) Geographical Information Systems and Landscape Archaeology, 1999; (series ed.) Archaeology of Mediterranean Landscapes, 5 vols, 1999–2000; (ed jtly) Economies Beyond Agriculture in the Classical World, 2001; (jtly) Leptiminus (Lamta): a Roman port city in Tunisia: the east baths, cemeteries, kilns, Venus mosaic, site museum and other studies, Report No 2, 2001, the urban survey, Report No 3, 2011; (jtly) The Archaeology of Fazzan, Vol. 1, Synthesis, 2003, Vol. 2, Gazetteer, Pottery and Other Finds, 2007, Vol. 3, Excavations by C. M. Daniels, 2010, Vol. 4, Survey and Excavations at Old Jarma, 2013; (ed jtly) The Libyan Desert: natural resources and cultural heritage, 2006; An Imperial Possession: Britain in the Roman Empire, 2006; (ed jtly) Cambridge Dictionary of Classical Civilization, 2006; (ed jtly) Archaeology and Desertification: the Wadi Faynan landscape survey, southern Jordan, 2007; (ed jtly) From Present to Past through Landscape, 2009; Imperialism, Power and Identity Experiencing the Roman Empire, 2011; 240 articles and papers. *Recreations:* family, book group. *Address:* School of Archaeology and Ancient History, University of Leicester, Leicester LE1 7RH. *T:* (0116) 252 2610, *Fax:* (0116) 252 5005. *E:* djm7@le.ac.uk.

MATTINSON, Deborah Susan; Founder Director, BritainThinks, and World Thinks, since 2010; *b* 17 Sept. 1956; *d* of late R. R. and J. M. Mattinson; *m* 1989, David Arnold Pelly; two *s* one *d. Educ:* Bristol Univ. (LLB). Account Manager, McCann Erickson, 1978–83; Account Dir, Ayer Barker, 1983–85; Co-founder, Gould Mattinson, 1985–90; Founder, GMA Monitor, 1990–92; Jt CEO, Opinion Leader Res., 1992–2007; Jt Chm., Chime Res. and Engagement Div., 2000–10. Comr, EOC, 2002–07. Chair, Young Women's Trust (formerly YWCA), 2012–. Trustee: Green Alliance, 2004–09; Dance Umbrella, 2008–14. *Publications:* Talking to a Brick Wall: how New Labour stopped listening to the voter and why we need a new politics, 2010. *Recreations:* family, reading, walking, theatre.

MATUSSEK, Thomas; Head of Public Affairs, Deutsche Bank AG, since 2011; Managing Director, Alfred Herrhausen Society, since 2013; *b* 18 Sept. 1947; *m* 1975, Ursula Schütten; one *s* two *d. Educ:* Sorbonne, Paris; Univ. of Bonn. Judge's Asst and Asst Lectr, Univ. of Bonn, 1973–75; entered German Foreign Service, 1975; Foreign Office, Bonn, 1975–77; London, 1977–80; Federal Chancellery, European Affairs, Bonn, 1980–83; New Delhi, 1983–86; Lisbon, 1986–88; Foreign Office, Bonn, 1988–92; Chief of Staff and Hd of Foreign Minister's Private Office, Bonn, 1992–94; Dep. Chief of Mission, Washington, 1994–99; Dir Gen., Political Affairs, Foreign Office, 1999–2002; Ambassador to UK, 2002–06; Permanent Representative of Germany to the UN, 2006–09; Ambassador of Germany to India, 2009–11. *Recreations:* mountaineering, ski-ing. *Address:* Deutsche Bank AG, Unter den Linden 13–15, 10117 Berlin, Germany. *Clubs:* Athenæum, Royal Automobile, Naval and Military, Travellers.

MATUTES JUAN, Abel; President, Fiesta Hotel Group S.L., since 2005; Chairman, Grupo de Empresas Matutes; *b* 31 Oct. 1941; *s* of Antonio Matutes and Carmen Juan; *m* Nieves Prats Prats; one *s* three *d. Educ:* University of Barcelona (Law and Economic Sciences). Prof., Barcelona Univ., 1963; Vice-Pres., Employers Organization for Tourism, Ibiza-Formentera, 1964–79; Mayor of Ibiza, 1970–71; Senator, Ibiza and Formentera in Alianza Popular (opposition party), 1977–82; Vice-Pres., Partido Popular (formerly Alianza Popular), 1979– (Pres., Economy Cttee); Mem., EEC, 1986–94; MEP for Spain, 1994–96; Pres., Commn for External Relations and Security, EP, 1994–96; Minister for Foreign Affairs, Spain, 1996–2000. Pres., Nat. Electoral Cttee; Spokesman for Economy and Finance, Grupo Popular in Congress (Parlt). Member: Bd, Banco Santander, 2002–; Adv. Bd, TUI. *Recreation:* tennis. *Address:* POB 416, Ibiza. *Clubs:* Golf Rocalliza (Ibiza); de Campo Tennis (Ibiza).

MAUCERI, John Francis; conductor, educator, writer and producer; Founding Director, Hollywood Bowl Orchestra, since 2006 (Director, 1991–97; Principal Conductor, 1997–2006); *b* 12 Sept. 1945; *s* of Gene B. Mauceri and Mary Elizabeth (*née* Marino); *m* 1968, Betty Ann Weiss; one *s. Educ:* Yale Univ. (BA, MPhil). Music Dir, Yale Symphony Orch., 1968–74; Associate Prof., Yale Univ., 1974–84; Music Director: Washington Opera, 1979–82; Orchestras, Kennedy Center, 1979–91; Amer. Symphony Orch., NYC, 1985–87; Scottish Opera, 1987–93; Teatro Regio, Torino, 1994–98; Pittsburgh Opera, 2001–06; Leonard Bernstein Fest., LSO, 1986; Conductor, Amer. Nat. Tour, Boston Pops Orch., 1987; co-Producer, musical play, On Your Toes, 1983; Musical Supervisor, Song and Dance, Broadway, 1985; Guest Conductor major orchestras, incl. NY Philharmonic, Chicago SO, LSO, ORF, LA Philharmonic, LPO, NY Philharmonic and opera houses, incl. La Scala, Royal Opera House, ENO, Metropolitan, NY, Deutsche Oper, Berlin, San Francisco Opera, Chicago Lyric; Conductor/arranger, Grammy Awards 50th Anniv., 2008; Creative Consultant, Walt Disney Educnl Prodns, 2009. Vis. Prof., Yale Univ., 2001. Dir, Charles Ives Soc., 1986–91 (Mem., 1986–); Mem., Adv. Bd, Amer. Inst. for Verdi Studies, 1986–; Consultant: for Music Theater, Kennedy Center for Performing Arts, Washington, 1982–91; Leonard Bernstein Orgn, 2006–; Trustee, Nat. Inst. for Music Theater, 1986–91. Member Advisory Board: Kurt Weill Edn, 1996–; Leonard Bernstein Center for Learning, 2006–; Film Music Soc., 2006–. Chancellor, Univ. of N Carolina Sch. of the Arts (formerly N Carolina Sch. of the Arts), 2006–13. Fellow, Amer. Acad. Berlin, 1999. Television appearances; numerous recordings (Grammy award for Candide recording, 1987; Edison Klassiek Award, 1991; Deutsche Schallplatten Prize, 1991, 1992, 1993, 1994; ECHO Award for Das Wunder der Heliane, 1994; Cannes Classical Award for Kurt Weill's Der Protagonist, 2003); soundtrack to film Evita, 1996; contrib. to film score DVD commentary, incl. El Cid, The Fall of the Roman Empire, The Adventures of Robin Hood, Bambi, Sunset Blvd, The Sea, Hawk, West Side Story. Antoinette Perry Award, League of NY Theatres and Producers, 1983; Drama Desk Award, 1983; Outer Critics Circle Award, 1983; Arts award, Yale Univ., 1985; Olivier award for Best Musical for Candide, adaptation for Scottish Opera/Old Vic prodn, 1988; Wavenden All Music Award for Conductor of the Year, 1989; Emmy Award, 1994, 1998, 2014; Soc. for Preservation of Film Music Award, 1995; Diapason d'Or, 1997 and 2007; Treasures of LA Award, 2007. Contrib., Huffington Post blogs. *Publications:* (contrib.) Sennets and Tuckets: a Bernstein celebration (ed Ledbetter), 1988; (contrib.) Atti di Convegno Internazionale: Verdi 2001, 2003; Celebrating West Side Story, 2007; various articles for Scottish Opera programmes, newspapers, magazines and jls. *Address:* c/o Columbia Artists Management, 1790 Broadway, New York, NY 10019–1412, USA. *W:* www.johnmauceri.com.

MAUDE, family name of **Viscount Hawarden** and **Baron Maude of Horsham**.

MAUDE OF HORSHAM, Baron *cr* 2015 (Life Peer), of Shipley in the County of West Sussex; **Francis Anthony Aylmer Maude;** PC 1992; Minister of State (Minister for Trade and Investment), Department for Business, Innovation and Skills and Foreign and Commonwealth Office, since 2015; *b* 4 July 1953; *s* of Baron Maude of Stratford-upon-Avon, TD, PC; *m* 1984, Christina Jane, *yr d* of late Peter Hadfield, Shrewsbury; two *s* three *d. Educ:* Abingdon Sch.; Corpus Christi Coll., Cambridge (MA (Hons) History; Avory Studentship; Halse Prize). Called to Bar, Inner Temple, 1977 (scholar; Forster Boulton Prize), Bencher, 2011. Councillor, Westminster CC, 1978–84. MP (C) Warwicks N, 1983–92; contested (C) Warwicks N, 1992; MP (C) Horsham, 1997–2015. PPS to Minister of State for Employment, 1984–85; an Asst Government Whip, 1985–87; Parly Under Sec. of State, DTI, 1987–89; Minister of State, FCO, 1989–90; Financial Sec. to HM Treasury, 1990–92; Shadow Chancellor, 1998–2000; Shadow Foreign Sec., 2000–01; Chm., Conservative Party, 2005–07; Shadow Minister for the Cabinet Office and Shadow Chancellor of the Duchy of Lancaster, 2007–10; Minister for the Cabinet Office and Paymaster Gen., 2010–15. Chm., Govt's Deregulation Task Force, 1994–97. Director: Salomon Brothers, 1992–93; Asda Gp, 1992–99; Man. Dir, 1993–97, Adv. Dir, 1997–98, Morgan Stanley & Co.; Dep. Chm., Benfield Gp, 2003–08; Chairman: Incepta Gp, 2004–06; Mission Marketing Gp, 2006–09. *Recreations:* ski-ing, cricket, reading, music. *Address:* House of Lords, SW1A 0PW.

MAUDSLAY, Richard Henry, CBE 2006; CEng, FREng; FIEE; Chairman, National Nuclear Laboratory, since 2009; *b* 19 Nov. 1946; *s* of Cecil Winton Maudslay and Charity Magdalen (*née* Johnston); *m* 1968, Rosalind Elizabeth Seville; two *d. Educ:* Christ's Hosp., Horsham; Edinburgh Univ. (BSc Electrical Engrg). CEng 1977; FIEE 1985; FREng 1994. Grad. trainee, Scottish Electrical Trng Scheme, 1968–69; Systems Analyst, Parsons Peebles, 1969–71; Systems Manager: Reyrolle Belmos, 1971–72; and Corporate Planner, Parsons Peebles, 1972–74; Prodn Manager, Parsons Peebles Power Transformers, 1974–78; Gen. Manager, Transformadores Parsons Peebles de Mexico, 1978–85; Managing Director: NEI Parsons, 1985–92; Rolls-Royce Industrial Power Gp, 1992–97 (Mem. Bd, Rolls-Royce Plc, 1994–97). Chm., Hardy & Greys Ltd, 1999–2013; Dep. Chm., Port of Blyth, 2004–14; non-executive Director: dominick hunter Gp plc, 2000–05; N G Bailey Gp Ltd, 2001–10. Mem. Bd, One NorthEast (RDA), 1999–2004 (Dep. Chm., 2002–04). Chairman: N E Sci. and Industry Council, 2004–08; Defence Sci. and Technol. Lab., MoD, 2005–08. Mem., Business Chamber, Enterprise Policy Gp, EC, 2007–12. Pres., BEAMA, 1996–98. Chm., British Mexican Soc., 2008–. *Recreations:* music, restoring and building houses, travel in Mexico. *Address:* Priorsgate House, Brinkburn, Longframlington, Northumberland NE65 8HZ.

MAUGER, Anita Joy, (Annie); Director, National Business Units, Chartered Institute of Housing, since 2015; *b* Jersey, 19 March 1963. *Educ:* Exeter Univ. (BA Hons Hist. 1984); Coll. of Librarianship, Wales (Postgrad. DipLib 1985); Leeds Metropolitan Univ. (MBA 2002). MCLIP 2004. Asst Librarian, Beds CC, 1986–87; Branch Librarian, E Lothian Council, 1987–88; various library roles, City of Edinburgh Council, 1988–95; Principal Librarian, Midlothian Council, 1995–99; Hd, Libraries and Heritage, City of York, 2000–03; Chief Exec., Yorks MLA, 2003–08; Acting CEO, Bradford Action for Refugees, 2009–10; management consultant, 2009–10; Chief Exec., CLIP, 2010–15. *Recreations:* reader, singer, swimmer. *Address:* Chartered Institute of Housing, 4th Floor, 125 Princes Street, Edinburgh EH2 4AD.

MAUGHAM, Jolyon Toby Dennis; QC 2015; *b* London, 1 July 1971; *s* of David Henry Benedictus, *qv* and Lynne Joyce Maugham and adopted *s* of Alan Barker; *m* 2007, Claire Elizabeth Prihartini; three *d. Educ:* Wellington High Sch., New Zealand; Durham Univ. (LLB); Katholieke Universiteit Leuven; Birkbeck Coll., Univ. of London (MA). BVC. Called to the Bar, Middle Temple, 1997; in practice as a barrister, 1997–. *Recreations:* windmilling, reading Beckett, tax policy, child rearing. *Address:* Devereux Chambers, 3 Devereux Court, WC2R 3JH. *T:* (020) 7353 7534. *E:* maugham@devchambers.co.uk.

MAUGHAN, Sir Deryck C., Kt 2002; Senior Advisor, Kohlberg Kravis Roberts & Company (Partner, 2005); *b* 20 Dec. 1947; *s* of Renwick Maughan and Muriel Maughan; *m* 1981, Va; one *d. Educ:* King's Coll., London (BA Hons 1969); Stanford Univ. (MS 1978). HM Treasury, 1969–79; Chief Exec., Salomon Bros, 1992–97; Vice Chm., Citigroup Inc., 1998–2004. Vice-Chm., NY Stock Exchange, 1996–2000. Harkness Fellow, 1977–78. Trustee, British Mus., 2013–. *Club:* Metropolitan (New York).

MAULEVERER, (Peter) Bruce; QC 1985; FCIArb 1997; a Recorder, 1985–2004; a Deputy High Court Judge, 1992–2004; *b* 22 Nov. 1946; *s* of late Major Algernon Arthur Mauleverer and Hazel Mary Mauleverer; *m* 1971, Sara (*née* Hudson-Evans); two *s* two *d*. *Educ:* Sherborne School; University College, Univ. of Durham (BA 1968); Birkbeck Coll., Univ. of London (MA Philos. 2007); Univ. of Buckingham (MA Mil. Hist. 2012). Called to the Bar, Inner Temple, 1969, Bencher 1993; Hd of Chambers, 4 Pump Ct, 1992–2000. Vice-Chm., Internat. Law Assoc., 1993–2014 (Hon. Sec.-Gen., 1986–93; Patron, 2014–). Vice-Pres., Internat. Social Sci. Council, UNESCO, 1998–2000. Trustee: UNICEF UK, 2002–08; Tavistock Centre for Couple Relationships, 2005–; Jubilee Sailing Trust, 2006–13 (Chm., 2009–13); MapAction, 2010–13; The Listen Charity, 2014–. *Recreations:* sailing, ski-ing, travel. *Address:* Eliot Vale House, 8 Eliot Vale, Blackheath, SE3 0UW. *T:* (020) 8852 2070. *Clubs:* Garrick, Royal Ocean Racing, Royal Yacht Squadron, Pilgrims, Ocean Cruising.

MAUNDER, Prof. Leonard, OBE 1977; BSc; PhD; ScD; FREng; FIMechE; Professor of Mechanical Engineering, 1967–92, now Emeritus (Professor of Applied Mechanics, 1961), Dean of the Faculty of Applied Science, 1973–78, University of Newcastle upon Tyne; *b* 10 May 1927; *s* of Thomas G. and Elizabeth A. Maunder; *m* 1958, Moira Anne Hudson (*d* 2005); one *s* one *d*. *Educ:* Bishop Gore Grammar Sch., Swansea; University Coll. of Swansea (BSc; Hon. Fellow, 1989); Edinburgh Univ. (PhD); Massachusetts Institute of Technology (ScD). Mem., Univ. Air Sqdn, UC Swansea, 1944–46. Instructor, 1950–53, and Asst Prof., 1953–54, in Dept of Mech. Engrg, MIT; Aeronautical Research Lab., Wright Air Development Center, US Air Force, 1954–56; Lecturer in Post-Graduate Sch. of Applied Dynamics, Edinburgh Univ., 1956–61. Christmas Lectr, Royal Instn, 1983. Member: NRDC, 1976–81; SRC Engrg Bd, 1976–80; Adv. Council on R&D for Fuel and Power, Dept of Energy, 1981–92; British Technology Gp, 1981–92; ACOST, 1987–93; Dep. Chm., Newcastle Hospitals Management Cttee, 1971–73. President: Internat. Fedn Theory of Machines and Mechanisms, 1976–79; Engrg, BAAS, 1980; Vice-Pres., IMechE, 1975–80; Chm., Engrg Educn (formerly Continuum) Exec. Bd, Royal Acad. of Engrg, 1997–2003. Hon. Foreign Mem., Polish Soc. Theoretical and Applied Mechanics, 1984. Hon. Fellow, UC, Swansea, 1989. *Publications:* (with R. N. Arnold) Gyrodynamics and Its Engineering Applications, 1961; Machines in Motion, 1986; numerous papers in the field of applied mechanics. *Address:* 46 Moorside South, Newcastle upon Tyne NE4 9BB.

MAUNSELL, (Caroline) Harriet, OBE 1994; non-executive Director, Pension Insurance Corporation, since 2012; *b* 22 Aug. 1943; *d* of Dr Geoffrey Sharman Dawes and Margaret Joan (*née* Monk); *m* 1986, Michael Brooke Maunsell, *qv*. *Educ:* Somerville Coll., Oxford (MA 1965). Called to the Bar, Middle Temple, 1973; Solicitor, 1978. Courtaulds Ltd, 1965–77; Lovell White & King, subseq. Lovells, 1977–97, Partner, 1980–97. Member: Occupational Pensions Bd, 1987–97 (Dep. Chm., 1992–97; Chm., 1993); Council, Occupational Pensions Adv. Service, 1990–93; OPRA, 1997–2005 (Chm., 2001–05). Co-founder and first Chm., Assoc. of Pension Lawyers, 1984–85 (Mem. cttees, 1984–97). Non-exec. Dir, Serious Fraud Office, 2004–09. Dir, Ambache Chamber Orchestra, 1996–2002; Council Mem., Cheltenham Ladies' Coll., 1998–2001; Member: Somerville Coll. Develt Bd, 2004–10 (Chm., 2005–10); With-Profits Cttee, Aviva (formerly Norwich Union), 2007–11. *Publications:* (with Jane Samsworth) Guide to the Pensions Act 1995, 1995. *Recreations:* reading, gardening, opera, travel. *Address:* 41 Colebrooke Row, N1 8AF.

MAUNSELL, Michael Brooke; Member, Determinations Panel, Pensions Regulator, 2005–12; *b* 29 Jan. 1942; *s* of Captain Terence Augustus Ker Maunsell, RN and Elizabeth (*née* Brooke); *m* 1st, 1965, Susan Pamela Smith (marr. diss. 1986; she *d* 2015); 2nd, 1986, (Caroline) Harriet Dawes (*see* C. H. Maunsell). *Educ:* Monkton Combe Sch.; Gonville and Caius Coll., Cambridge (MA, LLB). Admitted Solicitor, 1967; with Lovell White & King (Solicitors), 1967–88: Partner, 1971–88; Admin. Partner, 1978–83; Partner, 1988–97, Managing Partner, 1993–97, Lovell White Durrant; Sen. Fellow, British Inst. of Internat. and Comparative Law, 1998–2000. Dir, J. M. Jones & Sons (Holdings) Ltd, 1981–91. Chm., Educn and Trng Cttee, City of London Law Soc., 1978–91; Mem., London (No 13) Local, then Area, Legal Aid Cttee, 1971–89. Adminr, City Solicitors Educnl Trust, 2000–08. Trustee: Highgate Cemetery Charity, 1988–95; Kings Corner Project (Islington), 1997–2008; Richard Cloudesley's Charity, 2010– (Vice-Chair, 2013–); Dulwich Almshouse Charity, 2010–; Dulwich Estate, 2012–. Governor: Grey Coat Hosp., Westminster, 1997–2005; Bishopsgate Foundn, 2002–12 (Dep. Chm., 2007–08; Chm., 2008–11). Liveryman, City of London Solicitors' Co., 1973–. *Recreations:* opera, theatre, travel, good living. *Address:* 41 Colebrooke Row, N1 8AF. *T:* (020) 7226 7128.

MAUREY, Catherine Ésöhé, (Kiki), OBE 2013; executive coach-speaker and facilitator; Director, Kiki Maurey Consultancy Ltd, since 2007; *b* Parkstone, Poole, 11 June 1952; *d* of Ernest Danson Omoregie and Barbara Vivienne Omoregie (*née* Blewett). *Educ:* Univ. of Southampton (BSc Jt Hons Politics and Sociol. 1989); Univ. of Warwick Business Sch. (MBA 1991). Child minder and cleaning lady, 1972–81; admin posts commencing with temp. clerk typist, Health and Housing, New Forest DC, 1982–86; Econ. Develt Unit, Southampton CC, 1989–90; various pt-time roles, 1990–92, incl. Sen. Lectr, Univ. of Bournemouth, trng consultant to Exxon Chemicals Ltd; Dir, Business Ops and Mktg, Focus Consultancy Ltd, 1992–95; various sen. freelance contracts, 1995–97; Sen. Prog. Dir (pt-time), Southampton, Common Purpose, 1997–2000; various sen. freelance policy and prog. contracts, 2000–02, incl. Policy Innovation Unit, DfES and DoH; Sen. Fellow (pt-time), OPM, 2002–03; Women's Enterprise Champion and Consultant (pt-time), Small Business Service, DTI, 2003–06; Associate Dir, Strategy (pt-time), Prowess, 2004–05; various sen. freelance mgt and policy contracts, public, not-for-profit and private sectors, 2003–07. Non-executive Director: Southampton and SW Hampshire HA (Chm., Audit Cttee), 1997–2002; Learning and Skills Develt Agency, 2002–04; Mem. Bd, Nat. Ethnic Minority Business Task Force, 2007–09; Chm., S Central Connexions Partnership, 2002–05. *Recreations:* maximising fun in my professional and personal life; lover of books, gardening, birdwatching and my horses; regular contributor and author on 'lessons from life-n-leadership'. *Address:* Holly House, 31 Queens Road, Lyndhurst, Hants SO43 7BR. *T:* 07760 270392. *E:* kiki@kikimaurey.com.

MAURICE, Clare; Founder Partner, Maurice Turnor Gardner LLP, since 2009; *b* Frimley, Surrey, 25 Feb. 1954; *d* of Antony Colin Deans Rankin and Barbara Rankin (*née* Vernon); *m* 1980, Ian Maurice; two *d*. *Educ:* Sherborne Sch. for Girls; Univ. of Birmingham (LLB Hons). Admitted Solicitor, 1978; Partner, Allen & Overy LLP, 1985–2009. Dir, Symm Gp Ltd, 2009–. Chairman: Barts and the London Charity, 2001–09; Safe Lives (formerly Coordinated Action Against Domestic Abuse), 2011–. *Recreations:* theatre, the turf, travel, champagne. *Address:* 33 Norland Square, W11 4PU. *T:* (020) 7221 0962. *E:* clare.maurice@mtgllp.com. *Club:* Reform.

MAURICE, Rt Rev. Peter David; Bishop Suffragan of Taunton, 2006–15; *b* 16 April 1951; *s* of Eric and Pamela Maurice; *m* 1977, Elizabeth Maun; two *s* one *d*. *Educ:* Durham Univ. (BA 1972); Coll. of the Resurrection, Mirfield. Ordained deacon, 1975, priest, 1976; Curate, St Paul, Wandsworth, 1975–79; Team Vicar, Mortlake with E Sheen, 1979–85; Vicar, Holy Trinity, Rotherhithe, 1985–96; RD, Bermondsey, 1991–96; Vicar, All Saints, Tooting, 1996–2003; Archdeacon of Wells, 2003–06. *Recreations:* avid sports fan, enjoying holidays, birdwatching.

MAURICE, Dr Rita Joy; Director of Statistics, Home Office, 1977–89; *b* 10 May 1929; *d* of A. N. Maurice and F. A. Maurice (*née* Dean). *Educ:* East Grinstead County Sch.; University Coll., London. BSc (Econ) 1951; PhD 1958. Asst Lectr, subseq. Lectr in Economic Statistics, University Coll., London, 1951–58; Statistician, Min. of Health, 1959–62; Statistician, subseq. Chief Statistician, Central Statistical Office, 1962–72; Head of Economics and Statistics Div. 6, Depts of Industry, Trade and Prices and Consumer Protection, 1972–77. Member: Council, Royal Statistical Soc., 1978–82; Parole Bd, 1991–94; Retail Prices Index Adv. Cttee, 1992–94. *Publications:* (ed) National Accounts Statistics: sources and methods, 1968; articles in statistical jls. *Address:* 10 Fairfax Place, Swiss Cottage, NW6 4EH.

MAVOR, Prof. John, FREng; FRSE; Vice-President (Physical Science and Engineering), Royal Society of Edinburgh, 2004–07; Principal and Vice-Chancellor, Napier University, 1994–2002; *b* 18 July 1942; *s* of Gordon Hattersley Mavor and Wilhelmina Baillie McAllister; *m* 1968, Susan Christina Colton; two *d*. *Educ:* City Univ., London; London Univ. (BSc, PhD, DSc(Eng)); Edinburgh Univ. (MPhil 2007). FInstP; FIEEE; FIET. AEI Res. Labs, London, 1964–65; Texas Instruments Ltd, Bedford, 1968–70; Emihus Microcomponents, Glenrothes, 1970–71; University of Edinburgh: Lectr, 1971; Reader, 1979; Lothian Chair of Microelectronics, 1980; Head of Dept of Electrical Engrg, 1984–89; Prof. of Electrical Engrg, 1986–94; Dean, 1989–94, and Provost, 1992–94, Faculty of Sci. and Engrg. Hon. DSc: Greenwich, 1998; City, 1998. *Publications:* MOST Integrated Circuit Engineering, 1973; Introduction to MOS LSI Design, 1983; over 150 technical papers in professional electronics jls. *Recreations:* gardening, walking, steam railways. *Address:* 8 Heriot Row, Edinburgh EH3 6HU.

MAVOR, Katherine Lyndsay; Chief Executive, English Heritage, since 2015; *b* London, 30 March 1962; *d* of John Mavor and Jennifer Mavor; *m* 1989, Andrew Williams; two *s*. *Educ:* Westbourne Sch. for Girls, Glasgow; Trinity Coll., Oxford (MA Mod. Langs 1984; Hon. Fellow 2015); Poly of Central London (Postgrad. Dip. Mktg). Graduate trainee, Thomson Books, 1984–85; Product Manager, Macmillan Press, 1985–86; Publicity Manager, Unwin Hyman, 1987–88; Mktg Manager, Kogan Page, 1988–90; Mktg Dir, Regent Schs of English, 1990–94; Man. Dir, Anglo-Polish Interchange, 1994–97; Chief Executive: Language Line, 1998–2004; Project Scotland, 2005–09; Nat. Trust for Scotland, 2009–15. Trustee: Nat. Youth Th., 2012–; Saltire Endowment Trust, 2014–. DUniv Heriot-Watt, 2014. *Recreations:* hill walking, history, classical music, art, cinema, theatre, fiction, visiting heritage sites. *Address:* English Heritage, 1 Waterhouse Square, 138–142 Holborn, EC1N 2ST. *T:* (020) 7973 3000. *E:* Kate.Mavor@english-heritage.org.uk.

MAWBY, Colin (John Beverley); conductor and composer; Conductor, National Irish Chamber Choir, 1996–2001; *b* 9 May 1936; *e s* of Bernard Mawby and Enid Mawby (*née* Vaux); *m* 1987, Beverley Courtney; two *s*. *Educ:* St Swithun's Primary Sch., Portsmouth; Westminster Cathedral Choir Sch.; Royal Coll. of Music. Organist and Choirmaster of Our Lady's Church, Warwick St, W1, 1953; Choirmaster of Plymouth Cath., 1955; Organist and Choirmaster of St Anne's, Vauxhall, 1957; Asst Master of Music, Westminster Cath., 1959; Master of Music, 1961–75; Dir of Music, Sacred Heart, Wimbledon, 1978–81; Choral Dir, Radio Telefis Eireann, 1981–95. Conductor: Westminster Chamber Choir, 1971–78; Westminster Cathedral String Orchestra, 1971–78; New Westminster Chorus, 1972–80; Horniman Singers, 1979–80. Prof. of Harmony, Trinity Coll. of Music, 1975–81. Director (Catholic) Publisher, L. J. Cary & Co., 1963; Vice-Pres., Brit. Fedn of *Pueri Cantores*, 1966; Member: Council, Latin Liturgical Assoc., 1969; Adv. Panel, Royal Sch. of Church Music, 1974; Music Sub-Cttee, Westminster Arts Council, 1974. Hon. FGCM 1988. Broadcaster and recording artist; freelance journalism. KSG 2006. *Publications:* Church music including fifty Masses, anthems, motets, two children's operas and Holy Week music. *Recreation:* wine drinking. *Address:* 29b Lawrence Road, East Ham, E6 1JN. *E:* colinmawby@btinternet.com.

MAWBY, Peter John; lecturer and ornithologist; Headmaster, Lancaster Royal Grammar School, 1983–2001; *b* 17 Aug. 1941; *s* of Norman James Mawby and May Mawby (*née* Huse); *m* 1968, Gillian Fay Moore; one *s* one *d*. *Educ:* Sedbergh Sch.; Queens' Coll., Cambridge (DipEd 1964; MA 1966). Assistant Teacher: Shrewsbury Sch., 1964–65; St John's Sch., Leatherhead, 1965–68; Head of Biology, Edinburgh Acad., 1968–79; Head of Science, Cheltenham Coll., 1979–83. Member: Council, Brathay Exploration Gp, 1989–95; Court, Lancaster Univ., 1989–2001; Headteacher Mentoring Exec. Cttee, Grant-Maintained Schs' Centre, 1992–99. Consultant, Rydal Hall, Dio. of Carlisle, 2003–05. Chm., Lancs br., Cambridge Soc., 2006–; Pres., Old Lancastrian Club, 2006–07. *Publications:* (with M. B. V. Roberts) Biology 11–13, 1983; Biology Questions, 1985; Longman Science 11–14: Biology, 1991, 3rd edn 1996. *Recreation:* playing the 'cello. *Address:* Lowhill, Haverbreaks Road, Lancaster LA1 5BJ.

MAWDSLEY, Harry Paul, OBE 2003; JP; DL; Chairman, Magistrates' Association, 1999–2002; *b* 21 July 1939; *s* of Harry and Jessie Mawdsley; *m* 1970, Anne Horton Rigby (*d* 2014); two *s*. *Educ:* Univ. of Massachusetts (MSc 1969); Univ. of Manchester (MEd 1974). Teacher, Birmingham schs, 1961–66; Lectr, Alsager Trng Coll., Cheshire, 1966–85; Principal Lectr and Hd, Dept of Sport Sci., Crewe and Alsager Coll. of Higher Educn, 1985–88; Hd, Admissions and Mktg, Manchester Metropolitan Univ., 1988–99. Vice-Pres., British Univs Sports Assoc., 2000–. JP South Cheshire, 1975; DL Cheshire 2003. *Recreations:* jogging, gardening, foreign travel. *Club:* Army and Navy.

MAWER, Sir Philip (John Courtney), Kt 2002; Prime Minister's Independent Adviser on Ministerial Interests, 2008–11; *b* 30 July 1947; *s* of Eric Douglas and Thora Constance Mawer; *m* 1972, Mary Ann Moxon; one *s* two *d*. *Educ:* Hull Grammar Sch.; Edinburgh Univ. (MA Hons Politics 1971); DPA (London Univ. External) 1973. Senior Pres., Student Representative Council, 1969–70. Home Office, 1971; Private Sec. to Minister of State, 1974–76; Nuffield and Leverhulme Travelling Fellowship, 1978–79; Sec., Lord Scarman's Inquiry into Brixton disturbances, 1981; Asst Sec., Head of Industrial Relations, Prison Dept, 1984–87; Principal Private Sec. to Home Sec. (Rt Hon. Douglas Hurd), 1987–89; Under-Secretary, Cabinet Office, 1989–90; Secretary-General: Gen. Synod of C of E, 1990–2002; Archbishops' Council, 1999–2002; Parly Comr for Standards, 2002–07. Chm., Professional Regulation Exec. Cttee of Actuarial Profession, 2009–13; Member: Adv. Bd, Notarial Profession in Eng. and Wales, 2013–; Business Cttee, Gen. Council, Univ. of Edinburgh, 2014–. Dir, Ecclesiastical Insce Gp, 1996–2002, 2008–13 (Dep. Chm., 2010–13). Ind. Reviewer, Women Bishops Legislation, 2014–. Mem., All Churches Trust, 1992– (Dir, 2010–; Dep. Chm., 2013; Chm., 2013–); Trustee, Foundn for Church Leadership, 2003–10; Mem. Governing Body, SPCK, 1994–2002. Patron: Church Housing Trust, 1996–; Isabel Hospice, 2004–12. Hon. Lay Canon, St Alban's Cathedral, 2003–12. FRSA 1991–2007. Hon. FIA 2014. Hon. DLitt Hull, 2006; Hon. LLD Hertfordshire, 2007. *Recreation:* family and friends.

MAWHINNEY, family name of **Baron Mawhinney**.

MAWHINNEY, Baron *cr* 2005 (Life Peer), of Peterborough, in the county of Cambridgeshire; **Brian Stanley Mawhinney,** Kt 1997; PC 1994; *b* 26 July 1940; *s* of Frederick Stanley Arnot Mawhinney and Coralie Jean Mawhinney; *m* 1965, Betty Louise Oja; two *s* one *d*. *Educ:* Royal Belfast Academical Instn; Queen's Univ., Belfast (BSc); Univ. of Michigan, USA (MSc); Univ. of London (PhD). Asst Prof. of Radiation Research, Univ. of Iowa, USA, 1968–70; Lectr, subsequently Sen. Lectr, Royal Free Hospital School of Medicine, 1970–84. Mem., MRC, 1980–83. Mem., Gen. Synod of C of E, 1985–90. MP (C): Peterborough, 1979–97; Cambs NW, 1997–2005. PPS to Ministers in HM Treasury, Employment and NI, 1982–86; Under Sec. of State for NI, 1986–90; Minister of State: NI Office, 1990–92; DoH, 1992–94; Sec. of State for Transport, 1994–95; Minister without Portfolio, 1995–97; Opposition front bench spokesman on home affairs, 1997–98. Pres., Cons. Trade Unionists, 1987–90 (Vice-Pres., 1984–87); Chm. of Cons. Party, 1995–97. Mem., AUT. Contested (C) Stockton on Tees, Oct. 1974. Non-exec. dir of cos in England; Chm., Football League,

2003–10 (Hon. Pres., 2010–13); Jt Dep. Chm., England 2018 World Cup Bid, 2008–. Freedom, City of Peterborough, 2008. Hon. LLD QUB, 2008. *Publications:* (jtly) Conflict and Christianity in Northern Ireland, 1976; In the Firing Line, 1999; Just a Simple Belfast Boy (memoir), 2013. *Recreations:* sport, reading. *Address:* House of Lords, SW1A 0PW.

MAWHOOD, Caroline Gillian, (Mrs J. P. Nettel); Assistant Auditor General, National Audit Office, 1996–2009; *b* 17 July 1953; *d* of John Lennox Mawhood and Joan Constance Dick; *m* 1980, Julian Philip Nettel, *qv*; two *s*. *Educ:* Queen Anne's Sch., Caversham; Bristol Univ. (BScSoc Geography). CIPFA. Joined Exchequer and Audit Dept, 1976, Dep. Dir, 1989–92; Office of the Auditor General, Canada, 1992–93; Dir of Corporate Policy, Nat. Audit Office, 1993–95. Pres., CIPFA, 2008–09. Independent Member: Audit Cttee, DECC, 2010–; Debt Mgt Office, 2010–; Corp. of London, 2010–; Audit Progress Cttee, EC, 2011–; Food Standards Agency, 2013–14. Trustee, 2007–, Hon. Treas., 2009–, Breast Cancer Now (formerly Breakthrough Breast Cancer); Trustee, Wimbledon Guild Charity, 2012–. *Publications:* (contrib.) State Audit in the European Union, 1996; (contrib.) Protecting the Public Purse, 2015. *Recreations:* golf, tennis, swimming, bridge. *Clubs:* Roehampton, Wimbledon Park Golf, Royal Thames Yacht.

MAWREY, Richard Brooks; QC 1986; a Recorder of the Crown Court, since 1986; a Deputy High Court Judge, since 1995; *b* 20 Aug. 1942; *s* of Philip Stephen Mawrey and Alice Brooks Mawrey; *m* 1965, Gillian Margaret Butt, *d* of Francis Butt and Alice Margaret Butt; one *d*. *Educ:* Rossall School; Magdalen College, Oxford (BA, 1st class Hons Law, 1963; Eldon Law Scholar, 1964; MA 1967). Albion Richardson Scholar, Gray's Inn, 1964; called to the Bar, Gray's Inn, 1964, Bencher, 2004; Lectr in Law, Magdalen College, Oxford, 1964–65, Trinity College, Oxford, 1965–69. An Election Comr, 1995–. Co-Founder and Trustee, Historic Gardens Foundn, 1995–; Chm., Oxfordshire Gardens Trust, 2002–06. *Publications:* Computers and the Law, 1988; specialist editor: Consumer Credit Legislation, 1983; Butterworths County Court Precedents, 1985; Bullen & Leake & Jacob's Precedents of Pleadings, 13th edn 1990, 17th edn 2012; Butterworths Civil Court Pleadings, 1999–; Butterworths Commercial and Consumer Law Handbook, 2005–; Goode: Consumer Credit Law and Practice, 2006–; Blackstone's Guide to the Consumer Credit Act 2006, 2006; Encyclopaedia of Banking Laws, 2011–. *Recreations:* history, opera, cooking. *Address:* 2 Harcourt Buildings, Temple, EC4Y 9DB. *T:* (020) 7583 9020.

MAWSON, family name of **Baron Mawson**.

MAWSON, Baron *cr* 2007 (Life Peer), of Bromley-by-Bow, in the London Borough of Tower Hamlets; **Andrew Mawson,** OBE 2000; *b* 8 Nov. 1954; *s* of Jack and Mary Mawson; *m* 1975, Susan Barnes; two *s* one *d*. *Educ:* Manchester Univ. (BA 1979; MPhil 1987). Church Minister, United Reformed Church, 1984–. Founder, 1984, Chief Exec., 1984–96, now Pres., Bromley-by-Bow Centre; Co-Founder, 1998, Exec. Dir, 1998–2004, now Pres., Community Action Network. Founder Chm., 1996, now Pres., Stanton Guildhouse, Glos. Founder, 2006, Chm., 2012–, Water City CIC (formerly Water City Gp). Dir, Andrew Mawson Partnerships, St Paul's Way Transformation Project, 2007–; non-exec. Dir, Olympic Park Legacy Co., later London Legacy Develt Corp., 2009–12. Trustee, Legacy List, 2010–. Chm., SS Robin Trust. Chm., Blackheath Conservatoire, 2012–15. *Publications:* (jtly) Church and the City, 1975; (jtly) People before Structures, 1999; The Social Entrepreneur, 2008; The St Paul's Way Transformation Project: building the road as we walk it, 2012. *Recreation:* music. *Address:* House of Lords, SW1A 0PW. *T:* (020) 7620 6000. *E:* andrew@amawsonpartnerships.com.

MAXTON, family name of **Baron Maxton**.

MAXTON, Baron *cr* 2004 (Life Peer), of Blackwaterfoot in Ayrshire and Arran; **John Alston Maxton;** *b* Oxford, 5 May 1936; *s* of late John Maxton, agr. economist, and Jenny Maxton; *m* 1970, Christine Maxton; three *s*. *Educ:* Lord Williams' Grammar Sch., Thame; Oxford Univ. Lectr in Social Studies, Hamilton Coll. Chm., Assoc. of Lectrs in Colls of Educn, Scotland; Member: Educnl Inst. of Scotland; Socialist Educnl Assoc.; MSF. Joined Lab. Party, 1970. MP (Lab) Glasgow, Cathcart, 1979–2001. Opposition spokesman on health, local govt, and housing in Scotland, 1985–87, on Scotland, 1987–92; Scottish and Treasury Whip, 1984–85. Member: Scottish Select Cttee, 1981–83; Public Accounts Cttee, 1983–84; Culture, Media and Sport (formerly Nat. Heritage) Select Cttee, 1992–2001; Speaker's Panel of Chairmen, 1994–2001. *Recreations:* family, listening to jazz, gym and fitness, new technology.

MAXTON, Julie Katharine, PhD; Executive Director, Royal Society, since 2011; Visiting Fellow, University College, Oxford, since 2011; *b* Edinburgh, 31 Aug. 1955; *d* of Col Kenneth Maxton and Katriona Justine Maxton; *m* 1984, Major James Donald Carson, MBE, FTCL (*d* 2008); one *s*. *Educ:* St George's Sch., Edinburgh; University Coll. London (LLB Hons 1976); Univ. of Canterbury (LLM Hons); MA Oxon; Univ. of Auckland (PhD 1990). Called to the Bar, Middle Temple, 1978, Bencher, 2012; admitted to Bar of NZ, 1982; in practice as a barrister, 1982–2006, Mem., 4 New Sq., 2012–; Lectr in Law, Univ. of Canterbury, 1978–85; University of Auckland: Sen. Lectr in Law, 1986–91; Associate Prof. of Law, 1992; Prof. of Law, 1993–2006; Dean, Faculty of Law, 2001–06; Dep. Vice Chancellor, 2003–04; Registrar, 2006–11, Mem., Law Faculty, 2006–11, Univ. of Oxford; Fellow, University Coll., Oxford, 2006–11. Mem. Bd, Engrg UK, 2012–. Mem., Internat. Adv. Panel, National Univ. of Singapore, 2008–. Gov., Haberdashers' Aske's Sch., 2012–. *Publications:* articles in legal jls concerned with equity, trusts, commercial law, damages. *Recreations:* reading, music, sport. *Address:* Royal Society, 6–9 Carlton House Terrace, SW1Y 5AG. *T:* (020) 7451 2500, *Fax:* (020) 7930 2170. *E:* julie.maxton@royalsociety.org.

MAXWELL, family name of **Barons de Ros** and **Farnham**.

MAXWELL, Prof. David James, DPhil; Dixie Professor of Ecclesiastical History, University of Cambridge, since 2011; Fellow, Emmanuel College, Cambridge, since 2011; *b* Bushey, Herts, 8 Dec. 1963; *s* of John Maxwell and Teresa Maxwell (*née* Lucas); *m* 2002, Mandy Ridgway; two *s*. *Educ:* Watford Grammar Sch. for Boys; Univ. of Manchester (BA Hist. 1986); St Antony's Coll., Oxford (DPhil Hist. 1994). Hd of Hist. and House Master, Emmanuel Secondary Sch., Zimbabwe, 1987–90; Res. Fellow, Dept of Social Anthropol., Univ. of Manchester, 1994; University of Keele: Lectr in Internat. Hist., 1994–2001; Sen. Lectr in Hist., 2001–07; Prof. of African Hist., 2007–11. Ed., Jl of Religion in Africa, 1998–2005. Vice-Chm., Britain-Zimbabwe Soc., 1997–2000; Pres., African Studies Assoc. UK, 2014– (Vice-Pres., 2012–14). Trustee: Domboshawa Interdenominational Theol Coll., Harare, 2000–12; Southern African Book Develt Educn Trust, UK, 2002–08. *Publications:* Christians and Chiefs in Zimbabwe: a social history of the Hwesa people *c* 1870s–1990s, 1999; (ed with Ingrid Lawrie) Christianity and the African Imagination: essays in honour of Adrian Hastings, 2002; African Gifts of the Spirit: Pentecostalism and the rise of a Zimbabwean transnational religious movement, 2006; (ed with Patrick Harries) The Spiritual in the Secular: missionaries and knowledge about Africa, 2012. *Recreations:* walking, gardening, theatre, cinema, photography, family. *Address:* Emmanuel College, St Andrew's Street, Cambridge CB2 3AP. *T:* (01223) 334200.

MAXWELL, Dominic; *see* Maxwell-Scott, Sir D. J.

MAXWELL, Ian Robert Charles; Publisher, 1995–98, Editorial Consultant, since 1998, Maximov Publications; *b* 15 June 1956; *s* of late (Ian) Robert Maxwell, MC; *m* 1st, 1991, Laura Plumb (marr. diss. 1998); 2nd, 1999, Tara Dudley Smith (marr. diss. 2010); one *s*. *Educ:* Marlborough; Balliol Coll., Oxford (MA). Pergamon Press, 1978–83; Prince's Charitable Trust, 1983–84; British Printing & Communication Corporation, later Maxwell Communication Corporation, 1985–91 (Jt Man. Dir, 1988–91); Chm., Agence Centrale de Presse, 1986–89; Chairman and Publisher: Mirror Gp Newspapers, 1991 (Dir, 1987–91); The European Newspaper, 1991 (Dir, 1990–91). Mem., Nat. Theatre Develt Council, 1986–91; Pres., Club d'Investissement Media, 1988–91. Vice Chm., Derby County Football Club, 1987–91 (Chm., 1984–87). *Recreations:* music, ski-ing, water ski-ing, football.
See also K. F. H. Maxwell.

MAXWELL, Prof. James Rankin, PhD, DSc; FRS 1997; Senior Research Fellow, University of Bristol, 1999–2010 (Professor of Organic Geochemistry, 1990–99, now Emeritus); *b* 20 April 1941; *s* of John J. and Helen M. T. Maxwell; *m* 1964, Joy Millar Hunter; one *d* (one *s* decd). *Educ:* Univ. of Glasgow (BSc; PhD 1967); DSc Bristol 1982. Research Asst, Univ. of Glasgow, 1967; Postdoctoral Res. Chemist, Univ. of Calif, Berkeley, 1967–68; University of Bristol: Postdoctoral Fellow, 1968–69; Res. Associate, 1969–72; Lectr, 1972–78; Reader, 1978–90; Hd, Envmtl and Analytical Chem. Section, 1991–99. Geochemistry Fellow, Geochem. Soc., USA and European Assoc. Geochem., 1996. J. Clarence Karcher Medal, Univ. of Oklahoma, 1979; Treibs Medal, Geochem. Soc., USA, 1989. *Publications:* numerous papers in learned jls. *Recreations:* walking, gardening, cooking. *Address:* School of Chemistry, University of Bristol, Cantock's Close, Bristol BS8 1TS. *T:* (0117) 954 6339.

MAXWELL, His Honour John Frederick Michael; a Circuit Judge, 2005–13; *b* 20 May 1943; *s* of Frederic Michael and Mabel Doreen Maxwell; *m* 1986, Jayne Elizabeth Hunter; one *s* one *d*, and two step *s*. *Educ:* Dover Coll.; New Coll., Oxford (MA Juris.). Called to the Bar, Inner Temple, 1965; a Dep. Stipendiary Magistrate, 1978–90; Asst Recorder, 1990–95; a Recorder, 1995–2005. Standing Counsel to: HM Customs and Excise, 1995–2005; Revenue and Customs Prosecutions Office, 2005. Chm., Birmingham Karma Ling, 1991–; Trustee: Rokpa Trust, 1996–; Tara Trust, 2008–; Solihull SO. Mem., RYA. *Recreations:* music, yachting. *E:* john@maxwell100.plus.com. *Club:* Old Gaffers Assoc.

MAXWELL, John Hunter; Chairman, DX Services plc, 2004–06; *b* 25 Sept. 1944; *s* of late John Hunter Maxwell, OBE and of Susan Elizabeth Una Smith; *m* 1967, Janet Margaret Frew (marr. diss. 2010); three *s*. *Educ:* Melville Coll., Edinburgh; Dumfries Acad.; Edinburgh Univ. CA 1967. T. Hunter Thompson & Co., CA, Edinburgh, 1962–67; Regl Dir, Far East, Rank Xerox Ltd, 1967–83; Gp Financial Controller, Grand Metropolitan plc, 1983–86; Chief Executive: Provincial Gp, 1986–92; BPB Industries plc, 1992–93; non-exec. Dir, Alliance & Leicester, 1993–94; Corporate Develt Dir, Prudential Corp. plc, 1994–96; Dir Gen., AA, 1996–2000; Chm., Wellington Underwriting plc, 2000–03. Non-executive Director: RAC, 2000–10; Provident Financial, 2000–09; The Big Food Gp plc, 2001–05; Parity Gp plc, 2002–05; Royal & Sun Alliance plc, 2003–13; Homeserve plc, 2004–09; MSA, 2007–10; First Assist Ltd, 2009–. Chm., IAM, 2002–07 (Mem. Council, 1997–2007). CCMI (CIMgt 1992); FIMI 1997; FRSA 1997. Trustee, RAF Benevolent Fund, 2004–07. Gov., Royal Ballet Sch., 2000–06. Hon. Treas., Cruising Assoc., 1973–74. Freeman, City of London, 1998; Liveryman, Coachmakers' and Coach Harness Makers' Co., 1998–. *Recreations:* sailing, classic cars, travel, arts. *Address:* The Loft, The Street, Itchenor, W Sussex PO20 7AH. *Clubs:* Royal Automobile (Mem. Cttee, 2004–10), Royal Thames Yacht (Mem. Cttee, 2010–).

MAXWELL, Kevin Francis Herbert; Chairman, Avenue Partners Ltd, since 2009; *b* 20 Feb. 1959; *s* of late (Ian) Robert Maxwell, MC; *m* 1984, Pandora Deborah Karen Warnford-Davis (separated 2005); two *s* five *d*. *Educ:* Marlborough Coll.; Balliol Coll., Oxford (MA Hons). Chairman: Maxwell Communication Corporation, 1991 (Dir, 1986–91); Macmillan Inc., 1991 (Dir, 1988–91); Telemonde Inc., 1999–2002; Corunna Gp, 2007–09; Dir, Guinness Mahon Hldgs, 1989–92. Chm., Oxford United FC, 1987–92. Trustee, New Sch. for Social Research, NYC, 1989–92. *Recreations:* books, cooking, football.
See also I. R. C. Maxwell.

MAXWELL, Sir Michael (Eustace George), 9th Bt *cr* 1681 (NS), of Monreith, Wigtownshire; MRICS; *b* 28 Aug. 1943; *s* of Major Eustace Maxwell (*d* 1971) and late Dorothy Vivien, *d* of Captain George Bellville; *S* uncle, 1987. *Educ:* Eton; College of Estate Management. *Recreations:* microlights, curling, tennis, ski-ing. *Address:* 56 Queensmill Road, SW6 6JS. *Clubs:* Stranraer Rugby; Port William Tennis.

MAXWELL, Sir Nigel Mellor H.; *see* Heron-Maxwell.

MAXWELL, Prof. Patrick Henry, DPhil; FRCP, FMedSci; Regius Professor of Physic, University of Cambridge, since 2012; Fellow, Trinity College, Cambridge, since 2012; *b* 12 March 1962; *s* of Robert James Maxwell, *qv*; *m* 1989, Margaret Jane Hughes; two *s* one *d*. *Educ:* Eton (King's Schol.); Corpus Christi Coll., Oxford (BA Physiol Scis 1983; DPhil 1994; Hon. Fellow 2012); St Thomas's Hosp. Med. Sch., London (MB BS Distn 1986). MRCP 1989, FRCP 1995. House Officer, St Thomas' Hosp. and Worthing Hosp., 1986–87; Sen. House Officer, Hammersmith Hosp. Renal Unit, St Thomas' Hosp., Nat. Heart Hosp. and Nat. Hosp. for Neurology and Neurosurgery, 1987–89; Registrar, Lewisham Hosp. and Guy's Hosp., 1989–91; University of Oxford: MRC Trng Fellow, Inst. of Molecular Medicine, 1991–94; Clinical Lectr, 1994–96; Univ. Lectr, and Hon. Consultant Nephrologist, 1996–2000; Reader in Nephrology, 2000–02; Prof. of Nephrology, Imperial Coll., London, 2002–08; Hon. Consultant Physician, Imperial Coll. Healthcare NHS Trust (formerly Hammersmith Hosps), 2002–08; University College London: Prof. of Medicine, 2008–12; Hd, Div. of Medicine, 2008–11; Vice Dean for Experimental Medicine, 2009–11; Dean, Faculty of Med. Scis, 2011–12; Hon. Consultant Physician, Royal Free Hosp., 2008–12. Registrar, Acad. of Medical Scis, 2006–12. Sen. Investigator, NIHR, 2007–12; Exec., Francis Crick Inst., 2011–12. Director: Global Medical Excellence Cluster Ltd, 2009–; Imanova Ltd, 2011–12; Exec. Dir, Cambridge Univ. Health Partners, 2012–; non-exec. Dir, Cambridge Univ. Hosps NHS Foundn Trust, 2012–. Chairman: Physiological Scis Funding Cttee, Wellcome Trust, 2008–11; Scientific Advisory Board: Rosetrees Trust, 2010–; Lister Inst., 2013–; Chair, Molecular and Cellular Medical Bd, MRC, 2014–. Member: Renal Assoc.; Assoc. of Physicians of GB and Ire. Fellow, Faculty of Medicine, Imperial Coll. London, 2013–. FMedSci 2005. Mem., Editl Adv. Bd, BMA, 2013–. *Publications:* Medical Masterclass: nephrology, 2001, 2nd edn 2008; articles in learned jls on erythropoietin, HIF-1 and oxygen sensing. *Recreations:* sailing, losing to my children at chess. *Address:* School of Clinical Medicine, University of Cambridge, Box 111, Addenbrooke's Hospital, Hills Road, Cambridge CB2 0SP. *T:* (01223) 336738. *E:* regius@medschl.cam.ac.uk.

MAXWELL, Richard; QC 1988; a Recorder, since 1992; a Deputy High Court Judge, since 1998; *b* 21 Dec. 1943; *s* of Thomas and Kathleen Marjorie Maxwell; *m* 1966, Judith Ann Maxwell; two *s* two *d*. *Educ:* Nottingham High Sch.; Hertford College, Oxford (MA). Lectr in Law, 1966–68; called to the Bar, Inner Temple, 1968; in practice as a barrister, 1968–2009; Asst Recorder, 1989–92. *Recreations:* salt and freshwater fly fishing, golf, wine, single malt whisky, learning modern Greek, bowls. *Clubs:* Nottingham Squash Rackets; Darley Dale Flyfishers' (Chm., 2007–); Beeston Fields Golf; Queen Anne's Bowling Green; Peak Forest Angling, Derwent Fly Fishing.

MAXWELL, Robert James, CVO 1998; CBE 1993; FRCPE; Chairman, The Gloucestershire Partnership NHS Trust, 2002–08; *b* 26 June 1934; *s* of Dr George B. Maxwell, MC and Cathleen Maxwell; *m* 1960, Jane FitzGibbon; three *s* two *d*. *Educ:* Leighton Park Sch.; New Coll., Oxford (BA 1st Cl. Hons, MA; Newdigate Prize for Poetry); Univ. of Pennsylvania (MA); LSE (PhD); Univ. of Tromsø (Dip. in Health Econs). CGMA 2012. FCMA; FRCPE 1997; 2nd Lieut, Cameronians (Scottish Rifles), 1952–54. Union Corp., 1958–66; McKinsey & Co., 1966–75; Administrator to Special Trustees, St Thomas' Hosp.,

1975–80; Sec. and Chief Exec., The King's Fund, 1980–97. Pres., European Healthcare Management Assoc., 1985–87; Pres., Open Section, RSocMed, 1986–88; Chm. Council, Foundn for Integrated Medicine, 1998–2001. Chm., Court, LSHTM, 1985–95; Mem. Council, London Univ., 2004–08; Governor: NISW, 1981–98; UMDS, 1989–98; Director: Guy's and Lewisham Trust, 1990–93; Lewisham NHS Trust, 1993–98; Severn NHS Trust, 1998–2002; Mem., Bd of Management, Med. Defence Union, 1990–98 (Hon. Fellow, 1998). Chm., Leighton Park Sch., 1981–2001. FRSA 1995. Hon. FRCGP 1994; Hon. MRCP 1987; Hon. Mem., Assoc. of Anaesthetists, 1990. Trustee: Joseph Rowntree Foundn, 1994–2009; Thrive (formerly Horticultural Therapy), 1998–2009; Pharmacy Practice Res. Trust, 1999–2005. JP Inner London Youth and Family Courts (Chm.), 1971–98; JP S Glos, 1999–2004. DUniv Brunel, 1993; Hon. DLitt West of England, 1993. *Publications:* Health Care: the growing dilemma, 1974; Health and Wealth, 1981; Reshaping the National Health Service, 1988; Spotlight on the Cities, 1989; An Unplayable Hand?: BSE, CJD and British Government, 1997; (with B. Wannell) Persian Poems, 2012. *Recreations:* poetry, walking, stained glass, not quite catching up with correspondence. *Address:* Pitt Court Manor, North Nibley, Dursley, Glos GL11 6EL. *Clubs:* Brooks's, Royal Society of Medicine.

See also P. H. Maxwell.

MAXWELL, Simon Jeffrey, CBE 2007; Senior Research Associate, Overseas Development Institute, since 2009 (Director, 1997–2009); Director, Simon Maxwell Ltd, since 2010; Executive Chairman, Climate and Development Knowledge Network, since 2010; *b* 1 May 1948; *s* of Frederick Norman Maxwell and Ruth Maxwell (*née* Salinsky); *m* 1973, Catherine Elizabeth Pelly; three *s*. *Educ:* Lycée d'Anvers; Solihull Sch.; St Edmund Hall, Oxford (BA PPE 1970); Univ. of Sussex (MA Develt Econs 1973). United Nations Development Programme: Jun. Professional Officer, Nairobi, 1970–72; Asst Res. Rep., New Delhi, 1973–77; Agricl Economist, ODA, Santa Cruz, Bolivia, 1978–81; Fellow, Inst. of Develt Studies, Univ. of Sussex, 1981–97. World Economic Forum: Dep. Chm., Global Agenda Council on Humanitarian Affairs, 2010– (Chm., 2008–10); Mem., Global Agenda Council on Poverty and Econ. Develt, 2011–. Mem., Scientific Adv. Bd, EU Develt Corp., 2012–. Mem., Adv. Gp, IPPR, 2009–; Specialist Advr, H of C Select Cttee on Internat. Develt, 2010–. Member: Oxfam Field Cttee for Latin America, 1981–84; Ind. Gp on British Aid, 1982–; UN Adv. Gp on Nutrition, 1990–96; Program Adv. Panel, Foundn for Develt Co-operation, 1997–2009; Bd, Fair Trade Foundn, 2008–; Bd, Fundación para las Relaciones Internacionales y el Diálogo Exterior, 2011–. External Examiner, Wye Coll., Univ. of London, 1995–98; Gov., Inst. of Develt Studies, 1996–97. Mem. Council, Develt Studies Assoc. of UK and Ireland, 1998–2005 (Pres., 2001–05). Trustee, Action for Conservation through Tourism, 1998–2004; Patron, One World Media (formerly Broadcasting Trust), 1998–; Mem., Adv. Cttee, Charter 99, 1999–2002. Fellow, World Econ. Forum, 2003–; Hon. Fellow, Foreign Policy Assoc., NY, 2003–. *Publications:* numerous pubns on poverty, food security, aid and agricl develt. *Address:* 20 West Drive, Brighton, E Sussex BN2 0GD. *W:* www.simonmaxwell.eu.

MAXWELL, Stewart; *see* Maxwell, W. S.

MAXWELL, William, PhD; CPsychol; Chief Executive, Education Scotland, since 2012 (Interim Chief Executive, 2011); *b* Edinburgh, 14 Nov. 1957; *s* of Joseph Maxwell and Christine Maxwell; *m* Margaret; two *d*. *Educ:* High Sch. of Dundee; University Coll., Oxford (BA); Univ. of Glasgow (MAppSci); Univ. of Edinburgh (PhD). Area Principal Psychologist, Grampian Council, 1992–94; HM Inspectorate of Education: Inspector of Schs, 1994–2002; Chief Inspector of Educn, 2002–06; Hd, Educn, Information and Analytical Services, Scottish Exec., subseq. Scottish Govt, 2006–08; Chief Inspector of Educn and Trng Wales, HM Inspectorate for Educn and Trng in Wales, 2008–10; Sen. Chief Inspector of Educn, HM Inspectorate of Educn, 2010–11. FRSA. *Recreations:* climbing and mountaineering, cycling, the arts. *Address:* Education Scotland, Denholm House, Almondvale Business Park, Almondvale Way, Livingston EH54 6GA. *T:* (01506) 600366.

MAXWELL, (William) Stewart; Member (SNP) Scotland West, Scottish Parliament, since 2003; *b* 24 Dec. 1963; *s* of William Maxwell and Margaret Maxwell; *m* 1995, Mary Stevenson; one *d*. *Educ:* Glasgow Coll. of Technol. (BA Hons Soc. Sci.). Wilmax Ltd (family business), 1986–88, 1991–93; Admin. Officer, Scottish Training Foundn, 1988–91; Strathclyde Fire Brigade: Industrial Trng Manager, 1993–94; Sen. Admin. Officer, 1994–2001; Mgt Inf. System Project Manager, 2001–03. Scottish Parliament: Shadow Dep. Minister for Health, 2004–06; Shadow Minister for Sport, Culture and Media, 2006–07; Minister for Communities and Sport, 2007–09; Dep. Convener, Justice 1 Cttee, 2003–04; Member: Subordinate Legislation Cttee, 2003–07; Justice 2 Cttee, 2004–06; Enterprise and Culture Cttee, 2006–07; Justice Cttee, 2009–11; EU Cttee of the Regions, 2009–; Referendum (Scotland) Bill Cttee, 2013–14; Devolution (Further Powers) Cttee, 2014–; Convener, Educn and Culture Cttee, 2011–; Vice Pres., Eur. Alliance Gp, 2012–. Vice Convener, Publicity, 2003–04, Mem., NEC, 2003–04, SNP. Hon. Vice-Pres., Royal Envmtl Health Inst. of Scot., 2006–. *Recreations:* cinema, theatre, Rugby (debenture holder at Murrayfield), swimming, golf, reading, eating out, photography, scuba diving. *Address:* Scottish Parliament, Edinburgh EH99 1SP. *T:* (0131) 348 5000. *E:* Stewart.Maxwell.msp@scottish.parliament.uk.

MAXWELL DAVIES, Sir Peter, CH 2014; Kt 1987; CBE 1981; composer and conductor; Master of the Queen's Music, 2004–14; *b* 8 Sept. 1934; *s* of Thomas and Hilda Davies. *Educ:* Leigh Grammar Sch.; Manchester Univ. (MusB (Hons) 1956); Royal Manchester Coll. of Music. FRNCM 1978. Studied with Goffredo Petrassi in Rome (schol. 1957); Harkness Fellow, Grad. Music Sch., Princetown Univ., NJ, 1962–64. Dir of Music, Cirencester Grammar Sch., 1959–62; lecture tours in Europe, Australia, NZ, USA, Canada and Brazil; Visiting Composer, Adelaide Univ., 1966; Prof. of Composition, RNCM, 1975–80; Vis. Fromm Prof. of Composition, Harvard Univ., 1985. Founder and Co-Dir, with Harrison Birtwistle, of Pierrot Players, 1967–71; Founder and Artistic Director: The Fires of London, 1971–87; St Magnus Fest., Orkney Is, 1977–86 (Pres., 1986–); Artistic Dir, Dartington Hall Summer Sch. of Music, 1979–84; Associate Composer/Conductor: Scottish Chamber Orch., 1985–94 (Composer Laureate, 1994–); RPO, 1992–2000; Conductor/Composer, BBC Philharmonic Orch., 1992–2001. Retrospective Festival, South Bank Centre, 1990. President: Schs Music Assoc., 1983–; N of England Educn Conf., 1985; Composers' Guild of GB, 1986–; Making Music (formerly NFMS), 1989–; Cheltenham Arts Fests, 1994–96; SPNM, 1995–. Series for Schools Broadcasts, BBC Television. FRCM 1994; FRSAMD 1994; Fellow, British Acad. of Composers and Songwriters, 2005. Member: Accademica Filarmonia Romana, 1979; Royal Swedish Acad. of Music, 1993; Bavarian Acad. of Fine Arts, 1998. Hon. Member: RAM, 1979; Guildhall Sch. of Music and Drama, 1981; Royal Philharmonic Soc., 1987; RSA, 2001. Hon. FRIAS 1994. Hon. Fellow, Univ. of Highlands and Islands, 2004. Hon. DMus: Edinburgh, 1979; Manchester, 1981; Bristol, 1984; Open Univ., 1986; Glasgow, 1993; Durham, 1994; Hull, 2001; Oxford, 2005; Kingston, 2005; Cambridge, 2009; Hon. LLD Aberdeen, 1981; Hon. DLitt: Warwick, 1986; Salford, 1999; DUniv Heriot-Watt, 2002. Cobbett Medal, for services to chamber music, 1989; (first) Award, Assoc. of British Orchs, 1991; Gulliver Award, 1991; Charles Groves Award, NFMS, 1995; Dist. Musicians Award, ISM, 2001. Officier de l'Ordre des Arts et des Lettres (France), 1988. *Major compositions include: orchestral:* First Fantasia on an In Nomine of John Taverner, 1962, Second Fantasia, 1964; St Thomas Wake, 1968; Worldes Blis, 1969; Stone Litany, 1973; Symphony No 1, 1976; Black Pentecost, 1979; Symphony No 2, 1980; Sinfonia Concertante, 1982; Into the Labyrinth, 1983; Symphony No 3, 1985; An Orkney Wedding, with Sunrise, 1985; Violin Concerto, 1985; Concerto for trumpet and orch., 1988; Symphony No 4, 1989; Ojai Festival Overture, 1991; The Turn of the Tide, 1992; A Spell for Green Corn: The MacDonald Dances, 1993; Symphony No 5, 1994; Cross Lane Fair, 1994; The Beltane Fire, 1995; Symphony No 6, 1996; Concerto for piccolo, 1996; Concerto for piano, 1997; Mavis in Las Vegas, 1997; Sails in St Magnus, retitled Orkney Saga, I and II, 1997, III, 1999, V, 2000; Strathclyde Concertos: No 1, 1986; No 2, 1988; No 3, for horn, trumpet and orch., 1989; No 4, for clarinet and orch., 1990; No 5 for violin, viola and string orch., 1991; No 6, for flute and orch., 1991; No 7, for double bass and orch., 1992; No 8, for bassoon and orch., 1993; No 9, for woodwind and strings, 1994; No 10, for orch., 1996; A Reel of Seven Fishermen, 1998; Rome Amor, 1998; Horn Concerto, 1999; Symphony No 7, and No 8 (Antarctic), 2000; Violin Concerto No 2: Fiddler on the Shore, 2009; Symphony No 9, 2012; Symphony No 10, 2014; *instrumental and ensemble:* Sonata for trumpet and piano, 1955; Alma redemptoris mater, 1957; Revelation and Fall, 1966; Antechrist, 1967; Missa super L'Homme Armé, 1968; From Stone to Thorn, 1971; Ave Maris Stella, 1975; A Mirror of Whitening Light, 1977; Image, Reflection, Shadow, 1982; Trumpet Quintet, 1999; Crossing King's Reach, 2001; De Assumtione Beatae Mariae Virginis, 2001; Mass, 2001; Naxos Quartet No 1, 2002, No 2 and No 3, 2003, No 4 and No 5, 2004, No 6, No 7 and No 8, 2005; Piano Trio, 2002; Capstone for organ, 2013; String Quintet, 2015; *opera:* Taverner, 1970; The Martyrdom of Saint Magnus, 1976; The Two Fiddlers, 1978; The Lighthouse, 1979; Cinderella, 1979; Piano Sonata, 1981; Brass Quintet, 1981; Resurrection, 1987; The Doctor of Myddfai, 1995; *music theatre:* Eight Songs for a Mad King, 1969; Vesalii Icones, 1969; Miss Donnithorne's Maggot, 1974; Le Jongleur de Notre Dame, 1978; The No 11 Bus, 1984; The Great Bank Robbery, 1989; Mr Emmet Takes a Walk, 1999; *ballet:* Salome, 1978; Caroline Mathilde, 1990; *choral:* Five Motets, 1959; O Magnum Mysterium, 1960; Solstice of Light, 1979; The Three Kings, 1995; Job, 1997; The Jacobite Rising, 1997; Sea Elegy, 1998; Canticum Canticorum, 2001; Mass, 2002. *Address:* c/o Intermusica, Crystal Wharf, 36 Graham Street, N1 8GJ.

MAXWELL MACDONALD, Sir John (Ronald), 12th Bt *cr* 1682 (NS), of Pollok, Renfrewshire; *b* Edinburgh, 22 May 1936; *er s* of late John Maxwell Macdonald and Dame Anne Maxwell Macdonald, Btss (11th in line); *S* mother, 2011; *m* 1964, Eleanor Ruth Laird; two *s* one *d*. *Educ:* Winchester. Retired from land management. *Recreations:* fishing, sailing. *Heir: er s* John Ranald Maxwell Macdonald [*b* 16 Sept. 1965; *m* 1998, Emma Katherine Logie; one *s* two *d*]. *Address:* Gortinanane House, Tayinloan, Tarbert, Argyll PA29 6XG. *T:* (01583) 441223.

MAXWELL MARTIN, Anna; actor; *b* Beverley, E Yorks; *m* 2010, Roger Harry Michell, *qv*; two *d*. *Educ:* Beverley High Sch.; Liverpool Univ. (BA Hons Hist.). *Theatre* includes: Little Foxes, Donmar, 2001; National Theatre: Coast of Utopia, 2002; Honour, The Three Sisters, 2003; His Dark Materials, 2003–04; King Lear, 2014; Dumbshow, 2004, The Entertainer, 2006, Royal Court; Other Hands, Soho, 2006; Cabaret, Lyric, 2006; Measure for Measure, Almeida, 2010; Di and Viv and Rose, Hampstead, 2013; *films* include: The Hours, 2003; Enduring Love, 2004; Becoming Jane, 2007; *television* includes: North and South, 2004; Bleak House, 2005 (Best Actress, BAFTA, 2006); White Girl, 2008; Poppy Shakespeare, 2008 (Best Actress, BAFTA, 2009); Moonshot, 2009; On Expenses, 2010; South Riding, The Night Watch, 2011; Accused, 2012; The Bletchley Circle, 2012; Death Comes to Pemberley, 2013; Birthday, 2015; Midwinter of the Spirit, 2015. *Address:* c/o United Agents, 12–26 Lexington Street, W1F 0LE.

MAXWELL SCOTT, Sir Dominic James, 14th Bt *cr* 1642, of Haggerston, Northumberland; journalist (as Dominic Maxwell); chief theatre critic, The Times, 2013–15; *b* 22 July 1968; *s* of Sir Michael Fergus Maxwell Scott, 13th Bt and of Deirdre Moira, *d* of late Alexander McKechnie; *S* father, 1989; *m* 2004, Emma Jane, *d* of late Keith Perry; two *d*. *Educ:* Eton; Sussex Univ. Dir, Abbotsford Trust, 2008–11. *Heir: b* Matthew Joseph Maxwell Scott [*b* 27 Aug. 1976; *m* 2010, Melanie Louise, *d* of late Alan Greenall; two *s*].

MAXWELL-TIMMINS, Nicholas James; *see* Timmins.

MAY, family name of **Barons May** and **May of Oxford**.

MAY, 4th Baron *cr* 1935, of Weybridge, co. Surrey; **Jasper Bertram St John May;** Bt 1931; *b* 24 Oct. 1965; *o s* of 3rd Baron May and of Jillian Mary (*née* Shipton); *S* father, 2006. *Educ:* Harrow.

MAY OF OXFORD, Baron *cr* 2001 (Life Peer), of Oxford in the County of Oxfordshire; **Robert McCredie May,** OM 2002; AC 1998; Kt 1996; FRS 1979; Royal Society Research Professor, Department of Zoology, Oxford University, 1988–2002, now Emeritus; Fellow of Merton College, Oxford, 1988–2001, now Emeritus; President, Royal Society, 2000–05; *b* 8 Jan. 1936; *s* of Henry W. May and Kathleen M. May; *m* 1962, Judith (*née* Feiner); one *d*. *Educ:* Sydney Boys' High Sch.; Sydney Univ. BSc 1956, PhD (Theoretical Physics) 1959. Gordon Mackay Lectr in Applied Maths, Harvard Univ., 1959–61; Sydney Univ.: Sen. Lectr in Theoretical Physics, 1962–64; Reader, 1964–69; Personal Chair, 1969–73; Princeton University: Prof. of Biology, 1973–88; Class of 1877 Prof. of Zoology, 1975–88; Chm., Univ. Res. Bd, 1977–88; Chief Scientific Advr to the UK Govt and Hd of the OST, 1995–2000. Vis. Prof., Imperial Coll., 1975–88; visiting appointments at: Harvard, 1966; California Inst. of Technology, 1967; UKAEA Culham Lab., 1971; Magdalen Coll., Oxford, 1971; Inst. for Advanced Study, Princeton, 1972; King's Coll., Cambridge, 1976. Chm., Natural History Mus., 1994–98 (Trustee, 1991–93); Trustee: WWF (UK), 1990–94; Royal Botanic Gardens, Kew, 1991–96; Nuffield Foundn, 1993–2005. Non-exec. Dir, Dstl, 2005–13. Member: Smithsonian Council, USA, 1988–91; Jt Nature Conservation Council, 1989–95; Bd of Trustees, British Council, 2001–06; UK Climate Change Cttee, 2008–. Founder FMedSci 1998. Hon. Fellow: Amer. Soc. for Biochemistry, 1993; British Ecol Soc., 1995 (Pres., 1992–93); Australian Acad. of Technol Scis and Engrg, 2001; Linnean Soc., 2008; Hon. FInstP 2002; Hon. FREng 2005; Hon. FIBiol 2006. Overseas Mem., Australian Acad. of Sci., 1991; For. Associate, US Nat. Acad. of Scis, 1992. Honorary degrees from Uppsala, ETH Zürich, Yale, Princeton, Sydney, Oxford, Harvard and many other UK universities. Linnean Medal, 1991; Crafoord Prize, Royal Swedish Acad. of Scis, 1996; Swiss-Italian Balzan Prize, 1998; Japanese Blue Planet Prize, 2001; Copley Medal, Royal Soc., 2007. *Publications:* Stability and Complexity in Model Ecosystems, 1973, 2nd edn 1974; Theoretical Ecology: Principles and Applications, 1976, 3rd edn 2007; Population Biology of Infectious Diseases, 1982; Exploitation of Marine Communities, 1984; Perspectives in Ecological Theory, 1989; Infectious Diseases of Humans: dynamics and control, 1991; Extinction Rates, 1994; Evolution of Biological Diversity, 1999; Virus Dynamics, 2000; articles in mathematical, biol and physics jls. *Recreations:* tennis, running, bridge. *Address:* Department of Zoology, Tinbergen Building, South Parks Road, Oxford OX1 3PS.

MAY, Prof. Anthony Dormer, OBE 2004; FREng; Professor of Transport Engineering, University of Leeds, 1977–2009, now Emeritus; *b* 29 Feb. 1944; *s* of Albert James Gooding May and Beatrice Mary May; *m* 1968, Jennifer Margaret Caroline Hesketh. *Educ:* Bedford Sch.; Pembroke Coll., Cambridge (BA 1st cl. Hons (Mech. Scis) 1966, MA 1969); Yale Univ. 1967. CEng 1972; FICE 1993. Gp Planner Roads, GLC, 1967–77. Dir, MVA Ltd, 1985–2001. FREng 1995. *Publications:* over 80 papers in academic jls. *Recreations:* choral singing, canals, gardening, travel. *Address:* 10 Newton Terrace, York YO1 6HE. *T:* (01904) 621796.

MAY, Rt Hon. Sir Anthony (Tristram Kenneth), Kt 1991; PC 1998; Interception of Communications Commissioner, since 2013; President, Queen's Bench Division, High Court of Justice, 2008–11 (Vice-President, 2002–08); *b* 9 Sept. 1940; *s* of late Kenneth Sibley May and Joan Marguérite (*née* Oldaker); *m* 1968, Stella Gay Pattisson; one *s* two *d*. *Educ:*

Bradfield Coll.; Worcester Coll., Oxford (Trevelyan Scholar 1960, Hon. Scholar 1962; MA; Hon. Fellow, 1999). Called to the Bar, Inner Temple, 1967 (Scholar, 1965; Bencher, 1985; Reader, 2007; Treas., 2008); QC 1979; a Recorder, 1985–91; a Judge of the High Court of Justice, QBD, 1991–97; a Lord Justice of Appeal, 1997–2008; Dep. Hd of Civil Justice, 2000–03. Jun. Counsel to DoE for Land Commn Act Matters, 1972–75; Chm., Commn of Inquiry, Savings and Investment Bank Ltd, IoM, 1990. A Judge, Employment Appeal Tribunal, 1993–97; Judge in Charge, Non-Jury List, 1995–97. Chm., Security Vetting Appeals Panel, 1997–2000. Vice-Chm., Official Referees Bar Assoc., 1987–91. Mem., Civil Procedure Rule Cttee, 1997–2003. President: Technol. and Construction Bar Assoc., 2002–13; Soc. of Construction Law, 2004–12. Vice-Pres., Guildford Choral Soc., 1991– (Chm., 1980–91). Mem. Council, Wycombe Abbey Sch., 1997–2014. *Publications:* (ed) Keating on Building Contracts, 5th edn 1991, 6th edn 1995. *Recreations:* gardening, music, books, bonfires. *Club:* Garrick.

MAY, Dr Brian Harold, CBE 2005; guitarist, songwriter and producer; Owner, London Stereoscopic Company, since 2008; *b* Hampton, Middx, 19 July 1947; *s* of Harold and Ruth May; *m* 1st, 1976, Christine Mullen (marr. diss. 1988); one *s* two *d*; 2nd, 2000, Anita Dobson. *Educ:* Hampton Grammar Sch.; Imperial Coll. London (BSc 1974; PhD Astrophysics 2007). Founding Mem., Queen, 1970–; albums: Queen, 1973; Queen II, 1974; Sheer Heart Attack, 1974; A Night at the Opera, 1975; A Day at the Races, 1976; News of the World, 1977; Jazz, 1978; Live Killers, 1979; The Game, 1980; Flash Gordon Original Soundtrack, 1980; Hot Space, 1982; The Works, 1984; A Kind of Magic, 1986; The Miracle, 1989; Innuendo, 1991; Made in Heaven, 1995; (with Paul Rodgers) The Cosmos Rocks, 2008; solo albums: Back to the Light, 1993; Another World, 1998. Writer of music, Macbeth, for Red and Gold Th. Co., 1987; Prod. and Music Dir, We Will Rock You, Dominion Th., 2002 and worldwide. Trustee, Mercury Phoenix Trust, 1992–. Chancellor, Liverpool John Moores Univ., 2008–13 (Hon. Fellow, 2007). Hon. DSc: Herts, 2002; Exeter, 2007. *Publications:* (jtly) Bang! The Complete History of the Universe, 2006; A Survey of Radical Velocities in the Zodiacal Dust Cloud, 2008; (with E. Vidal) A Village Lost and Found, 2009; (jtly) Cosmic Tourist, 2012; (jtly) Diableries: stereoscopic adventures in Hell, 2013; (jtly) The Poor Man's Picture Gallery, 2014. *Address:* Duck Productions Ltd, PO Box 141, Windlesham, Surrey GU20 6YW.

MAY, Catherine Jean; Corporate Affairs Director, SABMiller plc, since 2012; *b* Shoreham-by-Sea, W Sussex, 14 Dec. 1964; *d* of Robert and Jean May; *m* 1999, Matthew Guarente; two *s*. *Educ:* King's Manor Sch.; Univ. of London (BA English). Partner, Luther Pendragon, 1997–2000; Corporate Relns Dir, Reed Elsevier plc, 2000–06; Corporate Affairs Dir, Centrica plc, 2006–12. Trustee: ENO, 2011–; Nat. Funding Scheme, 2012–. *Recreations:* opera, cookery, ski-ing, family. *E:* catherinemay.starst@hotmail.co.uk.

MAY, Charlotte Louisa, (Mrs Yemi Pearse); QC 2014; *b* Reading; *d* of Anthony and Catherine May; *m* 2000, Yemi Pearse; two *d*. *Educ:* Abbey Sch., Reading; Brasenose Coll., Oxford (BSc Biochem.); City Univ. (DipLaw (Commendation)). Called to the Bar, Inner Temple, 1995; in practice as barrister, specialising in intellectual property. *Publications:* (contrib.) The Modern Law of Copyright and Designs, 4th edn 2011. *Recreations:* swimming, tennis. *Address:* 8 New Square, Lincoln's Inn, WC2A 3QP. *T:* (020) 7405 4321. *E:* charlotte.may@8newsquare.co.uk. *Club:* Roehampton.

MAY, Christine; environmental business development and public affairs consultant; Member of Board, Accounts Commission for Scotland, since 2009; *b* Dublin, 23 March 1948; *m* William May; one *s* one *d*. *Educ:* Coll. of Catering and Domestic Sci., Dublin. Dip. Inst. Mgt. Catering manager, Dublin and London, 1965–81; Lectr, Fife Coll., 1987–94. Formerly Member, Board: Scottish Homes; Scottish Enterprise. Member (Lab): Kirkcaldy DC, 1988–96 (Leader, 1993–96); Fife Council, 1995–2003 (Leader, 1998–2003). MSP (Lab Co-op) Fife Central, 2003–07. Chair, Scottish Lib y and Information Council, 2005–11. Chair, Fife Historic Bldgs Trust, 2011–; Vice Chm., Fife Cultural Trust, 2012–. Mem. Bd, Queen's Hall, Edinburgh, 2012–. *E:* christinemay2@gmail.com.

MAY, David; *see* May, M. D.

MAY, Douglas James; QC (Scot) 1989; FRPS; an Upper Tribunal Judge (Administrative Appeals Chamber) (formerly a Social Security Commissioner and a Child Support Commissioner), 1993–2015; *b* 7 May 1946; *s* of Thomas May and Violet Mary Brough Boyd or May. *Educ:* George Heriot's Sch., Edinburgh; Edinburgh Univ. Advocate 1971. Temporary Sheriff, 1990–99. Mem., Tribunal Procedure Cttee, 2008. Contested (C): Edinburgh E, Feb. 1974; Glasgow Cathcart, 1983. Pres., Edinburgh Photographic Soc., 1996–99; Chm., Contemporary Distinctions Panel, RPS, 2010–. FRPS 2002. *Recreations:* golf, photography, travel, concert going. *Clubs:* Merchants of Edinburgh Golf (Captain, 1997–99), Bruntsfield Links Golfing Society, Luffness New Golf.

MAY, James Nicholas Welby; Director-General, UK Offshore Operators Association, 1997–2003; *b* 21 Feb. 1949; *s* of late Richard Percy May and of Caroline Rosemary Welby May (*née* Jack); *m* 1979, Diana Mary Tamplin; two *s*. *Educ:* Sherborne Sch., Dorset; Southampton Univ. (BSc 1970); College of Law. Called to the Bar, Lincoln's Inn, 1974. Programme Officer, UNEP, 1976–77; Project Officer, IUCN, 1977–78; Legal Officer, Friends of the Earth, 1978–79; Legal Adviser, NFU, 1980–89; Dir-Gen., British Retail Consortium, 1989–97. Sec., Footwear Distributors' Fedn, 1989–97; Member: Countryside Commn Common Land Forum, 1984–86; Nat. Retail Trng Council, 1989–97; Distributive Occupational Standards Council, 1993–97; Council, 1996–2003, Trade Assoc. Council, 1998–2003, CBI; Meteorological Cttee, 1997–99; HSE Open Govt Complaints Panel, 2003–05. Non-executive Director: Meteorological Office, 2000–07; Roehampton Club Members Ltd, 2011–; non-exec. Chm., Common Data Access Ltd, 2000–03; non-executive Member: Land Command Bd, 2004–07 (Chm., Audit Cttee, 2004–07); Defence Audit Cttee, 2005–07. Trustee, Sherborne Sch. Foundn, 1999–2004. *Recreations:* travel, tennis, ski-ing, golf. *E:* james.diana@blueyonder.co.uk. *Club:* Roehampton (Hon. Co. Sec., 2010–).

MAY, Jill Miranda; Panel Member non-executive Director, Competition and Markets Authority, since 2013; *b* London, 5 June 1961; *d* of John Langham and Irene Langham; *m* 1988, Mick May; two *s* four *d*. *Educ:* Benenden Sch.; Durham Univ. (BA Econs 1982). Corporate Finance, S. G. Warburg & Co. Ltd, 1982–95; Man. Dir, UBS AG, 2001–12. Dir, Langham Industries, 1996–. Panel Mem., Competition Commn, 2013–14; Mem. Complaints Cttee, IPSO, 2014–. Member: Council, Nat. Trust, 2011–14; Council, Durham Univ., 2012–; Cancer Research UK, 2015–. *Recreations:* travel, long-distance running, alpine walking, ski-ing. *Address:* 29 Palace Gardens Terrace, W8 4SB. *T:* (020) 7221 5779. *E:* jill.may50@gmail.com. *Clubs:* Hurlingham, 5 Hertford Street.

MAY, Air Vice-Marshal John Anthony Gerard, CB 1995; CBE 1993; Air Officer Training and Air Officer Commanding Training Group, Headquarters Personnel and Training Command, and Chief Executive, Training Group Defence Agency, 1994–97; *b* 12 Nov. 1941; *s* of late Anthony Frederick May and Beatrice Mary (*née* Niblett); *m* 1964, Margaret Anne Chester; two *s*. *Educ:* City of London Sch. Joined RAF 1961; flying trng, then Qualified Flying Instr, Linton-on-Ouse; Lightning aircraft, 1966; served with Nos 56, 5 and 19 Sqns; Staff Coll., Camberley, 1977; Chief Flying Instr, RAF Cranwell, 1979; Stn Comdr, Binbrook, 1985; Dep. Dir of Air Defence, MoD, 1987; Air Cdre Policy and Plans, RAF Support Comd, 1989; AOC No 38 Gp, and SASO, HQ Strike Comd, 1993–94. Vice-Chm. (Air), E Anglia RFCA, 2003–10. QCVSA 1971. *Recreations:* alpine ski-ing, classic cars. *Address:* 157 Sapley Road, Hartford, Huntingdon, Cambs PE29 1YT.

MAY, John Clive Cecil; Secretary General, Duke of Edinburgh's International Award Foundation, since 2011; *b* London, 17 Aug. 1964; *s* of John and Jennifer May. *Educ:* Wycliffe Coll.; Bristol Univ. (BA Jt Hons Drama and English 1985); Westminster Coll., Oxford (PGCE 1986); Open Univ. (MA Educn 1991). Teacher, Chadsmead Sch., Staffs, 1986–90; Dep. Hd, Scaynes Hill Sch., W Sussex, 1990–93; Hd, Handcross Sch., W Sussex, 1993–96; Hd, Manor Farm Sch., Bucks, 1996–99; Educn Dir, BITC, 1999–2003; Chief Executive Officer: Career Academies UK, 2003–09; Young Enterprise, 2009–11. Founding Dir and Mem., Adv. Bd, Teach First, 2002–14. Vice Chm., World Orgn of Scout Movement, 2008–14. Mem., Nat. Bd, UNICEF UK, 1992–98. Trustee: Scout Assoc., UK, 1982–2005; Marine Soc. and Sea Cadets, 2015–. FRSA. Queen's Award for Enterprise Promotion, 2008. *Recreations:* long distance running, hill walking, travel, theatre, Scouting. *Address:* Award House, 7–11 St Matthew's Street, SW1P 2JT. *T:* (020) 7222 4242. *E:* john.may@intaward.org. *Club:* Lansdowne.

MAY, Jonathan Charles; Executive Director, Policy and Strategy, Office of Fair Trading, 2006–10; *b* 12 Aug. 1949; *s* of Edward Kelly May and Sheila Joy May; *m* 1984, Florence Pauline Cowmeadow (marr. diss. 2009); one *s*; *m* 2014, Rolande Anderson. *Educ:* Reading Univ. (BA Hons Econ); LSE (MSc Econ). Res. Officer, LSE, 1973–75; Sen. Res. Officer, planning issues, DoE, 1975–84; overseas aid and Home Office expenditure work, 1984–94; Hd of competition, regulation and energy team, HM Treasury, 1994–99; Dir, UK Competition Policy, DTI, 1999–2001; Dir, Markets and Policy Initiatives, OFT, 2001–06 (Mem., Exec. Bd, 2006–10). Member: Competition Appeal Tribunal, 2011–; Financial Services Consumer Panel, 2012–; Consumer Focus Bd, 2013–; Enforcement Decisions Panel, Ofgem, 2014–; Special Advr, FIPRA Internat., 2011–. *Recreations:* family, friends, reading, relaxation, music.

MAY, Jonathan James Seaburne B.; *see* Bourne-May.

MAY, Juliet Mary; QC 2008; **Her Honour Judge May;** a Circuit Judge, since 2008; *b* London; *d* of Rt Hon. Sir John Douglas May, PC and Mary May; *m* 1988, (Jonathan) James (O'Grady) Cameron, *qv*; three *d*. *Educ:* Wycombe Abbey Sch.; Wadham Coll., Oxford (BA Psychol., Phil. and Physiol.); Inst. of Psychiatry (MPhil Clin. Psychol.); City Univ. (DipLaw); Inns of Court Sch. of Law (BVC). Sen. Clin. Psychologist, 1983–86; called to the Bar, Inner Temple, 1988, Bencher, 2010; in practice as barrister, specialising in commercial law, 1988–2008. *Address:* Southwark Crown Court, 1 English Grounds, SE1 2HU.

MAY, Prof. (Michael) David, DSc; FRS 1991; FREng; Professor, Department of Computer Science, Bristol University; *b* Holmfirth, 24 Feb. 1951; *s* of Douglas May. *Educ:* Queen Elizabeth's GS, Wakefield; King's Coll., Cambridge (BA 1972; MA 1976); DSc Southampton. Lectr, Dept of Computer Sci., Warwick Univ.; Technology Manager (Computer Architecture), Inmos Ltd, Bristol; co-founder and Chief Tech. Officer, XMOS Ltd. Vis. Prof. of Engrg Design, Oxford Univ., 1991. FREng 2010. *Publications:* (ed jtly) Networks, Routers and Transputers: function, performance and application, 1993. *Address:* Department of Computer Science, University of Bristol, Merchant Venturers' Building, Woodland Road, Bristol BS8 1UB. *T:* (0117) 954 5134; 9 Eaton Crescent, Clifton, Bristol BS8 2EJ. *T:* (0117) 974 2586.

MAY, Rt Hon. Theresa Mary; PC 2003; MP (C) Maidenhead, since 1997; Secretary of State for the Home Department, since 2010; *b* 1 Oct. 1956; *d* of Rev. Hubert Brasier and Zaidee Brasier (*née* Barnes); *m* 1980, Philip John May. *Educ:* St Hugh's Coll., Oxford (MA). Bank of England, 1977–83; Inter-Bank Res. Orgn, 1983–85; Assoc. for Payment Clearing Services, 1985–97 (Hd of European Affairs Unit, 1989–96). Mem. (C), Merton LBC, 1986–94. Contested (C): Durham NW, 1992; Barking, June 1994. Opposition frontbench spokesman on educn and employment, 1998–99; Shadow Secretary of State: for Educn and Employment, 1999–2001; for Transport, Local Govt and the Regions, 2001–02; for Transport, 2002; for Envmt and Transport, 2003–04; for the Family, 2004–05, also for Culture, Media and Sport, 2005; Chm., Cons. Party, 2002–03; Shadow Leader, H of C, 2005–09; Shadow Minister for Women, 2007–10; Shadow Sec. of State for Work and Pensions, 2009–10; Minister for Women and for Equalities, 2010–12. *Recreations:* walking, cooking. *Address:* House of Commons, SW1A 0AA. *Clubs:* Maidenhead Conservative; Leander.

MAYALL, Prof. James Bardsley Lawson, FBA 2001; Sir Patrick Sheehy Professor of International Relations, University of Cambridge, 1998–2004, now Emeritus; Fellow, 1998–2004, now Emeritus, and Director of Studies in Social and Political Sciences, since 2004, Sidney Sussex College, Cambridge (Vice-Master, 2003–04); *b* 14 April 1937; *s* of Robert Cecil Mayall and Rhoda Anne (*née* Stote); *m* 1st, 1964, Margaret Berry (marr. diss. 1990); one *d*; 2nd, 1991, Avril Doris Whalley. *Educ:* Shrewsbury Sch.; Sidney Sussex Coll., Cambridge (BA Hist. Tripos 1960; MA 1998). Sir John Dill Fellow, Princeton Univ., NJ, 1960–61; BoT, 1961–64; British High Commn, New Delhi, 1964–65; London School of Economics: Dept of Internat. Relns, 1966–98; Prof. of Internat. Relns, 1991–98, Prof. Emeritus, 1998–; Chm., Steering Cttee, Centre for Internat. Studies, 1991–98. Mem. Council, RIIA, 1992–98 (Associate Editor, Survey and Documents of Internat. Affairs, 1967–71). Chm., Adv. Bd, Inst. of Commonwealth Studies, Univ. of London, 2006–; Academic Advr, RCDS, 2008–13; Adv. Bd (Internat. Relns), William Grosvenor Partnership, 2014–. *Publications:* Africa and the Cold War, 1971; (Associate Ed.) Survey of International Affairs 1963, 1977; (ed jtly) A New International Commodity Regime, 1979; (ed jtly) The End of the Post-War Era: documents on Great Power relns 1968–75, 1980; (ed) The Community of States: a study in international political theory, 1982; Nationalism and International Society, 1990; (ed jtly) The Fallacies of Hope: the post Colonial record of the Commonwealth Third World, 1991; (ed) The New Interventionism 1991–94: United Nations experience in Cambodia, Former Yugoslavia and Somalia, 1996; World Politics: progress and its limits, 2000; (ed jtly) International Human Rights in the 21st Century: protecting the rights of groups, 2003; (with K. Srinivasan) Towards the New Horizons: world order in the Twenty First Century, 2009; (ed) The Contemporary Commonwealth, 1965–2009: essays to mark the centenary of the publication of The Round Table, 2009; (ed jtly) The New Protectorates: international tutelage and the making of liberal states, 2011. *Recreations:* cooking, gardening, watching cricket, walking the dog. *Address:* Sidney Sussex College, Sidney Street, Cambridge CB2 3HU. *T:* (01223) 767228. *Clubs:* MCC; Indian Internat. Centre (Delhi).

MAYALL, Lt Gen. Sir Simon (Vincent), KBE 2014; CB 2010; Prime Minister's Security Envoy to Iraq, 2014–15; *b* London, 7 March 1956; *e s* of Air Cdre Paul Vincent Mayall and Alexis Leonora Mayall. *Educ:* St George's Coll., Weybridge; Balliol Coll., Oxford (MA Hons Modern Hist.); King's Coll. London (MA Internat. Relns). Commnd 15th/19th King's Royal Hussars, 1979; served Sultan's Armed Forces, Oman, 1985–87; Staff Coll., then MoD, later Regtl Duty, 1987–93; MA to Dep. SACEUR, 1993–95; Defence Fellow, St Antony's Coll., Oxford, 1995–97; CO, 1st Queen's Dragoon Guards, 1997–99; Col, Army Plans, MoD, 1999–2001; Comdr, 1st Mechanised Bde, 2001–02; rcds, 2003; Dir, Army Plans, 2004–06; Dep. Comdr, Multi-Nat. Corps - Iraq, 2006–07; ACGS, 2007–09; DCDS (Ops), 2009–11; Defence Sen. Advr to the Middle East, 2011–14. Lieut, Tower of London, 2015–. Regtl Col, Queen's Dragoon Guards, 2008–; Dep. Col Comdt, AGC (Army Legal Services), 2009–15. Hon. Col, Univ. of London OTC, 2009–15. QCVS 2003. Officer, Legion of Merit (USA), 2007. *Publications:* Turkey, Thwarted Ambition, 1997, 2nd edn 2005. *Recreations:* theatre, history, travel, shooting, ski-ing, tennis. *Address:* 14 Earl's Court Square, SW5 9DN. *Clubs:* Garrick, Beefsteak, Cavalry and Guards, Chelsea Arts.

MAYBLIN, Andrea Doreen; *see* Levy, A. D.

MAYER, Anthony; *see* Mayer, R. A. J.

MAYER, (Anthony) David, FRCS; Consultant Hepatobiliary and Liver Transplant Surgeon, Queen Elizabeth Hospital, Birmingham, and Honorary Consultant Liver Transplant Surgeon, Birmingham Children's Hospital, 1990; Clinical Lead for Organ Retrieval, NHS Blood and Transplant, 2008; *b* 11 Jan. 1950; *s* of John Mayer and Sheila Mayer (*née* Lesser); *m* 1977, Helen Rastall; three *d*. *Educ:* Tonbridge Sch.; Univ. of Sussex (BSc 1971); Guy's Hosp., Univ. of London (MB BS 1976; MS 1986). FRCS 1980. House Officer, 1976–77, SHO, 1977, Guy's Hosp.; SHO, Brighton Gen. Hosp. and Royal Sussex Co. Hosp., 1978–80; Registrar, Scarborough Hosp., 1980–81; Res. Fellow, Leeds Gen. Infirmary, 1982–84; Registrar, Walsgrave Hosp., Coventry, 1985–86; Sen. Registrar, Queen Elizabeth Hosp., Birmingham, 1986–88; Vis. Fellow, UCSD, 1988–89. Hon. Sen. Lectr, Univ. of Birmingham, 1990. Chm., Liver Adv. Gp to UK Transplant, 2003–08; Pres., Transplantation Section, RSM, 2003–09. *Publications:* various articles on transplantation and surgery in med. jls, inc. Lancet, BMJ, New England Jl of Medicine and British Jl of Surgery. *Recreations:* cycling, music, literature, theatre. *Club:* Royal Society of Medicine.

MAYER, Prof. Colin Peter, FBA 2013; Peter Moores Professor of Management Studies, Saïd Business School (formerly School of Management Studies), University of Oxford, since 1994 (Peter Moores Dean, 2006–11); Fellow, Wadham College, Oxford, 1994–2006 and since 2011; *b* 12 May 1953; *s* of late Harold Charles Mayer and Anne Louise Mayer; *m* 1979, Annette Patricia Haynes; two *d*. *Educ:* St Paul's Sch.; Oriel College, Oxford (Hon. Fellow, 2006); Wolfson College, Oxford (MA, BPhil, DPhil); Harvard Univ. HM Treasury, 1976–78; Harkness Fellow, Harvard, 1979–80; Fellow in Economics, St Anne's College, Oxford, 1980–86 (Hon. Fellow, 1993); Price Waterhouse Prof. of Corporate Finance, City Univ. Business Sch., 1987–92; Prof. of Econs and Finance, Univ. of Warwick, 1992–94; Fellow, St Edmund Hall, Oxford, 2006–11. Chairman: ESF Network in Financial Markets, 1989–94; Oxford Economic Research Associates, subseq. OXERA Hldgs, Ltd, 1987–2010; non-exec. Dir, Aurora Energy Res., 2013–; Dir, Oxford Financial Res. Centre, 1998–2006. Delegate, OUP, 1996–2006 (Chm., Audit Cttee, 2002–06). Member: Competition Appeal Tribunal, 2011–; Natural Capital Cttee, DEFRA, 2012–. Mem. Exec. Cttee, REconS, 2002–06. Inaugural Fellow, European Corporate Governance Inst., 2002–. Gov., St Paul's Sch., London, 2002–11. Associate Editor: Jl of Internat. Financial Management; Jl of European Financial Management; Oxford Review of Economic Policy. *Publications:* (with J. Kay and J. Edwards) Economic Analysis of Accounting Profitability, 1986; (with J. Franks) Risk, Regulation and Investor Protection, 1989; (with A. Giovannini) European Financial Integration, 1991; (with X. Vives) Capital Markets and Financial Intermediation, 1993; (with T. Jenkinson) Hostile Takeovers, 1994; (with J. Franks and L. C. da Silva) Asset Management and Investor Protection, 2002; (with X. Freixas and P. Hartmann) Handbook of European Financial Markets and Institutions, 2008; Firm Commitment: why the corporation is failing us and how to restore trust in it, 2013; articles in economic and finance jls. *Recreations:* piano, jogging, reading philosophy and science. *Address:* Saïd Business School, University of Oxford, Park End Street, Oxford OX1 1HP. *T:* (01865) 288811.

MAYER, David; *see* Mayer, A. D.

MAYER, John; *see* Mayer, R. J.

MAYER, (Ralph) Anthony (Jeffrey), CBE 2000; Chairman, One Housing Group, since 2012; *b* 24 Feb. 1946; *s* of George Mayer and Margaret (*née* Jones); *m* 1971, Ann Gowen; one *s* one *d*. *Educ:* City of Bath Boys' Sch.; Lycée Michelet, Paris; St Edmund Hall, Oxford (BA Hons PPE). Ministry of Housing and Local Government, subseq. Department of the Environment, 1967–85: Asst Principal, 1967–72; seconded as Pvte Sec. to Parly Sec., CSD, 1971–72; Principal, 1972–81; seconded as Mem., CPRS, 1974–76, and as Prin. Pvte Sec. to Sec. of State for Transport, 1980–82; Asst Sec., 1981–85; Asst Dir, N. M. Rothschild and Sons, 1985–87; Man. Dir (Finance and Admin), Rothschild Asset Management, 1987–91; Chief Exec., Housing Corp., 1991–2000; Actg Chief Exec., Transport for London, 2000; Chief Exec., GLA, 2000–08; Chairman: Tenant Services Authy, 2008–12; London Pensions Fund Authy, 2009–12; One Housing Gp, 2012–. *Recreations:* hill walking, bridge, yachting. *Address:* 37 Copthall Gardens, Twickenham, Middlesex TW1 4HH.

MAYER, Prof. Roland George, PhD; Professor of Classics, King's College London, since 1996; *b* Annapolis, Md, 24 July 1947; *s* of Roland George Mayer, Jr and Mary Clare Devine; civil partnership 2014, David Munro. *Educ:* Univ. of Calif at Berkeley (BA 1967); Peterhouse, Cambridge (BA 1972; PhD 1977). Res. Fellow, Bedford Coll., Univ. of London, 1976–79; Lectr, 1979–88, Sen. Lectr, 1988–89, Birkbeck Coll., Univ. of London; Sen. Lectr, KCL, 1989–96. Editor, Classical Review, 1994–2001. *Publications:* Seneca: Phaedra, 2002; *edited:* Lucan, Civil War 8, 1982; Horace, Epistles 1, 1994; Tacitus, Dialogus, 2001; (with M. Coffey) Seneca, Phaedra, 1990: Horace, Odes Book I, 2012. *Recreations:* opera, South German Baroque churches. *Address:* Department of Classics, King's College London, Strand, WC2R 2LS. *T:* (020) 7848 2058. *E:* roland.mayer@kcl.ac.uk.

MAYER, Prof. (Roland) John, FRCPath; Professor of Molecular Cell Biology, 1986, now Emeritus, and Head of Molecular Cell Biology, School of Biomedical Sciences, 1997, University of Nottingham; *b* 30 April 1943; *s* of George and Ethel Mayer; *m* 1967, Elaine Ing; two *s*. *Educ:* Univ. of Birmingham (BSc 1st Cl., 1965; PhD 1968); DSc Nottingham 1980. Lectr, Sen. Lectr and Reader, Univ. of Nottingham, 1970–86. *Publications:* (with J. H. Walker) Immunochemical Methods in the Biological Sciences: enzymes and proteins, 1980; (with J. H. Walker) Immunochemical Methods in Cell and Molecular Biology, 1987; (with F. J. Doherty) Intracellular Protein Degradation, 1992; contribs to learned jls. *Recreation:* golf. *Address:* School of Molecular Medical Sciences, University of Nottingham Medical School, Queen's Medical Centre, Nottingham NG7 2UH. *T:* (0115) 970 9369.

MAYER, Thomas, CBE 1985; FREng; Chairman, Eldonray Ltd, 1990–2004; *b* 17 Dec. 1928; *s* of Hans and Jeanette Mayer; *m* 1st, 1956 (marr. diss. 1975); one *s* one *d*; 2nd, 1975, Jean Patricia Burrows. *Educ:* King's Sch., Harrow; Regent Street Polytechnic (BScEng). FIET (FIEE 1964); FRTS 1968; FREng (FEng 1987); CRAeS 1990. Broadcasting Div., Marconi Co. Ltd, 1948–68; Man. Dir, Marconi Elliott Micro-Electronics Ltd, 1968–69; Man. Dir, Marconi Communication Systems Ltd, 1969–81; Man. Dir, 1981–86, Chm., 1981–90, THORN EMI Electronics Ltd; Chief Exec., THORN EMI Technology Gp, 1986–88; Exec. Dir, THORN EMI plc, 1987–90. Chairman: THORN EMI Varian Ltd, 1981–89; Holmes Protection Gp, 1990–91; ITT Defence Ltd, 1993–97; Director: Thorn Ericsson, 1981–88; Systron Donner Corp., 1983–90; Inmos Corp., 1985–88; Babcock Thorn Ltd, 1985–90; THORN EMI Australia, 1987–88; non-executive Director: Devonport Management Ltd, 1990–97; Eurodis Electron (formerly Electron House) plc, 1991–2002. Chm., UK Nat. Widescreen Television Forum, DTI, 1991–97. Member: Council, IEE, 1971–74; Council, Electronic Engrg Assoc., 1974–75, 1981–87 (Pres., 1982–83); Nat. Electronics Council, 1983–98; SBAC, 1984–90 (Pres., 1987–88). FRSA 2011. Liveryman, Worshipful Co. of Engineers, 1984–. *Recreations:* golf, swimming, theatre. *Address:* 1590 A.D., Burton Lane, Monks Risborough, Bucks HP27 9JF. *T:* (01844) 344194. *Club:* Ellesborough Golf.

MAYER, Vera; Her Honour Judge Mayer; a Circuit Judge, since 2002; *b* 11 June 1948; *d* of Milan and Suzanna Mayer; two *d*. *Educ:* Bar-Ilan Univ., Israel (BA Psychol.); Inst. of Educn, Univ. of London (MSc Child Develt). Called to the Bar, Gray's Inn, 1978; Asst Recorder, 1998–2000; Recorder, 2000–02. Mem., Professional Conduct Cttee, Bar Council, 2000–02. *Recreations:* action-packed travel, photography, music, theatre. *Address:* Barnet County Court, St Mary's Court, Regent's Park Road, N3 1BQ. *E:* HHJudge.Mayer2@judiciary.gsi.gov.uk.

MAYER-SCHÖNBERGER, Prof. Viktor, Dr jur; Professor of Internet Governance and Regulation, since 2010, and Director of Advancement, Oxford Internet Institute, since 2012, University of Oxford; Fellow, Keble College, Oxford, since 2010; *b* Austria. *Educ:* Harvard Law Sch. (LLM 1989); Law Sch., Salzburg (Dr jur 1991); London Sch. of Econs and Pol Sci. (MSc Internat. Relns 1992). Founder, Ikarus Software, 1986–92; Asst Prof., 1999–2003, Associate Prof., 2003–08, Harvard Univ.; Associate Prof., Lee Kuan Yew Sch. of Public Policy, and Dir, Information and Innovation Policy Res. Centre, Nat. Univ. of Singapore, 2008–10. Advr to Minister of Finance, Austria, 2009–. Mem., Global Adv. Council, World Econ. Forum, 2010–. Mem., Trustworthy Computing Academic Adv. Bd, 2005–. *Publications:* Governance and Information Technology, 2007; Delete: the virtue of forgetting in the digital age, 2009; (with K. Cukier) Big Data: a revolution that will transform how we live, work and think, 2013. *Address:* Oxford Internet Institute, 1 St Giles, Oxford OX1 3JS. *E:* vms@acm.org.

MAYES, Maj.-Gen. Frederick Brian, CB 1995; FRCS; Director General, Army Medical Services, 1993–96; *b* 24 Aug. 1934; *s* of late Harry Frederick and Constance Enid Mayes; *m* 1962, Mary Anna Georgina Roche; one *s* two *d* (and one *s* decd). *Educ:* Wyggeston Grammar Sch., Leicester; St Mary's Hosp. Med. Sch. (MB BS London 1958). Commissioned Lieut RAMC, 1960; served Aden, E Africa, BAOR, UK; Consultant in Surgery, 1972; CO, BMH Hannover, 1984–87; CO, Cambridge Mil. Hosp., Aldershot, 1987–88; Consultant Surgeon, HQ BAOR, 1988–90; Comdr Med., HQ BAOR, 1990–93. QHS, 1991–96. Pres., St John's Ambulance, Germany, 1990. CStJ 1993. *Recreations:* off-shore sailing, bridge, mountaineering. *Address:* Mornington, 9 Searle Road, Farnham, Surrey GU9 8LJ. *T:* (01252) 715453.

MAYES, Ian; QC 1993; *b* 11 Sept. 1951; marr. diss.; two *s*. *Educ:* Highgate Sch. (Foundation Schol.); Trinity Coll., Cambridge. Called to the Bar, Middle Temple, 1974 (Harmsworth Schol.; Bencher, 2001). Dept of Trade Inspection, London Capital Group Ltd, 1975–77; Standing Counsel to Inland Revenue, 1983–93. Chm., Disciplinary Tribunal, Lloyd's of London. Mem., Justice Cttee on Fraud Trials. Chm., Art First. *Recreation:* photography. *Address:* Littleton Chambers, 3 King's Bench Walk North, Temple, EC4Y 7HR. *T:* (020) 7797 8600. *Club:* Garrick.

MAYES, Rt Rev. Michael Hugh Gunton; Bishop of Limerick and Killaloe, 2000–08; *b* 31 Aug. 1941; *s* of Thomas David Dougan Mayes and Hilary Gunton; *m* 1966, Elizabeth Annie Eleanor Irwin; one *s* two *d*. *Educ:* The Royal Sch., Armagh; Trinity Coll., Dublin (BA); Univ. of London (BD). Ordained, 1964; Assistant Curate: St Mark's, Portadown, 1964–67; St Columba's, Portadown, 1967–68; Missionary, Japan, 1968–74; Incumbent: St Michael's, Cork, 1975–86; Moviddy, Cork, 1986–88; Rathcooney, Cork, 1988–93; Archdeacon of Cork, Cloyne and Ross, 1986–93; Bishop of Kilmore, Elphin and Ardagh, 1993–2000. *Recreations:* reading, music, photography, walking. *Address:* 4 Langford Place, Langford Row, Cork, Ireland. *T:* (21) 4967688. *E:* mhg.mayes@gmail.com.

MAYFIELD, Sir Andrew Charles, (Sir Charlie), Kt 2013; Chairman, John Lewis Partnership, since 2007; *b* Hants, 25 Dec. 1966; *s* of Richard and Rosemary Mayfield; *m* 1993, Elizabeth Paton; one *s* two *d*. *Educ:* Radley Coll.; RMA, Sandhurst (Sword of Honour); Cranfield Sch. of Mgt (MBA). Captain, Scots Guards, 1986–91. Asst Product Manager, SmithKline Beecham, 1992–96; Consultant, McKinsey & Co., 1996–2000; John Lewis Partnership: Hd, Business Develt, 2000–01; Develt Dir, 2001–05; Man. Dir, 2005–07. Mem., UK Commn for Employment and Skills, 2007– (Chair, 2010–); Chm., British Retail Consortium, 2014–. Dir, Central Surrey Health Trustee Ltd, 2013–. Pres., Employee Ownership Assoc., 2011–. Mem. Council, Radley Coll., 2010–. Trustee, Scots Guards Charitable Fund, 2007–. Hon. Fellow, Univ. of Central Lancs, 2007. DUniv Loughborough, 2013; Hon. DBus London, 2013. *Recreations:* walking, ski-ing, sailing. *Address:* John Lewis Partnership, Partnership House, Carlisle Place, SW1P 1BY. *T:* (020) 7828 1000.

MAYFIELD, Rt Rev. Christopher John; Bishop of Manchester, 1993–2002; Hon. Assistant Bishop, Diocese of Worcester, since 2002; *b* 18 Dec. 1935; *s* of Dr Roger Bolton Mayfield and Muriel Eileen Mayfield; *m* 1962, Caroline Ann Roberts; two *s* one *d*. *Educ:* Sedbergh School; Gonville and Caius Coll., Cambridge (MA 1961); Linacre House, Oxford (Dip. Theology); MSc Cranfield Univ. 1984. Deacon 1963, priest 1964, Birmingham; Curate of St Martin in the Bull Ring, Birmingham, 1963–67; Lecturer at St Martin's, Birmingham, 1967–71; Chaplain at Children's Hospital, Birmingham, 1967–71; Vicar of Luton, 1971–80 (with East Hyde, 1971–76); RD of Luton, 1974–79; Archdeacon of Bedford, 1979–85; Bishop Suffragan of Wolverhampton, 1985–93. Dean of Retired Clergy, Dio. of Worcester, 2010–. Mem., H of L, 1998–2002. Treas., Worcester Civic Soc., 2009–. *Recreations:* family, gardening, walking. *Address:* 54 Primrose Crescent, St Peter's, Worcester WR5 3HT.

MAYHEW, family name of **Baron Mayhew of Twysden.**

MAYHEW OF TWYSDEN, Baron *cr* 1997 (Life Peer), of Kilndown in the co. of Kent; **Patrick Barnabas Burke Mayhew,** Kt 1983; PC 1986; QC 1972; DL; *b* 11 Sept. 1929; *o* surv. *s* of late A. G. H. Mayhew, MC; *m* 1963, Rev. Jean Elizabeth Gurney, OBE 1997, MA (Cantab), BD (Lond), FKC, *d* of John Gurney; four *s*. *Educ:* Tonbridge; Mons Officer Cadet Sch., Aldershot; Balliol Coll., Oxford (MA). President, Oxford Union Society, 1952. Commnd 4th/7th Royal Dragoon Guards, national service and AER, captain. Called to Bar, Middle Temple, 1955, Bencher 1980. Non-exec. Dir, Western Provident Assoc., 1997–2007 (Vice-Chm., 2000–07). Contested (C) Camberwell and Dulwich, 1970. MP (C): Royal Tunbridge Wells, Feb. 1974–1983; Tunbridge Wells, 1983–97. Parly Under Sec. of State, Dept of Employment, 1979–81; Minister of State, Home Office, 1981–83; Solicitor General, 1983–87; Attorney General, 1987–92; Sec. of State for NI, 1992–97. Mem., H of L, 1997–2015. Member of Executive: 1922 Cttee, 1976–79; Assoc. of Cons. Peers, 1998–2006. Chm., Prime Minister's Adv. Cttee on Business Appts, 2000–08. DL Kent, 2001. *Clubs:* Garrick, Pratt's, Beefsteak; Tunbridge Wells Constitutional.

MAYHEW, David Lionel, CBE 2011; Chairman: Cazenove Capital Holdings Ltd, 2005–13; JPMorgan Cazenove, 2010–11; Vice Chairman, JPMorgan, since 2010; *b* 20 May 1940; *s* of Lionel Geoffrey Mayhew and Biddy Vowe Mayhew; *m* 1966, Virginia Ann Wonnacott; two *s* one *d*. *Educ:* Eton Coll. With Panmure Gordon, 1961–69; Cazenove & Co., subseq. JPMorgan Cazenove Ltd, 1969–2011, Partner, 1971–2001; Chairman: Cazenove Gp, 2001–10; JPMorgan Cazenove Hldgs, 2005–10. Non-exec. Dir, Rio Tinto plc, 2000–10. Trustee: Royal Anniversary Trust, 2005–14; Game and Wildlife Conservation Trust, 2012–; Chm., Trustees, Alzheimer's Res. UK, 2012–. *Recreations:* farming, country pursuits. *Address:* c/o J.P. Morgan Cazenove, 25 Bank Street, E14 5JP. *Clubs:* Boodle's; Swinley Golf; New Zealand Golf.

MAYHEW, Jeremy Paul; Chairman, City Bridge Trust Committee, since 2014, Deputy Chairman, Policy and Resources Committee, since 2013, and Deputy Chairman, Finance Committee, since 2013, City of London Corporation (Chairman, Audit and Risk Management Committee, 2011–14); *b* Bristol, 1 Feb. 1959; *s* of late Yon Richard Mayhew and of Cora Angela Mayhew (*née* Lamboll). *Educ:* Clifton Coll., Bristol; Western Reserve Acad., Ohio (ESU Schol.); Balliol Coll., Oxford (MA PPE; scholar); Harvard Business Sch. (MBA High Dist. 1989). BBC Television: trainee asst producer, 1980–82; Asst Producer,

Current Affairs, 1982–84; independent prod./dir, documentary and current affairs for Channel 4, 1984–87; Strategy Consultant, Booz Allen & Hamilton, 1989–90; Special Advr to Sec. of State for Trade and Industry, then for Social Security, 1990–93; Hd, Strategy Develt, BBC, 1993–95; Dir, New Media, 1995–99, Dir, New Ventures and Strategy, 1999–2001, Dir, Bd, 1997–2001, BBC Worldwide Ltd; Dir and Hd, Strategy Practice, Human Capital consultancy, 2001–02; Sen. Advr, 2002–03 and 2008–09, Partner, 2003–08, Spectrum Strategy Consultants, later Spectrum Value Partners; Chm., 2008–11, Dep. Chm., 2011–12, Bd, Barbican Centre. Sen. Advr, Oliver & Ohlbaum Associates, 2010–11; Sen. Advr, PwC Consultancy, 2012–. Non-executive Director: Learning and Skills Develt Agency, 1999–2002; Strategic Rail Authy, 2000–06; London Develt Agency, 2008–12. Mem. (Public Rep.), Evaluation Cttee, ESRC, 2011–14; non-exec. Advr, Commissioning and Procurement, Mayor of London's Office for Policing and Crime, 2012–14; Mem., Regulatory Policy Cttee, 2012–. Mem., Ct of Common Council, City of London, 1996– (Chm., Educn Cttee, 2005–06). Mem. Council, London Chamber of Commerce and Industry, 1998–. Trustee: Hammersmith United Charities, 1991–96; British Friends of Harvard Business Sch., 1993–; City Arts Trust, 2001–; Thames Fest. Trust, 2004–08; Crossrail Art Foundn, 2014–; Governor: Sacred Heart Jun. Sch., 1990–96; City Literary Inst., 1998–2002; Clifton Coll., 2000–; London Guildhall Univ., 2000–02; London Metropolitan Univ., 2002–10; Prior Weston Primary Sch., Islington, 2014–; Mem. Court, City Univ., 1996–; Donation Gov., Christ's Hosp., 1998–. Constit. Officer, Hammersmith Cons. Assoc., 1990–93; Mem., Council, Bow Gp, 1990–93. Pres., Harvard Business Sch. Club of London, 1997, 1998. Sec. and Treas., Oxford Union Soc., 1979. Freeman, City of London, 1994; Liveryman, Loriners' Co., 1995– (Mem. Court, 2012–). *Recreations:* collecting political caricatures, theatre, cinema, art galleries, arguing. *Address:* City of London Corporation, PO Box 270, Guildhall, EC2P 2EJ. *T:* (020) 7600 4070, 07718 653215. *E:* jeremymayhew@btinternet.com. *Clubs:* Reform, Guildhall.

MAYHEW, Dame Judith; *see* Mayhew Jonas, Dame J.

MAYHEW, Kenneth; Professor of Education and Economic Performance, University of Oxford, 2008–14, now Emeritus (Reader in Economics, 1996–2008); Fellow and Tutor in Economics, Pembroke College, Oxford, 1976–2014, now Emeritus Fellow (Vicegerent, 2000–03); Extraordinary Professor, Maastricht University, since 2014; *b* 1 Sept. 1947; *s* of late Albert Chadwick Mayhew and Alice Mayhew (*née* Leigh). *Educ:* Manchester Grammar Sch.; Worcester Coll., Oxford (MA); London School of Economics (MScEcon). Economic Asst, HM Treasury, 1970–72; Res. Officer, Queen Elizabeth House, Oxford, 1972; Asst Res. Officer, then Res. Officer, Inst. of Economics and Statistics, Oxford, 1972–81; Economic Dir, NEDO, 1989–91; Dir, ESRC Centre on Skills, Knowledge and Orgnl Perf., subseq. Centre on Skills, Knowledge and Orgnl Perf., 1998–2014. Vis. Associate Prof., Cornell Univ., 1981. Advr, CBI, 1983. Mem., Armed Forces Pay Review Body, 2014–. Editor, Oxford Bull. of Econs and Stats, 1976–88; Associate Editor: Oxford Review of Economic Policy, 1984–; Oxford Economic Papers, 1997–; Mem., Editl Bd, Oxford Rev. of Educn, 2009–. *Publications:* Trade Unions and the Labour Market, 1983; (ed with D. Robinson) Pay Policies for the Future, 1983; (ed with A. Bowen) Improving Incentives for the Low Paid, 1990; (ed with A. Bowen) Reducing Regional Inequalities, 1991; (ed jtly) Providing Health Care, 1991; (ed jtly) Britain's Training Deficit, 1994; (ed jtly) The Economics of Skills Obsolescence, 2002; (ed jtly) Low Wage Work in the UK, 2008; reports and numerous articles on labour econs and industrial relns in learned jls. *Recreations:* travel, literature. *Address:* 3 Bitterell, Eynsham, Oxon OX29 4JL. *T:* (01865) 883547. *Club:* Reform.

MAYHEW, Prof. Leslie Dennis, PhD; Professor of Statistics, Cass Business School (formerly City University Business School), since 2002; Managing Director, Mayhew Harper Associates Ltd (formerly Mayhew Associates Ltd), since 2001; *b* 7 Nov. 1947; *s* of Charles and Violet Mayhew; *m* 1984, Karin Sigmund; two *s* one *d*. *Educ:* Birkbeck Coll., London (BSc Hons (1st class); PhD 1979). Dir of OR, later Business Develt Manager, Benefits Agency, and sen. post in Finance/Planning, DHSS, then DSS, 1979–93; Dir of Central Services and Prin. Estabts and Finance Officer, CSO, 1993–96; Gp Dir for Admin. Services and Registration, ONS, 1996–98; Prof. of Geography, Birkbeck Coll., London Univ., 1998–2001. Res. Schol., Internat. Inst. for Applied Systems Analysis, Vienna, 1980–82 and 1999–; Vis. Prof., Birkbeck Coll., London Univ., 1995–98. Mem., REconS, 2009. Hon. FIA 200. *Publications:* Urban Hospital Location, 1986; (jtly) The Economic Impacts of Population Ageing in Japan, 2004; (jtly) Unlocking the Potential, 2014; contrib. learned jls and periodicals in health, transport, geography and operational res. (current research: ageing, pensions, disability, neighbourhood statistics, demography, use of administrative data, health and social care). *Recreations:* tennis, music, travelling. *Address:* Faculty of Actuarial Science and Insurance, Cass Business School, 106 Bunhill Row, EC1Y 8TZ. *E:* lesmayhew@googlemail.com.

MAYHEW JONAS, Dame Judith, DBE 2002; Chairman, London & Partners, 2011–13; Senior Advisor, Tishman Speyer, since 2013; *b* 18 Oct. 1948; *m* 1st, 1976 (marr. diss. 1986); 2nd, 2003, Christopher William Jonas, *qv*. *Educ:* Univ. of Otago, NZ (LLM 1973). Barrister and Solicitor, NZ, 1973; admitted Solicitor, England and Wales, 1993. Lectr in Law, Univ. of Otago, 1970–73; Lecturer in Law and Sub Dean: Univ. of Southampton, 1973–76; King's Coll., London, 1976–89; Dir, Anglo French law degree, Sorbonne, Paris, 1976–89; Dir of Training and Employment Law, Titmuss Sainer Dechert, 1989–94; Dir of Educn and Trng, Wilde Sapte, 1994–99; Provost, King's Coll., Cambridge, 2003–06; Chancellor (formerly Provost), Bishop Grosseteste Univ. Coll., later Bishop Grosseteste Univ., 2008–. Chm., Private Investment Commn, 2000–06. Non-exec. Dir, Merrill Lynch & Co. Inc., USA, 2006–08 (Advr, 2003–06); Special Advisor: to Chm., Clifford Chance, 2000–03; City and Business Advr to Mayor of London, 2000–04. Mem., Adv. Cttee, Barclays Wealth UK Private Bank, 2012–13. Corporation of London: Mem., Court of Common Council, 1986–2004; Chm., Educn Cttee, 1989–95; Chm., 1997–2003, Dep. Chm., 2003–04, Policy and Resources Cttee. Director: Gresham Coll., 1990–2009; ESU, 1993–99; Geffrye Mus., 1995–99; Internat. Financial Services London (formerly British Invisibles), 1996–2004; City Disputes Panel, 1996–99; London First Centre, 1996–2002; London First, 1997–2003; 4Ps, 1997–2004; London Development Partnership, 1998–2000; London Develt Agency, 2000–04; Tower Hamlets Educn Business Partnership, 2001–03; Chm., New West End Co., 2008–13. Chairman: London-NY Dialogues, 1997–; Apeldoorn: British-Dutch Dialogues, 2010–. Trustee: Natural History Mus., 1998–2006; Imperial War Mus., 2008–; Global Trustee, Urban Land Inst., 2013–; Mem. Council, BM Develt Trust, 2001–02. Chairman: Royal Opera House, 2003–08; Ind. Schs Council, 2008–11; Sen. Advr, Chatham House, 2010–. Governor: London Guildhall Univ., 1992–99, 2000–03; Birkbeck Coll., London Univ., 1993–2004 (Chm., 1999–2003; Fellow, 2003)); Imperial Coll., London Univ., 2001–04. Fellow, London Business Sch., 2003; FCGI 2004; Hon. FICPD 2004. Hon. DLaws: Otago, 1998; City, 1999; London Metropolitan, 2003. *Recreations:* opera, ballet, gardening, tennis. *Address:* 25 Victoria Square, SW1W 0RB. *Club:* Guildhall.

MAYLAND, Rev. Canon Ralph, VRD 1962 and bar 1972; non-stipendiary Priest-in-Charge, Brancepeth, 1994–96; *b* 31 March 1927; *s* of James Henry and Lucy Mayland; *m* 1959, Rev. Jean Mary Goldstraw; one *d* and one adopted *d*. *Educ:* Cockburn High Sch., Leeds; Leeds City Training Coll.; Westminster Coll., London Univ.; Ripon Hall, Oxford. Schoolteacher, 1945–46; RN, 1946–51; perm. commn, RNR, 1952, Chaplain, 1961–82; 3rd yr student, 1951–52; schoolteacher, 1952–57; theol student, 1957–59. Curate of Lambeth, 1959–62; Priest-in-charge, St Paul's, Manton, Worksop, 1962–67; Vicar, St Margaret's, Brightside, 1968–72; Chaplain, Sheffield Industrial Mission, 1968–75; Vicar, St Mary's, Ecclesfield, 1972–82; Chaplain to Master Cutler, 1979–80; Canon and Treasurer, York Minster, 1982–94, Canon Emeritus, 1994–. Hon. Chaplain, HMS York, 1989–2011; Chaplain, 8th Destroyer Assoc., 2000–12. Life Mem., Royal Naval Assoc. *Recreation:* collecting Victorian children's literature. *Address:* 5 Hackwood Glade, Hexham, Northumberland NE46 1AL. *T:* (01434) 600339. *Club:* Nikaean.

MAYNARD, Prof. Alan Keith, OBE 2009; Professor of Health Economics, 1997–2014, now Emeritus, and Director, York Health Policy Group, 1998–2014, University of York; *b* 15 Dec. 1944; *s* of Edward Maynard and Hilda (*née* McCausland); *m* 1968, Elizabeth Shanahan; two *s* two *d*. *Educ:* Univ. of Newcastle upon Tyne (BA Hons 1st cl. 1967); Univ. of York (BPhil 1968). Asst Lectr and Lectr, Univ. of Exeter, 1968–71; University of York: Lectr in Econs, 1971–77; Sen. Lectr, then Reader in Econs and Dir, Grad. Programme in Health Econs, 1977–83; Prof. of Econs and Founding Dir, Centre for Health Econs, 1983–95; Sec., Nuffield Provincial Hosps Trust, 1995–96. Vis. Prof., LSE, 1995–2004; Hon. Prof., Univ. of Aberdeen, 2000–06; Adjunct Prof., Technol. Univ. of Sydney, 2003–. Founding Ed., Health Economics, 1992–. Mem., York HA, 1982–91; non-exec. Mem., York Hosp. NHS Trust, 1991–97; Chairman: York NHS Trust, 1997–2010; Vale of York NHS CCG, 2012–15. Member: ESRC, 1986–88; Health Services Res. Cttee, MRC, 1986–92; Police Foundn Inquiry into 1971 Misuse of Drugs Act, 1997–2000; UK Drug Policy Commn, 2008–12; Chm., Evaluation Panel, Fourth Health and Med. Res. Programme, EC, 1990–91; Specialist Advr, H of C Select Cttee on Health, 2006–10. FMedSci 2000. Hon. MFPHM. Hon. DSc Aberdeen, 2004; Hon. LLD Northumbria, 2006. *Publications:* Health Care in the European Community, 1976; (ed jtly) The Public Private Mix for Health, 1982, 2005; (with A. B. Atkinson and C. Trinder) Parents and Children, 1983; (ed jtly) Preventing Alcohol and Tobacco Problems, 1989; (ed jtly) Controlling Legal Addictions, 1990; (ed jtly) Competition in Health Care, 1991; (ed jtly) Purchasing and Providing Cost Effective Health Care, 1993; (ed with Iain Chalmers) Non Random Reflections on Health Services Research, 1997; (ed jtly) Being Reasonable about the Economics of Health, 1997; contrib. numerous articles to various jls. *Recreations:* walking, reading, watching cricket, football. *Address:* York Health Policy Group, Department of Health Sciences, University of York, Heslington, York YO10 5DD. *Club:* Royal Society of Medicine.

MAYNARD, Prof. Geoffrey Walter; Economic Adviser, Investcorp International Ltd, 1986–2003; Director of Economics, Europe and Middle East, Chase Manhattan Bank, 1977–86 (Economic consultant, 1974); Director, Chase Manhattan Ltd, 1977–86; *b* 27 Oct. 1921; *s* of Walter F. Maynard and Maisie Maynard (*née* Bristow); *m* 1949, Marie Lilian Wright; two *d*. *Educ:* London School of Economics. BScEcon; PhD. Served War, 1941–46, RAF. Lectr and Sen. Lectr, UC of S Wales, Cardiff, 1951–62; Economic Consultant, HM Treasury 1962–64; Economic Advr, Harvard Univ. Develt Adv. Gp in Argentina, 1964–65; University of Reading: Reader, 1966–68; Prof. of Economics, 1968–76; Vis. Prof. of Economics, 1976–. Fellow in Pol Economy, Johns Hopkins Univ., 1977–78. Editor, Bankers' Magazine, 1968–72; Under-Sec. (Econs), HM Treasury, 1972–74 (on leave of absence); Dep. Chief Economic Advr, HM Treasury, 1976–77; occasional consultant, IBRD, Overseas Develt Administration of FCO. Mem., Econ. Affairs Cttee, ESRC, 1982–85. Mem. Governing Body, Inst. of Develt Studies, Sussex, 1984–91; Mem. Council, Inst. of Fiscal Studies, 1988–2000. *Publications:* Economic Development and the Price Level, 1962; (jtly) International Monetary Reform and Latin America, 1966; (jtly) A World of Inflation, 1976; The Economy under Mrs Thatcher, 1988; chapters in: Development Policy: theory and practice, ed G. Papanek, 1968; Commonwealth Policy in a Global Context, ed Streeten and Corbet, 1971; Economic Analysis and the Multinational Enterprise, ed J. Dunning, 1974; Special Drawing Rights and Development Aid (paper), 1972; articles in Economic Jl, Oxford Economic Papers, Jl of Development Studies, World Development, etc. *Address:* 18 Mulberry Walk, St George's Park, Burgess Hill, West Sussex RH15 0SZ. *Club:* Reform.

MAYNARD, Paul Christopher; MP (C) Blackpool North and Cleveleys, since 2010; *b* Crewe, 16 Dec. 1975; *s* of Brian and Rosemary Maynard. *Educ:* University Coll., Oxford (BA Hons Modern Hist.). Special Advr to Dr Liam Fox, MP, 1999–2007. Contested (C) Twickenham, 2005. *Address:* House of Commons, SW1A 0AA.

MAYNARD, Roger Paul; Consultant, International Airlines Group, since 2011; Director of Investment and Alliances (formerly Investment and Joint Ventures), British Airways, 1996–2011; Director, Iberia, 2000–11; *b* 10 Feb. 1943; *s* of Leonard John Maynard and May Gertrude Blake; *m* 1st, 1966 (marr. diss. 2004); three *s* (including twin *s*); 2nd, 2011, Judith Lane. *Educ:* Purley Grammar Sch., Surrey; Queens' Coll., Cambridge (MA Hons Economics). Asst Principal, Bd of Trade, 1965; Second Secretary, UK Mission to UN and Internat. Organisations, Geneva, 1968; Principal: Dept of Industry, Shipbuilding Division, 1972; Dept of Trade, Airports Policy, 1975; Asst Sec., Dept of Industry, Air Division, 1978; Counsellor, Aviation and Shipping, British Embassy, Washington, 1982; British Airways: Vice Pres., Commercial Affairs, N America, 1987–89; Exec. Vice Pres., N America, 1989; Dir, Investor Relations and Marketplace Performance, 1989–91; Dir, Corporate Strategy, 1991–96. Chm., British Airways Pension Investment Mgt Ltd, 2005–09. Director: US Air, 1993–96; Qantas, 1993–2004; non-exec. Dir, AJW Aviation, 2011–14. Sen. Advr, L.E.K. Consulting, 2014–15. *Recreations:* cricket, golf, music. *Address:* 43 Rosebank, Holyport Road, Fulham, SW6 6LQ.

MAYNE, Ann, (Mrs Roger Mayne); *see* Jellicoe, P. A.

MAYNE, Prof. David Quinn, FRS 1985; FREng; Professor of Electrical and Computer Engineering, University of California, Davis, 1989–96, now Professor Emeritus; Senior Research Investigator, Department of Electrical and Electronic Engineering, Imperial College London, since 1996; *b* 23 April 1930; *s* of Leslie Harper Mayne and Jane Quin; *m* 1954, Josephine Mary Hess; three *d*. *Educ:* Univ. of the Witwatersrand, Johannesburg (BSc (Eng), MSc); DIC, PhD, DSc London. FIET, FIEEE; FREng (FEng 1987). Lectr, Univ. of Witwatersrand, 1950–54, 1956–59; R&D Engineer, British Thomson Houston Co., Rugby, 1955–56; Imperial College: Lectr, 1959–67, Reader, 1967–71; Prof. of Control Theory, 1971–89, now Prof. Emeritus; Sen. Sci. Res. Fellow, 1979–80; Hd of Dept of Electrical Engrg, 1984–88. Research Consultant, 1974–, at Univs of California (Berkeley, and Santa Barbara), Lund, Newcastle NSW, and Wisconsin. Res. Fellow, Harvard Univ., 1970; Vis. Prof., Academia Sinica, Beijing, Shanghai and Guangzhou, 1981; Hon. Prof., Beihang Univ., Beijing, 2006. Corresp. Mem., Nacional Acad. de Ingenieria, Mexico, 1983. FIC 2000; Fellow, IFAC, 2006. Hon. DEng Lund Univ., 1995. Heaviside Premium, IEE, 1981, 1985; Sir Harold Hartley Medal, Inst. of Measurement and Control, 1986; Control Systems Award, IEEE, 2009; High Impact Paper Award, 2011, Quazza Medal, 2014, IFAC. *Publications:* Differential Dynamic Programming, vol. 24 in Modern Analytic and Computational Methods in Science and Mathematics (with D. H. Jacobson, ed R. Bellman), 1970; Geometric Methods in System Theory, proc. NATO Advanced Study Inst., (ed. with R. W. Brockett), 1973; (with J. B. Rawlings) Model Predictive Control: theory and design, 2009; contribs to learned jls. *Recreations:* walking, cross-country ski-ing. *Address:* Department of Electrical and Electronic Engineering, Imperial College London, SW7 2BT.

MAYNE, Eric; Under Secretary, General Functions Group, Department of Economic Development, Northern Ireland, 1986–87, retired; *b* 2 Sept. 1928; *s* of Robert P. Mayne and Margaret Mayne; *m* 1954, Sarah Boyd (*née* Gray); three *s* two *d*. *Educ:* Bangor Grammar Sch.; Univ. of Reading (BSc); Michigan State Univ. (MS). Horticultural Advisor, Min. of Agriculture, NI, 1949–56; Kellogg Foundation Fellow, 1956–57; Horticultural Advisor, HQ Min. of Agriculture, NI, 1957–64; Principal Officer, 1964–67; Gen. Manager, NI Agric.

Trust, 1967–74; Sen. Asst Secretary, Dept of Agriculture, NI, 1974–79; Dep. Sec., Dept of Manpower Services, NI, 1979–82; Under Sec., Dept of Econ. Develt, NI, 1982–87. *Recreations:* gardening, winemaking.

MAYO, 11th Earl of, *cr* 1785; **Charles Diarmuidh John Bourke;** Baron Naas, 1776; Viscount Mayo, 1781; *b* 11 June 1953; *e s* of 10th Earl of Mayo and his 1st wife, Margaret Jane Robinson Harrison; S father, 2006; *m* 1st, 1975, Marie Antoinette Cronnelly (marr. diss. 1979); one *d*; 2nd, 1985, Marie Veronica Mannion; two *s*. *Educ:* St Aubyn's, Rottingdean; Portora Royal Sch., Enniskillen; QUB; Bolton Street Coll. of Technology, Dublin. *Heir: s* Lord Naas, *qv*. *Address:* Derryinver, Beach Road, Clifden, Co. Galway, Eire.

MAYO, Col (Edward) John, OBE 1976; Director General, Help the Aged, 1983–96; *b* 24 May 1931; *s* of late Rev. Thomas Edward Mayo, JP, and Constance Muriel Mayo; *m* 1st, 1961, Jacqueline Margaret Anne Armstrong, MBE 1985, Lieut WRAC (*d* 1993), *d* of late Brig. C. D. Armstrong, CBE, DSO, MC; one *s*; 2nd, 1998, Pamela Joyce Shimwell (MBE 2014). *Educ:* King's Coll., Taunton. Commissioned into Royal Regt of Artillery, 1951; served Malta and N Africa 36 HAA Regt, 1951–55; ADC to Governor of Malta, 1953–54; 2nd Regt RHA, BAOR, 1955–58; ADC to C-in-C BAOR/Comdr Northern Army Gp, 1958–60; 20 Field Regt, RA UK, 1960–61; Adjt 20 Field Regt, RA Malaya, 1961–63; Adjt 254 (City of London) Regt RA(TA), 1963–64; Instr RMA, Sandhurst, 1964–66; GSO3 Mil. Operations, MoD, 1966–68; Second in Comd 20 Heavy Regt, RA BAOR, 1968–70; GSO2 Instr Staff Coll., 1970–72; commanded 17 Trng Regt and Depot RA, 1972–74, and The Depot Regt RA, 1974–75; GSO1 Public Relations MoD, 1976–79; Col GS; Public Information BAOR, 1979–83; retired 1983. Dir, Executive Communication Consultants (IOM) Ltd, 1999–2008. Chm. Comrs, Jurby, IOM, 2002–04, 2008–09. Mem. Bd, HelpAge Sri Lanka, 1985–; Trustee: HelpAge Kenya, 1984–; HelpAge India, 1985–99; Global Cancer, 1998–2004; Combat Stress, 1993–2005. Patron: The Homeless Fund, 1996–2001; Gesture, 2002–03; Employers Retirement Assoc., 2003–. MCIPR (MIPR 1981). FRSA 1987. *Publications:* miscellaneous articles on military matters. *Recreations:* fishing, gardening, sailing, travelling, collecting and restoring antiques. *Address:* Ballamoar Castle, Sandygate, Isle of Man IM7 3AJ. *T:* (01624) 897504. *E:* mayo@manx.net. *Clubs:* Army and Navy, Special Forces, Woodroffe's, MCC.

MAYO, Rupert Charles; His Honour Judge Mayo; a Circuit Judge, since 2009; Resident Judge, Northampton Crown Court, since 2011; *b* Hemel Hempstead, 5 March 1963; *s* of late Philip Arthur Mayo and Jill Mary Mayo (*née* Jenkins); *m* 1990 (marr. diss. 2008); one *s* two *d*; *m* 2013, Vanessa Marshall; one *s*. *Educ:* Bedford Sch.; Durham Univ. (BA Hons Law and Politics). Called to the Bar, Gray's Inn, 1987; in practice in London and on Midland Circuit, principally in crime (fraud and serious offences) and regulatory work, London, 1987–2009; a Recorder, 2005–09. Trustee, Rutland Agricl Soc., 2006–. Chm., Cottesmore Hunt, 2004–06. Ed., Hong Kong Current Law, 1985–86. *Recreations:* sailing, cookery, shooting, keeping pigs and poultry, running. *Address:* Northampton Crown Court, 85–87 Lady's Lane, Northampton NN1 3HQ.

MAYO, Simon Andrew Hicks; Presenter: Drivetime Show, BBC Radio 2, since 2010; Kermode and Mayo's Film Review, BBC Radio Five Live, since 2001; *b* 21 Sept. 1958; *s* of Derek Leslie Mayo and Gillian Mary Mayo; *m* 1986, Hilary Mary Bird; two *s* one *d*. *Educ:* Solihull Sch.; Worthing Grammar Sch.; Warwick Univ. (BA Hons). Presenter: Breakfast Show, 1988–93, Morning Show, 1993–2001, Radio 1; Album Chart Show, Radio 2, 2001–; Radio 5 Live Afternoon Show, 2001–09; television: Scruples, 1988; Best of Magic, 1989; Confessions, 1994, 1995, 1996, 1997; The Big End, 1999; Winning Lines, 1998–2000; Dig!, 2005. Hon. Vice-Pres., Melchester Rovers, 1989. Hon. DLitt Warwick, 2005. *Publications:* (with S. Jenkins) Breakfast in the Holy Land, 1988; Confessions, 1991; Further Confessions, 1992; (with M. Wroe) Snogging, 1992; (with M. Wroe) The Big Match, 1993; Very Worst of Confessions, 1993; Classic Confessions, 1994; Itch (novel), 2012. *Recreations:* etymology, astronomy, the school run, walking in bad weather, thinking up quizzes. *Address:* c/o PBJ Management, 22 Rathbone Street, W1T 1LG.

MAYO, Simon Herbert; Vice President, Court of Appeal of the High Court, Hong Kong, 2000–03; *b* 15 Nov. 1937; *s* of late Herbert and Marjorie Mayo; *m* 1966, Catherine Yin Ying Young; one *s* one *d*. *Educ:* Harrow Sch. Admitted a solicitor, England and Wales, 1961, Hong Kong, 1963; called as barrister and solicitor, W Australia, 1967. Asst Legal Advr, GEC, 1961; Asst Solicitor, Deacons, Solicitors, Hong Kong, 1963; in private practice, WA, 1967; Asst Registrar, 1968, Registrar, 1976, Supreme Court of Hong Kong; a Judge of the High Court, Hong Kong, 1980–95; Justice of Appeal, Court of Appeal of Supreme, then High, Court, Hong Kong, 1995–2000. *Recreations:* golf, music, literature, walking. *Clubs:* Hong Kong, Sheko Country (Hong Kong).

MAYO, Simon Peter; QC 2008; a Recorder, since 2009; *b* London, 23 Sept. 1961; *s* of Peter and Anita Mayo. Called to the Bar, Inner Temple, 1985; in practice as barrister specialising in criminal law, 1985–. *Recreations:* Rugby, motorsport, running, cycling, swimming, travel. *Address:* 187 Fleet Street, EC4A 2AT. *T:* (020) 7430 7430.

MAYOR, His Honour Hugh Robert; QC 1986; a Circuit Judge, 1992–2007; *b* 12 Oct. 1941; *s* of George and Grace Mayor; *m* 1970, Carolyn Ann Stubbs; one *s* one *d*. *Educ:* Kirkham Grammar Sch.; St John's Coll., Oxford (MA). Lectr, Univ. of Leicester, 1964 (MA). Called to the Bar, Gray's Inn, 1968; a Recorder, 1982–92.

MAYOR ZARAGOZA, Federico; President, Fundación Cultura de Paz, Madrid, since 1999; *b* Barcelona, 27 Jan. 1934; *s* of Federico Mayor and Juana Zaragoza; *m* 1956, Maria Angeles Menéndez; two *s* one *d*. *Educ:* Madrid Complutense Univ. Granada University: Prof. of Biochemistry, 1963–73; Rector, 1968–72; Prof. of Biochemistry, Univ. Autónoma, Madrid, 1973. Dir, 1974–78, Scientific Chm., 1983–87, Molecular Biology Centre, Higher Council for Scientific Research. Under-Sec., Min. for Educn and Science, 1974–75; Pres., Commn for Study of Special Set of Rules for the four Catalan Provinces, 1976; Mem., Cortes (Parliament) for Granada, 1977–78; Dep. Dir-Gen., UNESCO, 1978–81; Minister for Educn and Science, Spain, 1981–82; Special Advr to Dir-Gen., UNESCO, 1982; Dir, Inst. of Sciences of Man, Madrid, 1983–87; Dir-Gen., UNESCO, 1987–99. Mem., European Parlt, 1987. Chair, Expert Gp, European Res. Council, 2003; Co-Chair, Alliance of Civilizations, UN, 2005–06. President: Initiative for Sci. in Europe, 2007–; Internat. Commn Against the Death Penalty, 2010–. *Address:* Mar Caribe, 15 Interland, Majadahonda, 28220 Madrid, Spain.

MAYOU, Prof. Richard Anthony, FRCP, FRCPsych; Professor of Psychiatry, University of Oxford, 1997–2004 and Fellow, Nuffield College, Oxford, 1976–2005, now Emeritus; *b* 23 Nov. 1940; *s* of Cecil Richard Mayou and Kathleen (*née* Batt); *m* 1981, Ann Foster (*née* Bowler) (*d* 2011); one step *s* one step *d*. *Educ:* King Edward's Sch., Birmingham; St John's Coll., Oxford (open scholar; BM, MSc, MA); Inst. of Psychiatry, London Univ. (MPhil). FRCPsych 1979; FRCP 1985. House Officer, Queen Elizabeth Hosp., Birmingham, 1966–67; House Physician, Hammersmith and Brompton Hosps, London, 1967–68; Registrar, then Sen. Registrar, Maudsley & Bethlem Royal Hosps, London, 1968–72; Lectr and Clinical Reader in Psychiatry, Oxford, 1973–97. Chm., Friends of Oxford Univ. Botanic Garden, 2004–. *Publications:* Shorter Oxford Textbook of Psychiatry, 1983, 4th edn 2001; Psychiatry Core Text, 1994, 3rd edn 2004; contribs to learned jls on psychological aspects of medical symptoms and disorders. *Recreations:* countryside, gardening, architecture, the arts. *Address:* Hill House, Shabbington, Aylesbury, Bucks HP18 9HQ. *T:* (01844) 201885. *E:* richard.mayou@nuffield.ox.ac.uk. *Club:* Athenæum.

MAYR-HARTING, Prof. Henry Maria Robert Egmont, DPhil, DD; FBA 1992; Regius Professor of Ecclesiastical History, University of Oxford, 1997–2003, now Emeritus; Co-Censor of Degrees, Christ Church, Oxford, since 2004 (Lay Canon, 1997–2003; Emeritus Canon, 2013); *b* 6 April 1936; *s* of Herbert Mayr-Harting and Anna Mayr-Harting (*née* Münzer), Prague; *m* 1968, Caroline Henry; one *s* one *d*. *Educ:* Douai School; Merton Coll., Oxford (BA Mod. Hist. 1957; MA; DPhil 1961; DD 2010). Asst Lectr and Lectr in Medieval History, Univ. of Liverpool, 1960–68; Fellow, and Tutor in Medieval History, 1968–97, Emeritus Fellow, 1997, St Peter's Coll., Oxford; Reader in Medieval History, Oxford Univ., 1993–97. Vis. Fellow, Peterhouse, Cambridge, 1983; Slade Prof. of Fine Art, Oxford Univ., 1987–88; Brown Foundn Fellow, Univ. of the South, Tennessee, 1992. Warburton Lect., Lincoln's Inn, 2008. Corresp. Mem., Austrian Acad. of Scis, 2001. Confrater, Douai Abbey, 2003. Hon. DLitt: Lawrence Univ., Wisconsin, 1998; Univ. of the South, Tennessee, 1999; UEA, 2009. *Publications:* The Acta of the Bishops of Chichester 1075–1207, 1965; The Coming of Christianity to Anglo-Saxon England, 1972, 3rd edn 1991; What to do in the Penwith Peninsula, Cornwall, in less than perfect weather, 1987, 2nd edn 1988; Ottonian Book Illumination: an historical study, 2 vols, 1991 (trans. German 1991), 2nd edn 1999; Two Conversions to Christianity: the Bulgarians and the Anglo-Saxons, 1994; Perceptions of Angels in History (inaugural lecture), 1998; (ed with Richard Harries) Christianity: two thousand years, 2001; Church and Cosmos in Early Ottonian Germany: the view from Cologne, 2007; Religion and Society in the Medieval West 600–1200: selected papers, 2010; Religion, Politics and Society in Britain 1066–1272, 2011; articles in learned jls, conference collections and Festschriften. *Recreations:* music, especially playing keyboard instruments; watching cricket. *Address:* St Peter's College, Oxford OX1 2DL; 29 Portland Road, Oxford OX2 7EZ. *Clubs:* Athenæum; Worcestershire County Cricket.

MAYS, Colin Garth, CMG 1988; HM Diplomatic Service, retired; Bursar, Yehudi Menuhin School, 1991–97; *b* 16 June 1931; *s* of William Albert Mays and Sophia May Mays (*née* Pattinson); *m* 1956, Margaret Patricia, *d* of Philemon Robert Lloyd and Gladys Irene (*née* Myers); one *s*. *Educ:* Acklam Hall Sch.; St John's Coll., Oxford (Heath Harrison Scholar, MA). Served in Army, 1949–51; entered HM Foreign (subseq. Diplomatic) Service, 1955; FO, 1955–56; Sofia, 1956–58; Baghdad, 1958–60; FO, 1960; UK Delegn to Conf. of 18 Nation Cttee on Disarmament, Geneva, 1960; Bonn, 1960–65; FO, 1965–69; Prague, 1969–72; FCO, 1972–77; Head of Information Administration Dept, 1974–77; Counsellor (Commercial), Bucharest, 1977–80; seconded to PA Management Consultants, 1980–81; Diplomatic Service Overseas Inspector, 1981–83; High Commissioner: Seychelles, 1983–86; Bahamas, 1986–91. *Recreations:* sailing, travel. *Club:* Travellers.

MAYSTADT, Dr Philippe; President, and Chairman, Board of Directors, European Investment Bank, 2000–11; President: Belgian Academy for Research and Higher Education, since 2014; International Center for European Education, since 2015; *b* 14 March 1948; *s* of Auguste Maystadt and Marie-Thérèse Deblon; *m* 1970, Suzanne Franquin; two *s* one *d*. *Educ:* Catholic Univ. of Louvain, Belgium (PhD Law 1970); Claremont Grad. Sch., LA (MA Public Admin). Asst Prof., Catholic Univ. of Louvain, 1970–77; MHR, Charleroi, Belgium, 1977–91, 1995–98; Mem., Senate, 1998–99; Sec. of State for Walloon Reg., 1979–80; Minister: for CS and Scientific Policy, 1980–81; of Budget, Scientific Policy and Planning, 1981–85; of Econ. Affairs, 1985–86; Dep. Prime Minister and Minister of Econ. Affairs, 1986–88; Minister of Finance, 1988–95; Minister of Finance and Foreign Trade, June–Sept. 1995; Dep. Prime Minister and Minister of Finance and Foreign Trade, 1995–98. Pres., Parti Social Chrétien, 1998–99. Chairman: G-10 Ministers of Finance, 1990–91; Council of Ministers of Economy and Finance of EC, 1993; Interim Cttee, IMF, 1993–98; Council of Governors, EBRD, 1997–98. Special Advr on Internat. Financial Reporting Standards, European Commn, 2013–14. Part-time Professor: Faculty of Law, Catholic Univ. of Louvain, 1989–; Faculty of Law, Econs and Finance, Univ. of Luxembourg, 2012–. *Publications:* (with A. Jacquemin) Les aspects juridiques de l'intervention de l'Etat dans la vie économique, 1975 (Prix spécial de l'Association des juristes d'entreprises); Ecouter et puis Décider, 1988; (with F. Dermine-Minet) Comprendre l'économie: le marché et l'Etat à l'heure de la mondialisation, 1998, 4th edn 2007; Europe: le continent perdu?, 2012.

MAZANKOWSKI, Rt Hon. Donald (Frank); PC (Can.) 1979; CC 2013 (OC 2000); AOE 2003; Deputy Prime Minister of Canada, 1986–93; Minister of Finance, 1991–93; *b* 27 July 1935; *s* of late Frank Mazankowski and Dora (*née* Lonowski); *m* 1958, Lorraine Poleschuk; three *s*. *Educ:* High Sch., Viking, Alberta. MP (Progressive Conservative), Vegreville, 1968–93; Minister for Transport and Minister responsible for Canadian Wheat Bd, 1979–80; Minister of Transport, 1984–86; Pres. of Queen's Privy Council for Canada, 1986–91; Minister of Agriculture, 1988–91; Minister responsible for Privatization, 1988; Govt House Leader and Pres. of Privy Council, 1986–91. Director: Shaw Communications Inc., 1993–2009; IMG Financial (formerly Investors Group) Inc., 1994–2010; Great West Life Assce Co., 1994–2010; Power Corp. of Canada, 1996–; Weyerhaeuser Co., 1997–2009; ATCO Gp, 1999–; Canadian Oilsands Trust, 2002–10; Dir and Trustee, Yellow Pages Gp, 2003–10. Chairman: Canadian Genetics Diseases Network, 1998–2004; Premier's Adv. Council on Health, Alberta, 2000–02. Hon. DEng Technical Univ. of Nova Scotia, 1987; Hon. LLD Alberta, 1993. *Address:* 80 Nottingham Inlet, Sherwood Park, AB T8A 6N2, Canada. *E:* donmaz@shaw.ca.

MBEKEANI, Nyemba W.; Chief Executive, Mkulumadzi Farm Bakeries Ltd, since 1981; Chairman, Spearhead Holdings Ltd, since 1987; *b* 15 June 1929; Malawi parentage; *m* 1950, Lois Moses (*née* Chikankheni); two *s* three *d*. *Educ:* Henry Henderson Institute, Blantyre; London Sch. of Economics (Economic and Social Administration, 1963). Local Government Officer, 1945–58; political detention in Malawi and Southern Rhodesia, 1959–60; Business Executive, 1960–61; Local Govt Officer, 1963–64; Foreign Service, 1964; High Commissioner for Malawi in London, 1964–67; Ambassador to USA and Permanent Rep. at the UN, 1967–72; Ambassador to Ethiopia, 1972–73; Gen. Manager, Malaŵi Housing Corp., 1973–81. Farmer, company director, tea broker, baker, confectioner. Chm., Petroleum Control Commn, 1987–93; Comr, Malaŵi Electoral Commn, 1998–99. Board Member: Lingadzi Farming Co., 1987–; Sable Farming Co., 1987–. Trustee, Small Farmers Fertilizer Revolving Fund, 1988–. Counsellor, Malaŵi Univ. Council, 1984–93; Chm., Malaŵi Polytechnic Bd of Govs, 1988–93. *Recreation:* flower gardening. *Address:* PO Box 2095, Blantyre, Malaŵi. *T:* 08831060; *Telex:* 44847 Lumadzi MI.

MBEKI, Thabo Mvuyelwa, Hon. GCMG 2000; President of South Africa, 1999–2008 (Deputy President, 1994–99); President, African National Congress, 1997–2007 (Deputy President, 1994–97); *b* 18 June 1942; *s* of late Govan and of Epainette Mbeki; *m* 1974, Zanele Dlamini. *Educ:* St John's High Sch., Umtata; Lovedale Inst.; Sussex Univ. (MA Econs; Hon. LLD 1995). Youth organiser, ANC, Johannesburg, 1961–62; left S Africa, 1962; worked in ANC Offices, London, 1967–70; mil. training, USSR, 1970; African National Congress: Asst Sec., Revolutionary Council, 1971–72; Mem., NEC, 1975–2007; Acting Rep., Swaziland, 1975–76; Rep. Nigeria, 1976–78; Political Sec., President's Office, 1978; Dir, Information and Publicity, 1984–89; Hd, Dept of Internat. Affairs, 1989–94 (Hd, delegn talks with S African Govt which led to unbanning of ANC and release of political prisoners, 1989; Mem., delegn concerning talks with S African Govt, 1990); Chm., 1993. Est. Thabo Mbeki Foundn, 2008.

M'BOW, Amadou-Mahtar; Director-General of Unesco, 1974–87; *b* 20 March 1921; *s* of Fara-N'Diaye M'Bow and N'Goné Casset, Senegal; *m* 1951, Raymonde Sylvain; one *s* two *d*. *Educ:* Univ. of Paris. Teacher, Rosso Coll., Mauritania, 1951–53; Dir, Service of Fundamental and Community Educn, Senegal, 1953–57; Min. of Education and Culture,

1957–58; Teacher at Lycée Faidherbe, St-Louis, Senegal, 1958–64; Prof., Ecole Normale Supérieure, Dakar, 1964–66; Minister of Educn, 1966–68; Mem. Nat. Assembly, Senegal, 1968–70; Minister of Culture, Youth and Sports 1968–70; Asst Dir-Gen. for Educn, UNESCO, 1970–74. Pres., Assises Nationales du Sénégale, 2008–. Member: Acad. des Sciences d'Outre-Mer, 1977; Acad. of Kingdom of Morocco, 1981; Hon. Mem., Royal Acad. Fine Arts, San Temo, Spain, 1977; For. Mem., Acad. of Athens, 1983. Hon. Professor: Ecole normale supérieure, Dakar, 1979; Ind. Univ. of Santo Domingo, 1978; Nat. Ind. Univ. of Mexico, 1979. Hon. Dr: Buenos Aires, 1974; Granada (Lit. and Phil.), Sherbrooke (Educn), West Indies (Laws), 1975; Open, Kliment Ohridski, Sofia, Nairobi (Lit.), 1976; Malaya (Lit.), Philippines (Laws); Venice (Geog.), Uppsala (Soc. Scis), Moscow (Soc. Scis), Paris I, 1977; Andes (Philos.), Peru (Educn Scis), Haiti, Tribhunvan Univ., Nepal (Lit.), State Univ., Mongolia, Khartoum (Law), Sri Lanka, 1978; Charles Univ., Prague (Phil.), Tashkent, Québec, 1979; Nat. Univ. of Zaïre, Madras, Belgrade, Ivory Coast, Sierra Leone, 1980; Univ. Gama Filho, Brazil, 1981; Nat. Univ. of Lesotho, 1981; Univ. of Benin, 1981; Technical Univ. of Middle East, Ankara, 1981; Univ. of Ankara, 1981, Univ. of Gand, Belgium, 1982; Nat. Univ. of Seoul, 1982; State Univ. of Kiev, 1982; Laval Univ., Quebec, 1982; Quaid-i-Azam Univ., Islamabad, 1983; Jawaharlal Nehru Univ., New Delhi, 1983; Aix-Marseilles Univ., 1983; Beijing Univ., China, 1983; Kim Il Sung Univ., PDR of Korea (Pedagogy), 1983; Lucknow Univ., India (Lit.), 1983; Chulalongkorn Univ., Thailand (Pedagogy), 1983; Sokoto Univ., Nigeria (Lit.), 1984; Malta Univ., 1986; Polytechnic Univ. of Catalonia, Cauca Univ. Popayan (Colombia), Univ. of Mayor, Real y Pontificia de San Francisco Xavier de Chuquisaca, Sucre (Bolivia), 1987; Grand Tribute, Univ. Candido Mendes, Brazil, 1981. Order of Merit, Senegal; Grand Cross: Order of the Liberator, Order of Andres Bello and Order of Francisco de Miranda, Venezuela; Order of Merit and Juan Montalvo National Order of Merit (Educn), Ecuador; Order of Miguel Antonio Caro y Rufino José Cuervo, Colombia; Order of Stara Planina, Bulgaria; Order of the Sun, Peru; Order of Merit of Duarte, Sanchez and Mella, Dominican Republic; National Order of the Lion, Senegal; Order of Alphonso X the Sabio, Spain; Order of the Southern Cross and Order of Merit of Guararapes, Brazil; Order of Distinguished Diplomatic Service Merit, Republic of Korea; Order of Sikatuna, Philippines; Order of Merit, Indonesia; Order of Merit, Syrian Arab Republic; Order of Merit, Jordan; Order of the Arab Republic of Egypt; Order of Felix Varela, Cuba; Grand Cross: Order of Nat. Flag (PDR of Korea); Order of Meritorious Action (Libya); Nat. Order of Andean Condor (Bolivia); Grand Order of Education (Bolivia); Grand Officer: National Order of Ivory Coast; National Order of Guinea; Order of Merit, Cameroon; National Order of Merit, Mauritania; Order of Independence, Tunisia; Commander: Order of Academic Palms; National Order of Upper Volta; Order of the Gabonese Merit; Order of Arts and Letters, France; Grand Medal, Order of the Inconfidência, State of Minas Gerais, Brazil; Medal: Order of Merit of Caetés, Olinda, Brazil; Order of Manual José Hurtado, Panama; Superior Decoration for Education, Jordan. Man and his World Peace Prize, Canada, 1978; Gold Medal of Olympic Order, 1981; Gold Medal of ALECSO (Arab Educnl, Cultural and Scientific Orgn), 1981; Internat. Dimitrov Prize, 1982; Gold Medal: Champion of Africa, 1986, of Andalucia, 1987. *Publications:* Le temps des peuples, ed R. Laffont, 1982; Where the Future Begins, 1982; Hope for the Future, 1984; Unesco: universality and international intellectual co-operation, 1985; numerous monographs, articles in educnl jls, textbooks, etc. *Address:* Assises Nationales du Sénégal - Bureau des Assises, Rue Kaolack X Louga, Point E, BP 22547, Dakar-Ponty, Senegal.

MBUBAEGBU, Stella Ngozi, CBE 2008; Principal and Chief Executive, Highbury College, Portsmouth, since 2001; *b* Obinagu, Nigeria, 27 Oct. 1955; *d* of Isaac and Patience Ene; *m* 1982, Chima Mbubaegbu; three *d. Educ:* Univ. of Benin (BA Hons English; MA); Univ. of Greenwich (PGCE); Univ. of Sheffield (MEd Dist.). Asst Registrar, W African Exams Council, 1983–89; Lectr, Sen. Lectr of Quality, then Manager, Southwark Coll., 1989–98; Dir, Planning and Quality, 1998–2000, Vice Principal, 2000–01, Croydon Coll. Mem. Bd, Learning and Skills Improvement Service, 2008; Chm., Further Educn Constituency Panel, Lifelong Learning UK, 2009. Chm., Black Leadership Initiative, 2002. Pres., Assoc. of Coll. Mgt, 2009. Fellow, Inst. for Learning, 2008; FRSA 2002. MInstD 2007. *Recreations:* reading, travel. *Address:* Highbury College, Tudor Crescent, Portsmouth, Hants PO6 2SA. *T:* (023) 9231 3215. *E:* stella.mbubaegbu@highbury.ac.uk.

MEACHER, family name of **Baroness Meacher**.

MEACHER, Baroness *cr* 2006 (Life Peer), of Spitalfields in the London Borough of Tower Hamlets; **Molly Christine Meacher;** Chairman, All Party Parliamentary Group for Drug Policy Reform, since 2011; *b* 15 May 1940; *d* of William F. and Lucy M. Reid; *m* 1991, Peter Richard Grenville Layard (*see* Baron Layard); two *s* two *d* by a former *m. Educ:* Berkhamsted Sch. for Girls; York Univ. (BScEcon); Univ. of London (DipSoc; CQSW). Campaign Dir and Res. Officer, CPAG, 1970–72; Projects Officer, Mental Health Foundn, 1973–78; Approved Social Worker, 1980–82; Mgr, Nat. Assoc. of CABx, 1982–84; Parly Officer, BASW, 1984–87; CEO, Campaign for Work, 1987–92; Advr to Russian Govt, 1991–94; Mem., later Dep. then Acting Chm., Police Complaints Authy, 1994–2002; Chairman: Security Industry Authy, 2002–04; E London NHS Foundn Trust (formerly E London and The City Mental Health NHS Trust), 2004–12; non-exec. Dir, Tower Hamlets Healthcare NHS Trust, 1994–98. Mental Health Act Comr, 1987–92; Comr, Marmot Commn on Inequalities in Health, 2008–10; Dir, Positive Mental Health, 2009–. Pres., Haemophilia Soc., 2013–. Trustee, Russian European Trust, 1998–2010. *Publications:* Scrounging on the Welfare, 1970; (jtly) To Him Who Hath, 1971; New Methods of Mental Health Care, 1979; (contrib.) The Mentally Disordered Offender, 1991. *Recreations:* music, golf, bridge, grandchildren. *Address:* House of Lords, SW1A 0PW. *E:* meachermc@parliament.uk.

MEACHER, Rt Hon. Michael (Hugh); PC 1997; MP (Lab) Oldham West and Royton, since 1997 (Oldham West, 1970–97); *b* 4 Nov. 1939; *s* of late George Hubert and Doris May Meacher; *m* 1st, 1962, Molly Christine (*née* Reid) (*see* Baroness Meacher) (marr. diss. 1987); two *s* two *d*; 2nd, 1988, Mrs Lucianne Sawyer. *Educ:* Berkhamsted Sch., Herts; New College, Oxford (Greats, Class 1 1962); LSE (DSA 1963). Sec. to Danilo Dolci Trust, 1964; Research Fellow in Social Gerontology, Univ. of Essex, 1965–66; Lecturer in Social Administration: Univ. of York, 1967–69; London Sch. of Economics, 1970. Parly Under-Secretary of State: DoI, 1974–75; DHSS, 1975–76; Dept of Trade, 1976–79; Mem., Shadow Cabinet, 1983–97; chief opposition spokesman on health and social security, 1983–87, on employment, 1987–89, on social security, 1989–92, on development and co-operation, 1992–93, on Citizen's Charter, 1993–94, on transport, 1994–95, on employment, 1995–96, on envmtl protection, 1996–97; Minister of State (Minister for the Envmt), DETR, 1997–2001, DEFRA, 2001–03. Mem., Treasury Select Cttee, 1980–83 (a Chm. of its sub-cttee). Chm., Labour Co-ordinating Cttee, 1978–83; Member: Campaign for Press Freedom; Labour Party NEC, 1983–88. Vis. Prof., Univ. of Surrey, Dept of Sociology, 1980–87. *Publications:* Taken for a Ride: Special Residential Homes for the Elderly Mentally Infirm, a study of separatism in social policy, 1972; Fabian pamphlets incl. The Care of the Old, 1969; Wealth: Labour's Achilles Heel, in Labour and Equality, ed P. Townsend and N. Bosanquet, 1972; Socialism with a Human Face, 1981; Diffusing Power: the key to Socialist revival, 1992; Destination of the Species: the riddle of human existence, 2010; The State We Need: keys to the renaissance of Britain, 2013; numerous articles. *Recreations:* music, sport, reading. *Address:* House of Commons, SW1A 0AA; 34 Kingscliffe Gardens, SW19 6NR.

MEACHIN, Andrew Philip; a District Judge (Magistrates' Courts), since 2012; *b* Nantwich, 12 July 1953; *s* of Jack Meachin and Brenda Meachin; *m* (marr. diss.); three *s* one *d. Educ:* King's Sch., Macclesfield; Coll. of Commerce, Aston Univ. Articled Clerk, Howarth Maitland & Son, Bury, Lancs, 1972–77; admitted solicitor, 1977; Solicitor and Partner, Wains (formerly Wain, Langstaff, Payne and Goalen), 1978–2012; Acting Stipendiary Magistrate, subseq. Dep. District Judge, 1999–2012. *Recreations:* cycling, walking, golf, theatre. *Address:* The Law Courts, Teesside TS1 2AS. *T:* (01642) 240301, *Fax:* (01642) 224010. *E:* apmeach@ntlworld.com. *Club:* Prestbury Golf.

MEAD, Deryk, CBE 2003; Chief Executive, NCH (formerly NCH Action for Children), 1996–2004; *b* 3 July 1945; *s* of Joe and Ruth Mead; *m* 1967, Susan Margaret Kay; two *s. Educ:* Univ. of Manchester (BSc, MSc); Univ. of Leeds (DipPSW); CQSW. Approved Sch. Officer, Burnley, 1969–74; Principal Officer, Social Services, Lancs, 1974–79; Deputy Director of Social Services: Rochdale, 1979–87; Cumbria, 1987–91; Dir of Social Services, Gloucestershire, 1991–96. Member: Meat Hygiene Bd, 2005–07; Bd, Passenger Focus, 2005; Bd, NHS Midlands and East (formerly W Midlands Strategic HA), 2007–; Public Mem., Network Rail, 2007. *Publications:* contrib. to numerous publications. *Recreations:* fell running, rock and ice climbing, sea kayaking.

MEAD, Dr Keith Owen, CB 2000; CEng, FIET; CMath, FIMA; Director of Technology and Engineering, Government Communications Headquarters, 1994–2000; *b* 14 Oct. 1945; *s* of Kenneth Stanley Mead and Constance Louise Mead; *m* 1971, Fiona McDonald McCall; one *s* one *d. Educ:* Southend High Sch. for Boys; Sussex Univ. (BSc); Liverpool Univ. (PhD 1971). CEng 1996, FIET (FIEE 1996); CMath 1996, FIMA 1996; ATCL (MusEd) 2001. Joined GCHQ, 1970; PSO, 1975; Asst Sec., 1987; RCDS 1990; Under Sec., 1994. Mem. Council, IMA, 1999–2002. *Publications:* maths res. papers in learned jls. *Recreations:* playing the piano, teaching and arranging music, walking. *E:* me@keithmead.name.

MEAD, Dr Timothy John; Registrary, University of Cambridge, 1997–2007, now Emeritus; Fellow, Wolfson College, Cambridge, 1997–2010, now Emeritus; Secretary, Cambridge Commonwealth and Overseas Trusts, 2008–10; Honorary Director, Cambridge European Trust, 2008–10; *b* 31 May 1947; *s* of Ernest Arthur Mead and Catherine Beryl Louisa Mead (*née* Midlane); *m* 1971, Anne Frances Glasson; one *s* one *d. Educ:* Queen Mary Coll., Univ. of London (BSc Hons 1969); Churchill Coll., Cambridge (PhD 1972). Admin. Asst, Univ. of Sheffield, 1972–75; University of Southampton: Asst Registrar, 1976–79; Asst Sec., 1979–82; Sen. Asst Registrar, 1982–86; Dep. Registrar and Academic Sec., Univ. of Nottingham, 1986–91; Registrar, 1991–97, and Sec., 1996–97, Univ. of Kent at Canterbury. Dir, Univs and Colls Staff Develt Agency, 1996–2004. Mem., Panel of Ind. Persons, Glos CC, 2013–. Treasurer: Mickleton Methodist Church, 2012–; Mickleton Soc., 2013–. Governor: Hills Rd Sixth Form Coll., Cambridge, 2001–08 (Chm., 2003–08); Addenbrooke's Hosp. NHS Foundn Trust, 2004–07. *Publications:* articles in Jl of Chemical Soc. *Recreations:* music, natural history. *Address:* 12 Sovereign Fields, Mickleton, Chipping Campden GL55 6RG. *E:* tais@themeads.fsnet.co.uk. *Club:* Oxford and Cambridge.

MEADE, family name of **Earl of Clanwilliam**.

MEADE, Eric Cubitt, FCA; Senior Partner, Deloitte Haskins & Sells, Chartered Accountants, 1982–85; *b* 12 April 1923; *s* of William Charles Abbott Meade and Vera Alicia Maria Meade; *m* 1960, Margaret Arnott McCallum (*d* 2008); two *s* one *d. Educ:* Ratcliffe College. FCA 1947. Served War, Hampshire Regt, 1942–46; N Africa, Italy, prisoner of war, 1944–45; Captain. Chartered Accountant, 1947. Mem. Council, Inst. of Chartered Accountants in England and Wales, 1969–79 (Chm., Parly and Law Cttee, 1974–76; Chm., Investigation Cttee, 1976–77); Chm., Consultative Cttee, Accountancy Bodies Ethics Cttee, 1977–83; Mem. Council, FIMBRA, 1986–87; Lay Mem., Solicitors Complaints Bureau, 1986–89; Mem., Audit Commn, 1986–89. *Recreations:* tennis, bowls. *Address:* 56 Hurlingham Court, Ranelagh Gardens, Fulham, SW6 3UP. *T:* (020) 7736 5382. *Club:* Hurlingham.

MEADE, Richard David; QC 2008; a Recorder, since 2010; a Deputy High Court Judge, since 2012; *b* London, 14 Nov. 1966; *s* of Prof. Thomas Wilson Meade, *qv*; *m* 2003, Sara Louise Payne; one *s* two *d. Educ:* William Ellis Sch., London; University Coll., Oxford (BA Juris.). Called to the Bar, Lincoln's Inn, 1991; in practice as barrister specialising in intellectual property, 1991–. *Publications:* (ed jtly) Kerly's Law of Trade Marks and Trade Names, 13th edn 2001, 14th edn 2005. *Recreations:* poker, family. *Address:* 8 New Square, Lincoln's Inn, WC2A 3QP. *Clubs:* Barracuda, Victoria Sporting.

MEADE, Prof. Thomas Wilson, DM; FRCP, FMedSci; FRS 1996; Emeritus Professor of Epidemiology, Department of Epidemiology and Population Health, London School of Hygiene and Tropical Medicine, since 2001; *b* 21 Jan. 1936; *s* of James Edward Meade, CB, FBA, and Elizabeth Margaret (*née* Wilson); *m* 1962, Helen Elizabeth Perks; one *s* two *d. Educ:* Westminster Sch.; Christ Church, Oxford; St Bartholomew's Hosp. Sen. Lectr, Dept of Public Health, LSHTM, 1968–70 (on secondment to Schieffelin Leprosy Research Sanatorium, S India, 1969–70); Dir, MRC Epidemiol. and Med. Care Unit, Northwick Park Hosp., then Wolfson Inst. of Preventive Medicine, 1970–2001, and Prof. of Epidemiol., St Bart's Hosp. Med. Coll., then St Bart's and The Royal London Hosp. Sch. of Medicine and Dentistry, 1992–2001, QMW, later QMUL. Member: MRC Physiological Systems and Disorders Bd, 1974–78; MRC Health Services Res. Panel and Cttee, 1981–90; Wellcome Trust Physiology and Pharmacology Panel, 1990–95; Council, Royal Soc., 1998–99. Founder FMedSci 1998. Hon. DSc QMUL, 2010. Internat. Balzan Prize, Fondazione Internazionale Premio E. Balzan, 1997; MRC Millennium Medal, 2002. *Publications:* papers on thrombosis and arterial disease. *Recreation:* allotment. *Address:* 28 Cholmeley Crescent, N6 5HA. *T:* (020) 8340 6260. *Club:* Leander (Henley-on-Thames).

See also R. D. Meade.

MEADES, Jonathan Turner; journalist, writer and television performer; *b* 21 Jan. 1947; *s* of late John William Meades and Margery Agnes Meades (*née* Hogg); *m* 1st, 1980, Sally Dorothy Renée (marr. diss. 1986), *d* of Raymond Brown; twin *d*; 2nd, 1988, Frances Anne (marr. diss. 1997), *d* of Sir William Bentley, KCMG; two *d*; 3rd, 2003, Colette Claudine Elizabeth, *d* of Michael Forder. *Educ:* King's Coll., Taunton; RADA; Bordeaux Univ. Editor, Event, 1981–82; Features Editor, Tatler, 1982–85; Restaurant Critic, The Times, 1986–2001. Columnist, The Times, 2001–05; contributor to magazines and newspapers, 1971–, including: Books and Bookmen, Time Out, Observer, Architects Jl, Sunday Times, Harpers and Queen, Vogue, Literary Review, Tatler, A La Carte, Independent, Sunday Correspondent, Mail on Sunday, Evening Standard. *Television: series:* The Victorian House, 1987; Abroad in Britain, 1991; Further Abroad, 1994; Even Further Abroad, 1997; Meades Eats, 2003; Abroad Again in Britain, 2006; Jonathan Meades: Abroad Again, 2007; Magnetic North, 2008; Jonathan Meades: Off Kilter, 2009; Jonathan Meades on France, 2012; Jonathan Meades: the Joy of Essex, 2013; Bunkers, Brutalism, Bloodymindedness: Concrete Poetry, 2014; *films:* Jerry Building, 1994; Heart Bypass, 1998; Travels with Pevsner: Worcestershire, 1998; Victoria Died in 1901 and is Still Alive Today, 2001; tvSSFBM EHKL, 2001; Joebuilding, 2006; *film script:* L'Atlantide, 1991. Hon. FRIBA 2013. *Publications:* This is Their Life, 1979; An Illustrated Atlas of the World's Great Buildings, 1980; Filthy English (short stories), 1984; Peter Knows what Dick Likes, 1989; Pompey (novel), 1993; The Fowler Family Business (novel), 2002; Incest and Morris Dancing, 2002; Museum Without Walls, 2012; Pidgin Snaps, 2013; An Encyclopaedia of Myself, 2014; The Plagiarist In The Kitchen, 2016. *Recreations:* buildings, mushrooms, woods. *Address:* c/o Anita Land Ltd, 10 Wyndham Place, W1H 2PU. *E:* jtm.juvarra@orange.fr. *Clubs:* Groucho, Academy.

MEADOW, Sir (Samuel) Roy, Kt 1997; FRCP, FRCPE, FRCPCH; Professor and Head of Department of Paediatrics and Child Health, University of Leeds, 1980–98, now Emeritus Professor; *b* 9 June 1933; *m* 1st, 1962, Gillian Margaret Maclennan; one *s* one *d*; 2nd, 1978,

Marianne Jane Harvey; 3rd, 2009, Donna Andrea Rosenberg. *Educ:* Wigan Grammar Sch.; Bromsgrove Sch.; Worcester Coll., Oxford (BA Hons Physiol. 1957; MA, BM BCh 1960); Guys Hosp. Med. Sch. DRCOG 1962; DCH 1963; MRCP 1964, FRCP 1974; FRCPE 1996; FRCPCH 1997. Partner GP, Banbury, 1962–64; junior appts at Guy's Hosp., Evelina Children's Hosp., Hosp. for Sick Children, London and Royal Alexandra Hosp., Brighton, 1964–67; MRC Sen. Res. Fellow, Birmingham Univ., 1967–68; Sen. Lectr and Consultant Paediatrician, Leeds Univ., 1970–80. Consultant Advr to CMO, DoH, 1997–2000. Blackwell Vis. Prof., NZ Paediatric Assoc., 1989; Kildorrery Lectr, Irish Paed. Assoc., 1987; Charles West Lectr, RCP, 1993. Chm., Assoc. for Child Psychology and Psychiatry, 1983–84; President: BPA, 1994–96 (Chm., Acad. Bd, 1990–94); (Inaugural), RCPCH, 1996–97. Enuresis Resource and Inf. Centre, 1996–2004. Editor, Archives of Diseases in Childhood, 1979–87. Dawson Williams Prize, BMA, 1994; James Spence Medal, RCPCH, 1999. *Publications:* Lecture Notes on Paediatrics, 1973, 7th edn 2001; Bladder Control and Enuresis, 1973; The Child and His Symptoms, 1978; ABC of Child Abuse, 1989, 4th edn as ABC of Child Protection, 2007; Paediatric Kidney Disease, 1992; reports and papers on teratogenicity of anticonvulsant drugs, Munchausen Syndrome by proxy child abuse, childhood urinary tract disorders and child abuse. *Recreation:* gardening.

MEADOWCROFT, Michael James; politician, writer and public affairs consultant; *b* 6 March 1942; marr. diss.; one *s* one *d*; *m* 2nd, 1987, Elizabeth Bee. *Educ:* King George V Sch., Southport; Bradford Univ. (MPhil 1978). Chm., Merseyside Regl Young Liberal Orgn, 1961; Liberal Party Local Govt Officer, 1962–67; Sec., Yorks Liberal Fedn, 1967–70; Asst Sec., Joseph Rowntree Social Service Trust, 1970–78; Gen. Sec., Bradford Metropolitan Council for Voluntary Service, 1978–83. Senior Vis. Fellow, PSI, 1989. Dir, Electoral Reform Consultancy Services, 1992–94. Columnist: The Times, 1986–87; Yorkshire Post, 2004–07; Clarinet and Saxophone Mag., 2007–09. Member: Leeds City Council, 1968–83; W Yorks MCC, 1973–76, 1981–83. Dir, Leeds Grand Theatre and Opera House, 1971–83; Chm., Leeds Library, 2008–. Chm., Liberal Party Assembly Cttee, 1977–81; Pres. Elect, 1987–88, Pres., 1993–2002, Liberal Party; Chair, Leeds Liberal Democrats, 2010–11. Contested (L) Leeds W, Feb. and Oct. 1974, 1987, 1992. MP (L) Leeds W, 1983–87. Chm., Electoral Reform Soc., 1989–93. Has undertaken 51 missions to 36 new and emerging democracies; Co-ordinator: UN Electoral Assistance Secretariat, Malawi, 1994; OSCE Internat. Observer Mission, Russian Presidential elecn, 1996, Bulgaria, 1996, Bosnia Refugee Vote, 1996; EU Observation Unit, Suriname Nat. Assembly elecns, 2000; EU Chief Observer, Zambian Presidential elecns, 2001; Advr on Jerusalem, EU Electoral Unit, Palestinian Assembly elecns, 1995–96; Consultant, Cttee for Free and Fair Elections, Cambodia, 1997; European Co-Dir, EC Support to Democratic Electoral Process in Cambodia, 1998; Post-Electoral Advr, Indonesian Assembly elecns, 1999; Consultant to: EC's TACIS project in Uzbekistan, 2002; Ind. Electoral Commn, Dem. Rep. of Congo, 2004–05; Electoral Commn, Benin, 2006; Nat. Democratic Inst. project, Bangladesh, 2008–12; IPU mission to Parliament of Oman, 2014. Trustee, Parly Outreach Trust, 2015–. Hon. Alderman, City of Leeds, 2002. Chevalier, Commanderie de Faugères, 1998. *Publications:* Liberal Party Local Government Handbook (with Pratap Chitnis), 1963; Success in Local Government, 1971; Liberals and a Popular Front, 1974; Local Government Finance, 1975; A Manifesto for Local Government, 1975; The Bluffer's Guide to Politics, 1976; Liberal Values for a New Decade, 1980; Social Democracy—Barrier or Bridge?, 1981; Liberalism and the Left, 1982; Liberalism and the Right, 1983; Liberalism Today and Tomorrow, 1989; The Politics of Electoral Reform, 1991; Diversity in Danger, 1992; The Case for the Liberal Party, 1992; (with E. Bee) Faugères: a guide to the Appellation, 1996, 3rd edn 2005 (French edn 2006); Focus on Freedom, 1997, 3rd edn 2001; (jtly) Philatelic Fiction: a bibliography, 2010; (ed) Freedom, Liberty and Fairness, 2011; Guide to the Artworks of the National Liberal Club, 2011; (ed jtly) The Leeds Yellow Book, 2015. *Recreations:* music (including jazz), French philately, Leeds political history. *Address:* Waterloo Lodge, 72 Waterloo Lane, Bramley, Leeds LS13 2JF. *T:* (0113) 257 6232. *E:* meadowcroft@bramley.demon.co.uk. *W:* www.bramley.demon.co.uk. *Clubs:* National Liberal (Archivist, 2009–); Armley Liberal, Upper and Lower Wortley Liberal (Leeds).

MEADOWS, Prof. (Arthur) Jack, FInstP; FCLIP; Professor of Library and Information Studies, Loughborough University, 1986–2001, now Emeritus Professor in Business Studies; *b* 24 Jan. 1934; *s* of Arthur Harold Meadows and Alice Elson; *m* 1958, Isobel Jane Tanner Bryant; one *s* two *d*. *Educ:* New Coll., Oxford (MA Physics; DPhil Astronomy); University Coll. London (MSc History and Philosophy of Science). Fulbright Schol., Vis. Fellow, Mt Wilson and Palomar Observatories, Asst Prof., Univ. of Illinois, 1959–61; Lectr, Univ. of St Andrews, 1961–63; Asst Keeper, British Mus., 1963–65; University of Leicester: Hd of Dept and Prof., Astronomy and History of Science Depts, 1965–86; Hd of Primary Communications Res. Centre, 1975–86; Hd of Office for Humanities Communication, 1982–86; Loughborough University: Hd, Library and Inf. Studies Dept, 1986–90; Hd, Computers in Teaching Initiative Centre for Liby and Inf. Studies, 1989–97; Pro-Vice-Chancellor, 1995–96. Hon. Life Vice-Pres., LA, 1995. Hon. FCLIP 2002. Hon. DSc City, 1995. *Publications:* Stellar Evolution, 1967; The High Firmament: a survey of astronomy in English literature, 1969; Early Solar Physics, 1970; Science and Controversy, 1972; Communication in Science, 1974; Greenwich Observatory: recent history (1836–1975), 1975; The Scientific Journal, 1979; (jtly) Dictionary of New Information Technology, 1982; (jtly) The Lamp of Learning: Taylor & Francis and the development of science publishing, 1984; (jtly) Maxwell's Equations and their Applications, 1985; Space Garbage, 1985; (jtly) Dictionary of Computing and Information Technology, 1987; The Origins of Information Science, 1987; (jtly) The History of Scientific Discovery, 1987; (jtly) Principles and Practice of Journal Publishing, 1987, rev. edn as Journal Publishing, 1997; Infotechnology, 1989; Innovation in Information, 1994; (jtly) Front Page Physics, 1994; (jtly) Project ELVYN, 1995; Communicating Research, 1998; Understanding Information, 2001; The Victorian Scientist, 2004; The Future of the Universe, 2007; Big Science, 2009; Background to Flight, 2011; about 250 articles. *Recreation:* sleeping in church services. *Address:* 47 Swan Street, Seagrave, Leics LE12 7NL. *T:* (01509) 812557.

MEADOWS, Graham David; Chief Executive, MC+TS-Europe sprl, since 2007; Special Adviser to European Commissioner for Social Policy, 2007–10, to Commissioner for Employment, Social Affairs and Inclusion, since 2010; *b* 17 Dec. 1941; *s* of late Albert Edward Meadows and Jessica Maude Titmus; two *d*; *m* 1995, Ruth Ringer. *Educ:* Edinburgh Univ. MA Hons Political Economy. Journalist, 1958–69, specialising latterly in agric. affairs; European corresp., Farmers' Weekly (based in Brussels), 1973–75; EC 1975–; Mem., agric. policy unit; adviser on agricl, fisheries and envmt policy, Office of Pres. of EEC (Gaston E. Thorn), 1981–84; Chef de Cabinet of Stanley Clinton Davis, Mem. of EEC responsible for transport, envmt and nuclear safety, 1985–89; Dir, 1989–2003, Acting Dir Gen., 2003–04, Dir-Gen., Regl Policy, 2004–06, Commn of European Communities. Hon. Prof., Sch. of City and Regional Planning, Cardiff Univ., 2007–12. DUniv Strathclyde, 2006. Emperor Maximilian Prize for Service to Eur. Regl Politics, CLRAE, 2007. *Recreations:* mountain walking, reading in the history of economic thought.

MEADOWS, Jack; *see* Meadows, A. J.

MEADOWS, Pamela Catherine, (Mrs P. A. Ormerod); Visiting Fellow, National Institute of Economic and Social Research, since 1998; Chairman, Synergy Research and Consulting, since 2004; *b* 9 Jan. 1949; *d* of late Sidney James Meadows, OBE and of Hilda Catherine (*née* Farley); *m* 1975, Paul Andrew Ormerod; one *s*. *Educ:* Kenya High Sch., Nairobi; Penrhos Coll., Colwyn Bay; Univ. of Durham (BA Econs 1970); Birkbeck Coll., Univ. of London (MSc Econs 1978). Research Officer, NIESR, 1970–74; Sen. Econ. Asst, then Econ. Advr, Home Office, 1974–78; Department of Employment: Econ. Advr, 1978–88; Grade 5, 1988–92; Chief Economic Advr, and Hd of Econs, Res. and Evaluation Div., 1992–93; Dir, PSI, 1993–98. Vis. Prof., Arbetslivsinstitutet, Stockholm, 1998–2000. Mem., Better Regulation Task Force, 1997–2000. Trustee, Employment Policy Inst., 1995–2000; Mem. Exec. Cttee, Public Mgt and Policy Assoc., 1998–2001. Gov., Birkbeck Coll., 1997–2001. *Address:* c/o National Institute of Economic and Social Research, 2 Dean Trench Street, Smith Square, SW1P 3HE.

MEADWAY, (Richard) John, PhD; Under Secretary, Department of Trade and Industry, 1989–96; *b* 30 Dec. 1944; *s* of late Norman Pardey Meadway and Constance Meadway (later Kellaway); *m* 1968, Rev. Dr Jeanette Valerie (*née* Partis); two *d*. *Educ:* Collyer's Sch., Horsham; Peterhouse, Cambridge (MA NatScis); Edinburgh Univ. (PhD); Oxford Univ. (MA). Asst Principal, Min. of Technology, 1970; Private Secretary: to Minister for Trade and Consumer Affairs, 1973; to Sec. of State for Prices and Consumer Protection, 1974; to the Prime Minister, 1976–78; Asst Sec., Dept of Trade, later DTI, 1979–89; Hd of Overseas Trade Div. 2, 1989–94, Hd of Export Control and Non-Proliferation Div., 1994–96, DTI. UK Gov., IAEA, 1994–96. Dir of Fitness to Practise, GMC, 1997–98. Chm., Newham Mind, 1998–2003. Trustee, Refugee Legal Centre, 1999–2006. FRSA 1995. *Publications:* papers on the amino-acid sequences of proteins. *Recreations:* reading, travel. *Address:* 4 Glebe Avenue, Woodford Green, Essex IG8 9HB. *T:* (020) 8504 1958. *Club:* Reform.

MEAGER, Michael Anthony; Director of Estates, Department of Health, 1989–91; *b* 15 Feb. 1931; *s* of Arthur Pattison Meager and Dora Edith Meager (*née* Greeves); *m* 1954, Val Cranmer Benson (*d* 2013); two *s* one *d*. *Educ:* Royal Naval Coll., Dartmouth; Clacton County High Sch.; Architectural Assoc. Sch. of Architecture. ARIBA 1955; AADip 1956. National Service, RE, 1955–57: commnd 1956, served Cyprus, 1956–57. HMOCS, Kenya, 1958–63; architect in private practice, 1964–66; Department of Health (formerly MoH and DHSS), 1966–91: Chief Archt, 1986–88; Dir of Health Building, 1988–89. *Club:* Royal Over-Seas League.

MEAGHER, Prof. Thomas Robert, PhD; Professor of Plant Biology, University of St Andrews, since 1999; *b* Oakland, Calif, 23 Nov. 1952; *s* of William Richard Meagher and Martha Meagher (*née* Bischoff); *m* 1977, Dr Laura Reinertsen. *Educ:* Univ. of S Florida (BA Hons Botany 1973); Duke Univ., N Carolina (PhD 1978). Duke University: teaching asst, Botany Dept, 1973–74; NIH Grad. traineeship, Univ. Prog. in Genetics, 1974–78; Res. Associate, 1978–82, Res. Scientist, 1983, Botany Dept; Temp. Instructor, Zool. Dept, 1984; Res. Scientist, Botany Dept, 1984–87; Asst Prof., 1987–90, Associate Prof., 1990–98, Prof., 1998–99, Rutgers Univ.; Dir, Centre for Evolution, Genes and Genomics, Univ. of St Andrews, 2004–12. Fulbright Schol., Dept of Pure Maths and Math. Stats, Univ. of Cambridge, 1982–83. Vis. Scientist, Univ. of Edinburgh, Royal Botanic Gdn, 1995–96; Hon. Prof., Scottish Crop Res. Inst., 2003–. Member: Sci. Adv. Council, 2004–09, Tree Health and Plant Biosecurity Task Force, 2012–, DEFRA. Natural Environment Research Council: Mem., 2007–; Chairman: Neomics Expert Wkg Gp, 2010; Adv. and Implementation Gp, Envmtl Omics Synthesis Centre, 2012–. Mem. Council, 2010–, Chair, Educn and Outreach Cttee, 2010–, Soc. for Study of Evolution. Trustee: Royal Botanic Gdn Edinburgh, 2013–; St Andrews Botanic Gdn, 2014–. Member, Editorial Board: Evolution, 1988–93, 2007–; Amer. Naturalist, 1990–93; Molecular Ecology, 1992–99; Jl of Evolutionary Biology, 1993–96; Heredity, 2000–; Ecology Letters, 2001–04. *Publications:* contributor: Plant Reproductive Ecology: patterns and strategies, 1988; Sexual Dimorphism in Plants, 1999; (with C. Vassiliadis) Genes in the Environment, 2003; contrib. learned jls incl. Amer. Naturalist, Amer. Jl of Botany, Annals of Botany, Biological Conservation, Biological Jl Linnean Soc., Biometrics, BioScience, California Jl of Sci. Educn, Conservation Letters, Crop Sci., Ecology, Ecol. Applications, Evolution, Evolutionary Ecology Res., Genetics, Genetic Res., Heredity, Jl of Evolutionary Biology, New Phytologist, Phil Transactions of Royal Soc., Proc. of Royal Soc., Theoretical and Applied Genetics, Theoretical Population Biology. *Recreation:* French horn (Mem., Scottish Vienna Horn Soc.). *Address:* School of Biology, University of St Andrews, St Andrews, Fife KY16 9TH. *T:* (01334) 463364, *Fax:* (01334) 463366. *E:* trm3@st-and.ac.uk.

MEAKINS, Prof. Jonathan Larmonth, OC 2000; MD; DSc; Nuffield Professor of Surgery, University of Oxford, 2002–08, now Emeritus; Fellow, Balliol College, Oxford, 2002; *b* 8 Jan. 1941; *s* of Jonathan Fayette Meakins and Mildred Dawson Meakins (*née* Larmonth); *m* 1972, Dr Jacqueline McClaran. *Educ:* McGill Univ. (BSc 1966); Univ. of Western Ontario (MD 1966); Univ. of Cincinnati (DSc 1972). Royal Victoria Hospital, Montreal: Consultant Surgeon, 1974–2002; Surgeon in Chief, 1988–98; McGill University: Asst Prof. of Surgery and Microbiol., 1974–79; Associate Prof., 1979–81; Prof. of Surgery and Microbiol., 1981–2002; Prof. and Chair of Surgery, 1988–93 and 1998–2002; Surgeon in Chief, McGill Univ. Health Centre, 1998–2002. Regent, 1993–2002, Vice Chair, 2000–02, Amer. Coll. of Surgeons. KM 1993. Hon. DSc McGill, 2015. *Publications:* Surgical Infection in Critical Care Medicine, 1985; (with J. C. McClaran) Surgical Care of the Elderly, 1988; (jtly) ACS Surgery: principles and practice, 1988, 5th edn 2003; (jtly) Host Defence Dysfunction in Trauma, Shock and Sepsis: mechanisms and therapeutic approaches, 1993; Surgical Infections: diagnosis and treatment, 1994. *Recreations:* tennis, golf, gardening, cooking, art history. *Clubs:* University (Montreal); Royal Montreal Golf, Montreal Indoor Tennis.

MEALE, Sir (Joseph) Alan, Kt 2011; MP (Lab) Mansfield, since 1987; *b* 31 July 1949; *s* of late Albert Henry and Elizabeth Meale; *m* 1983, Diana Gilhespy; one *s* one *d*. *Educ:* St Joseph's RC School; Ruskin College, Oxford; Sheffield Hallam Univ. (MA 1997). Seaman, British Merchant Navy, 1964–68; engineering worker, 1968–75; Nat. Employment Develt Officer, NACRO, 1977–80; Asst to Gen. Sec., ASLEF, 1980–83; Parly and Political Advisor to Michael Meacher, MP, 1983–87. An Opposition Whip, 1992–94; PPS to Dep. Leader of Lab. Party, 1994–97, to Dep. Prime Minister, 1997–98; Parly Under-Sec. of State, DETR, 1998–99. Mem., Select Cttee on Home Affairs, 1989–92; Chair, Cross Rail Select Cttee, 2005–08; Treas., Parly All Party Football Gp, 1989; Chairman: British Cyprus Cttee, 1992–; British Section, CPA Cyprus Gp, 2007–; Member: Parly Court of Referees, 1997–; Speaker's Panel, H of C, 2010–. Council of Europe: Mem., 2000–; First Vice-Pres., 2002–; President: Envmt, Agric., Local and Regl Democracy Cttee, 2008–; Eur. Prize Cttee, 2011–; Chief Whip, Council of Europe and Western EU British Delegn, 2007–; Mem., Socialist Bureau, 2011–; Leader, Labour Gp, 2012–; Mem., Eur. Interim Security and Defence Cttee, Western EU, 2012–. Fellow and Postgrad. Fellow, Industry and Parly Trust, 1989; Fellow, Armed Forces Parly Scheme (ranked Major). UK Parly Rep., Retired Mems Assoc., 2011–; Pres., Retired Miners Assoc., 2013–. Vice-Pres., Executive, Portland Coll. Trust, 1988–2011. Member: Exec., SSAFA, 1989–97; War Pensions Bd, 1989–97. Comr, Commonwealth War Graves Commn, 2002–10. Pres., Mansfield Town AFC, 2004–09. *Recreations:* reading, owner and breeder of thoroughbred horses, writing. *Address:* 85 West Gate, Mansfield, Notts NG18 1RT. *T:* (01623) 660531; House of Commons, SW1A 0AA. *Club:* Woodhouse Working Men's.

MEAR, Stephen; choreographer and director; Associate Choreographer, Chichester Festival Theatre, since 2009; *b* 19 Feb. 1964; *s* of Albert and Fay Mear; partner, Mark Smith. *Educ:* London Studio Centre. Dancer, later dance captain, in West End musicals, incl. 42nd Street, Cats, Follies, Some Like It Hot, Anything Goes, 1984–90; choreographer: Of Thee I Sing, Bridewell, 1999; A Little Night Music, Japan; Bouncers, Woman in Love, Derby Playhouse; Grapevine (world première); Shakers, Northampton Th. Royal; Love Off the Shelf, Harrogate Th.; Snoopy, Watermill Th., Newbury; Grease, Athens; Ruthie Henshall in

Concert, RFH and tour; She Loves Me, Canada; Gary Wilmot's Showstoppers Tour; Whitelight Tradeshow; Singin' in the Rain, W Yorks Playhouse, NT and tour, 2000, Châtelet Theatre, Paris, 2015; Stepping Out, Smoking with Lou Lou, Half a Sixpence, W Yorks Playhouse, 2000; (with Bob Avian) The Witches of Eastwick, Th. Royal, Drury Lane, 2001, Australian tour; Don Giovanni, Royal Opera House, 2002; Honk!, Japan and Singapore; The Three Musketeers, Rotterdam, 2003; Anything Goes, NT and Th. Royal, Drury Lane, 2003–04; Tonight's the Night, Victoria Palace, 2004; Acorn Antiques, Th. Royal, Haymarket and UK tour, 2005; On the Town, ENO, 2005; (with Matthew Bourne) Mary Poppins, Prince Edward, 2005, NY, UK and US tour, Netherlands and Australia (Olivier Award for Best Choreography; LA Drama Critics Award for Best Choreography, 2010; Helpmann Award for Best Choreography, Australia, 2011), Vienna and UK tour, 2015; Sinatra at the Palladium, 2006; The Little Mermaid, NY, 2007; Gigi, 2009, Hello Dolly, 2009 (Evening Standard Award for Best Choreography, 2009; Olivier Award for Best Choreography, 2010), Regents Park Open Air Th.; Sweet Charity, Menier Chocolate Factory Th., 2009–10, Th. Royal, Haymarket, 2010; Shoes (also dir), Sadler's Wells Th., 2010; Betty Blue Eyes, Novello Th., 2011; Crazy For You, Regents Park Open Air Th., Novello, 2011; Me and My Girl, Crucible, Sheffield, 2010; Stephen Ward, Aldwych Th., 2013; Ragtime, Milwaukee Repertory Th., 2013; Die Fledermaus, Metropolitan Opera, NY, 2013–14; City of Angels, Donmar Th., 2014; The Vote, Donmar Th., 2015; Dreamgirls, Milwaukee Repertory Th., 2015; Chichester Festival Theatre: Putting It Together, 2001; Just So, 2004 (also N Shore Music Th., Mass, USA); How to Succeed in Business Without Really Trying, 2005; Music Man, Funny Girl, 2008; The Grapes of Wrath, 2009; She Loves Me (also dir), 2011; Kiss Me, Kate, 2012; The Pajama Game, 2013 (also Shaftesbury Th., 2014); Gypsy, 2014 (also Savoy Th., 2015); Amadeus, 2014; Mack and Mable, 2015 (also UK tour). Choreographer, So You Think You Can Dance, BBC TV, 2010, Psychobitches, Sky Arts, 2012, and of several television adverts and music videos incl. Goldfrapp and Oasis. Carl Alan Award, Internat. Dance Teachers' Assoc., 2007; Dance Companion Award, Liverpool Inst. for Performing Arts, 2013. *Recreations:* theatre, film, music. *Address:* Chichester Festival Theatre, Oaklands Park, Chichester, W Sussex PO19 6AP. *E:* mearstephen@hotmail.com; Judy Daish Associates Ltd, 2 Saint Charles Place, W10 6EG. *T:* (020) 8964 8811. *E:* judy@judydaish.com.

MEARA, Ven. David Gwynne; Rector, St Bride's Church, Fleet Street, 2000–14; Archdeacon of London, 2009–14, now Archdeacon Emeritus; *b* 30 June 1947; *s* of Gwynne and Winifred Meara; *m* 1973, Rosemary Anne, *d* of John and Audrey Alexander; two *s* two *d*. *Educ:* Merchant Taylors' Sch., Northwood; Oriel Coll., Oxford (BA Lit. Hum. 1970; BA Theol. 1972; MA 1973); Cuddesdon Theol Coll., Oxford. Lambeth Dip. 1975. Ordained deacon, 1973, priest, 1974; Curate, Christchurch, Reading, 1973–77; Chaplain, Univ. of Reading, 1977–82; Vicar, Basildon, Aldworth and Ashampstead, 1982–94; RD, Bradfield, 1990–94; Rector, 1994–2000, Area Dean, 1996–2000, Buckingham; Priest-in-charge, London Guild Church of St Mary Aldermary, 2010–12. Sec., 1980–2000, Chm., 1990–2000, Oxford Diocesan Adv. Gp on Mission; Mem., Oxford DAC, 1998–2000. Hon. Canon, Christ Church Cathedral, Oxford, 1997–. Chaplain, Co. of Spectacle Makers, 2006–07. Liveryman: Turners' Co., 2012–; Co. of Stationers and Newspaper Makers, 2014–; Co. of Marketors, 2014–. Pres., Monumental Brass Soc., 2002–11. FSA 1994. Fellow, Soc. of Editors, 2014. Special Award, British Press Association 2010. *Publications:* The Foundation of St Augustine at Reading, 1982; Victorian Memorial Brasses, 1983; A. W. N. Pugin and the Revival of Memorial Brasses, 1991; Modern Memorial Brasses, 2008; Remembered Lives, 2013; The Kindersley Workshop in Oxfordshire, 2015; *contributions to:* Blue Guide to English Parish Churches, (Berkshire), 1985; Catalogue of Pugin Exhibition, V & A Mus., 1994; Catalogue of Pugin Exhibition, NY, 1995; Monumental Brasses as Art and History, 1996. *Recreations:* church-crawling, opera, theatre, art galleries, malt whisky. *Address:* Stonewalls Barn, 10 The Closes, Kidlington, Oxon OX5 2DP. *Club:* Athenæum.

MEARNS, Ian; MP (Lab) Gateshead, since 2010; *b* Newcastle upon Tyne, April 1957; partner, Anne. *Educ:* St Mary's RC Primary Sch., Forest Hall; St Mary's RC Tech. Sch., Newcastle upon Tyne. With Northern Gas, 1974–85. Chair: Educn Comm, UNESCO, 1993–2000; Scrutiny Policy Rev. Gp, NE Assembly. Council Rep., LGA (Vice-Pres., 2010–11; Vice-Chair: Envmt Bd; Culture Tourism and Sport Bd; Mem., Educn Exec.). Mem. (Lab) Gateshead Council, 1983–2010 (Dep. Leader, 2002–10). Mem., Educn Select Cttee, 2010–. *Address:* House of Commons, SW1A 0AA.

MEARS, Dr Adrian Leonard, CBE 2005; CPhys, FInstP; Director, Scienogy Ltd, 2005–13; *b* 27 May 1944; *s* of Leonard Mears and Marjorie (*née* Isaac); *m* 1969, Barbara Bayne; two *s*. *Educ:* Highgate Sch.; Christ Church, Oxford (DPhil, MA). Res. Associate, Univ. of Md, USA, 1969–71; joined RRE (later Royal Signals and Radar Establishment), 1971: worked on display technology, optoelectronics and lasers, 1971–81; Hd, Signal Processing, 1981–86; Dir of Science (Comd, Control, Communications and Inf. Systems), MoD, 1987–89; Dep. Dir and Commercial Dir, RSRE, 1990–91; Tech. and Quality Dir, DRA, 1991–95; Tech. Dir, 1995–2001, Chief Knowledge Officer, 1998–2000, DERA; Tech. Dir and Chief Tech. Officer, QinetiQ, 2001–04. *Recreations:* walking, theatre, music, local councillor. *Address:* 21 Collum End Rise, Leckhampton, Glos GL53 0PA. *T:* (01242) 521050.

MEARS, Martin John Patrick; solicitor in private practice; President of the Law Society, 1995–96; *b* 12 Feb. 1940; *s* of J. F. Mears and E. Mears; seven *c*. *Educ:* St Illtyd's College, Cardiff; Wadham Coll., Oxford (MA, BCL). Solicitor, 1966. Editor, legal satirical jl, Caterpillar. *Publications:* numerous articles in national, regional and legal press. *Recreations:* Law Society, journalism, travel, reading. *Address:* Mears Hobbs & Durrant, 92 High Street, Gorleston, Great Yarmouth, Norfolk NR31 6RH; Old Rectory, Haddiscoe, Norwich NR14 6PG. *Clubs:* Oxford and Cambridge; Norfolk (Norwich).

MEARS, Patrick Michael; tax adviser, since 1982; *b* London, 19 Jan. 1958; *s* of Alex Benjamin Albert Mears and Moira Mears; *m* 1st, 1983, Carol Anders (*d* 1987); one *d*; 2nd, 1995, Rachel Anderson; one *s*. *Educ:* Henley Grammar Sch.; London Sch. of Econs and Pol Sci. (LLB Hons 1979). Admitted solicitor, 1982; Allen & Overy: joined, 1980; Tax Partner, 1988–2011; Consultant, 2011–12. Chm., Adv. Panel, General Anti-Abuse Rule, HMRC, 2013–. Chm., LSE Alumni Assoc., 2013–. *Recreations:* theatre, fine art, tennis, bridge. *Address:* 15 Burbage Road, SE24 9HJ. *E:* patrick@mears.eu. *Clubs:* Dulwich Lawn Tennis, Old College Lawn Tennis and Croquet.

MEATH, 15th Earl of, *cr* 1627; **John Anthony Brabazon;** Baron Ardee (Ire.) 1616; Baron Chaworth (UK) 1831; *b* 11 May 1941; *er s* of 14th Earl of Meath, and Elizabeth Mary (*née* Bowlby); *S* father, 1998; *m* 1973, Xenia Goudime; one *s* two *d*. *Educ:* Harrow. Page of Honour to the Queen, 1956–58. Served Grenadier Guards, 1960–63. *Heir: s* Lord Ardee, *qv*. *Address:* Killruddery, Bray, Co. Wicklow, Ireland.

MEATH, Bishop of, (RC), since 1990; **Most Rev. Michael Smith;** *b* 6 June 1940; *s* of John Smith and Bridget Fagan. *Educ:* Gilson Endowed Sch., Oldcastle; St Finian's Coll., Mullingar; Lateran Univ., Rome (DCL 1966). Ordained priest, 1963; Curate, Clonmellon, 1967–68; Chaplain: St Loman's Hosp., 1968–74; Sacred Heart Hosp., 1975–84; Auxiliary Bp of Meath, 1984–88; Coadjutor Bp of Meath, 1988–90. Diocesan Sec., dio. of Meath, 1968–84; Sec., Irish Bishops' Conf., 1984– (Asst Sec., 1970–84). *Recreations:* golf, walking. *Address:* Bishop's House, Dublin Road, Mullingar, Co. Westmeath, Ireland. *T:* (44) 9348841, 9342039, *Fax:* (44) 9343020. *E:* bishop@dioceseofmeath.ie.

MEATH AND KILDARE, Bishop of, since 2013; **Most Rev. Patricia Storey;** *b* Northern Ireland, 30 March 1960; *d* of Norman and Eleanor Shaw; *m* 1983, Earl Storey; one *s* one *d*. *Educ:* Methodist Coll., Belfast; Trinity Coll., Dublin (MA Hons 1983; BTh 1994). Ordained deacon, 1997, priest, 1998; Curate, Ballymena, 1997–2000; Team Vicar, Glenavy, 2000–04; Rector, St Augustine's, Londonderry, 2004–13. Youth Worker Co-ord., C of I Youth Dept, 2000–04. *Recreations:* reading, dog-walking, book club, swimming, creative writing, eating out. *Address:* The Bishop's House, Moyglare, Maynooth, Co. Kildare, Ireland. *T:* (1) 6289825. *E:* patriciastorey56@yahoo.co.uk.

MEATH BAKER, (William John) Clovis, CMG 2013; OBE 2002; HM Diplomatic Service, retired; Director, Foreign and Commonwealth Office, 2013; *b* 11 May 1959; *s* of William Gregory Francis Meath Baker and Priscilla Ann Meath Baker (*née* Gurney); *m* 1985, Elizabeth Diana Woodham-Smith; four *d*. *Educ:* Eton (King's Schol.); Magdalen Coll., Oxford (MA). Short Service Commn, 2nd Goorkhas (Sirmoor Rifles), 1981–84. Entered FCO, 1985; Second, later First Sec. (Chancery and Inf.), and Consul, Kabul, 1988–89; FCO, 1989; First Secretary: and Consul, Prague, 1989–93; FCO, 1993–97; Consul (Pol), Istanbul, 1997–2000; First Sec., FCO, 2000–02; Counsellor: (Pol), Kabul, 2002; FCO, 2003; hcsc 2006; Dir, Intelligence Prodn, GCHQ, 2010–13. Deployable Civilian Expert, Stabilisation Unit, 2014–. Associate Fellow, RUSI. *Clubs:* Athenæum, Beefsteak.

MEDDINGS, Richard Henry; Group Finance Director, Standard Chartered plc, 2006–14 (Group Executive Director, 2002–14); *b* Wolverhampton, 12 March 1958; *s* of late Ronald Jack Meddings and Brenda Meddings; *m* Henrietta Took; two *s* one *d*. *Educ:* Wolverhampton Grammar Sch.; Exeter Coll., Oxford (BA Hons Modern Hist.). ACA. Price Waterhouse, 1980–84; Hill Samuel Bank, 1984–96; BZW, later CSFB, 1996–99; Gp Finance Dir, Woolwich plc, 1999–2000; Gp Financial Controller and Chief Operating Officer, Wealth Mgt, Barclays plc, 2000–02. Non-executive Director: 3i plc, 2008–14; Legal & General, 2014–; HM Treasury, 2014–; Deutsche Bank, 2015–. Mem. Bd, ICC UK, 2008–. Mem. Bd, Seeing is Believing, 2014– (Chm., 2004–14). *Recreations:* football, cricket, golf, fishing, history.

MEDHURST, Brian; Managing Director (International Division), Prudential Corporation plc, 1985–94; *b* 18 March 1935; *s* of late Eric Gilbert Medhurst and Bertha May (*née* Kinggett); *m* 1960, Patricia Anne Beer; two *s* one *d*. *Educ:* Godalming Grammar Sch.; Trinity Coll., Cambridge (MA). FIA 1962 (Mem. Council, 1982–87). Joined Prudential Assurance Co. Ltd, 1958; Deputy Investment Manager, 1972; Investment Manager, 1975; Jt Chief Investment Manager, 1981; Gen. Manager, 1982. *Recreations:* chess, golf, piano duets, tree felling. *Address:* Woodcroft, Yelverton, Devon PL20 6HY. *T:* (01822) 853337. *Club:* Yelverton Golf.

MEDINA, Earl of; Henry David Louis Mountbatten; *b* 19 Oct. 1991; *s* and *heir* of Marquess of Milford Haven, *qv*. *Educ:* Millfield.

MEDINA-MORA ICAZA, Eduardo; a Justice of the Supreme Court of Mexico, since 2015; *b* Mexico City, 30 Jan. 1957; *m* Laura; three *c*. *Educ:* National Autonomous Univ. of Mexico. Corporate Dir, Strategic Planning and Dep. Dir Gen., DESC Gp, 1991–2000; Dir Gen., Centre for Investigation and Nat. Security, 2000–05; Mem., Nat. Security Council, 2000–09; Minister (Sec.) of Public Security, 2005–06; Pres., Nat. Public Security Council, 2005–06; Attorney-Gen., 2006–09; Ambassador of Mexico to the Court of St James's, 2010–13. Chief Negotiator for Border Security Agreement Mexico-US, 2002; Chief Security Negotiator for Alliance for Prosperity and Security in N America, 2004–05; Ambassador of Mexico to USA, 2013–15; Member: High Level Gp on Border Security with Guatemala and Belize; Mexican security delegns in bilateral meetings with US, Canada, Colombia and Guatemala. Coordinator, legal adv. gp to Mexican Govt during N American Free Trade Agreement negotiations. Member: Mexican Barrister Assoc.; Amer. Bar Assoc.; Chatham House. *Publications:* Fisheries in the Exclusive Economic Zone, 1989; (jtly) Legitimate Use of Force, 2008. *Address:* Supreme Court, Pino Suárez 2, Colonia Centro, Delegación Cuauhtémoc, C.P. 06065, Mexico.

MEDLAND, Simon Edward; QC 2011; a Recorder, since 2005; *b* Liverpool, 1965; *s* of William John Medland and Beryl Margaret Rigby Medland; *m* 2000, T-J, *d* of M. Fairey, Pouzolles, France; one *s* one *d*. *Educ:* Mostyn Hse Sch., Parkgate; Wrekin Coll., Wellington; Univ. of Hull (BA); City Univ. (DipLaw); Inns of Court Sch. of Law. Called to the Bar, Middle Temple, 1991 (Ede and Ravenscroft Prize; Gottlieb Award); Circuit Jun., Chester, 2008–10. *Recreations:* playing the organ and the piano, ski-ing, historical research, shooting, supporting Tranmere Rovers FC. *Address:* Linenhall Chambers, 1 Stanley Place, Chester CH1 2LU. *T:* (01244) 348282; Exchange Chambers, Pearl Assurance House, Derby Square, Liverpool L2 9XX. *T:* 0845 300 7747. *Club:* City (Chester).

MEDLEY, George Julius, OBE 1989; Director, WWF-UK (World Wide Fund for Nature) (formerly World Wildlife Fund (UK)), 1978–93; *b* 2 Aug. 1930; *s* of late Brig. Edgar Julius Medley, DSO, OBE, MC and Norah Medley (*née* Templer); *m* 1952, Vera Frances Brand; one *s* one *d*. *Educ:* Winchester College; Wye College, Univ. of London. BSc (Hort.); London Business Sch. (Sen. Exec. Prog., 1968). Fruit farmer, 1952–56; Manager, Chemical Dept, Harrisons & Crosfield, Colombo, 1957–63; Dir, Fisons (Ceylon), 1960–63; Tech. Develt Manager, Tata Fison, Bangalore, 1963–64; Gen. Manager Pesticides Div., Tata Fison Industries, Bombay, 1964–68; Sales Manager, Western Hemisphere, Agrochemicals, Fisons Internat. Div., 1968–69; Overseas Manager, Fisons Agrochemical Div., 1970–71; Dep. Managing Dir, Glaxo Labs, India, 1972–73, Managing Dir, 1973–77. Chm., Alexis Productions Ltd, 1994–98; Director: Edward Jewson Services to Charities Ltd, 1993–2001; Tisbury Halls, 2006–11. Member: Radioactive Waste Management Adv. Cttee, 1991–98; UK Ecolabelling Bd, 1995–99. Vice-Pres., Organisation of Pharmaceutical Producers of India, 1974–77; Founder Mem. and Vice-Chm., Inst. of Charity Fundraising Managers, 1983 (Chm., 1984–85); Treasurer: Wilts Country Markets Ltd (formerly Wilts WI Market Soc.), 1993–99, 2004–07; Wilts Wildlife Trust, 1994–99 (Pres., 1999–2003); Trustee: Farming and Wildlife Adv. Gp, 1984–93; Internat. Inst. for Envmt and Develt, 1989–93; Falkland Islands Foundn, 1985–92. Member: Tisbury Parish Council, 2001–07 (Vice-Chm., 2002–07); Exec. Cttee, Wilts Village Halls Assoc., 2006–11. FCMI; FICFM 1988. Officer, Order of Golden Ark (Netherlands), 1993. *Publications:* contrib. to Strategic Planning Soc. Jl. *Recreations:* gardening, DIY. *Address:* Tyntes Place, Lady Down View, Tisbury, Wilts SP3 6LL. *T:* (01747) 870047.

MEDLICOTT, Michael Geoffrey; Chief Executive (formerly Managing Director), Servus (formerly Opus) Holdings plc, 1997–2001; *b* 2 June 1943; *s* of Geoffrey Henry Medlicott and Beryl Ann Medlicott (*née* Burchell); *m* 1st, 1973, Diana Grace Fallaw (marr. diss. 1998); one *s* three *d*; 2nd, 1999, Susan Caroline Whittall. *Educ:* Downside School; Lincoln College, Oxford (Scholar; MA). Management Trainee, P&O-Orient Lines, 1965–66; Shipping Asst, Mackinnon, Mackenzie & Co., Bombay, 1966–68, Tokyo, 1968–69; Asst to Management, P&O-Orient Lines, 1969–71; P&O Cruises: Develt Analyst, 1971–73; Asst Fleet Manager, 1973–75; Gen. Manager, Fleet, 1975–80; Gen. Manager, Europe, 1980–83; Dir, Europe, 1983–86; Man. Dir, Swan Hellenic, 1983–86; Man. Dir, P&O Air Holidays, 1980–86; Dir, P&O Travel, 1980–84; Chief Exec., BTA, 1986–93; Vice Pres., Europe, 1993–96, Europe and Asia, 1996–97, Delta Airlines Inc. Chairman: Delta Aeroflot Travel Enterprises (Moscow), 1996–97; Servus Facilities Mgt Ltd, 1998–2001; Servus b2b Ltd, 2000–01; Transaction Dir, Nomura Internat. Principal Finance Gp, 1997–2000; Director: Deltair UK Investments, 1995–96; Lesteris Ltd, 1995–96; Gatwick Handling Internat. Ltd, 1995–96; Grand Facilities Mgt Holdings Ltd, 1998–2000; Member, Board: Manchester Airport plc, 2002–04; Manchester Airports Gp plc, 2004–10; John Laing plc, 2004–06; Laing Rail Ltd,

2006–08; M40 Trains Ltd, 2006–08; OCS Gp Ltd, 2006– (Chm., Audit Cttee, 2008–12, 2013–; Mem., Audit, Nominations and Remuneration Cttees, 2008–); Myriad Healthcare Ltd (formerly Caring Homes Gp), 2010– (Chm., 2008–10, 2013–; Mem., Audit Cttee, 2008–13; Chairman: Risk Cttee, 2012–; Audit and Remuneration Cttees, 2013–); Chm., Investors Cttee, ING REIM Ltd Infrastructure Fund, 2007–09. Chm., European Travel Commn, 1992–93 (Chm., Planning Cttee, 1990–92). Member: Council of Management: Passenger Shipping Assoc., 1983–86; Heritage of London Trust, 1987–2008; London Tourist Bd, 1992–93; Council, Tidy Britain Gp, 1988–2008; Bd, British-Amer. Chamber of Commerce, 1996–97; Bd, Nat. Savings & Investments, HM Treasury, 2003–09 (Chm., Audit Cttee, 2005–07; Appts and Remuneration Cttee, 2007–09); Bd, CAA, 2010– (Member: Remuneration Cttee, 2010–; Audit Cttee, 2014–); Bd, CAA Internat., 2010–; Chm., Air Travel Trust, 2013–. Member: Adv. Panel, Languages Lead Body, Dept of Employment, 1990–93; Adv. Council, Univ. of Surrey Tourism Dept, 1991–93; Hon. Bd, Univ. Center of Hellenic and European Studies, Piraeus, 1994–. Trustee, British Travel & Educnl Trust, 1986–93. LEA Gov., Ecchinswell and Sydmonton C of E Primary Sch., 1999–2003. Mem., Royal Philatelic Soc. FRSA 1986. CRAeS 1994. Queen Mother's Birthday Award for Envmtl Improvement, 1993, 1995. *Publications:* (contrib.) Facility Management: risks and opportunities, 2000; (with Sir J. Marriott and R. A. Ramkissoon) Trinidad: a philatelic history to 1913, 2010 (4 Internat. Gold Medals, 2010, 2011 and 2012; Charles J. Peterson Literature Grand Award and Gold Medal, Nat. Philatelic Exhibns, 2011; contribs to British West Indies Study Circle Bulletin, 1970–. *Recreations:* philately, opera, travelling in perfect company. *Club:* Oxford and Cambridge.

MEDLYCOTT, Sir Mervyn (Tregonwell), 9th Bt *cr* 1808, of Ven House, Somerset; *b* 20 Feb. 1947; *s* of Thomas Anthony Hutchings Medlycott (*d* 1970) (2nd *s* of 7th Bt) and Cecilia Mary Medlycott, *d* of late Major Cecil Harold Eden; *S* uncle, 1986. Genealogist; FSG 1990; Pres., Somerset and Dorset Family History Soc., 1986– (Founder and Hon. Sec., 1975–77; Chm., 1977–84; Vice-Pres., 1984–86). *Heir:* none. *Address:* The Manor House, Sandford Orcas, Sherborne, Dorset DT9 4SB. *T:* (01963) 220206.

MEDVEDEV, Dmitry Anatolyevich, PhD; Prime Minister of Russia, since 2012; Chairman, United Russia Party, since 2012; *b* Leningrad, 14 Sept. 1965; *m* 1993, Svetlana Vladimirovna; one *s*. *Educ:* Leningrad State Univ. (PhD Law 1990). Lectr, St Petersburg State Univ., 1990–99; Advr to Chm., Leningrad CC, 1990–95; Expert Consultant to Cttee for Ext. Affairs, St Petersburg City Hall, 1990–95; Dep. Govt COS, 1999; Dep. COS, 1999–2000, First Dep. COS, 2000–03, COS, 2003–05, Presidential Exec. Office; First Dep. Prime Minister, 2005–08; President of Russia, 2008–12. Chm., 2000–01 and 2002–08, Dep. Chm., 2001–02, Bd of Dirs, OAO Gazprom. *Address:* Office of the Prime Minister, White House, 2 Krasnopresnenskaya Naberezhnaya, Moscow 103274, Russia.

MEDWAY, Lord; John Jason Gathorne-Hardy; *b* 26 Oct. 1968; *s* and *heir* of 5th Earl of Cranbrook, *qv*.

MEDWAY, Susan Clare; Director and Curator, Chelsea Physic Garden, since 2014; *b* Essex, 29 June 1965; *d* of Richard and Anne Whybrow; *m* 1997, John Medway. Hse steward, Uppark House, NT, 1994–97; Hse Manager, Chartwell, NT, 1997–2001; Property Manager, Sheffield Park Gdn and Estate, 2001–09; on secondment as Property Manager, Stowe Landscape Gdn, 2006–07; Gen. Manager, Sissinghurst Castle portfolio, 2009–11; Commercial and Ops Dir, Design Mus., 2011–14. *Recreations:* travel, gardening, museums, galleries, historic properties, sailing. *Address:* Chelsea Physic Garden, 66 Royal Hospital Road, SW3 4HS. *T:* (020) 7352 5646. *E:* smedway@chelseaphysicgarden.co.uk.

MEEK, Elizabeth Jane, CBE 2000; Chair, Centre for London, since 2011; *b* 5 Sept. 1950; *d* of Patrick and Gladys Cox; *m* 1975, Innes Meek; three *d*. *Educ:* John Port Sch., Etwall, Derbyshire; Univ. of Exeter (BA Hons English). Joined Civil Service (fast stream entry), 1972; Department of the Environment, then of Environment, Transport and the Regions, subseq. for Transport, Local Government and the Regions: Asst Private Sec. to Sec. of State, DoE, 1978–79; First Sec., British High Commn, Lagos, 1979–81 (on secondment); Govt link with Manchester Olympic Bid, 1991–93; Hd, London Policy Unit, 1993–94; Hd, Strategy and Co-ordination Unit, 1994–97, Dir, GLA Div. (setting up Mayor and Assembly of London), 1997–2000, Govt Office for London; Interim Dir Communications and Public Affairs, Transport for London, 2000–01 (on secondment); Regional Director: Govt Office for London, 2001–08; Govt Office for NW, 2008–11. Mem., Schizophrenia Commn, 2011–; Trustee, McPin Foundn, 2013–. Non-exec. Dir, Sanctuary Housing, 2011–. Mem. Bd, Film London, 2011–. Gov., Birkbeck, Univ. of London, 2011–. *Publications:* Survive Lagos, 1982. *Recreations:* mountain walking, ski-ing. *E:* zilkeem@gmail.com.

MEEK, Kingsley John Neville, (Kip); Senior Advisor, EE, since 2010; *b* Arusha, Tanzania, 18 April 1955; *s* of Charles Innes Meek and Nona Corry Meek (*née* Hurford); *m* 1986, Marian O'Connor; two *s* two *d*. *Educ:* Magdalen Coll., Oxford (BA 1st Cl. Hons Modern Hist.); London Business Sch. (MSc with Dist.). Boston Consulting Gp, 1977–79; McKinsey & Co., 1981–83; Dep. Dir, BT, 1983–85; Partner, Coopers & Lybrand, 1985–93; Man. Dir, Spectrum Strategy Consultants, 1993–2003. Chairman: Broadband Stakeholder Gp, 2007–10; South West Screen, 2010–12, Mem. Bd, RadioCentre, 2007–. Mem. Bd, Ofcom, 2004–07. Chm., Eur. Regulators Gp, 2007; Ind. Spectrum Broker, Govt Spectrum Modernisation Prog., 2009–10. *Publications:* (with R. Foster) Public Service Broadcasting in the United Kingdom, 2008; Report of the Independent Spectrum Broker, 2009. *Recreations:* tennis, bridge, Chelsea Football Club. *Address:* 51 Onslow Gardens, N10 3JY. *T:* (020) 8444 2032. *E:* kip.meek@ee.co.uk.

MEEK, Stephen Donald Andrew; Principal, Geelong Grammar School, Australia, since 2004; *b* 27 Nov. 1952; *s* of George Edward Meek and Joan Meek; *m* 1987, Christine Sanders; two *s*. *Educ:* St John's Sch., Leatherhead; St Andrews Univ. (MA 1st Cl. Hons Mediaeval and Modern Hist.); Worcester Coll., Oxford (PGCE). History teacher, Dulwich Coll., 1978–85; Sherborne School, 1985–95: Hd of Hist., 1985–90; Housemaster, School House, 1990–95; Headmaster, Hurstpierpoint Coll., 1995–2004. *Recreations:* house in France, golf, bridge. *Address:* Geelong Grammar School, 50 Biddlecombe Avenue, Corio, Vic 3214, Australia. *T:* (3) 52739247. *E:* principal@ggs.vic.edu.au.

MEEK, Stephen Graham; Acting Director General, Education Standards, Department for Education, 2012–13; *b* 4 Aug. 1965; *s* of Gerald Arthur Meek and Judith Ann Meek; *m* 1994, Juliet Louise Greer; one *s* (and one *s* decd). *Educ:* Rugby Sch.; Univ. of Edinburgh (MA Hons Pols and Hist. 1988); Univ. of Essex (MA Philos. 1989). HM Treasury, 1992–2005: Private Sec. to Economic Sec., 1994–95; Policy Advr, Social Security Team, 1997–2000; Hd, Home Financial Services Team, 2001–03; Hd, Educn, Trng and Culture Team, 2003–05; Prog. Dir for Children and Young People, LGA, 2005–06; Dir of Strategy, DFES, later DCSF, 2006–08; Dir, Young People: Qualifications Strategy and Reform, DCSF, later DFE, 2008–11.

MEEKE, (Robert) Martin (James); QC 2000; a Recorder, 1996; *b* 25 Dec. 1950; *s* of James Alexander Meeke and Mildred Alverta Meeke; *m* 1973, Beverley Ann Evans; one *s* one *d*. *Educ:* Allhallows Sch., Devon; Bristol Univ. (LLB Hons). Called to the Bar, Gray's Inn, 1973. *Address:* Colleton Chambers, Colleton Crescent, Exeter EX2 4DG. *T:* (01392) 274898.

MEESE, Edwin, III; lawyer; Ronald Reagan Distinguished Fellow in Public Policy, 1988, now Emeritus Fellow, and Chairman, Center for Legal and Judicial Studies, 2001–13, Heritage Foundation, Washington; Distinguished Visiting Fellow, Hoover Institution, Stanford University, California, since 1988; *b* Oakland, Calif, 2 Dec. 1931; *s* of Edwin Meese Jr and Leone Meese; *m* 1958, Ursula Herrick; one *s* one *d* (and one *s* decd). *Educ:* Oakland High Sch.; Yale Univ. (BA 1953); Univ. of Calif at Berkeley (JD 1958). Dep. Dist Attorney, Alameda County, 1959–67; Sec. of Legal Affairs to Gov. of Calif, Ronald Reagan, 1967–69; Exec. Assistant and C of S to Gov. of Calif, 1969–75; Vice-Pres., Rohr Industries, 1975–76; Attorney at Law, 1976–80; Dir, Center for Criminal Justice Policy and Management, Univ. of San Diego, 1977–81; Prof. of Law, Univ. of San Diego Law Sch., 1978–81; Counsellor to Pres. of USA, 1981–85; Attorney Gen. of USA, 1985–88. Hon. LLD: Delaware Law Sch.; Widener Univ.; Univ. of San Diego; Valparaiso Univ.; California Lutheran Coll.; Universidad Francisco Marroquin, Guatemala. *Publications:* With Reagan: the inside story, 1992; (jtly) Leadership, Ethics and Policing: challenges for the 21st century, 2003, 2nd edn 2009; contribs to professional jls. *Address:* The Heritage Foundation, 214 Massachusetts Avenue, NE, Washington, DC 20002–4999, USA.

MEESON, Nigel Keith; QC 2002; Head of Litigation, Conyers Dill & Pearman, Cayman Islands, since 2007; acting Judge of Grand Court, Cayman Islands, since 2007; *b* 10 Feb. 1959; *s* of Arthur Edward Meeson and Beryl Grace Meeson; *m* 1st, 1982, Beverley Christine Frank (marr. diss. 2006); two *d*; 2nd, 2007, Gaylene Brereton; one *d*. *Educ:* St Albans Sch., Herts; Magdalen Coll., Oxford (BA Hons Juris., MA). Called to the Bar, Middle Temple, 1982; Attorney, State Bar of Calif, 1990; Accredited Mediator, CEDR, 1993; FCIArb 2006; in practice as Barrister, 1983–2007; a Recorder, 2004–13; admitted to the Bar: of Cayman Is, 2007; of BVI, 2008. Vis. Lectr, UCL, 1994–2005. *Publications:* The Practice and Procedure of the Admiralty Court, 1986; Ship and Aircraft Mortgages, 1989; Admiralty Jurisdiction and Practice, 1993, 4th edn 2011; (contrib.) Ship Sale and Purchase, 2nd edn 1993, 3rd edn 1998; (contrib.) International Commercial Dispute Resolution, 2009; (contrib.) Cross Border Judicial Co-operation in Offshore Litigation, 2009; (contrib.) International Civil Fraud, 2014. *Recreations:* sailing, ski-ing, golf. *Address:* Conyers Dill & Pearman, Cricket Square, Hutchins Drive, PO Box 2681, Grand Cayman KY1-1111, Cayman Islands. *T:* 9453901, *Fax:* 9453902. *E:* nigel.meeson@conyersdill.com. *Club:* Bar Yacht.

MEEUWISSEN, Anthony, RDI 2013; freelance designer and illustrator, since 1967; *b* London, 26 June 1938; *s* of Henricus and Olive Meeuwissen; two *d*; *m* 2013, Marie-Beatrice Gwynn. *Educ:* Strode's Grammar Sch., Egham. Has undertaken commns from Penguin Books, Radio Times, Sunday Times Mag., Royal Mail, Pentagram Design. Collection of work, Dept of Prints and Drawings, V&A Mus., 1976; retrospective exhibn, Stroud Mus., 2009; exhibn, Corinium Mus., Cirencester, 2010. One Gold, Two Silver Awards, D&AD, 1972; Francobollo d'Oro award for world's most beautiful stamp (for Royal Mail 20½ p Christmas stamp, 1983), La XXXVI Fiera del Francobollo a Riccione, 1984. FRSA. *Publications:* (illustrator) The Witch's Hat, by Irwin Dermer, 1975; The Key of the Kingdom, 1992 (D&AD Gold Award, WH Smith Illustration Award, 1993); Remarkable Animals, 1997, miniature edn 2009. *Recreations:* country walks, reading, listening to music, visiting art galleries. *Address:* The Old House, St Chloe, Amberley, Stroud, Glos GL5 5AP. *T:* (01453) 873276. *E:* tonymeeuwissen@live.co.uk.

MEGAHEY, Leslie; writer and director, film, television and theatre; *b* 22 Dec. 1944; *s* of Rev. Thomas and Beatrice Megahey. *Educ:* King Edward VI Grammar Sch., Lichfield; Pembroke Coll., Oxford. BBC general trainee, 1965; radio drama, script editor, producer, 1967; director, producer, TV arts series, 1968–; Exec. Producer, Arena, 1978–79; Editor, Omnibus, 1979–81, Co-Editor, 1985–87; Head of Music and Arts, BBC TV, 1988–91; other *television:* The Orson Welles Story, 1982; Artists and Models, 1986; The RKO Story, 1987; Leonardo, 2003; numerous drama-documentaries; *films:* Schalcken the Painter, 1979; Cariani and the Courtesans, 1987; Duke Bluebeard's Castle (filmed opera), 1988; The Hour of the Pig, 1993; Earth (co-writer, narration script), 2007; *theatre:* (dir and co-author) Jack—a night on the town, Criterion, 1994, NY, 1996. Mem., Arts Council Adv. Panel, Film and TV, 1985–89. Awards: BAFTA, 1980; Prague, 1975; Asolo, 1985; NY, 1987; Banff, 1987; Royal Philharmonic, 1989; Prix Italia, 1989; Argentine Film Critics', 1999; Lifetime Achievement, Montréal FIFA Fest., 2001. *Address:* c/o The Agency, 24 Pottery Lane, W11 4LZ.

MEGAINEY, Zina Ruth; *see* Etheridge, Z. R.

MEGHIR, Prof. Konstantinos Ektor Dimitrios, (Costas), PhD; FBA 2005; Douglas A. Warner III Professor of Economics, Yale University, since 2010; *b* 13 Feb. 1959; *s* of John and Marie-Jose Meghir; *m* 1987, Sofia Skalistiri; one *s* one *d*. *Educ:* Univ. of Manchester (BA Econs, MA Econs; PhD 1985). Res. Schol., Internat. Inst. for Applied Systems Analysis, Vienna, 1982–83; Temp. Lectr, Univ. of Manchester, 1983–84; University College London: Res. Officer, 1984–85; Lectr, 1985–91; Reader, 1991–92; Prof. of Econs, 1992–2011; Hd, Dept of Econs, 2005–08. Dep. Res. Dir, 1991–2005, Co-Dir, 2005–11, ESRC Centre, Inst. of Fiscal Studies. Member, Council: REconS, 2007–12 (Mem. Exec., 2008–12); Econometric Soc., 2011– (Fellow, 2000). Bodossaki Foundn Prize, 1997; Frisch Prize, Econometric Soc., 2000. Jt Man. Ed., Econ. Jl, 1996–2001; Co-ed., Econometrica, 2001–06. *Publications:* contribs to learned jls. *Recreations:* sailing, ski-ing, photography. *Address:* Department of Economics, Yale University, 37 Hillhouse Avenue, CT 06511, USA. *T:* (203) 4323558, *Fax:* (203) 4326323. *E:* c.meghir@yale.edu.

MEHAFFEY, Rt Rev. James; Bishop of Derry and Raphoe, 1980–2002; *b* 29 March 1931; *s* of John and Sarah Mehaffey; *m* 1956, Thelma P. L. Jackson; two *s* one *d*. *Educ:* Trinity College, Dublin (MA, BD); Queen's University, Belfast (PhD). Curate Assistant: St Patrick's, Belfast, 1954–56; St John's, Deptford, London, 1956–58; Minor Canon, Down Cathedral, 1958–60; Bishop's Curate, St Christopher's, Belfast, 1960–62; Incumbent: Kilkeel, Diocese of Dromore, 1962–66; Cregagh, Diocese of Down, 1966–80. Freeman: City of London, 2002; City of Derry, 2015. Hon. DLitt Ulster, 1999. *Address:* 10 Clearwater, Londonderry BT47 6BE. *T:* (028) 7134 2624. *E:* james.mehaffey@btinternet.com.

MEHMET, Alper, MVO 1990; HM Diplomatic Service, retired; Ambassador to Iceland, 2004–08; *b* Cyprus, 28 Aug. 1948; *s* of late Bekir Mehmet and of Leman Mehmet; *m* 1968, Elaine Susan Tarrant; two *d*. *Educ:* Parmiter's Grammar Sch.; Bristol Poly. Entered Home Office, 1970; Immigration Service, 1970–79; Lagos, 1979–83; transf. to HM Diplomatic Service (first immigrant Mem. and Muslim to reach Ambassador rank); Asst Pvte Sec. to Parly Under-Sec. of State, FCO, 1983–85; Second Sec., Bucharest, 1986–89; Dep. Hd of Mission, Reykjavík, 1989–93; FCO, 1993–98; First Sec., Bonn, 1999, Berlin, 1999–2003. Special Advr on Iceland, FIPRA Internat., 2009–. Consultant, Stabilisation Unit (jt FCO, MoD and DFID), 2009–. UK Dir, Aqua Omnis Water Co., 2011–. Mem. Adv. Council and spokesman, Migration Watch UK, 2010– (Vice Chm., 2010–). Mem. Bd, FCO Assoc., 2013–. Trustee and Treas., City and Hackney Alcohol Service, 2010–12. Foundn Gov., 1995–, Foundn Trustee, 1997–, Vice Chm. Bd, 2013–, Parmiter's Sch. (Mem., Academy Bd, 2012–); Chm., Old Parmiter's Soc., 2014–. Public speaker, TV and radio commentator, and writer on immigration and social issues. *Recreation:* amateur dramatics (Mem., Chingford Amateur Dramatic and Operatic Soc.). *E:* alp.mehmet@ymail.com.

MEHTA, Bharat, OBE 2000; Chief Executive (formerly Clerk to the Trustees), Trust for London (formerly City Parochial Foundation), since 1998; *b* 5 March 1956; *s* of Maganlal Jinabhai Mehta and Rattanben Mehta; *m* 1990, Sally Anne Chambers; two *d*. *Educ:* Plymouth Poly. (BA Hons Psychology 1979); UCL (MSc Ergonomics 1981). Researcher, MRC, 1979–80; Community Develt Worker, Pensioners Link, 1981–84; Policy Officer, NCVO, 1984–86; Principal Officer, Waltham Forest LBC, 1987–89; Dir of Develt, 1989–93, CEO, 1993–98, Nat. Schizophrenia Fellowship. Chm., Active Community Unit Adv. Gp, Home Office, 2003–04. Dir, Social Justice and Human Rights Centre Ltd, 2011–. Member: HM

Treasury and Cabinet Office spending review of future role of third sector in econ. and social regeneration, 2006–07; Mental Health Foundn Commn on Ageing, 2011–13. Non-exec. Dir, N Middlesex Univ. Hosp. NHS Trust, 2005–09 (Vice Chm., 2008–09). Chm., Resource for London, 2011–. Patron, Revolving Doors Agency, 1998–. Member, Board: Joseph Rowntree Foundn, 2003–13; Social Justice and Human Rights Centre Ltd, 2011–; Home Gp, 2014–. Chair, Young Londoners Fund, 2009–10; Mem., Exec. Cttee, London Funders, 2011–. Chm., Governing Body, Bowes Primary Sch., 2000–05. Judge, Charity Awards, 2005–09. Fellow, British American Proj., 1996. FRSA 2003. *Publications:* contrib. British Jl of Psychology. *Recreations:* field hockey, swimming, history. *Address:* Trust for London, 6 Middle Street, EC1A 7PH. *Clubs:* Southgate Adelaide Hockey (Vice Pres., 2002–; Captain, 2008–), Griffins Hockey.

MEHTA, Prof. Goverdhan, Padma Shri 2000; PhD; FRS 2005; FNA; National Research Professor, since 2009, and Lily Grantee and Jubilant Bhartia Chair, University of Hyderabad; *b* 1943. *Educ:* Univ. of Rajasthan (MSc); Univ. of Pune (PhD). Res. Associate, Michigan State and Ohio State Univs, 1967–69; Lectr, then Asst Prof., Indian Inst. of Technol., 1969–77; Prof. of Chemistry, 1977–98, Founder Dean, 1977–86, Vice-Chancellor, 1994–98, Univ. of Hyderabad; Prof. of Chemistry and Dir, 1998–2005, CSIR Bhatnagar Fellow, Dept of Organic Chemistry, 2005–10, Indian Inst. of Science. President: INSA, 1999–2001; ICSU, 2005–08. *Address:* School of Chemistry, Central University PO, Hyderabad 500046, India.

MEHTA, Ved (Parkash), FRSL; writer; *b* Lahore, 21 March 1934; 2nd *s* of late Dr Amolak Ram Mehta (former Dep. Director General of Health Services, Govt of India), and Shanti Devi Mehta (*née* Mehra); naturalized citizen of USA, 1975; *m* 1983, Linn Fenimore Cooper Cary, *d* of late William L. Cary and of Katherine Cary; two *d*. *Educ:* Arkansas Sch. for the Blind; Pomona Coll. (BA 1956); Balliol Coll., Oxford (Hazen Fellow, 1956–59; BA Hons Mod. Hist. Oxon, 1959; MA 1962; Hon. Fellow, 1999); Harvard Univ. (MA 1961). Phi Beta Kappa, 1955. Harvard Prize Fellow, 1959–60; Residential Fellow, Eliot House, Harvard Univ., 1959–61; Guggenheim Fellow, 1971–72, 1977–78; Ford Foundn Travel and Study Grantee, 1971–76, Public Policy Grantee, 1979–82; MacArthur Prize Fellow, 1982–87. Staff writer, The New Yorker, 1961–94. Yale University: Rosenkranz Chair in Writing, 1990–93; Lectr in History, 1990, 1991, 1992; Lectr in English, 1991–93; Residential Fellow, 1990–93, Fellow, 1993–, Berkeley Coll. Vis. Schol., Case Western Reserve Univ., 1974; Beatty Lectr, McGill Univ., 1979; Vis. Prof. of Literature, Bard Coll., 1985, 1986; Noble Foundn Vis. Prof. of Art and Cultural History, Sarah Lawrence Coll., 1988; Vis. Fellow (Literature), Balliol Coll., 1988–89; Vis. Prof. of English, NY Univ., 1989–90; Arnold Bernhard Vis. Prof. of English and History, Williams Coll., 1994; Randolph Distinguished Vis. Prof. of English and History, Vassar Coll., 1994–96; Sen. Fellow, Freedom Forum, Media Studies Center, 1996–97; Fellow, Center for Advanced Study in Behavioral Scis, 1997–98. Mem. Council on Foreign Relations, 1979–. Member: Usage Panel, Amer. Heritage Dictionary, 1982; Johnsonians, 2006. Fellow, NY Inst. for Humanities, 1988–92. FRSL 2009. Official delegate, Jaipur Literature Fest., 2014. Hon. DLit: Pomona, 1972; Bard, 1982; Williams, 1986; Stirling, 1988; Bowdoin, 1995; Panjab Univ., Chandigarh, 2009. Assoc. of Indians in America Award, 1978; Silver Medal, Signet Soc., Harvard, 1983; Distinguished Service Award, Asian/Pacific Americans Liby Assoc., 1986; NYC Mayor's Liberty Medal, 1986; Centenary Barrows Award, Pomona Coll., 1987; Literary Lion Medal, 1990, Literary Lion Centennial Award, 1996, NY Public Liby; NY State Asian-American Heritage Month Award, 1991; Arkansas Traveler Award, Univ. of Arkansas, 2006. *Publications:* Face to Face, 1957 (Secondary Educn Annual Book Award, 1958; serial reading on BBC Light prog., 1958, dramatization on Home prog., 1959; reissued 1967, 1978); Walking the Indian Streets, 1960, rev. edn 1971; Fly and the Fly-Bottle, 1963, 2nd edn 1983 introd. Jasper Griffin; The New Theologian, 1966; Delinquent Chacha (fiction), 1967; Portrait of India, 1970, 2nd edn 1993; John Is Easy to Please, 1971; Mahatma Gandhi and His Apostles, 1977, reissued 1993; The New India, 1978; Photographs of Chachaji, 1980; A Family Affair: India under three Prime Ministers, 1982; Three Stories of the Raj (fiction), 1986; Rajiv Gandhi and Rama's Kingdom, 1995; A Ved Mehta Reader: the craft of the essay, 1998; Continents of Exile (autobiography): Daddyji, 1972; Mamaji, 1979; Vedi, 1982; The Ledge Between the Streams, 1984; Sound-Shadows of the New World, 1986; The Stolen Light, 1989; Up at Oxford, 1993; Remembering Mr Shawn's New Yorker: the invisible art of editing, 1998; All For Love, 2001; Dark Harbor, 2003; The Red Letters, 2004; Veritas, 2011; The Essential Ved Mehta, 2013; numerous translations, 1957–. Writer and commentator of TV documentary film Chachaji: My Poor Relation, PBS, 1978, BBC, 1980 (DuPont Columbia Award for Excellence in Broadcast Journalism, 1977–78). *Recreation:* listening to Indian and Western music. *Address:* 139 East 79th Street, New York, NY 10075, USA. *T:* (212) 7377487, *Fax:* (212) 4727220. *Clubs:* Century Association (NY) (Trustee, 1973–75; Mem. Wine Cttee, 2000–04); Tarratine (Dark Harbor, Maine).

MEHTA, Zubin; Music Director for life, Israel Philharmonic Orchestra (Musical Adviser, 1962–78); Artistic Director, Maggio Musicale Fiorentino, since 1986; General Music Director, Bavarian State Opera, 1998–2006; *b* 29 April 1936; *s* of Mehli Mehta; *m* 1st, 1958, Carmen Lasky (marr. diss. 1964); one *s* one *d*; 2nd, 1969, Nancy Kovack. *Educ:* St Xavier's Coll., Bombay; Musikakademie, Vienna. First Concert, Vienna, 1958; first prize internat. comp., Liverpool, 1958; US debut, Philadelphia Orch., 1960; debut with Israel and Vienna Philharmonic Orchs, 1961; apptd Music Director, Montreal Symphony Orch., 1961; European tour with this orch., 1962; guest conducting, major European Orchs, 1962; Music Director: Los Angeles Philharmonic Orch., 1962–78 (Hon. Conductor, 2006); New York Philharmonic, 1978–91. Opera debut, Montreal, Tosca, 1964; debut Metropolitan Opera, Aida, 1965; operas at Metropolitan incl.: Tosca, Turandot, Otello, Carmen, Mourning becomes Elektra (world première), Trovatore, etc. Tours regularly with Israel Philharmonic Orchs and occasionally with Vienna Phil. Orch.; regular guest conducting with Vienna Phil., Berlin Phil., Orch. de Paris. Hon. Doctorates: Colgate Univ.; Brooklyn Coll.; Westminster Coll.; Occidental Coll.; Sir George Williams Univ., Canada; Weizmann Inst. of Science, Israel; Tel-Aviv Univ. Holds numerous awards; Israel Wolf Foundn Prize, 1996; Praemium Imperiale, Japan Art Assoc., 2008. Padma Bhushan (India), 1967; Commendatore of Italy; Médaille d'Or Verneil, City of Paris, 1984; Presidential Medal of Distinction (Israel), 2012. *Publications:* The Score of My Life (memoir), 2008. *Address:* 27 Oakmont Drive, Los Angeles, CA 90049–1901, USA. *T:* (310) 4443111.

MEIER, Maj.-Gen. Anthony Leslie, CB 1995; OBE 1981; Director-General, Management and Support of Intelligence, Ministry of Defence, 1991–94; *b* 3 Sept. 1937; *s* of late Eric Leslie Francis Meier and Vera Madge Meier (*née* Terry); *m* 1973, Susanne Jennifer Manley; two *s* one *d*. *Educ:* Latymer Upper Sch.; RMA Sandhurst. Commissioned RASC, 1957, later RCT; regtl appts, Germany and on secondment to Brigade of Gurkhas, Far East, 1958–68; Staff Coll., 1969; MoD, 31 Sqn GTR, NDC, HQ BAOR, CO 8 Regt RCT, to 1981; Col GS Coord (COS), Staff Coll., 1981–84; NATO Defence Coll., Rome, 1984–85; HQ AFCENT, 1985–87; Dir of Intell. (Warsaw Pact), MoD, 1988–90. Dir, Macmillan Appeal for Brighton and Hove Hospice, 1994–96; non-exec. Dir, Eastbourne Hosps NHS Trust, 1994–2002. Adjudicator, Criminal Injuries Compensation Appeals Panel, 1997–2007. Chm., Bd of Govs, St Bede's Prep. Sch., Eastbourne, 1994–99; Dep. Chm., 1999–2008, Chm., 2008–, Bd of Govs, St Bede's Sch., Sussex; Special Comr, Duke of York's Royal Mil. Sch., 1998–2008 (Chm., 2003–08). *Publications:* Notes on the Soviet Ground Forces, 1972; articles in Internat. Defense Review. *Recreation:* sport. *Address:* c/o National Westminster Bank, 96 Terminus Road, Eastbourne, E Sussex BN21 3LX.

MEIER, His Honour David Benjamin; a Circuit Judge, 1993–2003; Designated Care Judge for Buckinghamshire; *b* 8 Oct. 1938; *s* of Arnold Meier, PhD and Irma Meier; *m* 1964, Kathleen Lesly Wilton; one *d*. *Educ:* Bury Grammar Sch.; King's College London (LLB). Admitted Law Society, 1964; Solicitor. Metropolitan Stipendiary Magistrate, 1985–93; a Recorder, 1991–93. Pres., Mental Health Tribunals, 1988–2000; Chairman: Juvenile Court, 1988–93; Family Panel, 1991–93. Pres., N Middx Law Soc., 1984–85. *Recreations:* riding, cricket, golf.

MEIER, Richard Alan; principal architect, Richard Meier & Partners Architects (formerly Richard Meier & Associates, New York), since 1963; *b* Newark, NJ, 12 Oct. 1934; *s* of Jerome Meier and Carolyn Meier (*née* Kaltenbacher); *m* 1978, Katherine Gormley (marr. diss. 1987); one *s* one *d*. *Educ:* Cornell Univ. (BAArch 1957). FAIA. Architect with: Frank Grad & Sons, NJ, 1957; Davis Brody & Wisniewski, NY, 1958–59; Skidmore, Owings & Merrill, 1959–60; Marcel Breuer & Associates, 1960–63. Adjunct Prof. of Architecture, Cooper Union, 1963–73; Visiting Professor: Yale Univ., 1975, 1977, 2008; Harvard Univ., 1977; UCLA, 1987, 1988. *Major works* include: Smith House, Darien, Conn, 1967, and houses in Harbor Springs, E Hampton, Malibu, Dallas, New York, Florida, Pittsburgh and Naples; Bronx Developmental Center, NY, 1977; Atheneum, New Harmony, 1979; High Mus. of Art, Atlanta, 1983; Mus. für Angewandte Kunst (formerly Kunsthandwerk), Frankfurt, 1984; Canal Plus HQ, Paris, 1992; City Hall and Central Liby, The Hague, 1995; Mus. of Contemp. Art, Barcelona, 1995; Getty Center, LA, 1997; 173/176 Perry St, NY, 2002; 66 Restaurant, NY, 2003; Center for Possibility Thinking, California, 2003; Jubilee Church, Rome, 2003; Burda Collection Mus., Baden-Baden, 2004; San Jose City Hall, 2005; 165 Charles St, NY, 2006; Ara Pacis Mus., Rome, 2006; Arp Museum, Rolandseck, Germany, 2007; Weill Hall, Ithaca, NY, 2008; On Prospect Park, NY, 2008; Saint-Denis, France, 2009; Italcementi i.Lab, Bergamo, 2012 (Greenbuilding Plus Award: Best New Building, 2010). *Exhibitions* include: XV Triennale, Milan, 1973; Mus. of Modern Art, NY, 1975, 1981; Princeton Univ., 1976; Cooper-Hewitt Mus., NY, 1976–77, 2009; Athens, 1982–83; Tokyo, 1988; Naples, 1991; Rome, 1993; Nagoya, 1996; Paris, 1999; London, 2007; Guggenheim, NY, 2010; Mumbai, 2010. 5 Architectural Record awards, 1964–77; 99 AIA Awards, 1968–2008; Pritzker Prize for Architecture, 1984; RIBA Gold Medal, 1988; 5 Progressive Architecture awards, 1979–95; AIA Gold Medal, 1997; Praemium Imperiale, Japan, 1997; Gold Medal for Architecture, AAAL, 2008; President's Medal, Architectural League of NY, 2009. Comdr, Ordre des Arts et Lettres (France), 1992 (Officier, 1984). *Publications:* On Architecture, 1982; Richard Meier, Architect, vol. 1 1984, vol. 2 1991, vol. 3 1999; vol. 4 2004; vol. 5 2009; Richard Meier Museums, 2006; Richard Meier Houses and Apartments, 2008; Richard Meier & Partners Complete Works: 1963–2008, 2008; contribs to professional jls. *Address:* 475 Tenth Avenue, Floor 6, New York, NY 10018–1120, USA.

MEIKLEJOHN, Dominic Francis, OBE 2007; HM Diplomatic Service; High Commissioner to Solomon Islands, Vanuatu and Nauru, 2012–15; *b* London, 14 Nov. 1967; *s* of David Meiklejohn and Eileen Meiklejohn; *m* 2008, Joanne Farrand; one *d*. *Educ:* Taunton Sch.; Merton Coll., Oxford (BA PPE). HM Customs and Excise; joined FCO, 1990; EC Dept, 1990–92; Hd, British Know-How Fund, British Embassy, Warsaw, 1993–96; OSCE Mission, Tirana, 1997; Hd, India Team, FCO, 1998–99; First Sec., Warsaw, 2000–03; Dep. Hd, Envmt Policy Dept, FCO, 2004; Deputy Consul-General: Basra, 2006–07; New York, 2008–12. *Recreations:* football, cricket, golf. *Address:* c/o Foreign and Commonwealth Office, King Charles Street, SW1A 2AH.

MEIN, Very Rev. James Adlington; Dean of the Episcopal Church, Diocese of Edinburgh, 2001–04, now Dean Emeritus; Rector of Christ Church, Morningside, 1990–2004; *b* 29 Dec. 1938; *s* of James Helliwell Mein and Kathleen Elsie Mein (*née* Dawson); *m* 1966, Helen Shaw (*née* Forrester-Paton); one *s* one *d*. *Educ:* Nottingham Univ. (BA Hons Theol. 1960); Westcott House, Cambridge. Ordained deacon, 1963, priest, 1964; Curate, St Columba, Edinburgh, 1963–67; Chaplain to Bp of Edinburgh, 1965–67; Sec., Christian Service Cttee, Malawi, 1967–72; Rector, St Mary, Grangemouth, 1972–82, with Bo'ness, 1976–82; Team Priest, Livingston, 1982–90; Canon, St Mary's Cathedral, Edinburgh, 1990–2001. *Recreations:* walking, golf, reading, television. *Address:* Cardhu, Bridgend, Linlithgow EH49 6NH. *T:* (01506) 834317. *E:* jim@meins.plus.com.

MEIRION-JONES, Prof. Gwyn Idris, FSA 1981; author and consultant on historic buildings; Professor Emeritus, London Metropolitan University; *b* 24 Dec. 1933; *e s* of late Maelgwyn Meirion-Jones and Enid Roberts, Manchester; *m* 1961, Monica (*d* 2003), *e d* of late George and Marion Havard, Winchester. *Educ:* North Manchester Grammar School; King's College London (BSc, MPhil, PhD). National Service, RAF Mountain Rescue, 1954–56. Schoolmaster, 1959–68; Lectr in Geography, Kingston Coll. of Technology, 1968; Sir John Cass College, later City of London Polytechnic: Sen. Lectr i/c Geography, 1969; Principal Lectr i/c, 1970; Head of Geography, 1970–89; Personal Chair, 1983–89, then Prof. Emeritus; Hon. Research Fellow, 1989–98. Leverhulme Research Fellow, 1985–87; Vis. Prof. of Archaeol., Univ. of Reading, 1995–2007. Dir, Soc. of Antiquaries, 2001–02. British Assoc. for the Advancement of Science: Sec., 1973–78, Recorder, 1978–83, Pres., 1992–93, Section H (Anthropology and Archaeology); Mem. Council, 1977–80; Mem. Gen. Cttee, 1977–83; Ancient Monuments Society: Mem. Council, 1974–79 and 1983–94; Hon. Sec., 1976–79; Vice-Pres., 1979–; Editor, 1985–94; Pres., Cambrian Archaeol Assoc., 2011–12. Member: Royal Commn on Historical Monuments of England, 1985–97; Adv. Cttee on Bldgs and Domestic Life, Welsh Folk Mus., 1991–95. Hon. Pres., Domestic Buildings Res. Gp (Surrey), 1991– (Pres., 1986–91). Editor, Medieval Village Res. Gp, 1978–86. Liveryman, Livery Co. of Wales (formerly Welsh Livery Guild), 2007–. Hon. Corresp. Mem., Soc. Jersiaise, 1980–90 and 1990–; Corresponding Member: Cie des Architectes en Chef des Monuments Historiques, 1989–; Soc. d'Histoire et d'Archéol. de Bretagne, 1997–. Exhibitions: vernacular architecture of Brittany, on tour 1982–89; Architecture vernaculaire en Bretagne (15e–20e siècles), Rennes and tour, 1984–89. *Publications:* La Maison traditionnelle (bibliog.), 1978; The Vernacular Architecture of Brittany, 1982; (with Michael Jones) Aimer les Châteaux de Bretagne, 1991 (trans. English and German); (with Michael Jones) Les Châteaux de Bretagne, 1992; (jtly) Manorial Domestic Buildings in England and Northern France, 1993; (jtly) La Ville de Cluny et ses Maisons XIe–XVe siècles, 1997; (jtly) The Seigneurial Residence in Western Europe AD *c* 800–1600, 2002; (dir, ed and contrib.) La Demeure Seigneuriale dans l'Espace Plantagenêt, XIe–XVIe siècles: salles, chambres et tours, Rennes, 2012; papers in sci., archaeol and ethnol jls. *Recreations:* food, wine, music, walking, fly-fishing. *Address:* 11 Avondale Road, Fleet, Hants GU51 3BH. *T:* (01252) 614300. *E:* gwynmj@orange.fr. *Clubs:* Athenæum; Royal Scots (Edinburgh).

MEISEL, Prof. John, CC 1999 (OC 1989); PhD; FRSC; President, Royal Society of Canada, 1992–95; Sir Edward Peacock Professor of Political Science, Queen's University, Canada, 1983–94, now Emeritus; Co-Editor (formerly Editor), International Political Science Review, 1979–95; *b* 23 Oct. 1923; *s* of Fryda S. Meisel and Anne Meisel (*née* Heller); *m* 1949, Murie A. Kelly (decd). *Educ:* Pickering Coll.; Univ. of Toronto (BA, MA); LSE (PhD). FRSC 1974. Political scientist; Queen's University, Canada: Instructor to Prof., 1949–79; Hardy Prof. of Political Science, 1963–79. Vis. Prof., Yale, 1976–77; Commonwealth Dist. Vis. Prof., UK, 1978. Chm., Canadian Radio-TV and Telecommunications Commn, 1980–83. President: Canadian Pol Sci. Assoc., 1973–74; Social Sci. Fedn of Canada, 1975–76. Hon. LLD: Brock; Calgary; Carleton; Queen's; Guelph; Toronto; Regina; DU Ottawa; Hon. DLitt Waterloo; Hon. DSS Laval. Canada Medals: Confedn Centennial, 1967; 125th Anniv. Confedn, 1992; Silver Jubilee Medal, 1977. *Publications:* The Canadian General Election of 1957, 1962; Papers on the 1962 Election, 1964; Working Papers on Canadian Politics, 1972;

(with Vincent Lemieux) Ethnic Relations in Canadian Voluntary Associations, 1972; Cleavages, Parties and Values in Canada, 1974; (with Jean Laponce) Debating the Constitution, 1994; A Life of Learning and Other Pleasures: John Meisel's tale, 2012; numerous articles in acad. jls. *Recreations:* visual and performing arts, hiking, bird watching, flower admiring, indoor gardening, printed word. *Address:* Colimaison, Tichborne, ON K0H 2V0, Canada. *T:* (613) 2792380; St Lawrence Place, Apt 615, 181 Ontario Street, Kingston, ON K7L 5M1, Canada. *E:* meiselj@queensu.ca.

MEIXNER, Helen Ann Elizabeth, (Mrs Helen Thornton), CMG 2001; Regional Director, South-East Europe and Director, Romania, 1997–2001, British Council; *b* 26 May 1941; *d* of Henry Gerard and Valerie Meixner; *m* Jack Edward Clive Thornton, CB, OBE (*d* 1996). *Educ:* Sydney C of E Grammar Sch. for Girls, Darlinghurst; Univ. of Queensland (BA 1961); Sch. of Slavonic and East European Studies, UCL (MA 2004). Teacher, Abbotsleigh Girls' Sch., Wahroonga, 1962; Educn Asst, ABC, 1963–64; joined British Council, 1966; Recruitment Unit, Zagreb Office, Exchanges, Courses, Staff Recruitment, Dir-Gen.'s and Personnel Depts; Head, Design, Production and Publishing Dept, 1984–86; Dep. Dir, Personnel and Head, Personnel Dept, 1986–91; Dir of Libraries, Books and Information Div., 1991–94; Dep. Dir, Professional Services and Head, Consultancy Gp, 1994–96; Dir, Central Europe, 1996–97. Member: Council, Ranfurly Liby Service, 1991–94; Exec. Cttee, VSO, 1995–97; Council, Book Aid Internat., 2001–08; Bd Mem., Sir John Cass's Foundn, 2009–. Dir, Cornerhouse, Manchester, 1993–95. Trustee, Anglo-Romanian Educnl Trust, 2002–09. Governor: Langford Primary Sch., Fulham, 2002–12 (Chm., 2008–11); Sir John Cass's Foundn and Redcoat Secondary Sch., 2010–; Anglia Ruskin Univ., 2013–. JP Inner London, 1988–98. *Recreations:* music, reading, walking, travel. *Address:* 131 Dalling Road, W6 0ET. *T:* (020) 8748 7692.

MELANESIA, Archbishop of, since 2009; **Most Rev. David Vunagi;** *b* Samasodu, St Ysabel, 5 Sept. 1950; *s* of late Douglas Vunagi and Rositer Vunagi; *m* 1978, Mary; two *s* one *d*. *Educ:* Univ. of the S Pacific (DipEd Sci. 1976); Univ. of PNG (BEd Biol. 1982); Melbourne Coll. of Divinity (BTh 1990); Vancouver Sch. of Theology (MTh 1998). Principal, Selwyn Coll., 1985–86; Founding Co-ordinator of Distance Educn, Solomon Islands Coll. of HE, 1991; Lectr in Biblical Studies, Bishop Patteson Theol Coll., Kohimarama, 1992; Principal, Selwyn Coll., 1993–96 and 1999; Sen. Priest, Lawe Region, Dio. of Ysabel, 1998; Mission Sec., Church of Melanesia, 2000; Bishop, Dio. of Temotu, 2001–09. *Recreations:* reading, listening to radio news. *Address:* Anglican Church of Melanesia, PO Box 19, Honiara, Solomon Islands. *T:* (677) 21892, 22339, *Fax:* (677) 21098, 22327. *E:* dvunagi@comphq.org.sb.

MELBOURNE, Archbishop of, since 2006, and Primate of Australia, since 2014; **Most Rev. Philip Leslie Freier,** PhD; *b* 9 Feb. 1955; *m* 1976, Joy Launder; two *s*. *Educ:* Qld Inst. of Technol. (BAppSc 1975); Univ. of Qld (DipEd 1976); St John's Coll., Morpeth (Associate Dip. in Theol 1984); Melbourne Coll. of Divinity (BD 1984); Univ. of Newcastle (MEdSt 1984); James Cook Univ., Townsville (PhD 2000). Teacher, Qld Educn Dept, 1976–81. Ordained deacon, 1983, priest, 1984; Deacon in Charge, Ch of the Ascension, Kowanyama, 1983–84, Priest in Charge, 1984–88; Rector: St Oswald, Banyo, 1988–93; Christ Ch, Bundaberg, 1993–99; Bishop of Northern Territory, 1999–2006. Area Dean: Brisbane N, 1992–93; the Burnett, 1995–98; Examining Chaplain to Archbp of Brisbane, 1993–99. Member: Diocesan Council, Dio. Carpentaria, 1986–88; Gen. Synod, 1987–98 (Mem., Missionary and Ecumenical Commn, 1995–98); Provincial Synod, 1987–98 (Mem., Standing Cttee, 1988–); Diocesan Council, Dio. Brisbane, 1991–94. *Publications:* Thaw Pathn a Palal Nguwl, 1978; (with E. J. Freier) Kupmari, A Picture Book, 1978; Science Program for Aboriginal Community Schools, 1980; (jtly) Mathematical Program for Schools in Aboriginal and Torres Strait Islander Communities, 1983; articles in jls. *Address:* The Anglican Centre, 209 Flinders Lane, Melbourne, Vic 3000, Australia.

MELBOURNE, Archbishop of, (RC), since 2001; **Most Rev. Denis James Hart;** *b* Melbourne, 16 May 1941; *s* of Kevin James Hart and Annie Eileen (*née* Larkan). *Educ:* Xavier Coll., Kew; Corpus Christi Coll., Werribee; Corpus Christi Coll., Glen Waverley. Ordained priest, 1967; Chaplain, Repatriation Hosp., Heidelberg, 1967–68; Asst Priest, N Balwyn, 1968; Asst Priest and Master of Ceremonies, St Patrick's Cathedral, Melbourne, 1969–74; Prefect of Ceremonies, Archdio. Melbourne, 1970–96; Advocate and Notary, Regional Matrimonial Tribunal, 1975–85; Exec. Sec., Nat. Liturgical Commn, Aust. Catholic Bps' Conf., 1975–90; Parish Priest, St Joseph's, W Brunswick, 1987–96; Vicar Gen. and Moderator of the Curia, 1996–2001; Aux. Bp, Archdio. Melbourne, 1997–2001; Titular Bp of Vagada, 1997–2001. Member: Congregation for Eastern Churches, 2014–; Pontifical Council for Culture, 2014–. Australian Catholic Bishops' Conference: Member: Commn for Liturgy, 2000–12; Permanent Cttee, 2002–; Chm., Cttee for Finance and Admin., 2002–12; Vice Pres., 2009–12; Pres., 2012–; Vice Pres., Internat. Commn for English in the Liturgy, 2008–. *Recreations:* walking, music, reading. *Address:* St Patrick's Cathedral, Melbourne, Vic 3002, Australia. *T:* (3) 99265612.

MELBOURNE, Assistant Bishops of; *see* Huggins, Rt Rev. P. J.; White, Rt Rev. P. R.

MELBOURNE, Dean of; *see* Loewe, Very Rev. A.

MELCHETT, 4th Baron *cr* 1928; **Peter Robert Henry Mond;** Bt 1910; Policy Director, Soil Association, since 2001; *b* 24 Feb. 1948; *s* of 3rd Baron Melchett and of Sonia Elizabeth Sinclair, *qv*; *S* father, 1973. *Educ:* Eton; Pembroke Coll., Cambridge (BA); Keele Univ. (MA). Res. Worker, LSE and Addiction Res. Unit, 1973–74. A Lord in Waiting (Govt Whip), 1974–75; Parly Under-Sec. of State, DoI, 1975–76; Minister of State, NI Office, 1976–79. Chm., working party on pop festivals, 1975–76; Chm., Community Industry, 1979–85; Chm., 1986–89, Exec. Dir, 1989–2000, Greenpeace UK. Special Lectr, Sch. of Biological Scis, Nottingham Univ., 1984–2002. Chairman: Wildlife Link, 1979–87; Greenpeace Japan, 1994–2001; Mem. Bd, Greenpeace Internat., 1989, 2001; Member: Govt Organic Action Plan Gp, 2002–08; BBC Rural Affairs Cttee, 2004–; Govt Sch. Meals Review Panel, 2005; Govt Rural Climate Change Forum, 2009–11. Vice-Pres., Ramblers' Assoc., 1984– (Pres., 1981–84). Hon DCL Newcastle, 2013. *Address:* Courtyard Farm, Ringstead, Hunstanton, Norfolk PE36 5LQ.

MELDING, David Robert Michael; Member (C) South Wales Central, since 1999, and Deputy Presiding Officer, since 2011, National Assembly for Wales; *b* 28 Aug. 1962; *s* of David Graham Melding and Edwina Margaret Melding (*née* King). *Educ:* Dwr-y-Felin Comprehensive Sch., Neath; UC Cardiff (BScEcon); Coll. of William and Mary, Virginia (MA). Cons. Res. Dept, 1986–89; Dep. Dir, Welsh Centre for Internat. Affairs, 1989–96; Manager, Carers Nat. Assoc. in Wales, 1996–99. *Publications:* Will Britain Survive Beyond 2020?, 2009; The Reformed Union: the UK as a federation, 2013. *Recreations:* swimming, reading, walking, pogoing to work. *Address:* National Assembly for Wales, Cardiff Bay, Cardiff CF99 1NA. *T:* 0300 200 7222. *E:* david.melding@assembly.wales.

MELDRUM, Sir Graham, Kt 2002; CBE 1994; QFSM 1989; FIFireE; Chairman, West Midlands Ambulance Service NHS Trust, since 2007; *b* 23 Oct. 1945; *s* of George Meldrum and Agnes (*née* Gordon); *m* 1964, Catherine Meier; one *s* one *d*. *Educ:* Inverurie Acad., Aberdeenshire. FIFireE 1995. Fireman to Station Officer, London Fire Bde, 1963–73; Instructor, in the rank of Asst Divl Officer, Fire Service Coll., 1973–74; Divl Officer III, Hants Fire Service, 1974–76; Tyne and Wear: Divl Officer II, 1976–79; Divl Officer I, 1979–80; Sen. Divl Officer, 1980–83; West Midlands: Asst Chief Officer, 1983–84; Dep. Chief Fire Officer, 1984–90; Chief Fire Officer, 1990–97; HM Chief Inspector of Fire Services, 1998–2007. Pres., Chief and Asst Chief Fire Officers' Assoc., 1994–95; Chairman: Fire Services Nat. Benevolent Fund, 1994; CACFOA (Research) Ltd, 1988–; CACFOA (Services) Ltd, 1988–. DUniv 1997. OStJ 1998. *Publications:* papers on fire engrg in jls. *Recreations:* computers, motor-cycling, railways, industrial archaeology, community work. *Address:* St Francis Chapel, Bridge Street, Kineton, Warwicks CV35 0JR.

MELDRUM, Hamish Robin Peter, FRCGP, FRCPE; Chairman of Council, British Medical Association, 2007–12 (Member, 2000–12); Deputy Chairman, BMJ Publishing Group, since 2014; *b* Edinburgh, 14 April 1948; *s* of James S. Meldrum and May I. Meldrum (*née* MacGregor); *m* 1974, Mhairi M. K.; two *s* one *d*. *Educ:* Stirling High Sch.; Edinburgh Univ. (BSc Med. Sci. 1969; MB ChB 1972). DRCOG 1977; FRCGP 2001; FRCPE. Hse physician, Edinburgh Royal Infirmary, 1972–73; Med. SHO, then Registrar, Torbay Hosp., Devon, 1973–76; GP trainee, Harrogate, 1976–78; Principal in Gen. Practice, Bridlington, E Yorks, 1978–2011. Mem., GPs Cttee, BMA, 1991–2012 (Chm., 2004–07). *Publications:* contrib. med. jls incl. BMJ. *Recreations:* sport (watching most, playing tennis, running, golf and keep fit), hill walking, music (varied), wine appreciation, good company and discussion. *Address:* Ardbeg, 4 Kinnear Road, Edinburgh EH3 5PE. *T:* (0131) 552 4191.

MELDRUM, James; Keeper, Registers of Scotland, 2003–09; *b* 9 Aug. 1952; *s* of late George and Marion Meldrum. *Educ:* Lenzie Academy; Glasgow Univ. (MA Hons). Joined Scottish Office 1973; Principal, 1979–86; Dep. Dir, Scottish Courts Admin, 1986–91; Head, Investment Assistance Div., Scottish Office Industry Dept, 1991–94; Registrar General for Scotland, 1994–99; Dir, Admin. Services, Scottish Exec., 1999–2002; Dir of Business Mgt and Area Business Manager, Glasgow, Crown Office and Procurator Fiscal Service, 2002–03. FRSA 2008. *Recreations:* reading, music, gardening. *Address:* 5 Roman Road, Kirkintilloch, Glasgow G66 1EE. *T:* (0141) 776 7071. *Club:* Royal Over-Seas League.

MELDRUM, Keith Cameron, CB 1995; veterinary consultant, since 1997; Chief Veterinary Officer, Ministry of Agriculture, Fisheries and Food, 1988–97; *b* 19 April 1937; *s* of Dr Walter James Meldrum and Mrs Eileen Lydia Meldrum; *m* 1st, 1962, Rosemary Ann (*née* Crawford) (marr. diss. 1980); two *s* one *d*; 2nd, 1982, Vivien Mary (*née* Fisher). *Educ:* Uppingham; Edinburgh Univ. Qualified as veterinary surgeon, 1961; general practice, Scunthorpe, 1961–63; joined MAFF, Oxford, 1963; Divl Vet. Officer, Tolworth, 1972, Leamington Spa, 1975; Dep. Regional Vet. Officer, Nottingham, 1978; Regional Vet. Officer, Tolworth, 1980; Asst Chief Vet. Officer, Tolworth, 1983; Dir of Vet. Field Service, 1986. UK Deleg., Office Internat. des Epizooties, 1988–97. Mem. Council, RCVS, 1988–97. Gov., Inst. of Animal Health, 1988–97. Trustee, Animal Health Trust, 2002–07. Hon. FRSPH (Hon. FRSH 2000). Bledisloe Vet. Award, RASE, 1995. *Recreation:* outdoor activities. *Address:* The Orchard, Swaynes Lane, Merrow, Guildford, Surrey GU1 2XX. *Club:* Farmers.

MELGUND, Viscount; Gilbert Francis Elliot-Murray-Kynynmound; *b* 15 Aug. 1984; *s* and *heir* of Earl of Minto, *qv*. *Educ:* Marlborough Coll.

MELHUISH, Prof. Edward Charles, PhD; Research Professor, Department of Education, University of Oxford, since 2012; *b* 3 April 1950; *s* of Robert Hector Melhuish and Elsie Beatrice Melhuish; one *s* four *d*. *Educ:* Univ. of Bristol (BSc); Univ. of London (PhD 1980). Researcher, Univ. of London, 1981–86; Lectr, UCNW, Bangor, 1987–94; Prof., Cardiff Univ., 1994–2000; Prof. of Human Develt (formerly Psychology), Birkbeck, 2001–15, and Dir, Inst. for the Study of Children, Families and Social Issues, 2010–12, Univ. of London. Vis. Prof., Univ. of Wollongong, 2014–. Consultant: OECD, WHO, EU. Exec. Dir, Nat. Evaluation of Sure Start, 2001–12. Trustee, WAVE Trust, 2013–; Advr, Save the Children Fund, 2014–. *Publications:* Day Care for Young Children: international perspectives, 1991; Early Childhood Care and Education, 2006; The National Evaluation of Sure Start: does area-based early intervention work?, 2007; Early Childhood Matters, 2010; (jtly) Assessing Quality in Early Childhood Education and Care, 2015. *Recreations:* reading, music, film, sailing, Rugby, travel, grandchildren.

MELHUISH, Sir (Michael) Ramsay, KBE 1993; CMG 1982; HM Diplomatic Service, retired; *b* 17 March 1932; *s* of late Henry Whitfield Melhuish and Jeanette Ramsay Pender Melhuish; *m* 1961, Stella Phillips; two *s* two *d*. *Educ:* Royal Masonic Sch., Bushey; St John's Coll., Oxford (BA). FO, 1955; MECAS, 1956; Third Sec., Bahrain, 1957; FO, 1959; Second Sec., Singapore, 1961; First Sec. (Commercial) and Consul, Prague, 1963; First Sec. and Head of Chancery, Bahrain, 1966; DSAO (later FCO), 1968; First Sec., Washington, 1970; Counsellor, Amman, 1973; Head of N America Dept, FCO, 1976; Counsellor (Commercial), Warsaw, 1979–82; Ambassador, Kuwait, 1982–85; High Comr, Zimbabwe, 1985–89; Ambassador, Thailand, 1989–92. Head, EC Monitor Mission, Zagreb, July–Dec. 1992. *Recreations:* tennis, golf. *Address:* Longwood Lodge, Leatherhead Road, Oxshott, Surrey KT22 0ET.

MELIA, Christine Hilary; Director, Italy, British Council, 2009–14; *b* Wirral, Cheshire, 24 March 1954; *d* of Peter Melia and Alice Shone; partner, Prof. Barrie Walsham Bycroft, *qv*. *Educ:* W Kirby Grammar Sch., Wirral; Nottingham Univ. (BA Jt Hons Geog. and Archaeol.). Joined British Council, 1979; London, 1979–85; Romania, 1985–88; London, 1988–90; Brazil, 1990–94; Caribbean, 1995; London, 1996–99; Spain, 1999–2004; Oxford, 2004–08. *Recreations:* travel, archaeology, food, wine, beekeeping, relaxing anywhere near the sea. *Address:* 4 Merrivale Square, Oxford OX2 6QX. *E:* christine.melia1@gmail.com. *Club:* Lansdowne.

MELIA, Dr Terence Patrick, CBE 1993; Chairman, Learning and Skills Development Agency, 2000–03; *b* 17 Dec. 1934; *s* of John and Kathleen Melia (*née* Traynor); *m* 1976, Madeline (*née* Carney); one *d*. *Educ:* Sir John Deane's Grammar Sch., Northwich; Leeds Univ. (PhD; J. B. Cohen Prize, 1961). CChem, FRSC. Technical Officer, ICI, 1961–64; Lectr, then Sen. Lectr, Salford Univ., 1964–70; Principal, North Lindsey Coll. of Technology, 1970–74; HM Inspector of Schools, 1974–92: Regional Staff Inspector, 1982–84; Chief Inspector, Further and Higher Educn, 1985–86; Chief Inspector, Higher Educn, 1985–91; Sen. Chief Inspector, HM Inspectorate of Schs, 1991–92; Chief Inspector, FEFC, 1993–96. Carried out, on behalf of Further Education Funding Council, subseq., Learning and Skills Council: official enquiries into: Bilston Coll., Melton Mowbray Coll., 1999; Sheffield Coll., 2000; Manchester Coll. of Arts and Technol., W Herts Coll., 2004; Strategic Area Reviews of Post-16 Educn, 2001–04. Vis. Prof., Leeds Metropolitan Univ., 1993–96. Chairman: Further Educn Staff Develt Forum, 1996–99; Further Educn Develt Agency, 1997–2000; Further Educn NTO, 1999–2001; Educn Policy Cttee, RSA Exams, 1996–99. Gov., Hills Road Sixth Form Coll., Cambridge, 2001–04. Hon. DSc Salford, 1998; Hon. DEd: Bradford, 2005; Plymouth, 2006. Plastics and Polymer Gp Prize, Soc. of Chemical Industry, 1964. *Publications:* Masers and Lasers, 1967; reports on official enquiries and strategic area reviews; papers on thermodynamics of polymerisation, thermal properties of polymers, effects of ionizing radiation, chemical thermodynamics, nucleation kinetics, thermal properties of transition metal compounds and gas kinetics. *Recreations:* golf, gardening.

MELINSKY, Rev. Canon (Michael Arthur) Hugh; Principal, Northern Ordination Course, 1978–88; *b* 25 Jan. 1924; *s* of late M. M. Melinsky and Mrs D. M. Melinsky; *m* 1949, Renate (*née* Ruhemann); three *d*. *Educ:* Whitgift Sch., Croydon; Christ's Coll., Cambridge (BA 1947, MA 1949); London Univ. Inst. of Education (TDip 1949); Ripon Hall, Oxford. Inter-Services Special Intelligence Sch., 1943–44; Japanese Intelligence in FE, 1944–46. Asst Master: Normanton Grammar Sch., 1949–52; Lancaster Royal Grammar Sch., 1952–57. Ordained deacon, 1957, priest, 1959; Curate: Wimborne Minster, 1957–59; Wareham, 1959–61; Vicar of St Stephen's, Norwich, 1961–68; Chaplain of Norfolk and Norwich Hosp.,

1961–68; Hon. Canon and Canon Missioner of Norwich, 1968–73; Chief Sec., ACCM, 1973–77. Chairman: C of E Commn on Euthanasia, 1972–75; Inst. of Religion and Medicine, 1973–77; Mem., Social Policy Cttee, C of E Bd for Social Responsibility, 1982–92; Mem. Cttee for Theological Educn, ACCM, 1985–88. Hon. Res. Fellow, Dept of Theol Studies, Manchester Univ., 1984. *Publications:* The Modern Reader's Guide to Matthew, 1963; the Modern Reader's Guide to Luke, 1963; Healing Miracles, 1967; (ed) Religion and Medicine, 1970; (ed) Religion and Medicine 2, 1973; Patterns of Ministry, 1974; (ed) On Dying Well, 1975, 2nd edn 2000; Foreword to Marriage, 1984; (contrib.) The Weight of Glory, 1991; The Shape of the Ministry, 1992; (contrib.) Tentmaking: perspectives on self-supporting ministry, 1998; A Code-breaker's Tale, 1998; Forming the Pathfinders: the career of Air Vice-Marshal Sydney Bufton, 2010. *Address:* 15 Parson's Mead, Norwich, Norfolk NR4 6PG. *T:* (01603) 455042.

MELLANBY, Carolyn Ann Fitzherbert; a District Judge (Magistrates' Courts), since 2009; *b* Shrewsbury, 30 April 1952; *d* of late Christopher Fitzherbert Jones and Eileen Eunice Jones (*née* Newport); *m* 1973, Alexander Robert Mellanby; one *s* one *d*. *Educ:* Hinchley Wood Co. Secondary Sch., Surrey; King's Coll., London (LLB 1973; AKC). Higher Rights of Audience (Criminal), 1994. Called to the Bar, Gray's Inn, 1975; Dep. Chief Clerk, Camberwell Green Magistrates' Court, 1977; Magistrates' Court Clerk, Hertford, 1977–78; Magistrate, Seychelles, 1982–85; Crown Prosecutor, Devon, 1986–89; admitted as solicitor, 1990; Partner, Ford Simey Solicitors, Exeter, 1990–2002; Solicitor and Hd, Family Dept, Christian Khan Solicitors, London, 2003–04; Consultant, Steel and Shamash Solicitors, London, 2004–09; Dep. Stipendiary Magistrate, later Dep. Dist Judge, 2000–09. Mem. and Examr, Children Panel, Law Soc., 1992–2009; Mem., Assoc. of Lawyers for Children, 1999–. *Recreations:* family, grandchildren, gardening, travel. *Address:* Luton and South Bedfordshire Magistrates' Court, Stuart Street, Luton, Beds LU1 5BL.

MELLARS, Sir Paul Anthony, Kt 2010; ScD; FBA 1990; Fellow, Corpus Christi College, Cambridge, since 1981 (President, 1992–2000); Professor of Prehistory and Human Evolution, Cambridge University, 1997–2007, now Emeritus; *b* 29 Oct. 1939; *s* of Herbert and Elaine Mellars; *m* 1969, Anny Chanut. *Educ:* Woodhouse Grammar Sch., Sheffield; Fitzwilliam Coll., Cambridge (Exhibnr; BA 1st Cl. Hons Archaeol. and Anthropol. 1962; MA 1965; PhD 1967; ScD 1988). FSA 1977. Sir James Knott Res. Fellow, Univ. of Newcastle upon Tyne, 1968–70; University of Sheffield: Lectr in Prehistory and Archaeol., 1970–75; Sen. Lectr, 1975–80; Reader, 1980–81; University of Cambridge: Lect, 1981–91; Reader in Archaeology, 1991–97. British Academy: Res. Reader, 1989–91; Reckitt Archaeol. Lectr, 1991; Vis. Prof., SUNY (Binghamton), 1974; Vis. Fellow, ANU, 1981; Danish Res. Council Vis. Lectr, Copenhagen and Aarhus Univs, 1985. President: Hunter Archaeol. Soc., 1975–80; Prehistoric Soc., 1998–2000 (Vice Pres., 1992–95); Chm., Archaeol. Sci. Cttee, Council for British Archaeol., 1980–87; Mem. Council, British Acad., 1994–97 (Chm., Archaeol. Sect., 1995). MAE 1999. Hon. Mem., Italian Inst. of Prehistoric & Proto-historic Sciences, 1997. *Publications:* (ed) The Early Postglacial Settlement of Northern Europe, 1976; Excavations of Oronsay, 1987; (ed) Research Priorities of Archaeological Science, 1987; (ed) The Human Revolution, 1989; (ed) The Emergence of Modern Humans, 1990; The Middle Palaeolithic: adaptation, behaviour & variability, 1991; (ed) The Origin of Modern Humans and the Impact of Science-based Dating, 1992; The Neanderthal Legacy, 1996; (ed) Modelling the Early Human Mind, 1996; Star Carr in Context, 1998; articles in archaeol. jls. *Recreations:* music, foreign travel. *Address:* Long Gable, Elsworth, Cambs CB23 4HX. *T:* (01954) 267275; Department of Archaeology, University of Cambridge, Downing Street, Cambridge CB2 3DZ. *T:* (01223) 333520.

MELLENEY, Clare Patricia; *see* Montgomery, C. P.

MELLING, Dr Jack; consultant and contractor, US Government Accountability Office, Washington, since 1998; *b* 8 Feb. 1940; *s* of John Melling and Mary (*née* Marsden); *m* 1967, Susan Ewart. *Educ:* Rivington and Blackrod Grammar Sch.; Manchester Univ. (BSc, MSc); Bath Univ. (PhD). FRPharmS 1977; FRSB (FIBiol 1979); FRCPath 1996; FRSC 2012. Res. Asst, Bath Univ., 1965–68; Lectr, Heriot-Watt Univ., 1968–69; SSO, then PSO, MoD, 1969–79; Dir, Vaccine Res. and Prodn Lab., PHLS, 1979–87; Dep. Dir, 1987–93, Dir, 1993–96, Centre for Applied Microbiology and Res., Porton Down; Dir, Biologicals Develt Center, Salk Inst. for Biol Studies, USA, 1996–2001; Dir (part-time), Karl Landsteiner Inst., Vienna, 2001–03; Sen. Project Manager (part-time), Battelle Meml Inst., Columbus, Ohio, 2001–05; Sen. Sci. Fellow, Center for Arms Control and Non-Proliferation, Washington, 2004–09. Visiting Professor: Rutgers Univ., 1979–84; Aston Univ., 1981–96; Westminster Univ., 1995–2005; Gastprofessor, Inst. for Social and Preventive Medicine, Univ. of Zürich, 1999–2006. Society of Chemical Industry: Mem. Council, 1983–86, 1998–2001; Sec., 1975–81, Chm., 1981–83, Biotechnology Gp; Chm. Pubns Cttee, 1999–2004; Hon. Treas., 2004–09; Chm., Bd of Trustees, 2009–15. Member: British Nat. Cttee for Microbiol., 1978–84; MRC Cttee on Develt of Vaccines and Immunol Products, 1979–96; Cttee on Safety of Medicines Biologicals Subcttee, 1982–99; Ind. Register Defence Scientific Adv. Council, 1994–98; Res. Adv. Cttee on Gulf War Veterans' Illnesses, US Dept of Veterans' Affairs, 2002–13. Sec., British Co-ordinating Cttee for Biotechnol., 1981–85; Sen. Scientific Advr, Internat. AIDS Vaccine Initiative, 1999–2006. Editor, Jl of Chem. Technol. and Biotechnol., 1985–; Mem. Editl Bd, Vaccine, 1983–. Lampitt Medal, SCI, 1993. *Publications:* Continuous Culture Applications and New Fields, 1977; Adhesion of Micro-organisms to Surfaces, 1979; The Microbial Cell Surface and Adhesion, 1981; Biosafety in Industrial Technology, 1994; papers in scientific jls. *Recreations:* ski-ing, shooting, walking. *Address:* US Government Accountability Office, 441 G Street NW, Washington, DC20548, USA. *E:* mellingj@gao.gov. *Clubs:* Athenæum, Royal Society of Medicine.

MELLITT, Prof. Brian, FREng; Chairman, Building Research Establishment, 1998–2010; *b* 29 May 1940; *s* of John and Nellie Mellitt; *m* 1961, Lyn Waring; one *s* one *d*. *Educ:* Loughborough Univ.; Imperial College, London Univ. (BTechEng, DIC). FIET, FIMechE, FIRSE; FREng (FEng 1990). Student apprentice, 1956, Junior Engineer, 1962, R&D Engineer, 1964, English Electric Co.; Lectr and Sen. Lectr, Huddersfield Polytechnic, 1966–67; Research Dept, British Rlys Bd, 1968–70; University of Birmingham: Lectr, 1971; Sen. Lectr, 1979; Prof., 1982; Head of Dept of Electronic and Electrical Engrg, 1986; Dean, Faculty of Engrg, 1987–88; Hon. Prof. of Electronic Engrg, 1989; Dir Engrg, London Underground Ltd, 1989–95; Dir, Metro Power, 1990–95; Dir of Engrg and Prodn, Railtrack PLC, 1995–99; Engrg Advr, Railtrack (UK), 1999–2000. Consultant Engineer, railway related organisations, 1972–. Chairman: BMCONSULT Ltd, 1999–; Metro-Consulting Ltd, 2000–02; SIRA Ltd, 2001–06; Director: Railway College Ltd, then Catalis Rail Trng, 1998–2000; Jarvis plc, 2002–09; Rail Advr, NM Rothschild, 1999–2003. President: Welding Inst., 2000–01; IEE, 2001–02 (Vice Pres., 1996–99; Dep. Pres., 1999–2001). Editor, IEE Procs (B), 1978–. Hon. Fellow, Assoc. of Project Managers, 1998. Hon. DTech Loughborough, 1991; Hon. DSc Huddersfield, 1998; Hon. DEng Birmingham, 1999. Leonardo da Vinci Award, Italian Assoc. for Industrial Design, 1989. *Publications:* contribs on electric railway topics to learned jls. *Recreation:* bridge. *Address:* The Priory, 36 Church Street, Stilton, Cambs PE7 3RF. *T:* (01733) 240573. *Club:* Athenæum.

MELLO, Prof. Craig C., PhD; Distinguished Professor, Program in Molecular Medicine, University of Massachusetts; Investigator, Howard Hughes Medical Institute, since 2000; *b* New Haven, Conn, 18 Oct. 1960; *s* of James and Sally Mello; *m* Margaret Hunter (marr. diss.); one *d*; *m* 1998, Edit Kiss; one *d*, and one step *s* one step *d*. *Educ:* Fairfax High Sch., Va; Brown Univ. (BS); Univ. of Colorado at Boulder; Harvard Univ. (PhD). Postdoctoral Fellow, Fred Hutchinson Cancer Res. Center, Seattle, 1990–94; joined Univ. of Massachusetts Medical Sch., 1994, Blais Univ. Chair in Molecular Medicine, 2003. (Jtly) Nobel Prize in Medicine, 2006. *Address:* Program in Molecular Medicine, University of Massachusetts Medical School, 373 Plantation Street, Worcester, MA 01605, USA.

MELLON, Sir James, KCMG 1988 (CMG 1979); HM Diplomatic Service, retired; Chairman, Charlemagne Capital (UK) Ltd (formerly Regent Europe Asset Management), since 2000; *b* 25 Jan. 1929; *s* of James Mellon and Margaret Traynor; *m* 1st, 1956, Frances Murray (*d* 1976); one *s* three *d*; 2nd, 1979, Mrs Philippa Shuttleworth (*née* Hartley). *Educ:* Glasgow Univ. (MA). Dept of Agriculture for Scotland, 1953–60; Agricultural Attaché, Copenhagen and The Hague, 1960–63; FO, 1963–64; Head of Chancery, Dakar, 1964–66; UK Delegn to European Communities, 1967–72; Counsellor, 1970; Hd of Sci. and Technol. Dept, FCO, 1973–75; Commercial Counsellor, East Berlin, 1975–76; Head of Trade Relations and Export Dept, FCO, 1976–78; High Comr in Ghana and Ambassador to Togo, 1978–83; Ambassador to Denmark, 1983–86; Dir-Gen. for Trade and Investment, USA, and Consul-Gen., New York, 1986–88. Chairman: Scottish Homes, 1989–96; Thamesmead Town, 1993–96; Regent Pacific Corp. Finance, 1999–2001. *Publications:* A Danish Gospel, 1986; Og Gamle Danmark, 1992; (ed and trans.) Per Federspiel, 2005. *Address:* Charlemagne Capital (UK) Ltd, 39 St James's Street, SW1A 1JD. *Club:* New (Edinburgh).

MELLOR, Christopher John; Director, Christopher Mellor Consulting, since 2012; *b* 3 March 1949; *s* of late John Whitaker Mellor and Mary Mellor (*née* Thompson); *m*; five *d*. Chartered Accountant, 1972. Various posts in local govt finance, 1967–79; with Anglian Water Authy, subseq. Anglian Water PLC, then awg plc, 1979–2003: Sen. Accountant, 1979–85; Principal Accountant, 1985–87; Hd, Privatisation Unit, 1987–88; Hd, Finance and Planning, 1988–90; Principal Accountant, then Head, Financial Planning, 1988–90; Gp Finance Dir, 1990–98; Gp Man. Dir, 1998–2000; Chief Exec., 2000–03; Dep. Chm., Monitor, Ind. Regulator of NHS Foundn Trusts, 2004–12; Interim Chm., Milton Keynes NHS Foundn Trust, 2013. Chm., NI Water Ltd, 2006–10; non-exec. Dir, Grontmij UK Ltd, 2004–10. Non-exec. Dir, Addenbrooke's Hosp. NHS Trust, 1994–98; interim Chm., Sherwood Forest Foundn Trust Hosp., 2012–13. *Recreations:* music, painting, golf.

MELLOR, Prof. David Hugh; Pro-Vice-Chancellor, University of Cambridge, 2000–01; Professor of Philosophy, University of Cambridge, 1986–99; Fellow, Darwin College, Cambridge, 1971–2005 (Vice-Master, 1983–87); *b* 10 July 1938; *s* of Sydney David Mellor and Ethel Naomi Mellor (*née* Hughes). *Educ:* Manchester Grammar School; Pembroke College, Cambridge (BA Nat. Scis and Chem. Eng, 1960; MA; PhD 1968; ScD 1990; MEng 1992); Univ. of Minnesota (Harkness Fellowship; MSc Chem. Eng, 1962). Technical Officer, ICI Central Instruments Lab., 1962–63; Cambridge University: Research Student in Philosophy, Pembroke Coll., 1963–68; Fellow, Pembroke Coll., 1964–68; Univ. Asst Lectr in Philosophy, 1965–70; Univ. Lectr in Philosophy, 1970–83; Univ. Reader in Metaphysics, 1983–85. Vis. Fellow in Philosophy, ANU, 1975; Radcliffe Trust Fellow in Philosophy, 1978–80. Hon. Prof. of Philosophy, Univ. of Keele, 1989–92. President: British Soc. for the Philos. of Science, 1985–87; Aristotelian Soc., 1992–93. Chm., Analysis Trust, 2000–08. Editor: British Journal for the Philosophy of Science, 1968–70; Cambridge Studies in Philosophy, 1978–82. FBA 1983–2008. Hon. FAHA, 2003. Hon. PhD Lund, 1997. *Publications:* The Matter of Chance, 1971; Real Time, 1981; Matters of Metaphysics, 1991; The Facts of Causation, 1995; Real Time II, 1998; Probability: a philosophical introduction, 2005; Mind, Meaning, and Reality, 2012; articles in Mind, Analysis, Philosophy of Science, Philosophy, Philosophical Review, Ratio, Isis, British Jl for Philosophy of Science, Jl of Philosophy. *Recreation:* theatre. *Address:* 25 Orchard Street, Cambridge CB1 1JS.

MELLOR, Rt Hon. David John; PC 1990; QC 1987; broadcaster, journalist and international business adviser; *b* 12 March 1949; *s* of late Mr and Mrs Douglas H. Mellor; *m* 1974, Judith Mary Hall (marr. diss. 1995); two *s*. *Educ:* Swanage Grammar Sch.; Christ's Coll., Cambridge (BA Hons 1970). FZS 1981. Called to the Bar, Inner Temple, 1972; in practice thereafter. Chm., Cambridge Univ. Conservative Assoc., 1970; contested West Bromwich E, Oct. 1974; MP (C) Putney, 1979–97; contested (C) same seat, 1997. PPS to Leader of Commons and Chancellor of the Duchy of Lancaster, 1981; Parly Under-Sec. of State, Dept of Energy, 1981–83, Home Office, 1983–86; Minister of State: Home Office, 1986–87; Foreign and Commonwealth Office, 1987–88; Dept of Health, 1988–89; Home Office, 1989–90; Privy Council Office (Minister for the Arts), 1990; Chief Sec. to the Treasury, 1990–92; Sec. of State for Nat. Heritage, 1992. Sec., Cons. Parly Legal Cttee, 1979–81; Vice-Chm., Greater London Cons. Members Cttee, 1980–81. Chairman: Sports Aid Foundn, 1993–97; Football Task Force, 1997–99. Special Trustee, Westminster Hosp., 1980–87; Trustee, Fund for the Replacement of Animals in Medical Experiments, 2004– (Co-Patron, 2005–). Mem. Council, NYO, 1981–; Mem. Bd, ENO, 1993–95; Pres., Bournemouth SO, 2000–09. Presenter: 6.06, 1993–99, Mellor, 1999–2001, BBC Radio 5; Vintage Years (series), BBC Radio 3, 1993–2000; The Midnight Hour, BBC2, 1997–99; New CD Show and David Mellor on Classic FM; David Mellor and Ken Livingstone Show, LBC, 2010–. Music Critic, Mail on Sunday, 2000–; columnist: The Guardian, 1992–94; The People, 1998–2003; sports columnist, Evening Standard, 1997–. BBC Radio Personality of the Year, Variety Club of GB, 1995. Hon. Associate, BVA, 1986. *Recreations:* classical music, reading, football.

MELLOR, Derrick, CBE 1984; HM Diplomatic Service, retired; re-employed at Foreign and Commonwealth Office, since 1984; Occasional Lecturer, School of Oriental and African Studies, since 1987; *b* 11 Jan. 1926; *s* of William Mellor and Alice (*née* Hurst); *m* 1954, Kathleen (*née* Hodgson); two *s* one *d*. Served Army, 1945–49. Board of Trade, 1950–57; Trade Commission Service, 1958–64: served Kuala Lumpur and Sydney; HM Diplomatic Service, 1964–: served Copenhagen, Caracas, Asunción (Ambassador, 1979–84) and London; Trng Consultant, FCO, 1987–. Project Dir for S Amer., GAP Activity Projects (GAP) Ltd, 1993–. Treasurer: Lord De La Warr Almshouses, 1995–2005; Wealden Cons. Party, 2000–. *Recreations:* tennis, golf, ski-ing. *Address:* Summerford Farmhouse, Withyham, E Sussex TN7 4DA. *T:* (01892) 770707. *Club:* Army and Navy.

MELLOR, Fiona; *see* MacCarthy, F.

MELLOR, Ian, MA; Headmaster, Stockport Grammar School, 1996–2005; *b* 30 June 1946; *s* of William Crompton Mellor and Annie Mellor; *m* 1969, Margery Ainsworth; three *s*. *Educ:* Manchester Grammar Sch.; Sidney Sussex Coll., Cambridge (MA, DipEd). Asst Modern Langs teacher, King's Sch., Chester, 1968–73; Head of Modern Languages: Kirkham Grammar Sch., Lancs, 1974–76; Bristol Grammar Sch., 1976–84; Dep. Head, Sale Boys' Grammar Sch., 1984–90; Head, Sir Roger Manwood's Sch., Sandwich, 1991–96. *Recreations:* Association football, cricket, reading, music of the 1960s, philatelic flaws and watermark varieties, bridge. *Address:* Bryn Issa, 10 Boot Street, Whittington, Shropshire SY11 4DG.

MELLOR, Dame Julie (Thérèse), DBE 2006; Parliamentary and Health Service Ombudsman, since 2012; *b* 29 Jan. 1957; *d* of Gp Capt. Edward Vernon Mellor and late Patricia Ann Mellor; *m* 1990, Nick Reed; one *s* one *d*. *Educ:* Winchester Co. High Sch. for Girls; Brasenose Coll., Oxford (BA Hons Exptl Psychol.; Hon. Fellow, 2003). Eleanor Emerson Fellow in Labour Educn, Cornell Univ., NY and teacher, Inst. for Educn Res. on Women and Work, 1979–81; Employee Relns Advr, Shell UK, 1981–83; Econ. Develt Officer, London Borough of Islington, 1983–84; Sen. Employment Policy Advr and Dep. Hd, Contract Compliance, Equal Opportunities Unit, ILEA, 1984–89; Equal Opportunities Manager, TSB Gp, 1989–91; Corporate Human Resources Dir, British Gas, 1992–96; owner and principal consultant, Julie Mellor Consultants, 1996–99; Chair, EOC, 1999–2005; Partner, PricewaterhouseCoopers, 2005–11. Mem., CRE, 1995–2002. Member: Minister's Nat. Adv. Council on Employment of Disabled People, 1993–95; Bd, Employers' Forum on

Disability, 2001–09; Bd, NCC, 2001–07; Bd, DIUS, later BIS, 2008–11. Trustee: Green Alliance, 2007–10; NESTA, 2012–. Chair, Fatherhood Inst. (formerly Fathers Direct), 2005–08. FCGI 2003. Hon. DPhil Anglia, 2003. *Recreations:* theatre, travel, food, family. *Address:* (office) Millbank Tower, Millbank, SW1P 4QP.

MELLOR, Very Rev. (Kenneth) Paul; Dean of Guernsey, Rector of St Peter Port and Priest-in-Charge of Sark, 2003–14; *b* 11 Aug. 1949; *s* of William Lewis and Frances Emma, (Peggy), Mellor; *m* 1972, Lindsey Helen Vinall; three *s*. *Educ:* Ashfield Sch., Kirkby-in-Ashfield; Southampton Univ. (BA Theol. 1971); Leeds Univ. (MA Theol. 1972); Cuddesdon Coll. Ordained deacon, 1973, priest, 1974; Curate: St Mary the Virgin, Cottingham, 1973–76; All Saints, Ascot, 1976–80; Vicar: St Mary Magdalen, Tilehurst, 1980–85; St Lalluwy, Menheniot, 1985–94; Canon Treasurer and Canon Residentiary, Truro Cathedral, 1994–2003 (Hon. Canon, 1990–94). RD, W Wivelshire, 1990–94; Chm., Truro Diocesan Bd for Mission and Unity, 1990–95. Member: Gen. Synod, 1994–; Cathedral Fabric Commn for England, 1995–2000. Hon. Canon, Winchester Cathedral, 2003–14, now Canon Emeritus. *Recreations:* walking, reading (esp. modern fiction), theatre, travel. *Address:* 10 Magdalene Court, Gigant Street, Salisbury, Wilts SP1 2DL. *E:* kpaulmellor@cwgsy.net.

MELLOR, His Honour Kenneth Wilson; QC 1975; a Circuit Judge, 1984–97; *b* 4 March 1927; *s* of Samuel Herbert Mellor; *m* 1957, Sheila Gale; one *s* three *d*. *Educ:* King's College Cambridge (BA 1949; LLB 1950; MA 1951). RNVR, 1944–47 (Sub Lieut). Called to the Bar, Lincoln's Inn, 1950. Dep. Chm., Hereford QS, 1969–71; a Recorder, 1972–84. Chm., Agricultural Land Tribunal (West Midlands).

MELLOR, Very Rev. Paul; *see* Mellor, Very Rev. K. P.

MELLOR, Ronald William, CBE 1984; FREng, FIMechE; Secretary, Institution of Mechanical Engineers, 1987–93; *b* 8 Dec. 1930; *s* of William and Helen Edna Mellor; *m* 1st, 1956, Jean Sephton (*d* 2010); one *s* one *d*; 2nd, 2012, Alison Rice. *Educ:* Highgate School; King's College London (BSc Eng). FIMechE 1980; FREng (FEng 1983). Commnd RA, 1950. Ford Motor Co.: Manager Cortina Product Planning, 1964; Manager Truck Product Planning, 1965; Chief Research Engineer, 1969; Chief Engine Engineer, 1970; Chief Body Engineer, Ford Werke AG, W Germany, 1974; Vice Pres. Car Engineering, Ford of Europe Inc., 1975–87; Dir, Ford Motor Co. Ltd, 1983–87. Mem., Bd of Govs, Anglia Polytechnic Univ., 1993–2002 (Hon. Fellow, 2004). Liveryman, Co. of Carmen, 1990–. Thomas Hawksley Lectr, IMechE, 1983. *Recreations:* yachting, dinghy sailing.

MELLOWS, Prof. Anthony Roger, OBE 2003; TD 1969; PhD, LLD; Solicitor of the Supreme Court, 1960–2001; Professor of the Law of Property in the University of London, 1974–90, now Emeritus; Lord Prior, Order of St John, 2008–14 (Vice Lord Prior, 2005–08); *b* 30 July 1936; *s* of L. B. and M. P. Mellows; *m* 1973, Elizabeth, DStJ, *d* of Ven. B. G. B. Fox, MC, TD, and of Hon. Margaret Joan Fox, *d* of 1st Viscount Davidson, PC, GCVO, CH, CB. *Educ:* King's Coll., London (AKC 1957; LLB 1957; LLM 1959; PhD 1962; BD 1968; LLD 1973; Fellow 1980). Commissioned Intelligence Corps (TA), 1959, Captain 1964; served Intell. Corps (TA) and (T&AVR) and on the Staff, 1959–71; RARO, 1971–91. Admitted a solicitor, 1960; private practice, 1960–2001; Sen. Partner, 1962–96, Consultant, 1996–2001, Alexanders; Consultant, Hunters, 2001–04. Asst Lectr in Law, King's Coll., London, 1962, Lectr, 1964, Reader, 1971; Dir of Conveyancing Studies, 1969; Dean, Fac. of Laws, Univ. of London, 1981–84, and of Fac. of Laws, KCL, 1981–85; Hd of Dept of Laws, KCL, 1984–87; Mem. Council, KCL, 1972–80. Mem., Archbishops' Millennium Adv. Gp, 1995–2000; Chm., Archbishops' Rev. of Bishops' Needs and Resources, 1999–2002. Chm., St John and Red Cross Defence Med. Welfare Service, 2001–05. Trustee: Kincardine Foundn, 1972–84; Nineveh Trust, 1985–90; London Law Trust, 1968– (Chm. Trustees); Lambeth Fund, 1995–2011; Marit and Hans Rausing Charitable Foundn, 1996–2006; Order of St John and British Red Cross Soc. Jt Cttee, 1987–2008 (Vice Chm. Trustees, 2001–08; Jt Pres., 2008–14); The Choral Foundn of the Chapels Royal, 2005–, Council of the Chapels Royal, 2011– (Vice-Chm.), HM Tower of London; The Constable's Fund, 2005–; Lambeth Trust, 2011–14. FRSA 1959. Freeman of the City of London, 1963. GCStJ 1991 (KStJ 1988; CStJ 1985; OStJ 1981; Mem. Council, 1981–88; Registrar, 1988–91; Chancellor, 1991–99; Dep. Lord Prior, 1999–2005); Grand Cross, Ordine Pro Merito Melitensi, SMO Malta, 2009 (Comdr 1999). British Red Cross Badge of Honour for Dist. Service, 2007. *Publications:* Local Searches and Enquiries, 1964, 2nd edn 1967; Conveyancing Searches, 1964, 2nd edn 1975; Land Charges, 1966; The Preservation and Felling of Trees, 1964; The Trustee's Handbook, 1965, 3rd edn 1975; Taxation for Executors and Trustees, 1967, 6th edn 1984; (jtly) The Modern Law of Trusts, 1966, 5th edn 1983; The Law of Succession, 1970, 4th edn 1983; Taxation of Land Transactions, 1973, 3rd edn 1982. *Address:* 22 Devereux Court, Temple Bar, WC2R 3JJ. *Club:* Athenæum.

MELLOWS, Heather Jean, (Mrs A. Johnson), OBE 2011; FRCOG; Consultant Obstetrician and Gynaecologist, Doncaster and Bassetlaw Hospitals NHS Foundation Trust, 1988–2011; Professional Adviser, Obstetrics and Gynaecology, Department of Health (on secondment), 2008–11 (Part-time Adviser, 2006–08 and 2011–12); *b* 13 March 1951; *d* of late A. Paul Mellows, DFC, MA, LLB and of Jean Mellows (*née* Wells); *m* 1982, Anthony Johnson (*d* 2012); two step *s*. *Educ:* Royal Free Hosp. Sch. of Medicine (MB BS 1974). FRCOG 1993; FFFP 2007. Regl Assessor in Obstetrics, Confidential Enquiry into Maternal Deaths, 1993–2008; Mem. Panel, Sec. of State's Inquiry into Quality and Practice within the NHS, arising from the actions of Rodney Ledward, 1999–2000 (reported, 2000). Co-Chm., Maternity Module, Children's Nat. Service Framework, 2002–04. Royal College of Obstetricians and Gynaecologists: Mem. Council, 1986–92, 1994–96 and 1999–2001; Chm., Hosp. Recognition Cttee, 1994–96; Jun. Vice Pres., 2001–04. *Address:* 8 Bedford Close, W4 2UE.

MELLY, Rear Adm. Richard Graham, (Dick); Clerk, Goldsmiths' Company, since 2005; *b* 31 Dec. 1953; *s* of Peter Emerson Melly and Shirley Julia Melly (*née* Higham); *m* 1987, Lynne Griffiths; two *d*. *Educ:* Winchester House Sch.; Stowe Sch.; Univ. of Manchester (BSc (Mech. Engrg) 1974); RNEC (MSc (Marine Engrg) 1980). CEng 1987–2007. Her Majesty's Ships: Devonshire, 1976–78; Hermes, 1980–82; Nottingham, 1988–90; staffing duties, MoD, 1993–95; Superintendent Ships, Portsmouth, 1995–98; rcds 2000; Dir, Naval Manning, 2001–03; COS to Second Sea Lord and C-in-C, Naval Home Comd, 2003–05. Trustee, Falkland Is Meml Chapel Trust, 2003–. Member: British Hallmarking Council, 2005–; Council, Goldsmiths Coll., 2005–. Trustee, Goldsmiths' Centre, 2007–. *Recreations:* ski-ing, computing, DIY. *Address:* The Goldsmiths' Company, Goldsmiths' Hall, Foster Lane, EC2V 6BN. *T:* (020) 7606 7010.

MELMOTH, Sir Graham (John), Kt 2002; Chief Executive, Co-operative Group Ltd (formerly Co-operative Wholesale Society), 1996–2002; *b* 18 March 1938; *s* of Harry James Melmoth and Marjorie Doris Melmoth (*née* Isitt); *m* 1967, Jennifer Mary Banning; two *s*. *Educ:* City of London Sch. FCIS 1972. National Service, 1957–59 (Lieut), RA. Asst Sec., Chartered Inst. of Patent Agents, 1961–65; Sec., BOC-AIRCO, 1965–69; Dep. Sec., Fisons, 1969–72; Sec., Letraset, 1972–75; CWS, then Co-operative Group Ltd: Sec., 1975–95; Director: Co-operative Bank plc, 1992–2003; Co-operative Press Ltd, 1994–98; Co-operative Insurance Soc. Ltd, 1996–2003. Chm., Ringway Developments plc, 1995–2002 (Dir, 1988–2002); Dir, Unity Trust Bank plc, 1992–98. Chairman: Manchester TEC Ltd, 1999–2001 (Dir, 1997–2001); Manchester Enterprises Ltd, 2001–03. Chm., NCVO, 2004–10; Pres., Gtr Manchester Centre for Vol. Orgns, 2011–13. Mem. Council, NACRO, 1998–2004. Trustee: New Lanark Conservation Trust, 1987–2004; Nat. Mus. of Labour History, 1995–2001; Charities Aid Foundn, 2004–10; CVS Cheshire East, 2013–. Pres., Internat. Co-operative Alliance, Geneva, 1995–97. CCMI (CIMgt 1997). FIGD 1996; FRSA 1996. *Recreations:* opera, theatre, Co-operative history. *Address:* Greengarth, Dockray, Cumbria CA11 0LS. *Club:* Reform.

MELROSE, Dianna Patricia; HM Diplomatic Service; High Commissioner to Tanzania, since 2013; *b* Bulawayo, S Rhodesia, 24 June 1952; *d* of late Gp Captain James F. C. Melrose and of Audrey Melrose (*née* Macqueen); *m* 1987, Chris Dammers (marr. diss.); two *s*. *Educ:* St Catherine's Sch., Bramley, Surrey; King's Coll. London (BA Hons Spanish and French); Inst. of Latin American Studies, Univ. of London (MA). Latin America Section, Noram Investment Services, 1973–74; C. E. Heath & Co., 1975–78; Specialist Tours Officer (Latin America), British Council, 1978–79; Oxfam: Policy Advr, 1980–84; Hd, Public Affairs Unit, 1984–92; Public Policy Dir, Oxfam UK, 1992–93; Policy Dir, Oxfam GB, 1993–99; Dep. Hd, 1999–2000, Hd, 2000–03, Policy Planning Staff, FCO; Hd, Extractive Industries Unit, 2003, Internat. Trade Dept, 2003–06, DFID; Hd, Enlargement and SE Europe Gp, FCO, 2006–08; Ambassador to Cuba, 2008–12. *Publications:* Bitter Pills: medicines and the third world poor, 1982; Nicaragua: the threat of a good example, 1985. *Recreations:* travel, reading, swimming. *Address:* c/o Foreign and Commonwealth Office, King Charles Street, SW1A 2AH. *E:* Dianna.Melrose@fco.gov.uk.

MELTON, Christopher; QC 2001; a Recorder, since 2005; *b* 15 Nov. 1958; *s* of Derek Edward and Margaret Melton; *m* 1990, Karen Jacqueline Holder; two *s* two *d*. *Educ:* Manchester Grammar Sch.; Bristol Univ. Called to the Bar, Gray's Inn, 1982; in practice, specialising in medical law. *Recreations:* running, golf, ski-ing, Francophile. *Address:* (chambers) 12 Byrom Street, Manchester M3 4PP. *Clubs:* Bowdon Lawn Tennis; Dunham Forest Golf.

MELVILL JONES, Prof. Geoffrey, FRS 1979; FRSC 1979; FCASI; FRAeS; Emeritus Professor, McGill University, since 1992; Adjunct Professor, since 1992, Research Professor, since 2001, University of Calgary; *b* 14 Jan. 1923; *s* of Sir Bennett Melvill Jones, CBE, AFC, FRS and Dorothy Laxton Jotham; *m* 1953, Jenny Marigold Burnaby; two *s* two *d*. *Educ:* King's Choir Sch.; Dauntsey's Sch.; Cambridge Univ. (BA, MA, MB, BCh). Appointments in UK, 1950–61: House Surgeon, Middlesex Hosp., 1950; Sen. Ho. Surg., Otolaryngology, Addenbrooke's Hosp., Cambridge, 1950–51; Scientific Flying Personnel MO, RAF, 1951; Scientific MO, RAF Inst. of Aviation Medicine, Farnborough, Hants, 1951–55; Scientific Officer (external staff), Medical Research Council of Gt Britain, 1955–61; McGill University: Dir, Aviation, later Aerospace Med. Res. Unit, 1961–88; Associate Prof., 1961–68; Full Prof., 1968–91; Hosmer Res. Prof. of Physiol., 1978–91. Fellow, Aerospace Medical Assoc., 1969; FCASI 1965; FRAeS 1981. First recipient, Dohlman Medal for research in the field of orientation and postural control, 1986; Robert Bárány Jubilee Gold Medal for most significant research on vestibular function during past 5 years; Ashton Graybiel Lectureship Award, US Navy, 1989; Stewart Meml Lectureship Award, RAeS, 1989; Buchanan-Barbour Award, RAeS, 1990; McLaughlan Medal, RSCan, 1991. *Publications:* Mammalian Vestibular Physiology, 1979 (NY); Adaptive Mechanisms in Gaze Control, 1985; research papers in physiological jls. *Recreations:* outdoor activities, music, gliding. *Address:* Department of Clinical Neurosciences, Faculty of Medicine, University of Calgary, 3330 Hospital Drive NW, Calgary, AB T2N 4N1, Canada. *T:* (403) 220 8764/7875, *Fax:* (403) 283 8731.

MELVILLE; *see* Leslie Melville, family name of Earl of Leven and Melville.

MELVILLE, 10th Viscount *cr* 1802; **Robert Henry Kirkpatrick Dundas;** Baron Duneira 1802; *b* 23 April 1984; *er s* of 9th Viscount Melville and of Fiona Margaret (*née* Stilgoe); *S* father, 2011. *Educ:* Marlborough. *Heir:* *b* Hon. James David Brouncker Dundas, *b* 19 Jan. 1986.

MELVILLE, Anthony Edwin; Headmaster, The Perse School, Cambridge, 1969–87; *b* 28 April 1929; *yr s* of Sir Leslie Galfreid Melville, KBE; *m* 1964, Pauline Marianne Surtees Simpson, *d* of Major A. F. Simpson, Indian Army; two *d*. *Educ:* Sydney Church of England Grammar Sch.; Univ. of Sydney (BA); King's Coll., Cambridge (MA). Sydney Univ. Medal in English, 1950; Pt II History Tripos, 1st cl. with dist., 1952; Lightfoot Schol. in Eccles. History, 1954. Asst Master, Haileybury Coll., 1953. *Recreations:* reading, gardening, music. *Address:* 4 Field Way, Cambridge CB1 8RW. *Club:* East India.

MELVILLE, Sir David, Kt 2007; CBE 2001; PhD; CPhys, FInstP; Vice-Chancellor, University of Kent, 2001–07; Chairman, Pearson Education Ltd, since 2012 (Board Member, since 2011); *b* 4 April 1944; *s* of late Frederick George Melville and Mary Melville; *m* (marr. diss.); one *s* two *d*; *m*. *Educ:* Clitheroe Royal Grammar Sch.; Sheffield Univ. (BSc 1st Cl. Hons 1965; PhD 1969); Columbia Univ. CPhys, FInstP 1978. Southampton University: Lectr in Physics, 1968–78; Sen. Lectr, 1978–84; Lancashire Polytechnic: Prof. of Physics and Head, Sch. of Physics and Astronomy, 1985–86; Asst Dir, 1986–89; Vice-Rector, 1989–91; Dir, Middlesex Polytechnic, 1991–92; Vice-Chancellor, Middlesex Univ., 1992–96; Chief Exec., FEFC, 1996–2001. ICI Res. Fellow, 1968; Visiting Professor: Univ. of Parma, Italy, 1974–80; Oporto Univ., Portugal, 1983; Univ. of Warwick, 1997–2003; Visiting Scientist: ICI Corporate Lab., Runcorn, 1975; Consiglio Nazionale delle Ricerche, Italy, 1976–80; Thames Gateway: Member: Further and Higher Educn Advrs Gp, 2002–10 (Co-Chm., 2008–10); Strategic Partnership, DCLG, 2006–10; Strategic Exec., 2009–10; Skills Envoy, 2008–11; Skills Commn, 2010–13; Higher Educn Commn, 2012–. Mem. Bd, British Non-Ferrous Metals Ltd, 1987–92. Vice-Chm., CVCP, 1995–96. Member: Council, BNF Metals Technol. Centre, 1986–92; SERC Materials Commn, 1988–92; SERC Condensed Matter Sub-Cttee, 1986–88; SERC Physics Cttee, 1988–92; SERC Metals and Magnetic Materials Cttee, 1988–92; Council for Industry and Higher Educn, 1994–96, 2001–07; Council, Inst. of Employment Studies, 1998–2001; Jt DfEE/DCMS Educn and Libraries Task Gp, 1999–2000; Bd, Higher Educn Stats Agency, 2002–07 (Chm., 2003–07); Bd, The Place, 2002–08; Kent Ambassadors, 2002–09; Bd, Higher Educn Prospects, 2002–07; DfES 14–19 Curriculum and Qualifications Adv. Cttee, 2003–04; DfES Foundn Degree Task Force, 2003–04; Kent Strategic Partnership, 2003–07; SE England Regl Assembly, 2003–06; SE England Sci., Engrg and Technol. Adv. Council, 2003–06; Bd, Lifelong Learning UK, 2004– (Chm., 2006–10); QCDA (formerly QCA) Quals and Skills Adv. Gp, 2004–10; DfES Rev. of Further Educn Colls, 2005–06; Bd, Medway Renaissance Partnership, 2005–07; Bd, Edexcel, 2005–11; Bd, ifs Sch. of Finance (formerly Inst. of Financial Services), 2005–11; DIUS Higher Educn Project Bd, 2006–08; BIS (formerly DIUS) Sci., Technol., Engrg and Math. High Level Strategy Gp, 2007–10; Adv. Bd, Black Leadership Initiative, 2007–10; Bd, Network for Black Professionals, 2010–. Chairman: SERC Magnetism and Magnetic Materials Initiative, 1989–91; UK and Republic of Ireland Chapter, Magnetics Soc., IEEE, 1988–93; Internat. Congress on Magnetism, Edinburgh, 1991; Health and Safety Cttee, Univs and Colleges Employers Assoc., 2003–07; Univs Race Equality Consultation Project, 2003–05; Univ. Vocational Awards Council, 2003–08; Higher Educn SE, 2003–06; Kent and Medway LSC, 2006–08; Cttee of Inquiry into Changing Learner Experience, 2008–09; Bd, Kent, Surrey and Sussex NHS Postgrad. Deanery, 2011–12; Bd, Health Educn Kent, Surrey and Sussex, 2012–13; Vice-Chm., Kent Public Service Bd, 2004–07. Member, Board: K Coll. (formerly W Kent Coll.), 2008–12; London S Bank Univ., 2009–12; Manchester Metropolitan Univ., 2011–. Hon. Pres., Co. of Middx Trust, 1992–; Trustee, Learning from Experience Trust, 2001–09; Vice-Chm., Trustees, Marlowe and Folkestone Academies, 2005–09; Patron: 157 Gp of FE Colls, 2007–; Comprehensive Future, 2008–; N Kent Thames Gateway Young Chamber, 2009–; Faversham Fest., 2010–13; Faversham Creek Trust, 2012–; Vice-Patron, Disabled Sailors Assoc., 2010–. DUniv: Middlesex, 1997; Derby, 2000; Hon.

DSc: Sheffield, 1997; Southampton, 2001; Hon. DCL Kent 2008. *Publications:* articles on magnetism, magnetic materials and biophysics in scientific and engrg jls; articles on educn and skills in nat. press. *Recreations:* sailing, golf.

MELVILLE, David; *see* Melville, R. D.

MELVILLE, James; *see* Martin, R. P.

MELVILLE, (Richard) David; QC 2002; **His Honour Judge Melville;** a Circuit Judge, since 2015; *b* 22 April 1953; *s* of Col Robert Melville and late Joan Emerton Melville (*née* Hawkins); *m* 1981, Catharine Mary Wingate; one *s* one *d*. *Educ:* Wellington Coll.; Pembroke Coll., Cambridge (BA 1974, MA 1978). Called to the Bar, Inner Temple, 1975, Bencher, 2007; Recorder, 2007–15. *Recreations:* sailing, ski-ing, painting, piano. *Address:* Plymouth Crown Court, 10 Armada Way, Plymouth, Devon PL1 2ER. *Clubs:* Bar Yacht; Royal Corinthian Yacht; Itchenor Sailing; West Wittering Sailing.

MELVILLE-ROSS, Timothy David, CBE 2005; Chairman, Higher Education Funding Council for England, since 2008; *b* 3 Oct. 1944; *s* of late Antony Stuart Melville-Ross and of Anne Barclay Fane; *m* 1967, Camilla Mary Harlackenden (marr. diss. 2013); two *s* one *d*. *Educ:* Uppingham School; Portsmouth College of Technology (Dip Business Studies). British Petroleum, 1963–73; Rowe, Swann & Co., stockbrokers, 1973–74; joined Nationwide Building Soc., 1974: Dir and Chief Gen. Man., 1985–87; Dir and Chief Exec., 1987–94; Dir Gen., Inst. of Dirs, 1994–99; Chm., Investors in People UK, 1999–2006. Dep. Chm., Monument Oil and Gas plc, 1997–99 (Dir, 1992–99); Chairman: NewsCast Ltd, 2000–04; Bank Insinger de Beaufort NV, 2000–05; DTZ Hldgs plc, 2000–11; Manganese Bronze plc, 2003–12 (Dir, 2000–12); Royal London Mutual Insce Ltd, 2005–13 (Dir, 1999–2013; Dep. Chm., 2002–05); Bovis Homes Gp plc, 2005–08 (Dir, 1998–2008); Homerton Univ. NHS Trust, 2013–. Member Council: Industrial Soc., 1986–95; Inst. of Business Ethics, 1994–. President: Chartered Mgt Inst., 2006–07; Inst. of Business Ethics, 2013–. Pro-Chancellor and Chm. of Council, Univ. of Essex, 2000–07 (Mem. Council, 1995–2007). Trustee, Uppingham Sch., 1988–2000. FRSA; FCIS; FCIB. *Recreations:* music, reading, bridge, tennis, the countryside.

MENARY, Andrew Gwyn; QC 2003; **His Honour Judge Menary;** a Circuit Judge, since 2013; *b* 29 March 1959; *m* 1st, 1982, Joy Michelle (marr. diss); one *s* one *d*; 2nd, 2010, Josephine Ann; two step *s*. *Educ:* BA Hons Law. Called to the Bar, Inner Temple, 1982; in practice as barrister, Liverpool, 1982–; a Recorder, 2002–13. *Recreations:* playing squash, walking in the Lake District, supporting Manchester United. *Address:* Queen Elizabeth II Law Courts, 1 Newton Street, Birmingham B4 7NA.

MENCHÚ, Rigoberta; human rights activist; Goodwill Ambassador, UNESCO, since 1996; *b* 9 Jan. 1959; *d* of late Vicente Menchú, Mayan resistance leader and founder, Cttee of Peasant Unity (CUC), Guatemala, and Juana Menchú; *m* 1995, Angel Canil. Works for indigenous peoples' rights; founded Rigoberta Menchú Tum Foundn, Guatemala City; Member: CUC; United Representation of Guatemalan Opposition; Five Hundred Years of Resistance Campaign; UN Working Group on Indigenous Populations; UN Internat. Indian Treaty Council. Pres., Indigenous Initiative for Peace, UN, 1999. Contested (Frento Amplio) Presidential elections, Guatemala, 2007 and 2011. Nobel Peace Prize, 1992. *Publications:* (with Elisabeth Burgos-Debray) I, Rigoberta Menchú, 1983 (trans. English 1984; in 12 other langs); (with Gianni Minà y Dante Liano) Rigoberta: grandchild of the Mayas, 1998 (trans. Italian and English).

MENDELSOHN, family name of **Baron Mendelsohn**.

MENDELSOHN, Baron *cr* 2013 (Life Peer), of Finchley in the London Borough of Barnet; **Jonathan Neil, (Jon), Mendelsohn;** Partner, Oakvale Capital LLP, since 2011; *b* London, 1966; *s* of Jeffrey and Evelyn Mendelsohn; *m* 1994, Nicola Clyne (*see* N. Mendelsohn); three *s* one *d*. *Educ:* Leeds Univ. (BA). Asst to Leader of the Opposition, 1995–97; Labour Party: Dir, Gen. Election Resources, 2007–10; Asst Treas., 2009–10. *Address:* House of Lords, SW1A 0PW. *T:* (020) 7219 3199.

MENDELSOHN, Nicola, (Lady Mendelsohn), CBE 2015; Vice-President of Europe, Middle East and Africa, Facebook, since 2013; *b* Manchester, 29 Aug. 1971; *d* of Barry Clyne and Celia Clyne; *m* 1994, Jonathan Mendelsohn (*see* Baron Mendelsohn); three *s* one *d*. *Educ:* Manchester High Sch. for Girls; Univ. of Leeds (BA Hons Eng. and Theatre Studies 1992). Account Manager, 1992–98, Business Develt Dir, 1998–2004, Bartle Bogle Hegarty; Dep. Chm., Grey London, 2004–08; Exec. Chm., Karmarama, 2008–13. Non-exec. Dir, Diageo, 2014–. Dir, Fragrance Foundn, 2001–11. Mem. Bd, Cosmetic Exec. Women, 2003–11; Chm., Corporate Bd, Women's Aid, 2007–13; Trustee, White Ribbon Alliance, 2011–13; Co-Chm., Creative Industries Council, 2012–. Dir, Baileys Women's Prize for Fiction (formerly Orange Prize for Fiction, then Women's Prize for Fiction), 2012–. Pres., Inst. of Practitioners in Advertising, 2011–13. Mem., Marketing Soc. *Recreations:* theatre, cinema, family, travel, charity work, feminism. *E:* nicola@redcapital.eu. *Clubs:* 30, Women in Advertising and Communications, London (Pres., 2008–09); Marketing Group of Great Britain.

MENDELSOHN, Robert Victor, JD; private investor and advisor to international businesses, since 2003; Chairman, Navigators Group, Inc., since 2013 (Director, since 2010); *b* NYC, 1946; *m* 1968, Patricia Fielding; one *s* one *d*. *Educ:* Georgetown Univ. (AB 1968); Harvard Univ. (JD 1971). Called to the Bar, NY, 1971; Attorney, Willkie Farr & Gallagher, NYC, 1971–74; Pres. and Dir, W. R. Berkley Corp., Greenwich, Conn, 1974–93; Chief Exec., 1994–97, Chm., 1997–2002, Royal & Sun Alliance USA, Inc., Charlotte, NC; Gp Chief Exec. and Dir, Royal & Sun Alliance Insce Gp plc, 1997–2002. Director: Amer. Insce Assoc., 1994–2003 (Chm., 1999–2000); Internat. Insce Soc., 1999–2005; Inspirica, Inc., 2011–. Chm. Council, Insce Co. Execs, 1998–2000. Mem., UK-China Forum, 1999. Mem., Bd of Regents, Georgetown Univ., Washington, 1999–2005; Dir, Georgetown Univ. Library, 2006–; Mem. Adv. Bd, Harvard Prog. on Corp. Governance, 2006–12. *Recreations:* golf, walking, ski-ing, sailing.

MENDELSON, Prof. Maurice Harvey; QC 1992; DPhil; barrister and arbitrator; Professor of International Law, University of London at University College London, 1987–2001, now Emeritus; *b* 27 Aug. 1943; *s* of William Maizel Mendelson and Anne (*née* Aaronson); *m* 1968, Katharine Julia Olga Kertesz; two *d*. *Educ:* St Marylebone Grammar Sch.; New Coll., Oxford (BA 1st Cl. Hons Jurisprudence 1964; MA; DPhil 1971). Called to the Bar, Lincoln's Inn, 1965 (Bencher, 2000); Internat. Law Fund Schol., 1966; Leverhulme European Res. Schol., 1966–67; Lectr in Laws, KCL, 1968–74; Kennedy Law Schol., Lincoln's Inn, 1970–73; Official Fellow and Tutor in Law, St John's Coll., Oxford, and Univ. Lectr in Law, Oxford, 1975–86. Fulbright Vis. Schol., Harvard Law Sch., 1977; Visiting Professor: Univ. of N Carolina, 1982; Univ. of Pennsylvania, 1986; Univ. of Paris II, 1993; Univ. of NSW, 1999; Univ. of Paris X, 2002–03. Mem., Bd of Editors, British Yearbook of Internat. Law, 1995–. Mem., Amer. Law Inst., 2000. FRGS 1995. Officier, Ordre de la Valeur (Cameroon), 2003. *Publications:* articles in internat. law jls, etc; reports to Internat. Law Assoc. *Recreations:* the arts, painting, swimming, tennis (Real and lawn). *Address:* Blackstone Chambers, Blackstone House, Temple, EC4Y 9BW. *T:* (020) 7583 1770. *Club:* Athenæum.

MENDES, Samuel Alexander, CBE 2000; Co-Founder, and Director, Neal Street Productions, since 2003; *b* 1 Aug. 1965; *s* of Valerie Hélène Mendes (*née* Barnett) and James Peter Mendes; *m* 2003, Kate Elizabeth Winslet, *qv* (marr. diss. 2010); one *s*. *Educ:* Magdalen Coll. Sch., Oxford; Peterhouse, Cambridge (BA English, 1st Cl. Hons). Asst Dir, Chichester Festival, 1987–88, Artistic Director, Minerva Studio Theatre, 1989: productions included: Summerfolk, 1989; Love's Labour's Lost, 1989; Artistic Dir, Donmar Warehouse Th., 1992–2002; productions at *Donmar Warehouse* include: Assassins, 1992; Translations, 1993; Cabaret, 1993, NY (Tony Award for Best Revival of Musical), 1998, 2014; Glengarry Glen Ross, 1994; The Glass Menagerie (Olivier Award), 1995; Company (Olivier Award), 1995; Habeas Corpus, 1996; The Fix, 1997; The Front Page, 1997; The Blue Room, 1998, NY, 1999; To the Green Fields and Beyond, 2000; Twelfth Night, 2002, NY, 2003; Uncle Vanya, 2002, NY, 2003; productions as freelance director: *Royal Shakespeare Co.:* Troilus and Cressida, 1990; The Alchemist, 1991; Richard III, 1992; The Tempest, 1993; *Royal National Theatre:* The Sea, 1991; The Rise and Fall of Little Voice, 1992; The Birthday Party, 1994; Othello, 1997; King Lear, 2014; The Cherry Orchard, Aldwych, 1989; London Assurance, Haymarket, 1989; Kean, Old Vic, 1990; The Plough and the Stars, Young Vic, 1991; Oliver!, Palladium, 1994; Gypsy, NY, 2003; The Vertical Hour, NY, 2006; The Winter's Tale, The Cherry Orchard, Old Vic, 2009; The Tempest, As You Like It, Old Vic, 2010; Richard III, Old Vic, 2011; Charlie and the Chocolate Factory, Th. Royal, 2013. *Films:* American Beauty, 1999 (Academy Award for Best Dir, 2000); Road to Perdition, 2002; Jarhead, 2006; Revolutionary Road, Away We Go, 2009; Skyfall, 2012 (Empire Award for Best Dir); Spectre, 2015; television, The Hollow Crown, 2012. Numerous other awards.

MENDONÇA, Nikki; President, OMD, Europe, Middle East and Africa, since 2007; *b* UK, 3 Dec. 1969; *d* of Dennis and Lorna Mendonça. *Educ:* Univ. of Wales Coll., Cardiff (BA Hons English and Spanish); Harvard Business Sch.; Stanford Univ. Grad. Sch. of Business. Media Manager, CIA Media Network UK, 1992–95; Gp Media Dir, Leo Burnett, 1995–98; Strategic Mktg Dir, Capital Radio, 1998–2002; Mktg and New Business Dir, OMD, EMEA, 2002–05; Business Develt Dir, Omnicom Media Gp EMEA, 2005–07. Mem. Bd, Internet Advertising Bureau Europe, 2015–. *Recreations:* travel, tennis. *E:* nikki.mendonca@omd.com.

MENDOZA, June Yvonne, AO 1989; OBE 2004; RP; ROI; artist; *d* of John Morton and Dot (*née* Mendoza), musicians; *m* 1960, Keith Ashley Victor Mackrell, *qv*; one *s* three *d*. *Educ:* Lauriston Girls' Sch., Melbourne; St Martin's Sch. of Art. Member: RP 1970; ROI 1968. Portraits for govt, regts, industry and commerce, academia, medicine, theatre, sport (e.g. Chris Evert for Wimbledon Mus.), and in public and private collections internationally. These include: Queen Elizabeth II; Queen Elizabeth the Queen Mother; Prince and Princess of Wales; Margaret Thatcher; John Major; Prime Minister of Australia, Sir John Gorton; Prime Minister of Fiji, Ratu Sir Kamisese Mara; Prime Minister of Singapore, Goh Chok Tong; former Prime Minister of Singapore, Lee Kuan Yew; Pres. of Iceland, Vigdis Finnbogadottir; Pres. of Philippines, Corazón Aquino; Donald Coggan, Robert Runcie, and George Carey, severally, while Archbishop of Canterbury; large group paintings include: The House of Commons in Session, 1986; House of Representatives, for new Parliament building in Canberra; private series of musicians include: Sir Yehudi Menuhin; Sir Georg Solti; Dame Joan Sutherland; Sir Colin Davis; Sir Charles Mackerras; Sir Michael Tippett. Lectures internationally; appearances on art programmes, TV and radio. Hon. Freeman, City of London; Hon. Mem., Barbers' Co. Hon. Mem., Soc. of Women Artists, 1986. Hon. DLitt: Bath, 1986; Loughborough, 1994; DUniv Open, 2003. *Address:* 34 Inner Park Road, SW19 6DD.

MENDOZA, Neil Francis Jeremy; Chairman, Victoria Private Investment Office, since 2010; *b* London, 2 Nov. 1959; *s* of Martin Mendoza and Dianne Mendoza; *m* 1993, Amelia Wallace; one *s* one *d*. *Educ:* Haberdashers' Aske's Sch.; Oriel Coll., Oxford (BA Geog. 1981). Banking Exec., Morgan Guaranty Trust Co. of New York, 1981–83; Dir, Albion Films, 1983–87; Co-Founder and Chief Exec., Forward Ltd, 1987–2001; Director: Hammer Films, 1998–2002; Cross Asset Mgt, 1998–2005; Golden Square Ltd, 2005–; Pencil Agency, 2011–. Member: Adv. Council and Steering Cttee, New Europe, 1999–2002; Steering Gp, No Campaign, 2000–02. Chairman: Landmark Trust, 2012–; Prince's Foundn for Children and the Arts, 2013–; Trustee, Forward Arts Foundn, 1994–2013; Shakespeare Schs Fest., 2010–15; Vice Chm., Soho Th., 2007–. *Recreations:* Shakespeare, bridge, barefoot running. *Address:* 50 Albemarle Street, W1S 4BD. *T:* (020) 7493 4361. *E:* mendoza.neil@gmail.com. *Clubs:* Garrick, Portland.

MENDUS, Prof. Susan Lesley, CBE 2013; FBA 2004; FLSW; Professor of Political Philosophy, University of York, 1996–2012, now Morrell Professor Emerita; *b* 25 Aug. 1951; *d* of John and Beryl Coker; *m* 1977, Andrew Mendus. *Educ:* UC of Wales, Aberystwyth (BA); Lady Margaret Hall, Oxford (BPhil). University of York: Lectr in Philos., 1975–90; Sen. Lectr in Political Philos., 1990–95; Dir, Morrell Studies in Toleration Prog., 1995–2000. FLSW 2010. *Publications:* Toleration and the Limits of Liberalism, 1989; Impartiality in Moral and Political Philosophy, 2002; Politics and Morality, 2009. *Recreations:* theatre, swimming, birdwatching. *Address:* 117 Osbaldwick Lane, York YO10 3AY. *T:* (01904) 413831. *E:* sue.mendus@york.ac.uk.

MENEM, Carlos Saúl; President of Argentina, 1989–99; *b* 2 July 1935; *s* of Saúl Menem and Mohibe Akil; *m* 1966, Zulema Fátima Yoma (marr. diss.); one *d* (one *s* decd); *m* 2001, Cecilia Bolloco (marr. diss. 2008); one *s*. *Educ:* Córdoba Univ. Legal Advr, Confederación General del Trabajo, La Rioja, 1955–70; lawyer, La Rioja, 1958; Gov., La Rioja, 1973–76, 1983–89; imprisoned, 1976–81. Pres., Partido Justicialista, La Rioja, 1963–. Vice Pres., Confedn of Latin American Popular Parties, 1990–. Founder, Juventud Peronista (Peronist youth gp), 1955. *Publications:* Argentina, Now or Never; Argentina Year 2000; (jtly) The Productive Revolution.

MENEVIA, Bishop of, (RC), since 2008; **Rt Rev. Thomas Matthew Burns,** SM; *b* Belfast, 3 June 1944; *s* of late William James Burns and Louisa Mary Burns (*née* McGarry). *Educ:* St Mary's Coll., Blackburn; Heythrop Coll., London Univ. (BD Hons 1973); Open Univ. (BA 1984). Joined SM, 1965; ordained, 1971; Curate, St Anne's, Whitechapel, 1973–74; Head of Econs, St Mary's GS, Sidcup, 1974–78; Head of Econs and Social Scis, St Mary's Sixth-Form Coll., Blackburn, 1979–86; Chaplain, RN, 1986–92; Bursar General, Marist Fathers, Rome, 1992–94; Chaplain, RN, 1994–98; VG 1998–2002; Princ. RC Chaplain, RN, and Dir, Trng and Progs, then Dir, Manning, Naval Chaplaincy Service, MoD, 1998–2002; RC Bishop of the Forces, 2002–08. Bishop Promoter and Trustee of the Apostleship of the Sea, 2003–; Bd Mem. and Trustee, St Luke's Centre, Manchester, 2005–. *Publications:* pamphlet, Index to the Laws of Rugby Football, 1997. *Recreations:* Rugby (advisor to referees), action novels, film-going. *Address:* Curial Office, 27 Convent Street, Greenhill, Swansea SA1 2BX. *T:* (01792) 644017.

MENHENNET, Dr David, CB 1991; Librarian of the House of Commons, 1976–91; Visiting Research Fellow, Goldsmiths College, London University, 1990–2002; *b* 4 Dec. 1928; *s* of William and Everill Menhennet, Redruth, Cornwall; *m* 1954, Audrey, *o d* of William and Alice Holmes, Accrington, Lancs; two *s*. *Educ:* Truro Sch., Cornwall; Oriel Coll., Oxford (BA 1st Cl. Hons 1952); Queen's Coll., Oxford. Open Scholarship in Mod. Langs, Oriel Coll., Oxford, 1946; Heath Harrison Trav. Scholarship, 1951; Bishop Fraser Res. Scholar, Oriel Coll., 1952–53; Laming Fellow, Queen's Coll., Oxford, 1953–54; Zaharoff Trav. Scholarship, 1953–54. MA 1956, DPhil 1960, Oxon. Liby Clerk, House of Commons Library, 1954; Asst Librarian i/c Res. Div., 1964–67; Dep. Librarian, 1967–76. Member: Study of Parliament Gp, 1964–90; Bd of Mgt, H of C, 1979–91. Chm. Adv. Cttee, Bibliographic Services, British Library, 1986–92 (Mem., 1975–86); Mem. Exec. Cttee, Friends of Nat. Libraries, 1991–96. FRSA 1966 (Life Fellow 2001). Freeman, City of London, 1990. Gen. Editor, House of Commons Library Documents series, 1972–90. *Publications:*

(with J. Palmer) Parliament in Perspective, 1967; The Journal of the House of Commons: a bibliographical and historical guide, 1971; (ed with D. C. L. Holland) Erskine May's Private Journal, 1857–1882, 1972; (contrib.) The House of Commons in the Twentieth Century, ed S. A. Walkland, 1979; (contrib.) The House of Commons: Services and Facilities 1972–1982, ed M. Rush, 1983; The House of Commons Library: a history, 1991, 2nd edn 2002; Essays and Articles on Bernardin de Saint-Pierre 1737–1814, 1998; articles in Lib. Assoc. Record, Parliamentarian, Parly Affairs, Polit. Qly, New Scientist, Contemp. Rev., Jl of Librarianship, Jl of Documentation, Book Collector. *Recreations:* U3A activities, visiting Cornwall, French literature. *Address:* Meadow Leigh, 3 Westfield Close, Bishop's Stortford, Herts CM23 2RD. *T:* (01279) 755815.

MENIN, Rt Rev. Malcolm James; Bishop Suffragan of Knaresborough, 1986–97; an Hon. Assistant Bishop, Diocese of Norwich, since 2000; *b* 26 Sept. 1932; *s* of Rev. James Nicholas Menin and Doreen Menin; *m* 1958, Jennifer Mary Cullen; one *s* three *d*. *Educ:* Dragon School; St Edward's School; University Coll., Oxford (MA); Cuddesdon Coll. Curate: Holy Spirit, Southsea, 1957–59; St Peter and St Paul, Fareham, 1959–62; Vicar of St James, Norwich, later St Mary Magdalene with St James, Norwich, 1962–86; RD Norwich East, 1981–86; Hon. Canon, Norwich Cathedral, 1982–86. *Recreations:* walking, photography, carpentry. *Address:* 32c Bracondale, Norwich NR1 2AN. *T:* (01603) 627987.

MENKES, Suzy Peta, (Mrs S. P. Menkes-Spanier), OBE 2005; International Vogue Editor, Condé Nast International, since 2014; *b* 24 Dec. 1943; *d* of late Edouard Gerald Lionel Menkès and Betty Curtis Lightfoot; *m* 1969, David Graham Spanier (*d* 2000); three *s* (one *d* decd). *Educ:* Univ. of Cambridge (MA). Editor, Varsity newspaper, Cambridge, 1966; Jun. Reporter, The Times, 1966–69; Fashion Editor, Evening Standard, 1969–77; Women's Editor, Daily Express, 1977–80; Fashion Editor: The Times, 1980–87; The Independent, 1987–88; Internat. Herald Tribune, later Internat. New York Times, 1988–2014. Freeman: City of Milan, 1986; City of London, 1987. Chevalier, Légion d'Honneur (France), 2005. British Press Awards Commendations, 1983 and 1984; Eugenia Sheppard Award for Fashion Journalism, Council of Fashion Designers of America, 1995; Special Recognition Award, British Fashion Awards, 2013; Fiorino d'Oro, City of Florence, 2013. *Publications:* The Knitwear Revolution, 1983; The Royal Jewels, 1985, 3rd edn 1988; The Windsor Style, 1987; Queen and Country, 1992. *Recreations:* family life, reading, opera, Royal history. *Address:* c/o Condé Nast International, 25 Maddox Street, W1S 2QN.

MENNELL, Stuart Leslie; Clerk, Hawkwell Parish Council, 2002–12; *b* 17 Oct. 1948; *s* of Albert Edward Mennell and Iris Mennell (*née* Jackson); *m* 1st, 1970, Margaret Hirst (*d* 2000); three *d*; 2nd, 2009, Tricia Stanford. *Educ:* Barlby High Sch., E Yorks. Ministry of Social Security, 1968–72; HM Customs & Excise: Preventive Duties, 1972–75; VAT, 1975–78; Regl Personnel Officer, 1978–82; Statistical Office, 1982–84; HQ Personnel Manager, 1984–86; Estate Manager, 1986–88; National Maritime Museum: Estabt Officer, 1988–89; Personnel & Corporate Planning Manager, 1989–93; Dir, Collections and Mus. Services Div., 1993–2001; Dir, Strategic Develts, 2001. MIPD 1989. *Recreations:* classic motor cycles, walking. *Address:* The Nest, Durham Road, Rochford, Essex SS4 3AE. *T:* (01702) 531155. *E:* stuart.mennell@btinternet.com.

MENNINI, Most Rev. Antonio; Apostolic Nuncio to the Court of St James's, since 2010; *b* Rome, 2 Sept. 1947. *Educ:* Pontifical Univ. (DTh). Ordained priest, Rome, 1974; entered Diplomatic Service of the Holy See, 1981; served in Uganda and Turkey; Italian and S African Desk, Section for Relns with States of the Secretariat of State, 1986–2000; Apostolic Nuncio to Bulgaria, 2000–02; apptd Titular Archbishop of Ferento, 2000; Representative of the Holy See to the Russian Fedn, 2002–11; Apostolic Nuncio to: Uzbekistan, 2002; Russian Fedn, 2009. *Address:* The Apostolic Nunciature, 54 Parkside, Wimbledon, SW19 5NE.

MENON, Prof. David Krishna, MD; PhD; FRCP, FRCA, FFICM, FMedSci; Professor of Anaesthesia, University of Cambridge, since 2000; Fellow, Queens' College, Cambridge, since 2002; *b* 21 Aug. 1956; *s* of Parakat Govindan Kutty Menon and Violet Rebecca Menon; *m* 1988, Wendy Humphreys; one *s*. *Educ:* Univ. of Madras (MB BS, MD 1992); RPMS, Univ. of London (PhD 1995). FRCA 1988; FRCP 1999. Residency in Internal Medicine, Jawaharlal Inst., Pondicherry, India, 1978–83; Registrar: in Medicine, Professorial Med. Unit, Leeds Gen. Infirmary, 1984–86; in Anaesthetics, Royal Free Hosp., London, 1987–88; MRC Res. Fellow, Robert Steiner Magnetic Resonance Unit, Hammersmith Hosp., 1989–91; Clinical Lectr, 1992–93, Lectr in Anaesthesia, 1993–2000, Univ. of Cambridge; Lead Consultant and Dir, Neurocritical Care, Addenbrooke's Hosp., 1997–2001. Sen. Investigator, NIHR, 2009–15. Co-Chair, Eur. Brain Injury Consortium, 2007–. Member: Council, Intensive Care Soc., 2002–09; Founding Bd, Faculty of Intensive Care Medicine, 2010–. Founder FMedSci 1998; FFICM 2011. *Publications:* Textbook of Neuroanaesthesia and Critical Care, 1998; contrib. to several textbooks, incl. Oxford Textbook of Critical Care, 1999, and Oxford Textbook of Medicine, 2001; contribs to various jls on topics of critical care and neurosciss. *Recreations:* basketball, science fiction, cooking. *Address:* University Department of Anaesthesia, Box 93, Addenbrooke's Hospital, Hills Road, Cambridge CB2 0QQ. *T:* (01223) 217889. *Club:* Royal Society of Medicine.

MENON, Prof. Mambillikalathil Govind Kumar, MSc, PhD; FRS 1970; Advisor to the Indian Space Research Organization, Department of Space, Government of India, since 2004 (Dr Vikram Sarabhai Distinguished Professor, 1999–2004); President, International Council of Scientific Unions, 1988–93; *b* 28 Aug. 1928; *s* of Kizhekepat Sankara Menon and Mambillikalathil Narayaniamma; *m* 1955, Indumati Patel; one *s* one *d*. *Educ:* Jaswant Coll., Jodhpur; Royal Inst. of Science, Bombay (MSc); Univ. of Bristol (PhD). Tata Inst. of Fundamental Research: Reader, 1955–58; Associate Prof., 1958–60; Prof. of Physics and Dean of Physics Faculty, 1960–64; Senior Prof. and Dep. Dir (Physics), 1964–66, Dir, 1966–75. Chm., Electronics Commn, and Sec., Dept of Electronics, Govt of India, 1971–78; Scientific Advr to Minister of Defence, Dir-Gen. of Defence Res. and Develt Orgn, and Sec. in the Ministry of Defence for Defence Res., 1974–78; Dir-Gen., Council of Scientific and Industrial Res., 1978–81; Sec. to Govt of India, Dept of Science and Technology, 1978–82, Dept of the Envmt, 1980–81; Chm., Commn for Addnl Sources of Energy, 1981–82; Mem., Planning Commn, 1982–89; Chm., Science Adv. Cttee to the Cabinet, 1982–85; Scientific Advr to the Prime Minister, 1986–89; Minister of State for Sci. and Technology, India, 1989–90; MP (Janata Dal) Rajasthan, Rajya Sabha, 1990–96. M. N. Saha Dist. Fellow, Nat. Acad. of Scis, India, 1994–99. Former Chancellor, NE Hill Univ., Shillong. Pres., India Internat. Centre, 1983–88, 2007–12; Member: UN Sec.-Gen.'s Adv. Cttee on Application of Sci. and Technol. to Develt, 1972–79 (Chm. for 2 yrs); Bd of Dirs, Internat. Fedn of Insts for Advanced Study, Stockholm, 1992–99. President: Indian Sci. Congress Assoc., 1981–82; Indian Statistical Inst., 1990–2012. Chairman: Indian Inst. of Technology, Bombay, 1997–2003; Indian Inst. of Technology, Delhi, 2003–06. Fellow: Indian Acad. of Sciences (Pres., 1974–76); Indian Nat. Science Acad. (Pres., 1981–82); Founding Fellow, Third World Acad. of Sciences; Hon. Fellow: Nat. Acad. of Sciences, India (Pres., 1987–88); Indian Inst. of Sciences, Bangalore; Hon. FInstP 1998; For. Hon. Member: Amer. Acad. of Arts and Scis; Russian Acad. of Scis; Mem., Pontifical Acad. of Scis, Vatican; Hon. Pres., Asia Electronics Union; Hon. Mem., Instn of Electrical & Electronics Engrs Inc., USA. Member: Governing Council, UN Univ., 1986–92; Bd, Inst. for Advanced Studies, UN Univ., Tokyo, 1996–2004 (Chm., 1996–2001). Hon. DSc: Jodhpur Univ., 1970; Delhi Univ., 1973; Sardar Patel Univ., 1973; Allahabad Univ., 1977; Roorkee Univ., 1979; Banaras Hindu Univ., 1981; Jadavpur Univ., 1981; Sri Venkateswara Univ., 1982; Indian Inst. of Tech. Madras, 1982; Andhra Univ., 1984; Utkal Univ., 1984; Aligarh Muslim Univ., 1986; Bristol Univ., 1990; N Bengal Univ., 1989; Indian Inst. of Technology, Kharagpur, 1990; Guru Nanak Dev Univ., 1996; Hon. Dr Engrg Stevens Inst. of Tech., USA, 1984; Hon. LLD IASE, Rajasthan, 2005. Royal Commn for Exhibn of 1851 Senior Award, 1953–55; Shanti Swarup Bhatnagar Award for Physical Sciences, Council of Scientific and Industrial Research, 1960; Khaitan Medal, RAS, 1973; Pandit Jawaharlal Nehru Award for Sciences, Madhya Pradesh Govt, 1983; G. P. Chatterjee Award, 1984; Om Prakash Bhasin Award for Science and Technol., 1985; C. V. Raman Medal, INSA, 1985; J. C. Bose Triennial Gold Medal, Bose Inst., 1983; (first) Ashutosh Mukherjee Gold Medal, Indian Science Congress Assoc., 1988; Gujar Mal Modi Foundn Award, New Delhi, 1994; Abdus Salam Award, Third World Acad. of Scis, 1997. National Awards: Padma Shri, 1961; Padma Bhushan, 1968; Padma Vibhushan, 1985. *Publications:* 150, on cosmic rays and elementary particle physics. *Recreations:* photography, bird-watching. *Address:* C-178 (First Floor), Sarvodaya Enclave, New Delhi 110017, India. *E:* mgkmenon@nic.in. *Clubs:* National Liberal; India International Centre (New Delhi).

MENON, Rajiv; QC 2011; *b* Newport, Wales, 19 April 1964; *s* of Dr Gopinath Menon and Dr Marioula Menon; *m* 1996, Anita Kirpal; two *c*. *Educ:* Dartmouth Coll. (BA 1987); London Sch. of Econs and Pol Sci. (MSc 1988); Coll. of Law (CPE 1992); Inns of Court Sch. of Law (BVC 1993). Called to the Bar, Middle Temple, 1993. *Address:* Garden Court Chambers, 57–60 Lincoln's Inn Fields, WC2A 3LS. *T:* (020) 7993 7803, *Fax:* (020) 7269 5669. *E:* rajivm@gclaw.co.uk.

MENSAH, Barbara; Her Honour Judge Mensah; a Circuit Judge, since 2005; a Judge of the Upper Tribunal (Immigration and Asylum Chamber) (formerly a Vice President, Immigration Appeal Tribunal, later a Senior Immigration Judge, Asylum and Immigration Tribunal), since 2003; *b* 6 March 1959; *d* of Benjamin Amponsah Mensah and Victoria (*née* Apomasu). *Educ:* Wadhurst Coll., Kent; Millfield Sch.; UC of Swansea (BSc Philos.); City Univ. (Dip Law); Council of Legal Educn (Bar Finals); Queen Mary and Westfield Coll., London (LLM). Called to the Bar, Lincoln's Inn, 1984, Bencher, 2005. Lawyer, International Tobacco (Ghana) Ltd, 1987–89; pt-time Sen. Lectr, Inns of Court Sch. of Law, 1990–2000; Immigration Adjudicator, 1995; Dep. District Judge (Magistrates' Courts), 1998; a Recorder, 2003–05. Member: Adv. Bd on Restricted Patients, 1999–2002; Legal Services Consultative Panel, 2000–02. Mem., Disciplinary Panel, Bar Council, 2001. Mem. (pt-time), Mental Health Tribunal, 2011–. ACIArb, 1994–2000. *Publications:* The Prison Guide (with Andrew Goodman), 1999; European Human Rights Case Locator 1960–2000, 2000; European Human Rights Case Summaries, 2001; contrib. to Inns of Court Sch. of Law Bar Manuals. *Recreations:* swimming, reading, music. *Address:* Luton Crown Court, 7 George Street, Luton, Beds LU1 2AA.

MENSAH, Evelyn Justina A.; *see* Asante-Mensah.

MENSCH, Louise; *b* London, 1971; *d* of Nicholas Bagshawe and Daphne Bagshawe (*née* Triggs); *m* Anthony LoCicero (marr. diss.); two *s* one *d*; *m* 2011, Peter Mensch. *Educ:* Sacred Heart Sch., Tunbridge Wells; Woldingham Sch., Surrey; Christ Church, Oxford (BA English). PR and Mktg Manager, EMI Classics and Sony Music, 1992–93; novelist, 1994–. MP (C) Corby, 2010–Aug. 2012. *Publications:* (as Louise Bagshawe): Career Girls, 1995; The Movie, 1996; Tall Poppies, 1997; Venus Envy, 1998; A Kept Woman, 2000; When She Was Bad, 2001; The Devil You Know, 2003; Monday's Child, 2004; Tuesday's Child, 2005; Sparkles, 2006; Glamour, 2007; Glitz, 2008; Passion, 2009; Desire, 2010; Destiny, 2011; (as Louise Mensch) Beauty, 2014. *Recreations:* reading, travel, music. *Club:* Groucho.

MENTETH, Sir Charles S.; *see* Stuart-Menteth.

MENTZ, Donald, AM 1994; Chief Executive Officer, Mentz International Trading, 2004; *b* 20 Oct. 1933; *s* of Stanley Mentz and Marie Agnes (*née* Bryant); *m* 1959, Mary Josephine (*née* Goldsworthy); one *s* two *d*. *Educ:* Hampton High School, Victoria; Dookie Agricultural College, Victoria (DDA); Melbourne Univ. (BAgrSc); Australian Nat. Univ. (BEcon). Dept of External Territories, Australia, 1969–73; Aust. Develt Assistance Bureau, Dept of Foreign Affairs, 1973–77; Dept of Business and Consumer Affairs, 1977–78; Dir of Operations, Asian Develt Bank, Philippines, 1979–81; Dep. Sec., Dept of Business and Consumer Affairs, Aust., 1981–82; Dep. Sec., Dept of Territories and Local Govt, 1983–84; Dir Gen., Commonwealth Agricl Bureaux, later CAB Internat., 1985–92; Man. Dir, Mentz Internat. Trading, 1993–99; Exec. Dir, Crawford Fund for Internat. Agricl Res., Aust., 1999–2001; Man. Dir, Mentak Granite and Marble Pty Ltd, 2000–03. *Recreations:* ski-ing, gardening. *Address:* 10 Bonwick Place, Garran, ACT 2605, Australia. *Clubs:* Athenæum; Commonwealth (Canberra).

MENZIES, Rt Hon. Lord; Duncan Adam Young Menzies; PC 2012; a Senator of the College of Justice in Scotland, since 2001; *b* 28 Aug. 1953; *s* of late Douglas William Livingstone Menzies and Margaret Adam (*née* Young); *m* 1979, Hilary Elizabeth McLauchlan Weston; two *s*. *Educ:* Cargilfield; Glenalmond (schol.); Wadham Coll., Oxford (schol.; MA); Edinburgh Univ. (LLB). Admitted Advocate, 1978; Standing Junior Counsel to Admiralty, 1984–91; QC (Scot.) 1991; Temp. Sheriff, 1996–97; Home Advocate Depute, 1998–2000. Chm., Scottish Planning, Local Govt and Envmtl Bar Gp, 1997–2001. Contested (C): Midlothian, 1983; Edinburgh Leith, 1987. Mem., von Poser Soc. of Scotland, 1996–. Founder, Scottish Wine Soc., 1976; Maître, Commanderie de Bordeaux à Edimbourg, 2012. *Recreations:* shooting, golf, wine. *Address:* Court of Session, Parliament House, Parliament Square, Edinburgh EH1 1RQ. *Clubs:* Saintsbury; New (Edinburgh); Honourable Company of Edinburgh Golfers.

MENZIES, Duncan Adam Young; *see* Menzies, Hon. Lord.

MENZIES, Mark; MP (C) Fylde, since 2010; *b* Irvine, 18 May 1971; *s* of Andrew Menzies and Mary Isobel Menzies. *Educ:* Keil Sch., Dumbarton; Univ. of Glasgow (MA Hons Econ. and Social Hist.). With Marks & Spencer plc, 1994–95; Mktg Manager, Asda Stores Ltd, 1995–2007; Hd, Local Mktg, Wm Morrison Supermarkets plc, 2008–10. Contested (C): Glasgow Govan, 2001; Selby, 2005. PPS to Minister for Energy, 2010–12, to Minister for Housing, 2012–13, to Minister for Internat. Develt, 2013–14. *Recreations:* ski-ing, walking, cinema. *Address:* House of Commons, SW1A 0AA. *T:* (020) 7219 7073, *Fax:* (020) 7219 2235. *E:* mark.menzies.mp@parliament.uk.

MENZIES, Lt-Gen. Robert Clark, CB 2002; OBE 1989; Surgeon General to the Armed Forces, 2000–02; *b* 1 June 1944; *s* of late Flt Lieut Robert Clark Menzies and Jane, (Jean), Reid Menzies; *m* 1st, 1967, Dr Joanna, (Joan), Letitia Lindsay Dunning (marr. diss. 2006); one *s* one *d*; 2nd, 2006, Dr Hansa Thakkar. *Educ:* Kilmarnock Acad.; Glasgow Univ. (MB ChB 1967). DMJ (Pathology) 1976; MRCPath 1980, FRCPath 1992; FFPH (FFPHM 1999); FRCPE 2000. OC, Med. Reception Stn, Warminster, 1969; Trainee Pathologist, Leishman Lab., Cambridge Mil. Hosp., 1971–72; Pathologist, BMH, Rinteln, 1973–75; Registrar in Pathology, Queen Alexandra Mil. Hosp., 1975–76; British Army Exchange Pathologist, Armed Forces Inst. of Pathology, Washington, 1976–78 (Chief, Missile Trauma Pathology Br. and Hon. Professional Lectr, George Washington Univ.); Sen. Registrar in Pathology, Leishman Lab., Cambridge Mil. Hosp., 1978–81; Lectr in Forensic Medicine, Charing Cross Hosp. Med. Sch., 1981–83; Consultant Pathologist, Leishman Lab., 1983–85; Prof. of Mil. Pathology, Royal Army Med. Coll. and RCPath, 1985–89; CO, BMH Rinteln, 1989–92; Dir of Army Pathology, 1992–94; CO, 217 (London) Gen. Hosp. RAMC(V), 1994–95; Commander Medical: HQ London Dist, 1995–96; HQ Land Comd, 1996–99; Dir Gen., AMS, 1999–2000. QHS 1996–2003. Chief Med. Officer, 2003–05, Actg Chief Comdr, 2005–06, St John Ambulance. Pres., Stapleford & Berwick St James Br., 2003–06, Heyford and District Br., 2012–, RBL. Chm., Upper Heyford Parish Council, 2011–14. Freeman, City of London, 1995. CStJ 2006 (Trustee and Dir, Priory of England and the Islands, Order of St John, 2004–06). *Publications:* articles on pathology, particularly forensic pathology, in jls. *Recreations:* walking, travelling, photography, reading, poetry, music. *Clubs:* Army and Navy; Clarendon (Oxford).

MEON, Archdeacon of The; *see* Collins, Ven. G. A.

MEPHAM, David John; UK Director, Human Rights Watch, since 2011; *b* Cambridge, 24 Dec. 1967; *s* of Ben Mepham and late Ann Mepham; *m* 2004, Charlotte Augst; one *s* one *d*. *Educ:* London Sch. of Economics (BSc 1st Cl. Hons Econ. 1989); St Antony's Coll., Oxford (MPhil Internat. Relns 1992). Speech writer and researcher, H of C, 1992–94; internat. policy specialist, Policy Dept, Labour Party, 1994–97; Hd, British Foreign Policy Prog., Saferworld, 1997–98; Special Advr to Sec. of State, DFID, 1998–2002; Associate Dir and Hd, Internat. Prog., IPPR, 2002–07; Dir of Policy, Save the Children UK, 2007–11. *Publications:* (ed) Progressive Foreign Policy, 2007; numerous policy reports and articles. *Recreations:* reading, cooking, country walks. *Address:* Human Rights Watch, 16–20 Ely Place, EC1N 6SN. *T:* (020) 7618 4726. *E:* mephamd@hrw.org.

MER, Francis Paul; Honorary Chairman, Board of Directors, Safran, since 2013 (Chairman, Supervisory Board, 2007–11; Vice Chairman, Board of Directors, 2011–13); Minister of Economy, Finance and Industry, France, 2002–04; *b* 25 May 1939; *s* of René Mer and Yvonne Casalta; *m* 1964, Catherine Bonfils; three *d*. *Educ:* Ecole Nationale Supérieure des Mines, Paris; Ecole Polytechnique. Mining engr, Ministry of Industry, 1966; tech. advr, Abidjan, 1967–68; joined St-Gobain Pont-à-Mousson Gp, 1970: St-Gobain Industries: Dir of Planning, 1971–73; Dir-Gen. Planning, 1973; Manager, 1974–78; St-Gobain Pont-à-Mousson: Dir of Planning, 1973; Asst Dir-Gen., 1978–82; Pres. Dir-Gen., Pont-à-Mousson SA, 1982–86; Pres. Dir-Gen., Usinor-Sacilor, 1986–2002; Chm., Usinor Gp, 2001–02; Co-Chm., Arcelor, 2002. Director: Credit Lyonnais, 1997–2002; Electricité de France, 1997; Air France, 1997–2002; Rhodia, 2004–11; Adecco, 2004–11. Chairman: Eurofer, 1990–97; IISI, 1997–98. President: French Steel Fedn, 1988–2002; Nat. Tech. Res. Assoc., 1991–2002; formerly President: Entreprise pour l'environnement; Cercle de l'industrie. Commandeur: Légion d'Honneur (France); Ordre Nat. du Mérite (France).

MERCADO, Anthony Raymond, CEng, FIET; Associate Partner, First Class Partnerships, since 2014; Director, MERCT Consulting Ltd, since 2014; *b* Johannesburg, 20 May 1951. *Educ:* Univ. of Witwatersrand (BSc Electrical Engrg). CEng 2002; FIET 2002. South African Rlys, 1974–88; Engrg Dir, GEC Traction, 1988–96; Operations Dir, Alstom Transport Systems, 1996–2000; Engrg Dir, Alstom Transport, 2000–04; Man. Dir, Alstom W Coast Train Care, 2005–08; Dir, Rail Technical and Professional, DfT, 2008–11; Customer Dir, 2011–14, Dir of Rail Develt Policy, 2013–14, Alstom Transport UK. *T:* 07801 772446. *E:* armercado51@gmail.com.

MERCER, Prof. Alan; Professor of Management Science (formerly of Operational Research), University of Lancaster, 1968–98, now Emeritus; *b* 22 Aug. 1931; *s* of Harold Mercer and Alice Ellen (*née* Catterall); *m* 1954, Lillian Iris (*née* Pigott); two *s*. *Educ:* Penistone Grammar Sch.; Cambridge Univ. (MA; DipMathStat); London Univ. (PhD). NCB, 1954–56; UKAEA, 1956–62; Armour & Co. Ltd, 1962–64; Univ. of Lancaster, 1964–: Chm., Sch. of Management and Organisational Scis, 1982–85. Mem., Central Lancashire Develt Corp., 1971–85; Mem., 1985–89, Chm., 1986–89, Warrington and Runcorn Develt Corp. Chm., Employers' Side of Whitley Council for New Towns Staff, 1979–89 (Mem., 1971–89); Mem., Management and Industrial Relns Cttee, SSRC, 1972–76, 1980–82; Chm., Industry and Employment Cttee, ESRC, 1984–87 (Vice Chm., 1982–84); Mem., NW Econ. Planning Council, 1973–79. Jt Editor, European Journal of Operational Research, 1977–98. *Publications:* Operational Distribution Research (jtly), 1978; Innovative Marketing Research, 1991; numerous papers in learned jls. *Recreations:* travel, sport. *Address:* South Cottage, Calton, Airton, Skipton, North Yorks BD23 4AD. *T:* (01729) 830542.

MERCER, (Christine) Ruth; Headmistress, Godolphin and Latymer School, since 2009; *b* Preston, 19 June 1962; *d* of George Mercer and Joan Evelyn Mercer (*née* Stopforth); *m* 1988, Colin B. Horsley; one *s* one *d*. *Educ:* Bedford Coll., London (BA Hons Hist. 1983); St Catherine's Coll., Oxford (PGCE 1984); Dept of Contg Educn, Univ. of Oxford (Adv. Dip. Local Hist. 2006). Hd of Hist. and Politics, Notting Hill and Ealing High Sch., 1992–98; Dep. Headmistress, Godolphin and Latymer Sch., 1998–2002; Headmistress, Northwood Coll., 2002–08. *Recreations:* travel, fell walking, genealogy, reading, history, swimming. *Address:* The Godolphin and Latymer School, Iffley Road, Hammersmith, W6 0PG. *T:* (020) 8741 1936.

MERCER, His Honour Geoffrey Dallas; a Circuit Judge, South Eastern Circuit, 1991–2005; *b* 17 Dec. 1935; *s* of Leon Dallas Mercer, FRCS and Veronica Kathleen Mary Lillian Mercer (*née* Pitt-Lancaster). *Educ:* Clifton Coll., Bristol; St John's Coll., Cambridge (MA, LLM). Called to the Bar, Gray's Inn, 1960; practised at the Bar, 1961–91; Hd of Chambers, 1985–91; an Asst Recorder, 1986; a Recorder, 1990. Former English Youth International and Cheshire County golfer. *Recreations:* golf, music. *Clubs:* Royal Automobile; Burhill Golf; Worplesdon Golf.

MERCER, Giles; *see* Mercer, R. G. G.

MERCER, Hugh Charles; QC 2008; barrister; *b* Barnard Castle, Co. Durham; *s* of Keith and Gabrielle Mercer; *m* 1995, Isabelle Corbeel; two *s* (one *d* decd). *Educ:* Downing Coll., Cambridge (BA 1984); Université Libre de Bruxelles (Licence spéciale en droit européen). Called to the Bar, Middle Temple, 1985, Bencher, 2012; in practice as barrister specialising in EU and internat. law; Chambers of Mark Littman, QC, 1987–95; Essex Court Chambers, 1995–; Eur. Circuit, Bar of England and Wales, 2001–. Hd, UK Delegn to Council of Bars and Law Socs of Europe, 2007–10; Chm., CCBE Perm. Delegn to Court of Justice of the UK, 2010–. *Publications:* Commercial Debt in Europe: recovery and remedies, 1991; European Civil Practice, 2004. *Recreations:* squash, mountain walking, gardening, scout leader. *Address:* Essex Court Chambers, 24 Lincoln's Inn Fields, WC2A 3EG. *T:* (020) 7813 8000, *Fax:* (020) 7813 8080. *Clubs:* Royal Automobile; Achille Ratti Climbing.

MERCER, Prof. Ian Dews, CBE 1996; Secretary General, Association of National Park Authorities, 1996–2001; Hon. Professor of Rural Conservation Practice, University of Wales, since 1991; *b* 25 Jan. 1933; *s* of Eric Baden Royds Mercer and Nellie Irene Mercer; *m* 1st, 1957, Valerie Jean Hodgson; four *s*; 2nd, 1976, Pamela Margaret Gillies (*née* Clarkson); one step *s* one step *d*. *Educ:* King Edward VI Sch., Stourbridge; Univ. of Birmingham (BA Hons). Sub-Lieut RNR, 1954–56. Field Centre appts, Preston Montford, 1956–57, Juniper Hall, 1957–59; Warden, Slapton Ley, 1959–68; Lectr, St Luke's Coll., Exeter, 1968–70; Warden, Malham Tarn Field Centre, 1970–71; County Conservation Officer, Devon CC; 1971–73; National Park Officer, Dartmoor, 1973–90; Chief Exec., Countryside Council for Wales, 1990–95. Chairman: Envmtl Trng Orgn, 1996–98; Devon Foot and Mouth Disease Inquiry, 2001–02; SW Forest Partnership, 2002–08; Dartmoor Commoners Council, 2004–13; Devon Rural Network, 2005–08; SW Uplands Fedn, 2006–; Napoli Public Inquiry, 2008; Member: England Cttee, Nature Conservancy Council, 1979–89; Inland Waterways, Amenity Adv. Council, 1995–2001; Devon and Cornwall Cttee, Nat. Trust, 1996–2005. President: Field Studies Council, 1986–2014; Devon Wildlife Trust, 1986– (Fellow, 2012); Vice-Pres., Council for Nat. Parks, 2001–. Governor: Univ. of Plymouth, 1996–2005; Stover Sch., 1996–2004 (Chm., 2003–04). FRAgS 1999; Hon. FLI 1997. Hon. LLD Exeter, 1994; Hon. DSc Plymouth, 1995. *Publications:* Nature Guide to the West Country, 1981; New Naturalist 111 – Dartmoor, 2009; chapters in books on conservation, education and national park matters. *Recreations:* painting, golf, teaching adults birds and landscape. *Address:* Ponsford House, Moretonhampstead, Devon TQ13 8NL. *T:* (01647) 440612. *Clubs:* Farmers; Symonds.

MERCER, Johnny; MP (C) Plymouth Moor View, since 2015; *b* Dartford, Kent, 17 Aug. 1981; *s* of Andrew Mercer and Margaret Mercer; *m* Felicity Cornelius; two *d*. *Educ:* Eastbourne Coll.; Royal Mil. Acad. Sandhurst. Intern, City of London, 2000–02; Officer, Army, 2002–14. *Address:* House of Commons, SW1A 0AA. *E:* johnny.mercer.mp@parliament.uk.

MERCER, Lesley; employment consultant, since 2014; Director, Employment Relations and Union Services, Chartered Society of Physiotherapy, 2005–14; *b* Clitheroe, Lancs, 6 Aug. 1954; *d* of Sqdn Ldr Donald Mercer and Jean Mercer; partner, 1980, Graham Taylor. *Educ:* Accrington High Sch.; Univ. of Nottingham (BA (Hons) Politics 1975). Asst Res. Officer, Merchant Navy and Airline Officers Assoc., 1977–79; Exec. Asst, 1979–85, Negotiations Officer, 1985–95, Soc. of Civil and Public Servants, subseq. Nat. Union of Civil and Public Servants; Sen. Negotiating Officer, 1995–2000, Asst Dir, 2000–05, CSP. Member: Industrial Tribunal Panel, 1989–2002; Central Arbitration Cttee, 2002–; Ind. Lay Chm., NHS Complaints Procedure, 1998–2002; ACAS Panel of Ind. Arbitrators, 2015–. Pres., 2012–13, Vice-Pres., 2013–14, TUC. Trustee Dir, Nautilus Internat., 2015–. Hon. FCSP 2012. DUniv Keele, 2015. *Recreations:* stained glass restoration, cycling, walking, gardening.

MERCER, Patrick John, OBE 1997 (MBE 1992); *b* 26 June 1956; *s* of late Rt Rev. Eric Arthur John Mercer and of Rosemary Wilma (*née* Denby); *m* 1990, Catriona Jane Beaton; one *s*. *Educ:* King's Sch., Chester; Exeter Coll., Oxford (MA Mod. Hist. 1980). Commnd 1st Bn Worcs and Sherwood Foresters, 1975: served NI, 1975–77; Captain: BAOR and W Belfast, 1980–83 (despatches); Instructor, Brecon, 1984–86; Major: Chief Instructor, Ugandan Sch. of Inf., 1986; Jun. Inf. Bn, Shorncliffe, 1986–88; sc, Camberley, 1988; Co. Comdr, Omagh, NI, 1989–90 (GOC's Commendation); SO2 G3 (Ops), HQ NI, 1991–92; Chief Instructor, Platoon Comdr's Course, 1993; Lieut Col, SO1 Instructor, Staff Coll., Camberley, 1994–95; CO, Tidworth, Bosnia, Canada, 1995–97; Col, Hd of Strategy, Army Trng and Recruitment Agency, 1997–99; Defence Corresp., Today prog., BBC Radio 4, 1999. Mem., KCL team tasked with writing defence policy for E Timor, 2000. MP for Newark, 2001–April 2014 (C, 2001–13, Ind, 2013–April 2014). Opposition front bench spokesman on home, constitutional and legal affairs, 2003–07, on homeland security, 2004–07; Chm., Counter-Terrorist Sub-Cttee, 2009–10. Hon. Col, Notts ACF, 2007–11. *Publications:* Inkermann: the soldiers' battle, 1997; Give Them a Volley and Charge, 1997; To Do and Die, 2009; Dust and Steel, 2010; Red Runs the Helmand, 2011; Doctor Watson's War, 2012; contrib. jls and newspapers. *Recreations:* water-colour painting, history, bird watching, country sports. *Club:* Newark Working Men's.

MERCER, Dr (Robert) Giles (Graham); Headmaster, Prior Park College, 1996–2009; *b* 30 May 1949; *s* of late Leonard and Florence Elizabeth Mercer; *m* 1974, Caroline Mary Brougham; one *s*. *Educ:* Austin Friars School, Carlisle; Churchill College, Cambridge (Scholar; 1st cl. Hist. Tripos, Pts I and II; MA); St John's College, Oxford (Sen. Schol., DPhil). Giorgio Cini Foundn Schol., Venice, 1973. Head of History, Charterhouse, 1974–76; Asst Principal, MoD, 1976–78; Dir of Studies and Head of History, Sherborne School, 1979–85; Headmaster, Stonyhurst Coll., 1985–96. Life Mem., Catholic Union, 1985; Mem., Catholic Record Soc., 2009–; Cttee, Assoc. of Papal Orders in GB, 2010–13. Chm., 2000–04, Vice-Pres., 2006–, Catholic Ind. Schs Conf.; Trustee: Bloxham Conf., 2008–10; Bath Preservation Trust, 2009–14; Clifton Dio., 2009–. Governor: All Hallows Prep. Sch., Shepton Mallett, 1999–2009; St Mary's Sch., Shaftesbury, 2005–07; St John's Catholic Primary Sch., Bath, 2012– (Chm., Curriculum Cttee, 2012–14; Chm. of Govs, 2014–); Downside Sch., 2015– (Vice-Chm., 2015–). Hon. Fellow, Rank Foundn, 2009. KSG 2004. *Publications:* The Teaching of Gasparino Barzizza, 1979. *Recreations:* art, music, travel, swimming, theatre, preparing a biography. *Address:* Inglewood, 84 Bloomfield Avenue, Bath BA2 3AD. *E:* giles.mercer530@gmail.com. *Club:* Oxford and Cambridge.

MERCER, Rev. Mgr Robert William Stanley, CR; Diocesan Bishop, Anglican Catholic Church of Canada, 1989–2005 (Assistant Bishop, 1988–89); *b* 10 Jan. 1935; *s* of Harold Windrum Mercer and Kathleen Frampton. *Educ:* Grey School, Port Elizabeth, S Africa; St Paul's Theological Coll., Grahamstown, SA (LTh). Deacon 1959, priest 1960, Matabeleland; Asst Curate, Hillside, Bulawayo, 1959–63; Novice, CR, 1963; professed, 1965; at Mirfield, 1963–66; at St Teilo's Priory, Cardiff, 1966–68; Prior and Rector of Stellenbosch, S Africa, 1968–70; deported from SA, 1970; Chaplain, St Augustine's School, Penhalonga, Rhodesia, 1971–72; Rector of Borrowdale, Salisbury, Rhodesia, 1972–77; Bishop of Matabeleland, 1977–87. Ordained deacon and priest, Personal Ordinariate of Our Lady of Walsingham (RC), 2012. Sub-Prelate, Order of St John of Jerusalem, 1981. *Address:* 3 The Limes, St Botolph's Road, Worthing, W Sussex BN11 4HY.

MERCER, Roger James, OBE 2005; FSA, FSAScot; FRSE; Secretary, Royal Commission on the Ancient and Historical Monuments of Scotland, 1990–2004; *b* 12 Sept. 1944; *o s* of Alan Mercer and Patricia (*née* Hicks); *m* 1970, Susan Jane Fowlie; one *s* one *d*. *Educ:* Harrow County Grammar Sch.; Edinburgh Univ. (MA). Inspector of Ancient Monuments, DoE, 1969–74; Lectr and Reader, Dept of Archaeology, Univ. of Edinburgh, 1974–89. Mem., Ancient Monuments Bd for Scotland, 1988–2004; Pres., Soc. of Antiquaries of Scotland, 2005–08 (Vice Pres., 1988–91); Vice President: Council for British Archaeology, 1990–94; Prehistoric Soc., 1989–92. British Acad. Readership, 1989; Hon. Professor of Archaeology: Univ. of Durham, 1996–; Univ. of Edinburgh, 1999–. Hon. FSAScot 2012 (FSAScot 1971); FSA 1976; FRSE 1995. Hon. MIFA 2004. *Publications:* Beaker Studies in Europe (ed), 1979; Hambledon Hill—a Neolithic Landscape, 1980; Grimes Graves—Excavations 1971–72, 1981; Carn Brea—a Neolithic Defensive Complex, 1981; (ed) Farming Practice in British Prehistory, 1981; Causewayed Enclosures, 1990; (with F. Healy) Hambledon Hill, Dorset, England, 2009; articles and reviews in learned jls. *Recreations:* music, books, good food. *Address:* Home House, 4 Old Church Lane, Duddingston, Edinburgh EH15 3PX. *T:* (0131) 661 2931.

MERCER, Ruth; *see* Mercer, C. R.

MERCHANT, Eileen; Headmistress, Putney High School (GDST), 1991–2002; *b* 20 Feb. 1944; *d* of Jeremiah and Ellen McGill; *m* 1966, John Richard Merchant, *qv*; two *s*. *Educ:* Sheffield Univ. (BSc 1st Cl. Chem.). Dir of Studies, Bedford High Sch., 1974–86; Dep. Hd, Latymer Sch., Edmonton, 1986–91. JP Wimbledon, 1999–2003, Sussex, 2005–14. *Recreations:* birdwatching, reading, walking.

MERCHANT, John Richard; Director of Resources, Voluntary Service Overseas, 1995–2003; *b* 4 June 1945; *s* of William Henry Merchant and Eileen Merchant; *m* 1966, Eileen McGill (*see* E. Merchant); two *s*. *Educ:* Gravesend Grammar Sch.; Sheffield Univ. (BSc); Cranfield Inst. of Technol. (MSc); Open Univ. (BSc). Lyons Bakery Ltd, 1966–69; Lectr, Cranfield Inst. of Technol., 1969–75; Statistician, MoD, 1975–79; Chief Statistician, CS Coll., 1979–82; Asst Sec., Cabinet Office (MPO), 1982–84; Principal Finance and Estabt Officer, DPP, 1984–86, Crown Prosecution Service, 1986–88; Under Sec., 1985; Sec. and Dir, Council Policy and Admin, SERC, 1988–94; Grade 3, Office of Public Service and Science, 1994. *Recreations:* Nigerian postal history, birdwatching.

MERCIECA, Most Rev. Joseph, STD, JUD; Archbishop of Malta, (RC), 1976–2006; *b* Victoria, Gozo, 11 Nov. 1928. *Educ:* Gozo Seminary; Univ. of London (BA); Gregorian Univ., Rome (STD); Lateran Univ., Rome (JUD). Priest, 1952; Rector of Gozo Seminary in late 1960s; Permanent Judge at Sacred Roman Rota and Commissioner to Congregation for the Sacraments and Congregation for the Doctrine of the Faith, 1969; Auxiliary Bishop of Malta, and Vicar-General, 1974–76. Consultor, Supreme Tribunal of Apostolic Segnatura suis, 1992–2008. *Address:* c/o Archbishop's Curia, PO Box 90, Marsa MRS 1000, Malta.

MEREDITH, Most Rev. Bevan; Archbishop of Papua New Guinea, Primate of the Province of Papua New Guinea, 1990–95; Bishop of New Guinea Islands, 1977–95; licensed to officiate, diocese of Brisbane; Hon. Assistant, St Faith's Parish, Strathpine, since 1995; *b* Alstonville, NSW, 14 Aug. 1927; 3rd *c* of Stanley Meredith and Edith Meredith (*née* Witchard). *Educ:* Univ. of Queensland; St Francis Theol Coll., Brisbane. Teacher, Slade Sch., Warwick, Qld and Housemaster, Highfields House, 1948–53; Staff, Martyrs' Meml Sch., PNG, 1954–58; deacon 1961, priest 1962, St Thomas, Toowong; Priest-in-charge, Managalas, PNG, 1963–67; Asst Bp of New Guinea, 1967–77. *Recreations:* music, photography, philately. *Address:* 23 Coronet Drive, Bray Park, Qld 4500, Australia. *T:* and *Fax:* (7) 38896993.

MEREDITH, David Michael; District Judge (Magistrates' Courts) (formerly Stipendiary Magistrate), Leicestershire, 1995–2011; *b* 2 May 1945; *s* of George and Phyllis Maude Meredith; one *s*; *m* 2008, Anne Marsden (*née* Middlebrook). *Educ:* King Edward VII Sch., Sheffield; St Edmund Hall, Oxford (BA, DipEd). Asst Teacher, Chorlton High Sch., 1969–70, and King Edward VII Sch., Sheffield, 1970–74; admitted solicitor, 1977; Articled Clerk and Asst Solicitor, 1975–81, Partner, 1981–95, Graysons, Sheffield. *Recreations:* football, bad golf, theatre, travel. *Clubs:* Vincent's (Oxford); Charnwood Forest Golf.

MEREDITH, Richard Alban Creed, MA; Head Master, Monkton Combe School, 1978–90; *b* 1 Feb. 1935; *s* of late Canon R. Creed Meredith; *m* 1968, Hazel Eveline Mercia Parry; one *s* one *d*. *Educ:* Stowe Sch.; Jesus Coll., Cambridge. Asst Master (Modern Langs), 1957–70, Housemaster, 1962–70, King's Sch., Canterbury; Headmaster, Giggleswick Sch., 1970–78. CMS Area Sec., dios of Derby, Leicester and Southwell, 1990–98. Reader, Church of England, 1957–. *Recreations:* walking, foreign travel, music, gardening. *Address:* Beacon Knoll, 334 Beacon Road, Loughborough LE11 2RD. *T:* (01509) 212008.

MERES, Lisa Moreen; *see* Opie, L. M.

MERIFIELD, Sir Anthony (James), KCVO 2000; CB 1994; The Ceremonial Officer, Cabinet Office, 1994–2000; *b* 5 March 1934; *s* of late Francis Bertram Merifield and Richardina (*née* Parker); *m* 1980, Pamela Pratt. *Educ:* Chesterfield Sch.; Shrewsbury Sch.; Wadham Coll., Oxford (MA). National Service, 1952–54, Royal Tank Regt. HM Overseas Civil Service, Kenya, 1958–65; Department of Health and Social Security: Principal, 1965–71; Asst Sec., 1971–77; Under Secretary, 1978–82; Under Sec., NI Office, 1982–85; Dir of Regl Liaison, NHS Management Bd, DHSS, subseq. NHS Management Exec., DoH, 1986–91; Head of Sen. and Public Appts Gp, Cabinet Office, 1991–94. Chm., KCH Charity (formerly Charitable Trust), 2004–12. *Address:* 49 Carson Road, SE21 8HT. *T:* (020) 8670 1546. *Clubs:* Athenæum; Achilles; Dulwich and Sydenham Hill Golf.

MERKEL, Dr Angela Dorothea; Member, Bundestag, since 1990; Chancellor, Federal Republic of Germany, since 2005; Chairman, Christian Democratic Union, since 2000; *b* Hamburg, 17 July 1954; *d* of Horst Kasner and Herlinde Kasner; *m* 1998, Prof. Dr Joachim Sauer. *Educ:* Univ. of Leipzig; Zentralinstitut für physikalische Chemie, East Berlin (Dr rer. nat. Physics 1986). Res. Associate in Quantum Chemistry, Zentralinstitut für Physikalische Chemie, East Berlin, 1978–90; joined Demokratischer Aufbruch, 1989, Press Spokesperson, 1990, Dep. Spokesperson for Govt of Lothar de Maizière, March–Oct. 1990; joined CDU, 1990; Dep. Federal Chm., 1991–98; Chm., CDU, Fed. State of Mecklenburg-Vorpommern, 1993–2000; Gen. Sec., CDU, 1998–2000; Chm., CDU/CSU Parly Gp, Bundestag, 2002–05. Federal Minister: for Women and Young People, 1991–94; for Environment, Nature Conservation and Nuclear Safety, 1994–98. *Publications:* Der Preis des Überlebens: Gedanken und Gespräche über zukünftige Aufgaben der Umweltpolitik, 1997; Europa und die deutsche Einheit: Zehn Jahre Wiedervereinigung: Bilanz und Ausblick, 2000; (with Hugo Müller-Vogg) Mein Weg: ein Gespräch mit Hugo Müller-Vogg, 2005. *Recreations:* reading, hiking, gardening. *Address:* c/o Bundeskanzleramt, Willy Brandt Strasse 1, 10557 Berlin, Germany. *T:* (30) 1840000, *Fax:* (30) 1840002357. *E:* internetpost@bundeskanzlerin.de.

MERLO, David, CEng, FIET; Director of Research, British Telecommunications plc, 1983–89; *b* 16 June 1931; *s* of Carlo G. Merlo and Catherine E. Merlo (*née* Stringer); *m* 1952, Patricia Victoria Jackson; two *s*. *Educ:* Kilburn Grammar Sch., London; London Univ. (BScEng 1st Cl. Hons 1954); W. B. Esson schol. of IEE, 1953, and IEE Electronics Premium, 1966. CEng 1967, FIEE 1973. Post Office Research Br., 1948; Executive Engineer, 1955; Sen. Scientific Officer, 1959; Principal Sci. Officer, 1967; Head of Division, 1974; Dep. Director of Research, 1977. Visiting Lecturer: Northampton Polytechnic, 1955–61; Regent Street Polytechnic, 1960–69; Governor, Suffolk College of Higher and Further Education, 1984–89. Served on numerous technical committees in telecommunications field. FRSA 1988. Patent award, 1970. *Publications:* miscellaneous contribs to learned jls. *Recreations:* reading, photography, wine. *Address:* Heather Lodge, Levington, Ipswich IP10 0NA. *T:* (01473) 659508.

MERRICK, Caragh; Member of Council, since 2013, and Treasurer, since 2014, University of Birmingham; *b* Belfast, 15 Nov. 1955; *d* of Robert Hagan Maginess and Daphne Anne Maginess (*née* Ferris); *m* 1983, John Edward Merrick. *Educ:* Belfast Royal Acad.; Univ. of St Andrews (MA). FCA 1982. Deloitte Haskins & Sells: Accountant, 1981–84; Manager, 1984–88; Sen. Manager, 1988–89; Audit Partner, Coopers & Lybrand Deloitte, then Coopers & Lybrand, later PricewaterhouseCoopers, 1990–2002; independent consultant, 2002–08. Trustee: RNT, 2002–08; RNT Foundn, 2009–13; Nat. Foundn for Youth Music, 2008–12 (Chm., Finance and Audit Cttee, 2008–12); Musicians' Benevolent Fund, later Help Musicians UK, 2010– (Hon. Treas., 2013–); UCAS, 2011– (Chm., Finance Cttee, 2012–). Mem. Council, RCA, 2006– (Chm., Audit Cttee, 2006–13; Treas., 2014–). FRSA. *Recreations:* theatre, ballet, music.

MERRICK, Prof. Linda, PhD; Principal, Royal Northern College of Music, since 2013; *b* Bristol, 11 May 1963; *d* of Dennis Francis Merrick and Joyce Grace Merrick; *m* 2002, Dr Martin Ellerby, composer. *Educ:* Hengrove Sch., Bristol; Royal Acad. of Music (GRSM Hons 1984; LRAM 1982; ARAM 1998); Univ. of Reading (MMus 1995); Birmingham Conservatoire, Univ. of Central England (PhD 2004). Hd, Music, LCM, 1997–2001; Royal Northern College of Music: Dir, Performance Studies and Sen. Tutor in Clarinet, 2001–02; Hd, Professional Performance Studies, 2002–04; Dep. Vice-Principal and Dir, Centre for Excellence in Teaching and Learning, 2004–06; Vice-Principal, 2006–12. Recordings include 21 CDs. FHEA 2004; FRNCM 2007; FLCM; FRSA. Hon. VCM 1984. *Publications:* Collaboration between Composer and Performers: British clarinet concertos 1990–2004, 2009. *Recreations:* travel, French literature, films and film music, walking, swimming, cooking. *Address:* Royal Northern College of Music, 124 Oxford Road, Manchester M13 9RD. *T:* (0161) 907 5273, 5382. *E:* linda.merrick@rncm.ac.uk.

MERRICKS, Walter Hugh, CBE 2007; a Gambling Commissioner, since 2012; *b* 4 June 1945; 2nd *s* of late Dick and Phoebe Merricks, Icklesham, Sussex; *m* 1982, Olivia Montuschi; one *s* one *d*, and one step *s*. *Educ:* Bradfield College, Berks; Trinity College, Oxford. MA Hons (Jurisp). Articled Clerk with Batt, Holden, 1968–70; admitted Solicitor, 1970; Hubbard Travelling Scholar, Montreal, 1971; Dir, Camden Community Law Centre, 1972–76; Lectr in Law, Brunel Univ., 1976–81; legal affairs writer, New Law Journal, 1982–85; Law Society: Sec., Professional and Public Relations, 1985–87; Asst Sec.-Gen. (Communications), 1987–95; Dir, Professional and Legal Policy, 1995–96; Insurance Ombudsman, 1996–99; Chief Ombudsman, Financial Ombudsman Service, 1999–2009; Chm., Office of Health Professions Adjudicator, 2009–12; Service Complaint Adjudicator, Legal Ombudsman, 2011–15; Service Complaint Reviewer, RICS, 2012–; Ind. Code Reviewer, British Copyright Council, 2013–; Associate, Verita, 2013–; Chm., IMPRESS: The Independent Monitor off the Press, 2015–. Member: Royal Commn on Criminal Procedure, 1978–81; Fraud Trials (Roskill) Cttee, 1984–86; Victim Support Wkg Party on Financial Compensation, 1992–93. Pres., British Insce Law Assoc., 2006–08; Chairman: British and Irish Ombudsman Assoc., 2001–04; Nat. Gamete Donation Trust, 2000–01; Internat. Network of Financial Ombudsman Schemes, 2007–09; Donor Conception Network, 2007–; Trustees, Acad. of Med. Royal Colleges, 2011–; Member: HFEA, 2002– (Chm., 2007–08); Bd (formerly Council), Ombudsman Service Ltd, 2010–15. Mem. Council, Justice, 2004– (Mem. Exec. Cttee, 2008–); Hon. FCII 2004. Hon. LLD London Guildhall, 2001. Achievement Award, British Insce Awards, 2004.

MERRILL, Alastair James Stuart; Vice Principal, University of St Andrews, since 2015; *b* Blackpool, 17 Jan. 1963; *s* of Howard Merrill and Catherine Merrill; *m* 1994, Janet Noakes; three *s*. *Educ:* Arnold Sch., Blackpool; Pembroke Coll., Cambridge (BA Hons Hist. 1985). FCIPS 2013. Fast stream, MoD, 1986–89; Second Sec., UK Delegn to NATO, 1989–91; Policy Officer, MoD, 1991–94; Civil Sec., UN Protection Forces, 1995; Dep. Dir of Private Office, HQ NATO, 1996–2001; Scottish Executive, later Scottish Government: Hd, Analytical Services, Educn Dept, 2001–03; Hd, Changing to Deliver, 2003–05; Hd, Police Div., 2005–08; Dir, Corporate Services, Scottish Prison Service, 2008–09; Commercial Dir and Chief Procurement Officer, 2009–15. *Recreations:* family, Boys' Brigade, sailing, motorcycling, choral singing. *Address:* University of St Andrews, College Gate, North Street, St Andrews, Fife KY16 9AJ. *T:* (01334) 462460. *E:* vpgov@st-andrews.ac.uk. *Club:* St Mary's Loch Sailing.

MERRILL, Dame Fiona Claire; *see* Reynolds, Dame F. C.

MERRIMAN, Air Vice-Marshal (Henry) Alan, CB 1985; CBE 1973; AFC 1957, and Bar 1961; DL; defence and aerospace consultant; *b* 17 May 1929; *s* of Henry Victor Merriman and Winifred Ellen Merriman; *m* 1965, Mary Brenda Stephenson; three *d*. *Educ:* Hertford Grammar Sch.; RAF Coll., Cranwell. Graduate, Empire Test Pilots Sch. FRAeS 1977. Commnd, 1951; Qual. Flying Instr, 263 F Sqdn, Empire Test Pilots Sch., Fighter Test Sqdn, A&AEE, Central Fighter Estabt, and RAF Staff Coll., 1952–63; Personal Air Sec. to Minister of Defence for RAF, 1964–66; Jt Services Staff Coll., 1966; OC Fighter Test Sqdn, A&AEE, 1966–69; HQ 38 Gp, 1969–70; Stn Comdr, RAF Wittering, 1970–72; RCDS, 1973; CO Empire Test Pilots Sch., 1974–75; Comdt, A&AEE, 1975–77; Dir, Operational Requirements (1), 1977–81; Mil. Dep. to Head of Defence Sales, 1981–84. Pres., Cambridge Br., RAFA, 2010–. Queen's Commendation for Valuable Services in the Air, 1956. DL Herts, 1995. *Recreations:* classic cars and aircraft, gardening. *Club:* Royal Air Force.

MERRIMAN, Huw William; MP (C) Bexhill and Battle, since 2015; *b* Brackley, Northants, 13 July 1973; *s* of Richard and Ann Merriman; *m* 2001, Victoria Powdrill; three *d*. *Educ:* Buckingham Co. Secondary Sch.; Aylesbury Coll. of Further Educn; Durham Univ. (BA Hons Law); Inns of Court Sch. of Law. Called to the Bar, Inner Temple, 1996; in practice as barrister, 1997; Man. Dir, Lehman Bros in Admin, 2008–15. Mem. (C), Wealden DC, 2007–15. Contested (C) NE Derbys, 2010. *Recreations:* cooking, gardening, beekeeping. *Address:* House of Commons, SW1A 0AA. *T:* (020) 7219 8712. *E:* huw.merriman.mp@parliament.uk. *Clubs:* Farmers; Bexhill Conservative.

MERRIMAN, Nicholas John, PhD; Director, Manchester Museum, University of Manchester, since 2006; *b* 6 June 1960; *s* of Michael and Pamela Merriman; *m* 1st (marr. diss.); two *s*; 2nd, 2010, Maria Balshaw May; one step *s* one step *d*. *Educ:* King Edward's Sch., Birmingham; St John's Coll., Cambridge (BA Archaeol. 1982; PhD 1989); Univ. of Leicester (Cert. Mus. Studies). AMA; FSA. Museum of London: Asst Keeper, Prehistory, 1986–91; Hd, Dept of Early London Hist. and Collections, 1991–97; University College London: Sen. Lectr, then Reader, in Mus. Studies, Inst. of Archaeol., 1997–2006; Curator, 1998–2006, Dir, 2006, Mus and Collections. Pres., Council for British Archaeol., 2005–08. Chm., Univ. Museums Gp, 2008–13. Chair: Collections Trust, 2014–; Rothesay Pavilion Trust, 2014–. FRSA. *Publications:* Beyond the Glass Case: the past, the heritage and the public in Britain, 1991; The Peopling of London, 1993; Making Early Histories in Museums, 1999; Public Archaeology, 2004. *Recreations:* running, family. *Address:* Manchester Museum, Oxford Road, Manchester M13 9PL. *T:* (0161) 275 2649, *Fax:* (0161) 275 2676. *E:* nick.merriman@manchester.ac.uk.

MERRITT, Prof. John Edward; Emeritus Professor, The Open University, since 1987; *b* 13 June 1926; *s* of Leonard Merritt and Janet (*née* Hartford); *m* 1948, Denise Edmondson; two *s*. *Educ:* Univ. of Durham (BA); Univ. of London (DipEdPsychol). AFBPsS; FRSA. Sandhurst, 1945–46; Trng Officer, Border Regt, 1946–48. Educnl Psychologist, Lancs LEA, 1957–59; Sen. Educnl Psychologist, Hull LEA, 1959–63; Lectr, Inst. of Educn, Univ. of Durham, 1964–71; Prof. of Teacher Educn, Open Univ., 1971–85, retd. Hon. Res. Fellow, Charlotte Mason Coll., Ambleside, 1986–88. Pres., UK Reading Assoc., 1969–70; Chm., 5th World Congress on Reading, Vienna, 1974; Mem., Nat. Cttee of Inquiry into Reading and Use of English (Bullock Cttee), 1973–75. Hon. FCP 1994. *Publications:* Reading and the Curriculum (ed), 1971; A Framework for Curriculum Design, 1972; (ed jtly) Reading Today and Tomorrow, 1972; (ed jtly) The Reading Curriculum, 1972; Perspectives on Reading, 1973; What Shall We Teach, 1974; Make Democracy Work, 2010; Installing Proactive Democracy: a guide for the not so dumb, 2011; The Republic of Soccon: the birth, decline and painful rebirth of democracy, 2011; numerous papers in educnl jls. *Recreations:* fell walking, orienteering, climbing, ski-ing, theatre. *Address:* Highfield, 5 Cross Street, Keswick, Cumbria CA12 4DE. *T:* (01768) 774875.

MERRITT, Lindsay; *see* Nicholson, L.

MERRITT, Prof. Neil; Vice-Chancellor, University of Portsmouth, 1992–94 (President, Portsmouth Polytechnic, 1991–92); *b* 3 March 1939; *s* of the late Leslie Alfred Merritt and Gladys Irene (*née* Green); *m* 1961, Jean Fisher (former Headmistress, Heathfield Sch., GPDST, Pinner); one *s* one *d*. *Educ:* Ilford County High Sch.; Univ. of Hull (LLB). Asst Lectr, City of London Coll., 1962–63; Lectr, Slough Coll., 1963–65; Staff Tutor, Further Educn Staff Coll., 1965–68; Head, Faculty of Management and Arts, Norfolk Coll. of Arts and Technology, 1968–73; Vice-Principal, Mid-Essex Technical Coll., 1973–74; Pro-Dir, Chelmer Inst. of Higher Educn, 1975–76; Vis. Prof. of Law, Indiana Univ., 1974 and 1976; Dir, Ealing Tech. Coll., later Ealing Coll. of Higher Educn, then Polytechnic of W London, 1977–91 (Prof. *ad hominem*, 1989). Secretary, then Chairman: Assoc. of Law Teachers, 1965–71; Standing Conf. of Principals, 1977–91; Member: Adv. Cttee on Legal Educn, 1972–76; CNAA Legal Studies Bd, 1978–84; Nat. Adv. Body for Public Sector Higher Educn Bd, 1982–88. Chm., Hillingdon Hosp. Trust, 1991–94. *Publications:* (with E. G. H. Clayton) Business Law, 1966; articles in professional jls on law, and higher educn policy. *Recreations:* history of polar exploration, 20th–21st century history of UK and USA, fine art, alleged interference in the kitchen.

MERRIVALE, 4th Baron *cr* 1925, of Walkhampton, Co. Devon; **Derek John Philip Duke;** *b* 16 March 1948; *s* of 3rd Baron Merrivale and of Colette, *d* of John Douglas Wise, Bordeaux, France; *S* father, 2007; *m* 1976, Guillemette Daras; one *s* three *d* (of whom one *s* one *d* are twins). *Heir: s* Hon. Thomas Duke [*b* 25 March 1980; *m* 2007, Diane Castel].

MERRON, Gillian Joanna; Chairman, Bus Users UK, since 2012; *b* 12 April 1959. *Educ:* Wanstead High Sch.; Univ. of Lancaster (BSc Hons (Mgt Scis) 1981). Business Develt Advr, 1982–85; Local Govt Officer, 1985–87; E Midlands full-time Official, NUPE and UNISON, 1987–95; Sen. Officer, UNISON, Lincolnshire, 1995–97. Mem., Lab. Pty, 1982–. MP (Lab) Lincoln, 1997–2010; contested (Lab) same seat, 2010. PPS to Minister of State for the Armed Forces, 1998–99, to Minister of State for Defence Procurement, 1999–2001, MoD, to Sec. of State for NI, 2001–02; an Asst Govt Whip, 2002–04; a Lord Comr of HM Treasury (Govt Whip), 2004–06; Parly Under-Sec. of State, DfT, 2006–07; a Parly Sec., Cabinet Office, and Minister for the E Midlands, 2007–08; Parly Under-Sec. of State, DFID, 2008, FCO, 2008–09; Minister of State (Minister for Public Health), DoH, 2009–10. Mem., Select Cttee on Trade and Industry, 1997–98. Vice-Chm., PLP Back bench Cttee on Foreign and Commonwealth Affairs, 1997–98; Chm., E Midlands Gp of Lab. MPs, 1999–2002; Associate, British-Irish Inter-Parly Body, 2001–02. Mem. Bd, Westminster Foundn for Democracy, 1998–2001. Grad., Armed Forces Parly Scheme (RAF), 1997–98; Fellow, Industry and Parlt Trust, 2002–. Dir (unpaid), E Midlands Sport, 2000–03. Mem. Bd of Nat. Officers, Liberal Judaism; a Vice Pres., Jewish Leadership Council, 2013–. *Recreations:* gym, running, films, Lincoln City FC.

MERRY, David Byron, CMG 2000; HM Diplomatic Service, retired; High Commissioner, Gaborone, 2001–05; *b* 16 Sept. 1945; *s* of late Colin Merry and Audrey Merry (*née* Handley); *m* 1967, Patricia Ann Ellis; one *s* two *d*. *Educ:* King Edward VII Sch., Sheffield; Ecclesfield Grammar Sch. Min. of Aviation, 1961–65; entered HM Diplomatic Service, 1965; Bangkok, 1969–73; Budapest, 1974–77; FCO, 1977–81; First Sec. (Econ.) and Civil Air Attaché, Bonn, 1981–85; Head of Chancery, E Berlin, 1985–88; FCO, 1989–93; Counsellor and Dep. Head of Mission, Manila, 1993–97; Dep. High Comr, Karachi, 1997–2000; FCO, 2000–01. *Recreations:* swimming, walking. *Address:* 22 Orchard Close, Hawley, Camberley, Surrey GU17 9EX.

MERRYLEES, Prof. Andrew, RSA 1991; RIBA; FRIAS, FCSD; architect, artist and planner; *b* 13 Oct. 1933; *s* of Andrew Merrylees and Mary McGowan Craig; *m* 1959, Maie Crawford; two *s* one *d*. *Educ:* Glasgow Sch. of Architecture (BArch 1956; DipTP 1957). RIBA 1958; FRIAS 1977; FCSD 1978. Joined Sir Basil Spence, Glover & Ferguson, 1952: student, 1952–57; architect, 1957–68; Associate, 1968; Partner, 1972–85; Principal, Andrew Merrylees Associates, then Andrew Merrylees Grierson & Robertson, subseq. Merrylees & Robertson, 1985–2000, merged with Hypostyle, 2001; consultant in private architectural practice, Hypostyle Architects, 2001–10. Consultant Architect: SCONUL, 1964–79; UC Dublin, 1973–91. Hon. Prof. of Architecture, Univ. of Dundee, 1998–. Member: Adv. Council for Arts in Scotland, 1989–97; Council, RIAS, 1991–94. Mem., Edinburgh Fest. Soc., 1979–. Trustee, RSA Foundn, 2012–. *Major projects* include: university buildings at Edinburgh (Civic Trust Award, for Univ. Liby, 1969; later listed by Historic Scotland), Heriot-Watt, Dublin, Liverpool, Newcastle and Aston in Birmingham; Scottish HQ for AA; Sorting Office for PO, Edinburgh (Art in Architecture Award, Saltire Soc., 1983); Nat. Liby of Scotland (SCONUL Award, 1996); British Golf Mus., St Andrews; Motherwell Heritage Centre. FRSA 1993. Winner, numerous design competitions, including: UC Dublin Liby; Liverpool Univ. Arts Liby; Conf. Centre, Heriot-Watt Univ.; John Logie Baird Visions Centre, Glasgow; Dundee Sci. Centre. Numerous awards, including: Bronze Medal, RIBA, 1968; Gold Medal, Royal Scottish Acad., 1984; Lifetime Achievement Award, RIAS, 2013. *Recreations:* interested in all art forms, drawing and painting has been life-long pursuit running in parallel with and informing design, exhibiting at Royal Scottish Academy, Scottish Arts Council, London, Warsaw, Paris and St Raphael. *W:* www.andrewmerrylees.com. *Club:* Scottish Arts (Edinburgh).

MERSEY, 5th Viscount *cr* 1916, of Toxteth; **Edward John Hallam Bigham;** Lord Nairne 1681; Baron Mersey 1910; *b* 23 May 1966; *s* of 4th Viscount Mersey and of Joanna (*née* Murray); *S* father, 2006; *m* 1st, 1994, Claire Haigh (marr. diss. 1996); 2nd, 2001, Clare, *d* of Robert Schaw Miller; two *d*. *Educ:* Eton; Balliol Coll., Oxford; Trinity Coll. of Music, London; Ludwig-Maximilians Univ., Munich. Composer. Recordings with Royal Scottish Nat. Orch., Scottish Ensemble and Polish Nat. Radio SO. *Heir: uncle* Hon. David Edward Hugh Bigham [*b* 14 April 1938; *m* 1965, Anthea Rosemary Seymour; three *s* one *d*]. *W:* www.nedbigham.com.

MERTHYR, 5th Baron *cr* 1911, of Senghenydd, co. Glamorgan; **David Trevor Lewis;** Bt 1896; *b* 21 Feb. 1977; *o s* of Trevor Oswin Lewis, CBE (disclaimed his peerage for life and did not use his title of baronet) and of Susan Jane Lewis (*née* Birt-Llewellin); *S* father, 2015; *m* 2002, Elizabeth Jane Widdows; two *d*. *Heir: uncle* Hon. Peter Herbert Lewis [*b* 25 March 1937; *m* 1974, Caroline Monica Cadogan; one *d*].

MERTON, Viscount; Thomas John Horatio Nelson; *b* 27 April 2010; *s* and *heir* of Earl Nelson, *qv*.

MERTON, Paul; *see* Martin, P. J.

MERTON, Prof. Robert C., PhD; School of Management Distinguished Professor of Finance, Sloan School of Management, Massachusetts Institute of Technology, since 2010; Resident Scientist, Dimensional Holdings Inc., since 2009; *b* 31 July 1944; *s* of late Robert K. Merton and Suzanne C. Merton; *m* 1966, June Rose (separated 1996); two *s* one *d*. *Educ:* Columbia Univ. (BS Engrg Math. 1966); California Inst. of Technology (MS Applied Math. 1967); MIT (PhD Econs 1970). Massachusetts Institute of Technology: Asst Prof., 1970–73, Associate Prof., 1973–74, Prof., 1974–80, of Finance; J. C. Penney Prof. of Management, 1980–88; George Fisher Baker Prof. of Business Admin, 1988–98, John and Natty McArthur University Prof., 1998–2010, now Univ. Prof. Emeritus, Harvard Business Sch. Mem., NAS, 1993; Fellow: Amer. Acad. of Arts and Scis; Econometric Soc.; Internat. Assoc. of Financial Engrs; Inst. for Quantitative Res. in Finance; Financial Mgt Assoc.; Amer. Finance Assoc. Hon. Professor: Hautes Etudes Commerciales, France, 1995; St Petersburg Univ. of Mgt and Econs, Russia, 2011. Hamilton Lect., RIA, 2010. Hon. LLD Chicago, 1991; Hon. DEconSc Lausanne, 1996; Dr *hc*: Paris Dauphine, 1997; Nacional Mayor de San Marcos, Peru, 2004; Universidad Católica de Chile, Santiago, 2014; Hon. Dr Mgt Sci., Nat. Sun Yat-sen Univ., Taiwan, 1998; Hon. DSc: Athens Univ. of Econs and Business, 2003; Claremont Graduate Univ., 2008; Chinese Univ. of Hong Kong, 2014; Hon. DPhil Nacional Federico Villarreal, Peru, 2004; Hon. DBA Macau, 2014. Leo Melamed Prize, Univ. of Chicago, 1983; Financial Engr of the Year Award, Internat. Assoc. of Financial Engrs, 1993; Internat. Prize, Accademia Nazionale dei Lincei, 1993; FORCE Award for Financial Innovation, Fuqua Sch. of Business, Duke Univ., 1993; Nobel Prize for Economics, 1997; Michael I. Pupin Medal for Service to the Nation, Columbia Univ., 1998; Distinguished Alumni Award, CIT, 1999; Nicholas Molodovsky Award, Assoc. for Investment Mgt and Res., 2003; Higher Standard Award, Professional Risk Managers' Internat. Assoc., 2006; Hall of Fame, Fixed Income Analysts Soc., 2007; Dist. Finance Educator Award, Financial Educn Assoc., 2008; Award for Foundational Contribs to Finance, Owen Sch. of Mgt, Vanderbilt Univ., 2008; Robert A. Muh Award in Humanities, Arts and Social Scis, MIT, 2009; Tjailing C. Koopmans Asset Award, Tilburg Univ., 2009; Award for Outstanding Contribs to Financial Econs, LECG, 2010; Kolmogorov Medal, Univ. of London, 2010; Melamed-Arditti Innovation Award, CME Gp, 2011; WFE Award for Excellence, World Fedn of Exchanges, 2013; Lifetime Achievement Award, Financial Intermediation Res. Soc., 2014. *Publications:* Continuous-Time Finance, 1990, rev. edn 1992; (jtly) Casebook in Financial Engineering: applied studies of financial innovation, 1995; (jtly) The Global Financial System: a functional perspective, 1995; (jtly) Finance, 2000; (jtly) Risk Management and International Financial Fragility, 2003; (jtly) The Derivatives Sourcebook: foundations and trends in finance, 2006; Financial Economics, 2nd edn 2009; contribs to scientific jls. *Address:* Sloan School of Management, Massachusetts Institute of Technology, 77 Massachusetts Avenue, E62–634, Cambridge, MA 02139, USA.

MERZ, (Joachim) Friedrich; Partner, Mayer Brown LLP, since 2005; *b* 11 Nov. 1955; *m* 1981, Charlotte Gass; one *s* two *d*. *Educ:* Univ. of Bonn. Mil. service, 1975–76. Practical trng in judicial and other legal work, Saarbrücken and Johannesburg, SA, 1982–85; magistrate, Saarbrücken, 1985–86; lawyer, 1986–: German Chemical Industry Assoc., Bonn, Frankfurt, 1986–89. Chm., Atlantik-Brücke e.V., 2009–. MEP (CDU/CSU) S Westfalia, 1989–94; Mem. (CDU/CSU) Bundestag, 1994–2009. Mem., Finance Cttee and Cttee for Eur. Affairs, Bundestag, 1994–2009. CDU/CSU Parliamentary Group: co-ordinator, on Finance Cttee, 1996–98; Dep. Chm., 1998–2000, 2002–04; Chm., 2000–02; Member: Bd, CDU Nordrhein-Westfalen, 1997–; Fed. Bd, 1998–2000, Presidium, 2002–04, CDU party.

MESHER, John; an Upper Tribunal Judge (Administrative Appeals Chamber) (formerly a Social Security Commissioner and Child Support Commissioner), 1993–2013; a Deputy Upper Tribunal Judge, since 2013; *b* 25 June 1947; *s* of late Percy Charles Mesher and Dorothy Mesher; *m* 1973, Hilary Anne Wilkens; one *s* one *d* (and one *d* decd). *Educ:* Bancroft's Sch.; University Coll., Oxford (BA Jurisp, BCL); Yale Law Sch. (LLM). Called to the Bar, Gray's Inn, 1970; Lectr in Laws, QMC, 1969–76; University of Sheffield: Lectr in Law, Sen. Lectr and Reader, 1976–93; Simmons & Simmons Res. Fellow in Pensions Law, 1988–93; Prof. Associate, 1993–. Part-time Chm. of Social Security, Medical, and Disability Appeals Tribunals, 1981–93, Pensions Appeal Tribunals, 1995–2004; Dep. Social Security Comr, 1991–93. Editor, Occupational Pensions Law Reports, 1992–97; Section Editor, Encyclopedia of Employment Law, 1991–97. *Publications:* Compensation for Unemployment, 1976; CPAG's Supplementary Benefit Legislation Annotated, 1983, 10th edn, as Income-Related Benefits: the Legislation, 1993; (contrib.) Rayden and Jackson on Divorce and Family Matters, 17th edn 1997; (contrib.) Social Security Legislation, vol. II, Income Support, Jobseeker's Allowance, State Pension Credit and the Social Fund, vol. v, Universal Credit, 2014; contribs to learned jls.

MESHOULAM, Melanie; *see* Clore, M.

MESIĆ, Stjepan, Hon. GCMG 2001; President, Republic of Croatia, 2000–10; *b* 24 Dec. 1934; *s* of Josip and Mandica Mesić; *m* 1961, Milka; two *d*. *Educ:* Univ. of Zagreb (LLB). Mayor, Orahovica, Croatia, 1967–71; MP Socialist Republic of Croatia, 1965–71; involved in Croatian Spring movt and served one-year jail sentence; Sec., 1990, Hd, Exec. Cttee, 1992, Croatian Democratic Union; Prime Minister, Socialist Republic of Croatia, May–Aug. 1990; last Pres., Yugoslavia, May–Dec. 1991; Speaker, Parlt of Republic of Croatia, 1992–94; Founder, Croatian Ind. Democrats Party (HND), 1994; Mem., Croatian Nat. Party (HNS), 1997–2000 (Exec. Vice-Pres. and Pres., Zagreb Br.). Charles Univ. Medal, 2001. Homeland War Meml Medal (Croatia), 1993; State Order of Star of Romania, 2000; Grand Star, Decoration of Honour for Merit (Austria), 2001; Golden Order, Gjergj Kastrioti Skënderbeu (Albania), 2001; Grand Cross, Order of Saviour (Greece), 2001; Order of White Double Cross, 1st class (Slovakia), 2001; Knight Grand Cross, Order of Merit with Grand Cordon (Italy), 2001; Grand Cross with Collar, Order of the Republic (Hungary), 2002; Dostyk Order, 1st degree (Kazakhstan), 2002; Order of the Crown (Malaysia), 2002. *Publications:* The Break-up of Yugoslavia: political memoirs, 1992, 2nd edn 1994. *Recreations:* Nanbudo, swimming. *Address:* c/o Office of the President of the Republic of Croatia, Pantovčak 241, 10 000 Zagreb, Croatia.

MESSEL, Prof. Harry, AC 2006; CBE 1979; BA, BSc, BMilSci; PhD (NUI) 1951; Professor and Head of the School of Physics, and Director of Science Foundation for Physics, University of Sydney, Australia, 1952–87, now Emeritus Professor; Chancellor, Bond University, 1992–97 (Executive Chancellor, 1993–96); *b* 3 March 1922. *Educ:* Rivers Public High Sch., Rivers, Manitoba. Entered RMC of Canada, 1940, grad. with Governor-General's Silver Medal, 1942. Served War of 1939–45: Canadian Armed Forces, Lieut, Canada and overseas, 1942–45. Queen's Univ., Kingston, Ont., 1945–48 (BA 1st Cl. Hons in Mathematics, 1948; BSc Hons in Engineering Physics, 1948); St Andrews Univ., Scotland, 1948–49; Institute for Advanced Studies, Dublin, Eire, 1949–51; Sen. Lectr in Mathematical Physics, University of Adelaide, Australia, 1951–52. CPhys, FInstP; FAAAS 1983. Mem., Aust. Atomic Energy Commn, 1974–81; Sen. Vice-Chm., Species Survival Commn, IUCN, 1978–2001 (Chm., Crocodile Specialist Gp, 1989–2004). Life Mem., Royal Instn of GB, 1991. FRSA 1972. Hon. DSc: Sydney; Royal Mil. Coll. of Canada, 2006; Hon. DHL Schiller Internat., 1994; DUniv Bond, 2008. ANZAAS Medal, 1995; Tall Poppy Award, NSW Australian Inst. of Political Sci., 2004; Sir Peter Scott Medal for Conservation Merit, IUCN/Species Survival Commn, 2004. *Publications:* Chap. 4, Progress in Cosmic Ray Physics, vol. 2, (North Holland Publishing Company), 1953; co-author and editor of: A Modern Introduction to Physics (Horwitz-Grahame, Vols I, II, III, 1959, 1960, 1962); Selected Lectures in Modern Physics, 1958; Space and the Atom, 1961; A Journey through Space and the Atom, 1962; The Universe of Time and Space, 1963; Light and Life in the Universe, 1964; Science for High School Students, 1964; Time, 1965; Senior Science for High School Students, 1966; (jt) Electron-Photon Shower Distribution Function, 1970; (jt) Multistrand Senior Science for High School Students, 1975; Australian Animals and their Environment, 1977; Time and Man, 1978; Tidal Rivers in Northern Australia and their Crocodile Populations (20 monographs), 1979–87; The Study of Populations, 1985; editor of: From Nucleus to Universe, 1960; Atoms to Andromeda, 1966; Apollo and the Universe, 1967; Man in Inner and Outer Space, 1968; Nuclear Energy Today and Tomorrow, 1969; Pioneering in Outer Space, 1970; Molecules to Man, 1971; Brain Mechanisms and the Control of Behaviour, 1972; Focus on the Stars, 1973; Solar Energy, 1974; Our Earth, 1975; Energy for Survival, 1979; The Biological Manipulation of Life, 1981; Science Update, 1983; The Study of Population, 1985; Highlights in Science, 1987; numerous papers published in: Proc. Physical Soc., London; Philosophical Magazine, London; Physical Review of America. *Recreations:* conservation, water ski-ing, hunting, fishing and photography. *Address:* 74 Montevideo Drive, Clear Island Waters, Qld 4226, Australia. *T:* (7) 55755873, *Fax:* (7) 55755874.

MESSERVY-WHITING, Maj.-Gen. Graham Gerald, CBE 2003 (MBE 1980); Member, War Pensions and Armed Forces Compensation Chambers, First-tier Tribunal (formerly Pensions Appeal Tribunal), since 2005; Honorary Senior Research Fellow, School of Government and Society, University of Birmingham, since 2010; *b* 20 Oct. 1946; *s* of late Gerald and Kathleen Messervy-Whiting; *m* 1969, Shirley Hitchinson; one *s*. *Educ:* Lycée Français de Londres; Army Staff Coll.; RAF Staff Coll. Commnd Intelligence Corps, 1967; Regtl duty, 1 KOSB, Germany, Libya, Cyprus, Hong Kong, 1968–82; jsdc 1984; Secretariat Chiefs of Staff, 1984–86; CO, Intelligence and Security Gp, Germany, 1986–88; Briefing Officer, SACEUR, 1988–91; rcds 1992; Mil. Advr to Lord Owen, 1992–93; Res. Fellow, KCL, 1993; Dir, Defence Commitments Staff, 1994–95; COS, WEU, 1995–98; Asst Dir, Ops, GCHQ, 1998–2000; C of S, EU Mil. Staff, 2000–03. Dep. Dir, Centre for Studies in Security and Diplomacy, Univ. of Birmingham, 2003–10. FRUSI 1996. Associate Fellow, Chatham House, 2003–07. *Publications:* contribs to academic pubns on Eur. security and defence issues. *Recreations:* travel, bridge. *Address:* School of Government and Society, University of Birmingham, Edgbaston, Birmingham B15 2TT. *E:* g.messervywhiting@bham.ac.uk. *Club:* Army and Navy.

MESSITER, Malcolm Cassan; oboist; Founder and Managing Director: Messiter Software, since 1985; Trans-Send International Ltd, since 1992; *b* 1 April 1949; *s* of late Ian and Enid Messiter; *m* 1972, Christine (marr. diss. 1998); one *d*. *Educ:* Bryanston Sch.; Paris Conservatoire; Royal Coll. of Music (ARCM Hons 1971). First Oboe: BBC Concert Orchestra, 1971–77; London Mozart Players, 1977–83; London Festival Orchestra, 1985–; many solo concerts. Several recordings. Founder: Virtual Orchestra Co. Ltd, 1999; Barnet Chamber Music Club, 2010. Owner, Just a Minute, BBC Radio 4, 2001–. *Publications:* personal computer software and manuals, guides to remote controlled model helicopters and aeroplanes. *Recreations:* wine, chamber music, model helicopters, oboe playing, automated harpsichords. *Address:* 47 Sutton Crescent, Barnet, Herts EN5 2SW.

MESTEL, Prof. Leon, PhD; FRS 1977; Professor of Astronomy, University of Sussex, 1973–92, now Emeritus; *b* 5 Aug. 1927; *s* of late Rabbi Solomon Mestel and Rachel (*née* Brodetsky); *m* 1951, Sylvia Louise Cole (*d* 2014); two *s* two *d*. *Educ:* West Ham Secondary Sch., London; Trinity Coll., Cambridge (BA 1948, PhD 1952). ICI Res. Fellow, Dept of Maths, Univ. of Leeds, 1951–54; Commonwealth Fund Fellow, Princeton Univ. Observatory, 1954–55; University of Cambridge: Univ. Asst Lectr in Maths, 1955–58; Univ. Lectr in Maths, 1958–66; Fellow of St John's Coll., 1957–66; Vis. Mem., Inst. for Advanced Study, Princeton, 1961–62; J. F. Kennedy Fellow, Weizmann Inst. of Science, Israel, 1966–67; Prof. of Applied Maths, Manchester Univ., 1967–73. Eddington Medal, 1993, Gold Medal, 2002, RAS. *Publications:* Magnetohydrodynamics (with N. O. Weiss), 1974 (Geneva Observatory); Stellar Magnetism, 1999, 2nd edn 2012; papers, revs and conf. reports on different branches of theoretical astrophysics. *Recreations:* reading, music. *Address:* 1 Highsett, Hills Road, Cambridge CB2 1NX. *T:* (01223) 355233.

MESTON, family name of **Baron Meston**.

MESTON, 3rd Baron *cr* 1919, of Agra and Dunottar; **James Meston;** QC 1996; **His Honour Judge Meston;** a Circuit Judge, since 1999; *b* 10 Feb. 1950; *s* of 2nd Baron Meston and Diana Mary Came, *d* of Capt. O. S. Doll; *S* father, 1984; *m* 1974, Jean Rebecca Anne, *d* of John Carder; one *s* two *d*. *Educ:* Wellington College; St Catharine's Coll., Cambridge (MA); Leicester Univ. (LLM). Barrister, Middle Temple, 1973; Jun. Counsel to Queen's Proctor, 1992–96; a Recorder, 1997–99. Legal Assessor, 1991–99, Sen. Legal Assessor, 1999, UKCC. Appeal Steward, BBB of C, 1993–2001. Pres., British Soc. of Commerce, 1984–92. *Heir: s* Hon. Thomas James Dougall Meston [*b* 21 Oct. 1977; *m* 2009, Anna Ching; one *s*]. *Address:* Queen Elizabeth Building, Temple, EC4Y 9BS. *Club:* Hawks (Cambridge).

METCALF, His Honour Christopher Sherwood John; a Circuit Judge, 2001–11; *b* 18 May 1945; *s* of Bernard Metcalf and Margaret Metcalf; *m* 1977, Pamela Falconer; two *s* two *d*. *Educ:* The Leys Sch., Cambridge; W Georgia Coll., USA (Rotary Internat. Schol. 1963). Called to the Bar, Middle Temple, 1972; in practice on Midland and Oxford Circuit, 1972–2001; Asst Recorder, 1991–95; Recorder, 1995–2001. Member: Mental Health Rev. Tribunal, 2001–; Parole Bd, 2002–. *Recreations:* foreign travel, church architecture, private enterprise, games, choral music.

METCALF, Sir David (Harry), Kt 2013; CBE 2008; PhD; Professor of Industrial Relations, London School of Economics, 1985–2009, now Emeritus Professor, Centre for Economic Performance; *b* 15 May 1942; *s* of Geoffrey and Dorothy Metcalf; *m* 1968, Helen Pitt (Dame Helen Metcalf, DBE, *d* 2003); one *s*. *Educ:* Manchester Univ. (BA Econ 1964; MA 1966); London Univ. (PhD 1971). Apprentice welder, English Electric, 1959–61; Lectr in Econs, LSE, 1967–75; Special Advr to Minister for Social Security, 1976–79; Prof. of Econs, Kent Univ., 1978–85. Comr, Low Pay Commn, 1997–2007; Dir, Starting Price Regulatory Commn, 2005–; Mem., Rev. Body on Sen. Salaries, 2009–15. Chm., Home Office Migration Adv. Cttee, 2007–16. Editor, British Jl Industrial Relns, 1990–95. *Publications:* Low Pay, Occupational Mobility and Minimum Wage Policy in Britain, 1983; New Perspectives on Industrial Disputes, 1993; Trade Unions: resurgence or demise?, 2005; articles in Econ. Jl, Industrial and Labor Relns Rev., etc. *Recreations:* horse-racing (owner and investor), watching Tottenham Hotspur FC. *Address:* 18 St Georges Avenue, N7 0HD. *T:* (020) 7607 5902. *E:* d.metcalf@lse.ac.uk. *Club:* MCC.

METCALF, Prof. David Michael, DPhil, DLitt; Professor of Numismatics, University of Oxford, 1996–98; Keeper of Heberden Coin Room, Ashmolean Museum, Oxford, 1982–98; Fellow of Wolfson College, Oxford, 1982–98, now Emeritus; *b* 8 May 1933; *s* of Rev. Thomas Metcalf and Gladys Metcalf; *m* 1958, Dorothy Evelyn (*née* Uren); two *s* one *d*. *Educ:* St John's College, Cambridge. MA, DPhil, DLitt. Asst Keeper, Ashmolean Museum, 1963. President: Royal Numismatic Soc., 1994–99 (Sec., and Editor, Numismatic Chronicle, 1974–84); UK Numismatic Trust, 1994–99. *Publications:* Coinage in South-eastern Europe 820–1396, 1979; Coinage of the Crusades and the Latin East, 1983, 2nd edn 1995; (ed with D. H. Hill) Sceattas in England and on the Continent, 1984; Coinage in Ninth-century Northumbria, 1987; Thrymsas and Sceattas in the Ashmolean Museum, Oxford: vol. 1, 1993, vol. 2, 1993, vol. 3, 1994; Corpus of Lusignan Coinage, vol. 2, 1996, vol. 1, 1998, vol. 3, 2000; Suevic Coinage, 1997; An Atlas of Anglo-Saxon Coin Finds, 1998; Byzantine Lead Seals from Cyprus, 2004; (with W. Op den Velde) The Monetary Economy of the Netherlands *c* 690–*c* 715, 2007; Byzantine Cyprus, 491–1191, 2009; (with W. Op den Velde) A Study of the 'Porcupine' Sceattas of Series E, vol. 1, 2009, vol. 2, 2010; Byzantine Lead Seals from Cyprus, vol. 2, 2014; articles on numismatics in various jls. *Address:* 20 The Shawl, Leyburn, N Yorks DL8 5DG.

METCALFE, Adrian Peter, OBE 2001; international sport and media consultant; *b* 2 March 1942; *s* of Hylton and Cora Metcalfe; *m* Catherine, Baroness von Delvig; one *s* one *d* by former marriage. *Educ:* Roundhay Sch., Leeds; Magdalen Coll., Oxford. Reporter, Sunday Express, 1964; Dep. Editor, World of Sport, ABC TV, 1965; Producer, Sports Arena, LWT, 1968; Presenter, CBS Sports Spectacular, 1972–76; Man. Dir, AMO Productions, 1976; Sen. Commissioning Editor, Sport and Features, Channel 4 TV, 1981; Commentator, ITV, 1966–87; Director of Programmes: Eurosport, 1989–91; Tyne Tees Television Ltd, 1991–92; Dir, Venue Production, Atlantic Olympic Games, 1994–96; Chm., API Television, 1996–98; Exec. Publr, worldsport.com, 1998–2000; Chm., AMDM Agency, 2003; Dir, World Professional Billiards and Snooker Assoc., 2004. GB Record, 400m, 45·7, ranked No 1 in the world at 400m, 1961; Gold Medal, 400m and 4×400m, World Student Games, 1963; Silver Medal, 4×400m, Tokyo Olympics, 1964; 7 British Records, 4 European Records, 1961–64. Pres., OUAC, 1962–63. Mem., UK Sport, 1998 (Chm., Major Events Steering Gp, 1999–2003); Life Vice-Pres. and Trustee, SportsAid (formerly Sports Aid Foundn), 1990. *Recreations:* still running, Russian culture.

METCALFE, Charles; wine and food presenter, writer and entertainer; *b* London, 15 April 1949; *s* of John Alan and Ann Monck Mason Metcalfe; *m* 1986, Kathryn McWhirter; one *s* two *d*. *Educ:* Eton Coll.; Christ Church, Oxford (MA Hons English Lang. and Lit.). Investment analyst, London Wall Gp, 1973–75; opera singer, tour guide and cook, 1975–83; Associate Ed., Wine Internat. mag., 1983–2005; Co-Chm., Internat. Wine Challenge, 1983–. TV presenter, 1987–; progs incl. This Morning, Great British Food, Simply Greek, Taste Today, Great Food Live. Hon. Pres., Assoc. of Wine Educators, 2002–; Chm. of Judges, Acad. of Chocolate Awards, 2015. Gran Orden de Caballeros del Vino, 1997; Comendador, Ordem do Mérito Empresarial (Classe do Mérito Agrícola) (Portugal), 2012. *Publications:* with Kathryn McWhirter: The Wines of Spain and Portugal, 1988; Sainsbury's The Wines of Spain and Portugal, 1991; Sainsbury's Pocket Food and Wine Guide, 1995; The Wine and Food Lover's Guide to Portugal, 2007; The Wine and Food Lover's Guide to Porto and Gaia, 2015. *Recreations:* cooking, environmental campaigning. *Address:* Old Inn House, London Road, Balcombe RH17 6JQ. *T:* (01444) 811682. *E:* charlesmetcalfe@btopenworld.com.

METCALFE, Prof. Ian Saxley, PhD; FREng; CEng, FIChemE; CChem, FRSC; Professor of Chemical Engineering, Newcastle University, since 2005; *b* Stockton-on-Tees, 7 Aug. 1961; *s* of Saxley Metcalfe and Margaret Metcalfe; *m* 2004, Maria Isabel Yorquez Ramirez; two *d*. *Educ:* Imperial Coll., London (BScEng 1982); Princeton Univ. (MA Chem. Engrg 1984; PhD Chem. Engrg 1987). CEng 1991; MIChemE 1991, FIChemE 2004; CChem 1992; MRSC 1992, FRSC 2012. Lectr, 1987–96, Sen. Lectr, 1996–97, Dept of Chem. Engrg, Imperial Coll., London; Prof. of Chemical Engrg, Univ. of Edinburgh, 1997–2001; Prof. of Chemical Engrg, UMIST, subseq. Univ. of Manchester, 2001–04, Vis. Prof., 2005–. FREng 2012. Exec. Editor, Chemical Engineering Science, 2001–13. *Publications:* Chemical Reaction Engineering: a first course, 1997. *Recreation:* dreaming of Buachaille Etive Mor on a sunny day. *Address:* School of Chemical Engineering and Advanced Materials, Merz Court, Newcastle University, Newcastle upon Tyne NE1 7RU. *T:* (0191) 222 5279. *E:* i.metcalfe@ncl.ac.uk.

METCALFE, Prof. James Charles, PhD; Professor of Mammalian Cell Biochemistry, University of Cambridge, 1996–2007, now Emeritus; Fellow, Darwin College, Cambridge, 1975–2000; *b* 20 July 1939; *s* of Cyril Tom Metcalfe and Olive Kate (*née* Ayling); *m* 1st, 1969, Susan Milner (marr. diss.); one *s* one *d*; 2nd, 1983, Aviva Miriam Tolkovsky. *Educ:* St Paul's Sch.; Sidney Sussex Coll., Cambridge (MA; PhD 1965). Research Fellow, Dept of Pharmacology, Cambridge Univ. and Dept of Pharmacology, Harvard Med. Sch., 1965–67; Mem. Scientific Staff, MRC Molecular Pharmacology Unit, Dept of Pharmacology, Cambridge, 1967–72; Res. Fellow, Dept of Chemistry, Stanford Univ., 1968; Perm. MRC appt, 1970; Div. of Molecular Pharmacology, NIMR, 1972–73; Univ. Lectr, Dept of Pharmacology, Cambridge, 1974; Sir William Dunn Reader, Dept of Biochem., Cambridge, 1974–96. Chm., Scientific Cttee, CRC, 1995–2000; Trustee and Chm., Scientific Cttee, EMF Biol Res. Trust, 2005–. Mem., EMBO, 1981. Fogarty Internat. Schol., NIH, 1979. Colworth Medal, Biochem. Soc., 1973. *Publications:* papers in scientific jls. *Recreations:* walking in France, reading, ski-ing. *Address:* Sanger Building, Department of Biochemistry, University of Cambridge, 80 Tennis Court Road, Old Addenbrookes Site, Cambridge CB2 1GA. *T:* (01223) 333633.

METCALFE, Prof. (John) Stanley, CBE 1993; Stanley Jevons Professor of Political Economy and Cobden Lecturer, School of Economic Studies, 1992–2008, now Professor Emeritus, Director, Policy Research in Engineering, Science and Technology, 1984–2008, and Co-executive Director, ESRC Centre for Research on Innovation and Competition, 1997–2006 (Executive Director, 1997), University of Manchester; *b* 20 March 1946; *m* 1967, Joan Shrouder; one *s* one *d*. *Educ:* Liverpool Collegiate High Sch.; Univ. of Manchester (BA 1967; MSc 1968). Lectr in Econs, Univ. of Manchester, 1967–74; Lectr, then Sen. Lectr in Econs, Univ. of Liverpool, 1974–80; University of Manchester: Prof. of Econs, 1980–2008, now Emeritus; Hd, Dept of Econs, 1986–89; Dean of Social Sci. Faculty, 1992–95; Mem. Court, 1992–2004 (Mem., Finance Cttee, 1977–2004); Interim Dean, Faculty of Med. and Human Scis, 2003–04. Vis. Prof. in Econs, Univ. of Queensland, 1996–; Adjunct Prof. of Econs, Curtin Univ. of Technol., 2008–. Vis. Fellow, Centre for Business Res., Cambridge Univ., 2007–. Member: ACARD, 1983–87; ACOST, 1987–92; MMC, 1991–97. President: Manchester Statistical Soc., 1992–94; Internat. J. A. Schumpeter Soc., 1999–2000. AcSS 2003. FRSA. *Publications:* (contrib.) The UK Economy, 1975; (jtly) Post Innovation Performance, 1986; (jtly) New Electronic Information: the UK database industry in its international context, 1987; (ed jtly) Barriers to Growth in Small Firms, 1989; The Enterprise Challenge: overcoming barriers to growth in small firms, 1990; (ed jtly) Evolutionary Theories of Economic and Technological Change, 1991; (ed jtly) Wealth from Diversity, 1996; Evolutionary Economics and Creative Destruction, 1998. *Address:* Manchester Institute of Innovation Research, University of Manchester, Harold Hankins Building, Booth Street West, Manchester M13 9QH.

METCALFE, Julian Edward, OBE 2014 (MBE 2000); Founder, 1986, Creative Director, 2003–08, Pret a Manger; Founder and Creative Director, Metcalfe's Food Company, since 2008; *b* 14 Dec. 1959; *s* of David Metcalfe and Alexa (*née* Boycun); one *d*; *m* 1st, 1993, Melanie Willson (marr. diss.); two *s*; 2nd, 2011, Brooke de Ocampo. *Educ:* Harrow; Central London Poly. (BSc). Founder, Itsu, 1997. *Recreation:* eating. *Address:* (office) 3rd Floor, 53 Parker Street, WC2B 5PT. *Club:* White's.

METCALFE, Julian Ross; HM Diplomatic Service, retired; Director of Advocacy, International Agency for Prevention of Blindness, 2010–12; *b* 24 Feb. 1956; *s* of late Patrick Ross Metcalfe and Marjory Gillian Metcalfe (*née* Gaze); *m* 1983, Rachel Mai Jones; one *d*. *Educ:* Horris Hill Sch.; Cheltenham Coll.; Univ. of Bristol (BSc Pols and Econs 1978); Univ. of Sussex (MA Econs 1981). Project Trust Volunteer, mentally handicapped children, S Africa, 1975; ODI Fellow serving as Health Planning Officer, Govt of Malaŵi, 1978–81; consultant, Commodities Res. Unit, 1982–83; FCO Econ. Advr, 1983–87; First Sec., Cairo, 1987–91; Southern Africa Dept, 1991–93, Eastern Adriatic Dept, 1993–95, FCO; Hd, UK Delegn, EC Monitoring Mission to Former Yugoslavia, 1995; Dep. Hd of Mission, Zagreb, 1995–97; Jt Hd, Eastern Adriatic Dept (dealing with Balkans), FCO, 1997–2000; Hd, Estate Strategy Unit, FCO, 2000–04; Dep. Perm. Rep. to the UN, Geneva, 2005–09. *Recreations:* camping, helping in garden. *E:* Julianmetcalfe@yahoo.com. *Club:* Royal Over-Seas League.

METCALFE, Stanley; *see* Metcalfe, J. S.

METCALFE, Stanley Gordon; Chairman: Queens Moat Houses plc, 1993–2001; Ranks Hovis McDougall PLC, 1989–93, retired (Managing Director, 1981–89, Chief Executive, 1984–89, and Deputy Chairman, 1987–89); *b* 20 June 1932; *s* of Stanley Hudson Metcalfe and Jane Metcalfe; *m* 1968, Sarah Harter; two *d*. *Educ:* Leeds Grammar Sch.; Pembroke Coll., Oxford (MA). Commnd Duke of Wellington's Regt, 1952. Trainee, Ranks, Hovis McDougall, 1956–59; Director, Stokes & Dalton, Leeds, 1963–66; Managing Director, McDougalls, 1966–69; Director, Cerebos Ltd, 1969–70; Managing Director: RHM Overseas Ltd, 1970–73; RHM Cereals Ltd, 1973–79; Director, Ranks Hovis McDougall Ltd, 1979. Member: Exec. Cttee, FDF, 1987–93 (Pres., 1990–92); Priorities Bd for R&D in Agriculture and Food, 1987–92; CBI President's Cttee, 1990–93; Council, Business in the Community, 1990–93. Chm., Adv. Bd, Inst. of Food Research, 1988–90. President, Nat. Assoc. of British and Irish Millers, 1978. *Recreations:* cricket, golf, theatre. *Address:* The Oast House, Lower Froyle, Alton, Hants GU34 4LX. *T:* (01420) 22310. *Clubs:* Boodle's, MCC; IZ, Arabs.

METCALFE, Stephen James; MP (C) South Basildon and East Thurrock, since 2010; *b* Walthamstow, 9 Jan. 1966; *s* of David John and Valerie Metcalfe; *m* 1988, Angela Claire Giblett; one *s* one *d*. *Educ:* Loughton Sch.; Buckhurst Hill Co. High Sch. Order Clerk, Burrup Matthieson, 1985–86; Metloc Printers Ltd: Sales Exec., 1986–87; Studio Manager, 1987–92; Dir, 1992–2011. Mem. (C) Epping Forest DC, 2003–07. Contested (C) Ilford S, 2005. PPS to Sec. of State for Justice, 2014–. Mem., Sci. and Technol. Select Cttee, 2010–15; Dep. Chm., Parly Scientific Cttee, 2014–. *Publications:* wine appreciation, theatre, Rugby, football. *Address:* House of Commons, SW1A 0AA. *T:* (020) 7219 7009. *E:* stephen.metcalfe.mp@parliament.uk.

METGE, Dame (Alice) Joan, DBE 1987; research anthropologist and writer; *b* 21 Feb. 1930; *d* of Cedric Leslie Metge and Alice Mary (*née* Rigg). *Educ:* Auckland Univ. (MA); London School of Economics (PhD). Jun. Lectr, Geography Dept, Auckland Univ., 1952; research and doctoral study, 1953–61; Lectr, Univ. Extension, Auckland Univ., 1961–64; University of Wellington: Sen. Lectr, Anthropology Dept, 1965–67, Associate Prof., 1968–88. Fifth Captain James Cook Res. Fellow, 1981–83. Hon. DLitt Auckland, 2001. Hutchinson Medal, LSE, 1958; Elsdon Best Meml Medal, Polynesian Soc., 1987; Te Rangi Hiroa Medal, Royal Soc. of NZ, 1997; Asia-Pacific Mediation Forum Peace Prize, 2006. *Publications:* A New Maori Migration, 1964; The Maoris of New Zealand, 1967, rev. edn 1976; (with Patricia Kinloch) Talking Past Each Other, 1978; In and Out of Touch, 1986; Te Kohao o Te Ngira, 1990; New Growth From Old, 1995; Korero Tahi-Talking Together, 2001; Tuamaka: the challenge of difference in Aotearoa New Zealand, 2010; Tauira: Maori methods of learning and teaching, 2015. *Recreations:* theatre, music, reading, gardening. *Address:* 3 Mariri Road, Onehunga, Auckland 1061, New Zealand. *T:* (9) 6345757.

METHAM, Patricia; education consultant, since 2014; National Lead for English, Office for Standards in Education, Children's Services and Skills, since 2013; *b* Cairo, 1 March 1945; *d* of John (Jack) Andrews and Jane Starrett Andrews; *m* 1st, 1966, Nicholas Hern (marr. diss.); two *d*; 2nd, 1986, Dr Tim Metham. *Educ:* Upper Chine Sch., Isle of Wight; Bristol Univ. (BA English and Drama). English and Drama Teacher: Dartford Girls' Grammar Sch., 1966–67; Sir Leo Schultz High Sch., Hull, 1967; Newland High Sch., Hull, 1967–72; Wimbledon High Sch., 1975–82 (School-Teacher Fellow, Merton Coll., Oxford, 1981); Head of English and Sixth Form, Francis Holland Sch., London, 1982–87; Head: Farlington Sch., Horsham, 1987–92; Ashford, Sch., 1992–97; Roedean Sch., 1997–2002; Principal, Internat. Regent's Sch., Thailand, 2003–05. HM Inspector of Schs, 2006–14. Vice Chm., Ind. Schs Exams Bd, 1999. JP, Horsham, then Ashford, 1991–97. *Publications:* editor of seven critical play texts. *Recreations:* theatre, choral singing, travel to centres of archaeological and cultural interest (in Europe, particularly), good food and good wine.

METHUEN, 8th Baron *cr* 1838; **James Paul Archibald Methuen-Campbell;** *b* Ludlow, 25 Oct. 1952; *s* of Christopher Paul Mansel Campbell Methuen-Campbell and Oona Methuen-Campbell (*née* Treherne); *S* cousin, 2014. *Educ:* Stowe Sch. Music critic, musicologist and author. *Publications:* Chopin Playing, 1981; (contrib.) Cambridge Companion to Chopin, 1992; Denton Welch: writer and artist, 2002; Claughton Pellew, 2015; past regular contribs to Records and Recording, Gramophone, The Times. *Recreations:* playing piano, photography. *Heir: half-b* Thomas Rice Mansel Methuen-Campbell, *b* 4 March 1977. *Address:* Corsham Court, Corsham, Wilts SN13 0BZ. *E:* jmethc@corc.fsbusiness.co.uk.

METHUEN, Richard St Barbe; QC 1997; a Recorder, since 2002; *b* 22 Aug. 1950; *s* of John Methuen and Rosemary Methuen; *m* 1974, Mary Catherine Griffiths, LLB, MA, *d* of David Howard Griffiths, OBE; one *s* two *d*. *Educ:* Marlborough College. Called to the Bar, Lincoln's Inn, 1972. Head of Chambers, 2000–05. Mediator in personal injury and clinical negligence work. *Address:* 12 King's Bench Walk, Temple, EC4Y 7EL. *E:* methuen@12kbw.co.uk.

METHUEN-CAMPBELL, family name of **Baron Methuen**.

METTERS, Dr Jeremy Stanley, CB 1994; FRCOG; Deputy Chief Medical Officer, Department of Health, 1989–99; HM Inspector of Anatomy, 1999–2005; *b* 6 June 1939; *s* of late Thomas Lee Metters and Henrietta Currey; *m* 1962, Margaret Howell; two *s* one *d*. *Educ:* Eton; Magdalene College, Cambridge; St Thomas' Hosp. (MB BChir 1963, MA 1965). MRCOG 1970, FRCOG 1982. House officer posts, St Thomas' Hosp. and Reading, 1963–66; Lectr in Obst. and Gyn., St Thomas' Hosp., 1968–70; Registrar in Radiotherapy, 1970–72; DHSS 1972; SPMO (Under Sec.), 1984; Dep. Chief Scientist, DHSS, later Dept of Health, 1986–89. Member: Council of Europe Cttee on Bioethics (formerly Ethical and Legal Problems relating to Human Genetics), 1983–89; ESRC, 1986–88. *Publications:* papers in med. and sci. jls. *Recreations:* DIY, steam preservation.

METTYEAR, His Honour Michael King; DL; a Circuit Judge, 1992–2015; *b* 22 Sept. 1946; *s* of Charles Frank Henry King and Vera May (*née* Moore); *m* 1984, Gail Stafford; one *s* one *d*. *Educ:* LLB London (external). Called to the Bar, Middle Temple, 1973; a Recorder, 1990–92; Hon. Recorder, Kingston upon Hull and ER of Yorks, 2003–14; a pt-time Justice of Grand Ct of Cayman Islands, 2012–. Member: Sentencing Adv. Panel, 1999–2004; Sentencing Guidelines Council, 2004–10. DL E Yorks, 2014. *Recreations:* tennis, travel, skiing.

METZ, David Henry, PhD; Visiting Professor, Centre for Transport Studies, University College London, since 2005; *b* 11 March 1941; *s* of Lewis and Esther Metz; *m* 1st, 1966, Marilyn Ann Yeatman (marr. diss. 1980); one *s*; 2nd, 1994, Monica Mary Threlfall. *Educ:* City of London Sch.; University Coll. London (BSc Chem., MSc Biochem.); King's Coll. London (PhD Biophysics). Virology Division, National Institute for Medical Research, 1967–76: Fellow, Helen Hay Whitney Foundn, 1967–69; Mem., MRC Scientific Staff, 1969–76; Res. Fellow, Dept of Microbiol., Harvard Med. Sch., and Children's Hosp. Med. Center, Boston, 1972–73; Dept of Energy, 1976–86; Dep. Dir-Gen., Office of Gas Supply, 1986–89; Dept of Energy, 1989–92; Chief Scientist, Dept of Transport, 1992–97; Dir, AgeNet, Wolfson Inst. of Preventive Medicine, 1997–2000. Vis. Prof., Centre for Ageing and Public Health, LSHTM, 2000–06. Non-executive Director: Camden and Islington Community Health Services NHS Trust, 2001–02; Camden PCT, 2002–11. Member: Mgt Bd, TRRL, 1993–96; Res. and Technol. Cttee, BR, 1994–96; Res. Adv. Council, NATS, 1997–99; Financial Services Consumer Panel, 2005–11. Mem. Mgt Bd, Oxford Dementia Centre, 1999–2001. *Publications:* Older, Richer, Fitter (with M. Underwood), 2005; The Limits to Travel, 2008; Peak Car: the future of travel, 2014; papers in sci. jls. *Address:* 32 Laurier Road, NW5 1SJ.

METZER, Anthony David Erwin; QC 2013; *b* Edgware, Middx, 19 July 1963; *s* of Kurt Metzer and Louise Taylor; *m* 1988, Dr Louise Sylvester; one *s* two *d*. *Educ:* Edgware Jun. Sch.; Haberdashers' Aske's Sch. for Boys; Wadham Coll., Oxford (BA Juris.); Inns of Court Sch. of Law. Called to the Bar, Middle Temple, 1987; in practice as a barrister, specialising in civil and criminal fraud, and civil actions against the police; Dr Johnson's Bldgs, 1988–90; Doughty St Chambers, 1990–2007; 23 Essex St, 2007–11; Argent Chambers, 2011–14; Hd of Chambers, Goldsmith Chambers, 2014–; Door Tenant, Exchange Chambers, 2014–; a part-time Immigration Judge, 2002–. *Publications:* (with Julian Weinberg) Criminal Litigation: first steps to survival, 1999. *Recreations:* theatre, music, football, cricket, meteorology. *Address:* Goldsmith Chambers, Goldsmith Building, Temple, EC4Y 7BL. *T:* (020) 7353 6802, *Fax:* (020) 7583 5255. *E:* a.metzer@goldsmithchambers.com.

MEWIES, Sandra Elaine, (Sandy); Member (Lab) Delyn, since 2003, and Commissioner, since 2011, National Assembly for Wales; *b* 16 Feb. 1950; *d* of Tom Oldland and Margaret Owens; *m* 1976, Paul Mewies; one *s*. *Educ:* Grove Park Girls' Grammar Sch.; Open Univ. (BA Hons). Journalist, 1967–87; marketing/PR, 1988–90; Community Care Co-ordinator, Clwyd, 1991–93; Lay Inspector of Schs, 1993–2002. Mem., Wrexham CBC, 1988–2004 (Mayor, 2000–01). Dir, Wales European Centre, 1997–2003; Bd Mem., N Wales Probation, 2000–03. Chm., Eur. and Ext. Affairs Cttee, 2003–10, Community and Culture Cttee, 2010–11, Nat. Assembly for Wales. Hon. Fellow, NE Wales Inst., later Glyndŵr Univ., 2002–. *Recreations:* reading, cooking. *Address:* National Assembly for Wales, Cardiff Bay, Cardiff CF99 1NA. *T:* 0300 200 7132, *Fax:* 0300 200 7285. *E:* sandy.mewies@assembly.wales; (constituency office) 64 Chester Street, Flint CH6 5DH. *T:* (01352) 763398.

MEXBOROUGH, 8th Earl of, *cr* 1766; **John Christopher George Savile;** Baron Pollington, 1753; Viscount Pollington, 1766; *b* 16 May 1931; *s* of 7th Earl of Mexborough, and Josephine Bertha Emily (*d* 1992), *d* of late Captain Andrew Mansel Talbot Fletcher; *S* father, 1980; *m* 1st, 1958, Lady Elizabeth Hariot (marr. diss. 1972; she *d* 1987), *d* of 6th Earl of Verulam; one *s* (one *d* decd); 2nd, 1972, Mrs Catherine Joyce Vivian, *d* of late J. K. Hope, CBE, DL; one *s* one *d*. *Educ:* MIMI. *Heir: s* Viscount Pollington, *qv*. *Address:* Old Manor House, Helmsley, York YO62 5AB. *T:* (01439) 771387. *Clubs:* White's; All England Lawn Tennis and Croquet; Air Squadron.

MEYER, Sir (Anthony) Ashley (Frank), 4th Bt *cr* 1910, of Shortgrove, Newport, Essex; *b* 23 Aug. 1944; *s* of Sir Anthony Meyer, 3rd Bt and Barbadee Violet Meyer (*née* Knight); *S* father, 2004; *m* 1966, Susan Mathilda (marr. diss. 1980), *d* of Charles Freestone; one *d*. *Educ:* Goldsmiths' Coll., London Univ. *Heir:* none.

MEYER, Catherine Irene Jacqueline, (Lady Meyer), CBE 2012; Founder and Chief Executive, Parents and Abducted Children Together, since 1999; *b* Baden-Baden, 26 Jan. 1953; *d* of late Maurice Laylle and of Olga Laylle; *m* 1997, Sir Christopher John Rome Meyer, *qv*; two step *s*, and two *s* by a previous marriage. *Educ:* Lycée Charles de Gaulle, London; University Coll. London (BA Hons). Account Executive: Merrill Lynch Inc., 1976–79; Dean Witter Ltd, 1979–80; E. F. Hutton and Co., 1980–85; Interdealer Broker, Tradition, 1992–93; Account Exec., Deutsche Bank, 1993–94; Sen. Account Exec., San Paulo Bank, 1994–96. Co-Founder, Internat. Centre for Missing and Exploited Children, 1998. Non-exec. Dir, LIFFE, 2003–08. Trustee, London Inst. for Math. Scis, 2013–14. Nat. Treas., Cons. Party, 2010–. *Publications:* Handbook on the Mechanism of the L.M.E. Option Market, 1982; Two Children Behind a Wall, 1997; They Are My Children Too, 1999. *Recreations:* ski-ing, porcelain painting, theatre. *Address:* c/o Parents and Abducted Children Together, 5/7 Vernon Yard, W11 2DX. *E:* cm@pact-online.org. *Clubs:* Walbrook, Ivy.

MEYER, Sir Christopher (John Rome), KCMG 1998 (CMG 1988); HM Diplomatic Service, retired; company director, consultant, writer and television documentary presenter; *b* 22 Feb. 1944; *s* of Flight Lieut R. H. R. Meyer (killed in action 1944) and late Mrs E. P. L. Meyer (subseq. Mrs A. B. Landells); *m* 1976, Françoise Elizabeth Hedges (marr. diss.), *d* of Air Cdre Sir Archibald Winskill, KCVO, CBE, DFC, AE; two *s*, and one step *s*; *m* 1997, Catherine Irene Jacqueline Laylle (*see* C. I. J. Meyer); two step *s*. *Educ:* Lancing College; Lycée Henri IV, Paris; Peterhouse, Cambridge (MA History; Hon. Fellow, 2002); Johns Hopkins Sch. of Advanced Internat. Studies, Bologna. Third Sec., FO, 1966–67; Army Sch. of Education, 1967–68; Third, later Second, Sec., Moscow, 1968–70; Second Sec., Madrid, 1970–73; First Sec., FCO, 1973–78; First Sec., UK Perm. Rep. to European Communities, 1978–82; Counsellor and Hd of Chancery, Moscow, 1982–84; Head of News Dept, FCO, 1984–88; Fellow, Center for Internat. Affairs, Harvard, 1988–89; Minister (Commercial), 1989–92, Minister and Dep. Hd of Mission, 1992–93, Washington; Press Sec. to Prime Minister (on secondment to Cabinet Office), 1994–96; Ambassador: to Germany, 1997; to USA, 1997–2003. Chm., Press Complaints Commn, 2003–09. Non-executive Director: GKN, 2003–10; Arbuthnot Banking Gp, 2007–; Member, International Advisory Board: British-American Business Inc., 2003–; Fleishman-Hillard, 2008–11; Chm., Adv. Bd, Pagefield, 2011–. Sen. Associate Fellow, RUSI, 2013–. Morehead-Cain Vis. Prof., Univ. of N Carolina, 2010. Documentary presenter: Mortgaged to the Yanks, 2006, Getting Our Way, 2010, BBC TV; Lying Abroad, 2006, How to Succeed at Summits, 2006, Corridors of Power, 2007, The Watchdog and the Feral Beast, 2009, BBC Radio 4; Networks of Power, Sky Atlantic, 2012. Gov., ESU, 2006–10. Pres., Printing Charity, 2011. Mem., Exec. Cttee, Pilgrims Soc., 2005–11. Trustee, Parents and Abducted Children Together, 2010–. Mem., Stationers' and Newspaper Makers' Co., 2009–; Freeman, City of London, 2009. *Publications:* DC Confidential, 2005; Getting Our Way, 2009; Only Child, 2013. *Clubs:* Garrick, Ivy, Walbrook; Metropolitan (Washington).

MEYER, Rabbi David; Executive Director, Partnerships for Jewish Schools, since 2015; *b* London, 23 June 1966; *s* of Benjamin Meyer and Maisie Meyer; *m* 1994, Meira K. Azose; three *s* two *d*. *Educ:* Hasmonean High Sch.; Kerem B'Yavneh Coll.; Jews' Coll. (BA Hons Jewish Studies 1989); Inst. of Educn, Univ. of London (PGCE 1990); City Univ. (MBA Mktg 1991); Kollel Pischei Teshuva (Rabbinical Ordination); Nat. Coll. for Sch. Leadership (NPQH 2007; Exec. Headteacher Cert. 2009). Ordained Rabbi, 1996; Exec. Dir, Jewish Assoc. for Business Ethics, 1996–97, Rabbinical Dir, 1997–2012; Hasmonean High School: Informal Educator and Dep. Headteacher, 1997–2005; Headteacher, 2005–09; Exec. Headteacher, 2009–15. Educnl consultant and lectr, 1994–; Educnl Programming, Yad Vashem, 1994–95; Sen. Lectr, Aish Hatorah, 1996–2000. *Recreations:* family, Daf Yomi, hiking, cycling, reading, trouble shooting, annoying his sister and brother, looking on the bright side of life. *Address:* Partnerships for Jewish Schools, Beit Meir, 44a Albert Road, NW4 2SJ.

MEYER, David Patrick; Strategy Consultant, Beacon Technology Services Ltd, since 2013; *b* Liverpool, 15 Nov. 1959; *s* of Denis Meyer and Joyce Meyer (*née* Harrison); *m* 1985, Emma Alden (marr. diss. 1993); one *d* (and one *d* decd). *Educ:* Brighton, Hove and Sussex Grammar Sch.; RMA Sandhurst; Army Staff Coll.; King's Coll. London (MA Internat. Studies 2006). FBCS 2006; CITP 2006. Royal Signals Officer, 1979–2010; CO 14th Signal Regt (Electronic Warfare), 1999–2001; Comdr, 11th Signal Bde, 2003–05; Dep. Chief Inf. Officer, MoD, 2008–10; Chief Inf. Officer, FCO, 2010–13. Mem., Ofcom Spectrum Adv. Bd, 2009– (Chm., 2010–). MInstD. *Recreations:* reading, politics, current affairs, technology. *E:* david@btsl.co.uk.

MEYER, Julie Marie, Hon. MBE 2012; Founder and Chief Executive Officer, Ariadne Capital, 2000–12; Founder, Entrepreneur Country, since 2009; Managing Partner, Ariadne Capital Entrepreneurs Fund, since 2011; *b* 28 Aug. 1966. *Educ:* Valparaiso Univ. (BA Dist. 1988); INSEAD (MBA 1997). Consultant: AC3, Paris, 1989–91; Meyer Gp, Paris, 1992–93; Account Manager, Cunningham Communication, 1994–97; Associate, Roland Berger & Partner, Paris, 1997; Co-Founder and Chief Marketing Officer, First Tuesday, 1998–2000; Asst Dir, NewMedia Investors, 1998–99. Member, Board of Directors: INSEAD, 2009–; Vestergaard Frandsen, 2010–; Group Silverline, 2012–; Quill; Taggster. *Recreations:* Pastis and Amaretto, any kind of sport, taking weekend trips, genealogy, carrying on family traditions, finding John Galt, building Entrepreneur Country. *Address:* Ariadne Capital, 17–19 Cockspur Street, SW1Y 5BL.

MEYER, Prof. Julienne Elizabeth, CBE 2015; PhD; Professor of Nursing Care for Older People, City University London, since 1999; Executive Director, My Home Life, since 2007; *b* Manchester, 31 Aug. 1956; *d* of Neil Meyer and Margaret Meyer; *m* 1979, Martin Davies; one *s*. *Educ:* Broad Oak Primary Sch.; Fallowfield C of E High Sch.; Leeds Poly. (BSc Nursing; RN); Garnett Coll., Roehampton (Cert Ed (FE); RNT); King's Coll. London (MSc Nursing; PhD Nursing 1995). Clin. nurse, Charing Cross Hosp., London, 1978–84; Nurse Tutor, West Thames Sch. of Nursing, 1984–87; Res. Fellow, 1987–90, Lectr in Nursing, 1990–96, KCL; Reader in Adult Nursing, City Univ. London, 1996–99. Adjunct Professor: Univ. of South Australia, 2003–10, 2013–; Griffith Univ., 2010–; Federation Univ. Australia, 2014–; Vis. Prof., Univ. of Wisconsin-Madison, 2011–. *Publications:* Lay Participation in Care in a Hospital Setting: an action research study, 2001; (ed jtly) Understanding Care Homes: a research and development perspective, 2008; articles in acad. and professional jls, 1998–. *Recreations:* family life, book club, film club, supper club. *Address:* Nursing Division, School of Health Sciences, City University London, Northampton Square, EC1V 0HB. *T:* (020) 7040 5791/5776. *E:* j.meyer@city.ac.uk.

MEYER, Michael Siegfried; Chairman, Remote Controlled Lighting Ltd, since 2001; General Partner, EMESS Capital LLP, since 2007; Executive Director, Domes of Silence Holdings Ltd, since 2005; *b* 2 May 1950; *s* of late Ernest Meyer and of Gretta Gillis; *m* 1st,

1984, Jill Benedict (marr. diss. 1990); one *d*; 2nd, 1994, Livia Hannah, *o d* of Maj.-Gen. Monty Green. *Educ:* South African College School, Cape Town. FCIS. Company Secretary, Heenan Beddow International, 1973–75; Director, 1976–79, Chief Exec., 1980–82, Chm. and Chief Exec., 1983–2000, EMESS plc; Man. Dir, Brilliant Hldgs GmbH, Germany, 1987–2000; Pres., Alsy Lighting Inc., 1988–2000; Chm., Supervisory Bd, Eclatec SA, France, 1989–2000; Chm. and CEO, Direct Message plc, 2002–05; Director: Meyer Leclerc & Co., 1982–2010; Design Trust, 1994–2001; Aluminium Shapes Ltd, 2002–; Windmill Extrusions Ltd, 2002–; Construct London, 2005–07; Partner, EMESS Capital 202 LLP, 2007–; non-executive Director: Royal Sovereign Group, 1986–90; Henderson Smaller Cos Investment Trust, 1990–2002; Walker Greenbank, 1991–97; Lontoh Coal Ltd, 2011–. FRSA. *Recreations:* watching cricket, Rugby, theatre and ballet. *Address:* Aluminium Shapes Ltd, 18–19 Princewood Road, Corby, Northants NN17 4AP. *Clubs:* Naval and Military, MCC, Lansdowne; Western Province Cricket (Cape Town); Wanderers (Johannesburg).

MEYER, Stephen Richard; Chief Inspector, Marine Accident Investigation Branch, Department for Transport (formerly Department for Transport, Local Government and the Regions), 2002–10; *b* 28 Aug. 1950; *s* of Ernest Frederick Meyer and Rita Agnes Meyer (*née* Humphreys); *m* 1977, Erica Michelle Diana, *d* of late Captain N. Hall, Jersey; two *d*. *Educ:* Merchant Taylors' Sch., Crosby; BRNC, Dartmouth. Joined RN, 1968; served HMS Tenby, Charybdis, Beachampton, Apollo, and USS Raleigh, 1969–74; loaned Sultan of Oman's Navy, i/c Sultan's Naval Vessel Al Mansur, 1975; comd HMS Bildeston, 1975–77; Flag Lieut to Adm. Sir Henry Leach, 1977–79; qualified principal warfare officer, 1980; served HM ships Coventry and Broadsword, 1980–83; commanded: HMS Galatea, 1985–86; HMS Liverpool, 1986–88; HMS Fearless, 1990–91; Head of Maritime Intelligence, 1992–93; Dir of Navy Plans, 1994–97; comd, HMS Illustrious, 1997–98; Head of Jt Force 2000 Study Team, 1998; Military Advr to High Representative, Sarajevo, 1999–2000; Comdr UK Task Gp, UK Maritime Forces, and Comdr Anti Submarine Warfare Striking Force, 2000–01; Chief of Staff, Permt Jt HQ, 2001–02; retd in rank of Rear-Adm. Mem., Safety Panel of Experts, Cruise Lines Internat. Assoc., 2012–. Trustee: CHIRP Charitable Trust, 2003–10; Blind Veterans UK, 2012–. *Recreations:* family, home, friends. *Address:* c/o Naval Secretary, Leach Building, Whale Island, Portsmouth PO2 8BY.

MEYLER, John William F.; *see* Forbes-Meyler.

MEYRIC HUGHES, Henry Andrew Carne; independent curator and consultant; President, International Foundation Manifesta (formerly European Visual Arts Manifestation), 1995–2007 (Founding Board Member, since 1993; Chairman, 1995–2006); Honorary President, International Association of Art Critics, Paris, since 2008 (President, 2002–08); *b* 1 April 1942; *s* of late Reginald Richard Meyric Hughes and of Jean Mary Carne Meyric Hughes (*née* Pratt); *m* 1968, Alison Hamilton Faulds; one *s* one *d*. *Educ:* Shrewsbury Sch.; Univs of Rennes and Munich; University Coll., Oxford (BA Hons); Univ. of Sussex (MA). British Council, 1968–92: Berlin, Lima, Paris, Milan, London; Dir, Fine Arts Dept, later Visual Arts Dept, 1986–92; Dir of Exhibns, South Bank Centre (Hayward Gall., Nat. Touring Exhibns, Arts Council Collection), 1992–96. British Comr, Venice Biennale and São Paulo Bienal, 1986–92; Official Comr, XXXIII Council of Europe exhibn, London, Barcelona and Berlin, 1995–96; Cypriot Pavilion, Venice Biennale, 2003; Co-curator: The Romantic Spirit in German Art, 1790–1990, Edinburgh, London, Munich, 1994; Blast to Freeze: British Art in the Twentieth Century, Wolfsburg and Toulouse, 2002–03; The Desire for Freedom: art in Europe since 1945, XXXth Council of Europe exhibn, Berlin, Milan, Tallinn, Krakow, Thessaloniki, Prague, Brussels and accompanying progs, 2012–15; Associate Curator, The Age of Modernism, Berlin, 1997. Dir, Riverside Trust, 1986–95; Mem. Court, RCA, 1986–92; Mem., Faculty of Fine Arts, British Sch. at Rome, 1988–94. Board Member: Internat. Assoc. of Curators of Contemp. Art, 1992–97; Konsthallen, Göteborg, 1995–2000; Inst. of Internat. Visual Arts, 1996–; Pres., British Sect., 1988–91, Mem., Adv. Bd, 2012–, AICA. Special Advr, Council of Europe exhibns, 2008– (Mem., Gp of Consultants, 2006–10). Pres. of Jury, Diploma examinations, École Nationale Supérieure des Beaux-Arts, Paris, 2004; Ext. Examiner, MA Curating Contemp. Art prog., RCA, 2011–13. Member: Cttee of Mgt, Matt's Gall., London, 1993–; Scientific Committee: Museum Moderner Kunst Stiftung Ludwig Wien, 2001–02; Galleria d'Arte Moderna, Bologna, 2001–05; Archive de la Critique d'Art, Rennes, 2002– (Mem., Adv. Bd, 2002–); Dox Centre for Contemporary Art, Prague, 2004–; Critique d'Art, 2010–. Trustee, Arnolfini Gall., Bristol, 2006–13. Chm., UK-China John Moores Critics Awards, 2012–13; Chair, Internat. Awards for Art Criticism, 2014–; Member, Jury: Turner Prize, 1988; Biennale de Cetinje, 2002; Caribbean Biennial, 2003; Gwangju Biennale, 2004 (Chm.); Premio Furla, Bologna, 2005; Dakar Biennial, 2006. Silver Medal, Czech Soc. for Internat. Cultural Relations, 1986. Officier, l'Ordre Nat. des Arts et des Lettres (France), 1997; Bundesverdienstkreuz (Germany), 2002. *Publications:* (contrib.) Il Dono/The Gift: generous offerings threatening hospitality in art, 2001; (ed jtly) From Art School to Professional Practice, 2008; (contrib.) Curare l'arte, 2008; (contrib.) Le Demi-siècle de Pierre Restany, 2009; (contrib.) Different Avant-Gardes in Central and East Europe after World War II, 2009; (ed jtly) AICA in the Age of Globalisation, 2010; (ed jtly) African Contemporary Art: critical concerns, 2011; (ed) The European Idea in Art and Art History, 2015; articles on visual arts and cultural relations, UK and overseas, 1966–, incl. contrib. to Burlington Mag., Critique d'Art, Manifesta Jl, THES. *Recreations:* music, Europe. *Address:* 13 Ashchurch Grove, W12 9BT. *T:* and *Fax:* (020) 8749 4098. *E:* henry.meyrichughes@tiscali.co.uk.

MEYRICK, Sir George (Christopher Cadafael Tapps Gervis), 7th Bt *cr* 1791, of Hinton Admiral; *b* 10 March 1941; *s* of Sir George David Eliott Tapps Gervis Meyrick, 6th Bt, MC and Ann, *d* of late Clive Miller; *S* father, 1988; *m* 1968, Jean Louise, *d* of late Lord William Montagu Douglas Scott and of Lady William Montagu Douglas Scott; two *s* one *d*. *Educ:* Eton; Trinity College, Cambridge (MA). FRICS. *Heir:* *s* George William Owen Tapps Gervis Meyrick [*b* 3 April 1970; *m* 2006, Candida Clark; one *s* two *d*]. *Address:* Hinton Admiral, Christchurch, Dorset BH23 7DU; Bodorgan, Isle of Anglesey LL62 5LW. *Club:* Boodle's.

MEYRICK, Rt Rev. Jonathan; *see* Lynn, Bishop Suffragan of.

MEYRICK, (Sir) Timothy (Thomas Charlton), (5th Bt *cr* 1880, of Bush, Pembrokeshire, but does not use the title); *b* 5 Nov. 1963; *s* of Sir David John Charlton Meyrick, 4th Bt and of Penelope Anne (*née* Marsden-Smedley); *S* father, 2004, but his name does not appear on the Official Roll of the Baronetage; *m* 2003, Natasha Domenica Bernabei. *Educ:* Eton; Bristol Univ. *Heir:* *b* Simon Edward Meyrick [*b* 20 Sept. 1965; *m* 1989, Jennifer Amanda Irvine; one *s* one *d*].

MICHAEL, Rt Hon. Alun (Edward); PC 1998; JP; Police and Crime Commissioner (Lab) for South Wales, since 2012; *b* 22 Aug. 1943; *m* 1966, Mary Crawley; two *s* three *d*. *Educ:* Colwyn Bay GS; Keele Univ. (BA Hons English and Phil.). Journalist, South Wales Echo, 1966–71; Youth and Community Worker, Cardiff, 1972–84; Area Community Education Officer, Grangetown and Butetown, 1984–87. Mem., Cardiff City Council, 1973–89 (sometime Chm., Finance, Planning, Performance Review, and Econ. Devel, and Chief Whip, Labour Gp). Dir, Cardiff and Vale Enterprise. Mem. (Lab and Co-op) Wales Mid and West, and First Sec. for Wales, Nat. Assembly for Wales, 1999–2000. MP (Lab and Co-op) Cardiff S and Penarth, 1987–Oct. 2012. An Opposition Whip, 1987–88; Opposition frontbench spokesman: on Welsh Affairs, 1988–92; on Home Affairs and the voluntary sector, 1992–97; Minister of State, Home Office, 1997–98; Sec. of State for Wales, 1998–99; Minister of State (Minister for Rural Affairs and Local Envmtl Quality, DEFRA, 2001–05; Minister of State, DTI, 2005–06. Chairman: Co-operative Parly Gp, 1988–92; Parly Friends of Co-operative Ideal, 1988–92; Member: Nat. Exec., Co-op. Party, 1988–92; Parly Cttee, Co-op. Union, 1988–94. Chairman: All-Party Gp on Alcohol Misuse, 1991–93, 1998–; All-Party, Penal Affairs Gp; Parly Friends of WNO, 1991–97; Jt Chm., All-Party Gp on Somalia, 1989–97; Vice-Chm., All-Party Penal Affairs Gp, 1991–97; Jt Sec., All-Party Gp for Further and Tertiary Educn, 1990–97; Sec., All-Party Panel for Personal Social Services, 1990–93. Formerly: Mem. Bd, Crime Concern; Vice-Pres., YHA; Mem. Exec., Nat. Youth Bureau. Formerly Vice-Pres., Bldg Socs Assoc. Dep. Chm., Cardiff Bay Opera House Trust, 1994–96; Mem. Bd, Cardiff and Vale Enterprise, 1982–93; plays leading role locally in community develt projects. FRSA 2003. JP Cardiff, 1972 (Chm., Cardiff Juvenile Bench, 1986–87; formerly Mem., S Glam Probation Cttee). *Recreations:* long-distance running, mountain walking, opera, listening to classical music, member of the Parliamentary Choir, reading. *Clubs:* Penarth Labour; Grange Stars; Earlswood.

MICHAEL, Sir Duncan, Kt 2001; PhD; FREng; Chairman, Ove Arup Partnership, 1995–2000 (Director, 1977–2002; Trustee, 1977–2006; Chairman of Trustees, 1995–2004); Trustee, Ove Arup Foundation, since 1995; *b* 26 May 1937; *s* of Donald Michael and Lydia Cameron MacKenzie; *m* 1960, Joan Clay; two *s* one *d*. *Educ:* Beauly Public School; Inverness Royal Academy. BSc Edinburgh; PhD Leeds. FICE 1975; FIStructE 1975; FREng (FEng 1984); FHKIE 1981; FRSE 2005. Engr, Dunoan Logan Contractors, 1955–58; Lectr, Leeds Univ., 1961; Engr, Ove Arup Partnership, 1962; Chm., Arup China/Hong Kong, 1978–88. Member: Council, IStructE, 1977–80, 1983–89; Jt Bd of Moderators of Engrg Instns, 1985–92; SE Asia Trade Adv. Group, BOTB, 1982–85; Civil Engineering Cttee, SERC, 1980–83; Council, Royal Acad. Engrg, 1994–2005 (Chm., Awards Cttee, 1995–99; Vice Pres., 1999–2005; new HQ project bd, 2004–12); Membership Cttee Panel, RSE, 2006–09; Vice-Chm., Council of Tall Buildings & Urban Habitat, 1980–96; Member: Educn and Trng Affairs Cttee, CBI, 1997–2003; State of the Nation Assessment Panel, ICE, 2000–03; Adv. Bd, Master of Research, Univ. of Dundee, 2000–07 (Chm., 2000–04); Supervisor, Arup/RAE Chair in Fire Safety, 2007–, Fellow, Sociology of Fire Safety, 2011–, Edinburgh Univ.; Chm., Engrg Adv. Bd, Aberdeen Univ., 1998–2012; Mentor: Professors of Design for Sustainable Engrg, Univ. of Cambridge, 2000–05; Imperial Coll., London, 2001–09; Member: Industrial Adv. Cttee, Churchill Coll., Cambridge, 2000–05; Academic Adv. Bd, Univ. of Highlands and Islands proj., 1999–2001; Bd, Housing Corp., 2000–08 (Chairman: Investment Cttee, 2002–08; Gold Awards Judging Panel, 2005–08); Mgt Bd, Scottish Res. Partnership in Engrg, 2007–11; Dir, GB Social Housing plc, 2010–; land assets advr to Chm., UCL Health Trust, 2005–08; Design Advr, Planning Cttee, London Bor. of Merton, 2007–. Fellowship of Engrg Vis. Prof., Aberdeen Univ., 1989–94; Vis. Prof., Leeds Univ., 1990–94. Trustee: Lydia Michael Trust, 2000–; Useful Simple Trust, 2009–. Pres., NW Wimbledon Residents' Assoc., 2010–. Fellow, Inst. of Scottish Shipbldrs and Engrs, 2000; Mem., Smeatonian Soc. of Civil Engrs, 2001. Hon. FRIBA 2009. Hon. DEng: Abertay Dundee, 1997; UMIST, 1999; Hon. DSc: Aberdeen, 2001; Robert Gordon, 2003; Strathclyde, 2005; Edinburgh, 2007. Gold Medal, IStructE, 2000. Jt Ed., Engrg and Philosophy Monist, 2006–09; Mem., Editl Adv. Bd, Philosophy of Engrg, 2009–. *Publications:* Skyscrapers, 1987; lectures and engineering papers in technical jls. *Recreations:* garden, lecturing, Scottish archaeology, opera. *Address:* 3 High Cedar Drive, SW20 0NU. *Clubs:* Caledonian, London Scottish Wimbledon.

MICHAEL, George; singer, songwriter and producer; *b* 25 June 1963; *né* Georgios Kyriacos Panayiotou; *s* of Jack Kyriacus Panayiotou and late Lesley Panayiotou. *Educ:* Bushey Meads Sch. Formed band, The Executive, 1981; co-singer, Wham!, 1981–86; solo singer, 1986–; nat. and internat. tours. *Albums include:* with Wham!: Fantastic, 1983; Make it Big, 1984; Music from the Edge of Heaven, 1985; The Final, 1986; solo: Faith, 1987; Listen Without Prejudice, 1989; Older, 1996; Songs from the Last Century, 1999; Patience, 2004. *Publications:* (with Tony Parsons) Bare: George Michael, his own story, 1990. *Address:* c/o Connie Filippello Publicity, 49 Portland Road, W11 4LJ; c/o Sony Music Entertainment UK, 9 Derry Street, W8 5HY.

MICHAEL, Prof. Ian David Lewis; King Alfonso XIII Professor of Spanish Studies, University of Oxford, 1982–2003, now Emeritus; Fellow, Exeter College, Oxford, 1982–2003, now Emeritus; *b* 26 May 1936; *o s* of late Cyril George Michael and Glenys Morwen (*née* Lewis). *Educ:* Neath Grammar Sch.; King's Coll., London (BA First Class Hons Spanish 1957; FKC 2002); PhD Manchester 1967. University of Manchester: Asst Lectr in Spanish, 1957–60; Lectr in Spanish, 1960–69; Sen. Lectr in Spanish, 1969–70; University of Southampton: Prof. of Spanish and Hd of Spanish Dept, 1971–82; Dep. Dean, Faculty of Arts, 1975–77, 1980–82; Sen. Curator and Chm., Univ. Library Cttee, 1980–82; Oxford University: Curator, Taylor Instn, 1994–2000; Chm., Faculty Bd of Mod. Langs, 1999–2000. Leverhulme Faculty Fellow in European Studies (at Madrid), 1977–78; first British-Spanish Foundn Vis. Prof., Complutensian Univ., Madrid, 1993–94. Member: Gp of Three for Spain (Humanities research review), Eur. Science Foundn, 1987; Welsh Acad. (Eng. Lang. Section), 1995–; Corresp. Mem., Royal Spanish Acad., 2009. Pres., Assoc. of Hispanists of GB and Ire., 1990–92; Pres., Oxford Medieval Soc., 2002–03; Mem., Oxford Soc., Madrid, 2004–; Trustee, Nat. Library of Spain, 2009–14. Comdr, Order of Isabel la Católica (Spain), 1986. *Publications:* The Treatment of Classical Material in the Libro de Alexandre, 1970; Spanish Literature and Learning to 1474, in, Spain: a Companion to Spanish studies, 1973, 3rd edn 1977; The Poem of the Cid, 1975, new edn 1984; Poema de Mio Cid, 1976, 2nd edn 1979; Gwyn Thomas, 1977; chapter on Poem of My Cid in New Pelican Guide to English Literature. I ii, 1983; (ed) Sound on Vision: studies on Spanish cinema, 1999; (ed) Context, Meaning and Reception of Celestina, 2000; Gonzalo de Berceo, Miracles of Our Lady, 2006; (with J. C. Bayo) Cantar de Mio Cid, 2008; articles in various learned jls and Festschriften; *as David Serafín:* Saturday of Glory, 1979 (John Creasey Meml Award, CWA, 1980); Madrid Underground, 1982; Christmas Rising, 1982; The Body in Cadiz Bay, 1985; Port of Light, 1987; The Angel of Torremolinos, 1988. *Recreations:* writing pseudonymous fiction; opera. *Address:* Calle Goya, 57 (buzón 10), 28001 Madrid, Spain. *T:* (91) 5769218. *E:* iandavidlm@gmail.com.

MICHAEL, Sir Jonathan, Kt 2005; FRCP; Chief Executive, Oxford Radcliffe Hospitals NHS Trust, since 2010; *b* 21 May 1945; *s* of late Ian Lockie Michael, CBE; *m* 1st, 1975, Jacqueline Deluz (marr. diss. 1992); one *s* three *d*; 2nd, 2005, Karen E. Young. *Educ:* Bristol Grammar Sch.; St Thomas's Hosp. Med. Sch., London Univ. (MB BS 1970). MRCS 1970; MRCP 1973, FRCP 1985. Consultant Physician and Nephrologist, Queen Elizabeth Hosp., Birmingham, 1980–2000; Med. Dir, 1994–97, Chief Exec., 1997–2000, University Hosp. Birmingham NHS Trust; Chief Exec., Guy's and St Thomas' Hosp. NHS Trust, then NHS Foundn Trust, 2000–07; Man. Dir, BT Health, BT Global Services, 2007–09. Chm., Inquiry into access to healthcare for people with learning disabilities, 2007 (report, Healthcare for All, 2008). Chairman: Assoc. UK Univ. Hosps, 2004–07; Bd of NHS Foundn Trust Network, 2006–07. Trustee, King's Fund, 2012–. Gov., Edgbaston High Sch. for Girls, Birmingham, 1988–2000 (Chm. Govs, 1997–2000; Vice-Pres., 2000–05). FKC 2005. *Publications:* contrib. articles on nephrology and medical science. *Address:* Oxford Radcliffe NHS Trust, Headley Way, Headington, Oxford OX3 9DU.

MICHAEL, Peter Anthony, CBE 1998; Director, Central Policy, HM Revenue and Customs, 2008–11; *b* 2 July 1954; *s* of Taxis Michael and Helen Marie Teresa Michael; *m* 1989, Joanne Elizabeth Angel; two *d*. *Educ:* Pierrepont Sch.; City of London Univ. (Dip. English Law 1976). HM Treasury: Policy Advr, Industrial Policy Div., 1978–79; Private Secretary: to Minister of State (Lords), 1981; to Minister of State (Commons), 1982; Board of Inland Revenue, later HM Revenue and Customs: Policy Adviser: Capital Taxes Div.,

1985–89; Internat. Div., 1989–90; Asst Dir, EC Unit, Internat. Div., 1990–98; Director: EU Div., 1998–2000; EU Coordination and Strategy, Internat., 2000–01; Tax Law Rewrite Project, 2001–03; Revenue Policy: Strategy and Co-ordination, 2003–05; Dep. Dir (formerly Dir, Policy Improvement and Professionalism), Central Policy, 2005–08. *Recreations:* music, fishing, IT.

MICHAEL, Sir Peter (Colin), Kt 1989; CBE 1983; Chairman: Classic FM, 1993–2008 (Director, 1991–2008); Pilot Investment Trust, 1993–97; *b* 17 June 1938; *s* of Albert and Enid Michael; *m* 1962, Margaret Baldwin; two *s*. *Educ:* Whitgift Sch., Croydon; Queen Mary Coll., Univ. of London (BSc Elec. Engrg; Fellow, 1983). Chairman: Micro Consultants Group, 1969–85; Quantel Ltd, 1974–89; Databasix Ltd, 1986–88; UEI plc, 1986–89 (Dep. Chm., 1981–85); Cray Electronics, 1989–93. Dir, Rutherford Asset Management, 1995–97; non-executive Director: GWR Gp plc, 1996–2005; Neverfail Holdings Ltd, 2001–; GCap Media plc, 2005–08. Chairman: Peter Michael Winery, Calif, 1982–; Donnington Valley Hotel, 1991–; The Vineyard at Stockcross, 1997–; Pelican Cancer Centre, 1999–; Virtual Music Stores Ltd, 2000–08. Member: Adv. Council for Applied R&D, 1982–85; NCB, 1983–86; ACARD Sub-Gp on Annual Review of Govt Funded R&D, 1985–86; Technol. Requirements Bd, DTI, 1986–88; Adv. Cttee, Royal Mint, 1999–2007; Modern Collection Cttee, 2006–09, Wine Sub-cttee, 2006–09, Goldsmiths' Co. Paper on City financing of electronics companies to PITCOM, 1988. Chairman: Royal Soc. of British Sculptors Appeal, 1992; Chelsea Harbour '93 Internat. Sculpture Exhibn Appeal; The Sculpture Company, 1995–99. Mem. Council, RCA, 2012–. Chm., Greenham Common Community Trust, 1996–. Humphrey Davies Lecture, QMC, 1984. Freeman, City of London, 1984; Liveryman, Goldsmiths' Co., 1988 (Freeman, 1984). CCMI (CBIM 1982). FRSA 1984. Hon. FBKSTS 1981. Hon. LLD Reading, 2004. The Guardian Young Businessman of the Year, 1982. *Recreations:* tennis, ski-ing, opera, classical music, wine, sculpture, writing rhyme. *Address:* (office) Buckingham House, West Street, Newbury, Berks RG14 1BE. *T:* (01635) 552502.

MICHAELS, Adrian Robert; Director, FirstWord Media Ltd, since 2014; *b* London, 8 Sept. 1969; *s* of Barry and Naomi Michaels; *m* 2000, Elena Lugli; two *d*. *Educ:* University Coll. Sch., Hampstead; Trinity Coll., Oxford (BA PPE). With Financial Times, 1993–2008: Americas Page Ed., 1997–99; NY corresp., 1999–2004; Milan corresp., 2004–08; Telegraph Media Group: Gp Foreign Ed., 2008–11; Editl Dir, Commercial, 2011–14. *Recreations:* golf, cheese. *Address:* FirstWord Media Ltd, 368 City Road, EC1V 2QA. *E:* info@firstword.co.uk. *Clubs:* MCC (Associate Mem.); Addington Golf.

MICHAELS, Prof. Leslie, MD; FRCPath, FRCP(C); Professor of Pathology, Institute of Laryngology and Otology, London University, 1973–90 (Dean, 1976–81); Emeritus Professor, Department of Histopathology, Royal Free and University College Medical School, University of London (formerly University College and Middlesex School of Medicine, then University College London Medical School), since 1990; *b* 24 July 1925; *s* of Henry and Minnie Michaels; *m* Edith (*née* Waldstein); two *d*. *Educ:* Parmiter's Sch., London; King's Coll., London; Westminster Med. Sch., London (MB, BS; MD). FRCPath 1963, FRCP(C) 1962. Asst Lectr in Pathology, Univ. of Manchester, 1955–57; Lectr in Path., St Mary's Hosp. Med. Sch., London, 1957–59; Asst Prof. of Path., Albert Einstein Coll. of Medicine, New York, 1959–61; Hosp. Pathologist, Northern Ont, Canada, 1961–70; Sen. Lectr, Inst. of Laryngol. and Otol., 1970–73. *Publications:* Pathology of the Larynx, 1984; Ear, Nose and Throat Histopathology, 1987, 2nd edn 2001; scientific articles in jls of medicine, pathology and otolaryngology. *Recreations:* reading, music, walking. *Address:* Romany Ridge, Hillbrow Road, Bromley, Kent BR1 4JL.

MICHAELS-MOORE, Anthony; *see* Moore.

MICHEL, Caroline Jayne, (Lady Evans of Temple Guiting); Chief Executive Officer, Peters Fraser & Dunlop, since 2007; *b* Harrogate, 4 April 1959; *d* of Wolfgang Michel and Valerie Michel (*née* Cryer); *m* 1991, Matthew Evans (*see* Baron Evans of Temple Guiting); two *s* one *d*. *Educ:* Oakdene Sch.; Univ. of Edinburgh (BA Sanskrit 1980; MA). Chatto & Windus; Jonathan Cape; Bloomsbury Publishing; Orion; Publisher: Vintage, 1993–2003; Harper Press, 2003–05; CEO William Morris Agency, 2005–07. Chair, BFI Trust, 2011– (Gov., BFI, 2003–09). Member: Adv. Cttee, Booker Prize Foundn, 1994–2001; Veuve Clicquot Business Woman Award Panel, 2011–; Govt Adv. Panel on public library service in England, 2014–. Trustee: Hay Festival, 2010–; Somerset House, 2013–. FRSA. *Recreation:* reading. *Address:* Peters Fraser & Dunlop, Drury House, 34–43 Russell Street, WC2B 5HA. *T:* (020) 7344 1055. *E:* cmichel@pfd.co.uk. *Clubs:* Groucho, Hurlingham, Ivy, 5 Hertford Street.

MICHEL, Prof. (Christopher) Charles, DPhil; FRCP; Professor of Physiology, Imperial College School of Medicine (formerly St Mary's Hospital Medical School), 1984–2000, now Emeritus; Senior Research Investigator, Imperial College London, since 2000; *b* 23 March 1938; *s* of late Maurice and May Michel; *m* 1965, Rosalind McCrink; one *s* one *d*. *Educ:* Leeds Grammar Sch.; Queen's Coll., Oxford (BA 1959, 1st cl. Physiol.; MA, DPhil 1962; BM BCh 1965). MRCP 1986, FRCP 1996. US Public Health Postdoctoral Res. Fellow, 1962; Oxford University: Deptl Demonstrator in Physiol., 1964–67; Univ. Lectr in Physiol., 1967–84; Fellow and Praelector in Physiol., Queen's Coll., 1966–84. Lectures: Oliver-Sharpey, RCP, 1985; Annual Prize Review, Physiol. Soc., 1987; Starling Centenary, World Congress for Microcirculation, 1996; Haliburton, KCL, 2000; Zweifach Meml, UCSD, 2001. Sec., Physiol Soc., 1980–83; Chm., RN Personnel Res. Cttee, 1991–96, Army Personnel Res. Cttee, 1993–94, MRC. Hon. Member: Amer. Physiol. Soc., 1993; Brit. Microcirculation Soc., 2001; Physiol Soc., 2001. Malpighi Prize, Eur. Soc. for Micro-circulation, 1984; Nishimaru-Tsuchiya Internat. Award, Japanese Soc. for Microcirculation, 2010. *Publications:* (ed with E. M. Renkin) American Handbook of Physiology: the microcirculation, 1984; articles in learned jls. *Recreations:* walking, ornithology, reading. *Address:* Sundial House, High Street, Alderney, Channel Islands GY9 3UG.

MICHEL, Prof. Dr Hartmut; Director, Max Planck Institut of Biophysics, Frankfurt am Main, since 1987; *b* Ludwigsburg, W Germany, 18 July 1948; *s* of Karl Michel and Frieda Michel; *m* (marr. diss.); one *s* one *d*. *Educ:* Universities of: Tübingen (Dip. in biochem.); Würzburg (PhD); Munich (habilitation for biochemistry, 1986). Res. associate with D. Oesterhelt, Univ. of Würzburg, 1977–79; group leader in D. Oesterhelt's dept, Max-Planck-Inst. of Biochemistry, Martinsried, until 1987. Mem., German Sci. Council, 2004–10. For. Mem., Royal Soc., 2005. Various prizes, including: Biophysics Prize of Amer. Phys. Soc., 1986; Otto Klung Prize for Chemistry, 1986; (jtly) Otto Bayer Prize, 1988; (jtly) Nobel Prize for Chemistry, 1988; Keilin Medal, Biochemical Soc., 2008. *Publications:* (ed) Crystallization of Membrane Proteins, 1990. *Recreations:* nature, wild life, physical exercise, readings on history and travel. *Address:* Max Planck Institut für Biophysik, Max von Laue Strasse 3, 60438 Frankfurt am Main, Germany. *T:* (69) 63031001, *Fax:* (69) 63031002.

MICHEL, Louis; Member (Mouvement Réformateur), European Parliament, since 2009; *b* 2 Sept. 1947; *m*; two *c*. German lang. teacher, 1968; Lectr, Inst. Supérieur de Commerce, St Louis; Prof. of Dutch, English and German Lit., Ecole Normale Provinciale, Jodoigne, 1968–78. MHR (PRL), Belgium, 1978–99; Mem., parly commns on Finance, Budget, Instnl Reforms, and Commn on supervising electoral expenditures; elected to Senate, 1999, 2003, 2004; Dep. Prime Minister and Minister of Foreign Affairs, Belgium, 1999–2004; Mem., European Commn, 2004–09. Mem., Benelux Interparly Consultative Council. Dep. Pres., Liberal Internat. Mem. Bd, ELDR. Liberal Reform Party (PRL): Sec.-Gen., 1980–82; Pres., 1982–90 and 1995–99; Pres., Parly Gp in Council of Walloon Reg., 1991–92; Parly Gp in House of Reps, 1992–95. Alderman, 1977–, Mayor, 1983–, Jodoigne. Comdr, Order of Leopold (Belgium), 1995; Grand-Croix: Order of Infante Dom Henrique (Portugal), 1999; Ordre of Orange-Nassau (Netherlands), 2000; Order of Isabel la Católica (Spain), 2000; Ordre Royal de l'Etoile Polaire (Sweden), 2001; Grand Officier, Légion d'Honneur, 2003. *Publications:* (with D. Ducarme) Le défi vert, 1980; (with P. Monfils) L'enfant, 1984; Libres et forts-projet éducatif pour réussir le futur, 1986; Wallons et optimistes, 1997; De echte Walen, 1997; Rendre Confiance, 1998; Objectif 100 La Wallonnie j'y crois!, 1998; Lettre aux citoyens de mon pays, 1999; L'axe du Bien, 2003; Horizons, 2004; L'Europe-Afrique: indispensable alliance; L'appui budgétaire; Jean Ray: une conscience; Les 100 raisons d'aimer l'Europe. *Address:* European Parliament, Rue Wiertz, 1047 Brussels, Belgium.

MICHELL, John; *see* Michell, M. J.

MICHELL, Keith; actor, since 1948; *b* Adelaide; *s* of Joseph Michell and Alice Maud (*née* Aslat); *m* 1957, Jeannette Sterke; one *s* one *d*. *Educ:* Port Pirie High Sch.; Adelaide Teachers' Coll.; Sch. of Arts and Crafts; Adelaide Univ.; Old Vic Theatre Sch. Formerly taught art. *Stage:* First appearance, Playbox, Adelaide, 1947; Young Vic Theatre Co., 1950–51; first London appearance, And So To Bed, 1951; Shakespeare Meml Theatre Co., 1952–56, inc. Australian tour, 1952–53 (Henry IV Part 1, As You Like It, Midsummer Night's Dream, Troilus and Cressida, Romeo and Juliet, Taming of the Shrew, All's Well That Ends Well, Macbeth, Merry Wives of Windsor); Don Juan, Royal Court, 1956; Old Vic Co., 1956 (Antony and Cleopatra, Much Ado about Nothing, Two Gentlemen of Verona, Titus Andronicus); Irma La Douce, Lyric, 1958, Washington, DC, 1960 and Broadway, 1960–61; The Chances, Chichester Festival, 1962; The Rehearsal, NY, 1963; The First Four Hundred Years, Australia and NZ, 1964; Robert and Elizabeth, Lyric, 1964; The King's Mare, 1966; Man of La Mancha, 1968–69, NY, 1970; Abelard and Heloise, 1970, Los Angeles and NY, 1971; Hamlet, Globe, 1972; Dear Love, Comedy, 1973; The Crucifer of Blood, Haymarket, 1979; On the Twentieth Century (musical), Her Majesty's, 1980; Pete McGynty and the Dreamtime (own adap. of Peer Gynt), Melbourne Theatre Co., 1981; Captain Beaky Christmas Show, Lyric, Shaftesbury Ave., 1981–82; The Tempest, Brisbane, 1982; opened Keith Michell Theatre, Port Pirie, with one-man show, 1982; Amadeus (UK tour), 1983; La Cage Aux Folles, San Francisco and NY, 1984, Sydney and Melbourne, 1985; Portraits, Malvern Fest. and Savoy, 1987; Aspects of Love, Edmonton and Toronto, 1991–92, Chicago, 1992; Scrooge, Melbourne, 1993; Caesar and Cleopatra, Edmonton, 1994; Brazilian Blue, Brisbane, 1995; various one-man shows, Family Matters, and All the World's a Stage, UK tour, S Australia Adelaide Fest. and Keith Michell Th., Port Pirie, 2000–04; Bernardino Ramazzini - The Artisan's Archangel, RSocMed London, 2005; *Chichester Festival Theatre:* Artistic Director, 1974–77; Tonight We Improvise, Oedipus Tyrannus, 1974; Cyrano de Bergerac, Othello, 1975; (dir and designed) Twelfth Night, 1976; Monsieur Perrichon's Travel, 1976; The Apple Cart, 1977; (dir and designed) In Order of Appearance, 1977; Murder in the Cathedral (Chichester Cathedral), 1977; Henry VIII, 1991; toured Australia with Chichester Co., 1978 (Othello, The Apple Cart); acted in: On the Rocks, 1982; Jane Eyre, 1986; The Royal Baccarat Scandal, 1988, transf. Theatre Royal Haymarket, 1989; Henry VIII, 1991; Monsieur Amilcar (Minerva), 1995. *Films include:* Dangerous Exile; The Hell Fire Club; Seven Seas to Calais; The Executioner; House of Cards; Prudence and the Pill; Henry VIII and his Six Wives; Moments, The Deceivers; Love/Lost. *Television includes:* Henry VIII in the Six Wives of Henry VIII (series), 1972; Keith Michell at Chichester, 1974; My Brother Tom, 1986; Captain James Cook, 1987; Murder She Wrote (series), 1990. Many recordings. First exhibn of paintings, 1959; subseq. one-man exhibns at John Whibley Gall., London, Wright Hepburn and Webster Gall., NY, Century Gall., Henley-on-Thames, Wylma Wayne Gall., London, Vincent Gall., Adelaide. Many awards. *Publications:* (ed and illus.) Twelve Shakespeare Sonnets (series of lithographs produced 1974), 1981; illus. and recorded Captain Beaky series, 1975; (compiled and illus.) Practically Macrobiotic, 1987, 3rd edn 2000. *Recreations:* gardening, photography, swimming, cooking.

MICHELL, Michael John; Head, Oil and Gas Division, Department of Trade and Industry, 1993–98; *b* 12 Dec. 1942; *s* of late John Martin Michell and of Pamela Mary Michell; *m* 1st, 1965, Pamela Marianne Tombs (marr. diss. 1978); two *s* (one *d* decd); 2nd, 1978, Alison Mary Macfarlane (marr. diss. 2005; she *d* 2013); two *s*; 3rd, 2005, Janice Margaret Bintcliffe. *Educ:* Marlborough College; Corpus Christi College, Cambridge (BA 1964). Min. of Aviation, 1964; Private Sec. to Sir Ronald Melville, 1968–69; Concorde Div., 1969–73; Sec. to Sandilands Cttee on inflation accounting, 1973–75; Private Sec. to Sec. of State for Industry, 1975–77; HM Treasury, 1977–80; Industrial Policy Div., Dept of Industry, 1980–82; RCDS 1983; Department of Trade and Industry: Head, Air Div., 1984–88; Chief Exec., Radio Div., subseq. Radiocommunications Agency, 1988–93. Director: Prestbury Enterprises Ltd, 1998–2011; Eni UK Ltd, 1999–2010.

MICHELL, Prof. Robert Hall, FRS 1986; FMedSci; Royal Society Research Professor at the University of Birmingham, 1987–2006, now Emeritus; *b* 16 April 1941; *s* of Rowland Charles Michell and Elsie Lorna Michell; two *s* one *d*. *Educ:* Crewkerne School, Somerset; Univ. of Birmingham (BSc Med. Biochem. and Pharmacol. 1962; PhD Med. Biochem. 1965; DSc 1978). Research Fellow, Birmingham, 1965–66, 1968–70, Harvard Med. Sch., 1966–68; Birmingham University: Lectr in Biochemistry, 1970–81; Sen. Lectr, 1981–84; Reader, 1984–86; Prof. of Biochemistry, 1986–87. Mem., Physiol. Systems and Disorders Bd, 1985–90, Chm., Grants Cttee B, 1988–90, MRC; Member: Fellowships Cttee, BHF, 1992–97; Fellowships Selection Panel, Lister Inst. of Preventive Medicine, 1999–2005; Fellowship Review Panel, Human Frontiers Sci. Prog., 1999–2001. Mem., Biochem. Panel, 1996 RAE, Biol Scis Panel, 2001 and 2008 RAEs, HEFCE. Member: Adv. Bd, Beit Meml Trust, 1993–2006; Council, Royal Soc., 1996–97; Adv. Bd, EMF Res. Trust, 2000–10. Pres., Med. Scis Sect., BAAS, 1993–94. Mem., EMBO, 1991. Morton Lectr, 2002, Hon. Mem., 2010, Biochem. Soc. Member, Editorial Boards: Jl Neurochem., 1974–80; Cell Calcium, 1979–89; Biochem. Jl, 1983–88; Current Opinion in Cell Biology, 1988–; Procs Royal Soc. B, 1989–97; Jl of Molecular Endocrinology, 1992–99; Molecular Membrane Biology, 1993–2007. FMedSci 2002. Chm. Govs, Cadbury Sixth Form Coll., 2010–. CIBA Medal, Biochemical Soc., 1988. *Publications:* (with J. B. Finean and R. Coleman) Membranes and their Cellular Functions, 1974, 3rd edn 1984; (ed with J. B. Finean) Membrane Structure, vol. 1 of New Comprehensive Biochemistry, 1981; (ed with J. W. Putney, Jr) Inositol Lipids in Cellular Signalling, 1987; (ed with M. J. Berridge) Inositol Lipids and Transmembrane Signalling, 1988; (ed jtly) Inositol Lipids and Cellular Signalling, 1989; contribs to Nature, Biochem. Jl and sci. jls. *Recreations:* birdwatching, wilderness, pottery. *Address:* 59 Weoley Park Road, Birmingham B29 6QZ. *T:* (0121) 472 1356.

MICHELL, Roger Harry; director; *b* 5 June 1956; *s* of H. D. Michell, DFC, and Jillian Green; *m* 1st, 1992, Kate Buffery (marr. diss. 2002); one *s* one *d*; 2nd, 2010, Anna Maxwell Martin, *qv*; two *d*. *Educ:* Clifton Coll., Bristol; Queens' Coll., Cambridge (BA Hons). With Royal Court Th., 1978–80, Royal Shakespeare Th., 1985–91. Judith E. Wilson Sen. Fellow, Cambridge Univ., 1990. *Plays* include: Private Dick, Edinburgh and Whitehall, 1980; The Catch, Royal Court, 1981; White Glove, Lyric, Hammersmith, 1982; Marya, Old Vic., 1990; My Night with Reg, Royal Court and Criterion, 1995; Some Sunny Day, Hampstead, 1996; Old Times, 2004, Betrayal, 2007, Donmar Warehouse; The Female of the Species, Vaudeville, 2008; Rope, Almeida, 2009; Tribes, Royal Court, 2010; Farewell to the Theatre, Hampstead, 2012; Birthday, Royal Court, 2012; Royal Shakespeare Company: Merchant of Venice, 1986; Dead Monkey, 1986; Hamlet, 1987; Temptation, 1987; Conversation, 1987; Constant Couple, 1988; Restoration, 1988; Some Americans Abroad, 1989; Redevelopment, 1989; Two Shakespearean Actors, 1990; Royal National Theatre: The Coup, 1991; Under Milk Wood, 1995; The Homecoming, 1997; Blue/Orange, 2000; Honour, 2003; Landscape with Weapon, 2007; *television* includes: Buddha of Suburbia, 1994; Ready When You Are,

Mr Patel, 1995; My Night with Reg, 1997; Michael Redgrave, My Father, 1998; *films:* Persuasion, 1995; Titanic Town, 1999; Notting Hill, 1999; Changing Lanes, 2002; The Mother, 2003; Enduring Love, 2004; Venus, 2007; Morning Glory, 2010; Hyde Park on Hudson, 2013; Le Week-End, 2013. *Address:* c/o Independent Talent Group Ltd, 40 Whitfield Street, W1T 2RH.

MICHELMORE, Clifford Arthur, CBE 1969; television broadcaster and producer; *b* 11 Dec. 1919; *s* of late Albert, (Herbert), Michelmore and Ellen Alford; *m* 1950, Jean Metcalfe (Broadcaster) (*d* 2000); one *s* one *d*. *Educ:* Cowes Senior Sch., Isle of Wight. Entered RAF, 1935; commnd 1940; left RAF 1947. Head, Outside Broadcasts and Variety, BFN, 1948; Dep. Station Dir, BFN, also returned to freelance as Commentator and Producer, 1949. Entered Television, 1950. Managing Director: Michelmore Enterprises Ltd, 1969–2000; Communication Consultants Ltd, 1969–84; RM/EMI Visual Programmes, 1971–81; Dir, CP Video, 1988–96. Introduced: "Tonight" series, 1957–65; 24 Hours series, 1965–68; General Election Results programmes, 1964, 1966, 1970; So You Think…, 1966–72; Our World, 1967; Apollo Space Programmes, 1960–70; Holiday, 1969–86; A Year to Remember, 1996–2000 (BBC Radio Two). Made films: Shaping of a Writer, 1977; Hong Kong: the challenge, 1978. FRSA 1975. Television Society Silver Medal, 1957; Guild of TV Producers Award, Personality of the Year, 1958; TV Review Critics Award, 1959; Variety Club Award, 1961. *Publications:* (ed) The Businessman's Book of Golf, 1981; Cliff Michelmore's Holidays By Rail, 1986; (with Jean Metcalfe) Two-Way Story (autobiog.), 1986; Some of These Days, 1987; contribs to Highlife, Financial Weekly; various articles on television, broadcasting and travel. *Recreation:* being with my grandchildren. *Address:* Northend Barn, South Harting, Petersfield, Hants GU31 5NR. *T:* (01730) 825665. *Club:* Royal Air Force.

MICHELS, Sir David (Michael Charles), Kt 2006; President, Institute of Hospitality, since 2012; *b* 8 Dec. 1946; *s* of Klaus Peter and Thelma Sadie Michels; *m* 1973, Michele Ann Arnold; one *s* one *d*. *Educ:* Hendon Coll. FIH. Grand Metropolitan, 1966–81; Ladbrokes: Sales and Marketing Dir, Hotels, 1981–83; Man. Dir, Leisure Div., 1983–85; Man. Dir, Ladbroke Hotels, 1985–87; Hilton International: Sen. Vice-Pres., Sales and Marketing, 1987–89; Dep. Chm., Hilton UK and Exec. Vice-Pres., Hilton Worldwide, 1989–91; Chief Exec., Stakis plc, 1991–99; Chief Executive: Hilton Internat. Hotels, 1999–2000; Hilton Gp plc, 2000–06. Sen. Eur. Strategist, Strategic Hotels & Resorts, 2007–. Dep. Chm., Marks and Spencer Gp plc, 2008–12; non-exec. Dir, British Land Co. plc, 2003–08; Sen. Ind. Dir, easyJet plc, 2006–11. Trustee, Anne Frank Trust. Hon. DLitt Glasgow Caledonian, 1993. *Recreations:* tennis, poker, reading.

MICHIE, Prof. Jonathan, DPhil; FAcSS; Professor of Innovation and Knowledge Exchange, and Director, Department for Continuing Education, University of Oxford, since 2008; President, Kellogg College, Oxford, since 2008; *b* 25 March 1957; *s* of late Prof. Donald Michie and (Dame) Dr Anne Laura McLaren, DBE, FRS; *m* 1988, Carolyn Grace Downs, *qv*; two *s*. *Educ:* Balliol Coll., Oxford (BA 1st Cl. Hons PPE); Queen Mary Coll., London (MSc Econ (Dist.)); DPhil Econ Oxon 1985. Lectr, Univ. of Oxford, 1983; Res. Officer, Econ. Dept, TUC, 1983–88; Expert to EC, Brussels, 1988–90; Fellow in Econs, St Catharine's Coll., Cambridge, 1990–92; Lectr in Accounting and Finance, Judge Business Sch., Univ. of Cambridge, 1992–97; Dir, Contracts and Competition Prog., ESRC, 1992–97; Sainsbury Prof. of Mgt, Birkbeck Coll., Univ. of London, 1997–2004; Prof. of Mgt and Dir, Business Sch., Univ. of Birmingham, 2004–08. Member: Enterprise and Skills Strategic Adv. Cttee, HEFCE, 2009–13; Econ. Adv. Panel, DEFRA, 2012–. Non-exec. Dir, Sandwell and W Birmingham Hosps NHS Trust, 2006–08 (Chm., Audit Cttee, 2006–08). Mem. Council, ACAS, 2007–14 (Chm., Audit Cttee, 2007–10). Member: Council, Univ. of Birmingham, 2005–08 (Mem., Investments Cttee, 2005–08); Nat. Exec. Cttee, Assoc. of Business Schs, 2005–08 (Treas., 2005–08); Bd, Oxford Univ. Soc., 2010– (Treas., 2010–); Finance Cttee, Univ. of Oxford, 2012–; Mem., Finance Cttee, 2013–, Pensions Trustee, 2013–, UCAS; Chm., Bd of Govs, UWC Atlantic Coll., 2015–. FAcSS (AcSS 2010) (Mem. Council, 2011–; Chm., Audit and Risk Mgt Cttee, 2011–). *Publications:* Wages in the Business Cycle, 1987; The Political Economy of Competitiveness, 2000; A Reader's Guide to Social Science, 2001; Systems of Production, 2002; The Handbook of Globalisation, 2003, 2nd edn 2011; The Political Economy of the Environment, 2011; Why the Social Sciences Matter, 2015. *Recreations:* supporting Manchester United, campaigning for supporter control of football clubs. *Address:* Kellogg College, Oxford OX2 6PN. *T:* (01865) 612003, *Fax:* (01865) 612001. *E:* jonathan.michie@kellogg.ox.ac.uk.

See also S. F. D. Michie.

MICHIE, Prof. Susan Fiona Dorinthea, DPhil; FBPsS, FAcSS; Co-Director, Centre for Outcomes Research and Effectiveness, since 2002, Director, Centre for Behaviour Change, since 2014, and Professor of Health Psychology, since 2005, University College London; *b* London, 19 June 1955; *d* of late Prof. Donald Michie and (Dame) Anne Laura Dorinthea McLaren, DBE, FRS; *m* 2009, Prof. Robert West; one *s* two *d*. *Educ:* St Anne's Coll., Oxford (BA Exptl Psychol. 1976); Inst. of Psychiatry, Univ. of London (MPhil Clin. Psychol. 1978); Wadham Coll., Oxford (DPhil Develtl Psychol. 1982). Chartered Clin. Psychologist 1978; Chartered Health Psychologist 1993; FBPsS 2001. Royal Free Hospital School of Medicine: Hon. Lectr in Develtl Psychol., 1987–91; Hon. Sen. Lectr in Health Psychol., 1991–2002; Sen. Res. Fellow in Clin. Health Psychol., Royal Free and UC Med. Sch., 1989–2002; King's College London: Dep. Dir, Psychol. and Genetics Res. Gp, 1993–2002; Res. Fellow, 1993–96; Sen. Res. Fellow, 1996–2001; Reader in Health Psychol., 2001–02; Reader in Health Psychol., UCL, 2002–05; Dir, Health Psychol. Res. and Hon. Consultant Clin. Psychologist, Camden and Islington Mental Health and Social Care Trust, Camden and Islington PCTs, 2002–. Fellow, Eur. Health Psychol. Soc., 2007; FAcSS 2012. *Publications:* (jtly) Preventive Medicine for Total Health, 1989; (jtly) The Psychological Care of Medical Patients: a practical guide, 2nd edn 2003; (ed jtly) Health Psychology in Practice, 2004; (jtly) Improving Health: changing behaviour, 2007; (jtly) The Behaviour Change Wheel: a guide to designing interventions, 2014; (jtly) An ABC of Behaviour Change Theories, 2014; over 300 jl articles, 25 books and book chapters, 350 conference abstracts. *Address:* Department of Clinical, Educational and Health Psychology, University College London, 1–19 Torrington Place, WC1E 7HB. *T:* (020) 7679 5930, *Fax:* (020) 7916 8511. *E:* s.michie@ucl.ac.uk.

See also J. Michie.

MICHIE, William; *b* 24 Nov. 1935; *m* 1st, 1957 (marr. diss. 1982); two *s*; 2nd, 1987, Judith Ann (*née* Frost); one step *s* one step *d*. *Educ:* Abbeydale Secondary Sch., Sheffield; Sheffield Polytechnic. Nat. Service, RAF, 1957–59. Formerly: apprentice electrician; maintenance electrician; Lab. Technician, Computer Applications; unemployed, 1981–83. Joined Labour Party, 1965; Co-op. Party, 1966. Mem., Unite (formerly AUEW, then AEU, then AEEU, then Amicus), 1952– (former Br. Trustee; former Standing Orders Cttee Deleg., Lab. Party Yorks Regl Conf.). Member: Sheffield City Council, 1970–84 (Chairman: Planning, 1974–81; Employment, 1981–83; Gp Sec./Chief Whip, 1974–83); South Yorks CC, 1974–86 (Area Planning Chm., 1974–81). MP (Lab) Sheffield, Heeley, 1983–2001. Member: Privileges Select Cttee, 1994–96; Members' Interests Select Cttee, 1993–96; Jt Cttee on Parly Privilege, 1997–2001. Chm., AEEU Parly Gp, 1997–2001 (Mem., 1983–2001). *Recreations:* darts, gardening, Sheffield Wednesday.

MICKELSON, Philip Alfred; golfer; *b* San Diego, 16 June 1970; *s* of Philip Mickelson and Mary Mickelson; *m* Amy McBride; one *s* two *d*. *Educ:* Arizona State Univ. Winner, Northern Telecom Open (as amateur), 1991; professional golfer, 1992–; wins include: Buick Invitational, 1993, 2000, 2001; Mercedes Championship, 1994, 1998; Northern Telecom Open, 1995; NEC World Series Golf, 1996; AT&T Pebble Beach Nat. Pro-Am, 1998, 2005; BellSouth Classic, 2000, 2005; PGA Tour Championship, 2000; US Masters Tournament, 2004, 2006, 2010; PGA Championship, 2005; Open, 2013; Member: US Ryder Cup Team, 1995, 1997, 1999 (winners), 2002, 2004, 2010, 2012; President's Cup Team, 1994 (winners), 1996 (winners), 1998, 2000 (winners), 2003. *Address:* c/o Gaylord Sports Management, 13845 North Northsight Boulevard, Suite 200, Scottsdale, AZ 85260, USA; c/o PGA Tour, 112 PGA Tour Boulevard, Ponte Vedra Beach, FL 32082, USA.

MICKLETHWAIT, (Richard) John; Editor-in-Chief, Bloomberg News, since 2015; *b* 11 Aug. 1962; *s* of late Richard Miles Micklethwait and of Jane Evelyn Micklethwait (*née* Codrington); *m* 1992, Fevronia Read; three *s*. *Educ:* Ampleforth Coll., York; Magdalen Coll., Oxford (BA Modern Hist.). The Economist: Finance corresp., 1987–90; W Coast Bureau Chief, 1990–93; Business ed., 1993–97; NY Bureau Chief, 1997–2000; US ed., 2000–06; Ed., 2006–15. Trustee, British Mus., 2011–. *Publications:* with Adrian Wooldridge: The Witch Doctors, 1996; A Future Perfect, 2000; The Company, 2003; The Right Nation, 2004; God is Back: how the global rise of faith is changing the world, 2009; The Fourth Revolution: the global race to reinvent the state, 2014. *Recreations:* sport, dog walking. *Address:* Bloomberg News, 731 Lexington Avenue, New York, NY 10022, USA. *Club:* Royal Automobile.

MICKLEWHITE, Sir Michael; *see* Caine, Sir Michael.

MIDDLE, Anne Hilary; Headteacher, Parkstone Grammar School, Poole, 2001–13; *b* 21 March 1952; *d* of late Louis Shinwell and of Sylvia Shinwell; *m* 2002, Keith Middle; one step *s* one step *d*. *Educ:* Univ. of Glasgow (MA; PGCE). John Kelly Girls' School, Brent, London: Teacher of Hist., 1973–80; responsible for teaching Econs, 1975–86; Hd of Careers, 1980–86; Dep. Dir, Sixth Form, 1983–86; Tiffin Girls' School, Kingston, London: Sen. Teacher, 1986–88; Hd, Middle Sch. and Careers, 1986–88; Dep. Headteacher, 1988–95; Headteacher, Queen Elizabeth Girls' Sch., Barnet, London, 1995–2001. Pres., Assoc. of Maintained Girls' Schs, 2004–05; Mem., GSHA, 2008–13. Chm., Delta Educnl Trust. *Recreations:* golf, reading, travel, antiques. *Address:* 31 Deverel Road, Charlton Down, Dorchester, Dorset DT2 9UD. *E:* annemiddle31@yahoo.co.uk. *Club:* Dorset Golf and Country (Bere Regis).

MIDDLE, Dr Jonathan Guy; Chairman, Association for Quality Management in Laboratory Medicine, since 2009; *b* Weston-super-Mare, 4 March 1949; *s* of Lionel Guy Middle and Joan Middle (*née* Bennett); *m* 1978, Fiona Anne Mulligan; two *d*. *Educ:* Weston-super-Mare Grammar Sch. for Boys; Fitzwilliam Coll., Cambridge (BA Hons Nat. Scis 1970); Univ. of Newcastle upon Tyne (PhD 1979); Univ. of West London (ALCM Jazz Saxophone Performance 2013). Res. Associate, CRC Labs, Univ. of Newcastle upon Tyne, 1973–76; Res. Officer, CRC Labs, Univ. of Nottingham, 1976–80; Basic Grade Clin. Biochemist, 1980–84, Sen. Grade Clin. Biochemist, 1984–87, Dept of Chemical Pathol., Royal Liverpool Hosp.; Principal Biochemist and Organiser UK Nat. External Quality Assessment Service for Steroid Hormones, Univ. Hosp. of Wales, Cardiff, 1987–96; Dep. Dir UK Nat. External Quality Assessment Service for Clin. Chemistry, Univ. Hosp. Birmingham, 1996–2010; Hon. Sen. Res. Fellow, Dept of Medicine, Univ. of Birmingham, 1996–2010. Member: BSI CH212, 2012–; ISO TC212 Wkg Gp 2, 2014–. STEM Ambassador for Sci., Sci., Technol., Engrg and Maths Network, 2011–. Fellow, Assoc. of Clin. Biochem., 2012. *Publications:* (contrib. chapter) Steroid Analysis, 1995, 2nd edn 2010; articles mainly in Annals of Clin. Biochem. *Recreations:* leading 'Second City Sax' saxophone quartet, playing saxophone in Birmingham University Music Society Saxophone Ensemble and Wind Band, playing keyboards in 'Earlswood' trio and other local bands. *Address:* Association for Quality Management in Laboratory Medicine, PO Box 15252, Birmingham B16 6HD. *E:* mail@aqmlm.org.uk.

MIDDLEBURGH, Rabbi Dr Charles Hadley; Rabbi: Dublin Jewish Progressive Congregation, 2002–11; Cardiff Reform Synagogue, 2004–14; Senior Lecturer in Rabbinics, since 2003, Director of Jewish Studies, since 2011, and Dean, since 2014, Leo Baeck College; Lecturer, Irish School of Ecumenics, Trinity College, Dublin, 2002–09; *b* 2 Oct. 1956; *s* of late Hyman Middleburgh and of Elizabeth Middleburgh; *m* 1984, Gilly Blyth. *Educ:* Brighton Coll.; University Coll. London (BA Hons, PhD 1982); Leo Baeck Coll. Lay reader, Brighton and Hove Progressive Synagogue, 1975–77; Minister, Kingston Liberal Synagogue, 1977–83; ordained 1986; Rabbi, Harrow and Wembley Progressive Synagogue, 1983–97; Exec. Dir, ULPS, 1997–2002; Rabbi, Progressive Judaism in Denmark, 2002–05. Leo Baeck College: Lectr in Bible, Aramaic, Rabbinic Practice, 1985–2002; Interim Dir of Rabbinic Studies, 2005–06; Hon. Dir of Studies, 2008–11. Patron, Dignity in Dying, 2004–. Occasional broadcaster, BBC Radio 4 and World Service, 1997–, RTE, Radio Eireann. FZS 1997. *Publications:* (Associate Ed.) Union of Liberal and Progressive Synagogues Daily, Sabbath and Festival Prayer Book, 1995; (ed jtly) Union of Liberal and Progressive Synagogues High Holy Days Prayerbook, 2003; (ed jtly) High and Holy Days: a book of Jewish wisdom, 2010; (ed jtly) A Jewish Book of Comfort, 2014. *Recreations:* animal photography, writing poetry, reading obsessively, playing with my grandchildren. *E:* charles.middleburgh@lbc.ac.uk. *W:* www.middleburgh.co.uk.

MIDDLEHURST, Tom; Member (Lab) Alyn and Deeside, National Assembly for Wales, 1999–2003; *b* 25 June 1936; *s* of late James Middlehurst and Agnes Middlehurst; *m* 1986, Patricia Mary; one *s* one *d* from a previous marriage. *Educ:* Ormskirk Grammar Sch.; Wigan Tech. Coll.; Liverpool Poly. Engrg apprentice, 1952–57; Underground Engr, NCB, 1957–63; engr, 1963–71; Local Govt Officer, Flintshire, later Clwyd, CC, 1971–93. Mem. (Lab), Alyn and Deeside DC, 1986–95; Mem. (Lab), Clwyd CC, 1993–95 (Chm., Housing Cttee; Chm., Personnel Cttee); Leader (Lab), Flintshire CC, 1995–99. Chm., Welsh Local Govt Assoc., 1997–99. National Assembly for Wales: Sec. for Post-16 Educn and Training, 1999–2000; Member: N Wales Cttee, 1999–2003; European Affairs Cttee, 2000–03; Local Govt and Housing Cttee, 2000–03; Envmt, Planning and Transport Cttee, 2000–03. Mem., Labour Party, 1961–; Mem. Bd of Dirs, Wales European Centre. Chairman: Welsh Crown Green Bowling Assoc., 2005–11; Flintshire Sports Council, 2005–11. Chm. Govs, Clwyd Theatr Cymru, 1995–99.

MIDDLESBROUGH, Bishop of, (RC), since 2008; **Rt Rev. Terence Patrick Drainey;** *b* Manchester, 1 Aug. 1949; *s* of Joseph Patrick Drainey and Mary Elizabeth Drainey (*née* Roebuck). *Educ:* Augustinian Theol Studium, Pontifical Univ. of Comillas, Valladolid (STB). Ordained priest, 1975; St Wulstan, Great Harwood, 1975–80; St Thomas of Canterbury, Higher Broughton, Salford, 1980–85; Immaculate Conception and St Philip Neri, Radcliffe, 1985–86; Priest (*fidei donum*), Archdiocese of Kisumu, Western Kenya, 1986–91; Parish Priest: Holy Cross, Patricroft, 1991–94; St Bernadette's, Whitefield, 1994–97; Spiritual Dir, 1997–2003, Dir of the Propaedeutic Prog., 1998–2003, Royal English Coll. of St Albans, Valladolid; Pres., St Cuthbert's Coll., Ushaw, 2003–07. Mem., Bishops' Conference Dept of Catholic Educn and Formation, 2008–; Bishops' Conference Liaison with: Seminary Rectors of Seminaries of England and Wales; National Conference of Vocation. Chairman: Nat. Office for Vocations; Caritas Social Action Network, 2014–. Appointed Papal Chaplain by His Holiness Pope Benedict XVI, 2006. *Recreations:* music, especially choral, walking, gardening. *Address:* (residence) Bishop's House, 16 Cambridge Road, Middlesbrough TS5 5NN. *T:* (01642) 818253; (office) Curial Office, 50a The Avenue, Linthorpe, Middlesbrough TS5 6QT. *T:* (01642) 850505.

MIDDLESEX, Archdeacon of; *see* Welch, Ven. S. J.

MIDDLETON, 13th Baron *cr* 1711; **Michael Charles James Willoughby;** DL; Bt 1677; *b* London, 14 July 1948; *s* of 12th Baron Middleton, MC and Janet (*née* Marshall-Cornwall); *S* father, 2011; *m* 1974, Hon. Lucy Corinna Agneta Sidney, *y d* of 1st Viscount De L'Isle, VC,

KG, KCMG, GCVO, PC; two *s* three *d*. *Educ:* Eton Coll.; Mons OCS; E Riding Coll. of Agriculture. Lieut, Coldstream Guards, 1967–71, QOY, 1971–75. Vice Pres., Europe, CLA, 2005–10. Jt Master, Middleton Hunt, 2009–13. DL ER Yorks, 2004. *Heir:* *s* Hon. James William Michael Willoughby [*b* 8 March 1976; *m* 2005, Lady Cara Mary Cecilia Boyle, *er d* of Earl of Cork and Orrery, *qv*; two *s* one *d*]. *Address:* North Grimston House, Malton, N Yorks YO17 8AX. *T:* (01944) 768204. *Clubs:* Cavalry and Guards, Pratt's.

MIDDLETON, Bishop Suffragan of, since 2008; **Rt Rev. Mark Davies;** *b* 12 May 1962; *s* of late Cyril and of Gwen Davies. *Educ:* UC of Ripon and York St John (BA Hons Leeds 1985); Coll. of the Resurrection, Mirfield (Cert. Pastoral Theol. 1986). Ordained deacon, 1989, priest, 1990; Asst Curate, Barnsley St Mary, 1989–92; Priest-in-charge, Barnsley St Paul, 1992–95; Rector of Hemsworth, 1995–2006; Asst Diocesan Dir of Ordinands, Wakefield, 1998–2006; RD, Pontefract, 2000–06; Archdeacon of Rochdale, 2006–08. Proctor in Convocation, 2000–06; Hon. Canon, Wakefield Cathedral, 2002–06. *Recreations:* music, food, walking. *Address:* The Hollies, Manchester Road, Rochdale OL11 3QY. *T:* (01706) 358550. *E:* bishopmark@manchester.anglican.org.

MIDDLETON, Bernard Chester, MBE 1986; self-employed book restorer and designer bookbinder, since 1953; *b* 29 Oct. 1924; *s* of late Regent Marcus Geoffrey Middleton and Doris Hilda Middleton (*née* Webster); *m* 1951, Dora Mary Davies (*d* 1997). *Educ:* Central Sch. of Arts and Crafts, London; apprenticed to British Museum Bindery (1940); City and Guilds of London Inst. (Silver Medal (1st prize) 1943). Served: Home Guard, 1941–43; RN, 1943–46. Craftsman-Demonstrator, RCA, 1949–51; Manager, Zaehnsdorf Ltd, 1951–53. Chief Examr in General Bookbinding, CGLI, 1957–63. Has conducted workshops for restoration of leather bindings in Belgium, Brazil, Switzerland, The Netherlands, USA and Venezuela; gold-tooled bindings are in many major libraries incl. BL, Royal Liby, The Hague, V&A Mus. and Wormsley Liby. Member: Art Workers Guild, 1961; Assoc. Internationale de Bibliophilie, 2002; Fellow, Designer Bookbinders, 1955 (Pres., 1973–75). FRSA 1951; FSA 1967. Hon. Fellow: Soc. of Bookbinders, 2002; Designer Bookbinders, 2011; Hon. Member: Guild of Book Workers, USA, 2003; Inst. of Conservation, 2006; Antiquarian Booksellers' Assoc., 2010. *Publications:* A History of English Craft Bookbinding Technique, 1963, 4th edn 1996; The Restoration of Leather Bindings, 1972, 4th edn 2004; You *Can* Judge a Book by Its Cover, 1994; Recollections: my life in bookbinding, 1995; Recollections: a life in bookbinding, 2000; A Bookbinder's Miscellany, 2015; contribs to craft jls and introductions to books and exhibn catalogues. *Recreations:* reading, enjoying the past from a safe distance. *Address:* 3 Gauden Road, Clapham, SW4 6LR. *T:* (020) 7622 5388, *Fax:* (020) 7498 2716. *E:* bcmiddleton@onetel.com.

MIDDLETON, Prof. Campbell Ross, PhD; Laing O'Rourke Professor of Construction Engineering, University of Cambridge, since 2011; *b* Sydney, 1959. *Educ:* Hutchins Sch., Hobart; Univ. of Tasmania (BE Hons 1981); Imperial Coll. London (MSc 1985; DIC); King's Coll., Cambridge (PhD 1993). FICE; MIE(Aust); CEng; CPEng. Dept of Main Roads, Tasmania, 1981–87; Engr, Ove Arup & Partners, London, 1987–88; University of Cambridge: Res. Asst, 1989–93; Sen. Res. Associate, 1993–94; Asst Dir of Res., 1995–99; Lectr, 1999–2000; Sen. Lectr, 2000–11. *Address:* Department of Engineering, Trumpington Street, Cambridge CB2 1PZ. *T:* (01223) 332726. *E:* prof@construction.cam.ac.uk.

MIDDLETON, David Fraser, CBE 2015; Chief Executive, Transport Scotland, since 2009; *b* 23 June 1956; *s* of late Fraser Middleton and Margaret Middleton; *m* 1992, Diane Lamberton; one *d*. *Educ:* Univ. of Glasgow (MA Hons (Modern Hist. and Political Econ.)). Joined Scottish Office, as administrative trainee, 1978: Private Sec. to successive Ministers of State, 1982–84; on secondment to Cabinet Office, 1984; Br. Hd, Finance Gp (Housing and Educn), 1984–89; Head, Whitfield Urban Partnership, Dundee, 1989–91; Hd of Div., Scottish Develt Dept, 1991–96; Hd Policy, Finance and Strategy Div., Roads Directorate, 1996–97; Hd, Personnel, 1997; Dir of Implementation, Scottish Exec., Jan.–June 1998; Head: Local Govt Gp, 1999–2001; Local Govt and External Relns, 2001–02; Rural Gp, Scottish Exec. Envmt and Rural Affairs Dept, 2002–06; Dir of Special Projects, UHI (on attachment), 2006–07; Deputy Chief Exec. and Dir of Corporate Services, Crown Office and Procurator Fiscal Service, Scottish Exec., then Scottish Govt, 2007; Hd, Scotland Office, 2007–09. *Recreations:* golf, gardening. *Address:* Transport Scotland, 58 Port Dundas Road, Glasgow G4 0HF. *Club:* Royal Musselburgh Golf.

MIDDLETON, (David) Miles, CBE 1992; Chairman: Isos Housing Group, 2005–11; Tees Valley Learning and Skills Council, 2000–04; Partner, Middleton Associates, since 1993; *b* 15 June 1938; *s* of late Harry Middleton and of Dorothy Hannah Middleton (*née* Nisbet); *m* 1st, 1962, Mary Gale (marr. diss. 1979); one *s* one *d*; 2nd, 1980, Elizabeth, (Bobbie), Lancaster; two step *s* two step *d*. *Educ:* Sedbergh Sch. ACA 1962, FCA 1972. Articled Clerk, Strachan & Co., 1956–61; Audit Sen., Coopers Brothers & Co., 1962–64; Coopers & Lybrand: Manager, Zürich, 1964–68; Newcastle upon Tyne office, 1968–71, 1986–90; Middlesbrough office, 1971–86; Partner, 1974; Sen. Partner, NE Practice, 1990–93. Chairman: Northern Enterprise Ltd, 1988–99; Hadrian's Wall Tourism Partnership, 2000–05. Member Board: Rural Develt Commn, 1992–99 (Chm., 1997–99); NE Regl Develt Agency, 1999–2001; Countryside Agency, 1999–2000; Milecastle Housing (formerly Tynedale Housing), 2000–05 (Chm., 2003–05). Pres., British Chamber of Commerce, 1990–92. *Address:* Stanegate, St Helen's Lane, Corbridge, Northumberland NE45 5JD. *T:* (01434) 633545. *Club:* Northern Counties (Newcastle upon Tyne).

MIDDLETON, Edward Bernard; Partner, PKF (UK) LLP, Chartered Accountants, 1979–2008; Director, London Cremation Company plc, since 2011; *b* 5 July 1948; *s* of Bernard and Bettie Middleton; *m* 1971, Rosemary Spence Brown; three *s*. *Educ:* Aldenham Sch., Elstree; Chartered Accountant, 1970. Joined London office of Pannell Kerr Forster, 1971; Nairobi office, 1973; Audit Manager, London office, 1975; seconded to DTI as Dir, Industrial Develt Unit, 1984–86. Dir, PKF Hotel Consultancy Services, 1996–2008. Mem. sub-cttee, Consultative Cttee of Accountancy Bodies, 1980–84. Hon. Treas., Hospitality Action (formerly Hotel and Catering Benevolent Assoc.), 1992–2009; Mem. Council, British Assoc. of Hospitality Accountants, 1997–2007. Trustee, ResCU, 2010–. Liveryman, 2004, Mem. of Ct, 2008–, Co. of Spectacle Makers (Trustee: Spectacle Makers Charity, 2009–12; Educn Trust, 2010–). *Recreations:* sailing, photography. *Address:* Barrans, Bury Green, Little Hadham, Ware, Herts SG11 2ES. *T:* (01279) 658684. *Clubs:* Reform; Yealm Yacht.

MIDDLETON, Dame Elaine (Madoline), DCMG 1998; MBE 1976; Executive Director, National Committee for Families and Children, Belize, 1994–98; *d* of Elstan Kerr and Leolyn Kerr Gillett; *m* 1961, Winston Middleton; one *s* two *d*. *Educ:* Belize Teachers' Trng Coll. (Teacher's Cert 1957); UC, Swansea (Dip. Social Welfare and Admin 1961; Dip. Applied Social Studies 1966); Univ. of the Union Inst., Ohio (BA in Social Work 1990). Primary Sch. Teacher, Salvation Army Sch. and Methodist Schs, Belize City, Dangriga and Gales Point, Manatee, 1947–57; Social Development Department, Belize: Probation Officer, 1957–62; Dep. Head, 1963–68; Head of Dept, 1969–81; Dir-Gen., Belize Red Cross Soc., 1981–83; lived and worked in USA, 1983–94. Member: Consortium for Belizean Develt, 1985–; Women's Commn of Belize, 1997–99. Sec., Bd of Mgt, Wesley Coll., 2000–07; Pres., YWCA of Belize, 2001–09. *Recreations:* reading, community work. *Address:* 16 4th Street, King's Park, Belize City, Belize. *T:* (2) 234760.

MIDDLETON, Jeremy Peter, CBE 2012; Board Member, North Eastern Local Enterprise Partnership, since 2012; *b* Burton on Trent, 19 Nov. 1960; *s* of Dennis Middleton and Vivienne Middleton; *m* 1988, Catherine Smith; one *s* two *d*. *Educ:* Univ. of Kent (BA Hons Hist.). Brand Manager, Procter and Gamble, 1984–88; Supervising Consultant, Price Waterhouse, 1988–90; Middleton Enterprises Ltd, 1990–; Co-Founder, 1990, Mem., Exec. Cttee, 1992–, Homeserve. Contested (C): Newcastle upon Tyne East and Wallsend, 1997; Hartlepool, Sept. 2004. Pres., 2008–09, Chm., 2009–12, Conservative Nat. Convention; Dep. Chm., Conservative Party, 2009–12. *Recreations:* ski-ing, trekking, cinema, tolerance. *E:* jeremy@middletonenterprises.com.

MIDDLETON, Sir John (Maxwell), Kt 2002; OBE 1978; Planter of Kulili Estates, Karkar Island; *b* 19 July 1930; *s* of William Maxwell Middleton and Alice Victoria (*née* Tregent); *m* 1961, Anna Maria Kadava; two *s*. *Educ:* Sydney C of E Grammar Sch. Chm., Dylup Plantation Ltd, 1977–86; Dir, Dylup Investment Corp., 1986–91; Foundn Dir, Ramu Sugar Ltd, 1981–2008. Mem., PNG House of Assembly and Parliament, 1968–77. Chairman: PNG Fiscal Commn, 1978–83; PNG Kokonas Indastri Koporasen (Copra Ind. Corp.), 2003–04. Mem. and Dep. Chm., PNG Cocoa Bd, 1978–92. *Publications:* (autobiog.) My Life on Karkar Island, 2012. *Recreations:* game fishing, sea activities. *Address:* Kulili Estates, PO Box 486, Madang 511, Papua New Guinea. *T:* 4237461, *Fax:* 4237473. *E:* wmm@global.net.pg. *Clubs:* Papua, Madang, Madang Country (PNG).

MIDDLETON, Rear-Adm. (John) Patrick (Windsor), CB 1992; Secretary, Royal Commission for the Exhibition of 1851, 1995–2002; *b* 15 March 1938; *s* of late Comdr John Henry Dudley Middleton, RN and Norna Mary Tessimond (*née* Hitchings); *m* 1962, Jane Rodwell Gibbs; one *s* one *d*. *Educ:* Cheltenham College; BRNC Dartmouth; RNEC Manadon. CEng, MIMechE, MIMarEST. Entered Royal Navy 1954; CSO(E) to Flag Officer Submarines, 1981; CSO(E) Falkland Islands, 1983; Captain Naval Drafting, 1984; Dir, In Service Submarines, 1987; CSO (Engrg), later (Support), to C-in-C Fleet, 1989–92, retd. Trustee, CARE for People with Learning Disabilities, 1993–2007 (Chm. Trustees, 1998–2007). Liveryman: Armourers and Brasiers' Co., 1971– (Mem. Ct of Assts, 1995–2015; Master, 2001–02). Gov., Chilmark and Fonthill Bishop Primary Sch., 2003–07. *Publications:* Admiral Clanky Entertains, 2010. *Recreations:* sailing, walking, gardening, writing. *Address:* Manora, Chilmark, Wilts SP3 5AH. *T:* (01722) 716231. *E:* mimanora@aol.com. *Club:* Royal Naval Sailing Association (Portsmouth).

MIDDLETON, Lawrence John, CMG 1985; PhD; HM Diplomatic Service; Ambassador to the Republic of Korea, 1986–90, retired; *b* 27 March 1930; *s* of John James Middleton and Mary (*née* Horgan); *m* 1963, Sheila Elizabeth Hoey; two *s* one *d*. *Educ:* Finchley Catholic Grammar Sch.; Regent Street Poly. (BSc (ext.) 1949); King's Coll., London (BSc Special Hons 1951, PhD 1954). Scientific Officer, ARC, 1954–60 and 1962–63; Asst Specialist, Univ. of Calif, Berkeley, 1959–60; on secondment as Cons. to FAO and to UN Cttee on Effects of Atomic Radiation, 1960–62 and to CENTO Inst. of Nuclear Science, 1963–65; Principal, Min. of Agriculture, 1966–68; First Sec., FO, 1968; Washington, 1969–71; Kuala Lumpur, 1971–74; Counsellor (Commercial), Belgrade, 1974–78; Dir of Research, FCO, 1978–80; Cabinet Office, 1980–82; Counsellor, UK Delegn to Conf. on Disarmament, Geneva, 1982–84; Sen. DS, RCDS, 1984–86. Mem. Council, 1994–2001, Vice-Pres., 1998–2001, Royal Asiatic Soc. (FRAS 1992); Chm., Anglo-Korean Soc., 1995–2002. Chm., N Oxford Defence Assoc., 1995–2000. *Address:* 12 Polstead Road, Oxford OX2 6TN.

MIDDLETON, Marc William; Partner, EY, since 2013; *b* London, 18 July 1961; *s* of William Middleton and Catherine Middleton; *m* 1990, Marcia Jenkins; three *s* one *d*. *Educ:* Haberdashers' Aske's Hatcham Sch.; Univ. of Manchester (BA Hons Mod. Langs). Partner and Man. Dir, N. M. Rothschild & Sons Ltd, 1984–2008; Man. Dir, Shareholder Executive, BIS, 2008–10; Vice-Chm., Macquarie Capital, 2010–12. *Recreations:* Rugby, football, running, ski-ing, theatre. *Clubs:* Riverside Racquets; Barnes Rugby Football.

MIDDLETON, Rev. Canon Michael John; Canon of Westminster, 1997–2004, now Canon Emeritus; Treasurer, 1997–2004, and Almoner, 2000–04, Westminster Abbey; *b* 21 July 1940; *s* of Bernard and Gladys Middleton; *m* 1965, Anne Elisabeth Parker; two *s* one *d*. *Educ:* Weymouth Grammar Sch.; St Cuthbert's Soc., Durham (BSc); Fitzwilliam Coll., Cambridge (MA); Westcott House, Cambridge. Ordained: deacon, 1966; priest, 1967; Curate, St George's Jesmond, Newcastle, 1966–69; Chaplain: St George's Grammar Sch., Cape Town, 1969–72; King's School, Tynemouth, 1972–77; Vicar, St George's, Jesmond, Newcastle, 1977–85; Rector of Hexham, 1985–92; Archdeacon of Swindon, 1992–97. Acting Archdeacon of Westmorland and Furness, 2012. Hon. Canon of Newcastle, 1990. Proctor in Convocation, 1980–92. *Recreations:* walking, Westerns. *Address:* 37 High Fellside, Kendal, Cumbria LA9 4JG. *T:* (01539) 729320.

MIDDLETON, Miles; *see* Middleton, D. M.

MIDDLETON, Rear-Adm. Patrick; *see* Middleton, Rear-Adm. J. P. W.

MIDDLETON, Sir Peter (Edward), GCB 1989 (KCB 1984); Director, 1991–2004, Chief Executive Officer, 1998–99, and Chairman, 1999–2004, Barclays Bank (Deputy Chairman, 1991–98; Chairman, BZW Banking Division, 1991–98); Chairman: Marsh Ltd, 2005–13; Burford Capital Ltd, since 2009; UK Chairman, Marsh & McLennan Companies, 2007–14 (Member, International Advisory Board, 2005–09); *b* 2 April 1934; *m* 1st, 1964, Valerie Ann Lindup (*d* 1987); one *d* (one *s* decd); 2nd, 1990, Constance Owen. *Educ:* Sheffield City Grammar Sch.; Sheffield Univ. (BA; Hon. DLitt 1984); Bristol Univ. Served RAPC, 1958–60. HM Treasury: Senior Information Officer, 1962; Principal, 1964; Asst Director, Centre for Administrative Studies, 1967–69; Private Sec. to Chancellor of the Exchequer, 1969–72; Treasury Press Secretary, 1972–75; Head of Monetary Policy Div., 1975; Under Secretary, 1976; Dep. Sec., 1980–83; Permanent Sec., 1983–91. Director: Bass PLC, 1992–2001; General Accident Fire & Life Assurance Corp. plc, later CGU plc, 1992–98; United Utilities PLC (formerly NW Water Gp), 1994–2007 (Vice-Chm., 1998–99; Chm., 1999–2000; Dep. Chm., 2000–07); MTS OJSC, 2005–07; Chairman: Camelot Gp plc, 2004–10; Barclays Asia Pacific Adv. Cttee, 2004–12; Three Delta Adv. Bd, 2006–11; Adv. Bd, Burford Advrs LLP, 2007–09; Mercer Ltd, 2009–14; Hamilton Ventures, 2009–; Hume Capital Securities plc, 2014–15; XCAP Securities plc, 2012–14; Burford Capital Hldgs (UK) Ltd (formerly Firstassist Legal Gp Hldgs Ltd), 2012–; Resort Gp, 2015–. Mem., Adv. Bd, Financial Dynamics, 2004–09; Sen. Advr, Fenchurch Adv. Partners, 2005–12; Mem., Adv. Bd, ST Telemedia, 2010–12. Chairman: Sheffield Urban Regeneration Co. Ltd (Sheffield 1), 2000–05; Creative Sheffield, 2006–11. Chm., CEDR, 2004–11. Dir, Internat. Monetary Conf., 2001–03; Mem. Adv. Council, Monetary Authy of Singapore, 2001–05. Member: Adv. Bd, Nat. Econ. Res. Associates 1991; Exec. Cttee, Centre for Econ. Policy Res. Pres., British Bankers' Assoc., 2004–06. Trustee, InterMedia Res. and Consulting Europe, 2011–14. Vis. Fellow, Nuffield Coll., Oxford, 1981–89. Dir, Inst. of Contemporary British History, 2001–03 (Chm., 1992–2001). Mem. Council, 1991–, Chancellor, 1999–2015, now Emeritus, Univ. of Sheffield (Pro-Chancellor, 1997–99; Hon. Prof., Mgt Sch., 2011–); Mem. Council, Manchester Business Sch., 1985–92; Governor: London Business Sch., 1984–90; Ditchley Foundn, 1985–; NIESR, 1991–2007. Dir, English Chamber Orch. and Music Soc., 1992–2003. Trustee, Philharmonia Trust Ltd, 2012–. Cdre, Civil Service Sailing Assoc., 1984–92. *Recreations:* hill walking, music, outdoor sports. *Address:* c/o Gill Herbert, Marsh & McLennan Companies, Tower Place East, Tower Place, EC3R 5BU. *Club:* Reform.

MIDDLETON, Prof. Richard, DPhil; FBA 2004; Professor of Music, University of Newcastle upon Tyne, 1998–2005, now Emeritus; *b* 4 Feb. 1945; *s* of Harold and Joan Middleton; *m* 1969, Jane Pescod Harding; three *d*. *Educ:* Clare Coll., Cambridge (BA 1966); Univ. of York (DPhil 1970). Staff Tutor in Music, Dept of Extramural Studies, Univ. of Birmingham, 1970–72; Open University: Lectr, 1972–79; Sen. Lectr, 1979–95; Reader in Music and Cultural Studies, 1995–97. Corresp. Mem., Amer. Musicological Soc., 2008. Hon.

DHL Chicago, 2006. *Publications:* Pop Music and the Blues, 1972; Studying Popular Music, 1990; (ed) Reading Pop, 2000; (ed jtly) The Cultural Study of Music: a critical introduction, 2003, rev. edn 2011; Voicing the Popular, 2006; Musical Belongings, 2009. *Recreation:* farming. *Address:* Lochhill Farm, Crossmichael, Castle Douglas DG7 3BE.

MIDDLETON, Richard Harry; interim Deputy Vice Chancellor, Middlesex University, 2015–Dec. 2016; Chair, Commonwealth Scholarship Commission, since 2015 (Member, 2009–15); *b* Cheltenham, 27 March 1955; *s* of Harry and Beryl Middleton; partner, 1989, Heather McAteer; one *s* one *d. Educ:* Cheltenham Grammar Sch.; Univ. of York (BA 1977); Univ. of London (MA 1979); Open Univ. (MBA 2000). Field Worker, CHAR, 1980–85; Housing Officer, GLC, 1985–86; Dir, Housing Advice Switchboard and Housing Services Agency, 1987–94; Gen. Manager, Health and Personal Social Services NI, 1994–97; Ops Dir, MRC, 1997–2002; Directorate Manager, Univ. Hosps of Leicester NHS Trust, 2002–07; Chief Operating Officer, Aston Univ., 2007–10; Interim Hd of Resources and Planning, Kingston Univ., 2011–13; Registrar, City Univ. London, 2013; Interim Acad. Registrar, Univ. of Beds, 2013–14; Prog. Manager, Student Educn Service, Univ. of Leeds, 2014–15. Consultant, Develt for Res. Up-take in Sub-Saharan Africa prog., 2012–. FRSA. *Publications:* Who's to Benefit?, 1985. *Recreations:* cycling, walking and talking in good company. *Address:* Commonwealth Scholarship Commission, c/o Association of Commonwealth Universities, Woburn House, Tavistock Square, WC1H 9HF. *E:* richard.middleton@cscuk.org.uk.

MIDDLETON, Timothy John; Director in the Legal Service, Council of the European Union, since 2003; *b* 15 Sept. 1953; *s* of William Smith Middleton and Brenda Mary Middleton; *m* 1983, Janet Kathleen Elliott; one *s* two *d. Educ:* King Edward VII Grammar Sch., Coalville, Leics; Balliol Coll., Oxford (MA Jurisprudence); Coll. of Law. Called to the Bar, Gray's Inn, 1977; Legal Asst, 1979–83, Sen. Legal Asst, 1983–85, MAFF; on secondment to Directorate Gen. VI (Agriculture), CEC, 1985–87; Lawyer: MAFF, 1987–89; Legal Secretariat to Law Officers, 1989–92; Legal Dir, Intervention Bd, 1992–94; Hd of a Legal Div., MAFF, 1994–97; Dep. Legal Advr, Home Office, 1997–2001; Solicitor to Equitable Life Inquiry, 2001–03. Governor: Broadwater Sch., Godalming, 1999–2003; Green Lane Infants Sch., Godalming, 1996–2000. Churchwarden, St John the Evangelist, Farncombe, 2000–03. *Recreations:* modern literature, theatre, cooking. *Address:* Council of the European Union, Rue de la Loi 175, 1048 Brussels, Belgium.

MIDGLEY, Darrell; Chief Information Officer, Department for Business, Innovation and Skills, since 2012; *b* Portsmouth, 13 March 1957; *s* of Norman Tomlinson Midgley and Joan Midgley; *m* 1981, Carole Patricia; one *s* one *d. Educ:* Portsmouth Northern Grammar Sch.; Bath Technical Coll. (HNC Engrg 1979); Kingston Poly. (MSc (Dist.) Adv. Manufg 1989). Ministry of Defence: Defence Fixed Networks Team Leader, 2002–06; Armoured Vehicle Pathfinder Team Leader, 2006; Satellite Team Leader, 2007–09; Hd, Networks, 2009–11. *Recreations:* sport, military history, family, gardening. *Address:* Department for Business, Innovation and Skills, 1 Victoria Street, SW1H 0ET. *T:* (020) 7215 6001. *E:* darrell.midgley@bis.gsi.gov.uk.

MIDGLEY, Prof. Paul Anthony, PhD; FRS 2014; Professor of Materials Science, University of Cambridge, since 2008; Fellow, Peterhouse, Cambridge, since 2000; *b* Welwyn Garden City, 22 March 1966; *s* of John Barry Midgley and Hazel Malvene Midgley; *m* 2015, Caroline Louise Harbord. *Educ:* Univ. of Bristol (BSc 1987; MSc 1988; PhD 1991). Royal Exhibn of 1851 Res. Fellow, 1991–93, Royal Soc. Univ. Res. Fellow, 1994–97, Univ. of Bristol; University of Cambridge: Asst Dir of Res., 1997–2000; Lectr, 2000–01; Sen. Lectr, 2001–03; Reader in Electron Microscopy, 2003–08; Lectr, Peterhouse, Cambridge, 2000–08. Pres., Eur. Microscopy Soc., 2008–12. *Publications:* contrib. papers to learned jls on electron microscopy and its application. *Recreations:* walking, cricket, cinema, badminton, art. *Address:* Department of Materials Science and Metallurgy, University of Cambridge, 27 Charles Babbage Road, Cambridge CB3 0FS. *T:* (01223) 334561, *Fax:* (01223) 334567. *E:* pam33@cam.ac.uk.

MIDLETON, 12th Viscount *cr* 1717 (Ire.); **Alan Henry Brodrick;** Baron Brodrick of Midleton, Co. Cork 1715; Baron Brodrick of Peper Harow 1796; Museum Manager, British Horological Institute, since 2001 (Chairman, 1999–2000); *b* 4 Aug. 1949; *s* of Alan Rupert Brodrick (*d* 1972) (*ggs* of 7th Viscount) and of Alice Elizabeth, *d* of G. R. Roberts; *S* uncle, 1989; *m* 1st, 1978, Julia Helen (marr. diss. 2002), *d* of Michael Pitt; two *s* one *d*; 2nd, 2002, Maureen Susan, *d* of Joseph Sime. *Educ:* St Edmund's School, Canterbury. Keeper of Horology, John Gershom Parkington Collection of Time Measurement Instruments, Bury St Edmunds, 1986–2002. British Horological Institute: FBHI; Mem. Council, 1993; Chm. Museum and Liby Cttee, 1994; Chm., Mus. Trust, 1995. *Recreation:* bicycling. *Heir: s* Hon. Ashley Rupert Brodrick, *b* 25 Nov. 1980.

MIDORI; *see* Goto, Mi Dori.

MIDWINTER, Eric Clare, OBE 1992; MA, DPhil; writer; *b* 11 Feb. 1932; *m*; two *s* one *d. Educ:* St Catharine's Coll., Cambridge (BA Hons History); Univs of Liverpool (MA Educn) and York (DPhil). Educational posts, incl. Dir of Liverpool Educn Priority Area Project, 1955–75; Head, Public Affairs Unit, Nat. Consumer Council, 1975–80; Dir, Centre for Policy on Ageing, 1980–91, Chm., 2002–10. Chairman: Council, Adv. Centre for Educn, 1976–84; London Transport Users Consultative Cttee, 1977–84; London Regl Passengers' Cttee, 1984–96; Community Educn Develt Centre, 1995–2001. Mem., POW Adv. Cttee on Disability, 1990–95. Vis. Prof. of Educn, Univ. of Exeter, 1993–2002. Pres., Assoc. of Cricket Statisticians and Historians, 1997–2004. Chm., Cricket Soc. Book of the Year Award, 2002–09. DUniv Open, 1989. *Publications:* Victorian Social Reform, 1968; Law and Order in Victorian Lancashire, 1968; Social Administration in Lancashire, 1969; Nineteenth Century Education, 1970; Old Liverpool, 1971; Projections: an education priority project at work, 1972; Social Environment and the Urban School, 1972; Priority Education, 1972; Patterns of Community Education, 1973; (ed) Teaching in the Urban Community School, 1973; (ed) Pre-School Priorities, 1974; Education and the Community, 1975; Education for Sale, 1977; Make 'Em Laugh: famous comedians and their world, 1978; Schools and Society, 1980; W. G. Grace: his life and times, 1981; Age is Opportunity: education and older people, 1982; (ed) Mutual Aid Universities, 1984; The Wage of Retirement: the case for a new pensions policy, 1985; Fair Game: myth and reality in sport, 1986; Caring for Cash: the issue of private domiciliary care, 1986; Redefining Old Age, 1987; The Lost Seasons: wartime cricket 1939–1945, 1987; (ed) Retired Leisure, 1987; Polls Apart? Older Voters and the 1987 General Election, 1987; New Design for Old, Function, Style and Older People, 1988; Red Roses Crest the Caps: a history of Lancashire cricket, 1989; Creating Chances: arts by older people, 1990; Old Order: crime and older people, 1990; Out of Focus: old age, the press and broadcasting, 1991; Brylcreem summer: the 1947 cricket season, 1991; An Illustrated History of County Cricket, 1992; Lifelines, 1994; The Development of Social Welfare in Britain, 1994; First Knock: cricket's opening pairs, 1994; European Year '93, 1995; 150 Years: a celebration: Surrey CCC, 1995; Thriving People: the growth and prospects of the U3A in the UK, 1995; Darling Old Oval: history of Surrey County Cricket Club, 1995; State Educator: the life and enduring influence of W. E. Forster, 1996; Pensioned Off: retirement and income examined, 1997; Yesterdays: the way we were, 1998; The Billy Bunter Syndrome: or why Britain failed to create a relevant secondary school system, 1998; (ed) MCC Yearbook, 1998, 1999, MCC Annual, 2000–06; From Meadowland to Multinational: a review of cricket's social history, 2000; Yesterdays: our finest hours, 2001; Quill on Willow: cricket in literature, 2001; Best-remembered: a hundred stars of yesteryear, 2002; As One Stage Door Closes: the story of John Wade, jobbing conjuror, 2002; Novel Approaches: a guide to the popular classic novel, 2003; 500 Beacons: the USA story, 2004; Red Shirts and Roses: the story of the two Old Traffords, 2005; The People's Jesters: Twentieth Century British comedians, 2006; Lord Salisbury, 2006; Parish to Planet: how football came to rule the world, 2007; George Duckworth, Warrington's Ambassador at Large, 2007; An Outline of Political Thought and Practice, 2008; I Say, I Say, I Say: the double act story, 2009; The Cricketer's Progress: Meadowland to Mumbai, 2010; Best-remembered II: cinema and radio, 2013; Guide to Cricket Lore, 2014; *relevant publication:* Variety is the Spice of Life: the worlds of Eric Midwinter, by Jeremy Hardie, 2015. *Recreations:* sport, comedy. *Clubs:* Savage, MCC; Lancashire CC.

MIDWINTER, Prof. John Edwin, OBE 1984; PhD; FRS 1985; FREng; Pender Professor of Electronic Engineering, University College London, 1991–2004, now Professor Emeritus; *b* 8 March 1938; *s* of Henry C. and Vera J. Midwinter; *m* 1961, Maureen Anne Holt; two *s* two *d. Educ:* St Bartholomew's Grammar Sch., Newbury, Berks; King's Coll., Univ. of London (BSc Physics, 1961; AKC 1961). PhD Physics, London (ext.), 1968. MInstP 1973; FIET (FIEE 1980; Hon. Fellow 2009); FIEEE 1983; FREng (FEng 1984). Joined RRE, Malvern, as Scientific Officer, 1961 (research on lasers and non-linear optics); Sen. Scientific Officer, 1964–68; Perkin Elmer Corp., Norwalk, Conn, USA, 1968–70; Res. Center, Materials Research Center, Allied Chemical Corp., Morristown, NJ, USA, 1970–71; Head of Optical Fibre Develt, PO Res. Centre, Martlesham, 1971–77; Head, Optical Communications Technol., British Telecom Res. Labs, 1977–84; University College London: BT Prof. of Optoelectronics, 1984–91; Head, Dept of Electronic Engrg, later of Electronic and Electrical Engrg, 1988–98; Vice Provost, 1994–99. Pres., IEE, 2000–01 (Vice Pres., 1994; Dep. Pres., 1998–2000; Chm., Electronics Div., 1991–92). Lectures: Bruce Preller, RSE, 1983; Clifford Patterson, Royal Soc., 1983; Cantor, RSA, 1984; lectures on climate change and low carbon living, 2006–. Hon. DSc: Nottingham, 2000; Loughborough, 2001; QUB, 2004. Electronics Div. Premium, 1976, J. J. Thompson Medal, 1987, Faraday Medal, 1997, IEE; Eric Sumner Award and Medal, IEEE, 2002. *Publications:* Applied Non-Linear Optics, 1972; Optical Fibers for Transmission, 1979 (Best Book in Technol. Award, Amer. Publishers' Assoc., 1980); over 200 papers on lasers, non-linear optics and optical communications. *Recreations:* country and mountain walking, ski-ing, public and schools lectures on climate change and renewable energy. *E:* john.midwinter@btopenworld.com.

MIDWINTER, Stanley Walter, CB 1982; Chief Planning Inspector (Director of Planning Inspectorate), Departments of the Environment and Transport, 1978–84; *b* 8 Dec. 1922; *s* of late Lewis Midwinter and Beatrice (*née* Webb); *m* 1954, Audrey Mary Pepper (*d* 1988); one *d. Educ:* Regent Street Polytechnic Sch.; Sch. of Architecture (DipArch, ARIBA 1948); Sch. of Planning and Res. for Regional Develt (AMTPI 1952, FRTPI 1965); Dip. in Sociol., Univ. of London, 1976. Served War, RE, 1942–46: N Africa, Italy, Greece. Planning Officer, LCC, 1949–54; Bor. Architect and Planning Officer, Larne, NI, 1955–60; joined Housing and Planning Inspectorate, 1960; Dep. Chief Inspector, 1976. Assessor at Belvoir Coalfield Inquiry, 1979. Town Planning Institute: Exam. Prize, 1952; Thomas Adams Prize, 1955; President's Prize, 1958. *Publications:* articles in TPI Jl.

MIELE, Claire Lizbeth; *see* Johnston, C. L.

MIERS, Sir (Henry) David (Alastair Capel), KBE 1985; CMG 1979; HM Diplomatic Service, retired; Chairman, Society of Pension Consultants, 1998–2006; *b* 10 Jan. 1937; *s* of late Col R. D. M. C. Miers, DSO, QO Cameron Highlanders, and Honor (*née* Bucknill); *m* 1966, Imelda Maria Emilia, *d* of Jean-Baptiste Wouters, Huizingen, Belgium; two *s* one *d. Educ:* Winchester; University Coll., Oxford. Tokyo, 1963; Vientiane, 1966; Private Sec. to Minister of State, FO, 1968; Paris, 1972; Counsellor, Tehran, 1977–79; Hd, Middle Eastern Dept, FCO, 1980–83; Ambassador to Lebanon, 1983–85; Asst Under-Sec. of State, FCO, 1986–89; Ambassador: to Greece, 1989–93; to Netherlands, 1993–96. Chairman: British-Lebanese Assoc., 1998–2012; Anglo-Hellenic League, 1999–2007.

MIESENBÖCK, Prof. Gero, MD; FRS 2015; Waynflete Professor of Physiology, since 2007, and Director, Centre for Neural Circuits and Behaviour, since 2011, University of Oxford; *b* 15 July 1965; *s* of Dr Gottfried and Hannelore Miesenböck; *m* 1997, Barrie Dolnick; one *d. Educ:* Univ. of Innsbruck (MD 1993); Umeå Univ., Sweden. Postdoctoral Fellow, 1992–98, Asst Mem. and Hd, Lab. of Neural Systems, 1999–2004, Meml Sloan-Kettering Cancer Center, NY; Asst Prof. of Cell Biol., Genetics and Neurosci., Weill Med. Coll. of Cornell Univ., NY, 1999–2004; Associate Prof. of Cell Biol. and Cellular and Molecular Physiol., Yale Univ. Sch. of Medicine, 2004–07. Member: EMBO, 2008; Austrian Acad. of Sci., 2014. FMedSci 2012. InBev-Baillet Latour Health Prize, 2012; Brain Prize, Grete Lundbeck Eur. Brain Res. Foundn, 2013; Gabbay Award, Rosenstiel Center, Brandeis Univ., 2013. *Publications:* contribs to learned jls. *Recreations:* literature, travel, hiking, ski-ing, history of science. *Address:* Centre for Neural Circuits and Behaviour, University of Oxford, Tinsley Building, Mansfield Road, Oxford OX1 3SR.

MIFFLIN, Helen; Her Honour Judge Mifflin; a Circuit Judge, since 2008; *b* Blaina, Blaenau, Gwent, 29 April 1960; *d* of Thomas George Mifflin and Sarah Elizabeth Mifflin; *m* 1986, Leslie Adrian Blohm, *qv*; two *d. Educ:* Univ. of Leicester (LLB Hons 1981); Inns of Court Sch. of Law. Called to the Bar, Lincoln's Inn, 1982; in practice as barrister specialising in family law (care proceedings and ancillary relief); Recorder, 2000–08. *Recreations:* musical theatre, reading, cooking. *Address:* Swansea Civil Justice Centre, Caravella House, Quay West, Quay Street, Swansea SA1 1SP. *T:* (01792) 485800.

MIFLIN, Dr Benjamin John, PhD; Chairman, Crop Evaluation Ltd, 2000–09; Director, 1994–99, Lawes Trust Fellow, 1999–2012, Rothamsted Research (formerly Institute of Arable Crops Research Rothamsted); *b* 7 Jan. 1939; *s* of late Stanley Miflin and Kathleen (*née* Davies); *m* 1964, Hilary Newman; three *d. Educ:* Univ. of Nottingham (BSc); Univ. of Illinois (MS); QMC and Imperial Coll., London (PhD 1965). FRAgS 1988; FRSB (FIBiol 1997). Lectr in Plant Scis (Plant Biochem.), Sch. of Agric., Univ. of Newcastle upon Tyne, 1965–73; Hd, Biochem. Dept, 1973–85, and Div. of Molecular Scis, 1983–85, Rothamsted Exptl Stn, Harpenden; Hd, Internat. R & D, Ciba-Geigy Seeds, Basle, 1986–93. Vis. Prof., Univ. of Nottingham, 1981–85 and 1994–2000. Mem., Adv. Cttee on Novel Foods and Processes, 1995–98. Corresp. Mem., Amer. Soc. of Plant Physiologists, 1986. *Publications:* (ed) The Biochemistry of Plants, Vol. 5, 1980, (ed with P. J. Lea) Vol. 16, 1990; (ed) Oxford Surveys of Plant Cell and Molecular Biology, Vols 1–7, 1984–91; numerous papers in field of plant biochem. and related subjects. *Recreations:* ski-ing, gardening, photography. *Address:* St Martin's, 51 Steyne Road, Seaford, E Sussex BN25 1HU.

MIFSUD BONNICI, Dr Carmelo, BA, LLD; Prime Minister of Malta, 1984–87; *b* 17 July 1933; *s* of Dr Lorenzo Mifsud Bonnici, and Catherine (*née* Buttigieg). *Educ:* Govt sch. and Lyceum, Malta; Univ. of Malta (BA, LLD); University Coll. London. Lectr in Industrial and Fiscal Law, Univ. of Malta, 1969–86. Legal Consultant, General Workers' Union, 1969–83; Dep. Leader, Labour Party, responsible for Party affairs, 1980–82; Designate Leader of the Labour Movement, 1982; co-opted to Parlt, 1983, Minister of Labour and Social Services, 1983; Sen. Dep. Prime Minister, 1983–84; Leader, Labour Party, 1984–92; MP First District, 1987–96. *Recreation:* reading. *Address:* Hamrun, Malta.

MIFSUD BONNICI, Dr Ugo; President of Malta, 1994–99; *b* 8 Nov. 1932; *m* 1959, Gemma Bianco; two *s* one *d. Educ:* Lyceum, Malta; Univ. of Malta (BA 1952; LLD 1955). Elected MP, 2nd Electoral Div., 1966–94; Shadow Minister of Educn, 1971–87; President: General Council, 1976; Admin. Council, 1976; Minister of: Educn, 1987–90; Educn and the Interior, 1990–92; Educn and Human Resources, 1992–94. Mem., Venice Commn, 2001–13.

Companion of Honour, Nat. Order of Merit (Malta). *Publications:* Biex il-Futur Jerga' Jibda, 1976; Il-Linja t-Tajba, 1980; Biex il-Futur Rega' Beda, 1992; Il-Manwal tal-President, 1997; Kif Sirna Repubblika, 1999; An Introduction to Comparative Law, 2004; An Introduction to Cultural Heritage Law, 2008; An Introduction to the Law of Education, 2014; Konvinzjoni u Esperjenza, 2015. *Recreations:* reading, writing, listening to music. *Address:* 18 Triq Erin Serracino Inglott, Cospicua, BML 1305, Malta. *Club:* Casino Maltese.

MILAŠINOVIĆ MARTINOVIĆ, Tanja, PhD; Ambassador of Bosnia and Herzegovina to the Republic of Austria, since 2012; *b* 28 June 1962; *d* of Rade and Radosava Milašinović. *Educ:* Univ. of Zagreb (MSc 1988); Univ. of Ljubljana (PhD 1992). Asst, Fac. of Mining, Geol. and Petroleum, Univ. of Zagreb, 1986–87; res. work, 1987–91, Asst, 1989–91, Inst. of Experimental Physics, Ludwig Maximilians Univ., Munich; Asst Prof., Faculties of Agric. and of Forestry, Univ. of Belgrade, 1992–98; Asst Minister, Min. of Foreign Econ. Affairs, Rep. of Srpska Govt, 1998–2001; Minister Counsellor and Chargé d'Affaires, Mission of Bosnia and Herzegovina to EU, Min. of Foreign Affairs, 2001–05; Ambassador of Bosnia and Herzegovina to the Court of St James's, 2005–08; Hd, Dept. for Western Europe, Min. of Foreign Affairs of Bosnia and Herzegovina, 2008–11. *Publications:* articles in learned jls. *Recreation:* tennis. *Address:* Embassy of Bosnia and Herzegovina, Tivoligasse 54, 1120 Vienna, Austria.

MILBANK, Prof. (Alasdair) John, PhD, DD; Research Professor of Religion, Politics and Ethics, and Director, Centre of Theology and Philosophy, University of Nottingham, since 2004; *b* 23 Oct. 1952; *s* of John Douglas Milbank and Jean Hyslop Milbank; *m* 1978, Alison Grant Legg; one *s* one *d*. *Educ:* Queen's Coll., Oxford (MA); PhD Birmingham 1986; DD Cantab 1998. Christendom Trust Teaching Fellow, Lancaster Univ., 1983–91; University of Cambridge: Lectr in Theol., 1991–96; Reader in Philosophical Theol., 1996–98; Fellow, Peterhouse, 1993–98; Frances Myers Ball Prof. of Philosophical Theol., Univ. of Virginia, 1999–2004. *Publications:* Theology and Social Theory, 1990, 2nd edn 2006; The Religious Dimension in Vico's Thought, Part I 1991, Part II 1992; The Word Made Strange: theology, language, culture, 1996; The Mercurial Wood (poems), 1997; (ed jtly) Radical Orthodoxy: a new theology, 1998; (with C. Pickstock) Truth in Aquinas, 2001; Being Reconciled: ontology and pardon, 2002; The Suspended Middle, 2005; The Legend of Death (poems), 2008; The Monstrosity of Christ, 2009; The Future of Love: essays in political theology, 2009; Paul's New Moment, 2010; Beyond Secular Order, 2013. *Recreations:* walking, poetry, photography, cinema, reading fiction, early music, archaeology. *Address:* Burgage Hill Cottage, Burgage, Southwell, Notts NG25 0EP. *T:* (01636) 819224, *Fax:* (office) (0115) 951 5887. *E:* john.milbank@nottingham.ac.uk. *Club:* Travellers.

MILBANK, Sir Anthony (Frederick), 5th Bt *cr* 1882; DL; farmer and landowner, since 1977; *b* 16 Aug. 1939; *s* of Sir Mark Vane Milbank, 4th Bt, KCVO, MC, and Hon. Verena Aileen, Lady Milbank (*d* 1995), *yr d* of 11th Baron Farnham, DSO; *S* father, 1984; *m* 1970, Belinda Beatrice, *yr d* of Brig. Adrian Gore, DSO; two *s* one *d*. *Educ:* Eton College. Brown, Shipley & Co. Ltd, 1961–66; M&G Securities Ltd, 1966–77. Chairman: Moorland Assoc., 1987–2001; Northern Uplands Moorland Regeneration Project, 1999–2001; Member: NCC Cttee for England, 1989–91; CLA Exec. Cttee, 1989–94; Council, RSPB, 1993–98, 2007–11. Pres., Yorks Wildlife Trust, 2000–03. High Sheriff of Durham, 1991–92; DL N Yorks, 1998. *Recreation:* various. *Heir: s* Edward Mark Somerset Milbank [*b* 9 April 1973; *m* 2008, Natalie Hicks-Löbbecke; two *s* one *d*]. *Address:* The Gate House, Barningham, Richmond, N Yorks DL11 7DW.

MILBANK, John; *see* Milbank, A. J.

MILBERG, Dr Joachim; Chairman, Supervisory Board, BMW AG, 2004–15 (Member, 2002–04); *b* Verl, Westfalia, 10 April 1943. *Educ:* Bielefeld State Engrg Coll.; Berlin Tech. Univ. (Dr ing 1971). Apprentice machine fitter, 1959–62; Res. Asst, Inst. Machine Tool and Prodn Technol., Berlin Tech. Univ., 1970–72; Exec. Manager, 1972–78, Hd, Automatic Turning Machines Div., 1978–81, Werkzeugmaschinenfabrik Gildemeister AG; Prof. of Machine Tools and Mgt Sci., Munich Tech. Univ., 1981–93; BMW AG: Member Board of Management: Prodn, 1993–98; Engrg and Prodn, 1998–99; Chm., Bd of Mgt, 1999–2002.

MILBORNE-SWINNERTON-PILKINGTON, Sir Thomas Henry; *see* Pilkington.

MILBOURN, Dr Graham Maurice; Director, National Institute of Agricultural Botany, 1981–90, retired; *b* 4 Sept. 1930; *s* of late Frank Milbourn, BSc and Winifred Milbourn; *m* 1956, Louise Lawson, BSc Hons; three *s*. *Educ:* Reading Univ. (BSc, MSc, PhD). Served RN, 1948–50. Asst Lectr, Reading Univ., 1953–56; SO, ARC Radiobiological Lab., 1956–61; Sen. Lectr, Crop Production, Wye Coll., London Univ., 1961–77; Prof. of Crop Production, Sch. of Agric., Edinburgh Univ., 1977–81. Vis. Prof., Silsoe Coll., Cranfield Univ. (formerly Inst. of Technology), 1991–2003. Pres., Assoc. Applied Biologists, 1991. *Publications:* papers on physiology of cereals and vegetables, uptake of radio-nucleides by crops. *Recreation:* sailing.

MILBURN, Rt Hon. Alan; PC 1998; Chairman, Social Mobility and Child Poverty Commission, since 2012; *b* 27 Jan. 1958; *m* 2007, Dr Ruth Briel; two *s*. *Educ:* Stokesley Comprehensive Sch.; Lancaster Univ. (BA). Co-ordinator, Trade Union Studies Information Unit, Newcastle, 1984–90; Sen. Business Development Officer, N Tyneside MBC, 1990–92. MP (Lab) Darlington, 1992–2010. Opposition front bench spokesman on health, 1995–96, on Treasury and econ. affairs, 1996–97; Minister of State, DoH, 1997–98; Chief Sec. to HM Treasury, 1998–99; Sec. of State for Health, 1999–2003; Chancellor, Duchy of Lancaster, 2004–05. Mem., Public Accounts Cttee, 1994–95; Chair, PLP Treasury Cttee, 1992–95. Govt's Ind. Reviewer on Social Mobility, 2010–12, and on Child Poverty, 2011–12. Chancellor, Lancaster Univ., 2015–.

MILBURN, Sir Anthony (Rupert), 5th Bt *cr* 1905; landowner; *b* 17 April 1947; *s* of Major Rupert Leonard Eversley Milburn (*yr s* of 3rd Bt) (*d* 1974) and of Anne Mary, *d* of late Major Austin Scott Murray, MC; *S* uncle, 1985; *m* 1977, Olivia Shirley, *y d* of Captain Thomas Noel Catlow, CBE, DL, RN; two *s* one *d*. *Educ:* Hawtreys, Savernake Forest; Eton College; Cirencester Agricultural Coll. MRICS. *Recreation:* sporting and rural pursuits. *Heir: s* Patrick Thomas Milburn [*b* 4 Dec. 1980; *m* 2009, Marina Louise, *o d* of Sir David Ralli, Bt, *qv*; one *s*]. *Address:* Bog House, Matfen, Newcastle upon Tyne NE20 0RF. *Club:* New (Edinburgh).

MILDMAY, Sir Walter John Hugh St J.; *see* St John-Mildmay.

MILDON, His Honour Arthur Leonard; QC 1971; a Circuit Judge, 1986–96; *b* 3 June 1923; *er s* of late Rev. Dr W. H. Mildon, Barnstaple; *m* 1950, Iva, *er d* of late G. H. C. Wallis, Plymouth; one *s* one *d*. *Educ:* Kingswood Sch., Bath; Wadham Coll., Oxford (MA). Pres., Oxford Univ. Liberal Club, 1948. Army Service, 1942–46: Lieut, 138th (City of London) Field Regt, RA; Captain, 1st Army Group, RA. Called to Bar, Middle Temple, 1950, Bencher, 1979, Lent Reader, 1999; Member of Western Circuit; Dep. Chm., Isle of Wight QS, 1967–71; a Recorder, 1972–85. Mem., Bar Council, 1973–74. Pres., Medico-Legal Soc., 1994–96. *Recreation:* sailing. *Address:* c/o 4 New Square, Lincoln's Inn, WC2A 3RJ. *T:* (020) 7822 2000.

See also D. W. Mildon.

MILDON, David Wallis; QC 2000; *b* 19 Sept. 1955; *s* of His Honour Arthur Leonard Mildon, *qv*; *m* 1983, Lesley Mary Richardson (*d* 2013); one *s* one *d*. *Educ:* Emmanuel Coll., Cambridge (LLB; MA). Called to the Bar, Middle Temple, 1980; in practice at the Bar, 1980–. *Recreations:* music, sailing. *Address:* Essex Court Chambers, 24 Lincoln's Inn Fields, WC2A 3EG. *T:* (020) 7813 8000.

MILDON, Russell; occasional speaker and consultant; Director, Common Market Organisations, European Commission, 2005–09; *b* 22 Aug. 1949; *s* of R. F. Mildon and J. Mildon (*née* Kröpfl); *m* 1973, Micheline Williams; two *s* one *d*. *Educ:* Royal Holloway Coll., London Univ. (Open Schol.; BSc Hons); Brunel Univ. (MTech). With Commission of the European Communities, 1974–: Statistics, studies and reports (Agricl), 1974–81; Gen. Affairs Gp, 1981–83; Private Sec. to Dep. Dir Gen., Agricl Markets, 1983–86; Advr to Vice-Pres., 1986–89; Head: Unit for Analysis of Situation of Agricl Holdings, 1989; Unit for Oilseeds and Protein Crops, 1989–93; Director: Internat. affairs relating to agric., 1993–96; orgn of markets in specialised crops, 1996–2001; Audit of Agricl Expenditure, Personnel and Admin, 2001–02; orgn of markets in crops, 2002–05. Occasional speaker and consultant. *Recreations:* wine and spirits, chess, travel.

MILEDI, Prof. Ricardo, MD; FRS 1970; Distinguished Professor, University of California, Irvine, since 1984; *b* Mexico City, 15 Sept. 1927; *m* 1955, Ana Carmen (Mela) Garces; one *s*. *Educ:* Univ. Nacional Autónoma, Mexico City. BSc 1945; MD 1955. Research at Nat. Inst. of Cardiology, Mexico, 1952–54; Rockefeller Travelling Fellowship at ANU, 1956–58; research at Dept of Biophysics, UCL, 1958–84. Fellow, Amer. Acad. of Arts and Scis, 1986; Mem., Nat. Acad. of Scis, 1989; Hon. Member: Hungarian Acad. of Scis, 1988; Mexican Acad. of Medicine, 1995; Corresp. Mem., Mexican Acad. of Scis, 1991; Titular Mem., Eur. Acad. of Arts, Scis and Humanities, 1992. Dr *hc*: Universidad del País Vasco, Spain, 1992; Univ. Nacional Autónoma de Mexico, 2007. Luigi Galvani Award, 1987; Internat. Prize for Science, King Faisal Foundn, 1988; Royal Medal, Royal Soc., 1998. *Address:* Laboratory of Cellular and Molecular Neurobiology, Department of Neurobiology and Behavior, 1215 and 1140 McGaugh Hall, University of California, Irvine, CA 92697–4550, USA. *T:* and *Fax:* (949) 8246090. *E:* rmiledi@uci.edu; 9 Gibbs Court, Irvine, CA 92612, USA. *T:* (714) 8562677.

MILEHAM, Peter; DL; National President, British Chambers of Commerce, 2006–08 (Director, 2002–08); *b* 31 March 1943; *s* of William John Mileham and Mary Margaret, (Mayda), Mileham (*née* Kerrigan); *m* 1973, Shelagh Frances Preston; two *d*. *Educ:* Scarborough Tech. Coll. (HND Bldg 1965); Hull and York Tech. Colls. MIOB. Dir, Liquid Plastics Ltd, Preston, 1973–2008. Chm., Preston and NW, Yorkshire Bank, 2005–12. Mem., Parly All Party Corporate Governance Gp, 2007–; Chm., Cons. Northern Transport Commn, 2009–. Director: NW Lancs Chamber of Commerce, 1992–2011; Creative Lancashire, 2013–. Vice Pres., Eurochambres Brussels, 2006–09. Dir, UK India Business Council, 2006–09. Mem. Council: Duchy of Lancaster Benevolent Fund, 2006–12; St John Ambulance, 2008–12. Dir, Bd of Trustees, Blackburn Cathedral, 2012–. Ambassador for Rosemere Cancer Care Foundn, Lancs and S Cumbria, 1980–; Citizens in Policing Ambassador, Lancs Constabulary, 2013–. Advr, Lionheart Trust, Glasgow, 2009–. Hon. Fellow, Univ. of Central Lancashire, 2009–. DL 2004, High Sheriff 2011–12, Lancs. Prestonian of the Year, Preston Guild, 2012. *Publications:* various papers and articles in leading construction industry press. *Recreations:* gardening, arts, classical music. *Address:* Bucklebury, 46 Lightfoot Lane, Fulwood, Preston PR2 3LR. *T:* (01772) 862220. *E:* peter.mileham@talktalk.net.

MILES, Anthony John; Executive Publisher, Globe Communications Corporation, Florida, USA, 1985–90; *b* 18 July 1930; *s* of Paul and Mollie Miles; *m* 1975, Anne Hardman. *Educ:* High Wycombe Royal Grammar Sch. On staff of (successively): Middlesex Advertiser; Nottingham Guardian; Brighton Evening Argus. Daily Mirror: Feature writer, 1954–66; Asst Editor, 1967–68; Associate Editor, 1968–71; Editor, 1971–74; Mirror Group Newspapers: Editorial Dir, 1975–84; Dep. Chm., 1977–79 and 1984; Chm., 1980–83. Dir, Reuters Ltd, 1978–84. Member: Press Council, 1975–78; British Exec. Cttee, IPI, 1976–84; Council, CPU, 1983–84; Life Vice-Pres., Newspaper Press Fund (Appeal Chm., 1982–83). *Address:* 6 Dukes Point, Dukes Head Yard, Highgate Village, N6 5JQ; Millennium Cottage, Dunster, Som TA24 6SY. *Clubs:* Garrick, Reform, Savile.

MILES, Barry; author; *b* Cheltenham, Glos, 21 Feb. 1943; *s* of Albert Miles and May Miles; *m* 1994, Rosemary Bailey; one *s*. *Educ:* Cirencester Grammar Sch.; Gloucestershire Coll. of Art (NDD 1963); Univ. of London (ATD 1964). Manager, Better Books, 1965; co-owner and Manager, Indica Books and Gall., 1965–70; co-Founder, publisher, editor, Mem. Editl Bd, International Times, 1966–74; audio archivist to Allen Ginsberg, 1970–72; archivist to William Burroughs, 1972; Editor, Time Out, 1978–79. Vis. Fellow, Liverpool John Moores Univ., 2007–. *Publications:* A Catalogue of the William S. Burroughs Archive, 1973; (with Joe Maynard) William S. Burroughs: a bibliography 1953–73, 1978; Ginsberg: a biography, 1989, 2nd edn 2002; William Burroughs: el hombre invisible, 1993; Paul McCartney: many years from now, 1997; (with Charles Perry) I Want to Take You Higher: the psychedelic era 1965–69, 1998; The Beatles: a diary, 1998; Jack Kerouac, King of the Beats: a portrait, 1998; The Beat Hotel: Ginsberg, Burroughs, and Corso in Paris, 1957–1963, 2000; In the Sixties, 2002; Hippie, 2003; Frank Zappa, 2004; Bukowski, 2005; Pink Floyd: the early years, 2006; Peace: 50 years of protest 1958–2008, 2008; The British Invasion, 2009; London Calling: a countercultural history of London since 1945, 2009; In the Seventies, 2011; William S. Burroughs: a life, 2014. *Recreations:* visiting art openings, drinking with friends in Soho. *Address:* c/o Antony Harwood Literary Agency, 103 Walton Street, Oxford OX2 6EB. *T:* (01865) 559615. *E:* james@antonyharwood.com. *Club:* Groucho.

MILES, Brian, CBE 1994; RD 1970; FNI; RNR (retired); Director, Royal National Lifeboat Institution, 1988–98; *b* 23 Feb. 1937; *s* of Terence Clifford Miles and Muriel Irene Terry; *m* 1964, Elizabeth Anne Scott; one *s* two *d*. *Educ:* Reed's School, Cobham; HMS Conway; Merchant Navy Cadet School. Master Mariner (Foreign Going) Cert. P&O Orient Lines: Cadet, 1954–57; Deck Officer, 1958–64; RNLI: Divl Inspector, 1964–73; Asst to Director, 1974–79; Ops Staff Officer, 1979–81; Dep. Dir, 1982–87. Chairman: Friends of Dolphin Trust, 1989–; Poole Arts Trust, 1996–2003; Member Council: Royal Nat. Mission to Deep Sea Fishermen, 1999–2012 (Dep. Chm., 2001–05, Chm., 2005–09); Dorset Br., BRCS, 2000–03. FNI 1989; CCMI (CIMgt 1994). Freeman, City of London, 1993; Mem., Master Mariners' Co., 1994–. Younger Brother, Trinity House, 1994. Comdr, Order of Lion (Finland), 1997. *Address:* 8 Longfield Drive, West Parley, Ferndown, Dorset BH22 8TY. *T:* (01202) 571739.

MILES, Caroline Valerie; *see* Pidgeon, C. V.

MILES, Prof. Christopher John; film director and producer; *b* 19 April 1939; *s* of late John Miles, MC and Clarice Baskerville (*née* Remnant); *m* 1967, Susan Helen Howard Armstrong; one *d*. *Educ:* Winchester Coll.; Institut des Hautes Etudes Cinématographiques, Paris. Dir, Milesian Film Productions, 1962–; *films* include: Six Sided Triangle, 1963; The Virgin and the Gypsy, 1970 (Best Film Award, US and UK Critics, 1970); Time for Loving, 1972; The Maids, 1974; That Lucky Touch, 1976; Alternative Three, 1977; Priest of Love: life of D. H. Lawrence, 1981; Lord Elgin and some stones of no value, 1985; Cyclone Warning Class 4, 1994; The Clandestine Marriage, 1999; *theatre:* Skin of our Teeth, Chicago, 1973; The Two Symposiums (Il Simposio antico e moderno), Italy, 2013; *television:* Zinotchka, 1973; Neck, 1978; Love in the Ancient World, 1996; Fire from Olympia, 2004. Prof. of Film and Television, RCA, 1989–93. Lecture tours: India, for British Council, 1985; USA, 1986. FRCA 1989. Patron, Marlowe Soc., 1995–. *Publications:* Alternative Three, 1977 (trans. 5 langs); (with John Julius Norwich) Love in the Ancient World, 1996; (contrib.) H of C Report on Film, 1982; contrib. Image et Son, D. H. Lawrence Soc. Jl. *Recreations:* film-making, long walks and sketching in Arcadia. *Address:* Calstone House, Calstone, Calne, Wilts SN11 8PY. *Club:* Garrick.

MILES, David, FSA, FSAScot; Chief Archaeological Advisor, English Heritage, 2005–08 (Chief Archaeologist, 1999–2005); *b* 6 Dec. 1947; *s* of Tom and Norah Miles; *m* 1969, Gwyn Morgan (*see* Gwyn Miles); one *s* one *d*. *Educ:* St Gregory's Grammar Sch., Huddersfield; King Edward VI Grammar Sch., Nuneaton; Birmingham Univ. (BA Hons). Dir of Excavations, M5 Excavation Cttee, 1970–71; Res. Asst, Bristol Univ., 1971–72; Director of Excavations: Abingdon Excavation Cttee, 1972–73; Upper Thames Excavation Cttee, 1973–74; Dep. Dir, 1974–87, Dir, 1987–99, Oxford Archaeological Unit. FSA 1984; FSAScot 2000. MCIfA (MIFA 1988). *Publications:* (with D. Benson) The Upper Thames Valley, 1974; An Introduction to Archaeology, 1977; (ed) The Romano-British Countryside, 1982; (ed with B. Cunliffe) Aspects of the Iron Age in Central Southern Britain, 1984; (ed with K. Branigan) The Economies of Romano-British Villas, 1987; (jtly) Two Oxfordshire Anglo-Saxon Cemeteries: Berinsfield and Didcot, 1995; (jtly) The Anglo-Saxon Cemetery at Butler's Field, Lechlade, Gloucestershire, 1998; (jtly) Uffington White Horse and its Landscape, 2003; The Tribes of Britain, 2005; (jtly) Iron Age and Roman Settlement in the Thames Valley, 2007; contrib. to learned jls, newspapers and magazines. *Recreations:* reading, gardening, arts. *Address:* 42 Reynolds Place, Blackheath, SE3 8SX; Pailler de la Devezette, 30460 Lasalle, France. *E:* david.miles66@btinternet.com.

MILES, Prof. David Kenneth, PhD; Professor of Economics, Imperial College London, since 2013; *b* 6 Oct. 1959; *s* of Kenneth Douglas Miles and Rebecca Owen; *m* 1997, Faye Dimdore; one *s* two *d*. *Educ:* Bishop Gore Sch., Swansea; University Coll., Oxford (BA PPE 1981); Nuffield Coll., Oxford (MPhil Econs 1983); Birkbeck Coll., London (PhD Econs 1993). Economist, Bank of England, 1983–89; Lectr, then Reader, Birkbeck Coll., London, 1989–93; Econ. Advr, Bank of England, 1993–94; Chief UK Economist, Merrill Lynch, 1994–96; Prof. of Financial Econs, 1996–2004, Vis. Prof., 2004–13, Imperial Coll. London; Man. Dir in Econ. Res. and Chief UK Economist, Morgan Stanley, 2004–09. Mem., MPC, Bank of England, 2009–15. Non-exec. Dir, FSA, 2004–09; Specialist Advr, Treasury Select Cttee, 1999–. Fellow, Centre for Econ. Policy Res., 1992–; Member, Council: NIESR, 2004–; REconS, 2010–. Gov., Pensions Inst., 2002–; Trustee, IFS, 2010–. Ed., Fiscal Studies, 1997–2004. *Publications:* Housing, Financial Markets and the Wider Economy, 1994; (with A. Scott) Macroeconomics: understanding the wealth of nations, 2001, 2nd edn 2004; (ed jtly) The Economics of Public Spending, 2003; The Miles Review of the UK Mortgage Market, 2004; (with A. Scott and F. Breedon) Macroeconomics: understanding the global economy, 2012; articles in econs jls and chapters in books. *Recreations:* cinema, squash, Rugby, children. *Address:* Imperial College Business School, Imperial College London, South Kensington Campus, SW7 2AZ.

MILES, Gwyn; Director, Somerset House Trust, 2006–14; *b* 17 Nov. 1947; *d* of Sir Morien Morgan, CB, FRS and of Lady Morgan (*née* Axford); *m* 1969, David Miles, *qv*; one *s* one *d*. *Educ:* Bristol Univ. (BSc Physiol.); Bath Univ. (DipEd); Museums Assoc. (Cert. in Conservation). Research Assistant: McGill Univ., Montreal, 1969; Bristol Univ., 1969–70; Science Teacher, St Mary Redcliffe and Temple Sch., Bristol, 1971; Department of Antiquities, Ashmolean Museum, Oxford: Conservator, 1972–82; Head of Conservation, 1982–85; Victoria and Albert Museum: Dep. Keeper of Conservation, 1985–89; Surveyor of Collections, 1989–95; Dir of Major Projects, 1995–2002; Dir, Projects and Estate, 2002–05. Trustee: The Making, 2004–12; Sainsbury Centre for the Visual Arts, 2011–. Hon. FRIBA 2011. *Publications:* Traditional Knitting in the British Isles, 1979; articles on conservation, collections management and gardening. *Recreations:* arts, architecture, gardening. *Address:* 42 Reynolds Place, Blackheath, SE3 8SX. *T:* (020) 8858 5580; Le Pailler de la Devezette, 30460 Lasalle, France.

MILES, Prof. Hamish Alexander Drummond, OBE 1987; Barber Professor of Fine Arts and Director of the Barber Institute, University of Birmingham, 1970–90, Professor at Large and Emeritus Director, 1990–91, Emeritus Professor, since 1992; *b* 19 Nov. 1925; *s* of J. E. (Hamish) Miles and Sheila Barbara Robertson; *m* 1957, Jean Marie, *d* of T. R. Smits, New York; two *s* two *d*. *Educ:* Douai Sch.; Univ. of Edinburgh (MA); Balliol Coll., Oxford. Served War: Army, 1944–47. Asst Curator, Glasgow Art Gallery, 1953–54; Asst Lectr, then Lectr in the History of Art, Univ. of Glasgow, 1954–66; Vis. Lectr, Smith Coll., Mass, 1960–61; Prof. of the History of Art, Univ. of Leicester, 1966–70. Trustee, National Galleries of Scotland, 1967–87; Mem., Museums and Galleries Commn, 1983–87. *Publications:* (jtly) The Paintings of James McNeill Whistler, 2 vols, 1980; sundry articles and catalogues. *Recreation:* woodland management. *Address:* 31 Drummond Place, Edinburgh EH3 6PW; Burnside, Kirkmichael, Blairgowrie, Perthshire PH10 7NA.

MILES, (Henry) Michael (Pearson), OBE 1989; Chairman: Schroders, 2003–12; Johnson Matthey PLC, 1998–2006 (Director, 1990–2006); London Mining plc, 2013–14; *b* 19 April 1936; *s* of late Brig. H. G. P. Miles and Margaret Miles; *m* 1967, Carol Jane Berg; two *s* one *d*. *Educ:* Wellington Coll. National Service, Duke of Wellington's Regt, 1955–57. Joined John Swire & Sons, 1958; Dir, John Swire & Sons (HK) Ltd, 1970–99 (Chm., 1984–88); Managing Director: John Swire & Sons (Japan) Ltd, 1973–76; Cathay Pacific Airways Ltd, 1978–84 (Chm., 1984–88); Chm., Swire Pacific, 1984–88; Exec. Dir, 1988–99, Advr to Board, 1999–2009, John Swire & Sons Ltd. Director: Baring PLC, 1989–95 (Jt Dep. Chm., 1994–95); Portals Holdings, 1990–95; BP, 1994–2006; ING Baring Hldgs Co., 1995–2002; BICC, 1996–2002. Chm., Hong Kong Tourist Assoc., 1984–88. Vice Pres., China Britain Business Gp, 1995–2000. Gov., Wellington Coll., 1988–2005. *Recreations:* golf, tennis. *Address:* 31 Roland Gardens, SW7 3PF. *Clubs:* White's; Queen's; Royal and Ancient Golf; Berkshire Golf; Sunningdale Golf.

MILES, Jenefer Mary; *see* Blackwell, J. M.

MILES, Prof. John Richard; Professor of Fashion and Textiles, Bath Spa University (formerly Bath Spa University College), 2002–13, now Emeritus; *b* 22 June 1944; *s* of Thomas William Miles and Hilda Mary Miles (*née* Davis); *m* 1963, Judith Bud (marr. diss.). *Educ:* Croydon Coll. of Art; Royal Coll. of Art (MDes). Set up design studio, Miles Calver and Pound (now Calver and Pound), 1973–78 (Director); Founder Dir, Peppermint Prints, 1978–82; founded John Miles Partnership, 1996. Head, Textiles and Fashion, Brighton Polytechnic, 1979–85; Design Dir, Courtaulds, 1985–87; Gen. Manager, Next, 1987–89; Prof. of Fashion and Textiles, RCA, 1989–97; Dir of Product Mkting, DMC, France, 1997–2000; Prof. of Design, Southampton Univ., 2001–02. Visiting Professor: Huddersfield Univ., 2010–; Univ. of Derby, 2014–. External examr to various univs, incl. Chief Ext. Examr, Staffs Univ., 2013–. Advr, Goldsmiths, Univ. of London, 2013–14. Consultant, Studio Claire and Lyn; Dir, Miles Whiston and Wright, 1989–96. Chm., Textile and Fashion Panel, CNAA, 1983–96; Mem., Industrial Lead Body, 1991–95. Governor, Winchester Sch. of Art, 1989–94. Hon. Dr of Design, Southampton, 1998. *Recreations:* gardening, films, cooking, reading. *Address:* The Old School House, 54 Main Street, South Rauceby, Sleaford, Lincs NG34 8QQ.

MILES, John Seeley, FCSD, FSTD; typographer and graphic designer; *b* 11 Feb. 1931; *s* of Thomas William Miles and Winifred (*née* Seeley); *m* 1955, Louise Wilson; one *s* two *d*. *Educ:* Beckenham and Penge Grammar Sch.; Beckenham School of Art. FCSD (FSIAD 1973); FSTD 1974. UN travelling schol. to Netherlands to practise typography and punch cutting under Jan van Krimpen and S. L. Hartz, 1954–55; Assistant to Hans Schmoller at Penguin Books, 1955–58; joined Colin Banks to form design partnership, Banks and Miles, 1958, Partner, 1958–96; Dir, Parsimony Press, 1999–2003. Consultant to: Zoological Soc., Regent's Park and Whipsnade, 1958–82; Expanded Metal Co., 1960–83; Consumers' Assoc., 1964–93; British Council, 1968–83; The Post Office, 1972–83; E Midlands Arts Assoc., 1974–79; Curwen Press, 1970–72; Basilisk Press, 1976–79; Enschedé en Zn, Netherlands, 1980–94; British Telecom, 1980–89; BAA, 1983–87; typographic advisor, HMSO, 1985–96; design advisor: Agricl Inf. Workshop, Udaipur, India, 1973; Monotype Corp., 1985–92; hon. design advisor: UEA, 1990–97; UNHCR, Geneva, 1994–99; Internat. Assoc. Univs, Paris, 2000–03; Aston-Mansfield Charities, 2001–03; Memorial Arts Charity, 2005–14; Southwell Minster, 2008–14. Designed banknote series Netherlands Antilles, 1987. Member: PO Design Adv. Cttee, 1972–76; Icograda Internat. Archive Cttee, 1993–2003. American Heritage Lectr, New York, 1960; held seminar, Graphic Inst., Stockholm, 1977 and 1986. Chairman: Wynkyn de Worde Soc., 1973–74; Arbitration Cttee, Assoc. Typographique Internationale, 1984–2002; Mem., Soc. Roy. des Bibliophiles et Iconophiles de Belgique, 1991–94. Governor, Central School of Arts and Crafts, 1978–85; External examiner: London Coll. of Printing, 1984–88; Technische Hoogschool Delft, 1986–87; Reading Univ., 1990–93; De Montfort Univ., 1994–99; Plymouth Univ., 2004–07. Mem. CGLI, 1986. Exhibitions: London, 1971, 1978; Amsterdam and Brussels, 1977; Hamburg, 1991. FRSA 1988. (With Colin Banks) Green Product Award, 1989; BBC Envmtl Award, 1990. *Publications:* The Puffin Noah's Ark, 1958; Design for Desktop Publishing, 1987; articles and reviews in professional jls. *Recreations:* gardening, painting, reading aloud. *Address:* Pit Cottage, Tunstall Common, Woodbridge, Suffolk IP12 2JR. *T:* (01728) 688889. *Club:* Double Crown.

MILES, Prof. Mervyn John, PhD; FRS 2011; CPhys, FInstP; Professor of Physics, since 1999, and Director, Centre for Nanoscience and Quantum Information, 2011–14, University of Bristol; *b* Worcester, 24 Nov. 1948; *s* of Edward John Miles and Olive Booth Miles (*née* Hockett); *m* 1973, Elizabeth Ann Callahan; two *s*. *Educ:* Worcester Royal Grammar Sch.; Univ. of Birmingham (BSc Hons; MSc Physics of Solids; PhD 1974). CPhys 1980; FInstP 2003. Alexander von Humboldt Fellow, Saarbrücken Univ., 1975–77; Res. Associate, Case Western Reserve Univ., 1977–78; Res. Asst, Physics Dept, Univ. of Bristol, 1978–81; SSO, 1981–86, PSO, 1986–89, BBSRC Inst. of Food Res., Norwich; Lectr, then Reader, Bristol Univ., 1989–99. Chief Scientific Advr, IOP Publishing, 2012–. *Publications:* contribs to scientific jls and chapters in books. *Recreations:* music, listening and playing (classical, jazz, rock, avant garde), half-marathon running, architectural studies. *Address:* H. H. Wills Physics Laboratory, University of Bristol, Tyndall Avenue, Bristol BS8 1TL. *T:* (0117) 928 8707, *Fax:* (0117) 925 5624. *E:* m.j.miles@bristol.ac.uk.

MILES, Michael; *see* Miles, H. M. P.

MILES, Oliver; *see* Miles, R. O.

MILES, Sir Philip John, 7th Bt *cr* 1859, of Leigh Court, Somersetshire; *b* 10 Aug. 1953; *o s* of Sir William Napier Maurice Miles, 6th Bt and Pamela (*née* Dillon); *S* father, 2010, but his name does not appear on the Official Roll of the Baronetage. *Educ:* Northease Manor, Lewes. High Sheriff, Wilts, 1999. *Heir:* none.

MILES, Raymond Reginald; Chief Executive, CP Ships Ltd, 1988–2005; *b* 2 Aug. 1944; *s* of Reginald Gonville Miles and Ellen Mary Miles (*née* Gower); *m* 1966, Susan Georgina Barrow, *d* of George Barrow; two *d*. *Educ:* Lanchester Poly. (BA Econs); London Business Sch. (MBA 1972). Ocean Group plc, Liverpool: Corporate Planner, 1972–75; Divl Finance Dir, 1975–78; Wilh. Wilhelmsen, Norway, USA and London: Exec. Vice Pres., Barber Blue Sea, 1978–86; Man. Dir, Global Equipt Mgt, 1986–88. Sen. Ind. Dir, Provident Financial plc, 2003–06; Sen. Ind. Dir, 2006–08, Chm., 2008–11, Southern Cross Healthcare Gp plc; Lead Ind. Dir, Stelmar Shipping Ltd, USA, 2004–05; Adv. Dir, Stena AB, Sweden, 2006–; Dep. Chm., Internat. Personal Finance plc, 2006–10; Adv. Dir, Survitec Gp, 2012–. Chm., World Shipping Council, 2001–05. Dir, W of England Protection and Indemnity Club, 1994–2004; Chm., Box Club, 2003–05. Trustee: Nat. Maritime Mus., Greenwich, 1998–2006; Nat. Maritime Mus., Cornwall, 2001–08; Garden Opera, 2003–10; Country Holidays for Inner City Kids, 2006–11; Chm., Devon Community Foundn, 2006–09. *Recreations:* Chelsea FC, opera, theatre, shooting. *E:* ray.miles@woodtown.org. *Club:* Reform.

MILES, (Richard) Oliver, CMG 1984; HM Diplomatic Service, retired; Senior Consultant, Al Shafie Miles Ltd, since 2011; *b* 6 March 1936; *s* of George Miles and Olive (*née* Clapham); *m* 1968, Julia, *d* of late Prof. J. S. Weiner; three *s* one *d*. *Educ:* Ampleforth Coll.; Merton Coll., Oxford (Oriental Studies). Entered Diplomatic Service, 1960; served in Abu Dhabi, Amman, Aden, Mukalla, Nicosia, Jedda; Counsellor, Athens, 1977–80; Head of Near East and N Africa Dept, FCO, 1980–83; Ambassador to: Libya, 1984; Luxembourg, 1985–88; Under-Sec. on loan to NI Office, Belfast, 1988–90; Asst Under Sec. of State (Economic), FCO, 1990–91; Dir Gen. of Jt Directorate, Overseas Trade Services, FCO/DTI, 1991–93; Ambassador to Greece, 1993–96. Dir and Sen. Consultant, 1997–2012, Chm., 2000–09, MEC Internat. Ltd. Non-exec. Dir, Vickers Defence Systems, 1990–93. Dep. Chm., Libyan British Business Council, 2004–. Chm., Host (Hosting for Overseas Students), 1998–2004; Pres., Soc. for Libyan Studies, 1998–2005. Dist. Vis. Prof., Amer. Univ., Cairo, 2005. *Recreations:* bird-watching, reading poetry, playing the flute. *Club:* Travellers.

MILES, Robert John; QC 2002; Attorney General, Duchy of Lancaster, since 2012; *b* 29 Nov. 1962; *s* of David and Marion Miles; *m* 1999, Lisabel Mary Macdonald. *Educ:* Christ Church, Oxford (MA, BCL). Called to the Bar, Lincoln's Inn, 1987, Bencher, 2007; in practice, specialising in company and commercial law. *Address:* 4 Stone Buildings, Lincoln's Inn, WC2A 3XT. *T:* (020) 7242 5524. *Club:* Garrick.

MILES, Roger Steele, PhD, DSc; Head, Department of Public Services, The Natural History Museum (formerly British Museum (Natural History)), 1975–94; *b* 31 Aug. 1937; *s* of John Edward Miles and Dorothy Mildred (*née* Steele); *m* 1960, Ann Blake; one *s* one *d*. *Educ:* Malet Lambert High Sch., Hull; King's Coll., Univ. of Durham (BSc, PhD, DSc). Sen. Res. Award, DSIR, 1962–64; Sen. Res. Fellow, Royal Scottish Museum, 1964–66, Sen. Scientific Officer, 1966–68; Sen. Sci. Officer, BM (Nat. Hist.), 1968–71, Principal Sci. Officer, 1971–74. Hon. Fellow, Columbia Pacific Univ., 1983. *Publications:* Palaeozoic Fishes, 2nd edn, 1971 (1st edn, J. A. Moy-Thomas, 1939); (ed, with P. H. Greenwood and C. Patterson) Interrelationships of Fishes, 1973; (ed, with S. M. Andrews and A. D. Walker) Problems in Vertebrate Evolution, 1977; (with others) The Design of Educational Exhibits, 1982, 2nd edn 1988; (ed with L. Zavala) Towards the Museum of the Future, 1994 (trans. Spanish and revised, 1995); papers and monographs on anatomy and palaeontology of fishes, articles on museums, in jls. *Recreations:* music, twentieth century art and architecture. *Address:* 3 Eagle Lane, Snaresbrook, E11 1PF. *T:* (020) 8989 5684.

MILES, Wendy Ann; *see* Henry, W. A.

MILES, Wendy Jane; QC 2015; Partner, Boies, Schiller and Flexner LLP, since 2014; *b* Te Aroha, NZ, 21 Oct. 1970; *d* of William John Miles and Barbara Mary Miles; *m* 2000, Kym Vincent McConnell; two *s*. *Educ:* Univ. of Canterbury, NZ (BA LLB 1994; LLM Hons 1998). Admitted solicitor, NZ and England, 1994; Associate, Russell McVeagh, Wellington, 1996–98; Associate, 1999–2004, Partner, 2005–14, Wilmer Hale. Vice-Pres., ICC Court of Internat. Arbitration, 2015–. Chair, Bd of Trustees, CIArb, 2014–; Sec., Arbitration Cttee, IBA, 2014–. *Recreations:* travel, reading, music, cycling. *Address:* c/o Boies, Schiller & Flexner (UK) LLP, 25 Old Broad Street, EC2N 1HQ. *T:* (020) 7614 0961. *E:* wmiles@bsfllp.com.

MILES, William; Chief Executive, West Yorkshire County Council, and Clerk to the Lieutenancy, West Yorkshire, 1984–86; *b* 26 Sept. 1933; *s* of William and Gladys Miles; *m* 1961, Jillian Anne Wilson; three *s*. *Educ:* Wyggeston School, Leicester; Trinity Hall, Cambridge (MA, LLM). Solicitor. Asst Solicitor, Leicester, Doncaster and Exeter County Boroughs, 1960–66; Asst Town Clerk, Leicester Co. Borough, 1966–69; Dep. Town Clerk,

Blackpool Co. Borough, 1969–73; City Legal Adviser, Newcastle upon Tyne, 1973–74; Chief Exec., Gateshead Borough Council, 1974–84. Mem., Local Govt Residuary Body (England), 1995–99. *Recreations:* bridge, hill walking, sport. *Address:* 3 St Stephen's Manor, Cheltenham GL51 3GF. *T:* (01242) 575840.

MILFORD, 4th Baron *cr* 1939, of Llanstephan, co. Radnor; **Guy Wogan Philipps;** QC 2002; Bt 1919; *b* 25 July 1961; *e s* of 3rd Baron Milford and Hon. Mary Makins (now Viscountess Norwich), *e d* of 1st Baron Sherfield, GCB, GCMG, FRS; *S* father, 1999; *m* 1996, Alice Sherwood; two *s. Educ:* Eton Coll. (KS; Captain of Sch.); Magdalen Coll., Oxford (Roberts-Gawen Scholar; BA 1st Cl. Classical Hon. Mods, 1st Cl. Lit.Hum.; MA); City Univ. (DipLaw). Called to the Bar, Inner Temple, 1986; in practice, 1987–. *Publications:* Bad Behaviour, 1988. *Heir: s* Hon. Archie Sherwood Philipps, *b* 12 March 1997. *Address:* Llanstephan House, Llanstephan, Brecon, Powys LD3 0YR. *T:* (01982) 560693. *E:* gmilford@outlook.com.

MILFORD, John Tillman; QC 1989; **His Honour Judge Milford;** a Circuit Judge, since 2002; *b* 4 Feb. 1946; *s* of late Dr Roy Douglas Milford, Strathtay, Perthshire, and Jessie Milford (*née* Rhind), JP; *m* 1975, Mary Alice, *d* of late Dr E. A. Spriggs of Wylam, Northumberland; three *d. Educ:* The Cathedral School, Salisbury; Hurstpierpoint; Exeter Univ. (LLB). Called to the Bar, Inner Temple, 1969, Bencher, 1998; in practice on NE Circuit, 1970–2002. Head, Trinity Chambers, Newcastle upon Tyne, 1985–99; a Recorder, 1985–2002; a Dep. High Court Judge, 1994–2002; Liaison Judge to Northumberland and N Tyneside Justices, 2003–11. Chm., Northumbria Area Judicial Forum, 2005–11. County Chairman: British Field Sports Soc. for South Northumberland, 1996–98; Countryside Alliance for South Northumberland, 1998–99; Regl Chm., Countryside Alliance for NE England, 1999–2002. Chairman: River Tyne Fishing Festival, 1997; Bywell Country Fair, 1999, 2000; Vice-Chm., Newcastle and Dist Beagles, 1999–2005. Trustee, Get Hooked on Fishing, 2003–13 (Chm., 2005–13). *Recreations:* fishing, shooting, gardening, ballet, collecting. *Address:* Trinity Chambers, The Custom House, Quayside, Newcastle upon Tyne NE1 3DE. *T:* (0191) 232 1927; The Law Courts, Quayside, Newcastle upon Tyne NE1 3LA. *Clubs:* Northern Counties (Newcastle upon Tyne) (Chm., 2003–07); Durham County (Durham).

MILFORD HAVEN, 4th Marquess of, *cr* 1917; **George Ivar Louis Mountbatten;** Earl of Medina, 1917; Viscount Alderney, 1917; *b* 6 June 1961; *s* of 3rd Marquess of Milford Haven, OBE, DSC, and of Janet Mercedes, *d* of late Major Francis Bryce, OBE; *S* father, 1970; *m* 1989, Sarah Georgina (marr. diss. 1996), *d* of late George Alfred Walker; one *s* one *d*; *m* 1997, Clare Wentworth-Stanley. *Heir: s* Earl of Medina, *qv*.

MILIBAND, Rt Hon. David (Wright); PC 2005; President and Chief Executive, International Rescue Committee, since 2013; *b* 15 July 1965; *s* of late Ralph Miliband and of Marion Miliband (*née* Kozak); *m* 1998, Louise Shackelton; two adopted *s. Educ:* Corpus Christi Coll., Oxford (BA 1st Cl. Hons PPE); Massachusetts Inst. of Technol. (Kennedy Schol.; MSC Political Sci.). Res. Fellow, Inst. of Public Policy Res., 1989–94; Head of Policy, Office of Leader of the Opposition, 1994–97; Dir of Policy, 1997, Head, 1998–2001, Prime Minister's Policy Unit. MP (Lab) South Shields, 2001–April 2013. Minister of State: DfES, 2002–04; Cabinet Office, 2004–05; Minister of State (Minister for Communities and Local Govt), ODPM, 2005–06; Sec. of State for Envmt, Food and Rural Affairs, 2006–07, for Foreign and Commonwealth Affairs, 2007–10. Sec., Commn on Social Justice, 1992–94. Vice Chm., Sunderland AFC, 2011–13. *Publications:* (ed) Re-inventing the Left, 1994; (ed jtly) Paying for Inequality: the economic cost of social injustice, 1994. *Recreation:* raising two sons. *Address:* International Rescue Committee, 122 East 42nd Street, New York, NY 10168, USA. *W:* www.davidmiliband.net. *Clubs:* Whiteleas Social, Cleadon Social.

See also Rt Hon. E. Miliband.

MILIBAND, Rt Hon. Edward; PC 2007; MP (Lab) Doncaster North, since 2005; *b* 24 Dec. 1969; *s* of late Ralph Miliband and of Marion Miliband (*née* Kozak); *m* 2011, Justine Thornton; two *s. Educ:* Corpus Christi Coll., Oxford (BA); London Sch. of Economics (MSc (Econ)). TV journalist; speechwriter and researcher for Harriet Harman, MP, 1993, for Rt Hon. Gordon Brown, MP, 1994–97; Special Advr to Chancellor of the Exchequer, 1997–2002; Lectr in Govt, Harvard Univ., 2002–04; Chm., Council of Econ. Advrs, HM Treasury, 2004–05. Parly Sec., Cabinet Office, 2006–07; Chancellor of the Duchy of Lancaster and Minister for the Cabinet Office, 2007–08; Sec. of State for Energy and Climate Change, 2008–10; Shadow Sec. of State for Energy and Climate Change, 2010; Leader of the Labour Party and Leader of the Opposition, 2010–15. *Address:* House of Commons, SW1A 0AA.

See also Rt Hon. D. W. Miliband.

MILINGO, Emmanuel; Former Archbishop of Lusaka (Archbishop, (RC), 1969–83); *b* 13 June 1930; *s* of Yakobe Milingo Chilumbu and Tomaide Lumbiwe Miti; *m* 2001, Maria Sung. *Educ:* Kachebere Seminary, Malawi; Pastoral Inst., Rome; University Coll., Dublin. Ordained priest, 1958; Curate: Minga Parish, Chipata Dio., 1958–60; St Mary's Parish, 1960–61; Chipata Cathedral, 1963–64; Parish Priest, Chipata Cathedral, 1964–65; Sec. for Communications at Catholic Secretariat, Lusaka, 1966–69. Founder, The Daughters of the Redeemer, Congregation for young ladies, 1971. Dep. Hd, Pontifical Council for Pastoral Care of Migrants and Itinerant Peoples, 1983–99. *Publications:* Amake-Joni, 1972; To Die to Give Life, 1975; Summer Lectures for the Daughters of the Redeemer, 1976; The Way to Daughterhood; My God is a Living God, 1981; Lord Jesus, My Lord and Saviour, 1982; Demarcations, 1982; The Flower Garden of Jesus the Redeemer; My Prayers Are Not Heard; Precautions in the Ministry of Deliverance. *Recreation:* music.

MILL, Douglas Russell; Principal, Douglas Mill Consulting, since 2008; Director, Professional Legal Practice, University of Glasgow, 2009–13; *b* 3 Jan. 1957; *s* of Alan M. L. Mill and Anna B. Mill (*née* Russell); *m* 1982, Christine Rankin; two *s* one *d. Educ:* Paisley Grammar Sch.; Glasgow Univ. (LLB, BA, MBA). Apprentice, Wright & Crawford, 1978–80; Partner: Cameron Pinkerton Haggarty, 1980–85; MacFarlane Young & Co., 1985–96; Sec., later Sec. and Chief Exec., Law Soc. of Scotland, 1997–2008. Dep. Dir, Univ. of Strathclyde Centre for Professional Legal Studies, 1993–96. DUniv Paisley, 2000. *Publications:* Successful Practice Management, 1992. *Recreations:* Rugby, golf. *Club:* Dunbar Golf.

MILL, Ian Alexander; QC 1999; *b* 9 April 1958; *s* of Ronald MacLauchlan Mill and Thelma Anita Mill; *m* 1987, Mary Emma Clayden; three *s. Educ:* Epsom Coll.; Trinity Hall, Cambridge (MA Classics and Law). Called to the Bar, Middle Temple, 1981; in practice at the Bar, 1982–. *Recreations:* cricket, golf, opera, theatre, good food and wine. *Address:* Blackstone House, Temple, EC4Y 9BW. *T:* (020) 7583 1770. *Club:* MCC.

MILLAIS, Sir Geoffroy Richard Everett, 6th Bt *cr* 1885, of Palace Gate, Kensington and Saint Ouen, Jersey; *b* 27 Dec. 1941; *s* of Sir Ralph Regnault Millais, 5th Bt and his 1st wife, Felicity Caroline Mary Ward (*née* Warner) (*d* 1994), *d* of Brig.-Gen. W. W. Warner, CMG; *S* father, 1992. *Heir: cousin* John Frederic Millais [*b* 17 Sept. 1949; *m* 1991, Susan Clayton; two *d*].

MILLAR, family name of **Baron Inchyra**.

MILLAR, Prof. Andrew John McWalter, PhD; FRS 2012; FRSE; Professor of Systems Biology, since 2004, and Associate Director, SynthSys, since 2012, University of Edinburgh; *b* London, 12 Oct. 1966; *s* of David McW. Millar and H. Josephine Millar; *m* 1998, Dr Karen J. Halliday; one *s* one *d. Educ:* Eur. Sch. of Luxembourg; Gonville and Caius Coll., Cambridge (BA 1st Cl. Hons Genetics 1988); Rockefeller Univ. (PhD 1994). Life Scis Res. Foundn post-doctoral Fellow, NSF Center for Biol Timing, Univ. of Virginia, 1994–95; Lectr, 1996–99, Reader, 1999–2002, Prof., 2002–04, Dept of Biol Scis, Univ. of Warwick; Founding Dir, Centre for Systems Biol., Univ. of Edinburgh, 2007–11. Theme Dir for Systems Biol., Scottish Univs Life Scis Alliance, 2007–09. Mem., EMBO, 2011–. FRSE 2013. *Publications:* (with P. J. Lumsden) Biological Rhythms and Photoperiodism in Plants, 1998; contrib. over 100 res. articles on biol rhythms and systems biol. *Recreations:* ski-ing, ice skating, reading to my children, travel, sailing. *Address:* SynthSys, University of Edinburgh, C. H. Waddington Building, King's Buildings, Edinburgh EH9 3BF. *T:* (0131) 651 3325, *Fax:* (0131) 651 9068. *E:* andrew.millar@ed.ac.uk.

MILLAR, Anthony Bruce; Chairman, Canadian Zinc (formerly San Andreas Resources) Corporation, 1994–2000; *b* 5 Oct. 1941; *s* of late James Desmond Millar and Josephine Georgina Millar (*née* Brice); *m* 1964, Judith Anne (*née* Jester); two *d. Educ:* Haileybury and Imperial Service College. FCA 1974 (ACA 1964). Asst to Group Management Accountant and Group Treasurer, Viyella Internat. Fedn, 1964–67; United Transport Overseas Ltd, Nairobi, and London (Dep. Group Financial Controller), 1967–72; Finance Dir, Fairfield Property Co. Ltd, 1972–75; Consultant, 1975–77; Managing Dir, Provincial Laundries Ltd, 1977–81; Dep. Chm., Hawley Group, 1981–82; Chm., 1982–92, Hon. Pres., 1992–2000, The Albert Fisher Gp. Freeman, City of London, 1993–; Liveryman, Fruiterers' Co., 1993– (Hon. Assistant and Mem. Ct, 2001–03). *Recreations:* swimming, walking, bridge, travel. *Address:* Frensham Vale House, Lower Bourne, near Farnham, Surrey GU10 3JB. *Club:* Mark's.

MILLAR, Betty Phyllis Joy; Regional Nursing Officer, South Western Regional Health Authority, 1973–84, retired; *b* 19 March 1929; *o d* of late Sidney Hildersly Millar and May Phyllis Halliday. *Educ:* Ursuline High Sch. for Girls; Dumbarton Academy; Glasgow Royal Infirm.; Glasgow Royal Maternity Hosp.; Royal Coll. of Nursing, London. RGN 1950; SCM 1953; NA (Hosp.) Cert. 1961. Theatre Sister, Glasgow Royal Infirm., 1953–54; Ward and Theatre Sister, Henry Brock Meml Hosp., 1954–55; Nursing Sister, Iraq Petroleum Co., 1955–57; Clinical Instructor, Exper. Scheme of Nurse Trng, Glasgow, 1957–60; Admin. Student, Royal Coll. of Nursing, 1960–61; 2nd Asst Matron, Glasgow Royal Infirm., 1961–62; Asst Nursing Officer, Wessex Regional Hosp. Bd, 1962–67; Matron, Glasgow Royal Infirm., 1967–69; Chief Regional Nursing Officer, SW Regional Hosp. Bd, 1969–73. WHO Fellowship to study nursing services in Scandinavia, 1967. Mem. Jt Bd of Clinical Nursing Studies, 1970–82. *Address:* Pinedrift, 45 Stoneyfields, Easton-in-Gordano, Bristol BS20 0LL. *T:* (01275) 372709.

MILLAR, Douglas George, CB 2007; Clerk Assistant, 2003–09, and Director General, Chamber and Committee Services, 2008–09, House of Commons; occasional consultant on parliamentary organisation, since 2009; *b* 15 Feb. 1946; *s* of late George Millar and Doris Mary Millar (*née* Morris); *m* 1st, 1967, Susan Mary Farrow (marr. diss. 1986); one *s* one *d*; 2nd, 1987, (Jane) Victoria Howard Smith; one *s* one *d. Educ:* City of Norwich Sch.; Bristol Univ. (BA Hons History 1967); Reading Univ. (MA Politics 1968). A Clerk, H of C, 1968–2009; Clerk of Defence Cttee, 1979–83; Clerk i/c Private Members' Bills and Divs, 1983–87; Clerk of Home Affairs Cttee, 1987–89; Principal Clerk and Clerk of Financial Cttees and Treasury and Civil Service Cttee, 1989–91; Sec. to Public Accounts Commn, 1989–91; Second Clerk, Select Cttees, 1991–94; Clerk of Select Cttees, 1994–97; Departmental Finance Officer, 1994–2003; Prin. Clerk, Table Office, 1998–2001; Clerk of Legislation, 2001–02. Jt Sec., Assoc. of Secs Gen. of Parlts, 1971–77. *Publications:* (ed jtly) Erskine May Parliamentary Practice, 2011; articles and reviews in parly and political jls. *Recreations:* watching Norwich City, family, golf, walking on the Norfolk coast, travelling. *Club:* Roehampton.

MILLAR, Sir Fergus Graham Burtholme, Kt 2010; DPhil; DLitt; FSA; FBA 1976; Camden Professor of Ancient History, University of Oxford, 1984–2002, now Emeritus Professor; Fellow of Brasenose College, Oxford, 1984–2002, Emeritus Fellow, 2002; *b* 5 July 1935; *s* of late J. S. L. Millar and of Jean Burtholme (*née* Taylor); *m* 1959, Susanna Friedmann; two *s* one *d. Educ:* Edinburgh Acad.; Loretto Sch.; Trinity Coll., Oxford (1st Cl. Lit. Hum.; Hon. Fellow, 1992); DPhil 1962, DLitt 1988, Oxon. Fellow: All Souls Coll., Oxford, 1958–64; Queen's Coll., Oxford, 1964–76 (Hon. Fellow, 1999); Prof. of Ancient History, UCL, 1976–84. Leverhulme Emeritus Fellow, Oriental Inst., Oxford, 2002–04, 2013–15; Sather Prof. of Classical Lit., Univ. of Calif, Berkeley, 2003. President: Soc. for the Promotion of Roman Studies, 1989–92 (Vice-Pres., 1977–89, 1992–2001; Hon. Vice-Pres., 2001); Classical Assoc., 1992–93; Pubns Sec., British Acad., 1997–2002. Schweich Lectr, British Acad., 2010. FSA 1978. Corresponding Member: German Archaeol. Inst., 1978; Bavarian Acad., 1987; Finnish Acad., 1989; Russian Acad., 1999; Amer. Acad. of Arts and Scis, 2003; Australian Acad. of Humanities, 2009. Ed., Jl of Roman Studies, 1975–79. Hon. DPhil Helsinki, 1994; Hon. DLitt: St Andrews, 2004; Jerusalem, 2012; Edinburgh, 2012. Conington Prize, Univ. of Oxford, 1963; Cultori di Roma Prize, Comune di Roma, 2005; Kenyon Medal for Classical Studies, British Acad., 2005. *Publications:* A Study of Cassius Dio, 1964; The Roman Empire and its Neighbours, 1967; (ed with G. Vermes) E. Schürer, history of the Jewish people in the Age of Jesus Christ (175 BC–AD 135), Vol. I, 1973, Vol. II, 1979, Vol. III, parts 1 and 2 (ed with G. Vermes and M. D. Goodman), 1986–87; The Emperor in the Roman World (31 BC–AD 337), 1977, 2nd edn 1992; (ed with E. Segal) Caesar Augustus: seven aspects, 1984; The Roman Near East, 1993; The Crowd in Rome in the Late Republic, 1998; Rome, the Greek World and the East, vol. I, 2002, vol. 2, 2004, vol. 3, 2006; The Roman Republic in Political Thought, 2002; A Greek Roman Empire: power and belief under Theodosius II (408–450), 2006; (jtly) Handbook of Jewish Literature from Late Antiquity, 2012; Religion, Language and Community in the Roman Near East, Constantine to Muhammad, 2013. *Address:* Oxford Centre for Hebrew and Jewish Studies, Clarendon Institute Building, Walton Street, Oxford OX1 2HG; 80 Harpes Road, Oxford OX2 7QL. *T:* (01865) 515782.

MILLAR, Fiona; writer, journalist, columnist, Education Guardian, since 2003; *b* London, 2 Jan. 1958; *d* of Robert Millar and Audrey Millar; partner, Alastair John Campbell, *qv*; two *s* one *d. Educ:* Camden Sch. for Girls; University Coll. London (BSc Econs and Econ. Hist.). Graduate trng scheme, Mirror Gp, 1980–82; Daily Express, 1982–88; freelance journalist, 1988–94; Office of the Leader of the Opposition, 1995–97; Special Advr to the Prime Minister, 1997–2003. Television programmes: writer and presenter, The Best for My Child, 2004; presenter: Involving Parents, 2005; The Parents' Guide, 2006; Admissions Code, 2007; The School Report, 2009. Chm., Comprehensive Future, 2008–12. Co-founder, Local Schs Network, 2010–. Mem., Ministerial Adv. Gp for Educn and Skills, Welsh Govt, 2010–13. Chairman: Trustees, Family and Parenting Inst., 2004–10; Nat. Youth Arts Trust, 2013–. Chairman of Governors: Gospel Oak Prim. Sch., 2000–10; William Ellis Sch., 2008–; Gov., Parliament Hill Sch., 2012–. *Publications:* (with Glenys Kinnock) By Faith and Daring, 1993; (with Melissa Benn) A Comprehensive Future, 2006; The Secret World of the Working Mother, 2009; A New Conversation with Parents, 2011. *Recreations:* swimming, reading, my children and friends, walking the dog, learning French. *Address:* 13 Estelle Road, NW3 2JX. *E:* fiona.millar1@btinternet.com.

See also G. J. Millar.

MILLAR, Gavin James; QC 2000; a Recorder, since 2003; *b* 10 July 1959; *s* of Robert and Audrey Millar; partner, Carmel Mary Elizabeth Fitzsimons; one *s* three *d. Educ:* St Peter's Coll., Oxford (BA Jurisprudence). Called to the Bar: Lincoln's Inn, 1981; NI, 2010. Founder Mem., Doughty St Chambers, 1990. Council of Europe Expert on Freedom of Expression, 2002–. Chair, Centre for Investigative Journalism, 2013–. Mem., Public Affairs Cttee, Bar

Council, 1995–97; Vice-Chm., Soc. of Labour Lawyers, 1999–2001. Mem. (Lab) Westminster CC, 1985–94. *Publications:* (jtly) Media Law and Human Rights, 2001, 2nd edn 2009. *Recreations:* family, football, painting. *Address:* Matrix Chambers, Griffin Building, Gray's Inn, WC1R 5LN. *Club:* Manchester United Football.

See also F. Millar.

MILLAR, Graeme Stewart, CBE 2006; FRPharmS; Director, Graeme Millar Ltd, since 1982; Chairman: Fletcher Jones Ltd, since 2000; Teko LLC, since 2011; *b* 20 Feb. 1955; *s* of Stewart and Louise Millar; *m* 1978, Fay Cooper Kennedy; three *s*. *Educ:* Heriot-Watt Univ. (BSc Hons Pharmacy). FRPharmS 1999. Director: Dunfermline Bldg Soc., 2001–09 (Vice Chm., 2007–09); Essentia Gp Ltd, 2003–08; Lomax Mobility Ltd, 2005–07. Dir, NCC, and Chm., Scottish Consumer Council, 2000–06; Chairman: Scottish Construction Forum, 2004–08; Scottish Food Adv. Cttee, 2006–11; Dir, Food Standards Agency, 2005–11. Non-exec. Dir, Scottish Rugby Union, 2006–08. Chairman: Sick Kids Friends Foundn, 2000–08; Lomond Centre, 2012. Mem. Adv. Bd, Reform Scotland, 2012–. Hon. Prof. of Pharmacy, Robert Gordon's Univ., Aberdeen, 2006–. *Recreations:* Rugby (spectator), golf, family and friends, good food and wine. *Address:* 2 Campbell Avenue, Edinburgh EH12 6DS. *T:* and *Fax:* (0131) 337 0608. *E:* millargraeme@yahoo.co.uk. *Clubs:* New (Edinburgh); Royal Burgess Golfing Society (Edinburgh); Golf House (Elie, Fife); Uphall Golf (West Lothian).

MILLAR, Prof. Jane Isobel, OBE 2001; DPhil; FBA 2014; Pro-Vice Chancellor, University of Bath, since 2006; *b* Tynemouth, 7 July 1953; *d* of Robert Coulson Millar and Margaret Elizabeth Millar; *m* 2008, Jeremy Andrew Toop Cooper. *Educ:* Univ. of Sussex (BA 1974); Brunel Univ. (MA 1980); Univ. of York (DPhil 1987). Res. Officer, DHSS, 1980–83; Res. Fellow, Social Policy Res. Unit, Univ. of York, 1983–85; Lectr in Social Policy, Univ. of Ulster, 1985–88; Lectr, 1988–91, Reader, 1991–94, Prof. of Social Policy, 1994–, Univ. of Bath. *Publications:* (with C. Glendinning) Women and Poverty in Britain, 1987, 2nd edn 1992; Poverty and the Lone-Parent Family: the challenge to social policy, 1989; Understanding Social Security, 2003, 2nd edn 2009; contrib. articles to learned jls incl. Jl Social Policy, Social Policy and Admin, Social Policy and Society. *Address:* Vice-Chancellor's Office, University of Bath, Bath BA2 7AY. *T:* (01225) 386141, *Fax:* (01225) 386626. *E:* j.i.millar@bath.ac.uk.

MILLAR, Rt Rev. Preb. John Alexander Kirkpatrick, (Sandy); Bishop, Church of Uganda, since 2005; an Honorary Assistant Bishop: (Bishop in Mission), Diocese of London, since 2006; Diocese of St Edmundsbury and Ipswich, since 2012; *b* 13 Nov. 1939; *s* of Maj.-Gen. Robert Kirkpatrick Millar of Orton, CB, DSO and Frances (*née* Beyts); *m* 1971, Annette Fisher; one *s* three *d*. *Educ:* Eton; Trinity Coll., Cambridge (BA 1962; MA 1966); Univ. of Durham (DipTh). Deacon 1976; priest 1977; Curate, 1976–85, Vicar, 1985–2005, Holy Trinity Brompton, with St Paul, Onslow Square; Area Dean, Chelsea, 1989–94; Prebendary, St Paul's Cathedral, 1997–2010; Priest-in-charge, St Mark's, Tollington Park, 2003–11. *Address:* Fairlawn, 37 Alde Lane, Aldeburgh IP15 5DZ. *T:* (01728) 452926.

MILLAR, John Stanley, CBE 1979; County Planning Officer, Greater Manchester Council, 1973–83; *b* 1925; *s* of late Nicholas William Stanley Millar and late Elsie Baxter Millar (*née* Flinn); *m* 1st, 1961, Patricia Mary (*née* Land) (*d* 1992); one *d*; 2nd, 1993, Christine (*née* Riley). *Educ:* Liverpool Coll.; Univ. of Liverpool. BArch, DipCD, PPRTPI, RIBA. Planning Asst, then Sen. Asst Architect, City of Liverpool, 1948–51; Sectional Planning Officer, then Dep. Asst County Planning Officer, Lancs CC, 1951–61; Chief Asst Planning Officer, then Asst City Planning Officer, City of Manchester, 1961–64; City Planning Officer, Manchester, 1964–73. *Publications:* papers in professional and technical jls. *Recreations:* walking, listening to music, travel, the sea. *Address:* 55 Stanneylands Drive, Wilmslow, Cheshire SK9 4EU. *T:* (01625) 523616.

MILLAR, Air Vice-Marshal Peter, CB 1998; Director of Administration, Magna Medica-Medical City Ltd, since 2014; *b* 20 June 1942; *s* of Air Cdre John Christopher Millar, RAF and Patricia Millar (*née* Allen); *m* 1966, Annette McMillan; one *s* two *d*. *Educ:* Malvern Coll.; RAF Coll., Cranwell. Served RAF: No 20 Sqn, Singapore, 1964–66; No 4 FTS, RAF Valley, 1967–69; Central Flying Sch., RAF Kemble, 1969–71; 560 Trng Sqn, Randolph AFB, Texas, 1971–74; RAF Staff Coll., 1974; Flight Commander: No 20 Sqn, Wildenrath, 1975–77; No 4 Sqn, Gutersloh, 1977–78; MoD, 1978–79; Sqn Comdr, No 233 OCU, RAF Wittering, 1979–82; USAF Air Warfare Coll., Maxwell AFB, Alabama, 1982–83; Brit. Defence Staff, Washington, 1983–84; Stn Comdr, RAF Wittering, 1985–86; RCDS 1987; on staff, UK Mil. Rep., NATO HQ, 1988–90; Dir NATO, MoD, 1990–93; HQ AAFCE, Ramstein AFB, Germany, 1993–95; Adminr, Sovereign Base Areas and Comdr, British Forces Cyprus, 1995–98; retd 1998. Dir of Security, Medical World Inc., and Dir, Internat. Admin, Medical Mall Ltd, 1998–99. Mem. Adv. Bd, World Challenge Expeditions Ltd, 2000–04; Dir, Ops, Intellectual Property Rights Protection Ltd, 2003–06. Chairman: Biotrans Consortium, 2004–08; Terrafuels Ltd, 2006–08; C-Green Fuels Ltd, 2006–12; Dir, Carbon Trading, 2005–08, Dir, Energy Sector, 2008–09, C-Questor Ltd; Sen. Vice Pres., Bio-Energy GHG Corp., 2010–12. Gov., Queen Alexandra's Hosp. Home, 2005–14. FRAeS 1997. *Recreations:* ski-ing, golf, off-shore sailing. *Club:* Royal Air Force.

MILLAR, Peter Carmichael, OBE 1978; Deputy Keeper of HM Signet, 1983–91; *b* 19 Feb. 1927; *s* of late Rev. Peter Carmichael Millar, OBE, DD and of Ailsa Ross Brown Campbell or Millar; *m* 1953, Kirsteen Lindsay Carnegie, *d* of late Col David Carnegie, CB, OBE, TD, DL, Dep. Gen. Manager, Clydesdale Bank; two *s* two *d*. *Educ:* Aberdeen Grammar Sch.; Glasgow Univ.; St Andrews Univ.; Edinburgh Univ. MA, LLB; WS. Served RN, 1944–47. Partner in law firms, Messrs W. & T. P. Manuel, WS, 1954–62; Aitken, Kinnear & Co., WS, 1963–87; Aitken Nairn, WS, 1987–92. Clerk to Soc. of Writers to HM Signet, 1964–83. Chairman: Church of Scotland Gen. Trustees, 1973–85; Mental Welfare Commn for Scotland, 1983–91; (part-time) Medical Appeal Tribunals, 1991–99; Pension Appeal Tribunals, 1992–99. Convener, Scottish Child and Family Alliance, later Children in Scotland, 1992–95. *Recreations:* golf, hill-walking, music. *Address:* 7/2 Brighouse Park Crescent, Edinburgh EH4 6QS. *T:* (0131) 336 2069. *Clubs:* New (Edinburgh); Hon. Co. of Edinburgh Golfers, Bruntsfield Links Golfing Society.

MILLAR, Robert Brandon, CA; Director, Ediston Residential, since 2013; *b* 30 March 1950; *m* 1975, Sandra Falconer; one *s* one *d*. *Educ:* George Heriot's Sch.; Edinburgh Univ. (MA Hons Econs). Gen. Mgt, BT, 1972–74; CA apprenticeship, Touche Ross & Co., 1974–78; Accountant, Bredero UK, 1978–79; Financial Controller, Castle Rock HA, 1979–83; Manager Registration, Housing Corp., 1983–89; Dir of Strategy, Scottish Homes, 1989–97; Finance Dir, Miller Homes, 1997–99; Chief Exec., Scottish Homes, subseq. Communities Scotland, 2000–03; Chief Exec., 2004–08, Develt Dir, 2008–12, New City Vision. *Recreation:* various sports. *Address:* Ediston Group, 39 George Street, Edinburgh EH2 2HN. *Club:* Merchants of Edinburgh Golf.

MILLAR, Prof. Robert Hamilton, (Robin), OBE 2015; PhD; FInstP; Salters' Professor of Science Education, University of York, 2006–14, now Emeritus; *b* Ballymena, NI, 7 July 1948; *s* of Robert and Margaret Millar; *m* 1973, Elizabeth Mackenzie; one *s* one *d*. *Educ:* Ballymena Acad.; Clare Coll., Cambridge (BA Natural Scis 1970); Univ. of Edinburgh (PhD Med. Physics 1973; DipEd 1974; MPhil 1981). MInstP 1984, FInstP 2013. School teacher, Lothian Regl Council, 1974–82; University of York: Lectr in Educn, 1982–90; Sen. Lectr, 1990–96; Prof. of Sci. Educn, 1996–2006. Pres., ASE, 2012. *Publications:* Doing Science: images of science in science education, 1989, 2011; Understanding Physics, 1989; (jtly) Young People's Images of Science, 1996; (jtly) Beyond 2000: science education for the future, 1998; (jtly) Science for Public Understanding, 2000; (ed jtly) Improving Science Education: the contribution of research, 2000; (ed jtly) Making a Difference: evaluation as a tool for improving science education, 2005; (jtly) Improving Subject Teaching: lessons from research in science education, 2006; Analysing Practical Science Activities to Assess and Improve their Effectiveness, 2010; contribs to learned jls in field of sci. educn. *Recreations:* hill-walking, choral singing, reading, photography. *Address:* Department of Education, University of York, Heslington, York YO10 5DD. *T:* (01904) 323469, *Fax:* (01904) 322605. *E:* robin.millar@york.ac.uk.

MILLAR, Robin John Christian, CBE 2010; musician and record producer; *b* London, 18 Dec. 1951; *s* of Dr Bruce Millar and Anne Millar; one *s* one *d*. *Educ:* Enfield Grammar Sch.; Queens' Coll., Cambridge (BA 1973; MA 1976). Chm., Scarlett Gp plc, 1982–90; Chm. and CEO, Whitfield Street Studios Ltd, 2004–07; Chm., Blue Raincoat Music Ltd, 2013–. Produced 44 number 1 records, incl. Diamond Life, by Sade; produced 1996 Olympic Games opening ceremony. Vis. Prof. and Lectr in commercial music, RAM, LCM, Surrey Univ. and Univ. of Modena. Hon. Prof., LCM, 2007–. Mem. Bd, Nat. Skills Acad. for Creative and Cultural, 2009–; Trustee, Creative and Cultural Skills UK, 2010–. Global Advr, Young Voices, 2011–. Hon. Patron, Music Producers Guild, 2000. Fellow, Assoc. of Professional Recording Services, 2009. *Recreations:* adventure, reading, sport. *W:* www.robinmillar.org.uk. *Club:* Groucho (Hon. Life Mem.).

MILLAR, Samira; *see* Ahmed, Samira.

MILLAR, Rt Rev. Preb. Sandy; *see* Millar, Rt Rev. Preb. J. A. K.

MILLARD, Anthony Paul; Founder and Chairman, Anthony Millard Consulting, since 2004; *b* 21 Sept. 1948; *s* of Leonard William Millard and Marjorie Ethel Millard (*née* Manley); *m* 1971, Lesley Margaret Baker; one *s* three *d*. *Educ:* Solihull Sch.; LSE (BSc Econ); Balliol Coll., Oxford (PGCE). Teaching in Zambia, 1971–74; Stagiaire (specialist trainee) with EC, 1974–75; Wells Cathedral School: Asst Master, 1975–77; Housemaster, 1977–86; Dep. Headmaster, 1982–86; Headmaster: Wycliffe Coll., Glos, 1987–93; Giggleswick Sch., 1993–2001. Man. Dir, Schools Div., Nord Anglia plc, 2002–03. Chairman: ISIS (Central), 1990–92; Services Cttee, HMC, 1995–2000; Boarding Schs Assoc., 2000 (Mem. Exec. Cttee, 1995–2001); Vice Chm., Bloxham Project Cttee, 1991–96; Mem. Council, ISCO, 1995–98. Contested (C) Wirral South, 2001. Chm., Internat. British Schs, 2011– (Chm. Govs, British Internat. Sch., NY, 2006–); Governor: Geneva English Sch., 2011–; Greensteds Sch., Nakuru, Kenya, 2015–. FRSA 1986. *Recreations:* travel, mountains, Shakespeare. *Address:* Brookside Cottage, Ewen, Cirencester, Glos GL7 6BU. *T:* (01285) 770365. *E:* anthony@ewenelite.com. *Club:* East India, Devonshire, Sports and Public Schools.

MILLARD, Dennis Henry; Chairman, Halfords plc, since 2009; *b* New York, 28 Feb. 1949; *s* of Harry and Edna Millard; *m* 1972, Paula; two *s* one *d*. *Educ:* Univ. of Natal, SA; Univ. of Cape Town Grad. Sch. of Business (MBA). CTA; CA (SA). Dir, Finance and Planning, Plate Glass Gp (SA), 1980–93; Finance Director: Medeva plc, 1994–96; Cookson Gp plc, 1996–2005. Chm., Connect (formerly Smiths News plc), 2006–15; non-executive Director: Exel plc, 2003–05; Xchanging plc, 2005–12; Debenhams plc, 2006–; Premier Farnell plc, 2007–15; Sen. Ind. Dir and Dep. Chm., Pets at Home Gp plc, 2014–. *Recreations:* surfing, golf, cycling. *Address:* Kingscote, Binfield Road, Wokingham, Berks RG40 5PP. *T:* (01344) 451216. *E:* dennis.millard@btinternet.com. *Clubs:* Sunningdale Golf; Durban Country (SA).

MILLARD, Keith Haverland; Group Chairman, Surrey, Vistage, since 2000; President, Institution of Mechanical Engineers, 2009–10; *b* Enfield, 20 Nov. 1942; *s* of Harold Millard and Kathleen Millard (*née* Hill); *m* 1966, Anne Sherrington; two *s*. *Educ:* Latymer Sch., Edmonton; Hendon Coll. of Technol.; Peterborough Tech. Coll. (HNC Mech. Engrg). CEng 1972; FIMechE 1977. Consulting engr, 1970–83; Man. Dir, Gilbert Associates, 1983–94; Business Develt Dir, Balfour Beatty Internat., 1994–96; Vice Pres., Parsons Corp., 1996–98. Institution of Mechanical Engineers: Trustee, 2004–09; Dep. Pres., 2007–09; Trustee, IMechE Pension Fund, 2010– (Chm., 2013–). Chief executive coach, 2000–. FInstD. Freeman, City of London, 2008; Liveryman, Engineers' Co., 2008. Paul Harris Fellow, Rotary Internat., 2008. *Recreations:* music, theatre, ski-ing, golf. *Club:* Rotary (Pres., Woking District, 1991–92).

MILLEDGE, Peter Neil; Counsel to the Chairman of Committees, House of Lords, since 2013 (Deputy Counsel, 2005–13); *b* 4 March 1955; *s* of late Frederick Milledge and Mary Kirkwood Milledge (*née* Cree); *m* 1979, Jennifer Miriam Greenall; two *s*. *Educ:* Newport (Essex) Grammar Sch.; King's Coll. London (LLB 1976). Called to the Bar, Middle Temple, 1977; joined Govt Legal Service, 1979; Legal Asst, 1979–82, Sen. Legal Asst, 1982–85, Asst Solicitor, 1985, DHSS; seconded to Law Officers' Dept, 1987–89; Asst Dir, Legal Services, DSS, subseq. DWP, 1989–2005. Governor: Newport Free GS, Saffron Walden, 2008–14; Joyce Frankland Acad., Newport, 2014–. *Publications:* (contrib.) Tribunals: practice and procedure, 1986; contribs to legal jls. *Recreations:* walking, gardening, local history, bellringing. *Address:* House of Lords, SW1A 0PW. *T:* (020) 7219 3211. *Club:* Civil Service.

MILLER, family name of **Baroness Miller of Chilthorne Domer**.

MILLER OF CHILTHORNE DOMER, Baroness *cr* 1998 (Life Peer), of Chilthorne Domer in the co. of Somerset; **Susan Elizabeth Miller;** *b* 1 Jan. 1954; *d* of Frederick Oliver Meddows Taylor and Norah Langham; *m* 1st, 1980, John Miller (marr. diss. 1998); one *d* (and one *d* decd); 2nd, 1999, Humphrey Temperley. *Educ:* Sidcot Sch.; Oxford Poly. David & Charles, Publishers, 1975–77; Weidenfeld & Nicholson, 1977; Penguin Books, 1977–79; bookshop owner, Sherborne and Yeovil, 1979–89. Lib Dem spokesman on envmt, food and rural affairs, H of L, 1999–2007, on home affairs, 2007–09; All Party Parliamentary Groups: Chairman: Street Children; Agroecology; Food and Health; Conservation and Wildlife. Member (Lib Dem): S Somerset DC, 1991–98 (Leader, 1996–98); Somerset CC, 1997–2005. Parish Councillor, Chilthorne Domer, 1987–. *Recreations:* horse riding, gardening, viniculture, reading, friends. *Address:* House of Lords, SW1A 0PW.

MILLER, Sir Albert (Joel), KCMG 2002; LVO 1994; MBE 1963; QPM 1970; CPM 1965; President, 1976–2003, Co-Chairman, 1998–2003, and Chief Executive Officer, 2006–08, Grand Bahama Port Authority Ltd; *b* 23 Feb. 1926; *s* of late Joseph Edward Miller and Nellie Miller; *m* 1949, Laurie; two *s* one *d*. *Educ:* private tutorage, St Augustine's Coll., Nassau. Joined Royal Bahamas Police Force, 1943: Detective Corporal, 1950; Detective Sergeant, 1953; Detective Inspector, 1955; Asst Supt, 1957; Dep. Supt, 1961; Supt, 1962; Asst Comr, 1964; Dep. Comr, 1968–71, resigned. Vice-Pres., 1971–74, Pres., 1974–, Bahamas Amusements Ltd. Hon. ADC to Governor of the Bahamas. *Recreations:* fishing, boating, swimming, reading. *Address:* PO Box F-44270, Freeport, Bahamas. *T:* (242) 3527770, *Fax:* (242) 3523702. *Clubs:* Les Ambassadeurs; Rotary of Freeport (Bahamas).

MILLER, Amelia, (Mrs Michael Miller); *see* Freedman, A.

MILLER, Prof. Andrew, CBE 1999; PhD; FRSE; Principal and Vice-Chancellor, Stirling University, 1994–2001, Professor Emeritus, since 2001; Secretary and Treasurer, Carnegie Trust for the Universities of Scotland, 2004–13; *b* 15 Feb. 1936; *s* of William Hamilton Miller and Susan Anderson (*née* Auld); *m* 1962, Rosemary Singleton Hannah Fyvie; one *s* one *d*. *Educ:* Beath High Sch.; Edinburgh Univ. (BSc Hons 1958; PhD 1962); Wolfson Coll., Oxford (MA 1967; Hon. Fellow, 1995). Postdoctoral Fellow, CSIRO, Melbourne, 1962–65; Tutor in Chemistry, Ormond Coll., Melbourne Univ., 1963–65; Staff Scientist, MRC Lab. of Molecular Biol., Cambridge, 1965–66; Lectr in Molecular Biophysics, Oxford Univ., 1966–83; Fellow, Wolfson Coll., Oxford, 1967–83; on secondment as Hd, EMBL, Grenoble, 1975–80; Edinburgh University: Prof. of Biochem., 1984–94; on secondment as Dir of Res.,

European Synchrotron Radiation Facility, Grenoble, 1986–91; Vice-Dean of Medicine, 1991–93; Vice-Provost of Medicine and Veterinary Medicine, 1992–93; Vice-Principal, 1993–94. Gen. Sec., RSE, 2001–05, 2007; Chm., RSE Scotland Foundn, 2007–09; Interim Chief Exec., Cancer Research UK, 2001–02. Chm., Internat. Centre for Math. Scis, Edinburgh, 2001–05. Leverhulme Emeritus Fellowship, 2001–03. Member: Action Gp on Standards in Scottish Schs, DFEE, 1997–99; Scottish Exec. Sci. Strategy Gp, 1999–2001; Bd, Food Standards Agency, 2003–05; Dep. Chm., Scottish Food Adv. Cttee, 2003–05. Dir, Scottish Knowledge plc, 1997–2002. Advr, Wellcome Trust, on UK-Wellcome-French-Synchrotron, 1999–2000. Mem. Council, Open Univ., 2001–05. FRSE 1986 (Mem. Council, 1997–2005). DUniv: Stirling, 2002; Open, 2007. Bicentennial Medal, RSE, 2007. *Publications:* (ed jtly) Minerals in Biology, 1984; numerous papers on collagen and muscle in scientific jls incl. Nature, Jl Molecular Biol. *Recreations:* music, walking, reading, wondering. *Address:* 5 Blackford Hill Grove, Edinburgh EH9 3HA.

MILLER, Andrew; QC 2014; *b* London, 11 Dec. 1962; *s* of Michael Irvine and Josephine Miller; *m* 1994, Laura Rodriguez Garcia; two *s*. *Educ:* Preston Manor High Sch., Wembley; Univ. of Southampton (LLB); Council of Legal Educn. FCIArb 1998. Called to the Bar, Inner Temple, 1989; in practice as a barrister, specialising in commercial, construction and insurance disputes. *Recreations:* travelling, theatre, diving, walking, cycling, ski-ing, gym and spinning. *Address:* 2 Temple Gardens, Temple, EC4Y 9AY. *T:* (020) 7822 1200, *Fax:* (020) 7822 1300. *E:* amiller@2tg.co.uk.

MILLER, Andrew Arthur; Chief Executive Officer, Guardian Media Group plc, 2010–15; *b* 10 July 1966; *s* of Sir Ronald Andrew Baird Miller, *qv*; *m* 1991, Helen Connolly; two *s* one *d*. *Educ:* Dollar Acad.; Univ. of Edinburgh (LLB Hons). CA 1991. CA trainee, Price Waterhouse, 1988–91; Costing Systems Manager, 1991–92, Factory Finance Manager and Brand Analyst, Detergents, 1992–94, Procter & Gamble; Corporate Finance Manager, Holiday Inn/Britvic Soft Drinks, Bass plc, 1994–95; Commercial Planning Manager, Walkers Snack Foods UK, 1996–97, Dir of Finance, Frito Lay Europe Ops, 1997–2000, Pepsico Gp; Man. Dir, Postanywhere, 2000–02; Gp Financial Controller, 2002–04, Chief Financial Officer, 2004–09, Trader Media Gp; Chief Financial Officer, Guardian Media Gp, 2009–10. Non-exec. Dir, Automobile Assoc., 2014–. *Recreations:* family, sport, the arts. *Club:* Caledonian.

MILLER, Dr Andrew Brooke; author; *b* Bristol, 1960; *s* of Kieth Wyndham Miller and Molly Anne Callard; one *d*. *Educ:* Middlesex Poly. (BA); Univ. of East Anglia (MA Creative Writing 1991); Lancaster Univ. (PhD Critical and Creative Writing 1995). *Publications:* Ingenious Pain, 1997 (James Tait Black Meml Prize, Premio Grinzane Cavour, Italy); Casanova, 1998; Oxygen, 2001; The Optimists, 2005; One Morning Like a Bird, 2008; Pure, 2011 (Costa Novel Award and Costa Book of Year, 2012); The Crossing, 2015. *Recreations:* aikido (Japanese martial art), playing the mandolin in a folk band, keeping chickens.

MILLER, Andrew Peter; *b* 23 March 1949; *s* of late Ernest William Thomas Miller and of Daphne May Miller; *m* Frances Ewan; two *s* one *d*. *Educ:* Hayling Island Secondary Sch.; LSE (Mature Student; Dip. Indust. Relations 1976). Lab. Technician, Dept of Geology, Portsmouth Poly., specialising in X-RF and X-RD analysis, 1967–76; Divl Officer, ASTMS, subseq. MSF, 1977–92. MP (Lab) Ellesmere Port and Neston, 1992–2015. PPS, DTI, 2001–05. Chairman: Regulatory Reform Select Cttee, 2005–10; Science and Technol. Select Cttee, 2010–15 (Mem., 1992–97); Parly and Scientific Cttee, 2010–15; Chm., 2005–10, Vice Chm., 2010–15, PITCOM, subseq. PICTFOR; Vice Chm., PLP Cttee on Science and Technol., 1993–97; Treas., 1997–2000, Vice Pres., 2000–03, Parlt and Sci. Cttee. Ldr, PLP Leadership Campaign Team, 1997–98. Dir, Eur. Informatics Market, 1996–98. Chm., Adv. Bd, Thornton Sci. Park, 2012–; Dir, Thornton Res. Properties Ltd, 2014–. Pres., Computing for Labour, 1993–. *Publications:* (jtly) North West Economic Strategy, 1987. *Recreations:* walking, photography. *Address:* Hollytree Cottage, Commonside, Alvanley, Cheshire WA6 9HB. *T:* (01928) 722642.

MILLER, Sir Anthony Thomas, 13th Bt *cr* 1705, of Chichester, Sussex; *b* 4 May 1955; *o s* of Sir Harry Miller, 12th Bt, and of Gwynedd Margaret Miller (*née* Sheriff); *S* father, 2007; *m* 1990, Barbara Battersby (*née* Kensington); two *s*, and two step *s* one step *d*. *Heir: s* Thomas Kensington Miller, *b* 26 Feb. 1994.

MILLER, Arjay; Dean, and Professor of Management, Graduate School of Business, Stanford University, 1969–79, now Dean Emeritus; Vice-Chairman, Ford Motor Company, 1968–69 (President, 1963–68); *b* 4 March 1916; *s* of Rawley John Miller and Mary Gertrude Schade; *m* 1940, Frances Marion Fearing; one *s* one *d*. *Educ:* University of California at Los Angeles (BS with highest hons, 1937). Graduate Student and Teaching Asst, University of California at Berkeley, 1938–40; Research Technician, Calif. State Planning Bd, 1941; Economist, Federal Reserve Bank of San Francisco, 1941–43. Captain, US Air Force, 1943–46. Asst Treas., Ford Motor Co., 1947–53; Controller, 1953–57; Vice-Pres. and Controller, 1957–61; Vice-Pres. of Finance, 1961–62; Vice-Pres., Staff Group, 1962–63. Mem. Bd of Dirs, Public Policy Inst., Calif; Trustee: Brookings Instn, Washington; Internat. Exec. Service Corps; Urban Inst. Mem. Bd of Dirs, SRI International; Mem., Trilateral Commn, 1977–87. Councillor, The Conference Board. Fellow, Amer. Acad. of Arts and Scis, 1990. Hon. LLD: Univ. of California (LA), 1964; Whitman Coll., 1965; Univ. of Nebraska, 1965; Ripon Coll., 1980; Washington Univ., St Louis, 1982. *Address:* 225 Mountain Home Road, Woodside, CA 94062, USA. *Clubs:* Bohemian, Pacific Union (San Francisco).

MILLER, Hon. (Arthur) Daniel; consultant; Premier, British Columbia, 1999–2000; *b* 24 Dec. 1944; *s* of Arthur William Miller and Evelyn Estelle Miller (*née* Lewis); *m* 1987, Beverly Gayle Ballard (*née* Bartram); three *s* two *d*. *Educ:* N Vancouver Secondary Sch. Millwright. Former Mem. Council, Prince Rupert City. Government of British Columbia: MLA (NDP) North Coast, 1986–2001; Minister of: Forests, 1991–93; Skills, Training and Labour, 1993–96; Municipal Affairs, 1996–97; Dep. Premier, 1996–99; Minister: of Employment and Investment, 1997–98; of Energy and Mines, and resp. for Northern Develt, 1998–2001. *Address:* 1234 Richardson Street, Victoria, BC V8V 3E1, Canada.

MILLER, Barry; Director General Service Personnel Policy, Ministry of Defence, 1999–2002; *b* 11 May 1942; *s* of Lt-Col Howard Alan Miller and Margaret Yvonne Richardson; *m* 1968, Katrina Elizabeth Chandler; one *s* one *d*. *Educ:* Lancaster Royal Grammar Sch. Ministry of Defence: Exec. Officer, RAE Farnborough, 1961; Asst Principal, MoD, London, 1965; Principal: Defence Policy Staff, 1969; Naval Personnel Div., 1969; Equipment Secretariat (Army), 1972; Defence Secretariat, 1973; CSD, 1975; Asst Secretary: Civilian Management, 1977; Defence Secretariat, 1980; RCDS 1984; Asst Sec., Management Services (Organisation), 1985; Director General: Defence Quality Assurance, 1986; Test and Evaluation, 1992; Asst Under Sec. (Finance), PE, 1994; Dir Gen., Finance, 1995; Command Sec. to Second Sea Lord and C-in-C Naval Home Command, and Asst Under-Sec. of State (Naval Personnel), 1996–99. Director: Royal Naval Film Corp., 1969–72; BSI, 1986–89; 3rd Gunwharf Gate Mgt Co. Ltd, 1997–99; RNM Functions Ltd, 2003–10. Hon. Dep. Sec., First Div. Assoc., 1969–73. Chairman: Finance Cttee, Greenwich Hosp., 1996–99; DHE Audit Cttee, 2002–04; Mem., Defence Estates Audit Cttee, 2004. Deputy Chairman: Trustees, Royal Naval Mus., Portsmouth, 2003–10; Governors, Royal Hosp. Sch., Holbrooke, 1996–99; Trustee, Nat. Mus. of RN, 2010–12 (Chm., Audit Cttee, 2010–12). Chairman: Friends of Torbay (Musical Weekend), 2007–11; Headway W Kent, 2014–; Mem. Council, Seafarers UK (formerly King George V Fund for Sailors), 2002–12 (Chm., Distribution Cttee, 2005–12); Trustee and Mem. Council, Tunbridge Wells Internat. Young Concert Artists Competition, 2003–10; Trustee, Midday Music, 2004–11; Trustee and Dir, Headway West Kent, 2011–; Trustee and Hon. Treas., Green Room Music, 1997–2011. *Club:* Civil Service (Chm., 1990–95).

MILLER, Bill; *b* 22 July 1954; *s* of George and Janet Miller; one *s* one *d*. *Educ:* Paisley Coll.; Kingston Poly. (BSc Land Econs). DipTP; MRICS. Surveyor, Glasgow DC, 1978–94. Councillor (Lab) Strathclyde, 1986–94. MEP (Lab) Glasgow, 1994–99, Scotland, 1999–2004. *Recreations:* record collecting, Kilmarnock Football Club, golf. *Club:* Castlemilk Labour (Glasgow).

MILLER, Carolyn, CBE 2013; consultant on international management, since 2013; Chief Executive, Merlin, 2005–13; *b* 20 Nov. 1951; *d* of Norman and Irene Miller. *Educ:* Southampton Univ. (BSc); City Univ., London (DipTP). Local govt, 1973–84; Sen. Advr to Ministry of Planning, Nicaragua, 1984–87; Save the Children: Prog. Dir, Mozambique/Angola, 1987–89; Hd, Southern Africa Regl Office, 1989–91; Dir, Asia, Latin America and Caribbean, ME, 1991–96; Dir of Progs, 1996–2001; Dir, Eastern Europe and the Western Hemisphere, subseq. Europe, ME and Americas, DFID, 2001–04. *Recreations:* walking, arts. *E:* carolyn.millerpersonal@gmail.com.

MILLER, Cheryl; *see* Miller, D. C.

MILLER, Christopher; *see* Miller, J. C.

MILLER, Colin Brown; Sheriff for South Strathclyde, Dumfries and Galloway, 1991–2010, recommissioned Sheriff, since 2010; *b* 4 Oct. 1946; *s* of late James Miller and Isabella Brown or Miller; *m* 1972, Joan Elizabeth Blyth; three *s*. *Educ:* Paisley Grammar Sch.; Glasgow Univ. (LLB 1967). Solicitor in private practice, 1969–91. Mem. Council, Law Soc. of Scotland, and Convener of various cttees, 1983–91. Dean, Faculty of Procurators in Paisley, 1991. *Recreations:* walking, family, railways, ships, motor vehicles, photography, visiting Australia. *Address:* Sheriffs' Chambers, Wellington Square, Ayr KA7 1EE. *T:* (01292) 268474.

MILLER, Hon. Daniel; *see* Miller, Hon. A. D.

MILLER, Prof. Daniel Malcolm Stuart, PhD; FBA 2008; Professor of Material Culture, Department of Anthropology, University College London, since 1995; *b* 1954; *m* Rickie Burman; one *s* one *d*. *Educ:* St John's Coll., Cambridge (BA 1976; PhD Anthropol. and Archaeol. 1984). Lectr, 1981–90, Reader, 1990–95, UCL. *Publications:* (ed with C. Tilley) Ideology, Power and Prehistory, 1984; Artefacts as Categories, 1985; Material Culture and Mass Consumption, 1987; (ed jtly) Domination and Resistance, 1989; (ed) Unwrapping Christmas, 1993; Modernity: an ethnographic approach, 1994; Acknowledging Consumption, 1995; (ed) Worlds Apart: modernity through the prism of the local, 1995; Capitalism: an ethnographic approach, 1997; A Theory of Shopping, 1998; (ed) Material Cultures, 1998; (with J. Carrier) Virtualism: a new political economy, 1998; (jtly) Shopping Place and Identity, 1998; (jtly) Commercial Cultures, 2000; (with D. Slater) The Internet: an ethnographic approach, 2000; The Dialectics of Shopping, 2001; (ed) Car Cultures, 2001; (ed) Consumption, 4 vols, 2001; Home Possessions, 2001; (with M. Bannerjee) The Sari, 2003; (ed with S. Küchler) Clothing as Material Culture, 2005; Materiality, 2005; (with H. Horst) The Cell Phone: an anthropology of communication, 2006; The Comfort of Things, 2008; Anthropology and the Individual, 2009; Stuff, 2009; (with Z. Búriková) Au Pair, 2010; (ed with S. Woodward) Global Denim, 2010; Tales from Facebook, 2011; Weinachten: das globale Fest, 2011; (with S. Woodward) Blue Jeans: the art of the ordinary, 2012; (with M. Madianou) Migration and New Media: transnational families, 2012; Consumption and its Consequences, 2012; (ed with H. Horst) Digital Anthropology, 2012; (with J. Sinanan) Webcam, 2014. *Address:* Department of Anthropology, University College London, 14 Taviton Street, WC1H 0BW.

MILLER, David; journalist and author; columnist: Daily Telegraph, 1997–2009; Daily Express, 2010–12; Chief Sports Correspondent, The Times, 1983–97; *b* 1 March 1935; *er s* of Wilfred Miller and Everilda Miller (*née* Milne-Redhead); *m* 1957, Marita Marjorie Malyon; one *s* one *d*. *Educ:* Charterhouse; Peterhouse, Cambridge (Nat. Sci. Tripos; CUAFC *v* Oxford, 1954–55). Sub-editor, The Times, 1956–59; Sports Correspondent: Daily Telegraph, 1960–73; Sunday Telegraph, 1961–73; Chief Sports Corresp., Daily Express, 1973–82. Has covered 23 Summer and Winter Olympic Games and 14 Football World Cups, attended 61 FA Cup Finals, over 430 England football internationals and 50 Wimbledon Championships. Member: Press Commn of IAAF, 1988–2004; FIFA Press Commn, 1993–97. Chm., Sports Writers' Assoc. of GB, 1981–84; Mem., Internat. Soc. of Olympic Historians, 1993–. Sports Writer of Year Award, What the Papers Say, 1986; Doug Gardner Services to Journalism Award, Sports Writers' Assoc., 2001; FIFA Centenary Jules Rimet Award, 2004; Vikelas Award, Internat. Soc. of Olympic Historians, 2015; Hall of Fame, Olympic Journalists Assoc., 2015. *Publications:* Father of Football: biography of Sir Matt Busby, 1970; World Cup, 1970; World Cup, 1974; The Argentina Story, 1978; Cup Magic, 1981; (with Sebastian Coe) Running Free, 1981; The World to Play For, 1982; Coming Back, 1984; England's Last Glory, 1986, updated 1996, 2006, 2014; Sports Writers' Eye (anthology), 1989; Stanley Matthews, 1990; Born to Run, 1992; (jtly) History of IAAF, 1992; Olympic Revolution: biography of Juan Antonio Samaranch, 1992 (trans. 8 langs); Our Sporting Times, 1996; (co-author) Opus: a history of Arsenal FC, 2007; (jtly) Olympic Guardians (1896–2010): biography of eight IOC presidents, 2010 (trans. French); (jtly) Centenary History, IAAF, 2012; (jtly) World History of Relays, IAAF, 2014; Official IOC books: Seoul '88; Albertville '92; Lillehammer '94; Atlanta '96; Nagano '98; Athens to Athens: official history, 1894–2004, of the International Olympic Committee and the Olympic Games, 2003, 4th edn as Athens to London, 1894–2012, 2012. *Recreations:* sailing, reading. *E:* dmiller2@btconnect.com. *Clubs:* Royal Thames Yacht; Hawks (Cambridge); Achilles; Corinthian Casuals Football; Pegasus Football (Oxford); Blakeney Sailing.

MILLER, Prof. David Andrew Barclay, FRS 1995; W. M. Keck Foundation Professor of Electrical Engineering, since 1997 (Professor of Electrical Engineering, since 1996), and Co-Director, Stanford Photonics Research Centre, since 1999, Stanford University; *b* 19 Feb. 1954; *s* of Matthew Barclay Miller and Martha Sanders Miller (*née* Dalling); *m* 1976, Patricia Elizabeth Gillies; one *s* one *d*. *Educ:* St Andrews Univ. (BSc Hons 1976); Heriot-Watt Univ. (PhD Phys 1979). FIEEE 1995. Res. Associate, 1979, Lectr, 1980–81, Heriot-Watt Univ.; Technical Staff, 1981–87, Head of Advanced Photonic Res. Dept, 1987–96, AT&T Bell subseq. Bell, Laboratories, Holmdel, NJ; Dir, E. L. Ginzton Lab., 1997–2006, Dir, Solid State and Photonics Lab., 1997–2009, Stanford Univ. Pres., IEEE Lasers and Electro-Optics Soc., 1995. Fellow: Amer. Phys. Soc.; Optical Soc. of America (Adolph Lomb Medal, 1986; R. W. Wood Prize, 1988); Corresp. FRSE 2002. MNAS 2008; Mem., NAE, 2010. Internat. Prize in Optics, Internat. Commn for Optics, 1991; Third Millennium Medal, IEEE, 2000. Hon. Dr Natural and Applied Scis, Free Univ. Brussels, 1997; Hon. DEng Heriot-Watt, 2003. *Publications:* Quantum Mechanics for Scientists and Engineers, 2009; numerous papers in learned jls. *Recreation:* clarinet and saxophone playing. *Address:* Ginzton Laboratory, 348 Via Pueblo Mall, Stanford University, Stanford, CA 94305–4088, USA. *T:* (650) 7230111; 815 San Francisco Court, Stanford, CA 94305, USA.

MILLER, Prof. David Leslie, DPhil; FBA 2002; Professor of Political Theory, University of Oxford, since 2002; Fellow in Social and Political Theory, Nuffield College, Oxford, since 1979; *b* 8 March 1946; *s* of Leslie Miller and Alice (*née* Renfrew); *m* 1982, Susan Deborah Hersh (marr. diss. 2009); two *s* one *d*. *Educ:* Canford Sch.; Selwyn Coll., Cambridge (BA, MA); Balliol Coll., Oxford (BPhil, DPhil 1974). Lecturer in Politics: Univ. of Lancaster,

1969–76; UEA, 1976–79; Jun. Proctor, Univ. of Oxford, 1988–89. *Publications:* Social Justice, 1976; Philosophy and Ideology in Hume's Political Thought, 1981; (with L. Siedentop) The Nature of Political Theory, 1983; Anarchism, 1984; (jtly) The Blackwell Encyclopaedia of Political Thought, 1986; Market, State and Community: theoretical foundations of market socialism, 1989; Liberty, 1991; (with M. Walzer) Pluralism, Justice and Equality, 1995; On Nationality, 1995; Principles of Social Justice, 1999; Citizenship and National Identity, 2000; (with S. Hashmi) Boundaries and Justice: diverse ethical perspectives, 2001; Political Philosophy: a very short introduction, 2003; National Responsibility and Global Justice, 2007; Justice for Earthlings, 2013. *Recreations:* tennis, hiking, theatre, music. *Address:* Nuffield College, Oxford OX1 1NF. *T:* (01865) 278569, *Fax:* (01865) 278621. *E:* david.miller@nuffield.ox.ac.uk.

MILLER, Prof. David Louis, MD; FRCP, FFPH; Professor of Public Health Medicine, St Mary's Hospital Medical School, University of London, 1983–95, now Emeritus Professor; *b* 16 Sept. 1930; *s* of John Henry Charles Miller and Muriel (*née* Rogers); *m* 1955, Wendy Joy Clark; three *s* one *d*. *Educ:* The Leys, Cambridge (Exhibnr); Peddie Sch., Hightstown, NJ, USA (Schol.); Clare Coll., Cambridge (BA 1952, MA 1955; MB, BChir 1955; MD 1965); St Thomas's Hosp. Med. Sch. (Scholar). DPH 1964; FRCP 1978 (MRCP 1973); FFPH (FFCM 1972). House Officer, St Thomas' Hosp., 1956–57; MO, RAF, 1957–60; Research Asst, RPMS, 1960–62; Epidemiologist, PHLS, 1962–71; US Public Health Service Internat. Res. Fellow, Johns Hopkins Sch. of Hygiene and Public Health, Md, 1965–66; Prof. of Community Medicine, Middlesex Hosp. Med. Sch., 1972–82. Hon. Sen. Res. Fellow, UMDS of Guy's and St Thomas' Hosp., then GKT, 1995–2002. Aneurin Bevan Meml Fellowship, Govt of India, 1981. Pres., Sect. Epidemiology, RSocMed, 1986–88; Acad. Registrar, FPHM, RCP, 1989–94. Life Mem., Soc. of Scholars, Johns Hopkins Univ., 1983. President: Central YMCA, 1986–2002 (Chm., 1977–99); Metropolitan Region of YMCAs, 2001–09. Gold Order Red Triangle, YMCA, 2013. *Publications:* (jtly) Lecture Notes on Epidemiology and Public Health Medicine, 1975, 5th edn 2004; Epidemiology of Diseases, 1982; pubns on epidemiology, esp. respiratory infections, vaccines, HIV and health services. *Recreations:* walking, music, youth and community. *Club:* Royal Society of Medicine.
See also R. C. W. Miller.

MILLER, His Honour David Quentin; a Circuit Judge, 1987–2000; *b* 22 Oct. 1936; *s* of Alfred Bowen Badger and Mair Angharad Evans. *Educ:* Ellesmere Coll., Shropshire; London Sch. of Econs and Pol Science, London Univ. (LLB Hons 1956). Called to the Bar, Middle Temple, 1958; admitted Barrister and Solicitor of the Supreme Court of NZ, 1959. In practice, SE Circuit, 1960–82; Metropolitan Stipendiary Magistrate, 1982–87; a Recorder, 1986–87. *Recreations:* history, walking, gardening, art, music, Trollope Society. *Address:* Highfields, Bullinghope, Hereford HR2 8EB. *T:* (01432) 273995.

MILLER, Sir Donald (John), Kt 1990; FRSE; FREng, FIMechE, FIET; Chairman, ScottishPower (formerly South of Scotland Electricity Board), 1982–92; *b* 9 Feb. 1927; *s* of John Miller and Maud (*née* White); *m* 1973, Fay Glendinning Herriot; one *s* two *d*. *Educ:* Banchory Academy; Univ. of Aberdeen (BScEng). FEng 1981. Metropolitan Vickers, 1947–53; British Electricity Authority, 1953–55; Preece, Cardew and Rider (Consulting Engrs), 1955–66; Chief Engr, North of Scotland Hydro-Electric Bd, 1966–74; Dir of Engrg, then Dep. Chm., SSEB, 1974–82. Chairman: Premium Trust, 1993–98; Nat. Cycle Network Steering Cttee, 1995–2001. Chm., Power Div., IEE, 1979. Hon. Mem., British Nuclear Energy Soc., 1989. DUniv Strathclyde, 1992; Hon. DSc Aberdeen, 1997. *Publications:* papers to IEE. *Recreations:* reading, gardening, sailing.

MILLER, (Dorothy) Cheryl, CBE 2002; Chief Executive (formerly Head of Paid Service), East Sussex County Council, 1994–2010; Managing Director, Cheryl Miller Associates Ltd, since 2011; *b* 31 Aug. 1954; *d* of Sidney Radcliffe and Dorothy (*née* Ainsworth); *m* 1976, Graham Edwin Miller; one *s* one *d*. *Educ:* Preston Park Sch., Lancs; Preston Sixth Form Coll.; Manchester Univ. (BA Hons). Admin. Trainee, CSD, 1975–77; HEO(D) and Asst Private Sec. to Lord Privy Seal and Leader of House of Lords, 1977–78; Personnel Policy Br., CSD, 1979–80; Mem., PM's Advr on Efficiency (Lord Rayner) Scrutiny Team, 1980; Cabinet Office: Head, CS Policy on Retirement and Redundancy Conduct and Discipline Br., 1980–84; Head, Constitutional Br., Machinery of Govt Div., 1984–85; Asst Dir, then Dep. Dir, then Hd, CSSB, 1986–90; Head, Staff Develt, DTI, 1991; County Personnel Officer, 1991–93 and Head, Exec. Office, 1992–93, E Sussex CC. Member: Royal Commn on Envmtl Pollution, 2000–03; Stakeholder Gp, Foresight Flood and Coastal Defence Project, OST, 2003–04; Geographic Inf. Panel, ODPM, later DCLG, 2005–08. Non-executive Director: Sussex Enterprise, 1994–2002; Wired Sussex, 1999–2002. Mem., SEEDA Adv. Council, 1998–2004. Chm., ACCE, 2000–01; Pres., SOLACE, 2004–05 (Vice-Pres., 2002–04). Chairman: E Sussex Youth Offending Bd, 2000–10; E Sussex Drug and Alcohol Action Team, 2000–06; Wokingham Improvement Bd, 2009–10; Slough Improvement Bd, 2011–14; Board Member: E Sussex Economic Partnership, 1996–2005; E Sussex Strategic Partnership, 2001–06; Brighton Univ., 2010–. Member: Hastings Academies Trust, 2011– (Chm., Audit Cttee, 2014–15; Trustee and Dir, 2015; Dep. Chm., Bd of Govs, 2015–); SE Council, Prince's Trust, 2011–13. *Recreations:* theatre, music, literature, women's equality issues.

MILLER, Ven. Geoffrey Vincent; Archdeacon of Northumberland, since 2005; *b* 26 Jan. 1956; *s* of late Harold and Vera Miller; *m* 1993, Elaine; one *s*. *Educ:* Sharston High Sch., Manchester; Durham Univ. (BEd 1978); St John's Coll., Nottingham (DPS 1983); Newcastle Univ. (MA with distinction 1994). Ordained deacon, 1983, priest, 1984; Curate, Jarrow, 1983–86; Team Vicar, St Aidan and St Luke, Billingham, 1986–92; Diocesan Urban Develt Officer, Dio. Durham, 1991–99; Community Chaplain, Stockton-on-Tees, 1992–94; Priest-in-charge, 1994–96, Vicar, 1996–99, St Cuthbert, Darlington; Diocesan Urban Officer and Residentiary Canon, St Nicholas Cathedral, Newcastle upon Tyne, 1999–2005. Chm., British Cttee, French Protestant Industrial Mission, 2000–. *Recreation:* looking on the brighter side. *Address:* 80 Moorside North, Fenham, Newcastle upon Tyne NE4 9DU. *T:* (0191) 273 8245, *Fax:* (0191) 226 0286. *E:* g.miller@newcastle.anglican.org.

MILLER, Rt Rev. Harold Creeth; *see* Down and Dromore, Bishop of.

MILLER, Iain George; Partner, Bevan Brittan LLP, since 2006; *b* Sunderland, 16 March 1963; *s* of late George Miller and of Margaret Miller; *m* 1990, Maria Frances Lewis (*see* Rt Hon. M. F. L. Miller); two *s* one *d*. *Educ:* Earl Haig Secondary Sch., Toronto; Loughborough Grammar Sch.; London Sch. of Econs and Pol Sci. (LLB Hons). Admitted as solicitor, 1988; articled clerk, 1986–88, Asst Solicitor, 1988–91, Stephenson Harwood; Asst Solicitor, Jaques & Lewis, 1991–94; Asst Solicitor, 1994–95, Partner, 1995–2006, Wright Son & Pepper. *Publications:* (with A. Hopper, QC) Gen. Ed., Cordery on Legal Services, looseleaf, 2011–; (ed jtly) Butterworths Guide to the Legal Services Act 2007, 2009; (jtly) Alternative Business Structures, 2012. *Recreations:* children, wife, Sunderland AFC and managing the stress caused by each of them. *Address:* Bevan Brittan LLP, Fleet Place House, 2 Fleet Place, Holborn Viaduct, EC4M 7RF. *T:* 0870 194 7827, *Fax:* 0870 194 7800. *E:* iain.miller@bevanbrittan.com.

MILLER, Ian Harper Lawson; Sheriff of Glasgow and Strathkelvin at Glasgow, since 2001; *b* 16 Jan. 1954; *s* of late Henry Young Miller and Jean Watson Harper Miller (*née* Lyall); *m* 1987, Sheila Matthews Howie; one *s* three *d*. *Educ:* Robert Gordon's Coll., Aberdeen; Univ. of Aberdeen (MA Hons Hist. 1976; LLB 1978). Solicitor, 1980–91; Partner, Burnett & Reid, Solicitors, Aberdeen, 1986–91; called to the Scottish Bar, 1992; Temp. Sheriff, 1998; Sheriff of Grampian Highland and Islands at Aberdeen, 1998–2001. Pt-time Tutor, Dept of Scots Law, Univ. of Aberdeen, 1981–91. Mem., Sheriff Court Rules Council, 1987–91. *Recreations:* reading, music, family life, golf. *Address:* Sheriff's Chambers, Glasgow Sheriff Court, 1 Carlton Place, Glasgow G5 9DA. *T:* (0141) 429 8888; 25 Wester Coates Avenue, Edinburgh EH12 5LS. *T:* (0131) 346 1853. *Clubs:* Royal Northern and University (Aberdeen); Royal Aberdeen Golf.

MILLER, Dr Jacques Francis Albert Pierre, AC 2003 (AO 1981); FRS 1970; FAA 1970; Head of Experimental Pathology Unit, Walter and Eliza Hall Institute of Medical Research, 1966–96; Professor of Experimental Immunology, University of Melbourne, 1990–97, now Emeritus; *b* 2 April 1931; French parents; *m* 1956, Margaret Denise Houen. *Educ:* St Aloysius' Coll., Sydney. BSc (Med.) 1953, MB, BS 1955, Sydney; PhD 1960, DSc 1965, London; BA Melbourne 1985. Sen. Scientist, Chester Beatty Res. Inst., London, 1960–66; Reader, Exper. Pathology, Univ. of London, 1965–66. Croonian Lectr, Royal Soc., 1992. For. Mem., Académie Royale de Médecine de Belgique, 1969; For. Associate, US Nat. Acad. Scis, 1982. Hon. MD Sydney, 1986. Langer-Teplitz Cancer Research Award (USA), 1965; Gairdner Foundn Award (Canada), 1966; Encyclopaedia Britannica (Australia) Award, 1966; Scientific Medal of Zoological Soc. of London, 1966; Burnet Medal, Austr. Acad. of Scis, 1971; Paul Ehrlich Award, Germany, 1974; Rabbi Shai Shacknai Meml Prize, Hadassah Med. Sch., Jerusalem, 1978; Saint-Vincent Internat. Prize for Med. Res., Italy, 1983; first Sandoz Immunology Prize, 1990; first Medawar Prize, Transplantation Soc., 1990; J. Allyn Taylor Internat. Prize for Medicine, John Robarts Res. Inst., 1995; Florey-Faulding Medal and Prize, Australian Inst. of Pol Sci., 2000; Copley Medal, Royal Soc., 2001; PM's Prize for Science, Australia, 2003. *Publications:* over 400 papers in scientific jls and several chapters in books, mainly dealing with thymus and immunity. *Recreations:* music, photography, art, literature. *Address:* Walter and Eliza Hall Institute of Medical Research, 1G Royal Parade, Parkville, Victoria 3050, Australia. *T:* (3) 93452555.

MILLER, James, CBE 1986; Chairman, Miller Group Ltd (formerly James Miller & Partners), 1970–99; *b* 1 Sept. 1934; *s* of Sir James Miller, GBE, and Lady Ella Jane Miller; *m* 1st, 1959, Kathleen Dewar; one *s* two *d*; 2nd, 1969, Iris Lloyd-Webb; one *d*. *Educ:* Edinburgh Acad.; Harrow Sch.; Balliol Coll., Oxford (MA Engrg Sci.). Joined James Miller & Partners, 1958; Board Mem., 1960; Man. Dir, 1970–91. Director: Life Assoc. of Scotland, 1981–93; British Linen Bank, 1983–99 (Chm., 1997–99); Britoil, 1988–90; Bank of Scotland, 1993–2000; Mem., Scottish Adv. Bd, British Petroleum, 1990–2001. Pres., FCEC, 1990–93 (Chm., 1985–86). Dir, Royal Scottish Nat. Orchestra, 1996–2002 (Chm., 1997–2002). Chm., Court, Heriot-Watt Univ., 1990–96. Hon. Consul for Austria, 1994–2003; Dean, Consular Corps in Edinburgh, Leith, 1999–2001. *Recreation:* shooting. *Address:* Alderwood, 49 Craigcrook Road, Edinburgh EH4 3PH. *T:* (0131) 332 2222. *Club:* City Livery.

MILLER, (James) Christopher, FCA; Chairman, Melrose plc, since 2003; *b* Birmingham, 25 Sept. 1951; *s* of James and Florence Miller; *m* 1974, Monica Stump; one *s* two *d*. *Educ:* Downside Sch.; Brasenose Coll., Oxford (MA Hons PPE). FCA 1977. Coopers & Lybrand, 1973–82; Associate Dir, Hanson plc, 1982–88; Chief Exec., Wassall plc, 1988–2000. *Recreations:* fishing, golf, ski-ing, shooting. *Address:* Melrose plc, Leconfield House, Curzon Street, W1J 5JA. *Clubs:* Boodle's; Sunningdale Golf, Royal St Georges Golf, Royal Wimbledon Golf.

MILLER, James Francis Xavier; Headmaster, Royal Grammar School, Newcastle upon Tyne, 1994–2008; *b* 3 March 1950; *yr s* of Lt-Col John Francis Miller and Barbara Mary Miller (*née* Cooke); *m* 1976, Ruth Ellen Rowland (*née* Macbeth); two *s*. *Educ:* Douai Sch.; Merton Coll., Oxford (BA Classical Mods and PPE; MA). Winchester College: Asst Master, 1972–89; Hd of Econs, 1978–82; Housemaster, 1982–89; Headmaster, Framlingham Coll., 1989–94. Chm., Amazing Grades Ltd (formerly study-links.com), 2000–09. Councillor, Winchester CC, 1976–83 (Chm., Health and Works Cttee, 1979–82). Governor: Hereford Sixth Form Coll., 2009–; King Edward's Sch. and King Edward's High Sch., Birmingham, 2009–12. Member: Eardisland Parish Council, 2011–14; Cttee, Hereford Historic Churches Trust, 2009–13. Trustee, Hereford Music Pool, 2014–. FRSA 1994. *Recreations:* opera, crosswords, theatre, trying to play the sax less badly, malt whisky, bridge, photographing Herefordshire's historic churches. *Address:* Orchard Cottage, Eardisland, Leominster, Herefordshire HR6 9BJ. *T:* (01544) 388454.

MILLER, Jane Elizabeth Mackay; QC 2000; **Her Honour Judge Miller;** a Circuit Judge, since 2010; *b* Rochester, Kent, 7 March 1956; *d* of Keith Mackay Miller and Edna Miller (*née* Rawlings); *m* 1982; three *s*. *Educ:* Maidstone Grammar Sch. for Girls; Univ. of Bristol (LLB). Called to the Bar, Inner Temple, 1979; Recorder, 1998–2010; Jt Hd of Chambers, 3 Pump Court, Temple, 2005–10. *Recreations:* gardening, cooking, violin playing, tennis, ski-ing. *Address:* Winchester Combined Court Centre, The Law Courts, Winchester, Hants SO23 9DL. *T:* (01962) 814100.

MILLER, Very Rev. John Dunlop; Minister, Castlemilk East Parish Church, Glasgow, 1971–2007; Moderator of the General Assembly of the Church of Scotland, 2001–02; *b* 11 Nov. 1941; *s* of Rev. Ian Robert Newton Miller and Dr Jessie Sinclair Miller (*née* Dunlop); *m* 1968, Mary Glen Robertson; one *s* two *d*. *Educ:* Kilmarnock Acad.; Merchant Taylors' Sch.; Corpus Christi Coll., Oxford (BA 1964); New Coll., Edinburgh (BD 1967); Union Theol Seminary, NY (STM 1970). Ordained 1971. Hon. DD Glasgow, 2001. *Publications:* Ministry and Mission in Working Class Areas, 1976; Buildings and Mission in Working Class Areas, 1986; Reflections on the Beatitudes, 2002; Silent Heroes, 2004; A Simple Life, 2014. *Recreation:* cycling. *Address:* 98 Kirkcaldy Road, Glasgow G41 4LD.

MILLER, John Harmsworth, CBE 2006; architect in private practice; *b* 18 Aug. 1930; *s* of Charles Miller and Brenda Miller (*née* Borrett); *m* 1st, 1957, Patricia Rhodes (marr. diss. 1975; she *d* 2015); two *d*; 2nd, 1985, Su Rogers. *Educ:* Charterhouse; Architectural Assoc. Sch. of Architecture (AA Dip. Hons 1957). ARIBA 1959. Private practice, Colquhoun and Miller, 1961–90, John Miller and Partners, 1990–; works include: Forest Gate High Sch., West Ham (Newham), 1965; Chemistry Labs, Royal Holloway Coll., London Univ., 1970; Melrose Activity Centre, Milton Keynes Develt Corp. (Commendation, Steel Awards, 1975); Pillwood House, Feock, Cornwall (RIBA Regional Award, 1975); housing, Caversham Road/Gaisford Street, Camden, 1978; single person flats, Hornsey Lane, Haringey, 1980; Oldbrook, Milton Keynes (Silver Award, Architectural Design, 1987; Highly Commended, Housing Design and Civic Trust Awards); Whitechapel Art Gall. extension, 1985 (RIBA Regl Award, 1988; Civic Trust Award, 1988); Gulbenkian Gall. for RCA, 1989; Stevens Bldg for RCA, and Nomura Gall. and bookshop for Tate Gall., 1991; Queen's building, UEA (RIBA Nat. Award) and new 20th century galls for Nat. Portrait Gall., 1993; Elizabeth Fry building, UEA, 1995 (RIBA Regl Award); Ramphal building, Warwick Univ., 1996; Serpentine Gall., 1998; Shackleton Meml Library, Scott Polar Res. Inst., Cambridge Univ., 1999 (RIBA Regl Award); Tate Gall. Centenary Develt, Tate Britain, 2001 (RIBA Nat. Award); Library, Newnham Coll., Cambridge, and Courtyard Develt, Fitzwilliam Mus., Cambridge, 2004 (RIBA Nat. Award, 2005); Playfair Project, Nat. Galls of Scotland, 2004; Brindley Arts Centre, 2005 (RIBA Nat. Award; Civic Trust Award); Business Sch., Warwick Univ., 2008. Exhibition Designs: Dada and Surrealism Reviewed, 1978; Ten Modern Houses, 1980; Picasso's Picassos, 1981; Adolf Loos, 1985; Matisse Picasso, 2002; Anthony Caro, 2006. Tutor: RCA and AA, 1961–73; Cambridge Sch. of Arch., 1969–70; Prof. of Environmental Design, RCA, 1975–85, Fellow 1976, Hon. Fellow, 1985. FRSA 1985. Vis. Prof., Sch. of Arch., UC Dublin, 1985. Visiting Critic: Cornell Univ. Sch. of Arch., Ithaca, 1966, 1968 and 1971; Princeton Univ. Sch. of Arch., NJ, 1970; Dublin Univ. Sch. of Arch., 1972–73; Univ. of Toronto, 1985. Trustee, De La Warr Pavilion, Bexhill, 2002–08.

European Prize for Architecture, 1988. *Publications:* Custom and Innovation, 2009; contribs to architect. jls. *Address:* Apt 10, The Beauchamp Building, Brookes Market, EC1N 7SX. *T:* (020) 7242 2404.

MILLER, Most Rev. John Michael; *see* Vancouver, Archbishop of, (RC).

MILLER, Jonathan; Foreign Affairs Correspondent, Channel 4 News, since 2003; *b* 21 Oct. 1962; *s* of John Miller and Sheila Rankin; *m* 1994, Cornelia Dobb; one *d*. *Educ:* Monkton Combe Sch., Bath; Durham Univ. (BA Hons Geog.). Journalist, South mag., 1986–89; freelance journalist, SE Asia, 1989–92; journalist, BBC World Service, 1992–94; Indochina Corresp., 1994–95, Bangkok Corresp., 1995–97, BBC; ind. film-maker, 1997–2003. Specialist Journalist of the Year, 2006, Internat. News Award, 2006, RTS; TV News Award, Amnesty Internat., 2006 and 2009; Internat. News Coverage Award (Lebanon), 2007, (Congo) 2009, RTS; Broadcast Journalist of the Year Award, One World, 2009. *Recreations:* travelling, photography, cooking curry, mountain walking. *Address:* Channel 4 News, ITN, 200 Gray's Inn Road, WC1X 8XZ. *T:* (020) 7430 4606. *E:* jonathan.miller@itn.co.uk.

MILLER, Sir Jonathan (Wolfe), Kt 2002; CBE 1983; stage director, writer and broadcaster; *b* 21 July 1934; *s* of late Emanuel Miller, DPM, FRCP; *m* 1956, Helen Rachel Collet; two *s* one *d*. *Educ:* St Paul's Sch.; St John's Coll., Cambridge (MB, BCh 1959; Hon. Fellow 1982). FRCP 1997; FRCPE 1998. Research Fellow: in Hist. of Med., UCL, 1970–73; in Neuropsychol., Univ. of Sussex. Associate Director, Nat. Theatre, 1973–75; Artistic Dir, Old Vic, 1988–90. Mem., Arts Council, 1975–76. Vis. Prof. in Drama, Westfield Coll., London, 1977; Fellow, UCL, 1981–. Co-author and appeared in Beyond the Fringe, 1961–64; stage directing in London and NY, 1965–67; *television:* Editor, BBC Monitor, 1965; directed films for BBC TV (incl. Alice in Wonderland), 1966; Exec. Producer, BBC Shakespeare series, 1979–81; writer and presenter, TV series, including: The Body in Question, 1978; Madness, 1991; Opera Works, 1997; Jonathan Miller's Brief History of Disbelief, 2004; *radio:* Self-Made Things (series), Radio 4, 2005; *stage:* School for Scandal, 1968, The Seagull, 1969, The Malcontent, 1973, Nottingham Playhouse; King Lear, The Merchant of Venice, Old Vic, 1970; The Tempest, Mermaid, 1970; Hamlet, Arts Theatre, Cambridge, 1970; Danton's Death, 1971, School for Scandal, 1972, Measure for Measure, 1974, Marriage of Figaro, 1974, The Freeway, 1974, Nat. Theatre; The Taming of the Shrew, 1972, The Seagull, 1973, Chichester; Family Romances, 1974, The Importance of Being Earnest, 1975, All's Well That Ends Well, 1975, Greenwich; Three Sisters, Cambridge, 1976; She Would If She Could, Greenwich, 1979; Long Day's Journey Into Night, Haymarket, 1986; The Taming of the Shrew, RSC, Stratford, 1987, Barbican, 1988; (jtly adapted and directed) The Emperor, Royal Court, 1987 (televised, 1988); Andromache, One Way Pendulum, Bussy D'Ambois, The Tempest, Candide, Old Vic, 1988; King Lear, The Liar, Old Vic, 1989; The Way of the World, Gate Theatre, Dublin, 1992; A Midsummer Night's Dream, Almeida, 1996; As You Like It, Gate Theatre, Dublin, 2000; The Cherry Orchard, Crucible, Sheffield, 2007; Hamlet, Tobacco Factory, Bristol, 2008; Rutherford & Son, nat. tour, 2013; King Lear, Viaduct, Halifax, 2015; *film:* Take a Girl Like You, 1970; *operas:* Arden Must Die, Sadler's Wells Theatre, 1974; The Cunning Little Vixen, Glyndebourne, 1975 and 1977; English National Opera: The Marriage of Figaro, 1978; The Turn of the Screw, 1979, 1991; Arabella, 1980; Otello, 1981; Rigoletto, 1982, 1985, 1995; Don Giovanni, 1985; The Magic Flute, 1986; Tosca, 1986; The Mikado, 1986, 1988, 1993, 2004, 2006; The Barber of Seville, 1987, 2006, 2013; Der Rosenkavalier, 1994; Carmen, 1995; La Traviata, 1996; The Elixir of Love, 2010, 2011; La Bohème, 2013; Kent Opera: Così Fan Tutte, 1975; Rigoletto, 1975; Orfeo, 1976; Eugene Onegin, 1977; La Traviata, 1979; Falstaff, 1980, 1981; Fidelio, 1982, 1983, 1988; La Scala: La Fanciulla del West, 1991; Manon Lescaut, 1992; Maggio Musicale, Florence: Don Giovanni, 1990; Così fan Tutte, Tosca, 1991; Marriage of Figaro, 1992; Idomeneo, 1996; Metropolitan Opera, New York: Katya Kabanova, 1991; Pelléas et Mélisande, 1995; Marriage of Figaro, Vienna State Opera, 1991; Roberto Devereux, Monte Carlo, 1992; Die Gezeichneten, Zürich, 1992; Maria Stuarda, Monte Carlo, 1993; The Secret Marriage, Opera North, 1993; Falstaff, Zürich, 1993; L'Incoronazione di Poppea, Glimmerglass Opera, 1994; Così fan tutti, Royal Opera House, and Rome, 1995; The Beggar's Opera, Wilton's Music Hall, 1999; Don Pasquale, Royal Opera House, 2004 and 2010; La Clemenza di Tito, Zürich, 2005; St Matthew Passion, Brooklyn Acad. of Music, 2006; *exhibitions:* Mirror Image: Jonathan Miller on reflection, Nat. Gall., 1998; Metal, wood and paper constructions, Boundary Gall., 2003. Hon. Fellow, RA, 1991; Hon. DLitt: Leicester, 1981; Cambridge, 1996. Silver Medal, Royal TV Soc., 1981; Albert Medal, RSA, 1990. *Publications:* McLuhan, 1971; (ed) Freud: the man, his world, his influence, 1972; The Body in Question, 1978; Subsequent Performances, 1986; (ed) The Don Giovanni Book: myths of seduction and betrayal, 1990; On Reflection, 1998. *Recreation:* deep sleep. *E:* jwmiller@btinternet.com.

MILLER, Judith Henderson; author and publishing consultant; *b* 16 Sept. 1951; *d* of Andrew and Bertha Cairns; *m* 1978, Martin John Miller (marr. diss. 1992; he *d* 2013); two *d*. *Educ:* Galashiels Acad.; Edinburgh Univ. (MA Hons English, 1973). Copywriter, WHT Advertising, Auckland, NZ, 1973–74; Editor, Lyle Publications, Galashiels, 1974–75; Occupational Guidance Officer, Dept of Employment, 1975–79; Man. Dir and Editor, Miller Publications, 1979–98; with Martin Miller opened Chilston Park Hotel, 1985; Man. Dir, MJM Publishing Projects, 1985–92; Co-Founder, Miller's Magazine, 1991. Television appearances include The House Detectives, The Art and Antiques Hour, The Antiques Trail, The Martha Stewart Show, Antiques Roadshow. *Publications:* Miller's Antiques and Collectables: the facts at your fingertips, 1993; Miller's Classic Motorcycles Price Guide, annually, 1993–98; Miller's Art Nouveau and Art Deco Buyer's Guide, 1995; Miller's Pine and Country Furniture Buyer's Guide, 1995; Period Kitchens, 1995; Period Fireplaces, 1995; How to Make Money out of Antiques, 1995; Period Soft Furnishings, 1996; Country Finishes and Effects, 1997; Miller's Clocks and Barometers Buyer's Guide, 1997; Wooden Houses, 1997; Care and Repair of Antiques and Collectables, 1997; The Style Sourcebook, 1998; Classic Style, 1998; Miller's Antiques Encyclopaedia, 1998; Period Details Sourcebook, 1999; A Closer Look at Antiques, 2000; Colour, 2000; Dorling Kindersley Antiques Price Guide, annually, 2003–; Collectables Price Guide, annually, 2003–; (with John Wainwright) Dorling Kindersley Collectors Guide to Costume Jewellery, 2003; Art Nouveau, 2004; Twentieth Century Glass, 2004; Arts and Crafts, 2005; Art Deco, 2005; Dorling Kindersley Furniture, 2005; Twentieth Century Roadshow, 2005; Buy, Keep or Sell, 2005; Tribal Art, 2006; Handbags, 2006; Perfume Bottles, 2006; Sixties Style, 2006; Metal Toys, 2006; Decorative Arts, 2006; Antiques Detective, 2007; with Martin Miller: Miller's Antiques Price Guide, annually 1979–98; The Antiques Directory—Furniture, 1985; Period Details, 1987; Miller's Pocket Antiques Fact File, 1988; Period Style, 1989; Understanding Antiques, 1989; Miller's Collectables Price Guide, annually 1989–98; Country Style, 1990; Miller's Collectors Cars Price Guide, annually 1991–98; Miller's Art Deco Checklist, 1991; Furniture Checklist, 1991; Period Finishes and Effects, 1992; Victorian Style, 1993. *Recreations:* antiques!, bridge. *Club:* Groucho.

MILLER, Julian Alexander, CB 2003; Deputy National Security Adviser, Cabinet Office, 2010–15; *b* 14 July 1955; *s* of Allan Douglas Stewart Miller and Mavis Jean Miller; *m* 1986, Roslin Mair; one *s* one *d*. *Educ:* Farnham Grammar Sch.; Sussex Univ. (BSc); Leeds Univ. (PhD 1980). Joined MoD, 1980: on loan to CSD, 1988; Private Sec. to Armed Forces Minister, 1990–92; on loan to FCO as First Sec., then Counsellor, UK Delegn to NATO, 1992–96; Hd, Resources and Programmes, Army, then Prog. Develt, 1996–99; Private Sec. to Defence Sec., 1999–2001; on loan to Cabinet Office as Chief, Assessments Staff, 2001–03; Dir Gen., Service Personnel Policy, 2003–06, Dir (formerly Dir Gen.), Resources and Plans, 2006–09, MoD; Dir, Foreign and Defence Policy, Cabinet Office, 2009–10. *Recreations:* reading, photography.

MILLER, Kenneth William, FCA; non-executive Director, Colt Group (Chairman, 2000–14); *b* 4 Feb. 1939; *s* of Albert William Miller and Winifred (*née* Ashworth); *m* 1st, 1964, Carol Susan Hislop (marr. diss. 1987); one *s* one *d*; 2nd, 1988, Jean Helen McPhail McInnes. *Educ:* Surbiton County Grammar Sch. FCA 1961. Company Sec., Hunting Associated Industries, 1965–73; Asst Finance Dir, Hunting Gp, 1969–73; Commercial Dir, E. A. Gibson & Co. Ltd, 1973–78; Hunting Petroleum Services plc: Dir, 1978–87; Man. Dir, 1987–89; Chief Exec., Hunting plc, 1989–2000. *Recreations:* reading, sport, music. *Address:* Colt Group, New Lane, Havant, Hants PO9 2LY. *T:* (023) 9245 1111. *Club:* Royal Automobile.

MILLER, Leszek; Deputy (Dem. Left Alliance) for Łódź, 1991–2005; Prime Minister of Poland, 2001–04; *b* Zyrardów, 3 July 1946; *m* 1969, Aleksandra Borowiec; one *s*. *Educ:* Higher Sch. of Social Scis, Warsaw (MPolSci.). Electrician, Enterprise of Linen industry, Zyrardów, 1963–70; became social and trade union activist, 1970; Polish United Workers' Party (PUWP): Youth Div., 1977–84, staff mem., 1988–99, Central Cttee; First Sec., Voivodeship's Cttee, 1985–88; Mem., Politburo Central Cttee, 1989–90. Minister: of Labour and Social Policy, 1993–96; and Hd, Council of Ministers' Office, 1996; of Internal Affairs and Admin, 1997. Socialdemocracy party, now Democratic Left Alliance: Gen. Sec., 1990–93; Vice-Chm., 1993–97; Chm., 1997–2001. Goodwill Ambassador, Polish Cttee, UNICEF, 2000–. Golden Cross of Merit, 1979; Kt's Cross, Polonia Restituta (Poland), 1984. *Recreations:* angling, literature.

MILLER, Ven. Luke Jonathan; Archdeacon of London, since 2015; Priest-in-charge, St Andrew-by-the-Wardrobe with St Ann, Blackfriars, since 2015; *b* Scunthorpe, 27 June 1966; *s* of Paul Richard Miller and Hilary Jane Miller; *m* 1995, Jacqueline Ann Blunden; three *s*. *Educ:* Haileybury; Sidney Sussex Coll., Cambridge (Barcroft Exhibn; Taylor Scholarship; BA 1987, MA 1991 (History Tripos)); St Stephen's House, Oxford Honour Sch. of Theol. (BA 1990, MA 1993). Ordained deacon, 1991, priest, 1992; Asst Curate, St Matthew, Oxhey, 1991–94; Asst Curate, 1994–95, Vicar, 1995–2011, St Mary the Virgin, Tottenham; Area Dean, East Haringey, 2005–11; Priest-in-charge, Holy Trinity, Winchmore Hill, 2011–12; Archdeacon of Hampstead, 2011–15. Local Vicar, Soc. of the Holy Cross, Chapter of Christ the King, 2003–12. Member, Council: St Stephen's House, 2008– (Chm., Finance and Gen. Purposes, 2008–); Haileybury, 2006–. Gov., Mulberry Primary Sch., 1996–2011 (Chair, 2001–11). Pres., Haileybury Soc., 2011. *Publications:* The Sorrow of Nature: the Way of the Cross with George Congreve and St Thérèse of Lisieux, 2014. *Recreations:* painting, reading, gardening.

MILLER, Prof. Marcus Hay, PhD; Professor of Economics, University of Warwick, since 1974; *b* 9 Sept. 1941; *s* of J. Irvine Miller and Rose H. (*née* Moir); *m* 1967, Margaret Ellen Hummel (marr. diss.; she *d* 2001); two *d*. *Educ:* Price's Sch., Fareham, Hants; University Coll., Oxford (BA 1st Cl. PPE); Yale Univ. (Henry Fellowship, MA, PhD Econ). Lecturer, London School of Economics, 1967–76; Prof. of Economics, Univ. of Manchester, 1976–78. Economist, 1972–73, Houblon-Norman Fellow, 1981–82, Bank of England; Vis. Associate Prof. of Internat. Finance, Univ. of Chicago, 1976; Vis. Prof. of Public and Internat. Affairs, Princeton Univ., 1983; Res. Fellow, Centre for Economic Policy Res., 1983– (Co-Dir, Internat. Macroeconomics Prog., 1986–91); Vis. Fellow, Inst. for Internat. Econs, Washington, 1986–. Member, Academic Panel, HM Treasury, 1976– (Chm., 1979–80); Adviser, House of Commons Select Cttee on the Treasury and Civil Service, 1980–81. Mem. Management Cttee, NIESR, 1980–91. *Publications:* joint editor: Monetary Policy and Economic Activity in West Germany, 1977; Essays on Fiscal and Monetary Policy, 1981; Targets and Indicators: a blueprint for the international co-ordination of economic policy, 1993; Exchange Rate Targets and Currency Bands 1992; The Asian Financial Crisis, 1999; articles in professional jls, mainly on domestic and internat. macroecons. *Recreations:* sailboarding, contemporary dance. *Address:* Department of Economics, University of Warwick, Coventry CV4 7AL. *E:* marcus.miller@warwick.ac.uk. *Club:* Reform.

MILLER, Rt Hon. Maria (Frances Lewis); PC 2012; MP (C) Basingstoke, since 2005; *b* 26 March 1964; *d* of John and June Lewis; *m* 1990, Iain George Miller, *qv*; two *s* one *d*. *Educ:* London Sch. of Econs (BSc Hons Econs 1985). Advertising Exec., Grey Advertising, 1985–90; Advertising and Mktg Manager, Texaco, 1990–95; Director: Grey Advertising, 1995–2000; Rowland Co., then PR21, 2000–02. Shadow Minister: for Education, 2005–06; for Family Welfare incl. CSA, 2006–07; for Family, 2007–10; Parly Under-Sec. of State, DWP, 2010–12; Sec. of State for Culture, Media and Sport and Minister for Women and for Equalities, 2012–14. Chm., Women and Equalities Select Cttee, 2015–. Pres., Wolverhampton NE Cons. Assoc., 2001–; Chm., Wimbledon Cons. Assoc., 2002–03. *Recreation:* three children. *Address:* House of Commons, SW1A 0AA. *T:* (020) 7219 3000. *E:* maria.miller.mp@parliament.uk.

MILLER, Michael A.; *see* Ashley-Miller.

MILLER, Rev. Canon Paul; Chaplain of the Isles of Scilly, since 2012; Chaplain to the Queen, since 2005; *b* 24 Feb. 1949; *s* of late Sidney George Miller and Florence Lilian Miller; *m* 1976, Lynette Jane Warren; three *s*. *Educ:* Cannock Sch., Chelsfield; Bromley Grammar Sch. for Boys; Oak Hill Theol Coll. Ordained deacon 1974, priest 1975; Assistant Curate: Upton, dio. Exeter, 1974–77; Farnborough, dio. Guildford, 1977–78; Vicar: St Luke, Torquay, 1978–86; Green Street Green and Pratts Bottom, 1986–2001; Rural Dean of Orpington, 1996–2001; Vicar of Shortlands, Bromley, 2001–12; Area Dean of Beckenham, 2009–12. Hon. Canon, Rochester, 2000–12, now Canon Emeritus; Anglican Ecumenical Borough Dean, Bromley, 2006–12. SBStJ 1984. *Recreations:* cricket, golf, football, travel, philately. *Address:* The Chaplaincy, Church Road, St Mary's, Isles of Scilly TR21 0NA. *T:* (01720) 423911. *E:* paulmiller@roundisland.net.

MILLER, Sir Peter (North), Kt 1988; Chairman, Lloyd's, 1984–87; Chairman, The Miller Insurance Group Ltd (formerly Thos R. Miller & Son (Holdings)), 1971–83 and 1988–96; *b* 28 Sept. 1930; *s* of Cyril Thomas Gibson Risch Miller, CBE and Dorothy Alice North Miller, JP; *m* 1991, Jane Herbertson; one *s* and two *s* one *d* by previous marriage. *Educ:* Rugby (1st XV and Capt. of running); Lincoln Coll., Oxford (MA Hons; full blue, cross country; Hon. Fellow, 1992); City Univ. (DSc). National Service, Intelligence Corps, 1949–50. Joined Lloyd's, 1953; qualified as barrister, 1954; Partner, Thos R. Miller & Son (Insurance), 1959, Sen. Partner, 1971–96. Dep. Chm., Lloyd's Insurance Brokers' Assoc., 1974–75, Chm. 1976–77; Mem., Cttee of Lloyd's, 1977–80 and 1982–89 (Mem. Council of Lloyd's, 1983–89); in charge of team responsible for passage of Lloyd's Bill (Fisher), 1980–82. Member: Baltic Exchange, 1966–; Insurance Brokers' Registration Council, 1977–81; Vice-Pres., British Insce Brokers' Assoc., 1978–96; Chm., British Cttee of Bureau Veritas, 1980–2002. Chm. of Trustees, Lloyd's Tercentenary Foundn, 1989–2007. One of HM's Lieutenants for the City of London, 1987–. Mem., Chief Pleas, Sark, 1969–2009. Mem., Rector's Council, Lincoln Coll., Oxford, 1992–2009. Commendatore, Ordine al Merito della Repubblica Italiana, 1989. Hon. DSc City, 1987. *Recreations:* all sport (except cricket), including tennis, running, sailing; wine, music, old churches, gardening. *Address:* c/o Miller Insurance Group, Dawson House, 5 Jewry Street, EC3N 2PJ. *Clubs:* Travellers; Vincent's (Oxford); Thames Hare and Hounds.

MILLER, Air Cdre Richard Albert, OBE 1976; FRAeS; Chairman, DGB Sterling (formerly Dinol (GB)) Ltd, 1998–2006; *b* 12 July 1936; *s* of Albert and Emily Kate Miller; *m* 1959, Beryl Marjorie Thompson (*d* 2010); one *s* one *d*. *Educ:* Northampton Grammar Sch.; Coll. of Art, Nottingham; Open Univ. (DipEd, BA Hons); Poly. of E London (MA, MSc). Royal Air Force, 1956–82, Pilot; Flying Duties, 1957–70; RAF Advanced Staff Course, 1970; MoD, 1971–72; OC 36 Sqn, RAF Lyneham, 1973–75; Station Comdr, RAF Benson and Dep. Captain of Queen's Flight, 1976–78; ADC to the Queen, 1976–78; RAF Diamond Jubilee Fellow, Univ. of S Calif and Fitzwilliam Coll., Cambridge, 1979; Dir, Dept of Air Warfare, RAF Coll., 1980; Dir, Air Staff Briefing, MoD, 1981–82; Dir, PR (RAF), MoD, 1982–84; retired (Air Cdre). Executive Air Weapons, BAe Inc., USA, 1985–86; Dir, Defence Procurement Management Gp, 1986–88, Dean, Continuing Educn, 1987–89, Dir, Sch. of Defence Management, 1988–95, RMCS; Dir of Strategic Mgt, Sch. of Defence Mgt, RMCS, Cranfield Univ., 1995–97. Visiting Professor: Cranfield Univ., 1997–2006; Bath Univ., 1999–2010. FCMI 1981. Freedom, City of London, 1982. QCVSA 1965, 1970. *Recreations:* French cultural and language studies, computing. *Address:* 32 Adam Court, Ravenscroft Road, Henley-on-Thames, Oxfordshire RG9 2BJ. *T:* (01491) 578281. *Club:* Royal Air Force.

MILLER, Richard Charles William; Humanitarian Director, ActionAid International, since 2015; *b* 5 March 1962; *s* of Prof. David Louis Miller, *qv*; *m* 1992, Sally Gardner; three *s*. *Educ:* Leys Sch., Cambridge; Univ. of Bristol (BSc Hons Soc. Admin and Pols 1984). Catholic Agency for Overseas Development: Africa Progs Officer, 1986–92; Dep. Dir, 1992–98; S Africa Regl Rep., 1998–2003; Exec. Dir, ActionAid UK, 2004–15. Mem., Adv. Bd, Traidcraft Exchange, 1986–89. Trustee: IVS, 1984–87; Disasters Emergency Cttee, 2004–15; ActionAid Netherlands (formerly Netherlands Inst. for Southern Africa), 2008–14; ActionAid USA, 2012–. Gov., Downlands Sch., Hassocks, 2009–. *Recreations:* family, travel, music, watching my sons play sport. *Address:* ActionAid UK, 33–39 Bowling Green Lane, EC1R 0BJ. *T:* (020) 3122 0514. *E:* richard.miller@actionaid.org.

MILLER, Richard Hugh; QC 1995; *b* 1 Feb. 1953; *s* of Sir Stephen James Hamilton Miller, KCVO, FRCS and Lady (Heather) Miller. *Educ:* Charterhouse; Univ. of Sussex (BSc Chem. Physics). Called to the Bar, Middle Temple, 1976, Bencher, 2007 (Chm., Finance Cttee and Mem., Exec. Cttee, 2012–); in practice at the Bar, specialising in patent matters; Hd of Chambers, Three New Square Intellectual Property, 2012–. Chm., Intellectual Property Bar Assoc., 2005–11 (Vice-Chm., 2004–05); Member: Bar Council, 2006–11 (Member: European Cttee, 2005–11 (Co-Chm., 2009–11); Professional Practice Cttee, 2008–13; Access to the Bar Cttee, 2009–10; Ethics Cttee, 2014–); Council, UK Gp, Internat. Assoc. for Protection of Intellectual Property, 2006–; Patents Sub-Gp, Council of Bars and Law Socs of Europe, 2008–; Working Gp for reform of Patents County Court, 2009. *Publications:* (ed jtly) Terrell on the Law of Patents, 14th edn 1994 to 17th edn 2011. *Recreations:* travel, films. *Address:* Three New Square Intellectual Property, Lincoln's Inn, WC2A 3RS. *T:* (020) 7405 1111.

MILLER, Richard Morgan; Chief Executive, Willis Corroon Group plc, 1990–94; *b* Nashville, Tenn, 1931; *m* 1953, Betty Ruth Randolph; one *s* two *d*. *Educ:* Montgomery Bell Acad., Nashville; Vanderbilt Univ., Nashville (BA 1953); Wharton Sch., Univ. of Pennsylvania. Served Korean War, 1953–55, Lt US Marine Corps; retired from US Marine Corps Reserve, 1960, Capt. Salesman, Dominion Insce Agency, 1955–58; established Richard M. Miller & Co., 1958, Pres., 1958–70; merger with Synercon Corp., 1970: Founder, Dir, Pres. and Chief Exec. Officer, 1970–76 (also Pres. and Chief Exec. Officer subsid. cos); Synercon Corp. merged into Corroon & Black Corp., 1976: Exec. Vice-Pres., Chief Operating Officer and Dir, 1976–78; Pres., Chief Operating Officer and Dir, 1978–88; Chief Exec. Officer, Pres. and Dir, 1988–89; Chm. Bd, Chief Exec. Officer and Dir, 1990–93; Corroon & Black Corp. merged into Willis Faber plc, 1990. Member, National Associations of: Casualty and Surety Agents; Insurance Brokers; Surety Bond Producers; Mem., Nat. Fedn of Independent Business; Director: Consumer Benefit Life Insce Co.; Meridian Insce Co. (Bermuda); Third Nat. Bank; Third Nat. Corp. Trustee and Member Executive Committee: Insce Inst. of America; Amer. Inst. for Property and Liability Underwriters. *Recreation:* golf. *Clubs:* City Midday, New York Athletic (New York); Belle Meade Country, Cumberland, Nashville City, Tennessee (Nashville, Tennessee); John's Island (Florida); Mid Ocean (Bermuda).

MILLER, Robert Alexander Gavin D.; *see* Douglas Miller.

MILLER, Robin Anthony; a Recorder of the Crown Court, 1978–2003; *b* 15 Sept. 1937; *s* of William Alexander Miller, CBE, BEM, and Winifred Miller; *m* 1962, Irene Joanna Kennedy; two *s* one *d*. *Educ:* Devonport High Sch., Plymouth; Wadham Coll., Oxford (MA). Called to the Bar, Middle Temple, 1960. *Address:* Flat 6, 1 Walker Terrace, West Hoe, Plymouth, Devon PL1 3BN. *T:* (01752) 604487.

MILLER, Sir Robin (Robert William), Kt 2003; Chairman: Edge Performance VCT, since 2005; Butler, Tanner & Dennis, since 2010; Director, Robin Miller Consultants Ltd. Joined East Midlands Allied Press as jun. reporter, Motor Cycle News, 1965; various sen. editl roles; Man. Dir, Mag. Div., 1974; Mem. Bd, 1976–2003; Chief Exec., 1985–98 and 2001–03, non-exec. Chm., 1998–2001, Emap plc. Chairman: Entertainment Rights plc, 2008–09; Setanta, 2009. Non-executive Chairman: HMV Gp, 2004–05; Boosey & Hawkes Music Publishers Ltd; GetMeMedia, 2009–; non-executive Director: Moss Bros plc, 1998–2001; Channel 4 TV, 1999–2006; Mecom Gp plc, 2005–09; Racing Post; former non-exec. Dir, Horserace Totalisator Bd. Chm., E Regl Sports Bd, Sport England, 2003–05; Mem. Panel, UK Sports Inst., 2000–. Trustee: Golf Foundation; Riders for Health. *Address:* (office) 3rd Floor, Albemarle House, Albemarle Street, W1S 4HA.

MILLER, Sir Ronald (Andrew Baird), Kt 1993; CBE 1985; CA; *b* 13 May 1937; *m* 1965, Elizabeth Ann Gordon; one *s* one *d*. *Educ:* Daniel Stewart's Coll.; Univ. of Edinburgh (BSc). With Dawson Internat., 1968–95: Dir, 1976; Chm. and Chief Exec., 1982–91; Exec. Chm., 1991–95. Director: Securities Trust of Scotland, 1983–2001; Christian Salvesen, 1987–97; Aggreko, 1997–2002; Mem. Bd, Scottish Amicable, 1997–2003 (Dir, Scottish Amicable Life Assce Soc., 1987–97, Dep. Chm., 1994–97). Chairman: British Knitting and Clothing Export Council (later British Fashion Exports), 1993–97 (Mem., 1987–98; Vice Pres., 1997–); Scottish Textile Assoc., 1992–95 (Mem., 1992–98); Cttee of Chairmen of Scottish Higher Educn Instns, 1999–2001; Member: N Amer. Adv. Gp, DTI, 1986–96; ScotBIC, 1990–95; Quality Scotland, 1991–95; Scottish Council, CBI, 1992–95; British Apparel and Textile Confedn, 1993–95; SHEFC, 1992–95; Quality Assurance Agency for Higher Educn, 1997–2003 (Chm., Scottish Cttee, 1998–2003); Walpole Cttee, 1992–95; SCOTrust, 1994–99. Mem. Court, Edinburgh Napier (formerly Napier) Univ., 1992–2001 (Chm. Court, 1998–2001; Chm., Develt Trust, 2001–). Liveryman, Woolmen's Co., 1992–. FRSA; CCMI. DSc *hc* Heriot-Watt, 1992; DUniv Napier, 2001. *Club:* Caledonian.

See also A. A. Miller.

MILLER, Ronald Kinsman, CB 1989; Solicitor of Inland Revenue, 1986–90, retired; part-time Chairman, VAT and Duties Tribunals, 1991–2002; *b* 12 Nov. 1929; *s* of William Miller and Elsie May Kinsman; *m* 1952, Doris Alice Dew (*d* 2009); one *s* one *d*. *Educ:* Colchester Royal Grammar Sch. Served RN, 1948–50. Called to the Bar, Gray's Inn, 1953. Joined Inland Revenue, 1950; Asst Solicitor, 1971; Law Officers' Dept, 1977–79; Principal Asst Solicitor, 1981–86. *Recreations:* gardening, reading, music. *Address:* 4 Liskeard Close, Chislehurst, Kent BR7 6RT. *T:* (020) 8467 8041. *Club:* Athenæum.

MILLER, Dr Roy Frank; Vice-Principal, 1985–98, Hon. Research Fellow in Physics, since 1998, Royal Holloway and Bedford New College, University of London; *b* 20 Sept. 1935; *s* of Thomas R. Miller and Margaret Ann Tattum; *m* 1961, Ruth Naomi Kenchington; one *s*. *Educ:* Wembley County Grammar Sch.; University Coll. SW England, Exeter; Royal Holloway Coll. BSc, PhD; CPhys, FInstP. Teacher, Halbutt Secondary Modern Sch., 1957; Royal Holloway College: Demonstrator, 1957, Asst Lectr, 1960, Lectr, 1963, Sen. Lectr, 1973, Physics Dept; Vice-Principal, 1978–81; Acting Principal, 1981–82; Principal, 1982–85; Hon. Fellow, 2000. Research Associate and Teaching Fellow, Case Western Reserve Univ., Ohio, USA, 1967–68. Mem. Senate, Univ. of London, 1981–85; Chm., Bd, Inst. of Classical Studies, Univ. of London, 1983–2001; Trustee and Governor, Strode's Foundn, Strode's Coll., Egham, 1982–. MRI. *Publications:* articles in Jl Phys C, Phil. Mag., Vacuum, Proc. Royal Soc. A. *Recreations:* mountaineering, squash, music. *Club:* Athenæum.

MILLER, Sidney James, MA; Citizens' Advice Bureau Adviser, Bedford, since 1996; *b* 25 Jan. 1943; *s* of Sidney Tomsett Miller and Mary Ada Miller (*née* Marshall); *m* 1971, Judith Branney (*née* Passingham); three *s* one *d*. *Educ:* Clifton Coll., Bristol; Jesus Coll., Cambridge (MA); Harvard Univ.; De Montfort Univ. VIth Form Classical Master and House Tutor, Clifton Coll., Bristol, 1965–68; Asst Master and Classical Tutor, Eton Coll., 1968–73, Head of Classical Dept, 1971–73; Dep. Headmaster (Organisation), Bridgewater Hall, Stantonbury Campus, Milton Keynes, 1974–77; Headmaster, Kingston Grammar Sch., Kingston upon Thames, 1977–86; Head Master, Bedford Sch., 1986–88; Professional Officer, Sch. Exams and Assessment Council, 1988–89; HEO, DES, later DFE, 1989–95. Mem., Gen. Synod of C of E, 1994–95. Dir, Bedford Concern for the Homeless and Rootless, 1996–2008 (Chm., 2005–08); Member: Community Resettlement Support Project, 2009–; Friends For Life, 2009–13. Official Prison Visitor, 2009–; Ind. Custody Visitor, 2009–13. Founder Mem., Bedford Millennium Probus Club, 1999– (Chm., 2007–08). Mem., Walk Uganda Christian mission gp, 2002–. *Publications:* (ed jtly) Greek Unprepared Translation, 1968; (ed jtly) Inscriptions of the Roman Empire AD14–117, 1971; article in Didaskalos, 1972. *Recreations:* watching sports, learning languages, exercising at gym. *Address:* 33A Bushmead Avenue, Bedford MK40 3QH. *Clubs:* MCC; Achilles; Bedford Rugby.

MILLER of Glenlee, Sir Stephen (William Macdonald), 8th Bt *cr* 1788, of Glenlee, Kirkcudbrightshire; FRCGP; General Practitioner, since 1986; *b* 20 June 1953; *s* of Sir Macdonald Miller of Glenlee, 7th Bt and Marion Jane Audrey Pettit, (Audrey, Lady Miller of Glenlee); *S* father, 1991; *m* 1st, 1978, Mary (*d* 1989), *d* of G. B. Owens; one *s* one *d*; 2nd, 1990, Caroline Clark (*née* Chasemore); one step *s* one step *d*. *Educ:* Rugby Sch.; St Bartholomew's Hosp. MB; FRCS 1981; MRCGP 1986, FRCGP 1995. Surgical Registrar, Sheffield, 1979–81; Orthopaedic Registrar, Newcastle, 1982–84. Vice-Chm., Northern Locality, Devon CCG, 2014–. *Publications:* various papers in med. jls. *Recreations:* gardening, fishing. *Heir:* *s* James Stephen Macdonald Miller, *b* 25 July 1981. *Address:* Burrowland, Sandford, Crediton, Devon EX17 4EL.

MILLER, Prof. William Lockley, PhD; FBA 1994; FRSE; Edward Caird Professor of Politics, Glasgow University, 1985–2009, now Emeritus; *b* 12 Aug. 1943; *s* of William Lockley Miller and Florence Ratcliffe; *m* 1967, Fiona Thomson; two *s* one *d*. *Educ:* Edinburgh Univ. (MA 1st Cl. Maths and Nat. Phil. 1965); Newcastle Univ. (PhD Computing 1970). Lectr in Politics, Sen Lectr and Prof., Strathclyde Univ., 1968–85. Vis. Prof. in Politics, Virginia Tech., Blacksburg, 1983–84. FRSE 1999. *Publications:* Electoral Dynamics, 1977; The End of British Politics?, 1981; The Survey Method, 1983; (with Martin Harrop) Elections and Voters, 1987; Irrelevant Elections?, 1988; (jtly) How Voters Change, 1990; Media and Voters, 1991; (jtly) Alternatives to Freedom, 1995; (jtly) Political Culture in Contemporary Britain, 1996; (jtly) Values and Political Change in Postcommunist Europe, 1998; (jtly) Models of Local Governance, 2000; (jtly) A Culture of Corruption?, 2001 (Ukrainian edn, 2004); (ed) Anglo-Scottish Relations from 1900 to Devolution and Beyond, 2005; (jtly) Multicultural Nationalism: Islamophobia, Anglophobia and devolution, 2006; (jtly) The Open Economy and its Enemies: public attitudes in east Asia and eastern Europe, 2006. *Recreation:* hill walking. *Address:* Department of Politics, Adam Smith Building, The University, Glasgow G12 8RT. *T:* (0141) 339 8855.

MILLER SMITH, Charles; Chairman: Firstsource Solutions UK Ltd, since 2008 (non-executive Director, since 2001); Edge International Management Ltd, since 2014; *b* 7 Nov. 1939; *s* of William Smith and Margaret Pettigrew Brownlie Wardrope; adopted grandfather's surname, Miller Smith, 1963; *m* 1st, 1964, Dorothy Agnes Wilson Adams (*d* 1999); one *s* two *d*; 2nd, 2004, Debjani Jash (marr. diss. 2010). *Educ:* Glasgow Acad.; St Andrews Univ. (MA). ACCA. Unilever: Financial Dir, Vinyl Products, 1970–73; Head of Planning, 1974; Finance Dir, Walls Meat Co., 1976; Vice-Chm., Hindustan Lever, 1979–81; Speciality Chemicals Group, 1981; Chief Executive: PPF Internat., 1983; Quest Internat., 1986; Financial Dir, Unilever Board, 1989; Exec., Unilever Foods, 1993–94; Imperial Chemical Industries: Dir, 1994–2001; Chief Exec., 1995–99; Chm., 1999–2001; Dep. Chm., 1999–2000, Chm., 2000–07, Chm., Adv. Bd, 2007–09, Scottish Power plc. Non-executive Director: Midland Bank, 1994–96; HSBC Hldgs plc, 1996–2001; Premier Foods plc, 2009–; Advr, Goldman Sachs, 2002–05; Sen. Advr, 2005, Consultant, 2014–, Warburg Pincus; Sen. Advr, Deutsche Bank (RREEF Infrastructure), 2007–11. Mem. Mgt Bd, MoD, 2002–07. Hon. LLD St Andrews, 1995. *Recreations:* reading, walking. *Address:* 8 Stack House, Cundy Street, SW1W 9JS. *Club:* National.

MILLETT, family name of **Baron Millett**.

MILLETT, Baron *cr* 1998 (Life Peer), of St Marylebone in the City of Westminster; **Peter Julian Millett,** Kt 1986; PC 1994; a Lord of Appeal in Ordinary, 1998–2004; a non-permanent Judge, Court of Final Appeal, Hong Kong, since 2000; *b* 23 June 1932; *s* of late Denis Millett and Adele Millett; *m* 1959, Ann Mireille, *d* of late David Harris; two *s* (and one *s* decd). *Educ:* Harrow; Trinity Hall, Cambridge (Schol.; MA; Hon. Fellow, 1994). Nat. Service, RAF, 1955–57 (Flying Officer). Called to Bar, Middle Temple, 1955, *ad eundem* Lincoln's Inn, 1959 (Bencher, 1980, Treas., 2004), Singapore, 1976, Hong Kong, 1979; at Chancery Bar, 1958–86; QC 1973; a Judge of the High Court of Justice, Chancery Div., 1986–94; a Lord Justice of Appeal, 1994–98. Examr and Lectr in Practical Conveyancing, Council of Legal Educn, 1962–76. Junior Counsel to Dept of Trade and Industry in Chancery matters, 1967–73. Mem., General Council of the Bar, 1971–75. Outside Mem., Law Commn on working party on co-ownership of matrimonial home, 1972–73; Mem., Dept of Trade Insolvency Law Review Cttee, 1977–82. Pres., West London Synagogue of British Jews, 1991–95. Editor-in-Chief, Encyc. of Forms and Precedents, 1988–. Hon. Fellow, QMUL, 2012. Hon. LLD London, 2000. *Publications:* contrib. to Halsbury's Laws of England; articles in legal jls. *Recreations:* philately, bridge, The Times crossword. *Address:* House of Lords, SW1A 0PW; 18 Portman Close, W1H 6BR. *T:* (020) 7935 1152; St Andrews, Kewhurst Avenue, Cooden, Bexhill-on-Sea, East Sussex TN39 3BH.

See also Hon. R. L. Millett.

MILLETT, Alexandra; *see* Healy, A.

MILLETT, Anthea Christine, CBE 2000; Commissioner, Civil Service Commission, 2007–12; *b* 2 Nov. 1941; *d* of Rupert Millett and Lucy Millett. *Educ:* Erdington Grammar School for Girls, Birmingham; Bedford Coll., Univ. of London (BA Hons). Teacher: Channing School, Highgate, 1963–65; Bournville Grammar Tech. Sch., Birmingham, 1965–67; Solihull High Sch., 1967–71 (Head of Dept); Dep. Head, Tile Hill Comprehensive Sch., Coventry, 1972–77; HM Inspectorate of Schools, subseq. OFSTED, 1978–95: Chief Inspector, 1987–92; Dir of Inspection, 1993–95; Chief Exec., TTA, 1995–99. Chairman:

Wilts HA, 2000–02; Avon, Glos and Wilts Strategic HA, 2002–06. Mem., Cttee of Enquiry, Mgt and Govt of Schools, 1975–77. FRGS; FRSA. *Recreations:* travel, walking, gardening, DIY.

MILLETT, Prof. Martin John, DPhil; FSA; FBA 2006; Laurence Professor of Classical Archaeology, since 2001, and Head of School of Arts and Humanities, since 2014, University of Cambridge; Fellow, Fitzwilliam College, Cambridge, since 2001; *b* 30 Sept. 1955; *s* of John Millett and Sybil Vera Millett (*née* Paine); *m* 2005, Joanna Story; one *s* one *d*. *Educ:* Inst. of Archaeology, Univ. of London (BA 1977); Merton Coll., Oxford (DPhil 1983). FSA 1984. Asst Keeper of Archaeol., Hants Co. Mus. Service, 1980–81; University of Durham: Lectr, 1981–91; Sen. Lectr, 1991–95; Prof. of Archaeol., 1995–98; Prof. of Classical Archaeol., Univ. of Southampton, 1999–2001. Vice-Pres., British Acad., 2010–14. Dir, 2001–07, Treas., 2007–11, Soc. of Antiquaries. Asst Ed., 1986–89, Ed., 1989–94, Archaeological Jl. *Publications:* The Romanization of Britain, 1990; Roman Britain, 1995; ed monographs and papers on Roman archaeology; contrib. numerous articles to learned jls. *Recreations:* food, wine, house restoration, the outdoors. *Address:* Faculty of Classics, University of Cambridge, Sidgwick Avenue, Cambridge CB3 9DA. *T:* (01223) 335161, *Fax:* (01223) 335409. *E:* mjm62@cam.ac.uk.

MILLETT, Peter Joseph, CMG 2013; HM Diplomatic Service; Ambassador to Libya, since 2015; *b* 23 Jan. 1955; *m* 1981, June Harnett; three *d*. Entered FCO, 1974; Vice Consul, Caracas, 1978–80; Second Sec., Doha, 1981–85; FCO, 1986–89; First Sec., UK Repn to EU, Brussels, 1989–93; Hd, Personnel Policy, FCO, 1993–96; Dep. Hd of Mission, Athens, 1997–2001; Dir, Security, FCO, 2002–05; High Comr to Cyprus, 2005–10; Ambassador to Jordan, 2011–15. *Address:* c/o Foreign and Commonwealth Office, King Charles Street, SW1A 2AH.

MILLETT, Hon. Richard (Lester); QC 2003; a Recorder, since 2010; a Deputy High Court Judge (Chancery Division), since 2013; *b* 29 Sept. 1961; *s* of Baron Millett, *qv*; *m* 1988, Patricia Mary Natalie Spencer; one *s* two *d*. *Educ:* Harrow Sch.; Trinity Hall, Cambridge (BA Hons Classical Tripos Pt 1, Law Tripos Pt 2; lightweight rowing blue, 1983). Called to the Bar, Lincoln's Inn, 1985 (Megarry Prize for Landlord and Tenant Law), Bencher, 2013; Standing Jun. Counsel to the Crown (Treasury A Panel), 2001–03. *Publications:* (with G. Andrews) The Law of Guarantees, 1992, 7th edn 2015; Atkin's Court Forms, vol. 21, Guarantee and Indemnity, 2015; contrib. Law Qly Rev., Halsbury's Laws of England, Jl of Internat. Business and Law. *Recreations:* Alpinism, gastronomy, fishing, shooting, music. *Address:* 53 Gloucester Avenue, NW1 7BA. *T:* (020) 7267 9804; Slivericks House, Ashburnham, Battle, E Sussex TN33 9PE; Essex Court Chambers, 24 Lincoln's Inn Fields, WC2A 3EG. *Clubs:* Royal Automobile; Leander (Henley-on-Thames).

MILLGATE, Prof. Michael Henry, PhD; FRSC; FRSL; University Professor of English, Emeritus, Toronto University, since 1994; *b* 19 July 1929; *s* of Stanley Millgate and Marjorie Louisa (*née* Norris); *m* 1960, Jane, *d* of Maurice and Marie Barr. *Educ:* St Catharine's Coll., Cambridge (MA); Michigan Univ.; Leeds Univ. (PhD). Tutor-Organizer, WEA, E Lindsey, 1953–56; Lectr in English Lit., Leeds Univ., 1958–64; Prof. of English and Chm. of the Dept, York Univ., Ont, 1964–67; Prof. of English, Toronto Univ., 1967–94 (University Prof., 1987–94). Killam Sen. Res. Schol., 1974–75, Killam Res. Fellow, 1986–88; John Simon Guggenheim Meml Fellow, 1977–78. FRSC 1982; FRSL 1984. Pierre Chauveau Medal, RSC, 1999. *Publications:* William Faulkner, 1961; (ed) Tennyson: Selected Poems, 1963; American Social Fiction, 1964; (ed jtly) Transatlantic Dialogue, 1966; The Achievement of William Faulkner, 1966; (ed jtly) Lion in the Garden, 1968; Thomas Hardy: his career as a novelist, 1971; (ed jtly) The Collected Letters of Thomas Hardy, vols I-VIII, 1978–2012; Thomas Hardy: a biography, 1982, rev. and expanded edn as Thomas Hardy: a biography revisited, 2004; (ed) The Life and Work of Thomas Hardy, 1985; (ed) William Faulkner Manuscripts 20, 21, 22 and 23, 1987; (ed) New Essays on Light in August, 1987; (ed) Thomas Hardy: selected letters, 1990; Testamentary Acts: Browning, Tennyson, James, Hardy, 1992; (ed jtly) Thomas Hardy's 'Studies, Specimens &c' Notebook, 1994; (ed) Letters of Emma and Florence Hardy, 1996; Faulkner's Place, 1997; (ed) Thomas Hardy's Public Voice, 2001; (ed jtly) Thomas Hardy's Poetical Matter Notebook, 2009. *Address:* 1 Balmoral Avenue, Apt 809, Toronto, ON M4V 3B9, Canada. *T:* (416) 920 3717.

MILLIDGE, Jonathan Varley; Group Human Resources Director, Royal Mail Group, since 2014; *b* Birmingham, 16 March 1964; *s* of Christopher and Kathleen Millidge; *m* 1989, Judith Stillwell; one *s* one *d*. *Educ:* Oakham Sch.; Royal Holloway Coll., Univ. of London (BA Hons). Dir, Resources, SSL, 1997–98; Gen. Manager West, Post Office Ltd, 1998–2000; HR Dir, Parcel Force, 2000–03; Royal Mail Group: Dir, Employee Relns, 2003–07; HR Dir, 2007–10; Company Sec., 2010–14. Chm., Nat. Design Consultancy, 2001–14. Trustee, Royal Mail Defined Contribution Plan, 2008–. FCMA 1995; FCIPD 2010. *Recreations:* travel, woodland management. *Address:* (office) 100 Victoria Embankment, EC4Y 0HQ. *T:* (020) 7449 8112, *Fax:* (020) 7530 7104. *E:* jon.millidge@royalmail.com.

MILLIGAN, Andrew, OBE 2015; Head, Global Strategy, Standard Life Investments, since 2000; *b* London, Nov. 1956; *s* of Owen and Bunty Milligan; *m* 1984, Rosemary; two *s*. *Educ:* Finchley Catholic Grammar Sch.; Bristol Univ. (BSc Econs and Econ. Hist. 1979). HM Treasury, incl. roles in social security, North Sea oil and gas, and IMF/World Bank divs, 1979–86; Econ. Advr, Lloyds Bank, 1986–91; Internat. Economist, Smith New Court, 1991–94; Chief Economist, New Japan Securities Europe, 1994–96; Dir, Econ. Res., Aviva/Morley Fund Mgt, 1996–2000. Mem., Governing Bd, Technol. Strategy Bd, 2007–14. Member: Court, Heriot-Watt Univ., 2011–; Bd, Edinburgh Business Sch., 2015–. Mem. Bd, Work Place Chaplaincy Scotland, 2011–. Mem. Council, Soc. of Business Economists, 1990– (Fellow, 2008). FRSA. *Recreations:* croquet in the summer, Rugby in the winter. *Address:* Standard Life Investments, 1 George Street, Edinburgh EH2 2LL. *T:* (0131) 245 8394. *E:* andrew_milligan@standardlife.com.

MILLIGAN, Eric; JP; Member (Lab), City of Edinburgh Council, since 1995; Convener, Lothian and Borders Police Board, 2003–07; *b* 27 Jan. 1951; *m* Janis. *Educ:* Tynecastle High Sch.; Napier Coll. Former printer. Member (Lab): Edinburgh DC, 1974–78; Lothian Regl Council, 1978–96 (Chm., Finance Cttee, 1980–82, 1986–90; Convener, 1990–96); Convener, Edinburgh City Council, 1995–96; Lord Provost and Lord-Lieutenant of Edinburgh, 1996–2003. Mem., COSLA, 1980–82, 1986–96 (Pres., 1988–90). Convener, Edinburgh Licensing Bd. Dir, Edinburgh Fest. Soc., 1996–2003; Chm., Edinburgh Military Tattoo Ltd, 1996–2003. Trustee, Royal Yacht Britannia. JP Edinburgh, 1996. Hon. FRCSE 2000. Hon. DBA Napier, 1999; DUniv Heriot-Watt, 2004. Chevalier, Ordre Nat. du Mérite (France), 1996; Gold Medal, Mayor of Paris, 2015. *Recreations:* watching football and Rugby as played by Heart of Midlothian FC and Boroughmuir RFC, listening to music. *Address:* c/o City of Edinburgh Council, City Chambers, High Street, Edinburgh EH1 1YJ. *T:* (0131) 200 2000. *Clubs:* New, Royal Scots (Edinburgh); Boroughmuir Rugby Football.

MILLIGAN, Iain Anstruther; QC 1991; *b* 21 April 1950; *s* of late Wyndham Macbeth Moir Milligan, MBE, TD; *m* 1979, Zara Ann Louise Spearman; one *s* two *d*. *Educ:* Eton; Magdalene College, Cambridge (MA); College of Law. Called to the Bar, Inner Temple, 1973, Bencher, 2002. Head of Chambers, 1999–2014. *Recreations:* farming, forestry, walking. *Address:* 20 Essex Street, WC2R 3AL. *T:* (020) 7842 1200; Dunesslin, Dunscore, Dumfries DG2 0UR. *T:* (01387) 820345.

MILLIGAN, June Elizabeth, PhD; Director General, Local Government and Communities (formerly Public Services and Local Government Delivery), Welsh Government (formerly Welsh Assembly Government), 2010–15; *b* Glasgow, 23 June 1959; *d* of Thomas Edward Cole and Enid Charlton Cole; *m* 1980, Brian Milligan; one *s* one *d*. *Educ:* Univ. of Glasgow (MA 1st Cl. Hons 1979; PhD 1982; BD 2008). Asst Prison Gov., 1983–85, Prison Gov. Grade V, 1985–89, Home Office; joined Welsh Office, 1989; First Sec., UK Repn to EU, Brussels, FCO, 1993–96; Principal Private Sec. to Sec. of State for Wales, 1996–99; Hd of Devolved Admins Dept, FCO, 2000; Welsh Assembly Government: Hd, Envmt, 2000–06; Business Develt Dir, 2006–09; Dir, Social Justice and Local Govt Dept, 2010. *Recreations:* celebrating life and love, constantly learning.

MILLIGAN, Scott Gregor; Director of Legal Services and Chief Legal Adviser, Department of Energy and Climate Change, 2008–13; *b* 28 Oct. 1951; *s* of late Gregor Stormont Milligan and Marylla Milligan (*née* Jolles); *m* 1984, Elizabeth Mary Cliff; one *s* two *d*. *Educ:* Christ's Hosp. Sch.; Mansfield Coll., Oxford (BA Modern Hist. 1973). Called to the Bar, Middle Temple, 1975; joined Govt Legal Service, 1977; Legal Asst, 1977–81, Sen. Legal Asst, 1981–85, Dept of Employment; Asst Solicitor, advising Dept of Employment, Treasury Solicitor's Dept and Dept of Energy, 1985–92; Asst Solicitor, DTI, 1992–2001; Dir, Legal Services Gp, DTI, then BERR, 2001–08. Chm., Whitehall Prosecutors' Gp, 2001–04. Trustee, Kingston Friends' Trusts, 2001–. *Recreations:* cycling, singing, Spring Grove Fringe theatre.

MILLIGAN, His Honour Timothy James; a Circuit Judge, 1991–2008; *b* 16 March 1940; *s* of Dr Peter James Wyatt Milligan and Rosemary Elizabeth Ann (*née* Dutton); *m* 1976, Sally Marcella (*née* Priest) (marr. diss. 1999); two step *s*. *Educ:* Frilsham House Prep. School; Winchester Coll.; Grenoble Univ. (1st and 2nd Foreigner's Degrees). Articled Clerk, Taylor Garrett, 1960–65; admitted Solicitor, 1967; Asst Solicitor, Leeds Smith, Beds, 1967–69; Asst Solicitor, then Partner, Triggs Turner, Guildford, 1969–73; Solicitor, then Partner, Warner & Richardson, Winchester, 1973–91; HM Coroner, Central Hants, 1982–91; a Recorder of the Crown Court, 1988–91. Hon. Mem., Coroners Soc. of GB, 1991; Mem. of various Old Wykehamist clubs and assocs. Chm. Disciplinary Cttee of Rackets Cttee, Tennis and Rackets Assoc., 1998–. *Recreations:* rackets, cricket, football, reading, music, theatre, cinema. *Clubs:* MCC; Hampshire CC (Mem. Cttee, 1993–); Jesters; Tennis and Rackets Association (Mem., Rackets Cttee, 1988–98).

MILLIKEN, Rt Hon. Peter (Andrew Stewart), OC 2014; PC (Can.) 2012; Special Adviser, Cunningham Swan, Carty, Little & Bonham, since 2011; Fellow, School of Policy Studies, Queen's University, Kingston, Ont, since 2011; Speaker, House of Commons, Canada, 2001–11; *b* Kingston, Ont, 12 Nov. 1946; *s* of John Andrew Milliken and Catherine Margaret (*née* McCuaig). *Educ:* Queen's Univ. (BA Hons 1968); Wadham Coll., Oxford (BA 1970, MA 1978); Dalhousie Univ. (LLB 1971). Called to the Bar, Ont., and Solicitor, Supreme Court of Ont., 1973; in practice with Cunningham Swan, Carty, Little & Bonham, 1973–88. MP (L) Kingston and the Islands, 1988–2011. Parly Sec. to Govt House Leader, 1993–96; Dep. Chm., Cttees of Whole House, 1996–97; Dep. Speaker and Chm., Cttees of Whole House, 1997–2001. Mem., Coroners' Council, Ont., 1985–88. *Address:* 2626 Leeman Road, Elginburg, ON K0H 1M0, Canada.

MILLIKEN-SMITH, Mark Gordon; QC 2006; a Recorder of the Crown Court, since 2004; *b* 4 July 1963; *s* of John Michael Milliken-Smith and Gillian Frances Milliken-Smith (*née* Woods, now Bird); *m* 1991, Sybella Anne Wilson; one *s* one *d*. *Educ:* Wellington Coll.; Univ. of Bristol (LLB Hons 1985). Called to the Bar, Gray's Inn, 1986; in practice, specialising in criminal law, fraud, sports law and professional discipline. *Recreations:* family and variously watching, playing and coaching sport, particularly cricket and Rugby. *Address:* 2 Bedford Row, WC1R 4BU. *T:* (020) 7440 8888, *Fax:* (020) 7242 1738. *E:* mmilliken-smith@2bedfordrow.co.uk. *Clubs:* MCC; Hankley Common.

MILLING, Amanda Anne; MP (C) Cannock Chase, since 2015; *b* Burton upon Trent, 12 March 1975; *d* of Humphrey and Patricia Milling. *Educ:* Moreton Hall Sch.; University Coll. London (BSc Hons Econs). Researcher, SW1 Res., 1997–99; Quaestor Research and Marketing Strategists: Sen. Res. Exec., 1999–2000; Res. Manager, 2000–03; Associate Dir, 2003–06; Res. Dir, 2006–10; Dir, Optimisa Res., 2010–14. *Recreation:* running. *Address:* House of Commons, SW1A 0AA. *T:* (020) 7219 8356. *E:* amanda.milling.mp@parliament.uk.

MILLINGTON, Anthony Nigel Raymond, OBE 2011; Director General, Tokyo Office, European Automobile Manufacturers Association, since 1995; *b* 29 Jan. 1945; *m* 1969, Susan Carolyn (*née* Steilberg); two *s*. *Educ:* Ipswich School; Univ. of Grenoble; Trinity College, Cambridge (BA); Univ. of Chicago. HM Diplomatic Service, 1968–94: FCO, 1968; Tokyo, 1969–76; FCO, 1976–80; Paris, 1980–84; Japanese National Defence College, 1984–85; Head of Chancery, Tokyo, 1985–88; Head of Far Eastern Dept, FCO, 1989–90; Rolls-Royce PLC, 1990; Pres., Rolls-Royce (Far East) Ltd, 1990–94 (on leave of absence); FCO, 1994. Mem., Japanese Prime Minister's Regulatory Reform Commn, 1998–2002. Advr to Bd of Dirs, Japan Automobile Importers' Assoc., 2001–. Chm., Automobile Cttee, Eur. Business Council in Japan, 2010–. Chm. Bd of Trustees, British Sch. in Tokyo, 2004–10; Mem. Council, Japan-British Soc., 2010– (Exec. Dir, 2013–); Dir, ESU, Japan, 2012–. *Recreations:* tennis, walking in the countryside. *Address:* c/o European Automobile Manufacturers Association, PO Box 564, Ark Mori Building, 1–12–32 Akasaka, Minato-ku, Tokyo 107–6030, Japan. *T:* (3) 35054963, *Fax:* (3) 35054871. *E:* anrm@gol.com. *Clubs:* Royal Automobile; Tokyo Lawn Tennis; Foreign Correspondents' (Tokyo), American (Tokyo).

MILLINGTON, Christopher John; QC 2001; a Recorder, since 1995; *b* 31 Oct. 1951; *s* of Dennis Millington and Christine Millington; *m* 1976, Jane Elisabeth Bucknell; one *s* one *d*. *Educ:* Birmingham Univ. (LLB, LLM). Called to the Bar, Gray's Inn, 1976; in chambers, Birmingham, 1976–. *Recreations:* tennis, golf, travel, music, especially rock guitar. *Address:* St Philip's Chambers, 55 Temple Row, Birmingham B2 5LS. *T:* (0121) 246 7000. *Clubs:* Edgbaston Priory Tennis, Blackwell Golf.

MILLINGTON, Tamara; *see* Ingram, T.

MILLION, Clive Ernest; His Honour Judge Million; a Circuit Judge, since 2009; *b* 7 Sept. 1946; *s* of Arthur Ernest Million and Phyllis May Million; *m* 1st, 1975, Pauline Margaret Lock (*d* 2011); three *s*; 2nd, 2012, Linda June Bone; one step *s* two step *d*. *Educ:* St Dunstan's Coll.; Birmingham Coll. of Art and Design (BA Hons Industrial Design (Engrg) 1969). Called to the Bar, Middle Temple, 1975; District Judge, Principal Registry, Family Div., 1993–2009; Asst Recorder, 1995–99; Recorder, 1999–2009. Mem., Parole Bd of England and Wales, 2010–. *Publications:* Family Law: tips & traps, 2009. *Recreations:* anything legal, but non-legal. *Address:* East London Family Court, 6th and 7th Floor, 11 Westferry Circus, E14 4HD. *T:* (020) 3197 2886.

MILLON, Charles; Ambassador of France to UN Food and Agriculture Organization, 2003–07; *b* Belley, Ain, 12 Nov. 1945; *s* of Gabriel Millon and Suzanne Millon (*née* Gunet); *m* Chantal Delsol; six *c*. *Educ:* Lamartine Instn, Belley; Saint-Marie Sch., Lyon. Asst Lectr, 1969; legal and fiscal consultant, 1969–. Deputy (UDF-PR) for Belley-Gex, elected 1978, 1981, 1986, 1988, 1993, 1995, 1997; Mem., Regl Council for Rhône-Alpes, elected 1981, 1986 (Pres., 1988–98); Mem., Gen. Council of the Ain (Canton of Belley), 1985–88; French National Assembly: Vice-Pres., 1986–88; Mem., Foreign Cttee, 1988; Pres., Parly Gp of UDF, 1989–95; Minister of Defence, 1995–97. Pres., Departmental Fedn, PR and UDF,

1983–85; Mem., Pol Bd, PR, 1984–95. Founder, 1998, Pres., 1998–99, Leader, 1999–2003, Droite Libérale Chrétienne. Mayor of Belley, 1977–2001; Municipal Councillor and Urban Community Councillor, Lyon, 2001–08. Associate: Intelstrat, Paris; Cross Invest, London; Founding Adminr, Institut Thomas More. *Publications:* L'extravagante histoire des nationalisations, 1984; L'alternance-Vérité, 1986; La tentation du conservatisme, 1995; La Paix Civile, 1998; Lettre d'un ami impertinent à Jacques Chirac, 2002.

MILLS; *see* Platts-Mills.

MILLS, family name of **Viscount Mills**.

MILLS, 3rd Viscount *cr* 1962; **Christopher Philip Roger Mills;** Bt 1953; Baron 1957; Regional Director, Environment Agency Wales; *b* 20 May 1956; *s* of 2nd Viscount Mills and Joan Dorothy (*d* 1998), *d* of James Shirreff; *S* father, 1988; *m* 1980, Lesley Alison, *er d* of Alan Bailey. *Educ:* Oundle School; Univ. of London (BSc Hons Biol Scis; MSc Applied Fish Biology); Plymouth Poly. Biologist at Salmon Research Trust of Ireland, 1980–89; National Rivers Authority: Technical Asst, 1989–91; Area Fisheries, Recreation and Ecology Manager, NW Region, 1991–95; Area Manager, Thames Reg., 1995–96; Area Manager, Thames Reg., Envmt Agency, 1996. Member Council: Inst. of Fisheries Mgt, 1993; RSPB, 1995–2000. *Publications:* papers in Aquaculture, Aquaculture and Fisheries Management, Fish Biology. *Recreations:* flyfishing, fine wines.

MILLS, Dame Anne (Jane), DCMG 2015; CBE 2007; PhD; FRS 2013; FMedSci; Professor of Health Economics and Policy, since 1995, and Deputy Director and Provost (formerly Vice-Director), since 2011, London School of Hygiene and Tropical Medicine; *b* 26 Jan. 1951; *d* of Maurice and Anthea Mills; *m* 1979, Patrick Corran; two *s*. *Educ:* Aston Clinton Primary Sch.; Aylesbury High Sch.; Oxford High Sch.; St Hilda's Coll., Oxford (MA Hist. and Econs 1973); Leeds Univ. (Dip. Health Services Studies 1976); PhD Health Econs London Univ. 1990. Fellow, ODI, 1973–75; Res. Officer, Nuffield Inst. for Health Services Studies, 1976–79; London School of Hygiene and Tropical Medicine: Lectr, 1979–86, Sen. Lectr, 1986–92, Reader, 1992–95, in Health Econs; Hd, Faculty of Public Health and Policy, 2006–11. Co-Chm., Wkg Gp 5, Commn on Macroecons and Health, 2000–02. Foreign Associate, Inst. of Medicine, 2006–. Pres., Internat. Health Econs Assoc., 2012–. FMedSci 2009. Prince Mahidol Award for Medicine, 2009. *Publications:* (with K. Lee) Policy Making and Planning in the Health Sector, 1982; (ed with K. Lee) The Economics of Health in Developing Countries, 1983; (ed jtly) Health System Decentralization Concepts, Issues and Country Experience, 1990; (ed with K. Lee) Health Economics Research in Developing Countries, 1993; (ed jtly) Private Health Providers in Developing Countries: serving the public interest?, 1997; (ed) Reforming Health Sectors, 2000; (jtly) The Challenge of Health Sector Reform: what must governments do?, 2001; (ed jtly) International Public Health, 2001, 3rd edn as Global Health: diseases, programs, systems and policies, 2011; (ed jtly) Priorities in Health, 2006; (ed jtly) Disease Control Priorities in Developing Countries, 2nd edn 2006; (ed jtly) Health, Economic Development and Household Poverty: from understanding to action, 2007; (ed jtly) Good Health at Low Cost: 25 years on, 2011. *Recreations:* music, walking, cooking. *Address:* London School of Hygiene and Tropical Medicine, Keppel Street, WC1E 7HT. *T:* (020) 7927 2354, *Fax:* (020) 7636 7679. *E:* anne.mills@lshtm.ac.uk.

MILLS, Carole Denise; Chief Executive, Milton Keynes Council, since 2014; *b* Coventry, 7 Dec. 1963; *d* of Peter and Pauline Mills; *m* (marr. diss.); one *s*; *m* 2011, Paul Humphrey; two step *s*. *Educ:* Wolverhampton Poly. CPFA 1992. Coventry HA, 1983–86; Coventry CC, 1986–88; Walsall Metropolitan Borough Council: various posts, 1988–2002; Actg Chief Financial Officer, 2002–03; Exec. Dir, Corporate Services, 2003–07. Chartered Institute of Public Finance and Accountancy: Mem. Council, 2007–08, 2009–10, 2012–15; Vice Pres., 2005–07, Pres., 2007–09, Midlands. Chm., Finance Adv. Gp, W Midlands, LGA, 2004–07; Nottingham City Council: Corporate Dir of Resources, 2007–08; Dep. Chief Exec., Corporate Dir of Resources and Chief Finance Officer, 2008–14; Actg Chief Exec., 2012. Accredited peer, LGA (formerly IDeA), 2005–. Gov., Bishop Vesey Grammar Sch., 2003–07 (Chm., Finance and Estates Cttee, 2005–07). *Recreations:* professional networks, coaching and mentoring, yoga, active CIPFA member. *Address:* Lichfield. *T:* (office) (01908) 252200. *E:* carole727mills@btinternet.com.

MILLS, David John; Chief Executive, Post Office Ltd, 2002–05; Senior Independent Director, One Savings Bank plc, 2011–14; *b* 9 Feb. 1944; *s* of John Henry Mills and Violet Germaine Mills; *m* 1967, Lesley Jacqueline Wand; one *s* two *d*. *Educ:* London Business Sch. (Dist. Sloan Fellow). Joined Midland Bank, later HSBC, 1962; Gen. Manager, HSBC, 1989–2002; Dir, Royal Mail Gp Hldgs, 2002–05. Chm., My Home Move Ltd, 2006–11; Director: Camelot Gp plc, 2003–06; Cardpoint plc, 2007–08; Payzone plc, 2007–10. Dir, PIA, 1995–2000. Chm., Employers' Forum on Disability Ltd, 2004–07; Mem., Nat. Disability Council, 1993–95. Trustee, RADAR, 2004–09; Vice Pres., Vitalise, 2005. *Recreations:* family, wine, fishing, motorsport. *E:* david@davidjmills.com. *Club:* Royal Automobile.

MILLS, Geoffrey Thomas; Headmaster, Latymer School, 1983–98; *b* 13 Nov. 1935; *s* of Thomas Henry Mills and Margaret Jane (*née* Lewington); *m* 1970, Dorothy Anne Williams; one *s* three *d*. *Educ:* Enfield Grammar Sch.; Clare Coll., Cambridge (MA). Nat. Service, Corporal Clerk, RASC, 1954–56. Foreign lang. asst, Lyons, France, 1960–61; teacher of French and Spanish, Guthlaxton Grammar Sch., Leicester, 1961–62; Hd of Spanish, Sweyne Grammar Tech. Sch., Rayleigh, Essex, 1962–65; Head of Modern Languages: Coborn Sch. for Girls, Bow, 1965–69; Woodhouse Grammar Sch., Finchley, 1969–73; Dir of Studies, Longdean Sch., Hemel Hempstead, 1973–78; Headmaster, Manhood High Sch. and Community Centre, Selsey, W Sussex, 1978–83. Ind. Chm., Standards Cttee, London Borough of Enfield, 1999–2010. Freeman, London Bor. of Enfield, 2012. *Recreations:* golf (Blue, 1958), bridge, crosswords, reading. *Address:* 59 Wades Hill, Winchmore Hill, N21 1BD. *T:* (020) 8360 7335. *Club:* Mid Herts Golf (Wheathampstead).

MILLS, Sir (George) Ian, Kt 2001; FCA, FIC, CMC, FIHM; Commissioner, London Region, NHS Executive, Department of Health, 2001–03; Member, NHS Appointments Commission, 2001–03; *b* 19 Nov. 1935; *s* of George Haxton Mills and Evelyn Mary (*née* Owen); *m* 1968, Margaret Elizabeth Dunstan; one *s* one *d* (and one *s* decd). *Educ:* Taunton's Grammar Sch., Southampton. FCA 1960; FIC (FIMC 1964); LHSM 1985; FIHM 1990; CMC 2000. Articled to Beal, Young & Booth, Southampton, 1954–60; Price Waterhouse, London, 1960–65; seconded to World Bank team assisting Govt of Pakistan Treasury, 1962; Chief Accountant, Univ. of Ibadan, Nigeria, 1965–68; rejoined Price Waterhouse, 1968; London Office, 1968–70; Newcastle upon Tyne Office, as Manager i/c Northern and Scottish Management Consultancy Ops, 1970–73; Partner, 1973; London Office, 1973–85: i/c Africa Management Consultancy Services, 1975–83; Nat. Dir, Central Govt Services, 1983–85; Nation Health Service Management Board, 1985–89: Dir of Financial Management, 1985–88; Dir of Resource Management, 1988–89; rejoined Price Waterhouse, 1989; Sen. Partner, Business Development Europe, 1989–91. Chairman: Lewisham and N Southwark HA, 1991–93; SE London HA, 1993–96; SE London Commissioning Agency, 1991–93; Lambeth, Southwark and Lewisham Health Commn, then HA, 1993–96; N Thames, then London, Reg., NHS Exec., DOH, 1996–2001. Mem., NHS Policy Bd, then Sec. of State for Health's Regl Chairmen's Adv. Cttee, 1996–2001. Mem., Ind. Remuneration Panel, London Borough of Lewisham, 2001–10 (Chm., 2001–10). Member: Blackheath Preservation Trust Ltd, 1991–2004; Bd of Govs, UMDS of Guy's and St Thomas' Hosps, 1991–96; IHSM Consultants, 1992–96; Bd of Govs, St Christopher's Hospice, 1993–2003 (Chm., 2000–03); Delegacy, KCH Med. Sch., 1993–96; Bd of Trustees, Blackheath Historic Bldgs Trust, 2003–11 (Chm., 2003–11); Bd of Trustees, Age Exchange Theatre Trust, 2008–14 (Chm., 2008–14). Trustee, SE London Community Foundn, 1995–2000; Chm. and Trustee, Talk About Art Initiative, 2014–. FRSA. Member: Editl Adv. Bd, Health Services Jl, 1992–96; Editl Bd, British Jl of Health Care Mgt, 1996–2003. *Publications:* St Margaret, Lee: a new guide, 1996; Rebirth of a Building, 2000; Craftsmen of St Margaret, 2006; articles in financial, educnl and med. jls. *Recreations:* classical music, photography, travel, heritage. *Address:* 60 Belmont Hill, SE13 5DN. *T:* (020) 8852 2457. *Club:* Royal Society of Arts.

MILLS, Gloria Helenly, CBE 2005 (MBE 1999); National Secretary, UNISON, since 2006; *b* 1958; *d* of James and Olga Mills. *Educ:* Open Univ. (Prof. Cert. Mgt 2003; Prof. Dip. Mgt 2004; MBA 2007). MCIPD 2004. NUPE: Regl Area Officer, 1985; Sen. Nat. Officer, Equal Rights, 1987; UNISON: Dir of Equal Opportunities, then of Equalities, 1993–2006; Nat. Organiser (Equalities), 1999–2006; Mem., Sen. Mgt Gp, 2004–. Trades Union Congress: Member: Women's Cttee, 1989–; General Council, 1994–; Exec. Cttee, 2000–; Pres., 2005–06; Chairman: Race Relns Cttee, 1995, 2000–; Women's Conf., 1999; Mem., Gen. Council, ITUC, 2006–. Member: Race Relns Forum, 1998–2003, Race Equality Adv. Panel, 2003–, Home Office; Race, Employment and Educn Forum, DFEE, 1998–2001; Employment Appeal Tribunal, 2000–; Commn for Racial Equality, 2002–07; Adv. Cttee on Equal Opportunities, EC, 2011–. Mem., Race Equality Adv. Gp, FA, 2007. Public Services International: Exec. Bd, 2002–; Chm., ETUC Women's Cttee, 2003 (Vice Pres., 2010–); Vice-Chm., World Women's Cttee, 2004; Pres., Women and Gender Equality Cttee, Eur. Public Services Confedn, 2010–. Mother of Chapel: NATSOPA, 1980–85; SOGAT, 1982–85. FRSA 1998. MCMI 2008. Hon. LLD Staffordshire, 2006. *Publications:* various articles on race equality and gender inc. article on combating institutional racism in Industrial Law Jl. *Recreations:* reading, cricket, football, Arsenal. *Address:* UNISON, 130 Euston Road, NW1 2AY. *T:* (020) 7121 5409. *E:* glormlls@aol.com, g.mills@unison.co.uk.

MILLS, Harold Hernshaw, CB 1995; Chairman, Caledonian MacBrayne Ltd, 1999–2006; *b* 2 March 1938; *s* of late Harold and Margaret Mills; *m* 1973, Marion Elizabeth Beattie, MA. *Educ:* Greenock High Sch.; Univ. of Glasgow (BSc, PhD). Cancer Research Scientist, Roswell Park Memorial Inst., Buffalo, NY, 1962–64; Lectr, Glasgow Univ., 1964–69; Principal, Scottish Home and Health Dept, 1970–76; Asst Secretary: Scottish Office, 1976–81; Privy Council Office, 1981–83; Scottish Development Dept, 1983–84; Under Sec., Scottish Develt Dept, 1984–88; Prin. Finance Officer, Scottish Office, 1988–92; Sec., Scottish Office Envmt Dept, 1992–95; Sec. and Hd of Dept, Scottish Office Develt Dept, 1995–98. Mem. Bd, Home in Scotland, 1998–2004 (Chm., 2000–04). Director: Northlink Orkney and Shetland Ferries Ltd, 2000–09; Edinburgh City Centre Partnership, 2002–06; Northlink Ferries Ltd, 2006–09. Chairman: LandTrust, 1998–2014 (Mem. Bd, 1998–); Edinburgh World Heritage Trust, 1999–2006; Trustee: Scottish Maritime Mus., 1998–; Edinburgh Old Town and South Side Trust, 1999–2006; Viewpoint Trust, 2008–; Scottish Waterways Trust, 2012–14; Dir, City of Adelaide Charitable Trust, 2005–. Gov., Queen Margaret UC, Edinburgh, 1998–2004. *Publications:* scientific papers in jls of learned socs on the crystal structure of chemical compounds. *Address:* 21 Hatton Place, Edinburgh EH9 1UB. *T:* (0131) 667 7910.

MILLS, Sir Ian; *see* Mills, Sir G. I.

MILLS, Prof. Ian Mark, OBE 2015; FRS 1996; Professor of Chemical Spectroscopy, University of Reading, 1966–95, now Emeritus; *b* 9 June 1930; *s* of John Mills, MD and Margheurita Alice Gertrude Mills (*née* Gooding); *m* 1957, Margaret Mary Maynard; one *s* one *d*. *Educ:* Leighton Park Sch.; Univ. of Reading (BSc); St John's Coll., Oxford (DPhil). Res. Fellow, Univ. of Minnesota, 1954–56; Res. Fellow in Theoretical Chem., Corpus Christi Coll., Cambridge, 1956–57; University of Reading: Lectr in Chemistry, 1957–64; Reader, 1964–66; Leverhulme Emeritus Res. Fellow, 1996–98. Mem. and Chm. of various cttees, IUPAC, 1985–2000; Royal Society of Chemistry: Vice-Pres., Faraday Div., 1984–86; Mem., British Nat. Cttee for IUPAC, 1992–2000 (Chm., 1998–2000); Mem. Council, Royal Instn, 2000–03. Pres., Consultative Cttee on Units, Bureau Internat. des Poids et Mesures, 1995–2014 (Hon. Mem., 2014); Chm., Cttee on Symbols and Units, BSI, 1996–2003. Hon. DSc Reading, 2015. Lomb Medal 1960, Fellow 1974, Lippincott Medal 1982, Optical Soc. of America; Spectroscopy Award, RSC, 1990. Editor, Molecular Physics, 1972–77 and 1995–2004. *Publications:* (ed jtly) Quantities, Units and Symbols in Physical Chemistry, 1988, 3rd edn 2006; papers in learned jls. *Recreations:* walking, sailing, socialising with many friends. *Address:* 57 Christchurch Road, Reading RG2 7BD. *T:* (0118) 987 2335. *E:* i.m.mills@reading.ac.uk; mills704ian@gmail.com; School of Chemistry, University of Reading RG6 6AD. *T:* (0118) 378 8456.

MILLS, John Frederick, CBE 2008; Director, Rural Policy, Department for Environment, Food and Rural Affairs, 2003–07; *b* 6 Sept. 1950; *s* of Henry Alfred Mills and Jean Margaret Aitchison; *m* 1st, 1974, Jean Marie Correia (*d* 1999); one *s* three *d*; 2nd, 2003, Imogen Stephanie Nicholls. *Educ:* Highgate Sch.; The Queen's Coll., Oxford (MA, BLitt (Mod. Hist.)); Merton Coll., Oxford (Domus Sen. Schol.). Department of Trade and Industry, 1974–92: Private Sec. to Minister of State for Industry, 1976–78; seconded to Govt of Hong Kong, 1981–85; Hd of Internat. Telecommunications Policy, 1986–89; Mem., Prime Minister's Policy Unit, 1989–92; Dir of Consumer Affairs, OFT, 1992–95; Chief Executive: Cornwall CC, 1995–99; Policy and Resources Dept, States of Jersey, 1999–2003. Income Tax Comr of Appeal, Jersey, 2009–. Non-executive Director: Royal Cornwall Hosps NHS Trust, 2007–09; Port of London Authy, 2008–14 (Vice Chm., 2009–14). Member: Commn for Rural Communities, 2009–13; Jersey Financial Services Commn, 2009–14; Ports of Jersey, 2010–; Office of Channel Is Financial Services Ombudsman, 2014–. Mem., OFT Adv. Panel, 2001–03. Gov., Highgate Sch., 1993– (Treasurer and Chm., 1999–). *Address:* Le Picachon, Les Varines, Jersey JE2 7SB. *T:* (01534) 732374.

MILLS, Sir Jonathan Edward Harland, Kt 2013; AO 2011; FRSE; Director, Edinburgh International Festival, 2007–14; *b* 21 March 1963; *s* of Dr Frank Mills, AO and Elayne Mary Mills. *Educ:* Univ. of Sydney (BMus Composition); RMIT Univ. (MArch Acoustic Design); studied composition with Peter Sculthorpe, Sydney, and piano and composition with Lidia Arcuri-Baldecchi and Bruno Bettinelli, Italy. FRSE 2010. Artistic Dir, Blue Mountains Fest., 1988–90; Composer-in-Residence and Res. Fellow in Envmtl Acoustics, RMIT Univ., 1992–97; Artistic Advr, Brisbane Biennial Internat. Music Fest., 1995–97; Artistic Dir, Melbourne Fest. (incl. Dir, Melbourne's Millennium Eve celebrations, 31 Dec. 1999 and Federation Fest., 2001), 2000–01; Composer-in-Residence, Bundanon Trust, 2002; Dir, Alfred Deakin Innovation Lects, 2003–05; Artistic Advr, Recital Centre and Elisabeth Murdoch Hall, Melbourne, 2005–06. Adjunct Professor: Envmtl Acoustics, RMIT Univ., 1998–2003; La Trobe Univ., 2004–07; Vice Chancellor's Fellow, Univ. of Melbourne, 2006; Visiting Professor: Edinburgh Napier Univ., 2008–; Edinburgh Univ., 2008–. Member: Australian Internat. Cultural Council, 1998–2003; Australian Heritage Commn, 2002–04; New Media Arts Bd, 2003–05, Maj. Performing Arts Bd, 2005, Australia Council; Australian Heritage Council, 2004–06; Board Member: Synergy Percussion, 2001–06; Melbourne Recital Hall, 2004–05; Art Exhibns Australia, 2005; Chairman: Commonwealth Govt Review into Australian Youth Orch. and Australian Nat. Acad. of Music, 2004–05; Review of Opera for Victoria Govt, 2005; Arts Adv. Panel, British Council, 2012–. Member Jury: Pratt Prize for Music Th., 2002–; Ian Potter Foundn Music Commns, 2003–05; Gustav Mahler Internat. Conducting Competition, Bamberg, 2010. Patron, Leigh Warren & Dancers, 2001–. Works and performances include: Ethereal Eye (electro-acoustic dance opera), 1996; The Ghost Wife (chamber opera, libretto by Dorothy Porter), 1999; Sandakan

Threnody (for solo tenor, chorus and orch.), 2001, theatrical version, 2004; The Eternity Man (chamber opera, libretto by Dorothy Porter), 2003; various other works for radio, film, theatre and concert perf. FRSA. DUniv: Stirling, 2008; Queen Margaret Univ., 2009; Dr *hc* Edinburgh, 2012. Centenary Medal, Australia, 2002; Prix Italia, 2005. Chevalier, Ordre des Arts et des Lettres (France), 2014. *Address:* c/o Edinburgh International Festival, The Hub, Castlehill, Edinburgh EH1 2NE.

MILLS, Sir Keith (Edward), GBE 2013; Kt 2006; DL; Deputy Chairman, London Organising Committee, 2012 Olympic Games, 2005–13; Chairman, KEM Management Ltd, since 2000; *b* 15 May 1950; *s* of Edward James Mills and Margaret Katherine Mills; *m* 1974, Maureen Elizabeth Simmons; one *s* one *d*. *Educ:* St Martin's, Brentwood. Mktg Exec., Economist newspaper, 1969–74; Mktg Manager, Financial Times, 1974–77; Account Dir, Newton & Godin Advertising, 1977–80; Man. Dir, Nadler & Larimer Advertising, 1980–84; Chm. and CEO, Mills Smith & Partners, 1984–89; CEO, Air Miles UK Ltd, 1988–92; Chairman: Loyalty Management Gp, 1992–2007; Loyalty Management UK Ltd, 2001. Internat. Pres. and CEO, London 2012 Ltd, 2003–06. Dir, AT Racing Ltd, 2006–; non-executive Director: Tottenham Hotspur plc, 2007–; Wordeo, 2013–. Chairman: Trustees, Sported Foundn (formerly Inspired By Sport Foundn), 2008–; Invictus Games CIC, 2014; Trustee: RA, 2013–; 1851 Trust, 2014–. DL Kent, 2008. Hon. PhD: Loughborough, 2006; Bath, 2011; Anglia Ruskin, 2011; Essex, 2013; Canterbury Christ Ch, 2014. *Recreations:* sailing, ski-ing, music, travelling. *Address:* 34 Hans Place, SW1X 0JZ. *T:* (office) (020) 7389 1900, *Fax:* (020) 7839 3772. *E:* k.mills@kemmanagement.co.uk. *Clubs:* Royal Thames Yacht, Royal Yacht Squadron; New York Yacht.

MILLS, Lawrence William Robert; Managing Owner, Oscar Mills & Associates, since 1994; Director, Kids' Gallery Co. Ltd, Hong Kong, since 2005; *b* London, 7 May 1934; *m* 1992, Amira Hamdy (*née* Elsayed); one *d* and two *d* by previous marriage. *Educ:* Reigate Grammar Sch., Surrey; Open Univ. (MBA 1997; LLB Hons 2004). National Service: RN, 1953; Intell. Corps, 1954. Formerly, Jun. Exec., K. F. Mayer Ltd, London. Hong Kong Govt (Mem. of HMOCS): Exec. Officer, Cl. II, 1958; Asst Trade Officer, 1960; Trade Officer, 1964; Sen. Trade Officer, 1968; Principal Trade Officer, 1969; Asst Dir of Commerce and Industry, 1971; Chief Trade Negotiator, 1974–75, 1977–79, 1981–83; Counsellor (Hong Kong Affairs), UK Mission, Geneva, 1976–77; Comr of Trade Industry and Customs, 1977; Director of Trade, Hong Kong, 1977–79, 1981–83; Comr of Industry, 1979–81; Regional Sec., Hong Kong and Kowloon, 1983; Official MLC, Hong Kong, 1983; retired from Hong Kong Govt Service, 1983. Chief Exec., Laws Fashion Knitters Ltd, Hong Kong and Sri Lanka, 1983–85; Dir Gen., Fedn of Hong Kong Industries, 1985–89; Chief Exec., Dubai Commerce and Tourism Promotion Board, 1989–93; Sen. Enterprise Advr, UN Develt Prog., China, 1994–97; Gen. Manager, Mohamed Hareb Al Otaiba, Dubai, 1997–98; Instnl/Mkting Advr, USAID/DAI Market Access Prog. for West Bank and Gaza Strip, on secondment as Chief Operating Officer, Palestine Trade Center, 1999–2000; Advr, EU Assistance Project, Jordan Tourism Bd, Amman, 2001–02. *Publications:* Protecting Free Trade - The Hong Kong Dilemma 1947–1997, 2012. *Recreations:* music (classical jazz), writing, reading. *Address:* 21/F Coda Plaza, 51 Garden Road, Central, Hong Kong. *Clubs:* Naval and Military; Hong Kong (Hong Kong).

MILLS, Leif Anthony, CBE 1995; General Secretary, Banking, Insurance and Finance Union (formerly National Union of Bank Employees), 1972–96; Chairman, Covent Garden Market Authority, 1998–2005; *b* 25 March 1936; *s* of English father and Norwegian mother; *m* 1958, Gillian Margaret Smith (*d* 2003); two *s* two *d*. *Educ:* Balliol Coll., Oxford. MA Hons PPE. Commnd in Royal Military Police, 1957–59. Trade Union Official, Nat. Union of Bank Employees, 1960–96: Research Officer, 1960; Asst Gen. Sec., 1962; Dep. Gen. Sec., 1968. Mem. various arbitration tribunals; Member: TUC Non-Manual Workers Adv. Cttee, 1967–72; TUC Gen. Council, 1983–96 (Pres., 1994–95); Office of Manpower Economics Adv. Cttee on Equal Pay, 1971; Cttee to Review the Functioning of Financial Instns, 1977–80; CS Pay Res. Unit Bd, 1978–81; Armed Forces Pay Review Body, 1980–87; Monopolies and Mergers Commn, 1982–91; Financial Reporting Council, 1990–96; Ind. Review Cttee on Higher Educn Pay & Conditions, 1998–99; Chairman: TUC Financial Services Cttee, 1983–96; TUC Educn and Training Cttee, 1989–94. Member: BBC Consultative Gp on Social Effects of Television, 1978–80; Council, NCVQ, 1992–96; Bd, Investors in People, 1992–96; PIA Ombudsman Council, 1994–2000 (Dep. Chm., 1997–2000); Bd, Employment Tribunal Service, 1996–2001; Council, Consumers' Assoc., 1996–2002. Contested (Lab) Salisbury, 1964, 1965 (by-elecn). Mem. Governing Body, London Business Sch., 1988–92. Trustee, Civic Trust, 1988–96. FRGS 1992. *Publications:* biography (unpublished), Cook: A History of the Life and Explorations of Dr Frederick Albert Cook, SPRI ms 883, Cambridge, 1970; (published) Frank Wild, Antarctic explorer, 1999; Men of Ice: two polar biographies, 2008; The Redoubtable Mrs Smith: a trade union novel, 2010; The Adventures of Mrs Smith: some trade union stories, 2011. *Recreations:* rowing, chess. *Address:* 31 Station Road, West Byfleet, Surrey KT14 6DR. *T:* (01932) 342829. *Clubs:* Oxford and Cambridge; Oxford University Boat, Weybridge Rowing (Pres., 2008–).

MILLS, Rt Rev. Murray John; Bishop of Waiapu, 1991–2002; Waiapu Diocesan Archivist, since 2008; *b* 29 May 1936; *s* of Robert Claude Mills and Mabel Winifred Mills; *m* 1961, Judith Anne Cotton; two *s* three *d*. *Educ:* Auckland Univ. (BA, MA); St John's Theol Coll. (LTh (First Cl. Hons)). Ordained: Deacon, 1960; Priest, 1961 (dio. of Auckland); Assistant Curate: Papakura, 1960–63; Whangarei, 1963–65; Vicar: Bay of Islands, 1965–70; Matamata, 1970–75; Archdeacon of Waikato, 1976–81; Vicar-Gen., dio. of Waikato, 1978–84; Vicar: Tokoroa, 1981–84; St John's Cathedral, Napier (dio. of Waiapu) and Dean of Waiapu, 1984–91. Examining Chaplain to Bishop of Waikato, 1974–84; Advr in Christian Educn, 1976–81. Liaison Bp, Oceania Mission to Seafarers, 1998–2002; Pres., Conf. of Churches in Aotearoa, NZ, 2000–03. Mem., Assoc. of Christian Spiritual Dirs, 2003–. *Publications:* History of Christ Church, Papakura, 1961. *Recreations:* tramping, gardening, drama, politics, music, reading. *Address:* 12 Clyde Road, Napier, New Zealand. *T:* (6) 8350884. *E:* muju@Xtra.co.nz.

MILLS, Neil McLay; Chairman, Sedgwick Group plc, 1979–84; *b* 29 July 1923; *yr s* of late L. H. Mills; *m* 1950, Rosamund Mary Kimpton (*d* 2012), *d* of Col and Hon. Mrs A. C. W. Kimpton; two *s* two *d*. *Educ:* Epsom Coll.; University Coll. London. Served War, 1940–46: commnd RN; Lieut RNVR; Coastal Forces (mentioned in despatches, 1944). Joined Bland Welch & Co. Ltd, 1948; Exec. Dir, 1955; Chm., 1965–74; Chm., Bland Payne Holdings Ltd, 1974–79. Underwriting Mem. of Lloyd's, 1955–91. Director: Montagu Trust Ltd, 1966–74; Midland Bank Ltd, 1974–79; Wadlow Grosvenor International Ltd, 1984–88; Threadneedle Publishing Co., 1987–93. Vice-President: Insurance Inst. of London, 1971–84; British Insurance Brokers Assoc., 1978–84 (Mem., Internat. Insurance Brokers Cttee); Mem. Cttee, Lloyd's Insurance Brokers Assoc., 1974–77. Member: Church Army Board, 1957–64 (Vice-Chm., 1959–64); Council, Oak Hill Theol Coll., 1958–62. Trustee and Governor, Lord Mayor Treloar Trust, 1975–81. Freeman, City of London, 1984; Liveryman, Insurers' Co., 1984–86. *Recreation:* reading and reflecting. *Address:* The Old Post House, 23 Broad Street, Alresford, Hants SO24 9AR. *T:* (01962) 732464, *Fax:* (01962) 732511. *Club:* Pilgrims.

MILLS, Nigel John; MP (C) Amber Valley, since 2010; *b* Jacksdale, 1974; *s* of John and Rosemary Mills; *m* 2013, Alice Elizabeth Ward. *Educ:* Univ. of Newcastle upon Tyne (BA Classics). ACA 2000. Tax Adviser: PricewaterhouseCoopers, 1998–2010; Deloitte, 2010. Mem. (C) Amber Valley BC, 2004–11; Heanor and Loscoe Town Council, 2007–11. Member, Select Committee: on Admin, 2010–; on NI Affairs, 2011–; on Work and Pensions, 2012–15; Public Accounts, 2015–. *Address:* House of Commons, SW1A 0AA.

MILLS, Oliver Arthur Seymour; care and health improvement adviser; independent consultant; National Programme Director, Towards Excellence in Adult Social Care, 2011–14; *b* 11 Oct. 1951; *s* of Seymour Herbert Hatten Mills and Mary Patricia Mills; *m* 1990, Janice Reay; two *s*, and one step *d*. *Educ:* Tonbridge Sch.; Univ. of Warwick (BA Hons Hist. 1973); Wadham Coll., Oxford (MSc Applied Soc. Studies 1979; CQSW 1979). Social worker, London Bor. of Camden, 1980–84; Team Leader, London Bor. of Lewisham, 1984–87; Kent County Council, 1987–2011: Social Services Directorate: Asst Dir, 1992–98; Dir, Ops, 1998–2005; Strategic Dir, Social Services, 2005–06; Man. Dir, Adult Social Services, 2006–11. Chm., SE Region, ADASS, 2007–11. Trustee, Football Beyond Borders, 2013–. *Recreations:* playing tennis, music, allotment. *Address:* 8 Grove Hill Gardens, Tunbridge Wells, Kent TN1 1SS. *E:* oasmills@btinternet.com.

MILLS, Sir Peter (Frederick Leighton), 3rd Bt *cr* 1921; *b* 9 July 1924; *s* of Major Sir Frederick Leighton Victor Mills, 2nd Bt, MC, RA, MICE, and Doris (*née* Armitage); *S* father, 1955; *m* 1954, Pauline Mary, *d* of L. R. Allen, Calverton, Notts; one *s* (one adopted *d* decd). *Educ:* Eastbourne Coll.; Cedara Coll. of Agriculture, University of Natal (BSc Agric.). Served HM Forces, 1943–47. CS, Fedn Rhodesia and Nyasaland, 1953; with Rhodesia Min. of Agric., 1964, Zimbabwe Min. of Agric., 1980–90. *Heir:* *s* Michael Victor Leighton Mills [*b* 30 Aug. 1957; *m* 1981, Susan, *d* of J. Doig, Harare, Zimbabwe].

MILLS, Rev. Peter Watson, CB 2010; Minister, Largoward with St Monans, since 2013; *b* 9 Feb. 1955; *s* of late Peter Watson Mills and of Janet (*née* Lonsdale); *m* 1979, Sheila Anderson; two *d*. *Educ:* Arbroath High Sch.; Christ's Coll., Univ. of Aberdeen (BD 1983, CPS 1983). Police Constable, Grampian Police, 1974–78. Licensed 1983, ordained, 1984; Asst Minister, Montrose, 1983–84; RAF Chaplain, 1984–2009; Principal Chaplain, C of S and Free Churches, 2001–06; Chaplain-in-Chief and Dir Gen. Chaplaincy Services, 2006–09; Minister, St Andrew's, Corby, 2009–13. Clerk, Presbytery of England, 2010–13; Chair, Churches Together, Corby District, 2010–13. QHC 2001–10. Hon. DD Aberdeen, 2009. *Recreations:* computing, reading, music, electric guitar. *Address:* The Manse, St Monans KY10 2DD. *Club:* Royal Air Force.

MILLS, Peter William; QC (Can.) 1985; company director and business consultant, since 1999; *b* 22 July 1942; *s* of Joseph Roger Mills and Jane Evelyn (*née* Roscoe); *m* 1967, Eveline Jane (*née* Black); two *s*. *Educ:* Dalhousie Univ. Law Sch. (JD (LLB 1967)); Dalhousie Univ. (BComm). ICD.D 2005. Barrister and solicitor, Ont, Canada; with McInnes, Cooper and Robertson, Halifax, 1967; Solicitor, Canadian Pacific Ltd, Montreal and Toronto, 1967–71; Dir, Cammell Laird Shipbuilders Ltd, 1971–76; Mem., Org Cttee for British Shipbuilders, 1976–77; Manager, Currie, Coopers & Lybrand Ltd, Toronto, 1977–79; The Woodbridge Co. Ltd: Gen. Counsel, 1980–98; Vice-Pres., 1980–87; Dir, 1982–98; Sen. Vice-Pres., 1988–98. Director: Corporate Develt, FP Publications Ltd, 1979–80; Augusta Newsprint Co., 1981–2011; Hudson's Bay Co., 1985–2006; Markborough Properties Inc., 1986–97; Cambridge Shopping Centres Ltd, 1997–2001; Cadillac Fairview Corp. Ltd, 2001–12; Torstar Corp., 2004–06; Jacques Whitford Ltd, 2007–09. Dir, St John's Rehabilitation Hosp. Foundn, 2002–03; Chm., Hudson's Bay Co. History Foundn, 2005–06. Dir, Canadian Inst. of Chartered Accts, 2004–10. *Recreations:* golf, sailing, travel, reading. *Address:* 390 Glencairn Avenue, Toronto, ON M5N 1V1, Canada. *Fax:* (416) 4820754. *E:* pwmills@sympatico.ca. *Club:* York Downs Golf and Country (Toronto).

MILLS, Richard Michael; Chairman and Chief Executive, Delfont Mackintosh Theatres Ltd, 1991–96; *b* 26 June 1931; *s* of Richard Henry Mills and Catherine Keeley; *m* 1st, 1960, Lynda Taylor (marr. diss. 1967); one *d*; 2nd, 1983, Sheila White; two *s*. Commenced working in the theatre as an Assistant Stage Manager in 1948, and worked in every capacity, including acting and stage management. Joined Bernard Delfont Ltd, 1962; Dir, 1967; Dep. Chm., 1970–79; Chm., 1979–91; Chief Exec., 1970–91; Managing Director: Prince of Wales Theatre, 1970–96; Prince Edward Theatre, 1978–96. Director: EMI Film & Theatre Corp., 1970–81; Trust House Forte Leisure, 1980–83; First Leisure Corp., 1983–93. Member: Nat. Theatre Bd, 1976–91; Finance and Gen. Purposes Cttee, NT, 1976–91; Drama Panel, Arts Council of GB, 1976–77; English Tourist Bd, 1982–85. Pres., Stage Golfing Soc., 2004–05. Shows worked on in the West End, 1948–62, include: I Remember Mama, Tuppence Coloured, Medea, Adventure Story, Anne Veronica, The Devil's General, I Capture the Castle, No Escape, Misery Me, Three Times a Day, The Sun of York, To my Love, Be my Guest, Hunter's Moon, The Iceman Cometh, Brouhaha, Detour after Dark, The Ginger Man, Sound of Murder, Will You Walk a Little Faster, Pool's Paradise, Belle, Come Blow your Horn. Whilst Gen. Manager and Dir with Bernard Delfont Ltd: Never Too Late, Pickwick, 1962; Caligula, Maggie May, Little Me, Our Man Crichton, 1963; The Roar of the Greasepaint (NY), Pickwick (NY), Twang, Barefoot in the Park, 1964; The Owl and the Pussycat, The Matchgirls, Funny Girl, Joey Joey, The Odd Couple, 1965; Queenie, Sweet Charity, The Four Musketeers, 1966; Golden Boy, Look Back in Anger (revival), 1967; Mame, Cat Among the Pigeons, 1968; Carol Channing, Danny La Rue at the Palace, 1969; Kean, Lulu, 1970; Applause, The Unknown Soldier and his Wife, 1971. With Lord Delfont presented in the West End: The Good Old Bad Old Days, Mardi Gras, Brief Lives, Queen Daniella, Cinderella, Henry IV, Harvey, Sammy Cahn's Songbook, Streetcar Named Desire, Good Companions, It's All Right if I Do It, Charley's Aunt, An Evening with Tommy Steele, Gomes, The Wolf, Danny La Rue Show, Beyond the Rainbow, Dad's Army, Plumber's Progress, Paul Daniels Magic Show, Underneath the Arches, Little Me, The Best Little Whorehouse in Texas, and over 200 pantomimes and summer season shows. *Recreations:* golf, poker. *Clubs:* Royal Automobile; Richmond Golf.

MILLS, Robert Ferris; Under Secretary, Department of Finance and Personnel, Northern Ireland, 1990–96, retired; *b* 21 Sept. 1939; *s* of Robert and Rachel Mills; *m* 1st, 1968, Irene Sandra Miskelly (marr. diss. 1978); one *s* one *d*; 2nd, 1984, Frances Elizabeth Gillies; two step *d*. *Educ:* Sullivan Upper School, Holywood, Co. Down; Queen's Univ., Belfast (BA Hons). Inland Revenue, 1961–64; Min. of Commerce, NI, 1964–68; Dept of Housing and Local Govt, 1968–71; Dept of the Environment, NI, 1971–75; Asst Sec., 1975–83, Under Sec., 1983–90, Dept of Health and Social Services, NI. *Recreations:* golf, tennis, travel, the arts.

MILLS, Simon Yarnton; Managing Director, Sustaincare Community Interest Co., since 2008; *b* Lyons, France, 2 Nov. 1949; *s* of Hamilton and Vlasta Mills; partner, 1988, Rachel Charlesworth (now Mills); one *s* one *d* and two step *d*. *Educ:* Sacred Heart Coll., Auckland, NZ; Churchill Coll., Cambridge (BA Med. Scis Tripos 1970). Nurseryman and horticultural consultant, 1970–77; herbal practitioner, 1977–; Pres., Nat. Inst. of Medical Herbalists, 1983–88; Founder Chm., Council for Complementary and Alternative Medicine, 1985–89; Founder Director: Centre for Complementary Health Studies, Univ. of Exeter, 1987–2000; MSc Prog. in Herbal Medicine, Maryland Univ. of Integrative Health (formerly Tai Sophia Inst., Md), 2000–; Sen. Teaching Fellow, Peninsula Med. Sch., Exeter, 2003–08; Project Lead, Integrated Self Care in Family Practice prog., DoH, 2008–11. Specialist Advr, H of L Select Cttee on Complementary and Alternative Medicine, 1999–2000. Professional Mem., Herbal Medicine Adv. Cttee, 2005–09. Chm., British Herbal Medicine Assoc., 1999–2004. *Publications:* Alternatives in Healing, 1988; Out of the Earth, 1991; (with K. Bone) Principles and Practice of Phytotherapy, 2000, 2nd edn 2013; (with K. Bone) The Essential Guide to Herbal Safety, 2005. *Recreations:* gardening, walking, finding good country pubs. *Address:* Notaries House, Chapel Street, Exeter EX1 1EZ. *T:* (01392) 423210, *Fax:* (01392) 424864. *E:* simon.mills@sustaincare.net. *Club:* Royal Society of Medicine.

MILLS, Stratton; *see* Mills, W. S.

MILLS, Rt Hon. Dame Tessa (Jane Helen Douglas); *see* Jowell, Rt Hon. Dame T. J. H. D.

MILLS, (William) Stratton; Senior Partner, 1974–2000, Consultant, 2000–05, Mills, Selig, Solicitors, Belfast (Partner, 1959–2000); company director; Chairman, Hampden Group PLC (formerly Hampden Homecare plc), 1992–99; *b* 1 July 1932; *o s* of late Dr J. V. S. Mills, CBE, Resident Magistrate for City of Belfast, and Margaret Florence (*née* Byford); *m* 1959, Merriel E. R. Whitla, *o d* of late Mr and Mrs R. J. Whitla, Belfast; three *s*. *Educ:* Campbell Coll., Belfast; Queen's Univ., Belfast (LLB). Vice-Chm., Federation of University Conservative and Unionist Assocs, 1952–53 and 1954–55; admitted a Solicitor, 1958. MP (UU) Belfast N, Oct. 1959–Dec. 1972; MP (Alliance) Belfast N, April 1973–Feb. 1974; PPS to Parly Sec., Ministry of Transport, 1961–64; Member: Estimates Cttee, 1964–70; Exec. Cttee, 1922 Cttee, 1967–70, 1973; Hon. Sec. Conservative Broadcasting Cttee, 1963–70, Chm., 1970–73; Mem., Mr Speaker's Conference on Electoral Law, 1967. Mem., One Nation Gp, 1972–73. Member: Adv. Bd, Public Records Office, NI, 1996–2008; Bd, Historic Bldgs Council for NI, 2004–10. Chm., Ulster Orchestra Soc. Ltd, 1980–90; Mem. Bd, Castleward Opera, 1988–98; Dir, Opera Rara, 1998–. Mem. Council, Winston Churchill Meml Trust, 1990–95. Arnold Goodman Award, for encouragement of business sponsorship of the arts, 1990. *Address:* 17 Malone Park, Belfast BT9 6NJ. *T:* (028) 9066 5210. *Clubs:* Carlton, MCC; Reform (Belfast); Royal County Down Golf.

MILLS-EVANS, Carole Denise; *see* Mills, C. D.

MILLSON, Tony; JP; HM Diplomatic Service, retired; Counsellor, Foreign and Commonwealth Office, 2001–03; *b* 25 Nov. 1951; *s* of Donald Millson and Joan (*née* Whittle). *Educ:* Grimsby Wintringham Grammar Sch. Entered HM Diplomatic Service, 1970; MECAS, 1973; Third Sec. (Commercial), Tripoli, 1974–76; Third, later Second Sec. (Devlt), Amman, 1976–80; FCO, 1980–83; Second Sec., BMG Berlin, 1983–86; First Sec., FCO, 1986–88; Hd of Chancery, Kuwait, 1988–90; FCO, 1991–93; Ambassador to Macedonia, 1993–97; Counsellor, FCO, 1997–98; High Comr, The Gambia, 1998–2000; Dep. High Comr, Abuja, 2000–01. JP London, 2004; Chm., Balham Youth Court, 2011. *Recreations:* reading, listening to music, surfing the web. *Address:* 7 George Mathers Road, Kennington, SE11 4RU. *T:* (020) 3524 6719.

MILLWARD, Michael Timothy Lawrence; Director, Rabat Office, and Representative to Morocco, Algeria, Mauritania and Tunisia, UNESCO, since 2014; *b* Bath, 5 July 1954; *s* of Lawrence Millward and Alison Millward (*née* Griffiths); *m* 1979, Michelle Rey; one *s*. *Educ:* Wallington High Sch. for Boys; Salford Univ. (BSc Hons Mod. Langs 1976). FTCL 1972. Teacher, English to foreigners, 1976–78; translator, 1978–84; Language Reviser, UNESCO, 1985–89; Asst Exec. Dir, ICSU, 1989–93; UNESCO: Liaison Officer, NGOs, External Relns, 1994–99; Sen. Liaison Officer, Office of Dir-Gen., 1999–2003; Dir, Exec. Office, Science Sector, 2003–05; Interim Dir, UNESCO Inst. for Stats, then Interim Dir, UNESCO Office, Venice, 2005–06; Sec., Gen. Conference of UNESCO, 2006–08; Dep. Dir, 2008–09, Dir, 2009–13, Governing Bodies Secretariat, and Sec., Gen. Conf. and Exec. Bd, 2009–13, UNESCO. Mem., Les Musicales du Luberon. *Recreations:* music, literature, theatre, travel, cuisine. *Address:* Bureau de l'UNESCO de Rabat, Avenue Ain Khalwiya, Souissi, Rabat, Morocco. *T:* 537755722, *Fax:* 537657722. *E:* m.millward@unesco.org.

MILMAN, Andrée, (Mrs David Milman); *see* Grenfell, A.

MILMAN, Sir David (Patrick), 10th Bt *cr* 1800, of Levaton-in-Woodland, Devonshire; educational consultant, since 1999; *b* 24 Aug. 1945; *er s* of Lt-Col Sir Derek Milman, 9th Bt and Christine Margaret Milman (*née* Whitehouse); *S* father, 1999; *m* 1969, Christina Hunt; one *s* one *d*. *Educ:* London Univ. (Teacher's Cert. 1st cl. 1968; BEd (Hons) 1969; MA 1976). Headteacher, 1981–89; Headteacher Trng Co-ordinator, ILEA, 1988–89; Asst Dir, Sch. Mgt South, 1989–91; Area Advr, 1991–93, Sen. Area Advr, 1993–98, NW Kent; District Adv. Officer, Dartford, 1998–99. *Publications:* Teachers' Guidelines to Take Part Readers Series, 1973; Take a Look Series, 1974; What do you think?, 1976; Senior Manager's Personal Profile, 1991. *Recreations:* ornithology, reading. *Heir: s* Thomas Hart Milman, *b* 7 Oct. 1976. *Address:* 71 Camden Road, Sevenoaks, Kent TN13 3LU. *T:* (01732) 459089.

MILMINE, Rt Rev. Douglas, CBE 1983; an Assistant Bishop, diocese of Chichester, since 1992; *b* 3 May 1921; *s* of Alexander Douglas Milmine and Rose Gertrude Milmine (*née* Moore); *m* 1945, Margaret Rosalind, *d* of Edward and Gladys Whitley, Kilmorie, Meadfoot, Torquay; three *s* one *d*. *Educ:* Sutton Valence School; St Peter's Hall, Oxford (MA 1946); Clifton Theological Coll. RAFVR, 1941–45; POW, 1943–45. Deacon 1947, priest 1948; Curate: SS Philip and James, Ilfracombe, 1947–50; St Paul's, Slough, 1950–53; missionary with South American Missionary Society: Maquehue, Chile, 1954; Temuco, 1955–60; Santiago, 1961–68; Archdeacon of N Chile, Bolivia and Peru, 1964–68; Hon. Canon of Chile, 1969–72; Midland Area Sec. of SAMS, 1969–72; Bishop in Paraguay, 1973–85; retired 1986. *Publications:* Stiff Upper Smile (autobiog.), 1993; La Comunión Anglicana en América Latina, 1993. *Recreation:* study of current affairs. *Address:* 1c Clive Court, 24 Grand Parade, Eastbourne, East Sussex BN21 3DD. *T:* (01323) 734159. *E:* doug2022@talktalk.net.

MILMO, His Honour John Boyle Martin; QC 1984; a Circuit Judge, 2004–13; *b* 19 Jan. 1943; *s* of late Dermod Hubert Francis Milmo, MB BCh and Eileen Clare Milmo (*née* White). *Educ:* Downside Sch.; Trinity Coll., Dublin (MA, LLB). Called to the Bar, Lincoln's Inn, 1966, Bencher, 1992; a Recorder, 1982–2004; a Dep. High Ct Judge, 1993–2004. Mem., Parole Bd, 2005–. Mem., Bar Council, 1992–2002 (Chm., Legal Aid and Fees Cttee, 1996–97). Chm., Adv. Bd, Criminal Justice Res. Centre, Nottingham Univ., 2014–. Trustee, Historic Singers Trust, 2004–. *Recreations:* opera, discography. *Club:* United Services (Nottingham).

MILMO, Patrick Helenus; QC 1985; *b* 11 May 1938; *s* of Sir Helenus Milmo; *m* 1968, Marina, *d* of late Alexis Schiray and of Xenia Schiray, rue Jules Simon, Paris; one *s* one *d*. *Educ:* Downside; Trinity Coll., Cambridge (BA 1961; MA 1997). Harmsworth Scholar; called to the Bar, Middle Temple, 1962 (Bencher, 1994; Reader, 2005). Part-time employment judge, 1998–2010. Asst Comr, Parly Boundary Commn, 2000–08. Dep. Chm., Disciplinary Cttee, RPSGB, 2008–10; Chm., Fitness to Practise Cttee, Gen. Pharmaceutical Council, 2010–. *Publications:* (ed jtly) Gatley on Libel and Slander, 9th edn 1998 to 11th edn 2009. *Recreations:* wine, horse-racing, cinema. *Address:* 5 Gray's Inn Square, Gray's Inn, WC1R 5AH; 7 Baalbec Road, N5 1QN.

MILNE, family name of **Baron Milne**.

MILNE, 3rd Baron *cr* 1933, of Salonika and of Rubislaw, co. Aberdeen; **George Alexander Milne;** self-employed chair caner (Ablecaner); *b* 1 April 1941; *s* of 2nd Baron Milne, TD and of Cicely Abigail Milne (*née* Leslie); *S* father, 2005. *Educ:* Winchester. Liveryman, Grocers' Co. *Recreations:* sailing, bicycling, golf. *Heir: b* Hon. Iain Charles Luis Milne [*b* 16 Sept. 1949; *m* 1987, Berta Guerrero; two *s*]. *T:* (020) 8977 9761. *E:* george.milne2@btinternet.com. *Club:* Pilgrims.

MILNE, Alexander Hugh; QC 2010; a Recorder, since 2007; *b* Hull, 20 April 1959; *s* of Michael Oliver Milne and Maureen Milne; *m* 1993, Sian Elizabeth Fleet; one step *s* one step *d*. *Educ:* Nottingham Univ. (BA Hons Law 1980). Called to the Bar, 1981; Bencher, Gray's Inn, 2015; Claims Corresp., W of England Protection and Indemnity Club, 1982–86; Campaigns Officer, British Section, Amnesty Internat., 1986; Blick & Co., Solicitors, 1986–87; barrister in private practice, specialising in criminal, regulatory and disciplinary law and public enquiries, 1987–. Sen. Trial Counsel to Office of Prosecutor, Special Tribunal for Lebanon, 2013–. Alternate Comr, Disciplinary Bd for Counsel, Internat. Criminal Ct, 2015. Associate MCIArb 2011; Supporting Mem., London Maritime Arbitrators Assoc., 2012–. *Recreations:* golf (in warmer climes), dog-walking. *Address:* 18 Red Lion Court, EC4A 3EB. *T:* (020) 7520 6000, *Fax:* (020) 7520 6248/9. *E:* alex.milne@18rlc.co.uk.

MILNE, David Calder; QC 1987; a Recorder, 1994–2006 (Assistant Recorder, 1989–94); *b* 22 Sept. 1945; *s* of late Ernest and Helena Milne; *m* 1st, 1978, Rosemary Bond (marr. diss. 1999); one *d*; 2nd, 2013, Amanda Robin Shepherd (*née* Clezy). *Educ:* Harrow Sch.; Oxford Univ. (MA). ACA 1969; FCA 1974. Articled to Whinney Murray & Co., chartered accountants, 1966–69; called to the Bar, Lincoln's Inn, 1970, Bencher, 1996. Trustee: Wildfowl and Wetlands Trust, 2002–11; British Trust for Ornithology, 2009–12. Hon. Fellow, Chartered Inst. of Taxation, 2009. *Recreations:* natural history, music, golf, Rugby. *Address:* (chambers) 16 Bedford Row, WC1R 4EF. *T:* (020) 7414 8080. *E:* dmilne@pumptax.com. *Clubs:* Garrick, Hurlingham, Gnomes; Walton Heath Golf.

MILNE, Maj. Gen. John, CB 2000; Regimental Controller, Royal Artillery, since 2009; *b* 13 Oct. 1946; *s* of Donald William Milne and Evelyn (*née* Ayrer); *m* 1970, Cherrill Rosemary Tookey; two *s* one *d*. *Educ:* Lowestoft Grammar Sch.; Royal Coll. of Defence Studies. Commnd, Royal Artillery, 1966: helicopter pilot, 1970–74; Mil. Asst, COS Northern Army Gp, 1980–82; Comdr, 2 Field Regt, 1986–88; Dep. Comdr, 7 Armd Bde, Saudi Arabia, 1990; Comdr, 1 Artillery Bde, 1992–93; Dir, Army Recruiting, 1994–97; Dep. Comdr for Logistics, Stabilisation Force, Bosnia Herzogovina, 1997; Dir for Support, Allied Land Forces, Central Europe, 1998–99; COS Kosovo Force, Pristina, 1999–2000. Col Comdt, RA, 2001–07. Registrar, St Paul's Cathedral, 2001–08. Chm. of Trustees, Royal Sch. Hampstead, 2004–15; Trustee, Haig Homes, 2010–. Freeman, City of London, 2001; Liveryman, Masons' Co., 2002–. FCMI (FInstM 1993). Bronze Star (US), 1991. *Recreations:* tennis, golf, bridge. *Address:* Lloyds Bank, 174 Fleet Road, Fleet, Hants GU51 4DD.

MILNE, Sir John (Drummond), Kt 1986; Chairman, Alfred McAlpine plc, 1992–96; *b* 13 Aug. 1924; *s* of Frederick John and Minnie Elizabeth Milne; *m* 1948, Joan Akroyd (*d* 2014); two *s* two *d*. *Educ:* Stowe Sch.; Trinity Coll., Cambridge. Served Coldstream Guards, 1943–47. APCM (now Blue Circle Industries): management trainee, 1948; Asst to Director i/c Overseas Investments, 1953; President, Ocean Cement, Vancouver, 1957; Director, APCM, 1964, Man. Dir and Chief Exec., 1975; Blue Circle Industries: Chm. and Managing Director, 1983; Chm., 1983–90 (non-exec., 1987–90). DRG plc (formerly The Dickinson Robinson Group): Dir, 1973–89; Chm., 1987–89; Director: Royal Insurance, 1982–95; Witan Investment Co., 1988–96; Avon Rubber, 1989–95; Solvay & Cie SA, 1990–96. *Recreations:* golf, shooting. *Address:* Chilton House, Chilton Candover, Hants SO24 9TX. *Clubs:* Boodle's, MCC; Berkshire Golf, Swinley Forest Golf.

MILNE, Judith Frances; *see* English, J. F.

MILNE, Nanette Lilian Margaret, OBE 1994; Member (C) Scotland North East, Scottish Parliament, since 2003; *b* 27 April 1942; *d* of Harold G. Gordon and Hannah L. C. Gordon (*née* Stephen); *m* 1965, Alan Ducat Milne; one *s* one *d*. *Educ:* Aberdeen High Sch. for Girls; Univ. of Aberdeen (MB ChB 1965). FFARCS 1969. Medical Officer, Grampian Health Board, later Aberdeen Royal Hospitals NHS Trust: anaesthetics, 1966–73; oncology research, 1980–92. Mem. (C), City of Aberdeen DC, 1988–96, Aberdeen CC, 1995–99. Vice-Chm., Scottish Cons. and Unionist Party, 1989–93. JP Aberdeen, 1993–2007. *Publications:* contrib. to BMJ on cardiovascular effects of laparoscopy and on colorectal cancer. *Recreations:* gardening, sports. *Address:* Scottish Parliament, Holyrood, Edinburgh EH99 1SP. *T:* (0131) 348 5652. *E:* nanette.milne.msp@scottish.parliament.uk.

MILNE, Nikola Caroline; *see* Stewart, N. C.

MILNE, Ronald Robert, FRSE; FCLIP; George Lyndon Hicks Fellow, National Library of Singapore, since 2015; library and heritage professional; *b* 14 Feb. 1957; *s* of Robert Hally Milne and Joyce (*née* McRobbie). *Educ:* Perth Acad.; Berwickshire High Sch.; Univ. of Edinburgh (MA 1979); University Coll. London (MA 1984); MA Oxon 2003. FCLIP (FLA 2001). SCONUL trainee, Cambridge Univ. Liby, 1981–82; Sen. Liby Asst, Univ. of London Liby Resources Co-ordinating Cttee, 1983–85; Asst Librarian, Glasgow Univ. Liby, 1985–90; Sub-Librarian, Trinity Coll., Cambridge, 1990–94; Asst Dir of Liby Services, KCL, 1994–98; Dir, Res. Support Libraries Prog., 1998–2002; Dep. to Dir, Univ. Liby Services and to Bodley's Librarian, 2002–04, Acting Dir and Bodley's Librarian, 2004–07, Oxford Univ.; Fellow, Wolfson Coll., Oxford, 2003–07; Dir of Scholarship and Collections, British Liby, 2007–09; Associate Chief Librarian (Research Collections), Alexander Turnbull Liby, Nat. Liby of NZ, 2009–11; Dep. Chief Exec. and Heritage Services Br. Manager, 2011–13, Dir, Heritage Projects, 2013–14, Min. for Culture and Heritage, NZ. FRSA 2000; FRSE 2006. *Publications:* contribs to professional jls and books. *Recreations:* tramping, listening to music, photography. *Address:* National Library of Singapore, 100 Victoria Street, Singapore 188064. *E:* ronaldmilne@gmail.com. *Clubs:* Reform; New Zealand Alpine.

MILNE, Lt Col Simon Stephen, MBE 1996; FRGS; Regius Keeper, Royal Botanic Garden Edinburgh, since 2014; *b* Dundee, 30 Jan. 1959; *s* of Stephen Milne and Susan Milne (*née* Cox); *m* 1993, Françoise Sevaux; one *s* two *d*. *Educ:* Univ. of St Andrews (BSc 1979); RNC Greenwich. Royal Marines, 1976–2000: 2nd Lt 1976; served: 41 and 45 Commandos; Comacchio Gp; HQ 3 Cdo Bde; HQ Cdo Forces; Dept of Comdt Gen.; Directorate of Navy Plans, MoD; Rapid Response Force Operational Staff, Bosnia; HQ NI. Dir, Sir Harold Hillier Gardens and Arboretum, 2000–04; Chief Exec., Scottish Wildlife Trust, 2004–14. Mem., HM Bodyguard, Hon. Corps of Gentlemen at Arms, 2012–. FRGS 1990. *Publications:* articles on conservation and biodiversity. *Recreations:* ski-ing, country pursuits, gardening, ornithology. *Address:* Royal Botanic Garden Edinburgh, 20A Inverleith Row, Edinburgh EH3 5LR. *Club:* Army and Navy.

MILNE, Prof. William Ireland, PhD; FREng, FIET, FIMMM; Professor of Electrical Engineering, since 1996, and Director, Centre for Advanced Photonics and Electronics, since 2005, University of Cambridge; Fellow, Churchill College, Cambridge, since 1977; *b* 15 Feb. 1948; *s* of William Ireland Milne and Jenelia Foy Kelso Milne (*née* Reid); *m* 1st, 1971, Jennifer Stovell (marr. diss. 1991); one *s* one *d*; 2nd, 1992, Catharina Jacqueline Ann Baker; one step *s* one step *d*. *Educ:* Forfar Acad.; St Andrews Univ. (BSc Hons 1970); Imperial Coll., London DIC, PhD 1973). FIET (FIEE 1989); FIMMM (FIM 1999). Sen. Scientist, then Principal Scientist, Plessey Res. Centre, Caswell, 1973–76; Engineering Department, University of Cambridge: Asst Lectr, 1976–80; Lectr, 1980–90; Reader, 1990–96; Hd, Electrical Div., 1999–2014. Visiting Professor: Tokyo Inst. of Technol., 1985 (Dist. Vis. Prof., 2014); Nanyang Technol Univ., Singapore, 1993; Gifu Univ., Japan, 2001; South East Univ., Nanying, 2007–; Shizuoka Univ., 2010–; Hong Kong Poly. Univ., 2014; Dist. Vis. Prof., Nat. Univ. of Singapore, 2008; Hon. Prof., Coll. of Sci. and Technol. of Huazhang Normal Univ., 2007–; Dist. Vis. Scholar, Kyung Hee Univ. Seoul, 2009–; Erskine Fellow, Univ. of Christchurch, NZ, 2015. FREng 2006. Hon. DEng Univ. of Waterloo, Toronto, 2003. J. J. Thomson Medal, IET, 2008; NANOSMAT Prize, 2010. *Recreations:* golf, tennis, travel. *Address:* Electrical Division Building, Engineering Department, Cambridge University, 9 J. J. Thomson Avenue, Cambridge CB3 0FA.

MILNE-WATSON, Sir Andrew (Michael), 4th Bt *cr* 1937, of Ashley, Longbredy, co. Dorset; Partner, GM-W Fabrics, since 2009; *b* 10 Nov. 1944; *o s* of Sir Michael Milne-Watson, 3rd Bt, CBE and Mary Lisette Gunion Milne-Watson (*née* Bagnall); *S* father, 1999;

m 1st, 1970, Beverley Jane Gabrielle Cotton (marr. diss. 1981); one *s* one *d*; 2nd, 1983, Gisella Stafford (*née* Tisdall); one *s*. *Educ:* Eton. Sales and Mgt Trainee, Sidney Flavel & Co. Ltd, 1965–68; Mgt Trainee, E Midlands Gas Bd, 1968–69; Ogilvy & Mather (UK): Trainee, 1969; Account Mgr, 1970; Account Dir, 1973–79; Managing and Client Service Director: Mathers Advertising Ltd, 1979–82; Phoenix Advertising Ltd, 1982–84; Dep. Chm., Lewis Broadbent Advertising Ltd, 1984–87; founded: Minerva Publications Ltd, 1987–89; MW Communications Ltd, 1989–90; Dir of Advertising and Mktg, Inc. Publications, 1990–93; Proprietor, A. D. R. Associates Ltd, 1993–2009. Liveryman, Grocers' Co. *Recreations:* cooking, gardening, building renovation. *Heir: s* David Alastair Milne-Watson [*b* 24 Aug. 1971; *m* 2000, Sandra M. Geraldi, Campinas, Brazil]. *Address:* 164 Rivermead Court, SW6 3SF. *T:* 07768 514310. *Club:* Garrick.

MILNER, family name of **Baron Milner of Leeds**.

MILNER OF LEEDS, 3rd Baron *cr* 1951; **Richard James Milner;** *b* 16 May 1959; *s* of 2nd Baron Milner of Leeds, AE and Sheila Margaret (*née* Hartley); *S* father, 2003; *m* 1988, Margaret, *y d* of G. F. Voisin; two *d*. *Educ:* Charterhouse; Surrey Univ. (BSc). Freeman, City of London, 1988; Liveryman, Clothworkers' Co., 1988. Mem., Vins Sans Frontières, Jersey. *Heir:* none. *Address:* Roche d'Or, Trinity, Jersey, CI JE3 5JA.

MILNER, Prof. (Arthur) David, PhD; FRS 2011; FRSE; Professor of Cognitive Neuroscience, 2000–08, now Emeritus, and Director, Neuroimaging Centre, 2011–14, University of Durham; *b* 16 July 1943; *s* of Arthur Milner and Sarah Ellen Milner (*née* Gaunt); *m* 1965, Christine Armitage; two *s*. *Educ:* Bradford Grammar Sch.; Lincoln Coll., Oxford (Open Schol.; BA 1965; MA 1970); Inst. of Psychiatry, London (DipPsych 1966; PhD 1971). Res. Asst, Inst. of Psychiatry, London, 1966–70; University of St Andrews: Lectr, 1970–82, Sen. Lectr, 1982–85, in Psychology; Reader in Neuropsychology, 1985–90; Prof. of Neuropsychology, 1990–2000; Chm., Dept of Psychology, 1983–88; Dean, Faculty of Science, 1992–94; Head, Sch. of Psychology, 1994–97. Hon. Prof., Univ. of Edinburgh, 2015–. FRSE 1992. *Publications:* The Neuropsychology of Consciousness, 1992; (with M. A. Goodale) The Visual Brain in Action, 1995, 2nd edn 2006; Comparative Neuropsychology, 1998; Cognitive and Neural Bases of Spatial Neglect, 2002; (with M. A. Goodale) Sight Unseen, 2004 (BPsS Book Award, 2005), 2nd edn 2013; The Roots of Visual Awareness, 2004; sci. articles in learned jls and books, mainly on brain mechanisms underlying visual perception, visual guidance of movement, and bilateral co-ordination. *Recreations:* walking, cinema, jazz. *Address:* Department of Psychology, University of Durham, Science Laboratories, South Road, Durham DH1 3LE. *T:* (0191) 334 9148.

MILNER, Prof. Brenda (Atkinson), CC 2004 (OC 1984); GOQ 2009 (OQ 1985); FRS 1979; FRSC 1976; Professor, Department of Neurology and Neurosurgery, McGill University, since 1970; Dorothy J. Killam Professor, Montreal Neurological Institute, since 1993 (Head of Neuropsychology Research Unit, 1970–91); *b* 15 July 1918; *d* of Samuel Langford and Clarice Frances Leslie (*née* Doig). *Educ:* Univ. of Cambridge (BA, MA, ScD); McGill Univ. (PhD). Experimental Officer, Min. of Supply, 1941–44; Professeur Agrégé, Inst. de Psychologie, Univ. de Montréal, 1944–52; Res. Associate, Psychology Dept, McGill Univ., 1952–53; Lectr, 1953–60, Asst Prof., 1960–64, Associate Prof., 1964–70, Dept of Neurology and Neurosurgery, McGill Univ. Hon. LLD: Queen's Univ., Kingston, Ont, 1980; Cambridge, 2000; Hon. DSc: Manitoba, 1982; Lethbridge, 1986; Mount Holyoke, 1986; Toronto, 1987; McGill, 1991; Wesleyan, 1991; Acadia, 1991; St Andrews, 1992; Hartford, 1997; McMaster, 1999; Memorial, 2002; Columbia, 2002; Ryerson, 2008; Hon. DSocSc Laval, 1987; Hon. Dr Montreal, 1988; Hon. DHumLit Mount St Vincent, 1988; DU Ottawa, 2004. Izaak Walton Killam Prize, Canada Council, 1983; Hermann von Helmholtz Prize, Inst. for Cognitive Neuroscience, USA, 1984; Ralph W. Gerard Prize, Soc. for Neuroscience, 1987; Wilder Penfield Prize, PQ, 1993; Metropolitan Life Foundn award, 1996; John. P. McGovern Award, AAAS, 2001; D. O. Hebb Award, Canadian Soc. for Brain, Behaviour and Cognitive Sci., 2001; Neurosci. Award, NAS, 2004; Gairder Foundn Award in Health Res., 2005; Pearl Meister Greengard Prize, 2011; Balzan Prize, Internat. Balzan Prize Foundn, 2012; Dan David Prize, Dan David Foundn, 2014. Grand Dame of Merit, Order of Malta, 1985. *Publications:* mainly articles in neurological and psychological jls. *Address:* Montreal Neurological Institute, 3801 University Street, Montreal, QC H3A 2B4, Canada. *T:* (514) 3988503, *Fax:* (514) 3988540.

MILNER, David; *see* Milner, A. D.

MILNER, Rt Rev. Ronald James; Bishop Suffragan of Burnley, 1988–93; Hon. Assistant Bishop, diocese of Southwell and Nottingham (formerly diocese of Southwell), since 1994; *b* 16 May 1927; *s* of Maurice and Muriel Milner; *m* 1950, Audrey Cynthia Howard; two *s* two *d* (and one *d* decd). *Educ:* Hull Grammar School; Pembroke Coll., Cambridge (MA); Wycliffe Hall, Oxford. Ordained deacon, 1953, priest, 1954; Succentor, Sheffield Cathedral, 1953–58; Vicar: Westwood, Coventry, 1958–64; St James, Fletchamstead, Coventry, 1964–70; Rector of St Mary's, Southampton, 1970–73; Rector of the Southampton Team Ministry, 1973–83; Archdeacon of Lincoln, 1983–88. *Recreations:* ornithology, walking, music. *Address:* 7 Crafts Way, Southwell, Notts NG25 0BL.

MILNER, Dr Simon Trevor; Director of Policy, UK, Middle East and Africa, Facebook, since 2014; *b* 23 April 1967; *s* of Trevor Winston Milner and Christine Mary Milner; *m* 1991, Sarah Wells; two *s* one *d*. *Educ:* Bradford Grammar Sch.; Wadham Coll., Oxford (BA Hons Hist. and Econs); London Sch. of Econs (MSc Industrial Relns, PhD Industrial Relns 1993). London School of Economics: Res. Officer, Centre for Econ. Performance, 1990–94; Lectr, Dept of Industrial Relns, 1994–95; Sec., Commn on Public Policy and British Business, IPPR, 1995–97; Sen. Advr, Policy and Planning, 1997–99, Secretary, 2000–05, BBC; BT plc: Hd, Ext. Relns, Equality of Access Office, 2005–08; Dir, Media and Convergence Policy, 2008–09; Dir, Gp Industry Policy, 2009–11; Dir of Policy, UK and Ireland, Facebook, 2012–14. *Publications:* New Perspectives on Industrial Disputes, 1993. *Recreations:* children, football, camping, festivals.

MILNER, Sir Timothy William Lycett, (Sir Tim), 10th Bt *cr* 1717, of Nun Appleton Hall, Yorkshire; *b* 11 Oct. 1936; *er s* of Sir (George Edward) Mordaunt Milner, 9th Bt and Barbara Audrey (*d* 1951), *d* of Henry Noel Belsham; *S* father, 1995. *Heir: b* Charles Mordaunt Milner [*b* 18 May 1944; *m* 1965, Lady Charlene French, *e d* of 3rd Earl of Ypres; three *s*]. *Address:* c/o Natte Valleij, Box 4, Klapmuts 7607, South Africa.

MILNER-GULLAND, Prof. Robert Rainsford, (Robin), FBA 2002; FSA; Professor of Russian and East European Studies, 1993–2001, Research Professor in Russian, 2001–09, School of Humanities (formerly School of European Studies), University of Sussex, now Professor Emeritus; *b* 24 Feb. 1936; *s* of late Laurence Harry Milner-Gulland and Ruth (Nancy) Milner-Gulland (*née* Bavin); *m* 1966, Alison Margaret Taylor; one *s* two *d*. *Educ:* Westminster Sch. (Schol.); New Coll., Oxford (Schol., then Sen. Schol.; BA Modern Langs, MA); Moscow Univ. University of Sussex: Asst Lectr, then Lectr, Sch. of Eur. Studies, 1962–74; Reader in Russian and E Eur. Studies, 1974–93. Member: Cttee, British Univs Assoc. of Slavists, 1970–78; Sussex Historic Churches Trust, 2002–; Res. Cttee, Sussex Archaeological Soc., 2005–. FSA 1988. Coronation Medal, 1953. *Publications:* Soviet Russian Verse: an anthology, 1964; (with M. Dewhirst) Russian Writing Today, 1974; (with J. Bowlt) An Introduction to Russian Art and Architecture, 1980; Cultural Atlas of Russia, 1989, 2nd edn 1998; (ed and trans.) The Life of Zabolotsky, 1994; The Russians, 1997, 2nd edn 1999; (ed and trans.) Icon and Devotion, by O. Tarasov, 2002; (ed and trans.) Framing Russian Art, by O. Tarasov, 2011; contrib. articles to learned jls on many aspects of Russian studies and on Romanesque art of Sussex. *Recreations:* walking, archaeology. *Address:* Arts Building, University of Sussex, Falmer, Brighton, Sussex BN1 9QN. *T:* (home) (01903) 892602. *E:* r.r.milner-gulland@sussex.ac.uk.

MILNES, Rodney; *see* Blumer, Rodney Milnes.

MILNES COATES, Prof. Sir Anthony (Robert), 4th Bt *cr* 1911; BSc, MB BS, MD; FRCPath, FRCP; Professor of Medical Microbiology, St George's, University of London (formerly St George's Hospital Medical School), since 1989; *b* 8 Dec. 1948; *s* of Sir Robert Edward James Clive Milnes Coates, 3rd Bt, DSO, and Lady Patricia Ethel, *d* of 4th Earl of Listowel; *S* father, 1982; *m* 1978, Harriet Ann Burton; one *s* two *d*. *Educ:* Eton; BSc London 1970; St Thomas's Hospital, London Univ. (MB BS 1973; MD 1984). MRCS 1973; MRCP 1978, FRCP 1998; FRCPath 1999. MRC Trng Res. Fellow, Dept of Bacteriology, RPMS, 1979–82; Sen. Registrar in Bacteriology, RPMS, 1982–84; Sen. Lectr (Hon. Consultant), Dept of Medical Microbiology, London Hosp. Medical Coll., 1984–90. Councillor, 1980–, Mayor, 2002–03, Royal Borough of Kensington and Chelsea. *Heir: s* Thomas Anthony Milnes Coates, *b* 19 Nov. 1986. *Address:* Hereford Cottage, 135 Gloucester Road, SW7 4TH. *Club:* Brooks's.

MILNOR, (Margaret) Dusa; *see* McDuff, M. D.

MILROY, Prof. (Ann) Lesley, PhD; Fellow, Faculty of Linguistics and Philology (formerly Centre for Linguistics and Philology), University of Oxford, since 2005; Hans Kurath Collegiate Professor of Linguistics, University of Michigan, 2000–05, now Professor Emerita; *b* 5 March 1944; *d* of Thomas Keddie Cross and Janet Elizabeth Cross; *m* 1965, Prof. James R. D. Milroy; three *s*. *Educ:* Univ. of Manchester (BA 1st Cl. Hons English 1965; MA 1967); Univ. of Belfast (PhD 1979). Various lecturing posts, Ulster Poly., 1972–82; Sen. Simon Research Fellow, Univ. of Manchester, 1982–83; University of Newcastle upon Tyne: Lectr in Linguistics, 1983–85; Sen. Lectr, 1985–88; Prof. of Sociolinguistics, 1988–98 (on leave of absence, 1994–98); Prof. of Linguistics, Univ. of Michigan, 1994–2000. Vis. Fellow, Univ. of Canterbury, Christchurch, NZ, 1992. *Publications:* Language and Social Networks, 1980, 2nd edn 1987; Observing and Analysing Natural Language, 1987; (with J. Milroy) Authority in Language: investigating language prescription and standardisation, 1987, 4th edn 2012; (with R. Lesser) Linguistics and Aphasia: psycholinguistic and pragmatic aspects of intervention, 1993; (ed with J. Milroy) Real English: the grammar of English dialects in the British Isles, 1993; (ed with P. Muysken) One Speaker, Two Languages: cross-disciplinary perspectives on codeswitching, 1995; (with M. Gordon) Sociolinguistics: method and interpretation, 2003; contrib. articles to learned jls. *Recreations:* swimming, walking, reading. *Address:* Stable Cottage, Hempton Road, Deddington, Oxon OX15 0TL.

MILROY, Very Rev. Dominic Liston, OSB; MA; Headmaster, Ampleforth College, 1980–92; *b* 18 April 1932; *s* of Adam Liston Milroy and Clarita Burns. *Educ:* Ampleforth Coll.; St Benet's Hall, Oxford (1st Cl. Mod. Langs, MA). Entered Ampleforth Abbey, 1950; teaching staff, Ampleforth Coll., 1957–74; Head of Mod. Langs, 1963–74; Housemaster, 1964–74; Prior of Internat. Benedictine Coll. of S Anselmo, Rome, 1974–79. Chm., HMC, 1992. Mem., Chevetogne Gp (Eur. Monasticism), 1993–2010. Hon. Prior, Chester Cathedral, 1995–. Chm., Ampleforth RC Primary Sch., 1996–2010. *Address:* Ampleforth Abbey, York YO62 4EN. *T:* (01439) 766714.

MILROY, Lesley; *see* Milroy, A. L.

MILROY, Lisa Katharine, RA 2005; painter; Head of Graduate Painting, Slade Sch. of Fine Art, University College London, since 2009; *b* Vancouver, 16 Jan. 1959; *d* of Reginald Charles Milroy and Leona Vera Milroy (*née* Demchuk); *m* 2011, Lewis Biggs, *qv*. *Educ:* St Martin's Sch. of Art; Goldsmiths' Coll., Univ. of London (BA 1st Cl. Hons Fine Arts 1982). *Solo exhibitions* include: Nicola Jacobs Gall., London, 1984, 1986, 1988; Cartier Art Foundn, Paris, 1984; John Berggruen Gall., San Francisco, 1989, 1992; Kunsthalle Bern, 1990; Galerie Luis Campaña, Frankfurt, 1991, Cologne, 1993, 1997, 2003; Waddington Galls, London, 1993, 1998; Galerie Jennifer Flay, Paris, 1993, 1996, 1999; Gall. Shoko Nagai, Tokyo, Kyoto City Univ. of Arts, 1994; British Sch. at Rome, 1995; Travel Paintings, Chisenhale Gall., London, Ikon Gall., Birmingham, Fruitmarket, Edinburgh, 1995–96; Alan Cristea Gall., London, 1998, 2000, 2003, 2005, 2009; Sadler's Wells Th., London, 2000; Tate Gall., Liverpool, 2001; Galerie Xippas, Paris, 2005, 2007; New Art Centre Sculpture Park and Gall., Roche Court, Wilts, Galerie Lelong, Zürich, 2006, 2009; Ikon Gall., Birmingham, 2007; *group exhibitions* include: Sydney Biennale, 1986, 1998; John Moores Liverpool Exhibns, Walker Art Gall., Liverpool, 1985, 1987, 1989, 2002, 2004; Carnegie Internat., 1991; Tate Gall., 1992, 1995; Calouste Gulbenkian Foundn, Lisbon, 1992, 1997; Vienna and Hamburg, 1993; Scottish Nat. Gall. of Modern Art, Edinburgh, 1995; Tate Gall., Liverpool, 1996, 1998; Whitechapel Art Gall., 2000; Jerwood Space, London, 2002; Galerie Lelong, Zürich, 2004; Tate Modern, 2004; Today Mus., Beijing, 2009; *work in public collections* including: Arts Council of GB; British Council; Calouste Gulbenkian Foundn, Lisbon; Contemporary Art Soc.; Metropolitan Mus. of Art, NY; Tate Gall., London; Tokyo Metropolitan Art Collection. Advr, Rijksakademie Van Beeldende Kunsten, Amsterdam, 1995–. Artist Trustee, Tate Gall., 2013–; Trustee, Nat. Gall., 2015–. 1st prize, John Moores, 1987; D&AD Silver Award for Royal Mail Millennium Stamp, 2000. *Recreation:* hiking. *Address:* c/o Royal Academy of Arts, Burlington House, Piccadilly, W1J 0BD.

MILSOM, Stroud Francis Charles; QC 1985; FBA 1967; Professor of Law, Cambridge University, 1976–90; Fellow of St John's College, Cambridge, since 1976; *b* 2 May 1923; *yr s* of late Harry Lincoln Milsom and Isobel Vida Collins; *m* 1955, Irène (*d* 1998), *d* of late Witold Szereszewski, Wola Krysztoporska, Poland. *Educ:* Charterhouse; Trinity Coll., Cambridge. Admiralty, 1944–45. Called to the Bar, Lincoln's Inn, 1947, Hon. Bencher, 1970; Commonwealth Fund Fellow, Univ. of Pennsylvania, 1947–48; Yorke Prize, Univ. of Cambridge, 1948; Prize Fellow, Fellow and Lectr, Trinity Coll., Cambridge, 1948–55; Fellow, Tutor and Dean, New Coll., Oxford, 1956–64; Prof. of Legal History, London Univ., 1964–76. Selden Society: Literary Dir, 1964–80; Pres., 1985–88. Mem., Royal Commn on Historical Manuscripts, 1975–98. Vis. Lectr, New York Univ. Law Sch., several times, 1958–70; Visiting Professor: Yale Law Sch., several times, 1968–; Harvard Law Sch. and Dept of History, 1973; Charles Inglis Thomson Prof., Colorado Univ. Law Sch., 1977. Maitland Meml Lectr, Cambridge, 1972; Addison Harris Meml Lectr, Indiana Univ. Law Sch., 1974; Vis. Prof. and Wilfred Fullagar Lectr, Monash Univ., 1981; Ford's Lectr, Oxford, 1986; Carpentier Lectr, Columbia Univ., 1995. Foreign Mem., Amer. Phil Soc., 1984. Hon. LLD: Glasgow, 1981; Chicago, 1985; Cambridge, 2003. Ames Prize, Harvard, 1972; Swiney Prize, RSA/RCP, 1974. *Publications:* Novae Narrationes (introd., trans. and notes), 1963; introd. reissue Pollock and Maitland, History of English Law, 1968; Historical Foundations of the Common Law, 1969, 2nd edn 1981; The Legal Framework of English Feudalism, 1976; Studies in the History of the Common Law (collected papers), 1985; A Natural History of the Common Law, 2003. *Address:* St John's College, Cambridge CB2 1TP; 113 Grantchester Meadows, Cambridge CB3 9JN. *T:* (01223) 354100. *Club:* Athenæum.

MILTON, Rt Hon. Anne (Frances); PC 2015; MP (C) Guildford, since 2005; Treasurer of HM Household (Deputy Chief Whip), since 2015; *b* 3 Nov. 1955; *d* of late Patrick Turner and Nesta Turner; *m* Dr Graham Henderson; three *s* one *d*. *Educ:* Haywards Heath Grammar Sch.; St Bartholomew's Hospital Sch. of Nursing (RGN 1977). Staff Nurse, 1977–78, Research Nurse, 1978–81, St Bartholomew's Hosp.; District Nursing Sister: City and Hackney HA, 1981–83; St Thomas' Hosp., London, 1983–85; Med. Advr on Housing for E London and City HA, 1985–2000; self-employed med. advr to social housing providers,

2000–05. Parly Under-Sec. of State, DoH, 2010–12; a Lord Comr of HM Treasury (Govt Whip), 2012–14; Vice-Chamberlain of HM Household (Govt Whip), 2014–15. *Publications:* contrib. Lancet. *Recreations:* gardening, reading, music. *Address:* House of Commons, SW1A 0AA. *T:* (020) 7219 8392. *E:* anne.milton.mp@parliament.uk.

MILTON, Maj.-Gen. Anthony Arthur, CB 2002; OBE 1995; Commandant General Royal Marines, and Commander United Kingdom Amphibious Forces, 2002–04; *b* 19 Aug. 1949; *s* of W. W. Milton; *m* 1972, Nova Mary Biscombe; three *d. Educ:* King Edward VI Sch., Chelmsford; St John's Coll., Cambridge (MPhil Internat. Relns; Fellow Commoner, 2007). Commnd Royal Marines, 1967; Subaltern, 42, 45 and 40 Commando, serving in Far East, Norway, Caribbean, Cyprus and NI, 1970–76; exchange tour with USMC, 1976–78; CTC, Lympstone, 1978–81; Army Staff Coll., 1982; MoD, 1983–84; Equerry to the Duke of Edinburgh, 1983–84; Co. Comdr, 42 Commando, 1985–86; COS, 3 Commando Bde, 1987–89; MoD, 1991–92; CO, 40 Commando, Norway and NI, 1992–94; rcds 1995; Comdr, 3 Commando Bde, 1995–97; Dir, N Atlantic and Western Europe, 1997–98; ADC to the Queen, 1997–99; Dir Gen., Jt Doctrine and Concepts, MoD, 1999–2002. SW Regl Chm., Campaign to Protect Rural England, 2009–15. Vis. Fellow, Cambridge Univ., 2007. FRGS 1992. Freeman, City of London, 2004. Liveryman, Plaisterers' Co., 2004. *Publications:* academic articles. *Recreations:* travel, music, mountains. *Club:* Army and Navy.

MILTON, Derek Francis, CMG 1990; HM Diplomatic Service, retired; student of Polish affairs; *b* 11 Nov. 1935; *s* of Francis Henry Milton and Florence Elizabeth Maud Kirby; *m* 1st, 1960, Helge Kahle; two *s*; 2nd, 1977, Catherine Walmsley. *Educ:* Preston Manor County Grammar Sch., Wembley; Manchester Univ. (BA Hons Politics and Modern History, 1959). RAF, 1954–56. Colonial Office, 1959–63; Asst Private Sec. to Commonwealth and Colonial Sec., 1962–64; Commonwealth Prime Ministers' Meeting Secretariat, 1964; First Secretary: CRO (later FO), 1964–67; UK Mission to UN, New York, 1967–71; Rome, 1972–75; FCO, 1975–77; Counsellor: Civil Service Res. Fellow, Glasgow Univ., 1977–78; Caracas, 1978–79; Dept of Trade, 1980–82; Overseas Inspectorate, 1982–84; Minister-Counsellor, Mexico City, 1984–87; RCDS, 1988; High Comr, Kingston, Jamaica, and non-resident Ambassador to Haiti, 1989–95. Americas Res. Gp, Res. Analysts, FCO, 1995–99 (on contract). *Recreations:* QPR Football Club, travel, swimming. *Address:* 31 Park Road, Beckenham BR3 1QG.

MILVERTON, 2nd Baron *cr* 1947, of Lagos and of Clifton; **Rev. Fraser Arthur Richard Richards;** Rector of Christian Malford with Sutton Benger and Tytherton Kellaways, 1967–93; *b* 21 July 1930; *s* of 1st Baron Milverton, GCMG, and Noelle Benda, *d* of Charles Basil Whitehead; *S* father, 1978; *m* 1957, Mary Dorothy, BD, *d* of late Leslie Fly, ARCM, Corsham, Wilts; two *d. Educ:* De Carteret Prep. Sch., Jamaica; Ridley Coll., Ontario; Clifton Coll.; Egerton Agric. Coll., Kenya; Bishops' Coll., Cheshunt. Royal Signals, 1949–50; Kenya Police, 1952–53. Deacon 1957, priest 1958, dio. Rochester; Curate: Beckenham, 1957–59; St John Baptist, Sevenoaks, 1959–60; Great Bookham, 1960–63; Vicar of Okewood with Forest Green, 1963–67. Chaplain, Wilts ACF, 1968–81. Trustee and Dir, Voice (UK) Ltd. Former Gov., Clifton Coll. *Recreations:* family, reading, current affairs and history; enjoys music and walking; interested in tennis, swimming, cricket and Rugby Union. *Heir: b* Hon. Michael Hugh Richards [*b* 1 Aug. 1936; *m* 1960, Edna Leonie (*d* 2001), *y d* of Col Leo Steveni, OBE, MC; one *s*].

MILWARD, Timothy Michael, FRCS; Consultant Plastic Surgeon to Leicester Royal Infirmary, Pilgrim Hospital, Boston, and Lincoln County Hospital, 1976–2002, now Emeritus; *b* 24 March 1937; *s* of Francis John and Rosemary Gwendoline Milward; *m* 1970, Susan Isabel; four *d* (incl. twins). *Educ:* Rugby Sch.; Clare Coll., Cambridge (MB, BCh, MA); St Thomas' Hosp. President: British Assoc. of Aesthetic Plastic Surgeons, 1987–88; BAPS, 1996; Mem., Senate of Surgery of GB and Ireland, 1995–98. Fellow, Acad. of Experts. *Publications:* contrib. British Jl of Plastic Surgery. *Recreations:* squash, tennis, walking with friends, silversmith. *Address:* Spire Leicester Hospital, Gartree Road, Leicester LE2 2FF. *T:* (0116) 265 3678, *Fax:* (0116) 265 3679.

MIMPRISS, Peter Hugh Trevor, CVO 2001; Charities Adviser to HRH the Prince of Wales, 2004–06; *b* 22 Aug. 1943; *s* of Hugh Trevor Baber Mimpriss and Gwyneth Mary Mimpriss (*née* Bartley); *m* 1st, 1971, Hilary Ann Reed (marr. diss. 1992); two *d*; 2nd, 1992, Elisabeth Lesley Molle. *Educ:* Sherborne Sch. Admitted solicitor, 1967. Joined Allen & Overy, 1968; Partner, 1972–2002; univ. solicitor, Univ. of London, 1995–2002; Dir, Edmond J. Safra Philanthropic Foundn, 2002–04. Chairman: Charity Law Assoc., 1992–97; Chariguard Gp of Common Investment Funds, 1994–2000. Director: Leeds Castle Foundn, 1980–2006; Chatham Historic Dockyard Trust, 1986–2000; Weston Park Foundn, 1986–2001; Lawcare (formerly Solcare), 1997–2002; PYBT, 1997–99; Prince's Regeneration Trust, 2002–08; Member, Council: Prince's Trust, 1998–2007; King George Jubilee Trust, 2000–06; Queen's Trust (formerly Queen's Silver Jubilee Trust), 2000–; Trustee: Inst. of Philanthropy, 2000–07; World Trade Centre Disaster Fund, 2001–06; Prince of Wales Arts and Kids Foundn, later Prince's Foundn for Children and the Arts, 2004–08; Prince's Sch. of Traditional Arts, 2005–08; Autism Speaks (formerly Nat. Alliance of Autism Res.), 2005–08 (Dep. Chm., 2005–08); Sir Edward Heath Charitable Foundn, 2005–10; Jewish Mus., 2006–11; John Ellerman Foundn, 2009–13; St Helena's Hospice, 2012–15; Medical Detection Dogs, 2015–. Hon. DCL Durham, 2003. *Recreations:* walking, maritime history, vintage cars, collecting books. *Clubs:* Athenæum, Garrick.

MIMS, Prof. Cedric Arthur, MD, FRCPath; Professor of Microbiology, Guy's Hospital Medical School, London, 1972–90; *b* 9 Dec. 1924; *s* of A. H. and Irene Mims; *m* 1952, Valerie Vickery; two *s* two *d. Educ:* Mill Hill Sch.; University Coll. London (BSc (Zool)); Middlesex Hosp. Med. Sch. (MB, BS, MD). Medical Research Officer, East African Virus Research Inst., Entebbe, Uganda, 1953–56; Research Fellow and Professorial Fellow, John Curtin Sch. of Med. Research, Australian Nat. Univ., Canberra, 1957–72; Rockefeller Foundn Fellow, Children's Hosp. Med. Centre, Boston, USA, 1963–64; Visiting Fellow, Wistar Inst., Philadelphia, USA, 1969–70. *Publications:* (jtly) The Biology of Animal Viruses, 1974; Mims' Pathogenesis of Infectious Disease, 1976, 5th edn 2000; (with D. O. White) Viral Pathogenesis and Immunology, 1984; (jtly) Medical Microbiology, 1993, 4th edn 2008; When We Die, 1998; The War Within Us, 2000; Love and Old Age, 2003; Fouling the Nest, 2006; The Story of Food, 2008; The Story of Childbirth, 2009; Celebrating the Human Hand, 2010; Lying, Walking, Running, 2014; Mightier Than the Sword: the story of the penis, 2014; The Enchanting World of Smell, 2014; numerous papers on the pathogenesis of virus infections. *Address:* 1/10 Murray Crescent, Griffith, ACT 2603, Australia.

MINA, Jacqueline Kathleen, OBE 2012; goldsmith and jewellery designer; *b* 5 Feb. 1942; *d* of John Frederick Bartlett and Kay Crome and step *d* of Emanuel Hurwitz; *m* 1966, Michael Christou Minas; one *d. Educ:* Hornsey Coll. of Art and Crafts; Royal Coll. of Art (DesRCA 1965). Has worked from own studio/workshop, 1965–. Part-time teaching posts include: Harrow Sch. of Art, 1965–70; Farnham Sch. of Art and Design, 1965–75; RCA, 1972–94; Leicester Coll. of Art, 1975–84. External examiner: Edinburgh Coll. of Art, 1989–91; Glasgow Sch. of Art, 1992–96; Bucks UC, 1997–2000. Member: Jury, Jerwood Prize for Applied Arts (Jewellery), 2007; Selection Panel, Contemp. Applied Arts. Mem., Assoc. for Contemporary Jewellery, 1997. FRSA 1999. Freeman, 1985, Lady Liveryman, 1995, Co. of Goldsmiths. Trustee, Bishopsland Educnl Trust, 2001. Work in exhibitions in UK, Europe and USA, including: Oxford Gall., 1980; Byzantium, NY, 1985; V&A Mus., 1985; Goldsmiths' Hall, London, 1997; Crafts Council Shop at V&A, 2000; World Craft Forum, Kanazawa, Japan, 2003; Collect, annually, V&A Mus., 2004–08, Saatchi Gall., London, 2008–11; Orgold, Flow Gall., 2004, Scottish Gall., Ruthin Crafts Centre, Wales, 2005; L'or, Bijoux d'Europe, France, 2005; The Goldmark, Thomas Goode, London, 2006; Diamonds, Contemp. Applied Arts, London, 2008, 2010; Kath Libbert Jewellery Gall., Salts Mill, 2009; Cox & Power, London, 2009; V&A Mus., 2009; Dovecot Gall., Edinburgh, 2010; Goldsmiths' Hall (retrospective), 2011; Contemp. Applied Arts, Scottish Gall., Ruthin Craft Centre (solo touring exhibn), 2011; Lesley Craze Gall., London, 2014; Out of Sight, Contemp. Applied Arts, London, 2014; Masters of Modern Jewellery, Beetles+Huxley Gall., London, 2014; group exhibitions: Silver, Savile Club, 2013; Contemp. Silver, Drapers' Hall, 2014; Collect, Saatchi Gall., 2014; Goldsmiths' Fair, 2014; 30 Years in the Making, Lesley Craze Gall., London, 2014; A Showcase of New Work, Scottish Gall., Edinburgh, 2015; Ringing the Changes, Victoria Sewart Gall., Plymouth, 2015; Premio Internazionale Mario Pinton, Oratoriio di San Rocco, Padua, Italy, 2015; work in public collections in UK and USA, including: Cooper Hewitt Mus., NY; Goldsmiths' Hall; Nat. Mus. of Scotland, Edinburgh; V&A Mus.; Crafts Council, London; Cleveland Contemp. Jewellery Collection, Middlesbrough Inst. of Modern Art; Mus. of Art & Design, NY City. Jerwood Prize for Applied Arts (Jewellery), Jerwood Foundn, 2000. *Publications:* (contrib.) V&A 150th Anniversary Album, 2007; contrib. articles to jls incl. Crafts mag., Jewellery Studies, Findings. *Recreations:* music (appreciation), contemporary dance (appreciation), gardening, cooking, swimming, grannying. *Address:* c/o The Goldsmiths' Company, Goldsmiths' Hall, Foster Lane, EC2V 6BN. *T:* (020) 7606 7010, *Fax:* (020) 7606 1511.

MINCHIN, Timothy David; musician, composer, songwriter, actor and comedian; *b* Northampton, 7 Oct. 1975; *s* of Dr David Minchin and Ros Minchin; *m* 2002, Sarah Gardiner; one *s* one *d. Educ:* Univ. of Western Australia (BA Eng. and Theatre 1995); Western Australia Acad. of Performing Arts (Dip. Contemporary Music 1998). Comedy shows include: Dark Side, Melbourne Internat. Comedy Festival, Edinburgh Fringe Fest. (Perrier Award for Best Newcomer), 2005; Ready For This?, Edinburgh Fringe Fest., 2008, UK tour, 2008–09, Australia and NZ tour, 2009; Tim Minchin and the Heritage Orchestra, UK tour, 2010–11, Australia tour, 2011; Tim Minchin vs the Orchestra, Australia tour, 2012; appearances on major UK, Australian and US TV shows. Composer of music and lyrics for Matilda The Musical, RSC, 2010, transf. West End, 2011, NY, 2013, Sydney, 2016. Performer: (as Judas Iscariot), Jesus Christ Superstar, O2 Arena, 2012, Australian tour, 2013; Rosencrantz and Guildenstern are Dead, Sydney Th. Co., 2013. *Publications:* (with D. C. Turner and T. King) Storm, 2014. *Address:* c/o Caroline Chignell, PBJ Management, 22 Rathbone Street, W1T 1LG. *T:* (020) 7287 1112.

MINDHAM, Prof. Richard Hugh Shiels, MD; FRCP, FRCPsych; Nuffield Professor of Psychiatry, 1977–2000, now Emeritus, and Dean, Faculty of Medicine, Dentistry and Health, 1996–97, University of Leeds; *b* 25 March 1935; *s* of Thomas Raper Mindham and Winifred Gertrude Mindham; *m* 1971, Barbara Harris Reid; one *s* one *d. Educ:* Guy's Hosp. Medical Sch.; Inst. of Psychiatry, Univ. of London; Univ. of Leeds (MA Hist. and Theory of Architecture 2004). MD 1974; FRCPsych 1977; FRCPE 1978; FRCP 2000. Nottingham University Medical School: Sen. Lectr in Psychiatry, 1972–76; Reader, 1976–77; Dean of Postgrad. Studies, Univ. of Leeds, 1994–96. Vis. Prof., Johns Hopkins Univ., 1982. Chief Examr, RCPsych, 1995–98. *Publications:* papers on psychiatry, psychopharmacology and Parkinson's disease. *Recreations:* music, architecture, walking. *E:* r.h.s.mindham@gmail.com. *Clubs:* Royal Society of Medicine; Western (Glasgow).

MINFORD, Prof. (Anthony) Patrick (Leslie), CBE 1996; Professor of Applied Economics, Cardiff Business School, Cardiff University, since 1997; *b* 17 May 1943; *s* of Leslie Mackay Minford and Patricia Mary (*née* Sale); *m* 1970, Rosemary Irene Allcorn; two *s* one *d. Educ:* Horris Hill; Winchester Coll. (scholar); Balliol Coll., Oxford (schol.; BA); London Sch. of Economics (grad. studies; MScEcon, PhD). Economic Asst, Min. of Overseas Development, London, 1966; Economist, Min. of Finance, Malawi, 1967–69; Economic Adviser: Director's Staff, Courtaulds Ltd, 1970–71; HM Treasury, 1971–73, and HM Treasury Delegn in Washington, 1973–74; Visiting Hallsworth Fellow, Manchester Univ., 1974–75; Editor, NIESR Review, 1975–76; Edward Gonner Prof. of Applied Econs, Liverpool Univ., 1976–97. Vis. Prof., Cardiff Business Sch., 1993–97. Dir, Merseyside Develt Corp., 1988–89. Mem., Monopolies and Mergers Commn, 1990–96. Mem., HM Treasury's Panel of Economic Forecasters, 1993–96. Mem. Bd, WNO, 1993–98. *Publications:* Substitution Effects, Speculation and Exchange Rate Stability, 1978; (jtly) Unemployment—Cause and Cure, 1983, 2nd edn 1985; (jtly) Rational Expectations and the New Macroeconomics, 1983; (jtly) The Housing Morass, 1987; The Supply Side Revolution in Britain, 1991; (jtly) The Cost of Europe, 1992; Rational Expectations Macroeconomics, 1992; Markets Not Stakes, 1998; (jtly) Britain and Europe: choices for change, 1999; (jtly) Advanced Macroeconomics: a primer, 2002; (jtly) Money Matters: essays in honour of Alan Walters, 2004; (jtly) Should Britain Leave the EU?: an economic analysis of a troubled relationship, 2005; An Agenda for Tax Reform, 2006; articles in learned jls on monetary and internat. economics. *Address:* Cardiff Business School, Cardiff University, Cardiff CF10 3EU.

MINGAY, (Frederick) Ray, CMG 1992; Chief Executive, Trade Development Services, since 1997; consultant to various companies and other organisations; *b* 7 July 1938; *s* of Cecil Stanley and Madge Elizabeth Mingay; *m* 1963, Joan Heather Roberts (*d* 2001); three *s* one *d. Educ:* Tottenham Grammar Sch.; St Catharine's Coll., Cambridge (Open Exhibnr; MA); London Univ. (Postgrad. Pub. Admin.); Min. of Educn Cert. of Teaching Competence. Nat. Service, 1959–61: 2nd Lieut RAEC; attached RIF, Kenya. Administration, St Thomas' Hosp., 1961; schoolmaster, 1961–62; Min. of Transport, 1962–64; BoT, 1964; Chrysler (UK) Ltd, 1968–70; Consul (Commercial), Milan, 1970–73; Asst Sec., Dept of Trade, 1973–78; Counsellor (Commercial), Washington, 1978–83; Under Secretary: Mechanical and Electrical Engrg Div., DTI, 1983–86; Regl Investment and Develt Div., DTI, 1986–88; Consul-Gen., Chicago, 1988–92; Head of Overseas Trade Div. DTI, 1992–93; Dir-Gen., Export Promotion, DTI, 1993–97 (concurrently Asst Under Sec. of State, FCO (Jt Export Promotion Directorate), 1993–96). Mem., Business Appts Panel, later Public Appts Assessor, DTI, subseq. BERR, then BIS, 2002–12; Ind. Mediator, 2006–; OCPA Accredited Ind. Public Appts Assessor, 2008–12. Dir, Cove Holidays Ltd, 1977–80; non-executive Director: Aalco, 1983–87; Amari World Steel, 1987–88. Mem., BOTB, 1993–97. Mem., Mid-West Marshall Scholar Selection Cttee, 1988–92. Churchill Fellow, Westminster Coll., Fulton, Mo, 1991. Trustee, St Andrew's Youth Club, Westminster, 2008–. FCMI; FRSA. Hon. Citizen, Minneapolis, 1990. *Club:* Reform.

MINGHELLA, Loretta Caroline Rose, OBE 2010; Chief Executive (formerly Director), Christian Aid, since 2010; *b* Isle of Wight, 4 March 1962; *d* of Edward Minghella and late Gloria Alberta Minghella, MBE; *m* 1992, Christopher Parsons; one *s* one *d. Educ:* Medina High Sch.; Clare Coll., Cambridge (BA Hons Law 1984); Coll. of Law. Admitted solicitor, 1987. Articled clerk, then solicitor, Kingsley Napley, 1985–89; Legal Advr, DTI, 1989–90; Securities and Investments Board, later Financial Services Authority: Asst Dir, 1990–93; Hd, Enforcement Law and Policy, 1993–98; Hd, Enforcement Law, Policy and Internat. Co-operation, 1998–2004; Chief Exec., Financial Services Compensation Scheme, 2004–10. Chm., Enforcement Cttee, IOSCO, 2003–04. Trustee, Disasters Emergency Cttee, 2010–. *Publications:* (jtly) Blackstone's Guide to the Financial Services and Markets Act 2000, 2001. *Recreations:* singing, theatre, ice cream tasting. *Address:* Christian Aid, PO Box 100, SE1 7RT. *T:* (020) 7523 2356.

MINGINISH, Hon. Lord; Roderick John MacLeod; Chairman, Scottish Land Court, and President, Lands Tribunal for Scotland, since 2014; *b* Uig, Isle of Skye, 7 Dec. 1952; *s* of Roderick MacLeod and Chirsty Mary MacLeod (*née* Morrison); *m* 1980, Lorna Jane

Robertson; one *s*. *Educ:* Portnalong Junior Secondary Sch.; Portree High Sch.; Univ. of Edinburgh (LLB Hons 1975). Admitted Solicitor, 1979, Advocate, 1994; Sheriff, 2000; Dep. Chm., Scottish Land Court, 2006–14; QC (Scot.) 2013. Chm., Bd of Dirs, Sabhal Mòr Ostaig, 2005–15. *Recreations:* walking, cycling, bird watching. *Address:* Scottish Land Court, George House, 126 George Street, Edinburgh EH2 4HH. *T:* (0131) 271 4357.

MINGOS, Prof. (David) Michael (Patrick), DPhil; FRS 1992; CChem, FRSC; Principal, St Edmund Hall, Oxford, 1999–2009; Professor of Chemistry, University of Oxford, 2000–09, now Emeritus; *b* 6 Aug. 1944; *s* of Vasso Mingos and Rose Enid Billie Hayes (*née* Griffiths); *m* 1967, Stacey Mary Hosken; one *s* one *d*. *Educ:* Univ. of Manchester (BSc); Univ. of Sussex (DPhil). CChem 1983; FRSC 1983. Fulbright Fellow, Northwestern Univ., 1968–70; ICI Fellow, Sussex Univ., 1970–71; Lectr, QMC, 1971–76; University of Oxford: Lectr, 1976–90; Reader, 1990–92; Fellow, Keble Coll., 1976–92 and by special election, 1993 (Hon. Fellow, 1999); Univ. Assessor, 1991–92; Sir Edward Frankland BP Prof. of Inorganic Chemistry, Imperial Coll., Univ. of London, 1992–99; Dean, Royal Coll. of Sci., 1996–99. Dist. Prof., Xi'an Petroleum Inst., China, 1994–; Wilhelm Manchot Res. Prof. and prize, Munich, 1995; Vis. Prof., Imperial Coll., London, 1999–2002; Univ. of Auckland Foundn Visitor, 2000. Univ. of Sussex 50th Anniv. Fellow, 2012. Lee Meml Lecture, Univ. of Chicago, 1997. Vice Pres., Dalton Div., RSC, 1993–96. Gov., Harrow Sch., 1994–2004. Hon. DSc: UMIST, 2000; Sussex, 2001. Corday Morgan Medal, 1980, Tilden Medal, 1988, Chemistry of Noble Metals Award, 1983, RSC; M. J. Collins Prize, for innovation in microwave chemistry, CEM Corp., 1996; Alexander von Humboldt Stiftung Forschungspreis, 1999. Regl Editor, Jl of Organometallic Chem., 1996–2006; Member, Editorial Board: Transition Metal Chem., 1975–2006; Structure and Bonding, 1983– (Man. Ed., 2002–); New Jl of Chem., 1986–96; Jl of Organometallic Chem., 1991–; Chemical Soc. Rev., 1992–97; Advances in Inorganic Chem., 1992–2000; Inorganic Chemistry, 1997–99. *Publications:* Introduction to Cluster Chemistry, 1990; Essentials of Inorganic Chemistry 1, 1995; Essential Trends in Inorganic Chemistry, 1997; (ed) Structural and Electronic Paradigms in Cluster Chemistry, 1997; Essentials of Inorganic Chemistry 2, 1998; (ed) Liquid Crystals, Vols 1 and 2, 1999; (ed) Supramolecular Assembly via Hydrogen Bonds, Vols 1 and 2, 2004; (Ed.-in-Chief) Comprehensive Organo-metallic Chemistry III, Vols 1–13, 2007; (ed and contrib.) Nitrosyl Complexes in Inorganic Chemistry, Biochemistry and Medicine, vols 1 and 2, 2014; (ed and contrib.) Gold Clusters, Colloids and Nano-particles, vols 1 and 2, 2014; contribs to jls of learned socs. *Recreations:* cricket, tennis, walking. *Address:* Inorganic Chemistry Laboratory, University of Oxford, South Parks Road, Oxford OX1 3QR. *T:* (01865) 272316. *E:* michael.mingos@seh.ox.ac.uk.

MINHINNICK, Dame Ngâneko (Kaihau), DNZM 2013; JP; Guardian of Ngati Te Ata tribe, New Zealand, since 1981; *b* Waiuku, Aotearoa, NZ, 16 Aug. 1939; *d* of Henare and Wheriko Kaihau; *m* 1956, Eden Minhinnick; four *s* two *d* (and one *s* decd). *Educ:* Waiuku High Sch. Kaitiaki (protector) of Tahuna Marae, 1957–; Sec., Tahuna Marae Trustees, 1957–. Took Manukau Claim (for protection of natural resources of Manukau Harbour) to Waitangi Tribunal, 1985; travelled to UN, to ensure, at internat. level, that indigenous people were heard by decision-makers, 1987–96; activist for conservation and Maori rights, 1997–2003. Mem., Auckland Regl Council, 1986–88. Mem., NZ Conservation Authy, 2000–. JP Waiuku 1970. *Address:* 78 King Street, Waiuku 2123, New Zealand. *T:* (9) 2357513. *Clubs:* Whanau, Marae, Manawhenua.

MINKOWSKI, Prof. Christopher Zand, PhD; Boden Professor of Sanskrit, University of Oxford, since 2005; Fellow of Balliol College, Oxford, since 2005; *b* 13 May 1953; *s* of late Prof. Jan M. Minkowski and Anne Shreve Minkowski. *Educ:* Gilman Sch., Baltimore; Harvard Coll. (AB English 1975; Harvard Nat. Schol.; Editl Bd, Lampoon); Univ. of Delhi (Dip. Hindi 1976); Harvard Univ. (AM 1980; PhD Sanskrit and Indian Studies 1986). Vis. Asst Prof. of Asian Langs and Lits, Univ. of Iowa, 1984–85; Instructor in Sanskrit, Brown Univ., 1985–87; Jun. Res. Fellow in Indology, Wolfson Coll., Oxford, 1988–89; Asst Prof., then Associate Prof., subseq. Prof., of Asian Studies and Classics, Cornell Univ., 1989–2006. Fulbright Res. Schol., Poona Univ., 1996–97; Mem., Sch. of Historical Studies, Inst. for Advanced Study, Princeton, 2010; Dir d'études invité, École des hautes études en sciences sociales, Paris, 2011; Gastwissenschaftler, Max-Planck-Institut für Wissenschaftsgeschichte, Berlin, 2012. *Publications:* Priesthood in Ancient India, 1991; numerous articles in learned jls on Vedic ritual, religion and literature, Sanskrit epics, hist. of astronomy and cosmology, and intellectual hist. of early Mod. S Asia. *Recreations:* walking, gardening, further adventures in the improbable. *Address:* Balliol College, Oxford OX1 3BJ.

MINN, U Kyaw Zwar; Ambassador of the Republic of the Union of Myanmar to the Court of St James's, since 2013, and (non-resident) to Ireland, Norway, and Sweden, since 2014; *b* Yangon, 2 June 1958; *s* of U Kyaw Min and Daw Ye Ye; *m* 1985, Aye Minn Myat; one *s*. *Educ:* Defence Studies Acad. (BSc); Nat. Defence Coll., Myanmar (MA Defence Studies); Lockland Airforce Base, Texas (Dip. Amer. Eng. Lang.); Fort Lec, Va (Dip. Aerial Delivery and Material Officer Course). Served in Defence Service (Myanmar Army) up to rank of Col, 1977–2008; Minister Counsellor, Min. of Foreign Affairs, 2008–10; Ambassador: to Myanmar Mission, NY, 2010–11; to France, 2011–13, and (non resident) to Andorra, Spain and Swiss Confederation, 2012–13. Dist. Service Medal; Gen. Service Medal; People's War Medal; State Peace and Tranquility Medal; Maing Yan/Me Tha Waw Battle Star; Conquest over Threat Medal; Service Medal; Campaign Star. *Recreations:* painting, golf, socialising. *Address:* Embassy of the Republic of the Union of Myanmar, 19A Charles Street, W1J 5DX. *T:* (020) 7148 0749, *Fax:* (020) 7409 7043. *E:* ambassadoroffice@myanmarembassylondon.com. *Clubs:* Travellers; Brocket Hall Golf.

MINOGUE, (Elizabeth) Ann, (Lady Stevenson of Balmacara); Partner, Macfarlanes LLP, since 2013; *b* Harrogate, 17 Oct. 1955; *d* of John Minogue and Jean Minogue; *m* 1991, Robert Wilfrid, (Wilf), Stevenson (*see* Baron Stevenson of Balmacara); one *s* two *d*. *Educ:* Aylesbury High Sch.; Clare Coll., Cambridge (BA 1977). Admitted solicitor, 1980; Partner: McKenna & Co., then Cameron McKenna, 1985–2001; Linklaters LLP, 2001–09; Ashurst LLP, 2009–13. President: British Council for Offices, 2005–06; City Property Assoc., 2012–14. Governor: London Contemporary Dance Trust, 1998–2004; City Univ., London, 2000–09; London Metropolitan Univ., 2009– (Vice Chair, 2014–). *Publications:* (ed jtly) Construction Law Handbook, subseq. ICE Manual of Construction Law, 2010. *Recreations:* Irish history, Russian, family. *Address:* Macfarlanes LLP, 20 Cursitor Street, EC4A 1LT. *T:* (020) 7849 2912. *E:* ann.minogue@macfarlanes.com.

MINSON, Prof. Anthony Charles, PhD; Professor of Virology, University of Cambridge, 1991–2010, now Emeritus; Fellow of Wolfson College, Cambridge, since 1982; Chairman, Cambridge University Press, 2010–12; *b* 8 Feb. 1944; *s* of Charles Minson and Esney Minson (*née* Lewis); *m* 1976, Jennifer Mary Phillips; one *s* one *d*. *Educ:* Ilford High Sch.; Birmingham Univ. (BSc); Australian Nat. Univ. (PhD 1969). Lectr, Univ. of Birmingham, 1974–76; Res. Fellow, 1976–82, Lectr, 1982–91, Pro-Vice-Chancellor, 2003–09, Univ. of Cambridge. Mem. Council, Soc. of Gen. Microbiol., 1990–93, 2003–06. Mem., Governing Body, Inst. of Animal Health, 1997–2003. Trustee: Animal Health Trust, 2007–; Lister Inst., 2010–. FMedSci 2002. *Publications:* scientific papers on biology and pathogenesis of animal and plant viruses. *Recreation:* sailing. *Address:* Department of Pathology, University of Cambridge, Tennis Court Road, Cambridge CB2 1QP. *T:* (01223) 333690, *Fax:* (01223) 333346. *E:* acm8@admin.cam.ac.uk.

MINTER, Graham Leslie, LVO 1983; HM Diplomatic Service, retired; Associate, Day Associates, since 2011; South America country coordinator, Amnesty International, since 2012; *b* 4 Jan. 1950; *s* of Norman Leslie Minter and Beryl Winifred Minter; *m* 1975, Peter Anne Scott; one *s* two *d*. *Educ:* Orange Hill County Grammar Sch. HM Diplomatic Service, 1968–2005: FCO, 1968–71; Anguilla, 1971–72; Latin American Floater, 1973–75; Asunción, 1975–78; FCO, 1978–79; First Secretary: (Econ.), Mexico City, 1979–84; FCO, 1984–90; Canberra, 1990–94; FCO, 1994–98; Ambassador to Bolivia, 1998–2001; Dep. Hd, Economic Policy Dept, FCO, 2002–04; Gp Hd, Global Business Gp, FCO, 2004–05. Sen. Consultant, Internat. Business Leaders' Forum, 2005–11. *Recreations:* travel, music, walking, reading, genealogy, birdwatching, table tennis, tennis, football. *Address:* Ringlestone, Goudhurst Road, Marden, Kent TN12 9JY.

MINTER, Susan Anne, FCIHort; horticultural consultant, since 2005; *b* Hammersmith, 6 April 1949; *d* of Harry and Norah Minter; civil partnership 2006, Penelope Ruth Hammond. *Educ:* N London Collegiate Sch.; Girton Coll., Cambridge (BA Hons Hist. 1971); Univ. of Calif, Berkeley (Fulbright Travel Schol.). FCIHort (FIHort 2003). Editor of encyclopaedias, Fabbri & Partners, then freelance, 1972–82; Supervisor, Palm House, Royal Botanic Gdns, Kew, 1985–91; Curator, Chelsea Physic Gdn, 1991–2001; Horticultural Dir, Eden Project, 2001–05. Hon. Sec., Chartered Inst. of Horticulture (formerly Inst. of Horticulture), 2007– (Pres., 2010–12). Chair, Herb Soc., 2008–13; Mem., Tender and Ornamental Plants Cttee, RHS, 1992–2012. Trustee: Horniman Mus. and Gdns, 1999–2009 (Mem., Gdns Cttee, 2009–12); Xplore, 2015–. Govt Ambassador for Diversity in Public Appts, 2009–. Devon NHS Health Champion, 2015–. FLS 1991. Veitch Meml Medal, RHS, 2013. *Publications:* The Greatest Glasshouse: the rainforests recreated, 1990; The Healing Garden, 1993, rev. edn 2004; The Apothecaries Garden: a history of Chelsea Physic Garden, 2000; The Well-Connected Gardener, 2010. *Recreations:* travel, photography, films/exhibitions, body-boarding, cliff walking, gardening, taking specialist gardening tours in UK and Europe. *Address:* c/o Chartered Institute of Horticulture, Capel Manor College, Bullsmoor Lane, Enfield, Middx EN1 4RQ. *T:* (01992) 707025. *E:* ioh@horticulture.org.uk. *Club:* Oxford and Cambridge.

MINTO, 7th Earl of, *cr* 1813; **Gilbert Timothy George Lariston Elliot-Murray-Kynynmound;** Bt 1700; Baron Minto, 1797; Viscount Melgund, 1813; *b* 1 Dec. 1953; *s* of 6th Earl of Minto, OBE and Lady Caroline, *d* of 9th Earl of Jersey; *S* father, 2005; *m* 1983, Diana, *yr d* of Brian Trafford; two *s* one *d* (and one *s* decd). *Educ:* Eton; North East London Polytechnic (BSc Hons 1983). MRICS. Lieut, Scots Guards, 1972–76. Mem., Royal Co. of Archers, Queen's Body Guard for Scotland, 1983–. *Heir:* *s* Viscount Melgund, *qv*. *Clubs:* White's, Shikar.

MINTO, Dr Alfred, FRCPsych; Consultant Psychiatrist (Rehabilitation), Southern Derbyshire Health Authority, 1988–90, retired 1991; *b* 23 Sept. 1928; *s* of Alfred Minto and Marjorie Mavor Goudie Leask; *m* 1949, Frances Oliver Bradbrook; two *s* two *d*. *Educ:* Aberdeen Central Sch.; Aberdeen Univ. (MB ChB 1951); MA History, Univ. of Nottingham, 1996. DPM RCS&P London 1961; MRCPsych 1972, FRCPsych 1974. House Physician, Huddersfield Royal Inf., 1952; Sen. House Officer/Jun. Hosp. Med. Officer, Fairmile Hosp., Wallingford, 1952–56; Sen. Registrar, St Luke's Hosp., Middlesbrough, 1956–59; Sen. Hosp. Med. Officer, 1959–63, Conslt Psychiatrist, 1963, Mapperley Hosp., Nottingham; Conslt Psychiatrist i/c, Alcoholism and Drug Addiction Service, Sheffield RHB, 1963–68; Conslt Psychiatrist, St Ann's and Mapperley Hosps, 1968–81; Med. Dir, Rampton Hosp., 1981–85; Associate Prof. of Psychiatry, Univ. of Calgary, and Clinical Dir of Forensic Psychiatry, Calgary Gen. Hosp., Alberta, 1986–87. Clinical Teacher, Nottingham Univ. Med. Sch., 1971–85; Special Lectr in Forensic Psych., Nottingham Univ., 1982–85. Conslt Psychiatrist, CS Comrs, 1964–85. *Publications:* Key Issues in Mental Health, 1982; papers on alcoholism, community care, toxoplasmosis. *Recreations:* books, people. *Address:* 76 Walsingham Road, Nottingham NG5 4NR.

MINTON, Kenneth Joseph, CBE 1995; Executive Chairman, 4 Imprint plc, 2004–10; Director: Solvay SA, 1996–2006; Pay Point plc, 2004–08; *b* 17 Jan. 1937; *s* of late Henry Minton and Lilian Minton (*née* Moore); *m* 1961, Mary Wilson; one *s*. *Educ:* Leeds Univ. (BSc 1st cl. Hons Mining Engrg). Management positions with: Unilever, UK and France, 1960–68; Laporte plc, 1968–95 (Chief Exec. and Man. Dir, 1979–95); Chm., SGB Gp plc, 1997–2000 (non-exec. Dir, SGB, 1997–2000); Executive Chairman: Arjo Wiggins Appleton plc, 1997–2001; Inveresk plc, 2001–02; non-executive Director: Caradon plc, 1991–99; Jeyes Gp plc, 1989–98 (Chm., 1993–96); John Mowlem & Co. PLC, 1994–98 (Chm., 1995–98); Sentrachem Ltd, 1996–97; Tomkins plc, 2000–06. Mem. Bd, CEFIC, 1991–95. Trustee, Industry and Parlt Trust, 1998– (Founder Mem., 1977; Chm., Mgt Council, 1993–96). Pres., SCI, 1996–98. SCI Centenary Medal, 1994. KSG 2006. *Recreations:* gardens, fine art, walking, South Africa, charities. *Address:* 7 Midway, St Albans, Herts AL3 4BD.

MINTON, Yvonne Fay, CBE 1980; mezzo-soprano; *er d* of R. T. Minton, Sydney; *m* 1965, William Barclay; one *s* one *d*. *Educ:* Sydney Conservatorium of Music. Elsa Stralia Scholar, Sydney, 1957–60; won Canberra Operatic Aria Competition, 1960; won Kathleen Ferrier Prize at s'Hertogenbosch Vocal Competition, 1961. Joined Royal Opera House as a Principal Mezzo-Soprano, 1965. Major roles include: Octavian in Der Rosenkavalier; Dorabella in Così fan Tutte; Marina in Boris Godunov; Helen in King Priam; Cherubino in Marriage of Figaro; Orfeo in Gluck's Orfeo; Sextus in La clemenza di Tito; Dido in The Trojans at Carthage; Kundry in Parsifal; Charlotte in Werther; Countess Geschwitz in Lulu. Recordings include Octavian in Der Rosenkavalier, Mozart Requiem, Elgar's The Kingdom, etc. Guest Artist with Cologne Opera Company, Oct. 1969–. Hon. RAM 1975. *Recreations:* reading, gardening. *Address:* c/o Ingpen and Williams, 7 St George's Court, 131 Putney Bridge Road, SW15 2PA. *T:* (020) 8874 3222.

MINZLY, Angela Christine Mary; *see* Heylin, A. C. M.

MIODOWNIK, Prof. Mark Andrew, PhD; Professor of Materials and Society, and Director, Institute of Making, University College London, since 2012; *b* London, 25 April 1969; *s* of Peter Miodownik and Kathleen Miodownik; *m* Ruby Wright; one *s*. *Educ:* St Catherine's Coll., Oxford (BA 1st Cl. 1992; PhD Turbine Jet Engine Alloys 1996). Worked in engrg res. instns, USA, Ireland and UK; former Hd, Materials Res. Gp, KCL. Has made radio progs for BBC Radio 4; television series: materials sci. consultant, Wonderstuff, 2011; presenter: How It Works, 2012; Everyday Miracles, 2014. Writer on materials sci. and engrg issues. Mem., Editl Bd, Interdisciplinary Sci. Reviews. *Publications:* (jtly) Computational Materials Engineering, 2007; Stuff Matters: the strange stories of the marvellous materials that shape our man-made world, 2013. *Address:* Mechanical Engineering Department, University College London, Gower Street, WC1E 6BT. *Club:* Royal Automobile.

MIQUEL, Raymond Clive, CBE 1981; Chairman and Managing Director, Lees Foods plc (formerly Lees Group Ltd), 1992–2009; Chairman, Scottish Sports Council, 1987–91; Member, Sports Council, 1988–91; *b* 28 May 1931; *m* 1958; one *s* two *d*. *Educ:* Allan Glen's Sch., Glasgow; Glasgow Technical Coll. Joined Arthur Bell & Sons Ltd as Works Study Engineer, 1956; Production Controller, 1958; Production Director, 1962; Dep. Man. Dir, 1965; Man. Dir, 1968–85; Dep. Chm., 1972; Chm., 1973–85. Chairman: Towmaster Transport Co. Ltd, 1974–86; Canning Town Glass Ltd, 1974–86; Wellington Importers Ltd, USA, 1984–86; Gleneagles Hotels PLC, 1984–86; Chm. and Chief Exec., Belhaven plc, 1986–88. Dir, Golf Fund Plc, 1989–94. Vis. Prof. in Business Develt, Glasgow Univ., 1985–. Member: British Internat. Sports Cttee, 1987–91; Sport and Recreation Alliance (formerly CCPR), 1984–. Governor, Sports Aid Foundn, 1979–2000. Sponsor: Raymond Miquel

Teaching Fellowship in Entrepreneurial Mgt, Glasgow Univ. Business Sch., 2010; Professor Raymond Miquel Enterprise Initiative, Adam Smith Business Sch., Univ. of Glasgow, 2013. CCMI (CBIM 1981). *Publications:* Business as Usual: the Miquel way (autobiog.), 2000, 2nd edn 2012. *Address:* Whitedene, Caledonian Crescent, Gleneagles, Perthshire, Scotland PH3 1NG.

MIRMAN, Sophie, (Mrs R. P. Ross); Joint Managing Director, Trotters Childrenswear and Accessories, since 1990; *b* 28 Oct. 1956; *d* of late Simone and Serge Mirman; *m* 1984, Richard Philip Ross; one *s* two *d. Educ:* French Lycée, London. Marks & Spencer, 1974–81; Gen. Manager, 1981–82, Man. Dir, 1982–83, Tie Rack; Co-Founder, Sock Shop International, 1983; Chm. and Joint Man. Dir, Sock Shop International plc, 1983–90. *Recreations:* family, sport. *Address:* Unit 7, Hurlingham Business Park, Sulivan Road, SW6 3DU. *T:* (020) 7371 5973.

MIRO, Victoria; Founder, and Director, Victoria Miro Gallery, since 1985; *b* 1 July 1945; *d* of Montagu and Jane Cooper; *m* 1970, Warren Miro; one *s* one *d. Educ:* Slade Sch. of Fine Art. Represents artists, including Chris Ofili, Peter Doig, Isaac Julien, Doug Aitken, Yayoi Kusama, Grayson Perry, Ian Hamilton Finlay. *Recreations:* food, fashion. *Address:* Victoria Miro Gallery, 16 Wharf Road, N1 7RW. *T:* (020) 7336 8109, *Fax:* (020) 7251 5596. *E:* victoria@victoria-miro.com.

MIRON, Stephen Gabriel; Group Chief Executive, Global Radio, since 2008; *b* Kingston upon Thames, 8 May 1965; *s* of Roger Miron and Josephine Miron (now Kaye); *m* 2005, Suzanne Grover; two *d. Educ:* Hampton Sch. Advertising Exec., Independent Television Pubns, 1985–88; Advertising Manager, Mail on Sunday, 1988–98; Commercial Dir, Independent Newspapers, 1998–2001; Managing Director: Associated New Ventures, 2002–03; Mail on Sunday and Mail Digital, 2003–08. Non-exec. Dir, Universal Music Ops, 2013–; Mem., Adv. Bd, Bartle Bogle Hegarty, 2013–. Member: Marketing Gp of GB; 30 Club. Pres., NABS. *Recreations:* golf, family, gym, cars, gadgets, Twitter. *Address:* Global Radio, 30 Leicester Square, WC2H 7LA. *T:* (020) 7766 6077. *E:* stephen.miron@thisisglobal.com. *Clubs:* Soho House, George, Alfred, Ivy; Wisley Golf.

MIRRÉ, Federico; Ambassador of the Argentine Republic to the Court of St James's, 2003–08; Permanent Representative to International Maritime Organisation, 2003–08; *b* 7 Aug. 1938; *s* of Emilio Juan Mirré and Marie Teresa (*née* Gavaldá-Lavin); *m* 1966; two *d*; *m* 2002, Cecilia Duhau. *Educ:* Manuel Belgrano Sch. of Marist Brothers; Univ. of Buenos Aires (LLB); Inst. of Foreign Service, Buenos Aires. Asst Prof. of Public Internat. Law, Univ. of Buenos Aires, 1977–79; Counsellor, Delegn to Papal Mediation, Vatican, 1979–81; Southern Patagonia Diplomatic Liaison Officer with Internat. Red Cross, 1982; Mem., Delegn to British-Argentine Negotiations on Malvinas, Berne, 1984; Minister, Paris, 1985–88; Ambassador to Ivory Coast, Burkina Fasso and Niger, 1988–91; Agent for Argentina on Laguna del Desierto boundary case with Chile, 1991–94; Ambassador to Norway and Iceland, 1994–99; Legal Advr, Min. of Foreign Affairs, 1999; Dir, Internat. Security, Min. of Labour, 2000–02; Hd, Dept of Western Europe, Min. of Foreign Affairs, 2002–03. Dir, Fundación Andina, 1991–94. Pres., Professional Assoc. of Foreign Service, 1992–94. Ed., Perspectiva Internacional, 1991–94. *Recreations:* photography, golf, sailing. *E:* femirre@gmail.com. *Club:* White's.

MIRREN, Dame Helen, DBE 2003; actress; *b* 26 July 1945; *m* 1997, Taylor Hackford. *Theatre includes: RSC:* Troilus and Cressida, Much Ado About Nothing, 1968; Richard III, Hamlet, The Two Gentlemen of Verona, 1970; Miss Julie, 1971; Macbeth, 1974; Henry VI parts I, II and III, 1977; Antony and Cleopatra, The Roaring Girl, 1983; *other:* Teeth 'n' Smiles, Royal Court, 1974; The Bed Before Yesterday, Lyric, 1976; Measure for Measure, Riverside, 1979; The Duchess of Malfi, Manchester Royal Exchange, 1980; Faith Healer, Royal Court, 1981; Extremities, Duchess, 1984; Two Way Mirror, Young Vic, 1988; Sex Please, We're Italian, Young Vic, 1991; A Month in the Country, Albery, and Roundabout, Broadway, 1994; Antony and Cleopatra, RNT, 1998; Collected Stories, Haymarket, 1999; Orpheus Descending, Donmar, 2000; Dance of Death, NY, 2001; Mourning Becomes Electra, NT, 2003; Phèdre, NT, 2009; The Audience, Gielgud Th., 2013 (Olivier Award for Best Actress), NY, 2015 (Tony Award for Best Actress in a Leading Role). *Films include:* Age of Consent, 1969; Savage Messiah, 1971; O Lucky Man, 1973; Caligula, 1977; The Long Good Friday, 1980; Excalibur, 1981; Cal, 1984; 2010, 1985; White Nights, Heavenly Pursuits, 1986; The Mosquito Coast, 1987; Pascali's Island, When the Whales Came, 1988; Bethune: The Making of a Hero, 1989; The Cook, The Thief, his Wife and her Lover, 1989; The Comfort of Strangers, 1989; Where Angels Fear to Tread, 1990; The Madness of King George, 1994; Some Mother's Son, 1996; Teaching Mrs Tingle, 1998; Greenfingers, The Pledge, 2001; Last Orders, Gosford Park, 2002; Calendar Girls, 2003; The Clearing, 2004; The Queen, 2006 (Best Actress, Oscar award, 2007); Inkheart, 2008; State of Play, 2009; The Last Station, Red, 2010; Brighton Rock, The Tempest, Arthur, The Debt, 2011; Hitchcock, Red 2, 2013; The Hundred-Foot Journey, 2014; Woman in Gold, 2015. *TV includes:* Prime Suspect (7 series), 1991–96, 2003, 2006 (Emmy Award, 2007); Painted Lady, 1997; Ayn Rand, 1998; Losing Chase; The Roman Spring of Mrs Stone; Elizabeth I; (dir) Happy Birthday (USA); Phil Spector, 2013 (Screen Actors Guild Award, 2014). Fellow, BAFTA, 2014. *Publications:* In the Frame: my life in words and pictures, 2007. *Address:* c/o PO Box 71253, SW11 9FX.

MIRRLEES, Sir James (Alexander), Kt 1997; FBA 1984; Professor of Political Economy, University of Cambridge, 1995–2003; Fellow of Trinity College, Cambridge, since 1995; Distinguished Professor-at-large, since 2002, and Master, since 2009, Morningside College, Chinese University of Hong Kong; *b* 5 July 1936; *s* of late George B. M. Mirrlees; *m* 1961, Gillian Marjorie Hughes (*d* 1993); two *d*; *m* 2001, Patricia Wilson. *Educ:* Douglas-Ewart High Sch., Newton Stewart; Edinburgh Univ.; Trinity Coll., Cambridge. MA Edinburgh Maths, 1957; BA Cantab Maths, 1959; PhD Cantab Econs, 1963. Adviser, MIT Center for Internat. Studies, New Delhi, 1962–63; Cambridge Univ. Asst Lectr in Econs and Fellow of Trinity Coll., 1963, University Lectr, 1965; Adviser to Govt of Swaziland, 1963; Res. Assoc., Pakistan Inst. of Develt Econs, Karachi, 1966–67; Edgeworth Prof. of Econs, and Fellow, Nuffield Coll., Oxford Univ., 1968–95. Visiting Professor: MIT, 1968, 1970, 1976, 1987; Univ. of California, Berkeley, 1986; Yale Univ., 1989; Laureate Prof., Univ. of Melbourne, 2005–. Mem., Treasury Cttee on Policy Optimisation, 1976–78. Mem., Scottish Council of Econ. Advrs, 2007–10. Chm., Tax by Design: the Mirrlees review, 2011. Econometric Society: Fellow, 1970; Vice-Pres., 1980, Pres., 1982; Chm., Assoc. of Univ. Teachers of Econs, 1983–87; President: Royal Economic Soc., 1989–92; European Economic Assoc., 2000. For. Hon. Mem., Amer. Acad. of Arts and Scis, 1981; Hon. Mem., Amer. Economic Assoc., 1982; Foreign Associate, US Nat. Acad. of Scis, 1999. Hon. FRSE, 1998. Hon. DLitt: Warwick, 1982; Portsmouth, 1997; Oxford, 1998; Hon. DSocSc Brunel, 1997; Hon. DSc: Edinburgh, 1997; Cambridge, 2015; Hon. Dr York, 2014. Nobel Prize for Economics, 1996; Royal Medal, RSE, 2009. *Publications:* (jtly) Manual of Industrial Project Analysis in Developing Countries, 1969; (ed jtly) Models of Economic Growth, 1973; (jtly) Project Appraisal and Planning, 1974; Welfare, Incentives and Taxation, 2006; articles in economic jls. *Recreations:* reading detective stories and other forms of mathematics, playing the piano, travelling, listening. *Address:* c/o Trinity College, Cambridge CB2 1TQ; Morningside College, Chinese University of Hong Kong, Shatin, N.T., Hong Kong.

MIRSKY, Prof. Rhona Mary, PhD; Professor of Developmental Neurobiology, 1990–2004, now Emeritus, and Principal Research Associate, Department of Cell and Developmental Biology, since 2004, University College London; *b* 29 May 1939; *d* of Thomas Gibson Pearson and Lynda Pearson (*née* Williams); *m* 1963, Jonathan Mirsky (marr. diss. 1985); *m* 2006, Kristján R. Jessen. *Educ:* New Hall, Cambridge (BA 1961; PhD 1964). Biochemistry Department, Dartmouth Medical School, USA: Instr, 1966–69; Asst Prof., 1969–73; Res. Associate (Asst Prof.), 1973–75; University College London: Vis. Scientist, 1974, Associate Res. Fellow, 1975–81, MRC Neuroimmunology Project, Dept of Zoology; Lectr, 1981–85, Reader, 1985–90, Dept of Anatomy and Develtl Biology. Mem. Council, MRC, 1998–2001. FMedSci 2001. *Publications:* numerous papers in scientific jls. *Address:* Department of Cell and Developmental Biology, University College London, Gower Street, WC1E 6BT. *T:* (020) 7679 3380.

MIRVIS, Chief Rabbi Ephraim; Chief Rabbi of the United Hebrew Congregations of the Commonwealth, since 2013; *b* Johannesburg, 1956; *s* of Rabbi Dr Lionel Mirvis and Freida Mirvis; *m* Valerie; four *s* (one *d* decd). *Educ:* Herzlia High Sch., Cape Town; Yeshivat Kerem BeYavne, Israel; Yeshivat Har Etzion, Israel; Univ. of South Africa (BA Educn and Classical Hebrew); Yaacov Herzog Teachers Coll., Israel. Rabbinic ordination, Machon Ariel, Jerusalem, 1978–80; Chief Rabbi of Ireland, 1984–92; Rabbi, Western Marble Arch Synagogue, 1992–96; Sen. Rabbi, Finchley Utd Synagogue (Kinloss), 1996–2013. Associate Pres., Conf. of European Rabbis (Mem., Steering Cttee). Chm., Irish Nat. Council for Soviet Jewry, 1984–92; Pres., Irish Council of Christians and Jews, 1985–92; Chm., Rabbinical Council of Utd Synagogue, 1999–2002. *Address:* Office of the Chief Rabbi, 305 Ballards Lane, N12 8GB. *T:* (020) 8343 6301.

MIRZOEFF, Edward, CVO 1993; CBE 1997; television director, executive producer and consultant; *b* 11 April 1936; *s* of late Eliachar Mirzoeff and Penina (*née* Asherov); *m* 1961, Judith Topper; three *s. Educ:* Hasmonean Grammar Sch.; Queen's Coll., Oxford (Open Scholarship in Mod. History; MA). Market Researcher, Social Surveys (Gallup Poll) Ltd, 1958–59; Public Relns Exec., Duncan McLeish & Associates, 1960–61; Asst Editor, Shoppers' Guide, 1961–63; with BBC Television, 1963–2000: director and producer of film documentaries incl. (with Sir John Betjeman) Metro-land, 1973, Target Tirpitz, 1973, A Passion for Churches, 1974, and The Queen's Realm, 1977; Police - Harrow Road, 1975; The Regiment, 1977; The Front Garden, 1979; The Ritz (BAFTA Award for Best Documentary), 1981; The Englishwoman and The Horse, 1981; The Venetian Dance Master, 1984; Elizabeth R (British Video Award), 1992; Torvill and Dean: facing the music, 1994; Treasures in Trust, 1995; John Betjeman - the last laugh, 2001; Series Editor: Bird's-Eye View, 1969–71; Year of the French, 1982–83; In At The Deep End, 1983–84; Just Another Day, 1983–85; Real Lives, 1985; Editor, 40 Minutes, 1985–89 (BAFTA Awards for Best Factual Series, 1985, 1989; Samuelson Award, Birmingham Fest., 1988); Executive Producer: Fire in the Blood, Pandora's Box, 1992; The Ark, 1993; True Brits, 1994; Situation Vacant, 1995; The House, 1996 (Royal Philharmonic Soc. Music Award for Radio, TV and Video, 1996; BPG Award for Best Documentary Series, 1996; Internat. Emmy, 1996); Full Circle with Michael Palin, 1997; The 50 Years War: Israel and the Arabs, 1998; Children's Hospital, 1998–2000; Michael Palin's Hemingway Adventure, 1999; Queen Elizabeth the Queen Mother, 2002; The Lord's Tale, 2002; A Very English Village, 2005. Chm., BAFTA, 1995–97 (Trustee, 1999–2006; Vice-Chm., TV, 1991–95); Trustee, David Lean BAFTA Foundn, 2006–11. Chm., Grierson (formerly Grierson Meml) Trust, 2002–06 (Trustee, 1999–2009; Vice-Chm., 2000–02; Patron, 2010–15). Mem., Salisbury Cathedral Council, 2002–10. Dir, Dirs' and Producers' Rights Soc., 1999–2007. Vice-Pres., Betjeman Soc., 2006– (Betjeman Lect., 2014). BFI TV Award, 1988; Alan Clarke Award for Outstanding Creative Contribn to Television, BAFTA, 1995. *Publications:* articles for The Oldie, Standpoint. *Recreation:* lunching with friends. *Address:* 9 Westmoreland Road, SW13 9RZ. *T:* (020) 8748 9247. *Club:* Garrick.

MISCAMPBELL, Gillian Margaret Mary, OBE 1982; DL; Chairman, Stoke Mandeville Hospital NHS Trust, 1995–2001; *b* 31 Dec. 1935; *d* of late Brig. Francis William Gibb and Agnes Winifred Gibb; *m* 1958, Alexander Malcolm Miscampbell (*d* 2010); three *s. Educ:* St Leonard's Sch. Member: Area Manpower Bd, 1985–88; Milton Keynes Develt Corp. Bd, 1990–92. Chm., Aylesbury Vale HA, 1981–93; Mem., Bucks HA, 1993–95. Mem. (C), Bucks CC, 1977–93 (Chm., 1989–93; Chm., Educn Cttee, 1985–89). Chm., Aylesbury Cons. Assoc., 1975–78; Vice Chm., Nat. Women's Adv. Cttee, Cons. Party, 1979–80. University of Buckingham: Mem. Council, 1985–2005 (Vice Chm., 1994–2005); Chm., F and GP Cttee, 1993–98. Chm., Cancer Care and Haematol. Fund, Stoke Mandeville Hosp., 2004–09. Dir, Buckinghamshire Foundn, 1999–2006; Chm., Aylesbury Grammar Sch. Foundn, 2005–14. DL Bucks, 1993. DUniv Buckingham, 1998. *Address:* Rosemount, 15 Upper Street, Quainton, Aylesbury, Bucks HP22 4AY. *T:* (01296) 655318.

MISKA, Prof. Eric Alexander, PhD; Herchel Smith Professor of Molecular Genetics, University of Cambridge, since 2013; *b* Bitburg, Germany, 29 June 1971; *s* of Siegfried Miska and Erica (*née* Steindorf); *m* 2000, Ines Alvarez Garcia; one *s* one *d. Educ:* St Wilibrord Gymnasium, Bitburg; Trinity Coll., Dublin (BA Biochem. 1996); King's Coll., Cambridge (PhD Pathol. 2000). Wellcome Trust Prize Fellow, Bob Horvitz Lab., 2000–03, Howard Hughes Med. Inst. Res. Associate, 2003–04, MIT; Gp Leader, Wellcome Trust/Cancer Res. UK Gurdon Inst., Univ. of Cambridge, 2005–; Fellow, Pembroke Coll., Cambridge, 2006–13. *Publications:* many res. papers and review articles in leading scientific jls, particularly in areas of non-coding RNA. *Recreations:* running, hiking, cycling, opera. *Address:* Wellcome Trust/Cancer Research UK Gurdon Institute, University of Cambridge, Tennis Court Road, Cambridge CB2 1QN. *T:* (01223) 767220. *E:* eric.miska@gurdon.cam.ac.uk. *W:* www.ericmiskalab.org.

MISKIN, Charles James Monckton; QC 1998; a Recorder, since 1998; *b* 29 Nov. 1952; *s* of late Nigel Monckton Miskin and Hilda Meryl Miskin (*née* Knight); *m* 1st, 1982, Karen Elizabeth Booth (marr. diss. 1995); one *s* three *d*; 2nd, 2005, Angharad Jocelyn Start; one *s* two *d. Educ:* Charterhouse Sch. (Sutton Prizewinner); Worcester Coll., Oxford (Open Exhibnr; BA Hons Juris. 1974; MA 1978). Called to the Bar, Gray's Inn, 1975, Bencher, 2005; in practice as barrister, 1977–, Hd of Chambers, 2003–06; Mem., S Eastern Circuit; Asst Recorder, 1992–98; Standing Counsel to Inland Revenue, 1993–98. Mem., Criminal Bar Assoc., 1977–. Chm., Bar Theatrical Soc., 1986–. Liveryman: Wax Chandlers' Co., 1975–; Armourers' and Braziers' Co., 1986–. *Recreations:* travel, opera, history, the children, laughter. *Address:* 23 Essex Street, WC2R 3AA. *T:* (020) 7413 0353. *Clubs:* Travellers, Hurlingham.

MISRA, Arnu Kumar; Chief Operating Officer, Matalan Retail Ltd, since 2013; *b* 8 Jan. 1962; *s* of Kulbushan Misra and Pushpa Misra; *m* 1990, Neelam Bhardwaj; one *s. Educ:* Univ. of Bradford (BSc 1st Cl. Hons 1983); Bradford Mgt Centre (MBA 1987); INSEAD (AMP 2005). MMM Logistics Consultancy, 1987–89; various exec. and sen. exec. roles, ASDA Gp plc, 1990–2003; Chief Operating Officer, 2003–05, CEO 2005–08, Cannons Gp; Exec. Vice Pres., Operations, Loblaw, 2009–11; New Business Dir, Asda, 2011–12. *Recreations:* fair-weather cricket, hill walking, spinning.

MISTRY, Cyrus Pallonji, FICE; Chairman, Tata Sons Ltd, since 2012 (Director, since 2006); *b* Mumbai, India, 4 July 1968; *s* of Pallonji S. Mistry and Patsy P. Mistry; *m* Rohiqa C.; two *s. Educ:* Cathedral and John Connon Sch., Mumbai; Imperial Coll. London (BSc Civil Engrg 1990); London Business Sch. (MSc Mgt 1997). Dir, Shapoorji Pallonji & Co. Ltd, 1991; Man. Dir, Shapoorji Pallonji Gp, 1994; Chairman: Tata Steel; Tata Motors; Tata Consulting Services; Tata Power; Indian Hotels Co.; Tata Global Beverages; Tata Chemicals. *Recreation:* playing golf occasionally. *Address:* Tata Sons Ltd, Bombay House, 24 Homi Mody Street, Mumbai 400 001, India. *T:* 2266658282, *Fax:* 2266657559. *E:* Chairman@tata.com.

MISTRY, Dhruva, Hon. CBE 2001; RA 1991; FRBS; sculptor, painter and printmaker; *b* Kanjari, Gujarat, 1 Jan. 1957; *s* of Pramodray and Kantaben Mistry. *Educ:* Maharaja Sayajirao Univ. of Baroda (MA 1981); RCA (British Council schol.; MA 1983). Freelance Sculptor Agent, Nigel Greenwood Gall., London, 1983–97; Artist-in-residence, Kettle's Yard, and Fellow of Churchill Coll., Cambridge, 1984–85; Sculptor-in-residence, V&A Mus., 1988; Prof., Hd of Sculpture and Dean, Faculty of Fine Arts, MS Univ. of Baroda, 1999–2002. Solo exhibitions include: Art Heritage, New Delhi, 1981, transf. to Jehangir Art Gall., Bombay, 1982, 2005; Contemp. Art Gall., Amdavad, 1983; Kettle's Yard Gall., Cambridge, 1985; Walker Art Gall., Liverpool, 1986; Nigel Greenwood Gall., London, 1987, 1990; Collins Gall., Glasgow, 1988; Laing Art Gall., Newcastle-upon-Tyne, 1989; Modern Art Gall., Fukuoka Art Mus., Fukuoka, 1994; Royal Acad., Friends Room, 1995; Meghraj Gall., London, 1996; Bothy Gall., Yorks Sculpture Park, W Bretton 1997; Nazar Gall., Vadodara, 1998; Gall. Espace, New Delhi, 1999; Limerick City Gall. of Art, Limerick, 2000; Sakshi Gall., Mumbai, 2001, 2005; Queen's Gall., British Council, New Delhi 2001; Rabindra Bhavan, Lalit Kala Akademi, New Delhi, 2005; Bodhi Art, Travancore Palace and Art Pilgrim, New Delhi, 2007; Harmony Art Foundn, Mumbai, 2008; Hatheesing Centre, Ahmedabad, 2010; Grosvenor Vadehra Art Gall., London, 2011; group exhibitions include: Royal Acad., London, 1982, 1996; Hayward Gall., London, Twinning Gall., NY, 1985; Kettle's Yard, Cambridge, 1987; Business Design Centre, London, 1995; Sakshi Gall., Mumbai, 2000; Lalit Kal Akademi, Delhi, 2001; Grosvenor Gall., London, 2005, 2007, 2009; Royal Acad. Summer Exhibns: 1988, 2008, 2010. Rep. Britain at 3rd Rodin Grand Prize Exhibn, Japan, 1990. Works in public collections including: Lalit Kala Akademi, New Delhi; Tate Gall., Arts Council, British Council and V&A Mus., British Liby, British Mus., London; Nat. Mus. of Wales, Cardiff; Fukuoka Asian Art Mus., Japan; open air collections include sculptures at Goodwood, Yorks Sculpture Park and Hakone Open Air Mus., Japan; works of art for: Victoria Square, Birmingham, commnd by Birmingham CC, 1992; Tamano City Project, Uno, Japan, 2002; LNG Petronet, Dahej, 2003; Delhi Univ., 2005. FRBS 1993. DUniv UCE, 2007. Madame Tussaud's Award for Art at RCA, 1983; Jack Goldhill Award, Royal Acad. of Arts, 1991; Award for Design of Humanities Prize Medal, 1994; Design and Pres.'s Award for Victoria Square Sculptures, 1995; Landscape Inst. and Marsh Fountain of the Year Award, 1995; Award of Excellence, Gujarat Gaurav Samiti, 2006; Triveni Award, Vadodora, 2014. *Recreations:* photography, reading, walking. *Address:* (office) 76 Anu Shakti Nagar, Sama, Vadodara-390008, Gujarat, India. *T:* (265) 2712949, (mobile) (91) 9376214606. *E:* dhruva@dhruvamistry.com. *W:* www.dhruvamistry.com.

MISTRY, Rohinton, FRSL; author; *b* Bombay, 1952; *m* 1975, Freny Elavia. *Educ:* Villa Theresa Prim. Sch., Bombay; St Xavier's High Sch., Bombay; Bombay Univ. (BSc Maths and Econs 1973); Univ. of Toronto (BA Eng. and Philos. 1983). Bank clerk, Toronto, 1975–85. FRSL 2009. DUniv Ottawa, 1996; Hon. DLitt: Toronto, 1999; York, 2003; Ryerson, 2012. Canada-Australia Literary Award, 1995; Trudeau Fellowship, Trudeau Foundn, 2004; Guggenheim Fellowship, 2005; Neustadt Internat. Prize for Literature, 2012. *Publications:* Tales From Firozsha Baag (short stories), 1987; *novels:* Such a Long Journey, 1991 (Gov. Gen.'s Award for Fiction, Canada, 1991; Commonwealth Writers' Prize for Best Book, 1992); A Fine Balance, 1995 (Giller Prize, Canada, 1995; Commonwealth Writers' Prize for Best Book, 1996; Winnifred Holtby Award, RSL, 1997; LA Times Fiction Prize, 1997); Family Matters (Kiriyama Pacific Rim Book Prize for Fiction), 2002; short stories and travel essays in literary periodicals and anthologies; works translated into 30 langs. *Address:* c/o Westwood Creative Artists Ltd, 94 Harbord Street, Toronto, ON M5S 1G6, Canada. *E:* bruce@wcaltd.com.

MITCALFE, (Joan) Kirsteen; Vice Lord-Lieutenant of Moray, 2005–11; *b* 23 July 1936; *d* of Douglas and Jenny Mackessack; *m* 1959, Hugh Mitcalfe; four *d*. *Educ:* Oxenfoord Castle Sch., Midlothian; Open Univ. (BA Hons). Secretary: Moray and Nairn Br., Pony Club, 1971–96; Forres Br., Riding for the Disabled, 1972–90; Burgie Internat. Horse Trials, 1988–2003. Gov., Gordonstoun Sch., 1981–94. Voluntary work with hospice movt, WRVS and as church sec. *Recreations:* ski-ing, fishing, travelling, music. *Address:* Thunderton Cottage, 79 Findhorn, Moray IV36 3YF. *T:* (01309) 690775. *E:* k.mitcalfe@btinternet.com.

MITCHARD, (Gerald Steven) Paul; QC 2008; Director, Career Planning and Professionalism, Faculty of Law, Chinese University of Hong Kong, since 2014; *b* Paulton, 2 Jan. 1952; *s* of Gerald Mitchard and Janet Mitchard; *m* 1987, Dorothy Grant; two *s*. *Educ:* Lincoln Coll., Oxford (MA Juris. 1974). Slaughter and May, 1977–84; Simmons & Simmons: Partner, 1984–99; Head of Litigation, 1993–99; Partner, Wilmer, Cutler & Pickering, 1999–2001; Head, Eur. Arbitration and Litigation, 2001–09, Global Co-head and Head of Asia, Internat. Arbitration and Litigation Gp, 2009–14, Skadden, Arps, Slate, Meagher & Flom (UK) LLP. Vis. Prof. of Law, China Univ. of Politics and Law, Beijing, 2012–15. *Recreations:* hiking, reading, scuba diving. *Address:* Faculty of Law, Chinese University of Hong Kong, Shatin, New Territories, Hong Kong. *Club:* Vincent's (Oxford).

MITCHELL, family name of **Baron Mitchell**.

MITCHELL, Baron *cr* 2000 (Life Peer), of Hampstead in the London Borough of Camden; **Parry Andrew Mitchell;** *b* 6 May 1943; *s* of Leon and Rose Mitchell; *m* 1st, 1972, Doreen Hargreaves (marr. diss.); one *d*; 2nd, 1988, Hannah Ruth Lowy; two *s* (twins). *Educ:* Christ's Coll., Finchley; Univ. of London (BSc ext.); Columbia Univ., NY (MBA). Chm., United Leasing plc, 1976–87. Opposition spokesperson, BIS, 2012–13. Mem., H of L Select Cttee on Sci. and Technol., 2003–07, on EU, Sub-Cttee B, Internal Market, 2007–09. Enterprise Advr to Labour Party, 2013–; Chm., Lab. Digital, 2013–. Chairman: Syscap plc, 1992–2006; Weizmann UK, 2005–09; Instant Impact Ltd, 2014–. Chairman: eLearning Foundn, 2006–10; Coexistence Trust, 2008–12; Founder Trustee, Lowy Mitchell Foundn. *Recreations:* gym obsessive, cyclist in the hills of Umbria, jazz night and day, opera, theatre and the cinema. *Address:* House of Lords, SW1A 0PW. *T:* 07515 339792. *E:* parrym@mac.com.

MITCHELL, Rt Hon. Andrew (John Bower); PC 2010; MP (C) Sutton Coldfield, since 2001; *b* 23 March 1956; *s* of Sir David Bower Mitchell and Pamela Elaine (*née* Haward); *m* 1985, Sharon Denise (*née* Bennett); two *d*. *Educ:* Rugby; Jesus Coll., Cambridge (MA History). 1st RTR (Short Service (Limited) Commission), 1975; served with UNFICYP. Pres., Cambridge Union, 1978; Chm., Cambridge Univ. Conservatives, 1977; rep. GB in E-SU American debating tour, 1978. Internat. and Corp. business, Lazard Brothers & Co., 1979–87, Consultant, 1987–92; Dir, Lazard Gp Cos, 1997–2009. Senior Strategy Adviser: Boots Co., 1997–2001; Accenture (formerly Andersen Consulting), 1997–2009; Investec, 2013–. Director: Miller Insce Gp, 1997–2001; Commer Gp, 1998–2002; Financial Dynamics Holdings, 1998–2002. Advr to Bd, Hakluyt, 1998–2001. Contested (C) Sunderland South, 1983. MP (C) Gedling, 1987–97; contested (C) same seat, 1997. A Vice-Chm., Cons. Party, with special responsibility for candidates, 1992–93; an Asst Govt Whip, 1992–94; a Lord Comr of HM Treasury (Govt Whip), 1994–95; Parly Under Sec. of State, DSS, 1995–97; Opposition front bench spokesman: economic affairs, 2003–04; police and home affairs, 2004–05; Shadow Sec. of State for internat. devélt, 2005–10; Sec. of State for Internat. Devélt, 2010–12; Parly Sec. to HM Treasury (Govt Chief Whip), 2012. Sec., One Nation Gp of Conservative MPs, 1989–92, 2005–. Chm., Coningsby Club, 1983; President: Islington North Conservatives, 1996–2006 (Chm., 1983–85); Gedling Cons. Assoc., 2004–. Vice-Chm., 1998–2010, Trustee, 2010–, Alexandra Rose Charity. Member Council: SOS Sahel, 1991–2010; GAP, 2000–05. *Recreations:* ski-ing, music, travel, wine. *Address:* 30 Gibson Square, N1 0RD. *T:* (020) 7226 5519; 8 Tudor Road, Sutton Coldfield B73 6BA. *T:* (0121) 355 5519. *Clubs:* Cambridge Union Society (Cambridge); Carlton and District Constitutional (Gedling); Sutton Coldfield Conservative.

MITCHELL, Andrew Jonathan, CMG 2013; Director, Insight, M-is plc, since 2015; *b* 7 March 1967; *s* of Michael John Mitchell and Patricia Anne Mitchell; *m* 1996, Helen Sarah Anne Magee; two *s* one *d*. *Educ:* St Mary's Coll., Crosby, Liverpool; Queen's Coll., Oxford (BA 1st Cl. Hons Mod. Langs 1990; Laming Scholar, Queen's Coll. Bursary, Markham Prize for French). Joined FCO, 1991; Second Sec., Bonn, 1993; First Sec., FCO, 1996; Dep. Hd of Mission, Kathmandu, 1999; Counsellor, FCO, 2002–07; Ambassador to Sweden, 2007–11; FCO Dir for 2012 Olympic and Paralympic Games, London, FCO, 2011–12; Dir, Prosperity, FCO, 2012–14. *Recreations:* enjoy cricket, Rugby and soccer, keen walker, reader of history, sciences, politics and current affairs. *Clubs:* MCC, Army and Navy, Soho House; Vincent's (Oxford).

MITCHELL, Andrew Robert; QC 1998; a Recorder, since 1999; *b* 6 Aug. 1954; *s* of late Malcolm Mitchell and of Edna Audrey Mitchell; *m* 1st, 1982, Patricia Ann Fairburn (marr. diss. 1991); 2nd, 1992, Carolyn Ann Blore; one *s* one *d*. *Educ:* Haberdashers' Aske's Sch.; Council of Legal Educn. Called to the Bar, Gray's Inn, 1976, Bencher, 2005; in practice at the Bar, 1976–; Asst Recorder, 1995–99. Head: Furnival Chambers, 1990–2008; Chambers of Andrew Mitchell QC, 2008–. Mem., Gen. Council of Bar, 2003–11 (Treas., 2008–11). Mem. (C) Haringey LBC, 1984–94 (Leader of the Opposition, 1989–91). Contested (C) Islington S and Finsbury, 1987. Gov., Highgate Primary Sch., 1984–99 (Chm. of Govs, 1997–98). *Publications:* Confiscation and Proceeds of Crime, 1993, 3rd edn (ed jtly) 2002–; Concise Guide to Criminal Procedure Investigations Act 1996, 1997; (contrib.) Administrative Court: practice *v* procedure, 2006. *Recreations:* watching football and cricket, trying to keep fit. *Address:* 33 Chancery Lane, WC2A 1EN. *T:* (020) 7440 9950. *E:* arm@33cllaw.com. *Clubs:* Royal Automobile, MCC.

MITCHELL, Angus; *see* Mitchell, J. A. M.

MITCHELL, His Honour Anthony Paul; a Circuit Judge, 2000–12; *b* 9 Aug. 1941; *s* of Arthur Leslie Mitchell and Ivy Muriel Mitchell (*née* Simpson); *m* 1st, 1972, Shirley Ann Donovan (marr. diss. 1985); one *s* one *d*, and one step *s* one step *d*; 2nd, 1989, Julia Fryer (*d* 2000); one step *s* one step *d*; 3rd, 2003, Bethan Henderson; one step *s* one step *d*. *Educ:* Whitgift Sch., Croydon; Coll. of Law, London. Articled, Routh Stacey & Co.; qualified, 1965; admitted Solicitor, 1966; Partner, Toller Hales Collcutt, 1969–2000; Dep. Dist Judge, 1982–2000; Asst Recorder, 1991–95; Recorder, 1995–2000. *Recreations:* time with family and friends, theatre, opera, cinema, walking, watching sport, keeping fit; Christianity and supporting my church and its musical tradition; Southern Burgundy, its wines and its weather, supporting National Youth Advocacy Service and its work with young people and vulnerable young adults, and still things spiritual with a small 's'. *Club:* Lansdowne.

MITCHELL, Austin Vernon, DPhil; *b* 19 Sept. 1934; *s* of Richard Vernon Mitchell and Ethel Mary Mitchell; *m* 1st, Patricia Dorothea Jackson (marr. diss.); two *d*; 2nd, Linda Mary McDougall; one *s* one *d*. *Educ:* Woodbottom Council Sch.; Bingley Grammar Sch.; Manchester Univ. (BA, MA); Nuffield Coll., Oxford (DPhil). Lectr in History, Univ. of Otago, Dunedin, NZ, 1959–63; Sen. Lectr in Politics, Univ. of Canterbury, Christchurch, NZ, 1963–67; Official Fellow, Nuffield Coll., Oxford, 1967–69; Journalist, Yorkshire Television, 1969–71; Presenter, BBC Current Affairs Gp, 1972–73; Journalist, Yorkshire TV, 1973–77; Co-presenter, Target, Sky TV, 1989–98. MP (Lab) Grimsby, April 1977–1983, Great Grimsby, 1983–2015. PPS to Minister of State for Prices and Consumer Protection, 1977–79; Opposition front bench spokesman on trade and industry, 1987–89. Member, Select Committee: on Treasury and Civil Service, 1983–87; on agric., 1997–2001; on envmt, food and rural affairs, 2001–05; Public Accounts, 2006–15. Mem., Public Accounts Commn, 1997–2015. Chair, Yorks and Humber Seafood Gp, Yorks Forward, 2007–11. Mem., OT Prophets. Associate Ed., House Magazine. ONZM 2001. *Publications:* New Zealand Politics In Action, 1962; Government By Party, 1966; The Whigs in Opposition 1815–1830, 1969; Politics and People in New Zealand, 1970; Yorkshire Jokes, 1971; The Half-Gallon Quarter-Acre Pavlova Paradise, 1974; Can Labour Win Again, 1979; Westminster Man, 1982; The Case for Labour, 1983; Four Years in the Death of the Labour Party, 1983; Yorkshire Jokes, 1988; Teach Thissen Tyke, 1988; Britain: beyond the blue horizon, 1989; Competitive Socialism, 1989; Accounting for Change, 1993; Election '45, 1995; Corporate Governance Matters, 1996; The Common Fisheries Policy: end or mend?, 1996; (with David Wienir) Last Time: Labour's lessons from the sixties, 1997; (with Anne Tate) Fishermen: the rise and fall of deep water trawling, 1997; Parliament in Pictures, 1999; Farewell My Lords, 1999; Austin Mitchell's Yorksher, 2002; Pavlova Paradise Revisited, 2002; Austin Mitchell's Yorkshire Sayings, 2004; Taming the Corporations, 2005; The Pensions Scandal, 2007; Grand Book of Yorkshire Humour, 2009; Calendar Boy, 2014. *Recreation:* worriting (*sic*). *Address:* 13 Bargate, Grimsby, NE Lincs DN34 4SS. *T:* (01472) 342145. *E:* austinmitchellexmr@gmail.com.

MITCHELL, Bryan James, CB 2006; Director, Business and Information Management Directorate, Welsh Assembly Government, 2003–05; *b* 1 March 1945; *s* of Herbert Mitchell and Hilda (*née* Grant); *m*; four *d*. *Educ:* Robert Clack Technical Sch., Dagenham; Open Univ. (BA). MoT, 1967–74; CSD, 1974–76; DoE, 1976–78; Welsh Office, 1978–99; Dep. Clerk to Nat. Assembly for Wales, 1999–2000; Welsh Assembly Government, 2000–05.

MITCHELL, Charles Julian Humphrey; *see* Mitchell, Julian.

MITCHELL, Charlotte Isabel; *b* 3 May 1953; *d* of (John) Angus (Macbeth) Mitchell, *qv* and Ann Katharine (*née* Williamson), MA, MPhil, author; *m* 1st, 1972 (marr. diss. 2000); one *s* one *d*; 2nd, 2002, Paul Southall. *Educ:* St George's Sch. for Girls, Edinburgh; Birmingham Coll. of Art (DipAD 1974); Dip Wine and Spirits 1991. Exhibn organiser, Scottish Craft Centre, 1974–76; Director: Real Foods Ltd, 1976–97; Go Organic Ltd, 1998–2003; organic food consultant, Waitrose plc, 1998–2002; Disability Equality Trainer, Capability Scotland, 2004–05. Trustee, 1987–2005, Dir, 1990–92, Chm., 1990–97, Hon. Vice-Pres., 2006–, Soil Assoc. Trustee, Knockando Wool Mill, Speyside, 2004–. Hon. Mem., BBC Scotland Adv. Council for Rural and Agricl Affairs, 1994–98. *Publications:* The Organic Wine Guide, 1987. *Recreations:* food, wine, music, books, gardening.

See also J. J. Mitchell.

MITCHELL, His Honour Christopher Richard; a Circuit Judge, 2003–12; Resident Judge, Basildon Combined Court Centre, 2007–11; *b* 16 Sept. 1942; *e s* of late Anthony Geoffrey Fulton Mitchell and of Cynthia Grace Mitchell (*née* Charlton); *m* 1980, Elisabeth Jeanne Antonine Pineau, *e d* of late Jean Pineau; one *d*. *Educ:* St Dunstan's Coll.; King's Coll. London (LLB 1964). Treasury Solicitor's Dept, 1965–69; called to the Bar, Gray's Inn, 1968; in practice at the Bar, London and S Eastern Circuit (crime), 1969–2003; Asst Recorder, 1987–91, Recorder, 1991–2003; Immigration Appeal Adjudicator, 1998–2003. Asst Comr, Parly Boundary Commn, 1993–94. *Recreations:* hill-walking, books, European railways, cycling, wooding. *Address:* c/o Amber Mercele, Hollis Whiteman Chambers, Lawrence Pountney Hill, EC4R 0EU. *T:* (020) 7933 8855.

MITCHELL, David Charles; His Honour Judge David Mitchell; a Circuit Judge, South Eastern Circuit, since 2001; Designated Civil Judge, London, since 2007; a Senior Circuit Judge, since 2010; Senior Resident Judge, Central London Civil Justice Centre, since 2011; *b* 4 May 1950; *s* of Charles and Eileen Mitchell; *m* 1973, Susan Cawthera; one *s* one *d*. *Educ:* state schs; St Catherine's Coll., Oxford (MA Juris.). Called to the Bar, Inner Temple, 1972; barrister-at-law, Bradford Chambers, 1972–99, Pump Court, Temple, 1999–2001; specialised in civil and family law, crime and personal injury; Asst Recorder, 1989–93; a Recorder, 1993–2001; Chm., Mental Health Rev. Tribunal (Restricted Panel), 2003–05; Designated Civil Judge: Kent, 2003–07. Course Dir, Judicial Studies Bd Civil Refresher Course,

2008–11. *Recreations:* hill-walking, ski-ing, the theatre, listening to classical music, anything connected with France. *Address:* Central London Civil Justice Centre, Thomas More Building, Royal Courts of Justice, Strand, WC2A 2LL.

MITCHELL, David James Stuart; freelance comedy actor and writer, since 1996; *b* Salisbury, 14 July 1974; *s* of Ian Douglas Mitchell and Kathryn Grey Mitchell (*née* Hughes); *m* 2012, Victoria, *d* of late Alan Coren and of Anne Coren; one *d*. *Educ:* Abingdon Sch.; Peterhouse, Cambridge (BA Hons 1996). *Television* includes: as actor and writer: Blunder, 2006; with Robert Webb: Bruiser, 2000; The Mitchell and Webb Situation, 2001; Peep Show, 2003– (Best Comedy Performance, BAFTA, 2008); That Mitchell and Webb Look, 2006–; Would I Lie to You?, 2007–; The Bubble, 2010; 10 O'Clock Live, 2011–; as actor: Jam & Jerusalem, 2006–09; Ambassadors, 2013; The Incredible Adventures of Professor Branestawm, 2014; host, Was It Something I Said?, 2013; *radio:* (with Robert Webb) That Mitchell and Webb Sound, 2003–; The Unbelievable Truth, 2007–; *film:* Magicians, 2007. Columnist, The Observer, 2008–. *Publications:* (with R. Webb) This Mitchell and Webb Book, 2009; Back Story, 2012; Thinking About It Only Makes It Worse, 2014. *Recreations:* walking, talking. *Address:* c/o Michele Milburn, Milburn Browning Associates, The Old Truman Brewery, 91 Brick Lane, E1 6QL. *T:* (020) 3582 9370, *Fax:* (020) 3582 9377. *E:* Michele@milburnbrowning.com.

See also G. R. P. Coren.

MITCHELL, David McKenzie, MD; FRCP; Consultant Physician, St Mary's Hospital, Paddington, since 1987, and Medical Director, Imperial College Healthcare NHS Trust (formerly St Mary's NHS Trust), since 1998; *b* 27 July 1948; *s* of John Bernard Mitchell and Elizabeth Mitchell; *m* 1st, 1977, Elizabeth Gaminara (marr. diss. 2005); one *s* one *d*; 2nd, 2009, Jennifer Leigh Hardyment. *Educ:* Mostyn House Sch.; Oundle Sch.; Gonville and Caius Coll., Cambridge (MB BChir 1974; MD 1983); Middlesex Hosp.; London Univ. (BA (Philos.) 1983, ext.); Keele Univ. (MBA 1998). FRCP 1991. Trng posts in gen. and respiratory medicine, Hammersmith Hosp., Brompton Hosp., UCH, London Chest Hosp., 1973–87; Res. Fellow in Immunology, ICRF, 1980–82. Liveryman, Musicians' Co., 2005. *Publications:* Respiratory Medicine Revision, 1986; AIDS and the Lung, 1990; Recent Advances in Respiratory Medicine, 1991; papers on various aspects of respiratory medicine. *Recreations:* playing jazz saxophone, classical music, opera, philosophy, travel. *Address:* Imperial College Healthcare NHS Trust, Praed Street, W2 1NY. *T:* (020) 7886 1082, *Fax:* (020) 7886 7833. *E:* david.mitchell@imperial.nhs.uk. *Club:* Athenæum.

MITCHELL, David William, CBE 1983; Chairman, 2001–04, Hon. President, 2005–10, Scottish Conservative and Unionist Party; *b* 4 Jan. 1933; *m* 1965, Lynda Katherine Marion Guy; one *d*. *Educ:* Merchiston Castle School, Edinburgh. Nat. Service, 1950–52 (commnd RSF; seconded to 4th Nigerian Regt, RWAFF). Western RHB, 1968–75; Director: Mallinson, Denny (Scotland), 1975–89; Hunter Timber (Scotland), 1989–92; Jt Man. Dir, M & N Norman (Timber) Ltd, 1992–96. Chm., Cumbernauld New Town Develt Corp., 1987–97. Member: Exec. Cttee, Scottish Council Develt and Industry, 1979–95; Scottish Council, CBI, 1980–85; Scottish Exec. Cttee, Inst. of Directors, 1984–91. President: Timber Trade Benevolent Soc., 1974; Scottish Timber Trade Assoc., 1984. Pres., Scottish Cons. and Unionist Assoc., 1980–82; Treasurer, Scottish Cons. Party, 1990–93, 1998–2001. Gov., Craighalbert Centre for Children with Motor Neurone Disease, 1992–95. *Recreations:* golf, shooting, fishing. *Address:* The Old Mill House, Symington, Ayrshire KA1 5QL. *T:* (01563) 830851. *Clubs:* Western (Glasgow); Royal and Ancient Golf, Prestwick Golf; Queen's Park Football.

MITCHELL, Donald Charles Peter, CBE 2000; PhD; FRCM; musicologist; Life President and Director, Britten Estate Ltd, since 2000 (Chairman, 1986–2000); Trustee, Britten-Pears Foundation, 1986–2000, now Trustee Emeritus; *b* 6 Feb. 1925; *s* of Frederick George Mitchell and Kathleen Mary Mitchell (*née* Charles); *m* 1956, Kathleen Livingston (*née* Burbidge); one step *s* and two foster *s*. *Educ:* Brightlands Prep. Sch.; Dulwich Coll.; Univ. of Durham (1949–50); Univ. of Southampton (PhD 1977). Advisory Reader (new fiction), Gainsborough Pictures (1928) Ltd, 1942–43; Non-Combatant Corps, 1943–45; Asst Master, Oakfield Sch., London, 1946–48; Founding Editor, Music Survey, 1947, Jt Editor, 1949–52; Music Critic: Musical Times, 1953–57; Musical Opinion, 1953–57; Head of Music Dept, Faber & Faber, 1958; Editor, Tempo, 1958–62; Music Staff, Daily Telegraph, 1959–64; Music Advr, Boosey & Hawkes, 1963–64; Music Critic, Listener, 1964; Man. Dir, Faber Music, 1965–71 (Vice-Chm., 1976–77; Chm., 1977–86, Pres., 1988–95); founding Prof. of Music, Univ. of Sussex, 1971–76; Executor, Benjamin Britten's estate, 1976. Guest Artistic Dir, Aldeburgh Fest., 1991. Visiting Professor of Music: Univ. of Sussex, 1977; Univ. of York, 1991; KCL, 1995–99; Hon. Res. Fellow, RCM, 2000–; Hon. Prof., Shanghai Conservatory of Music, 2006. Britten-Pears School for Advanced Musical Studies: Chm., Educn Cttee, 1976; Dir of Study Courses, 1977; Dir of Academic Studies, 1977–90; Hon. Dir, 1995. Director: Performing Right Soc., 1973 (Jt Dep. Chm., 1987–89, Chm., 1989–92, Hon. Mem. Council, 1992); Music Copyright (Overseas) Services Ltd, 1977–92; English Music Theatre, 1973; Nexus Opera, 1986–91; Chm. Exec. Cttee, Mahler Fest., Concertgebouw, Amsterdam, 1995. Member: BBC Central Music Adv. Council, 1967; Council, Aldeburgh Foundn, 1977–94; Adv. Bd, Musical Quarterly, NY, 1985; Adv. Bd, Kurt Weill Edition, NY, 1992; Editl Bd, Muziek & Wetenschap, 1997–2002. Vice-Pres., CISAC, 1992–94. Gov., 1988, Council of Honour, 2000–, RAM (Hon. RAM 1992); Gov., NYO, 1989–90. FRCM 2004. Hon. DMus Srinakharinwirot, Bangkok, 2001. Gustav Mahler Medal of Honor, Bruckner Soc., USA, 1961; Medal of Honour, Internat. Gustav Mahler Soc.; Gustav Mahler Medal of Honour, Vienna, 1987; Royal Philharmonic Soc. Award, 1992; Univ. of Toronto Distinguished Visitor Award, 1999; Charles Flint Kellogg Award, NY, 2002. *Publications:* (jtly) Benjamin Britten: a commentary on his works, 1952, 2nd edn 1972; (jtly) The Mozart Companion, 1956, 2nd edn 1965; Gustav Mahler: the early years, 1958, 4th edn 2003; The Language of Modern Music, 1963, 4th edn 1993; Alma Mahler: Gustav Mahler Memories and Letters, 1968, (jtly) 4th edn 1990; (jtly) The Faber Book of Nursery Songs, 1968; (jtly) The Faber Book of Children's Songs, 1970; Gustav Mahler: the Wunderhorn years, 1975, 3rd edn 2005; (jtly) Benjamin Britten: pictures from a life 1913–1976, 1978; Britten and Auden in the Thirties: the year 1936, (T. S. Eliot Meml Lectures), 1981, 2nd edn 2000; Gustav Mahler: songs and symphonies of life and death, 1985, 2nd edn 2002; Benjamin Britten: Death in Venice, 1987; (jtly) Letters from a Life: selected letters and diaries of Benjamin Britten, vols 1 and 2, 1991, vol. 3, 2004, vol. 4, 2008; Cradles of the New: writings on music 1951–1991, ed Mervyn Cooke, 1995; Gustav Mahler: the world listens, 1995; (jtly) Mahler's Seventh Symphony, facsimile edn 1995; (ed) New Sounds, New Century: Mahler's Fifth Symphony and the Royal Concertgebouw Orchestra, 1997; (jtly) The Mahler Companion, 1999; Discovering Mahler: writings on Mahler 1955–2005, 2007; articles in jls. *Recreations:* travelling, reading, cooking, collecting pottery and paintings, studying the classical music of Thailand. *Address:* 83 Ridgmount Gardens, Torrington Place, WC1E 7AY. *T:* (020) 7580 1241. *Club:* Garrick.

MITCHELL, His Honour Fergus Irvine; a Circuit Judge, 1996–2014; *b* 30 March 1947; *s* of Sir George Irvine Mitchell, CB, QC (Scot.) and Elizabeth Mitchell (*née* Leigh Pemberton), JP; *m* 1972, Sally Maureen, *yr d* of Sir Derrick Capper, QPM and Muriel Capper; one *s* one *d*. *Educ:* Tiffin Boys' Sch., Kingston-upon-Thames. Called to the Bar, Gray's Inn, 1971; Asst Recorder, 1989; Recorder, 1993. Member: Gen. Council of the Bar, 1992–95; Professional Conduct Cttee, 1993–95; Bar Race Relations Cttee, 1994–95. Chm., Lord Chancellor's Adv. Cttee, SW London, 2000–11; Magistrates' Liaison Judge, SW London, 2000–13. Mem., Mental Health Tribunal Restricted Patients Panel, 2000–. *Recreations:* France, opera.

MITCHELL, Rear-Adm. Geoffrey Charles, CB 1973; retired 1975; Director, The Old Granary Art and Craft Centre, Bishop's Waltham, Hants, 1975–86; *b* 21 July 1921; *s* of William C. Mitchell; *m* 1st, 1955, Jocelyn Rainger (*d* 1987), Auckland, NZ; one *s* two *d*; 2nd, 1990, Dr Hilary Gardiner. *Educ:* Marlborough College. Joined RN 1940; Captain 1961; Director Officer Recruiting, 1961–63; Captain (F), 2nd Frigate Sqdn, 1963–65; Director Naval Ops and Trade, 1965–67; Comdr, NATO Standing Naval Force Atlantic, 1968–69; Director Strategic Policy, to Supreme Allied Comdr Atlantic, 1969–71; Rear Adm. 1971; Dep. Asst Chief of Staff (Ops), SHAPE, 1971–74; Chm., RNR and Naval Cadet Forces Review Bd, 1974–75. *Recreations:* golf, painting, music, languages, sailing. *Address:* 10 Nelson Close, Stockbridge, Hants SO20 6ES. *T:* (01264) 810365.

MITCHELL, George Edward, CBE 2006; Chairman, The Malcolm Group, since 2006; *b* 7 April 1950; *m* 1971, Agnes Rutherford; three *d*. *Educ:* Forrester High Sch., Edinburgh. Joined Bank of Scotland, 1966: held a wide range of posts, incl. periods in Hong Kong, NY and London; Chief Exec., Bank of Scotland Retail Bank, 1999–2000; Chief Exec., Corporate, HBOS, 2001–05, Gov., 2003–05, Bank of Scotland. Director: Intrinsic Financial Services, 2006–; BUPA, 2007–. *Recreations:* football, tennis.

MITCHELL, Hon. George John, Hon. GBE 1999; lawyer; Partner, DLA Piper LLP, since 2005 (Chairman, 2005–08, now Emeritus); *b* 20 Aug. 1933; *s* of George and Mary Mitchell; *m* 1959, Sally L. Heath (marr. diss.); one *d*; *m* 1994, Heather MacLachlan; one *s* one *d*. *Educ:* Bowdoin Coll. (BA 1954); Georgetown Univ. (LLB 1960). Served US Army, 1954–56 (1st Lieut). Admitted to Bar of Maine and of Washington, 1960, to DC Bar, 1960; Trial Attorney, Anti-Trust Div., Dept of Justice, Washington, 1960–62; Exec. Asst to Senator Edmund Muskie, 1962–65; Partner, Jensen, Baird, Gardner, Donovan & Henry, Portland, 1965–77; US Attorney, Maine, 1977–79; US Dist Judge, N Maine, 1979–80; US Senator (Democrat) from Maine, 1980–95; Majority Leader, US Senate, 1988–95. Chm., Irish Peace Talks, 1995–98; Special US Envoy to the Middle East, 2009–11. Chm., Walt Disney Co., 2004. Chancellor, QUB, 1999–2009. Hd, Internat. Adv. Council, Thames Water, 1999–. Hon. LLD: QUB, 1997; Cambridge, 2010. Presidential Medal of Freedom (USA), 1999. *Publications:* (jtly) Men of Zeal: a candid inside story of the Iran-Contra Hearings, 1988; World on Fire, 1990; Not For America Alone: the triumph of democracy and the fall of communism, 1997; Making Peace, 1999. *Address:* DLA Piper LLP, 1251 Avenue of the Americas, New York, NY 10020–1104, USA.

MITCHELL, Gordon Scotland; Director, Starburst Consulting Ltd, since 2006; *b* 30 Dec. 1956. *Educ:* Univ. of Edinburgh (MA Hons); Univ. of Newcastle upon Tyne (BPhil); Bristol Business Sch., UWE (MBA 1997). Posts in nat. voluntary sector, 1982–92; Hd, Policy and Corporate Relns, Newport CBC, 1992–97; Chief Executive: Bracknell Forest BC, 1998–2003; Nottingham CC, 2003–06. Non-exec. Dir, Glos Hosps NHS Foundn Trust, 2009– (Vice Chm., 2012–). Governor: Nottingham Trent Univ., 2004–09; Glos Coll., 2008–. *Recreations:* good food and wine, lying in the sun. *Address:* 36 William Bancroft Building, Roden Street, Nottingham NG3 1GH.

MITCHELL, Gregory Charles Mathew; QC 1997; PhD; a Recorder, since 2000; *b* 27 July 1954; *s* of John Matthew Mitchell, *qv*; three *s* one *d*. *Educ:* King's Coll., London (BA Hons; PhD); City Univ. (Dip. Law). Called to the Bar, Gray's Inn, 1979, Bencher, 2005. *Recreations:* ski-ing, scuba diving, tennis. *Address:* 3 Verulam Buildings, Gray's Inn, WC1R 5NT. *T:* (020) 7831 8441.

MITCHELL, Harry; QC 1987; Company Secretary, The Wellcome Foundation Ltd, 1976–92, and Wellcome plc, 1985–92; *b* 27 Oct. 1930; *s* of Harry and Lily Mitchell; *m* 1960, Mrs Megan Knill (*née* Watkins); one step *s* one step *d*. *Educ:* Bolton School; Corpus Christi College, Cambridge (BA). FCIS. Called to the Bar, Gray's Inn, 1968. Asst District Comr, Colonial Service, Sierra Leone, 1954–59; Company Sec., Asbestos Cement, Bombay, 1960–64; Asst Company Sec., British Aluminium Co., 1964–66; Legal Manager/Exec. Dir Legal, Hawker Siddeley Aviation, 1966–76. Chm., Bar Assoc. for Commerce, Finance and Industry, 1984–85 (Vice-Pres., 1986–); Mem. Senate of Inns of Court and Bar and Bar Council, 1978–81, 1983–86; Part-time Immigration Adjudicator, 1992–2002. Director: Berkeley Square Pension Trustee Co. Ltd, 2004–08; Berkeley Square Common Investment Fund Ltd, 2005–08. Mem., Adv. Council and Hon. Legal Advr, Migrationwatch UK, 2003–. Mem., CBI London Regional Council, 1990–92. Board Member: Sarsen Housing Assoc., Devizes, 1994–2006 (Chm., 1995–2001); Silbury Gp Ltd, 2003–05; Ridgeway Community Housing Assoc., 2003–04. Trustee, Migraine Trust, 1995–2005. *Publications:* Remote Corners: a Sierra Leone memoir, 2002; articles in New Law Jl, Business Law Review and Jl of Immigration, Asylum and Nationality Law; numerous legal briefing papers on immigration and asylum law. *Recreations:* playing piano, opera, reading, travel. *Address:* The Mount, Brook Street, Great Bedwyn, Marlborough, Wilts SN8 3LZ. *T:* (01672) 870898. *E:* harrymitchellqc@hotmail.com.

MITCHELL, Iain Grant; QC (Scot.) 1992; barrister; *b* 15 Nov. 1951; *s* of late John Grant Mitchell and Isobel (*née* Gilhespie). *Educ:* Perth Acad.; Edinburgh Univ. (LLB Hons 1973). Called to the Scottish Bar, 1976; Temp. Sheriff, 1992–97; called to the Bar, Middle Temple, 2012. Vice-Chm., 2001–07, Chm., 2007–, Scottish Soc. for Computers and Law. Chm., IT Gp, Faculty of Advocates, 1999–; Mem., IT Cttee, 2011–, Cttee on Surveillance, 2015–, Bar Council; UK Rep., IT Cttee, 2011–, Chm., Wkg Pty on Surveillance, 2015–, CCBE. Exec. Ed., Scottish Parlt Law Rev., 1999–2003; Joint Editor: E-Law Rev., 2001–04; Internat. Free and Open Source Law Rev., 2009–. Cons. local govt cand. on various occasions, 1973–82; contested (C): Falkirk W, 1983; Kirkcaldy, 1987; Cumbernauld and Kilsyth, 1992; Dunfermline East, 1997; Dundee E, Scottish Parlt, 1999; Scotland, EP elecns, 1999; Edinburgh North & Leith, 2001; Falkirk W, Scottish Parlt, 2003. Hon. Secretary: Scottish Cons. & Unionist Assoc., 1993–98; Scottish Cons. & Unionist Party, 1998–2001; Chm., Edinburgh Central Cons. Assoc., 2003–05. Chairman: N Queensferry Community Council, 2007–10 and 2012–; N Queensferry Community Trust, 2012–. Member, Executive Committee: Scottish Council, European Movement, 1992–; Perth Civic Trust, 1999–2002. Director: Scottish Baroque Ensemble Ltd, 1985–2003 (Chm., 1999–2003); Cappella Nova, 2007–; Chairman: Trust for an Internat. Opera Theatre of Scotland, 1984–; N Queensferry Arts Trust, 2005–; N Queensferry Railway Station Preservation Trust, 2006–; Perthshire Public Arts Trust, 2007– (Trustee, 2000–07); Mem., Forth Bridge Meml Cttee, 2005–. Vis. Lectr, Inst. for Information, Telecommunications and Media Law, Westfälische Wilhelms-Univ., Germany. Reader, 2005–, Mem., Ch and Society Council, 2009–, Ch of Scotland. FSA (Scot) 1974; FRSA 1988. Freeman, City of London, 2010–; Liveryman, Information Technologists' Co., 2010– (Freeman, 2008–09); Mem., Merchant Co. of Edinburgh, 2006–. *Publications:* (contrib.) Electronic Evidence, 2nd edn 2010, 3rd edn 2012; (contrib.) FOSS Law Book, 2011; (contrib.) Open Source Software: law, policy and practice, 2013. *Recreations:* music and the arts, photography, cinema, walking, travel, finding enough hours in the day. *Address:* Advocates' Library, Parliament House, High Street, Edinburgh EH1 1RF. *T:* (0131) 226 5071. *Club:* Scottish Arts (Edinburgh).

MITCHELL, James; Social Security Commissioner, 1980–95; a Child Support Commissioner, 1993–95; *b* 11 June 1926; *s* of James Hill Mitchell and Marjorie Kate Mitchell (*née* Williams); *m* 1957, Diane Iris Mackintosh (*d* 2012); two *d*. *Educ:* Merchiston Castle Sch., Edinburgh; Brasenose Coll., Oxford, 1944–45 and 1948–51 (Open Exhibnr, BCL, MA). Served RAFVR, 1945–48. Assistant Master, Edge Grove Preparatory Sch., Herts, 1952–55;

called to the Bar, Middle Temple, 1954; private practice as barrister/solicitor, Gold Coast/ Ghana, 1956–58; practice as barrister, London, 1958–80. Most Hon. Order of Crown of Brunei, 3rd Cl. 1959, 2nd Cl. 1972. *Recreations:* walking, railways, the Jacobites.

MITCHELL, Rt Hon. Sir James (Fitz Allen), KCMG 1995; PC 1985; Prime Minister of St Vincent and the Grenadines, 1984–2000; *b* 15 May 1931; *s* of Reginald and Lois Mitchell; *m* (marr. diss.); four *d.* *Educ:* Imperial College of Tropical Agriculture (DICTA); University of British Columbia (BSA). MRSB (MIBiol 1965); CBiol 1973. Agronomist, 1958–65; owner, Hotel Frangipani, Bequia, 1966–, and other cos; Chm., Quatre Isle Resort, 2005–. MP for Grenadines, 1966–2001; Minister of Trade, Agriculture and Tourism, 1967–72; Premier, 1972–74; Minister of Foreign Affairs, 1984–92; Minister of Finance, 1984–98. Founder and Pres., New Democratic Party, 1975–2000; Chm., Caribbean Democrat Union, 1991–; Vice-Chm., Internat. Democrat Union, 1992– (Co-Chair, Nicaragua Observer Team and Hungary Observer Team, 1990); Chm., Caribbean Community, 2000. Chm., Commonwealth Observer Gp, Lesotho Gen. Election, 2002. Mem., Inter Action Council, 2008–. Alumni Award of Distinction, 1988, Centenary Award, 2008, Univ. of BC. Chevalier d'honneur, Chaîne des Rôtisseurs, 1995. Order of the Liberator (Venezuela), 1972; Order of Propitious Clouds (Taiwan), 1995; Gran Cruz, Order of Infante Dom Henrique (Portugal), 1997; Grand Cross, Order of Knights of Malta, 1998. *Publications:* World Fungicide Usage, 1967; Caribbean Crusade, 1989; Guiding Change in the Islands, 1996; A Season of Light, 2001; Beyond the Islands (autobiog.), 2006. *Recreation:* planting trees. *Address:* Bequia, St Vincent, West Indies. *T:* 4583255. *Clubs:* St Vincent Nat. Trust; Bequia Sailing.

MITCHELL, (Janet) Margaret; JP; Member (C) Scotland Central, Scottish Parliament, since 2003; *b* 15 Nov. 1952; *d* of late John Aitken Fleming and of Margaret McRae Fleming (*née* Anderson); *m* 1978, Henry Thomson Mitchell. *Educ:* Coatbridge High Sch.; Hamilton Teacher Training Coll. (DipEd); Open Univ. (BA); Strathclyde Univ. (LLB; DipLLP); Jordanhill Coll. (Dip Media Studies). Primary school teacher, Airdrie and Bothwell, 1974–93. Mem. and Cons Gp Leader, Hamilton DC, 1988–96. Non-exec. Dir, Stonehouse and Hairmyres NHS Trust, 1993–97; Special Advr to David McLetchie, MSP and James Douglas Hamilton, MSP, 1999–2002. Scottish Cons. justice spokesman, 2003–07 and 2013–; Scottish Parliament: Convener: Dyslexia Cross Party Cttee, 2007–; Cross Party Gp on Adult Survivors of Childhood Sexual Abuse, 2011–; Caribbean Cross Party Gp, 2011–; Co-Convener, Taiwan Cross Party Gp, 2011– (Mem., 2009–11); Vice-Convener, Tibet Cross Party Gp, 2008–11; Member: Equal Opportunities Cttee, 2011– (Convener, 2007–11); Justice Cttee, 2013– (Mem., Sub-cttee on Policing, 2013–). Mem., Scottish Cons. Party Exec., 2002–03. Hon. Member: Psoriasis Scotland Arthritis Link Volunteers, 2004–; Bd of Advrs, ThinkScotland.org, 2007–. JP South Lanarks, 1990. *Recreations:* music, cycling, photography. *Address:* Huntly Lodge, Fairfield Place, Bothwell G71 8RP; Scottish Parliament, Edinburgh EH99 1SP. *E:* Margaret.Mitchell.msp@scottish.parliament.uk. *Club:* New (Edinburgh).

MITCHELL, Jeremy George Swale Hamilton; consumer policy adviser; *b* 25 May 1929; *s* of late George Oswald Mitchell and late Agnes Josephine Mitchell; *m* 1st, 1956, Margaret Mary Ayres (marr. diss. 1988); three *s* one *d*; 2nd, 1989, Janet Rosemary Powney. *Educ:* Ampleforth; Brasenose and Nuffield Colls, Oxford (MA). 2nd Lt, RA, 1948–49. Dep. Research Dir, then Dir of Information, Consumers' Assoc. (Which?), 1958–65; Asst Sec., Nat. Econ. Develt Office, 1965–66; Scientific Sec., then Sec., SSRC, 1966–74; Under Sec., and Dir of Consumer Affairs, Office of Fair Trading, 1974–77; Under Sec. and Dir, Nat. Consumer Council, 1977–86. Member: Economic Develt Cttee for the Distributive Trades, 1981–86; Independent Cttee for Supervision of Telephone Information Services, 1989–97; Direct Mail Services Standards Bd, 1990–95; Bd, PIA, 1994–2000; Scottish Consumer Council, 1995–2000; Telecoms Ombudsman Service Council, 2002–06; Scottish Solicitors' Discipline Tribunal, 2004–08; Consumer Panel, OFCOM, 2006–08; Chm., Scottish Adv. Cttee on Telecommunications, 1998–2003; Comr for Scotland, Broadcasting Standards Commn, 1999–2000. *Publications:* (ed) SSRC Reviews of Research, series, 1968–73; (ed jtly) Social Science Research and Industry, 1971; Betting, 1972; (ed) Marketing and the Consumer Movement, 1978; (ed jtly) The Information Society, 1985; (ed) Money and the Consumer, 1988; Electronic Banking and the Consumer, 1988; The Consumer and Financial Services, 1990; Banker's Racket or Consumer Benefit?, 1991; (ed jtly) Television and the Viewer Interest, 1994; Shrapnel and Whizzbangs, 2008. *Recreations:* Swinburne, racing. *Address:* 19 Eglinton Crescent, Edinburgh EH12 5BY.

MITCHELL, John; *see* Mitchell, R. J.

MITCHELL, (John) Angus (Macbeth), CB 1979; CVO 1961; MC 1946; Secretary, Scottish Education Department, 1976–84; *b* 25 Aug. 1924; *s* of late John Fowler Mitchell, CIE and Sheila Macbeth, MBE; *m* 1948, Ann Katharine Williamson, MA, MPhil, author; two *s* two *d.* *Educ:* Marlborough Coll.; Brasenose Coll., Oxford (Junior Hulme Scholar); BA Modern Hist., 1948. Served Royal Armoured Corps, 1943–46: Lieut, Inns of Court Regt, NW Europe, 1944–45; Captain East African Military Records, 1946. Entered Scottish Education Dept, 1949; Private Sec. to Sec. of State for Scotland, 1958–59; Asst Sec., Scottish Educn Dept, 1959–65; Dept of Agriculture and Fisheries for Scotland, 1965–68; Scottish Development Dept, 1968; Asst Under-Secretary of State, Scottish Office, 1968–69; Under Sec., Social Work Services Gp, Scottish Educn Dept, 1969–75; Under Sec., SHHD, 1975–76. Chairman: Scottish Marriage Guidance Council, 1965–69; Working Party on Social Work Services in NHS, 1976; Working Party on Relationships between Health Bds and Local Authorities, 1976; Consultative Cttee on the Curriculum, 1976–80; Stirling Univ. Court, 1984–92; Scottish Action on Dementia, 1985–94; Vice-Convener, Scottish Council for Voluntary Orgs, 1986–91; Member: Commn for Local Authority Accounts in Scotland, 1985–89; Historic Buildings Council for Scotland, 1988–94. Mem., Dementia Services Develt Trust, 1988–2000. Hon. Vice-Pres., Scottish Genealogy Soc., 2007–. Hon. Fellow, Edinburgh Univ. Dept of Politics, 1984–88. Hon. LLD Dundee, 1983; DUniv Stirling, 1992. Kt, Order of Oranje-Nassau (Netherlands), 1946. *Publications:* Procedures for the Reorganisation of Schools in England (report), 1987; Monumental Inscriptions in SW Midlothian, 2005. *Recreations:* old Penguins, genealogy, gravestones. *Address:* Saint Margaret's Care Home, 8 East Suffolk Road, Edinburgh EH16 5PJ. *T:* 07903 831963. *E:* 31kinnear@googlemail.com.
See also C. I. Mitchell, J. J. Mitchell.

MITCHELL, Dr John Francis Brake, OBE 2001; FRS 2004; FRMetS; FIMA; Principal Research Fellow, Meteorological Office, since 2010; *b* 7 Oct. 1948; *s* of Norman Brake Mitchell and Edith Alexandra Mitchell (*née* Reside); *m* 1973, Catriona Rogers; one *s* two *d.* *Educ:* Down High Sch., Downpatrick; Queen's Univ., Belfast (BSc Applied Maths 1970; PhD Theoretical Physics 1973). FRMetS 1973. Joined Meteorological Office, 1973: HSO, 1973–75; SSO, 1975–78; PSO, 1978–88; Grade 6, 1988–2002; Chief Scientist, 2002–07; Dir, Climate Sci., 2007–10. Vis. Prof., Sch. of Maths, Meteorol. and Physics, Univ. of Reading, 2004–; Hon. Prof. of Envmtl Scis, UEA, 2003–; Hon. Vis. Prof., Sch. of Engrg, Univ. of Exeter, 2007–12. Symons Meml Lectr, RMetS, 2003. Mem., NERC, 2007–09. Member, Editorial Board: Climate Dynamics, 1994–; Proc. Royal Soc. A, 2013–. MAE 1998; FIMA 2003. L. G. Groves Trust Fund Prize for Meteorol., 1984; (jtly) Mumm Gerbier Award, 1997 and 1998; Hans Oeschger Medal, European Geophysical Soc., 2004; Symons Gold Medal, RMetS, 2011. *Publications:* contrib. scientific papers on climate and climate change. *Recreations:* sport, outdoor pursuits, photography. *Address:* Meteorological Office, Fitzroy Road, Exeter EX1 3PB. *T:* (01392) 884604, *Fax:* 0845 300 1300. *E:* john.f.mitchell@metoffice.gov.uk.

MITCHELL, John Gall; QC (Scot.) 1970; a Deputy Social Security Commissioner and a Deputy Child Support Commissioner, 1999–2001 (a Social Security (formerly National Insurance) Commissioner, 1979–99; a Child Support Commissioner, 1993–99); *b* 5 May 1931; *s* of late Rev. William G. Mitchell, MA; *m* 1st, 1959, Anne Bertram Jardine (*d* 1986); three *s* one *d*; 2nd, 1988, Margaret, *d* of late J. W. Galbraith. *Educ:* Royal High Sch., Edinburgh; Edinburgh Univ. (MA, LLB). Commn, HM Forces, 1954–56 (Nat. Service). Advocate 1957. Standing Junior Counsel, Customs and Excise, Scotland, 1964–70; Chairman: Industrial Tribunals, Scotland, 1966–80; Legal Aid Supreme Court Cttee, Scotland, 1974–79; Pensions Appeals Tribunal, Scotland, 1974–80. Hon. Sheriff: of Lanarkshire, 1970–74; of S Strathclyde, 1975–79. *Address:* Rosemount, Park Road, Dalkeith, Midlothian EH22 3DH.

MITCHELL, John Logan; QC (Scot.) 1987; *b* 23 June 1947; *s* of Robert Mitchell and Dorothy Mitchell; *m* 1973, Christine Brownlee Thomson; one *s* one *d.* *Educ:* Royal High School, Edinburgh (Past Pres., Former Pupils' Club); Edinburgh Univ. (LLB Hons). Called to the Bar, 1974; Standing Junior Counsel: to Dept of Agriculture and Fisheries for Scotland, 1979; Forestry Commission for Scotland, 1979; Advocate Depute, 1981–85. *Recreation:* golf. *Address:* 17 Braid Farm Road, Edinburgh EH10 6LE. *T:* (0131) 447 8099. *Clubs:* Mortonhall Golf, Craigielaw Golf, Luffness New Golf.

MITCHELL, John Matthew, CBE 1976; DPhil; Assistant Director-General, 1981–84, Senior Research Fellow, 1984–85, British Council; retired; *b* 22 March 1925; *s* of Clifford George Arthur Mitchell and Grace Maud Jamson; *m* 1952, Eva Maria von Rupprecht; three *s* one *d.* *Educ:* Ilford County High Sch.; Worcester Coll., Oxford; Queens' Coll., Cambridge (MA). DPhil Vienna. Served War, RN, 1944–46. British Council: Lectr, Austria, 1949–52 and Egypt, 1952–56; Scotland, 1957–60; Dep. Rep., Japan, 1960–63; Reg. Dir, Zagreb, 1963–66; Reg. Rep., Dacca, 1966–69; Dep. Controller, Home Div., 1969–72; Rep., Federal Republic of Germany, 1973–77; Controller, Educn, Medicine and Sci. Div., 1977–81. Vis. Fellow, Wolfson Coll., Cambridge, 1972–73; former Lectr, univs of Vienna, Cairo and Tokyo. Fellow, Chartered Inst. of Linguists, 1989 (Chm. Council, 1996–99; Pres., 2004–07; Vice-Pres., 2007–). *Publications:* International Cultural Relations, 1986; Selected Poems, 2009; verse, short stories and trans. from German and French. *Recreations:* golf, theatre, cinema, opera. *Address:* The Cottage, Pains Hill Corner, Pains Hill, Limpsfield, Surrey RH8 0RB. *T:* (01883) 723354. *Club:* Tandridge Golf.
See also G. C. M. Mitchell.

MITCHELL, Jonathan James; QC (Scot.) 1992; *b* 4 Aug. 1951; *s* of (John) Angus (Macbeth) Mitchell, *qv* and Ann Katharine (*née* Williamson); *m* 1987, Melinda McGarry; one *s* one *d.* *Educ:* Marlborough Coll.; New Coll., Oxford (BA); Edinburgh Univ. (LLB). Advocate, 1979; Temp. Sheriff, 1988–95. Dep. Social Security Comr, 1994–2002. Mem., Scotch Malt Whisky Soc. *Publications:* Eviction and Rent Arrears, 1994. *T:* 07739 639343, *Fax:* (0131) 220 2654. *E:* jonathanmitchell@mac.com. *W:* www.jonathanmitchell.info.
See also C. I. Mitchell.

MITCHELL, Julian, FSA; FRSL; writer; *b* 1 May 1935; *s* of late William Moncur Mitchell and of Christine Mary (*née* Browne). *Educ:* Winchester; Wadham Coll., Oxford. Nat. Service in Submarines, 1953–55; Temp. Acting Sub-Lieut, RNVR. Member: Literature Panel, Arts Council, 1966–69; Welsh Arts Council, 1988–92 (Chm. Drama Cttee, 1989–92). Curator: Joshua Gosselin exhibn, Chepstow, 2003; Wye Tour and its Artists, Chepstow, 2010. Wolfson Lecture, Oxford, 2003. John Llewellyn Rhys Prize, 1965; Somerset Maugham Award, 1966. Television plays include: Shadow in the Sun; A Question of Degree; Rust; Abide With Me (Internat. Critics Prize, Monte Carlo, 1977); Survival of the Fittest; Consenting Adults (Scottish BAFTA 2007); adaptations of: Persuasion; The Alien Corn; Staying On; The Good Soldier; The Mysterious Stranger; The Weather in the Streets; Inspector Morse; series, Jennie, Lady Randolph Churchill, 1974; television documentary: All the Waters of Wye, 1990. Films: Arabesque, 1965; Vincent and Theo, 1990; Wilde, 1997. Theatre: Adelina Patti, 1987. FRSL 1985; FSA 2010. *Publications: novels:* Imaginary Toys, 1961; A Disturbing Influence, 1962; As Far As You Can Go, 1963; The White Father, 1964; A Circle of Friends, 1966; The Undiscovered Country, 1968; *biography:* (with Peregrine Churchill) Jennie: Lady Randolph Churchill, 1974; *autobiography:* A Disgraceful Anomaly, 2003; *translation:* Henry IV (Pirandello), 1979 (John Florio Prize, 1980); *plays:* Half-Life, 1977; The Enemy Within, 1980; Another Country, 1981 (SWET play of the year, 1982; filmed, 1984); Francis, 1983; After Aida (or Verdi's Messiah), 1986; Falling Over England, 1994; August, 1994 (adapted from Chekhov's Uncle Vanya; filmed, 1996); The Good Soldier (adapted from Ford Madox Ford), 2010; Family Business, 2011; The Welsh Boy (adapted from James Parry's The True Anti-Pamela), 2012; *screenplay:* Wilde, 1997; (adapted from Ivy Compton-Burnett): A Heritage and Its History, 1965; A Family and a Fortune, 1975; (contrib.) History and Fiction, ed by R. L. O. Tomlin, 2005; contribs to: Welsh History Review, The Monmouthshire Antiquary; Gwent County History. *Recreation:* local history. *Address:* 25 Rylett Road, W12 9SS. *E:* julian.mitchell606@btinternet.com.

MITCHELL, Prof. Juliet Constance Wyatt, (Lady Goody), FBA 2010; writer, since 1962; psychoanalyst, since 1978; Director, Expanded Doctoral School in Psychoanalytic Studies, Psychoanalysis Unit, University College London, since 2010; *b* Christchurch, NZ, 4 Oct. 1940; *d* of Leonard Huskins and Marjorie Editta Mitchell; *m* 1962, Frances Rory Peregrine Anderson; *m* 1977, Dr Martin Rossdale; one *d*; *m* 2000, Sir John Rankine, (Sir Jack), Goody, FBA (*d* 2015); one step *s* four step *d.* *Educ:* King Alfred Sch., London; St Anne's Coll., Oxford (MA). University of Cambridge: Lectr of Gender Studies, 1996–2000; Prof. of Psychoanalysis and Gender Studies, 2000–09; Founder Dir, Centre for Gender Studies, 1998–; Fellow, Jesus Coll., Cambridge, 1996–2008, now Emeritus. Andrew Mellon Vis. Prof., Courtauld Inst. of Fine Art, 2011–12. Emeritus Leverhulme Scholar, 2011–. *Publications:* Women's Estate, 1972; Psychoanalysis and Feminism, 1974, 2nd edn 2000; (with A. Oakley) The Rights and Wrongs of Women, 1976; Women: the longest revolution, 1984; (with J. Rose) Lacan and the école freudienne, 1984; Selected Melanie Klein, 1986; (with A. Oakley) What is Feminism?, 1986; Before I Was I: essays of Enid Balint, 1993; (with A. Oakley) Who's Afraid of Feminism?, 1997; Mad Men and Medusas, 2000, 2nd edn 2010; Siblings: sex and violence, 2003, 2nd edn 2010; contribs to learned jls. *Recreations:* reading, swimming, theatre. *Address:* Jesus College, Cambridge CB5 8BL. *T:* (01223) 305271. *E:* jcwm2@cam.ac.uk.

MITCHELL, Katrina Jane, (Katie), OBE 2009; freelance director; Associate Director, Royal National Theatre, since 2003; *b* 23 Sept. 1964; *d* of Michael and Sally Mitchell. *Educ:* Magdalen Coll., Oxford (MA Eng. Lit. and Lang.). Asst Dir, 1989–90, Associate Dir, 1996–98, RSC; Associate Dir, Royal Court Th., 2001–04. Productions directed: Gate Theatre, Notting Hill: Vassa Zheleznova, 1991; Women of Troy, 1991; The House of Bernarda Alba, 1992; Royal Shakespeare Company: The Dybbuk, 1992; Ghosts, 1993; Henry VI, 1995; Easter, 1995; The Phoenician Women, 1996; Beckett Shorts, 1997; Uncle Vanya, 1998; Royal Court: Live Like Pigs, 1993; The Country, 2000; Mountain Language, Ashes to Ashes, 2001; Nightsongs, Face to the Wall, 2002; Forty Winks, 2004; The City, 2008; 2071, 2014, transf. Deutches Schauspielhaus, Hamburg, 2014; Abbey Theatre, Dublin: The Last Ones, 1993; Iphigenia at Aulis, 2001; National Theatre: Rutherford and Son, 1994; Machine Wreckers, 1995; The Oresteia, 1999; Ivanov, 2002; Three Sisters, 2003; Iphigenia at Aulis, 2004; A Dream Play, 2005; The Seagull, Waves, 2006; Women of Troy, 2007; Some Trace of Her…, 2008; Pains of Youth, 2009; Cat in the Hat, 2009; Welsh National Opera: Don Giovanni, 1996; Jenufa, 1998; Katya Kabanova, 2001; Jephtha, 2003, restaged, ENO, 2005; The Sacrifice, 2007; Endgame, 1996, Four Quartets, 2009, Donmar Warehouse; The Maids, 1999, The Cherry Orchard, 2014, The Way Back Home, 2014, Young Vic; Easter,

2001, Krapp's Last Tape, 2004, The Maids, 2008, Royal Dramatic Th., Stockholm; Request Programme, Schauspielhaus, Cologne, 2008; After Dido, ENO/Young Vic, 2009; Parthenogenesis, ROH, 2009; Al Gran Sole Carico D'Amore, Salzburg Fest., 2009; Idomeneo, ENO, 2010; The Trial of Ubu, Hampstead Th., 2012; Written on Skin, Aix-en-Provence Fest., 2012, ROH, 2013; Hansel and Gretel, RNT, 2012; Fräulein Julie, Barbican, 2013; television: Widowing of Mrs Holroyd, 1995; Turn of the Screw, 2004. *Address:* c/o Leah Schmidt, The Agency, 24 Pottery Lane, W11 4LZ.

MITCHELL, Madeleine Louise; solo concert violinist; chamber musician; Professor, Royal College of Music, since 1994; Director: London Chamber Ensemble, since 1994; Red Violin Ltd, since 1997 (Artistic Director, Red Violin Festival, 1997, 2007); *b* 2 March 1957; *d* of Desmond Mitchell and Evelyn Mitchell (*née* Jones); one *d*. *Educ:* Hornchurch Grammar Sch.; Royal Coll. of Music (Jun. Exhibnr; Open Foundn Scholar; GRSM (1st Cl. Hons); ARCM (Performance Hons), ARCM (Teacher Hons)); Eastman Sch. of Music, NY (Fulbright/ITT Fellow); Univ. of Rochester (MMus Performance and Lit.). Violinist and violist, Sir Peter Maxwell Davies' The Fires of London, 1985–87; Leader, Bridge String Quartet, 2000–07. Performed as soloist in over 40 countries in recitals and concertos with Royal Philharmonic, BBC Ulster, St Petersburg Philharmonic, Polish Radio Symphony, Württemberg Chamber, Czech Radio, Munich Chamber, Academy of London, Orch. of the Swan, Orch. de Bahia Brazil, Welsh Chamber Orch., BBC Nat. Orch. of Wales. Numerous internat. festivals and venues incl. BBC Proms, Wigmore Hall, Moscow Conservatoire, Vienna Schönberg Centre, Singapore Victoria Hall; Artist-in-Residence, Canberra Music Fest., 2013. TV and radio broadcasts, and recordings. Mem., Council, RCM, 2013–. FRSA 2000. Tagore Gold Medal, RCM, 1978. *Recreations:* art galleries, opera, gardens, the sea, cycling. *E:* mlmfrsa@aol.com.

MITCHELL, Margaret; *see* Mitchell, Jane M.

MITCHELL, Michael James Ross, PhD; Director General, National Networks (formerly Rail, then Rail and National Networks), Department for Transport, 2005–10; *b* 22 Feb. 1948; *s* of James and Margaret Mitchell; *m* 1971, Jillian Mary Tomory; two *s*. *Educ:* Univ. of Aberdeen (MA Hons 1970; PhD 1993); Univ. of Edinburgh (MBA 1987). CMILT (MCIT 1977). With BR, 1970–86 (Area Manager, Coventry, 1978–80); Eastern Scottish Omnibuses Ltd, 1986–94 (Ops Dir, 1990–94); Man. Dir, Grampian Regl Transport, later FirstBus plc, 1994–97; FirstGroup plc: Divl Dir, 1997; Man. Dir, First Great Western, 1998; Dir, Rail, 1999; Chief Operating Officer, 2001–04; Business Develt Dir, 2004–05. *Publications:* Aberdeen Suburban Tramways, 1980, revd edn 1981; Aberdeen District Tramways, 1983; Fae Dee to Don and Back Again: 100 years of Aberdeen transport, 1998; Aberdeenshire Tramways, 2013; Montrose and Bervie Railway, 2015. *Recreations:* vintage bus restoration, photography, travel.

MITCHELL, Michelle Elizabeth; Chief Executive Officer, Multiple Sclerosis Society, since 2013; *b* Ellesmere Port, 13 March 1972; *d* of James Alexander Graham Mitchell and Elizabeth Mitchell; partner, Sean McKee; one *s* one *d*. *Educ:* Sutton High Sch.; Univ. of Manchester (BA Hons Econs 1994); University Coll. London (MSc Pols and Public Admin 1997); INSEAD (Internat. Exec. Prog.); Harvard Univ. (Innovations in Govt). Political advr roles, UK Parlt, 1994–97; Hd, Parly Unit, Charter 88, 1997–2000; Govt Affairs Advr, NSPCC UK, 2000–02; Age Concern, later Age UK: Hd, Public Affairs, 2002–07; Communications Dir, 2007–10; Charity Dir, 2010–12; Charity Dir Gen., 2012–13. Chm., Trustees, Fawcett Soc., 2005–08; Trustee: Young Women's Trust, 2013–; King's Fund, 2014–; Dir, Power to Change Trust, 2014–. Nat. Commng Support, 2013–; Mem., Multiple Sclerosis Internat. Fedn, 2013–. MCIPR. *Recreations:* yoga, cooking. *Address:* Multiple Sclerosis Society, 372 Edgware Road, NW2 6ND. *T:* (020) 8438 0738, *Fax:* (020) 8438 0701. *E:* michelle.mitchell@mssociety.org.uk.

MITCHELL, Very Rev. Patrick Reynolds, KCVO 1998; Dean of Windsor, 1989–98; Register, Order of the Garter, 1989–98; Domestic Chaplain to the Queen, 1989–98; *b* 17 March 1930; *s* of late Lt-Col Percy Reynolds Mitchell, DSO; *m* 1st, 1959, Mary Evelyn (*née* Phillips) (*d* 1986); three *s* one *d*; 2nd, 1988, Pamela, *d* of late A. G. Le Marchant and *widow* of Henry Douglas-Pennant; one step *s* one step *d* (and two step *s* decd). *Educ:* Eton Coll.; Merton Coll., Oxford (MA Theol); Wells Theol Coll. Officer in Welsh Guards (National Service), 1948–49. Deacon, 1954; priest, 1955; Curate at St Mark's, Mansfield, 1954–57; Priest-Vicar of Wells Cathedral and Chaplain of Wells Theological Coll., 1957–60; Vicar of St James', Milton, Portsmouth, 1961–67; Vicar of Frome Selwood, Somerset, 1967–73; Dean of Wells, 1973–89; Director of Ordination Candidates for Bath and Wells, 1971–74. Res. Fellow, Merton Coll., Oxford, 1984. Chm., Cathedral Libraries and Archives Assoc., 1997–2001. Member: Adv. Bd for Redundant Churches, 1978–92; Cathedrals Adv. Commn for England, 1981–91. Governor, Wellington Coll., 1994–98. Hon. Freeman, City of Wells, 1986. FSA 1981. *Address:* Wolford Lodge, Dunkeswell, Honiton, Devon EX14 4SQ. *T:* (01404) 841244.

MITCHELL, Paul England; Consultant, Taylor Wessing LLP, since 2011; *b* St Albans, 2 Nov. 1951; *s* of late Ronald England Mitchell and Katia Patricia Mitchell; *m* 1984, Catherine Anne Ros-Jones (marr. diss. 2002); one *s* one *d*. *Educ:* Canford Sch.; Bristol Univ. (LLB Hons). Admitted as solicitor, 1976. Joynson-Hicks & Co., subseq. Taylor Joynson Garrett, then Taylor Wessing LLP: articled clerk, 1974–76; Asst Solicitor, 1976–78; Partner, 1978–2011. Chm., British Copyright Council, 2005–13; Trustee, Copyright Soc. of USA, 2009–12. Director: Rambert Dance Co., 2002–13; Dancers Career Develt, 2008–; Roald Dahl Mus. and Story Centre, 2010– (Chm., 2014–). Trustee, Royal Ballet Benevolent Fund, 2014–. Freeman: City of London, 1993; Fishmongers' Co., 1993. FRSA. *Publications:* (with D. Lester) Joynson-Hicks on UK Copyright, 1989. *Recreations:* family, walking, reading, food and wine, contemporary dance, sailing. *Address:* 74 Palace Road, SW2 3JX. *T:* (020) 8671 1564, *Fax:* (020) 8674 2378. *E:* paulm75@hotmail.com. *Club:* Garrick.

MITCHELL, (Richard) John; His Honour Judge John Mitchell; a Circuit Judge, since 2005; *b* 28 Oct. 1948; *s* of Kenneth Frank Mitchell and Edith Mitchell; *m* 1977, Marlene Le Saint; two *s*. *Educ:* Brentwood Sch.; Peterhouse, Cambridge (MA 1972). Called to the Bar, Middle Temple, 1972, Bencher, 2012; a District Judge, 1999–2005. Foundn Gov., Addey and Stanhope Sch., 2010–. *Publications:* Children Act Private Law Proceedings: a handbook, 2003, 3rd edn 2012; Adoption and Special Guardianship, 2009. *Recreations:* walking, theatre. *Address:* Central London County Court, Thomas More Building, Royal Courts of Justice, Strand, WC2A 2CC.

MITCHELL, Sarah Jane; Strategic Director, Adult Social Care, Surrey County Council, 2009–14; *b* St Margaret's Bay, Dover, 30 Sept. 1960; *d* of John Mitchell (Master Mariner) and Hilda Mitchell, QARANC; *m* 2007, Adam Clow; two *s*. *Educ:* Univ. of Essex (BA Hons Sociol. 1982); Univ. of Southampton (CQSW; DASS 1984); Portsmouth Univ. (MBA 1993). Hampshire County Council Social Services: Social Worker, 1984–87; Project Manager, 1987–88; Team Manager, 1988–91; Service Manager, 1990–93; Prin. Advr, Mental Health, 1993–94; Care Mgt Co-ordinator, 1994–96; Inspector, Social Services Inspectorate, 1996–97, Hd of Policy, NHS Exec., 1997–98, DoH; Asst Dir, Older People, Portsmouth CC, 1999–2004; Owner, SJM Consulting, 2004–06; Dir, Community Services, IoW Council, 2006–09. *Recreations:* raising two boys, scuba diving - dived around the world with whale sharks in Australia and in the Galapagos, camping, travelling, horseriding, politics.

MITCHELL, Prof. Stephen, DPhil; FBA 2002; Leverhulme Professor of Hellenistic Culture, University of Exeter, 2002–11, now Emeritus Professor; *b* 26 May 1948; *s* of David and Barbara Mitchell; *m* 1974, Matina Weinstein; three *s*. *Educ:* St John's Coll., Oxford (BA 1970; MA, DPhil 1975). Lectr, 1976, Sen. Lectr, 1984, Reader, 1989, Prof., 1993–2001, UC of Swansea, subseq. Univ. of Wales, Swansea; Dir, Exeter Turkish Studies, Univ. of Exeter, 2009–11. Vis. Fellow, Inst. of Advanced Study, Princeton, 1983–84; British Acad. Res. Reader, 1990–92. Hon. DTheol Humboldt Univ., Berlin, 2006. *Publications:* Anatolia: land, men and gods in Asia Minor, 1993; Cremna in Pisidia: an ancient city in peace and in war, 1995; Pisidian Antioch: the site and its monuments, 1998; A History of the Later Roman Empire 284–641, 2007, 2nd edn 2015; One God: Pagan monotheism in the Roman Empire, 2010; The Greek and Latin Inscriptions of Ankara, 2012. *Recreations:* walking, travel, wine. *Address:* British Institute at Ankara, c/o British Academy, 10 Carlton House Terrace, SW1Y 5AH. *E:* mitchank@gmail.com.

MITCHELL, Hon. Sir Stephen (George), Kt 1993; a Judge of the High Court of Justice, Queen's Bench Division, 1993–2003; President, National Security Appeals Panel, Information Tribunal, 2004–07; *b* 19 Sept. 1941; *s* of Sydney Mitchell and Joan Mitchell (*née* Dick); *m* 1978, Alison Clare (*née* Roseveare) (*d* 1998); two *d*. *Educ:* Bedford Sch.; Hertford Coll., Oxford (MA). Called to the Bar, Middle Temple, 1964, Bencher, 1993; Second Prosecuting Counsel to the Crown, Inner London Crown Court, 1975; Central Criminal Court: a Junior Prosecuting Counsel to the Crown, 1977; a Senior Prosecuting Counsel to the Crown, 1981–86; QC 1986; a Recorder, 1985–89; a Circuit Judge, 1989–93. Dep. Chm., Security Vetting Appeals Panel, 2001–04. Mem., Judicial Studies Bd, 1991–93. *Publications:* (ed) Phipson on Evidence, 11th edn, 1970; (ed) Archbold's Criminal Pleading Evidence and Practice, 1971–88; The Marks on Chelsea-Derby and Early Crossed-batons Useful Wares 1770–c1790, 2007, 1st Supplement, 2009. *Address:* Royal Courts of Justice, Strand, WC2A 2LL.

MITCHELL, Stephen Graham; Director, Parkfield House Communication Services Ltd, since 2014; *b* 14 July 1949; *s* of Derek Mitchell and Phyllis Mitchell (*née* Rigden); *m* 1977, Barbara Gilder; one *s* one *d*. *Educ:* Loughborough Grammar Sch.; Manchester Univ. (BA Hons). Reporter, Thompson Newspapers, Newcastle Jl, S Wales Echo, The Times, 1971–74; BBC: producer, reporter, Radio Newsroom, and Duty Editor, Today prog., 1974–84; Dep. Foreign News Ed., 1985; Ed., Parly Output, 1986–88; Ed., then Man. Ed., Radio Newsroom, 1988–93; Ed., Radio News Progs, 1993–97; Dep. Hd, News Progs (Bimedia), 1997–99; Hd, Radio News, 2000–07; Hd of News Progs, BBC, 2007–13; Dep. Dir, BBC News, 2008–13. Dir, NCTJ, 2012–. *Recreations:* theatre, reading. *Address:* 30 Amenbury Lane, Harpenden, Herts AL5 2DF.

MITCHELL, Stuart Robert; Chief Executive, SIG plc, since 2013; *b* Watford, 22 Dec. 1960; *s* of Arthur Robert Mitchell and Margaret Patricia Mitchell; *m* 1987, Tracey Victoria Webb; one *s* one *d*. *Educ:* Tadcaster Grammar Sch.; Univ. of Manchester Inst. of Sci. and Technol. (BSc Mgt Scis). J. Sainsbury plc: joined as graduate trainee, 1981; Trading Dir, 2000–03; Man. Dir, 2003–04; Man. Dir, A. S. Watson, Taiwan, 2005–06; CEO, Wilkinsons Hardware Stores Ltd, 2006–12. Non-exec. Dir, Enactus (formerly SIFE), 2011–. *Recreations:* ski-ing, golf, travel, sailing, cookery. *Address:* The Oaks, Oaks Road, Reigate, Surrey RH2 0LE. *E:* sr.mitchell@hotmail.co.uk. *Clubs:* Royal Automobile; Dorking Rugby (Dir, 2014–).

MITCHELL, Terence Croft; Keeper of Western Asiatic Antiquities, British Museum, 1985–89; *b* 17 June 1929; *s* of late Arthur Croft Mitchell and Evelyn Violet Mitchell (*née* Ware). *Educ:* Holderness School, New Hampshire, USA; Bradfield Coll., Berks; St Catharine's Coll., Cambridge (MA 1956). REME Craftsman, 1947–49. Asst Master, St Catherine's Sch., Almondsbury, 1954–56; Resident Study, Tyndale House, Cambridge, 1956–58; European Rep., Aust. Inst. of Archaeology, 1958–59; Dept of Western Asiatic Antiquities, British Museum, 1959, Dep. Keeper, 1974, Acting Keeper, 1983–85. Chm., Faith and Thought (formerly Victoria Inst.), 1986–2009; Vice Chm., British Inst. at Amman for Archaeology and History, 1990–93. Lay Chm., Chelsea Deanery Synod, 1981–84; Mem., Gideon Assoc., 1974–. Editor, Palestine Exploration Fund Monograph Series, 1990–2000. *Publications:* Sumerian Art at Ur and Al-'Ubaid, 1969; (ed) Sir Leonard Woolley, Ur Excavations VIII, The Kassite Period and the Period of the Assyrian Kings, 1965; VII, The Old Babylonian Period, 1976; (ed) Music and Civilization, 1980; chapters on Israel and Judah in Cambridge Ancient History, vol. 3, part 1, 1982, part 2, 1991; The Bible in the British Museum: interpreting the evidence, 1988, rev. edn 1996, rev. and enlarged edn 2004; (with Ann Searight) Catalogue of the Western Asiatic Seals in the British Museum: Stamp Seals III, 2007; articles and reviews. *Recreations:* music, reading, landscape gardening. *Address:* 32 Mallord Street, Chelsea, SW3 6DU. *T:* (020) 7352 3962. *Club:* Athenæum.

MITCHELL, Valerie Joy, OBE 2001; Chairman, Cultural Affairs Committee, English-Speaking Union of the Commonwealth, since 2009 (Director-General, 1994–2009); *b* 2 March 1941; *d* of Henry Frederick Twidale and Dorothy Mary (*née* Pierce), MBE; *m* 1st, 1962, Henri Pierre Eschauzier (marr. diss. 1970); two *s*; 2nd, 1972, Graham Rangeley Mitchell; one *d*. *Educ:* Beaufront Sch., Camberley; McGill Univ., Montreal (BA Hons). PA to Asst Dean of Arts and Sci., McGill Univ., Montreal, 1962–64; PR Consultant to Mayer-Lismann Opera Workshop, 1970–80; English-Speaking Union: Asst, Educn Dept, 1980–83; Dir of Branches and Cultural Affairs, 1983–94; Dep. Dir-Gen., 1989–94; Sec.-Gen., Internat. Council of ESU Worldwide, 1994–2009. Member: Internat. Cttee, Shakespeare Globe Centre, 2000–05 and 2014–; Exec. Cttee, European Atlantic Gp, 2001–; Pilgrims Soc., 2003–; Council, Shakespeare's Globe, 2014–; Trustee: Shakespeare Globe Trust, 2006–14; Longborough Fest. Opera, 2006–; Prince Galitzine-St Petersburg Trust, 2007–; Harvard House Meml Trust, 2008–. FRSA 1987. *Recreations:* music, theatre, tennis, walking. *Address:* 2 Glenside Gardens, Shady Bower, Salisbury SP1 2RF.

See also S. A. Price.

MITCHELL, Warren; actor; *b* 14 Jan. 1926; *s* of Montague and Annie Misell, later Mitchell; *m* 1952, Constance Wake; one *s* two *d*. *Educ:* Southgate Co. Sch.; University Coll., Oxford; RADA. Demobbed RAF, 1946. First professional appearance, Finsbury Park Open Air Theatre, 1950; Theophile in Can-Can, Coliseum, 1954; Crookfinger Jake in The Threepenny Opera, Royal Court and Aldwych, 1956; Mr Godboy in Dutch Uncle, Aldwych, 1969; Satan in Council of Love, Criterion, 1970; Herbert in Jump, Queen's, 1971; Ion Will in The Great Caper, Royal Court, 1974; The Thoughts of Chairman Alf, Stratford E, 1976; Willie Loman in Death of a Salesman, Nat. Theatre, 1979; Ducking Out, Duke of York's, 1983; Harpagon in The Miser, Birmingham Rep., 1986; Max in The Homecoming, 1991; West Yorkshire Playhouse: King Lear, 1996; Visiting Mr Green, 2000; Art, Wyndhams, 2000; The Price, Tricycle, 2002, Apollo, 2003 (Best Supporting Actor, Olivier Awards, 2004); *films include:* Diamonds Before Breakfast; Assassination Bureau; Best House in London; Till Death Us Do Part; Moon Zero Two; Whatever Happened to Charlie Farthing; Jabberwocky; Stand Up Virgin Soldiers; Meetings with Remarkable Men; Norman Loves Rose; The Chain; *television:* Alf Garnett in Till Death Us Do Part, BBC, 1966–78, and In Sickness and in Health, BBC, 1985, 1986; The Thoughts of Chairman Alf (series), 1998; Shylock in Merchant of Venice, BBC, 1981; Till Death (series), ITV, 1981; The Caretaker, BBC, 1981; So You Think You've Got Troubles (series), BBC, 1994; Wall of Silence, BBC, 1995; Death of a Salesman, BBC, 1996; Gormenghast, BBC, 2000. TV Actor of the Year Award, Guild of Film and TV Producers, 1966; Actor of Year Award: Evening Standard, 1979; Soc. of West End Theatres, 1979; Plays and Players, 1979. *Recreations:* sailing, tennis, playing clarinet. *Address:* c/o The Artists Partnership, 101 Finsbury Pavement, EC2A 1RS.

MITCHELL COTTS, Sir Richard Crichton; *see* Cotts.

MITCHELL-INNES, Alistair Campbell; Chairman, Next Pension Trustees Ltd, 1991–2005; *b* 1 March 1934; *s* of Peter Mitchell-Innes; *m* 1957, Penelope Ann Hill; one *s* two *d*. *Educ:* Charterhouse; Stanford Business Sch. (Executive Program). Dir, Brooke Bond Gp plc, 1979–84; Chief Exec., Nabisco Gp Ltd, 1985–88; Chief Exec., Isosceles plc, 1991–93; Dep. Chm., H. P. Bulmer (Holdings) plc, 1990–2001; Chairman: Sidney C. Banks plc, 1994–2000; Anglo & Overseas Trust PLC, 1996–2004. Non-exec. Dir, 1989–2004, Dep. Chm., 2002–04, Next plc. *Recreations:* golf, cricket, military history. *Address:* 9 Market Street, Rye, E Sussex TN31 7LA. *Clubs:* Caledonian, MCC; Berkshire Golf; Rye Golf.

MITCHELL KILPATRICK, Reginald; Director, Local Government Department, Welsh Government, since 2011; *b* London, 1963; *s* of Thomas and Mary Kilpatrick; *m* 1994, Joanna Clare Mitchell; one *s* one *d. Educ:* Oathall Comprehensive Sch., Haywards Heath; Univ. of Glamorgan (BSc Behavioural Sci. 1987); Sheffield Hallam Univ. (Postgrad. Dip. Applied Stats 1991); Cardiff Business Sch. (MPA 2011). Asst Statistician, Local Govt, Educn and Demography, 1988–91, Hd of Educn Statistics, 1991–94, Welsh Office; Dir, Wales Cancer Registry, 1994–96; Welsh Government: Head: of Health Financial Mgt, 1996–99; of Museums Policy, Wales Millennium Centre Project Lead, 1999–2002; Sponsorship Br., Welsh Develt Agency, 2002–03; Deputy Director: Assembly Budget Planning and Mgt, 2003–07; Local Govt Policy, 2007–11. *Recreations:* modern literature, contemporary music, learning the guitar, creating stained glass. *Address:* Welsh Government, Cathays Park, Cardiff CF10 3NQ. *T:* (029) 2082 5913. *E:* reg.kilpatrick@wales.gsi.gov.uk.

MITCHELL-THOMSON, family name of **Baron Selsdon**.

MITCHESON, Thomas George Moseley; QC 2014; *b* London, 6 June 1972; *s* of George Anthony Mitcheson and Lavinia Anne Mitcheson (*née* Moseley); *m* 2003, Elizabeth Adair Peltzer Dunn; one *s* one *d. Educ:* Eton Coll.; Trinity Coll., Cambridge (BA 1st Cl. Hons Natural Scis 1994); City Univ. (DipLaw 1995); Inns of Court Sch. of Law. Called to the Bar, Inner Temple, 1996; in practice at Intellectual Property Bar; Standing Counsel to Comptroller Gen. of Patents, 2009–14. Chm., Old Etonian Housing Assoc., 2010–. *Recreations:* family, singing (London Oriana Choir Mem., 1998–), the beaches of North Norfolk, golf. *Address:* Three New Square, Lincoln's Inn, WC2A 3RS. *T:* (020) 7405 1111, *Fax:* (020) 7405 7800. *E:* clerks@3newsquare.co.uk.

MITCHINER, Dr John Edward; HM Diplomatic Service, retired; High Commissioner to Sierra Leone, and Ambassador (non-resident) to Liberia, 2003–06; *b* 12 Sept. 1951; *s* of late Geoffrey Morford Mitchiner and Ursula Angela Mitchiner (*née* Adolph); *m* 1983, Elizabeth Mary Ford, MA, MNIMH. *Educ:* John Fisher Sch., Purley; Beaumont Coll., Old Windsor; Bristol Univ. (BA 1972); Sch. of Oriental and African Studies, London Univ. (MA 1973; PhD 1977). ACU Res. Fellow, Visva-Bharati Univ., Santiniketan, 1977–78; Bipradas Palchaudhuri Fellow, Calcutta Univ., 1978–79; joined FCO, 1980; Third, later Second Sec. (Information), Istanbul, 1982–85; FCO, 1985–87; Second Sec. (Develt), New Delhi, 1987–91; Second, later First Sec. (Political), Berne, 1991–95; Head, Japan Section, FCO, 1995–96; Ambassador to Armenia, 1997–99; Dep. High Comr, Kolkata, India, 2000–03. MRAS. *Publications:* Studies in the Indus Valley Inscriptions, 1978; Traditions of the Seven Rsis, 1982, 2nd edn 2000; The Yuga Purana, 1986, 2nd edn 2002; Guru: the search for enlightenment, 1992; contribs to learned jls. *Recreations:* sheep farming, bridge, tennis, family history. *Address:* Bower Farm, Whitland SA34 0QX.

MITCHISON, Avrion; *see* Mitchison, N. A.

MITCHISON, Prof. Denis Anthony, CMG 1984; Professor of Bacteriology, Royal Postgraduate Medical School, 1971–84, Professor Emeritus, London University, since 1984; at St George's, University of London (formerly St George's Hospital Medical School), since 1993; Director, Medical Research Council's Unit for Laboratory Studies of Tuberculosis, 1956–84; *b* 6 Sept. 1919; *e s* of Baron Mitchison, CBE, QC, and late Naomi Margaret Mitchison, CBE, writer; *m* 1st, 1940, Ruth Sylvia (*d* 1992), *d* of Hubert Gill; two *s* two *d*; 2nd, 1993, Honora (*d* 2012), *d* of Christopher Carlin. *Educ:* Abbotsholme Sch.; Trinity Coll., Cambridge; University Coll. Hosp., London (MB, ChB). House Physician: Addenbrooke's Hosp.; Royal Berkshire Hosp.; Asst to Pathologist, Brompton Hosp.; Prof. of Bacteriology (Infectious Diseases), RPMS, 1968–71. Member, Scientific Advisory Committee: TB Alliance, 1998–2008; Medicine in Need, 2006–. FRCP; FRCPath. *Publications:* numerous papers on bacteriology and chemotherapy of tuberculosis. *Address:* 14 Marlborough Road, Richmond, Surrey TW10 6JR. *T:* (020) 8940 4751.

See also N. A. Mitchison.

MITCHISON, Prof. (Nicholas) Avrion, FRS 1967; Jodrell Professor of Zoology and Comparative Anatomy, University College London, 1970–89, Emeritus Professor, 1990 and Hon. Senior Fellow, Institute of Ophthalmology, since 1998 (Hon. Fellow, 1993; Senior Fellow, Department of Immunology, 1996–98); *b* 5 May 1928; 3rd *s* of Baron Mitchison, CBE, QC, and late Naomi Margaret Mitchison, CBE, writer; *m* 1957, Lorna Margaret, *d* of Maj.-Gen. J. S. S. Martin, CSI; two *s* three *d. Educ:* Leighton Park Sch.; New Coll., Oxford (MA 1949). Fellow of Magdalen College, 1950–52; Commonwealth Fund Fellow, 1952–54; Lecturer, Edinburgh Univ., 1954–61; Reader, Edinburgh Univ., 1961–62; Head of Div. of Experimental Biology, Nat. Inst. for Med. Research, 1962–71; Scientific Dir, Deutsches Rheuma-Forschungszentrum Berlin, 1990–96. Hon. Member: German Soc. of Immunol., 1996; German Soc. of Rheumatol.; Foreign Hon. Mem., American Acad. of Arts and Scis, 1987; Foreign Associate, NAS, 1990; Foreign Mem., Polish Acad. Arts and Scis, 1998. Hon. MD Edinburgh, 1977; Hon. PhD Weizmann Inst., 1994. Scientific Medal, ZSL, 1962; Paul Ehrlich and Ludwig Darmstaedter Prize, 1975; Sandoz Prize in Basic Immunol., Novartis, 1995; Robert Koch Gold Medal, 2001. *Publications:* articles in scientific journals and over 200 articles cited in PubMed. *Address:* 13 Framfield Road, N5 1UU. *T:* (020) 7359 5344; Department of Immunology, University College London, The Cruciform Building, Gower Street, WC1E 6BT. *E:* n.mitchison@ucl.ac.uk.

See also D. A. Mitchison.

MITFORD, family name of **Baron Redesdale**.

MITFORD-SLADE, Patrick Buxton, OBE 2000; Partner, Cazenove & Co., 1972–96; *b* 7 Sept. 1936; *s* of late Col Cecil Townley Mitford-Slade and Phyllis, *d* of E. G. Buxton; *m* 1964, Anne Catharine Stanton (separated 2000), *d* of late Major Arthur Holbrow Stanton, MBE; one *s* two *d. Educ:* Eton Coll.; RMA Sandhurst. Commissioned 60th Rifles, 1955, Captain; served Libya, NI, Berlin and British Guyana; Adjt, 2nd Green Jackets, KRRC, 1962–65; Instructor, RMA Sandhurst, 1965–67. Stockbroker, Cazenove & Co., 1968–96; Man. Dir, Cazenove Money Brokers, 1986–96. Non-executive Director: Clive Securities Group Ltd, 1996–99; John Govett Holdings Ltd, 1996–97; Clive Discount Co. Ltd, 1996–98; Investec Bank (UK) Ltd, 1996–98; AIB Asset Management Hldgs Ltd, 1997–98; SG Hambros Bank (formerly SG Hambros Bank & Trust Co.) Ltd, 2001–08. Asst Sec., Panel on Takeovers and Mergers, 1970–72; Mem., Stock Exchange, 1972–86, Internat. Stock Exchange, 1986–92 (Mem. Council, 1976–91; Dep. Chm., 1982–85); Chairman: City Telecommunications Cttee, 1983–92; Securities Industry Steering Cttee on Taurus, 1988–90; Money Brokers Assoc., 1990–96; Dep. Chm., Stock Borrowing and Lending Cttee, 1996–98. Vice Pres., St Luke's Healthcare for the Clergy (formerly St Luke's Hosp. for the Clergy), 2012– (Hon. Treas., 1994–2001; Chm., 2001–11). Vice Pres., Officers' Assoc., 1985– (Chm., 1985–2000); Mem., Benevolent and Strategy Cttee, RBL, 1998–2005; Hon. Recorder, Royal (formerly British) Commonwealth Ex-Services League, 2005– (Hon. Treas., 1993–2005). Chairman: Royal Green Jackets Administrative Trustees, 2005–08 (Trustee, 1996–2008); The Rifles Regtl Trustees, 2007–13. Jt Pres., Reed's Sch., 2009– (Gov., 2001–08; Chm., 2002–08). *Recreations:* shooting, fishing. *Address:* The White House, Wivelrod, Alton, Hants GU34 4AR. *Club:* Army and Navy.

MITHANI, Abbas; His Honour Judge Mithani; a Circuit Judge, since 2006; *b* 27 Feb. 1958; *s* of late Hussein Mithani and of Lailabanu Mithani; *m* 1982, Sajeda Nurmohomed; two *s* one *d. Educ:* Univ. of Newcastle upon Tyne (LLB Hons); Univ. of Keele (LLM). Admitted solicitor (with Hons), 1981; Licensed Insolvency Practitioner, 1987; Civil Higher Court Advocate, 1994; Dep. Bankruptcy Registrar, 1994. Dep. Dist Judge, 1993–99; Dist Judge, 1999–2006; a Recorder, 2000–06. Hon. Prof. of Law, Univ. of Birmingham, 2000–07 and 2009–15; Visiting Professor of Law: Newcastle Univ., 2008–; Kingston Univ., 2009–. Mem. Court, Newcastle Univ., 2005–. Hon. QC 2009. Asian Jewel Award for Legal Excellence for Central Britain, Inst. of Asian Professionals, 2003; Lifetime Achievement Award, Soc. of Asian Lawyers, 2009. *Publications:* Islamic Wills, 1994; Mithani and Wheeler, 1995, 2nd edn as Mithani: Directors' Disqualification, 1998; *contributor:* Encyclopaedia of Forms and Precedents, 5th edn; Atkin's Court Forms, 2nd edn; Civil Court Service, 2000–; Kelly's Draftsman, 18th edn 2002; numerous contribs to Law Soc.'s Gazette, Insolvency Law and Practice and other jls on commercial litigation, insolvency and directors' duties. *Recreations:* keen interest in history and literature, watching all kinds of sports.

MITHEN, Prof. Steven John, PhD; FBA 2004; FSA, FSAScot; Professor of Early Prehistory, since 2000, and Deputy Vice Chancellor, since 2014, University of Reading; *b* 16 Oct. 1960; *s* of William Mithen and Patricia Mithen; *m* 1985, Susan Orton; one *s* two *d. Educ:* Slade Sch. of Fine Art; Univ. of Sheffield (BA 1st cl. Hons (Prehist. and Archaeol.) 1983); Univ. of York (MSc (Biol Computation) 1984); Univ. of Cambridge (PhD (Archaeol.) 1987). University of Cambridge: Res. Fellow in Archaeol., Trinity Hall, 1987–90; Lectr in Archaeol. (temp.), 1989–91; Res. Associate in Archaeol., McDonald Inst., 1991–92; University of Reading: Lectr, 1992–96, Sen. Lectr, 1996–98, in Archaeol.; Reader in Early Prehistory, 1998–2000; Hd, Sch. of Human and Envmtl Scis, 2003–08; Dean, Faculty of Sci., 2008–10; Pro Vice Chancellor, 2010–14. FSAScot 1993; FSA 1998. *Publications:* Thoughtful Foragers: a study of prehistoric decision making, 1990; The Prehistory of the Mind: a search for the origins of art, science and religion, 1996; (ed) Creativity in Human Evolution and Prehistory, 1998; (ed) Hunter-Gatherer Landscape Archaeology: the Southern Hebrides Mesolithic Project 1988–1998, 2 vols, 2001; After the Ice: a global human history 20,000–5,000 BC, 2003; The Singing Neanderthals, 2005; The Early Prehistory of Wadi Faynan, 2007; To The Islands, 2010; (ed) Water, Life and Civilization, 2011; Thirst: water and power in the ancient world, 2012; articles in jls incl. Antiquity, Jl of Archaeol Sci., Jl of Human Evolution, Current Anthropol. and Levant. *Recreation:* family. *Address:* University of Reading, PO Box 217, Reading RG6 6AH. *T:* (0118) 987 5123, *Fax:* (0118) 931 4404. *E:* s.j.mithen@reading.ac.uk.

MITSAKIS, Prof. Kariofilis; Professor of Modern Greek Literature, University of Athens, 1978–99, now Emeritus; *b* 12 May 1932; *s* of Christos and Crystalli Mitsakis; *m* 1966, Anthoula Chalkia; two *s. Educ:* Univs of Thessaloniki (BA, PhD), Oxford (MA, DPhil) and Munich. Scientific Collaborator, National Research Foundn of Greece, 1959–62; Associate Prof. of Byzantine and Modern Greek Literature, Univ. of Maryland, 1966–68; Chm. of Dept of Comparative Literature, Univ. of Maryland, 1967–68; Sotheby and Bywater Prof. of Byzantine and Modern Greek Language and Literature, Univ. of Oxford, 1968–72; Prof. of Modern Greek Lit., Univ. of Thessaloniki, 1972–75; Dir, Inst. for Balkan Studies, Thessaloniki, 1972–80. Hon. DLitt and Ph Johannesburg, 2001. Gottfried Herder Prize, Vienna Univ., 2000. *Publications:* Problems Concerning the Text, the Sources and the Dating of the Achilleid, 1962 (in Greek); The Greek Sonnet, 1962 (in Greek); The Language of Romanos the Melodist, 1967 (in English); The Byzantine Alexanderromance from the Cod. Vindob. theol. gr. 244, 1967 (in German); Byzantine Hymnography, 1971 (in Greek); Petrarchism in Greece, 1973 (in Greek); Introduction to Modern Greek Literature, 1973 (in Greek); Homer in Modern Greek Literature, 1976 (in Greek); George Viziynos, 1977 (in Greek); Modern Greek Prose: the Generation of the '30s, 1978 (in Greek); Modern Greek Music and Poetry, 1979 (in Greek and English); March Through the Time, 1982; The Living Water, 1983; Points of Reference, 1987 (in Greek); The Cycles with their trails that rise and fall, 1991 (in Greek); The Boston Essays, 1993 (in Greek); The Oxford Essays, 1995 (in Greek); The Alexanderromance, 2001 (in Greek); Modern Greek Miscellany, 2001 (in Greek); In Imagination and in Word: studies on the poet C. P. Cavafy, 2001 (in Greek); Pan the Great: studies on the poet A. Sikelianos, 2001 (in Greek); contribs to Balkan Studies, Byzantinisch-Neugriechische Jahrbücher, Byzantinische Zeitschrift, Comparative Literature Studies, Diptycha, Etudes Byzantines-Byzantine Studies, Glotta, Hellenika, Jahrbuch der Oesterreichischen Byzantinischen Gesellschaft, Nea Hestia, etc. *Recreations:* music, travelling. *Address:* 25 Troados Street, Aghia Paraskevi, 153 42 Athens, Greece.

MITTAL, Lakshmi Niwas; President and Chief Executive Officer, ArcelorMittal, since 2006 (Chairman and Chief Executive Officer, Mittal Steel Company Ltd, 2004–06); *b* 15 June 1950; *s* of Mohan Lal and Guta Mittal; *m* 1971, Usha; one *s* one *d. Educ:* St Xavier's Coll., Calcutta (BCom). Founded The LNM Group, Indonesia, 1976 (Chm.); subseq. expanded operations into Trinidad and Tobago, Mexico, Canada, Germany, Kazakhstan, USA, France, Algeria, Romania, S Africa and Czech Repub.; former Chm. and CEO, Ispat Internat. NV and LNM Holdings NV; Chm. and CEO of many group mem. cos. Has championed development of integrated mini-mills and use of direct reduced iron (DRI) as scrap substitute for steelmaking. Founder, LNM Foundn for charitable progs in India. Steelmaker of the Year, New Steel Magazine, 1996; Willy Korf Steel Vision Award, American Metal Market/World Steel Dynamics, 1998. *Recreations:* yoga, swimming. *Address:* ArcelorMittal, 7th Floor, Berkeley Square House, Berkeley Square, W1J 6DA.

MITTER, Prof. Rana Shantashil Rajyeswar, PhD; FBA 2015; Professor of History and Politics of Modern China, since 2008, and Deutsche Bank Director, China Centre, since 2013, University of Oxford; Fellow, St Cross College, Oxford, since 2001; *b* Cambridge, 11 Aug. 1969; *s* of Partha and Swasti Mitter; *m* 2004, Katharine Wilson; one *d. Educ:* King's Coll., Cambridge (BA 1992; PhD 1996); Harvard Univ. (Kennedy Schol.). Jun. Lectr, Univ. of Oxford and Jun. Res. Fellow, Wolfson Coll., Oxford, 1996–99; Lectr in Hist., Warwick Univ., 1999–2001; Lectr in Hist. and Politics of Modern China, Univ. of Oxford, 2001–08. Presenter, Night Waves, and Free Thinking, BBC Radio 3, 2007–. *Publications:* The Manchurian Myth: nationalism, resistance and collaboration in modern China, 2000; A Bitter Revolution: China's struggle with the modern world, 2004 (THES Young Acad. Author of Year, 2005); Modern China: a very short introduction, 2008, 2nd edn 2016; China's War with Japan, 1937–45: the struggle for survival, 2013 (RUSI/Duke of Westminster's Medal for Mil. Lit., 2014; US edn as Forgotten Ally, 2013). *Recreations:* biographies of long-forgotten 1970s politicians, reminiscences of best-forgotten 1970s television programmes. *Address:* China Centre, University of Oxford, Dickson Poon Building, Canterbury Road, Oxford OX2 6LU. *E:* rana.mitter@orinst.ox.ac.uk.

MITTING, Hon. Sir John Edward, Kt 2001; **Hon. Mr Justice Mitting;** a Judge of the High Court of Justice, Queen's Bench Division, since 2001; *b* 8 Oct. 1947; *s* of late Alison Kennard Mitting and Eleanor Mary Mitting; *m* 1977, Judith Clare (*née* Hampson); three *s. Educ:* Downside Sch.; Trinity Hall, Cambridge (BA, LLB). Called to the Bar, Gray's Inn, 1970, Bencher, 1996; QC 1987; a Recorder, 1988–2001; Chm., Special Immigration Appeal Commn, 2007–12. *Recreations:* wine, food, bridge. *Address:* Royal Courts of Justice, Strand, WC2A 2LL. *Club:* Garrick.

MITTLER, Prof. Peter Joseph, CBE 1981; MA, PhD, MEd; CPsychol; FBPsS, FIASSID; Professor of Special Education, University of Manchester, 1973–95, now Emeritus (Dean, Faculty of Education and Director, School of Education, 1991–94; Hon. Research Fellow, since 2009); *b* 2 April 1930; *s* of Dr Gustav Mittler and Gertrude Mittler; *m* 1st, 1955, Helle Katscher (marr. diss. 1997); three *s*; 2nd, 1997, Penelope Anastasia Platt. *Educ:* Merchant

Taylors' Sch., Crosby; Pembroke Coll., Cambridge (MA); PhD London; MEd Manchester. Clinical Psychologist, Warneford and Park Hosps, Oxford, 1954–58; Principal Psychologist, Reading Area Psychiatric Services, 1958–63; Lectr in Psychology, Birkbeck Coll., Univ. of London, 1963–68; Manchester University: Dir, Hester Adrian Res. Centre, 1968–82; Dir, Centre for Educnl Guidance and Special Needs, Dept of Educn, 1977–91; Dep. Dir, Sch. of Educn, 1989–91. Vis. Prof., Manchester Metropolitan Univ., 1996–97; Distinguished Vis. Prof., Univ. of Hong Kong, 1997–98; Fellow, Centre for Policy Studies, Dartington, 1995–. Chm., Nat Develt Gp for Mentally Handicapped, 1975–80; Mem., Schs Exams and Assessment Council, 1988–90. Pres., Internat. League of Socs for Persons with Mental Handicap, 1982–86 (Vice-Pres., 1978–82); Mem., Prince of Wales Adv. Gp on Disability, 1984–90; Chm. Trustees and Council, British Inst. of Learning Disabilities, 1995–97; Advr on disability to UN, UNESCO, WHO, ILO, UNICEF. *Publications:* ed, Psychological Assessment of Mental and Physical Handicaps, 1970; The Study of Twins, 1971; ed, Assessment for Learning in the Mentally Handicapped, 1973; ed, Research to Practice in Mental Retardation (3 vols), 1977; People not Patients, 1979; (jtly) Teaching Language and Communication to the Mentally Handicapped, (Schools Council), 1979; (ed jtly) Advances in Mental Handicap Research, 1980; (ed) Frontiers of Knowledge in Mental Retardation (2 vols), 1981; (ed jtly) Approaches to Partnership: professionals and parents of mentally handicapped people, 1983; (ed jtly) Aspects of Competence in Mentally Handicapped People, 1983; (ed jtly) Staff Training in Mental Handicap, 1987; (jtly) Inset and Special Educational Needs: running short, school-focused inservice courses, 1988; (ed jtly) Special Needs Education (World Yearbook of Education), 1993; Teacher Education for Special Educational Needs, 1993; (jtly) Innovations in Family Support for People with Learning Difficulties, 1994; (ed jtly) Teacher Education for Special Needs in Europe, 1995; (ed) Changing Policy and Practice for People with Learning Disabilities, 1995; (jtly) Disability and the Family, 1995; Working Towards Inclusive Education: social contexts, 2000; (jtly) Promoting the Human Rights of Children with Disabilities, 2007; Thinking Globally Acting Locally: a personal journey, 2010; Overcoming Exclusion: social justice through education, 2012; papers in psychol and educnl jls. *Recreations:* music, Italy. *Address:* 8 Drayton Manor, Parrs Wood Road, Manchester M20 5GJ. *E:* Peter.Mittler@manchester.ac.uk.

MIURIN, Fields W.; *see* Wicker-Miurin.

MIYAKE, Kazunaru, (Issey); fashion designer; *b* 22 April 1938. *Educ:* Tama Art Univ., Tokyo; Chambre Syndicale de la Couture, Paris. Assistant Designer: Guy Laroche, Paris, 1966–68; Hubert de Givenchy, Paris, 1968–69; Designer, Geoffrey Beene, NY, 1969–70; established Miyake Design Studio, Tokyo, 1970; first Paris fashion show, 1973; Founder: Pleats Please, 1993; A-POC, 1999. Co-Dir, 21_21 Design Sight, Tokyo, 2012–. *Exhibitions:* Bodyworks - Fashion Without Taboos, Tokyo, San Francisco, LA, London, 1985; Musée des Arts Décoratifs, Paris, 1988; Issey Miyake Making Things, Paris, 1998, NY, 1999, Tokyo, 2000. Numerous awards. Hon. Dr: RCA, 1993; Lyon, 1999. Chevalier, Légion d'honneur (France), 1993; Bunka Korosha (Japan), 1998; Order of Culture (Japan), 2010. *Publications:* East Meets West, 1978; Issey Miyake Bodyworks, 1983. *Address:* Issey Miyake Inc., 1–12–10 Tomigaya Shibuya-ku, Tokyo 151–8554, Japan.

MKAPA, Benjamin William; President, United Republic of Tanzania, 1995–2005; *b* 12 Nov. 1938; *s* of William Matwani and Stephania Nambanga; *m* 1966, Anna Joseph Maro; two *s*. *Educ:* Lupaso Primary Sch.; Ndanda Secondary Sch.; Kigonsera Seminary; St Francis Coll., Pugu (Cambridge Sch. Cert.); Makerere UC (BA Hons 1962); Sch. of Internat. Affairs, Columbia Univ. Admin. Officer, subseq. Dist Officer, then Foreign Service Officer, Dodoma, 1962; Managing Editor: The Nationalist and Uhuru, 1966–72; The Daily News, and The Sunday News, 1972–74; Press Sec. to President, 1974–76; Founding Dir, Tanzania News Agency, 1976; High Comr to Nigeria, 1976–77; nominated MP, 1977–82, 1984–85; elected MP for Nanyumbu, 1985, re-elected 1990; Minister for Foreign Affairs, 1977–82, 1984–90; Minister for Information and Culture, 1980–82; High Comr to Canada, 1982–83; Ambassador to USA, 1983–84; Minister for Information and Broadcasting, 1990–92; Minister for Science, Tech. and Higher Educn, 1992–95. Chm., 1996–2006, Mem., 1977–, Chama cha Mapinduzi (Revolutionary Party). Co-Chm., World Commn on Social Dimension of Globalisation, 2002; Chm., Southern African Develt Community, 2003–04; Member: Commn for Africa, 2004; UN Commn on Legal Empowerment of the Poor, 2006–08; African Union Panel of Eminent Persons, 2008. Chm., South Centre, Geneva; Co-Chairman: Investment Climate Facility for Africa; Africa Emerging Markets Forum. Member, Bd of Trustees: African Wildlife Foundn; Aga Khan Univ. Member: Club of Madrid; InterAction Council; Africa Forum. Global Leadership Award, Jane Goodall Inst., 2007. *Address:* Office of the Former President, PO Box 7652, Dar es Salaam, Tanzania.

MLINARIC, David, CBE 2009; interior decorator and designer, 1964–2004; founded David Mlinaric Ltd, 1964, became Mlinaric, Henry and Zervudachi Ltd, 1989; *b* 12 March 1939; *s* of Franjo and Mabel Mlinaric; *m* 1969, Martha Laycock; one *s* two *d*. *Educ:* Downside Sch.; Bartlett Sch. of Architecture; University Coll. London. Private and commercial interior designing and decorating, often in historic bldgs. Work includes: British Embassies in Washington, 1982, Paris, 1983; rooms in Nat. Gall. and NPG, London, 1986; Spencer House, London, 1990; Royal Opera House, Covent Garden; British Galls, V&A Mus.; Waddesdon Manor, 2000; Chatsworth House, 2006. Fellow, BIDA. Hon. Fellow, RCA, 1987. *Publications:* (with M. Cecil) Mlinaric on Decorating, 2008. *Recreations:* gardening, sightseeing. *Address:* Manor House, Spargrove, Evercreech, Shepton Mallet, Somerset BA4 6HQ.

MO, Timothy Peter; writer; *b* 30 Dec. 1950; *s* of Peter Mo Wan Lung and Barbara Helena Falkingham. *Educ:* Convent of the Precious Blood, Hong Kong; Mill Hill School; St John's Coll., Oxford (BA; Gibbs Prize 1971). *Publications:* The Monkey King, 1978 (Geoffrey Faber Meml Prize, 1979); Sour Sweet, 1982 (Hawthornden Prize, 1983; filmed, 1989); An Insular Possession, 1986; The Redundancy of Courage, 1991 (E. M. Forster Award, Amer. Acad. and Inst. of Arts and Letters, 1992); Brownout on Breadfruit Boulevard, 1995; Renegade or Halo^2 (James Tait Black Meml Prize), 1999; Pure, 2012. *Recreations:* scuba diving, weight training, gourmandising. *E:* timothymo@eudoramail.com.

MOATE, Sir Roger (Denis), Kt 1993; *b* 12 May 1938; *m* 1st; one *s* one *d*; 2nd, Auriol (*née* Cran) (MBE 2003); one *d*. *Educ:* Latymer Upper Sch., Hammersmith. Insurance Broker; with J. H. Minet, in S Africa and Kenya, 1957–60; Director: Walker Moate & Co., 1961–66; Alexander Howden Insce Brokers Ltd, 1967–70. Contested (C) Faversham, 1966. MP (C) Faversham, 1970–97; contested (C) Sittingbourne and Sheppey, 1997. Mem., Select Cttee on Agric., 1995–97. Hon. Sec., British-Amer. Parly Gp, 1974–81; Chm., British-Norwegian Parly Gp, 1987–97. Chm., Brentford and Chiswick Young Conservatives; Vice-Chm., Greater London Area Young Conservatives, 1964. Comdr, Royal Norwegian Order of Merit, 1994. *Recreations:* tennis, gardening. *Address:* New Calico, Newnham, Sittingbourne, Kent ME9 0LN.

MOBARIK, Baroness *cr* 2014 (Life Peer), of Mearns in the County of Renfrewshire; **Nosheena Shaheen Mobarik,** CBE 2014 (OBE 2004); Co-founder and Director, M Computer Technologies, 1997–2013; *b* Pakistan, 1957; *d* of Muhammed Tufail Shaheen; *m* Iqbal Mobarik; one *s* one *d*. *Educ:* Strathclyde Univ. Founder and Convenor, Scotland Pakistan Network; Chm., Pakistan Britain Trade Investment Forum; Chm., CBI Scotland, 2011–13.

MOBED, Rohinton; Chief Executive Officer, Elsevier, since 2012; *b* London, 29 May 1959; *s* of Yazdi Mobed and Goolcher Mobed; *m* 1990, Suzanne Taylor; two *d*. *Educ:* Trinity Coll., Cambridge (BA Engrg 1980); Imperial Coll. London (MSc Petroleum Engrg 1987). Schlumberger, 1980–2004: Vice Pres., Asia, GeoQuest, 1997–98; Mktg Manager, Asia, 1998–99; Vice Pres., Data Mgt, 2000–01; IHS: Pres., IHS Energy, 2004–07; Co-Pres. and Chief Operating Officer Energy, 2007–08; Co-Chm., 2008–09; Pres., Academic, Cengage Learning, 2009–10; Hd, sci. and technol. businesses, Elsevier, 2011–12. *Address:* Elsevier, c/o RELX Group, Grand Buildings, 1–3 Strand, WC2N 5JR. *T:* (020) 7930 7077. *E:* r.mobed@elsevier.com. *Club:* Oxford and Cambridge.

MOBERLY, Dr Patricia Jane; JP; Chairman, Guy's and St Thomas' Hospital NHS Foundation Trust (formerly NHS Trust), 1999–2011. *Educ:* Univ. of Liverpool (BA Hons Eng. Lang. and Lit.); King's Coll., London (PhD 1985). Teacher: Chikola Sch., Zambia; Roan Sch., Greenwich; Mary Datchelor Sch., Camberwell; Sen. Teacher and Hd, Sixth Form, Pimlico Sch., 1974–98. Mem., Lambeth BC, 1971–78. Member: Lambeth Southwark and Lewisham AHA, 1976–81; Lambeth DHA, 1981–90. Mem., GMC, 2002–. Governor: Maudsley and Bethlem Hosp., 1976–78; UMDS, 1988–90. Member: Nat. Cttee, Anti-Apartheid Movement; Cttee on Standards in Public Life, 2012–. JP Inner London, 1976. Hon. DSc South Bank, 2008.

MOBERLY, Sir Patrick (Hamilton), KCMG 1986 (CMG 1978); HM Diplomatic Service, retired; Ambassador to South Africa, 1984–87; *b* 2 Sept. 1928; *yr s* of G. H. Moberly; *m* 1955, Mary Penfold; two *s* one *d*. *Educ:* Winchester; Trinity Coll., Oxford (MA). HM Diplomatic Service, 1951–88; diplomatic posts in: Baghdad, 1953; Prague, 1957; Foreign Office, 1959; Dakar, 1962; Min. of Defence, 1965; Commonwealth Office, 1967; Canada, 1969; Israel, 1970; FCO, 1974; Asst Under-Sec. of State, 1976–81; Ambassador to Israel, 1981–84. *Recreations:* opera, congenial travel. *Address:* 38 Lingfield Road, SW19 4PZ.

MOCATTA, Jane; *see* Bewsey, J.

MOCHAN, Charles Francis; HM Diplomatic Service, retired; High Commissioner to Fiji, and also (non-resident) to Kiribati, Tuvalu and Nauru, 2002–06; *b* 6 Aug. 1948; *s* of Charles Mochan and Margaret Mochan (*née* Love); *m* 1970, Ilse Sybilla Carleon Cruttwell; one *s* one *d*. *Educ:* St Patrick's High Sch., Dumbarton. MoD (Navy), 1966; joined FCO 1967; Port Elizabeth, S Africa, 1970–72; Kingston, Jamaica, 1972–74; FCO, 1974–77; Seoul, 1977–80; Second, later First Sec., Helsinki, 1981–84; FCO, 1984–87; Dep. High Comr, Mauritius, 1988–91; FCO, 1991–95; Consul-Gen., Casablanca, 1995–98; Ambassador to Republic of Madagascar, 1999–2002, and concurrently to Federal Islamic Republic of Comoros, 2001–02. *Recreations:* soccer, ornithology, music, walking, golf.

MODARRESSI, Anne, (Mrs T. M. Modarressi); *see* Tyler, A.

MODOOD, Prof. Tariq, MBE 2001; PhD; FAcSS; Professor of Sociology, Politics and Public Policy, since 1997 and Director, Centre for the Study of Ethnicity and Citizenship, since 1999, University of Bristol; *b* Karachi, 4 Oct. 1952; *s* of Mirza Sabhuddin Modood and Nafeesa Modood; *m* 1979, Glynthea Thompson; two *d*. *Educ:* Univ. of Durham (BA Hons Philos. and Pol 1974, MA Politics 1975); University Coll., Swansea (PhD Philos. 1984). Temp. Lectr in Politics, Univ. of Bristol, 1980–81; Temp. Lectr in Social Philos., QUB, 1981–82; HM Inspector of Taxes, Oxford, 1982–83; Temp. Lectr in Politics, University Coll., Swansea, 1984–85; Equal Opportunities Officer, London Bor. of Hillingdon, 1987–89; Principal Employment Officer, Commn for Racial Equality, 1989–91; Gwilym Gibbon Res. Fellow, Nuffield Coll., Oxford, 1991–92; Hallsworth Res. Fellow, Univ. of Manchester, 1992–94; Prog. Dir, PSI, London, 1993–97. FAcSS (AcSS 2004). *Publications:* Not Easy Being British: colour, culture and citizenship, 1992; (jtly) Ethnic Minorities in Britain: diversity and disadvantage—the fourth national survey of ethnic minorities, 1997; Multicultural Politics: racism, ethnicity and Muslims in Britain, 2005; (ed jtly) Ethnicity, Social Mobility and Public Policy in the US and UK, 2005; Multiculturalism: a civic idea, 2007, 2nd edn 2013; (ed with Geoffrey Levey) Secularism, Religion and Multicultural Citizenship, 2009; Still Not Easy Being British: struggles for a multicultural citizenship, 2010; (ed with John Salt) Global Migration, Ethnicity and Britishness, 2011; (ed jtly) European Multiculturalisms: cultural, religious and ethnic challenges, 2012. *Recreations:* badminton, cycling, swimming, films, novels. *E:* t.modood@bristol.ac.uk.

MOELLER, Prof. Scott David; Professor in the Practice of Finance, Cass Business School, City University London, since 2010; *b* NJ, USA, 22 March 1954; *s* of Paul and Dorothy Moeller; *m* 2001, Dr Daniela Schwartz; two *s* two *d*. *Educ:* Yale Univ. (BA 1976; MA 1976; MBA 1978). Associate, then Sen. Associate, Booz Allen Hamilton, 1977, 1978–84; Morgan Stanley, 1984–96: Sen. Associate, then Vice Pres., NY; Exec. Dir, Tokyo; Geschäftsführer, Frankfurt; Man. Dir, Deutsche Bank, London, 1996–2001; Chief Exec., Executive Educn, Cass Business Sch., City Univ. London, 2002–10. *Publications:* (with C. Brady) Intelligent M & A: navigating the mergers and acquisitions minefield, 2007; Surviving M & A: make the most of your company being acquired, 2009; (ed) Finance Essentials: the practitioner's guide, 2012. *Address:* Cass Business School, City University London, 106 Bunhill Row, EC1Y 8TZ. *Fax:* (020) 7040 5168. *E:* scott.moeller@city.ac.uk.

MOERAN, Fenner Orlando; QC 2014; *b* London, 14 Aug. 1972; *s* of Edward and Jacky Moeran; *m* 2002, Emma Judge; one *s* one *d*. *Educ:* University Coll. Sch.; Univ. of Bristol (BSc Politics and Philosophy); City Univ. (DipLaw). Called to the Bar, Lincoln's Inn, 1996. *Recreations:* family, walking. *Address:* 3 Stone Buildings, Lincoln's Inn, WC2A 3XL.

MOFFAT, Captain (Alexander) Iain (Black), RD 1980 (and Bar 1988); CEng, MICE; FGS; RNR retired; Vice Lord-Lieutenant for Northumberland, 2002–13 (Acting Lord-Lieutenant, 2009); Professorial Fellow in Dam Engineering, University of Newcastle upon Tyne, since 2004 (Visiting Fellow, 2000–04); *b* 29 March 1938; *s* of late Alexander Moffat and Margaret D. H. Moffat (*née* Black); *m* 1963, Madeline Wright; one *s* one *d*. *Educ:* Edinburgh Acad.; Univ. of Edinburgh (BSc). CEng, MICE 1970; FGS 1987. Civil Engr posts, 1962–66; University of Newcastle upon Tyne: Lectr, 1966–74; Sen. Lectr, 1974–2000; Dep. Head, Dept of Civil Engrg, 1991–98. Vis. Sen. Lectr, Univ. of Durham, 1998–2001. Chm., 1994–2003, Pro-Chm., 2003–12, Northumbrian Univs Mil. Educn Cttee; Mem., ICE Panel for Historic Engrg Works, 2005–10. ICE Smeaton Lect., 2010. Vice-Chm. (RN and RM), RFCA for N of England, 1996–2003. Trustee, HMS Trincomalee Trust, 2008–. CO, Tyne Div., RNR, HMS Calliope, 1982–86. DL Northumberland, 1990. *Publications:* (jtly) Hydraulic Structures, 1990, 4th edn 2007; numerous contribs/papers to professional jls and conf. proc. in UK and overseas on issues in dam engrg, geotechnics, etc. *Recreations:* walking, history (technology (development of the submarine), naval, military, social (19th and 20th Century)), travel, reading. *Address:* 43 Bishops Hill, Acomb, Hexham, Northumberland NE46 4NH. *T:* (01434) 605243. *E:* aibmoffat@hotmail.co.uk.

MOFFAT, Alistair Murray; author and broadcaster; *b* 16 June 1950; *s* of John and Ellen Moffat; *m* 1976, Lindsay Anne Reid Thomas; one *s* two *d*. *Educ:* Kelso High Sch.; St Andrews Univ. (MA Hons); Edinburgh Univ. (CertEd); London Univ. (MPhil). Administrator, Edinburgh Festival Fringe, 1976–81; Scottish Television, subseq. Scottish Media Group: Arts Corresp., 1981–86; Controller of Features, 1987–90; Dir of Progs, 1990–93; Chief Exec., then Man. Dir, Scottish Television Enterprises, 1993–99. Chm., Scottish TV Regl Bd, 1999–2003. Rector, St Andrews Univ., 2011–14. *Publications:* The Edinburgh Fringe, 1978; Kelsae: a history from earliest times, 1985; Remembering Charles Rennie Mackintosh, 1989; Arthur and the Lost Kingdoms, 1999; The Sea Kingdoms, 2001; The Borders, 2002; Homing, 2003; Heartland, 2004; Before Scotland, 2005; Tyneside, 2005; East Lothian, 2006; The Reivers, 2007; Fife: a history, 2007; The Wall, 2008; Edinburgh, a History, 2008; Tuscany: a history, 2009; The Faded Map, 2010; The Highland Clans, 2010; The Scots: a genetic journey, 2011; Britain's Last Frontier, 2012; The British: a genetic journey, 2013; Hawick: a history from earliest times, 2014; Bannockburn: the battle for a nation, 2014; The Great Tapestry of Scotland, 2014; The Making of the Great Tapestry of Scotland, 2014; Scotland: a history from earliest times, 2015. *Recreation:* apprentice groom. *Address:* The Henhouse, Selkirk TD7 5EY.

MOFFAT, Anne; *b* 30 March 1958; *d* of Francis Hunter Moffat and late Wilma Hoxton Moffat; *m* 1984, David Adair Harold Picking (marr. diss. 2003); one *s*; *m* 2009, Lawrence Mulligan McCran. *Educ:* Woodmill High Comprehensive Sch. Nurse: Fife Health Bd, 1975–80; NI Eastern Health and Social Service, 1980–83 (staff nurse, 1982–83); staff nurse, then nursing sister, E Kent Community Health Care NHS Trust, 1984–2001. MP (Lab) E Lothian, 2001–10. Mem., NEC, COHSE, 1990; Mem., NEC, 1993–2001, Nat. Pres., 1999–2000, UNISON. Mem. (Lab), Ashford BC, 1994–98.

MOFFAT, Sir Brian (Scott), Kt 1996; OBE 1982; Deputy Chairman, HSBC Holdings plc, 2001–08 (Director, 1998–2008); *b* 6 Jan. 1939; *s* of Festus and Agnes Moffat; *m* 1964, Jacqueline Mary Cunliffe; one *s* one *d* (and one *s* decd). *Educ:* Hulme Grammar School. FCA. Peat Marwick Mitchell & Co., 1961–68; British Steel Corp., then British Steel plc, subseq. Corus Gp, 1968–2003: Man. Dir, Finance, 1986–91; Chief Exec., 1991–99; Chm., 1993–2003. Non-executive Director: Enterprise Oil, 1995–2002; Bank of England, 2000–06; Macsteel Global Hldgs (formerly Nosmas Investment Hldgs) BV, 2003–; Macstel Hldgs Luxembourg sàrl BV, 2011–. Hon. DSc: Warwick, 1998; Sheffield, 2001. *Recreations:* farming, fishing, shooting. *Club:* Flyfishers'.

MOFFAT, David Andrew, PhD; FRCS; Consultant Neurotologist and Skull Base Surgeon, Addenbrooke's Hospital, Cambridge, 1981–2012, now Hon. Emeritus Consultant; Associate Lecturer, University of Cambridge, since 1981 (Lecturer, 1981); *b* 27 June 1947; *s* of late Graham and Myra Moffat; *m* 1970, Jane Elizabeth; two *s* one *d*. *Educ:* St Nicholas Sch., Northwood; London Hospital Med. Coll. (BSc Hons 1968; MB BS 1971); Hon. MA Cantab 1984; Radbout Univ., Nijmegen (PhD 2012). MRCS 1971, FRCS 1977; LRCP 1971. Consultant Surgeon, Westminster Hosp., 1979–80. Chm., Intercollegiate Specialty Bd and Panel of Examiners, 1998–2001; Mem., Specialist Adv. Cttee in Otolaryngology, 2001–06. Hunterian Prof. of Surgery, RCS, 2009–11. Master, British Academic Conf. in Otolaryngology, 2006–09. Hon. Mem., German ENT Soc. Gold Medal, Internat. Fedn of Oto-rhino-laryngol Socs, 2013. *Publications:* (ed jtly) Recent Advances in Otolaryngology, 7, 1995, 8, 2007; Clinical Aspects and Outcomes of Lateral Skull Base Surgery, 2012; 30 chapters in textbooks; 188 papers in learned jls on neurology and skull base surgery including acoustic neuroma, meningioma, glomus jugulare tumours, squamous cell carcinomas of temporal bone, Ménière's disease, electrophysiology. *Recreations:* theatre, ballet, opera, motoring, golf, ski-ing. *Address:* Department of Neuro-otology and Skull Base Surgery, Box 48, Addenbrooke's Hospital, Cambridge University Hospitals NHS Foundation Trust, Hills Road, Cambridges CB2 0QQ. *T:* and *Fax:* (01223) 364114. *E:* dam26@cam.ac.uk. *Club:* Gog Magog.

MOFFAT, Rev. Canon George; Rector, Priory Church of St Mary and St Cuthbert, Bolton Abbey, 2007–12; Hon. Chaplain to the Queen, 2000–16; *b* 31 July 1946; *s* of George and Mary Moffat; *m* 1975, Peta Ollen; two *d*. *Educ:* Edinburgh Theol Coll.; New Coll., Edinburgh (BD 1977); Open Univ. (BA Hons 1987); Bradford Univ. (MA 2004). Ordained deacon, 1972, priest, 1973; Curate: Christ Church, Falkirk, 1973–76; St Peter, Lutton Place, Edinburgh, 1976–81; Anglican Chaplain, Edinburgh Univ., 1977–81; Curate, St Leonard and All Saints, Heston, 1981–84; Vicar, St Mary the Virgin, S Emsall, 1984–93; Team Rector, Manningham, 1993–2007. Hon. Canon, Bradford Cathedral, 2002–12. Non-exec. Dir, Bradford City Teaching PCT, 2003–06. *Recreations:* country walking, supporting creative modern dance, managing rough woodland and establishing a cider and perry orchard. *Address:* Fir Cottage, The Stenders, Mitcheldean GL17 0JE. *T:* (01594) 543668. *E:* rev.g.moffat@gmail.com.

MOFFAT, Captain Iain; *see* Moffat, Captain A. I. B.

MOFFATT, Prof. (Henry) Keith, ScD; FRS 1986; FRSE; Professor of Mathematical Physics, University of Cambridge, 1980–2002, now Professor Emeritus (Head of Department of Applied Mathematics and Theoretical Physics, 1983–91); Fellow, Trinity College, Cambridge, 1961–76, and since 1980; *b* 12 April 1935; *s* of late Frederick Henry Moffatt and Emmeline Marchant Fleming; *m* 1960, Katharine, (Linty), Stiven, *d* of late Rev. D. S. Stiven, MC, DD; one *s* two *d* (and one *s* decd). *Educ:* George Watson's Coll., Edinburgh; Edinburgh Univ. (BSc); Cambridge Univ. (BA, PhD, ScD). Lectr in Maths, Cambridge Univ., and Dir of Studies in Maths, Trinity Coll., 1961–76 (Tutor, 1971–75, Sen. Tutor, 1975); Prof. of Applied Maths, Bristol Univ., 1977–80; Dir, Isaac Newton Inst. for Mathematical Scis, Cambridge Univ., 1996–2001. Visiting appts, Stanford Univ. and Johns Hopkins Univ., 1965, Univ. of Paris VI, 1975–76, Institut de Mécanique, Grenoble, 1986, Univ. of California, San Diego, 1987, Santa Barbara, 1991, Ecole Polytechnique Palaiseau, 1992–99, Kyoto Univ., 1993; Blaise Pascal Internat. Chair, Ecole Normale Supérieure, Paris, 2001–03. Pres., IUTAM, 2000–04. Mem. Council and Trustee, African Inst. for Math. Scis, 2003–12; Member: Scientific Adv. Bd, Inst. for Math. Scis, Singapore, 2002–10; Council, Internat. Centre for Mech. Scis, 2002–10; Information, Communication and Emergent Technologies Panel, Science Foundn Ireland, 2008–11; Bd, African Inst. for Math. Scis—Next Einstein Initiative, 2009–; Conseil d'Enseignement et Recherche, Ecole Polytechnique, 2009–13. Co-editor, Journal of Fluid Mechanics, 1966–83. Foreign Mem., Royal Netherlands Acad. of Arts and Scis, 1991; Associé Etranger, Acad. des Sciences, Paris, 1998; Socio Straniero, Acad. Nazionale dei Lincei, Rome, 2001; Foreign Member: Nat Acad. of Scis, USA, 2008; Acad. of Scis, Lisbon, 2010. MAE 1994. FRSE 1988; Fellow, Amer. Phys. Soc., 2003. Hon. FIMA 2007. D*hc* Inst. Nat Polytechnique de Grenoble, 1987; Hon. DSc: SUNY, 1990; Edinburgh, 2001; Eindhoven Tech. Univ., 2006; Glasgow, 2007. Panetti-Ferrari Prize and Gold Medal, 2001; Euromech Fluid Mechanics Prize, 2003; Sen. Whitehead Prize, LMS, 2005; Hughes Medal, Royal Soc., 2005; David Crighton Medal, LMS/IMA, 2010. Officier des Palmes Académiques, 1998. *Publications:* Magnetic Field Generation in Electrically Conducting Fluids, 1978; (ed jtly) Topological Fluid Mechanics, 1990; Topological Aspects of the Dynamics of Fluids and Plasmas, 1992; Tubes, Sheets and Singularities in Fluid Dynamics, 2003; (ed jtly) A Voyage Through Turbulence, 2011; (ed jtly) Environmental Hazards: the fluid dynamics and geophysics of extreme events, 2011; (ed jtly) Fundamental Problems of Turbulence, 2014; papers in fluid mechanics and dynamo theory in Jl Fluid Mech. and other jls. *Recreations:* baking bread, poetry. *Address:* Trinity College, Cambridge CB2 1TQ.

MOFFATT, Laura Jean; *b* 9 April 1954; *d* of Stanley and Barbara Field; *m* 1975, Colin Moffatt; three *s*. *Educ:* Hazelwick Comprehensive Sch., Crawley; Crawley Coll. of Technology. SRN, 1975–97. Mem. (Lab), Crawley BC, 1984–97 (Mayor, 1989–90). Contested (Lab) Crawley, 1992. MP (Lab) Crawley, 1997–2010. Parliamentary Private Secretary: to Lord Chancellor, 2001–04; to Sec. of State, DWP, 2005–06; to Minister of State, DfES, 2006; to Sec. of State, DfES, 2006–07; to Sec. of State, DoH, 2007–09; Asst Regl Minister for the SE, 2009–10. *Recreations:* pets, walking, holidays with family.

MOFFETT, David Leslie; owner, Matrix Sports, New Zealand, since 2005; Managing Director, The Moffett Partnership, since 2013; *b* 17 May 1947; *s* of Henry Albert Moffett and Barbara Moffett, later Pinkney; *m* 1970, Lauren Jacqueline Dartnell; one *s* one *d*. *Educ:* Nairobi Primary Sch.; Prince of Wales Sch., Nairobi; Brisbane Boys' Coll. Man. Dir, Pacific Waste Management, Sydney, 1981–86; Exec. Dir, NSW Rugby, 1992–95; Chief Executive Officer: SANZAR, 1995–96; NZ RFU, 1996–99; Nat. Rugby League, Australia, 1999–2001; Sport England, 2002; Welsh Rugby Union, 2002–05. *Recreations:* walking, reading, cycling, photography.

MOFFETT, Peter; actor (stage name Peter Davison); *b* 13 April 1951; *s* of Claude and late Sheila Moffett; *m* 2003, Elizabeth Heery; two *s*, and one *d* from previous marriage. *Educ:* Winston Churchill Comprehensive Sch., Woking; Central Sch. of Speech and Drama (Acting Dip.). *Television* series: All Creatures Great and Small, 1978; Dr Who, 1981–84; A Very Peculiar Practice, 1986–87; Campion, 1989; Ain't Misbehavin', 1993; At Home with the Braithwaites, 2000; Last Detective, 2003; Too Good to be True, 2003; Distant Shores, 2005; The Complete Guide to Parenting, 2006; Fear, Stress and Anger, 2007 (Best Comedy Actor, Monte Carlo TV Fest., 2007); Unforgiven, 2009; Law and Order: UK, 2011–14; Pat and Cabbage, 2013; writer and dir, The Five(ish) Doctors (for BBC Dr Who 50th anniv.), 2013; *stage:* King Arthur in Spamalot, Palace Th., 2007; Legally Blonde, Savoy, 2010; The Vertical Hour, Park Th., 2014; Gypsy, Savoy Th., 2015. Top Man of Year Award, Multi-coloured Swap Shop, 1982. *Recreation:* sailing down the Thames.

MOFFITT, Prof. Terrie Edith, PhD; FBA 2004; FMedSci; Knut Schmidt Nielsen Professor of Psychology and Neuroscience, since 2008, and Nannerl O. Keohane University Professor, since 2013, Duke University; *b* 9 March 1955; *d* of Terry W. Moffitt and Glenda Macon Moffitt; *m* 1990, Prof. Avshalom Caspi, *qv*. *Educ:* Univ. of NC, Chapel Hill (BA 1977); USC (PhD 1984). Postdoctoral Fellow, UCLA, 1984; Res. Asst Prof., USC and Vis. Scholar, Univ. of Otago, NZ, 1985–86; Prof., Dept of Psychol., Univ. of Wisconsin, Madison, 1987–2007; Associate Dir, Dunedin Multidisciplinary Health and Develt Study, Dunedin Sch. of Medicine, Univ. of Otago, 1991–; Prof. of Social Behaviour and Develt, Inst. of Psychiatry, KCL, 1997–; Prof., Dept of Psychol. and Neurosci., Duke Univ., 2007–08. Trustee, Nuffield Foundn, 2011–. MAE 2005; FMedSci 1999; Fellow: Amer. Soc. of Criminology, 2003; Amer. Psychopathol Assoc., 2005; Amer. Acad. of Pol and Social Sci., 2008; Assoc. for Psychol Sci., 2009; FKC 2010. Early Career Contribn Award, 1993, Dist. Career Award in Clin. Child Psychol., 2006, Amer. Psychol Assoc.; Stockholm Prize in Criminology, 2007; Klaus-Grawe Prize in Clin. Psychol., Klaus Grawe Foundn, 2009; NARSAD Ruane Prize, Brain and Behaviour Res. Foundn, 2010; Klaus J. Jacobs Prize, Jacobs Foundn, 2010. *Publications:* Sex Differences in Antisocial Behaviours, 2001; over 300 articles in jls incl. Science, Lancet, JAMA, Proc. NAS, Archives of General Psychiatry, etc. *Recreations:* trekking and camping in the world's 'orange' countries on a scale from 'blue' (Scandinavia) to 'red' (Angola and Iran), working on her 250-acre farm in North Carolina. *Address:* Duke University, Box 104410, Suite 201 Grey House, 2020 Main Street, Durham, NC 27708, USA. *E:* terrie.moffitt@duke.edu. *W:* www.moffittcaspi.com.

MOGER, Christopher Richard Derwent; QC 1992; a Recorder, since 1993 (an Assistant Recorder, 1990–93); a Deputy High Court Judge, since 1999; arbitrator; *b* 28 July 1949; *s* of late Richard Vernon Derwent Moger and Cecile Eva Rosales Moger (*née* Power); *m* 1st, 1974, Victoria Trollope (marr. diss. 1991); three *s*; 2nd, 1991, Prudence Da Cunha. *Educ:* Sherborne School; Bristol Univ. (LLB Hons). FCIArb 1997. Called to the Bar, Inner Temple, 1972, Bencher, 2001. Member: Western Circuit; London Common Law Bar Assoc.; Commercial Bar Assoc.; Hong Kong Internat. Arbitration Centre; Kuala Lumpur Regl Centre for Arbitration; Arbitration Chambers Hong Kong, 2012–. *Recreations:* fishing, walking. *Address:* 4 Pump Court, Temple, EC4Y 7AN. *T:* (020) 7842 5555. *Club:* Garrick.

MOGFORD, Jeremy Lewis; Managing Director: Mogford Ltd, since 1998; Mogford Hotels Ltd, since 1998; *b* 9 Oct. 1947; *s* of Peter Charles Mogford and Pamela Margaret Mogford (*née* Bennett); *m* 1971, Hilary Jane Raymond; one *s* one *d*. *Educ:* Canford Sch.; Royal Grammar Sch., High Wycombe; Univ. of Surrey (BSc Hotel and Catering Admin). MIH (MHCIMA 1971). Founder, owner and Man. Dir, 1973–97, Consultant, 1997–, Browns Restaurants Ltd; Director: Peachey Productions, 1998–2000; Ruso Ltd, 2001–; RTLS (formerly RFTRAQ) Ltd, 2007– (Chm., 2014–). Mem. Exec. Cttee, Restaurant Assoc. of GB, 1998–2003. Dir and Sponsor, Discerning Eye Art Exhibn, 1995–97; Sponsor, Oxford Lit. Fest., 1995; Jt Chm., ROX (Backing Oxford Business), 1999–; Chm., Oxford High St Assoc., 2008–. Trustee, Fest. of Photography, Oxford, 2015–. Sponsor, annual short story competition, Jeremy Mogford Prize for Food and Drink Writing, 2013–. DUniv Oxford Brookes, 2001. Independent Gp Restaurateur of the Year, Caterer and Hotelkeeper mag., 1997. *Recreations:* topiary, fly fishing, 20th century British art. *Address:* c/o Mogford Ltd, 36 St Giles, Oxford OX1 3LD. *Clubs:* Garrick, Groucho, Soho House, 5 Hertford Street.

MOGG, family name of **Baron Mogg**.

MOGG, Baron *cr* 2008 (Life Peer), of Queen's Park in the County of East Sussex; **John Frederick Mogg,** KCMG 2003; European Adviser to Gas and Electricity Markets Authority, since 2013 (non-executive Chairman and Member, 2003–13); *b* 5 Oct. 1943; *s* of Thomas W. Mogg and Cora M. Mogg; *m* 1967, Anne Smith; one *d* one *s*. *Educ:* Bishop Vesey's Grammar Sch., Sutton Coldfield; Birmingham Univ. (BA Hons). Rediffusion Ltd, 1965–74; Principal: Office of Fair Trading, 1974–76; Dept of Trade (Insurance Div.), 1976–79; First Sec., UK Perm. Representation, Brussels, 1979–82; Department of Trade and Industry: Asst Sec., Minerals and Metals Div., 1982–85; PPS to Sec. of State for Trade and Industry, 1985–86; Under Secretary: European Policy Div., 1986–87; Industrial Materials Market Div., 1987–89; Dep. Hd, European Secretariat, Cabinet Office, 1989–90; Dep. Dir Gen., DGIII, EC, 1990–93; Dir Gen., DGXV, subseq. DG Internal Mkt, EC, 1993–2003. Chairman: Eur. Regulators' Gp for Electricity and Gas, 2005–11; Internat. Confedn of Energy Regulators, 2009–; Bd of Regulators, Agency for Co-operation of Regulators, 2010–; Adv. Bd, EU Observatory on IP Infringements, 2012–; Mem., Internat. Adv. Panel, Singapore, 2006–; Mem. Adv. Council, Electric Power Res. Inst., 2012–. Pres., Council of Eur. Energy Regulators, 2005–. Special Advr to Pres., Office for Harmonization in Internal Market, 2009–. Chm., Govs, Univ. of Brighton, 2006–. Trustee, Brighton Philharmonic Orch., 2006–12. *Address:* House of Lords, SW1A 0PW.

MOGG, Jacob William R.; *see* Rees-Mogg.

MOGGACH, Deborah; novelist, journalist and script-writer; *b* 28 June 1948; *d* of late Richard Alexander Hough, writer and of Helen Charlotte (*née* Woodyatt); *m* 1971, Anthony Austin Moggach (marr. diss. 1988); one *s* one *d*. *Educ:* Camden Sch. for Girls; Bristol Univ. (BA Hons English); Inst. of Educn, Univ. of London (BEd English). Mem., Exec. Cttee, English PEN, 1992–95; Chm., Soc. of Authors, 1999–2001 (Mem., Broadcasting Cttee, 1995–97, Mgt Cttee, 1998–2000). Television includes: Crown Court, 1983; To Have and to Hold, 1986; Stolen, 1990; Goggle Eyes (adaptation; Writers' Guild Award for Best Adapted Serial), 1993; Seesaw, 1998; Close Relations, 1998; Love in a Cold Climate (adaptation), 2001; Final Demand, 2003; Diary of Anne Frank, 2009; stage play, Double Take, Liverpool Playhouse, 1990, Chichester Fest. Theatre, 1993; film script, Pride and Prejudice (adaptation), 2005. Young Journalist of the Year, Westminster Arts Council, 1975. FRSL 1998. Hon. DLitt Bristol, 2005. *Publications:* You Must Be Sisters, 1978; Close to Home, 1979; A Quiet Drink, 1980; Hot Water Man, 1982; Porky, 1983; To Have and To Hold, 1986; Smile and other stories, 1987; Driving in the Dark, 1988; Stolen, 1990; The Stand-In, 1991; The Ex-Wives, 1993; Changing Babies, 1995; Seesaw, 1996; Close Relations, 1997; Tulip Fever, 1999; Final Demand, 2001; These Foolish Things, 2004 (filmed as The Best Exotic Marigold Hotel, 2012); In The Dark, 2007; Heartbreak Hotel, 2013; Something to Hide, 2015. *Recreation:* walking around London looking into people's windows. *Address:* c/o Curtis Brown, 28–29 Haymarket, SW1Y 4SP. *T:* (020) 7396 6600.

MOGGRIDGE, Harry Traherne, (Hal), OBE 1986; PPLI; FCIHort; RIBA; Consultant, Colvin and Moggridge, Landscape Consultants (established 1922), since 1997 (Partner, 1969–97; Senior Partner, 1981–97); *b* London, 2 Feb. 1936; *s* of late Lt-Col Harry Weston Moggridge, CMG, and Helen Mary Ferrier Taylor; *m* 1963, Hon. Catherine Greville Herbert, *yr d* of 2nd Baron Hemingford; two *s* one *d*. *Educ:* Tonbridge Sch.; Architectural Assoc. (Dip.); evening lectures in landscape design under Prof. P. Youngman. RIBA 1962. Notts CC, 1960; Asst to Geoffrey Jellicoe, 1961–63; Site architect for Sir Wm Halcrow & Ptrs, Tema Harbour, Ghana, 1964–65; Landscape asst, GLC, 1966–67; own practice; entered into partnership with late Brenda Colvin, CBE, PPILA, 1969, continuing in partnership with Christopher Carter, ALI, and staff of fifteen. Prof. of Landscape Architecture, Univ. of Sheffield, 1984–86. Member: Royal Fine Art Commn, 1988–99; Nat. Trust Architectural Panel, 1991–2009. Mem. Council, Landscape Inst., 1970–83 (Hon. Sec., Vice Pres., Pres. 1979–81) and 1987–93 (Deleg. to Internat. Fedn of Landscape Architects, 1980–90 and 2002–06; Chm., Internat. Cttee, 1986–92); Chm., Landscape Foundn, 1995–99. Mem., ICOMOS-IFLA Internat. Cttee on Cultural Landscapes, 2000–; Mem., ICOMOS-UK Cultural Landscapes and Historic Gdns Cttee, 2003–; IFLA Rep., UNESCO Historic Urban Landscape Wkg Gp, 2006–09. Chm., Penllergare Trust, 2000–12. Landscape works include: Brenig Reservoir, Clwyd; White Horse Hill, a new car park and restoration of grass downland; Gale Common Hill, Yorkshire, woods and fields over 100 million cubic metres of waste ash and shale built over 60 years; quarries; countryside studies; reclamation; public and private gardens; restoration of historic parks (e.g. Blenheim, Knole, Castle Hill, Dinefwr, Aberglasney garden), creation of new parks and consultancy for Inner Royal Parks of London; master plans for RHS Wisley Gdns and for Welsh Nat. Botanic Gdns. FRSA. VMH 2000; President's Medal, Landscape Inst., 2002; Europa Nostra Medal, 2003. *Publications:* numerous articles and chapters of books describing works or technical subjects. *Recreations:* looking at pictures, gardens, buildings, towns, landscapes and people in these places; walking, theatre, grandchildren. *Address:* Filkins, Lechlade, Glos GL7 3JQ. *T:* (01367) 860225. *Club:* Farmers.
See also Lady Goodhart.

MOGRA, Shaykh Ibrahim; Imam, Leicester, since 1990; Member, Executive Committee, Muslim Council of Britain, since 2002; *b* Malawi, 9 Oct. 1965; *s* of Umar Mogra and Zubaydah Ibrahim; *m* 1990, Rayhanah Sulayman; four *s*. *Educ:* Darul-Ulum, Holcombe (Al-Alimiyyah 1990); Al-Azhar Univ., Cairo (Licentiate 1992); Sch. of Oriental and African Studies, Univ. of London (MA 1998). Dir and Principal, Khazinatul-Ilm, Madaris of Arabic and Muslim Life Studies, Leicester, 1994–. Chm., Religions for Peace UK, 2009–; Co-Chm., Christian Muslim Forum, 2011–; Member: Eur. Council of Religious Leaders, 2005–; Imams and Rabbis for Peace, 2005–; Niwano Peace Prize Cttee, Japan, 2008–. Chaplain, Canary Wharf, 2013–. *Recreations:* football, cricket, swimming, DIY, keeps tropical fish. *E:* ibrahimmogra@hotmail.com. *W:* www.twitter.com/IbrahimMogra.

MOGREN, Dr Håkan Lars; Deputy Chairman, AstraZeneca PLC, 1999–2009; *b* 17 Sept. 1944; *s* of late Ivan and Märta Mogren; *m* 1975, Anne Marie (*née* Hermansson); two *s*. *Educ:* Royal Inst. of Technol., Stockholm (DSc Biotechnol. 1969). President and Chief Executive Officer: AB Marabou (Sweden), 1977–88; Astra AB (Sweden), 1988–99. Chairman: Reckitt Benckiser plc, 2001–03; Affibody AB, 2002–05; Vice Chm., Gambro AB, 1996–2006; Director: Investor AB, 1990–2010; Norsk Hydro ASA, 2001–07; Groupe Danone SA, 2003; Mem. Supervisory Bd, Rémy-Cointreau SA, 2003–08. Chairman: Res. Inst. of Industrial Econs, Sweden, 1993–2003; Sweden-Japan Foundn, Sweden, 1998–2003 (Dir, 1991–); Sweden-America Foundn, Sweden, 2000–; British-Swedish Chamber of Commerce, Sweden, 2001–03; Dir, Marianne and Marcus Wallenberg Foundn, 1999–. Member: Swedish Gastronomic Acad., 1985–; Royal Swedish Acad. of Engrg Scis, 1988–. Hon. DSc Leicester, 1998. King's Medal with Ribbon, Order of Seraphims (Sweden), 1998; Chevalier, Légion d'Honneur (France), 1995.

MOHAN, Dominic James; Adviser to Chief Executive, News Corporation, since 2013; *b* Bath, 26 May 1969; *s* of Michael and Deborah Mohan; *m* 1998, Michelle Knee; two *s* one *d*. *Educ:* Neale-Wade Sch., March; Univ. of Southampton (BA); Rutgers Univ., NJ. Reporter: Sunday Mirror, 1992–94; News of the World, 1994–95; The Sun: showbiz reporter, 1996–97; Dep. Ed., 1997–98, Ed., 1998–2003, showbiz; Asst Ed. and columnist, 2003–04; Associate Ed. (Features), 2004–07; Dep. Ed., 2007–09; Ed., 2009–13; Ed., The Sun on Sunday, 2012–13; columnist, Bizarre, 1998–2003. DJ, Virgin Radio, 2002–04 (Sony Gold Radio Award, 2003). Hugh Cudlipp Award, BPA, 2005. *Recreations:* football (Bristol City and Arsenal FC), my children, music, film. *Clubs:* Ivy, Soho House; Arsenal Football.

MOHYEDDIN, Zia; actor; President and Chief Executive Officer, National Academy of Performing Arts, Pakistan (Chairman, 2004); *b* 20 June 1931. *Educ:* Punjab University (BA Hons). Freelance directing for Aust. broadcasting, 1951–52; RADA, 1953–54; Pakistan stage appearances, 1956–59; UK stage, 1959–71; Dir Gen., Pakistan Nat. Performing Ensemble, to 1977; producer and dir, Central TV, 1980–94; *stage:* appearances include: A Passage to India, 1960; The Alchemist, 1964; The Merchant of Venice, 1966; Volpone, 1967; The Guide, 1968; On The Rocks, 1969; Measure for Measure, 1981; Film, Film, Film, 1986; *films:* Lawrence of Arabia, 1961; Sammy Going South, 1963; The Sailor from Gibraltar; Khartoum, 1965; Ashanti, 1982; Assam Garden, 1985; Immaculate Conception, 1992; The Odyssey; Doomsday Gun, 1993; L'Enfant des Rues, 1994; *television series:* The Hidden Truth, 1964; Gangsters, 1979; Jewel in the Crown, 1983; King of the Ghetto, 1986; Mountbatten, 1988; Shalom Salaam, 1989; creator, Family Pride, Channel Four, 1990. *Recreations:* reading, bridge, watching cricket. *Address:* c/o National Academy of Performing Arts, Old Hindu Gymkhana Building, M. R. Kiyani Road, Karachi, Pakistan. *Club:* Savile.

MOI, Daniel arap; President of Kenya, 1978–2002; Minister of Defence, 1979–2002; *b* Rift Valley Province, 2 Sept. 1924. *Educ:* African Inland Mission Sch., Kabartonjo; Govt African Sch., Kapsabet. Teacher, 1946–56. MLC, 1957; Mem. for Baringo, House of Representatives, 1963–78; Minister for Educn, 1961; Minister for Local Govt, 1962–64; Minister for Home Affairs, 1964–67; Vice-Pres. of Kenya, 1967–78. Chm., Kenya African Democratic Union (KADU), 1960; Pres., Kenya African Nat. Union (KANU) for Rift Valley Province, 1966; Pres. of KANU, 1978–2003. Chm., Rift Valley Provincial Council. Former Member: Rift Valley Educn Bd; Kalenjin Language Cttee; Commonwealth Higher Educn Cttee; Kenya Meat Commn; Bd of Governors, African Girls' High Sch., Kikuyu. EGH, EBS. *Address:* c/o State House, PO Box 40530, Nairobi, Kenya.

MOIR, Arthur Hastings; Clerk to the Northern Ireland Assembly, 2001–07; *b* 18 Oct. 1948; *s* of Arthur Moir and Kathleen Moir (*née* Hastings); *m* 1987, Catherine Quinn; three *d*. *Educ:* Belfast Royal Acad.; Queen's Univ., Belfast (LLB Hons 1971). Admitted solicitor, 1974; Partner: Alex Stewart & Son Solicitors, 1978–84; McConnell and Moir Solicitors, 1984–88; Legal Advr, Land Registry of NI, 1988–93; Registrar of Titles and Land Purchase Trustee, 1993–2001; Chief Exec., Land Registers of NI, 1995–2001. Part-time legal consultant and expert witness, 2007–. Mem., Soc. of Expert Witnesses, 2009–. Chm., N Down CAB, 2011–14. *Publications:* The Land Registration Manual, 1994, 2nd edn 2005; Moir on Land Registration, 2011. *Recreations:* reading, writing, playing bridge, losing golf balls. *Address:* Lincoln Building, Great Victoria Street, Belfast BT2 7SL.

MOIR, Sir Christopher Ernest, 4th Bt *cr* 1916, of Whitehanger, Fernhurst, co. Sussex; *b* 22 May 1955; *e s* of Sir Ernest Ian Royds Moir, 3rd Bt and of Margaret Hanham, *d* of George Eric Carter; *S* father, 1998; *m* 1983, Mrs Vanessa Kirtikar, *yr d* of V. A. Crosby; twin *s*, and one step *d*. *Educ:* King's College Sch., Wimbledon. FCA 1976. *Heir: er s* Oliver Royds Moir, *b* 9 Oct. 1984. *Address:* Three Gates, 174 Coombe Lane West, Kingston upon Thames, Surrey KT2 7DE.

MOIR, Dorothy Carnegie, CBE 2003; MD; FRCP, FFPH; Hon. Clinical Senior Lecturer in Public Health, Aberdeen University, since 2008; *b* 27 March 1942; *d* of Charles Carnegie Coull and Jessie Coull (*née* Ritchie); *m* 1970, Alexander David Moir; three *s*. *Educ:* Albyn Sch. for Girls, Aberdeen; Aberdeen Univ. (MB ChB 1965; MD 1970); Open Univ. (MBA 2000). FFPH (FFPHM 1988); FRCP 1996; FICS 2001. Resident Med. House Officer, Aberdeen Royal Infirmary, 1965–66; Resident Surg. House Officer, Royal Aberdeen Children's Hosp., 1966; Res. Fellow in Therapeutics, 1966–69, Lectr in Community Medicine, 1970–79, Univ. of Aberdeen; Community Medicine Specialist, Grampian Health Bd, 1979–88; Unit MO, Acute Services, Aberdeen Royal Infirmary, 1984–88; Director of Public Health and Chief Administrative Medical Officer: Forth Valley Health Bd, 1988–94; Lanarkshire Health Bd, 1994–2008; Hon. Consultant in Public Health Medicine, Grampian Health Bd, Aberdeen, 2008–13. *Publications:* (jtly) The Prescription and Administration of Drugs in Hospital: a programmed learning text, 1970, 3rd edn 1988; many articles in med. and pharmaceut. jls. *Address:* Medical School, Aberdeen University, Polwarth Building, Foresterhill, Aberdeen AB25 2ZD.

MOIR, James William Charles, CBE 2003; LVO 2002; Controller, BBC Radio 2, 1995–2003; *b* 5 Nov. 1941; *s* of William Charles Moir and Mary Margaret Moir (*née* Daly); *m* 1966, Julia (*née* Smalley); two *s* one *d*. *Educ:* Gunnersbury Catholic Grammar School; Univ. of Nottingham (BA). Joined BBC TV Light Entertainment Group, 1963; Producer, Light Entertainment, 1970, Exec. Producer, 1979; Head of Variety, 1982–87; Head of Gp, 1987–93; Dep. Dir, Corporate Affairs, BBC, 1993–95. BBC Royal Liaison, 1992–2003. Chm., EBU Working Pty on Light Entertainment, 1992–94. Mem., Internat. Media Centre, Univ. of Salford, 2001–. Trustee, Symphony Hall, Birmingham, 1996–. Hon. Mem. Council, NSPCC, 1990–. Hon. Pres., Students' Union, Univ. of Nottingham, 2002–05. FRTS 1990; Fellow, Radio Acad., 1998 (Outstanding Contrib. to Music Radio, 2001). Hon. DLitt Nottingham, 2004. Gold Badge of Merit, British Acad. Composers & Songwriters, 1993; Outstanding Contrib. to Broadcasting, BPG, 2002; Sandford St Martin Trust Radio Award for services to religious broadcasting, 2002. KSG 2004. *Address:* The Lawn, Elm Park Road, Pinner, Middx HA5 3LE. *Clubs:* Reform, Garrick.

MOIR, Judith Patricia; Her Honour Judge Moir; a Circuit Judge, since 1999; *b* 2 Dec. 1954; *d* of Norman and Stephanie Edwardson; *m* 1977, Charles Geoffrey Moir; two *s* one *d*. *Educ:* Central Newcastle High Sch.; Somerville Coll., Oxford (BA Jurisp.). Called to the Bar, Gray's Inn, 1978; in practice at the Bar, NE Circuit, 1978–99. *Recreation:* family. *Address:* Newcastle Combined Court Centre, Quayside, Newcastle upon Tyne NE1 3LA.

MOISEIWITSCH, Prof. Benjamin Lawrence, (Benno); Professor of Applied Mathematics, Queen's University of Belfast, 1968–93, now Emeritus; *b* London, 6 Dec. 1927; *s* of Jacob Moiseiwitsch and Chana Kotlerman; *m* 1953, Sheelagh Mary Penrose McKeon; two *s* two *d*. *Educ:* Royal Liberty Sch., Romford; University Coll., London (BSc, 1949, PhD 1952). Sir George Jessel Studentship in Maths, UCL, 1949; Queen's University, Belfast: Lectr and Reader in Applied Maths, 1952–68; Dean, Faculty of Science, 1972–75; Hd, Dept of Applied Maths and Theoretical Physics, 1977–89. MRIA 1969. *Publications:* Variational Principles, 1966, repr. 2004; Integral Equations, 1977, repr. 2005; How to Solve Applied Mathematics Problems, 2011; articles on theoretical atomic physics in scientific jls. *Address:* 21 Knocktern Gardens, Belfast, Northern Ireland BT4 3LZ. *T:* (028) 9065 8332.

MOLE, Christopher David; *b* 16 March 1958; *m* 1996, Shona Gibb; two *s*. *Educ:* Dulwich Coll.; Univ. of Kent (BSc 1979). Technologist, Plessey Res., 1979–81; Res. Manager, BT Labs, Martlesham, 1981–98. Mem. (Lab) Suffolk CC, 1985–2001 (Leader of Council, 1993–2001); Mem., Gen. Assembly, LGA. Dep. Chm., E of England Develt Agency, 1998–2001. MP (Lab) Ipswich, Nov. 2001–2010; contested (Lab) same seat, 2010. PPS to Minister for Local Govt, 2005–06, 2007–08; an Asst Govt Whip, 2008–09; Parly Under-Sec. of State, DfT, 2009–10. Mem., Select Cttee, ODPM, 2003–05, on Sci. and Technol., 2007.

MOLE, His Honour David Richard Penton; QC 1990; a Circuit Judge, 2002–13; *b* 1 April 1943; *s* of late Rev. Arthur Penton Mole and Margaret Isobel Mole; *m* 1969, Anu-Reet (*née* Nigol); three *s* one *d*. *Educ:* St John's School, Leatherhead; Trinity College, Dublin (MA); LSE (LLM). City of London College, 1967–74 (Sen. Lectr, 1971); called to the Bar, Inner Temple, 1970; Standing Junior Counsel to Inland Revenue in rating valuation matters, 1984; a Recorder, 1995–2002; Jt Hd of Chambers, 2000–02; authorised to act as High Ct Judge in Admin Ct, 2004. Legal Mem., Lands Tribunal, 2006–09; a Judge of the Upper Tribunal (Lands Chamber), 2009–13, Dep. Judge of the Upper Tribunal, 2013–15; Mem., Parole Bd, 2003–13. Part-time cartoonist, 1979–83. *Publications:* contribs to Jl of Planning Law. *Recreations:* walking, drawing, painting, flying.
See also S. G. Mole.

MOLE, Stuart Gordon, CVO 2009; OBE 1984; Director-General, Royal Commonwealth Society, 2000–09; Senior Associate, Sarlsdown Associates, since 2009; *b* 15 Jan. 1949; *s* of late Rev. Arthur Penton Mole and Margaret Isobel Mole; *m* 1st, 1971 (marr. diss. 1977); 2nd, 1982, Katherine Madeleine Anthea Little (marr. diss. 1996); two *s*; partner, Helen Catherine Vines; one *d*. *Educ:* St Paul's Cathedral Choir Sch.; St John's Sch., Leatherhead (music schol.); Univ. of Nottingham (BA 1970); Hertford Coll., Oxford (PGCE 1971); Birkbeck Coll., Univ. of London (MSc 1974). Lectr, Chelmsford Coll., 1971–75; Parly Press Officer, Liberal Party, 1975–77; Dir, OUTSET youth and disability charity, 1977–80; Hd, Office of Leader of Liberal Party, 1980–83; political lobbyist and speechwriter, 1983–84; Commonwealth Secretariat: Special Asst to Sec.-Gen., 1984–90; Dir, Sec.-Gen's Office, 1990–2000. Sen. Res. Fellow, Inst. of Commonwealth Studies, Univ. of London, 2010– (Mem. Adv. Council, 2013–). Mem. (Lib Dem), Chelmsford BC, 1972–87 (Chm., P & R Cttee, 1983–87). Contested: (L) Chelmsford, Feb. and Oct. 1974, 1979, 1983, 1987; (Lib Dem) N Essex and S Suffolk, European Parlt, 1994. Hd, Leader's Gen. Election Campaign Tour, 1993. Dir and Mem. Editl Bd, The Round Table: Commonwealth Jl of Internat. Affairs, 1994– (Chm., 2011–). Pres., Bath and Dist Royal Commonwealth Soc., 2009–. Hon. Fellow in Politics, 2009, doctoral res. student (pt-time), 2013–, Univ. of Exeter. Patron, Commonwealth Resounds, 2009–. *Recreations:* choral music, singing. *Address:* c/o Sarlsdown Associates, 5a Sarlsdown Road, Exmouth, Devon EX8 2HY. *Clubs:* Royal Over-Seas League; Bristol Commonwealth Society.
See also D. R. P. Mole.

MOLESWORTH, family name of **Viscount Molesworth**.

MOLESWORTH, 12th Viscount *cr* 1716 (Ire.); **Robert Bysse Kelham Molesworth;** Baron Philipstown 1716; businessman; *b* 4 June 1959; *s* of 11th Viscount Molesworth and Anne Florence (*née* Cohen; *d* 1983); *S* father, 1997. *Educ:* Cheltenham; Sussex Univ. (BA Philosophy). *Recreations:* ballroom dancing, travel, carpentry. *Heir: b* Hon. William John Charles Molesworth, *b* 20 Oct. 1960.

MOLESWORTH, Allen Henry Neville; management consultant; *b* 20 Aug. 1931; *s* of late Roger Bevil Molesworth (Colonel RA), and of Iris Alice Molesworth (*née* Kennion); *m* 1970, Gail Cheng Kwai Chan. *Educ:* Wellington Coll., Berks; Trinity Coll., Cambridge (MA). FCA. 2nd Lt, 4th Queen's Own Hussars, Malaya, 1950. Project Accounts, John Laing & Sons (Canada) Ltd, 1954–58; Singleton Fabian & Co., Chartered Accountants, 1959–63;

Consultant: Standard Telephones & Cables Ltd, 1963–67; Coopers & Lybrand Associates Ltd, 1967–76: India, 1970; Kuwait, 1971; France, 1972; New Hebrides, 1972; Laos, 1974; Tonga, 1975; Financial and Admin. Controller, Crown Agents, 1976–84; Chief Accountant, British Telecom Property, 1984–90. *Recreations:* shooting, ski-ing, music, restoring antiques. *Address:* c/o Lloyds, 8–10 Waterloo Place, SW1Y 4BE. *Clubs:* 1900, Coningsby.

MOLESWORTH-ST AUBYN, Sir William, 16th Bt *cr* 1689, of Pencarrow, Cornwall; *b* 23 Nov. 1958; *s* of Sir Arscott Molesworth-St Aubyn, 15th Bt, MBE and of Iona Audrey Armatrude, *d* of Adm. Sir Francis Loftus Tottenham, KCB, CBE; *S* father, 1998; *m* 1988, Carolyn, *er d* of William Tozier; two *s* one *d*. *Educ:* Harrow. Late Captain, The Royal Green Jackets. *Heir: s* Archie Hender Molesworth-St Aubyn, *b* 27 March 1997.

MOLINA, Prof. Mario Jose, PhD; Professor, Department of Chemistry and Biochemistry, University of California, San Diego, since 2004; President, Mario Molina Center, Mexico City, since 2004; *b* 19 March 1943; *s* of Roberto Molina-Pasquel and Leonor Henriquez de Molina; *m* 2006, Guadalupe Alvarez. *Educ:* Univ. Nacional Autónoma de México (Ingeniero Químico 1965); Univ. of Calif, Berkeley (PhD 1972). Asst Prof., Univ. Nacional Autónoma de México, 1967–68; Res. Associate, Univ. of Calif, Berkeley, 1972–73; Res. Associate, 1973–74, Asst Prof., 1975–79, Associate Prof., 1979–82, Univ. of Calif, Irvine; Sen. Res. Scientist, Jet Propulsion Lab., Calif, 1983–89; Prof., Dept of Earth, Atmospheric and Planetary Scis and Dept of Chemistry, MIT, 1989–2004. Mem., US Nat. Acad. of Scis, 1993. Tyler Ecology and Energy Prize, USA, 1983; (jtly) Nobel Prize for Chemistry, 1995. *Publications:* articles in jls and chapters in books. *Recreations:* music, tennis. *Address:* Department of Chemistry and Biochemistry, University of California, San Diego, 9500 Gilman Drive MC 0356, La Jolla, CA 92093, USA.

MOLITOR, Edouard, Hon. KCMG 1976; Grand Officier, Ordre du Mérite (Luxembourg), 1990; Grand Officier, Ordre de la Couronne de Chêne, 1996; Officier, Ordre Civil et Militaire d'Adolphe de Nassau, 1977; Ambassador of Luxembourg: to Italy, 1993–96; to Malta, 1995–96; Permanent Representative to UN Food and Agriculture Organisation, 1993–96; *b* Luxembourg City, 14 Feb. 1931; *s* of Joseph Molitor and Lucie Michels; *m* 1960, Constance Scholtes; three *s*. *Educ:* Univs of Grenoble, Nancy and Paris. Dr en droit. Barrister, Luxembourg, 1955–60; joined Diplomatic Service, 1960 (Political Affairs); First Sec. and Rep. to UNESCO, Paris, 1964–69; Counsellor and Consul-Gen., Brussels, 1969–73; Dir of Protocol and Juridical Affairs, Min. of Foreign Affairs, 1973–78; Mem., Commn de Contrôle, EC, 1973–77; Ambassador to the Holy See, 1976–79; Ambassador to Austria, 1978–89; Perm. Rep. to UNIDO, IAEA, 1978–89; Head of Luxembourg Delegn, MBFR Conf., 1978–89 and at CSCE Conf., Vienna, 1986–89; Ambassador to UK, Ireland and Iceland, and Perm. Rep. to Council of WEU, 1989–92. Mem., Rotary Club, Luxembourg. Foreign Decorations from: Norway, 1964; Italy, W Germany, Belgium, 1973; Greece, 1975; Denmark, Tunisia, Senegal, Netherlands, France, 1978; Vatican, Austria, 1989; Iceland, 1990; Italy 1996. *Recreations:* swimming, music, literature. *Address:* 23 rue d'Orval, 2270 Luxembourg.

MØLLER, Dr Per Stig; Commander, First Class, Order of Dannebrog (Denmark), 2002; MP (C) Gentofte, 1983–87, Frederiksberg, since 1987, Denmark; *b* 27 Aug. 1942; *s* of Poul and Lis Møller. *Educ:* Univ. of Copenhagen (MA Comparative Lit. 1967, PhD 1973). Cultural Ed., Radio Denmark, 1973–74; Lectr, Sorbonne, Paris, 1974–76; Dep. Hd, Culture and Society Dept, 1974 and 1976–79, Chief of Progs for Dir of Progs, 1979–84, Radio Denmark; Vice-Chm., 1985–86, Chm., 1986–87, Radio Council. Commentator, Berlingske Tidende, 1984–2001. Minister for the Envmt, 1990–93; Mem., Foreign Policy Cttee, 1994–2001; Chm., Security Policy Cttee, 1994–96; foreign policy spokesman, 1998–2001; Minister for Foreign Affairs, 2001–10; Minister for Culture, 2010–11. Mem., Council of Europe, 1987–90, 1994–97 and 1998–2001. Danish Conservative Party: Mem., Exec. Cttee, 1985–89 and 1993–98; Chm., 1997–98; Political Leader, Parly Party, 1997–98. Chm., Popular Educn Assoc., 1983–89. Georg Brandes Award, Soc. of Danish Lit. Critics, 1996; Einar Hansen Res. Fund Award, 1997; Cultural Award, Popular Educn Assoc., 1998; Raoul Wallenberg Medal, 1998; Kaj Munk Award, 2001; Rosenkjær Award, 2001; Robert Schuman Medal, 2003. Chevalier, Ordre National du Lion (Senegal), 1975; Grosskreuz des Verdienstordens (Germany), 2002; Comdr, Ordre National (Benin), 2003; Grand Cross, Order of Crown of Oak (Luxembourg), 2003; Gold Nersornaat (Greenland), 2005; Order of Stara Planina, 1st Cl. (Bulgaria), 2006; Comdr Grand Cross, Order of Polar Star (Sweden), 2007; Grand Cross, Order of South Cross (Brazil), 2007; Grand Cross of Comdr, Order for Merits to Lithuania, 2007. *Publications:* La Critique dramatique et littéraire de Malte-Brun, 1971; Malte-Bruns litterære Kritik og dens Plads i Transformationsprocessen, 1973; Erotismen, 1973; København-Paris t/r, 1973; På Sporet af det forsvundne Menneske, 1976; Livet i Gøgereden, 1978; Fra Tid til Anden, 1979; Tro, Håb og Fællesskab, 1980; Midt i Redeligheden, 1981; Orwells Håb og Frygt, 1983; Nat uden Daggry, 1985; (jtly) Mulighedernes Samfund, 1985; Stemmer fra Øst, 1987; Historien om Estland, Letland og Litauen, 1990; Kurs mod Katastrofer?, 1993; Miljøproblemer, 1995; Den naturlige Orden - Tolv år der flyttede Verden, 1996; Spor. Udvalgte Skrifter om det åbne Samfund og dets Værdier, 1997; Magt og Afmagt, 1999; Munk, 2000; Mere Munk, 2003; Samtale fremme forståelsen, 2010. *Address:* Folketinget, Christiansborg, 1240 Copenhagen, Denmark.

MOLLET, Richard James; Chief Executive, Publishers Association, since 2010; *b* Swansea, 9 Jan. 1970; *s* of Keith Mollet and Helen Mollet; *m* 2000, Nicola Laffan; three *s*. *Educ:* Olchfa Comp. Sch., Swansea; Worcester Coll., Oxford (BA Hons PPE 1992). Officer, RN, 1988–96; Account Dir, Ludgate Communications, 1996–2000; Dir, PPS Ltd, 2000–02; Associate Director: Fleishman-Hillard, 2002–05; Edelman, 2005–06; Dir, Public Affairs, BPI, 2006–10. Chair, Alliance for IP (formerly Alliance Against IP Theft), 2010– (Vice Chm., 2010–12). Member, Board: Book Industry Communications Ltd, 2010–; Publishers' Licensing Soc.; Copyright Licensing Agency. Chm. Trustees, World Book Day Ltd, 2011–. Contested (Lab) Surrey SW, 2010. *Recreations:* song writing, performing music, football (playing and watching), snowboarding, tennis, chess, reading, literature, film, theatre. *Address:* Talbot Mead, Ballsdown, Chiddingfold, Surrey GU8 4XJ. *T:* 07778 660304. *E:* rmollet@publishers.org.uk, mollets@btinternet.com.

MOLLON, Prof. John Dixon, DSc; FRS 1999; Professor of Visual Neuroscience, 1998–2011, Distinguished Teaching Fellow, since 2011, University of Cambridge; Fellow, since 1996, and President, since 2013, Gonville and Caius College, Cambridge; *b* 12 Sept. 1944; *s* of Arthur Greenwood Mollon and Joyce Dorothy Mollon. *Educ:* Scarborough High Sch.; Hertford Coll., Oxford (BA 1966; DPhil 1970). Sen. Schol., Wadham Coll., Oxford, 1967–69; Post-doctoral Fellow, Bell Telephone Labs, NJ, 1970; Lectr in Psychology, Corpus Christi Coll., Oxford, 1971–72; University of Cambridge: Univ. Demonstrator, 1972–76; Lectr, 1976–93, Reader, 1993–98, in Exptl Psychology. Hon. Sec., Experimental Psychology Soc., 1974–78. President: Cambridge Philosophical Soc., 2012–13; International Colour Vision Soc., 2011–. Fellow, Optical Soc. of America, 1984. *Publications:* (with H. B. Barlow) The Senses, 1982; (with L. T. Sharpe) Colour Vision: physiology and psychophysics, 1983; (with J. Pokorny and K. Knoblauch) Normal and Defective Colour Vision, 2003. *Recreations:* collecting antiquarian books and oak and walnut furniture, historical research. *Address:* Gonville and Caius College, Cambridge CB2 1TA.

MOLLOY, Francie; MP (SF) Mid Ulster, since March 2013; *b* Derrymagowan, Co. Tyrone, 16 Dec. 1950; *m*; two *s* two *d*. *Educ:* St Patrick's Intermediate Sch., Dungannon; Newry Further Educn Coll. Apprentice fitter/welder, Felden Govt Trng Centre, Belfast; fitter/welder, Planet/Powerscreen, Ulster; full-time political activist, 1980; Dir of Elections for Bobby Sands, 1981. Mem. (SF) Dungannon and S Tyrone BC, 1985–89 and 1993 (Mayor, 2001–02 and 2005–06; Dep. Mayor, 2003–04). Mem. (SF) NI Assembly, 1998–2013. Chm., Finance and Personnel Cttee, 1999–2003, Dep. Speaker, 2006–07 and 2007–11, Principal Dep. Speaker, 2011–13, NI Assembly. Contested (SF) NI, EP, 1994. *Address:* c/o Sinn Féin, 55 Falls Road, Belfast BT12 4PD.

MOLLOY, Michael John; writer; *b* 22 Dec. 1940; *s* of John George and Margaret Ellen Molloy; *m* 1964, Sandra June Foley; three *d*. *Educ:* Ealing School of Art. Sunday Pictorial, 1956; Daily Sketch, 1960; Daily Mirror, 1962–85: Editor, Mirror Magazine, 1969; Asst Editor, 1970; Dep. Editor, 1975; Editor, Dec. 1975–1985; Editor, Sunday Mirror, 1986–88; Mirror Group Newspapers: Director, 1976–90; Editor in Chief, 1985–90. Exhibitions of paintings: Galerie Aalders, S France, 2001; Walton Gall., London, 2003. *Publications:* The Black Dwarf, 1985; The Kid from Riga, 1987; The Harlot of Jericho, 1989; The Century, 1990; The Gallery, 1991; Sweet Sixteen, 1992; Cat's Paw, 1993; Home Before Dark, 1994; Dogsbody, 1995; The Witch Trade, 2001; The Time Witches, 2002; Wild West Witches, 2003; The House on Falling Star Hill, 2004; Peter Raven Under Fire, 2005; Peter Raven and the Pirate Raid, 2015. *Recreations:* reading, writing, painting. *Club:* Savile.

MOLONEY, Patrick Martin Joseph; QC 1998; **His Honour Judge Moloney;** a Circuit Judge, since 2007; Designated Civil Judge, East Anglia, since 2009; *b* 2 July 1953; *s* of late Dr Eamon Moloney and Jean Moloney (*née* Handley); *m* 2003, Sarah Harrison; one step *s* two step *d*. *Educ:* Prior Park Coll., Bath; St Catherine's Coll., Oxford (Open Schol.; BA Hons Jurisp. 1973; BCL 1974). Vis. Asst Prof., Univ. of British Columbia, 1974–75; called to the Bar, Middle Temple, 1976 (Harmsworth Schol.; Bencher, 2006); in practice at the Bar, specialising in libel law, 1978–2007; a Recorder, 2000–07. Mem. Bar, NI, 1999. FRGS 2003. *Publications:* (contrib. jtly) Halsbury's Laws of England, 1997. *Recreation:* independent travel. *Address:* Cambridge County Court, 197 East Road, Cambridge CB1 1BA.

MOLONEY, Dr Timothy John; QC 2010; *b* Ashton-under-Lyne, 10 Aug. 1965; *s* of James Moloney and Marie Moloney; *m* 1994, Tanya Burgess; one *s* one *d*. *Educ:* Loreto Sixth Form Coll., Manchester; Univ. of Birmingham (LLB Law and Politics 1987; PhD Law 1990). Lectr in Law, Univ. of Birmingham, 1990–92. Called to the Bar, Middle Temple, 1993; in practice as a barrister, 1994–. *Publications:* Rook and Ward on Sexual Offences, 3rd edn 2004, 4th edn 2010; (jtly) Blackstone's Guide to the Criminal Procedure Rules 2005, 2005, 2nd edn 2010; (contrib.) Blackstone's Criminal Practice, 2007–. *Recreations:* country walks, Benjamin Britten, Patrick Heron, The Fall, watching sport. *Address:* 54 Doughty Street, WC1N 2LS. *T:* (020) 7404 1313. *E:* t.moloney@doughtystreet.co.uk.

MOLONY, Sir Peter John, 4th Bt *cr* 1925, of the City of Dublin; *b* 17 Aug. 1937; *s* of Sir Joseph Molony, KCVO, QC and Carmen Mary Molony (*née* Dent, later Slay); *S* cousin 2014, but his name does not appear on the Official Roll of the Baronetage; *m* 1964, Elizabeth Mary Chaytor; three *s* one *d* (and one *s* decd). *Heir: s* John Benjamin Molony [*b* 19 Oct. 1966; *m* 2002, Rosemary McGrath; one *s* one *d*].

MOLYNEUX, Anne, MBE 2015; **Her Honour Judge Molyneux;** a Circuit Judge, since 2007; *b* Southport, 12 Jan. 1959; *d* of Robert Molyneux and Audrey Molyneux (*née* Young); *m* 2006, George Jonathan Morris; one *s* one *d* by a previous marriage. *Educ:* Univ. of Sheffield (LLB Hons 1979); Chester Coll. of Law. Admitted solicitor, 1983; Recorder, 2000–07. Mem., 2003–07, Judicial Mem., 2010–, Parole Bd. Mem., Law Soc. *Recreations:* walking, reading (Mem., Ealing and Fulham Book Club), family. *Address:* Isleworth Crown Court, 36 Ridgeway Road, Isleworth, Middx TW7 5LP. *E:* HHJudge.Molyneux@hmcourts-service.gsi.gov.uk.

MOLYNEUX, Prof. David Hurst, DSc; Professor of Tropical Health Sciences, University of Liverpool, 1991–2008, now Emeritus (Director, Liverpool School of Tropical Medicine, 1991–2000); *b* 9 April 1943; *s* of Reginald Frank Molyneux and Monica Foden Molyneux; *m* 1969, Anita Elisabeth Bateson; one *s* one *d*. *Educ:* Denstone Coll.; Emmanuel Coll., Cambridge (BA 1965; PhD 1969; MA 1969; DSc 1992). FRSB (FIBiol 1984). Lectr, Dept of Parasitology, Liverpool Sch. of Tropical Medicine, 1968–77; seconded as Research Officer to Nigerian Inst. for Trypanosomiasis, Kaduna, 1970–72, as Project Manager to UNDP/WHO, Bobo Dioulasso, Burkina Faso, 1975–77; Prof. of Biology, Univ. of Salford, 1977–91. Dir, DFID/Glaxo SmithKline Lymphatic Filariasis Support Centre, 2000–08. Member: WHO Cttees incl. Onchocerciasis, Guinea worm, Parasitic Diseases; Internat. Commn on Disease Eradication, 2001–. Mem., Bd of Trustees, 1999–2008, Chm. Bd, 2005–08, Pres., 2005–07, JRS Biodiversity Foundn (formerly Biosis, subseq. JRS Foundn), Philadelphia. Trustee, Nat. Museums and Galls on Merseyside, 1995–2000. President: British Soc. of Parasitology, 1992; RSTM&H, 2007–09. Mem., Governing Body, Inst. of Animal Health, 2001–09. Hon. FRCP 2006. Hon. Fellow, Liverpool John Moores Univ., 2010; Hon. Internat. Fellow, American Soc. of Tropical Med., 2014. Hon. DSc Georgetown, Washington, 2010. Chalmers Medal, 1987, Manson Medal, 2013, RSTM&H; Wright Medal, British Soc. of Parasitology, 1989; McKay Medal, Amer. Soc. of Tropical Medicine, 2007. *Publications:* The Biology of Trypanosoma and Leishmania: parasites of man and domestic animals (with R. W. Ashford), 1983; (ed) Control of Human Parasitic Diseases, 2006; numerous contribs to professional jls. *Recreations:* golf, music, travel, primitive art. *Address:* Liverpool School of Tropical Medicine, Pembroke Place, Liverpool L3 5QA. *T:* (0151) 705 3291; Kingsley Cottage, Town Well, Kingsley, Cheshire WA6 8EZ. *T:* (01928) 788397. *Club:* Delamere Forest Golf (Captain, 2007–08).

MOLYNEUX, Helena; Chair, Practical Action, since 2013 (Trustee, since 2008); *b* 17 Aug. 1948; *d* of Joseph and Mary Molyneux. *Educ:* Manchester Univ. (BSc); Cranfield Inst. of Technol. (MBA). FCIPD (FIPD 1994). United Biscuits, 1969–73; Univ. of Sierra Leone, 1973–76; Bank of America: Personnel Manager, Bank of Amer. Internat., 1979–80; Divl Personnel Manager, NT & SA, San Francisco, 1980–82; Head, Employee Relns and Personnel Planning, Eur., ME and Africa Div., 1982–87; Bankers Trust Co.: Head, Employee Relns and Staffing, Eur., 1987–89; Dir, Corporate Personnel, Eur., 1989–93; Dir of Personnel, British Council, 1993–2000; Consultant: HelenaMolyneux Consulting, 2000–04; Telos Partners Ltd, 2004–12. Vice-Chm., 1997–2001, Chm., 2001–08, Progressio (formerly Catholic Inst. for Internat. Relations). *Recreations:* Dorset, international development.

MOLYNEUX, Prof. Maxine Deirdre, PhD; Professor of Sociology, University College London, since 2012 (Founding Director, Institute of the Americas, 2012–14); *b* Pakistan, 24 May 1948; *d* of Cyril James Molyneux and Sarah Jane Jamieson; *m* 1979, Prof. Fred Halliday, FBA (*d* 2010); one *s*. *Educ:* Walsingham House Sch., India; Northlands, Argentina; British Sch., Uruguay; Univ. of Essex (BA Hons Sociol. 1975; PhD Sociol. 1983). AIL 1967. Lectr in Sociol., Univ. of Essex, 1976–92; pt-time Lectr, MSc Course in Develt, 1980–82, Lectr in Political Sociol., 1992–94, Birkbeck Coll., Univ. of London; School of Advanced Study, University of London: Lectr, 1994–96, Sen. Lectr, 1996–99, Prof. of Sociol., 2000–12, Inst. of Latin Amer. Studies, subseq. Inst. for the Study of the Americas; Dir, Inst. for the Study of the Americas, 2008–12. Member: HEFCE RAE Americas Panel, 2001; LAC Areas Panel, British Acad., 2008–; Scientific Council, GIS Institut des Amériques, Paris, 2010–. Mem., Exec. Cttee, Latin Amer. Studies Assoc., 2010–13. Mem., Bd of Trustees, Canning House, 2008–14. Series Ed. and Man. Ed., Palgrave Studies of the Americas, 2008–. *Publications:* La Voz de la Mujer: Periódico Comunista-Anárquico, 1997; State Policies and the Position of Women in Democratic Yemen, 1982; (with Fred Halliday) The Ethiopian Revolution, 1982; (ed with E. Dore) The Hidden Histories of Gender and the State in Latin America, 2000; (ed with N. Craske) Gender and the Politics of Rights and Democracy in Latin America, 2002; Women's Movements in International Perspective, 2000 (Movimientos de Mujeres en América Latina: Estudio Comparativa y Teórico, 2003); (with Sian Lazar) Doing the Rights

Thing: rights-based development and Latin American NGOs in Latin America, 2003; (ed with S. Razavi) Gender Justice, Development and Rights, 2003; (ed with Andrea Corwall) The Politics of Rights: dilemmas for feminist praxis, 2007. *Recreations:* music, art, travel, good food. *Address:* 17 Onslow Gardens, N10 3JT.

MOLYNEUX, Peter Douglas, OBE 2005; designer, producer and programmer of computer games; Creative Director, 22 Cans Ltd, since 2012; *b* 5 May 1959; *s* of George and Myrna Molyneux; *m* 2007, Emma Margaret Douglas; one *s. Educ:* Bearwood Coll., Wokingham; Farnborough Tech. Coll.; Southampton Univ. (BSc Computer Scis). Co-founder, Bullfrog Prodns, Guildford, 1987; Co-founder and Man. Dir, Lionhead Studios, 1997–2012; designer and programmer: Populous, 1989; Powermonger, 1990; Populous 2, 1991; Black & White, 2001; designer and producer: Syndicate, 1993; (and programmer) Theme Park, 1994; Magic Carpet, 1994; (and programmer) Dungeon Keeper, 1997; designer: Fable, 2004; Fable: The Lost Chapters, 2005; Black & White 2, 2005; The Movies, 2005; Black & White: Battle of the Gods, 2006; Fable 2, 2008; Fable 3, 2010; Curiosity, 2012; Godus, 2013. Fellow, BAFTA, 2011. Hon. DTech: Abertay Dundee, 2003; Bournemouth, 2005; Southampton, 2007; DUniv Surrey, 2007. Chevalier, Order of Arts and Letters (France), 2007. *Recreation:* playing poker and board games. *Address:* 22 Cans, 6 Stirling House, Stirling Road, Surrey Research Park, Guildford GU2 7RF. *T:* (01483) 484962. *E:* pmolyneux@22cans.com. *W:* www.twitter.com/pmolyneux.

MONAGHAN, Carol, (Mrs Feargal Dalton); MP (SNP) Glasgow North West, since 2015; *b* Glasgow, 2 Aug. 1972; *m* Feargal Dalton; one *s* two *d. Educ:* Univ. of Strathclyde (BSc Hons Laser Physics and Optoelectronics 1993); PGCE Physics and Maths. Teacher, Glasgow schs; Hd of Physics and Hd of Sci., Hyndland Secondary Sch., until 2015. Lectr, Univ. of Glasgow; consultant, Scottish Qualifications Authy. Mem., Sci. and Technol. Select Cttee, 2015–. *Address:* House of Commons, SW1A 0AA.

MONAGHAN, Charles Edward, CA; Chairman, Aegon UK, 1999–2005; President, Institute of Chartered Accountants of Scotland, 1999–2000; *b* 20 June 1940; *s* of Charles Monaghan and Elspeth Margaret Monaghan; *m* 1971, Dorothy Evelyn Hince; one *s. Educ:* Loretto Sch.; Edinburgh Univ. (BSc). CA 1965. Unilever, 1965–98: Ops Mem., E Asia Pacific, 1991–95; Head, Exec. Cttee Secretariat, 1996–98; Dir, Scottish Equitable, 1995. *Recreations:* squash, ski-ing, golf. *Address:* 10 Wool Road, Wimbledon, SW20 0HW. *T:* (020) 8946 8825. *Clubs:* Caledonian, Wimbledon; Royal Wimbledon Golf.

MONAGHAN, Karon; QC 2008; *b* London, 21 June 1963. *Educ:* Ealing Coll. of Higher Educn (LLB). Called to the Bar, Inner Temple, 1989; in practice as barrister specialising in equality law. *Publications:* Equality Law, 2007, 2nd edn 2013. *Address:* Matrix Chambers, Griffin Building, Gray's Inn, WC1R 5LN.

MONAGHAN, Dr Paul William; MP (SNP) Caithness, Sutherland and Easter Ross, since 2015; *b* Montrose, 1965; *s* of William Monaghan and Margaret Monaghan (*née* Innes); partner, Stephanie Anderson; one *d. Educ:* Inverness Royal Acad.; Univ. of Stirling (BA Hons 1st Psychol. and Sociol.; PhD Social Policy 2004). MBPsS 1999. Hd, Planning and Develt, Northern Constabulary, 2003–08; Dir and Gen. Manager, Highland Homeless Trust, 2008–15. FInstLM 2007. *Recreations:* travel, cycling. *Address:* House of Commons, SW1A 0AA. *T:* (020) 7219 8485. *E:* paul.monaghan.mp@parliament.uk.

MONAHAN, Erwin James, (Erwin James); writer; columnist, Guardian, since 1998; *b* Clevedon, 18 April 1957; *s* of Erwin James Monahan and Jeanie Monahan; two *d. Educ:* Ilkley Grammar Sch.; Open Univ. (Dip. Eur. Hum.; BA; MUniv). Drifter, criminal, 1972–82; fugitive in French Foreign Legion, 1982–84; life prisoner, 1984–2004. Develt Manager, Prisoners' Advice Service, 2004–06. Trustee: Prison Reform Trust, 2005–; Alternatives to Violence Project Britain, 2009–11; Turnkey Trust, 2012–13. Patron: Create, 2007–; Blue Sky, 2008–; Reader Orgn, 2012–; Writers in Prison Foundn, 2012–; Human Writes, 2014–; Prison Phoenix Trust, 2015–. FRSA. *Publications:* (as Erwin James) A Life Inside: a prisoner's notebook, 2003; The Home Stretch: from prison to parole, 2005; (contrib.) Humane Prisons, 2006; Redeemable: a memoir of darkness and hope, 2016. *Address:* c/o DGA, 55 Monmouth Street, WC2H 9DG. *T:* 07828 421707. *E:* erwin.james@theguardian.com.

MONBIOT, George Joshua; freelance author and journalist, since 1987; columnist, The Guardian, since 1995; Founder, Rewilding Britain, 2015; *b* 27 Jan. 1963; *s* of Raymond Geoffrey Monbiot, *qv. Educ:* Brasenose Coll., Oxford (BA, MA Zool.). BBC radio producer, 1985–87. Vis. Fellow, Green Coll., Oxford, 1993–95; Visiting Professor: Univ. of E London, 1997–99; Univ. of Bristol, 1999; Hon. Professor: Univ. of Keele, 1999–2000; Oxford Brookes Univ., 2003–. Hon. Fellow, Univ. of Cardiff, 2007. DU Essex, 2007. Sony Award for Radio Production, 1987; Lloyds Nat. Screenwriters Award, 1987; Sir Peter Kent Award, 1991; UN Global 500 Award, 1995; OneWorld Trust Media Award, 1996; Thomson Reuters Zoological Record Award, ZSL, 2013. *Publications:* Poisoned Arrows, 1989, 2nd edn 2003; Amazon Watershed, 1991; No Man's Land, 1994, 2nd edn 2003; Captive State, 2000, 2nd edn 2001; The Age of Consent, 2003, 2nd edn 2004; Heat, 2006; Bring on the Apocalypse: six arguments for global justice, 2008; Feral: searching for enchantment on the frontiers of rewilding, 2013 (Best Gen. Biology Book, Soc. of Biol. Book Awards, 2014; Nonfiction Award, Orion Book Awards, 2015). *Recreations:* natural history, kayaking, ultimate frisbee, apple growing, gardening, cooking, conversation. *Address:* Y Goeden Eirin, Newtown Road, Machynlleth SY20 8EY. *T:* (01654) 702758. *E:* george@monbiot.info.

MONBIOT, Raymond Geoffrey, CBE 1994 (MBE 1981); Deputy Chairman, Conservative Party, 2003–06; Chairman, Rotherfield Management Ltd, 1988–2011; *b* 1 Sept. 1937; *s* of Maurice and Ruth Monbiot; *m* 1961, Rosalie Vivien Gresham (*née* Cooke), OBE; one *s* one *d* (and one *d* decd). *Educ:* Westminster Sch.; London Business Sch. From pastry chef to Man. Dir of three subsids, J. Lyons & Co. Ltd, 1956–78; Man. Dir, Associated Biscuits, 1978–82; Chm., Campbell's Soups UK, 1982–88. Chm., Nat. Cons. Convention, 2003–06; Chm., Finance Cttee, 2004–06, Treas., Regl Develt, 2007–11, Cons. Party. Chm., Northants and Berks, Duke of Edinburgh Award Industrial Projects, 1976–86. Fellow, Mktg Soc. Freeman, City of London; Liveryman, Butchers' Co. David Ogilvy Award for Mktg, Campbell's Soups UK, 1985. *Publications:* How to Manage Your Boss, 1981; The Burnhams Book of Characters, 2002; The Characters of North Norfolk, 2003; More Characters of North Norfolk, 2006; Retirement is for Younger People, 2012. *Recreations:* gardening, cooking, writing, growing heritage apples. *Address:* Eastgate House, Burnham Market, Norfolk PE31 8HH. *T:* (01328) 730928. *E:* rotherfieldmgmnt@btconnect.com. *Club:* Farmers.

See also G. J. Monbiot.

MONCADA, Sir Salvador, Kt 2010; FRCP, FMedSci; FRS 1988; Professor Emeritus of Experimental Biology and Therapeutics, Wolfson Institute for Biomedical Research (formerly Institute for Strategic Medical Research (Cruciform Project)), University College London (Director, 1996–2011); Professor of Translational Medicine and Strategy, since 2013 and Director, Institute of Cancer Sciences, since 2014, University of Manchester; *b* 3 Dec. 1944; *s* of Dr Salvador Eduardo Moncada and Jenny Seidner; *m* 1st, 1966; one *d*; 2nd, 1998, HRH Princess Esmeralda of Belgium; one *s* one *d. Educ:* Univ. of El Salvador (DMS 1970); London Univ. (DPhil 1973; DSc 1983). FRCP 1994. GP, Social Service of El Salvador, 1969; Associate Prof. of Pharmacol. and Physiol., Univ. of Honduras, 1974–75; Wellcome Research Laboratories, 1971–73 and 1975–95: Sen. Scientist, 1975–77; Hd of Dept of Prostaglandin Res., 1977–85; Dir, Therapeutic Res. Div., 1984–86; Dir of Res., Wellcome Foundn, 1986–95. Croonian Lect., Royal Soc., 2005. Mem., British Pharmacol Soc., 1974 (Hon. Fellow, 2012). Founder FMedSci 1998. Associate Fellow, Third World Acad. of Sciences, 1988; For. Associate, Nat. Acad. of Scis, USA, 1994. Dr *hc:* Univ. of Complutense de Madrid, 1986; Univ. of Honduras, 1987; Univ. of Cantabria, 1988; Hon. DSc: Sussex, 1994; Mt Sinai Sch. of Medicine, NY, 1995; Nottingham, 1995; Univ. Pierre & Marie Curie, Paris, 1997. Peter Debeye Prize (jtly), Limburg Univ., 1980; Prince of Asturias Prize for Science and Technology, 1990; Royal Medal, Royal Soc., 1994; Amsterdam Prize for Medicine, 1997. *Publications:* (Scientific Ed.) British Medical Bulletin, 39 pt 3: Prostacyclin, Thromboxane and Leukotrienes, 1983; Nitric oxide from L-arginine: a bioregulatory system, 1990; (ed jtly) The Biology of Nitric Oxide, pts 3 and 4, 1994, pt 5, 1996, pt 6, 1998, pt 7, 2000; (ed jtly) Nitric Oxide and the Vascular Endothelium, 2006. *Recreations:* music, literature, theatre. *Address:* Faculty of Medical and Human Sciences, University of Manchester, Room 1.008, Core Technology Facility, 46 Grafton Street, Manchester M13 9NT.

MONCASTER, John Anthony; Master of the Senior (formerly Supreme) Court, Chancery Division, 1992–2011; *b* Louth, Lincs, 15 Oct. 1939; *oc* of Jack Moncaster and Muriel (*née* Butterick); *m* 1966, Gillian Ann, *o d* of Rev. Royston York; two *s* two *d.* Called to the Bar, Gray's Inn, 1961; practised at Chancery Bar. *Recreation:* books. *Address:* 24 Minster Yard, Lincoln LN2 1PY.

MONCK, family name of **Viscount Monck.**

MONCK, 7th Viscount *cr* 1801; **Charles Stanley Monck;** *S* father, 1982 but does not use the title. *Heir: b* Hon. George Stanley Monck.

MONCK, Elizabeth Mary, (Lady Monck), PhD; Senior Research Officer, Thomas Coram Research Unit, Institute of Education, 1997–2008; *b* 7 Aug. 1934; *d* of Geoffrey Dugdale Kirwan and Molly Kirwan (*née* Morrow); *m* 1960, Sir Nicholas Jeremy Monck, KCB (*d* 2013); three *s. Educ:* Godolphin Sch., Salisbury; Newnham Coll., Cambridge (MA); UCL (PhD 1996). MRC Social Psychiatry Res. Unit, Inst. Psychiatry, 1957–62; EIU, 1969–73; Research Officer: Centre for Envmtl Studies, 1974–80; Acad. Dept Child Psychiatry, Inst. Child Health, 1980–95; Associate, Newnham Coll., Cambridge, 1997–2003; Hon. Associate, 2011. Mem., ILEA, 1986–90. Mem., 1990–93, Chm., 1993–97, Regl Customer Service Cttee (Thames), OFWAT; Ind. Mem., Cttee on Chemicals and Materials in Public Water Supply, Drinking Water Inspectorate, 1998–2001; Reporting Mem., Competition Commn, 1999–2004. Trustee: National Gall., 1993–99; Family Rights Group, 2005–15; National Gall. Trust, 2009–. *Publications:* books include: (with R. Dobbs) The Great Ormond Street Adolescent Life Events Dictionary of Contextual Threat Ratings, 1985; (ed and contrib.) Emotional and Behavioural Problems in Adolescents: a multi-disciplinary approach to identification and management, 1988; (with A. Kelly) Managing Effective Schools, 1992; (with V. Wigfall and J. Reynolds) The Role of Concurrent Planning: making permanent placements for young children; (with A. Rushton) Enhancing Adoptive Parenting: a test of effectiveness. *Recreations:* walking, gardening, listening to music, painting, travel.

MONCKTON, family name of **Viscounts Galway** and **Monckton of Brenchley.**

MONCKTON OF BRENCHLEY, 3rd Viscount *cr* 1957; **Christopher Walter Monckton;** Director: Christopher Monckton Ltd, consultants, 1987–2006; Monckton Enterprises Ltd, since 2009; *b* 14 Feb. 1952; *s* of 2nd Viscount Monckton of Brenchley, CB, OBE, MC and Marianna Laetitia (*née* Bower); *S* father, 2006; *m* 1990, Juliet Mary Anne, *y d* of Jørgen Malherbe Jensen. *Educ:* Harrow; Churchill Coll., Cambridge (BA 1973, MA 1977); University Coll., Cardiff; Dip. Journalism Studies (Wales), 1974. Standing Cttee, Cambridge Union Soc., 1973; Treas., Cambridge Univ. Conservative Assoc., 1973. Reporter, Yorkshire Post, 1974–75, Leader-Writer, 1975–77; Press Officer, Conservative Central Office, 1977–78; Editor-designate, The Universe, 1978, Editor, 1979–81; Managing Editor, Telegraph Sunday Magazine, 1981–82; Leader-Writer, The Standard, 1982; Special Advr to Prime Minister's Policy Unit, 1982–86; Asst Editor, Today, 1986–87; Consulting Editor, 1987–92, Chief Leader-Writer, 1990–92, Evening Standard. Chief Policy Advr, Sci. and Public Policy Inst., Washington DC, 2007–. Dep. Leader, 2010, Hd of Policy, 2011, Leader, Scotland, 2012–13, UKIP. Freeman, City of London, and Liveryman, Worshipful Co. of Broderers, 1973–. Member: Internat. MENSA Ltd, 1975–; St John Amb. Brigade (Wetherby Div.), 1976–77; Hon. Soc. of the Middle Temple, 1979–; RC Mass Media Commn, 1979–; Sec. to Econ., Forward Strategy, Health, and Employment Study Gps, Centre For Policy Studies, 1980–82. Visiting Lecturer: in Business Studies, Columbia Univ., NY, 1980; St Andrews Univ., 1996; Hartford Univ., 2008, 2012; Rochester Univ., 2008; Prague Sch. of Econs, 2011; Princeton Univ., 2012; Nerenberg Lectr in Math., Univ. of W Ontario, 2012. Expert Reviewer, Intergovtl Panel on Climate Change, 2013; Non-Intergovtl Panel on Climate Change, 2014. Trustee, Hales Trophy for Blue Riband of Atlantic, 1986–. Gov., London Oratory Sch., 1991–96. Editor, Not the Church Times, 1982. Kt SMO, Malta, 1973; OStJ 1973. DL Greater London, 1988–96. Intelligence Medal, Army of Colombia, 2013. *Publications:* The Laker Story (with Ivan Fallon), 1982; Anglican Orders: null and void?, 1986; The Aids Report, 1987; Sudoku X, 2005; Sudoku X-mas, 2005; Sudoku Xpert, 2005; Junior Sudoku X, 2005; Sudoku Xtreme, 2005; (contrib.) Evidence-Based Climate Science, 2011; contrib. articles in Physics and Society, Jl of Chartered Insce Inst. of London, Annual Procs of Seminars on Planetary Emergencies, Energy & Envmt, Coordinates Jl of Marine Navigation, Chinese Sci. Bulletin. *Recreation:* romance. *Heir: b* Hon. Timothy David Robert Monckton [*b* 15 Aug. 1955; *m* 1984, Jennifer Carmody; three *s*]. *T:* 07814 556423. *E:* monckton@mail.com. *Clubs:* Brooks's, Beefsteak, Pratt's.

See also Hon. R. M. Monckton.

MONCKTON, Hon. Rosa(mond) Mary, (Hon. Mrs Dominic Lawson); Chairman, Asprey & Garrard UK Ltd, 2002–05 (Chief Executive, 2000–02); Co-Founder, Campaign for Learning Disabled, 2014; *b* 26 Oct. 1953; *d* of 2nd Viscount Monckton of Brenchley, CB, OBE, MC; *m* 1991, Hon. Dominic Ralph Campden Lawson, *qv*; two *d. Educ:* Ursuline Convent, Tildonk, Belgium. Asst Man. Dir, Cartier, London, 1979; Sales and Exhibn Manager, Tabbah Jewellers, Monte Carlo, 1980; Promotions Manager, Asprey, 1982–85; Man. Dir, 1986–97, Pres., 1997–2000, Tiffany, London. Dir, Aurum Hldgs Ltd, 2014–. Chm., KIDS, 1999–2004 (Pres., 2004–); Mem., Diana, Princess of Wales Meml Cttee, 1997–2004 (Chm., Fountain Design Cttee, 2001–02). Presenter of TV documentaries including: When a Mother's Love is not Enough, 2008; Tormented Lives, 2010; Letting Go, 2012. Liveryman, Goldsmiths' Co., 2000–. *Address:* Cox's Mill, Dallington, Heathfield, E Sussex TN21 9JG.

MONCKTON-ARUNDELL, family name of **Viscount Galway.**

MONCREIFF, family name of **Baron Moncreiff.**

MONCREIFF, 6th Baron *cr* 1873, of Tulliebole, co. Kinross; **Rhoderick Harry Wellwood Moncreiff;** Bt (NS) 1626, (UK) 1871; *b* 22 March 1954; *o s* of 5th Baron Moncreiff and Enid Marion Watson (*née* Locke); *S* father, 2002; *m* 1982, Alison Elizabeth Anne, *d* of J. D. A. Ross; two *s. Heir: s* Hon. Harry James Wellwood Moncreiff, *b* 12 Aug. 1986.

MONCREIFFE of that Ilk, Hon. Peregrine David Euan Malcolm; *b* 16 Feb. 1951; *s* of Sir Iain Moncreiffe of that Ilk, 11th Bt, CVO, DL, QC (Scot.) and Countess of Erroll, 23rd in line; *m* 1988, Miranda Fox-Pitt; two *s* four *d. Educ:* Eton; Christ Church, Oxford (MA Modern Hist.). Lieut, Atholl Highlanders, 1978. Investment banker: with White Weld & Co. Ltd/Credit Suisse First Boston Ltd, 1972–82; Lehman Brothers Kuhn Loeb/Shearson Lehman, 1982–86; E. F. Hutton & Co., 1986–88; Chief Exec., Buchanan Partners Ltd, 1990–99. Mem., Royal Commn on Ancient and Historical Monuments of Scotland, 1989–94. Chm., Scottish Ballet, 1988–90. Trustee, Save the Rhino, 1991–2000. Mem.,

Royal Co. of Archers (Queen's Body Guard for Scotland), 1979–. Freeman, City of London; Liveryman, Co. of Fishmongers, 1987–. *Address:* Highfield Place, La Pouqelaye, St Helier, Jersey JE2 3GG. *Clubs:* White's, Turf, Pratt's; New (Edinburgh); Leander (Henley); Brook (New York).

MONCRIEFF, Rear Adm. Ian, CBE 2010; DL; Chief Executive, United Kingdom Hydrographic Office, 2011–15 (National Hydrographer, 2006–10; Chief Operating Officer, 2010–11); *b* 5 Jan. 1955; *s* of Donald and Ellen Moncrieff; *m* 1986, Marion McLennan; two *s*. *Educ:* Kirkham High Sch.; Preston VI Form Coll.; Univ. of Keele (BA Hons Geog. and Geol. 1977); BRNC Dartmouth. Served in HM Ships Sheffield, Arrow, Yarnton and Nottingham, 1978–85; qualified as Principal Warfare Officer and specialist in communications, 1985; Principal Warfare Officer, HMS Glasgow, 1986; i/c new entry radio operator trng, HMS Mercury, 1986–88; Royal Cypher Officer and Flag Lieut, HMY Britannia, 1988–90; Desk Officer, Directorate of Naval Plans and Progs, MoD, 1990–92; CO, HMS Nottingham, 1992–94; DACOS Policy and Progs to C-in-C Fleet, 1994–97; Comdr, HMS Invincible, 1997–98; Captain 1998; CSO Plans and Policy to CGRM, 1998–2001; CO, HMS Endurance, 2001–03; Cdre 2003; Dir, Navy Communications and Inf. Systems, 2003–04; hcsc 2005; Comdr British Forces South Atlantic, 2005–06; Rear Adm., 2006; retd 2010. Non-exec. Dir and Marine Mem. Bd, PLA. Mem. Council, RNLI, 2007–13. Mem., Hon. Co. of Master Mariners, 2000–. Younger Brother, Trinity House, 2007–. MInstD 1996. Cert. Co. Direction, IoD, 2011. Trustee, Falklands Conservation, 2010–. DL Somerset, 2015. *Recreations:* wildlife photography, fly fishing. *Address:* Port of London Authority, London River House, Royal Pier Road, Gravesend, Kent DA12 2BG.

MONCRIEFF, Lucy Ann S.; *see* Scott-Moncrieff.

MONCRIEFF, Dame Suzanne Elizabeth, (Dame Suzie), DNZM 2012 (ONZM 1998); sculptor; Founder and Director, World of WearableArt Ltd, since 1987; *b* Ashburton, NZ, 7 June 1949; *d* of John Dick and Dorothy Dick; one *d*. *Educ:* Waimea Coll. (Sch. Cert.); Univ. Entrance English. Hon. DFA Massey, NZ, 2014. *Address:* World of WearableArt Ltd, 95 Quarantine Road, Annesbrook, Nelson 7011, New Zealand.

MOND, family name of **Baron Melchett**.

MONDALE, Walter Frederick; American Ambassador to Japan, 1993–96; *b* Ceylon, Minnesota, 5 Jan. 1928; *s* of Rev. Theodore Sigvaard Mondale and Claribel Hope (*née* Cowan); *m* 1955, Joan Adams (*d* 2014); two *s* (one *d* decd). *Educ:* public schs, Minnesota; Macalester Coll., Univ. of Minnesota (BA *cum laude*); Univ. of Minnesota Law Sch. (LLB). Served with Army, 1951–53. Admitted to Minn. Bar, 1956; private law practice, Minneapolis, 1956–60; Attorney-Gen., Minnesota, 1960–65; Senator from Minnesota, 1965–76; Vice-Pres., USA, 1977–81; Counsel with Winston & Strawn, 1981–87; Partner with Dorsey & Whitney, 1987–93. Democratic Candidate for Vice-Pres., USA, 1976, 1980; Democratic Candidate for Pres., USA, 1984. Chm., Nat. Democratic Inst. for Internat. Affairs, 1987–93. Mem., Democratic Farm Labor Party. *Publications:* The Accountability of Power, 1975. *Address:* c/o Dorsey & Whitney LLP, # 1500, 50 South 6th Street, Minneapolis, MN 55402–1498, USA.

MONDS, Prof. Fabian Charles, CBE 1997; PhD; Professor of Information Systems, 1987–2000, now Emeritus, and Pro-Vice-Chancellor (Planning), 1993–2000, University of Ulster; Chairman, Northern Ireland Centre for Trauma and Transformation, since 2002; *b* 1 Nov. 1940; *s* of Edward James Monds and Mary Brigid (*née* McPoland); *m* 1967, Eileen Joan Graham; two *d*. *Educ:* Queen's Univ., Belfast (BSc; PhD). CEng, MIET, MBCS. Vis. Asst Prof., Purdue Univ., USA, 1965, 1966; Lectr, 1967–77, Sen. Lectr, 1977–78, Reader, 1978–86, QUB; Dean, Faculty of Informatics, 1989–93, Provost, Magee Coll., Londonderry, 1995–2000, Univ. of Ulster. Gov. for NI, BBC, 1999–2006; Chairman: NI Inf. Age Initiative, 1999–2002; Univ. of Ulster Sci. Res. Parks Ltd, 1999–2002; NI Industrial Res. and Technol. Unit, 2000–01; Omagh 2010 Task Force, 2001–02; Invest Northern Ireland, 2002–05; Omagh Enterprise Co., 2008–14; Co-Chm., US-Ireland R&D Partnership, 2005–14; Vice-Chm., North West Regl Coll., 2008–15. Trustee, UK Teaching Awards Trust, 1999–2006. CCMI. *Publications:* Minicomputer Systems, 1979; (with R. McLaughlin) An Introduction to Mini and Micro Computers, 1981, 2nd edn 1984; The Business of Electronic Product Development, 1984; two patents; contrib. learned jls. *Recreation:* general aviation.

MONE, family name of **Baroness Mone**.

MONE, Baroness *cr* 2015 (Life Peer), of Mayfair in the City of Westminster; **Michelle Georgina Mone,** OBE 2010; *b* Glasgow, 8 Oct. 1971; *née* Allan; *m* Michael Mone (marr. diss. 2011); one *s* two *d*. Work as a model; office junior to Hd, Sales and Mktg for Scotland, Labatt Brewers, until 1995; Founder and Mem. Bd, Ultimo, 1996–2015; co-owner, Ultimo Brands Internat. Chair, Mone Review (to encourage business start-ups in disadvantaged areas), 2015–. Mem., Bd of Dirs, Prince's Scottish Youth Business Trust, 2001–. *Publications:* My Fight to the Top (autobiog.), 2015. *Address:* House of Lords, SW1A 0PW.

MONE, Rt Rev. John Aloysius; Bishop of Paisley, (RC), 1988–2004, now Emeritus; *b* 22 June 1929; *s* of Arthur Mone and Elizabeth Mone (*née* Dunn). *Educ:* Holyrood Secondary School, Glasgow; Séminaire Saint Sulpice, Paris; Institut Catholique, Paris (Faculty of Social Studies). Skill level one, British Sign Language, 2006. Ordained Priest, Glasgow, 1952; Assistant Priest: St Ninian's, Knightswood, Glasgow, also hosp. and sch. chaplain, 1952–74; Our Lady and St George's, Glasgow, 1975–79; Parish Priest, St Joseph's, Tollcross, Glasgow, 1979–84; Auxiliary Bishop of Glasgow, 1984–88. Episcopal Vicar, Marriage, 1981–83; Dir, Ministry to Priests Prog., 1982–84. Asst Chaplain, Inverclyde Royal Hosp., Greenock, 2008–. Scottish National Chaplain, Girl Guides, 1971–; Dir, Scottish Catholic Internat. Aid Fund, 1974–2011 (Chm., 1974–75, Pres./Treas., 1984–2004); Chm., Scottish Catholic Marriage Advisory Council, 1982–84; President: Scottish Justice and Peace Commn, 1987–2004; Pastoral and Social Care Commn, 1996–2004. Advr to Nat. Child Protection Team, 2004–. Pres., Paisley Family Soc., 2007–. *Recreations:* watching soccer (attending if possible), playing golf (when time!), playing the piano. *Address:* 30 Esplanade, Greenock, Renfrewshire PA16 7RU.

MONEO VALLÉS, Prof. José Rafael, (Prof. Rafael Moneo); architect; Josep Lluis Sert Professor of Architecture, Graduate School of Design, Harvard University, since 1991; *b* Tudela, Spain, 9 May 1937; *s* of Rafael Moneo and Teresa Vallés; *m* 1963, Belén Feduchi; three *d*. *Educ:* Tech. Sch. of Madrid (degree in arch., 1961). Fellow, Spanish Acad., Rome, 1963–65; Asst Prof., Technical Sch. of Architecture, Madrid, 1966–70; Prof. of Architectural Theory, Technical School of Architecture, Barcelona, 1970–80; Prof. of Composition, Tech. Sch. of Madrid, 1980–85; Chm., Dept of Architecture, Harvard Univ., 1985–90. Projects include: Diestre Factory, Zaragoza, 1967; Pamplona Bull Ring, 1967; Urumea Residential Building, San Sebastián, 1971; (with Ramón Bescós) Bankinter Bank, Madrid, 1976; Logroño Town Hall, 1976; Nat. Mus. of Roman Art, Mérida, 1986; Previsión Española Insurance Co., Seville, 1987; Bank of Spain, Jaén, 1988; San Pablo Airport, Seville, 1992; Architectural Assoc. of Tarragona, 1992; Atocha Railway Stn, Madrid, 1992; Thyssen-Bornemisza Mus., Madrid, 1992; Pilar and Joan Miró Foundn, Palma de Mallorca, 1992; Davis Art Mus., Wellesley Coll., Mass, 1993; (with Manuel de Solá-Morales) Diagonal Buildings, Barcelona, 1993; Don Benito Cultural Centre, Badajoz, 1997; Museums of Modern Art and Architecture, Stockholm, 1998; Town Hall extension, Murcia, 1998; Barcelona Concert Hall, 1999; Kursaal Auditorium and Congress Centre, San Sebastián, 1999; Potsdamer Platz Hotel and office building, Berlin; Audrey Jones Beck Building, Mus. of Fine Arts, Houston, 2000; Cathedral of Our Lady of the Angels, Los Angeles, 2002; (with Belén Moneo) new studios, Cranbrook Acad. of Art, 2002; Arenberg Campus Liby, Catholic Univ. Leuven, 2002; Chivite Winery, Arinzano, Navarra, 2002; Gregorio Marañón Mother's and Children's Hosp., Madrid, 2003; Gen. and Royal Archive of Navarra, Pamplona, 2003; Art and Nature Centre, Beulas Foundn, Huesca, 2004; (with José Antonio Martínez Lapeña and Elías Torres) apts, Sabadell, 2005; (with Alberto Nicolau) apts, La Haya, 2006; extension, Bank of Spain, Madrid, 2006; extension, Prado Mus., Madrid, 2007; Lab. for Integrated Sci. and Engrg, Harvard Univ., 2007; Mus. of Roman Th., Cartagena, 2008; Aragonia commercial center, apts, hotel and offices, 2008; Panticosa Resort Hotels, 2008; Novartis Lab., Basel, 2008; Chace Center, RI Sch. of Design, 2008; Liby, Univ. of Deusto, Bilbao, 2009; (with Moneo/Brock Architects) NW Sci. Bldg, Columbia Univ., 2010; extension to Atocha Rlwy Stn, Madrid, 2010; parish ch, Riberas de Loiola, San Sebastian, 2011. Gold Medal for Achievement in Fine Arts (Spain), 1992; Gold Medal: French Acad. of Architecture, 1996; Internat. Union of Architects, 1996; Pritzker Prize, 1996; Royal Gold Medal, RIBA, 2003. *Publications:* (jtly) Grand Hyatt Berlin, 2000; (jtly) Theoretical Anxiety and Design Strategies in the Work of Eight Contemporary Architects, 2004; Rafael Moneo: remarks on 21 works, 2010; articles in learned jls. *Address:* Calle Cinca 5, Madrid 28002, Spain; Department of Architecture, Harvard Graduate School of Design, 48 Quincy Street, Cambridge, MA 02138, USA.

MONEY-COUTTS, family name of **Baron Latymer**.

MONHEMIUS, Prof. (Andrew) John, PhD; CEng; Roy Wright Professor of Mineral and Environmental Engineering, 1996–2004, now Professor Emeritus, and Dean, Royal School of Mines, 2000–04, Imperial College of Science, Technology and Medicine, London University; Director, Anglo Asian Mining plc, since 2009; *b* 3 Oct. 1942; *s* of Frank Andre Monhemius and Edna Rowlands Monhemius; *m* 1966, Johanna Werson; one *s* one *d*. *Educ:* Univ. of Birmingham (BSc); Univ. of British Columbia (MASc); Imperial Coll., Univ. of London (PhD; DIC). CEng. Royal School of Mines, Imperial College: Lectr, 1966–86; Reader, 1986–96. Vis. Prof. of Extractive Metallurgy, Federal Univ. of Rio de Janeiro, 1973–75. FIMMM (FIMM 1984). Mem., Chaps Club. *Publications:* (ed with J. E. Dutrizac) Iron Control in Hydrometallurgy, 1986; more than 130 papers in scientific and tech. jls and conf. procs. *Address:* 64 South Western Road, Twickenham TW1 1LQ. *E:* j.monhemius@ic.ac.uk. *Club:* Twickenham Yacht.

MONK, (David) Alec (George); Chairman, Charles Wells Ltd, 1998–2003 (Director, 1989–2003); *b* 13 Dec. 1942; *s* of Philip Aylmer and Elizabeth Jane Monk; *m* 1965, Jean Ann Searle; two *s* two *d*. *Educ:* Jesus College, Oxford (MA (PPE); Hon. Fellow, 1999). Research Staff, Corporate Finance and Taxation, Sheffield Univ., 1966 and London Business Sch., 1967; Senior Financial Asst, Treasurer's Dept, Esso Petroleum Co., 1968; various positions with The Rio Tinto-Zinc Corp., 1968–77, Dir, 1974–77; Vice-Pres. and Dir, AEA Investors Inc., 1977–81; Chm. and Chief Exec., The Gateway Corp. (formerly Dee Corp.) PLC, 1981–89; CEO, Tri-Delta Corp. Ltd, 1990–93. Dir, Scottish Eastern Investment Trust, 1985–98. Mem., NEDC, 1986–90. Pres., Inst. of Grocery Distribution, 1987–89. Poole Harbour Comr, 2009–12. Vis. Indust. Fellow, Manchester Business Sch., 1984. Hon. Fellow, St Hugh's Coll., Oxford, 1985; Foundn Fellow, New Hall, Cambridge, 2001. Hon. LLD Sheffield, 1988. *Publications:* (with A. J. Merrett) Inflation, Taxation and Executive Remuneration, 1967. *Recreations:* sports, reading.

MONK, Fiona Beverley; Regional Employment Judge, Birmingham, since 2011; *b* London, 8 Sept. 1963; *d* of Ian and Beverley Monk; *m* 2009; two *d*; one step *s*. *Educ:* Chelmsford Co. High Sch. for Girls; Warwick Univ. (LLB Hons); Brunel Univ. (MA Law and Discrimination). Admitted solicitor, 1988; solicitor, Coventry Law Centre, 1989–97; Employment Judge, pt-time, 2000–07, full-time, 2007–11. Adjudicator (pt-time), Law Soc., 2005–07. *Recreations:* running, cooking, reading, family, theatre, holidays.

MONK, Heath Jon; Chief Executive, Future Leaders Trust, since 2007; *b* Hastings, E Sussex, 22 July 1970; *s* of Michael Monk and Molly Monk; *m* 1996, Lucy Katharine Knowling; two *s* one *d* (incl. twin *s*). *Educ:* Christ's Hospital Sch.; Queen's Coll., Oxford (BA Hons 1st Cl. Eng. Lang. and Lit. 1992); Univ. of Sheffield (PGCE 1994). Teacher of English and Drama, Bennett Meml Diocesan Sch., 1994–96; Asst Housemaster, Sevenoaks Sch., 1996–2000; Dep. Dir, DFEE, subseq. DFES, later DCFS, 2000–07. Advr, New Schs Network, 2010–; Trustee, Teaching Leaders, 2011–. *Recreations:* sport, cricket, golf, football (West Ham United), baseball (Seattle Mariners), cooking, theatre. *Address:* Future Leaders Trust, 65 Kingsway, WC2B 6TD. *T:* 07795 066301. *E:* heath.monk@future-leaders.org.uk. *Club:* Cooden Beach Golf.

MONK, Joanne Elizabeth; *see* Wheeler, J. E.

MONK, Richard Gordon, CMG 2009; OBE 2000; QPM 1995; international police leader and adviser, since 1996; *b* Barnet, Herts, 4 July 1944; *s* of Ernest and Thelma Monk; *m* 1988, Barbara Marshall; four *s* one *d*. *Educ:* E Barnet Grammar Sch.; Metropolitan Police Cadet Corps; Univ. of Durham (BA Hons Politics). Joined Metropolitan Police, 1963; Chief Superintendent, Brixton, 1986–88; Comdr, Metropolitan Police, 1988–91; Asst Chief Constable, Devon and Cornwall Constabulary, 1991–94; Asst Inspector, HM Inspectorate of Constabulary, 1994–98; Police Advr, Administrator of Sovereign Base Area, Cyprus, 1996–98; Police Comr, UN Internat. Police Task Force in Bosnia, 1998–99; Mem., UN Sec. Gen.'s Panel on Peace Ops, 2000; Dir and Sen. Police Advr to Sec. Gen., OSCE, 2002–06; Advr, US Inst. for Peace in Nepal, 2007; Police Comr, nat. and UN internat. police in Kosovo, 2007–08. Hon. Prof., Kyrgyzstan Nat. Police Acad., 2003–; Mem. Adv. Council, Internat. Network to Promote the Rule of Law, US Inst. of Peace, 2005–; Mem., Strategic Develt Bd, Durham Global Security Inst., Durham Univ., 2010–. Member: Council, NACRO, 1988–94; Funding Panel, Nat. Assoc. of Victim Support Schemes, 1988–94. Trustee, then Chm., Lucy Faithfull Foundn, 1993–98 (Patron, 1998–); Trustee, Suzy Lamplugh Trust, 1999–2005. Freeman, City of London, 2000. Liveryman, Co. of Security Professionals, 2008– (Founder, 1998–, Chm., 1999–2002 and 2008–12, Co. of Security Professionals' Trustees). Graduate, FBI Nat. Acad., 1985; Chm., FBI European Chapter, 1996. Hon. DCL Durham, 2009. UN Medals, Bosnia, 1998, Kosovo, 2007. *Publications:* Study on Policing in the Former Republic of Yugoslavia, 2001; Trends in Policing: interviews with police leaders across the globe, 2010. *Recreations:* travelling, classic cars and motor cycles, fitness training, attending senior common room, St Chad's College, Durham University. *Address:* 19 Rivermead, East Molesey, Surrey KT8 9AZ. *T:* (020) 8941 9600. *E:* richard.monk@virgin.net.

MONK, Dame Susan Catherine Hampsher-; *see* Leather, Dame S. C.

MONK BRETTON, 3rd Baron *cr* 1884; **John Charles Dodson;** DL; *b* 17 July 1924; *o s* of 2nd Baron and Ruth (*d* 1967), 2nd *d* of late Hon. Charles Brand; *S* father, 1933; *m* 1958, Zoë Diana Scott; two *s*. *Educ:* Westminster Sch.; New Coll., Oxford (MA Agric.). DL E Sussex, 1983. *Heir:* *s* Hon. Christopher Mark Dodson [*b* 2 Aug. 1958; *m* 1988, Karen, *o d* of B. J. McKelvain, Fairfield, Conn; two *s* one *d*]. *Address:* Chemin de la Becque 24, 1814 La Tour de Peilz, Switzerland. *T:* (21) 9442912.

MONKHOUSE, Richard Graham; JP; Chairman, Magistrates' Association, since 2013; *b* Carlisle, 30 July 1946; *s* of Philip Monkhouse and Margaret Monkhouse; *m* 1979, Jayne Pittilla, OBE. *Educ:* Altrincham Grammar Sch.; Bradford Univ.; Newcastle Poly. (DMS 1974). Actuarial student, NEL, 1968–71; Actuarial Asst, MPA, 1971–72; PA to Gen.

Manager, Slater Walker Insurance, 1972–73; Gp Product Manager, United Africa Co., 1974–84; Mktg Manager, Elcometer Instruments, 1984–94; self-employed Statistical Process Control consultant, 1994–. Magistrates' Association: Trustee, 2008–; Dep. Chm., 2011–13. JP Trafford, 1997 (Bench Chm., 2005–07). *Recreations:* sports, football (Man Utd), Rugby League (Wigan), music (choral, opera, classical), reading, cooking. *Address:* Magistrates' Association, 28 Fitzroy Square, W1T 6DD. *T:* (020) 7387 2353, 07761 211466. *E:* Richard.Monkhouse@magistrates-association.org.uk, rgm2@btinternet.com.

MONKS, family name of **Baron Monks**.

MONKS, Baron *cr* 2010 (Life Peer), of Blackley in the County of Greater Manchester; **John Stephen Monks;** General Secretary, European Trades Union Confederation, 2003–11; *b* 5 Aug. 1945; *s* of Charles Edward Monks and Bessie Evelyn Monks; *m* 1970, Francine Jacqueline Schenk; two *s* one *d. Educ:* Ducie Technical High Sch., Manchester; Nottingham Univ. (BA Econ). Joined TUC, 1969; Hd of Orgn and Industrial Relns Dept, 1977–87; Dep. Gen. Sec., 1987–93; Gen. Sec., 1993–2003. Member: Council, ACAS, 1979–95; ESRC, 1988–91. Vice-Chm., Learning and Skills Council, 2001–04. Chm. Trustees, People's History Museum (formerly Nat. Museum of Labour History), 2004– (Trustee, 1988–). Vis. Prof., Manchester Business Sch., Univ. of Manchester (formerly at UMIST, then at Sch. of Mgt, Univ. of Manchester), 1996–. Pres., BALPA, 2011–. Non-exec. Dir, Thompsons' Solicitors, 2010–; Trustee Dir, NOW: Pensions, 2011–. *Recreations:* hiking, music, cycling. *Address:* House of Lords, SW1A 0PW.

MONKS, Prof. Paul Steven, DPhil; Professor of Atmospheric Chemistry and Earth Observation Science, University of Leicester, since 2007; *b* St Helens, Lancs, 25 May 1967; *s* of Ken Monks and Barbara Monks; *m* 2002, Alison Riding; two *d. Educ:* Cowley High Sch., St Helens; Univ. of Warwick (BSc Hons 1988); Univ. of Oxford (DPhil 1992). NAS/Nat. Res. Council Resident Res. Associate, NASA, Goddard Space Flight Centre, Greenbelt, 1992–94; Sen. Res. Associate, Sch. of Envmtl Scis, UEA, 1994–96; Lectr, 1996–2002, Reader, 2002–07, Dept of Chem., Univ. of Leicester. Chm., Air Quality Expert Gp, DEFRA, 2009–; Member: Space Leadership Council, 2010–; Council, NERC, 2011–; Envmtl Pollution and Atmospheric Chem. Scientific Steering Cttee, 2014–. Co-Chm., Internat. Geosphere-Biosphere Prog.-Internat. Global Atmospheric Chem. proj., 2008–14. FRMetS 2004; FRSC 2004. *Publications:* over 200 articles in learned jls on physical chem. and atmospheric sci. *Recreations:* tennis, family, wine tasting (rare varieties), heritage steam, musicals, Italy. *Address:* Department of Chemistry, University of Leicester, Leicester LE1 7RH. *T:* (0116) 252 2141, 07554 333020, (Secretary) (0116) 252 3403, *Fax:* (0116) 252 3789.

MONKSWELL, 5th Baron *cr* 1885; **Gerard Collier;** *b* 28 Jan. 1947; *s* of William Adrian Larry Collier and Helen (*née* Dunbar); *S* to disclaimed barony of father, 1984; *m* 1974, Ann Valerie Collins; two *s* one *d. Educ:* Portsmouth Polytechnic (BSc Mech. Eng, 1971); Slough Polytechnic (Cert. in Works Management 1972). Massey Ferguson Manufg Co. Ltd: Product Quality Engineer, 1972; Service Administration Manager, 1984–89; Customer Advr, B&Q, 2001–06; self-employed, 2006–. Mem. (Lab), Manchester City Council, 1989–94. Mem., H of L, 1985–99. *Recreations:* politics, swimming, movies. *Heir: s* Hon. James Adrian Collier, *b* 29 March 1977. *Address:* 183 Egerton Road South, Manchester M21 0XD.

MONMOUTH, Bishop of, since 2013; **Rt Rev. Richard Edward Pain;** *b* 1956; *m* 1982, Juliet Morgan; two *s. Educ:* Bristol Univ. (BA 1979); Univ. of Wales, Cardiff (BD 1984); St Michael's Coll., Llandaff. Ordained deacon, 1984, priest, 1985; Curate, Caldicot, 1984–86; Priest-in-charge, 1986–88, Vicar, 1988–91, Cwmtillery; Vicar: Six Bells, 1988–91; Risca, 1991–98; Overmonnow with Wonastow and Michel Troy, 1998–2003; Monmouth with Overmonnow, 2003–08; Priest-in-charge, Mamhilad with Monkswood and Glascoed Chapel, 2008–13; Archdeacon of Monmouth, 2008–13. Warden of Ordinands, Dio. of Monmouth, 2001–06; Canon, St Woolos Cath., Newport, 2003. *Address:* Bishopstow, Stow Hill, Newport NP20 4EA. *T:* (01633) 263510, *Fax:* (01633) 259946.

MONMOUTH, Dean of; *see* Tonge, Very Rev. L.

MONRO, (Andrew) Hugh; educational consultant; Head, Bristol Cathedral School, 2007–08; Founding Principal, Bristol Cathedral Choir School Academy, 2008–09; *b* 2 March 1950; *s* of late Andrew Killey Monro, FRCS and Diana Louise (*née* Rhys); *m* 1974, Elizabeth Clare Rust; one *s* one *d. Educ:* Rugby School; Pembroke College, Cambridge (MA; PGCE). Graduate trainee, Metal Box, 1973; Haileybury College, 1974–79; Noble & Greenough School, Boston, Mass, 1977–78; Loretto School, 1979–86; Headmaster: Worksop College, 1986–90; Clifton College, 1990–2000; Master, Wellington College, 2000–05. *Recreations:* American literature, Cornish churches. *Club:* Hawks (Cambridge).

MONRO, Maj.-Gen. Hon. Seymour Hector Russell Hale, CBE 1996; LVO 2010; DL; Executive Chairman and Director, Highland Military Tattoo, since 2013; *b* 7 May 1950; *s* of Rt Hon. Lord Monro of Langholm, AE, PC, DL and (Elizabeth) Anne (*née* Welch); *m* 1977, Angela Sandeman; three *s. Educ:* Cargilfield Sch.; Glenalmond Coll.; RMA, Sandhurst. MA to Comdr 1st Br. Corps, 1982–84; Co. Comdr, 1st Bn Queen's Own Highlanders, 1984–86; Instr, All Arms Tactics, Warminster, 1986–87; Directing Staff, Army Staff Coll., 1987–89; CO, 1st Bn, Queen's Own Highlanders, 1989–91; Col, Gen. Staff, MoD, 1991–94; Comdr, 39 Inf. Bde, 1994–95; Pres., Regular Commns Bd, 1996–97; Dep. Chief, Jt Ops, HQ SFOR, 1997; Dir, Infantry, 1998–2001; Dep. Comdr, NATO Rapid Deployable Corps (Italy), 2001–03. ADC to the Queen, 1998–2001. Adjutant, Queen's Body Guard for Scotland, 2001–09. Dir, CairnGorm Mountain Ltd, 2009–14. Dir, Atlantic Salmon Trust, 2004–08; Chairman: Highlands and Islands Bd, Prince's Trust, 2004–07; Highland Heritage Appeal, 2007–13; Findhorn, Nairn and Lossie Fisheries Trust, 2008–. Mem. Council, Glenalmond Coll., 1993–2003. Pres., Forres and Dist Pipe Band, 2012–. Hon. Air Cdre, No 2622 (Highland) Sqdn, RAuxAF, 2008–. DL Moray, 2011. *Recreations:* shooting, fishing, stalking, golf, photography, conservation, travel, vintage cars. *Address:* Kirkton, Dallas, Moray IV36 2RZ. *Club:* New (Edinburgh).

MONRO, Stuart Kinnaird, OBE 2007; PhD; FRSE; Scientific Director: Our Dynamic Earth, Edinburgh, 2004–14; Scottish (formerly Edinburgh) Consortium for Rural Research, since 2009; *b* 3 March 1947; *s* of William Kinnaird Monro and Williamena Milne Monro; *m* 1971, Shiela Dowie Wallace; three *s* one *d. Educ:* Aberdeen Acad.; Univ. of Aberdeen (BSc 1970); Univ. of Edinburgh (PhD 1982; Hon. Fellow 2005). FGS 1990; CGeol 1991; FHEA 2007 (ILTM 2001). Principal Geologist, British Geol Survey, 1970–2004; Tutor in Earth Scis (pt-time), Open Univ., 1982–2009. Vis. Prof., 2008–14, Hon. Prof., 2014–, Sch. of Geoscis, Univ. of Edinburgh. Member: Scottish Sci. Adv. Council (formerly Adv. Cttee), 2003–09 (Ind. Co-Chm., 2007–09); Young People's Cttee, RSE, 2005–08; non-exec. Dir, Edinburgh Internat. Sci. Fest., 2004–; Trustee, Nat. Mus Scotland (formerly Nat. Mus of Scotland), 2005–13. Member: Council, Open Univ., 1994–2002; Court, Univ. of Edinburgh, 2007–14 (Vice-Convener, 2011–14). President: Westmorland Geol Soc., 1994–2005; Edinburgh Geol Soc., 2006–07; Mem. Council, Geol Soc. of London, 2009–. Hon. Geol Advr, John Muir Trust, 2005–. FRSSA 1998 (Pres., 2002–05); FRSE 2010; FSAScot 2011; FRSGS 2014. DUniv Open, 2011; Hon. DSc: Heriot-Watt, 2014; Edinburgh. Dist. Service Award, Geol Soc. of London, 2009. *Publications:* Geology of the Irvine District, 1999; various scientific papers and reports. *Recreations:* theatre, travel, the great outdoors—especially the rocks! *Address:* 34 Swanston Grove, Edinburgh EH10 7BW. *T:* (0131) 445 4619. *E:* stuart.monro@blueyonder.co.uk. *Clubs:* Rotary, Twenty (Edinburgh).

MONRO DAVIES, His Honour William Llewellyn; QC 1974; a Circuit Judge, 1976–99; *b* 12 Feb. 1927; *s* of Thomas Llewellyn Davies and Emily Constance Davies; *m* 1956, Jean (*d* 2014), *d* of late E. G. Innes; one *s* one *d. Educ:* Christ Coll., Brecon; Trinity Coll., Oxford (MA, LitHum). Served in RNVR, 1945–48 (Sub-Lt). Called to the Bar, Inner Temple, 1954. Mem., Gen. Council of the Bar, 1971–75. A Recorder of the Crown Court, 1972–76. *Recreations:* the theatre and cinema; watching Rugby football.

See also N. A. Stewart.

MONROE, Dame Barbara, DBE 2010; Chief Executive, St Christopher's Hospice, London, 2000–14; *b* Cowley, 6 April 1951; *d* of Robert Jones and Phyllis Jones; *m* 1975, Jeremy Monroe; one *s* one *d. Educ:* Oxford High Sch. GPDST; St Anne's Coll., Oxford (BA Hons 1973); Univ. of Exeter (BPhil, CQSW 1975). Probation Officer, Inner London Probation Service, 1974–76; Social Worker: Avon Social Services, 1976–80; Atkinson Morley's Hosp., 1982–87; St Christopher's Hospice: Principal Social Worker, 1987–89; Dir, Social Work, 1989–97; Dir, Patient and Family Services, 1997–2000. Hon. Prof., Internat. Observatory on End of Life Care, Lancaster Univ., 2009–14; Hon. Sen. Lectr, Faculty of Medicine and Health Scis, Univ. of Auckland, 2006–14. Ind. Mem., Community, Voluntary and Local Services Honours Cttee, 2013–. Chm., Childhood Bereavement Network, 2000–09; Vice Chm., Commn on Future of Hospice Care, 2011–13; Mem., Internat. Work Gp on Death, Dying and Bereavement, 1997–2014. Special Comr, Royal Hosp. Chelsea, 2013–. Trustee, Marie Curie Cancer Care, 2014–. FRSA. *Publications:* (jtly) Good Practices in Palliative Care: a psychosocial perspective, 1998; (ed with D. Oliviere) Patient Participation in Palliative Care: a voice for the voiceless, 2003; (ed with D. Oliviere) Death, Dying and Social Differences, 2004, 2nd edn (ed with D. Oliviere and S. Payne) 2011; (ed with F. Kraus) Brief Interventions with Bereaved Children, 2004, 2nd edn 2010; (ed with D. Oliviere) Resilience in Palliative Care: achievement in adversity, 2007. *Recreations:* my family, theatre, walking, books, wine and the maintenance always of a half full glass.

MONSON, family name of **Baron Monson**.

MONSON, 12th Baron *cr* 1728; **Nicholas John Monson;** Bt 1611; investor relations consultant, since 2007; *b* London, 19 Oct. 1955; *e s* of 11th Baron Monson and of Emma, *o d* of late Anthony Devas, ARA, RP; *S* father, 2011; *m* 1st, 1981, Hilary Martin (marr. diss. 1996); one *d* (one *s* decd); 2nd, 2002, La Ilustrisima Maria Victoria Nicklin Perez; 3rd, 2010, Silvana Fernandes, *widow* of Nicholas Jessen. *Educ:* Eton Coll.; Kingston Poly. Journalist, 1978–; author, 1984–; PR Dir, 1986; Chairman: Sinovation plc, 2003–06; Grenfell Consulting Ltd, 2010–. *Publications:* (with Debra Scott) The Nouveaux Pauvres, 1984; (with Sarah Goodall) The Palace Diaries, 2006. *Recreation:* reading. *Heir: b* Hon. Andrew Anthony John Monson [*b* 12 May 1959; *m* 1993, Emily Wheeler-Bennett; two *d*]. *Address:* Flat B, 318 Old Brompton Road, SW5 9JH. *E:* grenfell@consultant.com. *Club:* Travellers.

MONSON, (John) Guy (Elmhirst); Managing Partner and Chief Investment Officer, Sarasin & Partners LLP, since 2008; *b* London, 11 Sept. 1962; *s* of Hon. Jeremy David Alfonso John Monson and Patricia Mary, *yr d* of late Maj. George Barker, MFH; *m* 1995, Lady Olivia Rose Mildred FitzRoy, *y d* of 11th Duke of Grafton, KG; two *d. Educ:* Eton Coll.; Lady Margaret Hall, Oxford (BA PPE 1984). Joined Sarasin Investment Management Ltd, 1984; Dir, 1989–; Chief Investment Officer, 1993–2007; CEO, 2007; Chief Investment Officer, Bank Sarasin Gp, 1997–2007; Partner, Bank Sarasin & Co., 2001–02. *Recreation:* steam engines. *Address:* Sarasin & Partners LLP, Juxon House, 100 St Paul's Churchyard, EC4M 8BU. *T:* (020) 7038 7000. *Clubs:* White's, Pratt's.

MONSON, Prof. John Rowat Telford, MD; FRCS, FRCSE, FRCSI, FACS; Chief, Division of Colorectal Surgery, and Vice-Chairman of Surgery, University of Rochester Medical Center, Rochester, New York, since 2008 (Vice Chairman, Quality and Surgical Outcomes, since 2011 and Director, Surgical Health Outcomes and Research Enterprise, since 2012); *b* 14 Jan. 1956; *s* of Desmond Monson and Ann Monson; *m* 1980, Aideen White, MB; two *s* one *d. Educ:* Sandford Park Secondary Sch., Dublin; Trinity Coll. Dublin (MB BCh, BAO 1979; MD 1987). FRCSI 1983; FRCS 1987; FACS 1992; FRCSE (*ad hominem*) 2004. Pre-registration house officer, Royal City of Dublin Hosp., 1979; pre-Fellowship surgical trng, Dublin, 1980–83; post Fellowship surgical trng, Leeds, 1983–84; Res. Fellow, Univ. of Leeds, 1984–86; Sen. Registrar, Surgical Trng, Dublin, 1986–89; Fellow in Surgical Oncology, Mayo Clinic, USA, 1989–90; Asst Dir and Sen. Lectr in Surgery, St Mary's Hosp. Med. Sch., London, 1990–93; Prof. of Surgery and Hd of Dept, Academic Surgical Unit, 1993–2008, Hon. Prof., 2008–, Univ. of Hull. Surgical Res. Soc. Internat. Travelling Fellow, 1986; Edward Halloran Bennett Travelling Fellow in Surgery, 1989; James IV Assoc. Internat. Fellow, 1996. Visiting Professor: UCLA; Univ. of Texas; Monash Univ.; Australasian Coll. of Surgeons, 2009; Sir Edwin Tooth Vis. Prof., Univ. of Queensland, 2003. Mem. Council, British Jl of Surgery, 1997–2004. Vice-Pres., British Assoc. of Surgical Oncology, 1997; Hon. Sec., Surgical Res. Soc. of GB and Ireland, 1998–2004; Member: James IV Assoc. of Surgeons, 1999– (Dir, 2000–); Exec. Council, Amer. Soc. of Colon and Rectal Surgeons, 2014– (Chm., Res. Cttee, 2012–); Pres., Multidisciplinary Internat. Rectal Cancer Soc., 2012–13; Vice Pres., Optimizing Surgical Treatment of Rectal Cancer Internat. Collaborative, 2012–. Member: Special Adv. Cttee for Gen. Surgery in UK, 2000–06; Health Innovation Council, 2007–; Advr, NHS Modernisation Agency, 2002–; Bd Mem., BUPA Foundn, 2006–09; Nat. Co-ordinator, Laparoscopic Colorectal Trng Prog., DoH, 2008–09. Examiner, Intercollegiate Bd in Gen. Surgery, 2000–; Ext. Examiner, Univ. of Malaysia, 2001. 14th Millin Lectr, RCSI, 1990; Robert Smith Lectr, RCSI, 2006; Johnson and Johnson Lectr, RCSI, 2010; Gerhard Buess Lectr, 2012. Fellow, Amer. Soc. of Colon and Rectal Surgeons, 1995. Hon. FRCSGlas, 1998; Hon. Fellow: Soc. of Univ. Surgeons, USA, 2002; Assoc. of Surgeons of GB and Ireland, 2011. Section Ed., Media, Book Revs and For Debate, Diseases of Colon and Rectum, 2010– (Media Ed., 2008–); Mem., Editl Bd, Annals of Surgery, 2014–. *Publications:* (ed with A. Darzi) Laparoscopic Inguinal Hernia Repair, 1994; (ed jtly) Atlas of Surgical Oncology, 1994; (with A. Darzi) Laparoscopic Colorectal Surgery, 1995; (ed jtly) Surgical Emergencies, 1999; 290 contribs on subjects of colorectal surgery, tumour immunology and laparoscopic surgery in jls incl. Lancet, Brit. Jl Surgery and Brit. Jl Cancer. *Recreations:* wine, classic cars, historic motor racing, armchair sport, bad golf. *Address:* Division of Colorectal Surgery, University of Rochester Medical Center, 601 Elmwood Avenue, Rochester, NY 14642, USA. *T:* (585) 2733678.

MONTAGNIER, Prof. Luc; Professor, Pasteur Institute, Paris, 1985–2000 (Head of Viral Oncology Unit, 1972–2000); Director of Research, Centre national de la recherche scientifique, since 1974; *b* 18 Aug. 1932; *s* of Antoine Montagnier and Marianne (*née* Rousselet); *m* 1961, Dorothea Ackermann; one *s* two *d. Educ:* Collège de Châtellerault; Univ. de Poitiers; Univ. de Paris. Asst, 1955–60, Attaché, 1960, Head, 1963, Head of Research, 1967, Faculty of Science, Paris; Head of Lab., Inst. of Radium, 1965–71. Dist. Prof. and Dir, B. and G. Salick Center for Molecular and Cellular Biol., Queens Coll., CUNY, 1997–2001. Co-discoverer of AIDS virus, 1983. Nobel Prize in Physiology or Medicine, 2008. Grand Officier, Légion d'honneur (France); Commandeur, Ordre national du Mérite (France). *Publications:* Vaincre le Sida, 1986; Des virus et des hommes, 1994; Virus, 2000; Les Combats de la vie, 2008; Le Nobel et Le Moine, 2009; scientific papers on research into AIDS, molecular biology, virology, etc. *Address:* 1 rue Miollis, 75732 Paris Cedex 15, France.

MONTAGNON, Peter James; Associate Director, Institute of Business Ethics, since 2013; *b* Egham, 29 May 1950; *s* of Philip Montagnon and Barbara Montagnon (*née* Shuttleworth); *m* 1973, Isabel Mary; one *s* one *d. Educ:* St John's Coll., Cambridge (BA Modern and Medieval Langs 1972). Financial journalist, Reuters, 1972–80; Financial Times: Capital Mkts Ed.,

1980–86; World Trade Ed., 1986–91; Lex Column, 1991–94, Hd of Lex, 1993–94; Asia Ed., 1994–2000; Dir of Investment Affairs, ABI, 2000–10; Sen. Investment Advr, Financial Reporting Council, 2010–13. Vis. Prof. of Corporate Governance, Cass Business Sch., 2008–. Member: Bd, Internat. Corporate Governance Network, 2005–09 (Chm., 2007–09); Eur. Corporate Governance Forum, 2005–11; Corporate Governance Adv. Bd, Norges Bank Investment Mgt, 2013–; Bd, Hawkamah Inst. of Corporate Governance, Dubai, 2013–. Mem. Council, RIIA, 2011–. *Publications:* (contributing ed.) European Competition Policy, 1990. *Recreations:* languages, travel, current affairs. *Address:* Dormans Cross House, Hollow Lane, Dormansland, Lingfield, Surrey RH7 6NU. *T:* (01342) 835462.

MONTAGU; *see* Douglas-Scott-Montagu.

MONTAGU, family name of **Duke of Manchester**, **Earl of Sandwich**, and **Baron Swaythling**.

MONTAGU OF BEAULIEU, 4th Baron *cr* 1885; **Ralph Douglas-Scott-Montagu;** *b* 13 March 1961; *s* of 3rd Baron Montagu of Beaulieu and Elizabeth Belinda Douglas-Scott-Montagu (*née* Crossley); *S* father, 2015; *m* 2005, Ailsa Camm. *Heir: half-b* Hon. Jonathan Deane Douglas-Scott-Montagu, *b* 11 Oct. 1975.

MONTAGU, Jennifer Iris Rachel, CBE 2012; LVO 2006; PhD; FBA 1986; FSA; Curator of the Photograph Collection, Warburg Institute, 1971–91, now Hon. Fellow; *b* 20 March 1931; *d* of late Hon. Ewen Edward Samuel Montagu, CBE, QC. *Educ:* Brearley Sch., New York; Benenden Sch., Kent; Lady Margaret Hall, Oxford (BA; Hon. Fellow 1985); Warburg Inst., London (PhD). FSA 2008. Assistant Regional Director, Arts Council of Gt Britain, North West Region, 1953–54; Lecturer in the History of Art, Reading Univ., 1958–64; Asst Curator of the Photograph Collection, Warburg Inst., 1964–71. Slade Prof., and Fellow of Jesus Coll., Cambridge, 1980–81; Andrew W. Mellon Lectr, Nat. Gall. of Art, Washington, 1991; Invited Prof., Collège de France, 1994. Member: Academic Awards Cttee, British Fedn of University Women, 1963–89; Executive Cttee, National Art-Collections Fund, 1973–2005; Consultative Cttee, Burlington Magazine, 1975–; Cttee, The Jewish Museum, 1983–; Reviewing Cttee on Export of Works of Art, 1987–96. Trustee: Wallace Collection, 1989–2001; BM, 1994–2001. Hon. Academician, Accademia Clementina, Bologna, 1988. Serena Medal for Italian Studies, British Acad., 1992; Accademica Cultora, Accademia di San Luca, Rome, 2000; Premio Cultori di Roma, 2001; Premio Daria Borghese, 2001; Socio Onorario dell'Università e Nobil Collegio degli Orefici Gioiellieri Argentieri dell'Alma, Città di Roma, 2003. Chevalier de la Légion d'honneur (France), 1999; Ufficiale dell'Ordine al Merito (Italy), 2003; Comdr, Ordre des Arts et des Lettres (France), 2013 (Officier, 1991). *Publications:* Bronzes, 1963; (with Jacques Thuillier) Catalogue of exhibn Charles Le Brun, 1963; Alessandro Algardi, 1985 (special Mitchell Prize); Roman Baroque Sculpture: the industry of art, 1989; The Expression of the Passions, 1994; Gold, Silver and Bronze: metal sculpture of the Roman Baroque, 1996; (ed and contrib.) Algardi: l'altra faccia del Barocco, 1999; (ed and contrib.) Ori e argenti: Capolavori del '700 da Arrighi a Valadier, 2007; Antonio Arrighi: a silversmith and bronze founder in Baroque Rome, 2009; articles in learned periodicals. *Address:* 10 Roland Way, SW7 3RE. *T:* (020) 7373 6691; Warburg Institute, Woburn Square, WC1H 0AB.

MONTAGU, Sir Nicholas (Lionel John), KCB 2001 (CB 1993); Chairman, Financial Ombudsman Service, since 2012; *b* 12 March 1944; *s* of late John Eric Montagu and Barbara Joyce Montagu, OBE; *m* 1974, Jennian Ford Geddes, *o d* of late Ford Irvine Geddes, MBE; two *d*. *Educ:* Rugby Sch.; New Coll., Oxford (MA). Asst Lectr 1966–69, Lectr 1969–74, in Philosophy, Univ. of Reading; Department of Social Security (formerly Department of Health and Social Security): Principal, 1974–81 (seconded to Cabinet Office, 1978–80); Asst Sec., 1981–86; Under Sec., 1986–90; Deputy Secretary, 1990 (seconded to Dept of Transport, 1992–97): Public Transport, 1992–94; Infrastructure, 1994–95; Railways, 1995–97; Hd, Econ. and Domestic Secretariat, Cabinet Office, 1997. Chm., Board of Inland Revenue, 1997–2004. Adviser: IDDAS, 2005–11; Equiniti, 2010–12; Dir, Xafinity, 2005–10; Mem., Adv. Bd, PricewaterhouseCoopers, 2009–11; non-exec. Dir, PIC Hldgs, 2006–11; Chairman: With-Profits Cttee, Aviva UK Life (formerly Norwich Union), 2007–11. Chairman: Council, QMUL, 2009–; Cttee of Univ. Chairs, 2011–14. DUniv: Middlesex, 2001; Bradford, 2003; Hon. DLitt Reading, 2012. *Publications:* Brought to Account (report of Rayner Scrutiny on National Insurance Contributions), 1981; The Pale Yellow Amoeba (report of peer review of DCMS), 2000; articles in newspapers and magazines. *Recreations:* cooking, walking, shopping.

MONTAGU DOUGLAS SCOTT, family name of **Duke of Buccleuch**.

MONTAGU-POLLOCK, Sir Giles Hampden; *see* Pollock.

MONTAGU STUART WORTLEY, family name of **Earl of Wharncliffe**.

MONTAGUE, family name of **Baron Amwell**.

MONTAGUE, Sir Adrian (Alastair), Kt 2006; CBE 2001; Chairman, Aviva, since 2015 (Senior Independent Director, since 2013); *b* 28 Feb. 1948; *s* of late Charles Edward Montague and Olive Montague (*née* Jones); *m* 1st, 1970, Pamela Evans (marr. diss. 1982; she *d* 2000); one *s* two *d*; 2nd, 1986, Penelope Webb (marr. diss. 2009); one *s*; 3rd, 2015, Innes Daubeney. *Educ:* Trinity Hall, Cambridge (MA). Admitted Solicitor, 1973; with Linklaters & Paines, Solicitors, 1971–94 (Partner, 1979); Dir, Kleinwort Benson, subseq. Dresdner Kleinwort Benson, 1994–97; Chief Exec., Private Finance Initiative Task Force, HM Treasury, 1997–2000; Deputy Chairman: Partnerships UK, 2000–01; Network Rail, 2001–04; Chairman: British Energy Gp plc, 2002–09; Michael Page Internat., 2002–11; Cross London Rail Links Ltd, 2004–05; Friends Provident plc, later Friends Provident Gp plc, 2005–09 (Ind. Dir, 2004–09); Infrastructure Investors Ltd, 2005–09; London First, 2009–11 (non-exec. Dir, 2007–11); Anglian Water Gp, 2009–15; 3i Gp plc, 2010–15; Hurricane Exploration, 2011–13; Adv. Gp, Green Investment Bank, 2011–12 (Dep. Chair, 2012–13; Sen. Ind. Dir, 2012–13). Non-executive Director: CellMark AB, 2000–; Skanska AB, 2007–15. Mem., Strategic Rail Authy, 2000–01. Chm. Adv. Bd, Reform, 2010–12. Trustee, Historic Royal Palaces, 2007–13.

MONTAGUE, Robert Joel, CBE 1990; Founder, Chairman and Chief Executive, Axis Intermodal Ltd, since 1999; Founder, The North American Guitar, 2010; *b* 22 June 1948; *s* of late Robert and of Freda Montague; *m* 1972 (marr. diss.); two *s* one *d*; *m* 1990, Silke Kruse; two *s* one *d*. *Educ:* Bedstone Sch., Shropshire; Caius Sch., Brighton. Esso Petroleum Co. Ltd, 1964–69; Cables Montague Ltd, 1969–80; Founder, Chm. and Chief Exec., Tiphook plc, 1978–94. *Recreations:* children, fishing, opera, ballet, guitar.

MONTAGUE, Air Cdre Ruth Mary Bryceson; Director, Women's Royal Air Force, 1989–94; *b* 1 June 1939; *d* of late Griffith John Griffiths and Nancy Bryceson Griffiths (*née* Wrigley); *m* 1966, Roland Arthur Montague. *Educ:* Cavendish Grammar Sch. for Girls, Buxton; Bedford Coll., Univ. of London (BSc). Commissioned RAF, 1962; UK and Far East, 1962–66; UK, 1966–80; HQ Strike Command, 1980–83; RAF Staff Coll., 1983–86; Dep. Dir, WRAF, 1986–89. ADC to the Queen, 1989–94. Mem., Council and F and GP Cttee, RAF Benevolent Fund, 1994–2003; Chm., Adv. Bd, Princess Marina House Care Home, 2003–07. Mem. Council, Royal Holloway, London Univ., 1994–2003 (Hon. Fellow, 2006). FRSA 1993. Badge, Order of Mercy, 2008. *Recreations:* cookery, tapestry, gardening, swimming, world travel. *Address:* c/o National Westminster Bank, PO Box 873, 7 High Street, Marlow, Bucks SL7 1BZ. *Club:* Royal Air Force.

MONTAGUE, Sarah Anne Louise, (Mrs C. Brooke); Presenter, Today Programme, BBC Radio 4, since 2002; *b* 8 Feb. 1966; *d* of Col John and Mary Montague; *m* 2002, Christoph Brooke; three *d*, and one step *d*. *Educ:* Blanchelande Coll., Guernsey; Univ. of Bristol (BSc Hons Biol.). County Natwest, 1987–89; Charles Tyrwhitt Shirts, 1990–91; Channel TV, 1991–94; Reuters, 1994–95; Sky News, 1995–97; BBC, 1997–: BBC News 24, 1997–2001; Hardtalk, 1999–; BBC Newsnight, 2000; BBC Breakfast, 2001–02. *Recreations:* musicals, diving, ski-ing, jigsaws, gardens. *E:* Sarah.Montague@bbc.co.uk.

MONTEAGLE OF BRANDON, 7th Baron *cr* 1839; **Charles James Spring Rice;** *b* 24 Feb. 1953; *o s* of 6th Baron Monteagle of Brandon and of Anne Spring Rice (*née* Brownlow); *S* father 2013; *m* 1987, Mary Teresa Glover; four *d*. *Educ:* Harrow. *Heir: uncle* Hon. Michael Spring Rice [*b* 18 Feb. 1935; *m* 1959, Fiona Sprot; one *s* one *d*].

MONTEFIORE; *see* Sebag-Montefiore.

MONTEITH, Brian; Editor, ThinkScotland.org; *b* 8 Jan. 1958; *s* of Donald MacDonald Monteith and Doreen Campbell Monteith (*née* Purves); *m* 1984, Shirley Joyce Marshall (marr. diss.); twin *s*; *m* Jacqueline Anderson. *Educ:* Portobello High Sch.; Heriot-Watt Univ. Chm., Fedn of Conservative Students, 1982–83; Public Relations Consultant: Michael Forsyth Associates, London, 1983–84 and 1985–86; Dunseath Stephen Associates, Edinburgh, 1984–85; Man. Dir, Leith Communications Ltd, 1986–91; PR Dir, Forth Mktg Ltd, 1991–94; Scottish Dir, Communication Gp, 1994–96; sole proprietor and Consultant, Dunedin PR, 1996–99. Scottish Parliament: Mem., Scotland Mid and Fife, 1999–2007 (C 1999–2005, Ind 2005–07); Convener, Audit Cttee, 2003–07; Cons. spokesman on educn, culture and sport, 1999–2003, on finance and local govt, 2003–05. Mem., Tuesday Club. Chm. Trustees, ESU Scotland. *Publications:* Paying the Piper: from a taxing lament to a rewarding jig, 2007; The Bully State: the end of tolerance, 2009; The Full Monty, 2009. *Recreation:* football. *Club:* Duddingston Golf (Edinburgh).

MONTEITH, Very Rev. David Robert Malvern; Dean of Leicester, since 2013; *b* Enniskillen, NI, 5 June 1968; *s* of Thomas Malvern and Mary, (Molly), Louise (*née* Johnston); civil partnership 2008, David Hamilton. *Educ:* Portora Royal Sch., Enniskillen; St John's Coll., Durham (BSc Zool. 1989); St John's Coll., Univ. of Nottingham (BTh 1992; MA Mission and Ministry 1993). Ordained deacon, 1993, priest, 1994; Asst Curate, All Saints', Kings Heath, Birmingham, 1993–97; Asst Curate, 1997–2000, Associate Vicar, 2000–02, St Martin-in-the-Fields; Priest-in-charge, Holy Trinity, Wimbledon, 2002–09; Area Dean of Merton, Dio. of Southwark, 2004–09; Team Rector, Merton Priory Team, 2009; Canon Chancellor, Leicester Cath., 2009–13. Chair of Trustees, St Philip's Centre for Interfaith Dialogue, Leicester, 2012–. *Recreations:* visual arts, contemporary poetry, theatre, gardening. *Address:* St Martins House, 7 Peacock Lane, Leicester LE1 5PZ. *T:* (0116) 261 5356. *E:* david.monteith@leccofe.org.

MONTGOMERIE, family name of **Earl of Eglinton**.

MONTGOMERIE, Lord; Hugh Archibald William Montgomerie; Business Sales Consultant, Dell Computers, since 2004; *b* 24 July 1966; *s* and *heir* of 18th Earl of Eglinton and Winton, *qv*; *m* 1991, Sara Alexandra (marr. diss. 1998), *e d* of Niel Redpath; *m* 2001, Carol Anne Robinson, *yr d* of R. Donald Robinson Jr, Brentwood, Tenn; one *s* two *d*. *Educ:* Univ. of Edinburgh (MBA 2000). RN officer, 1988–92. Ops Manager, Gander & White Shipping Ltd, 1996–97. Intelligence Officer, 51 Highland Bde, 1997–98. Project Manager, ReServ Construction Co. Inc., 2000–04. Bd Mem., Soc. of Scottish Armigers. *Heir: s* Hon. Rhuridh Seton Archibald Montgomerie, *b* 4 March 2007.

MONTGOMERIE, Colin Stuart, OBE 2005 (MBE 1998); professional golfer, since 1987; *b* Glasgow, 23 June 1963; *s* of James Montgomerie; *m* 1st, 1990, Eimear Wilson (marr. diss. 2004); one *s* two *d*; 2nd, 2008, Gaynor Knowles. *Educ:* Strathallan Sch., Perth; Leeds Grammar Sch.; Houston Baptist Univ., Texas. Wins include: Scottish Amateur Stroke-Play Championship, 1985; Scottish Amateur Championship, 1987; Portuguese Open, 1989; Scandinavian Masters, 1991, 1999, 2001; Dutch Open, 1993; Volvo Masters, 1993, (jtly) 2002; Spanish Open, 1994; English Open, 1994; German Open, 1994, 1995; Lancôme Trophy, 1995; Alfred Dunhill Cup, 1995; Million Dollar Challenge, 1996; European Masters, 1996; Dubai Desert Classic, 1996; Irish Open, 1996, 1997, 2001; King Hassan II Trophy, 1997; European Grand Prix, 1997; World Cup (Individual), 1997; World Championship of Golf, 1997; PGA Championship, 1998, 1999, 2000; German Masters, 1998; British Masters, 1998; Benson & Hedges Internat. Open, 1999; Loch Lomond Invitational, 1999; BMW Internat. Open, 1999; Cisco World Matchplay, 1999; French Open, 2000; Skins Game, USA, 2000; Australian Masters, 2001; TCL Classic, 2002; Macau Open, 2003; Caltex Masters, Singapore, 2004; Dunhill Links Championship, 2005; Hong Kong Open, 2006; European Open, 2007; World Cup (Team), 2007; Senior USPGA Championship, 2014, 2015; 1st in European Order of Merit, annually, 1993–99, 2005. Member: Alfred Dunhill Cup team, 1988, 1991–2000; World Cup Team, 1988, 1991–93, 1997–99, 2006–07, 2008; Ryder Cup team, 1991, 1993, 1995, 1997, 1999, 2002, 2004, 2006, Captain, 2010; UBS Cup Team, 2003, 2004; Seve Trophy team, 2000, 2002, 2003, 2005, 2007. Coach of the Year, BBC Sports Personality of the Year, 2010. *Publications:* (with Lewine Mair) The Real Monty (autobiog.), 2002; The Thinking Man's Guide to Golf, 2003; Monty: the autobiography, 2012. *Address:* c/o IMG, McCormack House, Burlington Lane, W4 2TH.

MONTGOMERIE, Timothy Hugh; Comment Editor, The Times, 2013–14; *b* Barnstaple, N Devon, 24 July 1970. *Educ:* King's Sch., Gütersloh, Germany; Univ. of Exeter (BA Econs and Geog. 1992). COS to Rt Hon. Iain Duncan Smith, 2003; Founder, Centre for Social Justice, 2004; Founder and Ed., conservativehome.com, 2005–13. *Recreation:* season ticket holder at Manchester United.

MONTGOMERY, family name of **Viscount Montgomery of Alamein**.

MONTGOMERY OF ALAMEIN, 2nd Viscount *cr* 1946, of Hindhead; **David Bernard Montgomery,** CMG 2000; CBE 1975; Chairman, Baring Puma Fund, 1991–2002; *b* 18 Aug. 1928; *s* of 1st Viscount Montgomery of Alamein, KG, GCB, DSO, and Elizabeth (*d* 1937), *d* of late Robert Thompson Hobart, ICS; *S* father, 1976; *m* 1st, 1953, Mary Connell (marr. diss. 1967); one *s* one *d*; 2nd, 1970, Tessa, *d* of late Gen. Sir Frederick Browning, GCVO, KBE, CB, DSO, and Lady Browning, DBE (Dame Daphne du Maurier). *Educ:* Winchester; Trinity Coll., Cambridge (MA). Shell International, 1951–62; Dir, Yardley International, 1963–74; Man. Dir, Terimar Services (Overseas Trade Consultancy), 1974–99; Dir, Korn/Ferry International, 1977–93; Chm., Antofagasta (Chile) and Bolivia Railway Co., 1980–82; Dir, NEI, 1981–87. Mem., Exec. Cttee, British Gp, IPU, 1987–99, 2008–13; Deleg., OSCE Parly Assembly, 1991–2000. Elected crossbench Mem., H of L, 2005–15; Chm., London Gp, H of L, 2007–12. Editorial Adviser, Vision Interamericana, 1974–94. Chm., Economic Affairs Cttee, Canning House, 1973–75; Pres., British Industrial Exhibition, São Paulo, 1974. Councillor, Royal Borough of Kensington and Chelsea, 1974–78. Hon. Consul, Republic of El Salvador, 1973–77. President: Anglo-Argentine Soc., 1977–87; Anglo-Belgian Soc., 1994–2006; Chairman: Hispanic and Luso Brazilian Council, 1978–80 (Pres., 1987–94); Brazilian Chamber of Commerce in GB, 1980–82; European Atlantic Gp, 1992–94 (Pres., 1994–97). Pres., Cambridge Univ. Engrs Assoc., 2001–06. Patron: D-Day and Normandy Fellowship, 1980–95; 8th Army Veterans Assoc., 1985–2002. President: Redgrave Theatre, Farnham, 1977–89; Restaurateurs Assoc. of GB, 1982–90 (Patron, 1991–99); Acad. of Food and Wine Service, 1995–98; Centre for International Briefing, Farnham Castle, 1985–2003. Pres., Amesbury Sch., 1992– (Gov., 1976–92). Gran Oficial:

Orden Bernardo O'Higgins (Chile), 1989; Orden Libertador San Martin (Argentina), 1992; Orden Nacional Cruzeiro do Sul (Brazil), 1993; Orden de Isabel la Católica (Spain), 1993; Commander's Cross, Order of Merit (Germany), 1993; Order of Aztec Eagle (Mexico), 1994; Order of Leopold II (Belgium), 1997; Orden de San Carlos (Colombia), 1998; Orden del Libertador (Venezuela), 1999. *Publications:* (with Alistair Horne) The Lonely Leader: Monty 1944–45, 1994. *Heir: s* Hon. Henry David Montgomery [*b* 2 April 1954; *m* 1980, Caroline (*d* 2014), *e d* of Richard Odey, Hotham Hall, York; three *d*]. *Address:* 2/97 Onslow Square, SW7 3LU. *T:* (020) 7589 8747. *Clubs:* Garrick, Canning.

MONTGOMERY, Alan Everard, CMG 1993; PhD; HM Diplomatic Service, retired; Associate Member, General Medical Council, 2009–12; *b* 11 March 1938; *s* of Philip Napier Montgomery and Honor Violet Coleman (*née* Price); *m* 1st, 1960, Janet Barton (*d* 1994); one *s* one *d*; 2nd, 1999, Florence Belle Liebst. *Educ:* Royal Grammar Sch., Guildford; County of Stafford Training Coll. (Cert. of Educn); Birkbeck Coll., London (BA Hons, PhD). Served Middx Regt, 1957–59. Teacher, Staffs and ILEA, 1961–65; Lectr, Univ. of Birmingham, 1969–72; entered FCO, 1972; 1st Secretary: FCO, 1972–75; Dhaka, 1975–77; Ottawa, 1977–80; FCO, 1980–83; Counsellor GATT/UNCTAD, UKMIS Geneva, 1983–87; Counsellor, Consul-Gen. and Hd of Chancery, Jakarta, 1987–89; Head of Migration and Visa Dept, FCO, 1989–92; Ambassador to the Philippines, 1992–95; High Comr to Tanzania, 1995–98. Trade Policy Advr, Commonwealth Business Council, 1998–99. Mem., Fitness to Practise Cttee (formerly Professional Conduct Cttee), GMC, 2000–08, 2009–12; Lay Member: Immigration Services Tribunal, 2001–08; Complaints Commn, 2001–04, Professional Standards Cttee, 2004–05, Rules Cttee, 2006, Gen. Council of the Bar; Professional Conduct Panel, RICS, 2003–07; Professional Conduct Panel, British Assoc. for Counselling and Psychotherapy, 2003–08; Ind. Mem., Surrey Police Authy Misconduct Tribunals, 2004–10. Mem. Bd, FARM Africa, 1998–2001. Gp Leader, RCDS Africa tour, 2001–03. *Publications:* (contrib.) Lloyd George: 12 essays, ed A. J. P. Taylor, 1971; (contrib.) Commonwealth Banking Almanac, 1999; contrib. Cambridge Hist. Jl, 1972. *Recreations:* historic buildings, jazz, theatre, opera, gardening.

MONTGOMERY, Sir (Basil Henry) David, 9th Bt *cr* 1801, of Stanhope; CVO 2007; Lord-Lieutenant of Perth and Kinross, 1996–2006; Chairman, Forestry Commission, 1979–89; *b* 20 March 1931; *s* of late Lt-Col H. K. Purvis-Montgomery, OBE, and of Mrs C. L. W. Purvis-Russell-Montgomery (*née* Maconochie Welwood); *S* uncle, 1964; *m* 1956, Delia, *o d* of Adm. Sir (John) Peter (Lorne) Reid, GCB, CVO; one *s* four *d* (and one *s* decd). *Educ:* Eton. National Service, Black Watch, 1949–51. Member: Nature Conservancy Council, 1973–79; Tayside Regional Authority, 1974–79. Comr, Mental Welfare Commn for Scotland, 1990–91. Trustee, Municipal Mutual Insurance Ltd, 1980–96. Hon. LLD Dundee, 1977. DL Kinross-shire, 1960, Vice-Lieutenant 1966–74; JP 1966; DL Perth and Kinross, 1975. *Heir: s* James David Keith Montgomery [*b* 13 June 1957; *m* 1983, Elizabeth, *e d* of late E. Lyndon Evans, Pentyrch, Mid-Glamorgan; one *s* one *d*. Served The Black Watch, RHR, 1976–86]. *Address:* Home Farm, Kinross KY13 8EU. *T:* (01577) 863416.

MONTGOMERY, Vice Adm. Sir Charles (Percival Ross), KBE 2012 (CBE 2006); Director General, UK Border Force, Home Office, since 2013; *b* 12 April 1955; *s* of Phillip Stuart Montgomery and Eileen Beryl Montgomery; *m* 1982, Adrienne Julie; three *s* one *d*. *Educ:* Univ. of Sheffield (BEng Hons 1976). CO HMS Beaver, 1991–93; Directorate of Defence Policy, 1993–95; Private Sec. to Sec. of State, 1995–97; Trng Dir, Naval Recruiting and Trng Agency, 1997–2000; Hd, NRTA Estate Rev. Team, 2000; Asst Dir of Naval Staff (Strategy), 2000–02; rcds, 2003; Dir Naval Personnel Strategy, 2003–06; Cdre Maritime Warfare Sch. and CO HMS Collingwood, 2006–07; Naval Sec. and COS (Personnel) to C-in-C Fleet, 2007–10; Second Sea Lord and C-in-C Naval Home Comd, 2010–12; Flag ADC to the Queen, 2010–12. Chm. Bd, Greenwich Hosp., 2010–12. Younger Brother, Trinity House, 2007–. President: RN Hockey Assoc., 2009–12; RN Lawn Tennis Assoc., 2010–12; Combined Services Lawn Tennis Assoc., 2010–12; Combined Services Hockey Assoc., 2011–12; RN Benevolent Trust, 2013–; Vice-Pres., RN Rugby Union; Smile Support, 2013–. Patron, Battleback, 2010–. CCMI 2012; FCIPD 2012. Hon. Freeman, Wheelwrights' Co., 2014. Hon. DEng Sheffield, 2012. *Recreations:* cricket, golf, Rugby, hockey, gardening, outdoor pursuits. *Address:* Home Office, 2 Marsham Street, 3rd Floor, Fry Building, SW1P 4DF. *Clubs:* Royal Navy of 1765 and 1785; St Cross Cricket (Winchester); Army and Navy.

MONTGOMERY, Clare Patricia; QC 1996; a Recorder, since 2000; a Deputy High Court Judge, since 2003; a Judge of the Courts of Appeal of Jersey and Guernsey, since 2007; *b* 29 April 1958; *d* of Stephen Ross Montgomery and Ann Margaret Barlow; *m* 1991, Victor Melleney; two *d*. *Educ:* Millfield Sch.; UCL (LLB). Called to the Bar, Gray's Inn, 1980, Bencher, 2002. An Asst Recorder, 1999–2000. Mem., Supplementary Panel (Common Law), 1992–96. *Publications:* (ed) Archbold Criminal Pleading Evidence and Practice, annually, 1993–2014; (ed) Fraud: criminal law and procedure, 2008; (ed) The Law of Extradition and Mutual Assistance, 2013. *Address:* Matrix Chambers, Gray's Inn, WC1R 5LN. *T:* (020) 7404 3447.

MONTGOMERY, Sir David; *see* Montgomery, Sir B. H. D.

MONTGOMERY, David, CMG 1984; OBE 1972; Foreign and Commonwealth Office, 1987–91; *b* 29 July 1927; *s* of late David Montgomery and Mary (*née* Walker Cunningham); *m* 1955, Margaret Newman; one *s* one *d*. RNVR, 1945–46; Royal Navy, 1946–48. Foreign Office, 1949–52; Bucharest, 1952–53; FO, 1953–55; Bonn, 1955–58; Düsseldorf, 1958–61; Rangoon, 1961–63; Ottawa, 1963–64; Regina, Saskatchewan, 1964–65; FCO, 1966–68; Bangkok, 1968–72; Zagreb, 1973–76; FCO, 1976–79; Dep. High Comr to Barbados, 1980–84, also (non-resident) to Antigua and Barbuda, Dominica, Grenada, St Kitts and Nevis, St Lucia, St Vincent and the Grenadines, 1980–84; FCO, 1984–85. *Address:* Ross Court, Putney Hill, SW15.

MONTGOMERY, David John; Chief Executive Officer, Local World Ltd, since 2013 (Executive Chairman, 2012–13); *b* 6 Nov. 1948; *s* of William John and Margaret Jean Montgomery; *m* 1st, 1971, Susan Frances Buchanan Russell (marr. diss. 1987); 2nd, 1989, Heidi Kingstone (marr. diss. 1997); 3rd, 1997, Sophie Countess of Woolton, *d* of Baron Birdwood; one *s* one *d*. *Educ:* Queen's University, Belfast (BA Politics/History). Sub-Editor, Daily Mirror, London/Manchester, 1973–78; Assistant Chief Sub-Editor, Daily Mirror, 1978–80; Chief Sub-Editor, The Sun, 1980; Asst Editor, Sunday People, 1982; Asst Editor, 1984, Editor, 1985–87, News of the World; Editor, Today, 1987–91 (Newspaper of the Year, 1988); Man. Dir, News UK, 1987–91; Chief Exec., 1991, Dir, 1991–, London Live Television; Chief Exec., Mirror Gp Newspapers, 1992–99; Exec. Chm., 2000–09, Chief Exec., 2009–11, Mecom UK Mgt Ltd, later Mecom Gp plc. Director: Satellite Television PLC, 1986–91; News Group Newspapers, 1986–91; Caledonian Publishing Co. (Glasgow Herald & Times), 1991–92; Donohue Inc., 1992–95; Newspaper Publishing (The Independent, Independent on Sunday), 1994–98; Scottish Media Gp (formerly Scottish Television), 1995–99; Press Assoc., 1996–99; Chairman: Tri-mex Gp, 1999–2002; Yava, 2000–03; Africa Lakes plc, 2000–07; West 175 Media plc, 2002–06; Moyle Hldgs Ltd, 2003–08; NI Energy Hldgs, 2005–08; Berliner Verlag (Germany), 2005–09; Media Gp Limburg (Netherlands), 2006–08; RSDB (Netherlands), 2006–09; Royal Wegener (Netherlands), 2009–11. Pres., Integrated Educn Fund Develt Bd (NI), 2000–. Member: QUB Foundn Bd, 2002–05; Campaign for Peace and Democratic Reconstruction for NI, 2002–; Chm., Team NI, 2003–08. *Address:* 15 Collingham Gardens, SW5 0HS.

MONTGOMERY, Prof. Hugh Edward, MD; FRCP; Director, Institute for Human Health and Performance, since 2005, and Professor of Intensive Care Medicine, since 2008, University College London; *b* Plymouth, 20 Oct. 1962; *s* of Nelson and Bridget Montgomery; *m* 2001, Mary Limebury; two *s*. *Educ:* Plymouth Coll.; Middlesex Hosp., Univ. of London (BSc Physiol./Neuropharmacol. 1984; MB BS 1987; MD 1997). FRCP 2007; FFICM 2011. House Physician, Whittington Hosp., 1987; House Surgeon, Battle Hosp., Reading, 1988; Senior House Officer: Hammersmith Hosp., 1988–89; St Bartholomew's Hosp., 1989–90; Intensive Care Unit and Chronic Respiratory Unit, St Thomas' Hosp., 1990; MO, CJM Hosp., Kwazulu, Africa, 1990–91; Registrar: Medical and Cardiol., St Peters Hosp., Chertsey, 1991–92; Cardiol., St George's Hosp., 1992–93; BHF Res. Fellow and Clin. Lectr, Hatter Inst., 1993–95; Sen. Registrar, Intensive Care Unit, UCLH 1995–97, 1997–98; University College London: Res. Fellow, Cardiovascular Genetics, 1995–96; Lectr, Intensive Care, 1996–97; Res. Fellow, Cardiol., 1997–98; SHO, Dept of Anaesthetics, St Helier's Hosp., Surrey, 1997; Specialist Registrar, Cardiol. and Gen. Medicine, 1998–2000; Consultant Intensivist: UCLH, 2002–06; Whittington Hosp., 2006–. Leader, Project Genie, 2004–; London Leader, GLA, 2008–09. Member: Bd, UK Climate and Health Council, 2008–; Steering Gp, Natural Capital Initiative, 2009–. TV writer and presenter: Royal Instn Christmas Lectures, 2007; Who Sank the Mary Rose?, 2008. *Publications:* (ed) 100 Questions in Cardiology, 2000; My First MRCP Book, 2003; (ed) Puzzling Out Medicine series (10 books), 2005; (ed) Surviving Prescribing, 2006; *for children:* The Voyage of the Arctic Tern, 2002; Cloudsailors, 2005; The Genie in the Bottle, 2006; contrib. book chapters and scientific jls incl. Nature. *Recreations:* mountaineering, hill-walking, diving, writing. *Address:* UCL Institute for Human Health and Performance, 1st Floor, 170 Tottenham Court Road, W1T 7HA. *E:* h.montgomery@ucl.ac.uk.

MONTGOMERY, John; Sheriff of South Strathclyde, Dumfries and Galloway, since 2003, at Ayr since 2005; *b* 17 Sept. 1951; *s* of Robert and Jessie Montgomery; *m* 1978, Susan Wilson Templeton; one *s* three *d*. *Educ:* Stevenston High Sch.; Ardrossan Acad.; Glasgow Univ. (LLB Hons). NP. Solicitor, 1976–2003. Temp. Sheriff, 1995–99; Sheriff (pt-time), 2000–03. *Recreations:* family, walking, gardening, travel. *Address:* Sheriff Court, Wellington Square, Ayr KA7 1DR.

MONTGOMERY, John Duncan; Member, Monopolies and Mergers Commission, 1989–95; *b* 12 Nov. 1928; *s* of Lionel Eric Montgomery and Katherine Mary Montgomery (*née* Ambler); *m* 1956, Pauline Mary Sutherland; two *d*. *Educ:* King's College Sch., Wimbledon; LSE (LLB, LLM). Admitted Solicitor 1951; Treasury Solicitor's Dept, 1960–68; Legal Adviser, Beecham Products, 1974–75; Head, Legal Div., Shell UK, 1975–88 and Company Sec., Shell UK, 1979–88. Former Chm., Youth Orgns, Merton. Freeman, City of London, 1987; Mem., Loriners' Co., 1988. JP SW London, 1985–98. *Recreations:* dinghy sailing, photography. *Address:* 6 White Lodge Close, Sutton, Surrey SM2 5TQ. *Clubs:* MCC; Surrey CC.

MONTGOMERY, John Matthew; Clerk of the Salters' Company, 1975–90; *b* 22 May 1930; *s* of Prof. George Allison Montgomery, QC, and Isobel A. (*née* Morison); *m* 1956, Gertrude Gillian Richards (*d* 2008); two *s* one *d*. *Educ:* Rugby Sch.; Trinity Hall, Cambridge (MA). Various commercial appointments with Mobil Oil Corporation and First National City Bank, 1953–74. Member Council: Surrey Trust for Nature Conservation Ltd, 1965–89 (Chm., 1973–83; Vice-Pres., 1983–); Royal Soc. for Nature Conservation, 1980–89; Botanical Soc. of British Isles, 1991–95; Founder Mem., London Wildlife Trust, 1981–. Member, Executive Committee: Nat. Assoc. of Almshouses, 1980–91; Age Concern Gtr London, 1985–96 (Chm., 1988–91; Vice-Pres., 1996–2001). *Recreation:* various natural history interests. *Address:* 36 Gibson Court, 33 Manor Road North, Hinchley Wood, Esher, Surrey KT10 0AW. *T:* (01372) 749805.

MONTGOMERY, Prof. Jonathan Robert; Professor of Health Care Law, University College London, since 2013; Chairman: Nuffield Council of Bioethics, since 2012; Health Research Authority, since 2012; *b* 29 July 1962; *s* of Robert William Montgomery and Margaret Elizabeth Montgomery (*née* Exell); *m* 1986, Elsa Mary Wells Harnett; two *d*. *Educ:* King's College Sch., Wimbledon; Gonville and Caius Coll., Cambridge (BA 1983; LLM 1984). Lectr, 1984–98, Reader, 1998–2001, Prof. of Health Care Law, 2001–13, Univ. of Southampton. Non-exec. Dir, 1992–98, Chm., 1998–2001, Southampton Community Health Services NHS Trust; Chairman: W Hants NHS Trust, subseq. Hants Partnership NHS Trust, 2001–04; Hants and IoW Strategic HA, 2004–06; Hampshire PCT, 2006–13. Member: Med. Ethics Cttee, BMA, 2003–08; Ethics Adv. Gp to Care Records Develt Bd, NHS Prog. for IT, 2004–06; Working Party on Ethics of Public Health, Nuffield Council on Bioethics, 2006–07; Cttee on the Ethical Aspects of Pandemic Influenza, 2006–; Organ Donation Taskforce, 2008–09; Morecambe Bay Investigation, 2014. Chairman: Adv. Cttee on Clinical Excellence Awards, 2005–14; Working Party on a Strategy for Brain Tissue Banking, UK Clinical Res. Collaboration, 2007–08; Scientific Steering Cttee, Brain Banks UK, 2009–12; Human Genetics Commn, 2009–12. Comr, Commn of Inquiry into the Future of Adult Social Care, Hants CC, 2008. Chm., Winchester Diocesan Council for Social Responsibility, 1997–98; Lay Examining Chaplain for Bishop of Portsmouth, 2003– Patron, CISters (Childhood Incest Survivors), 2004–. Trustee, TADIC (Teenage Drop-in Centre, Hedge End), 2008–10. General Editor: (with G. Howells) Butterworths Family Law Service, 1996–; Butterworths Family and Child Law Bulletin, 1997–2006; Consultant Ed., Halsbury's Laws of England: Medical Professions vol., 5th edn 2011. Hon. FRCPCH 2005. *Publications:* Health Care Law, 1997, 2nd edn 2003; (with P. Alderson) Health Care Choices: making decisions with children, 1996; numerous book chapters and contribs to learned jls. *Recreations:* family and friends, active member of the Church of England, church youth work, lacrosse (Cambridge Univ. Lacrosse Club, 1982–84; Southampton Univ. Men's Lacrosse Club, 1984–88, 2007–08; Southampton City Lacrosse Club, 2008–). *Address:* Faculty of Laws, University College London, 104 Bentham House, Endsleigh Gardens, WC1H 0EG. *E:* Jonathan.Montgomery@ucl.ac.uk.

MONTGOMERY, Joseph, CB 2006; Chairman, Re Ltd, since 2015; *b* 1 Feb. 1961. *Educ:* Becket Sch., Nottingham; Aston Univ. (BSc 1983). Asst Sec., Cadbury Trust, 1986–89; Leader, Deptford Task Force, DTI, 1989–92; Chief Exec., Deptford City Challenge, 1992–94; Dir, Leisure, Economy and Envmt, 1994–99, Exec. Dir for Regeneration, 1999–2001, Lewisham BC; Director General: Neighbourhood Renewal Unit, DTLR, then at ODPM, subseq. Tackling Disadvantage Gp, ODPM, then at DCLG, 2001–06; Regions (formerly Places) and Communities, DCLG, 2006–11; Chief Exec. for Europe, Urban Land Inst., 2011–14. *Address:* Re Ltd, North London Business Park, Oakleigh Road South, N11 1NP.

MONTGOMERY, Kristina Aileen; QC 2013; **Her Honour Judge Montgomery;** a Circuit Judge, since 2014; *b* 17 Jan. 1971; *d* of Stuart Montgomery and Eva Montgomery; *m* 2006, Matthew Barnes; one *s*. Called to the Bar, Middle Temple, 1993; a Recorder, 2010–14. *Address:* Oxford Combined Court and Family Hearing Centre, St Aldates, Oxford OX1 1TL.

MONTGOMERY, Susannah; HM Diplomatic Service; Lead, Good Governance Fund, Foreign and Commonwealth Office, since 2015. *Educ:* Univ. of Cambridge. Joined FCO, 1995; Vice Consul, Almaty, 1996; Second Sec. (Pol), Moscow, 1997; Actg Hd of Mission, Minsk, 1998; Second Sec. (Pol), UK Mission to the UN, NY, 1999–2000; on secondment to DFID, 2001; Ops Manager, Finance Directorate, FCO, 2002–04; Hd, Nuclear Safety, Sci. and Envmt Team, Moscow, 2004–05; Strategic Policy Advr, Policy Planners, FCO, 2005–07; Hd, Eur. Prog. Team, FCO, 2007–08; High Comr, Gambia, 2008–09; Advr, Parly Relations

Team, 2010; Communications Manager, Paris, 2011; Ambassador to Slovakia, 2011–14. *Recreation:* archery. *Address:* c/o Foreign and Commonwealth Office, King Charles Street, SW1A 2AH.

MONTGOMERY CAMPBELL, Sir Philip Henry; *see* Campbell.

MONTGOMERY CUNINGHAME, Sir John Christopher Foggo, 12th Bt *cr* 1672, of Corsehill, Ayrshire and Kirktonholm, Lanarkshire; Director, Primentia Inc., and other companies; *b* 24 July 1935; 2nd *s* of Col Sir Thomas Montgomery-Cuninghame, 10th Bt, DSO (*d* 1945), and of Nancy Macaulay (his 2nd wife), *d* of late W. Stewart Foggo, Aberdeen (she *m* 2nd, 1946, Johan Frederik Christian Killander); *b* of Sir Andrew Montgomery-Cuninghame, 11th Bt; *S* brother, 1959; *m* 1964, Laura Violet, *d* of Sir Godfrey Nicholson, 1st Bt; three *d. Educ:* Fettes; Worcester Coll., Oxford (MA). 2nd Lieut, Rifle Brigade (NS), 1955–56; Lieut, London Rifle Brigade, TA, 1956–59. *Recreation:* fishing. *Heir:* none. *Address:* The Old Rectory, Brightwalton, Newbury, Berks RG20 7BL.

MONTI, Dr Mario; Senator-for-Life, Italy, since 2011; Prime Minister of Italy, 2011–13; *b* 19 March 1943; *m* 1970, Elsa Antonioli; one *s* one *d. Educ:* Bocconi Univ. (Dr); Yale Univ. Bocconi University, Italy: Asst, 1965–69; Prof. of Monetary Theory and Policy, 1971–85; Prof. of Economics and Dir, Economics Inst., 1985–94; Founder, Paolo Baffi Centre for Monetary and Financial Economics, 1985; Rector, Innocenzo Gasparini Inst. of Economic Res., 1989–94; Pres., 1994–. Mem., European Commn, 1995–2004. Chm., 2005–08, Hon. Pres., 2008–, Brussels European and Global Econ. Lab. (Bruegel). *Address:* Italian Senate, Piazza Madama, 00186, Rome, Italy.

MONTREAL, Bishop of, since 2004; **Rt Rev. Barry Bryan Clarke;** *b* Montreal, 10 Oct. 1952; *m* 1997, Leslie James; one *d* from previous marriage. *Educ:* McGill Univ. (BTh 1977); Montreal Theol Coll. (Dip. Min. 1978). Ordained 1978; Asst Curate, St Matthias, Westmount, 1978–80; Rector: Trinity Church, St Bruno, 1980–84; St Michael and All Angels, 1984–93; St Paul's, Lachine, 1993–2004. Regional Dean: Ste Anne, 1988–92; Pointe Claire, 1997–2003; Archdeacon, St Lawrence, 2003–04. *Address:* (office) 1444 Union Avenue, Montreal, QC H3A 2B8, Canada. *T:* (514) 8436577, *Fax:* (514) 8433221. *E:* bishops.office@montreal.anglican.ca.

MONTROSE, 8th Duke of, *cr* 1707; **James Graham;** Lord Graham 1445; Earl of Montrose 1505; Bt (NS) 1625; Marquis of Montrose 1644; Duke of Montrose, Marquis of Graham and Buchanan, Earl of Kincardine, Viscount Dundaff, Lord Aberuthven, Mugdock, and Fintrie 1707; Earl and Baron Graham (Eng.) 1722; *b* 6 April 1935; *e s* of 7th Duke of Montrose, and Isobel Veronica (*d* 1990), *yr d* of Lt-Col T. B. Sellar, CMG, DSO; *S* father, 1992; *m* 1970, Catherine Elizabeth MacDonell (*d* 2014), *d* of late Captain N. A. T. Young, and of Mrs Young, Ottawa; two *s* one *d. Educ:* Loretto. Elected Mem., H of L, 1999; Opposition Whip, H of L, 2001–11; Opposition spokesman on Scottish affairs, 2001–11. Captain, Royal Company of Archers (Queen's Body Guard for Scotland), 2005–14 (Mem., 1965–). Area Pres., Scottish NFU, 1986 (Mem. Council, 1981–86 and 1987–90); President: RHASS, 1997–98; Nat. Sheep Assoc., 2011–. ARAgS 2009, FRAgS 2013. OStJ 1978. *Heir: s* Marquis of Graham, *qv. Address:* Auchmar, Drymen, Glasgow G63 0AG. *T:* (01360) 660307.

MONTY, Simon Trevor; QC 2003; a Recorder, since 2010; a Deputy High Court Judge, since 2013; *b* 9 Dec. 1959; *s* of Cyril Monty and Gina (*née* Dixon); *m* 1985, Susan Andrea Goldwater; two *s* one *d. Educ:* Alleyn's Sch., Dulwich; Manchester Univ. (LLB Hons 1981). Called to the Bar, Middle Temple, 1982, Bencher, 2004; in practice as barrister, 1983–, specialising in professional negligence litigation. *Publications:* (contrib.) Jackson & Powell's Professional Liability Precedents, 2000. *Recreations:* ski-ing, music, walking. *Address:* Four New Square, Lincoln's Inn, WC2A 3RJ. *T:* (020) 7822 2000, *Fax:* (020) 7822 2001. *E:* s.monty@4newsquare.com.

MOODY, Prof. Christopher John, PhD, DSc; CChem, FRSC; Sir Jesse Boot Professor of Chemistry and Head, Organic Chemistry, University of Nottingham, since 2005; *b* Manchester, 30 Dec. 1951; *s* of Geoffrey Moody and Sheila Moody; *m* 1976, Barbara Moore; three *d. Educ:* Manchester Grammar Sch.; King's Coll. London (BSc 1973); Univ. of Liverpool (PhD 1976); Univ. of London (DSc 1989). Royal Soc. Postdoctoral Fellow, ETH, Zürich, 1976–77; Sen. Chemist, Roche, 1977–79; Lectr, then Reader, Imperial Coll. London, 1979–89; Professor of Organic Chemistry: Loughborough Univ., 1990–96; Univ. of Exeter, 1996–2005. *Publications:* (with L. M. Harwood) Experimental Organic Chemistry, 1989, 2nd edn 1999; (with G. H. Whitham) Reactive Intermediates, 1992; over 400 papers in learned jls. *Recreations:* sport, walking. *Address:* School of Chemistry, University of Nottingham, University Park, Nottingham NG7 2RD. *T:* (0115) 846 8500, *Fax:* (0115) 951 3564.

MOODY, Clare Miranda; Member (Lab) South West Region and Gibraltar, European Parliament, since 2014; *b* Chipping Norton, 30 Oct. 1965; *d* of Raymond and Joan Moody. *Educ:* Univ. of Kent (BA Industrial Relns). Trade union officer, UNIFI, Amicus then Unite, 1994–2014. Advr, Prime Minister's Policy Unit, 10 Downing St, 2008–10. Contested (Lab): SW Reg., EP, 2004; Salisbury, 2005. *Address:* European Parliament, 60 Rue Wiertz, 1047 Brussels, Belgium.

MOODY, David Barker, CVO 2014; Lord-Lieutenant of South Yorkshire, 2004–15; *b* 7 April 1940; *s* of Norman William Barker Moody and Dorothy Moody (*née* Beetham); *m* 1966, Carolyn Susan Lindop Green; one *s* two *d* (and one *d* decd). *Educ:* Worksop Coll.; Pembroke Coll., Oxford (MA Mod. Hist.); London Business Sch. (Sloan Fellow 1971). Asst Master, Sussex House Prep. Sch., 1959–60; graduate apprentice, United Steel Cos Ltd, 1963–64; Samuel Fox & Company Limited: Mgt Develt Officer, 1964–70; Manager Billet Finishing, 1970–72; Sales Manager, 1972–75; Commercial Dir, Spartan Redheugh Ltd, 1975–81; Chm. and Man. Dir, Spartan Sheffield Ltd, 1981–99; Chm., J. Shipman Properties Ltd, 1998–. Chm., S Yorks Investment Fund, 2001–10; President: Sheffield Chamber of Commerce and Industry, 1998–99; S Yorks Community Foundn, 2004–15; Army Benevolent Fund S Yorks, 2004–15; Wentworth Castle and Stainborough Park Heritage Trust, 2004–; Friends of Sheffield Cathedral, 2006–15 (Vice-Pres., 2004–06); Vice-Pres., S and W Yorks, RBL, 2004–15. Governor: Worksop Coll., 1975–2010 (Chm. of Govs, 1992–2001); Ranby House Sch., 1975–2010 (Chm. of Govs, 1992–2001); Fellow and Dir, Woodard Schs Ltd, 1981–2005. High Sheriff, S Yorks, 2003–04. *Recreations:* Burgundy, grandchildren, landscape, Romanesque, Schubert. *Address:* Ivas Wood, Round Green Lane, Stainborough, Barnsley, Yorks S75 3EL. *T:* (01226) 205325, *Fax:* (01226) 785420. *E:* davidmoody@stainborough.freeserve.co.uk. *Club:* Royal Over-Seas League.

MOODY, Ian Charles Hugh, OBE 1996; DL; Commissioner-in-Chief, St John Ambulance, 1991–95; *b* 25 April 1928; *s* of William Thomas Charles Moody and Roberta (*née* Baxter); *m* 1952, Angela de Lisle Carey (*d* 2007); one *s* two *d. Educ:* Cheltenham Coll.; RMA, Sandhurst. Served RWF, 1947–50. Industrial relations and personnel appointments with: Compania Shell de Venezuela, 1951–54; Shell Trinidad Ltd, 1954–59; Shell BP Nigeria Ltd, 1959–60; PT Shell Indonesia, 1960–64; Pakistan Shell Oil Ltd, 1964–68; Personnel Manager, Shell Nigeria Ltd, 1968–72; Employee Relations, Shell Internat. Petroleum Co. Ltd, 1974–76; Personnel Manager, Shell Internat. Trading Co., 1976–83; retd 1983. St John Ambulance, Devon: Comr, 1983–88; Comdr, 1988–91; Chm., 1995–98. Chm., E Devon Cons. Assoc., 1997–2000. FCIPD. DL Devon, 1991. KStJ 1991. *Recreations:* cricket, sailing, gardening. *Address:* The Queen Anne House, The Strand, Lympstone, Devon EX8 5JW. *T:* (01395) 263189. *Club:* MCC.

MOODY, Neil Robert; QC 2010; *b* Winchester, 1 Aug. 1965; *s* of Geoffrey and Janet Moody; *m* 1995, Nicola Ball; one *s* two *d. Educ:* Maidstone Grammar Sch.; University Coll., Oxford (BA 1987; MA 1992); Poly. of Central London (Dip. Law 1988). Called to the Bar, Gray's Inn, 1989; in practice as barrister, 1990–, specialising in commercial and common law. *Recreations:* ski-ing, sailing. *Address:* 2 Temple Gardens, EC4Y 9AY. *T:* (020) 7822 1200. *E:* nmoody@2tg.co.uk. *Clubs:* MCC; Salterns Sailing (Lymington).

MOODY-STUART, Sir Mark, KCMG 2000; PhD; FGS; FRGS; Director, Shell Transport and Trading Company plc, 1991–2005 (Chairman, 1997–2001); Chairman: Anglo American plc, 2002–09; Hermes Equity Ownership Services, since 2009; *b* 15 Sept. 1940; *s* of Sir Alexander Moody-Stuart, OBE, MC and Judith (*née* Henzell); *m* 1964, Judith McLeavy; three *s* one *d. Educ:* Shrewsbury Sch.; St John's Coll., Cambridge (MA, PhD; Hon. Fellow, 2001). Joined Shell, 1966; worked for various Shell companies in: Holland, 1966; Spain, 1967; Oman, 1968; Brunei, 1968–72; Australia, 1972–76; UK, 1977–78; Brunei, 1978–79; Nigeria, 1979–82; Turkey, 1982–86; Malaysia, 1986–89; Holland, 1990–94; Gp Man. Dir, 1991–2001, Chm., Cttee of Man. Dirs, 1998–2001, Royal Dutch/Shell Group. Director: HSBC Hldgs plc, 2001–10; Accenture, 2001–15; Saudi Aramco, 2007–; Zamyn, 2010–. Co-Chm., G-8 Task Force on Renewable Energy, 2000–01. Member: UN Sec.-Gen's Adv. Council on Global Compact, 2001–04; Bd, Global Reporting Initiative, 2001–07; UN Global Compact Bd, 2006– (Vice Chm., 2007–); Chairman: Global Business Coalition for HIV/AIDS, TB and Malaria, 2002–11; Global Compact Foundn, 2006–; Innovative Vector Control Consortium, 2008–; Hon. Co-Chm., Internat. Tax and Investment Center, 2011–. Vice-Pres., 1997–2001, Pres., 2001–08, Liverpool Sch. of Tropical Medicine; Mem. Bd, Internat. Inst. for Sustainable Develt, 2002–11. Gov., Nuffield Hosps, 2001–08. Trustee, St George's House, Windsor, 2011–. Mem., Soc. of Petroleum Engrs, 1990–; FGS 1966 (Pres., 2002–04); FInstPet 1997 (Cadman Medal, 2001); FRGS 1999. Hon. FIChemE 1997. Hon. DBA Robert Gordon, 2000; Hon. LLD Aberdeen, 2004; Hon. DSc London, 2007. *Publications:* Responsible Leadership: lessons from the front line of sustainability and ethics, 2014; papers in Geol Mag., Jl of Sedimentary Petrology, Bull. Amer. Assoc. Petrology and Geol., Norsk Polarinstitut, Proceedings of Geologists' Assoc., Corporate Environmental Strategy, Jl Corporate Citizenship. *Recreations:* sailing, travel, reading. *Address:* 9 Gun House, 122 Wapping High Street, E1W 2NL. *Clubs:* Travellers, Cruising Association.

MOOLLAN, Sir (Abdool) Hamid (Adam), Kt 1986; GOSK 2010; QC (Mauritius) 1976; Chairman, Law Reform Commission, Mauritius, 1996–2003; *b* 10 April 1933; *s* of Adam Sulliman Moollan and Khatija Moollan; *m* 1966, Sara Sidiot; three *s. Educ:* Soonee Surtee Musalman Society Aided School; Royal College School; King's College London (LLB); Faculté de Droit, Univ. de Paris. Called to the Bar, Middle Temple, 1956; joined Mauritian Bar, 1960. Chm., Bar Council, Mauritius, 1970, 1993, 2010–11. Mem., Presidential Commn for reform of judicial and legal system, Mauritius, 1997. *Recreations:* tennis, horse racing, hunting, fishing. *Address:* (home) 61 Floreal Road, Vacoas, Mauritius. *T:* 6864983; (chambers) 43 Sir William Newton Street, Port-Louis, Mauritius. *T:* 2126913. *E:* sirhamid@chambers.sirhamid.intnet.mu. *Clubs:* Royal Over-Seas League; Mauritius Gymkhana, Mauritius Turf.

MOON, Angus; *see* Moon, P. C. A.

MOON, Madeleine; MP (Lab) Bridgend, since 2005; *b* 27 March 1950; *d* of Albert Edward and Hilda Ironside; *m* Stephen John Moon (*d* 2015); one *s. Educ:* Madeley Coll. (Cert Ed 1971); Keele Univ. (BEd 1972); University Coll., Cardiff (CQSW, DipSW 1980). Social Services Directorate: Mid Glamorgan CC, 1980–96; City and Co. of Swansea, 1996–2002; Care Standards Inspectorate for Wales, 2002–05. Member (Lab): Porthcawl Town Council, 1990–2000 (Mayor, 1992–93, 1995–96); Ogwr BC, 1991–96; Bridgend CBC, 1995–2005. PPS to Minister of State, DCSF, 2007–08, to Minister of State, DECC, 2008–10. Member: Envmt, Food and Rural Affairs Select Cttee, 2005–07; Defence Select Cttee, 2009–. *Recreations:* travel, theatre, films, reading, walking, looking for things I have put in a safe place! *Address:* House of Commons, SW1A 0AA. *E:* moonm@parliament.uk.

MOON, Mary Marjorie; Head Mistress, Manchester High School for Girls, 1983–94; *b* 28 Sept. 1932; *d* of Clement Alfred Moon and Mabel Moon (*née* Berks). *Educ:* King Edward's Grammar Sch. for Girls, Camp Hill, Birmingham; Univ. of Manchester (BA Hons, MEd); Univ. of London Inst. of Education (PGCE); Buckinghamshire New Univ. (BA Creative Arts 2013). Asst English Teacher, 1955–59, Head of English Dept, 1959–63, Orme Girls' Sch., Newcastle-under-Lyme; Head of English, Bolton Sch. (Girls' Div.), 1963–71; Head Mistress, Pate's Grammar Sch. for Girls, Cheltenham, 1971–83. Mem. Court, Univ. of Manchester, 1985–2000. *Recreations:* photography, sketching, travel. *Address:* 18 South Parade, Bramhall, Stockport, Cheshire SK7 3BH.

MOON, Michael, RA 1994; artist; *b* 9 Nov. 1937; *s* of Donald and Marjorie Moon; *m* 1977, Anjum Khan; two *s. Educ:* Chelsea Sch. of Art; RCA. One-man shows include: Tate Gall., 1976; Waddington Galls, London, 1969, 1970, 1972, 1978, 1984, 1986, 1992; Macquarie Galls, Sydney, 1982; Christine Abrahams Gall., Melbourne, 1983; Pace Prints, NY, 1987; Kass/Meridien Gall., Chicago, 1988; Linda Goodman Gall., Johannesburg, 1994; Alan Cristea Gall., 1996; Serge Sirocco Gall., San Francisco, 1997; work in public collections include: Tate Gall.; Australian Nat. Gall., Canberra; Mus. of WA, Perth; Art Gall. of NSW, Sydney; Power Inst., Sydney; Walker Art Gall., Liverpool; Birmingham City Art Gall.; V&A Mus. *Address:* 61 Kirkwood Road, SE15 3XU. *T:* (020) 7639 6651.

MOON, Sir Peter Wilfred Giles Graham-, 5th Bt *cr* 1855; *b* 24 Oct. 1942; *s* of Sir (Arthur) Wilfred Graham-Moon, 4th Bt, and 2nd wife, Doris Patricia, *yr d* of Thomas Baron Jobson, Dublin; *S* father, 1954; *m* 1st, 1967, Sarah Gillian Chater (marr. diss.) (formerly *m* Major Antony Chater; marr. diss. 1966), *e d* of late Lt-Col Michael Lyndon Smith, MC, MB, BS, and Mrs Michael Smith; two *s*; 2nd, 1993, Mrs Terry de Vries, Cape Town, S Africa; 3rd, 1997, Noodaeng Samigran, Thailand; one *d. Recreations:* shooting, golf. *Heir: s* Rupert Francis Wilfred Graham-Moon, *b* 29 April 1968. *Clubs:* Royal Cork Yacht; Ecurie Cod Fillet.

MOON, (Philip Charles) Angus; QC 2006; barrister; *b* 17 Sept. 1962; *s* of Charles Moon and Liggy Quyke; *m* 1996, Florence; one *s* three *d. Educ:* King's Coll., Taunton; Christ's Coll., Cambridge (BA 1984). Called to the Bar, Middle Temple, 1986; in practice as a barrister, 1986–, specialising in medical and employment law. Editor, Medical Law Reports (Life Sciences Law Medical), 1998–. *Publications:* medical law reports. *Recreation:* novels of Elmore Leonard. *Address:* Serjeants' Inn Chambers, 85 Fleet Street, EC4Y 1AE. *T:* (020) 7427 5000.

MOON, Richard John, PhD; HM Diplomatic Service; UK Member, Advisory Committee on Administrative and Budgetary Questions, United Nations, New York, since 2011; *b* 3 Jan. 1959; *s* of late John Frederick Moon and Caroline Bowden Moon; *m* 1987, Sandra Sheila Francis Eddis (*d* 2009); one *s* one *d. Educ:* Chace Sch., Enfield; Wadham Coll., Oxford (MA); London Sch. of Econs (PhD 1994). Joined FCO, 1983; Second Sec., Jakarta, 1984–88; First Sec., FCO, 1988–93, Rome, 1993–97; FCO, 1997–99; UK Mission to UN, NY, 1999–2005; UK Delegn to OECD, Paris, 2005–07; Ambassador to Latvia, 2007–09; Project Dir, Strategy and Resource Gp, FCO, 2009–10. *Recreations:* history of art, marathon running. *Address:* c/o Foreign and Commonwealth Office, King Charles Street, SW1A 2AH.

MOON, Sir Roger, 6th Bt *cr* 1887, of Copsewood, Stoke, Co. Warwick; retired; *b* 17 Nov. 1914; *s* of Jasper Moon (*d* 1975) (*ggs* of 1st Bt) and Isabel (*née* Logan); *S* brother, 1988, but his name does not appear on the Official Roll of the Baronetage; *m* 1950, Meg (*d* 2000), *d* of late Arthur Mainwaring Maxwell, DSO, MC; three *d. Educ:* Sedbergh. Coffee planter, Kenya,

1933–35; Rubber planter, Malaya, 1939–41 and 1946–63; Oil palms planter, Malaya, 1963–67. *Recreation:* gardening. *Heir: b* Humphrey Moon [*b* 9 Oct. 1919; *m* 1st, 1955, Diana Hobson (marr. diss. 1964); two *d*; 2nd, 1964, Elizabeth Anne (*d* 1994), *d* of late George Archibald Drummond Angus and *widow* of H. J. Butler; one *d*]. *Address:* The Barn House, Wykey, Ruyton-XI-Towns, Shropshire SY4 1JA.

MOONCEY, Ebraham Mohamed; His Honour Judge Mooncey; a Circuit Judge, since 2009; *b* Jogwad, Gujarat, India; *s* of late Mohamed Gantawalla-Patel and Amina Patel; *m*; four *c*. *Educ:* Charnwood Primary Sch. and Jun. Sch., Leicester; Stoneygate Coll., Leicester; Linwood Secondary Modern Sch., Leicester; Gateway Sixth Form Coll., Leicester; Kingston Poly. (LLB Hons); Inns of Court Sch. of Law. Called to the Bar, Gray's Inn, 1983; a Recorder, 2004–09. Mem., Criminal Sub-cttee, Council of Circuit Judges, 2014–. *Recreations:* tennis, gardening.

MOONEY, Bel; writer and broadcaster; *b* 8 Oct. 1946; *d* of Edward and Gladys Mooney; *m* 1st, 1968, Jonathan Dimbleby, *qv* (marr. diss. 2006); one *s* one *d*; 2nd, 2007, Robin Allison-Smith. *Educ:* Trowbridge Girls' High School; University College London (1st cl. Hons, Eng. Lang. and Lit., 1969; Fellow 1994). Freelance journalist, 1970–79; columnist: Daily Mirror, 1979–80; Sunday Times, 1982–83; The Listener, 1984–86; The Times, 2005–07; Daily Mail, 2007–; Ed., Proof mag. (SW Arts), 2000–01; *television:* interview series: Mothers By Daughters, 1983; The Light of Experience Revisited, 1984; Fathers By Sons, 1985; Grief, 1995; various series for BBC Radio 4 (Sandford St Martin Trust award for Devout Sceptics, 1994) and films for BBC TV and Channel 4. Member, Board: Friends of Gt Ormond St, 1994–98; Theatre Royal, Bath, 2009–14. Governor, Bristol Polytechnic, 1989–91. Hon. Fellow, Liverpool John Moores Univ., 2002. Hon. DLitt Bath, 1998. *Publications: novels:* The Windsurf Boy, 1983; The Anderson Question, 1985; The Fourth of July, 1988; Lost Footsteps, 1993; Intimate Letters, 1997; The Invasion of Sand, 2005; *for children:* Liza's Yellow Boat, 1980; I Don't Want To!, 1985; The Stove Haunting, 1986; I Can't Find It!, 1988; It's Not Fair!, 1989; A Flower of Jet, 1990; But You Promised!, 1990; Why Not?, 1990; I Know!, 1991; The Voices of Silence, 1994; I'm Scared!, 1994; I Wish!, 1995; The Mouse with Many Rooms, 1995; Why Me?, 1996; The Green Man, 1997; Joining the Rainbow, 1997; I'm Bored, 1997; I Don't Want to Say Yes!, 1998; You Promised You Wouldn't be Cross, 1999; It's Not My Fault, 1999; So What?, 2002; Kitty's Big Ideas, 2002; Kitty's Friends, 2003; Mr Tubs is Lost, 2004; Who Loves Mr Tubs?, 2006; Big Dog Bonnie, 2007; Best Dog Bonnie, 2007; Bad Dog Bonnie, 2008; Brave Dog Bonnie, 2008; Busy Dog Bonnie, 2009; Bright Dog Bonnie, 2010; *miscellaneous:* The Year of the Child, 1979; Differences of Opinion (collected journalism), 1984; (with Gerald Scarfe) Father Kismass and Mother Claws, 1985; Bel Mooney's Somerset, 1989; From This Day Forward (Penguin Book of Marriage), 1989; Perspectives for Living, 1992; Devout Sceptics, 2003; (ed) Mothers and Daughters, 2006; Small Dogs Can Save Your Life (memoir), 2010; Lifelines (collection), 2015. *Recreations:* family, books, art, churches, the countryside, riding pillion on a Harley-Davidson. *Address:* c/o Daily Mail, 2 Derry Street, W8 5TS. *T:* (020) 7938 6000.

MOONEY, Kevin Michael; Partner, Simmons & Simmons, since 1972; *b* Hammersmith, 14 Nov. 1945; *s* of John Mooney and Bridget Mooney; *m* 1972, Maureen O'Hara; two *s* one *d*. *Educ:* Cardinal Vaughan Grammar Sch., Kensington; Univ. of Bristol (LLB). Admitted solicitor, 1971. Chairman: Ind. Panel on Classification of Borderline Products, 2008–13; Ind. Panel on the Advertising of Medicines, 2009–13; Rules Cttee, Unitary Patent Court, 2012–. Member: EC Expert Cttee on the Unitary Patent System, 2009–12; Expert Gp advising Preparatory Cttee on implementation of Unitary Patent Court, 2014–. *Recreations:* golf, farming in Majorca, supporting Queens Park Rangers. *Address:* 11 Trafalgar Road, Twickenham, Middx TW2 5EJ. *T:* (020) 8894 3398, (020) 7825 4480, *Fax:* (020) 7628 2070. *E:* kevin.mooney@simmons-simmons.com.

MOONEY, Patricia L.; *see* Lewsley-Mooney.

MOONIE, family name of **Baron Moonie**.

MOONIE, Baron *cr* 2005 (Life Peer), of Bennochy in Fife; **Lewis George Moonie;** *b* 25 Feb. 1947; *m* 1971, Sheila Ann Burt; two *s*. *Educ:* Grove Acad., Dundee; St Andrews Univ. (MB ChB 1970); Edinburgh Univ. (MSc 1981). MRCPsych 1979; MFCM 1984. Psychiatrist, Ciba-Geigy, Switzerland, and Organon Internat., Netherlands; Sen. Registrar (Community Medicine), subseq. Community Medicine Specialist, Fife Health Bd. Mem., Fife Regl Council, 1982–86. MP (Lab and Co-op) Kirkcaldy, 1987–2005. Opposition front bench spokesman on technology, 1990–92, on science and technol., 1992–97, and on industry, 1994–97; Parly Under-Sec. of State, 2000–03, and Minister for Veterans Affairs, 2001–03, MoD. Member: Social Services Select Cttee, 1987–89; Treasury Select Cttee, 1998–2000; H of C Commn, 1997; H of L Select Cttee on Econ. Affairs, 2007–12; Chm., Finance and Services Cttee, 1997–2000. Non-exec. Dir, Bwin.Party plc (formerly PartyGaming), 2007–. *Address:* House of Lords, SW1A 0PW.

MOONMAN, Eric, OBE 1991; Chairman, Essex Radio Group, 1991–2002; Visiting Professor, University of Liverpool, 2007–09 (Visiting Fellow, 2005–07); *b* 29 April 1929; *s* of late Borach and Leah Moonman; *m* 1st, 1962, Jane (marr. diss. 1991); two *s* one *d*; 2nd, 2001, Gillian Louise Mayer. *Educ:* Rathbone Sch., Liverpool; Christ Church, Southport; Univ. of Liverpool (DipSocSc 1955; Sen. Hon. Fellow, 2005); Univ. of Manchester (MSc 1967). Human Relations Adviser, British Inst. of Management, 1956–62; Sen. Lectr in Industrial Relations, SW Essex Technical Coll., 1962–64; Sen. Research Fellow in Management Sciences, Univ. of Manchester, 1964–66. MP (Lab) Billericay, 1966–70, Basildon, Feb. 1974–1979; PPS to Minister without Portfolio and Sec. of State for Educn, 1967–68. Chairman: All-Party Parly Mental Health Cttee, 1967–70 and 1974–79; New Towns and Urban Affairs Cttee, Parly Labour Party, 1974–79. Exec. Mem., Former Mems of Parlt Assoc., 2006–. Dir, Centre for Contemporary Studies, 1979–90; Dir, Nat. Hist. Mus. Develt Trust, 1990–91. Vis. Prof. of Mgt and Inf., City Univ., 1992–2011. Sen. Vice-Pres., Bd of Deputies, 1985–91, 1994–99; Pres., Zionist Fedn, 2001– (Chm., 1975–80). Member: Stepney Council, 1961–65 (Leader, 1964–65); Tower Hamlets Council, 1964–67. Chm., Islington HA, 1981–90; Mem., Bloomsbury and Islington HA, 1990–92; Chair, City of Liverpool Continuing Health Care Rev., 1996–2009. Mem. Adv. Council, Centre for Counter-Terrorism, Washington, 1998–; Advr on Counter-Terrorism, ITV News and Ind. Radio News, 2001–11. Mem., Council, Toynbee Hall Univ. Settlement, 1960–95 (Chm., Finance Cttee, 1980–95); Governor, BFI, 1974–80. Consultant, Internat. Red Cross (Namibia), 1991–95. Trustee: Balfour Diamond Jubilee Trust, 1985–2000; Winnicott Trust, 1990–93; Everton Former Players' Foundn, 2011–. FRSA. *Publications:* The Manager and the Organization, 1961; Employee Security, 1962; European Science and Technology, 1968; Communication in an Expanding Organization, 1970; Reluctant Partnership, 1970; Alternative Government, 1984; (ed) The Violent Society, 1987; Learning to Live in the Violent Society, 2006. *Recreations:* football (Chm., Everton Supporters' Club London Assoc., 1992–2014), theatre, music, cinema. *Address:* 1 Beacon Hill, N7 9LY.

MOOR, Jonathan Edward, CBE 2011; FCA; Director General, Resources and Strategy, Department for Transport, since 2013; *b* 23 June 1964; *s* of late Rev. David Drury Moor and Evangeline Moor (*née* White); *m* 1990, Sara Louise Stratton (marr. diss. 2015); three *d*. *Educ:* Canford Sch.; Univ. of Kent at Canterbury (BA Hons (Geog.) 1985). ACA 1989, FCA 2000. Trainee, subseq. Audit Manager, Touche Ross & Co., 1985–91; Audit Manager, Dist Audit, 1991–94; Audit Commission: Resources Sen. Manager, 1994–97; Associate Dir of Finance and Corporate Planning, 1997–2000; Finance Dir, 2000–03; Department for Transport: Finance Dir, 2003–04, Dir of Strategy and Resources, 2004–05, Driver, Vehicle and Operator Gp; Dir of Airports Strategy, 2006–08; Dir Gen., Civil Aviation, 2009–13. *Recreations:* travel, DIY, family. *Address:* Department for Transport, Great Minster House, 33 Horseferry Road, SW1P 4DR. *T:* (020) 7944 4597. *E:* jonathan.moor@dft.gsi.gov.uk.

See also Hon. Sir P. D. Moor.

MOOR, Hon. Sir Philip Drury, Kt 2011; **Hon. Mr Justice Moor;** a Judge of the High Court of Justice, Family Division, since 2011; Family Division Liaison Judge for Wales, since 2012; *b* 15 July 1959; *s* of late Rev. David Drury Moor and Evangeline Moor (*née* White); *m* 1987, Gillian Stark; two *d*. *Educ:* Canford Sch.; Pembroke Coll., Oxford (MA; Hon. Fellow 2014). Called to the Bar, Inner Temple, 1982, Bencher, 2004; QC 2001; a Recorder, 2002–11; a Dep. High Ct Judge, 2009–11. Hd of Chambers, 2007–11. Member: Cttee, Family Law Bar Assoc., 1987–2009 (Actg Treas., 2000–01; Vice-Chm., 2002–03, Chm., 2004–05); Gen. Council of the Bar, 1987–89, 2004–05 (Mem., 2002–03, Vice-Chm., 2003, Professional Standards Cttee); Council of Legal Educn, 1988–91 (Mem. Bd of Examrs, 1989–92). Chm., Inner Temple Scholarship Cttee, 2010–12. Gov., Royal Russell Sch., Croydon, 2009–. Trustee, Gingerbread, 2010–11. *Recreations:* cricket, Association football, Rugby football. *Address:* Royal Courts of Justice, Strand, WC2A 2LL. *Club:* MCC.

See also J. E. Moor.

MOOR, Dr Robert Michael, FRS 1994; Head of Protein Function Laboratory, Babraham Institute, 1996–99; *b* 28 Sept. 1937; *s* of Donald C. Moor and Gwendolen (*née* Whitby); *m* 1962, Felicia Alison Elizabeth Stephens; four *d*. *Educ:* Estcourt, Natal, S Africa; Gonville and Caius Coll., Cambridge Univ. (PhD 1965; ScD). Senior Scientist, ARC Unit of Reproductive Physiology and Biochemistry, 1965–86; Head, Dept of Molecular Embryology, AFRC Inst. of Animal Physiology and Genetics Res., 1986–93; Dep. Dir, Babraham Inst., 1993–97. Hon. Fellow, Italian Vet. Assoc., 1990. Hon. Dr Univ. of Milan, 1990. *Publications:* numerous contribs to learned jls. *Recreations:* mountaineering, music. *Address:* 19 Thornton Close, Cambridge CB3 0NF. *T:* (01223) 276669. *Club:* Alpino Italiano (Milan).

MOORBATH, Prof. Stephen Erwin, DPhil, DSc; FRS 1977; Professor of Isotope Geology, Oxford University, 1992–96, now Emeritus Professor; Professorial Fellow of Linacre College, 1990–96, now Emeritus Fellow (Fellow, 1970–90); *b* 9 May 1929; *s* of Heinz Moosbach and Else Moosbach; *m* 1962, Pauline Tessier-Varlêt; one *s* one *d*. *Educ:* Lincoln Coll., Oxford Univ. (MA 1957, DPhil 1959). DSc Oxon 1969. Asst Experimental Officer, AERE, Harwell, 1948–51; Undergrad., Oxford Univ., 1951–54; Scientific Officer, AERE, Harwell, 1954–56; Research Fellow: Oxford Univ., 1956–61; MIT, 1961–62; Sen. Res. Officer, 1962–78, Reader in Geology, 1978–92, Oxford Univ. Wollaston Fund, Geol Soc. of London, 1968; Liverpool Geol Soc. Medal, 1968; Murchison Medal, Geol Soc. of London, 1978; Steno Medal, Geol Soc. of Denmark, 1979. *Publications:* contribs to scientific jls and books. *Recreations:* music, philately, travel, linguistics. *Address:* 53 Bagley Wood Road, Kennington, Oxford OX1 5LY. *T:* (01865) 739507.

MOORCOCK, Michael John; author, since 1956; *b* 18 Dec. 1939; *s* of Arthur Moorcock and June Moorcock (*née* Taylor); *m* 1st, 1962, Hilary Bailey (marr. diss. 1978); one *s* two *d*; 2nd, 1978, Jill Riches (marr. diss. 1983); 3rd, 1983, Linda Mullens Steele. *Educ:* Michael Hall, Sussex; Pitman's Coll., Surrey. Ed., Tarzan Adventures, 1956–58; Asst Ed., Sexton Blake Liby, 1959–61; travelled as singer/guitarist in Scandinavia and W Europe, 1961–62; ed. and pamphlet writer for Liberal Party pubns dept, 1962–63; Ed., New Worlds, 1963–80 (Publisher, 1980–); writer and vocalist for Hawkwind, 1971–; writer, vocalist and fretted instruments for Deep Fix; vocalist and instrumentalist for Robert Calvert; writer for Blue Oyster Cult, and associated with various other bands. Has made recordings. *Publications:* books include: Byzantium Endures, 1981; The Laughter of Carthage, 1984; Mother London, 1988; Jerusalem Commands, 1992; Blood, 1994; Fabulous Harbours, 1995; The War Amongst the Angels, 1996; Tales from the Texas Woods, 1997; King of the City, 2000; (with Storm Constantine) Silverheart, 2000; London Bone, 2001; The Dreamthief's Daughter, 2001; Firing the Cathedral, 2002; The Skrayling Tree, 2003; The Life and Times of Jerry Cornelius, 2003; The Vengeance of Rome, 2006; The Metatemporal Detectives, 2007; Elric: the stealer of souls, 2008; The Best of Michael Moorcock, 2009; Hawkmoon: the mad god's amulet, 2010; Into the Media Web: selected short non-fiction, 1956–2006, 2010; The Whispering Swarm, 2015; various omnibus edns of novels; ed numerous anthologies, collections and short stories. *Recreations:* walking, mountaineering, travel. *Address:* c/o Morhaim, 30 Pierrepont Street, Brooklyn, NY 11201, USA. *T:* (718) 222 8400; c/o Nomads Association, 21 Honor Oak Road, Honor Oak, SE23 3SH; c/o Hoffman, 77 Boulevard St Michel, 75005 Paris, France. *Club:* Royal Over-Seas League.

MOORCRAFT, Dennis Harry; Under-Secretary, Inland Revenue, 1975–81; *b* 14 Aug. 1921; *s* of late Harry Moorcraft and Dorothy Moorcraft (*née* Simmons); *m* 1945, Ingeborg Utne (*d* 2000), Bergen, Norway; one *s* one *d*. *Educ:* Gillingham County Grammar Sch. Tax Officer, Inland Revenue, 1938. RNVR, 1940–46. Inspector of Taxes, 1948; Sen. Inspector of Taxes, 1956; Principal Inspector of Taxes, 1963. *Recreations:* gardening, garden construction, croquet, music.

MOORCROFT, David Robert, OBE 1999 (MBE 1983); Co-Founder, pointfourone sports consultancy, 2007; Chief Executive, UK Athletics, 1997–2007; *b* 10 April 1953; *s* of Robert Moorcroft and Mildred Moorcroft (*née* Hardy); *m* 1975, Linda Ann, *d* of John Ward; one *s* one *d*. *Educ:* Woodlands Comp. Sch.; Tile Hill Coll. of Further Educn; Loughborough Univ. (BEd 1976). School teacher, 1976–81. Athlete: Olympic Games: finalist, 1,500m, Montreal, 1976; semi-finalist, 5,000m, Moscow, 1980; finalist, 5,000m, Los Angeles, 1984; Commonwealth Games: Gold Medal, 1,500m, Edinburgh, 1974, Edmonton, 1978; Gold Medal, 5,000m, Brisbane, 1982; European Championships: Bronze Medal, 1,500m, Prague, 1978; Bronze Medal, 5,000m, Athens, 1982; Europa Cup: Gold Medal, 5,000m, Zagreb, 1981; set world record for 5,000m, Oslo, 1982, European record for 3,000m, Crystal Palace, 1982. Commentator, BBC TV and radio, 1983–97. Chief Executive: Coventry Sports Foundn, 1981–95 (Trustee, 1995–); British Athletic Federation Ltd, 1997; UK Athletics 98, 1998; Dir of Sport, Join In, 2012–.

MOORCROFT, Sir William, KBE 2008; Principal, Trafford College (formerly South Trafford College), since 2003; *b* Liverpool, 17 Feb. 1958; *s* of Robert and Diane Jane Moorcroft; *m* 1990, Wendy Anne Clarehugh; one *s*. *Educ:* Manchester Metropolitan Univ. (MA Mgt); Bolton Inst. (Cert Ed). MHCIMA 1992. Exec. Chef, Littlewoods Orgn, 1979–83; Lectr, Southport Coll., 1983–91; Nat. Chief Verifier, City & Guilds, 1991–94; Hd of Dept, 1994–97, Vice Prin., 1997–2002, South Trafford Coll., subseq. Trafford Coll. Member, Board: Learning and Skills Improvement Service, 2008–; Lancs County Cricket Foundn. *Recreation:* golf. *Address:* Trafford College, Manchester Road, Altrincham WA14 5PQ. *Club:* Southport and Ainsdale Golf.

MOORE, family name of **Earl of Drogheda** and **Baron Moore of Lower Marsh**.

MOORE, Viscount; Benjamin Garrett Henderson Moore; *b* 21 March 1983; *s* and *heir* of Earl of Drogheda, *qv*. *Educ:* Pro Corda; Eton; Peterhouse, Cambridge; Universität der Kunste Berlin. *Address:* 40c Ledbury Road, W11 2AB.

MOORE OF LOWER MARSH, Baron *cr* 1992 (Life Peer), of Lower Marsh in the London Borough of Lambeth; **John Edward Michael Moore;** PC 1986; *b* 26 Nov. 1937; *s* of Edward O. Moore; *m* 1962, Sheila Sarah Tillotson (*d* 2008); two *s* one *d*. *Educ:* London Sch. of Economics (BSc Econ). Nat. Service, Royal Sussex Regt, Korea, 1955–57 (commnd). Chm. Conservative Soc., LSE, 1958–59; Pres. Students' Union, LSE, 1959–60. Took part in expedn from N Greece to India overland tracing Alexander's route, 1960. In Banking and Stockbroking instns, Chicago, 1961–65; Democratic Precinct Captain, Evanston, Ill, USA, 1962; Democratic Ward Chm. Evanston, Illinois, 1964; Dir, 1968–79, Chm., 1975–79, Dean Witter Internat. Ltd. An Underwriting Mem. of Lloyds, 1978–92. Councillor (C), London Borough of Merton, 1971–74; Chm., Stepney Green Cons. Assoc., 1968. MP (C) Croydon Central, Feb. 1974–1992. A Vice-Chm., Conservative Party, 1975–79; Parly Under-Sec. of State, Dept of Energy, 1979–83; HM Treasury: Economic Sec., June–Oct. 1983; Financial Sec., 1983–86; Secretary of State: for Transport, 1986–87; for Social Services, 1987–88; for Social Security, 1988–89. Chairman: Credit Suisse Asset Mgt, 1991–2000; Energy Saving Trust Ltd, 1992–95 (Pres., 1995–2001); Director: Marvin & Palmer Associates Inc., 1989–2014; Monitor Inc., 1990–2006 (Chm., Monitor Europe, 1990–2006); Gartmore Investment Management, 1990–92; GTECH Corp., 1992–2001; Swiss American Inc., 1992–96; Blue Circle Industries, 1993–2001; Camelot PLC, 1994–96; Rolls-Royce plc, 1994–2005 (Dep. Chm., 1996–2003, Chm., 2003–05); BEA Associates, USA, 1996–98; Private Client Bank (formerly Private Client Partners), Zurich, 1999–2003; Chm. Trustees, Rolls-Royce Pension Fund, 1998–2007. Member: Adv. Bd, Sir Alexander Gibb & Partners, 1990–95; Supervisory Bd, ITT Automotive Europe GmbH (Germany), 1994–97. Mem. Council, Inst. of Dirs, 1991–2002. Mem. Ct of Governors, LSE, 1977–2002. *Address:* House of Lords, SW1A 0PW.

MOORE, Alan Edward, CBE 1980; Deputy Chairman: Lloyds TSB Group plc, 1998–2003 (Director, 1995–2003); Lloyds Bank Plc, 1998–2003 (Director, 1989–2003); TSB Bank plc, 1998–2003; *b* 5 June 1936; *s* of late Charles Edward and Ethel Florence Moore; *m* 1961, Margaret Patricia Beckley; one *s* one *d. Educ:* Berkhamsted Sch. FCIB, FCIS, FCT. Glyn Mills & Co., then Williams & Glyn's Bank, London, 1953–74; Dir Gen., Bahrain Monetary Agency, 1974–79; Dir and Treas., Lloyds Bank Internat., 1980–84; Dir of Treasury, Lloyds Bank, 1985–88; Dir of Corporate Banking and Treasury, Lloyds Bank, 1988–94; Dep. Chief Exec. and Treas., Lloyds Bank, 1994–98; Dep. Gp Chief Exec. and Treas., Lloyds TSB Gp plc, 1995–98. *Recreations:* photography, railway history, travel.

MOORE, Anthony Michael Frederick, (Anthony Michaels-Moore); baritone; *b* 8 April 1957; *s* of John Moore and Isabel (*née* Shephard); *m* 1st, 1980, Ewa Migocki (marr. diss. 2004); one *d*; 2nd, 2010, Emily Doyle Schluter; one *d. Educ:* Newcastle Univ. (BA Hons 1978); Royal Scottish Acad. of Music and Drama. First British winner, Pavarotti Comp., 1985. *Débuts:* Opera North, 1986; Royal Opera House, Covent Garden, 1987; Vienna State Opera, 1993; La Scala, Milan, 1993; Paris Opera, 1994; Buenos Aires, 1996; Metropolitan, NY, 1996; San Francisco, 1997; Chicago, 2000; Glyndebourne, 2001. *Rôles* include: Marcello, Belcore, Escamillo, Posa, Hamlet, Falke, Lescaut, Simon Boccanegra, Scarpia, Figaro, Orestes, Onegin, Rigoletto, Macbeth, Montforte, Ford, Ezio, Iago. Recordings incl. Carmina Burana, Lucia di Lammermoor, Falstaff, Aroldo, and La Favorite. Royal Philharmonic Soc. Award, 1997. *Recreations:* road bikes, cricket, swimming, spicy food. *Address:* c/o Intermusica, Crystal Wharf, N1 8GJ.

MOORE, Prof. Brian Cecil Joseph, PhD; FRS 2002; FMedSci; Professor of Auditory Perception, University of Cambridge, 1995–2014, now Emeritus; Fellow of Wolfson College, Cambridge, 1983–2013, now Emeritus; *b* 10 Feb. 1946; *s* of Cecil George Moore and Maria Anna Moore. *Educ:* St Catharine's Coll., Cambridge (BA Nat. Sci. 1968; PhD Exptl Psychol. 1971). Lectr in Psychology, Reading Univ., 1971–77; Vis. Prof., Brooklyn Coll., NY, 1973–74; University of Cambridge: Lectr in Experimental Psychology, 1977–89; Reader in Auditory Perception, 1989–95. FMedSci 2001. Fellow, Acoustical Soc. of America, 1985; Hon. Fellow, Belgian Soc. of Audiology, 1997; Hon. Fellow, British Soc. of Hearing Aid Audiologists, 1999. *Publications:* An Introduction to the Psychology of Hearing, 1977, 6th edn 2012; Frequency Selectivity in Hearing, 1986; Perceptual Consequences of Cochlear Damage, 1995; Hearing, 1995; Cochlear Hearing Loss, 1998, 2nd edn 2007; The Perception of Speech: from sound to meaning, 2007; Multistability in Perception: binding sensory modalities, 2012; Auditory Processing of Temporal Fine Structure: effects of age and hearing loss, 2014. *Recreations:* music, playing the guitar, bridge, fixing things. *Address:* Department of Experimental Psychology, University of Cambridge, Downing Street, Cambridge CB2 3EB. *T:* (01223) 333574.

MOORE, Charles Hilary; journalist and author; Consulting Editor, The Telegraph Group, since 2004; *b* 31 Oct. 1956; *s* of Richard and Ann Moore; *m* 1981, Caroline Mary Baxter; twin *s* and *d. Educ:* Eton Coll.; Trinity Coll., Cambridge (MA Hons History). Joined editorial staff of Daily Telegraph, 1979, leader writer, 1981–83; Assistant Editor and political columnist, 1983–84, Editor, 1984–90, The Spectator; weekly columnist, Daily Express, 1987–90; Dep. Editor, Daily Telegraph, 1990–92; Editor: The Sunday Telegraph, 1992–95; The Daily Telegraph, 1995–2003. Chm., Policy Exchange, 2005–11. Chm., Rectory Soc., 2005–. Mem. Council, Benenden Sch., 2000–09. Hon. PhD Buckingham, 2006. Luca de Tena Prize, 2011. *Publications:* (ed with C. Hawtree) 1936, 1986; (with A. N. Wilson and G. Stamp) The Church in Crisis, 1986; (ed with Simon Heffer) A Tory Seer: the selected journalism of T. E. Utley, 1989; Margaret Thatcher: the authorized biography, vol. 1: not for turning, 2013 (Elizabeth Longford Prize for Histl Biog., Paddy Power Political Book of Year, 2014). *Recreation:* hunting. *Address:* c/o The Daily Telegraph, 111 Buckingham Palace Road, SW1W 0DT. *T:* (020) 7931 2000. *Clubs:* Beefsteak, White's.

MOORE, Cicely Frances, (Mrs H. D. Moore); *see* Berry, C. F.

MOORE, David James Ladd; Partnership Secretary, Freshfields, 1993–98; *b* 6 June 1937; *s* of James and Eilonwy Moore; *m* 1968, Kay Harrison; two *s. Educ:* King Edward VI Sch., Nuneaton; Brasenose Coll., Oxford (BA); Birkbeck Coll., Univ. of London (BA (History of Art) 2003; MA History 2005). PO, 1961–67 (Asst Principal 1961, Principal 1966); Cabinet Office, 1967–69; HM Treasury, 1969–80 (Asst Sec. 1973); Under Secretary: Cabinet Office, 1980–82; HM Treasury, 1982–83; Inland Revenue (Principal Finance Officer), 1983–85; HM Treasury, 1985–93. *Recreations:* cinema, tennis, history of art, theatre. *Address:* 183 Hampstead Way, NW11 7YB.

MOORE, Prof. David Robert, PhD; Professor of Otolaryngology, University of Cincinnati, since 2013; Director, Communication Sciences Research Center, Cincinnati Children's Hospital, since 2013; *b* 19 July 1953; *s* of William Leonard Moore and Joan Moore (*née* Kerr); *m* 1976, Victoria Doloughan (marr. diss. 2014); one *d. Educ:* Monash Univ., Victoria (BSc; PhD). NIH Internat. Fellow, Univ. of Calif, Irvine, 1983–84; University of Oxford: MRC Sen. Fellow, 1986–89; Res. Lectr, 1989–96; Reader, 1996–99; Prof. of Auditory Neurosci., 1999–2002; Dir, MRC Inst. of Hearing Res., 2002–13. Co-Founder, NIHR Nottingham Hearing Biomed. Res. Unit, 2008. Vis. Prof., Univ. of Washington, Seattle, 1992; Vis. Schol., Center for Neural Sci., NY Univ., 1997. *Publications:* numerous peer-reviewed scientific contribs to internat. jls. *Recreations:* food and wine, cycling, family interests. *Address:* Communication Sciences Research Center, Cincinnati Children's Hospital Medical Center, 3333 Burnet Avenue, Cincinnati, OH 45229–3039, USA. *Club:* Yarragon Axe (Victoria, Australia).

MOORE, Derry; *see* Drogheda, Earl of.

MOORE, Most Rev. Desmond Charles, KBE 1996; former Bishop of Alotau, Papua New Guinea (RC); *b* Adelaide, 12 May 1926; *s* of Edwin John Moore and Margaret Mary Leahy. *Educ:* Christian Brothers Sch., Adelaide; Adelaide Univ.; Sacred Heart Monastery, Croydon, Vic. Entered novitiate, 1950, professed mem., 1951–, Congregation of Missionaries of the Sacred Heart of Jesus; ordained priest, 1957; Bursar and Assistant to Novice Master, St Mary's Towers Monastery, Douglas Park, 1958–61; Assistant to Parish Priest, Port Moresby, PNG, 1961–62; first Parish Priest, Boregaina Village, Rigo, 1962–67; Parish Priest, St Joseph's, Boroko, and Religious Superior, Missionaries of the Sacred Heart of Jesus, dio. of Port Moresby, 1967–70; cons. Bishop of Sideia, 1970, name of dio. changed to Alotau, 1977; retired, 2001. *Address:* Sacred Heart Monastery, 1 Roma Avenue, Kensington, NSW 2033, Australia. *T:* (2) 96627188. *T:* and *Fax:* (2) 93865206. *E:* desmondmoore@gmail.com.

MOORE, (Douglas) Marks; His Honour Judge Marks Moore; a Circuit Judge, since 2007; *b* 31 Jan. 1950; *s* of Douglas Moore and Josephine Moore (*née* Ritchie); *m* 1st, 1983, Susan Clayton (marr. diss. 2010); one *s* three *d*; 2nd, 2013, Maria Paris-Ketting. *Educ:* Regent House Sch., NI; Queen's Univ., Belfast (BA 1972; Dip. Soc. Anthropol. 1973); RMA Sandhurst; Inns of Court Sch. of Law. Subaltern, Irish Guards, 1974–76. Called to the Bar, 1979; Tenant in Chambers of Roy Amlot, QC, 6 King's Bench Walk; Recorder, 1998–2007; Senior Trial Attorney, Office of the Prosecutor: Internat. Criminal Tribunal for Rwanda, 2001–03, with responsibility for prosecution of former members of Hutu Govt and for the Special Investigation concerning alleged atrocities committed by the Rwandan Patriotic Front; Internat. Criminal Tribunal for Yugoslavia, The Hague, 2005–07, with responsibility for prosecution of former sen. Yugoslav officers involved in atrocities in Vukovar, Croatia. *Recreations:* fishing, golf, squash. *Address:* Isleworth Crown Court, 36 Ridgeway Road, Isleworth TW7 5LP. *Club:* Muthaiga Country (Kenya).

MOORE, Sir Francis Thomas, (Sir Frank), Kt 1983; AO 1991; Chairman, Asia-Pacific Economic Cooperation International Centre for Sustainable Tourism, since 2000; *b* 28 Nov. 1930; *m* 1972, Norma Shearer; two *s. Educ:* Nudgee Coll. Licensed Valuer, 1952–2008; Man. Dir, Radio Broadcasting Network of Queensland, 1957–78; Director: Universal Telecasters Qld Ltd, 1961–80; Trust Co. Australia Ltd, 1983–96; Chm., Nature Resorts Ltd, 1997–2002. Chairman: Queensland Tourist and Travel Corp., 1979–90; Tourism Council of Australia (formerly Australian Tourism Industry Assoc.), 1983–95; Nat. Centre for Studies in Travel and Tourism, 1987–94; Taylor Byrne Tourism Gp, 1990–2002; Tourism Forecasting Council, 1996–2003; Co-op. Res. Centre for Sustainable Tourism, 1997–2008; Dir, Gold Coast Airport Ltd, 2001–04; Mem., World Travel and Tourism Council, 1992–. *Address:* GPO Box 1150, Brisbane, Qld 4001, Australia.

MOORE, (Georgina) Mary; Principal, St Hilda's College, Oxford, 1980–90, Hon. Fellow, 1990; *b* 8 April 1930; *yr d* of late Prof. V. H. Galbraith, FBA, and late Georgina Rosalie Galbraith (*née* Cole-Baker); *m* 1963, Antony Ross Moore, CMG (*d* 2000); one *s. Educ:* The Mount Sch., York; Lady Margaret Hall, Oxford (BA Modern History 1951; MA; Hon. Fellow, 1981). Joined HM Foreign (later Diplomatic) Service, 1951; posted to Budapest, 1954; UK Permanent Delegn to United Nations, New York, 1956; FO, 1959; First Secretary, 1961; resigned on marriage. Mem., Council for Industry and Higher Educn, 1986–90. A Trustee: British Museum, 1982–92; Rhodes Trust, 1984–96; Pilgrim Trust, 1991–2005 (Chm., 1993–2005). JP Bucks, 1977–82. Hon. LLD Mount Holyoke Coll., 1991. Under the name Helena Osborne writes plays for television and radio. *Publications:* (as Helena Osborne): *novels:* The Arcadian Affair, 1969; Pay-Day, 1972; White Poppy, 1977; The Joker, 1979. *Recreations:* theatre, travel. *Address:* Touchbridge, Brill, Aylesbury, Bucks HP18 9UJ. *T:* and *Fax:* (01844) 238247. *Club:* University Women's.

MOORE, Gillian, MBE 1994; Head of Classical Music, Southbank Centre, since 2011; *b* 20 Feb. 1959; *m* 2001, Bruce Nockles; one *s* one *d. Educ:* Univ. of Glasgow (BMus Hons 1980); Univ. of York (MA 1981). Educn Officer, London Sinfonietta, 1983–93; Hd of Educn, Southbank Centre, 1993–98; Artistic Dir, ISCM World Music Days, 1998; Dir, London Sinfonietta, 1998–2006; Hd of Contemporary Culture, Southbank Centre, 2006–11. Member, Council: RCM; Royal Philharmonic Soc. Hon. ARAM, 2003. FRCM. Hon. FGS. Hon. DMus Brunel, 2006. *Address:* Southbank Centre, Belvedere Road, SE1 8XX. *T:* (020) 7921 0897. *E:* gillian.moore@southbankcentre.co.uk.

MOORE, Graham, QPM 1997; Chief Constable, West Yorkshire Police, 1998–2002; *b* 15 Jan. 1947; *s* of Graham and Kate Moore; *m* 1965, Susan Fletcher; one *s* one *d. Educ:* Brunts GS, Mansfield; Warwick Univ. (BA Hons Philosophy and Lit. 1975). Professional musician; Police Constable, Birmingham City Police, 1969–72; Inspector of Taxes, Inland Revenue, 1975–77; joined W Midlands Police, 1977; Asst Chief Constable, S Yorks Police, 1991–94; Dep. Chief Constable, Cambs Constabulary, 1994–98. *Recreations:* music, reading, tennis, shooting.

MOORE, Prof. Henrietta Louise, PhD; FBA 2007; Professor of Culture, Philosophy and Design, and Director, UCL Institute for Global Prosperity, University College London, since 2014; *b* Saunderton, 18 May 1957; *d* of Stephen Andrew Moore and Josephine Anne Jane Mary Moore. *Educ:* Univ. of Durham (BA Archaeol. and Anthropol. 1979); Newnham Coll., Cambridge (PhD 1983). Field Dir, UNA, Burkina Faso, 1983–84; Curatorial Asst for Anthropol., Univ. Mus. of Archaeol. and Anthropol., Cambridge, 1984–85; Lectr in Soc. Anthropol., Univ. of Kent, Canterbury, 1985–86; Lectr in Soc. Anthropol., 1986–88, Manager, African Studies Centre, 1987–90, Univ. of Cambridge; Lectr and Dir of Studies in Soc. Anthropol., Girton Coll., 1986–88; Fellow and Lectr in Anthropol. and Soc. and Pol Scis, Pembroke Coll., 1989–90; London School of Economics and Political Science: Lectr, 1990–93, Reader, 1993–97, in Soc. Anthropol.; Prof. of Soc. Anthropol., 1997–2008; Dir, Gender Inst., 1994–99; Dir, Culture and Communication Prog., Centre for Global Governance, 2005–11; Gov., 1999–2005; Dep. Dir, 2002–05; William Wyse Prof. of Social Anthropology, Univ. of Cambridge, 2008–14; Fellow, Jesus Coll., Cambridge, 2009–14. Fellow: Centre for Globalization and Policy Res., Sch. of Public Affairs, UCLA, 2005–11; Goodenough Coll., Univ. of London, 2005–; Maj. Res. Fellow, Leverhulme Trust, London, 2007–10. Visiting Professor: Univ. of Bergen, 1988; Univ. of Bremen, 1990; Univ. of Calif, Berkeley, 1994, 1997; Univ. of Porto, 2004; Vis. Lectr, Univ. of Witwatersrand, 1992. Co-Founder and Chm. Bd, SHM Productions Ltd, 1996–; Founder Trustee, SHM Foundn, 2007–. Member: Adv. Bd for Global Coalition on Africa, Min. of For. Affairs, Netherlands, 1994–95; Educn Cttee, Catholic Inst. for Internat. Relns, 1995–98; Bd of Res. Counsellors, Foundn for Advanced Studies on Internat. Devel t, Tokyo, 1996–99; Bd of Social Enterprise, London, 2002–04; Scientific Council, Eur. Res. Council, 2009–13; Chm. Wkg Gp, Best Practice for Social Enterprise, DTI, 2001–02. FRAI 1981 (Mem. Council, 1989–92); Member: African Studies Assoc., 1986– (Mem. Council, 1986–89); Assoc. of Social Anthropologists of UK and Commonwealth, 1986– (Hon. Sec., 1991–94); Amer. Assoc. of Anthropologists, 2004–; Council, British Acad., 2012–. Trustee, Barbican Centre, 2011–. FRSA 2000; FAcSS (AcSS 2001); MInstD 2002. *Publications:* Space, Text and Gender: an anthropological study of the Marakwet of Kenya, 1986, 2nd edn 1996; Feminism and Anthropology, 1988; (with M. A. Vaughan) Cutting Down Trees: gender, nutrition and change in the Northern Provinces of Zambia, 1890–1990, 1994 (Herskovits Prize, African Studies Assoc., USA, 1995); A Passion for Difference: essays in anthropology and gender, 1994; (ed) The Future of Anthropological Knowledge, 1996; (ed) Promoting the Health of Children and Young People: setting a research agenda, 1998; (ed jtly) Those Who Play with Fire: gender and fertility in Africa, 1999; (ed) Anthropological Theory Today, 1999; (ed with D. T. Sanders) Magical Interpretations, Material Realities: modernity, witchcraft and the occult in post colonial Africa, 2001; (with Ed Mayo) The Mutual State and How to Build It, 2001; (ed with D. T. Sanders) Anthropology in Theory: issues in epistemology, 2005; The Subject of Anthropology: gender, symbolism and psychoanalysis, 2007; (ed with David Held) Cultural Politics in a Global Age: uncertainty, solidarity and innovation, 2008; Still Life: hopes, desires and satisfactions, 2011; (ed with N. Long) Sociality: new comparative approaches, 2012; (ed with P. Aggleton, P. Boyce and R. Parker) Understanding Global

Sexualities, 2012; (ed with M. Kaldor and S. Selchow) Global Civil Society 2012: ten years of critical reflection, 2012; (ed with N. Long) The Social Life of Achievement, 2013. *Recreations:* relaxing, thinking, theatre, opera, walking. *Address:* UCL Institute for Global Prosperity, University College London, Gower Street, WC1E 6BT. *Club:* Groucho.

MOORE, Rt Rev. Henry Wylie; General Secretary, Church Missionary Society, 1986–89; Assistant Bishop, Durham, 1990–94; *b* 2 Nov. 1923; *m* 1951, Betty Rose Basnett; two *s* three *d. Educ:* Univ. of Liverpool (BCom 1950); Wycliffe Hall, Oxford; MA (Organization Studies) Leeds, 1972. LMS Railway Clerk, 1940–42. Served War with King's Regt (Liverpool), 1942–43; Rajputana Rifles, 1943–46. Curate: Farnworth, Widnes, 1952–54; Middleton, 1954–56; CMS, Khuzistan, 1956–59; Rector: St Margaret, Burnage, 1960–63; Middleton, 1963–74; Home Sec. and later Executive Sec., CMS, 1974–83; Bishop in Cyprus and the Gulf, 1983–86. *Recreation:* family life. *Address:* Fernhill Cottage, Hopesay, Craven Arms, Shropshire SY7 8HD.

MOORE, James Antony Axel Herring, OBE 1998; Executive Director, US-UK Educational Commission (Fulbright Commission), 1993–2002; *b* 26 April 1940; *s* of late Lieut A. D. W. Moore, RN (killed HMS Audacity, 1941) and Agneta Moore (*née* Wachtmeister); *m* 1964, Marianne Jerlström; two *s* one *d. Educ:* Wellington Coll.; Trinity Coll., Cambridge (MA); London Univ. Inst. of Educn (PGCE). Teacher: Norway, 1962–63; Thailand, 1964–67; British Council: Warsaw, 1967–70; Beirut, 1971–73; Ottawa, 1973–75; London, 1975–80; Chinese lang. trng, 1980–81; Director: Manila, 1981–85; Copenhagen, 1985–89; General Manager, Fellowships and Scholarships, 1990–93. *Recreations:* music, ski-ing, walking, languages. *Address:* 7 Brook Lane, Lindfield, Haywards Heath RH16 1SF.

See also Vice-Adm. Sir M. A. C. Moore.

MOORE, Jeremy Patrick; Director General, Strategy, Policy and Analysis, Department for Work and Pensions, since 2013; *b* London, 24 July 1956; *s* of James Patrick Moore and Jocelyn Ann Inrig; *m* 1989, Barbara Joan Richards. *Educ:* St George's Coll., Weybridge; London Sch. of Econs and Pol Sci. (BSc Econ; Bassett Meml Prize, 1978; MSc 1979); Alliance Française, Paris; London Univ. ext. (BA Italian 2009; Dr Guenther Prize, 2009). Res. admin posts, 1980–87, Principal Finance Officer, 1987–89, ESRC; policy posts, 1989–93, Dep. Dir, and Hd, Student Support Policy, 1993–98, DES, then DfE, later DfEE; Hd, Envmt, Transport and Regions Spending Team, HM Treasury, 1998–2000; Hd, Structural Unemployment Policy Div., DfEE, 2000–01; Department for Work and Pensions: Dep. Dir, Strategy and Planning, 2001–04; Director: Planning and Performance Mgt, 2005–09; Labour Market Policy, 2009–11; Disability Policy, and Office for Disability Issues, 2011–13. Non-exec. Dir, Student Loans Co., 1994–98. *Recreations:* French and Italian culture and literature, visiting Canada, Turkish language. *Address:* 12 Grandison Road, SW11 6LW. *E:* jeremypmoore@btinternet.com; Department for Work and Pensions, Caxton House, Tothill Street, SW1H 9NA. *E:* jeremy.moore@dwp.gsi.gov.uk.

MOORE, John, (Jonathan Moore); actor; writer; director; *b* 25 Nov.; *s* of Richard and Nora Moore. *Educ:* St Elphege's, Wallington; Roundshaw Sch., Wallington; Croydon Art Coll. *Writer: plays:* 1st play aged 11, Hornus' Poem; Sea Change, 1977; Obstruct the doors, cause delay and be Dangerous…, 1980; Street Captives, Edinburgh Fest., transf. Royal Exchange, 1981; Treatment, Donmar, 1982 (Edinburgh Fest. Fringe First award; also BBC TV Film); The Hooligan Nights (NT commn), 1985; Behind Heaven, Royal Exchange (commd), transf. Donmar, 1986; Regeneration, 1989; This Other Eden, Soho Th., 1990; Fall From Light, 2002; Mad God (adaptation of The Bacchae, commd by Royal Exchange), 2003–05, 2014; Inigo (also dir), White Bear Th., transf. Pleasance Main House, 2015; *television:* Crown Court (Granada TV), 1982; *libretto:* Stewart Copeland's Horse Opera (televised, also actor), 1992; *directed:* Turnage's Greek (world premiere; co-writer of adaptation from play), Munich Biennale (Best Libretto award), Edinburgh Internat. Fest., 1988, ENO, 1990 (dir. BBC TV film, Royal Phil. Soc. Best Film award); Elegy for Young Lovers, La Fenice, Venice, 1989; 63 Dream Palace, Munich Biennale (Best Dir award) and German TV, 1990; Baa Baa Black Sheep, Opera North, Cheltenham Fest., BBC TV, 1993; Cask of Amontillado, Holders, Barbados, 1993; East and West (also writer of text), Almeida, 1994; Life with An Idiot, ENO, Scottish Opera, 1995; James MacMillan's Ines de Castro, Scottish Opera, Edinburgh Internat. Fest., BBC TV, 1996; Dance Marathon, Basel Ballet, 1996; Inkle and Yarico, Holders Easter Season, Barbados, 1997; Mottke the Thief (also writer of adaptation from novel by Schalom Asch), Bonn Opera, 1998; Nyman's Facing Goya, Santiago del Compostela, Perrelada Fest., 2001; Die Versicherung, State Th., Darmstadt, 2002; Magic Flute (also trans. of spoken text), Scottish Opera, 2003; Sex, Chips and Rock 'n' Roll, Royal Exchange, 2005; The Soldier's Tale (also actor), Savannah Fest., Georgia, 2006; The Ballad of Elizabeth Sulky Mouth, Greenwich, 2006; The Revenger's Tragedy, Royal Exchange, 2008; House of Bernarda Alba, Battersea Arts Centre Main House, 2009; Crimes in Hot Countries, RADA, 2009; Our Lady of Sligo, RADA, 2010; Shadowball, Mermaid Th., 2010; Faith and Cold Reading, Live Th., Newcastle, 2011; Tell Tale Heart, ROH, 2011; Ashes and Sand, RADA, 2011; The Acid Test, RADA, 2012; Betrayal, RADA, 2013; Glengarry Glenross, Jacksons Lane Th., 2012; What You Will, Shakespeare's Globe, Cultural Olympiad, 2012; Sonnet Walks, Shakespeare's Globe, 2013–14; Unprotected, Courtyard Th., Hoxton, 2014; A Midsummer Night's Dream, Oval House, 2015; *actor: theatre* includes leading roles in: Class Enemy, Oxford Playhouse, transf. Young Vic, 1979; The Gorky Brigade, Royal Court, 1980; I Die for None of Them (one-man play), Edinburgh Fringe Fest., 1980, 1981 (Fringe First Award); Treatment, Gate, 1981, Donmar, 1982, Edinburgh Fest., 1986; Venice Preserv'd, Almeida, 1982; Arrivederci Millwall, Albany Empire, 1985; Behind Heaven, Royal Exchange, Donmar, 1986; The Art of Success, RSC, 1987; The Idiot, Barbican, 1990; Narrator, The Raven, Teatro Manzoni, Milan, 1990, Teatro Dell'Elfo, Milan, 2012; Dead Funny, Salisbury Playhouse, Th. Clwyd, 1998; Misalliance, 1998, The School of Night, 1999, Chichester Fest. Th.; A Midsummer Night's Dream, 2001, Macbeth, 2002, Arcola; Round the Horne, West End and No 1 UK tour, 2004; 2Graves (one-man play), Edinburgh Fest., transf. Arts Th., 2006; Holding Fire!, Shakespeare's Globe, 2007; Don Juan Comes Back From The War, New Diorama Th., 2014; *television* includes leading roles in: Treatment, 1984; Inside Story, 1986; Bleak House, 1986; Jack the Ripper (series), 1988; Roger Roger (two series), 1999, 2003; The People's Harry Enfield, 2001; Foyle's War, 2003; Cruel Train, 2004; City of Vice (series), 2007, Criminal Justice (series), 2008; Midsomer Murders (series), 2008; Sharpe's Peril (series), 2009; Holby City, 2013; *films* include: My Beautiful Laundrette, 1985; Golden Brown, 2011; 2 Graves, 2013. Collaborated on theatre pieces with Ludovico Einaudi, Stewart Copeland, Daniel Hope, band Test Dept, master percussionist Stomu Yamashta, jazz pianist Uri Caine, Eddy Grant, and mems of rock band Killing Joke and Jah Wobble; contrib. to BBC TV and radio arts discussion progs. Founder Mem. And Dir, New London Actors, 1980–84. Writer-in-Residence, Albany Empire, Deptford, 1985. Vis. Sen. Lectr, RCM, 2006; Guest Lectr, 2006, Vis. Lectr, 2010, Drama Centre, London; Vis. Lectr, RADA, 2009–13. Mem., Artistic Adv. Cttee, RADA, 2013–. Directed Shakespeare and screen acting workshops, Actor's Centre. *Publications:* Jonathan Moore: three plays, 2002. *Recreations:* meditation, interior landscape gardening, football. *Address:* (writing and directing) c/o Julia Kreitman, The Agency, 24 Pottery Lane, Holland Park, W11 4LZ. *T:* (020) 7727 1346. *E:* info@theagency.co.uk; (acting) c/o Meg Poole, Richard Stone Partnership, Suite 3, De Walden Court, 85 New Cavendish Street, W1W 6XD. *T:* (020) 7497 0869; (opera directing) Performing Arts, 6 Windmill Street, W1T 2JB. *T:* (020) 7255 7362. *E:* sam@performing-arts.co.uk. *W:* www.jonathanmooreuk.com.

MOORE, Hon. John Colinton, AO 2004; *b* Rockhampton, Qld, 16 Nov. 1936; *s* of Thomas R. Moore and Doris (*née* Symes); *m* 1st, 1965 (marr. diss.); two *s* one *d;* 2nd, 1980, Jacqueline Sarah, *d* of Hon. Sir William John Farquhar McDonald and Evelyn S. McDonald. *Educ:* Southport Jun. Sch., Qld; Armidale Sch., NSW; Univ. of Queensland (BCom; AAUQ). AASA. Stockbroker, 1960; Mem., Brisbane Stock Exchange, 1962–74. Former Director: Wm Brandt & Sons (Aust.); Phillips; First City; Brandt Ltd (PFCB Ltd); Merrill Lynch, Pierce, Fennell & Smith (Aust.) Ltd; Citi-national Ltd; Agricl Investments Aust. Ltd. MP (L) Ryan, Qld, 1975–2001; Fed. Minister for Business and Consumer Affairs, 1980–82; Opposition spokesman: for Finance, 1983–84; for Communications, 1984–85; for Northern Develt and Local Govt, 1985–87; for Tspt and Aviation, 1987; for Business and Consumer Affairs, 1987–89; for Business Privatisation and Consumer Affairs, 1989–90; Shadow Minister for Industry and Commerce, and Public Admin, 1995–96; Minister for Industry, Sci. and Tourism, 1996–98; Vice-Pres., Exec. Council, 1996–98; Minister for Defence, 1998–2001. Member: various Govt cttees, 1984–96; various internat. delegns. Queensland Liberal Party: Vice-Pres. and Treas., 1967–73; Pres., 1973–76 and 1984–90; Mem., Qld State Exec., Liberal Party of Aust., 1966–91 and 1996–98. Mem. Council, Order of Australia, 1996–98. Mem., Anti-Cancer Council of Qld, 1972. *Recreations:* tennis, cricket, reading, golf. *Address:* 6/49 River Esplanade, Mooloolaba, Qld 4557, Australia. *Clubs:* Queensland, Brisbane, Tattersall's (Brisbane); Queensland Turf.

MOORE, John David; Headmaster, St Dunstan's College, Catford, 1993–97; *b* 16 Feb. 1943; *s* of John and Hilda Moore; *m* 1966, Ann Medora; one *s* one *d. Educ:* St John's Coll., Cambridge (BA Classics 1965; MA 1969); CertEd Cambridge Univ., 1966. Classics Master, Judd Sch., Tonbridge, 1966–69; trainee commodity trader, Gill and Duffus Ltd, 1969–70; English Master, Skinners' Sch., Tunbridge Wells, 1970–74; Head of General Studies and English Master, King's Sch., Macclesfield, Ches., 1974–80; Dep. Headmaster, Carre's Grammar Sch., Sleaford, Lincs, 1981–86; Headmaster, Ilford County High Sch. for Boys, London Borough of Redbridge, 1986–93. Member Committee: S Lakeland Carers, 1998–2001 (Chm., 1999–2001); Old Bradfordian Assoc., 1999– (Pres., 2003–06). Governor: Heron Hill Primary Sch., Kendal, 1998–2007; King's Sch., Macclesfield, 2000–12 (Mem., Govs' Educn Sub-Gp, 1998–2012; Chm., Educn Cttee, 2006–12). Freeman, City of London, 1996. *Publications:* Haec Egimus - All This We Did: a history of Bradford Grammar School, 1949–63, 2011. *Recreations:* cricket, walking, theatre, music. *Address:* 12 Undercliff Road, Kendal, Cumbria LA9 4PS.

MOORE, Prof. John Halstead Hardman, PhD; FBA 1999; George Watson's and Daniel Stewart's Professor of Political Economy, University of Edinburgh, since 2000; Professor of Economic Theory, London School of Economics, since 1990 (quarter-time since 2000); *b* 7 May 1954; *s* of Frank Moore, OBE and Audrey Jeanne Moore (*née* Halstead); *m* 1986, Dr Susan Mary Hardman; one *s* one *d. Educ:* Dorking County Grammar Sch.; Fitzwilliam Coll., Cambridge (BA 1st cl. Hons Maths 1976; MA 1983); LSE (MSc 1980; PhD 1984). Exec. Engr, Dundee Telephone Area, 1976–78; Temp. Lectr in Econs, LSE, 1980–81; Lectr, Birkbeck Coll., London Univ., 1981–83; Lectr, 1983–87, Reader, 1987–90, LSE. Vis. Asst Prof., MIT, 1986–87; Vis. Prof., Princeton Univ., 1991–92; Prof., St Andrews Univ., 1997–2000 (quarter-time); Leverhulme Personal Res. Prof., 1998–2003; ESRC Professorial Fellow, 2004–07. Ed., Rev. of Economic Studies, 1987–91. Lectures: Walras-Bowley, 1996, Marschak, 2002, Econometric Soc.; Clarendon, Oxford Univ., 2001; Schumpeter, European Econ. Assoc., 2006; Max Weber, European Univ. Inst., 2006; Bernoulli, Univ. of Basel, 2007; Keynes Lectr, British Acad., 2007. Fellow: Econometric Soc., 1989 (Pres., 2010); Royal Soc. of Edinburgh, 2003. Foreign Hon. Member: Amer. Econ. Assoc., 2001; Amer. Acad. of Arts and Scis, 2002. Yrjö Jahnsson Award, European Econ. Assoc., 1999. *Publications:* articles on econs. *Recreations:* music, mountains. *Address:* School of Economics, University of Edinburgh, 31 Buccleuch Place, Edinburgh EH8 9JT; London School of Economics, Houghton Street, WC2A 2AE.

MOORE, Sir John (Michael), KCVO 1983; CB 1974; DSC 1944; Chairman, Lymington Harbour Commission, 1993–99 (Deputy Chairman, 1990–93); Second Crown Estate Commissioner, 1978–83; *b* 2 April 1921; *m* 1986, Jacqueline Cingel, MBE. *Educ:* Whitgift Middle Sch.; Selwyn Coll., Cambridge. Royal Navy, 1940–46. Royal Humane Society Bronze Medal, 1942. Ministry of Transport, 1946; Joint Principal Private Sec. to Minister (Rt Hon. Harold (later Lord) Watkinson), 1956–59; Asst Sec., 1959; Under-Sec. (Principal Estabt Officer), 1966; Under-Sec., DoE, 1970–72; Dep. Sec., CSD, 1972–78. *Recreations:* sailing, remembering walking hills and mountains (Kilimanjaro). *Address:* Court Lodge, Court Close, Ridgeway Lane, Lymington, Hants SO41 8NQ. *T:* (01590) 679963. *Club:* Royal Lymington Yacht.

MOORE, Jonathan; *see* Moore, John.

MOORE, Dame Julie, DBE 2012; Chief Executive, University Hospitals Birmingham NHS Foundation Trust, since 2006 (Executive Director of Operations, 2002–06); *b* Liverpool, 18 Aug. 1958; *d* of Edward James and Kathleen Mary Moore; civil partnership 2006, Lesley Ann Patterson. *Educ:* BSc; Univ. of Leeds (MA Health Services Studies). Registered Nurse, then nurse manager, later nursing dir, Leeds; gen. mgt posts, 1977–98; Dir, Leeds Teaching Hosps NHS Trust, 1998–2002. Hd, Educn and Trng Gp, NHS Future Forum, 2011–. Member: Commn on Living Standards; MoD/DoH Partnership Bd; Ind. Mem., OSCHR. Member: Nat. Organ Donation Taskforce, 2007–08; Nuffield Steering Gp on New Frontiers in Efficiency, 2009. Member: Internat. Adv. Bd, Univ. of Birmingham Business Sch.; Bd, Mktg Birmingham. *Recreations:* travel, music, history. *Address:* University Hospitals Birmingham NHS Foundation Trust, PO Box 9551, Main Drive, Queen Elizabeth Medical Centre, Birmingham B15 2PR. *T:* (0121) 371 4311. *E:* Julie.moore@uhb.nhs.uk.

MOORE, Katharine Elizabeth; Her Honour Judge Katharine Moore; a Circuit Judge, since 2014. *Educ:* Downing Coll., Cambridge (BA 1994). Called to the Bar, Middle Temple, 1995; a Recorder, 2009–14. *Address:* Norwich Crown Court, The Law Courts, Bishopsgate, Norwich NR3 1UR.

MOORE, Mark Jonathan, MA; Head of College, Clifton College, since 2005; *b* 25 April 1961; *s* of Dennis and Sheila Moore; *m* 1989, Joanna Hawley; two *s* two *d. Educ:* Wolverhampton Grammar Sch.; Downing Coll., Cambridge (BA Hons English 1983; PGCE 1984; MA 1987). Assistant Master: Marlborough Coll., 1984–87; Eton Coll., 1987–94; Hd of English, Radley Coll., 1994–2005. *Recreations:* ball games, reading, talking. *Address:* Clifton College, Bristol BS8 3JH. *T:* (0117) 315 7000, *Fax:* (0117) 315 7101. *Clubs:* Jesters; Hawks (Cambridge).

MOORE, Marks; *see* Moore, D. M.

MOORE, Martin Luke; QC 2002; *b* 25 April 1960; *s* of late Brig. Peter Neil Martin Moore, DSO (and two Bars), MC, and Enid Rosemary Moore; *m* 1985, Caroline Mary Mason; three *d. Educ:* Winchester Coll.; Lincoln Coll., Oxford (BA Hons). Called to the Bar, Lincoln's Inn, 1982, Bencher, 2010; in practice, specialising in company law litigation and advice. *Address:* Hurst Farm, Hurst Lane, Privett, Hants GU34 3PL. *T:* (01420) 588660; Erskine Chambers, 33 Chancery Lane, WC2A 1EN. *T:* (020) 7242 5532. *E:* mmoore@erskinechambers.com.

MOORE, Mary; *see* Moore, G. M.

MOORE, Vice Adm. Sir Michael (Antony Claës), KBE 1997; LVO 1981; Chief Executive (formerly Director General), Institution of Mechanical Engineers, 1998–2007; *b* 6 Jan. 1942; *s* of Lieut A. D. W. Moore, RN (killed HMS Audacity, 1941) and Agneta Moore (*née* Wachtmeister); *m* 1969, Penelope Jane, JP, *d* of Rear-Adm. Frederick Charles William Lawson, CB, DSC and Bar; one *s* three *d. Educ:* Wellington Coll.; RNC Dartmouth. Swedish Naval Interpreter. Joined RN, 1960; served HM Ships Gurkha, Britannia and Ashton, 1963–67; Flag Lieut to Comdr FEF, Singapore, 1967–68; i/c HMS Beachampton, 1969; qualified as Navigator, 1970; HM Ships Tenby, Brighton, Plymouth and Tartar (i/c), 1970–77; Naval Ops, MoD, 1977–79; HMY Britannia, 1979–81; Captain, 1981; Naval Asst to Chief of Fleet Support, MoD, 1981–82; i/c HMS Andromeda, and Capt. 8th Frigate Sqn, 1983–84; i/c Ops, Northwood MHQ, 1985–87; Dir, Naval Warfare, MoD, 1988–90; Rear Adm., 1990; Maritime Advr to SACEUR, 1990–93; Vice Adm. 1994; C of S to Comdr Allied Naval Forces Southern Europe, 1994–97. Chm., Forces Pension Soc. (formerly Officers' Pension Soc.), 2006–11. Dir, Tall Ships Youth Trust, 2010–; Pres., Friends of RN Mus. and HMS Victory, 2012–. Hon. Fellow: Swedish Royal Soc. of Naval Scis, 1992; IMechE 2006. Younger Brother, Trinity House, 1988. *Address:* Churchill Cottage, Castle Street, Portchester, Hants PO16 9QW.

See also J. A. A. H. Moore.

MOORE, Prof. Michael Arthur, DPhil; FRS 1989; Professor of Theoretical Physics, University of Manchester, 1976–2011, now Emeritus; *b* 8 Oct. 1943; *s* of John Moore and Barbara Atkinson; *m* 1967, Susan Eadington; three *s* one *d. Educ:* Huddersfield New Coll.; Oriel Coll., Oxford (BA 1964; DPhil 1967). Prize Fellow, Magdalen Coll., Oxford, 1967–71; Res. Associate, Univ. of Illinois, USA, 1967–69; Lectr in Physics, Univ. of Sussex, 1971–76. *Publications:* papers in scientific jls. *Recreation:* tennis. *Address:* The Schuster Laboratory, The University, Manchester M13 9PL.

MOORE, Rt Hon. Michael (Kenneth), ONZ 2000; PC 1990; Director-General, World Trade Organisation, 1999–2002; Ambassador of New Zealand to the United States of America, since 2010; *b* 28 Jan. 1949; *m* 1975, Yvonne (*née* Dereany). *Educ:* Dilworth Sch.; Bay of Islands College (only Minister in Labour Govt without a degree). Worked as social worker, builder's labourer, meat freezing worker and printer; MP (Lab) Eden 1972–75 (youngest NZ MP ever elected); MP (Lab) Papanui, later named Christchurch North, then Waimakariri, 1978–99; spokesperson on housing, regional, small town and community development, the environment, tourism, recreation and sport, overseas trade and marketing, external relations and trade, finance; Minister of Foreign Affairs and Trade, 1990; trade missions led incl. Japan, Europe, Soviet Union, Pakistan, Turkey; Prime Minister of NZ, Sept.–Oct. 1990; Leader of the Opposition, 1990–93. Adjunct Prof., Faculty of Law and Mgt, La Trobe Univ., 2003–. Hon. DCom: Lincoln, NZ; Auckland Univ. of Technol.; Hon. DEc People's Univ. of China; Hon. Dr Canterbury, Christchurch; Hon. DIur La Trobe. *Publications:* On Balance, 1980; Beyond Today, 1981; A Pacific Parliament, 1982; The Added Value Economy, 1984; Hard Labour, 1987; Fighting for New Zealand, 1993; Children of the Poor, 1996; A Brief History of the Future, 1998; A World Without Walls, 2003; Saving Globalization, 2009. *Address:* New Zealand Embassy, 37 Observatory Circle NW, Washington, DC 20008, USA.

MOORE, Rt Hon. Michael (Kevin); PC 2010; *b* 3 June 1965; *s* of Rev. (William) Haisley Moore and Geraldine Anne, (Jill), Moore; *m* 2004, Alison Louise Hughes; one *d. Educ:* Strathallan Sch.; Jedburgh Grammar Sch.; Univ. of Edinburgh (MA Jt Hons Politics and Modern Hist.). CA 1991. Research Asst to Archy Kirkwood, MP, 1987–88; with Coopers & Lybrand, Edinburgh, 1988–97 (a Manager, corporate finance). MP (Lib Dem) Tweeddale, Ettrick and Lauderdale, 1997–2005, Berwickshire, Roxburgh and Selkirk, 2005–15; contested (Lib Dem) same seat, 2015. Lib Dem spokesman on defence, 2005–06; on foreign affairs, 2006–07, on internat. devel t, 2007–10; Sec. of State for Scotland, 2010–13. Mem., Select Cttee on Scottish affairs, 1997–99. Gov. and Vice-Chm., Westminster Foundn for Democracy, 2002–05. Mem. Council, Chatham House, 2004–10. Parly Vis. Fellow, St Antony's Coll., Oxford, 2003–04. Gov., Ditchley Foundn, 2010–. *Recreations:* jazz, music, films, Rugby, hill-walking.

MOORE, Michael Rodney Newton, CBE 1996; Chairman, Which? Ltd, 1997–2008; Director, HBOS Financial Services, 2001–09; *b* 15 March 1936; *s* of Gen. Sir Rodney Moore, GCVO, KCB, CBE, DSO, PMN and Olive Marion (*née* Robinson); *m* 1986, Jan, *d* of Paul and Lilian Adorian; one *s. Educ:* Eton; Magdalen College, Oxford (MA); Harvard Business Sch. (MBA). Nat. Service Commission, Grenadier Guards, 1957–59, serving in Cyprus, Lebanon, UK. Called to the Bar, Gray's Inn, 1961; practised until 1964; joined Hill Samuel & Co., 1966 (Dir, 1970–71); subseq. Chm./Dir, various UK, USA & Swedish cos; Chairman: Tomkins, 1984–95; Quicks Gp, 1992–2002; Linx Printing Technologies, 1993–2005; London Internat. Gp, 1994–99; Warm Zones, 2001–04; Dir, Sir John Soane's Mus. Soc., 2004–05. Mem. Council of Mgt, Consumers' Assoc., 1997–2003. Trustee, Public Concern at Work, 1996–2003. Chm., NSPCC, 1988–95. *Recreations:* visiting ruins, opera, photography, reading. *Clubs:* Garrick, Pratt's, Boodle's.

MOORE, Michael S.; *see* Stuart-Moore.

MOORE, Miranda Jayne, (Mrs J. M. Haslam); QC 2003; *b* 4 Jan. 1961; *d* of Bryan John Moore and Anne Rosemary Janet Spokes Moore; *m* 1987, Jonathan Mark Haslam; one *s* one *d. Educ:* Univ. of Aston (BSc 1st Cl. Hons Business Studies). Called to the Bar, Lincoln's Inn, 1983, Bencher, 2012; in practice as barrister, specialising in criminal law, 1984–. *Recreations:* dancing, theatre, shopping. *Address:* 5 Paper Buildings, Temple, EC4Y 7HB. *T:* (020) 7583 6117. *E:* clerks@5pb.co.uk.

MOORE, (Sir) Norman Winfrid, (3rd Bt *cr* 1919; has established his claim but does not use the title); Senior Principal Scientific Officer, Nature Conservancy Council, 1965–83 (Principal Scientific Officer, 1958–65); Visiting Professor of Environmental Studies, Wye College, University of London, 1979–83; *b* 24 Feb. 1923; *s* of Sir Alan Hilary Moore, 2nd Bt; *S* father, 1959; *m* 1950, Janet (*d* 2014), PhD, *o d* of late Mrs Phyllis Singer; one *s* two *d. Educ:* Eton; Trinity Coll., Cambridge (MA); Univ. of Bristol (PhD). Served War, 1942–45, Germany and Holland (wounded, POW). *Publications:* The Bird of Time, 1987; Oaks, Dragonflies and People, 2002; scientific papers and articles. *Heir: s* Peter Alan Cutlack Moore [*b* 21 Sept. 1951; *m* 1989, Pamela Edwardes; one *s* one *d. Educ:* Eton; Trinity Coll., Cambridge (MA); DPhil Oxon]. *Address:* The Farm House, 117 Boxworth End, Swavesey, Cambridge CB24 4RA.

MOORE, Sir Patrick (William Eisdell), Kt 1992; OBE 1982; FRCS, FRACS; Consultant Surgeon, Honorary Staff, Auckland Hospital Board, now retired; *b* 17 March 1918; *m* 1942, Doris McBeth (Beth) Beedie; four *s. Educ:* Auckland Grammar Sch.; Otago Univ. (MB ChB); Univ. of London (DLO). Medical Officer, 28 Bn, 2 NZEF. Consultant Surgeon, Green Lane Hosp., 1951; Reader in Otolaryngology, Auckland Med. Sch., 1975–84. Vice-Pres., NZ League for Hard of Hearing, 1952–77; President: Deafness Res. Foundn, 1963–90; NZ Otolaryngological Soc., 1968–70; NZ Hunts Assoc., 1984–89; Founder and Patron, Hearing House of NZ, 1966; Master of Pakuranga Hunt, 1975–84; Auckland Cttee, NZ Racing Conf., 1976–84. Fellow, Selwyn Coll., Univ. of Otago, 2007. Augusta Award, Auckland Grammar Sch., 2008. *Publications:* A Great Run, 1972; So Old So Quick (autobiog.), 2004. *Recreation:* writing. *Address:* Binswood, 229 Remuera Road, Auckland 1050, New Zealand. *T:* (9) 5202679. *Club:* Northern (Auckland).

MOORE, Philip John, BMus; FRCO; Organist and Master of the Music, York Minster, 1983–2008, now Organist Emeritus; President, Royal College of Organists, since 2015; *b* 30 Sept. 1943; *s* of late Cecil and Marjorie Moore; one *s* two *d. Educ:* Maidstone Grammar Sch.; Royal Coll. of Music (ARCM, GRSM); BMus Dunelm. FRCO 1965. Asst Music Master, Eton Coll., 1965–68; Asst Organist, Canterbury Cathedral, 1968–74; Organist and Master of the Choristers, Guildford Cathedral, 1974–83. Hon. FRSCM 2005; Hon. FGCM 2006; Hon. Fellow, Acad. of St Cecilia, 2007. Hon. Dr York, 2014. Order of St William of York, 2008. *Publications:* anthems, services, cantatas, organ music, song cycles, chamber music, orchestral music. *Recreations:* collecting fountain pens, collecting Imari, cooking, log fires, architecture, cars, art, reading. *Address:* Rectory Cottage, Barton-le-Street, Malton YO17 6PN.

MOORE, Philip Wynford, TD 1994; Group Finance Director, Liverpool Victoria Friendly Society, since 2010; *b* 5 Jan. 1960; *s* of Cecil Philip John Moore and late Christine Margaret Moore; *m* 1995, Amanda Lawson; two *d. Educ:* St Albans Sch.; Clare Coll., Cambridge (BA Maths 1982; MA 1986). AIA 1986, FIA 1988. Life Dept, Commercial Union Insce Co., 1982–87; Managing Consultant, William M. Mercer, 1987–89; Coopers & Lybrand: leader of life actuarial practice, London, 1989–95; Partner, Financial Instns Gp, Coopers & Lybrand Consulting (East Asia), leader, E Asia Insce Consultancy practice, Hong Kong, 1995–98; Finance Dir and Actuary, National Provident Instn, 1998–2000; Corp. Dir of Finance and Hd of Mergers and Acquisitions, AMP (UK) plc, 2000–03; Gp Finance Dir, 2003–06, Gp Chief Exec., 2007, Friends Provident plc; Interim Chief Finance Officer, HMRC, 2008; Gp Finance Partner, 2008–10, and Chief Risk Officer, 2009–10, Pensions Corp. LLP. Non-executive Director: RAB Capital plc, 2009–11 (Chm., Audit Cttee, 2009–11); Towergate Insurance Ltd (formerly Towergate Partnership Co. Ltd), 2011– (Chm., Audit Cttee, 2011–; Sen. Ind. Dir, 2013–). Mem., Educn Leadership Team, BITC, 2006–10. Trustee: Childhood Eye Cancer Trust, 2007–13 (Chm., 2008–13); RBL, 2014– (Chm., Finance Cttee, 2014–). Gov., Aylward Acad., 2011– (Chm., Achievement and Standards Cttee, 2014–). *Recreations:* family, flying (private pilot's licence), ski-ing, running. *Address:* Liverpool Victoria Friendly Society, County Gates, Bournemouth BH1 2NF. *Club:* Honourable Artillery Company.

MOORE, Air Vice-Marshal Richard Charles, MBE 1989; Director, D&MM Associates Ltd, since 2014; Air Officer Administration, and Air Officer Commanding Directly Administered Units, 2003–05; *b* 5 Aug. 1950; *s* of Ernest William Moore and Hilda Margaret Moore (*née* Edwards); *m* 1977, Judith Ellen Owen; two *s. Educ:* Open Univ. (BSc Systems); RAF Staff Coll. Joined RAF, 1970; OC 16 Sqdn, 1983–85, 6 Wing, 1988–91, RAF Regt; MoD Staff appts, Regt 26 (RAF), 1985–88, Air Plans (LTC), 1991–95; Officer Commanding: Defence Nuclear Biol and Chem. Centre, 1995–97; RAF Honington, 1997–99; Comdt Gen., RAF Regt, 1999–2001; Team Leader, Ground Based Air Defence Integrated Project, Defence Procurement Agency, 2001–03. Dir, Network Enabled Solutions, QinetiQ Ltd, 2008–14. Chm., RAF Bobsleigh, Luge and Skeleton Bobsleigh Assoc., 1997–2006. *Recreation:* offshore sailing. *Address:* c/o RAF High Wycombe, Bucks HP14 4UE.

MOORE, Richard Hobart John de Courcy, FCA; Managing Partner, 1987–2004, and Senior Partner, since 1989, Moore Stephens; Chairman, Moore Stephens International Ltd, since 2005; *b* 31 Aug. 1949; *s* of late Hobart Harold de Courcy Moore and of Elizabeth Helen Moore; *m* 1977, Lucy Annabelle Sefton-Smith; one *s* one *d. Educ:* Stowe Sch. FCA 1979. Partner, Moore Stephens, 1975–. Comr, Royal Hospital Chelsea, 2006–12. Treas., Shipwrights' Co., 1989–. *Recreations:* Real tennis, cricket. *Address:* 11 Chelsea Park Gardens, SW3 6AF. *T:* (020) 7352 7594. *Clubs:* Boodle's, MCC, Hurlingham, Queen's.

MOORE, Richard Peter; HM Diplomatic Service; Ambassador to Turkey, since 2014; *b* Tripoli, Libya, 9 May 1963; *s* of John Robert Moore and (Norah) Patricia Moore (*née* Buckley); *m* 1985, Margaret Patricia Isabel, (Maggie), Martin; one *s* one *d. Educ:* St George's Coll., Weybridge; Worcester Coll., Oxford (BA (Hons) PPE); Kennedy Sch. of Govt, Harvard Univ. (Kennedy Schol.); Stanford Graduate Sch. of Business (Stanford Exec. Prog. 2007). Joined FCO, 1987; Third Sec., Hanoi, 1988; Second Sec. (Pol), Ankara, 1990; Consul (Pol and Press), Istanbul, 1991–92; Desk Officer, Iran, FCO, 1992–95; First Sec., Islamabad, 1995–98; Section Hd, Security Policy Gp, FCO, 1998–2001; Counsellor, Kuala Lumpur, 2001–05; Dep. Dir, Middle East, 2005–08, Dir, Progs and Change, 2008–10, Dir, Europe, Latin America and Globalisation, 2010–12, FCO. *Recreations:* golf, watching cricket and Rugby, reading, TV, travel. *Address:* British Embassy, Şehit Ersan Caddesi 46/A, Çankaya, Ankara, Turkey. *E:* richard.moore@fco.gov.uk. *Clubs:* Vincent's, MCC.

MOORE, Robert Jeffery; His Honour Judge Moore; a Circuit Judge, since 1995; Ethnic Minorities Liaison Judge for South Yorkshire and Humberside (formerly Sheffield), 1998–2004; *b* 1947; *s* of Jeffery Moore and Doreen Moore; *m* 1979, Susan Elaine Hatcliffe; two *s. Educ:* Loughborough Grammar Sch.; Univ. of Manchester (LLB Hons 1968); Council of Legal Educn (Bar Finals 1969). Called to the Bar, Gray's Inn, 1970; practised on North Eastern Circuit, from Sheffield, 1971–80 and from 11 Kings Bench Walk, Temple, 1980–95. Mem., Written Examinations and Interview Panel, Judicial Appts Commn, 2008–11. *Recreations:* travel, especially with family, Leicester Tigers Rugby club, golf. *Address:* The Law Courts, 50 West Bar, Sheffield S3 8PH. *Clubs:* Sloane; Sickleholme Golf (Bamford).

MOORE, Sir Roger (George), KBE 2003 (CBE 1999); actor; *b* London, 14 Oct. 1927; *m* 1st, Doorn van Steyn (marr. diss. 1953); 2nd, 1953, Dorothy Squires (marr. diss. 1969; she *d* 1998); 3rd, Luisa Mattioli (marr. diss.); two *s* one *d*; 4th, 2002, Kristina Tholstrup. *Educ:* RADA. Special Ambassador for UNICEF, 1991–. Golden Globe World Film Favourite Award, 1980. Stage début, Androcles and the Lion. *TV series include:* Ivanhoe, 1958; The Alaskans, 1960–61; Maverick, 1961; The Saint, 1962–69 (dir some episodes); The Persuaders, 1972–73; The Man Who Wouldn't Die, 1992; The Quest, 1995; *films include:* The Last Time I Saw Paris, 1954; The Interrupted Melody, 1955; The King's Thief, 1955; Diane, 1956; The Miracle, 1959; Rachel Cade, 1961; Gold of the Seven Saints, 1961; The Rape of the Sabine Women, 1961; No Man's Land, 1961; Crossplot, 1969; The Man Who Haunted Himself, 1970; Live and Let Die, 1973; The Man With The Golden Gun, 1974; Gold, 1974; That Lucky Touch, 1975; Street People, 1975; Shout at the Devil, 1975; Sherlock Holmes in New York, 1976; The Spy Who Loved Me, 1976; The Wild Geese, 1977; Escape to Athena, 1978; Moonraker, 1978; North Sea Hijack, 1979; The Sea Wolves, 1980; Sunday Lovers, 1980; For Your Eyes Only, 1980; The Cannonball Run, 1981; Octopussy, 1983; The Naked Face, 1983; A View to a Kill, 1985; Bed and Breakfast, 1989; Bullseye!, 1989; Fire, Ice and Dynamite, 1990; The Quest, 1997; Boat Trip, 2002; A Princess for Christmas, 2011. *Publications:* James Bond Diary, 1973; Roger Moore: my word is my bond, 2008; Bond on Bond, 2013; Last Man Standing, 2014. *Address:* Pinewood Studios, Iver Heath, Bucks SL0 0NH.

MOORE, Prof. Roger Kenneth, PhD; Professor of Spoken Language Processing, University of Sheffield, since 2004; *b* Swanage, 26 Feb. 1952; *s* of Kenneth Moore and Rosemary Moore; *m* 1987, Jenifer Younger; one *s. Educ:* Swanage Grammar Sch.; Univ. of Essex (BA Hons Computers and Communications Engrg 1973; MSc 1974; PhD 1976). FIOA 1987. Postdoctoral Researcher, UCL, 1976–80; Section Leader, RSRE, 1980–85; Hd, Speech Res. Unit, DERA, 1985–99; Chief Scientific Officer, 20/20 Speech Ltd, 1999–2004. Visiting Professor: Psychol. and Lang. Scis, UCL, 1990–; Bristol Robotics Lab., UWE, 2011–. Fellow, Internat. Speech Communication Assoc., 2008. Editor-in-Chief, Jl of Computer Speech and Lang., 1985–. *Publications:* (jtly) The Eagles Handbook of Standards and Resources for Spoken Language Systems, 1997; (jtly) Handbook of Multimodal and Spoken Dialogue Systems: resources, terminology and product evaluation, 2000; over 25 articles in acad. jls incl. Nature Scientific Reports, Speech Communication, Computer Speech and Lang., Phonetics, Connection Sci., IEEE Trans. on Computers, Artificial Intelligence Res. *Recreations:* photography, running. *Address:* Department of Computer Science, University of Sheffield, Regent Court, 211 Portobello, Sheffield S1 4DP. *T:* (0114) 222 1807. *E:* r.k.moore@sheffield.ac.uk.

MOORE, Rosalyn Elaine, (Mrs Stephen Littler); Chief Nursing Officer, Scotland, and Director for Patients, Public and Health Professions, Scottish Government, 2010–14; *b* Castleford, 1 March 1957; *d* of Harold Moore and Sheila Moore (*née* Turner); *m* 1998, Stephen Littler; one *s* two *d. Educ:* Normanton Grammar Sch.; Leeds Metropolitan Univ. (BSc Hons Nursing); Open Univ. (MA Educn and Leadership). SRN 1981; RNT 1989. Staff Nurse, Castleford and Normanton District Hosp., 1981–84; Paediatric Staff Nurse, Pontefract and Pinderfields Hosps, 1984–87; Nurse Tutor, Pinderfields Hosp., Wakefield, 1987–89; Hd, Adult Nursing, later Postgrad. Educn, Leeds Coll. of Health, subseq. Univ. of Leeds, 1989–96; Asst Dir of Nursing and Professional Develt Lead, Pinderfields and Pontefract NHS Trust, 1996–99; Chief Nurse and Ops Manager, NHS Direct, W Yorks, and Dep. Dir, W Yorks Metropolitan Ambulance Service, 1999–2002; Nat. Dir for Quality and Learning, and Dep. Clin. Dir, NHS Direct, 2002–04; Professional Nursing Officer, DoH, 2004–09; Dir of Nursing, NHS Connecting for Health, 2009–10.

MOORE, Rear-Adm. Simon, CB 2000; Chief Executive, Action Medical Research (formerly Action Research), 2001–09; *b* 25 Sept. 1946; *s* of Ronald and Christine Moore; *m* 1978, Catherine Sarcelet; three *d. Educ:* Brentwood Sch. Joined RN 1964; in command, HM Ships: Walkerton, 1974–75; Rhyl, 1983; Berwick, 1984–85; Asst Dir, Defence Policy, MoD, 1988–91; in command, HMS Fearless, 1991–93; Captain, BRNC, Dartmouth, 1993–95; Dir, Intelligence Regl Assessments, 1995–97; ACDS (Ops), MoD, 1997–2000. Pres., London Flotilla, 1999–2005. Gov., Hurstpierpoint Coll., 2001–13 (Chm. of Govs, 2003–13). Trustee: Assoc. of Med. Res. Charities, 2008–13; British Youth Opera, 2008–; SGS Foundn Trust, 2014–. Chm., Chanctonbury Chorus, 2010–. Liveryman, Curriers' Co., 2006–. *Recreations:* music, choral singing, theatre.

MOORE, Prof. Stuart Alfred; JP; DL; Robert Ottley Professor of Quantitative Studies, University of Manchester, 1992–97, now Emeritus Professor; *b* 9 Oct. 1939; *s* of Alfred Moore and Kathleen (*née* Dodd); *m* 1966, Diana Mary Connery; two *s* one *d. Educ:* Stockport Sch.; Manchester Univ. (MA Econs 1967). University of Manchester: Computer Asst, 1960–64; Lectr, then Sen. Lectr in Econ. Stats, 1964–92; Dean, Fac. of Econ. and Social Studies, 1980–83; Pro Vice-Chancellor, 1985–90, 1997–2000; Dep. Vice-Chancellor, 1990–96; Actg Vice-Chancellor, 1990–92; Chairman: Central Manchester Healthcare NHS Trust, 1992–2001; Stockport PCT, 2001–06; Bench, Manchester City Magistrates, 2006–08. JP City of Manchester, 1996; DL Greater Manchester, 2007. Hon. DSocSc Manchester, 2001. *Publications:* various papers in learned jls. *Recreations:* gardening, photography, travel, thrillers, films. *Address:* 2 Carisbrooke Avenue, Hazel Grove, Stockport SK7 5PL.

MOORE, Terence, CBE 1993; business consultant, 1995; Group Managing Director and Chief Executive Officer, Conoco Ltd, 1987–95; *b* 24 Dec. 1931; *s* of Arthur Doncaster Moore and Dorothy Irene Gladys (*née* Godwin); *m* 1955, Tessa Catherine (*née* Wynne); two *s* one *d. Educ:* Strand Sch., London; BScEcon, Univ. of London; Harvard (AMP). ACII 1958; AICS 1959. Shell Internat. Petroleum Co., 1948–64; Locana Corp. Ltd (investment bank), 1964–65; Conoco Ltd, 1965–95: Dep. Man. Dir, Marketing and Operations, 1975; Man. Dir, Supply and Trading, Europe, 1979. Director: Conoco Pension Trustees Ltd, 1996–2003; James Fisher & Son plc, 1998–2004. Pres., Oil Industries Club, 2003–09; Hon. Sec., Inst. of Petroleum, 1995–2001. Gov., Greenwich Theatre, 1991–97 (Vice Chm. Govs, 1992–93). Chm., St Katherine and Shadwell Trust, 1999. *Publications:* articles in industry jls. *Recreations:* music, theatre, walking, family and friends. *Address:* 67 Merchant Court, Thorpes Yard, 61 Wapping Wall, E1W 3SJ. *T:* and *Fax:* (020) 7481 0853. *E:* t.moore@talktalk.net.

MOORE, Prof. Terry, PhD; FRAS, FRIN, FCInstCES; Professor of Satellite Navigation, since 2001, Director, Nottingham Geospatial Institute (formerly Institute of Engineering Surveying and Space Geodesy), since 2003, and Associate Dean, Faculty of Engineering, since 2011, University of Nottingham; *b* 3 May 1961; *s* of Colin Leonard and Edna Moore; *m* 1985, Ingrid Tamara Rejent; one *s* one *d. Educ:* Univ. of Nottingham (BSc 1st Cl. Civil Engrg 1982; PhD Space Geodesy 1986). FRAS 1983; FRIN 1995; FCInstCES 2009. University of Nottingham: Res. Fellow, 1985–88; Lectr, 1989–97; Reader in Satellite Navigation, 1997–2000; Dep. Hd, Sch. of Civil Engrg, 2008–10. Special Prof., Chinese Acad. of Surveying and Mapping, 2004–. Vice Pres., Royal Inst. of Navigation, 2008–10, 2014–. Associate Fellow, Remote Sensing and Photogrammetry Soc., 2001. Fellow, US Inst. of Navigation, 2013. Harold Spencer-Jones Gold Medal, Royal Inst. of Navigation, 2013. *Publications:* chapters in: Sovereign Limits Beneath the Oceans: delimiting the new continental shelf, 1999; Guidelines for the use of GPS in Surveying and Mapping, 2003; contrib. papers to learned jls incl. Jl Navigation, Survey Rev., IEE Digest, GPS Solutions, Internat. Hydrographic Rev., Advances in Astronautical Scis, Hydro Internat., IALA Bulletin, Jl Surveying Engrg, Jl Satellite Positioning, Navigation and Communication, Jl British Interplanetary Soc., Navigation, Prequisas, Revista Brasileira de Cartografia, Space Communications Jl. *Recreations:* mountaineering, hill walking and other outdoor activities, travelling and caravanning, music: listening, singing and playing guitar, reading, sport, Sheffield United FC. *Address:* Nottingham Geospatial Institute, Nottingham Geospatial Building, University of Nottingham Innovation Park, Nottingham NG7 2TU. *T:* (0115) 951 3886, *Fax:* (0115) 951 3881. *E:* terry.moore@nottingham.ac.uk. *Club:* Austrian Alpine (Section Britannia).

MOORE, Trevor Charles; HM Diplomatic Service, retired; Strategic Development Consultant, Diocese of London, since 2014; *b* Freetown, Sierra Leone, 19 Jan. 1958; *s* of Samuel Robert William Moore and Janet Joan Moore; *m* 1991, Diane Elizabeth Burns; three *s. Educ:* Manchester Univ. (BA Jt Hons American and Russian Studies). Joined HM Diplomatic Service, 1980; Third Sec., Belgrade, Yugoslavia, 1983–86; Vice-Consul, NY, 1986–87; Second Sec., (Pol-Mil.), Washington, 1987–89; FCO, London, 1989–97; First Sec. (Comprehensive Nuclear Test Ban Treaty), Vienna, 1997–2001; Deputy Head: Latin America and Caribbean Dept, FCO, 2001–04; Counter-Proliferation Dept, FCO, 2004–07; Human Rights, Democracy and Governance Gp, FCO, 2007–08; Ambassador to Tajikistan, 2009–12; Finance Directorate, FCO, 2012; Special Projects Officer, Syria Team, FCO, 2012–13. *Recreations:* walking (Gold Duke of Edinburgh Award), reading (American and Russian literature), opera.

MOORE, Maj. Gen. William Hewitt, CBE 2004; Chief Executive Officer, The Portman Estate, since 2011; *b* 24 Feb. 1958; *s* of Brian and Eileen Moore; *m* 1986, Jane Moore; two *s. Educ:* Univ. of Salford (BA Hons Pols and Hist. of Industrial Soc. 1979). Battery Comdr 1 Parachute Battery (Bull's Troop), RHA, 1992–94; Directing Staff, Army Staff Coll., 1994–96; CO 7th Parachute Regt, RHA, 1996–98; Col Force Develt, 1998–2001; Commander: Sierra Leone Armed Forces, 2001; 19 Mechanised Bde, 2001–03; Dir Equipment Capability (Ground Manoeuvre), MoD, 2004–07; Dir Gen. Logistics, Support and Equipment, HQ Land Forces, 2007–08; Dep. Comdg Gen. Multi Nat. Corps, Iraq, 2009; Dir (Battlespace Manoeuvre) and Master Gen. of the Ordnance, 2010–11. Dir, Inter Services T20, Lord's, 2010–12. Trustee, Malvern Coll., 2005–14. FCMI. CMgr 2011. QCVS 2001. Cross of Merit (Czech Republic), 2003; Officer, Legion of Merit (USA), 2011. *Publications:* articles in RUSI, British Army Rev. *Recreations:* cricket, hill walking, ski-ing, cycling, rock music, outwitting the dog.

MOORE, Sir William (Roger Clotworthy), 3rd Bt *cr* 1932; TD 1962; DL; *b* 17 May 1927; *s* of Sir William Samson Moore, 2nd Bt, and Ethel Cockburn Gordon (*d* 1973); *S* father, 1978; *m* 1954, Gillian, *d* of John Brown, Co. Antrim; one *s* one *d. Educ:* Marlborough; RMC, Sandhurst. Lieut Royal Inniskilling Fusiliers, 1945; Major North Irish Horse, 1956. Grand Juror, Co. Antrim, 1952–68. Prison visitor, 1968–72. Mem., Parole Bd for Scotland, 1978–80. High Sheriff, Co. Antrim, 1964; DL Co. Antrim, 1990. *Heir: s* Richard William Moore [*b* 8 May 1955; *m* 1985, Karyn Furness; three *d.* Lieut Royal Scots, 1974]. *Address:* Moore Lodge, Ballymoney, Co. Antrim, Northern Ireland BT53 7NT. *Club:* Kildare Street and University (Dublin).

MOORE-BICK, Maj. Gen. John David, CBE 1997 (OBE 1991); DL; FICE; FCIL; General Secretary, Forces Pension Society, 2007–15; *b* 10 Oct. 1949; *s* of late John Ninian Moore-Bick and Kathleen Margaret Moore-Bick (*née* Beall); *m* 1973, Anne Horton; one *d. Educ:* Stonegate Sch.; Skinners'; St Catherine's Coll., Oxford (BA (Forestry), MA). Commissioned RA (V) 1969, regular commission, 1971; transf. to RE, 1972; served 45 Commando Gp, Junior Leaders' Regt RE and 23 Amphibious Engr Sqdn, 1972–79; Führungsakademie der Bundeswehr, 1979–82; HQ UKLF, 1982–84; Falkland Is, 1984–85; 26 Armd Engr Sqdn, 1985–86; Asst to Chm., NATO Mil. Cttee, 1986–88; 21 Engr Regt, Germany, and Gulf War, 1988–91; Chief Engr, Multi National Airmobile Div., 1991; Col Army Plans, MoD, 1991–94; Chief Engr, ARRC, 1994–95 and Implementation Force, Sarajevo, 1995–96; Dir, Army Staff Duties, MoD, 1996–99; Leader, MoD Study into Future of Shrivenham/Watchfield, 1999; MA to High Rep., Sarajevo, 2000; GOC UK Support Comd (Germany), 2001–03; Special Defence Advr, Serbia and Montenegro, 2003–04. Hon. Colonel: 39 (Skinners') Signal Regt, 2001–06; Sussex ACF, 2007–; Col Comdt, RE, 2002–12; Sqdn Col, 56 Signal Sqdn (V), 2011–14. Chm., RE Assoc., 2007–12. Patron, Eastbourne Scottish Pipe Band, 2006–; Chm., Blythe Sappers, 2010. Chm. Govs, Skinners' Sch., 2005–15. FICE 1997; FCIL (FIL 2003). Liveryman, Skinners' Co., 1988– (First Warden, 2007–08; Master, 2008–09). DL E Sussex, 2006. 1st Cl. Service Order (Hungary), 1996. *Recreations:* Eastern Europe and Germany, Kent and Sussex Weald. *Address:* Castle Well, Ewhurst Green, E Sussex TN32 5TD. *Club:* Army and Navy.

See also Rt Hon. Sir M. J. Moore-Bick.

MOORE-BICK, Rt Hon. Sir Martin (James), Kt 1995; PC 2005; **Rt Hon. Lord Justice Moore-Bick;** a Lord Justice of Appeal, since 2005; *b* 6 Dec. 1946; *s* of late John Ninian Moore-Bick and Kathleen Margaret Moore-Bick (*née* Beall); *m* 1974, Tessa Penelope Gee; two *s* two *d. Educ:* The Skinners' Sch., Tunbridge Wells; Christ's Coll., Cambridge (MA; Hon. Fellow, 2009). Called to the Bar, Inner Temple, 1969, Bencher, 1992 (Treas., 2015); QC 1986; a Recorder, 1990–95; a Judge of the High Ct of Justice, QBD, 1995–2005; Dep. Hd of Civil Justice, 2007–12; Vice-Pres., Court of Appeal, Civil Div., 2014–. Chm., Legal Services Consultancy Panel, 2005–09. *Recreations:* early music, gardening, reading. *Address:* Royal Courts of Justice, Strand, WC2A 2LL.

See also Maj. Gen. J. D. Moore-Bick.

MOORE-BRABAZON, family name of **Baron Brabazon of Tara**.

MOORE-BRIDGER, Timothy Peter, MA; Headmaster, King Edward VI Grammar School, Stratford-upon-Avon, 1997–2010; *b* 11 May 1945; *s* of Harry Charles and Winifred Jane Moore-Bridger; *m* 1980, Iwona Elzbieta Joanna (*née* Barycz); one *s* two *d. Educ:* Oswestry Sch., Shropshire; Queens' Coll., Cambridge (MA Mod. and Medieval Langs). Asst Master teaching French, Latin, Italian, Ancient History, St Paul's Sch., Barnes, 1967–88; Dep. Headmaster, Nottingham High Sch., 1988–97. Trustee: Shakespeare Birthplace Trust, 1997–2010; Hampton Lucy Grammar Sch. Trust, 2001–10. Gov., Oswestry Sch., 2011– (Vice Chm., 2013–). *Recreations:* attending and supporting RSC productions, singing in Stratford-upon-Avon Choral Society, gardening.

MOORE-GILLON, Dr John Christopher, FRCP; Consultant Physician, King Edward VII's Hospital Sister Agnes, since 2007; *b* London, 2 Jan. 1953; *s* of John Alec Moore-Gillon and Daphne Moore-Gillon; *m* 1980, Victoria Kirby, FRCS; one *s* two *d. Educ:* Tiffin Sch.; St Catharine's Coll., Cambridge (BA 1973); St Thomas's Hosp. Med. Sch. (MB (Dist.) BChir 1976; MD 1987); Univ. of London ext. (LLB 2003). MRCP 1978, FRCP 1992. Hse Officer, St Thomas's and Kingston Hosps, 1976–77; Sen. Hse Officer, St Thomas's and Royal Brompton Hosps, 1977–78; Med. Registrar, Kingston and St Thomas's Hosps, 1978–80; Res. Fellow, 1980–83, Lectr, 1983–88, Dept of Medicine, St Thomas's Hosp. Med. Sch.; Sen. Registrar, London Chest Hosp., 1985–88; Sen. Lectr and Hon. Consultant Physician, Med. Coll. of St Bartholomew's Hosp., 1988–92; Consultant Physician: St Bartholomew's Hosp., 1992–2010; Royal London Hosp., 1998–2010, now Emeritus Consultant. Hon. Sec., British Thoracic Soc., 1992–94; British Lung Foundation: Chm., 1994–99; Pres., 2001–07; Vice-Pres., 2007–; Hon. Med. Advr, 2010–. Liveryman, Soc. of Apothecaries, 1989 (Sen. Warden, 2013–14; Master, 2014–15). *Publications:* contrib. book chapters, rev. articles and scientific papers on respiratory medicine. *Recreations:* music, theatre, time with family and friends. *Address:* 37 Devonshire Street, W1G 6QA. *T:* (020) 7935 1977, *Fax:* (020) 7486 1978. *E:* drjohn.moore-gillon@btconnect.com. *Clubs:* Athenæum, Garrick.

MOORE-GWYN, Alison Frances, LVO 2013; Chief Executive Officer, Fields in Trust (National Playing Fields Association), 2004–12; *b* 25 March 1950; *d* of late Clifford George White and Joyce Beatrice White (*née* Lawley); *m* 1974, David Moore-Gwyn; two *s* one *d. Educ:* Berkhamsted Sch. for Girls; Girton Coll., Cambridge (BA 1971). Admitted solicitor, 1976; served articles, Clifford Turner. Trustee, NPFA, 1990–2004 (Chm., 2000–04). Trustee: Orders of St John Care Trust, 2000–10; St Endellion Easter Fest., 2004–. Gov., Berkhamsted Collegiate Sch., 1979–2013 (Vice Chm., 1997–2013). Trustee: Countryside Educn Trust, 2014–; Fortune Centre for Riding Therapy, 2014–; Vintage Music, 2014–. Mem., New Forest Beekeeping Assoc. *Recreations:* singing and enjoyment of music, fine art, reading, travel, gardening, sailing in fine weather only. *E:* alisonmooregwyn@gmail.com. *Club:* Beaulieu River Sailing.

See also D. C. S. White.

MOORE-WILTON, Maxwell William, AC 2001; Chairman and Director, Sydney Airports Ltd (formerly Macquarie Airports Management Ltd, then MAp Airports Ltd), since 2006; Chairman, Southern Cross Media Group (formerly Executive Chairman, Macquarie Media Group), since 2007; *b* 27 Jan. 1943; *s* of William Moore-Wilton and Cavell Little; *m* 1966, Janette Costin; one *s* one *d. Educ:* St Joseph's Coll., Qld; Univ. of Queensland (BEc). Commonwealth Department of Trade, Australia, 1964–78: Minister, Delegn for Trade Negotiations, Geneva, 1974–76; First Asst Sec., Policy Develt/Commodity Policy, 1976–78; Dep. Sec., Commonwealth Dept of Primary Industry, 1980–81; Gen. Manager, Australian Wheat Bd, Melbourne, 1981–84; Man. Dir, Australian Nat. Line, Melbourne, 1984–88; Chm., NSW Egg Corp., 1987–89; Chief Exec., Maritime Services Bd of NSW, 1989–91; Dir-Gen., NSW Dept of Transport, 1991–94; Chief Exec., Roads and Traffic Authy of NSW, 1994–95; Chm., Public Transport Corp., Vic, 1995–96; Nat. Dir, Policy Co-ordination and Priorities Rev., Australian Stock Exchange Ltd, 1995–96; Sec., Dept of Prime Minister and Cabinet, Australia, 1996–2002; Exec. Chm. and CEO, 2003–06, Chm., 2006–, Southern Cross Airports Corp. Hldgs (formerly Sydney Airport Corp.) Ltd; Exec. Dir, Macquarie Bank, 2006–08. Centenary Medal, Aust., 2003. *Recreations:* reading, swimming. *Address:* 8 Beatrice Street, Clontarf, NSW 2093, Australia. *Club:* Australian (Sydney).

MOOREHEAD, Caroline Mary, OBE 2005; FRSL; writer; *b* 28 Oct. 1944; *d* of Alan Moorehead and Lucy (*née* Milner); *m* 1967, Jeremy Swift (marr. diss. 2001); one *s* one *d. Educ:* Sorbonne, Paris; University Coll. London (BA Hons 1965). Reporter, Time magazine, 1968–70; Feature Writer, Telegraph magazine, 1970–71; Feature Ed., TES, 1971–74; Feature Writer, The Times, 1973–85; Human Rights Columnist and Feature Writer, Independent, 1985–91; Associate Producer, BBC human rights TV series, 1988–99. Royal Literary Fund Fellow, 2003–05. Trustee: Council, PEN, 1992–97; London Liby, 1994–97; Index on Censorship, 1994–2005; British Inst. for Human Rights, 1995–2004; Soc. of Authors,

1996–99; RSL, 1996–2001; Helen Bamber Foundn, 2005–; Interights, 2005; Mem., Eminent Persons Mission to USSR, 1994; Co-Founder, Africa and Middle East Refugee Assistance, 2003–. FRSL 1998. *Publications:* Fortune's Hostages, 1980; Sidney Bernstein: a biography, 1984; Freya Stark: a biography, 1987; (ed) Beyond the Rim of the World: the letters of Freya Stark, 1989; Troublesome People, 1991; (ed) Betrayed: children in today's world, 1994; Schliemann and the Lost Treasures of Troy, 1994; Dunant's Dream: war, Switzerland and the Red Cross, 1998; Iris Origo: Marchesa of the Val d'Orcia, 2000; Martha Gellhorn: a life, 2003; Human Cargo: a journey among refugees, 2005; (ed) Letters of Martha Gellhorn, 2006; Dancing to the Precipice: Lucie de la Tour du Pin and the French Revolution, 2009; Humanity in War, 2009; A Train in Winter, 2011; Village of Secrets: defying the Nazis in Vichy France, 2014. *Recreations:* travel, music. *Address:* c/o Clare Alexander, Aitken Alexander Associates, 291 Gray's Inn Road, WC1X 8EB.

MOORES, Sir Peter, Kt 2003; CBE 1991; philanthropist; Founder and Patron, Peter Moores Foundation, 1964–2014; Founder, Compton Verney Art Gallery; *b* 9 April 1932; *s* of Sir John Moores, CBE; *m* 1960, Luciana Pinto (marr. diss. 1984); one *s* one *d*. *Educ:* Eton; Christ Church, Oxford; Wiener Akademie der Musik und darstellende Kunst. Worked in opera at Glyndebourne and Vienna State Opera. Founded Peter Moores Foundn to support opera, visual arts, educn, health, youth, social and envmtl projects, 1964, closed down in 2014 with Swansong Project, supporting eight UK opera cos, 2014–15 (final prodn at Glyndebourne, 2015); pioneer of opera recordings in English trans. incl. The Ring of the Nibelungen, Mary Stuart, Julius Caesar, Falstaff, The Makropulos Case (all ENO), Idomeneo, Duke Bluebeard, Don Carlos (Opera North), Carmen (new critical edn), Il Trovatore, Tosca, Der Rosenkavalier; rare 19th century Italian opera in original lang. with Opera Rara, incl. Maria Padilla, Emilia di Liverpool, Rosmonda d'Inghilterra, Ricciardo e Zoraide, Rossini's Otello, Zoraida di Granata; contemporary English lang. recordings incl. Gawain, The Tempest (Royal Opera), Flight, The Sacrifice, Into the Little Hill, Written on Skin. Peter Moores Foundn Scholarships awarded to promising young opera singers. Estab. Transatlantic Slave Trade Gallery, Merseyside Maritime Mus., 1994. Endowed Faculty Dirship and Chair of Mgt Studies, 1992, and Lecturership in Chinese Business Studies, 2004, Oxford Univ. Benefactor, Chair of Tropical Horticulture, Univ. of WI, Barbados, 1995. Founded: Compton Verney House Trust, 1993 to house six perm. art collections and exhibns; Peter Moores Charitable Trust, 1998. Dir, The Littlewoods Orgn, 1965–93 (Chm., 1977–80). Director: Singer & Friedlander, 1978–92; Scottish Opera, 1988–92; Trustee, Tate Gall., 1978–85; Governor of the BBC, 1981–83. DL Lancs, 1992–2013. Hon. FRNCM, 1985. Hon. MA Christ Church, 1975; Hon. DLitt: WI, Barbados, 2008; Warwick, 2011. Gold Medal of the Italian Republic, 1974; Stauffer Medal, Germany, 2008; Prince of Wales Medal for Arts Philanthropy, Arts & Business Cymru, 2012. *Recreation:* opera. *Address:* c/o Katamor, 3 Vernon Street, Liverpool L2 2AY. *Club:* Boodle's.

MOORES, Dame Yvonne, DBE 1999; Chief Nursing Officer and Director of Nursing, Department of Health, 1992–99; *b* 14 June 1941; *d* of late Tom Abraham Quick and Phyllis Quick (*née* Jeremiah); *m* 1st, 1969, Bruce Holmes Ramsden; 2nd, 1975, Brian Moores. *Educ:* Itchen Grammar Sch., Southampton; Royal South Hampshire Hosp. (RGN); Southampton Gen. Hosp. (RM). Ward Sister, Whittington Hosp. and Royal Hampshire County Hosp., 1964–70; Principal Nursing Officer: N London HMC, 1971–72; W Manchester, 1973–74; Dist Nursing Officer, N Manchester, 1974–76; Area Nursing Officer, Manchester AHA, 1976–81; Chief Nursing Officer: Welsh Office, 1982–88; Scottish Office, Home and Health Dept, 1988–92. Vice-Chm., NHS Supply Council, 1979–82; Pres., Infection Control Nurses Assoc., 1987–90; Mem., WHO Global Adv. Gp for Nursing and Midwifery, 1992–97 (Chair, 1994–97); Vis. Prof., Sheffield Univ., 1996–99. Chm., Macmillan Cancer Unit Appeal, Calderdale, 2000–01. Dep. Chair, Cttee of Univ. Chairs, 2003–04. Bd Mem., Leadership Foundn for Higher Educn, 2005–07. Non-executive Director: NHBC, 2004–11 (Chm., Pensions Bd, 2007–); Poole Hosp. NHS Trust, 2006–14 (Vice-Chm., 2010–14). Mem. Council, Southampton Univ., 1994–2006 (Chm., 2000–06); Pro-Chancellor, Bournemouth Univ., 2006–13. Mem., Internat. Award Cttee, Princess Srinagarindra Award, 2000–. Patron: Assoc. for Continence Advice, 2005–11; Poole Hosp. Africa Link, 2010–; Forest Holme Hospice Charity, 2015–. Mem., Policy Steering Cttee, Ferndown Golf Club, 2007–10. Hon. Fellow, Coll. of Med., Univ. of Wales, 1995. Hon. FRSPH (Hon. FRSH); Hon. FFPHM 1996; Hon. FRCP. Hon. DSc: Portsmouth, 1993; Huddersfield, 1997; Bradford, 1998; DUniv: Central England, 2001; Southampton, 2006; Hon. DCL Northumbria, 1995; Hon. MA De Montfort, 1995; Hon. DEd Bournemouth, 2014. *Recreations:* bridge, golf, knitting, cooking. *Address:* The Chapter House, 43 Golf Links Road, Ferndown, Dorset BH22 8BT.

MOOREY, Adrian Edward; independent consultant, since 2003; *b* 4 May 1946; *s* of Edward Alfred Moorey and Lily Elizabeth Moorey; *m* 1st, 1969, Sandra Ann Jeffrey (marr. diss.); one *s*; 2nd, 1987, Lesley Nicola Hancock; one *s* one *d*. *Educ:* Sir Joseph Williamson's Mathematical Sch., Rochester. Advertising and Marketing Asst, Lonsdale-Hands Orgn, 1964–67; Asst Information Officer, 1967–69, Inf. Officer, 1969–72, Home Office; Press Officer, PM's Office, 1973; Department of Employment: Sen. Press Officer, 1974–75; Chief Press Officer, 1976–81; Head of Inf., 1982–86; Director of Information: DTI, 1987–90; Home Office, 1990–94; Dir, Corporate and Govt Affairs, Cable and Wireless plc, 1995–99; Corporate Communications Dir, CAA, 1999–2001; Dir of Communications, NATS, 2001–03. *Recreations:* cricket, golf. *Address:* Ellesmere House, 56 Bloomfield Avenue, Bath BA2 3AE.

MOORHEAD, Prof. Richard Lewis; Professor of Law and Professional Ethics, and Director, Centre for Ethics and Law, University College London, since 2012; *b* Ashington, Northumberland, 12 Feb. 1969; *s* of Lewis Moorhead and Elizabeth Dalton; *m* 2011, Dr Leanne Smith; one *s* two *d*. *Educ:* Hanley Castle High Sch.; Univ. of Warwick (LLB Hons Law). Admitted solicitor, 1995. Res. Associate, Univ. of Liverpool, 1990–91, 1992–93; trainee solicitor, 1993–95, solicitor, Irwin Mitchell, 1995–96; Res. Fellow, Inst. of Advanced Legal Studies, 1996–97; Lectr, Univ. of Birmingham, 1997–98; Res. Fellow, 1998–2000, Sen. Res. Fellow, 2000–02, Inst. of Advanced Legal Studies; Cardiff University: Sen. Lectr, 2002–04; Prof. of Law, 2004–12. Member: Legal Services Consultative Panel, 2001–06; Civil Justice Council, 2006–11. *Publications:* After Universalism: reengineering access to justice, 2003; Litigants in Person in First Instance Proceedings, 2005; Judgecraft, 2007; Damage-based Contingency Fees in Employment Cases, 2008; Something for Nothing, 2009; Designing Ethics Indicators for Legal Services, 2012. *Recreations:* reading, films, poetry. *Address:* Faculty of Laws, University College London, Bentham House, Endsleigh Gardens, WC1H 0EG. *T:* (020) 7679 1409. *E:* r.moorhead@ucl.ac.uk.

MOORHOUSE, Barbara Jane; Chief Operating Officer, Westminster City Council, 2011–13 (Strategic Director, Finance and Performance, 2010–11); *b* 21 Nov. 1958; *d* of Andre and Rosalind Moorhouse; *m* 2001, Mike Brittain. *Educ:* St Catherine's Coll., Oxford (BA Hons PPE 1981). FCMA 1990; ACT 1999. European Finance Dir, Courtaulds plc, 1986–90; Regulatory Dir, South West Water plc, 1991–95; Finance Dir, Johnson Controls Inc., 1995–96; Gp Finance Dir, Morgan Sindall plc, 1997–98; Interim Exec., Mondex Internat., Jigsaw plc and Energis plc, 1998–2000; Gp Finance Dir, Kewill Systems plc, 2000–02; Chief Financial Officer, Scala Business Solutions NV, 2003–04; Dir Gen., Finance, DCA, subseq. Finance and Commercial, MoJ, 2005–07; Dir Gen., Corporate Resources, DfT, 2007–09. Non-executive Director: CSA, 2003–06; OPM, 2009– (Chm., 2012–); Mem., Financial Reporting Rev. Panel, 2004–; Ind. Dir, Lending Standards Bd, 2014–. Lay Mem., Strategy and Finance, W Hants CCG, 2013–. *Recreations:* horse-riding, ballroom dancing, walking, skiing. *Address:* OPM Group, 252B Gray's Inn Road, WC1X 8XG.

MOORHOUSE, Judith Helen, OBE 2008; Chair, General Teaching Council England, 2004–09; *b* Eastleigh, Hants, 31 Oct. 1949; *d* of Edward and Joan Moorhouse. *Educ:* Coll. of Sarum St Michael, Salisbury (Cert Ed). Teacher of English: Fairoak Sch., Hants, 1971–72; Shackleton Sch., Fallingbostel, W Germany, 1972–73; Toynbee Sch., Eastleigh, 1973–74; Teacher of English, 1974–2010, Hd of Year, 1995–2010, Richmond Sch., N Yorks. National Union of Teachers: Exec. Mem., 1998–2004, 2008–10; Chm., Educn and Equal Opportunities Cttee, 2000–04; Pres., 2006–07. Mem., Governing Council, Nat. Coll. for Sch. Leadership, 2005–09; Specialist Schools and Academies Trust: Mem. Council, 2004–07; Trustee, 2007–12; Chm., Finance and Gen. Purposes Cttee, 2010–12. Non-exec. Dir, Teachers Assurance, 2008–11; Trustee/Director: Teachers Gp Educnl Trust, 2013–; Richmond N Yorks YMCA, 2014–. Nat. Examr of Accounts, NUT, 2012–. *Recreations:* basking on Greek beaches, far-flung travel, trade unionism and equal rights, singing - from blues to requiem masses, indiscriminate reading. *Address:* 67 Frenchgate, Richmond, N Yorks DL10 7AE. *T:* (01748) 825106, 07909 542283. *E:* judy@hmoorhouse.plus.com.

MOORHOUSE, (Kathleen) Tessa; a District Judge (formerly Registrar), Family Division of the High Court of Justice, 1982–2004; a Deputy District Judge, since 2004; *b* 14 Sept. 1938; *d* of late Charles Elijah Hall, MRCVS and Helen Barbara Hall; *m* 1959, Rodney Moorhouse. *Educ:* Presentation Convent, Derbyshire; Leeds Univ.; King's Coll., London. Called to the Bar, Inner Temple, 1971. Asst, Jardine's Bookshop, Manchester, 1953–56; student, Leeds Univ., 1956–59; teacher of educationally subnormal, 1959–61; student, King's Coll., London, 1961–62; Classifier, Remand Home, 1962–64; Lectr in Law, 1964–71; barrister in practice, 1971–82. *Address:* 1st Avenue House, 42–49 High Holborn, WC1V 6NP. *T:* (020) 7947 6000; Coram Chambers, Fulwood Place, WC1V 6HG.

MOORHOUSE, Michael George Currer; His Honour Judge Moorhouse; a Circuit Judge, since 2001; *b* 29 June 1946; *s* of Reginald Currer Moorhouse and Betty Moorhouse; *m* 1970, Jane Mary Ross; one *s* three *d*. *Educ:* Ampleforth Coll. Admitted solicitor, 1970; in private practice, 1970–2001; Partner, R. C. Moorhouse Co., subseq. Keeble Hawson Moorhouse, 1975–2001. *Recreations:* gardening, sport, walking. *Address:* Middlesbrough Combined Court, Russell Street, Middlesbrough TS1 2AE.

MOORHOUSE, Tessa; *see* Moorhouse, K. T.

MOOSA, Nazo; Managing Director, C5 Capital, since 2013; *b* Kabul, Afghanistan, 1 Feb. 1970; *d* of Mahbuba Moosa and M. Daoud Moosa. *Educ:* Univ. of Calif, Los Angeles (BA 1992); Columbia Business Sch. (MBA 1999). Associate, JH Partners, 1999; Dir, Carlyle Gp, 2000–12. Member, Board: Transics, 2004–06; LBi (formerly Big Mouth Media), 2006–12; Metrasens, 2013–; Arts Council England, 2013–; Charity Commn, 2013–. *Address:* 7 Vigo Street, W1S 3JR. *T:* 07799 472292.

MORAES, Claude Ajit; Member (Lab) London Region, European Parliament, since 1999; Deputy Leader, European Parliamentary Labour Party, since 2009; *b* 22 Oct. 1965; *s* of H. I. Moraes and Theresa (*née* Aranha); *m* Bharti Patel; one *s*. *Educ:* St Modan's High Sch., Stirling; Univ. of Dundee (LLB 1988); Birkbeck Coll., Univ. of London (MSc 1989). Res. Asst to John Reid, MP and Paul Boateng, MP, 1987–89; postgrad. study in internat. law, LSE, 1990–91; Nat. Policy Officer, TUC, 1989–92; Dir, Jt Council for Welfare of Immigrants, 1992–98; Chief Exec., Immigrants' Aid Trust, 1992–98. European Parliament: Socialist and Democrat Gp spokesperson on Civil Liberties, Justice and Home Affairs, 2009–14; Chm., Civil Liberties, Justice and Home Affairs Cttee, 2014–. Comr, CRE, 1998–99. Mem., Council, Liberty, 1997–2005. Columnist, Tribune, 1998–2005. Patron, Refugee Therapy Centre, 2000–. Contested (Lab) Harrow W, 1992. FRSA 1998. MEP of Year, Justice and Civil Liberties, Dods and Parliament Mag., 2011. *Publications:* (jtly) Social Work and Minorities: European perspectives, 1998; (jtly) The Politics of Migration, 2003; (jtly) The European Union after the Treaty of Lisbon, 2012; contributed: Full Employment and the Global Economy, 2004; Perspectives on Migration, 2005; Immigration under Labour, 2010; Roma: a European minority, 2011; contrib. jls and nat. newspapers. *Recreations:* Scottish literature, chess, films, listening to BBC Radio 4 and 6, World Service, BBC London Radio and my MP3 player. *Address:* European Parliament, Rue Wiertz, 1047 Brussels, Belgium. *T:* (Brussels) (2) 2845553, *T:* (020) 7609 5005. *E:* office@claudemoraes.com.

MORAHAN, Christopher Thomas, CBE 2011; television, film and theatre director; *b* 9 July 1929; *s* of Thomas Hugo Morahan and Nancy Charlotte Morahan (*née* Barker); *m* 1st, 1954, Joan (*née* Murray) (decd); two *s* (one *d* decd); 2nd, 1973, Anna (*née* Wilkinson, acting name Anna Carteret); two *d*. *Educ:* Highgate; Old Vic Theatre School. Directing for ATV, 1957–61; freelance director in TV for BBC and ITV, 1961–71; Head of Plays, BBC TV, 1972–76; Associate, National Theatre, 1977–88; Director, Greenpoint Films, 1983–2003. Trustee, Cherub Theatre, 2005–13. *Stage:* Little Murders, RSC, Aldwych, 1967; This Story of Yours, Royal Court, 1968; Flint, Criterion, 1970; The Caretaker, Mermaid, 1972, Everyman Th., Liverpool and Bath, 2009, transf. Trafalgar Studios, 2010, Adelaide Fest., San Francisco, Brooklyn Acad., NY, 2012; Melon, Th. Royal, Haymarket, 1987; A Letter of Resignation, Comedy, 1997; Quartet, Albery, 1999; The Importance of Being Earnest, Australia and NZ, 2000; Naked Justice, W Yorks Playhouse, 2001; The Dwarfs, Tricycle, 2003; Oldworld, tour, 2003; Hayfever, Clwyd Theatr Cymru, 2004; Daisy Miller, tour, 2005; The Rivals, Bath, 2005; The Linden Tree, Orange Tree Th., Richmond, 2006; Present Laughter, An Ideal Husband, Clwyd Theatr Cymru, 2006; Legal Fictions, tour, 2007, Savoy, 2008; Pack of Lies, tour, 2009; The White House Murder Case, Orange Tree Th., Richmond, 2012; Chichester Festival: Major Barbara, 1988; The Handyman, 1996; Racing Demon, 1998; The Importance of Being Earnest, Semi-Detached, The Retreat from Moscow, 1999; Heartbreak House, 2000; The Winslow Boy, Hock and Soda Water, 2001; The Ragged Trousered Philanthropists, 2010, and Everyman Th., Liverpool; Stevie, 2014; for National Theatre: State of Revolution, 1977; Brand, Strife, The Philanderer, 1978; Richard III, The Wild Duck, 1979; Sisterly Feelings, 1980; Man and Superman, 1981; Wild Honey (London Standard, Olivier, British Theatre Assoc. and Plays and Players Awards for Best Dir of the Year), 1984; The Devil's Disciple, 1994; *films:* Clockwise, 1986; Paper Mask, 1990; *television: films:* The Gorge, 1967; In the Secret State, 1985; After Pilkington, 1987 (Special Jury Prize, San Francisco Film Fest., 1987, Prix Italia, 1987); Troubles, 1988; The Heat of the Day, 1989; Old Flames, 1990; Can You Hear Me Thinking?, 1990; Common Pursuit, 1992; The Bullion Boys, 1993 (Internat. Emmy Award, 1994); Summer Day's Dream, 1994; It Might Be You, 1995; Element of Doubt, 1996; The Dwarfs, 2003; HR, 2007; *series:* Emergency Ward 10; The Orwell Trilogy; Talking to a Stranger; Fathers and Families; Jewel in the Crown (Internat. Emmy Award, BAFTA Best Series Dir Award, BAFTA Desmond Davis Award, 1984; Primetime Emmy Award, 1985); Ashenden, 1991; Unnatural Pursuits, 1992 (Internat. Emmy Award, 1993); Peacock Spring, 1996; A Dance to the Music of Time, 1997. Best Play direction award, SFTA, 1969. *Recreations:* photography, bird watching. *Address:* c/o Sheperd Management, 45 Maddox Street, W1S 2PE. *T:* (020) 7495 7813. *Club:* Garrick.

MORAN, 3rd Baron *cr* 1943; **James McMoran Wilson;** Founder and Chairman, Source Squared, since 2006; *b* York, England, 6 Aug. 1952; *s* of 2nd Baron Moran, KCMG and Shirley Rowntree Wilson (*née* Harris); *S* father, 2014; *m* 1980, Hon. Jane Hepburne-Scott, *d* of 10th Lord Polwarth, TD; two *s*. *Educ:* Eton Coll.; Trinity Coll., Cambridge (BA 1974; MA 1979). With Econ. Intelligence Dept, Bank of England, 1974–75; First Nat Bank of Boston, 1977–83; Partner, Boston Ventures, 1983–2005. *Recreations:* fishing, sailing, running. *Heir: er s* Hon. David Andrew McMoran Wilson, *b* 6 Nov. 1990. *Address:* 65 Upland Road, Brookline, MA 02445, USA. *Clubs:* Flyfishers'; Somerset (Boston).

MORAN, Andrew Gerard; QC 1994; a Recorder, since 1997; Deemster, High Court of Isle of Man, since 2002; a Deputy High Court Judge, since 2005; *b* 19 Oct. 1953; *s* of Francis Michael Moran and Winifrede Moran; *m* 1977, Carole Jane Sullivan; six *s* one *d*. *Educ:* West Park Grammar Sch., St Helens, Lancs; Britannia Royal Naval Coll., Dartmouth; Balliol Coll., Oxford (BA Law). Called to Bar, Gray's Inn, 1976, Bencher, 2005. Maritime and Commercial Arbitrator, London and Singapore, 2007–. *Recreations:* family, sport, travel, sailing. *Address:* Stone Chambers, 4 Field Court, Gray's Inn, WC1R 5EF. *T:* (020) 7440 6900.

MORAN, Catherine Elizabeth, (Caitlin); author; columnist, The Times, since 1992; *b* Brighton, 5 April 1975; *d* of John Moran and Margaret Moran; *m* 1999, Peter Paphides; two *d*. *Educ:* none. Melody Maker, 1992–95; presenter, Naked City, Channel 4, 1992–93; co-writer, Raised by Wolves, Channel 4, 2015. Columnist of the Year, 2010, Critic of the Year, 2011, Interviewer of the Year, 2011, British Press Awards; Columnist of the Year, British Soc. of Mag. Editors' Awards, 2013, 2014. *Publications:* The Chronicles of Narmo, 1990; How To Be a Woman, 2011 (Book of the Year, Galaxy Book Awards); Moranthology, 2012; How to Build a Girl, 2014. *Recreations:* hair biggening, cava, eyeliner, The Struggle. *E:* (literary agent, Georgia Garrett) Georgia@rcwlitagency.com, (screenwriting agent, Nick Marston), nick@curtisbrown.co.uk.

MORAN, Christopher John; Chairman, Christopher Moran Group of Companies, since 1970; *b* 16 Jan. 1948; *s* of late Thomas Moran and Iva Mary Moran (*née* Alcock); *m* 1981, Helen Elisabeth Taylor (marr. diss. 1999); two *s* (twins). *Educ:* Owen's Grammar Sch. Chm., C&UCO Properties Ltd, 2009–. Chairman: Finance Bd, LSO, 2004–; Co-operation Ireland (GB), 2004–; Co-operation Ireland, 2006–; Member: Consultative Cttee, Dulwich Picture Gall., 1993–96; Thames Adv. Bd, 1994–97; Adv. Council, LSO, 2008–. Trustee: UCL Hosps Charitable Foundn, 1999– (Chm., 2003–); Exec. Cttee, CCJ, 2003– (Vice Chm., 2008–); Mary Rose Trust, 2004–; LSO Endowment Trust, 2007–; Prince's Charities Council, 2009–. Hon. LLD Ulster. FRSA 2005. *Recreations:* architecture, opera, art, politics, country pursuits. *Address:* c/o Crosby Hall, Cheyne Walk, SW3 5AZ.

MORAN, David John; HM Diplomatic Service; Ambassador to Switzerland and (non-resident) to Liechtenstein, since 2014; *b* 22 Aug. 1959; *s* of late Thomas Henry Moran and of Donna Lois Moran (*née* Zastrow); *m* 1993, Carol Ann Marquis. *Educ:* Stoke Brunswick Sch.; Tonbridge Sch.; Willamette Univ., Salem, Oregon (BA); Univ. of Sussex (MA). Oregon State Employment Div., 1979–80, 1982–83; DTI, 1985; ODA, 1985–88; Second Sec., E Africa Office, ODA, Nairobi, 1988–91; Hd of Section, Econ. Relns Dept, FCO, 1991–93; First Sec., Moscow, 1993–96; Head: France and Switzerland Section, FCO, 1996–98; EU Charter of Rights Section, EU Dept (Internal), 1998–2000; Dep. UK Perm. Rep. to OECD, Paris, 2001–05; Ambassador to Uzbekistan, 2005–07; Counsellor, FCO, 2007–08; on loan to Cabinet Office, 2008–09; Ambassador to Kazakhstan and (non-resident) to Kyrgyz Republic, 2009–12; Chargé d'Affaires to Georgia (with personal rank of Ambassador), 2013. *Recreations:* writing and listening to music, reading, theatre, swimming, football. *Address:* c/o Foreign and Commonwealth Office, King Charles Street, SW1A 2AH.

MORAN, Rt Rev. Mgr John, CBE 1985; Principal RC Chaplain and Vicar General (Army), 1981–85; *b* 3 Dec. 1929; *s* of Thomas Moran and Gertrude May (*née* Sheer). *Educ:* De La Salle Coll., Sheffield; Ushaw Coll., Durham. Ordained Priest, Leeds Diocese, 1956; Curate, Dewsbury, 1956–60; Prison Chaplain, Armley, 1960–61; commissioned Army Chaplain, 1961; service in BAOR, Singapore, Malaya, Hong Kong, UK; Chaplain, RMA Sandhurst, 1968–70, Staff Chaplain, 1970–71; Senior Chaplain, HQ BAOR, 1977–79, and HQ UKLF, 1979–80. *Recreations:* music, rivers, clocks.

MORAN, Air Vice-Marshal Manus Francis; Royal Air Force, retired; *b* 18 April 1927; *s* of John Thomas Moran and Katherine Mary (*née* Coyle); *m* 1955, Maureen Elizabeth Martin, *o d* of Martin Dilks; one *s* three *d* (and one *s* decd). *Educ:* Mount St Joseph Abbey, Roscrea; University College Dublin (MB ChB, BAO 1952; MCh 1964); DLO, RCP and RCS, 1963. St Vincent's Hosp., Dublin, 1952; GP, Lutterworth, 1953–54; joined RAF 1954; Department of Otorhinolaryngology: served London, 1955–56; Wroughton, 1956–58; Weeton, 1958–59; Akrotiri, 1959–61; Halton, 1963–65; Consultant in ORL, RAF, 1965; served Changi, Singapore, 1965–68; Vis. Consultant, Johore Bahru Gen. Hosp., 1966–68; Nocton Hall, 1968–75; Wegberg, 1975–78; Wroughton, 1978–83; Consultant Adviser in ORL (RAF), 1983–88; Dean of Air Force Medicine, 1988–90; Sen. Consultant, RAF, 1990–91; Civilian Consultant in ORL, RAF Hosp., Wroughton, 1991–95. QHP, 1988–91. Lectr in ORL, IAM Farnborough, for Dip. in Aviation medicine, RCP, 1983–88. Consultant: Nuffield Hosp., Leicester, 1992–2000; Met. Police, 1994–2003. Chm., Gen. Cttee, 8th British Acad. Conf. in ORL, 1987–91. Member: Irish Otological Soc.; Midland Inst. of Otology (Vice-Pres., 1971, 1975); Otology Section, RSM (Vice-Pres., Section of Laryngology, 1988–91, Pres., 1991–92); Council, British Assoc. of Otolaryngologists, 1983–88; Joseph Soc., BMA; BS Cttee on Auditory Alarms in med. monitoring equipment, 1983–88; Bd, Co-operation North, 1992–97. Chm., Marston Meysey Charitable Trust, 1989–91 (Vice-Chm., 1987–89); Special Trustee, Royal Nat. Throat, Nose and Ear Hosp., 1993–99. Mem. Editl Bd, Amer. ENT Jl, 1982–92. FRAeS 1996. Hon. FRCSI 1991. Liveryman, Apothecaries' Soc. (Chm., Livery Cttee, 1994–96); Freeman, City of London. CStJ 1990. Med. Soc. (UCD) Gold Medal, 1951; Lady Cade Medal, RCS, 1980. *Publications:* Upper Respiratory Problems in Yellow Nail Syndrome (jtly), 1976; contribs to learned jls on ORL applied to aviation medicine, uraemic rhinitis, vestibular dysfunction, acoustic trauma and hearing conservation. *Recreations:* preservation of rural amenities, walking, poetry, theology, power boating. *Address:* The Old Forge House, Marston Meysey, Cricklade, Wilts SN6 6LQ. *T:* (01285) 810511. *Club:* Royal Air Force.

MORAN, Margaret; *b* 24 April 1955; *d* of Patrick John, (Jack), Moran and Mary (*née* Murphy). *Educ:* Birmingham Univ. (BSocSc). Dir, Housing for Women, 1987–97. Mem., Lewisham BC, 1984–96 (Chairman: Housing Cttee, 1985–91; Direct Lab. Cttee, 1991; Leader, 1995–96). Dep. Chm., AMA, 1994 (Chm., Housing Cttee, 1992). Contested (Lab) Carshalton and Wallington, 1992. MP (Lab) Luton S, 1997–2010. PPS to Minister for Cabinet Office, 1999–2003; an Asst Govt Whip, 2003–05. Member: NI Select Cttee, 1997–98; Public Admin Select Cttee, 1999.

MORAN, Prof. Michael John, PhD; FBA 2004; W. J. M. Mackenzie Professor of Government, University of Manchester, 1990–2011, now Emeritus; *b* 13 April 1946; *s* of Michael Moran and Bridget Moran (*née* Brennan); *m* 1967, Winifred, *d* of Vincent and Ellen Evaskitas; two *s*. *Educ:* Irish Christian Brothers, Kilrush; Cardinal Newman Secondary Mod. Sch., Birmingham; Univ. of Lancaster (BA 1967); Univ. of Essex (MA; PhD 1974). Lectr, Manchester Polytech., 1970–79; University of Manchester: Lectr, 1979–90; Dean, Faculty of Econ. and Social Studies, 1995–98. Ed., Political Studies, 1993–99; Co-Ed., Government and Opposition, 2000–06. *Publications:* scholarly monographs, student text books and contribs to learned jls. *Recreations:* operas, movies, mountains. *Address:* 14 Gladstone Street, Glossop, Derbyshire SK13 8LX. *E:* michael.moran@manchester.ac.uk.

MORAN, Rt Rev. Peter Antony; Bishop of Aberdeen, (RC), 2003–11; *b* 13 April 1935; *s* of Joseph Moran and Gertrude Moran (*née* O'Callaghan). *Educ:* St Aloysius' Coll., Glasgow; Pontifical Gregorian Univ., Rome (PhL 1955; STL 1959); Univ. of Glasgow (MA Hons (Classics) 1963); Univ. of Aberdeen (MEd 1968). Ordained priest, 1959; schoolmaster, Blairs Coll., Aberdeen, 1964–86; Parish Priest: Blairs, 1979–93; Inverurie, 1993–2003; Diocesan Administrator, Aberdeen, 2002–03. *Recreations:* modern languages, dinghy sailing, walking, music, sketching.

MORAN, Terence Anthony, CB 2007; Chief Operating Officer, 2011–13, and Second Permanent Secretary, 2012–13, Department for Work and Pensions; *b* Rotherham, 23 April 1960; civil partnership 2010, Stuart Hayes. *Educ:* St Joseph's Prim. Sch., Rawmarsh; Rawmarsh Comp. Sch.; Harvard Business Sch. (AMP 2006). Joined Civil Service, 1977; clerical asst, DHSS, 1977; Private Secretary: to Dir, Social Security Ops, 1990–91; to Chief Exec., Benefits Agency, 1992–96; Area Dir, Yorks, Benefits Agency, 2001–02; Dir, NW Reg., Jobcentre Plus, 2002–04; Chief Exec., Disability and Carers Service, 2004–07; Interim Chief Exec., Pension Service, 2007–08; Chief Exec. and Dir Gen., Pension, Disability and Carers Service, 2008–10, Dir Gen., Universal Credit, 2010–11, DWP. Chm., Together for Short Lives, 2014–; Trustee: Nat. Bd, Victim Support, 2006–08; Nat. Bd, Social Care Inst. for Excellence, 2013–. Volunteer: Speakers for Schs; Marie Curie UK. *Recreations:* sports, music, gardening, walking, baking.

MORAN, Vincent John; QC 2011; a Recorder, since 2010; *b* Dartford, 6 Feb. 1966; *s* of John and Anne Moran; *m* 1997, Alison Thraves; two *s* two *d*. *Educ:* Dartford Grammar Sch.; Clare Coll., Cambridge (BA 1987); City Univ. (DipLaw 1990). Called to the Bar, Gray's Inn, 1991; in practice as a barrister, specialising in construction law and professional negligence. *Publications:* (ed) Chitty on Contracts, 29th edn 2004, 30th edn 2008. *Recreations:* cricket, history, The Edgar Wallace. *Address:* Keating Chambers, 15 Essex Street, WC2R 3AA. *T:* (020) 7544 2600. *E:* vmoran@keatingchambers.com.

MORATINOS CUYAUBÉ, Miguel Angel, Knight, Order of Civil Merit (Spain); Minister of Foreign Affairs, Spain, 2004–10; *b* 8 June 1951; *m* Dominique Maunac; three *c*. *Educ:* Madrid (Law and Political Sci. degree); Diplomatic Sch. (Dip. Internat. Studies). Spanish Diplomatic Service: Dir-Hd, E Europe Co-ordination Desk, 1974–79; First Sec., 1979–80, Chargé d'affaires, 1980–84, Yugoslavia; Political Advr, Rabat, 1984–87; Dep. Dir Gen. for N Africa, 1987–91; Director General: Inst. for Co-operation with the Arab World, 1991–93; of Foreign Policy for Africa and ME, 1993–96; Ambassador, Israel, 1996; EU Special Rep. for the ME Peace Process, 1996–2003. Comdr, Order of Ouissam Alaouite (Morocco). *Publications:* The European Security and the Mediterranean, 1990; Mediterranean: a forgotten sea, 1990; Mediterranean and Middle East, 1995. *Recreations:* tennis, football.

MORAUTA, Rt Hon. Sir Mekere, KCMG 2009; Kt 1991; Chairman, Papua New Guinea Sustainable Development Program Ltd, since 2012; *b* 12 June 1946; *s* of Morauta Hasu and Morikoai Elavo; *m* Roslyn; two *s*. *Educ:* Univ. of Papua New Guinea (BEcon); Flinders Univ., SA. Res. Officer (Manpower Planning), Dept of Labour, 1971; Economist, Office of the Economic Advr, 1972; Sec. for Finance, Govt of PNG, 1973–82; Man. Dir, PNG Banking Corp., 1983–92; Gov., Bank of Papua New Guinea, 1993–94; Executive Chairman: Delta Seafoods, 1994–97; Morauta and Associates (Publishing), 1994–97. MP Moresby NW, 1997–2012 (People's Democratic Movement, 1997–2002, PNG Party, 2002–12); Minister: for Planning and Implementation, PNG, 1997–98; for Fisheries and Marine Resources, 1998–99; Prime Minister and Minister for Treasury, 1999–2002; Leader of the Opposition, 2007–10; Minister for Public Enterprises, 2011. Chm., Nat. Airline Commn, 1992–94. Mem. Bd, Angco; formerly Director: Highlands Gold (PNG); PNG Associated Industries; Thomas Nationwide Transport (PNG); James Barnes PNG; numerous public and commercial bodies. Former Mem. Fund Raising Cttees, Salvation Army and Red Cross. Hon. DTech Univ. of Technology, PNG, 1987; Hon. DEc PNG, 2001. *Publications:* numerous papers on economic and allied subjects.

MORAY, 21st Earl of, *cr* 1562; **John Douglas Stuart;** Lord Abernethy and Strathearn, 1562; Lord Doune, 1581; Lord St Colme, 1611; Baron Stuart (GB), 1796; *b* 29 Aug. 1966; *o s* of 20th Earl of Moray and of Lady Malvina Murray, *er d* of 7th Earl of Mansfield and Mansfield; *S* father, 2011; *m* 2000, Catherine Jane, *d* of Prof. Wilfred Alan Lawson; two *s*. *Educ:* Loretto School, Musselburgh; University Coll. London (BA Hist. of Art). *Heir:* *s* Lord Doune, *qv*. *Address:* Doune Park, Doune, Perthshire FK16 6HA; Darnaway Castle, Forres, Moray.

MORAY, ROSS AND CAITHNESS, Bishop of, since 2007; **Rt Rev. Mark Jeremy Strange;** *b* 2 Nov. 1961; *s* of Edward Strange and Dorothy Strange (*née* Tinker); *m* 1983, Jane Elizabeth; one *s* two *d*. *Educ:* Aberdeen Univ. (LTh); Lincoln Theol Coll. (Cert. in Ministry and Mission). Cathedral Verger, Worcester Cathedral, 1984–87; ordained deacon, 1989, priest, 1990; Curate, St Barnabas and Christchurch, Worcs, 1989–92; Vicar, St Wulstan, Warndon, Worcs, 1992–98; Rector, Holy Trinity, Elgin, 1998–2007; Priest-in-charge: St Margaret's, Lossiemouth, 1998–2007; St Michael's, Dufftown, 2004–07; St Margaret's, Aberlour, 2004–07. Canon, 2000–07, Provost, 2014–, St Andrew's Cathedral, Inverness. Convenor, Scottish Episcopal Youth Network, 2002–; Synod Clerk, Moray, Ross and Caithness, 2003–07. Moray Scout Association: Area Comr, 1998–2001; Area Chaplain, 2001–09; Chaplain, Elgin ATC, 2004–07. Chair, Elgin Community Planning Workers Gp, 2002–09. *Recreations:* hill-walking, beach-combing, whisky-tasting. *Address:* Bishop's House, Arpafeelie, North Kessock, Inverness IV1 3XD. *E:* bishop@moray.anglican.org.

MORAY, ROSS AND CAITHNESS, Dean of; *see* Simpson, Very Rev. A. J.

MORBEY, Gillian Ann, OBE 1995; Chief Executive, Sense and Sense International, since 2010; *b* Glasgow, 11 June 1953; *d* of Henry and Valerie Kay; *m* 1973, Jerry Morbey; one *s* one *d*. *Educ:* BA Hons Psychol. 1984. RGN 1974. Student Nurse, 1971–74, Staff Nurse, 1974–81, NHS; CEO, Sense Scotland, 1985–2010. Mem., All Party Disability Gp, 1994. Vice Chair, then Chair, Glasgow Council for Voluntary Sector, 1989–95. Mem., Nat. Disability Council, 2000. Pres., Deafblind Internat., 2011–. Trustee, Family Fund Trust, 1995–97 (Vice Chair, 1997–2001). Scottish Social Entrepreneur of Year, 2005. *Recreations:* walking, gardening, reading. *Address:* Sense, 101 Pentonville Road, N1 9LG. *T:* 0845 127 0060, *Fax:* 0845 127 0061. *E:* Gillian.Morbey@sense.org.uk.

MORCOM, Christopher; QC 1991; *b* 4 Feb. 1939; *s* of late Dr Rupert Morcom and Mary Morcom (*née* Carslake); *m* 1966, Diane, *d* of late Jose Antonio Toledo and Winifred Anne (*née* Wardlaw); one *s* two *d*. *Educ:* Sherborne Sch.; Trinity Coll., Cambridge (BA Hons 1961; MA 1964). Called to the Bar, Middle Temple, 1963 (Cert. Honour, Astbury Scholar; Bencher, 1996); Barrister, Mauritius, 1979–. Member: Senate, Law Soc. Jt Wkg Party on Intellectual Property Law, 1976–; Standing Adv. Cttee on Industrial Property, 1990–2001; Council, Intellectual Property Inst., 1991–. Chm., Competition Law Assoc., 1985–99. Pres., Ligue Internationale du Droit de la Concurrence, 1996–98 (Vice Pres., 1994–96; Hon. Pres., 2000). Chm., Bar Musical Soc., 1991–2008. *Publications:* Service Marks: a guide to the new law, 1987; A Guide to the Trade Marks Act 1994, 1994; (jtly) The Modern Law of Trade Marks, 2000, 4th edn 2012; legal articles in Law Soc. Gazette, Counsel, European Intellectual Property Rev. *Recreations:* music, walking. *Address:* Hogarth Chambers, 5 New Square, Lincoln's Inn, WC2A 3RJ. *T:* (020) 7404 0404. *Clubs:* Athenæum, Noblemen and Gentlemen's Catch.

MORDAUNT, Penelope Mary; MP (C) Portsmouth North, since 2010; Minister of State, Ministry of Defence, since 2015; *b* Torquay, 4 March 1973; *d* of John Edward Patrick Mordaunt and late Jennifer Mordaunt and step *d* of Sylvia Mordaunt. *Educ:* Oaklands RC Comprehensive Sch., Waterlooville; Reading Univ. (BA Hons Philosophy 1995). Aid worker, 1991–92; spokesman, Freight Transport Assoc., 1997–99; Hd, Foreign Press, George Bush's presidential campaign, 2000; Hd of Broadcasting, Cons. Party, 1999–2001; Director: RBKC, 2001–03; Media Intelligence Partners, 2004–06; Diabetes UK, 2006–09. Dep. Dir, Big Lottery Fund, 2003–05. Parly Under-Sec. of State, DCLG,

2014–15. *Recreations:* astronomy, painting, hospital volunteer, RNR, dance and music. *Address:* House of Commons, SW1A 0AA. *T:* (020) 7219 7129, *Fax:* (020) 7219 3592. *E:* penny.mordaunt.mp@parliament.uk.

MORDAUNT, Sir Richard (Nigel Charles), 14th Bt *cr* 1611; (does not use the title at present); documentary film producer; founder: Lusia Films UK, 1965; Coolamon Films Australia, 1994; *b* 12 May 1940; *s* of Lt-Col Sir Nigel John Mordaunt, 13th Bt, MBE, and Anne (*d* 1980), *d* of late Arthur F. Tritton; *S* father, 1979; *m* 1st, 1964, Myriam Atchia (decd); one *s* one *d*; 2nd, 1995, Diana Barbara (*née* Davis); one step *d*. *Educ:* Wellington. Producer, award-winning documentaries, England and Australia, 1965–. *Heir: s* Kim John Mordaunt, *b* 11 June 1966.

MORDEN, Jessica; MP (Lab) Newport East, since 2005; *b* 29 May 1968; *d* of Mick and Margaret Morden. *Educ:* Croesyceiliog Comp. Sch., Cwmbran; Univ. of Birmingham (BA Hons Hist. 1989). Researcher: to Huw Edwards, MP, 1991–92; to Llew Smith, MP, 1992–93; Organiser, SE Wales, Welsh Lab. Party, 1993–98; Elections Officer, Labour Party, 1998–99; Gen. Sec., Welsh Labour Party, 1999–2005. *Recreations:* gym, film. *Address:* House of Commons, SW1A 0AA. *T:* (020) 7219 6213, (constituency) (01633) 841725. *E:* jessica.morden.mp@parliament.uk. *Club:* Ringland Labour (Newport).

MORDUE, Jane Margaret; strategic management consultant and coach, since 2001; Chief Executive, Comparative Clinical Science Foundation, 2005–15; *b* 8 June 1953; *d* of late James Gibson Jones and Margaret Jones (*née* Finlayson); *m* 1st, 1990, Prof. Alan Osborn Betts (*d* 2005); 2nd, 2007, Howard James Mordue. *Educ:* Univ. of Leeds (BA); Cornell Univ. (EDP); INSEAD (AMP). MHSM. PA to Man. Dir, Fairclough Ltd, Leeds, 1976–79; University of London: PA to Principal and Information Officer, RVC, 1979–85; Admin. Assistant to Vice-Chancellor and Dep. Public Relations Officer, 1985–88; Sec., BPMF, 1988–96; Sec.-Gen., Law Soc., 1996–2000; Chm., Thames Valley Strategic HA, 2002–04. Vice-Chm., Gangmasters Licensing Authy, 2005–15. Mem. Cttee, Healthwatch England, 2012–. Mem., Bd of Trustees, 2008–13, Vice Chm., 2010–13, Citizens Advice (Chm., SE Area (formerly Region) Cttee, 2004–09); Chm., Rotary District 1260 Vocational Cttee, 2014–. CDir 2003. FRSA 1996; FIHM 2003. *Recreations:* travel, music, photography. *Club:* Institute of Directors.

MORE, Michael John, CBE 2008; PhD; Chief Executive, Westminster City Council, 2008–13; *b* 21 May 1955; *s* of late Norman More and of Kathleen Mary More; *m* 1982, Sue Jordan; two *s*. *Educ:* Univ. of Hull (BA 1st Cl. Hons; PhD 1982). CPFA 1985. Audit trainee, Nat. Audit Office, 1981–86; Cambridgeshire County Council: Audit Manager, 1986–90; Asst Dir, 1990–96; Hd of Finance, 1996–99; Dir of Resource Mgt, 1999–2002, Chief Exec., 2002–08, Suffolk CC; Clerk to Lord Lieut of Suffolk, 2002–08. Non-exec. Dir, Univ. Campus, Suffolk, 2005–08. Chm., Prince's Trust, Suffolk, 2006–08. Mem., Olympic Games Transport Bd, 2010–12; Mem. Bd and Chm., Audit Cttee, Cambridge Univ. Hosps NHS Foundn Trust, 2013–. Trustee: Ipswich Town FC Sports and Educn Trust, 2004–08; Addenbrooke's Charitable Trust, 2015–. FRSA. DUniv: E Anglia, 2009; Essex, 2009. *Publications:* press articles and papers in various analytical philosophy jls. *Recreations:* family, gardens, music, reading, analytical philosophy and logic, horse racing, football.

MOREAU, Jeanne; Officier de la Légion d'Honneur, 1991 (Chevalier, 1975); Commandeur, Ordre National du Mérite, 2007 (Chevalier, 1970; Officier, 1988) actress; *b* 23 Jan. 1928; *d* of Anatole-Désiré Moreau and Kathleen Moreau (*née* Buckley); *m* 1949, Jean-Louis Richard (marr. diss.); one *s*; *m* 1977, William Friedkin (marr. diss.). *Educ:* Collège Edgar-Quinet; Conservatoire national d'art dramatique. *Theatre:* Comédie Française, 1948–52; Théâtre National Populaire, 1953; Le Récit de la Servante Zerline, 1986–89; La Celestine, 1989; co-dir, Attila, Paris Opera, 2001; *films* include: Les amants, 1958; Les liaisons dangereuses, 1959; Le Dialogue des Carmélites, 1959; Moderato cantabile, 1960; Jules et Jim, 1961; La Baie des Anges, 1962; Journal d'une femme de chambre, 1963; Viva Maria, 1965; Mademoiselle, 1965; The Sailor from Gibraltar, 1965; The Immortal Story, 1966; Great Catherine, 1967; The Bride wore Black, 1967; Monte Walsh, 1969; Chère Louise, 1971; Nathalie Granger, 1972; La Race des Seigneurs, 1974; Mr Klein, 1976; Lumière (also Dir), 1976; Le Petit Théâtre de Jean Renoir, 1976; Madame Rosa, 1978; L'Intoxe, 1980; Querelle, La Truite, 1982; L'Arbre, 1983; Sauve-toi Lola, Le Paltoquet, Le Miracule, 1986; La Nuit de l'Océan, 1987; Ennemonde, 1988; Jour après Jour, 1988; Nikita, 1989; La Comédie d'un Jour, 1989; Anna Karamazoff, 1989; La Femme Fardée, Until the End of the World, 1990; La Vielle Qui Marchait Dans La Mer, Le Pas Suspendu de la Cigogne, The Map of the Human Heart, L'Amant, 1991; A Demain, L'Absence, 1992; Je m'appelle Victor, 1992; I Love You I Love You Not, 1995; The Proprietor, 1997; Un amour de sorcière, 1997; A tout jamais, 1999; Time to Leave, 2006; Désengagement, 2008; Visage, 2009; Une Estonienne à Paris, 2012; *television* plays and series: Huis Clos, BBC, 1984; The Last Seance, Granada, 1984; Le Tiroir Secret, 1985; We Shall Meet Again, BBC, 1992; The Clothes in the Wardrobe, BBC, 1993; A Foreign Field, BBC, 1993; The Great Catherine, 1994. Chm. Jury, Cannes Film Festival, 1975 and 1995. Fellow, BAFTA, 1996; Hon. Acad. Award, 1998; Festival Trophy, Cannes Film Festival, 2015. Mem., Acad. des Beaux Arts, 2000. Commandeur des Arts et des Lettres, 1985 (Chevalier, 1966). *Recreation:* reading.

MORELAND, Claire Josephine, MA; DL; Principal, Chetham's School of Music, 1999–Aug. 2016; *b* 2 Aug. 1958; *d* of late Peter Alfred White and of Eileen Beatrice White (*née* Kidston); *m* 1st, 1982, John Moreland (marr. diss. 1999); one *s*; 2nd, 2004, Richard Hickman (marr. diss. 2011). *Educ:* Devonport High Sch. for Girls; St Hugh's Coll., Oxford (MA Modern Langs, PGCE). Asst teacher, Sevenoaks Sch., 1981–84; Hd of German, Croydon High Sch. for Girls, 1984–88; Rugby School: asst teacher, 1988–92; Housemistress, 1992–97; Dep. Head, 1997–99. DL Gtr Manchester, 2012. *Publications:* Schreib mir Bitte, 1982. *Recreations:* literature, music, outdoor pursuits, finding silver linings. *Address:* Chetham's School of Music, Long Millgate, Manchester M3 1SB. *T:* (0161) 834 9644. *Clubs:* University Women's, East India.

MORELAND, Robert John; management consultant; Member, Economic and Social Committee, European Community, 1986–98 (Chairman, Regional Policy and Town and Country Planning Section, 1990–98); *b* 21 Aug. 1941; *s* of late Samuel John Moreland and Norah Mary, (Molly) (*née* Haines). *Educ:* Glasgow Acad.; Dean Close Sch., Cheltenham; Univ. of Nottingham (BA Econs); Inst. of World Affairs, Conn, and Warwick Univ. (postgrad. work). Civil Servant, Govt of NS, Canada, 1966–67, Govt of NB, 1967–72; Sen. Economist, W Central Scotland Planning Study, 1972–74; Management Consultant, Touche Ross and Co., London, 1974–. Member (C): for Knightsbridge, Westminster CC, 1990–98 (Chief Whip, 1993–94; Chm. of Envmt, 1994–95; Chm., Planning and Envmt, 1995–97); Gloucester CC, 2001–02. Contested (C): Pontypool, Oct. 1974; GLA, 2000. Mem. (C) Staffs, European Parlt, 1979–84, contested same seat, 1984; Chm., Eur. Cttee, Bow Gp, 1977–78; Dep. Chm., Conservative Gp for Europe, 2006–09 (Vice-Chm., 1985–88, 2003–06; Treas., 2000–03). Dep. Chm., 1998–2000, Chm., 2000–, London Europe Soc. Treas., European Movement, 2003–08. Dir, Albert Meml Trust, 1997–2000. Gov., Archbishop Tenison's Sch., Kennington Oval, 1992– (Chm., 2003–11). Mem. Bd, S Wales and Severn Partnership, Canal and River Trust, 2012–. *Publications:* Climate Change, 2000; contrib. to Crossbow. *Recreations:* tennis, ski-ing, watching cricket and Rugby, golf. *Address:* 3 The Firs, Heathville Road, Gloucester GL1 3EW. *T:* 07803 012683. *Clubs:* MCC; Gloucestershire CC.

MORENO, Glen Richard; Chairman: Pearson plc, since 2005; Virgin Money, since 2015; *b* 24 July 1943; *s* of John Moreno and Ellen (*née* Oberg); *m* 1966, Cheryl Eschbach. *Educ:* Stanford Univ. (BA with Dist. 1965); Univ. of Delhi (Rotary Foundn Fellow 1966); Harvard Law Sch. (JD 1969). Gp Exec., Citigroup, 1969–87; Pres., 1987–92, Dir, 1987–, Fidelity Internat.; Senior Independent non-executive Director: Man Gp plc, 1994–2009; Lloyds Banking Gp, 2010–12; Acting Chm., UK Financial Investments Ltd, 2009. Dep. Chm., Financial Reporting Council, 2010–14. Sen. Advr, HSBC, 2014–. Gov., Ditchley Foundn, 1983–. Dir, RADA, 2007–. *Recreations:* reading, shooting, Angus cattle breeder, vintner. *Address:* Pearson plc, 80 Strand, WC2R 0RL. *T:* (020) 7010 2306, *Fax:* (020) 7010 6601. *E:* glen.moreno@pearson.com. *Clubs:* Farmers, National Liberal.

MORETON, family name of **Earl of Ducie**.

MORETON, Lord; James Berkeley Moreton; *b* 6 May 1981; *s* and *heir* of 7th Earl of Ducie, *qv*.

MOREY, Anthony Bernard Nicholas, CBE 1993; HM Diplomatic Service, retired; *b* 6 Dec. 1936; *s* of late Bernard Rowland Morey and Madeleine Morey; *m* 1961, Agni Campbell Kerr; two *s* one *d*. *Educ:* Wimbledon Coll. Nat. service, 1955–57. FO, 1957–60; Kuwait, 1960–62; FO, 1962–65; Madras, 1965–66; FO, 1966; Tehran, 1967; Kabul, 1968–71; FCO, 1971–72; Washington, 1972–76; Zagreb, 1976–80; Lagos, 1980–83; seconded to Guinness Mahon, 1983–85; Counsellor and Consul General, Moscow, 1985–88; Dep. High Comr, Madras, 1989–91; Ambassador to Mongolia, 1991–93; Dep. High Comr, Calcutta, 1993–96. *Recreations:* gardening, music, cats. *Address:* Lattice House, Castleton, Sherborne, Dorset DT9 3SA. *Club:* Royal Calcutta Turf.

MOREY, Caroline; *see* Douglas, C.

MORFEY, Dr Kathryn Margaret Victoria; Consultant, Warner Goodman & Streat, 2000–02 (Associate Solicitor, 1991–2000); *b* 26 May 1942; *d* of Sidney Charles Waterton and Catherine Margaret Waterton (*née* Lilley); *m* 1963, Christopher Leonard Morfey; one *d* (one *s* decd). *Educ:* Newnham Coll., Cambridge (BA 1963; MA 1968); Univ. of Southampton (PhD 1968; LLB 1977). Admitted Solicitor, 1980. Lecturer: Univ. of Bristol, 1963; Univ. of Southampton, 1967–69; Nat. Childbirth Trust Orgnr, 1970–75; solicitor in private practice, 1980–2002. Mem., Sch. Admission Appeal Panel, 2003–. Member: Gen. Synod, C of E, 1990–2000; Legal Adv. Commn, C of E, 1991–93; Cathedrals Fabric Commn for England, 1991–96; Cathedrals Statutes Commn, 1996–2000; Vice-Pres., Winchester Diocesan Synod, 1997–2003. Gov., King Alfred's Coll. of Higher Educn, 1992–99. *Recreations:* visiting other people's gardens, choral music.

MORGAN; *see* Elystan-Morgan.

MORGAN, family name of **Baron Morgan**.

MORGAN, Baron *cr* 2000 (Life Peer), of Aberdyfi in the co. of Gwynedd; **Kenneth Owen Morgan,** FBA 1983; FRHistS; Principal, then Vice-Chancellor, University College of Wales, Aberystwyth and Professor in the University of Wales, 1989–95, Emeritus Professor, 1999 (Research Professor, 1995–99); Vice-Chancellor, then Senior Vice-Chancellor, University of Wales, 1993–95; *b* 16 May 1934; *s* of David James Morgan and Margaret Morgan (*née* Owen); *m* 1st, 1973, Jane Keeler (*d* 1992); one *s* one *d*; 2nd, 2009, Elizabeth Gibson, Bordeaux. *Educ:* University College School, London; Oriel College, Oxford (MA, DPhil 1958, DLitt 1985; Hon. Fellow, 2003). University College (later University of Wales), Swansea: Lectr in History Dept, 1958–66 (Sen. Lectr, 1965–66); Hon. Fellow, 1985; Hon. Prof., 1995–; Fellow and Praelector, Modern Hist. and Politics, Queen's Coll., Oxford, 1966–89 (Hon. Fellow, 1992); Faculty Lectr, 1995–2009. Supernumerary Fellow, Jesus Coll., Oxford, 1991–92. Amer. Council of Learned Socs Fellow, Columbia Univ., 1962–63; Visiting Professor: Columbia Univ., 1965; Univ. of S Carolina, 1972; Univ. of Witwatersrand, 1997, 1998 and 2000; Vis. Benjamin Meaker Prof., Univ. of Bristol, 2000; Vis. Prof., Inst. of Contemporary British History, KCL, 2011–; Vis. Lectr, Univ. of Texas, 1994, 1999, 2007, 2010, 2014. Lectures: O'Donnell, Univ. of Wales, 1981; Neale, UCL, 1986; Dodd, UCNW (Bangor), 1992, Univ. of Wales, Bangor, 2005; BBC (Wales), 1995; Prothero, RHistS, 1996; Merlyn-Rees, Univ. of Glamorgan, 2002; Presidential, Univ. of Rouen, 2003; Ford Special, Univ. of Oxford, 2005; London Guildhall, 2006; Gresham Coll., 2007; Speaker's House, 2011, 2015; Soc. des Anglicistes de l'Enseignement Supérieur, Limoges, 2012; KCL Constitutional Law, 2012; Keir Hardie Meml, 2014; Hist. of Parlt Trust, 2016. Member: Bd of Celtic Studies, 1972–2003; Council, Nat. Library of Wales, 1991–95. Member: H of L Select Cttee on the Constitution, 2001–04, 2015–; Jt Select Cttee on Draft Constitutional Renewal Bill, 2008. Chairman: Fabian Soc. Commn on the Monarchy, 2002–03; University Cttee on Student Radicalisation, 2015. Trustee: History of Parlt Trust, 2002–; Cttee for Defence of British Univs, 2013–. Mem., Yr Academi Gymreig. FRHistS 1964 (Mem. Council, 1983–86). Editor, Welsh History Review, 1961–2003; Jt Editor, 20th Century British History, 1994–99. Hon. Mem., Gorsedd of Bards, Nat. Eisteddfod, 2008. Founding FLSW 2010. Hon. Fellow: Univ. of Wales, Cardiff, 1997; Trinity Coll., Carmarthen, 1998. Hon. DLitt: Wales, 1997; Glamorgan, 1997; Greenwich, 2004. Gold Medal, Hon. Soc. of Cymmrodorion, 2009; Lifetime Achievement Award, All-Party Parly Gp on Hist. and Archives, 2014; Welsh Parliamentarian of Year Award, 2014. *Publications:* Wales in British Politics, 1963, 3rd edn 1980; David Lloyd George: Welsh radical as world statesman, 1963, 2nd edn 1982; Freedom or Sacrilege?, 1966; Keir Hardie, 1967; The Age of Lloyd George, 1971, 3rd edn 1978; (ed) Lloyd George: Family Letters, 1973; Lloyd George, 1974; Keir Hardie: radical and socialist, 1975 (Arts Council prize, 1976), 3rd edn 1997; Consensus and Disunity, 1979, 2nd edn 1986; (with Jane Morgan) Portrait of a Progressive, 1980; Rebirth of a Nation: Wales 1880–1980, 1981, new edn 1998 (Arts Council prize, 1982); David Lloyd George, 1981; Labour in Power 1945–1951, 1984, 2nd edn 1985; (ed jtly) Welsh Society and Nationhood, 1984; (ed) The Oxford Illustrated History of Britain, 1984, new rev. edn 2009; (ed) The Sphere Illustrated History of Britain, 1985; Labour People, 1987, new edn 1992; (ed) The Oxford History of Britain, 1989, new edn 2010; The Red Dragon and the Red Flag, 1989; The People's Peace: British History 1945–1990, 1991, new edn as The People's Peace: British History since 1945, 2001; Academic Leadership, 1991; Modern Wales: politics, places and people, 1995; Britain and Europe, 1995; Steady As She Goes, 1996; (ed) The Young Oxford History of Britain & Ireland, 1996, rev. edn 2005; Callaghan: a life, 1997; (ed jtly) Crime, Protest and Police in Modern British Society, 1999; The Twentieth Century, 2000; The Great Reform Act, 2001; Universities and the State, 2002; Michael Foot: the life, 2007; Ages of Reform, 2011; (contrib.) The Global Lincoln, 2011; Eminent Parliamentarians, 2012; (ed) David Lloyd George, 2013; Revolution to Devolution, 2014; Labour Leaders, 2015; Kenneth O. Morgan: my histories, 2015; many articles, reviews etc; many contribs to Oxford DNB. *Recreations:* music, architecture, sport, travel. *Address:* The Croft, 63 Millwood End, Long Hanborough, Witney, Oxon OX29 8BP. *T:* (01993) 881341. *Club:* Reform.

MORGAN OF DREFELIN, Baroness *cr* 2004 (Life Peer), of Drefelin in the County of Dyfed; **Delyth Jane Morgan;** Chief Executive, Breast Cancer Now, since 2015; *b* 30 Aug. 1961; *d* of late Julian Morgan and of Ann Morgan; *m* 1991, Jim Shepherd; one *d*. *Educ:* Bedford Coll., London, then UCL (BSc Physiol.; Fellow, 2005). Campaigns Co-ordinator, Shelter, 1986–88; Director: Workplace Nurseries Campaign, 1988–92; Commns, Nat. Asthma Campaign, 1992–96; Chief Executive: Breakthrough Breast Cancer, 1996–2005; Breast Cancer Campaign, 2011–15. Founding Mem., Long Term Conditions Alliance (Vice-Chm., 1996; Chm., 1996–98; Trustee, 1994–2000); Chm., DoH Primary Task Gp, Patient Choice, 2003; Member: NHS Nat. Cancer Taskforce, 2000–05; NHS Modernisation Bd, 2002–05. A Baroness in Waiting (Govt Whip), 2007–10; Parly Under-Sec. of State, DIUS, 2008, DCSF, 2008–10. House of Lords: Member: Select Cttee on Merit of Statutory

Instruments, 2005–07; Jt Cttee on Draft Children (contact) and Adoption Bill, 2005–; Vice Chair, All Party Gp on Breast Cancer, 2005–07. Mem. Exec. Council, Assoc. Med. Res. Charities, 1999–2004. Fellow, Cardiff Univ., 2005. *Address:* House of Lords, SW1A 0PW.

MORGAN OF ELY, Baroness *cr* 2011 (Life Peer), of Ely in the City of Cardiff; **(Mair) Eluned Morgan;** Director of Development (formerly Head of Low Carbon Business Development) for Wales, SSE plc (formerly Scottish and Southern Energy plc), 2009–13; *b* 16 Feb. 1967; *d* of late Rev. Bob Morgan and of Elaine Morgan; *m* 1996, Rev. Dr Rhys Jenkins, one *s* one *d. Educ:* Atlantic Coll.; Univ. of Hull (BA). Stagiaire with Socialist Gp, Europe. Parlt, 1990; with S4C, 1991; researcher and reporter, Agenda TV, 1992; documentary researcher, BBC TV, 1993. MEP (Lab) Mid and W Wales, 1994–99, Wales, 1999–2009; Mem., Industry, Res. and Energy Cttee, EP, 2004–09. Shadow spokesperson for Wales and Foreign Affairs, H of L, 2013–. Chm., Cardiff Business Partnership, 2013–14; Welsh Chm. and Trustee, Live Music Now, 2013–. Hon. Distinguished Prof., 2010, and Fellow, 2012–, Cardiff Univ. *Recreations:* walking, reading.

MORGAN OF HUYTON, Baroness *cr* 2001 (Life Peer), of Huyton in the County of Merseyside; **Sally Morgan;** Chairman, Office for Standards in Education, Children's Services and Skills, 2011–14; *b* 28 June 1959; *d* of Albert Edward Morgan and Margaret Morgan; *m* 1984, John Lyons; two *s. Educ:* Belvedere Girls' Sch., Liverpool; Durham Univ. (BA Geog. Hons); Univ. of London (PGCE, MA Educ.). Secondary Sch. Teacher, 1981–85; Labour Party: Student Organiser, 1985–87; Sen. Targetting Officer, 1987–93; Dir, Campaigns and Elecns, 1993–95; Head of Party Liaison for Leader of the Opposition, 1995–97; Pol Sec. to the Prime Minister, 1997–2001; Minister of State, Cabinet Office, 2001; Dir of Pol and Govt Relations, Prime Minister's Office, 2001–05. Mem. Bd, Olympic Delivery Authy, 2005–14. Non-executive Director: Dixons Carphone (formerly Carphone Warehouse) plc, 2005–; Southern Cross Healthcare Plc, 2006–11; Infinis Energy plc, 2014–; Countryside Properties, 2015–. Advr to Bd, Absolute Return for Kids, 2005–; Member, Advisory Panel: Lloyds Pharmacy, 2006–10; Virgin Hldg Co., 2011–. Mem. Council, KCL, 2014–. *Recreations:* relaxing with family and friends, cooking, gardening.

MORGAN, Alasdair Neil; Member (SNP) Scotland South, Scottish Parliament, 2003–11 (Galloway & Upper Nithsdale, 1999–2003); *b* 21 April 1945; *s* of Alexander Morgan and Emily Morgan (*née* Wood); *m* 1969, Anne Gilfillan; two *d. Educ:* Breadalbane Acad., Aberfeldy; Univ. of Glasgow (MA Hons 1968); Open Univ. (BA Hons 1990). IT Project Manager, Lothian Reg., 1986–96; IT Consultant, W Lothian Council, 1996–97. Contested (SNP) Dumfries, 1992. MP (SNP) Galloway and Upper Nithsdale, 1997–2001. Mem., Select Cttee on Trade and Industry affairs, 1997–2001. Scottish Parliament: Mem., Rural Affairs Cttee, 1999–2000; Convenor, Justice I Cttee, 2000–01; Mem., Finance Cttee, 2001–03; Convenor, Enterprise and Culture Cttee, 2003–04; Vice Convenor, Finance Cttee, 2004–05; Mem., European and External Relations Cttee, 2007–08; Dep. Presiding Officer, 2007–11; Mem., Rural Affairs and Envmt Cttee, 2008–11. Scottish National Party: Nat. Treas., 1983–90; Sen. Vice Convenor, 1990–91; Nat. Sec., 1992–97; Vice Pres., 1997–2004; Leader, Parly Gp, 1999–2001; Chief Whip, Scottish Parly Gp, 2005–07. Trustee, Scottish Parly Pension Fund, 2009–. Mem., Electoral Commn, 2014–. *Recreation:* hill walking. *Address:* 2 Park Place, Dunfermline KY12 7QJ.

MORGAN, Alastair William James; HM Diplomatic Service; Ambassador to the Democratic People's Republic of Korea, since 2015; *b* Camberley, 28 May 1958; *s* of Col Geoffrey Charles Purday Morgan, OBE, DL and Dr Barbara Hillary Morgan; *m* 1998, Ayako Nakamura; one *s* two *d. Educ:* St Andrew's Sch., Pangbourne; Sherborne Sch.; Trinity Coll., Cambridge (BA 1979; MA 1983). Lectr, Yakushuin Univ., Tokyo, 1983–85; with Department of Trade and Industry, later Department for Business, Innovation and Skills, 1985–: Insce Div., 1985–86; Aerospace Div., 1986–88; Private Sec. to Minister for Trade and Industry, 1988–89; Principal, Financial Services Div., 1991; Japanese lang. trng, 1991–92; First Sec., Tokyo, 1992–96; Hd, UK Mergers Section, DTI, 1996–99; Actg Chief Exec. and Dir of Ops, Invest in Britain Bureau, 1999–2001; Sen. Advr to Japanese Min. of Econ., Trade and Industry, Tokyo, 2001–02; Counsellor, Tokyo, 2002–06; Mandarin lang. trng, 2006; Counsellor, Beijing, 2007–10; Consul-Gen., Guangzhou, 2010–14. *Recreations:* walking, reading, oriental languages. *Address:* c/o Foreign and Commonwealth Office, King Charles Street, SW1A 2AH. *E:* alastair.morgan@fco.gov.uk.

MORGAN, Anthony Hugh, CMG 1990; HM Diplomatic Service, retired; Consul-General, Zürich, Director of British Export Promotion in Switzerland and Consul-General, Liechtenstein, 1988–91; *b* 27 March 1931; *s* of late Cyril Egbert Morgan and late Muriel Dorothea (*née* Nash); *m* 1957, Cicely Alice Voysey (*d* 2011); two *s* one *d. Educ:* King's Norton Grammar Sch.; Birmingham Univ. (BA 1952). Served HM Forces (RAF Educn Br.), 1952–55. Joined HM Foreign (later Diplomatic) Service, 1956; Cairo, then Cyprus, 1956; Khartoum, 1957; FO, 1959; Saigon, 1962; Second Sec., 1963; UK Delegn to NATO, 1965; First Sec., 1968; FCO, 1969; First Sec. and Head of Chancery, Calcutta, 1973; FCO, 1976; Dep. Head of Inf. Policy Dept, 1977; Counsellor: (Information), Brussels, 1977–79; (Commercial), Copenhagen, 1979–82; Vienna, 1982–88. Comdr, Order of Dannebrog, Denmark, 1979. *Recreations:* listening to music, looking at pictures. *Club:* Royal Air Force.

MORGAN, Arthur William Crawford, (Tony Morgan); Chief Executive, Industrial Society, 1994–2000; *b* 24 Aug. 1931; *s* of Arthur James and Violet Morgan; *m* 1955, Valerie Anne Williams; three *s. Educ:* Hereford High Sch.; Westcliff High Sch. Chm. and Chief Exec. Officer, Purle Bros Holdings, 1964–71; Dep. Chm., Wimpey Waste Management, 1974–81; Dir, Redland plc, 1971–73; Founder and Dir, Morgan Hemingway Investment Bank, 1973–78; working in California for non-profit organisations, incl. Hunger Project and Breakthrough Foundn, 1981–84; Chm., Wistech, 1984–90; Dir, Wraytech UK, 1996–99. Governor, BBC, 1972–77. Non-exec. Chm., Octopus Apollo VCT3 (formerly Octopus Protected VCT) plc, 2006–12 (non-exec. Dir, 2012–); non-executive Director: Alexander Corp., 1990–99; Quickheart Ltd, 2001–; Phoenix Venture Capital Trust, 2003–10; Re-Energy plc, 2006–09; Partner, Latitude Strategy Consulting, 2000–05. Sailed Olympic Games, Tokyo; Silver Medal, Flying Dutchman, 1964; Jt Yachtsman of the Year, 1965; Member: British Olympic Yachting Appeal, 1970; Royal Yachting Assoc. Council, 1968–72. Chairman: Hunger Project Trust, 1984–89; Youth at Risk, 1996–. FRSA. *Publications:* various technical papers. *Recreations:* squash, ski-ing, sailing, gardening, rowing. *Address:* The Old Dairy, Model Farm, Sutton Road, Cookham SL6 9QX. *T:* (01628) 529635. *Club:* Royal Thames Yacht.

MORGAN, Most Rev. Barry Cennydd; *see* Wales, Archbishop of.

MORGAN, Bill; *see* Morgan, J. W. H.

MORGAN, Brian David Gwynne, FRCS, FRCOphth; Consultant Plastic Surgeon, University College Hospital, London and Mount Vernon Hospital, 1972–98; *b* 2 March 1935; *s* of Brig. John Gwynne Morgan and Ethel Lilian Morgan; *m* 1962, Sally Ann Lewis; one *s* two *d. Educ:* Wycliffe Coll., Glos; University College Hosp., London (MB BS). FRCS 1963; FRCOphth 1995. University College Hospital: pre-registration house appts, 1959–61; Casualty Officer, 1961; Registrar in Surgery, St Richard's Hosp., Chichester, 1962–64; Registrar in Surgery, 1964–66, Sen. Registrar, 1967, UCH; Plastic Surgery Registrar and Sen. Registrar, Mt Vernon Hosp., 1967–70; Consultant Plastic Surgeon, Shotley Bridge, Durham, 1970–72. Hon. Archivist, British Assoc. of Plastic, Reconstructive and Aesthetic Surgeons, 1999–. Mem. Council, RCS, 1991–99 (Trustee, Hunterian Collection, 2000–). Fellow, UCL, 1992. *Publications:* Essentials of Plastic and Reconstructive Surgery, 1986. *Recreations:* water-colour painting, sailing, jazz trombone. *Address:* Stockers House, Stockers Farm Road, Rickmansworth, Herts WD3 1NZ. *T:* (01923) 773922, *Fax:* 07006 077506. *E:* brianandsallymorgan@btinternet.com.

MORGAN, Bruce; District Judge (Magistrates' Courts), West Mercia, 2003–11; *b* 30 March 1945; *s* of Francis William Morgan, DFC, and Phyllis Marie Morgan; *m* 1988, Sandra Joy Beresford; twin *d. Educ:* Oswestry School; Open Univ. (BA 1994). Solicitor of Supreme Court. Articled Clerk, Stourbridge, Worcs, 1964–69; Asst Solicitor, London, SE10, 1969–72; Partner with Lickfolds Wiley & Powles, 1973–86. Member: London Criminal Courts Solicitors Assoc. Cttee, 1971–73; Criminal Law Cttee, Westminster Law Soc., 1981–86; No 14 Area Regl Duty Solicitors Cttee, 1986–87; Metropolitan Stipendiary Magistrate, 1987–89; Stipendiary Magistrate, subseq. Dist Judge (Magistrates' Courts), W Midlands, 1989–2003. Ind. Prison Adjudicator, 2001–13. Member: Birmingham Magistrates' Court Cttee, 1990–93; Birmingham Magistrates' Bench Cttee, 1990–2003; Midland Mem., Nat., subseq. HM, Council of Dist Judges (Magistrates' Courts) (formerly Jt Council of Stipendiary Magistrates), 1995–2003; Member: W Mercia Area Judicial Forum, 2005–11; W Mercia Judicial Issues Gp, 2005–11. Member: British Acad. of Forensic Sci., 1970; Legal Medico Soc., 1970–2012; Our Soc., 1994–. Vice Chm., Cleobury North PCC, 1996–2010. Member: Ludlow Rotary Club, 1969–98; Knighton Rotary Club; Chm., Greenwich Round Table, 1983–84. Governor, Oswestry Sch., 1996–2013 (Vice Chm., 1996–2000, 2007–13). *Publications:* various articles in legal journals. *Recreations:* tennis, cricket, gardening, attending auctions, cooking. *Clubs:* Reform; Worcestershire Cricket.

MORGAN, Vice-Adm. Sir (Charles) Christopher, KBE 1996; Director General, Chamber of Shipping, 1997–2003; Director, CM Shipping Consultants Ltd, 2003–09; *b* 11 March 1939; *s* of late Captain Horace Leslie Morgan, CMG, DSO, RN and Kathleen Hilda Morgan; *m* 1970, Susan Caroline Goodbody; three *d. Educ:* Clifton College; BRNC Dartmouth. Joined RN, 1957; served Brunei, 1962–66; HMS Greatford in Comd, 1966; Specialist Navigation Course, 1967; HMS Eskimo in Comd, 1976; NDC 1978; Comdr Sea Training, 1979; MoD, 1981–83; RCDS, 1984; Captain 5th Destroyer Sqdn (HMS Southampton), 1985–87; Staff, Jt Service Defence Coll., 1987–89; Naval Sec., 1990–92; Flag Officer, Scotland, Northern England and NI, 1992–96. Younger Brother of Trinity House, 1977. Governor: Clifton Coll., 1994–; Sherborne Sch. for Girls, 2004–10. Chm. Trustees, Royal Naval Benevolent Soc., 1996–2005; Gov., Tancred Soc., 1996–. Member, Council: King George's Fund for Sailors, 1997–2003; RNLI, 2002–10 (Vice-Pres., 2009–); Chm., Bubbly charity, 2005–14. Freeman, Co. of Master Mariners, 1999; Liveryman, Shipwrights' Co., 2000. FCMI; FRIN 1996; MInstD 1996. *Recreations:* family, golf, tennis, Rugby, wine, gardening. *Address:* c/o Lloyds, 75 Cheap Street, Sherborne, Dorset. *Clubs:* Army and Navy; Royal North Devon Golf, Sherborne Golf.

MORGAN, Rt Hon. Sir (Charles) Declan, Kt 2004; PC 2009; Lord Chief Justice of Northern Ireland, since 2009; *b* 14 Jan. 1952; *m*; three *c. Educ:* St Columb's Coll., Londonderry; Peterhouse, Cambridge (BA 1974; Hon. Fellow, 2010); Queen's Univ., Belfast. Called to the Bar, NI, 1976; QC (NI) 1993; Sen. Crown Counsel, 2002–04; a Judge of the High Ct of Justice, NI, 2004–09. Chairman: Law Reform Adv. Cttee, 2004–07; NI Law Commn, 2007–09; NI Judicial Appts Commn, 2009–. Hon. Bencher, Middle Temple, 2012. *Address:* Royal Courts of Justice, Chichester Street, Belfast BT1 3JF.

MORGAN, Charles Peter Henry; DL; Chairman and Chief Executive Officer, Morgan Motor Co. Ltd, 2009–13; *b* 29 July 1951; *s* of Peter and Jane Morgan; *m* 2003, Kira Kopylova; one *s* one *d*, and one *s* two *d* from previous marriage. *Educ:* Sussex Univ. (BA Hons Hist. of Art 1971); Coventry Univ. (MBA Engrg Mgt 1994). News film cameraman, ITN, 1974–82; Co-founder and Dir, Television News Team Ltd, 1982–85; Morgan Motor Co. Ltd: Marketing Dir, 1985–99; Man. Dir, 1999–2004; Dir, Corporate Strategy, 2004–09. Hon. DBA Coventry, 2003. Silver Nymph award for news TV film, Montreux Internat. TV Fest., 1978. DL Worcs 2010. Hon. MA Worcester, 2008; Hon. DTech Loughborough, 2009; Hon. DBus Southampton Solent, 2010; DUniv Birmingham City, 2011. *Publications:* (with Gregory Houston Bowden) Morgan 100 Years, 2008 (German Motor Press Club Book Prize, 2010). *Recreations:* ski-ing, architecture and design, painting. *Address:* c/o Morgan Motor Co. Ltd, Pickersleigh Road, Malvern Link, Worcs WR14 2LL. *T:* (01684) 573104. *E:* charles.morgan@morgan-motor.co.uk. *Clubs:* Academy; British Racing Drivers'; St Moritz Tobogganing.

MORGAN, Christine Lesley; Head of Radio, BBC Religion and Ethics, since 2009; *b* 4 May 1958; *d* of Gerald Potts and Brenda Austin Potts (*née* Bell); *m* 1st, 1979, Christopher Harry Morgan (marr. diss. 1987); 2nd, 2000, Paul Vallely, *qv*; one *s. Educ:* Ormskirk Grammar Sch.; Southport Coll.; FE Teaching Dip. AEWVH 1987. Joined WRAF, 1976: HQ Strike Comd, 1976–78; Personal Staff of Chief of Air Staff, MoD, 1978–79; Design Team, Airmen's Comd Sch., Hereford, 1979–80; Personnel Asst to Purchasing Dir, H. P. Bulmer Ltd, 1980–83; Lectr in Business Studies, Royal Nat. Coll. for the Blind, 1983–87 (devised RNCB Nat. Work Experience Scheme, 1987); joined BBC Religious Broadcasting, 1987; Producer, Radio 4 Sunday, 1991–93; Producer, 1992–2004, Ed., 2004–, Thought for the Day; Series Producer: Sunday Radio 4, 1993–95; Heart and Soul, BBC TV, 1995; Producer: The Choice, 1995; File on 4, 1995–96; Heart of the Matter, BBC TV, 1998 (Series Producer, 1999–2001); Everyman, Letters to the Yorkshire Ripper, BBC TV, 2001; The Celibacy Debate, BBC TV; Exec. Producer, Music and Worship Progs, Religion and Ethics, 2002–04; Exec. Producer, Religion and Ethics, BBC Radio, 2004–09; Editor: Faith in Africa, 2005; Humphrys in Search of God, 2006; The King James Bible, 2011; The People's Passion, 2012. MA Lambeth, 2008. Sanford St Martin Award, 1992, 2007, 2011; Sony Bronze Award, 1995; Silver Award, Med. Radio of the Year, 1998; VLV New Prog. Award, 2007; Jerusalem Trust Award, 2007. *Recreation:* Thomas. *Address:* BBC Religion and Ethics, Dock House, MediaCityUK, Salford M50 2LH.

MORGAN, Rt Rev. Christopher Heudebourck; Area Bishop of Colchester, 2001–13; an Honorary Assistant Bishop, Diocese of Chichester, since 2014; *b* 23 March 1947; *m* 1975, Anne Musgrave; one *s* one *d. Educ:* City of Bath Boys' Sch.; Kelham Theol Coll.; Lancaster Univ. (BA 1973); Heythrop Coll., London (MTh 1991). Ordained deacon, 1973, priest, 1974; Curate, St James the Great, Birstall, 1973–76; Chaplain to EC staff, and Asst Chaplain, Holy Trinity Ch, Brussels, 1976–80; Team Vicar, St George, Redditch, and part-time Industrial Chaplain, 1980–85; Vicar, Sonning, 1985–96; Gloucester Diocesan Officer for Ministry, and a Residentiary Canon, Gloucester Cathedral, 1996–2001. Principal, Berks Christian Trng Scheme, 1985–89; Dir, Pastoral Studies, St Albans and Oxford Diocesan Ministry Course, 1992–96. *Recreations:* hill walking, improving at golf, music, grandchildren. *Address:* 6 Wellington Court, Grand Avenue, Worthing, W Sussex BN11 5AB.

MORGAN, Claire; *see* Durkin, C.

MORGAN, David; *see* Morgan, F. D.

MORGAN, David Leslie; Chairman, M&G Group plc, 1997–98; *b* 23 Dec. 1933; *s* of Captain Horace Leslie Morgan, CMG, DSO, RN and Kathleen Hilda Morgan (*née* Bellhouse); *m* 1965, Clare Jean Lacy; one *s* one *d. Educ:* Clifton Coll., Bristol; University Coll., Oxford (BA Hons PPE 1957). Worked in FE, for Shell, and later stockbroking in Malaysia, 1957–65; banking and investment management, Deltec Internat., London and NY, 1965–70; Dir, E. D. Sassoon, 1970–72; M&G Group, 1972–98: Dir, 1973–91, Man. Dir, 1991–95, Chm., 1995–97, M&G Investment Management; Dep. Gp Man. Dir, 1991–94; Dep. Chm.

and Man. Dir, 1994–97. MCSI (MSI 1993). FRSA 1993. *Recreations:* walking, wine, theatre. *Address:* 2 Orme Square, W2 4RS. *Clubs:* Royal Automobile; Royal North Devon Golf; Royal Mid Surrey Golf.

MORGAN, Prof. David Owen, PhD; FRS 2012; Professor, since 1997, and Vice Chair, since 1998, Department of Physiology, and Professor, Department of Biochemistry and Biophysics, since 1997, University of California, San Francisco. *Educ:* Univ. of Calgary (BSc Animal Biol. 1980); Univ. of California, San Francisco (PhD 1986). Postdoctoral Fellow, 1986–89, Asst Prof., 1989–95, Associate Prof., 1995–97, University of California, San Francisco. *Publications:* The Cell Cycle: principles of control, 2006; articles in jls. *Address:* Department of Physiology, Box 2200, University of California at San Francisco, 600 16th Street, San Francisco, CA 94158–2517, USA.

MORGAN, David Thomas; land and development consultant; *b* 22 Jan. 1946; *s* of Janet Catherine and Noel David Morgan; *m* 1968, Quita Valentine; two *d*. *Educ:* Alleyne's Grammar School, Stevenage; Univ. of Newcastle upon Tyne (BA Hons Land Use Studies 1968). MRTPI 1971–2008. Somerset CC, 1968–70; Worcs CC, 1970–71; Peterborough Develt Corp., 1971–81; Housing Develt Manager, 1981–85, Dir, Planning Services, 1985–87, LDDC; Chief Exec., Black Country Develt Corp., 1987–98. Mem., Inland Waterways Amenity Adv. Council, 1997–2006. *Recreation:* painting and drawing. *Address:* 3 Riverside Court, Caunsall, near Kidderminster, Worcs DY11 5YW. *T:* (01562) 851688.

MORGAN, Prof. David Vernon, PhD, DSc; FREng, FInstP, FIET, FCGI, FLSW; Professor of Microelectronics, 1985–2010, and Distinguished Research Professor, 2003–10, now Honorary, University of Wales Cardiff; *b* 13 July 1941; *s* of late David Vernon Grenville Morgan and Isabel Lovina Benson Williams (formerly Morgan; *née* Emanuel); *m* 1965, Jean Anderson; one *s* one *d*. *Educ:* UCW, Aberystwyth (BSc; Hon. Fellow, 2006); Gonville and Caius Coll., Cambridge (PhD); Leeds Univ. (DSc). CPhys; FREng (FEng 1966). Fellow, Univ. of Wales, at Cavendish Labs, Cambridge, 1966–68; Harwell Fellow, AERE, 1968–70; University of Leeds: Lectr, 1970–77; Sen. Lectr, 1977–80; Reader, 1980–85; Head of Electronics, 1988–94, Head, Cardiff Sch. of Engrg, 1995–2003, UWCC, subseq. Univ. of Wales Cardiff. Editor, Solid State Devices and Circuits series, 1975–95; Founding Editor, Design and Measurement in Electronic Engineering series, 1986–95. FCGI 1998; FLSW 2011. Papal Cross Pro Ecclesia et Pontifice, 2004. *Publications:* Channelling Theory Observation and Application, 1971; Solid State Electronics, 1972; An Introduction to Semiconductor Microtechnology, 1983, 2nd edn 1990; more than 200 papers in learned jls. *Recreations:* Rugby, golf, hill walking, yoga. *Address:* Cardiff School of Engineering, Cardiff University, Queen's Buildings, Newport Road, Cardiff CF24 3AA. *T:* (029) 2087 4424.

MORGAN, David Wynn; His Honour Judge David Wynn Morgan; a Circuit Judge, since 2000; *b* 18 April 1954; *s* of late Arthur Islwyn Lewis Morgan and of Mary Morgan (*née* Wynn); *m* 1982, Marian Eléna Lewis; one *s* one *d*. *Educ:* Kingswood Sch., Bath; Balliol Coll., Oxford (BA Jurisprudence). Called to the Bar, Gray's Inn, 1976; practised on Wales and Chester Circuit, 1977–2000; Asst Recorder, 1991–95, Recorder, 1995–2000. Mem., Parole Bd, 2002–09. *Recreations:* music, reading, being in Pembrokeshire. *Address:* The Crown Court, Cathays Park, Cardiff CF10 3PG.

MORGAN, Rt Hon. Sir Declan; *see* Morgan, Rt Hon. Sir C. D.

MORGAN, Prof. Derec Llwyd, DPhil, DLitt; FLSW; Vice-Chancellor and Principal, University of Wales, Aberystwyth, 1995–2004; Senior Vice-Chancellor, 2001–04, Professor Emeritus, since 2004, University of Wales; *b* 15 Nov. 1943; *s* of Ewart Lloyd Morgan and Margaret Morgan; *m* 1965, Jane Edwards; one *d*. *Educ:* Amman Valley GS; UCNW, Bangor (BA; Hon Fellow, 1996); Jesus Coll., Oxford (DPhil; Hon. Fellow, 1999); DLitt Wales, 1999. Res. Fellow, Univ. of Wales, 1967–69; Lectr, UCW, Aberystwyth, 1969–74; University College of North Wales, Bangor: Lectr, 1975–80, Sen. Lectr, 1980–83, Reader, 1983–89, Dept of Welsh; Dir, Research Centre Wales, 1985–89; Prof. of Welsh, 1989–95, and Vice-Principal, 1994–95, UCW, Aberystwyth. Supernumerary Fellow, 1997–98, Welsh Supernumerary Fellow, 2003–04, Jesus Coll., Oxford. Member: Bd of Celtic Studies, Univ. of Wales, 1990–96; Court and Council, Nat. Library of Wales, 1995–2007; Governing Body, Inst. of Grassland and Environmental Res., 1995–2004. Member: Gen. Adv. Council, BBC, 1984–90; Broadcasting Council for Wales, 1990–95; ITC, 1999–2003. Chm., Rowntree Commn on Rural Housing in Wales, 2007–08. Royal National Eisteddfod of Wales: Chm. Council, 1979–82, 1985–86; Chm. Exec. Cttee, Ynys Môn, 1983; Pres. Court, 1989–93. Chairman: All-Wales Cultural Forum, 1999; Celtic Film and Television Festival, 2000; Sir Kyffin Williams Trust, 2006–; Exec. Cttee, James Pantyfedwen Foundn, 2011–; Anglesey Language Forum, 2013–. Non-executive Director: PO Bd, Wales and the Marches, 1996–2000; Menter a Busnes, 1997–2000. Trustee, James Pantyfedwen Foundn, 2004–. Founding FLSW 2010 (Mem. Council, 2009–12). Hon. Fellow, Trinity UC, 2009. DUniv Wales, 2006. *Publications:* Y Tân Melys, 1966; Pryderi, 1970; Barddoniaeth Thomas Gwynn Jones: astudiaeth, 1972; Kate Roberts, 1974, 2nd edn 1991; (ed) Cerddi '75, 1975; Iliad Homer, 1976; (ed) Adnabod Deg, 1977; Gwna yn Llawen, Ŵr Ieuanc, 1978; Y Diwygiad Mawr, 1981 (trans., The Great Awakening in Wales, 1988); Williams Pantycelyn, 1983; Pobl Pantycelyn, 1986; (ed) Glas y Nef: cerddi ac emynau John Roberts Llanfwrog, 1987; Cefn y Byd, 1987; (ed) Emynau Williams Pantycelyn, 1991; (ed) Meddwl a Dychymyg Williams Pantycelyn, 1991; Ni cheir byth wir lle bo llawer o feirdd, 1992; Charles Edwards, 1994; Y Beibl a Llenyddiaeth Gymraeg, 1998; John Roberts Llanfwrog: pregethwr, bardd, emynydd, 1999; (contrib.) Gogoneddus Arglwydd, Henffych Well, 2000; Nid hwn mo'r llyfr terfynol: Hanes Llenyddiaeth Thomas Parry, 2004; (ed) Kyffin: a celebration, 2007; Tyred i'n Gwaredu, 2010; (ed) Daniel Owen's Fireside Tales, 2011; Y Brenhinbren: bywyd a gwaith Thomas Parry 1904–1985, 2013; (ed) Emlyn Hooson: essays and reminiscences, 2014. *Recreations:* cricket, gardening, fortunes and misfortunes of Swansea City AFC, reading. *Address:* Carrog Uchaf, Tregaian, Llangefni, Anglesey LL77 7UE. *Clubs:* Premier (Glamorgan County Cricket); Rygbi Llangefni.

MORGAN, Dianne; *see* Edwards, Dianne.

MORGAN, Douglas, IPFA; County Treasurer, Lancashire County Council, 1985–92; *b* 5 June 1936; *s* of late Douglas Morgan and Margaret Gardner Morgan; *m* 1960, Julia (*née* Bywater); two *s*. *Educ:* High Pavement Grammar Sch., Nottingham. IPFA 1963 (4th place in final exam. and G. A. Johnston (Dundee) Prize). Nat. Service, RAF, 1954–56. Nottingham CBC, 1952–61; Herefordshire CC, 1961–64; Berkshire CC, 1964–67; Asst Co. Treas., W Suffolk CC, 1967–70; Asst, later Dep., Co. Treas., Lindsey CC, 1970–73; Dep. Co. Treas., Lancashire CC, 1973–85. Chm., NW & N Wales Region, CIPFA, 1985–86; Pres., NW & N Wales Region, Students' Soc., CIPFA, 1989–90. Treas., Lancs Cttee, Royal Jubilee & Prince's Trust, 1985–92; Hon. Treasurer: Lancs Playing Fields Assoc., 1985–92; NW Region Library System and NW Sound Archive, 1986–92; Mem., Exec. Cttee, Lancs Union of Golf Clubs, 1998–2002. FRSA. *Publications:* articles for Public Finance & Accountancy and other local govt jls. *Recreations:* golf and "collecting" golf courses, jazz. *Address:* 8 Croyde Road, St Annes-on-Sea, Lancs FY8 1EX. *T:* (01253) 725808. *Club:* Fairhaven Golf (Centenary Captain, 1995–96).

MORGAN, (Evan) Roger; Senior Clerk, Science & Technology Committee, House of Lords, 1999–2003; *b* 18 April 1945; *s* of late Evan and Stella Morgan; *m* 1st, 1967 (marr. diss.); one *s* one *d*; 2nd, 1997, Lesley Greene (*née* Smith). *Educ:* Whitgift Sch., South Croydon; Battersea Coll. of Advanced Technol. Main career spent within DES, then Dept for Educn, later Dept for Educn and Employment: Under Sec., Further Educn, 1991–94, Internat. Relns and Youth, 1994–95; Asst Dir, Internat. Dept for Educn and Employment, 1995–97. Various voluntary post-retirement positions, 2003–. *Recreations:* making music, cycling, local history. *E:* morgan.roger@btopenworld.com.

MORGAN, Francis Vincent; General Secretary, Association of Governing Bodies of Independent Schools (formerly Governing Bodies Association and Governing Bodies of Girls' Schools Association), 1998–2003; *b* 22 June 1936; *s* of Joseph Michael Morgan and Monica Morgan; *m* 1965, Annette Mary Tolhurst; one *s*. *Educ:* St Edward's Coll., Liverpool; Univ. of Liverpool (Oliver Lodge Prize; BSc 1958); St John's Coll., Cambridge (PGCE 1959); Chelsea Coll., Univ. of London (MEd 1974). Asst master, Stonyhurst Coll., 1959–62; various posts, Redrice Sch., Andover, 1962–68; Lectr in Physical Scis, Homerton Coll., Cambridge, 1968–70; Schs Advr, Borough of Southend-on-Sea, 1970–73; Head: Sacred Heart Sch., Tunbridge Wells, 1973–78; St Mary's Catholic Sch., Bishop's Stortford, 1978–84; Schs Officer, Archdio. Westminster, 1984–86; Dir of Educn, RC Dio. Brentwood, 1986–90; Dir, United Westminster Schs and Royal Foundn of Grey Coat Hosp., 1990–98. Mem., Ind. Schs Pension Scheme Cttee, 1996–2001. Governor: Stonyhurst Coll., 1986–91; New Hall Sch., Chelmsford, 1992–2001 (Chm., 1995–2001); Westminster Cathedral Choir Sch., 1998–2010; Sutton Valence Sch., 1998–2004; St Mary's Sch., Ascot, 2002–11; St Mary's Sch., Cambridge, 2010–14 (Chm., 2012–14); Trustee: St Mary's Sch., Hampstead, 1992–2001; United Westminster Schs, 2000–06; Eastern Counties Educnl Trust (formerly Royal Eastern Counties Schs), 2002–12. *Recreations:* books, music, chess, bridge. *Address:* 34 Ashley Road, Newmarket, Suffolk CB8 8DA. *T:* (01638) 602313. *Club:* Athenæum.
See also J. A. Morgan.

MORGAN, Prof. Frank, OBE 2012; Vice-Chancellor, Bath Spa University (formerly Bath College of Higher Education, then Bath Spa University College), 1996–2011; *b* Stockport, 23 Nov. 1952; *s* of George Morgan and Hilda Morgan; *m* 1989, Gurcharan Kaur Dhillon; two *s*. *Educ:* Bridge Hall Sch., Stockport; University Coll. London (BA 1974); City Univ. Business Sch. (MSc 1976); Preston Poly. (CPFA 1981). Greater Manchester Transport, 1976–80; Accountant, London Bor. of Southwark, 1980–83; Hd, Finance, North East London Poly., 1983–86; Dep. Dir, Bath Coll. of Higher Educn, 1986–96. Gov., Bridgwater Coll., Som. *Recreations:* studying seventeenth century French plays, watching Rugby League, exploring England's industrial heritage.

MORGAN, (Frederick) David, OBE 2008; DL; President, International Cricket Council, 2008–10 (Director, since 2003); *b* 6 Oct. 1937; *s* of Frederick Barlow Morgan and Caroline Morgan (*née* Constable); *m* 1960, Ann Cruickshank; one *s*. *Educ:* Thomas Richards Technical Sch., Tredegar; Henley Management Coll. (Gen. Mgt Prog. 1975). British Steel: Works Manager, Hot Sheet Finishing and Cold Rolling, Llanwern, 1977–84; Regl Sales Manager, SW and Wales, Strip Products, 1984–85; Commercial Manager, Electricals, 1985–90; Commercial Dir, European Electrical Steels, 1991–2001. Dir, Newport Develt Bd, 1997–2002. Chm., Wkg Party on setting up ECB (reported 1996); Dep. Chm., 1997–2002, Chm., 2003–07, ECB; conducted review of business of domestic cricket in England and Wales (reported 2012). DL Gwent, 2009. Hon. Fellow, Univ. of Wales, 2011. Chancellor's Medal, Univ. of Glamorgan, 2004. *Recreations:* grandchildren, music, Church liturgy, Rugby, wine, newspapers. *Address:* 49 Old Hill Crescent, Christchurch, Newport NP18 1JL. *T:* (01633) 420485. *E:* fdm53a@gmail.com. *Clubs:* MCC (Pres., 2014–); Glamorgan CC, Worcestershire CC, Surrey CC (Hon. Life Vice-Pres., 2010).

MORGAN, Geoffrey Thomas, CB 1991; Under Secretary, Cabinet Office, 1985–91; *b* 12 April 1931; *s* of late Thomas Evan Morgan and Nora (*née* Flynn); *m* 1960, Heather, *d* of late William Henry Trick and of Margery Murrell Wells; two *d*. *Educ:* Roundhay Sch. National Service, Royal Signals, 1950–52; joined Civil Service, 1952; served in Mins of Supply and Aviation, 1952–65; HM Treasury, 1965–68 and 1981–83; CSD, 1968–81; seconded to Arthur Guinness Son & Co., 1970–72; Cabinet Office, 1983–91; Adviser to: World Bank in Washington, 1977–78; UN in NY, 1987–88; official missions to: People's Republic of China in Beijing, 1988, 1991; Govt of Hungary in Budapest, 1990–2000; Govt of Jamaica in Kingston, 1991; South Africa, 1991–95; Czech Republic, 1996–2000; Chile, 1998. Chm., Public Admin Cttee, WEU, 1990–91. Advr, Coopers & Lybrand, subseq. PricewaterhouseCoopers, 1991–2000. Panel Chm., CSSB, 1991–95; Chm., Internat. Adv. Panel, Civil Service Coll., 1998–2001. Trustee, Whitehall and Industry Gp, 1991–94. Trustee, Twickenham Mus., 2002–14. FRSA 1996. *Recreation:* enjoying life with grandchildren. *E:* morganongreen@gmail.com. *Clubs:* Athenæum; Lensbury (Teddington).

MORGAN, Dame Gillian (Margaret), DBE 2004; FRCP, FFPH; Permanent Secretary, Welsh Government (formerly Welsh Assembly Government), 2008–12; Chair, NHS Providers, since 2014; *b* 23 July 1953. *Educ:* University Coll. Hosp. Medical Sch. (MB BS 1976). DRCOG 1981; FFPH (FFPHM 1996); FRCP 1998; MRCGP 2008; CCMI 2008. Leicestershire Health Authority: Dir of Quality and Contracts, 1989–91; Dir of Public Health, 1991–94; Chief Exec., North and East Devon HA, 1995–2002; Chief Exec., NHS Confederation, 2002–08. Chairman: Compli With Us Ltd, 2012–13; Clinical Bd, London Cancer Alliance, 2012–13; Alzheimer's Soc., 2013–15; Foundn Trust Network, 2014–. Advr, de Poel, 2013–. Hon. Fellow, Trinity Univ. Coll., 2009. Hon. DSc City, 2006. *Recreation:* sailing.

MORGAN, Sir Graham, Kt 2000; independent health care advisor, since 2007; *b* 20 Aug. 1947; *s* of Islwyn and Phyllis Morgan; civil partnership 2006, Raymond Willetts. *Educ:* Treorchy Secondary Modern Sch.; Llandough Hosp. (RGN 1969). Staff Nurse: Llandough Hosp., Cardiff, 1969; Royal Marsden Hosp., 1970–72; Charge Nurse, St Mary's Hosp., Paddington, 1972–74; Nursing Officer, KCH, 1974–83; Asst Dir of Nursing, St Charles' Hosp., 1983–91; Special Nurse Advr, 1991–94, Dir of Nursing and Quality, 1994–99, Central Middlesex Hosp.; Exec. Dir of Nursing, 1999–2005, Dir of Clinical Strategy, 2005–07, NW London Hosps NHS Trust. Ordained priest, 1984; NSM, St Michael and All Angels, Bedford Park, 2003–. Dir and Trustee, St Margaret's Convent and St Mary's Nursing Home (formerly St Mary's Convent and Nursing Home), Chiswick, 2006–. *Publications:* (with Amanda Layton) Nuts and Bolts of Protocols, 1998; articles in various health care jls. *Recreations:* opera, dining out. *Address:* 24 Charleville Court, Charleville Road, W14 9JG. *Club:* National Liberal.

MORGAN, His Honour Hugh Marsden; a Circuit Judge, 1995–2010; *b* 17 March 1940; *s* of late Hugh Thomas Morgan, Cyncoed, Cardiff and Irene Morgan (*née* Rees); *m* 1967, Amanda Jane Tapley; two *s* one *d*. *Educ:* Cardiff High Sch.; Magdalen Coll., Oxford (Demy; BCL; MA Jurisp.). Tutor in Jurisprudence, St Edmund Hall and Pembroke Coll., Oxford, 1963–64. Called to the Bar, Gray's Inn, 1964; in practice: Midland Circuit, 1965–71; SE Circuit, 1971–95; Asst Recorder, 1983–87; Recorder, 1987–95. Member: Matrimonial Causes Rule Cttee, 1989–91; Family Proceedings Rule Cttee, 1991–93; Fees and Legal Aid Cttee, Senate and Bar Council, 1976–82; London Family Justice Council, 2005–10. Mem., Wine Cttee, SE Circuit, 1986–88. Mem. Cttee, Family Law Bar Assoc., 1976–89. *Recreations:* dabbling in artistic pursuits with friends, enjoying opera, ballet, cinema, lunching, wining and dining, family, travel. *Address:* c/o Judicial Secretariat, 2nd Floor, Rose Court, Southwark Bridge Road, SE1 9HS.

MORGAN, Rt Hon. (Hywel) Rhodri; PC 2000; Member (Lab) Cardiff West, National Assembly for Wales, 1999–2011; First Minister (formerly First Secretary) for Wales, 2000–09; *b* 29 Sept. 1939; *s* of late Thomas John and Huana Morgan; *m* 1967, Julie Edwards (*see* Julie Morgan); one *s* two *d*. *Educ:* St John's College, Univ. of Oxford (Hons cl. 2, PPE 1961); Harvard Univ. (Masters in Govt 1963). Tutor Organiser, WEA, S Wales Area, 1963–65; Research Officer, Cardiff City Council, Welsh Office and DoE, 1965–71; Economic Adviser,

DTI, 1972–74; Indust. Develt Officer, S Glamorgan County Council, 1974–80; Head of Bureau for Press and Inf., European Commn Office for Wales, 1980–87. MP (Lab) Cardiff West, 1987–2001. Opposition spokesman on: Energy, 1988–92; Welsh Affairs, 1992–97. Sec. for Economic Develt, Nat. Assembly for Wales, 1999–2000. Chancellor, Swansea Univ., 2011–. *Publications:* Cardiff: half and half a capital, 1994. *Recreations:* long-distance running, wood carving, marine wildlife. *Address:* Lower House, Michaelston-le-Pit, Dinas Powys, South Glamorgan CF64 4HE. *T:* (029) 2051 4262.

MORGAN, Ven. Ian David John; Archdeacon of Suffolk, since 2012; *b* Hereford, 6 Jan. 1957; *s* of David and Margaret Morgan; *m* 1991, Tracey; two *s* one *d.* *Educ:* Wallingford Sch.; LTCL 1975; Univ. of Hull (BA Hons Music 1978); Ripon Coll., Cuddesdon. Ordained deacon, 1983, priest, 1984; Curate: Holy Trinity, Hereford, 1983–86; St Nicholas and St Mary de Haura, Shoreham by Sea, 1986–88; Producer, Presenter and Sen. Producer, BBC Local and Network Radio, 1988–92; Vicar, All Hallows, Ipswich, 1992–95; Rector, St Mary at Stoke and St Peter, Stoke Park with St Francis and St Clare (SW Ipswich Team Ministry), 1995–2012; Rural Dean of Ipswich, 2008–12. Hon. Canon, St Edmundsbury Cath., 2009–. Chair of Governors: Stoke High Sch., 1996–2012; Suffolk One Sixth Form Coll., 2011–. Musical Dir, Abbot Consort of Voices, 2005–13. *Recreations:* supporter of Welsh Rugby, England cricket and Brighton and Hove Albion, cooking, Rotary (Pres., Ipswich Club, 2007–08), falling asleep whilst reading at the beach hut. *Address:* Glebe House, The Street, Ashfield cum Thorpe, Stowmarket, Suffolk IP14 6LX. *T:* (01728) 605497. *E:* archdeacon.ian@cofesuffolk.org.

MORGAN, Sir Ian Parry David H.; *see* Hughes-Morgan.

MORGAN, Ioan, CBE 2007; Principal, Warwickshire College, 1997–2010; *b* 4 April 1953; *s* of John and Marjorie Morgan; *m* 1976, Sandra Evans; two *s* one *d.* *Educ:* Univ. of Wales, Aberystwyth (BSc Hons 1975); London Univ. (CertEd 1978). CBiol 1980. Principal: Cambridgeshire Coll. of Agric. and Hort., 1985–89; Pembrokeshire Coll., 1989–97. Chm., 157 Gp of Colls, 2006. Mem., Commn for Skills and Employment, 2007–09; Further Educn Strategic Advr, Pearson/Educn Develt Internat., 2010–; Interim Principal: Dearne Valley Coll., Rotherham, 2012; Lewisham Southwark Coll., 2014–15; Peterborough Coll., 2015. Freelance consultant in further educn, 2010–. FCGI. *Recreations:* dogs, countryside, Rugby, cricket, travel. *T:* (01926) 633236. *E:* Ioan.Morgan@live.co.uk.

MORGAN, Jane Sara; *see* Gandee, J. S.

MORGAN, Janet; *see* Balfour of Burleigh, Lady.

MORGAN, Jeremy; *see* Morgan, T. J.

MORGAN, John; *see* Morgan, W. J.

MORGAN, John Alfred; Director, Eleco Holdings plc, 1997–2001; *b* 16 Sept. 1931; *s* of late Alfred Morgan and Lydia Amelia Morgan; *m* 1959, Janet Mary Sclater-Jones; one *d.* *Educ:* Rugeley Grammar Sch.; Peterhouse, Cambridge (BA). Investment Research, Cambridge, 1953–59; Investment Manager, S. G. Warburg & Co. Ltd, 1959–67; Director: Glyn, Mills & Co., 1967–70; Williams & Glyn's Bank Ltd, 1970–76; Rothschild Asset Management, 1976–78; Central Trustee Savings Bank Ltd, 1982–86; Zurich Life Assce Co. Ltd, 1970–87; Sealink UK Ltd, 1983–85; Caviapen Investments Ltd, 1993–97; Yamaichi Bank (UK) plc, 1994–98. Gen. Manager, British Railways Pension Funds, 1978–86; Chief Exec., IMRO, 1986–93. Chm., Post Office Users' Nat. Council, 1978–82. *Recreations:* music, contemporary art. *Club:* Reform.

MORGAN, His Honour John Ambrose; a Circuit Judge, 1990–2003; a Deputy Circuit Judge, 2003–09; *b* 22 Sept. 1934; *s* of Joseph Michael Morgan and Monica Morgan; *m* 1970, Rosalie Mary Tyson; two *s.* *Educ:* St Edward's Coll., Liverpool; Univ. of Liverpool (Emmott Meml Scholar 1953; Alsopp Prizewinner 1953; LLB 1955). Law Soc. Finals 1957 (Local Govt Prize). Nat. Service, RAF, 1958–60. Admitted Solicitor, 1958; practised in local govt and private practice, 1960–70; called to the Bar, Gray's Inn, 1970; N Circuit, 1970–90; Dep. Stipendiary Magistrate, 1982; Asst Recorder, 1983; Recorder, 1988. Chm. of Govs, St Edward's Coll., Liverpool, 1987–95. *Recreations:* Rugby Union football (Pres., Liverpool RFU, 1980–82), golf, cricket, music, amateur operatics. *Address:* Tarnbrick, 80 Beech Lane, Liverpool L18 3ER. *Clubs:* Athenæum (Liverpool) (Pres., 2010); Liverpool St Helen's Rugby Football, Woolton Golf, Sefton Cricket (Pres., 2003–06).

See also F. V. Morgan.

MORGAN, John Christopher; Chief Executive, Morgan Sindall Group plc, 1994–99 and since 2012 (Executive Chairman, 2000–12); *b* 31 Dec. 1955; *m* 1984, Rosalind Kendrew; two *s* one *d.* *Educ:* Peter Symonds Grammar Sch., Winchester; Univ. of Reading (BSc Estate Mgt 1977); Open Univ. (MBA 1994). Chairman: Morgan Lovell, 1977–94; Johnsons Freshly Squeezed Juice Ltd, 1985–96; Genetix plc, 2000–08. *Address:* Morgan Sindall Group plc, Kent House, 14–17 Market Place, W1W 8AJ. *T:* (020) 7307 9200.

MORGAN, John William Harold, (Bill), CBE 1998; FREng; Chairman, Trafford Park Urban Development Corporation, 1990–98; Director: AMEC plc, 1983–91 (Chairman, 1984–88); Hill Samuel & Co., 1983–89; *b* 13 Dec. 1927; *s* of John Henry and Florence Morgan; *m* 1952, Barbara (*née* Harrison); two *d.* *Educ:* Wednesbury Boys' High Sch.; Univ. of Birmingham (BScEng, 1st Cl. Hons). FIMechE, MIET. National Service commn with RAF, 1949–51. Joined English Electric Co., Stafford, as design engr, subseq. Chief Development Engr (Machines), 1953; Chief Develt Engr (Mechanical), 1957; Chief Engr (DC Machines), 1960; Product Div. Manager, 1962; Gen. Manager, Electrical Machines Gp, 1965; Man. Dir, English Electric-AEI Machines Gp (following merger with GEC/AEI), 1968; Asst Man. Dir and main board dir, GEC plc, 1973–83. Chm., Staffordshire Cable, 1989–93; Dep. Chm., Petbow Holdings, 1983–86; Director: Simon Engineering, 1983–88; Pitney Bowes, 1989–92; Tekdata, 1989–99; UMIST Ventures, 1989–2001. Additional Mem., Monopolies and Mergers Commn (Electricity Panel), 1992–98. FREng (FEng 1978; Mem. Council, 1987–90). FRSA 1988. Hon. DSc Salford, 1997. S. G. Brown award for an outstanding contrib. to promotion and development of mechanical inventions, Royal Society, 1968. *Recreations:* craft activities, particularly woodworking. *Address:* Sparrows, Shelley, Ipswich, Suffolk IP7 5RQ. *T:* (01206) 337552.

MORGAN, Jonathan; Managing Consultant, Insight Wales Consulting Ltd, since 2011; Consultant, Practice Solutions Ltd, since 2011; *b* 12 Nov. 1974; *s* of Barrie and Linda Morgan. *Educ:* Bishop of Llandaff Church in Wales Sch., Cardiff; Cardiff Univ. (LLB Hons Law & Politics; MSc Econ European Policy). European Funding Officer, Cardiff Further Educn Coll., 1998–99. National Assembly for Wales: Mem. (C) S Wales Central, 1999–2007, Cardiff N, 2007–11; contested (C) Cardiff N, 2011. *Recreations:* theatre, golf, music. *Club:* Merthyr Conservative (Merthyr Tydfil).

MORGAN, Julie; Member (Lab) Cardiff North, National Assembly for Wales, since 2011; *b* 2 Nov. 1944; *d* of late Jack Edwards and of Grace Edwards; *m* 1967, Rhodri Morgan, *qv*; one *s* two *d.* *Educ:* Howell's Sch., Llandaff; KCL (BA Hons); Manchester Univ.; Cardiff Univ. (DipSocAdmin, CQSW). Sen. Social Worker, Barry, S Glam. Social Services, 1980–83; Principal Officer and Develt Officer, W Glam. CC, 1983–87; Asst Dir, Child Care, Barnardo's, 1987–97. Member (Lab): S Glam. Council, 1985–96; Cardiff UA, 1996–97. Contested (Lab) Cardiff N, 1992. MP (Lab) Cardiff North, 1997–2010; contested (Lab) same seat, 2010. *Address:* Lower House, Michaelston-le-Pit, Dinas Powys CF64 4HE; National Assembly for Wales, Cardiff Bay, Cardiff CF99 1NA. *W:* www.juliemorgan.org.

MORGAN, Karen Jane, OBE 1999; DL; Chairman and Trustee, The Converging World, since 2007; *b* 28 June 1945; *d* of Walter Anderson Caldwell and Jean Drummond Caldwell (*née* Hislop); *m* 1st, 1977, (Malcolm) John Methven (later Sir John Methven; he *d* 1980); three step *d*; 2nd, 1988, Andrew John Mantle Morgan; two step *s* two step *d.* *Educ:* St Leonard's Sch., St Andrews; Univ. of Edinburgh (BSc 1st Cl. Hons Chemistry). ICI Ltd, 1968–81. Director: Latchways Ltd, 1982–85; Southdown Bldg Soc., 1990–92 (Vice-Chm., 1991–92); Associate, Solomon Hare LLP, 1993–2005. Dir, Wessex Water Services Ltd, 1998–2005. Member: Bd, NRA, 1989–95; Bd, EA, 1995–98; Envmt Cttee, RSA, 1999–2005; Council, NERC, 2002–08. Trustee, 1992–2007, Vice-Chm., 2001–07, Water Aid; Chm., EcoAlert Ltd, 2007–10; Chm. and Dir, Sustainable Engine Systems Ltd, 2010–13; Chm., Aspire Glos Ltd, 2015–. Mem. Council, CNAA, 1982–88; Comr, Fulbright Commn, 1983–87; Mem., Bd of Govs, Bristol Poly., 1989–92; University of West of England: Mem., 1992–2003, Dep. Chm., 1994–97, Chm., 1998–2003, Bd of Govs; Pro Chancellor, 2004–10; Mem., 1998–2003, Dep. Chm., 2000–02, Cttee of Univ. Chairmen; Member: Commn on Univ. Career Opportunity, 1999–2000; Jt Equality Steering Gp, 2001–03; Equality Challenge Unit Mgt Bd, 2003–06. Dir, At-Bristol, 2000–11; Trustee, Plymouth Marine Lab., 2005–12. Chm., Appeal Cttee, 2004–07, Vice Pres., 2007–, Penny Brohn Cancer Care (formerly Bristol Cancer Help Centre). Member: Governing Body, Colston's Collegiate Sch., 2004–13 (Chm., 2010–13); Governing Council, RAU (formerly RAC), Cirencester, 2004–13 (Vice Chm., 2005–10); Council, RSA, 2005–09; Adv. Bd, Cabot Inst., Univ. of Bristol, 2010–; Council, Univ. of Gloucestershire, 2012–. Trustee: Bath Festivals Trust, 1993–98; Colston's Foundn, 2010–; Friends of Cotswolds, 2014–; Patron, Ruskin Mill Trust, 2015–. FRSA 1998. Hon. DEd UWE, 2004. DL Glos, 2007. Freeman, 2001–03, Liveryman, 2003–12, Co. of Water Conservators; Mem., Soc. of Merchant Venturers, 2003–; Mem., Hon. Co. of Glos, 2008–. *Publications:* (contrib.) Time of Flight Mass Spectrometry, 1969. *Recreations:* music, sailing, skiing, travelling, water. *Address:* Little Skiveralls, Chalford Hill, Stroud, Glos GL6 8QJ. *Clubs:* Reform; Kandahar Ski; Downhill Only Ski; Royal Western Yacht, Clyde Cruising.

MORGAN, Lisa Jayne; Founder Director, Morgan-Knox Ltd, since 2010; *b* 28 May 1970; *m*; two step *d.* Buyer, Tandy, 1989–93; Gp Software Buyer, Dixons, 1993–97; GAME Group, 1997–2010: Hd, Buying, Electronics Boutique, 1997–98; Buying and Mktg Dir, 1998–2000; Commercial Dir, 2000–03; Dep. Chief Exec., 2003–06; Chief Exec., 2006–10. *Recreations:* horses, cooking, spending time with family.

MORGAN, Dr Llewelyn William Goronwy; Lecturer in Classical Languages and Literature, University of Oxford, since 2002; Tutorial Fellow in Classics, Brasenose College, Oxford, since 1997; *b* St Helens, 25 June 1968; *s* of William Geraint Morgan and Jill Morgan; *m* 1995, Andrea Mae Swinton; two *s.* *Educ:* Liverpool Coll.; Corpus Christi Coll., Oxford (BA 1990; MA); Trinity Coll., Cambridge (PhD 1995). Lectr, Dept of Classics, UCD, 1994–97. Philip Leverhulme Prize, 2004. *Publications:* Patterns of Redemption in Virgil's Georgics, 1999; Musa Pedestris: metre and meaning in Roman poetry, 2010; The Buddhas of Bamiyan, 2012. *Recreations:* walking the dog, reading Kipling, anything but marking, Twitter. *Address:* Brasenose College, Oxford OX1 4AJ. *T:* (01865) 277890. *E:* llewelyn.morgan@bnc.ox.ac.uk.

MORGAN, Loraine; District Judge (Magistrates' Courts) (formerly Metropolitan Stipendiary Magistrate), since 1995; *b* 2 Dec. 1953; *d* of late Enrico Bellisario and Elizabeth Bellisario (*née* Coyle); *m* 1976, Captain Dai Morgan, RN. *Educ:* St Augustine's Priory, Ealing; Univ. of Exeter; Coll. of Law, Guildford. Admitted Solicitor, 1981; Partner, Reynolds & Hetherington, Fareham, 1982–86, Allsworth & Spears, Fareham, 1986–88; Solicitor Advocate, 1988–95; Co-founder and Dir, Just Advocates Ltd, 1991–95; Plate Judge Advocate, 1996–2001; Asst Recorder, 1998–2000; a Recorder, 2000. Mem., Crown Court Rules Cttee, 1994. Vice-Pres., Bracton Law Soc., 1974–75; Cttee Mem., Hampshire Inc. Law Soc., 1990–94; Sec. and Chm., Southampton Criminal Courts Solicitors' Assoc., 1990–94; Vice-Chm., Criminal Law Solicitors' Assoc., 1991–94. *Recreations:* good wine, good food, the company of good friends. *Address:* c/o Southampton and New Forest Magistrates' Court, 100 The Avenue, Southampton SO17 1EY. *T:* (023) 8038 4200. *Clubs:* Lansdowne, Army and Navy.

MORGAN, Marilynne Ann, CB 1996; Solicitor to the Departments for Work and Pensions (formerly of Social Security) and of Health, and Head of Law and Special Policy Group, Department for Work and Pensions (formerly Department of Social Security), 1997–2004; *b* 22 June 1946; *d* of late J. Emlyn Williams and Roma Elizabeth Williams (*née* Ellis); *m* 1970, Nicholas Alan, *e s* of Rear-Adm. Sir Patrick Morgan, KCVO, CB, DSC. *Educ:* Gads Hill Place, Higham-by-Rochester; Bedford Coll., Univ. of London (BA Hons History). Called to the Bar, Middle Temple, 1972, Bencher, 2002 (Lent Reader, 2012). Res. Asst, Special Historical Sect., FCO, 1967–71; Department of Health and Social Security: Legal Asst, 1973; Sen. Legal Asst, 1978; Asst Solicitor, 1982; Under Sec. and Principal Asst Solicitor, 1985–91, DSS, 1988–91, DoE, 1991–92; Department of the Environment: Solicitor and Legal Advr, 1992–97; Chm., Departmental Task Force, 1994–95; Sen. Dir, Legal and Corporate Services Gp, 1996–97. Non-exec. Dir, Treasury Solicitor's Dept, 2004–10. Vice-Chm. 1983–84, Chm. 1984–86, Legal Sect. of Assoc. of First Div. Civil Servants. Mem., General Council of the Bar, 1987–92. Hon. Legal Advr, CS Sports Council, 2006–. Trustee/Director: Alzheimer's Soc., 2003–09 (Chm., Nominations Cttee, 2005–11); Ambache Orchestra, 2003–06; Alzheimer's Brain Bank UK, 2006–11; Bucks Historic Churches Trust, 2013–; Trustee, Middle Temple Charity Funds, 2014–; Chm., Friends of Bucks Historic Churches, 2008–. *Publications:* contributor, Halsbury's Laws of England, 1982, 1986; articles in learned jls. *Recreation:* homely pursuits. *Club:* University Women's (Trustee, 2009–; Chm. Trustees, 2011–).

MORGAN, Martin Gerard; Principal Social Worker, Child Care Social Services, Belfast Trust, since 2008; *b* 25 Oct. 1966; *s* of Robert Morgan and Kathleen Morgan; *m* 2001, Dympna O'Hara. *Educ:* Queen's Univ., Belfast (BA Hons Inf. Mgt; MSW; DipSW). Child Protection Investigation Team, 2002–03, Sen. Social Worker, 2005–08, Child Care Social Services. Mem. (SDLP), Belfast City Council, 1993–2005; Lord Mayor of Belfast, 2003–04. Pt-time columnist on NI politics. *Recreations:* golf, athletics, reading political biographies.

MORGAN, Prof. Mary Susanna, PhD; FBA 2002; Professor of the History and Philosophy of Economics, London School of Economics and Political Science, University of London, since 1999. *Educ:* LSE (BSc 1978; PhD 1984). Res. Asst to Economist, Citibank, London, 1973–75; Exchange Control Dept, Bank of England, 1978–79; Res. Officer, Dept of Econs, LSE, 1979–82, 1983–84; Lectr, Dept of Econs and Related Studies, Univ. of York, 1984–87; Vis. Asst Prof., Dept of Econs, Duke Univ., 1987; Lectr, Dept of Econ. History, 1988–94, Reader in History of Econs, 1994–99, LSE. Prof. of History of Econ. Thought and Philosophy of Econ. Sci., Univ. of Amsterdam (part-time), 1992–99. *Publications:* (ed jtly) The Probabilistic Revolution, vol. II: ideas in the sciences, 1987; The History of Econometric Ideas, 1990; (ed jtly) Higgling: transactors and their markets in the history of economics, 1994; (jtly) The Foundations of Econometric Analysis, 1995; (ed jtly) From Interwar Pluralism to Post-War Neoclassicism, 1998; (jtly) Methodology and Tacit Knowledge, 1999; (ed jtly) Models as Mediators, 1999; (ed jtly) Empirical Models and Policy Making, 2000; (ed jtly) The Age of Economic Measurement, 2001; (ed jtly) How Well Do Facts Travel?, 2011; The World in a Model: how economists work and think, 2012; articles in jls. *Address:* Department of Economic History, London School of Economics and Political Science, Houghton Street, WC2A 2AE.

MORGAN, Matthew Spencer Richard; Headmaster, Sir Thomas Rich's School, Gloucester, since 2013; *b* Oxford, 28 Sept. 1975; *s* of Richard Arthur George Morgan and Diana Elizabeth Morgan. *Educ:* Bedford Sch.; Royal Holloway, Univ. of London (BSc Hons 1997); Hughes Hall, Cambridge (PGCE 1998); Oxford Brookes Univ. (MA Educn (Distinction) 2002). NPQH 2006; CGeog 2009. Teacher of Geog., 1998–2003, Sen. Teacher, 2003–07, Royal Latin Sch., Buckingham; Dep. Headmaster, Sir Thomas Rich's Sch., 2007–13. FRGS 2006. *Publications:* articles in Teaching Geography, 2000–07. *Recreations:* walking, cooking, conducting. *Address:* Sir Thomas Rich's School, Oakleaze, Longlevens, Gloucester GL2 0LF. *T:* (01452) 338431. *E:* mm@strs.org.uk.

MORGAN, Michael David; Development Director, Anglia Housing Association Group, 1993–98; *b* 19 Jan. 1942; *s* of Edward Arthur and Winifred Maud Morgan; *m* 1980, Ljiljana Radojcic; three *d. Educ:* Royal Liberty Sch., Romford; Prince Rupert Sch., Wilhemshaven, FRG; Coll. of Estate Management, London Univ. (BSc Est. Man.). FRICS. Sheffield City Council, 1964–67; Derby Borough Council, 1967–70; Telford Develt Corp., 1970–92 (Chief Exec. and Gen. Manager, 1986–92, retd). *Recreations:* cricket, jogging, gardening. *Address:* Red Roofs, Ashton Road, Kingsland, Shrewsbury SY3 7AP. *T:* (01743) 352800.

MORGAN, Prof. Michael John, PhD, ScD; FRS 2005; Professor of Visual Psychophysics, City University, since 2000; *b* 25 Aug. 1942; *m* 1996, Prof. Linda Partridge (*see* Dame L. Partridge). *Educ:* Queens' Coll., Cambridge (BA 1964; PhD 1969; ScD 1994). Asst in Res., 1965–71, Lectr, 1971–78, Univ. of Cambridge; Fellow, Queens' Coll., Cambridge, 1967–74; Professor of Psychology: Univ. of Durham, 1978–81; UCL, 1981–89; Professorial Fellow, Univ. of Edinburgh, 1989–93; Prof. of Visual Psychophysics, UCL, 1993–2000. *Publications:* Molyneux's Question: vision, touch and the philosophy of perception, 1977; The Space Between Our Ears, 2003; contrib. learned jls. *Address:* Department of Optometry and Visual Science, City University, Northampton Square, EC1V 0HB.

MORGAN, Rt Hon. Nicola (Ann); PC 2014; MP (C) Loughborough, since 2010; Secretary of State for Education, and Minister for Women and Equality, since 2014; *b* Kingston upon Thames, 10 Oct. 1972; *d* of Peter M. Griffith and Jennifer C. Griffith; *m* 2000, Jonathan Morgan; one *s. Educ:* Surbiton High Sch.; St Hugh's Coll., Oxford (MA Law); Guildford Law Sch. Admitted as solicitor, 1996; in practice as solicitor, specialising in corporate law: Theodore Goddard, 1994–97; Allen & Overy, 1998–2002; Travers Smith, 2002–10. An Asst Govt Whip, 2012–13; Economic Sec., 2013–14, Financial Sec., 2014, HM Treasury. *Recreations:* running, ski-ing, spending time with family. *Address:* House of Commons, SW1A 0AA. *T:* (020) 7219 7224, (constituency) (01509) 262723. *E:* nicky.morgan.mp@parliament.uk.

MORGAN, Patrick; HM Diplomatic Service, retired; Ambassador to El Salvador, 1999–2003; *b* 31 Jan. 1944; *s* of Matthew Morgan and Margaret (*née* Docherty); *m* 1966, Marlene Collins Beaton (*d* 2011); two *s* two *d. Educ:* St Columba's High Sch., Greenock. BoT, 1963–64; CRO, 1964–65; FCO, 1965–67; British Embassy: Bonn, 1967–69; Kuwait, 1969–71; La Paz, 1972–75; FCO, 1975–79; British Embassy: Washington DC, 1979–83; Jakarta, 1983–86; FCO, 1987–92; Ambassador to Honduras, 1992–95; Counsellor and Dep. Hd of Mission, Abu Dhabi, 1995–98; Counsellor, FCO, 1998–99. Governor, Al Khubairat Community Sch., Abu Dhabi, 1995–98. *Recreations:* swimming, reading, music, travel. *Address:* 4 Den Close, Beckenham, Kent BR3 6RP.

MORGAN, Hon. Sir Paul (Hyacinth), Kt 2007; **Hon. Mr Justice Morgan;** a Judge of the High Court, Chancery Division, since 2007; *b* 17 Aug. 1952; *s* of Daniel Morgan and Veronica Mary (*née* Elder); *m* 1980, Sheila Ruth Harvey; three *s. Educ:* St Columb's Coll., Londonderry; Peterhouse, Cambridge (BA 1974; MA 1979). Called to the Bar, Lincoln's Inn, 1975, Bencher, 2001. QC 1992; a Dep. High Court Judge, 2001–07. Dep. Chm., Agricl Land Tribunal, 1999–2007. *Publications:* (ed jtly) Megarry on Rent Acts, 11th edn, 1988; (ed jtly) Woodfall on Landlord and Tenant, 28th edn, 1990; (ed jtly) Gale on Easements, 18th edn 2008, 19th edn (ed) 2012; (ed jtly) Fisher & Lightwood's Law of Mortgage, 13th edn 2010 and 14th edn 2014. *Address:* Rolls Building, 7 Rolls Building, Fetter Lane, EC4A 1NL.

MORGAN, Prof. Peter John, PhD; FRSE; Director, Rowett Institute of Nutrition and Health (formerly Rowett Research Institute), since 1999, and Professor, since 2008, University of Aberdeen (Vice-Principal, 2008–14); *b* 23 Feb. 1956; *s* of Dr John W. W. Morgan and Patricia M. Morgan; *m* 1991, Prof. Denise Kelly; one *s* one *d. Educ:* Queen Mary Coll., London (BSc); Univ. of Aberdeen (PhD 1981). FRSE 2002. AFRC post-doctoral res. asst, Dept of Zool., Univ. of Aberdeen, 1981–85; Rowett Research Institute, Aberdeen: SSO, 1985–89; PSO, 1989–96; Leader, Molecular Neuroendocrinology Res. Gp, 1991–97; Head, Molecular Neuroendocrinology Unit and Mem., Sen. Mgt Gp, 1997–99. Hon. Prof., Dept of Zoology, Univ. of Aberdeen, 1999–2008. Trustee, Rowett Res. Inst. Charity, 2008–. *Recreations:* music (pianist), squash, swimming, travel. *Address:* Rowett Institute of Nutrition and Health, University of Aberdeen, Greenburn Road, Bucksburn, Aberdeen AB21 9SB. *T:* (01224) 438663.

MORGAN, Peter William Lloyd, MBE 2003; Director-General, Institute of Directors, 1989–94; *b* 9 May 1936; *s* of late Matthew Morgan and of Margaret Gwynneth (*née* Lloyd); *m* 1964, Elisabeth Susanne Davis; three *d. Educ:* Llandovery Coll.; Trinity Hall, Cambridge. Joined IBM UK Ltd, 1959; Data Processing Sales Dir, 1971–74; Gp Dir of Marketing, IBM Europe, Paris, 1975–80; Executive Director: IBM UK Ltd, 1983–87; IBM UK Holdings Ltd, 1987–89; National Provident Institution: Dir, 1990–99; Chm., 1996–99; Underwriting Mem., 1987–, Ext. Mem. Council, 2000–09, Lloyd's. Chairman: South Wales Electricity PLC, 1996 (Dir, 1989–96); Pace Micro Technology plc, 1996–2000; Director: Hyder Consulting (formerly Firth Holdings) plc, 1994–2009; Baltimore Technologies plc (formerly Zergo Holdings), 1994–2003 (Dep. Chm., 1998–2000; Chm., 2000–03); Assoc. of Lloyd's Mems, 1997– (Chm., 2010–12); Oxford Instruments plc, 2000–09; Strategic Thought Gp plc, 2004–12 (Chm., 2004–09). Public Mem., Network Rail, 2012–. Mem., European Econ. and Social Cttee, Brussels, 1994–2002, 2006–. Liveryman, Co. of Inf. Technologists, 1992– (Master, 2002–03). Radical of the Year, Radical Soc., 1990. *Publications:* Alarming Drum, 2005. *Recreations:* history, travelling, gardening, country house opera, drinking wine, watching Rugby, walking dogs. *Address:* Fairwood, Grayswood Road, Haslemere, Surrey GU27 2BU. *Club:* Oxford and Cambridge.

MORGAN, Piers Stefan; Presenter, Piers Morgan Live, CNN, 2011–14; *b* 30 March 1965; *s* of Glynne and Gabrielle Pughe-Morgan; *m* 1st, 1991, Marion Elizabeth Shalloe (marr. diss. 2008); three *s*; 2nd, 2010, Celia, *d* of George Gordon Harvey Walden, *qv*; one *d. Educ:* Chailey Comprehensive Sch.; Lewes Priory Sixth Form Coll.; Harlow Journalism Coll. With Lloyd's of London, 1985–87; Reporter, Surrey and S London Newspapers, 1987–89; Showbusiness Editor, The Sun, 1989–94; Editor: News of the World, 1994–95; Daily Mirror, 1995–2004. Judge, TV series: America's Got Talent, 2006–10; Britain's Got Talent, 2007–10; Presenter, TV Series: Piers on…, 2009; Piers Morgan's Life Stories, 2009–; When Piers Met…, 2009. Editor of the Year, Newspaper Focus Awards, 1994. *Publications:* Private Lives of the Stars, 1990; Secret Lives of the Stars, 1991; Phillip Schofield: to dream a dream, 1992; Take That: our story, 1993; Take That: on the road, 1994; Va Va Voom: a fan's diary of Arsenal's invincible season, 2004; The Insider: the private diaries of a scandalous decade, 2005; Don't You Know Who I Am?, 2007; God Bless America: misadventures of a big mouth Brit, 2009; Shooting Straight, 2013. *Recreations:* cricket, Arsenal FC.

MORGAN, Rt Hon. Rhodri; *see* Morgan, Rt Hon. H. R.

MORGAN, Richard Hugo Lyndon; QC 2011; *b* London, 30 April 1963; *s* of John and Anne Lyndon Morgan; *m* 1996, Monica Marie Coombs; one *s* one *d. Educ:* St Edward's Sch., Oxford; St Edmund Hall, Oxford (sent down); Univ. of Buckingham (LLB 1985); Fitzwilliam Coll., Cambridge (LLM 1987). Called to the Bar, Gray's Inn, 1988; in practice as barrister, 1989–. Trustee/Dir, Action for Stammering Children (formerly Assoc. for Res. into Stammering in Childhood), 2006–13. *Recreations:* travel, casual sport, family and friends. *Address:* Maitland Chambers, 7 Stone Buildings, Lincoln's Inn, WC2A 3SZ. *T:* (020) 7406 1200, *Fax:* (020) 7406 1300. *E:* rmorgan@maitlandchambers.com.

MORGAN, Richard Martin, MA; Warden, Radley College, 1991–2000; *b* 25 June 1940; *s* of His Honour Trevor Morgan, MC, QC, and late Leslie Morgan; *m* 1968, Margaret Kathryn, *d* of late Anthony Agutter and of Mrs Launcelot Fleming; three *d. Educ:* Sherborne Sch.; Caius Coll., Cambridge (MA, DipEd); York Univ. Assistant Master, Radley Coll., 1963; Housemaster, 1969; Headmaster, Cheltenham College, 1978–90. Member, Adv. Council, Understanding British Industry, 1977–79. Pres., Mencap, S Wilts, 2004–12; Chm., Prince's Trust, Salisbury, 2004–08. Governor: Clifton Coll., 2001– (Chm., 2014–); Sherborne Sch., 2002–10. JP Glos, 1978–90. *Recreations:* reading, music, Anthony Powell Soc. *Address:* Warmans, Bodenham, Salisbury, Wilts SP5 4EV. *T:* (01722) 338868. *Clubs:* Free Foresters, Jesters'.

MORGAN, Robin Milne; Principal: Daniel Stewart's and Melville College, Edinburgh, 1977–89; The Mary Erskine School, 1979–89; *b* 2 Oct. 1930; *o s* of Robert Milne Morgan and Aida Forsyth Morgan; *m* 1955, Fiona Bruce MacLeod Douglas (*d* 2008); three *s* one *d. Educ:* Mackie Academy, Stonehaven; Aberdeen Univ. (MA); London Univ. (BA, External). Nat. Service, 2nd Lieut The Gordon Highlanders, 1952–54; Asst Master: Arden House Prep. Sch., 1955–60; George Watson's Coll., 1960–71; Headmaster, Campbell Coll., Belfast, 1971–76. *Recreations:* music, archaeology, fishing, entertaining my ten grandchildren. *Address:* 1c Old Mansion House, Newbyth, East Linton, E Lothian EH40 3DU.

MORGAN, Robin Richard; author and journalist; Editor, The Sunday Times Magazine, 1992–93 and 1995–2009; Chief Executive Officer, Iconic Images Inc., since 2013; *b* 16 Sept. 1953; *s* of Raymond Morgan and Jean Edith Bennett; *m*; two *s* one *d. Educ:* King Edward VI Grammar Sch., Stourbridge, W Midlands. County Express, Stourbridge, 1971–73; Evening Echo, Hemel Hempstead, 1973–79; Sunday Times, London, 1979–89: Reporter, 1979–83; Dep. News Editor, 1983–85; Insight Editor, 1985–87; Features Editor, Sunday Times, 1987–89; Editor, Sunday Express, 1989–91; Associate Editor, Sunday Times, 1991–92; Editorial Dir designate, Reader's Digest, 1993–94. Contributing Editor: GQ Magazine, 1999–2003; Departures Magazine, 2009–. Campaigning Journalist of the Year: (commended) 1982; (winner) 1983. *Publications:* (jtly) The Falklands War, 1982; (jtly) Rainbow Warrior, 1986; (jtly) Bullion, 1988; (ed) Manpower, 1988; (jtly) Ambush, 1989; (jtly) The Book of Movie Biographies, 1997; (ed) Sinatra: Frank and friendly, 2007; The Eltonography, 2008; All About Bond, 2012; (jtly) 1963: The Year of the Revolution: how youth changed the world, 2013. *Recreations:* cinema, US politics, modern American fiction, travel. *Address:* Iconic Images Inc., 1 Great Cumberland Place, W1H 7AL.

MORGAN, Prof. Rodney Emrys; Professor of Criminal Justice, University of Bristol, 1990–2001, now Emeritus; Visiting Professor: Cardiff University, 2008–13; University of Sussex, since 2012; *b* 16 Feb. 1942; *s* of William Emrys Morgan and Jessmine Lilian (*née* Reed); *m* 1966, Karin Birgitta Lang; three *s. Educ:* Haberdashers' Aske's Sch., Mill Hill; Paston Sch., N Walsham; Univ. of Southampton (BSc; Dip. Applied Social Studies). Lectr, Univ. of Southampton, 1971–72; Lectr, then Sen. Lectr, Univ. of Bath, 1972–89; University of Bristol: Reader, 1989–90; Dean of Law, 1992–95. HM Chief Inspector of Probation for England and Wales, 2001–04; Chm., Youth Justice Bd for England and Wales, 2004–07; Advr on criminal justice inspection, MoJ, 2007–11. Visiting Fellow: Univ. of Oxford, 1985–87; Human Rights Implementation Centre, Univ. of Bristol, 2013–; Centre for Internat. Prison Studies, Univ. of Essex, 2013–; Visiting Professor: Univ. of WA, 1991; Univ. of Freiburg, 1995; Univ. of Onati, 1996; Harvard Univ., 1996; LSE, 2007–11. Mem., Daniel Morgan Ind. Panel, 2014–. Mem., Academic Adv. Cttee, Cumberland Lodge, 2010–. Trustee: King's Coll. Centre for Criminol Res., 2003–11; Inst. for Criminal Policy Res., Birkbeck, Univ. of London, 2003–12; Police Foundn, 2006–; Dance Utd, 2006–; Bath Philharmonia, 2007–; Bath Alcohol and Drugs Adv. Service, 2007–12; Bath Festivals Trust, 2008–13; Pres., Mentoring Plus, 2007–. *Publications:* (ed jtly) Oxford Handbook of Criminology, 1994, 5th edn 2012; The Politics of Sentencing Reform, 1995; The Future of Policing, 1997; Preventing Torture, 1998; Protecting Prisoners, 1999; Crime Unlimited, 1999; Combating Torture in Europe, 2001; Handbook of Probation, 2007; contrib. numerous articles to law, social policy and criminology jls. *Recreations:* sailing, theatre, music, walking, gardening, taking risks. *Address:* Beech House, Lansdown Road, Bath BA1 5EG. *T:* (01225) 316676. *E:* karin.rod@freeuk.com.

MORGAN, Roger; *see* Morgan, E. R.

MORGAN, Roger Hugh Vaughan Charles, CBE 1991; Librarian, House of Lords, 1977–91; *b* 8 July 1926; *s* of late Charles Langbridge Morgan, and Hilda Vaughan, both novelists and playwrights; *m* 1st, 1951, Harriet Waterfield (marr. diss. 1965), *d* of Gordon Waterfield; one *s* one *d* (and one *s* decd); 2nd, 1965, Susan Vogel Marrian, *d* of Hugo Vogel, Milwaukee, USA; one *s. Educ:* Downs Sch., Colwall; Phillips Acad., Andover, USA; Eton Coll.; Brasenose Coll., Oxford (MA). Grenadier Guards, 1944–47 (Captain, 1946). House of Commons Library, 1951–63; House of Lords Library, 1963–91. Burgess of Laugharne, 2004. *Recreations:* painting, photography, cooking. *Address:* 30 St Peter's Square, W6 9UH. *T:* (020) 8741 0267. *Clubs:* Garrick, Beefsteak.

See also Dowager Marchioness of Anglesey.

MORGAN, Sarah Mary; QC 2011; a Recorder, since 2009; *b* Pembroke, 17 Sept. 1964; *d* of Malcolm Morgan and Georgina Morgan (*née* Duhig). *Educ:* Brunel Univ. (LLB Hons). Called to the Bar, Gray's Inn, 1988. *Recreations:* being, as often as possible, in the Caribbean Sea. *Address:* 1 Garden Court, Temple, EC4Y 9BJ. *T:* (020) 7797 7900, *Fax:* (020) 7797 7929. *E:* morgan@1gc.com.

MORGAN, Shan Elizabeth, CMG 2012; HM Diplomatic Service; Deputy Permanent Representative, UK Representation to the European Union, since 2012; *b* 12 March 1955; *d* of Air Cdre Alun Morgan, CBE and Yvonne Morgan (*née* Davies). *Educ:* South Park High Sch., Lincoln; High Wycombe Grammar Sch.; Royal Latin Sch.; Univ. of Kent (BA Hons 1977). Manpower Services Commn, subseq. Employment Dept, then DfES, 1977–97; Eur. Commn DG V, 1984–87; Pvte Sec. to Perm. Sec., Dept of Employment, 1990–92; Govt Office for London, 1992–94; UK Govt Deleg. to ILO Governing Body, 1994–97; seconded to FCO, 1997; First Sec., Labour and Social Affairs, Paris, 1997–2001; Counsellor, Social, Envmtl and Regl Affairs, UK Perm. Repn, Brussels, 2001–06; transferred FCO, 2006; Dir, EU, FCO, 2006–08; Ambassador to Argentina and (non-resident) to Paraguay, 2008–12. FRSA. Hon. DCL Kent, 2014. *Recreations:* walking, learning Welsh, cycling. *Address:* c/o Foreign and Commonwealth Office, King Charles Street, SW1A 2AH.

MORGAN, Stephen Peter, OBE 1992; Chairman: Redrow plc, since 2009 (Chairman, Redrow Group plc, 1974–2000); Bridgemere Group of Companies, since 1996; *b* 25 Nov. 1952; *s* of Peter and Mary Morgan; *m* 1st, 1973, Pamela Borrett; one *s* one *d*; 2nd, 2002, Fiona Elspeth, (Didy), Boustead (marr. diss. 2013); one *s* one *d. Educ:* Colwyn High Sch.; Liverpool Poly. Founded Redrow Gp plc, 1974. Owner, Carden Park Hotel, nr Chester, 2006–; owner and Chm., Wolverhampton Wanderers FC, 2007–. Chm. Trustees, Morgan Foundn, 2002–.

FCIOB 2000. Hon. Fellow: John Moores Univ., 1993; NE Wales Inst. of Higher Educn, 1993; Cardiff Univ., 2005; Wolverhampton Univ., 2010. *Publications:* The Redrow Way, 1999. *Recreations:* football, Rugby, ski-ing, walking, golf.

MORGAN, Terence Keith, CBE 2009; FREng, FIET; Chairman, Crossrail, since 2009; *b* 28 Dec. 1948; *s* of Keith and Ivy Morgan; *m* 1970, Ann Jones; one *s* one *d*. *Educ:* Univ. of Birmingham (MSc 1977). FIET (FIEE 1990); FREng (FEng 1995). Leyland Bus Co., 1980–85; Production Dir, Land Rover, 1985–91; Man. Dir, Land Rover Vehicles, Rover Gp, 1991–95; BAE Systems: Man. Dir, Royal Ordnance, 1995–97; Gp HR Dir, 1997–2000; Gp Man. Dir Ops, 2000–02; CEO, Tube Lines Ltd, 2002–09. *Recreations:* Rugby, golf. *Address:* Crossrail, 25 Canada Square, E14 5LQ.

MORGAN, (Thomas) Jeremy; QC 2003; *b* 18 Aug. 1948; *s* of Thomas Morgan and Jean Morgan (*née* Campbell); *m* 1998, Delia Dumaresq; one *d*, and one step *s*. *Educ:* Loretto Sch.; Exeter Coll., Oxford (BA Greats); Univ. of Kent (BA Law). FCIArb 1998. Admitted solicitor, 1976; Solicitor: Garratt Lane Law Centre, Wandsworth, 1976–80; Southwark Law Project, 1980–82; sole practitioner, 1982–89; called to the Bar, Middle Temple, 1989; in practice as barrister, 1990–2013. Mem., Treasury Panel of Counsel, 1997–2003. *Recreations:* Italy, cinema, windsurfing, ballet.

MORGAN, Most Rev. Thomas Oliver; Archbishop of Saskatoon and Metropolitan of the Ecclesiastical Province of Rupert's Land, 2000–03; Interim Rector and Dean, St John's Cathedral, Saskatoon, 2006–07 and 2011–12; *b* 20 Jan. 1941; *s* of Charles Edwin Morgan and Amy Amelia (*née* Hoyes); *m* 1963, Lillian Marie (*née* Textor); two *s* one *d*. *Educ:* Univ. of Saskatchewan (BA 1962); King's College, London (BD 1965); Tyndale Hall, Bristol (GOE 1966). Curate, Church of the Saviour, Blackburn, Lancs, 1966–69; Rector: Porcupine Plain, Sask, Canada, 1969–73; Kinistino, 1973–77; Shellbrook, 1977–83; Archdeacon of Indian Missions, Saskatchewan, 1983–85; Bishop of Saskatchewan, 1985–93; Bishop of Saskatoon, 1993–2003. Hon. DD Coll. of Emmanuel and St Chad, Saskatoon, 1986.

MORGAN, Tony; *see* Morgan, A. W. C.

MORGAN, Rt Rev. Mgr Vaughan Frederick John, CBE 1982; Parish Priest, St Teresa's Charlbury, 1997–2007; *b* Upper Hutt, New Zealand, 21 March 1931; *o s* of late Godfrey Frederick Vaughan Morgan and Violet (Doreen) Vaughan Morgan. *Educ:* The Oratory Sch., S Oxon; Innsbruck Univ. Ordained, 1957; Archdiocese of St Andrews and Edinburgh, 1959–62; entered Royal Navy as Chaplain, 1962; Prin. RC Chaplain (Naval), and Vicar Gen. for RN, 1979–84; Chaplain, The Oratory Sch., 1984–97. Chaplain to High Sheriff of Oxfordshire, 2000–01. Prelate of Honour to HH Pope John Paul II, 1979. *Publications:* contribs to journals. *Recreations:* music, swimming, painting, heraldry. *Address:* Flat 28, Diamond Court, 153 Banbury Road, Oxford OX2 7AA. *T:* (01865) 516672. *Club:* Army and Navy.

MORGAN, Prof. William Basil; Professor of Geography, 1971–92, Professor Emeritus, since 1988, and Head of Geography Department, 1982–87, King's College London; *b* 22 Jan. 1927; *s* of William George Morgan and Eunice Mary (*née* Heys); *m* 1954, Joy Gardner (*d* 2004); one *s* one *d*. *Educ:* King Edward's Sch., Birmingham; Jesus Coll., Oxford (MA); PhD Glasgow. Assistant, Glasgow Univ., 1948; Lecturer: University Coll., Ibadan, Nigeria, 1953; Univ. of Birmingham, 1959; Reader in Geography, KCL, 1967. Participant in various UN university res. projects and conferences. *Publications:* (with J. C. Pugh) West Africa, 1969; (with R. J. C. Munton) Agricultural Geography, 1971; Agriculture in the Third World: a spatial analysis, 1978; (with R. P. Moss) Fuelwood and rural energy production and supply in the humid tropics, 1981; contribs to geographical and other learned jls and to various conf. collections. *Recreation:* development geography. *Address:* 57 St Augustine's Avenue, South Croydon, Surrey CR2 6JQ. *T:* (020) 8688 5687. *E:* williammorgan@sky.com.

MORGAN, Prof. (William) John, PhD; Professor of Comparative Education, since 1995 and UNESCO Professor of Political Economy of Education, since 2005, University of Nottingham; *b* Rhymney, Wales, 4 Nov. 1946; *s* of late Glyndwr Morgan and Kathleen Morgan (*née* Evans); *m* 1975, Joyce Roberts; one *s* one *d*. *Educ:* Lewis Sch., Pengam; University Coll. of Swansea (Open Scholar; BA Jt Hons 1968; PGCE 1969); Jesus Coll., Oxford (Postgrad. Res.); University Coll., Cardiff (MEd 1979; Naughton Faculty Prize); Univ. of Nottingham (PhD 1994). Tutor Organiser, WEA, 1971–73; Lectr, then Sen. Lectr, Coll. of Technol., Cardiff, 1973–79; University of Nottingham: Lectr, then Sen. Lectr, 1979–95; Actg Dir, Inst. of Asian Pacific Studies, 1996–99; Dir, Centre for Comparative Educn Res., 1999–2009. Hon. Res. Fellow, University Coll. of Swansea, 1987; Visiting Professor: Univ. of Kerala, 1994; Centre for Adv. Studies in Soc. Scis, Univ. of Cordoba, 1996; Comparative Educn Soc. of Asia and Waseda Foundn, 1998; Univ. of Debrecen, 2005; Univ. of Helsinki, 2009; Inst. of Higher Educn, Beihang Univ., China, 2014; Vis. Professorial Fellow, Commonwealth Studies Inst., Sch. of Advanced Study, Univ. of London, 2002–05; Dist. Prof., Internat. Inst. of Adult and Lifelong Educn, 2008; Sen. Fellow, China Policy Inst., 2008; Hon. Prof., Cardiff Univ., 2014. Mem., Commonwealth Scholarship Commn, 2002–08 (Chair: Academic Staff Fellowships Cttee; Professional Fellowships Cttee); Steering Cttee, UNESCO Peace Prog. for Palestinian Higher Educn, 2007; Chm., UK Nat. Commn, UNESCO, 2010–13 (Dir, 2007–10); Convener, UNESCO Dir Gen.'s Consultation for Europe and N America, 2010; Co-Chair, UNESCO Dir Gen.'s Sen. Experts' Panel on Rethinking Educn in the 21st Century, 2013. Member, Executive Committee: Council for Educn in the Commonwealth, 1999–2002; British Assoc. of Internat. and Comparative Educn, 2002–05; Internat. Adv. Bd, Centre for Res. in Contg Educn and Lifelong Learning, Univ. of Hong Kong, 2007. Hon. Sec., Internat. Soc. for Comparative Adult Educn, 1990–93. Gov., Portland Coll. for the Disabled, 1991–93 (Chm., Educn and Trng Cttee, 1991–93). Patron, Landmine Disability Support Trust, 2007–. James A. Draper Meml Lectr, New Delhi, 2009. FRSA 1979; FRAI 1989; FLSW 2012. Hon. DSc Inst. of Sociol., Russian Acad. of Scis, 2010. Vice Chancellor's Achievement Medal, Univ. of Nottingham, 2014. Mem., editl bds of various internat. jls. *Publications:* (ed) The Welsh Dilemma: some essays on nationalism in Wales, 1973; (with N. T. Scott) Unemployed Graduates: a wasted national resource, 1987; (ed) Politics and Consensus in Modern Britain, 1988; (ed with B. Hake) Adult Education, Public Information and Ideology, 1989; Social Welfare in the British and West German Coal Industries, 1989; (ed jtly) Access and Delivery in Continuing Education: a guide to contemporary literature, 1992; (ed with P. Preston) Raymond Williams: politics, education, letters, 1993; (ed jtly) Access and Delivery in Continuing Education: first supplement, 1995; (ed with J. Muckle) Post-school Education and the Transition from State Socialism, 2001; (ed with S. W. Livingstone) Law and Opinion in 20th Century Britain and Ireland, 2003; Communists on Education and Culture, 2003; (jtly) Teacher Mobility, Brain Drain and Educational Resources in the Commonwealth, 2006; Place, Inequality and Recognition: key concepts in contemporary citizenship, 2008; (ed with B. Wu) Higher Education Reform in China, 2011; (with A. Guilherme) Buber and Education, 2013; (ed with B. Wu) Chinese Higher Education Reform and Social Justice, 2015; articles in jls and book chapters. *Recreations:* reading, music, Rugby, grandchildren. *Address:* School of Education, University of Nottingham, Jubilee Campus, Nottingham NG8 1BB. *T:* (0115) 951 3717, *Fax:* (0115) 846 6600. *E:* john.morgan@nottingham.ac.uk. *Club:* Royal Over-Seas League.

MORGAN HUGHES, David; *see* Hughes, His Honour David M.

MORGAN-WEBB, Dame Patricia, DBE 2000; Co-founder and Chief Executive, Morgan Webb Education Ltd, 2003–11; *m* 1992, Christopher J. Webb. Principal and Chief Exec., Clarendon Coll., 1991–98; Chief Exec., New Coll. Nottingham, 1998–2003. Member: Bd, QCA, 1997–2002; E Midlands Regl Cttee, FEFC; Derbys Learning and Skills Council, 2000. Mem. Bd, E Midlands Develt Agency, 1998–2004; Dir, Gtr Nottingham TEC. Gov., Walsall Coll., 2012–; Dir, Bd, St George's Free Sch., Newtown, Birmingham, 2013–. Trustee, S Staffs CAB, 2013–; Pres., Root and Renewal Foundn, 2013–. *Address:* Church Hill Cottage, Church Hill, Longdon Green WS15 4PU.

MORIARTY, Clare; Permanent Secretary, Department for Environment, Food and Rural Affairs, since 2015; *b* 6 April 1963; *d* of Michael John Moriarty, *qv*; *m* 2001, James MacDonald; two *d*, and one step *s* two step *d*. *Educ:* North London Collegiate Sch.; Balliol Coll., Oxford (BA Hons Maths 1985). FCCA 1995. Joined DHSS, 1985; Cycle Internat., Ecole Nat. d'Admin, Paris, 1990–91; Prin. Private Sec. to Sec. of State for Health, 1994–97; Hon. Sen. Res. Fellow, Sch. of Public Policy, UCL, 1997–98; Hd, NHS Foundn Trust Unit, DoH, 2002–04; Whole Systems Dir, Portsmouth and SE Hampshire Health and Social Care Community, 2004–05; Constitution Dir, DCA, later MoJ, 2005–08; Dir (Projects), DoH, 2008–09; Dir Gen., Corporate Support Functions, later Corporate Gp, DfT, 2009–12; Dir Gen., Rail Gp, then Rail Exec., DfT, 2013–15. *Recreations:* family, singing, cycling, mountain walking, restoring and maintaining hill farm in Connemara, Ireland. *Address:* Department for Environment, Food and Rural Affairs, Nobel House, 17 Smith Square, SW1P 3JR.

MORIARTY, Gerald Evelyn; QC 1974; a Recorder of the Crown Court, 1976–98; *b* 23 Aug. 1928; *er s* of late Lt-Col G. R. O'N. Moriarty and Eileen Moriarty (*née* Moloney); *m* 1961, Judith Mary, *er d* of Hon. William Robert Atkin; four *s*. *Educ:* Downside Sch.; St John's Coll., Oxford (MA). Called to the Bar, Lincoln's Inn, 1951, Bencher, 1983. *T:* (020) 7727 4593. *Club:* Reform.

MORIARTY, Brig. Joan Olivia Elsie, CB 1979; RRC 1977; Matron-in-Chief and Director of Army Nursing Services, 1976–80; *b* 11 May 1923; *d* of late Lt-Col Oliver Nash Moriarty, DSO, RA, and Mrs Georgina Elsie Moriarty (*née* Moore). *Educ:* Royal Sch., Bath; St Thomas' Hosp. (nursing); Queen Charlotte's Hosp. (midwifery). SRN. VAD, Somerset, 1941–42; joined QAIMNS (R), 1947; Reg. QAIMNS (later QARANC), 1948, retired Jan. 1981; appts incl.: Staff Captain, WO; Instr, Corps Trng Centre; Liaison Officer, MoD; served in UK, Gibraltar, BAOR, Singapore, Malaya, Cyprus; Matron, Mil. Hosp., Catterick, 1973–76; Comdt, QARANC Trng Centre, Aldershot, 1976. Major 1960; Lt-Col 1971; Col 1973; Brig. 1977. QHNS, 1977–80. OStJ 1977.

MORIARTY, Prof. Michael, PhD; FBA 2006; Drapers Professor of French, since 2011, and Head, Department of French, since 2012, University of Cambridge; Fellow, Peterhouse, Cambridge, since 2011; *b* 27 May 1956; *s* of Martin Moriarty and Ellen Moriarty (*née* O'Connor); *m* 1992, Morag Elizabeth Shiach; two *s*. *Educ:* Warwick Sch.; St John's Coll., Cambridge (BA 1978, MA 1982; PhD 1984). Asst Lectr, 1986–90, Lectr, 1990–95, Dept of French, Univ. of Cambridge; Res. Fellow, 1982–85, Lectr in French and Dir of Studies in Mod. Langs, 1985–95, Gonville and Caius Coll., Cambridge; Prof. of French Lit. and Thought, 1995–2005, Centenary Prof., 2005–11, QMUL. Member: Panel 51 (French), RAE 2001; Sub-panel 52 (French), RAE 2008. Chevalier, Ordre des Palmes Académiques (France), 2010. *Publications:* Taste and Ideology in Seventeenth Century France, 1988; Roland Barthes, 1991; Early Modern French Thought: the Age of Suspicion, 2003; Fallen Nature, Fallen Selves: Early Modern French Thought II, 2006; Disguised Vices: theories of virtue in early modern French thought, 2011 (R. H. Gapper Book Prize, Soc. of French Studies, 2012); (ed with N. Hammond) Evocations of Eloquence: rhetoric, literature and religion in early modern France, essays in honour of Peter Bayley, 2012; contrib. articles to French Studies, Romance Studies, etc. *Recreations:* walking, listening to music, crosswords. *Address:* Peterhouse, Trumpington Street, Cambridge CB2 1RD. *T:* (01223) 338254. *E:* mm10005@cam.ac.uk.

MORIARTY, Michael John, CB 1988; Deputy Chairman, Radio Authority, 1994–2000 (Member, 1991–2000); Deputy Under-Secretary of State and Principal Establishment Officer, Home Office, 1984–90; *b* 3 July 1930; *er s* of late Edward William Patrick Moriarty, OBE, and May Lilian Moriarty; *m* 1960, Rachel Milward, *d* of late J. S. Thompson and Isobel F. Thompson; one *s* two *d*. *Educ:* Reading Sch., Reading; St John's Coll., Oxford (Sir Thomas White schol.; MA Lit. Hum.). Entered Home Office as Asst Principal, 1954; Private Sec. to Parliamentary Under-Secretaries of State, 1957–59; Principal, 1959; Civil Service Selection Bd, 1962–63; Cabinet Office, 1965–67; Asst Sec., 1967; Private Sec. to Home Sec., 1968; Head of Crime Policy Planning Unit, 1974–75; Asst Under-Sec. of State, 1975–84; seconded to NI Office, 1979–81; Broadcasting Dept, 1981–84. UK Representative, 1976–79, and Chm., 1978–79, Council of Europe Cttee on Crime Problems. Sub-Treas., 1991–, Mem. Council, 2001–06, Chichester Cathedral; a Church Comr, 1996–98. Gov., Chichester Central C of E Jun. Sch., 2008–11 (Chm. of Govs, 2001–05). *Recreations:* music, walking, local interests. *Address:* 22 Westgate, Chichester, West Sussex PO19 3EU. *T:* (01243) 789985.
See also C. Moriarty.

MORIARTY, Stephen; QC 1999; *b* 14 April 1955; *s* of George William Moriarty and Dorothy Violet Moriarty (*née* Edwards); *m* 1988, Dr Susan Clare Stanford. *Educ:* Chichester High Sch. for Boys; Brasenose Coll., Oxford (BCL, MA; Vinerian Schol. 1978). Univ. Lectr in law, and Fellow and Tutor in Law, Exeter Coll., Oxford, 1979–86; called to the Bar, Middle Temple, 1986, Bencher, 2009; in practice at the Bar, 1986–; Hd, Fountain Court Chambers, 2013–. Chm., Commercial Bar Assoc., 2011–13. Mem., Bar Council, 2011–13. *Recreations:* theatre, opera, cycling. *Address:* Fountain Court Chambers, Fountain Court, Temple, EC4Y 9DH. *T:* (020) 7583 3335. *Club:* Reform.

MORICE, Prof. Peter Beaumont, DSc, PhD; FREng, FICE, FIStructE; Professor of Civil Engineering, University of Southampton, 1958–91, now Emeritus; *b* 15 May 1926; *o s* of Charles and Stephanie Morice; *m* 1st, 1952, Margaret Ransom (marr. diss. 1986); one *s* two *d*; 2nd, 1986, Rita Corless (*née* Dunk) (*d* 2006). *Educ:* Barfield Sch.; Farnham Grammar Sch.; University of Bristol; University of London. Surrey County Council, 1947–48; Research Div., Cement and Concrete Assoc., 1948–57. Vis. Prof., Ecole Nat. des Ponts et Chaussées, Paris; Mem. Foundn Cttee, Sultan Qaboos Univ., Oman, 1980–86. FREng (FEng 1989). Compagnon du Beaujolais, 1987. Order of Sultan Qaboos (Oman), 1986. *Publications:* Linear Structural Analysis, 1958; Prestressed Concrete, 1958; papers on structural theory in various learned journals. *Recreations:* sailing, DIY, reading, listening to music. *Address:* 12 Abbotts Way, Highfield, Southampton SO17 1QT. *T:* (023) 8055 7641, 07429 492356; La Vieille Boucherie, 1545 rue des Tonneliers, 46140 Douelle, France. *T:* 647225200.

MORISON, Hugh, CBE 2002; Chief Executive (formerly Director General), Scotch Whisky Association, 1994–2003; *b* 22 Nov. 1943; *s* of Archibald Ian Morison and Enid Rose Morison (*née* Mawer); *m* 1st, 1971, Marion Smithers (marr. diss. 1993); two *d*; 2nd, 1993, Ilona Bellos (*née* Roth). *Educ:* Chichester High School for Boys; St Catherine's Coll., Oxford (MA English Language and Literature; DipEd). Asst Principal, SHHD, 1966–69; Private Sec. to Minister of State, Scottish Office, 1969–70; Principal: Scottish Educn Dept, 1971–73; Scottish Economic Planning Dept, 1973–74; Offshore Supplies Office, Dept of Energy, 1974–75; Scottish Economic Planning Dept, 1975–82, Asst Sec., 1979; Gwilym Gibbon Res. Fellow, Nuffield Coll., Oxford, 1982–83; Scottish Development Dept, 1983–84; Under Secretary: SHHD, 1984–88; Industry Dept for Scotland, subseq. Scottish Office Industry Dept, 1988–93. Director: The Weir Gp, 1989–93; Praban na Linne Ltd, 2005–06. Member: Health Appts Adv. Cttee (Scotland), 1995–2000; Exec. Cttee, Barony Housing Assoc., 1996–2010 (Chm., 2005–09). Chm., Scottish Business and Biodiversity Gp, 1998–2003. Prés., 2001–03, Prés. d'honneur, 2003–, Confédn Eur. des Producteurs de Spiritueux. Gov., UHI (formerly UHI Millennium Inst.), 2004–13. Chm., Letterfearn Moorings Assoc., 2001–. *Publications:* The Regeneration of Local Economies, 1987; (with Ilona Bellos) Dauphiné, 1991; The Feelgood

Fallacy, 2008. *Recreations:* hill walking, cycling, sailing, playing the euphonium, looking at ruins. *Address:* 12 Sunbury Place, Edinburgh EH4 3BY. *T:* (0131) 225 6568. *Club:* New (Edinburgh).

MORISON, Prof. John William Edgar, PhD; Professor of Jurisprudence, Queen's University, Belfast, since 1996; *b* 8 March 1958; *s* of John Edgar Morison and Ellen McCracken Morison; *m* 1984, Susan Royal; two *d. Educ:* Brackenber House; Campbell Coll.; University of Wales, Cardiff (LLB 1979; PhD 1985). Queen's University, Belfast: Lectr in Law, 1984–94; Reader in Law, 1994–96; Hd, Sch. of Law, 2003–07. Mem., NI Judicial Appointments Commn, 2003–12; Ind. Bd Mem., NI Legal Services Commn, subseq. Legal Services Agency NI, 2014–. Dir, European Public Law Centre, Athens, 1996–. MRIA 2009. *Publications:* (with P. Leith) The Barrister's World and the Nature of Law, 1992; (with S. Livingstone) Reshaping Public Power: Northern Ireland and the British constitutional crisis, 1995; (ed jtly) Judges, Transition and Human Rights, 2007; (ed jtly) Values in Global Administrative Law, 2011. *Recreations:* collecting art, dog walking. *Address:* School of Law, Queen's University, Belfast BT7 1NN. *E:* j.morison@qub.ac.uk.

MORISON, Hon. Sir Thomas (Richard Atkin), Kt 1993; a Judge of the High Court of Justice, Queen's Bench Division, 1993–2007; *b* 15 Jan. 1939; *s* of Harold Thomas Brash Morison and Hon. Nancy Morison; *m* 1963, Judith Rachel Walton Morris (marr. diss. 1992); one *s* one *d*; *m* 1993, Caroline Yates. *Educ:* Winchester Coll.; Worcester Coll., Oxford, 1959–62 (MA). Passed final Bar examinations, 1959; called to the Bar, Gray's Inn, 1960, Bencher, 1987; pupil in Chambers, 1962–63; started practice, 1963; QC 1979; a Recorder, 1987–93. *Recreations:* reading, gardening, cooking. *Club:* Oriental.

MORITZ, Sir Michael J., KBE 2013; venture capitalist; President and Chairman, Sequoia Capital, since 2012 (Managing Partner, 1986–2012); *b* Cardiff, 12 Sept. 1954; *s* of Prof. Alfred. Moritz and Doris Moritz; *m* Harriet Heymen; two *c. Educ:* Howardian High Sch., Cardiff; Christ Church, Oxford (BA 1976); Wharton Sch., Univ. of Pennsylvania (MBA). Journalist, Time Inc.; Co-founder, Technologic Partners; Partner and venture capitalist, Sequoia Capital Israel, 1986. Chm., LUXIM Corp.; directorships include: Flextronics Internat. Ltd, 1993–2005; Yahoo!, 1995–2003; Saba Software, 1998–2006; eToys Inc., 1998–; PayPal, 1999–2002; Google Inc., 1999–2007; RedEnvelope Inc., 1999–2005 (Chm., 2003–05); GameFly Inc., 2002–; 24/7 Customer, 2003–; Green Dot Corp., 2003–; Kayak Software Corp. (formerly Kayak.com), 2005–; Sugar Inc., 2007–; Kiarna AB, 2010–; LinkedIn Corp., 2011–; Zappos.com Inc.; Nightfire Software Inc.; Maplebear Inc., 2013–. Hon. Fellow, Cardiff Univ., 2010. *Publications:* (with B. Seaman) Going for Broke: the Chrysler Story, 1981; The Little Kingdom: the private story of Apple Computer, 1984; Return to the Little Kingdom: Steve Jobs, the creation of Apple and how it changed the world, 2009; (with Sir Alex Ferguson) Leading, 2015. *Address:* Sequoia Capital, 3000 Sand Hill Road, Building 4, Suite 250, West Menlo Park, CA 94025, USA.

MORLAND, Charles Francis Harold; Chairman, Refugee Legal Centre, 2006–08; *b* 4 Sept. 1939; *s* of Sir Oscar Morland, GBE, KCMG, and Alice, *d* of Rt Hon. Sir Francis Oswald Lindley, GCMG, PC; *m* 1964, Victoria Longe (*d* 1998); two *s. Educ:* Ampleforth Coll.; King's Coll., Cambridge (MA). American Dept, FO, 1963–64; Local Dir, Oxford and Birmingham, Barclays Bank, 1964–79; on secondment as Under Sec. to Dept of Industry, 1979–81; Dir, Barclays Merchant Bank, then Barclays de Zoete Wedd, 1981–87; Man. Dir, Riggs AP Bank, 1987–89; Chm., Belmont Bank, 1991–93. Chm., Oxford Policy Inst., 1996–2005; Dir, British Inst. in Paris, 1997–2002. Chairman: Leonard Cheshire, 2000–05; Ryder Cheshire Foundn, 2005–07; Director: Centre for Accessible Environments, 2006–09; Employment Opportunities for People with Disabilities, 2006–09. *Recreations:* travel, cooking. *Address:* Aisle Barn, Chipley Park, Wellington, Som TA21 0QU. *T:* (01823) 401513.

See also M. R. Morland.

MORLAND, Edward; Chief Executive, Health & Safety Laboratory, since 2005; *b* 23 June 1957; *s* of Albert Edward Morland and Eva Doris Morland; *m* 1977, Lynda Hockenhull; one *s* one *d. Educ:* Wade Deacon Grammar Sch.; Manchester Poly. (BSc 1st Cl. Hons Physics 1982); UMIST (MSc Mgt Sci. 1994). FInstP 2006. Res. Scientist, UKAEA, 1975–92; Mktg Manager, AEA Technology, 1992–97; Commercial Dir, then Ops Dir, 1997–2003, Chief Exec., 2003–05, AEA Rail. FRSA 2005; FRSocMed 2007. *Publications:* (jtly) Mechanical Testing, 1988. *Recreations:* reading history, supporting Manchester United, playing strategy games, hill walking with my wife. *Address:* Health & Safety Laboratory, Harpur Hill, Buxton, Derbyshire SK17 9JN. *T:* (01298) 218001. *E:* eddie.morland@hsl.gov.uk.

MORLAND, Martin Robert, CMG 1985; HM Diplomatic Service, retired; consultant with Hardcastle and Co. Ltd, 1996–2002; *b* 23 Sept. 1933; *e s* of Sir Oscar Morland, GBE, KCMG and late Alice, *d* of Rt Hon. Sir Francis Oswald Lindley, PC, GCMG; *m* 1964, Jennifer Avril Mary Hanbury-Tracy; two *s* one *d. Educ:* Ampleforth; King's Coll., Cambridge (BA). Nat. Service, Grenadier Guards, 1954–56; British Embassy, Rangoon, 1957–60; News Dept, FO, 1961; UK Delegn to Common Market negotiations, Brussels, 1962–63; FO, 1963–65; UK Disarmament Delegn, Geneva, 1965–67; Private Sec. to Lord Chalfont, 1967–68; European Integration Dept, FCO, 1968–73; Counsellor, 1973–77, Rome (seconded temporarily to Cabinet Office to head EEC Referendum Information Unit, 1975); Hd of Maritime Aviation and Environment Dept, FCO, 1977–79; Counsellor and Head of Chancery, Washington, 1979–82; seconded to Hardcastle & Co. Ltd, 1982–84; Under-Sec., Cabinet Office, 1984–86; Ambassador to Burma, 1986–90; Ambassador and UK Perm. Rep. to Office of UN and other internat. orgns, Geneva, 1990–93; Dir, Public Affairs, BNFL, 1994–96. Mem. Cttee, Supporters of Nuclear Energy, 2005–11. Chm. Govs, Westminster Cathedral Choir Sch., 2001–08. Chm., Prospect Burma, 1994–2012. *Address:* Prospect House, Shaftesbury Road, East Knoyle, Salisbury SP3 6AR. *E:* m.morland731@btinternet.com.

See also C. F. H. Morland.

MORLAND, Sir Michael, Kt 1989; a Judge of the High Court of Justice, Queen's Bench Division, 1989–2004; *b* 16 July 1929; *e s* of Edward Morland, Liverpool, and Jane Morland (*née* Beckett); *m* 1961, Lillian Jensen, Copenhagen; one *s* one *d. Educ:* Stowe; Christ Church, Oxford (MA). 2nd Lieut, Grenadier Guards, 1948–49; served in Malaya. Called to Bar, Inner Temple, 1953, Bencher 1979; Northern Circuit; QC 1972; a Recorder, 1972–89; Presiding Judge, Northern Circuit, 1991–95. Mem., Criminal Injuries Compensation Bd, 1980–89. Mem., Gardiner Cttee on measures to deal with terrorism in NI, 1974; Chairman: Cttee of Inquiry for DHSS in case of Paul Brown, 1980; Public Inquiry for NI Office into death of Rosemary Nelson, 2004–11.

MORLAND, Sir Robert (Kenelm), Kt 1990; General Manager, Exports: Tate & Lyle Sugars, 1987–93; Tate & Lyle International, 1987–93; Director, Tate & Lyle Norway A/S, 1987–93; *b* 7 April 1935; *s* of late Kenelm and Sybil Morland; *m* 1st, 1960, Eve Charters (marr. diss. 1965); one *s*; 2nd, 1972, Angela Fraser; one *s. Educ:* Birkenhead Sch.; Rydal Sch., Colwyn Bay. Joined Tate & Lyle, 1953; held various managerial positions. Member: Cheshire Riverboard Authy, 1962–65; Birkenhead Nat. Assistance Bd, Adv. Cttee, 1962–65. Dir, 1996–98, Associate non-exec. Dir, 1999–2001, Kingston and Richmond HA; Bd Mem., Thames Health Primary Care Gp, 1999–2001; non-executive Director: Teddington, Twickenham and Hamptons PCT, 2001–02; Richmond and Twickenham PCT, 2002–04; Age Concern, Richmond upon Thames, 2004–05, Glos, 2005–11. Member: Birkenhead CBC, 1959–65; Richmond upon Thames BC, 1968–71. Contested (C) Birkenhead, 1964. Chairman: Birkenhead Young Conservatives, 1955–58; Kew Conservatives, 1971–74; Richmond and Barnes (now Richmond Park) Cons. Assoc., 1975–79 (Dep. Pres., 1985–98); Cons. Docklands Action Cttee, 1990–92; Greenwich and Lewisham Cons. Action Gp, 1993–94; Dep. Chm., Nat. Trade and Industry Forum, Cons. Party, 1991–96; Vice-President: Gtr London Conservatives, 1990– (Dep. Chm., 1978–81; Jt Hon. Treas., 1981–87; Chm., 1987–90); Newham S Cons. Assoc., 1989–96; Member: Cons. Nat. Union Exec. Cttee, 1978–93; Cons. Bd of Finance, 1981–87. Ind. Mem., Standards Cttee, Cotswolds Conservation Bd, 2005–12. Dir, Friends of the Cotswolds, 2007–12. Chairman: St Mary's Drama Gp, Hampton, 1999–2001 (Vice Chm., 1996–99); Friends of St Edward's Parish Ch, Stow-on-the-Wold, 2008–14; N Cotswold Probus, 2013–14. Vice Pres., Gloucestershire CCC, 2007–. *Recreations:* theatre, travel, cricket, horseriding. *Club:* Carlton.

MORLEY; *see* Hope-Morley, family name of Baron Hollenden.

MORLEY, 6th Earl of, *cr* 1815; **John St Aubyn Parker,** KCVO 1998; JP; Lt-Col, Royal Fusiliers; Lord-Lieutenant of Devon, 1982–98; *b* 29 May 1923; *e s* of Hon. John Holford Parker (*y s* of 3rd Earl), Pound House, Yelverton, Devon; *S* uncle, 1962; *m* 1955, Johanna Katherine, *d* of Sir John Molesworth-St Aubyn, 14th Bt, CBE; one *s* one *d. Educ:* Eton. 2nd Lt, KRRC, 1942; served NW Europe, 1944–45; Palestine and Egypt, 1945–48; transferred to Royal Fusiliers, 1947; served Korea, 1952–53; Middle East, 1953–55 and 1956; Staff Coll., Camberley, 1957; Comd, 1st Bn Royal Fusiliers, 1965–67. Director: Lloyds Bank Ltd, 1974–78; Lloyds Bank UK Management Ltd, 1979–86; Chm., SW Region, Lloyds Bank, 1989–91 (Chm., Devon and Cornwall Regl Bd, 1974–89). Chm., Plymouth Sound Ltd, 1974–94. Mem., Devon and Co. Cttee, Nat. Trust, 1969–84; President: Plymouth Incorporated Chamber of Trade and Commerce, 1970–2008; Cornwall Fedn of Chambers of Commerce and Trader Assocs, 1972–79; West Country Tourist Bd, 1971–89. Governor: Seale-Hayne Agricl Coll., 1973–93; Plymouth Polytechnic, 1975–82 (Chm., 1977–82). Pres., Council of Order of St John for Devon, 1979–98. DL 1973, Vice Lord-Lieutenant, 1978–82, Devon. JP Plymouth, 1972. Hon. Colonel: Devon ACF, 1979–87; 4th Bn Devonshire and Dorset Regl, 1987–92. *Heir: s* Viscount Boringdon, *qv. Address:* Pound House, Yelverton, Devon PL20 7LJ. *T:* (01822) 853162.

MORLEY, Dame Carol Mary; *see* Black, Dame C. M.

MORLEY, Catherine; *see* Pepinster, C.

MORLEY, David Howard; Global Senior Partner, Allen & Overy LLP, Solicitors, since 2008; *b* 21 Sept. 1956; *s* of Glyn and Yvonne Morley; *m* 1982, Sue (*née* Radcliffe); two *s* two *d. Educ:* St John's Coll., Cambridge (BA 1979). Admitted solicitor, 1982. Joined Allen & Overy, 1980: Partner, 1988; Hd, Banking Practice, 1998–2003; Worldwide Man. Partner, 2003–08. *Recreations:* cycling, ski-ing, sailing. *Address:* Allen & Overy, One Bishops Square, E1 6AD. *T:* (020) 3088 3000. *E:* david.morley@allenovery.com.

MORLEY, David John; HM Diplomatic Service, retired; High Commissioner to The Gambia, 2011–14; *b* Reading, 23 Oct. 1954; *s* of John Morley and Jean Morley; *m* 1978, Jacqueline Ann Wells. *Educ:* St Peter's Primary Sch., Reading; Bulmarshe Grammar Sch., Reading. Joined FCO, 1973; Third Sec., Kaduna, 1980–83; Second Sec., Moscow, 1990–93; Dep. High Comr, Mbabane, 1997–99; First Sec., UK Delegn to NATO, Brussels, 1999–2001; Adminr, Tristan da Cunha, 2007–10. *Recreations:* fishing, walking, travelling, dining.

MORLEY, Elliot Anthony; *b* 6 July 1952; *m* 1975; one *s* one *d. Educ:* St Margaret's C of E High Sch., Liverpool. Special needs teacher, comprehensive sch., Hull; head of individual learning centre, until 1987. Mem., Kingston upon Hull City Council, 1979–85; Chair, Hull City Transport Cttee, 1981–85. Contested (Lab) Beverley, 1983. MP (Lab) Glanford and Scunthorpe, 1987–97, Scunthorpe, 1997–2010. Opposition front bench spokesman on food, agriculture and rural affairs, 1989–97; Labour spokesperson on animal welfare, 1992–97; Parly Sec., MAFF, then DEFRA, 1997–2003; Minister of State (Minister for the Envmt), DEFRA, 2003–06. Mem., Select Cttee for Agriculture, 1987–90; Dep. Chair, PLP Educn Cttee, 1987–90. Vice-Pres., Wildlife and Countryside Link, 1990–97; Member of Council: RSPB, 1989–93; British Trust for Ornithology, 1992–95 (Vice-Pres., until 2009). Hon. Pres., N Lincs RSPCA, until 2010. Hon. Vice-Pres., Assoc. of Drainage Authorities, until 2010. Hon. Fellow, Univ. of Lincoln (formerly Lincs and Humberside Univ.). Hon. FICE. *Recreations:* ornithology, the environment, the countryside.

MORLEY, Iain Charles; QC 2009; *b* Dublin, 21 Oct. 1965; *s* of Charles Trevor Morley and Teresa Ann Morley (*née* Forken); *m* 1989, Jillian Helen Prickett (separated); two *s* one *d. Educ:* Lady Margaret Hall, Oxford (MA 1987). Called to the Bar: Inner Temple, 1988, Bencher, 2010; Eire, 1993; Pegasus Schol. 1993; in practice specialising in criminal law, London, 1989–2004; Prosecutor, UN Internat. Criminal Tribunal for Rwanda, Arusha, Tanzania, 2005–09; Sen. Trial Counsel, Special Tribunal for Lebanon, The Hague, 2009–12. Exec. Mem., SE Circuit, 2013–. Member: Inner Temple Advocacy Cttee, 1993–; Internat. Cttee, Advocacy Training Council, 2012–; Chair, Inner Temple Student Socs, 2013–. *Publications:* The Devil's Advocate, 2005, 2nd edn 2009. *Recreations:* cinema, opera, travels, fell-walking. *Address:* (chambers) 23 Essex Street, WC2R 3AA. *T:* (020) 7413 0353. *E:* iainmorley@23es.com.

MORLEY, Malcolm A.; artist; *b* 7 June 1931. *Educ:* Camberwell Sch. of Arts and Crafts; Royal Coll. of Art (ARCA 1957). *One man exhibitions:* Kornblee Gall., NY, 1957, 1964, 1967, 1969; Galerie Gerald Piltzer, Paris, 1973; Stefanotty Gall., NY, 1973, 1974; Clocktower Gall., Inst. for Art & Urban Resources, 1976; Galerie Jurka, Amsterdam, 1977; Galerie Jollenbeck, Cologne, 1977; Nancy Hoffman Gall., NY, 1979; Suzanne Hilberry Gall., Birmingham, Mich, 1979; Xavier Fourcade, NY, 1981, 1982, 1984, 1986; Galerie Nicholine Pon, Zurich, 1984; Fabian Carlsson Gall., London, 1985; Pace Gall., NY, 1988, 1991; Anthony d'Offay Gall., London, 1990; Tate Gall., 1991; Mary Boone Gall., NY, 1993, 1995; Sperone Westwater, NY, 1999, 2005, 2009, 2011, 2015; retrospective: Whitechapel Art Gall., also shown in Europe and USA, 1983–84; Centre Georges Pompidou, Paris, 1993; Fundacio La Caixa, Madrid, 1995; Hayward Gall., 2001; *major exhibitions:* Wadsworth Atheneum, Hartford, Conn, 1980; Akron Art Mus., 1982; *work in collections:* Met. Mus. of Art, NY; Detroit Inst. of Art; Hirshhorn Mus. and Sculpture Gdn, Washington; Louisiana Mus., Humlebaek, Denmark; Neue Galerie der Stadt Aachen; Mus. of Contemp. Art, Chicago; Munson-Williams-Proctor Inst., Utica, NY; Mus. of Modern Art, NY; Mus. Moderner Kunst, Vienna; Nat. Gall. of Art, Washington; Mus. of Contemp. Art, LA; Wadsworth Atheneum, Hartford; Centre Georges Pompidou, Paris; Nelson-Atkins Mus., Kansas City; Ludwig Forum for Internat. Art, Aachen, Vienna, Budapest; Mus. van Hedendaagse Kunst, Utrecht. First Turner Prize, Tate Gall., 1984; Painting Award, Skowhegan Sch. of Painting and Sculpture, 1992. *Relevant publication:* Malcolm Morley, by Jean-Claude Lebensztejn, 2001. *Address:* Sperone Westwater, 257 Bowery, New York, NY 10002, USA.

MORLEY, Michael John; Chief Executive, Coutts & Co., London, since 2009; *b* Bushey, Middx, 18 May 1957; *s* of John Lewis Morley and Jean Elizabeth Bentley Morley (*née* Morris); *m* 1991, Conchita Amell de la Morena; two *s. Educ:* Merchant Taylors' Sch., Northwood; Christ's Coll., Cambridge (BA Mod. and Medieval Langs 1979). Lloyds Bank Internat., 1980–86; Hd, Fixed Income, Enskilda Securities, 1986–94; Man. Dir and Hd, UK Private Banking, Merrill Lynch, 1994–2002; CEO, Barclays Wealth Internat., 2002–07; Man. Dir, Singer and Friedlander Investment Mgt, 2007–08. *Recreations:* playing the piano, ski-ing, walking around London, my family. *Address:* Coutts & Co., 440 Strand, WC2R 0QS. *T:* (020) 7753 1505, *Fax:* (020) 7753 1028. *E:* michael.morley@coutts.com.

MORLEY, Oliver Charles Fenton; Chief Executive, Driver and Vehicle Licensing Agency, Department for Transport, since 2013; *b* London, 22 June 1971; *s* of Michael and Delia Morley; *m* 1997, Susan Dandridge; two *s* two *d*. *Educ:* Jesus Coll., Cambridge (BA Econs 1993); London Business Sch. (MBA 1998). Shipping Exec., Maersk Line, 1993–96; Consultant, CSC Index/Kalchas, 1998–99; Reuters: Hd, Treasury Strategy, 2000–02; Hd, Sales Ops, 2002–04; Hd, Nordic Sales, 2005–06; Hd, Customer Experience, 2007–08; Dir, Commercial Services, 2008–10, Chief Exec., Keeper of the Public Records and Historical Manuscripts Comr, 2010–13, Nat. Archives. *Recreations:* food, wine, history, ski-ing, running. *Address:* Driver and Vehicle Licensing Agency, Longview Road, Swansea SA6 7JL.

MORNINGTON, Earl of; Arthur Gerald Wellesley; *b* 31 Jan. 1978; *er s* and *heir* of Duke of Wellington, *qv*; *m* 2005, Jemma Madeleine, *d* of John Edward Aitken Kidd; two *s* one *d* (of whom one *s* one *d* are twins). *Educ:* Eton Coll.; Christ Church, Oxford. A Page of Honour to HM Queen Elizabeth the Queen Mother, 1993–95. *Heir: s* Viscount Wellesley, *qv*. *Address:* The Old Rectory, Stratfield Saye, Hants RG7 2DA.

MORPHET, David Ian; author; *b* 24 Jan. 1940; *s* of late Albert and Sarah Elizabeth Morphet; *m* 1968, Sarah Gillian Sedgwick; two *s* one *d*. *Educ:* King James's Grammar Sch., Almondbury, Yorks; St John's Coll., Cambridge (History Schol.; English Tripos, class I, Pts I and II). Foreign Office, 1961; Vice Consul, Taiz, 1963; Doha, 1963–64; FO, 1964–66; Asst Private Sec. to Foreign Secretary, 1966–68; First Sec., Madrid, 1969–72; Diplomatic Service Observer, CS Selection Board, 1972–74; transf. to Dept of Energy, 1974; Asst Sec., 1975; Dep. Chm., Midlands Electricity Board (on secondment), 1978–79; Under-Secretary: Electricity Div., 1979–83; Energy Policy Div., 1983–85; Atomic Energy Div., 1985–89; UK Governor: Internat. Energy Agency, Paris, 1983–85; IAEA, Vienna, 1985–89. Director: BICC Cables Ltd, 1981–89; Planning and Develt, Balfour Beatty Ltd, 1989–91; Govt Affairs, BICC plc, 1992–95; Barking Power Ltd, 1993–2001; Dir Gen., Railway Forum, 1997–2000. Chm., Export Finance Cttee, CBI, 1992–96; Mem. Council, CBI, 1995–96 and 1997–2001. Founder Mem. and Chm., Nat. Schizophrenia Fellowship, 1977–83. *Publications:* Louis Jennings, MP: editor of The New York Times and Tory democrat, 2001; (ed) St John's College, Cambridge: excellence and diversity, 2007; *poetry:* Seventy-Seven Poems, 2002; The Angel and the Fox, 2003; Approaching Animals from A to Z, 2004; 39 Ways of Looking, 2005; The Silence of Green, 2007; The Maze: a daydream in five cantos, 2009; The Intruders and Other Poems, 2010; Lyrics from the Periodic Table, 2011; A Sequence from the Cyclades, 2012; Night Train to Utopia, 2013; Satires and Legacies, 2014; Homecoming by Microlight: landscapes and satires, 2015. *Address:* 11 Daisy Lane, SW6 3DD. *Club:* Athenæum.

MORPHET, Richard Edward, CBE 1998; Keeper, Modern Collection, Tate Gallery, 1986–98; *b* 2 Oct. 1938; *s* of Horace Taylor Morphet and Eleanor Morphet (*née* Shaw); *m* 1965, Sarah Francis Richmond, (Sally Morphet, CMG) (*d* 2014); two *d*. *Educ:* Bootham Sch., York; London Sch. of Economics (BA Hons History). Fine Arts Dept, British Council, 1963–66; Tate Gallery: Asst Keeper, 1966–73; Dep. Keeper, Modern Collection, 1973–86. Exhibitions (curator and author/editor of catalogue) include: Richard Hamilton, Tate, 1970; Bernard Cohen, Hayward, 1972; William Turnbull, Tate, 1973; Art in One Year: 1935, Tate, 1977; Meredith Frampton, Tate, 1982; Cedric Morris, Tate, 1984; The Hard-Won Image, Tate, 1984; Richard Hamilton, Tate, 1992; R. B. Kitaj, Tate, 1994; Encounters: New Art from Old, National Gallery, 2000; other exhibition catalogues include: Roy Lichtenstein, Tate, 1968; Andy Warhol, Tate, 1971; Howard Hodgkin, Arts Council, 1976; Leonard McComb, Serpentine, 1983; contribs to exhibn catalogues on Late Sickert, Hayward, 1981 and The Art of Bloomsbury, Tate, 1999. *Publications:* Jonathan Leaman, 2002; contrib. books on Eric Ravilious, 1983, Anthony Gross, 1992, and Ann Stokes, 2009; contrib. Apollo, Burlington Mag., Studio International, TLS, etc. *E:* richard.morphet@dgdns.fsnet.co.uk.

MORPHY, Leslie Ann, OBE 2010; Chief Executive, Crisis UK, 2006–14; *b* 23 Jan. 1949; *d* of Hugh Webster Morphy and Grace Clara Morphy; *m* 1981, Bob Deffee; one *s* one *d* (and one *d* decd). *Educ:* London Sch. of Econs (BSc Econ); Birkbeck Coll., London (MSc). Researcher, Penguin, 1971–72; Mgr, NUS, 1972–78; freelance consultancy, 1983–89; Dir, Broadcasting Support Services, 1978–83; Hd, R&D, Basic Skills Agency, 1989–96; Dir, Prince's Trust, 1996–2006. Non-executive Director: Home Gp, 2013–; Surrey and Borders Partnership NHS Foundn Trust. Trustee, Bliss, 2004–11; Chair, Newborn Vietnam. Gov., Oxford Brookes Univ., 2011– (Vice Chair, 2013–). *Recreations:* being with my family, theatre, reading novels, growing things. *Address:* 4 West Park Road, Kew Gardens, Richmond, Surrey TW9 4DA. *T:* 07867 515541. *E:* lmorphy@blueyonder.co.uk.

MORPURGO, Michael Andrew Bridge, OBE 2006 (MBE 1999); DL; writer; Joint Founder Director, Farms for City Children, since 1976; Children's Laureate, 2003–05; *b* 5 Oct. 1943; *s* of Tony Valentine Bridge and late Catherine Noel Kippe (*née* Cammaerts), and step *s* of late Jack Eric Morpurgo; *m* 1963, Clare (MBE 1999), *d* of Sir Allen Lane, founder, Penguin Books; two *s* one *d*. *Educ:* King's Sch., Canterbury; RMA Sandhurst; King's Coll., London (AKC, BA 1967; FKC 2001). Primary school teacher, 1967–75; with Clare Morpurgo founded Farms for City Children and opened Nethercott House farm, 1976; opened Treginnis Isaf, 1989, Wick Court, Glos, 1998. Co-writer/presenter, The Invention of Childhood (series), BBC Radio 4, 2006. DL Devon, 2015. Hon. DEd: Plymouth, 2002; UCE, 2007; Hon. DLitt: Exeter, 2004; Herts, 2006; Hon. MA Worcester, 2007 (with Clare Morpurgo). Bookseller Assoc. Writer of the Year, 2005. Chevalier des Arts et des Lettres, 2004. *Publications:* over 100 books for children, including: Friend or Foe, 1978; (with Ted Hughes) All Around the Year, 1979; The Nine Lives of Montezuma, 1980; The White Horse of Zennor, 1982; War Horse, 1984 (performed NT, 2007–08; filmed, 2012); Twist of Gold, 1986; Mr Nobody's Eyes, 1989; Why the Whales Came (Silver Pencil award, Holland), 1989 (screenplay, When the Whales Came, 1991; performed Alibi Th., 1995); My Friend Walter, 1990 (screenplay, 1994); Little Foxes, 1992; The Marble Crusher, 1992; King of the Cloud Forests, 1992 (Cercle d'Or, Montreuil, 1994; Prix Sorcière, 1995); The War of Jenkins Ear, 1992 (Best Book award, Amer. Liby Assoc., 1996); Blodin the Beast, 1993; Waiting for Anya, 1993; The Sandman and the Turtles, 1994; The Dancing Bear, 1995; The Wreck of the Zanzibar, 1995 (Whitbread Children's Award, and Children's Book Award, Fedn of Children's Books, 1996; IBBY Honour Book, 1998); Arthur High King of Britain, 1995; Sam's Duck, 1996; Muck and Magic, 1996; The Butterfly Lion, 1996 (Writers' Guild Award, 1996; Smarties Prize, 1997); The Ghost of Grania O'Malley, 1996; Robin of Sherwood, 1997; Farm Boy, 1997; Red Eyes at Night, 1997; Beyond the Rainbow Warrior, 1997; Escape from Shangri-la, 1998; Joan of Arc of Domrémy, 1998; Wartman, 1998; The Rainbow Bear, 1999 (Children's Book Award, Nat. Assoc. of Teachers of English); Kensuke's Kingdom, 1999 (Children's Book Award, Prix Sorcière, Prix Lire au Collège; performed Polka Th., 2002); Wombat Goes Walkabout, 1999 (Prix Sorcière); Animal Stories, 1999; Dear Olly, 2000; The Silver Swan, 2000; Black Queen, 2000; Tom's Sausage Lion, 2000; From Hereabout Hill, 2000; Billy the Kid, 2000 (performed Unicorn Th., 2006); Classic Boys' Stories, 2000; Toro! Toro!, 2001; More Muck and Magic, 2001; Because a Fire was in my Head, 2001; Out of the Ashes, 2001 (Children's Book Award); The Last Wolf, 2002; The Sleeping Sword, 2002; Cool, 2002; Mr Skip, 2002; Gentle Giant, 2003; Private Peaceful, 2003 (Children's Book Award, Blue Peter Award, Prix Sorcière; performed Bristol Old Vic, 2004); Little Albatross, 2003; Dolphin Boy, 2004; It's a Dog's Life, 2004, (with Patrick Benson), 2010; Sir Gawain and the Green Knight, 2004; Aesop's Fables, 2004; Cockadoodle-doo Mr Sultana!, 2004; (with Jane Feaver) Cock Crow, 2004; The Best Christmas Present in the World, 2004; The Amazing Story of Adolphus Tips (Sheffield Book Award), 2005 (theatre adaptation, 2015); I Believe in Unicorns, 2005; (with Michael Foreman) Beowulf, 2006; Singing for Mrs Pettigrew, 2006; Alone on a Wide Wide Sea, 2006 (Ind. Booksellers' Children's Book of Yr, 2007); (with Quentin Blake) On Angel Wings, 2006; (with Michael Foreman) The Mozart Question, 2007; Born to Run, 2007; (with Emma Chichester Clark) Hansel and Gretel, 2008; (with Michael Foreman) Kaspar, Prince of Cats, 2008; (with Christian Birmingham) This Morning I Met a Whale, 2008; Running Wild, 2009; (with Emma Chichester Clark) Best of Times, 2009; (with Michael Foreman) Not Bad for a Bad Lad, 2010; (with Michael Foreman) The Elephant in the Garden, 2010; Shadow, 2010; (with Emma Chichester Clark) The Pied Piper of Hamelin, 2011 (musical adaptation, 2015); A Medal For Leroy, 2012; Jo-Jo the Melon Donkey, 2013; Listen to the Moon, 2014; (with Michael Foreman) An Eagle in the Snow, 2015; libretti: Solar, 1981; Scarecrow (music by Phyllis Tate), 1982; *relevant publication*: Michael Morpurgo: war child to war horse, 2012. *Recreations:* dreaming, travelling. *Address:* c/o David Higham Associates, 7th Floor, Waverley House, 7–12 Noel Street, W1F 8GQ. *Club:* Chelsea Arts.

MORPUSS, Guy; QC 2008; barrister, since 1991; *b* Worcester, 13 March 1969; *s* of Richard and Rosemarie Morpuss; *m* 1999, Julie Davies; two *s*. *Educ:* Hillcrest High Sch., South Africa; Univ. of Birmingham (LLB 1st Cl. Hons). Called to the Bar, Lincoln's Inn, 1991; in practice as barrister specialising in commercial litigation. *Recreations:* running, travelling, ski-ing, music. *Address:* Macfarlanes LLP, 20 Cursitor Street, EC4A 1LT.

MORRELL, David William James; Scottish Legal Services Ombudsman, 1991–94; *b* 26 July 1933; *s* of Rev. W. W. Morrell, MBE, TD and Grace Morrell; *m* 1960, Margaret Rosemary Lewis; two *s* one *d*. *Educ:* George Watson's Coll., Edinburgh; Univ. of Edinburgh (MA Hons, LLB). Law Apprentice, Edinburgh, 1954–57; Admin. Asst, Univ. of Durham, 1957–60; Asst Registrar and Graduate Appts Officer, Univ. of Exeter, 1960–64; Sen. Asst Registrar, Univ. of Essex, 1964–66; Academic Registrar, 1966–73, Registrar, 1973–89, Univ. of Strathclyde; Lay Observer for Scotland, 1989–91. OECD Consultant on management in higher educn, 1990. Vice-Chm., Lomond Healthcare NHS Trust, 1995–99 (Chm., 1995–96); Mem., Argyll and Clyde Health Bd, 1999–2001. Governor: Univ. of Paisley (formerly Paisley Coll.), 1990–2002 (Vice-Chm., 1992–97, Chm., 1997–2002); Scottish Centre for Children with Motor Impairments, 1994–97; Chm., Conf. of Scottish Centrally-Funded Colls, 1997–2000. DUniv Paisley, 2005. *Publications:* papers on higher education and on provision of legal services. *Recreations:* hill-walking, fishing. *Address:* 29 Barclay Drive, Helensburgh, Dunbartonshire G84 9RA. *T:* (01436) 674875.

MORRELL, Leslie James, OBE 1986; JP; Chairman, Northern Ireland Water Council, 1982–93; *b* 26 Dec. 1931; *s* of James Morrell; *m* 1958, Anne Wallace, BSc; two *s* one *d*. *Educ:* Portora Royal Sch., Enniskillen; Queen's Univ., Belfast. BAgric 1955. Member: Londonderry CC, 1969–73; Coleraine Bor. Council, 1973–77; Mem. (U) for Londonderry, NI Assembly, 1973–75; Minister of Agriculture, NI Exec., 1973–74; Dep. Leader, Unionist Party of NI, 1974–80. Mem., BBC Gen. Adv. Cttee, 1980–86; Chm., BBC NI Agricl Adv. Cttee, 1986–91. Chm., NI Fedn of Housing Assocs, 1978–80; Member, Board: Oaklee Homes, 2003–09; Oaklee Housing Trust, 2006–; Company Sec., Choice Housing Ireland (formerly Oaklee Trinity) Ltd, 2014–. Hon. Secretary: Oaklee Homes Gp (formerly Housing Assoc., then Homes Gp), 1992–2014 (James Butcher Housing Assoc. (NI), 1981–92 (Chm., 1976–81)); James Butcher Retirement Homes Ltd, 1985–95; Oaklee Care and Support Services Ltd, Oaklee Enterprises and Oaklee Employment Services, 2009–. Mem. Exec., Assoc. of Governing Bodies of Voluntary Grammar Schs, 1978–84; Chm., Virus Tested Stem Cutting Potato Growers Assoc., 1977–88. JP Londonderry, 1966. *Address:* Dunboe House, Castlerock, Coleraine BT51 4UB. *T:* (028) 7084 8352.

MORRELL, Paul Dring, OBE 2009; Principal, Paul Morrell Consulting, since 2007; *b* Doncaster, Yorks, 28 Feb. 1948; *s* of David Dring Morrell and Joan Hannah Morrell (*née* Rankin); *m* 1978, Shirley Irene Betney. *Educ:* Oundle Sch.; Coll. of Estate Mgt, Univ. of Reading (BSc 1970). ARICS 1975, FRICS 1986; FICE 2011. Davis Langdon, chartered quantity surveyors, 1971–2007, Sen. Partner, 1999–2004. Chief Construction Advr, BIS, 2009–12. Mem., CABE, 2000–08 (Dep. Chm., 2007–08). Mem., Mgt Bd, British Council for Offices, 1999–2008 (Pres., 2004–05). Mem. Bd, Siobhan Davies Dance Co., 2002– (Chm., 2007–); Gov., RSC, 2006– (Mem. Bd, 2006–13); Trustee and Mem. Bd, Bristol Old Vic Th., 2013–; Trustee and Dep. Chm., Garden Bridge Trust, 2013–. Vis. Prof., Nottingham Trent Univ., 2012–. Hon. FRIBA 2000; Hon. FAPM 2012; Hon. FABE 2012. *Publications:* regular columnist on matters relating to construction incl. Building Mag. and Building Design. *Recreations:* sailing, opera, theatre, contemporary dance. *Address:* 4 Caithness Road, W14 0JB. *T:* (020) 7602 6082. *E:* paul.morrell@btinternet.com.

MORRELL, Rev. His Honour Peter Richard; a Circuit Judge, 1992–2009; *b* 25 May 1944; *s* of Frank Richard Morrell and Florence Ethel Morrell; *m* 1970, Helen Mary Vint Collins; two *d*. *Educ:* Westminster Sch.; University Coll., Oxford (MA). Admitted Solicitor, 1970; called to the Bar, Gray's Inn, 1974; a Recorder, 1990–92. C of E Reader, 2005–07, ordained deacon, 2008, priest, 2009, Peterborough Dio. *Recreations:* shooting, fishing, Spain. *Address:* Swallow Cottage, Nassington, Peterborough PE8 6QT. *T:* 07860 573597.

MORREY, Rev. William Reginald; Faith Communities Adviser, Action for Children, since 2008; *b* 24 March 1953; *s* of Claude William Morrey and Joan Morrey; *m* 1976, Vicki Mountford; two *s*. *Educ:* Birmingham Univ. (BA Theol. 1974); Queen's Coll., Birmingham; Westhill Coll., Birmingham (Cert. in Community and Youth Work 1976). Minister: Bideford, 1976–79; Ecclesall, Sheffield, and Chaplain to Children's Hosp., 1979–84; Halifax, 1984–87; Supt Minister, Bangor and Chaplain to UCNW, Bangor, and to RAF Valley, 1987–94; Co-ordinator, Council for Methodism in Wales, 1994–97; Chm., S Wales Dist, Methodist Ch, 1997–2007; Chair, Wales Synod, Methodist Ch in Wales, 2007–08. Pres., Methodist Conference, 2004–05; Chair, Methodist Council, 2006–09. Foundn Trustee, N Wales Deaf Assoc., 1994–; Chm., NCH Cymru, 2005–07; Faith Communities Advr, Action for Children, 2008–14. Chm., Amelia Trust Farm, 2011–. *Publications:* Seeing is Hearing: reflections on being deafened, 1995. *Recreations:* badminton, squash, walking, watching Rugby. *Address:* c/o Methodist Church Conference Office, 25 Marylebone Road, NW1 5JR.

MORRICE, Graeme; *b* Edinburgh, 23 Feb. 1959. *Educ:* Mauldeth Road Primary Sch.; Parrs Wood High Sch.; Broxburn Acad.; Napier Univ. (SHND Business Studies). Mem. (Lab) W Lothian Council, 1987–2012 (Leader, 1995–2007). MP (Lab) Livingston, 2010–15; contested (Lab) same seat, 2015.

MORRICE, Jane; Northern Ireland Member, since 2006, and Vice President, since 2013, European Economic and Social Committee; Deputy Chief Equality Commissioner for Northern Ireland, since 2008; *b* 11 May 1954; *d* of George Eric Morrice and Irene (*née* Cleland); *m* 1988, Paul Robinson (*d* 2009); one *s*. *Educ:* Univ. of Ulster (BA Hons W Eur. Studies 1977). Journalist, Brussels, specialising in internat. economy and Third World; business and labour relns corresp., 1980–87; BBC TV and Radio in NI, 1987–92; Head, Eur. Commn Office in NI, 1992–97; Mem., Eur. Commn Task Force preparing special support prog. for peace and reconciliation in NI and border counties of Ireland, 1992–97; Mem. (NI Women's Coalition) N Down, 1998–2003, and Dep. Speaker, 1999–2002, NI Assembly. Mem., NI Adv. Cttee, Ofcom, 2004–07. Bd Mem., Laganside Corp., 1998–2007. *Publications:* North/South Dialogue, 1984; The Lomé Convention From Politics to Practice, 1985. *Recreations:* writing, swimming, tennis, photography. *Address:* 18 Ballyholme Esplanade, Bangor, Co. Down BT20 5LZ.

MORRICE, Philip; HM Diplomatic Service, retired; director and consultant, various companies in Australia and UK; Director, TFG International Pty Ltd, since 2001; *b* 31 Dec. 1943; *s* of late William Hunter Morrice and Catherine Jane Cowie; *m* 1988, Margaret Clare

Bower; one *s* one *d*. *Educ:* Robert Gordon's College, Aberdeen; Univ. of Besançon; École Nat. d'Administration, Paris; London Business Sch. Entered HM Diplomatic Service, 1963; served Kuala Lumpur, 1964–67; CO, later FCO, 1967–69; Caracas, 1969–72; First Sec., UK Delegn to OECD, Paris, 1973–75; First Sec. (Energy), UK Perm. Rep. to EC, Brussels, 1975–78; FCO, 1978–81; First Sec. (Commercial), later Counsellor (Comm.), Rome, 1981–85; Counsellor (Econ. and Comm.), Lagos, 1986–88; Minister-Counsellor, Consul-Gen. and Dir of Trade Promotion, Brasilia, 1988–92; Director, Anglo-Taiwan Trade Cttee, subseq. British Trade and Cultural Office, Taipei (on secondment), 1992–95; Consul-Gen., Sydney, and Dir Gen. of Trade and Investment Promotion in Australia, 1995–99. Dir, KPMG Consulting, 1999–2001. *Publications:* The Schweppes Guide to Scotch, 1983; The Whisky Distilleries of Scotland and Ireland, 1987; The Teacher's Book of Whisky, 1993; numerous articles. *Recreations:* travel, tennis, golf, sailing. *Address:* TFG International Pty Ltd, Level 8, 139 Macquarie Street, Sydney, NSW 2000, Australia. *T:* (2) 93634389, 0408664021. *E:* philip.morrice@tfginternational.com. *Clubs:* Royal Automobile; Union (Sydney); Royal Sydney Yacht Squadron; Royal Sydney Golf.

MORRILL, Rev. Prof. John Stephen, DPhil; FRHistS; FBA 1995; Professor of British and Irish History, University of Cambridge, since 1998; Fellow, Selwyn College, Cambridge, since 1975; *b* 12 June 1946; *s* of William Henry Morrill and Marjorie (*née* Ashton); *m* 1968, Frances Mead (*d* 2007); four *d*. *Educ:* Altrincham County Grammar Sch.; Trinity Coll., Oxford (BA 1967; MA, DPhil 1971; Hon. Fellow, 2006). FRHistS 1977. Keasbey Lectr in Hist., 1970–71, Jun. Res. Fellow, 1971–74, Trinity Coll., Oxford; Coll. Lectr in Hist., St Catherine's Coll., Oxford, 1973–74; Lectr in Mod. Hist., Univ. of Stirling, 1974–75; Cambridge University: Asst Lectr and Lectr, Faculty of History, 1975–92; Reader in Early Modern Hist., 1992–98; Dep. Dir, Centre for Arts, Humanities and Social Scis, 2001–04; Selwyn College, Cambridge: Dir of Studies in Hist., 1975–91; Tutor, 1979–91; Admissions Tutor, 1983–87; Sen. Tutor, 1987–91; Vice Master, 1994–2004. Vice-President: RHistS, 1993–97; British Acad., 2001–09; Mem., AHRB, 1999–2004 (Convenor, History Panel, 1999–2002; Chair, Res. Cttee, 2002–04). Ordained permanent deacon, RC Ch, 1996. Foreign Mem., Finnish Acad. of Arts and Scis, 2002. Centenary Fellow, Historical Assoc., 2006. FRSA 2008. Hon. MRIA 2010. Hon. DLitt UEA, 2002; DUniv Surrey, 2002. *Publications:* Cheshire 1630–1660, 1974; The Revolt of the Provinces 1630–1650, 1976, rev. edn 1980; The Cheshire Grand Jury 1625–1659, 1976; (with G. E. Aylmer) The Civil Wars and Interregnum: sources for local historians, 1979; Seventeenth-Century Britain, 1980; (ed) Reactions to the English Civil War, 1982; (ed) Land Men and Beliefs, 1985; Charles I, 1989; Oliver Cromwell and the English Revolution, 1990; (ed) The National Covenant in its British Context, 1990; (ed) The Impact of the English Civil War, 1991; (ed) Revolution and Restoration, 1992; The Nature of the English Revolution, 1993; (with P. Slack and D. Woolf) Public Men and Private Conscience in Seventeenth-Century England, 1993; (ed) The Oxford Illustrated History of Tudor and Stuart Britain, 1996; (with B. Bradshaw) The British Problem 1534–1707: state formation in the Atlantic Archipelago, 1996; Revolt in the Provinces: the English people and the tragedies of war, 1998; (jtly) Soldiers and Statesmen of the English Revolution, 1998; Oliver Cromwell, 2007; contribs to learned jls. *Recreations:* classical music, whisky and whiskey, cricket. *Address:* Selwyn College, Cambridge CB3 9DQ; 1 Bradford's Close, Bottisham, Cambs CB25 9DW. *T:* (01223) 811822.

MORRIS; *see* Temple-Morris, family name of Baron Temple-Morris.

MORRIS, family name of **Barons Killanin, Morris, Morris of Aberavon, Morris of Handsworth, Morris of Kenwood** and **Naseby**.

MORRIS, 3rd Baron *cr* 1918; **Michael David Morris;** *b* 9 Dec. 1937; *er* twin *s* of 2nd Baron Morris and Jean Beatrice (later Lady Salmon; she *d* 1989), *d* of late Lt-Col D. Maitland-Makgill-Crichton; *S* father, 1975; *m* 1st, 1959, Denise Eleanor (marr. diss. 1962), *o d* of Morley Richards; 2nd, 1962, Jennifer (marr. diss. 1969), *o d* of Squadron Leader Tristram Gilbert; two *d*; 3rd, 1980, Juliet (marr. diss. 1996), twin *d* of Anthony Buckingham; two *s* one *d*; 4th, 1999, Nicola Mary, *o d* of Colin Morgan Watkins. *Educ:* Downside. *Heir: s* Hon. Thomas Anthony Salmon Morris, *b* 2 July 1982.

MORRIS OF ABERAVON, Baron *cr* 2001 (Life Peer), of Aberavon in the County of West Glamorgan and of Ceredigion in the County of Dyfed; **John Morris,** KG 2003; Kt 1999; PC 1970; QC 1973; Chancellor, University of South Wales (formerly University of Glamorgan), 2001–13; Lord-Lieutenant of Dyfed, 2002–06; *b* Nov. 1931; *s* of late D. W. Morris, Penywern, Talybont, Cardiganshire and Mary Olwen Ann Morris (later Lewis); *m* 1959, Margaret M., *d* of late Edward Lewis, OBE, JP, of Llandysul; three *d*. *Educ:* Ardwyn, Aberystwyth; University Coll. of Wales, Aberystwyth; Gonville and Caius Coll., Cambridge (LLM; Hon. Fellow); Academy of International Law, The Hague; Holker Senior Exhibitioner, Gray's Inn. Commissioned Royal Welch Fusiliers and Welch Regt. Called to the Bar, Gray's Inn, 1954, Bencher, 1985; a Recorder, 1982–97. MP (Lab) Aberavon, Oct. 1959–2001. Parly Sec., Min. of Power, 1964–66; Jt Parly Sec., Min. of Transport, 1966–68; Minister of Defence (Equipment), 1968–70; Sec. of State for Wales, 1974–79; opposition spokesman on legal affairs and Shadow Attorney Gen., 1979–81 and 1983–97; Attorney General, 1997–99. Member: Cttee of Privileges, 1994–97; Select Cttee on Implementation of Nolan Report, 1995–97; Adv. Cttee on Business Appointments, 2002–09. Dep. Gen. Sec. and Legal Adviser, Farmers' Union of Wales, 1956–58. Member: UK Delegn Consultative Assembly Council of Europe and Western European Union, 1963–64, 1982–83; N Atlantic Assembly, 1970–74. Chairman: Nat. Pneumoconiosis Jt Cttee, 1964–66; Jt Review of Finances and Management, British Railways, 1966–67; Nat. Road Safety Advisory Council, 1967. Mem. Council, Prince's Trust (Cymru), 2002–08. Pres., London Welsh Trust, 2001–09. Patron, London Welsh Lawyers, 2010–; Trustee, Foundn of St George's, Windsor, 2013–. David Lloyd George Meml Lect., Criccieth Fest., N Wales, 2007; Youard Lect., Swansea Univ., 2011; Annual Lect. for Political Archives, Nat. Liby of Wales, 2013. Hon. Fellow: UCW, Aberystwyth; Trinity Coll., Carmarthen; UC, Swansea; Univ. of Wales, Lampeter, 2009. Hon. LLD: Wales, 1985; S Wales, 2014. Lifetime Achievement Award, Wales Yearbook Awards, 2011. *Publications:* Fifty Years in Politics and the Law, 2011. *Address:* House of Lords, SW1A 0PW.

See also D. W. Morris.

MORRIS OF BOLTON, Baroness *cr* 2004 (Life Peer), of Bolton in the County of Greater Manchester; **Patricia Morris,** OBE; DL; *b* 16 Jan. 1953; *d* of late James Sydney Whittaker, Bolton; *m* 1978, His Honour William Patrick Morris, *qv*; one *s* one *d*. *Educ:* Bolton Sch. Girls' Div.; Clifton and Didsbury Colls of Educn. Personal Assistant: to N Regl Dir, Slater Walker Ltd, 1974–75; to Chevalier Dr Harry D. Schultz, 1975; Fund Manager, PPS, 1975–77; Technical Analyst: Foster & Braithwaite, 1977–78; Charlton, Seal, Dimmock & Co., 1979–83; Policy and Political Advr to a Cons. MEP, 1999–2001. Mem., Cons. Women's Nat. Cttee, 1989; Vice-Chm., Cons. Party, 2001–05. Contested (C) Oldham Central and Royton, 1992. Opposition Whip, H of L, 2004–10; opposition spokesman on women, 2005–10, on children and families, 2005–08, on educn, 2005–08, H of L. Dep. Chm., Salford Royal Hosps NHS Trust, 1993–97; Advr to Abbot of Ampleforth, 1998–2004. President: Nat. Benevolent Instn, 2006–; World Travel Market, 2009–; Co-Chm., Women in Public Policy, 2007–; Patron, OXPIP, 2006–; Trustee: Disability Partnership, 2007–; UNICEF, 2007–; Transformation Trust, 2009–. Mem. Cttee, Patrons and Associates, Manchester City Art Galls, 1982–94; Mem., Manchester N Valuation and Community Charge Tribunal, 1988–92; Chm., Bolton Cancer Res. Campaign, 1992–95; Mem. Bd Mgt, 1994–97, Dir, 1997–2002, Bolton Lads' and Girls' Club. Gov. and Trustee, Bolton Sch., 1992–. Chancellor, Univ. of Bolton, 2010–13. DL Greater Manchester, 2008. *Address:* House of Lords, SW1A 0PW.

MORRIS OF HANDSWORTH, Baron *cr* 2006 (Life Peer), of Handsworth in the County of West Midlands; **William Manuel Morris,** Kt 2003; OJ 2002; General Secretary, Transport and General Workers Union, 1992–2003 (Deputy General Secretary, 1986–92); *b* 19 Oct. 1938; *s* of William and Una Morris; *m* 1957, Minetta (*d* 1990); two *s*. *Educ:* Mizpah Sch., Manchester, Jamaica; Handsworth Tech. Coll. Hardy Spicer Engineering, 1954. Joined TGWU, 1958: Shop Steward, 1962; Mem. Gen. Exec. Council, 1971–72; Dist Officer, Nottingham, 1973; Dist Sec., Northampton, 1976; Nat. Sec., Passenger Services, 1979–85. Mem., TUC Gen. Council, 1988–2003. Non-exec. Dir, Bank of England, 1998–2006. Chm., Morris Inquiry, Metropolitan Police Authy, 2004. Member: Commn for Racial Equality, 1977–87; IBA Gen. Adv. Council, 1981–86; Bd, ITF, 1986–2003; Road Transport ITB, 1986–92; Prince's Youth Business Trust, 1987–90; BBC General Adv. Council, 1987–88; Employment Appeals Tribunal, 1988–2009; Economic and Social Cttee, EC, 1990–92; NEDC, 1992; ACAS, 1997–2003; Royal Commn on H of L reform, 1999; Commn for Integrated Transport, 1999–2005; Architects' Registration Bd, 2001–05; Panel on Takeovers and Mergers, 2005–. Chair, Midland Heart Housing Assoc., 2007–14. Vice Chm., Jamaica Nat. Money Services, 2007–11. Vis. Prof., Thames Valley Univ., 1997–2005. Chancellor: Univ. of Technology, Jamaica, 2000–10; Staffordshire Univ., 2004–11. Member: Governing Body, Atlantic Coll., 1994–2004; Court: Luton Univ., 1994–2006; Univ. of Northampton (formerly Nene Coll., later UC Northampton), 1996–2005. Member: Bd of Govs, London South Bank (formerly S Bank) Univ., 1997–2005; Univ. Assembly, Greenwich Univ., 1997–2001; Trustee Bd, Open Univ. Foundn, 1997–2006. Mem., Cricket Bd for England and Wales, 2004–15. Trustee, Performances Birmingham Ltd, 2008–15. DL Stafford, 2008. Hon. FRSA, 1992; Hon. FCGI, 1992. Hon. LLD: South Bank, 1994; Teesside, 1997; Univ. of Technol., Jamaica, 2000; Luton, 2000; Birmingham, Warwick, 2002; Nottingham, 2005; DUniv: Leeds Metropolitan, 1996; Middlesex, Stafford, 2002; Hon. DLitt: Westminster 1997; Hull, 2007; Hon. DBA Greenwich, 1997; Hon. Dr Thames Valley, 1997; Hon. DLit, London South Bank, 2007; MUniv Open, 1995; Hon. MA UC Northampton, 2001. *Recreations:* walking, gardening, watching sports. *Address:* House of Lords, SW1A 0PW. *E:* morrisw@parliament.uk.

MORRIS OF KENWOOD, 3rd Baron *cr* 1950, of Kenwood; **Jonathan David Morris;** company director; *b* 5 Aug. 1968; *s* of 2nd Baron Morris of Kenwood and of Hon. Ruth (CBE 2014), *d* of Baron Janner; *S* father, 2004; *m* 1996, Melanie, *d* of Robin Klein; two *s*. *Educ:* St Paul's Sch.; Leicester Univ. *Heir: s* Hon. Benjamin Julian Morris, *b* 5 Nov. 1998.

MORRIS OF YARDLEY, Baroness *cr* 2005 (Life Peer), of Yardley in the county of West Midlands; **Estelle Morris;** PC 1999; *b* 17 June 1952; *d* of Rt Hon. Charles Richard Morris, PC and of Pauline Morris. *Educ:* Whalley Range High Sch., Manchester; Coventry Coll. of Educn (TCert); BEd Warwick Univ. Teacher, 1974–92. Councillor, Warwick DC, 1979–91 (Labour Gp Leader, 1981–89). MP (Lab) Birmingham, Yardley, 1992–2005. An Opposition Whip, 1994–95; opposition front-bench spokesman on educn, 1995–97; Parly Under-Sec. of State, 1997–98, Minister of State, 1998–2001, DFEE; Sec. of State for Educn and Skills, 2001–02; Minister of State (Minister for the Arts), DCMS, 2003–05. Hon. Fellow, St Martin's Coll., Lancaster, 2006. Hon. DLitt: Warwick, 2002; Bradford, 2005; Chester, 2011; Hon. DEd: Wolverhampton, 2004; Manchester Metropolitan, 2007; Hon. DArts Leeds Metropolitan, 2004; DUniv: Birmingham, 2006; Open, 2011. *Address:* House of Lords, SW1A 0PW.

MORRIS, Alan Douglas; independent consultant on anti-corruption and regulatory compliance; Director, Anti-Corruption Advisory, PricewaterhouseCoopers, 2007–11; *b* 15 Sept. 1956; *s* of Leslie John Morris and Gladys Josephine Morris; *m* 1st, 1984, Barbara Caroline Alexandra Welsh (marr. diss. 1998); two *d*; 2nd, 1999, Anne Marie Stebbings (marr. diss. 2008). *Educ:* John Ruskin Grammar Sch., Croydon; Magdalene Coll., Cambridge (MA, LLM). FCMA. Joined Tate & Lyle, 1978; Esso Petroleum, 1981–84; Financial Controller: RBC Systems, 1984–87; MI Group, 1987–88; Simmons & Simmons: Finance Dir, 1988–96; Man. Dir, 1997–99; PricewaterhouseCoopers: Hd of Operations—Legal, 2000–04; Hd of Performance Improvement Consulting, Gatwick Region, 2004–07. Liveryman, Drapers' Co., 2005– (Mem., Ct of Assts, 2011–; Chm., Multi-Academy Trust). *Recreations:* acting, shooting, bridge, reading. *Address:* The Thatched Cottage, High Street, Lindfield, West Sussex RH16 2HU. *Club:* MCC.

MORRIS, Albert, FCIB; Director, 1989–94, and Deputy Group Chief Executive, 1992–94, National Westminster Bank; *b* 21 Oct. 1934; *m* 1987, Patricia Lane (*d* 2005). *Educ:* Skerry's Coll., Liverpool; City of Liverpool Coll. of Commerce; Admin. Staff Coll., Henley; MIT. National Westminster Bank: Head of Money Transmission, 1979–83; Dep. Gen. Manager, 1983–85, Gen. Manager, 1985–88, Management Services Div.; Chief Exec., Support Services, 1989–92. Director: NatWest Estate Management & Development Ltd, 1989–94; National Westminster Life Assce Ltd, 1992–94; Regent Associates, 1995–; Metroline plc, 1997– (Chm., 1997–2000); Chairman: BACS Ltd, 1985–94; Centre-file Ltd, 1988–94; Lorien plc, 1998–2007; Macro 4 plc, 2000–07; Inbucon Ltd, 2007–08. Founding Mem., 1985–87 and Mem. Council, 1990–94, UK Banking Ombudsman Scheme; Chm., APACS, 1993–94 (Dep. Chm., 1991–93; Dir, APACS Admin Ltd, 1987–94). Mem. Adv. Council, Sema Group, 1995–96; Special Advr, Ibos Ltd, 1995–96; non-exec. Mem., DSS Departmental Bd, 1993–97; Mem., Adv. Bd, Integral Specialist Services Ltd. Hon. Treas., Kingwood Trust, 1996–2000. CCMI; FCIB 1984 (Mem. Council, 1989–); FRSA 1989. Freeman, City of London, 1992; Liveryman, 1992–, Trustee, 2002–, Charity Dir and Chm. of Audit Cttee, Co. of Information Technologists. *Recreations:* golf, work, politics. *Address:* Stonebridge, 74 West Common, Harpenden, Herts AL5 2LD.

MORRIS, Air Marshal Sir Alec, KBE 1982; CB 1979; FREng; *b* 11 March 1926; *s* of late Harry Morris; *m* 1946, Moyna Patricia (*d* 2000), *d* of late Norman Boyle; one *s* one *d* (twins). *Educ:* King Edward VI Sch., East Retford; King's Coll., Univ. of London; Univ. of Southampton. Commnd RAF, 1945; radar duties, No 90 (Signals) Gp, 1945–50; Guided Weapons Dept, RAE, 1953–56; sc 1957; exchange duty, HQ USAF, 1958–60; space res., Min. of Supply, 1960–63; DS, RAF Staff Coll., 1963–65; OC Eng, No 2 Flying Trng Sch., Syerston, 1966–68; Asst Dir, Guided Weapons R&D, Min. of Tech., 1968–70; OC RAF Central Servicing Develt Estabt, Swanton Morley, 1970–72; SASO, HQ No 90 (Signals) Gp, 1972–74; RCDS, 1974; Dir of Signals (Air), MoD, 1975–76; Dir Gen. Strategic Electronic Systems, MoD (PE), 1976–79; Air Officer Engineering, RAF Strike Command, 1979–81; Chief Engineer, RAF, 1981–83. Exec., BAe, 1983–91, retd. FREng (FEng 1989). *Recreations:* tennis, gardening. *Address:* The Old Rectory, Church Street, Semington, Wilts BA14 6JW. *Clubs:* Royal Air Force; Bath and County (Bath).

MORRIS, Alfred Cosier, CBE 2003; DL; Chairman, Higher Education Associates Ltd, since 2011; *b* 12 Nov. 1941; *s* of late Stanley Bernard Morris, Anlaby, E Yorks, and Jennie Fletcher; *m* 1970, Annette, *er d* of Eamonn and May Donovan, Cork, Eire; one *d*. *Educ:* Hymers Coll., Hull (E Riding Scholar); Univ. of Lancaster (MA Financial Control 1970). FCA; FSS. Articled clerk to Oliver Mackrill & Co., 1958–63; Company Sec., Financial Controller and Dir, several cos, 1963–71; Sen. Leverhulme Res. Fellow in Univ. Planning and Orgn, Univ. of Sussex, 1971–74; Vis. Lectr in Financial Management, Univ. of Warwick, 1973; Group Management Accountant, Arthur Guinness Ltd, 1974–76; Management Consultant, Deloitte Haskins & Sells, 1976–77; Financial Adviser, subsids of Arthur Guinness, 1977–80; Dep. Dir, Polytechnic of the South Bank, 1980–85, Acting Dir, 1985–86; Dir, Bristol Poly., 1986–92; Vice Chancellor: UWE, Bristol, 1992–2005; Univ. of Wales, Lampeter, 2008–09; (interim) London Metropolitan Univ., 2009–10. Strategic Advr, Kaplan UK, 2010–11. Adviser to H of C Select Cttee on Educn, Sci. and Arts, 1979–83. Chm., PCFC Cttee on Performance

Indicators in Higher Educn, 1989–90; Member: CNAA, 1988–93; HEFCW, 1992–2000 (Chm., Audit Cttee, 1997–2000); Higher Educn Quality Council, 1992–94; South West Arts, 1994–2000; Bd, Westec, 1995–98; FEFCE, 1997–99 (Chm., Audit Cttee, 1997–99). Dir, Bristol and West, 1992–2002. Dir, SW Urban Regeneration Fund, 2003–08. Chairman: Bristol Old Vic Trust, 1992–94; Patrons of Bristol Old Vic, 1993–2008; Mem. Council, Bristol Old Vic Theatre Sch., 2006–10; Chm., N Bristol NHS Trust, 2006–08; Mem., SW of England RDA, 1998–2002; Trustee: Bristol Cathedral Trust, 1988–2007; John Cabot's Matthew Trust, 1996–2002; Bristol Charities, 2006–; Mem. Exec. Cttee, Bristol Soc., 1992–. President: City Acad. Bristol, 2003–06; Hartpury Coll., Glos, 2008–; Dir, eUnivs Holding Co., 2002–04. Mem. Council, Clifton High Sch., 1995–2004. Patron: DAVAR, 1999–2010; Fast Track Trust, 2000–10; Bristol Drugs Project, 2002–10; Trustee: Quartet Community (formerly Gtr Bristol) Foundn, 1999–2004 (Chm., 1999–2000); Patrons of the RWA, 2000–06; Mem. Council, RWA, 2009–10. Ringer, Antient Soc. of St Stephen's Ringers, 2007–; Mem., Soc. of Merchant Venturers of Bristol, 2004–; Pres., Dolphin Soc., 2008–09; Chair, Trinity St David Trust, 2009–10. DL, 2002, High Sheriff, 2006–07, Glos. Hon. Fellow: Humberside Univ., 1990; RWA, 2001. Hon. LLD: Bristol, 1993; UWE, 2006; Gloucestershire, 2007. *Publications:* (ed jtly and contrib.) Resources and Higher Education, 1982; articles and contribs to jls on higher educn. *Recreations:* sailing, wind-surfing. *Address:* Park Court, Sodbury Common, Old Sodbury BS37 6PX. *T:* 07837 949996. *Club:* Salcombe Yacht.

MORRIS, Sir Allan Lindsay, 11th Bt *cr* 1806, of Clasemont, Glamorganshire; *b* 27 Nov. 1961; *o s* of Sir Robert Morris, 10th Bt and of Christine Morris (*née* Field); *S* father, 1999, but his name does not appear on the Official Roll of the Baronetage; *m* 1986, Cheronne Denise, *e d* of Dale Whitford; two *s* one *d*. *Heir: er s* Sennen John Morris, *b* 5 June 1995. *Address:* Georgetown, Halton Hills, ON, Canada.

MORRIS, Prof. Andrew, MD; FRCPE, FRCPGlas, FMedSci; FRSE; Professor of Medicine, Director, Usher Institute of Population Health Science and Informatics, and Vice-Principal of Data Science, University of Edinburgh, since 2014; Chief Scientist, Health Department, Scottish Government, since 2012; *b* York, 7 Oct. 1964; *s* of David Morris and Beryl Morris; *m* 1994, Elspeth Riddell; one *s* two *d*. *Educ:* Royal Grammar Sch., Newcastle Upon Tyne; Robert Gordon160's Coll., Aberdeen; N Berwick High Sch.; Univ. of Glasgow (MB ChB 1987; MSc Clin. Pharmacol. 1992; MD 1994). FRCPE 1994; FRCPGlas 1994. Lectr in Medicine, Univ. of Glasgow, 1990–94; University of Dundee: Sen. Lectr, 1994–96; Reader, 1996–2000; Prof. of Diabetic Medicine, 2000–10; Prof. of Medicine, 2010–14; Dean of Medicine, 2012–14; Hon. Prof., 2014–; Lead Clinician for Diabetes, Scotland, 2002–06. Mem., Assoc. of Physicians of GB and Ire., 2004. FRSE 2006; FMedSci 2009. *Publications:* 300 articles in jls on diabetes, epidemiology informatics and genetics. *Recreation:* golf. *Address:* School of Molecular, Genetic and Population Health Sciences, University of Edinburgh, Medical School, Teviot Place, Edinburgh EH8 9AG. *T:* (0131) 651 7849. *E:* Andrew.Morris@ed.ac.uk. *Club:* Royal and Ancient St Andrews.

MORRIS, Andrew Bernard; Chief Executive, Academy for Chief Executives Ltd, since 2011 (Chairman, 2009–11); *b* 16 Oct. 1952; *s* of Sam and Golda Morris; *m* 1976, Jennifer Maizner; one *s* two *d*. *Educ:* Christ's Coll., London; Coll. for Distributive Trades; Harvard Business Sch. Sales and Marketing Dir, City Industrial Ltd, 1980–84; Jt Man. Dir, 1984–86, Man. Dir, 1986–89, Sales and Mktg Dir, 1989–99, Business Design Centre; CEO, 1999–2004, non-exec. Chm., 2004, Earls Court & Olympia Gp Ltd; Chief Exec., NEC Gp, 2004–06. Non-executive Director: Business Design Centre, 1999–; Ingenious Media Live VCT, 2005–. Non-executive Chairman: Brand Events, 2007–11; World Photography Awards, 2007–. *Recreations:* tennis, cycling, reading, contemporary art.

MORRIS, Andrew James; HM Diplomatic Service, retired; High Commissioner, Kingdom of Tonga, and Consul for Pacific Islands under American sovereignty South of the Equator, 1994–98; *b* 22 March 1939; *s* of late Albert Morris and of Clara Morris; *m* 1961, Ann Christine Healy; two *s*. Served Army, 1960–64. Entered FO, 1964; served Kuwait, Salisbury, Sofia, Muscat, and San Francisco, 1965–78; Consul, Los Angeles, 1978–82; FCO, 1982–86; First Sec., Kaduna, 1986–89; Dep. High Comr, Port Moresby, 1989–93; First Sec., FCO, 1993–94. *Recreations:* golf, travel.

MORRIS, Anne; *see* Molyneux, A.

MORRIS, Anne Marie; MP (C) Newton Abbot, since 2010; *b* London, 1957; *d* of late John Backes and of Margaret Agg; partner, Roger Kendrick. *Educ:* Hertford Coll., Oxford (BA PPP/Juris.); Open Univ. (MBA 1997); Harvard Univ. (Leadership Prog. 2004). Admitted solicitor, 1982; trainee solicitor, Withers, London, 1981–83; Corporate Finance Lawyer, Norton Rose, London, 1983–85; Corporate, Commercial, Banking Lawyer, Crossman Block, London, 1985; Asset Finance Lawyer, Sinclair Roche & Temperley, Singapore, 1986–88; Corporate Finance Lawyer, 1988–90, Hd, Educn and Trng, 1990–93, Allen & Overy; Dir, Professional and Business Develt, Baker & McKenzie, 1993–95; Dir, Mktg and Business Develt, Simmons & Simmons, 1995–97; Mktg Dir, Tax and Legal Services, EMEA, PricewaterhouseCoopers, 1997–99; Global Marketing Director: Ernst & Young, 1999–2002; Linklaters, 2002–05; Man. Dir, Manteion Ltd, 2005–. Mem., W Sussex CC, 2005–07 (Chm., Health Overview and Scrutiny Cttee). PPS, BIS, 2015–. Founder and Chair, All Party Parly Gp for Micro Businesses, 2011–15; Chair, All Party Parly Gp for Small Businesses, 2015. Sec., Bolney Br., Arundel and S Downs Cons. Assoc., 2003. Member: Cttee, Nat. Legal Educn and Trng Gp, 1990–94 (Chm., 1990–94); Lord Chancellor's Adv. Gp on Legal Educn, 1992–93; Cttee, Nat. Professional Services Mktg Gp, 1994–97; wkg party to develop personal mgt standards, Law Soc., 1994–95; Bd, Eur. Mentoring and Coaching Council, 2008–09; Work and Pensions Select Cttee, 2012–15; Specialist Assessor, Law, HEFC, 1992–93. Mem. Bd of Studies, Oxford Inst. of Legal Practice, 1990–2004; non-exec. Mem. Bd, Southampton Univ., 2005–06. Associate Gov., Rydon Sch., 2010–; former Gov., Newton Abbot Coll. FRSA 2000; FCIM 2002; MInstD 2001. *Address:* Templer House, Sandford Orleigh, Newton Abbot, Devon TQ12 2SQ. *T:* (01626) 368277. *E:* annemarie@annemariemorris.co.uk.

MORRIS, Anthony Paul; QC 1991; **His Honour Judge Anthony Morris;** a Senior Circuit Judge, since 2003; *b* 6 March 1948; *s* of late Isaac Morris Morris and Margaret Miriam Morris; *m* 1975, Jennie Foley; two *s*. *Educ:* Manchester Grammar Sch.; Keble Coll., Oxford (MA). Called to the Bar, Gray's Inn, 1970, Bencher, 2001; practising on Northern Circuit, 1970–2003. A Recorder of the Crown Court, 1988–2003. *Recreations:* travel, the arts, tennis, golf, bridge, Manchester United FC, Aldeburgh. *Address:* Central Criminal Court, Old Bailey, EC4M 7EH. *Clubs:* Garrick; Old Bailey Judges' Golfing Society.

MORRIS, Air Marshal Sir (Arnold) Alec; *see* Morris, Air Marshal Sir Alec.

MORRIS, Carolyn; *see* Quinn, C.

MORRIS, Air Vice Marshal Christopher Brian, CB 2012; QHS 2006; Chief of Staff Health (HQ Air Command), and Director General Medical Services, Royal Air Force, 2009–12; *b* Wrexham, 5 March 1952; *s* of Richard L. Morris and Patricia Morris; *m* 1975, Linda Goodman; two *s*. *Educ:* Hurstpierpoint Coll.; King's Coll. London; Westminster Med. Sch. (MB BS 1975); Birmingham Univ. (MMedSci 1995). DAvMed 1986; FFOM 2003. Joined RAF, 1972; med. cadet, 1972–75; SMO, RAF Laarbruch, 1988–91; Comd Flight Med. Officer (HQ Strike Comd), 1991–94; OC, Aviation Medicine Trng Centre, 1995–99; Asst Dir, Med. Policy (Surgeon Gen.'s Dept), 2000–03; ACOS Health, HQ Personnel and Trng Comd, then HQ Air Comd, 2006–09. OStJ 2007. Cdre, Fisher Owners Assoc. Pres., RAF Medical Bd, 2003–06. Richard Fox Linton Meml Prize, RAF Medical Services, 1993. *Recreation:* offshore sailing. *Address:* Cornwall. *Club:* Royal Air Force.

MORRIS, Rev. Dr Colin; writer and broadcaster; *b* 13 Jan. 1929; *o s* of Daniel Manley Morris and Mary Alice Morris, Bolton, Lancs; *m* 1985, Sandy James. *Educ:* Bolton County Grammar Sch.; Lincoln and Nuffield Colls, Oxford; Univ. of Manchester. Served RM, 1947–49. Student, Nuffield Coll., Oxford, 1953–56; ordained into Methodist ministry, 1956; Missionary, Northern Rhodesia, 1956–60; President: United Church of Central Africa, 1960–64; United Church of Zambia, 1965–68; Minister of Wesley's Chapel, London, 1969–73; Gen. Sec., Overseas Div., Methodist Church, 1973–78; Pres. of the Methodist Conference, 1976–77; Hd of Religious Programmes, BBC TV, 1978–84; Dep. Hd, 1978–79, Hd, 1979–87, Religious Broadcasting, BBC; Special Adviser to Dir-Gen., BBC, 1986–87; Controller, BBC NI, 1987–90; Dir, Centre for Religious Communication, Westminster Coll., Oxford, 1991–93. Chairman: Community and Race Relations Unit, BCC, 1974–76; Bd of Trustees, Refugee Legal Centre, 1993–95; Mem., Lord Chancellor's Adv. Cttee on Legal Educn and Conduct, 1991–94. Presenter, Sunday, BBC Radio 4, 1994–97. Lectures: Willson, Univ. of Nebraska, 1968; Cousland, Univ. of Toronto, 1972; Voigt, S Illinois Conf. United Methodist Church, 1973; Hickman, Duke University, North Carolina, 1974; Palmer, Pacific NW Univ., 1976; Heslington, Univ. of York, 1983; Hibbert, BBC Radio 4, 1986; William Barclay Meml, Glasgow, 1986; Univ. of Ulster Convocation, 1988; St Cuthbert's, Edinburgh, 1990; Studdert-Kennedy, Univ. of Leeds, 1994; Coll. of Preachers, 1995; Randall Preaching, Toronto, 1996; Hanna-Loane Lecture, 50th Anniversary Ulster Surgeon's Club, 2005. Select Preacher, Univ. of Cambridge, 1975, 2009, Oxford, 1976. Holds several hon. degrees. Officer-Companion, Order of Freedom (Zambia), 1966. *Publications:* Black Government (with President K. D. Kaunda), 1960; Hour After Midnight, 1961; Out of Africa's Crucible, 1961; End of the Missionary, 1961; Church and Challenge in a New Africa, 1965; Humanist in Africa (with President K. D. Kaunda), 1966; Include Me Out, 1968; Unyoung, Uncoloured, Unpoor, 1969; What the Papers Didn't Say, 1971; Mankind My Church, 1971; The Hammer of the Lord, 1973; Epistles to the Apostle, 1974; The Word and the Words, 1975; Bugles in the Afternoon, 1977; Get Through Till Nightfall, 1979; (ed) Kaunda on Violence, 1980; God-in-a-Box: Christian strategy in the TV age, 1984; A Week in the Life of God, 1986; Drawing the Line: taste and standards in BBC programmes, 1987; Starting from Scratch, 1990; Let God be God: TV sermons, 1990; Wrestling with an Angel, 1990; Start Your Own Religion, 1992; Raising the Dead: the art of preacher as public performer, 1996; God in the Shower: thoughts for the day, 2002; Bible Reflections Round the Year, 2005; Thing Shaken, Things Unshaken: reflections on faith and terror, 2006; Snapshots: episodes in a life, 2007; Just Round the Corner: glimpses of the afterlife, 2014; *relevant publications:* Spark in the Stubble, by T. L. Charlton, 1969; Bullet-Point Belief: the best of Colin Morris, by Rosemary Foxcroft, 2007. *Recreations:* writing, walking, music. *Address:* Tile Cottage, 8 Houndean Rise, Lewes, E Sussex BN7 1EG. *E:* colinmmorris@aol.com.

MORRIS, Rev. Prof. Colin, FBA 2007; Professor of Medieval History, University of Southampton, 1969–92, now Emeritus; *b* 16 Sept. 1928; *s* of Henry Morris and Catherine Victoria Morris; *m* 1956, Brenda Gale; two *s* one *d*. *Educ:* Queen's College, Oxford (BA Modern Hist. 1st cl. 1948; BA Theol. 1st cl. 1951; Hon. Fellow, 2009); Lincoln Theol Coll. Ordained deacon, 1953, priest, 1954. Fellow and Chaplain, Pembroke Coll., Oxford, 1953–69, now Emeritus. Pres., Ecclesiastical Hist. Soc., 1998–2000. FRHistS 1970. *Publications:* The Discovery of the Individual, 1972; The Papal Monarchy: the Western Church from 1050 to 1250, 1989; (ed with P. Roberts) Pilgrimage: the English experience from Becket to Bunyan, 2002; The Sepulchre of Christ and the Medieval West, 2005. *Recreations:* travel, liturgy, family and friends. *Address:* 83 James Weld Close, Southampton SO15 2YA. *T:* (023) 8033 3944. *E:* pr.colin.morris@gmail.com.

MORRIS, David; *see* Morris, William D.

MORRIS, David; MP (C) Morecambe and Lunesdale, since 2010; *b* Leigh, Lancs, 3 Jan. 1966; *s* of Captain Alan Lewis Morris and Vera White; *m* (marr. diss.); two *s*. *Educ:* St Andrew's Sch., Nassau. Company director, 1990–2010. Contested (C): Blackpool S, 2001; Carmarthen W and S Pembrokeshire, 2005. Mem., Select Cttee on Sci. and Technol., 2010–14, on Political and Constitutional Reform, 2014–15. Chairman, All-Party Groups: Bahamas, 2014–; Bovine TB, 2014–; Coastal and Marine, 2014–. UK Govt Self Employment Ambassador, 2014–. Chm., Cons. Friends of Nuclear Energy, 2010–. Lt Comdr, RN, Parly Armed Forces Scheme, 2010. Master Mariner, 2014. *Recreations:* music, classic cars. *Address:* House of Commons, SW1A 0AA. *T:* (020) 7219 7234.

MORRIS, His Honour David Griffiths; a Circuit Judge, 1994–2012; *b* 10 March 1940; *s* of Thomas Griffiths Morris and Margaret Eileen Morris; *m* 1971, Carolyn Mary (*née* Miller); one *s* one *d*. *Educ:* Abingdon Sch.; King's Coll., Univ. of London (LLB Hons). Called to the Bar, Lincoln's Inn, 1965, Bencher, 1999. Pupillage in London (Temple and Lincoln's Inn), 1965–67; Tenant in London Chambers (Temple), 1967–72; Tenant in Cardiff Chambers, 1972–94; Asst Recorder, 1979–84; Local Junior for Cardiff Bar, 1981–87; Head of Chambers, 1984–94; a Recorder, 1984–94. Judicial Member: Gwent Probation Bd, 1998–; Gwent Courts Bd, 2004–07; SE Wales Courts Bd, 2007–. Founder Member: Llantwit Major Round Table and 41 Clubs; Llantwit Major Rotary Club (Pres., 1984–85); Llanmaes Community Council, 1982–84; Mem., Bd of Trustees, Torfaen Mus. Trust, 2011–. *Recreations:* Rugby Union football, cricket, swimming, theatre, reading, gardening, family. *Address:* Bryn Hafren, Newport Road, Castleton, Cardiff CF3 2UN. *T:* (01633) 681244. *Clubs:* Cardiff and County, United Services Mess (Cardiff); Pontypool Rugby Football (Past Pres.).

MORRIS, David Richard, CEng, FIMechE; Chairman, Northern Electric plc, 1989–97; *b* 25 July 1934; *s* of Frederick George Morris and Marjorie Amy (*née* Brown); *m* 1961, (Ann) Carole Birch; two *s* one *d*. *Educ:* Imperial College (BScEng). ACGI. Graduate Engrg apprenticeship, D. Napier & Son, Divl Chief Develt Engr and Gen. Manager, 1956–69, English Electric; Divl Gen. Manager and Divl Dir, General Electric Co., 1969–75; Subsid. Co. Man. Dir, Sears Holdings plc, 1975–80; Delta Group plc: Divl Man. Dir, 1980–84; Gp Exec. Dir, 1984–88. FRSA. *Recreations:* sailing, golf, tennis, gardening.

MORRIS, Capt. David Simon, RN; Clerk to the Salters' Company, since 2006; *b* 4 Feb. 1951; *s* of late Basil Charles Owen Morris and Alice Joan Morris (*née* Crump); *m* 1987, Susie Turner; two *d*. *Educ:* Sedbergh Sch.; BRNC, Dartmouth. Joined RN, 1971; specialised in submarines and navigation; served in HM Ships Albion, Norfolk, Olympus, Repulse, Resolution, Osiris, Ocelot, 1972–81; Flag Lieut to Flag Officer Submarines, 1978–80; qualified Submarine Commnd, 1983; Exec. Officer, HMS Churchill, 1983–85; Defence Intelligence, MoD, 1985–87; commanded: HMS Onyx, 1987–89; HMS Revenge, 1991; HMS Renown (P), 1992–94; Dir, UK Strategic Targeting Centre, 1994–96; Cabinet Office, 1996–99; Dep. ACOS (Progs and Policy) to C-in-C Fleet, 1999–2001; Asst Dir, Directorate of Naval Ops and Strategic Plans, MoD, 2001–04; Navy Job Evaluation Judge, 2004–05. FCMI 2004; MNI 2004–09. Technical Deleg. (Alpine, Constituent), 1995–; Chairman: Combined Services Winter Sports Assoc. (Alpine), 1999–2004; British Alpine Racing Ski Club, 2008–10; Dir, Kandahar Ski Club, 2001–06. Freeman, Master Mariners' Co., 2004–11. Friend of RN Submarine Mus., 1999–. *Recreations:* ski-ing, vintage cars and boats, sailing, tennis, countryside. *Address:* Salters' Hall, 4 Fore Street, EC2Y 5DE. *T:* (020) 7588 5216, *Fax:* (020) 7638 3679. *E:* clerk@salters.co.uk. *Clubs:* Hurlingham, Royal Navy of 1765 and 1785; Kandahar Ski.

MORRIS, Prof. David William, PhD; FRAgS; sheep farmer, since 1983; agricultural consultant, since 1986; *b* 7 Dec. 1937; *s* of late David William Morris and Mary Olwen Ann Lewis; *m* 1966, Cynthia Cooper; one *s* one *d*. *Educ:* Ardwyn Grammar Sch.; UC of Wales (BSc Agric.); Univ. of Newcastle upon Tyne (PhD). FRAgS 1974. Develt Officer, Agric. Div., ICI, 1963–64; Asst Dir, Cockle Park Exptl Farm, Newcastle upon Tyne Univ., 1964–68; Farms Manager for Marquis of Lansdowne, Bowood, Wilts, 1968–70; Principal, Welsh Agricl Coll., Aberystwyth, 1970–83; Prof. of Agric., UC Wales, Aberystwyth, 1979–83. Churchill Fellowship, 1973. Chm., Lleyn Sheep Soc., 2005–07 (Treas., 2010–14); Hon. Life Mem., British Charollais Sheep Soc., 2001. John Gittins Meml Award, Royal Welsh Agricultural Soc., 2014. *Publications:* Practical Milk Production, 1976, 3rd edn 1977; (with M. M. Cooper) Grass Farming, 5th edn 1984. *Recreation:* farming. *Address:* Yr Ostrey, St Clears, Carmarthen, Carmarthenshire SA33 4AJ. *T:* (01994) 230240.

See also Baron Morris of Aberavon.

MORRIS, Sir Derek (James), Kt 2003; DPhil; Provost of Oriel College, Oxford, 2004–13 (Fellow and Tutor in Economics, 1970–98, now Hon. Fellow); *b* 23 Dec. 1945; *s* of Denis William and Olive Margaret Morris; *m* 1975, Susan Mary Whittles; two *s*. *Educ:* Harrow County Grammar Sch.; St Edmund Hall, Oxford (MA; Hon. Fellow); Nuffield Coll., Oxford; DPhil. Research Fellow, Centre for Business and Industrial Studies, Warwick Univ., 1969–70; Tutor and Sen. Tutor, Oxford University Business Summer Sch., 1970–78; Visiting Fellow, Oxford Centre for Management Studies, 1977–81; Economic Dir, Nat. Economic Develt Office, 1981–84; Oxford University: Sir John Hicks Res. Fellow, 1991–92; Chm., Social Studies Bd, 1993–94; Reader in Econs, 1996–98; Chm., Competition (formerly Monopolies and Mergers) Commn, 1998–2004 (Mem., 1991–2004; Dep. Chm., 1995–98). Vis. Lectr, Univ. of Calif, Irvine, 1986–87. Mem., Cttee of Inquiry into the Future of Cowley, 1990; Chm., Morris Review of Actuarial Profession, 2004–05; Mem., Cttee on Standards in Public Life, 2008–14. Gov., NIESR, 1997–. Chm., Oxford Economic Forecasting, 1984–98; Dir, Oxford China Economics Ltd, 1993–97; non-exec. Dir, then Chm., Lucida plc, 2009–14; Sen. Consultant, Frontier Economics, 2009–. Chm., Trustees, OUP Pension Fund, 2006–. Member Editorial Board: Oxford Economic Papers, 1984–97; Annual Register of World Events, 1985–97; Asst Editor, Jl of Industrial Economics, 1984–87; Associate Editor, Oxford Review of Economic Policy, 1985–98. Hon. Fellow, TCD, 2004. Hon. DCL: UC Dublin, 2004; UEA, 2005; Hon. DSc Cranfield, 2006. *Publications:* (ed) The Economic System in the UK, 1977, 3rd edn 1985; (with D. Hay) Industrial Economics, Theory and Evidence, 1979, 2nd edn 1991; (with D. Hay) Unquoted Companies, 1984; (ed jtly) Strategic Behaviour and Industrial Competition, 1987; (with D. Hay) State-Owned Enterprises and Economic Reform in China 1979–87, 1993; articles on unemployment, trade policy and performance, productivity growth, industrial policy, macroeconomic policy, the Chinese economy, exchange rates, profitability, the stock market and corporate control. *Recreations:* ski-ing, Rugby, reading history. *Clubs:* Reform, Oxford and Cambridge.

MORRIS, Desmond John, DPhil; writer on animal and human behaviour; artist; *b* 24 Jan. 1928; *s* of late Capt. Harry Howe Morris and Dorothy Marjorie Fuller Morris (*née* Hunt); *m* 1952, Ramona Baulch; one *s*. *Educ:* Dauntsey's Sch.; Birmingham Univ. (BSc); Magdalen Coll., Oxford (DPhil). Postdoctoral research in Animal Behaviour, Dept of Zoology, Oxford Univ., 1954–56; Head of Granada TV and Film Unit at Zool Soc. of London, 1956–59; Curator of Mammals, Zool Soc. of London, 1959–67; Dir, Inst. of Contemp. Arts, London, 1967–68; Research Fellow, Wolfson Coll., Oxford, 1973–81. Chm. of TV programmes: Zootime (weekly), 1956–67; Life (fortnightly), 1965–68; TV series: The Human Race, 1982; The Animals Roadshow, 1987–89; The Animal Contract, 1990; Animal Country, 1991–95; The Human Animal, 1994; The Human Sexes, 1997. Solo exhibitions of paintings in England, France, Belgium, Holland, Spain, Portugal and USA, 1948–; works in public collections in England, Scotland, Italy, Israel and USA. Hon. FLS 2006; Hon. FZS 2012. Hon. DSc Reading, 1998. *Publications:* (Jt Ed.) International Zoo Yearbook, 1959–62; The Biology of Art, 1962; The Mammals: A Guide to the Living Species, 1965; (with Ramona Morris) Men and Snakes, 1965; (with Ramona Morris) Men and Apes, 1966; (with Ramona Morris) Men and Pandas, 1966; The Naked Ape, 1967; (ed) Primate Ethology, 1967; The Human Zoo, 1969; Patterns of Reproductive Behaviour, 1970; Intimate Behaviour, 1971; Manwatching: a field guide to human behaviour, 1977; (jtly) Gestures: their origins and distribution, 1979; Animal Days (autobiog.), 1979; The Giant Panda, 1981; The Soccer Tribe, 1981; Inrock (novel), 1983; The Book of Ages, 1983; The Art of Ancient Cyprus, 1985; Bodywatching: a field guide to the human species, 1985; The Illustrated Naked Ape, 1986; Catwatching, 1986; Dogwatching, 1986; The Secret Surrealist, 1987; Catlore, 1987; The Human Nest-builders, 1988; The Animals Roadshow, 1988; Horsewatching, 1988; The Animal Contract, 1990; Animal-Watching, 1990; Babywatching, 1991; Christmas Watching, 1992; The World of Animals, 1993; The Human Animal, 1994; The Naked Ape Trilogy, 1994; Bodytalk: a world guide to gestures, 1994; The Illustrated Catwatching, 1994; Illustrated Babywatching, 1995; Catworld: a feline encyclopedia, 1996; Illustrated Dogwatching, 1996; The Human Sexes, 1997; Illustrated Horsewatching, 1998; Cool Cats: the 100 cat breeds of the world, 1999; Body Guards: protective amulets and charms, 1999; The Naked Eye: travels in search of the human species, 2000; Dogs: the ultimate dictionary of over 1,000 dog breeds, 2001; Peoplewatching, 2002; The Nature of Happiness, 2004; The Naked Woman: a study of the female body, 2004; Watching: encounters with humans and other animals, 2006; The Naked Man: a study of the male body, 2008; Baby: the amazing story of the first two years of life, 2008; (with S. Parker) Planet Ape, 2009; Owl, 2009; Child: how children think, learn and grow in the early years, 2010; Monkey, 2013; The Artistic Ape: three million years of art, 2013; Leopard, 2014; Headworks, 2014; Bison, 2015; numerous papers in zoological jls. *Recreations:* book-collecting, archæology. *Address:* c/o Jonathan Cape, Random Century House, 20 Vauxhall Bridge Road, SW1V 2SA. *W:* desmond-morris.com.

MORRIS, Desmond Victor; HM Diplomatic Service, retired; *b* 26 June 1926; *s* of late John Walter Morris and Bessie (*née* Mason); *m* 1st, 1951, Peggy Iris Mumford; two *d*; 2nd, 1961, Patricia Irene Ward, *d* of Charles Daniel and Emma Camwell; one *d*. *Educ:* Portsmouth Southern Secondary Sch. for Boys; Durham Univ. Served RAF, 1945–48. Joined HM Diplomatic Service, 1948; served at Seattle, Budapest, Saigon, Addis Ababa, Berne, Ankara and Pretoria; Dep. High Comr, Georgetown, 1973–78; Dep. Head of Accommodation and Services Dept, FCO, 1979–82; Consul-Gen. and Counsellor (Administration), Washington, 1982–86.

MORRIS, Dr Elizabeth Mary, OBE 2000; PhD; Senior Associate, Scott Polar Research Institute, since 2006; Professor of Ice Physics, University of Reading; *b* London, 7 Sept. 1946; *d* of James Creed Morris and Jessie Margaret Morris. *Educ:* Univ. of Bristol (BSc Physics; PhD Physics 1972). Institute of Hydrology: Higher SO, 1975–76; Sen. SO, 1976–80; Principal SO, 1980–86; British Antarctic Survey: Hd, Ice and Climate Div., 1986–99; Res. Activities Co-ordinator, 1999–2000; Arctic Sci. Advr, NERC, 2000–06 (on secondment). Vis. Prof., Earth Systems Sci. Centre, Univ. of Reading, 1996–2010. President: Internat. Commn on Snow and Ice, 1995–2001; Internat. Glaciological Soc., 2002–05. Hon. Dr Bristol, 2015. Polar Medal, 2003. *Publications:* contrib. papers to learned jls on glacier flow, snow physics, boundary layer meteorology and hydrology. *Recreations:* climbing, communal living. *Address:* Scott Polar Research Institute, University of Cambridge, Lensfield Road, Cambridge CB2 1ER. *T:* (01223) 336568. *E:* emm36@cam.ac.uk. *Clubs:* Cambridge Climbing and Caving; Austrian Alpine.

MORRIS, Frances Mary; Director of Collection (formerly Head of Collections), International Art, Tate, since 2007; *b* London, 13 Jan. 1959; *d* of Alan Croft Faulkner Morris and Elizabeth Villar; *m* 1989, Martin Caiger-Smith; two *s* one *d*. *Educ:* King's Coll., Cambridge (BA 1st cl. 1982); Courtauld Inst. of Art (MA Hist. of Art 1983). Curator, Tate Gall., 1987–97; Art Prog. Curator, Tate Gall. of Modern Art, 1997–2000; Hd of Displays, and Curator, Modern and Contemp. Art, Tate Modern, 2000–07. Mem., Internat. Cttee for Mus and Collections of Modern Art, ICOM, 2000–. *Publications:* Paris Post War: art and existentialism, 1993; (with S. Morgan) Rites of Passage, 1995; (with R. Flood) Zero to Infinity: Arte Povera 1962–72, 2001; (with Christopher Green) Jungles in Paris, 2005; Tate Modern: the handbook, 2006; Louise Bourgeois, 2007; Yayoi Kusama, 2012. *Recreations:* sailing, walking. *Address:* 35 Aldebert Terrace, SW8 1BH. *T:* (020) 7735 2459. *E:* frances.morris@tate.org.uk.

MORRIS, Hon. Frederick Reginald; President of the High Court, Republic of Ireland, 1998–2001; *b* 1 Dec. 1929; *s* of Michael Archdale Morris and Mary Archdale Morris (*née* Guiry); *m* 1965, Valerie Rose Farrell; two *d*. *Educ:* Glenstall Abbey Sch.; University Coll., Dublin; King's Inns, Dublin. Called to the Irish Bar, 1959 (Bencher, 1990), Inner Bar, 1973, Hon. Bencher, King's Inns, 2001; called to the Bar, Middle Temple, 1969, Hon. Bencher, 1999; Judge, High Court in Ireland, 1990–98; Mem., Council of State, 1998–2001. Chm., Tribunal of Inquiry into allegations of misconduct by mems of An Garda Siochana. Trustee, Acad. of Eur. Law, Trier. Freeman, City of Waterford, 1963. *Recreations:* sailing, golf, Rugby. *Address:* 17 Leeson Village, Upper Leeson Street, Dublin 4, Republic of Ireland; Four Courts, Dublin 7, Republic of Ireland. *Clubs:* Royal Irish Yacht (Dun Laoghaire); Milltown Golf (Dublin), Blainroe Golf (Co. Wicklow); University College Dublin Rugby.

MORRIS, Gareth; *see* Morris, John G.

MORRIS, Prof. Gareth Alun, DPhil; FRS 2014; Professor of Physical Chemistry, University of Manchester, since 1998; *b* Harrogate, 6 July 1954; *s* of Mervyn Morris and Margaret Alice Morris (*née* Burley); *m* 1983, Mary Isabella Ayre Care; two *d*. *Educ:* Royal Grammar Sch., Newcastle upon Tyne; Magdalen Coll., Oxford (MA Nat. Sci.; DPhil 1978). CChem 1986; MRSC 1986. Fellow, Magdalen Coll., Oxford, 1978–81; Izaak Walton Killam Postdoctoral Res. Fellow, Univ. of British Columbia (on leave of absence), 1978–79; Lectr, 1982–89, Reader, 1989–97, in Physical Chem., Univ. of Manchester. Leverhulme Res. Fellow, 1996–97; Vis. Prof., Univ. Pierre et Marie Curie, 2010. *Publications:* approx. 210 articles in learned jls, book chapters. *Recreations:* literature, music (especially guitar and lute), allotments, birdwatching. *Address:* School of Chemistry, University of Manchester, Oxford Road, Manchester M13 9PL. *T:* (0161) 275 4665. *E:* g.a.morris@manchester.ac.uk.

MORRIS, Gillian Susan, PhD; barrister in private practice; *b* 30 March 1953; *d* of late Edgar and Eve Morris; partner, David Millett. *Educ:* Univ. of Bristol (LLB Hons 1974); Churchill Coll., Cambridge (PhD 1978). Lectr in Law, Nottingham Univ., 1977–79; Sen. Lectr in Law, Poly. of N London, 1980–88; Lectr, 1988–91, Reader, 1991–93, Prof. of Law, 1993–2003, Prof. Associate, 2003–08, Brunel Univ. Honorary Professor: Univ. of Warwick, 2007–12; UCL, 2013–. Called to the Bar, Inner Temple, 1997. Labour Law Expert for ILO, 1990–; Legal Expert Advr to EC, later EU, 1991–. Chair, Rev. Body for Nursing and Other Health Professions, later NHS Pay Rev. Body, 2005–11; Deputy Chair: Central Arbitration Cttee, 2000–; Police Negotiating Bd and Police Adv. Bd for England and Wales, 2005–14; Mem., Panel of Arbitrators, ACAS, 2007–. *Publications:* Strikes in Essential Services, 1986; (with S. Fredman) The State as Employer: labour law in the public services, 1989; (with T. J. Archer) Trade Unions, Employers and the Law, 1992, 2nd edn 1993; (with S. Deakin) Labour Law, 1995, 6th edn 2012; (with T. J. Archer) Collective Labour Law, 2000; contrib. articles to legal jls. *Recreations:* walking, swimming, travel, the arts. *Address:* Matrix Chambers, Griffin Building, Gray's Inn, WC1R 5LN. *Club:* Lansdowne.

MORRIS, Grahame; MP (Lab) Easington, since 2010; *b* 13 March 1961; *s* of late Richard and Constance Morris; *m* 1986, Michelle Hughes; two *s*. *Educ:* Peterlee Howletch Secondary Sch.; Newcastle Coll. (BTEC ONC); Newcastle Poly. (BTEC HNC Med. Lab. Scis). Med. lab. SO, Sunderland Royal Infirmary, 1980–87; researcher and constituency caseworker to John Cummings, MP, 1987–2010. Non-exec. Dir, City Hosps Sunderland NHS Trust, 1997–2005. Mem. (Lab) Easington DC, 1987–2003. Mem., Health Select Cttee, 2010–15. *Address:* House of Commons, SW1A 0AA.

MORRIS, Grant, OBE 1994; RCNC; Commercial Director, NATO Eurofighter and Tornado Management Agency, 2008–11; *b* 28 May 1951; *s* of Lesley and Gena Morris; *m* 1975, Amanda Morgan; two *s* one *d*. *Educ:* Univ. of Bath (BSc Hons Engrg 1974). RCNC 1976; CEng, MIMechE 1979; MCIPS 2003. Proj. Manager, HMS Ocean, 1994–96; MoD, 1996; HQ QMG, 1997; Internat. Relns, MoD, 1997–2000; rcds, 2001; Dir Commercial, 2002–06, Dir Gen. Commercial, 2006–07, Defence Logistics Orgn; Dir Gen. Commercial, Defence Equipment and Support, MoD, 2007–08. Member: RYA; RNSA. *Recreations:* sailing, diving, cookery, travel, ski-ing, mountain biking. *Address:* Foxborough Cottage, North Road, Bath BA2 6HW. *E:* foxys.morris@gmail.com.

MORRIS, Prof. Howard Redfern, FRS 1988; Professor of Biological Chemistry, Imperial College London, 1980–2001, now Professor Emeritus and Senior Research Investigator; Founder Chairman and Chief Scientific Officer, BIOPHARMASPEC Group, since 2014; *b* 4 Aug. 1946; *s* of Marion Elizabeth and Herbert Morris, Bolton, Lancs; *m* 1st, 1969, Lene Verny Jensen (marr. diss.); two *d*; 2nd, 1988, Maria Panico; one *s* one *d*. *Educ:* Univ. of Leeds (BSc 1967; PhD 1970). SRC Fellow, Cambridge, 1970–72; Scientific Staff, MRC Lab. of Molecular Biol., Cambridge, 1972–75; Imperial College: Lectr, Dept of Biochem., 1975–78; Reader in Protein Chem., 1978–80; Hd, Dept of Biochem., 1985–88; Chm., Div. of Life Sciences, 1985–88. Founder Chm. and Chief Scientific Officer, M-Scan Gp, analytical chem. and biochem. consultants, 1979–2010. Visiting Professor: Univ. of Virginia, 1978; Soviet Acad. of Scis, 1982; Univ. of Naples, 1983; Life Scis Div., E. I. Dupont, USA, 1984–85; Dow Lectr in Analytical Chem., Univ. of British Columbia, 1989–90. Royal Soc. Rep. to Council, Inst. of Cancer Res., 1994–98 (Council Mem. and Trustee, 1994–2004); Mem., Audit Cttee, Inst. of Cancer Res., 2013–. Mem., EMBO, 1979–. Dr *hc* Univ. of Naples, Federico II, 2005; Hon. DSc Leeds, 2015. BDH Gold Dist. Medal and Prize for Analytical Biochem., Biochem. Soc., 1978; Medal and Prize for macromolecules and polymers, RSC, 1982; Gold Medal for dist. contribs to biopolymer sequencing and mass spectroscopy, Univ. of Naples/CNR Italy, 1989; Rector's Award for Excellence in Teaching, 1996, 2001; Blaise Pascale Medal and Prize for Life Scis and Medicine, Eur. Acad. of Scis, 2010; Franklin Medal and Prize for contribs to mass spectrometer design, Inst. of Physics, 2012; Royal Medal, Royal Soc., 2014. *Publications:* (ed) Soft Ionisation Biological Mass Spectrometry, 1981; some 450 contribs to learned jls, on mass spectrometry, incl. develt of Q-TOF instrumentation, protein, glycoprotein and natural product structure elucidation, including Enkephalin (the first endorphin), SRS-A leukotrienes, interleukin 2 and calcitonin gene related peptide. *Recreations:* travel, guitar. *Address:* Department of Life Sciences, Faculty of Natural Sciences, Sir Ernst Chain Building, Imperial College London, SW7 2AZ. *T:* (020) 7594 5221, *Fax:* (020) 7225 0458. *E:* h.morris@imperial.ac.uk.

MORRIS, Ian; *see* Morris, His Honour James I.

MORRIS, Prof. Ian Matthew, PhD; Jean and Rebecca Willard Professor of Classics, Stanford University, since 1995; Fellow, Stanford Archaeology Center, since 2000; *b* Stoke-on-Trent, Staffs, 27 Jan. 1960; *s* of Noel and Barbara Morris; *m* 1989, Kathy St John. *Educ:* Alleynes Comprehensive Sch., Stone; Birmingham Univ. (BA 1st Cl. Hons 1981); Cambridge

Univ. (PhD 1985). Res. Fellow, Jesus Coll., Cambridge, 1985–87; Asst Prof., 1987–90, Associate Prof., 1990–95, Hist. and Classics, Univ. of Chicago. Dir, Stanford excavations at Monte Polizzo, Sicily, 2000–07. Guggenheim Fellow, 2002–03; Nat. Fellow, Hoover Instn, 2013–14. Corresp. FBA 2013. Hon. Dr: De Pauw, 2012; Birmingham, 2014. *Publications:* Burial and Ancient Society, 1987; Death-Ritual and Social Structure in Classical Antiquity, 1992 (trans. Greek, 1997); (ed) Classical Greece: ancient histories and modern archaeologies, 1994; (with B. Powell) A New Companion to Homer, 1997; Archaeology as Cultural History, 2000 (trans. Spanish, 2007); (with B. Powell) The Greeks: history, culture and society, 2005, 2nd edn 2009; (with J. Manning) The Ancient Economy: evidence and models, 2005; (jtly) The Cambridge Economic History of the Greco-Roman World, 2007; (with W. Scheidel) The Dynamics of Ancient Empires, 2009; Why the West Rules - for Now, 2010; The Measure of Civilization, 2013; War! What is it Good For?, 2014. *Recreations:* dogs, cats, trying not to get lost, war games. *Address:* Department of Classics, Building 110, Stanford University, Stanford, CA 94305, USA. *T:* 8313380653. *E:* imorris@stanford.edu.

MORRIS, James; *see* Morris, Jan.

MORRIS, Air Vice-Marshal James, CBE 1984 (OBE 1977); Chief Executive, Scottish Society for the Prevention of Cruelty to Animals, 1991–2001; *b* 8 July 1936; *s* of late James and Davina Swann Morris; *m* 1959, Anna Wann Provan; three *s*. *Educ:* Kirkcaldy High Sch.; Edinburgh Univ. (BSc). Commnd RAF, 1957; Flying/Staff Duties, RAF, USN, RN, 1960–72; Sqn Comdr 201 Sqdn, 1975–77; psc 1978; Station Comdr RAF Kinloss, 1981–84; Dir Operational Requirements (Air), MoD, 1986–89; AO Scotland and NI, 1989–91. President: Scottish Area, RAFA, 1991–2006; Scottish Union Jack Assoc., 1995–2006. Regl Chm., Scottish and NI Air Cadets, 1995–97. HM Comr, Queen Victoria Sch., Dunblane, 1995–2005. Mem., Governing Bd, Scottish Food Quality Certification Ltd, 1998–2001; Chm., Mgt Bd, RAF Benevolent Fund Home, Alastrean House, 2001–05. *Recreation:* golf. *Address:* 22 The Inches, Dalgety Bay, Fife KY11 9YG. *Club:* Royal Air Force.

MORRIS, James; MP (C) Halesowen and Rowley Regis, since 2010; *b* Nottingham, 4 Feb. 1967; *m* 1995, Anna Mellitt; one *s* one *d*. *Educ:* Univ. of Birmingham (BA Eng. Lit.); Univ. of Oxford (postgrad.); Cranfield Sch. of Mgt (MBA). IT/software entrepreneur, 1996–2006; Managing Director: Torington Interactive, 1996–2001; Vice-Versa Ltd, 2001–06; Chief Exec., Localis, 2008–10. *Publications:* (ed jtly) Big Ideas: building on Conservative fundamentals, 2008; (ed jtly) Million Vote Mandate, 2008; (ed jtly) Can Localism Deliver?, 2009. *Recreations:* spending time with family, cricket, theatre, music. *Address:* House of Commons, SW1A 0AA. *T:* (020) 7219 7080. *E:* james.morris.mp@parliament.uk.

MORRIS, His Honour (James) Ian; a Circuit Judge, 1994–2007; *b* 6 Feb. 1944; *s* of late Thomas Orlando Morris and Pearl Morris; *m* 1st, 1966, Maureen Burton (marr. diss. 1978); one *s* one *d*; 2nd, 1979, Christine Dyson (*d* 1980); 3rd, 1982, Alison Turner (marr. diss. 1988); 4th, 1998, Jane Boddington. *Educ:* King Henry VIII Grammar Sch., Coventry; Corpus Christi Coll., Oxford (BA Jurisp. 1967; MA 1970). Called to the Bar, Inner Temple, 1968; Asst Recorder, 1984, Recorder, 1988–94, Midland and Oxford Circuit. Chairman: Sandwell AHA Enquiry, 1979; Bromsgrove Hosp. Enquiry, 1982; RHA Counsel, Cttee of Enquiry, Legionnaires' Disease, Stafford, 1985. Founder and first Chm., Birmingham Cancer Support Gp, 1984. Executive Chairman: link-global ltd, 2007–; Warmamask Ltd, 2007–15. Exec. Chm., Bromsgrove Internat. Young Musicians' Competition, 2013–. Hon. Pres., Council of Valuation Tribunal Members in England, 2006–10. *Publications:* Just a Grain of Sand (poetry), 2004; Palmers Hill (historical fiction), 2009; contrib. Internat. Jl of Child Abuse and Neglect. *Recreations:* writing, music, walking. *Address:* c/o Worcester Crown Court, Foregate Street, Worcester.

MORRIS, Jan, CBE 1999; MA Oxon; FRSL; writer; *b* 2 Oct. 1926. Commonwealth Fellow, USA, 1953; Editorial Staff, The Times, 1951–56; Editorial Staff, The Guardian, 1957–62. Fellow, Yr Academi Gymreig; Mem., Gorsedd of Bards, Nat. Eisteddfod of Wales. Hon. FRIBA 1998. Hon. Fellow: UCW, 1992; UCNW, 2003; Hon. Student, Christ Church, Oxford, 2002. Hon. DLitt: Wales, 1993; Glamorgan, 1996. PEN Lifetime Award, 2005; Wales World-Wide Award, Ninnau and Cambria magazines, 2007. *Publications:* (as James Morris or Jan Morris): Coast to Coast, 1956; Sultan in Oman, 1957; The Market of Seleukia, 1957; Coronation Everest, 1958; South African Winter, 1958; The Hashemite Kings, 1959; Venice, 1960, 3rd edn 1993; The Upstairs Donkey, 1962 (for children); The World Bank, 1963; Cities, 1963; The Presence of Spain, 1964, rev. edn (as Spain), 1988; Oxford, 1965, 2nd edn 1986; Pax Britannica, 1968; The Great Port, 1970; Places, 1972; Heaven's Command, 1973; Conundrum, 1974; Travels, 1976; Farewell the Trumpets, 1978; The Oxford Book of Oxford, 1978; Destinations, 1980; My Favourite Stories of Wales, 1980; The Venetian Empire, 1980, 2nd edn 1988; The Small Oxford Book of Wales, 1982; A Venetian Bestiary, 1982; The Spectacle of Empire, 1982; (with Paul Wakefield) Wales, The First Place, 1982; (with Simon Winchester) Stones of Empire, 1983; The Matter of Wales, 1984, revd edn as Wales, 1998; Journeys, 1984; Among the Cities, 1985; Last Letters from Hav, 1985; (with Paul Wakefield) Scotland, The Place of Visions, 1986; Manhattan '45, 1987; Hong Kong, 1988, 3rd edn 1996; Pleasures of a Tangled Life, 1989; (with Paul Wakefield) Ireland, Your Only Place, 1990; Sydney, 1992; O Canada!, 1992; Locations, 1992; (ed) Travels with Virginia Woolf, 1993; (with Twm Morys) A Machynlleth Triad, 1994; Fisher's Face, 1995; Fifty Years of Europe: an album, 1997; Lincoln: a foreigner's quest, 1999; (with Twm Morys) Our First Leader, 2000; Trieste and the Meaning of Nowhere, 2001; A Writer's House in Wales, 2002; A Writer's World, 2003; Hav, 2006; Europe, 2006; Contact!, 2009; Ciao, Carpaccio!, 2014. *Address:* Trefan Morys, Llanystumdwy, Gwynedd, Cymru/Wales LL52 0LP. *T:* (01766) 522222. *E:* jan.morris1@yahoo.com.

MORRIS, Rev. Dr Jeremy Nigel; Master, Trinity Hall, Cambridge, since 2014; *b* London, 22 Jan. 1960; *s* of David and Diana Morris; *m* 1992, Alexandra Davidson; one *s* two *d*. *Educ:* Balliol Coll., Oxford (BA 1981; DPhil 1985); Clare Coll., Cambridge (BA 1992); Westcott House, Cambridge (Cert. of Theol. for Ministry 1993). Scholarship Officer, Assoc. of Commonwealth Univs, 1985–87; Sen. Admin. Officer, LSE, 1987–90; Curate, St Mary's, Battersea, 1993–96; Vice-Principal, Westcott House, Cambridge, 1996–2001; Dean: Trinity Hall, Cambridge, 2001–10; of Chapel, King's Coll., Cambridge, 2010–14. *Publications:* Religion and Urban Change: Croydon 1840–1914, 1993; (ed with N. Sagovsky) The Unity We Have and the Unity We Seek, 2003; F. D. Maurice and the Crisis of Christian Authority, 2005; The Church in the Modern Age, 2007; (ed with D. Dormor) An Acceptable Sacrifice?: homosexuality and the Church, 2007; To Build Christ's Kingdom: an F. D. Maurice reader, 2007; contrib. articles to jls incl. Anglican Histl Rev., Histl Jl, Jl Ecclesiastical Hist., Theol. *Recreations:* piano, walking, historic buildings, riding. *Address:* Trinity Hall, Trinity Lane, Cambridge CB2 1TJ. *T:* (01223) 332540, *Fax:* (01223) 765157. *E:* master@trinhall.cam.ac.uk.

MORRIS, John Cameron; QC (Scot.) 1996; Sheriff of South Strathclyde, Dumfries and Galloway at Airdrie, since 1998; *b* 11 April 1952; *s* of Thomas and Louise Morris. *Educ:* Allan Glen's Sch., Glasgow; Strathclyde Univ. Solicitor, Scotland, 1976–84; admitted Advocate, Scottish Bar, 1985; called to the Bar, Inner Temple, 1990. Crown Counsel, Scotland, 1989–92. Temp. Sheriff, 1992–98; Temp. High Ct Judge, 2008–. *Recreations:* golf, music, reading. *Address:* Sheriff Court House, Graham Street, Airdrie ML6 6EE. *T:* (01236) 751121.

MORRIS, Prof. (John) Gareth, CBE 1994; FRS 1988; FRSB; FLSW; Professor of Microbiology, University of Wales, Aberystwyth, 1971–2000, now Emeritus; *b* 25 Nov. 1932; *s* of Edwin Morris and Evelyn Amanda Morris (*née* Griffiths); *m* 1962, Áine Mary Kehoe (*d* 2013); one *s* one *d*. *Educ:* Bridgend Grammar Sch.; Univ. of Leeds; Trinity Coll., Oxford. DPhil. FRSB (FIBiol 1971). Guinness Res. Fellow, Univ. of Oxford, 1957–61; Rockefeller Fellow, Univ. of Calif at Berkeley, 1959–60; Tutor in Biochem., Balliol Coll., Oxford, 1960–61; Lectr, subseq. Sen. Lectr, Univ. of Leicester, 1961–71. Vis. Associate Prof., Purdue Univ., USA, 1965. Member: UGC, 1981–86; Royal Commn on Environmental Pollution, 1991–99. FLSW 2011. *Publications:* A Biologist's Physical Chemistry, 1968, 2nd edn 1974; contribs on microbial biochemistry and physiology. *Recreations:* gardening, walking. *Address:* Cilgwyn, 16 Lôn Tyllwyd, Llanfarian, Aberystwyth, Dyfed SY23 4UH. *T:* (01970) 612502.

MORRIS, John Michael Douglas; General Secretary, 1986–99, and Company Secretary, 1990–99, Hon. Consultant, since 2000, British Boxing Board of Control; *b* 10 Aug. 1935; *s* of Charles Edward Douglas Morris and Mary Kathleen (*née* Murphy); *m* 1958, Jill Margaret Walker; two *s* two *d*. *Educ:* Towcester GS; John Fisher Sch.; Dulwich Coll. Reporter, Northampton Chronicle & Echo, 1953–60; Sports sub-editor, Evening Standard, 1960–67; Gp Sports Editor, United Newspapers, 1967–77; freelance writer and publican, 1977–79; John Morris Sports Agency, Northampton, 1979–86. Co. Sec., European Boxing Union, 1991–99; Mem., Bd of Govs, World Boxing Council, 1986–99 (Consultant, 2000–). Commissioner of the Year: World Boxing Council, 1987, 1989, 1994, and 1997; World Boxing Assoc., 1988. Pres., Nat. Schs Amateur Boxing Assoc., 2002–. Chair, Towcester and Dist Local History Soc., 2007–; Chair of Trustees, Northampton Town FC Charitable Foundn, 2009–. *Publications:* Play Better Tennis (instructional booklet), 1969; Come in No 3: biography of cricketer David Steele, 1977; Box On: biography of boxing referee Harry Gibbs, 1981. *Recreations:* amateur drama, reading, all sport. *Address:* 44 Alchester Court, Towcester, Northants NN12 6RP. *T:* (01327) 358590. *E:* john@morris2736.fsnet.co.uk.

MORRIS, Sir Keith (Elliot Hedley), KBE 1994; CMG 1988; HM Diplomatic Service, retired; *b* 24 Oct. 1934; *m* 1st, Maria del Carmen Carratala (*d* 2008); two *s* two *d*; 2nd, 2013, Maria Samuel; one step *d*. Entered Foreign Office, 1959; served Dakar, Algiers, Paris, Bogota; First Sec., FCO, 1971–76; Counsellor (Commercial), Warsaw, 1976–79; Minister-Counsellor, Mexico City, 1979–84; Head of Personnel Policy Dept, FCO, 1984–85; rcds, 1986; Minister (Commercial) and Consul-Gen., Milan, 1987–90; Ambassador to Colombia, 1990–94. Mem., Internat. Adv. Bd, Parra Rodriguez Sanin (formerly Parra, Rodriguez & Cavelier, then Rodriguez y Cavelier), Bogota, 2003–. Dir, British and Colombian Chamber of Commerce, 1999– (Chm., 1996–99). Mem., Adv. Bd, Internat. Council on Security and Devlt, 2008–. *Recreations:* history, hill walking. *Club:* Polish Hearth.

MORRIS, Kenneth; Managing Director, Nirvana Europe Ltd, since 1999; *b* 17 April 1947; *s* of Thomas and Phyllis Morris; *m* 1988, Veronica Ann Young; two *s*. *Educ:* George Stephenson Grammar Sch., West Moor, Newcastle upon Tyne. Group Accountant, Newcastle upon Tyne CBC, 1972; Management Accountant, Tyne and Wear CC, 1974; Chief Accountant, 1976, Dep. Dir of Finance, 1982, Gateshead MBC; County Treasurer, 1988, Man. Dir, 1992–99, Northumberland CC. *Recreations:* sport, reading, music. *Address:* 3 Bank Top, Earsdon, Whitley Bay, Tyne and Wear NE25 9JS. *T:* (0191) 253 4907; (office) Saville Exchange, Howard Street, North Shields, Tyne and Wear NE30 1SE. *T:* (0191) 257 1750.

MORRIS, Mali, RA 2010; artist; *b* Caernarfon, N Wales, 5 Feb. 1945; partner, Stephen Lewis. *Educ:* Univ. of Newcastle upon Tyne (BA Hons Fine Art 1968); Univ. of Reading (MFA 1970). Lectr in Painting, Sunderland Poly., 1970–72; Sessional Lectr, Dept of Fine Art, Univ. of Reading, 1975–90; Sen. Lectr (pt-time) in Painting, Chelsea Coll. of Art, London Inst., then Univ. of the Arts London, 1991–2005. Vis. Lectr at many UK college depts of fine art, 1972–90. External Examiner: Manchester Poly.; Slade Sch. of Art, 1996–99; Wimbledon Sch. of Art, 1999–2003; RCA, 2003–06; Univ. of Newcastle upon Tyne, 2012–14; Slade Sch. of Art, UCL, 2014–. Chm., Selection Panel, Jerwood Contemporary Painters, 2009; Selector and Mentor, Jerwood Painting Fellowships, 2012–13; Selection Panel, John Moores Painting Prize China, 2014. First solo exhibns, Serpentine Gall., 1977 and Ikon Gall., Birmingham, 1979; *solo exhibitions* include: Gall. Saoh, Tokyo, 2000; Spica Mus., Tokyo, 2004; Omotesando Gall., Tokyo, 2005; Robert Steele Gall., NY, 2005, 2007; Poussin Gall., London, 2005, 2008; Friends Room, Royal Acad., 2010; The Cut, Halesworth, 2011; Mostyn Gall., Llandudno, 2012; Eagle Gall., London, 2012; *group exhibitions* include: Walker Art Gall., Liverpool, 1980, 1989, 2003; Whitechapel Gall., 1977, 1983, 1985, 1986, 1988, 1992, 1994; Hayward Gall., 1980; Serpentine Gall., 1987; Barbican, 1988; Antwerp, 1997; RA Summer Show, 2008–15; Ruskin Gall., Cambridge, 2009; Brown Gall., London, 2010; Hidde van Seggelen Gall., London, 2012; Lion and Lamb Gall., London, 2012; Ikon Gall., Birmingham, 2014; Pulchri, The Hague, 2014; Pallant House, Chichester, 2014; Flowers NY, USA, 2014; Kapil Jarawala Gall., London, 2014; *work in public collections* incl. Arts Council England, British Council, Contemp. Arts Soc., Govt Art Collection, Whitworth Art Gall., Manchester, Nat. Mus. Wales, Cardiff, RA, Pallant House, Chichester, Fitzwilliam Mus., Cambridge. Trustee, Poetry London, 2013–. *Publications:* Mali Morris New Paintings, 1992; Mali Morris Paintings, 1994; The Singular and the Painterly, Mali Morris's Recent Work, 2002; Mali Morris New Paintings, 2008; (contrib.) A Sore Head, 2015; exhibn catalogues; contribs to Turps Banana, RA Mag. *W:* www.malimorris.co.uk.

MORRIS, Mark William; American choreographer, director and dancer; Founder and Artistic Director, Mark Morris Dance Group, since 1980; *b* Seattle, 29 Aug. 1956; *s* of William Morris and Maxine Crittenden Morris. Dir of Dance, Théâtre Royal de la Monnaie, 1988–91; Jt Founder, White Oak Dance Project, 1990; has choreographed more than 120 modern dance works for Mark Morris Dance Gp, including: L'Allegro, il Penseroso ed il Moderato, 1988; Dido and Aeneas (opera), 1988; The Hard Nut, 1991; Four Saints in Three Acts, 2000; V, 2001; All Fours, 2003; Mozart Dances, 2007; Socrates, 2010; choreography for other companies includes: ballets: Drink to Me Only With Thine Eyes, Amer. Ballet Theatre, 1988; Ein Herz, Paris Opera Ballet, 1990; Gong, Amer. Ballet Th., 2001; Sylvia, San Francisco Ballet, 2004; operas: Nixon in China, Houston Grand Opera, 1987; Orfée et Euridice, Seattle Opera, 1988; The Death of Klinghoffer, Théâtre de la Monnaie, 1991; The Indian Queen, ENO, 2015; dir, Die Fledermaus, Seattle Opera, 1990; dir and choreographed, Platée, Royal Opera, 1997; King Arthur, ENO, 2006. Fellow, MacArthur Foundn. *Address:* Mark Morris Dance Group, 3 Lafayette Avenue, Brooklyn, NY 11217–1415, USA.

MORRIS, Michael Clough; a District Judge (Magistrates' Courts), since 2002; *b* 28 Dec. 1946; *s* of Alfred Morris and Mary Morris, MBE, JP; *m* 1973, Hilary; three *s* one *d*. *Educ:* Calday Grange Grammar Sch., W Kirby; Univ. of Leeds (LLB Hons). Admitted solicitor, 1972; Partner, Wilkes Partnership, Birmingham, 1977–2002; Dep. Stipendiary Magistrate, 1995–2002. Birmingham Law Society: Chm., Criminal Law Cttee, 1994–2001; Dep. Vice Pres., 2001–02. Exec. Gov., Solihull Sch., 2006– (Vice-Chm., Govs, 2010–). *Recreations:* fell-walking, golf, Freemasonry. *Address:* Walsall Magistrates' Court, Stafford Street, Walsall WS2 8HA.

MORRIS, Michael Jeremy, MBE 2012; Director, Cultural Industry Ltd, since 1988; Co-Director, Artangel, since 1991; *b* 30 March 1958; *s* of Lawrence and Monica Morris; *m* 1991, Sarah Culshaw; one *s* one *d*. *Educ:* Oundle Sch.; Keble Coll., Oxford (BA Hons); British Assoc. for Counselling and Psychotherapy (Postgrad. Dip. Psychodynamic Marital and Couple Therapy 2008). Dir, Performing Arts, ICA, 1984–88. Director: Artangel Media Ltd, 2000–; Shockheaded Peter Ltd, 2000–02. Mem., Arts Adv. Panel, British Council, 1983–86. Artistic Associate: Lyric Th., 1999–2004; RNT, 2003–; Manchester Internat. Fest., 2006–. Associate Producer, Ex Machina/Robert Lepage, 1999–. Mem. Council, Tate Modern, 2005–. Trustee, Longplayer Trust, 2001–. Ambassador, School of Life, London, 2008–. Hon. Fellow, Goldsmiths, Univ. of London, 2012. Chevalier, Ordre National du Québec, 2002.

Publications: (with J. Lingwood) Off Limits: 40 Artangel projects, 2002. *Recreations:* collecting unusual stringed instruments, accordions and cookery books, table tennis. *Address:* Artangel, 31 Eyre Street Hill, EC1R 5EW. *T:* (020) 7833 4974. *E:* info@artangel.org.uk. *Club:* Two Brydges.

MORRIS, Michael Sachs; Director-General, British Insurance Brokers' Association, 1980–85; *b* 12 June 1924; *s* of late Prof. Noah Morris, MD, DSc, and Hattie Michaelis; *m* 1952, Vera Leonie, *er d* of late Paul and Lona Heller; one *s* one *d.* *Educ:* Glasgow Acad.; St Catharine's Coll., Cambridge. Wrangler, 1948. Scientific Officer, Admty Signals Estabt, 1943–46; Asst Principal, BoT, 1948; idc 1970; Under Secretary: Insurance Div., DoT, 1973; Shipping Policy Div., DoT, 1978–80. Chm., Consultative Shipping Gp, 1979–80. Mem., Barnet Health Authy, 1985–90. *Recreation:* sitting in the sun. *Address:* 5 Sunrise View, The Rise, Mill Hill, NW7 2LL. *T:* (020) 8959 0837. *Club:* Oxford and Cambridge.

MORRIS, Norma Frances, PhD; Research Fellow, University College London, since 1995; *b* 17 April 1935; *d* of Henry Albert Bevis and Lilian Eliza Bevis (*née* Flexon); *m* 1960, Samuel Francis Morris; one *s* two *d.* *Educ:* Ilford County High Sch. for Girls; University College London (BA, MA); Univ. of Twente, Netherlands (PhD). Assistante Anglaise, Paris, 1956–57; Asst Lectr, Univ. of Hull, 1959–60; MRC, 1960–95, Admin. Sec., 1989–95. Member: Nat. Biol Standards Bd, 1990–98; Gen. Chiropractic Council, 2002–04 (Chm., 1998–2002); British Acupuncture Accreditation Bd, 2004–14; Bd, Campaign for Sci. and Engrg, 2004–14; Compass Collaborative Adv. Gp, 2007–11. Trustee, Patients' Assoc., 2004–06. *Publications:* contribs to sci. policy and med. sociol. books and jls. *Recreations:* canoeing, opera, edible fungi. *Address:* Department of Science and Technology Studies, University College London, Gower Street, WC1E 6BT. *T:* (020) 7696 3703.

MORRIS, Peter Christopher West; solicitor; consultant with Sussex Defence Solicitors, 2008–14; *b* 24 Dec. 1937; *s* of C. T. R. and L. B. Morris; *m* 1st, 1959, Joy (marr. diss.); two *s* one *d*; 2nd, 1987, Terese; one step *s* two step *d.* *Educ:* Seaford Coll.; Christ's Coll., Cambridge, 1958–61 (MA, LLB). Hockey Blue, 1959, 1960, 1961; Hockey for Wales, 1962–65. National Service, 1956–58. Admitted Solicitor, 1965; Partner with Wild Hewitson & Shaw, 1967; a Recorder of the Crown Court, 1980–84; voluntary removal from Roll of Solicitors, 1982; Barrister, Middle Temple, 1982–84; company dir, 1985–93; name restored to Roll of Solicitors, 1993; Partner with Morris and Rogers, 1998–2003, with Morris and Warren, 2003–05 (Consultant, 2005–07). *Recreations:* golf, Arsenal Football Club. *Club:* Hawks (Cambridge).

MORRIS, Sir Peter (John), AC 2004; Kt 1996; FRS 1994; President, Royal College of Surgeons of England, 2001–04; Nuffield Professor of Surgery, Chairman, Department of Surgery and Director, Oxford Transplant Centre, Oxford University, 1974–2001, now Emeritus Professor; Fellow of Balliol College, 1974–2001, now Emeritus Fellow; Director, Centre for Evidence in Transplantation, Royal College of Surgeons of England and London School of Hygiene and Tropical Medicine, and Hon. Professor, London School of Hygiene and Tropical Medicine, since 2005; *b* 17 April 1934; *s* of Stanley Henry and Mary Lois Morris; *m* 1960, Mary Jocelyn Gorman; three *s* two *d.* *Educ:* Xavier Coll., Melbourne; Univ. of Melbourne (MB, BS, PhD). FRCS, FRACS, FACS, FRCP, FRCSGlas. Jun. surg. appts at St Vincent's Hosp., Melbourne, Postgrad. Med. Sch., London, Southampton Gen. Hosp. and MGH Boston, 1958–64; Research Fellow, Harvard Med. Sch., 1965–66; Asst Prof. in Surgery, Med. Coll. of Virginia, 1967; 2nd Asst in Surgery, Univ. of Melbourne, 1968–69, 1st Asst 1970–71; Reader in Surgery, Univ. of Melbourne, 1972–74. WHO Consultant, 1970–84; Cons. to Walter and Eliza Hall Inst. of Med. Res., 1969–74. Chairman: Nat. Kidney Res. Fund, 1986–90; Council, British Heart Foundn, 2003–09; Inst. of Health Scis, Oxford Univ., 2000–04; Member: MRC, 1983–87; Oxford RHA, 1988–90; Council, RCS, 1991–2004 (Vice Pres., 2000–01); Council, ICRF, 1995–2001. President: Transplantation Soc., 1984–86; British Soc. for Histocompatibility and Immunogenetics, 1993–95; Eur. Surgical Assoc., 1996–98; Internat. Surgical Soc., 2001–03; Medical Protection Soc., 2007–. Hunterian Prof., RCS, 1972. Lectr, Coll. de France, 1982; Rudin Prof., Columbia Univ., NY, 1983; USA Nat. Kidney Foundn Prof., 1986; Nimmo Vis. Prof., Univ. of Adelaide, 1993; Ho Tam Kit Hing Vis. Prof., Univ. of Hong Kong, 1994; Waltman Walters Vis. Prof., Mayo Clinic, 1994; G. T. Diethelm Prof., Univ. of Alabama, 2002; Honorary Professor: LSHTM, 2005; Warwick Univ., 2007. Lectures: Gibson, Columbia Univ., 1969; Deryl Hart, Duke Univ., 1979; Finlayson, RCPSG, 1984; Kinmonth, RCS, 1986; Loewenthal, Univ. of Sydney, 1987; Marjorie Budd, Univ. of Bristol, 1989; Champ Lyons, Univ. of Alabama, 1989; Fraser Meml, Univ. of Edinburgh, 1990; Bennett, TCD, 1991; Graham, Washington Univ., 1991; Murdoch Meml, Aberdeen Univ., 1991; Shaw, RCPE, 1991; Pybus Meml, N of Eng. Surg. Soc., 1992; Gallie, Royal Coll. of Physicians and Surgeons, Canada, 1992; Agnew, Univ. of Penn, 1993; Grey Turner, Internat. Surg. Soc., 1993; Gordon Taylor, RCSEd, 1995; Fred Belzer, Univ. of Wisconsin, 1998; Martin, Emory Univ., 1999; Ceppellini, Eur. Foundn for Immuno-Genetics, 1999; Paul Russell, Harvard Med. Sch., 2000; Dist. Lectr, Stanford Univ., 2001; Syme Oration, RACS, 2002; Rienhoff, Johns Hopkins Med. Sch., 2003; Hunterian Oration and Medal, RCS, 2005; Pehr Edman, St Vincent's Med. Res. Inst., Melbourne Univ., 2005; Bryant Stokes, Royal Perth Hosp., 2006; Dunphy, UCSF, 2008; Raj Yadav Oration, Delhi, 2008; Alexander, Univ. of Cincinnati, 2010; Halford Oration, Melbourne Univ., 2012. Pres., Med. Protection Soc., 2007–15; Governor: PPP Foundation (formerly PPP Healthcare Med. Trust), 1998–2003; Garfield Weston Foundn, 1998–; Trustee, Roche Organ Transplantation Res. Foundn, 1998–2004. Chm., Order of Australia Assoc., UK/Europe, 2008–13. Founder FMedSci 1998. Hon. Fellow: Amer. Surgical Assoc., 1982; Asian Surg. Soc., 1989; German Surgical Soc., 2003; Acad. of Med., Singapore, 2004; RCSI, 2006; Hon. FACS 1986; Hon. FRACS, 1995; Hon. FRCSE 1995; Hon. FDSRCS 2003; Hon. Mem., Amer. Soc. of Transplant Surgeons, 1993; Foreign Member: Inst. of Medicine, Nat. Acad. of Sci., 1997; Amer. Phil Soc., 2002. Hon. DSc: Hong Kong, 1999; Imperial Coll. London, 2003; Hon. DLaws Melbourne, 2012. Selwyn Smith Prize, Univ. of Melbourne, 1971; Cecil Joll Prize, RCS, 1988; Lister Medal, RCS, RCSE, Irish Coll. of Surgeons and Royal Soc., 1997; Maharshi Sushruta Award, Inst. of Kidney Disease, Ahmedabad, 2004; Neil Hamilton Fairley Medal, RCP, 2005; Medawar Prize, Transplantation Soc., 2006; Pioneer Award, Amer. Soc. of Transplant Surgeons, 2006; Internat. Surgical Soc. Prize, 2007. Editor, Transplantation, 1979–2014. *Publications:* Kidney Transplantation: principles and practice, 1979, 7th edn 2014; Tissue Transplantation, 1982; Transient Ischaemic Attacks, 1982; (ed jtly) Progress in Transplantation, vol. 1 1984, vol. 2 1985, vol. 3 1986; (ed) Oxford Textbook of Surgery, 1994, 2nd edn 2000; (ed) Transplantation Reviews, 1987–2002; numerous sci. articles and chapters in books concerned mainly with transplantation and surgery. *Recreations:* golf, tennis, cricket. *Address:* 19 Lucerne Road, Oxford OX2 7QB. *Clubs:* Oxford and Cambridge, MCC; Frilford Heath Golf (Oxford); Oxfordshire County Cricket; Melbourne Cricket (Melbourne); Barwon Heads Golf (Barwon Heads, Vic.).

MORRIS, Reyahn; *see* King, R.

MORRIS, Richard Charles; HM Diplomatic Service; Ambassador to Nepal, since 2015; *b* Worcester, 1 Nov. 1967; *s* of John and Kathleen Morris; *m* 1992, Alison Waring; two *s* one *d.* *Educ:* University Coll. of Wales, Aberystwyth (BA Hons English Lit.); Univ. of Illinois (Schol.); Aston Univ. (MBA). Entered FCO, 1990; Assistant Desk Officer: Non-Proliferation and Defence Dept, 1990–91; Cultural Relns Dept, 1991–92; temp. duty to UKMIS to UN, NY, 1993; Third Sec. (Pol), Ottawa, 1993–96; Second Sec. (Pol), Bridgetown, 1996–2000; Head: Resource Accounting and Budgeting Team, FCO, 2000–01; Assistance Gp, Consular Directorate, FCO, 2001–04; Dep. Hd of Mission and Consul Gen., Mexico City, 2005–08; Consul-Gen., Sydney and Dir-Gen., Trade and Investment, Australasia, 2008–12; Hd, Pacific Dept, FCO, 2013–15. FCIM; FRSA. *Recreations:* long distance running, reading. *Address:* Foreign and Commonwealth Office, King Charles Street, SW1A 2AH. *E:* Richard.morris@fco.gov.uk.

MORRIS, Richard Francis Maxwell; Chief Executive, Associated Board of the Royal Schools of Music, 1993–2009; *b* 11 Sept. 1944; *s* of late Maxwell Morris and Frederica (*née* Abelson); *m* 1st, 1974, Sarah Quill (marr. diss. 1978); 2nd, 1983, Marian Sperling; two *d.* *Educ:* Eton Coll.; New Coll., Oxford (MA); Coll. of Law, London; Acad. of Exec. Coaching (Dip. 2010). Solicitor, Farrer & Co., 1967–71; Legal Advr and Banker, Grindlay Brandts, 1971–75; Corporate Finance Manager, S. G. Warburg & Co., 1975–79; Hodder and Stoughton: Group Finance Dir, 1979; Man. Dir, Educnl and Acad. Publishing, 1987; Jt Man. Dir, 1989–91; Dir, The Lancet, 1986–91; Man. Dir, Edward Arnold, 1987–91. Director: Invicta Sound, 1984–91; Southern Radio, 1991–92; Magma Poetry, 2010–15; Mem., Develt Bd, Arvon Foundn, 2008–. Mem. Council, Kent Opera, 1985–90; Founder, Almaviva Opera, 1989–. Chairman: Music Educn Council, 1998–2001 (Mem. Exec. Cttee, 1995–); Henri Oguike Dance Co., 2009–12; Dep. Chm., Steering Bd, GLA Music Educn Prog., 2010–; Co-Founder and Vice-Chm., Mayor of London's Fund for Young Musicians, 2011–. Trustee: Council for Dance Educn and Trng, 1999–2005; Kent Music (formerly Kent Music Sch.), 2001–14; Yehudi Menuhin Sch., 2004– (Dep. Chm., 2010–11; Chm., 2011–); Music Preserved, 2010–14; Music Mark, 2014–. Hon. RCM 1994; Hon. RNCM 2001; Hon. FRAM 2007. Music Teacher Lifetime Achievement Award, 2015. *Recreations:* music, poetry, visual arts, golf. *Address:* Holdfast House, Edenbridge, Kent TN8 6SJ. *T:* (01732) 862439. *Club:* Athenæum.

MORRIS, Prof. Richard Graham Michael, CBE 2007; FRS 1997; Professor, since 1993, Royal Society Wolfson Professor, since 2006, of Neuroscience, and Director, Centre for Cognitive and Neural Systems, since 2005, Edinburgh University (Chairman, Department of Neuroscience, 1998–2002); Head, Neuroscience and Mental Health, Wellcome Trust, 2007–10 (Senior Neuroscience Adviser, 2010); *b* 27 June 1948; *s* of Robert Walter and Edith Mary Morris; *m* 1985, Hilary Ann Lewis (marr. diss. 2011); two *d*; partner, Mónica Muñoz-Lopez; one *s.* *Educ:* Trinity Hall, Cambridge (BA 1969; MA 1971); Univ. of Sussex (DPhil 1973). FRSE 1994. Addison Wheeler Fellow, Univ. of Durham, 1973–75; BM (Nat. History), 1975–76; BBC Science and Features Dept, 1977; Lectr, Univ. of St Andrews, 1977–86; Reader, Dept of Pharmacology, Univ. of Edinburgh, 1986–93. Visiting Professor: MIT, 1991; Nat. Centre for Biol Scis, Bangalore. Royal Society Leverhulme Fellow, 1996; Gatsby Res. Fellow, 1997. Lectures: Lansdown, Univ. of Victoria, BC, 1994; Segerfalk, Univ. of Lund, 1995; Swammerdam, 1996, Frijda, 2004, Netherlands Royal Acad.; Decade of the Brain, BNA, 1998; Feigen, Stanford Univ., 1998; Henry Dryerre Prize, RSE, 1998; Jerzy Konorski, Gdansk, 1999; Zotterman (and medal), Swedish Physiol. Soc., 1999; American Med. Alumnus, St Andrews Univ., 2003; Craik, Univ. of Cambridge, 2004; Presidential, Soc. for Neurosci., 2009; Indian Inst. of Science, Bangalore, 2012; Kavli Prize Ceremony, Oslo, 2014; Plenary, British Neurosci. Assoc., 2015. Invited Lectr, Peking Univ. and Chinese Nat. Acad. of Sci., Beijing, 2001, 2002. Member: Neuroscis Grants Cttee, MRC, 1981–85; Neuroscis and Mental Health Bd, MRC, 1993–97; Innovation Bd, MRC, 1997–2000; Strategy Develt Gp, MRC, 2000–04; Scottish Sci. Adv. Council, 2004–06; President's Adv. Gp, Weizmann Inst., Israel; Bd of Rev. Eds, SCIENCE Mag., 2007–. Member, Scientific Advisory Board: Alzheimer's Res. Trust; RIKEN Brain Scis Inst., Japan; MPI Martinsried, Germany; Picower Inst., MIT; Branco Weiss Sci. in Soc. Fellowship, Switzerland; Shanghai Inst. for Neurosci. Chm., Brain Res. Assoc., 1990–94; Guarantor of Brain; Hon. Sec., Exptl Psychol. Soc., 1985–89; Pres., Fedn of European Neurosci. Socs, 2006–08. Chm., Univ. Res. Fellowships Cttee B, 2011–14, Hooke Cttee, 2013–, Royal Soc. Mem., RYA. Founder FMedSci 1998; Foreign Fellow: Amer. Acad. of Arts and Scis, 2004; Amer. Assoc. for the Advancement of Sci., 2007; Norwegian Acad. of Sci. and Letters, 2007. Outstanding Achievement in Neurosci., British Neurosci. Assoc., 2002; EJN Prize, Fedn of Eur. Neuroscis, 2004; Feldberg Prize, Feldberg Foundn, 2006; Santiago-Grisolia Award, Valencia, 2007; Fondation IPSEN, Neuronal Plasticity Prize, 2013; Royal Medal, RSE, 2014. *Publications:* (ed) Parallel Distributed Processing, 1988; The Hippocampus Book, 2007; contrib. to academic jls and books. *Recreation:* sailing. *Address:* Centre for Cognitive and Neural Systems, University of Edinburgh College of Medicine, 1 George Square, Edinburgh EH8 9JZ. *T:* (0131) 650 3520. *E:* r.g.m.morris@ed.ac.uk.

MORRIS, Richard Keith, OBE 2003; FSA; archaeologist, writer, composer; Research Professor, University of Huddersfield, since 2010; *b* 8 Oct. 1947; *s* of John Richard Morris and Elsie Myra (*née* Wearne); *m* 1972, Jane Whiteley; two *s* one *d.* *Educ:* Denstone Coll., Staffs; Pembroke Coll., Oxford (MA); Univ. of York (BPhil). FSA 1982; MIFA 1986, Hon. MIFA 2001. Musician, 1971–72; Res. Assistant, York Minster Archaeol. Office, 1972–75; Churches Officer, 1975–77, Res. Officer, 1978–88, Council for British Archaeol.; Hon. Lectr, Sch. of History, Univ. of Leeds, 1986–88; Lectr, Dept of Archaeol., Univ. of York, 1988–91; Dir, Council for British Archaeology, 1991–99 (Hon. Vice-Pres., 2001); Dir, Inst. for Medieval Studies, 2003–10, Prof. for Research in the Historic Envmt, 2007–10, Univ. of Leeds. Comr, English Heritage, 1996–2005; Chairman: Ancient Monuments Adv. Cttee for England, 1996–2000; Historic Settlements and Landscapes Adv. Cttee, 2001–03; Bede's World, 2001–08; English Heritage Adv. Cttee, 2003–05; Heritage Lottery Fund Expert Panel, 2005–11; Blackden Trust, 2005–. Trustee: Nat. Heritage Meml Fund, 2011–; York Archaeological Trust, 2011–. Pres., Soc. for Church Archaeol., 2001–05. Hon. Vis. Prof., Univ. of York, 1995. Frend Medal, Soc. of Antiquaries of London, 1992. *Publications:* Cathedrals and Abbeys of England and Wales, 1979; The Church in British Archaeology, 1983; Churches in the Landscape, 1989; (jtly) Guy Gibson, 1994; Cheshire, VC, OM, 2000; (jtly) Breaching the German Dams, 2008; (jtly) The Archaeology of English Battlefields, 2012; Time's Anvil: England, archaeology and the imagination, 2013. *Recreations:* aviation history, natural history, dog walking, gliding. *Address:* 13 Hollins Road, Harrogate HG1 2JF. *T:* (01423) 504219.

MORRIS, Air Vice-Marshal Richard Vaughan, CBE 2000; AFC 1991; Chief of Staff and Deputy Commander-in-Chief, HQ Personnel and Training Command, Innsworth, 2000–01; *b* 24 Sept. 1949; *s* of Edgar Morris and Iona Morris (*née* Clement); *m* 1969, Sheena Blundell; two *s.* *Educ:* John Bright Grammar Sch., Llandudno. XV Sqn, Laarbruch, 237 OCU, Honington, 16 Sqn, Laarbruch, 1971–80; Tri-Nat. Tornado Trng Estabt, Cottesmore, 1980–82; PSO to ACAS, MoD, 1984–87; OC 14 Sqn, Bruggen, 1988–91; Comdr, British Forces Op. Jural, 1992; Station Comdr, Honington, 1993–94; Policy HQ Allied Forces Northwestern Europe, 1994; rcds, 1995; Comdt, Air Warfare Centre, Waddington, 1996–98; SASO, HQ 1 Gp, High Wycombe, 1998–2000; Comdr, British Forces Op. Desert Fox, 1998, Op. Allied Force, 1999; retired 2002. *Recreations:* golf, hill walking. *Address:* c/o Lloyds Bank, 65 High Street, Stamford PE9 2AT. *Club:* Royal Air Force.

MORRIS, Robert Matthew, CVO 1996; Assistant Under Secretary of State, Home Office, 1983–97; *b* 11 Oct. 1937; *s* of late William Alexander Morris and of Mary Morris (*née* Bryant); *m* 1965, Janet Elizabeth Gillingham; two *s* one *d.* *Educ:* Handsworth Grammar Sch.; Christ's Coll., Cambridge; Open Univ. (PhD 2004). S Staffords Regt, 1956–58. Joined Home Office, 1961; Asst Private Sec. to Home Sec., 1964–66; CSD, 1969–71; Sec. to NI (Compton) Inquiry, 1971; Principal Private Sec. to Home Sec., 1976–78; Sec. to UK Prison Services Inquiry (May Cttee), 1978–79; Head of Crime Policy Planning Unit, 1979–81; Asst Under Sec. of State, Fire and Emergency Planning, 1983, Immigration Policy, Nationality and Passports, 1986, Criminal Justice and Constitutional, 1991; Registrar, Baronetage, 1991–96.

Mem. Council, Internat. Social Service UK, 1998–2005. Sec. to (Hurd) Review of See of Canterbury, 2000–01. Governor: Mayfield Sch., 1978–83; Spencer Park Sch., 1980–86. Hon. Sen. Res. Fellow, Constitution Unit, Sch. of Public Policy, subseq. Dept of Political Sci., UCL, 1999–. *Publications:* Church and State in 21st Century Britain: the future of Church establishment, 2009; Reforming the Police in the Nineteenth Century, 2014; articles on criminal justice (especially police) history, and constitutional politics of religion. *Address:* 4 Desenfans Road, SE21 7DN.

MORRIS, Rt Rev. Roger Anthony Brett; *see* Colchester, Area Bishop of.

MORRIS, Rear-Adm. Roger Oliver, CB 1990; Hydrographer of the Navy, 1985–90; *b* 1 Sept. 1932; *s* of Dr Oliver N. Morris and H. S. (Mollie) Morris (*née* Hudson). *Educ:* Mount House School, Tavistock; Royal Naval College, Dartmouth. Entered Royal Navy, 1946, commissioned 1952; specialized in Hydrographic Surveying, 1956; commanded HM Ships Medusa, Beagle, Hydra, Fawn, Hecla, Hydra, 1964–80; RCDS 1978; Director of Hydrographic Plans and Surveys, 1980–81; Asst Hydrographer, 1982–84. Chm. of Council, Soc. for Nautical Res., 1989–94; Vice-Pres., Royal Inst. of Navigation, 1991–92; Pres., World Ship Soc., 1997–2000. *Publications:* Charts and Surveys in Peace and War, 1995. *Recreations:* heraldry, opera, bird watching. *Address:* Orchard House, Quantock View, Bishops Lydeard, Somerset TA4 3AW.

MORRIS, Sean Robert; His Honour Judge Sean Morris; a Circuit Judge, since 2008; *b* Bingley, W Yorks, 17 Oct. 1958; *s* of John Morris and Margaret Morris. *Educ:* Fulneck Sch., Leeds; Benton Park Grammar Sch., Leeds; Leeds Poly. (BA Hons Law). Pres., Students Union, 1981–82. Called to the Bar, Lincoln's Inn, 1983; in practice as barrister specialising in crime, 6 Park Square Chambers, Leeds, 1983–2008; a Recorder of the Crown Court, 2003–08; Resident Judge, Lincoln Crown Court, 2010–14. Hon. Recorder of Lincoln, 2011–14. *Recreations:* cooking, eating real curry, walking to country pubs. *Address:* Newcastle-upon-Tyne Combined Court Centre, The Law Courts, The Quayside, Newcastle-upon-Tyne NE1 3LA.

MORRIS, Simon C.; *see* Conway Morris.

MORRIS, Stephen Nathan; QC 2002; a Recorder, since 2000; a Deputy High Court Judge, since 2004; *b* 18 May 1957; *s* of late Jack Ellis Morris and June Audrey Morris (*née* Livingstone). *Educ:* Bradford Grammar Sch.; Christ's Coll., Cambridge (BA 1979, MA 1982). Called to the Bar, Lincoln's Inn, 1981; in private practice at the bar, 1983–; Jun. Counsel to the Crown (A Panel), 1999–2002; Asst Recorder, 1998–2000. *Publications:* (contrib.) Plender: European Court Practice and Precedent, 1998; (contrib.) Bar Council Practitioners' Handbook of EC Law, 1998; (contrib.) Bellamy & Child: European Community Law of Competition, 5th edn 2001. *Recreations:* ski-ing, theatre, gardening, cooking. *Address:* 20 Essex Street, WC2R 3AL. *T:* (020) 7842 1200. *Club:* Royal Automobile.

MORRIS, Thomas Alun, (Tom); Artistic Director, Bristol Old Vic, since 2009; *b* Stamford, Lincs, 1964; *s* of Michael and Rosemary Morris; *m* 2011, Kate McGrath; one *s* one *d*. *Educ:* Stonyhurst Coll.; Pembroke Coll., Cambridge (BA Hons English Lit. 1982; MA 1986). Formerly broadcaster and arts journalist for Independent, Sunday Times, Guardian, BBC Radio 4 and Time Out; Artistic Dir, Battersea Arts Centre, 1995–2004; Associate Dir, NT, 2004–09. Productions include: as *writer/adaptor*: with Carl Heap: Tom Tom, 1987; Battersea Arts Centre: Ben Hur, 2002; Jason and the Argonauts, 2003; The World Cup Final 1966, and tour, 2004; The Wooden Frock, Kneehigh Th., 2004; with Emma Rice: (also dir) Disembodied, nat. tour, 2005; Nights at the Circus, Lyric, Hammersmith, 2006; (with David Glass) A Matter of Life and Death by Samuel Beckett, NT, 2007; as *director*: Battersea Arts Centre: All that Fall, 1996; Trio, 1996; Othello Music, 1997; Oedipus the King, 1998; Macbeth, 1999; To the Island with the Goose, 1999; Unsung, 2000; Oogly Boogly, tour, 2004; (with Marianne Elliott) (also prod.) War Horse, Olivier, 2007, transf. NY, 2011 ((jtly) Tony Award for Best Direction, 2011); Bristol Old Vic: Juliet and Her Romeo, 2011; Swallows and Amazons, transf. Vaudeville and tour, 2011; The Little Mermaid, 2013; A Midsummer Night's Dream, 2014; World Cup Final 1966, 2014; opera: Battersea Arts Centre: Passions, 2001; Kombat Opera Klubneit, 2002; Newsnight: the opera, 2003; The Death of Klinghoffer, ENO, 2012; as *producer*: Matters of Life and Death Season, Battersea Arts Centre, 2000; Jerry Springer: the opera, 2001; Coram Boy, Olivier, 2005. *Recreations:* cricket, journalism, unusual music. *Address:* Bristol Old Vic, King Street, Bristol BS1 4ED.

MORRIS, Timothy Colin; HM Diplomatic Service; Ambassador to the Republic of South Sudan, since 2015; *b* 17 Sept. 1958; *s* of late Maj. Charles Anthony Morris and of Sheila Ann Margaret Morris (*née* Watson); *m* 1996, Patricia Tena; three *s*. *Educ:* Winchester Coll.; Queen's Coll., Oxford (BA 1st Cl. Hons Modern Langs (French and Spanish) 1981). Joined HM Diplomatic Service, 1981; Japanese lang. trng, 1982–84; Second Sec., Commercial, Tokyo, 1984–87; FCO, 1987–89; Hd, Exports to Japan Unit, DTI, 1989–91; First Sec. and Hd, Political Section, Madrid, 1991–95; Dep. Hd, UN Dept, FCO, 1996–98; Counsellor, Trade and Investment, Tokyo, 1998–2002; Dep. Hd of Mission, Lisbon, 2003–04; Hd, Internat. Orgns Dept, FCO, 2005–08; Ambassador to Morocco and (non-resident) to Mauritania, 2008–12; Hd of Sahel Task Force, FCO, 2012–13; UK Special Envoy for S Sudan, 2014; temp. Hd of Mission, Kinshasa, 2014–15. *Recreations:* music, literature. *Address:* c/o Foreign and Commonwealth Office, King Charles Street, SW1A 2AH. *Club:* Oxford and Cambridge.

MORRIS, Rev. Canon Timothy David; Priest Ministry Developer, Pembina Hills Parish, Diocese of Rupert's Land, Canada, 2008–10; *b* 17 Aug. 1948; *s* of Joseph Ernest and Mabel Elizabeth Morris; *m* 1st, 1972, Dorothy Helen Ralph (marr. diss. 1987); one *d*; 2nd, 1988, Irene Elizabeth Lyness. *Educ:* King Edward's Grammar Sch., Bath; Coll. of Estate Management, London Univ. (BSc Econs); Trinity Coll., Bristol and Bristol Univ. (DipTh). Asst Estate Surveyor, Min. of Public Building and Works, Edinburgh, 1969–72; Curate, St Thomas's Church, Edinburgh, 1975–77; Rector: St James's Episcopal Church, Leith, Edinburgh, 1977–83; St Ninian's, Troon, Ayrshire, 1983–85; St Peter's, Galashiels, 1985–2002; Church of the Good Shepherd, Murrayfield, 2002–08; Priest, St Salvador's Church, Stenhouse, 2003–08; Dean, Dio. Edinburgh, Episcopal Ch in Scotland, 1992–2001. Hon. Canon, St Mary's Cathedral, Edinburgh, 2002–. HM Lay Inspector of Educn, 2003–08. Chm., Bd of Mgt, Positive Help, Edinburgh, 2003–08. *Recreations:* music, Rugby Union, cricket, gardening, curling, cross-country ski-ing. *Address:* 2 The Firs, Foulden Newton, Berwick-upon-Tweed TD15 1UL. *T:* (01289) 386615.

MORRIS, Prof. Timothy John, PhD; Professor of Management Studies, Oxford University, and Fellow, Green Templeton College (formerly Templeton College), Oxford, since 2002; *b* 21 Jan. 1953; *s* of Ernest Joseph Morris and Dorothy Beatrice Morris; *m* 1999, Dr Helen Margaret Lydka; one *s* one *d* (and one *d* decd). *Educ:* Eltham Coll., London; Jesus Coll., Cambridge (BA Hons 1975); London Sch. of Econs (MSc 1980; PhD 1984); Nuffield Coll., Oxford; MA Oxon 2002. Faculty, London Business Sch., 1988–2000; Prof. of Organisational Behaviour, Imperial Coll. London, 2000–02; Dir, Clifford Chance Centre for Mgt of Professional Service Firms, Oxford Univ., 2003–05 and 2007–08. *Publications:* (jtly) The Car Industry: labour relations and industrial adjustment, 1985; Innovations in Banking: business strategies and employee relations, 1986; (jtly) Union Business, 1993; (jtly) Career Frontiers: new conceptions of working lives, 2000; numerous articles in scholarly jls. *Recreations:* cycling, theatre, cinema, running. *Address:* Saïd Business School, Oxford OX1 1HP. *T:* (01865) 288954, *Fax:* (01865) 288805. *E:* tim.morris@sbs.ox.ac.uk.

MORRIS, Sir Trefor (Alfred), Kt 1996; CBE 1992; QPM 1985; HM Chief Inspector of Constabulary, 1993–96; Chairman, Police Information Technology Organisation, 1996–2000; Adviser, British Transport Police Committee, 1996–2001; *b* 22 Dec. 1934; *s* of late Kenneth Alfred Morris and Amy Ursula (*née* Burgess); *m* 1958, Martha Margaret (*née* Wroe); two *d*. *Educ:* Ducie Technical High School, Manchester; Manchester University (Dip. Criminology); Nat. Exec. Inst., USA. Constable to Chief Superintendent, Manchester City Police, Manchester and Salford Police, Greater Manchester Police, 1955–76; Asst Chief Constable, Greater Manchester Police, 1976–79; Dep. Chief Constable, 1979–84, Chief Constable, 1984–90, Herts; HM Inspector of Constabulary, 1990–93. Trustee, Police Foundn, 1993–96. Pres., Police Mutual Assurance Soc., 1994–97. Member: St Albans Diocesan Synod, 1989–96; PCC, St Mary's Church, Abergavenny, 1997–; Governing Body, Church in Wales, 2003–09. Chairman: St Mary's Priory Develt Trust, 1999–; St Mary's Priory House Co. Ltd, 2009–. Churchwarden, St Mary's Priory Church, 2010–13. Vice President: Herts Scouts, 1989–; Police Athletics Assoc.; Pres., Luton, N Herts Inst. of Mgt; Pres., Beaufort Male Choir, 2010–13. Chm., Bryn-y-Cwm Community Forum, 2004–08. Dir, Abergavenny Food Fest. Co. Ltd, 1999–. Trustee, Hospice of the Valleys, 1997–2005. CCMI (CBIM 1986). FRSA 1993. OStJ 1984. *Recreations:* music, golf, wine, walking, gardening, medieval history. *Clubs:* Royal Over-Seas League; Monmouthshire Golf (Captain, 2005–06).

MORRIS, Ulrike Luise; *see* Tillmann, U. L.

MORRIS, Warwick; HM Diplomatic Service, retired; consultant on Asian Affairs; *b* 10 Aug. 1948; *e s* of late Clifford Morris and Patricia Morris (*née* O'Grady), JP; *m* 1972, Pamela Jean Mitchell, MBE; one *s* two *d*. *Educ:* Bishop's Stortford Coll. VSO, Cameroon, 1967–68; entered Diplomatic Service, 1969; Third Sec., Paris, 1972–74; Korean lang. trng, Yonsei Univ., Seoul, 1975–76; Second Sec., Seoul, 1977–79; FCO, 1979–83; First Sec., 1982; First Sec. (Commercial), Mexico City, 1984–87; Head of Chancery, Seoul, 1988–91; Dep. Head, Far Eastern Dept, FCO, 1991–93; Counsellor, 1993, Head, 1994, Permanent Under Sec.'s Dept, FCO; Econ. and Commercial Counsellor, New Delhi, 1995–98; RCDS, 1999; Ambassador: to Vietnam, 2000–03; to South Korea, 2003–08. Korea and Vietnam Advr to Lloyd's, 2008–12; non-executive Director: PCA Life Korea, 2008–13; Prudential Vietnam, 2013–. Member, Board: Locate in Kent, 2009– (Chm., 2012–); Kent Ambassador, 2010–. Hon. Pres., British Korean Law Assoc., 2008–; Chm., Anglo-Korean Soc., 2011–. Hon. Fellow, Robinson Coll., Cambridge, 2011. *Recreations:* sport, travel, philately. *Address:* Rosewood, Stonewall Park Road, Langton Green, Kent TN3 0HD.

MORRIS, Prof. (William) David, PhD, DSc(Eng); Professor of Mechanical Engineering, University of Wales, Swansea (formerly University College of Swansea), 1985 (Head of Department, 1985–91 and 1995); *b* 14 March 1936; *s* of late William Daniel and Elizabeth Jane Morris; *m* 1959, Pamela Eira Evans; two *s* one *d*. *Educ:* Queen Mary College, London (1st Cl. Hons BSc Eng); UC of Swansea, Wales (PhD); Univ. of London (DSc(Eng)). CEng, FIMechE, FIET. Bristol Siddeley Engine Co., 1958–60; James Clayton Res. Fellow, Univ. of Wales, Swansea, 1960–63; Lectr, Dept of Mech. Engrg, Univ. of Liverpool, 1963–67; Lectr, 1967–72, Reader, 1972–79, Sch. of Engrg, Univ. of Sussex; J. H. Fenner Prof. of Mech. Engrg and Head, Dept of Engrg Design, Univ. of Hull, 1979–85; Vice Principal, UC Swansea, 1991–93. *Publications:* Differential Equations for Engineers and Applied Scientists, 1979; Heat Transfer and Fluid Flow in Rotating Coolant Channels, 1981. *Recreations:* oil painting, DIY, walking.

MORRIS, His Honour William Patrick; a Circuit Judge, 1995–2012; Resident Judge, Bolton Crown Court, 2002–12; Honorary Recorder of Bolton, 2008–12; *b* 17 March 1947; *s* of His Honour Sir William Gerard Morris and Mollie Morris; *m* 1978, Patricia Whittaker (*see* Baroness Morris of Bolton); one *s* one *d*. *Educ:* Ampleforth Coll.; Gonville and Caius Coll., Cambridge (BA 1968, MA). Called to the Bar, Lincoln's Inn, 1970; a Recorder, 1988–95. *Recreations:* fishing, gardening, walking, watching Bolton Wanderers.

MORRISON, family name of **Viscount Dunrossil** and of **Baron Margadale**.

MORRISON, Alasdair; Chairman, MG Alba, 2008–11; Director, UBC Group, since 2007; *b* 18 Nov. 1968; *m*; one *s* one *d*. Former Western Isles correspondent, BBC; former Editor, New Gael newspaper. Mem. (Lab) Western Isles, Scottish Parlt, 1999–2007. Dep. Minister for Enterprise in the Highlands and Islands and Gaelic, 1999–2001, for Enterprise and Lifelong Learning and Gaelic, 2001, Scottish Exec. Dir, Harris Tweed Hebrides LLP, 2011–12. Contested (Lab) Western Isles, 2015.

MORRISON, Sir (Alexander) Fraser, Kt 1998; CBE 1993; Deputy Chairman, Clydesdale Bank plc, 1999–2004 (Director, 1994–2004); Chairman: Teasses Capital Ltd, since 2003; Vermilion Holdings, since 2007; Duthus Investments Ltd, since 2013; *b* 20 March 1948; *s* of late Alexander Ferrier Sharp Morrison and of Catherine Colina (*née* Fraser); *m* 1972, Patricia Janice Murphy; one *s* two *d*. *Educ:* Tain Royal Acad.; Univ. of Edinburgh (BSc Hons Civil Engrg). CEng, FICE 1993; Eur Ing 1993; MCIHT (MIHT 1982); FCIOB 1995. Morrison Construction Gp, subseq. Morrison: Dir, 1970; Man. Dir, 1976–96; Chm., 1984–96; Exec. Chm., 1996–2000. Director: Shand Ltd, 1978–89; Alexander Shand Holdings Ltd, 1982–86; RMJM Ltd, 2007–13 (Chm., 2007–13); Chm., Ramco Hldgs, 2005–13. Chm., Highlands & Islands Enterprise, 1992–98. Federation of Civil Engineering Contractors: Chm., Scottish Sect., 1991–92; Chm., Nat. Fedn, 1993–94; Vice Pres., 1994–96. Chm., American Patrons, Nat. Liby and Galls of Scotland, 2011. Chairman: Bd of Governors, Univ. of Highlands and Is Project, 1998–2001; Council St Leonard's Sch., St Andrews, 1999–2007. Internat. Pres., Chief Execs Orgn, 2009–10 (Dir, 2003–). FRSA 1990; FScotvec 1994. Hon. DTech: Napier, 1995; Glasgow Caledonian, 1997; DUniv Open, 2000. *Recreations:* shooting, golf, music, art. *Address:* Teasses House, near Ceres, Leven, Fife KY8 5PG. *T:* (01334) 828048; 14 East 75th Street, New York, NY 10021, USA. *T:* (212) 744 2697. *Clubs:* New (Edinburgh); Royal & Ancient Golf (St Andrews).

MORRISON, Alistair Neil; photographer of celebrities and dignitaries; *b* Lima, Peru, 4 Nov. 1956; *s* of James and Eileen Morrison; *m* 1st, 1980, Janis Anne Edwards (marr. diss. 1990); one *s* one *d*; 2nd, 2005, Louise Mary Bader; one *s* one *d*. *Educ:* Ardingly Coll., Sussex; Harrow Coll. (BA Hons Photography, Film and TV). Photographs exhibited in NPG, London; exhibitions: Twenty for Today, 1985, Olympians, 1992, NPG; Time to Reflect, 2000; Retrospective, New Lodge, Windsor, 2006; Nudes: a country collection, Linley, Belgravia, 2008. *Publications:* Time to Reflect I, 2000; Time to Reflect II, 2008. *Recreations:* art and photography galleries, all music, sun, sea, sand. *Address:* New Lodge, Drift Road, Windsor, Berks SL4 4RR.

MORRISON, Amanda Mary; *see* Doyle, A. M.

MORRISON, (Andrew) Neil, CBE 1997; QFSM 1989; HM Chief Inspector of Fire Services for Scotland, 1994–99; *b* 8 Sept. 1937; *e s* of late Andrew Steel Morrison and Margueritta Wilkin Caird; *m* 1963, Kathleen Rutherford; one *s*. *Educ:* Arbroath High Sch.; Dundee Coll. of Technol. FIFireE 1991. Angus Fire Brigade: Fireman, 1962–70; Leading Fireman, 1970–71; Sub-officer, 1971–74; Station Officer, 1974–75; Tayside Fire Brigade: Station Officer, 1975–76; Asst Divl Officer, 1976; Divl Officer, Grade III, 1976–79; Divl Officer, Grade I, 1979–80; Grampian Fire Brigade: Dep. Firemaster, 1980–85; Firemaster, 1985–93. Hon. DTech Robert Gordon Univ., 1994. *Recreations:* curling, golf, hill-walking, swimming. *Address:* 18 Slateford Gardens, Edzell, Angus DD9 7SX. *T:* (01356) 648768.

MORRISON, Rt Rev. Angus, PhD; Moderator of the General Assembly of the Church of Scotland, 2015–May 2016 (reverts to title Very Rev. May 2016); Chaplain to the Queen in Scotland, since 2006; *b* 30 Aug. 1953; *s* of Norman Morrison, MBE and Mary Ann Morrison; *m* 1983, Marion Jane Matheson; three *s* one *d*. *Educ:* Glasgow Univ. (MA Hons 1976); London Univ. (BD Hons 1993 ext.); Edinburgh Univ. (PhD 2001). Minister, Free Presbyterian Church of Scotland: Oban, 1979–86; Edinburgh, 1986–89; Minister: Associated Presbyterian Chs, Edinburgh, 1989–2000; St Columba's Old Parish Ch, Stornoway, 2000–11; Orwell and Portmoak Parish Ch, Kinross-shire, 2011–15. Moderator: Gen. Assembly, Associated Presbyterian Chs, 1998–99; C of S Presbytery of Lewis, 2003–04; Chaplain, Nicolson Inst., Stornoway, 2003–; Chaplain to Lord High Comr to Gen. Assembly of C of S, 2005, 2006; Convener, C of S Mission and Discipleship Council, 2005–09. Mem., C of S Special Commn on Same-Sex Relationships and the Ministry, 2009–11. Vis. Scholar, Princeton Theol Seminary, 2009; Vis. Lectr, United Theol Coll., Bangalore, 2012. *Publications:* (contrib.) Dictionary of Scottish Church History and Theology, 1993; (contrib.) Oxford DNB; (ed) Tolerance and Truth: the spirit of the age or the spirit of God?, 2007; (contrib.) Dizionario di Teologia Evangelica, 2007. *Recreations:* walking, reading, listening to music. *Address:* Church of Scotland, 121 George Street, Edinburgh EH2 4YN. *E:* angusmorrison3@gmail.com.

MORRISON, Anne Catherine; Chair, British Academy of Film and Television Arts, since 2014; *b* 18 Aug. 1959; *d* of late George Charles Morrison and of Persis Mae Morrison (*née* Ross); *m* 1989, Robert John Jarvis Johnstone; one *d*. *Educ:* Richmond Lodge Sch., Belfast; Churchill Coll., Cambridge (MA Eng. Lit). Gen. Trainee, BBC, 1981–83; Researcher and Dir, Documentary Features, BBC TV, 1983–87; Prod., Holiday, 1987–88; Series Prod., Crimewatch UK, 1988–90; Chief Assistant, Documentary Features, 1990–92; Exec. Prod., Taking Liberties, and Rough Justice, 1992; Dep. Head, 1992–94, Hd, 1994–96, Features, BBC TV; BBC Production: Head of Consumer and Leisure, 1996–98; Head of Features and Events, 1998–2000; Controller, Leisure and Factual Entertainment, 2000–01, General Factual Gp, 2001–02, Documentaries and Contemp. Factual, 2002–06, Network Production, 2006–09, BBC TV; Dir, BBC Acad., 2009–14. Trustee: BAFTA, 2010– (Dep. Chm., 2013–14; Mem., TV Cttee, 2008–13; Chm., Learning and Events Cttee, 2010–14); Charleston Trust, 2015–. *Recreations:* reading, dancing, films, improving my Italian. *Address:* BAFTA, 195 Piccadilly, W1J 9LN.

MORRISON, Blake; *see* Morrison, P. B.

MORRISON, Chloe Anthony, (Toni); writer; *b* 18 Feb. 1931; *d* of George Wofford and Ella Ramah Wofford (*née* Willis); *m* 1958, Harold Morrison (marr. diss. 1964); two *s*. *Educ:* Howard Univ.; Cornell Univ. (MA 1955). Lectr in English and Humanities: Texas Southern Univ., 1955–57; Howard Univ., 1957–64; Associate Prof. of English, NY State Univ. Coll., Purchase, 1971–72; Professor of Humanities: SUNY, Albany, 1984–89; Princeton Univ., 1989–. An Editor, Random House, NY, 1965. Numerous literary awards, incl Pulitzer Prize for Fiction, 1988; Nobel Prize for Literature, 1993; Presidential Medal of Freedom (USA), 2012. *Publications:* The Bluest Eye, 1970; Sula, 1974; Song of Solomon, 1977; Tar Baby, 1983; Beloved, 1987; Jazz, 1992; Playing in the Dark: whiteness and the literary imagination, 1992; (ed) Race-ing Justice, En-gendering Power, 1993; (ed jtly) Birth of a Nationhood, 1997; Paradise, 1998; Love, 2003; A Mercy, 2008; (jtly) Peeny Butter Fudge (for children), 2009; (jtly) Little Cloud and Lady Wind (for children), 2010; Home, 2012; Desdemona (play), 2012; God Help the Child, 2015. *Address:* c/o Amanda Urban, International Creative Management, 730 5th Avenue, New York, NY 10019, USA.

MORRISON, Dennis John; Regional Director, Government Office for the East Midlands, 1998–2002; Special Professor, Faculty of the Built Environment, University of Nottingham, 2000–10; *b* 20 May 1942; *s* of Leonard Tait Morrison and Alice Morrison; *m* 1967, Frances Joan Pollard; one *s* one *d*. *Educ:* Ashton-upon-Mersey Boys' School; Lymm Grammar School; Manchester Univ. (BA, DipT&CP). MRTPI. Planning appointments: Lancs CC, 1966–70; Welsh Office, Cardiff, 1970–75; NW Region, DoE, Manchester, 1975–81; Regional Controller, NW Enterprise Unit, DoE, 1981–84; Regional Controller (Urban and Economic Affairs), Merseyside Task Force, Liverpool, 1984–89; Regl Dir, Depts of Envmt and Transport, E Midlands Region, 1989–94; Dir, Envmt and Transport, Govt Office for E Midlands, 1994–97; Regl Dir, Govt Office for Merseyside, 1997–98. Mem., Adv. Bd, Highways Agency, 1999–2003; Bd Mem., Industrial Trust E Midlands, 2000–10. Non-exec. Dir, Independent Decision Makers Ltd, 2002–09. Mem., Exec. Cttee, Liverpool Cathedral, 1986–. Trustee, 2005–14, Arkwright Soc. (Vice. Pres., 2008–). FRGS. *Recreations:* antiquarian book collecting, horology, antique barometer restoration, hill walking, gardening, cooking, people watching. *Address:* Bowdon, Cheshire.

MORRISON, Sir Fraser; *see* Morrison, Sir A. F.

MORRISON, Fraser; *see* Morrison, R. F.

MORRISON, Sir George Ivan, (Sir Van), Kt 2015; OBE 1996; singer and songwriter; *b* Belfast, 31 Aug. 1945; *s* of George Morrison and Violet Morrison; *m* 1967, Janet Planet (marr. diss. 1973); one *d*; *m* Michelle Rocca; one *s* one *d*. Singer with Them, 1964–67; solo singer, 1967–. *Albums include:* with Them: Them, 1965; Them Again, 1966; solo: Blowin' Your Mind, 1967; Astral Weeks, 1968; Moondance, 1970; His Band and Street Choir, 1970; Tupelo Honey, 1971; St Dominic's Preview, 1972; Hard Nose the Highway, 1973; Veedon Fleece, 1974; A Period of Transition, 1977; Wavelength, 1978; Into the Music, 1979; Common One, 1980; Beautiful Vision, 1982; Inarticulate Speech of the Heart, 1983; A Sense of Wonder, 1985; No Guru, No Method, No Teacher, 1986; Poetic Champion Compose, 1987; Irish Heartbeat, 1988; Avalon Sunset, 1989; Enlightenment, 1990; Hymns to the Silence, 1991; Bang Master, 1991; Too Long in Exile, 1993; A Night in San Francisco, 1994; Days Like This, 1995; How Long Has This Been Going On, 1995; The Healing Game, 1996; Tell Me Something, 1996; The Philosopher's Stone, 1998; The Masters, 1999; Back on Top, 1999; Down the Road, 2002; What's Wrong with this Picture, 2003; Magic Time, 2005; Keep it Simple, 2008; Duets: reworking the catalogue, 2015. Hon. Freeman, Belfast, 2013. *Address:* Exile Productions Ltd, 2nd Floor, 88–90 Baker Street, W1U 6TQ.

MORRISON, Graham, RIBA; Partner, Allies and Morrison, Architects, since 1983; *b* 2 Feb. 1951; *s* of Robert Morrison and Robina Sandison Morrison. *Educ:* Brighton Coll.; Jesus Coll., Cambridge (MA; DipArch 1975). RIBA 1976. *Projects completed* include: Clove Bldg, London, 1990 (RIBA Award 1991); Sarum Hall Sch., London, 1995 (RIBA Award, Civic Trust Award, 1996); Nunnery Square, Sheffield, 1995 (RIBA Award 1996); British Embassy, Dublin, 1995 (RIBA Award 1997); Rosalind Franklin Bldg, Newnham Coll., Cambridge, 1995 (RIBA Award 1996); Abbey Mills Pumping Station, Stratford (RIBA Award), 1997; Rutherford Information Services Bldg, Goldsmiths Coll., London, 1997 (RIBA Award 1998); Blackburn Hse, London, 1999 (RIBA Award 2000); Blackwell, Cumbria, 2003 (RIBA Award, Civic Trust Award, 2003); extension to Horniman Mus., 2004 (RIBA Award, Civic Trust Award, 2004); 85 Southwark Street, London, 2004 (London Civic Trust Award, Bldg of Year Award, RIBA London, Nat. Winner for Corporate Workplace Bldg, British Council for Offices Awards, 2004); BBC Media Village, White City, 2003 (RIBA Award 2005; Civic Trust Award 2006); Fitzwilliam Coll. Gatehouse and Auditorium, 2004 (RIBA Award 2005; Civic Trust Award 2007); City Lit, 2004 (Civic Trust Award 2006); The Finlay Bldg, Merton Coll., 2004 (Civic Trust Award 2007); Girton Coll. Liby, Cambridge, 2005 (RIBA Award 2006; Civic Trust Award 2007); Farnborough Business Park, Hants, 2006 (RIBA Award 2007); WWT Vis. Centre and Footbridge, Welney, 2006 (Civic Trust Award 2007); Planetarium, Royal Observatory, Greenwich, 2007 (RIBA Award 2008; Civic Trust Award 2008); Bankside 123, 2007 (RIBA Award 2010); Paradise Street, Liverpool One, 2009 (RIBA Award 2009); Charles Street Car Park, Sheffield, 2009 (RIBA Award 2009); One Vine Street, The Quadrant, Regent Street, 2009 (RIBA Award 2009); Highbury Square, 2009 (RIBA Award 2010); Mint Hotel, Leeds (RIBA Award 2011); Royal Albert Meml Mus., 2013 (RIBA Award 2013); Simon Smith Bldg, 2013 (RIBA Award 2013); Masterplan London 2012 Stratford (RIBA Nat. Award 2013); Rambert London, 2014 (RIBA Award 2014); Ash Court, Girton Coll., Cambridge, 2014 (RIBA Award 2014). *Exhibitions* include: New British Architecture, Japan, 1994; Allies and Morrison Retrospective, USA Schs of Architecture, 1996–98, Helsinki, Delft and Strasbourg, 1999. Architects to Royal Fest. Hall, 1994– (RIBA Award 2008; RIBA Design for London Space Award, 2008). Lectures in Canada, Finland, India, Ireland, Japan, S Africa, UK, USA. Special Prof. of Architecture, Univ. of Nottingham, 2004–05. Member: RIBA Council, 1991–94; Architecture Adv. Cttee, Arts Council, 1996–97; Royal Fine Art Commn, 1998–99; Design Review Cttee, CABE, 2000–04; Historic England (formerly English Heritage): Member: London Adv. Cttee, 2001–11; CABE and Urban Panel, 2009–11; Comr, 2011–; Adv. Cttee, 2013–. External Examiner: Univ. of Cambridge, 1994–97; Univ. of Portsmouth, 2003–05. Dir, RIBA Jl, 1993–97. Masterplanning Architect of the Year and Public Bldg Architect of the Year, 2007, Masterplanning and Public Realm Architect of the Year, 2015, Education Architect of the Year, 2015, Bldg Design Awards. *Publications:* Allies and Morrison, 1996; Allies and Morrison 1, 2011; The Fabric of Place, 2014. *Address:* Allies and Morrison, 85 Southwark Street, SE1 0HX. *T:* (020) 7921 0100.

MORRISON, Howard Andrew Clive, CBE 2007 (OBE 1988); QC 2001; **His Honour Judge Morrison;** a Circuit Judge, since 2004; a Judge of the International Criminal Court, The Hague, since 2011; *b* 20 July 1949; *s* of Howard Edward Morrison and Roma Morrison; *m* 1980, Kathryn Margaret Moore; one *s* one *d*. *Educ:* London Univ. (LLB); Inns of Court Sch. of Law. Volunteer, Ghana, 1968–69, Desk Officer, Zambia and Malawi, 1975–76, VSO. Subaltern, Queen's Regt, 1970–74. Called to the Bar: Gray's Inn, 1977, Bencher, 2008; Fiji, 1988; Eastern Caribbean, 1990; in practice on Midland and Oxford Circuit, 1977–85; Resident Magistrate, then Chief Magistrate, Fiji, 1985–87; concurrently Sen. Magistrate for Tuvalu and locum Attorney Gen. of Anguilla, 1988–89; in practice on Midland and Oxford Circuit, 1989–2004; a Recorder, 1994–2004; engaged in defending in UN War Crime Tribunals, The Hague and Arusha, 1998–2004; Sen. Judge, Sovereign Base Areas, Cyprus, 2007–; Judge, Special Tribunal for Lebanon, 2010; Permanent Judge, UN Internat. Criminal Tribunal for former Yugoslavia, The Hague, 2010–. Advocacy Teacher/Trainer, Gray's Inn, 1994–. Holding Redlich Dist. Vis. Fellow, Monash Univ., 2007; Hon. Prof. of Law, Leicester Univ., 2012–; Sen. Fellow, Lauterpacht Centre for Internat. Law, Cambridge Univ., 2013–. Lectures on internat. humanitarian law, Europe, Africa, Middle East, USA and Australia. Member: Race Relations Cttee, 1996–2002, Equal Opportunities Cttee, 2002–03, Bar Council; IBA; Commonwealth Judges and Magistrates Assoc.; Justice; British Inst. for Internat. and Comparative Law; Adv. Bd, Jl of Internat. Criminal Law, 2008–; Adv. Bd, Internat. Criminal Law Network, 2012–. Member, Bar: Fiji; E Caribbean. FRGS 1991. Hon. LLD Leicester, 2014. *Publications:* numerous legal articles, mainly on internat. criminal law. *Recreations:* travel, scuba diving, flying, sailing. *Address:* c/o 36 Bedford Row, WC1R 4JH.

MORRISON, Air Marshal Ian Craig, CBE 2011; FRAeS; FCMI; Director General, Saudi Arabian Programme, since 2012; *b* Lancs, 15 Oct. 1959; *s* of Thomas David Morrison and Patricia Morrison; *m* 1996, Samantha Jayne McKie Edwards; one *s* one *d*. *Educ:* Winton High Sch.; Eccles Sixth Form Coll.; Open Univ.; Royal Coll. of Defence Studies. Commnd officer RAF, 1979; RAF aircrew and mil. duties incl. qwi, 1979–2000, RAF Staff Coll., 1995–96; Comdr XXV (Fighter) Sqn, 2000–03; Principal SO to UK CDS, MoD, 2003–04; Station Comdr, RAF Leeming, 2004–06; Dep. Comdr British Forces, Afghanistan, 2006; Dir RAF Operation Trng, 2007–09; Comdr Air Command Coordination Exec., ISAF HQ Kabul, Afghanistan, 2008; Asst COS, Air Capability, 2009–11; COS Capability HQ Air Comd, 2011–12. Trustee: Queen's Cottages Almshouse charity, 2011–; Harrison Homes Charity, 2012–. Upper Liveryman, Hon. Co. of Air Pilots (formerly GAPAN), 2011. FRAeS 2011; FCMI 2012; FInstD 2012. *Recreations:* dinghy sailing, running, fly fishing, family, martial arts. *Address:* UK MoD Team Riyadh, BFPO 5421, Riyadh, Saudi Arabia. *Club:* Royal Air Force.

MORRISON, Dr James, RSA 1992 (ARSA 1973); RSW 1968; painter in oil and water colours; *b* 11 April 1932; *s* of John Morrison and Margaret Thomson; *m* 1955, Dorothy McCormack (*d* 2005); one *s* one *d*; partner, Ann Keddie. *Educ:* Hillhead High Sch., Glasgow; Glasgow Sch. of Art (DA). Vis. Artist, Hospitalfield House, 1962, 1963; Duncan of Jordanstone College of Art, Dundee: Member of Staff, 1965–87; Head of Dept, 1978–87; Mem. Board, 1988–. Council Mem., Soc. of Scottish Artists, 1964–67; Keeper of the Collection, Royal Scottish Acad., 1992–. Mem., Inst. of Contemporary Scotland, 2000. Painting in Europe, USA and Canada, 1968–; painting in the High Arctic, 1990–96; painting in Africa, 1998; one-man exhibitions: Scotland, London, Italy, Germany, Canada, 1956–; Scottish Gall., Edinburgh, 2012; Fleming Gall., London, 2013; numerous works in public and private collections, UK and overseas. Torrance Award, RGI, 1958; Arts Council Travelling Award, 1968. DUniv Stirling, 1986. *Publications:* Aff the Squerr, 1976, 2nd edn 1990; Winter in Paris, 1991. *Recreation:* playing recorder in a chamber music group. *Address:* Craigview House, Usan, Montrose, Angus DD10 9SD. *T:* (01674) 672639.

MORRISON, James; *see* Morrison, J. J. H.

MORRISON, Janet Rachel; Chief Executive, IndependentAge, since 2007; *b* 13 April 1964; *d* of Alastair and Jennifer Morrison; one *s* one *d*. *Educ:* Univ. of Nottingham (BA Hons Pols 1985); Virginia State Univ. (MA Pol Sci. 1986). Dir, Policy and Res., NCVO, 1995–97; Sen. Policy Advr, BBC, 1997–99; Dep. Chief Exec., NESTA, 1999–2007. Member: Deregulation Task Force for Charities, 1994; Deakin Commn Charity Law Cttee, 1995. Chm., Baring Foundn, 2014– (Trustee, 2008–; Vice Chm., 2010–14). Mem., Campaign to End Loneliness, 2011–. *Recreations:* family, arts, comedy, walking, travel. *Address:* 27 Muswell Road, N10 2BS. *T:* (020) 8374 1728; IndependentAge, 6 Avonmore Road, W14 8RL. *T:* (020) 7605 4205.

MORRISON, Jasper, RDI 2001; designer; *b* 11 Nov. 1959; *s* of Alec and Dinah Morrison; *m* 2011, Junko Tamura. *Educ:* Kingston Polytechnic; RCA (MA Design). Established Office for Design, 1986. *Publications:* Jasper Morrison: designs, projects and drawings 1981–1989, 1990; A World Without Words, 1992, 2nd edn 1998; A New Tram for Hanover, 1997; Everything But the Walls, 2002, 2nd edn 2006; (with Naoto Fukasawa) Super Normal, 2007; The Good Life, 2014. *Address:* 24B Kingsland Road, E2 8DA. *T:* (020) 7739 2522.

MORRISON, Ven. John Anthony; Archdeacon of Oxford, 1998–2005, now Archdeacon Emeritus; a Residentiary Canon of Christ Church, Oxford, 1998–2005, now Canon Emeritus; *b* 11 March 1938; *s* of late Major Leslie Claude Morrison and Mary Sharland Morrison (*née* Newson-Smith); *m* 1968, Angela, *d* of late Major Jonathan Eric Bush; two *s* one *d*. *Educ:* Haileybury; Jesus Coll., Cambridge (BA 1960; MA 1964); Lincoln Coll., Oxford (MA 1968); Chichester Theol Coll. Deacon 1964, priest 1965; Curate: St Peter, Birmingham, 1964–68; St Michael-at-the-Northgate, Oxford, 1968–74; Chaplain, Lincoln Coll., Oxford, 1968–74; Vicar, Basildon, Berks, 1974–82; RD Bradfield, 1978–82; Vicar, Aylesbury, Bucks, 1982–89, Team Rector, 1989–90; RD Aylesbury, 1985–89; Archdeacon of Buckingham, 1990–98. Examining Chaplain to Bishop of Oxford, 1972–78. Mem., Gen. Synod, 1980–90, 1998–2000. Sen. Treas., Corp. of Sons of the Clergy, 2005–08 (Treas., 2002–08). County Chaplain: Bucks, 1990–98, Oxon, 1998–2007, RBL; Bucks, 1990–98, Oxon, 1998–2007, St

John Ambulance. Master, Spectacle Makers' Co., 2006–07. Hon. Chaplain, 007 Past Masters Assoc., 2007–. *Address:* 39 Crown Road, Wheatley, Oxford OX33 1UJ. *T:* (01865) 876625. *E:* morrison039@btinternet.com. *Clubs:* Leander (Henley-on-Thames); Vincent's (Oxford).

MORRISON, (Jonathan) James (Howard), CMG 2015; Director, Policy Coordination, Secretariat General, European Commission, since 2014; *b* Sale, Cheshire, 31 Dec. 1967; *s* of Kenneth and Norma Morrison; *m* 1994, Helen Pope; three *d. Educ:* Stockport Grammar Sch.; Birmingham Univ. (BA Hons); Ashridge Business Sch. (MBA). Home Office, 1989–91; HM Diplomatic Service, 1991–2008: UN Dept, 1991–94; Third, later Second, then First Sec., UK Perm. Repn, Brussels (Ext. Relns), 1994–99; press spokesman on EU issues, FCO, 1999–2000; Private Sec. to Minister for Europe, 2000–03; Eur. corresp. and Hd, Common Foreign and Security Policy Dept, 2003–04; Counsellor, UK Perm. Repn, Brussels, 2004–05; on loan to Ashridge Business Sch. as Strategy Tutor and Prog. Manager, 2006–07; Sen. Advr to Minister for Europe, 2007–08; Chef de Cabinet, Eur. Comr for Trade, EC, 2009; COS to EU High Rep. for Foreign and Security Policy and Vice Pres. of EC, 2009–14. *Recreations:* walking, classic cars, family. *Address:* European Commission, Rue de la Loi 200, 1040 Brussels, Belgium. *E:* james.morrison@ec.europa.eu.

MORRISON, Sir Kenneth (Duncan), Kt 2000; CBE 1990; Chairman, 1956–2008, and Managing Director, 1956–97 and 2002–08, William Morrison Supermarkets plc; *b* 20 Oct. 1931; *m* 1st, Edna (decd); one *s* two *d*; 2nd, Lynne; one *d*. Career in grocery retailing; co. now has over 100 stores. Pres., Yorkshire Agricultural Soc., 2010–11. *Address:* c/o William Morrison Supermarkets plc, Hilmore House, Gain Lane, Bradford BD3 7DL.

MORRISON, Leslie; Chief Executive Officer, Invest Northern Ireland, 2001–09; *b* 29 Jan. 1948. *Educ:* Queen's Univ., Belfast (BA Hons Mod. Languages 1971). Man. Dir, J. P. Morgan & Co., 1983–2001. *Address:* c/o Invest Northern Ireland, Bedford Square, Bedford Street, Belfast BT2 7ES. *T:* (028) 9023 9090.

MORRISON, Hon. Mary Anne, GCVO 2013 (DCVO 1982; CVO 1970); Woman of the Bedchamber to the Queen, since 1960; *b* 17 May 1937; *o d* of 1st Baron Margadale, TD. *Educ:* Heathfield School.

MORRISON, Murdo, FRAeS; Editor, Flight International, since 2001 (Managing Editor, 2001); *b* 22 June 1964; *s* of late John and of Mairi Morrison; *m* 1994, Juliet Parish; one *s* one *d. Educ:* Nicolson Inst., Stornoway; Glasgow Univ. (MA Hons Politics 1986); University Coll., Cardiff (Dip. Journalism 1987). Journalist, Commercial Motor, 1987–92; Editor, Car & Accessory Trader, 1992–94; Dep. Editor, Printweek, 1994–95; Editor: Planning Week, 1995; Motor Trader, 1995–2001. Governor, Middle Street Primary Sch., Brighton, 1998–2006 (Chm. of Govs, 2001–06). FRAeS 2010. *Recreations:* football, spending time with my children, music. *Address:* Reed Business Information, Quadrant House, The Quadrant, Sutton, Surrey SM2 5AS. *T:* (020) 8652 4395, *Fax:* (020) 8652 3850. *E:* murdo.morrison@flightglobal.com.

MORRISON, Neil; *see* Morrison, A. N.

MORRISON, Nigel Murray Paton; QC (Scot.) 1988; Sheriff of Lothian and Borders at Edinburgh, since 1996; Appeal Sheriff, Sheriff Appeal Court, since 2015; *b* 18 March 1948; *o s* of late David Paton Morrison, FRICS, FLAS and Dilys Morrison. *Educ:* Rannoch School. Called to the Bar, Inner Temple, 1972; admitted Scottish Bar, 1975; Asst Editor, Session Cases, 1976–82; Asst Clerk, Rules Council, 1978–84; Clerk of Faculty, Faculty of Advocates, 1979–87; Standing Junior Counsel to Scottish Develt Dept (Planning), 1982–86; Temporary Sheriff, 1982–96; Second (formerly Junior) Counsel to Lord President of Court of Session, 1984–89; First Counsel to Lord President, 1989–96; Counsel to Sec. of State under Private Legislation Procedure (Scotland) Act 1936, 1986–96. Chairman: Social Security Appeal Tribunals, 1982–91; Medical Appeal Tribunals, 1991–96. Dir of Judicial Studies, Judicial Studies Cttee, 2000–04. Pres., Sheriffs' Assoc., 2011–13 (Vice Pres., 2009–11). Trustee, Nat. Library of Scotland, 1989–98. Editor: Greens Civil Practice Bulletin, 1995–2003; Greens Litigation Styles, 1998–2003. *Publications:* (jtly) Greens Annotated Rules of the Court of Session, 1994; (ed jtly) Sentencing Practice, 2000; contribs to Stair Memorial Encyclopaedia of the Laws of Scotland, Macphail on Sheriff Court Practice, 2nd edn. *Recreations:* music, riding, being taken for walks by my dogs. *Address:* Sheriff Court House, 27 Chambers Street, Edinburgh EH1 1LB. *T:* (0131) 225 2525. *Club:* New (Edinburgh).

MORRISON, (Philip) Blake, FRSL; poet, novelist and critic; *b* 8 Oct. 1950; *s* of Arthur Blakemore Morrison and Agnes O'Shea; *m* 1976, Katherine Ann Drake; two *s* one *d. Educ:* Ermysted's Grammar Sch., Skipton; Nottingham Univ. (BA); McMaster Univ. (MA); University College London (PhD; Fellow, 2006). FRSL 1988. Poetry and fiction editor, TLS, 1978–81; Dep. Literary Editor, 1981–86, Literary Editor, 1987–89, Observer; Literary Editor, 1990–94, Staff writer, 1994–95, Independent on Sunday. Prof. of Creative and Life Writing, Goldsmiths Coll., London Univ., 2003–. Writer: of plays, The Man with Two Gaffers, 2006, Lisa's Sex Strike, 2007; We Are Three Sisters, 2011; of opera libretto, Elephant and Castle, 2007. Eric Gregory Award, 1980; Somerset Maugham Award, 1984; Dylan Thomas Meml Prize, 1985; E. M. Forster Award, 1988. *Publications:* The Movement: English poetry and fiction of the 1950s, 1980; (ed jtly) The Penguin Book of Contemporary British Poetry, 1982; Seamus Heaney, 1982; Dark Glasses, 1984; The Ballad of the Yorkshire Ripper, 1987; The Yellow House, 1987; And When Did You Last See Your Father, 1993 (Waterstone's/Volvo/Esquire Non-Fiction Award, 1993; J. R. Ackerley Award, 1994); The Cracked Pot, 1995; (ed jtly) Mind Readings, 1996; As If, 1997; Too True, 1998; Dr Ox's Experiment (opera libretto), 1998; Selected Poems, 1999; The Justification of Johann Gutenberg, 2000; Things My Mother Never Told Me, 2002; Oedipus and Antigone (translations), 2003; South of the River, 2007; The Last Weekend, 2010 (televised 2012); We are Three Sisters, 2011; A Discoverie of Witches (poetry), 2012; This Poem…, 2013; Shingle Street (poetry), 2015; (contrib.) Dear Stranger: letters on the subject of happiness, 2015. *Recreations:* football, tennis, running. *Address:* c/o United Agents, 12–26 Lexington Street, W1F 0LE. *T:* (020) 3214 0800.

MORRISON, Richard Duncan; Columnist, since 1999, Chief Music Critic, since 2001, The Times; *b* 24 July 1954; *s* of Donald and Mary Morrison; *m* 1st, 1977, Marian Plant (marr. diss. 2011); two *s* one *d*; 2nd, 2013, Anna Louise Elisabeth Tilbrook. *Educ:* University Coll. Sch.; Magdalene Coll., Cambridge (MA). Asst Editor, Classical Music magazine, 1977–83; Dep. Editor, Early Music magazine, 1984–88; The Times: Music Critic, 1984–89; Dep. Arts Editor, 1989–90; Arts Editor, 1990–99. Dir of Music, St Mary, Hendon, 1976–. FRSA 1995. *Publications:* Orchestra: the LSO: a century of triumphs and turbulence, 2003. *Recreations:* walking, organ-playing. *Address:* 8 Avenue Road, N6 5DW. *T:* (020) 8351 7603.

MORRISON, (Robert) Fraser; His Honour Judge Fraser Morrison; a Circuit Judge, since 2009; *b* Hitchin, 10 Feb. 1952; *s* of Robert Morrison and Mary Morrison; *m* 1975, Sheila Joanna Brand; two *s*. Admitted solicitor, 1975; solicitor in private practice, 1975–2008; Asst Recorder, 1995–99; Dep. Dist Judge, 1997–2009; Recorder, 1999–2009. *Recreations:* sport, good company. *Address:* Wood Green Crown Court, Woodall House, Lordship Lane, N22 5LF. *Club:* Hertford.

MORRISON, Hon. Sara Antoinette Sibell Frances, (Hon. Mrs Sara Morrison); *b* 9 Aug. 1934; *d* of 2nd Viscount Long and of Laura, Duchess of Marlborough; *m* 1954, Hon. Charles Andrew Morrison (marr. diss. 1984; he *d* 2005); one *s* one *d. Educ:* in England and France. Gen. Electric Co., 1975–98 (Dir, 1980–98); Non-executive Director: Abbey National plc (formerly Abbey Nat. Building Soc.), 1979–95; Carlton TV, 1992–98; Kleinwort Charter Trust, 1993–2002. Chairman: Nat. Council for Voluntary Orgns (formerly Nat. Council of Social Service), 1977–81; Nat. Adv. Council on Employment of Disabled People, 1981–84. County Councillor, then Alderman, Wilts, 1961–71; Chairman: Wilts Assoc. of Youth Clubs, 1958–63; Wilts Community Council, 1965–70; Vice-Chairman: Nat. Assoc. Youth Clubs, 1969–71; Conservative Party Organisation, 1971–75; Member: Governing Bd, Volunteer Centre, 1972–77; Annan Cttee of Enquiry into Broadcasting, 1974–77; Nat. Consumer Council, 1975–77; Bd, Fourth Channel TV Co., 1980–85; Video Appeals Cttee (Video Recordings Act, 1984), 1985–; Governing Council, Family Policy Studies Centre, 1983–99; Nat. Radiological Protection Bd, 1989–97; Council, PSI, 1980–93; Governing Body, Imperial Coll., London, 1986–2002 (Hon. Fellow 1993); UK Round Table on Sustainable Develt, 1995–98; Chm., WWF UK, 1998–2002; Dep. Chm., 2000–05, Vice Pres. Emeritus, 2005–, WWF Internat.; Chm., Council, Univ. of Bath, 2004–06. Life FRSA 1986; FCGI 2005. Hon. DBA Coventry, 1994; Hon. LLD De Montfort, 1998; Hon. DSc Buckingham, 2000. *Address:* Wyndham's Farm, Wedhampton, Devizes, Wilts SN10 3RR. *T:* (01380) 840221; 16 Groom Place, SW1X 7BA. *T:* (020) 7245 6553.

MORRISON, Stephen Roger; non-executive Chairman, All3Media, 2013–14 (Chief Executive, 2003–12); *b* 3 March 1947; *s* of Hyman Michael Morrison and Rebecca (*née* Zolkwer); *m* 1979, Gayle Valerie Broughall; three *d. Educ:* High Sch., Glasgow; Edinburgh Univ. (MA Hons); Nat. Film Sch., Beaconsfield (ANFS). BBC Scotland (Radio and TV), 1970; Granada Television: Producer/Dir, Northern Documentary Unit, 1974; Ed., Granada Regl Progs, 1977; Hd of Arts and Features, 1981; Dir of Programmes, 1987–92; Man. Dir, Broadcasting, 1992–94; Man. Dir, 1993–94; Man. Dir, LWT, 1994–96; Chief Exec., Granada Media Gp, 1996–2002. Feature Films Producer: The Magic Toyshop, 1986; The Fruit Machine, 1988; (Exec. Producer) My Left Foot, 1989 (2 Acad. Awards); (Exec. Producer) The Field, 1990; Jack and Sarah, 1995; August, 1996. *Recreations:* walking, reading, films and theatre, talking and dining, touring delicatessens. *Club:* Garrick.

MORRISON, Toni; *see* Morrison, C. A.

MORRISON, Van; *see* Morrison, G. I.

MORRISON, William Charles Carnegie, CBE 1993; CA; UK Deputy Senior Partner, Peat Marwick McLintock, later KPMG Peat Marwick, 1987–93; *b* 10 Feb. 1938; *s* of late William and Grace Morrison; *m* 1st; two *d*; 2nd, 1977, Joceline Mary (*née* Saint). *Educ:* Kelvinside Acad., Lathallan; Merchiston Castle Sch. Thomson McLintock & Co., subseq. KMG Thomson McLintock: qual. CA (with distinction), 1961; Partner, 1966; Jt Sen. Partner, Glasgow and Edinburgh, 1974–80; UK managing partner, 1980–87. Director: Thomas Cook & Son Ltd, 1971–72; Scottish Amicable Life Assce Soc., 1973–87, 1993–97; Securities Trust of Scotland, 1976–80; Brownlee & Co., 1978–80; Bank of Scotland, 1993–97; Chm., British Linen Bank Group Ltd, 1994–97; Mem. Bd, Scottish Amicable, 1997–2008. Pres., Inst. of Chartered Accountants of Scotland, 1984–85 (Vice-Pres., 1982–84). Chairman: Auditing Practices Bd of UK and Ireland, 1991–94; Exec. Cttee, The Accountants' Jt Disciplinary Scheme, 1993–2010; Mem., Financial Reporting Council, 1991–95. Vice Pres., Scottish Council (Develt and Industry), 1982–93 (mem. various cttees; Fellow, 1993); Member: Scottish Telecommunications Bd, 1978–80; Scottish Cttee, Design Council, 1978–81. Vis. Prof. in Accountancy, Univ. of Strathclyde, 1983. Governor, Kelvinside Acad., 1967–80 (Chm. of Governors, 1975–80); Hon. Treasurer, Transport Trust, 1982–88; Trustee, Ind. Living Funds, 1993–2002. FRSA 1990. *Publications:* occasional professional papers. *Recreations:* vintage transport, model railways. *Address:* 87 Campden Hill Court, Holland Street, W8 7HW. *T:* (020) 7937 2972. *Club:* Caledonian.

MORRISON-BELL, Sir William (Hollin Dayrell), 4th Bt *cr* 1905; solicitor and farmer; *b* 21 June 1956; *s* of Sir Charles Reginald Francis Morrison-Bell, 3rd Bt and of Prudence Caroline, *d* of late Lt-Col W. D. Davies, 60th Rifles (she *m* 2nd, Peter Gillbanks); *S* father, 1967; *m* 1984, Cynthia Hélène Marie White; one *s* one *d. Educ:* Eton; St Edmund Hall, Oxford. *Heir: s* Thomas Charles Edward Morrison-Bell, *b* 13 Feb. 1985. *Address:* Highgreen, Tarset, Hexham, Northumberland NE48 1RP. *T:* (01434) 240223; 28 Batoum Gardens, W6 7QD. *T:* (020) 7602 1363.

MORRISON-LOW, Sir Richard Walter; *see* Low, Sir R. W. M.

MORRISSEY, David; actor, director and producer; Director, On The Corner Productions; *b* Liverpool, 21 June 1964; *s* of Joseph and Joan Morrissey; *m* 2006, Esther, *d* of Lucian Freud, OM, CH; two *s* one *d. Educ:* St Margaret Mary's Sch., Liverpool; De La Salle Grammar Sch., Liverpool; Royal Acad. of Dramatic Art. Actor: *stage* includes: Le Cid, Twelfth Night, UK tour and Donmar Warehouse, 1986; King John, Richard III, Edward IV, 1988, RSC; Peer Gynt, Nat. Th., 1990; Much Ado About Nothing, Queen's, 1993; Three Days of Rain, Donmar Warehouse, 1999; In a Dark Dark House, Almeida, 2008; Macbeth, Everyman, Liverpool, 2011; Hangmen, Royal Court, 2015; *films* include: Waterland, 1992; Being Human, 1993; Hilary and Jackie, 1998; Fanny and Elvis, 1999; The Suicide Club, Some Voices, 2000; Captain Corelli's Mandolin, 2001; Stoned, 2005; Derailed, Basic Instinct 2, 2006; The Reaping, The Water Horse, 2007; The Other Boleyn Girl, Is Anybody There?, 2008; Blitz, 2011; *television* includes: One Summer, 1983; Framed, 1992; Between the Lines, 1993; The Knock, Finney, 1994; Out of the Blue, 1996; Holding On, 1997; Our Mutual Friend, 1998; State of Play, The Deal, 2003 (Best Actor, RTS Awards); Blackpool, 2004; Cape Wrath, 2007; Sense and Sensibility, 2008; Red Riding, 2009; Mrs Mandela, 5 Days, U Be Dead, 2010; South Riding, 2011; The Field of Blood, 2011, 2013; The Walking Dead (series), 2012–14; The 7:39, The Driver, 2014; The Extant (series), 2015; director: *films:* Bring Me Your Love (also prod.), 2000; Don't Worry About Me (also writer and prod.), 2009; *television:* Sweet Revenge, 2001; Passer By, 2004; Thorne: Sleepyhead (also prod.), 2010; Thorne: Scaredy Cat (also prod.), 2010; Richard II, 2012; producer, Amy, 2015. *Recreations:* horse riding, tennis, golf, football. *Address:* c/o Troika, 10a Christina Street, EC2A 4PA. *T:* (020) 7336 7868. *E:* info@troikatalent.co.uk. *Clubs:* One Alfred Place, Garrick, Soho House.

MORRISSEY, Gerry Anthony; General Secretary, Broadcasting, Entertainment, Cinematograph and Theatre Union, since 2007; *b* 12 April 1960; *s* of Jimmy and Peggy Morrissey; *m* 1996, Susan Caird; one *s* one *d. Educ:* Christian Brothers Secondary Sch., Tipperary Town. Storeman, BBC, 1976–88; Broadcasting and Entertainments Trade Alliance, subseq. Broadcasting, Entertainment, Cinematograph and Theatre Union: full-time Union Official, 1988–91; Supervisory Official, 1991–99; Asst Gen. Sec., 1999–2007. Exec. Mem., Union Network Internat., 2002–; Pres., UNI MEI, 2011–. *Recreations:* tennis, badminton, running, Arsenal Football Club, National Hunt racing. *Address:* (office) Broadcasting, Entertainment, Cinematograph and Theatre Union, 373–377 Clapham Road, SW9 9BT. *T:* (020) 7346 0900. *E:* gmorrissey@bectu.org.uk.

MORRISSEY, Helena Louise, CBE 2012; Chief Executive Officer, Newton Investment Management, since 2001; Founder and Chair, 30% Club, since 2010; *b* Altrincham, Cheshire; *d* of Anthony Atkins and Jacqueline Atkins; *m* 1990, Richard Morrissey; three *s* six *d. Educ:* Fitzwilliam Coll., Cambridge (BA Hons 1987). Schroders, NY, 1987–90; Schroders Investment Mgt, 1991–93; Global Bond Fund Manager, 1994–2004, Head of Fixed Income, 1999–2001, Newton Investment Mgt. Mem., Practitioner Panel, FSA, 2007–13. Dir, Investment Mgt Assoc., 2005–12. Member: Corporate Bd, RA, 2006–; Endowment Fund Investment Bd, Univ. of Cambridge, 2012–; Ext. Mem., Financial Services Trade and Investment Bd, 2015–. *Address:* Newton Investment Management Ltd, 160 Queen Victoria Street, EC4V 4LA. *Club:* Reform.

MORRITT, Rt Hon. Sir (Robert) Andrew, Kt 1988; CVO 1989; PC 1994; Chancellor of the High Court, 2005–13; Vice-President of the Court of Protection, 2005–13; *b* 5 Feb. 1938; *s* of Robert Augustus Morritt, MBE and Margaret Mary Morritt (*née* Tyldesley Jones); *m* 1962, Sarah Simonetta, *d* of late John Ralph Merton, MBE; two *s*. *Educ:* Eton Coll.; Magdalene Coll., Cambridge (BA 1961; Hon. Fellow, 2009). 2nd Lieut Scots Guards, 1956–58. Called to the Bar, Lincoln's Inn, 1962 (Bencher, 1984; Treas., 2005); QC 1977. Junior Counsel: to Sec. of State for Trade in Chancery Matters, 1970–77; to Attorney-Gen. in Charity Matters, 1972–77; Attorney General to HRH The Prince of Wales, 1978–88; a Judge of High Court of Justice, Chancery Div., 1988–94; a Lord Justice of Appeal, 1994–2000; Vice-Chancellor of the Supreme Court, 2000–05. Vice-Chancellor of Co. Palatine of Lancaster, 1991–94. Member: Gen. Council of the Bar, 1969–73; Adv. Cttee on Legal Educn, 1972–76; Top Salaries Review Body, 1982–87. Pres., Council of the Inns of Court, 1997–2000. *Recreations:* fishing, shooting. *E:* ramorritt@outlook.com. *Club:* Garrick.

MORROW, Baron *cr* 2006 (Life Peer), of Clogher Valley in the county of Tyrone; **Maurice George Morrow;** Member (DemU) Fermanagh and South Tyrone, Northern Ireland Assembly, since 1998; Chairman, Democratic Unionist Party; *s* of Ernest and Eliza Jane Morrow; *m* 1976, Jennifer Reid; two *d*. *Educ:* Drumglass High Sch.; East Tyrone Coll. of Further and Higher Educn. Minister for Social Devel t, NI, 2000–01. Mem. (DemU) Dungannon and S Tyrone BC. *Address:* House of Lords, SW1A 0PW.

MORROW, Cdre Anthony John Clare, CVO 1997; RN; Clerk to the Butchers' Company, 2003–14; Extra Equerry to the Queen, since 1998; *b* 30 March 1944; *s* of late Capt. John Geoffrey Basil Morrow, CVO, DSC, RN and Dorothy April Bettine (*née* Mather); *m* 1st, 1969 (marr. diss. 1979); two *d*; 2nd, 1982 (marr. diss 2010); one *s* one *d*. *Educ:* Summer Fields, Oxford; Nautical Coll., Pangbourne; BRNC, Dartmouth. Entered RN, 1962: qualified Signals Officer, HMS Mercury, 1971; Lt-Comdr 1972; on staff of C-in-C Fleet, Signals Officer, HM Yacht Britannia, 1976–78; commanded HMS Lindisfarne, 1978–79; Comdr 1979; on staff, UK Mil. Rep. to NATO, 1980–83; commanded HMS Active, 1983–85; RN Exchange to CNO, US Navy, Washington, 1985–87; MoD, 1987–88; Capt. 1988; Captain, HMS Mercury, 1988–91; commanded Fourth Frigate Sqdn, HMS Active, 1991–93; ACOS, Plans and Policy, CINCHAN, Eastern Atlantic, 1993–94; Commodore Royal Yachts, 1995–98; retired 1998. Gen. Manager, W. & F. C. Bonham & Sons Ltd, 1999. Chm., Assoc. of Royal Yachtsmen, 1998–. Younger Brother, Trinity House, 1996. *Recreations:* outdoor activities, sports. *Clubs:* Royal Yacht Squadron, Royal London Yacht; Bosham Sailing; Imperial Poona Yacht.

MORROW, Graham Eric; QC 1996; **His Honour Judge Morrow;** a Circuit Judge, since 2006; *b* 14 June 1951; *s* of George Eric Morrow and Freda Morrow; *m* 1987, Rosalind Nola Ellis; one *s*, and two step *d*. *Educ:* Liverpool Coll. (Foundation Mem., 2006); Univ. of Newcastle upon Tyne (LLB). Called to the Bar, Lincoln's Inn, 1974; Asst Recorder, 1990; a Recorder, 1997–2006. Trustee, Royal Sch. for the Blind, Liverpool, 2003–. *Recreations:* cycling, swimming, ski-ing.

MORROW, Rev. Canon Dr Joseph John; Lord Lyon King of Arms, since 2014; Vice Lord-Lieutenant, City of Dundee, since 2009; *b* 12 Dec. 1954. Team Rector, St Martin's/St John's Ch, Dundee; Chaplain, St Paul's Cathedral, Dundee (now Hon. Canon); Chaplain, Glamis Castle. Solicitor in private practice and voluntary sector; joined Faculty of Advocates, 2000, non-practising Mem., 2007. First-tier Tribunal Judge (Asylum and Immigration). President: Mental Health Tribunal for Scotland, 2008– (Convener, 2005–08); Additional Support Needs Tribunals for Scotland, 2011–14. Mem. Bd, Scottish Children's Reporter Admin, 2002–. Mem. (Lab), Dundee CC, 2003–09. Grand Master, Grand Lodge of Scotland, 2004–05. CStJ (OStJ 1996). *Address:* Court of the Lord Lyon, HM New Register House, Edinburgh EH1 3YT.

MORSE, Prof. Christopher George John, (Robin); Professor of Law, King's College London, since 1992; *b* 28 June 1947; *s* of John Morse and Margaret Gwenllian Morse (*née* Maliphant); *m* 1983, Louise Angela Stott; one *s*. *Educ:* Malvern Coll.; Wadham Coll., Oxford (MA, BCL). Called to the Bar, Middle Temple, 1971; King's College London: Lectr in Law, 1971–88; Reader, 1988–92; Hd and Dean, Sch. of Law, 1992–93, 1997–2001; FKC 2000. Visiting Professor: John Marshall Law Sch., Chicago, 1979–80; Univ. of Leuven, 1982; Dir of Studies, Hague Acad. of Internat. Law, 1990. *Publications:* Torts in Private International Law, 1978; (ed jtly) Dicey and Morris on the Conflict of Laws, 11th edn 1987 to 15th edn 2012; (ed jtly) Benjamin's Sale of Goods, 3rd edn 1987 to 7th edn 2006; Public Policy in Transnational Relationships, 1991; (ed jtly) Chitty on Contracts, 27th edn 1994 to 31st edn 2012; articles in learned jls and contribs to books. *Recreations:* Swansea City Association Football Club, travel. *Address:* Dickson Poon School of Law, King's College London, Strand, WC2R 2LS. *T:* (020) 7848 5454.

MORSE, Sir Christopher Jeremy, KCMG 1975; Warden, Winchester College, 1987–97 (Fellow, 1966–82); Chancellor, Bristol University, 1989–2003; *b* 10 Dec. 1928; *s* of late Francis John Morse and Kinbarra (*née* Armfield-Marrow); *m* 1955, Belinda Marianne, *d* of Lt-Col R. B. Y. Mills; three *s* one *d* (and one *d* decd). *Educ:* Winchester; New Coll., Oxford (Hon. Fellow, 1979). 1st Class Lit. Hum. 1953. 2nd Lt KRRC, 1948–49. Fellow, All Souls Coll., Oxford, 1953–68, 1983–2011 (Hon. Fellow, 2011). Trained in banking at Glyn, Mills & Co., and made a director in 1964; Executive Dir, 1965–72, non-exec. Dir, 1993–97, Bank of England; Lloyds Bank: Dep. Chm., 1975–77; Chm., 1977–93; Lloyds Bank International: Chm., 1979–80; Dep. Chm., 1975–77 and 1980–85; Chm., Lloyds Merchant Bank Hldgs, 1985–88. Alternate Governor for UK of IMF, 1966–72; Chm. of Deputies of Cttee of Twenty, IMF, 1972–74; Chm., Cttee of London Clearing Bankers, 1980–82 (Dep. Chm., 1978–80); Mem., Council of Lloyd's, 1987–98; President: London Forex Assoc., 1978–91; Institut Internat. d'Etudes Bancaires, 1982–83; British Overseas Bankers' Club, 1983–84; BBA, 1984–91 (Vice-Pres., 1991–92); Internat. Monetary Conf., 1985–86; Banking Fedn of EC, 1988–90; CIB, 1992–93 (Vice-Pres., 1991–92); Vice-Pres., BITC, 1992–98. Mem., NEDC, 1977–81. Chm., City Communications Centre, 1985–87; non-executive Director: Alexanders Discount Co. Ltd, 1975–84; Legal & General Assce Soc., 1964 and 1975–87; ICI, 1981–93; Zeneca, 1993–99. Hon. Mem., Lombard Assoc., 1989. Governor, Henley Management Coll., 1966–85. Chairman: Per Jacobsson Foundn, 1987–99; Trustees, Beit Meml Fellowships for Med. Res., 1976–2003; GBA, 1994–99; Mem., British Selection Cttee, Harkness Fellowships, 1986–90. Pres., Classical Assoc., 1989–90. Freeman, City of London, 1978; Chm., City Arts Trust, 1976–79. FIDE Internat. Judge for chess compositions, 1975–; Pres., British Chess Problem Soc., 1977–79; Hon. Life Mem., British Chess Fedn, 1988; Hon. Master of Chess Composition, Perm. Commn for Chess Composition, FIDE, 2006. Pres., Crown and Manor Boys' Club, Hoxton, 2002–10. Hon. DLitt City, 1977; Hon. DSc Aston, 1984; Hon. LLD Bristol, 1989. *Publications:* Chess Problems: tasks and records, 1995, 2nd edn 2001. *Recreations:* poetry, problems and puzzles, coarse gardening, golf. *Address:* 102a Drayton Gardens, SW10 9RJ. *T:* (020) 7370 2265. *Club:* Athenæum.

MORSE, Robin; *see* Morse, C. G. J.

MORSHEAD, Timothy Francis; QC 2011; *b* London, 16 Dec. 1969; *s* of Rev. Ivo Morshead and Anne Morshead; *m* 2003, Penrose Foss; one *s* one *d*. *Educ:* Marlborough Coll.; Pembroke Coll., Oxford (BA 1991); City Univ. (DipLaw 1993). Called to the Bar, Lincoln's Inn, 1995; in practice as a barrister, specialising in commercial property and public law; Mem., Attorney Gen.'s Panel of Counsel, 2001–11. *Recreations:* bicycling, photography. *Address:* Landmark Chambers, 180 Fleet Street, EC4A 2HG. *T:* (020) 7430 1221.

MORSON, Basil Clifford, CBE 1987; VRD 1963; MA, DM Oxon; FRCS; FRCPath; FRCP; Civilian Consultant in Pathology to the Royal Navy, 1976–86, now Emeritus; Consulting Pathologist and Research Consultant to St Mark's Hospital, since 1986 (Consultant Pathologist, 1956–86); Director, WHO International Reference Centre for Gastrointestinal Cancer, 1969–86; *b* 13 Nov. 1921; *s* of late A. Clifford Morson, OBE, FRCS; *m* 1st, 1950, Pamela Elizabeth Gilbert (marr. diss. 1982); one *s* two *d*; 2nd, 1983, Sylvia Dutton, MBE (*d* 2014). *Educ:* Beaumont Coll.; Wadham Coll., Oxford; Middlesex Hosp. Medical Sch. House Surg., Middlesex Hosp., 1949; House Surg., Central Middlesex Hosp., 1950; Asst Pathologist, Bland-Sutton Institute of Pathology, Middlesex Hosp., 1950. Sub-Lt RNVR, 1943–46; Surgeon-Comdr RNR (London Div.), retd 1972. President: Sect. of Proctology, RSocMed, 1973–74; British Soc. of Gastroenterology, 1979–80 (Hon. Mem., 1987); British Div., Internat. Acad. of Pathology, 1979–81; Treas., RCPath, 1983–88 (Vice-Pres., 1978–81). Vis. Prof. of Pathology, Univ. of Chicago, 1959; Sir Henry Wade Vis. Prof., RCSE, 1970; Vis. Prof of Pathology, Univ. of Texas System Cancer Center, 1980 (Joanne Vandenberg Hill Award); Lectures: Lettsomian, Med. Soc., 1970; Sir Arthur Hurst Meml, British Soc. of Gastroenterology, 1970; Richardson, Massachusetts Gen. Hosp., Boston, 1970; Skinner, RCR, 1983; Shelley Meml, Johns Hopkins Univ., 1983; Kettle, RCPath, 1987. FRCS 1972; FRCP 1979 (MRCP 1973); Hon. Fellow: Amer. Soc. of Colon and Rectal Surgeons, 1974; Amer. Coll. of Gastroenterology, 1978; French Nat. Soc. of Gastroenterology, 1982; RSM, 1989; RACS, 1990. Hon. Mem., Pathological Soc. of GB and Ireland, 2006. John Hunter Medal, RCS, 1987; Frederick Salmon Medal, Sect. of Coloproctology, RSM, 1991; President's Award, British Div., Internat. Acad. of Pathol., 2005. *Publications:* Pathology of Alimentary Tract, in Systemic Pathology, ed W. St C. Symmers, 1966, 3rd edn 1987; (ed) Diseases of the Colon, Rectum and Anus, 1969; Textbook of Gastrointestinal Pathology, 1972, 5th edn 2014; Histological Typing of Intestinal Tumours, 1976; The Pathogenesis of Colorectal Cancer, 1978; Pathology in Surgical Practice, 1985; Colour Atlas of Gastrointestinal Pathology, 1988; numerous articles in medical journals. *Recreations:* gardening, ornithology, travel. *Address:* 14 Crossways Park, West Chiltington, W Sussex RH20 2QZ. *T:* (01798) 813528.

MORT, Timothy James; His Honour Judge Mort; a Circuit Judge, since 1996; *b* 4 March 1950; *s* of Dr Philip Mort and Sybil Mort; *m* 1979, Philippa Mary Brown; one *s* three *d*. *Educ:* Clifton Coll., Bristol; Emmanuel Coll., Cambridge (Schol.; MA Law Tripos 1971). Called to the Bar, Middle Temple, 1972; in practice, Northern Circuit, 1972–96. *Recreations:* tennis, Real tennis, music. *Address:* c/o Minshull Street Crown Court, Manchester M1 3FS. *Club:* Manchester Tennis and Racquet.

MORTENSEN, Prof. Neil James McCready, MD; FRCS; Professor of Colorectal Surgery, University of Oxford, since 1999; Fellow, Green Templeton College (formerly Green College), Oxford, since 2005; Consultant Colorectal Surgeon, John Radcliffe Hospital, Oxford, since 1986; *b* 16 Oct. 1949; *s* of late Peter Mortensen and of Rhoda Mortensen; *m* 1973, Jane Baker; one *s* two *d*. *Educ:* Hampton Sch.; Univ. of Birmingham Medical Sch. (MB ChB 1973); Univ. of Bristol (MD 1977). FRCS 1977. Consultant Sen. Lectr, Univ. of Bristol and Bristol Royal Infirmary, 1981–86; Reader in Colorectal Surgery, Univ. of Oxford, 1994–99. Treas. and Dir, 1996–2004, Chm., 2004–13, British Jl of Surgery Soc.; President: Assoc. of Coloproctology, GB and Ire., 2002–03; Coloproctology Sect., RSocMed, 2003–04. Trustee and Mem. Council, RCS, 2013–. FRCPSGlas 2007; Hon. FRCSE 2009. Editor in Chief: Bull. RCS; Colorectal Disease, 2015–. *Publications:* An Atlas of Rectal Endosonography, 1991; Restorative Proctocolectomy, 1993; Ulcerative Colitis and Crohn's Disease, 1993; Controversies in Inflammatory Bowel Disease, 2001; Anorectal and Colonic Disease, 2010; original articles on all aspects of colorectal surgery and colorectal disease. *Recreations:* Real tennis, opera, farming. *Address:* Department of Colorectal Surgery, Churchill Hospital, Oxford OX3 7LE. *T:* (01865) 235613.

MORTIMER, Hon. Barry; *see* Mortimer, Hon. J. B.

MORTIMER, Edward, CMG 2010; freelance writer and consultant; Distinguished Fellow, All Souls College, Oxford, since 2013; *b* Burford, 22 Dec. 1943; *s* of Robert Cecil Mortimer and Mary Hope Mortimer (*née* Walker); *m* 1968, Elizabeth Anne Zanetti; two *s* two *d*. *Educ:* Eton Coll.; Balliol Coll., Oxford (BA 1965; Hon. Fellow 2004). Asst d'Anglais, Lycée Faidherbe, St Louis-du-Sénégal, 1962; Fellow, All Souls Coll., Oxford, 1965–72, 1984–86, 2006–08; Asst Paris Corresp., 1967–70, Foreign Specialist and Leader Writer, 1973–85, The Times; For. Affairs Ed., FT, 1987–98; Chief Speechwriter and Dir of Communications, Exec. Office of the Sec.-Gen., UN, 1998–2006; Sen. Vice Pres. and Chief Prog. Officer, 2007–11, Sen. Prog. Advr, 2012–, Salzburg Global Seminar. Sen. Associate, Carnegie Endowment, NY, 1980–81. Res. Associate, IISS, 1990–91. Rapporteur, Gp of Eminent Persons, Council of Europe, 2011. Hd, Ind. Review, BBC coverage of Arab Spring, 2012. Pres., British Assoc. of Former UN Civil Servants, 2011–; Chair: Sri Lanka Campaign for Peace and Justice, 2009–15; Ind. Diplomat UK, 2012–; Children's Radio Foundn UK, 2015–. Leonard Stein Lectr, Balliol Coll., Oxford, 2012. Hon. Prof., Univ. of Warwick, 1993–98. Hon. DLitt Exeter, 1999. *Publications:* France and the Africans, 1969; Faith and Power: the politics of Islam, 1982; The Rise of the French Communist Party, 1984; Roosevelt's Children, 1987 (US edn as The World that F.D.R. Built, 1989); European Security after the Cold War, 1992; (ed with Robert Fine) People, Nation and State, 1999; (with T. Garton Ash and K. Öktem) Freedom in Diversity, 2013. *Recreations:* talking, walking, reading aloud, going to the theatre. *Address:* 79 Witney Street, Burford, Oxon OX18 4RX. *E:* edward.mortimer@all-souls.ox.ac.uk. *Clubs:* Groucho, Frontline.

MORTIMER, Hugh Roger, LVO 1992; HM Diplomatic Service, retired; Minister and Deputy Head of Mission, Berlin, 2005–09; *b* 19 Sept. 1949; *s* of Phillip Roger Mortimer and Patricia Henley Mortimer (*née* Moreton); *m* 1974, Zosia Rzepecka (marr. diss. 2000); one *d* (and one *d* decd); *m* 2009, Martina Manfreda. *Educ:* Cheltenham Coll.; Univ. of Surrey (BSc Linguistics and Regl Studies); King's Coll., London (MA War Studies). Joined HM Diplomatic Service, 1973: Third Sec., Rome, 1975–78; Third, later Second Sec., Singapore, 1978–81; FCO, 1981–83; Second, later First Sec., UK Mission to UN, NY, 1983–86; FCO, 1986–89; on attachment to German Foreign Ministry, 1990; Dep. Head of Mission, Berlin, 1991–94; FCO, 1994–95; rcds 1996; Dep. Head of Mission, Ankara, 1997–2000; Ambassador to Slovenia, 2001–05. *Recreations:* jogging, squash, sailing, guitar playing.

MORTIMER, James Edward; Deputy Director and Treasury Officer of Accounts, 1995–2000; *b* 9 Nov. 1947; *s* of late James Edward Mortimer and Renee Mabel Mortimer (*née* Horton); *m* 1969, Lesley Patricia Young. *Educ:* Latymer Upper Sch.; Wadham Coll., Oxford (MA, BPhil). HM Treasury, 1971–2000: Economic Advr, 1974–81; Principal, 1981–83; Grade 5, 1983–91; Under Sec., 1991–2000; Head of Aid and Export Finance Gp, 1991–95. *Recreations:* football, golf, cricket, birdwatching, cinema. *Address:* 21 Hogarth Way, Hampton, Middlesex TW12 2EL. *Clubs:* Royal Automobile; Old Latymerians Association.

MORTIMER, Hon. (John) Barry, GBS 1999; QC 1971; mediator and arbitrator; a Non-Permanent Judge, Court of Final Appeal, Hong Kong, since 1997; a Judge, since 2005, and President, since 2010, Court of Appeal, Brunei Darussalam; *b* 7 Aug. 1931; *s* of late John William Mortimer and Maud (*née* Snarr) Mortimer; *m* 1958, Judith Mary (*née* Page) (*d* 2013); two *s* two *d*. *Educ:* St Peter's School, York (Headmasters' Exhibitioner 1945); Emmanuel College, Cambridge; BA 1955, MA 1959. Commissioned into 4 RTR, 1951; served in Egypt, 1951–52; 45/51 RTR (TA), 1952–57. Called to the Bar, Middle Temple, 1956 (Bencher, 1980; Master Reader, 2003); Harmsworth Law Scholar 1957; Prosecuting Counsel on NE Circuit: to Post Office, 1965–69; to Inland Revenue, 1969–71; a Recorder, 1972–87; Judge,

Supreme Court of Hong Kong, 1985–93; a Justice of Appeal, Court of Appeal, Supreme (later High) Court of Hong Kong, 1993–99 (a Vice-President, 1997–99). Chancellor, Dio. of Ripon, 1971–85. Chairman: Mental Health Review Tribunal, 1983–85; Overseas Trust Bank (Compensation) Tribunal, 1986–87; Member: Bar Council, 1970–75; Senate, 1979–85; Law Reform Commn, Hong Kong, 1990–99 (Chm., Sub-cttee on Privacy and Data Protection); Judicial Studies Bd, 1996–99; Vice Chm., Advocacy Inst. of Hong Kong, 1997–99; Chm., Criminal Court Users Cttee, 1998–99; Dir of Advocacy, Middle Temple, 2004–06. Chm., Envmtl Impact Assessment Appeal Bd, Kowloon Canton Railway Corp. Spur Line Appeal, 2001. Dir, City Disputes Panel Ltd, 2000–05. Hon. Diplomate, Amer. Bd of Trial Advocates, 1994. *Recreations:* reading, shooting, tennis. *Address:* The Grange, Staveley, Knaresborough, N Yorks HG5 9LD; 21 Fl., HK Diamond Exchange Building, 8–10 Duddell Street, Central, Hong Kong. *Clubs:* Travellers; Hong Kong.

MORTIMER, Robin John David; Chief Executive, Port of London Authority, since 2014; *b* Norwich, 8 June 1972; *s* of David and Valerie Mortimer; *m* 1999, Katie Luther; one *s* one *d*. *Educ:* Norwich Sch.; Queen's Coll., Oxford (BA Modern Hist.); Sch. of Oriental and African Studies, Univ. of London (MSc Develt Studies 1999). Department of the Environment, later Department of the Environment, Transport and the Regions: fast stream postings in local govt finance and internat. trade and envmt, 1994–96; Private Sec. to Sec. of State, 1996–98; Policy Advr on Gt Lakes region, DFID, 1999–2000; Department of the Environment, Transport and the Regions, later Department for Environment, Food and Rural Affairs: Hd, Water Industry Team, 2000–01; Private Sec. to Sec. of State, 2001–03; Hd, Rural Strategy Div., 2004–06; Dep. Dir, Office of Climate Change, 2006–07; Dir, Envmt and Rural Gp, 2007–14. *Recreations:* running, music, reading, cooking, history. *Address:* Port of London Authority, Pinnacle House, 23–26 St Dunstan's Hill, EC3R 8HN.

MORTIMORE, Prof. Peter John, OBE 1994; PhD; FBPsS; independent educational consultant; Director, Institute of Education, London University, 1994–2000 (Professor of Education, 1990–2000, now Emeritus); *b* 17 Jan. 1942; *s* of late Claude Mortimore and Rose Mortimore; *m* 1965, Jo Hargaden; three *d*. *Educ:* Chiswick County Grammar Sch.; St Mary's Coll., Strawberry Hill; Birkbeck Coll., London Univ. (BSc; Hon. Fellow 2001); Inst. of Education (MSc; Hon. Fellow 2008); Inst. of Psychiatry (PhD). CPsychol 1989; FBPsS 1989. Teacher, Sacred Heart Sch., SE5, 1964–66; Teacher and Head of Dept, Stockwell Manor Sch., SW9, 1966–73; Res. Officer, Inst. of Psychiatry, 1975–78; Mem., HM Inspectorate, 1978; Inner London Education Authority: Dir, Res. and Stats Br., 1979–85; Asst Educn Officer (Secondary Schs), 1985–87; Prof. of Educn, Lancaster Univ., 1988–90; Dep. Dir, London Univ. Inst. of Educn, 1990–94; Pro-Vice-Chancellor, London Univ., 1999–2000; Prof. of Educn, Univ. of Southern Denmark, 2008–09. Member: Educn Res. Bd, SSRC, 1981–82; Educn and Human Develt Cttee, ESRC, 1982–85; Univ. of London Exams and Assessment Council, 1991; Trustee, VSO, 1992–2002. Consultant, OECD, 2003–07. Governor: SOAS, 1993–98; Birkbeck Coll., 1998–2000. Monthly columnist, Guardian Education, 2006–. Hon. FCP 1994; AcSS 2000. FRSA 1990. Hon. DLitt Heriot-Watt, 1998; Hon. PhD Southern Denmark, 2008. *Publications:* (jtly) Fifteen Thousand Hours: secondary schools and their effects on children, 1979; (jtly) Behaviour Problems in Schools, 1984; (jtly) Secondary School Examinations, 1986; (jtly) School Matters: the junior years, 1988; (jtly) The Primary Head: roles, responsibilities and reflections, 1991; The Secondary Head: roles, responsibilities and reflections, 1991; (jtly) Managing Associate Staff, 1994; (jtly) Planning Matters, 1995; (jtly) Living Education, 1997; (jtly) Forging Links, 1997; Road to Improvement, 1998; (jtly) Understanding Pedagogy, 1999; (jtly) Culture of Change, 2000; (jtly) Improving School Effectiveness, 2001; Education under Siege, 2013. *Recreations:* theatre, art, music, walking.

MORTIMORE, Simon Anthony; QC 1991; *b* 12 April 1950; *s* of late Robert Anthony Mortimore and Katherine Elizabeth Mackenzie Mortimore (*née* Caine); *m* 1983, Fiona Elizabeth Jacobson; one *s* one *d*. *Educ:* Westminster School; Exeter Univ. (LLB). Called to the Bar, Inner Temple, 1972. CEDR accredited mediator, 1997–. Mem., ACCA Disciplinary Panel, 2003–07. Chm., Peasmarsh Chamber Music Fest., 2012–. *Publications:* contribs to Bullen and Leake and Jacobs Precedents of Pleading, 13th edn 1990; Insolvency of Banks, 1996; (ed) Company Directors: duties, liabilities and remedies, 2009, 2nd edn 2013. *Recreations:* opera, general cultural interests, travel, golf. *Address:* 3–4 South Square, Gray's Inn, WC1R 5HP. *T:* (020) 7696 9900. *Clubs:* Hurlingham, Brooks's; Royal St George's Golf, Rye Golf.

MORTON, 22nd Earl of, *cr* 1458 (*de facto* 21st Earl, 22nd but for the Attainder); **John Charles Sholto Douglas;** Lord Aberdour, 1458; Lord-Lieutenant of West Lothian, 1985–2001; *b* 19 March 1927; *s* of Hon. Charles William Sholto Douglas (*d* 1960) (2nd *s* of 19th Earl) and Florence (*d* 1985), *er d* of late Major Henry Thomas Timson; *S* cousin, 1976; *m* 1949, Sheila Mary, *d* of late Rev. Canon John Stanley Gibbs, MC, Didmarton House, Badminton, Glos; two *s* one *d*. Director: Quickwing, 2001–07; B-Fuel-Wise, 2003–07. DL West Lothian, 1982. *Recreation:* polo. *Heir:* *s* Lord Aberdour, *qv*. *Address:* Dalmahoy, Kirknewton, Midlothian EH27 8EB. *Clubs:* Farmers; Edinburgh Polo, Dalmahoy Country.

MORTON, Alison Margaret; *see* Kinnaird, A. M.

MORTON, Rev. Andrew Queen; Minister of Culross Abbey, 1959–87; *b* 4 June 1919; *s* of Alexander Morton and Janet Queen; *m* 1948, Jean, *e d* of George Singleton and Jean Wands; one *s* two *d*. *Educ:* Glasgow Univ. MA 1942, BD 1947, BSc 1948. Minister of St Andrews, Fraserburgh, 1949–59. Dept of Computer Science, Univ. of Edinburgh, 1965–86. Hon. Res. Fellow, Glasgow Univ., 1990. FRSE 1973. *Publications:* The Structure of the Fourth Gospel, 1961; Authorship and Integrity in the New Testament, 1963; (with G. H. C. Macgregor) The Structure of Luke and Acts, 1965; Paul the Man and the Myth, 1965; (with S. Michaelson) The Computer in Literary Research, 1973; Literary Detection, 1979; (with S. Michaelson and N. Hamilton-Smith) Justice for Helander, 1979; (with James McLeman) The Genesis of John, 1980; (with S. Michaelson) The Cusum Plot, 1990; (with M. G. Farringdon) Fielding and the Federalist, 1990; Proper Words in Proper Places, 1992; The Authorship and Integrity of the New Testament Epistles, 1993; The Making of Mark, 1995; Gathering the Gospels, 1997; A Fresh Look at Matthew, 1998; Revelation, 1998; The Codex Sinaiticus Revisited, 2002; A Gospel Made to Measure, 2004; contrib. ALLC Jl; TLS. *Recreations:* thinking, talking. *Address:* 4A Manse Street, Aberdour, Burntisland, Fife KY3 0TT. *T:* (01383) 860131. *E:* aqmorton@btinternet.com.

MORTON, His Honour (David) Christopher; a Circuit Judge, 1992–2008; *b* 1 Dec. 1943; *s* of Rev. Alexander Francis Morton and Esther Ann Morton; *m* 1970, Sandra Jo Kobes; three *s* one *d*. *Educ:* Worksop Coll., Notts; Fitzwilliam Coll., Cambridge (BA, LLB). Called to the Bar, Inner Temple, 1968; Wales and Chester Circuit; practised in Swansea, 1969–92. *Recreations:* Welsh affairs, railways, family. *Club:* Royal Over-Seas League.

MORTON, George Martin; Principal (formerly Senior) Planner, Trafford Borough Council, 1986–99; *b* 11 Feb. 1940; *s* of Rev. Thomas Ralph Morton, DD, and Janet Maclay MacGregor Morton (*née* Baird). *Educ:* Fettes Coll. Edinburgh; Edinburgh Coll. of Art; Glasgow Univ. Member: Manchester City Council, 1971–74; Greater Manchester Council, 1973–77. Sec., Tameside and Glossop CHC, 1984–86. MP (Lab) Manchester, Moss Side, July 1978–1983; an Opposition Whip, 1979–83. *Address:* 4 St Annes Road, Manchester M21 8TD. *T:* (0161) 881 8195.

MORTON, Prof. John, OBE 1998; PhD; FRS 2011; FBPsS; Director, Cognitive Development Unit, Medical Research Council, 1982–98; Hon. Professor, University College London, since 1998 (Hon. Fellow, 2012); *b* 1 Aug. 1933; *s* of late Winston James Morton and Mary Winifred Morton (*née* Nutter); *m*; one *d*; *m* 3rd, 1985, Guinevere Tufnell. *Educ:* Nelson Grammar Sch.; Christ's Coll., Cambridge (BA, MA); Reading Univ. (PhD 1961). FBPsS 1974 (Hon. FBPsS 1997). Scientist, MRC Applied Psychology Unit, Cambridge, 1960–82. Res. Fellow, Univ. of Michigan, 1967; Res. Associate and Lectr, Yale Univ., 1967–68; Vis. Scientist, MSH Paris, 1974–75; Max Planck Ges., Nijmegen, 1977–80; Visiting Professor: Cornell Univ., 1980; UCL, 1982–98; Vis. Fellow, Tokyo Metropolitan Inst. of Gerontology, 1981. Pres., EPsS, 1998–2000 (Hon. Mem., 2001). MAE 1990. President's Award, BPsS, 1988; Ipsen Prize in neural plasticity, Ipsen Foundn, 2001. *Publications:* (ed) Biological and Social Factors in Psycholinguistics, 1971; (ed jtly) Psycholinguistics: Developmental and Pathological, Series I, 1977, Series II, 1979; (with M. Johnson) Biology and Cognitive Development, 1991; (ed jtly) Development Neurocognition, 1993; (ed jtly) The Acquisition and Dissolution of Language, 1994; (ed jtly) Cognitive Science: an introduction, 1996; Understanding Developmental Disorders: a causal modelling approach, 2004; articles in sci. jls. *Recreations:* theatre, cooking, Tower Theatre Company, chocolate, Burnley FC. *Address:* (office) Institute of Cognitive Neuroscience, University College London, Alexandra House, 17–19 Queen Square, WC1N 3AR. *T:* (020) 7679 1156.

MORTON, John, DPhil; FCGI; FRAeS; FIMMM; CEng; Chief Executive, Engineering and Technology Board, 2005–08; Senior Research Investigator, Imperial College London, since 2012; Senior Lecturer, University College, Oxford, since 2012 (Lecturer, 2009–12); *b* Gateshead, 11 Dec. 1949; *s* of John Morton and Emmeline Morton (*née* Watson); *m* 1977, Maria Rosario Larrarte; two *s*. *Educ:* Grammar Sch. for Boys, Gateshead; St Catharine's Coll., Cambridge (BA 1971); Exeter Coll., Oxford (DPhil 1975); Stanford Graduate Sch. of Business. CEng 1978. Vis. Researcher, Escuela Técnica Superior de Ingenieros de Caminos, Canales y Puertos, Madrid (Royal Soc. Study Visit Award), 1979; Lectr, Dept of Aeronautics, Imperial Coll. London, 1979–85; Sen. Res. Associate, NASA Langley Res. Center, USA, 1986; Prof., Dept of Engrg Sci. and Mechanics, 1986–93, Dir, Center for Composite Materials and Structures, 1991–93, Virginia Tech.; Defence Research Agency, subseq. Defence Evaluation and Research Agency: Dir, Structural Materials Centre, 1993–97; Dir, Mechanical Scis Sector, 1998–2001; Chief Operating Officer, Future Systems and Technol., QinetiQ, 2001–05. Sen. Res. Fellow, Dept of Engrg Sci., Univ. of Oxford, 2009–12. Man. Dir, Oxcomp Ltd, 2011–13; UK Vice-Pres., TEAMS SL, 2012–. Vis. Scientist, Univ. Libre de Bruxelles, 1992; Prof. invité, Ecole polytechnique fédérale de Lausanne, 1992; Vis. Prof., Dept of Aeronautics, Imperial Coll. London, 1995–. Mem., Foresight Panel for Materials, OST, 1994–97. Chm., Women into Sci., Engrg and Construction, 2007–08. Mem. Council, IMMM, 2004–08. FIMMM 1992; FRAeS 1998; FCGI 2008. Liveryman, Co. of Engineers, 2006. (Jtly) Donald Julius Groen Prize, 1991 and 1995, (jtly) William Sweet Smith Prize, 1991, IMechE. *Publications:* articles on fracture mechanics, structural mechanics and the mechanics of composite materials. *Recreations:* tennis, gardening. *Address:* 129 High Street, Odiham RG29 1NW. *E:* john.morton@univ.ox.ac.uk. *Club:* Oxford and Cambridge.

MORTON, John David Peter; writer and director for television and radio, since 1992; *b* Sutton Bonnington, Notts, 22 Jan. 1957; *s* of Harold and Josephine Morton; *m* 1997, Helen Atkinson Wood. *Educ:* Kingsbridge Sch., S Devon; Univ. of Leicester (BA Hons English Lit. 1979); Hughes Hall, Cambridge (PGCE 1980); Univ. of Kent (MA Modern English Lit. 1981). English teacher, Peter Symonds' Coll., Winchester, 1981–92. Writer for BBC Radio: People Like Us, 1995; Mightier than the Sword, 1995; The Sunday Format, 1996; writer for BBC TV, (with C. Langham) Kiss Me Kate, 1998; writer and director for BBC Television: People Like Us, 1999; The Gist, 2001; (with T. Roche) Broken News, 2005; Twenty Twelve, 2010; W1A, 2014. *Recreations:* walking, tennis, squash, thinking. *Address:* c/o Curtis Brown, Haymarket House, 28–29 Haymarket, SW1Y 4SP.

MORTON, Kathryn Mary Stuart, CB 2002; Solicitor and Director General, Legal Services, Department for Environment, Food and Rural Affairs, 2001–02; *b* 2 June 1946; *d* of late Samuel Stuart Morton and Joan Alice Bessie Morton (*née* Tapscott). *Educ:* Ealing Grammar Sch. for Girls; Univ. of Sussex (BA). Admitted Solicitor, 1980. Leverhulme Res. Scholarship, India, 1967–68; Res. Asst, Lancaster Univ., 1969–71; Res. Officer, ODI, 1971–74; Res. Associate, ODI, and free-lance economist, 1974–80; with Bird & Bird, 1978–82; OFT, 1982–85; DTI, 1985–97, Under Sec. (Legal), subseq. Dir, 1992–97; Legal Advr and Solicitor, MAFF, 1997–2002. *Publications:* Aid and Dependence, 1975; (with Peter Tulloch) Trade and Developing Countries, 1977. *T:* (020) 7226 2332. *E:* kmsmorton@waitrose.com.

MORTON, Keith Farrance; QC 2011; *b* London, 8 Feb. 1966; *s* of Ian Francis Morton and Edna Hilda Morton (*née* Farrance). *Educ:* Earlham High Sch., Norwich; Univ. of Hull (BSc Econs 1987); City Univ. (DipLaw 1989); Inns of Court Sch. of Law. Called to the Bar, Lincoln's Inn, 1990; Treasury Counsel (Civil), 1997–2011. *Recreations:* architecture, music, cycling. *Address:* Temple Garden Chambers, 1 Harcourt Buildings, Temple, EC4Y 9DA. *T:* (020) 7583 1315. *E:* kmorton@tgchambers.com. *Club:* Two Brydges.

MORTON, Prof. Keith William; Professor of Numerical Analysis, and Professorial Fellow of Balliol College, Oxford University, 1983–97, now Emeritus Professor, Oxford University and Emeritus Fellow, Balliol College; Professor of Mathematics (part-time), University of Bath, 1998–2005; *b* 28 May 1930; *s* of Keith Harvey Morton and Muriel Violet (*née* Hubbard); *m* 1952, Patricia Mary Pearson; two *s* two *d*. *Educ:* Sudbury Grammar Sch.; Corpus Christi Coll., Oxford (BA 1952; MA 1954); New York Univ. (PhD 1964). Theoretical Physics Div., AERE, Harwell, 1952–59; Res. Scientist, Courant Inst. of Mathematical Sci., NY Univ., 1959–64; Head of Computing and Applied Maths, Culham Lab., UKAEA, 1964–72; Prof. of Applied Maths, Reading Univ., 1972–83. Fellow, SIAM, 2011. IMA Gold Medal, 2002; De Morgan Medal, LMS, 2010. *Publications:* (with R. D. Richtmyer) Difference Methods for Initial-value Problems, 1967; (ed with M. J. Baines) Numerical Methods for Fluid Dynamics, Vol. I 1982, Vol. II 1986, Vol. III 1988, Vol. IV 1993, Vol. V 1995; (with D. F. Mayers) Numerical Solution of Partial Differential Equations: an introduction, 1994, 2nd edn 2005; Numerical Solution of Convection-Diffusion Problems, 1996; numerous articles on numerical analysis and applied maths in learned jls. *Recreations:* reading, walking, gardening, listening to music. *Address:* Roscarrock, 48 Jack Straw's Lane, Headington, Oxford OX3 0DW. *T:* (01865) 768823. *E:* morton@maths.ox.ac.uk.

MORTON, Patricia Ann; *see* Jacobs, P. A.

MORTON, Wendy; MP (C) Aldridge-Brownhills, since 2015; *b* Northallerton, 1967; *d* of Thomas and Edna Hunter; *m* 1990, David Morton. *Educ:* Wensleydale Sch., N Yorks; Open Univ. (MBA). Exec. Officer, FCO, 1987–89; sales and marketing: HMCO Europe; Centrostyle; Dir, DM Electronics Ltd, 1991–. *Recreations:* walking, running, cooking, Rotary. *Address:* House of Commons, SW1A 0AA. *T:* (020) 7219 8784. *E:* wendy.morton.mp@parliament.uk.

MORTON JACK, His Honour David; a Circuit Judge, 1986–2008; *b* 5 Nov. 1935; *o s* of late Col W. A. Morton Jack, OBE, and late Mrs Morton Jack (*née* Happell); *m* 1972, Rosemary, *o d* of F. G. Rentoul; four *s*. *Educ:* Stowe (scholar); Trinity Coll., Oxford (Cholmeley Schol., MA). 2nd Lieut, RIrF, 1955–57. Called to the Bar, Lincoln's Inn, 1962; a Recorder of the Crown Court, 1979–86. *Recreations:* country pursuits, sheep-keeping, reading, music, gardens.

MOSCO, Les; Chief Executive Officer (formerly Managing Director), Commercial Strategies (formerly Purchasing Strategies) Ltd, since 2003; *b* Manchester, 15 July 1954; *s* of late Bernard Mosco and Stella Mosco; *m* 1979, Barbara Baum; one *s* one *d.* *Educ:* Queen Elizabeth's Grammar Sch., Middleton, Manchester; Sheffield Univ. (BSc 1st Cl. Hons Physics). FCIPS 1992. Various posts, British Coal, 1975–89; Asst Sec., Scottish Office, 1989–92; Gp Purchasing Dir, Natwest Bank, 1992–98; Supply Chain Exec., Amerada Hess, 1998–2000; Supply Chain Dir, Railtrack, then Network Rail, 2000–03; Dir, Commercial, Defence Equipment and Support, 2007–11, Commercial, 2011–14, MoD. Trustee: Victim Support; Chiltern Soc. MInstD. *Recreations:* walking and cycling in the Chilterns and London, watching film (especially in Rex Cinema, Berkhamsted), travel, current affairs. *Address:* 3 Rothschild Court, Hamberlins Lane, Northchurch, Berkhamsted, Herts HP4 3TD. *T:* (01442) 865693, 07799 718283. *E:* lesmosco@hotmail.com.

MOSELEY, Elwyn Rhys, CBE 2003; Commissioner for Local Administration in Wales (Ombudsman), 1991–2003; *b* 6 Aug. 1943; *s* of late Rev. Luther Moseley and Megan Eiluned Moseley (*née* Howells); *m* 1968, Annick Andrée Guyomard; two *s* one *d.* *Educ:* Caterham Sch.; Queens' Coll., Cambridge (MA). Solicitor. Asst Solicitor, Newport CBC, 1969–72; Sen. Asst Solicitor, Cardiff CBC, 1972–74; Cardiff City Council: City Solicitor, 1974–91; Dep. Chief Exec., 1979–91; Dir of Admin. and Legal Services, 1987–91.

See also T. H. Moseley.

MOSELEY, His Honour Hywel; *see* Moseley, His Honour T. H.

MOSELEY, Joyce, OBE 2007; Chief Executive, Catch22 (formerly Rainer), 1999–2011; *b* 12 Jan. 1947; *d* of late Harry Moseley and Kathleen Moseley (*née* Dalton); *m* 1995, Anthony Allen. *Educ:* Manchester High Sch. for Girls; Bedford Coll., Univ. of London (BScSoc Hons 1968 and Applied Social Studies 1970); Univ. of Surrey (MSc Social Res. 1984). Social worker and Sen. Social Worker, London Borough of Ealing, Sen. Social Worker and Area Manager, London Borough of Islington, 1974–86; Asst Dir, Herts CC, 1986–91; Dir of Social Services, London Borough of Hackney, 1991–97; consultancy, 1997–99. Chm., HCT Gp, 2010–. Mem., Youth Justice Bd for England and Wales, 1998–2004; Chm., Transition to Adulthood Alliance, 2012–. Non-exec. Dir, Tavistock and Portman NHS Foundation Trust, 2009–14. Trustee, Warren House Gp, Dartington Social Res. Unit, 2012– (Chair, 2014–). *Publications:* Other People's Children, 1976; contrib. articles and chapters to social care pubns. *Recreations:* theatre, walking, food and wine. *Club:* Two Brydges.

MOSELEY, His Honour (Thomas) Hywel; QC 1985; a Circuit Judge, 1989–2004; *b* 27 Sept. 1936; *s* of late Rev. Luther Moseley and Megan Eiluned Moseley; *m* 1960, Monique Germaine Thérèse Drufin (separated 2009); three *d.* *Educ:* Caterham Sch.; Queens' Coll., Cambridge (MA, LLM). Called to the Bar, Gray's Inn, 1964; in private practice, Cardiff, 1965–89, and London, 1977–89; a Recorder, 1981–89. Lectr in Law, 1960–65, Prof. of Law, 1970–82, UCW, Aberystwyth. Mem., Insolvency Rules Cttee, 1993–97. *Publications:* (with B. Rudden) Outline of the Law of Mortgages, 4th edn 1967. *Recreation:* reading. *Address:* Nantceiro, Llanbadarn Fawr, Aberystwyth, Ceredigion SY23 3HW. *T:* (01970) 623532.

See also E. R. Moseley.

MOSER, Dr Michael Edward; specialist international advisor on environment, UN Development Programme, Iran, The Maldives and China, and other international organisations; *b* 16 July 1956; *s* of late Roger Michael Moser and Noreen Moser (*née* Wane); *m* 1983, Joanna Jocelyn Stewart-Smith; three *d.* *Educ:* Shrewsbury Sch.; Durham Univ. (1st cl. Hons Ecol.; PhD). David Lack Studentship, BOU, 1980–82; British Trust for Ornithology: Estuaries Officer, 1983–86; Dir of Develt, 1986–88; Dir, Internat. Waterfowl and Wetlands Res. Bureau, then Wetlands Internat., 1988–99; English Nature: Mem., Council, 1999–2006; Dep. Chm., 2004–05; Acting Chm., 2005–06; Mem., UK Jt Nature Conservation Cttee, 2001–06. Member, Council: Tour du Valat, Centre for Mediterranean Wetlands, Camargue, France, 1990–2014; RSPB, 2001–06; Chairman: N Devon UNESCO Biosphere Reserve Partnership, 2007–12; SW Forestry and Woodlands (formerly SW Region) Adv. Cttee, Forestry Commn, 2007–; N Devon Nature Improvement Area Steering Gp, 2013–; Member, Board: Devon Wildlife Trust, 2014–; MAVA Foundn for Nature, Switzerland, 2015–. *Publications:* (with C. M. Finlayson) Wetlands, 1991. *Recreations:* natural history, travel, fly fishing, woodland management. *Address:* West Week Farm, Week, Chulmleigh, Devon EX18 7EE.

MOSER, Philip Curt Harold; QC 2012; *b* Vienna, 20 July 1968; *s* of Peter Moser and Maud Moser (now Fuerst); *m* 2003, Anne, *d* of Prof. Olle Isaksson and Eva Isaksson; one *s* one *d.* *Educ:* Vienna Internat. Sch.; Robinson Coll., Cambridge (BA 1990; MA); Inns of Court Sch. of Law. Called to the Bar, Inner Temple, 1992, Bencher, 2012; Mediator, 2003; Jun. Counsel to the Crown, 2008–12. Arbitrator, CADR Switzerland, 2015. University of Cambridge: Supervisor in EC Law, Robinson Coll., 1995–97; Res. Associate, Centre for Eur. Legal Studies, 1996–98. Fellow, Eur. Law Inst., 2012–. Bar Council Rep. to Fedn of Eur. Bars, 2001–07; UK Mem., Council, Internat. Criminal Bar, 2003–07 (Chm., Election and Constitution Cttees, 2003–07); Member: Cttee, Bar Eur. Gp, 1998–; Bar Liaison Cttee, Inner Temple, 2003–12; Cttee, UK Assoc. of Eur. Law, 2005–; Internat. Relns Cttee, 2000–08, Training for the Bar Cttee, 2012–13, Bar Council. Gov., St Joseph's Sch., Camden, 1995–2003. Mem., Editl Bd, European Law Reports, 1999–2012; Ed., The European Advocate, 2000–. *Publications:* (ed) Making Community Law, 2008; contrib. chapters to books on EU Law and articles in legal jls. *Address:* Monckton Chambers, 1 & 2 Raymond Buildings, Gray's Inn, WC1R 5NR. *T:* (020) 7405 7211, *Fax:* (020) 7405 2084. *E:* pmoser@monckton.com.

MOSES, Rev. Alan; *see* Moses, Rev. L. A.

MOSES, Rt Hon. Sir Alan (George), Kt 1996; PC 2005; a Lord Justice of Appeal, 2005–14; Chairman, Independent Press Standards Organisation, since 2014; *b* 29 Nov. 1945; *s* of late Eric George Rufus Moses, CB and of Pearl Moses (*née* Lipton); *m* 1992, Dinah Victoria Casson, *qv*; two *s* one *d* by a previous marriage. *Educ:* Bryanston Sch.; University Coll., Oxford (Quondam Exhibnr; BA). Called to the Bar, Middle Temple, 1968, Bencher, 1994; Mem., Panel of Junior Counsel to the Crown, Common Law, 1981–90; Junior Counsel to Inland Revenue, Common Law, 1985–90; a Recorder, 1986–96; QC 1990; a Judge of the High Ct, QBD, 1996–2005; Presiding Judge, SE Circuit, 1999–2002. Mem., Ct of Appeal, Cayman Islands, 2015–. Prof of Law, 2006–15, Mem. Council, 2007–13, RA; Mem. Bd, Royal Acad. Schs, 2015–. Mem. Cttee, London Library, 2003–06. Chm., Spitalfields Music, 2009–. Trustee: Koestler Award Trust, 2004–06 (Advr, 2006–); Pilgrim Trust, 2006–. *Club:* Union Socialista La Serra (Italy).

MOSES, Dinah Victoria, (Lady Moses); *see* Casson, D. V.

MOSES, Very Rev. Dr John Henry, KCVO 2006; Dean of St Paul's, 1996–2006, now Emeritus; Dean, Order of St Michael and St George, and Dean, Order of the British Empire, 1996–2006; *b* 12 Jan. 1938; *s* of late Henry William Moses and Ada Elizabeth Moses; *m* 1964, Susan Elizabeth; one *s* two *d.* *Educ:* Ealing Grammar School; Nottingham Univ. (Gladstone Meml Prize 1958; BA History 1959; PhD 1965); Trinity Hall, Cambridge (Cert. in Education 1960); Lincoln Theological Coll. Deacon 1964, priest 1965; Asst Curate, St Andrew, Bedford, 1964–70; Rector of Coventry East Team Ministry, 1970–77; Examining Chaplain to Bishop of Coventry, 1972–77; Rural Dean of Coventry East, 1973–77; Archdeacon of Southend, 1977–82; Provost of Chelmsford, 1982–96. Vis. Fellow, Wolfson Coll., Cambridge, 1987. Mem., Gen. Synod, 1985–2005; Church Comr, 1988–2006; Mem., ACC, 1997–2005. Chm. Council, Centre for Study of Theology, Essex Univ., 1987–96; Rector, Anglia Poly. Univ., 1992–96. Select Preacher, Oxford Univ., 2004–05. Vice-Pres., City of London Fest., 1997–2006. Freeman, City of London, 1997; Liveryman: Feltmakers' Co., 1998–; Plaisterers' Co., 1999–; Masons' Co., 2005–; Hon. Freeman: Water Conservators' Co., 2000–; Weavers' Co., 2011–. Hon. Dr Anglia Poly. Univ., 1997; Hon. DD: Nottingham, 2007; Grad. Theol Foundn, Indiana, 2010. OStJ 2003. Order of Al Istiqlal of Hashemite (Jordan), 2002. *Publications:* The Sacrifice of God, 1992; A Broad and Living Way, 1995; The Desert, 1997; One Equall Light: an anthology of the writings of John Donne, 2003; The Language of Love, 2007; Divine Discontent: the prophetic voice of Thomas Merton, 2014. *Address:* Chestnut House, The Burgage, Southwell, Notts NG25 0EP. *T:* (01636) 814880. *E:* johnmoses.southwell@gmail.com. *Club:* Athenæum.

MOSES, Rev. (Leslie) Alan; Vicar of All Saints', Margaret Street, London, since 1995; *b* 3 Nov. 1949; *s* of Leslie Moses and Edna (*née* Watson); *m* 1971, Theresa Frances O'Connor; one *s* one *d.* *Educ:* Univ. of Hull (BA Hons History); Univ. of Edinburgh (BD Hons); Edinburgh Theol Coll.; King's Coll., London (MA Systematic Theol. 2001). Ordained deacon 1976, priest 1977; Asst Curate, Old St Paul's, Edinburgh, 1976–79; Rector, St Margaret of Scotland, Leven, 1979–85; Priest-in-Charge, St Margaret of Scotland, Edinburgh, 1986–92; Rector, Old St Paul's, Edinburgh, 1985–95; Priest-in-Charge, The Annunciation, Bryanston St, 2006–10. Area Dean of Westminster-St Marylebone, 2001–; Preb., St Paul's Cathedral, 2010–. Mem., Gen. Synod of C of E, 2001–05, 2009–10, 2010–. Chair, Hse of Clergy, Dio. of London, 2013–. Chm., USPG: Anglicans in World Mission (formerly USPG), 2006–09 (Trustee (formerly Gov.), 1997–2009; Hon. Vice-Pres., 2009). *Recreations:* reading, visiting museums, galleries, churches and other buildings, exploring places. *Address:* The Vicarage, 7 Margaret Street, W1W 8JQ. *T:* (020) 7636 1788, *Fax:* (020) 7436 4470.

MOSEY, Prof. David, PhD; Professor of Law and Director, Centre of Construction Law, King's College London, since 2013; *b* London, 28 Oct. 1954; *s* of Victor and Vera Mosey; *m* 1980, Cécile Baland; two *s.* *Educ:* University Coll., Cardiff (LLB Hons 1976); King's Coll. London (PhD 2007). Admitted Solicitor, 1980; Legal Advr, Govt of Kingdom of Bahrain, 1980–84; Partner, Trowers & Hamlins, Solicitors, 1984–2013 (Resident Partner, Sultanate of Oman, 1988–91; Hd of Projects and Construction, 1992–2013). Hon. Legal Advr to British Ambassador, Oman, 1988–91. Jt Hd, Nat. Change Agent Prog., UK Govt, 2005–11; Lead Mentor, Two Stage Open Book procurement, Cabinet Office, 2013–. Chair, British Scholarships for Oman, 1988–91. Mem., Poetry Soc., 2015–. *Publications:* PPC 2000: suite of standard form contracts for project partnering and alliancing, 2000, rev. edn 2015; Early Contractor Involvement in Building Procurement, 2009. *Recreations:* having a laugh with the legions of other performing drummers, guitarists and poets. *Address:* King's College London, The Old Watch House, Strand, WC2R 2LS. *T:* (020) 7848 1661. *E:* david.mosey@kcl.ac.uk. *Club:* Henley Sailing.

MOSEY, Roger; Master, Selwyn College, Cambridge, since 2013; *b* 4 Jan. 1958; *s* of late Geoffrey Mosey and Marie Mosey (*née* Pilkington). *Educ:* Bradford Grammar Sch.; Wadham Coll., Oxford (MA Mod. Hist. & Mod. Langs); INSEAD (AMP 1999). Producer, Pennine Radio, 1979; Reporter, BBC Radio Lincolnshire, 1980; Producer: BBC Radio Northampton, 1982; Today programme, BBC Radio Four, 1984; BBC New York office, 1986; Editor: PM prog., 1987; World At One, 1989; Today prog., BBC Radio Four, 1993 (Sony Radio Gold Awards, 1994, 1995); Controller, BBC Radio Five Live, 1996–2000 (Sony Radio Gold Award, 1998); Acting Dir, BBC Continuous News, 1999; Hd of TV News, BBC, 2000–05; Dir of Sport, BBC, 2005–09; Dir of London 2012, BBC, 2009–12; Acting Dir of TV, BBC, 2012–13; Editorial Dir, BBC, 2013. Dir, Parly Broadcasting Unit Ltd, 1999–2003; Mem. Exec. Bd, European Broadcasting Union, 2011–13. Board Member: Union Dance, 2001–05; Invictus Games, 2013–15. Trustee: Nat. Media Mus., 2008–13; RIBA, 2010–14; Syndic, Fitzwilliam Mus., 2015–. Chair, Council, Bishop Grosseteste Univ., 2013–. Fellow, Radio Acad., 1999; FRTS 2013. Hon. DLitt Lincoln, 2011; DUniv Bradford, 2013. *Publications:* Getting Out Alive, 2015; contrib. Guardian, Daily Telegraph, Independent, Times, New Statesman. *Recreations:* football (Arsenal and Bradford City), political history, music, walking with a basset hound. *Address:* Master's Lodge, Selwyn College, Cambridge CB3 9DQ. *T:* (01223) 335890. *E:* master@sel.cam.ac.uk.

MOSHINSKY, Elijah; Associate Producer, Royal Opera House, since 1979; *b* 8 Jan. 1946; *s* of Abraham and Eva Moshinsky. *Educ:* Melbourne Univ. (BA); St Antony's Coll., Oxford. Apptd to Royal Opera House, 1973: work includes original productions of: Peter Grimes, 1975; Lohengrin, 1978, 1997; The Rake's Progress, 1979; Macbeth, 1981; Samson et Dalila, 1981; Tannhäuser, 1984; Otello, 1987; Die Entführung aus dem Serail, 1987; Attila, 1990; Simon Boccanegra, 1991; Stiffelio, 1993; Aida, 1994; I Masnadieri, 1997; Il Trovatore, 2002; for ENO: Le Grand Macabre, 1982; The Mastersingers of Nuremberg, 1984; The Bartered Bride, 1985, 1986; for Australian Opera: A Midsummer Night's Dream, 1978; Boris Godunov, 1980; Il Trovatore, 1983; Werther, Rigoletto, 1990; Les Dialogues des Carmélites; for Metropolitan Opera, NY: Un Ballo in Maschera, 1980; Samson, 1987; Ariadne auf Naxos, 1993; Otello, 1994; The Makropulos Case, 1996; The Queen of Spades; Samson et Dalila, 1998; other opera productions include: Wozzeck, 1976; Antony and Cleopatra, Chicago, 1990; I Vespri Siciliani, Grand Théâtre, Geneva; La Bohème, 1989, La Forza del Destino, 1990, Scottish Opera; Beatrice and Benedict, 1994, Cavalleria Rusticana and Pagliacci, 1996, WNO; Die Meistersinger von Nürnberg, Holland Fest.; Benvenuto Cellini, 50th Maggio Musicale, Florence, 1987; The Turn of the Screw, Broomhill Opera, 2000; Giovanna d'Arco, Buxton, 2015. Producer: Three Sisters, Albery, 1987; Light up the Sky, Globe, 1987; Ivanov, Strand, 1989; Much Ado About Nothing, Strand, 1989; Another Time, Wyndham's, 1989; Shadowlands, Queen's, 1989; Cyrano de Bergerac, Theatre Royal, Haymarket, 1992; Lord of the Flies, 1995, Richard III, 1998, RSC; productions at National Theatre: Troilus and Cressida, 1976; The Force of Habit, 1976; productions for the BBC: All's Well That Ends Well, 1980; A Midsummer Night's Dream, 1981; Cymbeline, 1982; Coriolanus, 1984; Love's Labour's Lost, 1985; Ghosts, 1986; The Rivals, 1987; The Green Man, 1990; Genghis Cohn, 1993; Danton, 1994. Director: Matador, Queen's, 1991; Beckett, Haymarket, 1991; Reflected Glory, Vaudeville, 1992; Old Wicked Songs, Gielgud, 1996; The Female Odd Couple, Apollo, 2001; Sleuth, Apollo, 2002. *Recreations:* telephone conversation, writing film scripts. *Club:* Garrick.

MOSIEWICZ, Muriel Anita; *see* Robinson, Muriel A.

MOSIMANN, Anton, OBE 2004; DL; Owner, Mosimann's (formerly Belfry Club), since 1988; Principal, Mosimann Academy, London, since 1996; *b* 23 Feb. 1947; *s* of Otto and Olga Mosimann; *m* 1973, Kathrin Roth; two *s.* *Educ:* private school in Switzerland; youngest Chef to be awarded Chef de Cuisine Diplôme; 3 degrees. Served apprenticeship in Hotel Baeren, Twann; worked in Canada, France, Italy, Japan, Sweden, Belgium, Switzerland, 1962–; cuisinier at: Villa Lorraine, Brussels; Les Près d'Eugénie, Eugénie-les-Bains; Les Frères Troisgros, Roanne; Paul Bocuse, Collonges au Mont d'Or; Moulin de Mougins; joined Dorchester Hotel, 1975, Maître Chef des Cuisines, 1976–88. Channel Four TV series: Cooking with Mosimann, 1989; Anton Mosimann Naturally, 1991; Swiss TV series: Healthy Food, 1997; Swiss Regional Cooking, 1998. Mem., Internat. Adv. Bd, Ecole Hôtelière, Lausanne, 2011–. World Pres., Les Toques Blanches Internationales, 1989–93; Hon. Member: Chefs' Assoc., Canada, Chicago, Japan, Switzerland, S Africa; World Assoc. of Chefs' Socs, 2008; Cercle des Chefs de Cuisine, Berne, 2008; Club Chefs des Chefs, 2008. Freeman, City of London, 1999. DL Greater London, 2011. Royal Warrant Holder as Caterer to the Prince of Wales, 2000; Pres., Royal Warrant Holders' Assoc., 2006–07. Hon. Prof., Thames Valley Univ., 2004. Disciple d'Escoffier of Great Britain, 2008. Johnson & Wales

University, RI: Dr of Culinary Arts *hc*, 1990; Hon. DSc Bournemouth Univ., 1998. Restaurateur of the Year, 2000. Numerous Gold Medals in Internat. Cookery Competitions; Catey Chef Award, Caterer and Hotelkeeper, 1985; Personnalité de l'année award, 1986; Glenfiddich Awards Trophy, 1986; Chevalier, Ordre des Coteaux de Champagne, 1990; Grand Cordon Culinaire, Conseil Culinaire Français de Grande Bretagne, 1994; Swiss Culinary Ambassador of the Year, Hotel & Restaurant Assoc. of Switzerland, 1995; Catey Lifetime Achievement Award for Catering, Caterer and Hotelkeeper, 2004; Davos Tourism Award for World Econ. Forum, 2010; ICD Lifetime Achievement Award, 2010; Asia Pacific Brands Foundn, Brand Personality Award, 2010; Hon. Cross, Fedn Cuisinier Exclusive d'Europe, 2012; Médaille du Mérite, Société Suisse des Cuisiniers, 2012; Gastronomische Akademie Deutschlands Rumohr Ring, 2013. Officier, Ordre Nat. du Mérite Agricole (France), 2006 (Chevalier, 1988). *Publications:* Cuisine à la Carte, 1981; A New Style of Cooking, 1983; Cuisine Naturelle, 1985; Anton Mosimann's Fish Cuisine, 1988; The Art of Anton Mosimann, 1989; Cooking with Mosimann, 1989; Anton Mosimann Naturally, 1991; The Essential Mosimann, 1993; Mosimann's World, 1996; Mosimann's Fresh, 2006; Five Centuries of Culinary History, 2012; 25 Years of Mosimann's, 2013. *Recreations:* classic cars and participating in rallies around the world, collecting antiquarian cookery books, enjoying fine wine, passionate about food and travelling, especially to the food markets of the Far East. *Address:* c/o Mosimann's, 11B West Halkin Street, SW1X 8JL. *T:* (020) 7235 9625. *Clubs:* Garrick, Reform.

MOSLEY, family name of **Baron Ravensdale**.

MOSLEY, Max Rufus; President, 1993–2009, Honorary President, Fédération Internationale de l'Automobile, since 2009 (Member of Senate, 1993–2013); Chairman, Global New Car Assessment Programme, since 2011; *b* 13 April 1940; *s* of Sir Oswald Mosley, 6th Bt and Hon. Diana (*d* 2003), *d* of 2nd Baron Redesdale; *m* 1960, Jean Taylor; one *s* (and one *s* decd). *Educ:* abroad; Christ Church, Oxford (MA Natural Sciences). Sec., Oxford Union Society, 1961. Called to the Bar, Gray's Inn, 1964; Dir, March Cars, 1969–79; Legal Adviser, Formula One Constructors' Assoc., 1971–82; Pres., Fédn Internat. du Sport Automobile, 1991–93 (Pres., Manufacturers' Commn, FISA, 1986–91). Chm., Eur. New Car Assessment Prog., 1997–2004; EU Commission: Co-founder, e-Safety Forum, 2003; Mem., High Level Gp, CARS 21 (Competitive Automotive Regulatory System for the 21st century), 2005–09. Hon. Mem., ERTICO Intelligent Transport Systems Europe, 2007 (Vice-Chm., 1999–2001, Chm., 2001–04, Supervisory Bd; Pres. and spokesperson, 2004–07). Mem. Bd of Trustees, 2001–14, Chm., Programmes Cttee, 2001–12, FIA Foundn for the Automobile and Society; Patron, eSafety Aware, 2006–09. Hon. President: Automobile Users' Intergroup, EP, 1994–99; Nat. Road Safety Council NGO, Armenia, 2005. Founder Mem., Inst du Cerveau et de la Moelle Epinière, 2005. Hon. DCL Northumbria, 2005. Gold Medal, Castrol/Inst. of Motor Industry, 2000; Quattroruote Premio Speciale per la Sicurezza Stradale (Italy), 2001; Goldene VdM-Dieselring (Germany), 2001. Grande Ufficiale dell' Ordine al Merito (Italy), 1994; Order of Madarski Konnik, 1st degree (Bulgaria), 2000; Order of Merit (Romania), 2004; Huésped Ilustre de Quito (Ecuador), 2005; Chevalier de la Légion d'Honneur (France), 2005; Commandeur de l'Ordre de Saint Charles (Monaco), 2006. *Publications:* Formula One and Beyond (autobiog.), 2015. *Recreations:* snow-boarding, walking. *Address:* 7 Boulevard Des Moulins, 98000, Monaco.

MOSLEY, Nicholas; *see* Ravensdale, 3rd Baron.

MOSLEY, Stephen James; *b* Solihull, 22 June 1972; *m* 1997, Caroline Smith; one *s* one *d*. *Educ:* King Edward's Sch., Birmingham; Univ. of Nottingham (BSc Chem. 1993). With IBM (UK) Ltd, 1993–97; Director: Weblong Ltd, 1997–2010; Streamfolder Ltd, 2004–10; Severn Industrial Estates Ltd, 2004–10. Member (C): Chester CC, 2000–09; Cheshire CC, 2005–09. MP (C) City of Chester, 2010–15; contested (C) same seat, 2015.

MOSS, Ann; *see* Moss, J. A.

MOSS, Christopher John; QC 1994; **His Honour Judge Moss;** a Senior Circuit Judge, since 2002; *b* 4 Aug. 1948; *s* of John (Jack) Gordon Moss and Joyce (Joy) Mirren Moss (*née* Stephany); *m* 1st, 1971, Gail Susan Pearson (marr. diss. 1987); one *s* two *d*; 2nd, 1988, Tracy Louise Levy (marr. diss. 1997); one *s* one *d*; 3rd, 1999, Lisa Annette O'Dwyer; two *d*. *Educ:* Bryanston Sch.; University Coll. London (LLB). Called to the Bar, Gray's Inn, 1972, Bencher, 2002; a Recorder, 1993–2002. *Recreation:* playing the piano and accordion. *Address:* Central Criminal Court, Old Bailey, EC4M 7EH.

MOSS, David Christopher, FCILT; Chairman, Bradford on Avon Preservation Trust Ltd, since 2004; *b* 17 April 1946; *s* of Charles Clifford Moss and Marjorie Sylvia Moss (*née* Hutchings); *m* 1971, Angela Mary Wood; one *s*. *Educ:* King's Sch., Chester; Magdalene Coll., Cambridge (BA 1968; MA). Asst Principal, MPBW, 1968; Principal, 1972, DoE, and subseq. Dept of Transport and HM Treasury; Asst Sec., 1980, Dept of Transport and DoE; Under Sec., Internat. Aviation, Dept of Transport, 1988–93; Railtrack: Commercial Dir, 1993–95; European Affairs Dir, 1995–98; Dir Gen. (Europe), 1998–2001. Pres., European Civil Aviation Conf., 1990–93; Bd Chm., Jt Aviation Authorities, 1990–93. FCIT 1998. *Recreations:* opera, ecclesiastical architecture, wine. *Club:* Oxford and Cambridge.

MOSS, David John; Deputy Director, Workforce (formerly Programme Director, NHS Pay Reform), Department of Health, 2003–07; *b* 23 May 1947; *s* of late John Henry Moss and Doris (*née* Fenna); *m* 1975, Susan Elizabeth Runnalls; three *s*. *Educ:* Sevenoaks Sch.; St John's Coll., Cambridge (MA); Poly. of Central London (Dip. Management Studies). IPFA; MHSM; FCMA. Management Trainee and Management Accounting, Philips Lamps, 1968–73; Asst Finance Officer, St Thomas' Hosp., 1973–74; Dist Finance Officer, Enfield Health Dist, 1974–79; Dist Treasurer, E Dorset HA, 1979–86; General Manager: Poole Gen. Hosp., 1986–88; Southampton Gen. Hosp., 1988–91; Southampton Univ. Hosps, 1991–93; Chief Exec., Southampton Univ. Hosps Trust, 1993–2004. Chm., UK Univ. Hosp. Forum, 2001–03; Mem., Audit Commn, 2001–07. Chm., Bd of Govs, Ferndown Upper Sch., 2009–. FRSA 1994; FCMI. *Publications:* (jtly) Managing Nursing, 1984; articles in professional jls. *Recreations:* cricket, golf, tennis, Rugby, history, opera, walking.

MOSS, (Sir) David John E.; *see* Edwards-Moss.

MOSS, Sir David Joseph, KCVO 1998; CMG 1989; HM Diplomatic Service, retired; High Commissioner in Kuala Lumpur, 1994–98; *b* 6 Nov. 1938; *s* of Herbert Joseph and Irene Gertrude Moss; *m* 1961, Joan Lillian Moss; one *d* (one *s* decd). *Educ:* Hampton Grammar Sch.; Open Univ. (BA Hons 2007). CS Commn, 1956; FO, 1957; RAF, 1957–59; FO, 1959–62; Third Sec., Bangkok, 1962–65; FO, 1966–69; First Sec., La Paz, 1969–70; FCO, 1970–73; First Sec. and Head of Chancery, The Hague, 1974–77; First Sec., FCO, 1978–79, Counsellor, 1979–83; Counsellor, Hd of Chancery and Dep. Perm. Rep., UK Mission, Geneva, 1983–87; Asst Under-Sec. of State, FCO, 1987–90; High Comr, New Zealand, 1990–94. *Recreations:* reading, listening to music. *Club:* Royal Over-Seas League.

MOSS, Elaine Dora; Children's Books Adviser to The Good Book Guide, 1980–86; *b* 8 March 1924; *d* of Percy Philip Levy and Maude Agnes Levy (*née* Simmons); *m* 1950, John Edward Moss, FRICS, FAI; two *d*. *Educ:* St Paul's Girls' Sch.; Bedford Coll. for Women (BA Hons); Univ. of London Inst. of Educn (DipEd); University College London Sch. of Librarianship (ALA). Teacher, Stoatley Rough Sch., Haslemere, 1945–47; Asst Librarian, Bedford Coll., 1947–50; freelance journalist and broadcaster (Woman's Hour, The Times, TES, TLS, The Spectator, Signal, etc.), 1956–; Editor and Selector, NBL's Children's Books of the Year, 1970–79; Librarian, Fleet Primary Sch., ILEA, 1976–82. Eleanor Farjeon Award, 1976. *Publications:* texts for several picture books, incl. Polar, 1976; catalogues for Children's Books of the Year, 1970–79; Picture Books for Young People 9–13, 1981, 3rd edn 1992; Part of the Pattern: a personal journey through the world of children's books 1960–1985, 1986; (with Nancy Chambers) The Signal Companion, 1996. *Recreations:* walking, art galleries, reading, ballet. *Address:* 19 Kekewich House, 1 View Road, N6 4DJ.

MOSS, Gabriel Stephen; QC 1989; a Deputy High Court Judge, Chancery Division; *b* 8 Sept. 1949; *m* 1979, Judith; one *d*. *Educ:* University of Oxford (Eldon Schol. 1975; BA Jurisprudence 1971; BCL 1972; MA). Lectr, Univ. of Connecticut Law Sch., 1972–73; called to the Bar, Lincoln's Inn, 1974 (Hardwicke Schol., 1971; Cassel Schol., 1975; Bencher, 1998); admitted to: Bar of Gibraltar; Bar of E Caribbean Supreme Court, 2011. Jt DTI Inspector, Bestwood plc, 1989. Formerly (part-time) Lectr/Tutor, Oxford, LSE, Council of Legal Educn; Vis. Prof., Oxford Univ., 2011–. Member: Bd, Insolvency Res. Unit, Univ. of Sussex (formerly at KCL), 1991–; Insolvency Law Sub-Cttee, Consumer and Commercial Law Cttee, Law Soc., 1991–; Insolvency Cttee, Justice, 1993–; Insolvency Lawyers Assoc., 1999–. Fellow, Soc. of Advanced Legal Studies, 1998. Chm. Editl Bd, Insolvency Intelligence, 1994– (Mem., 1992–); Mem. Adv. Editl Bd, Receivers, Administrators and Liquidators Qly, 1993–. *Publications:* (ed with David Marks) Rowlatt on Principal and Surety, 4th edn 1982 to 6th edn 2011; (with Gavin Lightman) The Law of Receivers of Companies, 1986, 5th edn as The Law of Administrators and Receivers of Companies, 2011; (with Ian Kawaley *et al*) Cross-Frontier Insolvency of Insurance Companies, 2001; (with Ian Fletcher and Stuart Isaacs) The EC Regulation on Insolvency Proceedings, 2002, 3rd edn 2016; (with Bob Wessels) EU Banking and Insurance Insolvency, 2006. *Recreations:* classical music, foreign travel, tennis. *Address:* 3–4 South Square, Gray's Inn, WC1R 5HP. *T:* (020) 7696 9900, *Fax:* (020) 7696 9911. *E:* clerks@southsquare.com.

MOSS, Prof. (Jennifer) Ann, PhD; FBA 1998; Professor of French, University of Durham, 1996–2003, now Emeritus; *b* 21 Jan. 1938; *d* of John Shakespeare Poole and Dorothy Kathleen Beese (*née* Sills); *m* 1960, John Michael Barry Moss (marr. diss. 1966); two *d*. *Educ:* Barr's Hill Grammar Sch., Coventry; Newnham Coll., Cambridge (MA; PhD 1975). Asst Lectr, UCNW, 1963–64; Resident Tutor and part-time Lectr, Trevelyan Coll., Durham, 1966–79; University of Durham: Lectr in French, 1979–85; Sen. Lectr, 1985–88; Reader, 1988–96. Licensed Reader, C of E, 2005–10. *Publications:* Ovid in Renaissance France, 1982; Poetry and Fable, 1984; Printed Commonplace-Books and the Structuring of Renaissance Thought, 1996; Latin Commentaries on Ovid from the Renaissance, 1998; Les Recueils de lieux communs: apprendre à penser à la Renaissance, 2002; Renaissance Truth and the Latin Language Turn, 2003. *Recreations:* daughters and grandchildren, travel in Near and Middle East. *Address:* 7 Mountjoy Crescent, Durham DH1 3BA. *T:* (0191) 383 0672.

MOSS, John Ringer, CB 1972; adviser to companies in Associated British Foods Group, 1980–98; *b* 15 Feb. 1920; 2nd *s* of late James Moss and Louisa Moss; *m* 1946, Edith Bland Wheeler; two *s* one *d*. *Educ:* Manchester Gram. Sch.; Brasenose Coll., Oxford (MA). War Service, mainly India and Burma, 1940–46; Capt., RE, attached Royal Bombay Sappers and Miners. Entered Civil Service (MAFF) as Asst Princ., 1947; Princ. Private Sec. to Minister of Agric., Fisheries and Food, 1959–61; Asst Sec., 1961; Under-Sec., Gen. Agricultural Policy Gp, 1967–70; Dep. Sec., 1970–80. Mem., Economic Develt Cttee for Agriculture, 1969–70. Specialist Adviser to House of Lords' Select Cttee on European Communities, 1982–90. Chm. Council, RVC, 1983–90. *Recreations:* music, travel. *Address:* 16 Upper Hollis, Great Missenden, Bucks HP16 9HP. *T:* (01494) 862676.

MOSS, Kate; fashion model; *b* 16 Jan. 1974; *d* of Peter Edward Moss and Linda Rosina Moss (*née* Shephard); one *d* by Jefferson Hack; *m* 2011, Jamie Hince. *Educ:* Riddlesdown High Sch., Purley. Modelling contracts with Calvin Klein, 1992–2000, 2006–; campaigns incl. Burberry, Chanel, Dior, Dolce & Gabbana, Gucci, Katherine Hamnett, Rimmel, H. Stern, Versace, Louis Vuitton, Yves Saint Laurent, Alexander McQueen; fashion design collaborations with Topshop, 2007–10 and 2014–. Fashion Personality of the Year, 1995, Model of the Year, 2001, 2006, Special Recognition Award, 2013, British Fashion Awards. *Publications:* Kate, 1995. *Address:* c/o Storm Model Management, 5 Jubilee Place, SW3 3TD.

MOSS, Ven. Leonard Godfrey; Archdeacon of Hereford and Canon Residentiary of Hereford Cathedral, 1991–97, now Archdeacon Emeritus; *b* 11 July 1932; *s* of Clarence Walter Moss and Frances Lilian Vera Moss; *m* 1954, Everell Annette (*née* Reed) (*d* 2012); one *s* one *d* (and one *s* decd). *Educ:* Regent St Poly., London; King's Coll., London and Warminster (BD, AKC 1959). Quantity Surveyor's Asst, L. A. Francis and Sons, 1948–54; RE (National Service), 1954–56. Ordained: deacon, 1960; priest, 1961; Assistant curate: St Margaret, Putney, 1960–63; St Dunstan, Cheam, 1963–67; Vicar: Much Dewchurch with Llanwarne and Llandinabo, 1967–72; Marden with Amberley and Wisteston, 1972–84; Hereford Diocesan Ecumenical Officer, 1969–83; Prebendary of Hereford Cathedral, 1979–97; Bishop of Hereford's Officer for Social Responsibility and Non-Residentiary Canon of Hereford Cathedral, 1984–91; Priest-in-charge, Marden with Amberley and Wisteston, 1992–94. Proctor in Convocation, 1970–97. *Publications:* (contrib.) The People, the Land and the Church, 1987; articles and reviews in theol jls. *Recreations:* adult education, reading, listening to music, theatre. *Address:* 10 Saxon Way, Ledbury, Hereford HR8 2QY.

MOSS, Malcolm Douglas; *b* 6 March 1943; *s* of late Norman Moss and Annie Moss (*née* Gay); *m* 1965, Vivien Lorraine (*née* Peake) (*d* 1997); two *d*; *m* 2000, Sonya Alexandra McFarlin (*née* Evans); one step *s* one step *d*. *Educ:* Audenshaw Grammar Sch.; St John's Coll., Cambridge (BA 1965, MA 1968). Teaching Cert 1966. Asst Master, 1966–68, Head of Dept, 1968–70, Blundell's Sch.; Insurance Consultant, 1970–72, Gen. Manager, 1972–74, Barwick Associates; Chairman: Mandrake Gp plc, 1986–88; Mandrake Associates Ltd (formerly Mandrake (Insurance and Finance Brokers)), 1986–93 (Dir, 1974–94); Fens Business Enterprise Trust, 1983–87 (Dir, 1983–94). Mem., Cambs CC, 1985–88. MP (C) NE Cambs, 1987–2010. PPS to Minister of State, FO, 1991–93, to Sec. of State for NI, 1993–94; Parly Under-Sec. of State, NI Office and Minister for Health and Envmt, 1994–97; opposition front bench spokesman on NI, 1997–99; on MAFF, 1999–2001; opposition spokesman, for local govt and regions, 2001–02, for aviation and rural transport, 2002, for arts and tourism, 2002–03, for home and constitutional affairs, 2003–05, for tourism, licensing and gambling, 2005–06. Mem., Foreign Affairs Select Cttee, 2006–10; Treas., Swiss All Party Parly Gp, 1987–89; Sec., Anglo-Bermuda All Party Parly Gp, 1989–91; Sec., 1988–91, Vice Chm., 1991–93, Cons. Backbench Energy Cttee. Chairman: SLL White Horses Charity, 2010–; Nat. Casino Forum, 2011–. *Recreations:* tennis, ski-ing, amateur dramatics, gardening.

MOSS, Peter Jonathan; His Honour Judge Peter Moss; a Circuit Judge, since 2004; *b* 29 March 1951; *s* of John Cottam Moss and Joyce Alison Moss (*née* Blunn); *m* (marr. diss.); three *s*; *m* 2010, Tertia Elizabeth, *d* of Alan Norman Mackesy and Janice Emily Mackesy, Glos. *Educ:* Charterhouse. Called to the Bar, Lincoln's Inn, 1976. Legal Mem., Mental Health Review Tribunal, 1994–2009; Asst Recorder, 1999–2000, Recorder, 2000–04. *Recreations:* golf, cricket, ski-ing, fishing. *Address:* Guildford Crown Court, Bedford Road, Guildford GU1 4ST. *Clubs:* MCC; New Zealand Golf.

MOSS, His Honour Ronald Trevor; a Circuit Judge, 1993–2009; *b* 1 Oct. 1942; *s* of Maurice and Sarah Moss; *m* 1971, Cindy (*née* Fiddleman); one *s* one *d*. *Educ:* Hendon County Grammar School; Nottingham University (Upper Second BA; Hons Law). Admitted Solicitor, 1968; Partner, Moss Beachley, solicitors, 1973–84; Metropolitan Stipendiary Magistrate, 1984–93; Asst Recorder, 1986–90; Recorder, 1990–93; Luton Crown Court, 1993–2005, Resident Judge, 2001–05; Harrow Crown Court, 2005–09. Chm., Inner London

Juvenile Courts, subseq. Inner London Youth and Family Panel, 1986–93. Mem. Cttee, London Criminal Courts Solicitors' Assoc., 1982–84. *Recreations:* golf, bridge, Watford Football Club. *Club:* Moor Park Golf.

MOSS, Sir Stephen (Alan), Kt 2006; Chief Executive, Queen's Medical Centre, Nottingham, 2003–05; *b* 15 May 1947; *s* of George Ernest Moss and Dorothy May Moss. *Educ:* Kingsmead Sch., Hednesford; Wolverhampton Sch. of Nursing (RN; OND); Univ. of London (DN). Nursing Officer: Royal Hosp., Wolverhampton, 1973–75; Dudley Rd Hosp., Birmingham, 1975–77; Sen. Nursing Officer, subseq. Dir of Nursing, Derbys Royal Infirmary, 1977–84; Dir of Nursing, Queen's Med. Centre, Nottingham, 1984–2003. Member: Sheffield HA, 1987–91; Commn for Health Improvement, 1999–2004; Chm., Mid Staffs NHS Foundn Trust, 2009–12; non-executive Director: Derby Hosps NHS Foundn Trust, 2013–; Health Educn England, 2014–. Chm., Trust Nurses Assoc., subseq. Nurse Dirs Assoc., 1997–2003. Hon. LLD Nottingham, 2011. *Recreations:* walking, pottering, antiques, theatre, travel. *Address:* 7 Hall Lane, Nether Heage, Belper, Derbys DE56 2JW. *T:* (01773) 856170. *E:* stephenm0109@yahoo.com.

MOSS, Stephen Hodgson; freelance naturalist, author, broadcaster and wildlife television producer; *b* London, 26 April 1960; *s* of late Franco Clerici and Kathleen Mary Hodgson Moss; *m* 1st, 1985, Jane Freeth (marr. diss. 2001); two *s*; 2nd, 2001, Suzanne Dolan; two *s* one *d*. *Educ:* Hampton Grammar Sch., Middx; Gonville and Caius Coll., Cambridge (BA English 1982). Television producer, BBC Educn Dept, 1982–97; Series Producer, BBC Natural History Unit, 1997–2011. Programmes include: Birding with Bill Oddie, 1997, 1998, 2000; Big Cat Diary, 1998; Bill Oddie Goes Wild, 2001, 2002, 2003; Springwatch, 2005–11 (RTS Award, 2005); (co-presenter) A Guide to Garden, Woodland, Coastal, Farmland, Wetland, Mountain and Moorland Birds, BBC Radio 4, 2007–13; The Nature of Britain, 2007; Autumnwatch, 2008; Birds Britannia, 2010; Big British Wildlife Revival, 2013; Hive Alive, 2014. Pres., Somerset Wildlife Trust, 2014– (Vice-Pres., 2011–14). Author of Report for NT, Natural Childhood, 2012. Hon. Prof., Business Sch. and Sch. of History, Univ. of Nottingham, 2011–14. Dilys Breese Medal, British Trust for Ornithology, 2009. *Publications:* Birds and Weather, 1995; Attracting Birds to your Garden, 1997; The Garden Bird Handbook, 2003; How to Birdwatch, 2003; Understanding Bird Behaviour, 2003; A Bird in the Bush, 2004; How to Watch Wildlife, 2005; Everything You Always Wanted to Know about Birds, 2005; This Birding Life, 2005; Remarkable Birds, 2007; A Sky Full of Starlings, 2008; The Bumper Book of Nature, 2009; (contrib.) Handbook of the Birds of the World, vol. 14, 2009; Birds Britannia, 2011; Wild Hares and Hummingbirds: the natural history of an English Village, 2011; Springwatch Guide to British Wildlife, 2012; (ed) Hedgerows Heaped With May: the Daily Telegraph book of the countryside, 2013; The Great British Year, 2013; (with Brett Westwood) Tweet of the Day, 2014 (Thomson Reuters Award for Communicating Zoology, 2014). *Recreations:* birding, natural history, collecting wildlife books, family life. *Address:* Mill Batch, Blackford Road, Mark, Highbridge, Som TA9 4NR. *T:* (01278) 641283, 07712 528179. *E:* stephenmoss@live.com.

MOSS, Stephen Raymond; writer with The Guardian; *b* 30 July 1957; *s* of Raymond Moss and Catherine Moss (*née* Croome); *m* 1984, Helen Bonnick; one *s*. *Educ:* Balliol Coll., Oxford (BA Modern Hist. 1978); Birkbeck Coll., London (MA in Victorian Studies 1986). Editor with Kogan Page Publishers Ltd, 1979–81; Editor: Managing Your Business, 1981–83; Marketing and Direction, 1983–89; joined The Guardian, 1989: Dep. Arts Ed., 1991–93; Dep. Features Ed., 1994–95; Literary Ed., 1995–98. *Publications:* (ed) Wisden Anthology 1978–2006: cricket's age of revolution, 2006. *Recreations:* chess, cricket, music. *Address:* c/o The Guardian, Kings Place, 90 York Way, N1 9GU. *E:* stephen.moss@theguardian.com.

MOSS, Sir Stirling, Kt 2000; OBE 1959; FIE; racing motorist, 1947–62, retired; Managing Director, Stirling Moss Ltd; Director, Stirling Products Ltd; *b* 17 Sept. 1929; *m* 1st, 1957, Kathleen Stuart (marr. diss. 1960), *y d* of F. Stuart Molson, Montreal, Canada; 2nd, 1964, Elaine (marr. diss. 1968), 2nd *d* of A. Barbarino, New York; one *d*; 3rd, 1980, Susan, *y d* of Stuart Paine, London; one *s*. *Educ:* Haileybury and Imperial Service Coll. Brit. Nat. Champion, 1950, 1951, 1952, 1954, 1955, 1956, 1957, 1958, 1959, 1961; Tourist Trophy, 1950, 1951, 1955, 1958, 1959, 1960, 1961; Coupe des Alpes, 1952, 1953, 1954; Alpine Gold Cup (three consecutive wins), 1954. Only Englishman to win Italian Mille Miglia, 1955. Competed in 529 races, rallies, sprints, land speed records and endurance runs, finished in 387 and won 211; drove 108 different cars. Successes include Targa Florio, 1955; Brit. Grand Prix, 1955, 1957; Ital. GP, 1956, 1957, 1959; NZ GP, 1956, 1959; Monaco GP, 1956, 1960, 1961; Leguna Seca GP, 1960, 1961; US GP, 1959, 1960; Aust. GP, 1956; Bari GP, 1956; Pescara GP, 1957; Swedish GP, 1957; Dutch GP, 1958; Argentine GP, 1958; Morocco GP, 1958; Buenos Aires GP, 1958; Melbourne GP, 1958; Villarreal GP, 1958; Caen GP, 1958; Portuguese GP, 1959; S African GP, 1960; Cuban GP, 1960; Austrian GP, 1960; Cape GP, 1960; Watkins Glen GP, 1960; German GP, 1961; Modena GP, 1961. Twice voted Driver of the Year, 1954 and 1961. *Publications:* Stirling Moss's Book of Motor Sport, 1955; In the Track of Speed, 1957; Stirling Moss's Second Book of Motor Sport, 1958; Le Mans, 1959; My Favourite Car Stories, 1960; A Turn at the Wheel, 1961; All But My Life, 1963; Design and Behaviour of the Racing Car, 1964; How to Watch Motor Racing, 1975; Motor Racing and All That, 1980; My Cars, My Career, 1987; (with D. Nye) Fangio: a Pirelli album, 1991; Great Drives in the Lakes and Dales, 1993; (with C. Hilton) Stirling Moss's Motor Racing Masterpieces, 1994; All My Races, 2009; (with S. Taylor) My Racing Life, 2015; *relevant publications:* Stirling Moss, by Robert Raymond, 1953; Racing with the Maestro, by Karl Ludvigsen, 1997; Stirling Moss: the authorised biography, by Robert Edwards, 2001. *Recreations:* historic racing, designing, model making. *Address:* (business) Stirling Moss Ltd, 46 Shepherd Street, W1J 7JN; (residence) 44 Shepherd Street, W1J 7JN. *Clubs:* Royal Automobile; British Racing Drivers' (Silverstone); British Automobile Racing (Thruxton); British Racing and Sports Car (W Malling, Kent); Road Racing Drivers of America, 200 mph (Bonneville, USA); Internationale des Anciens Pilotes des Grand Prix (Bergamo); Chm. or Pres. of 36 motoring clubs.

MOSS, Timothy James; Registrar of Companies for England and Wales and Chief Executive, Companies House, since 2012; *b* London; *s* of Prof. James Moss and Mary Moss; *m* 1996, Rachel; one *s* one *d*. *Educ:* Gonville and Caius Coll., Cambridge (BA 1988); Swansea Univ. (MBA 2002). Location Manager, Delta Crompton Cables, 1990–99; Manufacturing Manager: Norsk Hydro, Alupres, 1999; Pirelli Cables, 1999–2002; Dep. Dir of Ops, 2002–04, Dir, Corporate Strategy, 2004–12, Companies House. *Address:* Companies House, Crown Way, Cardiff CF14 3UZ. *E:* tmoss@companieshouse.gov.uk.

MOSSE, Prof. David, DPhil; FBA 2013; Professor of Social Anthropology, since 2007, and Head, Department of Anthropology and Sociology, School of Oriental and African Studies, University of London; *m* 1981, Julia Caroline Cleves (marr. diss.; she *d* 2007); two *s*. *Educ:* Univ. of Oxford (BA; DPhil Social Anthropol.). Rural develt consultant; Regl Rep. for S India, Oxfam; social develt advr for internat. develt agencies incl. DFID; Lectr in Social Anthropol., 1997, Mem., Governing Body, 2013–, SOAS, Univ. of London. Member, Editorial Board: World Develt; Amer. Ethnologist; Jl Develt Studies. *Publications:* The Rule of Water: statecraft, ecology and collective action in South India, 2003; Cultivating Development, 2005; (ed with D. Lewis) The Aid Effect, 2005; (ed with D. Lewis) Anthropology Upstream, 2005; (ed with D. Lewis) Development Brokers and Translators, 2006; (ed) Adventures in Aidland, 2011; The Saint in the Banyan Tree, 2012; contribs to learned jls. *Address:* Department of Anthropology and Sociology, School of Oriental and African Studies, University of London, Thornhaugh Street, Russell Square, WC1H 0XG.

MOSSE, Katharine Louise, (Kate), OBE 2013; novelist, broadcaster and playwright; *b* 20 Oct. 1961; *d* of late Richard Hugh Mosse and Barbara Mary Mosse; *m* 2001, Gregory Charles Mosse (*né* Dunk); one *s* one *d*. *Educ:* New Coll., Oxford (BA Hons 1984, MA 1994). Publisher, 1984–92; Exec. Dir, Chichester Fest. Th., 1998–2001; presenter, BBC 4 and BBC2 TV and BBC Radio 4, 2000–. Dir, Mosse Associates Ltd, 2003–. Co-founder and Hon. Dir, Orange, later Women's, then Baileys Women's Prize for Fiction, 1996–; Co-dir, Chichester Writing Festival, 2006–12; Mem. Bd, RNT, 2011– (Dep. Chair, 2014–). Trustee, Weald and Downland Open Air Mus., Sussex, 2009–11; Patron, Fishbourne Centre, 2010–. Pres., Consort of Twelve, 2013–. Hon. MA UC Chichester, 2006. *Publications:* Becoming a Mother, 1993, rev. 8th edn 2014; The House: behind the scenes at the Royal Opera House, Covent Garden, 1995; Eskimo Kissing, 1996; Crucifix Lane, 1998; Labyrinth, 2005; Sepulchre, 2007; Syrinx (play), 2009; The Winter Ghosts, 2009; Endpapers (play), 2011; Chichester Festival Theatre at Fifty, 2012; Citadel, 2012; The Mistletoe Bride and Other Haunting Tales, 2013; The Taxidermist's Daughter, 2014. *Recreations:* family, swimming, walking, reading, theatre, cycling. *Address:* c/o Lucas Alexander Whitley Agency, 14 Vernon Street, W14 0RT. *E:* mark@lawagency.co.uk.

MOSSELMANS, Carel Maurits, TD 1961; Chairman: Rothschild International Asset Management, 1989–96; Janson Green Holdings Ltd, 1993–96; Janson Green Ltd, 1993–96 (non-executive Director, 1993–98); *b* 9 March 1929; *s* of Adriaan Willem Mosselmans and Jonkvrouwe Nancy Henriette Mosselmans (*née* van der Wyck); *m* 1962, Hon. Prudence Fiona McCorquodale, *d* of 1st Baron McCorquodale of Newton, KCVO, PC; two *s*. *Educ:* Stowe; Trinity Coll., Cambridge (MA Modern Langs and Hist.). Queen's Bays 2nd Dragoon Guards, 1947–49; City of London Yeomanry (Rough Riders), TA, 1949; Inns of Court and City Yeomanry, 1961; Lt-Col comdg Regt, 1963. Joined Sedgwick Collins & Co., 1952 (Dir, 1963); Director: Sedgwick Forbes Hldgs, 1978; Sedgwick Forbes Bland Payne, 1979; Chm., Sedgwick Ltd, 1981–84; Dep. Chm., 1982–84, Chm., 1984–89, Sedgwick Group plc; Chairman: Sedgwick Lloyd's Underwriting Agents (formerly Sedgwick Forbes (Lloyd's Underwriting Agents)), 1974–89; The Sumitomo Marine & Fire Insurance Co. (Europe), 1981–90 (Dir, 1975–81); Rothschild Asset Management, 1990–93 (Dir, 1989–99); Exco plc, 1991–96; Director: Coutts & Co., 1981–95; Tweedhill Fisheries, 1990–; Chm., Cttee of Mgt, Lionbrook Property Fund 'B' (formerly Five Arrows Property Unit Trust Managers Ltd), 1993–2003; Mem. Investors' Cttee, Lionbrook Property Partnership, 1997–2003; Chm., Indoor Golf Clubs plc, 1998–2004. Vice-Pres., BIIBA, 1987–89. *Recreations:* shooting, fishing, golf, music. *Address:* 15 Chelsea Square, SW3 6LF. *T:* (020) 7352 0621, *Fax:* (020) 7351 2489. *Clubs:* White's, Cavalry and Guards; Royal St George's Golf; Sunningdale Golf; Swinley Forest Golf; Royal & Ancient Golf (St Andrews).

MOSSON, Alexander Francis; Member (Lab), Glasgow City Council, 1984–2007; Lord Provost and Lord-Lieutenant of Glasgow, 1999–2003; *b* 27 Aug. 1940; *m* 1971, Maureen Sweeney; four *s* three *d*. *Educ:* St Patrick's Primary Sch.; St Mungo's Acad. Glasgow Corporation, 1955; apprentice boilermaker, Barclay Curle, 1956; plater, Alexander Stephens, 1959; insulating engineer, 1963. Active Trade Unionist from age of 17; Glasgow City Council: Convener, Environmental Services, 1995–99; Bailie, 1992–99; Dep. Lord Provost, 1996–99. Chm., Glasgow City Mktg Bureau, 2003–07. Hon. FRCPSGlas 2003; Hon. FCLIP Scotland, 2003. Hon. LLD: Glasgow, 2001; Caledonian, 2002; Strathclyde, 2003. OStJ 2000. Golden Jubilee Medal, 2002. *Recreations:* painting with water colours and oils, watching football, researching Scottish and Middle East politics and history. *Address:* 1 Danes Drive, Glasgow G14 9HZ.

MÖST, Franz W.; *see* Welser-Möst.

MOSTESHAR, Prof. Sa'id; barrister and attorney-at-law; Director, since 2008, and Professor of International Space Policy and Law (formerly Professor of International Space Law), since 2009, London Institute of Space Policy and Law; *b* Tehran, Iran; *s* of Mohammad Ali Mosteshar and Mahmonir Mosteshar. *Educ:* Univs of Southampton, London and Oxford; degrees and qualifications in physics, econometrics, law and accountancy. FCA 1972; MCIArb 2008; FRAeS 2013. Called to the Bar, Lincoln's Inn, 1975; admitted to State Bar of Calif and US Federal Bar, 1981; in practice as barrister: Chambers of Gerald Owen, QC, 1975–78; Chambers of Peter Whiteman, QC, 1978–82; Chambers of Sa'id Mosteshar, 1982–; on secondment: as Hd, Space Unit, Clifford Chance, 1986–88; as Chief Legal Officer and Actg CEO, Tachyon Inc., 2000–01. Prof. of Global Communications Policy, UCSD, 1995–2002; Sen. Associate Res. Fellow, Inst. of Advanced Legal Studies, London Univ., 2008–. Vis. Fellow, LLM Tutor, UCL, 1992–94. Advr to govts incl. UK and its Delegn, Legal Sub-cttee, Cttee on Peaceful Uses of Outer Space, UN, 2010–. Mem., UK Space Leadership Council, 2010–. Mem., Editl Bd, Space Regulation Liby, 2010–. *Publications:* Company Taxation, 1983; Satellite and Cable Television: international protection, 1984, 2nd edn 1986; Satellite Communications, 1986; (contrib.) Encyclopaedia of Information Technology, 1990; European Community Telecommunications Regulation, 1993; Research and Invention in Outer Space: liability and intellectual property rights, 1995; (contrib.) Outlook on Space Law in the Next Thirty Years, 1997; (contrib.) Air and Space Law in the Twenty-first Century, 2001; (contrib.) National Regulation of Space Activities, 2010; (contrib.) Earth Observation Evidence and the Law, 2012; (contrib.) Commercialisation of Space, 2015; contribs to econometrics, accountancy and legal jls. *Address:* Hardwicke Building, Lincoln's Inn, WC2A 3SB. *T:* (020) 7691 0055; Charles Clore House, Russell Square, WC1A 5DR. *E:* SM@SpaceLaw.co.

MOSTYN, 7th Baron *cr* 1831, of Mostyn, co. Flint; **Gregory Philip Roger Lloyd Mostyn;** Bt 1778; *b* London, 31 Dec. 1984; *o s* of 6th Baron Mostyn and of Denise Suzanne (*née* Duvanel); *S* father, 2011. *Educ:* Durham Univ. (BA Hons Modern Hist. 2006). With Interac, 2007, Ladbrokes, 2008–09, Sportradar, 2009–10. *Recreations:* pool, chess, snooker, football. *Heir: cousin* Roger Hugh Lloyd Mostyn [*b* 1 Dec. 1941; *m* 1967, Mary Frances Elderton (marr. diss.); three *s*]. *Address:* Mostyn Hall, Holywell CH8 9HN. *T:* 07745 862941. *E:* lordmostyn@mostynestates.co.uk.

MOSTYN, Hon. Sir Nicholas Anthony Joseph Ghislain, Kt 2010; **Hon. Mr Justice Mostyn;** a Judge of the High Court of Justice, Family Division, since 2010; *b* 13 July 1957; *s* of Jerome John Joseph Mostyn and Mary Anna Bridget Mostyn (now Learoyd); *m* 1981, Lucy Joanna Willis (marr. diss. 2012); three *s* one *d*. *Educ:* Ampleforth; Bristol Univ. (LLB). Called to the Bar, Middle Temple, 1980, Bencher, 2005; QC 1995; Asst Recorder, 1997–2000; Recorder, 2000–10; Dep. High Court Judge, 2000–10. Kt of Honour and Devotion, SMO Malta, 2003. *Publications:* Child's Pay, 1993, 3rd edn 2002; At a Glance, annually, 1992–. *Recreations:* Wagner, Southampton FC, ski-ing. *Address:* Royal Courts of Justice, Strand, WC2A 2LL. *Club:* MCC.

MOSTYN, Sir William Basil John, 15th Bt *cr* 1670, of Talacre, Flintshire; *b* 15 Oct. 1975; *s* of Sir Jeremy John Anthony Mostyn, 14th Bt and of Cristina, *o d* of Marchese Orengo, Turin; *S* father, 1988; *m* 2009, Sejal Asar; two *s*. *Heir: s* Rohan Jeremy Mostyn, *b* 27 July 2010. *Address:* 76 Chelmsford Road, South Woodford, E18 2PP.

MOTE, Ashley; author; Member (UK Ind, then Ind) South East Region, European Parliament, 2004–09; *b* 25 Jan. 1936; *m* 1972, Anna-Nicola Goddard; one *s* one *d*. *Educ:* City of London Freemen's Sch. Army, 1954–56. Journalist, Picture Post, then Farmers' Weekly, 1956–61; communications specialist, 1961–68; Unilever, 1968–72; founder, internat. marketing co., 1972–90. Writer and broadcaster; columnist, Compass, 2004–07. Mem., Hambledon Club (Pres., 1998–2007). *Publications:* The Glory Days of Cricket: biography of Broadhalfpenny Down, 1998, 2nd edn 2014; (ed) John Nyren's The Cricketers of my Time

- the original version, 1998; (jtly) The Winning Edge: the secrets and techniques of the world's best cricketers, 2001; Vigilance: a defence of British liberty, 2001; OverCrowded Britain: our immigration crisis exposed, 2003; J'Accuse…!, 2008; We Want Our Country Back, 2009; Light in Dark Places, 2010; A Mote in Brussels' Eye, 2010. *Address:* Inwood Kilns, Binsted GU34 4PB. *Club:* Victory Services.

MOTH, Rt Rev. (Charles Phillip) Richard; *see* Arundel and Brighton, Bishop of, (RC).

MOTHERWELL, Bishop of, (RC), since 2014; **Rt Rev. Mgr Joseph Toal;** *b* Inverness, 13 Oct. 1956; *s* of Patrick Toal and Mary Toal (*née* MacInnes). *Educ:* Royal Scots Coll., Valladolid, Spain (STB 1980). Ordained priest, 1980; Asst Priest, St Peter's, Daliburgh, S Uist, 1980–83; Prof., St Mary's Coll., Blairs, Aberdeen, 1983–86; Parish Priest: St Michael's, S Uist, 1986–91; St Kieran's, Campbeltown, 1991–93; St Mary's, Benbecula, 1993–99; Spiritual Dir, Royal Scots Coll., Salamanca, 1999–2004; Rector, Salamanca, 2004–08; Bishop of Argyll and the Isles, (RC), 2008–14. *Address:* c/o Diocese of Motherwell, Coursington Road, Motherwell ML1 1PP.

MOTHERWELL, Prof. William Branks, PhD, DSc; FRS 2004; FRSE 2007; Alexander Williamson Professor of Chemistry (first incumbent), University College London, 1993–2012, now Emeritus; Visiting Researcher, Imperial College London, since 2012; *b* 10 May 1947; *s* of James Motherwell, BEM and Mary Motherwell (*née* Jarvie); *m* 1977, Dr Robyn Suzanne Hay; one *d*. *Educ:* Univ. of Glasgow (BSc 1st cl. 1969; PhD 1972; Carnegie Schol.); Univ. of London (DSc 1999). CChem; FRSC 1999. ICI Fellow, Univ. of Stirling, 1972–75; Schering-Plough Fellow, Imperial Coll., London, 1975–77; chargé de recherche, Inst. de Chimie des Substances Naturelles, CNRS, Gif-sur-Yvette, 1977–83; Lectr, 1983–90, Reader, 1990–93, Imperial Coll., London. Visiting Professor: Univ. of Paris, 1993; Univ. of Auckland, 1996; Université Bordeaux, 1998; Univ. of Rouen, 2002. Mem., Exec. Editl Bd, Tetrahedron, 1993–2013. Corday-Morgan Medal, 1983, Bader Award, 1991, Tilden Medal, 1999, Royal Soc. of Chemistry. *Publications:* over 200 scientific papers in learned jls. *Recreations:* music, walking, golf. *Address:* Department of Chemistry, Christopher Ingold Laboratories, University College London, 20 Gordon Street, WC1H 0AJ. *T:* (020) 7679 7533. *E:* w.b.motherwell@ucl.ac.uk.

MOTION, Sir Andrew, Kt 2009; writer; Homewood Professor of the Arts, Johns Hopkins University, Baltimore, since 2015; Poet Laureate, 1999–2009; *b* 26 Oct. 1952; *s* of late Andrew Richard Motion and Catherine Gillian Motion; *m* 1st, 1973, Joanna Jane Powell (marr. diss. 1983); 2nd, 1985, Janet Elisabeth Dalley (marr. diss. 2009); two *s* one *d*; 3rd, 2010, Kyeong-Soo Kim. *Educ:* Radley Coll.; University Coll., Oxford (BA 1st Cl. Hons, MLitt; Hon. Fellow, 1999). Lectr in English, Univ. of Hull, 1977–81; Editor of Poetry Review, 1981–83; Poetry Editor, 1983–89, Editl Dir, 1985–87, Chatto & Windus; Prof. of Poetry, UEA, 1995–2003; Prof. of Creative Writing, RHUL, 2003–15. Mem., Arts Council of England, subseq. Arts Council England, 1996–99 (Chm., Literature Adv. Panel, 1996–2003); Chm., MLA, 2008–12. Co-founder and co-dir, Poetry Archive, 2005–. Pres., CPRE, 2012–15. FRSL 1982; FRSA 2000. Hon. Fellow, Homerton Coll., Cambridge, 2014. Hon. DLitt: Hull, 1996; Exeter, 1999; Brunel, 2000; Anglia, 2001; Sheffield Hallam, 2003; Sheffield, 2005; Aberdeen, 2006; Chester 2008; Robert Gordon, Aberdeen, 2009; DUniv Open, 2002. *Publications: poetry:* The Pleasure Steamers, 1978, 4th edn 1999; Independence, 1981; The Penguin Book of Contemporary British Poetry (anthology), 1982; Secret Narratives, 1983; Dangerous Play, 1984 (Rhys Meml Prize); Natural Causes, 1987 (Dylan Thomas Award); Love in a Life, 1991; The Price of Everything, 1994; Salt Water, 1997; Selected Poems, 1998; Public Property, 2002; The Cinder Path, 2009; The Customs House, 2012 (Wilfred Owen Prize, 2014); *criticism:* The Poetry of Edward Thomas, 1981; Philip Larkin, 1982; (ed) William Barnes: selected poems, 1994; Thomas Hardy: selected poems, 1994; Ways of Life: on places, painters and poets, 2008; *biography:* The Lamberts, 1986 (Somerset Maugham Award, 1987); Philip Larkin: a writer's life, 1993 (Whitbread Award, 1993); Keats, 1997; Wainewright the Poisoner, 2000; In the Blood (autobiog.), 2006; *novels:* The Pale Companion, 1989; Famous for the Creatures, 1991; The Invention of Dr Cake, 2003; Silver: return to Treasure Island, 2012; The New World, 2014. *Address:* c/o Faber & Faber, Bloomsbury House, 74–77 Great Russell Street, WC1B 3DA.

MOTO, Dr Francis; Ambassador of Malaŵi to Brazil, since 2010; *b* 28 Feb. 1952; *s* of Bwanali and Rufina Moto; *m* 1982, Elizabeth Inglis; three *s* one *d*. *Educ:* Univ. of Malaŵi (DipEd; BEd); SOAS, Univ. of London (MA); PhD University Coll. London 1989. Chancellor College, University of Malaŵi: Staff associate, 1977–80; Lectr, 1980–90; Sen. Lectr, 1990–99; Associate Prof., 1999–2006; Hd of Dept and Dean of Faculty, 1985–2006; Vice Principal, 1994–98, Principal, 1998–2005, Univ. of Malaŵi; High Comr to UK and Republic of Ireland, 2006–10. Mem. Bd, Malawi Privatisation Commn, 2003–05. Chm., Women and Law in Southern Africa (Trustee, Regl Bd), 1998–2005. Mem. Bd, Malawi Inst. of Educn, 1998–2005. Chm., Malawi Nat. Day of Educn, 2000–04. Malaŵi Govt Scholarship Award, 1972, 1978; Commonwealth Scholarship Award, 1986. *Publications:* Nzeru Umati Zako Nzokuuza, 1987; Gazing at the Setting Sun, 1994; Trends in Malawian Literature, 2001; Topics in Language, Power and Society, 2007; contribs to Studies in African Linguistics, Jl Contemporary African Studies, Jl Humanities, Jl Social Sci., Nordic Jl African Studies. *Recreations:* football, golf, lawn tennis, squash, dancing, table tennis. *Address:* Embassy of Malaŵi, SH 15 Q1 15, Conjunto 03, 7165–230 Casa Sul, Brazil. *Clubs:* Gymkhana (Zomba); Blantyre Sports; Lilongwe Golf, Limbe Country.

MOTSON, John Walker, OBE 2001; BBC TV Sports Commentator, since 1971; *b* 10 July 1945; *s* of late William and Gwendoline Motson; *m* 1976, Anne Jobling; one *s*. *Educ:* Culford Sch., Bury St Edmunds. Barnet Press, 1963–67; Morning Telegraph, Sheffield, 1967–68; BBC Radio Sport, 1968–71 and 2001–; BBC TV Sport, 1971–. Commentator: 29 FA Cup Finals, 1977–2008; 8 World Cup Final Series, including 6 Finals, 1974–; 8 European Championships, 1976–. Commentator of the Year, RTS, 2004. *Publications:* Second to None: great teams of post-war soccer, 1972; (with J. Rowlinson) History of the European Cup, 1980; Motty's Diary: a year in the life of a commentator, 1986; Match of the Day: the complete record, 1992, 1994; Motty's Year, 2004; Motson's National Obsession, 2004; Motson's FA Cup Odyssey, 2005; Motson's World Cup Extravaganza, 2006; Motty: 40 years in the commentary box (autobiog.), 2009. *Recreation:* running half-marathons. *Address:* c/o Jane Morgan Management, Argentum, 2 Queen Caroline Street, W6 9DX. *T:* (020) 3178 8071. *Club:* Cricketers'.

MOTT, Sir David Hugh, 4th Bt *cr* 1930, of Ditchling, co. Sussex; *b* 1 May 1952; *o s* of Sir John Harmar Mott, 3rd Bt and Elizabeth Mott (*née* Carson); *S* father, 2015, but his name does not appear on the Official Roll of the Baronetage; *m* 1st, 1980, Amanda Jane (marr. diss. 2007), *d* of Lt-Comdr D. W. P. Fryer, RN; two *s*; 2nd, 2013, Vivian Nanzhou Yuan, *d* of Chen Shangren. *Heir: s* Matthew David Mott, *b* 1982.

MOTT, Gregory George Sidney, CBE 1979; Managing Director, Vickers Shipbuilding and Engineering Ltd, 1979–84, retired; *b* 11 Feb. 1925; *s* of Sidney Cyril George Mott and Elizabeth Rolinda Mott; *m* 1949, Jean Metcalfe. *Educ:* Univ. of Melbourne (BMechE Hons). Trainee Manager, Vickers Armstrong Ltd Naval Yard, 1948–49; Supervising Engr, A. E. Turner and John Coates, London, 1950–52; Sen. Draughtsman, Melbourne Harbour Trust Comrs, 1952–56; joined Vickers Armstrong Ltd, Barrow, trng on submarine construction, 1956; seconded to Naval Section Harwell, for shielding design DS/MP1 (specialised in computer technol.), 1957–59; returned to Barrow as Project Manager, Dreadnought, 1959–61; Technical Manager, Nuclear, 1961–64; Projects Controller, 1964–67; Local Dir, Vickers Ltd Shipbuilding Gp, 1966; responsible for Special Projects Div., incl. Oceanics Dept, 1968–72; Man. Dir, Vickers Oceanics Ltd, on formation of company, 1972–75; Dir, Vickers Ltd Shipbuilding Gp, and Gen. Manager, Barrow Shipbuilding Works (retained directorship, Vickers Oceanics Ltd, resigned later), 1975–77; Dir, Vickers Shipbuilding Gp Ltd, 1977; Gen. Manager and Dir, Barrow Engrg Works, Vickers Shipbuilding Gp Ltd, 1978.

MOTT, John Charles Spencer, FREng; Chairman, William Sindall plc, 1990–94 (Director, 1989–94); *b* Beckenham, Kent, 18 Dec. 1926; *m* 1953, Patricia Mary (*née* Fowler); two *s*. *Educ:* Balgowan Central Sch., Beckenham, Kent; Brixton Sch. of Building; Battersea Polytechnic; Rutherford Coll. of Technology, Newcastle upon Tyne; Wolfson Coll., Cambridge (BA English 1999; MA English 2004). FICE, FIStructE. Served war, Lieut, Royal Marines, 1943–46. Indentured as Engr with L. G. Mouchel & Partners, 1949–52; joined Kier Ltd, 1952; Agent on heavy civil engrg contracts, 1952–63; Chairman: French Kier Holdings plc, 1974–86 (Dir, on merger, 1973, Chief Exec., 1974–84); May Gurney Hldgs Ltd, 1986–89. Director: Kier Ltd, 1963; J. L. Kier & Co. Ltd (Holding Co.), 1968; RMC plc, 1986–94. Mem. Council, Fellowship of Engrg, 1983–86; Mem. Council, 1973–75, 1986–87, and Vice Pres., 1986–87, ICE; Mem., Bragg Cttee on Falsework, 1972–74. *Address:* 91 Long Road, Cambridge CB2 8HE. *Club:* Danish.

MOTT, Prof. Martin Gerard, FRCP, FRCPCH; Cancer and Leukemia in Children Professor of Paediatric Oncology, 1990–2000, now Emeritus, and Dean of Clinical Medicine and Dentistry, 1997–2000, University of Bristol; *b* 30 Nov. 1941; *s* of Mervyn Gerard Mott and Frances Emily Davis; *m* 1964, Patricia Anne Green; one *s* two *d*. *Educ:* Wimbledon Coll.; Univ. of Bristol (BSc 1963; MB ChB 1966; DSc 1991). FRCP 1983; FRCPCH 1996. Research Fellow, Univ. of Texas (M. D. Anderson Hosp.), 1972; Vis. Asst Prof., Stanford Univ., 1974–76; Sen. Lectr, then Reader, Univ. of Bristol, 1976–90. Founder Mem., UK Children's Cancer Study Gp, 1977–. International Society of Paediatric Oncology: Hon. Sec., 1979–82; Pres., Eur. Continental Branch, 1999–2000; Mem., GMC, 1999–2000. *Publications:* numerous contribs to learned jls on topics relating to childhood cancer. *Recreations:* music, ornithology. *Address:* 6 Wyecliffe Road, Henleaze, Bristol BS6 4NH. *T:* (0117) 962 1476.

MOTT, His Honour Michael Duncan; a Circuit Judge, 1985–2006; a Deputy Circuit Judge, 2006–12; *b* 8 Dec. 1940; *s* of late Francis J. Mott and Gwendolen Mott; *m* 1970, Phyllis Ann Gavin; two *s*. *Educ:* Rugby Sch.; Caius Coll., Cambridge (Exhibnr, MA). Called to Bar, Inner Temple, 1963; practised Midland and Oxford Circuit, 1964–69; Resident Magistrate, Kenya, 1969–71; resumed practice, Midland and Oxford Circuit, 1972; a Deputy Circuit Judge, 1976–80; a Recorder, 1980–85. *Recreations:* golf, travel, music, running the village shop. *Club:* Cambridge Union Society.

MOTT, Philip Charles; QC 1991; a Recorder of the Crown Court, since 1987; a Deputy High Court Judge, since 1998; *b* 20 April 1948; *s* of Charles Kynaston Mott and Elsie (*née* Smith); *m* 1977, Penelope Ann Caffery (marr. diss. 2011); two *d*. *Educ:* King's Coll., Taunton; Worcester Coll., Oxford (MA). Called to the Bar, Inner Temple, 1970, Bencher, 2006; in practice on Western Circuit, 1970–, Leader, 2004–07. Chm., Mental Health Review Tribunal (Restricted Patients Panel), 2000–. Bar Council: Member: Legal Services Cttee, 2004–05; Advocacy Trng Council, 2004–; Carter Response Gp, 2005–07; Bar Policy and Research Group: Vice-Chm., 2006; Mem., Gen. Mgt Cttee, 2007–08. *Recreations:* the countryside, growing trees, sailing. *Address:* Outer Temple Chambers, 222 Strand, WC2R 1BA. *T:* (020) 7353 6381. *Clubs:* Bar Yacht, Percuil Sailing.

MOTTELSON, Prof. Ben R., PhD; Danish physicist; Professor, Nordic Institute for Theoretical Atomic Physics, Copenhagen, 1957, now Emeritus; *b* Chicago, Ill, USA, 9 July 1926; *s* of Goodman Mottelson and Georgia Mottelson (*née* Blum); *m* 1948, Nancy Jane Reno; three *c*; became a Danish citizen, 1971. *Educ:* High Sch., La Grange, Ill; Purdue Univ. (officers' trng, USN, V12 program; BSc 1947); Harvard Univ. (grad. studies, PhD 1950). Sheldon Trav. Fellowship from Harvard at Inst. of Theoretical Physics, Copenhagen (later, the Niels Bohr Inst.), 1950–51. His Fellowship from US Atomic Energy Commn permitted continuation of work in Copenhagen for two more years, after which he held research position in CERN (European Organization for Nuclear Research) theoretical study group, formed in Copenhagen. Visiting Prof., Univ. of Calif at Berkeley, Spring term, 1959. Mem., Royal Danish Acad. of Scis and Letters, 1958. Nobel Prize for Physics (jtly), 1975; awarded for work on theory of Atomic Nucleus, with Dr Aage Bohr (3 papers publ. 1952–53). *Publications:* Nuclear Structure, vol. I, 1969; vol. II, 1975 (with A. Bohr); (jtly) The Principle Behind Quantum Mechanics, 2004; contrib. Rev. Mod. Phys (jt), etc. *Address:* Nordisk Institut for Teoretisk Fysik, Blegdamsvej 17, 2100 Copenhagen, Denmark.

MOTTISTONE, 6th Baron *cr* 1933, of Mottistone, Southampton; **Christopher David Peter Seely;** *b* 1 Oct. 1974; *s* of 5th Baron Mottistone and Joyce Seely (*née* Cairns); *S* father, 2013.

MOTTRAM, Lesley Anne; a District Judge (Magistrates' Courts), since 2005; *b* 3 May 1952; *d* of Fred and Peggy Pugh; *m* 1981, Michael Martin; one *s*. *Educ:* Priory Sch. for Girls, Shrewsbury; LLB Hons. Admitted solicitor, 1976; solicitor, specialising in criminal advocacy, West Midlands, 1977–2005. *Address:* Victoria Law Courts, Corporation Street, Birmingham B4 6QA. *T:* (0121) 212 6600.

MOTTRAM, Sir Richard (Clive), GCB 2006 (KCB 1998); Chairman, Amey plc, since 2008; *b* 23 April 1946; *s* of John Mottram and Florence Yates; *m* 1971, Fiona Margaret Erskine; three *s* one *d*. *Educ:* King Edward VI Camp Hill Sch., Birmingham; Univ. of Keele (1st Cl. Hons Internat. Relns). Entered Home Civil Service, 1968, assigned to Ministry of Defence: Asst Private Sec. to Sec. of State for Defence, 1971–72; Cabinet Office, 1975–77; Ministry of Defence: Private Sec. to Perm. Under Sec., 1979–81; Private Sec. to Sec. of State for Defence, 1982–86; Asst Under Sec. of State, 1986–89; Dep. Under Sec. of State (Policy), 1989–92; Permanent Secretary: Office of Public Service and Sci., 1992–95; MoD, 1995–98; DETR, then DTLR, 1998–2002; DWP, 2002–05; Perm. Sec., Intelligence, Security and Resilience, and Chm., Jt Intelligence Cttee, Cabinet Office, 2005–07; Chm., DSTL, 2008–14. Pres., Commonwealth Assoc. for Public Admin and Mgt, 2000–02. Mem. Internat. Adv. Bd, Garda World, 2008–. Vis. Prof., LSE, 2008–. Governor: Ditchley Foundn, 1996– (Vice Chm., Council of Mgt, 2010–13); Ashridge Business Sch. (formerly Ashridge Mgt Coll.), 1998–2015. Trustee, Royal Anniversary Trust, 2010–. AcSS 2000. Hon. DLitt Keele, 1996. *Recreations:* cinema, theatre. *E:* rcmottram@googlemail.com.

MOTYER, Rev. John Alexander; Minister of Christ Church, Westbourne, Bournemouth, 1981–89, retired; *b* 30 Aug. 1924; *s* of Robert Shankey and Elizabeth Maud Motyer; *m* 1948, Beryl Grace Mays; two *s* one *d*. *Educ:* High Sch., Dublin; Dublin Univ. (MA, BD); Wycliffe Hall, Oxford. Curate: St Philip, Penn Fields, Wolverhampton, 1947–50; Holy Trinity, Old Market, Bristol, 1950–54; Tutor, Clifton Theol Coll., Bristol, 1950–54, Vice-Principal, 1954–65; Vicar, St Luke's, Hampstead, 1965–70; Dep. Principal, Tyndale Hall, Bristol, 1970–71; Principal and Dean of College, Trinity Coll., Bristol, 1971–81. Vis. Prof. in OT, Reformed Theol Seminary, Jackson, Mississippi, 1999; Jean Alexander Bernhardt Lectr, Lenoir, NC, 2000. DD Lambeth, 1997. *Publications:* The Revelation of the Divine Name, 1959; After Death, 1965, repr. 1997; The Richness of Christ (Epistle to the Philippians), 1966; The Tests of Faith (Epistle of James), 1970, 2nd edn 1975; (Old Testament Editor) New Bible Commentary Revised, 1970, New Bible Commentary 21st Century Edition, 1994; The Day of the Lion (Amos), 1975; The Image of God: Law and Liberty in Biblical Ethics (Laing Lecture), 1976; The Message of Philippians, 1984; The Message of James, 1985; The Prophecy of Isaiah, 1993; A Scenic Route Through the Old Testament, 1994; Look to the Rock: an Old Testament background to our understanding of Christ, 1996; (contrib.) An Exegetical & Expository Commentary: the Minor Prophets, vol. 3, 1998; Isaiah (Tyndale Old

Testament Commentaries), 1999; The Story of the Old Testament, 2001; The Message of Exodus: the days of our pilgrimage, 2005; Discovering the Old Testament, 2006; Treasures of the King: psalms from the life of David, 2007; Life 2: The Sequel: what happens when you die, 2008; Journey: psalms for pilgrim people (Psalms 120–136), 2009; Roots: let the Old Testament speak, 2009; Isaiah By the Day, 2011; Preaching: simple teaching on simply preaching, 2014; Loving the Old Testament, 2014; contributor: New Bible Dictionary; Expositor's Bible Commentary; Law and Life (monograph); New International Dictionary of New Testament Theology; Evangelical Dictionary of Theology. *Recreations:* reading, odd-jobbing. *Address:* 27 Georges Road West, Poynton, Cheshire SK12 1JY. *T:* (01625) 267461.

MOUATT, (Richard) Brian, CBE 1997; Chief Dental Officer, Department of Health, 1991–96; *b* 4 Sept. 1936; *m* 1962, Ursula Wälti; one *s* one *d*. *Educ:* Blundell's Sch.; Edinburgh Univ. (BDS 1960). MGDS RCS 1979; FFGDP (UK) 2001. RAF Dental Branch, 1960–65 (to Sqn Leader); Dept of Public Health, Bournemouth, 1965–68; FCO, Chief Dental Officer to Republic of Zambia under Overseas Aid Scheme contract, 1968–72; gen. dental practice, Dorset, 1972–84; Dept of Health, 1984–96. Hon. Sen. Res. Fellow, Eastman Inst. of Dental Surgery, 1990–2005; Hon. Sen. Lectr, King's Coll. Sch. of Medicine and Dentistry, 1992–2000; Hon. Sen. Advr, Internat. Child Oral Health, Dept of Dental Public Health, KCL, 2006–. Chairman: FDI Developing Countries Fund, 1999–2001; FDI World Dental Develt, 1999–2006; Dental Protection Ltd, 2001–06. Mem. Bd, Medical Protection Soc., 1998–2006. Pres., Commonwealth Dental Assoc., 2000–04 (Vice-Pres., 1996–2000). Advr to Sec. of State for Educn and Skills (formerly Educn and Employment) on educnl matters for GCC, 1997–2005. *Recreations:* travel, water colour painting, sailing. *Address:* 30 Crescent Walk, West Parley, Dorset BH22 8PZ. *T:* (01202) 875139. *E:* Mouatt@msn.com.

MOULD, Philip Jonathan Clifford, OBE 2005; art dealer, writer, broadcaster and conservationist; Director, Philip Mould Ltd (formerly Historical Portraits Ltd), since 1987; *b* Clatterbridge, Cheshire; *s* of Anthony Mould and Catherine Mould; *m* 2004, Catherine Mary Morgan; one *s*. *Educ:* Kingsmead Sch., Hoylake; Worth Abbey Sch., Crawley; Univ. of East Anglia (BA Hons). Works of Art Advr, H of C and H of L, 1988–2011. Television work includes: writer and presenter, Changing Faces, 1988; an expert, Antiques Roadshow, 2008–; co-presenter, Fake or Fortune, 2011–. Chm., Kids in Museums, 2011–; Mem., English Heritage Blue Plaques Panel, 2014–; Trustee, English Heritage Trust, 2011–. Pres., Plantlife, 2010– (Chm., Trustees, 2002–07). Patron, Fight for Sight, 2010–. FLS 2011. Hon. DLitt UEA, 2013. *Publications:* Sleepers: in search of lost old masters, 1995; Sleuth: the amazing quest for lost art treasures, 2009. *Recreations:* tennis, un-cleaned pictures, fishing, shooting, ancient meadows. *Address:* Philip Mould Ltd, 29 Dover Street, W1S 4NA. *T:* (020) 7499 6818. *E:* art@philipmould.com. *Clubs:* Garrick, Buck's.

MOULD, Timothy James; QC 2006; barrister; *b* 22 May 1960; *s* of John and Dorothy Mould; partner, Debbie Field; one *s* one *d*. *Educ:* Blueboys Sch., Minchinhampton; Wycliffe Coll. Jun. Sch.; Rugby Sch.; Queen's Coll., Oxford (BA Hons Lit. Hum. 1982); Poly. of Central London (Dip. Law 1986). Called to the Bar, Gray's Inn, 1987; in practice as a barrister, 1987–, specialising in planning and administrative law. *Publications:* (ed) Encyclopedia of Rating and Local Taxation, 2007. *Recreations:* music, cricket, keeping calm, travel, food and wine in Italy. *Address:* Landmark Chambers, 180 Fleet Street, EC4A 2HQ. *T:* (020) 7430 1221. *E:* tmould@landmarkchambers.co.uk.

MOULDEN, Peter Ronald; a Judge of the Upper Tribunal (Immigration and Asylum Chamber) (formerly a Vice President, Immigration Appeal Tribunal, later a Senior Immigration Judge, Asylum and Immigration Tribunal), since 2000; Resident Senior Immigration Judge, Field House, London, 2006–10; *b* 31 Jan. 1945; *s* of Ronald Charles and Kathleen Norah Bell Moulden; *m* 1970, Elaine Williams; one *s* one *d*. *Educ:* Cranleigh Sch. In practice as solicitor, 1969–99; Adjudicator, Immigration Appeal Tribunal, 1999–2000. Craft-owning Freeman, Co. of Watermen and Lightermen, 2006–. *Recreation:* boating.

MOULE, John Stuart; Warden, Radley College, since 2014; *b* Shrewsbury, 29 Sept. 1971; *s* of Barry and Sheila Moule; *m* 1993, Diana; one *s* two *d*. *Educ:* Orleton Park Comprehensive Sch.; Telford New Coll.; Lady Margaret Hall, Oxford (BA 1st Cl. Hons Hist.). Teacher, Dean Close Sch., Cheltenham, 1993–98; Hd of Hist., Stowe Sch., 1998–2005; Vice Master, 2006–08, Head Master, 2008–14, Bedford Sch. *Recreations:* theology, political biography, P. G. Wodehouse, armchair sports viewing, theatre. *Address:* Radley College, Abingdon, Oxon OX14 2HR. *Club:* East India.

MOULTON, Jonathan Paul; Chairman, Better Capital GP and 12 GP Ltd, since 2009; *b* 15 Oct. 1950; *s* of Cecil Moulton and Elsie Moulton (*née* Pointon); *m* 1974, Pauline Dunn; one *s* one *d*. *Educ:* Univ. of Lancaster (BA Chem.). FCA 1977. Coopers & Lybrand: Manager, Liverpool, 1972–78; Manager in M&A gp, NY, 1978–80; Citicorp Venture Capital: NY, 1980–81; Man. Dir, London, 1981–85 (Mem., French and German Investment Cttees); Founder and Managing Partner, Schroder Ventures, London, 1985–94 (Mem., French and German Investment Cttees); Dir in Charge of Leveraged Buy-outs, Apax Partners, London, 1994–97 (Mem., Internat. Operating Cttee); Founder and Man. Partner, Alchemy Partners LLP, 1997–2009. Mem., Regl Growth Fund, 2011–. Trustee, UK Stem Cell Foundn, 2005–. Fellow, Soc. of Turnaround Professionals, 2000. *Recreations:* tennis, bridge, chess. *Address:* Better Capital LLP, 39–41 Charing Cross Road, WC2H 0AR.

MOUND, Laurence Alfred, DSc; FRES; Hon. Research Fellow, CSIRO Australian National Insect Collection (formerly Division of Entomology, Commonwealth Scientific and Industrial Research Organisation, then CSIRO Entomology, the CSIRO Ecosystem Sciences), since 1996; Research Associate, Natural History Museum (formerly British Museum (Natural History)), since 1992 (Keeper of Entomology, 1981–92); *b* 22 April 1934; *s* of John Henry Mound and Laura May Cape; *m* 1st, 1958, Agnes Jean Solari (marr. diss. 1985); one *s* two *d*; 2nd, 1987, Sheila Helen Halsey (marr. diss. 1994); 3rd, 2004, Alice Wells. *Educ:* Warwick Sch.; Sir John Cass Coll., London; Imperial Coll., London (DIC); DSc London; Imperial Coll. of Tropical Agriculture, Trinidad (DipTA). Nigerian Federal Dept of Agricl Research, 1959–61; Rockefeller Studentship, Washington and Calif, 1961; Empire Cotton Growing Corp., Republic of Sudan, 1961–64; Sen. Scientific Officer, BM (NH), 1964–69; Australian CSIRO Research Award, 1967–68; PSO, 1969–75, Dep. Keeper, Dept of Entomology, BM (NH), 1975–81. Sec., 1976–88, Vice-Chm., 1988–92, Council for Internat. Congresses of Entomology; Consultant Dir, Commonwealth Inst. of Entomology, 1981–92. Hon. Prof., Sch. of Pure and Applied Biology, Univ. of Wales at Cardiff, 1990–96; McMaster Res. Fellow, CSIRO, 1995–96. Editor, Jl of Royal Entomological Soc. of London, 1973–81 (Vice-Pres., RES, 1975–76). Numerous expedns studying thrips in tropical countries. *Publications:* over 360 technical books and papers on biology of thrips and whitefly, particularly in Bull. of BM (NH), incl. Whitefly of the World (with S. H. Halsey), Thrips of Central and South America (with R. Marullo), and Evolution of Ecological and Behavioural Diversity (with B. Crespi and D. Morris). *Recreation:* thrips with everything. *Address:* c/o CSIRO Australian National Insect Collection, GPO Box 1700, Canberra, ACT 2601, Australia. *T:* (2) 62464280, *Fax:* (2) 62464264. *E:* laurence.mound@csiro.au.

MOUNSTEPHEN, Rev. Canon Philip Ian; Executive Leader, Church Mission Society, since 2012; *b* Crookham Village, Hants, 13 July 1959; *s* of Dennis Mounstephen and Ann Mounstephen; *m* 1984, Ruth Weston; one *d*. *Educ:* St Edward's Sch., Oxford; Southampton Univ. (BA 1980); Magdalen Coll., Oxford (PGCE 1981; BA 1987; CTh 1988). Ordained deacon, 1988, priest, 1989; Vicar, St James', W Streatham, 1992–98; Church Pastoral Aid Society: Hd, Pathfinders, 1998–2002; Hd of Ministry and Dep. Gen. Dir, 2002–06; Chaplain: St Michael's, Paris, 2007–12; RBL, Paris Br., 2007–12. Canon, Dio. of Europe, 2012. Gov., Univ. of Glos, 2004–12 (Chair, Audit Cttee, 2007–12, Vice-Chair, Council, 2011–12; Hon. Fellow, 2013). *Recreations:* music, theatre, cinema, gardening, record collecting. *Address:* Church Mission Society, Watlington Road, Oxford OX4 6BZ. *T:* (01865) 787400, *Fax:* (01865) 776375. *E:* philip.mounstephen@cms-uk.org.

MOUNT, Ferdinand; *see* Mount, W. R. F.

MOUNT, Peter William, CBE 2007; CEng; Chairman, Central Manchester and Manchester Children's University Hospitals NHS Trust, 2001–14; *b* 14 Jan. 1940; *s* of William J. and Bridie Mount; *m* Margery; three *c*. *Educ:* De La Salle Sch., Manchester; UMIST (BSc Tech); Univ. of Vienna (short prog.). MIMechE. Prodn Engr, Rolls Royce Ltd, 1961–66; Mgt Consultant, PricewaterhouseCoopers, 1966–72; Project Dir, Chloride Industrial Batteries, 1972–78; Man. Dir, Chloride Ireland, 1978–81; various Bd appts then CEO, Thorn EMI Fire Protection Ltd and Dir, Thorn Security Ltd, 1984–93. Chairman: Salford Royal Hosps NHS Trust, 1983–2001; Greater Manchester NHS Workforce, 1993–2004; NHS Confederation, 2003–07. Member: Audit Cttee, DoH, 2002–08; Bd, Sector Skills Develt Agency, 2002–06 (Chm., Audit Cttee, 2002–06). Dep. Chm., Oldham TEC, 1987–93. Mem. Court, subseq. Gen. Assembly, Univ. of Manchester, 1995–. Founder and Chm. Trustees, charity working with Uganda schs. Co-holder of patent relating to gold processing. RHS Award, 1990. *Publications:* (jtly) Absenteeism in Industry, 1980. *Recreations:* walking, ski-ing, cars, computers, making and fixing things, music, good food, taking grandchildren for walks in the park. *Address:* 6 The Ceal, Compstall, Stockport, Cheshire SK6 5LQ. *T:* (0161) 427 4260. *E:* pwmount@me.com.

MOUNT, (William Robert) Ferdinand, (3rd Bt *cr* 1921, of Wasing Place, Reading, Berks, but does not use the title); author and journalist; Editor, Times Literary Supplement, 1991–2002; *b* 2 July 1939; *s* of Robert Francis Mount (*d* 1969), 2nd *s* of Sir William Arthur Mount, 1st Bt, CBE and his 1st wife, Lady Julia Pakenham (*d* 1956), *d* of 5th Earl of Longford; *S* uncle, 1993; *m* 1968, Julia Margaret, *d* of late Archibald Julian and Hon. Mrs Lucas; two *s* one *d* (and one *s* decd). *Educ:* Eton; Christ Church, Oxford. Has worked for Sunday Telegraph, Conservative Research Dept, Daily Sketch, National Review, Daily Mail, The Times; Political Columnist: The Spectator, 1977–82 and 1985–87; The Standard, 1980–82; Daily Telegraph, 1984–90; Sunday Times, 1997–2004; Head of Prime Minister's Policy Unit, 1982–83. Vice-Chm., Power Commn, 2005–06. Chm., Friends of British Liby, 2013–. FRSL 1991 (Mem. Council, 2002–05); FSA 2009. *Publications:* Very Like a Whale, 1967; The Theatre of Politics, 1972; The Man Who Rode Ampersand, 1975; The Clique, 1978; The Subversive Family, 1982; The Selkirk Strip, 1987; Of Love and Asthma, 1991 (Hawthornden Prize, 1992); The British Constitution Now, 1992; Umbrella, 1994; The Liquidator, 1995; Jem (and Sam): a revenger's tale, 1998; Fairness, 2001; Mind the Gap, 2004; Heads You Win, 2004; The Condor's Head, 2007; Cold Cream: my early life and other mistakes, 2008; Full Circle: how the classical world came back to us, 2010; The New Few: or a very British oligarchy, 2012; The Tears of the Rajas: mutiny, money and marriage in India 1805–1905, 2015. *Heir: s* William Robert Horatio Mount [*b* 12 May 1969; *m* 1997, Deborah Grey; two *s*]. *Address:* 17 Ripplevale Grove, N1 1HS. *T:* (020) 7607 5398.

MOUNT CHARLES, Earl of; Alexander Burton Conyngham; Director, Slane Castle Irish Whiskey Ltd, since 2009; *b* 30 Jan. 1975; *s* and *heir* of Marquess Conyngham, *qv*; *m* 2007, Carina Suzanne, *d* of late Nicholas George Bolton; two *s* one *d*. *Educ:* Trinity Coll., Dublin (BA History of Art 1997); Univ. of Cape Town (MBA 2005). Pernod Ricard; Christie's. *Heir: s* Viscount Slane, *qv*. *Address:* Slane Castle, Co. Meath, Eire.

MOUNT EDGCUMBE, 8th Earl of, *cr* 1789; **Robert Charles Edgcumbe;** Baron Edgcumbe, 1742; Viscount Mount Edgcumbe and Valletort, 1781; Farm Manager, for Lands and Survey, New Zealand, 1975–84; *b* 1 June 1939; *s* of George Aubrey Valletort Edgcumbe (*d* 1977) and of Meta Blucher, *d* of late Robert Charles Lhoyer; *S* uncle, 1982; *m* 1960, Joan Ivy Wall (marr. diss. 1988); five *d*. *Educ:* Nelson College. Career from farm worker to farm manager, managing first farm, 1960; taking up family seat in Cornwall, 1984. *Recreations:* hunting game, restoring classic cars. *Heir: half-b* Piers Valletort Edgcumbe [*b* 23 Oct. 1946; *m* 1971, Hilda Warn (marr. diss.); two *d*]. *Address:* Empacombe House, Cremyll, Cornwall PL10 1HZ.

MOUNTAIN, Sir Edward (Brian Stanford), 4th Bt *cr* 1922, of Oare Manor, Co. Somerset, and Brendon, Co. Devon; *b* 19 March 1961; *er s* of Sir Denis Mortimer Mountain, 3rd Bt and Hélène Fleur Mary Mountain (*née* Kirwan-Taylor); *S* father, 2005; *m* 1987, Charlotte Sarah Jesson, *d* of His Honour Henry Pownall, QC; two *s* one *d*. *Educ:* King's School, Bruton; RMA Sandhurst; Sparshott Coll. (Dip. Farm Mgt); RAC, Cirencester (BSc Rural Land Mgt 1995). Commnd Army, 1981, Blues and Royals; Captain, 1983; Major, 1991. Joined Bidwells, 1995. Contested (C): Caithness, Sutherland and Ross, Scottish Parlt, 2011; Inverness, Nairn, Badenoch and Strathspey, 2015. *Recreations:* shooting, fishing. *Heir: s* Thomas Denis Edward Mountain, *b* 14 Aug. 1989. *Address:* Delfur Lodge, Orton, Morayshire IV32 7QQ. *T:* (01542) 860274.

MOUNTBATTEN, family name of **Marquess of Milford Haven**.

MOUNTBATTEN OF BURMA, Countess (2nd in line), *cr* 1947; **Patricia Edwina Victoria Knatchbull,** CBE 1991; CD; JP; DL; Viscountess Mountbatten of Burma, 1946; Baroness Romsey, 1947; Vice Lord-Lieutenant of Kent, 1984–2000; *b* 14 Feb. 1924; *er d* of Admiral of the Fleet 1st Earl Mountbatten of Burma, KG, GCB, OM, GCSI, GCIE, GCVO, DSO, PC, FRS, and Countess Mountbatten of Burma, CI, GBE, DCVO, LLD (*d* 1960) (Hon. Edwina Cynthia Annette Ashley, *e d* of 1st and last Baron Mount Temple, PC); *S* father, 1979; *m* 1946, 7th Baron Brabourne, CBE (*d* 2005); four *s* two *d* (and one *s* decd). *Educ:* Malta, England and New York City. Served War in WRNS, 1943–46. Colonel-in-Chief, Princess Patricia's Canadian Light Infantry, 1974–2007. Chm., Edwina Mountbatten Trust. President: Friends of Cassel Hosp.; Friends of William Harvey Hosp.; Shaftesbury Homes and Arethusa; Kent Branches of Save the Children and Relate; Kent Community Housing Trust; Dep. Pres., BRCS; Vice-President: NSPCC; FPA; Nat. Childbirth Trust; SSAFA; RLSS; Shaftesbury Soc.; Nat. Soc. for Cancer Relief; Kent Voluntary Service Council; The Aidis Trust; RCN; Royal Nat. Coll. for Blind; Mountbatten Community Trust. Hon. President: Soc. for Nautical Research; British Maritime Charitable Foundn; Patron: Commando Assoc.; Royal Naval Commando Assoc.; Legion of Frontiersmen of the Commonwealth; HMS Kelly Reunion Assoc.; Safer World Project; VADs (RN); Compassionate Friends; Nurses' Welfare Trust; SOS Children's Villages (UK); Sir Ernest Cassel Educational Trust; Vice-Patron, Burma Star Assoc. JP 1971 and DL 1973, Kent. Hon. DCL Kent, 2000. DStJ 1981. Meritorious Service Cross (Canada), 2007. *Heir: s* Baron Brabourne, *qv*. *Address:* Newhouse, Mersham, Ashford, Kent TN25 6NQ. *T:* (01233) 503636.

See also Hon. P. W. A. Knatchbull, A. A. S. Zuckerman.

MOUNTEVANS, 4th Baron *cr* 1945, of Chelsea; **Jeffrey Richard de Corban Evans;** Managing Director, Gas, H. Clarkson & Co., since 2001; Lord Mayor of London, 2015–Nov. 2016; *b* Gothenburg, Sweden, 13 May 1948; *yr s* of 2nd Baron Mountevans and Deirdre Grace (*d* 1997), *d* of John O'Connell, Cork; *S* brother, 2014; *m* 1972, Hon. Juliet, *d* of 2nd Baron Moran, KCMG; two *s*. *Educ:* Nautical Coll., Pangbourne; Univ. of Paris, Sorbonne; Pembroke Coll., Cambridge (BA Econs 1971). H. Clarkson & Co.: shipbroker, 1972–; tanker broker, 1972–79; Gas Div., 1979–2000; Dir, 1989; Hd, Gas and Specialized Tankers, 2000–01. Dir, Maritime London, 2011– (Chm., 2013–). Elected Mem., H of L, 2015. Mem. Council, White Ensign Assoc., 2003–; Trustee: Seafarers UK (King George's Fund for

Sailors), 2011–; Mansion House Scholarship Scheme, 2011–; St Paul's Cathedral Chorister Trust, 2013–; Pres., City of London Sea Cadet Corps, 2007–. Magistrate, Central London Bench, 2007–. Gov., City of London Acad., Islington, 2008–; Almoner, Christ's Hospital Sch., 2010–. Church Warden, St Lawrence Jewry next Guildhall, 2009–. Alderman, Ward of Cheap, City of London, 2007–; Sheriff, City of London, 2012–13. Liveryman: Shipwrights' Co., 1979– (Prime Warden, 2006–07); World Traders' Co., 2010–; Goldsmiths' Co., 2012–; Wheelwrights' Co., 2013–. *Recreations:* matters maritime, cross-country ski-ing, Antarctic exploration, Scandinavia, France. *Heir: s* Hon. Alexander Richard Andvord Evans [*b* 23 July 1975; *m* 2007, Emma Williams]. *Address:* Members Room, PO Box 270, City of London Corporation, Guildhall, EC2P 2EJ. *E:* jeffrey.evans@cityoflondon.gov.uk. *Clubs:* Ward of Cheap (Patron, 2007–), City Pickwick.

MOUNTFIELD, Helen; QC 2010; a Recorder, since 2010; a Deputy High Court Judge, since 2013; *b* London, 14 March 1967; *d* of Sir Robin Mountfield, KCB and of Anne Mountfield; *m* 2005, Damian Tambini; three *d*. *Educ:* Crown Woods Comp. Sch.; Magdalen Coll., Oxford (BA 1st Cl. Hons Mod. Hist.); City Univ. (DipLaw); King's Coll., London (Dip Eur. Law). Called to the Bar, Gray's Inn, 1991 (Reid and Holker Schol.), Bencher, 2014; Founder Mem., Matrix Chambers, 2000–. Mem., RSA Commn on Drugs Policy, 2010. Trustee: Birthrights, 2013–; Equal Rights Trust, 2014–. *Publications:* (jtly) Blackstone's Guide to the Human Rights Act 1998, 1998, 6th edn 2011; (contrib.) The White Book, 2006; (contrib.) Oxford Guide to the Law, 2009. *Address:* Matrix, Griffin Building, Gray's Inn, WC1R 5LN. *T:* (020) 7404 3447, *Fax:* (020) 7404 3448. *E:* helenmountfield@matrixlaw.co.uk.

MOUNTFIELD, Peter; Executive Secretary, Development Committee, World Bank, 1991–95; *b* 2 April 1935; *s* of late Alexander Stuart Mountfield and Agnes Elizabeth (*née* Gurney); *m* 1958, Evelyn Margaret Smithies (*d* 2010); three *s*. *Educ:* Merchant Taylors' Sch., Crosby; Trinity Coll., Cambridge (BA); Graduate Sch. of Public Admin, Harvard. RN, 1953–55. Asst Principal, HM Treasury, 1958; Principal, 1963; Asst Sec., 1970; Under Secretary: Cabinet Office, 1977; HM Treasury, 1980–91. *Recreations:* reading, walking, looking at buildings. *Address:* Marchants, Church Street, Seal, Sevenoaks, Kent TN15 0AR. *T:* (01732) 761848. *E:* petermountfield@hotmail.com.

MOUNTFORD, Carol Jean, (Kali); *b* 12 Jan. 1954; *m*; one *s* one *d*; *m* 1995, Ian Leedham. *Educ:* Crewe and Alsager Coll. (BA SocSc ext.). Civil Service posts, Dept of Employment, 1975–96. Mem., Dept of Employment Exec. Cttee, CPSA, 1986. Mem. (Lab) Sheffield CC, 1992–96. MP (Lab) Colne Valley, 1997–2010. Parliamentary Private Secretary: to Minister for Work, 2003–04; to Immigration Minister, 2004–05; to Chief Sec. to Treasury, 2005–06; to Sec. of State for Defence, 2006–08. Mem., Treasury Select Cttee, 2001–03.

MOUNTFORD, Roger Philip; Chairman: HgCapital Trust plc, since 2005 (non-executive Director, since 2004); Allied Domecq Pension Fund, since 2013; *b* Wimbledon, 5 June 1948; *s* of Stanley W. A. Mountford and Evelyn Mountford (*née* Richardson); *m* 1981, Jane Stanton; three *d*. *Educ:* Kingston Grammar Sch.; London Sch. of Econs and Pol Sci. (BSc Econ 1971); Stanford Business Sch. (MS Mgt 1980). ACIB 1976. Merchant banker, Hambros Bank, subseq. SG Hambros, 1971–2000: Dir, 1984–98; Man. Dir, 1998–2000; Man. Dir, Hambro Pacific Ltd, Hong Kong, 1983–89. Chairman: CAA Pension Scheme, 2003–13; Housing Finance Corp., 2007–13; non-executive Director: Dover Harbour Bd, 2001–12 (Chm., 2011–12); CAA, 2003–13; High Speed Two (HS2) Ltd, 2015–. Member: C of E Pensions Bd, 2012–; Finance Adv. Cttee, Westminster Abbey, 2013–. Chm., LSE Enterprise Ltd, 2004–14; Mem. Council, LSE, 2014–. Chm., Fedn of Cons. Students, 1970–71. FRSA. *Recreations:* opera, music, theatre. *Clubs:* Carlton, London Capital; Hong Kong, Hong Kong Jockey (Hong Kong).

MOUNTGARRET, 18th Viscount *cr* 1550 (Ire.); **Piers James Richard Butler;** Baron (UK) 1911; *b* 15 April 1961; *s* of 17th Viscount Mountgarret and Gillian Margaret (*née* Buckley); *S* father, 2004; *m* 1st, 1995, Laura Brown Gary (marr. diss. 2000); two *d*; 2nd, 2006, Fenella Mary, *d* of David and Mary Fawcus; one *d*. *Educ:* Eton; St Andrews Univ. *Heir: b* Hon. Edmund Henry Richard Butler [*b* 1 Sept. 1962; *m* 1988, Adelle Lloyd (marr. diss. 1989)].

MOUSLEY, Timothy John; QC 2003; **His Honour Judge Mousley;** a Circuit Judge, since 2013; *b* 29 April 1956; *s* of late James Silvester and Patricia Mary Mousley; *m* 1981 (marr. diss. 2008); two *d*; partner, Elisabeth. *Educ:* Peter Symonds Sch., Winchester; Univ. of Keele (BA Hons Law and Econs). Called to the Bar, Middle Temple, 1979; barrister on Western Circuit, 1980–2013; a Recorder, 1998–2013. *Recreations:* sport (watching), gardening. *Address:* The Law Courts, Islington Street, Swindon, Wilts SN1 2HG. *Clubs:* Southampton Football; Hampshire County Cricket; West Tytherley Wine.
See also W. H. Mousley.

MOUSLEY, William Howard; QC 2011; a Recorder, since 2009; *b* London, 9 Jan. 1963; *s* of James Silvester Mousley and Patricia Mary Mousley; *m* 1988, Elaine Claire Delves; one *s* one *d*. *Educ:* Montgomery of Alamein Sch., Winchester; Peter Symonds Coll., Winchester; Univ. of Warwick (LLB Hons Law 1985). Called to the Bar, Middle Temple, 1986; in practice as a barrister, specialising in criminal law, 1987–. Vice-Pres., Winchester RFC, 2009–. *Recreations:* singing and playing harmonica in "Foolish Behaviour", coaching and watching Rugby, cricket, embracing baldness. *Address:* 2 King's Bench Walk, Temple, EC4Y 7DE. *T:* (020) 7353 1746, *Fax:* (020) 7583 2051. *E:* wmousley@2kbw.com. *Clubs:* Winchester Rugby Football, Scrummagers Cricket.
See also T. J. Mousley.

MOUTRAY, Stephen; Member (DemU) Upper Bann, Northern Ireland Assembly, since 2003; *b* 25 Feb. 1959; *s* of William and Lena Moutray; *m* 1985, Myrtle Taylor; two *s* one *d*. *Educ:* Kingspark Primary Sch.; Lurgan Jun. High Sch.; Lurgan Coll. Company dir (retail); sub postmaster. Mem. (DemU), Craigavon BC, 2001–13. *Recreations:* walking, swimming, collecting autographed biographies, travelling. *Address:* 31 High Street, Lurgan, Co. Armagh BT66 8AH. *T:* (028) 3831 0088, *Fax:* (028) 3831 0099. *E:* stephenmoutray@btinternet.com.

MOVERLEY, Prof. John, OBE 2004; FRAgS, FIAgrE; Chairman: Amenity Forum, since 2009; West Midlands Advisory Committee, Forestry Commission, since 2010; Deer Initiative Partnership; self-employed consultant, writer and speaker on food issues; *b* Thornton, Yorks, 13 Feb. 1950; *s* of Robert John and Elsie Maria Moverley; *m* 1973, Elizabeth Ann; two *s*. *Educ:* Pocklington Sch.; St Catharine's Coll., Cambridge (Scholar; BA 1971; Wood Prize for Agric. 1971). FRAgS 2006; FIAgrE 2006. Mgt consultant, 1971–74; Lectr and Res. Fellow, Univ. of Nottingham, 1974–77; Sen. Lectr in Mgt, Bishop Burton and Shuttleworth Colls, 1977–86; Dep. Principal, Bicton Coll., 1986–88; Principal, Lincolnshire Coll. of Agric. and Hort., 1988–97; Principal and Chief Exec., Myerscough Coll., 1997–2005; Chief Exec., RASE, 2005–08. Director: Azurance Ltd, 2010–; Greenwatt Rural Services, 2010–. Member: Editl Bd, Internat. Supermarket News; Severn and Wye Flood and Coastal Cttee, 2012–; Trustee, Community Forest Trust, 2013–; Trustee and Mem. Bd, BASIS Registration Ltd, 2009–. Gov., Moreton Morrell C of E Sch., 2013–. Pro Vice Chancellor and Prof., De Montfort Univ., 1994–97. Hon. Fellow: Univ. of Central Lancashire, 2005; Myerscough Coll., 2005. *Publications:* Microcomputers and Agriculture, 1984; From Village Pump to Royal Appointment, 2012; numerous papers and articles. *Recreations:* sport, garden. *Club:* Farmers.

MOVERLEY SMITH, Stephen Philip; QC 2002; *b* 10 Jan. 1960; *s* of Philip Smith and Carol Smith (*née* Moverley); *m* 1990, Caroline Topping; three *s*. *Educ:* Reading Sch.; Pembroke Coll., Oxford (MA). Called to the Bar, Middle Temple, 1985; in practice, specialising in international trust, company and commercial litigation and arbitration. *Recreations:* sailing, tennis, mountain walking, cycling. *Address:* 24 Old Buildings, Lincoln's Inn, WC2A 3UP. *T:* (020) 7691 2424, *Fax:* 0870 460 2178. *E:* sms@xxiv.co.uk.

MOWAT, Ashley; *see* Mowat, N. A. G.

MOWAT, David John; MP (C) Warrington South, since 2010; *b* Rugby, 1957; *s* of John and Pat Mowat; *m* 1983, Veronica Mann; one *s* three *d*. *Educ:* Lawrence Sheriff Grammar Sch., Rugby; Imperial Coll., London (BSc Civil Engrg). ACA 1981. Chartered Accountant, 1981–2002, Partner, 1989–2002, Arthur Andersen, London; Global Man. Partner for Energy, Accenture, 2002–05. Mem. (C) Macclesfield BC, 2007–08. PPS to Financial Sec. to HM Treasury, 2012–. *Recreations:* chess, golf, Rugby Union and League, theatre. *Address:* (office) 1 Stafford Road, Warrington, Cheshire WA4 6RP. *T:* (01925) 231267; House of Commons, SW1A 0AA. *E:* david.mowat.mp@parliament.uk. *Clubs:* Carlton; Warrington.

MOWAT, David McIvor; JP; consultant, business columnist and commentator; Managing Director, Iatros Ltd, 1994–2015; *b* 12 March 1939; *s* of Ian M. Mowat and Mary I. S. Steel; *m* 1964, Elinor Anne Birtwistle (*d* 2008); three *d*. *Educ:* Edinburgh Academy; University of Edinburgh (MA); BA Open Univ., 1984. Chief Executive: Edinburgh Chamber of Commerce and Manufactures, 1967–90; Chamber Developments Ltd, 1971; Edinburgh's Capital Ltd, 1986; Who's Who in Business in Scotland Ltd, 1989–90. Dir, St Andrews Golf Club Manufacturing Ltd, 1994–2011. Dep. Chm., Edinburgh Tourist Gp, 1985–90. Pres., British Chambers of Commerce Execs, 1987–89. JP Edinburgh, 1969. FRSA. *Address:* 37 Orchard Road South, Edinburgh EH4 3JA. *T:* (0131) 332 6865.

MOWAT, Her Honour Mary Jane Stormont; a Circuit Judge, 1996–2014; *b* 7 July 1948; *d* of late Duncan McKay Stormont Mowat and Jane Archibald Mowat (*née* Milne); *m* 1973, Prof. the Hon. Nicholas Michael John Woodhouse, *qv*, 2nd *s* of 5th Baron Terrington, DSO, OBE; one *s*. *Educ:* Sherborne Sch. For Girls; Lady Margaret Hall, Oxford (MA). Called to the Bar, Inner Temple, 1973. *Recreations:* music, walking, reading, riding.

MOWAT, Prof. (Norman) Ashley (George), LVO 2009; FRCP, FRCPE, FRCPGlas; Consultant Physician and Gastroenterologist, Aberdeen Royal Infirmary, 1975–2008; Professor in Medicine, Aberdeen University Medical School, 2002–08; Physician to the Queen in Scotland, 2001–08; *b* 11 April 1943; *s* of William Mowat and Isabella Parker Mowat (*née* Mair); *m* 1966, Kathleen Mary Cowie; one *s* two *d*. *Educ:* Fordyce Acad.; Aberdeen Univ. (MB ChB). MRCP 1971, FRCP 1984; FRCPE 1991; FRCPGlas 2002. Hse Officer, SHO, then Registrar, Trng, Aberdeen Teaching Hosps, 1966–72; Lecturer: in Medicine, Aberdeen Univ., 1972–73; in Gastroenterol., and Res. Fellow, St Bartholomew's Hosp., London, 1973–74; Clinical Sen. Lectr in Medicine, Aberdeen Univ. Med. Sch., 1975–2002. Vis. Physician to Shetland Is, 1975–94. President: Scottish Soc. of Gastroenterology, 2002–04; Scottish Soc. of Physicians, 2004–05. *Publications:* (ed jtly) Integrated Clinical Sciences: Gastroenterology, 1985; numerous contribs to med. and gastroenterol. jls. *Recreations:* sailing, photography, golf, reading. *Address:* York House, York Place, Cullen, Buckie AB56 4UW.

MOWBRAY, 27th Baron *cr* 1283, **SEGRAVE,** 28th Baron *cr* 1283, **AND STOURTON,** 24th Baron *cr* 1448, of Stourton, co. Wilts; **Edward William Stephen Stourton;** *b* 17 April 1953; *s* of Charles Edward Stourton, CBE, 26th Baron Mowbray, 27th Baron Segrave and 23rd Baron Stourton, and Hon. Jane de Yarburgh Bateson, *oc* of 5th Baron Deramore; *S* father, 2006; *m* 1980, Penelope Lucy, *e d* of Dr Peter Brunet; one *s* four *d*. *Educ:* Ampleforth. *Heir: s* Hon. James Charles Peter Stourton, *b* 12 Dec. 1991.

MOWBRAY, John; *see* Mowbray, W. J.

MOWBRAY, Sir John Robert, 6th Bt *cr* 1880; DL; *b* 1 March 1932; *s* of Sir George Robert Mowbray, 5th Bt, KBE, and Diana Margaret, *d* of Sir Robert Heywood Hughes, 12th Bt; *S* father, 1969; *m* 1957, Lavinia Mary, *d* of late Lt-Col Francis Edgar Hugonin, OBE, Stainton House, Stainton in Cleveland, Yorks; three *d*. *Educ:* Eton; New College, Oxford. DL Suffolk, 1993. *Address:* The Hill House, Duffs Hill, Glemsford, Suffolk CO10 7PP. *T:* (01787) 281930.

MOWBRAY, (William) John; QC 1974; *b* 3 Sept. 1928; *s* of James Mowbray, sugar manufr and Ethel Mowbray; *m* 1960, Shirley Mary Neilan; one *s* three *d*. *Educ:* Upper Canada Coll.; Mill Hill Sch.; New Coll., Oxford (BA Jurisprudence 1952); Heythrop Coll. (BA Theol. 2008; MA Dist. 2009). Called to Bar, Lincoln's Inn, 1953 (Bencher, 1983); called to Bahamian Bar, 1971, to Eastern Caribbean Bar, 1992. Chairman: Chancery Bar Assoc., 1985–94; Westminster Assoc. for Mental Health, 1981–88 (Trustee, 1999–2011); Westminster Christian Council, 1986–87 (Vice-Chm., 1984–85). Trustee, IMPACT, 2002–. *Publications:* Lewin on Trusts, 16th edn 1964, 18th edn 2008; Estate Duty on Settled Property, 1969; articles in jls. *Recreations:* music, observing nature in Sussex garden. *Club:* Travellers.

MOWL, Colin John, CB 2004; Executive Director, Macroeconomics and Labour Market, Office for National Statistics, 2002–08; *b* 19 Oct. 1947; *s* of late Arthur Sidney and Ada Mowl; *m* 1980, Kathleen Patricia Gallagher; one *s* one *d*. *Educ:* Lawrence Sheriff Sch., Rugby; LSE (BSc Econs, MSc). Econ. Asst, MoT, 1970–72; Sen. Econ. Asst, Econ. Advr, HM Treasury, 1972–83; Res. Manager, Forex Research Ltd, 1983; HM Treasury: Sen. Econ. Advr, 1983–90; Grade 3, and Hd, Econ. Analysis and Forecasting Gp, later Dep. Dir, Macroecon. Policy and Prospects, 1990–95; Dep. Dir, subseq. Dir, Budget and Public Finances, 1995–2002. *Publications:* various Treasury working papers. *Recreations:* family, visiting France, sport, medieval and Second World War history of Normandy. *E:* colin.mowl@gmail.com.

MOWLL, Rev. (John) William (Rutley); Chaplain to the Queen, 2000–12; *b* 24 March 1942; *s* of Wilfred Rutley Mowll and Mary Giffard (*née* Holden); *m* 1966, Susan Frances Lisle Bullen; two *s*. *Educ:* Canterbury Cathedral Choir Sch.; King's Sch., Canterbury; Sarum Theol Coll. Ordained deacon, 1966, priest, 1967; Curate: Church of the Ascension, Oughtibridge, dio. Sheffield, 1966–69; St James, Hill, dio. Birmingham, 1969–72; Industrial Chaplain and Vicar, Upper Arley, 1973–78; Priest-in-Charge, 1978–81, Rector, 1981–83, Upton Snodsbury; Vicar, Boughton-under-Blean with Dunkirk, 1983–2007, also Hernhill, 1989–2007; Rural Dean, Ospringe, Faversham, 1995–2001; Hon. Minor Canon, Canterbury Cathedral, 1995–2002; Chaplain to High Sheriff of Kent, 2001–02. Occasional Lectr, Nat. Maritime Mus. Mem., Soc. for Nautical Res., 1986–; Life Mem., HMS Warrior 1860; Hon. Mem., Guild of Master Craftsmen, 1984–. Model ships on display: SS Great Britain, Brunel Inst. Library, Bristol; HMS Warrior 1860, Victory Gate, Portsmouth. *Publications:* SS Great Britain: the model ship, 1982; HMS Warrior 1860: building a working model warship, 1997; (contrib.) Building Model Warships of the iron and steel era (ed P. Beisheim), 2002; Thunderer: building a model Dreadnought, 2010; contrib. Ships in Scale mag., 2012–13, 2015–16. *Recreations:* practising musician, amateur playwright, engineer in miniature craftwork, specialising in model ships. *Address:* Holly Cottage, Water Lane, Ospringe, Faversham, Kent ME13 8TS. *T:* (01795) 597597. *Club:* Faversham Farmers'.

MOWSCHENSON, Terence Rennie; QC 1995; a Recorder, since 2000; a Deputy High Court Judge, since 2003; *b* 7 June 1953; *s* of Henry and Hanny Mowschenson; *m* 1992, Judith Angela Strang. *Educ:* Eagle Sch., Umtali, Rhodesia; Peterhouse, Marandellas, Rhodesia; Queen Mary Coll., London (LLB Hons 1975); Exeter Coll., Oxford (BCL Hons 1976). FCIArb. Called to the Bar, Middle Temple, 1977, Bencher, 2003; Asst Recorder, 1997–2000.

Part-time Judge (formerly Chairman): Claims Mgt Tribunal, 1996–; Financial Services and Markets Act Tribunal, 2002–; Pension Regulator Tribunal, 2005–. Chm., Barristers' Benevolent Assoc., 1999– (Hon. Sec., 1995–97, Hon. Treas., 1997–99). *Recreations:* opera, reading, travel. *Address:* Wilberforce Chambers, 8 New Square, Lincoln's Inn, WC2A 3QP. *T:* (020) 7306 0102. *Clubs:* Royal Automobile, Garrick.

MOXHAM, Prof. John, MD; FRCP; Professor of Respiratory Medicine, King's College London School of Medicine; Consultant Physician, King's College Hospital, since 1982; Director of Clinical Strategy, King's Health Partners Academic Health Sciences Centre, since 2009; *b* 9 Dec. 1944; *s* of late Wilson Moxham and Marie Moxham (*née* Bland), Evesham, Worcs; *m* 1978, Nicola Seaman; three *d. Educ:* Prince Henry's Grammar Sch., Evesham; LSE (BSc (Econ) 1967); UCH Med. Sch. (MB BS 1973; MD 1982). MRCP 1975, FRCP 1987. Lectr in Medicine, UCH, 1978–80; Sen. Registrar, Brompton and St James' Hosp., London, 1980–82. King's College School of Medicine and Dentistry, then Guy's, King's and St Thomas' School of Medicine, King's College London, subseq. King's College London School of Medicine: Prof. of Respiratory Medicine, 1990–; Dean: for Med. Student Admissions, 1991–96, Faculty of Clin. Medicine, 1997–98; KCH Campus, 1998–2000; Vice-Dean, 2000–03; Medical Dir, 2003–09. Chm., Consultants' Cttee, KCH, 1995–97; non-exec. Dir, KCH NHS Trust, 2000–03. Chm., Doctors for Tobacco Law, 1991–97; Chm., 1996–98, 2009–, Mem. Bd, 2006–, ASH; Mem., Ind. Inquiry into Access to Healthcare for People with Learning Disabilities, 2007–08. Thoracic Society: Scientific Meetings Sec., 1988–90; Mem. Exec., 1988–93; Chm., Tobacco Cttee, 1990–93. Bertram Louis Abrahams Lect., RCP, 2007; Moran Campbell Lect., British Thoracic Soc., 2013. Gov., James Allen's Girls' Sch., 2004–14. Eur. Respiratory Soc. Congress Award, 2012. Hon. MFPH 2015. *Publications:* (ed jtly) Textbook of Medicine, 1990, 4th edn 2002; res. papers on clinical physiol., particularly ventilatory failure and respiratory muscle function. *Recreations:* family, art, good beer, mooching around London. *Address:* 17 Maude Road, Camberwell, SE5 8NY. *T:* (020) 7703 4396. *E:* john.moxham@nhs.net.

MOXON, Most Rev. Sir David John, KNZM 2014; Archbishop of Canterbury's Representative to the Holy See, and Director, Anglican Centre in Rome, since 2013; *b* 6 Sept. 1951; *s* of John Rosher Moxon and Joan Moxon; *m*; two *s* two *d. Educ:* Freyberg High Sch., Palmerston North; Massey Univ. (MA Hons); Oxford Univ. (MA); Univ. of Waikato (Cert. Maori Studies 1991). Volunteer service abroad (school leaver scheme), 1970; Univ. Tutor, Educn Dept, Massey Univ., 1974–75; Curate, St Luke's, Havelock North, 1978–81; Vicar, St George's, Gate Pa, Tauranga, 1981–87; Dir, Theol Educn by Extension Unit, Anglican Church of Aotearoa, NZ and Polynesia, 1987–93; Bishop of Waikato, 1993–2013; Archbishop and Co-Primate, Anglican Church in Aotearoa, NZ and Polynesia, 2006–13. Fellow, St Margaret's Coll., Univ. of Otago, 2006. Hon. Fellow, St Peter's Coll., Oxford, 2006. Hon. LTh Aotearoa. Gold Duke of Edinburgh Award, 1969. *Recreations:* playing flute, reading, tramping, swimming. *Address:* Anglican Centre, Palazzo Doria Pamphilj, Piazza del Collegio Romano 2, 00186 Rome, Italy.

MOXON, Prof. (Edward) Richard, FMedSci; FRS 2007; Action Research Professor of Paediatrics, University of Oxford, 1984–2008, now Emeritus Professor; Fellow, Jesus College, Oxford, 1984–2008, now Emeritus; Head, Molecular Infectious Diseases Group, Institute of Molecular Medicine, John Radcliffe Hospital, Oxford, 1988–2008; Founder and Chairman, Oxford Vaccine Group, 1994–2008; *b* 16 July 1941; *s* of late Gerald Richard Moxon and of Margaret Forster Mohun; *m* 1973, Marianne Graham; two *s* one *d. Educ:* Shrewsbury Sch.; St John's Coll., Cambridge (Keasby Award, 1961; BA 1963); St Thomas' Hosp. (MB, BChir 1966); MA Oxon 1984. MRCP 1968, FRCP 1984; FRCPCH 1997. Surgical House Officer, Kent and Canterbury Hosp., 1966; Medical House Officer, Peace Meml Hosp., Watford, 1966; Pathologist, St Thomas' Hosp., 1967; Sen. House Officer in Paediatrics: Whittington Hosp., 1968; Hosp. for Sick Children, Gt Ormond St, 1969; Children's Hosp. Medical Center, Boston, Mass, USA: Asst Resident in Pediatrics, 1970; Res. Fellow in Infectious Diseases Div., 1971–74; Johns Hopkins Hosp., Baltimore, Md, USA: Asst Prof. in Pediatrics, 1974–80; Associate Prof. in Pediatrics, 1980–84; Chief, Eudowood Div. of Pediatric Infectious Diseases, 1982–84. Vis. Scientist, Washington Univ., St Louis, 1990–91; Burroughs-Wellcome Vis. Prof., Allegheny Univ. of Health Scis, Philadelphia, 1999. Lectures: Mitchell, RCP, 1992; Blackfan, Children's Hosp. Med. Center, Boston, Mass, 1994; Teale, RCP, 1998; Dolman, Univ. of BC, 1999; Hattie Alexander Meml, Columbia, 2005; Award, Eur. Soc. of Clin. Microbiol. and Infectious Diseases, 2007; Fred Griffith Review, Soc. for Gen. Microbiol., 2007. Convenor, BPA Immunology and Infectious Diseases Gp, 1984–89; Chm., MRC Sub-Cttee, Polysaccharide Vaccines, 1986–90; Member: Steering Gp, Encapsulated Bacteria, WHO, 1987–93. Amer. Soc. Clinical Investigation. Founder FMedSci 1998; Fellow: Amer. Soc. of Microbiol., 2001; Infectious Diseases Soc. of America, 2002. Bill Marshall Award, ESPID, 2005. *Publications:* (with D. Isaacs): Neonatal Infections, 1991; A Practical Approach to Pediatric Infectious Diseases, 1996; Longman Handbook of Neonatal Infections, 1999; contribs to: Mandell's Principles and Practice of Infectious Diseases, 2nd edn 1985, 4th edn 1995; Forfar and Arneil's Textbook of Paediatrics, 4th edn 1992, 5th edn 1998; Oxford Textbook of Medicine, 3rd edn 1996, 4th edn 2000; editorial adviser: Lancet's Modern Vaccines, 1991; Lancet's Vaccine Octet, 1997; Yu, Merigan, Barrière, Antimicrobial Therapy and Vaccines, 1998; Stearns' Evolution in Health and Disease, 1998; many articles in learned jls on molecular microbiol., paediatric vaccines and infectious diseases, esp. relating to *Haemophilus influenzae* and *Neisseria meningitidis. Recreations:* music, tennis, golf, wines. *Address:* 9A North Parade Avenue, Oxford OX2 6LX.

MOXON, Very Rev. Michael Anthony, LVO 1998; Dean and Rector of St Mary's Cathedral, Truro, 1998–2004, Dean Emeritus, 2011; *b* 23 Jan. 1942; *s* of Rev. Canon Charles Moxon and Phyllis Moxon; *m* 1st, 1969, Sarah-Jane Cresswell (marr. diss. 2010); twin *s* one *d*; 2nd, 2010 Nicola Susan Trewolla. *Educ:* Merchant Taylors' Sch., Northwood, Middx; Durham Univ.; Salisbury Theol Coll.; Heythrop Coll., London (BD 1978; MA 1996). Deacon, 1970; priest, 1971; Curate, Lowestoft gp of parishes, 1970–74; Minor Canon, St Paul's Cathedral, 1974–81; Sacrist of St Paul's, 1977–81; Warden of Coll. of Minor Canons, 1979–81; Vicar of Tewkesbury with Walton Cardiff, 1981–90; Canon, 1990–98, Canon Steward, 1994–97, Canon Treas., 1997–98, St George's Chapel, Windsor; Chaplain in Windsor Great Park, 1990–98. Chaplain to the Queen, 1986–98. Member: Gen. Synod of C of E, 1985–90; Council for the Care of Churches, 1986–90; C of E Bd of Educn, 2001–04. Chaplain, HQ Cornwall County Fire Brigade, 1998–2004. *Recreations:* music, reading, cricket, classic motor cars. *Address:* St Neots, 79 Moresk Road, Truro, Cornwall TR1 1BT.

MOXON BROWNE, Robert William; QC 1990; a Recorder, since 1991; a Deputy Judge of the Technology and Construction Court (formerly Deputy Official Referee), since 1992; a Deputy Judge of the High Court, since 1999; *b* 26 June 1946; *s* of late Kendall Edward Moxon Browne and Sheila Heron Moxon Browne; *m* 1968, Kerstin Elizabet Warne; one *s* one *d. Educ:* Gordonstoun School; University College, Oxford (BA). Called to the Bar, Gray's Inn, 1969; specialises in commercial and insurance law in London and on Western Circuit. Dir, Sirius Projects Ltd, 2005–. *Recreations:* walking, gardening, wine. *Address:* 2 Temple Gardens, EC4Y 9AY. *T:* (020) 7822 1200.

MOYERS, Bill D.; journalist; Founder and Managing Editor, Public Affairs Television Inc., since 1987; *b* 5 June 1934; *s* of John Henry Moyers and Ruby Moyers (*née* Johnson); *m* 1954, Judith Suzanne Davidson; two *s* one *d. Educ:* High Sch., Marshall, Texas; Univ. of Texas; Univ. of Edinburgh; Southwestern Theological Seminary. BJ 1956; MDiv 1959. Personal Asst to Senator Lyndon B. Johnson, 1959–60; Executive Asst, 1960; US Peace Corps: Associate Dir, 1961–63; Dep. Dir, 1963. Special Asst to President Johnson, 1963–66; Press Sec., 1965–67; Publisher of Newsday, Long Island, 1967–70; Exec. Ed., Bill Moyers' Jl, Public Broadcasting Service, 1971–76, 1978–81; editor and chief reporter, CBS Reports, 1976–79; Sen. News Analyst, CBS Evening News, 1981–86. Contributing Editor, Newsweek Magazine. Pres., Florence and John Schumann Foundn. Over thirty-five Emmy Awards, incl. most outstanding broadcaster, 1974; Lowell Medal, 1975; ABA Gavel Award for distinguished service to American system of law, 1974; ABA Cert. of Merit, 1975; Awards for The Fire Next Door: Monte Carlo TV Festival Grand Prize, Jurors Prize and Nymph Award, 1977; Robert F. Kennedy Journalism Grand Prize, 1978, 1988; Christopher Award, 1978; Sidney Hillman Prize for Distinguished Service, 1978, 1981, 1987; Distinguished Urban Journalism Award, Nat. Urban Coalition, 1978; George Polk Award, 1981, 1987; Alfred I. du Pont—Columbia Univ. Award, 1981, 1987, 1988, 1991, 2000; Peabody Award, 1977, 1981, annually 1986–89, 1999, 2000; Overseas Press Award, 1986; Regents Medal of Excellence, 1992; Walter Cronkite Award for Excellence in Journalism, 1995; Nelson Mandela Award for Health and Human Rights, 1996; Charles Frankel Prize in the Humanities, NEH, 1996; Peabody Award for Lifetime Achievement, 2004. *Publications:* Listening to America, 1971; Report from Philadelphia, 1987; The Secret Government, 1988; Joseph Campbell and the Power of Myth, 1988; A World of Ideas, 1989, 2nd edn 1990; Healing and the Mind, 1993; Language of Life, 1995; Genesis, 1996; Fooling With Words, 1999; Moyers on America, 2004; Moyers on Democracy, 2008; Bill Moyers' Journal, 2012. *Address:* (office) 250 West 57th Street, Suite 718, New York, NY 10107, USA.

MOYES, David William; Manager, Real Sociedad Football Club, since 2014; *b* 25 April 1963; *m* Pamela; one *s* one *d*. Football player: Celtic, 1980–83; Cambridge United, 1983–85; Bristol City, 1985–87; Shrewsbury Town, 1987–90; Dunfermline Athletic, 1990–93; Hamilton Academical, 1993; Preston North End, 1993–98; Manager: Preston North End, 1998–2002 (Div. 2 Champions, 2000); Everton FC, 2002–13; Manchester United FC, 2013–14. Manager of Year, League Managers Assoc., 2003, 2005.

MOYES, James Christopher; Founder and Director, Momart Ltd, Fine Arts Services and Shipping Co., 1971–2000; working artist in all media; *b* 29 April 1943; *s* of Albert Jack Moyes and Catherine Louise Moyes; *m* 1st, 1969, Elizabeth McKee (marr. diss. 1981); one *d*; 2nd, 1987, Joanna Margaret Price (marr. diss. 2000); two *d*; 3rd, 2006, Alison Jane Winfield-Chislett (marr. diss. 2010). *Educ:* Univ. of Kent (BA); Slade Sch. of Art (MA 1999). Visiting Lecturer: Essex Univ., 1988–; UEA, 1988–98; Associate Vis. Lectr in Mus. Studies, Leicester Univ., 1990–2000. Vice Chm., Contemporary Arts Soc., 1996–99. Royal Warrant Holder, 1993 (re-assigned to Momart 1999). *Recreation:* rowing. *Address:* Studio #4, Ropewalk Mews, 118 Middleton Road, E8 4LP. *Club:* Quintin Boat.

MOYES, Dr William; Chairman: Monitor, Independent Regulator of NHS Foundation Trusts, 2004–10; General Dental Council, since 2013; *b* 18 Sept. 1949; *s* of William Moyes and Catherine (*née* Brannan); *m* 1971, Dr Barbara Ann Rice; one *s. Educ:* Lawside Acad., Dundee; Univ. of Edinburgh (BSc Chem. 1971; PhD Theoretical Chem. 1975); London Business Sch. (Public Sector Mgt Prog. 1988). DoE, 1974–76; Dept of Transport, 1976–80; Cabinet Office Econ. Secretariat, 1980–83; Finance Div., Scottish Office, 1983–85; Scottish Educn Dept, 1985–87; Dept of Agric. and Fisheries for Scotland, 1987–90; Dir, Strategic Planning and Performance Mgt, Mgt Exec., NHS in Scotland, 1990–94; Hd, Infrastructure Finance, Bank of Scotland, 1994–2000; Dir-Gen., British Retail Consortium, 2000–04. Director: British Linen Investments Ltd, 1996–2000; Catalyst Healthcare Gp, 1996–2000; Summit Healthcare Gp, 1997–2000; Community Health Facilities (Oxford) Ltd, 1998–2000; Eurocommerce, 2001–04 (also Mem., Steering Cttee); BRC Trading Ltd, 2002–04; Skills Mart Ltd, 2002–04; Mem. Bd, Priory Hosp. Gp, 2011–. Mem. Bd, OFT, 2010–14; Associate, Inst. for Govt, 2010–13; Mem. Bd, Albertus Inst., 2015–. Lay Mem., Legal Services Bd, 2008–. Mem. Council, Univ. of Surrey, 2004–08. Dir, BLISS (Nat. Charity for Newborn), 2002–04. Trustee: Nuffield Trust, 2008–12; Catholic Trust for England and Wales, 2010–. Gov., Heythrop Coll., 2011– (Chm., Governing Body, 2012–14). *Publications:* contrib. papers to scientific jls. *Recreations:* good food, gardening, theatre, hill walking.

MOYLAN-JONES, Rear-Adm. Roger Charles, CEng, FIMechE; Director General Aircraft (Navy), 1992–95; *b* 18 April 1940; *s* of Brian Percy Jameson Moylan-Jones and Louie-Mae (*née* Brown); *m* 1961, Mary Howells; two *s* one *d. Educ:* King Edward VI Grammar Sch., Totnes; BRNC, Dartmouth; RNEC, Manadon (BSc Eng 1964). CEng, FIMechE 1990. Joined BRNC Dartmouth, 1958; service in 766, 890, 360 Sqdns and HMS Ark Royal, 1965–69; HMS Ganges, 1969–71; Air Engineering Officer, 706 Sqdn and 819 Sqdn; Staff of Flag Officer Carriers and Amphibious Ships, 1971–77; ndc 1978; Staff of: Flag Officer, Naval Air Comd, 1978–80; Dep. Chief of Defence Staff (OR), 1981–82; CSO to FONAC, 1983–84; Capt., HMS Daedalus, 1984–86; RCDS 1987; Director: Aircraft Support Policy (Navy), 1988–89; Naval Manning and Trng (Engrg), 1989–91. Capt., RN and Combined Services CC, 1969–73, 1982, 1983; Pres., RNCC, 1993–95 (Chm., 1985–89; Life Vice Pres., 1995). President: Devon Assoc. of Cricket Officials, 2009–; Devon CCC, 2010– (Chm., 1997–2010; Hon. Life Mem., 2014); Minor Counties Cricket Assoc., 2015–; Chm., Devon Cricket Bd, 1997–2003; Mem., ECB Mgt Bd, 2000–05; Dir, ECB Ltd, 2000–05. Trustee and Dir, England and Wales Cricket Trust, 2006–. *Recreations:* cricket, travel. *Clubs:* Army and Navy, MCC; I Zingari, Free Foresters, Forty.

MOYLE, Rt Hon. Roland (Dunstan); PC 1978; barrister-at-law; Deputy Chairman, Police Complaints Authority, 1985–91; *b* 12 March 1928; *s* of late Baron Moyle, CBE; *m* 1956, Shelagh Patricia Hogan; one *s* one *d. Educ:* Infants' and Jun. Elem. Schs, Bexleyheath, Kent; County Sch., Llanidloes, Mont.; UCW Aberystwyth (LLB); Trinity Hall, Cambridge (MA, LLM). Called to the Bar, Gray's Inn, 1954. Commnd in Royal Welch Fusiliers, 1949–51. Legal Dept, Wales Gas Bd, 1953–56; Industrial Relations Executive with Gas Industry, 1956–62, and Electricity Supply Industry, 1962–66. MP (Lab) Lewisham N, 1966–74, Lewisham E, 1974–83; PPS to Chief Secretary to the Treasury, 1966–69, to Home Secretary, 1969–70; opposition spokesman on higher educn and science, 1972–74; Parly Sec., MAFF, 1974; Minister of State, NI Dept, 1974–76; Minister for Health, 1976–79; opposition spokesman on health, 1979–80; deputy foreign affairs spokesman, 1980–83; opposition spokesman on defence and disarmament, 1983. Mem., Select Cttee on Race Relations and Immigration, 1968–72; Vice-Chm., PLP Defence Group, 1968–72; Sec., 1971–74, Mem. Exec. Cttee, 1971–83, British Amer. Parly Gp; Treas., British S Amer. Gp, 1970–74. Pres., Montgomeryshire Soc., 2003–04. *Recreation:* pottering. *Address:* 139 Lee Park, Blackheath, SE3 9HE.

MOYNE, 3rd Baron *cr* 1932, of Bury St Edmunds; **Jonathan Bryan Guinness;** *b* 16 March 1930; *s* of 2nd Baron Moyne and Hon. Diana (*née* Mitford, later Hon. Lady Mosley) (*d* 2003); *S* father, 1992; *m* 1st, 1951, Ingrid Wyndham (marr. diss. 1962); one *s* one *d* (and one *s* decd); 2nd, 1964, Suzanne Phillips (*née* Lisney); one *s* one *d. Educ:* Eton; Oxford (MA, Mod. Langs). Journalist at Reuters, 1953–56. Merchant Banker: trainee at Erlangers Ltd, 1956–59, and at Philip Hill, 1959–62; Exec. Dir, 1962–64, non-exec. Dir, 1964–91, Leopold Joseph; Dir, Arthur Guinness Son & Co. Ltd, 1961–88. CC Leicestershire, 1970–74; Chairman, Monday Club, 1972–74. *Publications:* (with Catherine Guinness) The House of Mitford, 1984; Shoe: the Odyssey of a Sixties Survivor, 1989; Requiem for a Family Business, 1997. *Heir: s* Hon. Valentine Guy Bryan Guinness [*b* 9 March 1959; *m* 1986, Lucinda Jane, OBE (marr. diss. 2013), *o d* of Sir Miles Rivett-Carnac, 9th Bt; two *d*]. *Address:* 12 Gloucester Road, Painswick, Stroud, Glos GL6 6RA.

See also Hon. D. W. Guinness, Earl of Wemyss and March.

MOYNIHAN, family name of **Baron Moynihan**.

MOYNIHAN, 4th Baron *cr* 1929, of Leeds, co. York; **Colin Berkeley Moynihan;** Bt 1922; Founding Partner, CMA Consultants, since 1994; Director, Rowan Companies Inc., 1996–2015; Chairman, British Olympic Association, 2005–12; *b* 13 Sept. 1955; *s* of 2nd Baron Moynihan, OBE, TD, and of June Elizabeth (who *m* 1965, N. B. Hayman), *d* of Arthur Stanley Hopkins; *S* half-brother, 1997; *m* 1992, Gaynor-Louise Metcalf; two *s* one *d*. *Educ:* Monmouth Sch. (Music Scholar); University Coll., Oxford (BA PPE 1977, MA 1982). Pres., Oxford Union Soc., 1976. Personal Asst to Chm., Tate & Lyle Ltd, 1978–80; Manager, Tate & Lyle Agribusiness, resp. for marketing strategy and develt finance, 1980–82; Chief Exec., 1982–83, Chm., 1983–87, Ridgways Tea and Coffee Merchants; external consultant, Tate & Lyle PLC, 1983–87. Chm. and CEO, Consort Resources Ltd, 2000–03; Exec. Chm., Clipper Windpower Marine Ltd, 2005–07; Chairman: Pelamis Wave Power (formerly Ocean Power Delivery), 2005–11; Hydrodec Gp plc, 2012–; Buckthorn Partners LLP, 2014–. Dir, Inst. of Petroleum, 2001–03. MP (C) Lewisham East, 1983–92; contested (C) Lewisham East, 1992. Political Asst to the Foreign Sec., 1983; PPS to Minister of Health, 1985, to Paymaster General, 1985–87; Parly Under Sec. of State (Minister for Sport), DoE, 1987–90; Parly Under-Sec. of State, Dept of Energy, 1990–92. Chm., All-Party Parly Gp on Afghanistan, 1986; Vice Chm., Cons. Food and Drinks Sub-Cttee, 1983–85; Sec. Cons. Foreign and Commonwealth Affairs Cttee, 1983–85. Member: Paddington Conservative Management Cttee, 1980–81; Bow Group, 1978–92 (Mem., Industry Cttee, 1978–79, 1985–87); Chm., Trade & Industry Standing Cttee, 1983–87. Elected Mem., H of L, 1999. Sen. Opposition spokesman on foreign affairs, H of L, 1999–2002; Chm., Cons. Campaigning Bd, 2004–05; special advr to Leader of the Opposition, 2003–05 (Treas., Leadership Campaign Fund, 2003). Chm., Sydney Olympic UK Business Task Force, 1995–97; Member: Sports Council, 1982–85; Major Spectator Sports Cttee, CCPR, 1979–82; CCPR Enquiry into Sponsorship of Sport, 1982–83; Exec. Cttee, Assoc. Nat. Olympic Cttees, 2006–10; IOC Internat. Relations Cttee, 2008–14; Dir, LOCOG, 2005–13; Steward, British Boxing Bd of Control, 1979–87. Trustee: Oxford Univ. Boat Club, 1980–84; Sports Aid Trust, 1983–87; Governor, Sports Aid Foundn (London and SE), 1980–82. Pres., British Water Ski, 2006–. Mem. Council, Royal Commonwealth Soc., 1980–82. Hon. Sec., Friends of British Council. Freeman, City of London, 1978; Liveryman, Worshipful Co. of Haberdashers, 1981 (Third Warden, 2013–14). Patron, Land & City Families Trust. Oxford Double Blue, Rowing and Boxing, 1976 and 1977; World Gold Medal for Lightweight Rowing, Internat. Rowing Fedn, 1978; Olympic Silver Medal for Rowing, 1980; World Silver Medal for Rowing, 1981. *Recreations:* collecting Nonesuch Books, music, sport. *Heir: s* Hon. Nicholas Ewan Berkeley Moynihan, *b* 31 March 1994. *Address:* Room 3–19, Millbank House, House of Lords, SW1A 0PW. *T:* (020) 7219 5879. *E:* moynihanc@parliament.uk. *Clubs:* Ivy; Kandahar Ski; Leander (Henley-on-Thames); Vincent's (Oxford).

MOYNIHAN, Sir Daniel, Kt 2012; EdD; Chief Executive, Harris Federation of London Schools, since 2005; *b* London, 29 Jan. 1960; *s* of Edmund and Bridget Moynihan; *m* 1987, Jane Margaret Iles; one *s* one *d*. *Educ:* St George's RC Sch., Maida Vale; University Coll. London (BSc Econ. 1982); Inst. of Educn, London Univ. (PGCE Dist. 1984; MA Educnl Admin 1996; EdD 2002). Head of Econs, Bishop Challoner Sch., 1984–88; Head of Business Studies, Kingsbury High Sch., Brent, 1988–90; Asst Principal, 1990–96, Vice Principal, 1996–99, Leigh City Technol. Coll., Dartford; Headteacher, Valentines High Sch., Ilford, 1999–2004; Principal, Harris City Technol. Coll., 2005–08. Mem., Educn Hons Cttee, Cabinet Office, 2013–. *Publications:* (with B. Titley) Economics: a complete course, 1987, 3rd edn 2000; Advanced Business, 1995, 2nd edn 2001; Intermediate Business, 1996; (with B. Titley) Economics: a complete course for Cambridge IGCSE and O Level, 2007, 2nd edn 2012. *Recreations:* art, history, politics, travel. *Address:* Harris Federation, 4th Floor, Norfolk House, Wellesley Road, Croydon CR0 1LH. *E:* Dan.moynihan@harrisfederation.org.uk, D.Moynihan1@btinternet.com.

MOYNIHAN, Jonathan Patrick, OBE 1994; Chairman and Joint Principal, Ipex Capital, since 2008; *b* Cambridge, 21 June 1948; *s* of Sir Noël Henry Moynihan and Margaret Mary Moynihan (*née* Lovelace); *m* 1980, Patricia Underwood; one step *d*. *Educ:* Balliol Coll., Oxford (Lazarus Fletcher and Agnes Ward Schol. in Maths; MA 1975; Foundn Fellow 1999); Poly. of N London (MSc 1974); Massachusetts Inst. of Technol. (SM 1977). Track Records, 1970–71; Relief and Rehabilitation Organiser: War on Want, Calcutta, 1971; SCF, Orissa and Bangladesh, 1971–72; Product Manager, Roche Products Ltd, London, 1972–76; Associate, McKinsey & Co., Amsterdam, 1977–79; Vice Pres., Strategic Planning Associates, Washington DC, 1979–81; Pres., Moynihan Strategy Consultants, NY, 1981–82; Man. Vice Pres., First Manhattan Consulting Gp, NY, 1982–92; Chief Exec., 1992–99, Exec. Chm., 1994–2013, PA Consulting Gp. Chairman: UbiNetics, 1995–2005; Cubiks, 1998–2005; Meridica, 2000–05; ImPAct Executives, 2000–03; Aegate, 2003–10 (non-exec. Dir, 2011–); ProcServe Ltd, 2006–; PlaqueTec Ltd, 2007–; Semblant Ltd, 2008–. Mem., Overseas and Welfare Cttee, SCF, 1972–76. Member: Dean's Council, Sloan Sch., MIT, 1997–2011; Dean's Adv. Gp, Saïd Business Sch., 1999–2006; Vice Chancellor's Circle, Oxford Univ., 2010–. Chm., Balliol Campaign Bd, 1995–2007. Founder Chm., Helen Bamber Foundn, 2005–07. Mem. Council, Royal Albert Hall, 2012–. Hon. Fellow, Gray's Inn, 2012–. Dist. Friend of Oxford, 2010–. *Recreation:* economics. *Address:* 41 Chelsea Square, SW3 6LH. *T:* (020) 7376 6767, *Fax:* (020) 7376 6777. *E:* jon@moyni.biz. *Clubs:* Travellers, Carlton, MCC, Academy.

MOZAYEN, (Ann) Rosemary; *see* Arnott, A. R.

MOZUMDER, Air Vice-Marshal Aroop Kumar, CB 2015; Commander Defence Primary Healthcare, Joint Forces Command, 2013–15; Director General Royal Air Force Medical Services, 2011–15; *b* London, 24 April 1956; *s* of Sailendra Mohon Mozumder and Gouri Mozumder; *m* 1984, Jane Edgcumbe; one *s* two *d*. *Educ:* Latymer Upper Sch.; Charing Cross Hosp. Med. Sch., London (MB BS 1979; MSc 1998). DRCOG 1983; DTM&H 1985; DAvMed 1993; DMCC 2004; FRCGP 2013. MO, Save the Children, 1984–86; Royal Air Force: MO, 1987–2015; Inspector Gen., Defence Med. Services, 2009–11. QHP 2008–15. Farmington Scholar, Harris Manchester Coll., Univ. of Oxford. GP Advr, Care Quality Commn. Trustee: Help for Heroes; Headley Court Charity. Pres., Faculty of Conflict and Catastrophe Medicine, Apothecaries' Soc., 2012– (Mem., Ct of Assts, 2012–). President: RAF Real Tennis, 2011–; RAF Lawn Tennis, 2013–. CDir 2014. OStJ 2001. *Publications:* (contrib.) Conflict and Catastrophe Medicine, 2nd edn 2008, 3rd edn (contrib. ed.) 2013. *Clubs:* Royal Air Force; Royal Society of Medicine.

MPALANYI-NKOYOYO, Most Rev. Livingstone; Archbishop of Uganda, 1994–2003; *b* 1937. *Educ:* Buwalasi Coll., Uganda; Legon Trinity Coll., Ghana; East Bond Coll., England. Car mechanic; chauffeur to Bishop Lutaaya, dio. of W Buganda; ordained deacon, 1969, priest, 1970; served in parish: Kasubi, 1969–75; Nsangi, 1975–77; Archdeacon of Namirembe, 1977–79; Suffragan Bishop: dio. of Namirembe, 1980–81; dio. of Mukono, 1981–94. *Address:* c/o PO Box 14123, Kampala, Uganda.

MPUCHANE, Samuel Akuna; in business in Botswana, since 1991; *b* 15 Dec. 1943; *s* of Chiminya Thompson Mpuchane and Motshidiemang Phologolo; *m* Sisai Felicity Mokgokong; two *s* one *d*. *Educ:* Univ. of Botswana, Lesotho and Swaziland (BA Govt and Hist.); Southampton Univ. (MSc Internat. Affairs). External Affairs Officer, 1969–70; First Secretary: Botswana Mission to UN, 1970–71; Botswana Embassy, Washington, 1971–74; Under Sec., External Affairs, 1974–76; on study leave, 1976–77; Dep. Perm. Sec., Min. of Mineral Resources and Water Affairs, 1977–79; Admin. Sec., Office of Pres., 1979–80; Perm. Sec., Min. of Local Govt and Lands, 1980–81; High Comr for Botswana in UK, 1982–85; Perm. Sec. for External Affairs, 1986–90. Director, 1991–: Builders World; Building Materials Supplies; Royal Wholesalers; Parts World; Trade World; Blue Chip Investments; Continental Star Caterers; Minaras Investments (Pty) Ltd; Keystone Investments (Pty) Ltd; 21st Century Hldgs (Pty) Ltd; Kan Bw (Pty) Ltd. Mem. Bd Trustees, Univ. of Botswana Foundn, 2000–. *Recreations:* playing and watching tennis, watching soccer.

MROZ, Ann Dorota; Digital Publishing Director, TSL Education, since 2012, and Editor, Times Educational Supplement, since 2013; *b* London, 31 Jan. 1959; *d* of Bolesław Mroz and Maria Mroz; one *d* one *s*. *Educ:* Orange Hill Grammar Sch., Edgware; London Coll. of Printing (NCTJ Proficiency Cert.); Henley Coll. (Cert. Mgt). Times Higher Education Supplement, later Times Higher Education, 1974–2012: Sub-Editor, later Chief Sub-Editor; Dep. Editor, 2007–08; Editor, 2008–12. FRSA. *Recreations:* riding hobby horses, swimming against the tide, sailing too close to the wind. *Address:* TES Global, 26 Red Lion Square, WC1R 4HQ. *T:* (020) 3194 3326. *E:* ann.mroz@tesglobal.com.

MSAKA, Bright, SC; Chief Secretary for the President and Cabinet, Malaŵi, since 2004; *m* Primrose; three *c*. NP; Practised law, specialising in commercial litigation and tort; Lectr in Law, Univ. of Malaŵi; Examr of Co. Law, ACCA; High Comr of Malaŵi in UK, and concurrently Ambassador to Finland, Iceland, Norway, Portugal, Spain, Sweden, 1998–2003. *Address:* Office of the President and Cabinet, Private Bag 301, Lilongwe 3, Malaŵi.

MTETEMELA, Most Rev. Donald Leo; MP, Constituent Assembly of Tanzania, since 2014; Archbishop of Tanzania, 1998–2008; *b* Nov. 1947; *s* of Weston Mtetemela and Anjendile Mtetemela; *m* 1970, Gladys Matonya; three *s* four *d*. *Educ:* Dodoma Secondary Sch.; St Philip's Theol Coll., Kongwa (LTh); Wycliffe Hall, Oxford; DipTh London Univ. Ordained, 1971; Pastor, 1971–82; Asst Bishop, Central Tanganyika, 1982–90; Bishop of Ruaha, 1990–2010. Chancellor, St John's Univ. of Tanzania. Member: Windsor Continuation Gp, 2008; Bd, CMS-Africa, 2012–; Advr, Primates Council, Global Anglican Future Conf., 2015–. Founder and Chm., Mama Bahati Foundn, 2006–.

MUBARAK, (Mohammed) Hosny, Hon. GCMG 1985; President of Egypt, 1981–2011 (Vice President, 1975–81; Prime Minister, 1981–82); *b* 4 May 1928; *m* Suzanne Thabet; two *s*. *Educ:* Military Acad.; Air Force Acad. Joined Egyptian Air Force, 1950; Flight Instr, 1952–59, Dir Gen., 1967–69, Air Force Acad.; COS, 1969–72, C-in-C, 1972–75, Air Force; Lt Gen. 1973. Chm., OAU, 1989–90. National Democratic Party: Vice Chm., 1976–81; Sec. Gen., 1981–82; Chm., 1982–2011.

MUCH, Ian Fraser Robert; Chief Executive, De La Rue plc, 1998–2004; *b* 8 Sept. 1944; *s* of Alan Fraser Much and Helen Isabella Much (*née* Barker); *m* 1978, Perena Amanda Richards; two *d*. *Educ:* Haileybury and ISC; Lincoln Coll., Oxford (MA Jurisp.). The Metal Box Co., 1966–73; Selkirk Metalbestos, 1974–78; Household International Inc., 1978–84; Factory Manager, Nampa, Idaho, 1978–80; Vice-Pres., Gen. Manager, Greensboro, N Carolina, 1980–84; BTR: Man. Dir, Dunlop Aviation Div., 1985–87; Gp Chief Exec., 1987–88; Dir, BTR Industries; T & N: Exec. Dir, 1988–98; Man. Dir, Engineering & Industrial, 1990–91, Bearings and Industrial, 1991–95; Chief Exec., Ops, 1995–96; Chief Exec., 1996–98. Non-executive Director: Manchester United plc, 2000–05; Chemring, 2004–; Simplyhealth (formerly HSA) Gp, 2005–09; Senior plc, 2005–; BTG plc, 2010–. Governor, Haileybury and ISC, 2005–. Chm., Campaign Cttee, Lincoln Coll., Oxford, 2005–10. *Recreations:* ski-ing, tennis, squash, golf, swimming, bridge, theatre.

MUCHLINSKI, Prof. Peter Thomas; Professor of International Commercial Law, School of Oriental and African Studies, University of London, since 2005; *b* 18 Oct. 1957; *s* of late Franciszek Ksawery Muchlinski and Maria Irena Muchlinska. *Educ:* London Sch. of Econs (LLB); Christ's Coll., Cambridge (LLM). Called to the Bar, Lincoln's Inn, 1981; Res. Officer, British Inst. of Human Rights, 1979–80; Lectr in Law, Univ. of Kent at Canterbury, 1981–83; Lectr in Law, 1983–96, Sen. Lectr, 1996–98, LSE; Drapers Prof. of Law, QMW, Univ. of London, 1998–2001; Prof. of Law and Internat. Business, Kent Law Sch., Univ. of Kent, 2001–05. Principal Advr on investment law, Div. of Investment and Enterprise, UNCTAD, 1997–. FRSA 1999. *Publications:* Multinational Enterprises and the Law, 1995, 2nd edn 2007; (ed jtly) Oxford Handbook of International Investment Law, 2008; contrib. articles to jls incl. Yearbook of Internat. Investment Law and Policy, Cambridge Jl of Economics, Modern Law Rev., Internat. and Comparative Law Qly, Internat. Affairs, Business Ethics Qly, Indiana Jl of Global Legal Studies, Yearbook of Japanese Assoc. of Internat. Econ. Law, Politeia, German Law Jl; Eur. Yearbook of Internat. Law. *Recreations:* gardening, history. *Address:* School of Law, School of Oriental and African Studies, Thornhaugh Street, Russell Square, WC1H 0XG. *T:* (020) 7898 4751.

MUDD, (William) David; consultant on tourism, transport and communications; cruise lecturer; *b* 2 June 1933; *o s* of Capt. W. N. Mudd and Mrs T. E. Mudd; *m*; one *s* one *d* (and one step *d*). *Educ:* Truro Cathedral Sch. Journalist, Broadcaster, TV Commentator; work on BBC and ITV (Westward Television). Editor of The Cornish Echo, 1952; Staff Reporter: Western Morning News, 1952–53 and 1959–62; Tavistock Gazette, 1963. Mem., Tavistock UDC, 1963–65. MP (C) Falmouth and Camborne, 1970–92. PPS, Dept of Energy, 1979–81; Mem., Transport Select Cttee, 1982–92. Secretary: Conservative West Country Cttee, 1973–76; Conservative Party Fisheries Sub-Cttee, 1974–75, 1981–82. Contested (Ind.) Falmouth and Camborne, 2005. Patron, Court Interpreters' Assoc., Supreme Court of Hong Kong, 1979–97. *Publications:* Cornishmen and True, 1971; Murder in the West Country, 1975; Facets of Crime, 1975; The Innovators, 1976; Down Along Camborne and Redruth, 1978; The Falmouth Packets, 1978; Cornish Sea Lights, 1978; Cornwall and Scilly Peculiar, 1979; About the City, 1979; Home Along Falmouth and Penryn, 1980; Around and About the Roseland, 1980; The Cruel Cornish Sea, 1981; The Cornish Edwardians, 1982; Cornwall in Uproar, 1983; Around and About the Fal, 1989; Around and About the Smugglers' Ways, 1991; Strange Stories of Cornwall, 1992; Dartmoor Reflections, 1993; The Magic of Dartmoor, 1994; Let the Doors be Lock'd, 2000; Better with a Pinch of Salt, 2003; Sugar 'n' Spice, 2005; The Sign of the Balloon, 2006; Clarence the Cornish Chough, 2008; How Zacci Met the Queen, 2011. *Recreations:* jig-saw puzzles, photography. *Address:* The Retreat, Down Park Drive, Tavistock, Devon PL19 9AH.

MUDDIMAN, Noel, CBE 1992 (OBE 1985); Director: CF Solutions Ltd, since 2004; Motability, 1995–2004 (Member of Council, since 2004); *b* 17 Dec. 1943; *s* of late Flora Muddiman (*née* Holdsworth), and step *s* of late Arthur George Muddiman; *m* 1969, Patricia Anne Sevage; two *s*. *Educ:* Borden Grammar Sch.; RMA, Sandhurst. Commnd RCT, 1965; regtl posts in Germany, UK, Singapore; Staff Coll., Camberley, 1975; ndc, 1981; CO, 25 Transport and Movements Regt, RCT, 1983–85; Head of Personnel and Logistics, Falkland Islands, 1985–86; Principal Logistic Planner, British Forces Germany, 1987–90; Commander: Transport and Movements, BAOR, 1990–92; Logistic Support Gp (ME), 1991; rcds, 1992; Comdt, Army Sch. of Transport, 1993–95, retd. Non-exec. Dir, Metropole Search Partners Ltd, 2012–. Norwegian Gulf War Medal, 1995. *Publications:* (jtly) Blackadder's War, 1995. *Recreations:* gardening, walking, photography.

MUDDIMER, Robert Michael; Deputy Chairman, Tomkins plc, 1996–97 (Director, 1986–97); Chairman, Gates Rubber Co., 1996–97; *b* 30 Jan. 1933; *m* 1959, Marguerite Conroy; two *s* one *d*. *Educ:* Kibworth Grammar Sch.; Univ. of Nottingham (BSc Mech. Eng 1956). FIET (FIMfgE 1966). Materials Mgt, Lansing Bagnall, 1965–68; Director: BTR Ind. Ltd, 1969–80; Molins Tobacco Ind. Ltd, 1981–86; Chm., Rank Hovis McDougall, 1992–96. *Recreations:* golf, sailing, wooden clockmaking.

MUDIE, Colin Crichton, RDI 1995; CEng; FRINA, FRIN; Principal Partner, Colin Mudie, Naval Architects and Yacht Designers, 1958–2014; *b* 11 April 1926; *s* of Hon. John Mudie and Janet Somerville Mudie (*née* Jack); *m* 1954, Rosemary Horder; one *s*. *Educ:* George Watson's, Edinburgh; Whitgift Sch.; University Coll., Southampton. CEng 1971; FRINA 1971; FRIN 1972 (Hon. FRIN 2004). Design apprentice: British Power Boat Co., Southampton, 1942–46; Laurent Giles & Partners Ltd, 1946–49; various marine projects incl. Sopranino voyage, 1951–52 and Small World transatlantic balloon flight, 1958–59. Winston Churchill Fellowship, 1968. Design work includes sail trng vessels, reproduction, expedition and exploration boats, power boats, sailing yachts, motor cruisers, etc; designer of sail trng ship, Young Endeavour, GB's gift to Australia for 1988 Bicentennial. Member: Cttee of Mgt, RNLI, 1987–2001 (Vice-Pres., 1997–2001, now Life Vice-Pres.); Council, RINA, 1988–97. Associate Mem., Acad. de Marinha, Portugal, 1995. FRSA 1996. Award for sail trng brig Royalist, Lloyd's Register of Shipping, 1971; Small Craft Medal, RINA, 1984; Award for sail trng barque Lord Nelson, British Design Council, 1993. *Publications:* Sopranino (with P. Ellam), 1954; Motor Boats and Boating, 1972; Power Boats, 1975; with Rosemary Mudie: The Story of the Sailing Ship, 1975; Power Yachts, 1977; The Sailing Ship, 1984; Sailing Ships, 2000; contrib. papers at various symposia, and articles and illustrations to professional, yachting and other jls. *Recreations:* sailing, motor boating, model making. *Address:* Bywater Lodge, Undershore Road, Lymington, Hants SO41 5SB. *T:* (01590) 672047. *Clubs:* Royal Lymington Yacht, Lymington Town Sailing; Ocean Cruising.

MUDIE, George Edward; *b* 6 Feb. 1945. *Educ:* state schs. Former Mem. (Lab) Leeds CC, and Leader of Council. MP (Lab) Leeds E, 1992–2015. Treasurer of HM Household (Dep. Chief Govt Whip), 1997–98; Parly Under-Sec. of State, DfEE, 1998–99; an Asst Govt Whip, 2009–10; Opposition Whip, 2010–13. Mem., Treasury Select Cttee, 2001–14.

MUELLBAUER, Prof. John Norbert Joseph, PhD; FBA 1997; Professor of Economics, University of Oxford, 1997–2011, now Emeritus; Senior Research Fellow: Nuffield College, Oxford, since 2011 (Fellow in Economics, 1981–2011); Institute for New Economic Thinking at Oxford Martin School, since 2011; *b* 17 July 1944; *s* of late Prof. Norbert J. Muellbauer and Edith Heinz; *m* 1999, Dr Janine Aron; one *d*; one *s* from previous marriage. *Educ:* King's Coll., Cambridge (MA 1965); Univ. of Calif at Berkeley (PhD 1975). Lectr in Economics, Univ. of Warwick, 1969–72; Lectr, 1972–75, Reader, 1975–77, Prof., 1977–81, in Economics, Birkbeck Coll., London Univ. Member: Gp of Outside Ind. Economists advising the Chancellor of the Exchequer, 1989; Retail Price Index Adv. Cttee, 1993–95; Fellow, Econometric Soc., 1976. Medal, Helsinki Univ., 1980. *Publications:* (with Angus Deaton) Economics and Consumer Behaviour, 1980; articles in Financial Times, Amer. Econ. Review, Econometrica, Econ. Jl, etc. *Recreations:* music, tennis. *Address:* Nuffield College, Oxford OX1 1NF. *T:* (01865) 278583.

MUELLER, Rudolf Gottfried, Hon. CBE 1997; Chairman, Chiltern Participations UK Ltd, 2004–06; *b* 28 May 1934; Swiss national; *m* Christiane Béroud; two *s*. *Educ:* primary and secondary schools, St Gallen, Switzerland; Internat. Management Inst., Geneva. Swiss Fed. Commercial Dip. 1953; grad. 1969 from Univ. of Geneva with dip. equivalent to MBA. James Capel & Co., 1969–77; joined Union Bank of Switzerland, 1977: Chm. and Chief Exec., UBS UK, 1989–96; Mem., Exec. Bd, UBS Gp, 1991–96; non-exec. Chm., UBS UK, 1996–98; Chairman: WJB Chiltern Gp plc (formerly Chiltern Gp plc), 1998–2003; WJB Chiltern Wealth Mgt Services Ltd, 2004–06. Non-executive Director: Lend Lease Corp. Ltd, 1996–2002; TI Gp, 1996–2000. Chm., Swiss Options Financial Futures Exchange, Zürich, 1986–88; Dir, London Stock Exchange, 1991–95. Chm., Bd of Trustees, Rix Centre, 2004–10. Member of Board: Internat. Mgt Inst., Kiev, 1993–2005; Royal Opera House Trust, 1992–97; Dir, Royal Opera House, 1996–98. Hon. DBA East London, 2005. *Recreations:* golf, ski-ing, hiking, oenology.

MUFF, family name of **Baron Calverley**.

MUGABE, Robert Gabriel; President of Zimbabwe, since 1988; President, Zimbabwe African National Union-Patriotic Front, since 1988; *b* Kutama, 21 Feb. 1924; *m* 1961, Sarah Francesca Hayfron (*d* 1992); one *s* decd; *m*.1996, Grace Marufu; two *s* one *d*. *Educ:* Kutama Mission School; Fort Hare Univ. (BA (Educ), BSc (Econ)); London Univ. (by correspondence: BScEcon; BEd; LLB; LLM; MSc(Econ)); Univ. of S Africa (by correspondence BAdm). Teacher, 1942–58: Kutama, Mapanzure, Shabani, Empandeni Mission, Hope Fountain Mission, Driefontein Mission, Mbizi Govt Sch., Mambo Sch., Chalimbana Trng Coll., Zambia; St Mary's Teacher Trng Coll., Ghana. Publ. Sec. of Nat. Dem. Party, 1960–61; Publicity Sec. and acting Sec.-Gen., Zimbabwe African People's Union, 1961–62. Political detention, 1962; co-founded and became Sec.-Gen. ZANU, Aug. 1963, but in detention in Rhodesia, 1964–74; escaped to Mozambique and led armed struggle from there, 1975–79. Prime Minister 1980–87, Minister of Defence and of Public Service, 1980–84, First Sec. of Politburo, 1984–87, Zimbabwe. Jt Leader (with Joshua Nkomo) of the Patriotic Front, Oct. 1976; Pres., ZANU, 1977–87. Chm., African Union, 2015. Attended Confs: Geneva Constitutional Conf. on Rhodesia, 1976; Malta Conf., 1978; Lancaster House Conf., 1979. Holds hon. degrees from many instns. *Address:* Office of the President, Private Bag 7700, Causeway, Harare, Zimbabwe.

MUGGERIDGE, Rev. Sara Ann, (Sally), (Mrs R. D. Williams); Chief Executive, Industry and Parliament Trust, 2003–10; *b* 10 Sept. 1949; *d* of John Raymond Muggeridge, MBE and Sylvia Barbara Ann (*née* Jenkins); *m* 1969, Richard David Williams; one *s* two *d*. *Educ:* Aida Foster Stage Sch.; S Hampstead High Sch.; Guildhall Sch. of Music and Drama (Cert. Acting); Westfield Coll., London (BA Hons); Henley Mgt Coll. (Co. of Marketors Award 1992; MBA); Univ. of Kent (Cert. Applied Christian Theol, 2010); Canterbury Christ Church Univ. (FdA Theol, 2013). Mktg Manager, British Telecom plc, 1985–91; Cable & Wireless plc: Mktg Dir, Mercury Communications, 1991–93; Mgt Develt Dir, 1993–96; HR Dir, Asia, 1996–99; Mgt Develt Dir, Pearson plc, 1999–2003. Non-exec. Dir, Total Upstream UK Ltd, 2010–15. Chartered Institute of Marketing: Mem. Council, 1985–95; Pres., CIM Singapore, 1996–98; Exec. Vice-Pres., 1999–2004; Mem., Academic Senate, 2007–13. Member: Bd, Southern Arts, 1992–96; Council for Excellence in Mgt and Leadership, 2000–02; Chartered Dir (formerly Professional Accreditation) Cttee, IoD, 2006–. Church Comr and Gov., C of E, 2014–; ordained deacon, 2015. Trustee: Pearson Gp Pensions Ltd, 1999–2003; Tutu Foundn UK, 2003–13 (Vice Patron, 2013–); Foundn for Church Leadership, 2003–11 (Vice Pres., 2011–). Internat. Pres., Malcolm Muggeridge Soc., 2003–. Mem. Council, Univ. of Kent, 2006–12. Fellow, Industry and Parlt Trust, 1995; FCIM 1988; FCIPD 1996; FRSA 1995; FInstD 2011. Hon. Life Mem., Acad. of Mktg, 2013. President's Award, CIM, 1999; Voluntary Sector Achiever of the Yr, Woman of the Yr Awards, 2007; World of Difference Award, Internat. Alliance of Women, 2015. *Films:* acted in The Hallelujah Handshake, 1970, and The Yes Girls, 1971; contrib. Timeshift: Malcolm Muggeridge (TV), 2003. Mem., House of Laity, Gen. Synod, 2010–. Freeman, City of London, 1995. Master, Marketors' Co., 2013. *Publications:* contributor: The Laterite Road, 2005; Conversion: the spiritual journey of a twentieth century pilgrim, 2005; Seeing Through the Eye, 2005; Something Beautiful for God, 2009. *Recreations:* churchwarden, choral singing, preaching, theatre and the arts, entertaining granddaughters. *E:* sally@sallymuggeridge.com. *Clubs:* Farmers, Kennel, City Livery.

MUGGLETON, Prof. Stephen Howard, PhD; FREng; Professor of Machine Learning, since 2001 and Royal Academy of Engineering/Syngenta Research Professor of Machine Learning, since 2013, Imperial College London; *b* Salisbury, Southern Rhodesia, 6 Dec. 1959; *s* of late Prof. Louis Miles Muggleton and (Alice) Sylvia Muggleton; *m* 1988, Thirza Ana Castello-Cortes; one *d*. *Educ:* George Watson's Coll., Edinburgh; Univ. of Edinburgh (BSc Hons 1983; PhD 1986). Res. Fellow, Turing Inst., Glasgow, 1987–92; Res. Fellow, Wolfson Coll., Oxford, 1992–97; EPSRC Advanced Res. Fellow, Computing Lab., 1992–97, Reader, 1997, Univ. of Oxford; Prof. of Machine Learning, Dept of Computing, Univ. of York, 1997–2001; Imperial College London: EPSRC Prof. of Computational Bioinformatics, 2001–06; Dir, Modelling, BBSRC Centre for Integrative Systems Biol., 2005–10; RAEng/Microsoft Res. Prof. of Machine Learning, 2007–12; Dir, Syngenta University Innovation Centre, 2008–. Hon. Lectr, Univ. of Strathclyde, 1991–92; Fujitsu Vis. Associate Prof., Univ. of Tokyo, 1993. FAAAI 2002; FBCS 2008; FIET 2008; FREng 2010; FRSB (FSB 2011); Fellow, Eur. Coordinating Cttee for Artificial Intelligence, 2014. Ed.-in-Chief, Machine Intelligence series, 2000–. *Publications:* Inductive Acquisition of Expert Knowledge, 1990; (ed) Inductive Logic Programming, 1992; (ed jtly) Machine Intelligence, vol. 13, 1994, vol. 14, 1995, vol. 15, 1999; (ed jtly) Elements of Computational Systems Biology, 2010; (ed jtly) Latest Advances in Inductive Logic Programming, 2015; articles in jls incl. New Generation Computing, Jl of Logic Programming, Machine Learning, Artificial Intelligence, AI Communications, Procs of Royal Soc., Nature, Jl Molecular Biol. *Recreations:* reading, walking, listening to music, watching films. *Address:* Department of Computing, Imperial College London, 180 Queen's Gate, SW7 2RH.

MUGHAL, Sajda, OBE 2015; Director, JAN Trust, since 2008; *b* Nairobi, Kenya; two *d*. *Educ:* sch. in N London; BA Business Mgt. Author of reports: Consent Matters: towards effective prevention of forced marriages within the Pakistani community in the UK, 2012; Internet Extremism: working towards a community solution, 2013. *Recreations:* reading, keeping fit, travelling, current affairs. *Address:* c/o JAN Trust, 8–10 Bedford Road, Wood Green, N22 7AU. *E:* info@jantrust.org.

MUHEIM, Franz Emmanuel; President, Swiss Red Cross, 1996–2001; Vice-President, International Federation of Red Cross and Red Crescent Societies, 1996–2001; Swiss Ambassador to the Court of St James's, 1989–94; *b* 27 Sept. 1931; *s* of Hans Muheim and Hélène (*née* Ody); *m* 1962, Radmila Jovanovic. *Educ:* Univs of Fribourg (LèsL), Geneva and Paris (arts degree). Joined Swiss Federal Dept of Foreign Affairs, 1960; served successively in Belgrade, Rabat and London, 1961–70; Council of Europe, UN and Internat. Orgns Sect., Dept of Foreign Affairs, Berne, 1971–77; Dep. Head of Mission, Minister Plenipotentiary, Washington, 1978–81; Dep. Dir of Political Affairs and Head of Political Div. Europe and N America, with rank of Ambassador, Berne, 1982–83; Dir, Internat. Orgns, Dept of Foreign Affairs, 1984–89. Head of Swiss delegns to internat. confs, *inter alia* UNESCO, ESA, Red Cross, Non-Aligned Movement. Fellow, Center for Internat. Affairs, Harvard Univ., 1981–82; Prof., Bologna Center, Johns Hopkins Univ., 1995–96. *Publications:* (ed jtly) Einblick in die Schweizerische Aussenpolitik: festschrift für Staatssekretär Raymond Probst, 1984; Multilateralism Today: festschrift zum 70. Geburtstag von a. Ständerat Franz Muheim, 1993. *Recreations:* walking, mountaineering, ski-ing, photography, music. *Address:* Es Chesaux, 1646 Echarlens, Switzerland. *T:* (026) 9152474, *Fax:* (026) 9152450.

MUIR, Prof. Alexander Laird, MD; FRCPE, FRCR, FRCSE; Professor of Postgraduate Medicine, University of Edinburgh, 1990–99; Honorary Consultant Physician, Edinburgh Royal Infirmary, 1974–99; Honorary Physician to the Army in Scotland, 1986–99; *b* 12 April 1937; *s* of Andrew Muir and Helena Bauld; *m* 1968, Berenice Barker Snelgrove, FRCR; one *s* one *d*. *Educ:* Morrison's Acad.; Fettes Coll.; Univ. of Edinburgh. MB ChB; MD 1970; FRCPE 1975 (MRCPE 1967); FRCR 1986; FRCSE 1994. MO, British Antarctic Survey, 1963–65; MRC Fellow, McGill Univ., 1970–71; Consultant Physician, Manchester Royal Infirmary, 1973–74; Edinburgh University: Sen. Lectr in Medicine, 1974; Reader in Medicine, 1981–89; Postgrad. Dean of Medicine, 1990–99. Physician to the Queen in Scotland, 1985–96. Canadian MRC Vis. Scientist, Univ. of British Columbia, 1982. Chm. and Med. Dir, Jt Cttee for Higher Med. Trng, 1998–2001; Mem., Admin of Radioactive Substances Adv. Cttee, 1986–91. Vice-Pres., RCPE, 1994–97. Founder FMedSci 1998. Member Editorial Board: Thorax, 1981–86; British Heart Jl, 1986–90. *Publications:* contribs on physiology and diseases of heart and lungs to medical books, symposia and jls. *Recreations:* gardening, reading, ski-ing, golf. *Address:* Tigh na Darroch, St Fillans, Perthshire PH6 2NG.

MUIR, Gregor; Executive Director, Institute of Contemporary Arts, since 2011; *b* London, 29 Nov. 1964; *s* of John and Maura Muir. *Educ:* Camberwell Sch. of Arts and Crafts (BA Hons Fine Art, Painting 1987). Ind. writer, critic and curator, 1987–93; ind. writer and curator, 1993–97; Dir, Lux Gall., Hoxton Sq., 1997–2001; Kramlich Curator of Contemp. Art, Tate, 2001–03; Dir, Hauser & Wirth, London, 2004–10. *Publications:* Lucky Kunst: the rise and fall of young British art, 2009, 2nd edn 2010. *Recreations:* art, food, music, architecture, travel. *Address:* Institute of Contemporary Arts, The Mall, SW1Y 5AH. *T:* (020) 7930 0493.

MUIR, (Sir) Richard James Kay, (4th Bt *cr* 1892, of Deanston, Perthshire); *S* father, 1994, but does not use the title and his name is not on the Official Roll of the Baronetage; *b* 25 May 1939; *s* of Sir John Harling Muir, 3rd Bt, TD and Elizabeth Mary, *e d* of Frederick James Dundas; *m* 1st, 1965, Susan Elizabeth (marr. diss. 1974), *d* of George A. Gardener; two *d*; 2nd, 1975, Lady Linda Mary Cole, *d* of 6th Earl of Enniskillen, MBE; two *d*. *Heir: b* Ian Charles Muir [*b* 16 Sept. 1940; *m* 1967, Fiona Barbara Elspeth, *d* of Major Stuart Mackenzie; three *d*].

MUIR, Richard John Sutherland, CMG 1994; HM Diplomatic Service, retired; *b* 25 Aug. 1942; *s* of John Muir and Edna (*née* Hodges); *m* 1966, Caroline Simpson; one *s* one *d*. *Educ:* The Stationers' Co.'s Sch.; Univ. of Reading (BA Hons). Entered HM Diplomatic Service, 1964; FO, 1964–65; MECAS, Lebanon, 1965–67; Third, then Second Sec. (Commercial), Jedda, 1967–70; Second Sec., Tunis, 1970–72; FCO, 1972–75; First Sec., Washington, 1975–79; seconded to Dept of Energy, 1979–81; Dir-Gen., British Liaison Office, Riyadh, 1981–85; FCO 1985–94: Hd of Information Dept, 1987–90; Principal Finance Officer and Chief Inspector, 1991–94; Ambassador: to Oman, 1994–99; to Kuwait, 1999–2002. Chairman: Anglo-Omani Soc., 2004–12; Sir William Luce Meml Fund, 2007–; Dir, Altajir Trust, 2007–. Order of Na'aman (1st Class) (Oman), 2013.

MUIR, Tom; Under Secretary, Textiles and Retailing Division, Department of Trade and Industry, 1992–94; *b* 15 Feb. 1936; *s* of late William and Maria Muir; *m* 1968, Brenda Dew; one *s* one *d*. *Educ:* King Edward VI Sch., Stafford; Leeds Univ. (BA Econs 1962). FCIS 1994. English Electric Co. Ltd, 1954–59; BoT, 1962–68; UK Perm. Delegn to OECD (on secondment to HM Diplomatic Service), 1968–71; DTI, 1972–75; UK Perm. Repn to EC, 1975–79 (on secondment); DoI, 1979–81; Dept of Trade, 1981–83; DTI, 1983–94: Under Sec., Insce Div., 1982–87, Overseas Trade Div. 4, 1987–89, Internat. Trade Policy Div., 1989–92. Dir, British Retail Consortium, 1995–97. Inquiry Sec., then Inquiry Manager, Competition Commn, 1999–2008. Chm., Fedn of British Artists (Mall Galls), 1998–2001. *Recreations:* walking, reading, looking at buildings and pictures, opera.

MUIR MACKENZIE, Sir Alexander (Alwyne Henry Charles Brinton), 7th Bt *cr* 1805; *b* 8 Dec. 1955; *s* of Sir Robert Henry Muir Mackenzie, 6th Bt and Charmian Cecil de Vere (*d* 1962), *o d* of Col Cecil Charles Brinton; *S* father, 1970; *m* 1984, Susan Carolyn, *d* of late John David Henzel Hayter; one *s* one *d*. *Educ:* Eton; Trinity Coll., Cambridge. *Heir: s* Archie Robert David Muir Mackenzie, *b* 17 Feb. 1989.

MUIR WOOD, Prof. David, PhD; FREng, FICE, FRSE; Professor of Civil Engineering, University of Bristol, 1995–2009, now Emeritus; Professor of Geotechnical Engineering, University of Dundee, 2009–14, now Emeritus; Professor affilierad, Geotechnical Engineering, Chalmers University of Technology, Gothenburg, Sweden, since 2014; *b* 17 March 1949; *s* of Sir Alan Muir Wood, FRS, FREng and Winifred L. Wood; *m* 1978, Helen

Rosamond Piddington; two *s*. *Educ:* Royal Grammar Sch., High Wycombe; Peterhouse, Cambridge (BA 1970, MA 1974; PhD 1974). FICE 1992; FREng (FEng 1998); FRSE 2012. University of Cambridge: res. student, Engrg Dept, 1970–73; William Stone Res. Fellow, Peterhouse, 1973–75; Fellow, Emmanuel Coll., 1975–87; Demonstrator/Lectr in Soil Mechanics, Engrg Dept, 1975–87; University of Glasgow: Cormack Prof. of Civil Engrg, 1987–95; Hd, Dept of Civil Engrg, 1991–93; Dean, Faculty of Engrg, 1993–94; University of Bristol: Hd, Dept of Civil Engrg, 1997–2002; Dean, Faculty of Engrg, 2003–07. Royal Soc. Res. Fellow, Norwegian Geotechnical Inst., Oslo, 1975; Royal Soc. Industry Fellow, Babtie Gp, 1995–96. Hon. Editor, Géotechnique, 1991–93. Associate, Geotechnical Consulting Gp, 1983–. Chm., Scottish Geotechnical Gp, 1991–93. Elder: Cairns Ch of Scotland, Milngavie, 1993–98; Monikie and Newbigging, Murroes and Tealing, Ch of Scotland, 2011–. (Jtly) British Geotechnical Soc. Prize, 1978. *Publications:* (with R. J. Mair) Pressuremeter Testing: methods and interpretation, 1987; Soil Behaviour and Critical State Soil Mechanics, 1990; (jtly) Piled Foundations in Weak Rock, 1999; Geotechnical Modelling, 2004; Soil Mechanics: a one-dimensional introduction, 2009; A very short introduction to civil engineering, 2012; contrib. numerous papers to professional jls and confs. *Recreations:* music, opera, travel. *Address:* University of Dundee, Division of Civil Engineering, Fulton Building, Dundee DD1 4HN. *T:* (01382) 385379. *E:* d.muirwood@dundee.ac.uk; Kirklands, Kirkton of Monikie, Broughty Ferry, Angus DD5 3QN. *T:* (01382) 370685.

MUIRDEN, Catherine Mary; Human Resources Director, Retail Operations, Co-operative Foods, since 2014; *b* Inverness, 19 Sept. 1962; *d* of Rev. John R. Muirden and J. Christine Muirden; *m* 1998, Werner Keschner; one *s*. *Educ:* Inverness Royal Acad.; Edinburgh Univ. (MA Gen. Arts 1984). Marks & Spencer: personnel mgt appts, 1984–93; Econ. and Strategic Develt Unit, London Bor. of Croydon (on secondment), 1993–94; store manager, 1994–98; Divl Personnel Manager, 1998–2000; Regl Hd of HR, 2000–02; Gp Hd of Recruitment, 2002–05; Divl Hd of HR, 2005–07; HR Dir, UK Retail and Business Bank, Barclays plc, 2007–14. Non-exec. Dir, Crieff Hydro Gp of Hotels, 2014–. Chair, Fruitmarket Gall., Edinburgh, 2014–. Trustee: Nat. Galleries of Scotland, 2012–; Elevation Networks, 2012–. FRSA 2006. *Recreations:* early morning swimming, cycling to catch up with son, gardening, good food and drink. *E:* kittykeschner@icloud.com.

MUIRHEAD, Alastair William; Managing Partner, Phoenix Equity Partners, since 2001; *b* Sheffield, 12 Sept. 1953; *s* of William Calliope Muirhead and Joan Andrade Muirhead; *m* 1980, Linda Anne; three *d*. *Educ:* Tonbridge Sch.; St John's Coll., Oxford (Schol.; MA Hons Natural Scis (Chem.)). Man. Dir, Charterhouse Bank, 1989–96; Partner, Phoenix Gp, 1996–97; Managing Director: Donaldson Lufkin & Jenrette, 1997–2000; Credit Suisse, 2000–01. Trustee, 2008–, Treas., 2013–, RHS. *Recreations:* gardening, hill walking, fly fishing, golf. *Address:* Phoenix Equity Partners, 25 Bedford Street, WC2E 9ES. *T:* (020) 7434 6999. *Club:* Hankley Common Golf.

MUIRHEAD, Geoffrey, CBE 2004; FCILT, FICE; Group Chief Executive, Manchester Airports Group, 2001–10; *b* 14 July 1949; *s* of John Thomas Muirhead and Irene Clarke; *m* 1972, Clare Elizabeth Parker; one *d*. *Educ:* Teesside Polytechnic. FCIT 1994; FICE 1998. Started career with British Steel; subseq. senior positions with William Press, Simon Carves, Fluor and Shand, incl. posts in Saudi Arabia, Belgium, Eire; Manchester Airport: Dir, Develt, 1988; Dir, Business Develt, 1992; Chief Exec., 1993–2001. Past Pres., Airports Council Internat. Europe. Mem., NW Business Leadership Team, 1993–2010 (Dep. Chm., 2006–10); Exec. Mem., NW Regl Assembly, 2006–08; Mem. Leaders Bd, 4NW. Associate Mem., Greater Manchester Chamber of Commerce and Industry, 2001 (Past Pres.). Chm., Ask Developments, 2010. Mem. Bd, Manchester Metropolitan Univ. FRSA 1996. Hon. DBA: Manchester Metropolitan, 2003; Teesside, 2005; Hon. DSc Salford, 2004. *Recreations:* golf, travel.

MUIRHEAD, Dame Lorna (Elizabeth Fox), DBE 2000; Lord-Lieutenant of Merseyside, since 2006; Midwifery Sister, Liverpool Women's Hospital (formerly Liverpool Maternity Hospital), 1966–69 and 1974–2005; President, Royal College of Midwives, 1997–2004; *b* 13 Sept. 1942; *d* of Donald Fox and Joan Mary (*née* Harper); *m* 1966, Ronald A. Muirhead; one *s* one *d*. *Educ:* in Shropshire and Warwickshire. SRN 1963; SCM 1965; MTD 1970; FRCOG 2001. Nurse trng, Hallam Hosp., W Bromwich, 1960–63; midwifery trng, Hallam Hosp. and Marston Green Maternity Hosp., 1964–65; Staff Midwife, Liverpool Maternity Hosp., 1965–66; Midwifery Sister Tutor, 1969–71; part-time Lectr, Liverpool Poly., 1975–80; Sen. Lectr, British Shipping Fedn med. course, 1975–85; frequent Lectr at Univ. and Royal Coll. Midwives seminars and study days, 1980–. DL Merseyside, 2003. Fellow, Royal Coll. Midwives, 2005. Hon. Fellow, Liverpool John Moores Univ., 2001. Hon. LLD Liverpool, 2010. CStJ 2008. *Publications:* chapter on A Midwife's Role in Epidural Analgesia, in Epidural Analgesia in Obstetrics, ed A. Doughty, 1980. *Recreations:* choral singing, music, poetry, restoration of old furniture. *Address:* 15 Ullet Road, Sefton Gate, Liverpool L17 3BL. *T:* (0151) 733 8710.

MUIRHEAD, Oona Grant, CBE 2000 (OBE 1992); Managing Director, Muirhead Ltd, since 2012; Adviser, Aegis Defence Services, since 2012; *b* 29 Jan. 1956; *d* of Michael and Marion Muirhead. *Educ:* Univ. of Birmingham (BA Hons Russian; Dip. Vocational Techniques for Prof. Linguist). Ministry of Defence, 1979–2003: Defence Intelligence Service, 1979; various policy and operational posts, 1985–95; (first) Pol Advr to Chief of Jt Ops, 1995–97; Dir, Inf. Strategy and News, 1997–2000; rcds, 2000; DG, Mgt and Orgn, 2001–03; Prog. Dir for Modernising Rural Delivery, DEFRA, 2003–05; Dir of Strategy and Communications, LGA, 2005–07; Dir, Land Use Proj., DEFRA, 2007; South East England Development Agency: Exec. Dir, Skills and Sustainable Prosperity Directorate, 2007–09; Gp Exec. Dir, Strategy and Resources, 2009–11; Chief Exec., 2011–12; Dir, 2012, Mem., Exec. Bd, 2013–Jan. 2016, Security in Complex Envmts Gp, ADS Gp Ltd. *Recreations:* gardening, golf, walking, decorating/DIY, opera, the Archers omnibus, keeping mental chewing-gum. *Address:* Aegis Defence Services Ltd, 1 London Bridge, SE1 9BG.

MUIRHEAD, William Donald; Sheriff of Lothian and Borders at Livingston, 2009–13 (at Linlithgow, 2000–09); *b* 21 March 1948; *s* of William Ingram Muirhead and Phyllis Jessie Muirhead; *m* 1976, Maria de los Angeles Cabieces; one *s* two *d*. *Educ:* Melville Coll.; Edinburgh Univ. (LLB Hons). Solicitor, Aitken Nairn WS, 1972–2000. Pt-time Sheriff, 1993–99. *Recreations:* golf, music, hill walking, fishing. *Club:* Bruntsfield Links Golf.

MUIRHEAD, William Mortimer, AM 2013; Agent General for South Australia in London, since 2007; Founding Partner, M&C Saatchi, since 1995; *b* Adelaide, 11 July 1946; *s* of Denis and Lorna Muirhead; *m* 1971, Jeanne Elizabeth Meins; three *s*. *Educ:* Armidale Sch., Armidale, NSW; St Dunstan's Coll., London. Jackson Wain/Leo Burnett, 1966–70; Account Exec., Ogilvy & Mather, 1970–72; Account Dir, subseq. Gp Account Dir, Saatchi & Saatchi, 1972–89; Chm. and Chief Exec., Saatchi & Saatchi Advertising UK, 1989–92; Chm., Saatchi & Saatchi Europe, 1992–94; Chief Exec. and Pres., Saatchi & Saatchi Advertising Worldwide, 1994–95. *Recreations:* tennis, ski-ing, golf, music, travel. *Address:* Australia Centre, Strand, WC2B 4LG. *T:* (020) 7520 9100. *E:* agent-general@south-aus.eu. *Clubs:* Royal Automobile, Thirty, South Australia.

MUIRHEAD-ALLWOOD, Sarah Kathryn, FRCS; Consultant Orthopaedic Surgeon: Royal National Orthopaedic Hospital, since 1991; King Edward VII's Hospital for Officers, since 1993; *b* 4 Jan. 1947; *c* of late Maj. W. R. Muirhead and of Joyce Muirhead (*née* Forster); *m* 1983; two *s*. *Educ:* Wellington; St Thomas' Hosp. Med. Sch. (BSc, MB BS). MRCS, FRCS, LRCP. St Thomas' Hospital: House Surg., 1971–72; Sen. House Officer, 1972–73; Anatomy Demonstrator, 1973; Sen. House Officer, Stoke Mandeville Hosp., 1973–74; Registrar: UCH, 1974–77; Charing Cross Hosp., 1977–78; Sen. Registrar, Queen Mary's Hosp., Roehampton, Westminster Hosp., Royal Nat. Orthopaedic Hosp., UCH, 1978–84; Consultant Orthopaedic Surgeon, Whittington Hosp., 1984–2004. Hon. Sen. Clin. Lectr, UCL, 1984; Hon. Consultant: St Luke's Hosp. for the Clergy, 1984; Hosp. of St John and St Elizabeth. Member: British Orthopaedic Assoc., 1980; BMA, 1983; British Hip Soc., 1989; European Hip Soc., 1993; Internat. Hip Soc., 2009. Freeman, City of London, 2009; Liveryman, Gold and Silver Wyre Drawers' Co., 2009. *Publications:* contributions to: Joint Replacement—State of the Art, 1990; Recent Advances in Orthopaedic Surgery, 1991; Gray's Anatomy, 1995. *Recreations:* golf, sailing. *Address:* The London Hip Unit, 4th Floor, 30 Devonshire Street, W1G 6PU. *T:* (020) 7908 3709. *E:* londonhip@aol.com.

MUIRHEAD-ALLWOOD, William Forster Gillespie; *see* Muirhead-Allwood, S. K.

MUKARJI, Dr (Satyanand) Daleep, Hon. OBE 2008; Chairman, Y Care International, since 2010; *b* 22 Feb. 1946; *m* Azra Latifi; one *s* two *d*. *Educ:* Christian Med. Coll., Vellore, India (MB BS); London Sch. of Hygiene and Tropical Med. (DTPH); LSE (MSc). Med. Superintendent, Mission Hosp., Andhra Pradesh, India, 1972; MO and Project Dir, Leprosy Hosp., Dichpalli, 1973; Programme Dir, Rural Unit for Health and Social Affairs, Christian Med. Coll., Vellore, 1977–85; Gen. Sec., Christian Med. Assoc. of India, 1985–94; Exec. Sec., Urban Rural Mission, 1994–96, Health, Community and Justice, 1997–98, WCC, Geneva; Dir, Christian Aid, 1998–2010; Chm., Overseas Develt Inst., 2010–12. *Recreations:* music, theatre, cinema. *Address:* Y Care International, Kemp House, 152–160 City Road, EC1V 2NP; 7 Torrington Grove, N12 9NA.

MUKHAMEDOV, Irek Javdatovich, OBE 2000; ballet dancer; Artistic Director, Slovenian National Theatre Ballet, since 2010; *b* 1960; *s* of Djavdat Rasulievich Mukhamedov and Rashida Nizamovna; *m* 1990, Maria Zubkhova; one *s* one *d*. *Educ:* Moscow Choreographic Inst. Soloist, Moscow Classical Co., 1978–81; Bolshoi Ballet, 1981–90; Principal, 1990–99, Guest Artist, 1999–2001, Royal Ballet Co.; founded Mukhamedov & Co., 1991; Artistic Co-ordinator, 2006–07, Artistic Dir, 2007–10, Greek Nat. Opera Ballet. Vice Pres., Arts Educnl Sch., Tring, 2002–. *Leading rôles* in ballets including: Spartacus, Ivan the Terrible, Raymonda, La Bayadère, La Fille mal gardée, Manon, Giselle, Mr Worldly Wise, Mayerling, Different Drummer, Fearful Symmetries, Nutcracker, Les Biches, Prodigal Son, Othello, Cheating, Lying, Stealing, L'Après-midi d'un faune, The Crucible; musical: On Your Toes; *rôles created* include: Boris in The Golden Age; Vershinin in Winter Dreams; the foreman in the Judas Tree. *Address:* c/o Slovenian National Opera and Ballet Theatre, Zupanĉiĉeva 1, 1000 Ljubljana, Slovenia.

MUKHERJEE, Pranab Kumar; President of India, since 2012; *b* 11 Dec. 1935; *s* of Kamda Kinkar Mukherjee, of an illustrious family which was involved actively in the Freedom Movement of India; *m* 1957, Suvra Mukherjee; two *s* one *d*. *Educ:* Vidyasagar Coll., Suri; Calcutta Univ. (MA (Hist. and Pol Sci.); LLB). Elected Mem., W Bengal, Rajya Sabha, 1969, re-elected 1975, 1981, 1993, 1999; Leader, Rajya Sabha, 1980–85; Mem., and Leader of the House, Lok Sabha, 2004–12. Dep. Minister, Mins of Industrial Develt and of Shipping and Transport, 1973–74; Minister of State, Finance Min., 1974–77; Cabinet Minister i/c of Mins of Commerce, Steel and Mines, 1980–82; became youngest Minister to hold Finance Portfolio in Independent India, 1982–85; Dep. Chm., Planning Commn, 1991–93; Commerce Minister, 1993–95; Minister of External Affairs, 1995–96 and 2006–09; Minister of Defence, 2004–06; Minister of Finance, 2009–12. Spokesman, All India Congress Cttee, 1991; Chm., Central Election Campaign Cttee of Congress Party, 1984, 1991, 1996, 1998. *Publications:* Crisis in Democracy; An Aspect of Constitutional Problems in Bengal, 1967; Mid-Term Poll, 1969; Beyond Survival: an emerging dimension of Indian economy, 1984; Off the Track: an analysis of Indian economy, 1987; Saga of Struggle and Sacrifice, 1992; Challenges before the Nation, 1992. *Recreations:* music, gardening, reading. *Address:* Office of the President, Rashtrapati Bhavan, New Delhi 110004, India.

MUKHERJEE, Shiv Shankar; High Commissioner for India in the United Kingdom, 2008–09; *b* Bihar, India, 1 Aug. 1949; *s* of Ananga Mukherjee and Sumita Devi Mukherjee (*née* Chakravarti); *m* 1972, Nalini Kapoor; one *s* one *d*. *Educ:* St Stephen's Coll., Univ. of Delhi (Postgrad. Chemistry 1970). Attaché, then Under Sec., Bangladesh, Min. of External Affairs, India, 1973–75; Second Sec., then First Sec., Damascus, 1975–79; First Sec., Brussels, 1979–82; Dep. High Comr, Lusaka, 1982–85; Counsellor (Press), Washington, 1985–88; Dir (Ext. Publicity), Min. of External Affairs, 1988–89; Hd, India Observer Mission, 1989–90, High Comr, 1990–92, Windhoek; Jt Sec. (Ext. Publicity), Min. of External Affairs, 1992–94; Dir Gen., Indian Council for Cultural Relns, 1994–95; Minister (Press Inf. and Culture), Washington, 1995–98; Ambassador, Cairo, 1998–2000; High Comr, Pretoria, 2000–04; Ambassador, Kathmandu, 2004–08. Member: India Habitat Centre, 1993–; India Internat. Centre, 1993–; IUCN Project Adv. Cttee. Hon. Fellow, SOAS, 2010. *Recreations:* reading, golf, chess. *Address:* c/o High Commission of India, India House, Aldwych, WC2B 4NA. *Clubs:* Delhi Press, Delhi Gymkhana.

MUKHERJEE, Tara Kumar, FLIA; Managing Director, Owl Financial Services Ltd, since 1988; President, Confederation of Indian Organisations (UK), since 1975; Chairman, European Multicultural Foundation, since 1996; *b* 20 Dec. 1923; *s* of Sushil Chandra Mukherjee and Sova Moyee Mukherjee; *m* 1951, Betty Patricia Mukherjee; one *s* one *d*. *Educ:* Scottish Church Collegiate Sch., Calcutta, India; Calcutta Univ. (matriculated 1939). Shop Manager, Bata Shoe Co. Ltd, India, 1941–44; Buyer, Brevitt Shoes, Leicester, 1951–56; Sundries Buyer, British Shoe Corp., 1956–66; Prodn Administrator, Priestley Footwear Ltd, Great Harwood, 1966–68; Head Stores Manager, Brit. Shoe Corp., 1968–70; Save & Prosper Group: Dist Manager, 1970–78; Br. Manager, 1978–84; Senior Sales Manager, 1984–85; Br. Manager, Guardian Royal Exchange PFM Ltd, 1985–88. Pres., India Film Soc., Leicester, 1958–70. Chairman: Leicester Community Centre Project, 1962–66; Charter 90 for Asians, 1990–; Mem., Brit. Eur. Movt, London, 2004–; Pres., EC Migrants Forum, Brussels, 1990–96. Dir, Coronary Prevention Gp, 1986–. Patron: London Community Cricket Assoc., 1987–; Asha Foundn, 1999–; Global Diplomatic Forum, 2011. FRSA. DUniv Middx, 2003. *Recreation:* cricket (1st Cl. cricketer; played for Bihar, Ranji Trophy, 1941; 2nd XI, Leics CCC, 1949). *Address:* Tallah, 51 Viking Way, Pilgrims Hatch, Brentwood, Essex CM15 9HY. *T:* and *Fax:* (01277) 263207. *Club:* (Gen. Sec.) Indian National (Leicester).

MUKWENA, Prof. Royson Mabuku, PhD; Director, Research and Postgraduate Studies, since 2013, and Dean, School of Social Sciences, since 2014, Mulungushi University, Zambia; *b* Kalomo Dist, Zambia, 29 Feb. 1960; *s* of Alexander Mukwena and Vailet Mukwena; *m* 1986, Ruth Kanjanga Phiri; two *s* one *d*. *Educ:* St Marks Secondary Sch.; Univ. of Zambia (BA Public Admin 1983, MA Public Admin 1988); Univ. of Manchester (PhD Public Admin 1998). Lectr, Nat. Inst. of Public Admin, Zambia, 1985–86; Personnel Officer, Zambia Electricity Supply Corp. Ltd, 1987–88; Lectr in Public Admin, Univ. of Zambia, 1988–93; University of Namibia: Lectr, 1998–2002; Prof. of Public Admin, 2002–05; Hd, Dept of Political and Admin. Studies, 2005; Dep. Dean, 2001–03, Actg Dean, 2004, Faculty of Econs and Mgt Sci.; High Comr to Tanzania, and Ambassador (non-resident) to Burundi, Rwanda, Uganda, Union of the Comoros and Internat. Conf. on Great Lakes Reg., 2005–09; High Comr in UK and (non-resident) Ambassador to the Holy See and Ireland, 2009–12; Exec. Dir, Orgn for Social Sci. Res. in Eastern and Southern Africa, 2012. *Publications:* (ed with D. Olowu) Governance in Southern Africa and Beyond: experiences of institutional and public policy reform in developing countries, 2004; (ed with T. O. Chirawu) Decentralisation and Regional and Local Government in Namibia, 2008; chapters in books; articles in learned jls. *Recreation:* soccer fan (Manchester United). *E:* roymukwena@yahoo.com.

MULCAHY, Sir Geoffrey (John), Kt 1993; Chairman: Javelin Group Ltd, since 2003; British Retail Consortium, 2006–09; *b* 7 Feb. 1942; *s* of Maurice Frederick Mulcahy and Kathleen Love Mulcahy; *m* 1965, Valerie Elizabeth; one *s* one *d*. *Educ:* King's Sch., Worcester; Manchester Univ. (BSc); Harvard Univ. (MBA). Esso Petroleum, 1964–74; Norton Co., 1974–77; British Sugar, 1977–83; Woolworth Holdings, subseq. Kingfisher, 1983–2002: Gp Man. Dir, 1984–86; Chief Exec., 1986–93; Chm., 1990–95; Chief Exec., 1995–2002. Non-executive Director: Instore plc, 2004–06; Homsway Gp (China), 2004–07; Chelsea and Westminster Hosp. Foundn Trust, 2011–. Operating Partner, Global Leisure Partners, 2009–. Trustee, Foundn for Credit, 2008–. *Recreations:* sailing, squash. *Address:* Javelin Group Ltd, 200 Aldersgate Street, EC1A 4HD. *Clubs:* Lansdowne, Royal Automobile, Royal Thames Yacht, Queen's; Royal Southern Yacht.

MULCAHY, Leigh-Ann Maria; QC 2009; *b* London, 15 Oct. 1969; *d* of William and Margaret Mulcahy; *m* 2010, Dr Mark Ford; one *d*. *Educ:* Becket Sch., Nottingham; Jesus Coll., Cambridge (BA 1991); York Univ., Canada (LLM); Inns of Court Sch. of Law; King's Coll. London (Postgrad. Dip. EU Law). Called to the Bar, Inner Temple, 1993; in practice as barrister, specialising in commercial, insce and public law; Jun. Counsel to Crown, 1998–2009; First Counsel to Welsh Govt, 2013. *Publications:* (Gen. Ed.) Human Rights and Civil Practice, 2001; (ed) The Law and Regulation of Medicine, 2008; (ed) Jackson and Powell on Professional Liability, 5th edn, 2002, 7th edn, 2011. *Recreations:* travel, fitness, theatre. *Address:* Four New Square, Lincoln's Inn, WC2A 3RJ. *T:* (020) 7822 2000. *Fax:* (020) 7822 2001. *E:* l.mulcahy@4newsquare.com.

MULCAHY, Prof. Linda Mary, PhD; Professor of Law, London School of Economics and Political Science, since 2010; *b* High Wycombe, 1 Jan. 1962; *d* of Seàn Mulcahy and Euphemia Shirley Mulcahy; *m* 1990, Richard Emmott; two *s*. *Educ:* Lady Verney High Sch.; Wycombe High Sch.; Univ. of Southampton (LLB Hons); London Sch. of Econs and Pol Sci. (LLM Legal Theory); Univ. of London (PhD 1993; Postgrad. Cert. Art Hist.). Research Assistant: Univ. of Bristol, 1986–88; Law Commn, 1987–88; Res. Fellow, Univ. of Oxford, 1988–92; Sen. Res. Fellow, South Bank Univ., 1992–96; Reader, Univ. of North London, 1996–2000; Anniversary Reader, Anniversary Chair and Dean of Arts, Birkbeck, Univ. of London, 2000–10. Pres., Socio-Legal Studies Assoc., 1998–2001. *Publications:* Disputing Doctors: the socio-legal dynamics of complaints about doctors, 2003; (ed with S. Wheeler) Feminist Perspectives on Contract, 2005; Contract Law in Perspective, 5th edn 2008; (with Carl Stychin) Legal Methods and Systems, 4th edn 2010; Legal Architecture: justice, due process and the place of law, 2010. *Recreation:* art history and design. *Address:* Law Department, London School of Economics and Political Science, Houghton Street, WC2A 2AE. *E:* l.mulcahy@lse.ac.uk.

MULCAIR, Hon. Thomas J.; PC (Can.) 2012; MP (NDP) Outremont, since 2007; Leader, New Democratic Party of Canada and Leader of the Opposition, since 2012; *b* Ottawa, 24 Oct. 1954; *s* of Harry Donnelly Mulcair and Jean Marie Mulcair (*née* Hurtubise); *m* 1976, Catherine Pinhas; two *s*. *Educ:* McGill Univ. (BCL 1976; LLB 1977). Legislative counsel, Québec Justice, 1978–80; Dir, Affaires juridiques, Conseil de la langue Française, 1980–83; Dir, Legal Affairs, Alliance Québec, 1983–85; Partner, Donald and Duggan, 1985–87; Legal Revisor, Attorney Gen. of Manitoba, 1985–87; Pres., Office des Professions du Québec, 1987–93. Mem., Nat. Assembly of Québec, 1994–2007; Minister of Sustainable Develt, Envmt and Parks, Québec, 2003–06. Pres., English-speaking Catholic Council, 1987 (Mem., Bd of Dirs, 1984–87); Member, Board of Directors: Council on Licensure, Enforcement and Regulation, 1991–95; Opération Enfant Soleil Children's Hosp. Telethon, 1991–2003; St Patrick's Soc. of Montreal, 1991–2003, 2007–; Montreal Oral Sch. for the Deaf, 1993–2003; La Marois Country Club, 1993–97. *Publications:* Bibliographie sur la rédaction et l'interprétation des textes législatifs, 1980. *Recreations:* swimming, ice hockey, snowshoeing, golf. *Address:* House of Commons, Centre Block, Ottawa, ON K1A 0A6, Canada. *T:* (613) 9470867, *Fax:* (613) 9470868. *E:* thomas.mulcair@parl.gc.ca.

MULDER, (Robert) Frederick, CBE 2012; PhD; Director, Frederick Mulder Ltd, dealers in European original prints, since 1972; *b* 24 June 1943; *s* of William Eldred Bowman and Kathleen Elsie Delarue; *m* 1971, Valerie Ann Townsend (marr. diss. 2000); one *s* one *d* (and one *s* decd); one *s*. *Educ:* Eston High Sch., Sask.; Univ. of Saskatchewan (BA Hons Eng. 1965); Brown Univ., Providence, RI (MA Philos. 1967; PhD Philos. 1971); Linacre Coll., Oxford. Dir, P. and D. Colnaghi, 1972–75. Chm. of Trustees, Frederick Mulder Foundn (formerly Frederick Mulder Trust), 1986–; Founding Chm., The Funding Network, 2002–12; Trustee: Gaia Foundn, 1988–91; Network for Social Change, 1995–98; Oxford Res. Gp, 2000–06. *E:* fm@frederickmulder.com.

MULDOON, Bristow Cook; Head of Policy Advice, Press and Parliamentary Affairs, Royal Society of Edinburgh, since 2007; *b* 19 March 1964; *s* of late Bristow Cook Muldoon and of Annie McKenzie Muldoon (*née* McCallum); *m* 1988, Catherine Sloan McMillan; three *s*. *Educ:* Cumbernauld High Sch.; Univ. of Strathclyde (BSc Hons Chem.); Open Univ. (BA Hons). Manager in rail industry, 1986–99; business analyst, Great North Eastern Rly, 1997–99. Member (Lab): Lothian Regl Council, 1994–96 (Vice-Chm., Econ. Develt); West Lothian Council, 1995–99 (Convener, Community Services). Mem. (Lab) Livingston, Scottish Parlt, 1999–2007. Non-exec. Dir, West Lothian NHS Trust, 1997–99. Member: Labour Party; Co-Op Party; TSSA. *Recreations:* golf, music, football, reading. *Club:* Uphall Golf.

MULDOON, Prof. Paul; Howard G. B. Clark Professor in the Humanities, Princeton University, since 1998; *b* Portadown, NI, 20 June 1951; *s* of late Patrick Muldoon and Brigid (*née* Regan); *m* 1987, Jean Hanff Korelitz; one *s* one *d*. *Educ:* St Patrick's Coll., Armagh; Queen's Univ., Belfast (BA Eng. Lang. and Lit. 1973). BBC Northern Ireland: Producer, Arts Progs (Radio), 1973–78, Sen. Producer, 1978–85; TV Producer, 1985–86; Judith E. Wilson Vis. Fellow, Cambridge Univ., 1986–87; Creative Writing Fellow, UEA, 1987; Lecturer: Sch. of the Arts, Columbia Univ., 1987–88; Creative Writing Program, Princeton Univ., 1987–88; Writer-in-residence, 92nd Street Y, NY, 1988; Roberta Holloway Lectr, Univ. of Calif, Berkeley, 1989; Vis. Prof., Univ. of Mass, Amherst, 1989–90; Princeton University: Lectr, 1990–95; Prof., 1995–98; Dir, Creative Writing Program, 1993–2002; Vis. Prof., Bread Loaf Sch. of English, Middlebury, Vt, 1997–; Prof. of Poetry, Univ. of Oxford, 1999–2004; Fellow, Hertford Coll., Oxford, 1999–2004, now Hon. Fellow. Pres., Poetry Soc. of GB, 1996–2005. Mem., Aosdána, 1980–. FRSL 1981; John Simon Guggenheim Meml Fellow, 1990; Fellow: American Acad. of Arts and Scis, 2000; American Acad. of Arts and Letters, 2008. Readings of work throughout Europe, USA and Canada, Japan and Australia. Eric Gregory Award, 1972; Sir Geoffrey Faber Meml Award, 1980 and 1991; T. S. Eliot Prize for Poetry, 1994; Award in Literature, AAAL, 1996; Poetry Prize, Irish Times, 1997; Shakespeare Prize, 2004. *Publications: poetry:* Knowing My Place, 1971; New Weather, 1973; Spirit of Dawn, 1975; Mules, 1977; Names and Addresses, 1978; Immram, 1980; Why Brownlee Left, 1980; Out of Siberia, 1982; Quoof, 1983; The Wishbone, 1984; Selected Poems 1968–83, 1986; Meeting the British, 1987; Selected Poems 1968–86, 1987; Madoc: a mystery, 1990; Incantata, 1994; The Prince of the Quotidian, 1994; The Annals of Chile, 1994; Kerry Slides, 1996; New Selected Poems 1968–94, 1996; Hopewell Haiku, 1997; The Bangle (Slight Return), 1998; Hay, 1998; Poems 1968–1998, 2001; Moy Sand and Gravel, 2002 (Pulitzer Prize, 2003); Horse Latitudes, 2006; Maggot, 2010; One Thousand Things Worth Knowing, 2015; *drama:* Monkeys (TV play), 1989; Shining Brow (opera), 1993; Six Honest Serving Men (play), 1995; Bandanna (opera), 1999; *essays:* Getting Round: notes towards an Ars Poetica, 1998; To Ireland, I, 2000; The End of the Poem, 2006; *for children:* The O-O's Party, 1981; The Last Thesaurus, 1995; The Noctuary of Narcissus Batt, 1997; *translations:* The Astrakan Cloak, by Nuala Ní Dhomhnaill, 1993; (with R. Martin) The Birds, by Aristophanes, 1999; *edited:* The Scrake of Dawn, 1979; The Faber Book of Contemporary Irish Poetry, 1986; The Essential Byron, 1989; The Faber Book of Beasts, 1997; contribs to poetry anthologies; works trans. into numerous langs. *Recreations:* tennis, electric guitar. *Address:* c/o Faber & Faber, Bloomsbury House, 74–77 Great Russell Street, WC1B 3DA. *Clubs:* Athenæum, Groucho.

MULDOON, Dame Thea (Dale), DBE 1993; QSO 1986; *b* 13 March 1927; *d* of Stanley Arthur and Annie Eveleen Flyger; *m* 1951, Rt Hon. Sir Robert David Muldoon, GCMG, CH, PC (*d* 1992); one *s* two *d*. *Educ:* Takapuna Grammar Sch. Associated with many charities. Chairman: North Shore sub-gp, Auckland Br., Govt Superannuitants Assoc., 2006; Friends of Couldrey House Charitable Trust, 2006. Founding Patron, North Shore Hospice; Patron: Hibiscus Coast Br., NZ Red Cross Soc.; several horticultural orgns; Vice Patron, NZ Foundn for Conductive Educn. *Recreations:* walking, gym.

MULDOWNEY, Diane Ellen, (Mrs Dominic Muldowney); *see* Trevis, D. E.

MULDOWNEY, Dominic John; composer; Music Director, Royal National (formerly National) Theatre, 1976–97; *b* 19 July 1952; *s* of William and Barbara Muldowney; *m* 1986, Diane Ellen Trevis, *qv*; one *d*. *Educ:* Taunton's Grammar School, Southampton; York Univ. (BA, BPhil). Composer in residence, Southern Arts Association, 1974–76; composer of chamber, choral, orchestral works, including work for theatre, ballet and TV. *Compositions include:* Piano Concerto, 1983; The Duration of Exile, 1984; Saxophone Concerto, 1985; Sinfonietta, 1986; Ars Subtilior, 1987; Lonely Hearts, 1988; Violin Concerto, 1989; Three Pieces for Orchestra, 1990; Percussion Concerto, 1991; Oboe Concerto, 1992; Trumpet Concerto, 1993; Concerto for 4 Violins, 1994; The Brontës (ballet), 1995; Trombone Concerto, 1996; Clarinet Concerto, 1997; Irish Love Songs, 1998; The Fall of Jerusalem (oratorio), 1999; Piano Concerto No. 2, 2002; Red Razzmatazz (opera), 2005; War Oratorio (film), 2007; Tsunami (song cycle), 2008; Checkpoint Charlie, 2009; Ostalgie, 2011; English Song Book, 2015; Krieg der Welten, 2015. *Recreation:* driving through France and across America.

MULFORD, Dr David Campbell; Vice-Chairman International, Credit Suisse, since 2009; *b* Rockford, Ill, 27 June 1937; *s* of Robert Lewis Mulford and Theodora Henie Moellenhauer Mulford; *m* 1985, Jeannie Louise Simmons; two *s*. *Educ:* Lawrence Univ., Wisconsin (BA Econs *cum laude* 1959); Univ. of Cape Town; Boston Univ. (MA Pol Sci. 1962; Dist. Alumni Award, 1992); St Antony's Coll., Oxford (DPhil 1966). Special Asst to Sec. and Under Sec., US Treasury, 1965–66; Man. Dir and Head, Internat. Finance, White, Weld & Co., Inc., 1966–74; Sen. Investment Advr, Saudi Arabian Monetary Agency, 1974–84, on secondment; Under Sec. and Asst Sec. for Internat. Affairs, US Treasury, 1984–92 (sen. advr on financial assistance to former Soviet Union states; head of internat. debt strategy; led US delegn to negotiate estabt of EBRD); Mem. Exec. Bd, 1992–2003, Chm. Europe, 1993–99, Chm. Internat., 1999–2003, Credit Suisse First Boston; US Ambassador to India, 2004–09. Mem., Council on Foreign Relations, 1972–; Affiliate, Center for Strategic and Internat. Studies, Washington, 1992–. Hon. LLD Lawrence, Wisconsin, 1984. Alexander Hamilton Award, USA, 1992. Légion d'Honneur (France), 1990; Order of May (Argentina), 1993; Officer's Cross, Medal of Merit (Poland), 1995. *Publications:* Northern Rhodesia General Election, 1962; Zambia: the politics of independence, 1967. *Recreations:* golf, running, canoeing. *Club:* Metropolitan (Washington).

MULGAN, Geoffrey John, CBE 2004; PhD; Chief Executive, National Endowment for Science, Technology and the Arts, since 2011; *b* 28 Aug. 1961; *s* of Anthony Philip Mulgan and Catherine Mulgan (*née* Gough); *m* 1998, Rowena Young; one *s* one *d*. *Educ:* Balliol Coll., Oxford (MA 1982); Central London Poly. (PhD 1990). Investment Exec., Greater London Enterprise, 1984–86; Harkness Fellow, MIT, 1986–87; Consultant, and Lectr in Telecommunications, Central London Poly., 1987–90; Special Advr to Gordon Brown, MP, 1990–92; Fellow, BFI, 1992–93; Co-Founder and Dir, Demos, 1993–97 (Chm., Adv. Council, 1998–); Mem., Prime Minister's Policy Unit, 1997–2000; Director: Perf. and Innovation Unit, Cabinet Office, 2000–02; Prime Minister's Forward Strategy Unit, 2001–02; Strategy Unit, Cabinet Office, 2002–04; Head of Policy, Prime Minister's Office, 2003–04; Dir, Inst. of Community Studies, later The Young Foundn, 2004–11; Dir, Big Society Capital, 2011. Co-Chair, London Enterprise Panel, Digital Creative, Sci. and Technol. Wkg Gp, 2013–. Member: Health Innovation Council, 2008–10; Prime Minister's Council on Social Action, 2008–10. Visiting Professor: UCL, 1996–; LSE, 2004–; Melbourne, 2006–; China Exec. Leadership Acad., 2009–. Mem., Design Council, 2006–10. Chairman: Involve, 2005–10; Social Innovation Exchange, 2010–; Studio Schs Trust, 2012–; Trustee: Political Qly, 1995–2005; Work Foundn, 2005–10. *Publications:* Saturday Night or Sunday Morning, 1987; Communication and Control, 1990; Politics in an Antipolitical Age, 1994; (ed) Life After Politics, 1997; Connexity, 1997; Good and Bad Power: the ideals and betrayals of government, 2006; The Art of Public Strategy, 2009; The Locust and the Bee: predators and creators in capitalism's future, 2013. *Recreation:* making music. *Address:* National Endowment for Science, Technology and the Arts, 1 Plough Place, EC4A 1DE.

MULGRAVE, Earl of; John Samuel Constantine Phipps; *b* 26 Nov. 1994; *s* and *heir* of Marquis of Normanby, *qv*.

MULHALL, Daniel; Ambassador of Ireland to the Court of St James's, since 2013; *b* Waterford, 8 April 1955; *s* of Thomas and Alice Mulhall; *m* 1982, Greta Lothian; one *s* one *d*. *Educ:* University Coll., Cork (BA 1975; HDE 1978; MA 1979). Entered Dept of Foreign Affairs, Ireland, 1978; Third Secretary: Dept of Foreign Affairs, 1978–80; New Delhi, 1980–83; Dept of Foreign Affairs, 1983–87; First Secretary: Vienna, 1987–89; Dept of Foreign Affairs, 1989–90; Perm. Repn of Ireland to EU, Brussels, 1990–94; on secondment to Forum for Peace and Reconciliation, 1994–95; Press Section, Dept of Foreign Affairs, 1995–98; Consul Gen., Edinburgh, 1998–2001; Ambassador to Malaysia, and concurrently to Laos, Thailand and Vietnam, 2001–05; Dir Gen., EU Div., Dept of Foreign Affairs, 2005–09; Ambassador to Germany, 2009–13. *Publications:* A New Day Dawning: a portrait of Ireland in 1900, 1999; contrib. articles to jls on hist. and lit. *Recreations:* Irish history, literature, sport. *Address:* Embassy of Ireland, 17 Grosvenor Place, SW1X 7HR. *T:* (020) 7235 2171, *Fax:* (020) 7245 6961. *Clubs:* Royal Automobile, Travellers, Caledonian.

MULHOLLAND, family name of **Baron Dunleath**.

MULHOLLAND, Clare, OBE 1998; Vice Chairman of Council, Communications Regulatory Agency (formerly Independent Media Commission), Bosnia and Herzegovina, 1998–2005; *b* 17 June 1939; *d* of James Mulholland and Elizabeth (*née* Lochrin). *Educ:* Notre Dame High Sch., Glasgow; Univ. of Glasgow (MA Hons). Gen. trainee, then Press Officer, ICI, 1961–64; Press Officer: Granada Television, 1964–65; TWW, 1965–68; Press Officer, then Educn Officer, HTV, 1968–71; Independent Broadcasting Authority, later Independent Television Commission, 1971–97: Reg. Exec., Bristol, 1971–77; Reg. Officer, Midlands, 1977–82; Chief Asst, Television, 1982–83; Dep. Dir of Television, 1983–91; Dir of Programmes, 1991–96; Dep. Chief Exec., 1996–97; internat. broadcasting consultant, 1998–2008. Member: Arts Council of GB, 1986–94; Scottish Film Prodn Fund, 1984–90; Lottery Film Panel, Arts Council of England, 1997–2000. FRTS 1988. *Recreations:* travel, theatre, cinema.

MULHOLLAND, Prof. Clive William, PhD; CSci; Principal and Vice Chancellor, University of the Highlands and Islands, since 2014. *Educ:* Univ. of Ulster (BSc 1st Cl. Hons 1988; PhD Biochem. 1993). CSci 2004. Academic, 1997–2001, Dir, Lifelong Learning,

2001–07, and Prof. of Technol. Enhanced Learning, Univ. of Ulster; Dep. Vice Chancellor, Univ. of S Wales (formerly Glamorgan), 2007–14. FIBMS 1992; FRSA 2012; SFHEA 2013. *Address:* Executive Office, University of the Highlands and Islands, Ness Walk, Inverness IV3 5SQ. *T:* (01463) 279215. *E:* clive.mulholland@uhi.ac.uk.

MULHOLLAND, Rt Hon. Frank; PC 2011; Lord Advocate for Scotland, since 2011; *b* 18 April 1959; *s* of Charles and Jean Mulholland; *m* 1988, Marie Quinn; one *s*. *Educ:* Columba High Sch., Coatbridge; Univ. of Aberdeen (LLB Hons; DipLP); Univ. of Edinburgh (MBA 1997). Trainee solicitor, Bird Semple & Crawford Heron, 1982–84; Procurator Fiscal Depute: Greenock, 1984–87; Glasgow, 1987–91; NP 1992; SSC 1993; Crown Office: Solicitor: High Court Unit, 1991–94; Appeals Unit, 1994–97; Advocate Depute, 1997–2000; Asst Procurator Fiscal, 2000–01, Procurator Fiscal, 2001–03, Edinburgh; Sen. Advocate Depute, 2003–06; QC (Scot.) 2005; Area Procurator Fiscal, Lothian and Borders, 2006–07; Solicitor Gen. for Scotland, 2007–11. Admitted Mem., Faculty of Advocates, 2008. Accredited advocacy trainer, Nat. Inst. for Trial Advocacy, 2006–. *Recreations:* football, golf, squash, military history. *Address:* Crown Office, 25 Chambers Street, Edinburgh EH1 1LD.

MULHOLLAND, Gregory Thomas; MP (Lib Dem) Leeds North West, since 2005; *b* 31 Aug. 1970; *m* 2004, Raegan Melita Hatton; three *d*. *Educ:* St Ambrose Coll., Altrincham; Univ. of York (BA 1991; MA 1995). Account handler, several marketing and sales promotion agencies, 1997–2002. Mem. (Lib Dem), Leeds CC, 2003–05 (Lead Mem., Corp. Services and Metro (W Yorks PTA)). *Address:* (office) Wainwright House, 12 Holt Park Centre, Holt Road, Leeds LS16 7SR; House of Commons, SW1A 0AA.

MULHOLLAND, James Malachi; QC 2011; a Recorder, since 2007; *b* Manchester, 24 July 1964; *s* of James Gerard Mulholland and Martina Veronica Mulholland (*née* Barron); *m* 2005, Kate Fowler; one *s* one *d*. *Educ:* Cardinal Langley Grammar Sch., Rochdale; Univ. of Leeds (LLB Hons 1985). Called to the Bar, Inner Temple, 1986; in practice as a barrister in criminal law, specialising in serious fraud work. *Recreations:* books, classical music, conversation, Manchester United. *Address:* 15 New Bridge Street, EC4V 6AU. *T:* (020) 7842 1900. *E:* james.mulholland@15nbs.com.

MULKEARNS, Most Rev. Ronald Austin, DD, DCL; Bishop Emeritus of Ballarat (RC); *b* 11 Nov. 1930. *Educ:* De La Salle Coll., Malvern; Corpus Christi Coll., Werribee; Pontifical Lateran Univ., Rome. Ordained, 1956; Coadjutor Bishop, 1968–71; Bishop of Ballarat, 1971–97.

MULKERN, John, CBE 1987; JP; international airport and aviation consultant, since 1987; *b* 15 Jan. 1931; *s* of late Thomas Mulkern and Annie Tennant; *m* 1954, May Egerton (*née* Peters); one *s* three *d*. *Educ:* Stretford Grammar Sch.; Dip. Govt Admin of Local Govt Exam. Bd, London; Harvard Business Sch. (AMP 1977). Ministries of Supply and Aviation, Civil Service, 1949–65: Exec. Officer, finally Principal, Audit, Purchasing, Finance, Personnel and Legislation branches; British Airports Authority, 1965–87: Dep. Gen. Man., Heathrow Airport, 1970–73; Dir, Gatwick Airport, 1973–77; Man. Dir and Mem. of Bd, 1977–87. Chairman: British Airports International Ltd, 1978–82; Manchester Handling Ltd, 1988–94; Granik Ltd, 1990–91 (Pres., 1992–94); Director: London Luton Airport Ltd, 1991–2000; Reliance Aviation Security Ltd, 1992–94. President: Western European Airports' Assoc., 1981–83; Internat. Civil Airports Assoc. (Europe), 1986; Chm., Co-ordinating Council, Airports Assocs, 1982; Mem. Bd, Airport Operators Council Internat., 1978–81. Mem., Surrey Probation Cttee, 1996–2001. Trustee: Surrey Springboard, 1997–2001; BAA Pension Trust Co. Ltd, 1997–2000. Mem., Middlesex and Surrey Soc., 1995–2009. FCILT 1973 (Mem. Council, 1979–82); CCMI (CBIM 1981); FInstD 1982. JP Surrey, 1988. *Recreations:* family pursuits, opera, classical recorded music.

MULL, Very Rev. Gerald S.; *see* Stranraer-Mull.

MULLALLY, Rt Rev. Dame Sarah Elisabeth; *see* Crediton, Bishop Suffragan of.

MULLALY, Terence Frederick Stanley; art historian and critic; *b* 14 Nov. 1927; *s* of late Col B. R. Mullaly (4th *s* of Maj.-Gen. Sir Herbert Mullaly, KCMG, CB, CSI) and Eileen Dorothy (*née* Stanley); *m* 1949, Elizabeth Helen (*née* Burkitt). *Educ:* in India, England, Japan and Canada; Downing Coll., Cambridge (MA). FSA 1977; FRNS 1981 (Mem. Council, 1993–95); FSAScot 1995. Archæological studies in Tripolitania, 1948, and Sicily, 1949; has specialised in study of Italian art, particularly Venetian and Veronese painting of 16th and 17th centuries; lecturer and broadcaster; Art Critic, Daily Telegraph, 1958–86. Vis. Prof., Finch Coll., NY, 1967–72. President: Brit. Section, Internat. Assoc. of Art Critics, 1967–73; British Art Medal Soc., 1986–98 (Vice Chm., 1982–86; Vice-Pres., 1998–); Member: Adv. Cttee, Cracow Art Festival, 1974, Palermo Art Festival, 1976; UK Delegn, Budapest Cultural Forum, 1985; Cttee, FIDEM Congress, 1992; Comitato Scientifico, Arte Documento; Council: Attingham Summer Sch. Trust, 1984–90; Derby Porcelain Internat. Soc., 1985–; Friends, Univ. of Cyprus, 1995– (Vice Chm., 1998–); Artistic Adviser, Grand Tours, 1974–90; Director: Grand Tours, 1980–90; Specialtours, 1986. Editor, Jl of British-Italian Soc., 1995–. FRSA 1969. Commendatore, Ordine Al Merito, Italy, 1974 (Cavaliere Ufficiale, 1964); l'Ordre du Mérite Culturel, Poland, 1974; Order of Merit of Poland (Silver Medal), 1978; Bulgarian 1300th Anniversary Medal, 1981; Sacro Militare Ordine Costantiniano di S Giorgio (Silver Medal), 1982; Premio Pietro Torta per il restauro di Venezia, 1983; Socio Straniero, Ateneo Veneto, 1986. *Publications:* Ruskin a Verona, 1966; catalogue of exhibition, Disegni veronesi del Cinquecento, 1971; contrib. to catalogue of exhibition Cinquant' anni di pittura veronese: 1580–1630, 1974; ed and contrib. to catalogue of exhibition, Modern Hungarian Medal, 1984; contrib. to Affreschi del Rinascimento a Verona: interventi di restauro, 1987; Caterina Cornaro, Queen of Cyprus, 1989; catalogue of exhibn, Zofia Demkowska, 1997; (jtly) Cyprus: the legacy, 1999; contribs to DNB and on history of art, to Burlington Magazine, Master Drawings, Arte Illustrata, Arte Documento, Antologia di Belle Arti, The Minneapolis Inst. of Arts Bulletin, Bull. Univ. of New Mexico Art Mus., British Numismatic Jl, Numismatic Chronicle, Jl of British Art Medal Soc., Apollo, etc. *Recreations:* numismatics, Eastern Europe. *Address:* Waterside House, Pulborough, Sussex RH20 2BH. *T:* (01798) 872104.

MULLAN, Prof. John Dermot, PhD; Professor of English, University College London, since 2005; *b* London, 6 Aug. 1958; *s* of Dermot Mullan and Antonia Mullan; *m* 2000, Harriet Stewart; one *s* two *d*. *Educ:* Downside Sch.; King's Coll., Cambridge (BA 1980; PhD 1984). Res. Fellow, Jesus Coll., 1984–87, Lectr, Fitzwilliam Coll., 1987–94, Cambridge; Lectr, 1994–98, Sen. Lectr, 1998–2005, in English, UCL. Vis. Prof., Univ. of Munich, 1993. *Publications:* Sentiment and Sociability, 1988; (ed) Eighteenth-Century Popular Culture, 2000; How Novels Work, 2006; Anonymity: a secret history of English literature, 2007; What Matters in Jane Austen?, 2012. *Recreations:* eating, walking, swimming in the sea. *Address:* Department of English Language and Literature, University College London, Gower Street, WC1E 6BT. *E:* j.mullan@ucl.ac.uk.

MULLARD, Prof. Christopher Paul, CBE 2005; PhD; DL; Chairman and Chief Executive Officer, Focus Consultancy, since 1994; *b* 23 Nov. 1944; *m* 1989, Mike-Madelaine Elmont; one *s* two *d*. *Educ:* Park House Secondary Modern Sch., Newbury; Westminster City Coll., London; Univ. of Durham (MA 1975; PhD 1980). Northern Sec., CARD, 1964–68; Principal Community Relns Officer, Tyne and Wear, 1968–73; researcher and pt-time Lectr in Sociol., Univ. of Durham, 1973–76; Sen. Lectr in Sociol., King Alfred's Coll., Winchester, 1976–77; Lectr, Dept of Sociol. of Educn, Univ. of London Inst. of Educn, 1977–80; Dir, Race Relns Policy and Practice Res. Units, Univ. of London Inst. of Educn and LSE, 1980–86; University of Amsterdam: Royal Prof. in Ethnic Studies and Educn, and Dir, Centre for Race and Ethnic Studies, 1984–91; Advr to Senate, 1991–94. Mem., Widening Participation and Student Opportunity Strategy Adv. Cttee (formerly Widening Access and Participation Strategy Adv. Cttee), HEFCE, 2010–14; Ext. Affiliate, PURAI—Global Indigenous Res. and Diaspora, Univ. of Newcastle, Australia, 2014–. Foundn Dir, Focus Inst. on Rights and Social Transformation, 2004–. Chairman: Bernie Grant Trust, 2000–11 (Trustee, 2012–); London Notting Hill Carnival Ltd, 2002–08; Commn on African and Caribbean Families in Britain, 2010–; Ladybird Economic Advancement Partnership, 2014–; Mem., Dep. Prime Minister's Bicentenary Adv. Gp on Commemorating the Abolition of the Slave Trade, 2006–; Patron: Caribbean Women Equality and Diversity Forum, 2001–; Caribbean Develt Trust (UK), 2005–; Internat. Judge, Shanghai Tourism Festival Parade, 2005–; African Fellowship Trust, 2015–. Vis. Prof., 2007–, Gov., 2008–, Royal Agricl Univ. (formerly Coll.). Hon. Consul for South Africa, 2006–. FRSA 2005; MInstD 1998. DL Wilts, 2007. Hon. LLD Exeter, 2009. *Publications:* Black Britain, 1973; Aborigines in Australia Today, 1974; Race, Power and Resistance, 1985; De Plurale Kubus, 1990; Antirassistische Erziehung, 1991. *Recreations:* gardening, theatre, golf, travel. *Address:* Elmsgate House, Steeple Ashton, Trowbridge, Wilts BA14 6HP. *Club:* Reform.

MULLARKEY, Thomas, MBE 1996; Chief Executive, Royal Society for the Prevention of Accidents, since 2006; *b* 1 April 1957; *s* of James and Delia Mullarkey; *m* 1982, Sue Hamilton; two *s*. *Educ:* Maidstone Grammar Sch.; Univ. of Lancaster (BA Orgn Studies 1978); Indian Defence Services Staff Coll. (MSc Defence Studies 1992). Army officer, RA, 1975–95, service in UK, Germany, NI, Canada, India and Rwanda (co-ordinated UN restoration plan); Gen. Manager Projs, SBC Warburg, 1995–96; Gen. Manager, then Dir, Special Projs, XVII Commonwealth Games, Manchester, 1996–2001; Chief Exec., Nat. Security Inspectorate, 2002–06. *Publications:* A Thousand Hills: a story of crisis in Rwanda, 2001. *Recreations:* sailing, the hills, Daimlers, writing, holding forth. *Address:* Royal Society for the Prevention of Accidents, 28 Calthorpe Road, Birmingham B15 1RP. *T:* (0121) 248 2000.

MULLEE, Patrick; HM Diplomatic Service; Ambassador to Ecuador, since 2012; *b* 8 Oct. 1954; *s* of Patrick and Teresa Mullee; *m* 1987, Joanna Louise, *d* of Philip Hughes Johnson and Diana Ruth Chase; two *d*. Joined FCO, 1974; Prague, 1976–77; Caracas, 1977–80; Latin America and Africa floater, 1980–84; Policy Planning Staff, FCO, 1985–88; Vice-Consul, San José, 1988–91; Second Sec. (Chancery/Inf.), Bridgetown, 1991–95; Second, later First Sec., Eastern Caribbean Desk, FCO, 1995–97; Dep. Hd, Personnel Mgt Unit, FCO, 1997–2000; Dep. Hd of Mission and HM Consul, Quito, 2000–03; HR Manager, Directorate Gen. for Defence and Intelligence, FCO, 2003–07; Ambassador to Uruguay, 2008–12. *Recreations:* football, golf, mountains. *Address:* c/o Foreign and Commonwealth Office, King Charles Street, SW1A 2AH. *Clubs:* Wanderers Masters Football (Barbados); Quito Golf and Tennis (Ecuador).

MÜLLER, Alex; *see* Müller, K. A.

MULLER, Franz Joseph; QC 1978; a Recorder of the Crown Court, 1977–2008; *b* England, 19 Nov. 1938; *yr s* of late Wilhelm Muller and Anne Maria (*née* Ravens); *m* 1985, Helena (High Sheriff, S Yorks, 2009–10), *y d* of Mieczyslaw Bartosz; two *s*. *Educ:* Mount St Mary's Coll.; Univ. of Sheffield (LLB). Called to the Bar, Gray's Inn, 1961, Bencher, 1994; called to NI Bar, 1982. Graduate Apprentice, United Steel Cos, 1960–61; Commercial Asst, Workington Iron and Steel Co. Ltd, 1961–63. Commenced practice at the Bar, 1964; Head of Chambers, 11 King's Bench Walk, Temple, 1984–2005. Non-executive Director: Richards of Sheffield (Holdings) PLC, 1969–77; Satinsteel Ltd, 1970–77; Joseph Rodgers and Son Ltd and Rodgers Wostenholm Ltd, 1975–77. Mem., Sen. Common Room, UC Durham, 1981. Member: Mgt Cttee, St Wilfred's Centre, Sheffield, 2011–; Cttees, Restoration of St Marie's Cathedral, Sheffield, 2011–13. *Recreations:* the Georgians, fell walking, being in Greece, listening to music. *Address:* Slade Hooton Hall, Laughton en le Morthen, S Yorks S25 1YQ; KBW, The Engine House, 1 Foundry Square, Leeds LS11 5DL. *T:* (0113) 297 1200.

MÜLLER, Herta; writer; *b* Nitzkydorf, Romania, 17 Aug. 1953; *m* Richard Wagner (marr. diss. 1988); *m* 1990, Dr Harry Merkle. *Educ:* Univ. of Timisoara (German and Romanian Lit.). Translator, machine construction factory, Timisoara, 1976–79. Emigrated to Germany, 1987. Awards include: Deutscher Kritikerpreis, 1992; Kleist Preis, 1994; Literaturpreis Aristeion, EU, 1995; Dublin Literary Award, Internat. IMPAC, 1998; Franz Kafka Literaturpreis, 1999; Nobel Prize for Literature, 2009; Franz Werfel Preis, 2010. *Publications:* Niederungen, 1982; Drückender Tango, 1984; Der Mensch ist ein großer Fasan auf der Welt, 1986; Barfüßiger Februar, 1987; Reisende auf einem Bein, 1989; Der Teufel sitzt im Spiegel, 1991; Eine warme Kartoffel ist ein warmes Bett, 1992; Der Wächter nimmt seinen Kamm, 1993; Hunger und Seide (essays), 1995; In der Falle. Bonner Poetikvorlesungen, 1996; Der Fremde Blick oder Das Leben ist ein Furz in der Laterne, 1999; Im Haarknoten wohnt eine Dame, 2000; Heimat ist das, was gesprochen wird, 2001; Der König verneigt sich und tötet, 2003; Die blassen Herren mit den Mokkatassen, 2005; Cristina und ihre Attrappe, oder Was (nicht) in den Akten der Securitate steht, 2009; Lebensangst und Worthunger, 2010; Immer derselbe Schnee und immer derselbe Onkel (essays), 2011; *novels:* Der Fuchs war damals schon der Jäger, 1992; Herztier, 1994; Heute wär ich mir lieber nicht begegnet, 1997; Atemschaukel, 2009; in Romanian: Este sau nu este Ion, 2005; works trans. into numerous languages. *Address:* Carl-Hanser-Verlag, Postfach 860420, 81631 München, Germany.

MÜLLER, Prof. (Karl) Alex, PhD; physicist at IBM Zurich Research Laboratory, since 1963; *b* 20 April 1927. *Educ:* Swiss Federal Institute of Technology, Zürich (PhD 1958). FInstP 1998. Battelle Inst., Geneva, 1958–63; Lectr, 1962, Titular Prof., 1970, Prof., 1987–2009, now Prof. Emeritus, Univ. of Zürich; joined IBM Res. Lab., Zurich, 1963; Manager, Physics Dept, 1973; IBM Fellow, 1982–85; researcher, 1985–. Hon. degrees from twenty European and American univs. Prizes and awards include Nobel Prize for Physics (jtly), 1987. *Publications:* over 500 papers on ferroelectric and superconducting materials. *Address:* Physik-Institut, Universität Zürich-Irchel, Winterthurerstrasse 190, 8057 Zürich, Switzerland.

MULLIGAN, (Margaret) Mary; Member (Lab) Linlithgow, Scottish Parliament, 1999–2011; *b* Liverpool, 12 Feb. 1960; *m* 1982, John Mulligan; two *s* one *d*. *Educ:* Notre Dame High Sch., Liverpool; Manchester Univ. (BA Hons Econs and Social Studies 1981). Retail and personnel mgt, 1981–86. Member (Lab): Edinburgh DC, 1988–95 (Chm., Housing Cttee, 1992–97; City of Edinburgh Council, 1995–99. Scottish Executive: PPS to First Minister, 2000–01; Dep. Minister for Health and Community Care, 2001–03, for Communities, 2003–04. Scottish Parliament: Chm., Educn, Sports and Culture Cttee, 1999–2000; Mem., Local Govt and Communities Cttee, 2008–11. Contested (Lab) Linlithgow, Scottish Parlt, 2011. *Recreations:* music, theatre, watching sports.

MULLIGAN, Prof. William, FRSE; Professor of Veterinary Physiology, 1963–86, and Vice-Principal, 1980–83, University of Glasgow, now Professor Emeritus; *b* 18 Nov. 1921; *s* of John Mulligan and Mary Mulligan (*née* Kelly); *m* 1948, Norah Mary Cooper one *s* one *d* (and one *d* decd). *Educ:* Banbridge Academy; Queen's Univ. of Belfast (BSc); PhD London. FRSB (FIBiol 1988). Assistant, Dept of Chemistry, QUB, 1943–45; Demonstrator/Lectr, St Bartholomew's Med. Coll., London, 1945–51; Sen. Lectr, Veterinary Biochemistry, Univ. of Glasgow, 1951–63; McMaster Fellow, McMaster Animal Health Laboratory, Sydney, Aust., 1958–60; Dean of Faculty of Veterinary Medicine, Univ. of Glasgow, 1977–80. Dr med. vet. *hc* Copenhagen, 1983. *Publications:* (jtly) Isotopic Tracers, 1954, 2nd edn 1959; numerous contribs to scientific jls on immunology and use of radiation and radioisotopes in animal science. *Recreations:* golf, tennis, gardening, pigeon racing, theatre. *Address:* 25 Woodland Way, Wivenhoe, Colchester, Essex CO7 9AT.

See also J. S. Pitt-Brooke.

MULLIN, Christopher John, (Chris); author, journalist, politician; *b* 12 Dec. 1947; *s* of Leslie and Teresa Mullin; *m* 1987, Nguyen Thi Ngoc, *d* of Nguyen Tang Minh, Kontum, Vietnam; two *d. Educ:* Univ. of Hull (LLB). Freelance journalist, travelled extensively in Indo-China and China; sub editor, BBC World Service, 1974–78; Editor, Tribune, 1982–84. Executive Member: Campaign for Labour Party Democracy, 1975–83; Labour Co-ordinating Cttee, 1978–82. Contested (Lab): Devon N, 1970; Kingston upon Thames, Feb. 1974. MP (Lab) Sunderland S, 1987–2010. Parliamentary Under-Secretary of State: DETR, 1999–2001; DFID, 2001; FCO, 2003–05. Chm., Home Affairs Select Cttee, 1997–99, 2001–03; Mem., Standards and Privileges Cttee, 2007–10. Chm., All Party Vietnam Gp, 1988–99; Sec., British Cambodia All Party Gp, 1992–99; Hon. Sec., British Tibet All Party Gp; Chm., PLP Civil Liberties Gp, 1992–97. Trustee: Prison Reform Trust, 2006–10; N of England Civic Trust, 2011–; Chillingham Wild Cattle Trust, 2014–; Patron: Joe Homan Charity, 2011–. Chm., Heritage Lottery Fund NE, 2011–; Pres., Northumbria Wildlife Trust, 2012–. Judge, Man Booker Prize, 2011. Mem. Council, Winston Churchill Meml Trust, 2012–. Vis. Lectr, Sch. of Geog., Politics and Sociol., Univ. of Newcastle, 2010–. Hon. Fellow, Sch. of Govt and Internat. Affairs, Univ. of Durham, 2010. Hon. LLD City, 1992; Hon. DLitt Sunderland, 2010; Hon. DLaws Hull, 2011; Hon. DCL Newcastle, 2011; Hon. Dr Essex, 2011. Editor: Arguments for Socialism, by Tony Benn, 1979; Arguments for Democracy, by Tony Benn, 1981. *Publications: novels:* A Very British Coup, 1982 (televised 1988); The Last Man Out of Saigon, 1986; The Year of the Fire Monkey, 1991; *non-fiction:* Error of Judgement—the truth about the Birmingham bombings, 1986, rev. edn 1997; A View from the Foothills (diaries), 2009; Decline and Fall: diaries 2005–2010, 2010; A Walk-On Part: diaries 1994–1999, 2011; pamphlets: How to Select or Reselect your MP, 1981; The Tibetans, 1981. *E:* chris@chrismullinexmp.com. *W:* www.chrismullinexmp.com.

MULLIN, John; Head of Sports News, Telegraph Media Group, since 2015; *b* Bellshill, 22 March 1963; *s* of John and Helen Mullin; *m* 1995, Maggie O'Kane; one *s* two *d. Educ:* Seafar Primary Sch., Cumbernauld; Hutchesons' Grammar Sch.; Glasgow Univ. (MA Politics and Econs 1984); City Univ., London (Dip. Newspaper Journalism 1985). The Guardian: reporter, 1990–96; Night Ed., 1996–97; Ireland corresp., 1997–2000; Dep. Ed., The Scotsman, 2000–03; Exec. Ed., The Independent, 2003–07; Dep. Ed., 2007–08, Ed., 2008–13, Independent on Sunday; Referendum Ed., BBC Scotland, 2013–14.

MULLIN, (William Arthur) Roger; MP (SNP) Kirkcaldy and Cowdenbeath, since 2015. *Educ:* Univ. of Edinburgh (MA Hons Sociol. 1977); Stow Coll., Glasgow (HNC Electrical and Electronic Engrg). Tutor in Social Scis, Univ. of Edinburgh, 1977–79; Lectr in Industrial Sociol., W Lothian Coll., 1979–80; Sen. Lectr and Depute Hd, Centre for Industrial Studies, Glenrothes Coll., 1980–85; Hd of Dept, Stevenson Coll. of FE, 1985–86; Sen. Partner, Roger Mullin Associates, 1986–99; Man. Dir, Inter-ed Ltd, 1993–2012; freelance writer, researcher, 2014–15. Consultant to orgns incl. UNESCO, UNFAO, UNIDO, UNDP, ILO, IBRD and Asian Develt Bank. Associate Lectr and Ext. PhD Supervisor, Open Univ., 1978–2002; MBA Ext. Lectr and thesis supervisor, Stirling Univ., 2001–15. Director: Red Lead Arts Ltd, Belfast, 2004–05; Momentous Change Ltd, 2012–14. Hon. Prof., Stirling Univ. Mgt Sch., 2010–15. Internat. Progs Advr, Australian Acad., 1996–97; Columnist, TES Scotland. Advr to Lifelong Learning Inquiry, Enterprise and Lifelong Learning Cttee, Scottish Parlt, 2001–02. Member: Industrial Adv. Panel, Inst. of Biomed. and Life Scis, Univ. of Glasgow, 1997–2003; Internat. Adv. Gp, ICOD Canada. Chm., Bd of Trustees, Stirling Univ. Student Union, 2010–11. Hon. Pres., Univ. of Paisley, 1995–98. MIPD 1988. *Publications:* (contrib.) Multi-Party Britain, 1979; (contrib.) The Referendum Experience, Scotland 1979, 1981; Career Goals and Educational Attainment: what is the link?, 2004; (contrib.) Public and Third Sector Leadership, 2014; contrib. Bull. Scottish Politics. *Address:* (office) East Shop, Law's Close, 343 High Street, Kirkcaldy, Fife KY1 1JN. *T:* (01592) 747359, (020) 7219 6069. *E:* roger.mullin.mp@parliament.uk.

MULLINS, Andrew Oliver; Chief Executive, Knowledge and Networking Division, Informa plc, since 2014; *b* Woolwich, 21 March 1964; *s* of Gerald Oliver Mullins and Caroline Sylvia Mary Mullins; *m* 1992, Lucinda Harriet Nelson; two *s. Educ:* Yardley Court Prep. Sch.; Cranbrook Sch.; Bristol Univ. (BSc Hons Econs). Brand manager, Unilever, 1986–95; Global Brand Dir and Man. Dir, UDV Amsterdam, Diageo, 1995–2001; Mktg Dir and Gen. Manager, News Internat., 2001–07; Managing Director: Associated Newspapers, 2007–09; Evening Standard Ltd, 2007–14; Independent Print Ltd, 2010–14; CEO, London Live ESTV, 2013–14 (non-exec. Dir, 2014–). Non-executive Director: Which?, 2011–; Evening Standard, 2014–; Independent Print Ltd, 2014–. *Recreations:* golf, cycling, ski-ing. *E:* andrew.mullins@informa.com. *Clubs:* Dulwich and Sydenham Golf, Band of Brothers Cricket.

MULLINS, Rt Rev. Daniel Joseph; Bishop of Menevia, (RC), 1987–2001, now Emeritus; *b* 10 July 1929; *s* of Timothy Mullins. *Educ:* Mount Melleray; St Mary's, Aberystwyth; Oscott Coll.; UC of S Wales and Mon, Cardiff (Fellow, University Coll., Cardiff). Priest, 1953; Curate at: Barry, 1953–56; Newbridge, 1956; Bargoed, 1956–57; Maesteg, 1957–60; Asst Chaplain to UC Cardiff, 1960–64; Sec. to Archbp of Cardiff, 1964–68; Vicar General of Archdiocese of Cardiff, 1968; Titular Bishop of Stowe and Auxiliary Bishop in Swansea, 1970–87. Pres., Catholic Record Soc. Hon. Fellow, St David's University Coll., Lampeter, 1987. *Recreations:* golf, walking. *Address:* 8 Rhodfa Gwendraeth, Kidwelly, Carms SA17 4SR.

MULLINS, Edwin Brandt; author, journalist and film-maker; *b* 14 Sept. 1933; *s* of late Claud Mullins and Gwendolen Mullins, OBE; *m* 1st, 1960, Gillian Brydone (*d* 1982); one *s* two *d*; 2nd, 1984, Anne Kelleher. *Educ:* Midhurst Grammar Sch.; Merton Coll., Oxford (BA Hons, MA). London Editor, Two Cities, 1957–58; Sub-editor and Art Correspondent, Illustrated London News, 1958–62; Art Critic: Sunday Telegraph, 1962–69; Telegraph Sunday Magazine, 1964–86; contributor, 1962–, to The Guardian, Financial Times, Sunday Times, Director, Apollo, Art and Artists, Studio, Radio Times, TV Times, Country Living. Scriptwriter and presenter of numerous TV documentaries for BBC, Channel 4 and RM Arts, Munich, incl. 100 Great Paintings, The Pilgrimage of Everyman, Gustave Courbet, Fake?, Prison, The Great Art Collection, A Love Affair with Nature, Masterworks, Paradise on Earth, Montparnasse Revisited, Dürer, Out of the Dark Ages—a tale of four Emperors, Georges de la Tour—Genius Lost and Found, Van Gogh in England, The Changing of the Avant-Garde. *Publications:* Souza, 1962; Wallis, 1967; Josef Herman, 1967; Braque, 1968; The Art of Elisabeth Frink, 1972; The Pilgrimage to Santiago, 1974, repr. 2001; (ed) Great Paintings, 1981; (ed) The Arts of Britain, 1983; The Painted Witch, 1985; A Love Affair with Nature, 1985; The Royal Collection, 1992; Alfred Wallis: Cornish Primitive, 1994; In Search of Cluny—God's Lost Empire, 2006; Avignon of the Popes: city of exiles, 2007; The Camargue: portrait of a wilderness, 2009; Roman Provence, a History and Guide, 2011; Van Gogh: the asylum year, 2015; *novels:* Angels on the Point of a Pin, 1979; Sirens, 1983; The Golden Bird, 1987; The Lands of the Sea, 1988; Dear Venus, 1992; With Much Love, 1993; All My Worldly Goods, 1994; The Outfit, 1995; The Devil's Work, 1996. *Recreation:* everything except football. *Address:* 27 Bracken Gardens, Barnes, SW13 9HW.

MULLIS, Dr Kary Banks; American biochemist; Founder and Chief Scientific Advisor, Altermune Technologies LLC, since 2010 (President, Altermune LLC, 2004–09); *b* 28 Dec. 1944; *s* of Cecil Banks Mullis and Bernice Alberta Fredericks (*née* Barker); *m* 1963, Richards Train Haley (marr. diss.); one *d*; *m* 1975, Cynthia Gibson (marr. diss.); two *s*; *m* 1997, Nancy Cosgrove. *Educ:* Georgia Inst. of Technol. (BS Chemistry 1966); Univ. of Calif, Berkeley (PhD Biochemistry 1973). Lectr in Biochemistry, Univ. of Calif, Berkeley, 1972; Postdoctoral Fellow: Kansas Med. Sch., 1973–76; Univ. of Calif, San Francisco, 1977–79; Scientist, Cetus Corp., Calif, 1979–86; Dir of Molecular Biology, Xytronyx, Inc., San Diego, 1986–88; Consultant, Specialty Labs Inc., and Amersham Inc., 1988. Member: American Chemistry Soc.; Inst. of Further Study (Dir, 1983–). Preis Biochemische Analytik, German Soc. Clin. Chemistry, 1990; Allan Award, American Soc. of Human Genetics, 1990; Nat. Biotechnology Award, 1991; Robert Koch Award, 1992; Japan Prize, Japanese Inst. for Sci. and Technology, 1993; (jtly) Nobel Prize for Chemistry, 1993. *Publications:* Dancing Naked in the Mind Field, 1999; articles in prof. jls.

MULLIS, Marjorie; *see* Allthorpe-Guyton, M.

MULLOVA, Viktoria; violinist; *b* 27 Nov. 1959; *d* of Juri Mullov and Raisa Mullova; one *s* two *d. Educ:* Central Music Sch., Moscow; Moscow Conservatory. First prize, Sibelius Competition, Helsinki, 1980; Gold Medal, Tchaikovsky Competition, Moscow, 1982; left USSR, 1983. Has performed with most major orchestras; many festival appearances. Recordings include: violin concertos: Bach, Brahms, Tchaikovsky, Sibelius, Mendelssohn, Stravinsky, Bartok No 2, Shostakovich No 1, Prokoviev No 2, Paganini No 1; Bach partitas; sonatas for violin and piano: Bach, Janácek, Prokofiev, Debussy, Brahms; Vivaldi, Four Seasons; Through the Looking Glass (arrangements of works by Miles Davis, Weather Report and Youssou N'Dour). *Address:* c/o Askonas Holt, Lincoln House, 300 High Holborn, WC1V 7JH.

MULQUEENY, Emma Elizabeth; Founder and Chair, Rewired State Group, since 2014 (Founder and Chief Executive Officer, Rewired State, 2009–14); *b* Sidcup, Kent, 12 July 1971; *d* of Ken Knight and Sara Nicholls; *m* (marr. diss.); two *d. Educ:* St James Independent Sch. for Girls; Univ. of Surrey. Jillaroo and gold mine work, Australia, 1992–97; freelance consultancy, 1997–2004; Manager: Online Content, Bd of Inland Revenue, 2004–06; Strategic Communication, Cabinet Office, 2005–07; Hub Mum, FCO, 2007–08; Hd, Digital, Home Office, 2008–10; Curator, Open Platform, The Guardian, 2010–11. Mem., Exec. Cttee, British Interactive Media Assoc., 2011–. Member: Lord Mayor of London's Digital Adv. Bd, 2011–; Adv. Bd, Design Council, 2011–; Mozilla Learning Adv. Gp, 2012–; Comr, Speaker's Commn on Digital Democracy, 2014–. FRSA 2014. Fellow, Openforum Acad., 2011–; Google Fellow, 2014. *Recreations:* cooking, reading, travelling. *Address:* Rewired State Group, 3 Waterside Mews, Guildford GU1 1LA. *T:* 07730 570647. *E:* emma@rewiredstate.org. *Club:* Blacks.

MULREADY, Rt Rev. David Gray; Bishop of North West Australia, 2004–11; *b* 13 Sept. 1947; *s* of Norman Benson Mulready and Edna Faith Mulready (*née* Osborne); *m* 1971, Maureen Jane Mulready (*née* Lawrie); two *s* one *d. Educ:* Newington Coll., Sydney; Moore Theol Coll., Sydney (ThL 1971); Melbourne Coll. of Divinity (DipRE 1973). Ordained deacon and priest, 1971; Assistant Minister: Camden, 1971–73; Eastwood, 1973–74; Rector: Tambar Springs, 1974–77; Walgett, 1977–81; Manilla, 1981–85; Gunnedah, 1985–89; State Dir, Bush Ch Aid Soc., 1989–93; Rector, Penrith, 1993–2000; Rector and Sen. Canon, St John's Cathedral, Parramatta, 2000–04. *Recreations:* family, gardening, photography, travel, reading. *Address:* 28 Croft Place, Gerringong, NSW 2534, Australia. *T:* (2) 42342346.

MULRONEY, Rt Hon. (Martin) Brian; PC (Can.) 1984; CC 1998; Senior Partner, Norton Rose Fulbright Canada LLP (formerly Ogilvy Renault, then Norton Rose OR), since 1993; *b* 20 March 1939; *s* of Benedict Mulroney and Irene O'Shea; *m* 1973, Mila Pivnicki; three *s* one *d. Educ:* St Francis Xavier Univ. (BA); Université Laval (LLL). Partner, Ogilvy, Renault (Montreal law firm), 1965–76; Pres., Iron Ore Co. of Canada, 1976–83. MP (Progressive Conservative): Central Nova, 1983–84; Manicouagan, 1984–88; Charlevoix, 1988–93. Leader of the Opposition, 1983–84; Prime Minister of Canada, 1984–93. Royal Comr, Cliche Commn investigating violence in Quebec construction industry, 1974. Director: Barrick Gold Corp.; Trizec Properties Inc. (formerly TrizecHahn Corp.); Archer Daniels Midland Co.; Cendant Corp.; Quebecor Inc.; Quebecor World Inc. Member, International Advisory Council: China Internat. Trust and Investment Corp.; J P Morgan Chase & Co.; Independent News and Media plc. Trustee, Montreal Heart Inst. Hon. LLD: St Francis Xavier Univ., 1979; Meml Univ., 1980. *Publications:* Where I Stand, 1983. *Recreations:* tennis, swimming.

MULRYNE, Prof. (James) Ronald, PhD; Professor of English, University of Warwick, 1977–2004, now Emeritus; *b* 24 May 1937; *s* of Thomas Wilfred Mulryne and Mary Mulryne; *m* 1964, Eithne Wallace; one *s* one *d. Educ:* St Catharine's Coll., Cambridge (BA 1958; MA 1960; PhD 1962). Fellow, Shakespeare Inst., Univ. of Birmingham, 1960–62; University of Edinburgh: Lectr, 1962–72; Reader in English Lit., 1972–77; Hd, Dept of English Lit., 1976–77; University of Warwick: Pro-Vice-Chancellor, 1982–87; Director: Centre for Study of Renaissance, 1993–2003; AHRB Centre for Study of Renaissance Elites and Court Cultures, 2000–03. Vis. Associate Prof., Univ. of Calif, San Diego, 1970–71; Sen. Vis. Res. Fellow, Jesus Coll., Oxford, 1987; Vis. Fellow, Magdalen Coll., Oxford, 1991. General Editor: Revels Plays, 1979–2004; Shakespeare's Plays in Performance, 1984–2004. Dir, Digitisation of Festival Books in the Collections of the British Library (on-line pubn), 2005. Founder Dir, Mulryne & Shewring Ltd, Publishers, 1989–. Chm., Drama and Theatre Bd, CNAA, 1972–78; Member: Council of Mgt, UCCA, 1984–87; Drama Panel and Chm., Drama Projects Cttee, Arts Council of GB, 1987–91; Drama and Dance Adv. Cttee, British Council, 1991–97 (Chm., 1993–97); Arts and Humanities Research Council (formerly Board): Convener, English Lang. and Lit. Panel, 2000–04; Mem., Res. Cttee, 2000–04; Mem. Bd of Mgt, 2002–04. Mem. Bd of Dirs, Birmingham Rep. Theatre, 1987–95; Governor, RSC, 1998–2003. Trustee, Shakespeare's Birthplace Trust, 1985–2004. Chm., Friends of Shakespeare's Church, Stratford-upon-Avon, 2013–. Gov., 1985–2011, Trustee, 1998–, King Edward VI Sch., Stratford-upon-Avon (Dep. Chm., 1998–99, Chm., 2001–11, of Govs). Chm. Community Forum, World Class Stratford proj., 2007–10; Convenor, Soc. for European Festivals Res., 2010–. Pres., Stratford-upon-Avon Choral Soc., 2014–. FEA 2002. Chevalier, Ordre des Palmes Académiques (France), 1992. *Publications:* edited: Thomas Middleton, Women Beware Women, 1975; John Webster, The White Devil, 1970; Thomas Kyd, The Spanish Tragedy, 1970, 2nd edn 1989; The Guild and Guild Buildings of Shakespeare's Stratford, 2012; Ceremonial Entries in Early Modern Europe, 2015; edited with Margaret Shewring: Theatre of the English and Italian Renaissance, 1991; Italian Renaissance Festivals and their European Influence, 1992; Theatre and Government Under the Early Stuarts, 1993; Making Space for Theatre, 1995; Shakespeare and the Japanese Stage, 1998; The Cottesloe at the National, 1999; (ed with Elizabeth Goldring) Court Festivals of the European Renaissance, 2002; (ed with Takashi Kozuka) Shakespeare, Marlowe, Jonson: new directions in biography, 2006; (Gen. Ed.) Europa Triumphans: festivals of the European Renaissance, 2004 (2 vols); numerous books and articles, mainly on Shakespeare, Elizabethan Drama, European Festivals of the Renaissance and W. B. Yeats. *Recreation:* theatre. *Address:* 3 Benson Road, Stratford-upon-Avon CV37 6UU. *T:* (01789) 205774.

MULVANEY, Prof. Derek John, AO 1991; CMG 1982; Professor of Prehistory, Australian National University, 1971–85, now Emeritus; *b* 26 Oct. 1925; *s* of Richard and Frances Mulvaney; *m* 1st, 1954, Jean Campbell (*d* 2004); four *s* two *d*; 2nd, 2006, Elizabeth Morrison. *Educ:* Univ. of Melbourne (MA); Clare Coll., Univ. of Cambridge (BA, MA 1959, PhD 1970). FAHA 1970; FSA 1977; Corresp. FBA 1983; FRAI 1996. Navigator, RAAF, 1943–46 (Flying Officer); Lectr and Senior Lectr in History, Univ. of Melbourne, 1954–64; Senior Fellow, ANU, 1965–70; Vis. Prof., Cambridge, 1976–77; Chair of Australian Studies,

Harvard, 1984–85; Mem. Council, Aust. Inst. of Aboriginal Studies, 1964–80 (Chm., 1982–84); Australian Heritage Commissioner, 1976–82; Mem., Cttee of Inquiry, Museums and National Collections, 1974–75; Sec., Australian Acad. of Humanities, 1989–96. Hon. DLitt Melbourne, 2005. ANZAAS medal, 1988; Grahame Clark Medal, British Acad., 1999. *Publications:* Cricket Walkabout, 1967, 2nd edn 1988; The Prehistory of Australia, 1969, 2nd edn 1975; Australians to 1788, 1987; Encounters in Place, 1989; Commandant of Solitude, 1992; (ed jtly) My Dear Spencer: the letters of F. J. Gillen to Baldwin Spencer, 1997; (with J. Kamminga) Prehistory of Australia, 1999; Paddy Cahill of Oenpelli, 2004; Digging up a Past, 2011; numerous excavation reports and historical articles. *Recreation:* gardening. *Address:* 128 Schlich Street, Yarralumla, ACT 2600, Australia. *T:* (2) 62812352.

MULVANY, Patrick Mowbray; Director, Kamayoq, since 2012; *b* Eastbourne, 12 July 1946; *s* of Brian Mulvany and Barbara Mulvany; *m* 1972, Annabel Royes; two *s* one *d* (and one *s* decd). *Educ:* Eastbourne Coll.; St John's Coll., Oxford (MA Agricl Sci. 1969). CBiol 1977. Develt worker, Catholic Inst. for Internat. Relns, Honduras, 1969–72; Higher Scientific Officer, Nat. Inst. for Res. in Dairying, Reading, 1973–79; Sen. Policy Advr, Practical Action (formerly Intermediate Technol. Develt Gp), 1979–2012. Chm., UK Food Gp, 2002–14. Evaluations of: GRAIN, 2007; Friends of the Earth Internat., 2008; Via Campesina, 2010; S Africa Develt Community Seed Security Network, 2013; Civil Soc. Mechanism/Cttee on World Food Security, 2014. Member: Biosci. for Society Strategy Panel, BBSRC, 2013–; Food Ethics Council, 2014–; ECOROPA, 2014–; Etc Group, 2015–. Trustee: Oxfam, 1986–92; Action Aid, 1994–2001; Catholic Inst. for Internat. Relns, 1980–85 and 1993–2001; Sustain: the alliance for better food and farming, 2009–. Co-Chm., Consultative Gp on Internat. Agricl Res.-NGO Cttee, 2002–03. *Publications:* contrib. books, jls, confs and papers on issues concerning governance of technol., agricl biodiversity and food sovereignty. *Recreations:* music, growing food, travel, family. *T:* (Kamayoq) (020) 7193 7283. *E:* kamayoq@kamayoq.org.

MULVEY, Prof. Laura Mary Alice, FBA 2000; Professor of Film and Media Studies, since 1999, and Director, Institute for the Moving Image, since 2013, Birkbeck College, University of London; *b* 15 Aug. 1941. *Educ:* St Paul's Girls' Sch.; St Hilda's Coll., Oxford (BA). Teacher of film studies and film practice; responsible for Birkbeck Coll. MA in Film and TV History and Theory. Co-director: six films with Peter Wollen; (with Mark Lewis) Disgraced Monuments, 1994. *Publications:* Visual and Other Pleasures, 1989, 2nd edn 2009; Citizen Kane, 1993, 2nd edn 2013; Fetishism and Curiosity, 1996, 2nd edn 2013; Death Twenty-four Times a Second: stillness and the moving image, 2006; articles and chapters in books. *Address:* School of History of Art, Film and Visual Media, Birkbeck College, 43 Gordon Square, WC1H 0PD.

MULVILLE, James Thomas; Managing Director, Hat Trick Productions, since 1985; *b* 5 Jan. 1955; *s* of late James Lawrence Mulville and of June Mulville; *m* 1st, 1974, Julia Kelly; 2nd, 1987, Denise O'Donoghue, *qv* (marr. diss. 1998); 3rd, 1999, Karen Page; three *s* one *d*. *Educ:* Alsop Comprehensive Sch., Liverpool; Jesus Coll., Cambridge (BA Hons; Pres., Cambridge Footlights, 1976–77). With BBC Light Entertainment as writer and producer, 1978–82; Jt Founder, Hat Trick Prodns, 1985; co-writer and performer: Who Dares Wins (series), Channel 4, 1983–88; Chelmsford 123, Channel 4, 1987–90; actor: That's Love, 1987–91; GBH, 1991. FRTS 2001. Hon. DLit Liverpool. *Publications:* (jtly) Who Dares Wins, 1986. *Recreations:* my children, family, friends, films, Everton Football Club, shooting. *Address:* c/o Hat Trick Productions, 33 Oval Road, NW1 7EA. *T:* (020) 7434 2451.

MUMBENGEGWI, Hon. Simbarashe Simbanenduku; MP, Republic of Zimbabwe, since 2005; Minister of Foreign Affairs, since 2005; *b* Chivi, Zimbabwe, 20 July 1945; *s* of late Chivandire Davis Mumbengegwi and Dzivaidzo Shuvai Mumbengegwi; *m* 1983, Emily; one *s* four *d*. *Educ:* Fletcher High Sch., Gweru, Zimbabwe; Monash Univ., Melbourne (BA Gen., BA Combined Hons, DipEd, MEd). Teacher, Dadaya Secondary Sch., Zvishavane, and schools in Melbourne, then Tutor in Politics at colls in Melbourne, 1966–78; MP: Midlands Province, 1980–85; Shurugwi Constituency, Midlands Province, 1985–90; Dep. Speaker and Chm. of Cttees, House of Assembly, Parlt of Zimbabwe, 1980–81; Dep. Minister of Foreign Affairs, 1981–82; Minister: of Water Resources and Develt, 1982; of Nat. Housing, 1982–84; of Public Construction and Nat. Housing, 1984–88; of Transport, 1988–90; Ambassador and Perm. Rep. of Zimbabwe to UN, NY, 1990–95; Vice-Pres., UN Gen. Assembly, 1990–91; Mem., UN Security Council, 1991–92 (Pres. at height of Gulf War, 1991, and 1992); Ambassador to Belgium, Netherlands, Luxembourg and Perm. Rep. to EU, Brussels, 1995–99; Perm. Rep. to Orgn for Prohibition of Chem. Weapons, The Hague, 1997–99 (Mem. Council, 1997–99); High Comr, later Ambassador, to UK, and Ambassador to Ireland, 1999–2005. Participated in numerous ministerial confs and Heads of State summits of OAU, 1981–94; Hd of delegns to all annual confs of UN Commn for Human Settlements, 1983–88; served on numerous UN and ACP cttees. Mem., Youth Leagues of Nat. Democratic Party, ZAPU and ZANU, 1960–64; ZANU activist in exile, 1966–72; Zimbabwe African National Union: Dep. Chief Rep., 1973–76, Chief Rep., 1976–78, Australia and Far East; Chief Rep. to Zambia, 1978–80; ZANU-Patriotic Front: Provincial Treas., Midlands Province, 1981–84; Mem., Central Cttee, 1984–94, 2006– (Dep. Sec. for Publicity and Inf., 1984–89). *Recreations:* reading, photography, jogging, tennis, golf, swimming. *Address:* Ministry of Foreign Affairs, PO Box 4240, Harare, Zimbabwe.

MUMFORD, family name of **Lady Herries of Terregles**.

MUMFORD, Rev. David Christopher; Rector, St Andrew's, Brechin, and St Drostan's, Tarfside, 2007–15; Dean of Brechin, 2008–12; *b* 14 Jan. 1947. *Educ:* Merton Coll., Oxford (MA 1974); York Univ. (MSW 1981; CQSW 1981); Lincoln Theol Coll. Ordained deacon, 1986, priest, 1987; Assistant Curate: St Mark's, Shiremoor, Newcastle, 1986–89; St Augustine's, North Shields, 1989–91; Vicar, St Anthony, Byker, 1991–97; Rural Dean, Newcastle E, 1996–97; Vicar, St Peters, Cowgate, 1997–2002; Internat. Co-ordinator, Internat. Fellowship of Reconciliation, 2002–07. *Address:* 10 Temple Mains Steading, Innerwick, Dunbar, E Lothian EH42 1EF. *E:* dmumford@phonecoop.coop.

MUMFORD, Peter Taylor; theatre lighting and stage designer; television director; Chairman, Association of Lighting Designers (UK), since 2011; *b* 12 Dec. 1946; *s* of late John and Doreen Mumford; *m* 1st, 1969, Mary Davida Becket (*d* 1992); three *s*; 2nd, 1995, Tana Marge Lester (marr. diss. 2009); one *d*; 3rd, 2009, Alexandra Thompson. *Educ:* Central Sch. of Art (DipAD Theatre Design). Founding Mem., exptl theatre gp, Moving Being, late 1960s; freelance theatre artist, lighting and designing operas, plays and ballets, worldwide, 1978–; lighting designs for numerous productions, including: Fearful Symmetries, Royal Ballet, 1994; The Glass Blew In, Siobhan Davies Dance Co., 1995 (Olivier Award for Outstanding Achievement in Dance (for lighting design)); The Merchant of Venice, NT, 1999; Vincent in Brixton, NT, transf. Playhouse Th., 2002, transf. NY, 2003; Bacchai, NT, 2003 (Olivier Award for Best Lighting Designer); Peter Pan, Northern Ballet Th., 2005; Midsummer Marriage, Lyric Opera, Chicago, 2005; Cinderella, for Scottish Ballet, 2005; Madame Butterfly, for ENO, 2005–06, and Metropolitan Opera, NY, 2006; Eugene Onegin, Royal Opera House, 2006; The Rose Tattoo, NT, 2007; The Hothouse, NT, 2007; Fiddler on the Roof, Savoy Th., 2007; The Seagull, Royal Ct, 2007, transf. NY, 2008; Carousel, Savoy Th., 2008; Peter Grimes, Metropolitan Opera, NY, 2008; A View from the Bridge, Duke of York's, 2009; E=mc^2, Sadler's Wells, 2009; All's Well That Ends Well, NT, 2009; Metropolitan Opera 125th Anniversary Gala, NY, 2009; Carmen, Metropolitan Opera, NY, 2010; A Midsummer Night's Dream, Rose Th., Kingston upon Thames, 2010; An Ideal Husband, Vaudeville, 2010; A Streetcar Named Desire, Guthrie Th., Minneapolis, 2010; Bedroom Farce, Duke of York's and tour, 2010; Capriccio, Grange Park Opera, 2010; Elegy for Young Lovers, ENO at Young Vic, 2010; Enlightenment, Hampstead Th., 2010; Faust, ENO, 2010; La Spinalba, Guildhall Sch. of Music and Drama, 2010; Pictures from an Exhibition, Sadler's Wells, 2010; Pieces of Vincent, Arcola Th., 2010; Sucker Punch, Royal Court, 2010 (Knight of Illumination Award, Best Lighting for Drama); Tosca, Grange Park Opera, 2010; Twelfth Night, NT, 2011; Lucrezia Borgia and The Damnation of Faust, ENO, 2011; Punch and Judy, Opera Genève, 2011; Much Ado About Nothing, Wyndhams, 2011; Top Hat, UK tour, 2011; Faust, Metropolitan Opera, 2011, Eugene Onegin, LA Opera, 2011; Ghosts, Almeida, 2013; Women on the Verge of a Nervous Breakdown, Playhouse, 2015; The Flying Dutchman, Opera North, 2015; dir/designer of concert version of Ring Cycle, Opera North, 2011–; also set and lighting designs for Northern Ballet; dir, dance and music films for TV, incl. adaptations of Matthew Bourne's Swan Lake, and series of short films, 48 Preludes and Fugues (J. S. Bach). *Recreation:* fly fishing when the opportunity arises. *Address:* Vuelvo Al Sur, South Dock Marina, Rope Street, SE16 7SZ. *E:* mumf1@mac.com. *W:* www.petermumford.info.

MUMMERY, Christopher John L.; *see* Lockhart-Mummery.

MUMMERY, Rt Hon. Sir John Frank, Kt 1989; PC 1996; DL; a Lord Justice of Appeal, 1996–2013; a Deputy Chairman, Takeover Appeal Board, since 2014; *b* 5 Sept. 1938; *s* of late Frank Stanley Mummery and Ruth Mummery (*née* Coleman), Coldred, Kent; *m* 1967, Elizabeth Anne Lamond Lackie, *d* of late Dr D. G. L. Lackie and Ellen Lackie (*née* Easterbrook), Edinburgh; one *s* one *d*. *Educ:* Oakleigh House, Dover; Dover County Grammar Sch.; Pembroke Coll., Oxford, 1959–63 (MA, BCL; Winter Williams Prize in Law; Hon. Fellow, 1989). National Service, The Border Regt and RAEC, 1957–59. Called to Bar, Gray's Inn (Atkin Schol.), 1964 (Bencher, 1985; Treas., 2005). Treasury Junior Counsel: in Charity Matters, 1977–81; Chancery, 1981–89; a Recorder, 1989; a Judge of the High Court, Chancery Div., 1989–96. President: Employment Appeal Tribunal, 1993–96; Investigatory Powers Tribunal, 2000–13; Clergy Discipline Tribunals, 2003–13; Chm., Clergy Discipline Commn, 2003–13; Mem., Court of Ecclesiastical Causes Reserved, 2006– (Mem., Faculty Rule Cttee, 2015). Member, Senate of Inns of Court and Bar, 1978–81; Pres., Council of Inns of Court, 2000–03. Member: Justice Cttee on Privacy and the Law, 1967–70; Legal Adv. Commn, Gen. Synod of C of E, 1988–; Council of Legal Educn, 1989–92; leader, Rev. of Competition Appeal Tribunal Procedure, 2014. Chm. Trustees, CAB, Royal Courts of Justice, 2003–13. Gov., Inns of Court Sch. of Law, 1996–2001; Mem. Council, Pegasus Scholarship Trust, 1997–2013; Mem. Adv. Bd, British Inst. of Internat. and Comparative Law, 2001–13. Trustee, Wye Rural Museum Trust, 2008–. DL Kent, 2008–13. Hon. Fellow, Soc. for Advanced Legal Studies, 1997; Hon. Mem., Soc. of Legal Scholars, 1998; Hon. President: Employment Law Bar Assoc., 2003–13; Charity Law Assoc., 2004–. Hon. Fellow, Oxford Inst. of Intellectual Property, 2013. Hon. LLD: De Montfort, 1998; City, 2002; Hon. Dr Canterbury Christ Church, 2014. *Publications:* (co-ed) Copinger and Skone James on Copyright, 12th edn 1980, 13th edn 1991. *Recreations:* walks with family, friends and alone.

MUNBY, Rt Hon. Sir James (Lawrence), Kt 2000; PC 2009; President of the Family Division, since 2013; *b* 27 July 1948; *s* of Denys Lawrence Munby and Mary Munby (*née* Dicks); *m* 1977, Jennifer Anne Lindsay Beckhough; one *s* one *d*. *Educ:* Magdalen College Sch., Oxford; Wadham Coll., Oxford (BA). Called to the Bar, Middle Temple, 1971 (Bencher, 2000); QC 1988; a Judge of the High Court of Justice, Family Div., 2000–09; a Lord Justice of Appeal, 2009–13. Chm., Law Commn, 2009–12. *Address:* c/o Royal Courts of Justice, Strand, WC2A 2LL.

MUNBY, Dr John Latimer, CMG 1997; OBE 1984; Director, British Council, Greece, 1990–97; *b* 14 July 1937; *s* of late Lawrence St John Munby and Jennie Munby; *m* 1961, Lilian Cynthia Hogg; two *s*. *Educ:* King's Sch., Bruton; Lincoln Coll., Oxford (BA Jurisp., MA); Inst. of Educn, London Univ. (PGCE); Univ. of Essex (MA Applied Linguistics, PhD). Nat. service, 2nd Lieut, 1955–57. Educn Officer, Govt of Tanzania, 1961–68; joined British Council, 1969; seconded to Advanced Teachers' Coll., Zaria, then Ahmadu Bello Univ., Nigeria, 1969–72; Director: English Teaching Inf. Centre, 1974–76; English Lang. Consultancies Dept, 1976–78; Representative: Kuwait, 1978–81; Singapore, 1981–85; Dep. Controller, Home Div., 1985–87; Controller, Libraries, Books and Information Div., 1987–90. FRSA 1982. *Publications:* Read and Think, 1968; Communicative Syllabus Design, 1978; contrib. various jls. *Recreations:* music, sport, wine. *Address:* c/o CPS Registry, The British Council, 10 Spring Gardens, SW1A 2BN. *T:* (020) 7930 8466.

MUNBY, Stephen Thurston, CBE 2010; Chief Executive, CfBT Education Trust, since 2012; *b* North Shields, 25 Aug. 1956; *s* of Robert Munby and Hilda Munby; *m* 2005, Jacqueline Rothery. *Educ:* Royal Grammar Sch., Newcastle upon Tyne; Univ. of Reading (BA Hons Philos.); Univ. of Birmingham (PGCE); Manchester Metropolitan Univ. (MEd). Teacher of History and English, Fairfax Sch., Sutton Coldfield, then Teacher of History, Lord Lawson High Sch., Gateshead, 1978–85; TVEI support teacher, 1985–86; Sen. Lectr, Sunderland Poly., 1986–87; consultant, assessment and recording of achievement, 1987–89; Inspector, then Manager, Sch. Adv. Service, Oldham BC, 1989–97; Asst Dir, Blackburn with Darwen BC, 1997–2000; Dir, Educn and Lifelong Learning, Knowsley BC, 2000–05; Chief Exec., Nat. Coll. for Sch. Leadership, 2005–12. Hon. DArts Bedfordshire, 2010; DUniv Bishop Grosseteste University Coll., Lincoln, 2011. *Publications:* Assessing and Recording Achievement, 1989. *Recreations:* supporting Newcastle United Football Club, listening to Leonard Cohen and Bob Dylan music. *Address:* CfBT Education Trust, 60 Queens Road, Reading, Berks RG1 4BS.

MUNDAY, Janice Margaret, CBE 2013; Director, Advanced Manufacturing and Services, Department for Business, Innovation and Skills, since 2010; *d* of late Richard Munday and of Margaret Elliott (*née* Rogers); partner, Martin Edward Stanley, *qv*; one *s* (and one *s* decd). Public Service Delivery, Cabinet Office, 1989–92; Accountancy Policy, DTI, 1992–95; Dir of Policy, Charity Commn, 1995–96; Department of Trade and Industry: Dir of Policy, Consumer Affairs, 1999–2000; Dir, Participation and Skills, then Head, Employment Relns, 2000–07 (Dir, Employment Relns, 2003–07); Dir, Business Support Simplification Project, then Solutions for Business/BSSP, later Solutions for Business, Low Carbon and Services, BERR, subseq. BIS, 2007–10. *Recreations:* enjoying London, gardening, dog walking. *Address:* Department for Business, Innovation and Skills, 1 Victoria Street, SW1H 0ET. *T:* (020) 7215 5702, *Fax:* (020) 7215 6768. *E:* janice.munday@bis.gsi.gov.uk.

MUNDAY, Stephen Charles Richard, CBE 2013; Executive Principal, Comberton and Cambourne Village Colleges, and Chief Executive and Executive Principal, Comberton Academy Trust, since 2011; *b* Barking, Essex, 4 Aug. 1964; *s* of Brian and Jill Munday; *m* 1989, Elizabeth Marion Darling; one *s* two *d*. *Educ:* Simon Langton Grammar Sch. for Boys, Canterbury; St John's Coll., Cambridge (BA Econs 1986); Inst. of Educn, Univ. of London (PGCE; MA). Teacher of Econs, 1987–94, Hd of Sixth Form, 1989–94, Bishop's Stortford High Sch.; Dep. Hd, Saffron Walden Co. High Sch., 1994–2000. Hon. DEd Anglia Ruskin, 2009. *Publications:* Current Developments in Economics, 1996; Markets and Market Failure, 2000; (with C. Bamford) Markets, 2001. *Recreations:* sport, especially golf and cricket, local church. *Address:* Comberton Village College, West Street, Comberton, Cambridge CB23 7DU. *T:* (01223) 262503. *E:* thecollege@comberton.cambs.sch.uk. *Club:* Gog Magog Golf (Cambridge).

MUNDELL, Prof. Carole Gibson, PhD; Professor of Extragalactic Astronomy, since 2007 and Head of Astrophysics, since 2015, University of Bath; *b* Sheffield, 17 Aug. 1969; *d* of Robert Mundell and Hilda Mundell (*née* Gibson); *m* 1998, Dr David Leslie Shone; two *s*.

Educ: Penketh High Sch., Warrington; Priestley Sixth-Form Coll., Warrington; Univ. of Glasgow (BSc Hons 1992); Univ. of Manchester (PhD 1995). PPARC Postdoctoral Res. Fellow, Jodrell Bank, Univ. of Manchester, 1995–97; Postdoctoral Res. Associate, Dept of Astronomy, Univ. of Maryland, 1997–99; Astrophysics Research Institute, Liverpool John Moores University: Royal Soc. Univ. Res. Fellow, 1999–2009; Res. Councils UK Fellow, 2005–11; Prof. of Extragalactic Astronomy, 2007–15. Royal Soc. Wolfson Res. Merit Award, 2011–16. Mem. Council, STFC, 2015–; Chair, Skills and Engagement Adv. Bd, 2015–. *Publications:* contrib. papers in fields of active galaxies and gamma ray bursts to peer-reviewed jls incl. Nature, Sci., Astrophysical Jl and Monthly Notices of RAS. *Recreations:* music, reading, walking, knitting, family. *Address:* Department of Physics, University of Bath, Claverton Down, Bath BA2 7AY. *E:* c.g.mundell@bath.ac.uk.

MUNDELL, Rt Hon. David (Gordon); PC 2010; MP (C) Dumfriesshire, Clydesdale and Tweeddale, since 2005; Secretary of State, Scotland Office, since 2015; *b* 27 May 1962; *s* of Dorah Mundell; *m* 1987, Lynda Jane Carmichael (marr. diss. 2012); two *s* one *d*. *Educ:* Lockerbie Acad.; Edinburgh Univ. (LLB Hons 1984); Univ. of Strathclyde Business Sch. (MBA 1991). Trainee Solicitor, Tindal Oatts, Glasgow, 1985–87; Solicitor, Maxwell Waddell, Glasgow, 1987–89; Sen. Corporate Lawyer, Biggart Baillie & Gifford, Glasgow, 1989–91; Group Legal Advr Scotland, BT, 1991–98; Head of Nat. Affairs, BT Scotland, 1998–99. MSP (C) S of Scotland, 1999–2005. Shadow Sec. of State for Scotland, 2005–10; Parly Under-Sec. of State, Scotland Office, 2010–15. Member: Law Soc. of Scotland, 1986–; Law Soc., 1992–. *Recreations:* family and friends, travel. *Address:* House of Commons, SW1A 0AA.

MUNDELL, Prof. Robert Alexander, CC 2003; PhD; Professor of Economics, Columbia University, since 1974; *b* 24 Oct. 1932; *s* of William Campbell Mundell and Lila Teresa Mundell; *m* 1st, 1957, Barba Sheff (*d* 1972); 2nd, 1998, Valerie S. Natsios; one *s*. *Educ:* Univ. of BC; MIT (PhD); London Sch. of Econs; Univ. of Chicago. Instructor, Univ. of BC, 1957–58; economist, Royal Commn on Price Spreads of Food Products, Ottawa, 1958; Asst Prof. of Econs, Stanford Univ., 1958–59; Prof. of Econs, Johns Hopkins Univ., Sch. of Advanced Internat. Studies, Bologna, 1959–61; Sen. Economist, IMF, 1961–63; Prof. of Internat. Econs, Grad. Inst. Internat. Studies, Geneva, 1965–75; Professor of Economics: Univ. of Chicago, 1966–71; Univ. of Waterloo, Ont., 1972–74. Vis. Prof. of Econs, McGill Univ., 1963–64, 1989–90; First Rockefeller Vis. Res. Prof. of Internat. Econs, Brookings Inst., 1964–65; Guggenheim Fellow, 1971; Annenburg Dist. Schol. in Residence, Univ. of Southern Calif, 1980; Richard Fox Vis. Prof. of Econs, Univ. of Penn, 1990–91. Ed., Jl Pol Econ., 1966–71. Pres., N American Econ. and Financial Assoc., 1974–78. Hon. Dr: Paris, 1992; People's Univ. of China, 1995. Nobel Prize for Econs, 1999. *Publications:* The International Monetary System: conflict and reform, 1965; Man and Economics, 1968; International Economics, 1968; Monetary Theory: interest, inflation and growth in the world economy, 1971; contrib. learned jls. *Recreations:* painting, tennis, hockey, ski-ing, history. *Address:* 35 Claremont Avenue #5N, New York, NY 10027, USA. *T:* (212) 7490630; Palazzo Mundell, Strada di Santa Columba 2–4, Santa Columba, Siena 53100, Italy. *Club:* Reform.

MUNDY, Prof. Anthony Richard, FRCP, FRCS; Professor of Urology, University of London, since 1991; Director, Institute of Urology (formerly Institute of Urology and Nephrology), University College London, since 1996; Medical Director, UCL Hospitals NHS Foundation Trust, since 2000; *b* 25 April 1948; *s* of Peter Gordon Mundy and Betty (*née* Hall); *m* 1st, 1970, Sheila Peskett; 2nd, 1975, Marilyn Ashton; one *s* one *d*; partner, Debra Hendley; one *d*. *Educ:* Mill Hill Sch.; St Mary's Hosp. Medical Sch., London (MB BS Hons 1971); MS London 1982. MRCP 1974, FRCP 1996; FRCS 1975. House Surgeon, St Mary's Hosp., London, 1971; House Physician, Barnet General Hosp., 1972; Casualty Officer, St Mary's Hosp., London, 1973; Surgical Registrar, Orsett Hosp., 1973–75; Guy's Hospital: Sen. Registrar, Surgery, 1975–78, Urology, 1978–81; Consultant Urologist, 1981–99; Consultant Urologist, St Peter's Hosps and UCL Hosps, 1986–. Vis. Consultant Urologist, St Luke's Hosp., subseq. Mater Dei Hosp., Malta, 1984–. Lectures: Pradke, Pune, India, 1992; Sir Ernest Finch, Sheffield, 1994; Bodo von Garrelts, Stockholm, 1995; Ballenger, Puerto Rica, 1996; Ian Aird, Imperial Coll., 1999; Grey Turner, Newcastle, 1999; C. E. Alken, Dusseldorf, 1999; Rovsing, Copenhagen, 2000; British Assoc. of Urol Surgeons, 2001, 2009; Hunterian Oration, RCS, 2007; Moynihan, RCS/Assoc. of Surgeons of GB and Ireland, 2009. Hon. Prof. of Medicine, Univ. of Crete, 2009–. Pres., British Assoc. of Urol Surgeons, 2006–08 (Mem. Council, 1990–93, 1995–2001; Vice-Pres., 2003–06); Member: Exec. Cttee, Eur. Assoc. of Urol., 1994–2000 (Mem., Acad., 2000–); Council, RCS, 2000–10; Founder Mem., Genito-Urinary Reconstructive Surgeons, 1984–; Convenor, Urol Res. Soc., 1984–. Fellow, Urological Soc. of Australia and NZ, 2011; Hon. FRACS 2013. Hon. Member, Urological Society: of Australasia, 1986; of HK, 1989; of Singapore, 1990; of Malaysia, 1994; of S Africa, 1998; of Holland, 1990; of Germany, 2011; Internat. Mem., Amer. Assoc. of Genito-Urinary Surgeons, 2004–. Hon. PhD Crete, 2009. St Peter's Medal, British Assoc. of Urol Surgeons, 2002. *Publications:* Urodynamics: principles, practice and application, 1984, 2nd edn 1994; Current Operative Surgery: Urology, 1987; Neuropathic Bladder in Childhood, 1991; Urodynamic and Reconstructive Surgery of the Lower Urinary Tract, 1994; Scientific Basis of Urology, 1999, 3rd edn 2010; Succeeding as a Hospital Doctor, 2000, 3rd edn 2007; articles on reconstructive urology in various urological jls. *Recreations:* home, wine, history. *Address:* Emblem House, Tooley Street, SE1 2PR. *T:* (020) 7403 1221, *Fax:* (020) 7403 1664. *E:* tony.mundy1@btinternet.com.

MUNDY, (James) Toby; Founding Director, Toby Mundy Associates Ltd, since 2014; Executive Director, Samuel Johnson Prize for Non-Fiction, since 2015; *b* London, 11 Nov. 1968; *s* of Stuart Mundy and Olga Mundy; *m* 1995, Charis Evans; one *s* one *d*. *Educ:* Royal Holloway Coll., Univ. of London (BA 1st Cl. Hons Eng. Lit.); Queen Mary and Westfield Coll., Univ. of London (MA Dist. Lit. and Lang.). Editor, HarperCollins Publishers, 1991–97; Publishing Dir, Weidenfeld & Nicolson, 1997–2000; Founder, Chm. and Chief Exec., Atlantic Books Ltd, 2000–14. Non-exec. Dir, Prospect Publishing Ltd, 2005. Trustee, Wimbledon Bookfest, 2014–; Mem., Adv. Bd, DEMOS, 2014–. Hon. DArt Bournemouth, 2004. *Recreations:* walking, food and wine, playing with my children, cinema, music. *Address:* Toby Mundy Associates Ltd, 6 Bayley Street, Bedford Square, WC1B 3HE. *T:* (020) 3713 0067. *E:* tobymundy@tma-agency.com. *Clubs:* Union, Century.

MUNDY, Jo A.; *see* Shapcott, J. A.

MUNDY, John Kennedy; Sheriff of Tayside, Central and Fife, since 2011; *b* Glasgow, 20 Sept. 1958; *s* of Thomas Mundy and Margaret Mundy; *m* 1987, Fiona Margaret Brown; two *s*. *Educ:* Montgomery of Alamein Sch., Winchester; Balfron High Sch., Stirlingshire; Univ. of Dundee (LLB, DipLP 1981). Admitted as solicitor, 1983; admitted to Faculty of Advocates, 1987. Legal Assessor: GMC, 2007–11; NMC, 2007–11; Chm., Investigating Cttee, Gen. Osteopathic Council, 2009–11. *Recreations:* euphonium, guitar, golf, curling. *Address:* Falkirk Sheriff Court, Main Street, Camelon, Falkirk FK1 4AR.

MUNDY, Toby; *see* Mundy, J. T.

MUNGLANI, Rajesh, FRCA; Consultant in Pain Medicine, West Suffolk Hospital, Bury St Edmunds, since 2000; *b* 31 Aug. 1962; *s* of Balwani Rai Munglani and Krishna Gulati; *m* 1989, Dr Jane Bolland; four *d*. *Educ:* St George's Hosp., Univ. of London (MB BS 1985); DCH 1989. FRCA 1990. Clin. Lectr, 1993–96, Lectr in Anaesthesia and Pain Mgt, 1997–2000, Univ. of Cambridge; Consultant in Anaesthesia and Pain Mgt, Addenbrooke's Hosp., Cambridge, 1997–2000. John Farman Prof., RCAnaes, 1997. Founder and Dir, Healing the Person Ltd, 2009. British Pain Society: Exec. Officer, Interventional Pain Medicine Special Interest Gp, 2010–; co-founder and Sec., Medicolegal Special Interest Gp, 2011–; Mem. Council, 2011–. Founder, Cambridge Annual Medico-Legal Conference, 2011–; co-founder, Cambridge Medico-Legal Forum, 2012–. Fellow, Faculty of Pain Medicine, RCAnaes, 2008–; Mem. Council, Pain Section, RSocMed, 2014–. Founder and Chief Ed., Jl of Observational Pain Medicine. *Publications:* Pain: current understanding, emerging therapies and novel approaches to drug discovery, 2001; contrib. numerous papers and chapters on scientific basis of chronic pain, spinal pain incl. whiplash and complex regional pain syndromes. *Recreations:* walking in the Lake District, reading. *Address:* Spire Cambridge Lea Hospital, 30 New Road, Impington, Cambridge CB24 9EL. *T:* (01223) 479024. *E:* sue.sanalitro@gmail.com.

MUNIR, (Ashley) Edward, PhD; Barrister; Under Secretary, Ministry of Agriculture, Fisheries and Food, 1982–92; *b* 14 Feb. 1934; *s* of late Hon. Sir Mehmed Munir Bey, Kt, CBE, and late Lady (Vessime) Munir; *m* 1960, Sureyya S. V. Dormen; one *s*. *Educ:* Brentwood Sch.; St John's Coll., Cambridge (MA 1957); King's Coll., London (PhD 1992). Called to the Bar, Gray's Inn, 1956. Practised as barrister, 1956–60, 1992–; Crown Counsel, 1960–64; entered Govt Legal Service, 1964; Asst Solicitor, MAFF, 1975–82. *Publications:* Perinatal Rights, 1983; Fisheries after Factortame, 1991; Mentally Disordered Offenders, 1993. *Recreations:* walking, music. *Address:* (chambers) 5 St Andrew's Hill, EC4V 5BY. *T:* (020) 7332 5400. *Club:* Oxford and Cambridge.

MUNN, Geoffrey Charles, OBE 2013; FSA, FLS; jewellery historian and writer; Managing Director, Wartski Ltd, since 1990; *b* Hastings, 11 April 1953; *s* of Stewart Hayden Munn and Heather Rosemary Munn (*née* Hollingsworth); *m* 1983, Caroline Watney, MA; two *s*. *Educ:* Steyning Grammar Sch., Sussex. Joined Wartski, 1972, Dir, 1981. Contributor, Antiques Roadshow, 1989–. Ambassador: Samaritans, 1990–; Pancreatic Cancer UK, 2011–; Patron: Lowestoft Samaritans, 1994–; Sotterley Chapel Preservation Trust, 2005–. Curator, loan exhibns at Wartski, and Tiaras exhibn at V&A Mus., 2002. Actor in film, Joe's Palace, 2007. Freeman, Goldsmiths' Co., 1986 (Liveryman, 2005; Mem., Ct of Assts, 2014). FSA 1991; FLS 2014. FRSA 2012. *Publications:* Castellani and Giuliano: revivalist jewellers of the nineteenth century, 1984; (with C. Gere) Artists' Jewellery: Pre-Raphaelite to Arts and Crafts, 1989, 2nd edn 1996; The Triumph of Love: jewellery 1530–1930, 1993; Tiaras: a history of splendour, 2001, 5th edn 2012; Tiaras Past and Present, 2002; Southwold: an earthly paradise, 2006; Wartski: the first one hundred and fifty years, 2015; contribs to specialist press on hist. of jewellery and drawings of J. W. M. Turner and D. G. Rossetti. *Recreations:* mudlarking and metal detecting, Bonsai, running, cycling, cooking, museums and art galleries. *Address:* Wartski, 14 Grafton Street, W1S 4DE. *T:* (020) 7493 1141, *Fax:* (020) 7409 7448. *E:* geoffrey@wartski.com. *Clubs:* Garrick, Arts; Southwold Sailors' Reading Room.

MUNN, Dr Helen Louise; Executive Director, Academy of Medical Sciences, since 2009; *b* Cardiff, 11 Jan. 1978; *d* of late William Munn and of Janet Munn; *m* 2008, Alex Grant; one *s* one *d*. *Educ:* Howell's Sch., Llandaff; Cheltenham Ladies' Coll.; Queen's Coll., Oxford (BSc Biol Scis); Univ. of Edinburgh (PhD Molecular Scis 2003). Joined Acad. of Med. Scis, 2004; Policy Officer, 2004–06; Policy Manager, 2006–07; Policy Dir, 2007–09. *Recreations:* theatre, travel, novels, friends. *Address:* Academy of Medical Sciences, 41 Portland Place, W1B 1QH. *T:* (020) 3176 2151. *E:* helen.munn@acmedsci.ac.uk.

MUNN, Meg; consultant; *b* 24 Aug. 1959; *d* of late Reginald Edward Munn and of Lillian Seward; *m* 1989, Dennis Clifford Bates. *Educ:* Univ. of York (BA Hons Language); Univ. of Nottingham (MA Social Work; CQSW); Open Univ. (Dip. Mgt Studies). Social Work Assistant, Berkshire, 1981–84; Social Worker, 1986–90, Sen. Social Worker, 1990–92, Nottinghamshire; Dist Manager, Barnsley, 1992–96; Children's Service Manager, Wakefield, 1996–99; Asst Dir of Children's Services, Social Services, York, 1999–2000. MP (Lab and Co-op) Sheffield, Heeley, 2001–15. PPS, DFES, 2003–05; Parliamentary Under-Secretary of State: DTI, 2005–06; DCLG, 2006–07; FCO, 2007–08. All Party Parliamentary Groups: Chairman: Kurdistan Region in Iraq, 2008–15; Methodist, 2010–15; Child Protection, 2010–15; Vice-Chairman: Women in Enterprise, 2010–15; Engrg and IT, 2010–15; Yorks and N Lincs, 2011–15. Chm., 2008–10, Vice-Chm., 2010–12, Westminster Foundn for Democracy; Pres., Co-operative Congress, 2006. Mem., Mgt Cttee, Wortley Hall Ltd, 1994–2000; Chm. Cttee, Barnsley Br., CRS Ltd, 1997–2001. CMgr 2012; FCMI. *Publications:* (ed jtly) Family Fortunes: the new politics of childhood, 2004. *Recreations:* tennis, swimming, gardening.

MUNNS, Victor George; Counsellor (Labour), Washington, 1983–86; *b* 17 June 1926; *s* of Frederick William Munns and Lilian Munns; *m* 1952, Pamela Ruth Wyatt; two *s*. *Educ:* Haberdashers' Aske's, Hatcham; University Coll., London (BA). Served HM Forces (Army Intell.), 1945–48. Min. of Labour Employment Service, 1951–61; ILO, Trinidad and Belize, 1962–63; Sec., Shipbldg Industry Trng Bd, 1964–66; Res. Staff, Royal Commn on Trade Unions, 1966; Principal, Dept of Employment (Indust. Trng and Indust. Relations), 1967–72; Dep. Chief Officer, Race Relations Bd, 1973–74; Sec., Health and Safety Commn, 1974–77; Asst Sec., Health and Safety Exec., 1977–82. Dir, Nailsworth Festival, 1992–96. *Club:* Royal Over-Seas League.

MUÑOZ-DEACON, Julio; Ambassador of Peru to the Court of St James's, since 2012, and to Ireland, since 2014; *b* 17 July 1950; *s* of Julio Ernesto Muñoz and Hortensia Deacon; *m* 1982, Marcela Chávez; one *s* one *d*. *Educ:* Pontifical Catholic Univ. of Peru (Arts and Humanities); Diplomatic Acad. of Peru (BA Internat. Relns 1978). Diplomatic Service, Peru: joined as Third Sec. of Chancery, Gen. Directorate of Protocol, 1974; Third Sec., 1976–78, Second Sec., 1978, Venezuela; Second Sec., 1979–82, First Sec., 1982, Perm. Mission to OAS, Washington, DC; Hd, Gen. Secretariat's Cabinet, 1982; First Sec., 1985, Counsellor, 1986, Minister Counsellor, 1988, Perm. Mission to Internat. Agencies, Geneva; Integration Dir, Under-Secretariat for Econ. Affairs, Cooperation and Integration, 1991; Sub-regl Orgns Dir, Gen. Directorate of Multilateral Affairs, 1992; Gen. Dir, Tech. Office of Integration, 1993; Minister, Belgium, Luxembourg and EU, 1994–96; Ambassador to Czech Republic, 1996–99; Econ. Orgns Dir, Under-Secretariat of Multilateral and Special Affairs, 1999–2000; Asia and Oceania Dir, Under-Secretariat of Europe, Africa, Asia and Oceania Affairs, 2000; Admin Gen. Dir, 2002; Advr on Admin to Minister of Foreign Affairs, 2002; Ambassador, Perm. Rep. to Council, ICAO, Montreal, 2002–07; Information Physical Security Advr to Minister of Foreign Affairs, 2007–08; Admin Under-Sec., 2008–09; Gen. Sec., Min. of Foreign Affairs, 2009–10; Ambassador to Germany, 2011–12. *Address:* Embassy of Peru, 52 Sloane Street, SW1X 9SP. *T:* (020) 7235 3802. *Clubs:* Travellers, Athenæum.

MUNRO, Sir Alan (Gordon), KCMG 1990 (CMG 1984); HM Diplomatic Service, retired; *b* 17 Aug. 1935; *s* of late Sir Gordon Munro, KCMG, MC and Lilian Muriel Beit; *m* 1962, Rosemary Grania Bacon; twin *s* two *d*. *Educ:* Wellington Coll.; Clare Coll., Cambridge (MA). MIPM. Mil. Service, 4/7 Dragoon Guards, 1953–55; Middle East Centre for Arab Studies, 1958–60; British Embassy, Beirut, 1960–62; Kuwait, 1961; FO, 1963–65; Head of Chancery, Benghazi, 1965–66 and Tripoli, 1966–68; FO, 1968–73; Consul (Commercial), 1973–74, Consul-Gen., 1974–77, Rio de Janeiro; Head of E African Dept, FCO, 1977–78; Head of Middle East Dept, FCO, 1979; Head of Personnel Ops Dept, FCO, 1979–81; Regl Marketing Dir (ME), MoD, 1981–83; Ambassador to Algeria, 1984–87; Dep. Under-Sec. of State, ME/Africa, FCO, 1987–89; Ambassador to Saudi Arabia, 1989–93. Director: Schroder Asseily & Co. Ltd, 1993–2000; Middle East Internat., 1997–2006; Dabbagh Gp (Jedda), 1998–2001; Internat. Trade & Investment Missions Ltd, 1998–2002; Advr, Tate and Lyle; Dir, Arab-British Chamber of Commerce, 2007– (Vice-Chm., 1993–2007). Gov., Imperial

Coll., 1994–2001; Chm., Imperial Coll. Trust, 2009–10. Chairman: Soc. for Algerian Studies, 1994–2010; Saudi-British Soc., 2002–11; Beit Trust for Central Africa; Vice Chm., BRCS, 1994–2001; Chm., Jt Cttee, Red Cross and St John, 2001–11. Order of King Abdul Aziz (Saudi Arabia), 1993; OStJ 2006. *Publications:* An Arabian Affair (Arab Storm): politics and diplomacy behind the Gulf War, 1996, 2nd edn 2006; (contrib.) Envoys to the Arab World, 2009; Keep the Flag Flying: a diplomatic memoir, 2012; reviews and articles on Middle East. *Recreations:* historic buildings, gardening, music, history. *Club:* Travellers.

MUNRO, Dr Alan James; Fellow, since 1962, and Master, 1995–2002, Christ's College, Cambridge; *b* 19 Feb. 1937; *s* of John Bennet Lorimer Munro, CB, CMG and Gladys, (Pat), Maie Forbes Munro (*née* Simmons); *m* 1960, Mary, *d* of John Gibson Robertson, Dumfries; two *s*. *Educ:* Edinburgh Acad.; Christ's Coll., Cambridge (BA 1960; MA; PhD 1964). Nat. Service, 2nd Lt Queen's Own Cameron Highlanders, 1955–57; Demonstrator, 1963–67, Lectr, 1967–68, Dept of Biochemistry, Cambridge Univ.; Scientific Officer, MRC Lab. of Molecular Biology, Cambridge, 1968–71; Lectr, 1971–80, Reader, 1980–89, in Immunology, Dept of Pathology, Cambridge Univ.; Jt Founder and Scientific Dir, Cantab Pharmaceuticals plc, 1989–95. Director: Babraham Inst. Ltd, 1996–2002; Blackwell Science Ltd, 1997–2001; Genome Research Ltd, 1997–2001; Blackwell Publishing Ltd, 2001–07; Paradigm Therapeutics Ltd, 2002–07; Chm., Lorantis Holdings Ltd, 2000–03. Fulbright Travel Schol. and Vis. Scientist, Salk Inst., La Jolla, Calif, 1965–66; Boerhaave Prof., Univ. of Leiden, 1976–77. Chm., Link Cttee on Cell Engrg, DTI, 1994–2002. Gov., Lister Inst. of Preventive Medicine, 1996–2002. *Publications:* (jtly) The Immune System, 1981; papers in scientific jls on immunology and molecular biology. *Address:* Christ's College, Cambridge CB2 3BU.

See also B. S. Munro.

MUNRO of Lindertis, Sir Alasdair (Thomas Ian), 6th Bt *cr* 1825; *b* 6 July 1927; *s* of Sir Thomas Torquil Alfonso Munro, 5th Bt and Beatrice Maude (*d* 1974), *d* of Robert Sanderson Whitaker; *S* father, 1985; *m* 1954, Marguerite Lillian, *d* of late Franklin R. Loy, Dayton, Ohio, USA; one *s* one *d*. *Educ:* Georgetown Univ., Washington, DC (BSS 1946); Univ. of Pennsylvania (MBA 1951); IMEDE, Lausanne. 2nd Lieut, USAF (previously US Army), 1946–53. Senior Vice-Pres., McCann-Erickson, New York, 1952–69; Pres., Jennings Real Estate, Waitsfield, Vermont, 1970–83. Founder, Dir (and Past Pres.), St Andrew's Soc. of Vermont, 1972–; Vice-Chm., Assoc. Bd of Directors, Howard Bank, Waitsfield, 1974–84; Founder, sometime Dir and Pres., Valley Area Assoc., Waitsfield, 1972–80. Chairman: Munro, Jennings & Doig, 1983–90; Highland Develt Gp, 1987–91. *Publications:* Scottish Antiques, 2004. *Recreations:* gardening, travel, collector/dealer in Scottish antiques, Scottish heritage matters. *Heir:* *s* Keith Gordon Munro [*b* 3 May 1959; *m* 1989, Jada Louise Elwell; one *s* one *d*]. *Address:* RiverRidge, Box 940, Waitsfield, VT 05673, USA.

MUNRO, Dr (Bruce) Sean, FRS 2011; Head, Division of Cell Biology, Medical Research Council Laboratory of Molecular Biology, Cambridge, since 2012; *b* Cambridge, 19 Aug. 1961; *s* of Dr Alan James Munro, *qv*; *m* 2004, Dr Katja Roeper; two *s*. *Educ:* Netherhall Sch.; University Coll., Oxford (BA 1983); Trinity Coll., Cambridge (PhD 1987). Postdoctoral Fellow, Harvard Univ., 1987–89; Mem., Scientific Staff, MRC Lab. of Molecular Biol., Cambridge, 1989–. Jun. Res. Fellow, Trinity Coll., Cambridge, 1986–92. Mem. EMBO 1997 (Mem. Council, 2000–06); FAAAS 2012. Dir, Co. of Biologists Ltd, 2012–. *Publications:* papers in scientific jls on molecular and cell biology. *Recreations:* entertaining my children, cooking, politics. *Address:* MRC Laboratory of Molecular Biology, Francis Crick Avenue, Cambridge CB2 0QH. *T:* (01223) 267028.

MUNRO, Colin Andrew, CMG 2002; HM Diplomatic Service, retired; international affairs consultant, since 2007; Associate, Ambassador Partnership LLP, since 2010; *b* 24 Oct. 1946; *s* of Capt. Frederick Bertram Munro and Jane Eliza (*née* Taylor); *m* 1967, Ehrengard Maria Heinrich; two *s*. *Educ:* George Watson's Coll., Edinburgh; Edinburgh Univ. (MA Hons Mod. Langs 1968); King's Coll., London (MA Internat. Studies 2002). Asst Principal, Bd of Inland Revenue, 1968–69; FCO, 1969–71; Third, later Second, Sec., Bonn, 1971–73; Second, later First, Sec., Kuala Lumpur, 1973–77; FCO, 1977; Private Sec. to Minister of State, 1979–80; Hd of Chancery, Bucharest, 1981–82; FCO, 1983; Asst Head of W European Dept, 1985–87; Dep. Hd of Mission, E Berlin, 1987–90; Consul Gen., Frankfurt, 1990–93; Hd of OSCE and Council of Europe Dept, FCO, 1993–97; Ambassador to Republic of Croatia, 1997–2000; Dep. High Rep., Mostar, 2001; rcds, 2002; UK Perm. Rep. to OSCE, Vienna, 2003–07. *Publications:* (contrib.) Korea and East Asia, 2013; contrib. Jl of Prince Albert Soc., Jl of Inst. of Contemp. British Hist., Jl of Vienna Univ. Inst. for Peace Research, Bulletin of German Historical Inst. London. *Recreations:* sports especially hockey, cricket, ski-ing, golf, history, music. *Clubs:* Reform; Royal Selangor (Kuala Lumpur); Rotary (Vienna North East).

MUNRO, Prof. Eileen Margaret, CBE 2012; PhD; Professor of Social Policy, London School of Economics and Political Science, since 2008; *b* Cirencester, 21 Oct. 1950; *d* of late Patrick Higgins and Margaret Higgins; *m* 1974, Alexander James Munro (marr. diss. 2000); three *d*. *Educ:* Cirencester Grammar Sch.; Univ. of Exeter (BA Hons Philos. 1971); Univ. of Edinburgh (Dip. Social Admin 1972); Univ. of Southampton (CQSW 1973); London Sch. of Econs and Pol Sci. (MSc Logic and Scientific Methods 1981; PhD 1990). Med. Social Worker, St Mary's Hosp., London, 1973–74; Social Worker, Leics Social Services Dept, 1974–75; Psychiatric Social Worker, Maudsley Hosp., London, 1975–79; London School of Economics and Political Science: Res. Fellow, 1993–95; Lectr, 1995–2003; Reader, 2003–08; Gov., 2007–. Zellerbach Prof., Univ. of Calif, Berkeley, 2005. Led ind. govt review of child protection in England, 2010–11 (report, Munro Review of Child Protection: a child-centred system, 2011). Hon. DLitt Tavistock Inst., UEL, 2012. *Publications:* Understanding Social Work: an empirical approach, 1998; Effective Child Protection, 2002, 2nd edn 2008; Child Protection, 2007; (jtly) Learning Together to Safeguard Children, 2008; articles in Children and Youth Services Rev., British Jl of Social Work, Child Abuse and Neglect, Health, Risk and Society, Risk Analysis, British Jl of Psychiatry, Jl of Forensic Psychiatry. *Address:* London School of Economics and Political Science, Houghton Street, WC2A 2AE. *T:* (020) 7955 7349, *Fax:* (020) 7955 7415. *E:* E.Munro@lse.ac.uk.

MUNRO, Graeme Neil, CVO 2005; FSAScot; Director and Chief Executive, Historic Scotland, 1991–2004; *b* 28 Aug. 1944; *s* of Daniel Munro and Nancy Kirkwood (*née* Smith); *m* 1972, Nicola Susan Wells (*see* N. S. Munro); one *s* one *d*. *Educ:* Daniel Stewart's Coll., Edinburgh; Univ. of St Andrews (MA Hons 1967). FSAScot 1990. Joined Scottish Office as Asst Principal, 1968; Scottish Development Department: Housing, 1968; Planning, 1968–70; Private Sec. to Head of Dept, 1971; Principal, Roads, 1972–74; Scottish Home and Health Department: Hosp. Services, 1974–76; Criminal Justice, 1976–79; Assistant Secretary: Dept of Agriculture and Fisheries for Scotland (Fisheries), 1979–83; NHS Funding, Scottish Home and Health Dept, 1983–87; Management and Orgn, Scottish Office Central Services, 1987–90; Dir, Historic Buildings and Monuments, Scotland, 1990–91. Member: Council, Cockburn Assoc. (Edinburgh Civic Trust), 2005–11 (former Mem., Mgt and Finance Cttee); Mgt Cttee, Rosslyn Chapel Trust, 2005– (Dep. Chm., 2007–); Trustee, Historic Scotland Foundn, 2007– (Chm., 2011–). Comr, Queen Street Gardens, 2011–. *Recreations:* gardening, walking, travel, reading, voluntary work in conservation and Third World fields. *Address:* 15 Heriot Row, Edinburgh EH3 6HP. *T:* (0131) 556 3201. *E:* gandnmunro@hotmail.com.

MUNRO, Sir Ian Kenneth, 17th Bt *cr* 1634, of Foulis-Obsdale, Ross-shire; *b* 5 April 1940; *s* of Sir Kenneth Munro, 16th Bt and Olive Freda (*née* Broome); *S* father, 2004, but his name does not appear on the Official Roll of the Baronetage. *Heir:* *cousin* Godfrey Roland Munro [*b* 1 July 1938; *m* 1985, Julie Pamela Gosling; two *s* one *d*].

MUNRO, Jamie Ross; Joint Founder and Managing Director, Greenbird Media Ltd, since 2012; *b* Reading, 14 June 1971; *s* of Ian and Pauline Munro; *m* Pippa Dalley; two *d*. *Educ:* Chiltern Edge Sch.; Henley Coll.; Wolverhampton Univ. (BA Hons). Sales Support Exec., BBC Worldwide (Americas), 1994–95; Sales Exec., BBC Library Sales, 1995–96; Publishing Licensing Manager, BBC Worldwide, 1996–98; Commercial Dir, Drama, Entertainment and Children's, BBC Commercial Agency, 1998–2005; involved in sale of Strictly Come Dancing and What Not To Wear to USA; Commercial Dir and Sen. Vice Pres., Internat. Prodn, Tiger Aspect Prodns, 2005–08 (progs incl. two series of Make Me a Supermodel); Jt Man. Dir, Shine TV, 2008–12. *Recreations:* karaoke, watching England and Harlequins play Rugby, TV. *Clubs:* Groucho, Soho House, Ivy.

MUNRO, Julia Henrietta; University Librarian, University of Reading, since 2001; *b* 21 Dec. 1952; *d* of Leslie H. and Joan B. Tebbitt; *m* 1975, Dr Peter M. G. Munro; one *s* one *d*. *Educ:* Imperial Coll., London (BSc 1975); City Univ. (MSc 1977); Univ. of Reading (MBA 2000). ARCS 1975; MCLIP 2002. Grad. trainee liby asst, Poly. of Central London, 1975–76; Assistant Librarian: Paediatric Res. Unit, Guy's Hosp. Med. Sch., 1977–79; Centre for Envmtl Technol., Imperial Coll., London, 1979–84; UCL, 1984–93; Dep. Librarian, Univ. of Reading, 1993–2001. Mem., Lifelong Learning UK Sector Skills Council, 2005–11. *Recreation:* family life with a neurotic Weimaraner and a punk cat. *Address:* University of Reading, Whiteknights, PO Box 223, Reading, Berks RG6 6AE. *T:* (0118) 378 8774, *Fax:* (0118) 378 6636. *E:* j.h.munro@reading.ac.uk.

MUNRO, Neil Christopher, CBE 2003; Head, Customer Contact Transformation Programme, HM Revenue and Customs, 2006–07; *b* 25 July 1947; *s* of late Alan and of Jean Munro; *m* 1987, Caroline Anne Virginia Smith; two *d*. *Educ:* Wallasey Grammar Sch.; St John's Coll., Oxford (BA Hons Mod. Hist., MA). MCIPD (MIPD 1993). Board of Inland Revenue, subsequently HM Revenue and Customs, 1970–2007: various posts in tax policy and mgt work; seconded to CBI as Head, Taxation Dept, 1978–80; Dep. Dir of Personnel, 1991–94; Director: Mgt Services, 1994–96; Tax Law Rewrite Project, 1996–2001; Revenue Policy: Corporate Services, 2001–05; Better Guidance Prog., 2005–06. *Recreations:* modern literature, music, football, cooking, family history. *Address:* 66 Lavington Road, Ealing, W13 9LS. *E:* neilmunro47@o2.co.uk.

MUNRO, Nicola Susan, CB 2006; Head of Scottish Executive Development Department, 2001–07; *b* 11 Jan. 1948; *d* of Ernest Derek Wells and Barbara Gurney Wells; *m* 1972, Graeme Neil Munro, *qv*; one *s* one *d*. *Educ:* Harrogate Grammar Sch.; Univ. of Warwick (BA Hons History). Scottish Office, later Scottish Executive, 1970–2007: Head of Div. (hosp. services, food, med. educn), Scottish Home and Health Dept, 1986–89; Head of Div. (urban and local economic policy), Scottish Office Industry Dept, 1989–92; Head of Div. (curriculum, assessment, careers service, educn industry links), Scottish Office Educn Dept, 1992–95; Under-Sec., Public Health Policy, Scottish Office, then Scottish Exec., Dept of Health, 1995–2000; Hd of Envmt Gp, Scottish Exec. Rural Affairs Dept, 2000–01. Member: Scottish Consumer Council, subseq. Consumer Focus Scotland, 2008–; Scottish Refugee Council, 2008–; Consumer Adv. Panel, Office of Rail and Road (formerly Rail Regulation), 2010–. *Recreations:* reading, travel, gardening, family, friends. *Address:* 15 Heriot Row, Edinburgh EH3 6HP.

MUNRO, Sarah Belinda McLeod; QC 2002; **Her Honour Judge Munro;** a Circuit Judge, since 2011; *b* Southampton, 29 Sept. 1960; *d* of John and Margaret Munro; *m* Chris Doe; one *s*. *Educ:* St Swithun's, Winchester; Univ. of Exeter (BA Hons Classics); Poly. of Central London (DipLaw); Council of Legal Educn. Called to the Bar, Inner Temple, 1984; Recorder, 2000–11. *Recreations:* golf, dog walking, cooking, watching sport, ski-ing. *Address:* Portsmouth Combined Court Centre, Winston Churchill Avenue, Portsmouth PO1 2EB.

MUNRO, Sean; *see* Munro, B. S.

MUNROE-BLUM, Prof. Heather Anne Elise Lilian, OC 2003; OQ 2009; PhD; FRSC; Principal and Vice-Chancellor, and Professor of Epidemiology and Biostatistics, McGill University, 2003–13, now Emeritus; Chairman, Canada Pension Plan Investment Board, since 2014 (Director, since 2011; Chairman, Corporate Governance Committee, since 2014); Director, Royal Bank of Canada, since 2011; *b* 25 Aug. 1950; *d* of Donald Munroe and late Dorothy Munroe; *m* 1970, Leonard Blum, screenwriter; one *d*. *Educ:* McMaster Univ. (BA, BSW 1974); Wilfrid Laurier Univ. (MSW 1975); Univ. of NC, Chapel Hill (PhD with Dist. 1983). Psychiatric Social Worker and Social Work Supervisor, McMaster Univ. Med. Centre and St Joseph's Hosp., 1975–79; McMaster University: Clinical Lectr, 1976–79, Asst Clinical Prof., 1979–84, Dept of Psychiatry; Asst Prof., Depts of Psychiatry and Clinical Epidemiol. and Biostatistics, 1984–89; University of Toronto: Prof., and Dean, Faculty of Social Work, 1989–93; Prof., and Vice-Pres., Res. and Internat. Relns, 1994–2002. Asst Prof., Dept of Social Work, Atkinson Coll., York Univ., 1982–84; Continuing Sen. Fellow, Massey Coll. 2010– (Associate Fellow, 1990–93; Associate Sen. Fellow, 1998–2000; Sen. Fellow, 2000–10). Director: Neurosci. Canada Partnership, 2001–05 (Hon. Mem., 2005–); Neurosci. Canada Foundn, 2001–; McGill Univ. Health Centre, 2003–13; Gairdner Foundn, 2014–. Member: Assoc. of Univs and Colls of Canada, 2003–13 (Chair, Standing Adv. Cttee on Univ. Res.; Mem., Exec. Cttee, 2007–13); Assoc. of Amer. Univs, 2003–13; Conf. des recteurs et des principaux des Univs de Québec, 2003–13 (Vice Pres., 2005; Pres., 2007–13); Adv. Bd, 2014–, Bd, 2015–, Center for Advanced Study in Behavioral Scis, Stanford Univ. Fellow, Assoc. for Clinical Psychosocial Res., 1991; FRSC, 2002. Dr *hc*: Montréal, 2004; Edinburgh, 2005; École Normale Supérieure de Lyon, 2005; Hon. LLD: Toronto, 2005; Wilfrid Laurier, 2005; McMaster, 2007; Hon. DSc: N Carolina at Chapel Hill, 2008; Ottawa, 2008; Hon. DLit: Glasgow, 2013; Western, 2014. Outstanding Alumni Award, Sch. of Public Health, Univ. of NC, Chapel Hill, 1992; Dist. Alumni Award, McMaster Univ., 1995. *Publications:* (jtly) Schizophrenia in Focus: a psychosocial approach to treatment and rehabilitation, 1983; (jtly) PDQ Epidemiology, 1989; (ed jtly) Borderline Personality Disorder: an empirical perspective, 1992; (with E. Marziali) Interpersonal Group Psychotherapy for Borderline Personality Disorder, 1994; Growing Ontario's Innovation System: the strategic role of university research, 1999; contribs to books and numerous articles in learned jls. *Club:* Mount Royal.

MUNROW, Roger Davis, CB 1993; Chief Master of the Supreme Court of Judicature (Chancery Division), 1986–92, retired (Master, 1985–86); *b* 20 March 1929; *s* of late William Davis Munrow, CBE and Constance Caroline Munrow (*née* Moorcroft); *m* 1st, 1957, Marie Jane Beresford (*d* 2001); three *d*; 2nd, 2001, Norma Eileen Boucher (*d* 2014). *Educ:* Bryanston School; Oriel College, Oxford (MA). Solicitor. Entered Treasury Solicitor's Dept as Legal Assistant, 1959; Senior Legal Assistant, 1965; Assistant Treasury Solicitor, 1973; Principal Asst Treasury Solicitor, 1981. *Recreation:* swimming. *Address:* 5 Mallard Close, Harnham, Salisbury, Wilts SP2 8JB.

MUNT, Tessa; *b* Surrey, 16 Oct. 1959; *m* 1992, Martin Munt; one *s* one *d* and one step *d*. *Educ:* Reigate Co. Sch. for Girls; Sutton High Sch. Lectr, SE Essex Coll. of Arts and Technol., 1992–94; Adminr, Holiday Explorers, 1994; supply teacher, Samuel Ward Upper Sch., Haverhill, 1994–95; Manager, Community Resource Unit, Suffolk Social Services, 1994–96; PA to Phil Edmonds, 1996–98; fee-earner: Franks Charlesly and Co., 1996–98; Jay Benning and Pelts, 1998–99; Forsters, 1999–. Contested (C): S Suffolk, 2001; Ipswich, Nov. 2001; Wells, 2005. MP (Lib Dem) Wells, 2010–15; contested (Lib Dem) same seat, 2015. PPS to Sec. of State for Business, Innovation and Skills, 2012–15. Member, Select Committee: on Educn, 2010–12; on Admin, 2010–15.

MURAD, Prof. Ferid, MD, PhD; University Professor, Department of Biochemistry and Molecular Biology, and Director, Institute of Molecular and Cellular Signalling, George Washington University, since 2011; *b* 14 Sept. 1936; *s* of John Murad and Josephine Bowman; *m* 1958, Carol A. Leopold; one *s* four *d*. *Educ:* DePauw Univ. (BA 1958); Sch. of Medicine, Western Reserve Univ. (MD 1965; PhD 1965). University of Virginia: Dir, Clin. Res. Center, Sch. of Medicine, 1971–81; Prof., Depts of Internal Medicine and Pharmacology, 1975–81; Stanford University: Prof., Depts of Internal Medicine and Pharmacology, 1981–88; acting Chm., Dept of Medicine, 1986–88; Adjunct Prof., Dept of Pharmacology, Northwestern Univ., 1988–96; Prof. and Chm., Dept of Integrative Biol., Pharmacol. and Physiol., Houston Medical Sch., 1997–2011, and Dir, Inst. of Molecular Med., Houston, 1999–2011, Univ. of Texas. Albert and Mary Lasker Foundn Award for Basic Research, 1996; Nobel Prize in Medicine or Physiology, 1998. *Publications:* papers, published lecture. *Recreations:* golf, carpentry. *Address:* Department of Biochemistry and Molecular Biology, George Washington University, 2300 Eye Street NW, Suite 530, Washington, DC 20037, USA. *Fax:* (202) 9945040.

MURAKAMI, Takashi; artist; *b* Tokyo, 1 Feb. 1962. *Educ:* Tokyo National Univ. of Fine Arts and Music (BFA 1986; MFA 1988; PhD 1993). Works include fine art pieces, design collaborations and curatorial projects. *Solo exhibitions* include: Bard Coll. Center for Curatorial Studies, NY, 1999; Mus. of Contemp. Art, Tokyo, and Mus. of Fine Arts, Boston, 2001; Fondation Cartier pour l'art contemporain, Paris, 2002; Rockefeller Center, NY, 2003; Fondazione Sandretto Re Rebaudengo, Turin, 2005; (retrospective) Mus. of Contemp. Art, LA, 2007; Gagosian Gall., London, 2009. Dir of film, Jellyfish Eyes, 2013. *Publications:* Superflat, 2000; (jtly) My Reality: contemporary art and the culture of Japanese animation, 2001; (ed) Little Boy: the arts of Japan's exploding subculture, 2004. *Recreation:* cactus growing. *Address:* Kaikai Kiki Co. Ltd, Marunuma Art Residence, 493 Kamiuchimagi, Asaka-city, Saitama 351–0001, Japan.

MURDIN, Paul Geoffrey, OBE 1988; PhD; FInstP; Senior Fellow, Institute of Astronomy, Cambridge University, since 2002; *b* 5 Jan. 1942; *s* of Robert Murdin and Ethel Murdin (*née* Chubb); *m* 1964, Lesley Carol Milburn; two *s* one *d*. *Educ:* Trinity School of John Whitgift; Wadham Coll., Oxford (BA Physics); Univ. of Rochester, NY (PhD Physics and Astronomy). FRAS 1970; FInstP 1992. Res. Associate, Univ. of Rochester, 1970–71; Sen. Res. Associate, Royal Greenwich Observatory, 1971–74; Sen. Res. Scientist, Anglo-Australian Observatory, NSW, 1975–78; Royal Greenwich Observatory: Prin. Sci. Officer, 1979–81; Hd of La Palma Operations, 1981–87; Hd of Astronomy Div., 1987–90; Dir, Royal Observatory, Edinburgh, 1991–93; Head of Astronomy, PPARC, and Dir of Sci., BNSC, 1994–2001. Sen. Mem., Wolfson Coll., Cambridge, 1990–; Vis. Prof., Liverpool John Moores Univ., 2002–. Mem. Bd of Trustees, Nat. Maritime Museum, 1990–2001. Pres., Faulkes Telescope Corp., 1999–2005. Member: Royal Astronomical Soc., 1963– (Councillor, 1997–99; Vice-Pres., 2000–01; Treas., 2001–11); European Astronomical Soc., 1991– (Vice-Pres., 1991–93; Pres., 1993–97). RAS Service Award, 2012. *Publications:* The Astronomer's Telescope (with Patrick Moore), 1963; Radio Waves from Space, 1969; (with L. Murdin) The New Astronomy, 1974; (with D. Allen and D. Malin) Catalogue of the Universe, 1980; (with D. Malin) Colours of the Stars, 1985; End in Fire, 1989; Encyclopedia of Astronomy & Astrophysics, 2001; Firefly Encyclopedia of Astronomy, 2004; Full Meridian of Glory, 2009; Secrets of the Universe, 2009; Pursuit of Gazelles, 2011; Mapping the Universe: the interactive history of astronomy, 2012; Are we being watched?: the search for life in the Cosmos, 2013; over 150 pubns in astronom. and other sci. jls, principally Monthly Notices of RAS. *Recreations:* writing, music, natural history, history of art. *Address:* Institute of Astronomy, Madingley Road, Cambridge CB3 0HA. *E:* paul@murdin.com.

MURDOCH, Prof. Alison Pamela, MD; FRCOG; FRSB; Professor of Reproductive Medicine, University of Newcastle upon Tyne, since 2003; Consultant Gynaecologist, Newcastle Hospitals NHS Trust, since 1991; *b* 12 Feb. 1951; *d* of John Peter Smith and Ruby Smith (*née* Easton); *m* 1972, Ian James Murdoch; two *s* two *d*. *Educ:* Univ. of Edinburgh (BSc 1972; MB ChB 1975; MD 1987). MRCOG 1982, FRCOG 2001; FRSB (FSB 2012). Early career researching in field of reproductive endocrinology; estabd clinic for infertility treatment, NE England, leading to regl clin. service, Newcastle Fertility Centre at Life. Res. interests now relate to human pre-implantation embryology, mitochondrial transfer techniques and regulatory issues of egg and embryo donation to res. Founder Mem., Newcastle Embryonic Stem Cell Gp, 2001–; Chm., British Fertility Soc., 2002–06; Member: Nuffield Council on Bioethics, 2007–13; Adv. Cttee on Safety of Blood, Tissues and Organs, 2013–. *Address:* Newcastle Fertility Centre at Life, International Centre for Life, Times Square, Newcastle upon Tyne NE1 4EP. *T:* (0191) 213 8213.

MURDOCH, Elisabeth, (Mrs M. R. Freud); Chairman, Shine Group (formerly Shine Ltd), 2001–14 (Chief Executive, 2001–12); *b* 22 Aug. 1968; *d* of Keith Rupert Murdoch, *qv* and Anna Murdoch Mann (*née* Torv); *m* 1st, 1994, Elkin Kwesi Pianim; two *d*; 2nd, 2001, Matthew Rupert Freud, *qv*; one *s* one *d*. *Educ:* Vassar Coll., NY (BA). Dir of Programming, KSTU-TV, 1994–95; Pres. and CEO, EP Communications, 1995–96; Man. Dir, BSkyB Plc, 1996–2001. Trustee, Tate, 2008–. McTaggart Lectr, Edinburgh Internat. TV Fest., 2012.

MURDOCH, His Honour Gordon Stuart; QC 1995; a Circuit Judge, 2002–15; *b* 7 June 1947; *s* of late Ian William Murdoch and Margaret Henderson McLaren Murdoch; *m* 1976, Sally Kay Cummings; two *s*. *Educ:* Falkirk High Sch.; Sidney Sussex Coll., Cambridge (MA, LLB). Called to the Bar, Inner Temple, 1970; a Recorder, 1995–2002. *Recreations:* music, walking.

MURDOCH, John Derek Walter; Director of Art Collections, The Huntington Library, Art Collections and Botanical Gardens, California, 2002–12; Visiting Scholar, Ecole du Louvre, 2013; *b* 1 April 1945; *s* of James Duncan and Elsie Elizabeth Murdoch; *m* 1st, 1967, Prue Smijth-Windham (marr. diss. 1986); one *s* two *d*; 2nd, 1990, Susan Barbara Lambert, *qv* (marr. diss. 2007); 3rd, 2007, Allison Browne Freeman; one *s* two *d*. *Educ:* Shrewsbury Sch.; Magdalen Coll., Oxford (BA); King's Coll., London (MPhil). Asst Keeper, Birmingham City Art Gall., 1969–73; Victoria & Albert Museum: Asst, then Dep. Keeper, Dept of Paintings, 1973–86; Keeper of Prints, Drawings, Photographs and Paintings, 1986–89; Asst Dir in charge of Collections, 1989–93; Dir, Courtauld Inst. Gall., 1993–2002. Vis. Fellow, British Art Center, Yale Univ., 1979. Trustee: William Morris Gall., Walthamstow, 1975–2002 (Dep. Chm., 1997–2002); Dove Cottage, Grasmere, 1982–2002. *Publications:* David Cox, 1970; Byron, 1974; English Watercolours, 1977; The English Miniature, 1981; Discovery of the Lake District, 1984; A Sort of National Property, 1985; Painters and the Derby China Works, 1986; Seventeenth Century Portrait Miniatures in the Collection of the Victoria and Albert Museum, 1997; contrib. to Rev. of English Studies, Jl of Warburg and Courtauld Insts, Burlington Magazine, Apollo. *Address:* 34 Effingham Street, Ramsgate, Kent CT11 9AT.

MURDOCH, (Keith) Rupert, AC 1984; publisher; Executive Chairman, News Corporation, United States, since 2013 (Chief Executive Officer, 1979–2013; Chairman, 1991–2013); Executive Chairman, 21st Century Fox, since 2013 (Chief Executive, 2013–15); *b* 11 March 1931; *s* of late Sir Keith Murdoch and Dame Elisabeth Joy Murdoch, AC, DBE; *m* Patricia Booker (marr. diss.); one *d*; *m* 1967, Anna Torv (marr. diss. 1999); two *s* one *d*; *m* 1999, Wendi Deng (marr. diss. 2013); two *d*. Dir, News International plc, UK, 1969–2012 (Chm., 1969–87 and 1994–95; Chief Exec., 1969–81; Man. Dir, 1982–83); Chm., News America Publishing Inc.; Dir, Times Newspapers Hldgs Ltd, 1981–2012 (Chm., 1982–90 and 1994–2012); Chm. and Chief Exec. Officer, Fox Entertainment Gp Inc., 1998–; Chm., British Sky Broadcasting, 1999–2007. KSG 1998. *Address:* News Corporation, 1211 Avenue of the Americas, New York, NY 10036, USA.

See also E. Murdoch.

MURDOCH, Susan Barbara; *see* Lambert, S. B.

MURE, James Douglas McFarlane Haye; QC (Scot.) 2009; *b* Edinburgh, 4 Dec. 1962; *s* of Douglas Mure and Betteane Mure; *m* 1992, Lesley Miller; one *s* two *d*. *Educ:* Edinburgh Acad.; Clare Coll., Cambridge (BA Hons Hist. 1984; MA 1987); Edinburgh Univ. (LLB 1991; DipLP 1992). HM Diplomatic Service, 1984–88; admitted Faculty of Advocates, 1995; Standing Jun. Counsel, 2001–07, First Standing Jun. Counsel, 2007–09, Scottish Exec., later Scottish Govt. *Recreations:* music, singing. *Address:* Faculty of Advocates, Parliament House, Edinburgh EH1 1RF.

MURE, Kenneth Nisbet; QC (Scot.) 1989; *b* 11 April 1947; *o s* of late Robert and Katherine Mure. *Educ:* Cumbernauld Jun. Sch.; Glasgow High Sch.; Glasgow Univ. (MA, LLB). CTA (Fellow). Admitted to Scots Bar, 1975; called to English Bar, Gray's Inn, 1990. Lectr, Faculty of Law, Glasgow Univ., 1971–83. Temp. Sheriff, 1983–99. A Tribunal Judge (Tax and Chancery; Criminal Injuries Compensation) (formerly Mem., CICAP, and Chm., VAT Tribunal), 2000–. *Address:* Advocates' Library, Edinburgh EH1 1RF.

MURERWA, Dr Herbert Muchemwa; Member of Senate (Zanu PF) Goromonzi, Zimbabwe, since 2008; Minister of Lands and Rural (formerly Land) Resettlement, since 2009; *b* 31 May 1941; *m* 1969, Ruth Chipo; one *s* four *d*. *Educ:* Harvard Univ.; EdD (Educational Planning). Economic Affairs Officer, UN Economic Commission for Africa, Addis Ababa, 1978–80; Permanent Sec., Min. of Manpower Planning, 1980–81; Permanent Sec., Min. of Labour and Social Services, 1982–84; High Comr for Zimbabwe in UK, 1984–90; MP (Zanu PF) Goromonzi, 1990–2008; Minister: for the Envmt and Tourism, 1990–95; of Industry and Commerce, 1995–96; of Finance, 1996–2000 and 2002–07; of Higher Educn and Technol., 2000–01; of Internat. Trade and Technol., 2001–02; of Higher and Tertiary Educn, 2004.

MURFIN, Dr David Edward; Principal in general medical practice, Ammanford, 1974–2006; *b* 15 June 1946; *s* of Leslie Walter Murfin and Elizabeth Ann Murfin; *m* 1972, Ann Margaret Lewis; one *s* one *d*. *Educ:* Gowerton Boys' Grammar Sch.; King's Coll. London; St George's Hosp., London. Adviser to ABPI, 1991–2006. Mem. Council, RCGP, 1984–90 and 1993–96 (Vice Chm., 1994–96); Mem., Standing Cttee on Medicines, RCPCH, 1996–2001. Mem. Cttee, Retired Fellows Soc., RSocMed, 2015–. *Recreations:* reading, walking, cycling. *Address:* Longmeadow, 30 Llandeilo Road, Llandybie, Ammanford, Carmarthen SA18 3JB. *T:* (01269) 850914.

MURFITT, Catriona Anne Campbell; Her Honour Judge Murfitt; a Circuit Judge, since 2007; *b* London, 16 Jan. 1958; *d* of Dr A. Ian Campbell Murfitt and Anne Murfitt (*née* Ritchie); partner, Iain Hutton-Jamieson. *Educ:* St Mary's Sch. Ascot; Leicester Poly. Sch. of Law (BA Hons Law). Called to the Bar, Gray's Inn, 1981; practised at Family Bar, 1 Mitre Court, then 1 Hare Court, 1981–2007; Asst Recorder, 1998–2000; Recorder, 2000–07. Mem. Cttee, Family Law Bar Assoc., 1997–2003; Mem., Professional Complaints and Conduct Cttee, Bar Council, 2001–04. *Recreations:* creating a garden, art, landscapes, architecture, sacred choral music, textiles, ski-ing. *Address:* c/o Chelmsford County Court, Priory Place, New London Road, Chelmsford, Essex CM2 0PP. *T:* (01245) 264670. *E:* catriona.murfitt@googlemail.com.

MURGATROYD, Prof. Walter, PhD; Professor of Thermal Power, Imperial College of Science and Technology, 1968–86, now Professor Emeritus; Rockefeller International Fellow, Princeton University, 1979; *b* 15 Aug. 1921; *m* 1952, Denise (*née* Schlumberger) (*d* 2014); one *s* one *d* (and one *s* decd). *Educ:* St Catharine's Coll., Cambridge. BA 1946, PhD 1952. Hawker Aircraft Ltd, 1942–44; Rolls Royce Ltd, 1944–46; Univ. of Cambridge, 1947–54; UK Atomic Energy Authority, Harwell, 1954–56; Head of Dept of Nuclear Engineering, Queen Mary Coll., Univ. of London, 1956–67, and Dean of Engineering, 1966–67. Member: British-Greek Mixed Commn, 1963–78; British-Belgian Mixed Commn, 1964–78; British-Austrian Mixed Commn, 1965–78. Specialist Adviser to H of C Select Cttee on Energy, 1980–90. *Publications:* contrib. to various scientific and technical journals. *Recreation:* music.

MURIA, Sir (Gilbert) John Baptist, Kt 1995; Chief Justice, Kiribati, since 2011; *b* 2 Feb. 1953; *s* of late John Baptist Manumate and of Adriana Gala; *m* 1982, Rosemary Kekealu; one *s* three *d*. *Educ:* Univ. of Papua New Guinea (LLB). Called to the Bar: PNG, 1980; Solomon Is, 1981. Sen. Crown Counsel, Solomon Is, 1980; Sen. Legal Officer, 1981–83; Chief Legal Officer, 1984–87; Dep. Public Solicitor, 1987–89; Public Solicitor, 1989–91; Actg Attorney Gen., 1989; Puisne Judge, High Court of Solomon Is, 1991–93; Chief Justice, Solomon Is, 1993–2003; a Judge of Supreme Court, Belize, 2007–10. *Address:* High Court of Kiribati, Betio, Tarawa, Republic of Kiribati.

MURIE, John Andrew, MD; FRCSGlas, FRCSE; Consultant Vascular Surgeon: Spire Murrayfield Hospital, since 1989; Royal Infirmary of Edinburgh, 1989–2014; Professor of Surgery, National University of Malaysia, 2011–14; *b* 7 Aug. 1949; *s* of John Andrew Murie and Jessie Murie (*née* Sutherland); *m* 1977, Edythe Munn; one *d*. *Educ:* Univ. of Glasgow (BSc 1st Cl. Hons Biochem. 1971; MB ChB Hons 1975; MD 1984); MA Oxon 1984. FRCSGlas 1979; FRCSE 1993. Clin. Reader in Surgery, Nuffield Dept of Surgery, Univ. of Oxford and Fellow, Green Coll., Oxford, 1984–89; Hon. Consultant Surgeon, John Radcliffe Hosp., Oxford, 1984–89; Clin. Dir, Gen. and Vascular Surgery, Royal Infirmary of Edinburgh, 1995–2000; Hon. Sen. Lectr, Univ. of Edinburgh, 1989–2011. British Journal of Surgery: Mem. Editl Team, 1989–96; Jt Sen. Ed., 1996–2002; Editor in Chief, 2002–10. Mem., Nat. Panel of Specialists, NHS Scotland, 2000–05. Member of Council: Assoc. of Surgeons of GB and Ireland, 1994–99 (Hon. Editl Sec., 1996–99); Vascular Surgical Soc. of GB and Ireland, 1998–2001; RCPSG, 1998–2006. *Publications:* (ed with J. J. Earnshaw) The Evidence for Vascular Surgery, 1999, 2nd edn 2006; contrib. numerous chapters in textbooks and papers in learned jls on general theme of surgery (particularly vascular surgery). *Recreations:* golf, reading, food and wine. *Address:* Spire Murrayfield Hospital, 122 Corstorphine Road, Edinburgh EH12 6UD. *T:* (0131) 334 0363; 28 Mortonhall Road, Edinburgh EH9 2HN.

MURLEY, Richard Andrew; Managing Director, since 2006 and Executive Vice Chairman, since 2010, N. M. Rothschild & Sons Ltd; *b* 7 Jan. 1957; *s* of Alan and Anne Murley; *m* 1986, Penelope Wiseman; two *s* one *d*. *Educ:* Christ Church, Oxford (MA). Admitted solicitor, 1981; with Linklaters & Paines, 1979–81; Dir, Kleinwort Benson Ltd, subseq. Dresdner Kleinwort Benson, 1981–98; Man. Dir, Goldman Sachs Internat., 1998–2006; Dir Gen., Panel on Takeovers and Mergers, 2003–05; Co-Hd, UK Investment Banking, N. M. Rothschild & Sons Ltd, 2006–10. Member: Financial Reporting Review Panel, 2003–14; Code Cttee, Panel on Takeovers and Mergers, 2012–. Dir, University Coll. London Hosps NHS Foundn Trust, 2008– (Chm., 2010–). Trustee, Crisis, 2012–. *Recreations:* golf, sailing, ski-ing. *Address:* N. M. Rothschild & Sons Ltd, New Court, St Swithin's Lane, EC4N 8AL. *T:* (020) 7280 5000.

MURNAGHAN, Dermot John; Presenter: Sky News Today, since 2008; Eggheads, BBC2; *b* 26 Dec. 1957; *s* of late Vincent Murnaghan and of Wendy Murnaghan (*née* Bush); *m* 1989, Maria Keegan; one *s* three *d*. *Educ:* Sussex Univ. (BA 1979, MA History 1980); City Univ. (Postgrad. Dip. Journalism, 1983). Presenter, Business Prog., Channel 4, 1984–88; correspondent, EBC Switzerland, 1988–89; presenter: Channel 4 Daily, 1989–92; Lunchtime

News, ITN, 1992–99; ITV Nightly News, 1999–2001; ITV Evening News, 2001–02; BBC Breakfast, 2002–07; presenter: The Big Story, ITV, 1993–97; Britain's Most Wanted, ITV, 1997–2002. Interview of the Year Award, RTS, 1998; Newscaster of the Year Award, TRIC, 2000. *Recreations:* running, film, football, sailing, chess. *Address:* Sky News, British Sky Broadcasting, Grant Way, Isleworth, Middx TW7 5QD.

MURPHY, Baroness *cr* 2004 (Life Peer), of Aldgate in the City of London; **Elaine Murphy,** MD, PhD; FRCPsych; Chairman, Council, St George's, University of London, 2006–10; academic psychiatrist, 1983–2006; *b* Nottingham, 16 Jan. 1947; *d* of Roger Lawson and Nell Lawson (*née* Allitt); *m* 1st, 1969, John Matthew Murphy (marr. diss. 2001); 2nd, 2001, Michael Alfred Robb, *qv*. *Educ:* Univ. of Manchester Med. Sch. (MB, ChB 1971; MD 1979); PhD UCL 2000. FRCPsych 1986. Prof. of Psychiatry of Old Age, UMDS of Guy's and St Thomas' Hosps, 1983–96; Res. Fellow, Wellcome Inst. for History of Medicine, 1996–2005; Dist Gen. Manager, Lewisham and N Southwark HA, 1988–90; Chairman: City and Hackney NHS Trust, 1996–99; E London and the City HA, 1999–2002; NE London Strategic HA, 2002–06. Vice-Chm., Mental Health Act Commn, 1988–94. Hon. Prof. of Old Age Psychiatry, QMW, 1995–2006. *Publications:* Dementia and Mental Illness in Older People, 1986, 2nd edn 1993; Affective Disorders in the Elderly, 1986; After the Asylums, 1991; The Moated Grange, 2015; papers on mental disorder, social policy and social history. *Recreations:* Italy, social history research. *Address:* House of Lords, SW1A 0PW.

MURPHY, Andrew John; Sheriff of Tayside Central and Fife at Falkirk, 1991–2005; *b* 16 Jan. 1946; *s* of Robert James Murphy and Robina Murphy (*née* Scott); *m* 1980, Susan Margaret Thomson; two *s* two *d*. *Educ:* Allan Glen's School, Glasgow; Edinburgh Univ. (MA, LLB). 2nd Lieut RA (V), 1971–73; Flt Lieut RAF, 1973–75. Admitted to Faculty of Advocates, Scottish Bar, 1970; called to Bar, Middle Temple, 1990; Crown Counsel, Hong Kong, 1976–79; Standing Junior Counsel to Registrar General for Scotland, 1982–85; Temporary Sheriff, 1983–85; Sheriff of Grampian, Highland and Islands at Banff and Peterhead, 1985–91. *Address:* c/o Amethyst Chambers, 86/87 Temple Avenue, EC4Y 0HP. *T:* (020) 7936 4966.

MURPHY, Brian Gordon; Building Societies' Ombudsman, 1992–99; *b* 18 Oct. 1940; *s* of Albert and Doris Murphy; *m* 1973, Judith Ann Parkinson. *Educ:* Mill Hill Sch. Articled Smiles & Co.; admitted Solicitor, 1966; with Roythorne & Co. and Russell & DuMoulin, Canada; Partner: Knapp Fishers, 1968–87; Farrer & Co., 1987–92. Pt-time Chm., Employment (formerly Industrial) Tribunals, 1991–92 and 2000–03. Vice-Chm., Incorp. Council of Law Reporting for Eng. and Wales, 1992–96; Mem. Council, Law Soc., 1982–93 (Chm., Employment Law Cttee, 1987–90); Pres., Westminster Law Soc., 1983–84. *Recreations:* golf, theatre, photography, travel. *Club:* Phyllis Court (Henley).

MURPHY, Christopher Philip Yorke; political lecturer; *b* 20 April 1947; *s* of Philip John and Dorothy Betty Murphy; *m* 1969, Sandra Gillian Ashton. *Educ:* Devonport High Sch.; The Queen's Coll., Oxford (MA). Formerly Associate Dir, D'Arcy MacManus & Masius. President, Oxford Univ. Conservative Assoc., 1967; held number of Conservative Party offices, 1968–72. Parish Councillor, Windlesham, Surrey, 1972–76. Contested (C): Bethnal Green and Bow, Feb. 1974, Oct. 1974. MP (C) Welwyn Hatfield, 1979–87. Vice-Chairman: Parly Urban and New Town Affairs Cttee, 1980–87; Parly Arts and Heritage Cttee, 1981–86; Mem., Select Cttee on Statutory Instruments, 1980–87 (rep of cttee on Commonwealth Delegated Legislation Cttee, 1980–87); UK Delegate to Council of Europe/WEU, 1983–87 (Hon. Associate, 1988). Vice-President: C of E Artistic Heritage Commn, 1984–87; C of E Youth & Drugs Commn, 1986–87. Member: Nat. Cttee for 900th Anniversary of Domesday Book, 1986; Chief Pleas of Sark (Parlt), 1989–90 (Vice-Pres., Internat. Cttee of Chief Pleas, 1989–90); Arts Council of Bailiwick of Guernsey, 1988–90; Council, Société Guernesiaise, 1988–90. Life Mem., CPA, 1987. Hon. Sec., Société Sercquiaise, 1988–90. Sec., Sodor & Man Diocesan Synod, and Bishop's Advr, 1991–2000; Chapter Clerk, St German's Cathedral, 1992–2000; Diocesan Sec., Dio. of Sodor and Man, 1993–2000; Secretary: Diocesan Bd of Finance, 1993–2000; Church Comrs for IOM, 1993–2000; Legislative Cttee, 1997–2000; DAC for Care of Churches, 1997–2000. FRSA. Freeman, City of London, 1984. Hon. Citizen, Cork, 1985. *Recreations:* arts, heritage, travel, conservation, walking. *Club:* Oxford Union Society.

MURPHY, Conor Terence; Member (SF) Newry and Armagh, Northern Ireland Assembly, 1998–July 2012 and since June 2015; *b* 10 July 1963; *m* Catherine; one *s* one *d*. *Educ:* St Colman's Coll., Newry; Univ. of Ulster; Queen's Univ., Belfast (MA). Mem. (SF), Newry and Mourne DC, 1989–97. Minister for Regl Develt, NI, 2007–11. Contested (SF) Newry and Armagh, 2001. MP (SF) Newry and Armagh, 2005–15. *Address:* Northern Ireland Assembly, Parliament Buildings, Ballymiscaw, Stormont, Belfast BT4 3XX.

MURPHY, Denis; *b* 2 Nov. 1948; *s* of late John Murphy and of Josephine Murphy; *m* (separated); one *s* one *d*. *Educ:* St Cuthbert's Grammar Sch., Newcastle upon Tyne; Northumberland Coll. Apprentice electrician, 1965–69; underground electrician, Ellington Colliery, 1969–94. Mem. (Lab) Wansbeck DC, 1990–97 (Leader, 1994–97). MP (Lab) Wansbeck, 1997–2010.

MURPHY, Dervla; writer; *b* 28 Nov. 1931; *d* of Fergus Murphy and Kathleen Rochfort-Dowling; one *d*. *Educ:* Ursuline Convent, Waterford. American Irish Foundn Literary Award, 1975; Christopher Ewart-Biggs Meml Prize, 1978; Irish Amer. Cultural Inst. Literary Award, 1985. *Publications:* Full Tilt, 1965, 11th edn 1995; Tibetan Foothold, 1966, 5th edn 2000; The Waiting Land, 1967, 7th edn 1998; In Ethiopia with a Mule, 1968, 7th edn 1994; On a Shoe String to Coorg, 1976, 7th edn 1995; Where the Indus is Young, 1977, 7th edn 1995; A Place Apart, 1978, 4th edn 1987; Wheels Within Wheels, 1979, 6th edn 2001; Race to the Finish?, 1981, 2nd edn 1982; Eight Feet in the Andes, 1983, 7th edn 1994; Muddling Through in Madagascar, 1985, 6th edn 1998; Ireland, 1985; Tales from Two Cities, 1987, 5th edn 1999; (ed) Embassy to Constantinople, the Travels of Lady Mary Wortley Montague, 1988; In Cameroon with Egbert, 1989; Transylvania and Beyond, 1992, 4th edn 1993; The Ukimwi Road, 1993, 3rd edn 1994; South from the Limpopo, 1997, 3rd edn 1998; Visiting Rwanda, 1998; One Foot in Laos, 1999, 2nd edn 2000; Through the Embers of Chaos: Balkan journeys, 2002, 2nd edn 2003; Through Siberia by Accident, 2005, 2nd edn 2006; Silverland: beyond the Urals, 2006, 2nd edn 2007; The Island that Dared: Cuban journeys, 2008, 2nd edn 2010; Encounters in Gaza, 2012; Between River and Sea: encounters in Israel and Palestine, 2015. *Recreations:* reading, music, cycling, swimming, walking. *Address:* The Old Market, Lismore, Co. Waterford, Ireland.

MURPHY, Fiona Clare; barrister, Doughty Street Chambers, since 2013; *b* Belfast, 17 June 1966; *d* of Eugene Murphy and Rosaleen Murphy; partner, 2001, Sam Craig. *Educ:* Dominican Coll., Fort William; London Sch. of Econs and Pol Sci. (LLB); Coll. of Law. Admitted Solicitor, 1993; Solicitor, B. M. Birnberg & Co., 1992–98; Founder Partner, Bhatt Murphy, 1998–2013; called to the Bar, Gray's Inn, 2013. Member: Police Action Lawyers Gp, 1990–; Inquest Lawyers Gp, 1992–. *Recreations:* art and architecture, open spaces. *Address:* Doughty Street Chambers, 53–54 Doughty Street, WC1N 2LS. *T:* (020) 7404 1313, *Fax:* (020) 7404 2283. *E:* f.murphy@doughtystreet.co.uk.

MURPHY, Foster; *see* Murphy, R. S. F.

MURPHY, Gerard Martin, PhD; Senior Managing Director, since 2008, and Chairman, since 2009, Blackstone Group International Partners LLP (formerly Blackstone Group International Ltd); *b* 6 Nov. 1955; *m*; two *s*. *Educ:* University Coll., Cork (BSc, PhD 1980); University Coll., Dublin (MBS 1983). Various exec. posts in Ireland, UK and USA, Grand Metropolitan plc, 1978–91; Chief Executive Officer: Greencore Group plc, 1991–95; NFC plc, subseq. Exel plc, 1995–2000; Carlton Communications plc, 2000–03; Kingfisher plc, 2003–08. Non-executive Director: Novar plc (formerly Caradon plc), 1997–2003; Abbey National plc, 2004–05; Reckitt Benckiser plc, 2005–08; British American Tobacco plc, 2009–. *Address:* Blackstone Group International Partners LLP, 40 Berkeley Square, W1J 5AL.

MURPHY, Prof. Gillian, PhD; FMedSci; Professor of Cancer Cell Biology, 2002–14, now Emeritus, and Deputy Head, Department of Oncology, 2002–14, University of Cambridge; Fellow of Wolfson College, Cambridge, 2003–13, now Emeritus; *b* 25 May 1946; *d* of Donald Ralph Emery and Joan Edwina Emery. *Educ:* Univ. of Birmingham (BSc Biochem.; PhD Biochem. 1971). Nato Sci. Fellow, 1972–74; Res. Fellow, 1974–87, Arthritis Res. Campaign Sen. Fellow, 1987–97, Strangeways Res. Lab., Cambridge; Prof. of Cell Biol., Dept of Biol Sci., UEA, 1995–2002 (Hon. Prof., Biol Scis, 2002). Hon. Vis. Prof. of Biochem., Univ. of Hong Kong, 2000. Member: Biochem. Soc., 1975; Amer. Soc. for Biochem. and Molecular Biol. FMedSci 2005. *Recreations:* gardening, walking, handicrafts, music. *Address:* Cancer Research UK Cambridge Institute, Li Ka Shing Centre, Robinson Way, Cambridge CB2 0RE. *E:* gm290@cam.ac.uk.

MURPHY, Ian Patrick; QC 1992; a Recorder, since 1990; *b* 1 July 1949; *s* of Patrick Murphy and Irene Grace (*née* Hooper); *m* 1974, Penelope Gay; two *d*. *Educ:* St Illtyd's Coll., Cardiff; LSE (LLB). Chartering Clerk, Baltic Exchange, 1970–71; called to the Bar, Middle Temple, 1972, Bencher, 2001; Asst Recorder, 1986–90. *Recreations:* golf, ski-ing, cricket. *Address:* Farrar's Building, Temple, EC4Y 7BD. *T:* (020) 7583 9241; 3 Llandaff Chase, Llandaff, Cardiff CF5 2NA. *Clubs:* Cardiff County; Royal Porthcawl Golf.

MURPHY, Rt Hon. James; PC 2008; *b* 23 Aug. 1967; *s* of Jim Murphy and Anne Murphy. *Educ:* Bellarmine Secondary Sch., Glasgow; Milnerton High Sch., Cape Town. Dir, Endsleigh Insurance, 1994–96; Project Manager, Scottish Lab. Party, 1996–97. MP (Lab) Eastwood, 1997–2005, E Renfrewshire, 2005–15; contested (Lab) same seat, 2015. PPS to Sec. of State for Scotland, 2001–02; an Asst Govt Whip, 2002–03; a Lord Comr of HM Treasury (Govt Whip), 2003–05; Parly Sec., Cabinet Office, 2005–06; Minister of State: DWP, 2006–07; (Minister for Europe), FCO, 2007–08; Sec. of State for Scotland, 2008–10; Shadow Sec. of State for Scotland, 2010, for Defence, 2010–13, for Internat. Affairs, 2013–14; Leader, Scottish Labour Party, 2014–15. Parly Spokesman, Scottish PFA. Chm., Labour Friends of Israel, 2001–02. Pres., NUS, 1994–96. *Publications:* (as Jim Murphy) The Ten Football Matches that Changed the World, 2014.

MURPHY, James Patrick; Sheriff of Glasgow and Strathkelvin, 1989–2001; *b* 24 Jan. 1932; *s* of Henry Francis Murphy and Alice (*née* Rooney); dual British/Irish citizenship; *m* 1956, Maureen Coyne; two *s* one *d*. *Educ:* Notre Dame Convent; St Aloysius' Coll., Glasgow; Univ. of Glasgow (BL 1953). RNVR, 1952–57. Admitted Solicitor, 1953; assumed partner, R. Maguire Cook & Co., Glasgow, 1959; founded, with J. Ross Harper, firm of Ross Harper & Murphy, Glasgow, 1961; Sheriff of N Strathclyde, 1976–89. Last Glasgow Convenor of Poor's Roll dating from 15th century, 1962–65. President: Glasgow Juridical Soc., 1962–63; Glasgow Bar Assoc., 1966–67; Sheriffs' Assoc., 1991–92; Mem. Council, Law Soc. of Scotland, 1974–76. Lectr and Convenor, Law Soc. of Scotland Post-qualifying Legal Educn. Advocacy course, Stirling Univ. 1971–90. Convenor, Legal Aid Cttee for administering Scottish Legal Aid Scheme, 1975. Examr, Glasgow Univ., 1990–94. Governor, St Aloysius' Coll., Glasgow, 1978–86. Pres., Woodend Bowling and Lawn Tennis Club, 2012–13. *Publications:* contribs to Bench Books, other people's books and legal jls. *Recreations:* cycling, books, book binding, history, calligraphy, footering. *Address:* 8 Kirklee Gate, Glasgow G12 0SZ.

MURPHY, Joe; Political Editor, London Evening Standard, since 2003; *b* Lincs, 20 Sept. 1964; *s* of J. F., (Frank), Murphy and Iris Dove; *m* 1997, Joy Copley; one *d*. Political Reporter, The Sun, 1992–94; Political Corresp./Political Editor, Mail on Sunday, 1994–2001; Political Editor, Sunday Telegraph, 1999–2001; Whitehall Editor, London Evening Standard, 2001–03. *Recreation:* sailing. *Club:* Minima Yacht.

MURPHY, (John) Philip; Vice-President and Global Head of Government and Public Affairs, BG Group, since 2013; *b* 3 June 1958; *s* of Robert Anthony Murphy and Cecily Vaughan Murphy (*née* Nicholson); *m* 1st, 1983, Elizabeth McManus (marr. diss. 1988); 2nd, 1991, Sophie Annabel Davies; one *s* one *d*. *Educ:* St Cuthbert's Grammar Sch., Newcastle upon Tyne; Hertford Coll., Oxford (BA 2nd Cl. Hons French and Latin); City Univ. (Postgrad. Dip. in Practical Journalism); LSE (Dip. Macro- and Micro-Econs). Reporter: Southern Evening Echo, Southampton, 1981–83; and local govt corresp., The Journal, Newcastle upon Tyne, 1983–86; Lobby Corresp., Thomson Newspapers, 1986–87; Political Editor: Yorkshire Post, 1987–96; Press Assoc., 1996–98; Exec. Dir (Communications), Arts Council of England, 1998–99; Asst Gen. Sec. and Dir of Media Communications, Labour Party, 1999–2000; Special Advr to Prime Minister, 2000–01; BG Group: Govt Affairs Manager, 2001–02; Hd of Govt and Public Affairs, and Dep. Hd of Policy and Corporate Affairs Dept, 2003–06; Hd of Policy and Corporate Affairs—Europe and Central Asia, 2006–11; Hd of Partner Relations (Europe), 2010–12; Vice-Pres., Corporate Policy, 2012–13. *Publications:* (with R. Caborn) Regional Government for England: an economic imperative, 1995. *Recreations:* football, golf, literature, late 19th and 20th century art, music. *Address:* BG Group, 100 Thames Valley Park Drive, Reading RG6 1PT. *Clubs:* Wisley Golf; Old Thorns Golf.

MURPHY, Sir Jonathan (Michael), Kt 2014; QPM 2007; Chief Constable, Merseyside Police, since 2010; *b* Liverpool, 17 June 1958; *s* of William Michael Murphy and Martha Iris Murphy; *m* 1981, Janet Astbury; one *s* one *d*. *Educ:* Liverpool Univ. (LLB Hons 1990); Cambridge Univ. (Dip. Applied Criminol. 2001). Merseyside Police: Police Cadet, 1975–76; Constable, Liverpool City and Operational Support Gp, 1976–82; Detective Constable, 1982–84; Uniform Patrol Sergeant, 1984–85; Detective Sergeant, 1985–92; Detective Inspector Force Intelligence, 1992–95; Head, Criminal Investigation Dept, Wallasey, 1995–96, Liverpool City Centre area, 1996–97; Detective Superintendent, 1997–98; Detective Chief Superintendent, 1998–99; Force Ops Manager, 1999–2001; Asst Chief Constable (Hd of Ops), Nat. Crime Squad, 2002–04; Dep. Chief Constable, Merseyside Police, 2004–07; Nat. Hd, Crime Business Area, ACPO, 2010– (Co-ordinator, Serious and Organised Crime, 2007–10). Fulbright Police Fellowship, Univ. of Calif, 1995. *Recreations:* ski-ing, reading. *Address:* Merseyside Police, PO Box 59, Liverpool L69 1JD. *T:* (0151) 777 8000, *Fax:* (0151) 777 8020. *E:* chief@merseyside.pnn.police.uk.

MURPHY, Laurence; QC (Scot.) 2000; *b* 12 April 1958; *s* of William John Murphy and Alison Boyd Spindlow or Murphy; *m* 1989, Christine Marie Cecile Germaine Boch; one *s* one *d*. *Educ:* Univ. of Glasgow (MA (Hons) 1980; LLB 1982). Solicitor, 1983–89; Advocate, 1990–. *Recreations:* golf, tennis, walking, music, travel. *Address:* Advocates' Library, Parliament House, Edinburgh EH1 1RF. *T:* (0131) 226 2881.

MURPHY, Michael James, (Mick); Member (SF) South Down, Northern Ireland Assembly, 1998–2003; *b* Banbridge, 6 Feb. 1942; *s* of Michael and Mary Theresa Murphy; *m* 1965, Carole Trainor; six *d*. *Educ:* Leganny Sch., Leitrim, Co. Down. Publican in Rostrevor, 1978–91. Elected Mem. (SF) Newry and Mourne DC, 1996–; Mem. (SF) NI Forum, 1996–98. Contested (SF) S Down, 2001. *Recreations:* Gaelic games, Irish culture.

MURPHY, Prof. Michael Joseph, FBA 2002; Professor of Demography, London School of Economics and Political Science, since 1997; *b* 19 March 1947. *Educ:* Trinity Coll., Cambridge (BA 1969); Univ. of York (BPhil). Statistician, CSO, 1971–78; Res. Fellow, LSHTM, 1978–80; Lectr, LSE, 1980–97. *Publications:* contrib. learned jls. *Address:* Department of Social Policy, London School of Economics and Political Science, Houghton Street, WC2A 2AE.

MURPHY, Michael Joseph Adrian; QC 1993; **His Honour Judge Murphy;** a Circuit Judge, since 1999; *b* 1 Oct. 1949; *s* of late Patrick Joseph Murphy, Hirwaun, Mid-Glam., and Frances Murphy; *m* 1973, Rosemary Dorothy Aitken; three *s* one *d.* *Educ:* Aberdare Grammar Sch., Mid-Glam.; Sheffield Univ. (LLB, MA). Called to the Bar, Inner Temple, 1973. A Recorder, 1989–99. *Address:* The Law Courts, 50 West Bar, Sheffield S3 8PH. *T:* (0114) 281 2400.

MURPHY, Dame Olwen; *see* Hufton, Dame O.

MURPHY, Patrick James, CMG 1985; HM Diplomatic Service, retired; Adviser on Central Europe, British Consultancy Charitable Trust, 2005–12; *b* 11 March 1931; *e s* of late Dr James Murphy and Cicely Mary (*née* Crowley); *m* 1st, 1959, Barbara May Healey-Purse (marr. diss. 1969); two *s*; 2nd, 1974, Jutta Ulrike Oehlmann; one *s.* *Educ:* Cranbrook School; Gonville and Caius College, Cambridge (BA; Geography Tripos). Served RAF, 1950–52. Oxford and Cambridge Far Eastern Expedition, 1955–56; BBC Gen. Overseas Service, 1956; Joined FO, 1957; Frankfurt, 1958; Berlin, 1959; FO, 1962; Second Sec. (Commercial), Warsaw, 1962; First Sec., FO, 1965; First Sec. (Commercial) and Consul, Phnom Penh, 1966; Consul, Düsseldorf, 1969; Consul, Hamburg, 1971; FCO, 1974; First Sec., Vienna, 1977; Counsellor, FCO, 1981–87. Advr, Sultanate of Oman, 1987–90; Consultant, HM Diplomatic Service, 1990–95; Regl Dir for Poland and the Baltic States, 1995–2005, Czech and Slovak Republics, 1997–2005, and Belarus, 2000–05, BESO. Mem. Council, Polish Corps of Volunteer Experts, 2006–. Officer's Cross, Order of Merit (Poland), 2000. *Recreations:* history, travel, wine, Irish life. *Address:* 260 Dacre Park, SE13 5DD. *T:* (020) 8852 2483. *Club:* Royal Air Force.

MURPHY, Patrick Wallace; agricultural consultant, 1996–2006; Under Secretary, Land Use, Conservation and Countryside Group, Ministry of Agriculture, Fisheries and Food, 1994–96; *b* 16 Aug. 1944; *s* of Lawrence Vincent Murphy and Agnes Dunn; *m* 1972, Denise Lillieth Fullarton-Fullarton; two *s.* *Educ:* St Chad's College, Wolverhampton; Trinity Hall, Cambridge (BA Hons). Joined MAFF, 1966; Asst Private Sec. to Minister of Agriculture, Fisheries and Food, 1970; First Sec. (Agriculture and Commercial), British Embassy, Washington, 1974–78; Controller of Plant Variety Rights, 1978–82; Head, Land Use and Tenure Div., 1982–86; Under Sec., 1986; Head, Milk and Potatoes Gp, 1986–89; Hd of Pesticides, Vet. Medicines, Emergencies and Biotechnol. Gp, 1989–93; Hd of EC Gp, 1993–94. Non-exec. Dir, IDV (UK), 1985–88. Chm., I'Anson Cricket Competitions, 2006–12. Chm., Elstead Parish Council, 2011–. *Recreations:* cricket, walking, gardening.

MURPHY, Rt Hon. Paul (Peter); PC 1999; *b* 25 Nov. 1948; *s* of late Ronald and Marjorie Murphy. *Educ:* St Francis RC Primary Sch., Abersychan; West Monmouth Sch., Pontypool; Oriel Coll., Oxford (MA; Hon. Fellow, 2000). Management Trainee, CWS, 1970–71; Lectr in History and Govt, Ebbw Vale Coll. of Further Education, 1971–87. Mem., Torfaen Borough Council, 1973–87 (Chm., Finance Cttee, 1976–86); Sec., Torfaen Constituency Labour Party, 1974–87. MP (Lab) Torfaen, 1987–2015. Opposition front bench spokesman for Wales, 1988–94; on NI, 1994; on for. affairs, 1994–95; on defence, 1995–97; Minister of State, NI Office, 1997–99; Secretary of State: for Wales, 1999–2002 and 2008–09; for NI, 2002–05. Chm., Intelligence and Security Cttee, 2005–08. Vis. Parly Fellow, St Antony's Coll., Oxford, 2006–07. Hon. Fellow, Glyndŵr Univ., Wrexham, 2009. DUniv S Wales, 2014. *Recreation:* music. *E:* murphyrighthon@aol.com. *Clubs:* Oxford and Cambridge; St Joseph's (St Dials).

[Created a Baron (Life Peer) 2015 but title not yet gazetted at time of going to press.]

MURPHY, Peter John; QC 2002; a Recorder, since 2000; *b* 20 May 1958; s of John James Murphy and Joan Murphy; *m* 1997, Ceri Louise Phillips; two *s* three *d.* *Educ:* Leicester Univ. (LLB Hons). Joined chambers, Cardiff, 1980; called to the Bar, Gray's Inn, 1980; an Asst Recorder, 1997–2000. *Recreations:* amateur dramatics and singing, numerous sporting activities incl. swimming, football and squash, avid reader. *Address:* 30 Park Place, Cardiff CF10 3BS. *T:* (029) 2039 8421.

MURPHY, Peter William; His Honour Judge Peter Murphy; a Circuit Judge, since 2007; a Resident Judge, Peterborough Crown Court and Honorary Recorder of Peterborough, since 2014; *b* Boston, Lincs, 10 Feb. 1946; *s* of William Joseph Murphy and Rhiannon Murphy (*née* Rees); *m* 1992, Christine Service; one *s*, and one step *s.* *Educ:* Queen Elizabeth's Grammar Sch., Blackburn; Downing Coll., Cambridge (BA 1966; LLB 1967; MA 1970). Called to the Bar: Middle Temple, 1968, Bencher, 2013; Calif, 1981; Texas, 1985; private practice, London, 1970–78; Principal Lectr, Inns of Court Sch. of Law, 1978–80; private practice, San Francisco, 1980–84; Prof. of Law, South Texas Coll. of Law, 1984–2007; Trial and Appellate Counsel, Internat. Criminal Tribunal for Former Yugoslavia, 1998–2007. Hon. Recorder of Peterborough, 2014–. Trustee, Amer. Inns of Court Foundn, 1985–99, now Emeritus. Founding Editor-in-Chief, Blackstone's Criminal Practice, 1991–2007. *Publications:* A Practical Approach to Evidence, 1980, 12th edn as Murphy on Evidence, 2012; Evidence Proof and Facts: a book of sources, 2003; *novels:* Removal, 2012; A Higher Duty, 2013; Test of Resolve, 2014; A Matter for the Jury, 2014; And is there Honey still for Tea?, 2015; numerous law review articles. *Recreations:* theatre, music, watching sports (Blackburn Rovers, Harlequins and Wales), chess, snooker. *Club:* Reform.

MURPHY, Philip; *see* Murphy, J. P.

MURPHY, Richard James, FCA; campaigner for tax reform; Director, Tax Research LLP, since 2005; *b* Romford, Essex, 21 March 1958; *s* of William Patrick Murphy and late Barbara Jean Murphy; *m* 1999, Jacqueline Anne Walsh; two *s.* *Educ:* Southampton Univ. (BScSoc Business Econs and Accountancy 1979). ACA 1982, FCA 1993. With Chartered Accountants, Peat Marwick Mitchell & Co., London, 1979–83, Shelley Pinnick & Co., London, 1983–84; Principal, R J Murphy & Co., London, 1985–89; Sen. Partner, Murphy Deeks Nolan, London, 1989–2000; Principal, Fulcrum, Chartered Accountants, 2000–. Adviser: Tax Justice Network, London, 2003–; TUC, 2008–; PCS, 2009–. Academic, visiting or research Fellowships at: Univ. of Portsmouth Business Sch., 1997–2000; Centre for Global Political Econ., Univ. of Sussex, 2005–08; Tax Res. Inst., Univ. of Nottingham, 2006–09. Dir, Fair Tax Mark, 2013–. FRSA. Blogger at www.taxresearch.org.uk/Blog. *Publications:* (jtly) Tax Havens: at the heart of globalization, 2009; The Courageous State, 2011; Over Here and Undertaxed, 2013; contrib. articles to jls incl. Accountancy, Accountancy Age, AccountingWEB (contrib. ed.), Tax Notes Internat. *Recreations:* my family, transport history, railway modelling, walking Hector, a cocker spaniel, holidaying in England, birdwatching. *Address:* Tax Research LLP, The Old Orchard, Bexwell Road, Downham Market, Norfolk PE38 9LJ. *T:* (01366) 383500. *E:* richard.murphy@taxresearch.org.uk. *W:* www.taxresearch.org.uk/Blog.

MURPHY, (Robert Somerville) Foster; Principal, Charitable Futures, 2002–14; Chief Executive, Abbeyfield Society, 1992–2002; *b* 1 June 1940; *s* of Robert Somerville Foster Murphy and Eva Constance (*née* Harvey); *m* 1964, Patricia Mary Hamilton; one *s* one *d.* *Educ:* Dublin Univ. (MA); Downing Coll., Cambridge (MA); London Univ. (Dip. SocScis (ext.)). Irish Sec., SCM, 1965–67; Youth Sec., BCC, 1967–72; Youth Sec., subseq. Head of Div., then Dep. Dir, NCVO, 1972–81; Dir, Volunteer Centre, UK, 1981–92. Board Member: Innisfree HA, 1993–99; Internat. Assoc. for Homes & Services for the Aging, 1994–2003; Centre for Policy on Ageing, 1997–2002 (Chm., 2000–02); Citizen's Advice Notes Trust, 2002–05; Abbeyfield Internat., 2002–11 (Vice Chm., 2005–09); Vegetarian Housing Assoc., 2004–07. Voluntary Advr, Officers' Assoc., 2003–. *Publications:* (jtly) Integrating Care, Housing and Community, 1998. *Recreations:* opera, gardening, keeping fit. *Address:* 64 Callander Road, SE6 2QE. *E:* foster.murphy@ukgateway.net.

MURPHY, Rory; Director, Carom Ltd, since 2005; *b* 23 April 1955; *s* of Philip Murphy and Noreen Murphy (*née* Sheahan); *m* 1976, Catherine Deane; two *s.* *Educ:* Bishop Bright RC Grammar Sch., Leamington Spa. Photographer, Pitt Rivers Mus., Oxford, 1972–84 (on secondment as Union Official, 1979–84); Nat. Sec., ASTMS, Ireland, 1984–87; Asst Gen. Sec., ASTMS, later MSF, 1987–89; Chief Exec., Finers, Solicitors, 1989–90; Dir of Industrial Relations, Royal Coll. of Midwives, 1990–95; Gen. Sec., NatWest Staff Assoc., 1995–99; Jt Gen. Sec., UNIFI, 1999–2004; Asst Gen. Sec., Amicus, 2004–05; Hd of Commercial Health and Wellbeing, First Assist, 2006–07; Dir of People Management, PBLSat, 2007–08; Trade Union and Govt Advr, Swiss Re, 2008–09. Mem. Adv. Bd, Good Corp. *Recreations:* football (Arsenal), theatre, art, archaeology.

MURPHY, Dr Simon Francis; non-executive Chairman, Sandwell Local Improvement Finance Trust Company Ltd, since 2005; *b* 24 Feb. 1962; *s* of Patrick Joseph Murphy and Mary Frances Murphy; *m* 1992, Bridget Lee Brickley; one *s* one *d* (and one *s* decd). *Educ:* Sacred Heart Coll., Droitwich; N Worcs Coll., Bromsgrove; UCW, Aberystwyth (BSc Econ 1983; PhD 1986). Tutor, Dept of Political Sci., UCW, Aberystwyth, 1984–86; Asst to Leader of Labour Gp, Wolverhampton MBC, 1986–89; Head of Research, Office of John Bird, MEP, 1989–94. MEP (Lab) Midlands W, 1994–99, W Midlands Reg., 1999–2004. Whip, 1996–98, Leader, 2000–02, European PLP; Vice-President: Socialist Gp, EP, 2000–02; Eurogroup for Animal Welfare & Conservation, 1997–99. Contested (Lab) Wolverhampton SW, 1992. Chief Exec., Birmingham Forward, 2004–06; City Region Dir, Urban West Midlands, 2006–11. Dir, W Midlands Develt Agency, 1997. Dir, Capital Ventures Mgt Ltd, 2004–06; non-exec. Dir, Eur. Bd, iSoft Gp plc, 2003–06; Dir and Trustee, Groundwork W Midlands, 2013– (Chm., Finance and Audit Cttee, 2014–); Exec. Consultant, Shakespeares LLP, 2011–14; Business Develt Consultant, Waterhouse Search, 2011–14; Associate, Deloitte, 2011–13; Interim Chief Executive Officer: Worcester Community Trust, 2013–15; Groundwork N Ireland, 2015. Member: Better Regulation Commn (formerly Task Force), 2005–06; MG Rover Task Force, 2005–06; Technol. Transfer Fund Investment Gp, Advantage W Midlands, 2005–06. Non-exec. Dir, Dudley and Walsall NHS Mental Mealth Trust, 2015–. Gov., Univ. of Wolverhampton, 1996–99. W Mercia Police and Crime Comr candidate (Lab), 2012. *Publications:* (contrib.) Contemporary Minority Nationalisms, ed M. Watson, 1990; (contrib.) European Governance, 2002; Views from the UK on democracy, participation and policy-making in the EU; articles in Waterlog Mag. *Recreations:* running, reading, cooking, fishing, watching sport, junior Rugby coaching, manager of U11 girls cricket team.

MURPHY, Stephen David; General Secretary, Union of Construction, Allied Trades and Technicians, since 2012; *b* Chesterfield, Derbys, 8 April 1961; *s* of Thomas and Avis Murphy; *m* 1987, Angela Phillips; two *d.* *Educ:* Newbold Green Sch., Chesterfield. C&G Bricklaying. Bricklayer, 1978–97; shop steward, 1989–97; Union of Construction, Allied Trades and Technicians: Develt Officer, 1997–2001; Regl Organiser, 2001–05; Regl Sec., Midlands, 2005–11, Yorks, 2011–12. Mem., Lab. Party, 1997–. *Recreations:* Sheffield Wednesday, hill walking. *Address:* UCATT House, 177 Abbeville Road, SW4 9RL. *T:* (020) 7622 2442.

MURPHY, Steven; Chief Executive Officer, Christie's International plc, 2010–14; *b* New York, 17 March 1954; *s* of Edward Murphy and Gloria Murphy (*née* Suglia); *m* 1978, Annie Pleshette; one *s* one *d.* *Educ:* Georgetown Univ., Washington, DC (BA Eng. Lit.). Div. Pres., Simon & Schuster, 1985–91; Pres., EMI Music/Angel Records, 1991–98; Exec. Vice Pres. and Man. Dir, Disney Publishing, 1998–2000; Chief Operating Officer, 2000–02, Chief Exec. and Pres., 2002–09, Rodale Inc. *Recreations:* horse riding, yoga, art, reading, music, theatre. *Clubs:* Arts, Harry's Bar, Annabel's, 5 Hertford Street.

MURPHY, Stuart Neil Luke; Director, Entertainment Channels, Sky, since 2012; *b* 6 Nov. 1971; *s* of David Francis Murphy and Patricia Mary Murphy (*née* Downing); *m* 2002 (marr. diss. 2005); two *s.* *Educ:* St Mary's RC Sch., Ilkley; Clare Coll., Cambridge (MA Pol Geog.). Joined BBC, 1993; worked on comedy, documentaries, entertainment shows, 1993–96; Producer: MTV Europe, 1997; Big Breakfast, Channel 4, 1997; BBC: Strategic Develt Exec., TV, 1998; Broadcast Develt Exec., 1999–2002; launched UK Play, music and comedy channel, 1999; Hd of Programming, 1999–2001, Channel Controller, 2001–03, BBC Choice; Launch Controller, BBC 3, 2003–05; commissioned Little Britain, Gavin and Stacey, Nighty Night, Bodies, The Mighty Boosh, Torchwood; Creative Director: RDF Media, 2006; Twofour Broadcast, 2006–09; Sky: Dir of Programming, Sky1, 2009–12; Launch Dir, Sky Atlantic, 2011; commissioned Got To Dance, Pineapple Dance Studios, A League of Their Own, Strike Back, An Idiot Abroad, Stella, Hunderby, Dracula, Penny Dreadful, Fortitude, The Last Panthers, Moone Boy, The Enfield Haunting. Board Director: Nickelodeon, 2013; Jaunt, 2014–; A&E Networks UK, 2015–; Jupiter Entertainment, 2015–. *Recreations:* dispensing faultless life wisdom to my nodding, ignoring teenage sons, boxing, theme parks, Russian, classical music, interior design, Rugby. *Address:* British Sky Broadcasting Ltd, Grant Way, Isleworth, Middx TW7 5QD. *Club:* Ivy.

MURPHY, Thomas, CBE 1991; Managing Director, Civil Aviation Authority, 1987–95; *b* 13 Nov. 1928; *s* of Thomas Murphy and Elizabeth Gray Murphy (*née* Leckie); *m* 1962, Sheila Jean Dorothy Young; one *s* three *d.* *Educ:* St Mirin's Acad., Paisley; Glasgow Univ. (MA Hons). Served Royal Artillery, 1951–53. Marks and Spencer, 1953–55; British Petroleum, 1955–86: appts in Territory of Papua New Guinea, Trinidad, Scotland, Algeria, USA, 1955–68; Asst Gen. Man., BP Tanker Co., 1968–76; Gen. Man., Gp Personnel, 1976–81; Advr, Organisation Planning, 1981–86. Non-executive Director: CAA, 1986–87; Parity plc, 1997–2001; Oriel Gp plc, 1998. Internat. Sen. Managers Programme, Harvard Business Sch., 1973. *Recreations:* walking, coarse golf, destructive gardening. *Address:* Woodruffe, Onslow Road, Sunningdale, Berks SL5 0HW. *T:* (01344) 623261. *Club:* Wentworth.

MURPHY, Thomas James; journalist, singer and actor; *b* 26 June 1956; *s* of James Murphy and Beatrice Murphy (*née* Strand); *m* 1976, Janet Sallis; four *s.* *Educ:* Salesian Sch., Chertsey; Sussex Univ. (BA History); Warwick Univ. (MBA); Royal Acad. of Music (Cert.). Kitchen porter and factory labourer, 1977; trainee journalist, Slough Observer, 1978; Sports editor, Buckinghamshire Advertiser, 1981; Editor: Staines Informer, 1983; East Grinstead Courier, 1984; Sub-editor, The Independent, 1986; Dep. Chief sub-editor, London Evening News, 1987; Editor, The Universe, 1988–90; journalist, The Times, 1990. *Recreation:* swimming.

MURPHY-O'CONNOR, His Eminence Cardinal Cormac; Archbishop of Westminster, (RC), 2000–09, now Archbishop Emeritus; *b* 24 Aug. 1932; *s* of late Dr P. G. Murphy-O'Connor and Ellen (*née* Cuddigan). *Educ:* Prior Park Coll., Bath; English Coll., Rome; Gregorian Univ. PhL, STL. Ordained Priest, 1956. Asst Priest, Portsmouth and Fareham, 1956–66; Sec. to Bp of Portsmouth, 1966–70; Parish Priest, Parish of the Immaculate Conception, Southampton, 1970–71; Rector, English College, Rome, 1971–77; Bishop of Arundel and Brighton, 1977–2000. Cardinal, 2001. Chairman: Bishops' Cttee for Europe, 1978–83; Cttee for Christian Unity, 1983–2000; Dept for Mission and Unity, Bishops' Conf. of England and Wales, 1993–2001; Jt Chm., ARCIC-II, 1983–2000; Pres., Catholic Bps' Conf. of England and Wales, 2000–09. Member: Congregation for the Sacraments and Divine

Worship, 2001–12; Admin of Patrimony of Holy See, 2001–12; Council for Study of Orgnl and Econ. Problems of the Holy See, 2001–12; Presidential Cttee, Pontifical Council for the Family, 2002–12; Pontifical Council for Culture, 2002–12. DD Lambeth, 1999. *Publications:* At the Heart of the World, 2004; The Human Face of God, 2004; An English Spring (memoir), 2015. *Recreations:* music, sport. *Address:* St Edward's, 7 Dukes Avenue, Chiswick, W4 2AA.

MURRAY; *see* Erskine-Murray.

MURRAY, family name of **Duke of Atholl, Earl of Dunmore** and **Earl of Mansfield and Mansfield**.

MURRAY, Rt Hon. Lord; Ronald King Murray; PC 1974; a Senator of the College of Justice in Scotland, 1979–95; *b* 15 June 1922; *s* of James King Murray, MIEE, and Muriel (*née* Aitken), Glasgow; *m* 1950, Sheila Winifred Gamlin; one *s* one *d*. *Educ:* George Watson's Coll., Edinburgh; Univ. of Edinburgh (MA (1st cl. hons Phil) 1948; LLB 1952); Jesus Coll., Oxford (Hon. Fellow, 1999). Served HM Forces, 1941–46; commnd in REME, 1942; India and SEAC, 1943–46. Asst in Moral Philosophy, Edinburgh Univ., 1949–52; called to Scottish Bar, 1953; QC (Scotland) 1967; Advocate-Depute, 1964–67; Senior Advocate-Depute, 1967–70. MP (Lab) Leith, Edinburgh, 1970–79; Lord Advocate, 1974–79. Vice-Chm., Edinburgh Univ. Court, 1990–93. Mem., Scottish Records Adv. Council, 1987–93. Hon. Pres., Leith Boys' Brigade, 1984–98. Dr *hc* Edinburgh, 1996. *Publications:* contrib. various jls and books. *Recreations:* sailing, astronomy. *Address:* 1 Inverleith Grove, Edinburgh EH3 5PB. *T:* (0131) 551 5330. *Clubs:* Royal Scots (Edinburgh); Royal Forth Yacht.

MURRAY, Bishop of The, since 2013; **Rt Rev. John Frank Ford;** *b* 14 Jan. 1952; *s* of Royston and Ivy Ford; *m* 1981, Bridget Barnard; three *s*. *Educ:* Charles Chute Sch., Basingstoke; Southampton Coll. of Technol.; Chichester Theol Coll.; University Coll., Chichester (MA 2004). Ordained deacon, 1979, priest, 1980; Curate, Christ Ch, Forest Hill, 1979–82; Vicar: St Augustine, Lee, 1982–91; Lower Beeding, and Domestic Chaplain to Bp of Horsham, 1991–94; Diocesan Missioner, Chichester, 1994–2000; Chichester Cathedral: Canon and Preb., 1997–2000; Precentor and Canon Residentiary, 2000–05; Bishop Suffragan of Plymouth, 2005–13. *Recreations:* cricket, theatre, food and wine, travel, Middle Eastern politics and culture. *Address:* c/o Diocesan Registrar, PO Box 394, Murray Bridge, SA 5253, Australia. *T:* (8) 85322270. *E:* bishop@murray.anglican.org.

MURRAY, Alan James; Chief Executive Officer, Hanson plc, 2002–07; *b* 12 May 1953; *s* of James and Elsie Murray; *m* 2002, Pamela Clark. *Educ:* Lancaster Univ. (BA Hons Econ.). FCMA 1988. Finance Dir, Burton Gp, 1985–88; Hanson plc, 1988–2007: Finance Director: ARC General Products and S Region, 1993–94; Hanson Brick UK, 1994–95; Asst Finance Dir, 1995–97; Finance Dir, 1997–98; Chief Exec., Hanson Building Materials America, 1998–2002. Non-executive Director: Internat. Power plc, 2007–11; HeidelbergCement AG, 2010–; Wolseley plc, 2013–. *Recreations:* cinema, music, travel.

MURRAY, Alexander, FRHistS; FBA 1995; Fellow and Praelector in Modern History, University College, Oxford, 1980–2001, now Emeritus Fellow; *b* 14 May 1934; second *s* of late Stephen Hubert Murray and Margaret (*née* Gillett). *Educ:* Bedales Sch., Petersfield; New Coll., Oxford (BA Mod. Hist.; BPhil European Hist.). FRHistS 1971. Served RA, 1953–55. Asst Lectr in Medieval Hist., Univ. of Leeds, 1961–63; University of Newcastle upon Tyne: Lectr, 1963–77; Sen. Lectr, 1977–80; Public Orator, 1973–76; Chm., Faculty of Modern Hist., Univ. of Oxford, 1992–93. Directeur des Études Associé, École des Hautes Études en Sciences Sociales, Paris, 1986; Vis. Prof. of Medieval Hist., Harvard Univ., 1989–90. Mem., NYO, 1951–53. Dir and Trustee, Magdalena Consort, 2010–. Gov., Bedales Sch., 1986–94. *Publications:* Reason and Society in the Middle Ages, 1978; The Violent Against Themselves, 1998; The Curse on Self-Murder, 2000; Doubting Thomas in Medieval Exegesis and Art, 2006; Conscience and Authority in the Medieval Church (essays), 2015; contrib. learned jls and collections. *Recreations:* music, walking. *Address:* University College, Oxford OX1 4BH.

MURRAY, Andrew, OBE 2013; professional tennis player, since 2005; *b* Dunblane, Scotland, 15 May 1987; *s* of William Murray and Judy Murray; *m* 2015, Kim Sears. Winner: singles titles: San Jose, 2006, 2007; St Petersburg, 2007, 2008; ATP Masters Series Madrid, 2008, 2015; ATP Masters Series Cincinnati, 2008, 2011; Marseille, 2008; Doha, 2008, 2009; Valencia, 2009, 2014; ATP World Tour Masters 1000 Canada, 2009, 2010; Queen's, London, 2009, 2011, 2013, 2015; ATP World Tour Masters 1000 Miami, 2009, 2013; Rotterdam, 2009; ATP World Tour Masters 1000 Shanghai, 2010, 2011; Tokyo, 2011; Bangkok, 2011; Brisbane, 2012, 2013; US Open, 2012; Wimbledon, 2013; Shenzhen Open, 2014; Vienna, 2014; Munich, 2015; doubles titles: Valencia, 2010; Tokyo, 2011. Gold Medal, Men's Singles, Silver Medal, Mixed Doubles, London Olympics, 2012. BBC Sports Personality of the Year, 2013. *Publications:* Andy Murray: seventy-seven: my road to Wimbledon glory, 2013. *Address:* c/o Matt Gentry, 77, Fulham Green, Chester House, 81–83 Fulham High Street, SW6 3JA. *T:* (020) 3543 1487, 07736 300694.

MURRAY, Andrew Robin; HM Diplomatic Service, retired; Ambassador to Uruguay, 1998–2001; *b* 21 Sept. 1941; *s* of Robert Alexander Murray and Jean Agnes Murray (*née* Burnett); *m* 1965, Irene Dorothy Foy; one *s* one *d*. *Educ:* Glenalmond; Edinburgh Univ. (MA Hons 1965). Economist with Govt of Ontario, Canada, 1966; investment analyst, ICFC, 1969; joined HM Diplomatic Service, 1973; First Sec., Islamabad, 1975–78; Head of Chancery, Buenos Aires, 1979–81; FCO, 1982–84; Counsellor, UKMIS to UN, 1984–88; Counsellor and Dep. Head of Mission, Caracas, 1988–91; FCO, 1991–93; Counsellor (Econ. and Commercial), Stockholm, 1993–97. *Recreation:* sporadic sport.

MURRAY, Ann, Hon. DBE 2002; mezzo-soprano; *b* Dublin, 27 Aug. 1949; *m* 1981, Philip Gordon Langridge, CBE (*d* 2010); one *s*. *Educ:* Royal Manchester Coll. of Music. Roles include: *for English National Opera:* Ariodante; Beatrice; Charlotte; Rosina; Xerxes; *for Royal Opera:* Cherubino; Composer; Donna Elvira; Dorabella; Idamante; Marcellina; Mrs Grose in The Turn of the Screw; Oktavian; The Witch in Hansel und Gretel; *other roles:* Cecilio; Cenerentola; Countess in The Queen of Spades; Iphigénie; Nicklausse; Sextus. Many recitals and concerts (European recital tours, 1990, 1993, 1994); festival appearances incl. Aldeburgh, Edinburgh, Munich, Salzburg, Glyndebourne. Prof. of Singing, RAM, 2010–. Hon. FRAM 1999. Hon. DMus NUI, 1997. *Address:* c/o Askonas Holt Ltd, Lincoln House, 300 High Holborn, WC1V 7JH.

MURRAY, Athol Laverick, PhD; FRHistS; Keeper of the Records of Scotland, 1985–90; *b* Tynemouth, Northumberland, 8 Nov. 1930; *s* of late George Murray and Margery Laverick; *m* 1958, Irene Joyce Cairns; one *s* one *d*. *Educ:* Royal Grammar Sch., Lancaster; Jesus Coll., Cambridge (BA, MA); Univ. of Edinburgh (LLB, PhD). Research Assistant, Foreign Office, 1953; Assistant Keeper, Scottish Record Office, 1953–83; Deputy Keeper, 1983–84. Consultant Archivist, Jersey Archives Steering Gp, 1990–92. Vice-Pres., Soc. of Antiquaries of Scotland, 1989–92; Chm., Scottish Records Assoc., 1997–2000. FRHistS 1971. *Publications:* The Royal Grammar School, Lancaster, 1951; Castle Tioram: the historical background, 1998; *Fasti Ecclesiae Scoticanae Medii Aevi*, 2003; articles in Scottish Historical Review, etc. *Address:* 33 Inverleith Gardens, Edinburgh EH3 5PR. *T:* (0131) 552 4465. *Club:* Civil Service.

MURRAY, Braham Sydney, OBE 2010; Founder Artistic Director, Royal Exchange Theatre, Manchester, 1975–2012; *b* London, 12 Feb. 1943; *s* of Sam Goldstein and Gertrude Goldstein (now Murray), and step *s* of Philip Murray; two *s* by Johanna Bryant. *Educ:* Clifton Coll., Bristol; University Coll., Oxford. Artistic Dir, Century Theatre Co., 1965–67; Founder Artistic Dir, '69 Theatre Co., 1968–75: productions include: Charley's Aunt, Mary Rose, Endgame, Erb, Catch My Soul, She Stoops to Conquer, all transf. London; Royal Exchange Theatre, Manchester, 1975–2012: notable productions include: The Dybbuk, 1978; The Three Musketeers (and co-writer), 1979; Andy Capp, 1982; Hamlet, 1983; Riddley Walker, 1986; Court in the Act!, 1986, transf. London; Your Home in the West, 1991; The Odd Women, 1992; The Brothers Karamazov, Maybe, 1993; Miss Julie, 1995; Peer Gynt, Bats (and co-writer), 1999; Snake in Fridge (world premiere), 2000; Hedda Gabler, Time and the Conways, 2001; Othello, 2002; Cold Meat Party (world premiere), 2003; The Happiest Days of Your Life, 2003; Anthony and Cleopatra, 2005; The Glass Menagerie, 2008; True Love Lies (world premiere), 2009; Haunted (world premiere), 2009, transf. NY, 2010, Sydney, 2011; The Bacchae, 2010; Wonderful Town, 2012; West End productions include: The Good Companions, The Black Mikado, The Cabinet Minister, Lady Windermere's Fan, Kill Me Now; other productions include: Hang Down Your Head and Die, Oxford, London and NY; Uncle Vanya, NY; Resurrection (world premiere), Houston Grand Opera; Talking Heads, Australia tour; Skelling the Opera (world premiere), The Sage, Gateshead; The Tempest, Singapore. Hon. BA: Manchester Metropolitan, 1996; Central Lancashire, 2008. *Publications:* The Worst it can be is a Disaster (autobiog.), 2007; How to Direct a Play, 2011; *translations and adaptations:* Have You Anything to Declare, 1980; Court in the Act!, by Veber, 1988; Keep an Eye on Amelie, by Feydeau, 1991; The Marriage of Figaro, by Beaumarchais, 2002; Triumph of Love, by Marivaux, 2007. *Recreations:* food, wine, reading, France, Tottenham Hotspur.

MURRAY, Christine; Editor, The Architectural Review, since 2015; *b* Oakville, Ont, 16 Nov. 1977; *d* of Norman Murray and Nerina Murray; *m* 2007, Richard Marks; one *s* one *d*. *Educ:* Univ. of Toronto (BA Eng. Lit. 2000); Concordia Univ., Montreal (MA Eng. Lit. and Creative Writing 2005). Res. Asst, Flare mag., 2000–01; Actg Editl Asst, i-D mag., 2001–03; Montreal Correspondent, Fashion Qly, 2003–05; Ukula Magazine: Fashion and Design Editor, 2005–07; Editl Dir, 2007; Architects' Journal: Sen. Editor, The Critics, 2007–08; Dep. Editor, 2008–10; Editor, 2010–15. *Recreations:* fact collecting, rearranging furniture, undermining authority, coffee, gazing thoughtfully in various directions. *Address:* The Architectural Review, 69–77 Paul Street, EC2A 4NW. *E:* christine.murray@emap.com.

MURRAY, Craig John; writer and broadcaster; *b* 17 Oct. 1958; *s* of Robert Cameron Brunton Murray and Poppy Katherine Murray (*née* Grice); *m* 1st, 1984, Fiona Ann Kennedy (marr. diss. 2008); one *s* one *d*; 2nd, 2009, Nadira Alieva; one *s*. *Educ:* Paston Grammar Sch.; Univ. of Dundee (MA Hons). HM Diplomatic Service, 1984–2004: Second Sec., Lagos, 1986–89; FCO, 1990–94; First Sec., Warsaw, 1994–98; FCO, 1998–99; Dep. High Comr, Ghana, 1999–2002; Ambassador to Republic of Uzbekistan, 2002–04. Rector, Dundee Univ., 2007–10. Hon. Res. Fellow, Sch. of Law, Univ. of Lancaster, 2006–10. Contested: (Ind.) Blackburn, 2005; (Put an Honest Man into Parliament) Norwich North, July 2009. *Publications:* Murder in Samarkand, 2006; Dirty Diplomacy, 2007; Influence Not Power, 2007; The Catholic Orangemen of Togo, 2008; Sikunder Burnes: master of the great game, 2015. *Recreations:* drinking, gossiping, reading, Celtic music, football, cricket. *Address:* 89/14 Holyrood Road, Edinburgh EH8 8BA. *W:* www.craigmurray.org.uk. *Clubs:* Gin Dobry (Poznan); Imperial (Ekaterinburg).

MURRAY, Dale Jane, CBE 2013; entrepreneur and business investor; *b* Palmerston North, NZ, 15 Jan. 1970; *d* of William Anderson and Beverley Ramsay; *m* 1997, Simon Murray; three *s*. *Educ:* Auckland Inst. of Technol. (Nat. Dip. Accountancy 1992); London Business Sch., Univ. of London (MBA 2001). FCA 1993. Accountant, Price Waterhouse, 1987–92; Manager, Accounting and Admin, BellSouth NZ Ltd, 1992–95; Finance Manager, Pearson Television Ltd, 1995–99; Jt Man. Dir, Omega Logic Ltd, 1999–2003; CEO, Eposs Ltd, 2003–05; business angel investor, 2006–12. Non-executive Director: Sussex Place Ventures, 2012–; UKTI, 2012–; BIS, 2013–. Fellow, Coll. of Chartered Accountants Australia and NZ, 2013. *Recreations:* family, ski-ing, cycling, gardening. *E:* info@dalemurray.net.

MURRAY, Sir David (Edward), Kt 2007; Chairman, Murray Capital Ltd, since 2012; director of companies; *b* 14 Oct. 1951; *s* of late David Ian Murray and of Roma Murray; *m* 1st, 1972, Louise V. Densley (*d* 1992); two *s*; 2nd, 2011, Kae A. Tinto. *Educ:* Fettes Coll.; Broughton High Sch. Formed: Murray International Metals Ltd, 1976; Murray International Holdings Ltd, 1981; Murray Foundn, 1997. Young Scottish Businessman of the Year, 1984. Chairman: UK2000 (Scotland), 1987; Rangers FC, 1988–2002, 2004–09. Gov., Clifton Hall Sch., 1987. DUniv Heriot-Watt, 1986; Dr *hc* Edinburgh, 2008. *Recreations:* watching sport, collecting and producing wine (Chevalier du Taste Vin, 2006). *Address:* Murray Capital Ltd, 26 Charlotte Square, Edinburgh EH2 4ET. *T:* (0131) 243 2100.

MURRAY, David Edward, FRICS; management consultant, since 1997; Deputy Chief Executive (Property), Crown Estate, 1993–97; *b* 22 Jan. 1944; *s* of late Thomas and Emily Murray; *m* 1968, Barbara Collins, *d* of late Sir Geoffrey and Lady Collins, Dorset; two *s*. *Educ:* Abbotsholme Sch., Derbys; Manor Park Sch., Hants; Hammersmith Sch. of Art & Building. AIQS 1970; Dip. Constr. Econs 1975; FRICS 1983. Sir Robert McAlpine & Sons, 1962–67; Planning & Transportation Dept, GLC, 1968–72; Royal County of Berkshire: Gp Quantity Surveyor, 1972–77; Co. Quantity Surveyor, 1977–88; Dir of Property, 1988–93. External Examiner: Coll. of Estate Mgt, 1978–92; Univ. of Portsmouth, 1994–98. Pres., Soc. of Chief Quantity Surveyors in Local Govt, 1979; Royal Institution of Chartered Surveyors: Chm., Quantity Surveyor's R&D Cttee, 1983–84; Mem., Divl Council, 1975–; Trng Advr, 1998–; Mem., several panels and wkg parties. *Publications:* Cost Effectiveness in Property Management, 1984; Artificial Intelligence in Property Portfolio Management, 1988; papers on property mgt and procurement to various UK confs. *Recreations:* sport (especially sailing), reading, music. *Address:* Highcroft, 18 Highclere Drive, Camberley, Surrey GU15 1JY. *T:* (01276) 24345. *Club:* Parkstone Yacht (Dorset).

MURRAY, Rt Rev. David Owen; Assistant Bishop of Perth, Southern Region, Western Australia, 1991–2006; Director, Centre for Spirituality, St George's Cathedral, Perth, since 2007; *b* 23 Dec. 1940; *s* of George Lawrence Murray and Winifred Eva (*née* Morgan); *m* 1971, Janet Mary Chittleborough; two *s*. *Educ:* Swanbourne State Sch.; Claremont High Sch.; St Michael's House, Crafers, SA (Kelham, Aust.) (ThL 1968). Jun. Postal Officer, 1955; Postal Clerk, 1957–65. Ordained deacon, 1968, priest, 1969; Asst Curate, Bunbury, 1968–70; Rector: Lake Grace, 1970–74; Jerramungup, 1974–79; Mt Barker, 1979–83; Chaplain to the Bishop of Bunbury, 1978–83; Rector: S Perth, 1983–88; Fremantle, 1988–94; Archdeacon of Fremantle, 1988–91; Administrator during Abp's absences, Dio. of Perth, 1995–2006; Pastoral Carer of Archbishop's Spiritual Dirs, Dio. of Perth, 2007–; permission to officiate, Dio. of Bunbury, WA, 2010–. Perth Diocesan Trustee, 1992–2006. Episcopal Rep. for Australia and NZ Adv. Council to Anglican Religious Communities, 1993–2006; Mem., ANZ Regl Cttee, St George's Coll., Jerusalem, 2000–06. Mem., Governance Cttee and Mgt Council, St Hilda's Anglican Sch. for Girls, Mosman Park, WA, 2002–04; Mem., Council of Mgt, Peter Carnley Anglican Community Sch., 2007– (Dep. Chm., 2007–15; Chair: Bldgs and Grounds Cttee, 2008–15; Future Cttee, 2010–15). Mem., Morsecodians Fraternity of WA. *Recreations:* bagpipe playing, bush walking, swimming, cycling, caravanning, theatre, opera, concerts, reading, entertaining, motorcycling, sailing. *Address:* The Mallee Hut, 29 Charnley Gardens, Waikiki, WA 6169, Australia.

MURRAY, Air Vice-Marshal Hon. David Paul, CVO 2012; OBE 1999 (MBE 1996); Controller, Soldiers, Sailors, Airmen and Families Association (formerly Soldiers, Sailors, Airmen and Families Association Forces Help), since 2012; *b* London, 8 April 1960; *s* of Baron Murray of Epping Forest, OBE, PC and of Heather Murray; *m* 1984, Moira Roche; one *s* one *d. Educ:* RAF Coll., Cranwell. Commnd RAF, 1980; Stn Comdr, RAF Halton, 2000–02; Comdr, Winchester Garrison and Comdt, Defence Coll. of Police, 2002–05; ACOS Trng, 2006–09; rcds 2009; Hd, Defence Personnel Strategy and Progs, MoD, 2009–10; ACDS (Personnel and Trng) and Defence Services Sec., 2010–12. *Recreations:* reading, walking, British history and politics. *Address:* Soldiers, Sailors, Airmen and Families Association, 4 St Dunstan's Hill, EC3R 8AD. *T:* (020) 7463 9205. *E:* david.m@ssafa.org.uk. *Club:* Royal Air Force.

MURRAY, Denis James, OBE 1997; Ireland Correspondent, BBC, 1988–2008; *b* 7 May 1951; *s* of late James and Helen Murray; *m* 1978, Joyce Linehan; two *s* two *d. Educ:* St Malachy's Coll., Belfast; Trinity Coll., Dublin (BA Respondency 1993); Queen's Univ., Belfast (HDipEd). Grad. Trainee, then Reporter, Belfast Telegraph, 1975–77; Belfast Reporter, RTE, 1977–82; BBC: Dublin Correspondent, 1982–84; NI Political Correspondent, 1984–88. *Publications:* (contrib.) BBC Guide to 1997 General Election, 1997. *Recreations:* music, reading, sport, family!

MURRAY, Diana Mary, FSA; FSAScot; Secretary, Royal Commission on the Ancient and Historical Monuments of Scotland, since 2004; *b* 14 Sept. 1952; *d* of Keith and Mary Collyer; *m* 1987, Robin Murray; two *d. Educ:* King Edward VI Camp Hill Sch. for Girls, Birmingham; Univ. of Cambridge (MA 1974). MCIfA (MIFA 1984); FSAScot 1977; FSA 1986. Royal Commission on the Ancient and Historical Monuments of Scotland: Res. Asst, 1976–83; Hd, NMRS recording section, 1983–90; Curator of Archaeology Record, 1990–95; Curator Depute, NMRS, 1995–2004. Chm., Inst. of Field Archaeologists, 1995–96. Trustee: Nat. Trust for Scotland, 2011–14; Royal Botanic Garden Edinburgh, 2014–; Scottish Waterways Trust, 2014–; Scottish Seabird Centre, 2014–. JP E Lothian, 2000–07. *Recreations:* choral singing, gardening. *Address:* Royal Commission on the Ancient and Historical Monuments of Scotland, John Sinclair House, 16 Bernard Terrace, Edinburgh EH8 9NX. *T:* (0131) 662 1456, *Fax:* (0131) 662 1477. *E:* diana.murray@rcahms.gov.uk; The Rowans, 15 Manse Road, Dirleton, East Lothian EH39 5EL. *E:* diana.murray@rowanberry.co.uk.

MURRAY, Rt Hon. Sir Donald (Bruce), Kt 1988; PC 1989; a Lord Justice of Appeal, Supreme Court of Northern Ireland, 1989–93; a Judge of the Restrictive Practices Court, 1987–93; *b* 24 Jan. 1923; *y s* of late Charles Benjamin Murray and late Agnes Mary Murray, Belfast; *m* 1953, Rhoda Margaret (*d* 2005), *oc* of late Thomas and Anna Parke, Londonderry; two *s* one *d. Educ:* Belfast Royal Acad.; Queen's Univ. Belfast (LLB Hons); Trinity Coll. Dublin (BA). 1st Cl., Certif. of Honour, Gray's Inn Prize, English Bar Final Exam., 1944. Called to Bar, Gray's Inn, 1945, Hon Bencher, 1987. Asst Parly Draftsman to Govt of NI, 1945–51; Asst Lectr, Faculty of Law, QUB, 1951–53. Called to NI Bar, 1953, and to Inner Bar, NI, 1964; Bencher, Inn of Court, NI, 1971; Chm., Gen. Council of Bar of NI, 1972–75; Judge of the High Court of Justice, NI, 1975–89. Dep. Chm., Boundary Commn for NI, 1976–84. Chairman: Incorporated Council of Law Reporting for NI, 1974–87 (Mem., 1971); Bd, SLS Legal Publications (NI), 1988–94. Member: UK Delegn to Commn Consultative des Barreaux des Pays des Communautés Européennes, 1972–75; Jt Standing Cttee of Bars of UK and Bar of Ireland, 1972–75; Deptl Cttee on Registration of Title to Land in N Ireland. Chm., Deptl Cttee on Reform of Company Law in NI; Inspector apptd to report on siting of new prison in NI. Mem., Ct of the General Synod of Church of Ireland. Chm., Opera Review Gp, Arts Council of NI, 1998. Hon. LLD QUB, 1996. *Publications:* articles in various legal periodicals. *Recreations:* playing the piano, DXing.

MURRAY, Duncan Law; Sheriff Principal of North Strathclyde, since 2014; *b* 5 May 1959; *s* of James Duncan Murray and Catherine Margaret Law or Murray; *m* 1988, Ianthe Elizabeth Lee Craig; two *s* one *d. Educ:* Aberdeen Grammar Sch.; Aberdeen Univ. (LLB Hons 1980). Robson McLean Paterson: apprentice, 1980–82; Asst, 1982–85; Partner, Robson McLean, 1985–2002; Partner, 2002–14, Chief Exec., 2011–13, Morton Fraser, Solicitors. Part-time Sheriff, 2006–14. Pres., Law Soc. of Scotland, 2004–05. *Recreations:* golf, ski-ing, hill-walking, family. *Address:* Sheriff Court House, St James Street, Paisley PA3 2HW. *T:* (0141) 847 6746, *Fax:* (0141) 889 1748. *Club:* Luffness New Golf.

MURRAY, Elaine Kildare, PhD; Member (Lab) Dumfriesshire, Scottish Parliament, since 2011 (Dumfries, 1999–2011); *b* 22 Dec. 1954; *d* of Kenneth and Patricia Murray; *m* 1986, Jeffrey Leaver; two *s* one *d. Educ:* Edinburgh Univ. (BSc 1st Cl. Hons Chemistry); Cambridge Univ. (PhD Physical Chemistry 1980). Res. Fellow, Cavendish Lab., Cambridge, 1979–82; Researcher, Royal Free Hosp., London, 1982–84; SSO, Inst. of Food Res., Reading, 1984–87; Asst to Alex Smith, MEP, 1990–93; Associate Lectr, Open Univ., 1992–99. Scottish Executive: Dep. Minister for Tourism, Culture and Sport, 2001–03; Shadow Minister for Enterprise, 2007–08, for Envmt, 2008–11, for Rural Affairs and Envmt, 2011–12, for Housing and Transport, 2012–14, for Community Safety, 2014–. Scottish Parliament: Vice Convener, Finance Cttee, 2007–08; Mem., Rural Affairs, Climate Change and Envmt Cttee (formerly Rural Affairs and Envmt Cttee), 2008–11; Mem. Finance Cttee, 2012–13; Mem., Infrastructure and Capital Investment Cttee, 2013–14; Vice Convenor, Justice Cttee, 2014–. *Recreations:* cooking, spending time with my family and pets, exercise, music, reading, gardening. *Address:* 5 Friars' Vennel, Dumfries DG1 2RQ. *T:* (constituency office) (01387) 279205. *E:* elaine.murray.msp@scottish.parliament.uk.

MURRAY, Gordon; *see* Murray, I. G.

MURRAY, Prof. Gordon Cameron, RIBA; PPRIAS; Partner, Ryder Architecture (formerly Director, GMA Ryder), since 2012; Professor of Architecture and Urban Design, University of Strathclyde, since 2007 (Visiting Professor, 2002–07; Head, School of Architecture and Building Science, 2007–12); *b* 26 July 1952; *s* of James and Jessie Murray; *m* 1975, Sharon Boyle; two *d. Educ:* Univ. of Strathclyde (BSc, BArch). MCIArb; RIBA 1988; MRTPI 2010; FRIAS. Assistant Architect: Richard Moira, Betty Moira & James Wann, 1974; Dept of Architecture and Related Services, 1975–77; Project Architect, Sinclair and Watt Architects, 1978–79; Sen. Architect, Cunningham Glass Partnership, 1979–87; Partner: Cunningham Glass Murray Architects, 1987–92; Glass Murray Architects, 1992–99; Partner, Gordon Murray + Alan Dunlop Architects, 2000–10; Principal, Gordon Murray Architects, 2010–12. External Examiner: Univ. of Ulster, 2004–08, Univ. of Bonn, 2011–. Chairman: Technologies' Excellence Gp, Curriculum for Excellence, 2009–10; Standing Council of Hds of UK Schs of Architecture, 2010–12. President: Glasgow Inst. of Architects, 1998–2000; RIAS, 2003–05. Mem. Bd, Lighthouse Trust, 2003–09. *Publications:* An Integrated Transport System for Greater Glasgow, 1977; (with A. Sloan) James Miller, Architect: a monograph, 1990; (contrib.) Challenging Contextualism: the work of gm+ad architects, 2002; Curious Rationalism, 2006; contribs to Herald, Scotsman, Architects' Jl, Prospect, Architectural Rev., Architectural Res. Qly. *Recreations:* cinema, art, saxophone, jazz, travel. *Address:* Ryder Architecture, 221 West George Street, Glasgow G2 2ND. *T:* (0141) 285 0230. *E:* gmurray@ryderarchitecture.com.

MURRAY, Rt Rev. Ian; Bishop of Argyll and the Isles, (RC), 1999–2008, now Bishop Emeritus; *b* 15 Dec. 1932; *s* of John Murray and Margaret Murray (*née* Rodgers). *Educ:* Blairs Coll., Aberdeen; Royal Scots Coll., Valladolid, Spain; BA Hons Open Univ. 1991. Ordained priest, 1956; Curate: Lochore, Fife, 1956–61; St Columba, Edinburgh, 1961–63; Vice-Rector, Royal Scots Coll., Spain, 1963–70; Chaplain, Stirling Univ., 1970–78; Parish Priest: St Bride, Cowdenbeath, 1978–85; St Ninian, Edinburgh, 1985–87; Rector, Royal Scots Coll., Valladolid, 1987–88, Salamanca, 1988–94; Parish Priest: Galashiels, 1994–96; St Francis Xavier, Falkirk, 1996–99; VG, Archdio. of St Andrews and Edinburgh, 1996–99. Prelate of Honour, 1989. *Address:* St Columba's, 9 Upper Gray Street, Edinburgh EH9 1SN. *T:* (0131) 667 3377.

MURRAY, Ian; MP (Lab) Edinburgh South, since 2010; *b* Edinburgh, 10 Aug. 1976; *s* of James Brownlie Murray and Lena Murray; partner, Hannah Catherine Woolfson. *Educ:* Wester Hailes Educn Centre; Univ. of Edinburgh (MA Hons Social Policy and Law). Investment Administrator: WM Co., 1998; AEGON UK, 1998–99; Dir, Ops, Worldart.com, 2000–02; Dir, 100mph Events Ltd, 2002–; Partner, Alibi Bars LLP, 2005–11. Mem. (Lab) Edinburgh CC, 2003–10. PPS to Shadow Sec. of State for Culture, Media and Sport, 2010–11; Shadow Minister for Employee Relns, Postal and Consumer Affairs, 2011–13, for Trade and Investment (incl. Employment Relns and Postal Affairs), 2013–15; Shadow Sec. of State for Scotland, 2015–. Member: Business, Innovation and Skills Select Cttee, 2010–11; Envmtl Audit Select Cttee, 2010–12. *Address:* (office) 31 Minto Street, Edinburgh EH9 2BT. *T:* (0131) 662 4520, *Fax:* (0131) 662 1990. *E:* ian.murray.mp@parliament.uk.

MURRAY, (Ian) Gordon; Chief Executive Officer and Technical Director, Gordon Murray Design Ltd, since 2007; *b* 18 June 1946; *s* of William and Roma Murray; *m* 1970, Stella Gane; one *s. Educ:* Natal Tech. Coll., SA. Moved to England, 1969, to work in motor racing; joined Brabham, 1970: design draughtsman, 1970–73; Chief Designer, 1973–74; Technical Dir, 1974–86 (design innovations incl. fan car, 1978, and hydro-pneumatic suspension, 1981; 22 Grand Prix wins; 2 World Drivers' Formula 1 Championships, first turbo-powered World Championship, 1983); Technical Dir, McLaren Internat., 1986–90 (29 Grand Prix wins; 2 World Drivers' Formula 1 Championships; 2 World Formula 1 Constructors' Championships); Technical Dir, McLaren Cars Ltd, 1990–2004: designed and prod McLaren F1 road car (Fastest Road Car, 1992; GTR version won 2 championships, and Le Mans 1995). Hon. Prof., Durban Inst. of Technology, 2003–. John Bolster Award, Autosport Awards for Technical Achievement, 2014. *Recreations:* motor-cycles, music, food and fine wine, architecture. *Address:* Gordon Murray Design Ltd, Wharfside, Broadford Park, Shalford, Surrey GU4 8EP.

MURRAY, Irena, (Mrs Eric Ormsby), PhD; Sir Banister Fletcher Director (formerly Librarian), British Architectural Library, Royal Institute of British Architects, 2004–13, now Senior Research Fellow; *b* 3 July 1946; *d* of Jiri and Hana Žantovský; *m* 1995, Dr Eric Ormsby; two step *s. Educ:* Charles Univ., Prague (BA 1968); Univ. of Western Ontario, London (MLS 1970); Ecole des Chartes, Paris; McGill Univ., Montreal (MArch 1991; PhD 2003). Bibliographer, Nat. Liby of Canada, 1972; Curator, Nat. Archives of Canada, 1973; McGill University: Librarian, 1973–80; Dir, Art and Arch. Liby, 1981–96; Chief Curator, Rare Books and Special Collections, 1996–2004. FRSA. Hon. FRIBA 2014. *Publications:* (ed) Moshe Safdie: buildings and projects 1967–1992, 1996; (trans.) Karel Teige, Modern Architecture in Czechoslovakia, 2000; (ed) Looking at European Architecture, 2007; (ed) Le Corbusier and Britain, 2008; (ed) Palladio and His Legacy: a transatlantic journey, 2010. *Recreations:* reading, writing, walking. *Address:* c/o Royal Institute of British Architects, 66 Portland Place, W1B 1AD. *T:* (020) 7307 3644, *Fax:* (020) 7307 3719.

MURRAY, Prof. James Dickson, FRS 1985; FRSE 1979; Professor of Mathematical Biology, 1986–92, now Emeritus Professor, and Director, Centre for Mathematical Biology, 1983–92, University of Oxford; Professorial Fellow, 1986–92, Hon. Fellow, 2001, Corpus Christi College, Oxford; Senior Scholar, Princeton University, since 2010; *b* 2 Jan. 1931; *s* of Peter and Sarah Murray; *m* 1959, Sheila (*née* Campbell); one *s* one *d. Educ:* Dumfries Acad.; Univ. of St Andrews (BSc 1953; Carstairs Medal; Miller Prize; PhD 1956); Univ. of Oxford (MA 1961; DSc 1968). CBiol, FRSB (FIBiol 1988); FIMA 2009. Lectr, Applied Maths, King's Coll., Durham Univ., 1955–56; Gordon MacKay Lectr and Res. Fellow, Tutor in Applied Maths, Leverett House, Harvard, 1956–59; Lectr, Applied Maths, UCL, 1959–61; Fellow and Tutor in Maths, Hertford College, Oxford, 1961–63; Res. Associate, Harvard, 1963–64; Prof. of Engineering Mechanics, Univ. of Michigan, 1964–67; Prof. of Maths, New York Univ., 1967–70; Fellow and Tutor in Maths, 1969–85, Sen. Res. Fellow, 1985–86, Corpus Christi Coll., Oxford; Reader in Maths, Univ. of Oxford, 1972–86. Vis. Fellow, St Catherine's Coll., Oxford, 1967; Guggenheim Fellow, Pasteur Inst., Paris, 1968; Visiting Professor: Nat. Tsing Hua Univ., 1975; Univ. of Florence, 1976; MIT, 1979; Winegard Prof., Univ. of Guelph, 1979; Univ. of Utah, 1979, 1985; Ida Beam Prof., Univ. of Iowa, 1980; Univ. of Heidelberg, 1980; CIT, 1983; Univ. of Angers, 1993; La Chaire Européenne, Univ. of Paris, 1994, 1995, 1996; Stan Ulam Vis. Schol., Univ. of Calif. Berkeley's Los Alamos Nat. Lab., 1985; Philip Prof., 1988–94, Boeing Prof., 1997–2000, Prof. Emeritus, 2000, Univ. of Washington (endowed Chair, James D. Murray Prof. of Applied Maths and Neuropathol., est. in perpetuity in his honour, 2007); Hon. Prof., City Univ. of Hong Kong, 2013. Lectures: Scott Hawkins, Southern Methodist Univ., Dallas, 1984; Lansdowne, Univ. of Victoria, 1990; Pinkham, Swedish Hosp., Seattle, 1992 and 1998; Dist. Lecture Series, Emory Univ., 1992; Curle, Univ. of St Andrews, 1994; Smith, St Catherine's Coll., Oxford, 1994; Class of '62, Williams Coll., 1995; Faculty, 1998, Boeing Distinguished, 2011, Univ. of Washington, 1998; Bakerian, Royal Soc., 2009; Rees, Univ. of Delaware, 2009; Sears, Woods Hole Oceanographic Inst., 2010; Leonardo da Vinci Prize Lectr and Medal, Eur. Acad. of Scis, Milan, 2011; Turing Centenary Conf., Microsoft Res. Lectr, Univ. of Cambridge, and Plenary Lectr, Univ. of Princeton, 2012; Inaugural Hooke, Univ. of Oxford, 2014; 21st Anniversary Pekeris, Weizmann Inst., 2014. Math. Comr, SERC, 1985–88; Founding Pres., European Soc. for Mathematical and Theoretical Biol., 1991–94; Member: Bd of Dirs, Soc. for Mathematical Biol., USA, 1986–89; ESF Network Cttee, 1991–94. For. Mem., Acad. des Scis, France, 2000; Hon. Mem., Edinburgh Mathematical Soc., 2008. Hon. DSc: St Andrews, 1994; Strathclyde, 1999; Hon. Dr Math: Milan, 2004; Waterloo, 2006; Hon. LLD Dundee, 2011. Naylor Lect. and Prize in Applied Math., London Math. Soc., 1989; Akira Okubo Prize, Soc. for Mathematical Biol., USA, 2005; Gold Medal, IMA, 2009; William Benter Prize in Applied Maths, City Univ. of Hong Kong, 2012. *Publications:* Asymptotic Analysis, 1974, 3rd edn 1996; Nonlinear Differential Equation Models in Biology, 1977 (trans. Russian 1983); (ed with S. Brenner and L. Wolpert) Theories of Biological Pattern Formation, 1981; (ed with W. Jäger) Modelling of Patterns in Space and Time, 1984; Mathematical Biology, 1989, 3rd edn in 2 vols, vol. I 2002 (trans. Polish 2006, Russian 2009, Japanese 2013), vol. II 2003 (trans. Russian 2010); (ed with H. G. Othmer and P. K. Maini) Experimental and Theoretical Advances in Biological Pattern Formation, 1993; (jtly) The Mathematics of Marriage, 2002; several hundred articles in learned jls on the application of maths in biomed. scis.

MURRAY, Janice; Director General (formerly Director), National Army Museum, since 2010; *b* Newcastle-upon-Tyne, 15 Aug. 1957; *d* of Harold and Irene Blair; *m* 1st, 1982, Terence Christopher Murray (*d* 2000); two *s*; 2nd, 2004, David John Stockdale. *Educ:* Dame Allan's Girls' Sch.; Univ. of Warwick (BA Hons Hist.); Univ. of Leicester (Postgrad. Cert. Mus. Studies). Curator, Mus. and Art Gall., St Helen's, 1982–86; Keeper of Human Hist., Dundee Art Galls and Museums, 1986–96; Arts and Heritage Manager, Dundee CC, 1996–2002; Dep. Hd, Nat. Rlwy Mus., York, 2002–08; Chief Exec., Royal Armouries, 2009–10. Mem. Bd, Internat. Cttee of Museums and Collections of Arms and Military History, 2013–. Mem. Cttee, British Friends of Normandy, 2011–. FRSA. *Recreations:* gardening, hardy plants, contemporary glass, bagging bargains. *Address:* National Army Museum, Royal Hospital Road, SW3 4HT. *T:* (020) 7881 2402, *Fax:* (020) 7823 6573. *E:* jmurray@nam.ac.uk. *Clubs:* Sloane, Army and Navy.

MURRAY, Dame Jennifer Susan, (Dame Jenni), DBE 2011 (OBE 1999); Presenter, Woman's Hour, BBC Radio 4, since 1987; *b* 12 May 1950; *d* of Alvin Bailey and Win Bailey (*née* Jones); *m* 1971, Brian Murray (marr. diss. 1978); partner, David Forgham-Bailey; two *s. Educ:* Barnsley Girls' High Sch.; Hull Univ. (BA Hons French/Drama). BBC Radio Bristol, 1973–78; BBC TV South, 1978–82; BBC Newsnight, 1982–85; BBC Radio 4 Today,

1985–87. Vis. Prof., London Inst., 2000–. TV documentaries include: Everyman: Stand By Your Man, 1987, Breaking the Chain, 1988, As We Forgive Them, 1989; The Duchy of Cornwall, 1985, Women in Politics, 1989; Here's Looking At You, 1991; Presenter: Points of View, 1993; This Sunday, 1993–95; Dilemmas, 1994; The Turning World, 1998–2001; The Message, BBC Radio 4, 2001. Weekly columnist, The Express, 1998–2000. Pres., Fawcett Soc., 2001–; Patron: FPA, 2002–; Breast Cancer Campaign; non-exec. Dir, The Christie, until 2014. Hon. DLitt Bradford, 1994; DUniv Open, 1999; Hon. Dr: Sheffield; Bristol; St Andrews; Huddersfield; Salford. *Publications:* The Woman's Hour Book of Humour, 1993; The Woman's Hour: a history of British women 1946–1996, 1996; Is It Me Or Is It Hot In Here, 2001; That's My Boy!, 2003; Memoirs of a Not So Dutiful Daughter, 2008; My Boy Butch, 2011; contrib. to newspapers and periodicals. *Recreations:* reading, theatre, riding. *Address:* c/o Woman's Hour, BBC, Broadcasting House, Portland Place, W1A 1AA. *T:* (020) 7765 4314.

MURRAY, John; *see* Dervaird, Hon. Lord.

MURRAY, Prof. John Joseph, CBE 1997; PhD; FDSRCS; FMedSci; Dean of Dentistry, University of Newcastle upon Tyne, 1992–2002, now Professor Emeritus; Clinical Director, Dental Hospital, Royal Victoria Infirmary NHS Trust, Newcastle upon Tyne, 1995–2002; *b* 28 Dec. 1941; *s* of late John Gerald Murray, Bradford, and Margaret Sheila (*née* Parle); *m* 1967, Valerie (*d* 2002), *d* of late Harry and Lillie Allen; two *s. Educ:* St Bede's Grammar Sch., Bradford; Univ. of Leeds (BChD 1966; MChD 1968; PhD 1970); FDSRCS 1973; MCCDRCS 1989. Res. Fellow in Children's and Preventive Dentistry, Leeds Univ., 1966–70; Sen. Lectr in Children's Dentistry, 1970–75, Reader, 1975–77, Inst. of Dental Surgery, London; University of Newcastle upon Tyne: Prof. of Child Dental Health, 1977–92; Dental Postgrad. Sub-Dean, 1982–92. Chm., Cleft Lip and Palate Cttee, Clinical Standards Adv. Gp, 1998. Chm., Educn Cttee, GDC, 1999–2003. Mem., Children's Task Force, DoH, 2002–05. Chm., Multi-professional Postgrad. Dental Educn Cttee, Northern Deanery, NHS North East, 2007–14. Founder FMedSci 1998. Hon. MFPHM 1998. John Tomes Medal, BDA, 1993; H. Trendley Dean Award, Internat. Assoc. Dental Res., 1997; Colyer Gold Medal, RCS, 1999. *Publications:* (jtly) The Acid Etch Technique in Paedodontics and Orthodontics, 1985; Fluorides in Caries Prevention, 1976, 3rd edn (jtly) 1991; Appropriate Use of Fluorides for Human Health, 1985; The Prevention of Dental Disease, 1983, 4th edn 2003 as The Prevention of Oral Disease. *Recreations:* golf, photography. *Address:* 6 Regency Way, Darras Hall, Ponteland, Newcastle upon Tyne NE20 9AU. *T:* (01661) 871035. *Club:* Ponteland Golf (Capt. 2006; Chm., 2007–10).

MURRAY, John Loyola; Hon. Mr Justice John Murray; Chief Justice of Ireland, 2004–11; Senior Ordinary Judge, Supreme Court of Ireland, since 2011; Chancellor, University of Limerick, since 2013; *b* 27 June 1943; *s* of Cecil Murray and Catherine (*née* Casey); *m* 1969, Gabrielle Walsh; one *s* one *d. Educ:* Crescent Coll.; Rockwell Coll.; University Coll. Dublin and King's Inns (Barrister-at-Law). Called to the Bar, Supreme Court, Ireland, 1967, Bencher, 1985; called to the Inner Bar, 1981; Attorney Gen. of Ireland, Aug.–Dec. 1982; in private practice at the Bar of Ireland, 1982–87; Attorney Gen., 1987–91; Judge of Court of Justice of European Communities, 1991–99; Judge, Supreme Court of Ireland, 1999–2004. Mem., Council of State, 1982, 1987–91, 2004–. Vis. Lectr, Georgetown Univ. Summer Sch., Heidelberg and Florence, 1994–2002; Vis. Prof. of Law, Univ. of Louvain, 1997–2000; Adjunct Prof. of Law, Univ. of Limerick, 2012–. Hon. Co-chair, Internat. Law Inst., Washington, 1996–. Chairman: Bd, Courts Service, 2004–11; Judicial Appts Adv. Bd, 2004–11. Chairperson: Anti-Fraud Cttee, Eur. Central Bank, 2000–03; Ethical Cttee, EC, 2004–07. Governor: Marsh's Liby, Dublin, 2004–; St Patrick's Hosp., Dublin, 2004–. Hon. LLD: Limerick, 1993; New England Sch. of Law, 2006. Grand Cross, OM (Luxembourg), 1991. *Publications:* legal articles in law jls and other pubns. *Clubs:* Athenæum; Stephen's Green, Fitzwilliam Lawn Tennis (Dublin); Royal Irish Yacht.

MURRAY, Kevin; Chairman, Good Relations Group, since 2012; *b* Bulawayo, Rhodesia, 9 June 1954; *s* of Ian and Shirley Murray; *m* 1978, Elisabeth Anne Mary Whalley; one *s* one *d. Educ:* Hyde Park High Sch., Johannesburg. The Star, Johannesburg: court reporter and crime reporter, 1973–76; Foreign corresp., Argus Co., London, 1977–78; Air corresp. and Transport Ed., 1978–80; News Ed., 1980–81; Gp Pubns Ed. and PR Exec., Barlow Rd Ltd, Johannesburg, 1981–82; Man. Ed., Leadership SA Mag., 1982–83; Dir, Mktg and Advertising, Churchill Murray Pubns, Johannesburg, 1984–85; Managing Director: Kestrel Pubns, 1985–87; Shearwater Communications, 1987–88; Gp Public Relns Manager, Bayer plc, UK, 1988–92; Director: Corporate Communications, UKAEA, 1992–94; Corporate Affairs, AEA Technol., 1994–96; of Communications, British Airways, 1996–98; Sen. Consultant, 1998–99, Man. Dir, 1999–2002, Bell Pottinger Consultants; Chief Exec., 2002–05, Chm., 2005–12, Bell Pottinger Gp. FCIPR 2005. *Publications:* The Language of Leaders, 2011. *Recreations:* golf, cinema, walking, cycling. *Address:* Good Relations Group, 26 Southampton Buildings, WC2A 1PQ. *T:* (020) 7861 8572, *Fax:* (020) 7491 9853. *E:* kmurray@chime.plc.uk. *Clubs:* Royal Automobile; Frilford Heath Golf.

MURRAY, Prof. Leo Gerard; Director, Cranfield School of Management, 1986–2003; *b* 21 May 1943; *s* of Patrick and Teresa Murray; *m* 1970, Pauline Ball; one *s* one *d. Educ:* St Aloysius' Coll., Glasgow; Univ. of Rennes; Glasgow Univ. (MA Hons 1965). British Petroleum Co., 1965–67; Courtaulds Gp, 1968–75; A. T. Kearney Ltd, 1975–79; Rothmans International Ltd, 1979–86: Man. Dir, Murray Sons & Co. Ltd, 1979–82; Dir, Overseas Mfg and Licensing, 1982–85; Dir, ME Region, 1985–86. Pro Vice-Chancellor, Cranfield Inst. of Technology, then Univ., 1992–95. Mem., Textile Sector Gp, NEDO, 1987–88. Chairman: ICL Cranfield Business Games Ltd, 1987–92; Cranfield Conference Centre, 1993–2003; Man. Dir, Cranfield Management Develt Ltd, 1993–2003; Chm., Fairmays Solicitors, 2001–03. Board Member: E of England Develt Agency, 2000–06; E of England Internat., 2004–06. Non-exec. Dir, Spectris plc, 2003–06. Director and Treasurer: Council of Univ. Management Schs, 1987–92; Assoc. of Business Schs, 1992–93 and 1999–2003; Bd Mem., Eur. Foundn for Mgt Develt, 2000–03; Membre: Conseil d'Orientation, Ecole Internat. d'Affaires, Marseilles, 1988–91; Conseil d'Admin, Univ. Technique de Compiègne, 1996–99; Conseil d'Admin, Reims Mgt Sch., France, 2009–12; Internat. Adv. Bd, Lingnan University Coll., China, 2010–. Vice-Pres., Strategic Planning Soc., 1992–99. Chairman: Bd, Euro-Arab Management Sch., Granada, Spain, 2003–06; Govs, Nat. Centre for Languages, 2004–05. Trustee: Blind in Business, 1992–2005; Macintyre Charitable Trust, 2003–08. FCIM 1988; FRSA 1989; CCMI 2000. *Recreations:* family, golf. *Address:* The Beeches, 2 Church Lane, Lathbury, Bucks MK16 8JY. *T:* (01908) 615574. *Club:* Woburn Golf and Country.

MURRAY, Leo Joseph, CB 1986; QC (Aust.) 1980; legislation consultant, since 1989; Parliamentary Counsel, Queensland, Australia, 1975–89; *b* 7 April 1927; *s* of William Francis Murray and Theresa Agnes Murray (*née* Sheehy); *m* 1957, Janet Barbara Weir (marr. diss. 1987); two *d. Educ:* St Columban's Coll., Brisbane; Univ. of Queensland (BA, LLB). Admitted Barrister, Supreme Court, Queensland, 1951; Asst Crown Prosecutor, 1958; Asst Parly Counsel, 1963. *Recreation:* golf. *Address:* 99 Red Hill Road, Nudgee, Qld 4014, Australia. *T:* (7) 32675786. *Clubs:* Irish, Nudgee Golf (Brisbane).

MURRAY, Leslie Allan, (Les), AO 1989; poet; *b* 17 Oct. 1938; *s* of late Cecil Allan Murray and Miriam Pauline Murray (*née* Arnall); *m* 1962, Valerie Gina Morelli; three *s* two *d. Educ:* Univ. of Sydney (BA 1969). Acting Editor, Poetry Australia, 1973–80; Editor, New Oxford Book of Australian Verse, 1985–97; Literary Editor, Quadrant, 1987–. Hon. doctorates from univs of New England, Stirling, NSW, ANU, La Trobe, Sydney and St Andrews. Petrarca Prize, Germany, 1995; T. S. Eliot Prize, 1997; Queen's Gold Medal for Poetry, 1998. *Publications:* Collected Poems, 1976, rev. edn 1998, US edn as The Rabbiters Bounty, 1992; The Boys Who Stole the Funeral (verse novel), 1980; The Paperbark Tree (selected prose), 1991; (ed) Fivefathers, 1995; Subhuman Redneck Poems, 1996; Killing the Black Dog: essays and poems, 1996 (trans. Swedish, 2008), 2nd edn with Afterword, 2009; A Working Forest (prose), 1997; Fredy Neptune (verse novel), 1998 (Mondello Prize, Italy, 2004) (trans. Dutch, 2000, Italian and German, 2004, Norwegian, 2007); Conscious & Verbal (verse), 1999; Learning Human: selected poems (NY Times and Amer. Nat. Liby Assoc. Notable Book award), 2001, updated edn 2003; Poems the Size of Photographs, 2002; New Collected Poems, 2002; Hell and After: the first important English-language Australian poets, 2004; The Biplane Houses (verse), 2006; Taller When Prone (verse), 2010; (ed) The Quadrant Book of Poetry 2001–10, 2011. *Recreations:* work, gossip, fine coffee, ruminative driving, film-going. *Address:* c/o Margaret Connolly & Associates, 16 Winton Street, Warrawee, NSW 2074, Australia.

MURRAY, Michael Thomas; HM Diplomatic Service, retired; *b* 13 Oct. 1945; *s* of late Robert Murray and Anne Clark Murray (*née* Leech); *m* 1968, Else Birgitta Margareta Paues; one *s* one *d. Educ:* Bedlington Grammar Sch. Joined FO, 1964; DSAO, 1964; Prague, 1967; Vienna, 1971; Vice-Consul (Commercial), Frankfurt, 1973; Second Sec. (Develt), Khartoum, 1977; FCO, 1980; First Sec. and Hd of Chancery, Banjul, 1983; FCO, 1988; First Sec. (Develt/Econ.), Lusaka, 1995; on loan to DFID, Lusaka, 1998; Dep. Consul Gen., Chicago, 1999; Ambassador to Eritrea, 2002–06. Member: Cttee, Friends of Bellingham Surgery, 2007–; New Leader Project, Northumberland Uplands Local Action Gp, 2008–. *Recreations:* living lightly; coarse, chemical-free horticulture; my logpile, golf, arts and crafts. *Address:* The Old Rectory, Falstone, Hexham, Northumberland NE48 1AE. *Clubs:* Laholms Golf (Sweden); Hexham Golf.

MURRAY of Blackbarony, Sir Nigel Andrew Digby, 15th Bt *cr* 1628; farmer; *b* 15 Aug. 1944; *s* of Sir Alan John Digby Murray of Blackbarony, 14th Bt, and of Mabel Elisabeth, *d* of late Arthur Bernard Schiele, Arias, Argentina; *S* father, 1978; *m* 1980, Diana Margaret, *yr d* of Robert C. Bray, Arias, Argentina; one *s* two *d. Educ:* St Paul's School, Argentina; Salesian Agricl Sch., Argentina; Royal Agricultural Coll., Cirencester. Farms dairy cattle, store cattle, crops and bees. *Heir: s* Alexander Nigel Robert Murray [*b* 1 July 1981. *Educ:* Univ. of Buenos Aires]. *Address:* Establecimiento Tinamú, cc 67, 2624 Arias, Provincia de Córdoba, Argentina. *T:* (03468) 441231, 449801.

MURRAY, Norman Loch, CA; FRSE; Chairman: Edrington Group Ltd, since 2013 (Director, 2012–13); Scottish Ballet, since 2013; President, Institute of Chartered Accountants of Scotland, 2006–07; *b* 17 March 1948; *s* of Thomas Loch Murray and May Fox Murray (*née* Davidson); *m* 1973, Pamela Anne Low; two *s. Educ:* George Watson's Coll., Edinburgh; Heriot-Watt Univ. (BA 1971); Harvard Business Sch. (PMD 1987). CA 1976. Grad. trainee, Scottish & Newcastle Breweries, 1971–73; CA apprentice, Arthur Young McLelland Moores & Co., Edinburgh, 1973–76; Dep. Manager, Peat Marwick Mitchell & Co., Hong Kong, 1976–80; Asst Lectr, Accountancy and Finance, Heriot-Watt Univ., 1980; Manager, Royal Bank Develt Capital Ltd, 1980–84; Dir, Charterhouse Develt Capital Ltd, 1984–89; Dep. Chief Exec., 1989–96, Chief Exec., 1996–97, Chm., 1998, Morgan Grenfell Private Equity Ltd; Director: Morgan Grenfell & Co. Ltd, 1989–98; Morgan Grenfell Asset Mgt Ltd, 1997–98. Non-executive Director: Taunton Cider Co. Ltd, 1991–93; Bristow Helicopter Gp Ltd, 1991–96; Penta Capital Partners Hldgs Ltd, 1999–2007; Robert Wiseman Dairies plc, 2003–11; Greene King plc, 2004–12; Chm., Cairn Energy plc, 2002–11 (Dir, 1999–2011); Dep. Chm., Cairn India Ltd, 2006–08; Chm., Petrofac Ltd, 2011–14. Mem. Council, 1992–97, Chm., 1997–98, British Venture Capital Assoc. Mem. Council, 1992–98, Sen. Vice-Pres., 2005–06, ICAS. Chm., Audit Firm Governance Wkg Gp, Financial Reporting Council, 2008–10 (reported, 2010). Chm., Governing Council, George Watson's Coll., 2004–09 (Gov., 1994–2004). Gov., St Columba's Hospice, 1998–2003 (Chm., Investment Cttee, 1998–2003). Hon. Prof., Heriot-Watt Univ., Edinburgh, 2008–. FRSE 2015. *Publications:* (jtly) Making Corporate Reports Valuable, 1988. *Recreations:* climbing and hill walking, classic cars, golf, squash, travel, silviculture, addressing the haggis. *Address:* Ettrick, 8 Pentland Avenue, Colinton, Edinburgh EH13 0HZ. *Clubs:* Harvard Business School of London; New (Edinburgh); Luffness New Golf; Royal Hong Kong Yacht.

MURRAY, Sir Patrick (Ian Keith), 12th Bt *cr* 1673; *b* 22 March 1965; *s* of Sir William Patrick Keith Murray, 11th Bt, and of Susan Elizabeth (who *m* 1976, J. C. Hudson, PhD), *d* of Stacey Jones; *S* father, 1977. *Educ:* Christ College, Brecon, Powys; LAMDA. *Heir: kinsman* Major Peter Keith-Murray, Canadian Forces [*b* 12 July 1935; *m* 1960, Judith Anne, *d* of late Andrew Tinsley; one *s* one *d*].

MURRAY, Rev. Paul B.; *see* Beasley-Murray.

MURRAY, Peter Gerald Stewart; Chairman, Wordsearch, 2004–14 (Managing Director, 1983–2004); Founder Director, London Architecture Biennale, 2004, 2006; Chairman, New London Architecture, since 2012 (Exhibition Director, 2005–12); Director, London Festival of Architecture, 2008, 2010, 2012; *b* 6 April 1944; *s* of Stewart and Freda Murray; *m* 1967, Jane Wood; two *s* two *d. Educ:* King's Coll., Taunton; Sch. of Architecture, Royal West of England Acad., Bristol; Dept of Architecture, Univ. of Bristol; Architectural Assoc. Sch. of Architecture. Editor, Building Design, 1974–79; Editor, RIBA Jl, and Man. Dir, RIBA Magazines Ltd, 1979–84; founded Wordsearch Ltd and launched Blueprint mag., 1983. Editor, Pidgeon Digital, 2007–; Editor-in-Chief, New London Qly, 2010–. Mem., Mayor of London's Design Adv. Gp, 2012–. Mem. Council, 1987–90, Hon. Sec., 1989–90, AA; Mem. Architecture Cttee, RA, 2000–06. Exhibition Co-organiser: New Architecture: the work of Foster, Rogers and Stirling, RA, 1986; Living Bridges: the inhabited bridge, past, present and future, RA, 1996; New City Architecture, Broadgate, 2004. Vis. Prof., IE Univ., Madrid, 2011–. Trustee, Bannister Fletcher, 1984–86. Dep. Chm., Bedford Park Soc., 1998– (Hon. Sec., 1998–2013); Chm., London Soc., 2014–. Trustee, Cycle to Cannes, charity cycle ride, 2009–14 (Dir, 2006–09). Academician, Acad. of Urbanism, 2012. FRSA 1990. Hon. FRIBA 2000. Liveryman, Chartered Architects' Co., 2008 (Mem. Ct of Assts, 2010–; Upper Warden, 2014–15). *Publications:* Modern Architecture in Britain, 1984; Contemporary British Architects, 1995; Living Bridges (exhibn catalogue), 1996; New Urban Environments, 1997; The Saga of Sydney Opera House, 2004; Architecture and Commerce, 2005; 50 Years of London Architecture, 2010; A Passion to Build, 2012. *Recreations:* cycling, wood turning, looking at buildings, sketching, London. *Address:* 31 Priory Avenue, Bedford Park, W4 1TZ. *E:* pgsmurray@mac.com. *Clubs:* Athenæum, Architecture (Hon. Sec., 1978–), Hurlingham.

MURRAY, Richard Dixon, CB 2012; Director of Policy, The King's Fund, since 2014; *b* Bristol, 23 March 1965; *s* of Gerald Roy Murray and Jean Margaret Murray; civil partnership 2012, Tom Johnston Penman. *Educ:* Wellsway Comp. Sch.; Brasenose Coll., Oxford (BA Mod. Hist. and Econs 1986). Sen. Lectr, London Guildhall Univ., 1990–93; Econ. Advr, DoH, 1993–98; McKinsey & Co., 1998–2002; Department of Health: Sen. Econ. Advr, 2002–06; Dir, Finance and Strategy, 2006–13, and Chief Economist and Dir of Strategy, 2011–13; Chief Economist, NHS Commissioning Bd, 2013–14. *Recreations:* RSPB, Victorian literature, travel, ballet. *Address:* The King's Fund, 11–13 Cavendish Square, W1G 0AN. *T:* (020) 7307 2598. *E:* r.murray@kingsfund.org.uk.

MURRAY, Sir Robert Sydney, (Sir Bob), Kt 2010; CBE 2002; FCCA; Chairman and Founder, Omega International Group, since 1992; *b* Newcastle upon Tyne, 3 Aug. 1946; *s* of Sydney and Elsie Murray; *m* Susan Diane Gorman; one *s* two *d. Educ:* Consett Jun. Sch.; Annfield Plain Secondary Mod. Sch.; Consett Tech. Coll.; Newcastle Poly.; Leeds Poly. FCCA 1972. Dir and Founder, Spring Ram, 1978–89; Director: FKI plc, 1991–99; Wembley

Nat. Stadium, 2002. Dir, 1984–2006, Chm., 1986–2006, Life Pres., 2006, Sunderland AFC. Director: Stadia Bd, Football Foundn, 2004; Academy 360, 2005–. Project Dir, Nat. Football Centre, 2008–. Chm. Trustees, Sunderland AFC Foundn of Light, 2001–. Chancellor, Leeds Beckett (formerly Leeds Metropolitan) Univ., 2013–. Hon. Fellow, Sunderland Univ., 1991. Hon. DBA: Sunderland Univ., 1997; Leeds Metropolitan, 2008. Internat. Ambassador for Derwentside, Derwentside Council, 1999; Worldwide Ambassador for Sunderland, 2005. Freedom, City of Sunderland, 2011. *Recreations:* children and family, keeping fit, swimming and walking, travel and boating, spending time with my many entertaining and loyal friends, helping to realise projects and to assist people in the communities in which I have lived, passionate about lifelong learning and education and helping the next generation achieve their potential, anything and everything to do with Sunderland and NE England, football and in particular Sunderland AFC. *E:* nichola@sirbobmurray.com.

MURRAY, Sir Robin (MacGregor), Kt 2011; MD; FRS 2010; Professor of Psychiatric Research, Institute of Psychiatry, Psychology and Neuroscience (formerly Institute of Psychiatry), King's College London, since 2009 (Professor of Psychiatry, 1999–2009); *b* 31 Jan. 1944; *s* of James Alistair Campbell Murray and Helen Murray; *m* 1970, Shelagh Harris (marr. diss. 2013); one *s* one *d*; *m* 2014, Marta Di Forti. *Educ:* Royal High Sch., Edinburgh; Glasgow Univ. (MB, ChB 1968; MD 1974). MRCP 1971; MRCPsych 1976; MPhil London, 1976; DSc London, 1989. Registrar, Dept of Medicine, Univ. of Glasgow/Western Infirmary, 1971; Sen. House Officer, successively Registrar and Sen. Registrar, Maudsley Hosp., 1972–76; Vis. Fellow, National Inst. of Health, Washington, DC, 1977; Institute of Psychiatry, 1978–: Sen. Lectr, 1978–82; Dean, 1982–89; Prof. of Psychol Medicine, KCL, 1989–99. Pres., Assoc. of European Psychiatrists, 1995–96. For. Mem., Inst. of Medicine, USA, 2004. Founder FMedSci 1998. *Publications:* (jtly) Essentials of Postgraduate Psychiatry, 1979; (jtly) Misuse of Psychotropic Drugs, 1981; Lectures on the History of Psychiatry, 1990; Schizophrenia, 1996; Neurodevelopment and Adult Psychopathology, 1997; Psychosis in the Inner City, 1998; (jtly) First Episode Psychosis, 1999; (ed jtly) Comprehensive Care of Schizophrenia, 2000; (jtly) An Atlas of Schizophrenia, 2002; Marijuana and Madness, 2004; articles on schizophrenia, depression, brain imaging and psychiatric genetics. *Recreations:* Scottish and Jamaican music, swimming, walking labrador.

MURRAY, Roger; Chairman, Fuerst Day Lawson Holdings, 1998–2008; *b* 8 June 1936; *s* of Donald Murray and Nancy (*née* Irons); *m* 1960, Anthea Mary (*née* Turnbull); one *s* three *d*. *Educ:* Uppingham Sch.; Brasenose Coll., Oxford (MA). RNVR (Sub-Lieut), 1954–56. Joined Cargill Inc., Minneapolis, 1959; President: Cargill Canada, 1973; Cargill Europe Ltd, 1982–97; Chm., Cargill plc, 1982–97; Mem., Management Cttee, Cargill Inc., 1986–97. Dir, various Canadian cos, 1975–82. Chairman: JP Morgan Fleming Emerging Markets IT, 1994–2003; Pacific Rim Palm Oil Ltd (Mauritius), 2001–05. Mem. Bd, Commonwealth Develt Corp., 1997–2000. Canadian and British citizen. Ind. Mem., Chatham House, 1999–. FRGS 1990. *Recreations:* sailing, ski-ing, mountaineering, golf. *Address:* 25 Addison Avenue, Holland Park, W11 4QS. *T:* (020) 7603 3904. *Clubs:* Denham Golf; Alpine; Royal Lake of the Woods Yacht (Kenora, Ont) (Cdre, 2008–11).

MURRAY, Ronald King; *see* Murray, Rt Hon. Lord.

MURRAY, Sir Rowland William, 15th Bt *cr* 1630, of Dunerne, Fifeshire; *b* 22 Sept. 1947; *s* of Sir Rowland William Patrick Murray, 14th Bt and Josephine Margaret Murray (*née* Murphy) (*d* 1989); *S* father, 1994, but his name does not appear on the Official Roll of the Baronetage; *m* 1970, Nancy Diane, *d* of George C. Newberry; one *s* one *d*. *Educ:* Georgia State Univ. (SB 1974). General Manager, Beverly Hall Furniture Galleries, retail furniture and accessories. *Recreations:* golf, gardening, travel. *Heir: s* Rowland William Murray IV, *b* 31 July 1979. *Address:* 2565 Habersham Road NW, Atlanta, GA 30305–3577, USA. *T:* (404) 2662408. *Clubs:* Midtown Atlanta Rotary, Atlanta High Museum of Art, Atlanta Botanical Gardens.

MURRAY, Ruth Hilary; *see* Finnegan, R. H.

MURRAY, Sara Elizabeth, OBE 2012; Founder and Chief Executive, Buddi, since 2004; *b* Lancs, 2 Nov. 1968; *d* of Anthony Murray and Patricia Murray; one *d*. *Educ:* Malvern Girls' Coll.; St Hilda's Coll., Oxford (BA Hons PPP 1990); Univ. of Lausanne (Adv. Dip. French 1992). Founder and Chief Executive Officer: Ninah Consulting, 1992–2003; Inspop.com Ltd, 1998–2002; Dir, Business Develt, Zenith Optimedia, 2002–03. Non-exec. Dir, Schering Health Care, 2002–07. Member: Governing Bd, Technol. Strategy Bd, 2009–; Business Sec.'s Entrepreneurs' Forum, 2010–. Mem., Founding Bd, Seedcamp, 2007–. Mem., Develt Council, NPG, 2011–. Hon. DBus Plymouth, 2011. Entrepreneur of the Year, Orange Nat. Business Awards, 2009. *Recreations:* Private Pilot Licence (Helicopters) - helicopter flying in perfect weather, sailing, fishing, shooting, ski-ing. *Address:* Buddi, 52 Warwick Square, SW1V 2AJ. *E:* sara@buddi.co.uk, sara@rhogroup.com. *Clubs:* Queen's, Groucho.

MURRAY, Sheryll; MP (C) South East Cornwall, since 2010; *b* Millbrook, Cornwall, 4 Feb. 1956; *d* of Edgar and Elaine Hickman; *m* 1986, Neil Murray (*d* 2011); one *s* one *d*. *Educ:* Torpoint Sch. Insce underwriter, 1972–88; GP receptionist, 1990–2010. Mem. (C) Cornwall CC, 2001–05. *Address:* Windsor Place, Liskeard, Cornwall PL14 4BH. *T:* (01579) 344428. *E:* sheryll@sheryllmurray.com.

MURRAY, Simon Anthony, CEng; consultant; non-executive Director, Highways Agency, since 2012; *b* 31 Aug. 1951; *s* of Frank Murray and Barbara (*née* Williams); *m* 1st, 1974, Anne Humphrey (marr. diss. 1982); 2nd, 1983, Lindsay Maxwell (marr. diss. 2004); two *s* one *d*. *Educ:* Welbeck Coll.; Imperial Coll., London (BSc). CEng 1978; MICE 1978; FCGI 1999. Ove Arup & Partners: S Africa, 1975–77; Kenya, Zimbabwe, Hong Kong and London, 1977–89; Dir, 1990–94; Man. Dir, Gp Technical Services, BAA plc, 1995–98; Dir, Major Projects and Investment, Railtrack plc, 1999–2001. Non-executive Director: Ascot Authority (Hldgs) Ltd, 2000–06; Manchester Airport Develts Ltd, 2002–04; Chm., Geoffrey Osborne Ltd, 2003–12. Mem., EPSRC, 1998–2001. *Recreations:* gym, wine, reading. *Address:* 150 Langton Way, Blackheath, SE3 7JS.

MURRAY, Susan Elizabeth, (Mrs M. Weston); non-executive Director, Compass Group plc, since 2007; *m* 1989, Michael Weston; one step *d*. *Educ:* Communications, Advertising and Mktg Dip. 1978. Colgate-Palmolive, 1979–82; General Foods, then Kraft General Foods, 1982–89; Duracell, 1989–92; Worldwide Pres. and CEO, Pierre Smirnoff Co., 1992–98; Chief Exec., Littlewoods Stores, Littlewoods, 1998–2004. Non-exec. Chm., Farrow and Ball, 2007–14; non-executive Director: Enterprise Inns plc, 2004–14; Imperial Tobacco Gp plc, 2004–14; Wm Morrison Supermarkets plc, 2005–10; SSL International plc, 2005–08; Pernod Ricard SA, 2010–14. Council Mem. and Dir, ASA, 2003–09. *Recreations:* cycling, walking, theatre. *E:* info@susan-murray.com. *Clubs:* Forum UK, Women's Advertising Club of London.

MURRAY WELLS, James Nicholas, OBE 2015; Industry Head, Retail, Google, since 2013; *b* Westminster, London, 21 March 1983; *s* of Simon Henry Murray Wells and Alison Benedict Murray Wells. *Educ:* Harrow Sch.; Univ. of the West of England (BA Hons Eng.). Founder and Executive Chairman, Glasses Direct, 2004–13. Co-Founder, StartUp Britain, 2011–13. Queen's Award for Enterprise Promotion, 2009. *Address:* Google, 1–13 St Giles High Street, WC2H 8AG.

MURRELL, Geoffrey David George, CMG 1993; OBE 1987; HM Diplomatic Service, retired; *b* 19 Dec. 1934; *s* of Stanley Hector Murrell and Kathleen Murrell (Martin); *m* 1962, Kathleen Ruth Berton; one *s* three *d*. *Educ:* Minchenden Grammar School, Southgate; Lincoln Coll., Oxford (BA French and Russian, MA). FCO Research Dept, 1959–61; Moscow, 1961–64; FCO, 1964–68; Moscow, 1968–70; Head, Soviet Section, FCO Research Dept, 1970–75; First Sec., Belgrade, 1975–78; Regional Dir, Soviet and East European Region, Research Dept, 1978–83; Counsellor, Moscow, 1983–87; Counsellor, Res. Dept, FCO, 1987–91; Minister-Counsellor, Moscow, 1991–94. *Publications:* Russia's Transition to Democracy, 1996. *Recreations:* guitar, Russian and Italian literature.

MURRELL, Prof. John Norman, PhD; FRS 1991; FRSC; Professor of Chemistry, University of Sussex, 1965–99, now Emeritus (Pro-Vice-Chancellor (Science), 1985–88); *b* London, 2 March 1932; *m* 1954, Dr D. Shirley Read; two *s* two *d*. *Educ:* Univ. of London (BSc); Univ. of Cambridge (PhD). University of Sussex: Dean, Sch. of Molecular Scis, 1979–84; Acad. Dir of Univ. Computing, 1984–85; Dean, Chemistry, Physics and Envmtl Sci., 1996–99. Chm., Science Bd Computing Cttee, SERC, 1981–84. Hon. DSc Coimbra, Portugal, 1992. *Publications:* Theory of Electronic Spectra of Organic Molecules, 1960; (jointly): Valence Theory, 1965; Semi-empirical Self-consistent-field-molecular Theory of Molecules, 1971; Chemical Bond, 1978; Properties of Liquids and Solutions, 1982; Molecular Potential Energy Surfaces, 1985; Introduction to the Theory of Atomic and Molecular Scattering, 1989; Grow and Eat Something Different: some less common vegetables and fruit, 2007; Molsbook: a history of the School of Molecular Science, 2009. *Address:* Department of Chemistry, University of Sussex, Falmer, Brighton BN1 9QJ.

MURRIN, Orlando Richard Charles; journalist, food writer and hôtelier; executive coach, mentor and trainer, since 2013; *b* 1 April 1958; *s* of Patrick John Murrin and Patricia Mary, *d* of W. J. Skardon, OBE, MI5. *Educ:* Blundell's Sch., Devon; Magdalene Coll., Cambridge (Exhibnr; BA Hons English; MA). Radio 3 Sub-Editor, Radio Times, 1980–83; Chief Sub Ed., Living mag., 1983–85; Asst Ed., Country Homes and Interiors, 1985–87; advertising copywriter, 1987–90; Dep. Ed., Living mag., 1990–93; Ed., Woman and Home, 1993–96; Ed., BBC Good Food mag., 1997–2004; founding Ed., Olive mag., 2004; Editl Dir, Food Gp, BBC Magazines, 2004–09. Proprietor (with Peter Steggall): Le Manoir de Raynaudes, a gastronomic maison d'hôtes, 2004–09; Langford Fivehead, boutique hotel, 2010–12. Project Unleash, trng, coaching, consulting, 2014–. Clever Cook column, Daily Express, 1997–2002. Pianist, Kettners Restaurant, 1983–2002. *Publications:* The Clever Cookbook, 1999; The Can't Go Wrong Cookbook, 2002; The No-cook Cookbook, 2003; A Table in the Tarn, 2008. *Recreations:* Hollywood musicals, Judy Garland, the Beatles, aromatic plants (especially poisonous). *Address:* 5a North Street, Heavitree, Exeter EX1 2RH. *Club:* Soho House.

MURRISON, Dr Andrew William; MP (C) South West Wiltshire, since 2010 (Westbury, 2001–10); *b* 24 April 1961; *s* of William Gordon Murrison, RD and Marion Murrison (*née* Horn); *m* 1994, Jennifer Jane Munden; five *d*. *Educ:* Harwich High Sch.; The Harwich Sch.; BRNC Dartmouth; Bristol Univ. (MB ChB 1984; MD 1996); Hughes Hall, Cambridge (DPH 1996). MFOM 1994. Med. Officer, RN, 1981–2000, 2003 (Surg. Comdr); Med. Officer, RNR; Consultant Occupational Physician, 1996–2001. Opposition front bench spokesman on health, 2003–05, on defence, 2005–10; PPS to Sec. of State for Health, 2010–12; Parly Under-Sec. of State, MoD, 2012–14, NI Office, 2014–15. Chm., All Party Parly Gp on Morocco, 2010–12. Prime Minister's Special Rep., Centenary Commemoration of First World War, 2011–. *Publications:* Tommy This an' Tommy That, 2011; contribs to various biomed. pubns. *Recreations:* sailing, ski-ing. *Address:* House of Commons, SW1A 0AA.

MURSELL, Rt Rev. (Alfred) Gordon; Bishop Suffragan of Stafford, 2005–10; *b* 4 May 1949; *s* of late Philip Riley Mursell and Sheena Nicholson Mursell; *m* 1989, Anne Muir. *Educ:* Ardingly Coll.; Brasenose Coll., Oxford (MA 1974; BD 1987). ARCM 1975. Ordained deacon, 1973, priest, 1974; Curate, St Mary Walton, Liverpool, 1973–77; Vicar, St John, E Dulwich, 1977–87; Tutor, Salisbury and Wells Theol Coll., 1987–91; Team Rector, Stafford, 1991–99; Provost, subseq. Dean, of Birmingham, 1999–2005. Hon. DD Birmingham, 2005. *Publications:* Theology of the Carthusian Life, 1988; Out of the Deep: prayer as protest, 1989; The Meditations of Guigo I, Prior of the Charterhouse, 1995; The Wisdom of the Anglo-Saxons, 1997; English Spirituality, 2001; (Gen. Ed.) The Story of Christian Spirituality: two thousand years, from East to West, 2001; Praying in Exile, 2005. *Recreations:* music, hill-walking. *Address:* The Old Manse, Borgue, Kirkcudbright DG6 4SH. *T:* (01557) 870307. *E:* gordon.mursell@btinternet.com. *Club:* Athenæum.

MURTHY, Krishnan G.; *see* Guru-Murthy.

MURTON, Dr John Evan; HM Diplomatic Service; Deputy High Commissioner, Nairobi, since 2013; Permanent Representative to United Nations in Nairobi, since 2013; *b* 18 March 1972; *s* of Stewart Anthony Murton and Marion Elizabeth Murton; *m* 1998, Sarah Elizabeth Harvey; two *s* one *d*. *Educ:* Sidney Sussex Coll., Cambridge (BA Geog. 1994); Darwin Coll., Cambridge (PhD 1997). Entered FCO, 1997; UN Dept, FCO, 1997; Japanese lang. trng, 1998; Second Sec., Global Issues, 2000–03, First Sec., Energy and Envmt, 2003–04, Tokyo; Dep. Dir, NATO Sec. Gen.'s Private Office, 2004–07; High Comr, Mauritius, and Ambassador to Madagascar and The Comoros, 2007–10; Hd, Indian Ocean Network, FCO, 2009–10; Hd, E Asia and Pacific Dept, FCO, 2010–13. *Recreations:* hiking, ski-ing, playing guitar badly. *Address:* c/o Foreign and Commonwealth Office, King Charles Street, SW1A 2AH. *E:* john.murton@fco.gov.uk.

MUSCAT, Hon. Dr Joseph, CH National Order of Merit (Malta), 2013; Prime Minister of Malta, since 2013; Leader, Labour Party, since 2008; *b* Pieta, Malta, 22 Jan. 1974; *s* of Saviour and Grace Muscat; *m* 2001, Michelle; twin *d*. *Educ:* St Francis Sch., State Primary Sch., St Paul's Bay; Stella Maris Sch., Balzan; St Aloysius Coll., B'Kara; Univ. of Malta (BCom Mgt and Public Policy; BA Hons Public Policy; MA Eur. Studies); Univ. of Bristol (PhD Mgt Res. 2007). Journalist, then Asst Hd of News, One Radio and One TV, 1992–97; Mkt Intelligence Manager, Inst. for Promotion of Small Enterprise, 1997–99; Investment Advr, Crystal Finance Investments, reps in Malta of UBS Bank, Switzerland, 2000–04; first Ed., maltastar.com, Lab. Party's online newspaper, 2001–04. Mem., Central Admin of Labour Party as Educn Sec., 2001–03; MEP (Lab), Malta, 2004–08; Leader of Opposition, Parlt of Malta, 2008–13. Mem., Nat. Exec., Labour Party, 1994–2001; Dep., then Actg Chairperson, Labour Youth Forum, 1997. Grand Cross, Order of Honour (Greece), 2013. *Address:* Auberge de Castille, Valletta, Malta. *T:* 22002400. *E:* joseph.muscat@gov.mt.

MUSCATELLI, Prof. (Vito) Antonio, PhD; FRSE; Principal and Vice-Chancellor, University of Glasgow, since 2009; *b* 1 Jan. 1962; *s* of Ambrogio and Rosellina Muscatelli; *m* 1986, Elaine Flood; one *s* one *d*. *Educ:* High Sch., Glasgow; Univ. of Glasgow (MA Hons; Logan Prize; PhD). University of Glasgow: Lectr, then Sen. Lectr, 1984–92; Daniel Jack Prof. of Pol Economy, 1994–2007; Dean, Fac. of Soc. Scis, 2000–04; Vice-Principal (Strategy and Budgeting, then Strategy and Advancement), 2004–07; Principal and Vice-Chancellor, Heriot-Watt Univ., 2007–09. Visiting Professor: Univ. of Parma, 1989; Catholic Univ. of Milan, 1991–97; Univ. of Bari, 1995–2004; Res. Fellow, CESifo Res. Inst. Munich, 1999–. Adv. Panel of Econ. Consultants, Sec. of State for Scotland, 1998–2000; Special Advr, H of C Treasury Select Cttee, 2007–10; Mem., Council of Econ. Advrs, Scottish Govt, 2015–; Chm., Commn of Urban Econ. Growth for Glasgow City Reg., 2015–. Member: Res. and Knowledge Transfer Cttee, SFC, 2005–08; HEFCE RAE Panel, 2001, 2008; Res. Grants Bd, ESRC, 2002–07; Bd, Glasgow City Mktg Bureau, 2009–; Bd, SFC, 2012–; Chair, Res. and Commercialisation Cttee, 2007–08, 2012–14, Convener, 2008–10, Universities Scotland; Vice-Pres., Universities UK, 2008–10; Director: Russell Gp of Univs, 2009–; Universitas 21 Gp of Univs, 2009–; Nat. Centre for Univs and Business, 2013–; Bd, Univs Superannuation Scheme, 2015–. Council, Royal Econ. Soc., 2002–06. Trustee, CASE, 2013–. Dir, High Sch. of Glasgow, 2000–. FRSE 2003; FAcSS (AcSS 2004); FRSA 1995. Editor, Scottish Jl of

Political Economy, 1989–2003. Hon. LLD McGill, 2012. Commendatore (Italy), 2009. *Publications:* (jtly) Macroeconomic Theory and Stabilisation Policy, 1988; (ed) Economic and Political Institutions in Economic Policy, 1996; Monetary Policy; Fiscal Policies and Labour Markets; Macroeconomic Policy Making in the EMU, 2004. *Recreations:* music, literature, football, strategic games. *Address:* University of Glasgow, Glasgow G12 8QQ.

MUSEVENI, Lt-Gen. Yoweri Kaguta; President of the Republic of Uganda, since 1986; *b* 1944; *s* of Amos and Esteri Kaguta; *m* 1973, Janet Kataaha; one *s* three *d*. *Educ:* primary and secondary schs in Uganda; Univ. of Dar-es-Salaam, Tanzania (BA). Asst Sec. for Research in President's Office, 1970–71; Hd of Front for National Salvation and anti-Idi Amin armed gp, 1971–79; Minister of Defence, 1979–80, and Vice Chm. of ruling Military Commn; Chm., Uganda Patriotic Movement; Chm., High Comd of Nat. Resistance Army, 1981–86. *Publications:* What is Africa's Problem? (essays), 1992; Sowing the Mustard Seed: the struggle for freedom and democracy in Uganda (autobiog.), 1997. *Recreations:* karate, football. *Address:* Office of the President, Parliamentary Buildings, PO Box 7168, Kampala, Uganda. *T:* (41) 234522/234503.

MUSGRAVE, Sir Christopher John Shane, 8th Bt *cr* 1782, of Tourin, Waterford; *b* 23 Oct. 1959; *er s* of Sir Richard Musgrave, 7th Bt and of Maria (*née* Cambanis); *S* father, 2000. *Educ:* Cheltenham. *Heir: b* Michael Shane Musgrave [*b* 30 Jan. 1968; *m* 2005, Juana, *d* of Juan Larreta; one *s*].

MUSGRAVE, Sir Christopher (Patrick Charles), 15th Bt *cr* 1611; *b* 14 April 1949; *s* of Sir Charles Musgrave, 14th Bt and of Olive Louise Avril, *o d* of Patrick Cringle, Norfolk; *S* father, 1970; *m* 1st, 1978 (marr. diss. 1992); two *d*; 2nd, 1995, Carol, *d* of Geoffrey Lawson. *Recreations:* drawing, painting, model-making, animals, gardening. *Heir: b* Julian Nigel Chardin Musgrave [*b* 8 Dec. 1951; *m* 1975 (marr. diss. 1999); two *d*]. *Address:* Barn Farm, Bunns Lane, Hambledon, Hants PO7 4QH.

MUSGRAVE, Rosanne Kimble, MA; educational consultant, since 2000; Headmistress, Blackheath High School (GDST), 1989–2000; *b* 31 Jan. 1952; *d* of late Gp Captain John Musgrave, DSO, and Joanne Musgrave. *Educ:* Cheltenham Ladies' Coll.; St Anne's Coll., Oxford (MA); MA Reading Univ.; PGCE London Univ. Assistant teacher of English: Latymer Grammar Sch., 1976–79; Camden School for Girls (ILEA), 1979–82; Head of English: Channing Sch., Highgate, 1982–84; Haberdashers' Aske's School for Girls, Elstree, 1984–89. Pres., GSA, 1999; Dir of Member Support, 2008–11, Dep. Gen. Sec., 2011–13, Ind. Schs Specialist, 2013–14, ASCL. Corporate Mem., Cheltenham Ladies' Coll., 1989; Gov., St Albans High Sch., 1996–. FRSA 1994. Freeman, City of London, 1993. *Recreations:* letterpress printing, cooking. *Address:* 14 Fortis Green, N2 9EL.

MUSGRAVE, Thea, CBE 2002; composer; *b* 27 May 1928; *d* of James P. Musgrave and Joan Musgrave (*née* Hacking); *m* 1971, Peter Mark, conductor, *s* of Irving Mark, NY. *Educ:* Moreton Hall, Oswestry; Edinburgh Univ.; Paris Conservatoire; privately with Nadia Boulanger. Dist. Prof., Queens Coll., CUNY, 1987–2002. *Works include:* Cantata for a summer's day, 1954; The Abbot of Drimock (Chamber opera), 1955; Triptych for Tenor and orch., 1959; Colloquy for violin and piano, 1960; The Phoenix and the Turtle for chorus and orch., 1962; The Five Ages of Man for chorus and orch., 1963; The Decision (opera), 1964–65; Nocturnes and arias for orch., 1966; Chamber Concerto No. 2, in homage to Charles Ives, 1966; Chamber Concerto No 3 (Octet), 1966; Concerto for orchestra, 1967; Music for Horn and Piano, 1967; Clarinet Concerto, 1968; Beauty and the Beast (ballet), 1968; Night Music, 1969; Memento Vitae, a concerto in homage to Beethoven, 1970; Horn concerto, 1971; From One to Another, 1972; Viola Concerto, 1973; The Voice of Ariadne (opera), 1972–73; Rorate Coeli, for chorus, 1974; Space Play, 1974; Orfeo I and Orfeo II, 1975; Mary, Queen of Scots (opera), 1976–77; Christmas Carol (opera), 1979; An Occurrence at Owl Creek Bridge (radio opera), 1981; Peripeteia (orchestral), 1981; Harriet, the Woman called Moses (opera), 1984; Black Tambourine for women's chorus and piano, 1985; Pierrot, 1985; For the Time Being for chorus, 1986; The Golden Echo, 1987; Narcissus, 1988; The Seasons (orchestral), 1988; Rainbow (orchestral), 1990; Simón Bolivar (opera), 1993; Autumn Sonata, 1993; Journey through a Japanese Landscape (marimba concerto), 1993; Wild Winter, 1993; On the Underground (vocal), 1994; Helios (oboe concerto), 1995; Phoenix Rising (orchestral), 1997; Lamenting with Ariadne, 2000; Pontalba (opera), 2003; Turbulent Landscapes (orchestral), 2004; Wood, Metal and Skin (percussion concerto), 2004; Journey Into Light (soprano and orch.), 2005; Voices of Power and Protest, 2006; Two's Company (concerto for percussion and oboe), 2007; Green (for 12 strings), 2007; Cantilena (for oboe and string trio), 2008; Poets in Love (for tenor, baritone and piano), 2009; Sunrise (for flute, viola and harp), 2009; Ithaca (for unaccompanied chorus); 2009; Towards the Blue (clarinet solo with wind quartet and string quartet), 2010; Dawn (oboe solo), 2012; Loch Ness—a postcard from Scotland (orchestral), 2012. Performances and broadcasts: UK, France, Germany, Switzerland, Scandinavia, USA, USSR, etc, Edinburgh, Cheltenham, Aldeburgh, Zagreb, Venice and Warsaw Festivals. Hon. MusDoc, CNAA. *Address:* c/o Novello & Co. Ltd, 14–15 Berners Street, W1T 3LJ.

MUSGROVE, Harold John; Chairman, Worcester Acute Hospitals NHS Trust, 1999–2003; *b* 19 Nov. 1930; *s* of Harold Musgrove; *m* 1959, Jacquelin Mary Hobbs; two *s* two *d*. *Educ:* King Edward Grammar Sch., Birmingham; Birmingham Tech. Coll. Nat. Cert. of Mech. Engrg. Apprentice, Austin Motor Co., 1945; held various positions, incl. Chief Material Controller (Commission as Navigator, RAF, during this period); Senior Management, Truck and Bus Group, Leyland Motor Corp., 1963–78; Austin Morris: Dir of Manufacturing, 1978–79; Man. Dir, 1979–80; Chm. and Man. Dir, 1980–81; Chm., Light Medium Cars Group, 1981–82; Chm. and Chief Exec., Austin Rover Gp, 1982–86; Chloride plc: Dir, 1989–92; Chm., Industrial Battery Sector, 1989–91; Chm., Power Supplies and Lighting Gp, 1991–92. Non-exec. Dir, Metalrax plc, 1986–2003. Chairman: W Midlands Ambulance Service, 1992–94; Birmingham Heartlands Hosp. NHS Trust, 1994–96; Birmingham Heartlands and Solihull (Teaching) NHS Trust, 1996–99. Pres., Birmingham Chamber of Industry and Commerce, 1987–88. Pres., Aston Villa FC, 1986–98. FIMI 1985. DUniv Birmingham, 2000. Midlander of the Year Award, 1980; IProdE Internat. Award, 1981; Soc. of Engineers Churchill Medal, 1982. *Recreations:* golf, soccer. *Address:* Orchard Cottage, Laverton, Broadway, Worcs WR12 7NA.

MUSHARRAF, Gen. Pervez; President of Pakistan, 2001–08; Chief of Army Staff, 1998–2007; *b* 11 Aug. 1943; *s* of late Syed Musharraf Uddin; *m* 1968, Sehba Farid; one *s* one *d*. *Educ:* St Patrick's High Sch., Karachi; Forman Christian Coll., Lahore. Pakistan Mil. Acad., 1961; commnd Artillery Regt, 1964; Dir Gen., Mil. Ops, 1993–95; Chm., Jt Chiefs of Staff Cttee, 1999–2001; Chief Exec. of Pakistan, 1999–2002. *Publications:* In the Line of Fire (autobiog.), 2006.

MUSKERRY, 9th Baron *cr* 1781 (Ire.); **Robert Fitzmaurice Deane;** Bt 1710 (Ire.); *b* 26 March 1948; *s* of 8th Baron Muskerry and Betty Fairbridge, *e d* of George Wilfred Reckless Palmer; *S* father, 1988; *m* 1975, Rita Brink, Pietermaritzburg; one *s* two *d*. *Educ:* Sandford Park School, Dublin; Trinity Coll., Dublin (BA, BAI). *Heir: s* Hon. Jonathan Fitzmaurice Deane, *b* 7 June 1986. *Address:* 725 Ridge Road, Berea, Durban 4001, South Africa.

MUSSON, Rear Adm. (John Geoffrey) Robin, CB 1993; Senior Naval Directing Staff, Royal College of Defence Studies, 1990–93; Chief Naval Supply and Secretariat Officer, 1991–93; *b* 30 May 1939; *s* of late Geoffrey William Musson and Winifred Elizabeth Musson (*née* Whyman); *m* 1965, Joanna Marjorie Ward; two *s* one *d*. *Educ:* Luton Grammar Sch.; BRNC, Dartmouth. Entered RN, 1957; served HM Ships: Bulwark, 1960–61; Decoy, 1961–62; 2nd Frigate Sqdn, 1964–65; HM Ships: Cavalier, 1966–67; Forth, 1967–69; Kent, 1975–76; NDC, 1979; MA, VCDS (Personnel and Logistics), 1980–81; Sec. to Chief of Fleet Support, 1982–83; CSO (Personnel and Admin), FONAC, 1984–86; Dir, Naval Officer Appts (Supply and WRNS), 1986–88; Captain, HMS Cochrane, 1988–90; retd, 1993. Admiralty Bd Gov., Royal Naval Benevolent Trust, 1995–2002. Gov. (formerly Mem. Cttee of Mgt), Royal Hosp. Sch., Holbrook, 1995–2002. Sec., Salisbury Dio. Sudan Link, 1995–2001. Freeman, City of London, 1993. *Recreations:* Scottish country dancing, mending things, history.

MUSSON, John Nicholas Whitaker; Warden of Glenalmond College (formerly Trinity College, Glenalmond), 1972–87; *b* 2 Oct. 1927; *s* of late Dr J. P. T. Musson, OBE and Gwendoline Musson (*née* Whitaker); *m* 1953, Ann Preist (*d* 2004); one *s* three *d*. *Educ:* Clifton Coll.; Brasenose Coll., Oxford (MA). Served with Welsh Guards and Lancs Fusiliers, 1945–48 (commnd); BA Hons Mod. Hist., Oxford, 1951; HM Colonial Service, later HM Overseas Civil Service, 1951–59: District Officer, N Nigeria; Lectr, Inst. of Administration, N Nigeria; Staff Dept, British Petroleum, London, 1959–61; Asst Master and Housemaster, Canford Sch., 1961–72. Chm., Scottish Div. HMC, 1981–83; Scottish Dir, ISCO, 1987–93. Governor: Clifton Coll., 1989– (Mem. Council, 1989–95); George Watson's Coll., Edinburgh, 1989–98. Mercy Corps Europe/Scottish European Aid: Dir and Trustee, 1996–2000; Country Dir (Bosnia and Herzegovina), resident in Sarajevo, 1998–99; Vice-Chm., Mercy Corps Scotland (Aid Internat.), 2000–07. *Recreations:* travel, art, history, swimming. *Address:* 47 Spylaw Road, Edinburgh EH10 5BP. *Club:* New (Edinburgh).

MUSSON, Rear Adm. Robin; *see* Musson, Rear Adm. J. G. R.

MUSTHAPHA, (Mohamed) Faisz; High Commissioner for Sri Lanka in the United Kingdom, 2002–05; *b* 5 Dec. 1940; *s* of Seyed Mohamed Musthapha and Masooda Musthapha; *m* 1967, Fathima Fatheena; one *s* one *d*. *Educ:* Trinity Coll., Kandy; Univ. of Ceylon (LLB); Sri Lanka Law Coll. Advocate of the Supreme Court of Sri Lanka, 1965–; President's Counsel, 1988; Dep. DPP, 1976–78. Chairman: and Mem., Finance Commn of Sri Lanka, 1987–90; Human Rights Commn, Sri Lanka, 1998–2000; Mem., Law Commn of Sri Lanka, 1997–2000. Dir, Amana Investments Ltd, 1996; Chm., Amana Thakaful Ltd (Risk Mgt Co.), 1998–. Mem., Council of Legal Educn, 1997–2000. Legal Advr, All Party Conf., 1987. Member: Sri Lanka Delegn to Thimpu Talks, Bhutan, 1987; Sri Lankan Gp, Internat. Court of Arbitration, The Hague, 1996. Mem., Bar Assoc. of Sri Lanka (Dep. Pres., 1986–98). Chm., Amal Internat. Sch., 1990–2000. *Publications:* contribs on Islam and law. *Recreations:* reading, bird watching, badminton. *Address:* 35 Kaviratne Place, Colombo 6, Sri Lanka. *T:* (11) 2586963, *Fax:* (11) 5555048. *E:* faiszmusthapha@sltnet.lk.

MUSTON, Rt Rev. Gerald Bruce; Bishop of North-West Australia, 1981–92; *b* 19 Jan. 1927; 3rd *s* of Stanley John and Emily Ruth Muston; *m* 1951, Laurel Wright; one *s* one *d*. *Educ:* N Sydney Chatswood High School; Moore Theological College, Sydney. ThL (Aust. Coll. of Theology). Rector, Wallerawang, NSW, 1951–53; Editorial Secretary, Church Missionary Society (Aust.), 1953–58; Rector, Tweed Heads, NSW, 1958–61; Vicar, Essendon, Vic, 1961–67; Rural Dean of Essendon, 1963–67; Rector of Darwin, NT, and Archdeacon of Northern Territory, 1967–69; Federal Secretary, Bush Church Aid Society of Aust., 1969–71; Bishop Coadjutor, dio. Melbourne (Bishop of the Western Region), 1971–81. *Recreations:* golf, reading. *Address:* 17/27 Beddi Road, Duncraig, WA 6023, Australia.

MUSTOW, Stuart Norman, CBE 1995; FCIHT; FREng, FICE; County Surveyor, West Midlands, responsible for road, transport planning and Birmingham Airport, 1974–86; consulting engineer, 1986–2000; *b* 26 Nov. 1928; *s* of Norman Eric Mustow and Mabel Florence Mustow (*née* Purcell); *m* 1964, Sigrid Hertha Young; two *s* one *d*. *Educ:* Aston Univ. (BSc). FCIHT; FREng (FEng 1982). Mil. service, RA; Local Govt Engineering, 1949–69; City Engineer and Surveyor, Stoke on Trent, 1969–74. Chm., Hazards Forum, 1999–2003. Mem., Engineering Council, 1995–97. President: Inst. Municipal Engrs, 1980–81; ICE, 1993–94; Vice-Pres., Royal Acad. of Engrg, 1995–99. Hon. DSc Aston, 1994; Hon. DEng Birmingham, 2000. *Publications:* papers in learned jls. *Recreations:* outdoor life, church, social work.

MUTHALAGAPPAN, Kumar Periakaruppan, OBE 2009; FCA; Director, Paramount Hotel Collection, since 1997; Managing Director, MeDiNova Clinical Research and Medical Services, since 2011; *b* India, 2 June 1960; *s* of Muthu and Meena Muthalagappan; *m* 1988, Kannahi Sivanantham; two *s* one *d*. *Educ:* Univ. of Warwick (BSc Hons Accounting and Financial Analysis). FCA 1996. Senior Manager, KPMG, 1983–97. Member Board: Heart of England Tourist Bd, 2000–04; Visit Britain, 2002–10. Member, Board: Olympic Delivery Authy, 2006–14; Advantage W Midlands, 2009–12; Alexandra Palace, 2010–12; Age UK (Mem. Fundraising Bd, 2012). Mem. Council, Univ. of Warwick, 2007–10. Chm., City of Birmingham Symphony Orch., 2007–12; Mem. Bd, Belgrade Th., 2000–04. *Recreations:* music, history, sport, gardening. *Address:* 149 Warwick Road, Kenilworth, Warwicks CV8 1HY. *T:* (01926) 851156, *Fax:* (01926) 854420. *E:* kumar@muthalagappan.com.

MUTI, Riccardo, Hon. KBE 2000; Music Director, Chicago Symphony Orchestra, since 2010 (Music Director designate, 2009–10); *b* 28 July 1941; *m* 1969, Cristina Mazzavillani; two *s* one *d*. *Educ:* Diploma in pianoforte, Conservatorio di Napoli; Diploma in conducting and composition, Milan. Principal Conductor, Orchestra Maggio Musicale Fiorentino, 1969–80; Principal Conductor, 1972–82, Music Dir, 1979–82, New Philharmonia, later Philharmonia Orchestra, London; Philadelphia Orchestra: Principal Guest Conductor, 1977–80; Principal Conductor and Music Dir, 1980–92; Conductor Laureate, 1992–2003; Music Dir, La Scala, Milan, 1986–2005. Concert tours in USA with Philadelphia Orch.; concerts at Salzburg, Edinburgh, Lucerne, Flanders, Vienna and Ravenna Festivals; concerts with Berlin Philharmonic, Vienna Philharmonic, Concertgebouw Amsterdam, NY Philharmonic, Bayerisches Rundfunk SO, Filarmonica della Scala, Israel Philharmonic, Boston SO, Chicago SO; opera in Florence, Salzburg, Vienna, Munich, Covent Garden, Milan, Ravenna, Venice. Founder, Luigi Cherubini Youth Orch., 2004. Hon. degrees from Univs of Bologna, Urbino, Milan, Lecce and Tel Aviv, and univs in England and USA. Recording prizes from France, Germany, Italy, Japan and USA. Accademico: dell'Accademia di Santa Cecilia, Rome; dell'Accademia Luigi Cherubini, Florence. Hon. Citizen: Milan; Florence; Sydney; Ravenna. Grande Ufficiale, Repubblica Italiana; Cavaliere, Gran Croce (Italy), 1991; Verdienstkreuz, 1st class (Germany), 1976; KM; Ehrenkreuz (Austria).

MUTTER, Anne-Sophie; violinist. *Educ:* studied with Prof. Aida Stucki in Switzerland. Début with Herbert von Karajan, Salzburg, 1977; soloist with major orchestras of the world; also plays with string trio and quartet; has given first performances and recorded many works for violin by contemporary composers incl. Lutosławski, Moret, Penderecki, Gubaidulina, Rihm, Dutilleux, Currier and Previn. Guest teacher, RAM, 1985. Founder: Rudolf Eberle Foundn, 1987; Anne-Sophie Mutter Foundn, 1997. Hon. Pres., Univ. of Oxford Mozart Soc., 1983. Hon. Mem., Beethoven Soc., 1996. Prizes and awards include: Jugend Musiziert Prize (FRG) for: violin, 1970 and 1974; piano, 1970; Künstler des Jahres Deutscher Schallplattenpreis, 1979; Grand Prix Internat. du Disque, Record Acad. Prize, Tokyo, 1982; Internat. Schallplattenpreis, 1993; Grammy, 1994, 1999, 2000, 2004; Siemens Music Prize, 2008. Bundesverdienstkreuz (1st Cl.), 1987; Cross of Honour for Sci. and Art (Austria), 2001. *Recreations:* graphic arts, sport.

MUTTRAM, Roderick Ian, FREng; Founder and Managing Director, Fourth Insight Ltd, since 2012; *b* 15 Jan. 1952; *s* of late Wilfred Reginald Muttram, DSC, RN and Dorothy May Muttram (*née* Best); *m* 1974, Jane Elisabeth Sinkinson; four *d*. *Educ:* St Bartholomew's Grammar Sch., Newbury; Victoria Univ. of Manchester (BSc Hons); Manchester Metropolitan Univ. (DMS). Gp Engrg and Quality Dir, Ferranti Instrumentation Gp, 1986–90; Dir and Gen. Manager, Defence Systems Div., Thorn EMI Electronics, 1990–93; Railtrack plc: Director: Electrical Engrg and Control Systems, 1994–97; Safety and Standards, 1997–2000; Dir, Railtrack Gp plc, 1997–2000; CEO, Railway Safety, 2000–03; ind. engrg and safety consultant, 2003; Vice-Pres., Bombardier Transportation (UK) Ltd, 2003–12. Chm., Rail Industry Trng Council, 2001–03. Chm., Supervisory Bd, Eur. Rail Res. Inst., Netherlands, 1994–2003; Vice-Chm., Eur. Rail Res. Adv. Council, 2004–05; Dir, Assoc. Européenne pour l'Interopérabilité Ferroviaire, 2004–06. Freedom, City of London, 2004; Liveryman, Co. of Engineers, 2005. FREng 2002; FInstD 2008; FRSA 2014. *Publications:* (contrib.) The Yellow Book on Engineering Safety Management, 1996; numerous conf. papers in UK, Japan, Australia, USA; contrib. numerous papers to Jl Rail and Rapid Transit (IMechE), Japan Railway Tech. Rev., IEE Summer Schs. *Recreations:* small bore rifle shooting, motor vehicle restoration. *Address:* Fourth Insight Ltd, The Cottage, The Street, Ewhurst, Cranleigh, Surrey GU6 7QA. *T:* (01483) 277218. *E:* rod.muttram@uk.transport.bombardier.com.

MUTTUKUMARU, Christopher Peter Jayantha, CB 2006; barrister; General Counsel, Department for Transport, 2011–13; *b* 11 Dec. 1951; *y s* of late Maj. Gen. Anton Muttukumaru, OBE and of Margaret Muttukumaru; *m* 1976, Ann Elisabeth Tutton; two *s*. *Educ:* Xavier Coll., Melbourne; Jesus Coll., Oxford (BA, MA). Called to the Bar, Gray's Inn, 1974, Bencher, 2010; in practice at the Bar, 1976–83 and 2014–; Treasury Solicitor's Dept, 1983–88; Law Officers' Dept, 1988–91; Head of Employment Litigation Sect., Treasury Solicitor's Dept, 1991–92; Sec., Scott Inquiry into Export of Defence and Defence-related Equipment to Iraq, 1992–96; Treasury Solicitor's Department: Dep. Legal Advr, MoD, 1996–98; Legal Advr to DCMS, 1998–99; Dir, Legal (Commercial, Envmt, Housing and Local Govt), DETR, 1999–2001; Legal Dir (Transport), DTLR, 2001–02; Legal Services Dir, 2002–11, Legal Advr, 2003–11, DfT. Mem. Adv. Bd, Law Sch., City Univ., 2008– (Vice Chm., 2012–). Gov., Eltham Coll., London, 1998–2012 (Vice-Chm., Govs, 2006–12). Hon. DLaws City, 2012. Mem., Editl Adv. Bd, Nottingham Law Jl. *Recreations:* reading, cricket (watching), photography, sunflowers. *Address:* Monckton Chambers, 1–2 Raymond Buildings, Gray's Inn, WC1R 5NR. *T:* (020) 7405 7211.

MWINYI, Ndugu Ali Hassan; President, United Republic of Tanzania, 1985–95; *b* 8 May 1925; *s* of late Hassan Mwinyi Chande and Asha Mwinyishehe; *m* 1960, Siti A. Mwinyi (*née* Abdulla); five *s* four *d*. *Educ:* Mangapwani Sch. and Dole Sch., Zanzibar; Teachers' Training Coll., Zanzibar; Durham Univ. Inst. of Education. Primary sch. teacher, head teacher, Tutor, Principal, Zanzibar, 1945–64; Acting Principal Sec., Min. of Educn, 1964–65; Dep. Gen. Manager, State Trading Corp., 1965–70; Minister of State, President's Office, Dar es Salaam, 1970–72; Minister for Health, 1972–75; Minister for Home Affairs, 1975–77; Ambassador to Egypt, 1977–81; Minister for Natural Resources and Tourism, 1982–83; Minister of State, Vice-President's Office, 1983; Vice-Pres., Union Govt, 1984. Chama Cha Mapinduzi (Revolutionary Party): Member, 1977; Nat. Exec. Cttee, 1982; Central Cttee, 1984; Vice-Chm., 1984–90; Chm., 1990–96; Mem., Afro-Shirazi Party, 1964. Chairman: Zanzibar Film Censorship Bd, 1964–65; E African Currency Bd, Zanzibar, 1964–67; Nat. Kiswahili Council, 1964–77; Tanzania Food and Nutrition Council, 1974–76. Mem., Univ. Council of Dar es Salaam, 1964–65. *Address:* c/o State House, Dar es Salaam, United Republic of Tanzania.

MYER, Sidney Baillieu, AC 1990; MA Cantab; Chairman, Myer Emporium Ltd, 1978–86 (Director, 1955–86); Deputy Chairman, Coles Myer Ltd, 1986–94; Director: Myer Foundation, since 1959 (Chairman, 1992–95; Vice-President, 1959–92); N. M. Rothschild Australia Holdings (formerly N. M. Rothschild & Son (Australia) Pty Ltd), 1993–2003; *b* 11 Jan. 1926; *s* of late Sidney Myer and late Dame (Margery) Merlyn Baillieu Myer, DBE; *m* 1955, Sarah J., *d* of late S. Hordern; two *s* one *d*. *Educ:* Geelong Grammar Sch.; Pembroke Coll., Cambridge (MA). Sub-Lieut, RANVR, 1944–46. Joined Myer Emporium, 1953. Director: Myer Family Office Ltd (formerly Myer Family Co. Pty Ltd), 1953; Elders IXL Ltd, 1972–90; Cadbury Schweppes Aust. Ltd, 1976–82; Commonwealth Banking Corp., 1979–83; Network Ten Holdings Ltd and associated Cos, 1985–87; Chm., Nat. Mutual Life Assoc. of Australasia, 1988–92 (Dir, 1978–85 and 1986–). Dir, Howard Florey Inst. of Experimental Physiology and Medicine, 1971–2002 (Pres., 1988–92); Part-time Mem. Executive, CSIRO, 1981–85. Pres., French Chamber of Commerce (Vic), 1962–64; Rep. Chm., Aust.-Japan Foundn, 1976–81; Member: Consultative Cttee on Relations with Japan, 1978–81; Aust.-China Council, 1979–81; Nat. Bicentennial Sci. Centre Adv. Cttee, 1986–89; Nat. Adv. Cttee on Ageing, 2002–04; Future Melbourne Reference Gp, 2007–; Chm., Asia Soc. AustralAsia Centre, 2009–; participant, Rural Industries and Communities Aust. 2020 summit, 2008. Councillor: Aust. Conservation Foundn, 1964–73; Vic. Coll. of Arts, 1973–78; Chm., Art Foundn of Vic., 1986–88; Vice-Pres., Nat. Gall. Soc. of Vic., 1964–68; Dir, Tasman Inst., 1990–98; Trustee: Sidney Myer Fund, 1958–2001 (Chm. Trustees, 1992–2001); Nat. Gall. of Vic., 1973–83, now Trustee Emeritus (Vice-Pres., 1977–83); Victorian Tapestry Foundn, 1995–; Chm., Commonwealth Research Centres of Excellence Cttee, 1981–82. Hon. LLD Melbourne, 1993. Centenary Medal (Australia), 2003. Officier de la Légion d'Honneur (France), 2007 (Chevalier, 1976). *Recreations:* tennis, ski-ing, viticulture. *Address:* Level 18, 8 Exhibition Street, Melbourne, Victoria 3000, Australia. *Clubs:* Leander (Henley-on-Thames); Australian (Melbourne).

MYERS, Anthea Elizabeth Joy; *see* McIntyre, A. E. J.

MYERS, Sir (Arthur) Douglas, KNZM 2010; CBE 1991; Chairman, Lion Nathan Ltd, 1997–2001 (Chief Executive, 1988–97); *b* Auckland, NZ, 29 Oct. 1938; *s* of Sir Kenneth Ben Myers, MBE and Margaret Myers (*née* Pirie); *m* 1st, 1971, Stephanie Overton (marr. diss. 1988); one *s* two *d*; 2nd, 1990, Barbara Tinai Lucas. *Educ:* King's Coll., Auckland; Gonville and Caius Coll., Cambridge (BA Hist. 1961); Harvard Business Sch. (Prog. for Mgt Develt). Man. Dir, family co., Campbell & Ehrenfield Co., 1965, bought outright, 1970; formation of NZ Wines & Spirits (Campbell & Ehrenfield Co. and Lion Breweries), 1971, Man. Dir, 1971–81; Man. Dir, Lion Breweries Ltd, 1982–88. Mem., NZ Business Roundtable, 1982– (Chm., 1990–97). Estabd annual scholarships to Gonville and Caius Coll., Cambridge, King's Coll., Auckland, Auckland Univ., Brown Univ., and NZ Business Roundtable. Trustee, Civitas, 2002–14. *Recreations:* fly fishing, reading, travelling, diving. *Address:* 9 Queripel House, 1 Duke of York Square, SW3 4LY. *T:* (020) 3006 7900.

MYERS, David; Director, Shared Services Programme, Cabinet Office, 2005–07; *b* 28 March 1965; *s* of Frederick Myers and Beryl Adelaide Myers; *m* 1991, Janice Adele Harrison; three *d*. *Educ:* Highfield Sch., Liverpool; Univ. of Lancaster (BA Hons Econ 1st Cl 1987). British Gas plc, 1988–90; Rolls-Royce plc, 1990–92; KPMG, 1992; ICI Pharmaceuticals, 1993–96; Change Prog. Manager, Mil. Aircraft, BAe, 1996–98; Dir of IT, BAe Regl Aircraft, 1998–2000; Dir of IT and Business Change, BAE SYSTEMS Avionics, 2000–02; e-Business Dir, DEFRA, 2003–05. *Recreations:* landscape gardening, following St Helens Rugby League, exploring West Indies.

MYERS, (Denis) Kevin, CBE 2015; Director-General, Regulation, Health and Safety Executive, since 2015; President, International Association of Labour Inspection, since 2014 (Secretary General, 2011–14); *b* 30 Sept. 1954; *s* of Stephen Myers and Bridget Myers (*née* McSweeney); *m* 1976, Jan Hannan; four *s* one *d*. *Educ:* St Bonaventure's Sch., Forest Gate; Luton Coll. of Technol. (BSc Hons Biochem. and Envmtl Biol.). Joined Health and Safety Exec., 1976, various posts in London, E Anglia and SW, 1976–93; Policy Officer, DG XI, Eur. Commn, 1993–95; Health and Safety Executive: Regl Dir, Home Counties Reg., 1997–2002, Chief Inspector of Construction, 2000–05; Dir, Hazardous Installations, 2005–08; Dep. Chief Exec., 2008–13 and 2014–15, Actg Chief Exec., 2013–14. Non-exec. Dir, Office for Nuclear Regulation, 2011–14; Mem., Singapore Govt Internat. Adv. Panel for Workplace Safety and Health, 2013–. Trustee, British Safety Council, 2009–. *Recreations:* family, Italy, football (West Ham United FC), cricket, opera. *Address:* Health and Safety Executive, Redgrave Court, Merton Road, Bootle, Merseyside L20 7HS. *T:* (0151) 951 4701, *Fax:* (0151) 951 3448.

MYERS, Sir Derek (John), Kt 2014; Chief Executive: Royal Borough of Kensington and Chelsea, 2000–13; London Borough of Hammersmith and Fulham, 2011–13; Lead Commissioner, Rotherham Metropolitan Borough Council, since 2015; *b* 15 Aug. 1954; *s* of Alfred and Elsie Myers; *m* 1992, Anne Mercer; one *s* one *d*. *Educ:* Univ. of Manchester (BA Econs 1976; Dip. Social Work 1977); Univ. of London (LLB 1988). Social Services: Essex CC, 1977–86; Hillingdon LBC, 1986–92; Dir of Social Services, 1992–97, Chief Exec., 1997–2000, London Borough of Hounslow; Town Clerk, RBK&C, 2000–11. Chm., Soc. of Local Authority Chief Execs, 2008–12. Mem., Adv. Bd, Public Health England, 2013–. Chm. Trustees, Shelter, 2013–; Trustee, Royal Botanic Gdns, Kew, 2013–. *Recreations:* tennis, cooking, hill-walking.

MYERS, Dominic Peter; European Publishing Director, Amazon Media EU, since 2014; *b* Street, 13 Aug. 1962; *s* of Neville and Pat Myers; *m* 2001, Heike Diederichs; three *d*. *Educ:* Wadham Coll., Oxford (BA Eng. Lang. and Lit. 1984). Marks & Spencer, 1986–91; Somerfield, 1992–98; Managing Director: Hasbro Interactive, 1999–2000; Blackwell UK, 2002–05; HMV Group: Strategy Dir, Waterstone's, 2006–07; Gp Develt Dir, 2007–10; Man. Dir, Waterstone's, 2010–11. Non-exec. Chm., txt2buy Ltd, 2011–12; Chm., Bounts.it, 2013–14; Dir, Bear and Horn Ltd, 2011–; non-exec. Dir, Sainsbury's eBooks, 2012–14. *Recreation:* three daughters - keeps me busy.

MYERS, Sir Douglas; *see* Myers, Sir A. D.

MYERS, Geoffrey, CBE 1984; CEng; FCILT; Chairman, TRANSAID, 1988–95; Vice-Chairman, British Railways Board, 1985–87 (Member, 1980–87); *b* 12 July 1930; *s* of Ernest and Annie Myers; *m* 1959, Patricia Mary (*née* Hall); two *s*. *Educ:* Belle Vue High Sch.; Bradford Technical Coll. (BScEng London). CEng, MICE 1963; FCILT (FCIT 1973). RE, 1955–57. British Rail: civil engrg positions, 1957–64; Planning Officer, N Eastern Reg., 1964–66; Divl Movements Manager, Leeds Div., 1966–68; Dir of Studies, British Transport Staff Coll., 1968–70; Divl Man., Sheffield, 1970–76; Dep. Gen. Man., Eastern Reg., 1976–77, Gen. Man., 1977–78; Dir of Strategic Develt, 1978–80; Dep. Chief Exec. (Railways), 1983; Jt Managing Dir (Railways), 1984–85. Pres. Council, CIT, 1986–87. Bd Mem., TRANSAID Worldwide, 1998–2000. Mem. Council, Save the Children (UK), 1993–2000; Pres., White Rose Children's Charity, 1995–. Hon. DEng Bradford, 1988. OStJ 1979. *Recreations:* golf, walking. *Address:* The Spinney, Lands Lane, Knaresborough, N Yorks HG5 9DE. *T:* (01423) 863719.

MYERS, Gordon Elliot, CMG 1979; Under-Secretary, Arable Crops, Pigs and Poultry Group, Ministry of Agriculture, Fisheries and Food, 1984–89, retired; *b* 4 July 1929; *s* of William Lionel Myers and Yvonne (*née* Arthur); *m* 1963, Wendy Jane Lambert; two *s* one *d*. *Educ:* Kilburn Grammar Sch.; University Coll., Oxford (BA 1st Cl. Hons Modern History). Asst Principal, MAFF, 1951; Principal, 1958; Asst Sec., 1966; Head successively of Land Drainage Div., Sugar and Tropical Foods Div., and EEC Div., 1966–74; Under-Sec., MAFF, 1975; Minister (Agriculture), Office of UK Perm. Rep. to EEC, 1975–79; Under-Sec., Food Policy Gp, 1980–85, Cereals and Sugar Gp, 1985–86, MAFF. Mem., Cttee on Simplification of Common Agricl Policy, EEC, 1990–94. Sec., Caribbean Banana Exporters Assoc., 1993–2010. *Publications:* Banana Wars: the price of free trade, 2004. *Address:* Woodlands, Nugents Park, Hatch End, Pinner, Middx HA5 4RA. *Club:* Oxford and Cambridge.

MYERS, John David; Chairman of Industrial Tribunals, 1982–97 (Regional Chairman for Newcastle, 1994–97); part-time Chairman of Employment Tribunals, 1998–2005; *b* 30 Oct. 1937; *s* of Frank and Monica Myers; *m* 1974, Anne McGeough (*née* Purcell), *widow* of J. T. McGeough; one *s*. *Educ:* Marist College, Hull; Hull University. LLB Hons. Called to the Bar, Gray's Inn, 1968. Schoolmaster, 1958–64; University, 1964–67; pupillage with J. D. Walker (later Judge Walker); practice at Hull, 1969–82 (Junior, NE Circuit, 1975–76). Northumberland worker, Age UK, 2004–13. *Recreations:* cooking, oenology, bridge. *Club:* Alnmouth Golf.

MYERS, Kevin; *see* Myers, D. K.

MYERS, Martin Trevor, FRICS; Chairman, Mountgrange Capital plc, 2002–09; Senior Partner, Mountgrange Real Estate Opportunity Fund, since 2007; *b* 24 Sept. 1941; *s* of Bernard Myers and Sylvia Marjorie Myers (*née* Pearman); *m* 1981, Nicole Josephine Yerna; one *s* one *d*. *Educ:* Arnold House, St John's Wood; Latymer Upper Sch.; Coll. of Estate Management, London Univ. (BSc). FRICS 1975. Jones Lang Wootton, 1965–83: Partner, 1969; Proprietary Partner, 1972; Chm. and Chief Exec., Arbuthnot Properties, 1983; merged with Imry Property Holdings, 1987, and with City Merchant Developers, 1988; Chief Exec. and Man. Dir, Imry Holdings Ltd, 1989–97; Exec. Dep. Chm., Trillium Gp, 1998–2001. Trustee, Royal Marsden Cancer Campaign, 2003–09. *Recreations:* golf, shooting, exercise. *Club:* Turf.

MYERS, Dr Norman, CMG 1998; Managing Director, Norman Myers' Scientific Consultancy, since 1982; *b* 24 Aug. 1934; *s* of John Myers and Gladys Myers (*née* Haworth); *m* 1965, Dorothy Mary Halliman (separated 1992); two *d*. *Educ:* Keble Coll., Oxford (BA 1957; MA 1963); Univ. of Calif, Berkeley (PhD 1973). Dist Officer, Kenya Colonial Admin, 1958–61; high sch. teacher, Nairobi, 1961–65; freelance writer, professional photographer and lectr on African wildlife, Kenya, 1966–69; consultant in envmt and develt, 1972–: projects for develt orgns and res. bodies, incl. World Bank, UN agencies, OECD, EC, US Depts of State and Energy, NASA, US Nat. Acad. of Scis. Hon. Vis. Fellow, Green Templeton (formerly Green) Coll., Oxford, 1992–; Adjunct Prof., Duke Univ., 1997–; Prof. at Large, Univ. of Vermont, 2007–; Ext. Fellow, 21st Century Sch., Oxford, 2008–; Vis. Prof., Univs of Kent, Utrecht, Cape Town, Calif, Texas, Michigan, Cornell, Harvard and Stanford. For. Associate, US NAS, 1994; FWAAS 1989; FAAAS 1990; FRSA 1993; FLS 1993; Fellow, Royal Instn, 1997; Ext. Fellow, Saïd Business Sch., Oxford Univ., 2005. Hon. DSc Kent, 2003. Numerous awards for work in environment and development, including Volvo Envmt Prize, 1992; Pew Fellowship in Envmt, 1994; UNEP Sasakawa Envmt Prize, 1995; Blue Planet Prize, Asahi Glass Foundn, Japan, 2001. *Publications:* The Long African Day, 1972; The Sinking Ark, 1979 (trans. Japanese and Hungarian); Conversion of Tropical Moist Forests, 1980; A Wealth of Wild Species, 1983; The Primary Source: tropical forests and our future, 1984, rev. edn 1992; The Gaia Atlas of Planet Management, 1984 (trans. 11 langs), 2nd edn 2005; (ed jtly) Economics of Ecosystem Management, 1985; Future Worlds: challenge and opportunity in an age of change, 1990; Population, Resources and the Environment: the critical challenges, 1991; (ed) Tropical Forests and Climate, 1992; Ultimate Security: the environmental basis of political stability, 1993, 2nd edn 1996; Scarcity or Abundance: a debate on the environment, 1994 (trans. Italian); Environmental Exodus: an emergent crisis in the global arena, 1995; (jtly) Biodiversity Hotspots, 1999; Towards a New Greenprint for Business and Society, 1999; Food and Hunger in Sub-Saharan Africa, 2001; (jtly) Perverse Subsidies: how tax dollars can undercut the environment and the economy, 2001; New Consumers: the influence of affluence on the environment, 2004; The Citizen is Willing but Society Won't Deliver: the problem of institutional roadblocks, 2008; contrib. numerous professional papers in scientific jls incl. Science, Nature, Population and Develt Rev., Jl Envmtl Econs & Mgt, Internat. Jl Social Econs. *Recreations:* professional photography, marathon running, mountaineering. *Address:* Upper Meadow, 2 Douglas Downes Close, Headington, Oxford OX3 8FS. *T:* (01865) 750387. *Club:* Achilles.

MYERS, Robert William; Chairman, Robert Myers Associates, Landscape Architects, since 2006; *b* London, 19 May 1969; *s* of His Honour Mark Myers and Katherine Myers; *m* 1997, Clare Burlton; three *s*. *Educ:* Highgate Sch., London; Girton Coll., Cambridge (BA Hons Geog. 1990); Univ. of Central England (Dip. Landscape Architecture). Dir, Elizabeth Banks Associates, 1998–2005. Major projects include: design of Wellcome Trust Genome Campus, Hinxton Hall, 1998; new courtyard and gdns, Southwark Cath., 2001; design of Duke of York Sq., King's Rd, Chelsea, 2003; design of gdns at Tregothnan, Cornwall, 2004; landscape strategy and plan for The Backs, Cambridge, 2007; gdns, Clare Coll., Cambridge, 2009; Hereford Cathedral Close, 2011; Exeter Cathedral Green, 2011; RHS Wisley Bowes-Lyon Rose Garden, 2012; Magic Rose Garden, Hampton Court Palace, 2012. RHS Chelsea Flower Show Gold Medals for: Sir Hans Sloane Gdn, 2003; Costiera dei Fiori Gdn, 2006; Fortnum and Mason Gdn, 2007; Cadogan Estates Gdn, 2008; CRUK Gdn, 2010; Brewin Dolphin Garden, 2013. CMLI 1994. *Recreations:* sailing, ski-ing, cricket, playing trumpet and jazz piano. *Address:* Robert Myers Associates, Hergest Estate Office, Ridgebourne Road, Kington, Herefordshire HR5 3EG. *T:* (01544) 232035, *Fax:* (01544) 232031. *E:* robert@robertmyers-associates.co.uk.

MYERS, Sir Rupert (Horace), KBE 1981 (CBE 1976); AO 1995; FTSE, FAA; Professor Emeritus; Vice-Chancellor and Principal, University of New South Wales, 1969–81; *b* 21 Feb. 1921; *s* of Horace Alexander Myers and Dorothy (*née* Harris); *m* 1944, Io Edwina King (*d* 2001); one *s* three *d*; *m* 2002, Nancy Marguerite Besley. *Educ:* Melbourne High Sch.; Univ. of Melbourne (BSc 1942; MSc 1943; PhD 1947). FTSE (FTS 1979); FAA 1997; CPEng, FIMMA, FRACI; FAIM; FAusIMM; FAICD. Commonwealth Res. Fellow, Univ. of Melbourne, 1942–47; Principal Res. Officer, CSIRO, AERE Harwell, 1947–52; University of New South Wales: Foundn Prof. of Metallurgy, 1952–81; Dean, Faculty of Applied Science, 1956–61; Pro-Vice-Chancellor, 1961–69. Chairman: NSW State Pollution Control Commn, 1971–89; Aust. Vice-Chancellors' Cttee, 1977–79; Cttee of Inquiry into Technol Change in Australia, 1979–80; Commonwealth Cttee of Review of Nat. Capital Develt Commn, 1982–83; Consultative Cttee for Nat. Conservation Strategy for Australia, 1983–85; Coastal Council of NSW, 1982–85; Cttee of Review of NZ Univs, 1987–88; Cttee of Review of Aust. Sci. and Technology Council, 1993; Cttee of Review, Co-operative Res. Centres Prog., 1995; Co-operative Res. Centre for Greenhouse Accounting, 1999–2003. Pres., Aust. Acad. of Technol Scis and Engrg, 1989–94 (Vice-Pres., 1985–88). Director: CSR Ltd, 1982–93; Energy Resources of Australia Ltd, 1982–97; IBM Australia Ltd, 1988–91. Member: Nat. Energy Adv. Cttee, 1980–82; Australian Manufacturing Council, 1980–82. Mem., Sydney Opera House Trust, 1976–83; Foundn Pres., Friends of Royal Botanic Gdns, Sydney, 1982–85. Hon. FIEAust, 1992. Hon. LLD Strathclyde, 1973; Hon. DSc Wollongong, 1976; Hon. DEng Newcastle, 1981; Hon. DLitt NSW, 1981. Centenary Medal, Australia, 2003. *Publications:* Technological Change in Australia, 1980; numerous on metallurgy and atomic energy (also patents). *Recreations:* bowls, music, working with silver. *Address:* 1303/30 Glen Street, Milsons Point, NSW 2061, Australia. *T:* and *Fax:* (2) 89203108.

MYERSON, His Honour Arthur Levey; QC 1974; a Circuit Judge, 1978–99; *b* 25 July 1928; *o s* of Bernard and Eda Myerson; *m* 1960, (Elaine) Shirley Harris; two *s*. *Educ:* Blackpool Grammar Sch.; Queens' Coll., Cambridge (BA 1950; LLB 1951); BA (Open Univ.) 1985. RAF, 1946–48. Called to the Bar, 1952; a Recorder of the Crown Court, 1972–78; Resident Judge, York Crown Court, 1996–99. Pres., HM Council of Circuit Judges, 1991. *Recreations:* walking, reading, fishing. *Address:* 20 Sandmoor Lane, Leeds LS17 7EA. *Club:* Moor Allerton Golf (Leeds).

See also D. S. Myerson.

MYERSON, (David) Simon; QC 2003; a Recorder, since 2001; *b* 22 Oct. 1962; *s* of His Honour Arthur Levey Myerson, *qv*; *m* 1987, Nicole Maurice; four *d*. *Educ:* Carmel Coll.; Downing Coll., Cambridge (MA). Called to the Bar, Middle Temple, 1986, Bencher, 2013. *Recreations:* walking, reading, sailing. *Address:* 12 Byrom Street, Manchester M3 4PP. *T:* (0161) 829 2100, *Fax:* (0161) 829 2101; St Paul's Chambers, 2nd Floor Trafalgar House, 29 Park Place LS1 2SP. *T:* (0113) 245 5866, *Fax:* (0113) 245 5807. *E:* simon.myerson@me.com.

MYERSON, Prof. Jeremy; Director, Helen Hamlyn Centre for Design, since 1999, and Helen Hamlyn Professor of Design, since 2008, Royal College of Art (Professor of Design Studies, 2003–08; Director, InnovationRCA, 2004–09); *b* 6 Aug. 1956; *s* of Alexander and Maxine Myerson; *m* 1986, Wendy Smith; two *s*. *Educ:* Hull Univ. (BA Hons); Royal Coll. of Art (MA). Editor: Creative Rev., 1984–86; Design Week, 1986–89; freelance writing and consultancy, 1989–95; Prof. of Contemporary Design, De Montfort Univ., 1995–98. Mem. Bd, Design Council, 2009–11. Trustee: Gordon Russell Trust, 1994–2011; Audi Design Foundn, 2004–10. *Publications:* (jtly) Conran Design Guides to Tableware, Lighting, Home Office and Kitchenware, 1990; Gordon Russell: designer of furniture, 1992; Beware Wet Paint: designs by Alan Fletcher, 1996; New Public Architecture, 1996; (jtly) New Workspace New Culture: office design as a catalyst for change, 1998; (jtly) The Creative Office, 1999; Making The Lowry, 2000; IDEO: masters of innovation, 2001; (jtly) Rewind: 40 years of design and advertising, 2002; (jtly) The 21st Century Office, 2003; Space to Work: new office design, 2006; New Demographics New Workspace, 2010; Life of Work: what office design can learn from the world around us, 2014. *Recreations:* architecture, jazz, football. *Address:* Royal College of Art, Kensington Gore, SW7 2EU. *T:* (020) 7590 4242, *Fax:* (020) 7590 4244. *E:* jeremy.myerson@rca.ac.uk.

MYERSON, Julie Susan Emilia; novelist and author; *b* Nottingham, 2 June 1960; *d* of late Geoffrey Pike and of Maritza Simpson (*née* Jackson); *m* 2005, Jonathan Scott Myerson; two *s* one *d*. *Educ:* Nottingham Girls' High Sch.; Univ. of Bristol (BA Hons English). Publicist, Press Office, National Th., 1983–87; publicist, Walker Books, 1988–93. *Publications:* Sleepwalking, 1994; The Touch, 1996; Me and the Fat Man, 1998; Laura Blundy, 2000; Something Might Happen, 2002; Home: the story of everyone who ever lived in our house, 2004; Not a Games Person, 2005; The Story of You, 2006; Out of Breath, 2008; The Lost Child, 2009; Then, 2011; The Quickening, 2013; The Stopped Heart, 2016. *Recreation:* gardening. *Address:* c/o Karolina Sutton, Curtis Brown Group, Haymarket House, 28–29 Haymarket, SW1Y 4SP.

MYERSON, Prof. Roger Bruce, PhD; Professor of Economics, since 2001, and Glen A. Lloyd Distinguished Service Professor, since 2007, University of Chicago; *b* Boston, Mass, 29 March 1951; *m* 1982, Regina Weber; one *s* one *d*. *Educ:* Harvard Univ. (AB *summa cum laude*, SM Applied Maths 1973; PhD Applied Maths 1976). Northwestern University: Asst Prof. of Managerial Econs and Decision Scis, 1976–79; Associate Prof., 1979–82; Prof., 1982–2001. Vis. Prof. of Econs, Univ. of Chicago, 1985–86, 2000–01; Vis. Researcher, Univ. Bielefeld, 1978–79. Fellow: Econometric Soc., 1983 (Mem. Council, 1996–2002, 2005–07; Vice Pres., 2007–08; Pres., 2009); American Acad. of Arts and Scis, 1993. (Jtly) Nobel Prize in Econ. Scis, 2007. *Publications:* Game Theory: analysis of conflict, 1991 (trans. Chinese, 2001); Probability Models for Economic Decisions, 2005; *contributor:* Auctions, Bidding and Contracts, 1983; Social Goals and Social Organization, 1985; Game Theoretic Models of Bargaining, 1985; The Shapley Value, 1988; The New Palgrave: allocation, information and markets, 1989; Negotiation Analysis, 1991; Rational Interaction, 1992; Political Economy: institutions, competition and representation, 1993; Handbook of Game Theory, vol. 2, 1994; Advances in Economic Theory and Econometrics, vol. 1, 1997; Economics of Transnational Commons, 1997; Passion and Craft: how economists work, 1998; contrib. articles to newspapers and papers to learned jls, incl. Internat. Jl Game Theory, Econometrica, Games and Econ. Behavior, Social Choice and Welfare, Jl Econ. Theory, Amer. Econ. Rev. *Address:* Department of Economics, University of Chicago, 1126 East 59th Street, Chicago, IL 60637, USA.

MYERSON, Simon; *see* Myerson, D. S.

MYKURA, Dr Hamish Finlayson; Executive Vice President, and Head of International Content, National Geographic Channels International, since 2012; *b* Edinburgh, 28 March 1962; *s* of Dr Walter Mykura and Alison Mykura; *m* 1997, Janey Patricia Winifred Walker, *qv*; twin *d*. *Educ:* George Heriot's Sch., Edinburgh; Univ. of Aberdeen (MA 1984); Univ. of Manchester (PhD 1989). Prodn trainee, BBC, 1989–91; documentaries producer, BBC Radio, 1991–92; prod. and dir, BBC TV, 1992–2000; Dir, Blakeway Prodns, 2000–01; Channel 4 Television: Commng Ed. for Hist., 2001–03; Hd of Hist., Sci. and Religion, 2003–07; Hd of Documentaries and More4, 2008–12. FRSA. *Recreations:* hill walking, travel writing, classic cars of the 1970s and 80s. *Address:* National Geographic Channel, 10 Hammersmith Grove, W6 7AP. *E:* hamish.mykura@fox.com.

MYKURA, Janey Patricia Winifred; *see* Walker, J. P. W.

MYLAND, Howard David, CB 1988; Deputy Comptroller and Auditor General, National Audit Office, 1984–89; *b* 23 June 1929; *s* of John Tarrant and Frances Grace Myland; *m* 1951, Barbara Pearl Mills (*d* 2013); two *s* one *d*. *Educ:* Fairfields Schs; Queen Mary's Sch., Basingstoke. Served Intelligence Corps, 1948–50. Entered Exchequer and Audit Dept, 1948; Dep. Dir of Audit, 1972; Dir of Audit, 1977; Dep. Sec. of Dept, 1979; an Asst Auditor Gen., National Audit Office, 1984. Mem., CIPFA, 1979–. Mem., Basingstoke Round Table, 1962–70. *Publications:* Public Audit Law—Key Development Considerations, 1992. *Recreations:* travel, classical music, contract bridge.

MYLES, David Fairlie, CBE 1988; tenant hill farmer; *b* 30 May 1925; *s* of Robert C. Myles and Mary Anne S. (*née* Fairlie); *m* 1951, Janet I. (*née* Gall) (*d* 2012); two *s* two *d*. *Educ:* Edzell Primary Sch.; Brechin High Sch. National Farmers Union of Scotland: Mem. Council, 1970–79; Convenor of Organisation and Publicity Cttee, 1976–79. MP (C) Banff, 1979–83; Sec., Cons. backbench Cttees on European Affairs and on Agriculture, Fisheries and Food (Jt Sec.); Mem., Select Cttees on Agriculture and on European Legislation. Contested (C) Orkney and Shetland, 1983. Councillor, Angus DC, 1984–96 (Leader, Cons. Gp, 1992–96). Chm., Dairy Produce Quota Tribunal for Scotland, 1984–97; Member: Exec., Angus Tourist Bd, 1984–92; North of Scotland Hydro-Electric Bd, 1985–88; Extra-Parly Panel (Scotland), 1986–95; Potato Marketing Bd, 1988–97. Dean, Guildry of Brechin, 1993–95; Lord Pres., Ct of Deans of Scotland, 1995–96; Session Clerk, Edzell/Lethnot Parish Church, 1996–2001. *Recreations:* curling, Scottish fiddle music, works of Robert Burns. *Address:* Dalbog, Edzell, Brechin, Angus DD9 7UU; (home) The Gorse, Dunlappie Road, Edzell, Brechin, Angus DD9 7UB. *Clubs:* Farmers; Brechin Rotary.

MYLES, Lynda Robbie; independent film producer, Pandora Productions, since 1991; Head, Fiction Direction, National Film and Television School, since 2004; *b* 2 May 1947; *d* of late Alexander Watt Myles and Kathleen Kilgour Myles (*née* Polson); *m* 1972, Dr David John Will (marr. diss. 1978). *Educ:* Univ. of Edinburgh (MA Hons Mental Philosophy). Dir, Edinburgh Internat. Film Fest., 1973–80; Curator of Film, Pacific Film Archive, Univ. of Calif, Berkeley, 1980–82; Film Consultant, Channel Four TV, 1982–83; Producer, Enigma Films, 1983–86; Sen. Vice-Pres., Creative Affairs (Europe), Columbia Pictures, 1986–88; Commng Ed. for Drama, BBC TV, 1989–91. Co-Exec. Dir, East-West Producers' Seminar, 1990–94. Producer: Defence of the Realm, 1986; The Commitments, 1991; The Snapper, 1993; The Van, 1995; The Life of Stuff, 1997; When Brendan Met Trudy, 2000; (jtly) Killing Me Softly, 2001. Chair (first), Women in Film and TV, 1990–91; Mem. Bd, Ateliers du Cinéma Européen, 1998–. Gov., BFI, 1993–96. BFI Award, 1981. *Publications:* (with M. Pye) The Movie Brats, 1978. *Address:* Pandora Productions, 20 Ossington Street, W2 4LY. *T:* (020) 7243 3013. *Club:* Groucho.

MYLNE, Dawn; *see* Chatty, D.

MYLNE, Nigel James; QC 1984; a Recorder, 1985–2004; *b* 11 June 1939; *s* of late Harold James Mylne and Dorothy Evelyn Mylne (later D. E. Hogg); *m* 1st, 1967, Julie Phillpotts (marr. diss. 1977); two *s* one *d*; 2nd, 1979, Judith Hamilton (marr. diss. 1997); one *s*; 3rd, 2009, Susan Walker, *d* of Maj. Derek Stuart Holmes. *Educ:* Eton College. National Service, 10th Royal Hussars, 1957–59. Called to the Bar, Middle Temple, 1963, Bencher, 1995. Immigration Judge, 1997–2009; Pres., Mental Health Review Tribunals, 1999–2009. *Recreation:* beekeeping. *Address:* Langleys, Brixton Deverill, Wiltshire BA12 7EJ. *T:* (01985) 840351. *E:* nigelmylne@btinternet.com. *Club:* Pratt's.

MYLONAS, Michael John; QC 2012; *b* 11 June. *Educ:* Haileybury Jun. Sch.; Eton Coll.; Univ. of Buckingham (LLB Hons 1987); Inns of Court Sch. of Law. Called to the Bar, Gray's Inn, 1988; in practice as a barrister, 1988–. *Publications:* (contrib.) Medical Law Reports, 2000–10; (contrib.) APIL, Clinical Negligence, 2007; (contrib.) Medical Treatment Decisions and the Law, 2010. *Recreations:* ski-ing, climbing, polo, aviation. *Clubs:* Lansdowne; Binfield Heath Polo (Chm., 2010–).

MYLREA, (Anthony) Paul; Director of Communications, University of Cambridge, since 2013; Fellow, Wolfson College, Cambridge, since 2013; *b* 21 March 1956; *s* of late Thomas Aloysius Mylrea and Joan Mylrea (*née* Wilcox, latterly Taylor, stage name Joan Campion); *m* 1986, Frances Lowndes; one *s* two *d*. *Educ:* St Bede's Coll., Manchester; Univ. of Birmingham (BA Hons French 1978); Open Univ. (MBA 2003). Reuters: Corresp., London, Germany, Luxembourg, Belgium and Brazil, 1982–90; Chief Corresp., Chile, Bolivia and Peru, 1990–94; UK Political Corresp., 1994–97; Dep. Editor, 1997–99, Editor, 1999–2002, www.alertnet.org; Hd, Media, Oxfam GB, 2002–04; Dir, Gp Media, Transport for London, 2004–07; Dir, Communications, DFID, 2007–10; Hd, Press and Media Relns, 2010–11, Dir of Communications, 2011–12, Dir of Public Affairs, 2012–13, BBC. Associate Lectr, OU Business Sch., 2005–13. *Recreations:* swimming in cold water, scuba diving. *Address:* University of Cambridge, The Old Schools, Trinity Lane, Cambridge CB2 1TN. *T:* (01223) 765539. *E:* paul.mylrea@admin.cam.ac.uk.

MYNERS, family name of **Baron Myners**.

MYNERS, Baron *cr* 2008 (Life Peer), of Truro in the County of Cornwall; **Paul Myners,** CBE 2003; Partner and UK Chairman, Cevian Capital, since 2011; Chairman of Court and Council, London School of Economics and Political Science, since 2015; *b* 1 April 1948; adopted *s* of late Thomas Russell Myners and of Caroline Molly Myners; *m* 1995, Alison Agnes Isabel Macleod (*see* Lady Myners); one *s* one *d*, and three *d* by a previous marriage. *Educ:* Truro Sch., Cornwall; Univ. of London Inst. of Educn (BEd); Stanford Sch. of Business (SEP 1995). Daily Telegraph, 1970–74; N. M. Rothschild & Sons Ltd, 1974–85 (Dir, 1979); Gartmore plc: Chief Exec., 1985–93, 1999–2000; Chm., 1987–2001; Chairman: Guardian Media Gp plc, 2000–08; Land Securities PLC, 2006–08; Edelman UK, 2015–; Chm. and Dir,

Nomad Hldgs Ltd, 2014–; non-exec. Chm., Autonomous Res. LLP, 2011–. Financial Services Sec., HM Treasury, 2008–10. Dep. Chm., PowerGen plc, 1999–2001; Exec. Dir, Nat. Westminster Bank, 1997–2000; non-executive Director: Orange plc, 1996–99; Coutts Group, 1997–2000; Guardian Newspapers Ltd, 2001–08; mmO$_2$ plc (formerly BT Wireless), 2001–04; Marks and Spencer, 2002–06 (Chm., 2004–06); Bank of New York, 2002–06; RIT Capital, 2010–; Ecofin Water and Power Opportunities plc, 2012–; Co-operative Gp, 2013–14; MegaFon, 2013–; Mem., Ct of Dirs, Bank of England, 2005–08; Advr, Govt of Singapore Investment Corp., 2006–08; Chm., Personal Accounts Delivery Authy, DWP, 2007–08. Member: Financial Reporting Council, 1995–2004; Company Law Review Consultative Cttee, 1998–2000; Commn on English Prisons, 2007–08; Commn on Vulnerable Employment, 2007–08; Chm., Low Pay Commn, 2006–08. Vis. Fellow, Nuffield Coll., Oxford, 2007–; Exec. Fellow, London Business Sch., 2013–. Mem., Adv. Council, LSO, 1993–2003. Trustee: Nat. and Cornwall Maritime Mus. Trust, 1998–2004; Royal Acad. Trust, 2000–03; Tate Gall., 2003–08 (Chm., 2004–08; Chm. Council, Tate St Ives, 2001–08); Glyndebourne, 2003–08; Smith Inst., 2003–08; Charities Aid Foundn, 2003–04; Nat. Gallery, 2007–08. FRSA 1994. Hon. LLD Exeter, 2003. Freeman, City of London, 1996. *Publications:* Developing a Winning Partnership, 1995; Creating Quality Dialogue, 1999; Institutional Investment in the UK: a review for HM Treasury, 2001. *Recreations:* family, contemporary art, opera, Rugby football. *Address:* House of Lords, SW1A 0PW. *Clubs:* City of London, Oriental; Hong Kong; Royal Cornwall Yacht.

MYNERS, Lady; Alison Agnes Isabel Myners; psychotherapeutic counsellor, since 2013; Chair, Institute of Contemporary Arts, since 2010; *b* Surrey, 20 Nov. 1959; *d* of Angus James Macleod and Mary McKay Macleod; *m* 1995, Paul Myners (*see* Baron Myners); one *s* one *d*, and three step *d*. *Educ:* Lady Eleanor Holles Sch., Hampton; City of London Poly. (Bi-lingual Sen. Sec. Dip.); Regent's Univ. London (Dip. Psychotherapy and Psychol. of Counselling). Chair, Corporate Develt Bd, Women's Aid, 2005–07. Chair: Royal Acad. Schs' Patrons, 2003–06; Contemp. Art Soc., 2006–10. Trustee, Royal Acad. of Arts, 2003–08, Emeritus Trustee, 2009. Mem. Cttee, Action on Addiction, 1997–2000. Mem., Adv. Bd, Prix Pictet, 2009–. Cultural Champion Award, Arts & Business, 2012. *Recreations:* family, art, tennis, cycling, walking. *Address:* Institute of Contemporary Arts, The Mall, SW1Y 5AH. *T:* (020) 7766 1401. *E:* alison.myners@ica.org.uk. *Clubs:* St Mawes Sailing; Trebah Tennis.

MYNORS, Charles Baskerville, PhD; author, since 1983; barrister, since 1988; Chancellor, Diocese of Worcester, since 1998; *b* Normandy, Surrey, 27 Aug. 1953; *s* of David Rickards Baskerville Mynors, OBE and Mary Laurence Mynors (*née* Garton); *m* 1978, Janet Lennox Mynors (*née* Wardrop); one *s* one *d* (and one *d* decd). *Educ:* Eton Coll.; Corpus Christi Coll., Cambridge (MA Architecture); Univ. of Sheffield (MA Town and Regl Planning); Poly. of Central London (DipLaw); Univ. of Cambridge (PhD Law 2010). MRTPI 1979, FRTPI 1989; MRICS 1986, FRICS 2008; IHBC 1997. Planning Officer, Royal Borough of Kensington and Chelsea, 1977–86; called to the Bar: Middle Temple, 1988; NI, 2002; in practice as a barrister, Francis Taylor Bldg, 1989–. Member: Estates Cttee, Middle Temple, 1998–; Bar Council Disability Gp, 2004–; Legal Adv. Commn, Gen. Synod, 2011–. Sen. Res. Fellow, De Montfort Univ., Leicester, 1995–98; Vis. Prof., Oxford Brookes Univ., 2005–; Vis. Lectr, Univ. of Bath, 2012–. Mem., Advisory Gp, Prince's Regeneration Trust, 2009–. Trustee: Overseas Bishoprics Fund, 1997– (Chair, 2013–); Tree Advice Trust, 2012–14; Chm., Complaints Appeal Bd, Inst. of Chartered Foresters, 2008–. Member, Editorial Board: Jl of Architectural Conservation, 1995–; Jl of Planning and Envmt Law, 1998–; Ed., 1991–96, Gen. Ed., 1996–98, Consultant Ed., 1998–2002, Planning and Envmtl Law Bulletin. *Publications:* Urban Conservation and Historic Buildings: a guide to the legislation, 1983; Planning Applications and Appeals: a guide for architects and surveyors, 1987; Listed Buildings and Conservation Areas, 1989, 5th edn as Listed Buildings and Other Heritage Assets, 2015; Planning Control and the Display of Advertisements, 1992; (contrib.) Law, Policy and Development in the Rural Environment, 1999; The Control of Outdoor Advertising and Graffiti, 2009; The Law of Trees, Forests and Hedges, 2002, 2nd edn 2011; (contrib.) Gardens and Landscapes in Historic Building Conservation, 2014; Changing Churches: a practical guide to the faculty system, 2015; numerous jl articles. *Recreations:* church activities, law reform, learning to play the harp. *Address:* Francis Taylor Building, Temple, EC4Y 7BY. *T:* (020) 7353 8415, *Fax:* (020) 7353 7622. *E:* charles.mynors@ftb.eu.com.

MYNORS, Sir Richard (Baskerville), 2nd Bt *cr* 1964, of Treago, Co. Hereford; landowner; *b* 5 May 1947; *s* of Sir Humphrey Charles Baskerville Mynors, 1st Bt and Lydia Marian (*d* 1992), *d* of Sir Ellis Minns, LittD, FSA, FBA; *S* father, 1989; *m* 1970, Fiona Bridget, *d* of late Rt Rev. G. E. Reindorp; three *d*. *Educ:* Marlborough; Royal College of Music (ARCM, ARCO); Corpus Christi Coll., Cambridge (MA). Asst Director of Music, King's School, Macclesfield, 1970–73; Director of Music: Wolverhampton Grammar School, 1973–81; Merchant Taylors' School, Crosby, 1981–88; Belmont Abbey Sch., Hereford, 1988–89. *Heir:* none. *Address:* Treago, St Weonards, Hereford HR2 8QB. *T:* (01981) 580208.

MYNOTT, Adam Robert John; Director of Media Affairs, Huawei Technologies, since 2014; *b* 21 Oct. 1957; *s* of Michael J. Mynott and Rosalind S. Mynott; *m* 1987, Carol Elizabeth Schug; two *s* one *d*. *Educ:* Eastbourne Coll.; Univ. of Exeter (BA Hons Philos. 1980); London Coll. of Printing (Postgrad. Dip. Radio Journalism 1982). BBC: Producer, Today Prog., 1986–90; gen. news reporter, 1990–94; Sports Corresp., 1994–2001; S Asia Corresp., Delhi, 2001–04; E Africa Corresp., Nairobi, 2004–08; World Affairs Corresp., 2008–11; Dir of Media Relns, G4S plc, 2011–14. *Publications:* The Battle for Iraq, 2003. *Recreations:* news and current affairs, starting DIY projects. *Address:* Huawei Technologies, 16 Old Queen Street, Westminster, SW1H 9HP. *E:* adam.mynott@gmail.com. *Clubs:* Free Foresters, Sou'westers.

MYNOTT, Dr (Roger) Jeremy; Chief Executive of the Press, Secretary of the Press Syndicate and University Printer, Cambridge University Press, 1999–2002; Fellow, Wolfson College, Cambridge, 1999–2009, now Emeritus; *b* 15 Feb. 1942; *s* of Clifford Harry Mynott and Margaret Mynott (*née* Ketley); *m* 2000, Diane Speakman. *Educ:* Colchester Royal Grammar Sch.; Corpus Christi Coll., Cambridge (BA 1964; MA 1968; PhD 1968). Schoolmaster, Magdalen Coll. Sch., Oxford, 1964–65; Cambridge University Press, 1968–2002: sub-editor, 1968–69; editor, 1969–73; sen. editor, 1973–75; Associate Dir, 1975–79; Editl Dir, Humanities and Social Scis, 1979–81; Dir, Publishing Develt, 1981–85; Press Editl Dir Worldwide, 1985–92; Man. Dir, Publishing Div. and Dep. Chief Exec., 1992–99. FRSA 1990. Founder Mem., New Networks for Nature, 2009–. *Publications:* Little Thurlow 2000, 1999; Walks Round the Thurlows, 2005; Birdscapes, 2009; Thurlow 2010, 2010; (ed and trans.) Thucydides: the War of the Peloponnesians and the Athenians, 2013. *Recreations:* natural history (especially ornithology), walking, philosophy. *W:* www.jeremymynott.org.

MYRES, Rear-Adm. John Antony Lovell, CB 1993; Hydrographer of the Navy, 1990–94; *b* 11 April 1936; *yr s* of late Dr John Nowell Linton Myres, CBE and Joan Mary Lovell Myres (*née* Stevens); *m* 1965, Alison Anne, *d* of late Lieut David Lawrence Carr, RN (killed in action 1941) and Mrs James Pertwee; three *s*. *Educ:* Winchester College. FRICS 1975–95; FRGS 1993–97; FRIN 1994–97. Entered RN 1954; specialised Hydrographic Surveying, 1959; CO HM Ships Woodlark, 1969–71, Fox, 1972–73, Hecla, 1974, 1978–79, 1981–82; Hydrographer, RAustN, 1982–85. Sec., UK Polar Medal Assessment Cttee, 1994–2011. Pres., Orders and Medals Res. Soc., 1997–2001. Vice Pres., RNLI, 2006–. Younger Brother of Trinity House, 1990. Freeman, City of London, 1990; Liveryman, Chartered Surveyors' Co., 1990–97. Guild Burgess of Preston, 1952. *Publications:* (jtly) British Polar Exploration and Research: a historic and medallic record with biographies, 2000; articles in professional jls. *Recreations:* naval and medallic history, gardening. *Address:* The Gables, 43 Abingdon Road, Dorchester-on-Thames, Oxfordshire OX10 7JZ. *Club:* Antarctic.

MYRTLE, Brig. Andrew Dewe, CB 1988; CBE 1979 (MBE 1967); Chief Executive and Secretary, Tennis and Rackets Association, 1989–2001; *b* 17 Dec. 1932; *s* of Lt-Col John Young Elphinstone Myrtle, DSO, KOSB (killed in action in World War II) and late Doreen May Lake; *m* 1973, Mary Rose Ford; two *d*. *Educ:* Horris Hill Prep. Sch.; Winchester Coll.; RMA, Sandhurst (Sword of Honour); Army Staff Coll. Co. Comdr, 1 KOSB, 1964–66; Bde Major, 24 Infantry Bde, 1966–68; Co. Comdr, 1 KOSB, 1968–69, CO, 1 KOSB, 1969–71; MA to Adjt Gen., 1971–74; Comdt, Jun. Div., Staff Coll., 1974–77; Comd 8 Infantry Bde, 1977–79; student, RCDS, 1979; DDMO, MoD, 1980–83; Asst Comdt, RMA, Sandhurst, 1983–85; Comdr Land Forces, Cyprus, 1986–88. Col, KOSB, 1980–85. ADC to the Queen, 1985–88. *Recreations:* golf, fly-fishing. *Address:* Pen Guen, Stonor, Henley-on-Thames, Oxon RG9 6HB. *Clubs:* MCC; Huntercombe Golf; Queen's.

N

NAAS, Lord; Richard Thomas Bourke; *b* 7 Dec. 1985; *s* and *heir* of Earl of Mayo, *qv*.

NADER, Ralph; author, lecturer, lawyer; *b* Winsted, Conn, USA, 27 Feb. 1934; *s* of Nadra Nader and Rose (*née* Bouziane). *Educ:* Gilbert Sch., Winsted; Woodrow Wilson Sch. of Public and Internat. Affairs, Princeton Univ. (AB *magna cum laude*); Harvard Univ. Law Sch. (LLB). Admitted to: Bar of Conn, 1958; Bar of Mass, 1959; US Supreme Court Bar, 1963. Served US Army, 1959. Law practice in Hartford, Conn, 1959–; Lectr in History and Govt, Univ. of Hartford, 1961–63; Lectr, Princeton Univ., 1967–68. Member: Amer. Bar Assoc., 1959–; AAAS, 1964–; Phi Beta Kappa. Has pursued actively better consumer protection and improvement in the lot of the American Indian; lobbied in Washington for safer food, drugs, air, water and against nuclear reactors; played very important role in work for passing of: National Traffic and Motor Vehicle Safety Act, 1966; Wholesome Meat Act, 1967; Occupational Safety and Health Act, 1970; Safe Drinking Water Act, 1974; Freedom of Information Act, 1974; National Cooperative Bank Act, 1978. Candidate for Presidency of the USA (Green) 1996 and 2000, (Ind) 2004 and 2008. Nieman Fellows Award, 1965–66; named one of the Ten Outstanding Young Men of the Year by US Jun. Chamber of Commerce, 1967. *Publications:* Unsafe at Any Speed: the designed-in dangers of the American automobile, 1965, rev. edn 1991; (jtly) What to do with Your Bad Car, 1971; Working on the System: a manual for citizen's access to federal agencies, 1972; (jtly) Action for a Change, 1972; (jtly) Whistleblowing, 1972; (jtly) You and Your Pension, 1973; (ed) The Consumer and Corporate Accountability, 1973; (co-ed) Corporate Power in America, 1973; (jtly) Taming the Giant Corporation, 1976; (co-ed) Verdicts on Lawyers, 1976; (jtly) Menace of Atomic Energy, 1977; (co-ed) Who's Poisoning America?, 1981; (jtly) The Big Boys: power and position in American business, 1986; (jtly) Winning the Insurance Game, 1990; (jtly) No Contest, 1996; Only the Super-Rich Can Save Us! (novel), 2009; Getting Steamed to Overcome Corporatism, 2011; The Seventeen Solutions: bold ideas for our American future, 2012; Unstoppable: the emerging left-right alliance to dismantle the corporate state, 2014; contrib. articles to many magazines; has weekly syndicated newspaper column. *Address:* PO Box 19312, Washington, DC 20036, USA.

NAGAI, Kiyoshi, PhD; FRS 2000; Member, since 1981, and Senior Scientist, MRC Laboratory of Molecular Biology; Fellow, Darwin College, Cambridge, since 1993; *b* 25 June 1949; *s* of Prof. Otoji Nagai and Naoko Nagai; *m* 1974, Yoshiko Majima; one *s* one *d*. *Educ:* Toin High Sch.; Osaka Univ. (BSc 1972; MSc 1974; PhD 1978). Thomas Usher Res. Fellow, Darwin Coll., Cambridge, 1981–83. Mem., EMBO, 2000. Novartis Medal and Prize, Biochem. Soc., 2000. *Publications:* (jtly) RNA: protein interactions, 1994; res. pubns and reviews in scientific jls. *Recreations:* playing cello in chamber groups, reading. *Address:* MRC Laboratory of Molecular Biology, Francis Crick Avenue, Cambridge CB2 0QH. *T:* (01223) 267077. *E:* kn@mrc-lmb.cam.ac.uk.

NAGANO, Kent George; conductor; Music Director, Montréal Symphony Orchestra, since 2006; Principal Guest Conductor and Artistic Advisor, Gothenburg Symphony Orchestra, since 2012; General Music Director, Hamburgische Staatsoper, since 2015; *b* 22 Nov. 1951; *s* of George Kimiyoshi Nagano and Ruth Okamoto; *m* Mari Kodama; one *d*. *Educ:* Univ. of Calif. Music Director: Opéra de Lyon, 1988–98; Hallé Orch., 1991–2000; Artistic Dir, Deutsches Symphonie-Orchester Berlin, 2000–06; Music Director: LA Opera, 2001–06; Bayerische Staatsoper, 2006–13. Has performed with: Boston Symphony Orch., 1984; Paris Opera (World Première, St François d'Assise, by Messiaen); Metropolitan Opera; Salzburg Fest.; Vienna Philharmonic; Berlin Philharmonic; NY Philharmonic; also World Premières: Death of Klinghoffer by John Adams, Brussels, Lyon and Vienna; L'Amour de loin by Saariaho; A White House Cantata by Bernstein; Das Gehege by Wolfgang Rihm; Alice in Wonderland by Unsuk Chin; Babylon by Jörg Widmann. Gramophone Record of Year, 1990; Gramophone Opera Award, 1993; Grammy Award, 1995, 2001, 2011. *Address:* c/o International Classical Artists, Dunstan House, 14a St Cross Street, EC1N 8XA. *T:* (020) 7902 0520.

NAGDA, Kanti; Manager, Sangat Advice Centre, Harrow, since 1998; *b* 1 May 1946; *s* of Vershi Bhoja Nagda and Zaviben Nagda; *m* 1972, Bhagwati Desai; two *s*. *Educ:* City High Sch., Kampala, Uganda; Coll. of Further Educn, Chippenham, Wilts; E African Univ., Uganda; Cassio Coll., Watford. Sec.-Gen., Confedn of Indian Organisations (UK), 1975–98; Manager, Sancroft Community Centre, 1982–98. Pres., Nat. Congress of Gujarati Orgns, 1992–95; Chair, NW London Community Foundn, 2011–12. Exec. Cttee Member: Harrow Community Relations Council, 1974–76; Gujarati Literary Acad. (GB), 1976–82. President: Uganda Art Circle, 1968–71; Anglo Indian Circle, 1973–82 and 1985–88; Indian Cricket Club, Harrow, 1976–80; Greenford (Willow Tree) Lions Club, 1988–89. Trustee, Karma Yoga Foundn, 2009–. Hon. Editorial Consultant, International Asian Guide & Who's Who, 1975–95; Asst Editor, Oshwal News, 1977–84. Mem., Rose of England Lodge, 2010–. *Publications:* Muratiyo Ke Nokar (Gujarati novel), Kenya 1967; stories and articles in newspapers and jls. *Recreations:* cricket, photography. *Address:* 170 Tolcarne Drive, Pinner, Middx HA5 2DR. *T:* (020) 8429 2636. *Club:* Greenford Lions (Sec., 2012).

NAGEL, William, CMG 2002; Chairman, W. Nagel (International Diamond Brokers), since 1955; *b* 17 Jan. 1925; *m* 1960, Ruth Marion Josephine Yvonne Tand; one *s* three *d*. *Educ:* University Coll. London (LLB Hons 1949). Called to the Bar, Lincoln's Inn, 1949; post-grad. res. in Public Internat. Law, Fitzwilliam House, Cambridge Univ., 1950–53; Public Internat. Law Course, Internat. Court of Justice, The Hague, 1954; apptd Official Broker, De Beers, 1959. Special Advr to Minister of Foreign Affairs, Romania, 1992. Member: ESU; Foreign Press. Assoc.; RIIA. Freeman, City of London, 1988. Comdr, Order of the Crown (Belgium), 1996; Officer's Cross, Order of Merit (Germany), 2000; Comdr, Nat. Order Serviciul Credincios (Romania), 2002. *Address:* 10 Ely Place, EC1N 6RY. *T:* (020) 7242 9636, *Fax:* (020) 7430 0990. *E:* wn@wnagel.com.

NAGLE, Terence John, FRICS; Director, Wynnstay Properties plc, since 1998; *b* 10 Nov. 1942; *s* of Richard and Bridget Nagle; *m* 1974, Elizabeth Mary Millett; two *s* two *d*. *Educ:* Ottershaw Sch.; St John's Seminary, Wonersh (BTh). FRICS 1964. Property Dir, 1984–93, Man. Dir, 1993–97, Brixton Estate plc. *Recreations:* gardening, sitting on committees. *Address:* Pitch Place House, Worplesdon, Guildford, Surrey GU3 3LQ. *T:* (01483) 232036.

NAGLER, Neville Anthony, OBE 2011; Executive Director, Taxation Disciplinary Board, 2007–15; *b* 2 Jan. 1945; *s* of late Gerald and Sylvia Nagler; *m* 1971, Judy Mordant; one *s* one *d*. *Educ:* Christ's Coll., Finchley; Jesus Coll., Cambridge (MA); Cert. in Public Services Mgt, 2000. Asst Principal, HM Treasury, 1967–70; Private Sec. to Chancellor of Exchequer, 1970–71; Principal, 1972; transferred to Home Office, 1975; Asst Sec., Race Relations and Equal Opportunities, 1980–83; Head, Drugs and Extradition Div., 1983–88; Asst Sec., Home Office Finance Div., 1988–91; Chief Exec., subseq. Dir Gen., 1991–2004, Interfaith Consultant, 2005–07, Bd of Deputies of British Jews; Dir, Sternberg Foundn, 2005–06. Vice Chm., Inter Faith Network for UK, 2005–07. Lay Member: Disciplinary Tribunals, Council of Inns of Ct, 2005–12; Investigation Cttee, CIMA, 2007–13; Mem., Lord Chancellor's Adv. Cttee for JPs in NW London, 2006–14. UK Rep. to UN Commn on Narcotic Drugs, 1983–88; Chm., Council of Europe Pompidou Gp, 1984–88. Haldane Essay Prize, Haldane Soc., 1979; Cert. of Appreciation, US Drug Enforcement Admin, 1988. *Publications:* articles in Public Administration and UN Jl of Narcotic Drugs. *Recreations:* wine-making, listening to music, theatre, walking. *Address:* 24 Dawlish Drive, Pinner, Middx HA5 5LN. *T:* (020) 8868 3103.

NAHM, Prof. Werner, PhD; FRS 2011; Senior Professor of Theoretical Physics, and Director, School of Theoretical Physics, Dublin Institute for Advanced Studies, since 2002; *b* 1949. *Educ:* Ludwigs Maximilian Univ., Munich (Dip. Physics 1970); Bonn Univ. (PhD 1972). Postdoctoral res., Bonn Univ., 1972–75; Fellow and staff mem., CERN, 1976–82; Heisenberg Fellow, Bonn Univ., 1982–86; Associate Prof., Univ. of Calif, Davis, 1986–89; Prof., Bonn Univ., 1989–2002. Ext. Scientific Mem., Max-Planck-Inst. für Mathematik. Gothenburg Lise Meitner Prize, Univ. of Gothenburg, 2012; Max Planck Medal for Theoretical Physics, German Phys. Soc., 2013. *Address:* School of Theoretical Physics, Dublin Institute for Advanced Studies, 10 Burlington Road, Dublin 4, Ireland.

NAHORSKI, Prof. Stefan Ryszard, PhD; FMedSci; Professor of Pharmacology, 1984–2006, now Emeritus, and Head of Department of Cell Physiology and Pharmacology, 1993–2006, University of Leicester; *b* 10 Dec. 1945; *s* of Stanislaw Nahorski and Linda Nahorska; *m* 1969, Catherine Mary Gower; one *s* two *d*. *Educ:* St Boniface's Coll., Plymouth; Univ. of Southampton (BSc Hons); Portsmouth Sch. of Pharmacy (PhD 1971). Research Asst, Portsmouth, 1968–71; MRC Fellow, Sheffield, 1971–75; University of Leicester: Lectr in Pharmacology, 1976–81; Reader, 1981–84. Gov., Cornwall Coll., 2008–12. Founder FMedSci 1998. John Vane Medal, British Pharmacological Soc., 2004. *Publications:* Pharmacology of Adrenoceptors, 1985; Transmembrane Signalling, 1990; numerous research papers to learned jls. *Recreations:* tennis, walking, watching (supporting) soccer, sea angling.

NAHUM, Peter John; art advisor and dealer, Leicester Galleries, London, since 1984; *b* 19 Jan. 1947; *s* of Denis E. Nahum and Allison Faith Nahum (*née* Cooke); *m* 1987, Renate Angelika Meiser. *Educ:* Sherborne. Peter Wilson's Sotheby's, 1966–84; British Paintings Dept, Sotheby's, Belgravia, 1971–84, Sen. Dir, 1977–84; regular contributor to Antiques Road Show, BBC TV, 1980–2001. *Publications:* Prices of Victorian Paintings, Drawings and Watercolours, 1976; Monograms of Victorian and Edwardian Artists, 1976; Cross Section, British Art in the 20th Century, 1988; British Art in the Twentieth Century, 1989; Burne-Jones, The Pre-Raphaelites & Their Century, 1989; Burne-Jones: a quest for love, 1993; Fairy Folk in Fairy Land, 1997; Pre-Raphaelite . Symbolist . Visionary, 2001; Medieval to Modern, 2003; The Ruralists: a celebration, 2007; Ancient Landscapes, Pastoral Visions, 2008; Past and Present: Edward Burne-Jones, his medieval sources and their relevance to his personal journey, 2009. *Recreations:* reading, art, sailing, photography and street photography, gardening, theatre, travel, walking. *Address:* 5 Bloomsbury Square, WC1A 2TA. *T:* (020) 7242 1126. *E:* peternahum@leicestergalleries.com.

NAILATIKAU, Brig.-Gen. Hon. Ratu Epeli, LVO 1977; OBE 1979; CSM 1995; MSD 1988; President of Fiji, since 2009; *b* 5 July 1941; *s* of Ratu Sir Edward Cakobau, KBE, MC, ED and Adi Lady Vasamaca Tuiburelevu; *m* 1981, Adi Koila Nailatikau (*née* Mara), *d* of Ratu Sir Kamisese Mara, GCMG, KBE, CF, MSD, PC; one *s* one *d*. *Educ:* Levuka Public Sch.; Queen Victoria Sch., Fiji; Wadham Coll., Oxford. Enlisted in Royal Fiji Military Forces, 1962; commnd Fiji Infantry Regt, 1963; seconded to First Bn, Royal NZ Infantry Regt, Malaysia and Borneo, 1966; ADC to Governor of Fiji, 1968–69; Foreign Service Course, Oxford Univ., 1969–70; Second Secretary: Fiji High Commn, Canberra, 1970–72; Fiji Mission to UN, 1973–74; Australian Army Staff Coll., Queenscliffe, 1976 (psc); CO Fiji Bn, Fiji Infantry Regt serving with UNIFIL, 1978–79; Jt Services Staff Coll., Canberra, Australia, 1980 (jssc); Sen. Plans Officer, UNIFIL HQ, 1981; CS, 1981–82, Comdr, 1982–87, Royal Fiji Mil. Forces; Ambassador of Fiji to UK, and concurrently Ambassador to Denmark, Germany, Israel, the Holy See and Egypt, 1988–96; Roving Ambassador to Pacific Island countries, 1998; Perm. Sec. for Foreign Affairs and External Trade, Fiji, 1999; Mem., Military Council, May–July 2000; Deputy Prime Minister and Minister for Fijian Affairs: Interim Govt, July 2000–March 2001; Caretaker Govt, March–Sept. 2001; Speaker, House of Reps, Fiji, 2001–06; Minister, Interim Government: for Foreign Affairs and External Trade, 2007–08; for Foreign Affairs, Internat. Co-operation and Civil Aviation, 2008; for Indigenous Affairs, Provincial Develt and Multi-Ethnic Affairs, 2008–09. Fiji Equerry: to the Prince of Wales during Fiji Independence visit, 1970; to the Queen during Jubilee visit, 1977. Hon. Col 1st Bn Fiji Infantry Regt, 1996. OStJ 1985. Civil Service Medal (Fiji), 1995. *Recreations:* golf, tennis. *Address:* Government House, Berkley Crescent, PO Box 2513, Government Buildings, Suva, Fiji. *T:* 3314244, *Fax:* 3301645.

NAIPAUL, Sir Vidiadhar Surajprasad, (Sir Vidia), Kt 1990; author; *b* 17 Aug. 1932; *m* 1st, 1955, Patricia Ann Hale (*d* 1996); 2nd, 1996, Nadira Khannum Alvi. *Educ:* Queen's Royal Coll., Trinidad; University Coll., Oxford (Hon. Fellow, 1983). Hon. Dr Letters Columbia Univ., NY, 1981; Hon. LittD: Cambridge, 1983; London, 1988; Oxford, 1992. British Literature Prize, 1993; Nobel Prize for Literature, 2001. *Publications:* The Middle Passage, 1962; An Area of Darkness, 1964; The Loss of El Dorado, 1969; The Overcrowded Barracoon, and other articles, 1972; India: a wounded civilization, 1977; The Return of Eva Perón, 1980; Among the Believers, 1981; Finding the Centre, 1984; A Turn in the South, 1989; India: a million mutinies now, 1990; Beyond Belief: Islamic excursions, 1998; Letters between a Father and Son, 1999; Reading & Writing: a personal account, 2000; The Writer and the World (collected essays), 2002; Literary Occasions (essays), 2003; A Writer's People, 2007; The Masque of Africa, 2010; *novels:* The Mystic Masseur, 1957 (John Llewellyn Rhys Memorial Prize, 1958); The Suffrage of Elvira, 1958; Miguel Street, 1959 (Somerset Maugham Award, 1961); A House for Mr Biswas, 1961; Mr Stone and the Knights Companion, 1963 (Hawthornden Prize, 1964); The Mimic Men, 1967 (W. H. Smith Award, 1968); A Flag on the Island, 1967; In a Free State, 1971 (Booker Prize, 1971); Guerrillas, 1975; A Bend in the River, 1979; The Enigma of Arrival, 1987; A Way in the World, 1994; Half a Life, 2001; Magic Seeds, 2004. *Address:* c/o The Wylie Agency, 17 Bedford Square, WC1B 3JA.

NAIRN, Martin John L.; *see* Lambie-Nairn.

NAIRN, Sir Michael, 4th Bt *cr* 1904; *b* 1 July 1938; *s* of Sir Michael George Nairn, 3rd Bt, TD, and Helen Louise, *yr d* of Major E. J. W. Bruce, Melbourne, Aust.; *S* father, 1984; *m* 1st, 1972, Diana (*d* 1982), *er d* of Leonard Francis Bligh, NSW; two *s* one *d*; 2nd, 1986, Sally Jane, *d* of Major W. P. S. Hastings. *Educ:* Eton; INSEAD. *Heir: s* Michael Andrew Nairn [*b* 2 Nov. 1973; *m* 2009, Maya, *er d* of Peter Gill, San Antonio, Texas]. *Club:* Caledonian.

NAIRN, Nicholas Cameron Abel; chef; Chief Executive Officer and owner: Nairn Enterprises, since 1990; Nick Nairn Consulting, since 2008; Chief Executive Officer, owner and Senior Tutor, Nick Nairn Cook School, Port of Menteith, since 2000, and Aberdeen, since 2012; *b* Stirling, 12 Jan. 1959; *s* of James Nairn and Irene Nairn; *m* 2001, Holly Anderson; one *s* one *d*. *Educ:* McLaren High Sch.; Glasgow Coll. of Nautical Studies (Deck Officer Cl. 1 1984). Naval officer, Merchant Navy, 1976–83; owner and Head Chef: Braeval Restaurant, 1986– (Michelin Star, 1991); Nairns Restaurant with Rooms, 1997–. Television presenter: Wild Harvest, 1996; Ready Steady Cook, 1996–2010; Landward, 2007–; Paul and Nick's Big Food Trip, 2012–. Founder Mem., Scottish Chefs Assoc., 1991; Fellow, Master Chefs of GB, 2003. DUniv Stirling, 2007. Scottish Chef of the Year, 1996. *Publications:* Wild Harvest, 1996; Wild Harvest 2, 1997; Island Harvest, 1998; Nick Nairn's Top 100 Salmon Recipes, 2002; New Scottish Cookery, 2002; (jtly) The Ready Steady Cook Book, 2003; Nick Nairn's Top 100 Chicken Recipes, 2004; (jtly) Great British Menu, 2006; Fish 'n' Tips, 2006; Nick Nairn Cook School, 2008. *Recreations:* hillwalking, cycling, mountain biking, spending time with my family. *Address:* Nick Nairn Cook School, Port of Menteith, Stirling FK8 3JZ. *T:* (01877) 389900. *E:* info@nicknairncookschool.com.

NAIRN, Sir Robert Arnold S.; *see* Spencer-Nairn.

NAIRN, Prof. Tom C.; Professor of Nationalism and Global Diversity, Royal Melbourne Institute of Technology, 2002–10; *b* 2 June 1932; *s* of David Robertson Nairn and Katherine Herd Cunningham; partner, Millicent Petrie. *Educ:* Dunfermline High Sch.; Univ. of Edinburgh (MA Philosophy 1956); Scuola Normale Superiore, Pisa; Univ. de Dijon. Lectr in Social Philosophy, Univ. of Birmingham, 1962–64; Lectr in Gen. Studies, Hornsey Coll. of Art, 1966–69; Fellow, Transnational Inst., Amsterdam, 1972–75; Dir, Scottish Internat. Inst., Edinburgh, 1976–80; work in commercial TV, Glasgow, 1992–94; Researcher with Ernest Gellner, Centre for Nationalism Studies, Prague Coll. of the Central European Univ., 1994–95; Lectr in Nationalism Studies, Grad. Sch., Univ. of Edinburgh, 1994–99. Inst. of Advanced Studies Fellow, University Coll., Durham Univ., 2009. *Publications:* The Beginning of the End (with Angelo Quattrocchi), 1968; The Left Against Europe, 1975; The Break-up of Britain, 1977, new edn 2003; The Enchanted Glass: Britain and Monarchy, 1988; Faces of Nationalism, 1998; Pariah: misfortunes of the British kingdom, 2001; (with Paul James) Global Matrix, 2005.

NAIRN-BRIGGS, Very Rev. George Peter; DL; Dean (formerly Provost) of Wakefield, 1997–2007, now Dean Emeritus; *b* 5 July 1945; *s* of Frederick and Gladys Nairn-Briggs; *m* 1968, Candida Vickery; one *s* one *d*. *Educ:* Slough Tech. High Sch.; King's Coll., London (AKC 1969); St Augustine's Coll., Canterbury. Local authority housing, 1963–64; Press Officer, MAFF, 1964–66; ordained deacon, 1970, priest, 1971; Curate: St Laurence, Catford, 1970–73; St Saviour, Raynes Park, 1973–75; Vicar: Christ the King, Salfords, 1975–81; St Peter, St Helier, dio. Southwark, 1981–87; Bishop's Advr for Social Responsibility, Wakefield, 1987–97; Canon Residentiary, Wakefield Cathedral, 1992–97. A Church Comr, 2004–07. Chm., Standards Cttee, Wakefield MDC, 2002–. Mem., Gen. Synod of C of E, 1980–2007. DL W Yorks, 2006. *Publications:* Love in Action, 1986; Serving Two Masters, 1988; It Happens in the Family, 1992; contrib. to magazines and jls. *Recreations:* reading, buying antiques, travel. *Address:* Abbey House, 2 St James Court, Park Avenue, Wakefield WF2 8DN. *T:* (01924) 291029.

NAIRNE, Alexander Robert, (Sandy), CBE 2011; Director, National Portrait Gallery, 2002–15; *b* 8 June 1953; *s* of Rt Hon. Sir Patrick Dalmahoy Nairne, GCB, MC, PC; partner 1981, *m* 2006, Sylvia Elizabeth, (Lisa), Tickner, *qv*; one *s* one *d*. *Educ:* Radley Coll.; University Coll., Oxford (BA Modern History and Economics 1974; MA; Hon. Fellow 2006). Asst Dir, Museum of Modern Art, Oxford, 1974–76; Research Asst and Asst Keeper, Tate Gallery, 1976–79; Dir of Exhibitions, Inst. of Contemporary Arts, 1980–83; writer and associate producer, State of the Art, TV series, Channel 4, 1985–87; Dir of Visual Arts, Arts Council, 1987–92; Sen. Res. Fellow, Getty Grant Prog., 1992–93; Dir, Public and Regl Services, 1994–98, Dir, Nat. Progs, 1998–2002, Tate Gall. Member: Fabric Adv. Cttee, St Paul's Cathedral, 1996– (Chm., 2011–); Adv. Gp, Govt Art Collection, 2002–; London Cultural Strategy Gp, 2009–10. Trustee, Artangel, 1993–2006. Vis. Fellow, Clark Art Inst., Mass, 2007. Gov., Middx Univ., 1994–2003 (Dep. Chm., 1999–2000); Member Council: RCA, 2001–10; British Sch. in Rome, 2001–10; Museums Assoc., 2005–08 (Vice Pres., 2006–08); Paul Mellon Centre, 2007–12; Mem. Art Gp, Maggie's Cancer Care Centres, 2010– (Chm., 2011–). Trustee, Clore Leadership Prog., 2014– (Chm., 2014–). Sen. FRCA 2010; FSA 2012. Hon. DArts: Middx, 2005; De Montfort, 2008; London, 2012. *Publications:* State of the Art, 1987; Thinking about Exhibitions, 1996; The Portrait Now, 2006; Art Theft and the Case of the Stolen Turners, 2011; 21st Century Portraits, 2013. *Recreation:* racing punting. *Address:* 43 Lady Somerset Road, NW5 1TY. *Clubs:* Chelsea Arts; Leander (Henley).

See also A. Nairne.

NAIRNE, Andrew; Director, Kettle's Yard, University of Cambridge, since 2011; *b* 10 Feb. 1960; *s* of Rt Hon. Sir Patrick Dalmahoy Nairne, GCB, MC, PC; *m* 1995, Nicola Dandridge, *qv*; two *s*. *Educ:* Radley Coll.; Univ. of St Andrews (MA Art Hist. 1983). Asst Curator, Kettle's Yard, Cambridge, 1984–85; Dep. Dir, Ikon Gall., Birmingham, 1985–86; Exhibns Dir, Centre for Contemp. Arts, Glasgow, 1986–92; Visual Arts Dir, Scottish Arts Council, Edinburgh, 1992–97; Dir, Dundee Contemp. Arts, 1997–2001; Dir, Modern Art Oxford, 2001–08; Exec. Dir, Arts (formerly Arts Strategy), Arts Council England, 2008–11. Vis. Fellow, Nuffield Coll., Oxford, 2002–10. Chm., Visual Arts and Galls Assoc., 2005–07. FRSA 1997. *Recreation:* running. *Address:* 15 Grazebrook Road, N16 0HU. *T:* 07795 580108.

See also A. R. Nairne.

NAIRNE, Nicola; *see* Dandridge, N.

NAIRNE, Sandy; *see* Nairne, A. R.

NAIRNE, Sylvia Elizabeth, (Lisa); *see* Tickner, S. E.

NAISH, Sir (Charles) David, Kt 1994; DL; FRAgS; Director, 1998–2007, Chairman, 2002–07, Arla Foods UK (formerly Express Dairies plc); *b* 28 July 1940; *s* of Charles Naish and Muriel (*née* Turner); *m* 1966, Victoria Cockburn Mattock; two *s* one *d*. *Educ:* Worksop Coll.; RAC, Cirencester (MRAC). Jt Man. Dir, J. B. Eastwood Ltd, 1969–73; Chm., Thornhill Country Produce Ltd, 1982–85. Chm., Aubourn Farming Ltd, 1998–2003; Director: Assured British Meat Ltd, 1997–2001; Dalgety Gp Ltd, 1998–2003; Wilson Gp Ltd, 1997–; Caunton Investments Ltd, 2002–; Hilton Food Gp plc, 2007– (Chm., 2010–); Produce Investments plc, 2009–. Chm., Silsoe Res. Inst., 1998–2006. President: NFU, 1991–98 (Dep. Pres., 1985–91); COPA, 1995–97. FRAgS 1986; FRSA 1992; FIGD 1996. DL Notts, 1991. Hon. DSc De Montfort, 1996; DUniv Essex, 1998. *Recreations:* shooting, vintage motor cars. *Address:* Edwinstowe, Notts NG21 9QE. *Club:* Farmers (Chm., 1980).

NAISH, Peter; Chief Executive, Wood Green Animal Shelter, 1997–2000; *b* 24 Jan. 1945; *s* of Frederick and Ida Naish; *m* 1970, Janet Kemp (marr. diss. 1996); one *s* two *d*. *Educ:* Hampton Grammar Sch.; King's Coll., London. Area Manager, Notting Hill Housing Trust, 1970–73; Chief Executive: Irwell Valley Housing Assoc., 1973–77; English Churches' Housing Gp, 1971–89; Research and Development for Psychiatry, 1989–91; CLS Care Services, 1991–94; Chief Exec., EOC, 1994–97. *Recreations:* walking, music, poetry.

NAISMITH, Prof. James Henderson, PhD; FRS 2014; FRSC, FRSB, FRSE, FMedSci; Professor of Chemical Biology, University of St Andrews, since 2001; *b* Bellshill, 26 July 1968; *s* of Duncan Naismith and Frances Naismith; *m* 1993, Rachel Middleton; one *s* one *d*. *Educ:* Hamilton Grammar Sch.; Univ. of Edinburgh (BSc 1st Cl. Chem. 1989); Univ. of Manchester (PhD Structural Chem. 1992). FRSC 2002; FRSB (FSB 2009). NATO Fellow, Lab. of Stephen Sprang, Univ. of Texas Southwestern, 1993–94; University of St Andrews: Lectr, 1995–98; Reader, 1998–2001; Dir, Biomed. Scis Res. Complex, 2011–. Mem., EMBO, 2009–. FRSE 2005; FMedSci 2012. *Publications:* papers in learned jls. *Recreations:* family, American Civil War, Chinese art, work. *Address:* Biomedical Sciences Research Complex, University of St Andrews, North Haugh, St Andrews, Fife KY16 9ST. *T:* (01334) 463401. *E:* bsrc-dir@st-and.ac.uk.

NAJIM, Omar; Head of Delivery Improvement, McKinsey Hospital Institute, since 2011; *b* Baghdad, 10 Nov. 1973; *m* 2009, Hadeel Alwash. *Educ:* Al-Mansour High Sch. for Boys, Baghdad; Univ. of Baghdad (MB ChB); Imperial Coll. London (MSc Surgical Technol.). Surgeon in training, NHS, 2001–07; Dep. Dir, Med. Workforce Develt, NHS NW, 2007–09; Leadership Fellow, NHS Inst. for Innovation and Improvement, 2009–10; Sen. Operation Manager, St George's Hosp. NHS Trust, London, 2010–11. Mem., BMA (Chm., Civil and Public Services Cttee). *Publications:* contribs to BMJ, British Jl Hosp. Medicine, Head and Neck Jl, Clin. Voice, Philosophy Now, Jl Neurosurgery. *Recreations:* horse-riding, fencing, reading, squash, creating stories about strangers.

NAKASONE, Yasuhiro; Prime Minister of Japan, 1982–87; Chairman, Institute for International Policy Studies (formerly International Institute for Global Peace), since 1988; Founder and President, Asia Pacific Parliamentary Forum, 1993–2003 (Hon. President, since 2004); *b* 27 May 1918; 2nd *s* of Matsugoroh Nakasone; *m* 1945, Tsutako Kobayashi (*d* 2012); one *s* two *d*. *Educ:* Faculty of Law, Imperial Univ. (graduate). Joined Min. of Home Affairs, 1941; commd as Lt-Comdr, 1945. Mem., House of Representatives (elected 20 consecutive times), 1947–2003; Minister of State, Dir-Gen. of Science and Technology Agency, 1959–60; Minister of Transport, 1967–68; Minister of State, Dir-Gen. of Defence Agency, 1970–71; Minister of Internat. Trade and Industry, 1972–74; Minister of State for Admin. Management Agency, 1980–82. Chm. Exec. Council, 1971–72, Sec. Gen., 1974–76, Liberal Democratic Party. Hon. DHL, Johns Hopkins, 1984; Hon. Dr Louis Pasteur, Strasbourg, 1999. Médaille de la Chancellerie, Univs of Paris. *Publications:* The Ideals of Youth, 1947; Japan Speaks, 1954; The New Conservatism, 1978; Human Cities—a proposal for the 21st century, 1980; Anthology of Haiku by Nakasone Yasuhiro, 1985; Politics and My Life (autobiog.), 1992; Tenchiyujou (autobiography), 1996; The Making of the New Japan, 1999; Japan: a state strategy for the twenty-first century, 2002; Japanese Prime Ministership as a Science, 2004; Meditations, 2004; Anthology of Haiku 2009 by Nakasone Yasuhiro, 2009; My Last Word on Conservatism, 2010; Japanese Foreign Policy since 1945, 2012. *Address:* Toranomon 3–2–2, 30 Mori Building, Minato-ku, Tokyo 105–0001, Japan.

NALL, Sir Edward William Joseph, 3rd Bt *cr* 1954, of Hoveringham, co. Nottingham; *b* 24 Oct. 1952; *er s* of Sir Michael Joseph Nall, 2nd Bt and of Angela Loveday Hanbury (*née* Coryton); *S* father, 2001; *m* 2004, Helen Fiona Batterbury (*née* Fergusson); one *d*. *Educ:* Eton. Commnd 13th/18th Royal Hussars (QMO), subseq. Light Dragoons, 1973; Major, 1985; retd, 1993. *Heir: b* Alexander Michael Nall [*b* 3 July 1956; *m* 1982, Caroline Jane Robinson; one *s* one *d*]. *Address:* Hoveringham Hall, Hoveringham, Nottingham NG14 7JR.

NALL-CAIN, family name of **Baron Brocket**.

NALLY, Edward; Partner, Fieldings Porter, Bolton, since 1982; *b* 18 Jan. 1956; *s* of Edward and Sarah Nally; *m* 1977, Julie Fagan; one *s* one *d*. *Educ:* De La Salle Grammar Sch., Salford; Nottingham Univ. (LLB Hons). Solicitor. Diocesan Solicitor, Salford RC Dio., 1983–. Dep. Vice-Pres., 2002–03, Vice-Pres., 2003–04, Pres., 2004–05, Law Soc. Member: Judicial Appts Commn, 2006–11; Legal Services Bd, 2011–. Chm. of Governors, Pendleton Sixth Form Coll., Salford, 2000–07. *Recreations:* golf, walking, avid Bolton Wanderers football supporter. *Address:* Fieldings Porter, Silverwell House, Silverwell Street, Bolton BL1 1PT. *T:* (01204) 540900, *Fax:* (01204) 397254. *E:* edward.nally@fieldingsporter.co.uk. *Club:* Royal Automobile.

NAMALIU, Rt Hon. Sir Rabbie (Langanai), KCMG 1996 (CMG 1979); GCL 2008; CSM 2006; PC 1989; MP for Kokopo (Pangu Pati), Papua New Guinea, 1982–2007; Chancellor, University of Natural Resources and Environment, Vudal, 2007–11; *b* 3 April 1947; *s* of Darius Namaliu and Utul Ioan; *m* 1978, Margaret Nakikus (*d* 1993); two *s*, and one step *d*; *m* 1999, Kelin Tavul (marr. diss. 2004); one *s* two *d*; *m* 2005, Darusila Watangia. *Educ:* Univ. of Papua New Guinea (BA); Univ. of Victoria, BC (MA). Senior Tutor, later Lectr in History, Univ. of Papua New Guinea, 1973; Principal Private Sec. to Chief Minister (Hon. Michael Somare), 1974–75; Vis. Pacific Fellow, Centre for Pacific Studies, Univ. of California, Santa Cruz, 1975; Provincial Comr, East New Britain Province, 1976; Chm., Public Services Commn, 1976–79; Exec. Officer to Leader of the Opposition (Rt Hon. Michael Somare), 1980–81; Minister for Foreign Affairs and Trade, 1982–84, for Primary Industry, 1985; Dep. Leader, 1985–88, Parliamentary Leader, 1988–93, Pangu Pati; Leader of the Opposition, May–July 1988; Prime Minister, PNG, 1988–92; Leader of the Opposition, 1992–93; Speaker of Nat. Parlt, 1994–97; Senior Minister of State, 1997–98; Minister: for Petroleum and Energy, 1998–99; for Foreign Affairs and Immigration, 2002–06; for the Treasury, 2006–07. Non-executive Director: Marengo Mining Ltd, 2008–; Bougainville Copper Ltd; Kina Securities Ltd; Interoil Corp. PNG; non-exec. Dir and Chm., Kina Asset Management Ltd; Chm., Kramer Ausenco, 2010–. Hon. LLD Univ. of Victoria, BC, 1983. *Recreations:* swimming, walking, reading, golf. *Address:* PO Box 144, Kokopo 613, East New Britain Province, Papua New Guinea. *E:* rnamaliu@datec.net.pg.

NANCOLLAS, Sarah Catherine; Chief Executive, Lepra (formerly LEPRA Health in Action), since 2010; *b* London, 8 Aug. 1961; *d* of Henry John Nancollas, MBE and late Freda Nancollas. *Educ:* Simon Langton Grammar Sch. for Girls; Univ. of Nottingham (BSc Hons Civil Engrg 1983). Shift Controller, Northfleet, 1983–85, Distribution Manager, Plymstock, 1985–87, Blue Circle Cement; Sen. Mgt Consultant, Price Waterhouse, 1987–89; Implementation Manager, 1989–91, Distribution Manager Gen. Chemicals, 1991–92, BP Chemicals; Transport Advr, Save the Children UK, 1993–98; Chief Exec., Transaid, 1998–2003; Exec. Dir, Project Hope, 2003–04; Chief Exec., Canon Collins Trust, 2004–10.

Trustee: DHL UK Foundn, 2004–11; Skillshare Internat., 2004–11; ILEP, 2010–. *Recreations:* landscape photography, watching athletics, Formula 1 and cricket. *Address:* Lepra, 28 Middleborough, Colchester, Essex CO1 1TG. *T:* (01206) 216700. *E:* sarahn@lepra.org.uk.

NANDY, Dipak; Head of Equal Opportunities, Social Services Department, Nottinghamshire County Council, 1992–2001; *b* 21 May 1936; *s* of B. C. Nandy and Leela Nandy; *m* 1st, 1964, Margaret Gracie (decd); 2nd, 1972, Hon. Luise Byers (marr. diss. 1991); two *d*. *Educ:* St Xavier's Coll., Calcutta; Univ. of Leeds (BA 1st Cl. Hons English Literature, 1960; C. E. Vaughan Research Fellowship, 1960–62). Lectr, English Literature, Univ. of Leicester, 1962–66; Lectr and Fellow of Rutherford College, Univ. of Kent at Canterbury, 1966–68; founder-Director, The Runnymede Trust, 1968–73; Vis. Fellow, Adlai Stevenson Inst. of International Affairs, Chicago, 1970–73; Research Fellow, Social and Community Planning Research, 1973–74; special consultant on discrimination, Home Office, 1975; Dep. Chief Exec., Equal Opportunities Commn, 1976–86; Chief Exec., Intermediate Technology Develt Gp, 1986–88; Hon. Lectr in Social Policy, Univ. of Birmingham, 1989–95; Financial and Admin. Dir, RSP, Queen Elizabeth House, Oxford, 1991. Member: Cttee of Inquiry into Future of Broadcasting, 1974–77; Council, Nat. Assoc. Citizens' Advice Bureaux, 1983–86; BBC: Chm., Asian Programmes Adv. Cttee, 1983–88; Mem., General Adv. Council. Member: Council, Northern Chamber Orch., 1980–84; Royal Nat. Theatre Bd, 1991–97; Governor, BFI, 1984–87. Mem. Ct, Leicester Univ., 2002–08. Trustee, CSV, 1981–91. Hon. Liaison, Employment and Labour Law Sect., Amer. Bar Assoc., 1980–. *Publications:* numerous essays in books, periodicals and newspapers on literature, political thought, race relations, urban problems, equality for women, broadcasting policy and development issues. *Recreations:* collecting records, opera, computing. *Address:* 8 Woodhedge Drive, Thorneywood, Nottingham NG3 6LU. *T:* (0115) 948 1631.

See also L. E. Nandy.

NANDY, Lisa Eva; MP (Lab) Wigan, since 2010; *b* Manchester, 9 Aug. 1979; *d* of Dipak Nandy, *qv*. *Educ:* Parrs Wood Comp. Sch., Manchester; Univ. of Newcastle upon Tyne (BA Hons Pols 2001); Birkbeck, Univ. of London (MSc Pols and Govt 2005). Researcher to Neil Gerrard, MP, 2001–03; Policy Researcher, Centrepoint, 2003–05; Policy Advr, Children's Soc., 2005–10. Mem. (Lab) Hammersmith and Fulham LBC, 2006–10. Shadow Minister for Children and Families, 2012–15; Shadow Sec. of State for Energy and Climate Change, 2015–. *Recreations:* theatre, Rugby League. *Address:* House of Commons, SW1A 0AA. *T:* (020) 7219 7188. *E:* lisa.nandy.mp@parliament.uk.

NANSON, Maj. Gen. Paul Anthony Edward, CBE 2015 (MBE 2002); QCVS 1996; Commandant, Royal Military Academy, Sandhurst, since 2015; *b* Ormskirk, Lancs, 10 May 1965; *s* of Roy and Pam Nanson; *m* 1998, Louise Hatfield; one *s* one *d*. *Educ:* Merchant Taylors' Sch., Crosby; Royal Mil. Acad. Sandhurst. Commnd 1986; Platoon Comdr, 3rd Bn RRF, then Trng Regt, Queen's Div., 1986–89; Adjt, 2nd Bn RRF, 1993–95; Co. Comdr, 2nd Bn, Royal Anglian Regt, 1996–98; acsc, 1998–2000; COS, 102 Logistics Bde, 2000–02; Co. Comdr, 1st Bn RRF, 2002–04; Mem., Directing Staff, JSCSC, 2004–06; CO, 1st Bn RRF, 2006–08; COS, 1st (UK) Armd Div., 2009–11; Comdr, 7th Armd Bde, 2011–13; Dir, Army Div., JSCSC, 2014–15. Col, RRF, 2015–. *Recreations:* hill walking, cooking, running, family. *Club:* Ormskirk Golf.

NAPIER, family name of **Lord Napier and Ettrick** and **Baron Napier of Magdala**.

NAPIER, 15th Lord *cr* 1627 (Scot.), **AND ETTRICK,** 6th Baron *cr* 1872 (UK); **Francis David Charles Napier;** (12th) Bt (Napier, formerly Scott) of Thirlestane (NS) 1666; Chief of the Name and Arms of Napier; established Napier Garden Planning, 1999; *b* 3 Nov. 1962; *er s* of 14th Lord Napier (and 5th Baron Ettrick), KCVO, and of Delia Mary (*née* Pearson); *S* father, 2012; *m* 1993, Zara Jane, *o d* of Hugh McCalmont, Newmarket, Suffolk; one *s* one *d*. *Educ:* Stanbridge Earls School; South Thames Coll., Wandsworth, 1986–87 (City and Guilds Computer Diploma); Otley Coll., Ipswich (Nat. Cert Hort. Garden Design and Construction 1999). With a Lloyd's agency, 1984–92; with Heath Bloodstock Ltd, 1992–97. Member: Standing Council of Scottish Chiefs, 2011–; Standing Council of the Baronetage, 2014–. Mem., Montrose Soc., 2010–. *Recreations:* travelling, horse-racing, cycling, gardening. *Heir: s* Master of Napier, *qv*. *Address:* Gowan Cottage, Westley Waterless, Newmarket, Suffolk CB8 0RQ. *Clubs:* Pratt's; Forest.

NAPIER, Master of; Hon. William Alexander Hugh Napier; *b* 10 June 1996; *s* and *heir* of Lord Napier and Ettrick, *qv*.

NAPIER OF MAGDALA, 6th Baron *cr* 1868; **Robert Alan Napier;** *b* 6 Sept. 1940; *s* of 5th Baron Napier of Magdala, OBE, and Elizabeth Marian, *y d* of E. H. Hunt, FRCS; *S* father, 1987; *m* 1964, Frances Clare, *d* of late Alan Frank Skinner; one *s* one *d*. *Educ:* Winchester College; St John's Coll., Cambridge (BA 1st cl. Hons 1962; MA 1966). *Heir: s* Hon. James Robert Napier, *b* 29 Jan. 1966. *Address:* The Coach House, Kingsbury Street, Marlborough, Wilts SN8 1HU. *T:* (01672) 512333. *Club:* Leander (Henley-on-Thames).

NAPIER, Brian William; QC (Scot.) 2002; PhD; *b* 9 Jan. 1949; *s* of George Napier and Isobella Ramsey Ross Napier; *m* 1st, 1971, Helen Marjorie Mercer (marr. diss. 2001); one *s* one *d*; 2nd, 2007, Elizabeth Clarke; one *s*. *Educ:* George Watson's Coll., Edinburgh; Univ. of Edinburgh (LLB 1971); Queens' Coll., Cambridge (MA 1974; PhD 1976). Res. Fellow, 1974, Fellow, 1974–89, Queens' Coll., Cambridge; Asst Lectr, 1975–79, Lectr, 1979–89, Univ. of Cambridge; Prof. of Law, Queen Mary and Westfield Coll., Univ. of London, 1989–96, Vis. Prof., 1996–; called to the Bar, Middle Temple, 1990 and Gray's Inn. Prof. Associé, Univs of Paris 1 and 2, 1980–81. Joint Editor: Harvey on Industrial Relations and Employment Law, 1988–; Transfer of Undertakings, 1999–. *Recreations:* walking, music. *Address:* c/o Faculty of Advocates, Parliament House, Edinburgh EH1 1RF. *T:* (0131) 260 5654.

NAPIER, Sir Charles Joseph, 6th Bt *cr* 1867, of Merrion Square, Dublin; Founder and Director, Kilmeston Communications, since 2012; *b* 15 April 1973; *o s* of Sir Robin Surtees Napier, 5th Bt and of Jennifer Beryl (who *m* 2001, Major Donald Black, MC (who *d* 2009)), *d* of H. Warwick Daw; *S* father, 1994; *m* 2003, Imelda Blanche Elisabeth, *d* of late John Trafford and of Amanda Trafford; two *s* one *d*. *Educ:* Eton; Univ. of Edinburgh (MA Hons; Fencing Blue). Scottish European Aid, 1995–96; Corporate Fundraiser, MIND, 1997–98; Appeal Dir, 1998–99, and Mem. Mgt Cttee, 2001–09, Downside Settlement, Bermondsey; public affairs, The Policy Partnership, 1999–2006; Account Dir, PPS Gp, 2006; Associate Director: Quintus Public Affairs, 2006–09; Luther Pendragon, 2009–12. Mem. (Lab), Hammersmith and Fulham LBC, 2002–06. Governor: Peterborough Primary Sch., Fulham, 2000–08; Brackenbury Primary Sch., Hammersmith, 2014–. Mem., ESU. *Recreations:* watching and playing most sports, fishing. *Heir: s* Finnian John Lennox Napier, *b* 14 Feb. 2006. *Address:* 35 Warbeck Road, W12 8NS. *Club:* Flyfishers'.

NAPIER, Iain John Grant; Chairman, McBride plc, since 2007; *b* 10 April 1949. *Educ:* Eastwood High Sch., Newton Mearns. FCMA. Whitbread plc; Ford Motor Co.; joined Bass plc, 1989; Mktg and Commercial Dir, Bass Leisure Retail, 1989–93; Gp HR Dir, 1993–94; Chief Exec., Bass Leisure Div., 1994–96; Chm., Chateaux Lascombes wine estate, Bordeaux; Chief Exec., Bass Brewers and Bass International Brewers, 1996–2000; Chm., Bass Ireland; Dir, Bass plc, until 2000; Mem. Exec. Mgt Cttee, Interbrew SA, until 2001; Chief Exec., Taylor Woodrow plc, 2002–07; Chm., Imperial Tobacco Gp plc, 2007–14 (non-exec. Dir, 2000–14; Jt Vice Chm., 2004–07). Former non-executive Director: BOC Gp plc; Perry Gp; Henderson Investors plc; St Modwens Properties plc; Tomkins plc; non-executive Director: Collins-Stewart plc, 2007–09; John Menzies plc, 2008– (Chm., 2010–); Molson Coors Brewing Co., 2008–.

NAPIER, John, RDI 1996; stage designer; *b* 1 March 1944; *s* of James Edward Thomas Napier and Lorrie Napier (*née* Godbold); *m* 1st, Andreane Neofitou; one *s* one *d*; 2nd, Donna King; one *s* one *d*; 3rd, Caroline McGee. *Educ:* Hornsey Coll. of Art; Central Sch. of Arts and Crafts. Designed 1st production, A Penny for a Song, Phoenix, Leicester, 1967; *London productions:* Fortune and Men's Eyes, 1968; The Ruling Class, The Fun War, Muzeeka, George Frederick (ballet), La Turista, 1969; Cancer, Isabel's a Jezebel, 1970; Mister, The Foursome, The Lovers of Viorne, Lear, 1971; Jump, Sam Sam, Big Wolf, 1972; The Devils (ENO), Equus, The Party, 1973; Knuckle, 1974; Kings and Clowns, The Travelling Music Show, 1978; The Devils of Loudon, Lohengrin (Covent Garden); King John, Richard II, Cymbeline, Macbeth, Richard III, 1974; Hedda Gabler, 1975; Much Ado About Nothing, The Comedy of Errors, King Lear, Macbeth, 1976; A Midsummer Night's Dream, As You Like It, 1977; The Merry Wives of Windsor, Twelfth Night, Three Sisters, Once in a Lifetime, 1979; The Greeks, Nicholas Nickleby (SWET award, Tony Award), 1980; Cats (Tony award), 1981, revival 2014; Henry IV Parts I and II, Peter Pan, 1982; Macbeth (Covent Garden), 1983; Starlight Express, 1984 (Tony Award, 1987); Les Misérables, 1985 (Tony Award, 1987); Time, 1986; Miss Saigon, 1989; Children of Eden, 1990; Trelawny of the 'Wells', 1993; Sunset Boulevard, 1993 (Tony Award, 1995); Burning Blue, 1995 (Olivier award, 1996); The Tower, 1995; Jesus Christ Superstar, 1996; Who's Afraid of Virginia Woolf?, 1996; An Enemy of the People, 1997; Peter Pan, 1997; Martin Guerre, 1998; Candide, 1999; South Pacific, 2001; Skellig, 2003; Aladdin, 2004, 2005; Equus, 2007, transf. NY, 2008; Disconnect, 2010; Birdsong, 2010; *Glyndebourne:* Idomeneo, 1983; *WNO:* Don Giovanni, 2011; *USA:* Siegfried & Roy Show (Las Vegas; also co-dir), 1990; Jane Eyre (NY), 2000; Nabucco (Met. Opera), 2001; film designs incl. Hook, 1991; numerous designs for stage productions in Europe, Japan, Australia, USA and for TV. Cameron Mackintosh Vis. Prof. of Contemporary Theatre, Univ. of Oxford, 2001. Hon. Fellow, London Inst., 2001. American Acad. of Achievement, 1994. *Recreation:* photography. *Address:* c/o Macnaughton Lord Representation, 44 South Molton Street, W1K 5RT.

NAPIER, John Alan; Chairman: RSA Insurance Group (formerly Royal & Sun Alliance Insurance Group) plc, 2003–12; Aegis Group plc, since 2008; *b* 22 Aug. 1942; *s* of late William Napier and Barbara Napier (*née* Chatten); *m* 1st, 1961, Gillian Reed (marr. diss. 1977); two *s* one *d*; 2nd, 1992, Caroline Denning; one *d*, and two step *s* one step *d*. *Educ:* Colchester Royal Grammar Sch.; Emmanuel Coll., Cambridge (MA Econs). Jun. and middle mgt, Internat. Publishing Corp. and Reed Internat., 1960–69; Managing Director: Index Printers, 1969–72; QB Newspapers, 1972–76; Exec. Dir (Australia), James Hardie Industries, 1976–86; Group Managing Director: AGB plc, 1986–90; Hays plc, 1991–98; Chairman: Booker plc, 1998–2000; Kelda Gp plc, 2000–08. *Recreations:* rural matters, outdoor activities, people, philosophy. *Address:* Aegis Media, Regent's Place, 10 Triton Street, NW1 3BF. *Club:* Reform.

NAPIER, Sir John Archibald Lennox, 14th Bt *cr* 1627 (NS), of Merchistoun; *b* 6 Dec. 1946; *s* of Sir William Archibald Napier, 13th Bt and of Kathleen Mabel, *d* of late Reginald Greaves; *S* father, 1990; *m* 1969, Erica, *d* of late Kurt Kingsfield; one *s* one *d*. *Educ:* St Stithians; Witwatersrand Univ., Johannesburg. MSc(Eng); PhD. *Heir: s* Hugh Robert Lennox Napier, *b* 1 Aug. 1977. *Address:* Merchistoun, PO Box 65177, Benmore 2010, Republic of South Africa.

NAPIER, Maj.-Gen. Lennox Alexander Hawkins, CB 1983; OBE 1970; MC 1957; Vice Lord-Lieutenant of Gwent, 1995–2004; Inspector of Public Inquiries, 1983–98; *b* 28 June 1928; *s* of Major Charles McNaughton Napier and D. C. Napier; *m* 1959, Jennifer Dawn Wilson; one *s* two *d*. *Educ:* Radley; RMA Sandhurst. Joined Army, 1946; commnd into South Wales Borderers, 1948; commanded 1st Bn S Wales Borderers and 1st Bn Royal Regt of Wales, 1967–70; Instructor, JSSC, 1970–72; served Min. of Defence, 1972–74; Brigade Commander, Berlin Infantry Bde, 1974–76; Prince of Wales's Division: Divisional Brigadier, 1976–80; Col Commandant, 1980–83; GOC Wales, 1980–83. Col, The Royal Regt of Wales, 1983–89; Hon. Col, Cardiff Univ. OTC, 1985–92. Chm., Central Rail Users Cttee, 1985–95. Gwent: DL 1983; High Sheriff 1988. OStJ 1969. *Recreations:* shooting, gardening. *Address:* Solva, 8 Monkswell Road, Monmouth NP25 3PF.

NAPIER, Michael; *see* Napier, T. M.

NAPIER, Paul James; Group Editorial Development Director, Johnston Press plc, since 2012; *b* 3 Oct. 1966; *s* of Dennis Napier and Brenda Napier (*née* Duthie); *m* 1996, Lara Katya Balmforth; one *s* one *d*. *Educ:* Kettering Boys' Sch.; Univ. of York (BA Hons English and Related Lit. 1989); Heriot-Watt Univ. (MBA 2000). Ed., Banbury Guardian, 1997–2001; Ed.-in-Chief, Bucks Herald, 2001; Editor: Scarborough Evening News, 2001–03; Hartlepool Mail, 2003–06; Yorkshire Evening Post, 2006–12. *Recreations:* family, reading, running. *Address:* Johnston Press plc, 108 Holyrood Road, Edinburgh EH8 8AS.

NAPIER, Robert Stewart, CBE 2011; Chairman, Homes and Communities Agency, since 2008; *b* 21 July 1947; *s* of Andrew Napier and Lilian V. Napier (*née* Ritchie); *m* 1977, Patricia Stewart; one *d*. *Educ:* Sedbergh School; Sidney Sussex College, Cambridge (BA 1969; MA 1971); Harvard Business School (AMP 1987). RTZ Corp., 1969–73; Brandts, 1973–75; Fisons, 1975–81; Redland: Finance Dir, 1981–87; Man. Dir, 1987–97; Chief Exec., 1991–97; Chief Exec., WWF-UK, 1999–2007. Director: United Biscuits (Hldgs), 1992–2000; Rentokil Initial plc, 1996–99; Anglian Water Services Ltd, 2002–15 (Chm., Anglian Water Gp, 2015); English Partnerships, 2004–08 (Chm., 2008); Lafarge UK Pension Trustees Ltd, 2014–; Chm., Met Office, 2006–12. Pres., Nat. Council of Building Material Producers, 1996–97; Chairman: CBI Transport Policy Cttee, 1995–97; Alliance of Construction Product Suppliers, 1996–97. Chm., Green Fiscal Commn, 2007–09. Trustee: World in Need, 1988–91; ACET, 1991–94; CRASH, 1994–99 (Chm., 1998–99); Baynards Zambia Trust, 1996–; Carbon Disclosure Project, 2005–11 (Chm., 2008–11); Watts Gall., 2006–; UNEP-World Conservation Monitoring Centre, 2007– (Chm., 2008–); S Georgia Heritage Trust, 2007–08. Mem., Oversight Cttee, 2012–14, Trustee, Bd, 2014–, RCS. Governor: Reigate Grammar Sch., 1995–2002; Sedbergh Sch., 1998–2011 (Chm., 2000–11). Hon. FRCS 2014. Hon. Organist, Grytviken Church, S Georgia. *Recreations:* hill walking, escaping to Scotland, the works of John Buchan.

NAPIER, (Thomas) Michael, CBE 2005; President, Law Society, 2000–01; Attorney-General's pro bono envoy, since 2002; Consultant, Michael Napier Consulting Ltd, since 2012; non-executive Director, Harbour Litigation Funding Ltd, since 2013; *b* 11 June 1946; *s* of late Montague Keith Napier and Mary Napier; *m* 1969, Denise Christine Willey; one *s* two *d*. *Educ:* Loughborough GS; Manchester Univ. (LLB 1967). Articled clerk, Moss Toone & Deane, Loughborough, 1968–70; admitted Solicitor, 1970; Asst Solicitor, W. H. Thompson, Manchester, 1970–72; Partner 1973, Chm. and Sen. Partner, 1983–2012, Irwin Mitchell; Jt Sen. Partner, Pannone Napier, 1985–94. Mem., Mental Health Act Commn, 1983–92 (Jt Vice-Chm., 1985–88; Chm., NE Reg., 1985–90). Vis. Prof., Nottingham Law Sch., 1992–. Jt Founder, 1990, Pres., 1994–96, Assoc. of Personal Injury Lawyers; Member: Council, Law Soc., 1993–2005; Council, Justice, 1995–2009; Civil Justice Council, 1998–2008. Bd Mem., Galleries of Justice, 2001–04. Chm., Adv. Cttee, Rampton Hosp., 1992–96. Trustee, Thalidomide Trust, 2001–14 (Vice Chm., 2007–14). Editorial Consultant: Personal Injury Compensation (formerly Personal Medical Injuries Law Letter), 1985–2012; Med. Law Rev., 1994–2012; Ind. Lawyer, 2002–08. Hon. Bencher, Gray's Inn, 2005; Hon.

QC 2006. Freeman, Co. of Cutlers in Hallamshire, 1992. FICPD 2004; FRSA 2005. Hon. LLD: Nottingham Trent, 2001; Sheffield, 2002; Coll. of Law, 2012. *Publications:* (jtly) Conditional Fees: a survival guide, 1995, 2nd edn 2001; (jtly) Recovering Damages for Psychiatric Injury, 1995; (Consulting Ed.) Litigation Funding, 1999; (contrib.) Blackstone's Civil Practice, 2004; contrib. legal books and jls. *Recreation:* mountain biking in Norfolk. *Address:* Windmill Hill, 18 Hindringham Road, Great Walsingham, Norfolk NR22 6DR. *T:* (01328) 820213. *Club:* Athenæum.

NAPOLITAN, Leonard, CB 1970; Director of Economics and Statistics, Ministry of Agriculture, Fisheries and Food, 1965–77; *b* 9 April 1919; *s* of Domenic and Rose G. Napolitan; *m* 1945, Dorothy Laycock; two *d. Educ:* Univ. of London (BSc Econ. 1944); LSE (MSc Econ. 1946). Asst Agric. Economist, Univ. of Bristol, 1947–48; joined Min. of Agric. and Fisheries as Agric. Economist, 1948. Pres., Agric. Econs Soc., 1974–75. FRSA. *Address:* 4 Rectory Gardens, Burway Road, Church Stretton, Shropshire SY6 6DP.

NAPTHINE, Hon. Denis Vincent; MLA (L) South West Coast, Victoria, Australia, since 2002 (Portland, 1988–2002); Premier of Victoria, 2013–14; Leader, Liberal Party of Victoria, 2013–14; *b* Winchelsea, Victoria, 6 March 1952; *s* of Len and Theresa Napthine; *m* 1977, Peggy Rayner; three *s. Educ:* Chanel Coll., Geelong; Univ. of Melbourne (BVSc; MVSc); Deakin Univ. (MBA). Vet, 1975–88, incl. Dist Veterinary Officer, Hamilton, Regl Veterinary Officer, SW Victoria, then Manager, Hamilton complex of Dept of Agric. and Rural Affairs, Victoria. Shadow Minister for Sport, Recreation and Racing, 1991–92; Parly Sec. for Health, 1992–96; Minister for Youth and Community Services, 1996–99; Leader of Opposition, 1999–2002; Shadow Minister: for Regl and Rural Develt, 2002, and for State and Regl Develt, 2002–04; for Rural and Regl Develt, 2004–05; for Water, and for Agric., 2005–06; for Regl and Rural Develt, 2006–08; for Ports and for Racing, 2006–10; for Regl Cities, 2008–10; Minister for Major Projects, and for Ports, 2010–13; Minister for Racing, and Minister for Regl Cities, 2010–14. Treas., 1999, Leader, 1999–2002, Liberal Party of Vic. *Recreations:* swimming, reading, horseracing. *Address:* 94 Liebig Street, Warrnambool, Vic 3280, Australia.

NARAIN, Sase, OR 1976; CMG 1969; SC (Guyana) 1985; JP (Guyana); solicitor/attorney-at-law; Speaker of the National Assembly, Guyana, 1971–92; Chairman, National Bank of Industry and Commerce (Guyana), 1986–93; *b* 27 Jan. 1925; *s* of Oudit and Sookdai Naraine; *m* 1952, Shamshun Narain (*née* Rayman); four *s. Educ:* Modern Educational Inst.; Gibson and Weldon Law Tutors. Solicitor, admitted in England and Guyana, 1957. Town Councillor, City of Georgetown, 1962–70; Member: History and Arts Council, 1969–; Republic Cttee of Guyana, 1969; Pres., Guyana Sanatan Dharma Maha Sabha, 1963–94. Comr for Oaths to Affidavits, 1961; Notary Public, 1968. Dep. Chm., Public Service Commn, Guyana, 1966–71; Mem., Police Service Commn, 1966–71. Chm., Berger Paints (Guyana), 1966–78; Dir, Pegasus Hotels of Guyana, 1987–90. Member: Nat. Awards Cttee of Guyana, 1970–92; Bd of Governors, President's Coll., Guyana, 1985–88. JP 1962. *Recreations:* golf, cricket, swimming. *Address:* 14b New Garden Street, Queenstown, Georgetown, Demerara, Guyana. *T:* (2) 261409. *Clubs:* Georgetown Cricket, Everest Cricket (Guyana).

NARASIMHA, Prof. Roddam, FRS 1992; DST Year-of-Science Professor, Engineering Mechanics Unit, and Academy Professor, CSIR Academy of Scientific and Industrial Research, Jawaharlal Nehru Centre for Advanced Scientific Research, since 2013 (Chairman, 1990–2009; INSA Golden Jubilee Research Professor, 1991–94; Professor Ramanathan Distinguished Professor, 1995–2000; Honorary Professor, 2009–13); *b* 20 July 1933; *s* of Prof. R. L. Narasimhaiya and Smt R. N. Leela Devi; *m* 1965, Dr Neelima S. Rao; two *d. Educ:* University Coll. of Engineering, Bangalore (BE 1953); Indian Inst. of Science (DIISc 1955; AIISc 1957); California Inst. of Technology (PhD 1961). Res. Fellow, CIT, 1961–62; Indian Institute of Science: Asst and Associate Prof., 1962–70; Prof., 1970–98, and Chm., 1982–84, Dept of Aerospace Engrg; Dean of Engrg Faculty, 1980–82; Chm., 1982–89, Prof., 1982–98, Centre for Atmospheric and Oceanic Scis (formerly Centre for Atmospheric Scis); Dir, Nat. Aeronautical Lab., subseq. Nat. Aerospace Labs, Bangalore, 1984–93; Dir, Nat. Inst. of Advanced Studies, Bangalore, 1997–2004. Chief Project Co-ordinator, Hindustan Aeronautics Ltd, 1977–79. Clark B. Millikan Vis. Prof., CIT, 1985–; Jawaharlal Nehru Vis. Prof., Cambridge, 1989–90. Member: Sci. Adv. Council to the Prime Minister, 1985–89 and 2004–14, to the Cabinet, 1997–99, to Govt of India, 2000–03; Space Commn, Govt of India, 1989–2012. Pres., Indian Acad. of Scis, 1992–94. Fellow: Indian Nat. Sci. Acad., 1979; Third World Acad. of Scis, Italy, 1989; Foreign Associate: US Nat. Acad. of Engrg, 1989; US Nat. Acad. of Sci., 2000; Hon. Fellow: Aer. Soc. of India, 1985; Indian Inst. of Sci., 2008; Foreign Hon. Mem., Amer. Acad. Arts and Scis, 1999; Distinguished Alumnus: CIT, 1986; Indian Inst. of Sci., 1988. Bhatnagar Prize in Engrg, CSIR, India, 1976; Gujar Mal Modi Award for Sci., 1990; Srinivasa Ramanujan Medal, Indian Sci. Congress, 1998; Fluid Dynamics Award, Amer. Inst. Aeronautics and Astronautics, 2000; Lifetime Contribution in Engrg Award, Indian Nat. Acad. of Engrg, 2003; Trieste Sci. Prize, Third World Acad. of Scis, 2008; Lifetime Excellence Award in Earth System Scis, Min. of Earth Scis, 2013. Kannada Rajyotsava Award, Karnataka, 1986; Padmabhushan, 1987, Padma Vibhushan, 2013, India. *Publications:* (ed) Computer Simulation, 1979; (ed) Turbulence Management and Relaminarisation, 1987; (ed) Developments in Fluid Mechanics and Space Technology, 1988; Surveys in Fluid Mechanics, vol. III, 1993; The Monsoon Trough Boundary Layer, 1997; Verses for the Brave, 2000; (ed) The Dynamics of Technology, 2003; (ed jtly) Encyclopaedia of Classical Indian Sciences, 2007; (ed) Nature and Culture, 2011; numerous sci. papers in learned jls. *Recreations:* history, walking, music. *Address:* Jawaharlal Nehru Centre for Advanced Scientific Research, Jakkur, Bangalore 560064, India. *T:* (80) 22082999, *Fax:* (80) 22082951.

NARASIMHAN, Prof. Mudumbai Seshachalu, PhD; FRS 1996; *b* 7 June 1932; *s* of Seshachalu Iyengar and Padmasani; *m* 1962, Sakuntala Raman; one *s* one *d. Educ:* Madras Univ. (BA Hons); Bombay Univ. (PhD 1960). Tata Institute, Bombay: Associate Prof., 1963–65; Prof., 1965–75; Sen. Prof., 1975–90; Prof. of Eminence, 1990–93; Hon. Fellow, 1994; Dir of Maths, Internat. Centre, subseq. Abdus Salam Internat. Centre, for Theoretical Physics, Trieste, 1992–98; Prof. of Geometry, Scuola Internazionale Superiore di Studi Avanzati, Trieste, 2000. S. S. Bhatnagar Prize in Mathematical Scis, CSIR, 1975; Meghnad Saha Award, Univ. Grants Commn, 1978; Award for Maths, Third World Acad. of Scis, 1987; Srinivasa Ramanujan Medal, INSA, 1988; C. V. Raman Birth Centenary Award, Indian Sci. Congress, 1994; King Faisal Internat. Prize for Sci., 2006. Chevalier, Ordre National du Mérite (France), 1989; Padma Bhushan (India), 1990. *Address:* TIFR Centre, PO Box 1234, IISc Campus, Bangalore 560012, India.

NARAYAN, Prof. Ramesh, FRS 2006; FAAAS; Thomas Dudley Cabot Professor of the Natural Sciences, Harvard-Smithsonian Center for Astrophysics, Harvard University; *s* of Prof. Gopalasamudram Narayana Ramachandran, FRS. *Educ:* St Patrick's Sch., Adyar; Madras Christian Coll.; National Aeronautical Labs, Bangalore; Calif Inst. of Technol. FAAAS 2010; NAS, 2013. Arizona Univ., 1986–91; joined Harvard Univ., 1991. *Publications:* articles in jls. *Address:* Harvard-Smithsonian Center for Astrophysics, 60 Garden Street, Cambridge, MA 02138, USA.

NARAYANAN, Ravi, Hon. CBE 2009; Chairman: Asia-Pacific Water Forum, since 2013 (Vice-Chairman, 2006–13); Water Integrity Network Association, since 2013; *b* 20 June 1943; *s* of Vaidyanatha and Kanti Narayanan; *m* 1973, Geetha Subramanan; one *s* one *d. Educ:* Delhi Univ. (BSc Hons); Peterhouse, Cambridge (BA 1966, MA 1968). Dir, ActionAid India, 1985–92; Hd, Internat. Ops, 1992–94, Dir, Asia Progs, 1994–99, ActionAid; Dir and Chief Exec., WaterAid, 1999–2005. Sen. Associate, Nat. Inst. of Advanced Studies, Bangalore, India. Mem., UK Delegn to Second World Water Forum, The Hague, 2000; NGO Advr to EC Delegn to World Summit of Sustainable Develt, Johannesburg, 2002. Member: World Panel on Financing Water Infrastructure, 2002–03; Millennium Project UN Taskforce on Water and Sanitation, 2004–05; Water Supply and Sanitation Collaborative Council, Geneva; Chm., Internat. Steering Cttee, Water Integrity Network, 2010–13. Life Mem., Internat. Water Acad., Norway, 2005. *Address:* 6 Palace Cross Road, Bangalore, 560020 Karnataka, India.

NAREY, Sir Martin (James), Kt 2013; Government Advisor on Adoption and Children's Social Care, since 2011; Member of Council, Advertising Standards Authority, since 2011; Chair, Portman Group, since 2013; *b* 5 Aug. 1955; *s* of John and Ellenor Narey; *m* 1978, Jan Goudy; one *s* one *d. Educ:* Sheffield Poly. (BA Public Admin). Assistant Governor: HM Young Offender Inst. Deerbolt, 1982–86; Frankland, 1986–90; Gov. IV, Prison Service HQ, 1990–91; Home Office: Private Sec. to Minister of State, 1991–92; Criminal Policy, 1992–94; Head, Co-ordination of Computerisation in the Criminal Justice System Unit, 1994–96; Head of Crime Prevention Agency, 1996; Reviewer of Delay in the Criminal Justice System, 1996–97; HM Prison Service: Head of Security Policy, 1997–98; Dir of Regimes, 1998–99; Dir-Gen., 1999–2003; Perm. Under-Sec. of State, Home Office, 2003–05 (Comr for Correctional Services, 2003–04, Chief Exec., Nat. Offender Mgt Service, 2004–05); Chief Exec., Barnardo's, 2005–11. Non-executive Board Member: Scarborough and NE Yorks NHS Trust, 2009–12; Fabrick Housing Assoc., Middlesbrough, 2012–; MoJ, 2015–. Chairman: End Child Poverty Coalition, 2006–09; Ind. Commn on Social Mobility, 2009; Portman Gp Complaints Panel, 2013; Adoption Leadership Bd, 2014–; Brain Tumour Charity, 2015–. Chm., Corp., Redbridge Coll., 2008–10. Visiting Professor: Sheffield Hallam Univ., 2006–; Durham Univ., 2011–; Vis. Scholar, Inst. of Criminol., Univ. of Cambridge, 2011–. DUniv Sheffield Hallam, 2003; Hon. LLD Teesside, 2007; Hon. DLitt, Manchester Metropolitan, 2012. Chartered Mgt Inst. Gold Medal for Leadership, 2003. *Publications:* review of delay in criminal justice system, report into security at the Maze Prison, report of Ind. Commn on Social Mobility, 2009; Adoption: a blueprint for the nation's lost children (Times report), 2011; Making the Education of Children's Social Workers Consistently Effective (DfE), 2014. *Recreations:* planning holidays, watching Middlesbrough FC. *Address:* 34 Bagdale, Whitby, N Yorks YO21 1QL. *E:* nareymartin@gmail.com.

NARUEPUT, Owart S.; *see* Suthiwart-Narueput.

NASEBY, Baron *cr* 1997 (Life Peer), of Sandy in the co. of Bedfordshire; **Michael Wolfgang Laurence Morris;** PC 1994; *b* 25 Nov. 1936; *m* 1960, Dr Ann Appleby (Dr Ann Morris, MB, BS, MRCS, MRCP); two *s* one *d. Educ:* Bedford Sch.; St Catharine's Coll., Cambridge (BA Hons Econs; MA). Trainee to Marketing Manager, UK, India and Ceylon, Reckitt & Colman Gp, 1960–63; Service Advertising Ltd, 1964–68; Marketing Exec. to Account Supervisor, Horniblow Cox-Freeman Ltd, 1968–71, Dir 1969–71; Dir, Benton & Bowles Ltd, 1971–81; Proprietor: A. M. International, 1980–92; Julius International Consultants, 1997–2008. Non-executive Director: Tunbridge Wells Equitable Friendly Soc., 1992–2005 (Chm., 1998–2005); Mansell plc, 1998–2003; Invesco Recovery Trust 2005 plc, 1998–2005 (Chm., 2003–05); Chm., Invesco Recovery Trust 2011 plc, 2005–11. Contested (C) Islington North, 1966. Islington Council: Councillor, 1968–70; Alderman, 1970–74; Chm. of Housing, 1968; Leader, 1969–71. MP (C) Northampton South, Feb. 1974–1997; contested (C) same seat, 1997. PPS to Minister of State, NI Office, 1979–81; Chm. of Ways and Means and Dep. Speaker, H of C, 1992–97. Member: Public Accounts Cttee, 1979–92; Select Cttee on Energy, 1982–85; Chairman's Panel, 1984–92; Mem. Council, Europe and Western European Union, 1983–91; Chairman: British Sri Lanka Cttee, 1975–92 and 1997–; British Singapore Cttee, 1985–92 (Vice-Chm., 1997–); British Malaysia Cttee, 1987–92; British Burma Cttee, 1989–92; British Maldives Cttee, 2004–09; formerly: Vice-Chm., British Indonesia Cttee; Treas., British ASEAN and Thai Cttees; Secretary: British Venezuela Cttee; Cons. Housing and Local Govt Cttee, 1974–76; Cons Trade Cttee, 1974–76; Cons. Environment Cttee, 1977–79; Vice-Chm., Cons. Energy Cttee, 1981–92; Founder, Parly Food and Health Forum. Captain, Parly Golf Soc., 1988–91 (Pres., 2009–). Chm. Trustees, Victoria County History for Northamptonshire, 1994–2008; Jt Patron, Naseby Battlefield Trust, 2005–13. Founder and Pres., UK Br., Cofradía del Vino Chileno, 2005–. Chm., Govs, Bedford Sch., 1989–2002 (Governor, 1982–2002). Hon. Fellow, Univ. of Northampton, 2007. Ratna (Sri Lanka), 2005; Bernnardo O'Higgins Medal (Chile), 2013. *Publications:* (jtly) Helping the Exporter, 1967; (contrib.) Marketing below the Line: Studies in Management, 1972; The Disaster of Direct Labour, 1978. *Recreations:* restoration work, cricket, tennis, golf, budgerigars, forestry. *Address:* Caesar's Camp, Sand Lane, Sandy, Beds SG19 2AD. *T:* (01767) 680388. *Clubs:* Carlton, MCC, Lord's Taverners; All England Lawn Tennis and Croquet; John O'Gaunt Golf; Northamptonshire CC (Patron, 2006–09, Pres., 2009–).

NASH, family name of **Baron Nash**.

NASH, Baron *cr* 2013 (Life Peer), of Ewelme in the County of Oxfordshire; **John Alfred Stoddard Nash;** Parliamentary Under-Secretary of State, Department for Education, since 2013; *b* Bahrain, 22 March 1949; *s* of Lewis John and Josephine Nash; *m* 1983, Caroline Jennifer Paul; one *s* one *d. Educ:* Milton Abbey Sch.; Corpus Christi Coll., Oxford (MA Law). Called to the Bar, Inner Temple, 1972. Chm., 1988–2002, non-exec. Partner, 2002–12, Sovereign Capital. Non-exec. Dir, DfE, 2010–13. Chm., British Venture Capital Assoc., 1988–89. Chairman: Future (charity), 2005–; Pimlico Acad., 2008–. *Recreation:* golf. *Address:* Department for Education, Sanctuary Buildings, Great Smith Street, SW1P 3BT. *Clubs:* Athenaeum, Turf.

NASH, Prof. Anthony Aubrey, PhD; Professor of Veterinary Pathology, since 1994, and Head, Centre for Infectious Diseases, University of Edinburgh; *b* 6 March 1949; *s* of Alfred Nash and Mabel Evelyn Nash (*née* Garrett); *m* 1979, Marion Eileen Bazeley; four *d. Educ:* Queen Elizabeth Coll., London (BSc Hons 1970); Univ. of Birmingham (MSc 1971; PhD 1976). Lecturer: in Immunology, Dept of Pathology, Univ. of Cambridge, 1984–94; in Pathology, Newnham Coll., Cambridge, 1987–94. Eleanor Roosevelt Fellow, Dept of Immunology, Scripps Clinic and Res. Foundn, Calif, 1989–90. Member Council: Soc. for Gen. Microbiology, 2000–04; BBSRC, 2002–05. FMedSci 1999; FRSE 2005. *Publications:* (jtly) Mims' Pathogenesis of Infectious Disease, 5th edn, 1999; over 100 articles in learned jls. *Recreations:* family, Leicester City Football Club. *Address:* Roslin Institute, University of Edinburgh, Easter Bush, Edinburgh EH25 9RG. *T:* (0131) 651 9177.

NASH, David John, OBE 2004; RA 1999; sculptor, primarily in wood; Research Fellow, University of Northumbria, 1999–2003; *b* 14 Nov. 1945; *s* of Lt-Col William Charles Nash and Dora Lillian Nash; *m* 1972, Claire Langdown; two *s. Educ:* Brighton Coll.; Kingston Sch. of Art (Higher DipAD); Chelsea Sch. of Art. Has worked in Blaenau Ffestiniog, 1967–; over 100 solo shows world wide; 100 works in internat. public collections incl. Tate Gall., Guggenheim, NY, Nat. Mus. of Wales and Metropolitan Mus., Japan. Hon. Dr: Art and Design, Kingston, 1998; Humanities and Letters, W Glamorgan, 2002. *Publications:* Wood Primer, 1987; Forms into Time, 1996; Black and Light, 2001; The Return of Art to Nature, 2003; (ed jtly) David Nash at the Yorkshire Sculpture Park, 2010; *relevant publication:* David Nash, by Norbert Lynton, 2007; David Nash: a natural gallery, by Michelle Payne, 2013. *Address:* Capel Rhiw, Blaenau Ffestiniog, Gwynedd, N Wales LL41 3NT.

NASH, David Percy, FCA; *b* 24 May 1940; *s* of Percy and Kathleen Nash; *m* 2011, Lindsey Jane Thomas; two *s* by a previous marriage. *Educ:* Enfield Grammar Sch. FCA 1962. ICI plc, 1965–87; Gp Finance Dir, Cadbury Schweppes plc, 1987–89; Gp Finance Dir, 1989–93,

Chm. and CEO, Food and Retailing Sector, 1993–95, Grand Metropolitan plc. Chairman: Kenwood Appliances plc, 1996–2001; Amicus Healthcare Gp Ltd, 1996–97; Niceopen Ltd, 1997; General Healthcare Gp Ltd, 1998–2000; Cable & Wireless Communications plc, 1998–2000; non-executive Director: IMRO, 1993–98; Cable and Wireless plc, 1995–2002 (Dep. Chm., 2002); Energy Gp plc, 1996–98; AXA UK plc, 1996–2001. Hon. Treas., Prince of Wales's Internat. Business Leaders' Forum, 1990–2007. *Recreations:* horseracing, cycling. *Club:* Royal Ascot Racing.

NASH, Ellison; *see* Nash, His Honour T. M. E.

NASH, Frances Clare, (Mrs A. N. Simpson); Director, Legal Services, Ministry of Defence, since 2009; *b* 29 Dec. 1960; *d* of late Prof. Walter Nash and Doreen Mary Nash (*née* Richardson); *m* 2012, Anthony Nicholas Simpson. *Educ:* Forest Fields Coll., Nottingham; Jesus Coll., Oxford (BA 1982, MA); University Coll. London (LLM 1994). Admitted solicitor, 1986; private practice, 1986–87; Legal Dept, MAFF, 1987–93; Legal Secretariat to Law Officers, 1993–95; Legal Dept, MAFF, 1995–99; Dep. Legal Advr, MoD, 1999–2002; Dir, Legal Services, DEFRA, 2002–04; Hd, European Div., Treasury Solicitor's Dept, 2004–08; Dir, Personal Tax and Ops, HMRC, 2008. *Recreations:* gardening, tropical fishkeeping, international travel. *Address:* Ministry of Defence, Whitehall, SW1A 2HB. *T:* (020) 7218 0723. *E:* Frances.Nash154@mod.uk.

NASH, John Edward; Member, Supervisory Board, Bank Winter AG, Vienna, since 1996; Chairman, S. G. Warburg Bank AG, 1980–87 (Director, 1977–87; Deputy Chairman, 1977–80); *b* 25 June 1925; *s* of Joseph and Madeleine Nash; *m* 1st, 1947, Ralda Everard Herring (*d* 2006); two *s* two *d*; 2nd, 2009, Fiona Hood-Stewart. *Educ:* Univ. of Sydney (BEc); Balliol Coll., Oxford (BPhil). Teaching Fellow in Economics, Sydney Univ., 1947. Exec. Dir, Samuel Montagu & Co. Ltd, 1956; also Director, 1960–73: British Australian Investment Trust; Montagu Trust Ltd; Midland Montagu Industrial Finance Ltd; Capel Court Corp. (in Melb.); resigned all directorships on appt to Brussels, 1973; Dir of Monetary Affairs, EEC, 1973–77; Director: Reckitt & Colman plc, 1966–73 and 1977–86; S. G. Warburg & Co. Ltd, 1977–86; Mem. Adv. Bd, Bank S. G. Warburg Soditic AG, 1987–94. Dir, Oxford Univ. Business Summer Sch., 1965; Research Fellow, Nuffield Coll., Oxford (part-time), 1966–69. Hon. Treasurer, PEP, 1964–73. Mem. Bd of Trustees, WWF Internat., 1979–92, 1993–94 (Hon. Treas., 1985–92). *Recreations:* golf, horse-racing, music. *Address:* Chalet Gstelli, 3785 Gsteig bei Gstaad, Switzerland. *T:* (33) 7551162, *Fax:* (33) 7551132. *Clubs:* Turf, MCC; University (Sydney).

NASH, Jonathan Scott; QC 2006; *b* 16 Oct. 1962; *s* of late Bryan Whatmore Nash and of Jean Nash (*née* Cowie); *m* 1st, 1995, Constance Chanteux (marr. diss. 2003); two *s*; 2nd, 2012, Magdalena Popowicz. *Educ:* Reigate Grammar Sch.; St John's Coll., Oxford (BA Modern Hist. 1984). Called to the Bar, Gray's Inn, 1986; in practice at the Bar, 1987–, specialising in commercial law. *Recreations:* music, tennis, books. *Address:* 3 Verulam Buildings, Gray's Inn, WC1R 5NT. *T:* (020) 7269 1106. *E:* jnash@3vb.com. *Clubs:* Travellers, Home House.

NASH, Prof. Jordan, PhD; Professor of Physics and Head, Department of Physics, Imperial College London, since 2014; *b* New York, 14 June 1962; *s* of Kenneth and Carole Nash; *m* 2014, Carmen Curreli; two *s* one *d*. *Educ:* Carnegie Mellon Univ. (BSc Physics 1983); Stanford Univ. (PhD Physics 1990). Imperial College London: Lectr in Physics, 1993–2000; Reader in Physics, 2000–07; Hd, High Energy Physics Gp, 2007–14. Sen. Staff Scientist, CERN, 2003–08. Mem., STFC, 2015–. *Publications:* contribs to jls as mem. of Mark II, ALEPH, BaBar and CMS experiments. *Recreations:* cycling, swimming, binge reading, programming. *Address:* Blackett Laboratory, Imperial College London, South Kensington Campus, SW7 2AZ. *E:* j.nash@imperial.ac.uk.

NASH, Pamela; *b* Bellshill, 1984; *d* of David Nash and late Kathleen Nash. *Educ:* St Margaret's Sch., Airdrie; Glasgow Univ. (MA Politics). Mem. for Airdrie and Shotts, Scottish Youth Parlt, 2007–09; Parly researcher to John Reid, MP, 2007–10. MP (Lab) Airdrie and Shotts, 2010–15; contested (Lab) same seat, 2015. PPS to Shadow Sec. of State for NI, 2010–13, to Shadow Sec. of State for Scotland, 2011–12, to Shadow Sec. of Internat. Devel t, 2013–15. Member: Select Cttee on Sci. and Technol., 2010–15, Scottish Affairs, 2012–15; All Party Parly Gp for MS, 2010–15, Africa, 2010–15, Great Lakes, 2010–15, British-American, 2010–15, UAE, 2010–15, UN, 2010–15; Chair, All Party Parly Gp on HIV and AIDS, 2011–15, Belarus, 2012–15, Youth Unemployment, 2013–15.

NASH, Peter Philip, DPhil; Director, Transmissible Spongiform Encephalopathies and Zoonoses, Department for Environment, Food and Rural Affairs, 2002–06; *b* 18 May 1948; *s* of late Harold and Joan Nash; *m* 1977, June Mobbs; one *s* one *d*. *Educ:* Grove Park Grammar Sch., Wrexham; Jesus Coll., Oxford (MA, DPhil 1972). MAFF, subseq. DEFRA, 1972–; Head: Envmtl Protection Div., 1988–93; Financial Policy Div., 1993–97; Milk, Pigs, Eggs and Poultry Div., 1997–99; BSE Div., 1999–2002. *Recreations:* country walking, foreign languages, voluntary teaching of bridge, art history, family history. *T:* (020) 8349 2318.

NASH, Philip; Commissioner of Customs and Excise, 1986–90; *b* 14 March 1930; *s* of late John Hollett Nash and Edith Grace Nash (*née* Knee); *m* 1953, Barbara Elizabeth Bangs; one *s*. *Educ:* Watford Grammar School. National Service, RAF, 1949–50. HM Customs and Excise, 1950–90; on loan to Civil Service College, 1970–73; Asst Sec. and Head of Management Services, 1978–81; Asst Sec., Customs Directorate, 1981–86; Director, Customs, 1986–90. *Recreation:* family history. *Address:* Nutwood, 37 Lower Golf Links Road, Broadstone, Dorset BH18 8BQ. *T:* (01202) 601898.

NASH, Ronald Peter, CMG 2004; LVO 1983; HM Diplomatic Service, retired; High Commissioner, Trinidad and Tobago, 2004–06; *b* 18 Sept. 1946; *s* of John Henry Nash and Jean Carmichael Nash (*née* McIlwraith); *m* 1976, Annie Olsen; three *s*. *Educ:* Harefield Secondary Modern Sch.; Southall Tech. Sch.; Southall Grammar Tech. Sch.; Manchester Univ. (BA Hons). MCIL (MIL 1991). FCO, 1970; Moscow, 1974–76; UK Delegn to MBFR, Vienna, 1976–79; FCO, 1979–83; New Delhi, 1983–86; FCO, 1986–87; Dep. Hd of Mission, Vienna, 1988–92; Dep. High Comr, Colombo and (non-res.) Malé, 1992–95; Co-ordinator, Peace Implementation Conf. for Bosnia, 1995; Review of Africa Devel t Prog., ODA, 1996; Hd, Human Rights Policy Dept, FCO, 1996–99; Ambassador: to Nepal, 1999–2002; to Afghanistan, 2002–03. Chm. Bd Dirs, Overseas Children's Sch., Colombo, Sri Lanka, 1994–95. *Address:* Ryecroft, 175 Hivings Hill, Chesham, Bucks HP5 2PN. *Clubs:* Royal Scots (Edinburgh); Berkhamsted Lawn Tennis and Squash.

NASH, Stephen Thomas, CMG 2000; HM Diplomatic Service, retired; Honorary Patron, British Georgian Society, since 2010 (Chairman, 2004–10); *b* 22 March 1942; *s* of Thomas Gerald Elwin Nash and Gwendolen Selina Nash (*née* Osmaston); *m* 2004, Rusudan Benashvili; one *d*; two *s* two *d* from former marriages. *Educ:* Cheltenham Coll.; Pembroke Coll., Cambridge (MA Econs and History); Sch. of Oriental and African Studies (Arabic Studies); Queen's Coll., Oxford (MA Ethnology). Asst Dir, British Council, Baghdad, 1965–67; FCO 1967; served Caracas, Bogotá, Bangkok (SEATO), Guatemala; Dep. High Comr, Belmopan, 1981–82; Head, Indo-China Section, FCO, 1984–86; Chargé d'Affaires, Managua, 1986–88; seconded to British Aerospace, 1989–91; EC Monitor Mission to former Yugoslavia, Zagreb, 1991; Chargé d'Affaires, Tirana, 1993–95; Ambassador: to Georgia, 1995–98; to Albania, 1998–99; to Latvia, 1999–2002. Dir-Gen., Canning House, 2002–03. OSCE Election Observation Missions: to Latvia, 2002, and 2006 (Dep. Head); to Serbia (Head of Mission), 2004; to USA (Dep. Head), 2004; to Romania (Head), 2004. Director: London Inf. Network on Conflicts and State-building, 2002–06; MEC Internat./Windsor Energy Gp, 2006–. Vice-Chm., Friends of Academic Res. in Georgia, 2003–; Board Member: Britain Estonia Latvia Lithuania Legal Assoc., 2002–07; Mark Rothko Internat. Arts Centre, Daugavpils, Latvia, 2003–; British Latvian Assoc., 2004–; Anglo-Albanian Assoc., 2006– (Chm., 2012–); Tbilisi Heritage Gp, 2011–. Gov., Dulwich Village C of E Infant Sch., 2008–12. Order of Honour (Republic of Georgia), 2011. *Recreations:* spending time with my children, choral singing, ski-ing, hill walking, gardening, viola-playing.

NASH, His Honour Timothy Michael Ellison; a Circuit Judge, 1994–2010; *b* 10 Dec. 1939; *s* of late Denis Frederick Ellison Nash, OBE, AE, FRCS and Joan Mary Andrew; *m* 1965, Gael Nash; one *s* one *d* (and two *s* decd). *Educ:* Dulwich Coll.; St Bartholomew's Hosp. Called to the Bar, Gray's Inn, 1964; Standing Counsel: DHSS, 1974–79; DTI, 1976–91; Asst Recorder, 1987–89; Recorder, 1990–94. Legal Assessor, GMC and Royal Dental Council, 1989–94; Chm., Home Office Police Appeal Tribunals, 1988–94. Metropolitan Police Special Constabulary, 1961–83. Examr, Dio. of Canterbury, 1990–94. *Recreation:* walking round in ever-increasing circles.

NASH, Ven. Trevor Gifford; Executive Co-ordinator, Advisers for Churches' Ministry of Healing in England, 1990–97 (Adviser, 1973–97); Hon. Chaplain, Winchester Cathedral, since 1998; *b* 3 May 1930; *s* of Frederick Walter Gifford Nash and Elsie Violet Louise Nash; *m* 1957, Wanda Elizabeth (*née* Freeston); four *d*. *Educ:* Haileybury College, Hertford; Clare Coll., Cambridge (MA); Cuddesdon Coll., Oxford. Curate: Cheshunt, 1955–57; Kingston-upon-Thames, 1957–61; Priest-in-Charge, Stevenage, 1961–63; Vicar, Leagrave, Luton, 1963–67; Senior Chaplain, St George's Hosp. Gp, London, 1967–73; Rector, St Lawrence with St Swithun, Winchester, 1973–82; Priest-in-Charge, Holy Trinity, Winchester, 1977–82; RD of Winchester, 1978–82; Archdeacon of Basingstoke, 1982–90, Archdeacon Emeritus, 1990; Hon. Canon of Winchester, 1980–. Pres., Guild of Health, 1993–97; Warden, Guild of St Raphael, 1995–98. RAChD (TA), 1956–61. *Recreations:* painting, music, walking. *Address:* Cottage D, Headbourne Worthy House, Bedfield Lane, Winchester, Hants SO23 7JG. *T:* (01962) 861759.

NASHA, Margaret Nnananyana, (Mrs Lawrence Nasha); MP (Democratic Party), Botswana, since 1994; Speaker of the National Assembly of Botswana, 2009–14; *b* 6 Aug. 1947; *d* of Sadinyana and Motlatshiping Ramontshonyana; *m* 1975, Lawrence Nasha; four *s*. *Educ:* Univ. of Botswana (BA 1976). Several posts as broadcaster, 1968–84; Dir of Information and Broadcasting, Botswana, 1985–89; High Comr in UK, 1989–93; Government of Botswana: Dep. Minister, 1994–97, Minister, 1997–98, of Local Govt, Lands and Housing; Minister: of Minerals, Energy and Water Affairs, 1998–99; of Local Govt, 1999–2002; of Lands and Housing, 2003; of Local Govt, until 2009; of Presidential Affairs and Public Admin, 2009. *Publications:* Madam Speaker, Sir!, 2014. *Recreations:* leisure walks, tennis. *Address:* PO Box 240, Gaborone, Botswana.

NASHEED, Mohamed; President of the Maldives, 2008–12; Chairman, Maldivian Democratic Party, 2005–08; *b* Male, Maldives, 17 May 1967. *Educ:* Majeediyya Sch., Male; Overseas Sch., Colombo; Dauntsey's Sch., Wilts; Liverpool Poly. (BA Maritime Studies 1989). Helped establish Sangu, political mag., 1990 (banned within a year); arrested and jailed, 1991–93 (Amnesty Internat. prisoner of conscience); rearrested 1994, 1995; imprisoned 1996–98; elected MP for Male, 1999, subseq. stripped of seat and imprisoned 2001–03; fled Maldives, 2003; co-founded Maldivian Democratic Party (MDP) (first opposition party) in exile in Sri Lanka, 2004; granted refugee status by British Govt, 2004; returned to Maldives, 2005 to establish MDP; MDP officially recognised by Govt, June 2005; initiated campaign of non-violent civil disobedience in Maldives to pressure Govt to speed up implementation of democratic reforms, 2005–08; arrested Aug. 2006 and charged with terrorism but charges later dropped. Anna Lindh Meml Fund Prize, 2009; UNEP Champions of the Earth Laureate, 2010.

NASMITH, Sir James Duncan D.; *see* Dunbar-Nasmith.

NASMYTH, Prof. Kim Ashley, PhD; FRS 1989; Whitley Professor of Biochemistry, since 2006, and Head, Department of Biochemistry, since 2007, University of Oxford; Fellow, Trinity College, Oxford, since 2006; *b* 18 Oct. 1952; *s* of James Nasmyth and Jenny Hughes; *m* 1982, Anna Dowson; two *d*. *Educ:* Eton Coll.; York Univ. (BA); Edinburgh Univ. (PhD). Jane Coffin Childs Postdoctoral Fellow, Dept of Genetics, Univ. of Washington, 1978–80; Robertson Fellow, Cold Spring Harbor Lab., NY, 1980–81; Staff Mem., MRC Lab. of Molecular Biol., Cambridge, 1982–87; Unofficial Fellow, King's Coll., Cambridge, 1984–87; Sen. Scientist, 1987–96, Dir, 1997–2005, Inst. of Molecular Pathology, Vienna. Hon. Prof., Univ. of Vienna, 1995–. FMedSci 2009. MAE 1993; Member: EMBO, 1985; Austrian Acad. of Scis, 1999; Foreign Hon. Mem., Amer. Acad. of Arts and Scis, 1999. *Recreations:* climbing, ski-ing. *Address:* Department of Biochemistry, University of Oxford, South Parks Road, Oxford OX1 3QU. *T:* (01865) 275263.

NASON, Prof. Guy Philip, PhD; Professor of Statistics, University of Bristol, since 2002; *b* Dartford, 28 Aug. 1966; *s* of Brian and Diana Nason; *m* 1999, Philippa Anne Coates; two *d*. *Educ:* Univ. of Bath (BSc; PhD 1992); Jesus Coll., Cambridge (Dip. Math. Stat. 1988). Postdoctoral res., Univ. of Bath, 1992–93; University of Bristol: postdoctoral res., 1993–94; Lectr in Stats, 1994–2000; Reader in Stats, 2000–02; Hd, Stats Gp, 2006–08; Hd, Sch. of Maths, 2008–12. Adv. Res. Fellow, 2000–05, Mem., Maths Strategic Adv. Panel, 2007–, Estabd Career Fellow, 2013–, EPSRC. Royal Statistical Society: Sec., Res. Section, 2002–04; Mem. Council, 2004–08; Guy Medal in Bronze, 2001. *Publications:* Wavelet Methods in Statistics with R, 2008; contrib. papers to learned jls. *Recreations:* fine wine, building gardens. *Address:* School of Mathematics, University of Bristol, Bristol BS8 1TW. *T:* (0117) 331 8411.

NASON, Justin Patrick Pearse, OBE 1980; HM Diplomatic Service, retired; *b* 29 March 1937; *s* of John Lawrence Nason and Catherine Agnes (*née* McFadden); *m* 2000, Jeannine Dubois. *Educ:* Ampleforth; University Coll., Oxford. National Service, RAF, 1956–58. BICC, 1962–63; entered HM Foreign Service, 1963; FO, 1964–65; Prague, 1965–67; FCO, 1967–71; First Sec., Pretoria and Cape Town, 1971–74; Head of Chancery, Saigon, 1974–75; FCO, 1975–79; Head of Chancery, Kampala, 1979–81; Nat. Defence Coll. of Canada, 1981–82; Dep. High Comr, Colombo, 1982–85; Barclays Bank (on secondment), 1986–87; Minister Counsellor, Mexico City, 1988–90; temp. duty, Accra, 1990–91; Ambassador to Guatemala, 1991–95. *Recreation:* golf. *Club:* Oxford and Cambridge.

NATALEGAWA, (Raden Mohammad) Marty (Muliana), DPhil; Minister of Foreign Affairs, Indonesia, 2009–14; *b* 22 March 1963; *s* of Raden Sonson Natalegawa and Siti Komariyah Natalegawa; *m* 1987, Sranya Bamrungphong; two *s* one *d*. *Educ:* Corpus Christi Coll., Cambridge (MPhil 1986); London Sch. of Econs (BSc Hons 1989); Australian National Univ. (DPhil 1993). Agency for Policy Analysis and Devel t, Dept of For. Affairs, 1986–90; Indonesian Perm. Mission to UN, NY, 1994–99, Hd of Political Sect., 1999; Department of Foreign Affairs: Dep. Dir, 1999–2000, Dir, 2001–02, for Internat. Orgns; Spokesperson of Dept, 2002–05; Chief of Staff, Office of Minister of For. Affairs, 2002–04; Dir Gen. for ASEAN Co-operation, 2003–05; Ambassador to UK and to Ireland, 2005–07; Perm. Rep. to UN, NY, 2007–09. Foreign Service Award, 1996, 2006; Public Relns Soc. Award, 2004. *Recreations:* classic cars, football, walks. *Address:* c/o Ministry of Foreign Affairs, Jalan Pejambon No 6, Jakarta Pusat, 10110, Indonesia. *E:* rm3n@yahoo.com.

NATH, Sarah Joanna; *see* Tabrizi, S. J.

NATHAN, family name of **Baron Nathan**.

NATHAN, 3rd Baron *cr* 1940, of Churt, Surrey; **Rupert Harry Bernard Nathan;** *b* 26 May 1957; *o s* of 2nd Baron Nathan and of Philippa Gertrude (*née* Solomon); *S* father, 2007; *m* 1st, 1987, Ann Hewitt (marr. diss. 1997); 2nd, 1997, Jane, *d* of D. Cooper; one *s* one *d*. *Educ:* Charterhouse; Durham Univ. (BA). *Heir: s* Hon. Alasdair Harry St John Nathan, *b* 27 Sept. 1999.

NATHAN, David Brian; QC 2002; *b* 29 Nov. 1948; *s* of Ephraim and Jenny Nathan; *m* Susan Mary Hayes; two *d*; one *s* one *d* from previous marriage. *Educ:* City of London Sch.; Manchester Univ. (LLB Hons). Called to the Bar, Middle Temple, 1971; in practice as barrister, specialising in all areas of criminal defence work, 1971–; Hd of Chambers, 9 Lincoln's Inn Fields, 2002. *Recreations:* reading, watching old movies. *Address:* 5 St Andrew's Hill, EC4V 5BZ.

NATHAN, Peter Joseph; His Honour Judge Nathan; a Circuit Judge, since 2005; Designated Family Judge for Surrey, since 2011; *b* 20 Dec. 1949; *s* of Laurence Nathan and Julia Nathan; *m* 1974, Denise Pomper; three *s*. *Educ:* Homefield Prep. Sch., Sutton; Wallington Independent Grammar Sch.; London Sch. of Economics (LLB Hons 1971, LLM 1972). Called to the Bar, Inner Temple, 1973; admitted solicitor, 1981; founder Mem., One Garden Court Family Law Chambers, 1989; Dep. Dist Judge, 1993–2005; a Recorder of the Crown Court, 2000–05. *Recreations:* walking, reading history, travel, gardening.

NATHAN, Sara Catherine; portfolio worker and freelance journalist, since 1998; *b* 16 Feb. 1956; *d* of late Derek Nathan and Mary Nathan (*née* Lavine); *m* 1984, Malcolm John Singer; one *s* one *d*. *Educ:* New Hall, Cambridge (BA Hons); Stanford Univ., Calif. (Harkness Fellow). News trainee, 1980–82; with BBC news and current affairs, incl. Results Ed., Election prog., 1992, Newsnight, Breakfast Time/News, Money Prog., 1982–93; Editor: The Magazine, BBC Radio 5, 1993–95; Channel 4 News, 1995–97; columnist, The Scotsman, 1999–2000. Chm., Animal Procedures Cttee, 2006–12. Lay Member: Professional Conduct Cttee, Bar Council, 1998–2004; Judicial Appts Commn, 2006–12; Member: HFEA, 1998–2005; Radio Authy, 1999–2003; Criminal Injuries Compensation Appeals Panel, 2000–06; Gambling Rev. Body, 2000–01; Regulatory Decisions Cttee, FSA, 2001–06; OFCOM, 2002–07 (Dep. Chm., Content Bd, 2003–06); Cttee, ICSTIS (Phonepay Plus), 2002–08; Youth Crime Commn, 2008–10; Solicitors Regulation Authy, 2010–14 (Chm., Standards Cttee); Bd, Assoc. for TV on Demand, 2010–12; Chm., Disciplinary Tribunals, Nursing and Midwifery Council, 2012–; Public Appts Assessor, 2012–. Chm., Children First Commn, Lambeth, 2000–02; Marshall Scholarship Comr, 2000–07. Trustee, Why Me?, 2010–. Chm., Churchfield Community Assoc., 2009–12. Mem., BAFTA. *Recreations:* cinema, gym, book club, running Acton Central Station bookswap, Playing Out. *Address:* 29 Goldsmith Avenue, W3 6HR.

NATHAN, Sellapan Ramanathan; *see* Sellapan, R.

NATHAN, Stephen Andrew; QC 1993; a Recorder, since 2000; *b* 30 April 1947; *s* of Frederick Emil Nathan and Margot Sophie Jeanette Nathan (*née* Welch); *m* 1999, Colleen Toomey; one *s*; one *d*. *Educ:* Hall Sch., Hampstead; Cranleigh Sch., Surrey (Schol.); New Coll., Oxford (BA Law 1968; MA 1972). Called to the Bar, Middle Temple, 1969, Bencher, 2005; in practice at the Bar, 1969–; Asst Recorder, 1989–2000. Chm., London Common Law and Commercial Bar Assoc., 2009–11; Member: London Court of Internat. Arbitration, European Users' Council, 2011–; CEDR Exchange 2012–; Internat. Council for Commercial Arbitration, 2013–. Dep. Chm., Guild of Guide Lectrs, 1975–76; Chairman: Ponsonby Residents' Assoc., 1995–99; W Hampstead Gardens and Residents' Assoc., 2011–. *Publications:* (jtly) Employee Competition: covenants, confidentiality and garden leave, 2007, 2nd edn 2011. *Recreations:* tennis, swimming, fine cooking. *Address:* Blackstone Chambers, Blackstone House, Temple, EC4Y 9BW. *T:* (020) 7583 1770. *Club:* Royal Automobile.

NATHANSON, Dr Vivienne Hilary; Senior Director, British Medical Association, since 2014; *b* 9 March 1955; *d* of Norman Eric Nathanson and Margaret Nathanson (*née* Milman). *Educ:* Birkenhead High Sch., GDST; Middx Hosp. Med. Sch., Univ. of London (MB BS 1978). FRCP 2008. Med. Registrar, Glan Clwyd Hosp., 1981–84; British Medical Association: mgt trainee, 1984–86; Hd, Med. Ethics and Internat. Affairs, 1987–90; Scottish Sec., 1990–95; Hd, Professional Resources and Res. Gp, then Dir of Professional Activities, 1996–2014. Prof., Sch. for Health, Univ. of Durham, 2004–. Hon. FFPH 2013. Hon. DSc Strathclyde, 2004. *Recreations:* bridge, opera. *Address:* British Medical Association, BMA House, Tavistock Square, WC1H 9JP. *T:* (020) 7383 6111; 214 Princess Park Manor, Royal Drive, N11 3FS.

NATKIEL, Rod; Managing Director and Head of Production, RNA (Rod Natkiel Associates) Ltd, since 1999; *b* 30 Jan. 1952; *s* of late Daniel Natkiel and Marjorie Jessie (*née* Pinkham); *m* 1976, Janet Ruth Sawtell; two *s*. *Educ:* Kingston Grammar Sch.; Univ. of Bristol (BA Drama); Univ. of Birmingham (MBA Dist.). Theatre dir and composer, 1973–; Dir/Producer, BBC TV Entertainment, 1978–84; freelance Exec. Producer/Producer/Dir/Writer in Entertainment and Features, Drama, News and Current Affairs for all major broadcasters, 1984–; Hd of Network TV and Radio, BBC Birmingham, 1992–99; Events Creator/Prod., 2000–. Vis. Prof. in TV Studies, Univ. of Central England, 1993–99. Mem., Arts Council of England, 1997–98; Chair: W Midlands Arts Bd, 1997–2001; Screen W Midlands, 2001–03. Mem. Bd, Variety Children's Charity, 1995–; Chm., Variety Club Midlands, 1997–2000. *Recreations:* squash, cricket, theatre, cinema, DIY. *Address:* 5 Vesey Road, Sutton Coldfield, W Midlands B73 5NP. *T:* (0121) 355 2197, *Fax:* (0121) 355 8033. *E:* rod@rodnatkiel.co.uk.

NATTRASS, Michael Henry, FRICS; Member (UK Ind) West Midlands Region, European Parliament, 2004–14; *b* 14 Dec. 1945. Property mgt; co-founder and Sen. Partner, Nattrass Giles, chartered surveyors, 1980–2007. Former Party Chm. and former Dep. Leader, UKIP. Contested (UK Ind) S Staffordshire, 2010.

NATWAR-SINGH, Kanwar; Padma Bhushan, 1984; MP (Congress Party) Bharatpur: Lok Sabha, 1984–89 and 1998–99; Rajya Sabha, 2002–08; Union Minister for External Affairs, India, 2004–05; *b* 16 May 1931; *s* of Govind Singhji and Prayag Kaur; *m* 1967, Princess Heminder Kumari, *e d* of late Maharaja Yadvindra Singhji of Patiala; one *s* (one *d* decd). *Educ:* St Stephen's Coll., Delhi Univ. (BA 1st cl. hons History 1951); Corpus Christi Coll., Cambridge, 1952–54 (Hon. Fellow 2005); Peking Univ. Joined Indian Foreign Service, 1953; 3rd Sec., Peking, 1956–58; Under Sec., Ministry of External Affairs, and Private Sec. to Sec. General, 1958–61; Adviser, Indian Delegn to UN, NY, 1961–66; Rapporteur, UN Cttee on Decolonisation, 1962–66; Rapporteur, UN Trusteeship Council, 1965; Alt. Deleg. of India to UN Session for 1962; Rep. of India on Exec. Bd of UNICEF, NY, 1962–66; Dep. Sec. to Prime Minister of India, 1966–67; Dir, Prime Minister's Secretariat, New Delhi, 1967–70; Jt Sec. to Prime Minister, 1970–71; Ambassador to Poland, 1971–73; Dep. High Comr in London, 1973–77; High Comr for India in Zambia and Botswana, 1977–80; Ambassador to Pakistan, 1980–82; Sec., Min. of External Affairs, India, 1982–84; Minister of State for Steel, 1984–85, for Fertilizers, 1985–86; Union Minister of State for Foreign Affairs, 1986–89. Attended Commonwealth Heads of Govt Meetings: Jamaica, 1975; Lusaka, 1979; Member: Commonwealth Cyprus Cttee, 1977; Indian Delegn to Zimbabwe Ind. Celebrations, 1980; Sec.-Gen., 7th Non-Aligned Summit, New Delhi, 1983; Chief Co-ordinator, Commonwealth Heads of State and Govt Meeting, New Delhi, 1983; Pres., UN Conf. on Disarmament and Develt, 1987; Leader, Indian Delegn to 42nd Session of UN Gen. Assembly, 1987. Dir, Air India, 1982–84. Exec. Trustee, UNITAR, 1981–86. Pres., All India Tennis Fedn, 1988–92. Hon. Res. Fellow, UCL. Hon. Dr Pol Sci. Seoul, 2005. E. M. Forster Literary Award, 1989. Comdr, Ordre Nat. du Lion (Senegal), 2005. *Publications:* E. M. Forster: A Tribute, 1964; The Legacy of Nehru, 1965; Tales from Modern India, 1966; Stories from India, 1971; Maharaja Suraj Mal, 1707–1763, 1981; Curtain Raisers, 1984; Profiles and Letters, 1997; The Magnificent Maharaja Bhupinder Singh of Patiala 1891–1938, 1997; Heart to Heart, 2003; Yours Sincerely, 2008; My China Diary, 1956–88, 2010; Walking with Lions, 2012; One Life is Not Enough (autobiog.), 2014; writes and reviews for national and international newspapers and magazines. *Recreations:* tennis, watching cricket, reading, writing, collecting books and reading them, good conversation followed by prolonged periods of reflective uninterrupted silence. *E:* knatwarsingh@yahoo.com. *Clubs:* Garrick, Royal Over-Seas League (Life Mem.); India International Centre (Life Mem.), Gymkhana (Life Mem; Pres., 1984) (Delhi).

NATZLER, David Lionel; Clerk of the House of Commons, and Head of the House of Commons Service, since 2015; *b* 16 Aug. 1952; *o s* of Pierre Jean Natzler and late Brenda Agnes Natzler (*née* Wrangham); *m* 1988, Hilary Joan Gauld Thompson; two *s* one *d*. *Educ:* Eton Coll.; Trinity Coll., Cambridge (BA 1973): Harvard Univ. (Kennedy Schol.). House of Commons: Clerk of Select Committee: on Social Services, 1981–85; on Defence, 1989–95; on Procedure, 1995–97; on Trade and Industry, 1997–2001; Principal Clerk, Select Cttees, 2001–04; Sec., H of C Commn, 2004–06; Principal Clerk, Table Office, 2006–08; Clerk of Cttees, 2008–09; Clerk of Legislation, 2009–11; Clerk Asst and Dir Gen., Chamber and Cttee Services, 2011–15; Actg Clerk of H of C, 2014–15. *Address:* House of Commons, SW1A 0AA. *T:* (020) 7219 1310. *E:* natzlerdl@parliament.uk.

NAUGHTIE, (Alexander) James; journalist and broadcaster; Special Correspondent, BBC Radio 4, from Jan. 2016; Books Editor, BBC News, from Jan. 2016; *b* 9 Aug. 1951; *s* of Alexander and Isabella Naughtie; *m* 1986, Eleanor Updale; one *s* two *d*. *Educ:* Keith Grammar Sch.; Aberdeen Univ. (MA Hons); Syracuse Univ., New York (MA). The Press and Journal, 1975–77; The Scotsman, 1977–84; The Guardian, 1984–88; Presenter: The World at One, BBC Radio 4, 1988–94; Opera News, BBC Radio 3, 1990–93; BBC Proms, 1992–2004; Today, BBC Radio 4, 1994–2015; Bookclub, BBC Radio 4, 1998–; The New Elizabethans, BBC Radio 4, 2012. Laurence M. Stern Fellow, Washington Post, 1981. Chancellor, Stirling Univ., 2008–. Patron: Southbank Sinfonia, 2003–; Borders Book Festival, 2005–. Ambassador, The Prince's Foundn for Children and the Arts (formerly Prince of Wales Arts and Kids Foundn), 2005–. Trustee: Booker Prize Foundn, 2010–; Great Tapestry of Scotland, 2012–. Hon. LLD: Aberdeen, 1990; St Andrews, 2001; DUniv Stirling, 2001; Hon. DLitt: Glasgow Caledonian, 2002; Napier, 2002; Edinburgh, 2006. Personality of the Year, Sony Radio Awards, 1991. *Publications:* (ed) Playing the Palace: a Westminster collection, 1984; The Rivals: the intimate story of a political marriage, 2001; The Accidental American, 2004; The Making of Music: a journey with notes, 2007; The New Elizabethans, 2012; The Madness of July (novel), 2014; contribs to newspapers, magazines, journals. *Recreations:* books, opera. *Address:* BBC News Centre, Broadcasting House, Portland Place, W1A 1AA. *Club:* Garrick.

NAUGHTON, Prof. John; academic and journalist; Vice President, Wolfson College, Cambridge, since 2011; Senior Research Fellow, Centre for Research in the Arts, Social Sciences and Humanities, University of Cambridge, since 2012; *b* 18 July 1946; *s* of late Peter Naughton and Pearl Naughton (*née* Moran); *m* 1st, 1968, Carol (marr. diss. 2001); two *s*; 2nd, 2002, Susan Pinniger (*d* 2002); one *s* one *d*; 3rd, 2012, Fiona Blackburn (*née* Haigh). *Educ:* University Coll., Cork (BE 1968); Emmanuel Coll., Cambridge (MA 1972). Open University: Lectr, then Sen. Lectr, 1972–2002; Prof. of Public Understanding of Technol., 2002–11, now Prof. Emeritus. Res. Fellow, Twente Univ. of Technol., Netherlands, 1997–98; Adjunct Prof., UC Cork. Television Critic: Listener, 1982–87; Observer, 1987–95; columnist, 1987–, technol. columnist, 1995–, Observer. FRSA. *Publications:* A Brief History of the Future: the origins of the internet, 1999; From Gutenberg to Zuckerberg, 2012; contrib. articles to jls, newspapers and mags. *Recreations:* photography, conversation, blogging, Provençal summers. *Address:* Wolfson College, Barton Road, Cambridge CB3 9BB. *Clubs:* Garrick, Groucho.

NAUGHTON, Philip Anthony; QC 1988; *b* 18 May 1943; *s* of late Francis and Madeleine Naughton; *m* 1968, Barbara, *d* of Prof. F. E. Bruce; two *s* one *d*. *Educ:* Wimbledon Coll.; Univ. of Nottingham (LLB). Called to the Bar, Gray's Inn, 1970, Bencher, 1997. Marketing and public relations posts with BP Chemicals Ltd and Air Products Ltd, 1964–71; in practice as barrister, 1971–2008, and as a mediator, 1992–2012. *Recreations:* walking, sailing. *Address:* Serjeants' Inn Chambers, 85 Fleet Street, EC4Y 1AE. *T:* (020) 7427 5000.

NAVARRETE LÓPEZ, Jorge Eduardo; Senior Researcher on International Affairs, National Autonomous University of Mexico, since 2004; *b* 29 April 1940; *s* of late Gabriel Navarrete and Lucrecia López; *m* 1st, 1962, María Antonieta Linares (marr. diss. 1973); one *s*; 2nd, 1976, María de Navarrete (*d* 1985); 3rd, 1987, Angeles Salceda (marr. diss. 1994); 4th, 1996, Martha López (marr. diss. 2007). *Educ:* Nat. Sch. of Economics, Nat. Autonomous Univ. of Mexico (equivalent BA Econ.); post-graduate studies in internat. economy. Center for Latin American Monetary Studies, Mexico, 1963–65; Nat. Foreign Trade Bank, Mexico, 1966–72; joined Mexican Foreign Service, 1972; Ambassador to: Venezuela, 1972–75; Austria, 1976–77; Yugoslavia, 1977–79; Dep. Perm. Rep. to UN, NY, 1979; Under Sec. (Economics), Min. of Foreign Affairs, Mexico, 1979–85; Ambassador to UK and Republic of Ireland, 1986–89; to China, 1989–93; to Chile, 1993–95; Under Sec. for Energy, 1995–97; Ambassador to Brazil, 1997–2000; Perm. Rep. to UN, NY, 2000–02; Ambassador to Germany, 2002–04. Former Mem., South Commn. Holds decorations from Argentina, Brazil, Dominican Republic, Ecuador, Federal Republic of Germany, Italy, Panama, Poland, Sweden, Venezuela. *Publications:* The International Transfer of Technology (with G. Bueno and M. S. Wionczeck), 1969; Mexico's Economic Policy, 2 vols, 1971, 1972; Cancun 1981: the international meeting on co-operation and development, 1982; The External Debt of Latin America: issues and policies, 1987; (ed) The Deconstruction of Mexican Foreign Policy, 2005; China: the third inflection, 2007; The Global Foot-print of China: international relations of a global power, 2011; numerous essays on Mexican and Latin American economic issues, in Mexican and foreign jls. *Recreation:* chess. *Address:* Sta Margarita 214, 03100 Mexico City, Mexico.

NAVRATILOVA, Martina; tennis player; commentator; *b* Prague, 18 Oct. 1956; *d* of late Jana Navratilova. Left Czechoslovakia, 1975; adopted American nationality, 1981; *m* 2014, Julia Lemigova. Professional player, 1975–94. Has won 167 singles and 178 doubles titles, including 18 Grand Slam singles titles (a record 9 Wimbledon singles wins) and 41 Grand Slam doubles titles. Pres., Women's Tennis Assoc., 1979–80, 1994–95. *Publications:* Martina (autobiog.), 1985; Shape Your Self, 2006; novels (with Liz Nickles): The Total Zone, 1994; Killer Instinct, 1995; Breaking Point, 1996. *Address:* c/o International Management Group, 1360 E 9th Street, Suite #100, Cleveland, OH 44114–1782, USA.

NAWAZ, Amjad; His Honour Judge Nawaz; a Circuit Judge, since 2008; *b* Jhelum, Pakistan, 10 Feb. 1958; *s* of Choudary Mohammed Azam and Shafia Begum; *m* 1983, Shamin Akhtar; two *s* four *d* (incl. triplets). *Educ:* Univ. of Aston in Birmingham (BSc 1st Cl. Hons Managerial and Admin Scis). Called to the Bar, Lincoln's Inn, 1983; in practice as barrister, specialising in crime, chancery and commercial law, 1983–2008; Recorder, 2002–08. *Recreations:* cricket (played at University level), squash, tennis, Manchester United fan. *Address:* Wolverhampton Crown Court, Pipers Row, Wolverhampton WV1 3LQ.

NAWAZ, Maajid; Chairman, Quilliam Foundation, since 2008; *m* 2014, Rachel Maggart. *Educ:* Sch. of Oriental and African Studies, Univ. of London (BA Law and Arabic); London Sch. of Econs and Pol Sci. (MSc Pol Theory). Hon. Associate, Nat. Secular Soc., 2014–.

Columnist, Daily Beast, 2015–. Contested (Lib Dem) Hampstead and Kilburn, 2015. FRSA 2009. *Publications:* Radical, 2012; (with S. Harris) Islam and the Future of Tolerance: a dialogue, 2015. *Address:* Quilliam Foundation, PO Box 60380, WC1A 9AZ. *T:* (020) 7182 7280. *E:* information@quilliamfoundation.org.

NAYAR, Kuldip; syndicated columnist; Member, Rajya Sabha, 1997–2003; President: Citizens for Democracy; Transparency International; *b* 14 Aug. 1924; *m* 1949, Bharti; two *s*. *Educ:* Northwestern Univ., USA (BA Hons, LLB, MSc in journalism; Hon. PhD(Phil.) 1998; Alumni Award, 1999). Press Officer to Home Minister, India, 1954–64; Editor and General Manager, United News of India, 1964–67; Delhi Editor, The Statesman, 1967–75; Editor, Indian Express News Service, 1975–81; syndicated columnist, 1981–; correspondent, The Times, London, 1968–89; High Comr in UK, 1990. Mem., Indian delegn to UN Gen. Assembly. Prof. Emeritus, Symbiosis Inst. of Mass Communication, Pune Univ., 2001. Numerous journalism and public service awards. *Publications:* Between the Lines, 1967; India: the critical years, 1968; India, the critical years, 1971; Distant Neighbours, 1972; The Supersession of Judges, 1974; India After Nehru, 1975; The Judgement, 1977; In Jail, 1978; A report on Afghanistan, 1980; The Tragedy of Punjab, 1985; India House, 1992; The Martyr Bhagat Singh's Experiments in Revolution, 2000; Wall at Wagah: Indo-Pak relations, 2003. *Recreations:* music (Indian and Western); cricket, hockey. *Address:* D7/2 Vasant Vihar, New Delhi 110057, India. *T:* 26142388.

NAYLER, Georgina Ruth; Director, Pilgrim Trust, since 1996; *b* 16 March 1959; *d* of late Dennis Nayler and of Yvonne Nayler (*née* Loader); partner, Simon Stillwell; one *s* one *d*. *Educ:* Brentwood County High Sch. for Girls; Univ. of Warwick (BA). Joined Nat. Heritage Meml Fund, 1982: Asst Dir, 1987–88; Dep. Dir, 1988–89; Dir, 1989–95. Mem., Historic Bldgs Council for Scotland, 1990–96. Mem., Adv. Bd, Faculty of Arts, Univ. of Warwick, 2003–10. Trustee: Charlotte Bonham-Carter Charitable Trust, 2008–; Pitzhanger Manor Trust, 2013– (Dep. Chm., 2014–). *Recreation:* gardening. *Address:* c/o The Pilgrim Trust, 55a Catherine Place, SW1E 6DY.

NAYLOR, (Andrew) Ross, MD; FRCSE, FRCS; Consultant Vascular Surgeon, since 1995, and Professor of Vascular Surgery, since 2003, Leicester Royal Infirmary; *b* 22 March 1958; *s* of Robert Charles Naylor and Patricia Mary Naylor; *m* 1982, May Bruce MacPherson; one *s* one *d*. *Educ:* Merchiston Castle Sch., Edinburgh; Univ. of Aberdeen (MBChB (commendation) 1981; MD 1990). FRCSE 1986; FRCS 1994. House Officer, Aberdeen Hosps, 1981–82; Lectr in Pathology, Aberdeen Royal Infirmary, 1982–83; Sen. House Officer, Surgery, Aberdeen Hosps, 1983–85; Surgical Registrar, Edinburgh Hosps, 1985–88; Res. Fellow in Surgery, Edinburgh Univ., 1988–90; Lectr in Surgery, Leicester Univ., 1991–93; Consultant Vascular Surgeon, Aberdeen Royal Infirmary, 1993–95. Reader in Surgery, Leicester Royal Infirmary, 1995–2003. Hunterian Prof., RCS, 2002. Member Council: Vascular Soc. of GB and Ireland, 2007– (Pres., 2011–12); European Soc. of Vascular and Endovascular Surgery, 2010–Sept. 2016. Associate Ed., 2008–11, Sen. Ed., 2011–13, Ed. in Chief, 2013–Sept. 2016, Eur. Jl of Vascular and Endovascular Surgery. *Publications:* (ed jtly) Carotid Artery Surgery: a problem based approach, 2000; 64 book chapters on mgt of vascular disease; 420 pubns in peer reviewed jls, mainly relating to mgt of carotid artery disease. *Recreations:* road cycling, ski-ing, gardening. *Address:* 9 Dalby Avenue, Bushby, Leicester LE7 9RE. *T:* (0116) 252 3252, *Fax:* (0116) 252 3179. *E:* arnaylor@hotmail.com.

NAYLOR, Bernard; University Librarian, Southampton University, 1977–2000; President, Library Association, 2001–02; *b* 7 May 1938; *s* of William Edward Naylor and Lilian Naylor (*née* Oakes); *m* 1967, Frances Gemma Trenaman; four *s* one *d*. *Educ:* Balliol Coll., Oxford (BA 1963; MA 1965); Sch. of Librarianship and Archive Administration, University Coll. London (Dip. Lib. 1966). MCLIP (ALA 1969). Asst, Foreign Accessions Dept, Bodleian Liby, 1964–66; Librarian and Bibliographer, Univ. of London Inst. of Latin American Studies, 1966–74; Sec., Library Resources Co-ordinating Cttee, Univ. of London, 1974–77; Co-ordinator of Inf. Services, 1988–93, of Acad. Support Services, 1998–2000, Southampton Univ. Member: British Liby Adv. Cttee on Lending Services, 1978–86 (Chm., 1981–85); Council, Standing Conf. of Nat. and Univ. Libraries, 1979–82, 1984–90 (Vice-Chm., 1984–86; Chm., 1986–88); British Council Libraries Adv. Cttee, 1982–96 (Chm., 1986–95); British Liby Bd, 1995–2001. Chm., Hants Area Tech. Res. Indust. Commercial Service Exec., 1981–2000. Trustee: Nat. MSS Conservation Trust, 1995–; Hansard Trust, 2002–; Liby Assoc. Benevolent Fund, 2002– (Chm., 2008–13). Chm., Laser Foundn, 2003–05. Gov., La Sainte Union Coll., Southampton, 1996–97. Mem., British Council, 1995. Hon. DLitt Southampton, 2006. *Publications:* Accounts of Nineteenth Century South America, 1969; Directory of Libraries and Special Collections on Latin America and the West Indies, 1975; articles in liby jls. *Recreations:* playing the piano (in private), learning foreign languages. *Address:* 12 Blenheim Avenue, Highfield, Southampton SO17 1DU. *T:* (023) 8055 4697.

NAYLOR, (Charles) John, OBE 1993; Secretary and Treasurer, then Chief Executive, Carnegie United Kingdom Trust, 1993–2003; Chair, Office of Scottish Charity Regulator, 2006–11; *b* 17 Aug. 1943; *s* of late Arthur Edgar Naylor, MBE and Elizabeth Mary Naylor; *m* 1968, Margery Thomson; two *s*. *Educ:* Royal Grammar Sch., Newcastle upon Tyne; Haberdashers' Aske's Sch., Elstree; Clare Coll., Cambridge (MA History). Jun. and sen. exec. posts in industry, 1965–75; Dir, YMCA National Centre, Lakeside, Cumbria, 1975–80; Dep. National Sec., 1980–82, Nat. Sec., 1982–93, National Council of YMCAs; mem. and chm. of YMCA European and world cttees, 1976–92. Jt Founder, Y Care Internat., 1984. Vice-Chm., Nat. Council for Voluntary Youth Services, 1985–88; Mem., Nat. Adv. Council for Youth Service, 1985–88. Chairman: Assoc. of Heads of Outdoor Educn Centres, 1979–80; MSC and DES Working Party on Residential Experience and Unemployment, 1980–81; DES Adv. Cttee for Innovation in Youth Work, 1986–92; Mem., Scottish Charity Law Review Commn, 2000–01. Member: Community Fund Scottish Cttee, 2003–04 (Chm., 2004–06); UK Bd, Big Lottery Fund, 2004–06; Audit and Risk Mgt Cttee, Nat. Trust for Scotland, 2011–. Chm., 1995–2000, Trustee, 2000–06, Brathay Exploration Gp; Trustee and Treas., The Tomorrow Project, 2000–13; Chm., Strange Town (youth theatre), 2011– (Vice Chm., 2007–11). Trustee: Med. Res. Scotland (formerly Scottish Hosps Endowment Res. Trust), 2005–13; Foundn Scotland (formerly Scottish Community Foundn), 2011–; Trustee and Director: Resilient Scotland Ltd, 2011–14; Jessica (Scotland) Trust, 2011–14. Mem. Council, UK Scout Assoc., 2005–10 (Chm., Develt Grants Bd, 2003–10); Jt Founding Convenor, Scottish Grant Making Trust Gp, 1994–2004; Chm., RSA Scotland, 2012–14; Pres., YMCA Scotland 2012–. Mem., Clare Coll., Cambridge Alumni Council, 2010–13. Kirk Elder, 1998–. CCMI; FRSA. *Publications:* contribs on youth, outdoors and grant making to UK periodicals and books. *Recreations:* the outdoors (partic. mountains), travel, performing and other arts, golf. *Address:* Orchard House, 25b Cramond Glebe Road, Edinburgh EH4 6NT.

NAYLOR, Prof. David, OC 2006; MD, DPhil; FRCPC, FRSC 2004; Professor of Medicine, University of Toronto, since 1996 (President, 2005–13, now President Emeritus); *b* 26 Oct. 1954; *s* of Thomas Naylor and Edna (*née* Aziz); *m* 1985, Ilse Treurnicht, DPhil. *Educ:* Univ. of Toronto (MD 1978); Hertford Coll., Oxford (Rhodes Schol. 1979; DPhil 1983). FRCPC 1986. Resident in internal medicine, Univ. of Western Ontario teaching hosps, 1983–86; MRC Res. Fellow, Clinical Epidemiol., Toronto Gen. Hosp., 1987–88; University of Toronto: Asst Prof., 1988–92, Associate Prof., 1992–96, of Medicine; Dean of Medicine and Vice Provost, Relns with Health Care Instns, 1999–2005; Founding Dir, Clinical Epidemiology Prog., Sunnybrook Health Scis Centre, Toronto, 1990–96; Founding CEO, Inst. for Clinical Evaluative Scis, 1991–98. Chairman: Nat. Adv. Cttee on SARS and Public Health, 2003; Nat. Adv. Panel on Healthcare Innovation, 2014–15; Member: Global Commn on Educating Health Professionals for the 21st Century, 2009–10; Federal Rev. of Res. and Develt (Jenkins Panel), 2010–11. Fellow, Canadian Acad. of Health Scis, 2005; For. Associate, Inst. of Medicine, NAS, 2005. Hon. Life Mem., Canadian Public Health Assoc., 2005. Member Editorial Board: BMJ, 1996–98; Jl of American Med. Assoc., 1998–; Canadian Med. Assoc. Jl, 1998–2000. Hon. DSc Manitoba, 2009; Hon. LLD Western, 2011. *Publications:* co-author of numerous books and chapters, and over 250 jl articles. *Recreations:* golf, piano. *Address:* c/o Simcoe Hall 206, University of Toronto, 27 King's College Circle, Toronto, ON M5S 1A1, Canada. *Club:* Scarboro Golf.

NAYLOR, Maj.-Gen. (David) Murray, CB 1992; MBE 1972; DL; Director-General, Territorial Army and Organisation, Ministry of Defence, 1989–92; *b* 5 March 1938; *s* of Thomas Humphrey Naylor and Dorothy Isobel Durning Naylor (*née* Holt); *m* 1965, Rosemary Gillian Hicks Beach; three *s*. *Educ:* Eton Coll. psc, rcds. Joined Scots Guards, 1956; commnd as National Service and later as Regular Officer; commanded: 2nd Bn Scots Guards, 1976–79; 22nd Armoured Bde, 1982–83; Dep. Mil. Sec. (A), 1985–87; GOC NE Dist and Comdr 2nd Inf. Div., 1987–89. Chm., N Yorks Ambulance Service NHS Trust, 1992–97. Mem. (C), N Yorks CC, 1997–2005. DL N Yorks, 1994. Mem., Merchant Adventurers Co. of York, 1998. Gov., St Peter's Sch., York, 1991–2005 (Chm. of Govs, 2000–05). Lay Chm., Southern Ryedale Deanery, 2008–13. Mem., Kohima Educnl Trust, 2003– (Chm., 2003–09). Trustee, Ryedale Fest., 2012–15. *Publications:* Among Friends: Scots Guards 1956–1993, 1995; England's Cathedrals by Train: discover how the Normans and Victorians helped to shape our lives, 2013. *Recreations:* shooting, walking, tennis, travel. *Address:* Minster Hill, Huttons Ambo, York YO60 7HJ. *T:* (01653) 695008; 07889 138381. *Club:* Cavalry and Guards.

NAYLOR, Prof. Ernest, OBE 1998; PhD, DSc; Lloyd Roberts Professor of Marine Zoology (formerly Lloyd Roberts Professor of Zoology), 1982–96, now Professor Emeritus, and Head of School of Ocean Sciences, 1992–96, University College of North Wales, Bangor; *b* 19 May 1931; *s* of Joseph and Evelyn Naylor; *m* 1956, Carol Gillian Bruce; two *d*. *Educ:* Swanwick Hall Grammar Sch.; Univ. of Sheffield (BSc); Univ. of Liverpool (PhD, DSc). FIBiol 1972–96. Commnd RAF, 1954–56 (Educn Br.). Successively Asst Lectr, Lectr, Sen. Lectr and Reader in Zoology, University Coll. of Swansea, Wales, 1956–71; Prof. of Marine Biology, Univ. of Liverpool, 1971–82; Dean of Sci., UCNW, Bangor, 1989–91. Visiting Professor: Duke Univ., USA, 1969, 1970; Univ. of Otago, NZ, 1982. Mem., NERC, 1976–82 (Mem., Marine Sci. and Technol. Bd, 1994–96); Specialist Adviser to H of L Select Sub-Cttee on Marine Sci. and Technology, 1985; Ind. Mem., Co-ordinating Cttee on Marine Sci. and Technology, 1988–91; Ind. Assessor, Inter-Agency Cttee on Marine Sci. and Technol., 1991–98; UK Rep., EC Adv. Cttee for Marine Science and Technol., 1989–96. President: Sect. D (Zoology), BAAS, 1982; Estuarine and Coastal Sciences Assoc., 1986–89 (Hon. Life Mem. 2001); Soc. for Exptl Biology, 1989–91 (Hon. Life Mem. 1997); Member Council: Marine Biol Assoc. of UK, 1977–80, 1982–85; Challenger Soc. for Marine Sci., 1997–98 (Hon. Life Mem. 2007). Founding Ed., Estuarine, Coastal and Shelf Science, 1972–2000. *Publications:* British Marine Isopods, 1972; (co-ed with R. G. Hartnoll) Cyclic Phenomena in Marine Plants and Animals, 1979; Chronobiology of Marine Organisms, 2010; over 160 papers in learned jls. *Recreations:* travel, gardening. *Address:* School of Ocean Sciences, Bangor University, Menai Bridge, Anglesey LL59 5AB. *T:* (01248) 382842. *E:* e.naylor@bangor.ac.uk.

NAYLOR, Jennifer Mary; *see* Higham, J. M.

NAYLOR, John; *see* Naylor, C. J.

NAYLOR, Maurice; *see* Naylor, W. M.

NAYLOR, Maj.-Gen. Murray; *see* Naylor, Maj.-Gen. D. M.

NAYLOR, Sir Robert (Antony), Kt 2008; Chief Executive, University College London Hospitals NHS Trust, since 2000; *b* 13 Nov. 1949; *s* of Francis Thomas Naylor and Kathleen Mary (*née* Donellan); *m* 1974, Jane Karen Evans; one *s* one *d*. *Educ:* Presentation Coll., Reading; Thames Poly. (BSc Hons Chem. London). Grad. mgt trainee, King's Fund, 1972–74; Hosp. Sec., National Hosp., Queen Sq., 1974–77; Dist Administrator, Enfield HA, 1977–84; Chief Exec., Birmingham Heartlands and Solihull NHS Trust, 1984–2000. Chm., Shelford Gp, 2013–14; Dir, UCL Partners, 2008–; Mem., Foundn Trust Network, 2009–15. Proprietor, Henley Hotel, 1988–2001. Hon. Sen. Fellow, Univ. of Warwick. *Recreations:* golf, scuba diving. *Address:* 4 Chester Terrace, Regent's Park, NW1 4ND. *T:* (office) (020) 3447 9890. *E:* robert.naylor@uclh.nhs.uk.

NAYLOR, Ross; *see* Naylor, A. R.

NAYLOR, (William) Maurice, CBE 1973; FIHM; Director, National Association of Health Authorities, 1981–84; *b* 20 Dec. 1920; *s* of Thomas and Agnes Naylor; *m* 1948, Maureen Ann, *d* of John and Mary Walsh; one *s* two *d*. *Educ:* St Joseph's Coll., Market Drayton; Manchester Univ. (BA Admin). FIHM (FHSM 1956, Hon. FHSM 1987). War service, 1941–46, 135 Field Regt RA (FE, POW (captured at fall of Singapore), 1942–45). Parly Asst, Town Clerk's Office, Manchester, 1950–55; Asst Sec., Manchester RHB, 1955–57; Dep. Sec., 1957–63, Sec., 1963–73, Sheffield RHB; Regl Administrator, Trent RHA, 1973–81. Institute of Health Services Management: Mem., Nat. Council, 1966–86; Chm., 1974; Pres., 1975–76; Chm. Educn Cttee, 1980–86. Member: Cttee on Hosp. Supplies Orgn, 1969; Steering Cttee on Reorgn of NHS, 1973–74; Cornwall AHA, 1982–84; Chm., Patient Transport Services Working Party, 1981. Trustee, NHS Pensioners Trust, 1991–99. JP Sheffield, 1970. Hon. MBA Sheffield, 1982. *Publications:* (contrib.) Challenges for Change, 1971; Organisation of Area Health Services, 1972; (contrib. and Chm., Editl Cttee) Health Care in the United Kingdom: its organisation and management, 1982; contrib. to professional jls. *Address:* 7 Hewitt Drive, Kirby Muxloe, Leicester LE9 2EB. *T:* (0116) 239 2606.

NAYLOR-LEYLAND, Sir Philip (Vyvian), 4th Bt *cr* 1895, of Hyde Park House; Chairman, Milton (Peterborough) Estates Co.; *b* 9 Aug. 1953; *s* of Sir Vivyan Edward Naylor-Leyland, 3rd Bt and Hon. Elizabeth Anne Fitzalan-Howard, *yr d* of 2nd Viscount FitzAlan of Derwent, OBE (she *m* 2nd, Sir Stephen Hastings, MC, and *d* 1997); *S* father, 1987; *m* 1980, Lady Isabella Lambton, *d* of Viscount Lambton (*d* 2006); four *s* two *d*. *Educ:* Eton; RMA Sandhurst; NY Univ. Business Sch.; RAC Cirencester. 2nd Lieut, Life Guards, 1973, Lieut, 1975–76. Chm., Peterborough Royal Foxhound Show Soc., 1995– (Vice-Chm., 1988–95); Pres., Nat. Coursing Club, 1988–. Jt Master, Fitzwilliam (Milton) Hunt, 1987–. *Heir: s* Thomas Philip Naylor-Leyland [*b* 22 Jan. 1982; *m* 2011, Alice Dawson; one *s* one *d*]. *Address:* Milton, Peterborough, Cambs PE6 7AA; Nantclwyd Hall, Ruthin, Denbighshire LL15 2PR. *Clubs:* White's; Air Squadron; Sunningdale Golf.

NAYSMITH, (John) Douglas, PhD; *b* 1 April 1941; *s* of late James Naysmith and Ina (*née* Vass); *m* 1966, Caroline (separated), *d* of late Sidney and Kate Hill; one *s* one *d*. *Educ:* Musselburgh Burgh Sch.; George Heriot's Sch., Edinburgh; Edinburgh Univ. (BSc, PhD). CBiol 1989, FRSB (FIBiol 1999). Res. Asst, Edinburgh Univ., 1966–69; Fellow, Yale Univ., 1969–70; Res. Immunologist, Beecham Res. Labs, 1970–72; University of Bristol: Res. Associate, 1972–76; Fellow, 1976–81; Lectr in Immunology, Dept of Pathology, 1981–95; Administrator, Registrar's Office, 1995–97. MP (Lab and Co-op) Bristol NW, 1997–2010. Mem. (Lab) Bristol City Council, 1981–98 and 2010–. FRSocMed 1980.

NAZARETH, Gerald Paul, GBS 2000; CBE 1985 (OBE 1976); Non-Permanent Judge, Hong Kong Court of Final Appeal, 1997; Justice, Bermuda Court of Appeal, 2001–10; *b* 27 Jan. 1932; *m* 1959, Elba Maria Fonseca; three *d*. *Educ:* Nairobi; St Xavier's College, Bombay; LLB Bombay Univ. Called to the Bar, Lincoln's Inn, 1962. Public Prosecutor, and Senior Crown Counsel, Kenya, 1954–63; Solicitor General, British Solomon Islands, 1963–73; Attorney General and Legal Advisor, Western Pacific High Commn, 1973–76; Hong Kong: Law Draftsman, 1976–84; MLC, 1979–84; QC, 1982; Judge of the High Court, 1985–91; Justice of Appeal, 1991–2000 and Vice-Pres., 1994–2000, Court of Appeal. Comr, Supreme Court, Brunei, 1989–93. Member: Law Reform Commn, Hong Kong, 1982–84 (Chm., Sub-Cttee on Copyright Law, 1987–92); Wkg Gp on Sino-British Jt Declaration on Hong Kong, Beijing, 1984. Vis. Fellow, ANU, 1972. Vice-Pres., Commonwealth Assoc. of Legislative Counsel, 1983–90. *Recreations:* music, reading, gardening, walking.

NAZARETH, Prof. Irwin, PhD; FRCGP; Professor of Primary Care and Population Sciences, since 2002, and Vice Dean, Primary Care, since 2007, University College London; Director, General Practice Research Framework, General Medical Council, since 2005; *b* Bombay, 12 Oct. 1958; *s* of Ignatius Nazareth and Caroline Rodrigue-Nazareth. *Educ:* Topiwala Nat. Medical Coll., Bombay (MB BS 1984); London (PhD 1997). LRCPE 1986; LRCSE 1986; LRCPSGlas 1986; DRCOG 1988; MRCGP 1989, FRCGP 2004. SHO, 1984–89; University College London: Sir Jules Thorne Res. Fellow, 1990–93; Lectr in Primary Care, 1994–95; Sen. Lectr in Primary Care Medicine, 1995–2002. *Publications:* contrib. key chapters in six books on med. practice and res.; over 200 original res. papers in scientific med. jls. *Recreations:* running, travel, music. *Address:* Department of Primary Care and Population Health, University College London Medical School, Rowland Hill Street, NW3 2NF.

NAZIR-ALI, Rt Rev. Dr Michael James; Bishop of Rochester, 1994–2009; President, Oxford Centre for Training, Research, Advocacy and Dialogue, since 2009; *b* 19 Aug. 1949; *s* of James and Patience Nazir-Ali; *m* 1972, Valerie Cree; two *s*. *Educ:* St Paul's School and St Patrick's Coll., Karachi; Univ. of Karachi (BA 1970, Econs Sociology and Islamic History); Fitzwilliam Coll. (PGCTh 1972; MLitt 1977; Hon. Fellow, 2006) and Ridley Hall, Cambridge; St Edmund Hall, Oxford (BLitt 1974; MLitt 1981; Hon. Fellow, 1999); ThD Aust. Coll. of Theol., NSW 1985; DHLitt Westminster Coll., Penn 2004; DD Lambeth, 2005. Assistant: Christ Church, Cambridge, 1970–72; St Ebbe's, Oxford, 1972–74; Burney Lectr in Islam, Cambridge, 1973–74; Tutorial Supervisor in Theology, Univ. of Cambridge, 1974–76; Assistant Curate, Holy Sepulchre, Cambridge, 1974–76; Tutor, then Sen. Tutor, Karachi Theol Coll., 1976–81; Assoc. Priest, Holy Trinity Cathedral, Karachi, 1976–79; Priest-in-charge, St Andrew's, Akhtar Colony, Karachi, 1979–81; Provost of Lahore Cathedral, 1981–84; Bishop of Raiwind, Pakistan 1984–86; Asst to Archbp of Canterbury, Co-ordinator of Studies and Editor for Lambeth Conf., 1986–89; Director-in-Residence, Oxford Centre for Mission Studies, 1986–89; Gen. Sec., CMS, 1989–94; Asst Bishop, Southwark, 1992–94; Canon Theologian, Leicester Cathedral, 1992–94. Took seat in H of L, 1999. Mem., HFEA, 1998–2003 (Chm., Ethics and Law Cttee, 1998–2003). Sec., Archbp's Commn on Communion and Women in the Episcopate (Eames Commn), 1988–98; Chm., Wkg Party on Women in Episcopate, 2001–04; Archbishops' nominee, CCBI, 1990–94; Chairman: C of E Mission Theol Adv. Gp, 1992–2001; House of Bishops' Theol. Gp, 2004–09; Member: ARCIC II, 1991–2010; C of E Bd of Mission, 1991–94, 1996–2001; Archbps' Council, 2000–05; House of Bishops' Standing Cttee, 2000–05; Internat. Anglican-Roman Catholic Commn for Unity and Mission, 2001–; Vis. Bishop for Anglican Relations, Dio. S Carolina, 2010–. Mem. Bd, Christian Aid, 1987–97. Vis. Prof., Univ. of Greenwich, 1996–; Sen. Fellow, Wycliffe Hall, Oxford, 2010–; Visiting Faculty: London Sch. of Theol.; Lahore Coll. of Theol.; Forman Christian Univ.; Alexandria Sch. of Theol. Paul Harris Rotary Fellow, 2005. Hon. DLitt: Bath, 2003; Greenwich, 2003; Hon. DD: Kent, 2004; Nashotah, 2010. *Publications:* Islam: a Christian perspective, 1983; Frontiers in Muslim-Christian Encounter, 1987; Martyrs and Magistrates: toleration and trial in Islam, 1989; From Everywhere to Everywhere, 1990; Mission and Dialogue, 1995; The Mystery of Faith, 1995; Citizens and Exiles: Christian faith in a plural world, 1998; Shapes of the Church to Come, 2001; Understanding My Muslim Neighbour, 2002; Conviction and Conflict, 2006; The Unique and Universal Christ, 2008; Triple Jeopardy for the West, 2012; How the Anglican Communion Came to be and Where it is Going, 2013; *edited:* Working Papers for the Lambeth Conference, 1988; The Truth shall Make you Free: report of the Lambeth Conference, 1988; Trustworthy and True: Pastoral letters from the Lambeth Conference, 1988; articles and contribs to jls. *Recreations:* cricket, hockey, table tennis, reading fiction, humour and poetry, writing poetry. *Address:* 70 Wimpole Street, W1G 8AX.

NDOMBET-ASSAMBA, Aloun; High Commissioner of Jamaica in the United Kingdom, and Ambassador (non resident) to Norway, Sweden, Denmark, Finland and Ireland, since 2012; *b* Spanish Town, Jamaica; *d* of James Wood and Gloria Wood; one *s*. *Educ:* Univ. of the West Indies (LLB Hons); Norman Manley Law Sch. (Legal Educn Cert.); Inst. of Mgt and Prodn (Dip. Human Resources Develt); Univ. of Pittsburgh (Heinz Fellow). Legal Officer and Corporate Sec., Jamaica Industrial Develt Corp., 1983–87; Personal Manager and Legal Advr, 1988–94, Gen. Manager, 1994–2002, City of Kingston Co-op Credit Union. Parliament of Jamaica: Senator, 1998–2002; Minister of State, Min. of Industry, Sci., Commerce and Technol., 2002; Minister of Industry and Tourism, 2002–05, of Tourism, Entertainment and Culture, 2005–07; MP, St Ann SE, 2002–07. Man. Partner, Aloun Ndombet-Assamba & Co., Attorneys-at-Law, 2008–12. Founding Member: Lions Club, New Kingston, 1991; Women's Leadership Initiative, 2001. *Recreations:* theatre, cinema, family, travel, art, history, culture, dancing, swimming. *Address:* Jamaican High Commission, 1–2 Prince Consort Road, SW7 2BZ. *T:* (020) 7808 8001, *Fax:* (020) 7584 5482. *E:* hc@jhcuk.com, alounassamba@gmail.com; Grierfield Great House, Moneague, St Ann PO, Jamaica.

NDUNGANE, Most Rev. (Winston Hugh) Njongonkulu; President and Founder, African Monitor, since 2006; Archbishop of Cape Town and Metropolitan of Southern Africa, 1996–2008; *b* Kokstad, 2 April 1941; *s* of Foster Tunyiswa Ndungane and Tingaza (*née* Gcanca); *m* 1st, 1972, Nosipho Ngcelwane (*d* 1986); one *s* one *d*; 2nd, 1987, Nomahlubi Vokwana. *Educ:* Lovedale High Sch., Alice, E Cape; Federal Theol Seminary, Alice (Associate, 1973); King's Coll., London (AKC, BD 1978; MTh 1979; FKC 1997). Ordained deacon, 1973, priest, 1974; Assistant Priest: St Mark's, Athlone, Cape Town, 1973–75; St Mark, Mitcham, 1975–76; St Peter's, Hammersmith, 1976–77; St Mary the Virgin, Primrose Hill, 1977–79; Asst Chaplain, St George's, Paris, 1979; Rector, St Nicholas, Elsies River, Cape Town, 1980–81; Provincial Liaison Officer, CPSA, 1981–84; Principal, St Bede's Coll., Umtata, 1985–86; Provincial Canon, 1987; Chief Exec. Officer, CPSA, 1987–91; Bishop of Kimberley and Kuruman, 1991–96. Vis. Scholar, Ch Divinity Sch. of the Pacific, Berkeley, 1990–91. Chairman: SACC Church Leaders' Forum, 1997–98; Nat. Poverty Hearings, 1998; Member: Budget Gp, USPG, 1981–86; ACC, and its Standing Cttee, 1981–90; Bd, SABC, 1993– (Chm., Religious Broadcasting Panel, 1995–). Chm. Council, Univ. of Cape Town, 2008–. Hon. DD: Rhodes Univ., 1997; Protestant Episcopal Seminary, Va, 2000; Episcopal Divinity Sch., Cambridge, Mass, 2007; Hon. DHL Worcester State Coll., Mass, 2000; Hon. DSocSc Natal, 2001; Hon. PhD: Cape Town, 2003; Walter Sisulu, 2011; Hon. DLitt Witwatersrand, 2012; Hon. Dr S Africa, 2008. Grand Counsellor, Order of Baobab (S Africa), 2008. *Publications* include: The Commuter Population for Claremont, Cape, 1973; Human Rights and the Christian Doctrine of Man, 1979; A World with a Human Face: a voice from Africa, 2003; contributions to: Peace and Peacemaking, 1984; Open to the Spirit, 1987; Doing Ethics in Context, 1994; Ethics and Values: a global perspective, 1997; Change and Challenge, 1998; articles in periodicals. *Address:* African Monitor, PostNet Suite 63, Private Bag x12, Tokai 7966, Cape Town, South Africa.

NEAGLE, Lynne; Member (Lab) Torfaen, National Assembly for Wales, since 1999; *b* Merthyr Tydfil, 18 Jan. 1968; *m* 1996, Huw George Lewis, *qv*; two *s*. *Educ:* Cyfarthfa High Sch., Merthyr Tydfil; Reading Univ. (BA Hons French and Italian). Vol. Housing Rights Worker, Shelter Cymru, 1991–93; Inf. Project Officer, Mid Glam Assoc. of Voluntary Orgns, 1993–94; Res. Asst to Glenys Kinnock, MEP, 1994–97; Carers Develt Officer, Voluntary Action Cardiff, 1997–99. *Recreations:* cinema, reading, swimming. *Address:* (office) 73 Upper Trosnant Street, Pontypool, Torfaen NP4 8AU.

NEAL, Prof. Bernard George, MA, PhD, ScD; FREng; Emeritus Professor, since 1982 and Fellow, since 1986, Imperial College, London University (Professor of Applied Science, 1961–72, of Engineering Structures, 1972–81, of Civil Engineering, 1981–82, and Head of Civil Engineering Department, 1976–82); *b* 29 March 1922; *s* of late Horace Bernard Neal, Wembley, and Hilda Annie Webb; *m* 1948, Elizabeth Ann, *d* of late William George Toller, Woodbridge, and Bertha Catharine Toller; one *s* one *d*. *Educ:* Merchant Taylors'; Trinity College, Cambridge (Schol.; BA Mech. Scis 1942 (Rex Moir Prize, Ricardo Prize in Thermodynamics, John Bernard Seely Prize in Aeronautics); MA 1947; PhD 1948; ScD 1965). FICE 1960; FIStructE 1966; FREng (FEng 1980). Volunteered RAF Aircrew (failed medical), 1940. Temp. Experimental Officer, Admiralty, 1942–45; Research Student, Univ. of Cambridge, 1945–48; Research Associate, Brown University, USA, 1948–49; Demonstrator, 1949–51, Lecturer, 1951–54, Univ. of Cambridge; Research Fellow, 1947–50, Staff Fellow, 1950–54, Trinity Hall, Cambridge; Prof. of Civil Engineering, University Coll. of Swansea, 1954–61. Pro-Rector, Imperial Coll., London, 1972–74. Dean of City and Guilds Coll., 1964–67; Visiting Prof., Brown Univ., USA, 1959–60. Pres., Welding Inst., 1998–2000 (Chm., Res. Bd, 1974–98; Hon. FWeldI 1996). Pres., Croquet Assoc., 2004–09 (Vice Pres., 1995–2004; Council Medal, 2010). Telford Premium, 1951, Manby Premium, 1952, Instn Civil Engineers. *Publications:* The Plastic Methods of Structural Analysis, 1956; Structural Theorems and their Applications, 1964; technical papers on theory of structures, strength of materials. *Recreations:* lawn tennis, croquet. *Address:* 41 Asquith Road, Cheltenham GL53 7EJ. *T:* (01242) 510624. *Clubs:* All England Lawn Tennis and Croquet (Mem. Cttee, 1982–96; Vice-Pres., 1996–), Hurlingham; Cheltenham Croquet (Pres., 1995–).

NEAL, Prof. David Edgar, CBE 2014; FRCS, FMedSci; Professor of Surgical Oncology, University of Cambridge, 2002–14, now Emeritus, and Senior Visiting Fellow, since 2014; Honorary Consultant Urological Surgeon, Cambridge University Hospitals NHS Trust, 2002–14; Global Senior Vice President, Research (Academic), Elsevier, since 2014; *b* 9 March 1951; *s* of Norman and Beth Neal; *m* 1972, Deborah Mary Heyworth; three *d*. *Educ:* University Coll. London (BSc 1st Cl. Hons Anatomy; MB BS, MS). FRCS 1980. Tutor and Lectr in Surgery, Univ. of Leeds, 1981–83; First Asst in Urology, 1983–87, Sen. Lectr in Urological Surgery, 1988–92, Consultant Urologist, 1992–, Freeman Hosp., Newcastle upon Tyne; Prof. of Surgery, 1992–2002 and Dir, Med. Res., 1997–2002, Univ. of Newcastle upon Tyne. Mem., King's Fund Mgt Cttee, 1996–2002. Member: Council, RCS, 2002–12; Postgraduate Medical Educn and Trng Bd, 2003–09; Council, Acad. of Medical Scis, 2006–09. Hon. Mem., Urological Soc. Australia, 1999; Corresp. Mem., Amer. Assoc. Genito-urinary Surgeons, 1999. FMedSci 1998. St Peter's Medal, Brit. Assoc. of Urological Surgeons, 2001. *Publications:* Tumours in Urology, 1994; (jtly) Basic Science in Urology, 1999; contrib. articles to The Lancet, Annals Oncol., EMBO Jl, Nature genetics, Cancer Cell; over 480 peer-reviewed pubns. *Recreations:* playing the classical guitar, maintenance of classic motor cycles. *Address:* Department of Oncology, Addenbrooke's Hospital, Cambridge CB2 0QQ.

NEAL, Hon. Sir Eric (James), AC 1988; Kt 1982; CVO 1992; Governor, South Australia, 1996–2001; Chancellor, Flinders University, 2002–10; *b* 3 June 1924; *s* of James and May Neal; *m* 1950, Thelma Joan, *d* of R. E. Bowden; two *s*. *Educ:* South Australian Sch. of Mines. CEng, CPEng; FIGEM, FAIM. Boral Ltd: Dir, 1972–92; Chief Exec., 1973–87; Man. Dir, 1982–87; Chairman: Atlas Copco Australia Pty Ltd, 1989–96; Metal Manufacturers Ltd, 1990–96 (Dir, 1987–96); Director: Westpac Banking Corp., 1985–92 (Dep. Chm., 1987–88; Chm., 1989–92); John Fairfax Ltd, 1987–88; BHP Co. Ltd, 1988–94; Coca Cola Amatil Ltd, 1987–96. Mem., Australian Adv. Council, Gen. Motors, 1987–94. Mem., Cttee apptd by Fed. Govt to advise on Higher Defence Orgn, 1982. Mem., Amer. Bureau of Shipping, 1976–90; first Nat. Pres., Aust. Inst. of Co. Dirs, 1990–92. Chm. Exec. Cttee, Duke of Edinburgh's Sixth Commonwealth Study Conf. 1986; Nat. Chm., Duke of Edinburgh's Award Scheme in Australia, 1984–92; Internat. Trustee, Duke of Edinburgh's Award Internat. Assoc., 1986–97. Chief Comr, City of Sydney, 1987–88. Chm., SA Govt Veterans' Adv. Council, 2008–. Hon. FIEAust 1985; Hon. Fellow, Aust. Inst. of Building, 1998; Emeritus Mem., Aust. Inst. of Mgt, 1998; Life FAICD 2000. Hon. DEng Sydney, 1989; DUniv: S Australia, 1996; Flinders, 2001. US Dept of Defense Medal for Dist. Public Service, 1992. *Recreations:* naval history, travel, reading, shipping. *Address:* 82/52 Brougham Place, North Adelaide, SA 5006, Australia. *Clubs:* Adelaide (Adelaide); Melbourne (Melbourne).

NEAL, Frederick Albert, CMG 1990; FCIL; aviation consultant; UK Representative on Council of International Civil Aviation Organization, Montreal, 1983–93; *b* 22 Dec. 1932; *s* of Frederick William George Neal and Frances Elizabeth (*née* Duke); *m* 1958, Gloria Maria Moirano. *Educ:* Royal Grammar Sch., High Wycombe; Sch. of Slavonic Studies, Cambridge; Birkbeck Coll., London (BA). FCIL (FIL 1965). Min. of Supply, 1953; Asst Defence Supply Attaché, Bonn, 1958–64; Principal, Min. of Technology (subseq. DTI), 1967; Asst Sec., DTI, 1974; Counsellor (Economic and Commercial), Ottawa, 1975–80; Asst Sec., Dept of Trade, 1980–83. *Recreations:* golf, bridge, music. *Address:* 2 Hambledon Court, 19B Crescent East, Hadley Wood, Herts EN4 0EY. *Clubs:* Royal Over-Seas League; Hadley Wood Golf.

NEAL, (Harry) Morton, CBE 1991; FIC; Chairman, St Anselm Development Company Ltd, since 1985; *b* 21 Nov. 1931; *s* of late Godfrey French Neal and Janet Bryce Morton; *m* 1954, Cecilia Elizabeth Crawford, *d* of late Col M. Crawford, DSO; one *s* three *d*. *Educ:* Uppingham Sch.; London Univ. (BScEng); City and Guilds Coll. (ACGI). Flying Officer, RAF, 1953. Chm., Connaught Hotel Ltd, 1980–94 (Dir, 1966–97); Dir, Savoy Hotel Ltd, 1982–93. Chm., Harry Neal Ltd, 1985–2009. Member of Lloyd's. Chm., City and Guilds of London Inst., 1979–91 (Vice Pres., 1999–2004); Member: TEC, then BTEC, 1982–94; Court of City Univ., 1982–91; Delegacy, St Mary's Hosp. Med. Sch., 1993–98; Board of Governors: Imperial Coll., London, 1988–2001; Willesden Tech. Coll., 1983–86; Francis Holland Sch., 1988–2006 (Vice-Chm., 1996–2005); Mgt Cttee, Courtauld Inst. of Art, 1983–99; Court, Univ. of Herts, 2006–. Trustee: Buckminster Estate, 1969–2005; Samuel Courtauld Trust, 1989–2006; Prince of Wales Inst. of Architecture, 1991–99 (Mem., Bd of Advrs, 1993–99). President: Greater London Middx W County (formerly NW County) Scout Council, 1983–2007; City and Guilds Coll. Assoc., 1994–95; Herts Agricl Soc., 2004; City and Guilds Assoc., 2006–08. Liveryman, Carpenters' Co., 1955– (Master, 1997–98). High Sheriff, Herts, 1999–2000. FCIOB, FRSA; FCGI 1983. Hon. Fellow, Courtauld Inst. of Art, 2007; Fellow, Univ. of Herts, 2015. Chevalier de Tastevin, 1981. *Recreations:* gardening, shooting. *Address:* Great Sarratt Hall, Sarratt, Herts WD3 4PD.

NEAL, Michael David; Headmaster, Cranborne Chase School, 1969–83; *b* 27 Jan. 1927; *s* of David Neal, FCA; *m* 1952, Barbara Lisette, *d* of late Harold Carter, MA; two *s* two *d*. *Educ:* Winchester; University Coll., Oxford (BA); BSc Open Univ. 1996. Rifle Bde, 1945–48

(Captain); Asst Master, RNC Dartmouth, 1952–54; Eton Coll., 1954–69 (Housemaster, 1963–69). Mem., Eton UDC, 1960–63. Sec., PCC, St Peter's, Titley, Hereford, 1984–. *Address:* Wegnall's Mill, Presteigne, Powys LD8 2LD. *T:* (01544) 267012.

NEAL, Morton; *see* Neal, H. M.

NEALE, Sir Gerrard Anthony, (Sir Gerry), Kt 1990; *b* 25 June 1941; *s* of Charles Woodhouse Neale and Phyllis Muriel Neale; *m* 1st, 1965, Deirdre Elizabeth McCann (marr. diss. 2013); one *s* two *d*; 2nd, 2013, Susan Lorraine Harper. Councillor, Borough of Milton Keynes, 1973–79, Mayor, 1976–77. Chm., Buckingham Constituency Cons. Assoc., 1974–76. Contested (C) N Cornwall, Oct. 1974, 1992; MP (C) N Cornwall, 1979–92. PPS to Minister for Consumer Affairs, 1981–82, to Minister of State for Trade, 1981–83, to Sec. of State for Transport, 1985–86, to Sec. of State for the Environment, 1986–87, to Sec. of State for Defence, 1987–89. *Publications:* novels: Squaring Circles, 2011; If You Want To Say Yes, Say Yes, 2013; Win Some Lose Some, 2014. *Recreations:* sailing, golf, painting, writing and lyric writing.

NEALE, Gordon William, OBE 2002; consultant on disability sport, since 2010; Director of Events, Disability Sport Events (formerly Chief Executive, Disability Sport England), 1998–2010; *b* 10 April 1945; *s* of William and Lily Neale; *m* 2000, Elizabeth (*née* Irvine); one *s* one *d*. *Educ:* Beechfield Secondary Sch.; North London Univ. HM Forces, 1960–86 (GSM, Borneo, Malaya, NI; UN medal, Cyprus); Sport Develt Officer: Lee Valley Regl Park, 1986–88; English Volleyball Assoc., 1988–90; Disability Sport England, 1990–2010. Member Board: British Volleyball Fedn, 2008–; English Volleyball Assoc., 2008–. Chm. of Trustees, Cedars Trust Sch. and Sports Coll., Gateshead, 2010–. A torchbearer, London 2012 Olympics; commentator, London 2012 Paralympics. Silver Jubilee Medal, 1977; Peter Wardale Trophy, Volleyball England, 2014. *Recreations:* volleyball, swimming, cycling, disability sport. *Address:* 30 Holly Avenue, Whitley Bay, Tyne and Wear NE26 1ED. *T:* (0191) 252 0165, 07768 288030. *E:* mrgneale@btinternet.com. *Club:* Comrades (Whitley Bay).

NEALE, Gregory David; journalist, historian, broadcaster; Editor, 2000–04, and Founding Editor/Editor at large, since 2004, BBC History Magazine; *b* 1 May 1954; *s* of Lawrence Edwin Neale and Jean Alicia Neale (*née* Gilbert). *Educ:* Birkbeck Coll., London (BA Hons Hist.); Pembroke Coll., Oxford (MSt Modern Hist.). Work on newspapers, including: The Times, 1982–86; Daily Telegraph, 1987–89; Sunday Telegraph, 1989–99. Resident historian, Newsnight and The World, BBC TV, 2005–06. Editor, Oxford Today, 2007–11. Centenary Fellow, Historical Assoc., 2006. Hon. Vis. Fellow, Univ. of York, 2012–14. Editor of the Year, BSME, 2000, 2002. *Publications:* The Green Travel Guide, 1998, 2nd edn 1999; (with Tim Gopsill) Journalists: 100 years of the NUJ, 2007. *Recreations:* chess, choral singing, reading, walking, thinking about gardening. *E:* greg.neale@btinternet.com. *Clubs:* Frontline; Sutton United Supporters.

NEALE, Rt Rev. John Robert Geoffrey, AKC; *b* 21 Sept. 1926; *s* of late Geoffrey Brockman Neale and Stella Beatrice (*née* Wild). *Educ:* Felsted Sch.; King's Coll., London Univ. Served War of 1939–45: Lieut RA; Army, 1944–48. Business, G. B. Neale & Co. Ltd, EC2, 1948–51. King's Coll. London, 1951–55 (Jelf Prize, 1954). Deacon, 1955, priest, 1956; Curate, St Peter, St Helier, Dio. of Southwark, 1955–58. Chaplain, Ardingly Coll., Sussex, 1958–63; Recruitment Sec., CACTM (ACCM), 1963–67; Archbishops' Rep. for ordination candidates, 1967–68; Canon Missioner, Dio. of Guildford, Hon. Canon of Guildford Cath. and Rector of Hascombe, Surrey, 1968–74; Dir, Post Ordination Trng, 1974–88; Suffragan Bishop (later Area Bishop) of Ramsbury, 1974–88; Hon. Canon of Salisbury Cathedral, 1974–88; Archdeacon of Wilts, 1974–80; Dir, Diocesan Ordinands, 1976–88; Sec., Partnership for World Mission, 1989–91; Honorary Assistant Bishop: Dio. of Bath and Wells, 1991–2008; Dio. of Bristol, 1991–2015; Dio. of Gloucester, 1996–2004. FIC 1991. *Publications:* Ember Prayer, 1965. *Recreation:* horticulture. *Address:* Flat 2, 40 High Street, Corsham, Wilts SN13 0HB. *T:* (01249) 714110.

NEALE, Keith Douglas; independent adviser to pension funds, since 2002; *b* 27 March 1947; *s* of Douglas Jeffrey and Dorothy Neale; *m* 1969, Mary Williamson; one *s* one *d*. East Midlands Electricity Board, 1964; Trainee Accountant, Blackwell RDC, 1965; County Treasurer's Dept, Lindsey CC, Lincs, 1968; Asst Dir of Finance, Humberside CC, 1974; Dep. County Treasurer, 1982–87, County Treasurer, 1987–2002, Essex; Treasurer: Essex Police Authy, 1995–2002; Essex Fire Authy, 1998–2002. Treasurer: E Anglia Tourist Bd, 1987–96; E of England Tourist Bd, 1996–2006. Pres., Soc. of County Treasurers, 1998–99 (Hon. Sec., 1991–97; Vice-Pres., 1997–98); Advr, Policy Cttee, ACC, 1993–97. Member: CIPFA, 1969– (Mem., Pensions (formerly Superannuation) Panel, 1994–2003); UK Steering Cttee on Local Govt Pensions (formerly Superannuation), 1991–2002; Cttee, Nat. Assoc. of Pension Funds Investment, 1995–2000; Public Sector and Not-for-Profit Cttee, Accounting Standards Bd, 1999–2002. Freeman, City of London, 1999. *Address:* Moorfield House, 14 Hay Green, Danbury, Essex CM3 4NU. *T:* (01245) 222822.

NEALE, Kenneth James, OBE 1959; FSA; consultant; author and lecturer; Assistant Under Secretary of State, Home Office, 1976–82; *b* 9 June 1922; *s* of late James Edward and Elsie Neale; *m* 1943, Dorothy Willett; three *s* one *d*. *Educ:* Hackney Downs (Grocers') Sch., London. Entered Civil Service as Clerical Officer, Tithe Redemption Commn, 1939. Intelligence Officer, Home Guard, 1940–41; Lieut, RNVR, 1941–46. Exec. Officer, Min. of Nat. Insce, 1947–51; Asst Princ., 1951–55, Principal, 1955–64, Colonial Office; Sec. for Interior and Local Govt, Cyprus, 1957; Dep. Admin. Sec., Cyprus, 1958–59; Central African Office, 1962–64; Asst Sec., Commonwealth Office, and Counsellor, Diplomatic Service, 1964–67; Home Office: Asst Sec., 1967–70; Dir, Industries and Supply, 1970–75; Controller, Planning and Develt, 1976–80; Dir, Regimes and Services, 1980–82. Member: Prisons Bd, 1967–69, 1976–82; European Cttee on Crime Problems, 1976–84; Council of Europe Steering Gp on Reform of the Russian Prison System, 1995–2001; Chairman: Council of Europe Select Cttee on Standard Minimum Rules for Treatment of Prisoners, 1978–80; Council of Europe Cttee for Co-operation in Prison Affairs, 1981–84; Consultant: Prison Service Coll., 1982–90; Council of Europe, 1984–2001; Open Univ., 1990–93. Chairman: Essex Archaeol and Historical Congress, 1984–87 (Pres., 1987–90; Vice Pres., 2002–); Sampfords Soc., 1984–2004; Friends of Historic Essex, 1986–2002 (Vice Pres., 2002–); Member: Council, Essex Soc. for Archaeol. and Hist. (formerly Essex Archaeol Soc.), 1984–87; Library, Museum and Records Cttee, Essex CC, 1986–96; Essex Adv. Bd, Victoria County Hist., 2002–08; President: Chingford Hist. Soc., 1971–89; Saffron Walden Hist. Soc., 2000–; Sampfords Soc., 2010–. Mem. Editl Bd, Essex Jl, 1989–2002. *Publications:* Discovering Essex in London, 1970, 2nd edn 1986; Victorian Horsham, 1975; Work in Penal Institutions, 1976; Essex in History, 1977, 2nd edn 1997; Her Majesty's Commissioners, 1978; (ed) Strategies for Education within Prison Regimes, 1986; (ed) An Essex Tribute, 1987; (contrib.) Imprisonment: European perspectives, 1991; (ed) Essex Heritage, 1992; (ed) Prison Service People, 1993; (ed jtly) Essex Wills 1558–1603, vols 8–12, 1993–2000; (ed) Essex: 'full of profitable thinges', 1996; Heritage Sampford: community archaeology, historical research and landscape evaluation, 2007; various articles and papers on autobiographical records, local history, archaeology, natural history, penology. *Recreations:* reading, local history, archaeology, natural history. *Address:* Honeysuckle Cottage, Great Sampford, Saffron Walden, Essex CB10 2RW. *T:* (01799) 586304.

NEALE, Mark Frost, CB 2010; Chief Executive, Financial Services Compensation Scheme, since 2010; *b* 7 July 1957; *s* of Sir Alan (Derrett) Neale, KCB, MBE and Joan Neale (*née* Frost); *m* 1988, Xanthe Waddington Lunghi; one *s* one *d*. *Educ:* Queen's Coll., Oxford (BA 1st Cl. Hons Modern Hist. 1979). CSD, 1980–83; DES, then DFE, 1983–95; HM Treasury, 1995–98; Head, Structural Unemployment Policy Div., DFEE, 1998–2000; Dir, Finance and Commercial and Corporate Services, Employment Service, 2000–01; Dir, Children, Poverty and Housing, then Children and Housing, DWP, 2001–03; Dir Gen., Security, Internat. and Organised Crime, Home Office, 2003–05; Man. Dir, Budget, Tax and Welfare, HM Treasury, 2005–10. Mem. Council, Univ. of Roehampton, 2010–. *Recreation:* watching Chelsea FC. *Address:* Financial Services Compensation Scheme, 5th Floor, Lloyds Chambers, Portsoken Street, E1 8BN. *Club:* Reform.

NEALE, Michael Cooper, CB 1987; FIMechE; *b* 2 Dec. 1929; *s* of late Frank and Edith Kathleen Neale; *m* 1956, Thelma Weare; one *s* two *d*. *Educ:* West Bridgford Grammar Sch., Nottingham; Queen Mary Coll., Univ. of London (BScEng 1st cl. Hons; MScEng). Postgraduate research on fuel injection in diesel engines, 1951–53; Engr Officer, Royal Air Force, 1953–56; joined Civil Service, 1956; Aeroplane and Armament Experimental Estabt, Boscombe Down, 1956–58; joined Nat. Gas Turbine Estabt, Pyestock, 1958; Asst Director of Engine Develt, MoD Headquarters, 1971; Dep. Director (R&D), Nat. Gas Turbine Estabt, 1973–80; Dir Gen. Engines (PE), MoD, 1980–87; Sec., Royal Commn for Exhibn of 1851, 1987–94; non-exec. dir of cos and industrial consultant, 1988–96. Hon. Treas., Castleton Church, Dorset, 2002–08. Silver medallist, RAeS, 1987. *Publications:* papers in Aeronautical Research Council reports and memoranda series and elsewhere in the technical press, mainly concerning engines. *Recreations:* old railways, cricket as it used to be played. *Address:* Quill Cottage, 32 Hound Street, Sherborne, Dorset DT9 3AA. *T:* (01935) 814332. *Club:* Athenæum.

NEAME, Gareth Elwin; Managing Director, Carnival Film and Television Ltd, since 2004; *b* Beaconsfield, 8 March 1967; *s* of late Christopher Elwin Neame and Heather Marilyn Neame (*née* Wade); *m* 1995, Karen Elizabeth Hughes (marr. diss. 2001; she *d* 2010). *Educ:* Univ. of Birmingham (BA Hons Eng. and Drama 1988). Various roles in film and TV develt and prodn, 1988–93; producer, BBC drama, 1994–2000; independent producer, 1998–99; Hd, Drama Commissioning, BBC, 2000–04. Television productions include: as Producer: Truth or Dare, 1996; The Woman in White, The Missing Postman, 1997; Getting Hurt, 1998; All the King's Men, 1999; Happy Birthday Shakespeare, Take a Girl Like You; as Executive Producer: The Wyvern Mystery, Paranoid, Lorna Doone, 2000; Station Jim, 2001; Clocking Off, 2001–02; Murder, Tipping the Velvet, The Hound of the Baskervilles, 2002; Spooks, 2002–04; Trust, Cambridge Spies, State of Play, 2003; Red Cap, 2003–04; New Tricks, 2003–05; Gunpowder, Treason and Plot, Bodies, Conviction, Outlaws, The Grid, 2004; Hustle 2004–05; The Rotters Club, Fingersmith, Rome, 20,000 Streets Under the Sky, 2005; Hotel Babylon, 2006–09; Sea of Souls, Life Line, Empathy, Whistleblowers, The Old Curiosity Shop, 2007; Midnight Man, Harley Street, 2008; The Philanthropist, 2009; Material Girl, 2010; Downton Abbey, 2010–15; Page Eight, 2011; The Hollow Crown, 2012; Murder on the Home Front, Dracula, 2013; The 7:39, Turks and Caicos, Salting the Battlefield, 2014. Mem. Council, BAFTA, 2004–06. Ambassador, GREAT Britain Campaign, 2014–. David L. Wolper Award for Outstanding Producer, Producers Guild of America, 2012. *Recreations:* arts, literature, film and television, countryside, fine wine, travel. *Club:* Savile.

NEAME, Jonathan Beale; DL; Chief Executive, Shepherd Neame Ltd, since 2003; *b* Whitstable, 30 Jan. 1964; *s* of Robert Harry Beale Neame, *qv*; *m* 1996, Lucilla Margaret Baker; one *d*. *Educ:* Harrow (Leaving Schol.); Pembroke Coll., Cambridge (Open Exhibnr in Classics; Harris Meml Schol.; BA Hons Classics 1985; MA 1989); City Univ. (Dip. Legal Educn). Called to the Bar, Middle Temple, 1987; Associate Consultant, COBA Gp, 1987–91; Shepherd Neame Ltd: Co. Sec., 1991–94; Tenanted Trade Dir, 1994–98; Trade Dir, 1998–99; Man. Dir, 1999–2003. Non-executive Director: Invicta Radio Ltd, 1999–2004 (Chm., 2001–04); St Austell Brewery Co. Ltd, 2002–. Chm., British Beer and Pub Assoc., 2012–. Trustee, Leeds Castle Foundn, 2011–. Mem., Stour Fishery Assoc. Mem., Ct Assts, Brewers' Co. DL Kent, 2013. *Recreations:* cricket, ski-ing, Real tennis, walking, country pursuits. *Address:* Pheasant Farm, Church Road, Oare, Faversham, Kent ME13 0QB. *T:* (01795) 535366. *E:* jneame@shepherdneame.co.uk. *Clubs:* United and Cecil, MCC, Lord's Taverners; Royal St George's Golf; Kent County Cricket.

NEAME, Robert Harry Beale, CBE 1999; DL; President, Shepherd Neame Ltd, brewers, since 2006 (Chairman, 1971–2005); *b* 25 Feb. 1934; *s* of Jasper Beale Neame and Violet Evelyn Neame; *m* 1st, Sally Elizabeth Corben; one *s* two *d* (and one *s* decd); 2nd, 1974, Yvonne Mary Mackenzie; one *d*. *Educ:* Harrow (Head of School). Joined Shepherd Neame, 1956; Dir, 1957–2006; Dir and Chm., Faversham Laundry, 1961–70. SE Regl Dir, National Westminster Bank, 1982–92; Dir, SE Adv. Bd, Royal Insurance Co., 1988–2000; Director: Folkestone Racecourse, 1985–99 (Chm., 1988–99); Marr Taverns PLC, 1992–96; non-executive Director: Mendocino Brewing Co. (USA), 1998–2004; Merrydown plc, 1998–2004. Chairman: SE England Tourist Bd, 1979–90 (Vice-Pres., 1990–2003); Gatwick Airport Consultative Cttee, 1990–95; Member: SE RHA, 1977–78; Canterbury and Thanet RHA, 1990–94; Inland Waterways Amenities Adv. Council, 1992–98. Chairman, British Section: IULA, 1986–89; CEMR, 1986–89; Vice Chm., Consultative Council of Regl and Local Authorities, 1989. Mem. (C) for Faversham, Kent CC, 1965–89 (Leader, 1982–84). Pres., Kent CCC, 2003–04. DL 1992, High Sheriff, 2001, Kent. Hon. Alderman, Kent CC. Hon. DCL Kent, 2009. *Recreations:* cricket, squash, rackets (Army Rackets Champion, 1954), golf, shooting, ski-ing. *Address:* Dane Court Farmhouse, Kits Hill, Selling, Faversham, Kent ME13 9QP. *T:* (01227) 752284. *Clubs:* Press; MCC, Free Foresters, I Zingari, Band of Brothers, Butterflies; Kandahar Ski; Escorts, Jesters.
See also J. B. Neame.

NEARS, Colin Gray, CBE 1998; television producer; Member of Council, and Chairman of Advisory Panel on Dance, Arts Council of Great Britain, 1982–90; *b* 19 March 1933; *s* of William Charles Nears and Winifred Mildred Nears (*née* Gray). *Educ:* Ipswich Sch.; King's Coll., Cambridge (MA). Admin. Asst, RIBA, 1956; BBC, 1958–87; Producer: Schools Television, 1960; Music and Arts, 1967; Editor, Review, 1971–72. Author and director of programmes on literature, the visual arts, music and dance. Director: Royal Opera House, 1995–98 (Mem., 1990–98, Dep. Chm., 1991–98, Ballet Bd); Birmingham Royal Ballet Bd, 1993–2002 (Chm., 1993–99); Gov., Royal Ballet Sch., 1993–2000; Trustee: Royal Ballet Benevolent Fund, 1992– (Chm., 2011–13); Dancers' Resettlement Fund, subseq. Dancers' Career Develt, 1991–2013; Member Board: Riverside Trust, 1991–93; Rambert Dance Co., 1993–2001. FRSA. BAFTA award for Best Specialised Programme, 1973; Prix Italia music prize, 1982. *Recreations:* reading, gardening. *Address:* 16 Ashchurch Terrace, W12 9SL. *T:* (020) 8749 3615.

NEARY, Prof. Ian James, DPhil; Professor in the Politics of Japan, University of Oxford, since 2008 (Director, Nissan Institute of Japanese Studies, 2006–14; Head, School of Interdisciplinary Area Studies, 2011–14); Fellow, St Antony's College, Oxford, since 2004; *b* 9 July 1951; *s* of Kenneth and Joan Neary; *m* 1979, Suzuko Anai; one *s* one *d*. *Educ:* King Edward VII Grammar Sch., Sheffield; Sheffield Univ. (BA); Kyushu Univ.; Sussex Univ. (DPhil). Lecturer: Dept of Hist. and Politics, Huddersfield Poly., 1979–84; Dept of Politics, Newcastle Univ., 1984–89; Prof. of Japanese Politics, Dept of Government, Essex Univ., 1989–2004; Lectr in Japanese Politics, Univ. of Oxford, 2004–08. Pres., British Assoc. Japanese Studies, 1991–94. *Publications:* Politics, Protest and Social Control: origins of Buraku liberation, 1989; (with J. Howells) Intervention and Technological Innovation: government and the pharmaceutical industry in the UK and Japan, 1995; Human Rights in Japan, S Korea and Taiwan, 2002; The State and Politics in Japan, 2002; The Buraku Issue and Modern Japan,

2010; articles on Japan and human rights in Japan Forum, Social Res., etc. *Recreations:* running, triathlons, gardening, Witney Music Society. *Address:* Nissan Institute of Japanese Studies, 27 Winchester Road, Oxford OX2 6NA. *T:* (01865) 274570, *Fax:* (01865) 274574.

NEARY, Prof. (James) Peter, DPhil; FBA 2008; Professor of Economics, University of Oxford, since 2006; Fellow, Merton College, Oxford, since 2006; *b* Drogheda, Ireland, 11 Feb. 1950; *s* of late Peter Austin Neary and of Anne Rosemary Neary (*née* Loughran); *m* 1st, 1972, Frances Ruane (marr. diss. 1997); two *s*; 2nd, 1997, Mairéad Hanrahan; two *d*. *Educ:* Christian Brothers, Drogheda; Clongowes Wood Coll.; University Coll., Dublin (BA 1970; MA 1971); Univ. of Oxford (MPhil 1976; DPhil 1978). Res. Asst, Econ. and Soc. Res. Inst., Dublin, 1970–72; Trinity College, Dublin: Asst Lectr, 1972–74; Lectr, 1978–80; Fellow, 1980; Heyworth Res. Fellow, Nuffield Coll., Oxford, 1976–78; Prof. of Political Economy, University Coll., Dublin, 1980–2006. Visiting Scholar: MIT, 1978; Inst. for Internat. Econ. Studies, Stockholm, 1979; Internat. Inst. for Applied Systems Analysis, Laxenburg, 1981; Visiting Professor: Princeton Univ., 1980; Univ. of Calif, Berkeley, 1982; Queen's Univ., Ont., 1986–88; Univ. of Ulster, Jordanstown, 1992–93; Ecole Polytechnique, Paris, 1999–2000. Chm., Economics and Econometric Sub-Panel, UK REF 2014, 2010–. ERC Advanced Grant, 2012–. Co-Editor, Jl of Internat. Economics, 1980–83; Associate Editor: Economic Jl, 1981–85; Econometrica, 1984–87; Rev. of Economic Studies, 1984–93; Economica, 1996–2000; Ed., European Economic Rev., 1986–90. Fellow: Centre for Econ. Policy Res., 1983; Econometric Soc., 1987 (Mem. Council, 1994–99); Member: Council, Royal Econ. Soc., 1984–89, 1992–97; Eur. Econ. Assoc., 1985–92 (Pres., 2002; Fellow, 2004); President: Irish Econ. Assoc., 1990–92 Internat. Trade and Finance Soc., 1999–2000; Econs Section, BAAS, 2005. MAE 1989; Mem., RIA, 1997. Gold Medal in Soc. Scis, RIA, 2006. *Publications:* Measuring the Restrictiveness of International Trade Policy (with J. E. Anderson), 2005; (ed jtly) Natural Resources and the Macroeconomy, 1986; (ed jtly) Theory, Policy and Dynamics in International Trade, 1993; (ed) Readings in International Trade, 1995; over 100 articles, mainly on internat. economics. *Recreations:* family, travel, reading, music. *Address:* Department of Economics, Manor Road Building, Oxford OX1 3UQ.

NEARY, Martin Gerard James, LVO 1998; conductor and organist; Organist and Master of the Choristers, Westminster Abbey, 1988–98; Conductor, Millennium Consort Singers, since 2007; *b* 28 March 1940; *s* of late Leonard Walter Neary and of Jeanne Marguerite (*née* Thébault); *m* 1967, Penelope Jane, *d* of Sir Brian Warren and Dame Josephine Barnes, DBE; one *s* two *d*. *Educ:* HM Chapels Royal, St James's Palace; City of London Sch.; Gonville and Caius Coll., Cambridge (Organ Schol.; MA Theol. and Music). FRCO. Organist, St Mary's, Hornsey Rise, 1958; St Margaret's, Westminster: Asst Organist, 1963–65; Organist and Master of Music, 1965–71; Prof. of Organ, Trinity Coll., London, 1963–72; Organist and Master of Music, Winchester Cathedral, 1972–87. Organ Advr to dio. of Winchester, 1975–87. Conductor, Twickenham Musical Soc., 1966–72; Founder and Conductor: St Margaret's Westminster Singers, 1967–71; English Chamber Singers; Conductor, Waynflete Singers, 1972–88; Dir, Southern Cathedrals Festival, 1972, 1975, 1978, 1981, 1984, 1987; Conductor, Aspen Music Festival, 1980; Artistic Director: Paulist Choristers of California, 1999–2003; Pacific Acad. of Ecclesiastical Music, 2006–09; Dir of Music, First Congregational Ch of LA, 2001–02; Guest Conductor: Australian Youth Choir, 1999–; BBC Singers; Netherlands Chamber Choir; Chief Guest Conductor: Grand Rapids Choir of Men and Boys, 2010–; Salzburg Global Seminar Faculty, 2011. Consultant, Millennium Youth Choir, RSCM, 1999–2001. President: Cathedral Organists' Assoc., 1985–88; RCO, 1988–90, 1996–98 (Mem. Council, 1982–; a Vice-Pres., 1990–); Organists Charitable Trust (formerly Organists' Benevolent League), 1988–; John Carpenter Club, 1997–98; Chm., Herbert Howells Soc., 1993–; Mem., Exec. Cttee, Help Musicians UK (formerly Musicians Benevolent Fund), 1993– (Chm., Church Services Cttee, 1993–99). Music Advr, John Lyon's Charity, 2005–. Many organ recitals and broadcasts in UK, incl. Royal Festival Hall; has conducted many premières of music by British composers incl. John Tavener's Ultimos Ritos, 1979, and Akathist, 1988, Jonathan Harvey's Hymn, 1979, and Passion and Resurrection, 1981; conducted John Tavener's Veil of the Temple, Holland Fest., 2005; with Martin Neary Singers perf. madrigals and graces at 10 Downing Street, 1970–74. Toured US and Canada, 1963, 1968, 1971, 1973, 1975, 1977, 1979, 1982, 1984, 1986, 1988, 1992, 1996, appearances incl. Carnegie Hall, Lincoln Center, Kennedy Center, Roy Thomson Hall, Walt Disney Hall; many European tours, including Russia, 1994, Ukraine, 1996; BBC Promenade Concerts, incl. organ soloist on First Night, 2004; sometime Conductor with: ECO; LSO; BBCSO; Bournemouth SO and Sinfonietta; Acad. of Ancient Music; Winchester Baroque Ensemble; Orch. of the Age of Enlightenment; Arts Council Contemporary Music Network Tour, 1993; many recordings, incl. Purcell, Music for Queen Mary, Tavener, Akathist, and The Choirboys. FRSCM 1997. Hon. FTCL 1969; Hon. RAM 1988. Hon. DMus: Southampton, 1997; Lambeth, 2012. Hon. Citizen of Texas, 1971. Prizewinner, St Alban's Internat. Organ Festival, 1963; Conducting Scholarship, Berkshire Music Center, USA, 1963; Diploma, J. S. Bach Competn, Leipzig, 1968; UK/USA Bicentennial Fellow, 1979–80; Artist-in-residence, Univ. of California at Davis, 1984, 2007. *Compositions* include: What is Man?; May the grace of Christ (Nat. Anthem arr.); O worship the Lord, 2000; All Saints Mass, 2004; Joy and Woe, 2009; Mass of the Redeemer, 2011; responses, descants, carol and hymn arrangements, incl. Make me a channel of your peace. *Publications:* edns of early organ music; contribs to organ jls. *Recreations:* watching cricket, grandparental duties. *Address:* 13 Parkwood Road, Wimbledon, SW19 7AQ. *T:* and *Fax:* (020) 3016 7439. *E:* martin@mneary.co.uk. *Club:* Garrick.

NEARY, Most Rev. Michael; *see* Tuam, Archbishop of, (RC).

NEARY, Peter; *see* Neary, J. P.

NEATE, (Francis) Vincent (Hugh), CA; Partner, since 2007, and Head, UK Climate Change and Sustainability, since 2010, KPMG LLP; *b* London, 22 Jan. 1968; *s* of Francis Webb Neate and Patricia Ann Neate; *m* 1990, Emma Jane Pentland; two *s*. *Educ:* Colet Court; St Paul's Sch., Barnes; Univ. of Liverpool (BA Hons Philosophy 1992). CA 1995. Accountant, James and Cowper, Newbury, 1992–95; KPMG, 1995–. Mem., Global Adv. Council, Cornerstone Capital Inc., 2014–. Chair, Professional Standards Cttee, Eur. Private Equity and Venture Capital Assoc., 2009–14. Mem. Council, RIIA, 2014. Chair of Trustees: Fight for Peace Internat. Ltd, 2005–; Fight for Peace UK Ltd, 2005–; Trustee, From Babies with Love Ltd, 2012–. *Recreations:* reading, dog walking, gardening, drawing, ski-ing, sailing. *Address:* KPMG LLP, 15 Canada Square, E14 5GL.

NEATH, Gavin Ellis, CBE 2007; Senior Vice President, Sustainability, Unilever plc, 2011 (Senior Vice President, Global Communications, 2008–11); *b* 5 April 1953; *s* of late Ronald William Neath and Frances Gillian Neath; *m* 2006, Ann; three *d*. *Educ:* Univ. of Manchester; Univ. of Warwick; Stanford Univ. BA American Studies; MSc Mgt Scis. Unilever: graduate trainee, 1977; Mktg Dir, Lever France, 1985–90; Category Dir Laundry, Lever Europe, 1990–94; Man. Dir, Lever Ponds (SA), 1994–98; Chm., Unilever Bestfoods UK, 1998–2004; Chm., 2004–06, Nat. Manager, 2006–08, Unilever UK. Pres., Food and Drink Fedn, 2005–07. Mem. Develt Bd, Royal Court Th., 2005–08. Dep. Chm., St Margaret's Film Club. FIGD. *Recreations:* theatre, cinema, cricket, Rugby.

NEAVE, Sir Paul (Arundell), 7th Bt *cr* 1795, of Dagnam Park, Essex; *b* 13 Dec. 1948; *s* of Sir Arundell Thomas Clifton Neave, 6th Bt and Richenda Alice Ione (*d* 1994), *d* of Sir Robert Joshua Paul, 5th Bt; *S* father, 1992; *m* 1976, Coralie Jane Louise, *e d* of Sir Robin Kinahan, ERD; two *s*. *Educ:* Eton. *Heir: s* Frederick Paul Kinahan Neave, *b* 25 Jan. 1981. *Address:* Queen's House, Monk Sherborne, Hants RG26 5HH.

NEBHRAJANI, Sharmila, OBE 2014; Chair, Human Tissue Authority, since 2014 (Member, 2005–07); Director, External Affairs, Medical Research Council, since 2015; *d* of Vir and Jayantee Nebhrajani. *Educ:* City of London Sch. for Girls; St Anne's Coll., Oxford (BA 1st Cl. Physiolog. Scis (Medicine); MA). Mem. ICAEW 1991. Mgt Consultant, Coopers & Lybrand, 1988–93; Strategic Planning Manager, Cable & Wireless, 1993–95; Asst Dir, Corporate Finance, Price Waterhouse, 1995–96; Hd, Corporate Planning, BBC, 1996–2000; Chief Operating Officer, BBC Future Media and Technol., 2000–08; Dir, Financial and Commercial Strategy, BBC, 2008–09; Dir of Finance and Contracting, NHS Sussex (formerly E Sussex Downs and Weald, and Hastings and Rother PCTs), 2009–11; Chief Exec., Assoc. of Medical Res. Charities, 2011–14. Vice Chm., Human Fertilisation and Embryology Authy, 1998–2008. Member: Olympic Lottery Distributor, 2006–08; Audit Cttee, RSC, 2008–10; a Charity Comr, 2007–12; Audit Cttee and Ethics Cttee, Inst. of Cancer Res., 2011–; Bd, Pension Protection Fund, 2012–; Bd, Parly and Health Service Ombudsman, 2013–15. Dir, Towen Watson Master Trust Ltd, 2015–. Mem. Council, Univ. of Sussex, 2011–. Yale World Fellow, 2007. Mem. Bd, BMJ, 2014–. *Address:* (office) 151 Buckingham Palace Road, SW1W 9SZ.

NEČAS, Petr; MP (Civic Democratic), Zlin Region, 1992–2013; Prime Minister, Czech Republic, 2010–13; Leader, Civic Democratic Party, 2010–13; *b* Uherské, Hradiště, 19 Nov. 1964; *m* Radka Nečasová (marr. diss. 2013); two *s* two *d*; *m* 2013, Jana Nagyova. *Educ:* J. E. Purkyně Univ., Brno; Dr rer. nat. Mem., Foreign Affairs Cttee, Parlt of Czech Republic, 1992; Leader, Perm. Delegn to IPU and Delegn to WEU Assembly, 1992–96; First Dep. Minister of Defence, 1995–96; Shadow Minister of Defence, 1998; Dep. Prime Minister and Minister of Labour and Social Affairs, 2006–09. Civic Democratic Party: Mem., 1991–; Dep. Chm., 1999–2010. *Recreations:* politics, art.

NEEDHAM, family name of **Earl of Kilmorey**.

NEEDHAM, Phillip; Chief Executive, ADAS Group (formerly ADAS Agency), 1995–2000; *b* 21 April 1940; *s* of Ephraim and Mabel Jessie Needham; *m* 1962, Patricia Ann (*née* Farr); two *s* two *d*. *Educ:* Dunstable Grammar Sch.; Univ. of Birmingham (BSc); Imperial Coll., London Univ. (MSc, DIC). National Agricultural Advisory Service, subseq. Agricultural Development and Advisory Service, MAFF: Soil Scientist, 1961; Regional Soil Scientist, Reading, 1979; Hd of Soil Science, London, 1982; Sen. Agricl Scientist, 1985; Dep. Dir of R&D, 1987; Dir, Farm and Countryside Service and Commercial Dir, 1988–92; Dir of Ops, 1992–95. *Publications:* contribs to books and jls on various aspects of crop nutrition and soil science. *Address:* 58 Harpsden Road, Henley-on-Thames, Oxon RG9 1EG.

NEEDLE, Clive John; independent public policy advisor, since 1999; Director and Policy Advisor, EuroHealthNet (formerly European Network of Health Promoting Agencies), Brussels, since 2000. *Educ:* Southend High Sch.; Aston Univ. MEP (Lab) Norfolk, 1994–99; contested (Lab) Eastern Region, 1999, 2004. EU Rep., Health Action Partnerships Internat., 2010–13; Chairman: EU/EC Mental Health Platform, 2005–07; EU Public Health and Agriculture Consortium, 2011–12. Mem., Adv. Cttee on Public Health, 2012–, Adv. Gp on Tobacco, 2014–, WHO for Europe. Columnist, Eastern Daily Press, 2004–07.

NEEL, Janet; *see* Baroness Cohen of Pimlico.

NEELY, Prof. Andrew David, PhD; Director, Cambridge Service Alliance, since 2008; Professor of Manufacturing Engineering, University of Cambridge, since 2015; *b* Guisborough, 3 June 1967; *s* of John David and Elizabeth Anne Neely; *m* 1994, Anna-Liese Stubbs; two *s* two *d*. *Educ:* St Peter's Sch., York; Univ. of Nottingham (BEng 1989; PhD 1993); MA Cantab 1999. Res. Asst, Univ. of Nottingham, 1989–92; University of Cambridge: Sen. Res. Associate, 1992–95; Univ. Lectr, 1995–2000; Fellow, Churchill Coll., Cambridge, 1996–99; Prof. of Operations Mgt, Cranfield Sch. of Mgt, 2000–12; Dep. Dir, UK Advanced Inst. of Mgt Res., 2003–12; Royal Acad. of Engrg Prof. of Complex Services, Univ. of Cambridge, 2011–15. *Publications:* Measuring Business Performance, 1998; The Performance Prism, 2002; Managing Performance in Turbulent Times, 2011. *Address:* Institute for Manufacturing, University of Cambridge, 17 Babbage Road, Cambridge CB3 0FS. *T:* (01223) 766141. *E:* adn1000@cam.ac.uk.

NEELY, William Robert Nicholas; Chief Global Correspondent, NBC News, since 2013; *b* 21 May 1959; *s* of late William John Neely and of Patricia (*née* Larney); *m* 1988, Marion Kerr; two *d*. *Educ:* St Malachy's Coll., Belfast; Queen's Univ., Belfast (BA Jt Hons Eng. Lit. and Hist.). Reporter: BBC NI, 1981–86; BBC Network, 1987–88; Sky News, Jan.–June 1989; ITN, 1989–90; ITN: Washington Correspondent, 1991–97; Europe Correspondent, 1997–2002; International Editor, 2002–13. RTS News Awards, 1998 (World Cup), 2000 (European Football Championships), 2011 (Haiti earthquake); Internat. Emmy News Award, 2009 (China earthquake); BAFTA News Awards, 2009 (China earthquake), 2010 (Haiti earthquake), 2011 (Cumbria killings); Broadcasting Journalist of the Year, London Press Club, 2011. *Address:* NBC News, 200 Gray's Inn Road, WC1X 8XZ.

NEESON, Liam; *see* Neeson, W. J.

NEESON, Séan; Member (Alliance) Antrim East, Northern Ireland Assembly, 1998–2011; *b* 6 Feb. 1946; *s* of Patrick and Mary Neeson; *m* 1978, Carol Henderson; two *s* two *d*. *Educ:* Queen's Univ., Belfast (BA); St Joseph's Coll. of Educn, Belfast (Postgrad. Dip. in Educn 1968); Univ. of Ulster, Jordanstown (Postgrad. Dip. in Mktg 1988). Teacher, Head of History Dept, St Comgall's High Sch., Larne, 1968–85; marketing and PR consultant, 1988–98. Mem. (Alliance) Carrickfergus Council, 1977–2013; Mayor of Carrickfergus, 1993–94; Mem., NI Assembly, 1982–86. Leader, Alliance Party of NI, 1998–2001. Representative for NI: on Congress of Local and Regl Authorities in Europe, 2002; on Nat. Adv. Cttee on Historic Ships, 2007. Mem. Bd, Nat. Museums and Galleries (NI), 1998–2008. *Publications:* articles on maritime heritage in jls. *Recreation:* study of British and Irish maritime heritage. *Address:* 44 Milebush Park, Carrickfergus, Co. Antrim BT38 7QR. *T:* (028) 9336 4105.

NEESON, William John, (Liam), OBE 2000; actor; *b* Ballymena, NI, 7 June 1952; *s* of late Barney Neeson and of Katherine Neeson; *m* 1994, Natasha Jane Richardson, actress (*d* 2009); two *s*. Winner, NI Youth Heavyweight Boxing Championship. *Theatre* includes: The Risen, Lyric Players' Theatre, Belfast, 1976; Of Mice and Men, Abbey Theatre, Dublin; The Informer, Dublin Theatre Fest.; Translations, NT; The Plough and the Stars, Royal Exchange, Manchester; Anna Christie, Broadway, 1993; The Judas Kiss, Playhouse Theatre, 1998; The Crucible, Broadway, 2002; *films* include: Excalibur, 1981; Krull, 1983; The Bounty, 1984; Duet for One, Lamb, The Mission, 1986; A Prayer for the Dying, Suspect, 1987; The Dead Pool, The Good Mother, 1988; Darkman, Crossing the Line (retitled The Big Man, 1991), 1990; Shining Through, Under Suspicion, Leap of Faith, Husbands and Wives, 1992; Ethan Frome, 1993; Schindler's List, Nell, 1994; Rob Roy, 1995; Before and After, Michael Collins (Best Actor Award, Venice Film Fest.), 1996; Les Misérables, 1998; Star Wars Episode One: the Phantom Menace, The Haunting, 1999; Gangs of New York, K-19: The Widowmaker, 2002; Love Actually, 2003; Kinsey, Kingdom of Heaven, Batman Begins, 2005; Breakfast at Pluto, 2006; Seraphim Falls, 2007; Taken, 2008; Chloe, Clash of the Titans, The A-Team, 2010; Unknown, 2011; The Grey, Wrath of the Titans, The Dark Knight Rises, Battleship, Taken 2, 2012; Non-Stop, A Million Ways to Die in the West, A Walk Among the Tombstones, Third Person, 2014; Taken 3, Run All Night, 2015; *television* includes: A Woman of Substance, 1984; Arthur the King, 1985; Miami Vice, 1986; Hold the Dream, 1986; Sweet As You Are, 1987; Next of Kin, 1989; Five Minutes of Heaven, 2009.

NEGARA BRUNEI DARUSSALAM, HM Sultan of; Hassanal Bolkiah Mu'izzaddin Waddaulah, DKMB, DK, PSSUB, DPKG, DPKT, PSPNB, PSNB, PSLJ, SPMB, PANB; Hon. GCMG; DMN, DK (Kelantan), DK (Johor), DK (Negeri Sembilan), DK (Pahang); Ruler of Negara Brunei Darussalam (formerly Brunei), since 1967; Prime Minister, Negara Brunei Darussalam, since its independence, Jan. 1984; Minister of Defence, since 1986 (Finance and Home Affairs Minister, 1984–86); *b* 15 July 1946; *s* of Sultan Sir Muda Omar 'Ali Saifuddien Sa'adul Khairi Waddien, DKMB, DK, GCVO, KCMG, PSSUB, PHBS, PBLI (*d* 1986); *m* 1st, 1965, Rajah Isteri Anak Saleha; two *s* four *d*; *m* 1981, Pengiran Isteri Hajjah Mariam (marr. diss. 2003); two *s* two *d*; *m* 2005, Azrinaz Mazhar Hakim (marr. diss. 2010); one *s* one *d*. *Educ:* Victoria Inst., Kuala Lumpur; RMA Sandhurst (Hon. Captain, Coldstream Guards, 1968; Hon. General 1984). Collar of the Supreme Order of the Chrysanthemum; Grand Order of Mugunghwa. *Address:* Istana Nurul Iman, Bandar Seri Begawan, Negara Brunei Darussalam.

NEGISHI, Prof. Ei-ichi, PhD; Herbert C. Brown Distinguished Professor of Chemistry, since 1999 and Director, Negishi-Brown Institute, since 2011, Purdue University; *b* Changchun, China, 14 July 1935; *m* Sumire Suzuki; two *d*. *Educ:* Shonan High Sch.; Univ. of Tokyo (BS 1958); Univ. of Pennsylvania (Fulbright Smith-Mund Scholar, 1960; PhD 1963). Res. chemist, Iwakuni Res. Labs, Teijin Ltd, 1958–60; Postdoctoral Associate, 1966–68, Asst, 1968–72, Purdue Univ.; Asst Prof., 1972–76, Associate Prof., 1976–79, Syracuse Univ.; Purdue Univ., 1979–. Hon. DSc Purdue, 2012. (Jtly) Nobel Prize in Chemistry, 2010. Order of Culture (Japan), 2010. *Publications:* Organometallics in Organic Synthesis, vol. I, 1980; (ed) Handbook of Organopalladium Chemistry for Organic Synthesis, 2 vols, 2002; over 400 res. papers. *Address:* H. C. Brown Laboratory of Chemistry, Purdue University, 560 Oval Dreive, West Lafayette, IN 47907–2084, USA.

NEHER, Prof. Dr Erwin; Research Director, Max-Planck-Institut für biophysikalische Chemie, Göttingen, 1983–2011, now Emeritus; *b* 20 March 1944; *s* of Franz Xaver Neher and Elisabeth Neher; *m* 1978, Dr Eva-Maria Ruhr; three *s* two *d*. *Educ:* Technical Univ., Munich (PhD); Univ. of Wisconsin. Research Associate: Max-Planck-Inst. für Psychiatrie, Munich, 1970–72; Max-Planck-Inst. für biophysikalische Chemie, 1972–75 and 1976–83; Yale Univ., 1975–76; Fairchild Scholar, CIT, 1988–89. For. Mem., Royal Soc., 1994. Nat. and internat. sci. awards: (jtly) Nobel Prize in Physiology or Medicine, 1991. *Publications:* Elektronische Messtechnik in der Physiologie, 1974; (ed) Single Channel Recording, 1983. *Address:* Max-Planck-Institut für biophysikalische Chemie, Am Fassberg, 37077 Göttingen, Germany. *T:* (551) 2011675.

NEIDLE, Prof. Stephen, PhD, DSc, CChem, FRSC; Professor of Chemical Biology and Cancer Research UK Professorial Fellow, UCL School of Pharmacy, University College London (formerly School of Pharmacy, University of London), since 2002 (Director of Research, 2004–12); *b* 1 July 1946; *e s* of Michael and Hetty Neidle; *m* 1971, Andrea Anne Finn; two *s* one *d*. *Educ:* Hendon County Sch.; Imperial Coll., London (BSc 1967; PhD 1970; DSc 1995). CChem, FRSC 1999. ICI Research Fellow, Univ. of London, 1970–72; Mem., Scientific Staff, Dept of Biophysics, KCL, 1972–85; Institute of Cancer Research, University of London: Reader, 1986–90; Prof. of Biophysics, 1990–2002; Dean, 1997–2002. Vis. Prof., Univ. of Rome, 2006; Dist. Visitor, Baptist Univ. of Hong Kong, 2011. Guggenheim Lect., Univ. of Reading, 2005. Cancer Research Campaign: career develt awardee, 1979–85; Life Fellow, 1985–; Dir, Biomolecular Structure Unit, 1985–. Bristol-Myers Squibb Lectr, SUNY, 1993; Paul Ehrlich Lectr, Société de Chimie Thérapeutique, France, 2004; Pfizer Lectr, 2010. Chairman: Chemical Biol. Forum and Mem. Council, RSC, 2002–06; Cancer Chem. Wkg Gp, Amer. Assoc. for Cancer Res., 2011–12; Member: Funding Cttee, French Nat. Cancer Inst., 2010–12; Royal Soc. Ind. Fellow Panel, 2011–; Wellcome Trust Peer Rev. Panel, 2012–. Chm., Bd of Tetrahedron Publications, 2011–14. Hon. Fellow, Sch. of Pharmacy, Univ. of London, 2007. Pfizer Lectr, UK, 2010; Kelland Lectr, EORTC, 2011. Award in Bio-organic and Medicinal Chem., 1999, Interdisciplinary Award, 2002, Sovnovsky Award in Cancer Therapy, 2009–10, RSC; Aventis Prize in Medicinal Chem., Aventis Pharma, France, 2004. *Publications:* DNA Structure and Recognition, 1994; (ed) Oxford Handbook of Nucleic Acid Structure, 1999; Nucleic Acid Structure and Recognition, 2002; Principles of Nucleic Acid Structure, 2007 (ed) Cancer Drug Design and Discovery, 2007, 2nd edn 2013; Therapeutic Applications of Quadruplex Nucleic Acids, 2011; approx. 475 articles on nucleic acid structure and on design of anti-cancer and anti-infective drugs, and 12 patent filings. *Recreations:* film noir, theatre, ping-pong, walking, absorbing Yiddish culture. *Address:* UCL School of Pharmacy, University College London, 29–39 Brunswick Square, WC1N 1AX. *T:* (020) 7753 5800.

NEIGHBOUR, Roger Harvey, OBE 2011; FRCGP; consultant in medical education, since 2003; *b* 9 June 1947; *s* of late Kenneth George Neighbour and Eileen Nora Neighbour (*née* Roberts). *Educ:* Watford Grammar Sch.; King's Coll., Cambridge (BA 1968, MA 1972); St Thomas' Hosp. (MB BChir 1971). MRCGP 1975, FRCGP 1987; DObstRCOG 1975. GP, Abbots Langley, Herts, 1974–2003. Trainer, 1977–94, and Course Organiser, 1979–86, Watford Vocational Trng Scheme. Pres., RCGP, 2003–06. Mem., 1984–2004, and Convener, 1997–2002, Panel of MRCGP Examrs. Hon. FRCP 2004; Hon. FRACGP 2006. Hon. DSc Hertfordshire, 2004. *Publications:* The Inner Consultation, 1987, 2nd edn 2004; The Inner Apprentice, 1992, 2nd edn 2004; (jtly) The Successful GP Registrar's Companion, 2003; I'm Too Hot Now, 2005; papers on med. assessment and educn, psychotherapy and Franz Schubert; contribs to British Jl of Gen. Practice, Educn for Primary Care. *Recreations:* playing the violin, music of Schubert, France, writing, armchair philosophy, trying to give up golf. *Address:* Argowan, Bell Lane, Bedmond, Herts WD5 0QS; Appt 26, La Falaise d'Hacqueville, 52 rue Saint Gaud, 50400 Granville, France.

NEIL, Alexander; Member (SNP) Airdrie and Shotts, Scottish Parliament, since 2011 (Central Scotland, 1999–2011); Cabinet Secretary for Social Justice, Communities and Pensioners' Rights, since 2014; *b* 22 Aug. 1951; *s* of late Alexander Neil and Margaret Gunning Neil; *m* Isabella Kerr; one *s*. *Educ:* Dundee Univ. (MA Hons Econs 1973). Marketing Manager: Digital Equipment Corp., 1979–83; Future Technology Systems, 1983–84; Dir, Cumnock and Doon Enterprise Trust, 1983–88; Economic and Business Advr, 1988–. Dir, Prince's Scottish Youth Business Trust, 1988–90; non-exec. Dir and Chm., Network Scotland Ltd, 1989–96. Minister for Housing and Communities, 2009–11, Cabinet Sec. for Infrastructure and Capital Investment, 2011–12, for Health and Wellbeing, 2012–14, Scottish Parlt. *Recreations:* reading, travel. *Address:* 26 Overmills Road, Hazelbank, Ayr KA7 3LQ. *T:* (01292) 286675.

NEIL, Andrew Ferguson; publisher, broadcaster and company chairman; Editor-in-Chief, since 1996, Chief Executive, since 1999, and Chairman, since 2008, Press Holdings Media Group (formerly European Press Holdings; owner of The Spectator, Spectator Australia, Spectator Life, Spectator Health and Apollo magazines), since 2004; *b* Paisley, 21 May 1949; *s* of James and Mary Neil. *Educ:* Paisley Grammar Sch.; Univ. of Glasgow (MA Hons Politics and Economics, 1971). Conservative Res. Dept, 1971–72; joined The Economist, 1973; Correspondent in Belfast, London, NY and Washington, covering politics and business, 1973–82; UK Editor, London, 1982–83; Editor, The Sunday Times, 1983–94; Exec. Editor and Chief Correspondent, Fox Network News, NY, 1994; columnist, The Sunday Times and Daily Mail, 1995–96; Contributing Editor, Vanity Fair, NY, 1995–; Ed.-in-Chief, 1996–2006, Publisher, 1999–2006, The Scotsman, Scotland on Sunday and Edinburgh Evening News. Exec. Chm., Sky TV, 1988–90; Co-Proprietor and Dir, CGA and Country Magazine, 1990–97; Chairman: World Media Rights, London, 2005–; ITP, Dubai, 2006–; Peters, Fraser and Dunlop, London, 2008–10. Appears regularly on various current affairs television and radio programmes in Britain and America; presenter, television: formerly of The Midnight Hour, Westminster On-Line, Is This Your Life?, The Andrew Neil Show, Despatch Box, Thursday Night Live; Straight Talk with Andrew Neil; currently of The Daily Politics, Sunday Politics, This Week with Andrew Neil, formerly presenter, radio, Sunday Breakfast. Lord Rector, St Andrews Univ., 1999–2002. FRSA 1997. Journalist of the Year, Political Studies Assoc., 2013. *Publications:* The Cable Revolution, 1982; Britain's Free Press: Does It Have One?, 1988; Full Disclosure, 1996; British Excellence, 1998. *Recreations:* dining out in London, New York, Dubai and the Côte d'Azur, cycling. *Address:* Glenburn Enterprises Ltd, 8 Cadogan Square, SW1X 0JU. *Club:* Royal Automobile.

NEIL, Hilary Anne; *see* Chapman, H. A.

NEIL, Ronald John Baillie, CBE 1999; Chief Executive, BBC Production, 1996–98; *b* 16 June 1942; *s* of John Clark Neil and Jean McMillan Taylor; *m* 1967, Isobel Anne Clark. *Educ:* High Sch. of Glasgow. Reporter, Daily Express, 1961; BBC, 1967–98: Newsreader/Reporter, Reporting Scotland, 1967; Producer, Nationwide and 24 Hours, 1969; Output Editor, Nationwide, 1973; Dep. Editor, Newsnight, 1979; Editor: That's Life, 1981; Newsnight, 1981; Breakfast Time, 1983; Six O'Clock News, 1984; TV News, 1985; Dep. Dir, 1987–88, Dir, 1988–89, News and Current Affairs; Man. Dir, Regl Broadcasting, BBC, 1989. Chm., Fundraising and Communications Cttee, 2005–, Dep. Chm. Trustees, 2008–, RNLI. *Recreations:* food, wine. *Club:* Reform.

NEIL-DWYER, Glenn, FRCS, FRCSE; Consultant Neurosurgeon, Southampton University Hospitals NHS Trust, 1987–2002, now Honorary Emeritus; *b* 17 May 1938; *s* of Glen Shamrock Neil-Dwyer and Violet Agatha Hussey; *m* 1966, Jennifer Susan Edith Taylor; three *s*. *Educ:* Ruthin Sch.; St Mary's Hosp., London (MB BS; MS 1974). FRCSE 1967; FRCS 1968. Sen. House Officer, Neurosurgery, Addenbrooke's Hosp., 1968–69; Registrar, then Sen. Registrar, Wessex Neurol Centre, Southampton, 1969–74; Consultant Neurosurgeon: Cornwall Regl Hosp. and UCH (Jamaica), 1974–75; Brook Gen. Hosp., London, 1975–87; Consultant Advr in Neurosurgery to the Army, 1992–2005. Pres., Soc. of British Neurol Surgeons, 1998–2000 (Medal, 2015); Member, Council: RCS, 1998–2000; Med. Defence Union, 2000–08; Sec., Eur. Assoc. Neurosurgical Socs, 1999–2003 (Medal of Honour, 2007). Fellow, MDU, 2008. *Publications:* contrib. numerous papers to peer-reviewed jls on neurosurgical topics. *Recreations:* golf, sport, walking, travel, opera. *Address:* Annesley Glade, Bank, Lyndhurst, Hants SO43 7FD. *T:* (023) 8028 3352. *Club:* MCC.

NEILAND, Prof. Brendan Robert; Gallery Artist, Redfern Gallery, since 1992; Keeper of the Royal Academy, 1998–2004; *b* 23 Oct. 1941; *s* of Arthur Neiland and Joan Agnes Bessie Whiley; *m* 1970, Hilary Vivienne Salter; two *d*. *Educ:* Birmingham Sch. of Art (DipAD Hons); Royal Coll. of Art (MA). RE 1988–92 (Hon. RE 1998). Prof. of Painting, Univ. of Brighton, 1996–98. Vis. Prof. of Fine Art, Loughborough Univ., 1999. Exhibited: Angela Flowers Gall., 1970–78; Fischer Fine Art, 1978–92; Redfern Gall., 1993; retrospective exhibition, Turlej Gall., Crakow, Poland and Sharjah Art Museum, UAE, 2006; solo exhibitions: Redfern Gall., 2014; Galerie Belvedere, Singapore, 2015. Scholar, Crabtree Foundn, 1982. FRSA 1996. Hon. DArts de Montfort, 2013. Silver Medal, RCA, 1969; John Moores XI Prize, 1978; Daler Rowney Award, RA Summer Exhibn, 1989. *Publications:* Upon Reflection, 1997. *Recreations:* listening to the cricket commentary on Radio 4, drinking fine wines. *Address:* 2 Granard Road, SW12 8UL. *T:* and *Fax:* (020) 8673 4597. *Clubs:* Chelsea Arts, Arts.

NEILD, Prof. Robert Ralph; Professor of Economics, University of Cambridge, 1971–84, now Emeritus; Fellow of Trinity College, Cambridge, since 1971; *b* 10 Sept. 1924; *o s* of Ralph and Josephine Neild, Letchmore Heath, Hertfordshire; *m* 1st, 1957, Nora Clemens Sayre (marr. diss. 1961); 2nd, 1962, Elizabeth Walton Griffiths (marr. diss. 1986); one *s* four *d* (incl. twin *d*); 3rd, 2004, Virginia Matheson. *Educ:* Charterhouse; Trinity Coll., Cambridge. Royal Air Force, 1943–44; Operational Research, 1944–45. Secretariat of United Nations Economic Commission for Europe, Geneva, 1947–51; Economic Section, Cabinet Office and Treasury, 1951–56; Lecturer in Economics, and Fellow, Trinity College, Cambridge, 1956–58; National Institute of Economic and Social Research: at first as Editor of its Quarterly Economic Review; then as Deputy Director of the Institute, 1958–64; MIT Center for International Studies, India Project, New Delhi, 1962–63; Economic Adviser to HM Treasury, 1964–67; Dir, Stockholm Internat. Peace Research Inst., 1967–71. Vis. Fulbright Prof., Hampshire Coll. and Five Colls, Amherst, Mass, USA, 1985. Mem., Fulton Cttee on Reform of CS, 1966–68; Vice-Chm., Armstrong Cttee on Budgetary Reform in UK, Inst. for Fiscal Studies, 1979–80. Director: Nat. Mutual Life Assce Soc., 1959–64; Investing in Success Equities Ltd, 1961–64, 1972–87. *Publications:* Pricing and Employment in the Trade Cycle, 1964; (with T. S. Ward) The Measurement and Reform of Budgetary Policy, 1978; Tax Policy in Papua New Guinea, 1980; How to Make Up Your Mind about the Bomb, 1981; An Essay on Strategy, 1990; (ed with A. Boserup) The Foundations of Defensive Defence, 1990; The English, the French and the Oyster, 1995; Public Corruption: the dark side of social evolution, 2002; Riches and Responsibility: the financial history of Trinity College, Cambridge, 2008; The Financial History of Cambridge University, 2012; articles on economics, defence and other subjects. *Recreations:* oysters, painting. *Address:* Trinity College, Cambridge CB2 1TQ.

NEILL, family name of **Baron Neill of Bladen**.

NEILL OF BLADEN, Baron *cr* 1997 (Life Peer), of Briantspuddle in the co. of Dorset; **Francis Patrick Neill,** Kt 1983; QC 1966; Chairman, Committee on Standards in Public Life, 1997–2001; Warden of All Souls College, Oxford, 1977–95; Vice-Chancellor, Oxford University, 1985–89; *b* 8 Aug. 1926; *s* of late Sir Thomas Neill, JP, and Lady (Annie Strachan) Neill (*née* Bishop); *m* 1954, Caroline Susan (*d* 2010), *d* of late Sir Piers Debenham, 2nd Bt, and Lady (Angela) Debenham; three *s* two *d* (and one *s* decd). *Educ:* Highgate Sch.; Magdalen College, Oxford (Hon. Fellow, 1988). Gibbs Law Scholar, 1949; Eldon Law Scholar, 1950. BA 1950; BCL 1951; MA 1972. Served Rifle Brigade, 1944–47 (Captain); GSO III (Training), British Troops Egypt, 1947. Fellow of All Souls Coll., Oxford, 1950–77, Sub-Warden 1972–74, Hon. Fellow, 1997; Lectr in Air Law, LSE, 1955–58. Called to the Bar, Gray's Inn, 1951; Bencher, 1971; Vice-Treas., 1989; Treas., 1990; Member, Bar Council, 1967–71, Vice-Chm., 1973–74, Chm., 1974–75; Chm., Senate of the Inns of Court and the Bar, 1974–75; a Recorder of the Crown Court, 1975–78; a Judge, Cts of Appeal of Jersey and Guernsey, 1977–94. Chm., Justice—All Souls Cttee for Rev. of Admin. Law, 1978–87. Chairman: Press Council, 1978–83; DTI Cttee of Inquiry into Regulatory Arrangements at Lloyd's, 1986–87; Feltrim Loss Review Cttee at Lloyd's, 1991–92; first Chm., Council for the Securities Industry, 1978–85; Vice-Chm., CVCP, 1987–89. Independent Nat. Dir, Times Newspaper Hldgs, 1988–97. Hon. Prof. of Legal Ethics, Birmingham Univ., 1983–84. Hon. LLD: Hull, 1978; Buckingham, 1994; Hon. DCL Oxon, 1987. *Publications:* Administrative Justice: some necessary reforms, 1988. *Recreation:* music and forestry. *Address:* 20 Essex Street, WC2R 3AL. *Clubs:* Athenæum, Garrick, Beefsteak, Oxford and Cambridge.

See also Rt Hon. Sir Christopher Geidt, Rt Hon. Sir Brian Neill.

NEILL, Alistair, FFA, FIA; General Manager, Scottish Widows' Fund & Life Assurance Society, 1988–92; President, Faculty of Actuaries in Scotland, 1990–92; *b* 18 Nov. 1932; *s* of Alexander Neill and Marion Wilson; *m* 1958, Mary Margaret Hunter; one *s* two *d*. *Educ:* George Watson's Coll., Edinburgh; Univ. of Edinburgh (John Welsh Math. Bursar; MA 1953); Univ. of Wisconsin (Fulbright Grantee; MS 1954); BSc Open Univ. 2001. Instructor Lieut, RN, 1958–60. Actuarial management posts in Scottish Widows' Fund, 1961–92. Chm., Pensions Cttee, ABI, 1986–92. *Publications:* Life Contingencies, 1977, 5th edn 1989. *Recreations:* golf, model railways. *Address:* 24 Bonaly Crescent, Edinburgh EH13 0EW. *T:* (0131) 441 2038.

NEILL, Alistair Klaas, GM 2012; Chief Executive, Herefordshire Council, since 2013; *b* 5 Nov. 1956; *s* of John and Woutertje Neill; *m* 1992, Kathryn Shapland; one *s* two *d*. *Educ:* Glasgow Univ. (MA English and Philos.; DMS in Business, distn). Marketing Manager, Unilever, 1983–88; Marketing Dir UK and CEO Asia-Pacific, BP, 1988–95; Pres. Internat. Ops, Masco Corp., 1995–2002; Chief Operating Officer, Northants CC, 2002–03; Chief Executive: Merthyr Tydfil CBC, 2003–10; Southampton CC, 2010–13. Conducted Capability Revs of DTI, later BERR, Prime Minister's Delivery Unit, 2007, and Cabinet Office, 2008. Lectr in Mgt, Warwick, Cardiff and HK Univs. MInstD 1992. Leading Wales Award, 2005, 2006; Nat. Police Public Bravery Award, 2012; Pride of Britain Award, 2012. *Publications:* Sick Pay Schemes, and Causes of Malingering, 1979. *Recreations:* my wife, children, walking in Brecon Beacons, France, playing guitar, singing woefully. *Address:* Herefordshire Council, Brockington, Hereford HR1 1SH. *T:* 07792 881727. *E:* alistair.neill@yahoo.co.uk. *Clubs:* Cardiff Business, Solent Business (Southampton).

NEILL, Rt Hon. Sir Brian (Thomas), Kt 1978; PC 1985; a Lord Justice of Appeal, 1985–96; a Justice of Appeal, 1997–98, and President, 1998–2003, Court of Appeal for Gibraltar; *b* 2 Aug. 1923; *s* of late Sir Thomas Neill and Lady (Annie Strachan) Neill (*née* Bishop); *m* 1956, Sally Margaret (*d* 2009), *d* of late Sydney Eric and Marguerite Backus; three *s*. *Educ:* Highgate Sch.; Corpus Christi Coll., Oxford (Hon. Fellow 1986). Rifle Brigade, 1942–46 (Capt.). MA Oxford. Called to the Bar, Inner Temple, 1949, Bencher, 1976. QC 1968; a Recorder of the Crown Court, 1972–78; a Judge of the High Court, Queen's Bench Div., 1978–84. A Judge of the Commercial and Admiralty Courts, 1980–84; a Judge of Employment Appeal Tribunal, 1981–84. Mem., Departmental Cttee to examine operation of Section 2 of Official Secrets Act, 1971; Chairman: Adv. Cttee on Rhodesia Travel Restrictions, 1973–78; IT and the Courts Cttee, 1985–96; Supreme Court Procedure Cttee, 1986–90; Civil Mediation Council, 2003–06. Hon. Mem., Ct of Assts, 1998– (Mem., 1972–98), Master, 1980–81, Turners' Co. Chm. of Trustees, Lord Slynn of Hadley European Law Foundn, 2003–12. Governor, Highgate Sch., 1969–90. *Publications:* (with Colin Duncan) Defamation, 1978, 4th edn (ed jtly), 2015. *Clubs:* MCC, Hurlingham, Garrick.

See also Baron Neill of Bladen.

NEILL, Rev. Bruce Ferguson; Church of Scotland Minister, Maxton and Mertoun: with St Boswells, 1996–2007; with Newtown, 2006–07; *b* 9 Jan. 1941; *s* of Thomas Ferguson Neill and Jane (*née* Bruce); *m* 1966, Ishbel Macdonald; two *s* one *d*. *Educ:* Lesmahagow Primary; Hamilton Academy; Glasgow Univ. and Trinity Coll., Glasgow (MA, BD). Probationer Asst, Drumchapel Old Parish Church, 1964–66; Minister, Dunfermline Townhill Parish Church, 1966–71; commnd as Chaplain, RN, 1971; Naval appts include: HMS Drake, 1972; RM, 1972; HMS Seahawk, 1974; HMS Cochrane, 1976; ships of 1st and 2nd Flotillas, 1979; HMS Dryad, 1981; Britannia RNC, 1983; HMS Cochrane, 1986; ships of Minor War Vessels Flotilla, 1989–91; Prin. Naval Chaplain, Church of Scotland and Free Churches, 1991–96. QHC, 1991–96. *Recreations:* gardening, hill walking, woodwork, model making.

NEILL, Sir (James) Hugh, KCVO 1996; CBE 1969; TD 1950; JP; Lord-Lieutenant for South Yorkshire, 1985–96; Chairman, James Neill Holdings, 1963–89; *b* 29 March 1921; *o s* of Col Sir Frederick Neill, CBE, DSO, TD, DL, JP, and Lady (Winifred Margaret) Neill (*née* Colver); *m* 1st, 1943, Jane Margaret Shuttleworth (*d* 1980); two *d*; 2nd, 1982, Anne O'Leary; one *s*. *Educ:* Rugby School. War service with RE and Royal Bombay Sappers and Miners, UK, Norway, India, Burma and Germany, 1939–46 (despatches, Burma, 1945). Mem., British Overseas Trade Bd, 1973–78; Pres., European Tool Cttee, 1972–76; Mem., Trent Regional Health Authority, 1974–80; Chm. Exec. Cttee, Sheffield Council for Voluntary Service, 1953–87; Mem. Council, CBI, 1965–83; Chm., E and W Ridings Regional Council, FBI, 1962–64; Pres., Nat. Fedn of Engrs Tool Manufrs, 1963–65; Pres., Fedn of British Hand Tool Manufrs, 1960–61. Pres., Sheffield Chamber of Commerce, 1984–85. FCMI. Hon. Col, 3rd Bn Yorks Vol., subseq. 3rd/4th Bn Yorks Vol., later 3rd Bn Duke of Wellington's, 1988–93. Chm., Yorks & Humberside TAVRA, 1991–94. Hon. Fellow, Sheffield City Polytechnic, 1978; Hon. LLD Sheffield, 1982. Master Cutler of Hallamshire, 1958; High Sheriff of Hallamshire, 1971; DL South Yorkshire, 1974, JP 1985. KStJ 1985. *Recreation:* golf. *Address:* Barn Cottage, Lindrick Common, near Worksop S81 8BA. *T:* (01909) 562806. *Clubs:* East India; Lindrick (Worksop); Royal and Ancient (St Andrews); Hon. Co. of Edinburgh Golfers (Muirfield).

NEILL, John Mitchell, CBE 1994; Chief Executive, since 1987, and Chairman, since 2012, Unipart Group of Companies; *b* 21 July 1947; *s* of Justin Bernard Neill and Johanna Elizabeth Neill; *m* 1975, Jacquelyn Anne, *d* of late Philip Brown; two *s*. *Educ:* George Heriot's Sch., Edinburgh; Univ. of Strathclyde (BA, MBA, DBA). Europe AC Delco: Planning Manager, 1969–71; Marketing Manager, 1972–73; British Leyland: Merchandising Manager, 1974–75, Sales and Marketing Dir, 1976, Parts Div.; Managing Director: Car Parts Div., 1977–78; BL Components, 1979–80; Unipart Gp, 1981–82; Gp Man. Dir, Unipart Gp Ltd, 1983–86. A Dir, Bank of England, 1996–2003. Chm., Atlantis Resources Ltd, 2013–; Dir, Charter International (formerly Charter) plc, 1994–2012; non-exec. Dir, Rolls-Royce plc, 2008–. Dir, BITC, 1992–. Vice President: Inst. of Mktg, 2002– (Pres., 2000–01; Dep. Pres., 2001–02); Inst. of Motor Industry; BEN; Pres., SMMT, 2000–01. Trustee, Nat. Motor Mus. *Address:* Unipart Group of Companies Ltd, Unipart House, Cowley, Oxford OX4 2PG.

NEILL, Most Rev. John Robert Winder; Archbishop of Dublin, and Primate of Ireland, 2002–11; *b* 17 Dec. 1945; *s* of Eberto Mahon Neill and Rhoda Anne Georgina Neill; *m* 1968, Betty Anne (*née* Cox); three *s*. *Educ:* Sandford Park School, Dublin; Trinity Coll., Dublin (Foundation Schol., BA 1st Cl., MA); Jesus Coll., Cambridge (MA, Gardiner Memorial Schol., Univ. of Cambridge); Ridley Hall, Cambridge (GOE). Curate Asst, St Paul's, Glenageary, Dublin, 1969–71; Lectr (Old Testament) in Divinity Hostel, 1970–71; Bishop's Vicar and Dio. Registrar, Kilkenny, 1971–74; Rector of Abbeystrewry, Skibbereen, Co. Cork, 1974–78; Rector of St Bartholomew's, and Leeson Park, Dublin, 1978–84; Lectr (Liturgy) in Theological Coll., 1982–84; Exam. Chaplain to Archbishop of Dublin, 1982–84; Dean of Christ Church Cathedral, Waterford, 1984–86; Archdeacon of Waterford, 1984–86; Bishop: of Tuam, Killala and Achonry, 1986–97; of Cashel and Ossory, 1997–2002; of Dublin and Glendalough, 2002–11. Sec., Irish House of Bishops, 1988–95; Mem., Central Cttee, WCC, 1994–2006; Pres., CTBI, 1999–2002. Hon. LLD NUI, 2003. *Publications:* contribs to Theology, New Divinity, Search, Doctrine and Life and Intercom. *Recreations:* photography, travel. *Address:* Knockglass, Annamult Road, Bennettsbridge, Co. Kilkenny, Ireland.

NEILL, Nigel John Dermot, (Sam), DCNZM 2007; OBE 1992; actor; *b* 14 Sept. 1947; *s* of Dermot Neill and Priscilla Beatrice Neill (Ingham); *m* 1989, Noriko Watanabe; two *s* two *d*. *Educ:* Christ's Coll., Canterbury, NZ; Canterbury Univ., NZ (BA 1971). Director, NZ Nat. Film Unit, 1973–78; freelance actor, 1978–. *Films* include: My Brilliant Career, 1979; A Cry in the Dark, 1988; Dead Calm, 1989; Death in Brunswick, 1991; The Piano, Jurassic Park, 1993; In the Mouth of Madness, 1995; Restoration, 1996; The Event Horizon, 1997; Dish, 2000; Jurassic Park III, 2001; Dirty Deeds, 2003; Angel, 2007; Dean Spanley, 2008; Skin, 2009; The Vow, 2012; A Long Way Down, 2014; *television* includes: Reilly: the Ace of Spies (series), 1983; Jessica, 2004; Mary Bryant (series), 2005; Merlin, 2006; The Tudors (series), 2007; Alcatraz (series), 2012; Peaky Blinders (series), 2013–. Wine producer, Two Paddocks Wine, Queenstown, NZ, 1973–. Hon. DLitt Canterbury, NZ, 2002. *Recreations:* drinking, idling, farming, dogs, ski-ing, fly fishing, reading, ukelele, conviviality and isolation. *Address:* c/o Shanahan Management, Level 3 Berman House, 91 Campbell Street, Surry Hills, Sydney, NSW 2010, Australia.

NEILL, Robert James Macgillivray; MP (C) Bromley and Chislehurst, since June 2006; *b* 24 June 1952; *s* of John Macgillivray Neill and Elsie May Neill (*née* Chaston); *m* 2009, Daphne White. *Educ:* London Sch. of Econs (LLB Hons 1973). Called to the Bar, Middle Temple, 1975; barrister in private practice, 1975–2006. Member (C): Havering BC, 1974–90 (Chm., Envmt and Social Services Cttees); Romford, GLC, 1985–86; Greater London Authority: Mem. (C) Bexley and Bromley, London Assembly, 2000–08; Leader, Cons. Gp, 2000–02, 2004–06; Chair, Planning and Spatial Develt Cttee, 2002–04. Shadow Minister for Local Govt, 2007–10; Parly Under-Sec. of State, DCLG, 2010–12. Mem., Select Cttee on Justice and Constitutional Affairs, 2006–10; Chm., Select Cttee on Justice, 2015–. Mem., UK Delegn to Parly Assembly of Council of Europe, 2012–. Vice Chm., Cons. Party, 2012–. Dep. Chm., Commn on London Governance, 2004–06. Leader, London Fire and Civil Defence Authy, 1985–87. Mem., Metropolitan Police Authy, 2004–08. Regl Chm., Gtr London Cons. Party, 1996–99 (Dep. Chm., 1993–96). Contested (C) Dagenham, 1983 and 1987. Mem., UK Delegn, Cttee of Regions of EU, 2002–08. Non-exec. Dir, NE London HA, 2002–06. *Recreations:* opera, travel, sailing. *Address:* House of Commons, SW1A 0AA. *Club:* Carlton.

NEILL, Sam; *see* Neill, N. J. D.

NEILSON, Ian (Godfrey), DFC 1944; TD 1951; *b* 4 Dec. 1918; *er s* of James Wilson Neilson, solicitor, Glasgow; *m* 1945, D. Alison St Clair Aytoun, Ashintully; one *s* one *d*. *Educ:* Glasgow Acad.; Glasgow Univ. (BL). Legal Trng, Glasgow, 1935–39; Territorial Army, 1938; commnd June 1939; War Service, 1939–45: Field Artillery; Air Observation Post, 1940; RA Staff, HQ 21 Army Gp, 1944; Lt-Col comdg War Crimes Investigation Unit, Germany, 1945–46; formed and commanded No 666 (Scottish) Sqdn, RAuxAF, 1948–53. Enrolled Solicitor, 1946. Royal Institution of Chartered Surveyors: Scottish Sec., Edinburgh, 1946–53; Asst Sec., London, 1953–61; Under-Sec., 1961–65; The Boys' Brigade: Brigade Sec., 1966–74; Officer, 5th Mid-Surrey Co., 1972–78; Nat. Hon. Vice-Pres., 1982–; Hon. Vice-Pres., W of England Dist, 1983–. Clerk to Governors of the Cripplegate Foundn, Cripplegate Educnl Foundn, Trustees of St Giles and St Luke's Jt Parochial Charities, and Governors of the Cripplegate Schs Foundn, 1974–81. Hon. Treasurer, Thames Youth Venture Adv. Council (City Parochial Foundn), 1968–76. Vice-Chm., British Council of Churches Youth Dept, 1971–74; Trustee: St George's Chapel, London Airport, 1978–97 (Chm., 1983–96); Douglas Haig Meml Homes, 1979–96; Mem., Nat. Council for Voluntary Youth Services, 1966–74; Pres., London Br., Glasgow Academical Club, 1977–79; Chm. of Governors, Lucas-Tooth Leadership Training Fund for Boys, 1976–83; Governor, Kingsway-Princeton Coll. of Further Educn, 1977–83. Elder, United Reformed Church, St Andrew's, Cheam, 1972–83; Lay Mem., Provincial Ministerial Cttee, URC, 1974–83; Dir and Jt Sec., URC Trust, 1982–95; Mem. Council: Christchurch, Marlborough, 1984–90, 1992–97; St Peter's and St Paul's Trust, Marlborough, 1985–2012. BIM: Hon. Sec., City of London Branch, 1976–79, Chm., 1979–81, Vice Pres., 1981–87; Chm., Inner London Branches Area Cttee, 1981–83; FCMI (FBIM 1980). Sen. Instr, Royal Yachting Assoc., 1977–87; Chm., Air Observation Post Officers Assoc., 2012– (Vice Pres. and Vice Chm., 1978–2012). Chm., Epsom Choral Soc., 1977–81; Mem., Marlborough Coll. Choral Soc., 1985–2003. Mem., Marlborough Probus Club, 1993 (Chm. 1998–99). Member: Soc. for Army Histl Res., 1997–; Air-Britain (Historians), 2006–. Freeman, City of London, 1975; Freeman, GAPAN, 1976–78, Liveryman, 1978–2004; Chm., Queenhithe Ward Club, 1977–78. Hon. Editor, Tower and Town, Marlborough, 1984–95; Compiler and Reader, Talking Newspaper for the Blind, Marlborough, 1987–2003. *Recreations:* music, gardening. *Address:* The Paddock, Kingsbury Street, Marlborough, Wilts SN8 1HZ. *T:* (01672) 515114. *Clubs:* Marlborough Golf; Chartered Surveyors' Golfing Society (Hon. Mem.).

NEILSON, John Stuart; Secretary and Registrar, Imperial College London, since 2012; *b* 31 May 1959; *s* of late Ian Neilson, ISO, and Dr Betty Neilson (*née* Harley); *m* 1985, Alison Christine Green; one *s* one *d*. *Educ:* St Paul's Sch.; Corpus Christi Coll., Cambridge (BA 1st Cl. Hons 1980; Prize for Mgt Studies, ICE, 1980). Joined Department of Energy, 1980: Second Private Sec. to Sec. of State for Energy, 1983–85; Principal, 1985; on secondment to Econ. Secretariat, Cabinet Office, 1988–89; Principal Private Sec. to Sec. of State for Energy, 1989–92; Department of Trade and Industry: Private Sec. to Minister for Energy, 1992–93; Asst Sec., 1993; Director: UK Communications Policy, 1993–97; Aerospace and Defence Industries Policy, 1997–2000; Man. Dir, Customers and Supply, Ofgem, 2000–05; Gp Dir, Sci. and Engrg Base Gp, Office of Sci. and Technol., then Res. Base, Office of Sci. and Innovation, DTI, later Res. Base, DIUS, subseq. BIS, 2005–11; Dir, Financial Mgt, MoD, 2011–12. Mem., Audit Cttee, Archbishop's Council, 2007–. Trustee, Royal Albert Hall, 2013–. *Address:* Faculty Building, South Kensington Campus, Imperial College London, SW7 2AZ. *T:* (020) 7594 7272. *E:* j.neilson@imperial.ac.uk. *Club:* Athenæum.

NEILSON, Margaret Marion; Sheriff of Grampian, Highland and Islands at Inverness, since 2009; *b* Falkirk, 21 Feb. 1958; *d* of Alistair Fleming Neilson and Agnes Margaret Neilson (*née* Ritchie). *Educ:* Edinburgh Univ. (MA Hons French, LLB, DipLP). Solicitor in private practice, 1984–2006; Chm., Social Security Tribunals (pt-time), 2002–09; Employment Judge (pt-time), 2005–09; Immigration Judge (pt-time), 2006–09; Sheriff (pt-time), 2006–09. *Recreations:* scuba diving, travel, pilates, hill walking. *Address:* The Sheriff Court, The Castle, Inverness IV2 3EG. *T:* (01463) 230782.

NEISH, Andrew Graham; QC 2009; barrister; *b* Changi, Singapore, 5 March 1964; *s* of late Andrew Stephen Neish and of Joan Neish (*née* Catterall); *m* 1991, Sara Atkinson (marr. diss. 2007); two *s*; *m* 2014, Monica Lagazio. *Educ:* Nunthorpe Grammar Sch., York; St Andrews Univ. (MA Hons English 1986); City Univ. (Dip. Law 1987). Called to the Bar: Lincoln's Inn, 1988; BVI, 1999. MCIArb 2011. *Recreations:* reading, music (listening only, all styles), football (watching only, especially West Ham United FC), cooking, food and wine, Chinese ceramics, gin, tea, coffee, London, Italophile. *Address:* 4 Pump Court, Temple, EC4Y 7AN. *T:* (020) 7842 5555. *E:* aneish@4pumpcourt.com.

NELIGAN, His Honour John Oliver; a Circuit Judge, 1996–2014; *b* 21 June 1944; *yr s* of late Desmond Neligan, OBE and Penelope Anne Stabb; *m* 1971, Mary Brigid Daniel; one *s* two *d*. *Educ:* Brickwall Sch., Northiam. Admitted Solicitor, 1969; called to the Bar, Middle Temple, 1975; practised on Western Circuit; Recorder, 1994–96. Asst Comr, Boundary Commn for England, 1992–95. Mem., Mental Health Review Tribunal, 2001–11. *Recreations:* walking, painting, gardening. *Address:* Cuttisbeare, Butterleigh, Cullompton, Devonshire EX15 1PL.

See also M. H. D. Neligan.

NELIGAN, His Honour Michael Hugh Desmond; a Circuit Judge, 1990–2005; *b* 2 Dec. 1936; *s* of late Desmond West Edmund Neligan, OBE and Penelope Anne, *d* of Henry Mason; *m* 1965, Lynn (*née* Maidment); three *d*. *Educ:* Bradfield College; Jesus College, Cambridge. Commissioned Royal Sussex Regt, 1960–62; served East Africa with 23rd and 4th Bns, King's African Rifles. Called to the Bar, Middle Temple, 1962; Prosecuting Counsel to the Crown, 1972; Metropolitan Stipendiary Magistrate, 1987–90. *Recreations:* gardening, dog-walking.

See also J. O. Neligan.

NELIS, Mary Margaret; Member (SF) Foyle, Northern Ireland Assembly, 1998–2004; *b* 27 Aug. 1935; *d* of Denis Elliott and Catherine Coyle Elliott; *m* 1955, William Nelis; eight *s* one *d* (and one *s* decd). *Educ:* Inch Island Nat. Sch.; St Eugene's Convent Sch., Derry; Univ. of Ulster; Magee Adult Educn Faculty. Factory worker, 1949–56; Teacher, NW Coll. of Technol., Derry, then Derry Youth & Community Workshop, 1975–83. Mem., Sinn Féin, 1980–. Mem. (SF) Derry CC, 1994. Community develt, 1960–: Literacy trainee and Soc.

Mem., Derry Reading Workshop, Cornhill High Sch., Derry, 1974–75; Founder Member: Foyle Hills Tenants' Assoc., 1968–73; Dove House, 1985–90; Founder Mem. and Man. Dir, Templemore Co-op., Derry, 1988–91. *Recreations:* painting, writing, music, children. *Address:* 35 Westland Avenue, Derry City, Co. Londonderry BT48 9JE. *T:* (028) 7128 6453.

NELL, family name of **Baroness O'Neill of Bengarve**.

NELLIST, David; caseworker, Citizens Advice Bureau, since 1997; *b* 16 July 1952; *m* 1984, Jane Warner; one *s* three *d*. Mem., Unite (formerly Amicus). Welfare Rights Advr, Robert Zara & Co., 1992–97. Member: (Lab) W Midlands CC, 1982–86; (Socialist) Coventry CC, 1998–2012 (Leader, Socialist Gp, 1999–2010). MP (Lab, 1983–91, Ind. Lab, 1991–92) Coventry SE; contested: (Ind. Lab) Coventry SE, 1992; (Socialist) Coventry S, 1997; (Socialist) Coventry NE, 2001; (Socialist Alternative) Coventry NE, 2005, 2010; (TUSC) Coventry NE, 2015. Contested (No2EU) West Midlands, European Parlt, 2009, 2014. Mem. Nat. Cttee, Socialist Party, 1997–; Chairman: Socialist Alliance, 1998–2001; Campaign for a New Workers' Party, 2006–; Nat. Chm., Trade Unionist and Socialist Coalition, 2010–. *Address:* 33 Coundon Road, Coventry CV1 4AR. *T:* (024) 7622 9311. *E:* dave@nellist.net. *W:* www.twitter.com/davenellist.

NELMES, Dianne Gwenllian, (Mrs I. McBride); media and broadcasting consultant; *b* Windlesham; *d* of late James Allen Nelmes and Celandine Nelmes (*née* Kimber); *m* 1986, Ian McBride. *Educ:* Holt Co. Girls' Sch., Wokingham; Newcastle upon Tyne Univ. (BA Hons Econs/Politics 1973; Pres., Students' Union, 1973–74). Professional Cert. NCTJ 1978. Thomson grad. trainee journalist, 1974–78; journalist, on-screen reporter/presenter, BBC TV NE, 1978–83; News Ed., journalist, World in Action, Granada TV, 1983–87; Producer/Dir, Brass Tacks, BBC TV, 1987–88; Granada TV, 1988–98: Launch Ed., This Morning, 1988–89; Exec. Producer, Entertainment, 1989–92; Ed., World in Action, 1992–93; Controller: Factual Progs, 1993–96; Lifestyle Progs (launched 5 satellite-digital channels), 1996–98; Daytime, ITV Network Ltd, 1998–2000; Documentaries and Features, ITV Network, 2000–03; Dir, Daytime and Regl Programming, Granada Media, then Dir, Lifestyle Programming, Granada, later Dir, Daytime and Lifestyle Programming, ITV Prodns, 2003–08; Man. Dir, Liberty Bell Prodns, 2008–13; Creative Dir, Dinamite Prodns, 2013. Vis. Prof., Media and Journalism, Newcastle Univ., 2008–11. Trustee, Refuge, 2006–; Lay Trustee, NUS, 2012–. FRTS 1996; FRSA 2002. Hon. DCL Newcastle, 2011. *Recreations:* canal boating, mountain walking, films.

NELMES, Prof. Richard John, OBE 2001; ScD, PhD; FRS 2003; FRSE; FInstP; Professor of Physical Crystallography, 1992–2010, now Emeritus, Senior Honorary Professorial Fellow, since 2010, and Chairman, Centre for Science at Extreme Conditions, since 2003, University of Edinburgh; Honorary Scientist, Science and Technology Facilities Council, ISIS Facility, Rutherford Appleton Laboratory, since 2010 (Senior Visiting Fellow, 1994–2010); *s* of late Arthur Nelmes and Mabel Nelmes; *m* 1994, Tricia, *d* of late Eric Baldwin and of Eva Baldwin. *Educ:* Whitgift Sch., Croydon; St John's Coll., Cambridge (MA; ScD); Univ. of Edinburgh (PhD). FInstP 2001. University of Edinburgh: SRS Postdoctoral Fellow, 1969–71; Postdoctoral Res. Fellow, 1971–76; Lectr, 1976–85; Sen. Lectr, 1985–89; Reader and Professorial Fellow, 1989–92; EPSRC Sen. Fellow, 1989–94. Chm., High Pressure Gp, 1990–96, Founding Chm., Commn on High Pressure, 1996–2002, Internat. Union of Crystallography. FRSE 1995. Duddell Medal and Prize, Inst. of Physics, 2007. *Publications:* articles in scientific jls. *Recreations:* driving remote northern roads, reverie, music. *Address:* ISIS Facility, Rutherford Appleton Laboratory, Chilton, Didcot, Oxon OX11 0QX. *T:* (01235) 445285; Centre for Science at Extreme Conditions, and SUPA, School of Physics and Astronomy, University of Edinburgh, Mayfield Road, Edinburgh EH9 3JZ. *E:* r.j.nelmes@ed.ac.uk.

NELSON, family name of **Earl Nelson** and **Baron Nelson of Stafford**.

NELSON, 10th Earl *cr* 1805; **Simon John Horatio Nelson;** Baron Nelson of the Nile and of Hillborough, Norfolk, 1801; Viscount Merton, 1805; *b* 21 Sept. 1971; *s* of 9th Earl Nelson and Maureen Diana (*née* Quinn); *S* father, 2009; *m* 1999, Anna Stekerova; one *s* one *d*. *Heir:* *s* Viscount Merton, *qv*.

NELSON OF STAFFORD, 4th Baron *cr* 1960; **Alistair William Henry Nelson;** Bt 1955; family farming business, since 2007; *b* 1973; *o s* of 3rd Baron Nelson of Stafford and of Dorothy Irene Nelson; *S* father, 2006; *m* 2010, Kirsty Anne, *d* of Peter William Snowball; one *d*. *Educ:* Ampleforth Coll.; Loughborough Univ. (BEng Hons Manufacturing, Engrg and Mgt). Mech. Applications Engr, European Gas Turbines, 1995–2000; Design Engr, Farm Force Engineering Ltd, 2000–07. *Recreations:* horse trials, horse racing, shooting, ski-ing. *Heir:* *uncle* Hon. James Jonathan Nelson [*b* 17 June 1947; *m* 1977, Lucy Mary Brown; three *d*].

NELSON (NZ), Bishop of, since 2007; **Rt Rev. Richard Ellena;** *b* 15 Jan. 1951; *s* of Victor Albert Ellena and Helen Mae Ellena; *m* 1972, Hilary Geoghegan; one *s* one *d*. *Educ:* Canterbury Univ. (BMus 1976); St John's Coll., Auckland (LTh 1984). Head, Dept of Music, Rangiora High Sch., Christchurch, 1976–82; ordained priest, 1985; Vicar: St Peter's, Kensington-Otipua, 1986–91; Blenheim Anglican Parish, 1992–2006; Archdeacon, Nelson and Marlborough, 2001–06; Vicar-Gen., Dio. of Nelson, 2002–06. *Recreations:* reading, walking, sailing. *Address:* PO Box 100, Nelson, New Zealand. *T:* (3) 5483124. *E:* bishop@nelsonanglican.nz.

NELSON, Anthony; *see* Nelson, R. A.

NELSON, Hon. Brendan John; Director, Australian War Memorial, since 2012; *b* Coburg, Vic, 19 Aug. 1958; *s* of Desmond John and Patricia Anne Nelson; *m* 1st, 1980, Deanna (marr. diss. 1981); 2nd, 1983, Kathleen (marr. diss. 1999); one *s* one *d*; 3rd, 1999, Gillian Adamson; one step *d*. *Educ:* Modbury High Sch.; St Ignatius Coll.; Univ. of Adelaide; Flinders Univ. (BM BS 1983). FAMA 1995. Gen. med. practitioner, 1985–95, private gen. practice, Hobart, 1991–95; Dir, Hobart and Launceston After Hours Med. Service Pty Ltd, 1987–91; med. columnist, Woman's Day mag., 1995–97. Fed. Pres., AMA, 1993–95 (Fed. Vice Pres., 1991–93; Pres., Tasmanian Br., 1990–92). MP (L) Bradfield, NSW, 1996–2009; Parly Sec. to Minister of Defence, 2001; Minister: for Educn, Sci. and Trng, 2001–06; for Defence, 2006–07; Leader, Parly Liberal Party and Leader of the Opposition, 2007–08. Chm., House of Reps Standing Cttee for Employment, Educn and Trng, 1997–98, for Employment, Educn and Workplace Relns, 1998–2001. Ambassador of Australia to EU, Belgium and Luxembourg, Ambassador to NATO, and Special Rep. to WHO, 2010–12. Chm., Sydney Airport Community Forum, 1998–2001. Hon. FRACP 1995. DUniv Flinders, 2011. Gold Medal, AMA, 1995; Centenary Medal, 2003; Bruce Shepherd Medal, Australian Doctors' Fund, 2011. *Recreations:* fishing, tennis, motorcycles, music, guitars. *Address:* Australian War Memorial, GPO Box 345, Canberra, ACT 2601, Australia.

NELSON, Cairns Louis David; QC 2010; a Recorder, since 2006; *b* Capel, Surrey, 1 March 1964; *s* of William and Freda Nelson; *m* 1998, Eleanor Jane Laws, *qv*; two *s* two *d*. *Educ:* King's Coll. London (LLB). Called to the Bar, Gray's Inn, 1987. *Address:* 23 Essex Street, WC2R 3AA.

NELSON, David Brian; Senior Executive and Joint Head of Design, Foster + Partners, since 2007; *b* 15 April 1951; *s* of Victor Henry Nelson and Edna Mary (*née* Elliot); *m* 1977, Caroline Georgette Evans; two *d*. *Educ:* Loughborough Coll. of Art; Hornsey Coll. of Art; Royal Coll. of Art (MA). Joined Foster Associates, 1976; Dir, 1984; Partner, 1991; Dep. Chm., 2004–05. Projects, in Asia, Europe, Australia and USA, include: Century Tower, Tokyo, 1991; Amer. Air Mus., Duxford, 1997; New German Parlt, Reichstag, Berlin, 1999; Stanford Univ. Labs, Calif, 2003; Petronas Univ. of Technol., Malaysia, 2004; McLaren Technology Centre for McLaren, 2005; new Supreme Court, Singapore, 2006; Deutsche Bank Place, Sydney, Australia, 2006; transport projects: Bilbao Metro, Spain, 1995; Canary Wharf Underground Stn, 1999; N Greenwich Transport Interchange, London, 2000; Florence High-speed Rly Stn, 2010. Hon. FRIBA 2002. *Recreations:* motorsport, aviation, travel. *Address:* Foster + Partners, Riverside Three, 22 Hester Road, SW11 4AN. *T:* (020) 7738 0455, *Fax:* (020) 7738 1107. *E:* dnelson@fosterandpartners.com. *Club:* Architecture.

NELSON, Eleanor Jane; *see* Laws, E. J.

NELSON, Eric Victor, LVO 1975; HM Diplomatic Service, retired; *b* 11 Jan. 1927; *s* of Victor H. H. and E. Vera B. Nelson (*née* Collingwood); *m* 1960, Maria Teresa (Marité) Paul (*d* 2008); one *d* (and one *d* decd). *Educ:* Western High School; George Washington University, Washington DC. Royal Air Force, 1945–48. Board of Trade, 1949; served FO, later FCO: Athens, Belgrade, Haiphong, Caracas; First Sec., Saigon, 1962; First Sec. and Consul, Bujumbura, 1964 (Chargé d'Affaires *ai*, 1966–67); FO 1968; First Sec. and Consul, Asunción, 1971; First Sec., Mexico City, 1974; FCO, 1978; seconded to Brunei Govt Service as Special Adviser to HM Sultan of Brunei, for Establishment of Brunei Diplomatic Service, 1981–84; Consul-Gen., Bordeaux, 1984–87. Order of the Aztec Eagle, Mexico, 1975. *Recreations:* photography, computer graphics, tourism, cartooning, pastel drawing, sculpture. *Address:* 8 Purberry Grove, Ewell, Surrey KT17 1LU.

NELSON, Fraser Andrew; Editor, The Spectator, since 2009; *b* Truro, 14 May 1973; *m* 2006, Linda; two *s* one *d*. *Educ:* Nairn Acad.; Dollar Acad.; Glasgow Univ. (MA Hist. and Politics); City Univ. (Dip. Newspaper Journalism). Journalist, Glasgow Herald, 1995; Business Corresp., The Times, 1995–2001; Political Editor: Scotsman, 2001–06; The Spectator, 2006–09. *Address:* The Spectator, 22 Old Queen Street, SW1H 9HP. *T:* (020) 7961 0201, *Fax:* (020) 7961 0250. *E:* editor@spectator.co.uk.

NELSON, Sir Jamie (Charles Vernon Hope), 4th Bt *cr* 1912, of Acton Park, Acton, Denbigh; *b* 23 Oct. 1949; *s* of Sir William Vernon Hope Nelson, OBE and Hon. Elizabeth Ann Bevil Cary, *er d* of 14th Viscount Falkland; *S* father, 1991, but his name does not appear on the Official Roll of the Baronetage; *m* 1983, Maralyn Beverly Hedge (*née* Pyatt); one *s*. *Heir:* *b* Dominic William Michael Nelson [*b* 13 March 1957; *m* 1981, Sarah, *e d* of late John Neil Hylton Jolliffe; three *s* one *d*].

NELSON, Dame Janet Laughland, (Dame Jinty Nelson), DBE 2006; PhD; FBA 1996; Professor of Medieval History, King's College, London, 1993–2007, Emeritus Professor, 2008; *b* 28 March 1942; *d* of William Wilson Muir and Elizabeth Barnes Muir (*née* Laughland); *m* 1965, Howard George Horatio Nelson (marr. diss. 2010); one *s* one *d*. *Educ:* Keswick Sch., Cumbria; Newnham Coll., Cambridge (BA 1964; PhD 1967). King's College, London: Lectr, 1970–87; Reader, 1987–93; Dir, Centre for Late Antique and Medieval Studies, 1994–2000; FKC 2001. Chm., Adv. Bd, Inst. of Histl Res., Univ. of London, 1998–2001. Vice-Pres., British Acad., 1999–2001; FRHistS 1982 (Pres., 2000–04); FSA 2014; Corresp. Fellow, Medieval Acad. of Amer., 2000. Hon. DLitt: UEA, 2004; St Andrews, 2007; QUB, 2009; Liverpool, Nottingham, York, 2010; Glasgow, 2012. *Publications:* Politics and Ritual in Early Medieval Europe, 1986; The Annals of St-Bertin, 1991; Charles the Bald, 1992; The Frankish World, 1996; Rulers and Ruling Families, 1999; (ed jtly) Rituals of Power, 2000; (ed jtly) The Medieval World, 2001; Courts, Elites, and Gendered Power in the Earlier Middle Ages, 2007; (ed jtly) Lay Intellectuals in the Carolingian World, 2007; (ed jtly) Reading the Bible in the Middle Ages, 2015; (ed jtly) Ravenna: change and exchange, 2015. *Recreations:* music, walking, spending time with grandchildren Elias, Ruth, Martha and Miriam. *Address:* 71 Oglander Road, SE15 4DD. *E:* jinty.nelson23@gmail.com.

NELSON, Jeremy, (Jez); Chief Executive Officer, Somethin' Else, since 2009 (Founder and Creative Director, 1991–2009); *b* London, 11 April 1964; *s* of Alan and Sheila Nelson; *m* 1997, Fran Plowright; two *s*. *Educ:* Dulwich Coll.; King's Coll., London (BSc Human Biol.); Highbury Coll., Portsmouth (Postgrad. Dip. Radio Journalism). Pirate radio DJ, 1980–84; freelance radio presenter and journalist, 1984–90; *radio:* presenter: Jazz FM, 1990–91; various BBC radio progs, 1991–, incl. Jazz on 3, 1999–; *television:* presenter, Tomorrow's World, 1996–2000; producer and exec. producer, TV documentaries, 1995–. Hon. ARAM. *Recreations:* family, jazz and all good music, Arsenal FC, swimming, cycling, Spain. *Address:* Somethin' Else, 20–26 Brunswick Place, N1 6DZ. *T:* (020) 7250 5500. *E:* jez@somethinelse.com.

NELSON, John Frederick, FCA; Chairman, Lloyd's, since 2011; *b* 26 July 1947; *s* of George Frederick Nelson and Betty Violet Roddick; *m* 1976, Caroline Vivien Hannam; two *s* one *d*. FCA 1970. Kleinwort Benson, 1971–86, Dir, 1980–86; Lazard Brothers: Man. Dir, 1986–99; Vice Chm., 1990–99; Chm., Credit Suisse First Boston Europe, 1999–2002. Non-executive Director: Woolwich plc, 1998–2000; BT Gp plc, 2002–08; Kingfisher plc, 2002–11 (Dep. Chm., 2002–06 and 2009–11; Jt Dep. Chm., 2006–07); Hammerson plc, 2004–13 (Chm., 2005–13); Cazenove Gp, 2008–10; JPMorgan Cazenove Holdings, 2008–10. Senior Advr, Charterhouse Capital Partners LLP, 2006–. Chm., Chichester Harbour Trust, 2013–. Dir, ENO, 2002–10. Trustee, Nat. Gall., 2010–. *Recreations:* sailing, opera, ski-ing, tennis. *Clubs:* Hurlingham; Royal Yacht Squadron; Bosham Sailing.

NELSON, John Graeme; Management Consultant, First Class Partnerships, since 1997 (Chairman, 1999–2012); *b* 19 June 1947; *s* of late Charles and Jean Nelson; *m* 1971, Pauline Dickinson; one *s* one *d* (and one *s* decd). *Educ:* Aylesbury and Slough Grammar Schs; Univ. of Manchester (BA Econ Hons). Management trainee, BR Western Reg., 1968; Asst Station Man., Liverpool Street, 1971; Area Passenger Man., Shenfield, 1973; Passenger Sales Officer, Leeds, 1977; Passenger Man., Sheffield Div., 1979; Personal Asst, Chief Exec. BRB, 1981; Parcels Man., Southern Reg., 1982; Nat. Business Man., Red Star Parcels, 1984; Gen. Man., BR Eastern Reg., 1987; Man. Dir, Network SouthEast, 1991; Gp Man. Dir, S and E, BR, 1994–97; Dir, London Develt, Railtrack, 1997. Director: First Class Insight Ltd, 1997–2003; Renaissance Trains Ltd, 1999–; Hull Trains, 1999–2014; Laing Rail, 2002–06; Wrexham, Shropshire & Marylebone Railway Ltd, 2006–09; Tracsis plc, 2007–; YourRail Ltd, 2008–09; Passenger Transport Ltd, 2011–; Member, Board: M40 Trains Ltd, 1998–2002; SE Trains (Hldgs) Ltd, 2003–06. Chm., Tees, E and N Yorks Ambulance Service NHS Trust, 1997–2002. Member, Advisory Board: Nat. Railway Mus., 2006–12; Yorks Rail Acad., 2007–09. *Publications:* Voters Limits: a history of London's parliamentary representation, 2015. *Recreations:* piano, football, painting, psephology. *Address:* 32 St Paul's Square, York YO24 4BD. *T:* (01904) 638659. *E:* john.nelson@post.com.

NELSON, Marjorie J.; *see* Jackson-Nelson.

NELSON, Michael Edward; Chairman, Reuter Foundation, 1982–90; General Manager, 1976–89, and Deputy Managing Director, 1981–89, Reuters Ltd; *b* 30 April 1929; *s* of late Thomas Alfred Nelson and Dorothy Pretoria Nelson; *m* 1960, Helga Johanna (*née* den Ouden); two *s* one *d*. *Educ:* Latymer Upper School; Magdalen College, Oxford (MA). Joined Reuters, London, as trainee financial journalist, 1952; assignments Asia, 1954–57; returned to London; Manager, Reuters Economic Services, 1962; Chairman, 1987–88: Reuters Asia; Reuters Europe; Reuters Overseas. Trustee: Visnews, 1990–92 (Chm., 1985–89); Internat. Inst. of Communications, 1989–95 (Chm., UK Chapter, 1989–92); Chm. Adv. Council, World Econ. Forum Jl, World Link, 1990–92. Mem., Newspaper Panel, MMC, 1989–95. External examiner, Journalism MA, Sheffield Univ., 1999–2001. Mem. Council, Internat.

Assoc. for Media and Hist., 2001–09. Trustee, St Bride's Church, 1989–2009. Vice-Pres., Music Fest. of Beaulieu-sur-Mer, 2005. Hon. Res. Fellow, Univ. of Kent, 1997–. *Publications:* War of the Black Heavens: the battles of western broadcasting in the cold war, 1997; Queen Victoria and the Discovery of the Riviera, 2001; Americans and the Making of the Riviera, 2007; Castro and Stockmaster: a life in Reuters, 2011. *Recreations:* walking, music, history. *Address:* 40 Addison Avenue, W11 4QP. *T:* (020) 7603 1115; Domaine de la Rose, 2 Chemin des Restanques, 06650 Opio, France. *T:* 493773263. *Club:* Garrick.

NELSON, Nicholas; Teacher, Newlands Girls' School, Maidenhead, 2001–10; *b* 20 Jan. 1947; *s* of late Peter Nelson and Margaret Nelson; *m* 1972, Charmian Alice (*née* Bell); one *s* two *d. Educ:* Pudsey Grammar Sch., Yorkshire; Reading Univ. (BA (Hons) History; CertEd 1992); Birkbeck, Univ. of London (Grad. Dip. French 2013). BOAC/British Airways air cargo mgt in Japan/UK, 1969–81; DHL International (UK) Ltd: Gen. Man., 1981; Man. Dir, 1982; Regional Dir (Europe), 1987; Man. Dir, Parcels, PO, then Royal Mail Parcelforce, 1987–91; teacher, 1992–95, Head Teacher, 1995–2000, Queens' Sch., Bushey; Dir, Resources and Planning, Design Council, 2001. *Recreations:* cricket, trying to learn French.

NELSON, Prof. Philip Arthur, PhD; CEng, FREng; FIMechE; Professor of Acoustics, University of Southampton, since 1994; Chief Executive, Engineering and Physical Sciences Research Council (on secondment), since 2014; *b* Bishops Stortford, 22 June 1952; *s* of David and Brenda Nelson; *m* 1979, Jennifer Mills; two *s. Educ:* Colchester Royal Grammar Sch.; Univ. of Southampton (BSc 1st Cl Hons Mech. Engrg; PhD Sound and Vibration Studies 1981). CEng 1992; FIMechE 1997; FREng 2002. Res. develt and consulting engr, Sound Attenuators Ltd, 1978–82; University of Southampton: Lectr, Inst. of Sound and Vibration Res., 1982–88; Sen. Lectr, 1988–94; Founder Dir, Rolls-Royce Univ. Technol. Centre in Gas Turbine Noise, 1999–2001; Dir, Inst. of Sound and Vibration Res., 2001–05; Pro Vice-Chancellor, 2005–13. Vis. Prof., Penn State Univ., 1995. FIOA 1997. *Publications:* (with S. J. Elliott) Active Control of Sound, 1992; (jtly) Active Control of Vibration, 1996; contribs to refereed scientific jls. *Recreations:* golf, theatre, cinema. *Address:* Polaris House, North Star Avenue, Swindon SN2 1ET. *T:* (01793) 444429. *E:* Philip.Nelson@epsrc.ac.uk. *Club:* Hockley Golf.

NELSON, Philip Raymond, CMG 2005; JP; HM Diplomatic Service, retired; *b* 7 April 1950; *s* of David George Nelson and Marjorie Lilian Nelson (*née* Roberts); *m* 1st, 1971, Cynthia Lesley Elson (marr. diss. 1978); 2nd, 1992, Lyndsay Ann Halper; two *s. Educ:* Collyer's Sch., Horsham; Lincoln Coll., Oxford (BA Hons 1971); Fletcher Sch. of Law and Diplomacy, Tufts Univ. (AM 1972). Joined HM Diplomatic Service, 1972; Budapest, 1974–76; Private Sec. to Sir Nicholas Henderson, Paris, 1976–79; First Secretary: Rome, 1980–83; Manila, 1990; Budapest, 1991–94; Counsellor, FCO, 1994–2005. JP Ealing, 2007, NW London Family Court, 2009. *Recreations:* ski(mountaineer)ing, sailing (skippered Jolene II in Fastnet Races 2011 and 2013), cycling, mathematics. *E:* ravenscourt@compuserve.com. *Club:* Royal Ocean Racing.

NELSON, (Richard) Anthony; *b* 11 June 1948; *o s* of late Gp Captain R. G. Nelson and of Mrs J. M. Nelson; *m* 1974, Caroline Victoria Butler; one *s* one *d. Educ:* Harrow Sch. (Head of School; Rothschild Scholar, 1966); Christ's Coll., Cambridge (MA (Hons) Economics and Law). N. M. Rothschild & Sons Ltd, 1969–73; Man. Dir, Salomon Smith Barney, 1997–2000; Vice-Chm., Citigroup Corporate and Investment Bank, then Citigroup Global Capital Markets, later Citigroup Global Markets, subseq. Citi, 2002–08; Chairman: Southern Water, 2002–04; Britain in Europe, 2005–07; ifs Proshare, 2007–08; Dir, Internat. Financial Services London, 2007–08. Chm., Gateway to London, 2002–08. Contested (C) E Leeds, Feb. 1974. MP (C) Chichester, Oct. 1974–1997. PPS to Minister for Housing and Construction, 1979–83, to Minister of State for the Armed Forces, 1983–85; Economic Sec., 1992–94, Minister of State, 1994–95, HM Treasury; Minister of State, DTI, 1995–97. Member: Select Cttee on Science and Technology, 1975–79; Select Cttee on Televising of Proceedings of the House, 1988–92. Dir, Chichester Fest. Th., 1983–92. Mem., Governing Body, ICC (UK), 2005–08. FRSA 1979. *Recreations:* Rugby, music. *Address:* The Old Vicarage, Easebourne, near Midhurst, W Sussex GU29 0AL.

NELSON, Richard Campbell; Director, Applus Technologies Holdings SLU, since 2009; President, International Federation of Inspection Agencies, since 1999; *b* 11 Feb. 1943; *s* of Campbell Louis Nelson and Pauline (*née* Blundell); *m* 1971, Rosemary Eleanor Sterling; one *s* three *d. Educ:* Rugby Sch.; London Business Sch. (MSc Econs). Chartered Accountant. Dir, 1972–84, Chief Exec., 1982–84, Esperanza Ltd, subseq. Transcontinental Services Ltd; Chief Exec., Inchcape Testing Services, 1984–96; Intertek Testing Services, later Intertek Group plc: Exec. Chm., 1996–2001; Chief Exec., 1996–2005; Dep. Chm., 2005–09. Chm., Holland Park Sch. Trust, 2005–. *Recreations:* golf, tennis, bridge. *Address:* Flat 3, 10 Observatory Gardens, W8 7HY. *T:* (020) 7937 3457, 07775 785655. *E:* richardcnelson1@gmail.com. *Club:* Turf.

NELSON, Dr (Richard) Stuart, FInstP; Consultant, β Technology Ltd, 1996–2001; *b* 1 May 1937; *s* of Richard and Winifred Emily Nelson; *m* 1965, Veronica Mary Beck; one *s* two *d. Educ:* Univ. of Reading (BSc 1st Cl. Hons Physics, 1958; DSc 1969). FInstP 1968. Joined UKAEA, Harwell, 1958; Div. Head, Materials Develt Div., 1981; Dir, Nuclear Power Res., 1984; Dir, Northern Res. Labs, 1987–90 (including Risley, Springfield and Windscale Labs); Mem. Bd, UKAEA, 1991–96; Man. Dir, Industrial Business Gp, 1991–94, Exec. Dir, Ops, 1994–96, AEA Technology. Vis. Prof., Univ. of Sussex, 1970–. *Publications:* The Observation of Atomic Collisions in Crystalline Solids, 1968; Ion Implantation, 1973; Innovation Business, 1999; 200 papers in scientific jls. *Recreations:* hockey (played for Berkshire), golf (Club Captain, 1998), tennis. *Address:* 5 Whitehills Green, Goring, Reading, Berks RG8 0EB.

NELSON, Hon. Sir Robert (Franklyn), Kt 1996; a Judge of the High Court of Justice, Queen's Bench Division, 1996–2008; arbitrator and mediator, since 2009; *b* 19 Sept. 1942; *s* of late Clarence William and Lucie Margaret Nelson; *m* 1968, Anne-Marie Sabina Hall; two *s. Educ:* Repton; St John's Coll., Cambridge (MA). Called to the Bar, Middle Temple, 1965 (Harmsworth Entrance Exhibn, 1963), Bencher, 1993; QC 1985; a Recorder, 1986–96. *Recreations:* cricket, opera, golf. *Address:* 3 Verulam Buildings, Gray's Inn, WC1R 5NT. *T:* (020) 7831 8441.

NELSON, Stephen Keith James; Asset Management Director, Infracapital, since 2013; *b* 5 Jan. 1963; *s* of late Bertram James Nelson, OBE and of Constance Nelson (*née* Dangerfield); *m* 1991, Catherine; one *s* one *d. Educ:* Tonbridge Sch. (Scholar); St John's Coll., Oxford (Open Scholar; MA 1st cl. Lit. Hum.). Diageo: Man. Dir, Guinness GB, 1999–2000; CEO, Guinness World Records, 2000–01; Pres., Diageo N America (SW), 2001–03; J Sainsbury plc: Trading Dir, 2003–04; Mktg Dir, 2004–05; Gp Retail Dir, BAA plc, 2005–06; CEO, BAA Ltd, 2006–08. Non-executive Director: Duchy Originals Ltd, 2009–; Office of Rail Regulation, 2011–15; Associated British Ports Hldgs, 2013–. *Recreations:* family, cycling, guitar, reading, museums, galleries.

NELSON, Stuart; *see* Nelson, R. S.

NELSON, Trevor Ricardo, MBE 2002; broadcaster, BBC, since 1996; *b* Hackney, 7 Jan. 1964; *s* of Andrew Laurent-Nelson and Willyana Nelson; *m* Anna-Marie (marr. diss.); one *s* one *d. Educ:* Central Foundn for Boys Grammar Sch., London; Kingsway Princeton Coll. G&M Records, 1984–87; Red Records, 1987–89; Soul II Soul Records, 1989–90; EMI/Cooltempo Records, Artists & Repertoire, 1993–98; broadcaster: Kiss FM, 1990–95; BBC Radio 1, 1996–; BBC Radio 2, 1998–; BBC 1Xtra, 2007–; MTV UK, 1998–2009. *Recreations:* massive sports fan, loves golf, big Chelsea FC fan. *Address:* c/o Money Management, 42A Berwick Street, W1F 8RZ.

NELSON-TAYLOR, Dame Nicola (Jane), DBE 2014; National Leader of Education, since 2010; Executive Headteacher, Walbottle Village Primary School and Beech Hill Primary School, Newcastle upon Tyne, since 2010; *b* Newcastle upon Tyne, 9 Dec. 1971; *d* of Raymond Benjamin Nelson and Elizabeth Ann Nelson; *m* 1999, Paul Taylor (marr. diss. 2013); one *s. Educ:* Northumbria Univ. (BEd Hons 1994); Univ. of Newcastle upon Tyne (MEd 2002); NPQH 2002. Sen. Teacher, Shiremoor Primary Sch., 1995–2003; Dep. Head Teacher, 2003–06, Head Teacher, 2006–10, Beech Hill Primary Sch. *Recreations:* marathon running, trekking, cycling, family, friends, enjoying life, feeling the fear and doing it anyway. *Address:* Beech Hill Primary School, Linhope Road, West Denton, Newcastle upon Tyne NE5 2LW. *T:* (0191) 267 8113, *Fax:* (0191) 264 1240. *E:* Dame.nicola@beechhill.newcastle.sch.uk.

NEOPTOLEMOS, Prof. John P., MD; FRCS, FMedSci; The Owen and Ellen Evans Chair of Surgery (formerly Cancer Studies), University of Liverpool, since 2006 (Professor of Surgery, 2004–10; Head, Department of Surgery, 1996–2004); Director, Liverpool Cancer Research UK Centre, since 2010; Hon. Consultant Surgeon, Royal Liverpool University Hospital, since 1996; *b* 30 June 1951; *m* 1974, Linda Joan Blaylock; one *s* one *d. Educ:* Owen's Grammar Sch., N London; Churchill Coll., Cambridge (MA); Guy's Hosp., London (MB BChir); Univ. of Leicester (MD 1985). FRCS 1981. Guy's Hosp., London, 1976–77; Leicester Royal Infirmary, 1978–84 and 1986–87; UCSD, 1984–85; Sen. Lectr, then Reader, Dept of Surgery, Univ. of Birmingham, and Consultant Surgeon, City Hosp., Birmingham, 1987–94; Prof. of Surgery, Queen Elizabeth Hosp., Birmingham, 1994–96. Hunterian Prof. of Surgery, RCS, 1987–88; Moynihan Travelling Fellow, Assoc. of Surgeons of GB and Ireland, 1988; RSM Travelling Prof., USA, 1989; British Council Lect. Tour of Thai Med. Schs, 1990; Vis. Prof., Med. Sch., Univ. of Hong Kong, 1994; Eybers Vis. Prof., Med. Sch., Univ. of Orange Free State, S Africa, 1994; Vis. Prof., Christchurch Med. Sch., Univ. of Otago, NZ, 1995; Ext. Examr, 1996–97, Wilson Wang Vis. Prof., 1997, Chinese Univ. of Hong Kong; Visiting Professor: Univ. of Singapore, 1998; Univ. of Heidelberg, 2002; Pearce Gould Vis. Prof., UCL, 2008. Honyman Gillespie Lect., Edinburgh, 2007. Clinical Cancer Lead, Pancreas Biomedical Res. Unit, 2007–, Sen. Investigator, 2011–, NIHR. Has made scientific contribs to aetiology, diagnosis and treatment of diseases of the pancreas and biliary tree. President: Pancreatic Soc. of GB and Ireland, 1994–95 (Mem. Cttee, 1987–90); Liverpool and NW Soc. of Surgeons, 2006–07. Mem. Cttee, Surgical Res. Soc., 1994–98. Chairman: Eur. Study Gp for Pancreatic Cancer, 1991–; Pancreas Cancer Sub Group, NCRI, 2004–; Treas., Eur. Digestive Surgery, 1997–2004; Member Council: Eur. Pancreatic Club, 1995–2002 (Sec., 1996–2002); United Eur. Gastroenterol. Fedn, 1997–2002 (Mem., Scientific Cttee, 2002–06); Member: World Council, Internat. Hepato-Pancreato-Biliary Assoc., 1995–98; World Council, Internat. Assoc. of Pancreatology, 1996–2004 (Pres., 2000–02); Pancreatic Cancer Progress Review Gp, Nat. Cancer Inst., 2000; Nat. Cancer Inst. Specialized Prog. of Res. Excellence for Pancreatic Cancer, 2002–03; NW Regl Res. and Develt Biomedical Res. Cttee, 2001–02; Adv. Bd, Deutsche Krebshilfe Cancer Centers, 2006–; Panel Acad. Advrs, Commonwealth Scholarship Commn, 2007–12; Sci. Strategy Adv. Gp, CRUK, 2008–; Scientific Res. Cttee, Nat. Cancer Inst., France, 2010–; Scientific Cttee, Italian Assoc. for Cancer Res., 2009–; Advr, Bundesministerium für Bildung und Forschung/Deutsche Forschungsgemeinschaft, 2006–. Hon. Member: S African Gastroenterology Soc., 1991; German Soc. for Surgery, 2012. FMedSci 2007. RCS USA Travelling Award, 1984; Rodney Smith Prize, RCS, 1987; Hirschberg Award for Pancreatic Cancer, American Pancreatic Assoc., 2005. *Publications:* Cancer of the Pancreas, 1990, 2006; Cancer: a molecular approach, 1993; Pancreatic Cancer: molecular and clinical advances, 1996; The Pancreas, 1998, 2nd edn 2008; Acute Pancreatitis, 1999; Exocrine Pancreas Cancer, 2005; Cancer of the Pancreas, 2006; Pancreatic Cancer, 2010; contrib. numerous scientific papers in peer-reviewed jls, incl. New England Jl of Medicine, Lancet, Clin. Oncol., GUT, Annals of Surgery, Cancer Res., Gastroenterol., Proc. NAS, USA, Oncogene, Jl Nat. Cancer Inst. *Recreations:* racquet ball, Latin and ballroom dancing (Mem., Merrall's Acad. of Dance, 2003–). *Address:* Section of Surgery and Oncology, Department of Molecular and Clinical Cancer Medicine, Royal Liverpool University Hospital, 5th Floor, UCD Building, Daulby Street, Liverpool L69 3GA. *T:* (0151) 706 4175, *Fax:* (0151) 706 5798. *E:* j.p.neoptolemos@liv.ac.uk. *Club:* Heswall Squash (Trustee, 2005–).

NESBIT, Martin Alistair; Head of Environment and Climate Governance, Institute for European Environmental Policy, since 2014; *b* Frimley, Surrey, 14 May 1965; *s* of James Stuart Alistair Nesbit and Pamela Scrivener Nesbit; partner, Lucy Johnson; one *s. Educ:* Woking Sixth Form Coll.; Clare Coll., Cambridge (BA 1987); Univ. of Bristol (MA 1989). DoE, 1988–98; UK Perm. Repn to EU, 1998–2002; DEFRA, 2002–08; DECC, 2008–09; Dir, EU and Internat. Affairs, DEFRA, 2009–14. *Recreations:* hill-walking, kayaking, long-distance paths. *Address:* Institute for European Environmental Policy, Floor 3, 11 Belgrave Road, SW1V 1RB. *W:* www.twitter.com/arrhenius.

NESBITT, Dermot William Gibson; Senior Lecturer, Queen's University, Belfast, 2007–12; Commissioner, Equality Commission, Northern Ireland, since 2009; *b* 14 Aug. 1947; *s* of William Cromwell Nesbitt and Georgina Nesbitt; *m* 1970, Margaret Oriel Patterson; one *s* one *d. Educ:* Queen's Univ., Belfast (BSc 1st cl. Hons Econs). School Teacher, 1969–74; Lectr, Ulster Poly., 1976; Queen's Univ., Belfast, 1976–98 (Sen. Lectr and Head, Dept of Accounting and Finance). Mem., NI Forum for Political Dialogue, 1996–98. Mem. (UU) S Down, NI Assembly, 1998–2007. Jun. Minister, assisting David Trimble, 1999–2002, Minister of the Envmt, 2002, NI. Contested (UU) S Down, 1997, 2001, 2005. *Publications:* over 20 academic publications. *Recreations:* gardening, family. *Address:* 21 Downpatrick Road, Crossgar, Downpatrick, Co. Down BT30 9EQ. *T:* (028) 4483 1561.

NESBITT, Judith; Director (formerly Head) of National and International Partnerships, Tate, since 2010; *b* 24 March 1962; *d* of Thomas Robert Cecil Nesbitt and Joan Nesbitt (*née* Fleming); *m* 2008, Prof. Guy Lennox Claxton. *Educ:* Univ. of York (BA Hons Eng./Hist. of Art 1983); Courtauld Inst., London (MA Hist. of Art 1985). Sen. Asst Keeper, City Art Gall., Leeds, 1986–91; Exhibns Curator, Tate Gall. Liverpool, 1991–95, curated: Roy Lichtenstein, Robert Gober, 1993; Ann Hamilton, 1994; Sigmar Polke, 1995; Dir, Chisenhale Gall., 1995–98, curated shows of: Michael Landy, Pipilotti Rist, Gillian Wearing, Sam Taylor-Wood, Wolfgang Tillmans, Yukinori Yanagi, Paul Noble, Thomas Hirshhorn; Hd of Programming, Whitechapel Art Gall., 1998–2000, co-curated, Examining Pictures, 1999; Hd of UK Content, Eyestorm.com, 2000–01; Tate Britain: Chief Curator, 2001–10; curated: Michael Landy Semi-Detached, 2004; Peter Doig, 2008; Chris Ofili, 2010. Non-exec. Dir, Film Video Umbrella, 2011–. Mem., Adv. Panel, Platform for Art, 2004–. Hon. FRCA 1998. *Recreation:* making a garden. *Address:* Tate Britain, Millbank, SW1P 4RG. *T:* (020) 7887 8960, *Fax:* (020) 7887 8850. *E:* judith.nesbitt@tate.org.uk.

NESBITT, Michael Charles, DBA; Member (UU) Strangford, Northern Ireland Assembly, since 2011; Leader, Ulster Unionist Party, since 2012; *b* Belfast, 11 May 1957; *s* of Alfred Charles Nesbitt and Brenda Norma Patrick; *m* 1992, Lynda Byrons; two *s. Educ:* Campbell Coll., Belfast; Jesus Coll., Cambridge (BA 1979); Queen's Univ., Belfast (DBA). BBC Northern Ireland: sports reporter, 1979–86; presenter, Good Morning Ulster, 1986–89; Man. Dir, Anderson Kenny PR, 1989–92; presenter and broadcast journalist, Ulster TV,

1992–2006. Comr for Victims and Survivors, NI, 2008–10. *Recreations:* literature, music, golf. *Address:* Northern Ireland Assembly, Parliament Buildings, Stormont, Belfast BT4 3XX; (office) 16 South Street, Newtownards BT23 4JT. *E:* mike.nesbitt@mla.niassembly.gov.uk.

NESBITT, Simon John; QC 2015; *b* Belfast, 27 Sept. 1966; *s* of Henry Nesbitt and Elizabeth Nesbitt; civil partnership 2007, Simon Buxton; one *d*. *Educ:* Pembroke Coll., Oxford (BA Hons 1990; MA). Admitted: Solicitor, 1994; avocat à la cour, Paris, 1997; Lovell White Durrant, subseq. Lovells LLP, then Hogan Lovells International LLP: Associate Solicitor, London and Paris, 1994–2002; Partner, 2002–13; Global Co-Hd, Internat. Arbitration, 2013–15; called to the Bar, Lincoln's Inn, 2015; arbitrator and barrister, Maitland Chambers, 2015–. FCIArb 2004. *Publications:* articles relating to arbitration in Arbitration Internat., PLC Mag., Eur. Lawyer. *Recreations:* horse riding, sailing. *Address:* Maitland Chambers, 7 Stone Buildings, Lincoln's Inn, WC2A 3SZ. *T:* (020) 7406 1200. *E:* snesbitt@maitlandchambers.com.

NESS, Air Vice-Marshal Charles Wright, CB 2009; CEng, FRAeS; Defence Adviser, Fujitsu, since 2012; *b* 6 Nov. 1957; *s* of Air Marshal Sir Charles Ernest Ness, KCB, CBE and Audrey Ness; one *d*. *Educ:* Mill Hill Sch.; Liverpool Univ. (BEng). CEng 1986; FRAeS 1998. Joined RAF, 1975; Sen. Engrg Officer, 111 Sqn, 1986–88; OC, Engrg and Supply Wing, RAF Coningsby, 1993–95; Dep. Dir, Logistics Policy (RAF), 1995–97; Hd, Aero Engines Multi-Disciplinary Gp, 1997–99; Air Cdre, Communications and Inf. Systems, 1999; COS, Equipment Support (Air), 2000–02; Harrier Integrated Project Team Leader, 2003–04; Dir, Logistics No 1 Gp, 2004–05; Hd, RAF Process and Orgn Review, 2005–06; COS, Strategy, Policy and Plans, RAF High Wycombe, 2006–07; Dir Gen., Combat Air, Defence Equipment and Support Orgn, 2007–08; Sen. Technical Advr to Charles Haddon-Cave, QC, 2008–09; Dir of Tech. Airworthiness, Military Aviation Authy, 2010–12. *Club:* Royal Air Force.

NESS, Patrick M.; novelist; *b* Fort Belvoir, Va, 1971; civil partnership 1999, *m* 2014, M. A. Nowell. *Educ:* Univ. of Southern Calif (BA English *summa cum laude* 1993). *Publications:* The Crash of Hennington, 2003; Topics About Which I Know Nothing, 2005; The Crane Wife, 2013; *for children*: The Knife of Never Letting Go, 2008 (Guardian Children's Fiction Prize); The Ask and the Answer, 2009 (Costa Children's Book of the Year, 2010); Monsters of Men, 2010 (Carnegie Medal, 2011); A Monster Calls, 2011 (Galaxy Nat. Book Award; Red House Children's Book Award, Carnegie Medal, 2012); More Than This, 2013; The Rest of Us Just Live Here, 2015. *Recreations:* distance running, theatre, overpaying for imported breakfast cereal, cat harmonica. *Address:* c/o Michelle Kass Associates, 85 Charing Cross Road, WC2H 0AA. *T:* (020) 7439 1624. *E:* office@michellekass.co.uk.

NESS, Robert; Director, Hong Kong, British Council, since 2012; *b* 30 March 1953; *s* of late Robert Mitchell Ness and of Mary Ness (*née* Connor); *m* 1st, 1985, Geraldine McKendrick (marr. diss. 2013); two *s* one *d*; 2nd, 2013, Soon ok Shin. *Educ:* Arbroath High Sch.; Edinburgh Univ. (MA Hons; DipEd); Moray House Coll. of Educn (PGCE). Teacher, Madrid, 1978–80; joined British Council, 1981: English Tuition Co-ordinating Unit, 1981–83; Overseas Educnl Appts Dept, 1983–86; Asst Rep., Austria, 1987–89; English Lang. Div., 1989–92; Dep. Dir, SA, 1992–97; Dir, Cyprus, 1997–2000; Dir, Portugal, and Cultural Counsellor, Lisbon, 2000–03; Regl Dir, E Europe, 2003–05; Head, UK Directorate, 2005–08; Dir, Colombia, 2008–12. *Recreations:* music (especially jazz, opera, chamber), books, running, travel. *Address:* British Council, 10 Spring Gardens, SW1A 2BN.

NESSLING, Paul William Downs; HM Diplomatic Service, retired; Research Analysts, Foreign and Commonwealth Office, 2008–11; *b* 26 Sept. 1945; *s* of late Herbert William Nessling and Mary Alice Nessling (*née* Perry); *m* 1975, Kathryn Lynne Freeman; one *d*. *Educ:* Latymer Upper Sch., Hammersmith. Mgt trainee, Midland Bank, 1962–63; buyer, BAT, 1965–66; Department of Trade and Industry, 1967–75: on secondment as Third Sec., Chicago, 1970; Asst Private Sec. to Sec. of State, 1972–74; Private Sec. to Minister of Prices, 1974–75; on secondment as Second Sec., Bahrain, 1975–79; joined HM Diplomatic Service, 1979; Second Secretary: FCO, 1979–81; Lisbon, 1981–82; and Consul, Warsaw, 1982–84; Hd of Chancery, Aden, 1984; First Secretary: (Aid) and Dep. UK Perm. Rep. to UNEP, Nairobi, 1984–87; FCO, 1987–89; (Commercial), Harare, 1989–93; (Commercial), Muscat, 1993–96; Sarajevo, 1996–97; Dep. Dir, Jt Export Promotion Directorate, FCO, 1997–98; Dep. High Comr, Lusaka, 1998–2001; High Comr, Kingdom of Tonga, 2002–06. *Recreations:* current affairs, tennis, travelling, reading, walking.

NETANYAHU, Binyamin; Prime Minister of Israel, since 2009; Member, Knesset, since 1988; *b* 21 Oct. 1949; *s* of late Cela and Benzion Netanyahu; *m* (marr. diss.); one *d*; *m* 3rd, 1991, Sara; two *s*. *Educ:* MIT (BA 1976; MBA). Mgt Consultant, Boston Consulting Gp, 1976–78; Exec. Dir, Jonathan Inst., Jerusalem, 1978–80; Sen. Manager, Rim Industries, Jerusalem, 1980–82; Dep. Chief of Mission, Washington, 1982–84; Perm. Rep. to UN, 1984–88; Deputy Minister: Ministry of Foreign Affairs, 1988–91; Prime Minister's Office, 1991–92; Prime Minister of Israel and Minister of Housing and Construction, 1996–99; Foreign Minister, 2002–03; Finance Minister, 2003–05; Leader of Opposition, 2006–09; Foreign Minister and Minister for Health, for Communications, for Regl Cooperation, 2015–. Leader, Likud, 1993–99 and 2005–. *Publications:* (ed) Self-Portrait of a Hero: the letters of Jonathan Netanyahu, 1981; Terrorism: how the West can win, 1986; A Place Among the Nations: Israel and the world, 1993; Fighting Terrorism, 1996. *Address:* The Knesset, Kiryat Ben-Gurion, Jerusalem 91950, Israel.

NETHERCOT, Prof. David Arthur, OBE 2006; PhD, DSc; FREng, FTSE, FIStructE, FICE; Professor of Civil Engineering, 1999–2011, now Emeritus, Head of Department of Civil and Environmental Engineering, 1999–2011, and Deputy Principal, Faculty of Engineering, 2008–11, Imperial College London (formerly Imperial College of Science, Technology and Medicine, University of London); *b* 26 April 1946; *s* of late Arthur Owen Martin Nethercot and Dorothy May Nethercot; *m* 1968, Hedd Dwynwen Evans; two *d*. *Educ:* Univ. of Wales Coll. of Cardiff (BSc, PhD, DSc). FIStructE 1989; FICE 1994; FREng (FEng 1993); FCGI 2001; FTSE 2010. ICI Fellow, Univ. of Wales, 1970–71; Lectr, 1971–81, Sen. Lectr, 1981–86, Reader, 1986–89, Univ. of Sheffield; Prof. of Civil Engrg, 1989–99, Hd of Dept, 1994–99, Univ. of Nottingham. Visiting Professor: Japan Soc. for Promotion of Science, Univ. of Nagoya, 1980; Swiss Federal Inst. of Tech., Lausanne, 1990. President: IStructE, 2003–04 (Mem. Council, 1986–89, 1991–97; Vice-Pres., 2001–03); IABSE, 2013–; Chm., Cttee on Bldg and Civil Engrg Structures, BSI, 2013–; Member: Cttee on Structural Use of Steel in Building, BSI, 1986–2006 (Chm., 1995–2006); Joint Bd of Moderators, 1993–2000 (Chm., 1996–98); Standing Cttee on Structural Safety, 1996–2001; Council, Royal Acad. of Engrg, 2000–03. Foreign Mem., NAE, 2015. FRSA 2002. Charles Massonnet Prize, Eur. Convention for Constructional Steelwork, 2008; Gold Medal, IStructE, 2009; Lynn Beedle Prize, Structural Stability Res. Council, 2015. *Publications:* (jtly) Design for Structural Stability, 1979, 2nd edn 1985; Limit States Design of Structural Steelwork, 1986, 3rd edn 2001; (jtly) Design of Members Subject to Combined Bending and Torsion, 1989; (jtly) Lateral Stability of Steel Beams and Columns: common causes of restraint, 1992; (jtly) The Behaviour and Design of Steel Structures to EC3, 3rd edn 2001, 4th edn 2008; (jtly) Designers Guide to EN 1993–1–1: Eurocode 3: design of steel structures, 2005, 3rd edn 2011; about 400 sci. papers on structural engrg. *Recreation:* sport. *Address:* Department of Civil and Environmental Engineering, Imperial College London, South Kensington Campus, SW7 2AZ. *T:* (020) 7594 6097, *Fax:* (020) 7594 6042.

NETHERTHORPE, 3rd Baron *cr* 1959, of Anston, W Riding; **James Frederick Turner;** *b* 7 Jan. 1964; *s* of 2nd Baron Netherthorpe, and Belinda, *d* of F. Hedley Nicholson; *S* father, 1982; *m* 1989, Elizabeth Curran Fahan, *d* of Edward Fahan, Connecticut; two *s* two *d*. *Educ:* Heatherdown Prep. Sch.; Harrow Sch. *Heir:* *s* Hon. Andrew James Edward Turner, *b* 24 March 1993. *Address:* Boothby Hall, Boothby Pagnell, Grantham, Lincs NG33 4DQ. *T:* (01476) 585482.

NETHSINGHA, Andrew Mark, FRCO; conductor; Director of Music, and Fellow, St John's College, Cambridge, since 2007; Director and Co-Founder, St John's Sinfonia, since 2011; *b* 16 May 1968; *s* of Lucian Nethsingha and late Jane (*née* Symons); *m* 1996, Lucy Kathleen Sellwood; one *s* two *d*. *Educ:* Exeter Cathedral Sch.; Clifton Coll. (Music Schol.); Royal Coll. of Music (ARCM); St John's Coll., Cambridge (Organ Student; BA 1990; MA 1994). FRCO 1987. Chorister, Exeter Cathedral, 1976–81; Organ Schol., St George's Chapel, Windsor Castle, 1986–87; Asst Organist, Wells Cathedral, 1990–94; Master of Choristers and Organist, Truro Cathedral, 1994–2002; Dir of Music, Gloucester Cathedral, 2002–07, Organist Emeritus, 2008. Musical Director: Three Spires Singers and Orch., 1994–2002; Gloucester Choral Soc., 2002–07; Artistic Dir, Gloucester Three Choirs Fest., 2002–07. Début: BBC Proms, 2009; Amsterdam Concertgebouw, 2009; Suntory Hall, Tokyo, 2012; Munich Herkulessaal, 2013. Pres., Cathedral Organists' Assoc., 2007–10. Hon. Fellow, N and Midlands Sch. of Music, 2006; Hon. FGCM, 2008; Hon. FRSCM, 2015. *Recreations:* family, reading, walking, travel. *Address:* St John's College, Cambridge CB2 1TP. *T:* (01223) 338683. *E:* an323@cam.ac.uk.

NETTEL, Caroline Gillian; *see* Mawhood, C. G.

NETTEL, Julian Philip; Director, Julian Nettel Consulting Ltd, since 2009; *b* 23 Oct. 1953; *s* of Leopold and Clare Nettel; *m* 1980, Caroline Gillian Mawhood, *qv*; two *s*. *Educ:* Univ. of Bristol (BA Hons Philosophy). DipHSM, MHSM 1977. Hosp. Sec., Westminster Hosp., 1983–86; General Manager, Whittington and Royal Northern Hosps, 1986–90; Ops Dir, KCH and Dulwich Hosp., 1990–92; Exec. in Residence, Faculty of Admin, Univ. of Ottawa, 1992–93; Chief Executive: Ealing Hosp. NHS Trust, 1994–99; St Mary's NHS Trust, London, 1999–2007; Barts and The London NHS Trust, 2007–09; Sen. Chief Exec. Associate, 2010–13, Chief Exec. Associate, 2015–, Harvey Nash plc; Sen. Advr, Parthenon Gp, 2010–12; Interim Man. Dir, NHS Inst. for Innovation and Improvement, 2011–12; Interim Chief Exec., Gt Ormond St Hosp. for Children NHS Foundn Trust, 2014. Mem., Expert Reference Gp on Renal Nat. Service Framework, DoH, 2001–03. Trustee, Wimbledon Coll. of Art Trust, 2009–. *Recreations:* painting, cycling, bridge, keeping fit, gardening, golf, jazz. *Address:* 35 Skeena Hill, SW18 5PW. *T:* (020) 8788 2017. *Clubs:* Royal Thames Yacht, Roehampton; Wimbledon Park Golf.

NETTLETON, Catherine Elizabeth, CMG 2015; OBE 1999; HM Diplomatic Service; Director of Protocol, Foreign and Commonwealth Office, 2015; *b* 13 March 1960; *d* of late Kenneth Arthur Nettleton and Olga Nettleton (*née* Musgrave). *Educ:* Exeter Univ. (BA Hons); Manchester Univ. (MA). Inland Revenue, 1982; FCO, 1983; full-time Mandarin lang. training, 1984; Vice Consul, Beijing, 1987–89; Second Sec., FCO, 1989–91; First Sec. (Political/Economic), Mexico City, 1991–95; First Sec., 1995–99, Counsellor, 1999–2000, FCO; Political/Economic Counsellor, Beijing, 2000–03; rcds, 2004; Hd, FCO Services: Presidencies, FCO, 2004–06; Ambassador to Peru, 2006–10; Ambassador to Venezuela, 2010–14. *Recreations:* walking, ski-ing, theatre. *Address:* c/o Foreign and Commonwealth Office, King Charles Street, SW1A 2AH.

NEUBERGER, family name of **Baroness Neuberger** and **Baron Neuberger of Abbotsbury**.

NEUBERGER, Baroness *cr* 2004 (Life Peer), of Primrose Hill in the London Borough of Camden; **Rabbi Julia Babette Sarah Neuberger,** DBE 2004; Chief Executive, The King's Fund, 1997–2004; a Civil Service Commissioner, 2001–02; Senior Rabbi, West London Synagogue, since 2011; *b* 27 Feb. 1950; *d* of late Walter and Alice Schwab; *m* 1973, Anthony John Neuberger; one *s* one *d*. *Educ:* South Hampstead High Sch.; Newnham Coll., Cambridge (BA, MA); Leo Baeck Coll., London (Rabbinic Dip.). Lectr and Associate Fellow, Leo Baeck Coll., 1979–97; Associate, Newnham Coll., Cambridge, 1983–96; Harkness Fellow, Harvard Univ., 1991–92; Associate Fellow, King's Fund Coll., 1993–97; Bloomberg Prof. of Philanthropy and Public Policy, Divinity Sch., Harvard Univ., 2006. Rabbi, South London Liberal Synagogue, 1977–89; Chm., Rabbinic Conf., Union of Liberal and Progressive Synagogues, 1983–85. Chm., Camden and Islington Community Health Services NHS Trust, 1993–97; Member: Council, N London Hospice Gp, 1984–91; Ethics Adv. Gp, RCN, 1986–93; BMA Ethics Cttee, 1992–94; NHS Health Adv. Service, 1993–97; Council, St George's Hosp. Med. Sch., 1987–93; Chairman: Patients' Assoc., 1988–91; RCN Commn on the Health Service, 1988; Adv. Cttee, UK Clearing House on Health Outcomes, Nuffield Inst., 1992–95; Sainsbury Centre for Mental Health review of training needs of mental health workers; Chair: Commn on the Future of Volunteering, 2006–08; Responsible Gambling Strategy Bd, 2008–12; One Housing Gp, 2009–12; Adv. Panel on Judicial Diversity, 2009–10; Prime Minister's Champion for Volunteering, 2007–09; Rev. of Liverpool Care Pathway, 2013–14. Member: Cttee on Standards in Public Life, 2001–04; Interim (formerly Voluntary) Licensing Authority for IVF, 1987–91; Human Fertilization and Embryology Authority, 1990–95; GMC, 1993–2001; MRC, 1995–2000; Exec., Anchor Housing Assoc. and Trust, 1985–87; Exec., NCVO, 1988–89; Exec., Unicef UK, 1989–91; Council, SCF, 1994–96; Bd, Citizenship Foundn, 1989–92; Council, St George's House, Windsor, 1989–94; Council, Runnymede Trust, 1989–97; Library and Information Commn, 1995–97; Bd, Inst. for Jewish Policy Res., 2006–11; DCMS Mem., Review of Funding of BBC, 1999; Governor, British Inst. of Human Rights, 1989–93; Trustee: Imperial War Mus., 1999–2006; Multifaith Secondary School Trust, 2001–; Booker Prize Foundn, 2002–11; Walter and Liesel Schwab Charitable Trust, 2003–; Urban Village, 2004–11; Jewish Care, 2004–07 and 2009–11; British Council, 2004–07; Liberal Democrats, 2005–08; New Philanthropy Capital, 2008–11; Social Market Foundn, 2012–. Member: Nat. Cttee, SDP, 1982–88; Policy Cttee, SDP, 1983–85; Convenor, SDP/Liberal Lawyers' Working Party on Legal Services, 1985–87; Mem., Editorial Bd, Political Qly, 1987–93. Presenter, Choices, BBC TV, 1986 and 1987. Chancellor, Univ. of Ulster, 1993–2000. Member Council: RHBNC, 1991–93; UCL, 1993–97; Mem. Visiting Cttee, Meml Church, Harvard Univ., 1994–2000; Governor: James Allen's Girls' Sch., 1994–97; Dulwich Coll. Prep. Sch., 1995–97. Judge: Booker Prize, 1994; Orange Prize, 2010. Hon. FCGI 1997; Hon. Fellow, Mansfield Coll., Oxford, 1998. DUniv: Humberside, 1992; Stirling, 1995; Open, 1997; Hon. DSc: Ulster, 1994; Oxford Brookes, 1995; London, 2006; Hon. DLitt: City, 1994; Teesside, 1995; Hon. LLD: Nottingham, 1996; QUB, 2000; Aberdeen 2002; Hon. Dr Sheffield Hallam, 2001; Hon. DD Cambridge, 2015. *Publications:* The Story of Judaism (for children), 1986, 2nd edn 1988; (ed) Days of Decision (4 in series), 1987; Caring for Dying Patients of Different Faiths, 1987, 3rd edn 2004; (ed with John A. White) A Necessary End, 1991; Whatever's Happening to Women?, 1991; Ethics and Healthcare: the role of Research Ethics Committees in the UK, 1992; (ed) The Things That Matter (anthology of women's spiritual poetry), 1993; On Being Jewish, 1995; Dying Well: a guide to enabling a better death, 1999, 2nd edn 2004; (ed with Bill New) Hidden Assets: values and decision-making in the NHS today, 2002; The Moral State We're In, 2005; Not Dead Yet, 2008; Is That All There Is?, 2011; contribs to various books on cultural, religious and ethical factors in nursing, reviews for variety of jls and newspapers. *Recreations:* sailing, Irish life, opera, setting up the old girls' network, children. *Address:* House of Lords, SW1A 0PW.

NEUBERGER OF ABBOTSBURY, Baron *cr* 2007 (Life Peer), of Abbotsbury in the county of Dorset; **David Edmond Neuberger,** Kt 1996; PC 2004; a Justice and President of the Supreme Court of the United Kingdom, since 2012; *b* 10 Jan. 1948; *s* of Prof. Albert Neuberger, CBE, FRS and Lilian Ida (*née* Dreyfus); *m* 1976, Angela, *d* of Brig. Peter Holdsworth; two *s* one *d*. *Educ:* Westminster; Christ Church, Oxford (MA). N. M. Rothschild & Sons, 1970–73; called to the Bar, Lincoln's Inn, 1974, Bencher, 1993; QC 1987; a Recorder, 1990–96; a Judge of the High Ct of Justice, Chancery Div., 1996–2004; Supervisory Chancery Judge, Midland, Wales and Chester, and Western Circuits, 2001–04; a Lord Justice of Appeal, 2004–06; a Lord of Appeal in Ordinary, 2007–09; a non-permanent Judge, Hong Kong Court of Final Appeal, 2010–; Master of the Rolls and Hd of Civil Justice, 2009–12. Chm., Adv. Cttee on Spoliation of Art, 1999–. Chm., Schizophrenia Trust, 2003–. Gov., Univ. of the Arts, London (formerly London Inst.), 2000–11. *Address:* Supreme Court of the United Kingdom, Parliament Square, SW1P 3BD. *Club:* Garrick.

NEVILL, family name of **Marquess of Abergavenny**.

NEVILL, Amanda Elizabeth, CBE 2015; Chief Executive Officer (formerly Director), British Film Institute, since 2003; *b* 21 March 1957; *d* of John Henry Howard King and Jill King (*née* Livett); *m* 1980, Dominic John Nevill (marr. diss. 1986); two *d*. *Educ:* Bar Convent, York; British Inst., Paris. Rowan Gall., London, 1978–79; Francis Kyle Gall., London, 1979–80; Bath Internat. Fest. Contemporary Art Fair, 1980–84; Adminr, 1985–90, Sec., 1990–94, Royal Photographic Soc.; Head, Nat. Mus. of Photography, Film and TV, 1994–2003. FRSA. Hon. FRPS 1994. Hon. DLit Bradford, 2000. *Address:* British Film Institute, 21 Stephen Street, W1T 1LN. *T:* (020) 7957 8903.

NEVILL, Prof. Bernard Richard, FCSD; designer; Professor of Textile Design, Royal College of Art, 1984–89 (Fellow, since 1984); Director, Bernard Nevill Ltd (own furnishing collections), 1990–98; *b* 24 Sept. 1934; *s* of R. G. Nevill. *Educ:* privately; St Martin's Sch. of Art; Royal Coll. of Art. FSIA 1970. Designed exhibn, Opera and Ballet, for Cotton Bd, Manchester, 1950; lectured in art, fashion, history of costume, textile design and fashion drawing, Shoreditch Coll., 1954–56 (resp. for first dress show staged at GLC Chm.'s annual reception, County Hall); Lectr, St Martin's Sch. of Art and RCA, 1959–74 (liaised between Fashion and Textile Schs, devising projs and themes for finale to RCA annual diploma show); lectured in theatre design and book illustration, Central Sch. of Art and Design, 1957–60; freelance illustrator, Good Housekeeping, Woman's Jl, Vogue, Harper's Bazaar, incl. covers for Queen and Sketch, 1956–60; freelance journalist, Vogue, Sketch and textile and fashion periodicals, 1956–66; Art Critic, Vogue, 1965–66; Designer (later Design Dir), Liberty Prints, 1961: for next decade, produced collections which became fashion landmarks and re-estabd Liberty's as major source of fashion textiles worldwide; collections designed: Islamic, 1963 (anticipated Eastern revival in fashion); Jazz, 1964 (first re-appraisal of Art Deco); Tango, 1966; Renaissance, 1967; Chameleon, 1969 (co-ordinated prints); Designer and Design Dir, Ten Cate, Holland, 1969–71; Design Consultant in dress fabrics to Cantoni (founders of cotton industry in Italy), 1971–84: printed velvets and cottons have placed Cantoni in forefront of internat. ready-to-wear; designed printed sheet collection for Cantoni Casa, 1977; textile consultant and designer of dress fabrics, Unitika Ltd, Japan, 1990–; dress fabric collections for KBC, Germany, 1993–; furnishing textile designs commnd by Pierre Frey, France, 1991–; furnishing collections produced by DMC Texunion, France, 1992–; designing own-label home textile and furniture collections, with Hodsoll McKenzie, 1999–2001; redesign and supervision of restoration of interiors: Lennoxlove Castle, 1988–89; Eastnor Castle, 1989. Designed: two collections for Internat. Wool Secretariat, 1975–77; English Country House Collection for Sekers Internat., 1981–82 (used this collection when redesigning Long Gall., Lutyen's British Embassy, Washington); Collections for Romanex de Boussac, France, 1982–87, including English Gardens, Botanic, Figurative Porcelain Prints and Printed Damasks; furnishing collection for restored Château de Bagnole, France. Designed costumes: films: Genevieve, 1953; Next To No Time, 1955; The Admirable Crichton, 1957; musical: Marigold, 1958; opera: Così fan tutte (Glyndebourne), 1962. Engaged in restoration of Fonthill Abbey and woodlands, 1976–. Mem., Adv. Panel, National Dip. of Design, 1964–66; Governor, Croydon Coll. of Art, 1966–67. FRSA 1966, resigned 1977. Book reviewer, TLS, 1987–. Illustrated articles on his work have appeared in the Press. *Recreations:* looking at large well-built walls and buildings; passionate conservationist and environmentalist, collector, bibliophil; tree-worship, chamber music.

NEVILLE, family name of **Baron Braybrooke**.

NEVILLE, Prof. Adam Matthew, CBE 1994; TD 1963; FREng; FRSE; arbitrator and consultant on concrete and structural design and failures, retired; Principal and Vice-Chancellor, University of Dundee, 1978–87; *b* 5 Feb. 1923; *m* 1952, Dr Mary Hallam Cousins; one *s* one *d*. *Educ:* Queen Mary Coll., London Univ. (BSc 1st cl. Hons; Hon. Fellow, QMW, 1997); MSc, PhD, DSc (Eng) London; DSc Leeds. FIStructE; FREng (FEng 1986); FRSE 1979. Served War, Polish Forces under British comd, MC; Major RE (TA), 1950–63. Lectr, Southampton Univ., 1950–51; Engr, Min. of Works, NZ, 1951–54; Lectr, Manchester Univ., 1955–60; Prof. of Civil Engrg, Nigerian Coll. of Technology, 1960–62; Foundn Dean of Engrg, Calgary Univ., 1963–67, also Foundn Dean of Graduate Studies, 1965–66; Vis. Prof., Swiss Federal Inst. of Technology, 1967–68; Prof. and Head of Dept of Civil Engineering, Univ. of Leeds, 1968–78. Partner (formerly Dir), A & M Neville Engineering, 1975–2009. Chm., Cttee of Principals of Scottish Univs, 1984–86. Former Chm., Permanent Concrete Commn, RILEM (Internat. Union of Testing and Res. Labs for Materials and Structures); Dir, Petroleum Recovery Res. Inst.; Advr to Canadian Govt on management of concrete research. Member Council: Concrete Soc., 1968–77, (Pres., 1974–75); IStructE, 1976–79; Faculty of Building, 1976–80; Royal Acad. (formerly Fellowship) of Engrg, 1989–95 (Vice-Pres., 1991–95); Open University, 1979–87; Council of Europe Standing Conference on Univ. Problems, 1980–87 (Pres., 1984–86); Member: Bd, Architectural Educn, ARC, 1980–87; Exec. Cttee, IUPC, 1979–90 (Vice-Chm., 1983–85); British Library Adv. Council, 1989–94; SERC Envmt Cttee, 1988–91; Athlone-Vanier Fellowships Bd, 1990–96; NAPAG, 1992–97. Trustee, Carnegie Trust for Univs of Scotland, 1978–87. Mem. Editorial Boards of various technical jls. Fellow: Amer. Concrete Inst., 1973 (Hon. Mem., 1986); Concrete Soc., 1994 (Hon. Mem., 2000); Hon. Fellow: Inst. of Concrete Technology, 1976; Singapore Concrete Inst., 1987; Hon. Mem., Brazilian Concrete Inst., 2007; Hon. For. Mem., Académie Royale des Sciences d'Outre-Mer, Belgium, 1974. Hon. LLD: St Andrews, 1987; Dundee, 1998; Calgary, 2011; Hon. DAppSci Sherbrooke, Quebec, 1999; Laurea Magistrale ad Honorem, Politecnico di Torino, 2011. IStructE Research Award, 1960; Reinforced Concrete Assoc. Medal, 1961; Senior Research Fellowship, Nat. Research Council of Canada, 1967; Stanton Walker Award (US) 1968; Medal of Univ. of Liège (Belgium), 1970; Arthur R. Anderson Award, 1972, Turner Medal, 2001, R. Philleo Award, 2011, Amer. Concrete Inst.; President's Medal, Soc. of Engrs, 1985; Medal, Inst. of Concrete Technology, 1993; Gold Medal, Concrete Soc., 2007; Sustained Achievement Medal, RAEng, 2008; Polish Concrete Award, Dni Betonu, 2012. OStJ 1983. *Publications:* Properties of Concrete, 1963, 5th edn 2011, trans. into 13 languages; (with J. B. Kennedy) Basic Statistical Methods, 1964, 3 edns; Creep of Concrete: plain, reinforced and prestressed, 1970; (with A. Ghali) Structural Analysis: a unified classical and matrix approach, 1971, 6th edn 2008 (trans. Chinese, Japanese); Hardened Concrete: physical and mechanical aspects, 1971; High Alumina Cement Concrete, 1975; (with W. H. Dilger and J. J. Brooks) Creep of Plain and Structural Concrete, 1983; (with J. J. Brooks) Concrete Technology, 1987, 2nd edn 2010 (trans. Spanish, Malay, Arabic); Neville on Concrete, 2003, 2nd edn 2007; Concrete: Neville's insights and issues, 2006, rev. edn 2014; numerous research papers on concrete and concrete structures. *Recreations:* ski-ing (reminiscing), travel (Travelers' Century Club Plaque, 1990). *Club:* Athenæum.

See also Dame E. L. Neville.

NEVILLE, Prof. (Alexander) Munro, MD; FRCPath; Associate Director (formerly Administrator), and Research Secretary, Ludwig Institute for Cancer Research, New York and London, 1985–2005; *b* 24 March 1935; *s* of Alexander Munro and Georgina Neville; *m* 1961, Anne Margaret Stroyan Black; one *s* one *d*. *Educ:* Hillhead High Sch.; Univ. of Glasgow (MB ChB 1959; PhD 1965; MD 1969); Harvard Med. Sch.; DSc London, 1985. MRCPath 1969, FRCPath 1981. Med. appts, Glasgow Royal and Victoria Infirmaries, 1960–65; Res. Fellow, Harvard Med. Sch., 1965–67; Sen. Lectr in Pathology, Univ. of Glasgow, 1967–70; Hon. Consultant Pathologist, Royal Marsden Hosp., 1970–85; Prof. of Experimental Pathology, Univ. of London, 1972–85; Dean, Inst. of Cancer Research, 1982–84; Dir, Ludwig Inst. for Cancer Research, London Branch, 1975–85. Visiting Professor: of Pathol., RPMS, 1992–2006; of Med. Oncology, Imperial Coll. London, 2006–10. Hon. Treas., RCPath, 1993–98. *Publications:* The Human Adrenal Cortex, 1982; numerous papers on oncology and pathology in primary jls. *Recreations:* golf, gardening, history. *Address:* 6 Woodlands Park, Tadworth, Surrey KT20 7TL. *T:* (01737) 844113. *E:* munroneville@btinternet.com. *Club:* Banstead Downs.

NEVILLE, Prof. Anne, PhD; FREng; FRSE; RAEng Chair in Emerging Technologies, since 2009, Professor of Tribology and Surface Engineering, since 2003, and Director, Institute of Functional Surfaces, since 2013, University of Leeds; *b* Dumfries, 21 March 1970; *d* of William Neville and late Doris Neville; *m* 1999, Mark McKelvie; one *d*. *Educ:* Maxwelltown High Sch., Dumfries; Univ. of Glasgow (BEng 1st Cl. 1992; PhD 1995). FREng 2010. Lectr, 1995–99, Reader, 1999–2002, Prof., 2002–03, Dept of Mech. and Chem. Engrg, Heriot-Watt Univ. Ed., Tribology: Materials, Surfaces and Interfaces, 2007–. Mem., REF 2014 Panel, Gen. Engrg, 2010–13. Consultant, Oilfield Corrosion, Clariant, 2010–. Royal Soc. Wolfson Res. Merit Award Holder, 2012–. FRSE 2005. Suffrage Sci. Award, MRC, 2015. *Recreations:* visiting islands on West coast of Scotland, hillwalking, family. *Address:* School of Mechanical Engineering, Woodhouse Lane, University of Leeds, Leeds LS2 9JT. *T:* (0113) 343 6812, 07789 712417. *E:* a.neville@leeds.ac.uk.

NEVILLE, Prof. Brian George Richard, FRCP, FRCPCH; Professor of Childhood Epilepsy, Institute of Child Health, University College London, Great Ormond Street Hospital for Children NHS Trust and National Centre for Young People with Epilepsy, 2008–09, now Emeritus (Prince of Wales's Professor, 2004–07); *b* 13 Feb. 1939; *s* of George Edward Neville and Louisa Nellie Neville; *m* 1964, Heather Maureen Gemmell; one *s* three *d*. *Educ:* St Dunstan's Coll., Catford; Guy's Hosp. Med. Sch., London (MB BS 1964). MRCP 1966, FRCP 1980; FRCPCH 1997. Consultant Paediatric Neurologist, Guy's Hosp., 1973–89; Prof. of Paediatric Neurology, Inst. of Child Health, UCL, 1989–2004; Hon. Consultant Paediatric Neurologist, Great Ormond St Hosp. for Children, Nat. Centre for Young People with Epilepsy and Nat. Hosp. for Neurology and Neurosurgery, 1989–. Hon. Paediatric Neurologist: Jersey, 1989–2004; Malta, 1992–. Sec., 1980–83 and Pres., 1986–89, British Paediatric Neurology Assoc.; Founder and Chm., Eur. Acad. of Childhood Disability, 1989–2002; Co-Founder and Chm., Eur. Soc. of Movt Analysis in Children, 1993–96. *Publications:* (ed jtly) Congenital Hemiplegia, 2000; (ed jtly) The Management of Spasticity Associated with the Cerebral Palsies in Children or Adults, 2000; articles in paediatric neurology, particularly epilepsy and disability. *Recreations:* music, church organist, cycling, walking. *Address:* UCL Institute of Child Health, Neurosciences Unit, 30 Guilford Street, WC1N 1EH. *T:* (020) 7837 7618, *Fax:* (020) 7833 9469. *E:* b.neville@ucl.ac.uk. *Club:* Royal Society of Medicine.

NEVILLE, Dame Elizabeth (Louise), DBE 2003; QPM 1996; DL; Chief Constable, Wiltshire Constabulary, 1997–2004; *b* 5 Feb. 1953; *d* of Prof. Adam Matthew Neville, *qv*; one *s* one *d* from former marriage. *Educ:* St Hilda's Coll., Oxford (MA; Hon. Fellow, 2006); University Coll. London (PhD). Metropolitan Police, 1973–86; Thames Valley Police, 1986–91; Asst Chief Constable, Sussex Police, 1991–94; Dep. Chief Constable, Northamptonshire, 1994–97. Non-exec. Dir, Serious Fraud Office, 2004–12. Member: Police Appeals Tribunal, 2004–08; Civil Nuclear Police Authy, 2005–12; Determinations Panel, Pensions Regulator, 2010–; Ind. Complaints Assessor, DVO Gp, subseq. Safety, Service Delivery and Logistics Gp, then Motoring and Freight Service Gp, DfT, 2004–10; Regulatory Decisions Cttee, Financial Conduct Authy, 2013–; Complaints Adjudicator, Assets Recovery Agency, 2004–08; Ind. Adjudicator, Companies House, 2007–; Appeal Officer, Regulator of Community Interest Cos, 2013–. Non-exec. Mem. Bd, Insolvency Service, 2013–. Sen. Advr, Olive Gp, 2006–07. Dir, Ajay Shopfit Maintenance Ltd, 2004–08. Trustee: Cumberland Lodge (formerly King George VI and Queen Elizabeth Foundn of St Catharine's), 2002– (Vice Chm., 2011–); Wiltshire Bobby Van. Patron, Swindon Sanctuary, 2004–. Mem., Bd of Govs, Stonar Sch., Wilts, 2005–11 (Vice Chm., 2011). High Sheriff, 2010–11, DL 2011, Wilts. Hon. Fellow, Univ. of Northampton, 2004. Hon. LLD Southampton Solent, 2004. *Recreations:* ski-ing, sailing. *Club:* Reform.

NEVILLE, Helen Margaret, PhD; FRSC; Vice President, Corporate Research and Development, Procter & Gamble, since 2010; *b* Hong Kong, 6 June 1963; *d* of Ray Coates and Yvonne Coates; *m* 1987, Mark Neville; one *s* two *d*. *Educ:* Durham Univ. (BSc Chem. 1984); Univ. of Southampton (PhD Organic Chem. 1987). Research and Development, Procter & Gamble: Tech. Brand Manager, Newcastle Tech. Center, 1987–89; Gp/Section Hd, 1989–97, Associate Dir, 1997–99, W Europe, Central and E Europe, Middle East and Africa; Associate Dir, Global Household Cleaning, 1999–2003, Dir, Global Hand Dish Washing, 2003–06, Brussels Innovation Center; Dir, Feminine Care, Schwalbach Tech. Center, 2006–07; Vice Pres., Hair Care, Darmstadt Innovation Center, 2007–10. Mem., EPSRC, 2013–. Mem. Council, RSC, 2013–. *Recreations:* travel, food and wine, fitness. *E:* neville.hm@pg.com.

NEVILLE, (John) Oliver, MA, PhD; Principal, Royal Academy of Dramatic Art, 1984–93; *b* 14 Aug. 1929; *s* of Frederick and Ethel Neville; *m* 1st, 1952, Shirley Hall; one *s* one *d*; 2nd, 1964, Pat Heywood. *Educ:* Price's Sch., Fareham; King's Coll., Cambridge (Le Bas Student; BA Eng. Lit., MA, PhD). After National Service, engaged in following with ultimate aim of becoming a theatre director: studied theatre design under Reginald Leefe, 1949–51; joined Old Vic Co., walking on in Tyrone Guthrie's Tamburlaine, with Donald Wolfit, 1951; studied singing with Clive Carey and Frank Titterton; seasons of rep. at York, Scarborough, Worthing, Bristol, Birmingham and Manchester, 1952–58; re-joined Old Vic Co., 1958 (roles included Warwick in Henry VI Trilogy and Claudius in Hamlet); toured America, Poland, Russia, India, Pakistan, Ceylon, with Old Vic and Bristol Old Vic, as stage dir, actor and dir; Associate Dir, Old Vic Co., 1960–62 (directed Macbeth and The Tempest); Director: Library Theatre, Manchester, 1963–66; Arts Theatre, Ipswich, 1966–69; Mature Student, Cambridge, 1969–76 (PhD on Ben Jonson's Masques and Poetry); Caroline Spurgeon Res. Fellow, Bedford Coll., London, 1977–79; Sen. Lectr in Drama, Univ. of Bristol, 1979–84. *Recreations:* mediaeval church architecture and stained-glass, gardening. *Address:* c/o Peters, Fraser & Dunlop, Drury House, 34–43 Russell Street, WC2B 5HA.

NEVILLE, Munro; *see* Neville, A. M.

NEVILLE, Oliver; *see* Neville, J. O.

NEVILLE, Air Vice-Marshal Patrick, CB 1988; OBE 1976; AFC 1960; Chief of Air Staff, Royal New Zealand Air Force, 1986–89, retired; *b* 23 Sept. 1932; *s* of Patrick Joseph Neville and Helena Neville; *m* 1954, Barbara Howell; one *s* one *d*. *Educ:* Purbrook Park County High Sch. (SchCert). Commnd 1951; Navigator: RAF, 1951–55; RNZAF, 1955; CO No 14 Sqdn RNZAF, 1966–69; Base Comdr, RNZAF Base Ohakea, NZ, 1969–70; Hon. ADC to Gov. Gen., 1972; Sen. ASO, Air HQ, ANZUK Force Singapore; later, Dep. Comdr NZ Force SE Asia in Singapore, 1973–75; RNZAF Air Staff, 1975–77; Base Comdr, RNZAF Base Auckland, 1978–79; AOC RNZAF Support Gp, 1980–82; Asst CDS for Operations and Plans, Defence HQ, Wellington, 1982–83; Hd of NZ Defence Liaison Staff, London, and Defence Attaché, FRG, 1984–86. Gp Captain 1973, Air Cdre 1980, Air Vice-Marshal 1986. FNZIM; FRAeS. *Recreations:* golf, fishing. *Address:* 12 Mark Place, Lynmore, Rotorua 3010, New Zealand. *T:* (7) 3459650. *Club:* Rotorua Golf.

NEVILLE, Richard; Editor, The Courier, since 2011; *b* Singapore, 2 March 1968; *s* of Brian Neville and Elspeth Neville (*née* Riddell); *m* 1997, Morag Stewart; two *s*. *Educ:* Balfron High Sch.; Napier Univ. (HND Journalism Studies). Reporter, Edinburgh Evening News, 1989–93; Asst Editor, Evening Press, York, 1993–95; reporter, Daily Record, 1995–96; News Editor, 1996–99, Dep. Editor, 1999–2000, The Scotsman; Dep. Editor, 2000–01, Editor, 2002–03, Business a.m.; Dep. Editor, Press and Journal, 2003–11. *Recreations:* hillwalking, auctions, music, whisky. *Address:* The Courier, 80 Kingsway East, Dundee DD4 8SL. *T:* (01382) 575270. *E:* rneville@thecourier.co.uk.

NEVILLE-JONES, Baroness *cr* 2007 (Life Peer), of Hutton Roof in the County of Cumbria; **(Lilian) Pauline Neville-Jones,** DCMG 1996 (CMG 1987); PC 2010; Prime Minister's Special Representative to Business on Cyber Security, 2011–14; *b* 2 Nov. 1939; *d* of Roland Neville-Jones and Dr Cecilia Emily Millicent Winn. *Educ:* Leeds Girls' High Sch.; Lady Margaret Hall, Oxford (BA Hons Mod. History). Harkness Fellow of Commonwealth Fund, USA, 1961–63; HM Diplomatic Service, 1963–96: Third Sec., Salisbury, Rhodesia, 1964–65; Third, later Second Sec., Singapore, 1965–68; FCO, 1968–71; First Sec., Washington, 1971–75; FCO, 1975–77; Mem. Cabinet, later Chef de Cabinet to Christopher Tugendhat, European Comr for Budget, Financial Control, Financial Instns and Taxation, 1977–82; Vis. Fellow, RIIA, and Inst. français des relations internationales, 1982–83; Head of Planning Staff, FCO, 1983–87; Minister (Econ.), 1987–88, Minister, 1988–91, Bonn; Dep. Sec., Cabinet Office (on secondment), 1991–94; Chm., Jt Intelligence Cttee, Cabinet Office, 1993–94; Political Dir and Dep. Under-Sec. of State, FCO, 1994–96; Sen. Advr to High Rep. for Bosnia (on secondment), 1996. Man. Dir, and Hd of Global Business Strategy, NatWest Markets, 1996–98; Vice Chm., Hawkpoint Partners Ltd, 1998–2000; Chm., QinetiQ Group plc, 2002–05. Shadow Security Minister and Nat. Security Advr to Leader of the Opposition, 2007–10; Minister of State (Minister for Security), Home Office, 2010–11. Chm., Information Assurance Adv. Council, 2002–07. Mem., EPSRC, 2013–. A Gov., BBC, 1998–2004. Member, Council: Oxford Univ., 2004–06; Lancaster Univ., 2014–; Mem. Adv. Council, City Univ., 2006–09. FRSA 1986. DUniv Open, 1998; Hon. DSc (Econ) London, 1999; Hon. DSc City, 2007. Chevalier, Légion d'Honneur, 2007. *Recreations:* antiques, cooking, gardening. *Address:* House of Lords, SW1A 0PW. *E:* nevillejonesp@parliament.uk.

NEVILLE-ROLFE, Baroness *cr* 2013 (Life Peer), of Chilmark in the County of Wiltshire; **Lucy Jeanne Neville-Rolfe,** DBE 2012; CMG 2005; FCIS; Parliamentary Under-Secretary of State, Department for Business, Innovation and Skills, since 2014, and Department for Culture, Media and Sport, since 2015; *b* 2 Jan. 1953; *d* of late Edmund and Margaret Neville-Rolfe; *m* Sir Richard John Packer, *qv*; four *s*. *Educ:* Somerville Coll., Oxford (BA PPE; MA; Hon. Fellow, 2003). FCIS 2010. Joined MAFF, 1973; Pvte Sec. to Minister of Agric., Fisheries and Food, 1977–79; EC Sheepmeat and Milk, 1979–86; Land Use, 1986–88; Food Safety Act, 1988–90; Head of Personnel, 1990–92; Mem., Prime Minister's Policy Unit, 1992–94; Under Sec., 1994; Dir, Deregulation Unit, DTI, then Better Regulation Unit, Cabinet Office, 1995–97; Tesco plc: Gp Dir of Corporate Affairs, 1997–2006, and Company Sec., 2003–06; Exec. Dir, Corporate and Legal Affairs, 2006–13. Non-executive Director: John Laing Construction, 1991–92; Bd of Mgt, FCO, 2000–05; Carbon Trust, 2008–13; ITV plc, 2010–14; Chm., Dobbies Garden Centres plc, 2007–11. Member: Dep. Prime Minister's Local Govt Funding Cttee, 2003–04; ESRC Panel on Cultures of Consumption, 2003–07; Corporate Leaders Gp on Climate Change, 2005–; Foresight Obesity Project, 2005–07; China Britain Business Council, 2005–13; UK India Business Council, 2008–13; Efficiency Bd, Cabinet Office, 2010–; Strategic Adv. Gp, UKTI, 2011–. Member: Bd of Mgt, British Retail Consortium, 1998–2012 (Dep. Chair, 2003–12); Econs and Eur. Cttees, CBI, 1998–; UNICE Task Force on Enlargement, 1999–2004. Pres., EuroCommerce, 2012–15 (Vice Pres., 1998–2008). Gov., London Business Sch., 2011–. *Recreations:* cricket, racing, gardening, art, architecture, theatre.

See also M. T. Neville-Rolfe.

NEVILLE-ROLFE, Marianne Teresa, CB 2000; Director, P&M Hill Ltd (formerly P&M Hill Consultants Ltd), since 2004; *b* 9 Oct. 1944; *d* of late Edmund Neville-Rolfe and Margaret (*née* Evans); *m* 1st, 1972, David William John Blake (marr. diss. 1992); 2nd, 2001, Peter Andrew Hill. *Educ:* St Mary's Convent, Shaftesbury; Lady Margaret Hall, Oxford (BA). CBI, 1965–73 (Head, Brussels Office, 1971–72); Principal, DTI, 1973, Asst Sec., 1982, Under Sec., Internal European Policy Div., 1987; Chief Exec., CS Coll., and Dir, Top Management Prog., OMCS, then OPSS, Cabinet Office, 1990–94; Regl Dir, Govt Office for NW, 1994–99; Chief Exec., New East Manchester Ltd, 2000; Exec. Dir, SEEDA, 2001–04. Mem., ESRC, 2000–03. Chm., Bd of Govs, Univ. of Bolton, 2008–13; Mem., Bd of Govs, Univ. of Middx, 2014–. *Recreations:* travel, ski-ing, cycling, opera. *Address:* Angle Croft, Somerford Booths, Congleton, Cheshire CW12 2JU.

See also Baroness Neville-Rolfe.

NEVIN, Michael Patrick; HM Diplomatic Service; High Commissioner to Malawi, since 2012; *b* 13 Jan. 1969; *m* 1997, Sawako; three *c*. Entered FCO, 1993; Asst Desk Officer, China and Taiwan, FCO, 1993–95; Riyadh, 1996; UK Mission to UN, NY, 1996; Osaka, 1996–99; Second Sec. (Chancery), Lilongwe, 1999–2003; FCO, 2003; Dep. High Comr and Counsellor (Political), Nairobi, 2008–12. *Address:* c/o Foreign and Commonwealth Office, King Charles Street, SW1A 2AH.

NEW, Maj.-Gen. Sir Laurence (Anthony Wallis), Kt 1990; CB 1986; CBE 1980; Lieutenant Governor and Captain General of the Isle of Man, and President of the Tynwald Court, 1985–90; International President, Association of Military Christian Fellowships, 1991–2002; *b* 25 Feb. 1932; *s* of Lt-Col S. W. New, MBE and Mrs C. M. New; *m* 1956, Anna Doreen Verity (CStJ, LISTD); two *s* two *d*. *Educ:* King William's College, Isle of Man. RMA Sandhurst, 1950–52; commissioned, RTR, 1952; service in Hong Kong, Germany, Malaya, Borneo; CO 4 RTR, 1971–73; Bde Major, 20th Armd Bde, 1969–70; Sec., Defence Policy Staff, 1970–71; Defence and Military Attaché, Tel Aviv, 1974–77; Col GS, MoD, 1977–79; Brig. GS (Intelligence), 1981–82; COS, Defence Intelligence Centre, Falklands Campaign, 1982; ACGS (Op. Reqs), 1983–84; ACDS (Land Systems), MoD, 1984–85; graduate Staff Coll., JSSC, RCDS. Col Comdt, RTR, 1986–93; Vice Pres., TA&VRA, 1985–90; Hon. Col I of M ACF, 1998–2002. Gen. Sec., Officers' Pensions Soc., 1990–95; Campaign Dir, War and Service Widows Parly Pensions Campaign, 1994–95. Consultant, Lagan Gp of Cos, 1998–2010; Director: Charles Brand (IOM) Ltd, 1999–2006; Lagan Construction (IOM) Ltd, 2006–10. Lectr, Sir John Cass Business Sch., City of London (formerly City Univ. Business Sch.), 1992–2002; Instructor, 2003–05, Team Dir, 2005–13, Pointman Leadership Inst.; Dir, Pointman Leadership Ltd UK, 2009–13. Licensed Reader, C of E, 1974–2013; Local Preacher, Methodist Church, IOM Dist, 2004–; Church Warden, St Peter upon Cornhill, 1986–95; Pres., Soldiers' and Airmen's Scripture Readers Assoc., 1985–99; Vice Pres., Officers' Christian Union, 1988–93. President: Manx Music Fest., 1985–90; Mananan Internat. Fest. of Music and the Arts, 1987–; Manx Nat. Youth Band, 1995–; Mannin Art Gp, 1996–2007; Friends of the Gaiety Theatre, 1996–2006. County Pres., St John Ambulance Brigade and Assoc., 1985–90, and 1999–2007; Patron: I of M Red Cross, 1985–90; Burma Star Assoc. (I of M), 1995–; Pres., Normandy Veterans Assoc. (I of M), 1997–; Vice-Pres., 4/7th RTR Old Comrades, 1997–2010. Pres., Fishermen's Mission, 1998–2007; Vice Patron, Royal Nat. Mission to Deep Sea Fishermen, 1999–; Patron: Choice of Living in Community Homes, 1999–2013; Friends of Chernobyl's Children, 1999–; Ramsey Lifeboat, 1999–. Chairman: Bishop Barrow's Trustees, 1985–90; Royal Jubilee and Prince's Trust (I of M), 1986–90; Pres., White House School, Wokingham, 1985–. Freeman, City of London, 1985. Church Warden, St Matthew's Church, Douglas, 2010–13. CCMI 2002 (FBIM 1979; CBIM 1986). KStJ 1986. Internat. Centurion Award, Washington, 2000. *Recreations:* family, music, water colour painting. *Address:* The Granary, Ballaquark Farm, Laxey, Isle of Man IM4 7PH. *E:* generalnew@manx.net. *Club:* Army and Navy.

NEW, Terence Michael John; sculptor; President, Royal British Society of Sculptors, 2012–15; *b* Prestatyn, 1945; *s* of John and Elizabeth New; *m* 2012, Diane Shiach; three *d*. *Educ:* Wimbledon Sch. of Art (Foundn 1965); Hornsey Coll. of Art (DipAD 1968); Royal Coll. of Art (MA Sculpture 1971). Hd of Sculpture, Inst. of Technol., WA, 1978–80; Hd of Sculpture, 1986–2001, Hd of Fine Art, 2001–10, Royal Acad. Schs, Royal Acad. *Recreations:* reading, travelling, music, swimming, chess, horticulture. *Address:* 59 Hans Road, SW3 1RN. *T:* (020) 7823 8392. *E:* tmjnew@gmail.com. *Clubs:* Chelsea Arts, Dover Street Arts; Polish Hearth.

NEW SOUTH WALES, Metropolitan of; *see* Sydney, Archbishop of.

NEWALL, family name of **Baron Newall.**

NEWALL, 2nd Baron *cr* 1946; **Francis Storer Eaton Newall;** DL; former company director and chairman of several companies; Chairman, British Greyhound Racing Board, 1985–97; *b* 23 June 1930; *o s* of 1st Baron (Marshal of the RAF Lord) Newall, GCB, OM, GCMG, CBE, AM; *S* father, 1963; *m* 1956, Pamela Elizabeth, *e d* of E. H. L. Rowcliffe, Pinkney Park, Malmesbury, Wilts; two *s* one *d*. *Educ:* Eton College; RMA Sandhurst. Commissioned into 11th Hussars (Prince Albert's Own), 1950; served in: Germany, 1950–53; Malaya, 1953–55; on staff of GHQ FarELF, Singapore, 1955–56; Adjt Royal Gloucestershire Hussars, 1956–58; retired 1961. Introduced Farriers Registration Acts and Betting Gaming and Lotteries Amendment Acts (Greyhound Racing) in House of Lords. Cons. Whip and front bench spokesman, 1976–79; Founder Mem., House of Lords all party Defence Study Group; official visits to NATO, SHAPE, Norway, Morocco, Bonn, Cyprus, BAOR, Qatar, Oman, Bahrain and Romania; Deleg. to Council of Europe and WEU, 1983–97. Mem., Select Cttee on Laboratory Animals Protection Bill. Former Pres., Soc. for Protection of Animals Abroad. Chm., British Moroccan Soc., 2000–05. Mem., Merchant Taylors' Co. (Master, 1985–86). DL Greater London, 1988. *Recreations:* sport, travel, meeting people. *Heir: s* Hon. Richard Hugh Eaton Newall [*b* 19 Feb. 1961; *m* 1st, 1996, Keira (marr. diss. 2010), *d* of Robert Glen; two *d*; 2nd, 2011, Samantha Durchslag; two *s*]. *Address:* Wotton Underwood, Aylesbury, Bucks HP18 0RZ. *Club:* Cavalry and Guards.

NEWALL, Peter; HM Diplomatic Service, retired; Ambassador to Senegal and, concurrently, to Mali, Guinea-Bissau and Cape Verde, 2004–07; *b* 20 March 1947; *s* of Bobbie and Clio Newall; *m* 1969, Marina (*née* McHugh); one *s* two *d*. *Educ:* Kent Coll., Canterbury. Joined HM Diplomatic Service, 1966; Attaché, Tehran, 1970–72; Entry Clearance Officer, New Delhi, 1972–75; Finance Dept, FCO, 1975–79; 2nd Sec. (Commercial), Belgrade, 1979–82; 1st Sec. (Commercial), Kuwait, 1982–85; Nuclear Energy Dept, FCO, 1985–89; HM Consul, Marseilles, 1989–90; Jt Mgt Officer, Geneva, 1990–95; Counter Terrorism Policy Dept, FCO, 1995–97; Non-Proliferation Dept, FCO, 1997–99; Jt Mgt Officer, Brussels, 1999–2004. Occasional election observer, EU and OSCE, 2007–11. *Recreations:* golf, ski-ing, cinema, fixing things, cycling, swimming.

NEWARK, Archdeacon of; *see* Picken, Ven. D. A.

NEWBERRY, Raymond Scudamore, OBE 1989; Director, Brazil, British Council, 1990–93; *b* 8 Feb. 1935; *s* of late James Henry Newberry and Doris Ada Newberry; *m* 1967, Angelina Nance (*d* 2007); one *s* one *d*. *Educ:* Bristol Grammar Sch.; Selwyn Coll., Cambridge (BA); Univ. of Leeds (DipESL); Univ. of Bristol (DipEd). National Service, 1953–55. Lectr, Coll. of Arts, Baghdad Univ., 1959–62; British Council posts, 1962–94: Lectr, Teheran, 1963–64; Educn Officer, Calcutta, 1964–66; Head of English Dept, Advanced Teacher Trng Coll., Winneba, Ghana, 1966–70; Advr on English Lang., Min. of Educn, Singapore, 1970–74; Rep., Colombia, 1975–80; Director: North and Latin American Dept, 1980–82; America and Pacific Dept, 1982–84; Rep., Australia, 1984–89. Consultant, London Film Commn, 1996–99. Hon. Mem., Soc. of Bookbinders, 2011. *Recreations:* bookbinding, golf. *Address:* Silverwood, Wildwood Close, Woking, Surrey GU22 8PL. *T:* (01932) 341826.

NEWBERY, Prof. David Michael Garrood, CBE 2012; FBA 1991; Professor of Economics, University of Cambridge, 1988–2010, now Emeritus; Fellow, Churchill College, Cambridge, since 1966; *b* 1 June 1943; *s* of late Alan James Garrood Newbery, OBE, RN, and Betty Amelia Newbery; *m* 1975, Dr Terri Eve Apter; two *d*. *Educ:* Portsmouth Grammar Sch.; Trinity Coll., Cambridge (BA, MA); PhD 1976, ScD 2001, Cantab. Economist, Treasury, Tanzania, 1965–66; Cambridge University: Asst Lectr, 1966–71; Lectr, 1971–86; Reader, 1986–88; Prof. of Applied Econs, 2003–10; Dir, Dept of Applied Econs, 1988–2003; Res. Dir, Electricity Policy Res. Gp, 2005–. Associate Prof., Stanford Univ., 1976–77; Div. Chief, World Bank, Washington, 1981–83; Fellow, Centre for Economic Policy Res., 1984–; Vis. Prof., Princeton, 1985; Vis. Scholar, IMF, 1987; Ford Vis. Prof., Univ. of California, Berkeley, 1987–88; Sen. Res. Fellow, Inst. for Policy Reform, Washington, DC, 1990–96; Res. Fellow, Control and Power Res. Gp, Imperial Coll. London, 2011–15. Member: Competition (formerly Monopolies and Mergers) Commn, 1996–2003; Single Electricity Mkt Cttee, Ire., 2012–. President: European Economic Assoc., 1996 (Vice-Pres., 1994); Internat. Assoc. for Energy Economics, 2013; Mem. Council, REconS, 1984–89; Fellow, Econometric Soc., 1989 (Frisch Medal, 1990). Bd Mem., Review of Economic Studies, 1968–79; Associate Editor: Economic Jl, 1977–2000; European Economic Review, 1988–93. *Publications:* Project Appraisal in Practice, 1976; (with J. E. Stiglitz) The Theory of Commodity Price Stabilization, 1981; (with N. H. Stern) The Theory of Taxation for Developing Countries, 1987; (with I. P. Székely) Hungary: an economy in transition, 1992; Tax and Benefit Reform in Central and Eastern Europe, 1995; Privatization, Restructuring and Regulation of Network Utilities, 2000; articles in learned jls. *Recreation:* walking. *Address:* 9 Huntingdon Road, Cambridge CB3 0HH. *T:* (01223) 360216.

NEWBERY, Freya Patricia; Her Honour Judge Newbery; a Circuit Judge, since 2014; *b* Rustington, 1964; *d* of David Newbery and Brit Holmsen; *m* 1990, Tim Wright; one *s* one *d*. *Educ:* Felpham Comprehensive Sch.; New Hall, Cambridge (BA 1985). Called to the Bar, Middle Temple, 1986. *E:* freyanewbery@gmail.com.

NEWBIGGING, Sir David (Kennedy), Kt 2011; OBE 1982; Member, Senior Advisory Board, Academic Partnerships Group, since 2015; Chairman, Academic Partnerships International (London), and Director, Academic Partnerships (Dallas), 2012–15; *b* 19 Jan. 1934; *s* of late David Locke Newbigging, CBE, MC and Bar, and Lucy Margaret; *m* 1968, Carolyn Susan (*née* Band); one *s* two *d*. *Educ:* in Canada; Oundle Sch., Northants. Joined

Jardine, Matheson & Co. Ltd, Hong Kong, 1954; Dir, 1967; Man. Dir, 1970; Chm. and Sen. Man. Dir, 1975–83; Chairman: Hongkong & Kowloon Wharf & Godown Co. Ltd, 1970–80; Jardine Matheson & Co. Ltd, 1975–83; Jardine Fleming Holdings Ltd, 1975–83; Hongkong Land Co. Ltd, 1975–83; Hongkong Electric Holdings Ltd, 1982–83 (Dir, 1975–83); Rentokil Gp plc, 1987–94 (Dir, 1986–94); Redfearn PLC, 1988; NM UK Ltd, 1990–93; Ivory & Sime plc, 1992–95 (Dir, 1987–95); Maritime Transport Services Ltd, 1993–95; Faupel plc (formerly Faupel Trading Gp plc), 1994–2005 (Dir, 1989–2005); Equitas Holdings Ltd, 1995–98; Thistle Hotels plc, 1999–2003; Friends Provident Life Office, subseq. plc, 1998–2005 (Dir, 1993–2005; Dep. Chm., 1996–98); Talbot Hldgs Ltd, 2003–07; Synesis Life Ltd, 2006–08; Deputy Chairman: Provincial Gp plc, 1985–91 (Dir, 1984–91); Benchmark Gp plc, 1996–2004; Director: Hongkong & Shanghai Banking Corp., 1975–83; Hong Kong Telephone Co., 1975–83; Safmarine and Rennies Holdings Ltd (formerly Rennies Consolidated Holdings), 1975–85; Provincial Insurance, 1984–86; Provincial Life Insurance Co., 1984–86; CIN Management, 1985–87; PACCAR (UK) Ltd, 1986–97; Internat. Financial Markets Trading Ltd, 1986–93; United Meridian Corp., USA, 1987–98; Wah Kwong Shipping Hldgs Ltd (Hong Kong), 1992–99; Market Bd, Corp. of Lloyd's, 1993–95; Merrill Lynch & Co. Inc., USA, 1997–2007; Ocean Energy Inc., USA, 1998–2003; PACCAR Inc., USA, 1999–2006; Wah Kwong Maritime Transport Hldgs Ltd, Hong Kong, 2008–. Dir, British Coal Corp. (formerly NCB), 1984–87. Mem., Internat. Council, Morgan Guaranty Trust Co. of NY, 1977–85; Mem. Supervisory Bd, DAF Trucks NV, 1997–2000. Chairman, Council of Trustees: Mission to Seafarers (formerly Missions to Seamen), 1993–2006; Cancer Research UK, 2004–10 (Dep. Chm., 2002–04). Chm. of Trustees, Wilts Community Foundn, 1991–97; Trustee, UK Trust for Nature Conservation in Nepal (formerly King Mahendra UK Trust for Nature Conservation), 1988–. Member: Hong Kong Exec. Council, 1980–84; Hong Kong Legislative Council, 1978–82. Chairman: Hong Kong Tourist Assoc., 1977–82; Hong Kong Gen. Chamber of Commerce, 1980–82; Steward, Royal Hong Kong Jockey Club, 1975–84. JP (unofficial) Hong Kong, 1971; DL Wilts, 1993–2009; High Sheriff, Wilts, 2003–04. *Recreations:* most outdoor sports; Chinese art. *Address:* 119 Old Church Street, SW3 6EA. *T:* (020) 7352 1558. *Clubs:* Boodle's; Hong Kong (Hong Kong); Bohemian (San Francisco).

NEWBIGIN, John Lesslie, OBE 2015; cultural entrepreneur; consultant, since 2005; *b* Liverpool, 13 Oct. 1947; *s* of Rt Rev. James Edward Lesslie Newbigin and Helen Stewart Newbigin (*née* Henderson); *m* 1978, Juliet Grimshaw (marr. diss. 1994); two *d*. *Educ:* Queens' Coll., Cambridge (BA Hons 1970). Youth worker, ILEA, 1972–73; writer in residence, Common Stock Th., 1973–74; community worker, Avenues Unlimited, 1975–81; Manager, Brixton Young Families Housing Aid Assoc., 1981–84; Dir, London Youth Fest., 1984–85; Policy Advr, Office of the Leader of the Opposition, 1986–92; Asst to Chm., Enigma Prodns, 1992–97; Special Advr, DCMS, 1997–2000; Hd, Corporate Relns, Channel 4 TV, 2000–05. Vis. Prof., UEL, 2006–; Adjunct Prof., Univ. of Technol., Sydney, 2009–; Hon. Prof., Hong Kong Univ., 2015–. Member Board: Keen Students Sch., 2000–12; First Light Movies Ltd, 2004–14; Cultural Industries Develt Agency, 2005–11; Mediabox, 2006–11; Becta, 2008–11; ThreeJohnsandShelagh Ltd, 2010–; Chm., CAV Networks Ltd., 2011–. Member Advisory Board: BT Connected Earth, 2003–12; John Smith Meml Trust, 2006–; Aluna, 2007–10; Arts and Creative Industries, British Council, 2012–. Chm. of Trustees, Culture 24, 2006–14; Chm., Creative England (formerly Screen England), 2010–; Trustee: Whitechapel Art Gall., 2002–10; Theatre Royal Stratford East, 2004–09; Big Art Proj., 2007–09; Bd Dir, Battersea Arts Centre, 2013–. *Recreations:* walking, talking, cycling, recycling. *Address:* 50 Cephas Avenue, E1 4AT. *T:* 07909 907739. *E:* john@newbigin.co.uk.

NEWBOLD, Yvette Monica, (Yve); Chair, Ethical Trading Initiative, 2000–05; *b* 6 July 1940; *d* of late Thomas Peter Radcliffe and of Anne Gertrude Radcliffe (*née* Flynn); *m* 1958, Anthony Patrick Newbold; three *s* one *d*. *Educ:* Blessed Sacrament Convent, Brighton; LLB London; Solicitor, 1970. Staff Counsel: IBM, 1968–71; Rank Xerox, 1972–79; Internat. Counsel, Xerox (USA), 1979–82; European Counsel, Walt Disney Productions, 1983–85; Co. Sec., Hanson, 1986–95; Chief Exec., Pro-Ned, 1995–97; Partner, Heidrick & Struggles, 1998–2000. Non-executive Director: BT, 1991–97; Coutts & Co., 1994–98. Chair, Inst. for Global Ethics, 2005–08 (Mem., Adv. Bd, 1997–2004); Member: Royal Commn on Criminal Justice, 1991–93; Sen. Salaries Rev. Body, 1994–97; BT Social Report Panel, 2002–05; Adv. Bd, FTSE4Good, 2003–. Governor, London Business Sch., 1990–97.

NEWBOROUGH, 8th Baron *cr* 1776 (Ire.), of Bodvean; **Robert Vaughan Wynn;** Bt 1742; landowner and organic farmer; *b* 11 Aug. 1949; *o s* of 7th Baron Newborough, DSC and Rosamund Lavington Wynn (*née* Barbour); *S* father, 1998; *m* 1st, 1981, Sheila Christine Massey (marr. diss. 1988); one *d*; 2nd, 1988, Susan Elizabeth Hall (*née* Lloyd); one step *s*. *Educ:* Milton Abbey. Chm. and Man. Dir, Wynn Electronics, 1982–89; Dir, Country Wide Communications, 1992–. Welsh Exporter of Year, True Taste Wales, 2012; Farmer of Year, 2013, Diversification Farmer of Year, 2013, Farmers Weekly; Regl Butcher of Year, Countryside Alliance, 2013. *Recreations:* ski-ing, sailing, golf, tennis. *Heir: cousin* Antony Charles Vaughan Wynn [*b* 2 May 1949; *m* 1st, 1973, Jane Slane Sloan (*née* Thompson) (marr. diss. 1986); 2nd, 1996, Mrs Victoria Jane Domenge, *e d* of Lt-Gen. Sir Derek Boorman, *qv*]. *Address:* Peplow Hall, Peplow, Market Drayton, Shropshire TF9 3JP. *T:* (01952) 840230.

NEWBURGH, 12th Earl of, *cr* 1660 (Scot.); **Principe Don Filippo Giambattista Francesco Aldo Maria Rospigliosi;** Viscount Kynnaird, Baron Levingston of Flacraig, 1660; 11th Prince Rospigliosi (Holy Roman Empire), 11th Duke of Zagarolo, 14th Prince of Castiglione, Marquis of Giuliana, Count of Chiusa, Baron of La Miraglia and Valcorrente, Lord of Aidone, Burgio, Contessa and Trappeto, and Conscript Roman Noble, Patrician of Venice, Genoa, Pistoia, Ravenna and Ferrara; *b* 4 July 1942; *s* of 11th Earl of Newburgh and of Donna Giulia, *d* of Don Guido Carlo dei Duchi Visconti di Mondrone, Count of Lonate Pozzolo; *S* father, 1986; *m* 1972, Baronessa Donna Luisa, *d* of Count Annibale Caccia Dominioni; one *d*. *Heir: d* Princess Donna Benedetta Francesca Maria Rospigliosi, Mistress of Newburgh [*b* 4 June 1974; *m* 1999, Piero Riccardo Maria Albertario; two *s*]. *Address:* Piazza Sant'Ambrogio 16, 20123 Milan, Italy.

NEWBY, family name of **Baron Newby**.

NEWBY, Baron *cr* 1997 (Life Peer), of Rothwell in the co. of West Yorkshire; **Richard Mark Newby,** OBE 1990; PC 2014; *b* 14 Feb. 1953; *s* of Frank and Kathleen Newby; *m* 1978, Rev. the Hon. Ailsa Ballantyne, *yr d* of Baron Thomson of Monifieth, KT PC; two *s*. *Educ:* Rothwell Grammar Sch.; St Catherine's Coll., Oxford (MA). HM Customs and Excise: Administration trainee, 1974; Private Sec. to Permanent Sec., 1977–79; Principal, Planning Unit, 1979–81; Sec. to SDP Parly Cttee, 1981; joined SDP HQ Staff, 1981; Nat. Sec., SDP, 1983–88; Exec., 1988–90, Dir of Corporate Affairs, 1991, Rosehaugh plc; Director: Matrix Public Affairs Consultants, subseq. Matrix Communications Consultancy Ltd, 1992–99; Flagship Gp, 1999–2001; non-exec. Dir, Elmwood Design Ltd, 2004–09; Chm., Live Consulting Ltd, 2001–12. Chair, Internat. Develt through Sport, UK, 2007–12; Chm., Sport for Life, 2009–12. Dep. Chm., Lib Dem Gen. Election Team, 1995–97; Chief of Staff to Rt Hon. Charles Kennedy, 1999–2006. Lib Dem spokesman on Treasury affairs, 1998–2010, Lib Dem Chief Whip, 2012–, H of L; Govt spokesman on HM Treasury, H of L, 2012–; Captain of the Yeoman of the Guard (Dep. Chief Whip, H of L), 2012–15. Member: Select Cttee on Monetary Policy Cttee of Bank of England, 1998–2000; Select Cttee on Economic Affairs, 2001–03; Ecclesiastical Cttee, 2002–12; Chm., All Party Social Enterprise Gp, 2010–12 (Dep. Chm., 2003); Co-Chair, Lib Dem Parly Treasury Policy Cttee, 2010–12; Treas., Associate Parly Gp on Corporate Responsibility, 2009–12. FRSA 2006. *Recreations:* family, football, cricket. *Address:* 3 Wharf Terrace, Deodar Road, SW15 2JZ. *Club:* MCC.

See also C. Thomson.

NEWBY, Sir Howard (Joseph), Kt 2000; CBE 1995; DL; Vice Chancellor, University of Liverpool, 2008–15; *b* 10 Dec. 1947; *s* of Alfred Joseph Newby and Constance Annie (*née* Potts); *m* 1st, 1970, Janet Elizabeth (*née* Craddock) (marr. diss. 2003); two *s*; 2nd, 2005, Sheila Mary Watt (*née* Mann); one step *s* one step *d*. *Educ:* John Port Grammar Sch., Etwall, Derbyshire; Atlantic Coll., St Donat's, Glamorgan; Univ. of Essex (BA, PhD). University of Essex: Lectr in Sociology, 1972–75; Sen. Lectr, 1975–79; Reader, 1979–83; Prof. of Sociology, 1983–88; Dir, Data Archive, 1983–88, Chm. and Chief Exec., 1988–94, ESRC; Vice-Chancellor, Southampton Univ., 1994–2001; Chief Exec., HEFCE, 2001–06; Vice Chancellor, UWE, 2006–08. Prof. of Sociology and Rural Sociology, Univ. of Wisconsin-Madison, 1980–83; visiting appointments: Univ. of NSW, 1976; Sydney, 1976; Newcastle upon Tyne, 1983–84. Chm., CEST, 1995–99; Pres., CVCP, 1999–2001. Member: UFC, 1991–93; Rural Develt Commn, 1991–99; South and West RHA, 1994–96; ESTA, 1997–98; Railway Heritage Cttee, 1999–2013. Chm. Bd, Nat. Railway Mus., 2008–15; Trustee: Sci. Mus. Gp (formerly Nat. Mus. of Sci. and Industry), 2007–15; Nat. Football Mus., 2008–12. Gov., BFI, 2008–12. Hon. Fellow, Univ. of Wales, Cardiff, 1996. Hon. DLitt: City of London Poly., 1991; South Bank Univ., 1992; Surrey, 1992; Portsmouth, 1992 (Hon. Fellow, Portsmouth Poly., 1991); Ulster, 1994; Stirling, 2002; DU: Essex, 2000; Leicester, 2002; Hon. DSocSci Southampton, 2002; DUniv Derby, 2006. DL Merseyside, 2014. *Publications:* (jtly) Community Studies, 1971; The Deferential Worker, 1977; (jtly) Property, Paternalism and Power, 1978; Green and Pleasant Land?, 1979, 2nd edn 1985; (jtly) The Problem of Sociology, 1983; (jtly) Aproximación Teorética a la Sociologia Rural, 1983; Country Life, 1987; The Countryside in Question, 1988; (jtly) Social Class in Modern Britain, 1988; *edited jointly:* The Sociology of Community, 1974; Doing Sociological Research, 1977; International Perspectives in Rural Sociology, 1978; The Rural Sociology of the Advanced Societies, 1980; Political Action and Social Identity, 1985; Restructuring Capital, 1985; The National Trust: the next hundred years, 1995; over 50 papers in learned jls. *Recreations:* sharing everything in married life, especially time with our family, walks and cycle rides, Derby County and railway interests.

NEWCASTLE, Bishop of, since 2015; **Rt Rev. Christine Elizabeth Hardman;** *b* 27 Aug. 1951; *d* of Wynford Atkins and Margaret Elizabeth Atkins; *m* 1971, Roger John Hardman; two *d*. *Educ:* Queen Elizabeth's Girls' Grammar Sch., Barnet; Univ. of London (BScEcon (ext.) 1973); Westminster Coll., Oxford (MTh 1994). Ordained deaconess 1984, deacon 1987, priest 1994; Deaconess, Markyate Street, 1984–88; Course Dir, St Albans MTS, later St Albans and Oxford Ministry Course, 1988–96; Vicar, Holy Trinity, Stevenage, 1996–2001; RD Stevenage, 1999–2001; Archdeacon of Lewisham, later Archdeacon of Lewisham and Greenwich, 2001–12, now Archdeacon Emeritus; Hon. Asst Priest, Southwark Cathedral, 2012–15. Mem., Gen. Synod, C of E, 2005–. Prolocutor, Lower House of the Convocation of Canterbury, 2010–. *Recreations:* cycling, running, cinema, theatre. *Address:* Diocesan Office, Church House, St John's Terrace, North Shields NE29 6HS. *T:* (0191) 270 4100.

NEWCASTLE, Assistant Bishop of; *see* White, Rt Rev. F.

NEWCASTLE, Dean of; *see* Dalliston, Very Rev. C. C.

NEWCASTLE, NSW, Bishop of, since 2014; **Rt Rev. Gregory Edwin Thompson;** *b* Muswellbrook, 1956. *Educ:* Ridley Coll. (ThL; DipMin; BTh Hons). Assistant: Nightcliff, 1982–83; St James Old Cathedral, 1984–85; ordained deacon, 1986, priest, 1986; Asst Curate, Heidelberg, 1986–88; Rector, Sanderson, 1988–93; Army Reserve Chaplain, 1989–95; State Sec., Bush Church Aid NSW, 1994–98; Gen. Licence, 1994–99; Bush Church Aid Nat. Res. Office, 1998–99; Rector, E Sydney, 1999–2004; Area Dean, Sydney City, 2001–04; Rector, Canberra, 2005–07; Bishop of the Northern Territory, 2007–13. Pres., Council of Churches, Northern Territory, 2009–13. Chair: Anglicare Northern Territory, 2009–13; Gen. Synod Long Service Leave Fund, 2010; Member: Gen. Synod Aboriginal & Torres Strait Islander Task Gp and Standing Cttee, 2010–13; Australian Bishops Council of E Asia, 2011–13. *Address:* Level 3, 134 King Street, Newcastle, NSW 2300, Australia. *T:* (2) 49263733, *Fax:* (2) 49261968. *E:* bishopgreg@newcastleanglican.org.au.

NEWCOMBE, Andrew Bennett; QC 2010; *b* Merton, London, 6 Feb. 1953; *s* of Guy Bennett Newcombe and Sheila Kathleen Newcombe (*née* Saunders); *m* 1992, Freda Bush. *Educ:* Kingston Grammar Sch.; Durham Univ. (BA 1974). Officer, Royal Marines, 1974–85: 42 Cdo RM, 1975–77; ADC to C-in-C AFNORTH, 1977–78; flying duties with Fleet Air Arm and 3 Cdo Bde Air Sqdn, 1979–84, served Falklands (despatches, 1982); Bde Intelligence Officer, 3 Cdo Bde, 1984–85. Called to the Bar, Middle Temple, 1987, King's Inns, Dublin, 1995; in practice as a barrister, 1987–. Liveryman, Gunmakers' Co., 2011–. *Recreations:* exercising the whippet, shooting, occasional polo, novice's interest in 17th and 18th century ceramics. *Address:* Francis Taylor Building, Temple, EC4Y 7BY. *T:* (020) 7353 8415, *Fax:* (020) 7353 7622. *E:* clerks@ftb.eu.com. *Club:* Naval and Military.

NEWCOME, Rt Rev. James William Scobie; *see* Carlisle, Bishop of.

NEWCOMEN, Nigel Thomas, CBE 2011; Prisons and Probation Ombudsman, since 2011; *b* London, 14 June 1955; *s* of Rosalind Newcomen; *m* 1978, Susie Gammon; three *s*. *Educ:* St Christopher, Letchworth; Kent Univ. (BA Hons); London Sch. of Econs and Pol Sci. (LLM); Surrey Univ. (MSc). Sessional Community Service Supervisor, 1976–78, Community Service Officer, 1978–79, Inner London Probation Service; Res. Officer, Univ. of Sussex, 1980–81; Sen. Community Service Officer (pt-time), 1981–85, Hd of Res. and Information, 1985–91, SW London Probation Service; Lectr (pt-time), Chelsea Coll., Univ. of London, 1982–85; Hd of Section, Directorate of Inmate Activities, 1991–93, Lead, Criminal Justice Bill Team, Directorate of Services, 1993–94, Prison Service; Hd of Protective Security, 1994, Private Sec. to Home Sec., 1994–96, Home Office; Business Manager, Directorate of Prison Health Care, 1996; Hd of Secretariat, 1996–99, Asst Dir and Hd of Gp, Sentence Mgt Gp, 1999–2003, Prison Service; Dep. Chief Inspector of Prisons, 2003–11. *Recreations:* travel, sport, arts, allotment gardening. *Address:* PO Box 70769, SE1P 4XY. *T:* (020) 7633 4124. *E:* nigel.newcomen1@ppo.gsi.gov.uk.

NEWDEGATE; *see* FitzRoy Newdegate, family name of Viscount Daventry.

NEWELL, Christopher William Paul; Principal Legal Advisor to Director of Public Prosecutions, 2005–09; *b* 30 Nov. 1950; *s* of Nicolas Gambier Newell and Edith Alice Newell (*née* Edgill); *m* 1998, Teresa Mary Martin; one *d*. *Educ:* Wellington College; Southampton Univ. (LLB Hons). Called to the Bar, Middle Temple, 1973; Department of Director of Public Prosecutions: Legal Asst, 1975–78; Sen. Legal Asst, 1978–79; Law Officers' Dept, 1979–83; Sen. Legal Asst, DPP, 1983–86; Asst DPP, 1986; Branch Crown Prosecutor, Crown Prosecution Service, 1986–87; Asst Legal Sec., Law Officers' Dept, 1987–89; Crown Prosecution Service: Dir of HQ Casework, 1989–93; Dir (Casework), 1993–96; Dir, Casework Evaluation, 1996–98; Dir, Casework, 1998–2005. Sen. Vice-Chm., Criminal Law Cttee, IBA, 2002–06 (Vice-Chm., 2000–02). Trustee: Nat. Deaf Children's Soc., 2001–08; Centre for Accessible Envmts, 2001–08 (Vice-Chm., 2004–08); Crime Reduction Initiatives, 2001–11; Friends of W Byfleet Health Centre, 2009– (Chm., 2012–). Mem., Wisley with Pyrford PCC, 2010– (Vice Chm., 2013–). Gov., Pyrford C of E Primary Sch., 2008–; Trustee, Friends of Pyrford Primary Sch., 2009–13 (Chm., 2012–13). *Recreations:* sport, travel.

NEWELL, David Richard; Chief Executive, Newsmedia Association, since 2014 (Director: Newspaper Society, 1997–2014; Newspaper Publishers Association, 2007–14); *b* 21 Sept. 1951; *s* of late Dick Newell and Davida Newell (*née* Juleff); *m* 1978, Cora Sue Feingold; one *d*. *Educ:* Shrewsbury Sch.; Birmingham Univ. (LLB Hons 1973); Southampton Univ. (MPhil 1976). US, UK and British Council res. grants, 1974–81. Admitted Solicitor, 1978; Lawford & Co., 1976–78; Lectr in Law, Leicester Univ., 1978–86 (Postgrad. Tutor, 1979–84; Dir, Employment Law Postgrad. prog., 1983–86); Hon. Legal Advr, Leicester Legal Advice Centre, 1979–84; Hd of Govt and Legal Affairs, 1984–96, Dep. Dir, 1992–97, Newspaper Soc. Sec., Parly and Legal Cttee, Guild of Editors, 1984–97; Member: Advertising Assoc. Cttees, 1984–; Council, Campaign for Freedom of Information, 1990–2010 (Award for campaigning against official secrecy, 1989); Employment and Media Cttees, Law Soc., 1990–97; Council, World Assoc. of Newspapers, 1997–; Chm., Legal Framework Cttee, 1995–98, Bd Mem., 1996–, European Newspaper Publishers' Assoc. Director: ABC, 1997–; Press Standards Bd of Finance, 1997–; Advertising Standards Bd of Finance, 1998–; Nat. Readership Survey, 2014–. Sec., Regulatory Funding Co., 2014–. Special Award, UK Press Gazette, 1988; Newspaper Industry Award, 2009. *Publications:* The New Employment Legislation: a guide to the Employment Acts 1980 and 1982, 1983; Understanding Recruitment Law, 1984; (jtly) How to Study Law, 1986, 7th edn 2014; (jtly) Financial Advertising Law, 1989; (jtly) Aspects of Employment Law, 1990; (jtly) Law for Journalists, 1991; (jtly) Tolley's Employment Law, 1994, 3rd edn 2010; (jtly) The Law of Journalism, 1995; research papers and articles on employment law, media and legal policy issues. *Recreations:* country and seaside walks, sailing, tennis. *Address:* Newsmedia Association, 292 Vauxhall Bridge Road, SW1V 1AE. *T:* (020) 7963 7480.

NEWELL, Donald, FRICS; Co-Chairman, Europe Middle East Africa Division, CB Richard Ellis Services Inc., USA, 1998–2000; *b* 31 Aug. 1942; *s* of Stephen Newell and Ida Laura Newell (*née* Hatch); *m* 1968, Rosemary Litler-Jones; one *s* two *d*. *Educ:* Cheshunt Grammar Sch. FRICS 1968. Lander Bedells & Crompton, 1961–68; Hillier Parker May & Rowden, Chartered Surveyors, 1968–98: Partner, 1973–98; Man. Partner, 1986–90; Sen. Partner, 1990–98. Director: Oncor Internat., USA, 1995–98; CB Hillier Parker, 1998–2000; non-executive Director: London Merchant Securities PLC, 1998–2007; Derwent London plc, 2007–11. Dir, Paddington Business Improvement Dist Ltd, 2005–10. Pres., Brit. Council for Offices, 1991–92. Liveryman, Co. of: Pattenmakers, 1979– (Master, 2004–05); Chartered Surveyors, 1993–. *Recreation:* sport. *Clubs:* Buck's, MCC.

NEWELL, Rev. Canon Edmund John, DPhil; Principal, King George VI and Queen Elizabeth Foundation of St Catherine's, Cumberland Lodge, since 2013; *b* 9 Sept. 1961; *s* of Kenneth Ernest Newell and late Mary Newell (*née* James); *m* 1989, Susan Georgina Greer; one *s* one *d*. *Educ:* Ilfracombe Sch.; University Coll. London (BScEcon 1983); Nuffield Coll., Oxford (DPhil 1988; MA 1989); Oxford Ministry Course; Ripon Coll., Cuddesdon. Prize Res. Fellow, 1987, British Acad. Postdoctoral Fellow, 1989–92, Nuffield Coll., Oxford. Ordained deacon, 1994, priest, 1995; Curate, Deddington with Barford, Clifton and Hempton, 1994–98; Domestic Chaplain and Res. Asst to Bp of Oxford, 1998–2001; Chaplain, Headington Sch., Oxford, 1998–2001; Canon Residentiary, 2001–08, Chancellor, 2003–08, St Paul's Cathedral; Residentiary Canon and Sub Dean, Christ Church, Oxford, 2008–13, now Hon. non-Residentiary Canon. Dir, St Paul's Inst., 2003–08. FRHistS 1998; FRSA 2008. *Publications:* (ed) Seven Words for the 21st Century, 2002; (ed with Claire Foster) The Worlds We Live In, 2005; (with Sabina Alkire) What Can One Person Do?, 2005; (ed) Seven Words for Three Hours: a Good Friday meditation in words and music, 2005; (with John N. Reynolds) Ethics in Investment Banking, 2011; Choice, 2012; contribs to books, articles in learned jls and newspapers. *Recreations:* sport, music, exploring coastlines and islands. *Address:* Cumberland Lodge, The Great Park, Windsor, Berks SL4 2HP.

NEWELL, Dame Jane; *see* Newell, Dame P. J.

NEWELL, Michael Cormac; film director; *b* 28 March 1942; *s* of Terence William Newell and Mollie Louise Newell; *m* 1979, Bernice Stegers; one *s* one *d*. *Educ:* St Albans Sch.; Magdalene Coll., Cambridge (MA). Television dir, Granada TV, 1964–70: Ready When You Are Mr Magill; Baa Baa Black Sheep; Charm; freelance television dir, 1970–80: Melancholy Hussar; Just Your Luck; Destiny; Mr and Mrs Bureaucrat; Gift of Friendship; *films* include: Man in the Iron Mask, 1976; The Awakening, 1979; Dance with a Stranger, 1984 (Prix de la Jeunesse, Cannes); Good Father, 1986 (Prix Italia); Sweet and Sour, 1988; Into the West, 1992; Four Weddings and a Funeral, 1994 (Best Dir, BAFTA Awards, 1995); An Awfully Big Adventure, 1995; Donnie Brasco, 1997; Pushing Tin, 1999; Mona Lisa Smile, 2004; Harry Potter and the Goblet of Fire, 2005; Love in the Time of Cholera, 2008; Prince of Persia: The Sands of Time, 2010; Great Expectations, 2012; executive producer, Photographic Fairies, 1997; Best Laid Plans, 200 Cigarettes, 1999; High Fidelity, Traffic, 2000. Hon. DA Herts, 2005. *Recreations:* walking, reading (anything but fiction). *Address:* c/o Independent Talent Group Ltd, 40 Whitfield Street, W1T 2RH.

NEWELL, Rt Rev. Phillip Keith, AO 1993; Bishop of Tasmania, 1982–2000; *b* 30 Jan. 1930; *s* of Frank James and Ada Miriam Newell; *m* 1959, Merle Edith Callaghan; three *s*. *Educ:* Univ. of Melbourne; Trinity Coll., Melbourne. BSc 1953; DiplEd(Hons) 1954; ThL(Hons) 1959; BEd 1960; MEd 1969; FACE 1990. Mathematics Master: Melbourne High School, 1954–56; University High School, 1957–58; Tutor in Physics, Secondary Teachers' Coll., 1957; Assistant Curate: All Saints, East St Kilda, Melbourne, 1960–61; S Andrew's, Brighton, Melbourne, 1962–63; Asst Priest, S James, King Street, Sydney, 1963–67; Chaplain, Sydney Hosp., 1963–67; Rector, Christ Church, St Lucia, Brisbane, 1967–82; Residentiary Canon, S John's Cathedral, Brisbane, 1973–82; Archdeacon of Lilley, Brisbane, 1976–82. GCSJ 1979; KStJ 1981; OMLJ 2004 (ChLJ 1992). *Publications:* Body Search, 1993; A Pocket Lent Book, 1996. *Recreations:* education, music (classical and light opera), singing, choral conducting, wine making, travel, cricket (spectator), tennis (occasional game). *Address:* 4 Howley Court, Howrah, Tas 7018, Australia. *T:* (3) 6247 1706.

NEWELL, Dame (Priscilla) Jane, (Lady Cuckney), DBE 2013 (OBE 1997); Chair, John Lewis Partnership Pensions Trust, since 2013 (Trustee, since 2012); *b* London, 13 April 1944; *d* of Arthur Ronald Watts and Sylvia Margaret Watts (*née* McNabb); *m* 1st, 1977, Prof. Kenneth Wyatt Newell (*d* 1990); 2nd, 2007, Baron Cuckney (*d* 2008). *Educ:* Merrow Grange Convent, Guildford; Victoria Univ. of Wellington, NZ (BA French and English; Sen. Schol. 1980; BA 1st Cl. Hons Linguistics; Postgrad. Schol. 1981). Internat. CS, WHO, 1965–77; Sch. Adminr, Liverpool Sch. of Tropical Medicine, 1984–92; Assessor: Recruitment and Assessment Services, Cabinet Office, 1994–97; Assessment Consultancy Unit, Home Office, 1994–2006. Non-executive Director: Royal Liverpool Univ. Hosp. Trust, 1992–95; United Utilities plc, 1996–2006; Synesis Life Ltd, 2007–08. Chair: United Utilities Pension Scheme, 1998–2005; Electricity Supply Pension Scheme (UU Gp), 1998–2005; Royal Mail Pension Plan, 2005–12; Royal Mail Defined Contribn Pension Plan, 2009–12. Dir, Liverpool Associates in Tropical Health Ltd, 1994–98. Chair, 1995–97, Vice Pres., 1997–2014, now Emeritus Vice Pres., Liverpool Sch. of Tropical Medicine; Pro-Chancellor and Chair, Bd of Govs, London South Bank Univ., 1999–2007. Vice Pres., Pensions Archive Trust, 2009–; Trustee: Maxwell Pensioners Trust, 1992–97 (Chair, 1995–97); GlaxoSmithKline Pension Plan, 1994–2004; Dixons Gp Pension Scheme (UU Gp), 1998–2005; Common Purpose Charitable Trust, 1995–97; Age UK, 2009–15. Patron, Hillcroft Coll., 2011–. Gov., Pensions Policy Inst., 2009–. JP: Liverpool, 1993–95; S Western Magistrates' Court, 1995–2013. Hon. LLD London South Bank, 2008. *Recreations:* gardening, cooking, music, walking. *E:* pjnonline@gmail.com. *Club:* Athenæum.

NEWELL, Robert Fraser, CVO 2011 (LVO 2000); Director-General, Royal Over-Seas League, 1991–2011; *b* 3 May 1943; *s* of late Horace and Henrietta Newell; *m* 1969, Shahnaz Bakhtiar; two *d*. *Educ:* University Coll. Sch. FIH (MHCIMA 1986, FHCIMA 1997). Hotel mgt positions in London, Iran and Kenya, 1965–75; Dir of Admin, Kenya Utalii Coll., Nairobi, 1975–79; Gen. Manager, Royal Over-Seas League, 1979–91. Vis. Lectr in Hotel Financial Mgt, Ecole Hôtelière de Lausanne, 1983–2001. Chm., Assoc. of London Clubs, 1992–95; Member: Club Secs and Managers Assoc., 1982–2011; Council of Commonwealth Socs Cttee (formerly Jt Commonwealth Socs Council), 1991–2011; Cttee, Eur. Atlantic Gp, 1993–2010; Cttee, Kenya Soc., 1996–; Council, Mayfair St James's Assoc., 2001–11. Mem., Adv. Bd, Spirit of Remembrance, 2011–. Volunteer, Chain of Hope, 2001–; Trustee, Bridge of Hope, 2012– (Chm. Trustees, 2013–). Fellow, Brit. Assoc. Hotel Accountants, 1997; FCMI (FIMgt 1983). *Recreations:* tennis, music, walking, grandchildren, Alpine-walking. *Address:* Pichlhofstrasse 6 - Top 8, Kaprun 5710, Austria. *Club:* Royal Over-Seas League (Hon.).

NEWENS, (Arthur) Stanley; *b* 4 Feb. 1930; *s* of Arthur Ernest and Celia Jenny Newens, Bethnal Green; *m* 1st, 1954, Ann (*d* 1962), *d* of J. B. Sherratt, Stoke-on-Trent; two *d*; 2nd, 1966, Sandra Christina, *d* of J. A. Frith, Chingford; one *s* two *d*. *Educ:* Buckhurst Hill County High Sch.; University Coll., London (BA Hons History); Westminster Training Coll. (Post-Graduate Certificate of Education). Coal face worker in N Staffs mines, 1952–55. Secondary Sch. Teacher, 1956–65, 1970–74. MP (Lab) Epping, 1964–70 (NUT sponsored); MP (Lab and Co-op) Harlow, Feb. 1974–1983; contested (Lab) Harlow, 1983 and 1987; MEP (Lab and Co-op) London Central, 1984–99. Chairman: Eastern Area Gp of Lab. MPs, 1974–83; Tribune Gp of MPs, 1982–83 (Vice-Chm., 1981–82); PLP Foreign Affairs Gp, 1982–83 (Vice-Chm., 1976–77); Dep. Leader, British Lab. Gp of MEPs, 1988–89 (Chm., 1985–87); Pres., EP Central Amer. and Mexico Delegn, 1994–96; Vice-Chm., Labour Action for Peace. Active Member: Labour Party, holding numerous offices, 1949–; NUM, 1952–55; NUT, 1956–. Pres., Liberation (Movement for Colonial Freedom), 1992– (Chm., 1967–92). Dir, London Co-operative Soc., 1971–77 (Pres., 1977–81); Mem., Central Exec., Co-op. Union, 1974–80. Sec., Harlow Council for Voluntary Service, 1983–84. Mem., Harlow Health Centres Trust, 1984–. Chairman: Harlow Civic Soc., 1999–; Gibberd Garden Trust, 1999–; President: Waltham Abbey Historical Soc., 1998–; Socialist History Soc., 2013– (Vice-Pres., 2005–13); Vice-Pres., Friends of Historic Essex, 1982–; Member: Adv. Bd, Modern Record Centre, 1974–85, 1999–2008; Council, London Record Soc., 2001–05; Council, Essex Soc. for Archaeol. and Hist., 2002– (Pres., 2005–08; Trustee, 2012–). *Publications:* The Case Against NATO (pamphlet), 1972; Nicolae Ceausescu, 1972; Third World: change or chaos, 1977; A History of North Weald Bassett and its People, 1985; A Short History of the London Co-op Society Political Committee, 1988; (with Ron Bill) Leah Manning, 1991; The Kurds, 1994; Pathfinders, 1998; A Brief History of 100 Years of the Labour Party in the Eastern Region, 2000; Chris Morris: a landworker's struggle, 2003; A History of Struggle: 50th anniversary of Liberation (Movement for Colonial Freedom), 2004; (ed) A. E. Newens, The Memoirs of an Old East-Ender, 2006; Arthur Morrison: the novelist of realism in East London and Essex, 2008; In Quest of a Fairer Society: my life and politics, 2013; pamphlets and articles. *Recreations:* local historical research, family, reading, gardening. *Address:* The Leys, 18 Park Hill, Harlow, Essex CM17 0AE. *T:* (01279) 420108. *E:* stannewens@hotmail.com.

NEWEY, Brian; *see* Newey, S. B.

NEWEY, Rev. Canon Edmund James; Residentiary Canon and Sub-Dean, Christ Church, Oxford, since 2013; *b* Reading, 23 Sept. 1971; *s* of (Sidney) Brian Newey, *qv*; *m* 2003, Emma Rose Helen Wagstaff; one *s* one *d*. *Educ:* Abingdon Sch.; Lincoln Coll., Oxford (BA Modern Langs 1995); Emmanuel Coll., Cambridge (BA Theol. 1999); Westcott House; Manchester Univ. (PhD 2008). Lang. Asst, Akademisches Gymnasium and Wirtschaftkundliches Realgymnasium der Ursulinen, Innsbruck, 1992–93; Asst Master, Bolton Sch. (Boys Div.), 1994–97; ordained deacon, 2000, priest, 2001; Asst Curate, Birch with Fallowfield, Manchester, 2000–03; Rector, St Mary, Newmarket and St Agnes, Exning, 2003–07; Vicar, St Andrew, Handsworth, 2007–13; Area Dean of Handsworth, 2011–13. *Publications:* Children of God: the child as source of theological anthropology, 2012; contribs to bks and learned jls. *Recreations:* walking and running on the fells, family and friends. *Address:* Christ Church, Oxford OX1 1DP. *T:* (01865) 276150. *E:* edmund.newey@lincoln.oxon.org. *Club:* Mercia Fell Runners.

NEWEY, Hon. Sir Guy (Richard), Kt 2010; **Hon. Mr Justice Newey;** a Judge of the High Court of Justice, Chancery Division, since 2010; *b* 21 Jan. 1959; *s* of His Honour John Henry Richard Newey, QC and of Mollie Patricia Newey (*née* Chalk); *m* 1986, Angela Clare Neilson; one *s* three *d*. *Educ:* Tonbridge Sch.; Queens' Coll., Cambridge (MA 1st Cl., LLM 1st Cl.); Council of Legal Educn (1st Cl. in Bar Exams). Called to the Bar, Middle Temple, 1982, Bencher, 2010; in practice at Chancery Bar, 1983–2010; QC 2001; a Dep. High Ct Judge, 2006–10; Jun. Counsel to the Crown, Chancery, and A Panel, 1990–2001; Jun. Counsel to Charity Comrs, 1991–2001; Chancery Supervising Judge for Midlands, Wales and Western Circuits, 2014–. Inspector into affairs of MG Rover, 2005–09. An Acting Deemster, 2003–09, Deemster, 2009–11, Isle of Man. Gov., New Beacon Educnl Trust Ltd, 2001–09. *Publications:* (contrib.) Directors' Disqualification, 2nd edn 1998; (contrib.) Civil Court Service, 1999. *Address:* Royal Courts of Justice, 7 Rolls Building, Fetter Lane, EC4A 1NL.

See also M. C. Newey.

NEWEY, Michael Clive, FRICS; Chief Executive, Broadland Housing Group, since 2003; President, Royal Institution of Chartered Surveyors, 2013–14; *b* Farnborough, Kent, 9 June 1963; *s* of His Honour John Henry Richard Newey, QC, and of Mollie Patricia Newey (*née* Chalk); *m* 1987, Catherine Louise Hern; one *s* one *d*. *Educ:* Tonbridge Sch., Kent; Portsmouth Poly. (BSc Urban Land Admin). FRICS 1996. Surveyor: Porter Cobb & Prall, later GA Property Services, 1986–88; Prudential Property Services, 1988; Principal Surveyor, Richard Ellis, 1988–94; Associate Dir, Savills, 1994–97; Develt Dir, Flagship Housing Gp, 1997–2000; Exec. Dir, Anglia Housing Gp, 2000–03; sabbatical on secondment as Special Advr on Community Housing, to Dept of Human Services, Govt of Victoria, 2008–09. Vis. Fellow, Royal Agricl Univ., 2013–. Member: Flats over Shops Steering Gp, DoE, 1991–94; Adv. Bd, Regeneration Investment Orgn, UKTI, 2013–. Royal Institution of Chartered Surveyors: Chairman: Jun. Orgn, 1992–93; Residential Policy, 1999–2003; Eur. Housing Forum, 2002–05; Public Affairs, 2003–07; Ind. Housing Commn, 2012–13; Dep. Chm., Mgt Bd, 2006–10. Chm., Theatre Royal Norwich, 2015–. FCIH 2010. Mem., Australasian Housing Inst., 2009–. Hon. DSc Portsmouth, 2015. *Recreations:* holidays with family, golf, Norwich City Football Club, reading, theatre, housing policy. *Address:* Broadland Housing Group, Jarrold Stand, Norwich City Football Club, Carrow Road, Norwich NR1 1HU. *T:* (01603) 750292. *E:* michael.newey@broadlandgroup.org. *Clubs:* 1913 Wilderness; Victory Services.

See also Hon. Sir G. R. Newey.

NEWEY, (Sidney) Brian; consultant in transport; Assistant to Chief Executive, Railways, British Rail, 1990–93, retired; *b* 8 Jan. 1937; *s* of Sidney Frank Newey and Edith Mary Newey; *m* 1967, Margaret Mary Stevens (*d* 1996); one *s*. *Educ:* Burton upon Trent Grammar Sch.; Worcester Coll., Oxford (MA Mod. History). British Rail: Traffic apprentice, Western Region, 1960; Stationmaster, Southall, Middx, 1964; Freight Marketing Manager, Western Region, 1971; Divl Manager, Birmingham, 1978; Dep. General Manager, London Midland Region, 1980; Gen. Manager, Western Region, 1985–87; Director, Provincial, 1987–90. Chm., Oxford Diocesan Bd of Finance, 2001–13. Member: Governing Body, Whitelands Coll., Roehampton, 2006–; Council, Univ. of Roehampton, 2011–. *Recreations:* fell walking, history, reading, village and church affairs. *Address:* Chestnut Cottage, The Green South, Warborough, Oxon OX10 7DN. *T:* (01865) 858322.

See also Rev. Canon E. J. Newey.

NEWFOUNDLAND, CENTRAL, Bishop of, since 2005; **Rt Rev. David Torraville;** *b* 29 May 1953; *s* of Rev. Canon Arnold Torraville and Nita Marie Torraville; *m* 1979, Karen Flemming; one *s* one *d. Educ:* Meml Univ. of Newfoundland (BA, BEd); Queen's Coll., St John's, Newfoundland (MDiv). Fellow in Pastoral Leadership Develt, Princeton Theol Seminary. Rector: Twillingate, 1985–89; Cathedral of St Martin, Gander, 1989–2000; Exec. Officer, Dio. Central Newfoundland, 2001–05. *Recreation:* flyfishing. *Address:* 34 Fraser Road, Gander, NL A1V 2E8, Canada. *T:* (office) (709) 2562372, *Fax:* (709) 2562396. *E:* bishopcentral@nfld.net. *Club:* Kiwanis Internat.

NEWHAM, Prof. Dianne Jane, PhD; Professor of Physiotherapy, King's College London, since 1993; *b* 31 July 1949; *d* of Geoffrey Newham and Denise Millicent Newham; partner, Terry N. Williams; one *s. Educ:* Nairobi Convent Sch., Kenya; Ockbrook Moravian Sch.; Prince of Wales Sch. of Physiotherapy (MCSP, SRP 1976); UCL (MPhil 1982); North London Poly. (PhD 1985). FCSP 2007. Lab. Asst, Boots Co. Ltd, 1967–70; VSO, Nigeria, 1970–72; University College London: Physiotherapist, 1976–79; Res. Physiotherapist, Dept of Medicine, 1979–82; Associate Res. Fellow, Medicine and Surgery, 1985–87; Lectr in Physiology, 1987–89; King's College, London: Reader, 1989–93; Hd of Physiotherapy, 1989–2000; Dir, Div. of Applied Biomedical Res., 2000–12. Mem., Working Gp on estabt of UK Acad. of Med. Scis, 1996–98. *Publications:* chapters on human muscle pain, skeletal muscle function and fatigue; original research papers in jls of physiology, physiotherapy and rehabilitation. *Recreations:* travel, gardening, food and wine. *Address:* Centre of Human and Aerospace Physiological Sciences, King's College London, Shepherd's House, Guy's Campus, SE1 1UL. *T:* (020) 7848 6320.

NEWHOUSE, Jonathan Edward; Chairman and Chief Executive, Condé Nast International, since 1991; *b* New York, 30 March 1952; *s* of Norman Newhouse and Alice Newhouse; *m* 1995, Ronnie Cooke; two *d. Educ:* Isidore Newman Sch.; Yale Univ. Exec. Vice Pres., New Yorker mag., 1985–88; Publisher, Details mag., 1988–89; Pres., Condé Nast Internat., 1989–2012. Officier, Ordre des Arts et des Lettres (France), 2008. *Address:* Condé Nast International, 25 Maddox Street, W1S 2QN. *T:* (020) 7851 1818. *E:* jonathan.newhouse@condenastint.com. *Club:* Yale.

NEWING, John Frederick, CBE 1999; QPM 1988; DL; Chief Constable, Derbyshire Constabulary, 1990–2000; *b* 1 March 1940; *s* of Frederick George Newing and Emily Beatrice Newing (*née* Bettles); *m* 1963, Margaret May Kilborn (*d* 2007); two *s* one *d. Educ:* Kettering Grammar Sch.; Leeds Univ. (BA Hons Social and Public Administration). Joined Metropolitan Police, 1963; Police Staff Coll., 1967–68; Bramshill Scholarship, Leeds Univ., 1969–72; Community Relations Br., 1974; Staff Officer to Commissioner, 1977; Chief Supt i/c Marylebone Div., 1980; Senior Command Course, Police Staff Coll., 1981; Comdr, Community Relations, 1982, Public Order Branch, 1984; Dep. Asst Comr i/c W London Area, 1985–87; seconded to Home Office Science and Technology Gp, 1987–90. Pres., ACPO, 1998–99. Chm., E Midlands Regl Bd, Crimestoppers, 2001–06. DL Derbyshire, 2000. *Publications:* articles in Policing and other professional jls. *Recreations:* reading, walking, voluntary youth work, such sports as age allows. *Address:* Glapwell, Derbys.

NEWING, Rt Rev. Dom Kenneth Albert, OSB; *b* 29 Aug. 1923; *s* of Albert James Pittock Newing and Nellie Louise Maude Newing; unmarried. *Educ:* Dover Grammar School; Selwyn College, Cambridge (MA); Theological College, Mirfield, Yorks. Deacon, 1955; priest, 1956; Assistant Curate, Plymstock, 1955–63; Rector of Plympton S Maurice, Plymouth, 1963–82; Archdeacon of Plymouth, 1978–82; Bishop Suffragan of Plymouth, 1982–88; joined Order of St Benedict, 1988; solemn (life) profession, 1989. *Address:* St Benedict's Priory, 19a The Close, Salisbury SP1 2EB. *T:* (01722) 335868.

NEWINGTON, Sir Michael (John), KCMG 1993 (CMG 1982); HM Diplomatic Service, retired; Ambassador to Brazil, 1987–92; *b* 10 July 1932; *er s* of late J. T. Newington, Spalding, Lincs; *m* 1956, Nina Gordon-Jones; one *s* one *d. Educ:* Stamford Sch.; St John's Coll., Oxford. MA. RAF, 1951–52, Pilot Officer. Joined Foreign Office, 1955; Economic Survey Section, Hong Kong, 1957–58; resigned 1958. ICI, 1959–60. Rejoined FO, 1960; Second, later First Sec. (Economic), Bonn, 1961–65; First Sec., Lagos, 1965–68; Asst Head of Science and Technology Dept, FCO, 1968–72; Counsellor (Scientific), Bonn, 1972–75; Counsellor and Consul-Gen., Tel Aviv, 1975–78; Head of Republic of Ireland Dept, FCO, 1978–81; Consul-Gen., Düsseldorf, 1981–85; Ambassador to Venezuela and concurrently (non-resident) to Dominican Republic, 1985–87. *Recreations:* gardening, cultivating olives. *Address:* Mas Bomuré, 83460 Taradeau, France; 2 Church Street, St Clements, Sandwich, Kent CT13 9EH.

NEWISS, Hilary Jane; Chair, National Voices, since 2014; *b* Keighley, 16 April 1956; *d* of Reginald Stewart Newiss and Winifred Newiss; *m* 1985, Sir Peter Lytton Bazalgette, *qv*; one *s* one *d. Educ:* Harrogate Coll.; Somerville Coll., Oxford (BA Hons PPP 1977). Articled Clerk, Herbert Smith, 1979–81; admitted as solicitor, 1981; Solicitor: Clifford Chance, 1981–88; Theodore Goddard, 1988–90; Partner, Denton Hall, 1990–99. Fee-paid Judge, First-tier Tribunals Service, 2011–. Member: Human Genetics Commn, 2000–06; Intellectual Property Adv. Cttee, 2001–05; Nat. Information Governance Bd, 2007–13; Adv. Panel for Public Sector Information, 2007–15. Trustee and non-executive Director, Roslin Foundn, 2006–; Charleston, 2006–15; Francis Crick Inst., 2011–; Trustee, Natural Hist. Mus., 2015–. *Publications:* (ed and contrib.) International Intellectual Property Litigation (loose-leaf), 1997. *Recreations:* tennis, opera, theatre, art and design. *Address:* National Voices, 1st Floor, Bride House, 18–20 Bride Lane, EC4Y 8EE. *E:* vikki@newbaz.com.

NEWLAND, Prof. Adrian Charles, CBE 2010; FRCP, FRCPath; Professor of Haematology, Barts and the London School of Medicine and Dentistry, Queen Mary (formerly St Bartholomew's and Royal London School of Medicine and Dentistry, Queen Mary and Westfield College), University of London, since 1992; Director of Pathology, Barts Health (formerly Barts and the London) NHS Trust, since 2004; *b* 26 Aug. 1949; *m* 1973, Joanna Mary Shaw; one *s* one *d. Educ:* City of Norwich Sch.; Downing Coll., Cambridge (MA 1975); London Hospital Med. Coll. (MB BCh 1975). MRCP 1976, FRCP 1992; FRCPath 1992. Hon. Consultant, Barts Health (formerly Royal Hosps, then Barts and the London) NHS Trust, 1981–; Dir of R and D, Barts and the London NHS Trust, 1997–2001; Dir, NE Thames Cancer Network, 2001–13. Chairman: NICE Diagnostic Assessment Prog., 2010–; Healthcare Forum, UK Accreditation Service, 2013–; Dep. Chm., Chemotherapy Clinical Reference Panel, 2013–. President: British Soc. for Haematology, 1998–99; RCPath, 2005–08; Internat. Soc. of Hematology, 2014–. Hon. Sec., Acad. of Medical Royal Colleges, 2007–10. Ed. in Chief, Hematology, 1995–. *Publications:* (jtly) Pocket Consultant Haematology, 1986; (ed jtly) Cambridge Medical Reviews, vols 14, 1991; numerous contribs in field of haematology incl. chapters in books; over 250 papers in learned jls. *Recreations:* good literature, fine wine, walking, foreign travel. *Address:* Department of Haematology, The Royal London Hospital, Whitechapel, E1 1BB. *T:* (020) 3246 0338, *Fax:* (020) 3246 0351. *E:* a.c.newland@qmul.ac.uk; Flat 109, Waterdale Manor House, 20 Harewood Avenue, NW1 6JX. *Clubs:* Athenæum, MCC.

NEWLAND, Prof. David Edward, MA; ScD; FREng, FIMechE, FIET; Professor of Engineering (1875), 1976–2003, now Emeritus, Head, Engineering Department, 1996–2002, and a Deputy Vice-Chancellor, 1999–2003, University of Cambridge; Fellow, Selwyn College, Cambridge, since 1976; consulting engineer; *b* 8 May 1936; *s* of late Robert W. Newland and Marion A. Newland (*née* Dearman); *m* 1959, Patricia Frances Mayne; two *s. Educ:* Alleyne's Sch., Stevenage; Selwyn Coll., Cambridge (Lyttleton Scholar, 1956; Mech. Sciences Tripos: Rex Moir Prize, 1956, Ricardo Prize, 1957; MA 1961; ScD 1990); Massachusetts Inst. of Technol. (ScD thesis on nonlinear vibrations, 1963). English Electric Co., 1957–61; Instr and Asst Prof. of Mech. Engrg, MIT, 1961–64; Lectr and Sen. Lectr, Imperial Coll. of Science and Technol., 1964–67; Prof. of Mech. Engrg, Sheffield Univ., 1967–76. Mem., Royal Commn on Envmtl Pollution, 1984–89. Visitor, Transport and Road Res. Lab., 1990–92; non-exec. Dir, Cambridge-MIT Inst., 2000–02. Past or present mem., cttees of IMechE, DTI, BSI, SERC, Design Council, Engrg Council and Royal Academy (formerly Fellowship) of Engineering, including: Mem., Editorial Panel, 1968–82 and Consultant Editor, 1983–87, Jl Mech. Engrg Sci., Proc. IMechE, Part C; Engrg Awards Panel, Design Council, 1977–79; Council, Fellowship of Engrg, 1985–88; Working Party on Engineers and Risk Issues, Engrg Council, 1990–94; Member: SRC Transport Cttee, 1969–72; Mech. Engrg and Machine Tools Requirements Bd, 1977, 1978; Chm., BSI Tech. Cttee on bellows expansion jts, 1976–85. Technical witness, Flixborough Inquiry, 1974–75, and other engrg and patents cases; investigations following Piper Alpha, Potters Bar and other accidents; Engrg Advr, London Millennium Bridge Trust, 2000–01. Pres., Selwyn Coll. Alumni Assoc., 2013–14. Governor, St Paul's Schs, 1978–93. Freeman, City of London, 2000; Liveryman, Engrs' Co., 2001. Churchwarden, Ickleton, 1979–87. Distinguished Alumni Lectr, MIT, 1999. FREng (FEng 1982). Hon. DEng Sheffield, 1997. Charles S. Lake award, 1975, and T. Bernard Hall prize, IMechE, 1991, for papers in IMechE Procs; Applied Mechanics Award for dist. contribs, ASME, 2002. *Publications:* An Introduction to Random Vibrations and Spectral Analysis, 1975, 3rd edn, as Random Vibrations, Spectral and Wavelet Analysis, 1993; Mechanical Vibration Analysis and Computation, 1989; Discover Butterflies in Britain, 2006; Britain's Butterflies, 2002, 3rd edn 2015; Britain's Day-flying Moths, 2013; technical papers, mostly in British and Amer. engrg jls. *Recreations:* nature photography, entomology, walking, music, cycling. *Address:* Selwyn College, Cambridge CB3 9DQ. *Club:* Athenæum.

NEWLAND, Martin; Adviser, Abu Dhabi Media, since 2014 (Editorial Director, 2009–11; Chief Publishing Officer, 2011–14); *b* 26 Oct. 1961; *s* of Edward and Elena Newland; *m* 1987, Bénédicte Smets; three *s* one *d. Educ:* Downside Sch.; Goldsmiths Coll., London Univ. (BA Hons (Hist.) 1984); Heythrop Coll., London Univ. (MTh 1986). News Editor, Catholic Herald, 1986–88; Daily Telegraph: reporter, 1989–93; Home Ed., 1993–98; Dep. Ed. and Launch Ed., National Post, Canada, 1998–2003; Ed., The Daily Telegraph, 2003–05; Ed. and Launch Ed., The National, Abu Dhabi, 2008–09. *Recreations:* music, fitness, martial arts.

NEWLANDS, David Baxter; Chairman: Paypoint plc, 1998–2014; HellermannTyton plc, since 2013; *b* 13 Sept. 1946; *s* of George Frederick Newlands and Helen Frederica Newlands; *m* 1973, Susan Helena Milne; two *s* two *d. Educ:* Edinburgh Acad. FCA 1969. Deloitte & Touche, 1963–86, Partner, 1977–86; Gp Finance Director: Saatchi & Saatchi, 1986–89; General Electric Co. plc, 1989–97. Non-executive Director: Weir Gp, 1997–2003; Global Software Services, 1998–2004; Tomkins plc, 1999–2010 (Chm., 2000–10); Standard Life Assce Co., 1999–2006 (Dep. Chm., 2004–06); London Regl Transport, 1999–2001; Britax Internat. plc, 1999–2001 (Chm., 2000–01); Chairman: Prospect Investment Mgt, 1999–2014; KESA Electricals, later Darty plc, 2003–12; OB10 (formerly Oxford Business Exchange), 2004–11; Impress Coöperative UA, 2007–10. Chm., Raeburn Place Foundn, 2014–. Chm. Trustees, SeeAbility, 2001–07. *Recreations:* golf, Rugby, bridge. *Address:* Lane End, Chucks Lane, Walton-on-the-Hill, Surrey KT20 7UB. *T:* (01737) 812582. *Clubs:* Caledonian, Royal Automobile; Walton Heath Golf (Dir, 2001–); Sutton and Epsom Rugby (Cheam); Golf House (Elie); Royal and Ancient Golf (St Andrews).

NEWLANDS, Gavin Andrew Stuart; MP (SNP) Paisley and Renfrewshire North, since 2015; *b* Paisley, 2 Feb. 1980; *s* of Gordon Newlands and Isabel Newlands; *m* 2008, Lynn Single; two *d. Educ:* Trinity High Sch., Renfrew. Business Analyst, McDonald's Restaurants Ltd, 2005–07; Asst Manager, then Business Analyst, later Business Manager, AG Restaurants Ltd, 2007–15. *Recreations:* spending time with family, Rugby, football (watching), golf. *Address:* (office) 6 Porterfield Road, Renfrew PA4 8HG. *T:* (0141) 378 0600. *E:* gavin.newlands.mp@parliament.uk. *Club:* Paisley Rugby.

NEWLANDS, Rev. Prof. George McLeod, PhD, DLitt; FRSE; Professor of Divinity, University of Glasgow, 1986–2008, Hon. Professorial Research Fellow, since 2008; Principal, Trinity College, Glasgow, 1991–97 and 2002–07; *b* 12 July 1941; *s* of George and Mary Newlands; *m* 1967, Mary Elizabeth Wallace; three *s. Educ:* Perth Acad.; Univ. of Edinburgh (MA 1st Cl. Classics (Vans Dunlop Scholar, 1963); BD 1st Cl. Eccles. Hist. (Cunningham Fellow, 1966); PhD 1970; DLitt 2005); Univ. of Heidelberg; Univ. of Zürich; Churchill Coll., Cambridge (MA). Ordained minister, C of S, 1970, and priest, C of E, 1982. Asst Minister, Muirhouse, Edinburgh, 1969–70; Lectr in Divinity, Univ. of Glasgow, 1969–73; Cambridge University: Lectr in Divinity, 1973–86; Fellow, Wolfson Coll., 1975–82; Fellow and Dean, Trinity Hall, 1982–86; Glasgow University: Dean, Faculty of Divinity, 1988–90; Dir, Centre for Theol., Lit. and the Arts, 1999–2002. Hensley Henson Lectr, Oxford, 1995. Vis. Prof., Univ. of Mainz, 1999; Vis. Scholar: Claremont Sch. of Theol., Calif, 2002; Princeton Theol Seminary, 2005, 2009. Hon. Fellow, Sch. of Divinity, Univ. of Edinburgh, 2010. Member: Doctrine Commn, C of E, 1983–86; Doctrine Cttee, Scottish Episcopal Ch, 2008–; Convener, Panel on Doctrine, C of S, 1995–99. Member: Eur. Cttee, World Alliance of Reformed Churches, 1987–95; Church and Nation Cttee, C of S, 1992–96; Unity, Faith and Order Commn, Action for Churches Together in Scotland, 1995–; Scottish Churches Initiative for Unity, 1995–2003; HEFCE RAE Panel for Theology and Religious Studies, 1996, 2001, 2008 (Chm.); Center of Theol Inquiry, Princeton, 1998; Netherlands RAE Panel, 1999. Founder Mem., Affirmation Scotland, 2006–. Pres., Soc. for Study of Theology, 2013–14. FRSA 2005; FRSE 2008. Member, Editorial Board: Theology in Scotland, 1996–; Conversations in Religion and Theol., 2007–11; Modern Believing, 2011–. *Publications:* Hilary of Poitiers, 1978; Theology of the Love of God, 1980; (ed) Explorations in Theology 8, 1981; The Church of God, 1984; Making Christian Decisions, 1985; God in Christian Perspective, 1994; Generosity and the Christian Future, 1997; (ed jtly) Scottish Christianity in the Modern World, 2000; John and Donald Baillie: transatlantic theology, 2002; The Transformative Imagination, 2004; (ed jtly) Fifty Key Christian Thinkers, 2004; (ed jtly) Believing in the Text, 2004; Traces of Liberality, 2006; Christ and Human Rights, 2006; (jtly) Faith and Human Rights, 2008; (jtly) Hospitable God, 2010; Spirit of Liberality, 2014; *festschrift:* The God of Love and Human Dignity: essays for George Newlands, by P. Middleton, 2007; contribs to theol pubns. *Recreations:* music, walking. *Address:* 49 Highsett, Cambridge CB2 1NZ. *Club:* New (Edinburgh).

NEWLING, Caro; Joint Founder and Director, Neal Street Productions Ltd, since 2003; *b* London, 12 April 1957; adopted *d* of John and Evelyn Newling; partner, Gary Hamilton Powell. *Educ:* Brighton and Hove High Sch.; Roedean Sch.; Warwick Univ. (BA Hons Th. Studies); Webber-Douglas Acad. of Dramatic Art. Sen. Press Officer, RSC, 1986–91; Co-Founder and Exec. Producer, Donmar Warehouse Th., 1992–2002; over 70 prodns for Donmar Warehouse, W End and NY; prodns for Neal Street Productions, London and NY, incl. The Bridge Project, Shrek The Musical, Charlie and the Chocolate Factory. Chair, Paines Plough, 2011–; Member: Bd, National Th., 2002–10; Bd of Mgt, Soc. of London Theatres, 2008– (Pres., 2014–). Chair, Linbury Biennial Prize for Stage Design, 2010–.

Recreation: walking the Sussex Downs and the Scottish hills with friends and dogs. *Address:* Neal Street Productions Ltd, 26–28 Neal Street, First Floor, Covent Garden, WC2H 9QQ. *T:* (020) 7240 8890. *E:* cnewling@nealstreetproductions.com.

NEWLOVE, family name of **Baroness Newlove**.

NEWLOVE, Baroness *cr* 2010 (Life Peer), of Warrington in the County of Cheshire; **Helen Margaret Newlove;** community reform campaigner; Victims' Commissioner, since 2012; *b* Salford, 28 Dec. 1961; *m* 1986, Garry Newlove (*d* 2007); three *d.* Campaigner against anti-social behaviour. Founder: Newlove Warrington, 2008; Nat. Licensed Trade Assoc., 2010. *Address:* House of Lords, SW1A 0PW.

NEWMAN, Rt Rev. Adrian; *see* Stepney, Area Bishop of.

NEWMAN, Andrew William; Chief Executive, Objective Productions, since 2011 (Chief Creative Officer, 2009–11); *b* Plymouth, 4 Nov. 1969; *s* of Alastair John Newman and Geraldine Newman; *m* 2002, Terry Louise Burgess; two *s.* *Educ:* St Paul's Sch., London; University Coll. London (BSc Psychol.). Researcher, 1992–93, Asst Producer, 1993–95, Big Breakfast and The Word, Planet 24 Prodns; Asst Producer and writer, Brasseye, Talkback Prodns, 1995–96; Producer: Big Breakfast, Planet 24 Prodns, 1996–97; The Sunday Show, BBC TV, 1997; The 11 O'Clock Show and Ali G, Talkback Prodns, 1998; Commng Editor, Channel 4, 1999–2000; Hd of Progs, E4, 2000–01; Controller of Entertainment, Channel Five, 2001–03; Hd of Entertainment, 2003–05, Hd of Entertainment and Comedy, 2005–09, Channel 4. Chm., TV Cttee, BAFTA, 2011– (Dep. Chm., 2009–11). Member: BAFTA; Magic Circle. *Recreations:* watching television, collecting vintage Vivienne Westwood clothes, entertaining children, loving and hating contemporary art, buying books on Francis Bacon, magic, photography, arguing, occasional journalism, going for lunch, watching more television. *Address:* c/o Objective Productions, 3rd Floor, Riverside Building, County Hall, Westminster Bridge Road, SE1 7PB. *T:* (020) 7202 2300, *Fax:* (020) 7202 2301. *E:* AndrewNewman@objectiveproductions.com. *Clubs:* Soho House, Ivy.

NEWMAN, Catherine Mary; QC 1995; a Recorder, since 2000; a Deputy High Court Judge, since 2008; Lieutenant-Bailiff (Judge) of the Royal Court of Guernsey, since 2001; *b* 7 Feb. 1954; *d* of Dr Ernest Newman and Josephine (*née* McLaughlin); one *s* one *d.* *Educ:* University Coll. London (LLB 1st Cl. Hons 1978). Called to the Bar, Middle Temple, 1979 (Harmsworth Schol.), Bencher, 2002; admitted to courts of Dubai Internat. Financial Centre, 2010; called to the Bar, BVI, 2011; in practice in business and commercial fields, Chancery Div., 1980–; Dep. Registrar in Bankruptcy, 1991–2000; an Asst Recorder, 1998–2000. Member: Bar Council, 1987–90; Public Interest Adv. Panel, Legal Services Commn, 2000–04; Council, UCL, 2008–11. Chm., Inns of Ct and Bar Educnl Trust, 2005–. Foundn Trustee, CAFOD, 2009–. Consulting Ed., French on Winding Up, 2008–. *Publications:* Bar Finals Guide, 1980, 3rd edn 1987; Insolvency Issues, 1999. *Recreation:* eating with friends. *Address:* Maitland Chambers, 7 Stone Buildings, Lincoln's Inn, WC2A 3SZ. *T:* (020) 7406 1200.

NEWMAN, Cathy; presenter, Channel 4 News, since 2011; *b* Guildford, 14 July 1974; *d* of David Newman and Julia Newman; *m* 2001, John O'Connell; two *d.* *Educ:* Lady Margaret Hall, Oxford (BA 1st Cl. Hons English 1995). Researcher/trainee writer, The Independent, 1995–96; reporter, Media Week, 1996–97; contrib., Book Pages, Daily Telegraph, 1996–97; Media Business Reporter, The Independent, 1997; Financial Times: Media Corresp., 1998–99; Political Corresp., 1999–2002; Chief Political Corresp., 2002–06; Political Corresp., Channel 4 News, 2006–11. Presenter, Sunday Prog., GMTV, 2000–05. Regular blogger, Daily Telegraph, 2012–. Judge, Baileys Women's Prize for Fiction, 2015. Laurence Stern Fellow, Washington Post, 2000. *Recreations:* playing the violin, gardening, watching Agatha Christie adaptations, matchmaking (unsuccessful), walking on Exmoor. *Address:* Channel 4 News, ITN, 200 Gray's Inn Road, WC1X 8XZ. *T:* (020) 7833 3000. *E:* cathy.newman@itn.co.uk. *Club:* Soho House.

NEWMAN, Charles William Frank; a District Judge, since 1991; *b* 30 May 1946; *s* of John Leonard Newman and Enid Mary Newman; *m* 1st, 1970, Clare Willatt (decd); one *d*; 2nd, 1986, Anna Elizabeth Meacock; two *s.* *Educ:* Hawthorne Road Primary Sch., Kettering; Kimbolton Sch.; Queen Mary Coll., London (LLB Hons 1968). Admitted solicitor, 1972; Registrar of Co. Court, 1987. Mem., Judicial Appts Commn, 2006–12. Gov., Queen's Sch., Chester, 2003–09. *Recreations:* cooking, wine, reading, walking in the Lakes. *Club:* Army and Navy.

NEWMAN, Ven. David Maurice Frederick; Archdeacon of Loughborough, since 2009; *b* Woking, 23 Aug. 1954; *s* of Frederick Newman and Peggy Newman; *m* 1982, Helen Greet; one *s* two *d.* *Educ:* Hertford Coll., Oxford (MA 1979); St John's Coll., Nottingham (DipTh 1977). Ordained deacon, 1979, priest, 1980; Assistant Curate: Christ Church, Orpington, 1979–83; St Mary's, Bushbury, W Midlands, 1983–86; Vicar, All Saints, Ockbrook, Derbyshire, 1986–97; Team Rector, Emmanuel, Loughborough and St Mary-in-Charnwood, 1997–2009; Rural Dean, Akeley E, Loughborough, 1999–2006. Hon. Canon, Leicester Cathedral, 2006–. *Publications:* What Are We About to Receive?, 1982; (ed) Taking on Faith in the City, 1986. *Recreations:* walking, sport, theatre. *Address:* The Archdeaconry, 21 Church Road, Glenfield, Leics LE3 8DP. *T:* (0116) 261 5321. *E:* dmfnewman@gmail.com.

NEWMAN, Edward; Chair, Health Scrutiny Committee (formerly Health and Wellbeing Committee), Manchester City Council, since 2011; *b* 14 May 1953; *m*; three *c.* Formerly in light engineering, cable making; postal worker, Manchester. Mem. (Lab), Manchester CC, 1979–85, 2002– (Mem. for Housing, then Neighbourhood Services, Exec. Cttee, 2004–08). MEP (Lab) Greater Manchester Central, 1984–99. Mem. Bd, Willow Park Housing Trust, Wythenshawe, Manchester, 2004–13 (Chm., 2008–11); Chm. Bd, Wythenshawe Community Housing Gp, 2013–. *Publications:* (contrib.) The European Ombudsman: origins, establishment, evolution, 2005. *Address:* 234 Ryebank Road, Chorlton cum Hardy, Manchester M21 9LU.

NEWMAN, Sir Francis (Hugh Cecil), 4th Bt *cr* 1912, of Cecil Lodge, Newmarket; *b* 12 June 1963; *s* of Sir Gerard Robert Henry Sigismund Newman, 3rd Bt and of Caroline Philippa, *d* of late Brig. Alfred Geoffrey Neville, CBE, MC; *S* father, 1987; *m* 1990, Katharine, *d* of Timothy Edwards; three *s* one *d.* *Educ:* Eton; Univ. of Pennsylvania (BA Econs). *Recreations:* family, collecting, field sports. *Heir: s* Thomas Ralph Gerard Newman, *b* 7 Jan. 1993. *Address:* Burloes Hall, Royston, Herts SG8 9NE. *Clubs:* Pratt's, Turf; Eton Vikings.

NEWMAN, Sir Geoffrey (Robert), 6th Bt *cr* 1836; Director, Blackpool Sands (Devon) Utilities Co. Ltd, since 1970; *b* 2 June 1947; *s* of Sir Ralph Alured Newman, 5th Bt, and Hon. Ann Rosemary Hope, *d* of late Hon. Claude Hope-Morley; *S* father, 1968; *m* 1980, Mary, *y d* of Colonel Sir Martin St John Valentine Gibbs, KCVO, CB, DSO, TD; one *s* three *d.* *Educ:* Heatherdown, Ascot; Kelly Coll., Tavistock. 1st Bn, Grenadier Guards, 1967–70; Lt, T&AVR, until 1979. Daniel Greenaway & Sons Ltd, 1973–75; Mem., Transglobe Expedition, 1977–79; Prodn Controller, Wadlow Grosvenor Internat., 1980–90. Vice Chm. and Dir, Dartmouth Tourist Inf. Centre, 1995–2003; Mem., Devon Assoc. of Tourist Attractions, 1995–. Chm., Dartmouth Swimming Pool, 1999–. Walk Leader/Guide, The Wayfarers, 1990–2005. Pres., Dartmouth and Kingswear Soc., 2001–; Chm., Marine Conservation Soc., 2002–10. Vice Pres., Dartmouth Rugby Football Club, 2005–; Trustee, Britannia Mus., Britannia RNC, 2007–; Chm., Dartmouth and Dist Indoor Pool Trust, 2008–. FRGS. *Recreations:* sub-aqua, sailing, all sports. *Heir: s* Robert Melvil Newman, *b* 4 Oct. 1985.

NEWMAN, Hon. Sir George (Michael), Kt 1995; a Judge of the High Court of Justice, Queen's Bench Division, 1995–2007; a Deputy High Court Judge, since 2007; Judge of the Court of Appeal: Bahamas, 2009–11; Cayman Islands, since 2013; Surveillance Commissioner, since 2010; arbitrator and mediator; *b* 4 July 1941; *s* of late Wilfred James Newman and Cecilia Beatrice Lily Newman; *m* 1966, Hilary Alice Gibbs (*née* Chandler); two *s* one *d.* *Educ:* Lewes County Grammar Sch.; St Catharine's Coll., Cambridge (Squire Schol.; BA Law). Called to the Bar, Middle Temple, 1965 (Blackstone Scholar; Bencher, 1989; Treas., 2009), Trinidad and Tobago, 1979, St Kitts and Nevis, 1989. QC 1981; a Recorder, 1985–95. Counsel and Constitutional Advr to Gov. Gen. of Fiji, 1987; Constitutional Advr to Pres. of Fiji, 1988–90. Chm., Security Vetting Appeal Panel, 2009–. Fellow, Inst. of Advanced Legal Studies, 1999. FRSA 1991. *Publications:* (jtly) contribs to Halsbury's Laws of England, 4th edn. *Recreations:* tennis, golf, the countryside. *Address:* 3 Hare Court, Temple, EC4Y 7BJ. *Club:* Rye Golf.

NEWMAN, Jeremy Steven, FCA; Chairman: Single Source Regulations Office, since 2014; Arkarius Group Ltd, since 2014; *b* 30 Sept. 1959; *s* of Harold and Marilyn Newman; *m* 1987, Judi Levy; one *s* one *d.* *Educ:* Haberdashers' Aske's Sch., Elstree; City of London Poly. (Dip. Accountancy with Dist.); Harvard Business Sch. (AMP; ISMP). FCA 1982. Stoy Hayward & Co., then BDO Stoy Hayward LLP, later BDO LLP, 1978–2011; Partner, 1986; Man. Partner, 2001–08; CEO, BDO Internat., 2008–11; Chm., Audit Commn, 2012–15. Member: Murray Cttee on Audit Firm Governance, 2008–09; Internat. Integrated Reporting Cttee, 2009–11; non-exec. Bd Mem. and Chm., Audit and Risk Cttee, CPS, 2012–; Lead non-exec. Bd Mem., Dep. Chm., and Chm., Audit and Risk Cttee, Govt Law Dept (formerly Treasury Solicitor's Dept), 2013–. Non-exec. Dir, Social Investment Business, 2013–; Trustee, Social Investment Business Foundn, 2013–. Hon. Treasurer: British ORT, 1986–95; Community Security Trust, 2000–09; Labour Friends of Israel, 2004–05; Trustee, various charitable trusts; Chm. of Trustees, Sacks Morasha (formerly Morasha) Jewish Primary Sch., 2007–; Founder Mem. and Gov., Leigh City Technology Coll., 1990–2008; Mem. Council and Finance Cttee, Open Univ., 2014–. Hon. Vis. Prof., Cass Business Sch., 2013–. *Recreations:* opera, cinema, reading, spending time with my wife and children, foreign travel. *E:* jeremysnewman@hotmail.com.

NEWMAN, John Arthur, FSA; Reader, Courtauld Institute of Art, University of London, 1987–2001; *b* 14 Dec. 1936; *s* of late Arthur Charles Cecil Newman and Wynifred Kate Newman (*née* Owles); *m* 1965, Margaret Banner; two *d.* *Educ:* Dulwich Coll.; University Coll., Oxford (MA); Courtauld Inst. of Art, London Univ. (Academic Dip. 1965). Lectr, Courtauld Inst. of Art, 1966–87. Mem., Historic Buildings Council for England, 1977–84; Comr, English Heritage, 1986–89; Chm., Adv. Bd for Redundant Churches, 2000–05; Mem., Royal Commn on Ancient and Historical Monuments of Wales, 2000–10. Pres., Soc. of Architectural Historians of GB, 1988–92. *Publications:* Buildings of England series: Kent (2 vols), 1969, rev. edns as: vol. I, Kent: West and the Weald, 2012, vol. II, Kent: North East and East, 2013; (with Nikolaus Pevsner) Dorset, 1972; Shropshire, 2nd edn 2006; (contrib.) The History of the King's Works, vol. V, 1975; (ed with Howard Colvin) Roger North on Architecture, 1981; (contrib.) The History of the University of Oxford, vol. III, 1986, vol. IV, 1997; Buildings of Wales series: Glamorgan, 1995; Gwent/Monmouthshire, 2000. *Address:* 29 Scotton Street, Wye, Ashford, Kent TN25 5BU.

NEWMAN, Prof. Judith Alice, OBE 2012; PhD; Professor of American Studies, University of Nottingham, since 2000; *b* 9 May 1950; *d* of Ellis Edward Newman and Alice Dorothy Elizabeth Newman (*née* Herringshaw); *m* 1978, Ian Revie (marr. diss. 1999); one *s*, and one step *s.* *Educ:* Univ. of Edinburgh (MA English, MA French); Clare Coll., Cambridge (PhD 1982). University of Newcastle upon Tyne: Lectr, 1976–91; Reader, 1991–95; Prof. of American and Postcolonial Literature, 1995–2000. Chairman: British Assoc. for American Studies, 1995–98 (Sec., 1993–95); American Studies Panel, 2001 RAE; Main Panel L, 2008 RAE; Member: AHRC Res. Panel for English, 2004–07 (Convenor, 2007–09); AHRC Peer Review Coll., 2004. Founding FEA 1999; AcSS 2000. *Publications:* Saul Bellow and History, 1984; John Updike, 1988; Nadine Gordimer, 1988, reprinted 2014; (ed) Dred: a tale of the Great Dismal Swamp, 1992, 2nd edn 1998; The Ballistic Bard, 1995; Alison Lurie, 2000; Nadine Gordimer's Burger's Daughter (critical essays), 2003; Fictions of America, 2007; (ed with Celeste-Marie Bernier) Public Art, Memorials and Atlantic Slavery, 2009; Utopia and Terror in Contemporary American Fiction, 2013; 100 scholarly essays in learned jls and collections. *Recreations:* family, gardening, genealogy, trips home to Caithness, walking Rottweiler, learning Spanish. *Address:* School of American and Canadian Studies, University of Nottingham, University Park, Nottingham NG7 2RD. *T:* (0115) 951 4351, *Fax:* (0115) 951 4270. *E:* Judith.Newman@nottingham.ac.uk.

NEWMAN, Sir Kenneth (Leslie), GBE 1987; Kt 1978; QPM 1982; Commissioner of the Metropolitan Police, 1982–87; non-executive director of various companies, 1987–2002; *b* 15 Aug. 1926; *s* of John William Newman and Florence Newman; *m* 1949, Eileen Lilian. *Educ:* London Univ. (LLB Hons). Served War, RAF, 1942–46. Palestine Police, 1946–48; Metropolitan Police, 1948–73; Comdr, New Scotland Yard, 1972; Royal Ulster Constab., 1973–79; Sen. Dep. Chief Constable, 1973; Chief Constable, 1976–79; Comdt, Police Staff Coll., and HM Inspector of Constabulary, 1980–82. Vis. Prof. of Law, Bristol University, 1987–88. Registrar, Imperial Soc. of Knights Bachelor, 1991–98. Chairman: Disciplinary Cttee, Security Systems Inspectorate, British Security Industry Assoc., 1987–97; Assoc. for Prevention of Theft in Shops, 1987–91; Pres., Assoc. of Police and Public Security Suppliers, 1993–2000; Vice Pres., Defence Manufacturers Assoc., 1987–2000. Trustee: Police Foundn, 1982– (Chm., Res. Cttee, 1991–98); Community Action Trust (Crime Stoppers), 1987–2003; World Humanity Action Trust, 1993–98. CCMI (FBIM 1977). Freeman of the City of London, 1983. KStJ 1987 (CStJ 1984). Communicator of the Year, BAIE, 1984. Order of: Bahrain, Class 2, 1984; the Aztec Eagle, Cl. 2, Mexico, 1985. King Abdul Aziz, Cl. 1, Saudi Arabia, 1987; Grand Officer: Order of Orange-Nassau, Netherlands, 1982; Grand Order of the Lion, Malaŵi, 1985; Order of Ouissam Alouite, Morocco, 1987; Commander: National Order of Legion of Honour, France, 1984; Order of Military Merit, Spain, 1986; Kt Comdr, Order of Merit, West Germany, 1986; Medal of Merit, Cl. 1, Qatar, 1985. *Recreations:* walking, reading, bridge.

NEWMAN, Kevin; Senior Executive Vice President, since 2003, and Head of Retail Banking and Wealth Management, since 2014, HSBC Bank USA; *b* 28 June 1957; *s* of John and Valerie Newman; *m* 1983, Catherine Stewart-Murray; two *s* one *d.* *Educ:* Keele Univ. (BA Amer. Studies and Politics); Essex Univ. (US Govt and Politics). Mars Gp Services, 1981–85; Inf. Centre Manager, Business Systems Manager and Management Inf. Systems Dir, Woolworth, 1985–89; First Direct: joined 1989; Ops Dir, 1990; Chief Exec., 1991–97; Global Delivery Dir, Citibank, 1997–2000; Hd, HSBC.com, 2001–03; Hd, Personal Financial Services, HSBC USA, 2003–09; Hd, One HSBC Prog., 2009–11; Gp Hd, Retail Banking, HSBC, 2011–14. *Recreations:* squash, tennis, ski-ing, golf, gym workout, American football, family.

NEWMAN, Dr Lotte Therese, (Mrs N. E. Aronsohn), CBE 1998 (OBE 1991); general practitioner since 1958; President, Royal College of General Practitioners, 1994–97; *b* 22 Jan. 1929; *d* of Dr George Newman and Dr Tilly Newman; *m* 1959, Norman Edward Aronsohn; three *s* one *d.* *Educ:* North London Collegiate Sch.; Univ. of Birmingham; King's College London and Westminster Hosp. Med. Schs. BSc 1951, MB BS 1957; LRCP, MRCS 1957; FRCGP 1977. Casualty Officer, Westminster Hosp.; Paediatric House Officer, Westminster Children's Hosp.; gen. medicine, St Stephen's Hosp. Director: Private Patients Plan, 1983–96; Private Patients Plan (Lifetime) plc, 1991–96; Gov., PPP Medical Trust, 1997–99. Mem. Council, 1980–94, Vice-Chm., 1987–89, former Provost, NE London Faculty and former

Examr, RCGP; Hon. Sec., 1981–86, Pres. elect, 1986–87, Pres., 1987–88, Medical Women's Fedn; Pres., Internat. Soc. of Gen. Practice, 1988–90; Eur. Regl Vice-Pres., World Orgn of Nat. Colls, Acads and Academic Assocs of GPs/Family Physicians, 1992–94; Member: GMC, 1984–99 (Chm., Registration Cttee, 1997–99); Council, BMA, 1985–89 (Member: Med. Ethics Cttee; General Med. Services Cttee, 1983–86 and 1988–91; Private Practice and Prof. Fees Cttee, 1985–89; Forensic Medicine Sub-Cttee, 1985–89; Visitor to Council, 1996–97); Adv. Cttee on Breast Cancer Screening, 1988–97; Home Office Misuse of Drugs Tribunal, 1993–; Disability Benefits Forum, 1998–99; Ind. Practice Forum, Acad. of Medical Royal Colls, 2002–03; Chm., Camden and Islington Local Med. Cttee, 1986–89 (Vice-Chm., 1983–86); Chm., Regional Co-ordinating Cttee of Area Local Med. Cttees, 1985–87; Lectr, Royal Army Med. Coll., 1976–89 (first woman to give Sir David Bruce Lecture in Gen. Practice, 1989); temp. Adviser, WHO; formerly UK rep., OECD and Mem., Expert Cttees studying Primary Health Care in Germany, Switzerland, Sweden. Med. Advr, St John Ambulance, 1999–2003. Mem., Parole Bd, 1992–94. Mackenzie Lectr, RCGP, 1991; Dame Hilda Rose Lectr, Med. Women's Fedn, 1994. Member: Hunterian Soc.; Hampstead Medical Soc.; Assurance Med. Soc., 1987–2006. FRSocMed 1977; Fellow: BMA, 1998; Royal NZ Coll. of Gen. Practitioners, 1998. Freeman, City of London; Liveryman, Apothecaries' Soc. of London. Sir David Bruce Medal, RAMC, 1990; Purkinje Medal for Services to Medicine, Czech Soc. of Gen. Practice, 1985; Jewish Women's Distinction Award, 1994. *Publications:* papers on: women doctors; multidisciplinary training and courses of Primary Health Care Team; breast feeding; ENT conditions and management of mental health handicap in gen. practice. *Recreations:* listening, music, boating. *E:* normanarons@gmail.com. *Clubs:* Royal Automobile, City Livery, Little Ship.

NEWMAN, Malcolm, CPFA; Director, Pragmatics, since 2006; *b* 2 April 1946; *s* of John George and Elizabeth Newman; *m* 1980, Marilyn Wilson; one *s* one *d*. *Educ:* Jarrow Grammar Sch. Clerk, Hebburn UDC, 1962–66; Newcastle upon Tyne City Council: various positions, 1966–71; Sen. Audit Asst, 1971–72; Sen. Management Accountant, 1972–73; Chief Accountant, 1973–77; Asst City Treas. (Accounting), 1977–79; Man. (Cons.) and Gen. Man., Wilson Johnson, 1979–80; Asst Finance Officer (Audit and Tech.), Sefton MDC, 1980–82; Hd of Financial Services 1982–85, Bor. Treas. 1985–87, London Borough of Southwark; City Treas., 1987–97, Dep. Chief Exec., 1990–97, Sheffield City Council; Dir, John Carlisle Partnerships, 1997–2006. Director: Hallamshire Investments plc, 1988–97; Northern Gen. Hosp. NHS Trust, 1997; Chm., START Fedn, 1994. Governor: Sheffield Hallam Univ. (formerly Sheffield Poly.), 1989–94; Silverdale Sch., 1993–97. *Recreations:* outdoors, jogging, Newcastle United, learning about myself.

NEWMAN, Nanette, (Mrs Bryan Forbes); actress and writer; *b* 29 May 1934; *d* of Sidney and Ruby Newman; *m* 1955, Bryan Forbes, CBE (*d* 2013); two *d*. *Educ:* Sternhold Coll., London; Italia Conti Stage Sch.; RADA. Appeared as a child in various films for Children's Film Foundn; other film appearances include: The L-Shaped Room, 1962; The Wrong Arm of the Law, 1962; Seance on a Wet Afternoon, 1963; The Wrong Box, 1965; The Whisperers, 1966; Deadfall, 1967; The Madwoman of Chaillot, 1968; The Raging Moon, 1971 (Variety Club Best Film Actress Award); The Stepford Wives, 1974; International Velvet, 1978 (Evening News Best Film Actress Award); The Mystery of Edwin Drood, 1992; *television:* Call My Bluff, What's My Line, London Scene, Stay with me till Morning, Jessie (title role), Let There Be Love, A Breath of Fresh Air, Late Expectations, The Endless Game, The Mixer; own series: The Fun Food Factory, 1977; Newman Meets, 2000–01; Celebrations, 2001; Patten on a Plate, 2001. *Publications:* God Bless Love, 1972 (repr. 16 times); Lots of Love, 1973 (repr. 7 times); Vote for Love, 1976 (repr. 4 times); All Our Love, 1978; Fun Food Factory, 1976 (repr. twice); Fun Food Feasts, 1978; The Root Children, 1978; The Pig Who Never Was, 1979; Amy Rainbow, 1980; The Facts of Love, 1980; That Dog, 1980, reissued 2011; Reflections, 1981; The Dog Lover's Coffee Table Book, 1982; The Cat Lover's Coffee Table Book, 1983; My Granny was a Frightful Bore, 1983, repr. 2003; A Cat and Mouse Love Story, 1984; Nanette Newman's Christmas Cook Book, 1984; Pigalev, 1985; The Best of Love, 1985; The Summer Cookbook, 1986; Archie, 1986; Small Beginnings, 1987; Bad Baby, 1988; Entertaining with Nanette Newman and her Daughters Sarah and Emma, 1988; Sharing, 1989; Charlie the Noisy Caterpillar, 1989; ABC, 1990; 123, 1991; Cooking for Friends, 1991; Spider the Horrible Cat, 1992; There's a Bear in the Bath, 1993; There's a Bear in the Classroom, 1996; The Importance of Being Ernest the Earwig, 1996; Take 3 Cooks, 1996; Up to the Sky and Down Again, 1999; To You With Love, 1999; Bedtime Stories, 2002; Good Baby, Bad Baby, 2003; Small Talk, 2004; Ben's Book, 2005; Eating In, 2005; What Will You Be, Grandma?, 2011. *Recreation:* painting. *Address:* c/o Lloyds Private Banking, 50 Grosvenor Street, W1K 3LF. *Fax:* (01344) 845174.

NEWMAN, Paul Lance; QC 2009; *b* London, 30 Nov. 1966; *s* of Philip Newman and Valerie Elizabeth Newman (*née* Da Costa); *m* 1999, Hermione Sarah Lock (marr. diss. 2014); three *s*. *Educ:* Downing Coll., Cambridge (BA 1989); Harvard Law Sch. (LLM). Hardwicke and Kennedy Schol., Lincoln's Inn, 1989; called to the Bar, Lincoln's Inn, 1991; in practice as barrister, 1992–. *Publications:* contribs to legal jls. *Recreations:* cricket, football (particularly following Tottenham Hotspur), sport, family. *Address:* Wilberforce Chambers, 8 New Square, Lincoln's Inn, WC1A 3QP. *T:* (020) 7306 0102, *Fax:* (020) 7306 0095. *E:* pnewman@wilberforce.co.uk. *Clubs:* Bentley Cricket (Vice-Pres.); Southgate Hockey (Oakwood).

NEWMAN, Vice Adm. Sir Roy (Thomas), KCB 1992 (CB 1991); JP; DL; Flag Officer Plymouth, and Commander Central Sub Area Eastern Atlantic, 1992–96; *b* 8 Sept. 1936; *s* of Mr and Mrs T. U. Newman; *m* 1960, Heather (*née* Macleod); four *s*. *Educ:* Queen Elizabeth's Grammar Sch., Barnet, Herts; Open Univ. (BA). Joined RN, 1954; specialised in anti-submarine warfare, 1963; joined Submarine Service, 1966; Comdr 1971, Captain 1979; commanded: HMS Onyx, 1970–71; HMS Naiad, 1978–79; First Submarine Sqn and HMS Dolphin, 1981–83; Seventh Frigate Sqn and HMS Cleopatra, 1984–85; Dir of Naval Warfare, 1986–88; Flag Officer Sea Trng, 1988–89; COS to C-in-C Fleet and Dep. Comdr Fleet, 1990–92. Pres., Royal Naval Assoc., 1996–2001 (Vice Patron, 2001–). Chm., Trustees, RN Submarine Mus., 1998–2005. Younger Brother, Trinity House, 1997. Freeman, Shipwrights' Co., 1996. JP SE Hants, 1996; DL Hants, 2001. *Recreations:* cricket, golf, music, art.

NEWMAN TAYLOR, Sir Anthony (John), Kt 2008; CBE 2003 (OBE 1992); FRCP; FFOM, FMedSci; Professor of Occupational and Environmental Medicine, Imperial College London, since 1992; *b* 11 Dec. 1943; *s* of Reginald John Newman Taylor and Violet Anne (*née* Hilliard); *m* 1st, 1968, Gillian Frances Crick (marr. diss.); two *s* one *d*; 2nd, 1986, Frances Victoria Costley; one *s*. *Educ:* Radley Coll.; St Bartholomew's Hosp. Med. Coll. (MB BS 1970; MSc 1979). FRCP 1986; FFOM 1987; FMedSci 1999. Postgrad. trng, St Bartholomew's and Brompton Hosps, 1970–77; Royal Brompton Hospital: Consultant Physician, 1977–2010; Med. Dir, 1994–2005; Dir of Research, 1997–2006; Acting Chief Exec., 1996, July–Oct. 2002 and June 2004–March 2005; Dep. Chief Exec., 2003–06; Faculty of Medicine, Imperial College London: Hd, 2006–08, Dir, R&D, 2012–, Nat. Heart and Lung Inst.; Dep. Principal, 2008–10; Principal, 2010–12; President's Envoy for Health, 2012–. Civilian Advr in Chest Medicine to RAF, 1983–2010. Chairman: Industrial Injuries Adv. Council, 1996–2008 (Mem., 1983–2008; Chm., Res. Wkg Gp, 1984–96); Ind. Medical Expert Gp, Armed Forces Compensation Scheme, 2010–; Member: MRC Cttee on toxic hazards in envmt and workplace, 1982–90; Bevan Commn, 2008–; Ind. Scrutiny Gp Armed Forces Compensation Scheme Rev., 2010–11; Central Adv. Cttee on Pensions and Compensation, MoD, 2011–; Adv. Bd, Centre for Blast Injuries Studies, RBL, 2012–. Advr in occupational medicine, Nat. Asthma Campaign, subseq. Asthma UK, 1994–2010. WHO Advr to Minister of Health, India on long term consequences of methyl isocyanate exposure to population of Bhopal, 1985; Advr to Dept of Health, Valencia on epidemic of lung disease in textile spray workers, 1994. Mem., Health Honours Cttee, 2005–12. Chm., Coronary Artery Disease Res. Assoc., 1998–2009 (Trustee, 2009–14). Chm., Colt Foundn, 2008– (Trustee, 2005–). Gov., Royal Brompton Hosp., 1994–2005; non-executive Director: Royal Brompton and Harefield Trust, subseq. Foundn Trust, 2006–12; Imperial Coll. Healthcare NHS Trust, 2012–. Gov., Chislehurst C of E Primary Sch., 1995–99. *Publications:* chapters in textbooks on respiratory disease and occupational and environmental lung disease; papers in Lancet, BMJ, Thorax, Amer. Jl of Respiratory Disease and Critical Care Medicine; Jl of Allergy and Clinical Immunology, etc. *Recreations:* history and politics, cricket. *Address:* 11 Waldegrave Road, Bickley, Kent BR1 2JP. *Clubs:* Athenæum, MCC.

NEWMARK, Brooks Phillip Victor; *b* 8 May 1958; *s* of late Howard Newmark and of Gilda Newmark (now Gourlay); *m* 1985, Lucy Keegan; four *s* one *d*. *Educ:* Bedford Sch.; Harvard Coll. (AB); Worcester Coll., Oxford (res. grad.); Harvard Business Sch. (MBA). Vice Pres., Shearson Lehman Brothers Inc., 1984–87; Director: Newmark Brothers Ltd, 1987–92; Stellican Ltd, 1992–98; Partner, Apollo Mgt LP, 1998–2005. Contested (C): Newcastle Central, 1997; Braintree, 2001. MP (C) Braintree, 2005–15. Opposition Whip, HM Treasury, 2007–08, Foreign Affairs, 2009–10; a Lord Comr of HM Treasury (Govt Whip), 2010–12; Parly Sec., Cabinet Office, 2014. Mem., Treasury Select Cttee, 2006–07, 2012–14. Founder: Women2win, 2005–; A Partner in Educn, 2009–; Million Jobs Campaign, 2012–14. Bd Dir, Harvard Univ. Alumni Assoc., 2005–15. Chm., United and Cecil Club, 2010–14. *Recreations:* football (Newcastle United supporter), running, ski-ing. *Clubs:* Beefsteak, Boodle's, White's; St Moritz Tobogganing.

NEWPORT, Viscount; Alexander Michael Orlando Bridgeman; *b* 6 Sept. 1980; *s* and *heir* of 7th Earl of Bradford, *qv*.

NEWPORT, Dr Ronald William; Head of Daresbury Laboratory, Council for the Central Laboratory of the Research Councils, 1995–96; *b* 3 Nov. 1933; *s* of Thomas Prescott Newport and Elsie Newport; *m* 1959, Joan Margaret Williams; one *s* one *d*. *Educ:* Nantwich and Acton County Grammar Sch.; Univ. of Liverpool (BSc 1955; PhD 1960). Res. Physicist, British Nat. Hydrogen Bubble Chamber, 1960–62; Science Research Council, subseq. Science and Engineering Council, later Engineering and Physical Sciences Research Council: Rutherford High Energy Laboratory, later Rutherford Appleton Laboratory: Res. Physicist, 1962–79; Div. Manager, Technol. Dept, 1979–81; Dep. Div. Head, Instrumentation Div., 1981–84; Project Manager, James Clerk Maxwell Telescope, 1981–87; Associate Dir for Technol., 1987–88; Head of Science Div., 1988–91, Associate Dir Progs, 1991–94, SERC; Dep. Dir, Daresbury and Rutherford Appleton Lab., 1994–95. Member: Steering Cttee, Institut Laue Langevin, 1989–92; Council, European Synchroton Radiation Facility, 1989–92 (Chm., 1993–95). MRI 1995; FRSA 1997; FRAS 2004. MacRobert Award, for James Clerk Maxwell Telescope, Fellowship of Engineering, 1988. *Publications:* various papers, mainly on instrumentation. *Recreations:* reading, walking, photography, travel. *Address:* 5 Chapel Lane, Sutton Courtenay, Abingdon, Oxon OX14 4AN. *T:* (01235) 848424.

NEWRY AND MORNE, Viscount; Robert Francis John Needham; Managing Director, Arctic Shores Ltd, since 2014; Principal Consultant, NewAtlantic Ltd, since 2014 (Managing Director, 2013–14); *b* 30 May 1966; *s* and *heir* to Earl of Kilmorey, *qv*; *m* 1991, Laura Mary, *o d* of Michael Tregaskis; one *s* one *d*. *Educ:* Sherborne Prep. School; Eton College; Lady Margaret Hall, Oxford (BA); Imperial Coll., London (MBA 1993). Management trainee, Benjamin Priest, 1988–90; Sales Man., Lewmar Marine Ltd, 1991–92; Asst Man., Business Develt, Inchcape Pacific Ltd, 1994–95; Business Develt Manager, Inchcape NRG, 1995–97; Dir, Ops, Inchcape NRG HK, 1998–2000; Exec. Dir, NRG Solutions, 1997–2000; Dir, Morne Consultancy Ltd, 2000; Associate Dir, Ricoh UK Ltd, 2001–03; Director: Collabra Net Solutions Ltd, 2000; Newfield Inf. Technol., 2003–13. Non-exec. Dir, Fenix Media Ltd, 2001–04. *Recreations:* running, conservation. *Heir:* *s* Hon. Thomas Francis Michael Needham, *b* 25 Sept. 1998.

NEWSAM, Malcolm; Commissioner for Children's Social Care, Rotherham Metropolitan Borough Council, since 2014; *b* Derby, 27 April 1955; *s* of Malcolm and Audrey Newsam; *m* 2007, Caroline Beddoe; two step *s*. *Educ:* Bemrose Grammar Sch.; Keble Coll., Oxford (BA Modern Hist. 1976); Leicester Univ. (MA Social Work 1982). Social worker, 1982–84, Social Services Manager, 1984–96, Derbyshire CC; Asst Dir, Derby CC, 1996–2002; Asst Rev. Dir, Audit Commn, 2002–03; Dir, Social Services, 2004–06, Dir, Children's Services, 2006–09, Beds CC; Interim Corporate Dir, Children's Services, Thurrock BC, 2009; Interim Exec. Dir, Schs, Children and Families, Essex CC, 2009–10; Interim Corporate Dir, Families and Social Care, Kent CC, 2011; Interim Dir of Children's Services, Peterborough CC, 2011–12, Improvement Consultant, Doncaster MBC, 2013; Associate Consultant, iMPOWER Consulting, 2013–14; Improvement Consultant, Haringey LBC, 2014; Project Dir, Doncaster MBC, 2013–14. *Recreations:* cinema, travel, restaurants, hill walking, Eastern religions and meditation. *Address:* MCBN Management Consultants Ltd, 59 Union Street, Dunstable, Beds LU6 1EX. *T:* (01908) 281590. *E:* malcolm.newsam@live.co.uk.

NEWSAM, Sir Peter (Anthony), Kt 1987; Chairman, Central London Connexions Board, 2002–05; Director, University of London Institute of Education, 1989–94; *b* 2 Nov. 1928; *s* of late W. O. Newsam and of Mrs D. E. Newsam; *m* 1st, 1953, Elizabeth Joy Greg (marr. diss. 1987; she *d* 2012); four *s* one *d*; 2nd, 1988, Sue Addinell; one *d*. *Educ:* Clifton Coll.; Queen's Coll., Oxford (MA, DipEd). Asst Principal, BoT, 1952–55; teacher, 1955–63; Asst Educn Officer, N Riding of Yorks, 1963–66; Asst Dir of Educn, Cumberland, 1966–70; Dep. Educn Officer: W Riding of Yorks, 1970–72; ILEA, 1972–76; Educn Officer, ILEA, 1977–82; Chm., CRE, 1982–87; Sec., ACC, 1987–89; Dep. Vice-Chancellor, Univ. of London, 1992–94; Chief Adjudicator, Sch. Orgn and Admissions, 1998–2002. Advr to Educn Select Cttee, 2002–05. *Address:* Greenlea, Church Lane, Thornton le Dale, Pickering, N Yorks YO18 7QL.

NEWSON, Prof. Linda Ann, OBE 2015; PhD; FBA 2000; Professor of Geography, King's College London, 1994–2011, now Emeritus; Director, Institute of Latin American Studies (formerly for the Study of the Americas), University of London, since 2012; *b* 2 Aug. 1946; *d* of Donald George Newson and Evelyn Maud Newson (*née* Lee). *Educ:* Grey Coat Hosp., Westminster; University Coll. London (BA 1967; PhD 1972). King's College, London: Lectr, 1971–87; Reader, 1987–94; Hd, Sch. of Humanities, 1997–2000; FKC 2001. Vis. Prof., Univ. of Calif, Berkeley, 1989. Fellow, Newberry Liby, Chicago, 1985 and 2000. Leverhulme Emeritus Fellow, 2011–13. Mem. Council, British Acad., 2007–10. C. O. Sauer Award, Conf. of Latin Americanist Geographers, USA, 1992; Back Award, RGS, 1993. *Publications:* Aboriginal and Spanish Colonial Trinidad: a study in culture contact, 1976; The Cost of Conquest: Indian societies in Honduras under Spanish rule, 1986; Indian Survival in Colonial Nicaragua, 1987; Patterns of Life and Death in Early Colonial Ecuador, 1995; (with S. Minchin) From Capture to Sale: the Portuguese slave trade to Spanish America in the early seventeenth century, 2007; Conquest and Pestilence in the Early Spanish Philippines, 2009; (ed with John P. King) Mexico City through History and Culture, 2009. *Address:* Institute of Latin American Studies, School of Advanced Study, University of London, Malet Street, WC1E 7HU. *T:* (020) 7862 8868.

NEWSON, Marc Andrew, CBE 2012; RDI 2006; designer; *b* Sydney, Australia, 20 Oct. 1963; *s* of Carol Conomos; *m* 2008, Charlotte Stockdale; two *d*. *Educ:* Sydney Coll. of the Arts. Solo exhibitions include: Design Works, Powerhouse Mus., Sydney, 2001; Kelvin 40, Fondation Cartier pour l'art contemporain, Paris, 2004; Groningen Mus., Netherlands, 2004; Design Mus., London, 2004–05; Gagosian Gall., NY, 2007, 2010, London, 2008;

Philadelphia Mus. of Art, 2013–14; group exhibitions include: Conrad Foundn Collection, Design Mus., London, 1996, (guest curator), 2001; Review Gall., Design Mus., London, 1998–99; Milan in a Van, V&A Mus., 2002; Somewhere Totally Else, Design Mus., London, 2003–04; Design Real, Serpentine Gall., 2009; Out of Hand, Mus. of Art and Design, NY, 2014; Design is a State of Mind, Serpentine Gall., 2014. Adjunct Professor in Design: Hong Kong Poly. Univ., 2007; Sydney Coll. of the Arts, 2007. Designer of Year Award, Design Miami, 2006; London Design Medal, London Design Fest., 2008. Hon. Dr Visual Arts Sydney. *Address:* Marc Newson Ltd, 7 Howick Place, SW1P 1BB. *T:* (020) 7932 0990, *Fax:* (020) 7630 6017. *E:* pod@marc-newson.com. *Clubs:* George, Groucho.

NEWSON-SMITH, Sir Peter (Frank Graham), 3rd Bt *cr* 1944, of Totteridge, co. Hertford; Director of Music, Clayesmore Preparatory School, 1979–2003; *b* 8 May 1947; *s* of Sir John Newson-Smith, 2nd Bt and of Vera, Lady Newson-Smith; *S* father, 1997; *m* 1974, Mary Ann Owens (*née* Collins); one *s* one *d*, and two step *s*. *Educ:* Dover Coll.; Trinity Coll. of Music, London. GTCL; LT (MusEd). Asst Dir of Music, Dover Coll. Jun. Sch., 1969–73; Director of Music: Westbourne House, Chichester, 1973–78; Hazelwood, Limpsfield, 1978–79. Hon. Treas., Music Masters' Assoc., 2002–06. Chm., Young Musicians of Muscat, 2002–07. Freeman, City of London, 1969; Liveryman, Musicians' Co., 1969–. *Recreations:* travel, DIY, gardening. *Heir: s* Oliver Nicholas Peter Newson-Smith, *b* 12 Nov. 1975. *Address:* Old Beech House, Burton Street, Marnhull, Dorset DT10 1PP.

NEWSUM, Jeremy Henry Moore; DL; FRICS; Executive Trustee, Grosvenor Estate, since 1993; Group Chief Executive, Grosvenor (formerly Chief Executive, Grosvenor Estate Holdings), 1989–2008 (non-executive Director, since 2008); *b* 4 April 1955; *s* of late Neill Henry Hillas Newsum and Jane Ridsdale Newsum (*née* Moore); *m* 1979, Gillian Lucy Ratcliff; three *d*. *Educ:* Rugby; Reading Univ. (BSc Estate Mgt). With: Grosvenor Estate Holdings, 1976–78; Savills, 1979–85; London Partner, Bidwells, 1985–87; with Grosvenor (formerly Grosvenor Estate Hldgs), 1987–. Non-exec. Dir, TR Property Investment Trust, 2002–08. Pres., British Property Fedn, 2001–02; Chm., Urban Land Inst., 2009–11. Chm., Cambridge Ahead, 2013–14, now Hon. Vice Chm. A Church Comr, 1993–2000. Mem. Council, Imperial Coll. London, 2004–. DL Cambs, 2014. *Recreation:* any sport. *Address:* Priory House, Swavesey, Cambs CB24 4QJ. *T:* (01954) 232084.

NEWTON, 5th Baron *cr* 1892, of Newton-in-Makerfield, Co. Lancaster; **Richard Thomas Legh;** *b* 11 Jan. 1950; *er s* of 4th Baron Newton and Priscilla Egerton-Warburton; *S* father, 1992; *m* 1978, Rosemary Whitfoot, *yr d* of Herbert Clarke; one *s* one *d*. *Educ:* Eton; Christ Church, Oxford (MA). Solicitor, May May & Merrimans, 1976–79. General Comr for Income Tax, 1983–. Mem., Wealden DC, 1987–99. Mem., Sussex Downs Conservation Bd, 1992–95, 1997–98. *Recreation:* bridge. *Heir: s* Hon. Piers Richard Legh, *b* 25 Oct. 1979. *Address:* Laughton Park Farm, Laughton, Lewes, East Sussex BN8 6BU. *T:* (01825) 840627. *Clubs:* Pratt's, MCC.

NEWTON, Air Vice-Marshal Barry Hamilton, CB 1988; CVO 2002; OBE 1975; an Extra Gentleman Usher to the Queen, since 2002 (a Gentleman Usher, 1989–2002); *b* 1 April 1932; *s* of Bernard Hamilton Newton, FCA; *m* 1959, Constance Lavinia, *d* of Col J. J. Aitken, CMG, DSO, OBE and Constance Marion Aitken (*née* Drake); one *s* one *d*. *Educ:* Highgate. RAF Coll. Cranwell, 1951; 109 (Pathfinder) Sqn; Flt Comdr, 76 Sqn (nuclear weapon trials Australia and Christmas Island); Flying Instructor, RAF Coll. Cranwell, 1959; Sqn Comdr, No 6 FTS, 1961; Personal Staff Officer to C-in-C RAF Germany/Comdr 2 ATAF, 1967; OC Ops Wing, RAF Cottesmore, 1969; Defence Policy Staff, 1972, 1978; ndc 1974; Cabinet Office, 1975, 1979; Air Cdre Flying Trng, HQ RAF Support Comd, 1982; ADC to the Queen, 1983–84; Sen. Directing Staff (Air), RCDS, 1984; Comdt, JSDC, 1986–88. Vice-Chm., Council of TAVRAs, 1989–99; (First) Hon. Air Cdre, 606 (Chiltern) Sqn, 1996–2007, Hon. Inspector-Gen., 2000–09, RAuxAF; Pres., UK Reserve Forces Assoc., 2005–13. Hon. Freeman, Lightmongers' Co., 2002; Freeman, City of London, 2002; Liveryman, Hon. Co. of Air Pilots (formerly GAPAN), 2007–. *Recreations:* military history, walking, philately. *Address:* c/o National Westminster Bank, Blue Boar Row, Salisbury, Wilts SP1 1DF. *Club:* Royal Air Force.

NEWTON, Clive Richard; QC 2002; *s* of Henry Newton and Winifred Newton; *m* 1986, Robin Jeanne Williams (marr. diss. 1999); two *s*. *Educ:* Harrow Co. Grammar Sch. for Boys; Wadham Coll., Oxford (maj. schol.; BA First Cl. Hons; MA; BCL). Called to the Bar, Middle Temple, 1968 (Major Harmsworth Entrance Exhibnr; Astbury Law Schol.; Archibald Safford Prizeman; (jtly) Criminal Law Prize, 1967), Bencher, 2012; *ad eundem* Lincoln's Inn, 1978, Inner Temple, 1984; Lecturer: Wadham Coll., Oxford, 1969–76 and 1980–82; Oriel Coll., Oxford, 1985–. Mem., Anglo-American Real Property Institute, 1992–2005. *Publications:* General Principles of Law, 1972, 3rd edn 1983; (with R. S. Parker) Cases and Statutes on General Principles of Law, 1980; (ed jtly) Jackson's Matrimonial Finance and Taxation, 5th edn 1992 to 9th edn 2012. *Recreations:* walking, swimming, cricket, theatre. *Address:* 1 King's Bench Walk, Temple, EC4Y 7DB. *T:* (020) 7936 1500, *Fax:* (020) 7936 1590. *E:* cnewton@1kbw.co.uk.

NEWTON, Clive Trevor, CB 1991; Independent Chairman, Disciplinary Committee, National Association of Funeral Directors, since 1995; *b* 26 Aug. 1931; *s* of late Frederick Norman and Phyllis Laura Newton; *m* 1961, Elizabeth Waugh Plowman; one *s* one *d*. *Educ:* Hove Grammar School for Boys. LLB London. Called to Bar, Middle Temple, 1969; certified accountant, 1962–. Examiner, Insolvency Service, Board of Trade, 1952, Sen. Examiner, 1963, Asst Official Receiver, 1967; Principal, Marine Div., BoT, 1969; Sen. Principal, Marine Div., Dept of Trade, 1973; Asst Director of Consumer Credit, Office of Fair Trading, 1974; Asst Sec., Regional Development Grants Div., Dept of Industry, 1978; Dir of Consumer Affairs, OFT, 1980; Under Sec., Head of Consumer Affairs Div., DTI, 1986–91. Member: Legislation Cttee, Nat. Fedn of Consumer Gps, 1991–2001 (Vice Chm., 1993–96); E Sussex Valuation Tribunal, 1998–2003. Chartered Association of Certified Accountants, subseq. Association of Chartered Certified Accountants: Mem., 1983–92, Chm., 1987–91, and 1997–99, Disciplinary Cttee; Chm., Authorisation Appeal Cttee, 1994–97, 1998–2001. Lay Performance Assessor, GMC, 1997–2001; Ind. Chm. Disciplinary Cttee, Nat. Assoc. for Pre-Paid Funeral Plans, 1995–2001; Chm., Compliance Cttee, Funeral Planning Authy Ltd, 2001–. Director: Concordia (YSV) Ltd, 1994–99; Kennington Oval Ltd, 2003–10. Vice Chm., Sussex Area Cttee, Sanctuary Housing Assoc., 1999–2002. *Recreation:* watching cricket. *Clubs:* Royal Automobile; Surrey County Cricket (Mem. Gen. Cttee, 2000–10; Treas., 2003–10; Hon. Life Vice Pres., 2009).

NEWTON, Derek Henry; Chairman, C. E. Heath plc, 1984–87; *b* 14 March 1933; *s* of Sidney Wellington Newton and Sylvia May Newton (*née* Peacock); *m* 1st, 1957, Judith Ann (*d* 1995), *d* of Roland Hart, Kingston, Surrey; two *d*; 2nd, 2012, Angela Mary, *d* of Sir George Robert Edwards, OM, CBE, FRS. *Educ:* Emanuel School. FCII. Commissioned Royal Artillery, 1952–54 (Lieut). Clerical, Medical & General Life Assurance Society, 1954–58; C. E. Heath Urquhart (Life & Pensions), 1958–83, Chm., 1971–84; Dir, C. E. Heath, 1975, Dep. Chm., 1983–84; Director: Glaxo Insurance (Bermuda), 1980–93; Glaxo Trustees, 1980–92; Clarges Pharmaceutical Trustees, 1985–92. Governor, BUPA Med. R&D, 1981–94. *Recreations:* cricket, golf. *Address:* Pantiles, Meadway, Oxshott, Surrey KT22 0LZ. *T:* (01372) 842273. *E:* derekhnewton@hotmail.com. *Clubs:* Royal Automobile, MCC; Surrey County Cricket (Chm., 1979–94; Pres., 2004).

NEWTON, Rev. Sir George (Peter Howgill), 4th Bt *cr* 1900, of The Wood, Sydenham Hill; Vicar, Holy Trinity, Aldershot, since 2003 (Priest-in-charge, 1999–2003); Rural Dean, Aldershot, since 2012; *b* 26 March 1962; *s* of Sir (Harry) Michael (Rex) Newton, 3rd Bt and Pauline Jane Newton; *S* father, 2008; *m* 1988, Jane Louise Rymer; two *d*. *Educ:* Sherborne; Pembroke Coll., Cambridge (MA Maths; Sen. Optimae); Oak Hill Coll. (BA Theol and Pastoral Studies 1993). Ordained deacon, 1993, priest, 1994. Curate, St Thomas', Blackpool, 1993–99. Liveryman, Girdlers' Co. *Recreations:* cricket, bridge. *Heir: uncle* Rev. Canon Christopher Wynne Newton [*b* 23 July 1925; *m* 1950, Margaret Ormerod; two *s*]. *Address:* 2 Cranmore Lane, Aldershot, Hants GU11 3AS. *T:* (01252) 320618. *E:* vicar@htca.org.uk.

NEWTON, Gillian Mary, CBE 2009; Chief Executive, Fire Service College, Department for Communities and Local Government (formerly Office of the Deputy Prime Minister), 2004–08; *b* 13 Oct. 1952; *d* of late Thomas Frank Newton and Florence Elizabeth Newton (*née* Johnston). *Educ:* Trinity Grammar Sch., Northampton; Univ. of Hull; St Thomas' Hosp., London (RGN 1975); South Bank Poly., London (DipEd 1984); Univ. of Surrey (MSc Educnl Studies 1988). Various posts incl. Ward Sister, and Asst Dir of Nurse Educn, NHS, 1975–93; Dir, Professional Develt, Frances Harrison Coll., Guildford, 1991–93; Head: Sch. of Health Studies, Univ. of Portsmouth, 1993–95; Educn, NHS Exec., DoH, 1995–2000; Trng and Develt, HM Prison Service, 2000–04. Member: Northants Police Authy, 2008–12; Northants Police Audit Cttee, 2012–14. Non-exec. Dir, E Midlands Ambulance Service NHS Trust, 2011–14. Trustee, Age UK (formerly Age Concern) Northants, 2009–12. *Publications:* (with C. Andrewes) Medical Nursing, 1984.

NEWTON, Ian; *see* Newton, R. E. I.

NEWTON, Prof. Ian, OBE 1999; FRS 1993; FRSE; Head, Avian (formerly Vertebrate) Ecology Section, NERC Institute of Terrestrial Ecology, 1989–99, now Emeritus Fellow, NERC Centre for Ecology and Hydrology; *b* 17 Jan. 1940; *s* of Haydn Edwin Newton and Nellie Newton (*née* Stubbs); *m* 1962, Halina Teresa Bialkowska; two *s* one *d*. *Educ:* Bristol Univ. (BSc Zoology 1961); Worcester Coll., Oxford (DPhil Ornithology 1964; DSc 1982). FRSE 1994. Dept of Zoology, Oxford, 1964–67; Nature Conservancy, Edinburgh, 1967–73; Institute of Terrestrial Ecology, Natural Environment Research Council: Edinburgh, 1973–79; Huntingdon, 1979–99; research on avian population ecology, incl. finches, waterfowl, birds of prey, impact of pesticides. President: BOU, 1999–2003 (Vice-Pres., 1989–93); British Ecological Soc., 1994–95; Chairman: Council, RSPB, 2003–08; Bd, Peregrine Fund, 2005–08; British Trust for Ornithol., 2009–13. Hon. Fellow, Amer. Ornith. Union, 1983. Hon. DSc Sheffield, 2006. Union Medal, BOU, 1988; President's Medal, British Ecological Soc., 1989; Gold Medal, RSPB, 1991; Elliott Coues Award, Amer. Ornith. Union, 1995; Marsh Award in Conservation Biology, Zool Soc. of London, 1995; Godman-Salvin Medal, BOU, 2010; Salim Ali Internat. Award for Nature Conservation, Bombay Natural History Soc., 2014. *Publications:* Finches, 1972; Population Ecology of Raptors, 1979; The Sparrowhawk, 1986; (ed) Lifetime Reproduction in Birds, 1989; Population Limitation in Birds, 1998; The Speciation and Biogeography of Birds, 2003; The Ecology of Bird Migration, 2008; Bird Migration, 2010; Bird Populations, 2013; papers in sci. jls. *Recreations:* apple growing, walking. *T:* (01529) 497255.

NEWTON, Jeremy; Chief Executive, Prince's Foundation for Children and the Arts, since 2008; *b* 14 June 1955; *s* of Arthur James Newton and Dorothy Burton Newton; *m* 1978, Mary Rose Colleran; one *s* one *d*. *Educ:* Manchester GS; St John's Coll., Cambridge (MA Hons Mod. and Medieval Langs). FCA 1989. Audit Supervisor, Coopers & Lybrand, 1976–80; Dep. Dir, 1980–84, Dir, 1984–90, Chief Exec., 1990–94, Eastern Arts Assoc., then Eastern Arts Bd; Nat. Lottery Dir, Arts Council of England, 1994–98; Chief Exec., NESTA, 1998–2005; Dir, Louise T. Blouin Foundn, 2005–07; Man. Dir, RADA, 2007–08. Chair: Youth Dance England, 2005–09; Nat. Assoc. of Youth Theatres, 2013–. Fellow, Judge Business Sch., Univ. of Cambridge, 2009–. Trustee, Geffrye Mus., 2014–; Mem. Bd, Cambridge Live, 2015–. DUniv Loughborough, 2006. *Recreations:* theatre, cinema, chess, lacrosse, stand-up comedy. *E:* jeremy.newton@childrenandarts.org.uk.

NEWTON, Rev. Dr John Anthony, CBE 1997; Associate Tutor, Wesley College, Bristol, 1995–2011; *b* 28 Sept. 1930; *s* of late Charles Victor Newton and of Kathleen Marchant; *m* 1963, Rachel, *d* of late Rev. Maurice H. Giddings and of Hilda Giddings, Louth, Lincs; four *s*. *Educ:* Grammar School, Boston, Lincs; University Coll., Hull; London Univ.; Wesley House, Cambridge. BA, PhD (Lond), MA (Cantab). Research Fellow, Inst. of Historical Research, London Univ., 1953–55; Housemaster and actg Chaplain, Kent Coll., Canterbury, 1955–56; trained for Methodist Ministry, Wesley House, 1956–58; Asst Tutor, Richmond Coll., Surrey, 1958–61, having been ordained, 1960; Circuit Minister at Louth, Lincs, 1961–64, and Stockton-on-Tees, 1964–65; Tutor at Didsbury Coll. (from 1967, Wesley Coll.), Bristol, 1965–72; taught Church History, St Paul's United Theol Coll., Limuru, Kenya, and Univ. of Nairobi, 1972–73; Principal of Wesley Coll., Bristol, 1973–78; Superintendent Minister, London Mission (W London) Circuit, 1978–86; Chm., Liverpool Dist of Methodist Church, 1986–95; Warden, John Wesley's Chapel, Bristol, 1995–2000. President of the Methodist Conference, 1981–82; Jt Pres., Merseyside and Region Churches' Ecumenical Assembly, 1987–95; Moderator, Free Church Federal Council, 1989–90 and 1993–94; a Pres., Churches Together in England, 1990–94. Hon. Canon, Lincoln Cathedral, 1988. Chm. of Governors, Westminster Coll., Oxford, 1979–88; Trustee, Wesley House, Cambridge, 1979–88. President: Chesterton Soc., 1991–; Wesley Historical Soc., 1996–. Governor, Rydal School, Colwyn Bay, 1986–95. Hon. Fellow, Liverpool John Moores Univ., 1993. Hon. DLitt Hull, 1982; DD Lambeth, 1995. *Publications:* Methodism and the Puritans, 1964; Susanna Wesley and the Puritan Tradition in Methodism, 1968; The Palestine Problem, 1972; Search for a Saint: Edward King, 1977; The Fruit of the Spirit in the Lives of Great Christians, 1979; A Man for All Churches: Marcus Ward, 1984; The Wesleys for Today, 1989; Heart Speaks to Heart: ecumenical studies in spirituality, 1994. *Recreations:* music, walking, book-collecting. *Address:* 3 College Road, Westbury-on-Trym, Bristol BS9 3EJ. *T:* (0117) 959 3225.

NEWTON, Sir John Garnar, 4th Bt *cr* 1924, of Beckenham Kent; *b* 10 July 1945; *s* of Sir Kenneth Garnar Newton, 3rd Bt, OBE, TD and Margaret Isabel, *d* of Rev. Dr George Blair, Dundee; *S* father, 2008; *m* 1972, Jacynth Anne Kay Miller; three *s* (incl. twins). *Educ:* Reed's Sch., Cobham. Trustee, Barnet Almshouses. Master, Leathersellers' Co., 2005–06. Gov., Colfe's Sch., Lewisham, 2007–. *Heir: er twin s* Timothy Garnar Newton [*b* 4 Sept. 1973; *m* 2004, Sarah Jane Howat].

NEWTON, Prof. (John) Michael, DSc; Professor of Pharmaceutics, School of Pharmacy, University of London, 1984–2001, now Emeritus (Fellow, School of Pharmacy, 2000); Hon. Professor, Department of Mechanical Engineering, University College London, since 2001; *b* 26 Dec. 1935; *s* of Richard and Dora Newton; *m* 1st, 1959, Janet Hinninghan (marr. diss. 1986); one *s* two *d*; 2nd, 2003, Fridrun Podczeck. *Educ:* Leigh Grammar Sch., Lancs; Sch. of Pharmacy, Univ. of London (BPharm; DSc 1990); Univ. of Nottingham (PhD). FRPharmS. Apprentice pharmacist, Royal Albert Edward Infirmary, Wigan, 1953–55; Demonstrator, Univ. of Nottingham, 1958–62; Sen. Lectr, Sunderland Polytechnic, 1962–64; Lectr, Univ. of Manchester, 1964–67; Sen. Scientist, Lilly Research Centre Ltd, 1968–71; Lectr, Univ. of Nottingham, 1972–78; Prof. of Pharmaceutics, Univ. of London, at Chelsea College, 1978–83. Mem., Medicines Commn, 1996–2000. Dist. Lectr, Nagai Foundn, Tokyo, 1997. Hon. Dr: Uppsala, 1995; Coimbra, 2013. Harrison Meml Medal, RPSGB, 1996. *Publications:* over 450 peer-reviewed pubns in sci. jls associated with pharmaceutical technology and engineering. *Recreations:* fell walking, long distance running (Belgrave Harriers), gardening.

NEWTON, (John) Nigel; Founder, and Chief Executive, Bloomsbury Publishing Plc, since 1986 (Chairman, 1986–2007); *b* 16 June 1955; *s* of late Peter Leigh Newton and Anne St Aubyn Newton; *m* 1981, Joanna Elizabeth Hastings-Trew; one *s* two *d*. *Educ:* Deerfield, Mass;

Selwyn Coll., Cambridge (BA 1976; MA). Asst to Sales Dir, Macmillan Ltd, 1976–78; Dep. Man. Dir, Sidgwick & Jackson Ltd, 1978–86. Chm., World Book Day, 2006; Pres., Book Aid Internat., 2008–. Chairman: Charleston Trust, 2010–; British Library Trust, 2012–. Trustee, IISS, 2012–. Former Mem. Council, Publishers Assoc. Mem., Visiting Cttee, Cambridge Univ. Library. Campaign mem., Rescue The Cuckmere Valley, 2002–. *Recreations:* walking, great views. *Address:* (office) 50 Bedford Square, WC1B 3DP. *T:* (020) 7631 5600. *E:* nigel.newton@bloomsbury.com. *Clubs:* Garrick, Beefsteak, MCC, Hurlingham.

NEWTON, Julia Carolyn; a District Judge (Magistrates' Courts), since 2010; *b* Morecambe, Lancs, 23 July 1955; *d* of Geoffrey Newton and Maureen Newton (*née* Wilkinson); *m* 1986, Mark Lanyon Hindley; three *d. Educ:* Univ. of Southampton (LLB 1976); Coll. of Law, Lancaster Gate. Admitted solicitor, 1979; a Dep. Dist Judge (Magistrates' Courts), 2003–10. *Address:* Highbury Corner Magistrates' Court, 51–53 Holloway Road, N7 8JA.

NEWTON, Rt Rev. Mgr Keith; First Ordinary, Personal Ordinariate of Our Lady of Walsingham, since 2011; *b* 10 April 1952; *s* of James Henry and Eva Newton; *m* 1973, Gillian Irene Newton (*née* Donnison); two *s* one *d. Educ:* Alsop High Sch., Liverpool; KCL (BD, AKC 1973); Christchurch Coll., Canterbury (PGCE 1974); St Augustine's Coll., Canterbury. Ordained deacon, 1975, priest, 1976; Curate, St Mary's, Gt Ilford, 1975–78; Vicar, i/c St Matthews, Wimbledon Team Ministry, 1978–85; Rector, St Paul's, Blantyre, Dio. Southern Malaŵi, 1985–86; Dean of Blantyre, 1986–91; Priest i/c, 1991–93, Vicar, 1993–2002, Holy Nativity, Knowle; Priest i/c, All Hallows, Easton, 1997–2002; Bishop Suffragan of Richborough, 2002–10; Provincial Episcopal Visitor, Canterbury, 2002–10. RD, Brislington, 1995–99; Area Dean, Bristol S, 1999–2001. Hon. Canon: Southern Malaŵi, 1986–2011; Bristol Cathedral, 2000–02. Ordained priest (RC), 2011; Protonotary Apostolic, 2011. *Recreations:* travel, theatre. *Address:* 24 Golden Square, W1F 9JR.

NEWTON, Lesley; Her Honour Judge Newton; a Circuit Judge, since 2001; a Senior Circuit Judge and Designated Family Judge, since 2014; *b* 4 April 1955; *d* of Archie Newton and Joan Newton (*née* Robinson); *m* 1987, David Anthony Hernandez, *qv*; one *s* one *d. Educ:* Univ. of Manchester (LLB 1976). Called to the Bar, Middle Temple, 1977; barrister on N Circuit, 1979–2001; Head, Young Street Chambers, Manchester, 1997–2001; Asst Recorder, 1995–99; Recorder, 1999–2001. Mem., Family Justice Council, 2004–11. Course Dir for Family Law, Judicial Coll., 2011–. *Address:* Manchester County and Family Court, The Civil Justice Centre, 1 Bridge Street West, Manchester M60 9DJ. *T:* (0161) 240 5000.

NEWTON, Margaret; Schools Officer, Diocese of Oxford, 1984–88, retired; *b* 20 Dec. 1927; 2nd *d* of F. L. Newton, KStJ, MB, ChB, and Mrs A. C. Newton, MBE, BA. *Educ:* Sherborne School for Girls; St Andrews Univ.; Oxford University. MA Hons St Andrews, 1950; Educn Dip. Oxon 1951. Asst Mistress, King Edward VI Grammar School, Handsworth, Birmingham, 1951–54; Classics Mistress, Queen Margaret's Sch., York, 1954–60 (House Mistress, 1957); House Mistress, Malvern Girls' College, 1960–64 (Head of Classics Dept, 1962); Headmistress, Westonbirt Sch., 1965–80; Gen. Sec., Friends of the Elderly, 1981–83. *Address:* 14 Lygon Court, Fairford, Glos GL7 4LX.

NEWTON, Michael; *see* Newton, J. M.

NEWTON, Nigel; *see* Newton, J. N.

NEWTON, Lt Gen. Sir Paul (Raymond), KBE 2012 (CBE 2003); Professor of Security and Strategy Studies, and Director, Strategy and Security Institute, University of Exeter, since 2012; *b* 29 June 1956; *s* of Maj. Raymond Newton and Gladys Newton (*née* Nash); *m* 1985, Jan Eardley; two *s* one *d. Educ:* Pembroke Coll., Cambridge (MPhil 1993); Army Staff Coll., Camberley. CO 2nd Bn Princess of Wales's Royal Regt, 1994–97; HCSC 1999; Comdr, 8 Inf. Bde, 2000–03; rcds 2003; CDS's Liaison Officer to US Jt Staff, 2003; Dep., Strategic Planning, HQ Multi-Nat. Force Iraq, 2004; ACOS Intelligence, UK PJHQ, 2005–06; Comdr, Force Strategic Engagement Cell, HQ Multi-Nat. Force Iraq, 2007; ACDS, Develt, Concepts and Doctrine, 2008–10; Comdr, Force Develt and Trng, 2010–12. Col Comdt, Queen's Div., 2010–. Founder, Paul Newton Consultants Ltd (formerly Paul Newton Strategic Consultancy), 2011–; Strategic Advr and Chm., Internat. Adv. Bd (Defence and Security), Babcock Ltd, 2012–. Sen. Associate Fellow, RUSI, 2010–. Honorary Colonel: Southampton Univ. OTC, 2008–12; 15 Psychol Ops Gp, 2010–14; Small Arms Sch. Corps, 2010–14. Officer, Legion of Merit (USA), 2004; First Oak Leaf Cluster (USA), 2007. *Recreations:* sailing, ski-ing, international relations, history. *Clubs:* Army and Navy; New Forest Workmen's.

NEWTON, Peter Marcus; HM Diplomatic Service, retired; Executive Director, Canada UK Chamber of Commerce, 2000–02; *b* 16 Sept. 1942; *s* of Leslie Marcus Newton and Edith Mary Newton; *m* 1972, Sonia Maria; two *s* one *d. Educ:* Hamilton Academy; Glasgow Univ. (MA Hons); McGill Univ. (postgrad. studies). Third Sec., CRO, later CO, 1965; Kinshasa, 1967; Lima, 1968; First Sec., FCO, 1972; First Sec. (Econ.), Tokyo, 1975; First Sec. and Head of Chancery, Caracas, 1979; FCO, 1981; Counsellor, FCO, 1985–87; Consul-Gen., Montreal, 1987–89; Dep. High Comr, Ottawa, 1989–92; Head of S Atlantic and Antarctic Dept, FCO, 1992–95; Ambassador to Guatemala, 1995–98. *Address:* 57 Sheen Court, Sheen Road, Richmond, Surrey TW10 5DF.

NEWTON, (Robert Edward) Ian; school inspector and educational consultant, since 1995; *b* 4 Aug. 1946; *o s* of John Newton and Ethel Albiston; *m* 1969, Rev. Canon Fiona Olive Pallant; one *s* one *d. Educ:* Dulwich Coll.; Oriel Coll., Oxford (BA Hons Nat. Sci. (Physics) 1967; MA 1973); Inst. of Education, London Univ. (Postgrad. CertEd 1968). Rugby School: Physics Teacher, 1968; Sixth Form girls' housemaster, 1976; Head of Physics, 1991; Headmaster, Bedales Sch., 1992–94. Admin. Officer, HMC/GSA Wkg Party on Univ. Admission, 1996–98; Charter Mark Award assessor, 1996–97; Reporting Inspector, Ind. Schs Inspectorate, 2000–. Qualified Yachtmaster Ocean, 2000–. Chm., Edward Barnsley Educnl Trust and Workshop Co., 1997–2000. Governor: Coventry Sch. Foundn, 1999–2003; Laxfield Sch., 2005–13. FRGS 2001. CFM 1983. *Publications:* Wave Physics, 1990. *Recreations:* sailing, playing the bassoon, walking. *Address:* Manor Farm Cottage, 67 Langham Road, Field Dalling, Holt NR25 7LG. *Club:* Royal Naval Sailing Association.

NEWTON, Hon. Sir Roderick Brian, Kt 2014; **Hon. Mr Justice Newton;** a Judge of the High Court of Justice, Family Division, since 2014; *b* 15 April 1958; *s* of late Brian Newton and of June Newton; *m* 1978, Clare Augusta Swanzy; two *s* two *d. Educ:* Bishop's Stortford Coll.; City of London Poly. (BA Hons 1980). Called to the Bar, Middle Temple, 1982; Asst Recorder, 1998–2000; Recorder, 2000–05; Circuit Judge, 2005–14. Tutor, Judicial Coll., 2010–. *Recreations:* gardening, horses, livestock, classical music, natural history. *Address:* Royal Courts of Justice, Strand, WC2A 2LL.

NEWTON, Sarah; MP (C) Truro and Falmouth, since 2010; an Assistant Government Whip, since 2015; *m* Alan Newton; one *s* two *d. Educ:* Falmouth Sch.; King's Coll. London (BA Hist.); Grad. Sch. of Internat. Studies, USA. Formerly: Mktg Officer for IBIS, then Citibank; Director: American Express; Age Concern England; Internat. Longevity Centre. Former Mem. (C) Merton LBC. Member: Admin Select Cttee, 2010–12; Welfare Reform Bill Cttee, 2011; Sci. and Technol. Select Cttee, 2012–15; Care Bill Cttee, 2014; Ecclesiastical Cttee, 2014–15. Dep. Chm., Cons. Party, 2012–. FRSA. *Address:* House of Commons, SW1A 0AA.

NEWTON DUNN, William Francis; Member, East Midlands Region, European Parliament, 1999–2014 (C, 1999–2000; Lib Dem, 2000–14); *b* 3 Oct. 1941; *s* of late Lt-Col Owen Newton Dunn, OBE, and Barbara (*née* Brooke); *m* 1970, Anna Terez Arki; one *s* one *d. Educ:* Marlborough Coll. (scholar); Gonville and Caius Coll., Cambridge (MA); INSEAD Business Sch., Fontainebleau (MBA). With Fisons Ltd (Fertiliser Division), 1974–79. MEP (C) Lincolnshire, 1979–94; contested (C) Lincolnshire and Humberside S, 1994. European Parliament: Cons. Spokesman: on Transport, 1984–87; on Rules of Procedure, 1987–89; on Political Affairs, 1989–91; Chm., 1979 Cttee (Cons. backbench MEPs), 1983–88; Mem. Bureau, Cons. MEP Gp, 1988–94; Dep. Leader, EDG, 1991–93; Chm. and Jt Leader, British Cons. MEP Sect., EPP, 1993–94; Chm., 2000–04; Whip, 2004–07, Lib Dem MEPs; Quaestor, 2009–12; Member: Develt Cttee, 2009–14; Organised Crime Cttee, 2012–14. Contested: (C) Carmarthen, Feb. 1974, Cardiff W, Oct. 1974; (Lib Dem) E Midlands Reg., EP, 2014. *Publications:* Greater in Europe, 1986; Big Wing: biography of Air Chief Marshal Sir Trafford Leigh-Mallory, 1992; The Man Who Was John Bull: biography of Theodore Hook, 1996; The Devil Knew Not (novel), 2000; Europe Needs an FBI, 2004; What Do MEPs Do, 2014; pamphlet on the EU's Democratic Deficit, 1986. *Recreations:* grandsons, writing. *Address:* 29 Old Palace Lane, Richmond TW9 1PQ. *T:* (020) 8948 0614. *E:* billnewtondunn@aol.com.

NEYROUD, Peter William, CBE 2011; QPM 2004; Chief Constable and Chief Executive, National Policing Improvement Agency, 2007–10 (Chief Constable and Chief Executive designate, 2006–07); Affiliated Lecturer and Resident Scholar, Jerry Lee Centre for Experimental Criminology, Institute of Criminology, University of Cambridge, since 2012; Research Associate, Centre for Criminology, Oxford, since 2011; Director, Peter Neyroud Research Associates Ltd, since 2011; *b* 12 Aug. 1959; *s* of John Arthur Lucien Neyroud and Penelope Mary Anne (*née* Edwards); *m* 1986, Sarah Longman; two *s* two *d. Educ:* Winchester Coll.; Oriel Coll., Oxford (MA Mod. Hist.); Portsmouth Univ. (MSc Prof. Studies); Wolfson Coll., Cambridge (Dip Applied Criminology). Joined as Constable, Hampshire Constabulary, 1980; Sergeant, Southampton and Basingstoke, 1984–86; Inspector, Southampton, 1987–91; Chief Inspector, E Hampshire, 1991–93; Staff to Pres., ACPO, 1993–95; Detective Supt and Dir of Intelligence, 1995–97; West Mercia Constabulary: Asst Chief Constable (Support), 1998–2000; Dep. Chief Constable, 2000–02; Chief Constable, Thames Valley Police, 2002–06. Member: Sentencing Guidelines Council, 2004–10; Ind. Review Panel, Parole Bd, 2006–11. Visiting Fellow: Nuffield Coll., Oxford, 2008–; Teesside Univ., 2011–; Bucks New Univ., 2014–; Leon Radzinowicz Vis. Fellow, Cambridge Univ., 2008–09; Visiting Professor: Chester Univ., 2011–; Edgehill Univ., 2014–. Trustee, Internet Watch Foundn, 2012–. Hon. LLD Portsmouth, 2006. *Publications:* Policing, Ethics and Human Rights, 2001; Participation in Policing, 2001; Police Ethics for the 21st Century, 2003; Dictionary of Policing, 2008; Science and Policing, 2011; Policing, Ethics and Values, 2012. *Recreations:* running, reading, writing, gardening, four children. *Address:* c/o Institute of Criminology, University of Cambridge, Sidgwick Avenue, Cambridge CB3 9DA. *E:* pwn22@cam.ac.uk.

NGALI, Mwanyengela; Permanent Secretary, Ministry of Energy, Kenya, 1999–2001; *b* 1 Jan. 1947; *s* of Ngali Maganga and Ruth Mkandoo; *m* 1970, Elizabeth Wuganga; two *s* three *d. Educ:* Alliance High Sch., Kikuyu, Kenya; Univ. of Nairobi (BCom). Sales exec., Voice of Kenya, 1971–72; sales rep., Esso Standard Kenya Ltd, 1972–73; joined Kenyan Diplomatic Service, 1974: Commercial Attaché: Washington, 1974–81; London, 1981–82; First Sec. and Actg High Comr, Kampala, 1983–84; Counsellor, Jeddah and Riyadh, 1984–87; Under-Sec., Min. of Commerce, 1987–92; Dir, Political Affairs, Min. of Foreign Affairs and Internat. Co-operation, 1992; Counsellor and Actg High Comr, London, 1992–93; High Comr, Canada, 1993–95; High Comr, London, and Ambassador to Republic of Ireland and Switzerland, 1996–99. Contested: (Kanu) Wundanyi, Kenya, 2002; (Nat. Unity) Wundanyi, Kenya, 2007; Taita/Taveta Governor, 2013. Director: Nat. Oil Corp. of Kenya, 2003–05; Investment Promotion Centre, 2004–05; iWay Africa (formerly Africa Online) Ltd, 2001– (Dep. Chm.); Greenheat Kenya Ltd, 2014–; Chm., Kenya Pipeline Co. Ltd, 2005–06. Chm., Taskforce on Internally Displaced People, 2004–; Ind. Interview Panellist, Electoral and Boundaries Commn, 2011–. *Publications:* Mwana Taabu na Michezo Mingine ya Kuigiza, 1970; Beyond Etiquette: the story of a career diplomat (autobiog.), 2013. *Recreations:* walking, tennis, cycling, reading. *Address:* POB 11048, 00100 Nairobi, Kenya. *T:* 722204198.

NGUYEN VAN THAO; Ambassador of Vietnam to the Court of St James's, since 2014; *b* Vietnam, 1964; *m* Nguyen Minh Hien; two *d. Educ:* Acad. of Finance, Vietnam (BA). Dep. Sec. Gen., Vietnam Chamber of Commerce and Industry, 1997–2007; CEO, APEC CEO Summit, Vietnam, 2006; Dir Gen., Dept of Admin and Finance, 2007–11; Asst Minister, Min. of Foreign Affairs, 2011–14. Permanent Member: Vietnam-US Soc.; Assoc. for Liaison with Overseas Vietnamese; Vice Pres., Vietnam Business and Software Assoc. *Recreation:* golf. *Address:* Embassy of Vietnam, 12–14 Victoria Road, W8 5RD. *T:* (020) 7565 2214. *E:* vanphong@vietnamembassy.org.uk.

NIAGARA, Bishop of, since 2008; **Rt Rev. Michael Bird;** *b* Oakville, Ont, 15 Nov. 1957; *m* 1980, Susan Elaine Bailey; two *s* one *d. Educ:* Univ. of Toronto (BSc 1980); Trinity Coll., Toronto (MDiv 1984). Ordained deacon, 1984, priest, 1984; Rector, Burin, Newfoundland, 1984–87; Asst Priest, St George's, St Catharines, 1987–89; Rector: St Paul's, Dunnville and Dunn Parish, 1989–94; St Cuthbert's, Oakville, 1994–98; St Luke's, Burlington, 1998–2007; Coadjutor Bishop of Niagara, 2007. Regl Dean, Trafalgar, 1997; Canon, Christ's Church Cathedral, Hamilton, 1999; Archdeacon of Trafalgar, 2005. *Address:* Cathedral Place, 252 James Street North, Hamilton, ON L8R 2L3, Canada. *T:* (905) 5271316, *Fax:* (905) 5271281. *E:* bishop@niagara.anglican.ca.

NIBLETT, Anthony Ian; His Honour Judge Niblett; a Circuit Judge, since 2002; *b* 11 June 1954; *s* of late A. W. Niblett and of J. A. Niblett (*née* McMickan); *m* 1991, Valerie Ann Ranger; one *s* one *d. Educ:* Varndean Grammar Sch., Brighton; Univ. of Birmingham (LLB Hons); Coll. of Law. Called to the Bar, Inner Temple, 1976; Barrister, SE Circuit, 1977–2002; Asst Recorder, 1993–98; a Recorder, 1998–2002. Member: Professional Conduct Cttee, Bar Council, 1993–97; S Eastern Circuit Cttee, 1995–98 and 2000–02; Sussex Probation Bd, 2007–10. Jun. (Sec.), Sussex Bar Mess, 1986–95. Gov., Varndean Coll., Brighton, 1997–2003. *Recreations:* reading history, theatre, gardening. *Address:* Lewes Combined Court Centre, The Law Courts, High Street, Lewes, E Sussex BN7 1YB.

NIBLETT, Robin, CMG 2015; DPhil; Director, Royal Institute of International Affairs (Chatham House), since 2007; *b* 20 Aug. 1961; *s* of Alan and Christine Niblett; *m* 1990, Trisha de Borchgrave; two *d. Educ:* Cottesmore Sch.; Charterhouse; New Coll., Oxford (BA Mod. Langs 1984; MPhil 1993; DPhil Internat. Relns 1995). Musician, 1985–87; Center for Strategic and International Studies, Washington, DC: Res. Associate, 1988–91; Eur. Rep., 1992–97; Dir, Strategic Planning, 1997–2000; Exec. Vice Pres. and Chief Operating Officer, 2001–06. Non-exec. Dir, Fidelity Eur. Values Investment Trust, 2010–. Mem. Council, ODI, 2010–14. *Publications:* (ed with W. Wallace) Rethinking European Order: West European responses, 1989–97, 2001; (ed) America and a Changed World: a question of leadership, 2010. *Recreations:* tae kwon do, tennis, electric guitar. *Address:* Royal Institute of International Affairs, Chatham House, 10 St James's Square, SW1Y 4LE. *T:* (020) 7957 5702.

NICE, Sir Geoffrey, Kt 2007; QC 1990; a Recorder, since 1987; Vice Chairman, Bar Standards Board, since 2009; *b* 21 Oct. 1945; *s* of William Charles Nice and Mahala Anne Nice (*née* Tarryer); *m* 1974, Philippa Mary Gross; three *d. Educ:* St Dunstan's College, Catford; Keble College, Oxford. Called to the Bar, Inner Temple, 1971, Bencher, 1996. Member: CICB, 1995–2002; Bd, Indict, 2001–04. Sen. Trial Attorney, 1998–2001, Principal Trial Attorney, Milosevic prosecution, 2002–06, Internat. Criminal Tribunal for Former Yugoslavia; Comr, Royal Court, Jersey, 2006–07. Gresham Prof. of Law, Gresham Coll., 2012–; Professorial Res. Fellow, Univ. of Buckingham, 2014–. Mem., Internat. Steering Gp and Chm. Trustees, Iran Tribunal, 2011–. Mem., Adv. Bd, Weidenfield Scholars, 2012–. Patron, Prisoners of Conscience, 2012–. Contested (SDP/Liberal Alliance) Dover, 1983, 1987. Hon. LLD Kent, 2005. *Address:* 1 Temple Garden Chambers, 1 Harcourt Buildings, Temple, EC4Y 9DA. *T:* (020) 7583 1315. *Club:* Reform.

Ní CHIONNA, Orna, (Lady Turner of Ecchinswell); Deputy Chairman, National Trust, since 2014 (Member of Council, since 2013; Trustee, since 2014); *b* Dublin, 21 Feb. 1956; *d* of Eoin Ó Cionna and Eibhlín Uí Chionna; *m* 1985, (Jonathan) Adair Turner (*see* Baron Turner of Ecchinswell); two *d*. *Educ:* Scoil Lorcáin, Dublin; Sion Hill, Dublin; University Coll., Dublin (BE Electronics 1977); University Coll., Cork (MEngSc Microelectronics 1980); Harvard Business Sch. (MBA with Dist. 1983). Stagiaire, EC, Brussels, 1978; Mktg Engr, Lake Electronics Ltd, Dublin, 1980–81; with McKinsey & Co., 1983–2001, Partner, 1990–2001. Non-executive Director: Northern Foods plc, 2002–11 (Chm., Remuneration Cttee, 2005–10; Sen. Ind. Dir, 2005–11); Bupa, 2003–08 (Sen. Ind. Dir, 2007–08); Bank of Ireland UK Hldgs plc, 2004–07; Royal Mail Gp (formerly Royal Mail Hldgs), 2010– (Chm., Remuneration Cttee, 2011–; Sen. Ind. Dir, 2011–); Saga plc, 2014–; Chm., Remuneration Cttee, 2010–13, Sen. Ind. Dir, 2011–13, HMV plc; Chm., Adv. Bd, Eden McCallum Ltd, 2009–; Mem., UK Retail and Consumer Adv. Bd, Apax Partners LLP, 2005–08. Chm., Soil Assoc., 2007–13 (Trustee, 2002–). Mem., 2010–, Chair, 2013–, Business Adv. Council, and Mem., Bd of Govs, 2013–, Saïd Business Sch., Oxford Univ. Non-exec. Dir, Greenham Common Community Trust, 2005–13. Trustee: Bristol & West Pension Fund, 2004–07; Sir John Soane Museum, 2012–. *Recreations:* garden design, music, languages. *Address:* c/o Eden McCallum LLP, 4 Lancer Square, Kensington Church Street, W8 4EH. *T:* (020) 7361 7000. *E:* orna.nichionna@edenmccallum.com.

NICHOL, Sir Duncan (Kirkbride), Kt 1993; CBE 1989; Chairman, HM Courts Service Board, 2008–11; Hon. Professorial Fellow, Manchester Centre for Healthcare Management, University of Manchester, 1999–2004 (Professor and Director, Health Services Management Unit, 1994–98); *b* 30 May 1941; *s* of James and Mabel Nichol; *m* 1972, Elizabeth Wilkinson; one *s* one *d*. *Educ:* Bradford Grammar Sch.; St Andrews Univ. (MA Hons). FHSM 1987; Hon. FFPHM 1991. Asst Gp Sec. and Hosp. Sec. to Manchester Royal Infirmary, 1969–73; Dep. Gp Sec. and Actg Gp Sec., Univ. Hosp. Management Cttee of S Manchester, 1973–74; Dist Administrator, Manchester S Dist, 1974–77; Area Administrator, Salford AHA(T), 1977–81; Regional Administrator, 1981–84, Regional Gen. Manager, 1984–89, Mersey RHA; Chief Exec., NHS Management Executive, 1989–94. Chairman: Parole Bd of England and Wales, 2004–08; QC Selection Panel, 2005–08; Skills for Justice, 2010–. Comr for Judicial Appts, 2001–06. Non-executive Director: HM Prisons Bd/Correctional Services Strategy Bd, 1994–2005; BUPA, 1994–2002; Primary Group, 2001–08; Deltex Medical, 2004–; Christie Hospital NHS Trust, 2008–12; UK Accreditation Service Ltd, 2009– (Chm., Clinical Pathology Accreditation (UK) Ltd, 2000); Chairman: B Plan Information Systems, 1999–2001; Synergy Health (formerly Synergy Healthcare), 2012– (Dir, 2002–); Acad. for Healthcare Science, 2012–; Countess of Chester Hosp. NHS Foundn Trust, 2012–. Member: Central Health Services Council, 1980–81; NHS Training Authy, 1983–85; Chm., Jt Prison and Probation Services Accreditation Panel for Offending Behaviour Progs, 1999–2005. Pres., Inst. of Health Services Management, 1984–85; Chm., Educn Cttee, King Edward's Hosp. Fund for London, 1987–94. Hon. DLitt Salford, 1990. *Publications:* contributed: Health Care in the United Kingdom, 1982; Management for Clinicians, 1982; Working with People, 1983; Managers as Strategists, 1987. *Recreations:* walking, golf. *Club:* Athenæum.

NICHOL, Prof. Lawrence Walter, DSc; FAA; Vice-Chancellor, Australian National University, 1988–93; *b* 7 April 1935; *s* of Lawrence Gordon Nichol and Mavis Lillian Nichol (*née* Burgess); *m* 1963, Rosemary Esther (*née* White); three *s*. *Educ:* Univ. of Adelaide (BSc 1956, Hons 1957; PhD 1962; DSc 1974). Postdoctoral Fellow, Clark Univ., Mass, 1961–62; Res. Fellow, ANU, 1963–65; Sen. Lectr, then Reader, Univ. of Melbourne, 1966–70; Prof. of Phys. Biochem., ANU, 1971–85; Vice-Chancellor, Univ. of New England, 1985–88. FRACI 1971–94; FAA 1981; Fellow, Royal Soc. of NSW, 1986. David Syme Res. Prize, 1966; Lemberg Medal, Aust. Biochem. Soc., 1977. *Publications:* Migration of Interacting Systems, 1972; Protein-Protein Interactions, 1981; over 100 papers in internat. sci. jls. *Recreations:* philately, cinema, art, Spanish language. *Address:* Unit 36, 171 Walker Street, North Sydney, NSW 2060, Australia.

NICHOLAS, (Angela) Jane (Udale), OBE 1990; Dance Director, Arts Council of Great Britain, 1979–89, retired; *b* 14 June 1929; *d* of late Bernard Alexander Royle Shore, CBE; *m* 1964, William Alan Nicholas (*d* 2014). *Educ:* Norland Place Sch.; Rambert Sch. of Ballet; Arts Educnl Trust; Sadler's Wells Ballet Sch. Founder Mem., Sadler's Wells Theatre Ballet, 1946–50; Mem., Sadler's Wells Ballet at Royal Opera House, 1950–52; freelance dancer, singer, actress, 1952–60; British Council Drama Officer, 1961–70; Arts Council of Great Britain: Dance Officer, 1970–75; Asst Dance Dir, 1975–79. Member: Exec. Cttee, Dance UK, 1989–98; Creative Dance Artists Trust, 1990–93; Riverside Arts Trust, 1991–97; Benesh Inst. Endowment Fund, 1992–2013; Bd, Birmingham Royal Ballet, 1993–2002. FRSA 1990. *Recreations:* pruning, weeding, collecting cracked porcelain. *Address:* 21 Stamford Brook Road, W6 0XJ. *T:* (020) 8741 3035.

NICHOLAS, Sir David, Kt 1989; CBE 1982; Editor and Chief Executive, 1977–89, Chairman, 1989–91, Independent Television News; *b* 25 Jan. 1930; *m* 1952, Juliet Davies (*d* 2013); one *s* one *d*. *Educ:* Neath Grammar School; University Coll. of Wales, Aberystwyth. BA (Hons) English. National Service, 1951–53. Journalist with Yorkshire Post, Daily Telegraph, Observer; joined ITN, 1960; Deputy Editor, 1963–77. Produced ITN General Election Results, Apollo coverage, and ITN special programmes. Dir, Channel Four TV, 1992–97. Chm., Sports News TV, 1996–2003. Visiting Editor: Graduate Sch. of Journalism, Berkeley, Calif, 1993; Sch. of Journalism, Univ. of Boulder, Colorado, 1994. Chm., Deptford Challenge Trust, 1996–2005. Mem. Council, Goldsmiths Coll., 1996–2003 (Hon. Fellow, 2004). FRTS 1980. Fellow, UC Aberystwyth, 1990. Hon. LLD Wales, 1990; Hon. DHL Southern Illinois, 2000. Producers' Guild Award 1967, on return of Sir Francis Chichester; Cyril Bennett Award, RTS, 1985; Judges' Award, RTS, 1991; News World Lifetime Achievement Award, 2001; Lifetime Achievement Award, RTS, 2012. *Recreation:* walking. *Clubs:* Garrick, Reform (Chm., Media Gp, 1998–2003).

NICHOLAS, Prof. David, PhD; Founder and Director, CIBER Research Ltd, since 2012; Professor, Tomsk State University, Russia, since 2014; *b* 14 March 1947; *s* of Roy and Rita Nicholas; *m* 1976, Kay Reeves; one *s* one *d*. *Educ:* Huish's Grammar Sch., Taunton; Poly. of N London (MPhil 1986); PhD City Univ. 1995. MCLIP (ALA 1968). Asst Librarian, Hackney Public Libraries, 1971; Librarian, Middleton St George Coll. of Educn, Co. Durham, 1972; Res. Fellow, Univ. of Bath and Poly. of N London, 1973–76; Res./Inf. Asst, Time-Life International, 1976–77; Poly., later Univ. of N London, 1978–97, Sen. Res. Tutor, 1990–97; Hd, Dept of Inf. Sci., City Univ., 1998–2004; Dir, Dept of Inf. Studies (formerly Sch. of Liby, Archive and Inf. Studies), 2004–11, Centre for Publishing, 2005–11, UCL; Prof. of Inf. Sci., Northumbria Univ., 2013–15. Adjunct Prof., Univ. of Tennessee, 2012–. *Publications:* Immunology: an information profile, 1985; Online Searching: its impact on information users, 1987; Assessing Information Needs, 2000; Digital Consumers, 2008; Information Science: critical concepts in political science, 2014. *Recreations:* cycling, gardening, travelling by train. *Address:* CIBER Research Ltd, 1 Westwood Farmhouse, Greenham, Newbury RG14 7RU. *E:* Dave.Nicholas@ciber-research.eu.

NICHOLAS, Hon. Garvin Edward Timothy; Attorney General of Trinidad and Tobago, since 2015; *b* Trinidad, 24 Jan. 1967; *s* of Edward and Simona Nicholas; *m* Dr Nicola Alcalá; one *s*. *Educ:* Trinity Coll., Trinidad; Oxford Brookes Univ. (LLB); Inns of Court Sch. of Law, City Univ. (Postgrad. DiplS). Local Govt Councillor, 1992–96. Chm., F and GP Cttee, Diego Martin Regl Corp., 1992–96; called to the Bar, Inner Temple, 2001; in practice as barrister, 2001–; Legal Counsel to Leader of the Opposition, Trinidad and Tobago, 2003; Temp. Senator, Upper Hse of Parlt, 2003–04; Leader, Movt for Nat. Develt, 2007–10; Press Sec., Office of Prime Minister, 2010; High Comr for Trinidad and Tobago in the UK, 2010–14. *Recreations:* golf, debating, politics, travel, charity. *E:* galnic@yahoo.com. *Club:* Rotary (Port of Spain W) (Past Pres.).

NICHOLAS, Jane; *see* Nicholas, A. J. U.

NICHOLAS, Sir John (William), KCVO 1981; CMG 1979; HM Diplomatic Service, retired; *b* 13 Dec. 1924; *m* 1st, 1944, Rita Jones (*d* 2000); two *s*; 2nd, 2002, Diana Grigson (*d* 2014). *Educ:* Birmingham Univ. Served 7th Rajput Regt, Indian Army, 1944–47; joined Home Civil Service, 1949; War Office, 1949–57; transf. to CRO 1957; First Sec., Brit. High Commn, Kuala Lumpur, 1957–61; Economic Div., CRO, 1961–63; Dep. High Comr in Malawi, 1964–66; Diplomatic Service Inspector, 1967–69; Dep. High Comr and Counsellor (Commercial), Ceylon, 1970–71; Dir, Establishments and Finance Div., Commonwealth Secretariat, 1971–73; Hd of Pacific Dependent Territories Dept, FCO, 1973–74; Dep. High Comr, Calcutta, 1974–76; Consul Gen., Melbourne, 1976–79; High Comr to Sri Lanka and (non-resident) to Republic of the Maldives, 1979–84.

NICHOLAS, Mark Charles Jefford; presenter and commentator, Cricket On Five, Channel 5 (formerly Channel 5, then Five), since 2006; *b* 29 Sept. 1959; *s* of late Peter Jefford Nicholas and of Anne Evelyn Nicholas (stage name Loxley; she later *m* Brian Widlake). *Educ:* Bradfield Coll. Professional cricketer, Hampshire CCC, 1977–95: county cap, 1982; captain, 1984–95; winning team: John Player Sunday League, 1986; Benson & Hedges Cup, 1988, 1992; NatWest Trophy, 1992. Advertising dept, The Observer, 1980; PR consultant, Hill & Knowlton (UK) Ltd, 1987–88; TV and radio commentator; presenter and commentator: Sky TV, 1999; Channel 4 cricket, 1999–2005. Former journalist, Daily Telegraph. Sports Presenter of the Year, RTS, 2006. *Address:* c/o Channel 5 Television, 10 Lower Thames Street, EC3R 6EN.

NICHOLAS, Michael Bernard, FRCO; organist, choral director and composer; *b* 31 Aug. 1938; *s* of Bernard Victor Herbert Nicholas and Dorothy (*née* Gilfillan); *m* 1975, Heather Grant Rowdon; two *s*. *Educ:* City of London Sch.; Trinity Coll. of Music (Jun. Exhibitioner); Jesus Coll., Oxford (MA). FRCO 1958 (CHM 1964). Organist and Choirmaster: Louth Parish Church, Lincs, 1960–64; St Matthew's Ch, Northampton, 1965–71; Organist and Master of Choristers, Norwich Cathedral, 1971–94 (Organist Emeritus, 2005); (part-time) Lectr in Music, UEA, 1971–94; Chief Exec., RCO, 1994–97. Conductor: Louth Choral and Orchestral Soc., 1960–64; Northampton Bach Choir and Orch., 1965–71; Norwich Philharmonic Chorus, 1972–94; Co-Founder and Co-Artistic Dir, Norwich Fest. of Contemporary Church Music, 1981–92; Musical Dir, Allegri Singers, 1994–2000; Organist and Dir of Music, All Saints' Church, Blackheath, 1995–99; Dir of Music, St Mary-le-Tower, Ipswich, 1999–2013; Founder and Conductor, Tower Chamber Choir, 2001–13. Member: Council, RSCM, 1978–87; Council, RCO, 1980–94 and 1998–2004; Council and Academic Bd, Guild of Church Musicians, 1995–. Pres., Stowmarket Concerts and Tower Chamber Choir; a Vice-President: Organ Club, 1995–; Church Music Soc., 2002–; Mem., Cathedral Organists' Assoc., 1971– (Pres., 1975–77). Hon. FGCM 1995. Hon. DMus UEA, 1995. *Publications:* Sightsinging, 1966; Muse at St Matthew's, 1968; various choral and organ compositions. *Recreations:* bridge, walking, reading. *Club:* Athenæum.

NICHOLAS, Shān; Director: Taprobane Management Services Ltd, since 2007; Lasting Transformation Ltd, since 2011; *b* 24 Oct. 1952; *d* of Kenneth Nicholas and Jane Nicholas (*née* Selliah); one *d* with Pal Luthra. *Educ:* London Sch. of Econs and Pol Sci. (BSc Econ 1974); London Sch. of Hygiene and Tropical Medicine (MSc Med. Demography 1977). Asst Dir, Runnymede Trust, 1978–85; Hd, Human Resource Develt, London Bor. of Hackney, 1986–94; Exec. Dir Corp. Develt and Co. Secretary, Stonham Housing, 1998–2005; Chief Exec., Princess Royal Trust for Carers, 2005–07; Interim Chief Executive: YWCA (England and Wales), 2007–08; Brook London, 2008–09; Interim Develt Dir, Criminal Justice, and Vice Chair, T2A Alliance, Barrow Cadbury Trust, 2009–10; Interim Chief Exec., Child Poverty Action Gp, 2010; Interim Dir, British Inst. of Human Rights, 2010; Consultant, Coll. of Social Work, 2011; Interim Chief Executive: Children's Soc., 2011–12; Refugee Council, 2012–13; British Assoc. for Adoption and Fostering, 2013; United Response, 2014. *Publications:* (contrib.) Britain's Black Population, 1980; articles for British and French jls on race and immigration. *Recreations:* arts, theatre, music, reading. *E:* shan.nicholas1@btopenworld.com.

NICHOLL, His Honour Anthony John David; a Circuit Judge, 1988–2003; *b* 3 May 1935; *s* of late Brig. and Mrs D. W. D. Nicholl; *m* 1961, Hermione Mary (*née* Landon); one *s* two *d*. *Educ:* Eton; Pembroke Coll., Oxford; Wycliffe Hall, Oxford (DBTS). Called to Bar, Lincoln's Inn, 1958. Practised in London, 1958–61, in Birmingham, 1961–88; Head of Chambers, 1976–87; Chm., Fountain Court Chambers (Birmingham) Ltd, 1984–88. A Recorder, 1978–88. Reader, Coventry Dio., 2003–. *Recreations:* history, theology, music, gardening, choral singing.

NICHOLL, Prof. Jonathan Paul, CBE 2015; DSc; Professor of Health Services Research, since 1994, and Dean, School of Health and Related Research, since 2010, University of Sheffield; *b* Bristol, 15 April 1953; *s* of late Capt. Jack Nicholl and Berry Nicholl; partner, Joanna Saunders; one *s* two *d*. *Educ:* Abingdon Sch.; Univ. of Bristol (BA Philos.); Univ. of North London (MSc Stats); Univ. of Sheffield (DSc Health Services Res. 2009). CStat 1998. Res. Associate, Transport Studies Gp, UCL, 1977–81; Statistician, 1981–93, Dir, 1993–2010, Medical Care Res. Unit, Univ. of Sheffield; Dir, NIHR Sch. for Public Health Res., 2012–. *Publications:* 200 res. articles, mainly in gen. med. jls. *Recreations:* cricket, gardening, cycling, thinking. *Address:* School of Health and Related Research, University of Sheffield, 30 Regent Street, Sheffield S1 4DA. *E:* j.nicholl@sheffield.ac.uk.
See also Air Vice Marshal S. M. Nicholl.

NICHOLL, Air Vice-Marshal Steven Mark, CB 2001; CBE 1991; AFC 1981; FRAeS; Director, Military Requirements, Military Air and Information, BAE SYSTEMS, 2002–11; *b* 15 Nov. 1946; *s* of late Capt. Jack Nicholl, BOAC and Berry Nicholl; *m* 1974, Suzanne Tucker; two *s* one *d*. *Educ:* Abingdon Sch.; Pembroke Coll., Oxford (BA Eng.). FRAeS 1993. RAF university cadetship, 1965; flying/staff duties, 1970–88; Gp Capt. Plans, HQ RAF Germany, 1989–91; OC RAF Leuchars, 1992–93; rcds 1994; Dir Air Ops, Dir Air Plans, 1995–98, ACDS OR Air, subseq. Capability Manager (Strike), 1998–2001, MoD; Dir, Military Requirements, MASS, BAE SYSTEMS, 2002–10. *Recreations:* family, golf, ski-ing, gliding, reading. *Address:* 1 Tythe Close, Stewkley, Bucks LU7 0HD. *Clubs:* Royal Air Force; Leighton Buzzard Golf.
See also J. P. Nicholl.

NICHOLLS, family name of **Baron Nicholls of Birkenhead**.

NICHOLLS OF BIRKENHEAD, Baron *cr* 1994 (Life Peer), of Stoke D'Abernon in the County of Surrey; **Donald James Nicholls,** Kt 1983; PC 1986; a Lord of Appeal in Ordinary, 1994–2007; Second Senior Lord of Appeal, 2002–07; *b* 25 Jan. 1933; *yr s* of late

William Greenhow Nicholls and Eleanor Jane; *m* 1960, Jennifer Mary, *yr d* of late W. E. C. Thomas, MB, BCh, MRCOG, JP; two *s* one *d*. *Educ:* Birkenhead Sch.; Liverpool Univ. (LLB 1st cl. hons); Trinity Hall, Cambridge (Foundn Schol.; BA 1st cl. hons with dist., Pt II Law Tripos, LLB 1st cl. hons with dist.; Hon. Fellow, 1986). 2nd Lieut, RAPC, 1951–53. Certif. of Honour, Bar Final, 1958; called to Bar, Middle Temple, 1958, Bencher, 1981, Treas., 1997; in practice, Chancery Bar, 1958–83; QC 1974; Judge of High Court of Justice, Chancery Div., 1983–86; a Lord Justice of Appeal, 1986–91; Vice-Chancellor, Supreme Court, 1991–94; a Non-permanent Judge, Hong Kong Court of Final Appeal, 1998–2004. Chairman: Lord Chancellor's Adv. Cttee on Legal Educn and Conduct, 1996–97; Jt Parly Cttee on Parly Privilege, 1997–99. Mem., Senate of Inns of Court and the Bar, 1974–76. Patron, Cayman Is Law Sch., 1994–2006. Pres., Birkenhead Sch., 1986–. Hon. LLD Liverpool, 1987. *Recreations:* walking, history, music. *Address:* House of Lords, SW1A 0PW. *Club:* Athenæum (Trustee, 1998–2011).

See also Hon. J. P. Nicholls.

NICHOLLS, Brian; Director, John Brown Engineering, 1979–91; *b* 21 Sept. 1928; *s* of late Ralph and Kathleen Nicholls; *m* 1961, Mary Elizabeth Harley; one *s* two *d*. *Educ:* Haberdashers' Aske's Sch., Hampstead; London Univ. (BSc Econ); Harvard Business Sch. George Wimpey & Co., 1951–55; Constructors John Brown Ltd, 1955–75; Director: CJB Projects Ltd, 1972–75; CJB Pipelines Ltd, 1974–75; Dep. Chm., CJB Mohandessi Iran Ltd, 1974–75; Industrial Adviser, Dept of Trade, 1975–78; Director: John Brown Engrg Gas Turbines, 1979–91; Rugby Power Co., 1990–91; Vice Pres., John Brown Power Ltd, 1987–90; consultant, Scottish Enterprise, 1991–98. Member: Council, British Rly Industry Export Gp, 1976–78; Overseas Projects Bd, 1976–78; BOTB, 1978. Member: Council, British Chemical Engineering Contractors Assoc., 1973–75; Trade and Industry Cttee, British Algerian Soc., 1974–75; Scottish Council (Develt and Industry), 1983–98 (Vice Pres., 1991–98; Fellow 1998). Columnist, Jazz Jl, 1952–58; Ed., Jazz News, 1957–59. Dep. Chm., Nat. Jazz Fedn, 1954–59; Dir, Scottish Opera, 1993–99. Freeman Mem., Incorp. of Coopers of Glasgow, 1991; Mem., Trades House of Glasgow, 1990. *Recreations:* travel, walking, music. *Address:* Blairlogie Park, Hillfoots Road, Blairlogie, by Stirling FK9 5PY. *T:* (01259) 761497.

NICHOLLS, Christine Stephanie, DPhil; writer; *b* 23 Jan. 1943; *d* of Christopher James Metcalfe, Mombasa, Kenya, and Olive Metcalfe (*née* Kennedy); *m* 1966, Anthony James Nicholls, *s* of Ernest Alfred Nicholls, Carshalton; one *s* two *d*. *Educ:* Kenya High School; Lady Margaret Hall, Oxford (BA); St Antony's Coll., Oxford (MA, DPhil). Henry Charles Chapman Res. Fellow, Inst. of Commonwealth Studies, London Univ., 1968–69; freelance writer for BBC, 1970–74; res. asst, 1975–76; Jt Editor, 1977–89, Editor, 1989–95, DNB; Editor, Sutton Pocket Biographies, 1996–2000. *Publications:* The Swahili Coast, 1971; (with Philip Awdry) Cataract, 1985; Power: a political history of the 20th Century, 1990; The Dictionary of National Biography: 1961–70, 1981; 1971–80, 1986; 1981–85, 1990; Missing Persons, 1993; 1986–90, 1996; (ed) The Hutchinson Encyclopedia of Biography, 1996; David Livingstone, 1998; The History of St Antony's College, Oxford, 1950–2000, 2000; Elspeth Huxley: a biography, 2002; Red Strangers: the white tribe of Kenya, 2005; A Kenya Childhood, 2011. *Recreations:* reading novels, playing the flute. *Address:* 27 Davenant Road, Oxford OX2 8BU. *T:* (01865) 511320.

NICHOLLS, Clive Victor; QC 1982; a Recorder, 1984–99; *b* 29 Aug. 1932; twin *s* of late Alfred Charles Victor Nicholls and of Lilian Mary (*née* May); *m* 1960, Alison Virginia, *d* of late Arthur and Dorothy Oliver; three *s* three *d*. *Educ:* Brighton Coll.; Trinity Coll., Dublin (MA, LLB); Sidney Sussex Coll., Cambridge (BA *ad eund*; LLM). Called to the Bar: Gray's Inn, 1957 (Bencher, 1990); Australian Capital Territories, 1991. Trustee, Bob Champion Cancer Trust, 1994– (Chm. Trustees, 1982–94). *Publications:* (jtly) The Law of Extradition and Mutual Assistance: international practice and procedure, 2002, 3rd edn 2012. *Recreations:* sailing, fishing. *Address:* 3 Raymond Buildings, Gray's Inn, WC1R 5BH. *T:* (020) 7400 6400. *Clubs:* Garrick; Royal Western Yacht (Plymouth).

See also C. A. A. Nicholls.

NICHOLLS, Colin Alfred Arthur; QC 1981; a Recorder, 1984–99; *b* 29 Aug. 1932; twin *s* of late Alfred Charles Victor Nicholls and of Lilian Mary (*née* May); *m* 1976, Clarissa Allison Spenlove, *d* of late Clive and of Theo Dixon; two *s*. *Educ:* Brighton Coll.; Trinity Coll., Dublin. MA, LLB. Called to the Bar, Gray's Inn, 1957 (Albion Richardson Schol.), Bencher, 1989. Mem., Commonwealth Expert Gp on Rule of Law, 2011; Chm., Commonwealth Working Gp on Cybercrime, 2012–. Auditor, 1956, and Hon. Mem., 1958–, TCD Historical Soc. Commonwealth Lawyers Association: Mem. Council, 1987–90; a Vice Pres., 1990–96; Hon. Treas., 1996–; Hon. Sec., 1999–2003; Pres., 2003–05; Hon. Life Pres., 2007. Fellow, Soc. of Advanced Legal Studies, 1998. Gov., FBA, 2001–07. Trustee: Commonwealth Human Rights Initiative, 1998–2007; Commonwealth Law Conf. Foundn, 2003–07. *Publications:* (jtly) Corruption and Misuse of Public Office, 2006, 2nd edn 2011. *Recreation:* painting (exhib. RHA, ROI and NEAC). *Address:* 3 Raymond Buildings, Gray's Inn, WC1R 5BH. *T:* (020) 7400 6400. *Club:* Garrick.

See also C. V. Nicholls.

NICHOLLS, David Alan, CB 1989; CMG 1984; Senior Political-Military Associate, Institute for Foreign Policy Analysis, Cambridge, Mass, USA, since 1991; *b* 28 Aug. 1931; *s* of Thomas Edward and Beatrice Winifred Nicholls; *m* 1955, Margaret (*née* Lewis); two *d*. *Educ:* Cheshunt Grammar School; St John's Coll., Cambridge (Schol., Wright's Prizeman 1952, 1953; BA Hons 1954; MA 1989). Served RAF (Flying Officer), 1950–51. Admiralty, 1954–64; Asst Principal, 1954; Private Sec. to Parliamentary Sec., 1958–59; Principal, 1959; MoD, 1964–75; Private Sec. to Minister of Defence for Admin, 1968–69; Asst Sec., 1969; Cabinet Office, 1975–77; Asst Under-Sec. of State, MoD, 1977–80; Asst Sec., Gen. for Defence Planning and Policy, NATO, 1980–84; Dep. Under Sec. of State (Policy), MoD, 1984–89. Vis. Fellow, Magdalene Coll., Cambridge, 1989–90; Associate Fellow, RIIA, 1990–93; Hon. Fellow, Graduate Sch. of Internat. Studies, Univ. of Birmingham, 1992–98. Chm., Defence and Security Cttee, London Chamber of Commerce and Industry, 1994–2004 (Mem., 1991–). Chm., Soc. for Italic Handwriting, 1987–97. Mem., Visiting Cttee, RCA, 1991–92. *Recreations:* sketching, printmaking. *Address:* c/o HSBC, Shrewsbury, Shropshire SY1 1SL. *Club:* National Liberal.

NICHOLLS, David Alan; novelist, screenwriter; *b* Southampton, 30 Nov. 1966; *s* of late Alan Nicholls and of Ann Nicholls; partner, Hannah Weaver; one *s* one *d*. *Educ:* Toynbee Comprehensive Sch.; Barton Peveril Coll.; Univ. of Bristol (BA). Actor (stage-name, David Holdaway), 1991–98; script ed., 1996–2000; writer, 1999–: *television:* I Saw You, 2000 and 2002; Cold Feet, 2000 (British Acad. TV Craft Award for Best New Writer); Rescue Me, 2002; Much Ado About Nothing (Shakespeare Re-told Series), 2005; Aftersun, 2006; (screenplay) Tess of the D'Urbervilles, 2008; The 7:39, 2014; *film screenplays:* Simpatico, 1999; Starter for 10, 2006; And When Did You Last See Your Father?, 2007; One Day, 2011; Great Expectations, 2012; Far from the Madding Crowd, 2015; *theatre:* Aftersun, Old Vic, 2006. UK Author of the Year, Nat. Book Awards, 2014. *Publications:* Starter for 10, 2003; The Understudy, 2005; One Day, 2009 (Popular Fiction Book of Year, Galaxy Nat. Book Awards, 2010); Us, 2014. *Address:* c/o Jonny Geller, Curtis Brown, 28 Haymarket, SW1Y 4SP. *T:* (020) 7393 4400.

NICHOLLS, Dr (Jill) Nicola, LVO 2012; Chair, Woodland Trust, since 2010; *b* Epping, Essex, 13 Feb. 1958; *d* of Alan and Barbara Keep; one *s* one *d*. *Educ:* Univ. of Bristol (BSc 1st Cl. Hons Chem.); Gonville and Caius Coll., Cambridge (PhD Inorganic Chem. 1982). Res. Fellow, Gonville and Caius Coll., Cambridge, 1982–85; with Charterhouse Bank, then a Dir, Charterhouse Develt Capital, 1985–2003. Non-executive Director: Cambridge Enterprise Ltd, 2006–11; BPP Univ. (formerly BPP University Coll. of Professional Studies), 2008–; Buro Happold Engrs Ltd, 2014–. Mem., Adv. Bd, Judge Business Sch., Univ. of Cambridge, 2004–13. Trustee, then Chair, Green-Works, 2002–10; Trustee, Landmark Trust, 2013–14. *Publications:* contribs to scientific jls. *Recreations:* dance (mostly watching), woods and trees, local issues. *Address:* Woodland Trust, Kempton Way, Grantham, Lincs NG31 6LL. *E:* nicolanicholls@woodlandtrust.org.uk.

NICHOLLS, Rt Rev. John; Bishop of Sheffield, 1997–2008; an Honorary Assistant Bishop: Diocese of Derby, since 2008; Diocese of Manchester, since 2012; *b* 16 July 1943; *s* of late James William and Nellie Nicholls; *m* 1969, Judith Dagnall; two *s* two *d*. *Educ:* Bacup and Rawtenstall Grammar School; King's Coll., London (AKC); St Boniface Coll., Warminster. Curate, St Clement with St Cyprian, Salford, 1967–69; Curate, 1969–72, Vicar 1972–78, All Saints and Martyrs, Langley, Manchester; Dir of Pastoral Studies, Coll. of the Resurrection, Mirfield, 1978–83; Canon Residentiary of Manchester Cathedral, 1983–90; Suffragan Bishop of Lancaster, 1990–97. Hon. Fellow, Univ. of Central Lancashire, 1997. DUniv Sheffield Hallam, 2007; Hon. LittD Sheffield, 2009. BGCStJ, 2007 (Prelate, 2007–15). *Publications:* (jtly) A Faith Worth Sharing? A Church Worth Joining?, 1995. *Recreations:* music (listening and singing), reading, films. *Address:* 75 Rowton Grange Road, Chapel-en-le-Frith, High Peak SK23 0LD. *T:* (01298) 938249. *E:* jnseraphim@gmx.com.

NICHOLLS, John; *see* Nicholls, R. J.

NICHOLLS, Prof. John Graham, FRS 1988; Professor of Neurobiology, International School for Advanced Studies, Trieste, since 1998; *b* 19 Dec. 1929; *s* of late Dr Nicolai and of Charlotte Nicholls; *m* (marr. diss.); two *s*. *Educ:* Berkhamsted Sch.; Charing Cross Hosp.; King's Coll. and University Coll., London. BSc (1st cl. Hons); PhD; MB, BS. Research and teaching in Neurobiology at: Oxford, 1962; Harvard, 1962–65; Yale, 1965–68; Harvard, 1968–73; Stanford, 1973–83; Biocenter, Basel, 1983–98. *Publications:* From Neuron to Brain (with S. Kuffler), 1976, 5th edn (with A. R. Martin, P. Fuchs, D. Brown, M. Diamond and D. Weisblat), 2012; The Search for Connections, 1987; Pioneers of Neurobiology: my brilliant eccentric heroes, 2015. *Recreations:* Latin American history, music. *Address:* Scuola Internazionale Superiore di Studi Avanzati, via Bonomea 265, Trieste 34136, Italy.

NICHOLLS, Hon. John (Peter); QC 2006; barrister; *b* 30 Nov. 1963; *s* of Baron Nicholls of Birkenhead, *qv*; *m* 1991, Divya Bhatia, *d* of late Captain and Mrs Rajindar Bhatia; one *s* one *d*. *Educ:* Winchester Coll.; Trinity Hall, Cambridge (BA 1st Cl. Law 1985). Called to the Bar, Middle Temple, 1986; in practice as a barrister, specialising in business and commercial fields, Maitland Chambers, 1987–. *Recreations:* sport, travel. *Address:* Maitland Chambers, 7 Stone Buildings, Lincoln's Inn, WC2A 3SZ. *T:* (020) 7406 1200, *Fax:* (020) 7406 1300. *E:* jnicholls@maitlandchambers.com. *Clubs:* Aula; Hawks (Cambridge); Lensbury; Bombay Gymkhana.

NICHOLLS, Jonathan William Nicholas, PhD; Registrary, University of Cambridge, since 2007; Fellow of Emmanuel College, Cambridge, since 2007; *b* Chelmsford, 16 June 1956; *s* of Arthur John Nicholas Nicholls and Cecily Mary Nicholls (*née* Cosgrove); *m* 1998, Susan Catherine Rasmussen; one step *s* one step *d*. *Educ:* Univ. of Bristol (BA 1st Cl. Hons Eng. 1978); Emmanuel Coll., Cambridge (PhD 1984); Harvard Univ. (Herchel Smith Scholar, 1981–82). University of Warwick: Admin. Officer, 1982–86; Asst Registrar, 1986–89; Sen. Asst Registrar, 1989–92; Academic Registrar, 1992–99; Registrar, 1999–2003; Registrar and Sec., Univ. of Birmingham, 2004–07. Director: Cambridge Univ. Health Partners Ltd, 2008–; Cambridge Ahead Ltd, 2013–. Gov., Cambridge Univ. Hosps NHS Foundn Trust, 2007–. Chm., Assoc. of Heads of Univ. Admin, 2013– (Dep. Chm., 2006–12). Gov., Hills Rd Sixth Form Coll., 2010–14. Trustee, Storey's Field Community Trust, 2013–. *Publications:* The Matter of Courtesy: medieval courtesy books and the Gawain-poet, 1984. *Recreations:* cycling, running, watching football and cricket, birds, books, music, grandchildren. *Address:* University of Cambridge, The Old Schools, Cambridge CB2 1TN. *T:* (01223) 332294. *E:* Registrary@admin.cam.ac.uk. *Club:* Oxford and Cambridge.

NICHOLLS, Rt Rev. Linda Carol; a Suffragan Bishop of Toronto (Area Bishop of Trent-Durham), since 2008; *b* Calgary, Alberta, 25 Oct. 1954; *d* of Gerald Nicholls and Carol Nicholls (*née* Neumann). *Educ:* Sir John A. Macdonald Collegiate, Scarborough; Royal Conservatory of Music (Associate Dip. Piano Perf. 1974); Univ. of Toronto (BMus 1976; BEd 1977); Wycliffe Coll., Univ. of Toronto (MDiv 1986; DMin 2002; DD 2008); Toronto Sch. of Theology (Cert. in Spiritual Direction, Jubilee Prog. 1996). Music and Maths Teacher, Woodstock Internat. Christian Sch., Mussoorie, India, 1977–82; ordained deacon, 1985, priest, 1986; Asst Curate, St Paul's L'Amoreaux, Scarborough, 1985–87; Incumbent: Parish of Georgina, St James', Sutton and St George, Sibbald Point, 1987–91; Holy Trinity, Thornhill, 1991–2005; Co-ordinator for Dialogue (Ethics, Interfaith Relations & Congregational Develt), Faith, Worship and Ministry Dept, Anglican Church of Canada, 2005–07; Mem., ARCIC III, 2011–; Co-Chm., Anglican-RC Dialogue in Canada, 2012–. Mem., Tapestry Chamber Choir, 2002–. *Recreations:* canoeing, hiking, singing. *Address:* Trent Durham Bishop's Office, 965 Dundas Street West, Suite 207, Whitby, ON L1P 1G8, Canada. *T:* (905) 6681558. *E:* lnicholls@toronto.anglican.ca. *Club:* Newmarket (Ontario).

NICHOLLS, Michael John Gadsby; QC 2006; barrister and author; *b* 29 April 1948; *s* of late Ronald Harry Nicholls and Betty Jean Nicholls (*née* Gadsby); *m* 1st, 1970, Marian Howe (marr. diss. 2006); 2nd, 2007, Debbie Taylor. *Educ:* Whitley Abbey Sch., Coventry; BRNC, Dartmouth; Inns of Court Sch. of Law. Served RN, 1967–72 (specialist in hydrographic survey), Lieut 1971. Called to the Bar, Middle Temple, 1975; Army Legal Services, 1975–80, Major 1979; Dep. Dir, Army Legal Services, BAOR (GSO2), 1979; admitted solicitor, 1980, and in private practice, 1980–83; on staff of Official Solicitor to Supreme Court and Head of UK Child Abduction Unit, 1983–98; returned to private practice, 1998; in practice England, Wales and Western Australia, specialising in internat. family law and medical ethics, incl. jurisdiction, recognition and enforcement, conflicts of laws, children's cases incl. status, surrogacy, abduction and relocation, and medical treatment disputes. Consultant to Family Law Cttee, Council of Europe. Vis. Lectr, Acad. of Eur. Law, Trier. Member: Internat. Family Law Cttee, Family Justice Council; Internat. Acad. of Matrimonial Lawyers; WA Bar Assoc.; Family Law Practitioners' Assoc. of WA; Mental Health Review Bd of WA. *Publications:* (contrib.) Principles and Practice of Forensic Psychiatry, 1990; (jtly) The Human Rights Act 1998: a special bulletin, 1998; (contrib.) The Legal Aspects of Munchausen's Syndrome by Proxy, 2001; (jtly) International Movement of Children: law, practice and procedure, 2004, 2nd edn 2016; (jtly) The New Brussels II Regulation, 2005; (jtly) The 1996 Hague Convention on the Protection of Children, 2012; contribs on internat. family law and medical ethics to learned jls. *Recreations:* walking on the beach, painting, fly-fishing. *Address:* 1 Hare Court, Temple, EC4Y 7BE. *T:* (020) 7797 7070. *Clubs:* Special Forces; Honourable Artillery Company Saddle, Royal Artillery Hunt Supporters.

NICHOLLS, Michael William Newbery, FRCPath; President, 1993–98, Vice-President, 1998–2007, Hon. Treasurer, 2000–06, Fellowship of Postgraduate Medicine; *b* 22 May 1931; *s* of William Stanley Nicholls, MBE and Florence May (*née* King); *m* 1957, Pamela Winifred Hemer (*d* 1997); two *s*. *Educ:* Xaverian Coll., London; UCL; UCH Med. Sch. (MB, BS 1957). MRCS, LRCP 1955; MRCPath 1968, FRCPath 1980. Resident hosp. posts and general practice, 1955–61; Asst Microbiologist and Registrar, UCH, 1961–70; Consultant Microbiologist, Chichester and Worthing HAs, 1972–90; Dean of Postgrad. Medicine, SE Thames Reg., Univ. of London, 1990–96; Chief Exec., Centre for Educn R and D, 1990–94; Hon. Sen. Lectr in Med. Microbiology, UMDS, 1991–95. Mem., Worthing HA, 1982–90.

Trustee and Chm., Selection Bd for Paediatricians, Tushinskaya Trust, 1998–. Vice Chm., W Sussex History of Medicine Soc., 2002–. Freeman, City of London, 1984; Mem., Livery Cttee, Soc. of Apothecaries, 1994. *Publications:* various contribs, usually of new or creatively provocative material on med. microbiol., med. educn and the needed reforms in postgrad. and continuing med. educn. *Recreations:* singing, chamber music, walking, history of medicine, cycling and lately, of necessity, multi-tasking, gardening and writing obituaries. *Address:* Creekside, Greenacres, Birdham, Chichester, W Sussex PO20 7HL. *T:* (01243) 512937. *Clubs:* Athenæum; Offshore Cruising (Southampton).

NICHOLLS, Nicola; *see* Nicholls, J. N.

NICHOLLS, Sir Nigel (Hamilton), KCVO 1998; CBE 1982; Clerk of the Privy Council, 1992–98; *b* 19 Feb. 1938; *s* of late Bernard Cecil Hamilton Nicholls and Enid Kathleen Nicholls (*née* Gwynne); *m* 1967, Isobel Judith, *d* of Rev. Canon Maurice Dean; two *s*. *Educ:* King's School, Canterbury; St John's College, Oxford (BA 1962; MA 1966). Asst Principal, Admiralty, 1962, MoD, 1964; Asst Private Sec. to Minister of Defence for RN, 1965–66; Principal, 1966; Directing Staff, RCDS, 1971–73; Asst Private Sec. to Sec. of State for Defence, 1973–74; Asst Sec., 1974; Defence Counsellor, UK Delegation to MBFR Talks, Vienna, 1977–80; Asst Under-Sec. of State, MoD, 1984; Under Sec., Cabinet Office, 1986–89; Asst Under-Sec. of State (Systems), MoD, 1989–92. Mem. Council, Malvern St James (formerly Malvern Girls' Coll.), 1999–2007 (Chm., 2003–07). Chm., Malvern Hills DFAS, 2003–06. Freeman, City of London, 1999; Liveryman, Woolmen's Co., 1999–. Companion, IMM, 1999. *Recreations:* choral singing, walking. *Address:* Apartment 4 Woodgate, 7 Albert Road North, Malvern, Worcs WR14 2BF. *Club:* Oxford and Cambridge.

NICHOLLS, Patrick Charles Martyn; Consultant: Dunn & Baker, solicitors, 1987–2001; CVS, solicitors, since 2003; *b* 14 Nov. 1948; *s* of late Douglas Charles Martyn Nicholls and Margaret Josephine Nicholls; *m* 1976, Bridget Elizabeth Fergus Owens; one *s* two *d*. *Educ:* Redrice Sch., Andover. Qualified solicitor, 1974; Partner, Dunn & Baker, 1976–87. Mem., E Devon District Council, 1980–84. MP (C) Teignbridge, 1983–2001; contested (C) same seat, 2001. PPS to Ministers of State: Home Office, 1984–86; MAFF, 1986–87; Parliamentary Under-Secretary of State: Dept of Employment, 1987–90; DoE, 1990; Opposition spokesman on health, 1997–98, on agric., 1998–99. Vice Chm., Social Security Select Cttee, 1990–93. Vice-Chm., Cons. Party, 1993–94. Vice Chm., Soc. of Cons. Lawyers, 1986–87. Steward, British Boxing Bd of Control, 1985–87. Columnist, Western Morning News, 2002–. Lectr on Anglo-American relns and British constitution, incl. for Educnl Cultural Exchanges Ltd, Anglo-American Inst. and ESU. MCIJ 2004. Freeman, City of London, 1996. *Recreations:* theatre, opera, historical research, ski-ing. *Address:* Whitehall Manor, Whitehall, Hemyock, Devon EX15 3UQ. *T:* (01823) 680100; CVS, solicitors, 17 Albemarle Street, W1S 4HP. *Clubs:* Carlton; Newport Yacht.

NICHOLLS, Paul Richard; QC 2012; *b* Chelmsford, 27 Nov. 1967; *s* of Michael Arthur Nicholls and Ann Nicholls; *m* 1994, Claire Hollinghurst; one *s* two *d*. *Educ:* Latymer Sch., Edmonton; Sheffield Univ. (LLB); Worcester Coll., Oxford (BCL). Called to the Bar, Inner Temple, 1992; in practice as a barrister, specialising in employment, public and commercial law, 1992–. *Publications:* (contrib.) Halsbury's Laws of England, Administrative Law, 4th edn 2001; (contrib.) Tolley's Employment Law Handbook. *Recreations:* country walks, real ale, cricket. *Address:* 11 King's Bench Walk, Temple, EC4Y 7EQ. *T:* (020) 7632 8500, *Fax:* (020) 7583 9123. *E:* nicholls@11kbw.com.

NICHOLLS, Prof. (Ralph) John; Consultant Surgeon, St Mark's Hospital, London, 1978–2006, now Emeritus; Hon. Professor of Colorectal Surgery, Imperial College London, since 1997; *b* 20 May 1943; *s* of Clifton Wilson Nicholls and Muriel Morten Nicholls (*née* Heathcote); *m* 1966, Stella Mary McBride; two *s* one *d* (and one *d* decd). *Educ:* Felsted Sch., Essex; Gonville and Caius Coll., Cambridge (BA 1964; MB 1968, BChir 1967, MChir 1978; MA 1999); London Hosp. Med. Coll. London Hosp. trng posts, 1966–78; MRC Res. Fellow, 1971–72; Alexander von Humboldt Fellow, 1976–77; Consultant Surgeon, St Thomas' Hosp., 1982–93; Clin. Dir, St Mark's Hosp., London, 1997–2001; Associate Med. Dir, NW London Hosps NHS Trust, 2005–06. Hon. Civilian Consultant in Surgery to RAF, 1999–2008; Consultant, Policlinico de Monza, Italy, 2006–. Chm. Trustees, Northwick Park Inst. for Medical Res., 2007–. Ed., Colorectal Disease, 1999–2014. Mem., Specialist Adv. Cttee in Gen. Surgery, Jt Cttee for Higher Surgical Trng, 1997–2003. President: Assoc. of Coloproctology of GB and Ireland, 1999–2000; Eur. Assoc. of Coloproctology, 2004; Sec., Div. of Coloproctology, Sect. of Surgery, Union Européene des Médecins Spécialistes, 1997–2003. Hon. FRCPSGlas 1992; Hon. FRCSE 2007; Hon. FRCP 2008; Hon. Fellow: Brazilian Soc. Surgery, 1982; Swiss Soc. Gastroenterol., 1990; Canadian Soc. of Colon and Rectal Surgery, 1995; Amer. Soc. Colon and Rectal Surgeons, 2008; Amer. Coll. of Surgeons, 2010. Membre d'Honneur: Assoc. Française de Chirurgie, 1997; Academie Nationale de Chirurgie, 2005; Hon. Member, Society of Surgery: of Yugoslavia, 2002; of Chile, 2003; of Italy, 2004; of Spain, 2004; Hon. Member: Colorectal Soc. of Australia, 2007; Argentine Soc. of Coloproctology, 2007; British Soc. of Gastroenterol., 2011. *Publications:* (ed jtly) Restorative Proctocolectomy, 1993; (ed with R. R. Dozois) Colorectal Surgery, 1997; (Associate Ed.) Corman's Colon and Rectal Surgery, 6th edn 2012; contribs to learned jls incl. Lancet, BMJ, British Jl Surgery, Annals of Surgery, Gut, Diseases of the Colon and Rectum, Colorectal Disease. *Recreations:* languages, travel, history, music. *Address:* 24 St Mark's Crescent, NW1 7TU. *T:* (020) 7267 4433. *Club:* Athenæum.

NICHOLLS, Robert Michael, CBE 1995; Chairman, General Pharmaceutical Council, 2009–14; Regional Health Commissioner, London, Appointments Commission, 2005–08 (Deputy Chair, 2007–08); *b* 28 July 1939; *s* of late Herbert Edgar Nicholls and Bennetta L'Estrange (*née* Burges); *m* 1961, Dr Deirín Deirdre (*née* O'Sullivan); four *s*. *Educ:* Hampton Sch.; University Coll. of Wales (BA 1961); Univ. of Manchester (DSA 1962). FHSM (AHA 1963; FHA 1993). Asst Sec., Torbay Hosp., 1964; House Governor, St Stephen's Hosp., Chelsea, 1966; Asst Clerk to the Governors, St Thomas' Hosp., 1968; Dep. Gp Sec., Southampton Univ. Hosp. Management Cttee, 1972; Dist Administrator, Southampton and SW Hampshire Health Dist, 1974; Area Administrator, Newcastle upon Tyne AHA(T), 1977; Regl Administrator, SW RHA, 1981; Dist Gen. Man., Southmead DHA, 1985; Regl Gen. Man., later Chief Exec., Oxford RHA, 1988–93; Exec. Dir, London Implementation Gp, NHS Mgt Exec., 1993–96; health care mgt consultant, 1996–2005; Chm., Nat. Clinical Assessment Authy, 2003–05. Vis. Prof. of Society and Health, Bucks New Univ., 2014–. Co-Chair, Prescribing for Excellence Ref. Gp, Scottish Govt, 2014–. Non-exec. Dir, Nestor Healthcare Gp plc, 1997–2003 (Sen. non-exec. Dir, 2001–03). Health Sector Reform Advr, British Council, 1997–2003. Member: Health Educn Council, 1984–87; CMO's Med. Educn Wkg Pty, 1992–93; GMC, 1996–2005 (Chm., Preliminary Proceedings Cttee, 2000–03); All Party Pharmaceutical Gp, 2009–14; Bd, Medical Educn England, 2010–12. Member: Clinical Adv. Bd, Oxford Univ. Med. Sch., 2001–08; Bd, Modernising Pharmacy Careers, 2010–13. National Council, Inst. of Health Service Management (formerly IHA): Mem., 1976–86; Pres., 1983–84. Associate Fellow, Templeton Coll., Oxford, 1996–2001. *Publications:* (contrib.) Resources in Medicine, 1970; (contrib.) Working with People, 1983; (contrib.) Rationing of Healthcare in Medicine, 1993; (contrib.) Doctors in Society, 2005. *Recreations:* bird-watching, jazz, opera, sport. *Address:* Thame, Oxon.

NICHOLLS, Stephen John; a District Judge (Magistrates' Courts), since 2011; *b* Bournemouth, 12 Dec. 1956; *s* of Deryck John Nicholls and Geraldine Mary Nicholls; *m* 1991, Lynne Brien; one *s* one *d*. *Educ:* St Peter's Sch., Southbourne; Dorset Inst. of Higher Educn (BA Hons). Admitted as solicitor, 1981; articled clerk, 1979–81, solicitor, 1979–91, J. W. Miller & Sons; Andrews McQueen, 1991–98; Law Chambers, 2001–11. Lectr (pt-time), Open Univ., 1998–2003. Asst Coroner, Dorset, 2009–. *Recreations:* cricket, visiting France, reading, photography. *Address:* Bournemouth Magistrates' Court, The Law Courts, Stafford Road, Bournemouth BH1 1LA. *T:* (01202) 745309, *Fax:* (01273) 811770.

NICHOLS, Rt Rev. Anthony Howard, PhD; Dean of Students and Lecturer in Biblical Studies, Trinity Theological College, Perth, 2003–13, now Honorary Lecturer; *b* 29 March 1938; *m* 1968, Judith Margaret Ross; two *s* two *d*. *Educ:* Univ. of Sydney (BA; MEd); Univ. of London (BD Hons); Macquarie Univ. (MA Hons); Moore Coll., ACT (Theol. scholar); PhD Univ. of Sheffield 1997. Latin and history teacher, 1960–63. Assistant Curate: St Paul's Chatswood, 1966; St Bede's, Drummoyne, 1967; Lectr, Biblical Studies, Moore Coll., Sydney, 1968–72; Lectr, Biblical Studies and Educn, 1972–81, Dean of Faculty of Theology, 1977–81, Satya Wacana Christian Univ., Salatiga, Indonesia; Principal: Nungalinya Coll., Darwin (Training Coll. for Aboriginal theol students), 1982–87; St Andrew's Hall, Melbourne (CMS Training Coll.), 1988–91; Bishop of NW Australia, 1992–2003. Vis. Lectr, Anglican Inst., Bandung, Indonesia, 2004–; Vis. Prof., Sabah Theological Seminary, Malaysia, 2012. Stephen Bayne Scholar, Univ. of Sheffield, 1985–86. *Publications:* Mission of the Soul: studies in the Psalms, 1996; Jesus in All the Scriptures, 2007; jl articles on Bible translation, missiology, Indonesian religions, Aboriginal culture, and philosophy of educn. *Address:* 62/60 Kalinda Drive, City Beach, WA 6015, Australia.

NICHOLS, Prof. Colin Graham, PhD; FRS 2014; Carl Cori Professor, since 2006, and Director, Center for Investigation of Membrane Excitability Diseases, since 2010, Washington University, St Louis; *b* Leicester, 27 Aug. 1960; *s* of Graham P. Nichols and Margaret A. Nichols (*née* Walker); two *s* by Diana L. (*née* Coleman). *Educ:* Kingswood Sch., Corby; Royal Grammar Sch., Worcester; Leeds Univ. (BSc 1982; PhD 1985). Postdoctoral Fellow, Univ. of Maryland, 1985–91; Washington University, St Louis: Asst Prof., 1991–96; Associate Prof., 1996–2000; Prof., 2000–. *Recreations:* cricket, theatre. *Address:* 6975 Dartmouth Avenue, St Louis, MO 63130, USA. *T:* (314) 3626630. *E:* cnichols@wustl.edu.

NICHOLS, Dinah Alison, CB 1995; Director, Pennon Group plc, 2003–13; a Crown Estate Counsellor, 2011–13 (Commissioner, 2003–11); *b* 28 Sept. 1943; *d* of late Sydney Hirst Nichols and Freda Nichols. *Educ:* Wyggeston Girls' Grammar Sch., Leicester; Bedford Coll., Univ. of London (Reid Arts Schol.; BA Hons History, 1965; Hon. Fellow, RHBNC, 1997). Ministry of Transport: Asst Principal, 1965–69; Asst Private Sec. to Minister, 1969–70; Principal, 1970–74; Cabinet Office, 1974–77; Asst Sec., DoE, 1978–83; Principal Private Sec. to Sec. of State for Transport, 1983–85; Under Sec., DoE, 1985–91; Dep. Sec., DoE, later DETR, then DEFRA, 1991–2002; Dir Gen., Envmt, 1996–2002. Director: John Laing ETE, 1987–90; Anglian Water plc, 1992–95; Shires Smaller Companies plc, 1999–2012. Sec. of State for the Envmt's Rep., Commonwealth War Graves Commn, 1993–97. Dir, Cities in Schs, 1996–2000; Mem. Bd, Toynbee Housing Assoc., 1996–2007; Chairman: Toynbee Partnership Housing Assoc., 2002–07; Groundwork N London (formerly Groundwork Camden & Islington), 2003–10; National Forest Co., 2005–11; Member: Policy Cttee, CPRE, 2009–13; Green Alliance; Aldersgate Gp; Ind. Mem., Governance Community, Nat. Trust, 2013–. Trustee: Travel Foundn, 2003–09; Keep Britain Tidy (formerly Envmtl Campaigns (ENCAMS)), 2005– (Chm., 2012–); Groundwork London, 2008–10; Land Trust, 2010–; SW Lakes Trust, 2014–. Winston Churchill Meml Fellow, 1969. Life FRSA. Liveryman, Water Conservators' Co., 2009–. *Recreations:* fell walking, choral singing (Goldsmiths Choral Union), classical music, theatre, cross country ski-ing, countryside. *Club:* Swiss Alpine (Assoc. of British Members).

NICHOLS, Jeremy Gareth Lane, MA; Headmaster, Stowe School, 1989–2003; Interim Headmaster, Aiglon College, Switzerland, 2007; *b* 20 May 1943; *yr s* of late Derek Aplin Douglas Lane Nichols and of Ruth Anne Baiss (formerly Nichols); *m* 1972, Patricia Anne, *d* of Cdre Alan Swanton, DSO, DFC and bar, RN; one *s* three *d*. *Educ:* Lancing Coll., Sussex; Fitzwilliam Coll., Cambridge (BA English Lit. 1966; MA); Perugia Univ. Assistant Master: Livorno Naval Acad., 1965; Rugby Sch., 1966–67; Eton Coll., 1967–89, House Master, 1981–89; Gilman Sch., Baltimore, USA, 1979–80. Chm., Assoc. of Educnl Guardians for Internat. Students, 1995–2002. Founding Mem. Bd and Pres., Model EP, 1994–2000. Advr Trustee, Manor Charitable Trust, 1989–2003. Mem. Council, Univ. of Buckingham, 2010–. Governor: Wellesley House Sch., 1985–2004; Papplewick Sch., 1988–2003; Aysgarth Sch., 1990–2004; Truro High Sch., 2004–; West Buckland Sch., 2004–. FCT (FCollP 1997); FRSA. *Recreations:* outdoor pursuits, sport, music, old cars. *Address:* Tresithick House, St Erme, Truro, Cornwall TR4 9AU. *Clubs:* Hawks (Cambridge); I Zingari, Free Foresters, Corinthian Casuals.

NICHOLS, John Roland; Director of Global Business Development, Chartered Institute for Securities and Investment (formerly Securities and Investments Institute), 2009–10; *b* 13 Nov. 1951; *s* of Richard Alan Nichols and Katherine Louisa Nichols (*née* Barham); *m* 1983, Suzanne, *d* of James Harry Davies, MBE, RA retd, and Helen Christine Davies, JP (*née* Berry); one *s* one *d*. *Educ:* Latymer Upper Sch., Hammersmith; Univ. of Surrey (BSc Hons). Admitted as solicitor, 1977; entered FCO, 1977: First Secretary: Budapest, 1979–82; FCO, 1982–85; Brasilia, 1985–89; FCO, 1989–93; Counsellor and Dep. High Comr, Dhaka, 1993–95; Consul-Gen., Geneva, 1995–97; Dep. Hd of Mission, Dir of Trade Promotion and Consul-Gen., Berne, 1997–2000; Dep. Chief Exec., and Dir of Communications, Internat. Financial Services, London (on secondment), 2000–03; Ambassador to Hungary, 2003–07; Ambassador to Switzerland and (non-resident) to Liechtenstein, 2008–09. Freeman, City of London, 2006; Freeman, 2008, Liveryman, 2013, Musicians' Co. (Ct Asst, 2014–; Chm., Yeoman Coordination Cttee, 2014–). Chm. Trustees, Music-at-Hill, 2014–; Trustee, London Arts Orch., 2014–. *Recreations:* trying hard to be more than a Sunday painter (Vice Chairman and programme organiser, Guildford Art Soc.), travel, cycling, gardening, opera, music (in the Musicians' Co., Chm. of extensive programme of outreach into London schools to introduce children to classical music), theatre.

NICHOLS, Judith Elaine; *see* Coello, J. E.

NICHOLS, Peter Richard, FRSL 1983; playwright since 1959; *b* 31 July 1927; *s* of late Richard George Nichols and Violet Annie Poole; *m* 1960, Thelma Reed; one *s* two *d* (and one *d* decd). *Educ:* Bristol Grammar Sch.; Bristol Old Vic Sch.; Trent Park Trng College. Actor, mostly in repertory, 1950–55; worked as teacher in primary and secondary schs, 1958–60. Mem., Arts Council Drama Panel, 1973–75. Playwright in residence, Guthrie Theatre, Minneapolis, 1976. *TV plays:* Walk on the Grass, 1959; Promenade, 1960; Ben Spray, 1961; The Reception, 1961; The Big Boys, 1961; Continuity Man, 1963; Ben Again, 1963; The Heart of the Country, 1963; The Hooded Terror, 1963; The Brick Umbrella, 1964; When the Wind Blows, 1964 (later adapted for radio); Daddy Kiss It Better, 1968; The Gorge, 1968; Hearts and Flowers, 1971; The Common, 1973; Greeks Bearing Gifts (Inspector Morse series), 1991; *films:* Catch Us If You Can, 1965; Georgy Girl, 1967; Joe Egg, 1971; The National Health, 1973; Privates on Parade, 1983; *stage plays:* A Day in The Death of Joe Egg, 1967 (Evening Standard Award, Best Play; Tony Award, Best Revival, 1985); The National Health, 1969 (Evening Standard Award, Best Play); Forget-me-not Lane, 1971; Chez Nous, 1973; The Freeway, 1974 (radio broadcast, 1991); Privates on Parade, 1977 (Evening Standard Best Comedy, Soc. of West End Theatres Best Comedy and Ivor Novello Best Musical Awards); Born in the Gardens, 1979 (televised 1986); Passion Play, 1980 (Standard Best Play award, 1981); A Piece of My Mind, 1986; Blue Murder, 1995; So Long Life, 2000; Nicholodeon (revue), 2000; Lingua Franca, 2010; *musical:* Poppy, 1982 (SWET Best Musical

Award). *Publications:* Feeling You're Behind (autobiog.), 1984; Diaries 1969–1977, 2000; some TV plays in anthologies; all above stage plays published separately and in 2 vols, Nichols: Plays One and Two, 1991; Love Fifteen (novel), 2014. *Recreations:* listening to jazz, looking at cities. *Address:* c/o Alan Brodie Representation, Paddock Suite, The Courtyard, 55 Charterhouse Street, EC1M 6HA.

NICHOLS, Sir Richard (Everard), Kt 1998; Senior Partner, Sedgwick Kelly Solicitors, 2000–02 (Partner, 1996–2000); Lord Mayor of London, 1997–98; *b* 26 April 1938; *s* of late Guy Everard Nichols and of Patricia Mary (*née* Hurst); *m* 1966, Shelagh Mary Loveband; two *s* one *d.* *Educ:* Christ's Hosp., Horsham. Nat. Service, commnd RE, 1956–58. Admitted solicitor, 1963; Asst Solicitor, Gunston & Smart, Hong Kong, 1963–64; Sen. Partner, 1976–96, Kelly Nichols & Blayney. Chancellor, Univ. of Ulster, 2002–10. Almoner, Christ's Hosp., 1984–2004; Gov., Hon. the Irish Soc., 2000–04. Alderman, Ward of Candlewick, 1984–2007; Sheriff, City of London, 1994–95. Master, Salters' Co., 1988. KStJ 1997. *Recreations:* wine, travel, coarse gardening. *Address:* Newhall Farm, Bucks Hill, Kings Langley, Herts WD4 9AH. *T:* (01923) 269882. *Club:* East India.

NICHOLS, His Eminence Cardinal Vincent Gerard; *see* Westminster, Archbishop of, (RC).

NICHOLSON OF WINTERBOURNE, Baroness *cr* 1997 (Life Peer), of Winterbourne in the Royal County of Berkshire; **Emma Harriet Nicholson;** *b* 16 Oct. 1941; *d* of Sir Godfrey Nicholson, 1st Bt and late Lady Katharine Constance Lindsay, 5th *d* of 27th Earl of Crawford; *m* 1987, Sir Michael Harris Caine (*d* 1999); one adopted *s* one step *c* (and one step *c* decd). *Educ:* St Mary's School, Wantage; Royal Academy of Music. LRAM, ARCM. Computer Programmer, Programming Instructor, Systems Analyst, ICL, 1962–66; Computer Consultant, John Tyzack & Partners, 1967–69; Gen. Management Consultant and Computer Consultant, McLintock Mann and Whinney Murray, 1969–74; joined Save the Children Fund, 1974, Dir of Fund Raising, 1977–85, Pres., Hatherleigh Dist Br; Founder and Bd Mem., Stichting Redt de Kinderen, Netherlands, 1982–88; Founder and Mem., Comité d'Honneur Sauvez Les Enfants, France, 1983; Consultant, 1985–87: World Assoc. of Girl Guides and Girl Scouts; The Duke of Edinburgh's Award Scheme; Foster Parents Plan UK; Westminster Children's Hosp. Contested (C) Blyth Valley, 1979. MP Devon West and Torridge (C, 1987–95, Lib Dem, 1995–97). PPS to Minister of State, Home Office, 1992–93, MAFF, 1993–95, to Financial Sec. to HM Treasury, 1995; Lib Dem spokesperson on Overseas Develt and Human Rights, 1996–97. Mem., Select Cttee on Employment, 1990–91; Founder and Jt Chm., All Party Parly Gp for Romanian Children; Chm., All Party Parly Gp on Foreign Affairs, 2010; Vice Chm., All Party Parly Gp on Penal Affairs, 1992, on Human Trafficking, 2010, on European Reform, 2010, for Georgia, 2010, for Jordan, 2014; Mem., All Party Parly Gp for Bulgaria, for Moldova, for Romania, for Saudi Arabia (Treas.), on Tackling Terrorism, on Transatlantic and Internat. Security, for Trinidad and Tobago, for UN, for Ahmadiyya Muslim Community, on British-Iraq (Chm., 2009); Treas., All Party Parly Gp for Islamic Finance; Chm., All Party Parly Gp for Oman, for Kuwait, for UNA Adv. Gp; Chm. and Founder, All Party Parly Gp on Euro Inf. Mkt Gp; Co-Dep. Chm., British-Iranian All Party Parly Gp; Treas., All Party Parly Gp for Positive Eur. Gp, for British Caribbean; Sec., All Party Parly Gp on Syria, for Human Rights; Mem., Parly Panel, RCN, 1990–92; Sec. then Chm., Cons. Backbench Envmt Cttee, 1990–91; Vice-Chm., Cons. Party, 1983–87. Alternate Mem., UK Delegn to WEU and Council of Europe, 1990–92. House of Lords: front bench spokesman on Data Protection, 1998; Prime Minister's Trade Envoy to Iraq, 2014; Mem., Select Cttee on Soft Power and the UK's Influence, 2013–14. MEP (Lib Dem) SE Region, 1999–2009. European Parliament: Vice-Chairman: Cttee on For. Affairs (Vice-Pres., 2007–09), Human Rights, Common Defence and Security Policy; Pres., Delegn for Relns with Iraq; Member: Cttee on Women's Rights and Equal Opportunities; For. Affairs Cttee; Subcttee for Human Rights; Euro-Mediterranean Parly Assembly (Vice-Pres., Cttee on Women's Rights); Delegns to Mashreq countries and Gulf States, and to Euro-Mediterranean Partnership; Delegn for Relns with Iran; Stability Pact for SE Europe Parly Gp: Substitute Member: Cttee on Budgets; Parly Co-op Cttee for Kazakhstan, for Kyrgyzstan, for Uzbekistan, for Tajikistan, for Turkmenistan, for Mongolia; Agriculture and Rural Develt Cttee; EP/Romania Jt Parly Cttee; Delegn for Relns with the Mashreq Countries; Rapporteur for Iraq, for Romania, for Kashmir; Shadow Rapporteur for Iraq, for EU-India Free Trade Agreement, for a Special Place for Children in EU Ext. Action; Member, EU Election Observation Missions to: Palestine, 2005; Lebanon, 2005, 2009; Afghanistan, 2005; Azerbaijan, 2005; Armenia, 2007; Pakistan, 2008; Chief Observer, EU Election Observation, Yemen, 2006; Member: UN Election Observation Missions, Iraq, 2005; Eur. Parlt Delegn, OSCE Internat. Election Observation Mission, Moldova, 2009; Council of Europe Delegn to OSCE Election Observation Mission, Kazakhstan, 2011; UK Delegn to Parly Assembly of Council of Europe and Eur. Security and Defence Assembly, 2010–; former Co-Chm., High Level Gps for Romanian Children and for Moldovan children; High Rep. of Pres. of Rep. of Molodova for Children, 2007–10; High Rep. of Prime Minister of Romania for Children, 2009. Fellow, Industry and Parlt Trust. Vis. Parly Fellow, St Antony's Coll., Oxford, 1995–96 (Sen. Associate Mem., 1997–98, 1998–99, 2001–). WHO Envoy for Health, Peace and Develt, E Mediterranean Reg., 2002. Hon. Advr to PM of Iraq in the field of health, 2008–14. Board Member: Middle East and N Africa Council, Amer. Bar Assoc.; Foundn for Dialogue Among Civilisations, 2007–13; Founder and Exec. Chm., Iraq Britain Business Council, 2009–; Board Member: Global Warming Policy Foundn, 2009–; Durham Global Security Inst. Strategic Adv. Bd, 2011–; Architecture Develt Agency, 2014–. Vice-Moderator, Movement for Ordination of Women, 1991–93. Founder and Pres., Caine Prize for African Writing; Founder and Mem., Parly Appeal for Romanian Children, until 2009; Trustee: Africa '95; Booker Prize Foundn; Chm., Booker Prize for Russian Fiction, 1999–. Dir, Shelter; Founder and Chm., AMAR Internat. Charitable Foundn (formerly AMAR Appeal), 1991–; Founder and Pres., Asociatia Children's High Level Gp, 2006–; Member: Exec. Bd, UNICEF UK; MRC; Mgt Bd, European Movement (Vice-Chm.); POW Adv. Trust on Disability; Council, PITCOM; Centre for Policy Studies; RIIA; Adv. Bd, Women of Tomorrow Awards; Adv. Bd Mem. and Judge, Franklin D. Roosevelt Internat. Disability Rights Award, 2011–13; RAM Appeal Cttee; Courts of Reading, Southampton, Exeter and Sussex Univs; Editl Panel, 300 Gp Newsletter. Vice President: Small Farmers' Assoc.; ADC; ADAPT (Founder and Chm.); Methodist Homes for the Aged; LEPRA; Farms for City Children; Local Govt Gp for Europe. Deputy Chairman: Duke of Edinburgh's Award 30th Anniv. Tribute Project, 1986–88; Duke of Edinburgh's Internat. Project '87, 1987–88. President: Plymouth and W Devon Cassette, Talking Newspaper; W Regl Assoc. for the Deaf; Vice Pres., Little Foundn; Co-Patron, Manningford Trust; Patron: Hospice Care Trust, N Devon; CRUSAID; Devon Care Trust; Wilsford Trust; Relatives and Residents Assoc. (former Mem., Mgt Bd); Vice Patron, Blind in Business (Patron, 1993–95); Chm. Adv. Cttee, Carnegie UK Trust Venues Improvement Programmes. Mem., Co. of Inf. Technologists. Non-exec. Dir, Jt Leasing Co., 2013– (Chm., Supervisory Bd, 2013–). Chm., Internat. Year of the Disabled, UNESCO, 1981; former Co-Chm., UNA Adv. Gp, UNESCO; Former Vice-President: Assoc. of District Councils; British Tinnitus Assoc.; Nat. Assoc. for Maternal and Child Welfare; Child Psychotherapy Trust; The Missing Persons Hotline; former Member, Council: Howard League for Penal Reform; Media Soc.; Industry Churches Forum; former Member: Mgt Bd, European Movement; Guild of Mgt Consultants; Forum UK; Inst. of Economic Affairs; Council for Arab British Understanding; Prince of Wales Adv. Trust on Disability; Adv. Council, Justis Legal Databases; Develt Cttee, Exeter Univ.; British Romanian Assoc.; London Business Women's Network; Adv. Council, United World Foundn; Adv. Council, Centre for Adoptive Identity Studies, Univ. of East London; former Patron: Cities in Schs; Internat. Cttee for a Free Iraq; Ecaterina Iliescu Meml Lect.; British Deaf Accord; Nat. Deaf Blind and Rubella Assoc.; AMANA; Soc. for Freedom of the City of London Municipality; Freedom Council; Reading Industrial Therapy Orgn; Women into IT Foundn; Women's Engineering Soc.; Women's Business Assoc.; Sense South West; Opera South West; PHAB South West; Devon Daycare Trust; Deaf Educn through Listening and Talking; Nat. Music and Disability Inf. Service; former Trustee: Covent Garden Cancer Res. Trust; Motor Neurone Disease Assoc.; World Meml Fund for Disaster Relief. FRSA. Hon. Dr: N London, 1998; Victor Babes Univ., Timisoara, Romania, 2002; Acad. of Econ. Studies, Bucharest; Univ. of Birmingham, 2004; Dimitrie Cantemir Christian Univ., Bucharest, 2006; Oklahoma City Univ., USA, 2010; Kingston Univ., 2014. *Publications:* Why does the West forget?, 1993; Secret Society, 1996; (ed jtly) The Iraqi Marshlands, 2002; (ed) The Southern Mesopotamian Marshlands, 2012; contrib. various periodicals. *Recreations:* music, chess, reading, walking. *Address:* House of Lords, SW1A 0PW. *Club:* Reform.

NICHOLSON, Dr Anthony Andrew, FRCR; Consultant Interventional Radiologist, Leeds Teaching Hospitals, since 2003; *b* Liverpool, 5 April 1950; *s* of William Bell Nicholson and Marguerita Fleming Nicholson; *m* 1975, Lesley Oxendale; one *s* three *d.* *Educ:* Hillfoot Hey High Sch., Liverpool; Univ. of Wales, Swansea (BSc Hons 1972); Gonville and Caius Coll., Cambridge (MSc 1974); Univ. of Sheffield (MB ChB Hons 1983). FRCR 1988. Consultant Interventional Radiologist, Hull and E Yorks Hosps, 1990–2003. Pres., British Soc. of Interventional Radiol., 1999–2001; Dean and Vice Pres., RCR, 2008–11. Co-Founder and active supporter, Families for Individual Needs and Dignity, 1992–. Hon. FRCSI 2010; Dist. Fellow, Cardiovascular and Interventional Soc. of Eur., 2010. *Publications:* Textbook of Endovascular Procedures, 2000; 15 book chapters; over 200 articles in jls. *Recreations:* cycling, Rugby Union, Everton Football Club, music, theatre, travel, gardening. *Address:* 75 Southfield, Hessle, East Yorks HU13 0EX. *T:* (0113) 392 2860. *E:* tonynick60@gmail.com.

NICHOLSON, Air Vice-Marshal Antony Angus, CBE 1997; LVO 1980; FRAeS; defence and security consultant, since 2004; *b* 27 June 1946; *s* of late Air Cdre Angus Archibald Norman Nicholson, CBE, AE and Joan Mary, *d* of Ernest Beaumont, MRCVS, DVSM; *m* 1980, Fenella Janet Fraser; one *s* one *d,* and one step *s.* *Educ:* Eton Coll.; Churchill Coll., Cambridge (MA). FRAeS 1998. Joined RAF, 1968: helicopter pilot, 28 Sqn (Hong Kong), 3 Sqn SOAF (Oman), and 230 Sqn (UK), 1970–75; OC 3 Sqn SOAF, 1975–77; Equerry to HRH Duke of Edinburgh, 1978–80; OC 72 Sqn, 1981–83; MoD, 1984–86; RAF Instr, Army Staff Coll., 1986–88; Stn Comdr, RAF Shawbury, 1988–90; rcds 1991; Air Cdre Flying Trng, 1993–96; Dir, Operational Requirements (Air), 1996–98; Dir Gen. Air Systems 1, Defence Procurement Agency, 1998–2000. Eurofighter Internat. Ltd, 2000–01; Director: Babcock Defence, 2001–04; Primeguild Ltd, 2006–. Trustee, Hants and IoW Air Ambulance, 2010–. DSM (Oman), 1977. *Recreations:* squash, hill walking, Gloucester RFC. *Address:* c/o Barclays Bank, High Street, Odiham, Hants RG29 1LL. *Club:* Army and Navy.

NICHOLSON, Sir Bryan (Hubert), GBE 2005; Kt 1987; Chairman, Financial Reporting Council, 2001–05 (Director and Deputy Chairman, 1993–96; Member, 1996–98); Senior Advisor, Penfida Partners LLP, since 2006; *b* 6 June 1932; *s* of late Reginald Hubert and Clara Nicholson; *m* 1956, Mary Elizabeth, *er d* of A. C. Harrison of Oxford; one *s* one *d* (and one *s* decd). *Educ:* Palmers School, Grays, Essex; Oriel College, Oxford (MA PPE; Hon. Fellow, 1989). 2nd Lieut, RASC, 1950–52; Unilever Management Trainee, 1955–58; Dist. Manager, Van den Berghs, 1958–59; Sales Manager, Three Hands/Jeyes Group, 1960–64; Sperry Rand: Sales Dir, UK, Remington Div., 1964–66; Gen. Manager, Australia, Remington Div., 1966–69; Managing Dir, UK and France, Remington Div., 1969–72; Dir, Ops, Rank Xerox (UK), 1972–76; Dir, Overseas Subsidiaries, Rank Xerox, 1976; Exec. Main Bd Dir, Rank Xerox, 1976–84; Chm., Rank Xerox (UK) and Chm., Rank Xerox GmbH, 1979–84; Chm., MSC, 1984–87; Chm. and Chief Exec., PO, 1987–92; Chairman: Girobank, 1987–89; BUPA, 1992–2001 (Vice Pres., 2001–05; Pres., 2005–); Varity Hldgs, later Varity Europe Ltd, 1993–96; Cookson Gp, 1998–2003; Accountancy Foundn, 2003–04 (Dir, 2000–03). Non-executive Director: Rank Xerox, 1984–87; Baker Perkins Holdings, 1982–84; Evode, 1981–84; Internat. Post Corp. SA, 1988–92; GKN, 1991–2000 (Sen. Ind. Dir, 1996–2000); Varity Corp., USA, 1993–96; LucasVarity, 1996–99; Equitas Hldgs Ltd, 1996–2005; Action Centre for Europe Ltd, 1996–2004; Newsquest plc, 1997–99; Victoria plc, 2012 (Sen. Ind.); non-executive Chairman: GOAL plc, 2001–02; EDI plc, 2004–06 (Dep. Chm., 2002–04; Sen. Ind. Dir, 2006–11); Member: Adv. Bd, Active Internat., 2001–; Eur. Adv. Bd, Proudfoot Consulting, 2006–09. Confederation of British Industry: Mem. Council, 1987–2002; Mem., President's Cttee, 1990–98; Dep. Pres., 1993–94, 1996–97; Pres., 1994–96; Chairman: Task Force on Vocational Educn and Training, 1988–89; Educn and Training Affairs Cttee, 1990–93; Global Counsellor, Conf. Bd, 1994–2007 (Emeritus, 2007); Chairman: CNAA, 1988–91; NICG, 1988–90; NCVQ, 1990–93; Interchange Panel, 1996–97; Pres., N of England Educn Conf., 1996. Department of Employment: Member: Adv. Cttee on Women's Employment, 1985–87; Women's Issues Wkg Gp, 1992–93; Race Relns Adv. Gp, 1985–87. Member: NEDC, 1985–92; Council, Inst. of Manpower Studies, 1985–93; Governing Council, Business in the Community, 1985–93; Council, Prince's Youth Business Trust, 1986–2002; Council, Industrial Soc., 1988–2002 (Chm., 1990–93); Adv. Council, Economic and Regional Analysis, 1998–2010; Prime Minister's Adv. Cttee on Business Appointments, 1998–2009; Editl Bd, European Business Jl, 1988–2005; Adv. Bd, Britain in Europe, 1999–2004; Council, Atlantic Coll., 1999–2002; Adv. Gp, Higher Educn Policy Inst., 2002–05. President: Involvement and Participation Assoc., 1990–94; ACFHE, 1992–93; AFC, 1993–94; Nat. Centre for Young People with Epilepsy, 2005–11, now Life Vice Pres., Young Epilepsy; Vice President: Re-Solv (Soc. for Prevention of Solvent Abuse), 1985–; NCH Action for Children (formerly Nat. Children's Home), 1989–2002; SRHE, 1992–2010. Observer, 2006–08, Mem., 2008–13, Public Interest Oversight Bd, Internat. Fedn of Accountants. Chancellor, Sheffield Hallam Univ., 1992–2001; Pro Chancellor and Chm. Council, Open Univ., 1996–2004. President: Oriel Soc., 1988–92; Open Univ. Foundn, 2004–12. Patron: Rathbone Community Industry (formerly Rathbone Soc.), 1987–; Inst. of Financial Accountants, 2012–; Vice Pres., Industrial Trust, 1999–2010; Trustee: Babson Coll., Mass, USA, 1990–96; Buxton Fest. Foundn, 2003–09; Internat. Accounting Standards Cttee Foundn, 2006–12. President: Wakefield Trinity Wildcats, 2000–11; Nomad Th., E Horsley, 2002–. UK Hon. Rep. for W Berlin, 1983–84. CCMI (CBIM 1985); Hon. CIPD 1994. FCGI (CGIA 1988); FCIM 1990; FRSA 1985. Freeman, City of London, 1988. Hon. Fellow: Manchester Metropolitan Univ. (formerly Polytechnic), 1990; SCOTVEC, 1994; Scottish Qualifications Authy, 1997; Open Univ., 2006; Hon. FCA, ICAEW, 2011. Hon. DEd CNAA, 1992; DUniv: Open, 1994; Sheffield Hallam, 2001; Hon. DLitt Glasgow Caledonian, 2000. *Recreations:* tennis, bridge, opera, political history. *Club:* Oxford and Cambridge (Chm., 1995–97).

NICHOLSON, Sir Charles (Christian), 3rd Bt *cr* 1912, of Harrington Gardens, Royal Borough of Kensington; *b* 15 Dec. 1941; *s* of Sir John Norris Nicholson, 2nd Bt, KBE, CIE and Vittoria Vivien (*d* 1991), *y d* of Percy Trewhella; *S* father, 1993; *m* 1975, Martha Don, *d* of Stuart Warren Don and *widow* of Niall Anstruther-Gough-Calthorpe; one step *s* one step *d.* *Educ:* Ampleforth; Magdalen Coll., Oxford. *Heir:* *b* James Richard Nicholson [*b* 24 Oct. 1947; *m* 1980, Sarah Hazel, *d* of Richard Alan Budgett; one *s* one *d*]. *Address:* Turners Green Farm, Elvetham, Hartley Wintney, Hants RG27 8BE. *Clubs:* Brook's's, Pratt's; Royal Yacht Squadron.

See also Sir E. H. Anstruther-Gough-Calthorpe, Bt.

NICHOLSON, Rev. David; Vicar, St John's, Cudworth, since 1997; a Chaplain to the Queen, since 2014; *b* Batley, W Yorks, 8 Oct. 1957; *s* of Percy and Winifred Nicholson. *Educ:* Batley Grammar Sch.; Salisbury and Wells Theol Coll. Ordained deacon, 1983, priest, 1984; Curate: Trevethin, Pontypool, 1983–85; Ebbw Vale, 1985–87; Vicar: St Stephen's, Newport, 1987–95; Abertillery, Cwmtillery and Six Bells, 1995–97. Hon. Chaplain, Mission to Seafarers, 1987–95. Mem. of Council, Additional Curates' Soc., 1994–. Governor: Churchfield Primary Sch., Cudworth, 1997–; Birkwood Primary Sch., Cudworth, 2002–; Cherry Dale Primary Sch., Cudworth, 2002–. Mem., SSC, 1997–. *Recreations:* travel, cooking, history, music, family and friends. *Address:* The Vicarage, St John's Road, Cudworth, Barnsley, S Yorks S72 8DE. *T:* (01226) 710279. *E:* FrNicholson@aol.com.

NICHOLSON, David John; public affairs consultant, Butler-Kelly Ltd, 1998–2012; *b* 17 Aug. 1944; *s* of late John Francis Nicholson and Lucy Warburton Nicholson (*née* Battrum); *m* 1981, Frances Mary, *d* of late Brig. T. E. H. Helby, MC; two *s* one *d*. *Educ:* Queen Elizabeth's Grammar School, Blackburn; Christ Church, Oxford (MA Hons Mod. Hist.). Dept of Employment, 1966; Research Fellow, Inst. of Historical Res., 1970; Cons. Res. Dept, 1972 (Head, Political Section, 1974–82); Assoc. of British Chambers of Commerce, 1982–87 (Dep. Dir-Gen., 1986–87). Contested (C) Walsall S, 1983; MP (C) Taunton, 1987–97; contested (C) same seat, 1997. PPS to Minister for Overseas Develt, 1990–92. Member: Select Cttee on Parly Comr for Admin, 1992–97; Public Accounts Cttee, 1992–94; Select Cttee on Employment, 1994–96; Select Cttee on Educn and Employment, 1996–97; Jt Sec., All-Party Parly Gp for Population and Develt, 1990–94; Treasurer: All-Party Parly Gp on Water, 1993–97; All-Party Parly Gp on Waste Management, 1995–97; Sec., Cons. Backbench Social Services Cttee, 1988–90; Chm., Cons. W Country Mems Cttee, 1994–95 (Vice-Chm., 1992–93); Sec., Cons. Backbench Agriculture Cttee, 1995–97. Pres., Taunton Horticultural and Floricultural Soc., 1992–. Mem., Central Council, Royal Over-Seas League, 2013–. *Publications:* (ed with John Barnes) The Diaries of L. S. Amery: vol. I, 1896–1929, 1980; vol. II, The Empire at Bay, 1929–45, 1988; (contrib.) International Encyclopedia of Military History (2 vols), 2006. *Recreations:* travel, gardening, music, old buildings. *Address:* Allshire, East Anstey, Tiverton, Devon EX16 9JG.

NICHOLSON, Frank; DL; Managing Director, Vaux Breweries Ltd, 1984–99; Director, Swallow Group plc (formerly Vaux Group), 1987–99; *b* 11 Feb. 1954; 5th *s* of late Douglas Nicholson, TD and Pauline Nicholson; *m* 1986, Lavinia Stourton; three *s*. *Educ:* Harrow Sch.; Magdalene Coll., Cambridge (MA). FRICS 1977. Assistant, Debenham, Tewson and Chinnocks, 1976–81; Tied Trade Dir, Vaux Breweries Ltd, 1981–84. Dir, Washington Develt Corp., 1985–88; Chairman: Sunderland Youth Enterprise Trust, 1986–2012; Wearside Opportunity, 1988–92; City of Sunderland Partnership, 1992–99. Dep. Chm., Sunderland Univ. (formerly Poly.), 1991–2002 (Hon. Fellow, 1991). Gov., Durham Sch., 1999–. DL 1995, High Sheriff, 1999–2000, Co. Durham. Prince of Wales Community Ambassador's Award, 1995; Queen's Award for Enterprise Promotion, 2010. *Recreation:* country sports. *Address:* Cocken House, Chester-le-Street, Co. Durham DH3 4EN. *T:* (0191) 388 0505. *Clubs:* Royal Automobile; Northern Counties (Newcastle); Chilton and Windlestone Workingmen's (Co. Durham).

See also Sir P. D. Nicholson.

NICHOLSON, Graham Beattie; Chief Legal Adviser and Adviser to the Governor, Bank of England, 2009–15; *b* Lowestoft, 22 Feb. 1949; *s* of John Arthur and Ena Patricia Nicholson; one *d*. *Educ:* Bloxham Sch., Banbury; Trinity Hall, Cambridge (BA Law 1971). Admitted as solicitor, 1974; Freshfields, later Freshfields Bruckhaus Deringer LLP, 1971–2008: Partner, 1980–2008; Hd, Co. Dept, 1986–90; Man. Partner, 1990–93. Director: City of London Sinfonia, 2002–10; Barbican Centre Trust, 2009–13. *Recreations:* chamber music, sailing, literature, wine, gardening. *Address:* Hoo Hall, Hoo, Woodbridge, Suffolk IP13 7QT. *T:* (01473) 737623. *E:* graham.nicholson1@btinternet.com. *Clubs:* Athenæum; Aldeburgh Yacht.

NICHOLSON, Jack; American film actor, director and producer; *b* 22 April 1937; *s* of John and Ethel May Nicholson; *m* 1961, Sandra Knight (marr. diss. 1966); one *d*. *Films include:* Cry-Baby Killer, 1958; Studs Lonigan, 1960; The Shooting (also produced); Easy Rider, 1969; Five Easy Pieces, 1970; The Last Detail, 1973; Chinatown, 1974; One Flew Over the Cuckoo's Nest, 1975 (Acad. Award for Best Actor, 1976); The Passenger, 1975; The Shining, 1980; The Postman Always Rings Twice, 1981; Reds, 1981; Terms of Endearment (Acad. Award for Best Supporting Actor), 1984; Prizzi's Honor, 1985; Heartburn, 1986; The Witches of Eastwick, 1986; Ironweed, 1987; Batman, 1988; The Two Jakes, 1991 (also dir.); A Few Good Men, 1992; Man Trouble, 1993; Hoffa, 1993; Wolf, 1994; The Crossing Guard, 1996; Mars Attacks!, 1997; Blood & Wine, 1997; As Good as it Gets (Acad. Award for Best Actor), 1998; The Pledge, 2001; About Schmidt, 2003; Anger Management, 2003; Something's Gotta Give, 2004; The Departed, 2006; The Bucket List, 2008; How Do You Know, 2011. *Address:* c/o Bresler Kelly & Associates, 11500 West Olympic Boulevard, Suite 510, Los Angeles, CA 90064–1529, USA.

NICHOLSON, James Frederick; farmer; Member for Northern Ireland, European Parliament, since 1989 (OUP, 1989–94; UU, 1994–2009; UCUNF, 2009–14; UU, since 2014); *b* 29 Jan. 1945; *s* of Thomas and Matilda Nicholson; *m* 1968, Elizabeth Gibson; six *s* one *d*. *Educ:* Aghavilly Primary Sch. Member: Armagh Dist Council, 1975–97 (Chm., 1994–95; Mayor of Armagh, March–June 1995); Southern Health and Social Services Bd, 1977–. Mem. (OU) Newry and Armagh, NI Assembly, 1982–86. Contested (OUP) Newry and Armagh, 1987. MP (OU) Newry and Armagh, 1983–85. *Address:* Ulster Unionist Party, European Office, Strandtown Hall, 2–4 Belmont Road, Belfast BT4 2AN. *E:* jim.nicholson@uup.org.

NICHOLSON, Rt Hon. Sir (James) Michael (Anthony), Kt 1988; PC 1995; a Lord Justice of Appeal, Supreme Court of Judicature, Northern Ireland, 1995–2007; *b* 4 Feb. 1933; *s* of late Cyril Nicholson, QC, DL and late Eleanor Nicholson (*née* Caffrey); *m* 1973, Augusta Mary Ada, *d* of late Thomas F. Doyle and of Mrs Elizabeth Doyle, Co. Cork; one *s* two *d*. *Educ:* Downside; Trinity College, Cambridge (MA). Called to the Bar of N Ireland, 1956; to English Bar, Gray's Inn, 1963 (Hon. Bencher, 1995); to Bar of Ireland, 1975; QC (NI), 1971; Bencher, Inn of Court of NI, 1978; Chm., Exec. Council of Inn of Court of NI and of Bar Council, 1983–85; High Court Judge, NI, 1986–95. Chm., Mental Health Review Tribunal (NI), 1973–76; Mem., Standing Adv. Commn for Human Rights (NI), 1976–78. High Sheriff, Co. Londonderry, 1972. President: Irish Cricket Union, 1978; NW ICU, 1986–93. *Recreations:* cricket, chess. *Address:* c/o Royal Courts of Justice, Chichester Street, Belfast, Northern Ireland BT1 3JF. *E:* jmanicholson@gmail.com. *Club:* MCC.

NICHOLSON, Prof. Jeremy Kirk, PhD; FRCPath, FMedSci; CBiol, FRSB, CChem, FRSC; Professor of Biological Chemistry, since 1998, Head, Department of Surgery and Cancer, since 2009, and Director, MRC-NIHR National Phenome Centre, since 2012, Imperial College London; *b* Lytham St Annes, Lancs, 19 Aug. 1956; *s* of James Nicholson and Mavis Nicholson (*née* Kirkland). *Educ:* Univ. of Liverpool (BSc Hons 1977); St Thomas's Hosp. Med. Sch., London (PhD 1980). CBiol 1982; MIBiol 1982, FRSB (FIBiol 2002); MRCPath 1992, FRCPath 1999; CChem 1993; FRSC 1993. RTZ Post Doctoral Res. Fellow, Dept of Chem., 1980–81, Lectr in Chem., 1981–82, Birkbeck Coll., Univ. of London; Lectr in Experimental Pathol. and Toxicol., Sch. of Pharmacy, Univ. of London, 1982–85; Birkbeck College, University of London: Lectr in Chem., 1985–89; Reader in Biol Chem., 1989–92; Prof. of Biol Chem., 1992–98; Imperial College London: Hd, Biol Chem., Biomedical Scis Div., Faculty of Medicine, 1998–2007; Hd, Dept of Biomolecular Medicine, Div. of Surgery, Oncol., Reproductive Biol. and Anaesthetics, Faculty of Medicine, 2007–09. Honorary Professor: of Molecular Systems Biol., Shanghai Jiao Tong Univ., 2005; of Analytical Chem., Inst. of Chemical Phys, Chinese Acad. of Scis, Dalian, 2005; Dept of Chem., Tsinghua Univ., Beijing, 2005; of Medicine, Zhe-Jaing Univ., Hongzhou, 2005; of Systems Biol., Shanghai Univ. of Traditional Chinese Medicine, 2005; of Biol Spectroscopy, State Key Lab. of Magnetic Resonance and Molecular and Atomic Phys, Chinese Acad. of Scis, Wuhan, 2006; Einstein Hon. Prof., Chinese Acad. of Scis, 2014; Honorary Director: Metabonomics Res. Centre, Inst. of Chem. Phys, Chinese Acad. of Scis, Dalian, 2006; Wuhan Key State Lab. of Magnetic Resonance Res., Chinese Acad. of Scis, Wuhan, 2006; Vis. Prof., Nanyang Technical Univ., Singapore, 2012. Fellow, British Toxicol Soc., 2006; FMedSci 2010. Hon. Member: Nat. Magnetic Resonance Soc., India, 2009; Soc. of Toxicology, USA, 2013; Hon. Fellow, Metabolomics Soc., USA, 2013. Lectures: Theophilus Redwood, RSC, 2007; NIH Stars in Cancer and Nutrition Dist., 2010; Robert E. Stowell, Univ. of Calif, Davis, 2014. SAC Silver Medal, 1992, SAC Gold Medal, 1997, Silver Medal for Chemical Biol., 2003, Interdisciplinary Prize, 2008, RSC; Jubilee Silver Medal, British Chromatographic Soc., 1994; Pfizer Internat. Acad. Innovation Award for Chemical and Medicinal Technol., 2002; Pfizer Global Discovery Chem. Discipline Prize, 2006; Thompson-Reuters ISI Highly Cited Researcher (Pharmacol. and Toxicol.), 2014. *Publications:* over 700 articles in major internat. jls on metabolic spectroscopy, disease diagnosis and systems medicine. *Recreation:* scuba diving. *Address:* Department of Surgery and Cancer, Sir Alexander Fleming Building, Faculty of Medicine, Imperial College London, Exhibition Road, SW7 2AZ. *T:* (020) 7594 3195, *Fax:* (020) 7549 3221. *E:* j.nicholson@imperial.ac.uk.

NICHOLSON, Jeremy Mark; QC 2000; FCIArb; *b* 21 March 1955; *s* of Eric Day Nicholson and Joy Nicholson; *m* 1987, Elizabeth Brooke-Smith; two *s*. *Educ:* Rugby Sch.; Trinity Hall, Cambridge (MA); Coll. of Law. Called to the Bar, Middle Temple, 1977 (Harmsworth Schol.); in practice at the Bar, 1978–; arbitrator, 2011–. FCIArb 2011. *Recreations:* sailing, travelling, walking, pursuing superficial interests. *Address:* 4 Pump Court, Temple, EC4Y 7AN. *T:* (020) 7842 5555. *Club:* Royal Automobile.

NICHOLSON, Prof. Keith, PhD; CChem, FRSC; Chief Executive Officer, Skaill Advisory Services, since 2000; *b* Lochinver; *m* Angela. *Educ:* Kelvin Hall Sch., Hull; Univ. of Manchester (BSc Hons; MSc); Univ. of Strathclyde (PhD 1983). CChem 1986; FRSC 1986. Certified Inf. Security Manager 2003; Certified Inf. Systems Auditor 2004. Consultant, Geoconsultancy Services, Glasgow, 1983–85; Lectr, Univ. of Papua New Guinea, 1986–87; Asst Prof., Geothermal Energy Inst., Univ. of Auckland, 1987–90; Prof. of Energy and the Envmt, Robert Gordon Univ. (formerly Inst. of Technol.), Aberdeen, 1991–99; Prof. of Energy and Envmtl Engrg, Univ. of Aalborg, 1999–2000. Chief Executive Officer: Envirosurveys, Auckland, 1987–90; TP Gp, 1991–2000. Technol. Advr, Scottish Govt, 2008–; Mem., Scottish Govt Cyber Security Adv. Bd, 2011–. Chm., Revenue Scotland, 2015–; non-executive Board Member: Scottish Natural Heritage, 2010– (Chm., Audit and Risk Cttee, 2010–); SEPA, 2011– (Mem., Audit Cttee, 2011–); SFC, 2012– (Member: Audit Cttee, 2012–; Res. and Knowledge Exchange Cttee, 2012–). Hon. Fellow, Univ. of Paisley, 2002–07. Fellow, Assoc. of Applied Geochemists, 1986. MInstD 2001. *Publications:* (ed) Geothermal Energy, 1987; (ed) Geothermal Energy, 1989; Doing Business on the Internet, 1993; Geothermal Fluids: chemistry and exploration techniques, 1993, 2nd edn 2011; (jtly) Skye: the complete visitor's guide, 1994; (ed) Manganese Mineralisation, 1997; (ed) Energy and the Environment, 1999; over 150 scientific papers and reports. *Recreations:* wildlife, hill-walking, photography, golf, archaeology, antiquarian books, malt whisky. *E:* knicholson@knicholson.co.uk.

NICHOLSON, Lindsay, (Mrs Mark Johansen), FRAS; Editorial Director, Good Housekeeping, since 2008; *b* 7 Aug. 1956; *d* of late Anthony Cuthbertson-Nicholson and of Sheila (*née* Pigram); *m* 1st, 1981, John Merritt (*d* 1992); one *d* (and one *d* decd); 2nd, 2004, Mark Johansen. *Educ:* University Coll. London (BSc Hons Astronomy and Physics). Editl trng scheme, Mirror Gp Newspapers, 1978–80; worked on magazines: Woman's Own, 1981–83; Honey, 1983–84; Living, 1984–85; Best, 1987–89; Woman, 1992–95; Editor-in-Chief: Prima (incl. Launch of Prima Baby and Your Home), 1995–99; Good Housekeeping mag., 1999–2006; Editl Dir, National Magazine Co., 2006–08. Chairman: BSME, 1997; Women in Journalism, 2002–04; Editl Trng Cttee, PPA, 2002–05; Press Complaints Comr, 2008–14. Mem. Council, UCL, 2014–. Trustee, Home-Start, 2000–08; Patron, The Way (Widowed and Young) Foundn, 2007–13. FRAS 2003. Hon. Vis. Prof., City Univ., 2007–. Churchwarden, St Bride's, Fleet St, 2012–13. Editor of Year, 1999, Chairman's Award, 2005, PPA; Mark Boxer Award, BSME, 2007. *Publications:* Living on the Seabed, 2005. *Recreations:* horse-riding, power walking. *Address:* Good Housekeeping, 72 Broadwick Street, W1F 9EP. *T:* (020) 7439 5247. *Club:* Groucho.

NICHOLSON, Margaret Anne Windham; *see* Heffernan, M. A. W.

NICHOLSON, Maria Bernadette; *see* Maguire, M. B.

NICHOLSON, Martin Buchanan, CMG 1997; HM Diplomatic Service, retired; Associate Fellow, Royal Institute of International Affairs, 1999–2002; *b* 12 Aug. 1937; 2nd *s* of late Carroll and Nancy Nicholson; *m* 1964, Raili Tellervo Laaksonen; one *s* one *d*. *Educ:* Oundle Sch.; St Catharine's Coll., Cambridge (BA 1961; MA 1964); Moscow Univ. (Post-grad.). Entered Foreign Office, 1963; served Moscow, 1965–68 and 1971; Prague, 1972–75; Research Dept, FCO, 1975–78 and 1981–86; Mem., UK Delegn to MBFR, Vienna, 1978–81; Advr on Soviet, later Russian, Affairs, Cabinet Office (on secondment), 1987–94; Minister-Counsellor, Moscow, 1994–97. Res. Associate, IISS, 1998–99. *Publications:* Towards a Russia of the Regions, 1999; Memories of Childhood, 2008; On the Fringes of Europe: student years, 2011; Activities Incompatible: memoirs of a Kremlinologist and a family man, 2013; articles on Soviet and Russian affairs in The World Today and Internat. Affairs. *Recreations:* memoirs, family history, playing the flute, gardening. *Address:* 13 Riverdale Gardens, Twickenham TW1 2BX. *T:* (020) 8892 8214.

See also Sir R. B. Nicholson.

NICHOLSON, Rt Hon. Sir Michael; *see* Nicholson, Rt Hon. Sir J. M. A.

NICHOLSON, Michael Thomas, OBE 1992; Senior Foreign Correspondent, ITN, 1991–98; *b* 9 Jan. 1937; *s* of Major Allan Nicholson and Doris Alice (*née* Reid); *m* 1968, Diana Margaret Slater; two *s*, and two adopted *d*. *Educ:* Leicester Univ. (BA). Joined ITN, 1963: News Editor, 1965–66; War Correspondent, 1968–94: Nigeria, Biafra, Beirut, Jordan, Cyprus, Congo, Israel, Indo-Pakistan, Rhodesia, Angola, Falklands, Gulf, Bosnia, Croatia; Southern Africa Corresp., 1977–81; Newscaster, 1982–86; Washington Corresp., Channel 4, 1989–90; reporter and presenter, Tonight prog., ITV, 1998–2009. Broadcasting Guild Award for coverage of Cyprus war, 1974; Silver Medal for coverage of Vietnam war, Monte Carlo Film/TV Fest., 1976; RTS Journalist of the Year, 1978, 1982, 1991; BAFTA award for coverage of Falklands War, 1982; Gold medallist, New York Film/TV Awards, 1992, 1998; RTS Sports News Journalist of the Year, 1998. Campaign Medals: Falklands War, 1982; Gulf War, 1991; Baghdad, Gulf War II, 2003. *Publications:* Partridge Kite, 1976; Red Joker, 1978; December Ultimatum, 1981; Pilgrims Rest, 1983; Across the Limpopo, 1986; A Measure of Danger, 1991; Natasha's Story, 1993 (filmed as Welcome to Sarajevo, 1996); A State of War Exists: reporters in the line of fire, 2012. *Recreations:* sailing, walking. *Address:* Lurgashall, W Sussex; c/o Peters Fraser and Dunlop, 34–43 Russell Street, WC2B 5HA.

NICHOLSON, Prof. Nigel, PhD; FBPsS; Professor of Organisational Behaviour, London Business School, since 1990; *b* Banbury, 1 June 1944; *s* of Hubert Nicholson and Barbara Nicholson (*née* Collard); two *s* two *d* by former marriages; *m* 2002, Adèle Nsengiyumva; one *s*. *Educ:* University Coll., Cardiff (BA Hons Psychol. 1975; PhD 1988). Sen. Res. Fellow, MRC/ESRC Social and Applied Psychol. Res. Unit, Univ. of Sheffield, 1972–90. FBAM 1994; Fellow, Internat. Assoc. of Applied Psychol., 1998; FFFI. *Publications:* Steel Strike, 1983; Managerial Job Change, 1988; Managing the Human Animal, 2000; (ed) Blackwell Encyclopedic Dictionary of Organisational Behaviour, 2004; Traders: risks, decisions and management in financial markets, 2005; Family Wars, 2008; The 'I' of Leadership, 2013; over 200 articles. *Recreations:* being a dad, playing jazz flute, tennis, reading, writing, music, advancing understanding of evolution on modern life and business. *Address:* 8 The Squirrels, Pinner, Middx HA5 3BD. *E:* nnicholson@london.edu.

NICHOLSON, Sir Paul (Douglas), KCVO 2011; Kt 1993; Chairman, Vaux Group, 1976–99 (Managing Director, 1971–92); Lord-Lieutenant, County Durham, 1997–2013; *b* 7 March 1938; *s* of late Douglas Nicholson, TD and Pauline Nicholson; *m* 1970, Sarah, *y d* of Sir Edmund Bacon, Bt, KG, KBE, TD; one *d*. *Educ:* Harrow; Clare College, Cambridge (MA). FCA. Lieut, Coldstream Guards, 1956–58; joined Vaux Breweries, 1965. Chm., Northern Investors Co., 1984–89; Director: Tyne Tees Television, then Yorkshire-Tyne Tees Television Hldgs, 1981–97; Northern Development Co., 1986–2000; Northern Electric, 1990–97; Scottish Investment Trust plc, 1998–2005; Steelite International plc, 2000–02. Chm., Urban Develt Corp. for Tyne and Wear, 1987–98. Chm., N Region, CBI, 1977–79; Chm., N Regional Bd, British Technology Group, 1979–84. Chm., Brewers and Licensed Retailers Assoc. (formerly Brewers' Soc.), 1994–96; Pres., NE Chamber of Commerce, 1995–96. High Sheriff, Co. Durham, 1980–81; DL Co. Durham, 1980. *Publications:* Brewer At Bay (memoirs), 2003. *Recreations:* deerstalking, riding and driving horses (winner, Liverpool Foxhunters' Steeplechase, 1963 and 1965; Pres., Coaching Club, 1990–97). *Address:* Quarry Hill, Brancepeth, Durham DH7 8DW. *T:* (0191) 378 0275. *Clubs:* Boodle's, Pratt's; Northern Counties (Newcastle upon Tyne).

See also F. Nicholson.

NICHOLSON, Paul James, OBE 2006; FRCP; Associate Medical Director, Global Medical Operations, Procter & Gamble, since 2011; *s* of James and Margaret Nicholson. *Educ:* Univ. of Newcastle upon Tyne (MB BS 1981). MRCGP 1986; AFOM 1986, MFOM 1992, FFOM 1998; DAvMed 1990; MIOSH 1994, FIOSH 1999; FRCP 2000. MO, RAF, 1981–91 (Sqdn Leader). Occupational Physician, ICI Chemicals & Polymers Ltd, Teesside, 1991–93; Sen. Corporate Med. Advr, Procter & Gamble UK and Ireland, 1993–2005; Associate Med. Dir, Procter & Gamble Beauty Care, EMEA, 2000–11. Faculty of Occupational Medicine: Mem. Bd, 1996–99, 1999–2000 and 2006–08; Mem., Fellowship Cttee, 1999–2003; Clin. Lead, Occupational Health Standards and Accreditation, 2008–11; Society of Occupational Medicine: Hon. Asst Ed., 1991–2000; Mem. Council, 1993–95, 1999–2002; Pres., 2000–01; British Medical Association: Mem., Occupational Medicine Cttee, 1996–2005, 2006–; Chair, 2008–; Fellow, 2015; British Occupational Health Research Foundation: Vice Chm., 2003–04, Chm., 2008–10, Occupational Asthma Res. Wkg Gp; Chm., Occupational Contact Dermatitis Res. Wkg Gp, 2008–10; Mem., Res. Cttee, 2008–11. *Publications:* (contrib.) BASICS Monographs on Immediate Care, 1986, 2nd edn 1990; Occupational Asthma: prevention, identification and management: systematic review and recommendations, 2010; Occupational Contact Dermatitis and Urticaria: prevention, identification and management: systematic review and recommendations, 2010; Occupational Health Service Standards for Accreditation, 2010; contrib. papers to jls on aeromedical helicopters, gender and pilots, unemployment, aging workers, cyanide antidotes, shiftwork, occupational asthma, occupational contact dermatitis, health risk communication, occupational health services and systematic reviews. *Address:* Procter & Gamble, Whitehall Lane, Egham, Surrey TW20 9NW. *E:* pjnicholson@doctors.org.uk.

NICHOLSON, Ralph Lambton Robb; Secretary, United Kingdom Atomic Energy Authority, 1984–86; *b* 26 Sept. 1924; *s* of Ralph Adam Nicholson and Kathleen Mary Nicholson (*née* Robb); *m* 1951, Mary Kennard; one *s* two *d*. *Educ:* Sherborne School; Cambridge Univ.; Imperial College, London (BSc; ACGI). FIChemE. Royal Engineers, 1943–47. Chemical engineer, Distillers Co., 1950–51; Wellcome Foundation, 1951–54; Fisons, 1954–58; planning and commercial manager, UKAEA, 1958–67; Dir, Min. of Technology Programmes Analysis Unit, 1967–71; Principal Programmes and Finance Officer, UKAEA, 1971–84. *Publications:* contribs to energy and management jls. *Recreations:* gardening, music, canals. *Address:* The Garth, Midgham, Reading, Berks RG7 5UJ. *T:* (0118) 971 2211.

NICHOLSON, Robin Alaster, CBE 1999; Director, Cullinan Studio (formerly Edward Cullinan Architects), since 1989 (Partner, 1979–89); *b* 27 July 1944; *s* of late Gerald Hugh Nicholson and Margaret Evelyn Nicholson (*née* Hanbury); *m* 1969, Fiona Mary Bird; three *s*. *Educ:* Eton Coll.; Magdalene Coll., Cambridge (MA); University Coll. London (MSc 1969). RIBA 1989. Architect: Evan Walker Associates, Toronto, 1966; James Stirling, Chartered Architects, 1969–76; Boza Lührs Muzard, Santiago, Chile, 1973; Tutor in Architecture: UCL, 1974–76; Poly of N London, 1976–79. Vis. Fellow, Univ. of Wales, 1984; Hon. Prof., Univ. of Nottingham, 2013–. 9th Happold Medal Lect., Construction Industry Council, 2013. Dir, RIBA Journals Ltd, 1993–97. Mem. Council, 1991–97, Vice Pres., 1992–94, RIBA; Chm., Construction Industry Council, 1998–2000; Mem. Bd, Movement for Innovation, 1998–2002; Mem., DETR, subseq. DTLR, then ODPM, Urban Sounding Bd, 2001–03; Comr, Commn for Architecture and the Built Envmt, 2002–10; Dir, NHBC, 2007–13. Chm., Cambs Quality Panel, 2010–. FRSA 1995. Hon. FIStructE 2002; Hon. FCIBSE 2013. *Recreations:* gardening, making things. *Address:* (office) 5 Baldwin Terrace, N1 7RU. *T:* (020) 7704 1975. *Club:* The Edge.

NICHOLSON, Sir Robin (Buchanan), Kt 1985; PhD; FRS 1978; FREng; *b* 12 Aug. 1934; *s* of late Carroll and Nancy Nicholson; *m* 1st, 1958, Elizabeth Mary Caffyn (*d* 1988); one *s* two *d*; 2nd, 1991, Yvonne, *d* of late Arthur and Gwendoline Appleby. *Educ:* Oundle Sch.; St Catharine's Coll., Cambridge (BA 1956; PhD 1959; MA 1960). FIMMM; MInstP; FREng (FEng 1980). University of Cambridge: Demonstrator in Metallurgy, 1960; Lectr in Metallurgy, 1964; Fellow of Christ's Coll., 1962–66, Hon. Fellow 1984; Prof. of Metallurgy, Univ. of Manchester, 1966. Inco Europe Ltd: Dir of Research Lab., 1972; Dir, 1975; Man. Dir, 1976–81; Co-Chm., Biogen NV, 1979–81. Chief Scientific Advr to Cabinet Office, 1983–85 (Central Policy Review Staff, 1981–83). Director: Pilkington Brothers, then Pilkington, plc, 1986–96; Rolls-Royce plc, 1986–2005; BP plc, 1987–2005. Chairman: CEST, 1987–90; ACOST, 1990–93. Member: SERC (formerly SRC), 1978–81; Council for Sci. and Technol., 1993–2000. Mem. Council: Royal Soc., 1983–85; Fellowship of Engrg, 1986–89; Gov., Exeter Univ., 2005–. Pres., Inst. of Materials, 1997–98. Foreign Associate, Nat. Acad. of Engrg, USA, 1983. CCMI. Founder MAE 1988. Hon. FIChemE; Hon. Fellow UMIST, 1988. Hon. DSc: Cranfield, 1983; Aston, 1983; Manchester, 1985; Hon. DMet Sheffield, 1984; Hon. DEng Birmingham, 1986; DUniv Open, 1987. Rosenhain Medallist, Inst. of Metals, 1971; Platinum Medal, Metals Soc., 1982. *Publications:* Precipitation Hardening (with A. Kelly), 1962; (jtly) Electron Microscopy of Thin Crystals, 1965; (ed and contrib. with A. Kelly) Strengthening Methods in Crystals, 1971; numerous papers to learned jls. *Recreations:* family life, gardening, music. *Club:* MCC.

See also M. B. Nicholson.

Ní CHUILÍN, Carál; Member (SF) Belfast North, Northern Ireland Assembly, since 2007; Minister for Culture, Arts and Leisure, since 2011; *b* New Lodge, Belfast. *Educ:* Open Univ. (BSc Social Scis 1994). Imprisoned on explosives charges, 1989; released, 1993. Co-ordinator, Tar Anall, support services for political ex-prisoners and families. Mem. (SF) Belfast CC, 2005–07. Formerly Co-chair: N Belfast Partnership Bd; Urban II. *Address:* Northern Ireland Assembly, Parliament Buildings, Stormont, Belfast BT4 3XX.

NICKELL, Sir Stephen John, Kt 2015; CBE 2007; FBA 1993; Warden, Nuffield College, Oxford, 2006–12; *b* 25 April 1944; *s* of John Edward Hilary Nickell and Phyllis Nickell; *m* 1976, Susan Elizabeth (*née* Pegden); one *s* one *d*. *Educ:* Merchant Taylors' Sch.; Pembroke Coll., Cambridge (BA; Hon. Fellow 2006); LSE (MSc). Maths teacher, Hendon County Sch., 1965–68; London School of Economics: Lectr, 1970–77; Reader, 1977–79; Prof. of Economics, 1979–84; Dir, Inst. of Econs and Stats, Prof. of Econs, and Fellow of Nuffield Coll., Oxford Univ., 1984–98; Sch. Prof. of Econs, LSE, 1998–2005. Member: Academic Panel, HM Treasury, 1981–89; ESRC, 1990–94; Monetary Policy Cttee, Bank of England, 2000–06; Bd, UK Statistics Authy, 2008–10; UK Budget Responsibility Cttee, 2010–; Chairman: Nat. Housing and Planning Advice Unit, 2006–09; Adv. Cttee on Civil Costs, 2007–10. President: Eur. Assoc. of Labour Economists, 1999–2002; REconS, 2001–04 (Mem. Council, 1984–94). Fellow, Econometric Soc., 1980. Hon. Member: Amer. Economic Assoc., 1997; Amer. Acad. Arts and Scis, 2006. Hon. Fellow, Nuffield Coll., Oxford, 2003. Hon. DSc Warwick, 2008. IZA Prize in Labor Econs, 2008. *Publications:* The Investment Decisions of Firms, 1978; (with R. Layard and R. Dornbusch) The Performance of the British Economy, 1988; (with R. Jackman and R. Layard) Unemployment, 1991; (with R. Jackman and R. Layard) The Unemployment Crisis, 1994; The Performance of Companies, 1995; articles in learned jls. *Recreations:* reading, cricket, cooking. *E:* steve.nickell@nuffield.ox.ac.uk.

NICKERSON, Rachel; *see* Campbell-Johnston, R.

NICKLAUS, Jack William; professional golfer, 1961–2000; *b* 21 Jan. 1940; *s* of Louis Charles Nicklaus and Helen (*née* Schoener); *m* 1960, Barbara Jean Bash; four *s* one *d*. *Educ:* Upper Arlington High Sch.; Ohio State Univ. Won US Amateur golf championship, 1959, 1961; became professional golfer, 1961; designs golf courses in USA, Europe, and Far East; Chm., Golden Bear Internat. Inc. Captained US team which won 25th Ryder Cup, 1983. *Major wins include:* US Open, 1962, 1967, 1972, 1980; US Masters, 1963, 1965, 1966, 1972, 1975, 1986; US Professional Golfers' Assoc., 1963, 1971, 1973, 1975, 1980; British Open, 1966, 1970, 1978, and many other championships in USA, Europe, Australia and Far East. Hon. Dr Athletic Arts Ohio State, 1972; Hon. LLD St Andrews, 1984. Presidential Medal of Freedom (USA), 2005. *Publications:* My 55 Ways to Lower Your Golf Score, 1962; Take a Tip from Me, 1964; The Greatest Game of All, 1969 (autobiog.); Lesson Tee, 1972; Golf My Way, 1974; The Best Way to Better Your Golf, vols 1–3, 1974; Jack Nicklaus' Playing Lessons, 1976; Total Golf Techniques, 1977; On and Off the Fairway, 1979 (autobiog.); The Full Swing, 1982; My Most Memorable Shots in the Majors, 1988; Jack Nicklaus: my story, 1997. *Address:* (office) 11780 US Highway #1, North Palm Beach, FL 33408, USA.

NICKLESS, Edmund Francis Paul, CSci, CGeol, FGS; Executive Secretary, Geological Society of London, 1997–2015; *b* 25 Jan. 1947; *e s* of Philip Wilfred Nickless and Gabrielle Frances Nickless (*née* Hughes); *m* 1970, Elisabeth Deborah Pickard; two *d*. *Educ:* Salvatorian Coll., Harrow; Queen Mary Coll., Univ. of London (BSc). FGS 1971; CGeol 1990; EurGeol 2002; CSci 2004. Various posts with British Geol Survey, London and Edinburgh, 1968–83; Sec., Earth Scis Directorate, NERC, Swindon, 1983–89; Envmtl Advr, Sci. and Technol. Secretariat, Cabinet Office, 1989–91; Asst Dir, British Geol Survey, 1991–97. FRSA 1998. *Publications:* various papers on geology in learned jls and official pubns of British Geol Survey. *Recreations:* listening to music, gardening, walking. *Address:* Ringrose House, Main Street, Belton-in-Rutland LE15 9LB. *T:* (01572) 717324. *Club:* Athenæum.

NICKLIN, Matthew James; QC 2013; a Recorder, since 2009; *b* Oxford, 1970; *s* of Hugh David James Nicklin and Gillian Gawith Nicklin. *Educ:* Tasker-Milward Sch., Haverfordwest; Newcastle Univ. (LLB (Hons) 1st Cl. 1992). Called to the Bar, Lincoln's Inn, 1993; in practice as barrister, specialising in defamation and privacy law, 1996–; Jt Hd of Chambers, 5RB, 2014–. Barrister Mem., Bar Standards Bd, 2007–13. FRSA 2010. *Publications:* The Law of Privacy and the Media, 2002, 2nd edn 2011. *Recreations:* scuba diving, travel. *Address:* 5 Gray's Inn Square, Gray's Inn, WC1R 5AH. *T:* (020) 7242 2902, *Fax:* (020) 7831 2686. *E:* matthewnicklin@5rb.com. *Clubs:* Century, Rushmore, Ivy.

NICKLIN, Susanna; Chairman, Marsh Agency Ltd, since 2013; *b* 26 June 1964; *d* of Philip and Hilary Nicklin; *m* 1997, Paul Marsh (*d* 2009); one *s* one *d*. *Educ:* Exeter Coll., Oxford (MA). Literary Agent, 1987–2002; Dir, English PEN, 2002–05; Dir, Literature, British Council, 2005–13. *Recreations:* walking, opera, family, friends, France. *Address:* c/o Marsh Agency Ltd, 50 Albermarle Street, W1S 4BD. *T:* (020) 7493 7361. *E:* susie@susienicklin.com.

NICKOLS, Herbert Arthur; Headmaster, Westonbirt School, Tetbury, Gloucestershire, 1981–86; *b* 17 Jan. 1926; *s* of Herbert and Henrietta Elizabeth Nickols; *m* 1953, Joyce Peake; two *s* one *d*. *Educ:* Imperial Coll., Univ. of London (BSc). ACGI. Res. Demonstrator, Imperial Coll., 1947–49; Housemaster, Sen. Science Master and later Dep. Headmaster, St Edmund's Sch., Canterbury, Kent, 1949–81. *Recreations:* music, travel, cricket. *Address:* 39 Carlton Leas, The Leas, Folkestone, Kent CT20 2DJ. *T:* (01303) 254749.

NICKSON, family name of **Baron Nickson**.

NICKSON, Baron *cr* 1994 (Life Peer), of Renagour in the District of Stirling; **David Wigley Nickson,** KBE 1987 (CBE 1981); FRSE; Vice Lord-Lieutenant of Stirling and Falkirk, 1997–2005; *b* 27 Nov. 1929; *s* of late Geoffrey Wigley Nickson and Janet Mary Nickson; *m* 1st, 1952, Helen Louise Cockcraft (*d* 2012); three *d*; 2nd, 2013, Mrs Eira Drysdale (*née* Govett). *Educ:* Eton; RMA, Sandhurst. Commnd Coldstream Guards, 1949–54. Joined Wm Collins, 1954; Dir, 1961–85; Jt Man. Dir, 1967; Vice Chm., 1976–83; Gp Man. Dir, 1979–82; Chm., Pan Books, 1982. Director: Scottish United Investors plc, 1970–83; General Accident plc, 1971–98 (Dep. Chm., 1993–98); Scottish & Newcastle (formerly Scottish & Newcastle Breweries) plc, 1981–95 (Dep. Chm., 1982–83; Chm., 1983–89); Clydesdale Bank, 1981–89 (Dep. Chm., 1990–91; Chm., 1991–98); Radio Clyde PLC, 1982–85; Edinburgh Investment Trust plc, 1983–94; Hambro's PLC, 1989–98; National Australia Bank Ltd, 1991–96. Mem., H of L, 1994–2015. Chm., Top Salaries, then Sen. Salaries, Rev. Body, 1989–95; Chairman: SDA, 1989–90, Scottish Enterprise, 1990–93; CBI in Scotland, 1979–81; Pres., CBI, 1986–88 (Dep. Pres., 1985–86). Member: Scottish Indust. Develt Adv. Bd, 1975–80; Scottish Econ. Council, 1980–94; NEDC, 1985–88; Scottish Cttee, Design Council, 1978–81; Nat. Trng Task Force, 1989–91. Chairman: Countryside Commn for Scotland, 1983–85; Scottish Adv. Cttee, ICRF, 1994–2001; Atlantic Salmon Trust, 1989–96 (Mem., Council of Management, 1982–; Vice-Pres., 1996–); Conon Dist Salmon Fishery Bd, 1994–2005; Sec. of State for Scotland's Atlantic Salmon Task Force, 1996; Pres., Assoc. of Scottish Dist Salmon Fishery Bds, 1996–2011 (Vice Chm., 1989–92); Dir, Countryside Alliance, 1998–2000. Chairman: Cromarty Firth Fisheries Trust, 1999–2012; Loch Lomond Shores Trust, 1999–2002. Trustee: Game Conservancy, 1988–91; Prince's Youth Business Trust, 1987–90; Princess Royal's Trust for Carers, 1990–94. Chancellor, Glasgow Caledonian Univ., 1993–2002. Capt., Queen's Body Guard for Scotland, Royal Co. of Archers. Freeman, City of London, 1999; Hon. Freeman, Fishmongers' Co., 1999. DL Stirling and Falkirk, 1982. CCMI (CBIM 1980); FRSE 1987. Hon. Fellow, Paisley Coll., subseq. Univ. of Paisley, 1992. DUniv Stirling, 1986; Hon. DBA Napier Polytechnic, 1990; DUniv Glasgow Caledonian, 1993. *Recreations:* fishing, shooting, bird watching, the countryside. *Address:* The River House, Doune, Perthshire FK16 6DA. *T:* (01786) 841614. *Clubs:* Boodle's, Flyfishers'.

NICKSON, John Denis; author; *b* Lytham St Annes, Lancs, 10 April 1947; *s* of Denis and Joan Nickson; *m* 2005, Simon Rew. *Educ:* Giggleswick Sch.; University Coll. London (BA Hons Anthropol. 1968). Actor and th. producer, 1968–75; fundraiser, London Samaritans, 1975–76; Dir, Information and Sponsorship, British Council, 1977–89; Dir of Develt, ENO, 1989–96; Director: RA Trust, Royal Acad. of Arts, 1996–2005; Tate Foundn, Tate, 2005–11. Gov., Atlantic Council, 1997–2010; Mem., Governing Council, RCM, 2012–. Trustee: London Music Masters, 2013–; Opera Rara, 2013–. *Publications:* Giving is Good for You: why Britain should be bothered and give more, 2013. *Recreations:* music, visual arts, reading, walking, talking, the weather. *T:* 07817 140540. *E:* johndnickson@gmail.com.

NICOL, family name of **Baroness Nicol**.

NICOL, Baroness *cr* 1982 (Life Peer), of Newnham in the County of Cambridgeshire; **Olive Mary Wendy Nicol;** *b* 21 March 1923; *d* of James and Harriet Rowe-Hunter; *m* 1947, Alexander Douglas Ian Nicol (CBE 1985); two *s* one *d*. Civil Service, 1943–48. Opposition Whip, 1983–87, Opposition Dep. Chief Whip, 1987–89, Dep. Speaker, 1995–2002, H of L; Member: H of L Science and Technol. Select Cttee, 1990–93; Envmt and Social Affairs sub-cttee, European Communities Cttee, 1993–95; Sustainable Develt Select Cttee, 1994–95; Select Cttee on Animals in Scientific Procedures, 2001–02; Member: Ecclesiastical Cttee, 1989–95; Sci. and Technol. Subcttee on Disposal of Nuclear Waste, 1998–99; Bd Mem., Parly OST, 1998–99. Trustee, Cambridge United Charities, 1967–86; Director, Cambridge and District Co-operative Soc., 1975–81, Pres. 1981–85; Member: Supplementary Benefits Tribunal, 1976–78; Cambridge City Council, 1972–82; Assoc. of District Councils, Cambridge Branch, 1974–76 and 1980–82; various school Governing Bodies, 1974–80; Council, Granta Housing Soc., 1975; Careers Service Consultative Group, 1978–81. JP Cambridge City, 1972–86. *Recreations:* reading, walking. *Address:* c/o House of Lords, SW1A 0PW.

NICOL, Hon. Sir Andrew (George Lindsay), Kt 2009; **Hon. Mr Justice Nicol;** a Judge of the High Court of Justice, Queen's Bench Division, since 2009; *b* 9 May 1951; *s* of late Duncan Rennie Nicol and Margaret (*née* Mason); *m* 2005, Camilla Palmer; two *s*. *Educ:* Selwyn Coll., Cambridge (BA, LLB); Harvard Law Sch. (LLM). Harkness Fellow, 1973–75; Special Assistant: to Dir of Housing and Community Develt, California, 1975–76; Allen Allen and Hemsley, solicitors, Sydney, NSW, 1976–77; Lectr in Law, LSE, 1977–87; called to the Bar, Middle Temple, 1978, Bencher, 2004; barrister, 1979–2009; QC 1995; Asst Recorder, 1998–2000; Recorder, 2000–09; Dep. High Court Judge, 2003–09; Presiding Judge, SE Circuit, 2011–14. Chm., Immigration Law Practitioners' Assoc., 1997–2000. *Publications:* (with G. Robertson) Media Law, 1984, 5th edn 2007; (with A. Dummett) Subjects, Citizens, Aliens and Others, 1990; (with G. Millar and A. Sharland) Media Law and Human Rights, 2001, 2nd edn 2009. *Recreations:* family, sailing, walking. *Address:* Royal Courts of Justice, Strand, WC2A 2LL.

NICOL, (Andrew) William; JP; BSc; FICE, FIMechE, FIET; Chairman, 1987–93, and Chief Executive, 1990–93, South Western Electricity plc; *b* 29 April 1933; *s* of Arthur Edward Nicol and Ethel Isabel Gladstone Nicol (*née* Fairley); *m* 1960, Jane Gillian Margaret Mann; one *s*. *Educ:* King's College School, Wimbledon; Durham Univ. (BSc). W. S. Atkins & Partners, 1960–67; Electricity Council, 1967–69; London Electricity Board, 1969–81; Dep. Chm., SE Electricity Board, 1981–87. Chairman: Trustees, NICEIC Pension Fund, 1986–93; South Western Enterprises, 1992–93. JP Surrey 1976. *Recreation:* Honourable Artillery Company. *Club:* Caledonian.

NICOL, Angus Sebastian Torquil Eyers; barrister, 1963–2013; a Recorder of the Crown Court, 1982–98; *b* 11 April 1933; *s* of late Henry James Nicol and Phyllis Mary Eyers; *m* 1968, Eleanor Denise Brodrick; two *d*. *Educ:* RNC, Dartmouth. Served RN, 1947–56. Called to the Bar, Middle Temple, 1963. A Chairman: Disciplinary Cttee, Potato Marketing Bd, 1988–96; VAT and Duties (formerly VAT) Tribunal, 1988–2005; Adjudicator and Special Adjudicator, Immigration Appellate Authy, 1998–2002; Mem., Appeals Cttee, later Disciplinary Tribunal, Taxation Disciplinary Bd, 2006–13. Founder Vice-Chm. and Mem. Council, Monday Club, 1961–68. Lectr in Gaelic, Central London Adult Educn Inst., 1983–96; Sen. Steward, Argyllshire Gathering, 1983, 1998; Dir, 1981–, and Jt Sec., 1984–, Highland Soc. of London; Conductor, London Gaelic Choir, 1985–91, 2012–; Chieftain of Clan MacNicol and Comr for all Territories of GB south of River Tweed, 1988–; President: Scottish Piping Soc. of London, 2006–08; Coisir Lunnainn (London Gaelic Choir), 2007–. Piping Correspondent, The Times, 1979–2014. FSA (Scot.). Lewis and Harris Gold Medal for Gaelic Poetry, Royal Nat. Mod, 2009. *Publications:* Gaelic poems and short stories in Gairm, etc. *Recreations:* music, Gaelic language and literature, shooting, fishing, sailing, gastronomy. *Address:* 30 Wellington Court, Maltings Place, Bagley's Lane, SW6 2BU.

NICOL, Dr Richard Charles, FREng, FIET; Director and Chief Executive Officer, Fynntek Ltd, research consulting, 2001–14; *b* 14 July 1948; *s* of George Nicol and Alice (*née* Ardley); *m* 1974, Rosemary Jane Greaves; one *s* one *d*. *Educ:* University Coll. London (BSc Eng; PhD 1976). FIET (FIEE 1994). Joined Post Office Res., 1970; British Telecommunications, 1976–88; Manager, Univ. Res. Prog., 1988–92; BT Laboratories, then BTexact Technologies: Divl Manager, Visual Telecomms, 1992–95; Hd, Centre for Human Communications, 1995–98; Hd of Res., 1998–2001. Chm., ICT (formerly Digital Communications) KTN, 2007–. Dir, Suffolk Develt Agency, 2000–09; Mem. Bd, Suffolk Learning and Skills Council, 2001–08. Chairman: of Corp., Suffolk New Coll. (formerly Suffolk Coll.), 2009–13 (Vice-Chm. Corp., 1995–2009); Suffolk New Acads Trust, 2013–14; Mem. Council, Univ. of Essex, 2006–11. FREng 2000. *Recreations:* sailing, football (Ipswich Town). *Club:* Ipswich and Suffolk.

NICOL, William; *see* Nicol, A. W.

NICOLI, Eric Luciano, CBE 2006; Chairman: R&R Music Ltd, since 2008; Nick Stewart & Associates Ltd, since 2010; Director, Cogniti Inc., since 2009; *b* 5 Aug. 1950; *s* of Virgilio and Ida Nicoli; *m* 1977, Rosalind West (marr. diss. 2005); one *s* one *d*; *m* 2006, Lucy Caldwell; two *d*. *Educ:* Diss Grammar Sch.; King's College London (BSc Hons 1st class Physics). Marketing, Rowntree Mackintosh, 1972–80; United Biscuits: Marketing, 1980–83; Business Planning, 1984; Managing Dir, Frozen Food Div., 1985, Biscuit and Confectionery Div., 1986–88; Chief Exec., Europe, 1989–90; Gp Chief Exec., 1991–99; Chm., HMV Gp plc, 2001–04 (Dir, 2000–04); Exec. Chm., Thorn EMI plc, then EMI Gp plc, 1999–2007 (Dir, 1993–2007; CEO, 2007); Chairman: Tussauds Gp, 2001–07 (Dir, 1999–2007); Vue Entertainment Ltd, 2006–10; Sen. Partner, Sunningdale Capital LLP, 2010–14. Non-exec. Dir, Greencore Gp plc, 2010–. Dep. Chm., BITC, 1991–2003. Chm., Per Cent Club, 1995–2007. Trustee, Comic Relief, 1999–2004; Chm., EMI Music Sound Foundn, 2003–09 (Trustee, 2001). *Recreations:* music, sport, food.

NICOLL, Alison Jane; *see* Watt, A. J.

NICOLL, Prof. Angus Gordon, CBE 2002; FRCP, FRCPCH, FFPH; Head, Influenza and Other Respiratory Viruses Programme, European Centre for Disease Prevention and Control, since 2011 (on secondment as National Expert, 2005–11); *b* 5 Aug. 1950; *s* of James Nicoll and Mary Laugharne; *m* 1982, Mary Grizel Braham; one *s* two *d*. *Educ:* Trinity Coll., Cambridge (MA; BChir 1976, MB 1977); Middlesex Hosp., LSHTM (MSc Epidemiol. 1985). Paediatric trng, London, Scotland and Nottingham; trng in public health, London and Africa; Sen. Lectr in HIV Epidemiol., LSHTM and in E Africa, 1987–91; Consultant, 1991–2011, Dir, Communicable Disease Surveillance Centre, 2000–05, HPA. Hon. Sen. Lectr, Inst. of Child Health, London, 1996–; Hon. Prof., LSHTM, 2001–. *Publications:* (ed jtly) Manual of Childhood Infections, 1987, 2001. *Recreations:* family, running and other outdoor pursuits, theatre, social history. *Address:* European Centre for Disease Prevention and Control, Granits väg 8, 17165 Solna, Sweden. *Clubs:* John Snow Society; St Albans Striders.

NICOLL, Douglas Robertson, CB 1980; retired; *b* 12 May 1920; *s* of James George Nicoll and Mabel Nicoll (*née* Styles); *m* 1st, 1949, Winifred Campion (*d* 1987); two *s*; 2nd, 1992, Mrs Cathryn Sansom. *Educ:* Merchant Taylors' School; St John's College, Oxford (MA 1946). FO (Govt Code & Cipher Sch., Bletchley Pk, deciphering German Enigma machine), 1941–45; FCO (GCHQ), 1946–80; Joint Services' Staff College, 1953; Under Secretary, 1977–80; Cabinet Office, 1980–81 (produced Nicoll Report on performance of Jt Intelligence Cttee which remains classified but conclusions published in *Cold War History*, 7:4, 2007). *Publications:* contrib. to DNB and Oxford DNB. *Recreations:* chess, bridge, National Hunt racing, politics. *Address:* c/o National Westminster Bank, 31 The Promenade, Cheltenham, Glos GL50 1LH. *Club:* Travellers.

NICOLL, Sir William, KCMG 1992 (CMG 1974); a Director General, Council of European Communities, 1982–91; *b* 28 June 1927; *s* of Ralph Nicoll and Christina Mowbray Nicoll (*née* Melville); *m* 1954, Helen Morison Martin; two *d*. *Educ:* Morgan Acad., Dundee; St Andrews Univ. Entered BoT, 1949; British Trade Comr, India, 1955–59; Private Sec. to Pres. of BoT, 1964–67; Commercial Inspector, FCO, 1967–69; DTI, 1969–72; Office of UK Perm. Rep. to European Communities, 1972–75; Under Sec., Dept of Prices and Consumer Protection, 1975–77; Dep. UK Rep. to EEC, 1977–82. Fulbright Fellow, George Mason Univ., Va, USA, 1991–92. Editor, European Business Jl, 1993–2002. Hon. LLD Dundee, 1983. *Publications:* (ed and contrib.) Competition Policy Enquiry, 1988; (with T. C. Salmon) Understanding the European Communities, 1990; (with T. C. Salmon) Understanding the New European Community, 1993; (ed jtly) Perspectives on European Business, 1995, 2nd edn 1998; (ed jtly) Europe 2000, 1996; Building European Union, 1997; Europe Beyond 2000, 1998; (with T. C. Salmon) Understanding European Union, 2000, Polish edn 2003; contributed to: Government and Industry, ed W. Rodgers, 1986; Britain and Europe, ed R. Butler, 1988; The State of the EC, ed G. Rosendahl, 1993; Margaret Thatcher, Prime Minister Indomitable, ed W. Thompson, 1994; Maastricht and Beyond, ed A. N. Duff, 1994; The Council of the EU, ed M. Westlake, 1996, 3rd edn 2006; Encyclopedia of the EU, ed D. Dinan, 1998; Britain, the Commonwealth and Europe, ed A. May, 2001; The EU Today, 2001; contribs to various jls on European subjects, to Oxford DNB and to local hist. studies. *Address:* Outback, Nackington Road, Canterbury, Kent CT4 7AX. *T:* (01227) 456495.

NICOLLE, Frederick Villeneuve, FRCSCan; Consultant Plastic Surgeon, Hammersmith Hospital, since 1970; Senior Lecturer, University of London and Royal Postgraduate Medical School, since 1970; *b* 11 March 1931; *s* of Arthur Nicolle and Alice Nicolle (*née* Cobbold); *m* 1957, Helia Immaculata Stuart-Walker; one *s* two *d*. *Educ:* Eton; Trinity Coll., Cambridge (BA; MB BChir 1956; MChir 1970). FRCSCan 1963. McLaughlin Travelling Fellow, Canada, 1964; Consultant Plastic Surgeon, Montreal Gen. Hosp. and Montreal Children's Hosp., 1964–69; Lectr, McGill Univ., 1964–69; returned to UK, 1970; in private practice in aesthetic and reconstructive plastic surgery, 1970–. Vis. Prof. in Plastic Surgery, China, Syria, S America, SA, Australia, NZ and guest lectr in many countries; Hon. Prof., Singapore Assoc. of Plastic Surgeons, 1980. President: Brit. Assoc. Aesthetic Plastic Surgery, 1984–86 (Mem., 1980–); Chelsea Clinical Soc., 1986; Internat. Alpine Surgical Soc., 1996, 1997; Treas., Internat. Soc. Aesthetic Plastic Surgery, 1986–94 (Trustee, 1992–94); Member: Brit. Assoc. Plastic Surgery, 1966; Internat. Soc. Plastic Surgery, 1971; Amer. Soc. Aesthetic Plastic Surgery, 1982. *Publications:* The Care of the Rheumatoid Hand, 1975; Aesthetic Rhinoplasty, 1996; chaps in numerous text books of plastic and reconstructive surgery; contrib. British Jl Plastic Surgery and Jl Aesthetic Surgery. *Recreations:* painting, ski-ing, shooting, fishing, tennis. *Address:* Chalet Tschariet, 116 Grubestrasse, 3778 Schonried, Switzerland. *T:* (33) 7448977. *Club:* White's.

NICOLLE, Stéphanie Claire; QC (Jersey) 1995; HM Solicitor General for Jersey, 1994–2008; *b* 11 March 1948; *d* of Walter Arthur Nicolle and Madeleine Claire Nicolle (*née* Vitel). *Educ:* Convent of the Faithful Companions of Jesus, Jersey; St Aidan's Coll., Univ. of Durham. Called to the Bar, Gray's Inn, 1976; called to the Jersey Bar, 1978; Crown Advocate, 1986–94. Adjunct Prof. of Immovable Property, Inst. of Law, Jersey, 2009–12. *Publications:* (with P. Matthews) The Jersey Law of Property, 1991; The Origin and Development of Jersey Law, 1998. *Address:* 11 Parade Road, St Helier, Jersey, Channel Islands JE2 3PL.

NICOLSON, family name of **Baron Carnock**.

NICOLSON, Adam; *see* Carnock, 5th Baron.

NICOLSON, John; MP (SNP) Dunbartonshire East, since 2015; *b* Glasgow, 1961; *s* of John Donald Nicolson and Marion Stant; partner, Juliano Zini. *Educ:* Univ. of Glasgow (MA Hons); Harvard Univ. (Harkness Fellow; Kennedy Schol.). Speech writer, US Senate, 1985–87; freelance journalist and broadcaster, 1987–2015: reporter for Newsnight, Assignment, Public Eye, Panorama, On the Record; presenter: News 24; BBC Breakfast; ITV News; contrib. The Times, Sunday Times, Observer, Sunday Telegraph, Guardian. SNP spokesperson on Culture, Media and Sport, 2015–. *Recreations:* travel, reading, music, cooking, art, exploring derelict buildings. *Address:* House of Commons, SW1A 0AA. *T:* (020) 7219 6857. *E:* john.nicolson.mp@parliament.uk.

NICOLSON, Juliet; writer; *b* Bransgore, Hants, 9 June 1954; *d* of Nigel Nicolson, OBE, author, and Philippa Janet, *d* of Sir (Eustace) Gervais Tennyson d'Eyncourt, 2nd Bt; *m* 1977, James Macmillan-Scott (marr. diss. 1995); two *d*; *m* 2009, Charles Vernon Anson, *qv*. *Educ:* Benenden Sch.; Westminster Tutors; St Hugh's Coll., Oxford (BA English Lit. 1976; MA). With Hamish Hamilton, 1976–81; Chatto & Windus, 1981–83; Atlantic Monthly Press/Grove Press, 1983–94; Ed Victor Ltd, Literary Agency, 1996–2000; writer and journalist, 2000–. *Publications:* The Perfect Summer: dancing into shadow in 1911, 2006; The Great Silence 1918–1920: living in the shadow of the Great War, 2009; Abdication, 2012. *Recreations:* talking, walking, cooking. *Address:* c/o Ed Victor Ltd, 6 Bayley Street, WC1B 3HE. *T:* (020) 7304 4100.

See also Baron Carnock.

NICOLSON, Margaret Mary; *see* Appleton, M. M.

NICOLSON, Roy Macdonald; Chief Executive, Scottish Amicable Life plc, 1997–2000; *b* 12 June 1944; *s* of Alan Neil Nicolson and Mary Nicolson; *m* 1972, Jennifer Margaret Miller; one *s* one *d*. *Educ:* Paisley Grammar School. FFA. Joined Scottish Amicable, 1960; Asst London Secretary, 1971; Asst Actuary, 1973; Pensions Manager (Operations), 1976; Asst Gen. Manager (Pensions), 1982; Gen. Manager (Systems), 1985; Dep. Chief Gen. Manager, then Man. Dir, 1990. Director: J. Rothschild Assurance Hldgs, 1991–99; St James's Place Capital, 1997–2000; Prudential Assurance Co., 1997–2000; Nat. Australia WM (Europe), 2001–04; Nat. Australia WM Hldgs, 2003–04; Nat. Australia Gp (Europe), 2004–12; Chairman: Advice First Ltd, 2002–04; BDO Stoy Hayward Wealth Mgt, 2004–10. *Recreations:* golf, bridge. *Address:* Ardgarten, Doune Road, Dunblane, Perthshire FK15 9HR. *T:* (01786) 823849.

NIEDUSZYŃSKI, Anthony John; Secretary to Monopolies and Mergers Commission, 1993–96; *b* 7 Jan. 1939; *er s* of Tadeusz Adolf Antoni Nieduszyński, LLD and Madaleine Gladys Lilian (*née* Huggler); *m* 1980, Frances, *yr d* of Wing Comdr Max Oxford, OBE; one *d*. *Educ:* St Paul's School (Foundation Scholar); Merton College, Oxford (Postmaster; 1st cl. Hon. Mods 1959; 1st cl. Lit Hum 1961; MA). Board of Trade, 1964; Private Sec. to Pres. of

BoT, 1967–68; Principal Private Sec. to Minister for Trade and Consumer Affairs, 1972–74 and to Sec. of State for Trade, 1974; Asst Sec., Dept of Prices and Consumer Protection, 1974, Dept of Industry, 1977, Home Office, 1982; Under Sec., DTI, 1985–93; Head: of Radiocommunications Div., 1985; of Air Div., 1988; of Business Task Forces Div. 2, 1990; of Aerospace Div., 1992. *Recreations:* Gregorian chant, growing olives in Tuscany, language, opera, grandchildren. *Address:* Clarendon House, 33 Strand, Topsham, Exeter, Devon EX3 0AY. *Clubs:* Farmers, Polish Hearth.

NIELSEN, Anne Hedensted; *see* Steffensen, A. H.

NIELSON, Poul; Member, European Commission, 1999–2004; *b* 11 April 1943; *s* of Svend and Esther Nielson; *m* 1967, Anne-Marie Jørgensen; one *s* two *d*. *Educ:* Århus Univ. (Masters degree in Political Sci. 1972). Nat. Chm., Social Democratic Student Movt, 1966–67; Chm., Foreign Affairs Cttee, SDP, 1974–79, 2009–; Mem., UN Sec. Gen.'s Adv. Bd on Water and Sanitation, 2004–. MP (SDP) Denmark, 1971–73, 1977–84, 1986–99; Minister of Energy, 1979–82; Minister for Develt Co-operation, 1994–99. Head of Section, Min. of Foreign Affairs, 1974–79, 1984–85; Cons. in Public Mgt, Danish Admin. Sch., 1985–86; Investment Cons., Danish Wage Earner Pensions Fund, 1985–88; Man. Dir, LD Energi A/S, 1988–94; Mem., Bd of Dirs, Denerco, Danop, Vestas and other cos, 1986–94. Adjunct Prof., Aalborg Univ., 2005–. Polio Eradication Champion Award, Rotary Internat., 1999. *Publications:* Power Play and Security, 1968; The Company Act and the Wage Earners, 1974; Politicians and Civil Servants, 1987; En hel Nielson (memoirs), 2011. *Recreations:* photography, literature, music, gardening.

NIEMAN, Sandra; *see* Horley, S.

NIENOW, Prof. Alvin William, FREng; Professor of Biochemical Engineering, University of Birmingham, 1989–2004, now Emeritus; *b* 19 June 1937; *o s* of late Alvin William Nienow and Mary May Nienow (*née* Hawthorn); *m* 1959, Helen Mary Sparkes; two *s* one *d*. *Educ:* St Clement Danes Grammar Sch.; University Coll. London (BSc Eng, 1st Cl. Hons; PhD; DSc Eng). FIChemE; CEng, FREng (FEng 1985); CSci 2003. Industry, 1958–61; Lectr and Sen. Lectr, 1963–80, Hon. Res. Fellow, 1980–, Dept of Chem. and Biochem. Engineering, UCL; University of Birmingham: Prof. of Chem. Engineering, 1980–89; Dir, SERC, later BBSRC, Centre for Biochem. Engrg, 1989–2000. Vis. Prof., Fellow and Lectr, China and Japan; Vis. Prof. of Biochem. Engrg, Loughborough Univ., 2009–. Eminent Speaker, Chemical Coll., IEAust, 1999; Plenary Lectr, Pharmaceutical Section, AIChE, 2009. Member: AFRC, 1987–90; Biotechnol. Directorate, SERC, 1990–93; Engrg Bd, SERC, then EPSRC, 1991–94; Planning and Resources Bd, BBSRC, 1994–96; Council, IChemE, 1984–89; Scientific Adv. Cttee, EFCE, 1987–94; Standing Cttee for Engrg, Royal Acad. of Engrg, 1996–98; Internat. Adv. Bd, Inst. of Chemical Process Fundamentals, Acad. of Scis, Czech Republic, 1996–; Peer Review Coll., Danish Council for Strategic Res., 2008–; numerous other scientific and engrg bodies. Consultant: BHR Gp Fluid Mixing Processes, 1985–; Rhône-Poulenc Conseil Technologique, 1988–2000 (Pres., 1998–2000). Mem., Governing Body, Silsoe Res. Inst., 1996–98. Hon. Mem., Czech Soc. of Chemical Engrg, 2008. Ed. (Europe and Africa), Jl Chem. Engrg, Japan, 2001–05. Dr *hc* W Pomeranian Univ. of Technol., 2010; Hon. DSc Loughborough, 2012. Moulton Medal, 1984, Donald Medal, 2000, IChemE; Jan E. Purkyne Medal, Czech Acad. of Science, 1993; Lifetime Contribution Award, Eur. Fedn of Chemical Engrg Wkg Party on Mixing, 2003; Special Contributions Medal, Szczecin Univ. of Technol., 2008. *Publications:* (jtly) Mixing in the Process Industries, 1985, 2nd edn revised 1997; (ed) 3rd International Conference on Bioreactor and Bioprocess Fluid Dynamics, 1993, 4th International Conference, 1997; (jtly) Biochemical Engineering Principles, 2005; numerous papers on mixing, fluidisation and biochem. engrg in learned jls. *Recreations:* sport, travel, dancing, music, real ale, ski-ing (Escapade Medal, Trois Vallées, 2012, 2015). *Address:* Department of Chemical Engineering, University of Birmingham, Edgbaston, Birmingham B15 2TT. *Clubs:* MCC; Edgbaston Priory, Reading Cricket.

NIGHTINGALE, Anne, MBE 2000; presenter, BBC Radio 1, since 1970; guest presenter, BBC Radio 2; *b* Osterley, W London; one *s* one *d*. *Educ:* Lady Eleanor Holles Sch., Hampton; Poly. of Central London (Dip. Journalism). Columnist, Cosmopolitan, 1975–78; Presenter, The Old Grey Whistle Test, BBC TV, 1978–82; regular broadcaster on BBC Radio 4; regular appearances as DJ at major music festivals, UK, Europe, USA and Asia. Music albums: Annie on One, 1995; y4K Presents: Annie Nightingale, 2007. Hon. DLitt Westminster, 2012. *Publications:* How to Form a Beat Group, 1965; Chase the Fade (autobiog.), 1982; Wicked Speed (autobiog.), 2000; contrib. The Guardian, The Times, Punch, Radio Times, etc. *Recreation:* studying architecture and tall buildings. *Address:* BBC Radio 1, W1W 6AJ. *E:* annienightingale@gmail.com.

NIGHTINGALE, Anthony John Liddell, CMG 2012; JP; Director, Jardine Matheson Holdings Ltd, since 1994; Managing Director, Jardine Matheson Group, 2006–12; *b* Huddersfield, 8 Nov. 1947; *s* of William John Nightingale and Rosemary Mabel Nightingale; *m* 1973, Christina Philomena de Souza; one *s* one *d*. *Educ:* Uppingham Sch.; Peterhouse, Cambridge (BA Hons Classics 1969). Joined Jardine Matheson Gp, 1969; various roles in Japan, Saudi Arabia and Hong Kong; Director: Jardine Cycle & Carriage Ltd, 1993– (Chm., 2002–12); Jardine Strategic Hldgs Ltd, 2006–; Dairy Farm Internat. Hldgs Ltd, 2006–; Hongkong Land Hldgs Ltd, 2006–; Mandarin Oriental Internat. Ltd, 2006–. Non-executive Director: Schindler Hldg AG, 2013–; Prudential plc, 2013–; Ind. non-exec. Dir, China Xintiandi Ltd, 2013–; Sen. Advr, Academic Partnerships Internat., 2012–14; Advr, Dickson Concepts, 2012–14. Chm., Hong Kong General Chamber of Commerce, 2003–05; Member: Hong Kong Port Develt Bd, 1991–98; Hong Kong Trade Develt Council, 2005–09; (Non-Official) Commn on Strategic Develt, 2006–12 and 2013–; Cttee on Strategic Enhancement of Hong Kong as an Internat. Financial Centre, 2010–; Cttee on Real Estate Investment Trusts, Securities and Futures Commn, 2011–; Adv. Council, Hong Kong Univ. of Sci. and Technol., 2013–. Hong Kong Rep., APEC Business Adv. Council, 2005–; Chm., Hong Kong-APEC Trade Policy Study Gp Ltd, 2010–. Vice Pres., Real Estate Developers Assoc. of Hong Kong, 2007–13. Chm., 1995–2005, Patron, 2012–, Hong Kong Tennis Foundn; Chm., Sailors Home and Missions to Seamen, 2006–. Member: Chongqing Mayor's Internat. Adv. Council, 2010–12; Adv. Panel, UK ASEAN Business Council, 2012–. Hon. Prof., Hong Kong Baptist Univ., 2012. JP Hong Kong, 2005. Silver Bauhinia Star (Hong Kong), 2007. *Recreations:* climbing, hiking, tennis, ski-ing, golf, poster and woodblock art. *Address:* Jardine Matheson Holdings Ltd, 9th Floor, One Exchange Square, Central, Hong Kong. *T:* 28438207, *Fax:* 28435393. *E:* ajn@jardines.com. *Clubs:* Hong Kong, Hong Kong Country, Shek O Country, Mariners', Hong Kong Jockey (Voting Mem.), China (Hong Kong).

NIGHTINGALE, Benedict; *see* Nightingale, W. B. H.

NIGHTINGALE, Caroline Ann; *see* Slocock, C. A.

NIGHTINGALE, Sir Charles (Manners Gamaliel), 17th Bt *cr* 1628; Grade 7, Department of Health, 1996–2007; *b* 21 Feb. 1947; *s* of Sir Charles Athelstan Nightingale, 16th Bt, and Evelyn Nadine Frances (*d* 1995), *d* of late Charles Arthur Diggens; *S* father, 1977. *Educ:* St Paul's School. BA Hons Open Univ., 1990. Entered DHSS as Executive Officer, 1969; Higher Executive Officer, 1977; Sen. Exec. Officer, DoH, 1989. *Heir:* *cousin* Edward Lacy George Nightingale, *b* 11 May 1938. *Address:* 16 Unity Grove, Harrogate HG1 2AQ.

NIGHTINGALE, Mary; Newscaster, ITV News, since 2001 (Lunchtime News, 18.30 and News at Ten); *b* 26 May 1963; *d* of late David Trewyn Nightingale and Jennifer Constance Mary Nightingale (*née* Tetley); *m* 2000, Paul Fenwick; one *s* one *d*. *Educ:* Oakdene Sch., Beaconsfield; St Margaret Sch., Exeter; King Edward VI Sch., Totnes; Bedford Coll., London (BA Hons English 1985). Presenter: World Business Satellite, TV Tokyo, 1990–94; World Business Report, BBC World Service TV, 1991–93; London Tonight and London Today, ITV, 1993–99; Reuters Financial Television, 1994; BBC Radio Five Live, 1994–97; Rugby World Cup, ITV, 1995; Newscaster, ITN World News, 1995; Presenter: Ski Sunday, BBC, 1996; Holiday, BBC, 1997–98; Wish You Were Here?, ITV, 1999–2001; Britain's Best Dish, 2011–12. Patron: Willow Foundn; Rainbow Trust; Mariposa Trust; Action for Children; Ambassador, Prince's Trust. Newscaster of the Year, TRIC, 2002, 2004. *Recreations:* travel, ski-ing, friends and family. *Address:* c/o ITN, 200 Gray's Inn Road, WC1X 8XZ.

NIGHTINGALE, Neil; Creative Director, BBC Earth, since 2009; *b* 6 Feb. 1960; *s* of Ivor and Ann Nightingale; *m*. *Educ:* Wadham Coll., Oxford (BA (Zool.) 1982). Freelance journalist; BBC: researcher; producer, 1989–95, credits include: The Natural World; Wildlife on One; Lost Worlds Vanished Lives; The Private Life of Plants; The Restless Year; One Life; Great Barrier Reef; Editor: The Natural World, 1995–2001; The Wildlife Specials, 1997–2001; Dir, Walking with Dinosaurs 3D, 2013; Dir and Producer, Enchanted Kingdom 3D, 2014; Executive Producer, 2001–03: Wild Africa; Wild Down Under; Congo; Wild New World; Wild Battlefields; Head, 2003–09, Exec. Producer, 2009–11, BBC Natural History Unit. *Publications:* New Guinea: an island apart, 1992; Wild Down Under, 2003. *Recreations:* sailing, diving, wildlife, travel.

NIGHTINGALE, Nicholas John; Secretary General, World Alliance of YMCAs, 1999–2002; *b* 29 Aug. 1942; *s* of late Christopher, (Toby), and of Muriel, (Buster), Nightingale; *m* 1968, Sue Lyth (Rev. Dr Sue Nightingale); one *s* two *d* (and one *d* decd). *Educ:* Brighton, Hove and Sussex GS; Trinity Coll., Dublin (BA, LLB 1964); Harvard Business Sch. (AMP 1983). Qualified as solicitor, 1968; Solicitor, Slaughter & May, 1970–74; Partner, Patterson Glenton & Stracey, 1974; Solicitor and Co. Sec., Rowntree Mackintosh, 1975–85; Exec. Dir, Rowntree plc, 1985–89; Co. Sec., Tate & Lyle, 1989–93; Nat. Sec., YMCA England (formerly Nat. Council, YMCAs), 1993–98. Director: Tom Smith Crackers, 1983–85; Original Cookie Co., 1985–89; Cookie Jar, 1989–98; Ellis Patents, 1990–. Chm., Service 9, Bristol Council of Social Service, 1966–70; Treas., YMCA Metropolitan Reg., 1992–93. Vice Chm., Yorks Rural Community Council, 1985–89. Member: Ecumenical Advocacy Cttee, Ecumenical Advocacy Alliance, 2000–02; Council, Assoc. for Prevention of Torture, 2001–08. Mem., York Merchant Adventurers, 1986– (Gov., 2011–April 2012). Chm., Yorks Churches Fair and Just Trade Proj. (formerly Yorks Churches Trade Justice Campaign), 2004–10. Trustee, Nat. Centre for Early Music, 2010–. Chm. Govs, Easingwold Sch., 2004–10. *Recreations:* family life, walking, singing, tennis, opera, croquet. *Address:* 27 East Mount Road, York YO24 1BD. *T:* (01904) 689742.

NIGHTINGALE, Roger Daniel; economist and strategist; *b* 5 June 1945; *s* of Douglas Daniel John Nightingale and Edna Kathleen Vincent; one *s* four *d*. *Educ:* Welwyn Garden City Grammar Sch.; Keele Univ. (BA double hons Maths and Econs); University Coll. London (MSc Stats). Economist, Hoare & Co., 1968; Datastream, 1972, Dir, 1975; Hoare Govett, 1976, Dir, 1980; Head of Economics and Strategy Dept, Smith New Court, 1988–90; founded Roger Nightingale & Associates Ltd, consultancy firm, 1990. *Publications:* articles in financial magazines and newspapers. *Recreations:* snooker, collecting dictionaries, European history. *Club:* Reform.

NIGHTINGALE, (William) Benedict (Herbert); theatre critic, The Times, 1990–2010; *b* 14 May 1939; *s* of late Ronald Nightingale and Hon. Evelyn Nightingale, *d* of 1st Baron Burghclere; *m* 1964, Anne Bryan Redmon; two *s* one *d*. *Educ:* Charterhouse Sch.; Magdalene College, Cambridge (BA Hons); Univ. of Pennsylvania. General writer and northern drama critic, The Guardian, 1963–66; Literary Editor, New Society, 1966–68; theatre critic, New Statesman, 1968–86; Sunday theatre critic, New York Times, 1983–84; Prof. of English, Theatre and Drama, Univ. of Michigan, 1986–89. Mem., Drama Panel, and New Writing Cttee, Arts Council, 1975–80. Gov., Goldsmiths' Coll., 1978–81. *Publications:* Charities, 1973; Fifty Modern British Plays, 1981; Fifth Row Center, 1985; The Future of the Theatre, 1998; What's So Flinking Bunny?, 2010; Great Moments in the Theatre, 2012; (with Martyn Palmer) Les Misérables: from stage to screen, 2013. *Address:* 40 Broomhouse Road, SW6 3QX. *Club:* Garrick.

NIGHY, William Francis, (Bill); actor; *b* 12 Dec. 1949; *s* of Alfred Martin Nighy and Catherine Josephine (*née* Whittaker); partner, Diana Quick; one *d*. *Educ:* St Francis of Assisi Primary Sch., Caterham; John Fisher Grammar Sch., Purley; Guildford Sch. of Dance and Drama. *Theatre includes:* acting debut in The Milk Train Doesn't Stop Here Anymore, Watermill Th., Newbury; Everyman Th., Liverpool, 1972–75; Landscape, Silence, Gateway Th., Chester; The Warp, ICA, 1979; Betrayal, Almeida, 1991; A Kind of Alaska, Donmar Warehouse, 1998; The Vertical Hour, NY, 2006; National Theatre: Illuminatus!, 1977; A Map of the World, 1984; Pravda, 1985; King Lear, 1986; Mean Tears, 1987; Arcadia, 1993; The Seagull, 1994; Skylight, 1997; Blue/Orange, 2000–01; *television includes:* Easter 2016, 1982; The Last Place on Earth, 1985; Antonia and Jane, The Men's Room, 1991; The Maitlands, 1993; Longitude, 2000; Auf Wiedersehen, Pet (series 3), 2002; State of Play (Best Actor award, BAFTA, 2004), The Lost Prince, The Canterbury Tales, Ready When You are Mr McGill, The Young Visiters, 2003; He Knew He Was Right, 2004; The Girl in the Café, 2005; Gideon's Daughter, 2006; Page Eight, 2011; Turks & Caicos, Salting the Battlefield, 2014; extensive work on BBC radio, inc. Lord of the Rings; *films include:* Fairy Tale, 1997; Still Crazy, 1998 (Peter Sellers Comedy Award, Evening Standard British Film Awards); Blow Dry, The Lawless Heart, Lucky Break, 2001; AKA, 2002; I Capture the Castle, Underworld, Love Actually, 2003 (Best Supporting Actor awards: Los Angeles Film Critics, 2003; BAFTA, and London Film Critics' Circle, 2004; Peter Sellers Comedy Award, Evening Standard British Film Awards, 2004); Shaun of the Dead, Enduring Love, 2004; The Hitchhiker's Guide to the Galaxy, The Constant Gardener, 2005; Pirates of the Caribbean: Dead Man's Chest, Stormbreaker, 2006; Notes on a Scandal, 2007; Valkyrie, The Boat that Rocked, Glorious 39, 2009; Astro Boy, Harry Potter and the Deathly Hallows, Pt 1, 2010; Chalet Girl, 2011; The Best Exotic Marigold Hotel, 2012; Jack the Giant Slayer, About Time, 2013; I, Frankenstein, Pride, 2014; The Second Best Exotic Marigold Hotel, 2015. *Recreations:* reading, rhythm and blues, walking the dog. *Address:* c/o Markham, Froggatt & Irwin Ltd, 4 Windmill Street, W1T 2HZ. *Club:* Garrick.

NIKOLAJEVA, Prof. Maria, PhD; Professor of Education, since 2008 and Director, Centre for Children's Literature, since 2010, University of Cambridge; *b* Moscow, 16 May 1952; *d* of Alexei Nikolajev and Natalia Nikolajeva (*née* Tiain); *m* 1981, Staffan Skott; two *s* one *d*. *Educ:* Moscow Linguistic Univ. (MA 1973); Stockholm Univ. (PhD 1988). Jun. Researcher, Film Research Inst., Moscow, 1974–81; Stockholm University: Post-doctoral Researcher, 1991–94; Sen. Lectr, 1994; Associate Prof., 1995–99; Prof., 1999–2008; Associate Prof., Åbo Akademi Univ., 1997– (Vis. Prof., 1998–99). Visiting Professor: Univ. of Massachusetts, Amherst, 1993; San Diego State Univ., 1999–2001; Hon. Prof., Univ. of Worcester, 2007. FEA 2013. *Publications:* Den förlorade tiden och andra fantastiska berättelser, 1985; Masjas ryska kokbok, 1986; (with Bo Dellensten) Upptäck datorn!, 1987; The Magic Code: the use of magical patterns in fantasy for children, 1988; Selma Lagerlöf ur ryskt perspektiv, 1991; (ed) Modern litteraturteori och metod i barnlitteraturforskningen, 1992; (ed) Voices from Far Away: current trends in international children's literature research, 1995; (ed) Aspects and Issues in the History of Children's Literature, 1995; (ed) Återkommande mönster i Selma Lagerlöfs författarskap, 1995; När Sverige erövrade Ryssland: en studie i kulturernas samspel, 1996; Children's Literature Comes of Age: toward a new aesthetic, 1998; Barnbokens byggklossar, 1998, 2nd edn 2004 (trans. Danish); (with Ulla Bergstrand) Läckergommarnas kungarike, 1999; From Mythic to Linear: time in children's literature, 2000; Bilderbokens pusselbitar, 2000 (trans. Danish); (with Carole Scott) How Picturebooks Work, 2001; The Rhetoric of Character in Children's Literature, 2002; The Aesthetic Approach to Children's Literature, 2005; (ed with Sandra Beckett) Beyond Babar: the European tradition in children's literature, 2006; Power, Voice and Subjectivity in Literature for Young People, 2009; Om hur jag växte upp under diktaturen (memoir), 2010; Reading for Learning: cognitive approaches to children's literature, 2014; *fiction:* Var är solen?, 1987 (trans. Finnish, Danish, Dutch); Vem sa det först?, 1989; Nedräkningen, 1993 (trans. Danish, Lithuanian); Det finns inga kungar, 1994; contribs to essay collections; articles in academic jls incl. Children's Lit. Assoc. Qly, Children's Lit. in Educn, The Lion and the Unicorn, Canadian Children's Lit., Marvels & Tales, Papers, Style, Para★doxa, Compar(a)ison, Neohelikon. *Recreations:* travel, nature, animal and bird watching, gardening, papermaking, doll-house decoration. *Address:* University of Cambridge, Faculty of Education, 184 Hills Road, Cambridge CB2 8PQ. *T:* (01223) 767600. *E:* mn351@cam.ac.uk.

NIKOLAYEVA-TERESHKOVA, Valentina Vladimirovna; *see* Tereshkova.

NIMMO, Very Rev. Dr Alexander Emsley; Dean of Aberdeen and Orkney, since 2008; *b* Glasgow, 28 Feb. 1953; *s* of Alexander Emsley Nimmo and Christina Agnes Nimmo (*née* Roff). *Educ:* Univ. of Aberdeen (BD 1976; PhD 1997); Univ. of Edinburgh (MPhil 1983). FSA (Scot.) 1993. Edinburgh Theol Coll., 1976–78; ordained deacon, 1978, priest 1979; Precentor, Inverness Cathedral, 1978–81; Priest-in-Charge, 1981–83, Rector, 1984, St Peter's, Stornoway; Rector: St Michael and All Saints, Edinburgh, 1984–90; St Margaret's, Aberdeen, 1990–. Canon, St Andrew's Cathedral, Aberdeen, 1996; Synod Clerk, 2001. Chaplain: Saughton Prison, Edinburgh, 1987–90; HM Theatre, Aberdeen, 1990–; Episcopal Vis. Chaplain, Peterhead Prison, 2004–07. Mem., 1745 Assoc. (Chm., 2011–14). *Publications:* (contrib.) Dictionary of Scottish Church History and Theology, 1993; (contrib.) After Columba - after Calvin, 1999; (contrib.) Sir Thomas Urquhart of Cromarty, 2011; (contrib.) Living with Jacobitism 1690–1788, 2014. *Recreations:* music, hill-walking, cooking, gardening, languages. *Address:* The Clergy House, St Margaret of Scotland, Gallowgate, Aberdeen AB25 1EA. *T:* (01224) 644969. *E:* alexander306@btinternet.com. *Club:* Aberdeenshire Theological.

NIMMO SMITH, Rt Hon. Lord; William Austin Nimmo Smith; PC 2005; a Senator of the College of Justice in Scotland, 1996–2009; *b* 6 Nov. 1942; *s* of late Dr Robert Hermann Nimmo Smith and Mrs Ann Nimmo Smith; *m* 1968, Jennifer Main; one *s* one *d*. *Educ:* Eton Coll. (King's Scholar, 1956); Balliol Coll., Oxford (BA Hons Lit. Hum. 1965); Edinburgh Univ. (LLB 1967). Admitted to Faculty of Advocates, 1969; Standing Junior Counsel to Dept of Employment, 1977–82; QC (Scot.) 1982; Advocate-Depute, 1983–86; Temp. Judge, Court of Session, 1995–96. Chairman: Medical Appeal Tribunals, 1986–91; Vaccine Damage Tribunals, 1986–91; Mem. (part-time), Scottish Law Commn, 1988–96. Chm. Council, Cockburn Assoc. (Edinburgh Civic Trust), 1996–2001. *Recreations:* mountaineering, music. *Address:* c/o Parliament House, Parliament Square, Edinburgh EH1 1RQ.

NINEHAM, Rev. Prof. Dennis Eric, DD (Oxon); BD (Cantab); Hon. DD (Birmingham); Hon. DD (BDS Yale); Professor of Theology and Head of Theology Department, Bristol University, 1980–86, now Emeritus; Honorary Canon of Bristol Cathedral, 1980–86, now Emeritus; *b* 27 Sept. 1921; *oc* of Stanley Martin and Bessie Edith Nineham, Shirley, Southampton; *m* 1946, Ruth Corfield, *d* of Rev. A. P. Miller; two *s* one *d* (and one *d* decd). *Educ:* King Edward VI Sch., Southampton; Queen's Coll., Oxford (Hon. Fellow, 1991). Asst Chaplain of Queen's Coll., 1944; Chaplain, 1945; Fellow and Praelector, 1946; Tutor, 1949; Prof. of Biblical and Historical Theology, Univ. of London (King's Coll.), 1954–58; Prof. of Divinity, Univ. of London, 1958–64; Regius Prof. of Divinity, Cambridge Univ., and Fellow, Emmanuel Coll., 1964–69; Warden of Keble Coll., Oxford, 1969–79, Hon. Fellow, 1980. FKC 1963. Examining Chaplain: to Archbishop of York and to Bishop of Ripon; to Bishop of Sheffield, 1947–54; to Bishop of Norwich, 1964–73; to Bishop of Bristol, 1981–. Select Preacher to Univ. of Oxford, 1954–56, 1971, 1990, 1992, 1994, and to Univ. of Cambridge, 1959; Proctor in Convocation of Canterbury: for London Univ., 1955–64; for Cambridge Univ., 1965–69. Mem. General Synod of Church of England for Oxford Univ., 1970–76; Mem., C of E Doctrine Commn, 1968–76. Roian Fleck Resident-in-Religion, Bryn Mawr Coll., Pa, 1974; Provost's Visitor, Trinity Coll., Toronto, 1992; Vis. Prof., Rikkyo Univ., Tokyo, 1994. Governor of Haileybury, 1966–93. *Publications:* The Study of Divinity, 1960; A New Way of Looking at the Gospels, 1962; Commentary on St Mark's Gospel, 1963; The Use and Abuse of the Bible, 1976; Explorations in Theology, no 1, 1977; Christianity Mediaeval and Modern, 1993; (Editor) Studies in the Gospels: Essays in Honour of R. H. Lightfoot, 1955; The Church's Use of the Bible, 1963; The New English Bible Reviewed, 1965; contrib. to: Studies in Ephesians (editor F. L. Cross), 1956; On the Authority of the Bible, 1960; Religious Education, 1944–1984, 1966; Theologians of Our Time, 1966; Christian History and Interpretation, 1967; Christ for us To-day, 1968; Christian Believing, 1976; The Myth of God Incarnate, 1977; Imagination and the Future, 1980; God's Truth, 1988; A Dictionary of Biblical Interpretation, 1990; Resurrection, 1994; Jesus in History, Thought and Culture, 2004. *Recreation:* reading. *Address:* 9 Fitzherbert Close, Iffley, Oxford OX4 4EN. *T:* (01865) 715941.
See also Very Rev. J. H. Drury.

NISBET, Andrew; Chairman, Nisbets plc, since 1983; *b* Bristol, 21 Aug. 1960; *s* of Peter and Mary Nisbet; *m* 1985, Anne Marie West; one *s* one *d*. *Educ:* King's Coll., Taunton. With Peter Nisbet & Co. Ltd, 1978–83, Nisbets plc, 1983–. Chm., Young Bristol, 2005–10. Trustee, Bristol Old Vic Th. Sch., 2009–. Mem., Soc. of Merchant Venturers, 2002–. High Sheriff, City of Bristol, 2012–13. *Address:* 22 Clifton Road, Clifton, Bristol BS8 1AQ. *Club:* Clifton.

NISBET, Douglas; *see* Nisbet, J. D.

NISBET, Prof. Hugh Barr, LittD; Professor of Modern Languages, University of Cambridge, 1982–2007, now Emeritus; Fellow, Sidney Sussex College, since 1982; *b* 24 Aug. 1940; *s* of Thomas Nisbet and Lucy Mary Hainsworth; *m* 1st, 1962, Monika Luise Ingeborg Uecker (marr. diss. 1981); two *s*; 2nd, 1995, Angela Maureen Parker (*née* Chapman). *Educ:* Dollar Acad.; Univ. of Edinburgh (MA, PhD 1965); Univ. of Cambridge (LittD 2009). University of Bristol: Asst Lectr in German, 1965–67; Lectr, 1967–72; Reader, 1972–73; Prof. of German Lang. and Lit., Univ. of St Andrews, 1974–81. Mem., Gen. Teaching Council for Scotland, 1978–81. President: British Soc. for Eighteenth Century Studies, 1986–88; MHRA, 2010. Governor, Dollar Acad., 1978–81. Jt Editor, Cambridge Studies in German, 1983–2008; Germanic Editor, 1973–80, Gen. Editor, 1981–84, Modern Language Rev. *Publications:* Herder and the Philosophy and History of Science, 1970; (ed with Hans Reiss) Goethe's Die Wahlverwandtschaften, 1971; Goethe and the Scientific Tradition, 1972; (ed) German Aesthetic and Literary Criticism: Winckelmann to Goethe, 1985; (ed with Claude Rawson) Cambridge History of Literary Criticism, 9 vols, 1989–2013; (ed with John Hibberd) Texte, Motive und Gestalten der Goethezeit, 1989; (ed with D. E. D. Beales) Sidney Sussex College, Cambridge: historical essays, 1996; (ed with Laurence Dickey) Hegel's Political Writings, 1999; Lessing: Eine Biographie, 2008 (Hamann-Forschungspreis, 2010; Einhard Prize for Biography, 2011), rev. and updated English edn as Gotthold Ephraim Lessing: his life, works and thought, 2013; *translations:* Kant, Political Writings, 1970, 2nd edn 1991; Hegel, Lectures on the Philosophy of World History, 1975, 2nd edn 1980; Hegel, Elements of the Philosophy of Right, 1991; Hegel, Political Writings, 1999; (and ed) Lessing, Philosophical and Theological Writings, 2005; articles and reviews on German literature and thought. *Recreations:* music, art history. *Address:* Sidney Sussex College, Cambridge CB2 3HU. *T:* (01223) 338877.

NISBET, (James) Douglas; Senior Partner, Glasgow, Ernst & Young, since 2002; President, Institute of Chartered Accountants of Scotland, 2009–10; *b* Glasgow, 2 June 1959; *s* of James Nisbet and Sybil Nisbet; *m* 1994, Lesley; one *s* five *d*. *Educ:* Univ. of Strathclyde (BA Accountancy and Operational Res. 1980). Chartered Accountant, 1983. Arthur Young McLelland Moores, later Ernst & Young: joined, 1980; Man. Partner, Scotland, 2002–07. Jun. Vice Pres., 2007–08, Sen. Vice Pres., 2008–09, ICAS. Mem. Council, CBI Scotland, 2003–09 and 2012–. *Recreations:* golf, football, keep fit. *Address:* Ernst & Young LLP, G1, 5 George Square, Glasgow G2 1DY. *T:* (0141) 226 9000, *Fax:* (0141) 226 9001. *E:* dnisbet@uk.ey.com.

NISBET-SMITH, Dugal, CBE 1996; Director, Newspaper Society, 1983–97; *b* 6 March 1935; *s* of David and Margaret Homeward Nisbet-Smith; *m* 1959, Dr Ann Patricia Taylor; one *s* two *d*. *Educ:* Southland Boys' High Sch., Invercargill, NZ. Journalist on Southland Daily News, NZ, 1952–56; Features writer and reporter, Beaverbrook Newspapers, London, 1956–60; variously Asst Editor, Gen. Manager and Man. Dir, Barbados Advocate Co., Barbados, WI, Gen. Manager, Sierra Leone Daily Mail Ltd, W Africa, Dep. Gen. Manager, Trinidad Mirror Co., 1960–66; Sen. Industrial Relations Manager, Mirror Gp Newspapers, London, 1966–68; Develt Manager, 1969–71, Production Dir, 1971–73, Man. Dir, 1974–78, Scottish Daily Record and Sunday Mail Ltd, Glasgow; joined Bd, Mirror Gp Newspapers, 1976; Dir/General Manager, 1978–80, Man. Dir, 1980–81, Times Newspapers Ltd; Publishing Advr to HH the Aga Khan, Aiglemont, France, 1981–83. *Recreations:* travel, sculpture, painting. *Address:* 2 Middleton Place, Langham Street, W1W 7TA. *T:* (020) 7636 6403.

NISH, David Thomas; Chief Executive, Standard Life plc, 2010–15; *b* Barrhead, 5 May 1960; *s* of Thomas Nish and Jean C. M. Nish (*née* Scott); *m* 1983, Caroline Smith; one *s* one *d*. *Educ:* Univ. of Glasgow (BAcc); ICAS. Joined Price Waterhouse, 1981, Partner, 1993–97; Scottish Power plc: Dep. Finance Dir, 1997–99; Finance Dir, 1999–2005; Exec. Dir, Infrastructure Div., 2005; Finance Dir, Standard Life plc, 2006–09. Non-exec. Dir, Green Investment Bank plc, 2012–. Dep. Chm., ABI, 2012–; Mem., Adv. Bd, TheCityUK, 2013–. *Recreations:* travel, cycling, trekking, watching Rugby.

NISSAN, Gwyneth; *see* Williams, Gwyneth.

NISSEN, Alexander David; QC 2006; a Recorder, since 2007; a Deputy High Court Judge, since 2013; *b* 30 Aug. 1963; *s* of Charles Nissen and Jillian Nissen (*née* Moss); *m* 1995, Sally Daniel. *Educ:* Mill Hill Sch.; Manchester Univ. (LLB Hons 1984). Called to the Bar, Middle Temple, 1985; in practice as barrister, specialising in construction and engrg law and related professional negligence disputes, 1989–. FCIArb 2000; Chartered Arbitrator, 2003. *Publications:* (contrib.) Keating on Building Contracts, later Keating on Construction Contracts, 5th edn 1991 to 9th edn 2012; contrib. articles in Construction Jl. *Recreations:* theatre, escaping exercise, Coronation Street, dreaming about good food. *Address:* Keating Chambers, 15 Essex Street, WC2R 3AA. *T:* (020) 7544 2600, *Fax:* (020) 7544 2700. *E:* anissen@keatingchambers.com.

NISSEN, David Edgar Joseph, CB 1999; Solicitor and Director General Legal Services, Department of Trade and Industry, 1997–2002; *b* 27 Nov. 1942; *s* of Tunnock Edgar Nissen and Elsie Nissen (*née* Thorne); *m* 1969, Pauline Jennifer (*née* Meaden); two *d*. *Educ:* King's School, Chester; University College London (LLB). Solicitor, admitted 1969. Asst Solicitor, W Midlands Gas Board, 1969–70; Prosecuting Solicitor, Sussex Police Authority, 1970–73; HM Customs and Excise, 1973–90: Asst Solicitor, 1983–87; Principal Asst Solicitor, 1987–90; Legal Advr to Dept of Energy (Principal Asst Treasury Solicitor), 1990–92; Solicitor to HM Customs and Excise, 1992–95; Legal Advr to Home Office, 1995–97. *Recreations:* photography, music, gardening.

NISSEN, George Maitland, CBE 1987; Chairman, Chiswick House Friends, since 2001; *b* 29 March 1930; *s* of Col Peter Norman Nissen, DSO, and Lauretta Maitland; *m* 1956, Jane Edmunds, *d* of late S. Curtis Bird, New York; two *s* two *d*. *Educ:* Eton; Trinity Coll., Cambridge (MA). National Service, KRRC, 1949–50, 2/Lieut. Sen. Partner, Pember & Boyle, Stockbrokers, 1982–86; Chairman: Foreign & Colonial Emerging Markets Trust (formerly CDFC Trust) plc, 1987–99; Liberty Syndicate Management Ltd, 1997–2002; Director: Morgan Grenfell Gp, 1984–87 (Advr, 1987–92); Festiniog Rlwy, 1993–2003; Ffestiniog Travel (formerly Festiniog Rlwy Hldgs), 1993–. Mem., Stock Exchange, 1956–92 (Dep. Chm., 1978–81; Mem. Council, 1973–91); Chairman: Gilt-Edged Market Makers Assoc., 1986–92; IMRO, 1989–92; Dir, The Securities Assoc., 1986–89; Mem., Inflation Accounting Steering Gp, 1976–80. Non-exec. Dir, Ealing, Hammersmith and Hounslow HA, 1993–96. Mem. Council, GDST (formerly GPDST), 1993–2008. Gov., Godolphin and Latymer School, Hammersmith, 1987–97; Trustee, Lucy Cavendish Coll., Cambridge, 1994–97; Pres., Reed's Sch., Cobham, 1995–. Chm. of Holding Trustees, CPRW, 1991–; Trustee, Chiswick House and Gardens Trust, 2005–. Chm., Book Guild, 1993–2010. Hon. FRAM 1994. *Recreations:* railways, music. *Address:* Swan House, Chiswick Mall, W4 2PS. *T:* (020) 8995 8306. *E:* g.nissen@talk21.com.

NITTVE, (Arvid) Lars (Olov); Executive Director, M+, Hong Kong, since 2011; *b* 17 Sept. 1953; *s* of Bengt and Ulla Nittve; *m* 1st, 1988, Anna Olsson (marr. diss. 1999); one *s*; 2nd, 2005, Shideh Shaygan. *Educ:* Stockholm Univ. (MA 1978). Res. Asst and Lectr, Dept of Art History, Stockholm Univ., 1978–85; Art Critic, Svenska Dagbladet, Stockholm, 1979–85; Sen. Curator, Moderna Museet, Stockholm, 1986–90; Director: Rooseum-Center for Contemporary Art, Malmö, 1990–95; Louisiana Mus. of Modern Art, Humlebæk, Denmark, 1995–98; Tate Gall. of Modern Art, subseq. Tate Modern, 1998–2001; Dir, Moderna Museet, Stockholm, 2001–10. Prof., Umea Univ., Sweden, 2010. Hon. Dr Umea, 2009. *Publications* include: Svenska Valaffischer, 1979; Ola Billgren, 1985; Jan Håfström: grammaticus, 1990; Ulrik Samuelson: exit, 1987; Landskapet i nytt ljus, 1987; The Sublime - Walter De Maria, 1992; Truls Melin, 1992; Rolf Hanson, 1995; Sunshine & Noir: art in LA 1960–1996, 1997; Fashination, 2004. *Address:* West Kowloon Cultural District, M+, 29/F, Tower 6, The Gateway, 9 Canton Road, Tsim Sha Tsui, Kowloon, Hong Kong. *T:* 22000000.

NIVEN, Alastair Neil Robertson, LVO 2012; OBE 2001; PhD; Associate Director, Iraq Britain Business Council, since 2013; *b* 25 Feb. 1944; *s* of late Harold Robertson Niven and Elizabeth Isobel Robertson Niven (*née* Mair); *m* 1970, Helen Margaret Trow; one *s* one *d*. *Educ:* Dulwich Coll.; Gonville and Caius Coll., Cambridge (MA); Univ. of Ghana (Commonwealth Schol.; MA); Univ. of Leeds (PhD). Lecturer in English: Univ. of Ghana, 1968–69; Univ. of Leeds, 1969–70; Lectr in English Studies, Univ. of Stirling, 1970–78; Dir Gen., Africa Centre, London, 1978–84; Chapman Fellow 1984–85, Hon. Fellow 1985, Inst. of Commonwealth Studies; Special Asst to Sec. Gen., ACU, 1985–87; Lit. Dir, Arts Council of GB, then of England, 1987–97; Dir of Literature, British Council, 1997–2001; Principal, King George VI and Queen Elizabeth Foundn of St Catharine's, Cumberland Lodge, 2001–13. Visiting Professor: Univ. of Aarhus, 1975–76; Sheffield Hallam Univ., 1998–2002; Vis. Fellow, Aust. Studies Centre, Univ. of London, 1985; Hon. Lectr, SOAS, 1979–85; Hon. Fellow: Univ. of Warwick, 1988; Harris Manchester Coll., Oxford, 2012. Editor, Jl of Commonwealth Literature, 1979–92. Chairman: Public Schools Debating Assoc. of Eng. and Wales, 1961–62; Literature Panel, GLAA, 1981–84; Welfare Policy Cttee, 1983–87, Exec. Cttee, 1987–92, UK Council for Overseas Student Affairs; Southern Africa Book Develt

Educn Trust, 1997–2003; Soc. of Bookmen, 2003–04; Bd, Border Crossings, 2013–; Sec. and Treas., Assoc. for Commonwealth Lit. and Lang. Studies, 1986–89; Member: Public Affairs Cttee, Royal Commonwealth Soc., 1979–99; Laurence Olivier Awards Theatre Panel, 1989–91; British Library Adv. Cttee for the Centre for the Book, 1990–97; Home Office Standing Cttee on Arts in Prisons, 1995–97. Trustee: Millennium Liby Trust, 1998–2008; Council for Educn in the Commonwealth, 2013–. President: Windsor WEA, 2003–13; English PEN, 2003–07. Judge: Booker Prize, 1994, Man Booker Prize, 2014; Forward Poetry Prizes, 1996; David Cohen British Literature Prize, 2000 (deviser of Prize, 1992); The Independent Foreign Fiction Prize, 2001; DSC Prize for South Asian Literature, 2012 (Mem., Mgt Cttee, 2012–14); Chairman of Judges: Eurasia Reg., 1994, 1995, Adv. Cttee, 1996–2006, Commonwealth Writers' Prize; Stakis Prize for Scottish Writer of Year, 1998; ESU Marsh Prize for Biography, 1999–2011. Chm. of Govs, Royal Sch., Windsor, 2004–08. Mem. Editorial Bd, Annual Register, 1988– (Chm., 2013–). *Publications:* The Commonwealth Writer Overseas (ed), 1976; D. H. Lawrence: the novels, 1978; The Yoke of Pity: the fiction of Mulk Raj Anand, 1978; D. H. Lawrence: the writer and his work, 1980; (with Sir Hugh W. Springer) The Commonwealth of Universities, 1987; (ed) Under Another Sky: the Commonwealth Poetry Prize anthology, 1987; (ed jtly) Enigmas and Arrivals: an anthology of Commonwealth writing, 1997; articles in Afr. Affairs, Ariel, Brit. Book News, Jl of Commonwealth Lit., Jl of Indian Writing in English, Jl of RSA, Lit. Half-Yearly, Poetry Review, TES, THES, World Lit. Written in English, etc; study guides on Elechi Amadi, Wm Golding, R. K. Narayan, Raja Rao. *Recreations:* theatre, travel. *Address:* 51 Hanover Gardens, SE11 5TN. *Club:* Athenæum.

See also C. H. R. Niven.

NIVEN, Dr Colin Harold Robertson, OBE 2007; Founding Principal: Sherborne Qatar, 2009; St George's British Connection School, Tbilisi, Georgia, 2012–13; Master of Schools (Shanghai, Beijing, Suzhou), for Dulwich College International, China, 2003–06; *b* 29 Sept. 1941; *s* of late Harold Robertson Niven and Elizabeth Isobel Robertson Niven (*née* Mair). *Educ:* Dulwich Coll. (Capt. of School); Gonville and Caius Coll., Cambridge (MA); Brasenose Coll., Oxford (DipEd); Nancy Univ. (LèsL); Lille Univ. (Dr de l'Univ.). Lycée Mixte, Châlons-sur-Marne, 1963–64; Samuel Pepys Comprehensive Sch., 1964; Sedbergh Sch., 1964; Fettes Coll., 1965–73 (Housemaster, 1971–73); Head of Mod. Langs, Sherborne Sch., 1973–83; Principal: Island Sch., Hong Kong, 1983–87; St George's English Sch., Rome, 1988–91; Vis. Fellow, Westminster Coll., Oxford, 1991; Dir of Internat. Liaison, Sherborne Internat. Study Centre, 1992; Headmaster, Alleyn's Sch., Dulwich, 1992–2002; Master, Dulwich Coll. Internat. Sch., Shanghai, 2003–05. Hon. Res. Fellow, Exeter Univ., 1981–83. Dir, West Heath Ltd, 2003–. Chm., European Div., 1990–91, Chm., London Div., 1998, HMC. Sen. Consultant, CfA (Charity Fundraising Appts), 2002–06. Pres., Marlowe Soc., 1996–2003; Chm., Friends of E. H. Shepard, 2002–08. Trustee, Dulwich Picture Gall., 1996–99. Vice-Pres., Rugby Fives Assoc., 2001–. Judge: Marsh Biography Awards, 2000–11, Children's Lit. in Translation Awards, 2008–; Duke of Edinburgh's Eng. Lang. Book Prize, 2004–13. Governor: Portsmouth GS, 1999–2003; Sherborne Sch. Internat. Coll., 2001–; Blackheath Nursery and Prep. Sch., 2006–; St Lawrence Coll., Ramsgate, 2008–13 (Vice-Pres., 2013–); ESU, 2011–; Chm. of Govs, Gavá Sch., Barcelona, 2015–; Trustee, Campion Sch., Athens, 2002–12; Member: Council, King's Coll., Madrid, 1999–2004 and 2006–; Educn Cttee, 1999–2009, Cttee, London Branch, 2006–, ESU. Patron, Ind. Schs MLA, 1998–2008. President: Edward Alleyn Club, 2005–06 (Vice-Pres., 2003); Dulwich Soc., 2011–; Alleyn Club, 2013–14 (Vice Pres., 2012–13). FRSA. Freeman, City of London, 1999. CCF Medal 1983. Officier, Ordre des Palmes Académiques (France), 2002. *Publications:* Voltaire's Candide, 1978; Thomas Mann's Tonio Kröger, 1980; Vailland's Un jeune homme seul (critical edn), 1983; Island School: the first twenty years, 1987. *Recreations:* theatre, sport, foreign travel, cats, opera (Mem. choir, Dorset Opera, 1978–91). *Address:* 9 Oakfield Gardens, Dulwich Wood Avenue, SE19 1HF. *T:* (020) 8670 6957. *E:* niven.dulwich@yahoo.com. *Clubs:* Royal Over-Seas League, English-Speaking Union.

See also A. N. R. Niven.

NIVISON, family name of **Baron Glendyne**.

NIX, Prof. John Sydney; Emeritus Professor, University of London, since 1989 (Professor of Farm Business Management, 1982–89, and Head, Farm Business Unit, 1974–89, Wye College); *b* 27 July 1927; *s* of John William Nix and Eleanor Elizabeth (*née* Stears); *m* 1st, 1950, Mavis Marian (*née* Cooper) (*d* 2004); one *s* two *d*; 2nd, 2005, Susan Marie (*née* Clement). *Educ:* Brockley County Sch.; University Coll. of the South-West. BSc Econ (London), MA Cantab. Instr Lieut, RN, 1948–51. Farm Economics Branch, Sch. of Agriculture, Univ. of Cambridge, 1951–61; Wye College: Farm Management Liaison Officer and Lectr, 1961–70; Sen. Tutor, 1970–72; Sen. Lectr, 1972–75; Reader, 1975–82; apptd to personal chair, the first in Farm Business Management in UK, 1982; Fellow, 1995. Founder Mem., Farm Management Assoc., 1965; formerly Member: Study Groups etc. for Natural Resources (Tech.) Cttee; Agric. Adv. Council; ARC Tech. Cttee; ADAS Exptl and Develt Cttee; Meat and Livestock Commn; Countryside Commn. Programme Advr, Southern Television, 1966–81; Specialist Advr, Select Cttee on Agric., 1990–91. British Institute of Management: Chm., Jl Cttee of Centre of Management of Agric., 1971–96; Chm., Bd of Farm Management, 1979–81; Nat. Award for outstanding and continuing contrib. to advancement of management in agric. industry, 1982 (1st recipient). President: Agricl Economics Soc., 1990–91; Kingshay Farming Trust, 1991–96; Assoc. of Ind. Crop Consultants, 1993–97; Guild of Agricl Journalists, 2000–02. CCMI (CBIM 1983). FRSA 1984; FRAgS 1985; FIAgrM 1993. Hon. Fellow, RASE, 2007. Liveryman, Farmers' Co., 1999–. Agricl Communicators Award (1st recipient), Hydro Agri (UK), 1999; Farmers' Club Cup, 2005; Lifetime Achievement Award, NFU, 2006; Award for Excellence, Agricl Econs Soc., 2011. *Publications:* Farm Management Pocketbook, 1966, 38th edn 2007; (with C. S. Barnard) Farm Planning and Control, 1973, 2nd edn 1979, Spanish edn 1984; (with W. Butterworth) Farm Mechanisation for Profit, 1983; (with G. P. Hill and N. T. Williams) Land and Estate Management, 1987, 4th edn 2003; articles in Jl of Agricl Econs, Jl of RASE, Farm Management, etc. *Recreations:* Rugby, cricket, old films, reading the papers. *Address:* Rhode Farm, Doddington, Kent ME9 0NN. *Club:* Farmers.

NIXON, Dr Anthony; motivational public speaker, since 1982; Business and Management Consultant, A. & M. Nixon Enterprises, since 1992; *s* of late David and Mariam Nixon; *m* 1975, Marion Audrey Farr; one *s* four *d*. *Educ:* Univ. of Peshawar (BA 1955); Univ. of Karachi (DipM 1959; MA Econ. 1960); Massachusetts Inst. of Technol. (Postgrad. Business and Mgt 1960); UCW, Aberystwyth (MSc Pol Econ. 1986); Leeds Poly. (Dip. Liby and Inf. Sci., 1966); Salford Univ.; Manchester Univ.; DipEd ACP 1958; Concordia Coll. and Univ., Delaware (PhD 2013). Chartered Librarian 1970. Local Govt Officer, Lancs CC, 1968–71; Chief College Librarian and Lectr, Burnley Coll. of Further and Higher Educn, 1972–93 (Mem., Acad. Bd and Bd Cttees); Chairman and Managing Director: A. & M. Nixon Enterprises Ltd, 1990–91; Costcutter Nixon Supermkt, 1993–96. Columnist, New Life (London weekly mag.), 1987–88. Probation Officer Volunteer and Exec. Cttee Mem., Rossendale Probation and Aftercare Service, 1975–81; Chairman: NHS Exec. Complaints Procedure, NW Reg., DoH, 1999–2003; Complaints Procedure, Cumbria and Lancs NHS Strategic HA, 2003; East Lancashire Hospitals NHS Trust: Mem., Patient and Public Involvement Forum, 2005–07; Mem., Develt Cttee for Rossendale, 2006–; Gov., 2009–; Gov. to Council of Govs, 2011; Patient-led Inspections, 2013–; Gov., Blackpool Teaching Hosps NHS Foundn Trust, 2014–. Lancashire Probation Board: Mem., 2001–07; Chairman: Audit and Assessment Cttee, 2002–04 (Mem., 2001–02); Complaints Appeal Panel, 2002–; Member: Performance Cttee, 2003–04; Information Security Gp, 2003–05; Risk Mgt Cttee, 2003–. Lay Assessor, Lancs Reg., Nat. Care Standards Commn (formerly Inspection Unit, Social Services, Lancs CC), 2000–06; Member: Local Involvement Network (LINKS), NHS Health & Social Care, Lancs CC, 2007–; Regl Adv. Cttee on Clinical Excellence Awards to Consultants, NHS Adv. Cttee on Clinical Excellence Awards, DoH, 2011–. Mem., Community Relns Council, 1980–92, Chm., Employment Panel, 1987–88, Hyndburn and Rossendale. Rossendale Borough Council: Ind. Mem., Ethics Cttee, 2004–, Standards Cttee, 2006–10; Mem., Rossendale Strategic Partnership Cttee, 2004–06. Dir, Exec. Trustee and Sec., Bd of Dirs, BHAF Ltd, Manchester, 1998–2001 (Chm., Finance Cttee); non-exec. Dir and Trustee, Burnley, Pendle and Rossendale Crossroads Ltd, 2005–06. Mem., Lancs Healthwatch, 2012–15. Cttee Mem., Rossendale Dist, CPRE, 2005–. Business Advr and Mentor, Prince's Business Trust, 1999–. Chm., E Lancs Reg., CS Fellowship, 2002–. Mem. Ct, Univ. of Manchester, 2002–04. Gov., Lancashire County Sch., Rossendale, 1980–93, 2004–. Mem., Univ. of Third Age, Padiham. Travelled extensively in Russian Fedn and Republics of Latvia, Estonia and Lithuania and met prominent govt and religious leaders, industrialists, trade union officials, etc in order to promote goodwill between Britain and former Soviet Union, 1987; organised exchange visits between British and Soviet families for first time during Soviet rule, 1987–91. Consultant: Collective Farm, Piraviena, Rumsiskes, Lithuania, 1988–90; Pedagogical Univ., Vilnius, Lithuania, 1997. Has given talks on local radio in Lancs and on various Russian, Lithuanian, Estonian and Latvian radio and TV stations. Gold Medal, Public Speaking and Presentational Skills, LAMDA, 1969. *Publications:* South Asia: detente and co-operation or confrontation?, 1982; (contrib.) Day of Peace 1917–87, 1987; Meeting People through Russia to the Baltics, 1990; No Life Without You, 2014; contrib. articles to Sunday Times, New Scientist, Educa, Satellite Technol. and British and foreign jls. *Recreations:* discussing politics and philosophising on national and international economic and social issues; travelling, reading, country walks, picnics, futurologist, creative writing, cooking, swimming, gym. *Address:* Rose Bungalow, 7 Flax Close, Helmshore, Rossendale, Lancs BB4 4JL. *E:* anthonynixon96@yahoo.co.uk. *Club:* Inter-Varsity (Manchester).

NIXON, David A., OBE 2010; Artistic Director, Northern Ballet, since 2001; *b* Windsor, Ont; *s* of David Nixon and Alice Nixon (*née* Charvel); *m* 1985, Yoko Ichino. *Educ:* National Ballet Sch. of Canada. Principal Dancer: Deutsche Oper Berlin, 1985–90; Nat. Ballet of Canada, 1989–91; Ballet Master, Deutsche Oper Berlin, 1994–95; Dir, BalletMet, Columbus, Ohio, 1994–2001. Guest artist: Birmingham Royal Ballet; Bayerisches Staatsoper, Munich; Hamburg Ballet; Royal Winnipeg; Japan Fest. Best Male Performance, 1987; Dir of Year, Dance Europe mag., 2003, 2006.

NIXON, Prof. John Forster, FRS 1994; Research Professor of Chemistry, 2003–11, now Emeritus, University of Sussex (Professor of Chemistry, 1986–2003); *b* 27 Jan. 1937; *s* of late Supt Edward Forster Nixon, MBE and Mary Nixon (*née* Lytton); *m* 1960, Dorothy Joan (Kim) Smith; one *s* one *d*. *Educ:* Univ. of Manchester (BSc 1st Cl. Hons Chem. 1957, MSc 1958; PhD 1960; DSc 1973). Research Associate in Chem., Univ. of Southern Calif., LA, 1960–62; ICI Fellow, Inorganic Chem. Dept, Univ. of Cambridge, 1962–64; Lectr in Inorganic Chem., Univ. of St Andrews, 1964–66; University of Sussex: Lectr in Chem., 1966–76; Reader, 1976–86; Subject Chm. in Chem., 1981–84; Dean, Sch. of Chem. and Molecular Scis, 1989–92. Vis. Associate Prof. in Chem., Univ. of Victoria, BC, Canada, 1970–71; Visiting Professor: Simon Fraser Univ., BC, 1976; IIT, Bangalore, 2005; IISER, Trivandrum, 2010; Vis. Fellow, ANU, 2004. Mem., Editl Bd, Phosphorus, Sulfur and Silicon, 1989–2006. Mem. Bd of Dirs, Internat. Council for Main Gp Chem., 2000–06. Member: Internat. Cttee on Phosphorus Chem., 1983, 2000–; IUPAC Commn on Inorganic Nomenclature, 1985–87; Inorganic Chem. Panel, SERC Cttee, 1986–89; EPSRC Cttee, 1997–98. Royal Soc. Leverhulme Trust Sen. Res. Fellow, 1993. Mem. Council, Dalton Div., RSC, 1994–99. Corday-Morgan Medal and Prize, Chem. Soc., 1973; Main Gp Element Medal, 1985, Tilden Lectr and Medal, 1992, Ludwig Mond Lectr and Medal, 2003, RSC; Geza Zemplen Medal, Budapest Technical Inst., 2003; Alexander von Humboldt Prize, 2004; Alexander von Humboldt Res. Award, 2009. FRSA 1992. *Publications:* (jtly) Phosphorus: the carbon copy, 1998; approx. 400 papers in various learned jls. *Recreations:* walking, watching cricket, theatre. *Address:* Department of Chemistry and Biochemistry, School of Life Sciences, University of Sussex, Brighton, Sussex BN1 9RQ. *T:* (01273) 678536.

NIXON, Patrick Michael, CMG 1989; OBE 1984; HM Diplomatic Service, retired; Regional Coordinator for Coalition Provisional Authority, Southern Iraq, 2004; *b* 1 Aug. 1944; *s* of late John Moylett Gerard Nixon and Hilary Mary (*née* Paterson); *m* 1968, Elizabeth Rose Carlton; four *s*. *Educ:* Downside; Magdalene Coll., Cambridge. Joined HM Diplomatic Service, 1965; MECAS, Lebanon, 1966; Cairo, 1968; Lima, 1970; FCO, 1973; Tripoli, Libya, 1977; British Inf. Services, New York, 1980; Asst, later Hd, Near East and N Africa Dept, FCO, 1983; Ambassador and Consul-Gen. at Doha, Qatar, 1987–90; Counsellor, FCO, 1990–93; High Comr to Zambia, 1994–97; Dir, FCO, 1997–98; Ambassador to UAE, 1998–2003. Governor: All Hallows Sch., Cranmore Hall, 2003–12 (Chm., 2005–12); Downside, 2005–12. *Address:* The Old Vicarage, Church Street, Maiden Bradley, Warminster, Wilts BA12 7HN. *E:* patricknixon82@gmail.com.

NIXON, Rev. Rosemary Ann; Vicar of Cleadon, 1999–2007; Pastor to the Community of Durham Cathedral, since 2011; *b* 25 May 1945; *d* of Edwin Nixon and Dorothy Hall. *Educ:* Bishop Grosseteste Coll. of Educn (CertEd); Trinity Coll., Bristol (DipTh (London); BD Hons (London)); Durham Univ. (MA); Edinburgh Univ. (MTh). School teacher, Denton, Manchester, 1966–69; Parish Worker, St Luke's, West Hampstead, 1973–75; Tutor, St John's Coll., Durham and Dir of St John's Coll. Extension Prog., 1975–89; ordained deacon, 1987, priest, 1994; Team Vicar and Dir of the Urban Studies Unit, Parish of Gateshead, 1990–92; Staff Mem., Edinburgh Theol Coll., 1992–95; Principal, Theol Inst., Scottish Episcopal Church, 1995–99. Hon. Canon, St Mary's Cathedral, Edinburgh, and Pantonian Prof. of Theol., Edinburgh, 1996–99. Mem., SOTS, 1981–. *Publications:* Who's the Greatest?: Sunday schools today, 1984; Jonah: working with the word, 1986; The Message of Jonah, 2003; articles in theol dictionaries and periodicals. *Recreations:* music, hill walking, photography, friends, art. *Address:* Charisholme, 6 Wearside Drive, Durham DH1 1LE. *T:* (0191) 384 6558.

NIXON, Sir Simon (Michael Christopher), 5th Bt *cr* 1906, of Roebuck Grove, Milltown, co. Dublin and Merrion Square, City of Dublin; *b* 20 June 1954; *s* of Major Cecil Dominic Henry Joseph Nixon, MC (*d* 1994), and of Brenda Nixon (*née* Lewis); *S* uncle, 1997; *m* 2002, Pauline Julia Jones. *Heir: b* Michael David Hugh Nixon, *b* 19 May 1957.

NIZAMI, Farhan Ahmad, CBE 2007; DPhil; Founder Director, Oxford Centre for Islamic Studies (formerly Islamic Trust), since 1985; Prince of Wales Fellow, Magdalen College, Oxford, since 1997; *b* 25 Dec. 1956; *s* of late Prof. Khaliq Nizami and Razia Nizami; *m* 1983, Farah Deba Ahmad; one *s* one *d*. *Educ:* Aligarh Muslim Univ., India (BA Hons History, 1st cl., 1977; Univ. Medal, 1977; Begam Khursheed Nurul Hasan Gold Medal, 1977; Nat. Schol., 1977–79; MA, 1st cl., 1979; Univ. Medal, 1979); Wadham Coll., Oxford (Oxford Overseas Schol.; Frere Exhibnr; DPhil 1983). Rothman's Fellow in Muslim Hist., 1983–85, Fellow, 1985–97, Emeritus Fellow, 1997, St Cross Coll., Oxford. Secretary: Bd of Trustees, Oxford Centre for Islamic Studies (formerly Islamic Trust), 1985–; Bd of Dirs, Oxford Trust for Islamic Studies, 1998–2013; Dir, Oxford Inspires, 2002–03; Chm., Oxford Endeavours Ltd, 2003–. Scholar Consultant to Christian-Muslim Forum, 2005–09. Member: Council, Al-Falah Prog., Univ. of Calif, Berkeley, 1997–2004; Adv. Council, Wilton Park, 2000–04 (Chm., 2004–09); Court, Oxford Brookes Univ., 2000–09; Adv. Bd, Dialogues Project, New School Univ., NY, 2003–; Internat. Adv. Panel, Universiti Teknologi, Malaysia, 2013–; Internat. Adv. Bd, Universiti Tun Abdul Razak, 2013–; Internat. Adv. Bd, Doha Center for Interfaith Dialogue, 2014–. Member: Archbp of Canterbury's Ref. Gp for Christian-Muslim

Relations, 2001–04; Academic Consultative Cttee, Cumberland Lodge, 2003–12; Steering Cttee C-100, World Econ. Forum, Davos, 2003–07; Internat. Adv. Panel, World Islamic Econ. Forum (formerly Business Forum, Organisation of the Islamic Conf.), Malaysia, 2004–08; Internat. Jury, Sharjah Prize for Arab Culture, UNESCO, 2012–. Hon. Vice Pres., Christian Muslim Forum, 2012–. Gov., Magdalen Coll. Sch., Oxford, 2005–10. Patron, Oxford Amnesty Lectures, 2003–. Founder Editor, Jl of Islamic Studies, 1990–; Series Editor, Makers of Islamic Civilization, 2004–. Class IV, Order of Crown (Brunei), 1992. *Recreations:* reading, cricket. *Address:* Oxford Centre for Islamic Studies, George Street, Oxford OX1 2AR. *T:* (01865) 278731.

NKOYOYO, Most Rev. Livingstone M.; *see* Mpalanyi-Nkoyoyo.

NOAKES, Baroness *cr* 2000 (Life Peer), of Goudhurst in the co. of Kent; **Sheila Valerie Noakes,** DBE 1996; company director; *d* of Albert Frederick Masters and Iris Sheila Masters (*née* Ratcliffe); *m* 1985, Colin Barry Noakes. *Educ:* Eltham Hill Grammar Sch.; Univ. of Bristol (LLB). FCA. Joined Peat Marwick Mitchell & Co., 1970; seconded to HM Treasury, 1979–81; seconded to Dept of Health as Dir of Finance, NHS Management Exec., 1988–91; Partner, Peat Marwick Mitchell & Co., subseq. KPMG Peat Marwick, then KPMG, 1983–2000; a Dir, Bank of England, 1994–2001 (Chm., Cttee of non-exec. Dirs, 1998–2001). Opposition spokesman, H of L, on work and pensions, 2001–10, on health, 2001–03, on HM Treasury, 2003–10. Non-executive Director: Hanson plc, 2001–07; Carpetright plc, 2001–14 (Dep. Chm., 2012–14); SThree (formerly Solutions in Staffing and Software) plc, 2001–07; John Laing plc, 2002–04; ICI plc, 2004–08; Severn Trent plc, 2008–14; Royal Bank of Scotland Gp plc, 2011–. Comr, Public Works Loan Bd, 1995–2001; Dep. Chm., Ofcom, 2014–. Member: Council, ICAEW, 1987–2002 (Pres., 1999–2000); Inland Revenue Management Bd, 1992–99; NHS Policy Bd, 1992–95; Chancellor of Exchequer's Private Finance Panel, 1993–97; Bd of Companions, Inst. of Mgt, 1997–2002; Public Services Productivity Panel, 1998–2000; Adv. Council, Inst. of Business Ethics, 1998–2003. Trustee, Thomson Reuters (formerly Reuters) Founders Share Co., 1998–2013. Mem. Bd, ENO, 2000–08. Governor: London Business Sch., 1998–2001; Eastbourne Coll., 2000–04; Marlborough Coll., 2000–02. Hon. DBA London Guildhall, 1999; Hon. LLD Bristol, 2000; Hon. DSc Buckingham, 2001. *Recreations:* ski-ing, horse racing, opera, early classical music. *Address:* House of Lords, SW1A 0PW. *T:* (020) 7219 5230. *Club:* Farmers.

NOAKES, John Edward, OBE 1993; FRCGP; Partner, group medical practice in Harrow, 1961–99; *b* 27 April 1935; *s* of Edward and Mary Noakes; *m* 1960, Margaret Ann Jenner; two *s* one *d*. *Educ:* Wanstead County High Sch.; Charing Cross Hospital Medical Sch. (MB BS); DObstRCOG. Trainer, Gen. Practice Vocational Trng Scheme, Northwick Park Hosp., 1974–82. Member: Brent Harrow Local Med. Cttee, 1972–97; Harrow HA, 1982–90; CMO's Wkg Gp on Health of Nation, 1990–98; Chm., Brent Harrow Med. Audit Adv. Gp, 1992–95. Non-exec. Director: HEA, 1995–2000; HDA, 2000–03. Mem. Council, RCGP, 1989–94 (Vice-Chm., 1990–92; Chairman: NW London Faculty, 1989–91; Maternity Care Task Gp, 1994). *Recreations:* music (mainly opera), horticulture (Alpine plants), exploring Britain's canal system in own Narrow Boat. *Address:* Old Church Cottage, Chapel Lane, Long Marston, Herts HP23 4QT.

NOAKES, Michael, RP; portrait and landscape painter; *s* of late Basil and Mary Noakes; *m* 1960, Vivien Noakes (*née* Langley), DPhil, FRSL, writer (*d* 2011); two *s* one *d*. *Educ:* Downside; Royal Academy Schs, London. Nat. Dipl. in Design, 1954; Certificate of Royal Academy Schools, 1960. Commnd: National Service, 1954–56. Has broadcast and appeared on TV on art subjects in UK and internationally; Art Correspondent, BBC TV programme Town and Around, 1964–68; subject of BBC films: (with Eric Morley) Portrait, 1977, 1978; (with JAK) Changing Places, 1989. ROI 1964 (Mem. Council, 1964–78; Vice-Pres. 1968–72; Pres., 1972–78; Hon. Mem. Council, 1978–; Fellow, 1996–); RP 1967 (Mem. Council, 1969–71, 1972–74, 1978–80, 1993–95, 2004, 2006–07); Mem., NS, 1962–76 (Hon. Mem., 1976–); Chm., Contemp. Portrait Soc., 1971; a Dir, Fedn of British Artists, 1981–83 (a Governor, 1972–83). Freeman, City of London. *Exhibited:* Nat. Portrait Gall. Permt Collection; Christie's (one man show); Royal Soc. of Portrait Painters; Royal Acad.; many other mixed exhibns with socs in UK and abroad. Judge, Miss World Contest, 1976. Platinum disc, 1977 (record sleeve design Portrait of Sinatra). *Portraits include:* The Queen and most other members of the Royal family, sometimes being commissioned several times; Margaret Thatcher when Prime Minister and again in retirement, Bill Clinton when President, Pope Benedict XVI (commissioned by the Vatican); other leading figures from academic life, the arts, the services, the City and numerous private commns for families. *Represented in collections:* the Queen and Royal Collection Windsor; Prince of Wales; British Mus.; Nat. Portrait Gall. (incl. Hugill Fund Purchase, RA, 1972); numerous Oxford and Cambridge colleges; County Hall, Westminster; various livery companies and Inns of Court; House of Commons; Univs of London, Nottingham, East Anglia; City Univ.; Frank Sinatra. Designed £5 coin for 50th birthday of the Prince of Wales, 1998. *Publications:* A Professional Approach to Oil Painting, 1968; (with Vivien Noakes) The Daily Life of The Queen, 2000; contributions to various art journals. *Recreation:* idling. *Address:* Eaton Heights, Eaton Road, Malvern WR14 4PE. *T:* (01684) 575530; (studio) Regent's Park, NW8. *Club:* Garrick.

NOBAY, Prof. (Avelino) Robert, PhD; Senior Research Associate, Financial Markets Group, London School of Economics and Political Science, 1996–2014; Brunner Professor of Economic Science, University of Liverpool, 1980–96; *b* 11 July 1942; *s* of Theodore Anastasio Nobay and Anna Gracia D'Silva; *m* 1st, 1965; two *s*; 2nd, 1987, Carole Ann McPhee. *Educ:* Univ. of Leicester (BA); Univ. of Chicago; PhD Southampton. Jun. Economist, Electricity Council, London, 1964–66; Res. Officer, NIESR, 1966–70; Sen. Lectr, Univ. of Southampton, 1970–80. Vis. Associate Prof., Univ. of Chicago, 1977–79; Adjunct Prof., Centre for Internat. Econ. Studies, Univ. of Adelaide, 2001–05. *Publications:* (with H. G. Johnson) The Current Inflation; (with H. G. Johnson) Issues in Monetary Economics. *Recreations:* sailing, golf, music.

NOBES, (Charles) Patrick; retired Headmaster and teacher of English; *b* 17 March 1933; *oc* of Alderman Alfred Robert Nobes, OBE, JP, and Marguerite Violet Vivian (*née* Fathers), Gosport, Hants; *m* 1958, Patricia Jean (*née* Brand) (marr. diss. 2004); three *s*. *Educ:* Price's Sch., Fareham, Hants; University Coll., Oxford. MA. With The Times, reporting and editorial, 1956–57; Head of English Dept, King Edward VI Grammar Sch., Bury St Edmunds, 1959–64; Head of English and General Studies and Sixth Form Master, Ashlyns Comprehensive Sch., Berkhamsted, 1964–69; Headmaster: The Ward Freman Sch., Buntingford, Herts, 1969–74; Bedales Sch., 1974–81; Weymouth Grammar Sch., 1981–85, later The Budmouth Sch., 1985–86; St Francis' Coll., Letchworth, 1986–87. Chairman: HMC Co-ed Schs Gp, 1976–80; Soc. of Headmasters of Independent Schs, 1978–80; Mem., SHA Council, 1985–86. Pres., Soc. of Old Priceans, 1999–. General Editor and adapter, Bulls-Eye Books (series for adults and young adults with reading difficulties), 1972–. *Publications:* Eighteen to Eighty (poems), 2012. *Recreations:* writing, cricket and hockey, King Arthur, Hampshire, music, First World War, Salisbury Cathedral.

NOBLE, Adam; *see* Noble, R. A.

NOBLE, Adrian Keith; freelance director; Artistic Director, Royal Shakespeare Company, 1991–2003; *b* 19 July 1950; *s* of late William John Noble and Violet Ena (*née* Wells); *m* 1991, Joanne Elizabeth Pearce; one *s* one *d*. *Educ:* Chichester High Sch. for Boys; Bristol Univ. (BA); Drama Centre, London. Associate Dir, Bristol Old Vic, 1976–79; Resident Dir, RSC, 1980–82; Guest Dir, Royal Exchange Theatre, Manchester, 1980–81; Associate Dir, RSC, 1982–90. Artistic Dir, Shakespeare Festival, San Diego, 2010–13; Mellon Vis. Artist and Thinker, Columbia Univ., 2014. *Stage productions include:* Ubu Rex, A Man's A Man, 1977; A View from the Bridge, Titus Andronicus, The Changeling, 1978; Love for Love, Timon of Athens, Recruiting Officer (Edinburgh Fest.), 1979; Duchess of Malfi, 1980, Paris 1981 (Critics Award for Best Dir, 1982); Dr Faustus, The Forest, A Doll's House, 1981 (Critics Awards for Best Dir and Best Revival, 1982); King Lear, Antony and Cleopatra, 1982; A New Way to Pay Old Debts, Comedy of Errors, Measure for Measure, 1983; Henry V, The Winter's Tale, The Desert Air, 1984; As You Like It, 1985; Mephisto, The Art of Success (and NY, 1989), Macbeth, 1986; Kiss Me Kate, 1987; The Plantagenets, 1988; The Master Builder, 1989; The Three Sisters, 1990; Henry IV, parts 1 and 2, 1991; The Thebans, 1991; Hamlet, Winter's Tale (Globe Award for Best Dir, 1994), 1992; King Lear, Travesties, Macbeth, 1993; A Midsummer Night's Dream, 1994; Romeo and Juliet, The Cherry Orchard, 1995; Little Eyolf, 1996; Cymbeline, Twelfth Night, 1997; The Tempest, The Lion, the Witch and the Wardrobe, 1998; The Family Reunion, 1999; The Seagull, The Secret Garden, 2000; Chitty Chitty Bang Bang (also NY, 2005), Pericles, 2002; Brand, A Woman of No Importance, 2003; The Home Place, Gate, Dublin, 2005; Summer and Smoke, 2006, Kean, 2007, Apollo; Hamlet, Stratford Fest., Canada, 2008; Hedda Gabler, Th. Royal, Bath, 2010, Hong Kong Fest., 2014; The King's Speech, Yvonne Arnaud, Guildford, Wyndham's and tour, 2012; The Tempest, Th. Royal, Bath, 2012; The Captain of Köpenick, NT, 2013; Who's Afraid of Virginia Woolf, Th. Royal, Bath, 2014; The Importance of Being Earnest, Vaudeville, 2015; *opera:* Don Giovanni, Kent Opera, 1983, Lyon, 2009; The Fairy Queen (Grand Prix des Critiques), 1989, Il Ritorno d'Ulisse in Patria (Grand Prix des Critiques), 2000, Aix-en-Provence Fest.; The Magic Flute, Glyndebourne, 2004; Falstaff, Gothenburg, 2005; Così fan Tutti, 2006, Marriage of Figaro, 2007, Lyon; Macbeth, Metropolitan Opera, 2007; Carmen, Opéra Comique, Paris, 2008; Alcina, Wiener Staatsoper, 2010; Xerxes, Theater an der Wien, 2011; Simon Bocanegra, Rome, 2012; Don Carlo, Bolshoi, Moscow, 2013; Hansel und Gretel, Staatsoper, Vienna, 2015; *film:* A Midsummer Night's Dream, 1996. Vis. Prof., Univ. of the Arts London (formerly London Inst.), 2001–. Hon. Bencher, Middle Temple, 2001. Hon. FGS. Hon. DLitt: Birmingham, 1994; Bristol, 1996; Exeter, 1999; Warwick, 2001. *Publications:* How to do Shakespeare, 2010. *Address:* c/o Duncan Heath, Independent Talent Group Ltd, 40 Whitfield Street, W1T 2RH.

NOBLE, Alison; *see* Noble, J. A.

NOBLE, Alistair William; Sheriff of Lothian and Borders at Edinburgh, since 2008; *b* 10 Jan. 1954; *s* of late William Alexander Noble and Alexanderina Noble (*née* Fraser); *m* 1986, Olga Helena Marr Wojtas. *Educ:* Aberdeen Grammar Sch.; Aberdeen Univ. (LLB). Admitted Advocate, 1978; Temporary Sheriff, 1986; Sheriff of N Strathclyde at Dunoon, 1992–99; Sheriff of Glasgow and Strathkelvin, 1999–2008. *Recreation:* reading. *Address:* Sheriff Court House, 27 Chambers Street, Edinburgh EH1 1LB. *T:* (0131) 225 2525.

NOBLE, Amelia Anne Doris, (Mrs S. Manchipp); graphic designer; Founder and Director, Amelia Noble & Partners, 2009; *b* 5 May 1973; *d* of David and Antonia Noble; *m* 2000, Simon Manchipp; one *s* one *d*. *Educ:* Bedgebury Sch., Goudhurst; London Guildhall Univ. (Foundn Course in Art and Design); Central St Martin's Coll. of Art and Design (BA Hons); Royal Coll. of Art (MA). Partner, Co-founder and Dir, Kerr/Noble, 1997–2008. Vis. Lectr, Central St Martins Coll. of Art and Design, 1997–2002. Clients include Liberty, V&A Mus., Shakespeare's Globe Th., British Council, Design Mus., Tate Modern, Grafik Mag., Charities Adv. Trust, RCA and Phaidon. Ext. Examr for BA Graphic Design and Illustration course, Cambridge Sch. of Visual and Performing Arts, 2012–. Mem., Sounding Bd, Design Council, 2014–. Freeman, Fishmongers' Co., 2004. *Recreations:* the arts, understanding telegraphic speech and enforced herpetology. *Address:* Amelia Noble & Partners, 44 Champion Hill, SE5 8BS. *T:* 07976 939859. *E:* mail@amelianoble.com. *Club:* Typographic Circle.

NOBLE, Andrew James, LVO 1995; HM Diplomatic Service; Ambassador to Algeria, since 2014; *b* 22 April 1960; *s* of Kenneth John Noble and late Rosemary Noble; *m* 1992, Helen Natalie Pugh; two *s* two *d*. *Educ:* Honley High Sch., Huddersfield; Gonville and Caius Coll., Cambridge (BA Hons Modern and Medieval Langs 1982). Entered HM Diplomatic Service, 1982; Third Sec., Bucharest, 1983–86; Federal Foreign Ministry, Bonn, 1986–87 (on secondment); Second Sec., Bonn, 1987–89; FCO, 1989–94; First Sec., Cape Town/Pretoria, 1994–98; Dep. Hd, Security Policy Dept, FCO, 1998–2001; Dep. Hd of Mission and Consul Gen., Athens, 2001–05; Hd, Security Strategy Unit, later Security Dir, then Dir, Security and Estates, FCO, 2005–09; Minister and Consul Gen., Berlin, 2010–14. *Recreations:* choral singing, cooking, my family. *Address:* c/o Foreign and Commonwealth Office, King Charles Street, SW1A 2AH. *E:* Andrew.Noble@fco.gov.uk.

NOBLE, Rt Rev. Brian Michael; Bishop of Shrewsbury, (RC), 1995–2010; *b* 11 April 1936; *s* of Thomas Joseph and Cecelia Noble. *Educ:* Ushaw Coll., Durham. Ordained priest for RC Diocese of Lancaster, 1960; parish appts, 1960–72; Chaplain, Lancaster Univ., 1972–80; Lectr, Pontificio Collegio Beda, Rome, 1980–87; Parish Priest, St Benedict's, Whitehaven, and Dean of West Cumbria, 1987–95. Canon of Lancaster Cath. Chapter, 1994; Ecumenical Canon, Chester Cathedral, 2003–15. Hon. DTheol Chester, 2010. *Recreations:* music, poetry, natural history, walking. *Address:* Laburnum Cottage, 97 Barnston Road, Barnston, Heswall, Wirral CH61 1BW.

NOBLE, David, CBE 1989; Under Secretary and Head of Administrative Division, Medical Research Council, 1981–89, retired; *b* 12 June 1929; *s* of late William Ernest Noble and Maggie (*née* Watt); *m* 1st, 1969, Margaret Patricia Segal (*d* 2009); 2nd, 2012, Betty Price. *Educ:* Buckhurst Hill County High Sch., Essex; University Coll., Oxford (BA Hons English, 1952). Admin. Assistant, UCH, 1952–58; Mem., Operational Res. Unit, Nuffield Provincial Hosps Trust, 1958–61; Project Sec., Northwick Park Hosp. and Clinical Res. Centre, NW Thames RHA and MRC, 1961–68; Medical Research Council: Principal, 1968–72; Asst Sec., 1972–81. Member: Nat. Biological Standards Bd, 1983–90; PHLS Bd, 1990–97 (Dep. Chm., 1996–97). *Publications:* contribs to literature on operation and design of hosps and res. labs. *Recreations:* music, reading, travel. *Address:* Wild Strawberries, The Street, Brightwell cum Sotwell, Wallingford OX10 0RP. *T:* (01491) 837553.

NOBLE, Sir David (Brunel), 6th Bt *cr* 1902, of Ardmore and Ardadan Noble, Cardross, Co. Dunbarton; sales consultant, Allied Maples Group Ltd, 1989–97; *b* 25 Dec. 1961; *s* of Sir Marc Brunel Noble, 5th Bt, CBE and Jennifer Lorna, *d* of late John Mein-Austin; *S* father, 1991; *m* 1st, 1987, Virginia Ann (marr. diss. 1993), *yr d* of late Roderick Wetherall; two *s*; 2nd, 1993, Stephanie (*née* Digby); two *s* one *d* (and one *s* decd). *Educ:* Eton Coll.; Cambridge Tutors, Croydon; Canterbury Coll.; Greenwich Univ. (BA). Sales Exec., Gabriel Communications Ltd, 1986–88. Patron, Special Needs Children, 1997–. *Recreations:* golf, photography, gardening. *Heir:* *s* Roderick Lancaster Brunel Noble, *b* 12 Dec. 1988. *Address:* Meridian Court, 4 Wheelers Lane, Linton, Maidstone, Kent ME17 4BL. *Club:* HAC.

NOBLE, David Clive; Finance Director (formerly Director General, Finance), Defence Equipment and Support, Ministry of Defence, 2007–12; *b* 11 Nov. 1955; *s* of Keith and Dorothy Noble; *m* 1982, Jennifer Bainbridge; two *s* one *d*. *Educ:* King Edward VI Sch., Southampton; Queen's Coll., Oxford (BA 1978). ACMA 1986. Finance Director: Rolls-Royce and Associates, 1995–98; Rolls-Royce Energy Ops, 1998–2001; Gp Finance Dir, Nedalo, 2002–03; Finance Dir, Defence Procurement Agency, 2003–07. Non-exec. Dir, Northampton Gen. Hosp. NHS Trust, 2013–. Mem., Audit Cttee, STFC, 2013–.

NOBLE, David Jonathan; Chief Parliamentary Counsel and Chief Executive, Parliamentary Counsel Office, New Zealand, since 2013 (Chief Parliamentary Counsel and Compiler of Statutes (on secondment from Treasury Solicitor's Department), 2007–11); *b* 19 April 1955; *s* of late Kevin Charles Noble and Dr Prudence Mary Noble (*née* Proudlove); *m* 1986, Diana Stuart Jeffery; one *s* one *d*. *Educ:* Wallington Grammar Sch. for Boys, Surrey; Univ. of Birmingham (MSocSc); Univ. of Warwick (LLB Hons; Lord Rootes Scholar). Res. Asst, Faculty of Laws, UCL, 1978–81; called to the Bar, Gray's Inn, 1981; Sen. Asst Solicitor, London Bor. of Camden, 1983–86; Solicitor, Nabarro Nathanson, 1986; Principal Solicitor, London Bor. of Camden, 1986–87; Sen. Principal Legal Asst, DoE, 1987–91; Nat. Expert, DG XI, EC, 1991–94; Asst Solicitor, DoE, 1994–96; Sen. Principal Jurist, DG XI, EC, 1996–98; Principal Estabt Officer, Legal Secretariat to Law Officers, 1998–2000; Dir of Legal Services, Food Standards Agency, 2000–01; Dep. Legal Advr, Home Office, 2001–04; Legal Advr, DFES, later DCSF, 2004–07; Dir, Central Adv. Div., Treasury Solicitor's Dept, 2011–13. Mem. Editl Bd, Environmental Law Rev. *Publications:* (contrib.) Discretion and Welfare, 1981; (contrib.) Protecting the European Environment: enforcing EC environmental law, 1996; (contrib.) Perspectivas de Derecho Comunitario Ambiental, 1997; articles pubd in Urban Law and Policy and Jl of Planning and Environmental Law. *Address:* Parliamentary Counsel Office, Level 12, Reserve Bank Building, 2 The Terrace, PO Box 18 070, Wellington 6160, New Zealand. *T:* (4) 4729639. *E:* david.noble@parliament.govt.nz. *Club:* Royal Over-Seas League.

NOBLE, Prof. Denis, CBE 1998; FMedSci; FRS 1979; Burdon Sanderson Professor of Cardiovascular Physiology, Oxford University, 1984–2004, now Professor Emeritus; Tutorial Fellow, 1963–84, Professorial Fellow, 1984–2004, now Emeritus, Balliol College, Oxford; *b* 16 Nov. 1936; *s* of George and Ethel Noble; *m* 1965, Susan Jennifer Barfield, BSc, BA, DPhil; one *s* one *d*. *Educ:* Emanuel Sch., London; University Coll. London (BSc, MA, PhD; Fellow 1985). Asst Lectr, UCL, 1961–63; Tutor in Physiology, Balliol Coll., and Univ. Lectr, Oxford Univ., 1963–84; Praefectus of Holywell Manor (Balliol Graduate Centre), 1971–89; Vice-Master, Balliol Coll., 1983–85. Founder Dir, Physiome Scis Inc., 1994–2003. Visiting Professor: Alberta, 1969–70; Univs of BC, Calgary, Edmonton, and SUNY at Stonybrook, 1990; Univ. of Auckland, 1990; Osaka Univ., 2005; Adjunct Prof., Xian Jiaotong Univ., China, 2003–07. Lectures: Darwin, British Assoc., 1966; Nahum, Yale, 1977; Bottazzi, Pisa, 1985; Ueda, Tokyo, 1985; Lloyd Roberts, London Med. Soc., 1987; Allerdale Wyld, Northern Industrial and Technical Soc., 1988; Bowden, UMIST, 1988; Annual, Internat. Science Policy Foundn, 1993; Rijlant, Internat. Congress of Electrocardiology, Japan, 1994; Frank May, Leicester Univ., 1996; Conf. Claude Bernard, Soc. de Physiologie, Lille, 1996; Stevenson, Univ. of Western Ontario, 1996; Larmor, Belfast, 2003; Magnes, Jerusalem, 2003; Conway, UCD, 2004. Chm., Jt Dental Cttee (MRC, SERC, Depts of Health), 1985–90. Hon. Sec., 1974–80, Foreign Sec., 1986–92, Hon. Mem., 1997, Physiol Soc.; Founder Mem., Save British Science; Pres., Med. Section, BAAS, 1991–92; Sec. Gen., IUPS, 1994–2001 (Pres., 2009–; Chm., IUPS Congress, Glasgow, 1993); Pres., Virtual Physiological Human Inst., 2012–. Member: Partnership Korea, DTI, 1995–2000; Korea Adv. Gp, UK Trade & Investment (formerly Trade Partners UK), DTI, 2000–06. Editor, Progress in Biophysics, 1967–; Cons. Ed., Jl of Experimental Physiology, 2004–; Chief Ed., Disease Models, 2004–07; Head, Physiol. Faculty, Faculty of 1000, 2004–. Founder FMedSci 1998; Hon. MRCP 1988; Hon. FRCP 1994; Hon. FIPEM 2001. MAE 1989; Hon. Member: Amer. Physiol. Soc., 1996; Japanese Physiol Soc., 1998; Hon. Foreign Mem., Acad. Royale de Médecine de Belgique, 1993. Hon. DSc: Sheffield, 2004; Bordeaux 2, 2005; Warwick, 2008. Scientific Medal, Zool Soc., 1970; Gold Medal, British Heart Foundn, 1985; Pierre Rijlant Prize, Belgian Royal Acad., 1991; Baly Medal, RCP, 1993; Hodgkin-Huxley-Katz Prize, Physiol Soc., 2004; Mackenzie Prize, British Cardiac Soc., 2005. *Publications:* Initiation of the Heartbeat, 1975, 2nd edn, 1979; Electric Current Flow in Excitable Cells, 1975; Electrophysiology of Single Cardiac Cells, 1987; Goals, No Goals and Own Goals, 1989; Sodium-Calcium Exchange, 1989; Ionic Channels and the Effect of Taurine on the Heart, 1993; The Logic of Life, 1993; (ed with J.-D. Vincent) Ethics of Life, 1997 (trans. French 1998); The Music of Life, 2006 (trans. French 2007, Spanish 2008, Italian, Japanese, Korean, 2009, Chinese, Slovenian, 2010); Selected Papers of Denis Noble: a journey in physiology towards enlightenment, 2012; papers mostly in Jl of Physiology; contribs on sci. res. and funding to New Scientist, nat. press, radio and TV. *Recreations:* Indian and French cooking, Occitan language and music, classical guitar. *Address:* 49 Old Road, Oxford OX3 7JZ. *T:* (office) (01865) 272528.

NOBLE, Gillian Mae, CB 1999; Director (formerly Deputy Director) (Law and Order, Health and Local Government), HM Treasury, 1995–2001; *b* Edinburgh, 18 Nov. 1947; *d* of John Noble and Jessie Mae Noble (*née* Bonnington). *Educ:* Aberdeen Univ. (MA Hons Econ. Sci. 1969); University Coll. London (MSc Public Sector Econs 1974). Joined MoT, subseq. DoE, as econ., 1969; transf. to HM Treasury, 1976; various posts dealing with: planning and control of public expenditure, 1976–84; pensions and social security, 1984–87; Asst Sec., 1986; Head: Banking Div., 1987–92; Educn Sci. and Nat. Heritage Div., 1992; Under Sec., 1993; Hd, Health, Social Services and Territorial Depts Gp, 1993–95. Lay Mem., Nat. Biol Standards Bd, 2002–09. Trustee: Meningitis Trust, 1996–2014; St George's Hospital Charity (formerly Charitable Foundn), 2001–09 (Chm., 2002–09); Trustee and Chm., CSIS Charity Fund, 2007–. *Recreations:* listening to music, visiting heritage properties.

NOBLE, Rt Rev. John Ashley; Bishop of North Queensland, 2002–07; Vicar, St Andrews with St Luke's, Clifton Hill, North Fitzroy, 2007–11; *b* 30 March 1944; *s* of Mowbray Lloyd Noble and Norma June (*née* Shucksmith); *m* 1969, Lorene May Christine Wardrop; one *s* one *d*. *Educ:* St Francis Theological Coll., Brisbane (ThL 1965); Univ. of Queensland (BA 1973); Mt Gravatt Teachers' Coll., Brisbane (Cert. in Teaching, Secondary 1973). Deacon 1965, priest 1968; Asst Curacies, 1965–69; History Subject Master, Queensland Dept of Educn, 1974–78; Asst Chaplain, St Peter's Coll., Adelaide, 1979–81; Chaplain, St Paul's Sch., Brisbane, 1981–82; Diocese of Brisbane: Rector, St John's, Dalby, 1982–84; Rector, St Barnabas', Sunnybank, 1984–88; Lectr, St Francis Theol Coll., 1989–93; an Asst Bishop, 1993–2002; Bishop of the Northern Region, 1993–99; Dir, Ministries Develt and Theol Educn, 1999–2002. *Recreations:* reading, music, computers. *Address:* 139 Aspinall Street, Golden Square, Vic 3555, Australia.

NOBLE, Prof. (Julia) Alison, OBE 2013; DPhil; CEng; FREng, FIET; Technikos Professor of Biomedical Engineering, University of Oxford, since 2011; Fellow of St Hilda's College, Oxford, since 2011; *b* Nottingham, 28 Jan. 1965; *d* of James Bryan Noble and Patricia Ann Noble; *m* 2001, Mark Louis Durand; two *d*. *Educ:* St Hugh's Coll., Oxford (BA Hons 1st Cl. Engrg Sci. 1986; DPhil Engrg Sci. 1989). CEng 1995; FIET 2001; FREng 2008. Res. Scientist, GE Corporate R&D Center, Schenectady, NY, 1989–94; University of Oxford: Lectr, 1995–2000, Reader, 2000–02, in Engrg Sci.; Prof. of Engrg Sci., 2002–11; Fellow, Wolfson Coll., Oxford, 2005–11. Sen. MIEEE 2006. *Publications:* articles in professional jls. *Recreations:* pilates, attending live concerts and sports events. *Address:* Institute of Biomedical Engineering, Department of Engineering Science, University of Oxford, Old Road Campus Research Building, off Roosevelt Drive, Headington, Oxford OX3 7DQ. *T:* (01865) 617690. *E:* alison.noble@eng.ox.ac.uk.

NOBLE, (Richard) Adam; Teacher, Cumnor House School, since 2014; *b* 9 June 1962; *s* of John Alfred Noble and late Susan Vera Noble (*née* Thornton); *m* 1994, Katrina Johnson (marr. diss. 2010); two *s*. *Educ:* Bolton Sch. (Boys' Div.); SSEES, Univ. of London (BA Hons); Moscow State Univ.; St Antony's Coll., Oxford (MPhil). Joined FCO, 1987; Third, then Second Sec. (Chancery), Moscow, 1987–89; Second, then First Sec., FCO, 1989–93; First Sec., The Hague, 1993–95; FCO, 1995–98; First Sec. (Political) New Delhi, 1998–2001; Hd, Res. Analysts, FCO, 2001–02; Dep. Consul-Gen. and Dep. Hd of Mission, Hong Kong, 2004–06; Chief Exec., Wilton Park, 2006–07; Hd, Res. Analysts, FCO, 2007–08. Teacher, Crawford Primary Sch., Camberwell, 2012–14.

NOBLE, Roy, OBE 2001; broadcaster, BBC Wales and S4C, since 1985 (part-time, 1980–85); Vice Lord-Lieutenant of Mid Glamorgan, since 2012; *b* Brynaman, Carmarthenshire, 8 Nov. 1942; *s* of Ivor Henry Noble and Sarah Hannah Noble (*née* Jones); *m* 1968, Elaine Evans; one *s*. *Educ:* Amman Valley Grammar Sch.; Cardiff Training Coll. (Teacher's Cert. 1964); University Coll., Cardiff (BEd (Hons) 1980). LCP 1979. Teacher, Bath, 1964–66, Glamorgan, 1966–74; Headteacher: Ysgol Thomas Stephens, Pontneddfechan, 1974–81; Llangattock Ch in Wales Primary Sch., Crickhowell, 1981–85; presenter: radio incl. daily and Sunday progs, BBC Radio Wales, 1985–; television: series incl. Noble Trails, Noble Guides, Common Ground; Welsh lang. broadcaster (pt-time), S4C. Chm., Wales Youth Agency, 1998–2001; Member: Welsh Assembly Partnership Forum for the Older Person, 2005–08; Wales Tourism Adv. Bd, 2014; President: Curiad Calon; Rhondda Cynon Taff Alzheimer's Soc.; former Pres., Llangollen Internat. Musical Eisteddfod; Vice-President: Age Cymru; Velindre Hosp. Cancer Res. Appeals; St Davids Foundn Hospice, Newport; Cynon Valley Cancer Support Gp; LATCH; Noah's Ark Appeal. Trustee, Order of St John Cymru Wales, 2008–. Pres., Tenby Male Choir; Vice-President: Cwmbach Male Choir; Cor Bro Ogwr; Morriston Orpheus Male Choir; Hon. Mem., Treorchy Male Choir. Vice Pres., Aberdare RFC; Patron, Brynamman RFC. Mem., S Wales Br., ESU (former Vice Chm.). DL Mid Glamorgan, 2007. Hon. Fellow, UWIC, 2002. Paul Harris Fellow, Rotary Internat., 2009. RVS (formerly WRVS) Champion in Wales, 2012–. Accepted into Gorsedd y Beirdd, Nat. Eisteddfod of Wales, 2008. Chancellor's Medal, Univ. of Glamorgan, 2009. CStJ 2011 (OStJ 2002); Comdr, St John Cymru Wales, 2011– (Trustee, 2011–15). *Publications:* Noble Expressions, 1992; Roy Noble's Book of Nicknames, 1997; Roy Noble's Wales, 1999; Y Bachan Noble (autobiog., Welsh), 2001; Noble Thoughts, 2002; Noble Ways: lay-bys in my life (autobiog.), 2010; articles in mags and nat. press. *Recreations:* travelling by car (touring), whisky, factual books, watching Rugby football, buses (qualified bus driver), battlefields (visited many in Britain, Europe and America). *Address:* Llys Aman, Lle Hyfryd, Llwydcoed, Aberdare, Rhondda Cynon Taff CF44 0UN. *T:* (01685) 874076. *E:* nobleroy@talktalk.net.

NOBLE, Sir Timothy (Peter), 4th Bt *cr* 1923, of Ardkinglas, co. Argyll; Chairman, Spark Energy Ltd, since 2010; *b* Gerrard's Cross, 21 Dec. 1943; *yr s* of Sir Andrew Napier Noble, 2nd Bt, KCMG and Sigrid, 2nd *d* of Johan Michelet; *S* brother, 2010; *m* 1976, Elizabeth Mary, *d* of late Alexander Wallace Aitken; two *s* one *d*. *Educ:* Eton Coll.; University Coll., Oxford (BA 1965; MA); INSEAD, Fontainebleau (MBA 1970). Called to the Bar, Gray's Inn, 1969. Chief Exec., 1982–2000, Chm., 2000–07, Noble Group Ltd. Chairman: Business Archives Council of Scotland, 1986–95; Royal Scottish Nat. Opera Endowment Trust, 1994–2001; British Ski Acad., 1997–2003; Dir, British Snowsport Fedn, 1993–98. *Publications:* Noble Blood, 2007. *Recreations:* ski-ing, tennis, golf, history, astronomy, wine, poetry. *Heir: s* Lorne Andrew Wallace Noble [*b* 13 July 1980; *m* 2009, Verity Anne Bertram]. *Address:* Ardnahane, Barnton Avenue, Edinburgh EH4 6JJ. *Clubs:* Bruntsfield Golf (Edinburgh); Summit (Scotland).

NOBLETT, Ven. William Alexander, CBE 2012; Chaplain-General and Archdeacon to HM Prisons, 2001–11; Chaplain to the Queen, since 2005; *b* Dublin, 16 April 1953; *s* of Joseph Henry and Hilda Florence Noblett; *m* 1986, Margaret Armour; one *s*. *Educ:* High Sch., Dublin; Salisbury and Wells Theol Coll.; Univ. of Southampton (BTh 1978); MTh Oxford 1999. Ordained deacon, 1978, priest, 1979; Curate, Sholing, Southampton, 1978–80; Rector, Ardamine Union, 1980–82; Chaplain, RAF, 1982–84; Vicar, Middlesbrough St Thomas, 1984–87; Chaplain of HM Prison: Wakefield, 1987–93; Norwich, 1993–97; Full Sutton, 1997–2001. Canon and Prebend, York Minster, 2001–12, now Canon Emeritus. Hon. Canon, Liverpool Cathedral, 2009–12. *Publications:* Prayers for People in Prison, 1998; Inside Faith: praying for people in prison, 2009. *Recreations:* reading, music. *Address:* 41 Westpit Lane, Strensall, York YO32 5RY.

NOCKLES, Gillian; *see* Moore, G.

NODDER, Timothy Edward, CB 1982; Deputy Secretary, Department of Health and Social Security, 1978–84; *b* 18 June 1930; *s* of Edward Nodder; *m* 1952, Sylvia Broadhurst; two *s* two *d*. *Educ:* St Paul's Sch.; Christ's Coll., Cambridge. Under-Sec., DHSS, 1972. *Recreation:* natural history. *Address:* 83 Oakley Street, SW3 5NP.

See also L. A. McLaughlin.

NOE, Prof. Thomas Harold, PhD; Ernest Butten Professor of Management Studies, Saïd Business School, University of Oxford, since 2008; Fellow of Balliol College, Oxford, since 2008; *b* Whittier, Calif, 24 Aug. 1957; *s* of Harold Noe and Mary Noe; *m* 1997, Dr Debrah Pozsonyi; one *s*. *Educ:* Whittier Coll. (BA Philos. and Hist. 1979); Univ. of Texas, Austin (PhD Finance 1987); Univ. of Oxford (MA 2008). Asst Prof., Georgia Inst. of Technol., 1988–91; Prof., Georgia State Univ., 1992–97; A. B. Freeman Prof. of Finance, Tulane Univ., 1997–2007. Associate Editor: Rev. of Financial Studies, 2003–06; Rev. of Corporate Finance Studies, 2010–; Co-Editor, Jl of Econs and Mgt Strategy, 2007–. *Publications:* many articles in learned jls incl. Amer. Econ. Rev., Jl of Financial Econs, Jl of Finance, Rev. of Financial Studies, etc. *Recreations:* weightlifting, book collecting (neo-Latin). *Address:* Balliol College, Broad Street, Oxford OX1 3BJ. *T:* (01865) 288933. *E:* thomas.noe@sbs.ox.ac.uk.

NOEL, family name of **Earl of Gainsborough**.

NOEL, Hon. Gerard Eyre Wriothesley, FRSL; author and lecturer; Editorial Director, Catholic Herald, 1976–81 and since 1984 (Editor, 1971–76 and 1982–84); *b* 20 Nov. 1926; *s* of 4th Earl of Gainsborough, OBE, TD, and Alice (*née* Eyre); *m* 1958, Adele, *d* of Major V. N. B. Were and Dr Josephine Were (*née* Ahern), OBE; two *s* one *d*. *Educ:* Georgetown, USA; Exeter Coll., Oxford (MA, Modern History). Called to Bar, Inner Temple, 1952. Director: Herder Book Co., 1959–66; Search Press Ltd, 1972–. Literary Editor, Catholic Times, 1958–61; Asst Editor, Catholic Herald, 1968–71. Sen. Res. Fellow, St Anne's Coll., Oxford, 1993–. Lects and lect. tours, UK, USA, Ireland and Spain; Vis. Lectr, Oxford Centre for Jewish Studies, 1992–93. Mem. Exec. Cttee, 1974–, Hon. Treasurer, 1979–81, Vice-Pres., 2004–, Council of Christians and Jews. Contested (L) Argyll, 1959. FRSL 1999. Liveryman, Co. of Stationers and Newspapermakers. Freeman, City of London. Gold Staff Officer at Coronation, 1953. *Publications:* Paul VI, 1963; Harold Wilson, 1964; Goldwater, 1964; The New Britain, 1966; The Path from Rome, 1968; Princess Alice: Queen Victoria's Forgotten Daughter, 1974; contrib. The Prime Ministers, 1974; The Great Lock-Out of 1926, 1976; The Anatomy of the Roman Catholic Church, 1980; Ena: Spain's English Queen, 1984; Cardinal Basil Hume, 1984; (jtly) The Anatomy of the Catholic Church: before and after Pope John Paul II, 1994; Stranger than Truth: life and its fictions, 1996; A Portrait of the Inner Temple, 2002; Sir Gerard Noel, MP and the Noels of Chipping Campden, 2004; Miles: a portrait of the 17th Duke of Norfolk, 2004; (contrib.) Here is Chelsea, 2004; (contrib.) Anglicanism and the Western Christian Tradition, 2004; A Volume on Vermouth, 2006; The Catholic Herald: 1966–2006, a scrapbook, 2006; The Renaissance Popes, 2006; New Light on Lourdes, 2008; Pius XII: the hound of Hitler, 2008; *translations:* The Mystery of Love, 1960; The Way to Unity after the Council, 1967; The Holy See and the War in Europe (Official Documents), 1968; contrib. Oxford DNB; articles in: Church Times, Catholic Times, Jewish Chronicle, Baptist Times, Catholic Herald, Literary Review, European, International Mind. *Recreations:* Romance languages, Renaissance popes, old films. *Address:*

(office) Herald House, Lamb's Passage, EC1Y 8TQ; Westington Mill, Chipping Campden, Glos GL55 6EB. *Clubs:* Pratt's, Garrick, White's.

See also R. J. B. Noel.

NOEL, Lynton Cosmas; barrister, retired 1994; *b* 25 Oct. 1928; *m* 1962, Teresa Angela Diamonda; one *s* one *d*. *Educ:* St Joseph's RC Sch., Grenada; Polytechnic/Holborn Coll. of Law, Languages and Commerce; Inns of Court Sch. of Law (LLB). Called to the Bar, Lincoln's Inn, 1976. Asst Head Teacher, 1956–60; Telephone Engr, GPO, 1960–67; practised law, 1976–84; Lectr in Law, Coll. of Law Studies, 1984; 1st Sec., Grenada High Commn, London, 1984–85; Chargé d'Affaires, Caracas, 1985–90; High Comr for Grenada in London, 1990–92; returned to practice at the Bar, 1992. *Recreations:* music, chess.

NOEL, Robert John Baptist; Lancaster Herald of Arms, since 1999; *b* 15 Oct. 1962; *s* of Hon. Gerard Eyre Wriothesley Noel, *qv*; *m* 2013, Rowena Hale; one *s*. *Educ:* Ampleforth; Exeter Coll., Oxford (MA Hebrew); St Edmund's Coll., Cambridge (MPhil Internat. Relns). Baltic Exchange, 1984–85; Christie's, 1988–91; Bluemantle Pursuivant, 1992–99. Vice-Chm., White Lion Soc., 1998–. Fellow, Purchase Soc., 1998. Officer of Arms Attendant, Imperial Soc. of Kts Bach., 2001–. *Address:* College of Arms, 130 Queen Victoria Street, EC4V 4BT. *T:* (020) 7332 0414, *Fax:* (020) 7248 6448. *Clubs:* Garrick, Pratt's, Chelsea Arts.

NOEL, Robert Montague; Chief Executive, Land Securities Group PLC, since 2012; *b* Bradford, 12 June 1964; *s* of Henry Noel and Elizabeth Noel; *m* 1992, Sophie Bourdaire; one *s* two *d*. *Educ:* Marlborough Coll.; Univ. of Reading (BSc 1986). FRICS 1989. Director: Nelson Bakewell Ltd, 1992–2002; Great Portland Estates plc, 2002–09; Man. Dir, London Portfolio, Land Securities Gp PLC, 2010–12. Dir, New West End Co., 2004–12. Chm., Westminster Property Assoc., 2009–11. Trustee, LandAid, 2010–. *Address:* Land Securities Group PLC, 5 Strand, WC2N 5AF. *T:* (020) 7413 9000.

NOEL-BUXTON, family name of **Baron Noel-Buxton**.

NOEL-BUXTON, 4th Baron *cr* 1930, of Aylsham, Norfolk; **Charles Connal Noel-Buxton;** *b* Kingston-upon-Thames, 17 April 1975; *s* of 3rd Baron Noel-Buxton and of Sarah Margaret Surridge Noel-Buxton (*née* Barrett, now Adam); S father, 2013. *Educ:* Eton Coll. *Heir: uncle* Hon. Simon Campden Buxton [*b* 9 April 1943; *m* 1981, Alison Dorothy Liddle; one *s* one *d*]. *Club:* MCC.

NOEL-PATON, Hon. (Frederick) Ranald; Chairman, Murray Global Return plc, 2000–05 (Director, 1998–2005); *b* 7 Nov. 1938; *s* of Baron Ferrier, ED and Joane Mary, *d* of Sir Gilbert Wiles, KCIE, CSI; *m* 1973, Patricia Anne Stirling; four *d*. *Educ:* Rugby School; Haverford Coll.; McGill Univ. (BA 1962). Various posts, British United Airways, 1965–70; various sen. exec. posts, British Caledonian Airways, 1970–86; John Menzies Plc: Gp Man. Dir, 1986–97; Dep. Chm., 1997–98. Dir, 1986–98, Chm., 1998–2004, Pacific Assets Trust plc; Director: General Accident plc, 1987–98; Macallan-Glenlivet plc, 1990–96; Royal Bank of Scotland Gp, 1991–93. Hon. DBA Napier, 1992. *Recreations:* fishing, walking, golf, gardening, bird watching, the arts. *Address:* Pitcurran House, Abernethy, Perthshire PH2 9LH. *Clubs:* Royal Perth Golfing Soc. and County and City (Perth); Royal and Ancient Golf (St Andrews); Hong Kong, Shek O Country (Hong Kong).

NOEST, Peter John, FRICS; Managing Director, P. H. Gillingham (Investments) Ltd, since 1987; Chief Executive Officer (formerly Managing Director), Capital Consultancy Group Ltd, since 1993; Chairman, P. H. Gillingham Group Ltd, since 2003; Chief Executive, Cotswold Adventure Park Ltd, since 2015; *b* 12 June 1948; *s* of late Major A. J. F. Noest and of Mrs M. Noest-Gerbrands; *m* 1st, 1972, Lisabeth Penelope Moody (marr. diss. 1993); one *s* (one *d* decd); 2nd, 1993, Jocelyn Claire (*d* 2003), *yr d* of late A. D. Spencer; one *s*. *Educ:* St George's Coll., Weybridge; Royal Agricl Coll., Cirencester (MRAC 1971). FRICS 1978 (ARICS 1973). Joined Knight Frank & Rutley, 1971; Partner i/c Dutch office, Amsterdam, 1972; London Partner, 1977; full equity Partner, 1981; Consultant, 1983, full equity Partner, 1984, Hampton & Sons; Dir, Hampton & Sons Holdings, 1987 (subseq. merged with Lambert Smith to form Lambert Smith Hampton); Dir, Lambert Smith Hampton, 1988–92. *Publications:* (contrib.) Office Development, ed by Paul Marber, 1985. *Recreations:* hunting, shooting, travel, photography, country life, wines and food, Gascony (www.thegasconyexperience.com), garden design, arboriculture, business pelmanism, creating synergy. *Address:* Manor Farmhouse, Withington, Cheltenham, Glos GL54 4BG.

NOGAMI, Yoshiji; President, Japan Institute for International Affairs, since 2008; Executive Adviser, Mizuho Bank, since 2008; *b* 19 June 1942; *s* of Hiroshi Nogami and Masako Nogami; *m* 1978, Geraldine Ann Woods McDermott; three *s*. *Educ:* Univ. of Tokyo (BA American Studies). Joined Min. of Foreign Affairs, Japan, 1966; Econ. Counsellor, Washington, 1985–88; Actg Dir, Japan Inst. for Internat. Affairs, Tokyo, 1988–91; Deputy Director-General: ME and African Affairs Bureau, 1991–93, Foreign Policy Bureau, 1993–94, Min. of Foreign Affairs; Consul Gen., Hong Kong, 1994–96; Dir Gen., Econ. Affairs Bureau, Min. of Foreign Affairs, 1996–97; Ambassador to OECD, 1997–99; Dep. Minister for Foreign Affairs, 1999–2001; Vice-Minister for Foreign Affairs, 2001–02; Sen. Vis. Fellow, RIIA, 2002–04; Ambassador of Japan to Court of St James's, 2004–08. Officier de la Légion d'Honneur (France), 2001. *Recreations:* golf, cookery. *Address:* c/o Mizuho Bank, 1–5–5 Otemachi, Chiyoda-ku, Tokyo 100–8176, Japan.

NOKES, Caroline; MP (C) Romsey and Southampton North, since 2010; *b* Lyndhurst, 26 June 1972; *d* of Roy James Perry, *qv*; one *d*. *Educ:* La Sagesse Convent, Romsey; Peter Symonds Coll.; Univ. of Sussex (BA Hons). Researcher for Roy Perry, MEP, 1994–2004; Chief Exec., Nat. Pony Soc., 2008–09. Mem. (C) Test Valley BC, 1999–2011 (Exec. Mem. for Leisure, 2001–10). *Recreations:* riding, cookery. *Address:* House of Commons, SW1A 0AA. *T:* (020) 7219 1468. *E:* caroline.nokes.mp@parliament.uk.

NOKES, Stephen Anthony; Headmaster, John Hampden Grammar School, High Wycombe, since 2000; *b* Portsmouth, 31 Aug. 1952; *s* of Alan and Sheila Nokes; *m* 1984, Diana Rose; two *s*. *Educ:* St John's Coll., Southsea; University Coll. Swansea (MA); St John's Coll., Oxford (PGCE 1978); Univ. of Hertfordshire (AdvDip 1982). Teacher of Hist., Chiswick Sch., 1978–86; Hd of Hist. and Pols, Chesham High Sch., 1986–89; Hd of Humanities, 1989–92, Sen. Teacher, 1992–96, Dep. Hd, 1996–99, Beaconsfield High Sch. Dir, Sheldon Erskine Ltd, appt consultants, 2008–. Chairman: Bucks Sch. Forum, 2008–10; Exec. Cttee, Grammar Sch. Heads' Assoc., 2015– (Vice Chm., 2011–15); founder Mem., Grammar Sch. Heads Assoc. (formerly Professional Assoc. of Selective Schs), 2007–; Member: High Achieving Sports Schs, 2007–; Internat. Boys' Schs Coalition, 2007–; Boys' Assoc. Selective Schs, 2010–. Chm., Thames Valley Politics Assoc., 1997–2000. Governor: Davenies Sch., Beaconsfield, 2005–; Westfield Sch., Bourne End, 2005–09; Aldenham Sch., Herts, 2009–; St Piran's Sch., 2013–. Patron, Old Hampdians, 2013–. Trustee, Causeway Foundn, 2014–. Freeman, Educators' Co., 2010–. *Publications:* (jtly) Guide to First World War Battlefield Sites, 1987. *Recreations:* watching, analysing, discussing sport especially Rugby; theatre, ballet and travel (with wife); collecting and driving sports and classic cars (with sons); watching movies, playing with techno gadgets (middle-aged male); shooting (clay). *Address:* John Hampden Grammar School, Marlow Hill, High Wycombe, Bucks HP11 1SZ. *T:* (01494) 529589, *Fax:* (01494) 447714. *E:* office@jhgs.bucks.sch.uk. *Club:* Lansdowne.

NOLAN, Benjamin; QC 1992; a Recorder, since 1989; a Deputy High Court Judge; *b* 19 July 1948; *s* of Benjamin Nolan and Jane Nolan (*née* Mercer); two *d*. *Educ:* St Joseph's Coll., Blackpool; Newcastle upon Tyne Polytechnic; LLB London, 1970. Called to the Bar, Middle Temple, 1971, Bencher, 2004. *Recreations:* travel, cooking, walking, swimming, gardening. *Address:* Dere Street Chambers, 33 Broad Chare, Newcastle upon Tyne NE1 3DQ. *T:* (0191) 232 0541.

NOLAN, Christopher Johnathan James; film director, screenwriter and producer; *b* London, 30 July 1970; *m* 1997, Emma Thomas; four *c*. *Educ:* Haileybury; University Coll. London (BA English Lit. 1993). *Films* include: Following, 1998; Memento, 2000; Insomnia, 2002; Batman Begins, 2005; The Prestige, 2006; The Dark Knight, 2008; Inception, 2010; The Dark Knight Rises, 2012; Man of Steel, 2013; Interstellar, 2014. *Address:* c/o William Morris Endeavor Entertainment, 9601 Wilshire Boulevard, Beverly Hills, CA 90210, USA.

NOLAN, Dominic Thomas; QC 2006; a Recorder, since 2005; *b* 16 Jan. 1963; *s* of late Dennis Nolan and of Patricia Nolan; *m* 1988, Catherine Lucy, (Kate), Allen; three *s*. *Educ:* St Teresa's Jun. Boys' Sch., Norris Green; St Edward's Coll., Liverpool; Univ. of Nottingham (LLB Hons 1984). Called to the Bar, Lincoln's Inn, 1985 (Hardwicke Scholar, Buchanan Prizeman, Student of the Yr, 1985), Bencher, 2013; Head, Ropewalk Chambers, 2009–12. Special Lectr, 2003–09, Hon. Prof. (formerly Special Prof.), 2009–, Sch. of Law, Univ. of Nottingham. *Recreations:* family, friends, music, National Hunt racing, cycling. *Address:* Hailsham Chambers, 4 Paper Buildings, Temple, EC4Y 7EX. *T:* (020) 7643 5000.

NOLAN, Hon. Michael Alfred Anthony; QC 2015; *b* Bexhill, 17 June 1955; *s* of Baron Nolan, PC and of Margaret Nolan; *m* 1984, Adeline Oh; two *s* one *d*. *Educ:* Ampleforth Coll., Yorks; St Benet's Hall, Oxford (MA); City Univ. (DipLaw). Called to the Bar, Middle Temple, 1981. Mem., Exec. Cttee, Commercial Bar Assoc., 1998–2001. *Publications:* (contrib.) Butterworth's Commercial Court and Arbitration Pleadings, 2005. *Recreations:* skiing, tennis, opera, theatre, cricket. *Address:* Quadrant Chambers, 10 Fleet Street, EC4Y 1AU. *T:* (020) 7583 4444, *Fax:* (020) 7583 4455. *Clubs:* Hurlingham, MCC.

NOLAN, Prof. Peter Hugh, CBE 2009; PhD; Chong Hua Professor of Chinese Development, and Director, Centre of Development Studies, Department of Politics and International Studies, University of Cambridge, since 2012; Fellow, Jesus College, Cambridge, since 1979; *b* 28 April 1949; *s* of Charles Patrick Nolan and Barbara Vere Nolan; *m* 1975, Siobāin Suzanne Mulligan; one *s* one *d*. *Educ:* St Boniface's Coll., Plymouth; Fitzwilliam Coll., Cambridge (Open Schol.; BA 1970); SOAS, Univ. of London (MSc 1971; PhD 1981). Res. Fellow, Contemporary China Inst., SOAS, Univ. of London, 1971–75; Lectr, Dept of Economic History, Univ. of NSW, 1976–78; Res. Officer, Inst. of Commonwealth Studies, Oxford Univ., 1978–79; Cambridge University: Asst Lectr, 1979–84, Lectr, 1984–97, Faculty of Econs and Politics; Dir of Studies in Econs, Jesus Coll., 1980–97; Chair, Develt Studies Cttee, 1995–2011; Sinyi Prof. of Chinese Mgt, Judge Inst. of Mgt Studies, subseq. Judge Business Sch., 1997–2012. Hon. Dr Copenhagen Business Sch., 2009. *Publications:* (jtly) Inequality: India and China compared 1950–1970, 1976; Growth Processes and Distributional Change in a South Chinese Province: the case of Guangdong, 1983; (ed jtly) Re-thinking Socialist Economics, 1986; The Political Economy of Collective Farms: an analysis of China's post-Mao rural economic reforms, 1988; (ed jtly) Market Forces in China: competition and small business—the Wenzhou debate, 1989; (ed jtly) The Chinese Economy and Its Future, 1990; State and Market in the Chinese Economy: essays on controversial issues, 1993; (ed jtly) China's Economic Reforms in the 1980s: the costs and benefits of incrementalism, 1994; (ed jtly) The Transformation of the Communist Economies: against the mainstream, 1995; China's Rise, Russia's Fall: politics and economics in the transition from Stalinism, 1995; Indigenous Large Firms in China's Economic Reforms: the case of Shougang Iron and Steel Corporation, 1998; Coca-Cola and the Global Business Revolution, 1999; China and the Global Economy, 2001; China and the Global Business Revolution, 2001; (in Chinese) Looking at China's Enterprises, 2002; China at the Crossroads, 2003; Transforming China, 2003; (jtly) The Global Business Revolution and the Cascade Effect, 2007; Integrating China, 2007; Capitalism and Freedom: the contradictory character of globalisation, 2007; Crossroads: the end of wild capitalism, 2009; Is China Buying the World?, 2012; Chinese Firms, Global Firms: industrial policy in the age of globalisation, 2014; Re-balancing China, 2014. *Recreations:* swimming, music, playing recorder. *Address:* Jesus College, Cambridge CB5 8BL. *T:* (01223) 339477.

NOLAN, Philip Michael Gerard, PhD; Chairman: John Laing plc, since 2010; Ulster Bank, since 2013; Affinity Water, since 2013; *b* 15 Oct. 1953; *m* 1978, Josephine Monaghan; two *s*. *Educ:* Queen's Univ., Belfast (BSc Geol. 1976; PhD 1980); London Business Sch. (MBA 1991). Lectr in Geol., Ulster Poly., 1979–81; joined BP, 1981: geologist, holding posts in exploration, appraisal and develt, in UK, US and Australia, 1981–87; BP Exploration, London: commercial and planning posts, Head Office, 1987–93; Manager, Acquisitions and Disposals, 1993–95; on secondment as Man. Dir, Interconnector (UK) Ltd, 1995–96; joined BG, 1996: Dir, East Area, 1996–97, Man. Dir, 1997–99, Chief Exec., 1999–2001, Transco; Dir, BG, 1999–2000; Chief Executive: Lattice Gp plc, 2000–01; eircom Ltd, 2002–06. Chm., Infinis Ltd, 2007–10; non-exec. Dir, De La Rue plc, 2000–09. *Recreations:* golf, watching football and Rugby, walking, listening to music, reading.

NOLAN, Rt Rev. William; *see* Galloway, Bishop of, (RC).

NOON, family name of **Baron Noon**.

NOON, Baron *cr* 2011 (Life Peer), of St John's Wood in the London Borough of Camden; **Gulam Kaderbhoy Noon,** Kt 2002; MBE 1996; Founder, Noon Products Ltd, 1989 (Chairman, 1989–2005, non-executive Chairman, since 2005); Chairman, Noon Group, since 1995; *b* Bombay, 24 Jan. 1936; *s* of Kaderbhoy Ebrahimjee and Safiabai Kaderbhoy; *m* 1998, Mohini Kent; two *d*. Joined family business, Royal Sweets, Bombay, 1953; Founder, Chm. and Man. Dir, Bombay Halwa Ltd, London, 1972–. Founder, Asian Business Assoc., 1995 (Chm.); Mem. Bd, 1998–, Pres., 2002–, London Chamber of Commerce and Ind.; Chm., London Internat. Trade Forum, 2002–. Director: Covent Garden Market Authy, 1995–2000; Britain in Europe, 2004–07; Transport for London, 2004–; Good Relations (India) Pvt Ltd, 2006–; Zee Telefilms Ltd, 2006–; Zee Entertainment Studios Ltd, 2008–; non-executive Director: Obento Ltd (Subway Restaurants), 2004–; NeutraHealth plc, 2004–; Casualty Plus Ltd, 2005–; Member, Advisory Board: Bridges Community Ventures Ltd, 2007– (non-exec. Dir, 2005–07); British Olympic Assoc., 2007–; Member: Adv. Council, Prince's Trust, 1996–; Ethnic Minority Business Forum, 2000–03; Adv. Bd on Naturalisation and Integration, Home Office, 2004–08. Founder Mem., Cancer Res. UK, 2002–; Mem. Bd, Care Internat. UK, 2002–06; Trustee: Noon Foundn, 1995–; Arpana Charitable Trust UK, 1996–; Memorial Gates Trust, 1998–; British Food Trust, 1999–; Maimonides Foundn, 2002–; Co-Existence Trust; Founder and Chief Trustee, Noon Hosp. and Res. Centre, 2008–. Hon. Life Vice-Pres., Surrey Cricket Club, 2005. Chancellor, Univ. of E London, 2012–. Fellow, Birkbeck, Univ. of London, 2012. MUniv Surrey, 1998; Hon. DBA: London Guildhall, 2001; Kingston, 2005; E London, 2009; DUniv: Middlesex, 2002; UCE, 2002; W London, 2011; Hon. LLD Warwick, 2010; Hon. DLitt De Montfort, 2011. Asian of the Year, 1994; Multicultural Achievement Award, Carlton TV, 2002; Best Business Leader, Sage Business Awards, 2003; Asian Business Award, 2004; Gold Medal, Pravasi Bharatiya Samman Award, 2006; Global Indian, Rajiv Gandhi Awards, 2007; Platinum Award for Lifetime Achievement, Asian Achievers Awards, 2012. *Recreations:* cricket, current affairs, cinema. *Address:* 25 Queen Anne's Gate, St James's Park, SW1H 9BU. *Clubs:* Reform, MCC.

NOON, Paul Thomas, OBE 2013; General Secretary, Prospect, 2002–12 (Joint General Secretary, 2001–02); *b* 1 Dec. 1952; *s* of Thomas Noon and Barbara Noon (*née* Grocott); *m* 1977, Eileen Elizabeth Smith; two *d*. MoD, 1971–74; Institution of Professional Civil

Servants: Asst Negotiations Officer, 1974–77; Negotiations Officer, 1977–81; Asst Sec., 1981–89; Asst Gen. Sec., 1989–99; Gen. Sec., Instn of Professionals, Managers and Specialists, 1999–2001. Mem., Gen. Council, 2001–12, Exec. Cttee, 2002–12, TUC. Board Member: Unions Today, 1999–2002; Trade Union Fund Managers, 2001– (Dep. Chm., 2012–); Unity Trust Bank, 2012–; Chairman: CCSU, 2001–03, 2009–11; Civil Service Housing Assoc., (Vice-Chm., 1999–2002). Mem. Bd, ETM Placements, 2006–07. Mem., Green Economy Council, 2011–12. Trustee, Skills for Growth, 2014–. *Recreations:* reading, politics, family. *Address:* 3 Warwick Close, Bexley, Kent DA5 3NL. *T:* 07446 834162. *E:* noon.p@sky.com.

NOONAN, Michael; Member of the Dáil (TD) (FG), since 1981; Minister for Finance, Ireland, since 2011; *b* Limerick, 22 May 1943; widower; three *s* two *d.* *Educ:* St Patrick's Teacher Training Coll., Dublin; University Coll. Dublin. Minister: for Justice, 1982–86; for Industry, Commerce and Trade, 1986; for Energy, 1987; for Health, 1994–97. Chm., Public Accounts Cttee. Leader, Fine Gael Party, 2001–02. *Address:* Department of Finance, Government Buildings, Upper Merrion Street, Dublin 2, Ireland. *T:* (1) 6767571. *E:* Minister@Finance.gov.ie.

NOONEY, David Matthew; Director, Civil Justice and Legal Services, Department for Constitutional Affairs, 2003–04; *b* 2 Aug. 1945; *m* 1973, Maureen Georgina Revell; one adopted *d.* *Educ:* St Joseph's Acad., Blackheath. FICMA. HM Treasury, 1965–86; on loan to Lord Chancellor's Dept as Management Accounting Advr, 1986–88, transf. to the Dept, 1989; Head, Resources Div., 1988–91; Head, Civil Business, 1991–93; Head, Legal Services and Agencies Div., 1993; Prin. Estabt and Finance Officer, then Dir, Corporate Services, CPS, 1993–98; on secondment to Welsh Office, 1998–99; Dir, Modernising Govt Prog., LCD, 1999–2003. *Recreations:* sport, theatre, crosswords, poetry.

NOORDHOF, Jennifer Jane; *see* Eady, J. J.

NORBROOK, Prof. David Gordon Ellis; Merton Professor of English Literature, University of Oxford, 2002–14, now Emeritus; Fellow of Merton College, Oxford, 2002–14, now Emeritus; *b* 1 June 1950. *Educ:* Univ. of Aberdeen (MA 1972); Balliol Coll., Oxford; Magdalen Coll., Oxford (Prize Fellow 1975; DPhil 1978). Oxford University: Lectr in English, 1978–98; Fellow and Tutor in English, Magdalen Coll., 1978–98, Emeritus Fellow, 1999; Prof. of English, Univ. of Maryland, 1999–2002. Visiting Professor: Graduate Center, CUNY, 1989; École des Hautes Études en Scis Sociales, Paris, 2009. *Publications:* Poetry and Politics in the English Renaissance, 1984, 2nd edn 2002; (with Henry Woudhuysen) The Penguin Book of Renaissance Verse, 1992; Writing the English Republic: poetry, rhetoric and politics 1627–1660, 1999 (James Holly Hanford Prize, Milton Soc. of America, 2000); (ed) Lucy Hutchinson's Order and Disorder, 2001; (ed jtly) The Works of Lucy Hutchinson, vol. 1: Translation of Lucretius, 2012; numerous articles and reviews. *Recreation:* (armchair) travel. *Address:* Merton College, Oxford OX1 4JD.

NORBURN, Prof. David, PhD; Director, The Management School, Imperial College of Science, Technology and Medicine, and Professor of Management, University of London, 1987–2003; *b* 18 Feb. 1941; *s* of late Richard Greville and Constance Elizabeth Norburn; *m* 1st, 1962, Veronica Ellis (marr. diss. 1975); one *s* one *d*; 2nd, 1975, Prof. Susan Joyce Birley, *qv.* *Educ:* Bolton Sch.; LSE (BSc); City Univ. (PhD); Harvard Business Sch. (Internat. Teachers Prog.). Salesman, Burroughs Corp., 1962–66; Management Consultant, Price Waterhouse, 1966–67; Sen. Lectr, Regent Street Polytechnic, 1967–70; Sen. Res. Fellow, City Univ., 1970–72; Lectr, Sen. Lectr, Dir, MBA programme, London Business Sch., 1972–82; Inaugural Chairholder, Franklin D. Schurz Prof. in Strategic Management, Univ. of Notre Dame, Indiana, 1982–85; Prof. of Strategic Management, Cranfield Inst. of Technology, 1985–87. Director: Newchurch & Co., 1985–97; Whurr Publishing Co. Ltd, 1994–2002; Com. Medica Ltd, 1999–2003; Management Diagnostics Ltd, 2001–08; Mainstream Hldgs (US), 2005–08. Director: Strategic Mgt Soc., 1993–2002; Bd of Companions, Inst. of Mgt, 1994–97. Freeman, Clockmakers' Co. CCMI; Chartered FSMS; FRSA. Editor, European Business Journal, 1988–2003. *Publications:* British Business Policy (with D. Channon and J. Stopford), 1975; (jtly) Globalisation of Telecommunications, 1994; (jtly) Fusion in Home Automation, 1994; (with Sir William Nicoll and R. Schoenberg) Perspectives on European Business, 1995; articles in professional jls. *Recreations:* antiquarian horology, competitive tennis, carpentry. *Address:* Beech House, Forest Grange, Horsham RH13 6HX.

NORBURN, Susan Joyce, (Mrs David Norburn); *see* Birley, S. J.

NORBURY, 7th Earl of, *cr* 1827 (Ire.); **Richard James Graham-Toler;** Baron Norwood 1797; Baron Norbury 1800; Viscount Glandine 1827; *b* 5 March 1967; *o s* of 6th Earl of Norbury and of Anne, *d* of Francis Mathew; *S* father, 2000.

NORBURY, Brian Martin; Under Secretary, Department of Education and Science, later Department for Education, 1984–94; *b* 2 March 1938; *s* of Robert Sidney Norbury and Doris Lilian (*née* Broughton). *Educ:* Churcher's Coll., Petersfield; King's Coll., London (BA; AKC 1959). National Service, RAEC, 1959–61. Asst Principal, WO, 1961; Private Sec. to Under Sec. of State for War, 1962; Asst Private Sec. to Dep. Sec. of State for Defence, 1964; Principal, MoD, 1965, Cabinet Office, 1969; Private Sec. to Sec. of the Cabinet, 1970–73; Asst Sec., MoD, 1973; Principal Private Sec. to Sec. of State for Defence, 1979–81; Under Sec., MoD, 1981. Lay Mem., Special Educnl Needs Appeals Tribunal, 1994–2003; Mem., Ind. Monitoring Bd (formerly Bd of Visitors), Pentonville Prison, 1994–2008 (Chm., 1999–2003, 2005–06). Trustee, Choice Support, 1999–2015. FRSA 1992. *Recreation:* remembering riding on top of Routemaster buses. *Address:* 6 The Red House, 49–53 Clerkenwell Road, EC1M 5RS. *Club:* Reform.

NORBURY, Caroline, MBE 2012; Founder and Chief Executive, Creative England, since 2011; *b* Kluang, Malaysia, 24 July 1966; *d* of Robert and Doreen Norbury; *m* 1986, Ed Barker; one *s* one *d.* *Educ:* Univ. of Essex (BA Govt 1988); City Univ., London (MA Cultural Leadership 2009). Dir, Signals Media, 1990–97; Chief Executive Officer: First Take Films, 1998–2001; South West Screen, 2001–11. *Address:* Creative England, 1st Floor, College House, 32–36 College Green, Bristol BS1 5SP. *T:* (0117) 933 8920. *E:* ceomail@creativeengland.co.uk.

NORBURY, Hugh Robert; QC 2012; *b* Edinburgh, 6 April 1970; *s* of Robert and Jane Norbury; *m* 1997, Cecilia Ivimy; two *s.* *Educ:* Eton Coll.; Worcester Coll., Oxford (BA PPE); City Univ. (CPE); King's Coll. London (LLM). Called to the Bar, Lincoln's Inn, 1995; in practice as barrister, specialising in chancery and commercial, especially fraud. *Recreations:* spending time with family and friends, running, ski-ing, tennis, wine, trees. *Address:* Serle Court, 6 New Square, Lincoln's Inn, WC2A 3QS. *T:* (020) 7242 6105. *E:* clerks@serlecourt.co.uk.

NORDEN, Denis, CBE 1980; scriptwriter and broadcaster; *b* 6 Feb. 1922; *s* of George Norden and Jenny Lubell; *m* 1943, Avril Rosen; one *s* one *d.* *Educ:* Craven Park Sch., London; City of London Sch. Theatre Manager, 1939–42; served RAF, 1942–45; staff-writer in Variety Agency, 1945–47. With Frank Muir, 1947–64: collaborated for 17 years writing comedy scripts, including: (for radio): Take It From Here, 1947–58; Bedtime with Braden, 1950–54; (for TV): And So To Bentley, 1956; Whack-O!, 1958–60; The Seven Faces of Jim, 1961, and other series with Jimmy Edwards; resident in TV and radio panel-games; collaborated in film scripts, television commercials, and revues; joint Advisors and Consultants to BBC Television Light Entertainment Dept, 1960–64; jointly received Screenwriters Guild Award for Best Contribution to Light Entertainment, 1961; together on panel-games My Word!, 1956–93, and My Music, 1967–. Since 1964, solo writer for television and films; Looks Familiar (Thames TV), 1973–87; It'll Be Alright on the Night (LWT), 1977–2005; It'll be Alright on the Day, 1983; In On The Act, 1988; Pick of the Pilots, 1990; Denis Norden's Laughter File, 1991–2005; Denis Norden's Trailer Cinema, 1992; Laughter by Royal Command, 1993; 40 Years of ITV Laughter, 1995; Legends of Light Music, 1995. Film Credits include: The Bliss of Mrs Blossom; Buona Sera, Mrs Campbell; The Best House in London; Every Home Should Have One; Twelve Plus One; The Statue; The Water Babies. Variety Club of GB Award for Best Radio Personality (with Frank Muir), 1978; Male TV Personality of the Year, 1980; Lifetime Achievement Award: Writers' Guild of GB, 1999; RTS, 2000. *Publications:* (with Frank Muir): You Can't Have Your Kayak and Heat It, 1973; Upon My Word!, 1974; Take My Word for It, 1978; The Glums, 1979; Oh, My Word!, 1980; The Complete and Utter My Word Stories, 1983; Coming to You Live! behind-the-screen memories of 50s and 60s Television, 1986; You Have My Word, 1989; Clips from a Life, 2008. *Recreations:* reading, loitering. *Club:* Saturday Morning Odeon.

NORDMANN, François; Swiss Ambassador to France, 2002–07, and to Monaco, 2006–07; *b* 13 May 1942; *s* of Jean and Bluette Nordmann; *m* 1980, Miriam Bohadana. *Educ:* Univ. de Fribourg (licencié en droit). Private Sec. to Foreign Minister, Switzerland, 1975–80; Counsellor and Perm. Observer, Mission to UN, NY, 1980–84; Ambassador to Guatemala, El Salvador, Honduras, Nicaragua, Costa Rica and Panama, 1984–87; Ambassador and Head of Swiss Perm. Delegn to UNESCO, Paris, 1987–92; Ambassador and Dir, Directorate of Internat. Orgns, Swiss Foreign Min., Berne, 1992–94; Ambassador to UK, 1994–99; Mission to Internat. Orgns, Geneva, 2000–02. Officier de la Légion d'Honneur (France), 2013. *Recreations:* reading, theatre, walking, golf. *Club:* Cercle de l'Union Interalliée (Paris).

NORFOLK, 18th Duke of, *cr* 1483; **Edward William Fitzalan-Howard;** DL; Earl of Arundel, 1139; Baron Beaumont, 1309; Baron Maltravers, 1330; Earl of Surrey, 1483; Baron FitzAlan, Clun, and Oswaldstre, 1627; Earl of Norfolk, 1644; Baron Howard of Glossop, 1869; Earl Marshal and Hereditary Marshal and Chief Butler of England; Premier Duke and Earl; *b* 2 Dec. 1956; *er s* of 17th Duke of Norfolk, KG, GCVO, CB, CBE, MC and Anne Mary Teresa, CBE (*née* Constable-Maxwell); *S* father, 2002; *m* 1987, Georgina, *y d* of Jack and Serena Gore; three *s* two *d.* *Educ:* Ampleforth Coll., Yorks; Lincoln Coll., Oxford. Chairman: Sigas Ltd, 1979–88; Parkwood Group Ltd, 1989–2002. DL W Sussex, 2002. *Recreations:* ski-ing, motor-racing, shooting. *Heir:* *s* Earl of Arundel and Surrey, *qv.* *Address:* Arundel Castle, West Sussex BN18 9AB. *T:* (01903) 883400. *Club:* British Racing Drivers' (Silverstone).

NORFOLK, Archdeacon of; *see* Betts, Ven. S. J.

NORFOLK, Ven. Edward Matheson; Archdeacon of St Albans, 1982–87, Emeritus since 1987; *b* 29 Sept. 1921; *s* of Edward and Chrissie Mary Wilson Norfolk; *m* 1947, Mary Louisa Oates (*d* 2010); one *s* one *d* (and one *s* decd). *Educ:* Latymer Upper School; Leeds Univ. (BA); College of the Resurrection, Mirfield. Deacon, 1946; priest, 1947; Assistant Curate: Greenford, 1946–47; King Charles the Martyr, South Mymms, 1947–50; Bushey, 1950–53; Vicar: Waltham Cross, 1953–59; Welwyn Garden City, 1959–69; Rector, Great Berkhamsted, 1969–81; Vicar, King's Langley, 1981–82. Hon. Canon of St Albans, 1972–82. *Recreations:* walking, bird-watching. *Address:* 5 Fairlawn Court, Brewery Lane, Sidmouth, Devon EX10 8UR.

NORFOLK, Lawrence William; writer, since 1988; *b* 1 Oct. 1963; *s* of Michael Norfolk and Shirley Kathleen (*née* Blake); *m* 1994, Vineeta Rayan; two *s.* *Educ:* KCL (BA Hons (English) 1986; AKC 1986). *Publications:* Lemprière's Dictionary, 1991 (Somerset Maugham Award, 1992); The Pope's Rhinoceros, 1996; In the Shape of a Boar, 2001; (with Neal White) Ott's Sneeze, 2002; John Saturnall's Feast, 2012. *Recreations:* swimming, skydiving, reading. *Address:* c/o Blake Friedmann Literary Agency, First Floor, Selous House, 5–12 Mandela Street, NW1 0DU.

NORGROVE, David; Chairman: Low Pay Commission, since 2009; Family Justice Board, since 2012; *b* 23 Jan. 1948; *s* of Douglas and Ann Norgrove; *m* 1977, Jenny Stoker; one *s* two *d.* *Educ:* Christ's Hosp.; Exeter Coll., Oxford (BA); Emmanuel Coll., Cambridge (DipEcon); London Sch. of Econs (MSc). HM Treasury, 1972–78 and 1980–85; First Nat. Bank of Chicago, 1978–80; Private Sec. to the Prime Minister, 1985–88; Marks and Spencer, 1988–2004, Exec. Dir, 2000–04; Chairman: The Pensions Regulator, 2005–10; Pensions First Gp LLP, 2011–14. Non-exec. Dir, Strategic Rail Authy, 2002–04. Chm., Rev. of Family Justice System, 2010–11. Trustee, BM, 2004–12 (Dep. Chm. of Trustees, 2010–12; Chm., Audit Cttee, 2005–12; Chm., British Mus. Co., 2004–05; Chm., Friends of BM, 2008–12). Chm., Amnesty Internat. Charitable Trust, 2009–14; Trustee: Hanover Trust, 1993–2003; Media Trust, 1998–2003; Mencap, 2000–03. Mem. Council, Univ. of Oxford, 2014–. *Recreations:* music, walking, ski-ing.

NORGROVE, Michael William, CBE 2009; Director of Excise, Customs, Stamps and Money Laundering, HM Revenue and Customs, 2009–12; *b* 16 Dec. 1952; *s* of Walter and Nellie Norgrove; *m* 1977, Lalita (*née* Shiner); one *s* one *d.* *Educ:* Palmer's Boys' Sch., Grays, Essex; Bedford Coll., London (BA 1974); King's Coll. London (MA 1975); St John's Coll., Oxford (PGCE 1978). Joined HM Customs and Excise as Exec. Officer, 1978, Admin. trainee, 1981; seconded to HM Treasury, 1985–87; Principal, 1986; seconded to UK Permanent Repn, Brussels, 1988–93; Asst Sec., 1992; Head, Financial Mgt Div., 1993–98; apptd Comr, HM Bd of Customs and Excise, 1998; Comr, Ops (Compliance), 1998–2001; Dir, Large Business Gp, 2001–02; Exec. Dir, Intelligence, HM Customs and Excise, subseq. HMRC, 2002–06; Dir, Central Compliance, 2006–08, Excise, Stamps and Money, 2008–09, HMRC. *Recreations:* Real tennis, bird watching, jazz.

NORLAND, Otto Realf; Director, Northern Navigation International Ltd, USA, 1991–2006; London representative, Deutsche Schiffsbank (formerly Deutsche Schiffahrtsbank) AG, 1984–2000; Chairman, Otto Norland Ltd, 1984–2000; *b* 24 Feb. 1930; *s* of Realph I. O. Norland and Aasta S. Sæther; *m* 1955, Gerd Ellen Andenæs; two *d* (one *s* decd). *Educ:* Norwegian University College of Economics and Business Administration, Bergen. ACIB 1956, FCIB 1970. Hambros Bank Ltd, 1953–84, Dir, 1964–84. Director: Alcoa of Great Britain Ltd, 1968–84 (Chm., 1978–84); Banque Paribas Norge A/S, Oslo, 1986–88. Dir, Aluminium Fedn Ltd, 1979–84 (Pres., 1982). Freeman, City of London, 2005; Liveryman, Shipwrights' Co., 2006. *Recreations:* travel, stamps, books (polar explorations). *Clubs:* Naval and Military, Den Norske; Norske Selskab, Bibliofilklubben, Shippingklubben (Oslo).

NORMAN, (Alexander) Jesse; MP (C) Hereford and South Herefordshire, since 2010; *b* London, 23 June 1962; *s* of Sir Torquil (Patrick Alexander) Norman, *qv*; *m* 1992, Kate, *d* of Baron Bingham of Cornhill (Life Peer), KG, PC; two *s* one *d.* *Educ:* Eton Coll.; Merton Coll., Oxford (Open Exhibnr; BA Classics); University Coll. London (MPhil; PhD Philosophy 2003). Project Dir, Sabre Foundn, 1989–91; Manager, then Asst Dir, 1991–97, Dir, 1997, BZW; Teaching Fellow and Lectr, UCL, 1998–2003; Lectr, Birkbeck Coll., London, 2003; Exec. Dir, Policy Exchange, 2005–06. Hon. Res. Fellow, UCL, 2005–10. Director: Classical Opera Co., 2004–; Roundhouse, 2007–. Trustee: Kindle Centre, 2007–10; Hay Fest., 2008–. Chm., Select Cttee on Culture, Media and Sport, 2015–. Patron: Herefordshire Riding for Disabled, 2009–; No 1 Ledbury Rd, 2010–; Music Pool, 2010–; Herefords Mind, 2011–. Pres., Hereford Hosp. Radio, 2011–; Vice President: Ross Horticl Soc., 2011–; Herefords and Glos Canal Trust, 2011–. *Publications:* The Achievement of Michael Oakeshott, 1992; Breaking the Habits of a Lifetime: Poland's first steps to the market, 1992; After Euclid: visual reasoning and the epistemology of diagrams, 2006; Compassionate Conservatism, 2006; Compassionate Economics, 2008; Churchill's Legacy, 2009; The Big Society, 2010; Edmund Burke: philosopher, politician, prophet, 2013; pamphlets, essays, journalism and academic articles. *Recreations:* music, especially jazz and opera, hill-walking, sports, cinema. *Address:* House of Commons, SW1A 0AA; Suite 3, Penn House, Broad Street, Hereford HR4 9AP. *E:* jesse.norman.mp@parliament.uk. *Club:* Westfields Football.

NORMAN, Rev. Canon Andrew; Principal, Ridley Hall Theological College, Cambridge, since 2009; *b* Cuckfield, W Sussex, 26 Jan. 1963; *s* of John Warden Norman and Anna Louise Norman; *m* 1991, Amanda Cullen; two *d. Educ:* University Coll., Oxford (MA PPE); Ridley Hall, Cambridge and Virginia Theol Seminary (Cert. in Theol. and Ministry 1995); Selwyn Coll., Cambridge (MA Theol. 1999); Newcastle Poly. (Postgrad. Dip. in Mgt Studies; Intermediate Dip. in French); Univ. of Birmingham (MPhil Missiology 2007). Lay Asst, St Luke's-in-the-City, Liverpool, 1986; Thomas De La Rue and Co. Ltd: Mgt Trainee, 1986–87; Production Controller, 1987–88; Project Manager, 1989; Sales Admin. Manager, 1990–92; ordained deacon, 1995, priest, 1996; Asst Chaplain, St Michael's, Paris, 1995–99; Associate Vicar, Christ Church, Clifton, Bristol, 2000–02; Archbishop of Canterbury's Asst Sec. for Anglican Communion & Ecumenism, 2002–04, Principal Sec. for Internat., Ecumenical and Anglican Communion Affairs, 2005–08. Hon. Provincial Canon, Canterbury Cathedral, 2005–; Hon. Canon, Ely Cathedral, 2012–. *Publications:* Anglican Mission en France, 1995. *Recreations:* current affairs, travel and related reading, savouring France. *Address:* Ridley Hall, Sidgwick Avenue, Cambridge CB3 9HG. *T:* (01223) 746580, *Fax:* (01223) 746581. *E:* ridleypa@hermes.cam.ac.uk.

NORMAN, Rear-Adm. Anthony Mansfeldt, CB 1989; Bursar and Fellow, St Catharine's College, Cambridge, 1989–97; *b* 16 Dec. 1934; *s* of Cecil and Jean Norman; *m* 1961, Judith Pye; one *s* one *d. Educ:* Royal Naval Coll., Dartmouth. MA Cantab 1992. Graduate ndc. Various sea/shore appts, 1952–73; Staff of Dir Underwater Weapons, 1973–74; student ndc, 1974–75; CO HM Ships Argonaut and Mohawk, 1975–76; Fleet Anti-Submarine Warfare Officer, 1976–78; CO (Captain), HMS Broadsword, 1978–80; Asst Dir Naval Plans, MoD, 1980–83; Captain: 2nd Frigate Sqdn, HMS Broadsword, 1983–85; Sch. of Maritime Ops, HMS Dryad, 1985–86; Dir Gen., Naval Personal Services, MoD (Navy), 1986–89. *Recreations:* tennis, hill walking, travel. *Address:* c/o National Westminster Bank, 208 Piccadilly, W1A 2DG. *Club:* Army and Navy.

NORMAN, Archibald John; Chairman: ITV plc, since 2010; Lazard London, since 2013; Hobbycraft Ltd, since 2014; *b* 1 May 1954; *s* of Dr Archibald Percy Norman, *qv*; *m* 1983, Vanessa Mary Peet; one *d. Educ:* Univ. of Minnesota; Emmanuel Coll., Cambridge (BA Hons Econs, MA); Harvard Business Sch. (MBA 1979). Citibank NA, 1975–77; McKinsey & Co. Inc., 1979–86, Principal 1984; Gp Finance Dir, Woolworth Holdings plc, later Kingfisher plc, 1986–91; Gp Chief Exec., 1991–96, Chm., 1996–99, Asda Group plc. Chairman: Chartwell Land plc, 1987–91; Energis plc, 2002–05; Aurigo Mgt, then Aurigo Mgt Partners LLP, 2006–10; HSS, 2007–12; non-exec. Chm., French plc, 1999–2001; non-exec. Dir, Geest plc, 1988–91; Director: Coles, Australia, 2007–; Target Ltd, Australia, 2013–; Member: British Railways Bd, 1992–94; Railtrack Gp Bd, 1994–2000; Advr, Wesfarmers, Australia, 2007–. Sen. Advr, Lazard & Co., 2004–13. Member: DTI Deregulation Taskforce, 1993–97; Anglo-German Deregulation Taskforce, 1995. MP (C) Tunbridge Wells, 1997–2005. Chief Exec. and Dep. Chm., Cons. Party, 1998–99 (a Vice-Chm., 1997–98); Opposition front bench spokesman on the envmt, transport and the regions, 2000–01. Gov., NIESR, 1997–. Trustee, Cystic Fibrosis Trust, 2009–12. Fellow, Marketing Soc. Hon. Dr: Leeds Metropolitan, 1995; York, 2012. Yorkshire Business Man of the Year, 1995; NatWest Retailer of the Year, 1996; Special Award, Inst. for Turnaround, 2010. *Recreations:* farming, horses, tennis, opera, football. *Address:* ITV plc, London Television Centre, Upper Ground, SE1 9LT.

NORMAN, Archibald Percy, MBE 1945; MD; FRCP, FRCPCH, FRCPI; Physician, Hospital for Sick Children, 1950–77, then Hon. Physician; Paediatrician, Queen Charlotte's Maternity Hospital, 1951–77, then Hon. Paediatrician; *b* 19 July 1912; *s* of Dr George Percy Norman and Mary Margaret MacCallum; *m* 1950, Aleida Elisabeth M. M. R. Bisschop; five *s. Educ:* Charterhouse; Emmanuel Coll., Cambridge. FRCP 1954; FRCPI 1995; FRCPCH 1996. Served War of 1939–45, in Army, 1940–45. Chairman: Med. and Res. Cttee, Cystic Fibrosis Res. Trust, 1976–84; E Surrey Cttee, Mencap Homes Foundn, 1987–92; Mem., Attendance Allowance Appeals Bd, 1978–84. Mem., Bd of Trustees, Children's Trust, 1987–98 (Chm., 1991–93). *Publications:* (ed) Congenital Abnormalities, 1962, 2nd edn 1971; (ed) Moncreiff's Nursing and Diseases of Sick Children, 1966; (ed) Cystic Fibrosis, 1983; contributions to medical journals. *Address:* White Lodge, Heather Close, Kingswood, Surrey KT20 6NY. *T:* (01737) 832626.

See also A. J. Norman.

NORMAN, Barry (Leslie), CBE 1998; author, journalist and broadcaster; *b* 21 Aug. 1933; *s* of late Leslie and Elizabeth Norman; *m* 1957, Diana (*d* 2011), *o d* of late A. H. and C. A. Narracott; two *d. Educ:* Highgate Sch. Entertainments Editor, Daily Mail, 1969–71, then made redundant; writer and presenter of Film 1973–81, and Film 1983–98, BBC1; presenter of: Today, Radio 4, 1974–76; Going Places, Radio 4, 1977–81; Breakaway, Radio 4, 1979–80; Omnibus, BBC1, 1982; The Chip Shop, Radio 4, 1984; How Far Can You Go?, Radio 4, 1990; writer and presenter of: The Hollywood Greats, BBC1, 1977–79, 1984, 1985; The British Greats, 1980; Talking Pictures (series), BBC1, 1988; Barry Norman's Film Night, BSkyB, 1998–2001. Dir, Nat. Film Finance Corp., 1980–85. Weekly columnist: The Guardian, 1971–80; Radio Times. Gov., BFI, 1996–2001. Hon. LittD: UEA, 1991; Hertfordshire, 1996. Richard Dimbleby Award, BAFTA, 1981; Columnist of the Year, 1991; Special Award: London Film Critics' Circle, 1995; Guild of Regl Film Writers, 1995. *Publications:* The Matter of Mandrake, 1967; The Hounds of Sparta, 1968; Tales of the Redundance Kid, 1975; End Product, 1975; A Series of Defeats, 1977; To Nick a Good Body, 1978; The Hollywood Greats, 1979; The Movie Greats, 1981; Have a Nice Day, 1981; Sticky Wicket, 1984; The Film Greats, 1985; Talking Pictures, 1988; The Birddog Tape, 1992; 100 Best Films of the Century, 1993; (with Emma Norman) Barry Norman's Video Guide, 1994; The Mickey Mouse Affair, 1995; (with Emma Norman) Barry Norman's Family Video Guide, 1996; Death on Sunset, 1998; And Why Not? (memoirs), 2002; Barry Norman's Book of Cricket, 2009; See You in the Morning, 2013. *Recreations:* watching first-class cricket, supporting Tottenham Hotspur. *Address:* c/o Curtis Brown Ltd, Haymarket House, 28–29 Haymarket, SW1Y 4SP. *T:* (020) 7396 6600. *Clubs:* MCC, Groucho, Lord's Taverners (Pres., 2011–12).

NORMAN, David Mark; Chairman, Norlan Resources Ltd, since 1998; *b* 30 Jan. 1941; *s* of late Mark Richard Norman, CBE and of Helen Norman (*née* Bryan); *m* 1966, Diana Sheffield; one *s* three *d. Educ:* Eton Coll.; McGill Univ. (BA); Harvard Business Sch. (MBA). Norcros Ltd, 1967–77, Dir of Ops and Main Bd Dir, 1975–77; Russell Reynolds Associates Inc., 1977–82: Exec. Dir, 1977–78; Man. Dir, 1978–82; Chairman: Norman Resources Ltd, 1982–83; Norman Broadbent Internat. Ltd, 1983–98; Chm. and Chief Exec., 1987–97, non-exec. Chm., 1997–98, BNB Resources plc. Chm., Royal Ballet Sch., 2000–09; Gov., Royal Ballet, 1996–2009. Trustee, Royal Botanic Gardens, Kew, 2002–07. Pres., Tennis and Rackets Assoc., 2011– (Chm., 1992–97). *Recreations:* golf, tennis, rackets, classical music, opera, ballet. *Address:* Burkham House, Alton, Hants GU34 5RS. *T:* (01256) 381437. *E:* dmnorman2@aol.com. *Clubs:* Boodle's; Queen's (Dir, 2007–; Chm., 2011), All England Lawn Tennis.

NORMAN, Rev. Dr Edward Robert Michael; Canon Residentiary, 1995–2004, and Chancellor, 1999–2004, York Minster; *b* 22 Nov. 1938; *o s* of Ernest Edward Norman and Yvonne Louise Norman. *Educ:* Chatham House Sch.; Monoux Sch.; Selwyn Coll., Cambridge (MA, PhD, DD). FRHistS. Lincoln Theological Coll., 1965. Deacon, 1965; Priest, 1971. Asst Master, Beaconsfield Sec. Mod. Sch., Walthamstow, 1957–58; Fellow of Selwyn Coll., Cambridge, 1962–64; Fellow of Jesus Coll., Cambridge, 1964–71; Lectr in History, Univ. of Cambridge, 1965–88; Dean of Peterhouse, Cambridge, 1971–88 (Emeritus Fellow); Dean of Chapel, Christ Church Coll., Canterbury, 1988–95. Wilkinson Prof. of Church History, Wycliffe Coll., Univ. of Toronto, 1981–82; Associated Schol., Ethics and Public Policy Center, Washington, 1986–; Hon. Prof., Univ. of York, 1996–2004. NATO Res. Fellow, 1966–68. Asst Chaplain, Addenbrooke's Hosp., Cambridge, 1971–78. Hon. Curate, St Andrew-by-the-Wardrobe, and St James Garlickhythe, City of London, 2005–12. Ordinariate of Our Lady of Walsingham, 2012–. Lectures: Reith, 1978; Prideaux, 1980; Suntory-Toyota, LSE, 1984. Six Preacher in Canterbury Cathedral, 1984–90. FRSA. *Publications:* The Catholic Church and Ireland, 1965; The Conscience of the State in North America, 1968; Anti-Catholicism in Victorian England, 1968; The Early Development of Irish Society, 1969; A History of Modern Ireland, 1971; Church and Society in Modern England, 1976; Christianity and the World Order, 1979; Christianity in the Southern Hemisphere, 1981; The English Catholic Church in the Nineteenth Century, 1983; Roman Catholicism in England, 1985; The Victorian Christian Socialists, 1987; The House of God: church architecture, style and history, 1990; Entering the Darkness: Christianity and its modern substitutes, 1991; An Anglican Catechism, 2001; Out of the Depths, 2001; Secularisation, 2002; Anglican Difficulties, 2004; The Mercy of God's Humility, 2004; The Roman Catholic Church, 2007. *Recreation:* watching television. *Address:* Flat 7, Oakland Court, Kings Road, Herne Bay, Kent CT6 5RL. *T:* (01227) 742400.

NORMAN, Ven. Garth; Archdeacon of Bromley and Bexley (formerly Bromley), 1994–2003, now Emeritus; *b* 26 Nov. 1938; *s* of Harry and Freda Norman; *m* 1977, Jacqueline Elisabeth (*née* Yunge-Bateman); one *s. Educ:* Henry Mellish Grammar Sch., Nottingham; Univ. of Durham (BA Hons Theol., DipTh, MA); Univ. of East Anglia (MEd); Univ. of Cambridge (PGCE). Deacon 1963, priest 1964; Curate, St Anne's, Wandsworth, 1963–66; Team Vicar, Trunch, Norfolk, 1966–71; Rector of Gimingham, 1971–77; Team Rector of Trunch, 1977–83; RD, Repps, 1975–83; Principal, Chiltern Christian Trng Scheme, Dio. of Oxford, 1983–88; Dir of Training, Dio. of Rochester, 1988–94; Hon. Canon of Rochester Cathedral, 1991–2003. *Recreations:* walking, music. *Address:* 12 Scotsdowne Road, Trumpington, Cambridge CB2 9HU. *T:* (01223) 844303.

NORMAN, George Alfred B.; *see* Bathurst Norman.

NORMAN, Geraldine Lucia, OBE 2011; Advisor to Director, State Hermitage Museum, St Petersburg, since 2012 (UK Representative, 2001–12); Chief Executive, Hermitage Foundation UK (formerly Secretary, then Chief Executive, Friends of The Hermitage), 2003–12; *b* 13 May 1940; *d* of Harold Hugh Keen and Catherine Eleanor Lyle Keen (*née* Cummins); *m* 1971, Frank Norman (*d* 1980). *Educ:* St Mary's Sch., Calne; St Anne's Coll., Oxford (MA). Teaching Asst, UCLA, 1961–62; Statistician, The Times, 1962–66; Econ. Writer, FAO, Rome, 1966–67; Sale Room Corresp., The Times, 1969–87; Art Market Corresp., The Independent, 1987–95. Exec. Dir, Hermitage Develt Trust, 1999–2001; Exec. Ed., Hermitage Mag., 2003–05. Medal in memory of 300 years of St Petersburg (Russian Fedn), 2005. News Reporter of Year, British Press Awards, 1976. *Publications:* (as Geraldine Keen) The Sale of Works of Art, 1971; Nineteenth Century Painters and Painting: a dictionary, 1977; (with Tom Keating and Frank Norman) The Fake's Progress, 1977; (as Florence Place) Mrs Harper's Niece, 1982; Biedermeier Painting, 1987; (with Natsuo Miyashita) Top Collectors of the World, 1993; The Hermitage: the biography of a great museum, 1997. *Recreations:* transcendental meditation, reading detective stories. *Address:* 5 Seaford Court, 220 Great Portland Street, W1W 5QR. *T:* (020) 7387 6067.

NORMAN, Gregory John, AO 1999 (AM 1987); golfer; Chairman and Chief Executive Officer, Great White Shark Enterprises LLC; *b* 10 Feb. 1955; *s* of M. Norman; *m* 1st, 1981, Laura Andrassy (marr. diss. 2007); one *s* one *d*; 2nd, 2008, Christine Marie Evert, *qv* (marr. diss. 2009). *Educ:* Townsville Grammar Sch.; High Sch., Aspley, Queensland. Professional golfer, 1976–; tournament wins include: Open, Turnberry, 1986; Open, Royal St George's, 1993; Australian Open, 1980, 1985, 1987, 1995, 1996; US PGA, 1993, 1994; Players' Championship, 1994; numerous awards and other wins in Australia, S Africa, USA. *Publications:* My Story, 1983; Shark Attack, 1988; Greg Norman's Better Golf, 1994; The Way of the Shark, 2006. *Address:* Great White Shark Enterprises LLC, 2041 Vista Parkway, Level 2, West Palm Beach, FL 33411, USA.

NORMAN, (Herbert) John (La French), FISOB; writer and organ consultant; *b* 15 Jan. 1932; *s* of late Herbert La French Norman, Hon. RCO, FRSA, and Hilda Caroline (*née* West); *m* 1956, Jill Frances Sharp; one *s* two *d. Educ:* Tollington Sch.; Imperial Coll., London (BSc 1953). ARCS 1953. Wm Hill & Son and Norman & Beard Ltd (organbuilders by appt to HM Queen), 1953–74; Dir, 1960–74; Man. Dir, 1970–74; Exec., IBM UK Ltd, 1974–90. Work on organs in cathedrals in Gloucester, Norwich, Lichfield, Southwell Minster, Chelmsford and Brisbane, Australia; also Bath Abbey and RCO. Organ Advr, Dio. London, 1975–; Organ Consultant to: Harrow Sch.; Lancing Coll.; Mill Hill Sch.; English and American Ch, Den Haag; Gibraltar Cathedral; Liberal Jewish Synagogue, St John's Wood; St Margaret's, Westminster; St Mary's Pro-cathedral, Dublin; St Helen's, Bishopsgate; St Mary's, Twickenham; Chapel of St Mary Undercroft, Houses of Parliament; Mullingar Cathedral, Ireland; St Lawrence, Whitchurch (Handel organ); Parish Churches of Oakham, Westbourne, Ashton-on-Ribble, Baldock, Bolton, Farnham, Coulsdon and Donaghadee (NI); Armenian Ch, Kensington; St Botolph, Aldersgate; Worcester Cathedral; St Mary-le-Bow, City of London; St Mary, Rye; St Peter, Notting Hill; St Swithun, Worcester; Edington Priory Ch; St John, Notting Hill; Holy Trinity, Bramley; Prichard-Jones Hall, Univ. of Bangor; Great Hall, QMUL; OBE Chapel, St Paul's Cathedral; St Michael, Sutton Court, Chiswick; West Wittering Parish Ch; St Mary, Finedon; St Boniface Anglican Ch, Antwerp, Belgium; Liverpool Anglican Cathedral. Founding Editor: Musical Instrument Technol., 1969–2002; The Organbuilder, 1983–2000; In Sight, 1991–95; Columnist, Organists' Rev., 1980–. Member: St Albans Diocesan Synod, 1980–86; Organs Cttee, Council for Care of Churches, 1987–2001; London DAC for Care of Churches, 1989–; Cathedrals Fabric Commn for England, 1991–2001. Chm., British Inst. of Organ Studies, 2006–11; Past Pres., Inst. of Musical Instrument Technol. Freeman, City of London; Liveryman, Musicians' Co., 1972–. Hon. FIMIT. *Publications:* (with Herbert Norman) The Organ Today, 1966, 2nd edn 1980; The Organs of Britain, 1984; (with Jim Berrow) Sounds Good, 2002; The Box of Whistles, 2007. *Recreations:* writing, music, architecture, travel. *Address:* 15 Baxendale, Whetstone, N20 0EG. *T:* (020) 8445 0801. *W:* www.jnorman.me.uk.

NORMAN, Prof. Jane Elizabeth, MD; Professor of Maternal and Fetal Health, and Director, Tommy's Centre for Maternal and Fetal Health Research, University of Edinburgh, since 2008; Hon. Consultant Obstetrician and Gynaecologist, Edinburgh Royal Infirmary, since 2008; *b* England, 1963. *Educ:* Edinburgh Univ. (MB ChB 1986; MD 1992). MRCOG 1992. Trng in obstetrics and gynaecol., Univ. of Edinburgh, 1986–92; University of Glasgow: Clin. Lectr, 1993; Personal Chair, 2006–07; Regius Prof. of Obstetrics and Gynaecol., 2007–08. FMedSci 2012. *Publications:* (with D. Hart) Gynaecology Illustrated, 5th edn, 2000; (ed with I. Greer) Preterm Labour: managing the risk in clinical practice, 2005; chapters in: Gynaecology by Ten Teachers, 17th edn 2000 and 18th edn 2006; Preterm Birth, 2004; Preterm Birth: Mechanisms, Mediators, 2007; Dewhurst's Textbook of Obstetrics and

Gynaecology, 2012; contrib. articles to jls incl. BMJ, PLOS Medicine, Lancet, British Jl Obstetrics and Gynaecol., Obstetrics and Gynaecol., Jl Reproductive Immunol., Amer. Jl Obstetrics and Gynaecol., Jl Clin. Endocrinol. and Metabolism. *Address:* MRC Centre for Reproductive Health, Queen's Medical Research Institute, 47 Little France Crescent, Edinburgh EH16 4TJ. *T:* (0131) 242 6623. *E:* jane.norman@ed.ac.uk.

NORMAN, Jesse; *see* Norman, (Alexander) Jesse.

NORMAN, Jessye; soprano, concert and opera singer; *b* Augusta, Ga, USA, 15 Sept. 1945; *d* of late Silas Norman Sr and Janie King Norman. *Educ:* Howard Univ., Washington, DC (BM *cum laude*). Peabody Conservatory, 1967; Univ. of Michigan, 1967–68 (MMus). Operatic début, Deutsche Oper, Berlin, 1969; La Scala, Milan, 1972; Royal Opera House, Covent Garden, 1972; NY Metropolitan Opera, 1983; American début, Hollywood Bowl, 1972; Lincoln Centre, NYC, 1973. Tours include North and South America, Europe, Middle East, Australia, Israel, Japan. Many international festivals, including Aix-en-Provence, Aldeburgh, Berlin, Edinburgh, Flanders, Helsinki, Lucerne, Salzburg, Tanglewood, Spoleto, Hollywood, Ravinia. Hon. Fellow: Newnham Coll., Cambridge, 1989; Jesus Coll., Cambridge, 1989. Hon. DMus: Howard Univ., 1982; Univ. of the South, Sewanee, 1984; Boston Conservatory, 1984; Univ. of Michigan and Brandeis Univ., Mass, 1987; Harvard Univ., 1988; Cambridge, 1989; Hon. DHL Amer. Univ. of Paris, 1989. Hon. RAM 1987. Musician of the Year, Musical America, 1982; prizes include: Grand Prix du Disque (Acad. du Disque Français), 1973, 1976, 1977, 1982, 1984; Grand Prix du Disque (Acad. Charles Cros), 1983; Deutscher Schallplattenpreis, 1975, 1981; Cigale d'Or, Aix-en-Provence Fest., 1977; IRCAM record award, 1982; Grammy, 1984, 1988. Commandeur de l'Ordre des Arts et des Lettres, France, 1984. *Publications:* Stand Up Straight and Sing! (memoir), 2014.

NORMAN, John; *see* Norman, H. J. La F.

NORMAN, Prof. Kenneth Roy, FBA 1985; Professor of Indian Studies, University of Cambridge, 1990–92, Emeritus Professor 1992; *b* 21 July 1925; *s* of Clement and Peggy Norman; *m* 1953, Pamela Raymont; one *s* one *d*. *Educ:* Taunton School; Downing College, Cambridge (MA 1954). Fellow and Tutor, Downing College, Cambridge, 1952–64; Lectr in Indian Studies (Prakrit), 1955–78, Reader, 1978–90, Univ. of Cambridge. Foreign Mem., Royal Danish Acad. of Sciences and Letters, 1983. *Publications:* Elders' Verses I (Theragāthā), 1969; Elders' Verses II (Therīgāthā), 1971; (trans.) Jain Cosmology, 1981; Pāli Literature, 1983; The Group of Discourses (Sutta-nipāta), Vol. I, 1984, Vol. II, 1992, 2nd edn 2001; Collected Papers: Vol. I, 1990, Vol. II, 1991, Vol. III, 1992, Vol. IV, 1993, Vol. V, 1994, Vol. VI, 1996, Vol. VII, 2001, Vol. VIII, 2007; Poems of Early Buddhist Monks, 1997; The Word of the Doctrine (Dhammapada), 1997; A Philological Approach to Buddhism, 1997; (with W. Pruitt) The Pātimokkha, 2001; (with W. Pruitt) Kaṅkhāvitaraṇī, 2003; (ed) Pāli Tipitakam Concordance, Vol. II 4–9, 1963–73; (ed) Critical Pāli Dictionary Vol. II 11–17, 1981–90. *Recreations:* pottery, reading. *Address:* 6 Huttles Green, Shepreth, Royston, Herts SG8 6PR. *T:* (01763) 260541.

NORMAN, Lisa Marie; *see* Harker, L. M.

NORMAN, Sir Nigel (James), 4th Bt *cr* 1915 of Honeyhanger, Shottermill, co. Surrey; *b* 5 Feb. 1956; *er s* of Sir Mark Annesley Norman, 3rd Bt and Joanna Camilla (*née* Kilgour); *S* father, 2013; *m* 1st, 1985, Joanna Naylor-Leyland (marr. diss. 1989); 2nd, 1994, Mrs Juliet Clare Louise Marriott (*née* Baxendale); three *s* one *d*. *Heir: s* Antony Richard St Valery Norman, *b* 10 March 1995.

NORMAN, Philip Frank William; author and journalist; *b* 13 April 1943; *s* of Clive and Irene Norman; *m* 1990, Sue Summers; one *d*. *Educ:* Ryde Sch., Isle of Wight. Trainee reporter, Hunts Post, Huntingdon, 1961–64; Reporter: Cambridge News, 1965; Northern Despatch, 1965; Northern Echo, 1965–66; Feature Writer, Sunday Times Mag., 1966–75; Atticus Columnist and Feature Writer, Sunday Times, 1976–82. Writer of musicals: This is Elvis: Viva Las Vegas, 2006 (2 national tours); Laughter in the Rain: the Neil Sedaka Story, 2010. *Publications:* Slip on a Fat Lady, 1970; Plumridge, 1971; Wild Thing, 1972; The Skaters' Waltz, 1979 (one of 20 Best Young British Novelists, 1983); Shout!: the true story of the Beatles, 1981, 4th edn 2003; The Road Goes on For Ever, 1982; The Stones, 1984, 6th edn 2012; Tilt the Hourglass and Begin Again, 1985; Your Walrus Hurt the One You Love, 1985; Awful Moments, 1986; Pieces of Hate, 1987; The Life and Good Times of the Rolling Stones, 1989; Words of Love, 1989; Days in the Life: John Lennon remembered, 1990; The Age of Parody, 1990; Elton, 1991, 3rd edn, as Sir Elton, 2000; Everyone's Gone to the Moon, 1995; Buddy: the biography, 1996; Babycham Night, 2003; John Lennon: the life, 2008; Mick Jagger, 2012; Macca: the life of Paul McCartney, 2016; contrib. Times, Guardian, Daily Mail, New York Times, Vanity Fair, Playboy, Cosmopolitan, GQ, Spectator, New Statesman etc. *Recreations:* literature, cinema. *Address:* 46 Willoughby Road, NW3 1RU. *E:* philip@philipnorman.com. *Clubs:* Groucho, Ivy.

NORMAN, Sir Ronald, Kt 1995; OBE 1987; DL; CEng; Chairman, Priority Sites, 1997–2001; *b* 29 April 1937; *s* of Leonard William Norman and Elsie Louise Norman (*née* Cooke); *m* 1st, 1961, Jennifer Mansfield (marr. diss. 1972); two *s* one *d*; 2nd, 1975, Joyce Lyons. *Educ:* Dulwich Coll.; King's Coll., London (BSc Eng.). CE; CEng, MICE 1966. Man. Dir, then Chm., Cecil M. Yuill Ltd, Developers, Hartlepool, 1965–86; Chm., R. Norman Ltd, Developers, Durham, 1986–93. Chm., Teesside Develt Corp., 1987–98. Pres., Cleveland Community Foundn, 1998–; Vice-Pres., Trincomalee Trust, 1998–. Pres., Durham Co. Scouts Assoc., 2006–. DL Cleveland, 1996. *Publications:* The Odd Man Out in the Alps, 2008. *Recreations:* mountain climbing (has climbed all the Munros in Scotland), book collecting, restoring antique books. *Address:* Sparrow Hall, Dalton-Piercy, Cleveland TS27 3HY. *T:* (01429) 273857.

NORMAN, Russell; restaurateur; Founder, Polpo Ltd, since 2009; *b* London, 9 Dec. 1965; *s* of Ernest Clifford Norman and Carole Julia Norman (*née* Giddy, now Beadle); *m* 2004, Jules McNally; one *s* two *d*. *Educ:* Heathland Sch., Hounslow; Sunderland Poly. (BA English); Inst. of Educn, Univ. of London (PGCE English and Drama). Maitre d', Joe Allen Restaurant, 1990–99; Hd of Drama, Bentley Wood High Sch., 1995–98; General Manager: Circus Restaurant, 1999–2002; Zuma Restaurant, 2002–06; Ops Dir, Caprice Hldgs Ltd, 2006–09. Presenter, TV series, The Restaurant Man, 2014. Columnist, Esquire Mag., 2015–. *Publications:* Polpo: a Venetian cookbook (of sorts), 2012; Spuntino: comfort food (New York style), 2015. *Recreations:* cooking, Scrabble. *Address:* c/o Cathryn Summerhayes, William Morris Endeavour, 100 New Oxford Street, WC1A 1HB. *T:* (020) 8929 8409. *E:* csummerhayes@wmeentertainment.com. *Club:* Groucho.

NORMAN, Susan Elizabeth, (Mrs J. C. Sheridan), OBE 2014; Chief Executive and Registrar, United Kingdom Central Council for Nursing, Midwifery and Health Visiting, 1995–2002; *b* 9 Aug. 1946; *d* of late Dr J. M. Norman and Betty Norman (*née* Colyer); *m* 1983, John Christopher Sheridan. *Educ:* St Nicholas Sch., Fleet, Hants; Dartington Hall, Devon; St Thomas' Hosp. (RGN); Bedford Coll., London (RNT); South Bank Univ. (BEd Hons). Student nurse, St Thomas' Hosp., 1965–69; Dist Nurse, RBK&C, 1969–71; Staff Nurse, Royal Marsden Hosp., 1972; Nursing Officer (Dist Nursing), Kensington and Chelsea, 1972–73; Staff Nurse, Montreal Gen. Hosp., 1974–75; Tutor Student, London Univ., 1975–77; Tutor and Sen. Tutor, Nightingale Sch., 1977–87; Principal Nursing Officer (Asst Sec.), DoH, London and Leeds, 1988–95. Vis. Prof., London South Bank (formerly S Bank) Univ., 2002–. President: Nat. Assoc. of Theatre Nurses, 2002–04; Nightingale Fellowship, 2007–; Chair: in touch Support, 2006–10; Florence Nightingale Mus. Trust, 2012–. FRSA 1997. Hon. DSc Plymouth, 2002. *Publications:* Nursing Practice and Health Care, 1989, 5th edn 2008. *Recreations:* music (singing and opera), walking, UK and France, eating out, volunteer gardener with Thrive.

NORMAN, Sir Torquil (Patrick Alexander), Kt 2007; CBE 2002; Chairman, Roundhouse Trust, 1996–2007; *b* 1933; *s* of Sir Henry Nigel St Valery Norman, 2nd Bt, CBE and Patricia Moyra Norman; *m* 1961, Lady (Elizabeth) Anne (*d* 2005), *d* of Alexander Victor Edward Paulet Montagu; three *s* two *d*. *Educ:* Eton; Trinity Coll., Cambridge (BA 1957). Served RAF. Investment banker, NY; Man. Dir, Berwick Timpo, toy co., until 1979; former Chm., Bluebird Toys. Set up Norman Trust; bought Roundhouse, 1996, re-launched as arts venue, 2006. *Publications:* Kick the Tyres, Light the Fires, 2012.
See also A. J. Norman.

NORMANBY, 5th Marquis of, *cr* 1838; **Constantine Edmund Walter Phipps;** Baron Mulgrave (Ire.) 1767; Baron Mulgrave (GB) 1794; Earl of Mulgrave and Viscount Normanby 1812; *b* 24 Feb. 1954; *e s* of 4th Marquis of Normanby KG, CBE and of Hon. Grania Guinness (OBE 2000), *d* of 1st Baron Moyne; *S* father, 1994; one *d* by Ms Sophie McCormick; *m* 1990, Mrs Nicola St Aubyn (*see* Marchioness of Normanby); two *s* one *d*. *Educ:* Eton; Worcester Coll., Oxford; City Univ. *Publications:* Careful with the Sharks, 1985; Among the Thin Ghosts, 1989; What You Want, 2014. *Heir: s* Earl of Mulgrave, *qv*. *Address:* Mulgrave Castle, Whitby, N Yorks YO21 3RJ. *Club:* Garrick.

NORMANBY, Marchioness of; Nicola Phipps; journalist, author; *b* 15 Feb. 1960; *d* of late Milton Shulman and of Drusilla Beyfus, *qv*; *m* 1st, 1987, Edward St Aubyn (marr. diss. 1990); 2nd, 1990, Earl of Mulgrave (*see* Marquis of Normanby); two *s* one *d*. *Educ:* St Paul's Girls' Sch.; Corpus Christi Coll., Oxford (BA Hons). Trustee: Nat. Gall., 2004–12; Garden Mus., Lambeth, 2013– (Curator, exhibn, Fashion and Gardens, 2014). *Publications:* (as Nicola Shulman): A Rage for Rock Gardening, 2002, 3rd edn 2004; Graven with Diamonds: the many lives of Thomas Wyatt, 2011, 3rd edn 2014. *Recreations:* singing, Latin, gardening. *Address:* Mulgrave Castle, Whitby, N Yorks YO21 3RJ.
See also A. Shulman.

NORMAND, Andrew Christie, CB 2001; SSC; FSAScot; Sheriff at Glasgow, since 2006; *b* 7 Feb. 1948; *m* 1975, Barbara Jean Smith; two *d*. *Educ:* George Watson's Coll., Edinburgh; Univ. of Edinburgh (MA 1968; LLB 1970); Queen's Univ., Kingston, Ont (LLM 1972). Admitted solicitor, 1974. Crown Office: Legal Asst, Edinburgh, 1974–76, 1977; seconded to Scottish Law Commn, 1976; Sen. Legal Asst, Edinburgh, 1977–78, Perth, 1978–81; Asst Solicitor, 1981–87; Procurator Fiscal, Airdrie, 1987–88; Dep. Crown Agent for Scotland, 1988–90; Regl Procurator Fiscal, Glasgow, 1990–96; Crown Agent for Scotland, 1996–2003; an all-Scotland Sheriff, 2003–06. *Address:* Sheriff Court of Glasgow and Strathkelvin, 1 Carlton Place, Glasgow G5 9DA.

NORMANTON, 6th Earl of, *cr* 1806; **Shaun James Christian Welbore Ellis Agar;** Baron Mendip, 1794; Baron Somerton, 1795; Viscount Somerton, 1800; Baron Somerton (UK), 1873; Royal Horse Guards, 1965; Blues and Royals, 1969; left Army, 1972, Captain; *b* 21 Aug. 1945; *er s* of 5th Earl of Normanton; *S* father, 1967; *m* 1970, Victoria Susan (marr. diss. 2000), *o d* of late J. H. C. Beard; one *s* two *d*; *m* 2009, Rosalind Bearnice (*d* 2011), *d* of late G. S. Nott. *Educ:* Eton. *Recreations:* shooting, scuba diving, motor boating. *Heir: s* Viscount Somerton, *qv*. *Address:* Ellingham Farm, Ellingham, Ringwood, Hants BH24 3PJ. *T:* (01425) 473477. *Clubs:* White's; Royal Yacht Squadron.

NORMINGTON, Sir David (John), GCB 2011 (KCB 2005; CB 2000); First Civil Service Commissioner and Commissioner for Public Appointments, since 2011; *b* 18 Oct. 1951; *s* of late Ronald Normington and of Kathleen Normington (*née* Towler); *m* 1985, Winifred Anne Charlotte Harris, *qv*. *Educ:* Bradford Grammar Sch.; Corpus Christi College, Oxford (BA Hons Mod. Hist.). Department of Employment, subseq. Department for Education and Employment: joined 1973; Private Sec. to Perm. Sec., 1976–77; Principal Private Sec. to Sec. of State for Employment, 1984–85; Employment Service Regional Dir for London and SE Region, 1987–89; Hd of Strategy and Employment Policy Div., 1990–92; Dir of Personnel and Develt, 1992–95, of Personnel and Support Services, 1995–97; Dir Gen., Strategy, Internat. and Analytical Services, 1997–98; Dir Gen. for Schs, 1998–2001; Permanent Secretary: DfEE, then DfES, 2001–05; Home Office, 2006–10. Mem. Council, Univ. of Warwick, 2011–. Trustee, NSPCC, 2012–. *Recreations:* gardening, ballet, walking, cricket. *Address:* Civil Service Commission, 1 Horse Guards Road, SW1A 2HQ. *E:* david.normington@csc.gsi.gov.uk.

NORMINGTON, Winifred Anne Charlotte, (Lady Normington); *see* Harris, W. A. C.

NORREY, Philip Julian, PhD; Chief Executive, Devon County Council, since 2006; *b* 9 July 1963; *s* of Harold and Dorothy Norrey; *m* 2003, Stephanie Ann Sloman. *Educ:* Colchester Royal Grammar Sch.; Univ. of Bristol (BA Hons Hist. 1984; PhD Hist. 1988). Audit Examiner, District Audit, 1989; graduate trainee, Somerset CC, 1990; Asst Dir of Educn, N Somerset DC, 1996–98; Dep. Dir, 1998–2003, Dir, 2003–06, of Educn, Devon CC. Chm., Assoc. of County Chief Execs, 2011–12. Hon. Fellow, Univ. of Exeter, 2003. *Publications:* contrib. Historical Jl. *Recreations:* cycling, food and wine, historical research, Burnley Football Club, railways, classical music, 70s and 80s TV drama. *Address:* c/o Devon County Council, County Hall, Topsham Road, Exeter EX2 4QD. *T:* (01392) 383201. *E:* phil.norrey@devon.gov.uk.

NORREYS, Lord; Henry Mark Willoughby Bertie; *b* 6 June 1958; *s* and *heir* of the Earl of Lindsey (14th) and Abingdon (9th), *qv*; *m* 1989, Lucinda, *d* of Christopher Moorsom; two *s*. *Educ:* Eton; Univ. of Edinburgh. Kt of Honour and Devotion, SMO Malta, 1995; Kt of Justice, Constantinian Order of St George, 1998; Kt, Order of St Maurice and St Lazarus, 1999. *Heir: s* Hon. Willoughby Henry Constantine St Maur Bertie, *b* 15 Jan. 1996. *Address:* The Old Dairy, Gilmilnscroft, Sorn, Mauchline, Ayrshire KA5 6ND. *Clubs:* Pratt's; Puffin's (Edinburgh).

NORRIE, family name of **Baron Norrie**.

NORRIE, 2nd Baron *cr* 1957; **George Willoughby Moke Norrie;** *b* 27 April 1936; *s* of 1st Baron Norrie, GCMG, GCVO, CB, DSO, MC, and Jocelyn Helen (*d* 1938), *d* of late R. H. Gosling; *S* father, 1977; *m* 1st, 1964, Celia Marguerite, JP (marr. diss. 1997), *d* of John Pelham Mann, MC; one *s* two *d*; 2nd, 1997, Mrs Pamela Ann McCaffry, *d* of Sir Arthur Ralph Wilmot, 7th Bt. *Educ:* Eton College; RMA Sandhurst. Commissioned 11th Hussars (PAO), 1956; ADC to C-in-C Middle East Comd, 1960–61; GSO 3 (Int.) 4th Guards Brigade, 1967–69; retired, 1970. Underwriting Mem. of Lloyd's, 1977–97. Director: Fairfield Nurseries (Hermitage) Ltd, 1976–89; International Garden Centre (British Gp) Ltd, 1984–86; Conservation Practice Ltd, 1989–91; Hilliers (Fairfield) Ltd, 1989–97; Advisor to: S Grundon (Waste) Ltd, 1991–2001; CH2M Hill Ltd (London), 1994–96. Non-exec. Dir, Philip T. English Internat. Financial Services Ltd, 2007–12. Mem., EC Cttee, Sub Cttee F (Environment), H of L, 1988–92. President: The Conservation Volunteers (formerly British Trust for Conservation Volunteers), 1987–2014; Internat. Cultural Exchange, 1988–2000; The Salespeople's Charity (formerly Commercial Travellers Benevolent Instn), 1992–; Royal British Legion (Newbury Branch), 1971–96; Nat. Kidney Fedn, 1994–2001; Vice President: Tree Council, 1990–2001; Council for Nat. Parks, 1990–. Member, Council: Winston Churchill Meml Trust, 1993–2010; Royal Scottish Forestry Soc., 2012–. Patron: Age Resource, 1991–2004; Faure-Alderson Romanian Appeal, 1993–2001; Janki Foundn, 1997–; UK Patron, RLSS, 1994– (Mem., Commonwealth Council, 1999–). Gov., Dunstan Park

Sch., Thatcham, 1989–94. Mem., British Soc. of Dowsers, 1999–. Sponsored: Swimming and Water Safety Bill, 1993 (enacted under statutory order, 1994); Nat. Parks Bill, 1993 (incorp. in Envmt Act, 1995). Freeman, City of London, 1999. Green Ribbon Political Award for services to the envmt, H of L, 1993. *Recreations:* fishing, golf. *Heir: s* Hon. Mark Willoughby John Norrie [*b* 31 March 1972; *m* 1st, 1998, Carol (marr. diss. 2012), *e d* of Michael Stockdale; two *s*; 2nd, 2014, Penelope Menzel; one *s*]. *Address:* Holehouse, Penpont, Thornhill, Dumfriesshire DG3 4AP. *T:* (01848) 600243. *Clubs:* Cavalry and Guards, MCC.

NORRIE, Prof. Alan William, PhD; FBA 2011; Professor of Law, University of Warwick, since 2009 (Head, School of Law, 2011–15); *b* Arbroath, Scotland, 14 Nov. 1953; *s* of Tom Norrie and Gertrude Norrie; *m* 1978, Gwen Chapman; two *s*. *Educ:* Bishop's Stortford Coll.; Methodist Coll., Belfast; Univ. of Edinburgh (LLB 1975); Univ. of Sheffield (MA Criminol. 1976); Univ. of Dundee (PhD 1985). Lectr, Univ. of Dundee, 1977–86; Lectr, 1987–91, Sen. Lectr, 1991–94, Univ. of Warwick; Drapers' Prof. of Law, QMW, 1994–97; Edmund-Davies Prof. of Criminal Law and Criminal Justice, KCL, 1997–2009. Leverhulme Major Res. Fellow, 2015–. *Publications:* Law, Ideology and Punishment, 1991; Crime, Reason and History, 1993, 3rd edn 2014; Punishment, Responsibility and Justice, 2000; Law and the Beautiful Soul, 2005; Dialectic and Difference, 2010. *Recreations:* reading, music, film, theatre, art, football, gardening, dog walking. *Address:* School of Law, University of Warwick, Coventry CV4 7AL. *T:* (024) 7615 1107. *E:* A.W.Norrie@warwick.ac.uk.

NORRIE, Her Honour Marian Farrow, (Mrs W. G. Walker); a Circuit Judge, 1986–2012; *b* 25 April 1940; *d* of Arthur and Edith Jackson; *m* 1st, 1964; two *d*; 2nd, 1983, (William) Guy Walker, CBE (*d* 2007); one step *s* two step *d*. *Educ:* Manchester High Sch. for Girls; Nottingham Univ. (LLB). Admitted Solicitor of Supreme Court, 1965; a Recorder, 1979–86. Consultant, Norrie, Bowler & Wrigley, Solicitors, Sheffield, 1983–86 (Sen. Partner, 1968–83). Member: Parole Bd, 1983–85; Appts Commn, Press Council, 1985.

NORRINGTON, Humphrey Thomas, OBE 2001; Vice Chairman, Barclays Bank, 1991–93; *b* 8 May 1936; *s* of Sir Arthur Norrington and Edith Joyce, *d* of William Moberly Carver; *m* 1963, Frances Guenn Bateson; two *s* two *d*. *Educ:* Dragon School, Oxford; Winchester; Worcester College, Oxford (MA). Barclays Bank: joined, 1960; general management, 1978–87; Dir, 1985–93; Exec Dir, Overseas Ops, 1987–91. Chm., Exec. Cttee, British Bankers' Assoc., 1990–91. Chm., Southwark Cathedral Develt Trust, 1986–93; Director: City Arts Trust, 1988–93; Mildmay Mission Hosp., 1992–2007 (Vice Pres., 2007–); World Vision UK, 1991–2005. Member, Archbishops' Commission: on Rural Areas, 1988–90; on Orgn of the C of E, 1994–95. Chm., Premier Christian Media Trust, 1999–2011; Trustee: Lambeth Trust (formerly Lambeth Fund), 1991–2014; Stewards' Trust, 2007–. Hon. Treas., RSPB, 1996–2003; Hon. Treas., 1997–2004, Vice Pres., 2005–, RCM. *Recreations:* music, countryside. *Address:* Hill House, Frithsden Copse, Berkhamsted, Herts HP4 2RQ. *T:* (01442) 871855. *Club:* Oxford and Cambridge.

See also Sir R. A. C. Norrington.

NORRINGTON, Sir Roger (Arthur Carver), Kt 1997; CBE 1990 (OBE 1980); Chief Conductor: Zurich Chamber Orchestra, since 2011; Camerata Academica Salzburg, 1997–2006, now Conductor Laureate; *b* 16 March 1934; *s* of late Sir Arthur Norrington and Edith Joyce, *d* of William Moberly Carver; *m* 1st, 1964, Susan Elizabeth McLean May (marr. diss. 1982); one *s* one *d*; 2nd, 1986, Karalyn Mary Lawrence; one *s*. *Educ:* Dragon Sch., Oxford; Westminster; Clare Coll., Cambridge (BA; Hon. Fellow, 1991); Royal Coll. of Music. Freelance singer, 1962–72. Principal Conductor: Kent Opera, 1966–84; Bournemouth Sinfonietta, 1985–89; Music Director: Orch. of St Luke's, NY, 1990–94; Schütz Choir of London, 1962–82; London Classical Players, 1978–98; Chief Conductor, Radio Sinfonie Orchester Stuttgart, 1998–2011. Prince Consort Prof., RCM, 1997. Guest conducts many British, European and American orchestras, appears at Covent Garden, Coliseum, Proms and festivals; broadcasts regularly at home and abroad. Débuts: British, 1962; BBC Radio, 1964; TV 1967; Germany, Austria, Denmark, Finland, 1966; Portugal, 1970; Italy, 1971; France and Belgium, 1972; USA, 1974; Holland, 1975; Switzerland, 1976. Many gramophone recordings. Hon. RAM 1988. FRCM 1992. DUniv York, 1991; Hon. DMus Kent, 1994. Cavaliere, Orden al Merito (Italy), 1981; Ehrenkreuz, 1st cl. (Austria), 1999. *Publications:* occasional articles in various musical journals. *Recreations:* gardening, reading, walking.

See also H. T. Norrington.

NORRIS, Brig. His Honour (Alaric) Philip, OBE 1982; a Circuit Judge, 1995–2008; *b* 20 Sept. 1942; *yr s* of late Charles Henry Norris and Maud Frances Norris (*née* Neild); *m* 1967, Pamela Margaret Parker; three *s*. *Educ:* Sir William Turner's Sch., Coatham, Redcar; Queens' Coll., Cambridge (MA); Dip. in Law and Amer. Studies, Univ. of Virginia, USA, 1979. Admitted Solicitor, 1968; commnd Army Legal Services, 1970; served MoD, SHAPE, BAOR, Berlin, NEARELF, NI, UKLF/Land Comd, USA and Geneva; retired, in rank of Brig., 1995. Asst Recorder, 1988–92, Recorder of the Crown Court, 1992–95. Liveryman, Fruiterers' Co., 2005–. *Recreations:* a bit of all sorts, but not golf. *Address:* c/o Woolwich Crown Court, 2 Belmarsh Road, SE28 0EY.

NORRIS, Hon. Sir Alastair Hubert, Kt 2007; FCIArb; **Hon. Mr Justice Norris;** a Judge of the High Court, Chancery Division, since 2007; Vice-Chancellor, County Palatine of Leicester, since 2013; *b* 17 Dec. 1950; *s* of Hubert John Norris and Margaret Murray (*née* Savage); *m* 1982, Patricia Lesley Rachel White; one *s* two *d*. *Educ:* Pate's Grammar Sch., Cheltenham; St John's Coll., Cambridge (MA). FCIArb 1991. Called to the Bar, Lincoln's Inn, 1973, Bencher, 2005; QC 1997; an Asst Recorder, 1998–2000; a Recorder, 2000–01; a Circuit Judge, 2001–07. *Recreation:* sailing. *Address:* Royal Courts of Justice, 7 Rolls Building, Fetter Lane, EC4A 1NL. *Clubs:* Gloucestershire County Cricket; Marlow Sailing, Teifi Boating.

NORRIS, Dan; *b* 28 Jan. 1960; *s* of David Norris and June Norris (*née* Allen). *Educ:* Chipping Sodbury Comprehensive Sch.; Univ. of Sussex (MSW). Researcher and author. Member (Lab): Bristol CC, 1989–92, 1995–97; Avon CC, 1994–96. Contested (Lab): Northavon, 1987; Wansdyke, 1992. MP (Lab) Wansdyke, 1997–2010; contested (Lab) NE Somerset, 2010. Member: Lab. Leadership Campaign Team, 1998–2000; Lab. Parly Campaign Team, 2000–01. An Asst Govt Whip, 2001–03; PPS to Sec. of State for NI, 2005–07, to Sec. of State for Foreign and Commonwealth Affairs, 2007–09; Parly Under-Sec. of State, DEFRA, 2009–10. Founder, Kidscape SW, 2000. Hon. Fellow, Sch. of Cultural and Community Studies, Univ. of Sussex, 1989. Mem., GMB. Ed., Liberal Demolition (qly jl), 2000. *Publications:* Violence Against Social Workers: the implications for practice, 1990; contribs to learned jls and newspaper articles. *Recreation:* photography.

NORRIS, David Owen, FRAM, FRCO; composer, pianist and broadcaster; *b* 16 June 1953; *s* of Albert Norris and Margaret Norris (*née* Owen); two *s*. *Educ:* Royal Academy of Music (FRAM 1986); Keble Coll., Oxford (MA; Hon. Fellow, 2006). FRCO 1972. Repetiteur, Royal Opera House, 1977–80; Asst Mus. Dir, RSC, 1977–79; Prof., Royal Acad. of Music, 1977–89; Dir, Petworth Fest., 1986–92; Artistic Dir, Cardiff Fest., 1992–95; Gresham Prof. of Music, 1993–97; Prof., 1999–2007, Vis. Prof., 2007–, RCM; AHRC (formerly AHRB) Fellow in Performing Arts, 2000–04, Prof., 2007–, Southampton Univ. Chm., Steans Inst. for Singers, Chicago, 1992–98. Concerts world-wide; tours of Australia, USA, Canada; radio and TV progs in GB and N America incl. progs on Radio 3 and Radio 4, and BBC2 films on Elgar, Britten and Vaughan Williams. Gilmore Artist, 1991. Recordings include: concertos by Elgar, Lambert, Phillips and Horowitz; complete piano music of Elgar, Dyson and Quilter; songs by Somervell, Quilter, Britten, Tippett, Trevor Hold, Mendelssohn and Schubert (incl. Kosegarten Liederspiel); 'The World's First Piano Concertos' on Square Piano; newly discovered items from Jane Austen's music collection; all Mendelssohn's Songs without Words. Compositions include: Think only this, 2002; Tomorrow nor Yesterday, 2005; Prayerbook, 2006; Piano Concerto in C, 2008; The Jolly Roger, 2008; Sterne, 2013; Symphony, 2013; Turning Points, 2015. *Address:* 17 Manor Road, Andover, Hants SP10 3JS.

NORRIS, Geoffrey; Chief Music Critic, Daily Telegraph, 1995–2009; *b* 19 Sept. 1947; *s* of Leslie and Vera Norris. *Educ:* Univ. of Durham (BA); Inst. Teatra, Muzyki i Kinematografii, Leningrad; Univ. of Liverpool. ARCM 1967. Lectr in Music History, RNCM, 1975–77; Commning Editor, Scholarly Music Books, OUP, 1977–83; Music Critic: The Times, 1983; Daily Telegraph, 1983–95. Prof., Rachmaninoff Music Inst., Tambov, 2005–. Mem., Critics' Circle. *Publications:* Rakhmaninov, 1976, 2nd edn, Rachmaninoff, 1993; (with Robert Threlfall) A Catalogue of the Compositions of S. Rachmaninoff, 1982; contribs to New Grove Dictionary of Music and Musicians, Oxford Companion to Music. *Recreation:* Italy. *Club:* Arts.

NORRIS, Gilbert Frank; Chief Road Engineer, Scottish Development Department, 1969–76; *b* 29 May 1916; *s* of Ernest Frank Norris and Ada Norris; *m* 1941, Joan Margaret Catherine Thompson (*d* 2005); one *s*. *Educ:* Bemrose Sch., Derby; UC Nottingham. FICE. Served with Notts, Bucks and Lindsey County Councils, 1934–39; Royal Engineers, 1939–46; Min. of Transport: Highways Engr in Nottingham, Edinburgh and Leeds, 1946–63; Asst Chief Engr, 1963–67; Dep. Chief Engr, 1967; Dir, NE Road Construction Unit, 1967–69. *Address:* Woodhead Lee, Lamlash, Isle of Arran KA27 8JU.

NORRIS, John Hallam Mercer, CBE 1987; Crown Estate Commissioner, 1991–99; Vice Lord-Lieutenant of Essex, 1992–2003; *b* 30 May 1929; *s* of late William Hallam Norris and Dorothy Edna Norris (*née* Mercer); *m* 1954, Maureen Joy Banyard; two *d*. *Educ:* Brentwood School. Mem., BSES Expedn, Newfoundland, 1947. Partner, W. H. Norris & Sons, 1963–. Chm., Essex River Authy, 1971–74; Member: Anglian Water Authy, 1974–85; Adv. Cttee, 1988, Board, 1989–94, NRA; Adv. Cttee, Envmt Agency, 1994–96; Founder Mem., Envmt Agency Bd, 1996–97; Chairman: Essex Land Drainage Cttee, 1974–89; Crouch Harbour Authy, 1981–88. President: CLA, 1985–87 (Mem., Exec. Cttee, 1973–; Chm., 1983–85); Essex Agricl Soc., 1989; Soc. of Old Brentwood, 2003–04. Chm., Chelmsford Cathedral Council, 2000–. FRAgS 1992; Hon. FIWEM 1992. DL Essex, 1989. *Recreations:* fishing, sailing. *Address:* Mountnessing Hall, Brentwood, Essex CM13 1UN. *T:* (01277) 352152. *Clubs:* Boodle's, Farmers.

NORRIS, John Robert, CBE 1991; PhD, DSc; Director, Group Research, Cadbury Schweppes Ltd, 1979–90; *b* 4 March 1932; *s* of Albert Norris and Winifred May Perry; *m* 1st, 1956, Barbara Jean Pinder (*d* 1994); one *s* one *d* (and two *s* decd); 2nd, 1998, Pauline Mary Corrigan. *Educ:* Depts of Bacteriology and Agriculture, Univ. of Leeds (BSc 1st Cl. Hons 1954, PhD 1957, DSc 1987). Lectr in Bacteriology, Univ. of Glasgow, 1957–63; Microbiologist, Shell Research Ltd, 1963–73 (Dir, Borden Microbiol Lab., 1970–73); Dir, Meat Res. Inst., ARC, 1973–79. Editor, Methods in Microbiology, 1969–92. *Publications:* papers in microbiol jls. *Recreations:* walking, wood carving, Yoga, photography. *Address:* Langlands, 10 Langley Road, Bingley, West Yorks BD16 4AB. *T:* (01274) 406973. *Club:* Farmers.

NORRIS, Prof. Kenneth John, DPhil; Director, Science, Zoological Society of London, since 2014; *b* Birmingham, 17 Nov. 1963; *s* of John Norris and Barbara Norris; *m* 1989, Tracy Evans; two *c*. *Educ:* University Coll. of Wales, Aberystwyth (BSc Envmtl Biol. 1985); Univ. of Oxford (DPhil 1989). Postdoctoral Researcher, Univ. of Oxford, 1989–92; Res. Biologist, RSPB, 1993–97; University of Reading: Lectr, 1997–2003; Reader in Applied Ecol., 2003–04; Prof. of Agro-ecol., 2005–14; Dir, Centre for Agri-Envmtl Res., 2005–14. *Publications:* over 100 scientific papers. *Recreations:* cycling, reading, rock music. *Address:* Institute of Zoology, Zoological Society of London, Regent's Park, NW1 4RY. *T:* (020) 7449 6244. *E:* ken.norris@ioz.ac.uk.

NORRIS, Philip; *see* Norris, Brig. His Honour A. P.

NORRIS, Rufus; theatre director; Director, National Theatre, since 2015 (Associate Director, 2012–15); *b* 16 Jan. 1965; *s* of Malcolm and Lauriston Norris; *m* 1994, Tanya Ronder; two *s*. *Educ:* North Bromsgrove High Sch.; Kidderminster Coll. of Further Educn; RADA (Dip.). Actor, 1989–92; director, 1992–; Artistic Dir, Arts Threshold, 1992–95; Asst Dir, Royal Court Th., 1996–97; Associate Dir, Young Vic Th., 2002–. Director: Afore Night Come, 2001, Sleeping Beauty, 2002, Young Vic; Festen, Lyric, 2004; Tintin, Barbican, 2005, Playhouse, 2007; Cabaret, Lyric, 2006; Vernon God Little, Young Vic, 2007; Death and the King's Horseman, NT, 2009; The Country Girl, Apollo, 2010; Don Giovanni, ENO, 2010; London Road, NT, 2011; Dr Dee, Manchester Internat. Fest., 2011, ENO, 2012; Feast, Young Vic, 2013; Table, NT, 2013; The Amen Corner, NT, 2013; Behind the Beautiful Forevers, NT, 2014; Everyman, NT, 2015; wonder.land, NT, 2015; films: King Bastard, 2009; Broken, 2009; London Road, 2015. Arts Foundn Fellow, 2001. *Address:* c/o Nick Marston, Curtis Brown, Haymarket House, 28–29 Haymarket, SW1Y 4SP.

NORRIS, Stephen Anthony; film producer and media consultant; *b* 14 June 1959; *s* of Roy Anthony Norris and Brenda Winifred Norris; *m* 1986, Susan Jennifer Boyle; two *s* one *d*. *Educ:* St Nicholas Grammar Sch. Warner Bros Productions, London, 1979–82; European Production, Warner Bros, LA, 1982–84; Dir of Ops, Enigma Productions, 1984–86; Sen. Vice Pres., Columbia Pictures, LA, 1986–88; Man. Dir, Enigma Productions Ltd, 1989–97; British Film Comr, 1998–2006; Man. Dir, Film, Framestore (formerly Framestore CFC), 2006–10; Chief Exec., Apollo Prodns, 2010–; Exec. Prod., Pinewood Films, 2011–. Dir, British Film and TV Producers Assoc., 1989–91; Vice Chm., Producers Alliance for Cinema and TV, 1991–93; Council Member: British Screen Adv. Council, 1998–2006; BAFTA, 1999–2005; Chm., UK Screen, 2010–. Associate Producer/Producer: Memphis Belle, 1990; Being Human, 1993; War of the Buttons, 1994; Le Confessional (Best Film, Canadian Acad., 1995); My Life So Far, 1998; Producer/Executive Producer: Triangle, 2009; Harry Brown, 2009; Me and Orson Welles, 2009; Heartless, 2010; A Fantastic Fear of Everything, 2012. *Recreations:* cinema, Rugby, my family, golf. *Address:* Pinewood Studios, Pinewood Road, Iver Heath, Bucks SL0 0NH.

NORRIS, Steven John, FRICS, FCILT, FCIHT; Chairman: Internet Corporation Ltd, since 2008; Soho Estates Ltd, since 2011; Base Communications Ltd, since 2011; BNP Paribas Real Estate UK, since 2013; London Resort Company Holdings, since 2014; Driver Group plc, since 2015; Partner, Norris McDonough LLP, since 2013; *b* 24 May 1945; *s* of John Francis Birkett Norris and Eileen Winifred (*née* Walsh); *m* 1969, Peta Veronica Cecil-Gibson (marr. diss.); two *s*; *m* 2000, Emma Courtney; one *s*. *Educ:* Liverpool Institute; Worcester College, Oxford. MA. Private company posts, 1967–90; Dir-Gen., Road Haulage Assoc., 1997–2000; Sen. Partner, Park Place Communications, 2001–13; Chairman: Jarvis plc, 2003–10; AMT-Sybex Gp Ltd, 2005–12; Saferoad BLG, 2007–13. Non-executive Director: initiate Consulting Ltd, 2003–14; Optare, 2014–; Sen. Ind. Dir, ITIS Hldgs Ltd, 1998–2011. Board Member: Transport for London, 2000–01 and 2008–12; London Develt Agency, 2008–12. Mem., Berks CC, 1977–85. Mem., Berks AHA, 1979–82; Vice-Chm., W Berks District HA, 1982–85. Contested (C) Oxford E, 1987. MP (C): Oxford E, 1983–87; Epping Forest, Dec. 1988–1997. PPS to Hon. William Waldegrave, MP, Minister of State, DoE, 1985–87, to Rt Hon. Nicholas Ridley, Sec. of State for Trade and Industry, 1990, to Rt Hon. Kenneth Baker, Home Sec., 1991–92; Parly Under-Sec. of State, Dept of Transport, 1992–96. Vice Chm., Cons. Party, 2000–01. Chairman: Grant Maintained Schools Trust, 1988–89; Crime Concern

Trust, 1988–91; Alcohol and Drug Addiction Prevention and Treatment, 1990–92; Prince Michael Road Safety Awards Scheme, 1997–2004; Urology Foundn, 2004–14; London Action Trust, 2006–11; East Side Young Leaders Acad., 2006–11. FCILT (FCIT 1997); FCIHT (FIHT 1997); FRICS 2013; Hon. CompICE 1996; Hon. Fellow, Assoc. for Project Mgt (Hon. Fellow, Assoc. of Project Managers, 2012). Freeman, City of London, 1985; Liveryman: Coachmakers' and Coach Harness Makers' Co., 1985–; Watermen and Lightermen's Co., 1997–; Co. of Carmen, 1998–. *Publications:* Changing Trains, 1996. *Recreations:* reading, not walking. *Address:* Norris McDonough LLP, 5–8 The Sanctuary, Westminster, SW1P 3JS. *Clubs:* Brooks's, Royal Automobile, Garrick, Arts.

NORRIS, Sydney George, CB 1996; Director of Finance, Prison Service, Home Office, 1996–97; *b* 22 Aug. 1937; *s* of late George Samuel Norris, FCA and Agnes Rosa Norris; *m* 1965, Brigid Molyneux FitzGibbon; two *s* one *d.* *Educ:* Liverpool Inst. High Sch. for Boys; University Coll., Oxford (MA); Trinity Hall and Inst. of Criminology, Cambridge (Dip. in Criminology); Univ. of California, Berkeley (MCrim). Intelligence Corps, 1956–58; Home Office, 1963–97; Private Sec. to Parly Under Sec. of State, 1966; Harkness Fellow, 1968–70; Sec., Adv. Council on Penal System, 1970–73; Principal Private Sec. to Home Sec., 1973–74; Asst Sec., 1974; seconded to HM Treasury, 1979–81; Asst Under Sec. of State, 1982; seconded to NI Office as Principal Estabt and Finance Officer, 1982–85; Dir of Operational Policy, Prison Dept, 1985–88; Police Dept, 1988–90; Principal Finance Officer, 1990–96. Parish Warden, Mortlake with East Sheen, 2002–06. Chm., Romney Street Gp, 2007–14. *Recreations:* fell walking, gardening, ski-ing, piano, running. *Address:* 58 East Sheen Avenue, SW14 8AU. *Clubs:* Athenæum, Thames Hare and Hounds.

NORRIS, William John; QC 1997; *b* 3 Oct. 1951; *s* of late Dr John Phillips Norris, QGM and Dr Joan Hattersley Norris; *m* 1987, Lesley Jacqueline Osborne; two *d.* *Educ:* Sherborne Sch.; New Coll., Oxford (MA). Called to the Bar, Middle Temple, 1974 (Benefactors' Scholarship). Chm., Personal Injury Bar Assoc., 2006–08. Mem., panel of chairmen, Sport Resolutions UK, 2005–; Legal Mem., Nat. Anti-Doping Panel, 2011–. Trustee, Injured Jockeys Fund, 2006–. Gen. Ed., Kemp and Kemp, The Quantum of Damages, 2004–. *Publications:* Perhaps It Will Brighten Up Later, 2004; 100 Years—Still Counting, 2011. *Recreations:* sailing (former Class Captain, XOD), shooting, racing, writing. *Address:* 39 Essex Street, WC2R 3AT. *T:* (020) 7832 1111. *Clubs:* Royal Cruising, Royal Lymington Yacht.

NORRISS, Air Marshal Sir Peter (Coulson), KBE 2000; CB 1996; AFC 1977; defence consultant; *b* 22 April 1944; *s* of Arthur Kenworthy Norriss and Marjorie Evelyn Norriss; *m* 1971, Lesley Jean McColl; two *s* one *d.* *Educ:* Beverley Grammar Sch.; Magdalene Coll., Cambridge (MA 1970); Harvard Business Sch. Joined RAF, 1966; Flying Instructor RAF Coll., Cranwell, 1969–71; Buccaneer Pilot, 1972–76; RAF Staff Coll., 1977; on Staff of RAF Minister, 1977–79; OC, No 16 Sqn, 1980–83; Head, RAF Presentation Team, 1984; Station Comdr, RAF Marham, 1985–87; ADC to the Queen, 1985–87; Higher Comd and Staff Course, 1988; on Staff, Operational Requirements, 1988–91; Dir Gen. Aircraft 2, 1991–95; Dir Gen. Air Systems 1, MoD (PE), 1995–98; Controller Aircraft, 1996–2000, and Dep. Chief of Defence Procurement (Ops), 1998–2000, MoD (PE, subseq. Defence Procurement Agency). Non-executive Director: DERA, 1998–2000; Turbomeca UK Ltd (formerly Microturbo Ltd), 2002–08 (Chm., 2002–07); Chemring Gp plc, 2004–13. Pres., RAeS, 2003–04. *Recreations:* golf, ski-ing. *Club:* Royal Air Force.

NORTH, family name of **Earl of Guilford.**

NORTH, Lord; Frederick Edward George North; *b* 24 June 2002; *s* and *heir* of Earl of Guilford, *qv.*

NORTH, Alan; *see* North, R. A.

NORTH, Air Marshal Sir Barry Mark, (Air Marshal Sir Baz), KCB 2015; OBE 2002 (MBE 1996); FRAeS; Deputy Commander for Capability and Personnel, Headquarters Air Command, since 2013; *b* Clatterbridge, Cheshire, 13 Sept. 1959; *s* of Robert and Doreen North; *m* 1985, Fiona Jane Walker; two *d.* *Educ:* Carre's Grammar Sch., Sleaford, Lincs; Trent Poly., Nottingham (HND Business Studies); King's Coll. London (MA Defence Studies). ADC to CDS, 1988–91; Officer Commanding: 78 Sqdn, 1991; Special Forces Flight 7 Sqdn, 1992–96; Personal Staff Officer to AOC 1 Gp, 1996–98; Wing Comdr, Ops, HQ Strike Comd, 1998–99; OC 33 Sqdn, 1999–2002; Dep. Asst COS, J1/5/6 and Hd, Jt Helicopter Comd, 2002–04; Station Comdr, RAF Aldegrove and Sen. RAF Officer, NI, 2004–06; Air Component Comdr and AOC 83 Expeditionary Air Gp, 2006; Dir, Air Resources and Plans, MoD, 2007–09; AOC, 22 Gp, RAF and COS Trng, HQ Air Comd, 2009–10; Asst Chief of the Air Staff, 2010–13. Non-exec. Dir, CAA, 2010–13. Liveryman, Gold and Silver Wyre Drawers' Co., 2003–; Upper Liveryman, Hon. Co. of Air Pilots (formerly GAPAN), 2010–. QCVS 2006. FRAeS 2014. Alumnus of the Year, Nottingham Trent Univ., 2011. *Recreations:* frightening the rough of the occasional golf course, pottering in the garden. *Club:* Royal Air Force.

NORTH, Prof. Douglass Cecil, PhD; Spencer T. Olin Professor in Arts and Sciences, Washington University, St Louis, since 1995; Bartlett Burnap Senior Fellow, Hoover Institution, Stanford University, since 2001; *b* 5 Nov. 1920; *s* of Henry North and Edith Saitta; *m* 1st, 1944, Lois Heister; three *s*; 2nd, 1972, Elisabeth Case. *Educ:* Univ. of California at Berkeley (BA, PhD). Acting Asst Prof., Asst Prof., Associate Prof. and Prof., Univ. of Washington, Seattle, 1950–83; Washington University, St Louis: Henry R. Luce Prof. of Law and Liberty and Prof. of Econs and of History, 1983–90. Peterkin Prof. of Political Economy, Rice Univ., 1979; Pitt Prof. of American Instns, Cambridge, 1981–82. Fellow, Amer. Acad. of Arts and Scis; Corresp. FBA, 1996; Dist. Fellow, AEA, 2009. Hon. degrees: Cologne 1988; Zürich 1993; Stockholm 1994; Colombia, 1998; St Louis, Missouri, 2003. (Jtly) Nobel Prize for Economics, 1993. *Publications:* The Economic Growth of the United States 1790–1860, 1961; Growth and Welfare in the American Past, 1966; (with Roger Miller) The Economics of Public Issues, 1971; (with Lance Davis) Institutional Change and American Economic Growth, 1971; (with Robert Thomas) The Rise of the Western World, 1973; Structure and Change in Economic History, 1981; Institutions, Institutional Change and Economic Performance, 1990; Understanding the Process of Economic Change, 2004; (with John Wallace and Barry Weingast) Violence and Social Orders: a conceptual framework for interpreting recorded human history, 2009. *Recreations:* tennis, hiking, music, photography. *Address:* Department of Economics, Seigle Hall 391, Washington University, Campus Box 1208, One Brookings Drive, St Louis, MO 63130–4899, USA.

NORTH, John Joseph; Associate, Department of Land Economy, University of Cambridge, since 1992 (Senior Visiting Fellow, 1985–92); *b* 7 Nov. 1926; *s* of Frederick James North and Annie Elizabeth North (*née* Matthews); *m* 1958, Sheila Barbara Mercer; two *s.* *Educ:* Rendcomb College; Univ. of Reading (BSc, DipAgric); Univ. of California (MS). FRSB (FIBiol 1972). Agricultural Adviser, Nat. Agricultural Advisory Service, 1951; Kellogg Fellowship, USA, 1954–55; Regional Agricultural Officer, Cambridge, 1972; Senior Agricultural Officer, 1976; Chief Agricl Officer, ADAS, MAFF, 1979. *Recreations:* golf, gardening. *Address:* 28 Hauxton Road, Little Shelford, Cambridge CB22 5HJ. *T:* (01223) 843369.

NORTH, Sir Jonathan; *see* North, Sir W. J. F.

NORTH, Sir Peter (Machin), Kt 1998; CBE 1989; DCL; FBA 1990; Principal of Jesus College, Oxford, 1984–2005; Pro-Vice-Chancellor, University of Oxford, 1988–93, and 1997–2005 (Vice-Chancellor, 1993–97); *b* Nottingham, 30 Aug. 1936; *o s* of late Geoffrey Machin North and Freda Brunt (*née* Smith); *m* 1960, Stephanie Mary (OBE 2000; JP, DL), *e d* of T. L. Chadwick; two *s* one *d.* *Educ:* Oakham Sch.; Keble Coll., Oxford (BA 1959, BCL 1960, MA 1963, DCL 1976; Hon. Fellow, 1984). National Service, Royal Leics Regt, 2nd Lieut, 1954–56. Teaching Associate, Northwestern Univ. Sch. of Law, Chicago, 1960–61; Lecturer: University Coll. of Wales, Aberystwyth, 1961–63; Univ. of Nottingham, 1963–65; Tutor in Law, 1965–76, Fellow, 1965–84, Keble Coll., Oxford. Mem., Hebdomadal Council, 1985–99. A Law Comr, 1976–84; called to the Bar, Inner Temple, 1992 (Hon. Bencher, 1987). Vis. Professor: Univ. of Auckland, 1969; Univ. of BC, 1975–76; Dir of Studies, Hague Acad. of Internat. Law, 1970 (general course in private internat. law, 1990); Lectures: Hague Acad. of Internat. Law, 1980; Horace Read Meml, Dalhousie Univ., 1980; Colston, Bristol Univ., 1984; Frances Moran Meml, TCD, 1984; Philip James, Leeds Univ., 1985; James Smart, 1988; MacDermott, QUB, 1991; Graveson, KCL, 1992; Douglas McK. Brown, Univ. of BC, 1998; F. A. Mann, 2000. Chairman: Road Traffic Law Review, 1985–88; Conciliation Project Adv. Cttee, 1985–88; Management Cttee, Oxford CAB, 1985–88; Appeal Cttee, Assoc. of Certified Accountants, 1990–93 (Mem., 1987–93); Ind. Review of Parades and Marches in NI, 1996–97; Standing Adv. Cttee on Private Internat. Law, 1998–2009; Ind. Cttee for Supervision of Standards of Telephone Inf. Services, 1999–2006; Review of Drink and Drug Driving Law, 2009–10; Member: Lord Chancellor's Adv. Cttee on Legal Educn, 1973–75; Social Scis and the Law Cttee, ESRC (formerly SSRC), 1982–85; Govt and Law Cttee, ESRC, 1985–87; Adv. Develt Council, Nat. Fisheries Mus., 1996–2000; Sen. Salaries Review Body, 2004–12; Accountancy Investigation and Disciplinary Bd Tribunal, 2005–13. Council Member: British Inst. of Internat. and Comparative Law, 1986–2005 (Chm., Private Internat. Law Section, Adv. Bd, 1986–92); Univ. of Reading, 1986–89; British Acad., 1996–99. Oxford University Press: Delegate, 1993–2008; Chm., Finance Cttee, 2005–08 (Mem., 1993–2005); Vice-Chm., Visitors, Ashmolean Mus., Oxford, 2006–07 (Visitor, 2004–07). Pres., Oxford Inst. of Legal Practice, 1999–2010; Mem., Inst. of Internat. Law, 1985; Mem., Internat. Acad. of Comparative Law, 1990. Hon. QC 1993. Hon. Fellow: UCNW, Bangor, 1988; Trinity Coll., Carmarthen, 1995; Univ. of Wales, Aberystwyth, 1996; Jesus Coll., Oxford, 2005. Hon. LLD: Reading, 1992; Nottingham, 1996; Aberdeen, 1997; New Brunswick, 2002; DHL Arizona, 2005. Mem., Editorial Cttee, British Yearbook of Internat. Law, 1983–; General Editor, Oxford Jl of Legal Studies, 1987–92. *Publications:* Cheshire, Private International Law, 8th edn 1970 to 14th edn as Cheshire and North's Private International Law (cons. ed.), 2008; (ed jtly) Chitty on Contracts, 23rd edn 1968 to 26th edn 1989; Occupiers' Liability, 1971, 2nd edn 2014; The Modern Law of Animals, 1972; Private International Law of Matrimonial Causes, 1977; Contract Conflicts, 1982; (with J. H. C. Morris) Cases and Materials on Private International Law, 1984; Private International Law Problems in Common Law Jurisdictions, 1993; Essays in Private International Law, 1993; Civil Liability for Animals, 2012; articles and notes in legal jls. *Recreations:* children, grandchildren, gardening, cricket. *Address:* 34 Woodstock Close, Oxford OX2 8DB. *T:* (01865) 557011; 5 Coln Manor, Coln St Aldwyns, Cirencester, Glos GL7 5AD. *T:* (01285) 750400.

NORTH, Rt Rev. Philip John; *see* Burnley, Bishop Suffragan of.

NORTH, Prof. (Richard) Alan, PhD; FRS 1995; Professor, University of Manchester, 2004–13, now Emeritus (Vice-President, 2004–11); *b* 20 May 1944; *s* of Douglas Abram North and Constance (*née* Ramsden); *m* 1st, 1969, Jean Valerie Aitken Hall (marr. diss. 1982); two *d*; 2nd, 1991, Annmarie Surprenant; two *s.* *Educ:* Univ. of Aberdeen (BSc; MB, ChB 1969; PhD 1973). Asst and Associate Prof., Dept of Pharmacol., Loyola Univ., Chicago, 1975–81; Massachusetts Institute of Technology: Associate Prof., Dept of Nutrition and Food Sci., 1981–84; Prof. of Neuropharmacol., Dept of Applied Biol Scis, 1984–86; Sen. Scientist, Vollum Inst., Oregon Health Scis Univ., Portland, 1987–93; Prin. Scientist, Geneva Biomedical Res. Inst., Glaxo Wellcome R&D (formerly Glaxo Inst. for Molecular Biol.), 1993–98; Prof. of Molecular Physiol., Inst. of Molecular Physiol., Univ. of Sheffield, 1998–2004; Dean, Faculty of Life Scis, 2004–08, Dean, Faculty of Med. and Human Scis, 2006–11, Univ. of Manchester; Dir, Manchester Academic Health Sci. Centre, 2008–10. Visiting Professor: Flinders Univ., 1983; Bogomoletz Inst., 1984; Frankfurt Univ., 1988; Univ. of Melbourne, 1991. Gaddum Lecture, British Pharmacol Soc., 1988. Mem., MRC, 2001–06. Pres., Physiol Soc., 2003–06. Ed.-in-Chief, British Jl of Pharmacol., 2000–04. FMedSci 2004. *Publications:* original res. papers in jls of physiol., pharmacol., neuroscience and biochem. *Recreation:* mountaineering. *Address:* University of Manchester, Michael Smith Building, Oxford Road, Manchester M13 9PT. *T:* (0161) 275 1499, *Fax:* (0161) 275 1498. *E:* r.a.north@manchester.ac.uk.

NORTH, Richard Conway; Deputy Chairman, Majid Al Futtaim Properties LLC, since 2014 (non-executive Director, since 2009); *b* 20 Jan. 1950; *s* of John and Megan North; *m* 1978, Lindsay Jean Buchanan; three *d.* *Educ:* Marlborough Coll.; Sidney Sussex Coll., Cambridge (BA 1971; MA 1974). FCA 1976; FCT 1993. Coopers & Lybrand, 1971–91: qualified as accountant, 1974; seconded to: NY, 1976–78; Midland Bank, 1981–82; Partner, 1983–91; Group Finance Director: Burton Gp plc, 1991–94; Bass, subseq. Six Continents, plc, 1994–2003; CEO, Hotel Div., Six Continents, subseq. InterContinental Hotels Gp plc, 2002–04; Chairman: Britvic Soft Drinks, 1996–2004; Woolworths Gp plc, 2007–08 (non-exec. Dir, 2006–07). Non-executive Director: ASDA Gp plc, 1997–99; Bristol Hotel Company Inc., 1997–98; Leeds United plc, 1998–2002; Felcor Lodging Trust Inc., 1998–2004; LogicaCMG (formerly Logica) plc, 2002–04; Majid Al Futtaim Gp LLC, 2006–09; Mecom plc, 2007–09. Chm., Payments Council, 2010–14. Member: Cttee, 100 Gp, 1996–2000; Exec. Cttee, World Travel and Tourism Council, 2004. Mem. Senate, ICAEW, 1991–2000. *Recreations:* golf, soccer, rock 'n' roll, history. *Clubs:* Athenæum, Hurlingham; Burhill Golf (Walton on Thames); Huntercombe Golf; Berkshire Golf.

NORTH, Prof. Robert, (Robert North Dodson); freelance choreographer; Professor and Director, Ballett Akademie, Munich, Germany, since 2007; Ballet Director, Krefeld and Mönchengladbach Theatres, Germany, since 2007; *b* 1 June 1945; *s* of Charles Dodson and Elizabeth Thompson; *m* 1st, 1978, Janet Smith (marr. diss.); 2nd, 1999, Sheri Cook. *Educ:* Pierrepont Sch. (A levels in Maths, Physics and Art); Central Sch. of Art; Royal Ballet Sch. Dancer and choreographer, London Contemporary Dance Co., 1966–81 (Jt Artistic Dir, 1980–81); seasons with Martha Graham Dance Co., 1967 and 1968; Teacher of Modern Dance, Royal Ballet Sch., 1979–81; Artistic Dir, Ballet Rambert, 1981–86; freelance work, Europe and USA, 1986–90; Ballet Dir, Teatro Regio, Turin, 1990–91; Artistic Dir, Gothenburg Ballet, 1991–96; Dir, Corps de Ballet, Arena di Verona, 1997–99; Artistic Dir, Scottish Ballet, 1999–2002. Has choreographed ballets for dance companies throughout the world, including: Royal Ballet; English National Ballet; Dance Theatre of Harlem; Royal Danish Ballet; San Francisco Ballet; Oakland Ballet; Finnish Nat. Ballet; Batsheva; Janet Smith and Dancers; La Scala, Milan; Rome Opera; Staatsoper Dresden; Györ Ballett; *ballets choreographed* include: Troy Game; Death and the Maiden; The Annunciation; A Stranger I Came; Running Figures; Pribaoutki; Colour Moves; Entre dos Aguas; full-length ballets: Carmen; Elvira Madigan; Romeo & Juliet; Living in America; Prince Rama and the Demons; Life, Love & Death; The Russian Story; The Snowman; The Cradle Will Rock; Eva; Ragazzi Selvaggi; Orlando; Carmina Burana; Bach; Wie Ihr's Wollt; Tschaikowskys Träume; Casanova; Fado/Bolero; Lost Children; Pictures from the New World; also choreography for films, television (incl. Lonely Town, Lonely Street, and For My Daughter (Golden Prague Award, 1983)), theatre, musicals and opera (Carmen, Royal Albert Hall). *Address:* c/o Val West, 49 Springcroft Avenue, N2 9JH.

NORTH, Sir Thomas (Lindsay), Kt 1982; FAIM, FRMIA; Chairman, G. J. Coles & Coy Limited, Melbourne, Australia, 1979–83, Hon. Chairman, 1983–84; *b* 11 Dec. 1919; *s* of John North and Jane (*née* Irwin); *m* 1944, Kathleen Jefferis; two *d*. *Educ:* Rutherglen, Vic. FAIM 1972. Joined G. J. Coles & Co. Ltd, 1938; Gen. Man., 1966; Dep. Man. Dir, 1969; Man. Dir, 1975–79; Dir, various G. J. Coles subsid. cos. Dep. Chm., KMart (Australia) Ltd, 1975–; Chairman: Island Cooler Pty Ltd, 1985–; Smurfit Australia Pty Ltd, 1986–. *Recreations:* horse racing, swimming. *Address:* Chiltern, 5/627 Toorak Road, Toorak, Vic 3142, Australia. *T:* (3) 98223161. *Clubs:* Athenæum, Royal Automobile of Victoria (Melbourne); Australian Armoured Corps (Sydney); Victorian Amateur Turf (Dep. Chm.), Victoria Racing, Moonee Valley Race; Melbourne Cricket.

NORTH, Sir (William) Jonathan (Frederick), 2nd Bt *cr* 1920; *b* 6 Feb. 1931; *s* of Muriel Norton (*d* 1989), 2nd *d* of Sir William Hicking, 1st Bt, and Hon. John Montagu William North (marr. diss. 1939; he *d* 1987), 2nd *s* of 8th Earl of Guilford; *S* grandfather, 1947 (under special remainder); *m* 1956, Sara Virginia, *d* of Air Chief Marshal Sir Donald Hardman, GBE, KCB, DFC; one *s* two *d*. *Educ:* Marlborough Coll. *Heir: s* Jeremy William Francis North [*b* 5 May 1960; *m* 1986, Lucy, *d* of G. A. van der Meulen, Holland; two *s* two *d*].

NORTHAM, Jeremy Philip; actor; *b* 1 Dec. 1961; *s* of late Prof. John and Rachel Northam; *m* 2005, Elizabeth L. Moro (marr. diss.). *Educ:* King's Coll. Sch., Cambridge; Bristol Grammar Sch.; Bedford Coll., London (BA Hons English); Bristol Old Vic Theatre Sch. *Theatre* includes: National Theatre, 1989–91: Hamlet, School for Scandal, The Voysey Inheritance (Olivier Award for Outstanding Newcomer); Royal Shakespeare Co., 1992–94: Loves Labour's Lost, The Country Wife, The Gift of the Gorgon; Old Times, Donmar Warehouse, 2004; Hay Fever, Noël Coward Th., 2012; *television* includes: Journey's End, Piece of Cake, 1988; Martin of Lewis, 2003; The Tudors, 2007; Fiona's Story, 2008; White Heat, 2012; *films* include: Wuthering Heights, Soft Top Hard Shoulder, 1992; Carrington, The Net, Voices, 1995; Emma, 1996; Mimic, Amistad, 1997; The Misadventures of Margaret, 1998; Gloria, The Winslow Boy, An Ideal Husband, Happy Texas, 1999; The Golden Bowl, 2000; Enigma, Gosford Park, 2001; Possession, 2002; Cypher, The Singing Detective, 2003; The Statement, Stroke of Genius, 2004; Guy X, 2005; A Cock and Bull Story, 2006; Dean Spanley, 2008; Glorious 39, 2009; Creation, 2009. Best Actor, Evening Standard Awards, 2000; Best Film Actor, Variety Club, 2000; Best British Actor, Critics Circle Award, 2000. *Address:* c/o Curtis Brown, 5th Floor, Haymarket House, 28–29 Haymarket, SW1Y 4SP.

NORTHAMPTON, 7th Marquess of, *cr* 1812; **Spencer Douglas David Compton;** DL; Earl of Northampton, 1618; Earl Compton, Baron Wilmington, 1812; *b* 2 April 1946; *s* of 6th Marquess of Northampton, DSO, and Virginia (*d* 1997), *d* of Lt-Col David Heaton, DSO; *S* father, 1978; *m* 1st, 1967, Henriette Luisa Maria (marr. diss. 1973), *o d* of late Baron Bentinck; one *s* one *d*; 2nd, 1974, Annette Marie (marr. diss. 1977), *er d* of C. A. R. Smallwood; 3rd, 1977, Hon. Mrs Rosemary Dawson-Damer (marr. diss. 1983); one *d*; 4th, 1985, Hon. Mrs Michael Pearson (marr. diss. 1988); one *d*; 5th, 1990, Pamela Martina Raphaela Kyprios (marr. diss. 2013); 6th, 2013, Tracy Goodman. *Educ:* Eton. DL Northants 1979. *Recreation:* freemasonry (Pro Grand Master, United Grand Lodge of England, 2001–09). *Heir: s* Earl Compton, *qv*. *Address:* Compton Wynyates, Tysoe, Warwicks CV35 0UD. *Club:* Turf.

NORTHAMPTON, Bishop of, (RC), since 2005; **Rt Rev. Peter John Haworth Doyle;** *b* 3 May 1944; *s* of John Robert Doyle and Alice Gertrude Doyle (*née* Haworth). *Educ:* St Ignatius Coll., Stamford Hill; Allen Hall Seminary. Ordained priest, 1968; Asst Priest, Portsmouth and Windsor, 1968–75; Adminr, St John's Cathedral, Portsmouth, 1975–87; Parish Priest: St Joseph's, Maidenhead, 1987–91; St Peter's, Winchester, 1991–2005. Canon, Portsmouth Cathedral, 1983–2005; VG, Dio. Portsmouth, (RC), 2001–05. Mem., Old Brotherhood, 1994–2005. *Recreations:* Rugby (played for Windsor and Portsmouth RFCs, now a spectator), golf, ski-ing. *Address:* Bishop's House, Marriott Street, Northampton NN2 6AW. *T:* (01604) 715635, *Fax:* (01604) 792186. *E:* admin@northamptondiocese.com.

NORTHAMPTON, Archdeacon of; *see* Ormston, Ven. R. J.

NORTHBOURNE, 5th Baron *cr* 1884; **Christopher George Walter James,** DL; FRICS; Bt 1791; Chairman: Betteshanger Farms Ltd, since 1975; Betteshanger Investments Ltd; *b* 18 Feb. 1926; *s* of 4th Baron Northbourne and Katherine Louise (*d* 1980), *d* of late George A. Nickerson, Boston, Mass; *S* father, 1982; *m* 1959, Aliki Louise Hélène Marie Sygne, *e d* of Henri Claudel, Chatou-sur-Seine, and *gd* of late Paul Claudel; three *s* one *d*. *Educ:* Eton; Magdalen Coll., Oxford (MA). Director: Anglo Indonesian Corp., 1971–96; Plantation & General (formerly Chillington Corp.) PLC, 1986–96; Center Parcs PLC, 1988–96 (Dep. Chm., 1988–96). Elected Mem., H of L, 1999. DL Kent, 1996. *Heir: s* Hon. Charles Walter Henri James [*b* 14 June 1960; *m* 1987, Catherine Lucy, *d* of Ralph Burrows; two *s* one *d*]. *Address:* 11 Eaton Place, SW1X 8BN. *T:* (020) 7235 6790; Coldharbour, Northbourne, Deal, Kent CT14 0LP. *T:* (01304) 611277. *Clubs:* Brooks's, Royal Yacht Squadron.

See also Hon. S. R. E. C. James.

NORTHBROOK, 6th Baron *cr* 1866; **Francis Thomas Baring;** Bt 1793; Trustee, Fortune Forum, since 2006; *b* 21 Feb. 1954; *s* of 5th Baron Northbrook and of Rowena Margaret, 2nd *d* of Brig.-Gen. Sir William Manning, GCMG, KBE, CB; *S* father, 1990; *m* 1st, 1987, Amelia Sarah Elizabeth (marr. diss. 2006), *er d* of Dr Reginald Taylor; three *d*; 2nd, 2013, Charlotte Lee, *d* of Thomas W. Pike. *Educ:* Winchester Coll.; Bristol Univ. (BA Hons 1976). FRGS 1986. Trainee accountant, Dixon Wilson & Co., 1976–80; Baring Brothers and Co. Ltd, 1981–89; Sen. Investment Man., Taylor Young Investment Management Ltd, 1990–93; Investment Man., Smith and Williamson Securities, 1993–95; Dir, Mars Asset Mgt Ltd, 1996–2006. Chm., Dido Films Ltd, 2002–07. Elected Mem., H of L, 1999; an Opposition Whip, 1999–2000. Trustee, Winchester Medical Trust, 1991–96. Mem., Gunmakers' Co. *Heir:* (to baronetcy) *kinsman* Peter Baring [*b* 12 Sept. 1939; *m* 1973, Rose, *d* of George Nigel Adams; one *s*]. *Address:* House of Lords, SW1A 0PW. *Clubs:* White's, Pratt's, Beefsteak.

NORTHCOTE, family name of **Earl of Iddesleigh**.

NORTHERN, Richard James, MBE 1982; HM Diplomatic Service, retired; consultant, since 2011; Director, RN4 Consultancy Ltd, since 2011; *b* 2 Nov. 1954; *s* of late James Wilfred Northern and of Margaret Northern (*née* Lammie); *m* 1981, Linda Denise Gadd; two *s* one *d*. *Educ:* Bedford Sch.; Jesus Coll., Cambridge (BA 1976; MA 1980). Joined HM Diplomatic Service, 1976: FCO, 1976–78; MECAS, Beirut and London, 1978–80; Third Sec. and Vice Consul, Riyadh, 1980–83; Second, later First, Sec. (Political/Inf.), Rome, 1983–87; First Secretary: FCO, 1987–92; (Economic), Ottawa, 1992–94; Dep. Consul Gen. and Dep. Dir for Trade and Investment, Toronto, 1994–97; Counsellor (Econ./Commercial), Riyadh, 1997–2000; Counsellor, FCO, 2000–01; Dir Gen. for Trade and Investment in Italy, and Consul Gen., Milan, 2001–06; Asst Dir, Human Resources, FCO, 2006–10; Ambassador to Libya, 2010–11. Sen. Consultant, Internat. Hosps Gp, 2011–; Sen. Adv, G4S, 2011–12. Trustee, British-Italian Soc. *Recreations:* tennis, music, languages, Italian wine, football. *Address:* c/o Morgan Cameron Ltd, 9 Thorney Leys Park, Witney OX28 4GE. *E:* richard@rn4consultancy.co.uk. *Clubs:* Oxford and Cambridge; Luton Town Football.

NORTHERN TERRITORY (AUSTRALIA), Bishop of the, since 2015; **Rt Rev. Dr Gregory David Anderson;** *b* Sydney, 1 Oct. 1961; *s* of Roger Barry Anderson and Shirley Mirrette Anderson (*née* Owen); *m* 1988, Annette Lorraine Eriksson; two *s* two *d*. *Educ:* James Ruse Agricultural High Sch.; Sydney Univ. (BA Hons; PhD); Moore Theol Coll. (BTh; DipMin; MA Theol.); Deakin Univ. (Master of Professional Educn and Trng). Lectr, Nungalinya Coll., Darwin, 1995–2001; ordained deacon, 2001, priest, 2002; Aboriginal Ministry Develt Officer, Dio. of the Northern Territory, 2001–06; Hd, Dept of Mission, Moore Theol Coll., 2007–14. *Recreations:* squash, singing, crosswords, gardening. *Address:* GPO Box 2950, Darwin, NT 0801, Australia. *T:* (8) 89417440, *Fax:* (8) 89417446. *E:* bishop@ntanglican.org.au.

NORTHESK, 15th Earl of, *cr* 1647; **Patrick Charles Carnegy,** PhD; Lord Lour 1639; Lord Rosehill and Eglismauldie 1647; writer, lecturer and broadcaster; *b* 23 Sept. 1940; *s* of Canon Patrick Charles Carnegy and Joyce Eleanor (*née* Townsley); *S* kinsman, 2010; *m* 2010, Jill Gomez, *qv*. *Educ:* Rugby; Trinity Hall, Cambridge (BA 1963; MA 1967; PhD 2008). Journalist, TES, 1964–69; Asst Ed., TLS, 1969–78; Ed., Faber & Faber Ltd, 1978–88; Dir, Faber Music Ltd, 1979–88; Dramaturg, ROH, 1988–92. Stratford theatre critic, The Spectator, 1998–. Leverhulme Res. Fellow, 1994–96. Mem., BBC Gen. Adv. Council, 1990–96. *Publications:* Faust as Musician: a study of Thomas Mann's novel Doctor Faustus, 1973; (ed) Christianity Revalued, 1974; Wagner and the Art of the Theatre, 2006 (Special Jury Prize, George Freedley Meml Award, 2006; Royal Philharmonic Soc. Award, 2007). *Heir: b* Colin David Carnegy [*b* 16 Aug. 1942; *m* 1973, Rosemary Frances Deschamps (*née* Chamier); three *s* one *d*]. *E:* patrick.carnegy@btopenworld.com.

NORTHESK, Countess of; *see* Gomez, J.

NORTHLAND, Viscount; courtesy title of heir to Earldom of Ranfurly, not used by current heir.

NORTHOLT, Archdeacon of; *see* Green, Ven. D. J.

NORTHOVER, Baroness *cr* 2000 (Life Peer), of Cissbury in the co. of West Sussex; **Lindsay Patricia Northover,** PhD; PC 2015; *b* 21 Aug. 1954; *d* of Maurice Charles Colin Granshaw and Patricia Winifred Granshaw (*née* Jackson); *m* 1988, Prof. John Martin Alban Northover, *qv* (separated); two *s* one *d*. *Educ:* Brighton and Hove High Sch.; St Anne's Coll., Oxford (exhibitioner; MA Modern History); Bryn Mawr Coll. (ESU schol.); Univ. of Pennsylvania (MA History and Philosophy of Sci. 1978; PhD 1981). Res. Fellow, UCL and St Mark's Hosp., 1980–83; Fellow, St Thomas's Hosp. Med. Sch., 1983–84; Lectr, Wellcome Inst. for the History of Medicine and UCL, 1984–91. Mem., cttee negotiating Liberal and SDP merger, 1987–88; Chair: SDP Health and Welfare Assoc., 1987–88; SDP Parly Cands' Assoc., 1987–88; Lib Dem Parly Cands' Assoc., 1988–91; Chair, Women Liberal Democrats, 1992–95. House of Lords: Lib Dem spokesperson on health, 2001–02, on internat. develt, 2002–10; govt spokesman on health, internat. develt and justice, and for women and equalities, 2010–12, on health, internat. develt, women and equalities, DCMS and DEFRA, 2012–13, on educn, internat. develt, women and equalities, and DEFRA, 2013–; lead govt spokesperson for DFID, 2011–; a Baroness in Waiting (Govt Whip), 2010–14; Parly Under-Sec. of State, DFID, 2014–15. Member: Select Cttee on Embryonic Stem Cell Res., 2001–02; Sub-Cttee on Foreign Affairs, Defence and Internat. Develt, 2003–04, on Economic and Financial Affairs and Internat. Trade, 2008–10, Select Cttee on EU. Sec., All-Party Gp on Overseas Develt, 2003–10; Mem. Council, Overseas Develt Inst., 2005–10. Mem. Exec., CPA, 2006–10 (Vice-Chair, 2008–10). Contested: (SDP/Alliance) Welwyn, Hatfield, 1983 and 1987; (Lib Dem) Basildon, 1997. Trustee: Tropical Health and Educn Trust, 2007–10; UNICEF UK, 2009–10; Liberal Democrats, 2009–11. Patron, Breast Cancer Campaign, 2002–09. Trustee, Bryn Mawr Coll. Assoc. (GB). *Publications:* academic books and contribs to learned jls. *Address:* House of Lords, SW1A 0PW.

NORTHOVER, Prof. John Martin Alban; Professor of Intestinal Surgery, Imperial College, London, since 2001; Consulting Surgeon, St Mark's Hospital for Intestinal and Colorectal Disorders, London, since 2012 (Senior Surgeon, 1984–2012); Consultant Surgeon, The London Clinic, since 1988; *b* 17 June 1947; *s* of William Joseph Northover and Peggy Vesta Northover (*née* Jacobs); *m* 1st, 1974, Sheila Ann Scott (marr. diss. 1987); two *s*; 2nd, 1988, Lindsay Patricia Granshaw (*see* Baroness Northover); two *s* one *d*. *Educ:* Southern Grammar Sch., Portsmouth; King's Coll. Hosp., London (MB BS Hons 1970; MS 1980). KCH and Middlesex Hosp. trng posts, 1970–84; Dir, Colorectal Cancer Unit, CRUK (formerly ICRF), 1985–2005. Res. Fellow, Univ. of Cape Town, 1976–77. Arris and Gale Lectr, RCS, 1979. Hon. Civilian Consultant Advr in Colorectal Surgery to the Army, 1998–2014. Chm., MRC Colorectal Cancer Trials Data Monitoring and Ethics Cttee, 1995–2008; Member: Adv. Cttee on Distinction Awards, NW London, 2001–03; NHS Bowel Screening Adv. Cttee, 2008–. Pres., Assoc. of Coloproctology of GB and Ireland, 2007–08; Vice-Pres., Internat. Soc. of Univ. Colon and Rectal Surgeons, 1998–99; Member: James IV Assoc. of Surgeons, 2001–11; Soc. of Pelvic Surgeons, 2004–10; Corresp. Mem., Surgical Res. Soc. of Southern Africa, 1989; Hon. Mem., Sect. of Colon and Rectal Surgery, RACS, 1992. *Publications:* (ed jtly) Pocket Examiner in Surgery, 1984, 2nd edn 1992; (ed with J. Kettner) Bowel Cancer: the facts, 1992; (ed with R. Phillips) Modern Coloproctology, 1993; (ed jtly) Current Surgical Practice, Vol. 8, 1998; (ed with W. Longo) Re-operative Colon and Rectal Surgery, 2003; Your Guide to Bowel Cancer, 2007; book chapters; numerous contribs to learned jls incl. Lancet, BMJ, British Jl Surgery, British Jl Cancer. *Address:* 116 Harley Street, W1G 7JL. *T:* (020) 7486 1008, *Fax:* (020) 7486 0665.

NORTHUMBERLAND, 12th Duke of, *cr* 1766; **Ralph George Algernon Percy;** DL; Bt 1660; Earl of Northumberland, Baron Warkworth 1749; Earl Percy 1766; Earl of Beverley 1790; Lord Lovaine, Baron of Alnwick 1784; Chairman, since 1992, and President, since 1995, Northumberland Estates; *b* 16 Nov. 1956; 2nd *s* of 10th Duke of Northumberland, KG, GCVO, TD, PC, FRS and Lady Elizabeth Diana Montagu-Douglas-Scott (*d* 2012), *er d* of 8th Duke of Buccleuch and Queensberry, KT, GCVO, PC; *S* brother, 1995; *m* 1979, Isobel Jane Miller (*see* Duchess of Northumberland); two *s* two *d*. *Educ:* Eton; Oxford Univ. MRICS (ARICS 1986). Land Agent with: Cluttons, 1979–82; Humberts, 1982–86; Northumberland Estates, 1986–96. DL Northumberland, 1997. *Recreations:* tennis, fishing, shooting, painting. *Heir: s* Earl Percy, *qv*. *Address:* Alnwick Castle, Alnwick, Northumberland NE66 1NG. *T:* (01665) 602456; Syon House, Brentford, Middlesex TW8 8JF. *T:* (020) 8560 2353.

NORTHUMBERLAND, Duchess of; (Isobel) Jane Miller Percy; Lord-Lieutenant of Northumberland, since 2009; *d* of John Walter Maxwell Miller Richard; *m* 1979, Ralph George Algernon Percy (*see* Duke of Northumberland); two *s* two *d*. Trustee, Alnwick Garden Trust. *Address:* Alnwick Castle, Alnwick, Northumberland NE66 1NG.

NORTHUMBERLAND, Archdeacon of; *see* Miller, Ven. G. V.

NORTHWAY, Eileen Mary, CBE 1990; RRC 1982 (ARRC 1969); Principal Nursing Officer and Matron-in-Chief, Queen Alexandra's Royal Naval Nursing Service, 1986–90, retired; *b* 22 July 1931; *d* of Ernest and Margaret Northway. *Educ:* St Michael's Convent, Newton Abbot. SRN 1952, SCM 1954; joined QARNNS 1956. QHNS, 1986–90. OStJ 1985. *Recreations:* gardening, reading.

NORTON, family name of **Barons Grantley** and **Rathcreedan**.

NORTON, 8th Baron *cr* 1878; **James Nigel Arden Adderley;** *b* 2 June 1947; *er s* of 7th Baron Norton, OBE and Betty Margaret, *o d* of James McKee Hannah; *S* father, 1993; *m* (marr. diss.); one *s* one *d*; *m* 1997, Frances Elizabeth Prioleau, *yr d* of George Frederick Rothwell; one *d*. *Educ:* Downside. FCA 1970. *Heir: s* Hon. Edward James Arden Adderley [*b* 19 Oct. 1982; *m* 2010, Sarah Jane Wilkinson]. *Address:* Chalet Petrus, rue de Patier 24, 1936 Verbier, Switzerland.

NORTON OF LOUTH, Baron *cr* 1998 (Life Peer), of Louth in the co. of Lincolnshire; **Philip Norton,** PhD; Professor of Government, since 1986, Director, Centre for Legislative Studies, since 1992, and Head, Department of Politics and International Studies, 2002–07, University of Hull; *b* 5 March 1951; *y s* of late George E. Norton and Ena D. Norton. *Educ:* Univ. of Sheffield (BA 1st cl. Hons; Nalgo Prize 1972; PhD); Univ. of Pennsylvania (MA; Thouron Scholar). Lectr, 1977–82, Sen. Lectr, 1982–84, Reader, 1984–86, Univ. of Hull. Member: Exec. Cttee, Study of Parlt Gp, 1981–93 (Acad. Sec., 1981–85); Exec. Cttee, British Politics Gp (USA), 1982–95, 2009–11 (Pres., 1988–90); Exec. Cttee, Political Studies Assoc. of UK, 1983–89; Society and Politics Res. Develt Gp, ESRC, 1987–90; Council, Hansard Soc., 1997– (Dir of Studies, 2002–). Chm., H of L Select Cttee on the Constitution, 2001–04; Co-Chair, Parly Univ. Gp, 2009–; Chair, All Party Parly Gp on Constitution, 2010–. Chairman: Cons. Pty Commn to Strengthen Parlt, 1999–2000; Standards Cttee, Kingston-upon-Hull City Council, 1999–2003. Co-Chm., Res. Cttee of Legislative Specialists, Internat. Political Sci. Assoc., 1994–2003. Pres., Politics Assoc., 1993–2008; Vice-Pres., Political Studies Assoc., 2002–. Trustee, Hist. of Parlt Trust, 1999–. Co-Chair, Higher Educn Commn, 2012–. Governor, King Edward VI Grammar Sch., Louth, 1988– (Warden, 1990–93). FRSA 1995; FAcSS (AcSS 2001). Assoc. Ed., Political Studies, 1987–93; Ed., Jl of Legislative Studies, 1995–. Hon. LLD Lincoln, 2011. *Publications:* Dissension in the House of Commons 1945–74, 1975; Conservative Dissidents, 1978; Dissension in the House of Commons 1974–79, 1980; The Commons in Perspective, 1981; (jtly) Conservatives and Conservatism, 1981; The Constitution in Flux, 1982; The British Polity, 1984, 5th edn 2010; Law and Order and British Politics, 1984; (ed) Parliament in the 1980s, 1985; (ed jtly) The Political Science of British Politics, 1986; (ed) Legislatures, 1990; (ed) Parliaments in Western Europe, 1990; (ed) New Directions in British Politics, 1991; (jtly) Politics UK, 1991, 8th edn 2013; (ed jtly) Parliamentary Questions, 1993; (jtly) Back from Westminster, 1993; Does Parliament Matter?, 1993; (ed) National Parliaments and the European Union, 1996; (ed jtly) The New Parliaments of Central and Eastern Europe, 1996; (ed) The Conservative Party, 1996; (ed) Legislatures and Legislators, 1998; (ed) Parliaments and Governments in Western Europe, 1998; (ed) Parliaments and Pressure Groups in Western Europe, 1999; (ed jtly) Parliaments in Asia, 1999; (ed) Parliaments and Citizens in Western Europe, 2002; Parliament in British Politics, 2005, 2nd edn 2013; (ed jtly) Post-Communist and Post-Soviet Parliaments: the initial decade, 2007; (ed jtly) The Internet and Parliamentary Democracy in Europe, 2008; (ed) A Century of Constitutional Reform, 2011; (ed) Eminent Parliamentarians, 2012; The Voice of the Backbenchers, 2013. *Recreations:* table-tennis, walking. *Address:* Department of Politics, University of Hull, Hull, East Yorkshire HU6 7RX. *T:* (01482) 465863. *Club:* Royal Over-Seas League.

NORTON, Maj. Gen. Sir George (Pemberton Ross), KCVO 2013; CBE 2008 (MBE 1998); Deputy Commander NATO Rapid Deployable Corps - Italy, since 2013; *b* London, 27 Nov. 1962; *s* of late Richard Glover Norton and Philippa Margaret Norton (*née* Fisher); *m* 1990, Alexandrine Freiin von Lüninck; three *d. Educ:* Summer Fields; Radley; St John's Coll., Cambridge (BA 1984; MA); RMA Sandhurst; German Armed Forces Staff Coll., Hamburg. HCSC; Commnd Grenadier Guards, 1985; regtl duty, 1985–93; MA to COS ACE RRC, 1995–97; Capt., Queen's Co., 1997–2000; Directing Staff, Staff Coll., 2000–02; CO 1st Bn Grenadier Guards, 2002–04; Dir Policy and Plans, Combined Forces Comd, Afghanistan, 2004; Sec. to Chiefs of Staff Cttee, MoD, 2005–06; Dep. Comdr, Task Force Helmand, Afghanistan, 2007; Comdr 38 (Irish) Bde, 2007–10; Dep. Comdr I Marine Expeditionary Force (Forward) and Regl Comd (SW), Afghanistan, 2010–11; GOC London Dist and Maj. Gen. Comdg Household Div., 2011–13. Regtl Lt Col, Grenadier Guards, 2012–. QCVS 2011. Bronze Star Medal (USA), 2004; Meritorious Honor Award (USA), 2011. *Recreations:* ski-ing, cricket, red wine. *Address:* Headquarters NATO Rapid Deployable Corps - Italy, Ugo Mara Barracks, BFPO 61. *Clubs:* Cavalry and Guards, MCC, Pratt's, Pitt, Buck's.

NORTON, Heather Sophia; Her Honour Judge Norton; a Circuit Judge, since 2012; *b* Thatcham, 24 Nov. 1966; *d* of Doris Norton; *m* 1996, Rev. Canon Nicholas Charles Papadopulos, *qv*; one *s* one *d. Educ:* Chichester High Sch. for Girls; Millfield Sch.; Birmingham Univ. (LLB Hons). Called to the Bar, Middle Temple, 1988; a Recorder, 2007–12. Trustee, Safe Partnership, 2001–13. *Publications:* (jtly) Pace: a practical guide to the Police and Criminal Evidence Act 1984, 2006, 4th edn 2015. *Recreations:* classical music, history, women's equality, walking in Wales, the novels of Georgette Heyer. *Address:* Canterbury Crown Court, The Law Courts, Chaucer Road, Canterbury, Kent CT1 1ZA. *E:* HHJudge.Norton@judiciary.gsi.gov.uk.

NORTON, Dame Hilary Sharon Braverman; *see* Blume, Dame H. S. B.

NORTON, Hugh Edward; non-executive Director: Inchcape plc, 1995–2004; Standard Chartered plc, 1995–2006; *b* 23 June 1936; *s* of late Lt-Gen. Edward F. Norton, CB, DSO, MC and I. Joyce Norton; *m* 1965, Janet M. Johnson (*d* 1993); one *s*; *m* 1998, F. Joy Harcup; one *s* one *d. Educ:* Winchester Coll.; Trinity Coll., Oxford (BA Hons Lit.Hum.). British Petroleum Co., 1959–95: Chief Exec., BP Exploration Co., 1986–89; Man. Dir, 1989–95. Trustee, Shelter, 2003–12. *Recreations:* painting, ornithology, tennis, travel, chess.

NORTON, James, FCIS; General Secretary, Arthritis and Rheumatism Council for Research, 1981–98; *b* 12 July 1931; *s* of James and May Norton; *m* 1956, Dora Ashworth; one *s. Educ:* West Hill Sch., Stalybridge; Open Univ. (BA Hons 2002); Univ. of Sheffield (MA Historical Res. 2005). FCIS 1972. Stalybridge, Hyde, Mossley and Dukinfield Tspt Bd, 1947–60; Wing Comdr, RAF, 1961–81. *Recreations:* walking, cricket, Manchester United. *Address:* 665 Chatsworth Road, Chesterfield S40 3PA. *T:* (01246) 566160. *Club:* Royal Air Force.

NORTON, Jim; *see* Norton, M. J.

NORTON, John Lindsey; Chairman, National Society for Prevention of Cruelty to Children, 1995–2001 (Hon. Treasurer, 1991–95); *b* 21 May 1935; *s* of Frederick Raymond Norton and Doris Ann Norton; *m* 1959, Judith Ann Bird; three *d. Educ:* Winchester College; Cambridge Univ. (MA). Blackburn Robson Coates & Co., 1959–63; BDO Binder Hamlyn, later Binder Hamlyn, 1963–96: Nat. Man. Partner, 1983–88; Chm., BDO Binder, 1988–92; Sen. Partner, Binder Hamlyn, 1993–96. Chairman: Barking Power Ltd, 1995–2011; Thames Valley Power Ltd, 1995–2011 (Dir, 1995–2011). *Recreations:* walking, gardening, golf. *Address:* Knowle Cottage, 1 Shorts Lane, Beaminster, Dorset DT8 3BD.

NORTON, Michael Aslan, OBE 1998; social entrepreneur; author; *s* of Richard and Helene Norton; *m* 1977, Hilary Sharon Braverman Blume (*see* Dame H. S. B. Blume); one *d*, and two step *s. Educ:* Charterhouse; King's Coll., Cambridge (MA Natural Scis). Investment Manager, Samuel Montagu & Co., 1964–67; Exec., New Enterprises, IPC, 1968; Publishing Exec., BPC Publishing, 1969–71; freelance writer, lectr, OU tutor and activist, 1971–75; Founder and Director: Directory of Social Change, 1975–94; Centre for Innovation in Voluntary Action, 1995–; Founder and Chm., Internat. Centre for Social Franchising, 2011–. Creator of first lang. teaching prog. in UK for non-English speaking immigrant families and children, 1965–70; Co-ordinator, Save Piccadilly Campaign, 1972–74; Co-Founder: Soho Housing Assoc., 1974; Changemakers, 1994 (Chm., 1994–); UnLtd, the Foundn for Social Entrepreneurs, 2001; UnLtd India, 2007; UnLtd SA, 2010; Buzzbnk (formerly BuzzBank), 2010 (Chm., 2010–); Founder: Books for Change, 1996; YouthBank, 1998; Booksline (India), 2000; Young Achievers Trust, 2006; Otesha Proj. UK, 2007; SmallWorks, 2011; Co-Founder, Internat. Centre for Social Franchising, 2012; Sponsor, Children's Develt Bank prog. for street banking in S Asia, 2004; Initiator: MyBnk children's banking and financial literacy prog. in UK, 2006; FoodCycle (formerly FoodWorks), youth volunteering prog., 2009–. Adjunct Prof., Univ. of Cape Town Graduate Sch. of Business, 2011–; Prof., China Philanthropy Res. Inst., Beijing Normal Univ., 2015. Hon. DLitt Wolverhampton, 2009. Karmaveer Award, Indian Confedn of NGOs, 2012; Beacon Fellow, 2013; UK Charity Award (Outstanding Achievement), 2014. *Publications:* The Community Newspaper Kit, 1975; The Mural Kit, 1976; Colour in your Environment, 1979; A Guide to the Benefits of Charitable Status, 1981; A Guide to Company Giving, 1984; The WorldWide Fundraisers Handbook, 1996, 3rd edn 2009; The Non-Profit Sector in India, 1997; Getting Started in Fundraising (India), 2000; (with Nina Botting) The Complete Fundraising Handbook, 4th edn 2001 to 5th edn 2007; Getting Started in Communication (India), 2003; 365 Ways to Change the World, 2005; Need to Know? Fundraising, 2007; The Everyday Activist, 2007; Writing Better Fundraising Applications, 1992, 4th edn (with M. Eastwood) 2010; Click2Change, 2012. *Recreations:* cycling, bridge, crosswords, dreaming up ideas to change the world, mentoring and supporting emerging social entrepreneurs.

NORTON, Michael James, (Jim), FREng; independent director and consulting engineer; *b* 15 Dec. 1952; *s* of Christopher Stephen Norton and Lilian Ivy Norton; *m* 1976, Barbara Foster; one *s. Educ:* Roan Sch., Blackheath; Sheffield Univ. (BEng Hons (Electronic Engrg) 1974; Mappin Medal, 1974). AMIEE 1974, FIET (FIEE 1997); FREng 2011. Post Office (Telecommunications), later British Telecommunications, 1970–87 (lastly, Sen. Man., Internat. Business); Practice Dir, Butler Cox plc, 1987–90; Marketing Dir, Cable & Wireless (Europe), 1990–93; Chief Exec., Radiocoms Agency, DTI, 1993–98; Dir, Electronic Commerce Team, Performance and Innovation Unit, Cabinet Office, 1999; Institute of Directors: Hd of Electronic Business Policy, 1999–2001; Sen. Policy Advr, e-Business and e-Govt, 2004–08; Ext. Examr, IoD Cert. in Co. Direction, 2008–; Chm., Deutsche Telekom Ltd, 2001–02. Non-executive Director: Securicor plc, 2000–02; 3i European Technology Trust, 2000–04; Zetex (formerly Telemetrix) plc, 2000–08 (Sen. Ind. Dir, 2003–08); F & C Capital & Income (formerly F & C PEP & ISA) Trust plc, 2001–14. Chm., UK Spectrum Policy Forum, 2013–. Mem., Commn on Nat. Security in 21st Century, IPPR, 2007–09. Mem., Ind. Rev. of UEA Climatic Res. Unit, 2010. Mem., Engrg Policy Cttee, 2014–, Mem., Finance Cttee, 2014–, RAEng. Ext. Bd Mem., POST, 2001–; Strategic Stakeholder Gp Mem., Nat. Hi-Tech Crime Unit, 2005–06; Council Mem., PICTFOR (formerly PITCOM), 2005–12 (Chm., Prog. Cttee, 2009–12). British Computer Society: Trustee, 2008–13; Vice Pres., 2008–11; Pres., 2011–12; Trustee Dir, BCS L&D Ltd, 2014–. Vis. Prof. of Electronic Engrg, Univ. of Sheffield, 1998–. Gov. and Mem. Audit Cttee, Coventry Univ., 2012–. FRSA 1993; FInstD 2001. Hon. DEng Sheffield, 2003; Hon. LLD Bath, 2012. *Recreations:* reading, music, amateur radio. *Address:* 179b Kimbolton Road, Bedford MK41 8DR. *W:* www.profjimnorton.com.

NORTON, Hon. Sir Nicholas John H.; *see* Hill-Norton.

NORTON, Maj. Peter Allen, GC 2006; CEng; private consultant in counter-threat, ordnance, munitions and explosives, since 2015; Member, Directing Staff and Lecturer in Explosive Ordnance Engineering and Counter-IED Technologies, Defence Academy College of Management and Technology, 2008–13; *b* 10 Dec. 1962; *m* 1st, 1994, Susan Ann Chapman (marr. diss. 2009); two *s*; 2nd, 2013, Dr Katherine Jane Eburn Hewins; one *d. Educ:* Cranfield Univ. (MSc Explosive Ordnance Engrg, 2008). CEng 2011. Enlisted RAOC, 1983; trained as Ammunition Technician; Instr, Improvised Explosive Device Disposal, Army Sch. of Ammunition, 1993–95; loan service, Royal Army of Oman, 1995–98; Royal Logistics Corps: Sen. Ammunition Technician, 1998; Conductor, 2002; commnd, 2002; 2nd i/c Combined Explosives Exploitation Cell, Iraq, 2005 (GC for outstanding bravery and leadership). Mem., Nat. Council, IExpE, 2010–14 (Chm., Tech. Cttee, 2011–14). Dir, Help for Heroes Recovery, 2011–; Chm., VC and GC Assoc., 2014– (Vice Chm., 2013–14); Trustee, VC and GC Benevolent Fund, 2007–. MIExpE 1991, FIExpE 2012; MCGI 2010. FBI Star, 2009; US Army Commendation Medal, 2009. *Recreations:* spending time with his children, photography, Open University studies.

NORTON, Sally; *see* Harrison, S.

NORTON-GRIFFITHS, Sir John, 3rd Bt *cr* 1922; FCA; *b* 4 Oct. 1938; *s* of Sir Peter Norton-Griffiths, 2nd Bt, and Kathryn (*d* 1980), *e d* of late George F. Schrafft; *S* father, 1983; *m* 1964, Marilyn Margaret, *er d* of late Norman Grimley. *Educ:* Eton. FCA 1966. *Heir: b* Michael Norton-Griffiths [*b* 11 Jan. 1941; *m* 1965, Ann, *o d* of late Group Captain Blair Alexander Fraser; one *s*].

NORWICH, 2nd Viscount *cr* 1952, of Aldwick; **John Julius Cooper,** CVO 1993; FRSL, FRGS, FSA; writer and broadcaster; *b* 15 Sept. 1929; *s* of 1st Viscount Norwich, PC, GCMG, DSO, and Lady Diana Cooper (*d* 1986), *d* of 8th Duke of Rutland; *S* father, 1954; *m* 1st, 1952, Anne (Frances May) (marr. diss. 1985), *e d* of late Hon. Sir Bede Clifford, GCMG, CB, MVO; one *s* one *d*; 2nd, 1989, Mollie Philipps, *e d* of 1st Baron Sherfield, GCB, GCMG, FRS. *Educ:* Upper Canada Coll., Toronto, Canada; Eton; University of Strasbourg; New Coll., Oxford. Served 1947–49 as Writer, Royal Navy. Entered Foreign Office, 1952; Third Secretary, British Embassy, Belgrade, 1955–57; Second Secretary, British Embassy, Beirut, 1957–60; worked in Foreign Office (First Secretary from 1961) and in British Delegation to Disarmament Conference, Geneva, from 1960 until resignation from Foreign Service 1964. Chairman: British Theatre Museum, 1966–71; Venice in Peril Fund, 1970–92; Colnaghi, 1992–96; Chm. Emeritus, World Monuments Fund Britain; Member: Exec. Cttee, National Trust, 1969–95 (Properties Cttee, 1970–87); Franco-British Council, 1972–79; Bd, English Nat. Opera, 1977–81. Curator, Sovereign Exhibn, London, 1992. Has made some thirty documentary films for television, mostly on history and architecture. Commendatore, Ordine al Merito della Repubblica Italiana, 1995; Stella della Solidarietà Italiana, 2001. *Publications:* (as John Julius Norwich): Mount Athos (with Reresby Sitwell), 1966; The Normans in the South (as The Other Conquest, US), 1967, new edn (incl. The Kingdom in The Sun) as The Normans in Sicily, 1992; Sahara, 1968; The Kingdom in The Sun, 1970; (ed) Great Architecture of the World, 1975; A History of Venice: vol. I, The Rise to Empire, 1977: vol. II, The Greatness and the Fall, 1981; Christmas Crackers: being ten commonplace selections, 1970–79, 1980; (ed) Britain's Heritage, 1982; (ed) The Italian World: history, art and the genius of a people, 1983; Fifty Years of Glyndebourne, 1985; A Taste for Travel (anthology), 1985; The Architecture of Southern England, 1985; Byzantium: vol. 1, The Early Centuries, 1988; vol. 2, The Apogee, 1991; vol. 3, The Decline and Fall, 1995; More Christmas Crackers 1980–89, 1990; Venice: a traveller's companion, 1990; (ed) The Oxford Illustrated Encyclopaedia of the Arts, 1990; (with H. C. Robbins Landon) Five Centuries of Music in Venice, 1991; (with C. Miles) Love in the Ancient World, 1997; (with Quentin Blake) The Twelve Days of Christmas, 1998; Shakespeare's Kings, 1999; Still More Christmas Crackers, 2000; Paradise of Cities: Venice in the 19th century, 2003; (ed) The Duff Cooper Diaries, 2005; The Middle Sea: a history of the Mediterranean, 2006; Trying to Please (memoirs), 2008; (ed) The Great Cities in History, 2009; The Popes: a history, 2011 (as Absolute Monarchs, US); A History of England in 100 Places, 2011; (ed) Darling Monster, 2013; Sicily: a history, 2015. *Recreations:* sight-seeing, nightclub piano. *Heir: s* Hon. Jason Charles Duff Bede Cooper, *b* 27 Oct. 1959. *Address:* 24 Blomfield Road, W9 1AD. *T:* (020) 7286 5050. *Club:* Beefsteak.

See also A. C. A. Cooper, Baron Milford.

NORWICH, Bishop of, since 1999; **Rt Rev. Graham Richard James;** *b* 19 Jan. 1951; *s* of late Rev. Lionel Dennis James and Florence Edith May James (*née* James); *m* 1978, Julie Anne Freemantle; one *s* one *d* (and one *d* decd). *Educ:* Northampton Grammar Sch.; Univ. of

Lancaster (BA 1972); Univ. of Oxford (DipTh 1974); Cuddesdon Theological Coll. Deacon 1975, priest 1976; Asst Curate, Christ the Carpenter, Peterborough, 1975–78; Priest-in-charge, later Team Vicar, Christ the King, Digswell, 1979–83; Selection Sec. and Sec. for Continuing Ministerial Educn, ACCM, 1983–85; Sen. Selection Sec., ACCM, 1985–87; Chaplain to Archbishop of Canterbury, 1987–93; Bishop Suffragan of St Germans, 1993–99. Hon. Canon: St Matthew's Cathedral, Dallas, Texas, 1989–; Truro Cathedral, 1993–99. Vice-Moderator, Churches Commn on Inter-Faith Relations, 1993–99; Chm., Rural Bishops Panel, C of E, 2001–06; Member: Gen. Synod of C of E, 1995–; Archbps' Council, 2006–10 (Chm., Ministry Div., 2006–12). Took seat in H of L, 2004. Mem., H of L Select Cttee on Communications, 2011–15. Chairman: Central Religious Adv. Cttee, BBC, 2004–08; Standing Conf. on Religion and Belief, BBC, 2009–11. Mem. Bd, Countryside Agency, 2001–06; Chm., Norfolk Community Foundn, 2005–08; Pres., Royal Norfolk Agricl Assoc., 2005. *Publications:* (contrib.) Say One for Me, 1992; (ed) New Soundings, 1997; Changing Rural Life, 2004; A Fallible Church, 2008; contribs to Theology; The Lent Factor, 2014. *Recreations:* theatre, discovering secondhand bookshops, cricket. *Address:* Bishop's House, Norwich NR3 1SB. *T:* (01603) 629001. *E:* bishop@dioceseofnorwich.org. *Clubs:* Athenæum; Norfolk.

NORWICH, Dean of; *see* Hedges, Very Rev. J. B.

NORWICH, Archdeacon of; *see* McFarlane, Ven. J. E.

NORWOOD, Mandi, (Mrs M. Norwood-Kelly); publishing consultant; Editorial Director, since 2011 and Senior Vice President, Niche Media, New York; *b* 9 Oct. 1963; *m* 1995, Martin Kelly; two *d.* Sub-editor, Look Now, 1983–84; Features Editor, Clothes Show, 1986; Dep. Editor, More!, 1986–90; Editor: Looks, 1989–90; Company, 1990–95; Cosmopolitan, 1995–2000; Editor-in-Chief: Mademoiselle, 2000–01; Shop Etc, 2004–06; Founding Partner, Trampoline Gp, Leadership and Mgt Consultancy, 2008–11. Ed. of Year, British Press Awards, 1993. *Publications:* Girls Just Want to Have Fun (short stories), 1999; How to be Number One in Your Own World, 2000; Sex and the Married Girl, 2003; The Hitched Chick's Guide to Modern Marriage, 2004; Rock Star Momma, 2007; Michelle Style, 2009. *Club:* Groucho.

NORWOOD, Her Honour Suzanne Freda, (Mrs John Lexden Stewart); a Circuit Judge, 1973–95; *b* 24 March 1926; *d* of late Frederic Francis Norwood and Marianne Freda Norwood (*née* Thomas); *m* 1954, John Lexden Stewart (*d* 1972); one *s. Educ:* Lowther Coll., Bodelwyddan; St Andrews Univ. MA English, MA Hons History. Called to Bar, Gray's Inn, 1951; practised at Bar, SE Circuit. Member: Parole Bd, 1976–78; Mental Health Review Tribunal, 1983–98 (Chm., Oxford and Anglia Area, 1994–98). Member: Greenwich and Bexley AHA, 1979–82; Greenwich DHA, 1982–85; Bexley DHA, 1985–90. Pres., Medico-Legal Soc., 1990–92. Hon. LLD St Andrews, 1996. *Recreations:* walking, housekeeping, opera. *Address:* 69 Lee Road, SE3 9EN.

NORWOOD-KELLY, Mandi; *see* Norwood, M.

NOSS, Dame Celia Mary; *see* Hoyles, Dame C. M.

NOSS, John Bramble; HM Diplomatic Service, retired; *b* 20 Dec. 1935; *s* of John Noss and Vera Ethel (*née* Mattingly); *m* 1957, Shirley May Andrews; two *s* one *d. Educ:* Portsmouth Grammar School. Foreign Office, 1954; RAF, 1955–57; served FO, Beirut, Copenhagen, FCO; Russian language training, 1965; Moscow, 1965–68; Santiago, 1968–70; FCO, 1970–73; First Sec. (Economic), Pretoria, 1974–77; First Sec. (Commercial), Moscow, 1977–78; FCO, 1978–81; Consul (Inward Investment), New York, 1981–85; High Comr, Solomon Is, 1986–88; Dep. Hd of Mission and Commercial Counsellor, Helsinki, 1988–91; Consul-Gen., Perth, 1991–93; Internat. Primary Aluminium Inst., 1994–97 (Dep. Sec. Gen., 1996–97). *Recreations:* family, reading, golf. *Address:* 8 Hither Chantlers, Langton Green, Tunbridge Wells, Kent TN3 0BJ. *T:* (01892) 862157.

NOSSAL, Sir Gustav (Joseph Victor), AC 1989; Kt 1977; CBE 1970; FRS 1982; FAA; Director, The Walter and Eliza Hall Institute of Medical Research, Melbourne, 1965–96; Professor of Medical Biology, University of Melbourne, 1965–96, now Professor Emeritus; *b* Austria, 4 June 1931; *m* 1955, Lyn B. Dunnicliff; two *s* two *d. Educ:* Sydney Univ. (1st Cl. Hons BScMed (Bacteriology), 1952; 1st Cl. Hons MB, BS 1954 (Mills Prize)); Melbourne Univ. (PhD 1960). FAA 1967; FRACP 1967; Hon. FRCPA 1971; FRACMA 1971; FRCP 1980; FTS 1981; Hon. FRSE 1983. Jun., then Sen. Resident Officer, Royal Prince Alfred Hosp., Sydney, 1955–56; Res. Fellow, Walter and Eliza Hall Inst. of Med. Res., 1957–59; Asst Prof., Dept of Genetics, Stanford Univ. Sch. of Medicine, Calif, 1959–61; Dep. Dir (Immunology), Walter and Eliza Hall Inst. of Med. Res., 1961–65. Vis. scientist and vis. professor to several univs and res. insts; has given many lectures to learned societies, assocs and univs. Dir, CRA Ltd, 1977–97. World Health Organisation: Member: Expert Adv. Panel on Immunology, 1967; Adv. Cttee Med. Res., 1973–80; Special Consultant, Tropical Disease Res. Prog., 1976; Chm., Global Programme for Vaccines and Immunization, 1993–2002. Chm., West Pac Adv. Co. Med. Res., 1976–80; Member: Aust. Science and Technol. Council, 1975–83; Bd, CSIRO, 1987–94; Prime Minister's Sci. and Engrg Council, 1989–98. Chairman: Felton Bequests' Cttee, 1977–; Vic Health Promotion Foundn, 1987–96; Bill and Melinda Gates Foundn Vaccine Prog., 1998–2003. President: Internat. Union of Immunological Socs, 1986–89; Australian Acad. of Science, 1994–98. Mem., Aust. Soc. of Immunology; Hon. Mem., Amer. (1975), French (1979), Indian (1976), Soc. of Immunology; Foreign Hon. Mem., Amer. Acad. of Arts and Scis, 1974. For. Associate, US Nat. Acad. of Scis, 1979; Fellow, New York Acad. of Scis, 1977; For. Fellow, Indian Nat. Sci. Acad., 1980. Hon. MD Johannes Gutenberg Univ., Mainz, 1981. Emil von Behring Prize, Philipps Univ., Marburg, Germany, 1971; Rabbi Shai Shacknai Memorial Prize, Univ. of Jerusalem, 1973; Ciba Foundn Gold Medal, 1978; Burnet Medal, Aust. Acad. of Sci., 1979; Robert Koch Gold Medal, Univ. of Bonn, 1996; Peter Wills Medal, Research Australia Awards, 2012. Mem. Editorial Bd of several med. jls. *Publications:* Antibodies & Immunity, 1968, rev. edn 1977; Antigens Lymphoid Cells & The Immune Response, 1971; Medical Science & Human Goals, 1975; Nature's Defences (Boyer Lectures), 1978; Reshaping Life: key issues in genetic engineering, 1984; Diversity and Discovery, 2007. *Recreations:* golf, literature. *Address:* Department of Pathology, University of Melbourne, Parkville, Vic 3010, Australia. *T:* (3) 83446946. *Club:* Melbourne (Melbourne).

NOTLEY, Maj.-Gen. Charles Roland Sykes, CB 1994; CBE 1991; President of the Ordnance Board, 1992–94; *b* 5 May 1939; *s* of late Major Henry Sykes Notley, 3rd Carabiniers, and Mrs Stephanie Paterson-Morgan; *m* 1965, Katherine Sonia Bethell; two *d. Educ:* Winchester Coll. Commnd 3rd Carabiniers, 1959; Command, Royal Scots Dragoon Guards, 1979–82; Dir, Op. Requirements (Land), MoD, 1986–89; Dir, Logistic Ops (Army), MoD, 1989–90; Vice-Pres., Ordnance Board, 1991–92. *Recreations:* equitation, sailing. *Address:* c/o Royal Bank of Scotland, 62 Threadneedle Street, EC2R 8LA. *Clubs:* Royal Ocean Racing; Royal Yacht Squadron (Cowes); Royal Cruising.

NOTT, Rt Hon. Sir John (William Frederic), KCB 1983; PC 1979; farmer, Trewinnard Manor, St Erth, Cornwall; *b* 1 Feb. 1932; *s* of late Richard Nott, Bideford, Devon, and Phyllis (*née* Francis); *m* 1959, Miloska Sekol Vlahovic, Maribor, Slovenia (OBE 2012); two *s* one *d. Educ:* King's Mead, Seaford; Bradfield Coll.; Trinity Coll., Cambridge. Lieut, 2nd Gurkha Rifles (regular officer), Malayan emergency, 1952–56; Trinity Coll., Cambridge, 1957–59 (BA Hons Law and Econs); Pres., Cambridge Union, 1959; called to the Bar, Inner Temple, 1959; Gen. Manager, S. G. Warburg & Co. Ltd, Merchant Bankers, 1959–66. MP (C) Cornwall, St Ives, 1966–83; Minister of State, HM Treasury, 1972–74; Cons. front bench spokesman on: Treasury and Economic Affairs, 1974–76; Trade, 1976–79; Sec. of State for Trade, 1979–81; Sec. of State for Defence, 1981–83. Chm. and Chief Executive, Lazard Brothers & Co. Ltd, 1985–90 (Dir, 1983–90); Chm., Hillsdown Hldgs plc, 1993–99 (Dir, 1991–99). Chairman: Etam plc, 1991–95; Maple Leaf Foods Inc., Canada, 1993–95; Dep. Chm., Royal Insurance PLC, 1986–91 (Dir, 1985–91); Director: AMEC plc, 1991–93; Apax Partners & Co. Capital Ltd, 1996–; Altium Capital Hldgs, 1996–; Chiswell Associates Ltd, 1999–2002; 30 St James Square Investments, 2001–; Adviser: Apax Partners, 1990–98; Freshfields, 1991–95. *Publications:* Here Today, Gone Tomorrow (autobiog.), 2002; Mr Wonderful Takes a Cruise, 2004; Haven't We Been Here Before? Afghanistan to the Falklands: a personal connection, 2007; Trewinnard—A Cornish History, 2013; Mr Wonderful seeks Immortality, 2014. *Recreations:* farming, fishing. *Address:* 31 Walpole Street, SW3 4QS. *T:* (020) 7730 2351, *Fax:* (020) 7730 9859. *Clubs:* Pratt's, Beefsteak, Buck's.

See also Rt Hon. H. G. W. Swire.

NOTT, Rt Rev. Peter John; Bishop of Norwich, 1985–99; Hon. Assistant Bishop, Diocese of Oxford, since 1999; *b* 30 Dec. 1933; *s* of Cecil Frederick Wilder Nott and Rosina Mabel Bailey; *m* 1961, Elizabeth May Maingot; one *s* three *d. Educ:* Bristol Grammar Sch.; Dulwich Coll.; RMA Sandhurst; Fitzwilliam House, Cambridge; Westcott House, Cambridge (MA). Curate of Harpenden, 1961–64; Chaplain of Fitzwilliam Coll., Cambridge, 1964–69; Fellow of Fitzwilliam Coll., 1967–69, Hon. Fellow, 1993; Chaplain of New Hall, Cambridge, 1966–69; Rector of Beaconsfield, 1969–77; Bishop Suffragan of Taunton, 1977–85. Archbishop's Adviser to HMC, 1980–85; President: SW Region, Mencap, 1978–84; Somerset Rural Music Sch., 1981–85; Royal Norfolk Agricl Assoc., 1996. Vice-Chm., Archbishops' Commn for Rural Areas, 1988–90. Trustee, Nat. Army Mus., 2001–09. Dean, Priory of England, Order of St John of Jerusalem, 1999–2003. KStJ 1999. *Publications:* Moving Forward in Prayer, 1991; Bishop Peter's Pilgrimage: his diary and sketchbook, 1996; Letter from Losinga and other sermons, 1999. *Address:* Westcot House, Westcot, Wantage, Oxon OX12 9QA. *T:* (01235) 751233.

NOTT, Roger Charles L.; *see* Lane-Nott.

NOTTINGHAM, Bishop of, (RC), since 2015; **Rt Rev. Patrick Joseph McKinney;** *b* 30 April 1954; *s* of Patrick and Bridget McKinney. *Educ:* St Mary's Coll., Oscott; Gregorian Pontifical Univ., Rome (LTh). Ordained priest, 1978; Asst Priest, Our Lady of Lourdes, Yardley Wood, Birmingham; Chaplain, St Thomas Aquinas Secondary Sch., Kings Norton; Teacher, Fundamental Theology, 1984–89, Rector and Lectr in Ecclesiology, 1989–98, St Mary's Coll., Oscott; Parish Priest, St John's, Great Haywood, 1998–2001; Episcopal Vicar, Archdiocese of Birmingham, 1998–2006; Parish Priest, Our Lady and All Saints, Stourbridge and Dean, Dudley Deanery, 2006–15. Chair, Ecumenical Commn, Archdiocese of Birmingham. Mem., Met. Chapter of St Chad, 1992–. Prelate of Honour, 1990. *Address:* Catholic Diocese of Nottingham, Willson House, 25 Derby Road, Nottingham NG15 5AW.

NOTTINGHAM, Archdeacon of; *see* Clark, Ven. S. E.

NOULTON, John David; transport consultant; *b* 5 Jan. 1939; *s* of John Noulton and Kathleen (*née* Sheehan); *m* 1961, Anne Elizabeth Byrne (*d* 2012); three *s* one *d. Educ:* Clapham Coll. ComplCE 1994. Asst Principal, Dept of Transport, 1970–72; Principal, DoE, 1972–78; Pvte Sec. to Minister of State, DoE, 1976–78; Asst Sec., Depts of the Environment and of Transport, 1978–85; Under Sec., Dept of Transport, 1985–89. British Co-Chm., Channel Tunnel Intergovtl Commn, 1987–89; Director: Transmanche Link, 1989–92; Public Affairs, Eurotunnel, 1992–2004. Special Advr to Chm., London Olympic Develt Authy, 2006. Chm., Council for Travel and Tourism, 2001–03. Trustee, 2004–09, Treas., 2006–09, Franco-British Council. *Recreations:* boating, swimming, walking, writing, Mediterranean gardening. *Address:* 74 Garricks House, Wadbrook Street, Kingston upon Thames, Surrey KT1 1HS. *T:* (020) 8546 3855. *Club:* Royal Motor Yacht.

NOURRY, Arnaud; Chairman and Chief Executive Officer, Hachette Livre, since 2003; *b* 7 Jan. 1961; *s* of Claude Nourry and Marie Paule Nourry (*née* Boiron); *m* 1996, Danielle Belforti; two *s* one *d. Educ:* Ecole Supérieure de Commerce, Paris (MBA 1982); Paris Univ. (3rd degree Sociology 1983). Consultant, Mensia, 1986–90; Hachette Livre: Project Manager, 1990–95; Dep. Finance Officer, 1995–97; Gen. Manager, Hatier textbook div., 1998–2002. Ordre National du Mérite (France), 2006. *Recreations:* classical music, tennis, wine. *Address:* Hachette Livre, 58 Rue Jean Bleuzen, CS 70007, 92178 Vanves Cedex, France. *T:* (1) 43923543, *Fax:* (1) 43923532. *E:* anourry@hachette-livre.fr.

NOURSE, Christopher Stuart; arts project manager and consultant, since 2004; *b* Salisbury, 13 Aug. 1946; *s* of late Rev. John Nourse and Helen Nourse (*née* Allison); civil partnership 2008, Charles Shu Ming Chan. *Educ:* Hurstpierpoint Coll., Sussex; Edinburgh Univ. (LLB); Inns of Court Sch. of Law. Life Officers' Assoc., 1970–72; various managerial positions with Royal Opera Hse, English Opera Gp and Royal Ballet New Gp, 1972–76; Gen. Manager, 1976–86, Admin. Dir, 1986–91, Sadler's Wells Royal Ballet, later Birmingham Royal Ballet; Asst to Gen. Dir, Royal Opera Hse, 1991–96; Admin. Dir, Royal Opera Hse Trust, 1996–97; Exec. Dir, Rambert Dance Co., 1997–2001; Man. Dir, English Nat. Ballet, 2001–03. Projects include: project manager, Appeal launch for A Statue for Oscar Wilde, NPG, 1997; Adminr, Nat. Dance Awards, 2004–10; project manager, Dance Proms, Royal Albert Hall, 2011–14. Exec. Dir, Frederick Ashton Foundn, 2011–. Non-executive Director: London Dance Network, 1998–2000 (Vice-Chm.); Dancers' Pension Scheme, 2006– (Chm., 2010–); Candoco Dance Co., 2008–14. Trustee: Nat. Youth Dance Trust, 2002–04; Youth Dance England, 2004–; Dame Margot Fonteyn Scholarship Fund, 2007– (Lead Trustee, 2007–); Cecchetti Soc., 2009–. Gov., Royal Ballet, 2008–. FRSA. *Recreations:* music, the performing and visual arts, ballroom dancing, the countryside, the Orient. *Address:* 278 Earl's Court Road, SW5 9AS.

NOURSE, Edmund Alexander Martin; QC 2015; *b* UK, 27 Jan. 1970; *s* of Dr Christopher Henry Nourse and Victoria Helen Mary Phillips; *m* 2005, Susan Julians; two *d. Educ:* Magdalen Coll., Oxford (BA 1st Cl. Hons Modern Hist.); City Univ. (DipLaw). Called to the Bar, Lincoln's Inn, 1994; in practice as barrister, specialising in commercial law, 1995–. *Recreations:* cricket, cooking, travel, photography. *Address:* One Essex Court, Temple, EC4Y 9AR.

NOURSE, Rt Hon. Sir Martin (Charles), Kt 1980; PC 1985; a Lord Justice of Appeal, 1985–2001; Vice-President, Court of Appeal (Civil Division), 2000–01; Acting Master of the Rolls, 2000; *b* 3 April 1932; *yr s* of late Henry Edward Nourse, MD, MRCP, of Cambridge, and Ethel Millicent, *d* of Rt Hon. Sir Charles Henry Sargant, Lord Justice of Appeal; *m* 1972, Lavinia, *yr d* of late Comdr D. W. Malim; one *s* one *d. Educ:* Winchester (Fellow, 1993–2006); Corpus Christi Coll., Cambridge (Hon. Fellow, 1988). National Service as 2nd Lieut, Rifle Bde, 1951–52; Lieut, London Rifle Bde Rangers (TA), 1952–55. Called to Bar, Lincoln's Inn, 1956, Bencher, 1978, Treas., 2001; Mem., General Council of the Bar, 1964–68; a Junior Counsel to BoT in Chancery matters, 1967–70; QC 1970; Attorney Gen., Duchy of Lancaster, 1976–80; a Judge of the Courts of Appeal of Jersey and Guernsey, 1977–80; Judge of the High Court of Justice, Chancery Div., 1980–85. Pres., Council of Inns of Court, 1992–95. Dep. Chm., Takeover Panel Appeal Bd, 2006–15. *Address:* Dullingham House, Dullingham, Newmarket, Cambs CB8 9UP.

NOUSS, Hunada, FCA; Chief Operating Officer, Children's Investment Fund Foundation, since 2013; *b* 19 Jan. 1959. *Educ:* Lady Margaret Hall, Oxford (BA Hons PPE, MA). FCA 1984; ATII 1985. Arthur Andersen, 1980–90; Dir of Tax and Treasury, Lowe Gp plc, 1990–92; Dir, Financial Planning, Diageo plc, and other roles, 1993–2001; Finance Dir, Burger King, 2001–05; Director-General: Finance and Corporate Services, DCLG, 2007–10; Finance, DWP, 2010–12. Non-exec. Dir, Gentoo Gp Ltd, 2013–. Trustee, Breast Cancer Campaign, 2009–15. Mem. Council, City Univ. London, 2011–. *Recreations:* photography, travel. *Address:* Children's Investment Fund Foundation, 7 Clifford Street, W1S 2FT.

NOUVEL, Jean Henri; architect, since 1966; *b* 12 Aug. 1945; *s* of Roger Nouvel and Renée Nouvel (*née* Barlangue); *m* 1992, Catherine Richard; one *d;* two *s* by Odile Fillion. *Educ:* Ecole Nationale Supérieure des Beaux Arts, Paris. Founder: Jean Nouvel and Associates, 1984–89; Jean Nouvel and Emmanuel Cattani, 1989–94; Ateliers Jean Nouvel, 1994–. Projects include: residential, educational, office and retail buildings in France; Institut du Monde Arabe, Paris, 1987; Hôtel de Saint-James, Bordeaux; Lyon Opera House, 1993; Fondation Cartier, Paris, 1994; Palais de Justice, Nantes, 2000; Cultural and Congress Centre, Lucerne, 2000; Gasometer, Vienna, 2001; Andel, Prague, 2001; Reina Sofia Mus. extension, Madrid, 2005; Guthrie Theater, Minneapolis, 2006; Musée du quai Branly, Paris, 2006; Pavilion B, Genoa Exhibition Centre, 2009; Copenhagen Concert Hall, 2009; Serpentine Gall. Summer Pavilion, 2010; One New Change, Cheapside, 2010; Baku Mus. of Modern Art, Azerbaijan, 2010; Montpelier City Hall, 2011; Tower, Doha, 2012; One Central Park, Sydney, 2014; Paris Philharmonie, 2015. Silver Medal, 1983, Gold Medal, 1998, French Acad. of Architecture; Grand Prix National d'Architecture, France, 1987; Praemium Imperiale, Japan Art Assoc., 2001; Royal Gold Medal, RIBA, 2001; Pritzker Architecture Prize, 2008. Commandeur, Ordre des Arts et des Lettres (France), 1997 (Chevalier, 1983); Chevalier: Ordre du Mérite (France), 1987; Légion d'Honneur (France), 2002. *Address:* Ateliers Jean Nouvel, 10 Cité d'Angoulême, 75011 Paris, France.

NOUY, Danièle Marcelle Blanche; Chevalier de la Légion d'Honneur 2008; Officier de l'Ordre du Mérite 2011; Chair, Supervisory Board, Single Supervisory Mechanism, since 2014; *b* Rennes, France, 30 July 1950; *d* of Georges Police and Marcelle Police (*née* Pensec); *m* 1972, Jean-Yves Nouy; two *d. Educ:* Inst. d'Études Politiques, Paris (degree in Pol Sci. and Public Admin 1971); Panthéon-Assas Univ., Paris (Postgrad. Cert. Law (Civil and Admin. Law) 1972). Banque de France: Supervisor of French credit instns, French Banking Supervision Commn, 1974–84; Rep. in NY, 1985–86; Policy Expert on Euromkts, Foreign Dept, 1986–87; Commission Bancaire: Hd, Res. Dept, 1987–90; Dir, Hd of supervision of French banks, 1990–94; Dir, Associate to Sec. Gen., 1994–96; Dep. Sec. Gen., 1996–98, Sec. Gen., 1998–2003, Basel Cttee on Banking Supervision; Secretary General: Commn Bancaire, 2003–10; French Prudential Supervision and Resolution Authy, 2010–13. Chair, Cttee of Eur. Banking Supervisors, 2006–08. *Publications:* (contrib.) Financial Supervision in the 21st Century, 2013; contrib. papers to Rev. d'Economie Financière, Rev. Banque, Financial Stability Rev., Jl Financial Stability, Risk, Débats Economiques et Financiers. *Address:* European Central Bank, 60640 Frankfurt am Main, Germany. *T:* (69) 13444100. *E:* officechairsb@ecb.europa.eu.

NOVOSELOV, Sir Konstantin S., Kt 2012; PhD; FRS 2011; Royal Society Research Fellow, since 2007, and Professor of Physics, since 2010, University of Manchester; *b* Nizhnii Tagil, Russia, 23 Aug. 1974; *s* of Sergey Novoselov and Tatiana Novoselova; *m* Irina Barbolina; two *d. Educ:* Moscow Inst. of Physics and Technol. (MSc *cum laude* 1997); Univ. of Nijmegen (PhD 2004). Researcher: Inst. for Microelectronics Technol., Chernogolovka, 1997–99; High Magnetic Field Lab., Univ. of Nijmegen, 1999–2001; Researcher, 2001–05, Leverhulme Res. Fellow, 2005–06, Univ. of Manchester. Special Prof., Radboud Univ. Nijmegen, 2013–. Hon. FRSC 2011; Hon. FInstP 2011. Hon. DSc Manchester, 2011. Europhysics Prize, Eur. Physics Soc. Condensed Matter Div., 2008; (jtly) Nobel Prize in Physics, 2010; Leverhulme Medal, Royal Soc., 2013. *Publications:* contrib. res. papers to jls incl. Nature, Science, Nature Materials, Nature Physics, Nature Nanotechnol., Rev. of Modern Physics, Physical Rev. Letters, Procs of NAS. *Address:* School of Physics and Astronomy, University of Manchester, Oxford Road, Manchester M13 9PL.

NOWAK, Paul; Assistant General Secretary, Trades Union Congress, since 2013; *b* Birkenhead, 18 May 1972; *s* of John and Ann Novak; *m* 1998, Vicky Mason; two *s* one *d. Educ:* Wirral Grammar Sch. for Boys; Liverpool John Moores Univ. (BA Hons Urban Studies); Harvard Univ. (Trade Union Prog. 2005). Clerical Asst, Cheshire CC, 1996–97; Trades Union Congress: Policy and Campaigns Officer, 1998–2000; Regl Sec., Northern, 2000–02; Nat. Organiser, 2002–11; Hd, Orgn and Services, 2011–13. Mem. Council, ACAS, 2011–. *Publications:* (contrib.) Union Organization and Activity, 2004; (contrib.) Union Revitalisation in Advanced Economies: assessing the contribution of Union organising, 2009. *Recreations:* family, playing guitar and ukelele (badly), Everton FC. *Address:* Trades Union Congress, Congress House, Great Russell Street, WC1B 3LS. *T:* (020) 7467 1231. *E:* pnowak@tuc.org.uk.

NOYER, Christian; Governor, Banque de France, 2003–15; Chairman, Bank for International Settlements, since 2010; *b* 6 Oct. 1950. *Educ:* Univ. of Rennes (lic. en droit 1971); Univ. of Paris (DèS droit 1972); Inst d'Etudes Politiques, Paris (Dip. 1972); Ecole Nat. d'Admin. Mil. service, Naval Officer, 1972. Entered Treasury, Min. of Finance, France, 1976; Financial Attaché, Perm. Repn to EEC, Brussels, 1980–82; French Treasury: Chief of Banking Office and of Export Credit Office, 1982–85; Advr to Minister for Econ. Affairs and Finance, 1986–88; Dep. Dir in charge of internat. multilateral issues, 1988–90; Dep. Dir in charge of debt mgt, monetary and banking issues, 1990–92; Dir responsible for public hldgs and public financing, 1992–93; Chief of Staff, Minister for Economic Affairs, 1993; Dir, Treasury, 1993–95; Chief of Staff to Minister for Econ. Affairs and Finance, 1995–97; Dir, Min. of Econ. Affairs, Finance and Industry, 1997–98; Vice-Pres., European Central Bank, 1998–2002; Special Advr, Min. of Economy, Finance and Industry, France, 2002–03. Pres., Prudential Supervision Authy, France, 2010–. Member: European Monetary Cttee, 1993–95, 1998 (Alternate Mem., 1988–90); Econ. and Financial Cttee, 1999–2002; OECD Working Party, 1993–95; Alternate Mem., G7 and G10, 1993–95. Alternate Gov., IMF and World Bank, 1993–95. Chm., Paris Club of Creditor Countries, 1993–97. Chevalier, Ordre Nat. du Mérite (France), 1994; Commandeur, Légion d'Honneur (France), 2012 (Chevalier, 1998; Officier, 2007); Commandeur, Ordre des Arts et des Lettres (France), 2011; Comdr, Ordre Nat. du Lion (Senegal), 1995; Grand Cross, Order of Civil Merit (Spain), 2002; Officier, Ordre Nat. de Valeur (Cameroon), 2007. *Publications:* Banks: the rules of the game, 1990; articles in jls.

NOYES, Dr Peter, CPsychol; Director, Noyes Consulting Ltd, since 2013; Vice Chancellor, University of Wales, Newport, 2007–12; *b* 4 Aug. 1956; *s* of Alfred and Nora Noyes; *m* 1980, Prof. Janet Martin; two *s* one *d. Educ:* Loughborough Univ. (BSc Hons Social Psychol. 1977; PGCE Primary Educn 1981); PhD Educnl Psychol. London Univ. 1984. CPsychol 1989. Child Care Officer, Marchant-Holliday Sch., 1981–82; teacher: Wadebridge Jun. Sch., 1982–83; Saltash Jun. Sch., 1983–86; Res. Associate, Univ. of Bristol, 1986–88; Cheltenham and Gloucester College of Higher Education: Hd, Dept of Community and Social Studies, Res. Dir and Hd of Psychol., 1988–92; Dean: Educn and Health, 1992–93; Business and Social Studies, 1993–96; University of Wales College, Newport, subsequently University of Wales, Newport: Dean, Educn, Humanities and Sci., 1996–97; Asst Principal, 1997–99; Dep. Vice Chancellor, 1999–2006. Mem., Student Experience and Teaching Quality Cttee, HEFCW, 2008–12; Chairman: Welsh Internat. Consortium, 2010–12; Univs Assoc. for Lifelong Learning, 2010–12; Dep. Chm., Higher Educn Wales, 2011–12. Mem. Council, Univ. of Wales, 2005–11. Member: Assoc. Sci. Educn, 1986–; British Educnl Res. Assoc., 1986–. Mem. Council, CBI, 2006–11. Gov., Olveston C of E Prim. Sch., 2013–. FRSA 2002. *Publications:* articles in educn and psychol. jls. *Recreations:* supporter of Brighton and Hove Albion FC, supporter of Bristol Rugby Club, horse racing, theatre. *Address:* The Cottage, Parsons Well, The Village, Bristol BS35 1NR. *T:* 07775 684598. *E:* noyes1956@hotmail.co.uk.

NOYORI, Prof. Ryoji, DEng; Fellow, RIKEN, since 2015 (President, 2003–15); University Professor, Nagoya University, since 2003; *b* Kobe, Japan, 3 Sept. 1938; *s* of Kaneki and Suzuko Noyori; *m* 1972, Hiroko Oshima; two *s. Educ:* Univ. of Kyoto (BSc 1961; MSc 1963; DEng 1967); Harvard Univ. Res. Associate, Dept of Industrial Chemistry, Univ. of Kyoto, 1963–68; Nagoya University: Associate Prof. of Chemistry, 1968–72; Prof. of Chemistry, 1972–2003; Dir, Chemical Instrument Centre, 1979–91; Dean, Graduate Sch. of Sci., 1997–99; Dir, Res. Centre for Materials Sci., 2000. Sci. Advr, 1992–96, Mem., Scientific Council, 1996–2015, Min. of Educn, Sci. and Culture, subseq. Educn, Culture, Sports, Sci. and Technol., Japan. For. Mem., Royal Soc., 2005. Numerous awards, incl. (jtly) Nobel Prize for Chemistry, 2001. *Publications:* Asymmetric Catalysis in Organic Synthesis, 1994; articles in scientific jls. *Address:* RIKEN, 2–1 Hirosawa, Wako, Saitama 351–0198, Japan; Department of Chemistry, Graduate School of Science, Nagoya University, Chikusa, Nagoya, Aichi 464–8602, Japan.

NSUGBE, Oba Eric; QC 2002; a Recorder, since 1999; Senior Advocate, Nigeria, 2005; *b* 23 Dec. 1962; *s* of Philip O. Nsugbe and Patricia Nsugbe; *m* 1994, Ambereen Laila (*née* Salamat); one *s* one *d. Educ:* St Edward's Sch., Oxford; Univ. of Hull (LLB Hons); Inns of Court Sch. of Law; Nigerian Law Sch. Called to the Bar, Gray's Inn, 1985, Bencher, 2005; Jt Hd of Chambers, 3 Pump Court, 2007–; barrister and solicitor, Nigeria, 1986. Mem., Judicial Studies Bd of England and Wales, 1996–2002. Bar Council: Member: Professional Conduct Cttee, 2001–; Pupillage and Trng Cttee, 2000–02; Response Cttee on Carter Reform of Legal Aid, 2006–07. Member: Glidewell Cttee on Judicial Appts and Silk, 2002–03; Cttee on reform of Silk, DCA, 2004–05. Gray's Inn Advocacy Trainer, 2004–07. Vis. Prof. of Law, City Univ., 2008–. FRSA 2006. *Recreations:* squash, football, jazz, travel, African art. *Address:* (chambers) 3 Pump Court, Temple, EC4Y 7AJ. *T:* (020) 7353 0711, *Fax:* (020) 7353 3319. *E:* oba.nsugbe@virgin.net.

NTAGALI, Most Rev. Stanley; *see* Uganda, Archbishop of.

NUGEE, Hon. Sir Christopher (George), Kt 2013; **Hon. Mr Justice Nugee;** a Judge of the High Court of Justice, Chancery Division, since 2013; *b* 23 Jan. 1959; *s* of late Edward George Nugee, TD, QC and Rachel Elizabeth Nugee; *m* 1991, Emily Thornberry, *qv;* two *s* one *d. Educ:* Radley Coll.; Corpus Christi Coll., Oxford (BA 1st Cl. Hons Lit. Hum 1981); City Univ. (Dip. Law (Distinction) 1982). Called to the Bar, Inner Temple, 1983 (Queen Elizabeth Schol., 1983; Eldon Law Schol., 1984), Bencher, 2003; in practice at the Bar, 1984–2013; QC 1998; a Recorder, 2002–13; a Dep. High Ct Judge, 2003–13; a Judge of the Cts of Appeal of Jersey and Guernsey, 2011–13. Member: Bar Council, 1991–93 (Mem., Professional Conduct Cttee, 1992–96); Cttee, Assoc. of Pension Lawyers, 1998–2002. *Recreations:* Tideway sculling, cycling, my family. *Address:* Royal Courts of Justice, Rolls Building, 7 Rolls Buildings, Fetter Lane, EC4A 1NL.

See also Maj. Gen. R. E. Nugee.

NUGEE, Emily; *see* Thornberry, E.

NUGEE, Maj. Gen. Richard Edward, CBE 2012 (MBE 1998); FRGS; Assistant Chief of Defence Staff (Personnel Capability) and Defence Services Secretary, since 2015; *b* Hampstead, 3 June 1963; *s* of late Edward George Nugee, TD, QC and Rachel Elizabeth Nugee; *m* 1990, Frances Renee Isabelle Bernard; two *s. Educ:* Radley Coll.; Durham Univ. (BA Hons Anthropol. 1985); City and Guilds Inst. 1994; King's Coll. London (MA Mil. Affairs 1995). Army Scholar, 1979; Cadet, 1982; commnd 1985; acsc 1995; JSCSC 2001; Comdr, 40 Regt (Lowland Gunners), RA, 2003; COS, Project Hyperion, 2005; HCSC 2006; Chief Jt Fires and Influence HQ, ARRC, 2006; Dir Manning (Army), 2009–12; Dir Gen. Personnel, Army, 2012–13; COS ISAF Jt Comd, 2013–15. Commodore: British Kiel Yacht Club, 2008–09; RA Yacht Club, 2011–13; Chm., Thorney Island Water Sports Centre, 2011–13. Trustee: Forces Trust, 2004– (Chm., 2012–); Nugee Foundn, 2007–. Inaugural Internat. Data Governance Award, DebTech Internat. LLC, Data Admin Newsletter and Wilshire Conferences Inc., 2010. *Publications:* contribs to magazines incl. British Army Rev., RA Jl, HR Dir. *Recreations:* family, offshore sailing, cycling, singing, theatre. *E:* richard@nugee.com.

See also Hon. Sir C. G. Nugee.

NUGENT, family name of **Earl of Westmeath.**

NUGENT, Sir Christopher George Ridley, 6th Bt *cr* 1806, of Waddesdon, Berks; *b* 5 Oct. 1949; *er s* of Sir Robin George Colborne Nugent, 5th Bt and of Ursula Mary, *d* of Lt-Gen. Sir Herbert Fothergill Cooke, KCB, KBE, CSI, DSO; *S* father, 2006, but his name does not appear on the Official Roll of the Baronetage; *m* 1985, Jacqueline Vagba; three *s. Educ:* Eton; Univ. of East Anglia. *Heir: s* Terence Nugent, *b* 1 March 1986.

NUGENT, Adm. Sir James Michael B.; *see* Burnell-Nugent.

NUGENT, Sir Nicholas (Myles John), 8th Bt *cr* 1795, of Ballinlough, co. Westmeath; *b* London, 17 Feb. 1967; *o s* of Sir John Edwin Lavallin Nugent, 7th Bt and of Penelope Anne, *d* of late Brig. Richard Nigel Hanbury, CBE, TD; *S* father, 2009; *m* 1999, Alice Mary, *d* of Peter Player; two *d* (and one *d* decd). *Educ:* Eton. Dir, Robert J. Goff & Co. plc, 2007–; non-exec. Dir, Kilcarn Stud Ltd. *Heir: cousin* Charles Rupert Nugent [*b* 24 Jan. 1962; *m* 1989, Louise Victoria Nixon; two *s* one *d*]. *Address:* Ballinlough Castle, Co. Westmeath.

NUGENT, Sir (Walter) Richard (Middleton), 6th Bt *cr* 1831, of Donore, Co. Westmeath; *b* 15 Nov. 1947; *er s* of Sir Peter Walter James Nugent, 5th Bt and of Anne Judith, *o d* of Major Robert Smyth, Gaybrook, Co. Westmeath; *S* father, 2002; *m* 1985, Kayoko Okabe. *Educ:* Headfort; Downside. FCA 1970. Deloitte, Plender, Griffiths & Co., 1967–74; Gp Tax Mgr, Europe, Carrier Corp., 1974–76; Chief Accountant, Swire Pacific Ship Mgt, 1977–79; Corporate Accountant, Asia Pacific, Everett Steamship Corp., SA, 1980–84; Dir of Finance, IMS Japan KK, 1986–2003. *Heir:* none. *Address:* 61–6 Yaguchi-dai, Naka-ku, Yokahama-shi 231–0831, Kanagawa-ken, Japan. *T:* (45) 6219283.

NUNBURNHOLME, 6th Baron *cr* 1906; **Stephen Charles Wilson;** *b* 29 Nov. 1973; *o s* of 5th Baron Nunburnholme and of Linda Kay (*née* Stephens); S father, 2000; *m* 2002, Chie Mannami, MA (RCA); two *s. Educ:* Nottingham Univ.; Univ. of Westminster. *Heir: s* Hon. Charles Taiyo Christobal Wilson, *b* 14 Sept. 2002.

NUNES, Prof. Terezinha, PhD; Professor of Educational Studies, since 2005, and Course Director for Masters in Child Development and Education, 2009–14, University of Oxford; Fellow, Harris Manchester College, Oxford, since 2005; *b* 3 Oct. 1947; *d* of Luiz Conzaga Nunes and Semíramis Oliveira Nunes; *m* 1st, 1973, David W. Carraher (marr. diss. 1990); one *s* one *d;* 2nd, 1995, Prof. Peter Elwood Bryant, *qv. Educ:* Univ. Federal de Minas Gerais (BS Psychol); City Univ. of New York (MA Psychol. 1975; PhD 1976). Accredited Psychologist. Res. asst, NY Infant Day Care Study, 1973–75; Adjunct Lectr, Dept of Psychol., Brooklyn Coll., NY, 1975; Hd, Inst. of Child Devlt, Belo Horizonte, Brazil, 1976–77; Associate Prof., 1976–78, and Hd, Centre of Applied Psychol., 1977, Dept of Psychol., Univ. Federal de Minas Gerais; University of Pernambuco: Associate Prof. and Course Tutor, Masters prog. in

Psychol., 1978–90; Hd, Pedagogical Centre, 1981–84; Res. Fellow, Sch. of Educn, Open Univ., 1990–91; Institute of Education, University of London: Lectr, 1991–93; Sen. Lectr, 1993–96; Course Tutor for Masters in Child Develt, 1993–98; Prof. of Educn, Child Develt and Learning, 1996–2000; Res. Tutor and Hd, Child Develt and Learning Acad. Gp, 1998–2000; Prof. of Psychol. and Hd of Dept, Oxford Brookes Univ., 2000–05. Fulbright Fellow, 1971–76; Vis. Fellow, Wolfson Coll., Oxford, 1988–89; British Acad. Res. Reader, 2003–04; Vis. Prof., Univ. Bandeirantes, São Paulo, Brazil, 2012. *Publications:* as Terezinha Carraher: O Método Clínico: usando os exames de Piaget, 1982; (jtly) Na Vida, Dez; Na Escola, Zero: os contextos culturais da aprendizagem de matemática, 1988; Sociedade e Inteligência, 1989; as Terezinha Nunes: (jtly) Dificuldades de aprendizagem da leitura: teoria e prática, 1992; (jtly) Street Mathematics and School Mathematics, 1993; (with P. E. Bryant) Children Doing Mathematics, 1996 (trans. Portuguese, Spanish and Greek); Developing Children's Minds Through Literacy and Numeracy: an inaugural lecture, 1998; (jtly) Introdução a Educação Matemática: os números e as operações numéricas, 2001, 2nd edn 2005; Teaching Mathematics to Deaf Children, 2004 (trans. Greek, 2012); (with P. E. Bryant) Improving Literacy Through Teaching Morphemes, 2006; (with P. E. Bryant) Children's Reading and Spelling: beyond the first steps, 2009; (with P. E. Bryant) Leitura e Escrita: além dos primeiros passos, 2014; papers in acad. jls on research on child develt, maths educn, literacy learning, working memory and deaf children's learning. *Recreations:* travelling, reading, cooking. *Address:* Department of Education, University of Oxford, 15 Norham Gardens, Oxford OX2 6PY. *T:* (01865) 284892, *Fax:* (01865) 274027. *E:* terezinha.nunes@education.ox.ac.uk.

NUNN, Very Rev. Andrew Peter; Dean of Southwark, since 2012; *b* Leicester, 30 July 1957; *s* of Peter Nunn and Jill Nunn (*née* Upton). *Educ:* Bushloe High Sch., Wigston; Guthlaxton Upper Sch., Wigston; Leicester Poly. (BA Hons Public Admin. 1979); Leeds Univ. (BA Hons Theol. and Religious Studies 1982); Coll. of the Resurrection, Mirfield. Ordained deacon, 1983, priest, 1984; Asst Curate, St James, Manston, 1983–87; Curate-in-charge, 1987–91, Vicar, 1991–95, St Hilda, Richmond Hill; Chaplain and PA to Bishop of Southwark, 1995–99; Southwark Cathedral: Priest Vicar, 1995–99; Vice Provost and Precentor, 1999–2000; Sub Dean and Precentor, 2000–10; Acting Dean of Southwark, 2010–11. Proctor in Convocation, Gen. Synod, 2005–10, 2010– (Chaplain, 2011–12); Sen. Selector and Bishop's Selection Advr (Vocation), 2006–12. Member: Liturgical Commn, 2011–12; Crown Nominations Commn, 2011–. Delegate from Archbishop's Council, TEAM Conf., S Africa, 2007. Chaplain, Agnes Stewart C of E High Sch., Leeds, 1987–95. Hon. Chaplain and Hon. Liveryman, Co. of Launderers, 2000–; Hon. Liveryman, Co. of Glaziers and Painters of Glass, 2012–; Hon. Chaplain: Whitsters Club, 2007–; Innholders' Co., 2014–. *Publications:* Lift Up Your Hearts, 2011. *Recreations:* reading, theatre, music, travelling, driving, friends. *Address:* Southwark Cathedral, London Bridge, SE1 9DA. *T:* (020) 7367 6700, *Fax:* (020) 7367 6725. *E:* andrew.nunn@southwark.anglican.org.

NUNN, Imogen Mary, (Lady Nunn); *see* Stubbs, I. M.

NUNN, John Francis, PhD, DSc, MD; FRCS, FRCA; FGS; Head of Division of Anaesthesia, Medical Research Council Clinical Research Centre, 1968–91; *b* 7 Nov. 1925; *s* of late Francis Nunn, Colwyn Bay; *m* 1949, Sheila, *d* of late E. C. Doubleday; one *s* two *d*. *Educ:* Wrekin Coll.; Birmingham Univ. (MD (Hons) 1970; PhD 1959; DSc 1992). FRCA (FFARCS 1955); FRCS 1983. MO, Birmingham Univ. Spitzbergen Expedition, 1948; Colonial Med. Service, Malaya, 1949–53; University Research Fellow, Birmingham, 1955–56; Leverhulme Research Fellow, RCS, 1957–64; Part-time Lectr, Postgrad. Med. Sch., Univ. of London, 1959–64; Consultant Anæsth., Hammersmith Hosp., 1959–64; Prof. of Anaesthesia, Univ. of Leeds, 1964–68. Member: Council, RCS, 1977–82 (Mem. Board, Faculty of Anaesthetists, Vice-Dean, 1977–79, Dean, 1979–82); Council, Assoc. of Anaesthetists, 1973–76 (Vice Pres., 1988–90); Pres., Sect. Anaesthesia, RSM, 1984–85. Hunterian Professor, RCS, 1960; Visiting Professor, various American Universities, 1960–98; British Council Lecturer: Switzerland, 1962; USSR, 1963; Czechoslovakia, 1969; China, 1974. Joseph Clover Lectr, RCS, 1968. Mem., Egypt Exploration Soc. FGS 2001. Hon. FFARCSI 1985; Hon. FRSocMed 1992; Hon. FANZCA 1993 (Hon. FFARACS); Hon. FRCA 1993. Hon. Dr: Turin, 1993; Uppsala, 1996. (1st) Sir Ivan Magill Gold Medal, Assoc. of Anaesthetists of GB and Ireland, 1988; Richardson Award, Geologists' Assoc., 1999. *Publications:* Applied Respiratory Physiology, 1969, 4th edn as Nunn's Applied Respiratory Physiology, 1993, (contrib.) 5th edn 2000 to 7th edn 2010; (ed jtly) General Anaesthesia, 3rd edn 1971, 5th edn 1989; Ancient Egyptian Medicine, 1996; (jtly) The Tale of Peter Rabbit (in ancient Egyptian hieroglyphs), 2005; several chapters in medical text-books, and publications in Journal Appl. Physiol., Lancet, Nature, British Journal Anæsth., etc. *Recreations:* Egyptology, model engineering. *Address:* 3A Dene Road, Northwood, Middx HA6 2AE. *T:* (01923) 826363.

NUNN, Sir Trevor (Robert), Kt 2002; CBE 1978; director; Artistic Director, Royal National Theatre, 1997–2003; *b* 14 Jan. 1940; *s* of late Robert Alexander Nunn and of Dorothy May (*née* Piper); *m* 1st, 1969, Janet Suzman (*see* Dame J. Suzman) (marr. diss. 1986); one *s*; 2nd, 1986, Sharon Lee Hill (marr. diss. 1991); two *d*; 3rd, 1994, Imogen Stubbs, *qv*; one *s* one *d*. *Educ:* Northgate Grammar Sch., Ipswich; Downing Coll., Cambridge (BA). Producer, Belgrade Theatre, Coventry; Royal Shakespeare Company: Chief Exec., 1968–86; Artistic Dir, 1968–78; Jt Artistic Dir, 1978–86; Dir Emeritus, 1986–. Major productions include: *theatre*: The Life and Adventures of Nicholas Nickleby, Aldwych, 1980, transf. NY, 1981–82 and 1986; Cats, New London, 1981, NY 1982, London revival 2014; Starlight Express, Apollo Victoria, 1984, NY 1987; Les Miserables, Queen's, 1985–, NY 1987–2003 and revival, 2006; Chess, Prince Edward, 1986, NY 1988 and 2003; Aspects of Love, Prince of Wales, 1989, NY 1990, Menier Chocolate Factory, 2010; Sunset Boulevard, Adelphi, 1993, NY 1994; Oklahoma!, RNT, 1998, NY 2002; My Fair Lady, RNT, then transf. Th. Royal, Drury Lane, 2001; South Pacific, RNT, 2001; Anything Goes, RNT, 2002, transf. Th. Royal, Drury Lane, 2003; The Woman in White, Palace, 2004, NY 2005; Acorn Antiques: the musical, Th. Royal, Haymarket, 2005; Porgy and Bess, Savoy, 2006; The Seagull, King Lear, RSC, 2007; Gone with the Wind, New London, 2008; Inherit the Wind, Old Vic, 2009; A Little Night Music, Garrick, 2009, NY 2009; Cyrano de Bergerac, Chichester, 2009; Birdsong, Comedy, 2010; Flare Path, Rosencrantz and Guildenstern Are Dead, The Tempest, The Lion in Winter, Th. Royal, Haymarket, 2011; Kiss Me, Kate, Chichester Fest., 2012, transf. Old Vic, 2012; All That Fall, Jermyn Street Th., A Chorus of Disapproval, Harold Pinter Th., 2012; Relative Values, Th. Royal, Bath, 2013, transf. Harold Pinter Th., 2014; Scenes from a Marriage, St James Th., 2013; Fatal Attraction, Th. Royal Haymarket, 2014; Volpone, Swan Th., Stratford, 2015; The Wars of the Roses, Rose Th., Kingston, 2015; *films:* Hedda, 1976; Lady Jane, 1986; Twelfth Night, 1996. Mem., Arts Council of England, 1994–96. Hon. MA: Newcastle upon Tyne, 1982; Warwick.

NUNNELEY, Sir Charles (Kenneth Roylance), Kt 2003; CA; Chairman: Nationwide Building Society, 1996–2002 (Director, 1994–2002; Deputy Chairman, 1995–96); National Trust, 1996–2003; *b* 3 April 1936; *s* of late Robin Michael Charles Nunneley and Patricia Mary (*née* Roylance); *m* 1961, Catherine Elizabeth Armstrong Buckley; one *s* three *d*. *Educ:* Eton Coll. CA 1961. Robert Fleming (merchant bankers), 1962–96: Dir, 1968–96; Dep. Chm., 1986–96; Chairman: Save & Prosper Gp, 1989–96; JP Morgan Income & Capital Investment Trust (formerly Fleming, then JP Morgan Fleming, Income & Capital Investment Trust) plc, 1992–2007; IMRO Ltd, 1992–97 (Dir, 1986–97); Monks Investment Trust plc, 1996–2005 (Dir, 1977–2005); Edinburgh Fund Managers Gp plc, 2003; Dep. Chm., Clerical Medical & General Life Assurance Soc., 1978–96 (Dir, 1974–96); Dir, Macmillan Ltd, 1982–96. Chm., Instnl Fund Managers' Assoc., 1989–92. National Trust: Member: Council, 1992–2003; Exec. Cttee, 1991–2003; Chm., Finance Cttee, 1991–96. Chm. Council, N Wessex Downs Area of Outstanding Natural Beauty, 2004–10. Mem., Adv. Bd, Aberdeen Select Charity Funds, 2011–. Mem. Court, Grocers' Co., 1975– (Master, 1982–83). Governor, Oundle Schs, 1975–99. *Recreations:* walking, theatre, photography. *Address:* 116 Rivermead Court, Ranelagh Gardens, SW6 3SD.

NURSAW, Sir James, KCB 1992 (CB 1983); QC 1988; HM Procurator General and Treasury Solicitor, 1988–92; *b* 18 Oct. 1932; *s* of William George Nursaw (*d* 1994); *m* 1959, Eira, *yr d* of late E. W. Caryl-Thomas, MD, BSc, Barrister-at-law; two *d*. *Educ:* Bancroft's School; Christ's Coll., Cambridge (Schol.; MA, LLB). Called to Bar, Middle Temple, 1955 (Blackstone Entrance Schol. and Prize, Harmsworth Schol.), Bencher, 1989. Senior Research Officer, Cambridge Univ. Dept of Criminal Science, 1958. Joined Legal Adviser's Branch, Home Office, 1959; Principal Asst Legal Advr, HO and NI Office, 1977–80; Legal Secretary, Law Officers' Dept, 1980–83; Legal Adviser, Home Office and NI Office, 1983–88. Counsel to Chm. of Cttees, H of L, 1993–2002. Liveryman, Loriners' Co. *Clubs:* Oxford and Cambridge, MCC.

NURSE, Sir Paul (Maxime), Kt 1999; PhD; FRS 1989; President, Royal Society, 2010–15; Director, Francis Crick Institute (formerly UK Centre for Medical Research and Innovation), since 2011; *b* 25 Jan. 1949; *s* of Maxime Nurse and Cissie Nurse (*née* White); *m* 1971, Anne Teresa (*née* Talbott); two *d*. *Educ:* Harrow County Grammar Sch.; Univ. of Birmingham (BSc): Univ. of East Anglia (PhD). Research Fellow, Univ. of Edinburgh, 1973–79; SERC Advanced Fellow and MRC Sen. Fellow, Univ. of Sussex, 1979–84; Hd of Cell Cycle Control Laboratory, Imp. Cancer Res. Fund, London, 1984–87; Oxford University: Fellow, 1987–93, Hon. Fellow, 1993–, Linacre Coll.; Iveagh Prof. of Microbiology, 1987–91; Royal Soc. Napier Res. Prof., 1991–93; Dir of Lab. Res., 1993–96, Dir Gen., 1996–2002, ICRF; Chief Exec., Cancer Res. UK, 2002–03; Pres., Rockefeller Univ., NY, 2003–10. Trustee, British Mus., 2012–. MAE 1992; Foreign Associate US NAS, 1995. Fleming Lectr, 1984, Marjory Stephenson Lectr, 1990, Soc. of Gen. Microbiology; Florey Lectr, Royal Soc., 1990; Wenner-Gren Lectr, Stockholm, 1993; Dunham Lectr, Harvard, 1994. President: Genetical Soc., 1990–94; British Sci. Assoc., 2014–15. Founder FMedSci 1998. Ciba Medal, Biochemical Soc., 1991; Feldberg Foundn Prize, 1991; (jtly) Louis Jeantet Prize for Medicine, Geneva, 1992; Gairdner Foundn Internat. Jt Award, 1992; Royal Soc. Wellcome Medal, 1993; Jimenez Diaz Meml Award, Madrid, 1993; Rosenstiel Award, Brandeis Univ., 1993; Pezcoller Award for Oncology Res., Trento, 1995; Royal Soc. Royal Medal, 1995; Dr Josef Steiner Prize, Steiner Cancer Foundn, Bern, 1996; Dr H. P. Heineken Prize, Netherlands, 1996; Alfred P. Sloan Jr Prize and Medal, General Motors Cancer Res. Foundn, 1997; Judd Award, Meml Sloan-Kettering Cancer Center, NY, 1998; Lasker Award, Albert and Mary Lasker Foundn, NY, 1998; (jtly) Nobel Prize for Physiology or Medicine, 2001. Hon. FREng 2012. Officer, Légion d'Honneur (France), 2002. *Publications:* numerous, in sci. jls, concerned with cell and molecular biology. *Recreations:* gliding, astronomy, talking. *Address:* Royal Society, 6–9 Carlton House Terrace, SW1Y 5AG.

NUSSBAUM, David Simon Matthew; Chief Executive, WWF-UK, since 2007; *b* Stoke on Trent, 13 July 1958; *s* of Gerald and Enid Nussbaum; *m* 1983, Kathleen Kinderman; two *s* two *d*. *Educ:* Queens' Coll., Cambridge (BA Theol. 1980; MA); Univ. of Edinburgh (MTh 1981); Heriot-Watt Univ. (Dip. Accounting (Distn) 1982); London Business Sch. (MSc Finance (Distn) 1998). CA 1985; CTA 1985. Audit Sen./Asst, 1982–86, Asst Manager, 1986–87, Price Waterhouse; Investment Controller, 3i plc, 1987–90; Commercial and Business Develt Manager, Reedpack Ltd, 1990–91; Corporate Develt Dir, 1991–92, Finance Dir, 1992–97, Field Group plc; Dir, Finance, Inf. and Planning, and a Dep. Chief Exec., Oxfam, 1997–2002; Transparency International: Man. Dir, 2002–03; Chief Exec., 2003–07; Transparency International UK: non-exec. Dir, 2008–; Chm., 2012–. Non-executive Director: Traidcraft plc, 1991–2006 (Chm., 1999–2006); Shared Interest, 2006–14; Low Carbon Accelerator, 2006–13. FRSA. MInstD. Hon. DCL Newcastle, 2011. *Publications:* (contrib.) Christianity and the Culture of Economics, 2001; (contrib.) Charities, Governance and the Law: the way forward, 2003. *Recreation:* Post-Christendom orthopraxis. *Address:* WWF-UK, Living Planet Centre, Rufford House, Brewery Road, Woking, Surrey GU21 4LL. *T:* (01483) 412202. *E:* dnussbaum@wwf.org.uk, dsmnussbaum@aol.com.

NÜSSLEIN-VOLHARD, Christiane, PhD; Director, since 1985, and Director of Department of Genetics, since 1990, Max Planck Institute for Developmental Biology; *b* 20 Oct. 1942; *d* of Rolf Volhard and Brigitte Volhard (*née* Haas). *Educ:* Univ. of Tübingen. Res. Associate, Max Planck Institute for Virus Research, 1972–74; EMBO Fellow: Biozentrum Basel Lab., 1975–76; Univ. of Freiberg, 1977; Head of Gp, European Molecular Biology Lab., Heidelberg, 1978–80; Gp Leader, Friedrich Miescher Lab., 1981–85, Scientific Mem., 1985–90, Max Planck Ges. Mem., Sci. Council, ERC, 2005–12. (Jtly) Nobel Prize for Physiology or Medicine, 1995. *Publications:* Coming to Life: how genes drive development, 2006; articles in learned jls. *Address:* Max-Planck-Institut für Entwicklungsbiologie, Spemannstraße 35/III, 72076 Tübingen, Germany.

NUTBEAM, Prof. Donald, PhD; FFPH; Vice-Chancellor, University of Southampton, since 2009; *b* 18 May 1955; *s* of late Walter Charles Nutbeam and Ada Rose Nutbeam; *m* 1978, Sarah Choules; one *s* one *d*. *Educ:* St Bartholomew's Grammar Sch., Newbury; Univ. of Southampton (MA; PhD 1988). FFPH 2003. Health Educn Officer, Portsmouth Health Dist, 1978–81; Res. Assistant, Wessex RHA, 1981–83; Res. Fellow in Health Promotion, Southampton Univ., 1983–85; Hd of Res., Welsh Heart Prog., Univ. of Wales Coll. of Medicine, 1985–88; Dir, Res. and Policy, Health Promotion Authy, Wales, 1988–90; University of Sydney, Australia: Prof. of Public Health, 1990–2000; Hd, Dept of Public Health and Community Medicine, 1997–2000; Associate Dean of Medicine, 1999–2000; Hd of Public Health, DoH, 2000–03; University of Sydney, Australia: Pro-Vice-Chancellor, 2003–06; Provost and Dep. Vice-Chancellor, 2006–09; Vis. Prof., 2009–. Visiting Professor: LSHTM, 2001–06; Nanjing Univ., 2010–. *Publications:* numerous contribs to scientific jls and texts. *Recreations:* sport, gardening, travel. *Address:* University of Southampton, Highfield, Southampton SO17 1BJ. *Club:* Athenæum.

NUTT, Prof. David John, DM; FRCP, FRCPsych, FMedSci; Edmond J. Safra Professor of Neuropsychopharmacology and Head, Centre for Neuropsychopharmacology (formerly Department of Neuropsychopharmacology and Molecular Imaging), Imperial College London, since 2008; *b* 16 April 1951; *s* of R. J. (Jack) Nutt and Eileen M. (*née* Baber); *m* 1979, Diana Margaret Sliney; two *s* two *d*. *Educ:* Bristol GS; Downing Coll., Cambridge (MB BChir); Guy's Hosp.; Lincoln Coll., Oxford (DM 1983). MRCP 1977, FRCP 2002; MRCPsych 1983, FRCPsych 1994; FMedSci 2002; FRSB (FSB 2012). Oxford University: Clinical Scientist, MRC Clinical Pharmacology Unit, 1978–82; Lectr, Dept of Psychiatry, 1982–84; Wellcome Sen. Fellow in Clinical Sci., 1985–86; Head, Section of Clinical Sci., Nat. Inst. of Alcohol Abuse and Alcoholism, NIH, 1986–88; Bristol University: Dir, Psychopharmacology Unit, 1988–2008; Prof. of Psychopharmacology, 1994–2009; Head: Div. of Psychiatry, 1995–97; Dept of Clinical Medicine, 1997–2003; Community Based Medicine, 2004–09; Dean of Clinical Medicine and Dentistry, 1999–2003. Chairman: Adv. Council on the Misuse of Drugs, 2008–09 (Chm., Technical Cttee, 2000–08); Ind. Scientific Cttee on Drugs, 2010–; Member: Ind. Inquiry into Misuse of Drugs Act 1971, 1997–2000 (reported, 2000); Cttee on the Safety of Medicines, 2001–; Lead Scientist, DTI Foresight Prog., Brain Science Addiction and Drugs, 2005–06. FMedSci 2002. John Maddox Prize for Standing up for Science, Sense about Science, 2013. *Publications:* Inverse Agonists, 1994; jointly: Hypnotics and Anxiolytics, 1995; Depression, Anxiety and the Mixed Conditions,

1997; Panic Disorder: clinical diagnosis, management and mechanisms, 1998; Generalized anxiety disorder: diagnosis, treatment and its relationship to other anxiety disorders, 1998; Atlas of Psychiatric Pharmacotherapy, 1999, rev. edn 2006, 2nd edn 2007; Milestones in Drug Therapy: anxiolytics, 2000; Post Traumatic Stress Disorder: diagnosis, management and treatment, 2000, (jtly) 2nd edn 2009; Clinician's Manual on Anxiety Disorder and Comorbid Depression, 2000; Anxiety Disorders: an introduction to clinical management and research, 2001; Mood and Anxiety Disorders in Children and Adolescents, 2001; Anxiety Disorders Comorbid with Depression: panic disorder and agoraphobia, 2002; Generalised Anxiety Disorder: symptomatology, pathogenesis and management, 2002; Anxiety Disorders, 2003; Calming the Brain, 2003; (jtly) Treating Depression Effectively, 2004, 2nd edn 2007; (jtly) Drugs and the Future: brain science, 2006; (jtly) Serotonin and Sleep: molecular, functional and clinical aspects, 2007; (jtly) Handbook of Fear and Anxiety, 2008; (jtly) Addiction, 2008; (with S. J. Wilson) Sleep Disorders, 2008; (jtly) The Neurobiology of Addiction, 2010; Drugs: without the hot air, 2012; (jtly) Substance Abuse, 2013. *Recreations:* gardening, grandchildren, swimming. *Address:* Burlington-Danes Building, Hammersmith Hospital, Du Cane Road, W12 0NN. *T:* (020) 7594 6628.

NUTTALL, Christopher Peter; Director of Research and Statistics, Home Office, 1989–99; *b* 20 April 1939; *s* of Barbara Goodwin and David Nuttall; *m* 1966, Caryn Thomas; two *s*; partner, Joy Louise Hutcheon, *qv*. *Educ:* Queen Elizabeth Grammar Sch., Wakefield; Univ. of Keele (BA); Univ. of California at Berkeley (MA). Home Office Res. Unit, 1963–75 (Principal Res. Officer, 1971–75); Dir of Res., 1975–80, Dir Gen., Res. and Stats, 1980–82, Min. of Solicitor Gen., Ottawa; Asst Dep. Solicitor Gen. of Canada, 1982–89; Asst Under-Sec. of State, Home Office, 1989. Consultant to Govt of Barbados on criminal justice res., inf. and policy, 2000–03. UN Human Rights Fellow, 1967–68. *Publications:* Parole in England and Wales, 1977; The Barbados Crime Survey, 2002; Sentencing in Barbados, 2003; Handbook for Crime Prevention in Southern Africa and the Caribbean, 2008; articles on parole, deterrence, crime prevention and imprisonment. *Recreations:* The United States, photography, taking baths, books. *Address:* 2, The Cottage, The Hill, Polstead, Suffolk CO6 5AH.

NUTTALL, David John; MP (C) Bury North, since 2010; *b* Sheffield, 25 March 1962; *s* of Roy Nuttall and Kathleen Nuttall; *m* 2004, Susan Smith (*née* Finn). *Educ:* Aston Comp. Sch., Rotherham; Univ. of London (LLB ext.). Admitted solicitor, 1990, NP, 1998; Taylor Son & Co., later Taylors, solicitors: trainee legal exec., 1980–88; Legal Exec. and Articled Clerk, 1988–90; Partner, 1990–98; Sen. Partner, 1998–2006; NP, Nuttall's Notaries, 2006–10. Contested (C): Sheffield Hillsborough, 1997; Morecambe and Lunesdale, 2001; Bury N, 2005; Yorkshire and the Humber, EP, 1999. *Recreations:* walking, watching cricket and football, bird watching. *Address:* House of Commons, SW1A 0AA. *T:* (020) 7219 7030. *E:* david.nuttall.mp@parliament.uk. *Club:* Salisbury Conservative (Bury).

NUTTALL, Rev. Derek, MBE 1990; Minister, United Reformed Church, Windsor, 1990–2003; *b* 23 Sept. 1937; *s* of Charles William Nuttall and Doris Nuttall; *m* 1965, Margaret Hathaway Brown (*d* 1993); two *s* one *d*; *m* 2000, Doreen Margaret Fox. *Educ:* Ironville Sch.; Somercotes Sch.; Overdale Coll., Selly Oak (Diploma). Semi-skilled worker in industry, 1953–60; office clerk, 1960–61; college, 1961–65; ministry in Falkirk, 1965–67; Vice Chm., Central Scotland Br., The Samaritans, 1966–67; ordained, 1967; ministry and community work in Aberfan, 1967–74: Gen. Sec., Community Assoc.; mem., church and community cttees; Nat. Organiser, 1974–78, Dir, 1978–90, Cruse—the Nat. Orgn for the widowed and their children, subseq. Cruse—Bereavement Care. Member: Exec., Internat. Fedn of Widow/Widower Orgns, 1980–90; Internat. Workgroup on Death and Dying, 1980–90; Internat. Liaison Gp on Disasters, 1986–90; Sec., Wkg Party on Social and Psychological Aspects of Disasters, 1989–91. Chm., Churches Together in Windsor, 1992–95; Convenor, Reading and Oxford Dist URC Pastoral Cttee, 1995–98. Chaplain: King Edward VII Hosp., Windsor, 1991–2003; Thames Valley Hospice, Windsor, 1993–2003. *Publications:* The Early Days of Grieving, 1986, rev. and expanded edn 2006; (contrib.) Interpreting Death, 1997; To Everything a Season: an exploration of loss and grief in the bible, 2010; articles and papers on bereavement and on needs of widows, widowers and bereaved children. *Recreations:* music, reading, writing, keeping up with the family's activities, enjoying East Sussex. *Address:* Lymewood, Tilsmore Road, Heathfield, East Sussex TN21 0XT. *T:* (01435) 866026.

NUTTALL, Graeme John, OBE 2014; Partner, Field Fisher Waterhouse LLP (formerly Field Fisher & Martineau), since 1988; *b* Bury, Lancs, 29 Dec. 1959; *s* of Geoffrey Nuttall and Anne Nuttall; *m* 1985, Elizabeth Jane; two *s*. *Educ:* Price's Grammar Sch., and Price's VI Form Coll., Fareham; Peterhouse, Cambridge (BA 1981). CTA. Field Fisher & Martineau: articled clerk, 1982–84; Solicitor, 1984–88. Govt's Independent Advr on Employee Ownership (pt-time), 2012 (report, Sharing Success: the Nuttall Review of Employee Ownership, 2012). *Publications:* Employee Ownership: legal and tax aspects, 1987; Nelson-Jones and Nuttall's Tax Tables, 1988, 5th edn 1992; Nuttall's Tax Tables 1994–95, 1994; (jtly) Sponsorship, Endorsement and Merchandising, 2nd edn 1998. *Recreations:* art, horse racing. *Address:* Field Fisher Waterhouse LLP, Riverbank House, 2 Swan Lane, EC4R 3TT. *T:* (020) 7861 4000, *Fax:* (020) 7488 0084. *E:* graeme.nuttall@fieldfisher.com.

NUTTALL, Sir Harry, 4th Bt *cr* 1922, of Chasefield, Bowdon, Chester; *b* 2 Jan. 1963; *s* of Sir Nicholas Keith Lillington Nuttall, 3rd Bt and Rosemary Caroline (*née* York); *S* father, 2007; *m* 1st, 1996, Kelly Marie Allen (marr. diss. 1999); 2nd, 2002, Dalit, *o d* of late Isaac Cohen, Stockholm; one *s* one *d*. *Heir:* *s* James Isaac Nuttall, *b* 2 Nov. 2005. *Clubs:* White's; British Racing Drivers'.

NUTTALL, Rt Rev. Michael; Bishop of Natal, 1982–2000; *b* 3 April 1934; *s* of Neville and Lucy Nuttall; *m* 1959, Dorris Marion Meyer; two *s* one *d*. *Educ:* Maritzburg Coll. (matric. 1951); Univ. of Natal (BA 1955); Rhodes Univ. (BA Hons in History 1956); MA (Cantab); MA, DipEd (Oxon); BD Hons (London). Teacher at Westville High Sch., Natal, 1958; Lectr in History, Rhodes Univ., 1959–62; Theological Student, St Paul's Coll., Grahamstown, 1963–64; ordained deacon, 1964, priest, 1965; Assistant Priest, Cathedral of St Michael and St George, Grahamstown, 1965–68; Lectr in Ecclesiastical History, Rhodes Univ., 1969–74; Dean of Grahamstown, 1975; Bishop of Pretoria, 1976–81. Pemberton Fellow, University Coll. Durham, 2001. Hon. DTheol Western Cape, 1998; Hon. DLitt Natal, 2000. *Publications:* Prayerfulness in the Spirit, 2002; Number Two to Tutu - a memoir, 2003; A Voice within Church and Society: a personal anthology, 2015; chapters in: Better Than They Knew, Volume 2 (ed R. M. de Villiers), 1974; Authority in the Anglican Communion (ed Stephen W. Sykes), 1987; Change and Challenge (ed J. Suggit and M. Goedhals), 1998; articles in Dictionary of S African Biography. *Recreations:* walking, bird watching. *Address:* 362 Amber Valley, Private Bag X30, Howick, 3290, South Africa.

NUTTALL, Prof. Patricia Anne, OBE 2000; PhD; Professor of Arbovirology, Department of Zoology, University of Oxford, since 2013; Fellow of Wolfson College, Oxford, 1974–77 and since 1990; *b* 21 Jan. 1953; *m* 1984, Robert Warden Cragg; twin *d*. *Educ:* Univ. of Bristol (BSc 1974); Univ. of Reading (PhD 1978); MA Oxon 1995. Worked in Australia and Slovakia; joined NERC Inst. for Virology and Envmtl Microbiol., subseq. CEH Oxford, 1980; acting Dir, 1995–97; Site Dir, 1997–2001; Director: NERC Centre for Ecology & Hydrology, 2001–11; Nat. Capability Integration, 2011–12, Special Projects, 2012–13, NERC. Hon. Professor: of Virology, Univ. of Oxford, 1996–; Univ. of Nankia, China, 2008; Vis. Prof. of Drug Discovery, Univ. of Oxford, 2010–13. Chm., Partnership for Eur. Envmtl Res., 2008–10. Ivanovsky Medal for Virology, Russian Acad. of Scis, 1996. Chevalier, Ordre de Mérite Agricole (France), 2009. *Address:* Department of Zoology, University of Oxford, South Parks Road, Oxford OX1 3PS. *T:* (01865) 271167. *E:* pat.nuttall@zoo.ox.ac.uk.

NUTTALL, Paul; Member (UK Ind) North West, European Parliament, since 2009; *b* Liverpool, 30 Nov. 1976; *m* 2008, Linda. *Educ:* Salvio High Sch.; Hugh Baird Coll.; N Lincs Coll.; Edge Hill Univ. (BA Hist.); Liverpool Hope Univ. (MA). Formerly Lectr in History. Chm., 2008–10, Dep. Leader, 2010–, UKIP. Contested (UK Ind) Bootle, 2015. *Address:* European Parliament, Rue Wiertz, 1047 Brussels, Belgium; (office) PO Box 2034, Liverpool L69 2DG.

NUTTALL, Peter Francis; a District Judge (Magistrates' Courts) (formerly Stipendiary Magistrate), Nottinghamshire, 1991–2009; *b* 20 Feb. 1944; *s* of Francis Nuttall and Dorothy May Nuttall (*née* Horning); *m* 1965, Wendy Anna Ida Griffiths; one *s* two *d*. *Educ:* Lewes County Grammar Sch. for Boys; Coll. of Law, Guildford and London. Articled Clerk, Uckfield, 1961, Harrow, 1964; Asst to Justices' Clerk, 1964–68; Dep. Clerk to Justices, Watford, 1968–73; Clerk to Justices, Pendle and Ribble Valley, 1973–85; Clerk to Bradford Justices, 1985–90. Chm., Yorks Region Mental Health Review Tribunal, 1986–90. *Recreations:* dinghy sailing, fruit growing, photography, painting, committed francophile.

NUTTALL, Simon James; Visiting Professor, 1995–2006, and Member of the Academic Council, 1997–2006, College of Europe, Bruges; *b* 6 Oct. 1940; *s* of John C. Nuttall and Amy L. Nuttall. *Educ:* Glossop Grammar Sch.; St John's Coll., Oxford (MA). HM Diplomatic Service, 1963–71; Office of Clerk of the Assembly, Council of Europe, 1971–73; Eur. Commn, 1973–95. Vis. Fellow, 1995–97, Acad. Visitor, 2000–04, LSE. *Publications:* European Political Co-operation, 1992; European Foreign Policy, 2000; articles on European foreign policy. *Recreations:* reading, writing. *Address:* Duck House, South Street, Sherborne, Dorset DT9 3LT; 14 Lesley Court, Strutton Ground, SW1P 2HZ. *Club:* Oxford and Cambridge.

NUTTER, Most Rev. Harold Lee, CM 1997; DD; Archbishop of Fredericton and Metropolitan of the Ecclesiastical Province of Canada, 1980–89, retired (Bishop of Fredericton, 1971, Bishop Emeritus, 1992); Vice-Chairman, New Brunswick Police Commission, 1988–98; *b* 29 Dec. 1923; *s* of William L. Nutter and Lillian A. Joyce; *m* 1946, Edith M. Carew; one *s* one *d*. *Educ:* Mount Allison Univ. (BA 1944); Dalhousie Univ. (MA 1947); Univ. of King's College (MSLitt 1947). Rector: Simonds and Upham, 1947–51; Woodstock, 1951–57; St Mark, Saint John, NB, 1957–60; Dean of Fredericton, 1960–71. Co-Chairman, NB Task Force on Social Development, 1970–71; Mem., Adv. Cttee to Sec. of State for Canada on Multi-culturalism, 1973. Member: Bd of Governors, St Thomas Univ., 1979–89; Bd of Regents, Mount Allison Univ., 1978–84; Vice-Chm., Bd of Governors, Univ. of King's Coll., 1971–89. Pres., Atlantic Ecumenical Council, 1972–74, 1984–86. Co-Chm., Dialogue New Brunswick, 1989–90. Hon. DD: Univ. of King's College, 1960; Montreal Diocesan Coll., 1982; Wycliffe Coll., 1983; Trinity Coll., Toronto, 1985; Hon. LLD, Mount Allison Univ., 1972. Golden Jubilee Medal, 2002. *Publications:* (jointly) New Brunswick Task Force Report on Social Development, 1971. *Address:* Apt 101, 103 North Street, Perth, ON K7H 3P3, Canada.

NUTTING, Diane Patricia, (Lady Nutting), OBE 1998; Chairman: Georgian Group, 1999–2014; Prince of Wales's Drawing School, 2005–08; *b* 8 Sept. 1941; *d* of Duncan and Patricia Kirk; *m* 1st, 1959, 2nd Earl Beatty, DSC (*d* 1972); one *s* one *d*; 2nd, 1973, John Nutting (*see* Sir John Nutting, Bt); one *s* one *d*. *Educ:* Moira House, Eastbourne. Director: Anglia Television, 1980–95; Chiltern Radio, 1985–95. Member: Council, Nat. Trust, 1985–2000 (Chm., Thames and Chiltern Region, 1984–97; Mem., Properties Cttee, 1991–); Royal Fine Art Commn, 1985–2000; Cathedrals Fabric Commn, 1990–2000; St Albans Fabric Commn, 1993–; Churches Preservation Trust, 1997–. Trustee: Nat. Heritage Meml Fund and Heritage Lottery Fund, 1991–97; British Architectl Liby Trust, 2002–; Kelmarsh Hall Charitable Trust, 2002–. Mem., Westminster CC, 1968–78 (Mem. Town Planning Cttee). JP Inner London, 1978. *Recreations:* history, architectural history. *Address:* The Manor House, Great Cheverell, Devizes, Wilts SN10 5YA; K3 Albany, Piccadilly, W1J 0AY. *Club:* Athenæum.

NUTTING, Sir John (Grenfell), 4th Bt *cr* 1903, of St Helens, Booterstown, co. Dublin; QC 1995; a Recorder of the Crown Court, since 1986; a Judge, 1995–2014, Senior Judge, 2014, Courts of Appeal of Jersey and Guernsey; a Deputy High Court Judge, since 1998; *b* 28 Aug. 1942; *s* of Rt Hon. Sir Anthony Nutting, 3rd Bt, PC and of Gillian Leonora (*née* Strutt); *S* father, 1999; *m* 1973, Diane Patricia, Countess Beatty (*see* D. P. Nutting); one *s* one *d*, and one step *s* one step *d*. *Educ:* Eton Coll.; McGill Univ. (BA 1964). Called to the Bar, Middle Temple, 1968, Hon. Bencher 1991; Jun. Treasury Counsel, 1981–86; First Jun. Treasury Counsel, 1987–88; Sen. Treasury Counsel, 1988–93; First Sen. Treasury Counsel, 1993–95. Mem., Bar Council, 1976–80, 1986–87; Chm., Young Bar, 1978–79; Vice Chm., Criminal Bar Assoc., 1995. Member: Lord Chancellor's Adv. Cttee on Legal Educn and Conduct, 1997–99; Appts Panel, Ind. Supervisory Authy for Hunting, 2001–05; Commissioner: for Interception of Communications (Jersey and Guernsey), 1999–2004; for Regulation of Investigatory Powers (Jersey and Guernsey), 2004–14. Chm., Inquiry into Former Armed Service Personnel in Prison, Howard League for Penal Reform, 2009–11 (Report, 2011). Chm., Helmsdale River Bd, and Helmsdale Dist Salmon Fishery Bd, 2001–. Pres., NE Milton Keynes Conservative Assoc., 1990–93. A Patron, Philharmonia Orch., 2001–10. Chm. of Govs, Burghley House Preservation Trust, 2009–; Trustee, Trust Hse Trust, 2010–; Mem., Provost's Appeals Panel, 2012–, Chm., Henry VI Soc., 2014–, Eton Coll. FRPSL 1970. *Recreations:* shooting, stalking, fishing. *Heir:* *s* James Edward Sebastian Nutting [*b* 12 Jan. 1977; *m* 2007, Antonia, *d* of Eugen von Boch; one *s* one *d*]. *Address:* The Manor House, Great Cheverell, Devizes, Wilts SN10 5YA; K3 Albany, Piccadilly, W1J 0AY; Achentoul, Kinbrace, Sutherland KW11 6UB. *Clubs:* White's, The Other.

NUTTON, Prof. Vivian, PhD; FBA 2008; Professor of the History of Medicine, University College London, 1993–2009, now Emeritus; *b* Halifax, Yorks, 21 Dec. 1943; *s* of Eli and Constance Nutton; *m* 1973, Christine Clements; one *s* two *d*. *Educ:* Elland C of E Prim. Sch.; Bradford Grammar Sch.; Selwyn Coll., Cambridge (BA 1965; PhD 1970; Hon. Fellow 2009). Res. Fellow, 1967–69, Fellow and Dir of Studies in Classics, 1969–77, Selwyn College, Cambridge; Historian (Ancient), Wellcome Inst., and Hon. Lectr, UCL, 1977–93. Visiting Professor: Johns Hopkins Univ., Baltimore, 1988; Russian People's Friendship Univ., Moscow, 1998; Vis. Fellow, Inst. for Advanced Study, Princeton, 2000; Hooker Dist. Vis. Prof., McMaster Univ., 2007; Hon. Prof., Dept of Classics and Centre for Hist. of Medicine, 2011–13, Prof., Dept of Classics, 2013–14, Univ. of Warwick. Corresp. Mem., Internat. Acad. of Hist. of Medicine, 1985; Member: Acad. Internat. d'Histoire des Scis, 1993; Academia Europaea, 2000; Deutsche Akademie der Wissenschaften (formerly Deutsche Akademie der Naturforscher Leopoldina), 2002; Fellow, Studio Firmano per la Storia della Medicina, 2003. Hon. FRCP 1999; Hon. Fellow, Faculty of the History and Philosophy of Medicine, Soc. of Apothecaries, 2014. *Publications:* Galen, On Prognosis: text, translation, commentary, 1979; (ed) Galen: problems and prospects, 1981; (ed jtly) Theories of Fever from Antiquity to the Enlightenment, 1981; John Caius and the Manuscripts of Galen, 1987; From Democedes to Harvey: studies in the history of medicine, 1988; (ed) Medicine at the Courts of Europe, 1500–1837, 1990; (jtly) The Western Medical Tradition, 800 BC to AD 1800, 1995 (Histoire de la lutte contre la maladie, 1999); (ed jtly) The History of Medical Education in Britain, 1995; Galen, On My Own Opinions: text, translation and commentary, 1999; (ed) The Unknown Galen, 2002; Ancient Medicine, 2004, 2nd edn 2012; (ed) Pestilential Complexities: understanding medieval plague, 2008; (trans. and ed) Girolamo Mercuriale, De arte gymnastica, 2008; (ed jtly) Girolamo Mercuriale: medicina e cultura nell'Europa del Cinquecento, 2008; Galen, On Problematical Movements, 2011; (trans. jtly) Galen, Psychological Writings, 2013; Rumbustious John: change and renewal in Victorian

Sandridge, 2014. *Recreations:* bellringing, singing, playing piano and organ. *Address:* Life Sciences Faculty, University College London, Gower Street, WC1E 6BT. *E:* ucgavnu@ucl.ac.uk.

NYE, Baroness *cr* 2010 (Life Peer), of Lambeth in the London Borough of Lambeth; **Susan Jane Nye;** Director, Government Relations, No 10 Downing Street, 2007–10; *b* London, 17 May 1955; *m* 1989, Gavyn Davies, *qv*; two *s* one *d*. *Educ:* Westcliff High Sch. for Girls. Sec., No 10 Downing St, 1976; Advr to Gordon Brown, MP, 1992–2007. *Address:* House of Lords, SW1A 0PW.

NYE, Prof. John Frederick, FRS 1976; Melville Wills Professor of Physics, University of Bristol, 1985–88 (Professor of Physics, 1969–88), now Professor Emeritus; *b* 26 Feb. 1923; *s* of Haydn Percival Nye and Jessie Mary, *d* of Anderson Hague, painter; *m* 1953, Georgiana Wiebenson; one *s* two *d*. *Educ:* Stowe; King's Coll., Cambridge (Maj. Schol.; MA, PhD 1948). Research, Cavendish Laboratory, Cambridge, 1944–49; Univ. Demonstrator in Mineralogy and Petrology, Cambridge, 1949–51; Bell Telephone Laboratories, NJ, USA, 1952–53; Lectr, 1953, Reader, 1965, Univ. of Bristol; Visiting Professor: in Glaciology, California Inst. of Technol., 1959; of Applied Sciences, Yale Univ., 1964; of Geophysics, Univ. of Washington, 1973. President: Internat. Glaciological Soc., 1966–69; Internat. Commn of Snow and Ice, 1971–75. For. Mem., Royal Swedish Acad. of Scis, 1977. Kirk Bryan Award, Geol. Soc. of Amer., 1961; Seligman Crystal, Internat. Glaciol Soc., 1969; Antarctic Service Medal, USA, 1974; NPL Metrology Award, 1986; Charles Chree Medal, Inst. of Physics, 1989. *Publications:* Physical Properties of Crystals, 1957, rev. edn 1985; Natural Focusing and Fine Structure of Light, 1999; papers on physics of crystals, glaciology, optics, microwaves, and applications of catastrophe theory in scientific jls. *Address:* 45 Canynge Road, Bristol BS8 3LH. *T:* (0117) 973 3769.

NYE, Rick; *see* Nye, R. C.

NYE, Robert; writer; *b* 15 March 1939; *s* of Oswald William Nye and Frances Dorothy Weller; *m* 1st, 1959, Judith Pratt (marr. diss. 1967); three *s*; 2nd, 1968, Aileen Campbell; one *d*, and one step *s* one step *d*. *Educ:* Southend High School, Essex. Freelance writer, 1961–; Poetry Critic, The Times, 1971–96; Chief Book Reviewer, The Scotsman, 1965–2000. FRSL 1977. *Publications: poetry:* Juvenilia 1, 1961; Juvenilia 2, 1963 (Eric Gregory Award, 1963); Darker Ends, 1969; Agnus Dei, 1973; Two Prayers, 1974; Five Dreams, 1974; Divisions on a Ground, 1976; A Collection of Poems 1955–1988, 1989; 14 Poems, 1994; Henry James and Other Poems, 1995; Collected Poems, 1995; The Rain and the Glass: 99 poems, new and selected, 2005 (Cholmondeley Award, 2007); Sixteen Poems, 2005; One or Two Swallows, 2008; An Almost Dancer: poems, 2005–2011, 2012; *fiction:* Doubtfire, 1967; Tales I Told My Mother, 1969; Falstaff, 1976 (The Guardian Fiction Prize, 1976; Hawthornden Prize, 1977); Merlin, 1978; Faust, 1980; The Voyage of the Destiny, 1982; The Facts of Life and Other Fictions, 1983; The Memoirs of Lord Byron, 1989; The Life and Death of My Lord Gilles de Rais, 1990; Mrs Shakespeare: the complete works, 1993; The Late Mr Shakespeare, 1998; *plays:* (with Bill Watson) Sawney Bean, 1970; The Seven Deadly Sins: A Mask, 1974; Penthesilea, Fugue and Sisters, 1976; *children's fiction:* Taliesin, 1966; March Has Horse's Ears, 1966; Wishing Gold, 1970; Poor Pumpkin, 1971; Out of the World and Back Again, 1977; Once Upon Three Times, 1978; The Bird of the Golden Land, 1980; Harry Pay the Pirate, 1981; Three Tales, 1983; Lord Fox and Other Spine-Chilling Tales, 1997; *translation:* Beowulf, 1968; *editions:* A Choice of Sir Walter Ralegh's Verse, 1972; William Barnes: Selected Poems, 1973; A Choice of Swinburne's Verse, 1973; The English Sermon 1750–1850, 1976; The Faber Book of Sonnets, 1976; PEN New Poetry 1, 1986; (jtly) First Awakenings: the early poems of Laura Riding, 1992; A Selection of the Poems of Laura Riding, 1994; Some Poems by Ernest Dowson, 2006; Some Poems by Thomas Chatterton, 2007; Some Poems by Clere Parsons, 2008; The Liquid Rhinoceros and other uncollected poems by Martin Seymour-Smith, 2009; Some Poems by James Reeves, 2009; contribs to British and American periodicals. *Recreation:* gambling. *Address:* Thornfield, Kingsland, Ballinhassig, Co. Cork, Ireland.

NYE, Roderick Christopher, (Rick); Director, Populus, since 2003; *b* 28 Feb. 1967; *s* of late Bertram Edward Nye and of Elsie Doreen Nye; *m* 1994, Diana Grace, *d* of John and Priscilla Douglas. *Educ:* Norton Knatchbull Sch., Ashford; American Univ., Washington; Univ. of Leeds (BA Hons 1989). Policy Advr to David Owen, 1989–90; Journalist, VNU Business Publications, 1990–92; Dep. Dir, 1992–95, Dir, 1995–99, Social Market Foundn; Dir, Cons. Res. Dept, 1999–2003. Mem. (C), Westminster CC, 1998–2002. *Publications:* Welfare to Work: the 'America Works' experience, 1996; (ed) The Future of Welfare, 1997. *Recreations:* United States, reading, sport (watching), Chelsea FC. *Address:* (office) 10 Northburgh Street, EC1V 0AT. *Club:* Sam's.

NYE, Simon Beresford; writer; *b* 29 July 1958; *s* of Dennis Beresford Nye and Sheila Elizabeth Nye; *m* 2011, Claudia Stumpfl; two *s* two *d*. *Educ:* Collyer's Sch., Horsham; Bedford Coll., London (BA French and German 1980). Writer: *television series:* Men Behaving Badly, 1992–99; Frank Stubbs Promotes, 1993–95; Is It Legal?, 1995–98; My Wonderful Life, 1997–98; How Do You Want Me?, 1998–99; Beast, 2000–01; The Savages, 2001; Wild West, 2002–03; Hardware, 2003–04; Carrie and Barry, 2004–05; Reggie Perrin, 2009–10; Just William, 2010; Warren United, 2014; *television films:* True Love, 1996; The Railway Children, 2000; Pollyanna, 2003; Pride, 2004; Beauty, 2004; Tunnel of Love, 2004; Open Wide, 2005; My Family and Other Animals, 2005; Catwalk Dogs, 2007; Tommy Cooper: not like that, like this, 2014; 4 ITV pantomimes, 1998–2002; *translations* of plays: Don Juan, 2002; Accidental Death of an Anarchist, 2003. *Publications:* Men Behaving Badly, 1989; Wideboy, 1991; The Best of Men Behaving Badly, 2000; various translations. *Recreation:* sitting in cafés. *Address:* c/o Knight Hall Agency, Lower Ground Floor, 7 Mallow Street, EC1Y 8RQ. *T:* (020) 3397 2901.

NYE, William James, LVO 2015; Secretary-General, Archbishop's Council and General Synod of the Church of England, since 2015; *b* Amersham, 28 March 1966; *s* of Lt Col Ralph Nye and Barbara Nye; *m* 2006, Dr Katherine Bartlett; one *d*. *Educ:* Christ's Hosp.; Clare Coll., Cambridge (BA 1987); Yale Univ. (MA 1989). HM Treasury, 1990–98; DCMS, 1998–2000; HM Treasury, 2001–02; Home Office: Finance Dir, 2002–05; Dir, Counter-Terrorism and Intelligence, 2005–07; Dir in Office for Security and Counter-Terrorism, 2007–08; Dir, Nat. Security Secretariat, later Dir, Strategy and Counter-terrorism, Nat. Security Secretariat, Cabinet Office, 2008–11; Principal Private Sec. to the Prince of Wales and the Duchess of Cornwall, 2011–15. *Address:* Church House, Great Smith Street, SW1P 3AZ. *Club:* Sussex County Cricket.

NYMAN, Bernard Martin; Sole Principal, BM Nyman & Co., solicitors and publishing lawyers, since 1999; *b* London, 27 Feb. 1954; *s* of Raymond Nyman and Jean Nyman; *m* 1986, Carole Stern; two *d*. *Educ:* Royal Liberty Sch.; Univ. of Sheffield (BA Hons Law 1975). Admitted solicitor, 1979; Solicitor, 1979–83, Partner, 1983–94, Rubinstein Callingham; Partner, Manches & Co., 1994–98. Trustee: Enid Blyton Trust for Children, 2000–08; Cleft Lip and Palate Assoc., 2003–14. *Publications:* The Encyclopaedia of Forms and Precedents, vol. 21 (pt 2), Copyright, 1991 to 2015; (contrib.) Character Merchandising, 2nd edn 1996; (contrib.) Copinger and Skone James on Copyright, 14th edn 1999 to 16th edn 2013. *Recreations:* jazz, cricket, football, reading, films, family, meditating, cuddling our cats. *Address:* BM Nyman & Co., 25 Limes Avenue, N12 8QN. *T:* (020) 3601 4163, *Fax:* (020) 8445 2852. *E:* bernie@bmnyman.co.uk.

NYMAN, Michael, CBE 2008; composer; *b* 23 March 1944; *s* of Mark and Jeanette Nyman; *m* 1970; two *d*. *Educ:* Royal Academy of Music; King's College London (BMus); Conservatorul Ciprian Porumbescu, Bucharest. FRAM 1991. Music critic, Spectator, New Statesman, The Listener, 1968–78; formed: Michael Nyman Band, 1977; MN Records, 2005. *Film scores include:* The Draughtsman's Contract, 1982; Drowning by Numbers, 1988; The Cook, The Thief, His Wife and Her Lover, 1989; Monsieur Hire, 1989; The Hairdresser's Husband, 1990; Prospero's Books, 1991; The Piano, 1992; Carrington, 1994; The Diary of Anne Frank, 1995; The Ogre, 1996; Gattaca, 1997; Ravenous, 1998; Wonderland, The End of the Affair, 1999; Act Without Words, 2000; The Claim, 2001; 24 Hours in The Life of a Woman, The Actors, 2002; Natalie, 2003; Detroit: Ruin of a City, 9 Songs, A Cock and Bull Story, The Libertine, 2005; Man on Wire, 2008; Everyday, 2012; *other compositions:* A Broken Set of Rules, Royal Ballet, 1983; The Man Who Mistook his Wife for a Hat (opera), 1986; String Quartets, 1985, 1988, 1990, 1995; Six Celan Songs, 1990–91; Noises, Sounds and Sweet Airs (opera), 1991; Where the Bee Dances, for saxophone and orch., 1991; Songs for Tony, 1993; The Piano Concerto, 1993; MGV (Musique à Grand Vitesse), 1993; Harpsichord Concerto, 1995; Trombone Concerto, 1995; After Extra Time, 1996; Double Concerto for Saxophone and Cello, 1997; Cycle of Disquietude, 1998; The Commissar Vanishes, 1999; Facing Goya (opera), 2000, revised 2002; Concerto for Saxophone Quartet and Orch., 2001; a dance he little thinks of, for orch., 2001; Violin Concerto, 2003; Man and Boy: Dada (opera), For John Peel (trio), Acts of Beauty (chamber ensemble), 2004; Love Counts (opera), Melody Waves, 2005; 11th Symphony: Hillsborough Memorial, 2014; ballet scores. *Video art:* Videofile, 2009; Images Were Introduced, 2013. Ivor Novello Classical Music Award, 2011. *Publications:* Experimental Music: Cage and Beyond, 1974, 2nd edn 1999; Sublime, 2008. *Recreation:* QPR. *Club:* Groucho.

NZIMBI, Most Rev. Benjamin Mwanzia; Archbishop of Kenya, 2002–09; Bishop of All Saints Cathedral Diocese, 2002–09; *b* 17 Oct. 1945; *s* of Paul Nzimbi Munuve and Martha Nditi Nzimbi; *m* 1974, Alice Kavula Nzimbi; three *s* two *d*. *Educ:* Univ. of Nairobi (BA Religious Studies and Philos. 1974); Trinity Coll., Nairobi; Hamline Univ., St Paul, USA (MA Mgt for Non-Profit 1999). Taught in secondary sch. and teachers' colls, 1974–84. Ordained, deacon, 1978, priest, 1979; Curate, All Souls Parish, Machakos, and Chaplain, Machakos Teachers' Coll., 1978–84; Vicar, St Francis Parish, Karen, Nairobi, 1984–85; Bishop: Machakos Dio., 1985–95; Kitui Dio., 1995–2002. Ombudsman, Jomo Kenyatta Univ. of Agriculture and Technol., 2013. *Address:* c/o Anglican Church of Kenya, PO Box 40502, 00100 Nairobi, Kenya.

O

OAKDEN, Edward Anthony, CMG 2006; HM Diplomatic Service; Ambassador to Jordan, since 2015; *b* 3 Nov. 1959; *s* of Richard Ralph Oakden and Patricia Jeanne Oakden; three *d*; *m* Dr Florence Eid. *Educ:* Repton Sch.; Cambridge Univ. (BA Hons Hist.). Entered FCO 1981; Second Secretary: Baghdad, 1984–85; Khartoum, 1985–88; Private Sec. to Ambassador and First Sec., Washington, 1988–92; Deputy Head: EU Dept (Ext.), 1992–94; Eastern Adriatic Dept, 1994; Private Sec. to Prime Minister, 1995–97; Deputy Head: EU Dept (Internal), 1994–98; of Mission, Madrid, 1998–2002; Hd, Security Policy Dept, 2002; Dir, Internat. Security, 2002–04; Dir, Defence and Strategic Threats, and Ambassador for Counter-terrorism, 2004–06; Ambassador to UAE, 2006–10; Man. Dir, UKTI, 2010–13 (on secondment); Dir, Middle East and North Africa, FCO, 2013–15. *Recreations:* family, running, swimming, history, classical music. *Address:* c/o Foreign and Commonwealth Office, King Charles Street, SW1A 2AH.

OAKELEY, Sir John (Digby Atholl), 8th Bt *cr* 1790, of Shrewsbury; Director, Dehler Yachts UK, 1988–98; *b* 27 Nov. 1932; *s* of Sir Atholl Oakeley, 7th Bt and of Mabel, (Patricia), *d* of Lionel H. Birtchnell; *S* father, 1987; *m* 1958, Maureen Frances, *d* of John and Ellen Cox; one *s* one *d*. *Educ:* private tutor. Own charter business, 1958–61; Contracts Manager, Proctor Masts, 1961–72; Managing Director: Freedom Yachts Internat. Ltd, 1981–88; Miller & Whitworth, 1972–81. *Publications:* Winning, 1968; Sailing Manual, 1980; Downwind Sailing, 1981. *Recreation:* yachting (holder of national, international, European and world titles; twice represented Great Britain in Olympic Games). *Heir: s* Robert John Atholl Oakeley [*b* 13 Aug. 1963; *m* 1989, Catherine Amanda, *d* of late William Knowles; one *s* one *d*]. *Address:* 10 Bursledon Heights, Long Lane, Bursledon, Hants SO31 8DB. *Club:* Royal Air Force Yacht (Hamble).

OAKES, Sir Christopher, 3rd Bt *cr* 1939, of Nassau, Bahama Islands; *b* 10 July 1949; *s* of Sir Sydney Oakes, 2nd Bt, and Greta (*d* 1977), *yr d* of Gunnar Victor Hartmann, Copenhagen, Denmark; *S* father, 1966; *m* 1978, Julie Dawn, *d* of Donovan Franklin Cowan, Regina, Canada; one *s* one *d*. *Educ:* Bredon, Tewkesbury; Georgia Mil. Acad., USA. *Heir: s* Victor Oakes, *b* 6 March 1983.

OAKES, (William) John, MA; Headmaster, Dartford Grammar School, since 2009; *b* Hindley, 17 Jan. 1956; *s* of Norman and Marion Oakes; *m* 1987, Amanda Percival; one *s* one *d*. *Educ:* Bishop Vesey's Grammar Sch.; Goldsmiths' Coll., Univ. of London (BSc; PGCE); Univ. of Greenwich (MA Outdoor Educn). Langley Park School for Boys: Hd of Geology, 1978–2001; Hd of Outdoor Educn, 1981–2001; Sen. Teacher, 1989–2001; Dartford Grammar School: Asst Headteacher, 2001–04; Dep. Headteacher, 2004–06; Hd of Sch. and Acting Headteacher, 2007–09. Member, Head Teacher Group: Internat. Baccalaureat Schs and Colls Assoc., 2009–; Kent and Medway Trng, 2009–; Confucius Classrooms, 2009– (Chm., Head Teacher Steering Gp, 2015–). *Recreations:* outdoor pursuits, Rugby, gardening, travel. *Address:* Dartford Grammar School, West Hill, Dartford, Kent DA1 2HW. *T:* (01322) 223039. *E:* head@dartfordgrammarschool.org.uk.

OAKESHOTT, family name of **Baron Oakeshott of Seagrove Bay**.

OAKESHOTT OF SEAGROVE BAY, Baron *cr* 2000 (Life Peer), of Seagrove Bay in the co. of Isle of Wight; **Matthew Alan Oakeshott;** Chairman, OLIM Property Ltd, since 2012; Joint Managing Director, Value and Income Trust plc, since 1986; *b* 10 Jan. 1947; *o s* of Keith Robertson Oakeshott, CMG and of Jill Oakeshott; *m* 1976, Dr Pippa Poulton; two *s* one *d*. *Educ:* Charterhouse (Sen. Foundn Scholar); University Coll. and Nuffield Coll., Oxford (BA 1st cl. Hons PPE). ODI/Nuffield Fellow, Kenya Ministry of Finance and Planning, 1968–70; Special Advr to Rt Hon. Roy Jenkins, MP, 1972–76; Investment Mgr, then Dir, Warburg Investment Management, 1976–81; Investment Mgr, Courtaulds Pension Fund, 1981–85; founder and Jt Man. Dir, OLIM Ltd (Independent Investment Managers), 1986–2012. Mem. (Lab) Oxford City Council, 1972–76. Member: SDP Nat. Cttee, 1981–82; SDP Nat. Economic Policy Cttee, 1981–83. Contested: (Lab) Horsham and Crawley, Oct. 1974; (SDP/Alliance) Cambridge, 1983. A Lib Dem spokesman on Treasury, 2001–11, and on Work and Pensions, 2003–10, H of L; Mem., Select Cttee on Economic Affairs, H of L, 2001–08; Chm., Business Adv. Gp, BIS, 2010–11. Gov., NIESR, 2010–. *Publications:* (contrib.) By-Elections in British Politics, 1973. *Recreations:* music, elections, Arsenal FC. *Address:* c/o House of Lords, SW1A 1AA.

OAKHAM, Archdeacon of; *see* Steele, Ven. G. J.

OAKLEY, Christopher John, CBE 1999; Chief Executive, MEF Comm V (formerly Comm VA MEF), since 2003; *b* 11 Nov. 1941; *s* of late Ronald Oakley and Joyce Oakley; *m* 1st, 1962, Linda Margaret Viney (marr. diss. 1986); one *s* two *d*; 2nd, 1990, Moira Jean Martingale (marr. diss. 2003); one *s*, and two adopted *d*; 3rd, 2004, Lisa Hanson; one step *d*. *Educ:* Skinners' School, Tunbridge Wells. Kent and Sussex Courier, 1959; Bromley and Kentish Times, 1963; Kent and Sussex Courier, 1963; Evening Argus, Brighton, 1966; Evening Echo, Basildon, 1969; Evening Post, Leeds, 1970; Dep. Editor, Yorkshire Post, 1976; Editor, Lancashire Evening Post, 1981; Dir, Lancashire Evening Post, 1981–83; Editor, Liverpool Echo, 1983–89; Dir, Liverpool Daily Post and Echo Ltd, 1984–89; Editor-in-Chief, 1989–91, Man. Dir, 1990–93, Chm., 1993–97, Birmingham Post & Mail; Gp Chief Exec., Midland Ind. Newspapers plc, 1991–97; Man. Dir, Mirror Regl Newspapers, 1997–98; Chief Exec., Regl Ind. Media, 1998–2002; Exec. Chm., HRM Partnership Ltd, 2002–03. Chairman: Coventry Newspapers, 1991–97; Midland Weekly Media, 1997; Newsco Insider Ltd, 2002–14; Chapter Eight Ltd, 2009–14; Royal Armouries Trading and Enterprises Ltd, 2010–12. Pres., Newspaper Soc., 1997–98; Hon. Vice Pres., Soc. of Editors. Nat. Appeals Chm., Newspaper Press Fund, 2000–01. Trustee: Royal Armouries, 2002–10; Television Trust for the Envmt, 2010–. Hon. Fellow, Univ. of Central Lancashire, 1998. *Address:* MEF Comm V, Dreve des Pins 40, 1420 Braine-l'Alleud, Belgium.

OAKLEY, Rev. Canon Mark David; Canon Chancellor, St Paul's Cathedral, since 2012 (Canon Residentiary and Treasurer, 2010–12); Deputy Priest in Ordinary to the Queen, since 1996; Canon Emeritus of Holy Trinity Pro-Cathedral, Brussels, since 2008; *b* 28 Sept. 1968; *s* of David Oakley and Sheila (*née* Cupples). *Educ:* Shrewsbury Sch.; King's Coll., London (BD 1st cl. 1990; AKC 1990); St Stephen's House, Oxford. Ordained deacon, 1993, priest, 1994; Asst Curate, St John's Wood Ch, 1993–96; Chaplain to the Bp of London, 1996–2000; Priest-in-charge, subseq. Rector, St Paul's, Covent Garden, 2000–05; Archdeacon of Germany and Northern Europe, and Chaplain of St Alban's, Copenhagen, 2005–08; Priest-in-charge, Grosvenor Chapel, Mayfair, 2008–10. Area Dean, Westminster St Margaret, 2004–05. Eric Abbott Meml Lectr, Eric Abbott Meml Trust, Westminster Abbey and Keble Coll., Oxford, 2002; Vis. Lectr, Dept of Theol. and Religious Studies, KCL, 2014. Univ. Sermon, Oxford, 2014. Pres., Shrops Horticl Soc., 2014–15. Governor: St Clement Danes Sch., 2000–05; City Literary Inst., 2002–05. Trustee, Civil Liberties Trust, 2014–. Patron, Tell MAMA, 2013–. Freeman, City of London, 1999. *Publications:* The Collage of God, 2001, 2nd edn 2012; (ed) John Donne: selected poetry and prose, 2004; (ed) Readings for Weddings, 2004, 2nd edn 2013; (ed) Readings for Funerals, 2015. *Recreations:* poetry, theatre, dog-walking, reading in the bath. *Address:* 6 Amen Court, EC4M 7BU. *E:* chancellor@stpaulscathedral.org.uk. *Club:* Garrick.

OAKLEY, Robin Francis Leigh, OBE 2001; Contributing Political Analyst, CNN, since 2009 (European Political Editor, 2000–09); *b* 20 Aug. 1941; *s* of Joseph Henry Oakley, civil engineer and Alice Barbara Oakley; *m* 1966, Carolyn Susan Germaine Rumball; one *s* one *d*. *Educ:* Wellington College; Brasenose College, Oxford (MA). Liverpool Daily Post, 1964–70; Sunday Express, 1970–79; Assistant Editor: Now! magazine, 1979–81; Daily Mail, 1981–86; Political Editor: The Times, 1986–92; BBC, 1992–2000. Presenter, The Week in Westminster, BBC Radio, 1987–92, 2000–05. Turf columnist: Spectator, 1995–; FT, 2003–06. Trustee, Thomson Foundn, 2001–14. *Publications:* Valley of the Racehorse: a year in the life of Lambourn, 2000; Inside Track: the political correspondent's life, 2001; Frankincense and More: the Barry Hills biography, 2010; The Cheltenham Festival: a centenary history, 2011; Clive Brittain: the smiling pioneer, 2012; Britain and Ireland's Top Racehorses of All Time, 2012; Tales from the Turf, 2013. *Recreations:* theatre, horse racing, sports, bird watching. *Address:* 24 Bridge End, Dorchester-on-Thames, Wallingford, Oxon OX10 7JP. *Club:* Royal Automobile.

See also B. M. G. Elkington.

OAKLEY, Prof. Stephen Phelps, PhD; FBA 2008; Kennedy Professor of Latin, and Fellow of Emmanuel College, University of Cambridge, since 2007; *b* 20 Nov. 1958; *s* of Julian Oakley and Jillian Oakley (now Marshallsay); *m* 1998, Ruth Mary Otway; two *s*. *Educ:* Bradfield Coll., Berks; Queens' Coll., Cambridge (BA Hons Classics 1980; MA 1983; PhD 1985). Res. Fellow, 1984–86, Official Fellow, 1986–98, Emmanuel Coll., Cambridge; Reader in Classics, 1998–2002, Prof. of Latin, 2002–07, Univ. of Reading. MAE 2012. Mem., Pontifical Acad. of Latin, 2014. *Publications:* The Hill Forts of the Samnites, 1995; A Commentary on Livy, books 6–10, Vol. 1 1997, Vol. 2 1998, Vol. 3 2005, Vol. 4 2005; contrib. learned jls. *Recreations:* gardening, exploring Dorset. *Address:* Emmanuel College, Cambridge CB2 3AP. *T:* (01223) 334200. *E:* spo23@cam.ac.uk.

OAKLEY, Dame Susan (Elizabeth Anne); *see* Devoy, Dame S. E. A.

OAKS, Agnes, CBE 2010; former freelance ballerina; Assistant to the Artistic Director, Estonian National Ballet, since 2009; *b* 29 May 1970; *d* of Juhan Oks and Valentina Oks; *m* 1990, Thomas Edur, *qv*; one *d*. *Educ:* Estonian State Ballet Sch.; Bolshoi Ballet Sch., Moscow; Royal Ballet Sch. (PDTC 2007). Principal Ballerina with: Estonian Opera Ballet, 1989–90; English Nat. Ballet, 1990–96; Birmingham Royal Ballet, 1996–97; Resident Guest Artist with English National Ballet, 1997–2009; has danced most classical ballets, inc. Swan Lake, Cinderella, Sleeping Beauty, The Nutcracker, Giselle, Coppélia, Romeo and Juliet, Don Quixote, and many others. Patron (with Thomas Edur): British Ballet Orgn, 2004–; English Nat. Ballet Sch., 2008–. 2001 Year Award, Achievements in Dance, Estonia, 2002; Unique Partnership Award (with Thomas Edur), Critics' Circle, 2003; Olivier Award, Achievements in Dance (with Thomas Edur), 2004; Best Female Dancer Award, Critics' Circle, 2008. Third Class Order of the White Star (Estonia), 2001. *Address:* c/o Estonian National Opera, Estonia av. 4, Tallinn 10148, Estonia.

OAKSHOTT, Sir Thomas Hendrie, 4th Bt *cr* 1959, of Bebington, co. Palatine of Chester; *b* Nairobi, 12 June 1959; *e s* of Hon. Sir Michael Arthur John Oakshott, 3rd Bt and Christina Rose Methuen Oakshott (*née* Banks) (*d* 1985); *S* father 2014. *Educ:* Rugby Sch.; Edinburgh Univ. (BMus 1983). FRCO; LRAM. *Heir: b* Charles Michael Oakshott [*b* 21 May 1961; *m* 1989, Anne Stapleton; one *s* two *d*]. *Address:* Warre House Cottage, Common Lane, Eton College, Windsor, Berks SL4 6DU.

OATEN, Mark; Chief Executive, International Fur Trade Federation, since 2011; *b* 8 March 1964; *s* of Ivor Condell Oaten and Audrey Oaten; *m* 1992, Belinda Fordham; two *d*. *Educ:* Hatfield Poly. (BA Hons 1986); Hertfordshire Coll. of FE, Watford (Dip in Public Relns 1989). Consultant, Shandwick Public Affairs, 1990–92; Consultant, 1992–95, Man. Dir, 1995–97, Westminster Public Relations. Dir, Oasis Radio, 1995–96. Mem. (Lib Dem) Watford BC, 1986–94. Contested (Lib Dem) Watford, 1992. MP (Lib Dem) Winchester, 1997–2010. PPS to Leader of Liberal Democrat Party, 1999–2001. Lib Dem spokesman: on disabilities, 1997–99; on foreign affairs and defence, 1999–2001; on Cabinet Office, 2001–02; on home affairs, 2003–10. Mem., Select Cttee on Public Admin, 1999–2001. Chm., All-Pty Prisoners of War Gp, 1998–2000; Sec., All-Pty EU Accession Gp, 2000–05; Co-Chm., All-Pty Adoption Gp, 2000–05; Treas., All-Pty Human Rights Gp, 2000–05. Chm., Lib Dem Parly Pty, 2001–03. Mem., Council of Europe, 2008–10. Director: British Healthcare Trades Assoc., 2008–11; Unlock, 2008. *Publications:* Coalition, 2007; Screwing Up, 2009. *Recreations:* gardening, cinema, swimming, football.

OATES, Baron *cr* 2015 (Life Peer), of Denby Grange in the County of West Yorkshire; **Jonathan Oates;** Chief of Staff to Deputy Prime Minister, 2010–15; *b* London, 1969; *s* of Rev. Canon John Oates, *qv*; civil partnership 2006, David Hill. *Educ:* Marlborough Coll.; Exeter Univ. (BA Hons Politics). Actg Dep. Head, St James' Secondary Sch., Zongoro, Zimbabwe, 1988; Political Consultant, Westminster Strategy, 1993–98; Parly Advr, Parliament of S Africa, 1999–2001; Policy Advr to Youth Justice Bd, 2001–02; Associate, Mark Bolland Associates Ltd, 2002–04; Dir, Bell Pottinger, 2004–07 and 2008–09; Dir of Communications, Lib Dems, 2007–08 and 2009–10. Election Agent to: Edward Davey, 1997; Jenny Tonge, 2001; Campaign Manager for Jeremy Browne, 2005. Mem., Royal Bor. of Kingston Council, 1994–98 (Dep. Leader, 1997–98). *Recreations:* running, poetry, politics.

OATES, Joan Louise, PhD; FBA 2004; Fellow, Girton College, Cambridge, 1971–95, Life Fellow, since 1995; Senior Fellow, McDonald Institute for Archaeological Research, Cambridge, since 1995; *b* 6 May 1928; *d* of Harold Burdette Lines and Beatrice Naomi Lines; *m* 1956, (Edward Ernest) David (Michael) Oates, FBA (*d* 2004); one *s* two *d*. *Educ:* Syracuse Univ., Syracuse, NY (BA 1950); Girton Coll., Cambridge (Fulbright Schol., Wenner-Gren Schol.; PhD 1953). Asst Curator, Metropolitan Mus. of Art, NYC, 1954–56; Lectr in Hist. and Archaeol. of Ancient Near East, Univ. of Cambridge, 1989–95. Guggenheim Fellow, 1966–67. Arents Medal, Syracuse Univ., 1991; John Coles Medal, British Acad., 2014. *Publications:* Babylon, 1976 (trans. German, Italian, Spanish, Polish, Lithuanian, Turkish, Hungarian, Arabic), rev. edn 2005; (ed jtly) Of Pots and Plans, 2002; with David Oates: The Rise of Civilization, 1976 (trans. Japanese, Hungarian, Arabic); Nimrud: an Assyrian City revealed, 2001, 2nd edn 2004; Excavations at Tell al Rimah: the pottery, 2001; Excavations at Tell Brak, vol. 1, Mitanni and Old Babylonian, 1997, vol. 2, Nagar in the 3rd Millennium BC, 2001; over 120 papers in jls and chapters in books. *Recreations:* snorkelling, walking, bird watching, painting. *Address:* 86 High Street, Barton, Cambridge CB23 7BG. *T:* (01223) 262273.

OATES, Rev. Canon John; Rector of St Bride's Church, Fleet Street, 1984–2000; Prebendary, St Paul's Cathedral, 1997–2001, now Prebendary Emeritus; *b* 14 May 1930; *s* of John and Ethel Oates; *m* 1962, Sylvia Mary, *d* of Herbert Charles and Ada Harris; three *s* one *d*. *Educ:* Queen Elizabeth School, Wakefield; SSM, Kelham. Curate, Eton College Mission, Hackney Wick, 1957–60, Founder, 59 Club, 1959; Development Officer, C of E Youth Council and mem. staff, Bd of Education, 1960–64; Development Sec., C of E Council for Commonwealth Settlement, 1964–65, Gen. Sec. 1965–70; Sec., C of E Cttee on Migration and Internat. Affairs, Bd for Social Responsibility, 1968–71; Vicar of Richmond, Surrey, 1970–84; RD, Richmond and Barnes, 1979–84; Area Dean, City of London, 1997–2000; permission to officiate, dios of London and Southwark, 2000–. Commissary: of Archbishop of Perth and Bishop of NW Australia, 1968–2000; to Archbishop of Jerusalem, 1969–75; to Bishop of Bunbury, 1969–. Hon. Canon, Bunbury, 1969–. Mem., Unilever Central Ethical Compliance Gp, 1991–97; Consultant, Creative Visions, USA, 2001–. Chapter Clerk, London City Deanery, 1994–97; Mem., Coll. of Canons, St Paul's Cathedral, 2001–. Chaplain: Inst. of Journalists, 1984–2000 (Life FCIJ 1995); Inst. of Public Relations, 1984–2000; Publicity Club of London, 1984–2000; London Press Club, 1984–2000; Co. of Marketors, 1984–2000; Co. of Stationers and Newspapermakers, 1989–2000; Co. of Turners, 1995–2001; Guild of St Bride, 2000–; Hon. Asst, St Cyprian's, Clarence Gate, 2001–. Freeman, City of London, 1985; Hon. Liveryman: Marketors' Co., 1999–; Turners' Co., 2000–. *Recreations:* broadcasting, walking, exploring. *Address:* 27 York Court, The Albany, Kingston upon Thames KT2 5ST. *T:* (020) 8974 8821. *E:* john.oates@blueyonder.co.uk. *Clubs:* Athenæum, Garrick.
See also Baron Oates.

OATES, (John) Keith; Deputy Chairman, 1994–99 and Managing Director, 1991–99, Marks and Spencer plc; Forestry Commissioner for England, since 2013 (non-executive Director, English Committee, 2007–13, Member, GB Board of Forestry Commissioners, since 2013, Forestry Commission); *b* 3 July 1942; *s* of late John Alfred Oates and Katherine Mary (*née* Hole); *m* 1968, Helen Mary (*née* Blake) (*d* 2015); one *s* three *d*. *Educ:* King's Sch., Chester; Arnold Sch., Blackpool; London School of Economics (BScEcon); Univ. of Manchester Inst. of Sci. and Technology (DipTech Industrial Admin); Bristol Univ. (MSc Management Accounting). FCT 1982. Work Study trainee, Reed Paper Gp, 1965–66; Budgets and Planning Man., IBM (UK) Ltd, 1966–73; Gp Financial Controller, Rolls Royce (1971) Ltd, 1973–74; Controller, Black and Decker Europe, 1974–78; Vice Pres., Finance, Thyssen Bornemisza NV, 1978–84; Finance Dir, Marks and Spencer plc, 1984–91 (Founder Chm., Marks and Spencer Financial Services). Chm., Phaunos Timber Fund Ltd, 2006–12; non-executive Director: John Laing plc, 1987–89; British Telecom, 1994–2000; Guinness, 1995–97; MCI Communications Corp., 1996–97; Diageo, 1997–2004; FSA, 1998–2001; Coutts Bank, Monaco, 2002–05. Gov., BBC, 1988–93. Member: Council, CBI, 1988–2000; Bd, London First, 1993–96; Sports Council of GB, 1993–97; English Sports Council, 1997–99; Public Mem., Network Rail, 2012–. Chm., Quality, Efficiency and Standards Team, 1999–2000. Chm., Eur. Council of Financial Execs, 1984; Mem., 100 Gp Chartered Accountants, 1985–93. Pres., UMIST Assoc., 1996–97. Mem. Council, Wycombe Abbey Sch., 1995–. Patron: Campaign for Resource, Bristol Univ., 1996–2002; London Christies Against Cancer, 1999–2001. DTI Innovation Lecture, 1997. CCMI (CIMgt 1992). FRSA 1993. Hon. LLD Bristol, 1998; Hon. DSc UMIST, 1998. *Recreations:* music, travel, fly fishing, ski-ing, spectator sports (esp. Association Football, athletics and cricket). *Club:* MCC.

OATES, Keith; *see* Oates, J. K.

OATES, Laurence Campbell, CB 2006; Official Solicitor to the Supreme Court, 1999–2006; Public Trustee, 2001–06; *b* 14 May 1946; *s* of late Stanley Oates and Norah Christine Oates (*née* Meek); *m* 1968, Brenda Lilian Hardwick; one *s* one *d*. *Educ:* Beckenham and Penge Grammar School; Bristol Univ. (LLB 1967). Called to the Bar, Middle Temple, 1968; Dept of Employment, 1976–80; Law Officers' Dept, 1980–83; Asst Treasury Solicitor, Dept of Transport, 1983–88; Lord Chancellor's Department: Under Sec. and Hd of Legislation Gp, 1988–92; Circuit Administrator, Midland and Oxford Circuit, 1992–94; Assoc. Head of Policy Gp, 1995–96; Dir, Magistrates' Courts' Gp, 1996–99. Lay Advr, RCPCH, 2007–. Trustee: Royal Hosp. for Neuro-disability, 2007–; Grange Centre, 2007–; Just Advocacy, 2007–; Woking CAB, 2014–; Citizens Advice Surrey, 2014–. Gov., Woking Coll., 2007–. *Recreations:* music, golf. *Address:* Cedar Waters, White Rose Lane, Woking, Surrey GU22 7JY.

OATLEY, Brian; Chairman, Invicta Community Care NHS Trust, 1997–2001; *b* 1 June 1935; *s* of Arnold and Vivian Oatley. *Educ:* Bolton School; King's College, Cambridge (BA, PGCE). Teacher, North Manchester Grammar School, 1959–64; Assistant, Senior Assistant and Deputy County Education Officer, Kent County Council, 1964–84, County Educn Officer, 1984–88. Chm., Maidstone Priority Care NHS Trust, 1991–97. Member: RHS; Kent Trust for Nature Conservation; Camden Choir. Gov., Kent Inst. of Art and Design, 1989–98. *Recreations:* music, travel, gardening, painting. *Address:* 6A Arundel Square, N7 8AT.

OATLEY, Michael Charles, CMG 1991; OBE 1975; international intelligence specialist, retired; *b* 18 Oct. 1935; *s* of Sir Charles Oatley, OBE, FRS and Lady Oatley (*née* Enid West); *m* 1st, Pippa Howden; two *s* one *d*; 2nd, Mary Jane Laurens; one *s*. *Educ:* The Leys Sch.; Trinity Coll., Cambridge. Served RN, 1953–55. HM Foreign, later Diplomatic, Service, 1959–91; a Man. Dir, Kroll Associates, 1991–94; Man. Dir, 1994–98, Chm., 1998–2001, Ciex Ltd. Director: Ovag Ltd, 2002–09; ICT Cambridge Ltd, 2004–06; Chm., Aurora (NI) Ltd, 2015–. *Address:* Castlebrook House, Nunney, Frome, Somerset BA11 4LN. *Clubs:* Chelsea Arts, Naval.

OBAMA, Barack Hussein, Jr, JD; President of the United States of America, since 2009; *b* Honolulu, 4 Aug. 1961; *s* of late Barack Obama and Ann Dunham; *m* 1992, Michelle Robinson; two *d*. *Educ:* Columbia Univ. (BA Pol Sci. 1983); Harvard Univ. (JD *magna cum laude* 1991). Ed.-in-Chief, Harvard Law Review. Writer and financial analyst, Business Internat. Corp., 1984–85; Dir, Developing Communities Project, Chicago, 1985–88; Exec. Dir, Project Vote, Illinois, 1992; Associate, Miner, Barnhill & Galland, PC, Chicago, 1993–96, Of Counsel, 1996–2004; Sen. Lectr, Law Sch., Univ. of Chicago, 1993–2004. Mem., Illinois Senate, Dist 13, Springfield, 1997–2005; US Senator (Democrat) from Illinois, 2005–08; US Senate: Member: Envmt and Public Works Cttee, 2005–06; Foreign Relns Cttee; Veterans' Affairs Cttee. Nobel Peace Prize, 2009. *Publications:* Dreams from My Father: a story of race and inheritance, 1995; Audacity of Hope: thoughts on reclaiming the American dream, 2006; Change We Can Believe In: Barack Obama's plan to renew America's promise, 2008; Of Thee I Sing: a letter to my daughters (for children), 2010. *Address:* The White House, Washington, DC 20500, USA.

OBAN (St John's Cathedral), Provost of; *see* McNelly, Very Rev. N.

OBASANJO, Gen. Olusegun; President of Nigeria, 1999–2007; Nigerian Head of State, Head of the Federal Military Government and Commander-in-Chief of the Armed Forces, Nigeria, 1976–79; Member, Advisory Council of State, 1979–2007; farmer; *b* Abeokuta, Ogun State, Nigeria, 5 March 1937; *m*; two *s* three *d*. *Educ:* Abeokuta Baptist High Sch.; Mons Officers' Cadet Sch., England. Entered Nigerian Army, 1958; commission, 1959; served in Zaire (then, the Congo), 1960. Comdr, Engrg Corps, 1963; Comdr of 2nd (Rear) Div. at Ibadan; GOC 3rd Inf. Div., 1969; Comdr, 3rd Marine Commando Div.; took surrender of forces of Biafra, in Nigerian Civil War, 1969–70; Comdr Engrg Corps, 1970–75. Political post as Federal Comr for Works and Housing, Jan.–July 1975. Chief of Staff, Supreme HQ, July 1975–Feb. 1976. Mem., Internat. Ind. Commn on Disarmament and Security; Mem., Africa Progress Panel, 2006–. Part-time Associate, Univ. of Ibadan. *Publications:* My Command (autobiog.), 1980; Africa in Perspective: myths and realities, 1987; Nzeognu, 1987; Africa Embattled, 1988; Constitution for National Integration and Development, 1989; Not My Will, 1990; Challenge of Leadership in African Development, 1990; Impact of Europe in 1992 on West Africa, 1990; Leadership Challenge of Economic Reforms in Africa, 1991; Challenge of Agricultural Production and Food Security in Africa, 1992. *Recreations:* squash, table tennis, billiards, snooker.

O'BEIRNE RANELAGH, John, (John Ranelagh), PhD; Director: Nordic World, 2006–14 (Executive Chairman, 2006–08); Vizrt, 2008–11 (Deputy Chairman, 2009–11); Consultant, TV 2 Norway, 1991–2014; Member, Independent Television Commission, 1994–99; *b* 3 Nov. 1947; *o s* of late James O'Beirne Ranelagh and Elaine Lambert O'Beirne Ranelagh; *m* 1974, Elizabeth Grenville, *y d* of Prof. Sir William Rede Hawthorne, CBE, FRS. *Educ:* St Christopher's Sch.; Cambridgeshire Coll. of Arts and Technology; Christ Church, Oxford (MA); Eliot Coll., Univ. of Kent (PhD). Chase Manhattan Bank, 1970; Campaign Dir, Outset Housing Assoc., 1971; Univ. of Kent Studentship, 1972–74; BBC TV, 1974; Conservative Res. Dept, 1975–79; Associate Producer, Ireland: a television history, BBC TV, 1979–81; Commissioning Editor, Channel Four TV Co., 1981–88 (Sec. to the Bd, 1981–83); Dep. Chief Exec. and Dir of Programmes, TV2 Denmark, 1988; Exec. Producer and writer, CIA, BBC TV/NRK/Primetime, 1989–92; Associate, Hydra Associates, 1989–91; Consultant, TVI Portugal, 1992–94; Director: Kanal Kaks, Estonia, 1995–97; TMS Ltd, 1999–2002; Barnimagen, 2000–01; Exec. Producer, Lykkelandet, 2003–04 (Gullruten Prize winner). Dir, Broadcasting Research Unit, 1988–90 (Mem., Exec. Cttee, 1984–87). Mem., Political Cttee, UNA, 1978–90. Governor, Daneford Sch., 1977–81. Kt 1st Cl., Royal Order of Merit (Norway), 2013. *Publications:* Science, Education and Industry, 1978; (with Richard Luce) Human Rights and Foreign Policy, 1978; Ireland: an illustrated history, 1981; A Short History of Ireland, 1983, 3rd edn 2012; The Agency: the rise and decline of the CIA, 1986 (Nat. Intelligence Book Award, and New York Times Notable Book of the Year, 1987); (contrib.) Freedom of Information, ed by Julia Neuberger, 1987; (contrib.) The Revolution in Ireland 1879–1923, ed D. G. Boyce, 1988; Den Anden Kanal, 1989; Thatcher's People, 1991; CIA: a history, 1992; (contrib.) In the Name of Intelligence: essays in honor of Walter Pforzheimer, 1994. *Recreations:* Bentley motor cars, reading. *Address:* The Garner Cottages, Mill Way, Grantchester, Cambridge CB3 9NB. *Clubs:* Travellers, Chelsea Arts, Groucho; Metropolitan (Washington).

OBORNE, Peter Alan; Contributing Editor, The Spectator, since 2006; *b* 11 July 1957; *s* of Brig. John Oborne and Margaret Oborne; *m* 1986, Martine Karmock; two *s* three *d*. *Educ:* Sherborne Sch.; Christ's Coll., Cambridge (BA Hist. 1978). N. M. Rothschild & Sons Ltd, 1981–84; Financial Weekly, 1985–86; Daily Telegraph, 1986; Reporter, Evening Standard, 1987–96; Asst Ed., Sunday Express, 1996–2001; Political Ed., Spectator, 2001–06; Political Columnist, Daily Mail, 2006–10; Chief Political Commentator, Daily Telegraph, 2010–15. Presenter, films (all for Channel 4) including: Mugabe's Secret Famine, 2003; Afghanistan: here's one we invaded earlier, 2003; Dirty Race for the White House, 2004; Iraq: the reckoning, 2005; Spinning Terror, 2006; Waiting for the Taliban, 2009; Holy Warriors, 2009; Inside the Pro-Israel Lobby, 2009; Wonderful World of Tony Blair, 2011; Unreported World: Vlad's Army, 2011. *Publications:* Alastair Campbell: New Labour and the rise of the media class, 1999, revd edn (with Simon Walters), 2004; Basil D'Oliveira: cricket and conspiracy, 2004; The Rise of Political Lying, 2005; The Use and Abuse of Terror, 2006; The Triumph of the Political Class, 2007; (with James Jones) Muslims Under Siege, 2008; (with Jesse Norman) Churchill's Legacy: the Conservative case for the Human Rights Act, 2009; (with Frances Weaver) Guilty Men, 2011; (with David Morrison) A Desperate Delusion: why the West is wrong about nuclear Iran, 2013; Wounded Tiger: a history of cricket in Pakistan, 2014. *Recreations:* reading, cricket, horse-racing. *Address:* 60 Elmwood Road, W4 3DZ. *E:* peter.oborne@btinternet.com.

O'BOYLE, Fionnuala Mary J.; *see* Jay-O'Boyle, F. M.

O'BRIEN, family name of **Baron Inchiquin**.

O'BRIEN, Anthony John; Director, Western Balkans, British Council, since 2012; *b* 17 Jan. 1951; *s* of Padraig and Sheila O'Brien; *m* 1975, Yolanda Lange; three *d*. *Educ:* Jesus Coll., Cambridge (BA Law 1971); Univ. of Manchester (DipTEO, PGCE 1975); Inst. of Educn, London (MA Educn 1986). Volunteer teacher of English, VSO, Aswan, Egypt, 1971–73; Lectr in ESP, Univ. of Tabriz, Iran, 1975–77; British Council: Dir of Studies, Morocco, 1978–82; Consultant, London, 1982–85; Dir, English Language Centre, Singapore, 1986–90, Hong Kong, 1990–94; Dir, Morocco, 1994–97; Dir, English Lang. Teaching, London, 1997–2002; Dir, Sri Lanka, 2002–06; Dir, Poland, 2006–11; Dir, Serbia, 2011–12. *Publications:* Nucleus: medicine, 1980; Teacher Development: evaluation and teacher profiles in TESOL, 1984; numerous articles for professional jls. *Recreations:* learning other cultures, travel, bird watching. *Address:* British Council, Terazije 8/2, 11000 Belgrade, Serbia. *E:* tony.obrien@britishcouncil.org.

O'BRIEN, Barry John; Chairman, European Mergers and Acquisitions, Jefferies International Ltd, since 2014; *b* Cardiff, 27 Oct. 1952; *s* of John, (Jack) and Patricia O'Brien; *m* 1984, Susan Bond; two *s* one *d*. *Educ:* St Illtyd's Coll., Cardiff; University Coll. London (LLB; Hon. Fellow, 2013). Admitted as solicitor, 1978; Articled Clerk, then Associate, Slaughter and May, 1976–84; with Freshfields, later Freshfields Bruckhaus Deringer LLP, 1984–2014, Partner, 1986–2014. Mem., Educn Leadership Team, Business in the Community, 2005–13. Vice Chm. Govs, 2003–14; Chm. Govs, 2014–, Arnold Hse Sch.; Chm. Govs, Haggerston Girls' Sch., 2008–; Mem., Arnold Foundn Bd, 2007–, Gov., 2012–, Rugby Sch. Liveryman, Solicitors' Co., 2013–. *Publications:* contribs to legal pubns. *Recreations:* family, sport (Welsh Rugby, Glamorgan cricket, Arsenal, golf and ski-ing), opera, contemporary art. *Address:* Jefferies International Ltd, Vintners Place, 68 Upper Thames Street, EC4V 3BJ. *T:* (020) 7029 8558. *E:* bobrien@jefferies.com. *Clubs:* Athenæum, Walbrook, MCC; Glamorgan County Cricket (Mem. Cttee, 2008–; Chm., 2011–); Brocket Hall; Loch Lomond; Highgate Golf.

O'BRIEN, Basil Godwin, CMG 1996; High Commissioner of the Bahamas to the United Kingdom, 1999–2007, and Ambassador to the European Union, Belgium, France, Germany and Italy, 1999–2008; *b* 5 Dec. 1940; *s* of late Cyril O'Brien and Kathleen O'Brien (*née* Brownrigg); *m* 1967, Marlene Devika Chand; two *s*. *Educ:* St John's Coll., Nassau; Univ. Tutorial Coll., London; London Inst. of World Affairs (Dip. Internat. Affairs, London Univ.). HEO, Min. of Ext. Affairs, Bahamas, 1969–70; Asst Sec., later Dep. Perm. Sec., Cabinet Office, 1970–78; Permanent Secretary: Min. of Tourism, 1978–86; Min. of Foreign Affairs, 1986–89; Min. of Agriculture, Trade and Ind., 1989–93; Min. of Educn, 1993–94; Sec. to Cabinet and Hd, Public Service, 1994–99. Permanent Representative: to IMO, London; to Internat. Orgn for Migration and WTO, Geneva; to Bureau of Internat. Expositions, Paris. Director: Source River Hldgs Co. Ltd; Source River Ltd; formerly: Director: Bahamas Hotel Trng Coll.; Bahamasair Hldgs Co. Past Chm., Bd of Govs, St John's Coll., Nassau. Past Mem., Anglican Central Educn Authy. Mem., La Chaîne des Rôtisseurs. *Recreations:* walking, swimming, gardening. *Clubs:* Royal Automobile, Royal Over-Seas League; Skal.

O'BRIEN, Most Rev. Brendan Michael; *see* Kingston (Ontario), Archbishop of, (RC).

O'BRIEN, Brian Murrough Fergus; Deputy Special Commissioner of Income Tax, 1991–2006; *b* 18 July 1931; *s* of late Charles Murrough O'Brien, MB, BCh and Elizabeth Joyce O'Brien (*née* Peacocke). *Educ:* Bedford Sch.; University Coll., Oxford (BA 1954, MA 1959). Nat. Service, Royal Inniskilling Fusiliers, 1950–51. Called to the Bar, Lincoln's Inn, 1955; Office of Solicitor of Inland Revenue, 1956–70; Asst Solicitor, Law Commn, 1970–80; Secretary, Law Commn, 1980–81. Special Comr of Income Tax, 1981–91. Mem., Senate of Inns of Court and Bar Council, 1977–80; Hon. Gen. Sec., 1962–67 and Chm., 1974–76, CS Legal Soc.; Chm., Assoc. of First Div. Civil Servants, 1979–81. Lay Chm., Westminster (St Margaret's) Deanery Synod, 1978–82. Trustee, St Mary's, Bourne St, 1968–2005. *Recreations:* music, travel. *Address:* Thornby Grange, Thornby, Northants NN6 8SG. *T:* (01604) 743646. *Club:* Reform.

O'BRIEN, David P., OC 2008; Chairman: EnCana Corporation, 2002–13 (Director, 1990); Royal Bank of Canada, 2004–14 (Director, 1996–2014); *b* 9 Sept. 1941; *s* of John L. O'Brien and Ethel; *m* 1968, Gail Baxter Corneil; one *s* two *d*. *Educ:* Loyola Coll. (BA Hons Econs 1962); McGill Univ. (BCL 1965). Associate and Partner, Ogilvy Renault (law firm), 1967–77; various mgt posts, 1978–85, Exec. Vice Pres., 1985–89, Petro-Canada; Pres. and CEO, Noverco Inc., 1989; Dir, 1990, Chm., 1992, PanCanadian Petroleum Ltd (Pres. and CEO, 1990–95); Dir, 1995–2001, Pres. and Chief Operating Officer, 1995–96, Chm., Pres. and CEO, 1996–2001, Canadian Pacific Ltd; Chm. and CEO PanCanadian Energy Corp., 2001–02. Director: TransCanada Pipelines Ltd, 2001–12; Molson Inc., 2002–12; Enerplus Resources Fund, 2008. *Recreations:* tennis, biking, golf. *Clubs:* Calgary Petroleum, Calgary Golf and Country, Glencoe Golf and Country (Calgary).

O'BRIEN, Prof. Denis Patrick, FBA 1988; Professor of Economics, University of Durham, 1972–97, now Emeritus; *b* Knebworth, Herts, 24 May 1939; *s* of Patrick Kevin O'Brien and Dorothy Elizabeth Crisp; *m* 1st, 1961, Eileen Patricia O'Brien (*d* 1985); one *s* two *d*; 2nd, 1993, Julia Stapleton; one *d*. *Educ:* Douai Sch.; University Coll. London (BSc (Econ) 1960); PhD Queen's Univ., Belfast, 1969. In industry, 1960–62; Queen's University, Belfast: Asst Lectr, 1963–65; Lectr, 1965–70; Reader, 1970–72. Dist. Fellow, History of Econs Soc., 2003. *Publications:* (with D. Swann) Information Agreements, 1969; J. R. McCulloch, 1970; Correspondence of Lord Overstone, 3 vols, 1971; (jtly) Competition in British Industry, 1974; (ed) J. R. McCulloch: Treatise on Taxation, 1975; The Classical Economists, 1975; Competition Policy, Profitability and Growth, 1979; (with J. Presley) Pioneers of Modern Economics in Britain, 1981; (with A. C. Darnell) Authorship Puzzles in the History of Economics, 1982; (with J. Creedy) Economic Analysis in Historical Perspective, 1984; Lionel Robbins, 1988; Thomas Joplin and Classical Macroeconomics, 1993; Methodology, Money and the Firm, 2 vols, 1994; The Classical Economists Revisited, 2004; History of Economic Thought as an Intellectual Discipline, 2007; The Development of Monetary Economics, 2007; (ed with J. Creedy) G. W. Norman: taxation and the promotion of human happiness, 2009; (ed with J. Creedy) Darwin's Clever Neighbour: George Warde Norman and his circle, 2010. *Recreation:* the violin.

O'BRIEN, Dermod Patrick; QC 1983; a Recorder of the Crown Court, 1978–2005; *b* 23 Nov. 1939; *s* of Lieut D. D. O'Brien, RN, and Mrs O'Brien (*née* O'Connor); *m* 1974, Zoë Susan Norris (marr. diss. 2003); two *s*. *Educ:* Ampleforth Coll., York; St Catherine's Coll., Oxford. BA (Jurisprudence); MA. Called to Bar, Inner Temple, 1962, Bencher, 1993; joined Western Circuit, 1963; in practice as a barrister, 2 Temple Gardens, 1963–2010, Head of Chambers, 1999–2003. Governor, Milton Abbey Sch., 1992–2012. *Recreations:* fishing, shooting, ski-ing, gardening. *Address:* Rodwell Manor, West Lambrook, Kingsbury Episcopi, Somerset TA13 5HA. *Clubs:* Boodle's; Piscatorial.

O'BRIEN, Edna; writer; *b* Ireland, 1930; marr. diss.; two *s*. *Educ:* Irish convents; Pharmaceutical Coll. of Ireland. Yorkshire Post Novel Award, 1971; Ulysses Medal, UCD, 2006; Lifetime Achievement Award, Irish Booksellers, 2009. *Publications:* The Country Girls, 1960 (screenplay for film, 1983; play, 2012); The Lonely Girl, 1962; Girls in Their Married Bliss, 1963; August is a Wicked Month, 1964; Casualties of Peace, 1966; The Love Object, 1968; A Pagan Place, 1970; A Pagan Place (play), 1971; Night, 1972; A Scandalous Woman (short stories), 1974; Mother Ireland, 1976; Johnnie I hardly knew you, 1977; Mrs Reinhardt and other stories, 1978; Virginia (play), 1979; The Dazzle, 1981; Returning, 1982; A Christmas Treat, 1982; A Fanatic Heart (selected stories), 1985; Tales for the Telling, 1986; Flesh and Blood (play), 1987; Madame Bovary (play), 1987; The High Road, 1988; Lantern Slides (short stories), (Los Angeles Times Award) 1990; Time and Tide, 1992 (Writers' Guild Award, 1993); House of Splendid Isolation, 1994; Down by the River, 1997; James Joyce, 1999; Wild Decembers, 1999; In The Forest, 2002; Iphigenia (play), 2003; Triptych (play), 2003; The Light of Evening, 2006; Byron in Love, 2009; Haunted (play), 2010; Saints and Sinners, 2011; Country Girl (memoir), 2012; The Love Object (short stories), 2013; The Little Red Chairs, 2016. *Recreations:* reading, theatre, film. *Address:* c/o Ed Victor, 6 Bayley Street, WC1B 3HE. *T:* (020) 7304 4100; c/o Angharad Wood, Tavistock Wood, 45 Conduit Street, W1S 2YN. *T:* (020) 7494 4767.

O'BRIEN, John Gerard; Chief Executive, London Councils, since 2007; *b* 18 Jan. 1960; *s* of Patrick and Bridget O'Brien; *m* 1990, Anne-Marie Boyce; one *s*. *Educ:* St Martin's Sch., Brentwood; Univ. of Warwick (BA Hons Hist. and Politics 1982). Grad. trainee, Basildon DC, 1982–84; Principal Asst, Westminster CC, 1984–88; Mgt Consultant, KPMG, 1988–99; Dir (Solutions), Improvement and Develt Agency for Local Govt, 1999–2003; Dir, Local Govt Perf. and Practice, ODPM, subseq. DCLG, 2003–06; Dir, Ind. Commn, LGA (on secondment), 2006–07. Chair, SOLACE Foundn, 2011–14. *Publications:* (with K. Ennals) The Enabling Role of Local Authorities, 1990. *Recreations:* family, friends, sport. *Address:* London Councils, 59½ Southwark Street, SE1 0AL. *Club:* Essex County Cricket.

O'BRIEN, His Eminence Cardinal Keith Michael Patrick; Archbishop of St Andrews and Edinburgh, (RC), 1985–2013, now Emeritus; *b* Ballycastle, Co. Antrim, 17 March 1938; *s* of late Mark Joseph O'Brien and Alice Mary (*née* Moriarty). *Educ:* St Patrick's High Sch., Dumbarton; Holy Cross Acad., Edinburgh; Edinburgh Univ. (BSc 1959, DipEd 1966); St Andrew's Coll., Drygrange; Moray House Coll. of Education, Edinburgh. Ordained priest, 1965; pastoral appointments: Holy Cross, Edinburgh, 1965–66; St Bride's, Cowdenbeath, 1966–71 (while Chaplain and teacher of Maths and Science, St Columba's High Sch., Cowdenbeath and Dunfermline); St Patrick's, Kilsyth, 1972–75; St Mary's, Bathgate, 1975–78; Spiritual Dir, St Andrew's Coll., Drygrange, 1978–80; Rector, St Mary's Coll., Blair, Aberdeen, 1980–85. Apostolic Adminr, Dio. Argyll and the Isles, 1996–99. Cardinal Priest, 2003. Hon. LLD Antigonish, Nova Scotia, 2004; Hon. DD: St Andrews, 2004; Edinburgh, 2004. KGCHS 2003 (Grand Prior, Scottish Lieutenancy, 2001–13); Bailiff Grand Cross of Honour and Devotion, SMO Malta, 2005. *Recreations:* music, hill walking. *E:* kpobrien247@gmail.com.

O'BRIEN, Prof. Kevin Donald, PhD; Professor of Orthodontics, University of Manchester, since 1996; Chairman, General Dental Council, 2011–13; *b* Edinburgh, 2 Feb. 1957; *s* of Frances Pagett; *m* 1979, Janet Miller; one *s* two *d*. *Educ:* King Edward VI Sch., Stourbridge; Univ. of Manchester (BDS 1979; MSc 1986; PhD 1991). FDSRCPSGlas 1984; DOrthRCS 1986; FDS RCS 2011. Gen. Dental Practitioner, 1979–84; hosp. trainee, 1984–87; MRC Fellow, 1987–91; Asst Prof., Univ. of Pittsburgh, 1991–92; University of Manchester: Sen. Lectr, 1992–96; Dean, Dental Sch., 2004–07; Associate Dean, Faculty of Med. and Human Sci., 2007–10. Member: Council, British Orthodontic Soc., 1998–2004; Dental Schs Council, 2004–07; Dental Prog. Bd, Health Educn England, 2011–13. Ed., Jl of Orthodontics, 2001–04. *Publications:* articles in Amer. Jl of Orthodontics, Eur. Jl of Orthodontics. *Recreations:* football spectator, walking, gardening. *Address:* School of Dentistry, J. R. Moore Building, University of Manchester, Manchester M15 6FH. *T:* (0161) 275 6620. *E:* kevin.obrien@manchester.ac.uk.

O'BRIEN, Margaret Anne; Director of Midwifery, Auckland District Health Board, New Zealand, since 2011; *b* 18 March 1955; *d* of Eric James Hues and Enid Dorothy Hues; *m* 1st, 1977, Malcolm Richard Elliott (marr. diss. 2006); one *s*; 2nd, 2007, Jarrard Michael O'Brien. *Educ:* Steyning Grammar Sch. Registered Nurse, 1976; Registered Midwife, 1979. Midwife, Southlands Hosp., Shoreham, 1979–95; Regl Officer, Royal Coll. of Midwives, 1995–97; Hd of Midwifery, Southampton Gen. Hosp., 1997–2000; Dir of Midwifery, 2000–08, and Gen. Manager, 2002–08, Queen Charlotte's and Chelsea Hosp., London; Dir of Midwifery and Hd of Nursing, Imperial Coll. NHS Healthcare Trust, 2008–11. Pres., Royal Coll. of Midwives, 2004–08 (Hon. Fellow, 2009). *Recreation:* exploring the different and unusual.

O'BRIEN, Rt Hon. Michael; PC 2009; QC 2005; *b* 19 June 1954; *s* of Timothy Thomas and Mary O'Brien; *m* 1987, Alison Munro; two *d*. *Educ:* BA Hons Hist. and Pol. Lectr in Law, Colchester Inst., 1981–87; solicitor, 1987–92; called to the Bar, Middle Temple, 2011; barrister, No5 Chambers, Birmingham, 2011–. MP (Lab) N Warwicks, 1992–2010; contested (Lab) same seat, 2010, 2015. Opposition spokesperson: HM Treasury, 1995–96; City, 1996–97; Parly Under-Sec. of State, Home Office, 1997–2001, FCO, 2002–03; Minister of State: (Minister for Trade, Investment and Foreign Affairs), FCO and DTI, 2003–04; (Minister for Energy, e-Commerce and Postal Services), DTI, 2004–05; Solicitor General, 2005–07; Minister of State: DWP, 2007–08; DECC, 2008–09; (Minister for Health Services), DoH, 2009–10. Member: Home Affairs Select Cttee, 1992–94; Treasury Select Cttee, 1994–95. Chm., Lab. Home Affairs Cttee, 1995–96. Parly Advr, Police Fedn, 1993–96. *E:* mob@no5.com.

O'BRIEN, Prof. Patrick Karl, DPhil; FBA 1990; Professor of Economic History, University of London, 1990–98; Professor of Global Economic History, London School of Economics, 2009–14; *b* 12 Aug. 1932; *s* of William O'Brien and Elizabeth Stockhausen; *m* 1959, Cassy Cobham; one *s* two *d*. *Educ:* London Sch. of Economics (Lilian Knowles Schol.; BSc 1958); Nuffield Coll., Oxford (DPhil). London University: Res. Fellow, 1960–63; Lectr, 1963–70; Reader in Econs and Econ. Hist., 1967–70; Oxford University: Univ. Lectr in Econ. Hist., 1970–84; Reader, 1984–90; Faculty Fellow, 1970–84, Professorial Fellow, 1984–90, Emeritus Fellow, 1991, St Antony's Coll.; Dir, Inst. of Historical Res., Univ. of London, 1990–98; Centennial Prof. of Econ. Hist., LSE, 1999–2009. Convenor: Eur. Res. Prog. on Regimes for Prodn, Develt and Diffusion of Useful and Reliable Knowledge in E and W from Accession of the Ming Dynasty 1368 to the Industrial Revolution 1756–1846, 2009–13; Leverhulme Trust Funded Network on Economic Outcomes Flowing from the Revolution and Napoleonic Wars 1793–1815, LSE, 2015–. Pres., Econ. Hist. Soc., 1999–2001. MAE 2002. Hon. Foreign Fellow, Amer. Historical Assoc., 2013. Hon. Dr: Carlos III, Madrid, 1998; Uppsala, 1999. *Publications:* The Revolution in Egypt's Economic System, 1966; The New Economic History of the Railways, 1977; (with C. Keyder) Economic Growth in Britain and France 1780–1914, 1978; (ed jtly) Productivity in the Economies of Europe in the 19th and 20th Centuries, 1983; (ed) Railways and the Economic Development of Western Europe 1830–1914, 1983; (ed) International Productivity Comparisons 1750–1939, 1986; The Economic Effects of the Civil War, 1988; (ed jtly) The Industrial Revolution and British Society, 1993; (ed) Industrialization: perspectives on the international economy, 1998; (ed) Philips Atlas of World History, 2000; Imperialism and Industrialization of Britain and Europe, 2000; (ed) Urban Achievement in Early Modern Europe, 2001; (ed) The Political Economy of British Historical Experience, 2002; (ed) Two Hegemonies: Britain 1846–1914 and the United States 1941–2001, 2002; contribs to many learned jls. *Recreations:* Western art, walking. *Address:* 13 Woodstock Close, Oxford OX2 8DB. *T:* (01865) 512004.

O'BRIEN, Prof. (Patrick Michael) Shaughn, DSc; MD; FRCOG; Foundation Professor of Obstetrics and Gynaecology, Keele University Medical School, since 1989; Consultant Obstetrician and Gynaecologist, since 1989, and Clinical Director, Obstetrics and Gynaecology, since 2012, University Hospital North Staffordshire; *b* 1 April 1948; *s* of late Patrick O'Brien and Joan O'Brien (*née* Edleston); *m* 1985, Sandie Louise Norman; one *s* one *d*. *Educ:* Boys' Grammar Sch., Pontypridd; Welsh Nat. Sch. of Medicine, Univ. of Wales (MB BCh 1972; MD 1979); DSc Keele, 2008. MRCOG 1979, FRCOG 1991. Res. Fellow, Univ. of Nottingham, 1974–76; Sen. House Officer, John Radcliffe Hosp., Oxford, 1976–77; Registrar: Brighton Sussex Co. Hosp., 1977–78; Middlesex Hosp., 1978–79; Clin. Lectr and Sen. Registrar, Univ. of Nottingham, 1979–84; Sen. Lectr and Consultant, Royal Free Hosp. Med. Sch., 1984–89. Postgrad. Clin. Tutor, N Staffs Hosp., 1996–2000; Chm., N Staffs Med. Inst., 2002–05; Specialty Gp Lead Reproductive Health West Midlands (North) Comprehensive Local Res. Network, 2012–; Clinical Lead, W Midlands (N) Comprehensive Local Res. Network, Reproductive Health and Childbirth, 2012. Mem., Council of Govs, Shrewsbury and Telford NHS Trust, 2012–. Vice Pres., 2004–07, Internat. Fellow, Council, 2008–, RCOG; Chm. and Founder, Internat. Soc. for Premenstrual Disorders, 2008–; Chm., British Soc. of Psychosomatic Obstetrics and Gynaecol., 2011–14. FRSocMed. Mem., Bd of Govs, Shrewsbury Girls' High Sch., GDST, 2012–. Founder and Foundn Editor-in-Chief, The Obstetrician and Gynaecologist, 1998–2004; Editor-in-Chief, Map of Medicine (Obstetrics and Gynaecol.), 2008–13. *Publications:* Premenstrual Syndrome, 1987; The Year Book of Obstetrics and Gynaecology, vol. 5, 1997, vol. 6, 1998, vol. 7, 1999, vol. 8, 2000; Problems of Early Pregnancy, 1997; Evidence Based Fertility, 1998; Gene Identification, Manipulation and Therapy, 1998; Fetal Programming, 1999; Hormones and Cancer, 1999; Introduction to Research Methodology, 1999, 2nd edn 2007; Placenta, 2000; Disorders of the Menstrual Cycle, 2000; Psychological Disorders in Obstetrics and Gynaecology, 2006; The Premenstrual Syndromes: PMS and PMDD, 2007; over 300 pubns inc. 40 chapters and numerous orig. res. papers, abstracts and revs on premenstrual syndrome, menopause, menstrual disorders (co-inventor of the menstrual pictograms), pre-eclampsia, GnRH analogues, gynaecological endocrinology. *Recreations:* classical music, jazz, play clarinet and saxophone, travel, ski-ing, sailing holidays, sculptures (2 exhibited, 2013, 4 exhibited, 2014, Weston Park Nat. Fine Art Competition). *Address:* Cardington House, Shrewsbury SY1 1ES. *T:* (01782) 672382.

O'BRIEN, His Honour Patrick William; a Circuit Judge, 1991–2014; a Deputy Circuit Judge, since 2014; *b* 20 June 1945; *s* of William C. O'Brien and Ethel M. O'Brien; *m* 1970, Antoinette Wattebot; one *s* two *d*. *Educ:* St Joseph's Academy, Blackheath; Queens' College,

Cambridge (MA, LLM). Called to the Bar, Lincoln's Inn, 1968, Bencher, 2003; practised SE Circuit; a Recorder, 1987. *Publications:* (contrib. jtly) Great Oxford: essays on the life and work of Edward de Vere, 17th Earl of Oxford, 2004. *Recreations:* cricket, choral singing, musical theatre. *Address:* Armigers, Thaxted, Dunmow, Essex CM6 2NN. *Clubs:* MCC; Norfolk (Norwich).

O'BRIEN, Prof. Paul, PhD; FRS 2013; CChem, FRSC; CEng, FIMMM; Professor of Inorganic Materials Chemistry, Manchester Materials Science Centre and School of Chemistry, University of Manchester, since 1999 (Head, School of Materials, 2013–14); *b* 22 Jan. 1954; *s* of Thomas O'Brien and Maureen O'Brien (*née* Graham); *m* 1979, Kym Evans. *Educ:* Cardinal Langley Grammar Sch., Middleton, Manchester; Univ. of Liverpool (BSc 1975); University Coll., Cardiff (PhD 1978). CChem, FRSC 1993; CEng, FIMMM (FIMM 2001). Lectr, Chelsea Coll., Univ. of London, 1978–84; Lectr, 1984–91, Reader in Inorganic Chem., 1991–94, QMC; Professor of Inorganic Chemistry: QMW, 1994; Imperial Coll., London, 1995–99; Res. Dean, Faculty of Sci. and Engrg, 2000–02, Hd, Dept of Chem., 2002–09, Acting Hd, Sch. of Materials, 2011–12, Univ. of Manchester. Vis. Prof. and Dist. MDI Schol., Molecular Design Inst., Dept of Chem., Georgia Inst. of Technol., 1997–99; Sumitomo Prof. of Materials Chem., Imperial Coll., London, 1997–99; Royal Soc. Amersham Internat. Res. Fellow, 1997–98; Dist. Vis. Schol., Inst. of Advanced Study, Durham Univ., 2011. A. G. Evans Meml Medal Lectr, Cardiff Univ., 2005. Fellow: Eur. Acad. of Scis, 2012; IUPAC; FRI; FLSW 2015; Corresp. Fellow, Worldwide Innovation Foundn, 2006. Hon. DSc: Zululand, Kwa Zulu, Natal, 2006; Liverpool, 2013; Aveiro, 2015. Potts Medal (Dist. Alumnus Award), Univ. of Liverpool, 2001; Kroll Medal and Prize, 2007, Colin Humphries Award, 2011, Platinum Medal Award, 2014, IMMM; 1st Peter Day Award in Materials Chem., RSC, 2009; Gold Medal, Soc. of Dyers and Colourists, 2015. Joint Editor: Advanced Chemistry Texts, 2003–; Nanoscience and Nanotechnology series, 2005–; Nanoscience Specialist Periodical Report, 2012–. *Publications:* (with A. C. Jones) CVD of Compound Semiconductors: precursor synthesis, development and applications, 1997; over 600 contribs to learned jls. *Recreations:* hill-walking, camping with my family and dog, reading, maintaining my elderly farmhouse/land, theatre, travel. *Address:* University of Manchester, School of Materials, Oxford Road, Manchester M13 9PL. *T:* (0161) 275 4653, (0161) 306 2279, *Fax:* (0161) 275 4616. *E:* paul.obrien@manchester.ac.uk.

O'BRIEN, Air Vice-Marshal Robert Peter, CB 1997; OBE 1983; Air Secretary, 1994–97, and Chief Executive, RAF Personnel Management Agency, 1997–98; *b* 1 Nov. 1941; *s* of Major Thomas Joseph O'Brien, MC, RE and Doris Winifred O'Brien; *m* 1964, Carole Evelyn Anne Wallace; two *s*. *Educ:* Salesian College, Farnborough; RAF College, Cranwell. BA (External) London 1962. Commissioned 1962; Pilot 31 Sqn (Canberras), 1963–66; Central Flying Sch./4FTS (Gnats), 1966–67; ADC to AOC 38 Gp, 1967–70; Flt Comdr, 15 Sqn (Buccaneers), 1970–73; Army Staff Coll., 1974; HQ RAF Germany, 1975–77; OC London UAS (Bulldogs), 1977–79; Chief Instr/TTTE (Tornados), 1980–83; Stn Comdr, RAF Marham, 1983–85; Air Staff, MoD, 1985–87; Dep. Comdr/COS HQ BF Cyprus, 1988–91; Dir of Infrastructure (RAF), MoD, 1991–92; Comdt, JSDC, 1992–94. ADC to the Queen, 1983–85. *Address:* c/o Lloyds, Cox's and King's Branch, PO Box 1190, 7 Pall Mall, SW1Y 5NA. *Club:* Royal Air Force.

O'BRIEN, Sir (Robert) Stephen, Kt 2013; CBE 1987; Chairman: Barts Health NHS Trust (formerly Barts and the London NHS Trust), since 2010; International Health Partners, since 2005; *b* 14 Aug. 1936; *s* of Robert Henry and Clare Winifred O'Brien; *m* 1st, 1958, Zoë T. O'Brien (marr. diss. 1989); two *s* two *d*; 2nd, 1989, Meriel Barclay. *Educ:* Sherborne Sch., Dorset. Joined Charles Fulton & Co. Ltd, 1956; Dir, 1964; Chm., 1973–82; Chief Exec., 1983–92, Vice-Chm., 1992–2003, Vice Pres., 2003–, BITC. Chm., Cranstoun, 1969–83 (Pres., 1983–88); Dir, Kirkland-Whittaker Co. Ltd, 1980–82. Chief Exec., London Forum, 1993–94; Vice-Chm., 1993–2005, Chief Exec., 1995–99, London First Centre, subseq. Think London; London First: Chief Exec., 1992–2002; Chm., 2002–05; Jt Pres., 2005. Chairman: Foreign Exchange and Currency Deposit Brokers Assoc., 1968–72; Project Fullemploy, 1973–91; Home Sec.'s Adv. Bd on Community Radio, 1985–86; Unitas Communications, 2007–13; London Works, 2013–. Ordained Deacon, 1971; Hon. Curate, St Lawrence Jewry, 1973–80; Chm., Christian Action, 1976–88. Vice-Chm., Church Urban Fund, 1994–2002. Pres., Esher Assoc. for Prevention of Addiction, 1979–90. Chm., UK 2000, 1988–92 (Mem. Bd, 1986–92); Director: Cities in Schools, 1989–95; Prince of Wales' Business Leaders Forum, subseq. Internat. Business Leaders Forum, 1990–2010; Member: Admin. Council, Royal Jubilee Trusts, 1984–89; Mgt Cttee, Action Resource Centre, 1986–91; Council, RSA, 1987–91; Trustee: Learning from Experience Trust, 1986–94; Immigrants Aid Trust, 1997–2007; PYBT, 1987–99; Mayor's Fund for London, 2008–; High St Fund, 2011–13; Barts Health Charity, 2012–; Chairman: Prince's Trust Regl Council for London, 2000–06; Tower Hamlets Primary Care Trust, 2005–10; Lord Mayor's Appeal Cttee, 2010–11. Chm., Unicorn Children's Th., 2006–09. Chm. Govs, UEL, 1999–2005. Hon. Fellow, QMUL, 2012. Hon. LLD Liverpool, 1994; Hon DSc City, 2000; DUniv: Middx, 2001; UEL 2005. *Recreations:* classical music, gardening, cooking. *Address:* Woodhouse, Compasses Road, Pattiswick, Essex CM77 8BB.

O'BRIEN, Prof. Sean Patrick, FRSL; freelance writer, since 1989; Professor of Creative Writing, Newcastle University, since 2006 (Visiting Professor, 2003–06); *b* 19 Dec. 1952; *s* of Patrick Francis O'Brien and Mary Irene O'Brien; partner, Ms Gerry Wardle. *Educ:* Selwyn Coll., Cambridge (BA 1974); Birmingham Univ. (MA 1977); Leeds Univ. (PGCE 1981). Teacher of English, Beacon Community Coll., Crowborough, 1981–89; Fellow in Creative Writing, Univ. of Dundee, 1989–91; Northern Arts Literary Fellow, Univs of Durham and Newcastle upon Tyne, 1992–94; Lectr on Writing (MA course), 1998, and Prof. of Poetry, 2003–06, Sheffield Hallam Univ. British Council Visiting Writer: Univ. of Odense, 1996; Hokudai Univ., Sapporo, 1997; Writer in Residence: South Bank Centre Poetry Internat., 1998; Univ. of Leeds, 1999; (with Julia Darling) Live Theatre Newcastle, 2001–03. External Examiner: MLitt, Univ. of St Andrews, 2003–06; MSc, Univ. of Edinburgh, 2006–10; MA, BA, Univ. of Manchester, 2007–10; BA, Univ. of Warwick, 2011–14; BA, Univ. of Lancaster, 2012–Sept. 2016. Specialist Advr to Scottish Arts Council, 2003–05. Vice Pres., Poetry Soc., 2006–11. Mem., Newcastle Lit. and Philosophical Soc., 1990. Mem., Vujonistas. FRSL 2007. Hon. DCL Northumbria, 2003; Hon. DLitt Hull, 2009. Gregory Award, 1979; Somerset Maugham Award, 1984; Cholmondeley Award, 1988; E. M. Forster Award, AAAL, 1993; Northern Writer of the Year, Northern Arts and New Writing North, 2001; Northern Rock Foundn Award, 2007. *Publications:* The Indoor Park, 1983; The Frighteners, 1987; HMS Glasshouse, 1991; Ghost Train (Forward Prize for Best Collection), 1995; (jtly) Penguin Modern Poets 5, 1995; The Deregulated Muse: essays on contemporary poetry in Britain and Ireland, 1998; (ed) The Firebox: poetry in Britain and Ireland after 1945, 1998; Downriver (Forward Prize for Best Collection), 2001; Cousin Coat: selected poems 1976–2001, 2002; The Birds, 2002; (jtly) Rivers, 2002; Keepers of the Flame, 2003; Laughter When We're Dead, in Live Theatre: six plays from the North East, 2003; (ed jtly) Ten Hallam Poets, 2005; (contrib.) Ellipsis 1 (short stories), 2005; The Inferno, a New Verse Version, 2006; The Drowned Book, 2007 (Forward Prize for Best Collection, 2007; T. S. Eliot Prize, 2007); The Silence Room (short stories), 2008; Afterlife (novel), 2009; (jtly) Night Train, 2009; November, 2011; Collected Poems, 2012; (ed jtly) Train Songs, 2013; The River Road, 2014; The Beautiful Librarians, 2015; (trans. with D. Hahn) Selected Poems of Corsino Fortes, 2015; Once Again Assembled Here (novel), 2016, Quartier Perdu (short stories), 2016. *Recreations:* reading, listening to music, walking the dog. *Address:* School of English Language, Literature and Linguistics, Percy Building, Newcastle upon Tyne NE1 7RU. *T:* (0191) 222 3875. *E:* sean.o'brien@newcastle.ac.uk.

O'BRIEN, Shaughn; *see* O'Brien, P. M. S.

O'BRIEN, Sir Stephen; *see* O'Brien, Sir R. S.

O'BRIEN, Rt Hon. Stephen (Rothwell); PC 2013; Under-Secretary-General for Humanitarian Affairs and Emergency Relief Coordinator, United Nations, since 2015; *b* Tanzania, 1 April 1957; *s* of David and Rothy O'Brien; *m* 1986, Gemma Townshend; two *s* one *d*. *Educ:* Sedbergh Sch.; Emmanuel Coll., Cambridge (MA); Chester Coll. of Law. Solicitor, Freshfields, 1981–88; Gp Internat. Dir and Gp Sec., Redland plc, 1988–98. MP (C) Eddisbury, July 1999–2015. PPS to Opposition spokesman on foreign affairs, 2000, to Chm. of Cons. Pty, 2000–01; an Opposition Whip, 2001–02; Shadow Financial Sec. to the Treasury, 2002; Shadow Paymaster Gen., 2002–03; Shadow Sec. of State for Industry, 2003–05; Shadow Minister for Skills and Higher Educn, 2005; Shadow Minister for Health, 2005–10; Parly Under-Sec. of State, DFID, 2010–12; Prime Minister's Envoy and Special Rep. for the Sahel, 2012–15. Member, Select Committee: on Educn and Employment, 1999–2001; on Envmt, Food and Rural Affairs, 2001. All Party Groups: Chairman: Malaria; Tanzania; Classical Music; Primary Headache Disorders; Roofing; Jt Chm., Minerals; Vice-Chairman: Aid, Trade and Debt; Member: Africa; British-American; Hong Kong. Introduced Private Members Bill on Honesty in Food Labelling, 2001 and 2003. Mem., Cons. Nat. Membership Cttee, 1999–2001; Secretary: Cons. Trade and Industry Cttee, 1999–2001; Cons. NI Cttee, 1999–2001. Associate Mem., British-Irish Inter-Parly Body, 2000–10. Mem., Internat. Investment Panel and SE Regl Council, CBI, 1995–98. UK Building Materials Producers, then Construction Products Association: Chm., Public and Parly Affairs Cttee, 1995–99; Member: Cttee of Mgt; Pres.'s Strategy Cttee; Econ. and Market Forecasting Panel, 1989–95; Parly Advr, Manufg Technologies Assoc., 2005–10. FCIS 1997 (Parly Advr, 2000–10). Director: Cambridge Univ. Careers Service, 1992–99; City of London Sinfonia, 2001–; Small Business Res. Trust, 2006–07. Chm., Malaria Consortium, 2006–10; Global Advocate, Roll Back Malaria Partnership, WHO, 2013–; Patron, Malaria No More UK, 2014–. Trustee, Bd, Liverpool Sch. of Tropical Medicine, 2006–10, 2013– (Vice Chm.); Dir/Trustee, Innovative Vector Control Consortium, 2008–10, 2015–. Chm., Chichester Cons. Assoc., 1998–99 (Vice-Pres., 1999–). Champions Award for Action on Malaria Control and Advocacy, 2015. *Recreations:* music (piano, conducting), fell-walking, historic vehicles. *Clubs:* Winsford Constitutional and Conservative; Cheshire Pitt.

O'BRIEN, Susan Joyce; QC (Scot.) 1998; Chairman, Faculty Services Ltd, 2005–07; *b* 13 Aug. 1952; *d* of Sir Frederick William Fitzgerald O'Brien, QC (Scot.) and Audrey Muriel O'Brien (*née* Owen); *m* 1978, Peter Ross, Professor of Evolutionary Computing, Napier Univ., now Emeritus; two *d*. *Educ:* St George's Sch., Edinburgh; Univ. of York (BA Hons 1973; BPhil 1976); Univ. of Edinburgh (LLB 1978). Admitted Solicitor, Scotland, 1980; Asst Solicitor, Shepherd & Wedderburn WS, 1980–86; WS 1983; admitted to Faculty of Advocates, 1987; Standing Junior Counsel to: Registrar Gen., 1991; Home Office, 1992–97; Keeper of the Registers, 1998; Temp. Sheriff, 1995–99. Chair: Caleb Ness Inquiry for Edinburgh and the Lothians Child Protection Cttee, report pub. 2003; Scottish Historical Child Abuse Inquiry, 2015–. Member: Investigatory Powers Tribunal, 2009–; Pensions Appeal Tribunals (Scotland), 2012–. Fee paid Employment Judge (formerly Chm., Employment Tribunal), 2000–. Mem., Panel of Legal Assessors for Gen. Teaching Council for Scotland, 2005–10. Reporter, Scottish Legal Aid Bd, 1999–2005. Gov., Heriot-Watt Univ., 2013–. *Address:* c/o Faculty of Advocates, Parliament Square, Edinburgh EH1 1RF. *T:* (0131) 226 5071.

O'BRIEN, Timothy Brian, RDI 1991; designer; Hon. Associate Artist, Royal Shakespeare Company, since 1988 (Associate Artist, 1966–88); *b* 8 March 1929; *s* of Brian Palliser Tiegue O'Brien and Elinor Laura (*née* Mackenzie); *m* 1997, Jenny Jones. *Educ:* Wellington Coll.; Corpus Christi, Cambridge (MA); Yale Univ. Design Dept, BBC TV, 1954; Designer, Associated Rediffusion, 1955–56; Head of Design, ABC Television, 1956–65 (The Flying Dutchman, 1958); partnership in stage design with Tazeena Firth, 1974–79; output incl.: The Bartered Bride, The Girl of the Golden West, 1962; West End prodns of new plays, 1963–64; London scene of Shakespeare Exhibn, 1964; Tango, Days in the Trees, Staircase, RSC, and Trafalgar at Madame Tussaud's, 1966; All's Well that Ends Well, As You Like It, Romeo and Juliet, RSC, 1967; The Merry Wives of Windsor, Troilus and Cressida (also Nat. Theatre, 1976), The Latent Heterosexual, RSC, 1968; Pericles (also Comédie Française, 1974), Women Beware Women, Bartholomew Fair, RSC, 1969; 1970: Measure for Measure, RSC; Madame Tussaud's in Amsterdam; The Knot Garden, Royal Opera; 1971: Enemies, Man of Mode, Merchant of Venice, RSC; 1972: La Cenerentola, Oslo; Lower Depths, The Island of the Mighty, RSC; As You Like It, OCSC; 1973: Richard II, Love's Labour's Lost, RSC; 1974: Next of Kin, NT; Summerfolk, RSC; The Bassarids, ENO; 1975: John Gabriel Borkman, NT; Peter Grimes, Royal Opera (later in Göteborg, Paris); The Marrying of Ann Leete, RSC; 1976: Wozzeck, Adelaide Fest.; The Zykovs, RSC; The Force of Habit, NT; 1977: Tales from the Vienna Woods, Bedroom Farce, NT; Falstaff, Berlin Opera; 1978: The Cunning Little Vixen, Göteborg; Evita, London (later in Australia, Austria, USA); A Midsummer Night's Dream, Sydney Opera House; 1979: The Rake's Progress, Royal Opera; 1981: Lulu, Royal Opera; 1982: La Ronde, RSC; Le Grand Macabre, ENO; 1983: Turandot, Vienna State Opera; 1984: The Mastersingers of Nuremberg, ENO; Tannhäuser, Royal Opera; 1985: Samson, Royal Opera; Sicilian Vespers, Grande Théâtre, Geneva; Old Times, Haymarket; Lucia di Lammermoor, Köln Opera; 1986: The Threepenny Opera, NT; Die Meistersinger von Nürnberg, Netherlands Opera; The American Clock, NT; 1987: Otello, and Die Entführung aus dem Serail, Royal Opera; 1988: Three Sisters, RSC; 1989: Cymbeline, RSC; Exclusive, Strand; 1990: King, Piccadilly; Love's Labours Lost, RSC; 1991: Twelfth Night, Tartuffe, Playhouse; War and Peace, Kirov, Leningrad; Beauty and the Beast, City of Birmingham Touring Opera; 1992: Christopher Columbus, RSC; 1993: Eugene Onegin, Royal Opera; Misha's Party, RSC; 1994: On Approval, Playhouse; The Clandestine Marriage, Queen's; 1995: The Merry Wives of Windsor, NT; The Merry Wives of Windsor, Oslo; 1996: Outis, La Scala, Milan; 1997: A Christmas Carol, Clwyd; 1998: Evita, US tour; 1999: Twelfth Night, Macbeth, Clwyd; 2001: Bedroom Farce, Clwyd; 2002: Romeo and Juliet, Clwyd; 2004: Werther, Lisbon; 2005: Ulysses Comes Home, Birmingham Opera Co.; 2006: Das Rheingold, Lisbon; 2007: Die Walküre, Lisbon; 2008: Siegfried, Lisbon, 2008; Macbeth, Clwyd, 2008; Götterdämmerung, Lisbon, 2009. Chm., Soc. of British Theatre Designers, 1984–91; Master, Faculty of RDI, 1999–2001. Trustee, Useful Simple Trust, 2008. (Jtly) Gold Medal for Set Design, Prague Quadriennale, 1975; (jtly) Golden Triga, for Best Nat. Exhibit, Prague Quadriennale, 1991. *Address:* The Level, Blackbridge Road, Freshwater Bay, Isle of Wight PO40 9QP. *E:* all@highwaterjones.com.

O'BRIEN, Sir Timothy John, 7th Bt *cr* 1849; *b* 6 July 1958; *s* of John David O'Brien (*d* 1980) and of Sheila Winifred, *o d* of Sir Charles Arland Maitland Freake, 4th Bt; *S* grandfather, 1982, but his name does not appear on the Official Roll of the Baronetage; *m* 2000, Susannah, *yr d* of Bryan Farr; three *d*. *Educ:* Millfield; Univ. of Hartford, Conn. *Heir:* *b* James Patrick Arland O'Brien [*b* 22 Dec. 1964; *m* 1992, Lianna Mace; two *s* one *d*].

O'BRIEN, Dame Una, DCB 2015 (CB 2011); Permanent Secretary, Department of Health, since 2010; *b* Solihull, 23 Dec. 1957; *d* of Patrick O'Brien and Margaret O'Brien. *Educ:* Convent HCJ, Birmingham; St Anne's Coll., Oxford (BA Hons Modern Hist.); Harvard Univ. (Kennedy Schol.); London Sch. of Econs (MSc Econ Internat. Relns). Parly res. asst to Lab. frontbench spokesmen on NI, 1980–82; Res. Officer, Inst. of Educn, Univ. of London, 1984–86; Corporate Services Manager, London Lighthouse, 1987–90; Department of Health, 1990–: Policy Manager, for people with physical disability, 1990–92; Performance Manager, NHS W Midlands, NHS Mgt Exec., 1992–93; Private Sec., Minister of State for Health,

1993–94; Principal Private Sec., Sec. of State for Transport, 1994–95; Dep. Dir, Prime Minister's Efficiency Unit, Cabinet Office, 1996–98; Sec., Public Inquiry into Paediatric Cardiac Surgery in Bristol (Kennedy Inquiry), 1998–2001; on secondment to NHS as Dir, Develt and Clin. Governance, UCL NHS Foundn Trust, 2002–05; Dir, Provider Reform, Policy, 2005–07; Dir Gen., Policy and Strategy, 2007–10. Gov., Jack Tizard Sch., Hammersmith, 2006–09. *Recreations:* travel, theatre, walking, the River Thames. *Address:* Department of Health, Richmond House, 70 Whitehall, SW1A 2NS. *T:* (020) 7210 5762. *E:* una.o'brien@dh.gsi.gov.uk.

O'BRIEN, Sir William, Kt 2010; JP; *b* 25 Jan. 1929; *m* Jean; three *d. Educ:* St Joseph's Sch., Castleford; Leeds Univ. (BEd 1961). Coalminer, 1945–83. Wakefield DC: Mem., 1973–83; former Dep. Leader and Chm., Finance and Gen. Purposes Cttee. Mem., NUM, 1945–; Local Branch Official, 1956–83. MP (Lab) Normanton, 1983–2005. Opposition front bench spokesman on the Environment, 1987–92, for Northern Ireland, 1992–96. Member: Public Accounts Cttee, 1983–88; Energy Select Cttee, 1986–88; Envmt, Transport and Regions Select Cttee, 1997–2005; Public Accounts Commn, 1997–2005. Chm., Dr Jackson Cancer Fund, Pontefract, 1996–; Sec., Pontefract Groups Together, 2006; Mem., Pontefract Town Centre Partnership, 2008–; Friend, Pontefract Castle Gp, 2009–; Sec., Pontefract Magna Carta Gp, 2013–. Governor: Carleton Community High Sch., 2006; Orchard Head Primary Sch., 2007. JP Wakefield, 1979. *Recreations:* reading, organising, gardening. *Address:* 29 Limetrees, Ferrybridge Road, Pontefract WF8 2QB.

O'BRIEN, Adm. Sir William (Donough), KCB 1969 (CB 1966); DSC 1942; Commander-in-Chief, Western Fleet, Feb. 1970–Sept. 1971, retd Nov. 1971; Vice-Admiral of the United Kingdom and Lieutenant of the Admiralty, 1984–86; *b* 13 Nov. 1916; *s* of late Major W. D. O'Brien, Connaught Rangers and I. R. Caroe (*née* Parnis); *m* 1943, Rita Micallef, Sliema, Malta; one *s* two *d. Educ:* Royal Naval Coll., Dartmouth. Served War of 1939–45: HM Ships Garland, Wolsey, Witherington, Offa, 1939–42; Cottesmore i/c, 1943–44; Arakan Coast, 1945. HMS Venus i/c, 1948–49; Commander 1949; HMS Ceylon, 1952; Admiralty, 1953–55; Captain, 1955; Captain (D) 8th DS in HMS Cheviot, 1958–59; HMS Hermes i/c, 1961–64; Rear-Admiral 1964; Naval Secretary, 1964–66; Flag Officer, Aircraft Carriers, 1966–67; Comdr, Far East Fleet, 1967–69; Admiral 1969. Rear-Admiral of the UK, 1979–84. Chairman: Kennet and Avon Canal Trust, 1974–91; King George's Fund for Sailors, 1974–86. Pres., Assoc. of RN Officers, 1973–88. *Address:* 16/17 Hays Park, near Shaftesbury, Dorset SP7 9JR. *T:* (01747) 830989.

O'BRIEN QUINN, James Aiden; *see* Quinn.

OBRIST, Hans Ulrich; Co-Director, Exhibitions and Programmes, and Director, International Projects, Serpentine Gallery, since 2006; *b* Zurich, 21 May 1968; *s* of Fritz Obrist and Ella Obrist (*née* Bernegger). *Educ:* Univ. of Gallen (Economy and Soc. Scis). Curator in Residence, Cartier Foundn, Paris, 1991; Founder and Head, Migrateurs prog., 1993–2006, Curator, 2000–06, Musée d'Art Moderne de la Ville de Paris; Curator, Museum in Progress, Vienna, 1993–2000. Lectr, Univ. of Lüneburg, 1993–2000; Prof., Univ. of Venice, 2000. Founder and Ed. in Chief, Point d'Ironie, 1997–. Has curated over 250 exhibitions. *Publications:* (ed) Gerhard Richter's Sils, 1992; (ed) Gerhard Richter's Text: schriften und interviews, 1993; (ed) Paul-Armand Gette's Nymphaeum, 1993; (ed) Bertrand Lavier's Argo, 1994; (ed) Christian Boltanski's Les Vacances à Berck-Plage (About 1975), 1995; (ed) Annette Messager's Nos Témoignages, 1995; (ed) Gerhard Richter's The Daily Practice of Painting: writings and interviews 1962–93, 1995; Do It, 1995; (ed) Gilbert & George's Oh, the Grand Old Duke of York, 1996; (ed jtly) The Words of Gilbert & George, with Portraits of the Artists from 1968 to 1997, 1997; (ed jtly) Unbuilt Roads, 107 Unrealised Projects, 1997; (ed jtly) Sogni/Dreams, 1999; (ed jtly) Weltwissen Wissenwelt: Das globale Netz von Text und Bild, 2000; (ed jtly) Interarchive: archival practices and sites in the contemporary art field, 2002; (ed jtly) Bridge the Gap?, 2002; Hans Ulrich Obrist: interviews, vol. 1, 2003; (ed) Do It, 2004; (ed jtly) Prefaces by Hans Ulrich Obrist 1989–2005, 2005; (ed jtly) Smithson Time: a dialogue, 2005; (ed jtly) Matthew Barney: drawing restraint 1987–2002 v.1, 2006; (jtly) Anri Sala, 2006; (with Pedro Reyes) El Aire Es Azul/The Air is Blue, 2006; (jtly) donststopdontstopdontstopdontstop, 2006; (with Robert Violette) The Words of Gilbert & George, 2006; (ed jtly) Barry Flanagan: sculpture 1965–2005, 2006; Hans Ulrich Obrist: everything you always wanted to know about curating but were afraid to ask, 2007; (with Nicolas Trembley) The Secret Files of Gilbert and George, 2007; (with Pedro Reyes) The Air is Blue—Art Meets Architecture: Luis Barragan revisited, 2007; The Future Will Be…, 2007; (jtly) Ryan Gander: intellectual colours, 2007; (with Adrian Notz) Merz World: processing the complicated order, 2007; (ed jtly) Rirkrit Tiravanija—A Retrospective, 2007; (jtly) Olafur Eliasson: the Goose Lake Trail (Southern Route), 2007; (jtly) Thomas Bayrle: 40 years of Chinese rock 'n' roll, 2007; Formulas for Now, 2008; (jtly) Susan Hefuna: Pars Pro Toto, 2008; (jtly) Victor Man, 2008; (with Dietmar Elger) Gerhard Richter: text, writings, interviews and letters, 2009; (ed) Susan Hefuna: Pars Pro Toto II, 2009; (jtly) Ways Beyond Art: Ai Weiwei, 2009; Hans Ulrich Obrist: interviews, vol. 2, 2010; (ed) London a Portrait of a City: Serpentine Gallery 24-hour interview marathon, 2010; (jtly) Marianne Heske: a doll's house, 2011; Ways of Curating, 2014; The Conversation Series: Rem Koolhaas, 2007; Yona Friedman, 2007; Wolfgang Tillmans, 2007; Gilbert and George, 2007; Zaha Hadid, 2007; Thomas Demand, 2007; John Chamberlain, 2007; Konrad Klapheck, 2007; Robert Crumb, 2007; Olafur Eliasson, 2008; Nancy Spero, 2008; Philippe Parreno, 2008; Dominique Gonzalez-Foerster, 2008; Christian Boltanski, 2009; Gustav Metzger, 2009; Enzo Mari, 2009; Ken Adam and Katharina Fritsch, 2009; John Baldessari, 2010; Yoko Ono, 2010; Hens-Peter Feldmann, 2010; Rosemarie Trockel, 2010; Jeff Koons, 2010; Cedric Price, 2010; Marina Abramovic, 2010; Lucien Hervé, 2011; Rirkrit Tiravanija, 2011; Cerith Wyn Evans, 2011; Dan Graham, 2012; Kazuyo Sejima, 2012; Claude Parent, 2012; Edouard Glissant, 2012; Lives of the Artists, Lives of the Architects, 2015; contributing editor for internat. art magazines incl. Artforum, Atlantica, Flash Art Internat., der Freund, Paradis Mag., Numero d and Trans. *Address:* Serpentine Gallery, Kensington Gardens, W2 3XA. *T:* (020) 7402 6075, *Fax:* (020) 7402 4103. *E:* information@serpentinegallery.org.

OBUNGE, Rev. Onimim Loloba, (Nims), MBE 2008; DL; Minister in Charge, Freedom's Ark Church, Tottenham, since 1993; Founder and Chief Executive, Peace Alliance, since 2001; *b* London, 2 Jan. 1965; *s* of late Ambassador Daye Dagogo Obunge and of Lady Emma Sokari Obunge; *m* 1996, Edosa Jacqueline Arthur; one *s* one *d. Educ:* Univ. of Jos, Nigeria (BSc Politics and Internat. Law 1986); Hampstead Bible Sch. Ordained Minister, 1990; Associate Pastor, Victory Ch, Finchley, then Sen. Pastor, Victory Ch, Tottenham, 1990–93. Chm., ind. adv. gp, London Criminal Justice Partnership, 2007–. Mem., Roundtable for Gun Crime, 2002–, Stop and Search Action Team, 2005–, Home Office. Member: London Adv. Bd, CRE, 2004–07; Adv. Bd, London Crime Stoppers, 2005–. Metropolitan Police Authority: Member: Trident Ind. Adv. Gp, 2002–; Stop and Search Security Panel, 2003; Ind. Adv. Gp, Operation Blunt, 2005–07. Borough of Haringey: Member: Local Strategic Partnership, 2005–; Crime Disorder Reduction Partnership, 2005–; Chm., Other Violent Crime Partnership Bd, 2006–. Mem. Bd, Spring Harvest, 2007–09. Ecumenical Bor. Dean, 2000–. Police Chaplain, Haringey Police, 2000–. Founder and Mem., Haringey Multifaith Forum (Chm., 2002–05); Founder, Haringey and London Week of Peace, 2001–. DL Greater London, 2009. *Recreations:* swimming, table tennis, lawn tennis. *Address:* The Peace Alliance/ Freedom's Ark, Tottenham Town Hall, Town Hall Approach, N15 4RY. *T:* (020) 8808 9439, (020) 8493 0050, *Fax:* (020) 8493 0058. *E:* info@peacealliance.org.uk.

O'BYRNE, Andrew John Martin; QC 2006; *b* 23 April 1950; *s* of late Andrew John O'Byrne and Winifred O'Byrne; *m* 1977, Anne Victoria Roby; two *s. Educ:* St Joseph's Coll., Blackpool; Univ. of Liverpool (LLB). Called to the Bar, Gray's Inn, 1978, Bencher, 2014; in practice, specialising in criminal law, incl. serious fraud. Mem., Bar Council, 2013–. Leader, Northern Circuit, 2014–. *Recreations:* family, reading, good wine, good company. *Address:* St Johns Buildings, 24a–28 St John Street, Manchester M3 4DJ. *T:* (0161) 214 1500, *Fax:* (0161) 835 3929.

O'CARROLL, Derek; Sheriff of South Strathclyde, Dumfries and Galloway at Airdrie, since 2014; *b* St Albans, 20 Jan. 1960; *s* of Maurice and Ita O'Carroll; *m* 2001, Julia Maguire; one *s. Educ:* Austin Friars Sch., Carlisle; Cults Acad., Aberdeen; Edinburgh Univ. (LLB Hons; DipLP). Solicitor, 1991–99; called to the Scottish Bar, 2000; Chairman: Social Security Tribunal, 1999–2007; Rent Assessment Cttee, 2002–07; Private Rented Housing Panel, 2002–07; Convener, Mental Health Tribunal, 2005–10; Sheriff (pt-time), 2006–10; All-Scotland Floating Sheriff, based in Edinburgh, 2010–14. Mem., Scottish Legal Aid Bd, 1998–2002. Dir, Faculty Services Ltd, 2003–07; Mem., Faculty of Advocates, 2000– (Mem. Council, 2005–08); Hon. Sec. Sheriffs' Assoc., 2015– (Mem. Council, 2011–14). *Publications:* contrib. articles and pubns on legal topics especially landlord and tenant/housing law, public law, employment/discrimination law. *Recreations:* travel, swimming, pool, keeping fit, good food and drink. *Address:* Sheriff Court House, Graham Street, Airdrie ML6 6EE. *E:* sheriffdocarroll@scotcourts.gov.uk.

O'CATHAIN, Baroness *cr* 1991 (Life Peer), of The Barbican in the City of London; **Detta O'Cathain,** OBE 1983; Managing Director, Barbican Centre, 1990–95; *b* 3 Feb. 1938; *d* of late Caoimhghin O'Cathain and Margaret O'Cathain; *m* 1968, William Bishop (*d* 2001). *Educ:* Laurel Hill, Limerick; University College, Dublin (BA). Aer Lingus, Dublin, 1961–66; Group Economist, Tarmac, 1966–69; Economic Advr, Rootes Motors, 1969–72; Sen. Economist, Carrington Vyella, 1972–73; Economic Advr, British Leyland, 1973–74; Dir, Market Planning, Leyland Cars, 1974–76; Corporate Planning Exec., Unigate, 1976–81; Milk Marketing Board: Head of Strategic Planning, 1981–83; Dir and Gen. Manager, 1984; Man. Dir Milk Marketing, 1985–88. Advr on Agricl Marketing to Minister of Agriculture, 1979–83. Member: British-Irish Parly Assembly, 2008–11; Council of Europe, 2009; WEU, 2009. Non-executive Director: Midland Bank, 1984–93; Channel 4, 1985–86; Tesco, 1985–2000; Sears, 1987–94; British Airways, 1993–2004; BET, 1994–96; BNP Paribas (formerly BNP) UK Holdings Ltd, 1995–2005; Thistle Hotels, 1996–2003; South East Water plc, 1998–2008; William Baird Plc, 2000–02; Allders plc, 2000–03. FCIM 1987 (Pres., 1998–2001); FRSA 1986. Hon. Fellow, Harris Manchester Coll., Oxford, 2008. Mem., Brooklands Mus. Trust, 2006–10 (Chm., Appeal Bd, 2007–10). Chm. Council, Chichester Cathedral, 2010–. Commander: Royal Norwegian Order, 1992; Order of the Lion (Finland), 1992; Mem., Order of Pres. of Azerbaijan, 2011. *Recreations:* music, reading, walking, gardening. *Address:* House of Lords, SW1A 0PW. *T:* (020) 7219 0662. *Club:* Athenæum.

O'CEALLAIGH, Dáithí; Director General, Institute of International and European Affairs, Dublin, 2010–13; Chairman, Press Council of Ireland, since 2010; *b* 24 Feb. 1945; *m* 1968, Antoinette Reilly; one *s* one *d. Educ:* University College Dublin (BA). Teacher, Zambia, 1968–71; entered Diplomatic Service, Ireland, 1973; Third Sec., 1973, First Sec., 1974, Dept of Foreign Affairs; First Sec., Moscow, 1975–77, London, 1977–82; First Sec., 1982–85, Counsellor, 1985, Anglo-Irish Div., Dublin; Counsellor, Anglo-Irish Secretariat, Maryfield, 1985–87; Consul General, New York, 1987–93; Ambassador, Finland and Estonia, 1993–98; Asst Sec., Admin Div., 1998–2000; Second Sec. General, Anglo-Irish Div., 2000–01, Dublin; Ambassador: to UK, 2001–07; to UN, Geneva, 2007–09. Hon. Prof., Inst. of Irish Studies, Univ. of Liverpool, 2007. Hon. Dr Geneva Sch. of Diplomacy and Internat. Relns, 2010. Comdr, First Class, Order of White Rose of Finland, 2004. *Publications:* (ed jtly) Britain and Europe: the endgame, an Irish perspective, 2015. *Recreations:* bird-watching, cinema, history, theatre, jazz, vintage cars. *Address:* 1 Vesey Place, Dun Laoghaire, Co. Dublin, Ireland.

OCEAN, Humphrey; *see* Butler-Bowdon, H. A. E.

OCKELTON, (Christopher) Mark (Glyn); a Vice President, Upper Tribunal (Immigration and Asylum Chamber) (formerly Deputy President, Immigration Appeal Tribunal, later Asylum and Immigration Tribunal), since 2000; a Recorder, since 2003; a Deputy High Court Judge, since 2008; *b* 11 July 1955; *s* of Denis William Ockelton and Elvire Mabel Louise Jeanne (*née* May); *m* 1992, Brigid Joan Oates; one step *s* one step *d. Educ:* Winchester Coll.; Peterhouse, Cambridge (BA 1976; MA 1980); BD London 1989. Called to the Bar, Lincoln's Inn, 1977 (Bencher, 2001); Lectr in Law, 1979–93, Sen. Lectr, 1993–96, Hon. Fellow, 1996–2003, Vis. Fellow, 2003–, Univ. of Leeds; Immigration Adjudicator, 1992–96; Chm., 1996–2000, Vice-Pres., Jan.–May 2000, Immigration Appeal Tribunal. Vis. Prof. of Law, Univ. of Louisville, 1984–85; Vis. Lectr, Univ. du Maine, France, 1989. Parish Clerk: St Mary's Ch, Whitby, 1994–; St Mary's Ch, Rotherhithe, 2004–. Dep. Chancellor, Dio. of Hereford, 2010–. Mem., Ancient Soc. of Coll. Youths, 1974–; Parish Clerks' Co., 2005–. Hon. Col, Commonwealth of Ky, 1985. *Publications:* The Tower, Bells and Ringers of Great St Mary's, Cambridge, 1981; Trusts for Accountants, 1987; Heydon and Ockelton's Evidence: cases and materials, 3rd edn 1991, 4th edn 1996; contrib. articles and reviews in legal, philosophical, antiquarian and campanological jls. *Recreations:* books, bells, buildings. *Address:* Upper Tribunal (Immigration and Asylum Chamber), Field House, 15–25 Bream's Buildings, EC4A 1DZ. *Club:* Athenæum.

OCKENDON, Prof. John Richard, FRS 1999; Professor of Mathematics, University of Oxford, 2008–10, now Emeritus; Fellow, St Catherine's College, Oxford, 1965–2010, now Emeritus; *b* 13 Oct. 1940; *s* of George and Doris Ockendon; *m* 1967, Hilary Mason; one *d. Educ:* Dulwich Coll.; St John's Coll., Oxford (MA; DPhil 1965). Lectr, Christ Church, Oxford, 1963–65; University of Oxford: Lectr in Applicable Maths, 1975–2008; Res. Dir, Oxford Centre for Industrial and Applied Maths, 1989–2009; Dir, Oxford Centre for Collaborative Applied Maths, 2008–10. Adv. Prof., Fudan Univ., Shanghai, 1999; Adjunct Prof., Univ. Teknologi Malaysia, 2014. Chair, Scientific Cttee, Smith Inst. Knowledge Transfer Network, 2001–08; Chief Mathematician and Tech. Dir, Smith Inst. for Industrial Maths and System Engrg, 2014–. SIAM Fellow, 2009. Gold Medal, IMA, 2006. *Publications:* (with C. Elliott) Free Boundary Problems, 1981; (with H. Ockendon) Viscous Flow, 1997; (jtly) Applied Partial Differential Equations, 1999; (with H. Ockendon) Waves and Compressible Flow, 2003; (jtly) Applied Solid Mechanics, 2008. *Recreations:* bird watching, Hornby-Dublo, old sports cars. *Address:* Mathematical Institute, University of Oxford, Andrew Wiles Building, Radcliffe Observatory Quarter, Woodstock Road, Oxford OX2 6GG. *T:* (01865) 270513.

OCONE, Prof. Raffaella, PhD; FIChemE; CEng, FREng; FRSE; FRSC; Professor of Chemical Engineering, Heriot-Watt University, since 1999; *b* Morcone, Italy, 14 Jan. 1960; *d* of Giuseppe Ocone and Franca Ocone (*née* Lombardi). *Educ:* Univ. di Napoli, Federico II (Laurea, Chem. Engrg); Princeton Univ. (MA 1989; PhD 1992). FIChemE 2003; CEng 2003; CSci 2005; FRSC 2009; FREng 2013. Lectr, Univ. di Napoli, Federico II, 1991–95; Reader, Univ. of Nottingham, 1995–99. Visiting Professor: Louisiana State Univ., 1992–93; Univ. Claude Bérnard, Lyon, 1994–95. FRSE 2006; FRSA 2009. Cavaliere, Ordine della Stella della Solidarità (Italy), 2006. *Publications:* (with G. Astarita) Special Topics in Transport Phenomena, 2002; contribs to scientific pubns. *Recreations:* reading, classical music, opera, fiction, gym, playing the piano badly; does not own a TV. *Address:* Chemical Engineering, School of Engineering and Physical Sciences, Heriot-Watt University, Edinburgh EH14 4AS. *T:* (0131) 451 3129. *E:* r.ocone@hw.ac.uk.

O'CONNELL, Sir Bernard, Kt 2004; management consultant, 2004–08; Principal and Chief Executive Officer, Runshaw College, Lancashire, 1984–2004; *b* 16 April 1945; *s* of Richard and Brigid O'Connell; *m* 1966, Jane; one *s* one *d*. *Educ:* London Univ. (BSc Econ.); Liverpool Univ. (MA, MEd); Manchester Univ. (Teacher's Cert.). Millbank Coll. of Commerce, 1968–79; Vice-Principal, Old Swan Tech. Coll., 1979–84. *Publications:* Creating an Outstanding College, 2005; college manuals. *Recreations:* watching Liverpool FC, travel, reading. *Address:* 28 Magazine Brow, Wallasey, Merseyside CH45 1HP. *T:* (0151) 639 1556. *E:* oconnellbernard@yahoo.co.uk.

O'CONNELL, Cathy; *see* Newman, C.

O'CONNELL, Enda; *see* O'Connell, P. E.

O'CONNELL, Sir Maurice (James Donagh MacCarthy), 7th Bt *cr* 1869, of Lakeview, Killarney and Ballybeggan, Tralee; *b* 10 June 1958; *s* of Sir Morgan Donal Conail O'Connell, 6th Bt and of Elizabeth, *o d* of late Major John MacCarthy O'Leary; *S* father, 1989; *m* 1993, Francesca, *d* of late Clive Raleigh; one *s*. *Heir: s* Morgan Daniel Clive MacCarthy O'Connell, *b* 17 Nov. 2003. *Address:* Lakeview House, Killarney, Co. Kerry, Ireland.

O'CONNELL, Prof. (Patrick) Enda, PhD; CEng, FREng; FICE; Professor of Water Resources Engineering, Newcastle University (formerly University of Newcastle upon Tyne), since 1984; *b* 3 April 1945; *s* of Patrick and Cecilia O'Connell; *m* 1974, Jane Rosemary; one *s* two *d*. *Educ:* University Coll., Galway (BEng 1st Cl. Hons (Civil)); Imperial Coll., London (DIC; PhD). Asst Lectr, 1968–69, Lectr, 1969–76, Dept of Civil Engrg, Imperial Coll., London; Section/Div. Hd, NERC Inst. of Hydrol., 1976–84; Dir, Water Resource Systems Res. Lab., Sch. of Civil Engrg and Geoscis, 1984–2009, Earth Systems Engrg, 2003–09, Univ. of Newcastle upon Tyne, later Newcastle Univ. FREng 2005. *Publications:* contrib. internat. jls incl. Jl Hydrol., Hydrological Processes, Hydrological Scis, Hydrol., Earth Systems Scis, Sci. of the Total Envmt, Water Resources Mgt, Water Resources Res. *Recreations:* walking in the Yorkshire Dales, ski-ing, salmon angling in the West of Ireland (Mem., Irish Internat. Trout Angling Team, 1967–69), enjoying the food and wines of Tuscany. *Address:* School of Civil Engineering and Geosciences, Newcastle University, Newcastle upon Tyne NE1 7RU. *T:* (0191) 222 6405, *Fax:* (0191) 222 6669. *E:* enda.oconnell@ncl.ac.uk.

O'CONNELL, Stephen; Member (C) Croydon and Sutton, London Assembly, Greater London Authority, since 2008; *b* Dulwich, 9 Sept. 1956; *s* of Ronald John and Phyllis Jean O'Connell; two *s*. *Educ:* Brockley Co. Grammar Sch. CeMAP 2000; CeFA 2001. Barclays Bank, 1976–2005. Mem. (C) Croydon Council, 2002– (Cabinet Member: Safety and Cohesion, 2006–08; Regeneration and Econ. Develt, 2008–10; Community Safety, 2010–11; Finance and Performance, 2011–14; Dep. Leader, 2006–08; Shadow Spokesman on Finance, 2014–15, on Safety and Justice, 2015–). Mem., Metropolitan Police Authy, 2008–12 (Chm., Finance Cttee, 2008–11); non-exec. Advr, Mayor's Office for Policing and Crime, 2013–. Trustee: Crystal Palace FC Foundn, 2013–; Purley Young People's Club, 2015–. FRSA. *Recreations:* dog walking, real ale, political literature, Crystal Palace Football Club. *Address:* Greater London Authority, City Hall, The Queen's Walk, SE1 2AA. *T:* (020) 7983 4405, *Fax:* (020) 7983 4419. *E:* Steve.O'Connell@london.gov.uk. *W:* www.steveoconnell.org, www.twitter.com/steveo_connell.

O'CONNOR, Biddie; *see* O'Connor, B. A.

O'CONNOR, Rev. Canon (Brian) Michael (McDougal); Dean of Auckland, New Zealand, 1997–2000; *b* 20 June 1942; *s* of Brian McDougal O'Connor and Beryl O'Connor; *m* 1968, Alison Margaret Tibbutt (marr. diss. 2004); two *s*. *Educ:* Lancing Coll.; St Catharine's Coll., Cambridge (BA, MA); Cuddesdon Coll., Oxford. Admitted Solicitor, 1964; Asst Curate, St Andrew, Headington, 1969–72; Sec., Oxford Dio. Pastoral Cttee, 1972–79; Vicar, Rainham, Kent, 1979–97; Rural Dean of Gillingham, 1981–88; Priest-in-charge, Little Missenden, 2002–04. Hon. Canon: of Rochester Cathedral, 1988–97; of Auckland Cathedral, 2000–. Church Comr, 1995–97. Member: General Synod, 1975–90 (Mem., Standing Cttee, 1985–90); Crown Appointments Commn, 1987–90; ACC, 1988–92. Deleg., WCC Assembly, Canberra, 1991. Commissary for Bishop: of Auckland, NZ, 1996–97; of Newcastle, NSW, 1996–. Exec. Officer, Ecclesiastical Law Soc., 2001–07. *Address:* 1 Steadys Lane, Stanton Harcourt, Witney, Oxon OX29 5RL. *T:* (01865) 882776. *E:* canonmichaeloc@aol.com.

O'CONNOR, Bridget Anne, (Biddie); Headmistress, Haberdashers' Aske's School for Girls, Elstree, since 2011; *b* Chesterfield, 28 April 1958; *d* of John O'Connor and Joan O'Connor (*née* Mears); *m* 1982, Simon Salem; one *d*. *Educ:* St Helena's Sch., Chesterfield; St Hugh's Coll., Oxford (BA Lit.Hum. 1980); Sidney Sussex Coll., Cambridge (PGCE 1981). Asst Classics Teacher and Form Tutor, Clarence Gate, Francis Holland Sch., 1981–84; Asst Classics Teacher, then Hd of Dept, Old Palace Sch., Croydon, 1984–91; Haberdashers' Aske's School for Girls, Elstree: Hd of Classics, 1991–97; Hd of Sixth Form, 1993–98; Dep. Headmistress, 1998–2002; Headmistress, Loughborough High Sch., 2002–11. *Recreations:* reading, cooking, art, gardening, walking. *Address:* Haberdashers' Aske's School for Girls, Aldenham Road, Elstree, Herts WD6 3BT. *T:* (020) 8266 2300. *E:* biddieoc@habsgirls.org.uk.

O'CONNOR, Christopher; Director, Chris O'Connor & Associates Ltd, since 2013; *b* Poynton, 21 April 1966; *s* of Patrick O'Connor and Veronica O'Connor; partner, Susan Chennell; one *d*. *Educ:* Salford Univ. (BEng Hons Electronic Engrg); Manchester Business Sch. (MBA). Design Engr, British Aerospace, 1989–91; Programme Manager: Hewlett-Packard, 1991–2000; Agilent Technologies, 2000–06; Dir, Bradford-i Business Transformation Prog., City of Bradford MDC, 2006–07; Dir, 2008–10, Chief Exec., Shared Services, 2010–13, DfT. *Recreations:* all forms of motorsport (watching), rallying (competing). *Address:* Chris O'Connor & Associates Ltd, Common Lodge, Moss Lane, St Michaels, Preston PR3 0TY. *T:* (01995) 679396. *E:* chris.oconnor@coassociates.co.uk.

O'CONNOR, Christopher Paul, OBE 2012; HM Diplomatic Service; Consul-General, Los Angeles, since 2013; *b* Epsom, 18 Dec. 1968; *m* Martha Dorothy Nelems; two *d*. *Educ:* Fitzwilliam Coll., Cambridge (BA Hons 1991); Durham Univ. (MA 1993). Entered FCO, 1993; Southern Eur. Dept, FCO, 1993–94; UN/Internat. Orgns Res. Gp, London, 1994–95; Attaché, Cairo, 1995–96; Second Sec., Riyadh, 1996–99; First Sec., UK Delegn to NATO, 1999; Sen. Policy Advr, Canadian Dept for Foreign Affairs, 1999–2000 (on secondment); Head: Political Section, Ottawa, 2000–03; ME Peace Process Team, FCO, 2003–05; Dep. Hd of Mission, Beirut, 2006–08; Ambassador to Tunisia, 2008–13. *Recreations:* learning languages, being a father. *Address:* c/o Foreign and Commonwealth Office, King Charles Street, SW1A 2AH.

O'CONNOR, His Eminence Cardinal Cormac M.; *see* Murphy-O'Connor.

O'CONNOR, Hon. Deirdre Frances; Judge, Federal Court of Australia, 1990–2002; President, Administrative Appeals Tribunal, 1990–94 and 1999–2002; *b* 5 Feb. 1941; *d* of D. A. Buff; *m* 1974, Michael John Joseph, SC; four *s* (and one *s* decd). *Educ:* Bethlehem Coll., Ashfield; Sydney Univ. (BA 1961; LLB 1st Cl. Hons 1974); DipEd New England 1963. Teacher of hist., various high schs and tech. colls, 1963–74; Lectr in Law, Univ. of NSW, 1974–75; Sen. Lectr in Law, Macquarie Univ., 1975–78; part-time Lectr on media and law, Aust. Film and TV Sch., 1975–80; admitted NSW Bar, 1980; Comr, NSW Law Reform Commn, 1983–85; Chm., Aust. Broadcasting Tribunal, 1986–90. President: Nat. Native Title Tribunal, 1993–94; Aust. Industrial Relns Commn, 1994–97. Mediator, NSW Workers Compensation Commn, 2002; Judicial Mem., NSW Parole Authy (formerly Parole Bd), 2003– (Alternate Chm.). Chm., Telephone Information Services Standards Council, 2010–. Mem., Aust. Inst. Judicial Admin, 1992–. Trustee, Internat. Inst. of Communications, 1989–92. Member, Council: Order of Australia, 1990–96; Univ. of Canberra, 1992–95. *Recreations:* reading, antiques.

O'CONNOR, Sir Denis (Francis), Kt 2010; CBE 2002; QPM 1996; HM Chief Inspector of Constabulary, 2009–12; *b* 21 May 1949; *m* 1972, Louise (*née* Harvey); one *s* two *d*. *Educ:* La Sainte Union Coll.; Southampton Univ. (BEd Hons 1974); Cranfield Inst. of Technol. (MSc 1985). Chief Supt, Notting Hill, 1990; Asst Chief Constable, Surrey Police, 1991; Dep. Chief Constable, Kent Constabulary, 1993; Asst Comr, SW Area, later S London, Metropolitan Police, 1997–2000; Chief Constable, Surrey Police, 2000–04; HM Inspector of Constabulary, 2004–09. Former Member: Criminal Justice Wkg Gp, Adv. Council on Misuse of Drugs; DoH Task Force on Effectiveness of Drugs Services; Mem., Ind. Inquiry into the Misuse of Drugs Act 1971, 1997–2000. Vice-Pres., ACPO, 2002–04. Radzinowicz Fellow, Inst. of Criminology, Univ. of Cambridge, 2013. Hon. DLaws Wolverhampton, 2013. *Publications:* Developing a Partnership Approach for Drugs Education, 1992; Management by Objectives on Trial, 1992; Community Policing: are good intentions enough?, 1994; Increasing Community Safety from Drug Related Crime, 1995; Criminal Justice: what works?, 1995; Drugs: partnerships for policy, prevention and education, 1998; Performance from the Outside-In, 2010; article in Criminal Justice Jl. *Recreations:* reading, walking, gardening.

O'CONNOR, Desmond Bernard, (Des), CBE 2008; entertainer and singer; *b* 12 Jan. 1932; *m* 1st, Phyllis; one *d*; 2nd, Gillian Vaughan; two *d*; 3rd, Jay; one *d*; 4th, Jodie Brooke Wilson; one *s*. Served RAF. Former Butlin's Red Coat, Filey; professional début, Palace Theatre, Newcastle upon Tyne, 1953; one-man shows, UK, Canada, USA and Australia, 1980–; Royal Variety Show appearances, incl. compère, 1997; musicals: Dreamboats and Petticoats, Playhouse, London, 2011–12; Wizard of Oz, London Palladium, 2012. *Television includes:* Spot the Tune, 1958; Sunday Night at the London Palladium; Take Your Pick, 1992, 1994, 1996; Pot of Gold, 1993, 1995; Countdown, 2007–08; own shows: The Des O'Connor Show, 1963 and 1970–76; Kraft Music Hall Presents: The Des O'Connor Show, 1970–71 (USA); Des O'Connor Tonight, 1977–2003; Des O'Connor Now, 1985; Fame in the Family, 2000–; Today with Des and Mel, 2002–06. Has made over 1,000 appearances at the London Palladium. No 1 single, I Pretend, 1968. Male TV Personality, TV Times, annually 1969–73; Lifetime Achievement Award, Nat. TV Awards, 2001; Grand Order of Water Rats Lifetime Achievement Award, 2012. *Publications:* Bananas Can't Fly (autobiog.), 2001; Laughter Lines: comic verse to celebrate life's little moments, 2014. *Address:* c/o Lake-Smith Associates, Suite 172, 43 Bedford Street, WC2E 9HA. *E:* Pat@lakesmith.co.uk.

O'CONNOR, Gillian Denise; *see* Brasse, G. D.

O'CONNOR, Gillian Rose; mining correspondent, Financial Times, 1999–2001; *b* 11 Aug. 1941; *d* of Thomas McDougall O'Connor and Kathleen Joan O'Connor (*née* Parnell). *Educ:* Sutton High School for Girls; St Hilda's College, Oxford. Editor, Investors Chronicle, 1982–94; Personal Finance Ed., FT, 1994–98. *Publications:* A Guide to Stockpicking, 1996. *Address:* Phlox Cottage, Wroxton Lane, Horley, Banbury OX15 6BB.

O'CONNOR, Michael, CBE 2000; Chief Executive, StepChange, since 2014; *b* London, 15 Dec. 1956; *s* of John and Kathleen O'Connor; partner, Elizabeth Owen. *Educ:* Univ. of Keele (BSc Hons Physics and Geol. 1979); Imperial Coll. London (MSc Social and Envmtl Aspects of Sci. and Technol. 1980; DIC). Civil Servant, DoH, HM Treasury and Cabinet Office, 1982–89; Dir, Coronary Prevention Gp, 1989–92; Consultant on public health policy, 1992–93; Dir for Developed Economies, Consumers Internat., 1993–96; Chief Executive: Millennium Commn, 1996–2006; Olympic Lottery Distributor, 2006–10; Consumer Futures (formerly Consumer Focus), 2010–14. Non-exec. Mem., Customer Fairness Cttee, British Gas, 2013–. Founding Mem., Coll. of Fellows, Keele Univ., 2013–. *Recreations:* art, walking, music, poetry. *Address:* StepChange, Lynton House, 7–12 Tavistock Square, WC1H 9LT. *E:* moconnorcf@gmail.com.

O'CONNOR, Rev. Canon Michael; *see* O'Connor, Rev. Canon B. M. McD.

O'CONNOR, Michael Thomas; freelance costume designer, since 1992; *b* London, 27 Oct. 1965; *s* of Thomas Patrick O'Connor and Patricia Theresa O'Connor (*née* Fraser); partner, John Phillip Usher. *Educ:* Slade Sch. of Fine Art (Fine Art foundn). Costumier, Bermans and Nathans, 1986–92. Member: Acad. of Motion Picture Arts and Scis, 2009–; BAFTA, 2009–. *Films include:* Assistant Costume Designer: Oscar and Lucinda, 1998; Topsy Turvy, 2000; Quills, 2001; Costume Designer: The Last King of Scotland, 2006; Brick Lane, 2007; The Duchess, 2008 (Academy Award, BAFTA Award, Costume Designers Guild Award, Phoenix Film Critics Soc. Award, Satellite Award, for Costume Design, 2009); Miss Pettigrew Lives For a Day, 2008; The Eagle, Jane Eyre, 2011; Invisible Woman, 2014; Suite Française, 2015.

O'CONNOR, Neil Brendan; Director, Fire Resilience and Emergencies, Department for Communities and Local Government, since 2011; *b* Hackney, 4 May 1963; *s* of John O'Connor and Eleanor, (Judy), O'Connor; *m* 2006, Juliet Mountford; three *s* one *d*. *Educ:* Finchley Catholic High Sch. Transport clerk, W H Malcolm Ltd, 1980; Clerical Officer, PSA, 1980–83; Department of the Environment: Clerical Officer, 1983–85; EO, 1985–90; HEO, 1990–97; Principal Officer (Grade 7), 1997–2002; Deputy Director: ODPM, 2002–06; Home Office, 2006–07; DCSF, 2007; Cabinet Office, 2007–08; Dep. Dir, 2008–09, Dir, 2009–11, DCLG. *Recreations:* classic minis (Mem., Mini Cooper Register), northern soul, football. *Address:* Department for Communities and Local Government, 2 Marsham Street, SW1P 4DF. *T:* 0303 444 1367. *E:* neil.o'connor@communities.gsi.gov.uk. *Club:* West Ham United Football.

O'CONNOR, Patrick Michael Joseph; QC 1993; *b* 7 Aug. 1949; *s* of Denis Bellew O'Connor and Ingelore Biegel; *m* 1986, Gillian Denise Brasse, *qv*; two *d*. *Educ:* St Francis Xavier's Grammar Sch., Liverpool; UCL (LLB Hons). Called to the Bar, Inner Temple, 1970, Bencher, 2008. *Publications:* articles in Criminal Law Review and other academic and professional jls. *Address:* Doughty Street Chambers, 53–54 Doughty Street, WC1N 2LS. *T:* (020) 7404 1313.

O'CONNOR, Ronald; Education Advisor, Abu Dhabi Education Council; *b* 1 Dec. 1950; *s* of John O'Connor and Mary O'Connor (*née* McDermott); *m* 1992, Marie Harvey Milne; one *s*. *Educ:* Stirling Univ. (BA (Hons), Dip Ed). Teacher, modern langs, Belmont Acad., Ayr, 1977–81; Principal Teacher, modern langs, 1981–83, Asst Head, 1983–88, Garnock Acad.; Educn Officer, 1988–93, Asst Dir of Educn, 1993–95, Strathclyde Regl Council; Glasgow City Council: Sen. Depute Dir of Educn, 1995–99; Dir of Social Work Services, 1999–2002; Dir of Educn Services, 2002–04; Exec. Dir (Educn, Training and Young People), 2004–07. *Recreations:* golf, football, reading.

O'CONNOR, Sandra Day; Associate Justice of the Supreme Court of the United States, 1981–2006; *b* 26 March 1930; *d* of Harry and Ada Mae Day; *m* 1952, John Jay O'Connor III (*d* 2009); three *s*. *Educ:* Stanford Univ. (BA 1950; LLB 1952). Legal appts in Calif and Frankfurt, 1952–57; in private practice, 1959–60; Asst Attorney-Gen., Arizona, 1965–69; Judge: Maricopa County Superior Ct, 1975–79; Arizona Ct of Appeals, 1979–81. Mem. Senate, Arizona, 1969–75 (majority leader, 1972–75). Director: Nat. Bank of Arizona, Phoenix, 1971–74; Blue Cross/Blue Shield, Arizona, 1975–79. American Bar Association:

Member: Exec. Bd, Central Eur. and Eurasian Law Initiative, 1990–; Exec. Cttee, Mus. of Law, 2000–; Adv. Commn, Standing Cttee on Law Library of Congress, 2002–; Commn on Civic Educn and Separation of Powers, 2005–; Mem., Adv. Cttee, Judicial, Amer. Soc. of Internat. Law, 2001–; Hon. Mem., Adv. Cttee for Judiciary Leadership Develt Council. Chm., Maricopa County Juvenile Detention Home, 1963–64; Pres., Heard Museum, Phoenix, 1968–74, 1976–81; Member: Nat. Bd, Smithsonian Assocs, 1981; Selection Cttee, Oklahoma City Nat. Meml and Mus., 2005–; Adv. Bd, Stanford Center on Ethics, 2005–; Adv. Bd, Smithsonian Nat. Mus. of Natural History, 2006–; Bd of Trustees, Rockefeller Foundn, 2006–; Co-Chm., Nat. Adv. Council, Campaign for Civic Mission of Schs, 2005–. Founder and Chair, iCivics Inc., 2009–. Trustee, Stanford Univ., 1976–81; Chancellor, Coll. of William and Mary, 2005–11. Hon. Bencher, Gray's Inn, 1982. *Publications:* Lazy B: growing up on a cattle ranch in the American Southwest, 2002; The Majesty of the Law: reflections of a Supreme Court Justice, 2003; (for children): Chico, 2005; Finding Susie, 2009.

O'CONNOR, Sean Michael; Editor, The Archers, BBC Radio, since 2013; *b* Bromborough, 11 Feb. 1968; *s* of Alan James O'Connor and Anne O'Connor; partner, 2007, R. H. Haywood. *Educ:* St Anselm's Coll., Birkenhead; University Coll. London (BA Hons Eng. Lang. and Lit.). Regl Theatre Young Director Scheme, Lyric Hammersmith, Queen's Th., Hornchurch, 1989–92; freelance theatre dir, 1992–99; TV producer, Eastenders, Footballers' Wives, Hollyoaks, Family Affairs, Minder, 1999–2009; film producer, Camberwell Prodns, 2010–. Producer, film, The Deep Blue Sea, 2011. Mem., BAFTA, 2004–. *Publications:* Straight Acting, 1998; (with Tom Morris) Juliet and her Romeo (adaptation), 2010; Handsome Brute, 2013. *Recreations:* theatre, opera. *Address:* The Archers' Office, BBC Birmingham, The Mailbox, 104 Wharfside Street, Birmingham B1 1RF. *E:* sean.o'connor@bbc.co.uk.

ODDIE, Bill; *see* Oddie, W. E.

ODDIE, His Honour Christopher Ripley; a Circuit Judge, 1974–94, sitting at Mayor's and City of London Court, 1989–94; *b* Derby, 24 Feb. 1929; *o s* of Dr and Mrs J. R. Oddie, Uttoxeter, Staffs; *m* 1957, Margaret Anne (*d* 2012), *d* of Mr and Mrs J. W. Timmis; one *s* three *d*. *Educ:* Giggleswick Sch.; Oriel Coll., Oxford (MA). Called to Bar, Middle Temple, 1954, Oxford Circuit. Contested (L) Ludlow, Gen. Election, 1970. A Recorder of the Crown Court, 1972–74. Chm., County Court Rule Cttee, 1985–87 (Mem., 1981–87). Member: Judicial Studies Bd, 1989–91; Cttee, Council of Her Majesty's Circuit Judges, 1989–91. Mem. Council, St Mary's Hosp. Med. Sch., 1980–88. Gen. Editor, Butterworth's County Court Precedents and Pleadings, 1988–92. *Recreations:* reading, opera, walking. *Address:* c/o 17 Ridgemount, Guildford, Surrey GU2 7TH. *T:* 07816 851733. *E:* isabellacox@uwclub.net.

ODDIE, William Edgar, (Bill), OBE 2003; writer, actor and broadcaster; *b* 7 July 1941; *m* 1st, Jean Hart (marr. diss.); two *d*; 2nd, Laura Beaumont; one *d*. *Educ:* Halesowen Grammar Sch.; King Edward's Sch., Birmingham; Pembroke Coll., Cambridge (BA 1963; MA 1967). Mem. Council, RSPB (Vice-Pres.). *Theatre* includes: writer and performer, Cambridge Circus (revue), Cambridge Footlights, transf. London, then NZ and Australia; performer: Tommy; Mikado, Coliseum, 1988; The Ghost Train, Lyric, Hammersmith, 1992; *television* includes: joint writer: Doctor in the House; Doctor at Large; Astronauts; writer and actor: TW3; BBC3; The Goodies (eight series), 1970–81; presenter: Ask Oddie; Who Do You Think You Are? (one prog. of series), 2004; The Truth About Killer Dinosaurs, 2005; wildlife programmes incl. Birding With Bill Oddie (three series); Bill Oddie Goes Wild; Britain Goes Wild; Springwatch (series), 2005, 2006, 2007 and 2008; Autumnwatch (series), 2006, 2007 and 2008; Bill Oddie: Back in the USA, 2007; Bill Oddie's Wild Side (series), 2008; Bill Oddie's Top 10 Frights and Delights, 2010; *radio* includes: jt writer, I'm Sorry I'll Read That Again; presenter, Breakaway. *Publications:* Little Black Bird Book, 1982; Gone Birding, 1983; (jtly) Big Bird Race, 1983; (jtly) The Toilet Book, 1986; Bird Watching With Bill Oddie, 1988; Bird Watching for Under Tens; Bill Oddie's Colouring Guides, 1991–92; Follow That Bird!, 1994; (jtly) Bird in the Nest, 1995; (jtly) Birding With Bill Oddie, 1997; Bill Oddie's Gripping Yarns: tales of birds & birding, 2000; One Flew into the Cuckoo's Egg, 2008; articles in jls. *Address:* c/o All Electric Productions, PO Box 1805, Andover, Hants SP10 3ZN. *T:* (01264) 771726. *E:* info@allelectricproductions.co.uk.

ODDIE, Dr William John Muir; Editor, Catholic Herald, 1998–2004; *b* 1 June 1939; *s* of John Male and Irene Oddie; *m* 1968, Cornelia; one *s* two *d*. *Educ:* Silcoates Sch., Yorks; Trinity Coll., Dublin (BA 1964; MA 1980); Leicester Univ. (PhD 1970); St Stephen's House, Oxford (MA Oxon 1981). Sec., Ancient Monuments Soc., 1970–72; ordained deacon, 1977, priest 1978; Asst Curate, Holy Trinity, Westbury on Trym, Bristol, 1978–80; Bp's Chaplain to Graduates, Oxford Univ., 1980–85; Librarian, Pusey House, Oxford, 1980–85; Fellow, St Cross Coll., Oxford, 1981–85; Rector, St Andrew's, Romford, 1985–87; received into RC Church, 1991; freelance journalist, Sunday Telegraph, Daily Telegraph, Daily Mail, Sunday Times, etc, 1987–98. Chm., G. K. Chesterton Soc., 2008–. *Publications:* Dickens and Carlyle: the question of influence, 1972; What will Happen to God? feminism and the reconstruction of Christian belief, 1984; After the Deluge: essays towards the desecularisation of the Church, 1987; The Crockford's File: Gareth Bennett and the death of the Anglican mind, 1989; The Roman Option: crisis and the realignment of English-speaking Christianity, 1996; John Paul the Great: maker of the post-conciliar Church, 2003; Chesterton and the Romance of Orthodoxy: the making of GKC, 1874–1908, 2008; The Holiness of G. K. Chesterton, 2010. *Recreations:* reading, music, travel, domestic pursuits. *Address:* 6 Sunningwell Road, Oxford OX1 4SX. *T:* (01865) 247450.

ODDSSON, Hon. Davíd, Hon. KBE 1990; Editor, Morgunbladid, since 2009; *b* 17 Jan. 1948; *s* of Oddur Ólafsson and Ingibjörg Kristín Lúdvíksdóttir; *m* 1970, Ástrídur Thorarensen; one *s*. *Educ:* Univ. of Iceland (grad. Lawyer). Reykjavík Theatre Co., 1970–72; Morgunbladid Daily, 1973–74; Almenna Bókafélagið Publishing House, 1975–76; Office Manager, 1976–78, Man. Dir, 1978–82, Reykjavík Health Fund; Mayor of Reykjavík, 1982–91; MP (Ind) Reykjavik, 1991–2005; Prime Minister of Iceland, 1991–2004; Foreign Minister, 2004–05; Chm., Bd of Govs, Central Bank of Iceland, 2005–09. Leader, Independent Party, 1991–2005. Hon. LLD Manitoba, 2000. Grand Cross, Order of Merit (Luxembourg). *Publications:* (trans.) Estonia: a study of imperialism, by Anders Küng, 1973; Róbert Elíasson Returns from Abroad (TV drama), 1977; A Policy of Independence, 1981; Stains on the White Collar (TV drama), 1981; Everything's Fine (TV drama), 1991; A Couple of Days without Gudny (short stories), 1997; Stolen from the Author of the Alphabet (short stories), 2002. *Recreations:* bridge, forestry, angling.

ODDY, (William) Andrew, OBE 2002; DSc; FSA; Keeper of Conservation, British Museum, 1985–2002; *b* 6 Jan. 1942; *s* of late William T. Oddy and Hilda F. Oddy (*née* Dalby); *m* 1965, Patricia Anne Whitaker; one *s* one *d*. *Educ:* Bradford Grammar Sch.; New Coll., Oxford (BA 1964; BSc 1965; MA 1969; DSc 1994). FSA 1973; FIIC 1974. Joined British Museum Research Lab., 1966, research into conservation and ancient technology; Head of Conservation, 1981. Member: Scientific Cttee, Internat. Congress on Deterioration and Preservation of Stone, 1976–91; Dept of Transport Adv. Cttee on Historic Wrecks, 1981–91; Council, Textile Conservation Centre, 1985–99; Cons. Cttee, Council for Care of Churches, 1985–90; Cons. Cttee, Cons. Unit, Mus. and Gall. Commn, 1987–92; Science-based Archaeol. Cttee, SERC, 1990–93; Council, Internat. Inst. for Conservation of Historic and Artistic Works, 1990–96 (Pres., 2001–07); Fabric Adv. Cttee, Cathedral and Abbey Church of St Alban, 1991–2010. Member: Council, RNS, 1975–78 and 2007–12 (Vice Pres., 2009–12); Res. Cttee, Soc. of Antiquaries of London, 2001–05. Trustee: Anna Plowden Trust, 1998–2006; Gabo Trust, 2002–10; Mercian Regiment Mus. (Worcs), 2012– (Editor, Friends' Newsletter, 2013–). Hon. Res. Fellow, UCL, 1992–2001. Lectures: Chester Beatty, RSA, 1982; Leventritt, Harvard Univ. Art Mus., 1996; Forbes Prize, Internat. Inst. for Conservation, 1996. Freeman, Goldsmiths' Co., 1986. *Publications:* editor: Problems in the Conservation of Waterlogged Wood, 1975; Aspects of Early Metallurgy, 1980; Scientific Studies in Numismatics, 1980; Metallurgy in Numismatics II, 1988; The Art of the Conservator, 1992; Restoration: is it acceptable?, 1994; joint editor: Conservation in Museums and Galleries, 1975; Metallurgy in Numismatics I, 1980; Aspects of Tibetan Metallurgy, 1981; A Survey of Numismatic Research 1978–1984, 1986; Metallurgy in Numismatics IV, 1998; Reversibility: does it exist?, 1999; Past Practice - Future Prospects, 2001; (jtly) Romanesque Metalwork: copper alloys and their decoration, 1986; (ed) Coinage and History in the Seventh Century Near East 2, 2010; (ed jtly) Coinage and History in the Seventh Century Near East 4, 2015; papers in learned jls. *Recreations:* family history, early Islamic coinage and history. *Address:* 5 Albany Terrace, Worcester WR1 3DU.

O'DELL, Mrs June Patricia, OBE 1990; equality campaigner; Chair and Board Member, Probus Women's Housing Society Ltd, 1996–2005; *b* 9 June 1929; *d* of Leonard Vickery, RN and Myra Vickery; *m* 1951 (marr. diss. 1963); one *s* two *d*. *Educ:* Edgehill Girls College; Plymouth Technical College. Estate Agent; Sen. Partner, Chesney's, Estate Agents, 1965–88; Dir, Eachdale Developments Ltd, 1988–98. Nat. Pres., Fedn of Business and Professional Women, 1983–85; Chm., Employment Cttee, Internat. Fedn of Business Professional Women, 1983–87; Dep. Chm., EOC, 1986–90; Member: Women's Nat. Commn, 1983–85; European Adv. Cttee for Equal Treatment between Women and Men, 1986–90; Authorised Conveyancing Practitioners Bd, 1991–95; Legal Aid Adv. Cttee, 1993–94. Non-exec. Dir, Aylesbury Vale Community Healthcare NHS Trust, 1991–98. Gov., Sir William Ramsay Sch., 2002–05. FRSA 1986 (Mem. Council, 1992–97). *Recreations:* music, particularly opera and choral; writing, literature, the countryside, equestrian events. *Address:* Gable End, High Street, Great Missenden, Bucks HP16 9AA.

ODELL, Prof. Peter Randon; Professor Emeritus, Erasmus University, Rotterdam (Director, Centre for International Energy Studies, 1981–91); *b* 1 July 1930; *s* of late Frank James Odell and late Grace Edna Odell; *m* 1957, Jean Mary McKintosh; two *s* two *d*. *Educ:* County Grammar Sch., Coalville; Univ. of Birmingham (BA, PhD); Fletcher Sch. of Law and Diplomacy, Cambridge, Mass (AM). FInstPet 1973–2003. RAF 1954–57. Economist, Shell International Petroleum Co., 1958–61; Lectr, LSE, 1961–65; Sen. Lectr, LSE, 1965–68; Prof. of Economic Geography, Erasmus Univ., 1968–81. Visiting Professor: LSE, 1983–2001; College of Europe, Bruges, 1983–90; Plymouth Univ., 1996–2003; Scholar in Residence, Rockefeller Centre, Bellagio, 1984; Killam Vis. Scholar, Univ. of Calgary, 1989; Vis. Scholar, Univ. of Cambridge, 1996–99. Stamp Meml Lectr, London Univ., 1975. Canadian Council Fellow, Univ. of Toronto, 1978. Special Advr to Sec. of State for Energy, 1977–79; Special Advr, Trade and Industry Select Cttee, H of C, 2001–02. Contested (Lib Dem) Suffolk, EP elecns, 1989. European Editor, Energy Jl, 1988–90. FRSA 1983; FRGS 1995; FEI 2003. Internat. Assoc. for Energy Econs Prize, for outstanding contribns to energy econs and its literature, 1991; RSGS Centenary Medal for res. on N Sea oil province, 1993; OPEC Lifetime Achievement Award for outstanding contrib. to petroleum industry, 2006. *Publications:* An Economic Geography of Oil, 1963, reprinted 2013; Natural Gas in Western Europe, 1969; Oil and World Power, 1970, 8th edn 1986; (with D. A. Preston) Economies and Societies in Latin America, 1973, 2nd edn 1978; Energy: Needs and Resources, 1974, 2nd edn 1977; (with K. E. Rosing) The North Sea Oil Province, 1975; The West European Energy Economy: the case for self-sufficiency, 1976; (with K. E. Rosing) The Optimal Development of the North Sea Oilfields, 1976; (with L. Vallenilla) The Pressures of Oil: a strategy for economic revival, 1978; British Oil Policy: a Radical Alternative, 1980; (with K. E. Rosing) The Future of Oil, 1980–2080, 1980, 2nd edn 1983; (ed with J. Rees) The International Oil Industry: an interdisciplinary perspective, 1986; Global and Regional Energy Supplies: recent fictions and fallacies revisited, 1991; Europe's Energy: resources and choices, 1998; Fossil Fuel Resources in the 21st Century, 1999; Oil and Gas: crises and controversies 1961–2000, Vol. 1, Global Issues, 2001, Vol. 2, Europe's Entanglement, 2002; Why Carbon Fuels will Dominate the 21st Century's Global Energy Economy, 2004; A New World Energy Order, 2007; Managing the UK's Remaining Oil and Gas Resources: a future role for the state?, 2010; An Energetic Life: the memoirs of Peter R. Odell, 1930–2010, 2011. *Address:* 7 Constitution Hill, Ipswich IP1 3RG. *T:* (01473) 253376. *E:* peterodell2@btinternet.com.

ODELL, Sir Stanley (John), Kt 1986; *b* 20 Nov. 1929; *s* of George Frederick Odell and Florence May Odell; *m* 1952, Eileen Grace Stuart; four *d*. *Educ:* Bedford Modern School. Chairman: Mid Beds Young Conservatives, 1953–59; Mid Beds Cons. Assoc., 1964–69 (Pres., 1991–2005); Beds Cons. European Constituency Council, 1979; E of England Provincial Council, Cons. Party, 1983–86 (Pres., 1991–93); Nat. Union of Cons. and Unionist Assocs, 1989–90 (Vice Chm., 1986–89); Pres., Bedford & Kempston Cons. Assoc., 2005–12. Chairman: S Beds Community Health Care NHS Trust, 1994–99; Beds and Luton Community Health Care NHS Trust, 1999–2001; Mary Seacole Homes for the Homeless in Luton, 1999–2012. Chm., Anglo-American Cttee, RAF Chicksands, 1987–96. Member of Court: Bedfordshire (formerly Luton) Univ., 1994–; Intelligence Corps, 2002–11. Chm., Biggleswade and Dist Young Farmers' Club, 1949–51; Founder Playing Mem., Biggleswade Rugby Club, 1949. Patron: Friends of Chicksands Priory, 1983–2008; Camphill, Beds, 1998–; John Bunyan Museum, Bedford, 1999–; Churchwarden, Campton Parish Church, 1978–91. Hon. Fellow, Univ. of Beds (Hon. Fellow, Luton Univ., 2002). *Recreations:* politics, shooting. *Address:* Woodhall Farm, Campton, Shefford, Beds SG17 5PB. *T:* (01462) 813230.

ODGERS, Anthony Louis; Deputy Chief Executive, Shareholder Executive, Department for Business, Innovation and Skills, since 2013; *b* 28 Sept. 1967; *s* of Ian and Juliet Odgers; *m* 1996, Tara Usher; two *s* two *d*. *Educ:* King's Sch., Canterbury; Gonville and Caius Coll., Cambridge (BA Natural Scis 1989; MA 1993); INSEAD (MBA). Deutsche Morgan Grenfell: Graduate Trainee, then Exec., Project Finance Advisory, 1989–93; Exec., then Asst Dir, Corporate Finance, 1995–99; Lehman Brothers: Sen. Vice Pres., UK and Communications M&A, 1999–2002; Man. Dir and Hd of Communications M&A, 2002–07; Deutsche Bank: Chief Operating Officer, Adv. Business, 2007–09; Hd, Restructuring Adv. (EMEA), 2009–10; Hd of Portfolio, Shareholder Exec., BIS, 2010–13. *Recreations:* swimming, table tennis, cricket (watching), cinema, traditional North London over-parenting. *Address:* 1 Victoria Street, SW1H 0ET. *T:* (020) 7215 3329. *E:* anthony.odgers@bis.gsi.gov.uk.

ODGERS, Sir Graeme (David William), Kt 1997; DL; Chairman, Kent Economic Board (formerly Kent and Medway Economic Board), 2001–09; *b* 10 March 1934; *s* of late William Arthur Odgers and Elizabeth Minty (*née* Rennie); *m* 1st, 1957, Diana Patricia Berge (*d* 2012); one *s* two *d* (and one *d* decd); 2nd, 2014, Susan Tait. *Educ:* St John's Coll., Johannesburg; Gonville and Caius Coll., Cambridge (Mech. Scis Tripos); Harvard Business Sch. (MBA, Baker Scholar). Investment Officer, Internat. Finance Corp., Washington DC, 1959–62; Management Consultant, Urwick Orr and Partners Ltd, 1962–64; Investment Executive, Hambros Bank Ltd, 1964–65; Director: Keith Shipton and Co. Ltd, 1965–72; C. T. Bowring (Insurance) Holdings Ltd, 1972–74; Chm., Odgers and Co. Ltd (Management Consultants), 1970–74; Dir, Industrial Develt Unit, DoI, 1974–77; Assoc. Dir (Finance), General Electric Co., 1977–78; Gp Finance Dir, 1979–86, Gp Man. Dir, 1983–86, Tarmac; British Telecommunications: pt-time Mem. Bd, 1983–86; Govt Dir, 1984–86; Dep. Chm. and Chief Finance Officer, 1986–87; Gp Man. Dir, 1987–90; Chief Exec., Alfred McAlpine plc, 1990–93; Chm., Monopolies and Mergers Commn, 1993–97. Non-executive Director: Dalgety, 1987–93; Nat. & Provincial Bldg Soc., 1990–93; Scottish and Southern Energy, 1998–2004. Chm., Locate in Kent, 1998–2006; Dep. Chm., Kent Partnership, 2001–09.

Pres., New Marlowe Th. Develt Trust, 2009–11 (Chm., 2007–09; Trustee, 2011–). Mem., Kent Ambassadors, 1998–. DL Kent, 2002. Freedom, City of Canterbury, 2015. Hon. Fellow, Canterbury Christchurch Univ., 2010. Hon. DLaws Greenwich, 2004; Hon. DCL Kent, 2005. Kent Invicta Award, 2009. *Recreation:* golf. *Address:* Cramond House, Harnet Street, Sandwich CT13 9ES. *Clubs:* Wildernesse (Sevenoaks); Royal Cinque Ports Golf.

ODITAH, Dr Fidelis Hilary Izuka; QC 2003; Senior Advocate of Nigeria, since 2004; *b* 27 March 1964; *s* of Augustine and Vera Oditah; *m* 1992, Precilla Osondu; two *s* two *d*. *Educ:* Univ. of Lagos (LLB); Magdalen Coll., Oxford (MA, BCL; DPhil 1989). Called to the Bar, Lincoln's Inn, 1992, Bencher, 2010; Fellow and Tutor in Law, Merton Coll., Oxford, and Travers Smith Braithwaite Lectr in Corporate Finance Law, Univ. of Oxford, 1989–97. Vis. Prof., Univ. of Oxford, 2000–. *Publications:* Legal Aspects of Receivables Financing, 1991; The Future for the Global Securities Markets, 1996; Insolvency of Banks, 1996; contrib. learned jls. *Recreations:* golf, tennis, music, reading. *Address:* 3–4 South Square, Gray's Inn, WC1R 5HP. *T:* (020) 7696 9900, *Fax:* (020) 7696 9911. *E:* fidelisoditah@southsquare.com.

ODLING-SMEE, John Charles, CMG 2005; Director, European II Department, International Monetary Fund, 1992–2003; *b* 13 April 1943; *s* of late Rev. Charles William Odling-Smee and Katharine Hamilton Odling-Smee (*née* Aitchison); *m* 1996, Carmela Veneroso. *Educ:* Durham School; St John's College, Cambridge (BA 1964); MA Oxon 1966. Junior Research Officer, Dept of Applied Economics, Cambridge, 1964–65; Asst Research Officer, Inst. of Economics and Statistics, Oxford, 1965–66; Fellow in Economics, Oriel College, Oxford, 1966–70; Research Officer, Inst. of Economics and Statistics, Oxford, 1968–71 and 1972–73; Economic Research Officer, Govt of Ghana, 1971–72; Senior Research Officer, Centre for Urban Economics, LSE, 1973–75; Economic Adviser, Central Policy Review Staff, Cabinet Office, 1975–77; Senior Economic Adviser, HM Treasury, 1977–80; Senior Economist, IMF, 1981–82; Under-Sec., HM Treasury, 1982–89; Dep. Chief Economic Advr, HM Treasury, 1989–90; Sen. Advr, IMF, 1990–91. *Publications:* (with A. Grey and N. P. Hepworth) Housing Rents, Costs and Subsidies, 1978, 2nd edn 1981; (with R. C. O. Matthews and C. H. Feinstein) British Economic Growth 1856–1973, 1982; articles in books and learned jls. *Address:* 3506 Garfield Street NW, Washington, DC 20007, USA. *T:* (202) 3383471. *E:* jodlingsmee@juno.com.

O'DOHERTY, Patrick; Principal, Lumen Christi College, Derry, since 2003 (Vice Principal, 1997–2003); *b* Londonderry, 10 Nov. 1956; *s* of Gerard and Agnes O'Doherty; *m* 1977, Darina; two *d*. *Educ:* St Columb's Coll., Derry; Queen's Univ., Belfast (BEd 1979); Univ. of Ulster (MSc Educn Mgt 1996). Professional Qual. for Headship NI 2001. St Columb's College: Teacher of English, 1979–82; Hd of Latin, 1982–88; Hd of English, 1988–97. *Recreations:* visiting Italy, classical civilizations.

ODONE, Cristina; writer and broadcaster; Deputy Editor, The New Statesman, 1998–2004; *b* 11 Nov. 1960; *d* of late Augusto and Ulla Odone; *m* 2005, Edward Lucas; one *d*. *Educ:* Worcester Coll., Oxford (MA). Freelance journalist, 1983–84; journalist: Catholic Herald, 1985–86; The Times diary, 1987; Vice-Pres., Odone Associates, Washington, 1988–92; Editor, The Catholic Herald, 1992–96 (Mem., Bd of Dirs, 2007–); television reviewer, 1996–98, columnist, 2010–, The Daily Telegraph; columnist, Observer, 2001–08. Res. Fellow, Centre for Policy Studies, 2009–. Mem., Ext. Adv. Panel, Faculty of Theology and Religion, Oxford Univ. Member: Adv. Bd, Citizens' Service Scheme, 1995–; Bd of Dirs, Longford Trust, 2003–. FRSA 1996. *Publications:* novels: The Shrine, 1996; A Perfect Wife, 1997; The Dilemmas of Harriet Carew, 2008; The Good Divorce Guide, 2009; non-fiction: In Bad Faith, 2008; What Real Women Want, 2009; Assisted Suicide, 2010. *Recreations:* walking, travelling. *Address:* c/o Curtis Brown Ltd, 5th Floor, Haymarket House, 28–29 Haymarket, SW1Y 4SP.

O'DONNELL, family name of **Baron O'Donnell**.

O'DONNELL, Baron *cr* 2012 (Life Peer), of Clapham in the London Borough of Wandsworth; **Augustine Thomas, (Gus), O'Donnell,** GCB 2011 (KCB 2005; CB 1994); Secretary of the Cabinet and Head of the Home Civil Service, 2005–11; *b* 1 Oct. 1952; *s* of Helen O'Donnell (*née* McClean) and James O'Donnell; *m* 1979, Melanie Joan Elizabeth Timmis; one *d*. *Educ:* Univ. of Warwick (BA Hons); Nuffield Coll., Oxford (MPhil). Lectr, Dept of Political Economy, Univ. of Glasgow, 1974–79; Economist, HM Treasury, 1979–85; First Sec. (Econ.), British Embassy, Washington, 1985–88; Sen. Economic Adviser, 1988–89, Press Sec., 1989–90, HM Treasury; Press Sec. to Prime Minister, 1990–94; Under Sec., Monetary Gp, 1994–95, Dep. Dir, Macroeconomic Policy and Prospects Directorate, 1995–96, HM Treasury; Minister (Economic), British Embassy, Washington, and UK Exec. Dir, IMF and World Bank, 1997–98; HM Treasury: Dir, Macroeconomic Policy and Prospects Directorate, 1998–2000; Man. Dir, Macroeconomic Policy and Internat. Finance, 2000–02; Hd of Govt Econ. Service, 1998–2003; Permanent Sec., 2002–05. Advr to CEO, TD Bank, 2012–; Sen. Advr, 2012–13, Chm., 2013–, Frontier Economics; non-exec. Dir and Strategic Advr, Brookfield Asset Mgt, 2013–. Mem., Economist Trust, 2012–. Visiting Professor: LSE, 2013–; UCL, 2013–. Hon. FBA 2014. *Publications:* articles in economic jls. *Recreations:* football, cricket, golf, tennis. *Address:* House of Lords, SW1A 0PW. *Club:* All England Lawn Tennis.

O'DONNELL, Prof. Barry, FRCS, FRCSI; President, Royal College of Surgeons of Ireland, 1998–2000; Professor of Paediatric Surgery, Royal College of Surgeons in Ireland, 1986–93, now Professor Emeritus; Consultant Paediatric Surgeon, Our Lady's Hospital for Sick Children, Dublin, 1957–93; *b* 6 Sept. 1926; *e s* of Michael J. O'Donnell and Kathleen O'Donnell (*née* Barry); *m* 1959, Mary Leydon, BA, BComm, BL, *d* of John Leydon, LLD, KCSG; three *s* one *d*. *Educ:* Christian Brothers College, Cork; Castleknock College, Dublin; University College, Cork (MB Hons 1949). MCh NUI, 1954. FRCS 1953, FRCSI 1953; FRCSEd *ad hominem* 1992; FRCPSGlas *qua surgeon* 1999. Ainsworth Travelling Scholar, Boston (Lahey Clinic and Boston Floating Hosp., 1955–56); Sen. Registrar, Hosp. for Sick Children, London, 1956–57. Vis. Prof. at many US univs, incl. Harvard, Columbia, Johns Hopkins, Michigan, Pennsylvania; Hunterian Prof., RCS, 1986. Jt Pres., British, Canadian and Irish Med. Assocs, 1976–77; President: British Assoc. of Paediatric Surgeons, 1980–82; Surgical Sect., Royal Acad. of Medicine of Ireland, 1990–92; Mem. Council, RCSI, 1972–77 and 1993–96 (Vice Pres., 1996–98); Chm., Jl Cttee, BMA, 1982–88. Director: Standard Chartered Bank, Ireland, 1977–90; West Deutsche Landesbank, 1990–96. Vicary Lect., RCS, 2013. Hon. FRCS 2007. Hon. Fellow: Amer. Acad. of Pediatrics, 1974; New England Surgical Assoc., 1996; Amer. Surgical Assoc., 1998; Coll. of Medicine of S Africa, 2001; Faculty of Nursing, RCPI, 2013; Hon. FACS 1999; Hon. Mem., Boston Surgical Soc., 2000. Silver Jubilee Medal, 1977; People of the Year Award, New Ireland Insce Co., 1984; Denis Browne Gold Medal, British Assoc. of Paediatric Surgeons, 1989; Urology Medal, American Acad. of Pediatrics, 2003; Dist. Alumnus Award, UC, Cork, 2004; Lifetime Achievement Award, Irish Medical Times, 2014. *Publications:* Essentials of Paediatric Surgery, 1961, 4th edn 1992; Abdominal Pain in Children, 1985; (ed jtly) Paediatric Urology, 3rd edn 1997; Terence Millin, 2003; Irish Surgeons and Surgery in the Twentieth Century, 2008. *Recreations:* repeating myself, incompetent golf. *Address:* 28 Merlyn Road, Ballsbridge, Dublin 4, Ireland. *T:* and *Fax:* 2694000. *E:* bodonnel@indigo.ie. *Clubs:* Royal Irish Yacht; Portmarnock Golf.

O'DONNELL, Sir Christopher (John), Kt 2003; Chair of Council, University of York, since 2008; *b* 30 Oct. 1946; *s* of Anthony John O'Donnell and Joan Millicent O'Donnell; *m* 1971, Maria Antonia Wallis; three *s* one *d*. *Educ:* Imperial Coll., London (BSc Eng Hons); London Business Sch. (MSc Econ). Man. Dir, Vickers Ltd Medical Engineering, 1974–79; Area Vice Pres., Europe, C. R. Bard, Inc., 1979–88; Man. Dir, Smith & Nephew Medical Ltd, 1988–93; Gp Dir, 1993–97, Chief Exec., 1997–2007, Smith & Nephew plc. Non-exec. Dir, BOC Gp, 2001–06. *Recreations:* flying, golf. *Address:* Wetherby, W Yorks.

O'DONNELL, Donal Gerard; Hon. Mr Justice O'Donnell; a Judge of the Supreme Court of Ireland, since 2010; *b* Belfast, 25 Oct. 1957; *s* of Rt Hon. Turlough O'Donnell, *qv*; *m* 1985, Mary Rose Binchy; two *s* two *d*. *Educ:* St Mary's, Belfast; University Coll., Dublin (BCL 1980); King's Inns (BL 1982); Univ. of Virginia (LLM 1983). Called to Irish Bar, 1982, Bar of NI, 1989; Sen. Counsel, 1995. Mem. (pt-time), Law Reform Commn, 2005–12. *Recreations:* golf, reading, walking. *Address:* The Supreme Court, Four Courts, Dublin 7, Ireland.

O'DONNELL, Fiona; *b* Nanaimo, Vancouver Is., Canada, 27 Jan. 1960; *d* of Pat Kenny and Gladys Kenny (*née* Miners); three *s* one *d*. *Educ:* Lochaber High Sch.; Glasgow Univ. Project manager, Stonham Housing Assoc.; Asst Manager, Capability Scotland, Upper Springland; Constituency Asst to Douglas Alexander, MP; researcher for Hugh Henry, MSP and Trish Goodman, MSP; researcher and PA, Mackay Hannah; organiser, then Develt Officer, Scottish Labour Party. MP (Lab) E Lothian, 2010–15; contested (Lab) same seat, 2015. Member: Co-op Party; GMB; Amnesty Internat.; RSPB. *Recreations:* swimming, food and wine with friends, housework.

O'DONNELL, Hugh Bede Butler; Member (Lib Dem) Scotland Central, Scottish Parliament, 2007–11; *b* 1 May 1952; *s* of late Hugh O'Donnell and Christina O'Donnell; *m* (separated); one *s* one *d*. *Educ:* Queen Margaret Coll., Edinburgh (BA Hons 1996); Southern Connecticut State Univ. Civil Servant, 1969–72; manager, Tesco Plc, 1972–85; agent, Prudential Portfolio Managers, 1985–95; support worker, Quarriers, 1995–99; Parly Aide to Donald Gorrie, MSP, 1999–2007. Non-exec. Dir, Social Enterprise, RECAP, 2003–10. Election Supervisor, UN Mission to Kosovo, 2001. *Recreations:* relaxing on island of Kos, failing to learn Greek, TV crime fiction, bad DIY, olive picking, the life of Alexander the Great, reading historical fiction, raging at the world.

O'DONNELL, Ian Francis George; Executive Director of Corporate Resources, London Borough of Ealing, since 2009; *b* London, 22 Jan. 1962; *s* of Bernard Francis O'Donnell and Joan Alice O'Donnell; *m* 1992, Jacquie Louise Duckworth; one *s* one *d*. *Educ:* Kent Coll., Canterbury; University Coll., London (BSc Econs). CIPFA 2000. Credit Controller, Ind Coope Ltd, 1984–85; Accts and Rechargeable Works Manager, London Bor. of Barnet, 1985–87; Credit Manager, Hay Mgt Consultants, Sydney, 1987–88; London Borough of Camden: Community Charge Manager, 1988–90; Local Revenues Manager, 1990–92; Hd of Exchequer, 1992–99; Hd, Client Financial Services, 1999–2003; Asst Dir of Finance, London Bor. of Lambeth, 2003–06; Dir of Finance, London Bor. of Waltham Forest, 2006–09. Expert Advr, on Debt, to Cabinet Office, 2011–12; Treas., W London Waste Authy, 2012–. Chm. Bd, Fighting Fraud Locally, 2012–. Trustee, Public Concern at Work, 2012–. Hon. Treas., Comics Creators' Guild, 1997–2002. Vice-Pres., Soc. of London Treasurers, 2015–. Freedom, City of London, 2012. *Recreations:* golf, game and sport angling, Arsenal FC, the arts. *Address:* Ealing Council, Perceval House, 14–16 Uxbridge Road, W5 2HL. *T:* (020) 8825 5269. *E:* odonnelli@ealing.gov.uk.

O'DONNELL, James Anthony; Organist and Master of the Choristers, Westminster Abbey, since 2000; *b* 15 Aug. 1961; *s* of late Dr (James Joseph) Gerard O'Donnell and of Dr Gillian Anne O'Donnell (now Womersley). *Educ:* Westcliff High Sch., Essex; Jesus Coll., Cambridge (Organ Scholar and Open Scholar in Music; BA 1982, MA; Hon. Fellow, 2011). Westminster Cathedral: Asst Master of Music, 1982–88; Master of Music, 1988–99. Prof. of Organ, 1997–2004, Vis. Prof. of Organ, 2004–, Vis. Prof. Choral Conducting, 2013–, RAM; Vis. Performance Fellow, Univ. of Aberdeen, 2013–. FRCO 1983 (Performer of the Year, 1987; Mem. Council, 1989–2003; Pres., 2011–13). Hon. FRSCM 2000; Hon. RAM 2001; Hon. FGCM 2001; Hon. FRCM 2009. Has made many recordings with Westminster Cathedral Choir and Choir of Westminster Abbey. Hon. DMus Aberdeen, 2013. Gramophone Record of the Year and Best Choral Recording awards, 1998 for masses by Martin and Pizzetti; Royal Philharmonic Soc. award, 1999. KCSG 1999. *Recreations:* opera, food, wine. *Address:* c/o The Chapter Office, 20 Dean's Yard, Westminster Abbey, SW1P 3PA. *Club:* Athenæum.

O'DONNELL, Dr Michael; author and broadcaster; *b* 20 Oct. 1928; *o s* of late Dr James Michael O'Donnell and Nora (*née* O'Sullivan); *m* 1953, Catherine Dorrington Ward (*d* 2007); one *s* one *d* (and one *d* decd). *Educ:* Stonyhurst; Trinity Hall, Cambridge (Lane Harrington Schol.); St Thomas's Hosp. Med. Sch., London (MB, BChir). FRCGP 1990. Editor, Cambridge Writing, 1948; Scriptwriter, BBC Radio, 1949–52. General Medical Practitioner, 1954–64. Editor, World Medicine, 1966–82. Member: GMC, 1971–97 (Chm., Professional Standards Cttee, 1995–97); Longman Editorial Adv. Bd, 1978–82. Mem., Alpha Omega Alpha Honor Med. Soc., 1995. Inaugural lecture, Green Coll., Oxford, 1981. John Rowan Wilson Award, World Medical Journalists Assoc., 1982; John Snow Medal, Assoc. of Anaesthetists of GB and Ireland, 1984. Scientific Adviser: O Lucky Man (film), 1972; Inside Medicine (BBC TV), 1974; Don't Ask Me (Yorkshire TV), 1977; Don't Just Sit There (Yorkshire TV), 1979–80; Where There's Life (Yorkshire TV), 1981–83. *Television plays:* Suggestion of Sabotage, 1963; Dangerous Reunion, 1964; Resolution, 1964; *television documentaries:* You'll Never Believe It, 1962; Cross Your Heart and Hope to Live, 1975; The Presidential Race, 1976; From Europe to the Coast, 1976; Did History Really Happen?, 1977, 1998; Chasing the Dragon, 1979; Second Opinion, 1980; Judgement on Las Vegas, 1981; Is Your Brain Really Necessary, 1982; Plague of Hearts, 1983; Medical Express, 1984; Can You Avoid Cancer?, 1984; O'Donnell Investigates…booze, 1985; O'Donnell Investigates…food, 1985; O'Donnell Investigates…the food business, 1986; O'Donnell Investigates…age, 1988; Health, Wealth and Happiness, 1989; What is this thing called health, 1990; The Skin Trade, 1991; Whose Blue Genes?, 1992; Out of Town, Out of Mind, 1993; Beyond belief, 1994; Way beyond belief, 1995; Dads, 1995; Still Beyond Belief, 1996; New Age Superstition, 1999; *radio:* contributor to Stop the Week (BBC), 1976–92; Chm., My Word (BBC), 1983–92; Presenter: Relative Values (BBC), 1987–97; The Bhamjee Beat, 1995; Utopia and Other Destinations, 1996–98; Murder, Magic and Medicine, 1998–2001; The Age-old Dilemma (series), 2007. Medical Journalists Assoc. Award, 1973, 1982, 1990, 1996, Lifetime Achievement Award, 2007; British Science Writers' Award, 1979. *Publications:* Cambridge Anthology, 1952; Europe Tomorrow, 1971; My Medical School, 1978; The Devil's Prison, 1982; Doctor! Doctor! an insider's guide to the games doctors play, 1986; The Long Walk Home, 1988; Dr Michael O'Donnell's Executive Health Guide, 1988; A Sceptic's Medical Dictionary, 1997; Medicine's Strangest Cases, 2002; Madness and Creativity in Literature and Culture, 2004; Dr Donovan's Bequest, 2006; The Barefaced Doctor, 2013; contrib. Punch, New Scientist, The Listener, The Times, The Guardian, Daily Telegraph, Daily Mail. *Recreations:* walking, listening to music, loitering (with and without intent). *Address:* Handon Cottage, Markwick Lane, Loxhill, Godalming, Surrey GU8 4BD. *T:* (01483) 208295. *E:* michaelodonnell3@mac.com. *Club:* Garrick.

O'DONNELL, Rt Hon. Turlough; PC 1979; Lord Justice of Appeal, Supreme Court of Northern Ireland, 1979–89; *b* 5 Aug. 1924; *e s* of Charles and Eileen O'Donnell; *m* 1954, Eileen McKinley; two *s* two *d*. *Educ:* Abbey Grammar Sch., Newry; Queen's Univ., Belfast (LLB). Called to Bar of Northern Ireland, 1947; called to Inner Bar, 1964; Puisne Judge, NI, 1971–79. Chairman: NI Bar Council, 1970–71, Council of Legal Educn, NI, 1980–90. *Recreations:* golf, folk music. *Address:* c/o Royal Courts of Justice (Ulster), Belfast BT1 3JF.
See also D. G. O'Donnell.

O'DONNELL BOURKE, Patrick Francis John; Group Finance Director, John Laing plc, since 2011; *b* 22 March 1957; *m* 1992, Jane; three *s*. *Educ:* Stonyhurst Coll.; Trinity Coll., Cambridge (BA 1979). ACA 1983. KPMG, 1979–86; Hill Samuel, 1986–87; Barclays de Zoete Wedd, 1987–95; Powergen: Hd of M&A, 1995–98; Gp Treas., 1998–2000; Gp Finance Dir, Viridian Gp, 2000–07; Gp Chief Exec., Viridian Gp Ltd, 2007–11. *Address:* John Laing plc, 1 Kingsway, WC2B 6AN.

O'DONOGHUE, Denise, OBE 1999; non-executive Director, ITV Studios UK (Managing Director, 2010–14); *b* 13 April 1955; *d* of late Micheal O'Donoghue and Maura O'Donoghue; *m* 1987, James Mulville, *qv* (marr. diss. 1998); *m* 2006, Michael Holland. *Educ:* St Dominic's Girls' Sch.; York Univ. (BA Hons). Coopers & Lybrand, 1979–81; Dir, IPPA, 1981–83; Holmes Associates, 1983–86; Managing Director: Hat Trick Films, 1995–2006; Hat Trick Hldgs, 2003–06. Non-exec. Dir, Big Talk Productions, 2013–. FRTS 1998; CCMI (CIMgt 1998). Awards from RTS, BAFTA, and Broadcasting Press Guild; Emmy Awards.

O'DONOGHUE, Hughie, RA 2009; artist; *b* Manchester, 5 July 1953; *s* of Daniel O'Donoghue and Sabina, (Sheila), O'Donoghue; *m* 1974, Clare Reynolds; two *s* one *d*. *Educ:* St Augustine's Grammar Sch., Manchester; Trinity and All Saints Coll., Leeds; Goldsmith's Coll., Univ. of London (MA). Artist in Residence: Nat. Gall., 1984–85; St John's Coll., Oxford, 2000; Eton Coll., 2013; *solo exhibitions* include: Haus der Kunst, Munich, 1997; Irish Mus. of Modern Art, Dublin, 1998–99, 2009; RHA Gall., Dublin, 1999; Fitzwilliam Mus., Cambridge and tour, 2001–03; Imperial War Mus., London and Manchester, 2003–04; Gemeentemuseum, The Hague; Centre Culturel Irlandais, Paris; Leeds Art Gall., 2009; DOX Mus., Prague, 2011; RA, 2012; Abbot Hall, Kendal, 2012; created stained glass windows for Henry VII Lady Chapel, Westminster Abbey, 2013. Mem., Aosdána, 2013–. Hon. LLD NUI, Cork, 2005. *Recreations:* walking the Atlantic coastline of County Mayo, following trials and tribulations of Manchester United. *Address:* c/o Marlborough Fine Art, 6 Albermarle Street, W1S 4BY. *T:* (020) 7629 5161. *E:* mfa@marlboroughfineart.com, odon@iol.ie. *Clubs:* Arts, Academicians' Room.

O'DONOGHUE, Gen. Sir Kevin, KCB 2005; CBE 1996; Chief of Defence Materiel, Ministry of Defence, 2007–10; Master General of Logistics, 2009–12; *b* 9 Dec. 1947; *s* of late Phillip James O'Donoghue and Winifred Mary O'Donoghue; *m* 1973, Jean Monkman; three *d*. *Educ:* Eastbourne Coll.; UMIST (BSc 1st Cl. Hons). Commnd RE, 1969; 23 Engr Regt, BAOR; Adjt 21 Engr Regt, 1974; Instructor, RMA Sandhurst, 1976; Staff Coll., Canada, 1978; Mil. Ops, MoD, 1979; MA to CGS, 1980; OC 4 Field Sqdn, 1982; Directing Staff, Staff Coll., Camberley, 1984; Comdr, 25 Engr Regt, BAOR, 1986–88; Dep. ACOS, HQ UKLF, 1988; Higher Comd and Staff Course, 1990; Comdr Corps RE, 1 (BR) Corps, 1990; Comd Engr, ACE Rapid Reaction Corps, 1992; NATO Defence Coll., 1993; Dir, Staff Ops, SHAPE, 1993; COS HQ QMG, 1996–99; ACGS, 1999–2001; UK Mil. Rep. to NATO and EU, 2001–02; DCDS (Health), 2002–04, Chief of Defence Logistics, 2004–07, MoD; Chief Royal Engr, 2004–09. Col, Royal Glos, Berks and Wilts Regt, 2001–07; Col Comdt, RE, 2002–09. Hon. Col Comdt, RLC, 2008–12. Chm., SSAFA (formerly SSAFA Forces Help), 2010–. Gentleman Usher to the Sword of State, 2013–. Chm. Govs, Eastbourne Coll., 2014–. Liveryman, Masons' Co., 2010–. *Recreations:* military history, furniture restoration, gardening. *Club:* Army and Navy.

O'DONOGHUE, (Michael) Peter (Desmond); York Herald, College of Arms, since 2012; *b* Sevenoaks, Kent; *s* of Michael John O'Donoghue and Elizabeth Anne Hawkins O'Donoghue (*née* Borley); *m* 2002, Catherine Ann Wolfe, PhD; one *s* one *d*. *Educ:* Dulwich Coll.; Gonville and Caius Coll., Cambridge (BA 1994). Independent genealogist, historian and archivist, 1994–2003; College of Arms: Res. Asst, 1994–2005; Bluemantle Pursuivant of Arms, 2005–12. Vice Pres., Assoc. of Genealogists and Researchers in Archives, 2011–. Freeman, City of London, 2005–; Liveryman, Armourers and Brasiers' Co., 2010–. Jt Editor, Coat of Arms, 2004–. FSA. *Publications:* The Electrical Contractors' Association 1901–2001, 2001; various articles in heraldic and genealogical jls and magazines. *Address:* College of Arms, Queen Victoria Street, EC4V 4BT. *T:* (020) 7332 0776. *E:* york@college-of-arms.gov.uk.

O'DONOGHUE, Most Rev. Patrick; Bishop of Lancaster, (RC), 2001–09; *b* 4 May 1934; *s* of Daniel O'Donoghue and Sheila O'Donoghue (*née* Twomey). *Educ:* St Edmund's Coll., Ware, Herts. Ordained priest, 1967; Asst priest, Willesden, 1967–70; Mem., Diocesan Mission Team, Westminster, 1970–73; Pastoral Dir, Allen Hall, 1973–78; Asst Administrator, Westminster Cathedral, 1978–85; Rector, Allen Hall, 1985–91; Administrator, Westminster Cathedral, 1991–93; Auxiliary Bishop of Westminster (Bishop in W London), 1993–2001. *Recreations:* football, theatre, country walking, the Arts. *Address:* 1 The Presbytery, Bantry, Co. Cork, Ireland.

O'DONOGHUE, Peter; *see* O'Donoghue, M. P. D.

O'DONOGHUE, Philip Nicholas, CBiol, FRSB; General Secretary, Institute of Biology, 1982–89; *b* 9 Oct. 1929; *s* of Terence Frederick O'Donoghue and Ellen Mary (*née* Haynes); *m* 1955, Veronica Florence Campbell; two *d*. *Educ:* East Barnet Grammar Sch.; Univ. of Nottingham (BSc; MSc 1959). FRSB (FIBiol 1975). Experimental Officer, ARC's Field Stn, Compton, 1952–55 and Inst. of Animal Physiology, Babraham, 1955–61; Scientific Officer, National Inst. for Res. in Dairying, Shinfield, 1962–66; Lectr in Exptl Vet. Science and later Sen. Lectr in Lab. Animal Science, Royal Postgrad. Med. Sch., Univ. of London, 1966–82. Hume Meml Lect., UFAW, 1990. Vice-Pres., Inst. of Animal Technicians, 1969–2001; Hon. Sec., Inst. of Biology, 1972–76; Member: TEC, 1973–79 (Chm., Life Sciences Cttee, 1973–80); Council, Section of Comparative Medicine, RSM, 1983–96 (Pres., 1985–86); President: Lab. Animal Sci. Assoc., 1989–91; Fedn of European Lab. Animal Sci. Assocs, 1990–95. Editor, Laboratory Animals, 1967–82. Lab. Animal Sci. Assoc. Award, 1994. *Publications:* (with V. F. O'Donoghue) Georgian Cookery: recipes and remedies from 18th century Totteridge, 2007; editor of books and author of articles chiefly on the law relating to and the effective use and proper care of laboratory animals. *Recreations:* music, local history, talking, limited gardening. *Address:* 21 Holyrood Road, New Barnet, Herts EN5 1DQ. *T:* (020) 8449 3692. *Clubs:* Athenæum, Royal Society of Medicine.

O'DONOHOE, Nicholas Peter; Chief Executive Officer, Big Society Capital, since 2011; *b* Liverpool, 10 April 1957; *s* of Niall O'Donohoe and Barbara O'Donohoe; *m* 2003, Stephanie Nicola Barwise, *qv*; one *s* two *d*, and two *d* by a previous marriage. *Educ:* Trinity Coll., Dublin (BA Hons); Wharton Sch., Univ. of Pennsylvania (MBA). Goldman Sachs, 1981–96: Resident Manager, Zurich, 1988–91; Exec. Dir, Equity Capital Mkts, 1991–93; Hd of Internat. Mktg, Goldman Sachs Asset Mgt, 1991–96; JP Morgan: Hd, Eur. Equity Sales, 1996–99; Hd, Eur. Equity, 1999–2002; Global Hd of Res., 2003–10; Mem., Investment Bank Global Mgt Cttee, 2004–11; Mem., Exec. Cttee, JP Morgan Chase, 2007–11. Mem. Bd, Think Forward Ltd, 2011–; Mem., Adv. Bd, Bridges Ventures, 2011–. Mem. Bd, Global Impact Investing Network, 2009–; Chairman: Social Innovation Council, WEF, 2013; UK Adv. Cttee, G8 Social Impact Investment Task Force, 2013–14. *Recreations:* tennis, cycling, ski-ing. *Address:* Big Society Capital, 72–78 Fleet Street, EC4Y 1HY. *T:* (020) 7186 2501. *E:* nickodonohoe@gmail.com. *Club:* Queen's.

O'DONOHOE, Stephanie Nicola; *see* Barwise, S. N.

O'DONOVAN, Kathleen Anne; Member of Court, Bank of England, 1999–2005 (Chairman, Audit Committee); *b* Warwicks, 23 May 1957. *Educ:* University Coll. London (BSc Econs). Joined Turquands Barton Mayhew, subseq. Ernst & Young, 1975; Partner, 1989–91; Finance Dir, BTR, then BTR Siebe, subseq. Invensys plc, 1991–2002. Co-founder, Bird & Co. Gp, 1981. Non-executive Director: EMI Gp, 1997–2007 (Chm., Audit Cttee, 1999–2007); Prudential plc, 2003–12 (Chm. Audit Cttee, 2006–12); Great Portland Estates plc, 2003–09; O_2, 2005–07; ARM Hldgs plc, 2006–; Trinity Mirror plc, 2007–13; DS Smith plc, 2012–.

O'DONOVAN, Michael; Chief Executive, Multiple Sclerosis Society, 2002–06; *b* 26 Sept. 1946; *s* of James and Mary O'Donovan; *m* 1969, Susan Mary (*née* O'Brien); three *s*. *Educ:* St Ignatius Coll., N15; Durham Univ. (BA Hons Mod. Hist.). Beecham Group: Gen. Manager, then Man. Dir, Toiletries and Household Div., 1981–85; Regl Man. Dir, Far East, 1985–89; SmithKline Beecham, subseq. GlaxoSmithKline: Vice-Pres., Over-the-Counter Medicine Develt, 1990–92; Vice-Pres., Strategic Planning, 1993–2001. Non-exec. Dir, Adler Europe, 2005–07; Treasurer: Eur. Patients' Forum, 2006–10; Exec. Cttee, Eur. MS Platform, 2006–12. Vice-Chm., Neurol Alliance, 2003–06 (Mem., 2003–06); Co-Chair, National Voices, service user alliance, 2008–09 (Trustee, 2009–12). Chairman: Central London Community Healthcare NHS, 2009–12; Heatherwood and Wexham Park NHS Foundn Trust, 2012–14; non-exec. Dir, Frimley Health NHS Foundn Trust, 2014–. Member: Adv. Cttee, Inst. of Complex Neurodisability, 2003–10; Bd, European Medicines Agency, 2009–12. Trustee, Long Term Conditions (formerly Medical Conditions) Alliance, 2005–08 (Chm., 2008). *Recreations:* keeping fit, modern history. *Club:* Royal Scots (Edinburgh).

O'DONOVAN, Rev. Canon Oliver Michael Timothy, DPhil; FBA 2000; FRSE; Professor of Christian Ethics and Practical Theology, University of Edinburgh, 2006–12, now Emeritus; *b* 28 June 1945; *s* of Michael and Joan M. O'Donovan; *m* 1978, Joan Elizabeth Lockwood; two *s*. *Educ:* University Coll. Sch., Hampstead; Balliol Coll., Oxford (MA, DPhil); Wycliffe Hall, Oxford; Princeton Univ. Ordained deacon 1972, priest 1973, dio. of Oxford. Tutor, Wycliffe Hall, Oxford, 1972–77; Prof. of Systematic Theology, Wycliffe Coll., Toronto, 1977–82; Regius Prof. of Moral and Pastoral Theology, Univ. of Oxford, 1982–2006; Canon of Christ Church, Oxford, 1982–2006. McCarthy Vis. Prof., Gregorian Univ., Rome, 2001; Hon. Prof., Sch. of Divinity, Univ. of St Andrews, 2013–. Member: C of E Bd for Social Responsibility, 1976–77, 1982–85; ARCIC, 1985–90; Anglican-Orthodox Jt Doctrinal Discussions, 1982–84; Gen. Synod of C of E, 2005–06. Pres., Soc. for the Study of Christian Ethics, 1997–2000. Hulsean Lectr, Cambridge Univ., 1993–94; Bampton Lectr, Oxford Univ., 2003. FRSE 2009. Hon. DD Wycliffe Coll., Toronto, 2002. *Publications:* The Problem of Self-Love in Saint Augustine, 1980; Begotten or Made?, 1984; Resurrection and Moral Order, 1986; On the Thirty Nine Articles, 1986, 2nd edn, 2011; Peace and Certainty, 1989; The Desire of the Nations, 1996; (with Joan Lockwood O'Donovan) From Irenaeus to Grotius, 1999; Common Objects of Love, 2002; The Just War Revisited, 2003; (with Joan Lockwood O'Donovan) Bonds of Imperfection, 2004; The Ways of Judgment, 2005; The Word in Small Boats: sermons from Oxford, 2010; Self, World and Time, 2013; Finding and Seeking, 2014; contrib. Jl of Theol Studies, Jl of Religious Ethics, Ethique, Studies in Christian Ethics, and Political Theol. *Address:* The University of Edinburgh, School of Divinity, New College, Mound Place, Edinburgh EH1 2LX.

O'DONOVAN, Prof. Peter Joseph, FRCS, FRCOG; Consultant Gynaecologist, since 1990, Lead Gynaecological Cancer, since 2006, Lead Intellectual Property, since 2007, Bradford Teaching Hospitals NHS Trust; Professor of Medical Innovation, since 2003, Director, Institute of Pharmaceutical Innovation, since 2008, University of Bradford; *b* 13 Dec. 1954; *s* of Patrick Joseph O'Donovan and Sheila Doreen O'Donovan; *m* 1988, Carmel Beirne; two *s* two *d*. *Educ:* Presentation Brothers' Coll., Cork; UC Cork, Nat. Univ. Ireland (MB BCh BAO). FRCS 1982; MRCOG 1986, FRCOG 1998. Bradford Teaching Hospitals NHS Trust: Dir, Post Grad. Med. Educn, 1997–2003; Dir, Merit Centre, 1997–. Mem., Medical Devices Agency, DoH, 2001–09. Dir, Medipex (NHS Innovation), 2004–. Dir, Eur. Acad. Gynaecol Surgery, 2007–. Pres., British Soc. for Gynaecological Endoscopy, 2002–04; Pres., Eur. Soc. Gynaecol Endoscopy, 2014– (Treas., 2006–12; Vice Pres., 2012–14). Ed. in Chief, Reviews in Gynaecological Practice, 2001–05; Ed., Gynecol Surgery, 2003–06. *Publications:* Recent Advances in Gynaecological Surgery, 2002; Conservative Surgery for Menorrhagia, 2003; Preserving Your Womb: alternatives to hysterectomy, 2005; Ambulatory Gynaecological Surgery, 2006; Complications in Gynaecological Surgery, 2008; Conservative Surgery for Abnormal Uterine Bleeding, 2007; Modern Management of Abnormal Uterine Bleeding, 2008. *Recreations:* food, walking, tennis, Rugby Union (as spectator), reading tabloid newspapers, writing, travel. *Address:* Cotswold, 3 Creskeld Crescent, Bramhope, Leeds LS16 9EH. *T:* (0113) 261 4259, (office) (01274) 364888. *E:* podonovan@hotmail.com.

O'DOWD, Sir David (Joseph), Kt 1999; CBE 1995; QPM 1988; DL; law enforcement consultant, 2002–10; HM Chief Inspector of Constabulary, 1996–2001; *b* 20 Feb. 1942; *s* of late Michael Joseph O'Dowd and Helen (*née* Merrin); *m* 1963, Carole Ann Watson; one *s* one *d*. *Educ:* Gartree High Sch.; Oadby, Leics; Univ. of Leicester (Dip. Social Studies); Open Univ. (BA); Univ. of Aston (MSc); FBI Nat. Acad., USA. Sgt, Inspector and Chief Inspector, CID, Leicester City Police, 1961–77; Supt, W Midlands Police, Coventry and Birmingham, 1977–84; Hd, Traffic Policing, Dir, Complaints and Discipline Investigation Bureau and Hd, Strategic Planning and Policy Analysis Unit, Metropolitan Police, 1984–86; Chief Constable, Northants Police, 1986–93; HM Inspector of Constabulary, 1993–96. British Chief Constables' Rep., Nat. Exec. Inst., FBI Acad., Washington, 1988. Dir, police extended interview scheme, 1992–93. Vis. Teaching Fellow, Mgt Centre, Univ. of Aston, Birmingham, 1988; Vis. Prof., UWE, 2002. Fellow, 1994, Gov., 2002–10, Univ. of Northampton (formerly Nene Coll., then UC Northampton). CCMI (CIMgt 1988). Freedom, City of London, 2008. DL 2002, High Sheriff, 2006–07, Northants. Hon. DSc Aston, 2003. OStJ 1999. *Recreation:* golf. *Clubs:* Northampton Golf (Harlestone, Northants), Aphrodite Hills Golf (Paphos, Cyprus) (Captain, 2015).

O'DOWD, John Fitzgerald; Member (SF) Upper Bann, Northern Ireland Assembly, since 2003; Minister of Education, since 2011; *b* Banbridge, Co. Down, 10 May 1967; *s* of Vincent and Bridie O'Dowd; *m* 1998, Mary; one *s* one *d*. *Educ:* Lismore Comp. Sch. Mem., Craigavon Council, 1997–2010. Contested (SF) Upper Bann, 2010. *Address:* Sheena Campbell House, 77 North Street, Lurgan, Co. Armagh BT67 9AH. *T:* (028) 3834 9675. *E:* johnodowd@sinn-fein.ie.

O'DRISCOLL, Most Rev. Percival Richard; Archbishop of Huron and Metropolitan of Ontario, 1993–2000; Bishop of Huron, 1990–2000; *b* 4 Oct. 1938; *s* of T. J. O'Driscoll and Annie O'Driscoll (*née* Copley); *m* 1965, Suzanne Gertrude Savignac; one *s* one *d*. *Educ:* Bishop's Univ., Lennoxville, Quebec (BA, STB); Huron Coll., London, Ont. (DD). Ordained deacon 1964, priest 1966; Assistant Curate: St Matthias, Ottawa, 1965–67; St John Evan, Kitchener, 1967–70; Religious Educn Dir, St Paul's Cathedral and Bishop Cronyn Memorial, London, 1970; Rector: St Michael & All Angels, London, 1970–75; St Bartholomew's, Sarnia, 1975–80; Rector, St Paul's Cathedral, and Dean of Huron, 1980–87; Suffragan Bishop of Huron, 1987–89; Coadjutor Bishop, 1989–90. *Recreations:* camping, hiking, photography. *Address:* 4–1241 Beaverbrook Avenue, London, Ontario, N6H 5P1, Canada. *Club:* London (Ontario).

O'DWYER, Martin Patrick; His Honour Judge O'Dwyer; a Circuit Judge, since 2007; *b* Wallasey, 24 Dec. 1955; *s* of Patrick O'Dwyer and Norah O'Dwyer (*née* Winterton). *Educ:* Merton Coll., Oxford (BA). Called to the Bar, Middle Temple, 1978; a Recorder, 1998–2007. *Recreations:* Dandie Dinmont terriers, gardening.

ŌE, Kenzaburo; Japanese writer; *b* 31 Jan. 1935; *m* 1960, Yukari Itami; two *s* one *d*. *Educ:* Tokyo Univ. (BA French Lit. 1959). Visited Russia and Western Europe to research and write series of essays on Youth in the West, 1961. Shinchosa Lit. Prize, 1964; Tanizaka Prize, 1967;

Nobel Prize for Literature, 1994. *Publications:* The Catch, 1958 (Akutagawa Prize); Nip the Buds, Shoot the Kids, 1958; Our Age, 1959; Screams, 1962; The Perverts, 1963; Hiroshima Notes, 1963; Adventures in Daily Life, 1964; A Personal Matter, 1964; The Silent Cry (original title, Football in the First Year of the Man'en Era), 1967; Teach us to Outgrow our Madness: four short novels, 1978; (ed) Fire from the Ashes: short stories about Hiroshima and Nagasaki, 1985; The Treatment Tower, 1990; Japan, the Ambiguous and Myself (lectures), 1995; A Quiet Life, 1998; Rouse Up O Young Men of the New Age!, 2002; Somersault, 2003; A Healing Family (biog. and autobiog.), 2007; The Changling, 2010. *Address:* Atlantic Books, 26–27 Boswell Street, WC1N 3JZ; 585 Seijo-Machi, Setagaya-Ku, Tokyo, Japan.

OEHLERS, Maj.-Gen. Gordon Richard, CB 1987; Director, Corps of Commissionaires, 1994–99; *b* 19 April 1933; *s* of late Dr Roderic Clarke Oehlers and Hazel Ethne Oehlers (*née* Van Geyzel); *m* 1956, Doreen, (Rosie), Gallant (*d* 2015); one *s* one *d*. *Educ:* St Andrew's School, Singapore. CEng, FIET. Commissioned Royal Corps of Signals, 1958; UK and Middle East, 1958–64; Adjutant, 4th Div. Signals Regt, 1964–66; Instructor, School of Signals, 1966–68; OC 7th Armd Bde HQ and Signals Sqdn, 1968–70; GSO2 (Weapons), 1970–72; CO 7th Signal Regt, 1973–76; Commander Corps Royal Signals, 1st (British) Corps, 1977–79; Dir, Op. Requirements 4 (Army), 1979–84; ACDS (Comd Control, Communications and Inf. Systems), 1984–87. Dir of Security and Investigation, British Telecom, 1987–94. Col Comdt, RCS, 1987–93; Hon. Col 31st (Greater London) Signal Regt (Volunteers), 1988–94. Chm., Royal Signals Instn, 1990–93. Pres., British Wireless Dinner Club, 1986–87. *Recreations:* interested in all games esp. badminton (Captain Warwicks County Badminton Team, 1954–56), lawn tennis (Chm., Army Lawn Tennis Assoc., 1980–86), golf. *Address:* c/o National Westminster Bank, 4 High Street, Petersfield, Hants GU32 3JF. *Club:* Liphook Golf (Captain, 1998–99).

OESTERHELT, Dr Jürgen; Ambassador of Germany to the Holy See, 1997–2000; *b* 19 Aug. 1935; *s* of Dr Egon Oesterhelt and Trude (*née* Pfohl); *m* 1963, Katharina Galeiski; one *s* one *d*. *Educ:* Munich Univ. (LLD 1959); State Bar Exam. 1962; Columbia Univ., NY (Master of Comparative Law 1963). Internat. lawyer in Paris, 1963–64; joined German Diplomatic Service, 1964; Moscow, 1965–66; UN, NY, 1967–71; Sofia, 1971–74; German Foreign Office, 1974–77; Athens, 1977–80; Foreign Office: Hd of Div., Legal Dept, 1980–85; Dir, Political Dept, 1985–86; Dir Gen., Legal Dept and Legal Advr to Foreign Minister, 1986–92; Ambassador to Turkey, 1992–95; Ambassador to the UK, 1995–97. Mem., Bd of Trustees, Anglo-German Foundn, 2003–09. Commander's Cross: Order of Merit (Germany), 1997 (Cross, 1988); Order of Phoenix (Greece), 1982; Order of White Rose (Finland), 1989; Grand Cross: Order of Merit (Austria), 1990; Order of Pius IX, 2000. *Recreations:* music, reading. *Address:* Auf der Königsbitze 4, 53639 Königswinter, Germany. *E:* juergen@oesterhelt.de.

OESTREICHER, Rev. Canon Dr Paul; Hon. Consultant, Centre for International Reconciliation, Coventry Cathedral, 1997–2005 (Director of the International Ministry of Coventry Cathedral, 1986–97); Canon Residentiary of Coventry Cathedral, 1986–97, now Canon Emeritus; Member of the Society of Friends (Quakers), since 1982; Quaker Chaplain to the University of Sussex, 2004–10, now Chaplain Emeritus; journalist; *b* Meiningen, Germany, 29 Sept. 1931; *s* of Paul Oestreicher and Emma (*née* Schnaus); *m* 1st, 1958, Lore Feind (*d* 2000); one *s* two *d* (and one adopted *s* decd); 2nd, 2002, Prof. Barbara Einhorn. *Educ:* King's High Sch., Dunedin; Univ. of Otago (BA Pol Sci. and German 1953); Victoria Univ., NZ (MA Hons Pol Sci. 1955); Lincoln Theol Coll. Fled to NZ with refugee parents, 1939; Editor, Critic (Otago Univ. newspaper), 1952–53; subseq. free-lance journalist and broadcaster; returned to Europe, 1955. Humboldt Res. Fellow, Bonn Univ., 1955–56, Free Univ. of Berlin, 1992–93; fraternal worker with German Lutheran Church at Rüsselsheim, trng in problems of industrial soc. (Opel, Gen. Motors), 1958–59; ordained 1959; Curate, Dalston, E London, 1959–61; Producer, Relig. Dept, BBC Radio, 1961–64; Assoc. Sec., Dept of Internat. Affairs, Brit. Council of Churches with special resp. for East-West Relations, 1964–69; Vicar, Church of the Ascension, Blackheath, 1968–81; Asst Gen. Sec. and Sec. for Internat. Affairs, BCC, 1981–86; Dir of (Lay) Trng, Dio. Southwark, 1969–72; Hon. Chaplain to Bp of Southwark, 1975–81; Public Preacher in Dio. Southwark, 1981–86; Hon. Canon of Southwark Cathedral, 1978–83, Canon Emeritus 1983–86. Vis. Fellow, 2010, Res. Associate, 2011–, Nat. Centre for Peace and Conflict Studies, Univ. of Otago. Member: Gen. Synod of C of E, 1970–86, 1996–97; Internat. Affairs Cttee, C of E, 1965–2001. Member: Brit. Council of Churches working parties on Southern Africa and Eastern Europe; Anglican Pacifist Fellowship, 1960– (Counsellor, 1998–); Exec. Cttee, Christian Peace Conf., Prague, 1964–68; Exec. Mem., Christian Concern for Southern Africa, 1978–81; Chm. of Trustees, Christian Inst. (of Southern Africa) Fund, 1984–95; Chairman: British Section, Amnesty International, 1974–79; Christians Aware, 1999–2000; Pres., Action by Christians against Torture, 2005–. Mem. Council, Keston Coll. (Centre for the Study of Religion and Communism), 1976–82. Vice-Chm., 1980–81, Vice-Pres. 1983–, Campaign for Nuclear Disarmament; Mem. Alternative Defence Commn, 1981–87; Vice-Chm., Ecumenical Commn for Church and Society in W Europe (Brussels), 1982–86. Trustee, Dresden Trust, 1993–2005. Companion, Community of the Cross of Nails, 2007–. Shelley Lectr, Radio NZ, 1987; Keynote speaker, WCC Internat. Ecumenical Peace Convocation, Kingston, Jamaica, 2011. Launched Oestreicher Leadership Prog., King's High Sch., Dunedin, 2013. Freeman, Meiningen, Germany, 1995. Hon. DLitt Coventry Polytechnic, 1991; Hon. LLD Sussex, 2005; DD Lambeth, 2008; Hon. DD Otago, 2009. Prize for Promotion of European Unity, Wartburg Foundn, 1997; Award of Merit, City of Coventry, 2002. Order of Merit, 1st Cl. (Germany), 1995; Order of Merit, Free State of Saxony, 2004. *Publications:* (ed English edn) Helmut Gollwitzer, The Demands of Freedom, 1965; (trans.) H. J. Schultz, Conversion to the World, 1967; (ed, with J. Klugmann) What Kind of Revolution: A Christian-Communist Dialogue, 1968; (ed) The Christian Marxist Dialogue, 1969; (jtly) The Church and the Bomb, 1983; The Double Cross, 1986. *Recreations:* addicted to newsprint, active and passive, Mozart, Bach, Johann Strauss, Father and Son and the cry of seagulls. *Address:* 97 Furze Croft, Furze Hill, Hove, E Sussex BN3 1PE. *T:* (01273) 728033. *E:* paul.oestreicher.nz@gmail.com; 42/8 Leeds Street, Te Aro, Wellington 6011, New Zealand.

O'FARRELL, Hon. Barry Robert; MP (L) Ku-ring-gai, since 1999 (Northcott, 1995–99); Premier of New South Wales, 2011–14; *b* Melbourne, 24 May 1959; *m* 1992, Rosemary Kent Cowan; two *s*. *Educ:* Australian National Univ. (BA 1979). State Dir, NSW Liberal Party, 1992–95. New South Wales Government: Shadow Minister, 1998–2007; Dep. Leader of the Opposition, 1999–2002, 2003–07; Leader of the Opposition, 2007–11; Minister for Western Sydney, 2011–14. Leader, NSW Liberal Party, 2007–14. *Recreations:* bushwalking, reading, family. *Address:* (office) 27 Redleaf Avenue, Wahroonga, NSW 2076, Australia. *T:* 94878588. *E:* kuringgai@parliament.nsw.gov.au.

O'FARRELL, Declan Gerard, CBE 2000; FCCA; Chief Executive Officer, Castletown Corporation Limited, since 2003; *b* 10 Feb. 1949; *s* of Bartholomew and Mary Carmel O'Farrell; *m* 1971, Jennie; one *s* three *d*. *Educ:* Finchley Catholic Grammar Sch. FCCA 1973. With British Tissues, 1967–81 (mgt trainee to Gp Mgt Accountant); financial analyst, Express Dairies, 1981; various financial posts with Express Foods Gp (Financial Controller, Distribn Div., until 1986); joined LT bus operations, 1986; Dir, 1989–2004, Man. Dir, 1989–94, Chief Exec., 1994–2003, Metroline (new bus co. subsid.), subseq. Metroline plc. Dir, NW London TEC, 1990–2001 (Chm., 1993–96); Founder Mem., London TEC Council. Chm., Business Link London, 1997–2001. Chairman: West Herts Coll., 2004–11; Herts Community NHS Trust (formerly Herts Community Health Services, NHS), 2010–. CCMI (CIMgt 2001); FRSA 2000. *Recreations:* gardening, golf, vintage bus.

O'FARRELL, Finola Mary Lucy, (Mrs S. Andrews); QC 2002; a Recorder, since 2006; *b* 15 Dec. 1960; *d* of John Stephen O'Farrell and Rosaleen Mary O'Farrell; *m* 1993, Stuart Andrews (*d* 2010); one *d*. *Educ:* St Philomena's Sch., Carshalton; Durham Univ. (BA Hons). Called to the Bar, Inner Temple, 1983; in practice, specialising in construction law. Mem., editl team, Keating on Building Contracts, 5th edn 1991, 6th edn 1995; Jt Ed., Construction Law Yearbook, 4th edn, 1999; Consulting Ed., Construction Law Reports, 2007–. *Publications:* (contrib.) Engineers' Dispute Resolution Handbook, 2006, 2nd edn 2011; (contrib.) ICE Manual of Construction Law, 2010. *Recreations:* horse riding, contemporary dance and art, theatre. *Address:* Keating Chambers, 15 Essex Street, Outer Temple, WC2R 3AA. *T:* (020) 7544 2600, *Fax:* (020) 7544 2700. *E:* fofarrell@keatingchambers.com.

O'FARRELL, Margaret Helen, (Maggie); author; *b* Coleraine, NI, 27 May 1972; *m* William Sutcliffe; one *s* two *d*. *Educ:* North Berwick High Sch.; Brynteg Comp. Sch.; New Hall Coll., Cambridge (BA Hons Eng. Lit. 1993). Editl Asst, Asst Arts Ed., then Dep. Literary Ed., Independent on Sunday, 1996–2000. *Publications:* After You'd Gone, 2000 (Betty Trask Award, 2001); My Lover's Lover, 2002; The Distance Between Us, 2004 (Somerset Maugham Award, 2005); The Vanishing Act of Esme Lennox, 2006; The Hand that First Held Mine (Costa Novel Award), 2010; Instructions for a Heatwave, 2013. *Address:* c/o A. M. Heath and Co., 6 Warwick Court, WC1R 5DJ.

O'FERRALL, Rev. Patrick Charles Kenneth, OBE 1989; Hon. Assistant Priest, St Andrew's, Farnham, since 2012; *b* 27 May 1934; *s* of late Rev. Kenneth John Spence O'Ferrall and Isoult May O'Ferrall; *m* 1st, 1960, Mary Dorothea (*d* 1997), 4th *d* of late Maj. C. E. Lugard and Mrs K. I. B. Lugard; one *s* two *d*; 2nd, 1999, Wendy Elizabeth Barnett (*née* Gilmore). *Educ:* Pilgrims Sch., Winchester (Cathedral Chorister); Winchester Coll. (Scholar); New Coll., Oxford (BA Lit.Hum. 1958; MA); Harvard Business Sch. (AMP 1983). Nat. Service, 1952–54, 2nd Lieut, Royal Fusiliers. Iraq Petroleum and associated cos, 1958–70; BP, 1971–73; Total CFP Paris (Total Moyen Orient), 1974–77; Total Oil Marine, London: Commercial Manager, 1977–82; Dir, Gas Gathering Pipelines (N Sea) Ltd, 1977–78; Project Co-ordination Manager, Alwyn N, 1983–85; Projects Co-ordination Manager, 1985–90; Dep. Chm., 1991–93, Chm., 1993–99, Lloyd's Register of Shipping. Mem., Offshore Industry Adv. Bd, 1992–94. Chm., City of London Outward Bound Assoc., 1993–97. Mem., Court of Common Council, Corp. of London, 1996–2001. Liveryman, Co. of Shipwrights, 1992–; Master, Coachmakers' and Coach Harness Makers' Co., 1993–94. FRSA 1993; CCMI (CIMgt 1994). Hon. FREng 2000. Lay Reader, 1961–2000; ordained deacon, 2000, priest, 2001; Curate (Ordained Local Minister), 2000–07, Hon. Asst Priest, 2007–12, SS Peter and Paul, Godalming. *Recreations:* music (playing violin and singing), tennis, golf, wine, crosswords, travel. *Address:* Pear Tree House, 66 Firgrove Hill, Farnham, Surrey GU9 8LW. *T:* (01252) 724498. *E:* patrickoferrall@gmail.com. *Clubs:* MCC, Aldgate Ward (Pres., 1998), Oxford and Cambridge.

OFFER, Prof. Avner, DPhil; FBA 2000; Chichele Professor of Economic History, University of Oxford, 2000–11; Fellow, All Souls College, Oxford, 2000–11, now Emeritus; *b* 15 May 1944; *s* of Zvi and Ivriyah Offer; *m* 1966, Leah Koshet; one *s* one *d*. *Educ:* Western Valley Sch., Yif'at, Israel; Hebrew Univ. (BA 1973); St Antony's Coll., Oxford; Merton Coll., Oxford (MA 1976; DPhil 1979). Mil. service, Israel, 1962–65; Kibbutz mem., 1965–67; Conservation Officer, Israel, 1967–69; Jun. Res. Fellow, Merton Coll., Oxford, 1976–78; Lectr in Econ. and Social Hist., 1978–90, Reader, 1990–91, Univ. of York; Reader in Recent Social and Econ. Hist., Univ. of Oxford, and Fellow, Nuffield Coll., 1992–2000. Hartley Fellow, Univ. of Southampton, 1981–82; Vis. Associate, Clare Hall, Cambridge, 1984; Res. Fellow, Inst. Advanced Study, ANU, 1985–88; Sen. Fellow, Rutgers Univ., 1991–92; Sen. Vis. Fellow, Remarque Inst., NY Univ., 1999; Leverhulme Major Res. Fellow, 2008–11; Principal Investigator, Inst. for New Econ. Thinking project on Nobel Prize in Econs, 2011–13. FAcSS (AcSS 2003). *Publications:* Property and Politics 1870–1914: landownership, law, ideology and urban development in England, 1981; The First World War: an agrarian interpretation, 1989; (ed) In Pursuit of the Quality of Life, 1996; The Challenge of Affluence: self-control and well-being in the United States and Britain since 1950, 2006; (ed) Insecurity, Inequality and Obesity in Affluent Societies, 2012; articles on land, law, empire, consumption and quality of life. *Recreations:* literature, classical music, visual arts. *Address:* 15 Hamilton Road, Oxford OX2 7PY. *T:* (01865) 553380.

OFFER, Ven. Clifford Jocelyn; Archdeacon of Norwich and Canon Residentiary (Canon Librarian) of Norwich Cathedral, 1994–2008; *b* 10 Aug. 1943; *s* of late Rev. Canon Clifford Jesse Offer and Jocelyn Mary Offer; *m* 1980, Dr Catherine Mary Lloyd; two *d*. *Educ:* King's Sch., Canterbury; St Peter's Coll., Oxford (sent down); Exeter Univ. (BA 1967); Westcott House, Cambridge. Ordained deacon, 1969, priest, 1970; Curate, St Peter and St Paul, Bromley, 1969–74; Team Vicar, Southampton City Centre, 1974–83; Team Rector, Hitchin, 1983–94. Vice Chm., then Chm., St Albans ABM, 1989–94; Chairman: Norwich Diocesan Adv. Bd for Mission and Ministry (formerly ABM), 1994–99, 2000–03; Norwich Course Mgt Cttee, 1999–2003; Norwich Bd of Ministry, 2003–08; Warden of Readers, Dio. Norwich, 1994–2008; Bishops' Advr (formerly Bishops' Selector), 1995–; Mem., Gen. Synod of C of E, 1999–2005. Mem., Council for E Anglia Studies, 2000–08. FRSA 1997. *Publications:* King Offa in Hitchin, 1992; In Search of Clofesho, 2002. *Recreations:* collecting naval buttons, ship-modelling, growing chrysanthemums. *Address:* Chase House, Peterstow, Herefordshire HR9 6JX. *T:* (01989) 567874.

OFFMANN, Karl Auguste; President, Republic of Mauritius, 2002–03; *b* 25 Nov. 1940; *s* of Laurent Wilford Offmann and Liliane Armoorgum; *m* 1969, Marie-Rose Danielle Moutou; two *s*. *Educ:* Mech. Engrg Apprenticeship Scholar 1956; Claver House, London (Dip. Social and Political Sci. 1975). Plant and Personnel Manager, L'Express, daily newspaper, 1963–79. Leader, Internat. Young Christian Workers Movement, 1957–79; politician, 1976–2002 (full–time, 1982–2002). Founder Mem., Africa Forum, 2006–. Grand Commander, Order of Star and Key of the Indian Ocean (Republic of Mauritius); Grand Croix 1st class, l'Ordre National à Madagascar. *Address:* P18 Cité Jules Koenig–Vuillemin, Beau–Bassin, Mauritius. *T:* 454 2880, *Fax:* 454 9634. *E:* offmann@intnet.mu.

OFFNER, Gary John; Director, Priority Markets and Partnerships, New South Wales Trade and Investment, since 2012; *b* 26 Oct. 1961; *s* of John Frederick Offner and Dorothy Offner; *m* 1993, Beth Frances Hickey. *Educ:* Christian Brothers Coll., Sutherland; Barristers' Admission Board (Dip. Law 1988); Univ. of Technology, Sydney (MBA 1993); Australian Inst. of Co. Dirs. Joined NSW Public Sector, 1980; admitted to NSW Bar, 1988; Advr to Minister for Natural Resources, 1988–89; Manager, Internat. Div., NSW Dept of State and Regl Develt, 1990–97; Official Rep. of NSW Govt in UK and Europe and Dir, NSW Govt Trade and Investment Office, 1997–2001; Dir, Strategic Markets, NSW Govt, 2001–03; Review Dir, NSW Premier's Dept, 2003; Dir, NSW Dept of State and Regl Develt, 2003–09; Dir, State and Regl Develt and Tourism, Industry and Investment, NSW, 2009–11. *Recreations:* golf, cricket, Rugby, sailing. *Address:* L47 MLC Centre, 19 Martin Place, Sydney, NSW 2000, Australia. *Club:* Sydney Cricket Ground.

OFFORD, Dr Matthew James, FRGS; MP (C) Hendon, since 2010; *b* Alton, Hants, 3 Sept. 1969; *s* of Christopher and Hilda Offord; *m* 2010, Claire Michelle Rowles. *Educ:* Amery Hill Sch., Alton; Nottingham Trent Univ. (BA Hons); Lancaster Univ. (MA); King's Coll. London (PhD 2011). FRGS 2005. Political analyst, BBC, 2001–10. Mem. (C) Barnet BC, 2002–10 (Dep. Leader, 2006–09). Chm., Hendon Cons. Assoc., 2004–07. Contested (C)

Barnsley E and Mexborough, 2001. *Recreations:* scuba diving, sailing, swimming, reading, travel, wine. *Address:* House of Commons, SW1A 0AA. *T:* (020) 7219 7083. *E:* matthew.offord.mp@parliament.uk.

OFIELD-KERR, Dr Simon Douglas; Vice-Chancellor, University for the Creative Arts, since 2011; *b* Newton Abbott, 28 Jan. 1966; *s* of late Derek Malcolm Ofield and of Patricia Ofield; civil partnership 2006, Anton Kerr; one *s*. *Educ:* Bishopshalt Sch., Hillingdon; Exeter Coll. of Art and Design (BA Hons Fine Art 1990); Univ. of Leeds (MA Social Hist. of Art 1992; PhD Hist. of Art 1997). Academic Gp Chair for Art, Philosophy and Visual Culture, Middlesex Univ., 1996–2006; Dean, Faculty of Art, Design and Architecture, Kingston Univ., 2006–11. Member, Executive Group: UK Arts and Design Instns Assoc., 2011–; GuildHE, 2013–. Gov., Kingston Grammar Sch., 2010–. FRSA 2006. Mem. Bd and Founder Ed., Jl of Visual Culture, 2002–. *Publications:* articles in Art History, Jl of Visual Culture, Oxford Art Jl, Visual Culture in Britain. *Address:* University for the Creative Arts, Falkner Road, Farnham, Surrey GU9 7DS. *T:* (01252) 892600. *E:* sofieldkerr@ucreative.ac.uk.

OFILI, Christopher; artist; *b* Manchester, 1968. *Educ:* Tameside Coll. of Technol.; Chelsea Sch. of Art (Christopher Head drawing scholarship 1989; BA); Hochschule der Künste, Berlin; Royal Coll. of Art (MA). British Council Travel Scholarship, Zimbabwe, 1992. Trustee, Tate, 2000–05. Solo exhibitions include: Kepler Gall., London, 1991; Victoria Miro Gall., London, 1996, 2000, 2002; Contemporary Fine Art, Berlin, 1997, 2005; Southampton City Art Gall., 1998; Serpentine Gall., London, 1998; Whitworth Art Gall., Manchester, 1998–99; Gavin Browns Enterprise, NY, 1999; Gall. Side 2, Japan, 2001; (as GB rep.) Venice Biennale, 2003; Studio Mus., Harlem, 2005; Tate Britain, 2005–07, 2010 (retrospective); Kestnergesellschaft, Hanover, 2006; David Zwirner, NY, 2007; New Mus., NY, 2014. Group exhibitions include: Cornerhouse Gall., Manchester, 1993; MOMA, Oxford, 1995; ICA, 1997; Mus. of Contemp. Art, Sydney, 1997; RA, 1997; Walker Art Gall., Liverpool, 1997; British Council touring exhibn, incl. Finland, Sweden and Czech Republic, 1997–2000; Tate Gall., 1998–99; 6th Internat. Biennale, Istanbul, 1999; Carnegie Mus. of Art, Pittsburgh, 1999–2000; Brooklyn Mus. of Art, NY, 1999; Saatchi Gall., 2000; South Bank Centre, 2000; Mus. of Contemp. Art, LA, 2001; Bronx Mus. of the Arts, NY, 2002 (and touring); Santa Monica Mus. of Art, Calif, 2002; MOMA, NY, 2002; Nat. Gall. and UK tour, 2003; Joslyn Art Mus., Omaha, 2004; Palais de Tokyo, 2005; ICA, Boston, 2005; MOMA, NY, 2005; MOMA, NY, V&A, Hayward Gall., London, 2006; MIMA, Middlesbrough, Gary Tatinsian Gall., Moscow, 2007; Metamorphosis: Titian, ROH and Nat. Gall., London, 2012. Hon. Fellow, Univ. of the Arts, London, 2004. Turner Prize, 1998; Southbank Award, Visual Arts, London, 2004. *Address:* c/o Victoria Miro Gallery, 16 Wharf Road, N1 7RW.

O'FLAHERTY, Prof. Coleman Anthony, AM 1999; Deputy Vice-Chancellor, University of Tasmania, Australia, 1991–93, Professor Emeritus 1993; *b* 8 Feb. 1933; *s* of Michael and Agnes O'Flaherty; *m* 1957, Nuala Rose Silke (*d* 1999). *Educ:* Nat. Univ. of Ireland (BE); Iowa State Univ. (MS, PhD). FICE; FIEI; FIE(Aust); FCIHT. Engineer: Galway Co. Council, Ireland, 1954–55; Canadian Pacific Railway Co., Montreal, 1955–56; M. W. Kellogg Co., USA, 1956–57; Asst Prof., Iowa State Univ., 1957–62; Leeds University: Lectr, 1962–66; Prof. of Transport Engineering, Inst. for Transport Studies and Dept of Civil Engineering, 1966–74; First Asst Comr (Engineering), Nat. Capital Develt Commn, Canberra, 1974–78; Dir and Principal, Tasmanian Coll. of Advanced Educn, subseq. Tasmanian State Inst. of Technology, 1978–90. Vis. Prof., Univ. of Melbourne, 1973. Chairman: Tasmanian Liby Adv. Bd, 1997–2006; Tasmania State Liby and Archives Trust, 1997–2006. Trustee, Tasmanian Mus. and Art Gall., 1993–2000. Dep. Nat. Pres., Assoc. Independent Retirees, 2007–10 (Pres., Tasmanian Div., 2005–07). Hon. LLD Tasmania, 1994. *Publications:* Highways, 1967, vol. I of 4th edn (Transport Planning and Traffic Engineering), 1997, vol. II of 4th edn (Highway Engineering), 2001; (jtly) Passenger Conveyors, 1972; (jtly) Introduction to Hovercraft and Hoverports, 1975; contribs to professional jls. *Recreation:* bush walking. *Address:* 22 Beach Road, Legana, Tasmania 7277, Australia. *T:* and *Fax:* (3) 63301990. *Club:* Launceston.

O'FLAHERTY, Stephen John, CMG 2003; Managing Director, Goldman Sachs International, since 2005; *b* 15 May 1951; *s* of late Brig. Denis O'Flaherty, CBE, DSO and of Jill O'Flaherty; *m* 1975, (Sarah) Louise Gray; one *s* two *d*. *Educ:* Douai Sch.; Jesus Coll., Oxford (BA). HM Diplomatic Service, 1975–2004: entered FCO, 1975; Second Sec., New Delhi, 1977–80; First Secretary: FCO, 1980–81; Prague, 1981–84; FCO, 1984–88; Vienna, 1988–92; Counsellor, FCO, 1992–2004. *Address:* (office) Peterborough Court, 133 Fleet Street, EC4A 2BB.

O'FLYNN, Patrick James; Member (UK Ind) Eastern Region, European Parliament, since 2014; *b* Cambridge, 29 Aug. 1965; *m* Carol Ann Rice; two *c*. *Educ:* Parkside Community Coll., Cambridge; Long Road Sixth Form Coll., Cambridge; King's Coll., Cambridge (BA Econs 1987); City Univ., London (Dip. Journalism). Reporter, Hull Daily Mail, 1989–92; reporter, 1992–93, political corresp., 1993–96, Birmingham Post; Dep. Political Ed., Sunday Express, 1996–98; Chief Political Commentator, 1998–2000, Political Ed., 2000–14, Daily Express. Dir of Communications, then Econs spokesman, UKIP, 2014–15. Contested (UK Ind) Cambridge, 2015. *Address:* European Parliament, 60 Rue Wiertz, 1047 Brussels, Belgium.

of MAR, family name of **Countess of Mar**.

O'GARRA, Dr Anne, FRS 2008; Associate Director, Francis Crick Institute, since 2015; Adjunct Professor, National Heart and Lung Institute, Imperial College London, since 2012; *b* Gibraltar, 4 Nov. 1954; *d* of late Louis O'Garra and Teresa O'Garra (*née* Azzopardi); *m* Dr Paulo Julio de Miranda Vieira. *Educ:* Chelsea Coll., Univ. of London (BSc 1st Cl. Hons Microbiol. and Biochem. 1980); Nat. Inst. for Med. Res. (PhD 1983). Postdoctoral Fellow, Div. of Immunol., NIMR, 1983–87; DNAX Research Institute, Palo Alto, California: Postdoctoral Fellow, 1987–89; Sen. Res. Associate, 1989–93; Staff Scientist, then Sen. Staff Scientist, 1993–98; Principal Staff Scientist, 1999–2001; Head, Div. of Immunoregulation, MRC Nat. Inst. for Med. Res., 2001–15. Mem., EMBO, 2009. FMedSci 2005; FAAAS 2006. *Publications:* contribs to scientific jls incl. Nature, Eur. Jl Immunol., Jl Exptl Medicine, Immunol., Immunity. *Address:* Francis Crick Institute, Mill Hill Laboratory, The Ridgeway, Mill Hill, NW7 1AA.

OGATA, Prof. Sadako, Hon. DCMG 2011; Special Advisor to President, Japan International Cooperation Agency (President, 2003–12); Co-Chair, Commission on Human Security, 2001–03; Chair, Advisory Board on Human Security, 2003–11, now Hon. Chair; *b* 16 Sept. 1927; *m*; one *s* one *d*. *Educ:* Univ. of the Sacred Heart, Tokyo (BA); Georgetown Univ. (MA); PhD California (Berkeley). Prof., 1980–90, Director of Internat. Relations, 1987–88, Dean, Faculty of Foreign Studies, 1989–90, Sophia Univ., Japan. Minister, Perm. Mission of Japan to UN, 1976–78; Chm. Exec. Bd, UNICEF, Japanese Rep. to UN Commn on Human Rights, 1982–85; UN High Comr for Refugees, 1991–2000. Hon. DCL Oxon, 1998; Hon. LLD Cantab, 1999. *Publications:* Defiance in Manchuria: the making of Japanese foreign policy 1931–1932, 1964; The Turbulent Decade: confronting the refugee crisis of the 1990s, 2005. *Address:* c/o Japan International Cooperation Agency, Nibancho Center Building, 5–25 Niban-cho, Chiyoda-ku, Tokyo 102–8012, Japan.

OGBORN, Prof. Miles, PhD; FBA 2012; Professor of Geography, Queen Mary, University of London. Formerly at St David's UC, Lampeter. Philip Leverhulme Prize, Leverhulme Trust, 2001; Dist. Histl Geographer, Assoc. of Amer. Geographers, 2009. *Publications:* Spaces of Modernity: London's geographies 1680–1780, 1998; (contrib.) Introducing Cultural Studies, 1999, 2nd edn 2008; (ed jtly) Cultural Geography in Practice, 2003; (ed with C. W. J. Withers) Georgian Geographies: essays on space, place and landscape in the Eighteenth Century, 2004; Indian Ink: script and print in the making of the English East India Company, 2007; Global Lives: Britain and the world, 1550–1800, 2008; (ed with C. W. J. Withers) Geographies of the Book, 2010; contribs to jls incl. Jl Histl Geog., Trans IBG, Hist. of Sci. *Address:* School of Geography, Queen Mary, University of London, Mile End Road, E1 4NS.

OGDEN, Sir Peter (James), Kt 2005; Founder and Chairman, The Ogden Trust, since 1994; *b* 26 May 1947; *s* of late James Platt Ogden and Frances Ogden (*née* Simmonds); *m* 1970, Catherine Rose Blincoe; two *s* one *d*. *Educ:* Rochdale Grammar Sch.; Univ. of Durham (BSc 1968; PhD 1971); Harvard Business Sch. (MBA 1973); Hughes Hall, Cambridge (MA 2002). Man. Dir, Morgan Stanley & Co., 1985; Chairman: Computacenter Ltd, 1985–97 (non-exec. Dir, 1997–); Dealogic Ltd, 1985–. Hon. FInstP 2010. Hon. DCL Durham, 2002; Hon. DSc Warwick, 2009. *Recreation:* sailing. *Address:* The Ogden Trust, Hughes Hall, Cambridge CB1 2EW. *T:* (01223) 761843, *Fax:* (01223) 761837. *E:* office@ogdentrust.com. *Club:* Royal Yacht Squadron (Cowes).

OGDEN, Prof. Raymond William, PhD; FRS 2006; George Sinclair Professor of Mathematics, University of Glasgow, 1984–2010 and since 2012; *b* 19 Sept. 1943; *s* of Arthur and Norah Ogden; *m* 1969, Susanne Thomas; two *s* two *d*. *Educ:* Gonville and Caius Coll., Cambridge (BA 1966; PhD 1970). SRC Postdoctoral Res. Fellow, UEA, 1970–72; Lectr, 1972–76, Reader, 1976–80, in Maths, Univ. of Bath; Prof. of Maths, Brunel Univ., 1981–84; 6th Century Chair in Engrg, Univ. of Aberdeen, 2010–12. *Publications:* Non-linear Elastic Deformations, 1984, 2nd edn 1997; (jtly) Nonlinear Theory of Electroelastic and Magnetoelastic Interactions, 2014; more than 200 articles in internat. scientific jls. *Recreations:* music, wine, learning languages, absorbing the sun in the Mediterranean. *Address:* School of Mathematics and Statistics, University of Glasgow, University Gardens, Glasgow G12 8QW. *E:* Raymond.Ogden@glasgow.ac.uk.

OGG, Derek Andrew; QC (Scot.) 1999; Senior Advocate Depute, 2007–11; Head, National Sexual Crimes Unit, Crown Office, Edinburgh, 2009–11; *b* 19 Sept. 1954; *s* of Alec and Elsie Ogg. *Educ:* Edinburgh Univ. (LLB 1978). Dip. in Master Advocacy, Nat. Inst. for Trial Advocacy, USA, 1996. Asst Solicitor, Ross & Connel Solicitors, Dunfermline, 1978–80; Partner and Founder, Hunter Burns & Ogg Solicitors, Edinburgh, Perth and Dunfermline, 1980–89; Standing Jun. Counsel, Scottish Office, 1983–88; called to the Scottish Bar, 1989; Jun. Counsel, 1989–99; Reserve Counsel, UN *Ad Hoc* Tribunal for War Crimes in Former Republic of Yugoslavia, The Hague, 1998–2004. Chm. (*ad hoc*), Discipline Tribunal, ICAS, 2001–. Chm., Faculty of Advocates Criminal Bar Assoc., 2003–05. Founder and Chm., Scottish Aids Monitor, 1983–93; Trustee, Nat. Aids Trust, 1987–90. Mem., Royal Philosophical Soc., Glasgow. Founding Fellow (FFCS) 2002, Hon. Fellow, 2004, Inst. for Contemporary Scotland. *Recreations:* hill-walking in Scotland, collecting and competing classic cars, supporter of Celtic Football Club, reading history, occasional broadcaster and commentator on public affairs on TV and radio in Scotland. *Address:* Rawcliffe House, 10 Rawcliffe Gardens, Mansionhouse Road, Glasgow G41 3DA. *E:* derekandrewogg@hotmail.com.

OGILVIE, (Dame) Bridget (Margaret), (Dr Bridget Ogilvie), AC 2007; DBE 1997; FRCPath, FMedSci; FRS 2003; FAA; FRSB; Director: Wellcome Trust, 1991–98; AstraZeneca (formerly Zeneca Group plc), 1997–2006; High Steward of University of Cambridge, 2001–09; *b* 24 March 1938; *er d* of late John Mylne Ogilvie and Margaret Beryl (*née* McRae). *Educ:* New England Girls' Sch., Armidale, NSW; Univ. of New England, Armidale (BRurSc 1960; Distinguished Alumni Award, 1994); PhD 1964, ScD 1981, Cambridge. FRSB (FIBiol 1985); FRCPath 1992. Parasitology Div., Nat. Inst. for Med. Res., London, 1963–81; Ian McMaster Fellow, CSIRO Div. of Animal Health, Australia, 1971–72; with Wellcome Trust, 1979–98: Co-ordinator, Tropical Med. Prog., 1979–81; Dep. Sec. and Asst Dir, 1981–84; Dep. Dir, Science, 1984–89; Dir, Science Progs, 1989–91. Director: Lloyds Bank, 1995; Lloyds TSB Gp, 1996–2000. Visiting Professor: Dept of Biology, Imperial Coll., London, 1985–92; UCL, 1998–. Member: Council for Science and Technol., 1993–2000; Commonwealth Scholarship Commn, 1993–2000; Adv. Council for Chemistry, Univ. of Oxford, 1997–2001; Australian Health and Med. Res. Strategic Review, 1998–99; Chairman: COPUS, 1998–2002; AstraZeneca Sci. Teaching Trust, 1998–2006; Medicines for Malaria Venture, 1999–2006; Adv. Cttee for Sci., Technol., Business, British Liby, 2000–02. Non-executive Director: Scottish Sci. Trust, 1999–2002; Manchester Technol. Fund, 1999–2004. Chm., Assoc. of Med. Res. Charities, 2002–07. Trustee: Sci. Mus., London, 1992–2003; RCVS Trust Fund, 1998–2001; NESTA, 1998–2002; Cancer Res. UK (formerly CRC), 2001–10; Sense about Science, 2002–; Centre of the Cell, UK, 2005–14. Chairman, Governing Body: Inst. for Animal Health, 1997–2003; Lister Inst., 2002–11. Founder FMedSci 1998; FAA 2008. Hon. Member: British Soc. for Parasitology, 1990; Amer. Soc. of Parasitologists, 1992; BVA, 1998; BAAS, 2005; Hon. FRCP 1996 (Hon. MRCP 1992); Hon. FRACP 1998; Hon. ARCVS 1993. Hon. Fellow: UCL, 1993; Girton Coll., Cambridge, 1993; St Edmund's Coll., Cambridge, 1999; Mansfield Coll., Oxford, 2010; Hon. FRVC 1994; Hon. FIBiol 1998; Hon. FRSocMed 1999. Hon. DSc: Nottingham, Salford, Westminster, 1994; Glasgow, Bristol, ANU, 1995; Buckingham, Dublin, Trent, Oxford Brookes, 1996; Greenwich, 1997; Auckland, NZ, Durham, Kent, 1998; Exeter, Imperial Coll., London, 1999; Leicester, 2000; Manchester, St Andrews, 2001; Wollongong, 2005; New England, 2015; Hon. LLD: TCD, 1996; Dundee, 1998; Hon. MD Newcastle, 1996; Dr *hc* Edinburgh, 1997. Lloyd of Kilgerran Prize, Foundn for Sci. and Technology, 1994; Wooldridge Meml Medal, BVA, 1998; Australian Soc. for Medical Res. Medal, 2000; Kilby Award, Kilby Awards Foundn, USA, 2003; Duncan Davies Meml Medal, Res. and Develt Soc., 2004; Ralph Doherty Meml Medal, Qld Inst. of Medical Res., 2006. *Publications:* contrib. scientific papers to parasitological and immunological jls. *Recreations:* the company of friends, looking at landscapes, music, gardening. *Address:* 79 Brondesbury Road, NW6 6BB. *Clubs:* Reform; Oxford and Cambridge; Queen's (Sydney).

OGILVIE, Ven. Gordon; Archdeacon of Nottingham, 1996–2006; *b* 22 Aug. 1942; *s* of late Gordon and Eliza J. Ogilvie (*née* Cullen); *m* 1967, Sylvia Margaret, *d* of late Rankin and Jessie Weir; one *s* one *d*. *Educ:* Hillhead High Sch., Glasgow; Glasgow Univ. (MA 1964); London Coll. of Divinity (ext. BD London Univ., 1967). Ordained deacon, 1967, priest, 1968; Asst Curate, Ashtead, 1967–72; Vicar, St James, New Barnet, 1972–80; Dir, Pastoral Studies, Wycliffe Hall, Oxford, 1980–87; Priest-in-charge, 1987–89, Team Rector, 1989–96, Harlow Town Centre with Little Parndon; Chaplain, Princess Alexandra Hosp., Harlow, 1988–96. Hon. Canon, Chelmsford Cathedral, 1993–96. *Recreations:* sport in general, piano, photography. *Address:* 49 Argyle Street, St Andrews, Fife KY16 9BX. *T:* (01334) 470185. *E:* gordon.ogilvie@virgin.net.

OGILVIE, Prof. Sheilagh Catheren, PhD; FBA 2004; Professor of Economic History, University of Cambridge, since 2004; *b* 7 Oct. 1958; *d* of Robert Townley Ogilvie and Sheilagh Stuart Ogilvie. *Educ:* Queen Elizabeth Sch.; Univ. of St Andrews (MA 1st cl. Hons 1979); Trinity Coll., Cambridge (PhD 1985); Univ. of Chicago (MA 1992). Res. Fellow, Trinity Coll., Cambridge, 1984–88; Univ. Asst Lectr, 1989–92, Univ. Lectr, 1992–99, Reader in Econ. History, 1999–2004, Faculty of Econs, Univ. of Cambridge. *Publications:* The Park Buffalo: the history of the conservation of the North American bison, 1979; (ed) Proto-Industrialization in Europe, 1993; (ed with Markus Cerman) Protoindustrialisierung in Europa: Industrielle Produktion vor dem Fabrikszeitalter, 1994; Germany: a new social and economic history, (ed) vol. 2, 1630–1800, 1996, (ed with Richard Overy) vol. 3, Since 1800, 2003; (ed with Markus Cerman) European Proto-Industrialization, 1996; State Corporatism and Proto-Industry: the Württemberg Black Forest 1590–1797, 1997; A Bitter Living: women, markets and social capital in Early Modern Germany, 2003; Institutions and European Trade: merchant guilds, 1000–1800, 2011; articles in Amer. Historical Rev., Bohemia, Český časopis historický, Comparative Studies in Soc. and Hist., Continuity and Change, Early Modern Women, Econ. Hist. Rev., Explorations in Econ. Hist., Histoire sociale/Social History, Histoires et sociétés rurales, Historical Jl, Historická Demografie, Jahrbuch für Wirtschaftsgeschichte, Jahrbuch für Regionalgeschichte, Jl of Econ. Hist., Jl of Econ. Perspectives, The History of the Family, Past & Present, Revue d'Allemagne et des pays de langue allemande, Social Hist. and Trans of RHistS, Zeitschrift für Agrargeschichte und Agrarsoziologie, Zeitschrift für württembergische Landesgeschichte. *Recreations:* indiscriminate reading, walking in Central European mountains, thinking, talking, counting. *Address:* Faculty of Economics, University of Cambridge, Sidgwick Avenue, Cambridge CB3 9DD. *T:* (01223) 335222, *Fax:* (01223) 335475. *E:* sco2@econ.cam.ac.uk.

OGILVIE-GRANT, family name of **Earl of Seafield**.

OGILVIE THOMPSON, Julian; Director: De Beers Consolidated Mines Ltd, 1966–2006 (Deputy Chairman, 1982–85 and 1998–2001; Chairman, 1985–97); De Beers SA, 2002–08; *b* 27 Jan. 1934; *s* of late Hon. N. Ogilvie Thompson, formerly Chief Justice of S Africa, and of Eve Ogilvie Thompson; *m* 1956, Hon. Tessa Mary Brand, *yr surv. d* of 4th Viscount Hampden, CMG and Leila, Viscountess Hampden; two *s* two *d. Educ:* Diocesan Coll., Rondebosch; Univ. of Cape Town; Worcester Coll., Oxford. MA. Diocesan Coll. Rhodes Scholar, 1953. Joined Anglo American Corp. of SA Ltd, 1956; Dir, 1970; Exec. Dir, 1971–82; Dep. Chm., 1983–90; Chm., 1990–2002; Anglo American plc: Chief Exec., 1999–2000; Chm., 1999–2002; Chairman: Anglo American Gold Investment Co. Ltd, 1976–90; Minorco SA (formerly Minerals and Resources Corp. Ltd), 1982–99; Vice Chairman: First Nat. Bank Ltd, 1977–90; Urban Foundn, 1986–95. Rhodes Trustee, 2002–15; Trustee, Mandela Rhodes Foundn, 2003–. Hon. LLD Rhodes, 1986. Comdr, Order of the Crown (Belgium), 1993; Grand Official, Order of Bernardo O'Higgins (Chile), 1996; Presidential Order of Honour (Botswana), 1997. *Recreations:* shooting, fishing, golf. *Address:* Froome, Froome Street, Athol Extension 3, Sandton, 2196, S Africa. *T:* (11) 8843925. *Club:* White's.

OGILVY, family name of **Earl of Airlie**.

OGILVY, Lord; David John Ogilvy; *b* 9 March 1958; *s* and *heir* of 13th Earl of Airlie, *qv*; *m* 1st, 1981, Hon. Geraldine Harmsworth (marr. diss. 1991), *d* of 3rd Viscount Rothermere; one *d*; 2nd, 1991, Tarka Kings; three *s. Educ:* Eton and Oxford (MA). Man. Dir, Richard L. Feigen UK Ltd, art dealers, 1982–2002. Trustee: Macmillan Trust, 2006–; Rothschild Foundn, 2013–. *Heir: s* Master of Ogilvy, *qv. Address:* Airlie Castle, Kirriemuir, Angus DD8 5NG.

OGILVY, Master of; David Huxley Ogilvy; *b* 11 Dec. 1991; *s* and *heir* of Lord Ogilvy, *qv*.

OGILVY, Sir Francis (Gilbert Arthur), 14th Bt *cr* 1626 (NS), of Inverquharity, Forfarshire; Chartered Surveyor; *b* 22 April 1969; *s* of Sir David John Wilfrid Ogilvy, 13th Bt and of Penelope Mary Ursula, *d* of Captain Arthur Lafone Frank Hills, OBE; *S* father, 1992; *m* 1996, Dorothy, *e d* of Rev. Jock Stein and Rev. Margaret Stein; three *s* one *d. Educ:* Edinburgh Acad.; Glenalmond; RAC, Cirencester (BSc Hons). MRICS. *Heir: s* Robert David Ogilvy, *b* 8 July 1999. *Address:* Winton House, Pencaitland, E Lothian EH34 5AT.

OGILVY, Hon. James (Donald Diarmid); Chairman, Foreign & Colonial Management Ltd, 1998–99 (Chief Executive, 1988–97); *b* 28 June 1934; *y s* of 12th Earl of Airlie, KT, GCVO, MC and Lady Alexandra Marie Bridget Coke, *d* of 3rd Earl of Leicester, GCVO, CMG; *m* 1st, 1959, June Ducas (marr. diss. 1978; she *d* 2001); two *s* two *d*; 2nd, 1980, Lady Caroline (*née* Child-Villiers), *d* of 9th Earl of Jersey. *Educ:* Eton Coll. Served 1st Bn, Scots Guards, Egypt, 1953–55 (2nd Lieut). Partner, Rowe & Pitman, 1959–86; Vice Chm., Mercury Asset Management plc, 1986–88. Chairman: Sutherlands (Holdings), 1998–2000; Off Plan Fund, 2004–05. Director: Foreign and Colonial Investment Trust, 1990–97; Foreign & Colonial Emerging Markets, 1995–98; Berkshire Capital Corp. UK, 1998–2006; Lord North Street Holdings Ltd, 2005–08; Black Sea Fund, 2005–06. Dir, 1974–76, Chm., 1976–83, Inst. for Obstetrics and Gynaecology; Gov., Queen Charlotte's and Chelsea Hosp. for Women, 1974–80. Chm., Garden Museum (formerly Museum of Garden History), 2002–11. A Page of Honour to King George VI, 1947–51. Mem., Queen's Body Guard for Scotland, Royal Co. of Archers. Grand Official, Nat. Order of the Southern Cross (Brazil), 1993. *Recreations:* shooting, golf. *Address:* Sedgebrook Manor, Sedgebrook, Grantham, Lincs NG32 2EU. *T:* (01949) 842337; Flat 20, Stack House, Cundy Street, SW1W 9JS. *Clubs:* White's, Pratt's, Turf, Boodles Ladies.

OGILVY-WEDDERBURN, Sir Andrew John Alexander, 7th Bt *cr* 1803, of Balindean, Perthshire (13th Bt *cr* 1704 but for the attainder, 1746); *b* 4 Aug. 1952; *s* of Sir (John) Peter Ogilvy-Wedderburn, 12th and 6th Bt, and late Elizabeth Katharine, *e d* of John A. Cox, Drumkilbo; *S* father, 1977; *m* 1st, 1984, Gillian Meade (marr. diss. 2014), *yr d* of Richard Adderley, Pickering, N Yorks; two *s* (twins) one *d* (and one *s* decd); 2nd, 2014, Fiona Margaret Anne, *d* of William Beaton, Earls Mill, Moray. *Educ:* Gordonstoun. QCVS 1996. *Heir: s* Peter Robert Alexander Ogilvy-Wedderburn, *b* 20 April 1987. *Address:* Silvie House, Alyth, Perthshire PH11 8NA.

OGIO, Sir Michael, GCMG 2011 (CMG 2001); CBE 1994; Governor-General of Papua New Guinea, since 2011; *b* PNG, 17 July 1943; *m* (*d* 2009); four *s* one *d. Educ:* Dip. Curriculum Develt; Australian Sch. of Pacific Admin (Dip. Sch. Admin). School teacher; sch. inspector. Mem., N Solomons, Provincial Govt, 1980–84 (Dep. Premier and Minister of Educn); Mem. (People's Democratic Movt) N Bougainville Open, Nat. Parlt, 1987–2002 and 2007–10; Minister: for Conservation; for Public Service, 1988; Minister, then Vice Minister, for Bougainville Affairs, 1992–94; Vice Minister for Corporate Affairs, 1997–98; Dep. Speaker, 1998; Minister for Forests, 1998–2000; Dep. Prime Minister, 2000–02; Minister for Higher Educn, Res. and Technol. KStJ. *Recreation:* formerly soccer in youth. *Address:* Government House, PO Box 79, Port Moresby, Papua New Guinea. *T:* 3214874, *Fax:* 3214543. *Club:* Papuan Royal.

OGLE, Very Rev. Catherine; Dean of Birmingham, since 2010; *b* Upminster, 12 May 1961; *d* of Henry Charles Ogle and Josephine Ogle (*née* Bathard); *m* 1990, Robin Goater; one *s. Educ:* Perse Sch. for Girls, Cambridge; Univ. of Leeds (BA 1982; MPhil 1985; MA 1991); Westcott House, Cambridge; Fitzwilliam Coll., Cambridge (BA 1987). Ordained deacon, 1988; Asst Curate, St Mary, Middleton, Leeds, 1988–91; Religious Progs Ed., BBC Radio Leeds, 1991–95; NSM, St Margaret and All Hallows, Leeds, 1991–95; ordained priest, 1994; Priest-in-charge, Woolley with W Bretton, 1995–2001; Vicar of Huddersfield, 2001–10; Chaplain, Univ. of Huddersfield, 2003–06. Mem. Council, Coll. of the Resurrection, Mirfield, 2008–10. Hon. Canon, Wakefield Cathedral, 2008. Hon. DLitt Aston, 2014. *Recreations:* painting, reading, theatre, walking, cooking, fashion, Radio 4. *Address:* 38 Goodby Road, Moseley, Birmingham B13 8NJ. *E:* dean@birminghamcathedral.com.

OGLESBY, Michael John, CBE 2011; Vice Lord-Lieutenant, Greater Manchester, 2008–14; Chairman, Bruntwood Ltd, since 2000; *b* Scunthorpe, 5 June 1939; *s* of George Oglesby and Alice Oglesby; *m* Jean; one *s* one *d. Educ:* De Aston Sch., Market Rasen; Aston Univ., Birmingham (BSc Building). Founder, 1978, CEO, 1980–2000, Bruntwood Estates Ltd. Chairman: MIDAS, 2004–; RNCM, 2004–12; Steering Bd, MCRC, 2005–. DL 2005, High Sheriff 2007, Gtr Manchester. Hon. LLD Manchester, 2006; Hon. DSc Aston, 2007. *Recreations:* sailing, ski-ing, theatre, music. *Address:* Bruntwood Ltd, City Tower, Piccadilly Plaza, Manchester M1 4BT.

OGLESBY, Peter Rogerson, CB 1982; *b* 15 July 1922; *s* of late Leonard William Oglesby and late Jessie Oglesby (*née* Rogerson); *m* 1st, 1947, Doreen Hilda Hudson (*d* 2006); three *d*; 2nd, 2012, Doreen Lilian Keeling. *Educ:* Woodhouse Grove Sch., Apperley Bridge. Clerical Officer, Admty, 1939–47; Exec. Officer, Min. of Nat. Insce, 1947–56; Higher Exec. Officer, MPNI, 1956–62, Principal 1962–64; Principal Private Secretary: to Chancellor of Duchy of Lancaster, 1964–66; to Minister without Portfolio, 1966; to First Sec. of State, 1966–68; to Lord President, 1968; Asst Sec., Cabinet Office, 1968–70, Asst Sec., DHSS, 1970–73; Sec., Occupational Pensions Bd, 1973–74; Under Sec., 1974–79; Dep. Sec., 1979–82, DHSS. Dir, Regency Final Gp, 1983–91. *Address:* 7 Roebuck Heights, North End, Buckhurst Hill, Essex IG9 5RF. *T:* (020) 8504 9104.

OGLEY, William David; Chief Executive, States of Jersey, 2003–11; *b* 26 May 1955; *s* of Thomas William and Olive Ogley; *m* 1976, Anne Dolores Walker; two *d. Educ:* Manchester Univ. (BA Hons Physics and Psych.); CIPFA (prize winner). Derbyshire CC, 1976–83 (to Principal Accountant, 1980–83); Group Accountant, Oxfordshire CC, 1983–85; Hertfordshire County Council: Sen. Asst County Treasurer, 1985–88 (Educn and Social Services); Dep. County Treasurer, 1988–90; Dir, Inf. Systems, 1990–91; Dir of Finance, 1991–93; Dep. Controller and Dir of Resources, Audit Commn, 1993–96; Chief Exec., 1996–2003. *Recreations:* tennis, gardening, sailing, family, reading.

OGMORE, 3rd Baron *cr* 1950, of Bridgend; **Morgan Rees-Williams;** *b* 19 Dec. 1937; *s* of 1st Baron Ogmore, PC, TD and (Alice Alexandra) Constance Rees-Williams (*née* Wills); *S* brother, 2004; *m* 1990, Beata Ewa Solska; two *s. Educ:* Mill Hill Sch. Lieut, The Welch Regt, 1956–58. *Heir: s* Hon. Tudor David Rees-Williams, *b* 11 Dec. 1991. *Address:* 50 Novello Street, SW6 4JB. *T:* (020) 7736 2734.

OGNALL, Hon. Sir Harry Henry, Kt 1986; DL; a Judge of the High Court of Justice, Queen's Bench Division, 1986–2000; *b* 9 Jan. 1934; *s* of Leo and Cecilia Ognall; *m* 1977, Elizabeth Young; two step *s* and two *s* one *d* of former marriage. *Educ:* Leeds Grammar Sch.; Lincoln Coll., Oxford (MA (Hons)); Univ. of Virginia, USA (LLM; Fulbright Scholar, 1956). Called to Bar (Gray's Inn), 1958; Bencher, 1983. Joined NE Circuit; a Recorder, 1972–86; QC 1973. Member: Criminal Injuries Compensation Bd, 1976; Planning Cttee, Senate of Inns of Court and Bar, 1980–83; Professional Conduct Cttee, 1985; Judicial Studies Bd (Chm., Criminal Cttee), 1986–89; Parole Bd, 1989–91 (Vice-Chm., 1990–91); a Judicial Mem., Proscribed Orgns Appeal Commn, 2001–09. Arbitrator, Motor Insurers' Bureau Agreement, 1979–85. Trustee, Martin House Hospice, 2002–10. DL W Yorks, 2000. *Recreations:* photography, bridge, grandchildren. *Club:* Ilkley Bowling.

O'GORMAN, Michelle Jane; *see* Corbett, M. J.

O'GRADY, Frances Lorraine Maria; General Secretary, Trades Union Congress, since 2012 (Deputy General Secretary, 2003–12); *b* 9 Nov. 1959; *d* of James and Margaret O'Grady; one *s* one *d. Educ:* Milham Ford Comprehensive Sch., Oxford; Manchester Univ. (BA Pols and Mod. Hist.); Middlesex Polytechnic (Dip Ind Relns and Trade Union Studies). Employment Rights Officer, Women and Employment Project, 1982–87; Health and Safety Officer, City Centre, London, 1987–88; Campaigns Officer, Health Rights, 1988–89; Sen. Researcher, TGWU, 1989–94; Trades Union Congress: Campaigns Officer, 1994–96; Dir, New Unionism, 1996–98; Hd, Orgn, 1998–2003. Member: Unite (TGWU); NUJ. *Publications:* (with Heather Wakefield) Women, Work and Maternity: the inside story, 1989. *Recreations:* labour history, cinema, Arsenal FC. *Address:* Trades Union Congress, Congress House, Great Russell Street, WC1B 3LS. *T:* (020) 7636 4030, *Fax:* (020) 7636 0632. *E:* fogrady@tuc.org.uk.

O'GRADY, Prof. Francis William, CBE 1984; TD 1970; MD, MSc; FRCP, FRCPath, FFPM; Foundation Professor of Microbiology, University of Nottingham, 1974–88, now Emeritus; *b* 7 Nov. 1925; *s* of Francis Joseph O'Grady and Lilian Maud Hitchcock; *m* 1951, Madeleine Marie-Thérèse Becquart; three *d. Educ:* Middlesex Hosp. Med. Sch., London (BSc 1st Cl. Hons; MB, BS Hons; MSc; MD). FRCP 1976; FRCPath 1972; FFPM 1989. House Physician, Middx and North Middx Hosps, 1951; Asst Pathologist, Bland-Sutton Inst. of Pathol., Middx Hosp., 1952–53, 1956–58 and 1961–62; Pathologist, RAMC, 1954–55, AER, 1956–72; Asst Prof. of Environmental Medicine, Johns Hopkins Univ., Baltimore, 1959–60; Reader, 1962–66, and Prof. of Bacteriology, 1967–74, Univ. of London; Bacteriologist, St Bartholomew's Hosp., 1962–74; Chief Scientist, DHSS, subseq. DoH, 1986–90. Hon. Consultant Microbiologist, PHLS, 1974–96. Mem., MRC, 1980–84, 1986–90; Chm., MRC Physiol Systems and Disorders Bd, 1980–82 (Mem., 1977–80; Mem., Grants Cttee, 1975–76); Chm., MRC Cttee on Hosp. Infection, 1977–80 (Mem., 1967–77). Member: Antibiotics Panel, Cttee on Med. Aspects of Food Policy, 1968–72; Sub-Cttee on Toxicity, Clin. Trials and Therapeutic Efficacy, 1971–75, and Sub-Cttee on Biol Substances, 1971–81, Cttee on Safety of Medicines; Jt Sub-Cttee on Antimicrobial Substances, Cttee on Safety of Medicines and Vet. Products Cttee, 1973–80; Cttee on Rev. of Medicines, 1975–81; Public Health Lab. Service Bd, 1980–86, 1993–96; Nat. Biological Standards Bd, 1983–87. Hon. Consultant Microbiologist to the Army, 1982–91. William N. Creasy Vis. Prof. of Clin. Pharmacology, Duke Univ., NC, 1979. Erasmus Wilson Demonstrator, RCS, 1967; Foundn Lectr, Univ. of Hong Kong, 1974; Sydney Watson Smith Lectr, RCPE, 1975; Jacobson Vis. Lectr, Univ. of Newcastle upon Tyne, 1979; Berk Lectr, British Assoc. of Urol Surgeons, 1980; Garrod Lectr, British Soc. for Antimicrobial Chemotherapy, 1983; Jenner Lectr, St George's Hosp. Med. Sch., 1988. Pres. Council, British Jl of Exper. Pathol., 1980–91 (Mem., 1968–80); Mem. Editorial Boards: Jl of Med. Microbiol., 1970–75; Pathologie Biologie, 1973–78; British Jl of Clin. Pharmacol., 1974–84; Drugs, 1976–88; Gut, 1977–83; Jl of Infection, 1978–83; Revs of Infectious Diseases, 1979–88. *Publications:* Airborne Infection: transmission and control, 1968; Antibiotic and Chemotherapy, 1968, 7th edn 1997; (ed) Urinary Tract Infection, 1968; (ed) Microbial Perturbation of Host Defences, 1981; papers on clin. and exper. infection and on antimicrobial chemotherapy. *Address:* Letheringsett Hall, Church Lane, Letheringsett, Holt NR25 7YA.

O'GRADY, Jeremy Robert; Founding Editor, since 1995, and Editor in Chief, since 2003, The Week magazine; *b* Wüppertal, Germany, 12 July 1953; *s* of Major Robert Hardress Standish O'Grady, MC and Hon. Joan O'Grady; *m* 2005, Hon. (Juliana) Caroline (Matilda) Law, *d* of Baron Coleraine, *qv*; three *s* one *d. Educ:* Ampleforth Coll.; Trinity Coll., Cambridge (BA Social and Pol Scis 1975); Cornell Univ. (MA Govt). Res. Officer, Child Welfare, London Bor. of Redbridge, 1979–82; Researcher, Inst. of Community Studies, 1982–84; Film Censor, BBFC, 1984–94. Res. Fellow, London Business Sch., 1991–93. Co-Founder, Intelligence Squared, 2002–. *Publications:* New Ways of Delivering Local Services, 1985. *Recreations:* arguing, hiking. *Address:* 2 Sterndale Road, W14 0HS. *E:* jeremy_ogrady@theweek.co.uk.

O'GRADY, Michael Gerard; QC (Scot.) 1999; Sheriff of Lothian and Borders at Edinburgh, since 2007; Temporary Judge, since 2004; *b* 19 Aug. 1954; *s* of Thomas Anthony O'Grady and Margaret Imelda O'Grady (*née* King); *m. Educ:* Univ. of Glasgow (MA, LLB). Solicitor in private practice, 1977–88; admitted to Faculty of Advocates, 1988; Advocate Depute, 1993–97; Standing Junior to FCO, 1997–99; Chm., Advocates' Criminal Law Gp,

1999–2000; Floating Sheriff of Glasgow and Strathkelvin, 2000–07. Examiner, Glasgow Graduate Law Sch., 2002–. *Recreations:* guitar, travel, reading, art. *Address:* Sheriff Court House, 27 Chambers Street, Edinburgh EH1 1LB. *Club:* Scottish Arts (Edinburgh).

O'GRADY, Paul James, MBE 2008; drag queen, entertainer, television and radio presenter, author and actor; *b* Birkenhead, 14 June 1955; *s* of late Patrick O'Grady and Mary, (Molly), O'Grady; one *d*. *Educ:* Redcourt St Anselm's; Corpus Christi High Sch., Birkenhead. *Television* series: The Lily Savage Show, 1997; Lily Savage's Blankety Blank, 1998–2002; Lily Live, 2000–01; Paul O'Grady's Orient, 2000; Paul O'Grady's America, 2001; Eyes Down, 2003; The Paul O'Grady Show, 2004–05, 2013–14; The New Paul O'Grady Show, 2006; Paul O'Grady Live, 2010–11; Paul O'Grady's For the Love of Dogs, 2012–15; Paul O'Grady's Working Class, 2013; Paul O'Grady's Animal Orphans, 2014–15; The Paul O'Grady Show, 2015; other television includes: Playhouse Presents: Nellie and Melba (co-writer), 2012; Little Crackers: Boo (writer), 2012; *radio:* presenter, Radio 2, 2009–; *theatre:* Prisoner Cell Block H - the Musical, 1995; Annie, 1998; Snow White; Aladdin; Child Catcher in Chitty Chitty Bang Bang, 2002. Hon. Fellow, Liverpool John Moores Univ., 2005. Hon. DArts De Montfort, 2010. *Publications:* At My Mother's Knee… and other low joints, 2008; The Devil Rides Out, 2010; Still Standing: the Savage years, 2012. *Recreations:* fire eating, smallholder, conservationist, gay activist. *Address:* c/o BM Creative Management Ltd, Second Floor, Aldwych House, 81 Aldwych, WC2B 4HN. *T:* (020) 7151 0152. *E:* bmcreative@dircon.co.uk.

OGSTON, Prof. Derek, CBE 1995; MD, PhD, DSc; FRCP; FRSE 1982; Professor of Medicine, 1983–97, and Vice Principal, 1987–97, University of Aberdeen; *b* 31 May 1932; *s* of Frederick John Ogston and Ellen Mary Ogston; *m* 1963, Cecilia Marie Clark; one *s* two *d*. *Educ:* King's Coll. Sch., Wimbledon; Univ. of Aberdeen (MA, PhD 1962; MD 1969; DSc 1975; MLitt 1999; BTh 2005). FRCP Edin. 1973; FRCP 1977; FRSB (FIBiol 1987). University of Aberdeen: Res. Fellow, 1959–62; Lectr in Medicine, 1962–69; Sen. Lectr in Med., 1969–75; Reader in Med., 1975–76; Regius Prof. of Physiology, 1977–83; Dean, Faculty of Medicine, 1984–87. MRC Trav. Fellow, 1967–68. Vice-Chm., Grampian Health Bd, 1993–97 (Mem., 1991–97); Mem., GMC, 1984–94. Member: Governing Body, Rowett Res. Inst., 1977–92; Court, Univ. of Aberdeen, 1998–2002. Hon. LLD Aberdeen, 2007. *Publications:* Physiology of Hemostasis, 1983; Antifibrinolytic Drugs, 1984; Venous Thrombosis, 1987; The Life and Work of George Smith, RSA, 2000; George Leslie Hunter 1877–1931, 2002; Working Children, 2003; Leslie Hunter: drawings and paintings of France and Italy, 2004; Children at School, 2005; (jtly) King's College, Aberdeen, 2009; (jtly) Stichill Parish: past and present, 2010; scientific papers on haemostasis. *Recreations:* music, travel, wildlife. *Address:* 64 Rubislaw Den South, Aberdeen AB15 4AY. *T:* (01224) 316587.

OGUNDEHIN, Michelle Aramide Janet; Editor-in-Chief: Elle Decoration UK, since 2004; Elle Decoration Country, since 2011; *b* Salford, 5 Nov. 1967; *d* of Aderemi and Barbara Ogundehin; *m* 1996, Eamonn Dunne (marr. diss. 1998); one *s*. *Educ:* Bartlett Sch. of Architecture, University Coll. London (BSc Hons Architecture 1989; DipArch 1992). Asst Ed., Blueprint, 1995–96; Sen. Ed., Blueprint Mag., 1996; Elle Decoration UK: Features Dir, 1997–98; Dep. Ed., 1998–99; Ed.-at-Large, 1999–2004; Ed.-in-Chief, Real Homes, 2007–08. Dir, MO:Studio Ltd, 2002–. Trustee, V&A Mus., 2008–; Dir, V&A Enterprises Bd, 2009–. Dir, South Coast Design Forum, 2008–13. FRSA 2009. *Publications:* (with P. Murray) Understanding Plans, 1997; Bringing Architecture Home, 2003; (contrib.) LA Lofts, 2006; Swarovski Crystal Palace, 2010. *Recreations:* Basset Hounds, Italy, good design, film, friends, family, food. *Address:* Elle Decoration, Hearst Magazines UK, 72 Broadwick Street, W1F 9EP. *T:* (020) 7534 2522. *E:* michelle.ogundehin@hearst.co.uk. *W:* www.mostudio.co.uk, www.twitter.com/MOgundehin.

OGUS, Prof. Anthony Ian, CBE 2002; FBA 2007; Professor of Law, University of Manchester, 1987–2008, now Emeritus; *b* 30 Aug. 1945; *s* of Samuel Joseph Ogus and Sadie Phyllis Ogus (*née* Green); *m* 1st, 1980, Catherine Klein (*d* 1998); 2nd, 2001, Helen Margaret Legard Owens. *Educ:* St Dunstan's Coll.; Magdalen Coll., Oxford (BA 1966; BCL 1967; MA 1970). Asst Lectr in Law, Univ. of Leicester, 1967–69; Tutorial Fellow in Law, Mansfield Coll., Oxford, 1969–75; Sen. Res. Fellow, Centre for Socio-Legal Studies, Wolfson Coll., Oxford, 1975–78; Prof. of Law, Univ. of Newcastle, 1978–87. Res. Prof., Univ. of Maastricht, 1997–2008; Erasmus Prof. of Private Law, Univ. of Rotterdam, 2008–11. Mem., Social Security Adv. Cttee, 1994–2008. Columnist, Opera Now. *Publications:* Law of Damages, 1973; (jtly) Law of Social Security, 1978, 5th edn 2002; (jtly) Policing Pollution, 1983; (jtly) Readings in the Economics of Law and Regulation, 1984; Regulation: legal form and economic theory, 1994; (jtly) Controlling the Regulators, 1998; (jtly) Economie du droit: le cas français, 2002; Costs and Cautionary Tales: economic insights for the law, 2006; Travels with my Opera Glasses, 2013; articles in legal periodicals. *Recreations:* theatre, opera, concerts, cycling, reading, walking. *Address:* Woodland House, Midgeley Lane, Goldsborough HG5 8NN. *T:* (01423) 864099. *Club:* Oxford and Cambridge.

O'HAGAN, 4th Baron *cr* 1870; **Charles Towneley Strachey;** *b* 6 Sept. 1945; *s* of Hon. Thomas Anthony Edward Towneley Strachey (*d* 1955; having assumed by deed poll, 1938, the additional Christian name of Towneley, and his mother's maiden name of Strachey, in lieu of his patronymic) and Lady Mary (who *m* 1981, St John Gore, CBE, FSA; she *d* 2000), *d* of 3rd Earl of Selborne, PC, CH; *S* grandfather, 1961; *m* 1995, Mrs Elizabeth Lesley Eve Macnamara (*née* Smith); two *d* from previous marriages. *Educ:* Eton; (Exhibitioner) New College, Oxford. Page to HM the Queen, 1959–62. Independent Member, European Parliament, 1973–75; Junior Opposition Whip, House of Lords, 1977–79; MEP (C) Devon, 1979–94. *Heir: brother* Hon. Richard Towneley Strachey, *b* 29 Dec. 1950. *Address:* The Granary, Beaford, Winkleigh, Devon EX19 8AB.

O'HAGAN, Dr Dara; Member (SF) Upper Bann, Northern Ireland Assembly, 1998–2003; *b* 29 Aug. 1964; *d* of Joseph and Bernadette O'Hagan. *Educ:* Univ. of Ulster (BA Hons Hist. and Politics 1991); Queen's Univ., Belfast (MSSc 1994; PhD 1998). Contested (SF) Upper Bann, 2001.

O'HAGAN, Leonard John Patrick, CBE 2012; DL; Chairman, Northern Ireland Water, since 2015; *b* Newry, Co. Down, 15 May 1954; *s* of late Leonard O'Hagan and of Ruby O'Hagan; *m* 1981, Maureen Dalzell; one *s* one *d*. *Educ:* St Colman's Coll., Newry; Queen's Univ., Belfast (BSc Econ). Jefferson Smurfit Group: PA to Sir Michael Smurfit, 1985–88; Man. Dir, Print and Distribution Div., 1988–90; Chief Operating Officer, Fitzwilton plc, 1990–99; CEO, Fitzwilton Ltd, 1999–2002. Chairman: Safeway Ireland, 1996–2000; Resource Services Gp, 2011–14; non-executive Director: Waterford Wedgwood UK plc, 1999–2002; Independent News and Media, 2012–. Chm., Belfast Harbour Comrs, 2007–14. Mem. Council, CBI, 1993–2000; Chm., CBI/IBEC Business Cttee, 1997–2001; Vice Pres., Ireland-US Business Council, 2008–. Chm., Metropolitan Arts Centre, 2010. FInstD 2002. DL Co. Down, 2010. Hon. DSc Ulster, 2011; Hon. DSc Econs QUB, 2013. *Recreations:* sailing, ski-ing, golf, art. *Clubs:* Royal North of Ireland Yacht, Royal St George Yacht.

O'HALLORAN, Sarah Jane; *see* Vaughan Jones, S. J.

O'HANLON, Michael David Peter, PhD; Director, Pitt Rivers Museum, Oxford, 1998–2015; Professorial Fellow, Linacre College, Oxford, 1998–2015, now Emeritus; *b* 2 July 1950; *s* of late Michael Charles O'Hanlon and Rosemary Alice O'Hanlon, Kitale, Kenya; *m* 1981, Linda Helga Elizabeth, *d* of (Anthony) Noble Frankland, *qv*; one *d*. *Educ:* Kenya; Plymouth Coll., Devon; Pembroke Coll., Cambridge (MA); University Coll. London (PhD 1985). Field res., Wahgi Valley, PNG Highlands, 1979–81; Curator, Pacific collections, Ethnography Dept, BM, 1983–98. Visitor: Mus. of Hist. of Sci., Oxford Univ., 1998–2015; Oxford Univ. Mus. of Nat. Hist., 2002–15; Mem., Cttee to Visit, Peabody Mus., Harvard, 2003–13; Trustee, Horniman Mus., 2010–14. Mem. Council, 1994–97, Hon. Sec., 1997–98, RAI. Reviews Editor, MAN, 1988–90; Mem., Editl Bd, Jl Material Culture, 1996–2015. *Publications:* Reading the Skin, 1989; Paradise: portraying the New Guinea Highlands, 1993; (ed with E. Hirsch) The Anthropology of Landscape, 1995; (ed with Robert L. Welsch) Hunting the Gatherers: ethnographic collectors, agents and agency in Melanesia 1870s–1930s, 2000; (ed with E. Ewart) Body Arts and Modernity, 2007; The Pitt Rivers Museum: a world within, 2014; contrib. articles and reviews in professional jls.

O'HARA, Brendan; MP (SNP) Argyll and Bute, since 2015; *b* Glasgow, 27 April 1963; *m* Catherine; two *d*. *Educ:* St Andrew's Secondary Sch., Carntyne; Univ. of Strathclyde (BA Econ. Hist. and Modern Hist. 1992). Work with Glasgow DC; television producer, STV, Sky Sports, BBC; TV programmes include: Comedy Connections; Movie Connections; The Football Years; Scotland's Greatest Album; Road to Referendum. Contested (SNP): Glasgow Springburn, 1987; Glasgow Central, 1992. *Address:* House of Commons, SW1A 0AA.

O'HARA, Edward; *b* 1 Oct. 1937; *s* of Robert Edward O'Hara and Clara O'Hara (*née* Davies); *m* 1962, Lillian Hopkins (decd); two *s* one *d*; *m* 2014, Margaret Gilbert (*née* Gartside). *Educ:* Magdalen Coll., Oxford (MA 1962); PGCE 1966, DipED (Adv.) 1970, London. Assistant Teacher: Perse Sch., Cambridge, 1962–65; Birkenhead Sch., 1966–70; Lectr and Principal Lectr, C. F. Mott Coll. of Educn, 1970–74; Principal Lectr and Sen. Tutor, Dean of Postgrad. Studies, City of Liverpool Coll. of Higher Educn, 1974–83; Head of Curriculum Studies, Sch. of Educn and Community Studies, Liverpool Polytechnic, 1983–90. Knowsley Borough Council: Mem., 1975–91; Mem., all Standing Cttees; Chairman: Youth Cttee, 1977–79 and 1981–82; Educn Cttee, 1978–79 and 1987–90; Econ. Devel and Planning Cttee, 1990–91. MP (Lab) Knowsley S, Sept. 1990–2010. Mem., Speaker's Panel of Chairmen, 1993–10. Co-Chm., All Pty Gp on Ageing and Older People, 1997–10; Chairman: All Pty MV Derbyshire Gp, 1997–2005; British-Greek Gp, IPU, 1997–2010; Argentine Gp, IPU, 2005–10. Member: Bd of Management, NFER, 1986–90; European Assoc. of Teachers; Socialist Educn Assoc.; Hon. Mem. and Parly Advr, Assoc. of Chief Educn Social Workers, 1992–93; Member: Labour Movement in Europe; Perm. Cttee of Assembly of European Regions, 1989–90; Merseyside Rep., Régions Européennes de Tradition Industrielle, 1989–90; Deleg., Council of Europe and WEU, 1997–2010: Gen. Rapporteur for Cultural Heritage and Museums Rapporteur, Council of Europe, 2003–10; Chair, Technol. and Aerospace Cttee and Mem., Presidential Cttee, 2004–09, Mem., Defence Cttee, 2009–10, WEU. Member: Fabian Soc.; Co-op Party; Socialist Educn Assoc. Chm., British Cttee for Reunification of Parthenon Marbles, 2011–. Mem., Bd of Management, Royal Liverpool Philharmonic Soc., 1987–90; Corresp. Mem., Foundn for Hellenic Culture. Trustee, Community Develt Foundn (Chm., 1997–2005); Vice-Chm., Develt Trust Bd, Nat. Wildflower Centre, 1996–2010. Former Vice-Pres., TS Iron Duke, Huyton. Governor: Knowsley Community Coll., 1975–2010; Prescot Co. Primary Sch., 1975–2008. Former Pres., Knowsley South Jun. FC. *Recreations:* music (classical, jazz, folk, esp. Rembetiko), reading, theatre, travel, Greek language and culture. *Address:* 69 St Mary's Road, Huyton, Merseyside L36 5SR. *T:* (0151) 489 8021.

O'HARE, John Edward; Master of Senior Courts Costs Office (formerly Supreme Court Taxing, later Costs, Office), since 1995; *b* 26 Feb. 1949; *s* of Kevin Mark Plunkett O'Hare and Kathleen Mary O'Hare; *m* 1st, 1970, Vivien Eleanor Harwood; one *s*; 2nd, 1993, Alison Jane Springett; one *s*. *Educ:* Bromley Boys' GS; Leicester Univ. (LLB). Called to the Bar, Lincoln's Inn, 1972; College of Law: Lectr, 1974–78; Sen. Lectr, 1978–85; Principal Lectr, 1985–95. *Publications:* Civil Litigation, 1980, 17th edn 2015; (ed) White Book Service, 1999–2015. *Recreations:* bridge, cycling. *Address:* Senior Courts Costs Office, Thomas More Building, Royal Courts of Justice, Strand, WC2A 2LL.

O'HARE, Kevin Patrick; Director, Royal Ballet, since 2012; *b* Hull, 14 Sept. 1965; *s* of Michael O'Hare and Anne Veronica O'Hare (*née* O'Callaghan). *Educ:* Royal Ballet Sch. Sadler's Wells Royal Ballet, subseq. Birmingham Royal Ballet: Dancer, 1984–90; Principal Dancer, 1990–2000; Company Manager, 2001–04; Royal Ballet: Company Manager, 2004–09; Admin. Dir, 2009–12. Mem., Bd of Dirs, Northern Ballet, 2015–; Mem. Bd, Dance UK, 2013–. Gov., Royal Ballet Sch., 2000–09, 2012. Major roles as dancer incl. Siegfried, Florimund, Albrecht, Romeo, Amynta in Sylvia; performed in works by Ashton, Balanchine, Cranko, MacMillan, Van Manen, Tharp and Tudor. Hon. DA Hull, 2014. *Address:* Royal Opera House, Covent Garden, WC2E 9DD. *T:* (020) 7212 9685. *E:* kevin.ohare@roh.org.uk. *Club:* Soho House.

O'HARE, Prof. Peter, PhD; Professor of Virology, Department of Medicine, Imperial College London, since 2010; *b* 9 Dec. 1956; *s* of Eugene and Sinéad O'Hare; *m* 1983, Jane Hillier; two *d*. *Educ:* St Columb's Coll., Derry; Sheffield Univ. (BSc 1978); NIMR, London (PhD 1981). Res. Fellow, NIMR, London, 1981–83; Damon-Runyon Res. Fellow, Johns Hopkins Univ. Medical Sch., 1983–86; Gp Leader, 1986–2010, Dir, 2002–10, Marie Curie Research Inst. Chm., Scientific Adv. Bd, Pancreatic Cancer UK, 2012–. MAE 2008. *Publications:* numerous articles on molecular and cell biology, virology and field of gene delivery, in learned jls, Nature, Cell etc. *Recreations:* passionate (though untalented) photographer, hiking, canoeing, vociferous supporter of Irish Rugby, history of science. *Address:* Department of Medicine, Imperial College London, St Mary's Campus, Norfolk Place, W2 1PG.

O'HEAR, Prof. Anthony, PhD; Professor of Philosophy (formerly Garfield Weston Professor of Philosophy), University of Buckingham, since 2003 (Head, Department of Education, 2003–09); Director, Royal Institute of Philosophy, since 1994; *b* 14 Jan. 1942; *s* of Hugo O'Hear and Ann Margery Hester O'Hear (*née* Gompertz); *m* 1981, Patricia Catherine Mary Patterson (Patricia Linton, in ballet); one *s* two *d*. *Educ:* St Ignatius Coll., Tottenham; Heythrop Coll.; Warwick Univ. (MA 1968; PhD 1971). Lecturer in Philosophy: Univ. of Hull, 1971–75; Univ. of Surrey, 1975–84; Prof. of Philosophy, Univ. of Bradford, 1985–2003. Vis. Res. Fellow, LSE, 2002–; Calouste Gulbenkian Vis. Prof., Catholic Univ. of Portugal, 2004–05; Vis. Scholar, Social Philosophy and Policy Center, Bowling Green State Univ., Ohio, 2010. Member: CATE, 1990–94; SCAA, 1993–97; TTA, 1994–97; Teachers' Standards Review Gp, 2011–12. Dir, Cuckoo Hall Academies Trust, 2012–; Gov., Heron Hall Free Sch., Edmonton, 2013–. Ed., Philosophy, 1995–. *Publications:* Karl Popper, 1980; Education, Society and Human Nature, 1981; Experience, Explanation and Faith, 1984; What Philosophy Is, 1985; The Element of Fire, 1988; Introduction to the Philosophy of Science, 1989; Jesus for Beginners, 1993; Beyond Evolution, 1997; After Progress, 1999; Philosophy in the New Century, 2001; Plato's Children, 2006; The Great Books, 2007; The Landscape of Humanity, 2008; (with Mark Sidwell) The School of Freedom, 2009; (with N. O'Hear) Picturing the Apocalypse: the Book of Revelation in the arts over two millennia, 2015. *Recreations:* music, visual arts, ski-ing, tennis. *Address:* University of Buckingham, Hunter Street, Buckingham MK18 1EG. *T:* (01280) 820219. *E:* anthony.ohear@buckingham.ac.uk. *Club:* Athenæum.

O'HIGGINS, Michael; Chair, NHS Confederation, since 2012; *b* Dublin, 1 Aug. 1954; *s* of William and Bridget Higgins; *m* 2011, Patricia Brown (*née* Swinfen). *Educ:* Trinity Coll. Dublin (BA Econs 1975); London Sch. of Econs and Pol Sci. (MSc Social Policy 1976). Reader in Social Policy, Univ. of Bath, 1978–87; Principal Adminr, OECD, Paris, 1987–88; Partner, Price Waterhouse Mgt Consultancy, 1989–96; Man. Partner, PA Consulting Gp, 1997–2006; Chair: Audit Commn, 2006–12; Pensions Regulator, 2011–14. Specialist Advr,

H of C Select Cttee on Social Services, 1980–88. Chm., Investec Structured Products Calculus VCT, plc, 2010–; non-executive Director: HM Treasury, 2008–14 (Chair, Audit Cttee, 2008–14); Oxford Med. Diagnostics, 2010–12; Network Rail, 2012– (Chair, Remuneration Cttee, 2013–). Visiting Fellow: Harvard Univ., 1984–85; ANU, 1986; Visiting Professor: LSE, 1992–98; Univ. of Bath, 2009–12. Chair, Centrepoint, 2004–11. *Publications:* (ed jtly) The Future of Welfare, 1986; (ed jtly) Poverty, Inequality and Income Distribution in Comparative Perspective: the Luxembourg Income Study, 1987; contrib. papers to jls incl. Rev. of Income and Wealth, Jl Social Policy, Public Admin, Political Qly, Policy & Politics, British Tax Rev. *Recreations:* sport, classical jazz music, cooking, wine, travel, modern art. *Address:* NHS Confederation, Floor 4, 50 Broadway, SW1H 0DB. *E:* chair@nhsconfed.org.

OHLSON, Sir Brian (Eric Christopher), 3rd Bt *cr* 1920; money broker, retired; *b* 27 July 1936; *s* of Sir Eric James Ohlson, 2nd Bt, and Marjorie Joan, *d* of late C. H. Roosmale-Cocq; *S* father, 1983. *Educ:* Harrow School; RMA Sandhurst. Commissioned into Coldstream Guards, 1956–61. Started money broking, 1961. *Recreations:* sport of kings, cricket, bowls, safaris, bridge, Real tennis. *Heir: b* Peter Michael Ohlson [*b* 18 May 1939; *m* 1968, Sarah, *o d* of Maj.-Gen. Thomas Brodie, CB, CBE, DSO; two *d*]. *Address:* 1 Courtfield Gardens, SW5 0PA. *Clubs:* MCC, Hurlingham, Queen's.

OISTRAKH, Igor Davidovich; violinist, violist and conductor; Professor, Royal Conservatoire, Brussels, since 1996; *b* Odessa, 27 April 1931; *s* of late David Oistrakh; *m* 1960, Natalia Nikolaevna Zertsalova, pianist, Hon. Artist of Russia; one *s*. *Educ:* Music Sch. and State Conservatoire, Moscow. FRCM. Many foreign tours (USSR, Europe, the Americas, Japan, Aust.); Prof., Internat. Summer Acad., Belgium, 1997–. Many gramophone recordings. Mem. jury of major violin competitions. Hon. President: César Franck Soc., Liège; Russian Br., Eur. String Teachers Assoc.; Hon. Member: Beethoven Soc., Bonn; Ysaye Foundn, Liège; Wieniawski Soc., Poznan; Heifetz Soc., USA; Mendelssohn and Schumann Foundns, Leipzig. 1st prize: Violin Competition, Budapest, 1949; Wieniawski Competition, Poznan, 1952; Igor Oistrakh internat. violin competition estabd Iserlohn, Germany, 1993. People's Artist of USSR, 1989.

OKA, Prof. Takeshi, PhD; FRS 1984; FRSC 1977; Professor of Chemistry, Astronomy and Astrophysics, 1981–2003, and Robert A. Millikan Distinguished Service Professor, 1989–2003, University of Chicago, now Emeritus Professor; *b* 10 June 1932; *s* of Shumpei and Chiyoko Oka; *m* 1960, Keiko Nukui; two *s* two *d*. *Educ:* University of Tokyo. BSc, PhD. Fellow, Japanese Soc. for Promotion of Science, 1960–63; National Research Council of Canada: Postdoctorate Fellow, 1963–65; Asst Research Physicist, 1965–68; Associate Research Physicist, 1968–71; Senior Research Physicist, 1971–75; Herzberg Inst. of Astrophysics, 1975–81. Centenary Lectr, Royal Soc., 1982; Chancellor's Distinguished Lectr, Univ. of California, 1985–86. Fellow, Amer. Acad. of Arts and Scis, 1987. Hon. DSc: Waterloo, 2001; London, 2004. Steacie Prize, Steacie Fund, NRSC, 1972; Earle K. Plyler Prize, Amer. Physical Soc., 1982; William F. Meggers Award, 1997, Ellis R. Lippincott Award, 1998, Optical Soc. of America; E. Bright Wilson Award in Spectroscopy, ACS, 2002; Davy Medal, Royal Soc., 2004. *Address:* Department of Chemistry, University of Chicago, 5735 S Ellis Avenue, Chicago, IL 60637, USA.

OKALIK, Paul; MLA for Iqaluit-Sinaa, Nunavut, since 2013; Minister of Justice, since 2013, and Minister of Health and for Immigration, since 2014, Nunavut, Canada; *b* 26 May 1964; one *s* two *d*. *Educ:* Iqaluit High Sch.; Carleton Univ. (BA); Univ. of Ottawa (LLB 1997). Called to the Bar, 1999. MLA for Iqaluit W, 1999–2011. Nunavut, Canada: Premier and Minister of Exec. and Intergovtl Affairs, 1999–2008; Minister of Justice, 2000–08; Speaker, 2010–11; Minister of Culture and Heritage, 2013–14, of Languages, 2013–14. *Address:* Legislative Assembly of Nunavut, PO Box 1200, 926 Federal Road, Iqaluit, NU X0A 0H0, Canada.

O'KELLY, Helen W.; *see* Watanabe-O'Kelly.

OKEOVER, Sir Andrew Peter Monro W.; *see* Walker-Okeover.

OKINE, Most Rev. Robert Garshong Allotey; Archbishop of West Africa, 1993–2003; Bishop of Koforidua-Ho, Ghana, 1981–2003; *b* 12 July 1937; *s* of late Robert Cudjoe Okine and Miriam Naadjah Decker; *m* 1967, Juliana Sakai (*née* Nerquaye-Tetteh); two *s* two *d*. *Educ:* Anglican Church schs, Gold Coast and Gambia; Methodist Boys' High Sch., Bathurst, The Gambia; Adisadel Coll., Cape Coast, Ghana; Theol Coll., SSM, Kelham (GOE 1964); Inst. of Pastoral Educn, London, Ont. (CertCPE 1972); Huron Coll., Univ. of W Ontario, Canada (BMin 1973); Vanderbilt Univ., Nashville, USA (MA 1975); George Peabody Coll. for Teachers, Nashville, USA (EdS 1975); Haggai Inst. for Advanced Leadership Trng, Singapore (Cert. Completion 1990). Ordained deacon 1964, priest 1965; Asst Curate, St Andrew's, Sekondi, 1964–66; Chaplain and teacher, Adisadel Coll., Cape Coast, 1966–68; Rector: St James, Agona-Swedru, 1968–69; Bishop Aglionby Meml Parish, Tamale, 1969–71; Assistant Priest: St Anne's, Byron, and St George's, London, Ont., Canada, 1971–73; Holy Trinity Episcopal Church, Nashville, USA, 1973–75; Christ Church Parish, Cape Coast, 1975–81; Headmaster, Acad. of Christ the King, 1976–81; Principal, St Nicholas Theol Coll., 1976–81; Archdeacon of Koforidua and Rector, St Peter's, Koforidua, Feb.–Oct. 1981. Hon. Canon, Cathedral Church of Most Holy Trinity, Accra, 1979–81. Chairman: Provincial Liturgical Commn, 1984–2003; Bd of Educn, Anglican Educn Unit, 1991–2003; Human Resources Develt Desk, Jt Anglican Diocesan Council, 1991–2003; Council, Anglican Provinces of Africa, 1999–2003; Mem., Anglican Peace and Justice Network, Global Anglican Consultative Council, 1996–2002. Founder, Kwabeng Anglican Secondary Technical Sch., 1983; Gov., Adisadel Coll., 1987–97. Patron, YMCA (Eastern), 1984–2003. Hon. DD W Ontario, 1982. Order of the Volta (Ghana), 2008. *Recreations:* entertaining, watching good movies, listening to all brands of music. *Address:* 10 Lizam Road (off ECOMOG), Haatso, Accra, Ghana.

OKOGIE, His Eminence Cardinal Anthony Olubunmi, CON 1999; DD; Archbishop of Lagos, (RC), 1973–2012; *b* Lagos, 16 June 1936. *Educ:* St Gregory's Coll., Lagos; St Theresa's Minor Seminary, Ibadan; St Peter and St Paul's Seminary, Ibadan; Urban Univ., Rome. Priest, 1966; appointments include: Acting Parish Priest, St Patrick's Church, Idumagbo, 1967–71; Asst Priest, and Master of Ceremonies, Holy Cross Cathedral, Lagos, 1967–71; Religious Instructor, King's Coll., Lagos, 1967–71; Director of Vocations, Archdiocese of Lagos, 1968–71; Manager, Holy Cross Group of Schools, Lagos, 1969–71; Auxiliary Bishop of Oyo, 1971–72; Auxiliary Bishop to Apostolic Administrator, Archdiocese of Lagos, 1972–73. Cardinal, 2003. Vice-Pres., 1983–88, Pres., 1988–94, Catholic Bishops Conf. of Nigeria; Roman Catholic Trustee of Christian Assoc. of Nigeria, 1974–; Member: State Community Relns Cttee, 1984–; Prerogative of Mercy, 1986–; Adv. Council on Religious Affairs, 1987–; Pontifical Council for Social Communications, 2003–; Congregation for the Evangelization of Peoples, 2003–; Council of Cardinals for Study of Organizational and Econ. Questions of Holy See, 2006–14. Special Envoy of HH Pope Benedict XVI, Nat. Eucharistic Congress, Ghana, 2005. Chm., Christian Assoc. of Nigeria, 1989–97. *Address:* c/o 19 Catholic Mission Street, PO Box 8, Lagos, Nigeria.

OKRI, Ben, OBE 2001; FRSL; novelist and poet; *b* 15 March 1959; *s* of Silver and Grace Okri. *Educ:* Univ. of Essex. Poetry Editor, West Africa, 1983–86; broadcaster and presenter, BBC, 1983–85; Fellow Commoner in Creative Arts, Trinity Coll., Cambridge, 1991–93. Vis. Prof., Sch. of English, Univ. of Leicester, 2012–14. Mem. Bd, RNT, 1999–2006. Member: Soc. of Authors, 1986–; Council, RSL, 1999–2004. FRSL 1998; FRSA 2003. Hon. DLitt: Westminster, 1997; Essex, 2002; Exeter, 2004; London, 2010; Hon. Dr of Utopia, Univ. voor het Algemeen Belang, Belgium, 2009; Hon. DArts Bedfordshire, 2010. Crystal Award, World Econ. Forum, Switzerland, 1995; Grinzane Prize for Africa, 2008; Internat. Literary Award of Novi Sad, 2008. *Publications:* Flowers and Shadows, 1980; The Landscapes Within, 1982; Incidents at the Shrine, 1986 (Commonwealth Prize for Africa, 1987; Paris Review Aga Khan Prize for fiction, 1987); Stars of the New Curfew, 1988; The Famished Road, 1991 (Booker Prize, 1991; Premio Letterario Internazionale Chianti-Ruffino-Antico Fattore, 1993; Premio Grinzane Cavour, 1994); An African Elegy, 1992; Songs of Enchantment, 1993; Astonishing the Gods, 1995; Birds of Heaven, 1995; Dangerous Love, 1996 (Premio Palmi, 2000); A Way of Being Free, 1997; Infinite Riches, 1998; Mental Fight, 1999; In Arcadia, 2002; Starbook, 2007; Tales of Freedom, 2009; A Time for New Dreams, 2011, Wild, 2012; The Age of Magic, 2014. *Recreations:* music, chess, theatre, art, good conversation, walking, silence. *Address:* c/o The Marsh Agency Ltd, 50 Albemarle Street, W1S 4BD. *Club:* PEN International (Vice-Pres., English Centre, 1997).

OLAH, Prof. George Andrew, PhD; Distinguished Professor of Chemistry and Director, Loker Hydrocarbon Research Institute, University of Southern California, since 1977; *b* 22 May 1927; *s* of Julius Olah and Magda Krasznai; *m* 1949, Judith Lengyel; two *s*. *Educ:* Technical Univ. of Budapest (PhD Chemistry 1949). Faculty Mem., Technical Univ. of Budapest, 1950–55; Associate Dir for Organic Chem., Central Res. Inst., Hungarian Acad. of Scis, 1955–56; Res. Scientist, Dow Chemical Co., 1957–65; Prof. and Chm., Dept of Chem., Case Western Reserve Univ., Cleveland, Ohio, 1965–77. For. Mem., Royal Soc., 1997. Numerous hon. doctorates. Nobel Prize in Chemistry, 1994; numerous awards. *Publications:* Theoretical Organic Chemistry, 2 vols, 1954; (ed) Friedel-Crafts and Related Reactions, 4 vols, 1963–65; (ed jtly) Carbonium Ions, 5 vols, 1968–75; Friedel-Crafts Chemistry, 1973; Carbocations and Electrophilic Reactions, 1973; Halonium Ions, 1975; (jtly) Superacids, 1985; (jtly) Hypercarbon Chemistry, 1987; (jtly) Nitration: methods and mechanism, 1989; (ed) Cage Hydrocarbons, 1990; (ed jtly) Electron Deficient Boron and Carbon Clusters, 1991; (ed jtly) Chemistry of Energetic Materials, 1991; (ed jtly) Synthetic Fluorine Chemistry, 1992; (jtly) Hydrocarbon Chemistry, 1994; A Life of Magic Chemistry (autobiog.), 2001; (jtly) Beyond Oil and Gas: the methanol economy, 2006; numerous scientific papers and 100 patents. *Address:* Loker Hydrocarbon Research Institute, University of Southern California, Los Angeles, LA 90089, USA. *T:* (213) 7405976.

OLAZÁBAL, José Maria; golfer; *b* Fuenterrabia, Spain, 5 Feb. 1966; *s* of Gaspar and Julia Olazábal. Professional golfer, 1985–; wins include: European Masters, 1986; Benson and Hedges Internat. Open, 1990, 2000; NE+-C World Series, 1990, 1994; The Internat. (USA), 1991; Grand Prix of Europe, 1991; Mediterranean Open, 1992, 1994; Volvo PGA Championship, 1994; US Masters, 1994, 1999; Dubai Desert Classic, 1998; French Open, 2001; Buick Invitational, 2002; Member: European Ryder Cup Team, 1987, 1989, 1991, 1993, 1997, 1999, 2006, 2008 (Vice-Captain), 2012 (Captain), 2014 (Vice-Captain); Spanish Team, Alfred Dunhill Cup, 1999, 2000; Continental Europe Team, Seve Trophy, 2013 (Captain); European Team, Royal Trophy, 2013 (Captain). *Address:* c/o 112 PGA Tour Boulevard, Ponte Vedra Beach, FL 32082, USA.

OLCAYTO, Rory Erol; Editor, Architects' Journal, since 2015; *b* Taplow, 11 May 1972; *s* of Ender Olcayto and Joan Olcayto (*née* St John); partner, Frances Balaam; one *d*. *Educ:* Colgrain Primary Sch., Helensburgh; Hermitage Acad., Helensburgh; Univ. of Strathclyde (BSc Hons Architectural Studies; MSc Computer Aided Building Design). Architectural asst, HD, Mimarlik, Istanbul, 1991; Dir, Strathclyde Winterschool 1994, 1993–94; architectural assistant: Quaternaire, Liege, 1994; Hamilton DC, 1994–95; lead artist, Inner Workings (videogames), 1997–99; 1st year studio leader, Dept of Arch. and Building Sci., Univ. of Strathclyde, 2000–02; architectural asst, Gordon Murray + Alan Dunlop Architects, 2001–03; Asst Ed., Project Scotland, 2003–06; Dep. Ed., Construction Manager, 2006–07; Sen. Reporter, Building Design, 2007–08; Architects' Journal: Features Ed., 2008–09; Dep. Ed., 2010–14; Actg Ed., 2014–15. FRSA. *Publications:* The Architecture of Rogers Stirk Harbour + Partners: British Museum World Conservation and Exhibitions Centre, 2014. *Recreations:* towns and cities on foot, forests and coastlines on bike, meze at home with family and friends, sketching and drawing with thick black pens; and these things: cinema, theatre, galleries, bookshops, swimming, tennis, late night telly, art, technology, history, magic, pop, politics, satire, lists. *Address:* College Place, London. *E:* rolcayto@yahoo.co.uk.

OLDENBURG, Claes Thure; artist; *b* Stockholm, 28 Jan. 1929; *s* of Gösta Oldenburg and Sigrid Elisabeth (*née* Lindfors); *m* 1st, 1960, Pat Muschinski (marr. diss. 1970); 2nd, 1977, Coosje van Bruggen (*d* 2009). *Educ:* Yale Univ. (BA 1951); Art Inst. Chicago. Apprentice reporter, City News Bureau, Chicago, 1950–52; became American citizen, 1953. First gp exhibn at Club St Elmo, Chicago, 1953; subseq. at local shows, Chicago and Evanston, 1953–56; moved to NY, 1956; has participated in numerous gp exhibns of contemp. art in USA and Europe, including: Dallas Mus. Contemp. Art, 1961, 1962; ICA, 1963; Mus. Mod. Art, NY, 1963, 1988, 1990, 1991; Washington Gall. Mod. Art, 1963; Tate Gall., 1964; Metropolitan Mus. Art, NY, 1969; one-man shows in USA and Europe, including: Reuben Gall., NY, 1960; Sidney Janis Gall., NY, 1964–70; travelling exhibitions: Tate Gall. and other European galls, 1970; Musée d'Art Moderne, Paris, 1977; Nat. Gall. of Art, Washington, 1995; Solomon R. Guggenheim Mus., NY, and galls in London, LA and Bonn, 1995–96; numerous commnd works in permanent collections in USA and Europe, incl. Centre Georges Pompidou, Paris, Museums of Contemp. Art, Chicago and LA, Tate Gall.; numerous outdoor works in corporate and private collections. Member: AAIL, 1975; Amer. Acad. Arts and Scis, 1978. Awards include: Brandeis Award for Sculpture, 1971; Medal, Amer. Inst. Architects, 1977; Wilhelm-Lehmbruck Sculpture Award, Duisburg, 1981; Wolf Foundn Prize, Israel, 1989; Lifetime Achievement Award, Internat. Sculpture Centre, 1994. *Publications:* Spicy Ray Gun, 1960; Ray Gun Poems, 1960; More Ray Gun Poems, 1960, 2nd edn 1973; Injun and Other Histories, 1960; Store Days, 1967; Notes, 1968; Constructions, Models and Drawings, 1969; Notes in Hand, 1971; Raw Notes, 1973; Log, May 1974–August 1976, 1976; (jtly) Il Corso del Coltello: Menu, 1985 (trans. Italian 1985); (jtly) Sketches and Blottings toward the European Desktop, 1990 (trans. Italian 1990); Multiples in Retrospect, 1991; (with Coosje van Bruggen) Large-Scale Projects, 1994; exhibn catalogues; contribs to books and jls. *Address:* c/o Pace Gallery, 32 E 57th Street, New York, NY 10022–2513, USA.

See also R. E. Oldenburg.

OLDENBURG, Richard Erik; Consultant, Sotheby's North and South America, since 2006 (Chairman, 1995–2000; Hon. Chairman, 2000–06); *b* 21 Sept. 1933; *s* of Gösta Oldenburg and Sigrid Elisabeth (*née* Lindforss); *m* 1st, 1960, Harriet Lisa Turnure (*d* 1998); 2nd, 2003, Mary Ellen Meehan. *Educ:* Harvard Coll. (AB 1954). Manager, Design Dept, Doubleday & Co., NYC, 1958–61; Man. Editor, Trade Div., Macmillan Co., NYC, 1961–69; Dir, Publications, 1969–72, Dir, 1972–94, Museum of Modern Art, NYC. *Address:* c/o Sotheby's, 1334 York Avenue, New York, NY 10021, USA.

See also C. T. Oldenburg.

OLDFATHER, Irene; Director, Health and Social Care Alliance Scotland, since 2012; *b* 6 Aug. 1954; *d* of Campbell and Margaret Hamilton; *m* 1978, Rodrick Oldfather; one *s* one *d*. *Educ:* Univ. of Strathclyde (BA Hons Politics 1976; MSc Res. 1983). Lectr in US Politics, Univ. of Arizona, 1978–79; Policy Planner, Glasgow CC, 1980–90; Political Researcher, MEP, 1990–97; freelance journalist, European affairs, 1994–98; part-time Lectr, Paisley Univ., 1996–98. Lead Consultant, Dementia, Big Lottery Life Changes Trust, 2011–12. MSP (Lab) Cunninghame S, 1999–2011. Scottish Parliament: Convenor: Cross Party Gp on Tobacco Control; Cross Party Gp on Alzheimer's and Dementia, 2007–11 (produced Charter of Rights for People with Dementia and Main Carers, 2009); Member: Eur. Cttee,

1999–2011 (Convenor, 2001–03, 2007–11; Vice-Convenor, 2003–07); Health and Community Care Cttee, 1999–2001. Contested (Lab) Cunninghame S, Scottish Parlt, 2011. Member: European Cttee of Regions, 1997–2011 (Vice Pres., Socialist Gp, 2001–11); European Econ. and Social Cttee, Oct. 2016–. Mem. (Lab) N Ayrshire Council, 2012–. *Publications:* res. paper for Scotland Europa. *Recreations:* going to ballet, reading, children, pets. *E:* iro_07@hotmail.com.

OLDFIELD, Bruce, OBE 1990; designer; *b* 14 July 1950; parents unknown; brought up by Dr Barnardo's, Ripon, Yorks. *Educ:* Ripon Grammar School; Sheffield City Polytechnic (Hon. Fellow 1987); Ravensbourne College of Art; St Martin's College of Art. Established fashion house, 1975; produced designer collections of high fashion clothes for UK and overseas; began exporting clothes worldwide, 1975; began making couture clothes for individual clients, 1981; opened first Bruce Oldfield retail shop, selling ready to wear and couture to international clientèle, 1984; opened addnl premises focusing on weddings, 2009; launched signature fragrance, 2011. Exhibitor: British Design Exhibn, Vienna, 1986; Australian Bicentennial Fashion Show, Sydney Opera House, 1988. Lectures: Fashion Inst., NY, 1977; Los Angeles County Museum, 1983; Internat. Design Conf., Aspen, Colorado, 1986 (Speaker and show). Vice Pres., Barnardo's. Trustee, Royal Acad., 2000–02. Gov., London Inst., 2000–02. Hon. Fellow RCA, 1990. Hon. DCL Northumbria at Newcastle, 2001; DUniv UCE, 2005; Hon. DLitt Hull, 2009. Designed for films: Jackpot, 1974; The Sentinel, 1976. *Publications:* (with Georgina Howell) Bruce Oldfield's Season, 1987; Bruce Oldfield: Rootless: an autobiography, 2004. *Recreations:* music, reading, driving, working. *Address:* 27 Beauchamp Place, SW3 1NJ. *T:* (020) 7584 1363. *E:* hq@bruceoldfield.com. *W:* www.bruceoldfield.com.

OLDFIELD, Michael Gordon, (Mike); musician and composer; *b* 15 May 1953; *s* of Dr Raymond Henry Oldfield and Maureen Bernadine Liston; four *s* two *d* (and one *s* decd). *Educ:* St Edward's, Reading; Presentation Coll., Reading. Records include: Tubular Bells, 1973 (over 16 million copies sold to date); Hergest Ridge; Ommadawn; Incantations; Platinum; QE2, 1980; Five Miles Out, 1982; Crises, 1983; Discovery, 1984; The Killing Fields (film sound track), 1984; Islands, 1987; The Wind Chimes (video album), 1988; Earthmoving, 1989; Amarok, 1990; Heaven's Open, 1991; Tubular Bells II, 1992; The Songs of Distant Earth, 1994; Voyager, 1996; Tubular Bells III, 1998; Music of the Spheres, 2008; Man on the Rocks, 2014. Extensive world wide concert tours, 1979–. Mem., Assoc. of Professional Composers. Freeman, City of London, 1982. Hon. Pict. *Publications:* Changeling (autobiog.), 2007. *Recreations:* helicopter pilot, squash, ski-ing, cricket. *Club:* Jacobs Larder (Ealing).

OLDFIELD, Richard John; Executive Chairman, Oldfield Partners LLP, since 2013 (Chief Executive, 2005–13); Vice Lord-Lieutenant of Kent, since 2011; *b* London, 11 Oct. 1955; *s* of Christopher Charles Bayley Oldfield and Bridget Ruth Pearl Oldfield (*née* Craigie); *m* 1st, 1982, Hon. Alexandra Frances Margaret (*d* 1995), *d* of 2nd Viscount Davidson; two *s* one *d*; 2nd, 1997, Amicia de Moubray; one *s*. *Educ:* Eton Coll.; New Coll., Oxford (BA Modern Hist.). With S. G. Warburg, then Mercury Asset Mgt, 1977–96, Dir, 1990–96; Chief Exec., Alta Advisers, 1997–2005. Dir, Keystone Investment Trust, 2001–10 (Chm., 2002–10). Chm., Oxford Univ. Endowment Mgt Ltd, 2007–14. Pres., Demelza Hospice Care for Children, 2005– (Chm., 2000–02; Trustee, 2000–05); Trustee: Leeds Castle Foundn, 2001–11; Canterbury Cathedral Trust, 2009–; Royal Marsden Cancer Charity, 2011–; Clore Duffield Foundn, 2013–. Seneschal, Canterbury Cathedral, 2014–. High Sheriff, Kent, 2008–09. *Publications:* Simple But Not Easy, 2007. *Address:* Doddington Place, Sittingbourne, Kent ME9 0BB. *E:* rjo@oldfieldpartners.com. *Clubs:* White's, Beefsteak.

OLDHAM, Prof. (Charles Herbert) Geoffrey, CBE 1990; Professorial Fellow, Science Policy Research Unit, University of Sussex, 1966–97, now Hon. Professor (Director, 1980–92); Science Adviser to President, International Development Research Centre, Ottawa, on secondment, 1992–96; *b* 17 Feb. 1929; *s* of Herbert Cecil Oldham and Evelyn Selina Oldham (*née* Brooke); *m* 1951, Brenda Mildred Raven; one *s* one *d* (and two *s* decd). *Educ:* Bingley Grammar Sch.; Reading Univ. (BSc Hons); Toronto Univ. (MA, PhD). Research geophysicist, Chevron Research Corp., 1954–57; Sen. Geophysicist, Standard Oil Co. of California, 1957–60; Fellow, Inst. of Current World Affairs, studying Chinese lang. and sci., 1960–66; Scientific Directorate, OECD, 1965–66; Dep. Dir, Science Policy Res. Unit, 1966–80; Associate Dir, Internat. Develt Res. Centre, Ottawa, 1970–80. Vis. Prof., Stanford Univ., 1979; Vis. Researcher, Aust. Sci. and Tech. Adv. Council, 1988. Chm., UN Adv. Cttee on Sci. and Tech. for Develt, 1991–92; UK Mem., UN Commn on Sci., Technol. and Develt, 1993–97; Member: WHO Adv. Cttee, Health Res., 1995–99; Adv. Cttee on Gender and Sci., Acad. of Scis of Developing World, 2009–12; Panel on Problems Facing Women Researchers in Canadian Univs, Council of Canadian Acads, 2011–12. Chm. Bd, SciDev.Net, 2001–08. Hon. LLD York, Canada, 2006. *Publications:* articles in jls on science, technology and Chinese development. *Recreations:* travel, esp. long distance train journeys, golf, U3A courses. *Address:* 7 Martello Mews, Seaford, E Sussex BN25 1JT.

OLDHAM, Gavin David Redvers; Founder, and Chairman, since 2014, Share plc (formerly The Share Centre (Holdings) Ltd) (Chief Executive, 1994–2013); Founder and Chairman, The Share Centre, since 1990 (Chief Executive, 1990–2013); *b* London, 5 May 1949; *s* of David George Redvers Oldham and Penelope Barbara Oldham (*née* Royle); *m* 1975, Virginia Russell; four *d*. *Educ:* Eton Coll.; Trinity Coll., Cambridge (BA 1971). FCSI. CSE Aircraft Services Ltd, 1971–76; Wedd Durlacher Mordaunt, later Barclays de Zoete Wedd, 1976–86: Partner, 1984–86; Secretariat, 1984–86; Founder and Chief Exec., 1986–89, Chm., 1989–90, Barclayshare. Lay Mem., Oxford dio., Gen. Synod, 1995–; Church Comr, 1998–2013 (Dep. Chm., Assets Cttee, 2013). Trustee, Personal Finance Educn Gp, 2003–14; Founder and Chm., Share Foundn, 2005–; Founder and Man. Dir, Share Radio, 2014–. MInstD 1988. *Recreations:* sailing, family tree, philosophical/theological discussion. *Address:* c/o Share plc, Oxford House, Oxford Road, Aylesbury, Bucks HP21 8SZ. *T:* (01296) 439100, *Fax:* (01296) 414410. *E:* gdro@btconnect.com, ceo@share.co.uk, gavin.oldham@shareradio.co.uk, gavin.oldham@sharefound.org. *Clubs:* Leander, Royal Motor Yacht.

OLDHAM, Geoffrey; *see* Oldham, C. H. G.

OLDHAM, Sir John, Kt 2003; OBE 2001; FRCGP; Chairman, Independent Commission on Whole Person Care, since 2013; *b* 17 Aug. 1953; *s* of Kenneth and Marian Oldham; *m* 1987, Julia Robinson. *Educ:* Manchester Univ. (MB ChB 1977); Manchester Business Sch. (MBA Dist. 1992); DCH London 1980. FRCGP 2002. House Officer, Manchester Royal Infirmary, 1978–79; SHO, Royal Manchester Children's Hosp., 1979–80; GP trainee, Darbishire House, Manchester, 1980–81; SHO, St Mary's Hosp., Manchester, 1981–84; Principal GP, Manor Hse Surgery, Glossop, 1984– (Sen. Partner, 1987–2010). Exec. Chm., Quest4Quality Ltd, 2007–10. Hd, Nat. Primary Care Develt Team, 2000–06; Founder and Chm., Improvement Foundn, 2006–07; Advisor (part-time): Mersey RHA, 1989–91; Primary Care Div., DoH, 1996–99; Med. Advr (pt-time), Derbys FHSA and N Derbys HA, 1990–96. Non-exec. Bd Mem., School Food Trust, 2005–09; non-exec. Dir, Internat. Soc. for Quality and Accreditation, 2008–12 (Treas., 2010–12); Mem., Nat. Quality Bd, NHS, 2009–14; Nat. Clinical Lead for Quality and Productivity, DoH, 2010–13. *Publications:* Sic Evenit Ratio Ut Componitur: the small book about large system change, 2004; contribs to BMJ. *Recreations:* hiking, cooking, blues music. *Address:* 2 Crofton Avenue, Chiswick, W4 3EW. *E:* john.oldham@quest4quality.co.uk.

OLDHAM, Peter Robert; QC 2010; *b* London, 2 April 1963; *s* of Alexander and Gillian Oldham; *m* 1990, Jane; one *s* one *d*. *Educ:* Corpus Christi Coll., Cambridge (BA Hist. 1984). Called to the Bar, Gray's Inn, 1990.

OLDLAND, Andrew Richard; QC 2011; a Recorder, since 2004; Partner, Michelmores LLP, since 2011; *b* Newbury, 11 May 1965; *s* of Michael and Alison Oldland; *m* 1997, Gretchen Holtz; one *s* two *d*. *Educ:* Bradfield Coll.; London Sch. of Econs and Pol Sci. (BSc Econ); City Univ. (DipLaw). Called to the Bar, Inner Temple, 1990, in practice as barrister, specialising in regulatory offences and financial crime; Standing Counsel, HMRC, 2008–11; A List Counsel, Serious Fraud Office, 2009–11. *Recreations:* sailing, walking, pole-vaulting. *E:* andrew.oldland@michelmores.com.

OLDMAN, Gary; actor; *b* 21 March 1958; *m* 1st, 1988, Lesley Manville, *qv* (marr. diss. 1990); one *s*; 2nd, 1991, Uma Thurman (marr. diss. 1993); 3rd, Donya Fiorentino (marr. diss. 2001); two *s*; 4th, 2008, Alexandra Edenborough. *Educ:* South East London Sch. for Boys; Rose Bruford Coll. of Speech and Drama (BA Theatre Arts 1979). *Theatre* includes: Greenwich Young People's Theatre; Theatre Royal, York; Glasgow Citizens' Theatre: Massacre at Paris, A Waste of Time, Desperado Corner, Chinchilla, 1980 (toured Europe and S America); Royal Court Theatre: Rat in the Skull, 1984; The Pope's Wedding, 1984; Women Beware Women, 1986; Serious Money, 1987; Royal Shakespeare Company: The Desert Air, 1985; The War Plays, 1985; Real Dreams, 1986; The Country Wife, Royal Exchange, Manchester, 1986; Entertaining Mr Sloane, Oldham Rep. Co., 1987; *films* include: Sid and Nancy, 1986; Prick Up Your Ears, 1987; Track 29, 1988; Paris By Night, 1989; State of Grace, 1990; JFK, Chattahoochee, 1991; Bram Stoker's Dracula, 1992; True Romance, 1993; Romeo is Bleeding, Immortal Beloved, The Professional, 1994; Murder in the First, The Scarlet Letter, 1995; The Fifth Element, Air Force One, 1997; Lost in Space, Nil By Mouth, 1998 (writer and dir; BAFTA Award for best original screenplay); Hannibal, The Contender, 2001; Harry Potter and the Prisoner of Azkaban, 2004; Batman Begins, Harry Potter and the Goblet of Fire, 2005; Backwoods, 2006; Harry Potter and the Order of the Phoenix, 2007; The Dark Knight, 2008; The Unborn, A Christmas Carol, 2009; The Book of Eli, 2010; Red Riding Hood, Harry Potter and the Deathly Hallows, Pt 2, Tinker, Tailor, Soldier, Spy, 2011; The Dark Knight Rises, 2012; Dawn of the Planet of the Apes, 2014; Child 44, 2015; *television* includes: Remembrance, 1982; Meantime, 1984; Heading Home, 1991; Fallen Angels: dead end for Delia, 1993.

O'LEARY, Catherine Elizabeth; Her Honour Judge O'Leary; a Circuit Judge, since 2009; *b* Manchester, 1957; *d* of Cornelius Rapheal O'Leary and Hannah Elizabeth Dennehy O'Leary (*née* Neville); *m* 1980, John Martyn Bennett; three *s*. *Educ:* Hollies Convent Grammar Sch.; Liverpool Univ. (LLB 1978). Called to the Bar, Gray's Inn, 1979; Dep. District Judge, 1992–98; District Judge, 1998–2009; Recorder, 2002–09. Mem., Women in Literature Book Club. *Recreations:* cooking, theatre, reading. *Address:* Liverpool Civil and Family Courts, 35 Vernon Street, Derby Square, Liverpool L2 2BX. *T:* (0151) 296 2200, *Fax:* (0151) 296 2201.

O'LEARY, Rt Hon. Elizabeth Mary; *see* Truss, Rt Hon. E. M.

O'LEARY, (Michael) John; Editor, Policy Review Magazine, 2008–11; *b* 11 Dec. 1951; *s* of Captain Daniel Joseph O'Leary, RN, and Sylvia Jane O'Leary; *m* 1977, Susan Berenice Whittingham; two *s* one *d*. *Educ:* Taunton Sch.; Sheffield Univ. (BA Politics 1973; Pres., Students' Union, 1973–74). Reporter, Evening Chronicle, Newcastle upon Tyne, 1975–78; Reporter/news editor, 1978–85, Dep. Editor, 1985–90, THES; Educn Corresp., 1990–93, Educn Editor, 1993–2002, The Times; Editor, THES, 2002–07. Mem., Govt Inquiry into Primary Sch. Test Standards, 1999. *Publications:* (ed) The Times Good University Guide, annually 1993–. *Recreations:* squash, tennis, travel, watching Arsenal. *Club:* Woodford Wells (Woodford).

O'LEARY, Peter Leslie; Under-Secretary, Inland Revenue, 1978–84; *b* 12 June 1929; *s* of Archibald and Edna O'Leary; *m* 1960, Margaret Elizabeth Debney; four *d*. *Educ:* Portsmouth Southern Grammar Sch.; University Coll., London (BA). Joined Inland Revenue as Inspector, 1952; Sen. Principal Inspector, 1974. *Recreations:* horology, gardening. *Address:* 17 Sleaford Road, Heckington, Sleaford, Lincs NG34 9QP.

OLIPHANT, Tuelonyana Rosemary D.; *see* Ditlhabi Oliphant.

OLISA, Kenneth Aphunezi, OBE 2010; Chairman, Restoration Partners, since 2006; Lord-Lieutenant of Greater London, since 2015; *b* Nottingham, 13 Oct. 1951; *s* of Charles Harry Olisa and Barbara Enid Olisa (*née* Blaskey); *m* 1976, Julia Berenice Sherwood; two *d*. *Educ:* High Pavement Grammar Sch., Nottingham; Fitzwilliam Coll., Cambridge (BA 1974; MA 1981). FBCS 2006. IBM: Systems Engr, 1974–76; Salesman, 1976–78; Series/1 Product Mktg Manager, 1978–80; Wang Labs Inc.: Product Mktg Dir, 1981–82; Sales Manager, 1982–84; Mktg Dir EMEA, 1984–86; Vice Pres., US and Worldwide Mktg, 1986–90; Sen. Vice Pres., EMEA, 1990–92; Chairman: Interregnum plc, 1992–2006; Metapraxis, 1993–2005; VossNet plc, 1994–97; DMATEK plc, 1996–98; GeoConference, 1996–2000; Callcentric, 1997–2000; Catalyst Solution, 1999–2000; Independent Audit, 2007–; Outsourcery, 2013–. Non-executive Director: Open Text Corp., 1998–2008; uDate.com, 2000–03; Eurasian Natural Resources Corp., 2007–10; Reuters Gp, 2004–08; Thomson Reuters Corp., 2008–. Dir, Thames Reach, 1992– (Chm., 1994–). Mem., Postal Services Commn, 2000–04. Mem. Bd, Ind. Parly Standards Authy, 2009–13. Mem., Women's Enterprise Taskforce, BERR, 2006–09; Dir, W Lambeth NHS Healthcare Trust, 1995–99. Founding Chm., Powerlist Foundn, 2010–. Dir, Inst. of Dirs, 2013–. Chm., Shaw Trust, 2013–; Trustee: Reuters Foundn, 2005–; BCS, Chartered Inst. for IT, 2007–14 (Chairman: Strategic Panels, 2007–10; Policy and Public Affairs Bd, 2010–12; BCS Learning and Develt, 2012–14); Gov., Peabody Trust, 1998–2007. 1869 Benefactor Fellow, Fitzwilliam Coll., Cambridge, 2012. Liveryman, Information Technologists' Co., 1993– (Master, 2010–11). Life Vice Pres., Fitzwilliam Soc., 2011; Mem., Guild of Cambridge Benefactors, 2012. *Recreations:* golf, ski-ing. *Address:* Restoration Partners, Linen Hall, 162–168 Regent Street, W1B 5TD. *E:* ken@olisa.com. *Clubs:* Oxford and Cambridge, Walbrook; Pyrford Golf.

OLIVER, Prof. Alexander Duncan, LittD; Professor of Philosophy, University of Cambridge, since 2012; Fellow, Gonville and Caius College, Cambridge, since 2004; *b* Bristol, 24 Aug. 1966; *s* of Michael John Oliver and Suzanne Nesta Newman; *m* 1988, Catrin Margaret Clare Hutton; one *s* one *d*. *Educ:* Bristol Grammar Sch.; Clare Coll., Cambridge (BA 1988; MA; PhD 1994; LittD 2014); Yale Univ. (Mellon Fellow; MA; MPhil 1990). Res. Fellow, Gonville and Caius Coll., Cambridge, 1993–94; University of Cambridge: Temp. Asst Lectr in Philosophy, 1994–95; Asst Lectr, 1995–97; Lectr, 1998–2000; Sen. Lectr, 2000–05; Reader, 2005–12; Director of Studies in Philosophy: Sidney Sussex Coll., 1993–97; Trinity Hall, 1995–98; Queens' Coll., 1996–2002; Gonville and Caius Coll., 2004–15; Dir, Grad. Studies, 1999, 2000, Chm., 2008–09, Faculty of Philosophy; Fellow: Gonville and Caius Coll., 1994–96; Queens' Coll., 1996–2004; Judge Business Sch., 2009–. Leverhulme Trust Maj. Res. Fellow, 2002–04; Mind Assoc. Sen. Res. Fellow, 2012–13. Mem., Knowledge Transfer Panel, AHRC, 2007–09. Mem., Analysis Trust Cttee, 1996– (Sec., 1996–2000). *Publications:* (ed with D. H. Mellor) Properties, 1997; (ed with J. Lear) The Force of Argument, 2010; (with T. Smiley) Plural Logic, 2013; contrib. articles to philosophical jls. *Recreations:* beer, Italy, labrador retrievers, reggae. *Address:* Gonville and Caius College, Cambridge CB2 1TA. *Clubs:* Athenæum; Elizabethan (Yale).

OLIVER, Prof. (Ann) Dawn (Harrison), PhD, LLD; FBA 2005; Professor of Constitutional Law, University College London, 1993–2008, now Emeritus; *b* 7 June 1942; *d* of Gordon and Mieke Taylor; *m* 1967, Stephen John Lindsay Oliver (*see* Sir S. J. L. Oliver); one *s* two *d*. *Educ:* Newnham Coll., Cambridge (BA 1964; MA 1967; PhD 1993; Associate Fellow, 1996–99); LLD Cantab 2011. Called to the Bar, Middle Temple, 1965 (Harmsworth

Schol.; Bencher, 1996; Treas., 2011); in practice at the Bar, 1965–69; Consultant, Legal Action Gp, 1971–76; University College London: Lectr in Law, 1976–87; Sen. Lectr, 1987–90; Reader in Public Law, 1990–93; Head of Law Dept, 1993–98; Dean, Faculty of Laws, 1993–98 and 2007; Hon. Fellow, 2001. Hon. Fellow, Soc. of Advanced Legal Studies, 1997–. Member: Wkg Party on Noise, DoE, 1990–91; Animal Procedures Cttee, Home Office, 2003–11. Member: Commn on Election Campaigns, Hansard Soc., 1990–91; Study of Parlt Gp, 1991– (Pres., 2010–15); Labour and Liberal Democrats Jt Consultative Cttee on Constitutional Reform, 1996–97; Royal Commn on Reform of the H of L, 1999; Fabian Soc. Commn on the future of the Monarchy, 2002–03; Convenor, UK Constitutional Law Gp, 2006–10. Bar Standards Board: Mem., Bar Vocational Course Rev., 2008; Chm., Bar Transfer Test Rev., 2012. Chm., Advertising Adv. Cttee, ITC, 1999–2003. Mem., Exec. Cttee, Internat. Assoc. of Constitutional Law, 2007–10. Trustee: Citizenship Foundn, 1990–94; British Inst. of Internat. and Comparative Law, 2012–. Hon. QC 2012. Editor, Public Law, 1993–2001. *Publications:* (ed jtly) The Changing Constitution, 1985, 8th edn 2015; (ed jtly) New Directions in Judicial Review, 1988; (ed jtly) Economical with the Truth: the press in a democratic society, 1990; Government in the United Kingdom: the search for accountability, effectiveness and citizenship, 1991; (jtly) The Foundations of Citizenship, 1994; (jtly) Public Service Reform: issues of accountability and public law, 1996; (ed jtly) Halsbury's Laws of England on Constitutional Law and Human Rights, 1996; (ed jtly) The Law and Parliament, 1998; Common Values and the Public-Private Divide, 1999; Constitutional Reform in the UK, 2003; (ed jtly) Human Rights and the Private Sphere, 2008; Justice, Legality and the Rule of Law: lessons from the Pitcairn prosecutions, 2009; (ed jtly) The Regulatory State: constitutional implications, 2010; (ed jtly) How Constitutions Change, 2011; (ed jtly) Parliament and the Law, 2013; articles and book chapters on constitutional and admin. law and on law and politics. *Recreations:* walking, London, Aldeburgh, travel, sketching. *Address:* 3 Lloyds Place, SE3 0QE.

OLIVER, Prof. David, MD; FRCP; FRSocMed; Consultant Physician, Geriatric and General Internal Medicine, Royal Berkshire NHS Foundation Trust, since 2004; Visiting Professor of Medicine for Older People, City University London, since 2009; Expert Clinical Advisor, NHS Emergency Care Intensive Support Team, since 2013; Senior Visiting Fellow, King's Fund, since 2013; *b* Manchester, 13 Jan. 1966; *s* of Dr Fred Oliver and Marlene Oliver; *m* 1992, Anne Sowdon. *Educ:* Manchester Grammar Sch.; Queen's Coll., Oxford (BA Physiol Scis 1987); Trinity Hall, Cambridge (MB BChir 1989); Univ. of London (MHM 1997; MD 2000; Dip. Med. Educn 2000); Univ. of Middlesex (MSc Health and Social Care Leadership 2004); Univ. of Manchester (MA Health Care Ethics and Law 2007). Dip. Geriatric Medicine. FRCP 2001. Trng posts, Newcastle Royal Victoria Infirmary, Epping Hosp., Manchester Royal Infirmary, Guy's Hosp., St George's Hosp., Conquest Hosp., Hastings, Kent, Canterbury Hosp. and St Thomas' Hosp., 1989–98; Consultant Physician, Clin. Dir and Lead Clinician, Queen Mary's Hosp., Sidcup, 1998–2004; Sen. Lectr, Sch. of Health and Social Care, Univ. of Reading, 2004–09; Clin. Dir, Royal Berks NHS Foundn Trust, 2004–10 (Lead Clinician, 2004–09); Specialist Clin. Advr to DoH, 2009–10; Nat. Clin. Dir for Older Peoples Services (England), DoH, 2009–13. Vis. Prof., Univ. of Surrey, 2014–. Chm., Speciality Cttee for Geriatric Medicine, RCP. Pres., British Geriatrics Soc., 2014–Nov. 2016. FRSocMed. Mem., Old Mancunians Assoc. *Publications:* (jtly) Making Health Care Systems Fit for an Ageing Population, 2014; over 100 book chapters; contrib. original papers, rev. articles, editls and commentary pieces to jls, incl. Health Service Jl; regular blogs for King's Fund and British Geriatrics Soc. *Recreations:* supporting Manchester City FC and the England cricket team, playing village cricket, theatre, travel, walking, angling, canoeing. *Address:* Royal Berkshire NHS Foundation Trust, Reading RG1 7AN. *E:* david.oliver@royalberkshire.nhs.uk; King's Fund, 11–13 Cavendish Square, W1G 0AN. *E:* d.oliver@kingsfund.org.uk. *Clubs:* Royal Society of Medicine, Civil Service.

OLIVER, Hon. David Keightley Rideal; QC 1986; *b* 4 June 1949; *o s* of Baron Oliver of Aylmerton, PC; *m* 1st, 1972, Marisa Mirasierras (marr. diss. 1987); two *s*; 2nd, 1988, Judith Britannia Caroline Powell (marr. diss. 2004); two *s*. *Educ:* Westminster School; Trinity Hall, Cambridge; Institut d'Etudes Européennes, Brussels. Called to the Bar, Lincoln's Inn, 1972, Bencher, 1994; Junior Counsel to Dir-Gen. of Fair Trading, 1980–86. *Recreations:* gardening, bird watching, shooting.

OLIVER, Dawn, (Lady Oliver); *see* Oliver, A. D. H.

OLIVER, Dame Gillian (Frances), DBE 1998; FRCN; Independent Consultant and Advisor for Nursing and Allied Health Professionals, Macmillan Cancer Relief, 2004–06 (Director of Service Development, 2000–04); *b* 10 Oct. 1943; *d* of Frank Joseph Power and Ethel Mary Power; *m* 1966, Martin Jeremy Oliver; three *d*. *Educ:* Brentwood County High Sch., Essex; Middlesex Hosp., London (RN); Open Univ. (BA 1979). FRCN 1998. Night Sister and Ward Sister, Clatterbridge Centre for Oncology, 1978–87; Advr in Oncology Nursing, RCN, 1987–89; Regl Nurse, Cancer Services, Mersey RHA, 1989–90; Dir of Patient Services, Clatterbridge Centre for Oncology, 1990–2000. Hon. Fellow, Liverpool John Moores Univ., 2006. *Recreations:* travel, music, literature. *Address:* 1 Well Close, Ness, Neston, Cheshire CH64 4EE.

OLIVER, Comdr James Arnold, RN; Clerk, Ironmongers' Company, 1990–2005 (Deputy Clerk, 1989–90); *b* 10 Aug. 1941; *s* of Capt. Philip Daniel Oliver, CBE, RN and Audrey Mary Oliver (*née* Taylor); *m* 1973, Anne Elise de Burgh Sidley. *Educ:* Sedbergh Sch.; BRNC. Joined RN, 1959; seaman officer, 1959–88; navigation specialist, 1969; Divl Officer, Dartmouth, 1971–73; served in minesweepers, frigates and HM Ships Ark Royal, 1973–74, Sheffield, 1976–78, and Fearless, 1984–86; CO, Barbados Coastguard, 1981–83. Clerk and Trust Manager, Ewelme Almshouse Charity, 2006–. Mem. Court, Ironmongers' Co., 2006–. FCMI (FIMgt 1994). *Recreations:* cruising under sail, country life, carriage driving.
See also Sir S. J. L. Oliver.

OLIVER, Sir (James) Michael (Yorrick), Kt 2003; DL; Chairman: Helios Underwriting plc (formerly Hampden Underwriting plc), since 2007 (Director, since 2007); Zirax plc, 2005–10; Europa Oil & Gas, 2004–10; Director, Hampden Capital plc, 2005–11; Lord Mayor of London, 2001–02; *b* 13 July 1940; *s* of George Leonard Jack Oliver and Patricia Rosamund Oliver (*née* Douglas); *m* 1963, Sally Elizabeth Honor Exner; two *d*. *Educ:* Brunswick Sch.; Wellington Coll. FCSI (MSI 1992). Rediffusion Ltd, 1959–63; Manager, Helios Ltd, 1965–70; Kitcat & Aitken, 1970–86 (Partner, 1977–86); Dir, Kitcat & Aitken & Co., 1986–90; Man. Dir, Carr Kitcat & Aitken, 1990–93; Dir, Lloyds Investment Managers Ltd, 1994–96; Dir, Investment Funds, Hill Samuel Asset Management Ltd, subseq. Scottish Widows Investment Partnership, 1996–2001. Director: Garbhaig Hydro Power Co., 1988–2010; German Investment Trust, 1994–97; German Smaller Cos Investment Trust, 1994–2001; Euro Spain Fund Ltd, 1996–2005; Portugal Growth Fund, 1996–2000; Hill Samuel UK Emerging Cos Investment Trust plc, 1996–2000; European Growth Fund, 2001–08; Chm., Central and Eastern European Fund Ltd, 2003–10. Dir, Centrepoint Soho, 1992–96. Trustee: UK Growth & Income Fund; Income Plus Fund, 1992–2004. Chm., St John Ambulance, City of London Centre, 1998–99, 2003–. Governor: Bishopsgate Foundn, 1983–2010 (Chm., 1985–88); King Edward's Sch., Witley, 1992–2007; Univ. of East London, 1999–2003; Chancellor, City Univ., 2001–02. Chm., Steering Cttee for Mus. of Port of London and Docklands, 1993–2009 (Chm., Trustees, 1996–98); Mem., Mus. of London Develt Council, 1991–96; Trustee: Geffrye Mus., 1992–97; Mus. of London, 2003–10. Gov., Hon. the Irish Soc. and Vice Adm. of the North, 2007–09. Common Councilman, City of London Corp., 1980–87; Alderman, Ward of Bishopsgate, 1987–2009; Sheriff, City of London, 1997–98. Liveryman, Ironmongers' Co., 1962– (Master, 1991–92). JP City of London, 1987; DL Cambs, 2004. FRGS 1962. Hon. LLD UEL, 1999; Hon. DLitt City, 2001. KStJ 2001. *Recreations:* archaeology, travel. *Address:* Paradise Barns, Bucks Lane, Little Eversden, Cambridge CB23 1HL. *T:* (01223) 263303. *Clubs:* City of London, East India.

OLIVER, Jamie Trevor, MBE 2003; chef; *b* May 1975; *s* of Trevor and Sally Oliver; *m* 2000, Juliette Norton; one *s* three *d*. *Educ:* Westminster Catering Coll. Began cooking at parents' pub, The Cricketers, Clavering, Essex; worked in France; head pastry chef, The Neal Street Restaurant, London; sous chef, River Café, London; consultant chef, Monte's, London, until 2002; established restaurants: Fifteen, London, 2002; Fifteen, Amsterdam, 2004; Fifteen, Cornwall, 2006; Jamie's Italian, 2008; Barbecoa, 2010; established: Recipease shops, Clapham Junction and Brighton, 2009; Jamie magazine, 2009; Jamie at Home party planning, 2009; Jamie Oliver's Fabulous Feasts event catering, 2010; Jamie's Wood Fired Ovens, 2010. Presenter, TV series: The Naked Chef (3 series), 1999–2001; Jamie's Kitchen, 2002; Return to Jamie's Kitchen, 2003; Jamie's School Dinners, 2005; Jamie's Great Escape, 2005; Jamie's Return to School Dinners, 2006; Jamie's Chef, 2007; Jamie at Home, 2007, 2008; Jamie's Ministry of Food, 2008; Jamie's American Road Trip, 2009; Jamie's Family Christmas, 2009; Jamie Does…, 2010; Jamie Oliver's Food Revolution (USA), 2010, 2011; Jamie's 30 Minute Meals, 2010; Jamie's Dream School, 2011; Jamie Cooks Summer, 2011; Jamie's Great Britain, 2011; Jamie's Summer Food Rave Up, 2012; Jamie's 15 Minute Meals, 2012; Jamie's Money Saving Meals, 2013, 2014; Jamie and Jimmy's Friday Night Feast, 2014; Jamie's Comfort Food, 2014; Jamie's Cracking Christmas, 2014; Jamie's Sugar Rush, 2015; Jamie's Super Food, 2015. *Publications:* The Naked Chef, 1999; The Return of the Naked Chef, 2000; Happy Days with the Naked Chef, 2001; Jamie's Kitchen, 2002; Jamie's Dinners, 2004; Jamie's Italy, 2005; Cook with Jamie: my guide to making you a better cook, 2006; Jamie at Home: cook your way to the good life, 2007; Jamie's Ministry of Food: anyone can learn to cook in 24 hours, 2008; Jamie's America, 2009; Jamie Does…, 2010; Jamie's 30 Minute Meals, 2010; Jamie's Great Britain, 2011; Jamie's 15 Minute Meals, 2012; Save with Jamie: shop smart, cook clever, waste less, 2013; Jamie's Comfort Food, 2014; Everyday Super Food, 2015. *Address:* Jamie Oliver Enterprises Ltd, 19-21 Nile Street, N1 7LL.

OLIVER, Rt Rev. John Keith; Bishop of Hereford, 1990–2003; Hon. Assistant Bishop, diocese of Swansea and Brecon, since 2004; *b* 14 April 1935; *s* of Walter Keith and Ivy Oliver; *m* 1961, Meriel Moore (*d* 2014); two *s* (and one *d* decd). *Educ:* Westminster Sch. (Fellow 2003); Gonville and Caius Coll., Cambridge (MA, MLitt); Westcott House. Asst Curate, Hilborough Group of Parishes, Norfolk, 1964–68; Chaplain and Asst Master, Eton College, 1968–72; Team Rector: South Molton Group of Parishes, Devon, 1973–82; Parish of Central Exeter, 1982–85; Archdeacon of Sherborne, 1985–90. Chm., ABM, 1993–98. Chaplain, 2003–13, Trustee, 2005–13, RABI; Trustee, Marches Energy Agency, 2004–13; President: Nat. Farm Attractions Network, 2009–13; Auto-Cycle Union, 2009–. Mem., Billy Wright Inquiry, Banbridge, NI, 2005–10. FRAgS 2012 (ARAgS 2007). Freeman, City of Hereford, 2002. *Publications:* The Church and Social Order, 1968; contribs to Theology, Crucible. *Recreations:* railways, music, architecture, motorcycling. *Address:* The Old Vicarage, Glascwm, Powys LD1 5SE. *Clubs:* Farmers, Oxford and Cambridge.

OLIVER, Ven. John Michael; Archdeacon of Leeds, 1992–2005; *b* 7 Sept. 1939; *s* of Frederick and Mary Oliver; *m* 1964, Anne Elizabeth Barlow; three *d*. *Educ:* Ripon Grammar Sch.; St David's Coll., Lampeter (BA 1962); Ripon Hall, Oxford. Ordained deacon, 1964, priest 1965; Asst Curate, St Peter, Harrogate, 1964–67; Senior Curate, Bramley, Leeds, 1967–72; Vicar: St Mary, Harrogate, 1972–78; St Mary with St David, Beeston, Leeds, 1978–92. Ecumenical Officer for Leeds, 1980–86; Rural Dean of Armley, 1986–92; Hon. Canon of Ripon, 1987–92. *Recreations:* cricket, theatre, cooking, a reluctant gardener. *Address:* 42A Chapel Lane, Barwick in Elmet, Leeds LS15 4EJ. *T:* (0113) 393 5019. *E:* olivers42@talktalk.net.

OLIVER, Jonathan Barnaby Larson; Group Director of Media Relations, Prudential plc, since 2012; *b* Burton upon Trent, 18 April 1973; *s* of John and Hilary Oliver; *m* 2006, Caroline Carberry; one *s* two *d*. *Educ:* Repton Sch., Derbys; Peterhouse, Cambridge (BA Hons Hist. 1994). Reporter, Leicester Mercury, 1995–96; Business corresp., Daily Express, 1996–2000; Dep. Political Ed., Mail on Sunday, 2000–08; Political Ed., Sunday Times, 2008–10; Dir, Media Relns, TLG Communications, 2010–12. *Recreations:* open air swimming, reading history, spending time with family. *Address:* (office) 12 Arthur Street, EC4R 9AQ. *E:* jonathan.oliver@prudential.co.uk.

OLIVER, Kaye Wight, CMG 2001; OBE 1994; HM Diplomatic Service, retired; High Commissioner to Lesotho, 1999–2002; *b* 10 Aug. 1943. Joined Dept of Customs and Excise, 1962; entered Diplomatic Service, 1965; served FCO, Kuala Lumpur, Lilongwe and Paris; First Sec., Nairobi, 1983–84; Head of Chancery and Consul, Yaoundé, 1984–87; FCO, 1987–90; Consul and Dep. Head of Mission, later Chargé d'Affaires, Kinshasa, Burundi and Rwanda, 1990–94; on secondment to ODA, 1994–95; Ambassador to Rwanda, 1995–98 and (non-resident) to Burundi, 1996–98. Member, Commonwealth Election Observer Group: to Kenya, 2002; to Nigeria, 2007; to Swaziland, 2008; to Rwanda, 2010; to Kenya, 2013. *Address:* 7 Elliott Road, Chiswick, W4 1PF.

OLIVER, Sir Michael; *see* Oliver, Sir J. M. Y.

OLIVER, Neil Paterson; author and broadcaster, since 2000; *b* Renfrew, Scotland, 21 Feb. 1967; *s* of Archibald Paterson Oliver and Norma Agnes Cameron Oliver (*née* Neill); *m* 2009, Trudi Alexandria Wallace; two *s* one *d*. *Educ:* Univ. of Glasgow (MA Hons Archaeol.); Napier Univ., Edinburgh (Dip. Journalism); Queen Margaret Coll., Edinburgh (Dip. Public Relns). Freelance field archaeologist, 1988–91; reporter, Dumfriesshire Newspapers Gp, 1991–94; Dep. Ed., E Lothian Courier, 1994–95; Press Officer, 1995–98, Internet Ed., 1998–2000, BT. Presenter, television series: Two Men in a Trench, 2002–03; Coast, 2005–; The Face of Britain, 2006; Scotland's History: the Top Ten, 2006; The History Detectives, 2007; A History of Scotland, 2008–09; A History of Ancient Britain, 2011; Vikings, 2012; Sacred Wonders of Britain, 2013; Coast Australia, 2014; The Celts, 2015. Patron, Assoc. of Lighthouse Keepers, 2008–. Hon. DLitt Abertay Dundee, 2011. *Publications:* (with A. Pollard) Two Men in a Trench I, 2002; (with A. Pollard) Two Men in a Trench II, 2003; Not Forgotten, 2005; Coast From the Air, 2007; Amazing Tales for Making Men Out of Boys, 2008; A History of Scotland, 2009; A History of Ancient Britain, 2011; Vikings: a history, 2012; Master of Shadows, 2015. *Recreations:* drinking tea, drinking wine, fantasising about one day moving the whole family to a small holding. *Address:* c/o Sophie Laurimore, Factual Management Ltd, 105 Tanners Hill, SE8 4QD. *T:* (020) 8694 1626.

OLIVER, Maj.-Gen. Richard Arthur, CB 1999; OBE 1986; Chief Executive, Year Out Group, 2000–14; *b* 16 July 1944; *s* of late Arthur R. L. and Betty Oliver; *m* 1972, Julia Newsum; three *s*. *Educ:* Repton Sch.; RMA, Sandhurst; RMCS (psc†). GSO2, Exercise Planning Staff, HQ BAOR, 1977–79; OC, 25 Field Sqdn Regt, 1979–81; GSO2, Exercise Planning Staff, HQ 3rd Armoured Div., 1981; Chief Logistic Plans, HQ 1st (Br.) Corps, 1982–83; CO, 36 Engr Regt, 1983–85; Col, Army Staff Duties 2, MoD (Army), 1985–88; hcsc, Army Staff Coll., 1988; Comdr, Berlin Infantry Bde, 1988–90; rcds 1991; Brig., AQ, HQ 1st (Br.) Corps, 1992; Deputy Chief of Staff: G1/G4 HQ Allied Comd Europe, Rapid Reaction Corps, 1992–94; HQ Land Comd, 1994–96; COS HQ Adjutant Gen. (PTC), 1996–99. Business Develt Advr, Granada Food Services, 1999–2000. Member: Nat. Bd, Race for Opportunity, BITC, 1998–99; Bd of Trustees (formerly Council), Cranstoun Drug Services, 2000– (Chm., 2001–); Pilot Bd, Young Volunteer Challenge, DfES, 2003–05; Travel Advice Review Gp, FCO, 2004–06; Consular Stakeholders Panel, FCO, 2007–11;

BS8848 Rev. Panel, BSI, 2007– (Chm., 2013–). FInstD 1998. *Publications:* (contrib.) The British Army and the Operational Level of War, 1989; articles in RUSI Jl and various educnl and travel mags. *Recreations:* gardening, fishing, shooting, indoor rowing, reading, water colours; beekeeping. *Address:* Queensfield, 28 Kings Road, Easterton, Devizes, Wilts SN10 4PX. *T:* (01380) 812368. *Club:* Army and Navy.

OLIVER, Dr Ronald Martin, CB 1989; RD 1973; FRCP; Deputy Chief Medical Officer (Deputy Secretary), Department of Health and Social Security, 1985–89, retired; *b* 28 May 1929; *s* of late Cuthbert Hanson Oliver and Cecilia Oliver; *m* 1957, Susanna Treves Blackwell; three *s* one *d*. *Educ:* King's Coll. Sch., Wimbledon; King's Coll., London; St George's Hosp. Med. Sch. (MB, BS 1952). MRCS, LRCP 1952; DCH 1954; DPH 1960; DIH 1961; MD London 1965; MFOM 1978; FRCP 1998 (MRCP 1987); MFCM 1987. Served RNR: Surg. Lieut, 1953–55; Surg. Lt-Comdr, retd 1974. St George's Hosp., London: House Surgeon and Physician, 1952–53; Resident Clin. Pathologist, 1955–56; trainee asst, gen. practice, 1956–57; Asst County MO, Surrey CC, 1957–59; MO, London Transport Exec., 1959–62; MO, later SMO, Treasury Med. Service (later CS Med. Adv. Service), 1962–74; seconded Diplomatic Service as Physician, British Embassy, Moscow, 1964–66; SMO, 1974–79, SPMO, 1979–85, DHSS; Chief Med. Advr, ODA, 1983–85. Gov., Manor House Sch., Little Bookham, 1991–99 (Chm., 1995–99). *Publications:* papers in med. jls on epidemiology of heart disease, public health, toxicology, and health service admin. *Recreations:* golf, travelling. *Address:* 4 Hawks Hill House, Guildford Road, Leatherhead, Surrey KT22 9GS. *T:* (01372) 362323. *Club:* Effingham Golf.

OLIVER, Simon Jonathan; His Honour Judge Oliver; a Circuit Judge, since 2010; a Designated Family Judge for Berkshire, since 2012; *b* Reading, 9 May 1958; *s* of John Michael Oliver and Shirley Mary Oliver; *m* 1983, Melanie Louise Joanna Stevens; two *s*. *Educ:* Reading Sch.; Univ. of Exeter (LLB 1980; MPhil 1998). Called to the Bar, Inner Temple, 1981; *ad eundem* Lincoln's Inn, 1984; in practice as barrister, specialising in family and educn law, 1981–2007; Recorder, 2003–10. Chair: (pt-time) Special Educnl Needs and Disability Tribunal, 1994–2007 (Actg Pres., 2008–09); Care Standards Tribunal, 2000–07 (Dep. Pres., 2007–10). Member: Stewards' Enclosure, Henley Royal Regatta, 1982–; Glyndebourne Fest. Soc., 2009–. Liveryman, Co. of Founders, 1985 (Mem., Ct of Assts, 2009–). FRSA. *Publications:* Special Educational Needs and the Law, 1996, 2nd edn 2007; Enforcing Family Finance Orders, 1999, 2nd edn 2012. *Recreations:* ski-ing, gardening, opera, making chutneys and piccalilli. *Address:* Reading County Court, 160–163 Friar Street, Reading RG1 1HE. *Clubs:* Leander (Henley-on-Thames); Surrey County Cricket.

OLIVER, Prof. Stephen George, PhD; FMedSci; Professor of Systems Biology and Biochemistry, since 2007, and Director, Cambridge Systems Biology Centre, University of Cambridge; Fellow, Wolfson College, Cambridge, since 2009; *b* 3 Nov. 1949; *s* of late Anthony George Oliver and Ivy Florence Oliver (*née* Simmons); *m* 1st, 1972, Rowena Philpott (marr. diss. 2008); one *d*; 2nd, 2009, Elaine Fenn. *Educ:* Univ. of Bristol (BSc Hons Microbiol. 1971); Nat. Inst. for Medical Research (PhD 1974). SRC Res. Fellow, Univ. of Calif, Irvine, 1974–77; Lectr in Microbiol., Univ. of Kent, Canterbury, 1977–81; Sen. Lectr in Applied Molecular Biol., 1981–87, Prof. of Biotechnol., 1987–99, UMIST; Prof. of Genomics, Univ. of Manchester, 1999–2007. Ed.-in-Chief, Yeast, 1985–. Chairman: MRC Bioinformatics and Mathematical Biol. Fellowships Panel, 2001–04; Wellcome Trust Molecules, Genes and Cells Funding Cttee, 2004–08. FMedSci 2002. Fellow, Amer. Acad. for Microbiol., 2000; FAAAS 2008; Mem. EMBO 2004. Hon. Member: Hungarian Acad. of Scis, 1998; British Mycol Soc., 2008. *Publications:* (ed with K. Gull) The Fungal Nucleus, 1981; (with T. A. Brown) Microbial Extrachromosomal Inheritance, 1985; (with J. M. Ward) A Dictionary of Genetic Engineering, 1985; (ed with M. F. Tuite) Biotechnology Handbooks—Saccharomyces, 1991; (jtly) The Eukaryotic Genome: organisation and regulation, 1997; (ed jtly) Encyclopedia of Microbiology, vols 1–4, 2000; (ed with J. I. Castrillo) Yeast Systems Biology, 2003; articles in scientific jls. *Recreations:* music, the outdoors, searching for hills to walk or bike up in East Anglia. *Address:* Cambridge Systems Biology Centre and Department of Biochemistry, University of Cambridge, Cambridge CB2 1GA.

OLIVER, Rt Rev. Stephen John; Area Bishop of Stepney, 2003–10; *b* 7 Jan. 1948; *s* of John Oliver and Nora Oliver (*née* Greenhalgh); *m* 1969, Hilary Joan Barkham (*d* 2010); two *s*. *Educ:* St Augustine's Coll., Canterbury; King's Coll. London (AKC 1970). Ordained deacon, 1971, priest, 1972; Asst Curate, Clifton, Nottingham, 1970; Vicar, Christ Church, Newark on Trent, 1975; Rector, St Mary Plumtree, Nottingham, 1979; Producer, Religious Programmes, BBC, 1985, Chief Producer, 1987; Rector of Leeds, 1991–97; Canon Residentiary, St Paul's Cathedral, 1997–2003. Mem., Liturgical Commn, Gen. Synod of C of E, 1991–2001. Hon. Canon, Ripon Cathedral, 1996. Chm., Praxis, 1997–2001; Member: Elida Gibbs Ethics Cttee, 1994–96; W Yorks Playhouse Community and Educn Cttee, 1991–96; Leeds Common Purpose Adv. Gp, 1994–96; Unilever Central Ethical Compliance Gp, 1997–2003. Trustee, More Than Gold, 2008–10. Chairman, Governors: Leeds Girls' High Sch., 1993–96; Agnes Stewart High Sch., 1993–96. Pres., Leeds Church Inst., 1991–96. *Publications:* Why Pray?, 1993; (ed) Pastoral Prayers, 1996; (contrib.) New SCM Dictionary of Liturgy and Worship, 2002; Guiding Stars, 2005; (ed) Inside Grief, 2013. *Recreations:* reading, theatre, flying, ski-ing. *Address:* Garden Cottage, Church Lane, Averham, Notts NG23 5RB.

OLIVER, Sir Stephen (John Lindsay), Kt 2007; QC 1980; President of First-tier Tax Chamber and Vice-President (Tax) of Upper Tribunal, 2009–11; Vice President (Finance) of Upper Tribunal, 2010–11 (Presiding Special Commissioner, and President, VAT and Duties (formerly Value Added Tax) Tribunals, 1992–2009); a fee-paid Judge of Upper Tribunal, 2011–13; *b* 14 Nov. 1938; *s* of late Philip Daniel Oliver and Audrey Mary Oliver; *m* 1967, Ann Dawn Harrison Taylor (*see* A. D. H. Oliver); one *s* two *d*. *Educ:* Rugby Sch.; Oriel Coll., Oxford (MA Jurisprudence). National Service, RN, 1957–59: served submarines; Temp. Sub-Lieut. Called to the Bar, Middle Temple, 1963; Bencher, 1987; a Recorder, 1989–91; Circuit Judge, 1991–92. Mediator, Pump Court Tax Chambers, 2012–. President: Financial Services and Mkts Tribunal, 2001–10; Pensions Regulator Tribunal, 2005–10. Asst Boundary Comr, Parly Boundary Commn, 1977. Chm., Blackheath Concert Halls Charity, 1986–92; Mem. Council, London Sinfonietta, 1993–2014. Trustee: Britten-Pears Foundn, 2001–09; TaxAid, 2007–13. *Recreations:* music, films, golf. *T:* (020) 7414 8080.

See also J. A. Oliver.

OLIVER-JONES, His Honour Stephen; QC 1996; a Circuit Judge, 2000–15; *b* 6 July 1947; *s* of Arthur William Jones and Kathleen Jones; *m* 1972, Margaret Anne Richardson; one *s* one *d*. *Educ:* Marling Sch., Stroud; UC, Durham Univ. (BA Hons). Lectr in Law, Durham Tech. Coll., 1968–70. Called to the Bar, Inner Temple, 1970, Bencher, 2010; Mem., Oxford, later Midland and Oxford, Circuit; an Asst Recorder, 1988–93; a Recorder, 1993–2000; Designated Civil Judge for W Midlands and Warwicks, 2002–09. Legal Mem., Mental Health Tribunal (formerly Pres., Mental Health Rev. Tribunal), 1997–. Mem., Civil Procedure Rule Cttee, 2002–08. *Recreations:* fly fishing, book collecting. *E:* soliverjones@msn.com. *Club:* East India.

OLIVIER, Lady; *see* Plowright, Dame J. A.

OLIVIER, Joan Sheila Ross; Headmistress, Lady Margaret School, Parsons Green, 1984–2006; *b* 30 April 1941; *m* 1966, John Eric Hordern Olivier; one *s*. *Educ:* Queen Mary Coll., Univ. of London (BA Hons); Hughes Hall, Cambridge (PGCE). Hd of History, Camden Sch. for Girls, 1965–73; Dep. Hd, Lady Margaret Sch., 1973–84. Chm., Wimbledon Br., NADFAS, 2012–15. JP Wimbledon, 1993–2011. *Recreations:* bad bridge, patchwork.

OLIVIERI, René; Chairman, The Wildlife Trusts, since 2012; *b* 1 May 1953; *m*; two *c*. *Educ:* Univ. of Oregon, Eugene (BA Political Scis); Johns Hopkins Univ. (MA Internat. Relns). Blackwell Publishers: Publisher, 1980–83; Editl and Mktg Dir, 1983–85; Dep. Man. Dir, 1985–88; Man. Dir, 1988–2000; CEO, 2000–07; Chief Operating Officer, Wiley-Blackwell, 2007–08; Chm., Tubney Charitable Trust, 2008–12. Chairman: InfoSource Inc., 1990–2000; NCC Blackwell, 1992–96; Polity Press, 1995–2000; Marston Book Services, 1998–2000. Non-exec. Dir, IOP Publishing, 2014–. Mem., HEFCE, 2008–14. Chairman: Belgrade Th., 2011–12; Blikbook, 2011–. *Publications:* articles in jls incl. THES, Res. Evaluation, Info. Services and Use. *Recreations:* theatre, horse riding, tennis, ski-ing, scuba diving, early music. *E:* rene.olivieri@mhcom.co.uk.

OLLERENSHAW, Eric, OBE 1991; *b* 26 March 1950; *s* of Eric and Barbara Ollerenshaw. *Educ:* London Sch. of Economics and Political Science (BSc Econs). History teacher, Northumberland Park Sch., Tottenham, Hendon Sch., Barnet, and Tom Hood Sch., Leytonstone, 1973–2000. Member (C): ILEA, 1986–90 (Leader, Cons. Gp, 1988–90); Hackney LBC, 1990–2007 (Leader, Cons. Gp, 1996); London Assembly, GLA, 2000–04 (Dep. Leader, 2000–02, Leader, 2002–04, Cons. Gp). MP (C) Lancaster and Fleetwood, 2010–15; contested (C) same seat, 2015. PPS to Baroness Warsi, 2010–15. Hd of Cities and Diversity, Cons. Party, 2005–10. Mem. Bd, London Develt Agency, 2004–08. *Recreations:* reading, listening to music.

OLLEY, (John) Brian; HM Diplomatic Service; High Commissioner to Cameroon, and Ambassador to Gabon, Chad and Equatorial Guinea, since 2013; *b* Moshi, Tanzania, 14 Feb. 1957; *s* of Bill Olley and Stella Olley; *m* 1989, Pascale Abadie; two *s* one *d*. *Educ:* King's Sch., Canterbury; Univ. of Nottingham (BSc 1st Cl. 1978; MSc 1984); Royal Mil. Acad. Sandhurst. Joined Army, 1980; Queen's Gurkha Engrs, 1980–83; various postings, Hong Kong, Nepal, Germany, London; sc 1990; CO 1RSME Regt, 1998–2000; joined FCO, 2001; Pol Officer and Hd, Security Sector Reform Section, Afghanistan Unit, Kabul and London, 2002–03; Hd, Pol and Public Affairs, Helsinki, 2004–08; Dep. High Comr, Cyprus, 2008–13. *Recreations:* tennis, golf, family. *Address:* British High Commission, Avenue Winston Churchill, PO Box 547, Yaoundé, Cameroon. *T:* 22220545. *E:* brian.olley@fco.gov.uk.

OLLILA, Jorma Jaakko, Hon. CBE 2007; Chairman, Board of Directors, Nokia Corporation, 2006–12 (Chief Executive Officer, 1992–2006, and Chairman, Group Executive Board, 1999–2006); Chairman, Outokumpu, since 2013; Advisory Partner, Perella Weinberg Partners, since 2014; *b* Seinäjoki, Finland, 15 Aug. 1950; *m* Liisa Annikki Metsola; two *s* one *d*. *Educ:* Univ. of Helsinki (MSc Political Sci. 1976); LSE (MSc Econ 1978); Helsinki Univ. of Technology (MSc Eng 1981). Citibank: Account Manager, Corporate Bank, Citibank NA, London, 1978–80; Account Officer, 1980–82, Mem. Bd of Mgt, 1983–85, Citibank Oy; Nokia: Mem., Gp Exec. Bd, 1985–2006; Vice-Pres., Internat. Operations, 1985–86; Sen. Vice-Pres., Finance, 1986–89; Dep. Mem., Bd of Dirs, 1989–90; President: Nokia Mobile Phones, 1990–92; Nokia, 1992–99. Chairman: Bd, MTV Oy, 1993–97; Royal Dutch Shell, 2006–15; Member Board: ICL plc, 1992–2000; Otava Books and Magazines Gp Ltd, 1996–; UPM-Kymmene, 1997–2008 (Vice-Chm., 2004–08); Ford Motor Co., 2000–08; Tetra Laval Gp, 2013–; Member Supervisory Board: Tietotehdas Oy, 1992–95; Pohjola Insurance Co. Ltd, 1992–97; NKF Holding NV, 1992–99; Oy Rastor Ab, 1992–93; Sampo Insurance Co. Ltd, 1993–2000; Merita Bank Ltd, 1994–2000. Chm. Supervisory Bd, Finnish Foreign Trade Assoc., 1993–98; Vice Chm. Bd, Finnish Sect., ICC, 1993–97; Member: Planning Bd for Defence Economy, 1992–96; Technol. Delegn, Ministry of Trade and Industry, 1992–95; Bd and Exec. Cttee, Confedn of Finnish Industry and Employers, 1992–2002 (Dep. Chm. Bd, 1995–2002); Council, State Technical Res. Centre, 1992–93; Bd, Econ. Inf. Bureau, 1993–97; Council, Centre for Finnish Business and Policy Studies, 1993–2001; Supervisory Bd, Foundn for Pediatric Res., 1993–98; Sci. and Technology Policy Council of Finland, 1993–2002; Council of Supervisors, Res. Inst. of Finnish Economy, 1993–2000; Exec. Bd, Assoc. for Finnish Cultural Foundn, 1993–99; Delegn, Finnish-Swedish Chamber of Commerce, 1993–99; Supervisory Bd, WWF Finland, 1995–97; Competitiveness Adv. Gp, EC, 1995–96; European Round Table of Industrialists, 1997– (Chm., 2005–09); GBDe Business Steering Cttee, 1999–. Overseas Adv. Trustee, American-Scandinavian Foundn, 1994–. Chm. Adv. Cttee, Helsinki Univ. of Technology, 1996– (Vice-Chm., 1993–95); Member: Council, Helsinki Sch. of Econs and Business Admin, 1993–98; Dean's Council, John F. Kennedy Sch. of Govt, Harvard, 1995–; Internat. Bd, United World Colls, 1995–; Bd of Dirs, Univ. of Helsinki, 2009–. Hon. PhD Helsinki, 1995; Hon. DSc Helsinki Univ. of Technol., 1998. Comdr 1st Cl., Order of White Rose (Finland), 1996; Order of White Star (Estonia), 1995; Comdr, Order of Orange (Nassau), 1995; Officer's Cross, Order of Merit (Hungarian Republic), 1996; Commander's Cross, Order of Merit, Germany, 1997, Poland, 1999. *Publications:* (with Harri Saukkomaa) Mahdoton menestys: kasvun paikkana Nokia (autobiog.), 2013.

OLMERT, Ehud; Prime Minister of Israel, 2006–09 (Acting, Jan.–April 2006, Interim Prime Minister, April–May 2006); Member, Knesset, 1973–98 and 2003–09; *b* Nahlat Jabotinsky, Binyamina, 30 Sept. 1945; *s* of Mordechai and Bella Olmert; *m* Aliza Richter; two *s* two *d*. *Educ:* Hebrew Univ. of Jerusalem (BA Psychol. and Philos. 1968; BA Law 1973). Military service, 1963, 13th Regt, Golani Bde, wounded, completed service at Hamahane newspaper, 1971. Started practising law, private law firm, 1975; Sen. Partner, Ehud Olmert and Associates Law Firm, 1978. Volunteer, Israel Defence Forces, 1979–82, completed officers' course, volunteered for reserve service in Lebanon. Knesset: Member, 1981–88: For. Affairs and Defence Cttee; Finance Cttee; Educn and Culture Cttee; Defence Budget Cttee; Minister: of Minority Affairs, 1988–90; of Health, 1990–92; of Industry, Trade and Labour, 2003–06; of Communications, 2003–05; of Finance, 2005 and 2007; of Welfare and Social Services, 2006–07; Vice Prime Minister, 2003. Mayor of Jerusalem, 1993–2003.

OLNER, William John; *b* 9 May 1942; *s* of Charles William Olner, miner and Lillian Olner; *m* 1962, Gillian Everitt. *Educ:* Atherstone Secondary Modern Sch.; North Warwicks Tech. Coll. Engineer, Rolls Royce, 1957–92. Nuneaton and Bedworth Borough Council: Cllr, 1972–92; Leader, 1982–87; Mayor, 1987–88; Chm., Envmtl Health Cttee, 1990–92. MP (Lab) Nuneaton, 1992–2010. Member: Envmt, Transport and the Regions (formerly Envmt) Select Cttee, 1995–2001; Foreign Affairs Select Cttee, 2001–05; DCLG (formerly ODPM) Select Cttee, 2005–10. Chm., Industry and Parlt Trust, 2007–10. Mem. (Lab) Warwicks CC, 2013– (Vice Chm., Regulatory Cttee, 2013–). *Recreations:* hospice movement, walking, current affairs. *Address:* 6 Cotswold Crescent, Nuneaton, Warwicks CV10 8PL.

O'LOAN, family name of **Baroness O'Loan**.

O'LOAN, Baroness *cr* 2009 (Life Peer), of Kirkinriola in the County of Antrim; **Nuala Patricia O'Loan,** DBE 2008; MRIA; Chair, Governing Authority, National University of Maynooth, since 2011; Member, International Contact Group for the Basque country, since 2011; *b* 20 Dec. 1951; *m* 1975, Declan O'Loan, *qv*; five *s*. *Educ:* King's College, London (LLB Hons); Coll. of Law. Solicitor of Supreme Ct of England and Wales. Articled Clerk, Stephenson Harwood, London, 1974–76; Law Lectr, Ulster Poly., 1976–80; University of Ulster: Law Lectr, 1985–92; Sen. Lectr, 1992–2000; Jean Monnet Chair in European Law, 1992–99; Police Ombudsman for NI, 2000–07. Special Comr, CRE, 2004–05. Chm., Formal Investigation into Human Rights, Equality and Human Rights Commn, 2008–09; Member: Ind. Gp for Dialogue and Peace, 2007–10; Ind. Rev. of Outsourcing Abuse, UK Border Agency, for Home Sec., 2009–10; Ind. Rev. Panel for Police Service of NI Investigation into matters arising out of Report of Police Ombudsman for NI into circumstances surrounding death of Raymond McCord, Jr and related matters, 2010–. Roving Ambassador and Special

Envoy for Conflict Resolution, Ireland, 2008–11; Special Envoy on UN Security Council Resolution 1325 on Women, Peace and Security, 2009–11. Lay Visitor, RUC Stations, 1991–97; Chm., NI Consumer Council for Electricity, 1997–2000; Member: Gen. Consumer Council for NI, 1991–96 (Convenor, Energy and Transport Gp, 1994–96); UK Domestic Coal Consumers' Council, 1992–95; Ministerial Working Gp on Green Economy, 1993–95; Northern HSS Bd, 1993–97 (Convenor for Complaints, 1996–97); Police Authy for NI, 1997–99; Legal Expert Mem., EC Consumers' Consultative Council, 1994–95. Mem., Club de Madrid NetPLUSS, 2011–. MRIA 2012. *Publications:* articles on European law, policing and consumer law, and faith issues. *Recreations:* music, reading. *Address:* 48 Old Park Avenue, Ballymena, Northern Ireland BT42 1AX. *T:* (028) 2564 9636. *E:* oloann@parliament.uk.

O'LOAN, Declan; Member (SDLP) North Antrim, Northern Ireland Assembly, 2007–11; *b* Ballymena, 5 Aug. 1951; *s* of Charles and Elizabeth O'Loan; *m* 1975, Nuala Patricia (*see* Baroness O'Loan); five *s*. *Educ:* Imperial Coll., London (BSc 1973); Fitzwilliam Coll., Cambridge (PGCE 1974); Univ. of Ulster (MBA 1989). Teacher of Maths: Ramsden Sch. for Boys, 1974–76; Rainey Endowed Sch., Magherafelt, Co. Derry, 1976–80; St Mary's Yala, Kenya, 1980–82; St Patrick's Iten, Kenya, 1982–83; Methodist Coll., Belfast, 1983–87; Teacher of Maths, 1987–2005, Hd of Maths, 1990–2005, St Louis Grammar Sch., Ballymena. Member (SDLP): Ballymena BC, 1993–2015 (Dep. Mayor, 2008–09; Chm., Audit and Scrutiny Cttee, 2011–12); Mid and E Antrim BC (formerly DC), 2014–. Northern Ireland Assembly: Member: Finance and Personnel Cttee, 2007–11; Cttee on Procedures, 2007–10; Assembly and Exec. Rev. Cttee, 2010; Chm., Cttee on Standards and Privileges, 2009–11; Dep. Chm., Culture, Arts and Leisure Cttee, 2010–11. Member: NI Community Relns Council, 2001–08; Indep. Panel of Victims and Survivors Service, NI, 2012–. Member: Bd, NI Assembly and Business Trust, 2007–11; Exec. Cttee, NI Assembly Br., CPA, 2009–11. Contested (SDLP): N Antrim, 2010, 2015; N Antrim, NI Assembly, 2011. Chm., Ballymena District Policing Partnership, 2010–12; Mem., Ballymena Policing and Community Safety Partnership, 2012–15. Hon. Consul for Romania in NI, 2010–. *E:* declanoloan@gmail.com.

O'LOGHLEN, (Sir) Michael, (7th Bt *cr* 1838, of Drumconora, Ennis); QC (Vic) 1991; *b* Melbourne, 21 May 1945; *e s* of Sir Colman Michael O'Loghlen, 6th Bt and of Margaret O'Loghlen (*née* O'Halloran); *S* father 2014, but his name does not yet appear on the Official Roll of the Baronetage; *m* 1st, 1967, Elizabeth Mary Clarke (marr. diss. 1988); three *s*; 2nd, 1989, Elizabeth Margaret Heslop (marr. diss. 2003); one step *s* one step *d*. *Educ:* Xavier Coll., Kew; Univ. of Melbourne (LLB). In practice, Victorian Bar, 1970–2010. Hon. Life Mem., Vic Compensation Bar Assoc., 2010 (former Chm.). *Heir: s* Hugh O'Loghlen, *b* 6 Dec. 1968. *Address:* PO Box 280, Apollo Bay, Vic 3233, Australia.

O'LONE, Marcus James, CVO 2013 (LVO 2003); Agent to the Queen, Sandringham, since 1998; *b* Belfast, 18 Nov. 1953; *s* of late Col Robert John O'Lone, DSO, OBE and Charmian O'Lone; *m* 1981, Elizabeth Mary Foster; one *s* two *d*. *Educ:* Wellington Coll., Crowthorne; Royal Agricultural Coll., Cirencester. FAAV 1980; FRICS 1986. Agent to the Marquess of Salisbury, 1977–95; Dep. Ranger, Windsor Great Park, 1995–98. Pres., NW Norfolk Scouts, 1998–; Vice Pres., Norfolk Scouts, 2005–. *Recreations:* shooting, fishing, golf. *Address:* Laycocks, Sandringham, Norfolk PE35 6EB. *T:* (01485) 540581. *Club:* Farmers.

OLSEN, Hon. John Wayne, AO 2007; Deputy Chairman and Chief Executive Officer, American Australian Association Ltd, since 2010; *b* 7 June 1945; *s* of S. J. Olsen; *m* 1968, Julie, *d* of G. M. Abbott; two *s* one *d*. *Educ:* Kadina Memorial High Sch.; Sch. of Business Studies, SA. Managing Dir, J. R. Olsen & Sons Pty Ltd, 1968–79. Pres., S Australia Liberal Party, 1976–79; South Australia Government: MP (L): Rocky River, 1979–85; Custance, 1985–90; Kavel, 1992–2002; Chief Sec. and Minister of Fisheries, 1982; Leader of the Opposition, 1982–90; Senator for SA, 1990–92; Shadow Minister of Industry, Trade, Regl Develt, Public Works and Small Business, 1992–93; Minister for Industry, Manufg, Small Business, Regl Develt and Minister for Infrastructure, 1993–96; Minister for State Develt, and for Multicultural and Ethnic, then Multicultural, Affairs, 1996–2001; Premier of SA, 1996–2001; Consul General for Australia: in LA, 2002–06; in NY, 2006–09. Chairman: SA Football Commn, 2010–; Adelaide Oval Stadium Mgt Authy, 2014–. Fellow, Nat. Inst. of Accts. *Recreation:* barefoot water ski-ing. *Address:* PO Box 133, Glenelg, SA 5045, Australia. *Club:* West Adelaide Football.

OLSSON, Curt Gunnar; Chairman, Skandinaviska Enskilda Banken, 1984–96; *b* 20 Aug. 1927; *s* of N. E. and Anna Olsson; *m* 1954, Asta Engblom; two *d*. *Educ:* Stockholm Sch. of Econs (BSc Econs 1950). Managing Director, Stockholm Group: Skandinaviska Banken, 1970–72; Skandinaviska Enskilda Banken, 1972–76; Man. Dir and Chief Exec., Head Office, 1976–82, and first Dep. Chm., 1982–84, Skandinaviska Enskilda Banken. Hon. Consul Gen. for Finland, 1989–99. Hon. DEcon, Stockholm, 1992. Kt Order of Vasa, Sweden, 1976; King Carl XVI Gustaf's Gold Medal, Sweden, 1982; Comdr, Royal Norwegian Order of Merit, 1985; Comdr, Order of the Lion, Finland, 1986.

OLSWANG, Simon Myers; Senior Partner, 1981–98, Chairman, 1998–2002, Olswang, solicitors (formerly Simon Olswang & Co.); non-executive company director and executive film producer; *b* 13 Dec. 1943; *s* of Simon Alfred Olswang and Amelia Olga Olswang; *m* 1969, Susan Jane Simon; one *s* two *d*. *Educ:* Bootham Sch., York; Newcastle upon Tyne Univ. (BAEcon). Admitted solicitor, 1968; Attorney at Law, California State Bar, 1978. Trainee, Asst Solicitor, then Partner, Brecher & Co., 1966–81; Founder, Simon Olswang & Co., 1981. Member: Entertainments Symposium Adv. Bd, UCLA, 1982–88; British Screen Adv. Council, 1985–2010 (Chm., Wkg Party on Convergence, 1994–99); non-exec. Director: Press Assoc., 1995–97; Amdocs Ltd, 2004–; DIC Entertainment Inc., 2005–08; Amiad Filtration Systems Ltd, 2009–; Mem., Adv. Bd, Palamon Capital Partners, 2002–. Member: Council, BFI, 1998–99; Bd, BL, 2001–08; Bd, Intellectual Property Inst., 2004–06. Chm. Govs and Trustee, Langdon Coll. of Further (Special) Educn, 1992–2009; Overseas Mem., Bd of Trustees, Council of Christians and Jews, 2006–12; Mem., Bd of Trustees, Tel Hai Academic Coll., 2012–. Executive Producer: Peter and the Wolf, 2008; The Flying Machine, 2011; Zaytoun, 2012. Blog, http://simonolswang.wordpress.com. *Publications:* (contrib.) Accessright: an evolutionary path for copyright into the digital era, 1995; (contrib.) Masters of the Wired World, 1988. *Recreations:* family, friends, sailing, theatre, cinema, travel, fruit-farming. *Address:* Moshav Almagor, Upper Galilee, Israel 12922. *Clubs:* Garrick (Overseas Mem.); Royal Motor Yacht (Overseas Mem.) (Poole).

OLSZEWSKI, Jan; Order of White Eagle (Poland), 2009; Political Adviser to President of Poland, 2006–10; *b* Warsaw, 20 Aug. 1930. *Educ:* Warsaw Univ. Mem., underground Boy Scouts during German occupation. Res. Asst, Legal Scis Dept, Polish Acad. Scis, 1954–56; Mem., editorial staff, Po Prostu, 1956–57 (periodical then closed down by authorities); subseq. banned from work as journalist; apprenticeship in legal profession, 1959–62; practised as trial lawyer, specialising in criminal law; served as defense counsel in political trials; suspended from the Bar, 1968, for defending students arrested for anti-communist demonstrations; returned as attorney, 1970. Co-Founder: (with Zdzisław Najder), Polish Independence Alliance, 1975–80; Workers' Defense Cttee, 1976–77; co-author of statute of Free Trade Unions, 1980, which he personally delivered to Gdansk shipyard; involved in formation of Solidarity, and legal advr, 1980; defense counsel at trials of Solidarity activists (incl. Lech Wałęsa), 1980–89; attorney for family of Fr Jerzy Popiełuszko at trial of his assassins, 1985; Mem., President Lech Wałęsa's Adv. Cttee, Jan.–Nov. 1991; MP Poland, 1991–93 and 1997–2005; Prime Minister of Poland (first non-communist govt), 1991–92; co-founder and Chm., Movement for Reconstruction of Poland, 1995–2011.

OLVER, Sir Richard (Lake), Kt 2013; FREng; Partner, Edgewater Energy LLC, since 2009; Director, EdgeMarc LLC, since 2012; Senior Advisor: C,D&R LLP, since 2008; HSBC, since 2011; *b* 2 Jan. 1947; *s* of Graham Lake Olver and Constance Evelyn Olver; *m* 1968, Pamela Kathleen Larkin; two *d*. *Educ:* City Univ. (BSc 1st Cl., Civil Eng); Univ. of Virginia Business Sch. FREng 2005; FICE 2010. British Petroleum: joined Engineering Dept, 1973, UK and overseas; Vice-Pres., BP Pipeline Inc., 1979; Divl Manager, New Technology, 1983; Divl Manager, Corporate Planning, 1985; Man. Dir, Central North Sea Pipelines, 1988; Gen. Manager, BP Gas Europe, 1988; Chief of Staff, BP, and Head, Corporate Strategy, 1990; Chief Exec., BP Exploration, USA, and Exec. Vice-Pres., BP America, 1992; Dep. CEO, 1995, CEO, 1998, BP Exploration; Chm., BP Amer. Adv. Bd, 1998; Man. Dir, BP Exploration and Production, 1998–2003; Dep. Gp Chief Exec., BP plc, 2003–04; Dep. Chm., TNK-BP (Russia), 2004–06; Chm., BAE SYSTEMS, 2004–14. Mem., Trilateral Commn, 2005–. UK Business Ambassador, 2008–. Member: PM's Business Adv. Gp, 2010–; India-UK CEO Forum, 2010–. Non-executive Director: Thomson-Reuters (formerly Reuters), 1997–2009. Hon. DSc: City, 2004; Cranfield, 2006. *Recreations:* sailing, downhill ski-ing, ballet, fine art. *Address:* C,D&R LLP, Cleveland House, 33 King Street, SW1Y 4AR. *E:* dick@sirrichardolver.com.

O'MAHONY, Patrick James Martin; His Honour Judge O'Mahony; a Circuit Judge, since 2004; *b* 18 April 1951; *s* of Patrick Noel and Elizabeth Nora O'Mahony; *m* 1979, Jane Tayler; one *s* two *d*. *Educ:* Stonyhurst Coll.; UCL (LLB (Laws) 1972). Called to the Bar, Inner Temple, 1973; in practice as barrister, London, 1973–83 and 1988–2004; Sen. Crown Counsel, Attorney Gen.'s Chambers, Hong Kong, 1983–88. Hon. Recorder of Margate, 2002–. *Recreations:* long distance running, horse racing, literary criticism. *Address:* c/o Circuit Secretariat, 2 Southwark Bridge, SE1 9HS. *Clubs:* Hong Kong Football; Red and Yellow Racing (Broadstairs).

O'MALLEY, His Honour Stephen Keppel; DL; a Circuit Judge, 1989–2010; *b* 21 July 1940; *s* of late D. K. C. O'Malley and Mrs R. O'Malley; *m* 1963, Frances Mary, *e d* of late James Stewart Ryan; four *s* two *d*. *Educ:* Ampleforth Coll.; Wadham Coll., Oxford (MA). Called to Bar, Inner Temple, 1962; Mem. Bar Council, 1968–72; Co-Founder, Bar European Gp, 1977; a Recorder, Western Circuit, 1978–89. Wine Treasurer, Western Circuit, 1986–89. DL Somerset, 1998. *Publications:* Legal London, a Pictorial History, 1971; European Civil Practice, 1989. *Address:* Heale House, Curry Rivel, Langport, Somerset TA10 0PN.

OMAND, Sir David (Bruce), GCB 2004 (KCB 2000); Visiting Professor, King's College London, since 2006; Security and Intelligence Co-ordinator and Permanent Secretary, Cabinet Office, 2002–05; *b* 15 April 1947; *s* of late J. Bruce Omand, JP, and of Esther Omand; *m* 1971, Elizabeth, *er d* of late Geoffrey Wales, RE, ARCA; one *s* one *d*. *Educ:* Glasgow Acad.; Corpus Christi Coll., Cambridge (BAEcon; MAEcon; Hon. Fellow, 2010); Open Univ. (BSc Maths/Physics 2007). Ministry of Defence: Asst Principal, 1970; Private Sec. to Chief Exec. (PE), 1973; Asst Private Sec. to Sec. of State, 1973–75, 1979–80; Principal, 1975; Asst Sec., 1981; Private Sec. to Sec. of State, 1981–82; on loan to FCO as Defence Counsellor, UK Delegn to NATO, Brussels, 1985–88; Asst Under Sec. of State (Management Strategy), 1988–91, (Programmes), 1991–92; Dep. Under Sec. of State (Policy), MoD, 1992–96; Dir, GCHQ, 1996–97; Permanent Under-Sec. of State, Home Office, 1998–2001; Chm., Centre for Mgt and Policy Studies, Cabinet Office, 2001–02. Non-exec. Dir, Finmeccanica UK Ltd, 2008–14; Sen. Ind. Dir, Babcock International plc, 2012– (non-exec. Dir, 2009–12). Mem., Global Commn on Internet Governance, 2014–. Trustee, Natural History Mus., 2006–14. Hon. PhD Birmingham, 2008. *Publications:* Securing the State, 2010. *Recreations:* opera, hill-walking. *Club:* Reform.

O'MARA, Margaret; Director, Human Resources, National Offender Management Service, Home Office, 2006–07; *b* 10 May 1951; *d* of Thomas Patrick and Madge O'Mara. *Educ:* St Hilda's Coll., Oxford (1st Cl. Hons Lit.Hum.); University Coll. London (MSc Econs of Public Policy). Entered HM Treasury, 1973; Private Sec. to Chancellor of Exchequer, 1982–85; Head: Economic Briefing Div., 1985–87; Monetary Policy Div., 1987–90; Public Expenditure Div., monitoring Dept of Employment, 1990–92; Arts Gp, then Libraries, Museums and Galls Gp, Dept of Nat. Heritage, 1992–95; Dir, Personnel and Support, then Personnel, HM Treasury, 1995–2000; Associate Dir, Policing and Security, NIO, 2000–03; Director: Organised Crime, 2003–04, Crime Reduction, 2004–06, Home Office. Member, Executive: Particular Baptist Fund, 2008–; Assoc. of Grace Baptist Churches (SE), 2009–. Dir, Grace Baptist Charities Ltd, 2009–. *Recreations:* walking, cooking, Irish history.

O'MORCHOE, David Nial Creagh, CB 1979; CBE 2007 (MBE 1967); (The O'Morchoe); Chief of O'Morchoe; *b* 17 May 1928; *s* of Nial Creagh O'Morchoe and Jessie Elizabeth, *d* of late Charles Jasper Joly, FRS, FRIS, MRIA, Astronomer Royal of Ireland; *S* father as Chief of the Name (O'Morchoe, formerly of Oulartleigh and Monamolin), 1970; *m* 1954, Margaret Jane, 3rd *d* of George Francis Brewitt, Cork; two *s* one *d*. *Educ:* St Columba's Coll., Dublin (Fellow 1983–2007; Chm. of Fellows, 1989–99); RMA Sandhurst. Commissioned Royal Irish Fusiliers, 1948; served in Egypt, Jordan, Gibraltar, Germany, Kenya, Cyprus, Oman; psc 1958, jssc 1966; CO 1st Bn RIrF, later 3rd Bn Royal Irish Rangers, 1967–68; Directing Staff, Staff Coll., Camberley, 1969–71; RCDS 1972; Brigade Comdr, 1973–75; Brig. GS, BAOR, 1975–76; Maj.-Gen. 1977; Comdr, Sultan of Oman's Land Forces, 1977–79, retired. Dep. Col, 1971–76, Col 1977–79, The Royal Irish Rangers. Pres., Republic of Ireland Dist, RBL, 1999–; SSAFA (formerly SSAFA/Forces Help Society, then SSAFA Forces Help): Chm., 1987–2010, Pres., 2010–, Rep. of Ireland Br.; Council Mem., 2002–10; Hon. Life Mem., 2010; Mem. Council, Concern, Dublin, 1984–2004 (Sec., 1989–98). Member: Church of Ireland Gen. Synod, 1993–2005; Rep. Church Body, 1994–2004. Founder Mem., Standing Council of Irish Chiefs and Chieftains, 1992 (Chm., 1994–98). Mem., Order of Friendly Brothers of St Patrick, 1980– (Grand Pres., 2002–08). KLJ 2010. *Recreations:* sailing, an interest in most sports. *Heir: s* Dermot Arthur O'Morchoe, *b* 11 Aug. 1956. *Address:* c/o Bank of Ireland, Gorey, Co. Wexford, Ireland. *Clubs:* Kildare Street and University, Friendly Brothers (Dublin); Irish Cruising.

ÖNAÇ, Aydin; Headmaster, St Olave's Grammar School, since 2010; *b* Derbyshire, 21 Dec. 1951; *s* of Yusuf Önaç and Muriel Önaç (*née* Hallam); *m* 1976, Tahera Khakoo (marr. diss. 1990); one *s* one *d*; *m* 2013, Saima Malik. *Educ:* Lady Manners Grammar Sch., Bakewell (Head Boy); Royal Coll. of Music (BMus; ARCM); University Coll. London (BSc 1st Cl. Hons Maths 1981). Concert pianist, 1973–; pupil of Cyril Smith; performances with LSO, LPO, with conductors incl. Sir Charles Groves; plays all Rachmaninov piano concertos. Teacher of Maths, Hemel Hempstead Sch., 1982–84; Hd, Maths, Bridgnorth Endowed Sch., 1984–90; Dep. Hd, The Chase, Malvern, 1990–2002; Headteacher: Tewkesbury Sch., 2002–06; Fortismere, Muswell Hill, 2006–10. Consultancy work for National Coll., 2007–09. FRSA 2008. *Recreations:* Rugby, squash, chess, rock climbing (incl. Kilimanjaro), travel, foreign languages, reading, charity, passionate about maths and music, favourite cities are London, Istanbul and Florence. *Address:* St Olave's Grammar School, Goddington Lane, Orpington, Kent BR6 9SH. *T:* (01689) 820101. *E:* headmaster@saintolaves.net.

OÑATE LABORDE, Santiago; Permanent Observer, Mission of Mexico to the Council of Europe, since 2013; *b* 24 May 1949; *s* of Santiago Oñate and Clara Laborde; *m* 1981, Laura Madrazo; three *d*. *Educ:* Universidad Nacional Autónoma de México (LLB 1972); postgrad. studies at Università degli Studi di Pavia, LSE and Univ. of Wisconsin-Madison. Prof. of Law, Universidad Autónoma Metropolitana-Azcapotzalco, Mexico, 1976–81; Vis. Prof., Law Sch., Univ. of Wisconsin-Madison, 1981–82. Mem. Congress, Chamber of Deputies, Mexico, 1985–88; Mem., Representative Assembly of Federal Dist, Mexico, 1988–91; Ambassador,

Permanent Rep. to OAS, Washington, 1991–92; Attorney Gen. for Protection of Envmt, 1992–94; COS, President's Office, 1994; Sec. of State for Labour, 1994–95; Pres., Nat. Exec. Cttee, Partido Revolucionario Institucional, 1995–96; Ambassador for Mexico: to UK, 1997–2001; to the Netherlands, 2001–03; Legal Advr, OPCW, 2004–13. UN Audiovisual Lecture series, The Chemical Weapons Convention: an overview, 2009. *Publications:* La Acción Procesal en la Doctrina y el Derecho Positivo Mexicano, 1972; El Estado y el Derecho, 1977; Legal Aid in Mexico, 1979; Los Trabajadores Migratorios Frente a la Justicia Norteamericana, 1983. *Recreations:* theatre, music, walking, nature protection. *Address:* (office) 8 Boulevard du President Edwards, 67000 Strasbourg, France. *Club:* University (Mexico).

ONDAATJE, Sir Christopher; *see* Ondaatje, Sir P. C.

ONDAATJE, Michael; *see* Ondaatje, P. M.

ONDAATJE, Sir (Philip) Christopher, OC 1993; Kt 2003; CBE 2000; President, Ondaatje Foundation, since 1975; *b* 22 Feb. 1933; *s* of Philip Mervyn Ondaatje and Enid Doris Gratiaen; *m* 1959, Valda Bulins; one *s* two *d*. *Educ:* Blundell's Sch., Tiverton; LSE. National and Grindlays Bank, London, 1951–55; Burns Bros, & Denton, Toronto, 1955–56; Montrealer Mag. and Canada Month Mag., 1956–57; Maclean-Hunter Publishing Co. Ltd, Montreal, 1957–62; Financial Post, Toronto, 1963–65; Pitfield Mackay, Ross & Co. Ltd, Toronto, 1965–69; Founder: Pagurian Corp. Ltd, 1967–89; Loewen, Ondaatje, McCutcheon & Co. Ltd, 1970–88. Mem. Adv. Bd, Royal Soc. of Portrait Painters, 1998–; Mem. Council, RGS, 2001–05. Trustee, Nat. Portrait Gall., 2002–09. Mem., Canada's Olympic Bob-Sled Team, 1964. FRGS 1992. Hon. LLD Dalhousie, 1994; Hon. DLitt: Buckingham, 2002; Exeter, 2003; Macquarie, 2011. *Publications:* Olympic Victory, 1964; The Prime Ministers of Canada (1867–1967), 1967, rev. edn (1867–1985), 1985; Leopard in the Afternoon, 1989; The Man-Eater of Punanai, 1992; Sindh Revisited: a journey in the footsteps of Sir Richard Francis Burton, 1996; Journey to the Source of the Nile, 1998; Hemingway in Africa, 2003; The Power of Paper, 2007; The Glenthorne Cat, 2008; The Last Colonial, 2012. *Recreations:* tennis, golf, adventure, photography. *Address:* Glenthorne, Countisbury, near Lynton, N Devon EX35 6NQ. *Clubs:* Travellers, MCC; Somerset County Cricket (Life Mem.); Chester Golf; Lyford Cay (Bahamas).
See also M. Ondaatje.

ONDAATJE, (Philip) Michael, OC 1988; writer; *b* 12 Sept. 1943; *s* of Philip Mervyn Ondaatje and Enid Doris Gratiaen. *Educ:* Dulwich Coll.; Univ. of Toronto; Queen's Univ., Canada. Prof., Dept of English, Glendon Coll., York Univ., 1971–. *Publications: poetry:* The Dainty Monsters, 1967; The Man with Seven Toes, 1968; There's a Trick I'm Learning to Do, 1979; Secular Love, 1984; The Cinnamon Peeler, 1991; (ed) The Long Poem Anthology, 1979; Handwriting, 1998; *prose:* Leonard Cohen (criticism), 1968; The Collected Works of Billy the Kid (poetry and prose), 1970; (ed) The Broken Ark, 1971; How to Train a Bassett, 1971; Rat Jelly, 1973; Coming Through Slaughter, 1976; Running in the Family (autobiog.), 1982; In the Skin of a Lion, 1987 (Trillium Award); (ed) From Ink Lake: an anthology of Canadian stories, 1990; Elimination Dance, 1991 (trans. French); The English Patient, 1992 (jt winner, Booker Prize; Trillium Award; filmed, 1997); Anil's Ghost, 2000; The Conversations: Walter Murch and the art of editing film, 2002; Divisadero, 2007; The Cat's Table, 2011. *Address:* Department of English, Glendon College, York University, 2275 Bayview Avenue, Toronto, ON N4N 3M6, Canada.
See also Sir P. C. Ondaatje.

O'NEIL, H. James, (Jim); Head, Global Financial Institutions Group, Bank of America Merrill Lynch, since 2014 (Co-Head, 2013–14); *b* New York, 1966; *s* of Henry O'Neil and Doris O'Neil. *Educ:* Univ. of Virginia (BS); Univ. of Chicago (MBA High Hons). Merrill Lynch & Co., subseq. Bank of America Merrill Lynch, 1993–2010, latterly Hd, Internat. Corporate Finance; Hd, Mkt Investments, 2010–12, Chief Exec., 2012–13, UK Financial Investments Ltd. *Address:* Bank of America Merrill Lynch, Financial Centre, 2 King Edward Street, EC1A 1HQ.

O'NEIL, Roger; Member, Advisory Board, Nevastar Finance Ltd, since 2009; *b* 22 Feb. 1938; *s* of James William O'Neil and Claire Kathryn (*née* Williams); *m* 1976, Joan Mathewson; one *s* one *d*. *Educ:* Univ. of Notre Dame (BS Chemical Engrg, 1959); Cornell Univ. (MBA 1961). Joined Mobil Corp., New York, 1961; Various staff and exec. positions in Japan, Hong Kong, Australia, Paris, Cyprus, London and New York, 1963–73; Chm., Mobil cos in SE Asia, Singapore, 1973–78; Manager, Planning, Mobil Europe Inc., London, 1978–81; Manager, Corporate Econs and Planning, Mobil Corp., New York, 1981–82; Gp Vice Pres., Container Corp. of America, Chicago, 1982–84; Pres., Mobil Oil Italiana SpA, Rome, 1984–87; Chm. and Chief Exec., Mobil Oil Co., London, 1987–91; Dir and Vice Pres., Mobil Europe, 1991–92; Exec. Vice Pres. and Mem. Exec. Cttee, Statoil, 1992–97. Sen. Oil and Gas Advr, Dresdner Kleinwort Benson, 1997–2003. Non-exec. Bd Mem., Enterprise Oil plc, 1997–2002. Vice-Pres., Inst. of Petroleum, 1989–93 (FInstPet 1988). Mem., Adv. Bd, Johnson Business Sch., Cornell Univ., 1990–. FRSA 1988. *Publications:* Along the Way: a story of places, people and the international oil business, 2011. *Recreations:* archæology, skiing, golf. *Address:* 3 Ormonde Gate, SW3 4EU. *Clubs:* Royal Automobile, Hurlingham; Royal Mid-Surrey Golf.

O'NEIL, William Andrew, CM 1995; CMG 2004; Secretary-General, International Maritime Organization, 1990–2003, now Emeritus; *b* Ottawa, 6 June 1927; *s* of Thomas Wilson and Margaret O'Neil (*née* Swan); *m* 1950, Dorothy Muir (decd); one *s* two *d*; *m* 2007, Olga Bosquez. *Educ:* Carleton Univ.; Univ. of Toronto (BASc Civil Engrg 1949). Engrg posts with Fed. Dept of Transport, 1949–55; Div. Engr, Regl Dir and Dir of Construction, St Lawrence Seaway Authy, 1955–71; Federal Department of Transport: Dep. Administrator, Marine Services, 1971–80; also Comr, Canadian Coast Guard, 1975–80; St Lawrence Seaway Authority, 1980–90: Pres. and Chief Exec. Officer; Dir, Canarctic Shipping Co.; Pres., Seaway Internat. Bridge Corp. Council of International Maritime Organization: Canadian Rep., 1972–90; Chm., 1980–90. Chm., Canadian Cttee, Lloyd's Register of Shipping, 1987–88; Mem. Bd, Internat. Maritime Bureau, 1991–. Chm., Governing Bd, Internat. Maritime Law Inst., Malta, 1991–2003. Chancellor, World Maritime Univ., 1991–2003. Member: Assoc. of Professional Engrs of Ont; ASCE; Engrg Alumni Hall of Dist., Univ. of Toronto, 1996. Hon. Freeman, Shipwrights' Co., 2002. FILT (FCIT 1994); FRSA 1992; Foreign Mem., Royal Acad. of Engrg, 1994. Hon. Titulary Mem., Comité Maritime Internat., 2001. Hon. LLD: Univ. of Malta, 1993; Meml Univ. of Newfoundland, Canada, 1996; Korea Maritime, 2002; Hon. DSc Nottingham Trent, 1994. Engrg Medal, 1972, Gold Medal, 1995, Assoc. of Professional Engrs of Ont; Distinguished Public Service Award, USA, 1980; Admirals' Medal, Admirals' Medal Foundn, Canada, 1994; NUMAST Award, 1995; Seatrade Personality of the Year Award, 1995; Silver Bell Award, Seamen's Church Inst., NY, 1997; Cdre Award, Conn Maritime Assoc., USA, 1998; Dioscuri Prize, Italian Naval League, 1998; Vice-Adm. Jerry Land Medal, Soc. of Naval Architects and Marine Engrs, USA, 1999; Halert C. Shepheard Award, Chamber of Shipping of America, 2000; Dist. Servs Medal, Directorate Gen. for Maritime Affairs, Colombia, 2001; Lifetime Achievement Award, Communications and IT in Shipping, 2002; 15 Nov. 1817 Medal, Uruguay, 2002. Ordre Nat. des Cèdres (Lebanon), 1995; Grand Cross, Order of Vasco Núñez de Balboa (Panama), 1998; Golden Jubilee Medal, 2002.

O'NEILL, family name of **Barons O'Neill**, **O'Neill of Clackmannan**, **O'Neill of Gatley** and **Rathcavan**.

O'NEILL, 4th Baron *cr* 1868; **Raymond Arthur Clanaboy O'Neill,** KCVO 2009; TD 1970; Lord-Lieutenant of County Antrim, 1994–2008; *b* 1 Sept. 1933; *s* of 3rd Baron and Anne Geraldine (she *m* 2nd, 1945, 2nd Viscount Rothermere, and 3rd, 1952, late Ian Fleming, and *d* 1981), *e d* of Hon. Guy Charteris; *S* father, 1944; *m* 1963, Georgina Mary, *er d* of Lord George Montagu Douglas Scott; three *s*. *Educ:* Eton; Royal Agricultural Coll. 2nd Lieut, 11th Hussars, Prince Albert's Own; Major, North Irish Horse, AVR; Lt-Col, RARO; Hon. Colonel: NI Horse Sqn, RYR, 1986–91; 69 Signal Sqn, NI Horse, 1988–93. Chairman: Ulster Countryside Cttee, 1971–75; NI Museums Council, 1993–98; Vice-Chm., Ulster Folk and Transport Mus., 1987–90 (Trustee, 1969–90); Member: NI Tourist Bd, 1973–80 (Chm., 1975–80); NI Nat. Trust Cttee, 1980–91 (Chm., 1981–91); Museums and Galleries Commn, 1987–94; President: Youth Action (formerly NI Assoc. of Youth Clubs), 1965–2007; Royal Ulster Agricl Soc., 1984–86 (Chm. Finance Cttee, 1974–83). DL Co. Antrim, 1967. *Recreations:* vintage motoring, railways, gardening. *Heir:* *s* Hon. Shane Sebastian Clanaboy O'Neill [*b* 25 July 1965; *m* 1997, Celia, *e d* of Peter Hickman; three *s*]. *Address:* Shanes Castle, Antrim, N Ireland BT41 4NE. *T:* (028) 9446 3264. *Club:* Turf.

O'NEILL OF BENGARVE, Baroness *cr* 1999 (Life Peer), of The Braid in the County of Antrim; **Onora Sylvia O'Neill,** CH 2014; CBE 1995; PhD; FBA 1993; FMedSci; Chairman, Equality and Human Rights Commission, since 2012; *b* 23 Aug. 1941; *d* of Hon. Sir Con O'Neill, GCMG and Rosemary Margaret (*née* Pritchard) (later Lady Garvey); *m* 1963, Edward John Nell (marr. diss. 1976); two *s*. *Educ:* St Paul's Girls' Sch.; Somerville Coll., Oxford (BA, MA; Hon. Fellow, 1993); Harvard Univ. (PhD). Asst, then Associate Prof., Barnard Coll., Columbia Univ., 1970–77; University of Essex: Lectr, 1977–78; Sen. Lectr, 1978–83; Reader, 1983–87; Prof. of Philosophy, 1987–92; Principal, Newnham Coll., Cambridge, 1992–2006. Hon. Prof. of Ethics and Political Philos., Faculty of Philos., Univ. of Cambridge, 2003. Member: Animal Procedures Cttee, 1990–94; Nuffield Council on Bioethics, 1991–98 (Chm., 1996–98); Human Genetics Adv. Commn, 1996–99; MRC, 2012–. Chm., Nuffield Foundn, 1998–2010 (a Trustee, 1997–2010). Fellow, Wissenschaftskolleg, Berlin, 1989–90. President: Aristotelian Soc., 1988–89; Mind Assoc., 2003–04; British Acad., 2005–09. FMedSci 2002; Fellow, Austrian Acad. Sci., 2003. Mem., Amer. Philos. Soc., 2003. Foreign Hon. Mem., Amer. Acad. of Arts and Scis, 1993; Hon. FRS 2007; Hon. MRIA 2003. Hon. Bencher, Gray's Inn, 2002. Hon. DLitt: UEA, 1995; Dublin, 2002; Ulster, 2003; Bath, 2004; DU Essex, 1996; Hon. LLD: Nottingham, 1999; Aberdeen, 2001; Harvard, 2010; Glasgow, 2010; UCL, 2010; NUI, 2011; Hon. DLit London, 2003; Hon. DCL Oxford, 2003; Hon. DLaw Cambridge, 2007; Hon. Dr: Stirling, 2005; QUB, 2005; Ludwig Maximilian Univ., Munich, 2006; Edinburgh, 2006; Heriot-Watt, 2007; Newcastle, 2008; York, 2009; Leeds, 2012; Sussex, 2012. *Publications:* Acting on Principle, 1976; Faces of Hunger, 1986; Constructions of Reason, 1989; Towards Justice and Virtue, 1996; Bounds of Justice, 2000; Autonomy and Trust in Bioethics, 2002; A Question of Trust, 2002; (with N. Manson) Rethinking Informed Consent in Bioethics, 2007; numerous articles on philosophy, esp. political philosophy and ethics in learned jls. *Recreations:* walking, talking. *Address:* House of Lords, SW1A 0PW.

O'NEILL OF CLACKMANNAN, Baron *cr* 2005 (Life Peer), of Clackmannan in Clackmannanshire; **Martin John O'Neill;** *b* 6 Jan. 1945; *s* of John and Minnie O'Neill; *m* 1973, Elaine Marjorie Samuel; two *s*. *Educ:* Trinity Academy, Edinburgh; Heriot-Watt Univ. (BA Econ.); Moray House Coll. of Education, Edinburgh. Insurance Clerk, Scottish Widows Fund, 1963–67; Asst Examiner, Estate Duty Office of Scotland, 1971–73; Teacher of Modern Studies: Boroughmuir High School, Edinburgh, 1974–77; Craigmount High School, Edinburgh, 1977–79; Social Science Tutor, Open Univ., 1976–79. MP (Lab): Stirlingshire E and Clackmannan, 1979–83; Clackmannan, 1983–97; Ochil, 1997–2005. Opposition spokesman on Scottish affairs, 1980–84, on defence matters, 1984–88, on energy, 1992–95; chief opposition spokesman on defence, 1988–92. Mem., Select Cttee, Scottish Affairs, 1979–80; Chm., Select Cttee on Trade and Industry, 1995–2005. FRSA. *Recreations:* watching football, reading, listening to jazz, the cinema. *Address:* House of Lords, SW1A 0PW.

O'NEILL OF GATLEY, Baron *cr* 2015 (Life Peer), of Gatley in the County of Greater Manchester; **Terence James, (Jim) O'Neill;** Commercial Secretary, HM Treasury, since 2015; Visiting Research Fellow, Breugel, since 2013; *b* Manchester, 17 March 1957; *s* of late Terence and Kathleen O'Neill; *m* 1983, Caroline; two *c*. *Educ:* Burnage High Sch., Manchester; Univ. of Sheffield (BA Econs 1978; MA 1979); Univ. of Surrey (PhD 1983). Economist: Bank of America, 1982–83; Internal Treasury Mgt, Marine Midland Bank, 1983–88; Swiss Bank Corp., 1988–95 (Hd of Global Res., 1991–95); Goldman Sachs: Economist and Partner, 1995–2013; Co-Hd, Global Econs Res. and Chief Currency Economist, 1995–2001; Hd, Global Econs Res., 2001–08; Chief Economist, 2001–10; Hd of Global Econs, Commodities and Strategy Res., 2008–10; Chm., Goldman Sachs Asset Mgt, 2010–13. Creator of acronym, BRICs (Brazil, Russia, India and China as the growth opportunities of the future), 2001. Chm., City Growth Commn, 2013–14. Non-exec. Dir, DFE, 2013–. Hon. DLitt Sheffield, 2014. *Publications:* The Growth Map: economic opportunity in the BRICs and beyond, 2011; The BRIC Road to Growth, 2013. *Recreations:* sport, tennis, running, football, travel.

O'NEILL, Aidan Mark Sebastian; QC (Scot.) 1999; *b* 27 Jan. 1961; *s* of John Joseph, (Jack), O'Neill and Teresa Josephine O'Neill (*née* Birt); civil partnership 2006, Douglas Edington, *s* of late Capt. J. A. R., (Jock), Edington and Mrs H. A. L. C. Edington. *Educ:* St Francis Xavier Coll., Coatbridge; Holy Cross High Sch., Hamilton; Langside Coll., Glasgow; Univ. of Edinburgh (LLB Hons 1st cl. 1982); Univ. of Sydney (LLM Hons 1st cl. 1987); European Univ. Inst., Florence (LLM 1993); Univ. of Edinburgh (LLD 2013). Admitted Faculty of Advocates, 1987; called to the Bar, Inner Temple, 1996; Standing Jun. Counsel to Educn Dept, Scottish Office, 1997–99; Associate Mem., 2000, Mem., 2010–, Matrix Chambers, Gray's Inn. Inaugural Univ. Center for Values, Law and Public Affairs Fellow in Law and Normative Inquiry, Princeton Univ., 2007–08; Chair, Edinburgh Centre for Constitutional Law, 2009–; Hon. Fellow, Sch. of Law, Univ. of Edinburgh, 2009. *Publications:* (jtly) EU Law for UK Lawyers: the domestic impact of EU law within the UK, 1994, 2nd edn 2011; Decisions of the European Court of Justice and their Constitutional Implications, 1994; Judicial Review in Scotland: a practitioner's guide, 1999; articles in jls incl. Modern Law Rev., European Human Rights Law Rev., Juridical Rev., Judicial Rev., Common Knowledge, Public Law, Northern Ireland Legal Qly, Edinburgh Law Rev., Legal Studies, Common Market Law Rev., Scots Law Times, The Tablet. *Address:* Matrix Chambers, Gray's Inn, WC1R 5LN. *T:* (020) 7404 3447, *Fax:* (020) 7404 3448.

O'NEILL, Prof. Alan, PhD; Professor of Meteorology, since 1993, and Director of Research, School of Mathematical and Physical Sciences, University of Reading, since 2014; *b* Merthyr Tydfil, 23 Sept. 1950; *s* of Bernard and Irene O'Neill; *m* 1973, Angela Portlock; one *s* one *d*. *Educ:* County Grammar Sch., Merthyr Tydfil; St Nicholas Grammar Sch., Northwood; Oriel Coll., Oxford (MA Physics); Open Univ. (MSc Maths); Univ. of Reading (PhD Meteorol. 1979). Hd, Stratospheric Res., Meteorological Office, 1974–93; SPSO (Individual Merit), 1990–93; Dir, Nat. Centre for Earth Observation, Univ. of Reading, 2008–13. *Publications:* contrib. papers to Qly Jl RMetS. *Recreations:* reading history, walking, music, theatre. *Address:* Department of Meteorology, University of Reading, Berks RG6 6BB. *E:* a.oneill@reading.ac.uk. *Club:* Meteorological.

O'NEILL, Alan Dennis; Chairman, Hertfordshire Learning and Skills Council, 2003–08; *b* 2 March 1945; *s* of Dennis O'Neill and Audrey Florence O'Neill; *m* 1969, Susan Fearnley; one *s* two *d*. *Educ:* King George V Sch., Southport; Bishopshalt Sch., Hillingdon; Univ. of

Birmingham (BSc Hons Physics 1966). Joined Kodak Ltd as res. scientist, 1966; Dir and Manager, Manufacturing Ops, 1991–96; Vice-Pres. and Chief Purchasing Officer, Eastman Kodak Co., 1996–98; Chm. and Man. Dir, Kodak Ltd, 1998–2001. *Recreations:* bee-keeping, running, ski-ing, golf. *Address:* St Michael's Croft, Woodcock Hill, Berkhamsted, Herts HP4 3TR.

O'NEILL, Brendan Richard, PhD; FCMA; Chief Executive, ICI plc, 1999–2003 (Chief Operating Officer, 1998–99; Director, 1998–2003); *b* 6 Dec. 1948; *s* of John Christopher O'Neill and Doris O'Neill (*née* Monk); *m* 1979, Margaret Maude; one *s* two *d*. *Educ:* West Park GS, St Helens; Churchill Coll., Cambridge (MA Nat. Sci. 1972); Univ. of East Anglia (PhD Chemistry 1973). FCMA (FCIMA 1983). Ford Motor Co., 1973–75; British Leyland, 1975–81; BICC plc, 1981–83; Gp Financial Controller, Midland Bank, 1983–87; Guinness plc: Dir of Financial Control, 1987; Finance Dir, 1988–90, Man. Dir, Internat. Reg., 1990–92, United Distillers; Man. Dir, Guinness Brewing Worldwide, 1993–97; Chief Exec., Guinness, Diageo plc, 1997–98. Director: Guinness plc, 1993–97; EMAP plc, 1995–2002; Diageo plc, 1997–98; Tyco International, 2003–; Rank Gp plc, 2004–07; Endurance Specialty Hldgs Ltd, 2004–14; Towers Watson (formerly Watson Wyatt), 2006–; Informa plc, 2008–. Mem. Council, 2000–07, Finance Cttee, 1994–2000, Cancer Res. UK (formerly ICRF). Trustee, Inst. of Cancer Research, 2015–. *Recreations:* music, reading, family.

O'NEILL, Brian Patrick; QC 2010; a Recorder, since 2002; *b* Dungannon, Co. Tyrone, 29 Nov. 1962; *s* of Patrick O'Neill and Bernadette O'Neill; *m* 2001, Charmaine Silveira; two *s* one *d*. *Educ:* St Patrick's Acad., Dungannon; Brunel Univ. (LLB Hons). Called to the Bar, Gray's Inn, 1987. *Recreations:* family, football, cooking. *Address:* 2 Hare Court, Temple, EC4Y 7BH. *T:* (020) 7353 5324. *E:* brianoneillqc@2harecourt.com. *Clubs:* Arsenal Football; Broomwood Football (Wandsworth); Battersea Ironsides Sports; Spencer Sports (Earlsfield).

O'NEILL, Dennis James, CBE 2000; operatic tenor; Director, Wales International Academy of Voice, University of Wales Trinity St David, since 2011; *b* 25 Feb. 1948; *s* of late Dr William P. O'Neill and Eva A. O'Neill (*née* Rees); *m* 1st, 1970, Ruth Collins (marr. diss. 1987); one *s* one *d*; 2nd, 1988, Ellen Folkestad. *Educ:* Gowerton Boys' Grammar Sch. FTCL 1969; ARCM 1971. Specialist in Italian repertoire and works of Verdi in particular; Début: Royal Opera House, Covent Garden, 1979; Vienna State Opera, 1981; Hamburg State Opera, 1981; San Francisco Opera, 1984; Chicago Lyric Opera, 1985; Paris Opera, 1986; Metropolitan Opera, NY, 1986; Bayerische Staatsoper, Munich, 1992; has performed worldwide in opera and concerts. Many recordings. Presenter, Dennis O'Neill, BBC TV, 1987, 1988, 1989. Vis. Prof., RAM, 2005 (Hon. RAM 2006). Dir, Wexford Fest. Artists Develt prog., 2005–; Dir (and Founder), Cardiff Internat. Acad. of Voice, Cardiff Univ., 2007–10. Fellow, Univ. of Wales Trinity St David, 2010. FLSW 2014. Hon. Fellow, Univ. of Cardiff, 1997; Hon. FRWCMD (Hon. FWCMD, 1993). Hon. DMus Glamorgan, 2003. Verdi medal, Amici di Verdi, 2005; Golden Jubilee Award, Welsh Music Guild, 2005. OStJ 2008 (SBStJ 2006). *Recreations:* dinner parties, Verdi. *Address:* c/o Ingpen & Williams, 7 St George's Court, 131 Putney Bridge Road, SW15 2PA. *T:* (020) 8874 3222.

O'NEILL, Prof. Hugh St Clair, PhD; FRS 2012; FAA; Laureate Professor, Research School of Earth Sciences, Australian National University, since 2014; *b* Farnborough, Hants, 5 Sept. 1953; *s* of Captain Barry O'Neill and Barbara O'Neill; *m* 1985, Marlene Quincey; one *s* one *d*. *Educ:* Wellington Coll.; St Edmund Hall, Oxford (BA 1975); Univ. of Manchester (PhD 1978). Res. Fellow, Res. Sch. of Earth Scis, ANU, 1981–86; Staff Scientist, Bayerisches Geoinstitut, Univ. of Bayreuth, Germany, 1987–94; Research School of Earth Sciences, Australian National University: Sen. Fellow, 1994–2004; Prof., 2004–12; Associate Dir, 2006–13; Distinguished Prof., 2012–14. FAA 2008; Australian Laureate Fellow, 2013. *Publications:* contrib. papers to learned scientific jls. *Recreations:* field work, walking, theatre, popular history.

O'NEILL, Jim; *see* Baron O'Neill of Gatley.

O'NEILL, John Joseph, (Jonjo); racehorse trainer, since 1987; *b* 13 April 1952; *s* of Thomas and Margaret O'Neill; *m* 1997, Jacqueline (*née* Bellamy); three *s* two *d*. *Educ:* Castletownroache Nat. Sch. National Hunt jockey, 1969–87: winner, 901 races; Champion Jockey, 1977–78, 1979–80; broke record for number of winners in one season, 149 in 1977–78; winner: Cheltenham Gold Cup: 1979 on Alverton; 1986 on Dawn Run; Champion Hurdle: 1980 on Sea Pigeon; 1984 on Dawn Run; has trained over 1,600 winners including: Gipsy Fiddler, Windsor Castle Stakes, Royal Ascot; Well Sharp, Ascot Stakes, Royal Ascot; Tominator, Northumberland Plate; Mini Sensation, Coral Welsh National, 2002; Synchronised, Coral Welsh National, 2011, Betfred Cheltenham Gold Cup, 2012; Butler's Cabin, Irish Grand National, 2007; Don't Push It, Grand National, 2010; Taquin de Seuil, Challow Novices' Hurdle, 2012; also 22 winners at Cheltenham National Hunt Fest., 19 winners at Aintree Fest. and 3 winners at Punchestown Fest. Ireland's People of Year Award, 1986. *Address:* Jackdaws Castle, Temple Guiting, Cheltenham, Glos GL54 5XU. *T:* (01386) 584209, *Fax:* (01386) 584219. *E:* reception@jonjooneillracing.com. *W:* www.jonjooneillracing.com.

O'NEILL, Mark William Robert, PhD; Director of Policy, Research and Development, Glasgow Life, since 2009; *b* 10 Nov. 1956; *s* of Michael O'Neill and Greta (*née* Desmond). *Educ:* University Coll., Cork (BA Hons 1976; HDipEd 1977); Leicester Univ. (Grad. Cert. Mus. Studies 1985); Getty Leadership Inst. (Mus. Mgt Inst. 1993); City of London Univ. (PhD 2011). Curator, Springburn Mus., 1985–90; Glasgow Museums, 1990–2005: Keeper of Social Hist., 1990–92; Sen. Curator of Hist., 1992–97; Hd, Curatorial Services, 1997–98; Head, 1998–2005; Hd, Glasgow Arts and Mus, 2005–09. FMA 1997. *Publications:* contrib. numerous articles on philosophy and practice of museums. *Recreations:* classical music, fiction, psychology. *Address:* Glasgow Life, 220 High Street, Glasgow G4 0QW. *E:* Mark.O'Neill@glasgowlife.org.uk.

O'NEILL, Martin Hugh Michael, OBE 2004 (MBE 1983); Manager, Republic of Ireland national football team, since 2013; *b* Kilrea, NI, 1 March 1952; *m* Geraldine; two *d*. Professional footballer: Nottingham Forest, 1971–81 (League Champions, 1978; European Cup winners, 1979 and 1980); Norwich City, 1981, 1982–83; Manchester City, 1981–82; Notts Co., 1983–85; Mem., NI team, 1971–84 (64 caps); Manager: Grantham Town, 1987–89; Shepshed Charterhouse, 1989; Wycombe Wanderers, 1990–95 (Vauxhall Conf. winners, promoted to Football League, 1992–93); Norwich City, 1995; Leicester City, 1995–2000; Celtic, 2000–05; Aston Villa, 2006–10; Sunderland, 2011–13.

O'NEILL, Michael Angus, CMG 2012; Assistant Secretary-General, United Nations Development Programme, since 2014; *b* 25 May 1965; *s* of Capt. Shane O'Neill and Jean O'Neill (*née* Macintosh Mayer); *m* 1991, Claire Naomi, *d* of Sir David (Gordon) Bannerman, *qv*; three *s* one *d*. *Educ:* Manchester Grammar Sch.; Brasenose Coll., Oxford (MA); LSE (MSc). MoD, 1988–91; Second Sec., UK Delegn to NATO, 1991–94; joined HM Diplomatic Service, 1994; Second, later First, Sec., FCO, 1994–98; Vis. Fellow, Inst. for Nat. Security Studies, Washington, DC, 1998–99; First Sec., Washington, 1999–2002; Counsellor, UK Mission to UN, NY, 2002–06; Counsellor, UK Perm. Repn to EU, Brussels, 2006–07; UK Special Rep. for Sudan, FCO, 2007–10; UK Sen. Rep., Southern Afghanistan and Head of Mission, Helmand Provincial Reconstruction Team, 2010–12; Ambassador to Qatar, 2012–13; Dir, Cabinet Office Nat. Security Secretariat, 2013–14. *Recreations:* travel, watching films and football, walking a chocolate labrador. *Address:* United Nations Development Programme, One Millennium Plaza, New York, NY 10017, USA.

O'NEILL, Prof. Michael Stephen Charles, DPhil; Professor of English Literature, University of Durham, since 1995; *b* 2 Sept. 1953; *s* of Peter and Margaret O'Neill; *m* 1977, Rosemary McKendrick; one *s* one *d*. *Educ:* Exeter Coll., Oxford (Open Exhibnr 1972, Open Scholar 1973; BA 1st Cl. Hon. Mods; 1st Cl. Hon. Schs 1975; MA 1981; DPhil 1981). University of Durham: Lectr, 1979–91; Sen. Lectr, 1991–93; Reader, 1993–95; Hd of Dept of English Studies, 1997–2000, 2002–05; Dir (Arts and Humanities), 2005–11, Acting Exec. Dir, 2011–12, Inst. of Advanced Study. Founding FEA 2000. Chm., Adv. Bd, Internat. Byron Soc., 2010–; Member, Advisory Board: Romantic Circles, 1994–; Romanticism, 1994–; Romanticism and Victorianism on the Net, 1996–; Wordsworth Circle, 2005–; Keats-Shelley Rev., 2010–. Trustee, Wordsworth Conf. Foundn, 2009–. Eric Gregory Award for Poetry, 1983; Cholmondeley Award, 1990. *Publications:* The Human Mind's Imaginings: conflict and achievement in Shelley's poetry, 1989; Percy Bysshe Shelley: a literary life, 1989; The Stripped Bed (poems), 1990; (with Gareth Reeves) Auden, MacNeice, Spender: the Thirties poetry, 1992; (ed and introd) Shelley, 1993; (ed) The Bodleian Shelley Manuscripts, vol. XX, The 'Defence of Poetry' Fair Copies, 1994; Romanticism and the Self-Conscious Poem, 1997; (ed with D. H. Reiman) Fair-Copy Manuscripts of Shelley's Poems in European and American Libraries, 1997; (ed) Keats: bicentenary readings, 1997; (ed) Literature of the Romantic Period: a bibliographical guide, 1998; (ed with Zachary Leader) Percy Bysshe Shelley: the major works, 2003; The Poems of W. B. Yeats: a sourcebook, 2004; (ed with Mark Sandy) Romanticism, 4 vols, 2006; (ed with Charles Mahoney) Romantic Poetry: an annotated anthology, 2007; The All-Sustaining Air: romantic legacies and renewals in British, American and Irish poetry since 1900, 2007; (jtly) Dante Rediscovered: from Blake to Rodin, 2007; Wheel (poems), 2008; (ed with Ash Amin) Thinking about Almost Everything, 2009; (ed) Cambridge History of English Poetry, 2010; (contrib.) The Cambridge Companion to the Epic, 2010; (ed with Madeleine Callaghan) Twentieth-Century British and Irish Poetry: Hardy to Mahon, 2011; (contrib.) A Companion to Romantic Poetry, 2011; (ed jtly) Venice and the Cultural Imagination, 2012; (with Michael D. Hurley) Poetic Form: an introduction, 2012; (ed jtly) The Complete Poetry of Percy Bysshe Shelley, vol. III, 2012 ((jtly) Richard J. Finneran Award, Soc. for Textual Scholarship, 2013); (ed jtly) The Oxford Handbook of Percy Bysshe Shelley, 2013; Gangs of Shadow (poems), 2014; (ed jtly) The Persistence of Beauty: Victorians to Moderns, 2015; contrib. The Wordsworth Circle, Essays in Criticism, The Charles Lamb Bulletin, Romanticism, PN Rev., TLS, London Mag., The Reader, etc. *Address:* Department of English Studies, University of Durham, Hallgarth House, 77 Hallgarth Street, Durham DH1 3AY. *T:* (0191) 334 2582, *Fax:* (0191) 334 2501. *E:* m.s.o'neill@dur.ac.uk.

O'NEILL, Michelle; Member (SF) Mid-Ulster, Northern Ireland Assembly, since 2007; Minister of Agriculture and Rural Development, since 2011; *m* Paddy O'Neill; one *s* one *d*. Pol Advr to Francie Molloy, NI Assembly, 1998–2005. Mem. (SF) Dungannon and S Tyrone BC, 2005– (Mayor, 2010–11). Formerly Member: Bd, E Tyrone Comhairle Ceantair; Mid Ulster Dáil Ceantair. *Address:* Northern Ireland Assembly, Parliament Buildings, Stormont, Belfast BT4 3XX.

O'NEILL, Paul Henry; Senior Advisor, The Blackstone Group, 2003–11; Chairman (non-executive), Value Capture LLC, since 2005; *b* 4 Dec. 1935; *m* 1955, Nancy Jo Wolfe; one *s* three *d*. *Educ:* Fresno State Coll., Calif (BA Econs); Indiana Univ. (MPA). Computer analyst, Veterans Admin, 1961–66; Asst Dir, Associate Dir and Dep. Dir, Office of Mgt and Budget, 1967–77; Vice-Pres., 1977–85, Pres., 1985–87, Internat. Paper Co.; Chm. and CEO, 1987–99, Chm., 1999–2000, Alcoa; Sec., US Treasury, 2001–02. Director: Eastman Kodak, 2003–06; TRW Automotive Hldgs, 2003–14; Nalco Co., 2003–07; Qcept, 2004–; Celanese Corp., 2004–13. Director: Peterson Inst. for Internat. Econs (formerly Inst. for Internat. Econs), 2003–12; Center for Global Develt, 2004–10. Mem. Bd of Trustees, RAND Corp., 2003–13 (formerly Chm.). *Recreation:* painting. *Address:* Suite 100, One North Shore Center, 12 Federal Street, Pittsburgh, PA 15212, USA.

O'NEILL, Robert James, CMG 1978; HM Diplomatic Service, retired; *b* 17 June 1932; *m* 1958, Helen Juniper; one *s* two *d*. *Educ:* King Edward VI Sch., Chelmsford; Trinity Coll., Cambridge (Schol.; 1st cl. English Tripos Pts I and II). Entered HM Foreign (now Diplomatic) Service, 1955; FO, 1955–57; British Embassy, Ankara, 1957–60; Dakar, 1961–63; FO, 1963–68, Private Sec. to Chancellor of Duchy of Lancaster, 1966, and to Minister of State for Foreign Affairs, 1967–68; British Embassy, Bonn, 1968–72; Counsellor Diplomatic Service, 1972; seconded to Cabinet Office as Asst Sec., 1972–75; FCO, 1975–78; Dep. Governor, Gibraltar, 1978–81; Under Sec., Cabinet Office and Mem., Jt Intelligence Cttee, 1981–84; Asst Under-Sec. of State, FCO, 1984–86; Ambassador to Austria, and concurrently Head of UK Delegn, MBFR, Vienna, 1986–89; Ambassador to Belgium, 1989–92; EC Presidency Rep. for Macedonia, 1992. EU Rep., OSCE Bosnia elections Task Force, 1995. Chm., Anglo-Austrian Soc., 2014–. *Publications:* (with N. Weaver) Edward Bawden in the Middle East, 2008. *Recreations:* diplomatic history, hill-walking. *Address:* 4 Castle Street, Saffron Walden, Essex CB10 1BP. *T:* (01799) 520291. *Club:* Travellers.

O'NEILL, Prof. Robert John, AO 1988; FASSA; Director, Lowy Institute for International Policy, 2003–12; Chairman, Australian Strategic Policy Institute, Canberra, 1999–2005; Chichele Professor of the History of War, and Fellow of All Souls College, University of Oxford, 1987–2001, now Emeritus Fellow; *b* 5 Nov. 1936; *s* of Joseph Henry and Janet Gibbon O'Neill; *m* 1965, Sally Margaret Burnard; two *d*. *Educ:* Scotch Coll., Melbourne; Royal Military Coll. of Australia; Univ. of Melbourne (BE); Brasenose Coll., Oxford (MA, DPhil 1965; Hon. Fellow, 1990). FASSA 1977; FIE(Aust) 1981–96; FRHistS 1990–2004. Served Australian Army, 1955–68; Rhodes Scholar, Vic, 1961; Fifth Bn Royal Australian Regt, Vietnam, 1966–67 (mentioned in despatches); Major 1967; resigned 1968. Sen. Lectr in History, Royal Military Coll. of Australia, 1968–69; Australian National University: Sen. Fellow in Internat. Relations, 1969–77, Professorial Fellow, 1977–82; Head, Strategic and Defence Studies Centre, 1971–82 (Adjunct Prof., 2001–); Dir, IISS, 1982–87; Dir of Graduate Studies, Modern History Faculty, Univ. of Oxford, 1990–92. Dep. Chm. Bd, Graduate Sch. of Govt, 2003–05, Chm., Internat. Academic Adv. Bd, US Studies Centre, 2009–11, Univ. of Sydney. Official Australian Historian for the Korean War, 1969–82. Dir, Shell Transport and Trading, 1992–2002. Chairman: Management Cttee, Sir Robert Menzies Centre for Australian Studies, Univ. of London, 1990–95; Bd, Centre for Defence Studies, KCL, 1990–95; Chm. Council, IISS, 1996–2001 (Mem. Council, 1977–82, 1992–94, Vice-Chm. Council, 1994–96). Governor: Ditchley Foundn, 1989–2001; Internat. Peace Acad., 1990–2001; Salzburg Seminar, 1992–97; Trustee: Imperial War Museum, 1990–98 (Chm. Trustees, 1998–2001); Commonwealth War Graves Commn, 1991–2001; Mem., Rhodes Trust, 1995–2001. Mem., Adv. Bd, Investment Co. of America, 1988–2010, and Dir, two other mutual funds, Capital Group, LA, 1992–2013. Pres., Rylstone and Dist Historical Soc., 2003–07; Mem. Exec. Cttee, Blackheath History Forum, 2009–. Chm., Round Table Moot, 1986–92. Hon. Col 5th (Volunteer) Royal Green Jackets, 1993–99. Foundn Fellow, Australian Inst. of Internat. Affairs, 2009. Hon. DLitt ANU, 2001. Centenary Medal (Australia), 2003; Nat. Volunteer Award (Australia), 2012. *Publications:* The German Army and the Nazi Party 1933–1939, 1966; Vietnam Task, 1968; General Giap: politician and strategist, 1969; (ed) The Strategic Nuclear Balance, 1975; (ed) The Defence of Australia: fundamental new aspects, 1977; (ed) Insecurity: the spread of weapons in the Indian and Pacific Oceans, 1978; (ed jtly) Australian Dictionary of Biography, Vols 7–14, 1979–97; (ed with David Horner) New Directions in Strategic Thinking, 1981; Australia in the Korean War 1950–1953, Vol. 1, Strategy and Diplomacy, 1981, Vol. II, Combat Operations, 1985; (ed with David Horner) Australian Defence Policy for the 1980s, 1982; (ed) Security in East Asia, 1984; (ed) The Conduct of East-West Relations in the 1980s, 1985; (ed) New

Technology and Western Security Policy, 1985; (ed) Doctrine, the Alliance and Arms Control, 1986; (ed) East Asia, the West and International Security, 1987; (ed) Security in the Mediterranean, 1989; (ed with R. J. Vincent) The West and the Third World, 1990; (ed with Beatrice Heuser) Securing Peace in Europe 1945–62, 1992; (ed jtly) War, Strategy and International Politics, 1992; (ed with John Baylis) Alternative Nuclear Futures, 1999; articles in many learned jls. *Recreations:* local history, walking.

O'NEILL, Sally Jane; QC 1997; a Recorder, since 2000; *b* 30 Sept. 1953; *d* of late Maj. John O'Neill, RA retd and Frances Agnes O'Neill (*née* Riley); *m* 1986, David Bloss Kingsbury. *Educ:* St Joseph's Convent, Stafford; Alleyne's Grammar Sch., Uttoxeter; Mid-Essex Technical Coll. (LLB 1975). Called to the Bar, Gray's Inn, 1976, Bencher, 2002; in practice at the Bar, 1976–. An Asst Recorder, 1997–2000. Chm., Criminal Bar Assoc., 2007–08. *Recreations:* gardening, tennis, ski-ing, sailing, bull dogs, P. G. Wodehouse. *Address:* Furnival Chambers, 32 Furnival Street, EC4A 1JQ. *T:* (020) 7405 3232.

O'NEILL, Susan Janet; *see* Watts, S. J.

O'NEILL, William Alan; Executive Vice President, News Corporation, 1990–2002; Director, News International plc, 1995–2002; *b* 22 May 1936; *s* of John O'Neill and Martha O'Neill (*née* Kitson); *m* 1962, Alene Joy Brown; one *s* one *d*. *Educ:* Sydney Tech. Coll. Gp Employee Relns Manager, News Ltd (Australia), 1977–80; Gen. Manager, 1981, Dir, 1981–90, Times Newspapers Ltd; Vice-Pres. (Personnel), News America Publishing, 1984–85; Exec. Vice-Pres., and Gen. Manager, New York Post, 1985–86, and Vice-Pres. (Human Resources), News Corp., 1986; Man. Dir, News Internat. Newspapers, 1987–90; Director: News Corp., 1987–90; News Gp Newspapers Ltd, 1987–90; Director and Executive Vice-President: News America Inc., 1990–2002; News America Publishing Inc., 1990–2002; CEO, News Internat. plc, 1995. Chm., Convoys Ltd, 1987–89; Dep. Chm., Townsend Hook, 1987–89; Director: Sky TV; Eric Bemrose Ltd. Life Mem., American-Australian Assoc. *Recreations:* travelling, genealogy. *Address:* 31 Wolfeton Way, San Antonio, TX 78218–6035, USA. *T:* (210) 8058871.

ONIONS, Jeffery Peter; QC 1998; *b* 22 Aug. 1957; *s* of late Derrick and Violet Onions; *m* 1987, Sally Louise Hine; one *d*. *Educ:* St Albans Sch.; St John's Coll., Cambridge (BA 1979, MA 1983; LLM (LLB 1980); hockey blue 1977–79). Called to the Bar, Middle Temple, 1981 (Astbury Schol.), Bencher, 2010; in practice at the Bar, 1981–. Mem., Bar Council, 1987–89. *Recreations:* cricket, wine, opera. *Address:* 1 Essex Court, Temple, EC4Y 9AR. *T:* (020) 7583 2000. *Clubs:* MCC, Middlesex CC, Surrey CC; Hawks (Cambridge); 1890.

O'NIONS, Sir (Robert) Keith, Kt 1999; PhD; FRS 1983; Rector, 2010–14, and President, 2013–14, Imperial College London; Chairman, Cambridge Enterprise, since 2014; *b* 26 Sept. 1944; *s* of William Henry O'Nions and Eva O'Nions; *m* 1967, Rita Margaret Bill; three *d*. *Educ:* Univ. of Nottingham (BSc 1966); Univ. of Alberta (PhD 1969). Post-doctoral Fellow, Oslo Univ., 1970; Demonstr in Petrology, Oxford Univ., 1971–72, Lectr in Geochem., 1972–75; Associate Prof., then Prof., Columbia Univ., NY, 1975–79; Royal Soc. Res. Prof., 1979–95, and Fellow, Clare Hall, 1980–95, Cambridge Univ. (Hon. Fellow, 1995); Oxford University: Prof. of Physics and Chemistry of Minerals, 1995–2004 (on leave of absence, 2000–04); Head, Dept of Earth Scis, 1995–99; Fellow, St Hugh's Coll., 1995–2004, now Hon. Fellow; Fellow, Wolfson Coll., 2004–10; Chief Scientific Advr, MoD, 2000–04; Dir Gen. of Res. Councils, Office of Sci. and Technol., later Dir Gen., Sci. and Innovation, DTI, subseq. DIUS, 2004–08; Dir, Inst. for Security Sci. and Technol., Imperial Coll. London, 2008–10. Vis. Prof., Univ. of Oxford, 2004–05. Mem. Bd, Agency for Sci., Technol. and Res., Singapore. Trustee: Natural History Mus., 1996–2006 (Chm., 2003–06); Nanyang Tech. Univ., Singapore. Hon. FREng 2005. Hon. Fellow, Indian Acad. of Scis, 1998; For. Fellow, Nat. Indian Sci. Acad., 2000; Mem., Norwegian Acad. of Sciences, 1980. Hon. doctorates from Univs of Abertay, Alberta, Cardiff, Edinburgh, Glasgow, Heriot-Watt, Paris, RHBNC, Loughborough, Nottingham and Birmingham. Macelwane Award, Amer. Geophys. Union, 1979; Bigsby Medal, Geol Soc. London, 1983; Holmes Medal, Eur. Union of Geosciences, 1995; Lyell Medal, Geol Soc. of London, 1995; Urey Medal, Eur. Assoc. Geochemistry, 2001. *Publications:* contrib. to jls related to earth and planetary sciences.

ONIONS, Robin William; His Honour Judge Onions; a Circuit Judge, since 2000; *b* 12 April 1948; *s* of late Ernest Onions, DFC, and Edith Margaret Onions; *m* 1970, Catherine Anne Graham; two *s*. *Educ:* Prestfelde Sch., Shrewsbury; Priory Grammar Sch., Shrewsbury; London Sch. of Econs (LLB 1970). Articled clerk, Royal Borough of Kingston upon Thames, 1971–73; admitted solicitor, 1973; J. C. H. Bowdler & Sons, Shrewsbury, subsequently Lanyon Bowdler: solicitor, 1974–76; Partner, 1977–2000; Sen. Partner, 1993–2000. Resident Judge, Shrewsbury Crown Court, 2005–14. Mem., Parole Bd, 2010–. *Recreations:* football, cricket, travel, gardening, keeping fit? *Address:* Shrewsbury Crown Court, The Shirehall, Abbey Foregate, Shrewsbury, Shropshire SY2 6LU.

ONN, Melanie; MP (Lab) Great Grimsby, since 2015; *b* Great Grimsby, 19 June 1979; *d* of Jacqueline Jagger; *m* 2014, Christopher Jenkinson; one *s*. *Educ:* Healing Comprehensive Sch., Grimsby; Franklin Coll., Grimsby; Middlesex Univ. (BA Hons Politics, Philosophy and Internat. Studies 2000). Labour Party: Facilities Adminr, 2000–03; Communications Officer to Gen. Sec., 2003–06; Compliance Officer, 2006–10; Hd of Compliance, 2010; Regl Organiser, Yorks and Humber, Unison, 2010–15. *Address:* House of Commons, SW1A 0AA. *T:* (020) 7219 6282; (office) 112 Cleethorpe Road, Grimsby, NE Lincs DN31 3HW. *T:* (01472) 359584. *E:* melanie.onn.mp@parliament.uk.

ONSLOW, family name of **Earl of Onslow**.

ONSLOW, 8th Earl of, *cr* 1801; **Rupert Charles William Bullard Onslow;** Bt 1660; Baron Onslow 1716; Baron Cranley 1776; Viscount Cranley 1801; *b* 16 June 1967; *s* of 7th Earl of Onslow and of Robin Lindsay Onslow (*née* Bullard); *S* father, 2011; *m* 1999, Leigh, *d* of late E. Jones-Fenleigh, one *d*. *Educ:* Eton; Western Kentucky Univ., USA. *Recreations:* photography, riding, shooting. *Heir: kinsman* Anthony Ernest Edward Onslow, *b* 30 May 1955. *Address:* Temple Court, Clandon Park, Guildford, Surrey GU4 7RQ.

ONSLOW, Andrew George; QC 2002; *b* 10 Feb. 1957; *s* of late John Onslow and of Susan Margaret Ursula Onslow; *m* 1991, Elizabeth Jane Owen; three *s* two *d*. *Educ:* Lancing Coll.; Corpus Christi Coll., Oxford (Open Schol.; BA 1st Cl. Hons Lit.Hum. 1979); City Univ. (Dip. Law 1981). Called to the Bar, Middle Temple, 1982; in practice, specialising in commercial law. *Address:* 3 Verulam Buildings, Gray's Inn, WC1R 5NT. *T:* (020) 7831 8441, *Fax:* (020) 7831 8479. *E:* aonslow@3vb.com.

ONSLOW, Sir Richard (Paul Atherton), 9th Bt *cr* 1797, of Althain, Lancashire; *b* Bournemouth, 16 Sept. 1958; *o s* of Sir John Roger Wilmot Onslow, 8th Bt and of Catherine Zoia (*née* Greenway, now Keefe); *S* father, 2009; *m* 1st, 1984, Josephine Anne Dean (marr. diss. 2003); one *s* one *d*; 2nd, 2014, Carol Anne, *y d* of late Harold Hillary. *Educ:* Cheltenham Coll.; Univ. of Leicester (BSc Hons). *Heir: s* Harry Alexander John Onslow, *b* 7 Oct. 1986.

ONTARIO, Bishop of, since 2011; **Rt Rev. Michael Douglas Oulton;** *b* Sackville, NB, 21 Dec. 1959; *s* of C. Robert Oulton and Lucy L. Oulton (*née* Sharpe); *m* 1980, Rev. Jeanie Lee Vautour; two *s* one *d*. *Educ:* Tantramor Regl High Sch., Sackville; Mt Allison Univ., Sackville (BA); Univ. of New Brunswick, Fredericton (LLB); Univ. of Toronto (Wycliffe Coll.) (MDiv). Associate Lawyer: Hicks Le Moine, Amherst, NS; Ove B. Samuelson, Sackville; ordained deacon, 1992, priest, 1993; Rector: Parish of Alberton, PEI, 1992–97; Parish of St Peter, Kingston, Ont, 1997–2004; Parish of Christ Ch, Belleville, Ont, 2004–11. *Recreations:* time with my family, hockey, golf. *Address:* Diocese of Ontario, 90 Johnson Street, Kingston, ON K7L 1X7, Canada. *T:* (613) 5444774, *Fax:* (613) 5473745. *E:* moulton@ontario.anglican.ca.

ONWURAH, Chinyelu Susan, (Chi); MP (Lab) Newcastle upon Tyne Central, since 2010; *b* Wallsend, 12 April 1965. *Educ:* Kenton Sch.; Imperial Coll., London (BEng Electrical Engrg 1987); Manchester Business Sch. (MBA 2002). CEng 2003. With Nortel, 1987–95; Cable & Wireless, 1995–99; Director: product strategy, Global Telesystems UK, 1999–2000; mkt devlt, Teligent, 2000–01; Partner, Hammatan Ventures, 2001–04; Hd, telecoms technol., Ofcom, 2004–10. Shadow Minister: for innovation and sci., BIS, 2010–13; Cabinet Office, 2013–15. *Address:* House of Commons, SW1A 0AA.

OPENSHAW, Hon. Dame Caroline Jane, (Lady Openshaw); *see* Swift, Hon. Dame C. J.

OPENSHAW, Hon. Sir (Charles) Peter (Lawford), Kt 2005; **Hon. Mr Justice Openshaw;** DL; a Judge of the High Court of Justice, Queen's Bench Division, since 2005; *b* 21 Dec. 1947; *s* of late Judge William Harrison Openshaw and Elisabeth Joyce Emily Openshaw; *m* 1979, Caroline Jane Swift (*see* Hon. Dame C. J. Swift); one *s* one *d*. *Educ:* Harrow; St Catharine's College, Cambridge (MA). Called to the Bar, Inner Temple, 1970, Bencher, 2003; practised on Northern Circuit, Junior 1973; Assistant Recorder, 1985; a Recorder, 1988–99; QC 1991; Hon. Recorder of Preston, 1999–2005; a Sen. Circuit Judge, 1999–2005; a Presiding Judge, N Eastern Circuit, 2009–12. Dir, Criminal Trng, Judicial Coll., 2013–. Mem., Criminal Procedure Rules Cttee, 2005–. Hon. Canon, Blackburn Cathedral, 2008–. DL Lancs, 2000. *Recreations:* fishing, gardening, village life. *Address:* Royal Courts of Justice, Strand, WC2A 2LL.

OPENSHAW, Prof. Peter John Morland, PhD; FRCP; FMedSci; Professor of Experimental Medicine and Head, Department of Respiratory Medicine, National Heart and Lung Institute, since 1997, and Director, Centre for Respiratory Infections, since 2008, Imperial College London; *b* Glastonbury, 11 Nov. 1954; *s* of William Arthur Openshaw and Susan Elizabeth (*née* Scott Stokes); *m* 1st, 1979, Clare Patricia Vaughan (*d* 1996); two *s* one *d*; 2nd, 2001, Evelyn Samuels Welch; one step *s* two step *d*. *Educ:* Sidcot and Bootham Quaker Schs; Guy's Hosp., Univ. of London (BSc 1976; Paediatric Prize, 1978; MB BS 1979; Gold Medal in Medicine 1979); PhD NIMR 1988. MRCP 1982, FRCP 1994. SHO, Brompton Hosp., 1981–82; Medical Registrar and Lectr, RPMS, 1983–85; Wellcome Trust Sen. Fellow in Clin. Sci., 1988–98; Hon. Physician, St Mary's Hosp., 1990–. Croonian Lect. on influenza, RCP, 2013. Member: Scientific Pandemic Influenza Adv. Cttee, DoH, 2007–; European Scientific Working Gp on Influenza, 2008– (Vice-Pres., 2008–); Jt Cttee on Vaccination and Immunisation subgroups on respiratory infections, 2009–; Scientific Adv. Gp on Emergencies, 2009–10. Dir, Mechanisms of Severe Acute Influenza Consortium, 2009–14. Mem., various Wellcome Trust funding panels, 1997–2010. Pres., British Soc. for Immunol., 2014– (Mem., Forum, 2009–). FMedSci 1999. Mem., Med. Res. Club, 1989– (Sec., 2004–09). Robert M. Chanock Lifetime Achievement Award, Internat. RSV Symposium, 2012. *Publications:* contrib. papers on viral immunology and respiratory medicine to jls incl. Nature Medicine, Jl Exptl Medicine. *Recreations:* fresh air, odd music, tying knots. *Address:* Respiratory Medicine, St Mary's Campus, Imperial College, Norfolk Place, Paddington, W2 1PG. *T:* (020) 7594 3854, *Fax:* (020) 7262 8913. *E:* p.openshaw@imperial.ac.uk.

OPIE, Alan John, OBE 2013; baritone; *b* 22 March 1945; *s* of Jack and Doris Winifred Opie; *m* 1970, Kathleen Ann Smales; one *s* one *d*. *Educ:* Truro Sch.; Guildhall Sch. of Music (AGSM); London Opera Centre. Principal rôles include: Papageno in The Magic Flute, Sadler's Wells Opera, 1969; Tony in the Globolinks, Santa Fe Opera, 1970; Officer in the Barber of Seville, Covent Garden, 1971; Don Giovanni, Kent Opera, and Demetrius, English Opera Gp, 1972; Prin. Baritone with ENO, 1973–96; *English National Opera:* Figaro; Papageno; Guglielmo; Beckmesser; Valentin; Lescaut in Manon; Eisenstein and Falke in Die Fledermaus; Danilo; Silvio; Junius in Rape of Lucretia; Cecil in Gloriana; Faninal in Der Rosenkavalier; Germont in La Traviata; Marcello and Schaunard in La Bohème; Kovalyov in The Nose; Strephon in Iolanthe; Grosvenor in Patience; Tomsky in Queen of Spades; Paolo in Simon Boccanegra; Harlequin in Ariadne auf Naxos; Dr Faust by Busoni; Sharpless in Madame Butterfly; Fiddler in Königskinder; Sancho in Don Quixote, 1994; Alfonso in Così fan Tutte, 1997; Falstaff, 1997 and 2004; Don Carlo in Ernani, 2000; title rôle in Rigoletto, 2003; Leon Klinghoffer in The Death of Klinghoffer, 2012; *Royal Opera, Covent Garden:* Hector in King Priam, 1985; Ping in Turandot, 1986; Mangus in The Knot Garden, 1988; Falke in Die Fledermaus, 1989; Paolo in Simon Boccanegra; rôles in Death in Venice, 1992; Sharpless in Madame Butterfly, 1993; Faninal in Der Rosenkavalier, 1995; Germont in La Traviata, 2001, 2002; Balstrode in Peter Grimes, 2004; Sulpice in La Fille du Regiment, 2012; *Glyndebourne Festival Opera*: Sid in Albert Herring, 1985, 1990; rôles in Death in Venice, 1989; Figaro in Le Nozze di Figaro, 1991; Balstrode in Peter Grimes, 1992; Dr Falke in Die Fledermaus, 2006; Vicar in Albert Herring, 2008; *Scottish Opera:* Baron in La Vie Parisienne, 1985; Storch in Intermezzo, 1986; Forester in Cunning Little Vixen, 1991; *Opera North:* Diomede in Troilus and Cressida, 1995; *Metropolitan Opera, NY:* Balstrode in Peter Grimes, 1994; Sharpless in Madama Butterfly, 1997; Fieramosca in Benvenuto Cellini, 2003; Forester in Cunning Little Vixen with NY Philharmonic Orch., 2011; *Welsh National Opera:* Frank in Die Fledermaus, 2011; Sharpless in Madama Butterfly, 2013; *La Scala, Milan:* title role, Outis, by Berio, world première 1996; Forester in Cunning Little Vixen, 2003; Kolenaty in The Makropoulos Case, 2008; Germont in La Traviata, Berlin, 2001, Toronto, 2007; Balstrode in Peter Grimes, Florence, Japan, Paris Bastille, 2002; Sharpless in Madame Butterfly, China, 2002, Los Angeles, 2004; Mao in Madame Mao (world première), Santa Fe, 2003; Rigoletto, Philadelphia, 2007, for Australian Opera, 2010; Pangloss in Candide, Naples, 2007; Scarpia in Tosca, Toronto, 2008; Falstaff, Strasbourg and Washington, 2009; Germont in Traviata, San Diego, 2010; Golaud in Pelleas and Melisande, 2010, Gianni Schicchi, 2012, Opera Holland Park; has also appeared at Bayreuth Fest., Berlin (Unter den Linden, Berlin Staatsoper, 1990) and in Amsterdam and Munich (rôles include Beckmesser), and at Buxton Fest. and in Brussels, Chicago, Vienna, Paris, Strasbourg, Dallas, Toronto and Sydney. Has made numerous recordings, esp. of operas of Benjamin Britten. Grammy Awards for recordings of Peter Grimes, 1996, and Die Meistersinger, 1997. *Address:* Chartwood Lodge, Punchbowl Lane, Dorking, Surrey RH5 4ED.

OPIE, Geoffrey James; freelance lecturer on 19th and 20th century art and design, 1989–2005, now retired; *b* 10 July 1939; *s* of Basil Irwin Opie and Florence Mabel Opie (*née* May); *m* 1st, 1964, Pamela Green; one *s* one *d*; 2nd, 1980, Jennifer Hawkins; one *s*. *Educ:* Humphry Davy Grammar School, Penzance; Falmouth Sch. of Art (NDD); Goldsmiths' Coll., London (ATC). Asst Designer, Leacock & Co., 1961; Curator, Nat. Mus. of Antiquities of Scotland, 1963; Designer, Leacock & Co., 1967; Curator, Victoria and Albert Mus., 1969, Educn Dept, 1978–89, Head of Educn Services, 1983–89. *Publications:* The Wireless Cabinet 1930–1956, 1979; (contrib.) Encyclopedia of Interior Design, 1997; contribs to various jls. *Recreations:* painting, literature, music, motorcycling.

OPIE, Iona Margaret Balfour, CBE 1999; FBA 1998; folklorist; *b* 13 Oct. 1923; *d* of late Sir Robert Archibald, CMG, DSO, MD, and of Olive Cant; *m* 1943, Peter Mason Opie (*d* 1982); two *s* one *d*. *Educ:* Sandecotes Sch., Parkstone. Served 1941–43, WAAF meteorological section. Hon. Mem., Folklore Soc., 1974. Coote-Lake Medal (jtly with husband), 1960. Hon. MA: Oxon, 1962; OU, 1987; Hon. DLitt: Southampton, 1987; Nottingham, 1991; DUniv Surrey, 1997. *Publications:* (with Peter Opie or using material researched with him): I Saw Esau, 1947, 2nd edn (illus. Maurice Sendak), 1992; The Oxford Dictionary of Nursery Rhymes, 1951, 2nd edn 1997; The Oxford Nursery Rhyme Book, 1955; The Lore and

Bishkek, 21 Erkindik Boulevard, Office 404, Bishkek 720040, Kyrgyz Republic. *T:* (312) 303637. *E:* ukin.kyrgyzrepublic@fco.gov.uk. *Clubs:* Travellers; Royal and Ancient Golf (St Andrews), Woking Golf; Lucifer Golfing Society.

ORDE, His Honour Denis Alan; author; a Circuit Judge, 1979–2001; *b* 28 Aug. 1932; *3rd s* of late John Orde, CBE, Littlehoughton Hall, Northumberland, and Charlotte Lilian Orde, County Alderman; *m* 1961, Jennifer Jane, *d* of late Dr John Longworth, Masham, Yorks; two *d*. *Educ:* Oxford Univ. (MA Hons). Served Army, 1950–52, 2nd Lieut 1951; TA, 1952–64 (RA), Capt. 1958. Pres., Oxford Univ. Conserv. Assoc., 1954; Mem. Cttee, Oxford Union, 1954–55; Vice-Chm., Fedn of Univ. Conserv. Assocs, 1955. Called to Bar, Inner Temple, 1956; Pupil Studentship, 1956; Profumo Prize, 1959; Bencher, 1998; Hd of Chambers, 1979. Assistant Recorder: Kingston upon Hull, 1970; Sheffield, 1970–71; a Recorder of the Crown Court, 1972–79; Liaison Judge to Magistrates, 1983–97; Dep. High Court Judge (Civil), 1983–2005; Resident Judge, Crown Court, 1986–2001; sat in NE and London. A Pres., Mental Health Review Tribunal (Restricted Cases), 2001–05. Chairman: Criminal Justice Liaison Cttee, Cos of Northumberland, Tyne and Wear and Durham, 1995–2000; Criminal Justice Strategy Cttee for Durham Co., 2000–01; Mem., Lord Chancellor's County Adv. Cttee, 1987–2001. Contested (C): Consett, 1959; Newcastle upon Tyne West, 1966; Sunderland South, 1970. Rep. for NE, Bow Gp, 1962–70. Mem., Chollerton PCC, 1980–91. Life Vice-Pres., Northumberland LTA, 1982–. Gov., Christ's Hospital, Sherburn, 1993–98. *Publications:* Nelson's Mediterranean Command, 1997; In the Shadow of Nelson: the life of Admiral Lord Collingwood, 2008; contrib. Oxford DNB and to magazines. *Recreations:* writing naval history, cricket, family history, biography. *Address:* Chollerton Grange, Chollerton, near Hexham, Northumberland NE46 4TG; Aristotle Court, 75 Plater Drive, Oxford Waterside, Oxford OX2 6QU. *Clubs:* Northern Counties (Newcastle); Oxford Univ. Cricket.

ORDE, Sir Hugh (Stephen Roden), Kt 2005; OBE 2001; QPM 2010; President, Association of Chief Police Officers of England, Wales and Northern Ireland, 2009–15; *b* 27 Aug. 1958; *s* of Thomas Henry Egil Orde and Stella Mary Orde; *m* 1st, 1985, Kathleen Helen (marr. diss. 2010); one *s*; 2nd, 2011, Denise Weston; one *s* one *d*. *Educ:* Univ. of Kent at Canterbury (BA Hons Public Admin and Mgt). Joined Metropolitan Police, 1977; Sergeant, Brixton, 1982; Police Staff Coll., 1983; Inspector, Greenwich, 1984–90 (Bramshill Schol., 1984–87); Staff Officer to Dep. Asst Comr, SW London, as Chief Inspector, 1990; Chief Inspector, Hounslow, 1991–93; Superintendent, Territorial Support Gp, 1993–95; Detective Chief Superintendent, Major Crimes, SW Area, 1995–98; Comdr, Crime, S London, 1998; Dep. Asst Comr (Comr's Comd), 1999–2002; Chief Constable, Police Service of NI, 2002–09. *Recreations:* marathon running, wine, gardening.

ORDE, Sir John (Alexander) Campbell-, 6th Bt *cr* 1790, of Morpeth; *b* 11 May 1943; *s* of Sir Simon Arthur Campbell-Orde, 5th Bt, TD, and Eleanor (*d* 1996), *e d* of Col Humphrey Watts, OBE, TD, Haslington Hall, Cheshire; *S* father, 1969; *m* 1973, Lacy Ralls (marr. diss. 1991), *d* of Grady Gallant, Nashville, USA; one *s* three *d*. *Educ:* Gordonstoun. *Heir: s* John Simon Arthur Campbell-Orde, JD [*b* 15 Aug. 1981; *m* 2006, Maura McClelland (marr. diss. 2009), JD, *o d* of Philip McClelland, Carlisle, PA].

ORDE-POWLETT, family name of **Baron Bolton**.

ORDIDGE, Prof. Roger John, PhD; FMedSci; Professor of Imaging Science, and Director, Melbourne Brain Centre Imaging Unit, University of Melbourne, since 2011; *b* 22 Aug. 1956; *s* of John Ordidge and Margaret Ordidge; *m* 1978, Claire Page; one *s* two *d*. *Educ:* Univ. of Nottingham (BSc Phys 1977; PhD Phys 1981). Develt Scientist, 1982–83, Sen. Develt Scientist, 1983–86, Oxford Research Systems; Lectr in Phys, Univ. of Nottingham, 1986–89; Prof. of Phys, Oakland Univ., Mich, 1989–93; Co-Dir, MR Research Lab., Henry Ford Hosp., Detroit, 1989–93; Joel Prof. of Physics Applied to Medicine, 1994–2011, Vice Dean for Res., Faculty of Engrg Scis, 2006–10, UCL. Institute of Neurology: Hon. Sen. Fellow, 1996–2011; Dir, Wellcome Trust High Field MR Res. Lab., 1999–2011. Fellow, Internat. Soc. of Magnetic Resonance in Medicine, 2001–. FMedSci 2006. *Publications:* approx. 190 res. papers on MRI and its applications in learned jls; eight patents on design of MRI scanners. *Recreations:* tennis, hiking, racquet sports in general, golf, exploring Australia. *Address:* Department of Anatomy and Neuroscience, Centre for Neuroscience, Royal Parade, University of Melbourne, Vic 3010, Australia. *T:* (3) 83441953. *E:* roger.ordidge@unimelb.edu.au.

O'REGAN, Hon. Sir Mark (Andrew), KNZM 2013; **Hon. Justice O'Regan;** a Judge, Supreme Court of New Zealand, since 2014; *b* Wellington, NZ, 30 Nov. 1953; *s* of Hon. Sir (John) Barry O'Regan and Cassie O'Regan; *m* 1985, Nicola Ann Saker; two *s* one *d*. *Educ:* St Patrick's Coll., Silverstream; Victoria Univ. of Wellington (BA 1974; LLM with distinction 1979). Admitted as barrister and solicitor of High Court, 1977; Station Manager, DHL Internat. SA, Paris, 1980–81; Solicitor, 1982–84, Partner, 1984–2000, Chapman Tripp, barristers and solicitors, Wellington; a Judge, High Court of NZ, Auckland, 2000–04; a Judge, 2004–14 and Pres., 2010–14, Court of Appeal of NZ. *Recreations:* walking, reading, golf. *Address:* Supreme Court of New Zealand, 85 Lambton Quay, Wellington 6011, New Zealand. *Club:* Wellington (Wellington).

O'REGAN, Sister Pauline Margaret, DCNZM 2001; CBE 1990; writer; *b* 28 June 1922; *d* of John Joseph O'Regan and Mary Margaret O'Regan (*née* Barry). *Educ:* Cronadun Primary Sch., W Coast, NZ; St Mary's High Sch., Greymouth; Univ. of Canterbury, Christchurch (MA Hist.). Entered Order of Sisters of Mercy, 1942; professed as Sister of Mercy, 1944; teacher, St Mary's Coll., Christchurch, 1945–49; Principal: Villa Maria Coll., Christchurch, 1950–66; Mercy Coll., Timaru, 1967–68; teacher, Aranui High Sch., Christchurch, 1973–77; community worker, Aranui, 1978–. Winston Churchill Fellow, 1979. Mem., Winston Churchill Meml Trust Bd, NZ, 1985–90. *Publications:* A Changing Order, 1986, 2nd edn 1995; (jtly) Community, 1989; Aunts and Windmills, 1991; There is Hope for a Tree, 1995; (jtly) Parish: for the people in the pews, 2000; Miles to Go, 2004, 2nd edn 2007. *Recreations:* cryptic crosswords, films, reading. *Address:* Christchurch, New Zealand.

O'REGAN, Sir Stephen Gerard, (Sir Tipene), Kt 1994; Ngai Tahu tribal leader; company director; *b* 23 Sept. 1939; *s* of Rolland O'Regan and Rena Ruhia O'Regan (*née* Bradshaw); *m* 1963, Sandra Ann McTaggart; one *s* four *d*. *Educ:* Marist Brothers Primary Sch.; St Patrick's Coll.; Victoria Univ. (BA (Hons) Pol Sci. and Hist.); Wellington Teachers' Coll. Sen. Lectr and Head of Dept of Social Studies and Maori, Wellington Teachers' Coll., 1968–83; founded Aoraki Consultant Services, 1983, now Principal Dir. Maori Fisheries Negotiator with Crown, 1987–92. Chairman: Mawhera Incorp., 1976–88; Sealord Group (formerly Sealord Products) Ltd, 1993–2002; Ngai Tahu Hldg Corp. Ltd, 1996–2000; Te Tapuae o Rehua Ltd, 1997–2005; Escorial Co. Ltd, 1999–2004; Clifford Bay Marine Farms Ltd, 2000–15; Dep. Chm., Transit NZ Authy, 2000–06; Director: Ngai Tahu Fisheries Ltd, 1986–90; Broadcasting Corp. of NZ, 1986–88; Television NZ Ltd, 1988–95; Whale Watch Kaikoura Ltd, 1988–2009; Moana Pacific Fisheries Ltd, 1990–95; Ngai Tahu Property Group Ltd, 1993–2000; Meridian Energy Ltd, 2000–05. Co-Chm., NZ Constitutional Adv. Panel, 2012–13. QEII Postgrad. Schol. in Maori, 1977–78; Lansdowne Fellow, Univ. of Victoria, BC, 1994; Canterbury University: Ngai Tahu Fellow (History), 1977–78; Vis. Lectr, NZ History, 1989–2000; Sen. Res. Fellow, 2001–04; Asst Vice-Chancellor (Maori), 2005–10; Adjunct Prof., 2011–; Vis. Fellow, Stanford Univ., 2009; Fellow, Univ. of Auckland, 2011 (Chm., Centre for Maori Research Excellence, 2006–15). Mem., Adv. Bd, Univ. of Otago Business Sch., 2003–15. Chairman: Ngai Tahu Maori Trust Bd, 1983–96 (Mem., 1974–96); Ngai Tahu Charitable Trust, 1983–97; Ngai Tahu Negotiating Gp, 1990–99; Maori Fisheries Commn, 1990–93; Treaty of Waitangi Fisheries Commn, 1993–2000; Dep. Chm., Fedn of Maori Authorities, 1986–88 (Exec. Mem., 1988–97); Member: Maori Adv. Cttee, NZ Historic Places Trust, 1977–90; NZ Geographic Bd, 1983–2013; Bd of Trustees, Nat. Mus. of NZ, 1984–94; NZ Conservation Authy, 1990–96; Bd, Law of the Sea Inst., 1995–2001; Bd of Trustees, Marine Stewardship Council, 2000–05; Trustee, Christchurch Arts Centre, 2010–13. Patron: Foundn for Res. on Marine Mammals, 2001; Christchurch Arts Fest., 1998–2015. Writer and presenter, Manawhenua: the Natural World of the Maori (TV documentary series), 1987. Dist. Fellow, Inst. of Dirs, NZ, 2001. Hon. DLitt Canterbury, 1992; Hon. DComm: Lincoln, 2004; Victoria, 2006. New Zealander of the Year, Nat. Business Review, 1993; Supreme Award, NZ Seafood Industry Council, 2002. *Publications:* New Myths and Old Politics, 2014; contribs to numerous books, articles in jls, reports, etc. *Address:* 342 Marine Parade, Christchurch 8061, New Zealand. *Clubs:* Royal Port Nicholson Yacht; Waikawa Boating.

O'REILLY, Sir Anthony (John Francis), Kt 2001; PhD; Chief Executive, Independent News & Media, 2004–09 (Executive Chairman, 2000–04); Chairman: Independent Newspapers PLC, 1980–2009; Waterford Wedgwood PLC, 1993–2009; *b* Dublin, 7 May 1936; *oc* of J. P. O'Reilly, former Inspector-General of Customs; *m* 1962, Susan (marr. diss.), *d* of Keith Cameron, Australia; three *s* three *d* (of whom two *s* one *d* are triplets); *m* 1991, Chryss Goulandris. *Educ:* Belvedere Coll., Dublin; University Coll., Dublin (BCL 1958); Bradford Univ. (PhD 1980). Admitted Solicitor, 1958. Industrial Consultant, Weston Evans UK, 1958–60; PA to Chm., Suttons Ltd, Cork, 1960–62; Chief Exec. Officer, Irish Dairy Bd, 1962–66; Man. Dir, Irish Sugar Bd, 1966–69; Man. Dir, Erin Foods Ltd, 1966–69; Jt Man. Dir, Heinz-Erin, 1967–70; Man. Dir, H. J. Heinz Co. Ltd, UK, 1969–71; H. J. Heinz Co.: Sen. Vice-Pres., N America and Pacific, 1971–72; Exec. Vice-Pres. and Chief Op. Off., 1972–73; Pres. and Chief Operating Officer, 1973–79; Pres., 1979–96; CEO, 1979–98; Chm., 1987–2000. Lectr in Business Management, UC Cork, 1960–62. Director: Robt McCowen & Sons Ltd, 1961–62; Agricl Credit Corp. Ltd, 1965–66; Nitrigin Eireann Teoranta, 1965–66; Allied Irish Investment Bank Ltd, 1968–71; Thyssen-Bornemisza Co., 1970–72; Independent Newspapers (Vice Chm., 1973–80); Nat. Mine Service Co., 1973–76; Mobil, 1979–88; Bankers Trust Co., 1980–90; Allegheny Internat. Inc., 1982–87; Washington Post, 1987–94; GEC, 1990–92; Chairman: Fitzwilliam Securities Ltd, 1971–77; Fitzwilton Ltd, 1978– (Dep. Chm., 1972–78); Atlantic Resources PLC, 1981. Member: Incorp. Law Soc.; Council, Irish Management Inst.; Hon. LLD: Wheeling Coll., 1974; Rollins Coll., 1978; Trinity Coll., 1978; Allegheny Coll., 1983. *Publications:* Prospect, 1962; Developing Creative Management, 1970; The Conservative Consumer, 1971; Food for Thought, 1972. *Recreations:* Rugby (played for Ireland 29 times), tennis. *Clubs:* Reform, Annabel's; Stephen's Green (Dublin); Duquesne, Allegheny, Fox Chapel, Pittsburgh Golf (Pittsburgh); Carlton (Chicago); Lyford Cay (Bahamas).

O'REILLY, Most Rev. Colm; Bishop of Ardagh and Clonmacnoise, (RC), 1983–2013, now Bishop Emeritus; *b* 11 Jan. 1935; *s* of John and Alicia O'Reilly. Ordained priest, 1960. *Address:* St Michael's, Longford, Ireland. *T:* (43) 46432.

O'REILLY, Sir John (James), Kt 2007; DSc, PhD; CEng, FREng; FRAeS; Director General, Knowledge and Innovation, Department for Business, Innovation and Skills, 2013–15; *b* 1 Dec. 1946; *s* of Patrick William and Dorothy Ann O'Reilly; one *s* one *d*. *Educ:* Brunel Univ. (BTech 1969; DSc 1991); Essex Univ. (PhD 1982). Student apprentice, RRE, Malvern, 1963–69; Lectr, then Sen. Lectr, Univ. of Essex, 1972–85; Prof. of Electronic Engrg, 1985–94, Hd, Sch. of Electronic Engrg and Computer Systems, 1985–93, UCNW, later Univ. of Wales, Bangor; Principal Res. Fellow, BT Labs, 1993–94; Prof. of Telecommunications, 1994–2001, Hd, Dept of Electronic and Electrical Engrg, 1997–2001, UCL; Chief Exec., EPSRC, 2001–06; Vice-Chancellor, Cranfield Univ., 2006–13. Chief Exec., IDB Ltd, 1986–94. Dir, ERA Foundn, 2008–; Chm., NICC Standards Ltd, 2008–. Comr, Royal Commn for the Exhibn of 1851, 2011–. Mem. Bd, Agency for Sci., Technol. and Res., Singapore, 2011–; Chm., Sci. and Engrg Res. Council, Singapore, 2012–. Pres., IEE, 2004–05 (Vice-Pres., 2000–02; Dep. Pres., 2002). Trustee, RAeS, 2013–. FREng 1993. Hon. FIChemE 2004; Hon. FIET 2011. Hon. Foreign Member: Acad. Hassan II des Scis et Techniques, 2006–; Lisbon Acad. of Scis, 2008–. *Publications:* Telecommunication Principles, 1984; Optimisation Methods in Electronics and Communications, 1984; (ed with K. W. Cattermole) Problems of Randomness in Communication Engineering, 1984; contrib. numerous jl and conf. papers. *Recreations:* music, theatre, gardening, cooking.

O'REILLY, Most Rev. Leo; *see* Kilmore, Bishop of.

O'REILLY, Air Vice-Marshal Patrick John, CB 1999; CEng, FIET, FRAeS; Director of Military Support, Claverham Ltd, 2000–06; *b* 26 April 1946; *s* of John Francis O'Reilly and Elizabeth O'Reilly (*née* Hammond); *m* 1974, Christine Adair Williamson; two *s*. *Educ:* Ryland Bedford Sch., Sutton Coldfield; Aston Univ. (BSc). Joined RAF 1969; numerous aircraft engrg appts in UK, Germany and the Falkland Is involving fast-jet and rotary aircraft; rcds 1991; Air Officer Wales, 1992–94; Dir Gen. Technical Services, and Pres. of Ordnance Bd, 1996–98, retd 1999. Pres., Wales, Midlands and SW Area, RAFA, 2008–. Liveryman, Engineers' Co., 2004 (Master, 2015–). *Recreation:* shooting. *Address:* Seend, Wilts. *Clubs:* Royal Air Force; Bath and County.

OREJA AGUIRRE, Marcelino; Member, European Commission, 1994–99; President, Institute of European Studies, San Pablo-CEU University, since 2000; *b* 13 Feb. 1935; *m* 1967, Silvia Arburua; two *s*. *Educ:* Univ. of Madrid (LLD). Prof. of Internat. Affairs, Diplomatic Sch., Madrid, 1962–70; Dir of Internat. Service, Bank of Spain, 1970–74; Minister of Foreign Affairs, 1976–80; Governor-Gen., Basque Country, 1980–82; Sec. Gen., Council of Europe, 1984–89; Mem. (Partido Popular) European Parlt, 1989–94 (Chm., Institutional Affairs Cttee, 1989–94). *Address:* 81 Nunez de Balboa, 28006 Madrid, Spain. *T:* (1) 5759101.

ORFORD, Julia Amanda; *see* Dias, J. A.

ORGAN, Bryan; *see* Organ, H. B.

ORGAN, Diana Mary; Trustee, Gloucestershire Young Carers (Strategic Lead, 2010); *b* 21 Feb. 1952; *d* of Jack Stanley Pugh and Vera Lillian Pugh; *m* 1975, Richard Thomas Organ; two *d*. *Educ:* Church of England Coll., Edgbaston; St Hugh's Coll., Oxford (BA Hons 1973); Bath Univ. (CertEd 1974). Special Needs Teacher, High Heath Special Sch., 1975; Remedial Teacher, Cardiff, 1976; Special Needs Teacher, Plymouth, 1977–78; Dep. Head, St German's Primary Sch., 1978–79; Head, Special Needs Units, Shepton Mallet, 1979–82; special needs posts, Somerset, 1982–92; Lab Gp policy researcher, Oxfordshire CC, 1993–95. MP (Lab) Forest of Dean, 1997–2005. Chief Exec., Young Gloucestershire, 2006–10. Trustee: Glos Envmtl Trust Co., 2005–; Community Foster Care, 2005; UK Youth, 2006–. Trustee, Nat. Waterways Trust, 2009–12. *Recreations:* gardening, cinema, sailing, swimming. *Address:* Gloucestershire Young Carers, 7 Twigworth Court Business Centre, Twigworth GL2 9GG. *T:* (01452) 733060.

ORGAN, (Harold) Bryan; painter; *b* Leicester, 31 Aug. 1935; *oc* of late Harold Victor Organ and Helen Dorothy Organ; *m* (marr. diss. 1981); *m* 1982, Sandra Mary Mills. *Educ:* Wyggeston Sch., Leicester; Coll. of Art, Loughborough; Royal Academy Schs, London. Lectr in Drawing and Painting, Loughborough Coll. of Art, 1959–65. One-man exhibns: Leicester Museum and Art Gallery, 1959; Redfern Gallery, 1967, 1969, 1971, 1973, 1975, 1978, 1980; Leicester 1973, 1976; New York, 1976, 1977; Turin, 1981. Represented: Kunsthalle, Darmstadt, 1968; Mostra Mercato d'Arte Contemporanea, Florence, 1969; 3rd Internat. Exhibn of Drawing,

Germany, 1970; São Paulo Museum of Art, Brazil; Baukunst Gallery, Cologne, 1977. Works in public and private collections worldwide. Portraits in National Portrait Gallery include: Dr Roy Strong, 1971; Lester Piggott, 1973; Harold Macmillan, 1980; Prince of Wales, 1981; Lady Diana Spencer, 1981; Lord Denning, 1982; Jim Callaghan, 1983; Duke of Edinburgh, 1983; other portraits include: Malcolm Muggeridge, 1966; Sir Michael Tippett, 1966; Mary Quant, 1969; Princess Margaret, 1970; Elton John, 1973; Lester Piggott, 1973; President Mitterrand, 1985; Richard Attenborough, 1985, 2003; Colin Cowdrey, 1996; Lord Woolf, 2002; Roy Jenkins, 2002; Martin Johnson, 2004; Lord Sugar, 2010. Hon. MA Loughborough, 1974; Hon. DLitt: Leicester, 1985; Loughborough, 1992. *Address:* c/o Redfern Gallery, 20 Cork Street, W1S 3HL. *T:* (020) 7734 1732.

ORGILL, Richard Michael James; Global Head of Corporate and Institutional Banking, HSBC Holdings plc, 1998–2001; *b* 14 Oct. 1938; *m* 1968, Anne Whitley; two *s* one *d*. *Educ:* Bryanston Sch. FCIB 1989. Gen. Manager and Chief Exec. Officer, Hongkong and Shanghai Banking Corp., Malaysia, 1985–89; Gen. Manager Internat., Hongkong and Shanghai Banking Corp., Hong Kong, 1989–90; Gen. Manager and Chief Exec. Officer, Hongkong Bank of Australia Ltd, 1990–93; Chief Operating Officer, 1993–94, Dir and Dep. Chief Exec., 1994–98, Midland Bank plc. Director: HSBC (formerly Midland) Bank plc, 1994–2001; Hongkong and Shanghai Banking Corp. Ltd, 1999–2001; HSBC Investment Bank Hldgs plc, 1999–2001; ICICI Bank UK Ltd, 2002–12.

ORHNIAL, Anthony Joseph Henry, CB 2007; Director, Personal Tax and Welfare Reform, HM Treasury, 2005–08; *b* 31 Oct. 1947; *s* of Antoine Orhnial and late Hilda Orhnial (later Mell); *m* 1982, Gertrud Wienecke; one *d*. *Educ:* St Edward's Coll., Malta; St Benedict's Sch., Ealing; London Sch. of Economics (BSc (Econ), MSc (Econ)). Research Asst, RTZ Services Ltd, 1970–71; Kingston Polytechnic, Kingston on Thames: Lectr, 1971–74; Sen. Lectr, 1974–84; Principal Lectr in Economics, 1984–88; Principal: Inland Revenue, 1988–91; HM Treasury, 1991–93; Asst Dir, 1993–2000, Dir, 2000–05, Personal Tax, Inland Revenue. Specialist Advr, Finance Bill Sub-Cttee, Econ. Affairs Cttee, H of L, 2010–. Vis. Lectr in Economics, Konstanz Univ., Germany, 1979–80. Trustee, Child Poverty Action Gp, 2010–. *Publications:* Limited Liability and the Modern Corporation, 1982; articles in Economica, Jl of Accounting Research, British Review of Economics. *Recreations:* travel, reading, cookery, furniture restoration. *Address:* 32 Marjorie Grove, SW11 5SJ.

O'RIORDAN, Rear-Adm. John Patrick Bruce, CBE 1982; DL; Chief Executive, St Andrew's Group of Hospitals, Northampton, 1990–2000; *b* 15 Jan. 1936; *yr s* of Surgeon Captain Timothy Joseph O'Riordan, RN and Bertha Carson O'Riordan (*née* Young); *m* 1959, Jane, *e d* of John Alexander Mitchell; one *s* two *d*. *Educ:* Kelly College. Nat. Service and transfer to RN, 1954–59; served in submarines, Mediterranean, Home and Far East; HM Ships Porpoise (i/c) and Courageous, NDC, HMS Dreadnought (i/c), MoD, 1960–76; Captain (SM), Submarine Sea Training, 1976–78; RCDS, 1979; HMS Glasgow (i/c), 1980–81; ACOS (Policy), Saclant, USA, 1982–84; Dir, Naval Warfare, MoD, 1984–86; Mil. Dep. Comdt, NATO Defence Coll., Rome, 1986–89. Consultant, Spencer Stuart and Associates, 1989. Director: Workbridge Enterprises Ltd, 1990–2000; Ind. Healthcare Assoc., 1993–2000; NXD O'Riordan Bond, 1999–2008. Chairman: SSAFA Forces Help (formerly SSAFA) Northants, 1996–2000; SSAFA Forces Help, Dumfriesshire and the Stewartry, 2000–08 (Chm., Scottish Resources Cttee, 2006–08). Patron: John Paul Jones Birthplace and Mus., 2012–; SW Scotland RNR, 2014–. JP Northants, 1991–2000; DL Northants, 1997. *Recreations:* sailing, Rugby football, stalking, fishing, painting. *Address:* Nether Crae, Mossdale, Kirkcudbrightshire DG7 2NL. *T:* (01644) 450644. *Clubs:* Army and Navy, Royal Navy of 1765 and 1785; Royal Yacht Squadron, Royal Naval Sailing Association.

See also Lt Gen. A. J. N. Graham.

O'RIORDAN, Marie; Editor-in-Chief, John Brown Media, since 2009; *b* 3 April 1960; *d* of Michael and Maura O'Riordan. *Educ:* University Coll. Dublin (BA English and Hist.; MA Modern English and American Lit.). More! magazine: Prodn Editor, 1990–92; Dep. Editor, 1992–94; Editor, 1994–96; Editor, Elle magazine, 1996–99; Gp Publishing Dir, EMAP Elan, 1999–2001; Ed., Marie Claire, 2001–08; Agony Aunt and Columnist, The Times, 2009–. EMAP Editor of Year, 1996; IPC Media Editor of Year, 2003 and 2005. *Recreations:* reading, movies, walking, travelling. *Clubs:* Soho House, Groucho.

O'RIORDAN, Prof. Timothy, OBE 2010; DL; FBA 1999; Professor of Environmental Sciences, University of East Anglia, 1980–2006, now Emeritus; *b* 21 Feb. 1942; *s* of late Kevin Denis O'Riordan and Norah Joyce O'Riordan (*née* Lucas); *m* 1967, Ann Morison Philip (*d* 1992); two *d*. *Educ:* Univ. of Edinburgh (MA 1963); Cornell Univ. (MS 1965); Univ. of Cambridge (PhD 1967). Asst Prof. and Associate Prof., Dept of Geography, Simon Fraser Univ., Canada, 1967–74; Reader, Sch. of Environmental Scis, UEA, 1974–80. Chm., Envmt Cttee, Broads Authy, 1989–98; Mem., UK Sustainable Develt Commn, 2000–08; Adviser: Envmtl Res. Directorate, EC, 1996–97; Accounting for Sustainability Project, 2007; Member, Environmental Advisory Council: Dow Chemicals, 1992–98; Eastern Group plc, 1995–2000; Asda plc, 2004–12; Advr, Anglian Water, 2006–. Pres., CPRE Norfolk, 2002–. Trustee, Norfolk Can Inspire, 2012–15. FRSA. DL Norfolk, 1998; Sheriff of Norwich, 2009–10. Gill Meml Award, RGS, 1982; Distinguished Friend of Oxford Univ., 2011. *Publications:* Environmentalism 1976, 2nd edn 1981; (jtly) Countryside Conflicts, 1986; (jtly) Sizewell B: an anatomy of the inquiry, 1987; (ed) Environmental Science for Environmental Management, 1994, 2nd edn 1999; (ed jtly) Interpreting the Precautionary Principle, 1994; (ed) The Politics of Climate Change in Europe, 1996; (ed) Ecotaxation, 1997; (ed jtly) The Transition to Sustainability, 1998; Globalism, Localism and Identity, 2000; (ed jtly) Reinterpreting the Precautionary Principle, 2001; (ed jtly) Biodiversity, Human Livelihoods, and Sustainability, 2002; Addressing Tipping Points for a Precarious Future, 2013. *Recreations:* swimming, bird watching, classical double bass playing. *Address:* Wheatlands, Hethersett Lane, Colney, Norwich NR4 7TT. *T:* (01603) 810534. *E:* t.oriordan@uea.ac.uk.

ORITA, Masaki; Professor of International Law, Chuo University, 2007, now Emeritus; Chairman, Institute of Foreign Studies, since 2005; *b* 29 July 1942; *s* of Saburo Orita and Saeko Orita; *m* 1967, Masako Okami; one *s*. *Educ:* Univ. of Tokyo (LLB 1965); St Catherine's Coll., Oxford (Dip. Econ. and Pol Sci.). Entered Ministry of Foreign Affairs, Japan, 1965; First Secretary: USSR, 1975–77; Japanese Delegn to OECD, 1977–79; Dep. Budget Examiner, Min. of Finance, Tokyo, 1979–81; Dir, Treaties Div., Min. of Foreign Affairs, 1981–84; Pol Counsellor, USA, 1984–87; Dir, Overseas Estabts Div., Minister's Secretariat, 1987–89; Dep. Dir-Gen., ME and African Affairs Bureau, 1989; Exec. Asst to Prime Minister of Japan, 1989–91; Consul-Gen., Hong Kong, 1992–94; Dir-Gen., Treaties Bureau, 1994–95, N American Bureau, 1995–97, Min. of Foreign Affairs; Ambassador to Denmark (and concurrently to Lithuania), 1997–2001; Ambassador to UK, 2001–04; Sen. Advr to Minister of Foreign Affairs, 2005–06; Ambassador and Special Envoy for UN Reform, 2005–06. Comdr, Order of Orange Nassau (Netherlands), 1991; Grand Cross, Order of Dannebrog (Denmark), 1998. *Address:* 1–29–5–203 Daizawa, Setagaya-ku, Tokyo 155–0032, Japan. *Clubs:* Kojunsha, Tokyo (Tokyo).

ORKNEY, 9th Earl of, *cr* 1696; **Oliver Peter St John;** Lord Dechmont, Viscount Kirkwall, 1696; Professor of Political Studies, 1998, and Senior Scholar, since 1999, University of Manitoba (Associate Professor, 1972–98); *b* Victoria, BC, 27 Feb. 1938; *s* of Lt-Col Frederick Oliver St John, DSO, MC (*d* 1977; *g s* of 5th Earl of Orkney) and of Elizabeth, *d* of E. H. Pierce; *S* kinsman, 1998; *m* 1st, 1963, Mary Juliet (marr. diss. 1985), *d* of W. G. Scott-Brown, CVO, MD, FRCS, FRCSE; one *s* three *d* (and one *d* decd); 2nd, 1985, Mrs Mary Barbara Huck, *d* of late Dr David B. Albertson; one step *s* three step *d*. *Educ:* Woodbridge Sch.; Univ. of British Columbia (BA 1960); LSE (MSc 1963); PhD London Univ. 1972. Lecturer: UCL, 1963–64; Univ. of Manitoba, 1964–66; Asst Prof., Univ. of Manitoba, 1966–72. Visiting Professor: Carleton Univ., 1981–82; Canadian Armed Forces, W Germany, 1985 and 1990–91; Univ. of Victoria, 1986, 2002; USAF Special Ops Sch., Florida, 1993–2003. Partner, Heartland Associates Inc., 1998–. Member: RIIA, 1962–64; Canadian Inst. of Internat. Affairs, 1964–2004. Regular radio and TV commentaries, Canada and USA. Outreach Award, Univ. of Manitoba, 1996; Stanton Award for Excellence in Teaching, 1997; Citizen of the Year award, St Andrew's Soc., Winnipeg, 2010. *Publications:* Fireproof House to Third Option, 1977; Mackenzie King to Philosopher King, 1984; Air Piracy, Airport Security and International Terrorism: winning the war against hijackers, 1991; (contrib.) Aviation Terrorism and Security, 1998; (ed and contrib.) From the Great War to the Global Village, 2005; numerous contribs to jls. *Recreations:* swimming, squash, tennis, photography, touring, farming. *Heir:* *s* Oliver Robert St John [*b* 19 July 1969; *m* 1997, Consuela Hazel Davies; one *s* one *d*]. *Address:* 597 Gertrude Avenue, Winnipeg, MB R3L 0M9, Canada. *E:* hrtland@mts.net.

ORMAN, Stanley, PhD; Chief Executive Officer, Orman Associates, Maryland, since 1996; *b* 6 Feb. 1935; *s* of Jacob and Ettie Orman; *m* 1960, Helen (*née* Hourman); one *s* two *d*. *Educ:* Hackney Downs Grammar School; King's College London. BSc (1st Cl. Hons) 1957; PhD (Organic Chem.) 1960. MICorr; FRIC 1969. Research Fellowship, Brandeis Univ., 1960–61; AWRE Aldermaston, research in corrosion and mechano-chemical corrosion, 1961–74, project work, 1974–78; Director Missiles, 1978–81, Chief Weapon System Engineer Polaris, 1981–82, MoD; Minister-Counsellor, Hd of Defence Equip. Staff, British Embassy, Washington, 1982–84; Dep. Dir, AWRE, MoD, 1984–86; Dir Gen., SDI Participation Office, MoD, 1986–90; Chief Exec. Officer, General Technology Systems Inc., 1990–95. Founder Chm., Reading Ratepayers' Assoc., 1974; Pres., Reading Hebrew Congregation, 1970–74. *Publications:* Faith in G.O.D.S.: stability in the nuclear age, 1991; An Uncivil Civil Servant, 2013; contrib. articles on free radical chemistry, materials science and mechano-chemical corrosion; over 225 articles on ballistic missile defence, nuclear warhead issues and defence policy in jls and other media. *Recreations:* sporting—originally athletics, now tennis; designing bow ties, embroidery. *Address:* 11420 Strand Drive #104, Rockville, MD 20852, USA. *E:* stanleyo11@verizon.net.

ORME, Howard Peter; Director General, Finance and Commercial, Department for Business, Innovation and Skills, since 2009; *b* Derby, 1960; *s* of Alan and Dorothy Orme; *m* 1984, Judith Harris; one *s* two *d*. *Educ:* Derby Comprehensive Sch.; St Edmund Hall, Oxford (MA). FCMA 2005. Unilever, 1982–2001; Allied Domecq, 2002–05; Dep. Finance Dir Gen., DWP, 2006–09. *Recreations:* music, log chopping, reading. *Address:* Department for Business, Innovation and Skills, 1 Victoria Street, SW1H 0ET.

ORME, Jeremy David, FCA; accountant; *b* 27 Dec. 1943; 2nd *s* of John Samuel Orme, CB, OBE, and of Jean Esther (*née* Harris); *m* 2001, Jennifer Anne Page, *qv*; two *s* from former marriage. *Educ:* Winchester Coll.; Christ Church, Oxford (MA). Robson Rhodes, chartered accountants, 1966–87, Man. Partner, 1982–87; Asst Sec. (on secondment), Dept of Transport, 1979–81; SIB, 1987–98 (investigations and enforcement roles); FSA, 1998–2001 (various roles concerned with financial crime). Member: National Bus Co., 1984–86 (Dep. Chm. 1985–86); Audit Commn for Local Authorities and NHS in England and Wales, 1989–2000 (Dep. Chm., 1997–2000); Chm., Financial Fraud Information Network, 1997–2000.

See also B. J. Coles.

ORME, Prof. Michael Christopher L'Estrange, MD; FRCP; Chairman, European Association for Clinical Pharmacology and Therapeutics, 2003–07 (Secretary, 1991–2003); Professor of Pharmacology and Therapeutics, Liverpool University, 1984–2001, now Emeritus; *b* 13 June 1940; *s* of Christopher Robert L'Estrange Orme and Muriel Evelyn Janet Orme; *m* 1967, Joan Patricia Abbott (*d* 2013); one *s*. *Educ:* Sherborne Sch.; Sidney Sussex Coll., Cambridge (MB BChir 1964; MA 1965; MD 1975); King's Coll. Hosp. FRCP 1980; FFPM 1989; FFSRH (FFFP 1994); FFPH (FFPHM 2000). House Officer and Registrar posts, KCH, Hammersmith Hosp., Brompton Hosp. and St Mary's Hosp., 1965–69; Sen. Registrar, Hammersmith Hosp., 1970–73; Wellcome Fellowship, Karolinska Inst., Stockholm, 1973–74; Liverpool University: Sen. Lectr, 1975–81; Reader in Clinical Pharmacology, 1981–84; Dean, Faculty of Medicine, 1991–96. Hon. Consultant Physician, Royal Liverpool and Broadgreen Univ. Hosps NHS Trust, 1975–2001; Dir of Educn and Trng, NW Regl Office, NHS Exec., 1996–2001. Gov., Glos Hosp. NHS Foundn Trust, 2008–10. Secretary: Clin. Sect., British Pharmacol Soc., 1982–88; Clin. Sect., Internat. Union of Pharmacol., 1987–93. Pres., Liverpool Medical Inst., 1994–95; Chm., Specialist Adv. Cttee on Clin. Pharmacol. and Therapeutics, 1991–93; Member: Internat. Adv. Bd, World Conf. on Clin. Pharmacol. and Therapeutics, 1989, 1992, 1996, 2000; WHO Scientific Working Gp on Drugs in Breast Milk, and on Filariasis, 1981–96. Gov., Birkenhead Sch., Wirral, 1990–2005. Founder FMedSci 1998. Hon. FRCGP 1998. Hon. Fellow, Univ. of Central Lancs, 2001. Hon. DSc Salford, 2000; Hon. MD: Internat. Med. Univ., Malaysia, 2004; Karolinska Inst., Stockholm, 2013. Paul Martini Prize, Paul Martini Stiftung, Germany, 1974. *Publications:* Self Help Guide to Medicine, 1988; (ed) Therapeutic Drugs, 1991; contribs to learned jls. *Recreations:* sailing, astronomy, cooking, walking. *Address:* Lark House, Clapton-on-the-Hill, Cheltenham, Glos GL54 2LG. *T:* (01451) 822238.

ORME, Canon Prof. Nicholas Ian, DPhil, DLitt, DD; FSA, FRHistS; Professor of History, University of Exeter, 1988–2007, now Emeritus; *b* 3 June 1941; *s* of late Edward and Kathleen Orme; *m* 1981, Rona Jane Monro; one *d*. *Educ:* Bristol Cathedral Sch.; Magdalen Coll., Oxford (MA 1966, DPhil 1969, DLitt 1986); DD Oxon 2008. FRHistS 1973; FSA 1982. Lectr, Univ. of Exeter, 1964–88. Research Fellow: Nuffield Foundn, 1991; Leverhulme Trust, 1993; British Acad., 1998; Vis. Res. Fellow, Merton Coll., Oxford, 1982; Vis. Scholar, St John's Coll., Oxford, 1997; Vis. Prof., Univ. of Minnesota, 1998; Vis. Lectr, Arizona State Univ., 2002. Chm. Council, 1996–2000, and Vice-Pres., 1996–, Devon and Cornwall Record Soc.; President: Somerset Archaeol Soc., 1997; Bristol and Glos Archaeol Soc., 2003; Devon History Soc., 2003–06; Devonshire Assoc., 2011–12. Licensed Reader, Church of England, 1993–; Lay Canon, Truro Cathedral, 2005–11, Emeritus Canon, 2011–. Corresp. Fellow, Medieval Acad. of America, 2003. *Publications:* English Schools in the Middle Ages, 1973; Education in the West of England 1066–1548, 1976; The Minor Clergy of Exeter Cathedral, 1980; Early British Swimming, 1983; From Childhood to Chivalry, 1984; Exeter Cathedral as it was 1050–1550, 1986; Education and Society in Medieval and Renaissance England, 1989; John Lydgate's Table Manners for Children, 1989; (ed) Unity and Variety: a history of the Church in Devon and Cornwall, 1991; (with M. Webster) The English Hospital: 1070 to 1570, 1995; White Bird Flying (children's stories), 1995; English Church Dedications, 1996; Education in Early Tudor England, 1998; The Saints of Cornwall, 2000; Medieval Children, 2001; (with David Lepine) Death and Memory in Medieval Exeter, 2003; (with John Chynoweth and Alexandra Walsham) Richard Carew's Survey of Cornwall, 2004; Medieval Schools, 2006; Cornish Wills 1342–1540, 2007; Cornwall and the Cross, 2007; The Cathedral Cat, 2008; Exeter Cathedral: the first thousand years, 2009 (Book of Yr, Devon Hist. Soc., 2011); Victoria County History of Cornwall, vol. 2, 2010; (with J. Cannon), Westbury-on-Trym: monastery, minister and college, 2010; Fleas, Flies and Friars: children's verse from Medieval England, 2011; The Church in Devon 400–1560, 2013; English School Exercises 1420–1530, 2013; The Churches of Medieval Exeter, 2014. *Recreations:* exercising, cycling, church-crawling. *Address:* c/o Department of History, University of Exeter, Amory Building, Rennes Drive, Exeter EX4 4RJ.

ORME, His Honour Robert Thomas Neil; a Circuit Judge, 1992–2014; *b* 25 Jan. 1947; *s* of Thomas Elsmore Orme and Iris Marguerita Orme; *m* 1971, Angela Mary Stokes; one *s* one *d. Educ:* Denstone Coll., Staffs; University Coll. London (LLB Hons). Called to the Bar, Gray's Inn, 1970; Midland and Oxford Circuit; Asst Recorder, 1984–88; Recorder, 1988–92. W Midlands Probation Cttee, 1996–2001; W Midlands Probation Bd, 2001–12; a Judge (formerly Pres.), Mental Health Review Tribunals, 2001–. Gov., Denstone Coll., Staffs, 2000–. Chm., Moseley Soc., 1993–2008; Trustee, Moseley Community Develt Trust, 2001–. *Recreations:* opera, theatre, keen interest in conservation.

ORMEROD, Prof. (Lawrence) Peter, MD, DSc; FRCP, FRCPE, FRCPGlas; Professor of Respiratory Medicine, Lancashire Postgraduate School of Medicine and Health, University of Central Lancashire, Preston, since 2000; Professor of Respiratory Medicine, Manchester University, since 2011; *b* 28 Aug. 1950; *s* of Milton Blackburn Ormerod and Dorothy Ormerod; *m* 1970, Pauline Morris; one *s* one *d. Educ:* Bacup and Rawtenstall Grammar Sch.; Univ. of Manchester (BSc Hons Pharmacol. 1971; MB ChB Hons 1974; MD 1986; DSc Med 2000). FRCP 1990; FRCPE 2010; FRCPGlas 2010. Jun. doctor posts, Manchester, 1974–77; Registrar, Respiratory and Gen. Medicine, Birmingham, 1977–78; Sen. Registrar, N Manchester Gen. Hosp., 1978–80; Consultant Gen. and Respiratory Physician, Royal Blackburn Hosp. (formerly Blackburn Royal Infirmary), 1981–2012. Pres., British Thoracic Soc., 2008–09. *Publications:* (with P. D. O. Davies) Case Presentations in Clinical Tuberculosis, 1999; over 125 articles, incl. over 100 on clinical, bacteriological and epidemiological aspects of tuberculosis, in learned jls. *Recreations:* league cricket player until 52, military history. *Address:* 28 Gregory Fold, Helmshore, Rossendale, Lancs BB4 4JW. *T:* (01706) 229594. *E:* pandpormerod@hotmail.com.

ORMEROD, Mark Edward, CB 2007; Chief Executive, UK Supreme Court, since 2015; *b* 3 Aug. 1957; *s* of Dr Thomas Edward Ormerod and late Dr June Anne (*née* Vaux). *Educ:* Oundle Sch.; Leeds Univ. (BA); Univ. de Tours (MèsL). Trainee accountant, Whinney Murray, 1980–81; joined Lord Chancellor's Department, 1981: Inner London Crown Court, 1981–83; posts at HQ, 1983–93; Principal Private Sec. to Lord Chancellor, 1993–96; Head: of Magistrates' Courts Div., 1996–97; of Criminal Justice Div., 1997–99; Dir, Criminal Justice, 1999–2001; career break, 2001–02; Director: Criminal Law and Policy, Home Office, 2002–04; Family Justice, DCA, 2004–05; Civil and Family Justice and Customer Services, HMCS, DCA, subseq. MoJ, 2005–08; Dir, Access to Justice Policy, MoJ, 2008–09; Chief Exec., Law Commn of England and Wales, 2009–11; Chief Exec., Probation Assoc., 2011–14; Founder Dir, Probation Inst., 2014–15. Sec., Sir Hayden Phillips' review of honours system, Cabinet Office, 2004. Gov., Aylwin Girls' Sch., 2002–06. *Recreations:* sailing, gardening, singing. *Address:* c/o Supreme Court of the United Kingdom, Parliament Square, SW1P 3BD.

ORMEROD, Pamela Catherine; *see* Meadows, P. C.

ORMEROD, Peter; *see* Ormerod, L. P.

ORMEROD, Prof. Stephen James, PhD; FIEEM; FLSW; FRSB; Professor of Ecology, Cardiff University, since 2001; Chairman of Council, Royal Society for the Protection of Birds, since 2012; *b* Burnley, Lancs, 24 Jan. 1958; *s* of Mathew Henry, (Harry), Ormerod and Marjorie Ormerod (*née* Crossley); *m* 2004, Dr Isabelle Durance; one *s*, and three step *s. Educ:* Burnley Grammar Sch.; Huddersfield Poly. (BSc 1st Cl. 1980); Univ. of Wales Inst. of Sci. and Technol. (MSc Applied Hydrobiol. 1981; PhD Freshwater Ecol. 1985). FIEEM 1987. University of Wales Institute of Science and Technology, then University of Wales College of Cardiff, later Cardiff University: Sen. Res. Associate, 1984–94; Lectr, 1994–95; Sen. Lectr, 1995–97; Reader in Ecol., 1997–2001. Vis. Prof., Univ. de Pau et des Pays de L'Adour, 1997–2001. Editor, 1999–2000, Chief Editor, 2000–04, Jl of Applied Ecol. Mem., Countryside Council for Wales, 1991–95; Dep. Chm., Ind. Envmt Adv. Panel, Welsh Water, 2012–. Mem. Council, 2003–, Chm., Wales Adv. Cttee, 2007–12, RSPB. Member, Council: Freshwater Biol Assoc., 2000–04; British Trust for Ornithol., 2011–12; Trustee, Assoc. of Rivers Trusts, subseq. Rivers Trust, 2008–12. Pres., Inst. of Ecol. and Envmtl Mgt, 2007–10 (President's Medal, 2010). Fellow, Winston Churchill Meml Trust, 1987. FRSB (FSB 2013). FLSW 2013. Marsh Award for Marine and Freshwater Ecol., ZSL, 2011. *Publications:* The Dippers (with S. J. Tyler), 1994; over 270 scientific papers on river and wetland ecology. *Recreations:* family, outdoors (especially birds and wildlife), arts, travel. *Address:* Cardiff School of Biosciences, Cardiff University, Museum Avenue, Cardiff CF10 3AX. *E:* ormerod@cardiff.ac.uk.

ORMESSON, Comte Jean d'; Chevalier des Palmes académiques, 1962; Commandeur des Arts et Lettres, 1973; Grand Officier de la Légion d'honneur, 2002 (Officier, 1988); Officier de l'Ordre national du Mérite, 1978; Membre Académie française 1973; President, International Council for Philosophy and Humanistic Studies (UNESCO), 1992–96 (Secretary-General, 1971–92; Deputy, 1950–71); writer and journalist; *b* 16 June 1925; 2nd *s* of Marquis d'Ormesson, French diplomat and Ambassador; *m* 1962, Françoise Béghin; one *d. Educ:* Ecole Normale Supérieure. MA (History), Agrégé de philosophie. Mem. French delegns to various internat. confs, 1945–48; Mem. staff of various Govt Ministers, 1958–66; Mem. Council ORTF, 1960–62; Mem. Control Cttee of Cinema, 1962–69; Mem. TV Programmes Cttee, ORTF, 1973–74. Mem., Brazilian Acad. of Letters, 1979. Diogenes: Dep. Editor, 1952–72; Mem. Managing Cttee, 1972–80; Editor, 1980–82; Editor-in-Chief, 1982–; Le Figaro: Dir, 1974–77; Editor-in-Chief, 1975–77. *Publications:* L'Amour est un plaisir, 1956; Du côté de chez Jean, 1959; Un amour pour rien, 1960; Au revoir et merci, 1966; Les Illusions de la mer, 1968; La Gloire de l'Empire, 1971 (Grand Prix du Roman de l'Académie française), Amer. edn (The Glory of the Empire), 1975, Eng. edn 1976; Au Plaisir de Dieu, 1974, Amer. edn (At God's Pleasure), 1977, Eng. edn 1978; Le Vagabond qui passe sous une ombrelle trouée, 1978; Dieu, sa vie, son œuvre, 1981; Mon dernier rêve sera pour vous, 1982; Jean qui grogne et Jean qui rit, 1984; Le Vent du soir, 1985; Tous les hommes en sont fous, 1986; Le Bonheur à San Miniato, 1987; Garçon de quoi écrire, 1989; Histoire du Juif errant, 1991; Tant que vous penserez à moi, 1992; La Douane de mer, 1994; Presque rien sur presque tout, 1996; Casimir mène la grande vie, 1997; Une autre histoire de la littérature française, vol. I 1997, vol. II 1998; Le rapport Gabriel, 1999; Voyez comme on danse, 2001; C'était bien, 2002; Et toi mon cœur, pourquoi bats-tu?, 2003; Une fête en larmes, 2005; Odeur du temps, 2007; La vie ne suffit pas, 2007; Qu'ai-je donc fait, 2008; C'est une chose étrange à la fin que le monde, 2010; La Conversation, 2011; C'est l'amour que nous aimons, 2012; Un jour je m'en irai sans en avoir tout dit, 2013; Comme un chant d'espérance, 2014; articles and essays, columns in Le Figaro, Le Monde, Le Point, La Revue des Deux Mondes, La Nouvelle Revue Française. *Recreation:* ski-navigation. *Address:* Académie française, 23 quai Conti, 75006 Paris, France.

ORMOND, Richard Louis, CBE 2001; Director, National Maritime Museum, 1986–2000 (Head of Picture Department, 1983–86); Director, John Singer Sargent catalogue raisonné project, since 1980; *b* 16 Jan. 1939; *s* of late Conrad Eric Ormond and Dorothea (*née* Gibbons); *m* 1963, Leonée Jasper; two *s. Educ:* Christ Church, Oxford (MA). Assistant Keeper, 1965–75, Dep. Director, 1975–83, Nat. Portrait Gallery. Kress Prof., Nat. Gall. of Art, Washington, 2001–02. Chm., Watts Gall., Compton, Surrey, 1985–. *Publications:* J. S. Sargent, 1970; Catalogue of Early Victorian Portraits in the National Portrait Gallery, 1973; Lord Leighton, 1975; Sir Edwin Landseer, 1982; The Great Age of Sail, 1986; F. X. Winterhalter and the Courts of Europe, 1987; (jtly) Frederic, Lord Leighton, 1996; (jtly) Sargent Abroad, 1997; (jtly) John Singer Sargent, vol. 1, the early portraits, 1998, vol. 2, portraits of the 1890s, 2002, vol, 3, the later portraits, 2003, vol. 4, figures and landscapes, 1874–1882, 2006, vol. 5, figures and landscapes, 1883–1899, 2010, vol. 6, Venetian figures and landscapes, 1898–1913, 2009, vol. 7, figures and landscapes, 1900–1907, 2012, vol. 8, figures and landscapes, 1908–1913, 2014; (jtly) John Singer Sargent (catalogue of exhibn at Tate Gallery), 1998; The Monarch of the Glen: Landseer in the Highlands, 2005; (jtly) Sargent's Venice, 2006; Edwin Landseer: the private drawings, 2009; (jtly) Sargent and the Sea, 2009; (jtly) G. F. Watts: the hall of fame, 2012. *Recreations:* cycling, opera, theatre. *Address:* 8 Holly Terrace, N6 6LX. *T:* (020) 8340 4684. *Club:* Garrick.

ORMONDROYD, Janet Eve Lynne; Chief Executive, Bristol City Council, 2008–12; *b* Baildon, W Yorks, 4 Sept. 1954; *d* of Rowland and Elsie Briggs; *m* 1st, 1973, Chris Ormondroyd; one *s* one *d*; 2nd, 1999, Doug Greenwood (*d* 2012). *Educ:* Salt Grammar Sch., Shipley; Bradford-Ilkley Coll. (BA Hons); Bradford Univ. (MA Managing Change). Dir, Bradford Council, 1988–2003; Dir, Local Govt Practice, ODPM, 2003–04; Chief Exec., Suffolk Coastal DC, 2004–05; Dep. Chief Exec., Hull CC, 2005–08; Interim Chief Exec., Rotherham MBC, 2014–15. Non-exec. Dir, Health and Social Care Inf. Centre, 2014. FRSA. *Recreations:* interior decorating, gardening, cooking, travelling, swimming.

ORMROD, Prof. (William) Mark, DPhil; FSA, FRHistS; Professor of Medieval History, since 1995 and Dean, Faculty of Arts and Humanities, since 2015, University of York; *b* 1 Nov. 1957; *s* of David F. Ormrod and Margaret S. Ormrod; partner, Richard M. Dobson. *Educ:* King's Coll., London (BA 1979; AKC 1979); Worcester Coll., Oxford (DPhil 1984). FRHistS 1990; FSA 2006. Lectr in Medieval Hist., Queen's Univ., Belfast, 1984–87; British Acad. Postdoctoral Res. Fellow, St Catharine's Coll., Cambridge, 1987–90; University of York: Lectr in Medieval Hist., 1990–95; Academic Co-ordinator for Arts and Humanities, 2010–15. Hon. Fellow, Historical Assoc., 2015. *Publications:* The Reign of Edward III, 1990, 2nd edn 2000; Political Life in Medieval England, 1995; (with Anthony Musson) The Evolution of English Justice, 1999; (ed) The Kings and Queens of England, 2001, 2nd edn 2004; (ed with Rosemary Horrox) A Social History of England, 2006; Edward III, 2011; contrib. to English Histl Rev., Speculum, etc. *Recreations:* music, theatre, literature, travel. *Address:* Vice-Chancellor's Department, University of York, York YO10 5DD. *T:* (01904) 322005, *Fax:* (01904) 323918. *E:* mark.ormrod@york.ac.uk.

ORMSBY, Irena; *see* Murray, Irena.

ORMSBY GORE, family name of **Baron Harlech**.

ORMSTON, Ven. Richard Jeremy; Archdeacon of Northampton, since 2014; *b* Sutton Coldfield, 17 Nov. 1961; *s* of Joseph and Mary Ormston; *m* 1988, Jacqueline Dakin; one *s* one *d. Educ:* Southlands Coll., London (BA 1983); Oak Hill Theol Coll. (BA 1987); Brunel Univ. (MTh 1998). Ordained deacon, 1987, priest, 1988; Asst Curate, St Mary, Rodbourne Cheney, 1987–91; Rector, Collingtree with Courteenhall and Milton Malsor, 1991–2001; Rural Dean, Wootton, 1996–2001; Rector, St Peter, Oundle, 2001–14; Rural Dean, Oundle, 2003–13. Hon. Canon, Peterborough Cathedral, 2003–. *Recreation:* supporting Northampton Saints RFC. *Address:* Westbrook, 11 The Drive, Northampton NN1 4RZ.

OROMBI, Most Rev. Henry Luke; Bishop of Kampala, 2003–12; Archbishop of Uganda, 2003–12; *b* 11 Oct. 1949; *s* of Luka Jalobo and Susan Jalobo; *m* 1972, Phoebe Orombi; two *s* one *d* (and one *d* decd). *Educ:* St John's Coll., Nottingham (BTh 1983). Ordained 1979; Diocesan Youth Pastor, Madi/W Nile, 1979–86; Archdeacon, Goli, 1987–93; Bishop of Nebbi, 1993–2003. *Recreations:* music, walking. *Address:* c/o PO Box 335, Nakasero, Kampala, Uganda. *T:* (41) 270218, *Fax:* (41) 251925. *E:* Orombih@yahoo.com.

O'RORKE, His Honour Richard Charles Colomb; a Circuit Judge, 1994–2010; *b* 4 June 1944; *s* of late Charles Howard Colomb O'Rorke and Jacqueline O'Rorke; *m* 1966, Jane Elizabeth Phoebe Harding; one *s* three *d. Educ:* Blundell's Sch.; Exeter Coll., Oxford. Called to the Bar, Inner Temple, 1968; Recorder, Midland and Oxford Circuit, 1987–94. *Recreations:* Japanese martial arts, literature and culture, gardening. *Address:* c/o HM Courts and Tribunal Service, PO Box 8793, Leicester LE1 8BN.

O'ROURKE, Andrew; Ambassador of Ireland, retired; *b* 7 May 1931; *s* of Joseph O'Rourke and Elizabeth (*née* O'Farrell); *m* 1962, Hanne Stephensen; one *s* two *d. Educ:* Trinity Coll., Dublin (BA, BComm). Joined diplomatic service, 1957; Third Sec., Berne, 1960; First Sec., London, 1964; First Sec., later Counsellor, Dept of Foreign Affairs, Dublin, 1969–73; Counsellor, later Dep. Perm. Rep., Perm. Rep. of Ireland to EEC, 1973–78; Sec.-Gen., Dept of For. Affairs, 1978–81; Perm. Rep. to EEC, 1981–86; Ambassador to: France, OECD and UNESCO, 1986–87; UK, 1987–91; Denmark, Norway and Iceland, 1991–96. Grand Cross: Order of Civil Merit, Spain, 1985; OM, Luxembourg, 1986; OM, Portugal, 1987. *Recreations:* walking, golf, European affairs. *Address:* 2 Sorrento Lawn, Dalkey, Co. Dublin, Ireland. *Club:* Kildare Street and University (Dublin).

See also K. H. O'Rourke.

O'ROURKE, Prof. Kevin Hjortshøj, PhD; FBA 2013; MRIA; Chichele Professor of Economic History, University of Oxford, since 2011; Fellow, All Souls College, Oxford, since 2011; *b* Bern, Switzerland, 25 March 1963; *s* of Andrew O'Rourke, *qv*; *m* 1993, Rosemary Byrne; two *s* two *d. Educ:* Trinity Coll., Dublin (BA); Harvard Univ. (AM; PhD 1989). Asst Prof., Columbia Univ., 1989–92; Lectr, then Sen. Lectr, UCD, 1992–2000; Prof. of Econs, TCD, 2000–11. Res. Dir, Centre for Econ. Policy Res., 2014– (Dir, Econ. History Prog., 2011–). Res. Vis. Associate Prof., Harvard Univ., 1989; Vis. Prof., Sciences Po, Paris, 2005. Pres., Eur. Historical Econs Soc., 2009–11; Vice Pres., Econ. Hist. Assoc., 2011–12. Mem., Municipal Council, Saint Pierre d'Entremont, 2008–. MRIA 2009. *Publications:* (with J. Williamson) Globalization and History, 1999; (with R. Findlay) Power and Plenty, 2007. *Recreations:* family, walking, reading, Shamrock Rovers FC. *Address:* All Souls College, High Street, Oxford OX1 4AL.

O'ROURKE, Patrick Jake; journalist, since 1970; author; *b* 14 Nov. 1947; *s* of Clifford Bronson O'Rourke and Delphine O'Rourke (*née* Loy); *m* 1st, 1990, Amy Lumet (marr. diss.); 2nd, 1995, Christina Mallon; one *s* two *d. Educ:* Miami Univ. (BA); Johns Hopkins Univ. (MA). Free-lance writer and ed., miscellaneous small press publications, 1970–73; National Lampoon: writer/editor, 1973–75; Man. Editor, 1975–77; Editor-in-Chief, 1977–81; free-lance writer, 1981–85; Foreign Corresp., Rolling Stone, 1986–2001; Contributing Ed., Weekly Standard, 1996–; Corresp., Atlantic Monthly, 2001–06; columnist, The Daily Beast, 2014–. H. L. Mencken Res. Fellow, Cato Inst., 1993–. *Publications:* Modern Manners, 1983; The Bachelor Home Companion, 1987; Republican Party Reptile, 1987; Holidays in Hell, 1988; Parliament of Whores, 1991; Give War a Chance, 1992; All the Trouble in the World, 1994; Age and Guile Beat Youth, Innocence and a Bad Haircut, 1995; Eat the Rich, 1998; The CEO of the Sofa, 2001; Peace Kills, 2004; On the Wealth of Nations, 2007; Driving Like Crazy, 2009; Don't Vote, It Just Encourages the Bastards, 2010; Holidays in Heck, 2011; The Baby Boom, 2014. *Address:* c/o Grove/Atlantic Press, 154 W 14th Street, New York, NY 10011, USA.

ORR, Dr Andrew William, FRCGP; author; Vice Lord-Lieutenant of Kincardineshire, since 2008; *b* London, 12 July 1946; *s* of Lt Col Harold Arthur Orr, RA and Joan Margaret Newland Orr (*née* Glossop); *m* 1971, Antonia Sybilla Atkinson; two *s* one *d. Educ:* Haileybury Coll.; St Bartholomew's Hosp. (MB BS 1971); DRCOG 1974; DCH 1977. MRCS 1971; LRCP 1971; MRCGP 1977, FRCGP 1999. RAMC, 1970–78, Regtl Med. Officer, Scots Guards; Capt. 1973; Major 1977; GP, Montrose, 1978–2006. Trainer and Tutor in Gen. Practice, Univ. of Dundee, 1984–2006; Exec., Angus Div. of Gen. Practice, 1987–2006; Member: E Scotland Postgrad. Cttee, 1989–2004; Scottish Intercollegiate Guidelines Network, 2001–03. Designer and Partner, Rank & File Stationery Products, 1987–97.

Consultant to offshore petroleum trng industries, 1993–2000. Founder, Montrose Day Care Centre, 1984; Chm., Montrose Heritage Trust, 2011–; Pres., Montrose Soc., 2012–. Mem., 1990–, Surgeon, 2010–, Queen's Bodyguard for Scotland (Royal Co. of Archers). Pres., TS Carron, Stonehaven Sea Cadets, 2012–. DL Kincardineshire, 2004. *Publications:* Sea Dog Bamse: World War II canine hero (with Angus Whitson), 2008; Skipshunden Bamse En Norsk Krigshelt, 2011; various med. res. and rev. articles. *Recreations:* collecting and conserving paintings and antiques, historical research and writing, field sports, fishing vessel 'Sybilla'. *Address:* Kirkside, St Cyrus, Montrose, Angus DD10 0DA. *E:* orrkirkside@btinternet.com.

ORR, Prof. Christopher John, MBE 2008; RA 1995; RE 1990; artist; Professor of Printmaking, and Director of Printmaking Department, Royal College of Art, 1998–2008, now Professor Emeritus; Treasurer, Royal Academy, since 2014; *b* 8 April 1943; *s* of Ronald Orr and Violet (*née* Townley); *m* 1984, Catherine Terris; one *s* one *d*. *Educ:* Royal Coll. of Art (MA; RCA 1967). Artist and teacher, 1967–. One man touring exhibitions: The Complete Chris Orr, 1976; Many Mansions, 1990. Work in public collections: British Council; Arts Council; V&A Mus.; Science Mus.; Govt Art Collection; BM; NPG. *Publications:* Many Mansions, 1990; The Small Titanic, 1994; Happy Days, 1999; Semi-Antics, 2001; The Disguise Factory, 2003; Cities of Holy Dreams, 2007; The Multitude Diaries, 2008; Chris Orr, The Making of Things, 2013. *E:* chrisorr@aol.com. *W:* www.chrisorr-ra.com. *Club:* Chelsea Arts.

ORR, Craig Wyndham; QC 2006; barrister; *b* 8 Jan. 1962; *s* of late Joseph Leonard Orr and of Dawyne Orr; *m* 1998, Jane Lloyd-Sherlock; two *s* one *d*. *Educ:* St Andrew's Coll., Grahamstown, SA; Rugby Sch.; Downing Coll., Cambridge (BA Hons 1984); University Coll., Oxford (BCL 1985). Called to the Bar, Middle Temple, 1986 (Fox Scholar 1986); in practice as a barrister, 1988–, specialising in commercial litigation. *Publications:* (jtly) Fountain Court Chambers' Carriage by Air, 2001; (contrib.) Professional Negligence and Liability, 2006–. *Recreations:* travel, wine, food. *Address:* One Essex Court, Temple, EC4Y 9AR. *T:* (020) 7583 2000.

ORR, David Campbell; Chief Executive Officer, National Housing Federation, since 2005; *b* Kirkconnel, Scotland, 27 March 1955; *s* of Jack and Janet Orr; *m* 1979, Carol Massey; one *s* two *d*. *Educ:* Univ. of Dundee (MA 1976). Dep. Warden, Community House Glasgow, 1976–77; Co-ordinator, Centrepoint, 1977–86; Chief Executive Officer: Newlon Housing Trust, 1986–90; Scottish Fedn of Housing Assocs, 1990–2005. Chair, Reall, 2014–; Senior Independent Director: Housing Finance Corp., 2005–14; Affordable Housing Finance, 2014–; Bd Mem., My Home Finance, 2010–. Pres., Housing Europe, 2008–10. *Recreations:* cinema, theatre, squash, hill walking, Heart of Midlothian FC, singing, family. *Address:* National Housing Federation, Lion Court, 25 Proctor Street, WC1V 6NY. *T:* (020) 7067 1021, *Fax:* (020) 7067 1011. *E:* david.orr@housing.org.uk.

ORR, David Malcolm, CBE 2010; FREng; External Board Member, Houses of Parliament, since 2013; Permanent Secretary, Department for Regional Development, Northern Ireland, 2011–12; President, Institution of Civil Engineers, 2007–08; *b* 19 Aug. 1953; *s* of James and Mabel Orr; *m* 1975, Vyvienne McKay; one *s* one *d*. *Educ:* Belfast Royal Acad.; Queen's Univ., Belfast (BSc 1974, MSc 1978). FICE 2002; FIEI 2006; FIAE 2007; FREng 2009. Joined Roads Service, NI, 1974: Chartered Civil Engr, 1974–2008; Dir, Network Services, 2001–06; Dir, Dept of Finance and Personnel, 2006–11. Vice Pres., ICE, 2004–07. *Recreations:* travel, cycling, local history.

ORR, Deborah Jane, (Mrs W. W. Self); newspaper columnist, The Guardian, since 2009; *b* 23 Sept. 1962; *d* of John Scott Orr and Winifred Meta Orr; *m* 1997, William Woodard Self, *qv*; two *s*, and one step *s* one step *d*. *Educ:* St Andrews Univ. (MA 1983). Dep. Editor, City Limits Magazine, 1988–90; Editor, Guardian Weekend Magazine, 1993–98; columnist, The Independent, 1998–2009. Columnist of the Year, What the Papers Say Awards, 1999. *Address:* The Guardian, Kings Place, 90 York Way, N1 9AG. *E:* Deborah.Orr@guardian.co.uk.

ORR, Iain Campbell; HM Diplomatic Service, retired; Founder, BioDiplomacy consultancy, 2002; *b* 6 Dec. 1942; *s* of late Rev. David Campbell Orr and Hilda Dora Moore; *m* 1978, Susan Elizabeth Gunter; one *s* one *d*. *Educ:* Kirkcaldy High Sch.; St Andrews Univ. (MA); Linacre Coll., Oxford (BPhil). Asst Lectr, Dept of Politics, Glasgow Univ., 1967–68; entered HM Diplomatic Service, 1968; language student, Hong Kong, 1969–71; Second, later First Sec., Peking, 1971–74; FCO, 1974–78; Asst Political Adviser, Hong Kong, 1978–81; Dublin, 1981–84; FCO, 1984–87; Consul-Gen., Shanghai, 1987–90. Dep. High Comr, Wellington, 1991–94; Counsellor, FCO, 1994–98; Dep. High Comr, Ghana, 1998–2000. Co-founder, Global Islands Network; Member: Adv. Council, World Land Trust, 2003–; Council, UK Overseas Territories Conservation Forum, 2006–. *Recreations:* natural history, islands, anthologies, reading poetry.

ORR, Prof. Jean Agnes, CBE 2004; Professor of Nursing, and Head, School of Nursing and Midwifery, Queen's University of Belfast, 1991–2008, now Emeritus; Chairman, WAVE Trauma Centre, since 2013; *b* 10 Sept. 1943; *d* of E. Smyth; *m* 1968, I. Orr. *Educ:* Ulster Poly. (BA Hons Social Admin 1976); Manchester Univ. (MSc 1978). RN 1965; Registered Health Visitor 1971. Nursing Officer, Down and Lisburn Trust, NI, 1976–77; Lectr, Ulster Poly., 1978–81; Lectr, 1981–89, Sen. Lectr, 1989–91, Manchester Univ. Subject Specialist Reviewer, QAA, 1999–2002. Member: Council of Deans and Hds of UK Univ. Faculties for Nursing, Midwifery and Health Visiting, 1991–2008; Bd, IVINUR (Internat. Virtual Nursing Sch.), 2004; NMC, 2006; Council, Pharmaceutical Soc. of NI, 2006. Adjunct Faculty Mem., Univ. of Mass, 1995; Mem. Bd, Univ. of Mass/Ghana Health Care Consortia, 1995; Ext. Academic Advr, Univ. Teknologi MARA, Malaysia, 2006. Patron, WAVE Trauma Centre, NI, 2001; Trustee: Early Childhood Develt Prog., 1985; Marie Curie Cancer Care UK, 2000. *Publications:* Learning to Care in the Community, 1985, 2nd edn 1993; Health Visiting, 1985, 2nd edn 1992; Women's Health in the Community, 1987; A Community Health Profile, 1994. *Recreations:* travelling, music, good food.

ORR, Sir John, Kt 2001; OBE 1992; QPM 1997; DL; Chief Constable of Strathclyde Police, 1996–2001; *b* 3 Sept. 1945; *s* of late Samuel Orr and of Margaret Orr (*née* Walker); *m* 1966, Joan Underwood; two *s* one *d*. *Educ:* James Hamilton Acad., Kilmarnock; Open Univ. (BA 1983); Glasgow Univ. (DipFM 1987). Cadet, Renfrew & Bute Constab., 1961–64; Kilmarnock Burgh Police, 1964–66; Cumbria Constab., 1966–69; Ayrshire Constab., 1969–75; Strathclyde Police, 1975–87; Detective Chief Supt and Jt Head, Strathclyde Police CID, 1987–90; Dep. Chief Constable, Dumfries and Galloway Constab., 1990–94; Asst Insp. of Constab. for Scotland, 1994–95. Pres., ACPO in Scotland, 1997–98; Chm. Crime Cttee, ACPO, 1998–2001; Mem., Scottish Crime Prevention Council, 1997–2001. Trustee, Crimestoppers Trust, 2001–04; Patron, Craighalbert Centre, Cumbernauld, 2001–; Chm. of Trustees, Cash for Kids' Charity, Radio Clyde, Glasgow, 2002–09. Chm., Kilmarnock FC, 2001–03 (Hon. Pres., 2003–). Advr, Royal Bank of Scotland Gp, 2001–09. Graduate, FBI Nat. Exec. Inst., Washington, 1997. Honorary President: Glasgow Bn, Boy's Bde, 1997–2004; Football Safety Officers Assoc. (Scotland), 2007–. DL Dumfries, 2001. Hon. LLD Glasgow Caledonian, 1998; DUniv Glasgow, 2001. Paul Harris Fellow, Rotary Internat., 1997. Lord Provost of Glasgow's Award for Public Service, 1998. *Recreations:* football, reading. *Address:* c/o Royal Bank of Scotland, 68 Whitesands, Dumfries DG1 2PG.

ORR, John Carmichael; Chairman: Molins plc, 1991–99; Waddington plc, 1997–99; *b* 19 Aug. 1937; *s* of John Washington Orr and Nora Margaret Orr (*née* Carmichael); *m* 1967, Janet Sheila Grundy; one *s* one *d*. *Educ:* King Edward's Sch., Birmingham; Trinity Hall, Cambridge (MA). Industrial & Commercial Finance Corporation Ltd, 1960–68; S. G. Warburg & Co. Ltd, 1969–81 (Dir, 1972–81); Finance Dir, Grand Metropolitan plc, 1981–87; Man. Dir, Merrill Lynch Europe Ltd, 1987–90. Non-executive Director: Sketchley plc, 1990–99; Throgmorton Trust plc, 1990–2002; Marston, Thompson & Evershed plc, 1992–96; Govett Strategic Investment Trust plc, 1992–97; Granada plc, 1992–2004; W. H. Smith plc, 1993–2004; Lazard Brothers & Co. Ltd, 1993–2002. Patron, Foundn for Liver Res. (formerly Liver Res. Trust), 2011– (Trustee, 1999–2010; Chm., 2003–10). *Recreations:* tennis, golf, opera, theatre. *Address:* 7 Kitson Road, SW13 9HJ. *T:* (020) 8563 9616. *Clubs:* Roehampton; Royal Wimbledon.

ORR, John Douglas, CBE 2010; FRCSEd, FRCPEd; consulting paediatric surgeon with medico-legal and expert witness practice; Consultant Paediatric Surgeon, Royal Hospital for Sick Children, Edinburgh, 1984–2009; President, Royal College of Surgeons of Edinburgh, 2006–09; *b* 11 July 1945; *s* of Sir John Henry Orr, OBE, QPM and Isobel Margaret Orr; *m* 1971, Elizabeth Erica Yvonne Miklinska; two *s* one *d*. *Educ:* George Heriot's Sch., Edinburgh; High Sch., Dundee; St Andrews Univ. (MB ChB 1969); Univ. of Stirling (MBA). FRCSEd 1975; FRCPEd; FRCPSGlas *ad eundem*. Sen. Surgical Registrar, Aberdeen Royal Infirmary, 1978–80; Sen. Paediatric Surgical Registrar, Edinburgh and Gt Ormond St Hosps, 1980–84; Med. Dir, Royal Hosp. for Sick Children, Edinburgh, 1996–2000; Associate Med. Dir, Lothian Univ. Hosps NHS Trust, 2000–05. Mem. Bd, NHS Quality Improvement Scotland, 2007–11. Hon. FRCSI; Hon. FRCS (Hong Kong); Hon. FRCS (Sri Lanka). *Recreations:* golf, gardening. *Address:* 428 Lanark Road, Edinburgh EH13 0LT. *Club:* Royal & Ancient Golf (St Andrews).

ORR-EWING, Hon. Sir (Alistair) Simon, 2nd Bt *cr* 1963, of Hendon, co. Middlesex; *b* 10 June 1940; *e s* of Baron Orr-Ewing, OBE and Joan Helen Veronica Orr-Ewing (*née* McMinnies); *S* to Btcy of father, 1999; *m* 1968, Victoria, *er d* of Keith Cameron; two *s* one *d*. *Educ:* Harrow; Grenoble Univ.; Trinity Coll., Oxford (BA Hons PPE). FRICS 1972. Trainee surveyor, 1968–72. Dir various private cos. Mem. (C), RBK&C Council, 1982–90 (Chm., Planning Cttee, 1986–88). *Recreations:* ski-ing, shooting, tennis. *Heir: er s* Archie Cameron Orr-Ewing [*b* 29 March 1969; *m* 1999, Nicola de Selincourt; three *s*]. *Address:* Fifield House, Fifield, Chipping Norton, Oxon OX7 6HH. *T:* (01993) 830305. *Clubs:* Boodle's, MCC.

ORR EWING, Sir Archibald Donald, 6th Bt *cr* 1886, of Ballikinrain, Stirlingshire, and Lennoxbank, co. Dunbarton; *b* 20 Dec. 1938; *er s* of Major Sir Ronald Archibald Orr Ewing, 5th Bt and Marion Hester, *yr d* of Col Sir Donald Walter Cameron of Lochiel, KT, CMG; *S* father, 2002; *m* 1st, 1965, Venetia Elizabeth Turner (marr. diss. 1972); 2nd, 1972, Nicola Jean-Anne Black; one *s*. *Educ:* Gordonstoun; Trinity Coll., Dublin (MA). Grand Master Mason of Scotland, 1999–2004 and 2005–08. *Heir: s* Alistair Frederick Archibald Orr Ewing, *b* 26 May 1982. *Address:* Cardross House, Port of Menteith, Stirling FK8 3JY.

ORR EWING, Major Edward Stuart, CVO 2007; landowner and farmer, since 1969; Lord-Lieutenant of Wigtown, 1989–2006; *b* 28 Sept. 1931; *s* of late Captain David Orr Ewing, DSO, DL and of Mary Helen Stuart Orr Ewing (*née* Noaks); *m* 1st, 1958, Fiona Anne Bowman (*née* Farquhar) (marr. diss. 1981); one *s* two *d*; 2nd, 1981, Diana Mary Waters. *Educ:* Sherborne; Royal Military Coll. of Science. Regular soldier, The Black Watch, 1950–69. DL Wigtown, 1970. *Recreations:* country sports, ski-ing, painting. *Address:* Dunskey, Portpatrick, Wigtownshire DG9 8TJ. *T:* (01776) 810211. *Club:* New (Edinburgh).

ORR-EWING, Hamish; Chairman, Rank Xerox Ltd, 1980–86; *b* 17 Aug. 1924; *o s* of Hugh Eric Douglas Orr-Ewing and Esme Victoria (*née* Stewart), Strathgarry, Killiecrankie, Perthshire; *m* 1st, 1947, Morar Margaret Kennedy; one *s* (one *d* decd); 2nd, 1954, Ann Mary Teresa Terry. *Educ:* Heatherdown, Ascot; Eton. Served War, Captain Black Watch. Salesman, EMI, 1950; Ford Motor Co., 1954; Ford Light Car Planning Manager, 1959–63; Leyland Motor Corp. Ltd, 1963–65; joined Rank Xerox, 1965; apptd to Bd as Dir of Product Planning, 1968; Dir of Personnel, 1970; Man. Dir, Rank Xerox (UK) Ltd, 1971; Reg. Dir for Rank Xerox Ops in UK, France, Holland, Sweden and Belgium, 1977; Chairman: Jaguar plc, 1984–85; White Horse Hldgs, 1987–91; Dir, Tricentrol PLC, 1975–86. Chairman: Work and Society, 1982–85; European Govt Business Relations Council, 1980–84; Member: MSC, 1983–85; Engrg Council, 1984–87; Envmt Awards Panel, RSA, 1987–94; President: Inst. of Manpower Studies, 1986–89; Inst. of Training and Develt, 1987–89. CBI: Member: Bd, Educn Foundn (UBI), 1982–87; Council, 1985–87; Chm., Educn and Trng Cttee, 1985–87. Trustee: Shaw Trust, 1985– (Pres., 2003–09); Roman Res. Trust, 1990–97. Governor: Interphil, 1985–94; New Coll., Swindon, 1984–95 (Chm. of Govs, 1986–92); Bradon Forest Sch., 1989–92. CCMI (CBIM 1981). *Recreations:* anything mechanical, country life, the Roman Empire. *Address:* Fox Mill Farm, The Fox, Purton, near Swindon, Wilts SN5 4EF. *T:* (01793) 770496.

ORR-EWING, Hon. Sir Simon; *see* Orr-Ewing, Hon. Sir A. S.

ORREGO-VICUÑA, Prof. Francisco; Professor of International Law: Heidelberg University Center in Santiago, Chile, since 2002; School of Law and Institute of International Studies, University of Chile, 1969–2010; Judge, International Monetary Fund Administrative Tribunal, since 2012; Judge (ad hoc), International Court of Justice, 2008–14; *b* 12 April 1942; *s* of Fernando Orrego Vicuña and Raquel Vicuña Viel; *m* 1965, Soledad Bauzá; one *s* two *d*. *Educ:* Univ. of Chile (Degree in Law); LSE (PhD). Admitted to legal practice, 1965. Sen. Legal Advisor, OAS, 1965–69 and 1972–74; Dir, Inst. of Internat. Studies, Univ. of Chile, 1974–83; Ambassador of Chile to UK, 1983–85. Pres., Chilean Council on Foreign Relations, 1989–2000. Judge, World Bank Admin. Tribunal, 1992–2009 (Vice-Pres., 1995–2001; Pres., 2001–04); Judge (ad hoc) Internat. Tribunal for the Law of the Sea, 2000–09. Mem. Panel of Arbitrators and Conciliators, ICSID, 1995–2010; Pres. Panel, UN Compensation Commn, 1998–2001; Arbitrator: Internat. Chamber of Commerce, 1999–; 20 Essex St Chambers, London, 2004–; WTO, 2010–; Member: Mem., London Court of Internat. Arbitration, 2001– (Vice-Pres., 2006–07); Perm. Court of Arbitration, 2010–. Medal of Merit, Univ. of Heidelberg, 2007. *Publications:* Derecho de la Integración Latinoamericana, 1969; Los Fondos Marinos, 1976; Antarctic Resources Policy, 1983; The Exclusive Economic Zone, 1984; Antarctic Mineral Exploration, 1988; The Exclusive Economic Zone in International Law, 1989; The Changing International Law of High Seas Fisheries, 1999; International Dispute Settlement in an Evolving Global Society, 2004; contrib. Amer. Jl of Internat. Law, Internat. and Comparative Law Quarterly and Annuaire Français de Droit Internat. *Recreations:* golf, ski-ing. *Address:* Avenida El Golf 40, 6th Floor, Santiago 755–0107, Chile. *T:* (2) 24416300. *Club:* Athenæum.

ORRELL, James Francis Freestone; His Honour Judge Orrell; a Circuit Judge, since 1989; *b* 19 March 1944; *s* of late Francis Orrell and Marion Margaret Orrell; *m* 1970, Margaret Catherine Hawcroft; two *s*. *Educ:* Ratcliffe; Univ. of York (BA History). Called to the Bar, Gray's Inn, 1968; Recorder, Midland and Oxford Circuit, 1988. *Address:* c/o Derby Combined Court Centre, Morledge, Derby DE1 2XE.

ORRELL-JONES, Keith; Chairman, Smiths Group (formerly Smiths Industries) plc, 1998–2004; *b* 15 July 1937; *m* 1961, Hilary Kathleen Pegram; four *s*. *Educ:* Newcastle-under-Lyme High Sch.; St John's Coll., Cambridge (BA 1961; MA 1967). Tarmac Civil Engineering, 1961–64; RMC plc, 1964–70; Marley plc, 1970–72; Area Manager, ARC, 1972–81; Pres., ARC America, 1981–87; Chief Exec., ARC, 1987–89; Dir, Consolidated Gold Fields, 1989; Pres., Blue Circle America, and Dir, Blue Circle Industries plc, 1990–92;

Gp Chief Exec., Blue Circle Industries, 1992–99; Chm., FKI plc, 1999–2004. Dir, Smiths Industries plc, 1992–98. FRSA 1989; CCMI (CIMgt 1992). *Address:* 6 Gerald Road, SW1W 9EQ. *Club:* Royal Automobile.

ORWIN, Peter David, OBE 1991; MC 1966; HM Diplomatic Service, retired; Director: Papea Ltd (formerly Welund Report), since 2008; Welund Horizon Ltd, since 2013; *b* 20 Dec. 1944; *s* of late John Antony Arnold Orwin and of Catherine Mary Orwin (*née* Rutherford); *m* 1977, Pamela Jane Heath; one *s* two *d*. *Educ:* Peter Symonds Sch.; RMA, Sandhurst. Commnd into Prince of Wales's Own Regt of Yorkshire, 1964; served Berlin, 1965; Aden, 1965–67; UK, 1968–69; Cyprus, 1969–70; UK/MoD, 1970–74; retd 1975; entered HM Diplomatic Service, 1975: First Secretary: Athens, 1977–84; Brasilia, 1984–87; FCO, 1987–89; First Sec., then Counsellor, Tel Aviv, 1989–93; Counsellor, FCO, 1993–96; Counsellor, The Hague, 1996–99. Security and Business Risks Advr, Syngenta (formerly Zeneca Agrochemicals), 1999–2009. Director: Drum-Cussac Ltd, 2001–02; PE-2 Ltd, 2004–06. Associate MInstD. *Recreations:* country pursuits, travel, sailing. *Address:* Cinderhill Oast, Mayfield, East Sussex TN20 6PY.

OSAMOR, Kate Ofunne; MP (Lab and Co-op) Edmonton, since 2015; *b* N London, 15 Aug. 1968. *Educ:* Creighton Comprehensive Sch.; Univ. of E London (BA Hons Third World Studies 2006). Big issue; NHS Exec. Asst, Camidoc GP Out of Hours, 2002–10; Black and Ethnic Minorities Labour, 2012–13; NHS Practice Manager: Sterndale Surgery, 2012–13; Park Lodge Med. Centre, 2013–15. Member: Petitions Select Cttee, 2015–; Educn Select Cttee, 2015–. Mem., Nat. Exec., Labour Party, 2014–. *Address:* House of Commons, SW1A 0AA.

OSBALDESTON, Prof. Michael David, OBE 2008; Professor and Director, Cranfield School of Management, Cranfield University, 2003–09, now Professor Emeritus; *b* 12 Feb. 1949; *s* of Richard Grahame Osbaldeston and Betty Osbaldeston (*née* McKenzie); *m* 1974, Valerie Davies; one *s* one *d*. *Educ:* Bishop Vesey's Grammar Sch.; Liverpool Univ. (BSc Hons); Liverpool Univ. Business Sch. (MBA). Consultant, Merrett Cyriax Associates, 1971–73; Researcher, Ashridge Res. Unit, 1973–76; Ashridge Management College, 1976–2000: Programme Dir, 1977–81; Dir, Ext. Relns, 1982–84; Dir of Studies, 1985–87; Dean, 1988–90; Chief Exec., 1990–2000; Dir of Global Learning, Shell Internat. Ltd, 2000–02. Non-executive Director: Chartwell Ltd, 1997–2001; Univ. of Stellenbosch Business Sch.-Exec. Develt Ltd, 2000–; Internat. Develt Advr, Skema Business Sch., France, 2009–; Associate Dir, 2011–12, Dir, 2012–, Quality Services, Eur. Foundn for Mgt Develt (Vice-Pres., 1997–2000). Vice-Pres., Ashridge Business Sch., 2009–. Gov., RAU (formerly RAC), 2009–. Vice-Pres., Strategic Planning Soc., 1995–2000. FCIPD (FIPD 1985); CCMI (CIMgt 1991). *Publications:* The Way We Work: a European study of changing practice in job design, 1979; (contrib.) Redesigning Management Development in The New Europe, 1998; contrib. numerous articles and papers in mgt jls. *Recreations:* sailing, theatre, France, grandfathering. *Address:* Oak House, 1 Dairymede, Speen, Princes Risborough, Bucks HP27 0TD. *T:* (01494) 488754; Cranfield University, Cranfield, Bedford MK43 0AL. *T:* (01234) 754403. *Club:* Athenæum.

OSBORN, Alec; *see* Osborn, W. A.

OSBORN, Frederic Adrian, (Derek), CB 1991; Chairman, Cynnal Cymru—Sustain Wales; *b* 14 Jan. 1941; *s* of late Rev. George R. Osborn and E. M., (Betty), Osborn, MBE; *m* 1st, 1971, Caroline Niebuhr Tod (*d* 2003); one *d* one *s*; 2nd, 2009, Linda Pritchard. *Educ:* Leys School, Cambridge; Balliol College, Oxford (BA Maths 1963; BPhil 1965). Min. of Housing and Local Govt, 1965–75; Dept of Transport, 1975–77; Department of the Environment, 1977–95: Under Sec., Finance, 1982–86, Housing Gp, 1986–87; Dep. Sec., Local Govt and Finance, 1987–89; Dir Gen., Envmtl Protection, 1990–95. Chm., EEA, 1995–2000; Co-Chm., UN Special Session on sustainable develt, 1997; Bd Mem. for England and Wales, Envmt Agency, 1996–98; Special Advr, H of C Envmtl Audit Cttee, 1998–99, 2001–05; Chairman: UNED-UK, 1996–2002; Internat. Inst. for Envmt and Develt, 1998–2004 (Vice-Chm., 2004–06); UK Round Table on Sustainable Develt, 1999–2000; Member: Sustainable Develt Commn, 2000–06; Bd, Inst. of Eur. Envmt Policy, 2002–; Eur. Econ. and Social Cttee, 2006–10 (Chm., Sustainable Develt Observatory, 2006–10). Mem. Bd, Severn Trent Plc, 1998–2006; Chm., Jupiter Global Green Investment Trust, 2001–06. Vis. Fellow, Green Coll., Oxford, 1996–97; Vis. Prof., Sch. of Public Policy, UCL, 1998–. Trustee, Stakeholder Forum for a Sustainable Future, 2015– (Chm., 2002–07; Pres., 2007–15). *Publications:* Earth Summit II, 1998; contribs to Jl of Envmtl Law, Pol Qly. *Recreations:* walking, piano, reading, bridge.

OSBORN, Sir John (Holbrook), Kt 1983; scientist, soldier, industrialist and politician, now retired; *b* 14 Dec. 1922; *s* of late Samuel Eric Osborn and Aileen Decima, *d* of Colonel Sir Arthur Holbrook, KBE, MP; *m* 1st, 1952, Molly Suzanne (*née* Marten) (marr. diss.); two *d*; 2nd, 1976, Joan Mary MacDermot (*née* Wilkinson) (*d* 1989); 3rd, 1989, Patricia Hine (*née* Read). *Educ:* Rugby; Trinity Hall, Cambridge (Part 2 Tripos in Metallurgy; MA); Diploma in Foundry Technology, Nat. Foundry Coll., 1949. Served in Royal Corps of Signals, 1943–47 (West Africa, 1944–46; Captain); served in RA (TA) Sheffield, 1948–55, Major. Joined 1947, and Technical Dir, 1951–79, Samuel Osborn & Co. Ltd, and associated companies. Chairman, Hillsborough Divisional Young Conservative and Liberal Association, 1949–53. MP (C) Hallam Div. of Sheffield, 1959–87 (NL and U, 1959–64); PPS to the Secretary of State for Commonwealth Relations and for the Colonies, 1963–64. Chairman: Cons. Parly Transport Cttee, 1970–74; Anglo-Swiss Parly Gp, 1981–87; (or Vice-Chm.) Anglo-Soviet Parly Gp, 1968–87; Vice Chm., Parly and Scientific Cttee, 1963–66, 1982 (Officer, 1959–87; Life Mem., 1987); Jt Sec., 1922 Cttee, 1968–87; Member: Science and Technol. Select Cttee, 1970–73; Educn, Science and Arts Select Cttee, 1979–83; Chm., All Party Channel Tunnel Gp, 1985–87; Individual Mem., Parly Gp for Energy Studies, 1987 (Chm., 1985–87; Vice-Chm., Cons. Parly Energy Cttee, 1979–81). Mem., UK Delegn to Council of Europe and WEU, 1973–75, 1980–87 (Hon. Associate, Council of Europe, 1987, WEU, 1990); Council of Europe: Vice Chm., Science and Technol. Cttee, 1981–87; Chm., Eur. Scientific Contact Gp, 1982–87. Chm., Econ. Affairs and Develt Sub-Cttee (North/South: Europe's role), 1985–87. Mem., European Parlt, 1975–79. Life Member, British Branch: CPA, 1987 (Mem., 1959–87); IPU, 1987 (Mem. Exec., 1968–75, 1979–83). Mem. Council, European Atlantic Gp, 1990. Mem., Interim (formerly Voluntary) Licensing Authy, MRC/RCOG, 1987–91. Chairman: Friends of Progress, 1989–95; Business and Develt Cttee, UK Chapter, Soc. for Internat. Develt, 1990–95. Mem., RIIA, 1985–. Freeman Co. of Cutlers in Hallamshire, 1987 (Asst Searcher, 1951–65; Searcher, 1965–70 and 1973–87). Fellow, Institute of British Foundrymen, 1948–72 (Member Council, Sheffield Branch, 1954–64); FIMMM (FIM 1986; MISI 1947); Fellow, Institute of Directors; Member Council: Sheffield Chamber of Commerce, 1956–89 (Hon. Life Mem., 1989); Assocs British Chambers of Commerce, 1960–62 (Hon. Secretary, 1962–64); British Iron and Steel Res. Association, 1965–68; CBI and Yorks and WR Br., CBI, 1968–79; Industrial Soc., 1963–79 (Life Mem.). Hon. Patron, Sheffield Inst. of Advanced Motorists, 1996– (Pres., 1960–96); Chm., H of C Motor Club, 1979–84. Mem., Court and Council Sheffield Univ., 1951–79. Trustee: Talbot Trust, 1950–98; Zackery Merton Trust, 1951–2002 (Chm., 1988–98). FRSA 1966. Travelled widely in business and politics. *Recreations:* golf, photography, gardening, walking. *Clubs:* Carlton, Royal Over-Seas League.

OSBORN, Rev. Lionel Edwin; Chair, Newcastle upon Tyne District of the Methodist Church, since 2001; President, Methodist Conference, 2011–12; Ecumenical Canon, St Nicholas' Cathedral, Newcastle; *b* Birmingham, 6 May 1952; *s* of John Edwin Osborn and Audrey Joan Osborn; *m* 1977, Charlotte Elizabeth Windows. *Educ:* Five Ways Grammar Sch., Birmingham; Wesley Coll., Bristol. Methodist Minister: Ripley, Derbyshire, 1976–81; Bury and Heywood, 1981–88; Bramhall, Cheshire, 1988–96; N Shields and Whitley Bay, 1996–2001. Chaplain, Northern League Football, 1998–. *Publications:* Light from Light: saints along the way, 2014; contrib. articles to Methodist pubns. *Recreations:* football, cricket, walking, reading, classical music. *Address:* 246 Wingrove Road North, Fenham, Newcastle upon Tyne NE4 9EJ. *T:* (0191) 273 9790. *E:* leo.osborn@talk21.com.

OSBORN, Madeleine Nasim; *see* Abas, M. N.

OSBORN, Sir Richard (Henry Danvers), 9th Bt *cr* 1662, of Chicksands Priory, Co. Bedford; fine art consultant; *b* 12 Aug. 1958; surv. *s* of Sir Danvers Lionel Rouse Osborn, 8th Bt, and Constance Violette, JP, OStJ (*d* 1988), *d* of late Major Leonard Frank Rooke, KOSB and RFC; *S* father, 1983; *m* 2006, Belinda Mary Elworthy; one *d*. *Educ:* Eton. Christie's, 1978–83; Consultant to P & D Colnaghi Ltd, 1984–86. Dir, Paul Mitchell Ltd (antique frames and picture conservation), 1991–2002. *Recreations:* cricket, tennis, squash, horse racing, Real tennis, golf. *Address:* 48 Lessar Avenue, SW4 9HQ. *Clubs:* Pratt's, MCC, Turf, White's; New Zealand Golf.

OSBORN, (Wilfred) Alec, MBE 2005; CEng, FIMechE; President, Institution of Mechanical Engineers, 2006–07; *b* 16 May 1939; *s* of Fredrick Osborn and Annie Osborn (*née* Wade); *m* 1963, Mary Jane Flanders; three *d*. *Educ:* Grantham Coll. for Further Educn. CEng 1969; FIMechE 1991. Student apprentice, Rubery Owen & Co., 1955–60; Design Engr, British Racing Motors, 1960–69; Perkins Engines: Design Engr, 1969–75; Chief Engineer: Applications Engrg, 1975–77; Test Ops, 1977–82; Product Engrg, 1982–2002; Consultant, 2002–04. Lectr (pt time), Stamford Coll. for Further Educn, 1963–73. Institution of Mechanical Engineers: Chm., Combustion Engines Gp, 1994–97; Vice Pres., 2002–04; Dep. Pres., 2004–06; Chm., Technical Strat. Bd, 2004–06; Member: Risk and Audit Cttee, 2008–15; Investigating Panel, 2011–; Chm., Trustee Bd Awards Cttee, 2012– (Vice Chm., 2010–12). Member: Quality Audit Cttee, Engrg Council UK, 2003–06; Dewar Trophy Tech. Cttee, RAC, 2005–; Industrial Adv. Cttee, Univ. of Leeds, 2008–. Freeman, City of London, 2002; Liveryman, Co. of Engineers, 2002–. Chairman: Govs, Deacon's Sch., Peterborough, 1997–2004; Interim Exec. Bd, Hereward Community Coll., Peterborough, 2002–04; Dir, Thomas Deacon City Acad., Peterborough, 2004–09; Gov., Grantham Coll., 2009–13. Trustee, Maudslay Scholarship Foundn, Pembroke Coll., Cambridge, 2007–. *Recreations:* golf, cricket, gardening, walking. *Address:* 61 The High Street, Thurlby, Bourne, Lincs PE10 0ED. *Clubs:* Farmers, MCC; Burghley Park Golf.

OSBORNE, Rt Hon. Lord; Kenneth Hilton Osborne; PC 2001; a Senator of the College of Justice in Scotland, 1990–2011; *b* 9 July 1937; *s* of Kenneth Osborne and Evelyn Alice (*née* Hilton); *m* 1964, Clare Ann Louise Lewis; one *s* one *d*. *Educ:* Larchfield Sch., Helensburgh; Merchiston Castle Sch., Edinburgh; Edinburgh Univ. (MA, LLB). Admitted to Faculty of Advocates in Scotland, 1962; QC (Scotland) 1976. Standing Junior Counsel to Min. of Defence (Navy) in Scotland, 1974–76; Advocate-Depute, 1982–84. Chairman: Disciplinary Cttee, Potato Marketing Bd, 1975–90; (part-time), VAT Tribunals, 1985–90; Medical Appeal Tribunals, 1987–90; Mem., Lands Tribunal for Scotland, 1985–87. Chm., Local Govt Boundary Commn for Scotland, 1990–2000. *Recreations:* ski-ing, fishing, gardening, music, cooking. *Address:* 42 India Street, Edinburgh EH3 6HB. *T:* (0131) 225 3094; Primrose Cottage, Bridgend of Lintrathen, by Kirriemuir, Angus. *T:* (01575) 560316. *Club:* New (Edinburgh).

OSBORNE, Dr Basil Alfred Herbert Ernst; Bishop of Amphipolis, 2006–09; Head of the Episcopal Vicariate of Orthodox Parishes of Russian Tradition in Great Britain and Ireland (Ecumenical Patriarchate), 2006–09; *b* Alexandria, Egypt, 12 April 1938; *s* of Alexander W. R. Osborne and Josephine Gerringer; *m* 1962, Rachel Vida Spitzer (*d* 1991); two *s* one *d*; *m* 2010, Jessica Mary, *widow* of John Aubrey Rose; one step *d*. *Educ:* State Univ. of New York at Buffalo (BA (Classics), 1963); Univ. of Cincinnati, Ohio (PhD (Classics), 1969). Ordained deacon, 1969, priest, 1973; consecrated bishop, 1993; Bishop of Sergievo, 1993–2006; Asst Bishop, 1993–2003, Administering Bishop, 2003–06, Russian Orthodox Dio. of Sourozh; VG, 1997–2003. A Pres., Churches Together in England, 1993–98; Chm., Oxfordshire Ecumenical Council, 1997–98. Chm. Bd of Dirs, Inst. for Orthodox Christian Studies, Cambridge, 1999–2003. Rep. of Russian Orthodox Church, Internat. Commn on Anglican-Orthodox Theol Dialogue, 2001–06. Editor: Sourozh: A Journal of Orthodox Life and Thought, 1980–2006; The Messenger, 2006–09. Phi Beta Kappa, 1963. *Publications:* The Light of Christ, 1992, 2nd edn 1996; Speaking of the Kingdom, 1993; The Healing Word, 2008. *Address:* 31 Warnborough Road, Oxford OX2 6JA. *T:* (01865) 557454.

OSBORNE, Rev. Canon Brian Charles; Vicar of Holy Trinity, Skirbeck, Boston, Lincolnshire, 1980–2003; Chaplain to the Queen, 1997–2008; *b* 17 May 1938; *s* of Walter and Gweneth Osborne; *m* 1968, Kathryn Ruth Grant; two *d*. *Educ:* St Andrews Univ. (MA Hons Classics); DipTh London Univ. 1980; Clifton Theol Coll. Ordained deacon, 1963, priest, 1964; Asst Curate, Holy Trinity, Boston, 1963–68; Priest-in-charge, 1968–71, Incumbent, 1971–75, St John's, New Clee, Grimsby; Vicar, St Augustine's, Derby, 1975–80. Pt-time Chaplain, Pilgrim Hosp., Boston, 1984–88. Rural Dean, Holland East, 1985–94; Hon. Canon of Lincoln, 1992–2006, now Canon Emeritus. Retired Clergy Advr, 2004–12. *Recreations:* reading, photography. *Address:* 3 Newlands Road, Haconby, Bourne, Lincs PE10 0UT. *T:* (01778) 570818.

OSBORNE, Charles (Thomas), FRSL; author and critic; *b* 24 Nov. 1927; *s* of Vincent Lloyd Osborne and Elsa Louise Osborne; *m* 1970, Marie Korbelářová (marr. diss. 1975); civil partnership 2006, Kenneth Thomson. *Educ:* Brisbane State High Sch. Studied piano and voice, Brisbane and Melbourne; acted in and directed plays, 1944–53; wrote poetry and criticism, published in Aust. and NZ magazines; co-owner, Ballad Bookshop, Brisbane, 1947–51; actor, London, provincial rep. and on tour, also TV and films (incl. The Dam Busters), 1953–57; Asst Editor, London Magazine, 1958–66; Asst Lit. Dir, Arts Council of GB, 1966–71, Lit. Dir, 1971–86; Chief Theatre Critic, The Daily Telegraph, 1987–91. Broadcaster, musical and literary progs, BBC, 1957–; Dir, Poetry International, 1967–74; Sec., Poetry Book Soc., 1971–84; opera critic, Jewish Chronicle, 1985–. Mem. Editorial Board: Opera, 1970–; Annual Register, 1971–87. Vice Pres., Richard Strauss Soc., 1994–. FRSL 1996. MInstD 2002. DUniv Griffith Univ., Australia, 1994. Gold Medal, Amici di Verdi, 1993; Commendatore dell'Ordine della Stella della Solidarietà Italiana (Italy), 2008. *Publications:* (ed) Australian Stories of Today, 1961; (ed) Opera 66, 1966; (with Brigid Brophy and Michael Levey) Fifty Works of English Literature We Could Do Without, 1967; Kafka, 1967; Swansong (poems), 1968; The Complete Operas of Verdi, 1969 (trans. Italian 1975; trans. French 1989); Ned Kelly, 1970; (ed) Australia, New Zealand and the South Pacific, 1970; (ed) Letters of Giuseppe Verdi, 1971; (ed) The Bram Stoker Bedside Companion, 1973; (ed) Stories and Essays by Richard Wagner, 1973; The Concert Song Companion, 1974; Masterpieces of Nolan, 1976; Masterpieces of Drysdale, 1976; Masterpieces of Dobell, 1976; Wagner and his World, 1977 (USA 1977; trans. Spanish 1985); Verdi, 1977 (trans. Spanish 1985); (ed) Dictionary of Composers, 1977; The Complete Operas of Mozart, 1978 (trans. Italian 1982); (ed) Masterworks of Opera: Rigoletto, 1979; The Opera House Album, 1979 (trans. Dutch 1981); W. H. Auden: the Life of a Poet, 1980; (ed with Kenneth Thomson) Klemperer Stories, 1980 (trans. German 1981); The Complete Operas of Puccini, 1981; The Life and Crimes of Agatha Christie, 1982, 2nd edn 1999; The World Theatre of Wagner, 1982; How to Enjoy Opera, 1983 (trans. Spanish 1985); The Dictionary of Opera, 1983 (trans. Finnish 1984; trans. Portuguese 1987); Letter to W. H. Auden and Other Poems, 1984;

Schubert and his Vienna, 1985 (trans. German 1986); Giving It Away (memoirs), 1986; (ed) The Collins Book of Best-Loved Verse, 1986; Verdi: a life in the theatre, 1987; The Complete Operas of Richard Strauss, 1988; Max Oldaker: last of the matinée idols, 1988; The Complete Operas of Wagner, 1990; The Bel Canto Operas, 1993; The Pink Danube (novel), 1998; First Nights, Second Thoughts, 2001; The Yale Opera Guide, 2004; novels, adapted from plays by Agatha Christie: Black Coffee, The Unexpected Guest, 1998; Spider's Web, 2000; The Importance of Being Earnest (novel, adapted from play by Oscar Wilde), 1999; poems in: The Oxford Book of Australian Verse, 1956; Australian Poetry, 1951–52, etc; The Queensland Centenary Anthology, 1959; Australian Writing Today, 1968; various jls; contrib.: TLS, Observer, Sunday Times, Times, Guardian, New Statesman, Spectator, London Mag., Encounter, Opera, Chambers Encyc. Yearbook, and Enciclopedia dello spettacolo; also cassettes. *Recreations:* travelling, planning future projects. *Address:* 125 St George's Road, SE1 6HY. *T:* (020) 7928 1534.

OSBORNE, Clive Maxwell Lawton; JP; Legal Adviser, Serious Organised Crime Agency, 2005–11; *b* 20 July 1955; *s* of Raymond Peter Osborne and Eileen Mary Osborne (*née* Lawton); *m* 1985, Ursula Frances Amanda Futcher; one *s* one *d*. *Educ:* Newcastle High Sch.; Christ Church, Oxford (Open Exhibnr; MA). Called to the Bar, Gray's Inn, 1978 (Holker Sen. Schol.), Bencher, 2009; joined Home Office, 1980; Asst Legal Advr, 1991–97; Legal Dir, DTI, 1997–99; Asst Legal Advr, NI Office, 1999–2001; Dep. Legal Advr, Home Office and NI Office, 2001–05. UK Pres., Camden Asset Recovery Inter-Agency Network, 2007. Pres., Old Newcastilian Club, 2014–15. Hon. Steward, Westminster Abbey, 2014. JP Cheshire, 2014. Freeman, City of London, 2014; Liveryman, Glaziers' Co., 2014. *E:* cmlosborne21@googlemail.com. *Clubs:* Travellers; Potters (Stoke-on-Trent).

OSBORNE, David Allan; HM Diplomatic Service, retired; Ambassador to Honduras, 1998–2002; *b* 31 Aug. 1942; *s* of Donald Stewart Osborne and Caroline Susie Osborne (*née* Stanbury); *m* 1966, Joan Marion Duck; two *d* (one *s* decd). *Educ:* St Albans Grammar Sch.; Central London Poly. (DMS). Joined Commonwealth Relations Office, 1961; Accra, 1963–65; FCO, 1966–68; Guatemala City, 1968–73; Bonn, 1973–74; Valletta, 1974–77; sabbatical, 1977–78; First Sec., FCO, 1978–79; Mexico City, 1979; San José (concurrently accredited to Managua and San Salvador), 1980–84; FCO, 1984–88; Dep. Consul Gen., São Paulo, 1988–91; EU Monitor, Croatia, 1991–92; FCO, 1992–94; Santiago, 1994–95; FCO, 1995–96; Chargé d'Affaires, Managua, 1997. Hon. Citizen of Honduras, 2002. EU Monitor Medal, 1992. *Recreations:* reading, walking, chess, indigenous cultures in Latin America, various sports. *Address:* Firlings, Firle Road, Seaford, East Sussex BN25 2HU.

OSBORNE, Douglas Leonard, FCIS; Chief Executive, Leukaemia Research Fund, 1989–2007; *b* 19 Oct. 1940; *s* of Leonard Osborne and Gladys Ellen (*née* Ward); *m* 1969, Barbara Helen Bartrop; one *s* one *d*. *Educ:* Royal Masonic Sch. ACIS 1967, FCIS 1985. London Association for the Blind: Asst Sec., 1965–75; Asst Dir, 1975–79; Dir, 1979–83; Administrator, Leukaemia Res. Fund, 1983–89. Trustee: BlindAid (formerly Metropolitan Soc. for the Blind), 1979–2013; Alternative Hair Charitable Foundn, 2012–; Beefy's Charity Foundn, 2013–. *Publications:* (ed jtly) Charities Administration, 1986, and Supplements, 1987–. *Recreations:* listening to music, cooking, travel, swimming. *Address:* 360 Topsham Road, Exeter, Devon EX2 6HF.

OSBORNE, Rt Hon. George (Gideon Oliver); PC 2010; MP (C) Tatton, since 2001; Chancellor of the Exchequer, since 2010; First Secretary of State, since 2015; *b* 23 May 1971; *s* and *heir* of Sir Peter George Osborne, Bt, *qv*; *m* 1998, Hon. Frances Victoria, *d* of Baron Howell of Guildford, *qv*; one *s* one *d*. *Educ:* St Paul's Sch., London; Davidson Coll., N Carolina (Dean Rusk Schol.); Magdalen Coll., Oxford (MA Hons Mod. Hist.). Freelance journalist, 1993; Hd, Pol Sect., Cons. Res. Dept, 1994–95; Special Advr, MAFF, 1995–97; Pol Office, 10 Downing St, 1997; Pol Sec. to Leader of Opposition, 1997–2001; Sec. to Shadow Cabinet, 1997–2001. An Opposition Whip, 2003; Opposition frontbench spokesman on Treasury, 2003–04; Shadow Chief Sec. to HM Treasury, 2004–05; Shadow Chancellor of the Exchequer, 2005–10. Member: Public Accounts Cttee, 2001–03, Public Accounts Commn, 2002–03, H of C; Select Cttee on Transport, 2003. Trustee, Arts and Business, 2006–10. Vice-Pres., E Cheshire Hospice, 2001–. *Address:* House of Commons, SW1A 0AA. *T:* (020) 7219 8214.

OSBORNE, Georgiana Louise; Lord-Lieutenant of Angus, since 2001; *b* 24 Aug. 1944; *d* of Richard Douglas Moore and June Louise Moore (*née* Peachey); *m* 1968, James Carnegy Osborne; three *s* one *d*. *Educ:* Wellington Diocesan Sch. for Girls (Nga Tawa), Marton, NZ; Victoria Univ. of Wellington (BA); Lausanne Univ. (Philips Overseas Schol. 1964). Dep. Pres., Angus Br., 1991–98, Pres., Tayside Br., 1999–2004, BRCS. JP Angus, 2001–08. Patron, 2003, Trustee, 2004–12, Angus Coll.; Trustee, Queen Mother's Memorial Fund for Scotland, 2003–08. Pres., Angus, Perth and Kinross Branch, 2006–09, Jt Pres., Dundee and Angus Branch, 2010–, SSAFA; Hon. Vice Pres., Dundee and Angus Bn, Boys' Bde, 2012–. Hon. Pres., Strathmore Assoc., 2013–; Hon. Vice Pres., Tayside SO, 2013–. Vice Pres., Black Watch Assoc., 2001–. Patron, Dorward House, Montrose, 2006–. Badge of Honour for Distinguished Service, 1996, for Outstanding Service, 2004, BRCS. *Recreations:* music and the arts in general, tennis, golf. *Address:* Balmadies, Guthrie, Forfar, Angus DD8 2SH. *T:* and *Fax:* (01307) 818242.

OSBORNE, Ven. Hayward John; Archdeacon of Birmingham, since 2001; *b* 16 Sept. 1948; *s* of Ernest and Frances Joy Osborne; *m* 1973, Sandra Julie Hollander; two *s* three *d*. *Educ:* Sevenoaks Sch.; New Coll., Oxford (BA 1970, MA 1973); King's Coll., Cambridge (PGCE); Westcott House Theol Coll., Cambridge. Ordained deacon, 1973, priest, 1974; Curate, Bromley Parish Ch, 1973–77; Team Vicar, Halesowen, 1977–83; Team Rector, St Barnabas, Worcester, 1983–88; Vicar, St Mary, Moseley, Birmingham, 1988–2001; Area Dean, Moseley, 1994–2001; Priest-in-charge, Allens Cross, 2008–10. Mem., Gen. Synod of C of E, 1998–2015. Hon. Canon, Birmingham Cathedral, 2000. *Recreations:* music, theatre, computing, photography. *Address:* Church of England Birmingham, 1 Colmore Row, Birmingham B3 2BJ. *T:* (0121) 426 0441.

See also K. F. Colvin.

OSBORNE, Helena; *see* Moore, G. M.

OSBORNE, Jana; General Secretary, National Federation of Women's Institutes, since 1996; *b* 11 Jan. 1953; *d* of Jan Koutny and Miloslava Koutna'; *m* 1978, Graeme Stephen Osborne. *Educ:* Charles Univ., Prague (BA Hons Modern Langs 1978); Poly. of Central London (Postgrad. Personnel Mgt Course); Kingston Univ. (LLM Employment Law, 2003). MIPD 1989. Journalist and interpreter, Nihon Denpa News, Prague, 1974–79; Personnel Officer, Bowater Industrial plc, 1987–88; Office Manager, Thorpac Gp plc, 1988–89; National Federation of Women's Institutes: Personnel Officer, 1989–92; Head of Personnel, 1992–95; Gen. Manager, 1995–96. *Recreations:* cycling, walking, music, literature, gardening. *Address:* (office) 104 New Kings Road, SW6 4LY. *T:* (020) 7371 9300.

OSBORNE, Very Rev. June; DL; Dean of Salisbury, since 2004; *b* 10 June 1953; *d* of Wilfred and Enid Osborne; *m* 1984, Paul Anthony Goulding, *qv*; one *s* one *d*. *Educ:* Manchester Univ. (BA Hons (Econ.) 1974); St John's Coll., Nottingham; Wycliffe Hall, Oxford; Birmingham Univ. (MPhil 1993). Lay Asst, St Aldates, Oxford, 1975–77; ordained dss, 1980, deacon, 1987, priest, 1994; Curate, St Martin in the Bull Ring, and Chaplain, Birmingham Children's Hosp., 1980–84; Minister-in-charge, St Paul with St Mark, Old Ford, 1984–95; Canon Treas., Salisbury Cathedral, 1995–2004. Mem., Dean Selection Panel, 2009–. DL Wilts, 2006. *Recreations:* supporting Manchester City FC, friendships. *Address:* The Deanery, 7 The Close, Salisbury, Wilts SP1 2EF. *T:* (01722) 555110, *Fax:* (01722) 555109. *E:* thedean@salcath.co.uk.

OSBORNE, Kenneth Hilton; *see* Osborne, Rt Hon. Lord.

OSBORNE, Prof. Michael John, FAHA; FAIM; Professor, Peking University, China, since 2003; Foundation Distinguished Professor, Institute for Advanced Study, La Trobe University, Australia, since 2006; Professorial Fellow, University of Melbourne, since 2009; *b* 25 Jan. 1942; *s* of Samuel Osborne and Olive May Osborne (*née* Shove); *m* 1st, 1978, Dawn Brindle (marr. diss. 2005); 2nd, 2009, Liang Wenquan; one *s*. *Educ:* Eastbourne Grammar Sch.; Christ Church, Oxford (MA); Catholic Univ. of Leuven (DPhil and Lett.). Lectr, Dept of Classics, Bristol, 1966–67; Lectr, then Sen. Lectr, Dept of Classics and Archaeology, Univ. of Lancaster, 1967–82; University of Melbourne: Prof. and Chm., Dept of Classical and Near Eastern Studies, 1983–90, now Prof. Emeritus; Dep./Associate Dean, Faculty of Arts, 1985–89; Pro-Vice-Chancellor and Vice-Pres., Academic Bd, 1989; Vice-Chancellor and Pres., La Trobe Univ., 1990–2006. Mem., Inst. for Advanced Study, Princeton, 1978–79; Visiting Professor: Maximilians Univ., Munich, 1973; Leuven, 1975, 1988; Vis. Fellow, other univs, 1972–85; Guest Prof., Hellenic Educn and Res. Centre, Athens, 2006–; Prof., Beijing Foreign Studies Univ., China, 2008–; Hon. Professor: Yunnan Univ., China, 1994; Kunming Med. Coll., China, 1995; Yunnan Normal Univ., China, 1997; Yunnan Agricl Univ., China, 2001; Harbin Med. Univ., China, 2001; Sichuan Univ., China, 2002. Chm., Victorian Vice-Chancellors' Cttee, 1993–94; Member: Bd of Dirs, Australian Vice-Chancellors' Cttee, 1994–96 (Chm., Students and Scholarships Cttee, 1995–96; Chm., Standing Cttee for Internat. Affairs, 1996–2004; Leader, delegn to Hungary, Czech and Slovak Republics, 1993, to S Africa, 1994, to China, 1998–); Business/Higher Educn Round Table (Mem., Task Force on Higher Educn, 1996–; Mem. Bd of Dirs, 1996–2003); Res. Cttee, Cttee for Econ. Devett of Australia, 1993–96; Bd of Dirs, Internat. Devett Program, 1996–99; Bd of Dirs, Grad. Careers Council of Australia, 1996–98; Co-Chm. Planning Cttee, Australian Educn Internat., 2000–02. President: Univ. Mobility in Asia Pacific Scheme, 2000–02; Internat. Network of Univs, 2000–06; Co-Pres., Peking Univ.-La Trobe Univ.-Beijing Foreign Studies Univ. Centre for China Studies, 2005–08; Chm., Nat. Centre for Hellenic Studies and Res., 1997–2005; Mem., Governing Bd, World Heritage Trng and Res. Inst. for Asia and Pacific Region, 2007–. FAHA 1985; FAIM 2000. Laureate: Royal Acad. of Sci., Letters and Fine Arts, Belgium, 1980; Acad. of Institutions and Cultures, Thessaloniki, 2013; Alexander S. Onassis Public Benefit Foundn Res. Fellow, 2001; Hon. Fellow: Hungarian Acad. of Engrg, 1998; Greek Epigraphic Soc., 2013; Corresp. Mem., Acad. of Athens, 1998. Hon. DLitt: Athens, 2001; La Trobe, 2007. Aristotle Award, Greece, 1998; Hon. Distinction, Hellenic Republic of Cyprus, 2000; Centenary Medal, Australia, 2003; Niki Award, Australia, 2005; Gold Crown of World Congress of Greeks of the Diaspora, Greece, 2006. *Publications:* Naturalization in Athens, 4 vols, 1981–83; Lexicon of Greek Personal Names, vol. II: Attica, 1994; The Foreign Residents of Athens, Studia Hellenistica Vol. 33, 1995; Correspondence between China and Great Britain: vol. I, railways and mines, 2006, vol. II, education, 2007, vol. III, commerce and trade, 2008, vol. IV, protocol, 2009, vol. V, territorial and legal issues, 2009; Athens in the Third Century BC, 2010; Inscriptiones Graecae, vol. II/III (3) Attica 300–229 BC, 2014; numerous articles in learned jls on Greek history, Greek epigraphy and Greek archaeology. *Recreations:* tennis, travel, Australian Rules football; Rugby League. *Address:* Institute for Advanced Study, Michael J. Osborne Centre, La Trobe University, Melbourne, Vic 3086, Australia. *T:* (4) 88022880. *Club:* Essendon Football.

OSBORNE, Prof. Nigel, MBE 2003; composer; Reid Professor of Music, 1990–2012, now Emeritus and Co-Director, Institute for Music in Human and Social Development, 2007–12, Edinburgh University; *b* 1948. *Educ:* St Edmund Hall, Oxford; studied at Warsaw Acad. and Polish Radio Exptl Studio. FRCM 1996. Staff of Music Dept, Nottingham Univ., 1978; Co-Editor-in-Chief, Contemporary Music Review. Initiator of programme of rehabilitation for refugee children in Balkans and Caucasus, 1992–. Queen's Award, Edinburgh Univ., 1997. *Compositions include:* Seven Words, 1971 (Radio Suisse Romande Prize); Heaventree, 1973 (Gaudeamus Prize); Kinderkreuzzug, 1974; I am Goya, 1977 (Radcliffe Award); Orlando Furioso, 1978; In Camera, 1979; Sinfonia, 1982; Sinfonia II, 1983; Zansa, 1985; The Electrification of the Soviet Union (opera), 1987; Violin Concerto, 1990; Terrible Mouth, 1991; The Sun of Venice, 1993; Art of Fugue, 1993; Sarajevo (opera), 1994; Evropa (first opera of war in Sarajevo), 1995; Oboe Concerto, 1998; String Quartet no 1, 1999; Widows (opera), 2000; The Piano Tuner, 2004; Differences in Demolition (opera), 2007; orchestral, choral, instrumental, ballet and electronic music; numerous recordings.

OSBORNE, Sir Peter (George), 17th Bt *cr* 1629; Chairman and Managing Director, Osborne & Little plc (design company), since 1967; *b* 29 June 1943; *s* of Lt-Col Sir George Osborne, 16th Bt, MC, and Mary (Grace) (*d* 1987), *d* of C. Horn; *S* father, 1960; *m* 1968, Felicity Alexandra, *d* of Grantley Loxton-Peacock; four *s*. *Educ:* Wellington Coll., Berks; Christ Church Coll., Oxford. *Heir:* *s* Rt Hon. George Gideon Oliver Osborne, *qv*. *Address:* 51 Lansdowne Road, W11 2LG. *Club:* White's.

OSBORNE, Rachel Claire Elizabeth, ACA; Finance Director, John Lewis, since 2011; *b* Sedgefield, Co. Durham, 2 March 1965; *d* of Stanley Osborne and Barbara Foster (*née* Roby); *m* 2012, Allan Bentley; two *s*. *Educ:* Joseph Rowntree Comp. Sch., York; St Peter's Sch., York; Christ's Coll., Cambridge (BA Vet. Medicine 1986). ACA 1990. Audit Manager, KPMG, London, 1988–91; Haircare Analyst, UK Forecaster and Sen. Analyst, Procter and Gamble, 1991–94; UK Finance Dir, then Dir, Strategy and Planning, Europe, PepsiCo, 1994–2003; Dir, Business Performance, Kingfisher, 2003–09; Chief Financial Officer, UK and Ire., SODEXO, 2010–11. *Recreations:* gardening, cooking, my children. *Address:* Windsor. *E:* rachelosborne999@gmail.com.

OSBORNE, Richard Ellerker; author and broadcaster; *b* 22 Feb. 1943; *s* of late William Harold Osborne and Georgina Mary Osborne (*née* Farrow); *m* 1985, Hailz-Emily Wrigley; one *s*. *Educ:* Worksop Coll.; Univ. of Bristol (BA, MLitt). Asst Master, Bradfield Coll., 1967–88 (Head of Sixth Form Gen. Studies, 1978–88; Head of English, 1982–88); presenter and contrib., BBC Radio 3, 1969–; Music Critic, The Oldie, 1992–. Mem., Critics' Panel, Gramophone, 1974–; Chm., Music Section, Critics' Circle, 1984–87. *Publications:* Rossini, 1985, 2nd edn 2007; Conversations with Karajan, 1989; Herbert von Karajan: a life in music, 1998; Till I End My Song, 2002; Karajan: Mensch und Mythos, 2008; Garsington Opera: a celebration, 2011; Music and Musicians of Eton, 2012; The Grange, Hampshire, 2012; (ed and trans.) Ferdinand Hiller Conversations with Rossini, 2015; contribs to newspapers, jls, music dictionaries and guides. *Recreations:* hill-walking, food and wine, reading in the garden, watching cricket. *Address:* 2 Vaughan Copse, Eton, Berks SL4 6HL. *E:* h.osborne@etoncollege.org.uk.

OSBORNE, Prof. Robin Grimsey, PhD; FBA 2006; Professor of Ancient History, University of Cambridge, since 2001 (Director, Museum of Classical Archaeology, 2008–14); Fellow, King's College, Cambridge, since 2001; *b* 11 March 1957; *s* of John Leonard Osborne and Joyce Elizabeth Osborne (*née* Warner); *m* 1st, 1979, Catherine Joanna Rowett (marr. diss.); two *d*; 2nd, 2014, Caroline Vout. *Educ:* Colchester Royal Grammar Sch.; King's Coll., Cambridge (BA 1979; PhD 1982; MA 1983). Jun. Res. Fellow, King's Coll., Cambridge, 1982–86; University of Oxford: Tutorial Fellow in Ancient Hist., Magdalen Coll., 1986–89; Univ. Lectr in Ancient Hist., 1989–96; Prof. of Ancient Hist., 1996–2001; Fellow and Tutor, 1989–2001, Emeritus Fellow, 2001–, Corpus Christi Coll. Chm., Council of Univ. Classical Depts, 2006–12. Chm., Sub-Panel 31, Classics and Byzantine Studies, REF 2014. President:

Soc. for Promotion of Hellenic Studies, 2002–06; Classical Assoc., 2012–13. Member, Editorial Board: Jl of Hellenic Studies; Jl of Mediterranean Archaeology; Omnibus; Past and Present. *Publications:* Demos: the discovery of classical Attika, 1985; Classical Landscape with Figures: the ancient Greek city and its countryside, 1987; (ed jtly) Art and Text in Ancient Greek Culture, 1994; (ed jtly) Placing the Gods: sanctuaries and the sacred landscape of ancient Greece, 1994; (ed jtly) Ritual, Finance, Politics: Athenian democratic accounts presented to David Lewis, 1994; Greece in the Making 1200–479 BC, 1996 (trans. Spanish 1998, Greek 2000), 2nd edn 2009; Archaic and Classical Greek Art, 1998; (ed jtly) Performance Culture and Athenian Democracy, 1999; (ed) The Athenian Empire, 4th edn 2000; (ed) Classical Greece, vol. 1, Short Oxford History of Europe, 2000 (trans. Spanish 2001, Polish 2002); (ed jtly) Greek Historical Inscriptions 403–323 BC, 2003; (ed) Studies in Ancient Greek and Roman Society, 2004; Greek History, 2004 (trans. Japanese 2011), 2nd edn 2014; (ed) The Old Oligarch, 2nd edn 2004; (ed jtly) Mediterranean Urbanization 800–600 BC, 2005; (ed jtly) Poverty in the Roman World, 2006; (ed jtly) Rethinking Revolutions through Classical Greece, 2006; (ed jtly) Art's Agency and Art History, 2007; (ed jtly) Classical Archaeology, 2007, 2nd edn 2012; (ed) Debating the Athenian Cultural Revolution: art, literature, philosophy and politics 430–380 BC, 2007; Athens and Athenian Democracy, 2010; The History Written on the Classical Greek Body, 2011; Athenian Democracy, 2014; numerous articles in learned jls. *Address:* King's College, Cambridge CB2 1ST. *E:* ro225@cam.ac.uk.

OSBORNE, Roy Paul; HM Diplomatic Service, retired; *b* 13 July 1951; *s* of Gilbert William Osborne and Jean Mary Osborne; *m* 1977, Vivienne Claire Gentry; two *d.* *Educ:* St Christopher's Junior Sch., Cowley; Magdalen Coll. Sch., Oxford. Entered FCO, 1970; served Oslo, Islamabad and Rome; FCO, 1981–85, Asst Private Sec. to Minister of State, 1983–85; Second Sec., Commercial/Aid, later First Sec., Head of Chancery and Consul, Yaoundé, 1985–89; First Sec., Press and Inf., Madrid, 1989–93; Section Head, Drugs and Internat. Crime, FCO, 1993–97; Ambassador to Nicaragua, 1997–2000; Dep. Hd, Overseas Territories Dept, 2001–04; Dir, Trade and Investment, Berne, 2005–09. *Recreations:* birdwatching, wild life conservation, gardening, tennis, travel. *Address:* Pear Tree Farm, Over Stowey, Som TA5 1JB. *T:* (01278) 734604.

OSBORNE, Sandra Currie; *b* 23 Feb. 1956; *d* of Thomas Clark and Isabella Clark; *m* 1982, Alastair Osborne; two *d.* *Educ:* Camphill Sen. Secondary Sch., Paisley; Anniesland Coll.; Jordanhill Coll.; Strathclyde Univ. (MSc). Community Worker, Glasgow; Women's Aid. Mem. (Lab), S Ayrshire Council, 1991–97. MP (Lab) Ayr, 1997–2005, Ayr, Carrick and Cumnock, 2005–15; contested (Lab) same seat, 2015.

OSBORNE, Steven; classical pianist; *b* Broxburn, Scotland, 12 March 1971; *s* of Ian Osborne and Jean Osborne (*née* McNeil); *m* 2004, Jean Johnson. *Educ:* St Mary's Music Sch., Edinburgh; Univ. of Manchester (MusB 1st cl. Hons 1991); Royal Northern Coll. of Music (GRNCM 1992; Postgrad. Dip. 1993; MusM 1994). Orchestral collaborations include: CBSO, NHK Symphony Orch., BBC SO, BBC Scottish SO, Scottish Chamber Orch., Munich Philharmonic, Berlin SO, Australian Chamber Orch.; performances at venues including: Carnegie Hall, Kennedy Center, Suntory Hall, Philharmonie Berlin, Concertgebouw Amsterdam, Royal Albert Hall, Wigmore Hall. Recordings include works by Debussy, Rachmaninov, Beethoven, Alkan, Britten, Tippett, Messiaen, Shostakovich, Liszt and Kapustin. Clara Haskil Prize, 1991; (jtly) First Prize, Naumburg Internat. Piano Competition, 1997; Best Concerto Recording (Britten), Gramophone Awards, 2009; Best Instrumental Recording (Mussorgsky/Prokofiev), Gramophone Awards, 2013; Instrumentalist of the Year, Royal Philharmonic Soc. Awards, 2013. *Recreations:* hill walking, tennis, pool, reading, jazz. *Address:* c/o Sulivan Sweetland, 1 Hillgate Place, Balham Hill, SW12 9ER. *T:* (020) 8772 3470. *E:* es@sulivansweetland.co.uk.

OSBORNE, Susan Edna, CBE 2005; independent management and nursing consultant, since 2009; *b* 7 Dec. 1952; *d* of late John Gilbertson Osborne and Edna Joan Osborne (*née* Boughen). *Educ:* Dame Alice Harpur Sch. for Girls, Bedford; University Coll. Hosp. (SRN 1974); Queen Charlotte's Hosp. for Women (SCM 1976); London Univ. (DipN); South Bank Univ. (MSc); King's Coll. London (MSc). Staff Nurse, Orthopaedic/Surgery, UCH, 1974–75; pupil midwife, Queen Charlotte's Hosp., 1975–76; Staff Nurse, Medicine, Radcliffe Infirmary, 1976–77; Night Sister, UCH, 1977–78; Sister, Intensive Therapy Unit, then Nursing Officer, Whittington Hosp., London, 1979–83; Sen. Nurse, Central Middx Hosp., 1983–86; Dep. Dir, Nursing Service, 1986–87, Acute Service Manager, 1987–89, Homerton Hosp.; Actg Regl Nurse, 1989–90, NHS Trust Develt Officer, 1990–91, NE Thames RHA; Chief Exec., Royal London Homeopathic Hosp. NHS Trust, 1991–94; mgt and nursing consultant, 1994–98; Dir, Nursing and Quality, Luton & Dunstable Hosp. NHS Trust, 1998–2000; Dir of Nursing Services, St Mary's NHS Trust, 2000–07; Dir of Nursing, Imperial Coll. Healthcare NHS Trust, 2007–08; Chief Nurse, NHS E of England, 2008–09. Non-exec. Dir, Homerton Univ. Hosp. NHS Foundn Trust, 2014–. Chm., Safe Staffing Alliance, 2014–15. Trustee, Cavell Nurses' Trust (formerly NurseAid), 2010–. *Publications:* numerous contribs to nursing and health services jls, incl. Jl Advanced Nursing, Nursing Times, Jl Nursing Mgt, Health Services Jl. *Recreations:* general socialising, theatre, the Archers, cats, golf, enjoying life.

OSBORNE, Trevor, FRICS; Chairman, Trevor Osborne Property Group Ltd, since 1973; *b* 7 July 1943; *s* of Alfred Osborne and Annie Edmondson; *m* 1st, 1969, Pamela Ann Stephenson (marr. diss. 1998); one *s* one *d*; 2nd, 2003, Barbara Jane Fitzpatrick (marr. diss. 2014). *Educ:* Sunbury Grammar School. South Area Estate Manager, Middx County Council, 1960–65; Partner, A. P. C., 1966–67; Principal, Private Property Interests, 1967–73; Chm., 1973–93, Chief Exec., 1981–93, Speyhawk plc; Chairman: St George, 1985–96; Hawk Development Management, 1992–98; Lucknam Park Ltd, 1991–95; Building & Property Management Services, 1993–96; non-exec. Dir, Redland, 1989–92. Pres., British Property Fedn, 1991–92 (Mem. Council, 1985–92); BPF Vis. Fellow, Land Mgt, Reading Univ., 1987–90; Vis. Fellow, Architecture and Planning, Oxford Brookes Univ., 2003– (Mem. Court, 2008–14). Founder Mem. and Chm., POW Urban Villages Forum, 1992–99; Member: Royal Opera House Devlt Bd, 1987–94 (Chm., ROH Development Ltd, 1994); Council of Advrs, Prince of Wales Inst. of Architecture (Trustee, 1991–93); Council, City Property Assoc., 1987–94; Royal Fine Art Commn, 1994–99 (Trustee, 2003–); Council Mem., Georgian Group, 2002–09; Chm., Adv. Bd, SE Excellence, 2006–09. Governor: Bournemouth Univ. Business Sch., 2008–11; Bath Spa Univ., 2013–. Formerly Mem., Wokingham DC (Leader, 1980–82); Trustee, Wokingham Cons. Assoc., 1982–91. Pres., Windsor Arts Centre; Chm., St Sebastian's Playing Field Trust; Director: London First, 1992–95; Buxton Fest., 2004–14; Bath Mozartfest Ltd, 2012–; Trustee, Holbourne Mus. Trust Co., 2008–14. Freeman, City of London; Liveryman, Chartered Surveyors' Co. Fellow, Duke of Edinburgh Award World Fellowship; FRSA. *Recreations:* travel, walking, art, theatre, opera, tennis. *Address:* Trevor Osborne Property Group Ltd, Rectory Lodge, Combe Hay, Bath BA2 7EG. *Clubs:* Athenæum, Arts.

OSBOURNE, Maj. Gen. Edward Alexander S.; *see* Smyth-Osborne.

OSEI, Isaac; MP (New Patriotic Party), Subin Constituency, Ghana, since 2009; *b* 29 March 1951; *s* of late Nana Osei Nkwantabisa I and of Eunice Rosina Osei; *m* 1980, Marian Fofo; two *s* two *d.* *Educ:* Achimota Sch.; Univ. of Ghana (BSc Hons Econs); Center for Devolt Econs, Williams Coll., Mass (MA Devolt Econs). Asst Econ. Planning Officer, Min. of Finance, Ghana, 1973–77; Chief, Commercial Ops, 1977–81, Projects, R&D, 1981–82, Ghana Tourist Develt Co.; Managing Consultant, Ghanexim Econ. Consultants, 1982–2000; High Comr for Ghana in UK, and Ambassador to Ireland, 2001–06; Chief Exec., Ghana Cocoa Bd, 2006–08. Chair, Bd of Govs, Commonwealth Secretariat, 2002–04. Director: E. K. Osei & Co. (Civil Eng. and Gen. Bldg Contractors), 1982–95; Kas Products Ltd (Quarry Masters), 1982–99; Intravenous Infusions Ltd, 1988– (Man. Dir, 1999–2001; Chm., 2007–). *Recreations:* from a distance, football and American football, reading. *Address:* Parliament House, Accra, Ghana. *E:* ikeosei@email.com.

OSGERBY, Jay, OBE 2013; RDI 2007; designer; Founding Director: Barber & Osgerby Ltd, since 1996; Universal Design Studio Ltd, since 2001; Map Project Office Ltd, since 2012; *b* Oxford, 23 Oct. 1969; *s* of Paul Osgerby and Wendy Osgerby (*née* Hickman); *m* 2000, Helen Louise Smith; one *s* two *d.* *Educ:* Ravensbourne Coll. (BA 1st cl. Hons Furniture and Product Design; Fellow, 2013); Royal Coll. of Art (MA Arch.). MCSD 2005. Tutor: Oxford Brookes Univ., 1993–97; Ravensbourne Coll., 1996–2000. Mem. Jury, workshop/conf., 2003, and Dip. and Masters course, Ecole cantonale d'art de Lausanne. Dir, workshop, Vitra Design Mus., 2004. Vis. Tutor and Ext. Examiner, RCA, 2008–12. Clients include: Vitra, B&B Italia, Knoll, Louis Vuitton, Flos, Established & Sons, Venini, Isokon and Cappellini; *commissions* include: furniture for De La Warr Pavilion, Bexhill-on-Sea, RIBA, Portsmouth Cathedral; torches for London 2012 Olympic and Paralympic Games; design of £2 coin for Royal Mint of London Underground. *Exhibitions* at: V&A; Sotheby's; Haunch of Venison, London; Design Miami/Basel; MOMA, NY; Internat. Furniture Fair, NY; Haute Definition, Paris; Musée de la Mode et du Textil, Paris; Design Mus.; Crafts Council; *work in permanent collections*: V&A; Metropolitan Mus. of Art, NY; Design Mus.; Art Inst. of Chicago; Indianopolis Mus. of Art. FRSA 2005. Hon. DA Oxford Brookes, 2012. Best New Designer, ICFF, NY, 1998; Jerwood Applied Arts Prize (jtly), Jerwood Foundn, 2004; Designer of the Future, Design Miami/Basel, 2006; Designer of Year, Maison & Objet, 2013. *Address:* Barber & Osgerby, 37–42 Charlotte Road, EC2A 3PG. *T:* (020) 7033 3884, *Fax:* (020) 7033 3882. *E:* mail@barberosgerby.com.

O'SHAUGHNESSY, family name of **Baron O'Shaughnessy**.

O'SHAUGHNESSY, Baron *cr* 2015 (Life Peer), of Maidenhead in the Royal County of Berkshire; **James Richard O'Shaughnessy;** Managing Director, Floreat Education, since 2013; *b* Taplow, Bucks, 26 March 1976; *s* of Michael O'Shaughnessy and Veronica O'Shaughnessy; *m* 2005, Lucy Sheppard; one *s* two *d.* *Educ:* Wellington Coll.; St Hugh's Coll., Oxford (BA PPE 1998; MA). Special Advr, Conservative Res. Dept, 2001–03; Hd, Res., LLM Communications, 2003–04; Dep. Dir, Policy Exchange, 2004–07; Dir, Policy and Res., Conservative Party, 2007–10; Dir, Policy, Prime Minister's Office, 2010–11. Gp Hd of Strategy, Wellington Coll., 2012–14; Chief Policy Advr, Portland Communications, 2012–; Advr, Character Lab., USA, 2014–. Dir, Mayforth Consulting, 2012–. Chm., Internat. Positive Educn Network, 2014–. Vis. Fellow, Policy Exchange, 2012–. Hon. Sen. Res. Fellow, Sch. of Educn, Univ. of Birmingham, 2012–. Chm. Govs, Garratt Park Sch., 2005–07; Gov., Lena Gardens Sch., 2013–. *Publications:* More Good School Places (with Charlotte Leslie), 2005; (ed) The Leadership Effect: can headteachers make a difference, 2007; Competition Meets Collaboration: helping school chains address England's long tail of educational failure, 2012. *Recreations:* family, reading, football, AFC Wimbledon. *E:* james@oshaughnessy.co.uk. *Club:* Black's.

O'SHEA, Colette; Managing Director, London Portfolio, Land Securities Group plc, since 2014; *b* Essex, 1 April 1968; *d* of Bernard O'Shea and Teresa O'Shea. *Educ:* Univ. of Reading (BSc 1989). FRICS 2012. Hd, Estates, Mercers' Co., 1999–2003; Develt Manager, 2003–08, Hd, Develt, London Portfolio, 2008–14, Land Securities Group plc. Non-exec. Dir, Genesis Housing Assoc., 2011–. Pres., British Council for Offices, 2014–15. *Recreations:* walking, running, cycling, design. *Address:* Land Securities Group plc, 5 Strand, WC2N 5AF. *T:* 07802 801569. *E:* colette.oshea@landsecurities.com.

O'SHEA, Michael Kent; Director, Export Control and Non-Proliferation, Department of Trade and Industry, 2002–04; *b* 12 March 1951; *s* of Donovan Henry Victor and Joan O'Shea; *m* 1988, Linda Beata Szpala (*d* 2005). *Educ:* Bristol Grammar Sch.; Corpus Christi Coll., Cambridge (BA 1st Cl. Hons History). Department of Trade and Industry, 1973–2004: Under Sec., Finance and Resource Mgt, 1992–96; Dir, Engrg Automotive and Metals, 1996–98; Dir, Engrg Industries, 1998–2002. *Recreations:* owning Theo's Charm, watching National Hunt racing and cricket, playing bridge, listening to Wagner, visiting Italy, walking, cooking, drinking good beer and wine. *Club:* Gloucestershire CC.

O'SHEA, Prof. Michael Roland, PhD; Professor of Neuroscience and Co-Director, Centre for Computational Neuroscience and Robotics (formerly Director, BBSRC Sussex Centre for Neuroscience), University of Sussex, since 1991; *b* 5 April 1947; *s* of Capt. Jack Arthur O'Shea and Ellen O'Shea (*née* Hughes); *m* 1977, Barbara Moore (marr. diss. 1991); (one *d* decd). *Educ:* Forest Hill Sch., London; Univ. of Leicester (BSc 1st Cl. Hons Biol Scis 1968); Univ. of Southampton (PhD Neurobiol. 1971). University of California, Berkeley: NATO Fellow, 1971–73; NIH Fellow, 1973–75; SRC Fellow, Univ. of Cambridge, 1975–77; Asst Prof., Univ. of Southern Calif., LA, 1977–79; Associate Prof., Brain Research Inst., Univ. of Chicago, 1979–85; Professor of: Neurobiol., Univ. of Geneva, 1985–88; Molecular Cell Biol., RHBNC, Univ. of London, 1988–91. *Publications:* The Brain: a very short introduction, 2005; numerous papers on neuroscience in learned jls. *Recreations:* classical music, mountaineering, modern poetry, triathlons, restoration of classic Lotus. *Address:* 29 Eldred Avenue, Brighton BN1 5EB. *T:* (01273) 678508; Sussex Neuroscience, School of Biological Sciences, University of Sussex, Brighton BN1 9QG.

O'SHEA, Sir Timothy (Michael Martin), Kt 2008; PhD; Principal and Vice-Chancellor, and Professor of Informatics and Education, University of Edinburgh, since 2002; *b* 28 March 1949; *s* of John Patrick O'Shea and Elisabeth Hedwig Oberhof; *m* 1982, Prof. Eileen Scanlon; two *s* two *d.* *Educ:* Royal Liberty Sch., Havering; Sussex Univ. (BSc); Leeds Univ. (PhD). Postgrad. res., Univs of Texas at Austin and Edinburgh; Open University: founder, Computers and Learning Res. Gp, 1978; Lectr, 1978–82, Sen. Lectr, 1983–87, Inst. of Educnl Technol.; Prof. of IT and Educn, 1987–97; Pro-Vice-Chancellor for QA and Res., 1994–97; Vis. Prof. of Computer Supported Collaborative Learning, 1998–2001; Master of Birkbeck Coll., and Prof. of Inf. and Communication Technologies, 1998–2002, Pro-Vice-Chancellor, 2001–02, Union Laurel, 2002, Fellow, Birkbeck Coll., 2003, Univ. of London. Vis. Scientist, Xerox PARC Calif, and Vis. Schol., Univ. of Calif, Berkeley, 1986–87. Chm., NATO prog. on Advanced Educnl Technol., 1988–90. Member: Bd, China-Britain Business Council, 2008–10; Strategy Commn, German Govt Exzellenzinitiative, 2009–13; Dep. Pres., French Govt Initiatives d'Excellence en Formations Innovantes, 2011–12. Chairman: London Metropolitan Network Ltd, 1999–2002; HERO Ltd, 2000–02; Scottish Inst. for Enterprise, 2009–; Mem. Bd, Scottish Enterprise, 2006–10 (Chm., Proof of Concept Stakeholders, 2004–10). Vice Convener, Univs Scotland, 2009–12 (Convener, Res. and Commercialisation Cttee, 2003–07). Director: Edexcel Foundn, 1998–2001 (Mem., Exec. Cttee, 1998–2001); Univs and Colls Staff Develt Agency, 1999–2000. Chm., Inf. Systems Sector Gp, CVCP, 1999. Member: HEFCE Cttee on Equal Opportunities, Access and Lifelong Learning, 1998; JISC, 2000–13 (Chm., 2008–13); Bd, UUK, 2001–04; Bd, British Council, 2003–09; Univ. Adv. Bd, Coursera, 2013–; Univ. Council, All-Party Parly Univ. Gp, 2013–. Convenor, Further and Higher Educn Sector Oversight Bd for Info. and Technol., Scottish Govt, 2013–. Pres., Psychol. Sect., BAAS, 1991–92; Chm., Artificial Intelligence Soc., 1979–82. Trustee, Eduserv, 1999–2000; Chm., Newbattle Abbey Coll. Trust, 2012–. Curator, Sch. of Advanced Study, London Univ., 1999–2002; Provost, Gresham Coll., 2000–02; Mem. Council, RCM, 2001; Governor: City Lit. Inst., 1998–2000; SOAS, 1998–2002; St George's Med. Sch.,

London Univ., 2000–02; Mem. Governing Council, Confucius Inst. HQ, 2007–. Chm., Bd of Dirs, Edinburgh Fest. Fringe, 2012–. Fellow, European Co-ordinating Cttee for Artificial Intelligence, 1999; FRSE 2004; FAcSS (AcSS 2009). Presenter and author, The Learning Machine (TV series), 1985. DUniv: Heriot-Watt, 2008; Strathclyde, 2011; Hon. LLD McGill, 2012; Hon. Dr St Petersburg Univ. of Humanities and Social Scis, 2013. *Publications:* include: Self-improving teaching systems, 1979; (jtly) Learning and Teaching with Computers, 1983; (jtly) Artificial Intelligence: tools, techniques and applications, 1984; (ed) Advances in Artificial Intelligence, 1985; (ed jtly) Intelligent Knowledge-based Systems: an introduction, 1987; (ed jtly) Educational Computing, 1987; (ed jtly) New Directions in Educnl Technology, 1992; contrib. learned jls. *Address:* University of Edinburgh, Old College, South Bridge, Edinburgh EH8 9YL.

OSHEROFF, Prof. Douglas Dean, PhD; Professor of Physics and Applied Physics, 1987, now Emeritus, and J. G. Jackson and C. J. Wood Professor of Physics, 1992, now Emeritus, Stanford University (Chairman, Department of Physics, 1993–96 and 2001–04); *b* 1 Aug. 1945; *s* of William and Bessie Anne Osheroff; *m* 1970, Phyllis Shih-Kiang Liu. *Educ:* California Inst. of Technology (BSc Physics 1967); Cornell Univ. (PhD Physics 1973). AT&T Bell Laboratories: Mem., technical staff, 1972–81; Hd, Solid State and Low Temp. Physics Res., 1981–87. MNAS, 1987; Mem., Amer. Acad. Arts and Scis, 1982. Fellow, APS. Sir Francis Simon Meml Award, 1976; Oliver E. Buckley Condensed Matter Physics Prize, 1981; Macarthur Prize Fellow Award, 1981; (jtly) Nobel Prize for Physics, 1996. *Publications:* contrib. chapters in books; numerous papers and articles in jls incl. Phys Rev., Phys Rev. Letters, Jl Low Temp. Phys. *Recreations:* photography, hiking, travel, music. *Address:* Department of Physics, Stanford University, Stanford, CA 94305–4060, USA.

OSIKENA, Josephine Onotseogboya; Director, Foreign Policy Centre, since 2010; *b* South Lambeth, London, 8 Feb. 1974; *d* of late Francis D. Osikena and Maria O. Osikena (*née* Odiodio). *Educ:* Lilian Baylis Sch., Kennington; London Guildhall Univ. (BA Hons French and Econs 1998); Sch. of Oriental and African Studies, Univ. of London (MSc Develt Studies 1999). British Council Lang. Asst, Academie de Créteil, France, 1996–97; various short-term co-ordinator roles including: BBC, 2000; Cendent Internat. Assignment Services, 2000–02; Land Securities Trillium, 2002–03; DEFRA, 2003; DfT, 2003; Cabinet Office, 2004; Healthcare Commn, 2004; Women's Nat. Commn, 2004; London Bor. of Tower Hamlets, 2005; Prog. Manager, 2005–08, Prog. Dir, 2008–10, Democracy and Internat. Develt, Foreign Policy Centre. French Interpreter (pt-time volunteer), Camden CAB, 2004–09. Mem., Clapham Soc., 2012–. *Publications:* (contrib.) US Strategy in Africa: AFRICOM, terrorism and security challenges, 2010; reports for Foreign Policy Centre. *Recreations:* international affairs, particularly socio-economic and political development across Africa and throughout the global African diaspora; attending jazz concerts and festivals, participating in local history lectures and walks, visiting public libraries, jogging, swimming, dancing (particularly salsa). *Address:* Foreign Policy Centre, Unit 1.9, 1st Floor, The Foundry, 17 Oval Way, Vauxhall, SE11 5RR. *T:* (020) 3752 5850/1. *E:* josephine.osikena@fpc.org.uk.

OSLER, Douglas Alexander, CB 2002; HM Senior Chief Inspector of Education (formerly of Schools), Scottish Executive (formerly Scottish Office), 1996–2002; *b* 11 Oct. 1942; *s* of Alexander Osler and Jane Brown; *m* 1973, Wendy Cochrane; one *s* one *d*. *Educ:* Univ. of Edinburgh (MA Hons Hist.); Moray House Coll. of Educn (Teaching Cert.). Teacher, Liberton High Sch., Edinburgh, 1965; Principal Teacher, History, Dunfermline High Sch., 1969; HM Inspector, Chief Inspector, Depute Sen. Chief Inspector of Schools, Scottish Office, 1974–95. Interim Scottish Prisons Complaints Comr, 2003; Reviewer, Parole Bd of Scotland, 2004; Ind. Reviewer, Scottish Courts Service, 2005. Chm., Inquiry into Child Abuse at Cabin Hill Sch., Belfast, 2004–05; Ind. Chm., Scottish Cons. Party Policy Adv. Gp, 2006; Chm. Comrs, S Eastern Educn and Liby Bd, NI, 2006–10; Ambassador, Scottish Adv. Cttee, Skillforce, 2014– (Vice-Chm., 2010–13). Chm., Assessment Bd, Caritas Awards, 2012–14. Chm., Royal Blind and Scottish War Blinded, 2008–14. ESU Fellowship, 1966; Internat. Leadership Fellowship, USA, 1989; Vis. Prof., Strathclyde Univ., 2003–05. Trustee, Scottish Schools Pipes and Drums Trust, 2014–. Book reviewer, Scotsman, 2011–15. KSG 2001. *Recreations:* golf, gardening, reading, Rotary International.

OSMOND, Prof. Charles Barry, PhD; FAA; FRS 1984; ML; Professor of Plant Science, University of Wollongong, 2011–13, now Hon. Visiting Professor; President and Executive Director, Biosphere 2 Center, Columbia University, 2001–03; Visiting Fellow, School of Biochemistry and Molecular Biology, Australian National University, since 2004; *b* 20 Sept. 1939; *s* of Edmund Charles Osmond and Joyce Daphne (*née* Krauss); *m* 1st, 1962, Suzanne Alice Ward; one *s* one *d* (and two *s* decd); 2nd, 1983, Ulla Maria Cornelia Gauhl (*née* Büchen). *Educ:* Morisset Central Sch.; Wyong High Sch.; Univ. of New England, Armidale (University Medal in Botany, 1961; BSc 1961, MSc 1963); Univ. of Adelaide (PhD 1965). FAA 1978. Post-doctoral Res. Associate, Botanical Sciences Dept, Univ. of Calif, LA, 1965; Royal Commn for Exhibn of 1851 and CSIRO Fellow, Botany Sch., Cambridge Univ., 1966; successively Res. Fellow, Fellow and Sen. Fellow, Dept of Environmental Biol., ANU, Canberra, 1967–78, Prof. of Biology, 1978–87; Exec. Dir, Biol Sciences Center, Desert Res. Inst., Reno, 1982–86; Arts and Scis Prof., Duke Univ., USA, 1987–91; Prof., 1991–2001, and Dir, 1991–98, Res. Sch. of Biol Scis, ANU, Canberra. Fulbright Sen. Scholar, Univ. of Calif, Santa Cruz, 1973–74; Carnegie Instn Fellow (Plant Biol.), Stanford, 1973–74; Richard Mereton Guest Prof., Technical Univ., Munich, 1974; Overseas Fellow, Churchill Coll., Cambridge, 1980. Mem., German Nat. Acad. Leopoldina, 2001. Goldacre Award, Aust. Soc. of Plant Physiologists, 1972; Edgeworth David Medal, Royal Soc. of NSW, 1974; Forschungspreis, Alexander von Humboldt Foundn, 1997; Clarke Medal, Royal Soc. of NSW, 1998. *Publications:* (ed jtly) Photosynthesis and Photorespiration, 1971; (ed jtly) Photorespiration in Marine Plants, 1976; (jtly) Physiological Processes in Plant Ecology, 1980; (ed jtly) Encyclopedia of Plant Physiology, Vols 12 A-D, Physiological Plant Ecology, 1981–83; (ed jtly) Photoinhibition, 1987; (ed jtly) New Vistas in Measurement of Photosynthesis, 1989; (ed jtly) Plant Biology of the Basin and Range, 1990; (ed jtly) Water and Life, 1992; (ed jtly) Nurturing Creativity in Research, 1997; articles on plant metabolic biology and its ecological implications in learned jls. *Recreation:* biological research. *Address:* PO Box 3252, Weston Creek, ACT 2611, Australia. *T:* (2) 62871487.

OSMOND, Richard George; Secretary, The Post Office, 1995–97; *b* 22 Jan. 1947; *s* of late Lt-Col Clifford George Osmond, OBE, RE and Florence Rose Osmond (*née* Baker). *Educ:* Merchant Taylors' Sch. (Exhibnr); Univ. of Exeter. FCIPD (FIPD 1988). Post Office, 1967–97: Dep. Sec., 1985; Controller, Corporate Personnel, 1986; Head of Community Affairs, 1989; Dir, Group Personnel, 1993. Dir, Headteachers into Industry, 1990–96; Mem., Adv. Bd, Centre for Educn and Industry, Univ. of Warwick, 1992–98, Hon. Associate Fellow, 1998–2001; Chm., Policy Adv. Cttee, Sch. Curriculum and Industry Partnership, 1995–97. Vis. Fellow, Inst. of Educn, London Univ., 1997–99. Diocesan Gov., Univ. of Winchester (formerly King Alfred's Coll., Winchester), 1999–2008; Chm. of Governors, Peter Symonds Coll., Winchester, 2000–04. Vice Pres., ACRE, 1997–2008. FRSA 1990 (Member: Early Learning Study, 1993–94; Educn Adv. Gp, 1996–2001). Member, Council: Friends of Cathedral Music, 1977–83, 2003–09; L'Amitié Henri Bosco, 2010–14. Freeman, City of London, 1989; Liveryman, Musicians' Co., 1990–. *Recreations:* church music, bird watching, bridge. *Address:* 10 Hazel Grove, Winchester SO22 4PQ. *T:* (01962) 850818. *Club:* Athenæum.

OSMOTHERLY, Sir Edward (Benjamin Crofton), Kt 2002; CB 1992; Clerk Adviser, European Scrutiny Committee, House of Commons, 2003–10; *b* 1 Aug. 1942; *s* of Crofton and Elsie Osmotherly; *m* 1970, Valerie (*née* Mustill); one *d* one *s*. *Educ:* East Ham Grammar School; Fitzwilliam College, Cambridge (MA). Asst Principal, Ministry of Housing and Local Govt, 1963–68 (Private Sec. to Parly Sec., 1966–67, to Minister of State, 1967–68); Principal, 1968–76; Harkness Fellow, 1972–73 (Guest Scholar, Brookings Instn, Washington DC; Exec. Fellow, Univ. of California at Berkeley); Asst Sec., DoE, 1976–79; seconded to British Railways Bd, 1979; Head of Machinery of Govt Div., CSD, 1980–81; Under Sec. (Railways), Dept of Transport, 1982–85; Under Sec., Dir of Personnel, Management and Training, Depts of the Environment and of Transport, 1985–89; Dep. Sec., Public Transport and Res. Dept, 1989–92, Prin. Establishment and Finance Officer, 1992–93, Dept of Transport; Local Govt Ombudsman, 1993–2001; Chm., Commn for Local Admin in England, 1994–2001; Mem., Adjudication Panel for England, 2002–03. Chm., Ind. Review of Govt Business Statistics, 1996. Chm., British and Irish Ombudsman Assoc., 1998–2001. *Recreation:* reading.

OSÓRIO, Antonio Mota de Sousa H.; *see* Horta-Osório.

OSOWSKA, Francesca, OBE 2015; Director, Scotland Office, since 2015; *b* Whitehaven, Cumbria, 25 July 1970; *d* of Thomas Osowski and Barbara Osowska (*née* Matthews, later Davis). *Educ:* St Bees Sch.; Churchill Coll., Cambridge (BA Econs 1992); Coll. of Europe, Bruges (MSc Eur. Econs). Govt economist, Employment Dept Gp, later DfEE, 1993–2001; Scottish Executive, later Scottish Government: Sen. Civil Servant, 2001–07; Principal Private Sec. to the First Minister of Scotland, 2007–09; Director: Culture, Ext. Affairs and Tourism, 2009–10; Housing, Regeneration and Commonwealth Games, 2011–12; Commonwealth Games and Sport, 2013–14. *Recreation:* triathlon (particularly in hot and sunny climes). *Address:* Scotland Office, 1 Melville Crescent, Edinburgh EH3 7HW. *T:* (0131) 244 9022. *E:* francesca.osowska@scotlandoffice.gsi.gov.uk. *Club:* Edinburgh Triathletes.

OST, Michael Stuart; Group Chief Executive, Coats Viyella plc, 1997–99; *b* 29 Oct. 1944; *s* of Peter Stuart Ost and Betty Constance Ost; *m* 1977, Judith Ann Latham; one *s*. *Educ:* Scarborough High Sch. for Boys; London School of Economics (BSc Econ). Univ. Apprentice, Rolls-Royce Aero Engines Ltd, 1963–67; Singer Co.: Corporate Auditor, NY, 1968–70; Financial Controller, Thailand, 1970–72; Mktg Dir, Brazil, 1972–75; Gen. Manager, Turkey, 1975–77; Vice Pres., Far East, Getz Corp., 1978–82; President: Singer Brazil, 1982–83; Latin America Div., Singer, 1983–84; Exec. Vice Pres., Carrier International, 1984–85; Pres., ETO Carrier, 1985–87; Group Chief Executive, McKechnie plc, 1987–97. Non-executive Director: Lex Service plc, 1993–2002; Porvair plc, 1999; Henlys Group plc, 2002 (Chm., 2003–04); non-exec. Dep. Chm., MG plc, 1999–2000. Chm., Pension Trustees, RAC plc, 2003–05. FRSA 1993; CCMI (CIMgt 1994). *Recreations:* golf, bridge, reading. *Clubs:* Savile, Royal Automobile; Landings (Savannah, USA); Worplesdon Golf.

OSTERLEY, Robin Marius; Chief Executive, Supporters Direct, since 2014; *b* 22 Feb. 1957; *s* of late Allan Osterley and of Barbara Dora Osterley; *m* Karen; two *s* two *d*. *Educ:* Monkton Combe Sch.; St Edmund Hall, Oxford (BA Hons 1979). Sen. Mktg Manager, ICL, 1982–93; Mktg Manager, Orch. of St John's, Smith Square, 1994; Man. Dir, Cala Records Ltd, 1994–96; Chief Exec., Making Music (formerly The National Federation of Music Societies), 1997–2013. Member: Exec. Cttee, Music Educn Council, 2001–13; Nat. Music Council, 2001–13 (Chm., 2001–09); Music Manifesto Partnerships and Advocacy Gp, 2009–11; Chair, Special Interest Gp for Arts and Heritage, 2008–13, Dir, 2011–13, ACEVO, 2008–; Dir, Voluntary Arts, 2011–13. Chm., Superact! CIC, 2014. Music Director: Stevenage Choral Soc., 2001–; Alyth Choral Soc., 2014–. Chm. Govs, Hunsdon JMI Sch., 2005–; Parent Gov. Rep., Oversight and Scrutiny Cttee, Herts CC, 2013–. *Recreations:* singing, conducting, bad piano playing, running slowly, never letting the grass grow under the feet. *E:* robinosterley@googlemail.com.

OSTLER, Catherine Emma, (Mrs Albert Read); Contributing Editor: Daily Mail, since 2011; Newsweek, since 2014; *d* of late John R. Ostler and of Patricia Ann Ostler; *m* 2003, Albert, *s* of Piers Paul Read, *qv*; one *s* two *d*. *Educ:* Cheltenham Ladies' Coll.; St Hilda's Coll., Oxford (BA English 1991; MA). Tatler, 1991–94, latterly Features Ed.; Features Writer, Mail on Sunday, 1994–96; Editor: Saturday Mag., Express, 1996–99; Times Weekend, 1999–2000; PeopleNews.com, 2000–01; ES Mag., 2002–09; Tatler, 2009–10. *Address:* Daily Mail, Northcliffe House, 2 Derry Street, W8 5TS.

OSTLER, Dr Nicholas David MacLachlan; Chairman, Foundation for Endangered Languages, since 1996; *b* Tunbridge Wells, Kent, 20 May 1952; *s* of Kenneth M. Ostler and Yvonne L. Ostler (*née* Jolly); *m* 1st, 1983, Olga M. Sarasti (marr. diss. 1988); one *d*; 2nd, 1997, Jane Dunn. *Educ:* Yardley Court Prep. Sch.; Tonbridge Sch., Kent; Balliol Coll., Oxford (BA Classics Mods, PPE 1975; MA 1987); Massachusetts Inst. of Technol. (PhD Linguistics 1979). Foreign Lectr, Toyama Univ., Japan, 1979–81; Consultant, Logica Ltd, 1982–83; Principal Consultant, Scicon Ltd, London, 1983–87; Sen. Consultant, Touche Ross Mgt Consultants, 1987–91; Dir, Linguacubun Ltd, 1991–2001; ind. author, 2001–. Res. Associate, SOAS, 2007–. Hon. Fellow (Linguistics), Lancaster Univ., 1999–; Academician, Russian Acad. Linguistics, 2004–. Ed., Ogmios, Foundn for Endangered Langs, 1995–2006. *Publications:* Empires of the World: a language history of the world, 2005; Ad Infinitum: a biography of Latin, 2007; The Last Lingua Franca: the rise and fall of world languages, 2010; contribs to Foundn for Endangered Langs procs. *Recreations:* whippets, using dead languages. *Address:* 129 High Street, Hungerford, Berks RG17 0DL. *T:* 07720 889319. *E:* nicholas@ostler.net.

OSTLERE, Dr Gordon; *see* Gordon, Richard.

OSTRIKER, Prof. Jeremiah Paul, PhD; Professor of Astronomy, Columbia University, since 2012; Treasurer, National Academy of Sciences, since 2008; Senior Researcher, Princeton University, since 2012; *b* 13 April 1937; *s* of Martin Ostriker and Jeanne (*née* Sumpf); *m* 1958, Alicia Suskin; one *s* two *d*. *Educ:* Harvard Univ. (AB Physics and Chem. 1959); Univ. of Chicago (PhD Astrophysics 1964). Postdoctoral Fellow, Univ. of Cambridge, 1964–65; Princeton University: Res. Associate and Lectr, 1965–66; Asst Prof., 1966–68; Associate Prof., 1968–71; Prof., Dept of Astrophysical Scis, 1971–2012; Chm., Dept of Astrophysical Scis, and Dir, Observatory, 1979–95; Charles A. Young Prof. of Astronomy, 1982–2002, Charles A. Young Professor Emeritus, 2012; Provost, 1995–2001; Dir, Princeton Inst. for Computational Sci. and Engrg, 2005–09; Plumian Prof. of Astronomy and Experimental Philosophy, Inst. of Astronomy, and Fellow of Clare Coll., Univ. of Cambridge, 2001–04. Mem., Editl Bd and Trustee, Princeton Univ. Press, 1982–84 and 1986. Trustee, 1997–2006, Hon. Trustee, 2007–, Amer. Mus. of Natural Hist. Mem., Amer. Philosophical Soc., 1994; Foreign Member: Royal Netherlands Acad. of Arts and Scis, 1999; Royal Soc., 2007. Hon. DSc Chicago, 1992. Henry Norris Russell Prize, AAS, 1980; Vainu Bappu Meml Award, INSA, 1993; Karl Schwarzschild Medal, Astronomische Ges., 1999; US Nat. Medal of Sci., 2000; Gold Medal for Astronomy, RAS, 2004; Catherine Wolfe Bruce Gold Medal, Astronomical Soc. of Pacific, 2011; James Craig Watson Medal, NAS, 2012; Open Science Champion of Change, The White House, 2013. *Publications:* Development of Large-Scale Structure in the Universe, 1991; (ed with J. N. Bahcall) Unsolved Problems in Astrophysics, 1997; (ed with A. Dekel) Formation of Structure in the Universe, 1999; (with S. Mitton) Heart of Darkness: unravelling the mysteries of the invisible universe, 2013; contribs to Astrophysical Jl and Nature on topics in theoretical astrophysics. *Recreations:* squash, bicycling, photography. *Address:* Princeton University, 109 Peyton Hall, Ivy Lane, Princeton, NJ 08544–1001, USA. *E:* ostriker@princeton.edu; Department of Astronomy, Columbia University, Mail Code 5246, 550 West 120th Street, New York, NY 10027, USA.

OSTROWSKI, Joan Lorraine; *see* Walley, J. L.

O'SULLIVAN, Alison Jane; Director, Children and Young People (formerly Children's Services), Kirklees Council, since 2006 (Director for Children and Adults, 2012–15); *b* 25 March 1955; *d* of Kenneth Attenborough and Hazel (*née* Wain, now Hart); *m* 1983, Patrick Joseph O'Sullivan; two *s*. *Educ:* John Port Comprehensive Sch., Etwall, Derbys; Univ. of Bradford (BA Hons (Applied Social Studies), CQSW, 1978); Huddersfield Poly. (DMS 1990). Bradford Social Services: social worker, Manningham area of Bradford, 1978–83; Team Manager, 1983–92; Sen. Manager, Children's Services, 1992–97; Assistant Director: Learning Disability, Physical Disability, and Sensory Impairment and Mental Health Services, 1997–99; Adult Services, 1999–2000; on secondment to Bradford AHA, as Jt Comr for Older People's Services, 2000–02; Dir of Social Services, Bradford CC, 2002–05. Pres., Assoc. of Dirs of Children's Services, 2015–April 2016 (Vice Pres., 2014–15). *Recreations:* building extensions, gardening, narrowboating, watching romantic comedies, ski-ing. *Address:* Kirklees Council, Civic Centre 3, High Street, Huddersfield HD1 2NF. *T:* (01484) 225242, *Fax:* (01484) 225237. *E:* alison.o'sullivan@kirklees.gov.uk.

O'SULLIVAN, David; Ambassador for the European Union to the United States of America, since 2014; *b* 1 March 1953; *s* of late Gerald and Philomena O'Sullivan; *m* 1984, Agnes O'Hare; one *s* one *d*. *Educ:* St Mary's Coll., Rathmines, Dublin; Trinity Coll. Dublin (MA 1975); Coll. of Europe, Bruges. Irish Diplomatic Service, 1977–79; entered European Commission, 1979: First Sec., Delegn to Tokyo, 1981–84; Mem., Cabinet of Comr Peter Sutherland, 1985–89; Hd, Educn and Trng Unit, 1989–93; Dep. Hd, Cabinet of Comr Padraig Flynn, 1993–96; Dir, Eur. Social Fund, 1996–99; Dir-Gen., Educn, Trng and Youth, Feb.–May 1999; Hd, Cabinet of Pres. Romano Prodi, 1999–2000; Sec.-Gen., 2000–05; Dir Gen. for Trade, 2005–10; Dir Gen. for External Relns, 2010; Chief Operating Officer, Eur. External Action Service, 2011–14. Vis. Prof., European Coll., Parma, 2013–. Hon. DPhil Dublin Inst. of Technol., 2005. Transatlantic Business Award, American Chamber of Commerce to EU, 2014. *Recreations:* tennis, music, cinema. *Address:* Delegation of the European Union to the United States of America, 2175 K Street NW, Washington, DC 20037, USA.

O'SULLIVAN, Michael Joseph, CMG 2008; Chief Executive, Cambridge International Examinations, since 2013; *b* 21 Dec. 1958; *s* of late Patrick Joseph O'Sullivan and of Mary Elizabeth O'Sullivan (*née* Herbert); *m* 1989, Moira Helen Grant; one *s* two *d*. *Educ:* Brasenose Coll., Oxford (BA Hons German and French); Wolfson Coll., Cambridge (MPhil Linguistics). VSO Teacher of English, Xiangtan, Hunan, China, 1982–84; joined British Council, 1985: E Europe and N Asia Dept, 1985–87; Asst Dir, China, 1987–90; UK planner, Corporate Affairs, 1991–93; Dir, S China (Hong Kong), 1993–95; Hd, Corporate Planning, 1995–97; Policy Dir, Asia Pacific, 1997–2000; Dir, China, 2000–05; Regl Dir, China, 2005–07; Sec. Gen., EU Chamber of Commerce, China, 2007–08; Dir, Cambridge Commonwealth Trust and Cambridge Overseas Trust, 2008–13. *Recreations:* cycling, travel, music, rowing. *Address:* Cambridge International Examinations, 1 Hills Road, Cambridge CB1 2EU.

O'SULLIVAN, His Honour Michael Neil; a Circuit Judge, 2004–13; *b* 5 Feb. 1943; *s* of Ernest George Patrick Sullivan (who changed family name to O'Sullivan by Deed Poll, 1967) and Dorothy Florence (*née* Piper); *m* 1972, Maria Colette Smith; one *s* two *d*. *Educ:* Beaumont Coll.; City of London Coll. Exporter, motor mechanic, asst works manager, advertiser, Co. Court Clerk and Trust Adminr, 1960–70; called to the Bar: Gray's Inn, 1970; King's Inns, Ireland, 1994. Asst Recorder, 1991–95, Recorder, 1995–2004. Member: Mental Health Tribunal, 2009–13; Parole Bd, 2010–. *Recreations:* Rugby Union (player, coach, club and internat. spectator), wood-turning, fly-fishing, reading and writing poetry, walking between interesting public houses. *Club:* Folkestone Rugby Football (Pres., 2008–14).

O'SULLIVAN, Prof. Patrick Edmund, OBE 1988; PhD; CEng; FInstE; Haden-Pilkington Professor of Environmental Design and Engineering, University College London, 1999–2002, now Emeritus; non-executive Director, Titon Holdings, 2002–15; *b* 28 March 1937; *s* of Daniel O'Sullivan and Margaret Cecilia (*née* Mansfield); *m* 1963, Diana Grimshaw; three *s* one *d*. *Educ:* Finchley Catholic Grammar Sch.; Leeds Univ. (BSc); Durham Univ. (PhD). FCIBSE 1975. University of Newcastle upon Tyne: DSIR Post-Doctoral Res. Fellow, 1963–64; Sen. Res. Fellow in Bldg Sci., 1964–66; Lectr, 1966–70; Sen. Lectr, 1970; Prof. of Architectural Sci., UWIST, 1970–89; Dean, Faculty of the Built Envmt, and Head, Bartlett Sch., UCL, 1989–99. Chm., Bldg Regulation Adv. Cttee, DETR, 2000–01. Chm., Friendly Trust, 2009–14. Hon. FRIBA; Hon. FCIBSE 2000. MIOA 1975. Gold Medal, RSH, 1999. *Publications:* Insulation and Fenestration, 1967; articles in learned jls. *Recreations:* swimming, riding, walking, theatre, bridge. *Club:* Farmers.

O'SULLIVAN, Patrick Henry Pearse, FCA; Chairman: Old Mutual, since 2010; ERS Syndicate Management Ltd, Lloyd's of London, since 2013; *b* 15 April 1949; *s* of Cornelius J. O'Sullivan and Marie Slowey; *m* 1974, Evelyn Holohan; two *s* one *d*. *Educ:* Trinity Coll., Dublin (BBS 1971); London Sch. of Econs (MSc Accounting and Finance 1975). FCA 1985. Arthur Andersen & Co., 1971–74; with Bank of America, working in Germany, San Francisco, LA, Miami and London, 1975–87; Gen. Manager, BA Futures Inc., London, 1987–88; Exec. Dir and Financial Controller, Goldman Sachs, 1988–89; Man. Dir, Internat. Financial Guaranty Insce Co., 1990–93; Hd, Internat. Banking and Structured Finance, 1994–96, Chief Operating Officer, 1996–97, Barclays/BZW; Chief Exec., Eagle Star Insce Co. Ltd, 1997–2002; Gp Finance Dir, 2002–07, Vice Chm. and Chief Growth Officer, 2007–09, Zurich Financial Services. Chairman: Farmers Gp Inc., 2007–09; Shareholder Exec., 2012–14; non-executive Director: Man Gp plc, 2007–13; Collins Stewart plc, 2007–09; COFRA Hldg AG, Switzerland, 2007–12; Bank of Ireland, 2009–15 (Dep. Gov., 2011–15). *Recreation:* golf. *Address:* Oak Gables, Daneshill, The Hockering, Woking, Surrey GU22 7HQ. *E:* patrick@o-sullivan.org; Old Mutual plc, 5th Floor, Millennium Bridge House, 2 Lambeth Hill, EC4V 4GG. *Clubs:* Royal Automobile, Mark's; Wisley.

O'SULLIVAN, Robert Michael; QC 2012; *b* Solihull, 9 April 1966; *s* of Dermot O'Sullivan and Valerie O'Sullivan (*née* Wetton). *Educ:* Dauntsey's Sch., Wilts; King's Coll. London (LLB; AKC). Called to the Bar, Lincoln's Inn, 1988; in practice as barrister, specialising in crime. *Recreations:* watching cricket, theatre. *Address:* 5 Paper Buildings, Temple, EC4Y 7HB. *T:* (020) 7583 6117. *Club:* MCC.

O'SULLIVAN, Ronnie; snooker player; *b* 5 Dec. 1975; *s* of Ronnie and Maria O'Sullivan. World Jun. Snooker Champion, Bangalore, 1991; turned professional, 1992; wins include: UK Championship, 1993 (youngest ever winner of a ranking event), 1997, 2001, 2007, 2014; British Open, 1994; Masters, 1995, 2005, 2007, 2009, 2014; Asian Classic, 1996; German Open, 1996; Regal Scottish Open, 1998, 2000; China Open, 1999, 2000; Regal Scottish Masters, 1998, 2000, 2002; Irish Masters, 2001, 2003, 2005, 2007; World Championship, 2001, 2004, 2008, 2012, 2013; Premier Snooker League, 1997, 2001, 2002, 2004, 2005, 2006, 2007, 2008, 2010; Welsh Open, 2004, 2005, 2014; Totesport Grand Prix, 2004; Shanghai Masters, 2009. Player of the Year and Fans' Player of the Year, World Snooker, 2014. *Publications:* Ronnie: the autobiography of Ronnie O'Sullivan, 2004; Running, 2013. *Address:* c/o Grove Leisure, 4 Redwing Court, Ashton Road, Romford RM3 8QQ.

O'SULLIVAN, Sally Angela; Chair, August Media, since 2005; *b* 26 July 1949; *d* of late Lorraine and Joan Connell; *m* 1st, 1973, Thaddeus O'Sullivan (marr. diss.); 2nd, 1980, Charles Martin Wilson, *qv* (marr. diss. 2001); one *s* one *d*. *Educ:* Ancaster House Sch.; Trinity Coll., Dublin (BA). Dep. Editor, Woman's World, 1977–78; Women's Editor: Daily Record, 1980; Sunday Standard, 1981; Editor, Options, 1982–88; Launch Editor, Country Homes & Interiors, 1986; Editor: She, 1989; Harpers & Queen, 1989–91; Editor-in-Chief: Good Housekeeping, 1991–95; Ideal Home, Homes & Ideas, Woman & Home, Homes & Gardens, Country Homes & Interiors, Beautiful Homes, Living, etc, 1996–98; Chief Exec., Cabal Communications, 1998–2003; Gp Editorial Dir, Highbury House Communications, 2003–05. Non-executive Director: London Transport, 1995–2000; Anglian Water, 1996–2001. Member: Broadcasting Standards Council, 1994–2003; Foresight Retail and Consumer Services Panel, 1999–2001. Dep. Chm., Elizabeth Finn Care, 2013– (Trustee, 2010–13). Hon. Fellow, Univ. of Central Lancashire, 2012. Magazine Editor of the Year, 1986 and 1994. *Recreations:* family, horses, farming.

O'SULLIVAN, (Thomas) Sean (Patrick); QC 2014; *b* Harrow, 19 Jan. 1974; *s* of Thomas and Christine O'Sullivan; *m* 2000, Samantha Goodhew; one *s* one *d*. *Educ:* Merchant Taylors' Sch., Northwood; Exeter Coll., Oxford (MA Mod. Hist.); City Univ. (CPE). Called to the Bar, Inner Temple, 1997; in practice as a barrister, specialising in commercial litigation, 4 Pump Court, 1997–. *Publications:* Civil Appeals, 2010, 2nd edn 2015. *Recreations:* tennis, golf, cricket, watching football. *Address:* 4 Pump Court, Temple, EC4Y 7AN. *T:* (020) 7842 5555. *Club:* Oxford and Cambridge.

O'SULLIVAN, Hon. Victoria; *see* Glendinning, Hon. Victoria.

O'SULLIVAN, Zoë Siobhan; QC 2015; *b* London, 10 Jan. 1968; *d* of T. R. O'Sullivan and Susan O'Sullivan; *m* 1999, Peter Thomas; three *s*. *Educ:* Lady Margaret Hall, Oxford (MA Hons English Lang. and Lit. 1991); City Univ., London (DipLaw 1992); Inns of Court Sch. of Law. Called to the Bar, Middle Temple, 1993; in practice as barrister, specialising in commercial law, 1994–. Associate, Westminster Abbey Inst., 2015–July 2016. *Recreations:* singing (Member, Bach Choir), classical music, ballet, running, family, travelling the Greek islands. *Address:* One Essex Court, Temple, EC4Y 9AR. *T:* (020) 7520 4620. *E:* zosullivan@oeclaw.co.uk.

OSWALD, Prof. Andrew John, DPhil; Professor of Economics, Warwick University, since 1996; *b* 27 Nov. 1953; *s* of late Ian Oswald and Joan Oswald (*née* Thomsett); *m* 1st, 1975, Coral Simpson (marr. diss. 2004); two *d*; 2nd, 2012, Amanda Goodall. *Educ:* Hollywood High Sch., Perth, Aust.; Currie High Sch., Edinburgh; Stirling Univ. (BA); Strathclyde Univ. (MSc); Nuffield Coll., Oxford (DPhil 1980). Lectr, Balliol Coll., Res. Officer at Inst. of Econs and Stats, and Jun. Res. Fellow, St John's Coll., Oxford Univ., 1979–82; Vis. Lectr, Princeton Univ., 1983–84; Jun. Res. Fellow, St John's Coll., Oxford, 1985–86; Sen. Res. Fellow, Centre for Lab Econs, LSE, 1987–98; De Walt Ankeny Prof. of Econs, Dartmouth Coll., USA, 1989–91; Sen. Res. Fellow, Centre for Econ. Performance, LSE, 1992–95; Jacob Wertheim Fellow, Harvard Univ., 2005; ESRC Professorial Fellow, 2006–09; Vis. Fellow, Cornell Univ., 2008; Vis. Prof., Univ. of Zurich, 2008. Acting Res. Dir, IZA Inst., Bonn, 2011–13. Mem., Bd of Editors, Science Jl, 2010–. Hon. Dr Basel, 2013. Tassie Medallion, Stirling Univ., 1975; Lester Prize, Princeton Univ., 1995; Medal, Univ. of Helsinki, 1996. *Publications:* (with A. Carruth) Pay Determination and Industrial Prosperity, 1989; (with D. Blanchflower) The Wage Curve, 1994; contrib. numerous articles to jls. *Recreations:* walking, racquet sports. *Address:* Economics Department, Warwick University, Coventry CV4 7AL. *T:* (024) 7652 3510.

OSWALD, Lady Angela Mary Rose, CVO 2001 (LVO 1993); Woman of the Bedchamber to HM Queen Elizabeth the Queen Mother, 1983–2002; *b* 21 May 1938; *d* of 6th Marquess of Exeter, KCMG, and Lady Mary Burghley, *d* of 7th Duke of Buccleuch, KT; *m* 1958, Sir (William Richard) Michael Oswald, *qv*; one *s* one *d*. *Educ:* Winceby House Sch., Bexhill. Extra Woman of the Bedchamber to HM Queen Elizabeth the Queen Mother, 1981–83. Freeman, City of London, 1995. *Address:* The Old Rectory, Weasenham St Peter, King's Lynn, Norfolk PE32 2TB. *T:* (01328) 838311.

OSWALD, Kirsten Frances; MP (SNP) East Renfrewshire, since 2015; *b* Dundee, 21 Dec. 1972; *d* of Ed and Helen Oswald; *m* Davinder Bedi; two *s*. *Educ:* Carnoustie High Sch.; Univ. of Glasgow (MA Hons Hist. 2005). HR, Motherwell Coll., 1998–2002; Hd of HR, South Lanarks Coll., 2002–15. SNP spokesperson on armed forces and veterans, 2015–. *Address:* House of Commons, SW1A 0AA.

OSWALD, Sir Michael; *see* Oswald, Sir W. R. M.

OSWALD, Richard Anthony; Deputy Health Service Commissioner, 1989–96; *b* 12 Jan. 1941; *s* of late Denis Geoffrey Oswald and Dorothy Lettice Oswald (*née* Shaw); *m* 1963, Janet Iris Penticost; three *s* one *d* (and one *d* decd). *Educ:* The Leys School, Cambridge. DipHSM, MHSM, 1966. NHS admin. posts, 1961–77; Dist Administrator, Leeds West, 1977–84; Gen. Manager, Leeds Western HA, 1985–89. Trustee: CHASE Children's Hospice Service, 1998–2005 (Chm., 1999–2001); St Mary's Historic House and Gardens Charitable Trust, 2006–14. Churchwarden, St Peter's Henfield, 2014–. *Recreations:* church, amateur theatre (Chm., Henfield Theatre Co., 2010–14), painting. *Address:* Croft Cottage, Nep Town Road, Henfield, W Sussex BN5 9DU. *T:* (01273) 492702.

OSWALD, Sir (William Richard) Michael, KCVO 1998 (CVO 1988 LVO 1979); National Hunt Advisor to the Queen, since 2003; Racing Manager for Queen Elizabeth the Queen Mother, 1970–2002; *b* 21 April 1934; *s* of Lt-Col William Alexander Hugh Oswald, ERD and Rose-Marie (*née* Leahy); *m* 1958, Lady Angela Mary Rose Cecil (*see* Lady A. M. R. Oswald); one *s* one *d*. *Educ:* Eton; King's College, Cambridge (MA). 2nd Lieut The King's Own Royal Regt, 1953; Captain, Royal Fusiliers (TA), 1957. Manager, Lordship and Egerton Studs, 1962–70; Manager, 1970–97, Dir, 1998–99, Royal Studs. Mem. Council, Thoroughbred Breeders' Assoc., 1964–2001 (Pres., 1996–2001); Chm., Bloodstock Industry Cttee, Animal Health Trust, 1989–2002; Trustee, British Equine Veterinary Assoc. Trust, 1998–2004. Mem., Jockey Club. Hon. Air Cdre, No 2620 (Co. of Norfolk) Sqdn, RAuxAF, 2001–. Hon. DSc De Montfort, 1997. *Recreations:* painting, military history. *Address:* The Old Rectory, Weasenham St Peter, King's Lynn, Norfolk PE32 2TB. *T:* (01328) 838311, *Fax:* (01328) 838264; The Royal Studs, Sandringham, Norfolk PE35 6EF. *T:* (01485) 540588. *Clubs:* Army and Navy, Royal Air Force.

See also Lt Col A. F. Matheson of Matheson, yr.

OTAKA, Tadaaki, Hon. CBE 1997; Permanent Conductor, NHK Symphony Orchestra, and Artistic Director, New National Theatre, Tokyo, 2010–14; Music Advisor and Chief Conductor, Sapporo Symphony Orchestra, 1998, now Hon. Music Director; Music Advisor and Principal Conductor, Kioi Sinfonietta, Tokyo, since 1995; *b* 8 Nov. 1947; *s* of Hisatada and Misaoko Otaka; *m* 1978, Yukiko. *Educ:* Toho Music Coll., Tokyo; Vienna Acad. Chief Conductor, Tokyo Philharmonic Orch., 1974–91, now Conductor Laureate; Conductor, Sapporo SO, 1981–86; Principal Conductor, BBC Nat. Orch. of Wales, 1987–95, now Conductor Laureate; Chief Conductor, Yomiuri Nippon SO, 1992–98; Dir, Britten Pears Orch., 1998–2001; Principal Guest Conductor, Melbourne SO, 2010–12. Suntory Award (Japan), 1992. *Recreations:* fishing, cooking, computer. *Address:* c/o Askonas Holt Ltd, Lincoln House, 300 High Holborn, WC1V 7JH. *T:* (020) 7400 1700.

OTAÑO, Marta; *see* Andreasen, M.

OTLEY, Prof. David Templeton, PhD; Distinguished Professor of Accounting and Management, Lancaster University Management School, 2000–11, now Emeritus; *b* 10 June 1944; *s* of late Frank Otley and Catherine Otley; *m* 1971, Shelagh Elizabeth Gill; one *s* one *d*. *Educ:* Wellington Grammar Sch.; Churchill Coll., Cambridge (BA 1966, MA 1970); Brunel Univ. (MTech 1971); Manchester Business Sch. (PhD 1976). CDipAF 1980. OR Scientist, NCB, 1966–69; University of Lancaster: Lectr in Financial Control, 1972–83; Sen. Lectr,

1983–86; Prof. of Mgt Control, 1987–88; KPMG Prof. of Accounting, 1988–2000; Associate Dean, 2002–11. Non-exec. Dir, Lancaster HA, 1992–94. Vice-Chm., Business and Mgt Panel, 1996 RAE; Chairman: Accounting and Finance Panel, 2001 RAE; Main Panel I, 2008 RAE; Hong Kong Business, Accounting, Economics and Finance Panel, 2014, RAE. Mem. Mgt Bd, ICAEW Centre for Business Performance, 1999–2011; Sen. Moderator, ICAEW Advanced Stage Examinations, 2001–08; Member: ESRC Res. Grants Bd, 1996–2001; ESRC Audit Cttee, 2002–08. Chm., Mgt Control Assoc., 1983–88, 2005–09. Pres., Mgt Accounting Sect., AAA, 2009–10. Gen. Editor, British Jl of Mgt, 1989–98. Fellow, British Acad. of Mgt, 1994. *Publications:* (with C. R. Emmanuel) Accounting for Management Control, 1985, 2nd edn 1990; Accounting Control and Organizational Behaviour, 1987; (jtly) Accounting for the Human Factor, 1989; (jtly) Management Control: theories, issues and practices, 1995, 2nd edn 2005; numerous contribs to acad. and prof. jls. *Address:* Lancaster University Management School, Lancaster LA1 4YX. *T:* (01524) 593636, *Fax:* (01524) 847321. *E:* d.otley@lancs.ac.uk. *Club:* Oxford and Cambridge.

O'TOOLE, Dr Barbara Maria, (Mo); Visiting Professor of Creativity and Innovation, Newcastle University Business School, since 2008; *b* 24 Feb. 1960. *Educ:* Convent of the Sacred Heart, Fenham, Newcastle upon Tyne; Newcastle upon Tyne Poly. (BA Hons 1983); Univ. of Newcastle upon Tyne (PhD 1994). Lecturer: Postgrad. Sch. for Advanced Urban Studies, Univ. of Bristol, 1991–94; in Politics, Univ. of Newcastle upon Tyne, 1994–97; Hd, Policy Promotion, Local Govt Internat. Bureau, 1997–99. MEP (Lab) NE Region, 1999–2004. Former Chm., Northern Film & Media; Man. Dir, MOPA Public Affairs, 2004–05; England Partnership Manager, NESTA, 2005–08. *Publications:* Prélèvement Obligatoire: a transitional comparison of European local taxation systems, 1991; Rebuilding the City: property led regeneration in the UK, 1992; An Evaluation of the Castlemilk Initiative for the Scottish Office, 1995; Regulation Theory and the British State, 1996.

O'TOOLE, Liam Bernard, PhD; Chief Executive Officer, Arthritis Research UK, since 2009; *b* Liverpool, 27 Nov. 1960; *s* of Bernard O'Toole and Anne O'Toole; *m* 1992, Sarah Davidson; two *s* one *d. Educ:* Tiffin Sch., Kingston upon Thames; University Coll. of North Wales, Bangor (BSc); Univ. of Sheffield (PhD 1988). Post-doctoral Res. Asst, Dept of Biol. and Pre-clinical Medicine, Univ. of St Andrews, 1987–89; Royal Soc./CNRS Exchange Fellow, Univ. of Nice, 1989; Res. Information Officer, British Diabetic Assoc., 1990–92; Medical Research Council: Res. Prog. Manager, Physiol Med. Infections Bd, 1992; Internat. Section Prog. Manager, 1992–94; Clin. Trials Manager, 1994–97; Prog. Manager, Molecular and Cellular Medicine Bd, 1997–2001; Admin. Dir, NCRI, 2001–04; CEO, UK Clinical Res. Collaboration, 2004–08; Hd, Office for Strategic Co-ordination of Health Res., 2007–09. Member, Committee: Adv. Bd to Wales Office for Res. and Devlt for Health and Social Care, 2007–; User Panel, EPSRC, 2008–09; Mem., Exec. Council, AMRC, 2012–. *Publications:* contrib. articles to Clin. Oncol., Nature Reviews Cancer, Annals of Oncol., Eur. Jl of Cancer. *Recreations:* family, Rugby, scuba diving, tennis. *Address:* Arthritis Research UK, 41 Portland Place, W1B 1QH; Arthritis Research UK, Copeman House, St Mary's Court, St Mary's Gate, Chesterfield, Derbys S41 7TD. *T:* 0300 790 0400.

O'TOOLE, Rt Rev. Mark Anthony; *see* Plymouth, Bishop of, (RC).

O'TOOLE, Mo; *see* O'Toole, B. M.

OTTAWA, Bishop of, since 2007; **Rt Rev. John Holland Chapman;** *b* Ottawa, 19 Jan. 1954; *s* of Ven. William Donald Chapman and Jean Chapman (*née* Holland); *m* 1976, Catherine Elizabeth Brabazon; two *s* one *d. Educ:* Carleton Univ., Ottawa (BA 1975); Huron Coll., Univ. of Western Ontario (MDiv 1978); Univ. of the South, Sewanee (DMin 1984); Huron Univ. Coll. (DD 2008). Ordained deacon, 1978, priest, 1978; Asst Curate, St Matthias', Ottawa, 1978–79; Chaplain, Huron Coll., 1979–83; Lectr, Huron Univ. Coll., 1983–87; Rector, St Jude's, London, Ont, 1987–99; Prof. in Pastoral Theol., 1999–2001, Dean of Theol., 2001–07, Huron Coll. *Address:* Bishop's Office, 71 Bronson Avenue, Ottawa, ON K1R 6G6, Canada.

OTTAWAY, Rt Hon. Sir Richard (Geoffrey James); Kt 2014; PC 2013; *b* 24 May 1945; *s* of late Professor Christopher Ottaway, PhD, FRCVS and Grace Ottaway; *m* 1982, Nicola E. Kisch. *Educ:* Backwell Secondary Modern School, Somerset; Bristol University. LLB (Hons). Entered RN as an Artificer apprentice, 1961; commissioned and entered RNC, Dartmouth, 1966; served with Western Fleet, HM Ships Beechampton, Nubian and Eagle, 1967–70; Bristol Univ., 1971–74; articled to Norton Rose Botterell & Roche, 1974; admitted Solicitor, 1977; specialist in international, maritime and commercial law; Partner, William A. Crump & Son, 1981–87. Dir, Coastal Europe Ltd, 1988–95. MP (C) Nottingham N, 1983–87; contested (C) same seat, 1987; MP (C) Croydon S, 1992–2015. PPS to Ministers of State, FCO, 1985–87, to Pres. of BoT, 1992–95, to Dep. Prime Minister, 1995; an Asst Govt Whip, 1995–96; a Lord Comr of HM Treasury (Govt Whip), 1996–97; an Opposition Whip, 1997; Opposition front bench spokesman on: local govt and London, 1997–98; defence, 1999–2000; Treasury, 2000–01; the envmt, 2004–05. Chm., Foreign Affairs Select Cttee, 2010–15 (Mem., 2003–04); Member: Standards and Privileges Select Cttee, 2001–04; Parly Intelligence and Security Cttee, 2005–10. Vice-Chm., 1922 Cttee, 2005–10. Chm., All-Party Parly Gp on Population and Development, 1992–95. A Vice-Chm., 1998–99, Mem. Bd, 2006–10, Cons. Party. *Publications:* (jtly) Road to Reform, 1987; (jtly) Privatisation 1979–1994, 1994; Has London lost its confidence?, 2002; papers on combating internat. maritime fraud, on financial matters and on the environment. *Recreations:* jazz, yacht racing. *Club:* Royal Thames Yacht.

OTTER, Stephen, QPM 2009; HM Inspector of Constabulary, since 2012; *b* Bethnal Green, 24 May 1962; *s* of Tony and Rosemary Otter; *m* 2005, Sophie Hamer; three *s* one *d. Educ:* London Sch. of Econs (MSc(Econ) Criminal Justice Studies); Fitzwilliam Coll., Cambridge (Postgrad. Dip. Applied Criminol.). Patrol Constable, Maidenhead, Thames Valley Police, 1982–85; Patrol Inspector, 1985–87, Detective Inspector, 1987–88, Tsim Sha Tsui, Royal Hong Kong Police; Metropolitan Police: Constable, 1989–91; Sergeant, 1991–93; Inspector, 1994–96; Chief Inspector, 1996–97; Superintendent, 1997–98; Bor. Comdr (Chief Superintendent), 1998–2001; Comdr, 2001–02; Asst Chief Constable, 2002–04, Dep. Chief Constable, 2004–07, Avon and Somerset Police; Chief Constable, Devon and Cornwall Constabulary, 2007–12. FRSA. *Recreations:* reading, listening to music, gardening. *Address:* HM Inspectorate of Constabulary, Globe House, 89 Eccleston Square, SW1V 1PN. *T:* (020) 3513 0512.

OTTOLENGHI, Yotam; food writer; chef/patron of Ottolenghi and NOPI, London; *b* Jerusalem, 14 Dec. 1968; *s* of Michael and Ruth Ottolenghi; civil partnership 2011, Karl Allen; one *s. Educ:* Tel Aviv Univ. (MA Philosophy and Comparative Lit. 1997); Cordon Bleu Cookery Sch., London. Pastry chef, The Capital, Knightsbridge, 1997; pastry section, Kensington Place and Launceston Place, London, 1998; Hd Pastry Chef, Baker & Spice, London, 1999–2000; opened Ottolenghi Deli, Notting Hill, 2002, Islington, 2004, Kensington, 2005, Belgravia, 2007; opened NOPI restaurant, 2011. Television series: Jerusalem on a Plate, 2011; Ottolenghi's Mediterranean Feasts, 2012; Ottolenghi's Mediterranean Island Feasts, 2013. *Publications:* Ottolenghi: The Cookbook, 2008; Plenty, 2010; (with Sam Tamimi) Jerusalem, 2012; Plenty More, 2014. *Recreations:* pilates, eating out, travelling.

OTTON, Sir Geoffrey (John), KCB 1981 (CB 1978); Second Permanent Secretary, Department of Health and Social Security, 1979–86, retired; *b* 10 June 1927; *s* of late John Alfred Otton and Constance Alma Otton; *m* 1952, Hazel Lomas (*née* White); one *s* one *d. Educ:* Christ's Hosp.; St John's Coll., Cambridge (MA). Home Office, 1950–71: (seconded to Cabinet Office, 1959–61; Principal Private Sec. to Home Sec., 1963–65); Dept of Health and Social Security, 1971–86. *Recreation:* music. *Address:* 72 Cumberland Road, Bromley, Kent BR2 0PW. *T:* (020) 8460 9610.

OTTON, Rt Hon. Sir Philip (Howard), Kt 1983; PC 1995; FCIArb; arbitrator and mediator; a Lord Justice of Appeal, 1995–2011; Judge of the Court of Appeal, Gibraltar, 2003–08; Judge of Civil and Commercial Court, Qatar, 2006–11; *b* 28 May 1933; *o s* of late Henry Albert Otton and Leah Otton, Kenilworth; *m* 1965, Helen Margaret, *d* of late P. W. Bates, Stourbridge; two *s* one *d. Educ:* Bablake School, Coventry; Birmingham Univ. (LLB 1954). Chartered Arbitrator 2007. 2nd Lieut, 3rd Dragoon Guards, 1955–57. Called to the Bar, Gray's Inn, 1955, Bencher 1983; QC 1975. Dep. Chm., Beds QS, 1970–72; Junior Counsel to the Treasury (Personal Injuries), 1970–75; a Recorder of the Crown Court, 1972–83; Judge of the High Court, QBD, 1983–95; Presiding Judge, Midland and Oxford Circuit, 1986–88; Judge in Charge of Official Referees Courts, 1991–95. Surveillance Comr, 2001–10. Chairman: Royal Brompton and National Heart and Lung Hospitals SHA, 1991–94; Royal Brompton and Harefield (formerly Royal Brompton Hosp.) NHS Trust, 1994–2002; Nat. Heart and Lung Inst., 1991–95. Non-exec. Dir, Equitable Life Assurance Soc., 2001–03. President: Soc. of Construction Law, 1995–2004; Bar Disability Panel, 1996–2001; Professional Negligence Bar Assoc., 1997–2001; Personal Injury Bar Assoc., 2000–02. Mem., Middle Temple, 2007–. Mem., Transitional Med. Bd, Imperial Coll. Sch. of Medicine, 1995–2002. Governor, Nat. Heart and Chest Hosps, 1979–85. Trustee: Migraine Trust, 1992–98; Media Standards Trust, 2007–13. Pres., Holdsworth Club, Birmingham Univ., 2000–01. Visitor, Univ. of Essex, 2001–05. Hon. Legal Advr, OStJ, 2001–08. Convenor, FA Premier League, 2004–; Formula 1 Internat. Court of Appeal, 2010–. Fellow: Inst. of Advanced Legal Studies, 1999; Amer. Law Inst., 2000; Hon. Fellow, Inst. of Judicial Admin, Birmingham Univ., 1995. Hon. Mem., Amer. Bar Assoc. FCIArb (Mediation) 1994; FRSocMed 1998. Hon. LLD: Nottingham Trent, 1997; Birmingham, 2007; DU Essex, 2006. Award of Merit, City of Coventry, 2005. *Recreations:* theatre, opera, music. *Address:* 20 Essex Street, WC2R 3AL. *T:* (020) 7583 9294, *Fax:* (020) 7583 1341. *E:* clerks@20essexst.com. *Clubs:* Garrick, Pilgrims.

OTTON-GOULDER, Catharine Anne; QC 2000; a Recorder, since 2000; a Deputy High Court Judge, since 2008; a Deemster, Isle of Man, since 2008; *b* 9 April 1955; *e d* of late Prof. Michael Douglas Goulder, DD and Alison Clare (*née* Gardner). *Educ:* Somerville Coll., Oxford (BA 1st Cl. Hons Lit. Hum. 1977). Admitted as solicitor, 1980; called to the Bar, Lincoln's Inn, 1983; Mem., Brick Court Chambers, 1984–; Asst Recorder, 1997–2000. Reader, C of E, 1998–. *Address:* Brick Court Chambers, 7–8 Essex Street, WC2R 3LD.

OTTOW, Prof. Annetje, PhD; Professor of Public Economic Law, Europa Institute, since 2007, and Dean, Faculty of Law, Economics and Governance, since 2014, Utrecht University; non-executive Director, Competitions and Markets Authority, since 2013; *b* 10 Aug. 1965; *m* Ton Tekstra; one *s. Educ:* Leiden Univ. (LLM *cum laude* 1988); Queen Mary Coll., Univ. of London (LLM 1990); Univ. of Amsterdam (PhD 2006). Admitted to Bar of Netherlands, 1990; Attorney: De Brauw Blackstone Westbroek, The Hague, Rotterdam and Brussels, 1990–95; Houthoff Buruma, 1995–2001, Partner, Regulatory and Competition Div., 1997–2001; Sen. Researcher and Lectr, Inst. for Information Law, Univ. of Amsterdam, 2001–06. Visiting Professor: Florence Sch. of Regulation, Eur. Univ. Inst. of Florence; Competition Law Center, George Washington Univ., 2012; Chinese Univ. of Hong Kong, 2013. Founder, Tijdschrift voor Toezicht, 2010. Non-Govtl Advr to Internat. Competition Network, 2009. Mem. Bd, Ind. Post and Telecommunications Authy, Netherlands, 2006–13 (Vice Pres., 2012–13); Chm. (Internal), Strategy Cttee, Authority Consumer Mkts, Netherlands, 2012–13. Member, Supervisory Board: VU Univ. Amsterdam and VU Univ. Med. Center, 2013–; Het Juridisch Loket, 2013–. *Publications:* (contrib.) EU Agencies in - and - the External Relations of the EU, 2014; (contrib. with C. A. Fonteijn) Mundi et Europae Civis: liber amicorum Jacques Steenbergen, 2014; Market and Competition Authorities: good agency principles, 2015; contribs to Jl Antitrust Enforcement, Eur. Contract Law, Utrecht Law Rev. *Recreations:* cycling, yoga. *Address:* Drift 15, 3512 BR Utrecht, Netherlands. *T:* 302537091. *E:* a.t.ottow@uu.nl.

OTTY, Timothy John; QC 2006; *b* 12 Aug. 1967; *s* of Neville and Jean Otty; *m* 1998, Gabriella Ricciardi; one *d. Educ:* Tower House Prep. Sch.; St Paul's Sch.; Trinity Coll., Cambridge (exhibnr, BA 1989, MA 1992); Inns of Court Sch. of Law. Volunteer worker: Mother Teresa's Home for destitute and dying, 1989; Royal Hosp. for Neurodisability, 1990–98. Called to the Bar, Lincoln's Inn, 1990 (Tancred Schol.; European Bursary Award); Virgin Islands, 2014. Stagiaire, Eur. Commn of Human Rights, 1993; Vice Chm., Bar Human Rights Cttee of England and Wales, 2005–10. Member: Attorney General's Treasury Panel, 2003–06; Exec. Cttee and Council, Commonwealth Lawyers' Assoc., 2005–; Exec. Cttee, Human Rights Lawyers Assoc., 2009–; Foreign Sec.'s Adv. Gp on Human Rights, 2010–15. Vis. Lecturer: LSE, 2006–14; Georgetown Univ., 2010; Vis. Fellow, Mansfield Coll., Oxford, 2009–10. Trustee, British Inst. of Internat. and Comparative Law, 2011–13. Chm., Human Dignity Trust, 2011–; Trustee, Irene Taylor Music in Prisons Trust, 2007–13. Mem., Editl Bd, Eur. Human Rights Law Rev., 2008–. Judges' Commendation, Bar Council Pro Bono Award, 2007; Liberty and Justice Human Rights Lawyer of the Year, 2008. *Publications:* (contrib.) Sweet & Maxwell's Human Rights Practice, 1st edn, 2001. *Recreations:* marathon running, golf, Liverpool FC, Italy, cinema, theatre, tennis. *Address:* Blackstone Chambers, Temple, EC4Y 9BW. *T:* (020) 7583 1770, *Fax:* (020) 7822 7350. *Clubs:* Athenæum; Serpentine Running.

OUDKERK, Daniel Richard; QC 2010; *b* 9 April 1969; *s* of Patrick Oudkerk and Ann Oudkerk; *m* 2001, Joanna Pollard; three *s. Educ:* Univ. of Bristol (LLB Hons). Called to the Bar, Inner Temple, 1992; in practice as barrister, specialising in commercial and employment law. *Recreations:* ski-ing, cycling, wild brown trout. *Address:* Essex Court Chambers, 24 Lincoln's Inn Fields, WC2A 3EG. *T:* (020) 7813 8000. *E:* doudkerk@essexcourt.net.

OUELLET, Hon. André; PC (Can.) 1972; QC (Can.) 1992; President and Chief Executive Officer, Canada Post Corporation, 1999–2004 (Chairman, 1996–99); *b* St Pascal, Quebec, 6 April 1939; *s* of Albert Ouellet and Rita Turgeon; *m* 1965, Édith Pagé; two *s* two *d. Educ:* Univ. of Ottawa (BA 1960); Univ. of Sherbrooke (LLL 1963). Called to the Bar. MP (L): Montreal-Papineau, 1967–88; Papineau-St-Michel, 1988–96; PMG, 1972–74; Minister: for Consumer and Corporate Affairs, 1974–76; of Urban Affairs, 1976–78; of Public Works, 1978–79; PMG 1980–84, and Minister for Consumer and Corporate Affairs, 1980–83; Minister of Labor, 1983–84; Minister of State for Regl Economic Devlt, 1984; Pres., Privy Council and Govt Leader in H of C, 1984; Minister of Foreign Affairs, 1993–96. Hon. Dr Ottawa, 1995. *Recreations:* golf, reading, theatre. *Address:* 17 Chase Court, Ottawa, ON K1V 9Y6, Canada.

OUELLET, His Eminence Cardinal Marc; Prefect of the Congregation for Bishops, and President, Pontifical Commission for Latin America, since 2010, PSS; *b* 8 June 1944. *Educ:* Amos Teacher Training Coll., Quebec; Grand Séminaire de Montréal (LTh Univ. of Montreal 1968); St Thomas Aquinas Pontifical Univ., Rome (LPh 1976); Gregorian Univ., Rome (Dr Dogmatic Theol. 1983). Ordained priest, 1968; Curate, St Sauveur, Val d'Or, 1968–70; teacher of philosophy, Major Seminary, Bogota; Faculty Member and Professor: Major Seminary, Manizales, Columbia, 1974; Grand Séminaire de Montréal; Major Seminary, Cali, Columbia, 1983 (Rector, 1984–89); Rector: Grand Séminaire de Montréal, 1990; St Joseph's Seminary, Edmonton, 1994; Titular Chair of Dogmatic Theol., John Paul II Inst.,

Lateran Pontifical Univ., 1996–2002; Sec., Pontifical Council for the Promotion of Christian Unity, 2001–03; Titular Bp, Agropoli, 2001; Cardinal, 2003; Archbishop of Quebec, (RC), and Primate of Canada, 2003–10.

OUGHTON, John Raymond Charles; executive coach and mentor; *b* 21 Sept. 1952; *s* of late Peggy Oughton. *Educ:* Reading Sch.; University Coll., Oxford (BA Mod. Hist. 1974). Joined MoD, 1974; Mem. UK Delegn, UN Law of Sea Conf., 1978; Asst Pvte Sec. to Minister of State for Defence, 1978–80; on secondment to Canadian Govt, 1980–81; Sales Policy, 1981–83; Office of Personal Advr to Sec. of State for Defence, 1984; Pvte Sec. to Minister for the Armed Forces, 1984–86; Sen. Principal, Directorate of Procurement Policy, 1986–87; Asst Sec., Dir of Procurement Policy, 1988–89; Head of Resources and Progs (Navy), 1990–93; Office of Public Service, Cabinet Office: Under Sec. and Head, Govt Efficiency Unit, 1993–98; Dir, Efficiency and Effectiveness Gp, 1996–98; Ministry of Defence: Dep. Under-Sec. of State, 1998; Hd, Chief of Defence Logistics Implementation Team, 1998–99; Dep. Chief of Defence Logistics, 1999–2003; Office of Government Commerce, HM Treasury: Dep. Chief Exec., 2003–04; Second Permanent Sec. and Chief Exec., 2004–07. Interim Man. Dir, KMG Gp, 2008. FRSA; FCIPS. *Recreations:* squash, tennis, travel, watching cricket and football. *Address:* 1 Adderley Grove, SW11 6NA. *T:* (020) 7223 5793. *E:* johnoughton@yahoo.co.uk. *Clubs:* Oxford and Cambridge; Tottenham Hotspur Football, Middlesex CC.

OULTON, Sir (Antony) Derek (Maxwell), GCB 1989 (KCB 1984; CB 1979); QC 1985; MA, PhD; Permanent Secretary, Lord Chancellor's Office, and Clerk of the Crown in Chancery, 1982–89; barrister-at-law; Life Fellow, Magdalene College, Cambridge, since 1995 (Fellow, 1990–95); *b* 14 Oct. 1927; *y s* of late Charles Cameron Courtenay Oulton and Elizabeth, *d* of T. H. Maxwell, KC; *m* 1955, Margaret Geraldine (*d* 1989), *d* of late Lt-Col G. S. Oxley, MC, 60th Rifles; one *s* three *d*. *Educ:* St Edward's Sch., Oxford; King's Coll., Cambridge (scholar; BA (1st Cl.), MA; PhD 1974). Called to Bar, Gray's Inn, 1952, Bencher, 1982–2002; in private practice, Kenya, 1952–60; Private Sec. to Lord Chancellor, 1961–65; Sec., Royal Commn on Assizes and Quarter Sessions, 1966–69; Asst Solicitor, 1969–75. Dep. Sec., 1976–82, and Dep. Clerk of the Crown in Chancery, 1977–82, Lord Chancellor's Office. Vis. Prof. in Law, Bristol Univ., 1990–91. Chm., Mental Health Foundn Cttee on the Mentally Disordered Offender, 1989–92. Trustee, Nat. Gallery, 1989–96. Pres., Electricity Arbitration Assoc., 1990–2001. *Publications:* (jtly) Legal Aid and Advice, 1971; (ed) Lewis, We the Navigators, 2nd edn 1994; contrib. Oxford DNB. *Address:* Magdalene College, Cambridge CB3 0AG. *T:* (01223) 332100.

OULTON, Claire Marion, MA; Headmistress, Benenden School, 2000–13; *b* 23 July 1961; *d* of Prof. L. Zisman and S. Zisman; *m* 1986, Nicholas Oulton; two *d*. *Educ:* Somerville Coll., Oxford (BA Hons History 1983; MA 1994); KCL (PGCE 1984). Teacher of History, Benenden Sch., 1984–88; Head of History, Charterhouse, 1988–94; Headmistress, St Catherine's Sch., Guildford, 1994–2000. Governor: Charterhouse, 2003–; John Wallis Acad., Ashford, 2010–.

OULTON, Sir Derek; *see* Oulton, Sir A. D. M.

OULTON, Rt Rev. Michael Douglas; *see* Ontario, Bishop of.

OUSELEY, Baron *cr* 2001 (Life Peer), of Peckham Rye in the London Borough of Southwark; **Herman George Ouseley,** Kt 1997; President, Different Realities Partnership Ltd, 2006–10 (Managing Director, 2000–06); non-executive Director, Focus Consultancy Ltd, 2000–10; *b* 24 March 1945; *m* 1972, Margaret Neill; one *s* one *d*. Various public service posts, 1963–86; Race Relations Adviser: Lambeth BC, 1979–81; GLC, 1981–84; Dir of Educn, 1986–88, Chief Exec., 1988–90, ILEA; Chief Exec., London Borough of Lambeth, 1990–93; Chm., CRE, 1993–2000. Member: Council, Inst. of Race Relations, 1990–; Council, FA, 2008–13; Chair: Kick It Out, 1994–; PRESET Educn and Employment Charitable Trust, 1997–; Patron: Presentation Housing Assoc., 1990–2000; Daneford Trust, 1998–; Helena Kennedy Foundn, 2003–. Non-exec. Dir, Brooknight Security, 1995–2005. Pres., LGA, 2001–04 (Vice Pres., 2010–). Trustee, Manchester United Foundn, 2007–. *Publications:* The System, 1981; pamphlets and articles on local government, public services, employment, training and race equality issues. *Address:* House of Lords, SW1A 0PW.

OUSELEY, Hon. Sir Duncan (Brian Walter), Kt 2000; **Hon. Mr Justice Ouseley;** a Judge of the High Court, Queen's Bench Division, since 2000; Lead Judge, Administrative Court, since 2010; *b* 24 Feb. 1950; *s* of late Maurice and Margaret Ouseley; *m* 1974, Suzannah Price; three *s*. *Educ:* Trinity Sch., Croydon; Fitzwilliam Coll., Cambridge (MA; Hon. Fellow, 2011); University Coll. London (LLM). Called to the Bar, Gray's Inn, 1973 (Atkin Scholar 1972); Bencher 2000; Junior Counsel to the Crown, Common Law, 1986–92; QC 1992; a Recorder, 1994–2000; QC (NI) 1997; Jt Hd of Chambers, 2000. Pres., Immigration Appeal Tribunal, 2003–05; Chm., Special Immigration Appeal Commn, 2003–06. Chairman, Examination in Public Shropshire Structure Plan, 1985, Hampshire Structure Plan, 1991. Vice-Chm. Planning and Envmt, Bar Assoc., 2000. *Recreations:* family, sport, music, wine. *Address:* Royal Courts of Justice, Strand, WC2A 2LL. *Club:* Garrick.

OUSTON, Hugh Anfield; Head, Robert Gordon's College, Aberdeen, 2004–14; *b* Dundee, 4 April 1952; *s* of Philip and Elizabeth Ouston; *m* 1988, Yvonne Caroline Young; two *s* two *d*. *Educ:* Glenalmond Coll.; Christ Church, Univ. of Oxford (BA Hons); Univ. of Aberdeen (DipEd). Teacher of History, N Berwick High Sch., 1977–84; Hd of History, Beeslack High Sch., 1984–92; Asst Hd, Dunbar Grammar Sch., 1992–97; Dep. Principal, George Watson's Coll., Edinburgh, 1997–2004. *Recreations:* bird watching, gardening, hill walking.

OUTHWAITE, Wendy Jane Tivnan; QC 2009; *b* Taplow, Bucks, 11 July 1965; *d* of Ian and Carol Guthrie; *m* 1994, Charles Outhwaite; three *s* one *d*. *Educ:* Wycombe Abbey; St Hugh's Coll., Oxford (MA Juris.); Institut d'Etudes Européennes, Brussels (License special en droit Européen). Called to the Bar, Lincoln's Inn, 1990; barrister specialising in torts and judicial review, 1990–2012. Producer of English sparkling wine, 2007–. *Publications:* The Civil Practitioner's Guide to the Human Rights Act, 2000; (contrib.) Healthcare Law: the impact of the Human Rights Act 1998, 2000; (contrib.) Burnett Hall on Environmental Law, 2nd edn 2008. *Recreations:* boxing, wine.

OUTLAW, Nathan Daniel; Chef Patron, Nathan Outlaw Restaurants Ltd, since 2009; *b* Maidstone, 7 March 1978; *s* of Clive and Sharon Outlaw; *m* 2001, Rachel Morris; one *s* one *d*. *Educ:* Holmesdale Sch., Snodland, Kent; Thanet Coll. Chef: Intercontinental Hotel, Hyde Park Corner, London, 1996–97; Chavot Restaurant, Fulham, 1997–98; 2nd chef, Seafood Restaurant, Padstow, Cornwall, 1998–99; sous chef, Lords of the Manor, Gloucester, 1999–2001; Head Chef, Vineyard at Stockcross, Berks, 2001–03; Chef/Proprietor, The Black Pig, Rock, Cornwall, 2003–04; Head Chef: St Ervan Manor, Padstow, 2005–06; Restaurant Nathan Outlaw, Marina Villa Hotel, Fowey, Cornwall, 2007–09; Proprietor/Chef: Nathan Outlaw Seafood Grill, St Enodoc Hotel, Rock, 2009–; Restaurant Nathan Outlaw, St Enodoc Hotel, Rock, 2010– (2 Michelin Stars, 2010); Outlaw's Fish Kitchen, Port Isaac, Cornwall, 2013–; The Mariners Public House, Rock, Cornwall, 2014–; Consultant and Chef, Outlaw's Seafood and Grill at The Capital Hotel, Knightsbridge, 2012–. *Publications:* Nathan Outlaw's British Seafood, 2012; Nathan Outlaw's Fish Kitchen, 2014. *Recreations:* collecting cookery books, Star Wars, spending time with family. *Address:* Nathan Outlaw Restaurants Ltd, St Enodoc Hotel, Rock, Cornwall PL27 6LA. *T:* (01208) 862737. *E:* mail@nathan-outlaw.com.

OUTRAM, Sir Alan James, 5th Bt *cr* 1858; MA; *b* 15 May 1937; *s* of late James Ian Outram and late Evelyn Mary Littlehales; *S* great-uncle, 1945; *m* 1976, Victoria Jean, *d* of late George Dickson Paton, Bexhill-on-Sea; one *s* one *d*. *Educ:* Spyway, Langton Matravers, Swanage; Marlborough College, Wilts; St Edmund Hall, Oxford. Harrow School: Asst Master, 1961–98; Housemaster, 1979–91; Under Master, 1992–96. Lt-Col TAVR. Pres., Dorset LTA, 1995–2005, now Life Vice-Pres. *Recreations:* golf, bridge, cycling. *Heir:* *s* Douglas Benjamin James Outram, *b* 15 March 1979. *Address:* Chase House, Moorside, Sturminster Newton, Dorset DT10 1HQ. *Club:* Vincent's (Oxford).

OVENDEN, Rev. Canon John Anthony, LVO 2007; Fellow and Dean of Chapel, Harris Manchester College, Oxford, since 2012; *b* 26 May 1945; *s* of Rev. Edward and Marjorie Ovenden; *m* 1974, Christine Ann Broadhurst; two *s* one *d*. *Educ:* St Paul's Cathedral Choir Sch.; Ardingly Coll.; Borough Rd Coll. of Educn; Salisbury and Wells Theol Coll.; Open Univ. (BA Hons 1980, 1993); King's Coll. London (MA 1996). Ordained deacon, 1974, priest, 1975; Assistant Curate: Handsworth, Sheffield, 1974–77; Uckfield, and Priest in Charge of Isfield, Sussex, 1977–80; Precentor and Sacrist, Ely Cathedral, 1980–85; Vicar, St Mary's, Primrose Hill, 1985–98; Canon of Windsor, Chaplain in the Great Park and Chaplain, Cumberland Lodge, 1998–2011 (Fellow, 2014); Canon Chaplain, 1998–2012, Canon Precentor, 2007–12, Canon Emeritus, 2012–, St George's Chapel. Chaplain to the Queen, 2002–15; Extra Chaplain, Mansfield Coll., Oxford, 2014–. Golden Jubilee Medal, 2002; Diamond Jubilee Medal, 2012. *Publications:* (contrib.) Christians and Muslims in the Commonwealth: a dynamic role in the future, ed Anthony O'Mahony and Ataullah Siddiqui, 2001. *Recreations:* theatre-going, music, walking, sport. *Address:* Harris Manchester College, Mansfield Road, Oxford OX1 3TD; Little Croft, Great Rissington, Cheltenham, Glos GL54 2LN.

OVENDEN, John Frederick; County Councillor, Kent, 1985–2001 (Leader, Labour Group, and Co-Leader of Council, 1994–97); *b* 17 Aug. 1942; *s* of late Richard Ovenden and Margaret Louise Ovenden (*née* Lucas); *m* 1963, Maureen (*née* White); one *d*. *Educ:* Salmestone County Primary Sch., Margate; Chatham House Grammar Sch., Ramsgate. Asst Exec. Engr, Post Office, 1961–74. MP (Lab) Gravesend, Feb. 1974–1979. Contested (Lab) Gravesham, 1983. Manager, Post Office, subseq. British Telecom, 1979–90. *Recreations:* cricket (Kent), reading, walking, gardening, jazz, modern history. *Club:* Gillingham Labour (Gillingham).

OVENDEN, Richard, FSA; Bodley's Librarian, University of Oxford, since 2014; Fellow, Balliol College, Oxford, since 2014; *b* Deal, Kent, 25 March 1964; *s* of Stanley and Betty Doreen Ovenden; *m* 1994, Lyn Youngson; two *d*. *Educ:* Sir Roger Manwood's Sch.; Durham Univ. (BA Hons 1985); University Coll. London (DipLib 1987; MA 1987). Asst Librarian, H of L Liby, 1987–89; Curator, Nat. Liby of Scotland, 1989–99; Hd, Special Collections, Edinburgh Univ. Liby, 1999–2002; Dir of Collections, Edinburgh Univ., 2002–03; Bodleian Library: Keeper, Special Collections, 2003–12; Dep. Librarian, 2012–14. Mem., American Philosophical Soc., 2015. FSA 2007. FRSA 2006. Hon. Fellow, St Hugh's Coll., Oxford, 2014. *Publications:* John Thomson (1837–1921): photographer, 1997; (jtly) A Radical's Books, 1999; contribs to jls on book history, history of photography, information sci. *Recreations:* photography, art galleries, cooking. *Address:* Bodleian Library, Broad Street, Oxford OX1 3BG. *T:* (01865) 277158. *E:* richard.ovenden@bodleian.ox.ac.uk. *Club:* Grolier (New York).

OVERBURY, Rupert Simon; His Honour Judge Overbury; a Circuit Judge, since 2007; Deputy Resident Judge, Ipswich Crown Court; *b* Aldershot, 26 Dec. 1957; *s* of late (Henry) Colin (Barry) Overbury, CBE and of Dawn Rhodes Overbury (*née* Dade, now Boyd); *m* 1996, Claire Elizabeth Brett; two *s*. *Educ:* Framlingham Coll.; Central London Poly. (BA Hons Law). Called to the Bar, Middle Temple, 1984; barrister, 3 New Square, Lincoln's Inn, 1984–93, 18 Red Lion Court, 1993–2007; Recorder, 2003–07; Diversity and Community Relations Judge for Suffolk. Chm., Trustee Bd, Saxmundham and Leiston CAB, 2006–13. Hon. Comdr, 48 Fighter Wing, USAF Judge Advocate Staff, 2015. *Recreations:* fly-fishing, shooting, travel, wood turning. *Address:* Ipswich Crown Court, 1 Russell Road, Ipswich, Suffolk IP1 2AG. *T:* (01473) 228585. *E:* hhjudge.overbury@judiciary.gsi.gov.uk.

OVEREND, Sandra; Member (UU) Mid-Ulster, Northern Ireland Assembly, since 2011; *b* Magherafelt, 11 May 1973; *d* of Billy and Glynis Armstrong; *m* 1997, Nigel Overend; two *s* one *d*. *Educ:* Cookstown High Sch.; Univ. of Ulster (BA Hons Business Studies). DipHE Accounting; Stonebridge Associated Colls PR. Asst accountant, 1996–98; Office Manager for Billy Armstrong, MLA, 1998–2011; Women's Develt Officer, UU Party, 2008–11. Contested (UU) Mid-Ulster, 2015. Chair, Bellagy Primary Sch. Parents' Assoc., 2010–. Mem., Select Vestry, Ballyscullion Parish Ch. *Recreations:* cycling, reading. *Address:* Mid-Ulster Constituency Office, 1 High Street, Moneymore, Co. Londonderry, Northern Ireland BT45 7PB. *T:* (028) 8674 8090. *E:* sandra.overend@mla.niassembly.gov.uk.

OVERY, Prof. Richard James, PhD; FRHistS; FBA 2000; Professor of History, Exeter University, since 2004; *b* 23 Dec. 1947; *s* of James Herbert Overy and Margaret Grace Overy (*née* Sutherland); *m* 1992, Kim Turner (marr. diss. 2004); two *d*, and one *s* two *d* from previous marriage. *Educ:* Sexey's Grammar Sch., Som; Gonville and Caius Coll., Cambridge (BA 1969; MA 1972; PhD 1977). Cambridge University: Res. Fellow, Churchill Coll., 1972–73; Lectr, Queens' Coll., 1973–79; Asst Univ. Lectr, 1976–79; King's College, London: Lectr, 1980–88; Reader, 1988–92; Prof. of Modern Hist., 1992–2004; FKC 2003. Chm., RAF Mus. Research Bd, 2013–. Trustee, RAF Mus., 1999–2003. Mem., Eur. Acad. for Scis and Arts, 2013. FRHistS 1997; FRSA 2006. T. S. Ashton Prize, Econ. Hist. Soc., 1982; Cass Prize, Business Hist. Soc., 1987; Samuel Eliot Morison Prize, Soc., for Mil. Hist., 2001; James Doolittle Award, MIT, 2010. *Publications:* William Morris, Viscount Nuffield, 1976; The Air War 1939–45, 1980; The Nazi Economic Recovery, 1982, 2nd edn 1996; Goering: the Iron Man, 1984, 2nd edn 2000; The Origins of the Second World War, 1987, 2nd edn 1998; The Road to War, 1989, 3rd edn 2009; War and Economy in the Third Reich, 1994; The Interwar Crisis 1919–1939, 1994; Why the Allies Won, 1995; The Penguin Atlas of the Third Reich, 1996, 2nd edn 2000; The Times Atlas of the Twentieth Century, 1996, 2nd edn 1999; Bomber Command 1939–45, 1997; Russia's War, 1998; (Gen. Ed.) The Times History of the World, 1999; The Battle, 2000; Interrogations: the Nazi elite in Allied hands 1945, 2001; The Dictators, 2004 (Wolfson History Prize, Hessell Tiltman Prize for History, 2005); The Morbid Age: Britain between the wars, 2009; 1939: countdown to war, 2009; The Third Reich: a chronicle, 2010; The Bombing War: Europe 1939–1945, 2013 (Cundill Award, 2014); A History of War in 100 Battles, 2014; contrib. to Econ. Hist. Rev., Jl of Strategic Studies, Past and Present, English Histl Rev., etc. *Recreation:* opera. *Address:* Department of History, University of Exeter, Amory Building, Rennes Drive, Exeter EX4 4RJ. *E:* r.overy@ex.ac.uk. *Club:* Academy.

OVEY, Rev. Dr Michael John; Principal, Oak Hill Theological College, London, since 2007; *b* Isle of Wight, 9 Dec. 1958; *s* of Kenneth John and Elizabeth Ruth Ovey; *m* 1987, Heather Elizabeth Jefferyes; two *s* one *d*. *Educ:* Balliol Coll., Oxford (BA 1981; BCL 1982); Trinity Coll. and Ridley Hall, Cambridge (BA 1991); Moore Coll., Sydney (MTh 2000); King's Coll. London (PhD 2005). Barrister, 1982–85; Parly Draftsman, 1985–88; ordained deacon, 1991, priest, 1992; Curate and Dir of Trng, All Saints, Crowborough, 1991–95; Junior Lectr, Moore Theol Coll., Sydney, 1995–98; Oak Hill Theological College, London: Kingham Hill Res. Fellow, 1998–2005; Lectr and College Dean, 2005–07. *Publications:* (with Dr S. Jeffery and Dr A. Sach) Pierced For Our Transgressions, 2007; (with Dr Dan Strange) Confident: why we can trust the Bible, 2015; (contrib.) One God in Three Persons, 2015; articles in Oak Hill Sch. Theol. Papers, IVP Dictionary of Apologetics, IVP Dictionary of Theology, Cambridge Papers, Churchman, Reformed Theol Rev.

OWADA, Hisashi; a Judge, since 2003, and President, 2009–12, International Court of Justice; *b* Niigata, Japan, 18 Sept. 1932; *s* of Takeo Owada and Shizuka Tamura; *m* 1962, Yumiko Egashira; three *d*. *Educ:* Univ. of Tokyo (BA 1955); Univ. of Cambridge (LLB 1956). Joined Foreign Service of Japan; Private Secretary: to Foreign Minister, 1971–72; to Prime Minister, 1976–78; Principal Legal Advr and Dir-Gen., Treaties Bureau, Foreign Ministry, 1984–87; Dep. Foreign Minister, 1989–91; Vice Foreign Minister, 1991–93; Advr to Foreign Minister, 1999–2003; Permanent Representative: to OECD, 1988–89; to UN, 1994–98 (Pres., Security Council, 1997, 1998). Sen. Advr to Pres., World Bank, 1998–2003. Judge, Perm. Court of Arbitration. Professor: Waseda Univ., Japan, 1999–2003; Leiden Univ.; Adjunct Professor: Tokyo Univ., 1963–88; Columbia Law Sch., 1994–98; Visiting Professor: Harvard Univ., 1979–81, 1987, 1989, 2000–02; NY Univ. Law Sch., 1994–98. Pres., Japan Inst. Internat. Affairs, 1999–2003. Mem., Institut de Droit Internat. (Pres., 2011–13). Hon. Fellow, Trinity Coll., Cambridge, 2002. Hon. Mem., Amer. Soc. of Internat. Law (Mem., Exec. Council). Bd Mem., UN Foundn; Lifetime Trustee, Aspen Inst.; Hon. Gov., Ditchley Foundn. Hon. LLD: Keiwa Coll., Japan, 2000; Banares Hindu, India, 2001; Waseda, Japan, 2004; Groningen, 2009; Cambridge, 2015. *Publications:* Practice of Japan in International Law, 1984; From Involvement to Engagement: a new direction for foreign policy of Japan, 1994; On Diplomacy, 1997; A Treatise on International Relations, 2003; In the Cause of Peace and Scholarship, 2008. *Recreations:* music, ski-ing, mountain walking. *Address:* International Court of Justice, Carnegieplein 2 (Peace Palace), 2517 KJ The Hague, Netherlands. *T:* (070) 3022323, *Fax:* (070) 3602385.
See also Emperor of Japan.

OWEN, family name of **Baron Owen**.

OWEN, Baron *cr* 1992 (Life Peer), of the City of Plymouth; **David Anthony Llewellyn Owen,** CH 1994; PC 1976; European Union Co-Chairman, International Conference on Former Yugoslavia, 1992–95; *b* Plympton, South Devon, 2 July 1938; *s* of Dr John William Morris Owen and Mary Llewellyn; *m* 1968, Deborah Schabert; two *s* one *d*. *Educ:* Bradfield College; Sidney Sussex College, Cambridge (BA 1959; MB, BChir 1962; MA 1963; Hon. Fellow, 1977); St Thomas' Hospital. FRCP 2005. St Thomas' Hospital: house appts, 1962–64; Neurological and Psychiatric Registrar, 1964–66; Research Fellow, Medical Unit, 1966–68. Contested (Lab) Torrington, 1964; MP (Lab 1966–81, SDP, 1981–92) Plymouth Sutton, 1966–74, Plymouth Devonport, 1974–92. PPS to Minister of Defence, Administration, 1967; Parly Under-Sec. of State for Defence, for RN, 1968–70; Opposition Defence Spokesman, 1970–72, resigned over EEC, 1972; Parly Under-Sec. of State, DHSS, 1974; Minister of State: DHSS, 1974–76; FCO, 1976–77; Sec. of State for Foreign and Commonwealth Affairs, 1977–79; Opposition spokesman on energy, 1979–80. Sponsored 1973 Children's Bill; ministerially responsible for 1975 Children's Act. Co-founder, SDP, 1981; Chm., Parly Cttee, SDP, 1981–82; Dep. Leader, SDP, 1982–83; Leader, SDP, 1983–87, resigned over issue of merger with Liberal Party, re-elected, 1988–92. Co-founder: Social Market Foundn, 1989; Charter 2010, 2009–10. Chm., New Europe, 1999–2005. Chairman: Decision Technology Internat., 1970–72; Middlesex Hldgs, subseq. Global Natural Energy plc, 1995–2006; Yukos International, 2002–05; Europe Steel, 2002–; Director: New Crane Publishing, 1992–2005; Coats Viyella plc, 1994–2001; Abbott Laboratories Inc., 1996–2011; Intelligent Energy, 2003–05; Hyperdynamics, 2009–14. Member: Ind. Commn on Disarmament and Security Issues, 1980–89; Ind. Commn on Internat. Humanitarian Issues, 1983–88; Carnegie Commn on Preventing Deadly Conflict, 1994–99; Eminent Persons Gp on Curbing Illicit Trafficking in Small Arms and Light Weapons, 1999–2003. Chm., Humanitas, 1990–2001. Governor, Charing Cross Hospital, 1966–68. Patron, Greenham Common Trust, 2004–; Pres., Enham Trust, 2004–12; Chm., Daedalus Trust, 2011–. President: Nat. Marine Aquarium, 2006–10; River Thames Soc., 2010–. Chancellor, Liverpool Univ., 1996–2009. *Publications:* (ed) A Unified Health Service, 1968; The Politics of Defence, 1972; In Sickness and in Health, 1976; Human Rights, 1978; Face the Future, 1981; A Future That Will Work, 1984; A United Kingdom, 1986; Personally Speaking to Kenneth Harris, 1987; Our NHS, 1988; Time to Declare (autobiog.), 1991; (ed) Seven Ages (anthology of poetry), 1992; Balkan Odyssey, 1995; The Hubris Syndrome, 2007, 2nd edn 2012; In Sickness and in Power, 2008, 3rd edn 2011; Time to Declare: second innings (autobiog.), 2009; Nuclear Papers, 2009; Europe Restructured: the Eurozone crisis and its aftermath, 2012; Bosnia and Herzegovina: the Vance-Owen Peace Plan, 2013; The Hidden Perspective: the military conversations 1906–1914, 2014; The Health of the Nation: NHS in peril, 2014; articles in Lancet, Neurology, Clinical Science, Brain, Qly Jl Med., Foreign Affairs, and Psychiatrist. *Recreation:* sailing. *Address:* 78 Narrow Street, Limehouse, E14 8BP. *T:* (020) 7987 5441, (office) (01442) 872617, *Fax:* (01442) 876108. *E:* davidowen@lorddavidowen.co.uk. *W:* www.lorddavidowen.co.uk.

OWEN, Albert; MP (Lab) Ynys Môn, since 2001; *b* 10 Aug. 1959; *s* of late William Owen and Doreen Owen (*née* Woods); *m* 1983, Angela Margaret Magee; two *d*. *Educ:* Holyhead Comprehensive Sch.; Coleg Harlech; Univ. of York (BA Hons Politics 1997). Merchant seafarer, 1975–92; full-time educn, 1992–97; Manager, Centre for the Unwaged (advice, trng and information centre), 1997–2001. *Recreations:* travel by train, cooking, gardening, walking, running, cycling. *Address:* House of Commons, SW1A 0AA; (constituency office) Ty Cledwyn, 18a Thomas Street, Holyhead, Anglesey LL65 1RR. *T:* (01407) 765750.

OWEN, (Alfred) David, OBE 1997; Group Chairman, 1975–2010, Consultant, since 2010, Rubery Owen Holdings Ltd; *b* 26 Sept. 1936; *m* 1966, Ethne (*née* Sowman); two *s* one *d*. *Educ:* Brocksford Hall; Oundle; Emmanuel Coll., Cambridge Univ. (MA). Joined Rubery Owen Gp, 1960; Gen. Man., Rubery Owen Motor Div., 1962–67; Dep. Man. Dir, Rubery Owen & Co. Ltd, 1967; Gp Man. Dir, Rubery Owen Holdings Ltd, 1969–81; Director: Severn Valley Railways (Holdings) plc, 1984–; Blackwell Sci. Ltd, 1993–2003; Welconstruct Gp (formerly Grimmitt Hldgs) Ltd, 2001–07; Darlaston Housing Trust Ltd, 2004–10; Walsall Housing Regeneration Community Agency, 2005–11; Jt Patron, BRM Assoc., 2013–. Warden, Birmingham Assay Office, 1999–2005. Member: Council, Univ. of Aston, 1981–2001; Bd, British Library, 1982–90; Bd, Nat. Exhibn Centre, 1982–2006; Bd, Castle Vale Housing Action Trust, 1993–2000. President: Comité de Liaison Eur. de la Distribn Ind. de Pièces de rechange et équipements pour Autos, 1988–90; Comité de Liaison de la Construction de Carrosseries et de Remorques, 1998–99; Commercial Trailer Assoc., 1992–2004. Treas., SMMT, 2001–. Chm., Charles Hayward Foundn, 2004–09. Dir, Library of Birmingham Trust, 2013–. Mem., Develt Bd, Aston Univ., 2013–. Hon. DSc Aston, 1988; DUniv Central England, 2000. *Recreations:* walking, photography, music, industrial archaeology, local history, collecting books. *Address:* Mill Dam House, Mill Lane, Aldridge, Walsall, West Midlands WS9 0NB. *T:* (office) (0121) 526 3131. *Club:* National.

OWEN, Arthur Leslie, (Les); non-executive director and financial services professional; Group Chief Executive, AXA Asia Pacific Holdings, 2000–06 (Board Member, 1998–2006); *b* 6 Feb. 1949; *s* of Arthur Llewellyn Owen and Annie Louise Owen (*née* Hegarty); *m* 1972, Valerie Emmott; three *d*. *Educ:* Holt High Sch., Liverpool; Univ. of Manchester (BSc Hons Maths); Inst. for Mgt Develt, Lausanne. FIA 1975; FIAA 2004–10; FPMI. Joined Sun Life Corp., 1971: Chief Gen. Manager, 1992–95; Gp Man. Dir, 1995–97; Chief Exec., AXA Sun Life plc, 1997–99; Board Member: Sun Life & Provincial Hldgs plc, 1996–2000; AXA Nichidan, Japan, 1999–2002; Alliance Bernstein (formerly Alliance Capital Management) (Australia & NZ), 2000–06; AXA Minmetals, China, 2002–06; Computershare plc, 2007–; Football Fedn of Aust., 2007–11; Discovery Hldgs, 2007–; Royal Mail Gp, 2010–; Chm., AXA China Region, 2002–06; non-exec. Chm., Jelf Gp plc, 2010–; non-executive Director: Just Retirement, 2010–14; CPP, 2010–15. Member Board: Western TEC, 1994–98; PIA, 1997–99. *Recreations:* sport, soccer, cricket, golf, gardening, reading. *Address:* Broadway Lea, Broadway, Shipham, Somerset BS25 1UE.

OWEN, Bernard Laurence; a Chairman of Industrial Tribunals, 1982–95; *b* 8 Aug. 1925; *s* of Albert Victor Paschal Owen and Dorothy May Owen; *m* 1950, Elsie Yarnold; one *s* two *d*. *Educ:* King Edward's School, Birmingham; solicitor. Commissioned Royal Warwickshire Regt, 1945, service in Sudan, Eritrea, Egypt; staff appts in GHQs Middle East and Palestine, 1946–47; retired 1947 (Major); qualified as solicitor, 1950; a Senior Partner, C. Upfill Jagger Son & Tilley, 1952–82. *Recreations:* gardening, photography, bird watching.

OWEN, David; *see* Owen, A. D.

OWEN, David Christopher; QC 2006; arbitrator and mediator; *b* 21 June 1958; *s* of late Kenneth and Barbara Owen; *m* 1985, Philippa Reid; one *s* one *d*. *Educ:* Marlborough Coll.; Merton Coll., Oxford (BA 1st Cl. Hons Hist.; MA). Administrator, Defence Procurement and Overseas Finance Divs, HM Treasury, 1979–81; called to the Bar, Middle Temple, 1983; Mediator Accreditation, CEDR, 2003. Mem., Magic Circle, 1978–; Associate Mem., Inner Magic Circle, 2013–. *Publications:* (ed jtly) MacGillivray on Insurance Law, 9th edn 1997 to 11th edn 2008. *Recreations:* magic, music, travel. *Address:* 20 Essex Street, WC2R 3AL. *T:* (020) 7842 1200, *Fax:* (020) 7842 1270. *E:* clerks@20essexst.com.

OWEN, David Harold Owen, OBE 1998; Registrar of the Privy Council, 1983–98; *b* 24 May 1933; *er* twin *s* of late Lloyd Owen Owen and Margaret Glyn Owen, Machynlleth, Powys; *m* 1st, 1961, Ailsa Ransome Wallis (*d* 1993); three *d*; 2nd, 1995, Julia (*née* Beck), *widow* of W. M. Lowe. *Educ:* Harrow Sch.; Gonville and Caius Coll., Cambridge. Called to the Bar, Gray's Inn, 1958. Served Royal Welch Fusiliers, 1951–53 (2nd Lieut). Campbell's Soups Ltd, King's Lynn, 1958–68; Lord Chancellor's Dept, 1969–80 (Private Sec. to Lord Chancellor, 1971–75); Chief Clerk, Judicial Cttee of Privy Council, 1980–83. *Recreations:* music, travel. *Address:* Whitelea, Stoney Lane, Bovingdon, Herts HP3 0DP. *Club:* Reform.
See also M. N. Gibbon.

OWEN, Prof. David Roger Jones, PhD, DSc; FRS 2009; FREng, FICE; Professor in Civil Engineering, Swansea University (formerly University of Wales, Swansea), since 1983; *b* Llanelli, 27 May 1942; *s* of Evan William Owen and Margaret Owen; *m* 1964, Janet Mary Pugh; two *d*. *Educ:* Univ. of Wales, Swansea (BSc 1963; MSc 1964); Northwestern Univ. (PhD 1967); Univ. of Wales (DSc 1983). FICE 1983; FREng 1996. Walter P. Murphy Res. Fellow, Northwestern Univ., 1966–67; Lectr, Sen. Lectr, then Reader, Univ. of Wales, Swansea, 1967–82. Founder and Chm., Rockfield Software Ltd, 1985–. Hon. DSc: Porto, 1996; Ecole normale supérieure, Cachan, 2008; Poly. Univ. of Catalonia, 2012. Foreign Member: US Nat. Acad. of Engrg, 2011; Chinese Acad. of Scis, 2011. Computational Mechanics Award, 2002, Gauss-Newton Medal, 2004, Internat. Assoc. for Computational Mechanics; Warner T. Koiter Medal, Amer. Soc. of Mechanical Engrs, 2003; Gold Medal, Univ. of Split, 2004; Premier Medal, Spanish Soc. for Computational Mechanics, 2005. *Publications:* (with E. Hinton) Finite Element Programming, 1977; (with E. Hinton) An Introduction to Finite Element Computations, 1979; (with E. Hinton) Finite Elements in Plasticity: theory and practice, 1980; (jtly) Computational Methods for Plasticity: theory and applications, 2008; over 400 articles in scientific jls. *Recreations:* tennis, flying, golf, walking. *Address:* 91 West Cross Lane, West Cross, Swansea SA3 5LU. *T:* (01792) 404935, *Fax:* (01792) 295676. *E:* d.r.j.owen@swansea.ac.uk.

OWEN, Sir Geoffrey (David), Kt 1989; Visiting Professor in Practice, Department of Management, London School of Economics and Political Science, since 2014 (Senior Fellow, 1998–2014); *b* 16 April 1934; *s* of late L. G. Owen and Violet Owen (*née* Chamberlain); *m* 1st, 1961, Dorothy Jane (*d* 1991); two *s* one *d*; 2nd, 1993, Miriam Marianna Gross, *qv*. *Educ:* Rugby Sch.; Balliol Coll., Oxford (MA). Joined Financial Times, 1958, feature writer, industrial correspondent; US Correspondent, 1961; Industrial Editor, 1967; Executive, Industrial Reorganisation Corp., 1967–69; Dir of Admin, Overseas Div., 1969, Dir of Personnel and Admin, 1972, British Leyland Internat.; Dep. Editor, 1974–80, Editor, 1981–90, Financial Times; Dir, Business Policy Prog., Centre for Econ. Performance, LSE, 1991–98. Dir, Laird Gp, 2000–06. Chm., Wincott Foundn, 1998–. *Publications:* Industry in the USA, 1966; From Empire to Europe, 1999; The Rise and Fall of Great Companies: Courtaulds and the reshaping of the man-made fibres industry, 2010.

OWEN, Gillian Frances, PhD; energy and utilities (formerly energy and environment) policy consultant, since 1988; Honorary Senior Research Associate, UCL Energy Institute, University College London, since 2015 (Senior Research Associate, 2011); *b* 26 May 1954; *d* of Iorwerth Ellis Owen and Edith Maud Owen; *m* 1980, David Ian Green. *Educ:* Newcastle upon Tyne (BA Librarianship/Social Scis 1976); Birkbeck Coll., Univ. of London (PhD Public Policy 1994). Asst Cataloguer, Clwyd CC, 1976–77; Asst Librarian, Coll. of Librarianship, Wales, 1978; Energy Advice Officer, City of Newcastle upon Tyne, 1979–81; Information and Develt Officer, 1981–84, Chief Officer, 1984–88, Nat. Energy Action. Sen. Res. Fellow, Centre for Mgt under Regulation, Univ. of Warwick, 2004–11; Research Prog. Leader, Monash Univ., Melbourne, 2012. Specialist Advr, Envmt Select Cttee, 1993–95; Mem., Monopolies and Mergers, subseq. Competition, Commn, 1992–2002; Expert Advr, Economic and Social Cttee, EC, 1996, 2002. Non-exec. Dir, Ofwat, 2006–12. Member: Bedfordshire Police Authy, 1994–2003; Adv. Bd, Ofgem, 1999–2000; Fuel Poverty Adv. Gp, 2002–12 (Dep. Chair, 2010–12); DEFRA Regulation Task Force, 2003–05; Consumer Challenge Panel, Australian Energy Regulator, 2013–; Expert Reference Panel, Energy White Paper (Australia), 2013–15; Bd, Energy Consumers Australia, 2014–; Chair, REAL Assurance Consumer Code, 2006–12; Vice Chm., Consumer Congress, 1987; Chm., Public Utilities Access Forum, 1995–2012. *Publications:* Public Purpose or Private Benefit: the politics of energy conservation, 1999. *Recreations:* travel, walking, cycling, art, design and architecture, theatre, cinema. *Address:* UCL Energy Institute, Central House, 14 Upper Woburn Place, WC1H 0NN.

OWEN, Gordon Michael William, CBE 1991; Chairman, NXT plc, 2001–05; *b* 9 Dec. 1937; *s* of late Christopher Knowles Owen and Mrs Margaret Joyce Milward (*née* Spencer); *m* 1963, Jennifer Pearl, (Jane), Bradford (marr. diss. 2001); one *s* one *d*; *m* 2001, Tina Elizabeth (*née* Davies). *Educ:* Cranbrook Sch. Cable & Wireless, 1954–91: Dir, 1986–91; Jt Man. Dir, 1987–88; Dep. Chief Exec., 1988–90; Gp Man. Dir, 1990–91; Chairman: Mercury Communications Ltd, 1990–91 (Man. Dir, 1984–90); Peterstar Communications, St Petersburg, 1992–94; Energis Communications Ltd, subseq. Energis plc, 1993–2002; Utility Cable plc, 1994–98; Acorn (formerly Acorn Computer) Group, 1996–98; Yeoman Gp plc, 1996–2004; Director: Portals Gp, 1988–95; London Electricity, 1989–97; Waste Gas Technology, 1993–2002; Olivetti SpA, 1996–2001. Chm., MacIntyre Care, 1993–2003. Chm., Acad. of St Martin in the Fields Orch., 2002–04 (Vice-Chm., 1994–2002). Chm. Bd of Govs, St Michael's Sch., Otford, 1994–2011. *Recreations:* beekeeping, stamp collecting, sailing, bad golf. *Address:* Sutton End House, Sutton, W Sussex RH20 1PY.

OWEN, Sir Hugo Dudley C.; *see* Cunliffe-Owen.

OWEN, Ivor Henri, CBE 1992; CEng, FIMechE; Director General, Design Council, 1988–93; *b* 14 Nov. 1930; *s* of Thomas and Anne Owen; *m* 1954, Jane Frances Graves; two *s* one *d*. *Educ:* Liverpool College of Technology; Manchester College of Science and Technology. Engineering apprentice, later design engineer, Craven Bros (Manchester), Stockport, 1947–57; Manufacturing Develt Engr, Steam Turbine Div., English Electric,

Rugby, 1957–62; Manager, Netherton Works, English Electric, Bootle, 1962–66 (hydro electric plant, steam turbine components, condensers, nuclear equipment); Manager, English Electric Computers, Winsford, 1966–69; Manager, Winsford Kidsgrove Works, ICL, 1969–70; Man. Dir, RHP Bearings, 1970–81; Thorn EMI: Chief Exec., Gen. Engineering Div., 1981–83; Chm., Appliance and Lighting Group, 1984–87; Dir, 1984–87. Chm., Ball Roller Bearing Manufrs Assoc., 1978–80; Vice-Pres., Fedn European Bearing Manufrs Assoc., 1978–80. Royal Acad. of Engrg Vis. Prof., Univ. of Bath, 1994–97. FRSA. *Recreations:* theatre, reading, running, gardening, motor cycling, silversmithing.

OWEN, Jane Caroline; HM Diplomatic Service; Chief Operating Officer, UK Trade & Investment, since 2014; *b* 15 April 1963; *d* of Thomas and Jeanne Owen; *m* 1998, David Donnelly; one *s* one *d*. *Educ:* Ellerslie Sch., Malvern; Trinity Coll., Cambridge (BA Hons 1986). English teacher, JET prog., Osaka, Japan, 1986; entered FCO, 1987; Mexico and Central American Dept, FCO, 1987; Japanese lang. trng, 1988–90; 2nd Sec., Commercial, Tokyo, 1990–93; Head: Exports to Japan Unit, DTI, 1993–96 (on secondment); Mediterranean and Asia Sect., EU Dept (External), FCO, 1996–98; Dep. Hd of Mission, Hanoi, 1998–2002; Dir of Trade Promotion, Tokyo, 2002–06; Counsellor, Climate, Science, Economy and Trade, 2006–08, Dir of Trade and Investment, 2008–10, New Delhi; Ambassador to Norway, 2010–14. *Recreations:* travelling, scuba diving, ski-ing, spending time with my family. *Address:* UK Trade & Investment, 1 Victoria Street, SW1H 0ET.

OWEN, Jennifer Ann, CBE 2010; Deputy Chief Executive, 2010–12, and Executive Director, Adults, Health and Community Wellbeing (formerly Adult Social Care), 2004–12, Essex County Council; *b* 23 Aug. 1954; *d* of Col John Edward Owen and Jean Wardle Owen; *m* 2001, Jeff Jerome; one *s*. *Educ:* Sheffield Poly. (BA Hons Applied Soc. Studies; CQSW, CMS 1976). Regl Dir, Social Services Inspectorate, DoH, 2001–04. Non-executive Director: Royal Free London (formerly Hampstead) NHS Foundn Trust, 2010–; Housing & Care 21. Pres., Assoc. of Dirs of Adult Social Services, 2009–10 (Vice-Pres., 2008–09); Trustee, Bd, SCIE, 2007–13. *Recreations:* theatre, country walks, travelling, company of friends.

OWEN, John Aubrey; Senior Partner, Inside Advice, consultancy services, since 2001; *b* 1 Aug. 1945; *s* of late Prebendary Douglas Aubrey Owen and Patricia Joan Owen (*née* Griggs); *m* 1971, Julia Margaret Jones; one *s* one *d*. *Educ:* City of London Sch.; St Catharine's Coll., Cambridge (MA). Joined Min. of Transport, 1969; Asst Private Sec. to Minister for Transport Industries, 1972; DoE, 1973–75; Dept of Transport, 1975–78; seconded to Cambridgeshire CC, 1978–80; DoE, 1980–2001: Regional Dir, Northern Regional Office, Depts of the Environment and Transport, 1987–91; Dir, Personnel Management, 1991–95. Dir, Regeneration, then Skills, Educn and Regeneration, later Skills, Enterprise and Communities, Govt Office for London, 1995–2001. Chm., Mosaic (formerly New Islington and Hackney) Housing Assoc., 2002–06; Dep. Chm., Family Mosaic Housing Assoc., 2006–. MInstD. *Recreations:* gardening, reading, watching cricket, genealogy. *Address:* 33 Valley Road, Welwyn Garden City, Herts AL8 7DH. *T:* (01707) 321768. *E:* johna.owen@ntlworld.com. *Club:* Middlesex CC.

OWEN, Prof. John Joseph Thomas, FRS 1988; Sands Cox Professor and Head of Department of Anatomy, University of Birmingham, 1978–2001; *b* 7 Jan. 1934; *s* of Thomas and Alice Owen; *m* 1961, Barbara Schofield Forster (marr. diss. 1992); two *s*. *Educ:* Univ. of Liverpool (BSc, MD); MA Oxon 1963. Lecturer: Univ. of Liverpool, 1960–63; Univ. of Oxford, 1963–72; Fellow, St Cross Coll., Oxford, 1968–72; Sen. Scientist, Imperial Cancer Res. Fund's Tumour Immunology Unit, UCL, 1972–74; Prof. of Anatomy, Univ. of Newcastle upon Tyne 1974–78. Vis. Scholar, Stanford Univ., USA, 2000–01; Greenberg Scholar, Oklahoma Med. Res. Foundn, USA, 2001–02. Medical Research Council: Mem., Physiol Systems and Disorders Bd, 1978–83; Chm., Grants Cttee, B, 1980–83; Mem., Cell Bd, 1991–94; Member: Wellcome Trust's Biochemistry and Cell Biology Panel, 1987–90; Council, Nat. Kidney Res. Fund, 1987–90; Council, Royal Soc., 1991–93. Founder FMedSci 1998. *Publications:* numerous contribs to sci. literature. *Recreations:* road and track cycling, dancing, Japanese studies, helping with my grandchildren.

OWEN, Prof. John Wyn, CB 1994; FLSW; Member, Administrative Council, Madariaga - College of Europe Foundation, since 2005; Professor, College of Medicine, Swansea University, since 2013; *b* 15 May 1942; *s* of late Idwal Wyn Owen and of Myfi Owen (*née* Hughes); *m* 1967, Elizabeth Ann (*née* MacFarlane); one *s* one *d*. *Educ:* Friars School, Bangor; St John's Coll., Cambridge (BA 1964, MA 1968); Hosp. Admin. Staff Coll. (DipHA 1967). Trainee, King Edward VII's Hosp. Fund for London, 1964–66; Dep. Hosp. Sec., West Wales Gen. Hosp., Carmarthen, 1966–67; Hosp. Sec., Glantawe HMC, Swansea, 1967–70; Staff Training Officer, Welsh Hosp. Bd, Cardiff, 1968–70; Divl Administrator, Univ. of Wales, Cardiff, HMC, 1970–72; St Thomas' Hospital: Asst Clerk, and King's Fund Fellow, 1972–74; Dist Administrator, St Thomas' Health Dist, Teaching, 1974–79; Trustee, Refresh, 1976–78; Hon. Tutor, Med. Sch., 1974–79; Praeceptor, Sch. of Health Administration, Univ. of Minnesota, 1974–79; Exec. Dir, United Medical Enterprises, London, 1979–85; Dir, NHS Wales, Welsh Office, 1985–94; Chm., Welsh Health Common Services Authy, 1985–94; Dir Gen., NSW Health Dept, Sydney, 1994–97; Sec., Nuffield Trust, 1997–2005. Personal Chair, Univ. of Wales, 2012; Professorial Fellow, Royal Soc. Public Health, 2012. Chairman: Olympic Health and Med. Working Cttee, 1994–97; DoH Change Mgt Gp on Nurse Regulation, 1999–2001; Member: Strategic Planning and Evaluation Cttee, Nat. Health and MRC, 1994–97; Australian Health Ministers' Adv. Council, 1994–97 (Chm., 1995–97); Health Adv. Bd, 1994–97; Public Health Assoc., 1994; Mgt Cttee, Nat. Breast Cancer Centre, 1995–97. Mem., Bd, 2006–, Chair, Global Health Cttee, 2007–13, UK Health Protection Agency; Member: Wales Bd, Health Protection Cttee, 2006–13; Health Protection Adv. Cttee, Welsh Assembly Govt, then Welsh Govt, 2010– (Chm., 2014–); Global Council, Health Action Partnership Internat., 2010; Adv. Bd, Global Health Section, Internat. Studies Assoc., 2014–; Vice-Chm., Nat. Heart Forum, 2007–. Sen. Associate, Judge Inst. of Mgt Studies, Univ. of Cambridge, 1997–2010; Adjunct Prof., Public Health, Univ. of Sydney, 2006–; Visiting Fellow: Univ. of NSW, 1979; LSE, 1997–2010. Trustee, RESEC, and Chair, RESEC Cymru/Wales, 2009–. Trustee, Florence Nightingale Museum Trust, 1983–90; Chm., Health Bldg Educn Gp, British Consultants' Bureau, 1983–85; Mem. Adv. Forum, Personnel Lead Body, 1992–94. Chm., Europe in the World, European Foundn Centre, 2004–05. Founder Mem., Med. Chapter, Australian Opera, 1995–97; Mem., NSW Cambridge Soc. Cttee, 1996–97; Sec., London Cambridge Soc., 1997–2004 (Chm., 2004–11); Chair, Wales Br., Britain Australia Soc., 2009–. Chm., Canada UK Colloquium, 2013; Mem. Bd, Canada UK Council, 2014–. Chm., UWIC, 2005–11; Member: Court, Univ. of Wales, 1998–2011; Council, Univ. of Wales Coll. of Medicine, 1997–2005. Mem., Inst. of Medicine, NAS, USA, 1998. FRGS 1968; FRSA 1998; FHSM 1992; FACHSE 1994; FRSocMed 1997; FRSPH 2013. CCMI 2005; Founding FLSW 2010 (Mem. Council, 2010–; Treas., 2012–). Hon. FFPHM 1991; Hon. MRCP 2002. Hon. Fellow: UCW, Aberystwyth, 1991; UCW, Bangor, 1992. Hon. Mem., Gorsedd of Bards, 2000. DUniv Glamorgan, 1999; Hon. DSc City, 2004. *Publications:* contribs to professional jls. *Recreations:* organ playing, opera, travel. *Address:* Newton Farm, Newton, Cowbridge CF71 7RZ. *T:* (01446) 775113. *Clubs:* Athenæum; Cardiff and County.

OWEN, John Wynne, CMG 1998; MBE 1979; DL; HM Diplomatic Service, retired; Chairman (non-executive): CLS Fabrication Ltd, 1989–2012; Autoport North America Inc., since 2004 (Director, since 2002); Iceman Capital Advisors Ltd, since 2006; Loriners' Investment Co. Ltd, since 2008; Fidelity China Special Situations plc, since 2010; *b* 25 April 1939; *s* of Thomas David Owen and Mair Eluned Owen; *m* 1st, 1962, Thelma Margaret Gunton (*d* 1987); one *s* two *d*; 2nd, 1988, Carol Edmunds; one step *d*. *Educ:* Gowerton Grammar Sch.; Westminster Coll., London. FO 1956; 2nd Lieut Royal Signals, 1958–60; served Djakarta, Saigon, Paris, San Salvador, to 1967; resigned 1967; business, 1967–70; reinstated 1970; FCO, 1970–73; Tehran, 1973–77; São Paulo, 1978–80; Peking, 1980–82; FCO, 1983; special leave, 1985; Chm., Gunham, Holdings Ltd, 1985–89; Counsellor, FCO, 1989–92; Consul Gen., Boston, 1992–95; Governor, Cayman Is, 1995–99. Non-executive Director: Scimitar Advrs, 1999–; Queensgate Bank Ltd, 2010–, Queensgate Trust Co. Ltd, 2010– (non-exec. Dir, Queensgate Bank and Trust Co., 2006–10). Chairman: British Laminated Plastics Fabricators' Assoc., 1987–90; Isle of Wight Strategic Partnership, 2006–08; IoW Chamber of Commerce, Trade and Industry, 2008–. Trustee: Grandparents Fedn, subseq. Grandparents Assoc., 2000–09 (Dep. Chm., 2002–09); Fidelity UK Foundn, 2006–; Fidelity Internat. Foundn, 2007–. Chm., Friends of the Cayman Is, 2006–. Fellow, Univ. of Wales, Aberystwyth, 2006. FCMI. Freeman, City of London, 1978; Liveryman, Loriners' Co., 1978– (Mem., Ct of Assts, 1999–; Master, 2005). DL Isle of Wight, 2007. *Recreations:* walking, art, reading, fly-fishing.

OWEN, Jonathan Robert, OBE 2014; social entrepreneur and author, since 2001; *b* Eaglescliffe, 2 June 1958; *s* of Toby and Gaie Owen; *m* 1997, Hiromi Takahashi. *Educ:* Eton Coll.; Queens' Coll., Cambridge (BA Modern Hist. 1980; MA); London Business Sch. (MSc 1986). Brand mgt, Procter & Gamble, 1980–83; Hd of Res., SDP, 1983–84; Partner: Cap Gemini, Mac Gp, 1986–98; Accenture (formerly Andersen Consulting), 1998–2001; owner, Auvian Ltd, 2001–. Co-Founder and Trustee: Teach First, 2002–; Start Up, 2005–; Future Leaders, 2006–; Teaching Leaders, 2008– (Chm., 2008–); Achievement for All, 2011–; Spark Inside, 2012– (Chm., 2012–); Stir Educn, 2013– (Chm., 2013–); Right to Succeed, 2015– (Chm., 2015–). FRGS; FRSA. *Publications:* Management Stripped Bare, 2002, 3rd edn 2012; Hardcore Management, 2004; How to Lead, 2005, 4th edn 2015; Leadership Skills Handbook, 2006, 3rd edn 2012; How to Manage, 2006, 4th edn 2015; Power at Work, 2008; Tribal Business School, 2008; Death of Modern Management, 2009; How to Sell, 2010; How to Influence, 2010; Leadership Rules, 2011; Management Rules, 2011; Mobile MBA, 2011; How to Coach, 2013; Quantitative Easing: the wrong sort of money; 2013; Mindset of Success, 2015. *Recreations:* tribes, extreme jogging, chocolate, opera. *Address:* Teaching Leaders, 65 Kingsway, WC2B 6TD. *T:* (020) 3116 0707. *E:* jo@ilead.guru.

OWEN, Les; *see* Owen, A. L.

OWEN, Lynette Isabel, OBE 2009; copyright and rights consultant; Copyright Director, Pearson Education Ltd, 2002–13; *b* 29 June 1947; *d* of Warwick Jack Burgoyne Owen and Betty Isabel Owen (*née* Drummond). *Educ:* Bedford Coll., London (BA Hons (English) 1968). Rights Asst, CUP, 1968–73; Rights Manager, Pitman Publishing Ltd, 1973–75; N American Sales Manager, Marshall Cavendish, 1975–76; Rights Manager, 1976–87, Rights Dir, 1988–94, Longman Gp UK; Rights and Contracts Dir, Addison Wesley, 1994–98; Rights Dir, Pearson Educn Ltd, 1998–2001. London Internat. Book Fair/British Council Lifetime Achievement Award for contribn to internat. publishing, 2003; (inaugural) Kim Scott Walwyn Prize, 2004. *Publications:* Selling Rights, 1991, 7th edn 2014; Clark's Publishing Agreements, contrib. 2nd and 3rd edns, gen. ed. and contrib. 4th edn 1993 to 9th edn 2013; handbooks on copyright and licensing for Eastern Europe, China, etc; numerous articles in Bookseller, Publishing News, Learned Publishing, etc. *Recreations:* theatre, music, art, reading. *Address:* 147B St Pancras Way, NW1 0SY. *T:* and *Fax:* (020) 7284 0470. *E:* lynetteowen@hotmail.co.uk.

OWEN, Michael James; football commentator, BT Sport, since 2013; former professional footballer; *b* 14 Dec. 1979; *s* of Terence Owen and Janette Owen; *m* 2005, Louise Bonsall; one *s* three *d*. *Educ:* Hawarden High Sch.; Idsall Sch.; Lilleshall Sch. of Excellence. Liverpool Football Club, 1996–2004: member, winning team: Worthington Cup, 2001; FA Cup 2001; UEFA Cup, 2001; Charity Shield, 2001; European Super Cup, 2001; player: Real Madrid, 2004–05; Newcastle Utd, 2005–09 (Captain, 2008–09); Manchester Utd, 2009–12; Stoke City, 2012–13. Mem., England Football Team, 1998–2008; Mem., World Cup team, 1998, 2002, 2006. Ambassador and Advr, Qipco British Champions' Series, Flat Racing, 2013–. Young Player of the Year, PFA, 1998; BBC Sports Personality of the Year, 1998; Ballon d'Or, France Football, 2001. *Publications:* (with Dave Harrison) Michael Owen: in person (autobiog.), 2000; Michael Owen's Soccer Skills, 2000; (with Paul Hayward) Michael Owen: off the record (autobiog.), 2004. *Address:* c/o MOM Sports, MOM House, Shay Lane, Hampton, Malpas, Cheshire SY14 8AD.

OWEN, Sir Michael (John), Kt 2014; PhD; FRCPsych, FMedSci; FLSW; Professor of Psychological Medicine and Head, Institute of Psychological Medicine and Clinical Neuroscience (formerly Department of Psychological Medicine, then Department of Psychological Medicine and Neurology), since 1998, Director, MRC Centre for Neuropsychiatric Genetics and Genomics, since 2009, School of Medicine, Cardiff University (formerly University of Wales College of Medicine, Cardiff); *b* 24 Nov. 1955; *s* of Dr John Robson Owen and Mary Gillian Owen (*née* Dowsett); *m* 1985, Dr Deborah Cohen; two *s* one *d*. *Educ:* Univ. of Birmingham (BSc Anatomical Studies 1977; PhD Neurosci. 1982; MB ChB 1983). MRCPsych 1987, FRCPsych 1997. University of Wales College of Medicine, Cardiff, then School of Medicine, Cardiff University: Sen. Lectr, Dept of Psychological Medicine and Inst. of Med. Genetics, 1990–95; Prof. of Neuropsychiatric Genetics, 1995–98; Pro Vice-Chancellor for Res., 2001–04; Dep. Pro Vice-Chancellor for Res., 2005–13; Chm., Div. of Community Specialties, School of Medicine, Cardiff Univ., 2002–05. Hon. Consultant Psychiatrist, Cardiff and Vale NHS Trust, 1990–; Dir, Neurosci. and Mental Health Res. Inst., 2010–14. FMedSci 1999; FLSW 2011. Strömgren Medal, Erik Strömgren Foundn, 2011; Lieber Prize, Brain and Behavior Res. Foundn, 2012; William K. Warren Dist. Res. Award, Internat. Congress on Schizophrenia Res., 2013. *Publications:* (jtly) Seminars in Psychiatric Genetics, 1994; (ed jtly) Psychiatric Genetics and Genomics, 2002; articles on psychiatric genetics and psychiatry. *Recreations:* walking, cycling, reading, sailing, fishing. *Address:* MRC Centre for Neuropsychiatric Genetics and Genomics, Hadyn Ellis Building, Cathays, Cardiff CF24 4HQ. *T:* (029) 2068 8320. *E:* owenmj@cardiff.ac.uk.

OWEN, Dr Myrfyn; Director General, Wildfowl and Wetlands Trust, 1992–97; ecological consultant, 1997–2009; *b* 8 April 1943; *s* of William Owen and Anne Mary Owen; *m* 1967, Lydia Marian Vaughan (*née* Rees); two *d*. *Educ:* Sir Hugh Owen Grammar Sch.; University Coll., Aberystwyth (BSc 1964); Univ. of Leeds (PhD 1967). Wildfowl Trust, later Wildfowl and Wetlands Trust: Ecologist, 1967; Conservation Res. Officer, 1974; Asst Dir (Res.), 1979; Head of Res., 1988; Dir, 1991–92. *Publications:* Wildfowl of Europe, 1976; Wild Geese of the World, 1980; Wildfowl in Great Britain, 1986; Waterfowl Ecology, 1990; numerous scientific papers. *Recreations:* gardening, cookery, cycling, wildlife. *Address:* Woodleigh House, 62 Woodmancote, Dursley, Glos GL11 4AQ. *T:* (01453) 543244.

OWEN, Nicholas David Arundel; Presenter: BBC News, since 2007; Classic FM, since 2010; *b* 10 Feb. 1947; *m* 1983, Brenda (*née* Firth); two *s* one *d*, and one step *s* one step *d*. Newspaper journalist, 1964–81; BBC TV, 1981–83; Presenter, ITN, 1984–2007. *Publications:* The Brighton Belle, 1972; History of the British Trolleybus, 1974; Diana, The People's Princess, 1997; Days Like This, 2012. *Recreations:* railways, reading, walking, golf, bridge. *Address:* BBC News Centre, Broadcasting House, Portland Place, W1A 1AA.

OWEN, Patricia, (Mrs Peter Owen); *see* Hodge, P.

OWEN, Peter Francis, CB 1990; Secretary General, Institute of Chartered Accountants in England and Wales, 2002–03 (Executive Director, 1998–2002); Executive Director, Better Government Initiative, since 2013; *b* 4 Sept. 1940; *s* of Arthur Owen and Violet (*née* Morris);

m 1963, Ann Preece; one *s* one *d*. *Educ:* The Liverpool Inst.; Liverpool Univ. (BA French). Joined MPBW, 1964; Cabinet Office, 1971–72; Private Sec. to successive Ministers of Housing and Construction, 1972–74; Asst Sec., Housing Policy Review, 1975–77, Local Govt Finance, 1977–80; Under Sec. and Regional Dir of Northern and Yorks and Humberside Regs, Depts of the Environment and of Transport, 1980–82; Under Secretary: Rural Affairs, DoE, 1983; Local Govt Finance Policy, DoE, 1984–86; Dep. Sec., Housing and Construction, DoE, 1986–90; Head of Econ. and Domestic Affairs Secretariat, Cabinet Office, 1990–94; Dep. Sec., Sch. Curriculum and Teachers, DFE, 1994–95; Dir Gen. for Schools, DfEE, 1995–98. *Recreations:* reading, gardening, French, classical guitar. *Address:* Oakmead, The Avenue, Hampton, Middlesex TW12 3RS.

OWEN, Philip W.; *see* Wynn Owen.

OWEN, Prof. Richard John, PhD; Chair, Responsible Innovation, since 2010, and Associate Dean (Research), since 2014, University of Exeter Business School (Director, Postgraduate Research, 2012–14); *b* Campbeltown, Scotland, 20 Oct. 1966; *s* of Gordon Owen and Maria Owen; *m* 1995, Therese Hassell; one *s* one *d*. *Educ:* Christ Coll., Brecon; Univ. of Wales (BSc; PhD 1997). Faculty Scientist, Bermuda Biological Station for Res., 1997–2003; Hd, Envmt and Human Health, Envmt Agency, 2003–08; Prof., Policy Studies Inst. and Univ. of Westminster, 2008–10. Strategic Advr, EPSRC, 2011–. FRSA 2010. *Publications:* contribs to books and articles in scientific jls. *Recreations:* Norfolk Terriers, country walks, travel. *Address:* University of Exeter Business School, Streatham Court, Rennes Drive, Exeter EX4 4PU. *T:* (01392) 723458. *E:* r.j.owen@exeter.ac.uk.

OWEN, Richard Wilfred, FCA; retired from Touche Ross, 1993; *b* 26 Oct. 1932; *s* of Wilfred Owen and Ivy (*née* Gamble); *m* 1966, Sheila Marie Kerrigan; three adopted *s* one adopted *d*, and one foster *s* one foster *d*. *Educ:* Gunnersbury Catholic Grammar Sch. Lloyds Bank, 1949–51; RAF Russian translator, 1951–53; accountancy articles, 1953–58; Thomson McLintock, 1958–62; Crompton Parkinson, 1962–64; Touche Ross & Co., 1964–93: admitted to Partnership, 1969; seconded to HM Treasury, 1971; Partner-in-Charge, Management Consultancy, 1974–87, Nat. Dir, Personnel, 1987–93; UK Chm., 1988–90; Eur. Dir, Management Consultancy, 1990–92. Pres., Management Consultancies Assoc., 1987. Chm., Cardinal Hume Centre, 1996–2002; Trustee, Isabel Hospice, 1994–2000. KSG 1997. *Recreation:* Salisbury Cathedral guide. *Address:* 26 The Close, Salisbury, Wilts SP1 2EJ.

OWEN, Rob, OBE 2015; Chief Executive, St Giles Trust, since 2007; *b* Woking, 27 July 1965; *s* of late John Owen and of Sue Owen; *m* 2000, Cindy Yendell; one *s* one *d*. *Educ:* Univ. of Liverpool (BA Hons); Henley Business Sch. (MBA). Nomura, 1987–90; Schroders, 1991–98; ABN-Amro, 1998–2001. *Publications:* Sports Sponsorship: going for gold, 2006. *Recreations:* running, snow boarding, family. *Address:* St Giles Trust, Georgian House, 64–68 Camberwell Church Street, SE5 8JB. *E:* Rob.Owen@StGilesTrust.org.uk. *Club:* Reform.

OWEN, Robert Frank; QC 1996; **His Honour Judge Owen;** a Circuit Judge, since 2009; a Deputy High Court Judge, since 2008; *b* 31 May 1953; *s* of Tudor Owen and Pat Owen; *m* 1980, Anna Shaw; three *s*. *Educ:* St Asaph Grammar Sch.; Poly. of Central London (LLB Hons). Called to the Bar, Gray's Inn, 1977, Bencher, 2007; Recorder, 2000–09. *Recreations:* coastal walking, sport. *Address:* Birmingham Civil Justice Centre, 33 Bull Street, Birmingham B4 6DS.

OWEN, Robert John Richard; Director, Stanhill Capital Ltd, since 2011; *b* 11 Feb. 1940; *s* of Richard Owen and Margaret Owen (*née* Fletcher); *m* (marr. diss.); two *s* one *d*; *m* Margaret Helen. *Educ:* Repton School; Oxford University. Foreign Office, 1961–68, incl. HM Embassy, Washington, 1965–68; HM Treasury, 1968–70; Morgan Grenfell & Co., 1970–79 (Dir, 1974); Lloyds Bank International, 1979–85 (Dir); Chm. and Chief Exec., Lloyds Merchant Bank, 1985–88; Comr for Securities, Hong Kong, 1988–89; Chm., Securities and Futures Commn, Hong Kong, 1989–92. Chairman: Techpacific Capital Ltd, 1999–2004; Internat. Securities Consultancy Ltd, 2000–; Crosby Asset Mgt Ltd (formerly Crosby Capital Partners Inc.), 2002–11; IB Daiwa Ltd, 2005–08; Repton Internat. Schs Ltd, 2013–; Sen. Advr, Nomura Internat. (Hong Kong) Ltd, 1993–2007; Dep. Chm., Nomura Asia Hldgs Ltd, 1994–97; Director: European Capital Co. Ltd, 1992–2001; Sunday Communications Ltd, 2000–07; Singapore Exchange Ltd, 2004–13; Citibank (Hong Kong) Ltd, 2004–; Repton Dubai Ltd, 2007–; Foremarke Dubai Ltd, 2013–; Repton Abu Dhabi Ltd, 2013–. Mem. Council and Mem. Regulatory Bd, Lloyd's of London, 1993–95; Bd Mem., Dubai Financial Services Authority, 2002–. Gov., Repton Sch., 1994–. *Recreations:* oriental paintings, mountain walking. *Address:* Mary Knoll House, Whitcliffe, Ludlow, Shropshire SY8 2HD.

OWEN, Hon. Sir Robert (Michael), Kt 2001; a Judge of the High Court, Queen's Bench Division, 2001–14; *b* 19 Sept. 1944; *s* of Gwynne Llewellyn Owen and Phoebe Constance Owen; *m* 1969, Sara Josephine Rumbold; two *s*. *Educ:* Durham Sch.; Exeter Univ. (LLB). Called to Bar, Inner Temple, 1968, Bencher, 1995; QC 1988. Judicial Mem., Transport Tribunal, 1985–97; Recorder, 1987–2000; Dep. High Court Judge, 1994–2000; Presiding Judge, Western Circuit, 2005–08. Chm., Litvinenko Inquiry, 2014–. DTI Inspector, 1991–92. Chairman: Gen. Council of the Bar, 1997; Civil Cttee, Judicial Studies Bd, 2004–08; Dir of Trng for Sen. Judiciary, 2010–12; Mem. Bd, Judicial Coll., 2011–12. Chm., London Common Law and Commercial Bar Assoc., 1994–95. Chairman: vCJD Trust, 2002–; Fowey Harbour Commn Consultative Gp, 2006–10; British Internat. 6m Assoc., 2014–. Trustee, Pestalozzi Internat. Village Trust, 2014–. Gov., Coll. of Law, 1998–2004. FRSA 1997. Hon. LLD Exeter, 2007. *Clubs:* Travellers, Les Six; Royal Yacht Squadron.

OWEN, Ruth Ellen, CBE 2010; Director General Personal Tax, HM Revenue and Customs, since 2012; *b* Kingston upon Thames, 12 Oct. 1968; *d* of Michael Owen and Penny Owen. *Educ:* Epsom High Sch.; Queen Mary and Westfield Coll., Univ. of London (BA Hons Politics 1990). Joined DSS, 1990; Business Strategy Dir, 2005–08, Chief Operating Officer, 2008–11, Jobcentre Plus; Work Services Dir and Dep. Chief Operating Officer, DWP, 2011–12. *Recreation:* supporting Manchester City Football Club. *Address:* HM Revenue and Customs, Room 2C/22, 100 Parliament Street, SW1A 2BQ. *T:* (020) 7147 2735. *E:* ruth.owen@hmrc.gsi.gov.uk.

OWEN, Susan Jane, CB 2010; Permanent Secretary, Department for Culture, Media and Sport, since 2013; *b* 3 June 1955; *d* of Glyn and Diana Owen; *m* 1987, Prof. Martin C. Albrow; one *s*, and three step *s*. *Educ:* Lady Eleanor Holles Sch.; Newnham Coll., Cambridge (MA); University Coll. Cardiff (MSc Econ. 1977). Lectr, UC Cardiff, 1979–88; HM Treasury: Econ. Advr, 1989–95; Asst Sec./Grade 5, EU Co-ordination, 1995–98; on secondment: Econ. Advr, Work/Family Balance Policy, No 10 Policy Unit, 1998–99; Econ. Counsellor, Washington, FCO, 1999–2002; Dir, EMU Policy, Euro Preparations and Debt Mgt, 2002–05; Dir of Ops, 2005; Dir Gen. for Corporate Performance, 2006–09, Actg Perm. Sec., 2008, DFID; Dir Gen. for Strategy (formerly Welfare and Wellbeing), DWP, 2009–13. Associate Fellow, Newnham Coll., Cambridge, 2011–14. *Publications:* contrib. articles to jls incl. Fiscal Studies, Work, Employment and Society, Jl Labour Economics. *Recreations:* family, friends, sport, theatre, cooking, gardening. *Address:* Department for Culture, Media and Sport, 100 Parliament Street, SW1A 2BQ. *T:* (020) 7211 6254. *Clubs:* Royal Automobile; Everton Football.

OWEN, Tim Wynn; QC 2000; a Recorder, since 2004; a Deputy High Court Judge, since 2010; *b* 11 Jan. 1958; *s* of Meurig Wynn Owen and Thelma Owen (*née* Parry); *m* 1992, Jemma Redgrave; two *s*. *Educ:* Atlantic Coll.; London Sch. of Economics (BA 1st Cl. Hons History 1979); PCL (Dip. Law 1982). Campaign Co-ordinator, Radical Alternatives to Prison, 1979–81; called to the Bar, Middle Temple, 1983 (Bencher, 2005); in practice at the Bar, 1984–; called to the Bar of Antigua and Barbuda, 1994. *Publications:* (jtly) Prison Law, 1993, 4th edn 2008. *Recreations:* film, travel. *Address:* Matrix Chambers, Griffin Building, Gray's Inn, WC1R 5LN. *T:* (020) 7404 3447.

OWEN, Trevor Bryan, CBE 1987; Chairman: Bethlem Royal and Maudsley Special Health Authority, 1988–94; Committee of Management, Institute of Psychiatry, 1990–97; *b* 3 April 1928; *s* of Leonard Owen, CIE and Dilys (*née* Davies Bryan); *m* 1955, (Jennifer) Gaie (*née* Houston); one *s* one *d*. *Educ:* Rugby Sch.; Trinity Coll., Oxford (Scholar; MA). Sch. Student, British Sch. of Archaeology, Athens, 1953–54; ICI, 1955–78: wide range of jobs culminating in, successively: Chm., J. P. MacDougall Ltd; Dir, Paints, Agricl and Plastics Divs; Co. Personnel Manager; Man. Dir, Remploy Ltd, 1978–88. Member: Higher Educn Review Gp, Govt of NI, 1979–81; CNAA, 1973–79; Continuing Educn Adv. Council, BBC, 1977–85; Council, CBI, 1982–88; Council, Industrial Soc., 1967–88; Council, Inst. of Manpower Studies, 1975–88 (Chm., 1977–78); Chm. Bd of Governors, Nat. Inst. for Social Work, 1985–91 (Mem., 1982–97; Mem., Working Party on Role and Tasks of Social Workers, 1981–82). Chm., Phab, 1988–91. *Publications:* Business School Programmes—the requirements of British manufacturing industry (with D. Casey and N. Huskisson), 1971; Making Organisations Work, 1978; The Manager and Industrial Relations, 1979; articles in jls. *Address:* 8 Rochester Terrace, NW1 9JN.

OWEN, Tudor Wyn, FRAeS; **His Honour Judge Owen;** a Circuit Judge, since 2007; *b* Aberdare, Glamorgan, 16 May 1951; *s* of late Abel Rhys Owen and Mair Owen (*née* Jenkins); *m* 1978 (marr. diss.). *Educ:* Aberdare Boys Grammar Sch.; King's Coll. London (LLB Hons 1973); Council of Legal Educn. Called to the Bar, Gray's Inn, 1974; in practice on SE Circuit, 1975–2007; DTI Inspector, 1987; Asst Recorder, 1991–93; Recorder, 1993–2007. Mem., SE Circuit Cttee, 1993–96. General Council of the Bar: Mem., 1988–94; Member: Professional Conduct Cttee, 1989–91; Professional Standards Cttee, 1991–92; Gen. Mgt Cttee, 1992–94; Vice-Chm., Bar Cttee, 1992–93. Mem., Criminal Bar Assoc. Cttee, 1986–92 (Treas., 1989–92). Panel Mem., Bar Disciplinary Tribunals, 1995–2007. Mem., Parole Bd, 2010–; Judicial Mem., Mental Health Review Tribunal, 2010–. UK delegate to European Air Sports, 2005–06. FRAeS 2003. Freeman, City of London, 2004; Liveryman, Hon. Co. of Air Pilots (formerly GAPAN), 2005 (Asst to Court, 2007–09; Warden, 2009–12; Master, 2013–14). *Recreations:* flying helicopters and WWII aeroplanes, racing historic Formula 1 cars, travel. *Address:* Snaresbrook Crown Court, 75 Hollybush Hill, E11 1QW. *E:* HHJudge.TudorOwen@judiciary.gsi.gov.uk. *Clubs:* Garrick, Royal Air Force; St Moritz Tobogganing.

OWEN, Ursula Margaret, OBE 2004; freelance publisher and writer; *b* 21 Jan. 1937; *d* of Emma Sophie Sachs (*née* Boehm) and Werner Sachs; *m* 1960, Edward Roger John Owen (marr. diss.); one *d*. *Educ:* Putney High Sch.; St Hugh's Coll., Oxford (BA Hons Physiol.); Bedford Coll., London (Dip. Soc. Studies). Psychiatric social worker, Littlemore Hosp., Oxford 1960–62; Lectr, English Lang., Amer. Univ. in Cairo, 1962–63; research work in mental health and physical disabilities, 1964–67; Editor, Frank Cass, 1971–73; Sen. Editor, Barrie & Jenkins, 1973–75; Virago Press: Founder-dir, 1974; Editl Dir, 1974–90; Jt Man. Dir, 1982–90; Dir, Paul Hamlyn Fund, 1990–92. Cultural Policy Advr to Lab. Party, 1990–92; Ed. and Chief Exec., Index on Censorship, 1993–2006. Dir, New Statesman and Society, 1983–90. Chm., Educn Extra, 1993–2002; Mem., Royal Literary Fund Cttee, 1989–94. Vice-Pres., Hay Fest., 2003–. Project Dir, 2006–09, Founder Trustee, 2010–, Free Word Centre. Mem. Bd, English Touring Opera, 2007–. Trustee: World Film Collective, 2009–; Women for Refugee Women, 2009–11; Carcanet Press, 2011–; Patron, Ledbury Poetry Fest., 2014–. Governor: Parliament Hill School, 1991–93; South Bank Centre, 2003–. *Publications:* (ed) Fathers: Reflections by Daughters, 1983; (ed with Mark Fisher) Whose Cities?, 1991. *Recreations:* music, reading, film, travel. *Address:* 1c Spencer Rise, NW5 1AR.

OWEN-JONES, David Roderic; His Honour Judge Owen-Jones; a Circuit Judge, since 2011; *b* Bangor, N Wales, 16 March 1949; *s* of John Eryl Owen-Jones, CBE, DL and Mabel Clara Owen-Jones (*née* McIlvride). *Educ:* Llandovery Coll.; University Coll. London (LLB 1970; LLM 1971). Called to the Bar, Inner Temple, 1972, Lincoln's Inn *ad eundem*, 1986; a Recorder, 2001–11. Mem., Lord Chancellor's Adv. Cttee on Appointment of JPs for Inner London, 1984–90. Vice Chm., Assoc. of Liberal Lawyers, 1986–94. Gov., Internat. Students House, 1995–2010 (Trustee, 1981; Fellow, 2010). Legal Advr to Hon. Soc. of Cymmrodorion, 2006–. Contested (Lib): Carmarthen, Feb. and Oct. 1974; Rugby and Kenilworth, 1983, 1987. FRSA 1984. Mem., Co. of Watermen and Lightermen, 2015. *Recreations:* theatre, travel, historical biography. *Address:* Basildon Crown Court, The Gore, Basildon, Essex SS14 2BU. *T:* (01268) 45800. *E:* hhjudge.owen-jones@judiciary.gsi.gov.uk. *Clubs:* National Liberal (Trustee, 1990–), Reform.

OWEN-JONES, Sir Lindsay Harwood, KBE 2005 (CBE 2000); Honorary Chairman, L'Oréal, 2011–13 (Chairman and Chief Executive Officer, 1988–2006; non-executive Chairman, 2006–11); *b* 17 March 1946; *s* of Hugh A. Owen-Jones and Esmee Owen-Jones (*née* Lindsay); *m*; one *d*; *m* 1994, Cristina Furno. *Educ:* Worcester Coll., Oxford (BA; Hon. Fellow, 2006); European Inst. of Business Admin. Product Manager, L'Oréal, 1969; Head, Public Products Div., Belgium, 1971–74; Manager, SCAD (L'Oréal subsid.), Paris, 1974–76; Marketing Manager, Public Products Div., Paris, 1976–78; Gen. Manager, SAIPO (L'Oréal subsid.), Italy, 1978–81; Pres., 1981–83, Chm., 1991–2011, COSMAIR (L'Oréal agent), USA; Vice-Pres., L'Oréal Mgt Cttee and Mem. Bd of Dirs, 1984; Pres. and Chief Operating Officer, 1984–88. Director: Air Liquide, 1994–2009; Sanofi-aventis, 1999; Ferrari, 2005–. Commandeur, Légion d'Honneur (France), 2005 (Officier, 1998). Hon. DSc Cranfield Sch. of Mgt, 2001. *Recreation:* private helicopter pilot.

OWENS, Ann Rosemarie; *see* Easter, A. R.

OWENS, Prof. David Howard, PhD; FREng; Professor of Control and Systems Engineering, and Head of Department, Automatic Control and Systems Engineering, University of Sheffield, 1999–2009, now Emeritus; *b* 23 April 1948; *s* of Maurice Owens and Joan Owens; *m* 1969, Rosemary Frost; one *s* one *d*. *Educ:* Imperial Coll., London (BSc 1st Cl. Hons Phys 1969; PhD 1973). CEng 1976; FIET (FIEE 1976); FIMechE 2001; CMath 1979; FIMA 1979; FREng 2008. SO, UKAEA Winfrith, 1969–73; Lectr, Sen. Lectr, then Reader, Dept of Control Engrg, Univ. of Sheffield, 1973–84; Prof. of Engrg Maths, 1984–87, Prof. of Mechanical Engrg, 1987–90, Strathclyde Univ.; Prof. and Hd, Sch. of Engrg and Computer Sci., Univ. of Exeter, 1990–99; Dean of Engrg and Convener of Deans, Univ. of Sheffield, 2002–06. Dir and Chm., Exeter Enterprises Ltd, 1995–99; Dir, Iter8 Control Systems, 2007–14. Chm., UK Automatic Control Council, 1999–2002; Ind. Mem., Nuclear Safety Adv. Cttee, HSE, 1995–2006. Vis. Prof., Univ. of Southampton, 2011–. Scientific Consultant, Italian Inst. of Technol., Genoa, 2012–. Governor: Sheffield Teaching Hosps NHS Foundn Trust, 2012–15; Henry Fanshawe Foundn, 2014–. Freeman, Co. of Cutlers in Hallamshire, 2007. *Publications:* Feedback and Multivariable Systems, 1979; Multivariable and Optimal Systems, 1981; Analysis and Control of Multipass Processes, 1982; Stability Analysis for Linear Repetitive Processes, 1992; Control Systems Theory and Applications for Linear Repetitive Processes, 2007; over 500 technical articles in areas of control and systems engrg. *Recreations:* reading, guitar, sketching, entertaining. *Address:* Department of Automatic Control and Systems Engineering, University of Sheffield, Mappin Street, Sheffield S1 3JD. *T:* (0114) 222 5684, *Fax:* (0114) 222 5661. *E:* d.h.owens@sheffield.ac.uk.

OWENS, Eleanor Jayne; Her Honour Judge Owens; a Circuit Judge, since 2014; *b* Norwich, 25 Aug. 1969; *d* of Peter Michael Slaughter and Veronica Audrey Slaughter. *Educ:* St Bedes Sch., Redhill; New Hall, Cambridge (BA 1991); Nottingham Trent Univ. (LLB Hons). Admitted solicitor, 1997; Legal Advr, Cumbria, 1991–96, Cambs, 1996–99; Legal Team Manager, Cambs, 1999–2013; Dep. Justices' Clerk, Cambs, 2013–14; a Recorder, 2009–14. *Recreations:* horse riding, gardening, reading, cinema, walking, opera. *Address:* Reading County and Family Court Hearing Centre, 160–163 Friar Street, Reading RG1 1HE. *T:* (0118) 987 0500. *E:* hhj.owens@judiciary.gsi.gov.uk.

OWENS, Prof. Ian Peter Farrar, PhD; Professor of Evolutionary Ecology, Imperial College London, since 2004; Director of Science, Natural History Museum, since 2011; *b* Sutton Coldfield, 1967; *s* of Peter and Sheila Owens; *m* 1992, Sally Ann Gibbins; two *s*. *Educ:* Univ. of Liverpool (BSc Zoology 1989); Univ. of Leicester (PhD Evolutionary Biol. 1992). Natural Hist. Mus. Scholar, Ornithological Section, Natural Hist. Mus., Tring, 1987; NERC Student, Univ. of Leicester, 1989–91; NERC Postdoctoral Res. Fellow, Inst. of Zool., Zool Soc. of London and UCL, 1992–95; Lectr in Ecol., 1995–98, Sen. Lectr in Ecol., 1998–2000, Univ. of Queensland; Imperial College London: Governors' Lectr in Biol., 2000–02; Reader in Evolutionary Ecol., Silwood Park, 2003–04; Dep. Dir, NERC Centre for Population Biol., 2004–10; Hd, Ecol. and Evolution Section, 2006–09; Hd, Div. of Biol., 2006–09; Hd, Dept of Life Scis, 2007–11. Member: NERC Peer Rev. Coll., 2002–07; NERC Steering Panel on Post-genomics and proteomics, 2004–; DEFRA Peer Rev. Panel, 2006–. Ed., Behavioral Ecology, 2001–07; Member, Editorial Board: Jl of Evolutionary Biology, 2001–06; Series B Biol Scis, Procs of Royal Soc., 2002–08; Ecology Letters, 2003–06; BMC Evolutionary Biology, 2006–; BMC Ecology, 2006–; Mem. Council, Encyclopedia of Life, 2012–. Member: Bd of Trustees, Nat. Biodiversity Network, 2012–; Council, British Trust for Ornithol., 2012–. External Examiner: Univ. of Lancaster, 2005–08; UEA, 2007–09; Univ. of Cambridge, 2009–12. Hon. Res. Fellow, Inst. of Zool., Zool Soc. of London, 2004. Scientific Medal, Zool Soc. of London, 2005. *Publications:* Evolutionary Ecology of Birds: life histories, mating systems and extinction (with P. M. Bennett), 2002; approx. 100 articles in scientific jls on ecology, evolution, animal behaviour and biodiversity. *Recreations:* bird watching, natural history, walking, photography. *Address:* Natural History Museum, Cromwell Road, SW7 5BD. *T:* (020) 7942 5374, *Fax:* (020) 7942 5765. *E:* i.owens@nhm.ac.uk.

OWENS, Jeffrey Phillip, CMG 2012; Visiting Professor, Vienna University, since 2012; Senior Tax Policy Advisor, Ernst & Young, since 2012; *b* Swansea, 26 Jan. 1946; *s* of Granville Philip Owens and Megan James Owens; *m* 1989, Janice Callaghan; two *s* two *d*. *Educ:* Inst. of Mgt Accountants; Univ. of Wales, Cardiff (BSc Econs); Queens' Coll., Cambridge (PhD Econs 1973); Alliance Français (Dip. Langue Français). Commercial trainee, British Steel, 1962–64; cost accountant, Tube Investments UK, 1964–66; Economist, 1972–80, Sen. Economist, 1980–86, Hd of Division, 1986–2001, Dir, Center for Tax Policy and Admin, 2001–12, OECD, Paris. Advr to govts and orgns, incl. EC, 2012–14, World Bank, 2014–. Dist. Fellow, 2012, Res. Fellow, 2013–, Internat. Tax and Investment Centre, Washington; Robert Schuman Fellow, Eur. Univ. Inst., Florence, 2013. Chm., SMU-TA Adv. Panel, Singapore. Mem., Franco-Welsh Soc. Internat. Tax Person of Year, Tax Notes jl, USA, 2011. *Publications:* Growth of Euro-Dollar Market, 1974; Local Government, 1991; Tax Systems in North Africa and European Countries, 1994; BRICS and the Emergence of International Tax Coordination, 2014. *Recreations:* sailing, ski-ing, gardening, cooking, cinema, travel, family, good wine, reading. *Address:* 23 avenue Onze Novembre, Meudon 92190, France. *T:* 778671068. *E:* jeffrey.p.owens@gmail.com. *Club:* St Quentin Sailing.

OWENS, Matthew, FRCO; conductor, composer and organist; Organist and Master of the Choristers, Wells Cathedral, since 2005; *b* 17 Jan. 1971; *s* of John Duncan Owens and Brenda Owens; *m* 2004, Alison Jane Darragh, PhD; two *s*. *Educ:* Chetham's Sch. of Music, Manchester; Queen's Coll., Oxford (BA Hons Music 1992; MA 1996); Royal Northern Coll. of Music (MusM 1994; PPRNCM 1994); Sweelinck Conservatorium, Amsterdam. FRCO 1994. Sub organist, Manchester Cathedral, 1996–99; Organist and Master of Music, St Mary's Episcopal Cathedral, Edinburgh, 1999–2004. Asst and Associate Dir, Nat. Youth Choir, 1993–2000; Organist, Musical Dir and Singer, BBC Daily Service, 1994–99; Artistic Dir and Conductor, Exon Singers, 1997–2011; Conductor, Wells Cathedral Oratorio Soc., 2005–; Founder and Artistic Director: Cathedral Commissions, 2006–; new music wells festival, 2008–. Tutor in Organ Studies: Chetham's Sch. of Music, 1994–99; RNCM, 1995–2000; Wells Cathedral Sch., 2006–13. Mem., Cathedrals' Liturgy and Music Gp, Assoc. English Cathedrals, 2008–13. Pres., Cathedral Organists' Assoc., 2010–13. Hon. FGCM 2012. *Publications:* The Holly and the Ivy, 2012; St Matthew Passion, 2013; Crux fidelis, 2014; Holy Trinity Blessing, 2015; Joseph Fili David, 2015; Magnificat and Nunc Dimittis 'Fauxbourdon Service', 2015; This Joyful Eastertide, 2015; educational articles, and reviews in Organists' Rev., Choir and Organ, Cathedral Music. *Recreations:* reading, concerts, opera, cooking, travel, film, art, politics, horseracing, walking Elsie the dog. *Address:* c/o Wells Cathedral Music Office, Chain Gate, Cathedral Green, Wells, Somerset BA5 2UE. *T:* (01749) 674483. *E:* musicoffice@wellscathedral.uk.net.

OWENS, Prof. Nicholas John Paul, PhD; CBiol, FRSB; FRGS; Professor of Ocean Science, Plymouth University, since 2012; Director, Scottish Association for Marine Science and Chief Executive Officer, SAMS Group, since 2015; *b* 17 Jan. 1954; *s* of Michael John Joseph Benedict Owens and Christine Mary Theresa Owens; *m* 1982, Susan Mary Forster (*d* 2015); four *s*. *Educ:* Univ. of Liverpool (BSc 1976); Univ. of Dundee (PhD 1981). MIBiol, CBiol 1983; FRSB (FIBiol 2009); FRGS 2009. Res. Scientist, Inst. for Marine Envmtl Res., 1979–92; University of Newcastle: Prof. of Marine Sci., 1992–2000; Hd, Dept of Marine Scis and Coastal Mgt, 1993–99; Director: NERC Plymouth Marine Lab., 2000–07; British Antarctic Survey, 2007–12; Sir Alister Hardy Foundn for Ocean Sci., 2012–15. Non-exec. Dir, CEFAS, DEFRA, 2012–15 (Chm., Sci. Adv. Cttee, 2012–15). Bd Dir, PML (formerly Plymouth Marine) Applications Ltd, 2001–07. Trustee: Nat. Marine Aquarium, 2002–09; Scottish Assoc. for Marine Sci., 2009–10. Hon. Prof., Univ. of Plymouth, 2006–12. Fellow, Marine Biol Assoc., 2015. *Publications:* over 100 articles in learned marine sci. jls. *Recreations:* game fishing, yachting, running, mountaineering, gardening. *Address:* Scottish Association for Marine Science, Scottish Marine Institute, Oban, Argyll PA37 1QA. *E:* nick.owens@sams.ac.uk. *W:* www.twitter.com/n1jpo. *Club:* Allen Valley Angling and Conservation.

OWENS, Prof. Susan Elizabeth, OBE 1998; PhD; FBA 2011; Professor of Environment and Policy, University of Cambridge, since 2004; Fellow of Newnham College, Cambridge, since 1981; *b* 24 Jan. 1954; *d* of Alfred Raymond Penrose and Patricia Mary Penrose (*née* Dorrell); *m* 1976. *Educ:* Stevenage Girls' Sch.; Univ. of East Anglia (BSc Hons, PhD). Res. Officer, Energy Panel, SSRC, 1979; Res. Fellow, Inst. of Planning Studies, Univ. of Nottingham, 1980–81; University of Cambridge: Asst Lectr in Geography, 1981–86; Lectr, 1986–2000; Reader in Envmt and Policy, 2000–04; Hd, Dept of Geography, 2010–13. King Carl XVI Gustaf Vis. Prof. of Envmtl Sci., Stockholm Resilience Centre and Royal Inst. of Technol., 2008–09; Hon. Prof., Univ. of Copenhagen, 2008–. Global Envmtl Change Programme Res. Fellow, ESRC, 1993–94. Member: UK Round Table on Sustainable Devel, 1995–98; Countryside Commn, 1996–99; Govt Adv. Panel on Integrated Transport Policy, 1997–98; Royal Commn on Envmtl Pollution, 1998–2008 (Special Advr, 1992–94); Steering Panel for OST review of Sci. in DEFRA, 2005–06; Res. Cttee (formerly Strategic Res. Bd), ESRC, 2007–11; Hazardous Substances Adv. Cttee, 2013–; Science Adv. Council, Stockholm Envmt Inst., 2013–; Chm., Governance Working Gp, European Envmtl and Sustainability Adv. Councils, 2003–06. Mem., sub-panel H31, Town and Country Planning, RAE 2008. Mem., Royal Soc. Sci. Policy Adv. Gp, 2008–13. Trustee, Miriam Rothschild and John Foster Human Rights Trust, 2007–10. FAcSS (AcSS 2002). Life Hon. MRTPI 2013 (Hon. MRTPI 2006). Dr *hc* Royal Inst. Technol., Stockholm, 2012. Back Award, RGS (with IBG), 2000. *Publications:* Energy, Planning and Urban Form, 1986; (jtly) Environment, Resources and Conservation, 1990; (ed jtly) Britain's Changing Environment from the Air, 1991; (jtly) Land Use Planning Policy and Climate Change, 1992; (jtly) Land and Limits: interpreting sustainability in the planning process, 2002, 2nd edn 2011; contrib. learned jls, incl. Trans Inst. of British Geographers, Land Use Policy, Town Planning Review, Political Qly, Jl of Risk Res., Envmt and Planning A, Govt and Policy (Envmt and Planning C), Envmtl Conservation, European Envmt, Global Envmtl Change, Jl Envmtl Law, Critical Policy Studies, Envmtl Sci. and Policy. *Recreations:* walking, literature. *Address:* Department of Geography, University of Cambridge, Downing Place, Cambridge CB2 3EN. *T:* (01223) 333399.

OWER, Dr David Cheyne, TD 1975; Senior Principal Medical Officer, Department of Health and Social Security, 1976–87; *b* 29 July 1931; *s* of Ernest Ower and Helen Edith Cheyne (*née* Irvine); *m* 1954, June Harris; two *s* two *d*. *Educ:* King's Coll. Sch., Wimbledon; King's Coll., London; King's Coll. Hosp. Med. Sch. (MB, BS 1954). DObstRCOG 1959; FFPH (FFCM 1983; MFCM 1976). Jun. hosp. appts, King's Coll. Hosp. and Kingston Hosp., 1955; RAF Med. Br., 1956–58; gen. practice, 1959–64; DHSS (formerly Min. of Health) Med. Staff, 1965–87. T&AVR, and RAMC(V), 1962–; Lt-Col RAMC(V); CO 221 (Surrey) Field Amb., 1973–75. *Recreations:* music, bridge, thinking about playing golf. *Address:* Bonshaw, Winchester Road, Alresford, Hants SO24 9EZ. *T:* (01962) 735152.

OWERS, Dame Anne (Elizabeth), DBE 2009 (CBE 2001); Chairman: Board, Clinks, since 2011; Independent Police Complaints Commission, since 2012; Board, Koestler Trust, since 2013; *b* 23 June 1947; *d* of William Spark and Anne Smailes Spark (*née* Knox); *m* 1st, 1968 (marr. diss.); two *s* one *d*; 2nd, 2005, Edmund Stephen Cook. *Educ:* Washington Grammar Sch., Co. Durham; Girton Coll., Cambridge (BA Hons 1968). Research and teaching in Zambia, 1968–71; work at JCWI, 1981–92 (Gen. Sec., 1986–92); Dir, Justice, 1992–2001; HM Chief Inspector of Prisons for England and Wales, 2001–10. Chm. Bd of Trustees, Refugee Legal Centre, 1994–98; Member: Lord Chancellor's Adv. Cttee on Legal Educn and Conduct, 1997–99; Home Office Task Force on Human Rights, 1999–2001; Legal Services Consultative Panel, 2000–01; non-exec. Dir, Criminal Cases Rev. Commn, 2010–14. Chm. Bd, Christian Aid, 2008–13. Hon. Fellow: South Bank Univ., 2005; Lucy Cavendish Coll., Cambridge, 2007. DUniv Essex, 2006; Hon. DCL Oxford, 2013. *Publications:* (ed jtly) Economic, Social and Cultural Rights, 1999; chapters and papers on immigration and nationality matters and on prisons. *Recreations:* music, walking, friends, family.

OWUSU, Elsie Margaret Akua, OBE 2003; RIBA; Founder and Principal, Elsie Owusu Architects, since 1989; Partner, Feilden & Mawson LLP, architects, since 2006; *b* 9 Dec. 1953; *d* of Paul Kofi Owusu and Joyce Ophelia Owusu; one *d*. *Educ:* Demonstration Sch., Legon, Ghana; Streatham Hill and Clapham Girls' High Sch.; Architectural Association Sch. of Architecture. RIBA 1989; Specialist Conservation Architect 2012. Design Team, Solon SE Housing Assoc., 1981–85; Women's Design Service, 1985–86; in private practice, Owusu and Teague, 1986–89. Lead architect: for Feilden & Mawson: interiors, UK Supreme Court, 2006–09; Green Park Underground Station (masterplan and conservation plan), 2008–09; for Elsie Owusu Architects: Lagos Bus Rapid Transit, 2008–10; pilot route of Accra Bus Rapid Transit, 2011–12; (with Sir Peter Blake) 60 Aden Grove, N16, 2012. Founder Member: Soc. of Black Architects, 1990 (first Chm., 1990–92); Black Internat. Construction Orgn, 1996–; Sec., Fedn of Black Housing Orgns, 1994–96 (Mem., Exec. Cttee, 1994–96); Member: Educnl Vis. Bd, RIBA, 1995–96; Haringey Employment Commn, 1996–97; Trafalgar Square Plinth Cttee, 1999–2000; Building Regulations Adv. Cttee, 2001–03; Enabling Panel, CABE, 2002–08; Adv. Bd, Ayebia Clarke Publishing, 2010–; Board Member: Arts Council of England, subseq. Arts Council England, 2002–09; Nat. Trust, 2002–04. Acting Chair, 2006–08, Chair, 2008–09, Aduna. Dir, JustGhana Ltd, 2007–. Vice-Pres., Women's Transport Seminar, 2005–07. Mem., Bd of Trustees, Royal African Soc., 2008–. Member: Bd of Governors, Middlesex Univ., 1996–2000; Corp., Coll. of NE London, 1996–2001. *Recreations:* reading, walking, drawing, dreaming. *Address:* 30 Chalfont Court, Baker Street, NW1 5RS. *T:* (020) 7486 2188.

OXBURGH, family name of **Baron Oxburgh**.

OXBURGH, Baron *cr* 1999 (Life Peer), of Liverpool in the county of Merseyside; **Ernest Ronald Oxburgh,** KBE 1992; PhD; FRS 1978; Chairman, 2OC, since 2006; Rector, Imperial College of Science, Technology and Medicine, 1993–2001; *b* 2 Nov. 1934; *m* Ursula Mary Brown; one *s* two *d*. *Educ:* Liverpool Inst.; University Coll., Oxford (BA 1957, MA 1960); Univ. of Princeton (PhD 1960). Departmental Demonstrator, 1960–61, Lectr in Geology, 1962–78, Univ. of Oxford; Fellow of St Edmund Hall, Oxford, 1964–78, Emeritus Fellow, 1978, Hon. Fellow, 1986; University of Cambridge: Prof. of Mineralogy and Petrology, 1978–91; Hd of Dept of Earth Scis, 1980–88; Fellow of Trinity Hall, 1978–82, Hon. Fellow, 1983; Queens' College: Pres., 1982–89; Professorial Fellow, 1989–91; Hon. Fellow, 1992; Chief Scientific Advr, MoD, 1987–93. Chairman: Shell Transport & Trading plc, 2004–05; Falck Renewables, 2007–11; Green Energy Options, 2011–. Chm., SETNET, 2001–05. Visiting Professor: CIT, 1967–68; Stanford and Cornell Univs, 1973–74; Sherman Fairchild Distinguished Vis. Scholar, CIT, 1985–86. Trustee, Natural History Mus., 1993–2002 (Chm. Trustees, 1999–2002). Chm., H of L Select Cttee on Sci. and Technol., 2001–05. Member: SERC, 1988–93; Hong Kong UGC, 1988–2002; Nat. Cttee of Inquiry into Higher Educn (Dearing Cttee), 1996–97. President: Eur. Union of Geosciences, 1985–87 (Hon. Fellow 1993); BAAS, 1995–96; Carbon Capture and Storage Assoc., 2005–; Inst. of Measurement and Control, 2012–15. FGS (Pres., 2000–02); Fellow: Geol. Soc. of America; Amer. Geophys. Union. Hon. Mem., Geologists' Assoc.; Foreign Corresp., Geologische Bundesanstalt, Austria and of Geological Soc. of Vienna; Foreign Member: Venezuelan Acad. of Scis, 1992; Deutsche Akad. der Naturforscher Leopoldina, 1994; Corresp. Mem., Australian Acad. of Sci., 1999; For. Associate, US Acad. of Scis, 2001. FIC 2003. Hon. FIMechE 1993; Hon. FCGI 1996; Hon FREng 2000. Hon. Fellow, Univ. Coll., Oxford, 1983. DSc (*hc*): Univ. of Paris, 1986; Leicester, 1990; Loughborough, 1991; Edinburgh, 1994; Birmingham, 1996; Liverpool, 1996; Southampton, 2003; Liverpool John Moores, 2006; Lingnan, Hong Kong, 2006; Newcastle upon Tyne, 2007; Leeds, 2009; Wyoming, 2011; Hon. DSc St Andrews, 2013. Bigsby Medal, Geol Soc., 1979; Sir George Thomson Gold Medal, Inst. of Measurement and Control, 2010; Public Service Medal, Singapore, 2010; Melchett Lectr and Medal, Inst. of Energy, 2014. Officier, Ordre des Palmes Académiques (France), 1995. *Publications:* contribs to Nature, Jl Geophys Res., Phil Trans Royal Soc., Annual Reviews, Science, Bull. Geol Soc. America, Jl Fluid Mechanics, Jl Geol Soc. London. *Recreations:* mountaineering, orienteering, reading, theatre. *Address:* c/o House of Lords, SW1A 0PW.

OXENBURY, Helen Gillian; children's writer and illustrator; *b* Suffolk, 2 June 1938; *d* of Thomas Bernard Oxenbury and Muriel (*née* Taylor); *m* 1964, John Burningham, *qv*; one *s* two *d*. *Educ:* Ipswich Sch. of Art; Central Sch. of Art. Stage designer, Colchester, 1960, Tel-Aviv, 1961; TV designer, London, 1963. *Publications: author and illustrator:* Number of Things, 1967; ABC of Things, 1971; Pig Tale, 1973; (with F. Maschler) A Child's Book of Manners: Verses, 1978; The Queen and Rosie Randall, 1979; 729 Curious Creatures, 1980; 729 Merry Mixips, 1980; 729 Puzzle People, 1980; 729 Animal Allsorts, 1980; Crazy Creatures, 1980; Assorted Animals, 1980; Bill and Stanley, 1981; Bedtime, 1982; Monkey See, Monkey Do, 1982; Holidays, 1982; Helping, 1982; Mother's Helper, 1982; Animals, 1982; Beach Day, 1982; Shopping Trip, 1982; Good Night, Good Morning, 1982; The Birthday Party, 1983; The

Dancing Class, 1983; Eating Out, 1983; The Car Trip, 1983; The Drive, 1983; The Checkup, 1983; First Day of School, 1983; First Day at Playschool, 1983; Playschool, 1983; Grandma and Grandpa, 1984; Our Dog, 1984; The Important Visitor, 1984; Helen Oxenbury Nursery Story Book, 1985; Tom and Pippo Go Shopping, 1988; Tom and Pippo's Day, 1988; Tom and Pippo in the Garden, 1988; Tom and Pippo Go for a Walk, 1988; Tom and Pippo Make a Mess, 1988; Tom and Pippo Read a Story, 1988; Tom and Pippo See the Moon, 1988; Tom and Pippo and the Washing Machine, 1988; Pippo Gets Lost, 1989; Tom and Pippo and the Dog, 1989; Tom and Pippo in the Snow, 1989; Tom and Pippo Make a Friend, 1989; Tom and Pippo on the Beach, 1993; It's My Birthday, 1994; First Nursery Stories, 1994; *illustrator:* The Great Big Enormous Turnip, 1968; The Quangle-Wangle's Hat, 1969; Letters of Thanks, 1969; The Dragon of an Ordinary Family, 1969; The Hunting of the Snark, 1970; Meal One, 1971; Cakes and Custard: Children's Rhymes, 1974; Balooky Klujypop, 1975; Animal House, 1976; Tiny Tim: Verses for Children, 1981; We're Going on a Bear Hunt, 1989; Farmer Duck, 1992; The Three Little Wolves and The Big Bad Pig, 1993; So Much, 1994; Alice in Wonderland, 1999; Franny B. Kranny, 2001; Big Momma Makes the World, 2002; Alice Through the Looking Glass, 2005; The Growing Story, 2007; Ten Little Fingers Ten Little Toes, 2008; There's Going to be a Baby, 2010; King Jack and the Dragon, 2012; Charley's First Night, 2013; Charley Meets Granpa, 2013. *Address:* c/o Greene and Heaton Ltd, 37 Goldhawk Road, W12 8QQ.

OXENBURY, Dame Shirley (Ann), DBE 1992 (OBE 1987); Personal Assistant to Rt Hon. Christopher Patten, 1997–2000; *b* 4 July 1936. *Educ:* Ensham County Sch., London, SW17. PA to Harold Fielding, 1965–70; Personal Assistant (at Conservative Central Office) to Chairman of the Conservative Party: Katharine Macmillan, Sara Morrison, Baroness Young, 1970–75; Lord Thorneycroft, 1975–81; Cecil Parkinson, 1981–83; John Gummer, 1983–85; Norman Tebbit, 1985–87; Peter Brooke, 1987–89; Kenneth Baker, 1989–90; Christopher Patten, 1990–92; Norman Fowler, 1992–94; Jeremy Hanley, 1994–95; Brian Mawhinney, 1995–97. Women's Transport Service (FANY), 1979–. *Recreations:* swimming, arts, learning languages. *T:* (020) 7798 8316.

OXFORD, Bishop of; *no new appointment at time of going to press.*

OXFORD, Archdeacon of; *see* Gorick, Ven. M. C. W.

OXFORD AND ASQUITH, 3rd Earl of, *cr* 1925; **Raymond Benedict Bartholomew Michael Asquith,** OBE 1992; Viscount Asquith 1925; Director: JKX Oil & Gas plc, since 1997; Zander Corporation Ltd, since 2002; Hansa Trust, since 2013; *b* 24 Aug. 1952; *er s* of 2nd Earl of Oxford and Asquith, KCMG and Anne Mary Celestine (*née* Palairet); *S* father, 2011; *m* 1978, Mary Clare, *e d* of Francis Pollen; one *s* four *d*. *Educ:* Ampleforth; Balliol College, Oxford. HM Diplomatic Service, 1980–97: FCO, 1980–83; First Sec., Moscow, 1983–85; Cabinet Office and FCO, 1985–92; Counsellor, Kiev, 1992–97. Elected Mem., H of L, 2014. *Heir: s* Viscount Asquith, *qv*. *Address:* The Manor House, Mells, Frome, Somerset BA11 3PN.

See also Hon. Sir D. A. G. Asquith.

OXFORD, Prof. John Sydney, PhD; FRCPE, FRSB; Professor of Virology, Queen Mary (formerly Barts and the Royal London Hospitals), University of London, 1988, now Emeritus; Founder, Retroscreen Virology Ltd, since 1990; Founder and Director, Oxford Media and Medicine Ltd, since 2011; *b* 6 March 1942; *s* of Sydney and Edith Oxford; *m* 1965, Gillian Claire Mason; one *s* four *d*. *Educ:* Univ. of Reading (BSc Hons 1963); Univ. of Sheffield (PhD 1966). FRCPE 2013; FRSB (FSB 2013). Lectr in Med. Microbiol., Univ. of Sheffield, 1966–70; Res. Fellow, John Curtin Sch. of Med. Res., ANU, 1970–73; Member, Scientific Staff: NIMR, Mill Hill, 1973–76; Nat. Inst. for Biol Standards and Control, S Mimms, 1976–88. Vis. Schol., Dept of Microbiol., Univ. of Melbourne, 1987–88. Chm., Global Hygiene Council, 2005–. Res. in location and analysis of lung samples from permafrost or lead coffin encased victims of 1918 Spanish influenza. Fellow, Strehlow Aboriginal Res. Foundn, Adelaide, 1990. MInstD 1993. Hon. DSc Kingston, 2011. *Publications:* (jtly) Influenza, the Viruses and the Disease, 1985; (jtly) Conquering Viral Disease, 1986; (jtly) Human Virology, 1993, 4th edn 2010; contrib. 250 scientific papers on influenza viruses with special emphasis on antivirals and vaccines. *Recreations:* literature and poetry, historical analysis of World War I and emergence of Spanish influenza in 1916; travelling the world as regards prevention of bird flu H5N1 and making science films and pieces for BBC, Channel 4 and National Geographic; spending special time with my wife, five children and family. *Address:* Blizard Institute, Queen Mary College, 4 Newark Street, E1 2AT. *E:* j.oxford@qmul.ac.uk. *Club:* Athenæum.

OXFUIRD, 14th Viscount of, *cr* 1651; **Ian Arthur Alexander Makgill,** MA; Bt 1627 (NS); Lord Makgill of Cousland, 1651; Managing Director, Ticon UK Ltd, management consultancy; *b* 14 Oct. 1969; *s* of 13th Viscount of Oxfuird, CBE and of Alison Campbell, *e d* of Neils Max Jensen, Randers, Denmark; *S* father, 2003; *m* 2009, Ruth Mairo, *d* of Samuel Fripp; one *s* one *d*. *Educ:* Canford Sch., Wimborne; Univ. of Plymouth (BA Hons Media); Univ. of Middlesex (MA Design for Computer Media). Project manager for business to consumer IT projects for Axon and Tesco; started mgt consultancy firm for public sector, Ticon UK Ltd, 2003. *Recreations:* boxing, ski-ing, contemporary art. *Heir: s* Master of Oxfuird, *qv*. *E:* ian.makgill@ticon.uk.com.

OXFUIRD, Master of; Hon. Max George Samuel Makgill; *b* 24 Aug. 2012; *s* and *heir* of Viscount of Oxfuird, *qv*.

OXLEY, Julian Christopher; Director and Secretary, 1984–89, Director-General, 1989–96, Guide Dogs for the Blind Association; *b* 23 Nov. 1938; *s* of Horace Oxley and Lilian Oxley (*née* Harris); *m* 1979, Carol (*née* Heath) (*d* 2010); one *d*; *m* 2014, Catherine Margaret (*née* Follows-Smith); one *s* two *d* from previous marriage. *Educ:* Clifton Coll., Bristol; Oriel Coll., Oxford (Organ Scholar, MA). FCA. Dir and Sec., Williams & James plc, 1970–84. Chm., Internat. Fedn of Guide Dog Schs, 1990–97. Non-exec. Dir, Heatherwood and Wexham Park Hosps NHS Trust, 1999–2006. Mem. Council, Gloucester Civic Trust, 1972–75. Chm. of Govs, Selwyn Sch., Gloucester, 1980–84. Trustee, Nat. Confedn of PTAs, 2002–09 (Chm., 2004–09). *Recreations:* music, old furniture, railway signalling and operation. *Address:* Cura, Main Road, Minsterworth, Gloucester GL2 8JH. *T:* (01452) 750797. *E:* julian.oxley@btinternet.com.

OXMANTOWN, Lord; Laurence Patrick Parsons; Founder, Oriental Parsons Consultants, Beijing; President, Citiarc Group; Partner and Marketing Director, Daisy Capital International, since 2012; *b* 31 March 1969; *s* and *heir* of Earl of Rosse, *qv*; *m* 2004, Anna, *d* of Qicai Lin; one *s* one *d*. *Educ:* Aiglon Coll., Switzerland; Univ. of Beijing Language Inst. Jones Lang Wootton, China, 1993–96; Vice Pres., Taihe Real Estate Gp, 1996–2001; Marketing Dir, Guohua Real Estate, 2002–04; Vice Pres., Zhongpu Real Estate, 2004–07; Man. Dir, China Horizon Real Estate Gp, Beijing, 2007–11. *Heir: s* Hon. William Yufan Charles Parsons, *b* 28 June 2008. *Address:* 1059 Le Leman Lake Villas, SE Baixing zhuang, Houshayou, Shunyi District, Beijing 101300, China.

OZ, Amos; Professor of Hebrew Literature, 1987–2005, now Emeritus, and Agnon Professor in Modern Hebrew Literature, since 1993, Ben-Gurion University of the Negev; *b* Jerusalem, 4 May 1939; *m* 1960, Nily Zuckerman; one *s* two *d*. *Educ:* Hebrew Univ. of Jerusalem (BA Hebrew Literature and Philosophy 1965). Teacher of Literature and Philosophy, Hulda High Sch. and Regl High Sch., Givat Brenner, 1963–86. Vis. Fellow, St Cross Coll., Oxford, 1969–70; Writer in Residence: Hebrew Univ. of Jerusalem, 1975–76, 1990; Tel Aviv Univ., 1996; Visiting Professor: Univ. of Calif at Berkeley, 1980; Oxford Univ., 1998; Writer in Residence and Visiting Professor of Literature: Boston Univ., 1987; Princeton Univ., 1997; Weidenfeld Vis. Prof. of Comparative European Literature, Univ. of Oxford, 1998. Member: Peace Now, 1977–; Catalan Acad. of Mediterranean, 1989; Acad. of Hebrew Language, 1991. Hon. Dr: Hebrew Union Coll., Cincinnati and Jerusalem, 1988; Western New England Coll., Mass, 1988; Tel Aviv, 1992; Brandeis, 1998. Bernstein Prize, 1983; Bialik Prize, 1986; Internat. Peace Prize, German Publishers' Union, 1992; Israel Prize for Literature, 1998. Officier de l'Ordre des Arts et des Lettres, 1984, Chevalier de la Légion d'Honneur, 1997 (France). *Publications: stories:* Where the Jackal Howls, 1965; Between Friends, 2013; *novels:* Elsewhere Perhaps, 1966; My Michael, 1968 (elected one of 100 masterpieces of the 20th century, Bertelsmann Club, Germany, 1999; elected one of best foreign bks in China, 1999); Touch the Water, Touch the Wind, 1973; A Perfect Peace, 1982; Black Box, 1987 (Prix Femina Etranger, Wingate Prize, 1988); To Know a Woman, 1989; The Third Condition, 1991; Don't Call it Night, 1994; Panther in the Basement, 1995; The Same Sea, 1999; Rhyming Life and Death, 2009; Scenes from Village Life, 2011; *for children:* Soumchi, 1977 (Ze'ev Award, Hans Christian Andersen Medal, 1978; Luchs Prize, Germany, Hamore Prize, France, 1993); Suddenly in the Depths of the Forest, 2010; *novellas:* Unto Death, 1971; The Hill of Evil Counsel, 1976; *anthology:* Other People, 1974; *essays:* Under This Blazing Light, 1978; In the Land of Israel, 1983; The Slopes of Lebanon, 1987; Report of the Situation, 1992; The Silence of Heaven, 1993; Israel, Palestine and Peace, 1994; The Real Cause of My Grandmother's Death, 1994; The Story Begins, 1996; All Our Hopes, 1998; How to Cure a Fanatic, 2006; (with Fania Oz-Salzberger) Jews and Words, 2012; *memoir:* A Tale of Love and Darkness, 2004; work translated into 33 languages; articles on literary, political and ideological topics in jls.

OZAWA, Seiji; Japanese conductor; Co-founder and Artistic Director, Tokyo Opera Nomori, since 2005; Music Director, Vienna State Opera, 2002–10; *b* Shenyang, China, 1 Sept. 1935; *m* 1st, Kyoko Edo; 2nd, Vera Ilyan; one *s* one *d*. *Educ:* Toho School of Music, Tokyo; studied with Hideo Saito, Eugène Bigot, Herbert von Karajan, Leonard Bernstein. Won Besançon Internat. Comp., 1959, Koussevitzky Meml Scholarship, 1960. Asst Conductor, NY Philharmonic Orch., 1961–62 and 1964–65; music dir, Ravinia Fest., Chicago, 1964–68; conductor, Toronto SO, 1965–69; music dir, San Francisco SO, 1970–76, music advisor, 1976–77; Artistic Advr, Tanglewood Fest., 1970–73; Music Dir, Boston SO, 1973–2002. Tours with Boston Symphony Orchestra: Europe, 1976, 1988, 1993; Japan, 1978; China (musical and cultural exchange), 1979; European music festivals, 1979, 1984, 1991; 14 USA cities (orchestra's hundredth birthday), 1982; Japan, 1982 and 1986; Far East, 1989, 1994; S America, 1992; tours with Vienna Philharmonic: Asia, 1993, 1996, 2000; Europe, 1997, 1998, 2000, 2001; Berlin Philharmonic: regular concerts; tours incl. US/Asia, 1993; Guest conductor with major orchestras in Canada, Europe, Far East and USA; Conductor: Saito Kinen Orch., Japan (European tours, 1987, 1989, 1991; Carnegie Hall, NY, 1991; Saito Kinen Fest., later Seiji Ozawa Matsumoto Fest., 1992–); Salzburg Fest. Opera highlights: La Scala, Milan; Covent Garden, London; Paris Opera (incl. world première of Messiaen's Saint François d'Assise); Vienna State Op. début, Eugene Onegin, 1988; many recordings (awards). Evening at Symphony, PBS television series with Boston Symphony Orch. (Emmy award). Hon. DMus: Univ. of Mass; New England Conservatory of Music; Wheaton Coll., Norton, Mass. Seiji Ozawa Hall inaugurated at Tanglewood, Mass, 1994. Inouye Award (first), for lifetime achievement in the arts, Japan, 1994; Praemium Imperiale, 2011. *Address:* Tokyo Opera Nomori, Jimbo-cho Mitsui Building 17F, Kanda Jimbo-cho 1–105, Chiyoda-ku, Tokyo 101–0051, Japan.

OZGA, Prof. Jennifer, PhD; FBA 2013; Professor of the Sociology of Education, University of Oxford, since 2010; Fellow, Green Templeton College. *Educ:* Univ. of Aberdeen (MA; MEd); Open Univ. (PhD). NUT; author and mgt of courses on educn for Open Univ. until 1991; Dean, Faculty of Educn, Bristol Poly., subseq. UWE, 1991–93; Prof. of Educn Policy and Dean of Social Scis, Keele Univ., 1993–2000; Prof. of Educnl Res. and Dir, Centre for Educnl Sociol., Univ. of Edinburgh, 2000–10. Vis. Prof., Univ. of Umeå, Sweden; Vis. Schol., Helsinki Univ., Finland. FAcSS (AcSS). Hon. Dr Turku, Finland. *Publications:* (with M. Lawn) Teachers, Professionalism and Class, 1981; (ed) Policy-making in Education, 1985; (ed jtly) Curriculum Policy: a reader, 1990; (ed) Women in Educational Management, 1992; (ed jtly) Work and Identity in the Primary School, 1997; Policy Research in Educational Settings, 2000; (ed with R. Lingard) The RoutledgeFalmer Reader in Education Policy and Politics, 2007; (ed jtly) Social Capital, Professionalism and Diversity, 2009; (ed jtly) Fabricating Quality in Europe: data and education governance, 2011; contribs to learned jls incl. World Yearbook of Educn, Educnl Rev., Jl Educn Policy, Critical Studies in Educn, Res. Papers in Educn, British Jl Sociol. of Educn, Eur. Educnl Res. Jl. *Address:* Department of Education, University of Oxford, 15 Norham Gardens, Oxford OX2 6PY.

P

PACEY, Stephen James; an Upper Tribunal Judge (Administrative Appeals Chamber) (formerly a Social Security and Child Support Commissioner), 1996–2013; *b* 5 July 1949; *s* of Randall Brown Pacey and May Pacey (*née* Oldknow); *m* 1978, Jessica Susan Turley; one *s*. *Educ:* Kimberley County Secondary Modern Sch.; Beeston Coll.; Trent Poly. (LLB 1971); Univ. of Huddersfield (LLM Dist. 2008). Admitted Solicitor, 1975 (Wolverhampton Law Soc. Centenary Prizeman, 1975). Directorate of Legal Affairs, CBI, 1971–72; Lectr in Law, Isleworth Poly., 1972–73; solicitor in private practice, 1975–87; consultant planning inspector, 1989–91; Chm., Independent Tribunal Service, 1991–96; Dep. Social Security and Child Support Comr, 1993–96. Chairman (part-time): Social Security Appeal Tribunals, 1984–91; Med. Appeal Tribunals, 1987–91; Industrial Tribunals, 1988–91; Registered Homes Appeal Tribunals, 1992–96; pt-time Immigration Judge, 1998. Freeman, City of London, 1984. *Recreations:* photography, literature, performing arts.

PACINO, Alfredo James, (Al); actor; *b* New York, 25 April 1940; *s* of Salvatore Pacino and late Rosa Pacino; one *d* by Jan Tarrant; twin *s* and *d* by Beverly D'Angelo. *Educ:* High Sch. of Performing Arts, NY; Actors Studio, NY. Has worked as mail delivery boy, messenger, cinema usher and bldg supt; actor, dir and writer, NY theatres; appeared in première of The Indian Wants the Bronx, Waterford, Conn, 1966, and NY, 1968; Broadway début, Does a Tiger Wear a Necktie?, 1969 (Tony Award, best supporting actor); film début, Me, Natalie, 1969; *theatre includes:* Camino Real, Lincoln Center Rep. Theater, 1970; The Basic Training of Pavlo Hummel, 1972, (title rôle) Richard III, 1973, Boston Theater Co.; Arturo Ui, 1975; Jungle of Cities, 1979; American Buffalo, 1981, transf. UK, 1984; Julius Caesar, 1988; Salome, 1992; Circle in the Square, 1992; Hughie (also dir), 1996; The Resistible Rise of Arturo Ui, Michael Schimmel Centre, NY, 2002; The Merchant of Venice, Delacorte Th., NY, 2010; Glengarry Glen Ross, Gerald Schoenfeld Th., NY, 2012; An Evening with Al Pacino, UK, 2013, 2015; *films include:* Panic in Needle Park, 1971; The Godfather, 1972 (Best Actor Award, Nat. Soc. of Film Critics, USA); Scarecrow, 1973; Serpico, The Godfather Part II, 1974; Dog Day Afternoon, 1975; Bobby Deerfield, 1977; And Justice for All, 1979; Cruising, 1980; Author! Author!, 1982; Scarface, 1983; Revolution, 1985; The Local Stigmatic, 1989 (also play, Actors Playhouse, NY, 1969); Sea of Love, The Godfather Part III, 1990; Frankie and Johnny, 1991; Glengarry Glen Ross, Scent of a Woman (Acad. Award for best actor, 1993), 1992; Carlito's Way, Two Bits, 1994; City Hall, Heat, 1995; Donny Brasco, Looking for Richard (also writer, prod. and dir), 1996; Devil's Advocate, 1997; Man of the People, 1999; Any Given Sunday, Insider, Chinese Coffee (also dir), 2000; Insomnia, Simone, 2002; The Recruit, 2003; People I Know, The Merchant of Venice, 2004; Two for the Money, 2006; Ocean's Thirteen, 2007; Righteous Kill, 2008; Stand Up Guys, 2013; Salomé (also dir), Wilde Salomé (documentary) (also writer and dir), 2014; The Humbling, 2014; Danny Collins, 2015; Manglehorn, 2015; *television includes:* Angels in America, 2004; You Don't Know Jack, 2010 (Golden Globe for Best Actor in TV mini-series, 2011); Phil Spector, 2013. Co-artistic Dir, Actors Studio Inc., NY, 1982–83; Mem., Artistic Directorate, Globe Theatre, 1997–. Cecil B. DeMille award for lifetime achievement, Golden Globe Awards, 2001. Fellow, BFI, 2014. *Address:* c/o United Talent Agency, 9336 Civic Center Drive, Beverly Hills, Los Angeles, CA 90210, USA.

PACK, Prof. Donald Cecil, CBE 1978 (OBE 1969); MA, DSc; CMath, FIMA; FEIS, FRSE; Professor of Mathematics, University of Strathclyde, Glasgow, 1953–82, Hon. Professor, 1982–86, Professor Emeritus, 1986 (Vice-Principal, 1968–72); *b* 14 April 1920; *s* of late John Cecil and Minnie Pack, Higham Ferrers; *m* 1947, Constance Mary Gillam (*d* 2010); two *s* one *d*. *Educ:* Higham Ferrers Primary Sch.; Wellingborough School; New Coll., Oxford. Lecturer in Mathematics, University College, Dundee, University of St Andrews, 1947–52; Visiting Research Associate, University of Maryland, 1951–52; Lecturer in Mathematics, University of Manchester, 1952–53. Royal Soc. European Res. Prog., Inst. Plasma Physics, Munich, 1967; Guest Professor: Technische Universität, Berlin, 1967; Bologna Univ. and Politecnico Milano, 1980; Technische Hochschule Darmstadt, 1981; other vis. appts at Warsaw Univ., 1977, Kaiserslautern, 1980, 1984. Member: Dunbartonshire Educn Cttee, 1960–66; Gen. Teaching Council for Scotland, 1966–73; Chairman: Scottish Certificate of Educn Examn Bd, 1969–77; Cttee of Inquiry into Truancy and Indiscipline in Schools in Scotland, 1974–77; Member: various Govt Scientific Cttees, 1952–84; Defence Scientific Adv. Council, 1975–80; Consultant, MoD, 1984–2001. DERA Vis. Fellow, 1999–2001. Member: British Nat. Cttee for Theoretical and Applied Mechanics, 1973–78; Internat. Adv. Cttee on Rarefied Gas Dynamics Symposia, 1976–88; Council, Gesellschaft für Angewandte Mathematik und Mechanik, 1977–83; Council, RSE, 1960–63; Scottish Arts Council, 1980–85; Hon. Mem., European Consortium for Mathematics in Industry, 1988. Founder Chm., NYO of Scotland, 1978–88 (Chm., Steering Cttee, 1978; Hon. Pres., 1988–); Mem., European Music Year UK Cttee (Chm., Scottish Sub-Cttee), 1982–86; a Founder and First Hon. Treasurer, IMA, 1964–72; Governor, Hamilton Coll. of Education, 1977–81; Pres., Milngavie Music Club, 1983–93 (Hon. Pres., 1994–2010). DUniv Strathclyde, 2014. Elder, Ch of Scotland, 1973–. *Publications:* papers on fluid dynamics. *Recreations:* music, gardening, golf. *Address:* 18 Buchanan Drive, Bearsden, Glasgow G61 2EW. *T:* (0141) 942 5764.

PACK, Maj.-Gen. Simon James, CB 1997; CBE 1994 (OBE 1990); Royal Marines, retired; International Teams Director, England and Wales Cricket Board, 1997–2001; Chief Operating Officer, Gill Jennings & Every LLP, 2002–10; *b* 10 July 1944; *s* of late Captain A. J. Pack, OBE, RN and Eloise Pack; *m* 1970, Rosemary-Anne Fuller; one *s* one *d*. *Educ:* Fernden Prep. Sch.; Hurstpierpoint Coll.; Ecole de Commerce, Switzerland (Dip. French). Commnd into RM, 1962; served 3 Cdo Bde, Malaya, Sarawak, 1963–66; HMS Zulu, 1966–68; ADC to Governor of Queensland, 1969–70; Adjt, 41 Cdo, NI and Malta, 1970–72; Instructor, Officers Tactics Wing, Warminster, 1972–75; 42 Cdo, Norway, Hong Kong, 1976–79; Directorate of Naval Plans, MoD, 1979–81; Directing Staff, Army Staff Coll., 1981–83; MoD, 1984–87; CO 45 Cdo Gp, 1987–89; COS, HQ Cdo Forces, 1989–90; Dir, Defence Commitments Staff, MoD, 1990–94; Comdr, British Forces, Gibraltar and NATO Comdr, Western Mediterranean, 1994–97. ADC to the Queen, 1990–94. Non-exec. Dir, Maritime Services Mgt Ltd, 1997–99. Dir, Friends of Gibraltar Heritage Soc., 2000–. Gov., Oratory Sch., Reading, 1991–2000. FCMI (FIMgt 1997). *Recreations:* watching cricket, golf, gardening, family bridge, opera. *Address:* Littlecroft, Privett, Hants GU34 3NR; 13A Prince of Wales Mansions, Prince of Wales Drive, SW11 4BG.

PACKER, Christopher Jonathan; Legislative Counsel to the General Synod, since 2014; *b* Amersham, 28 May 1970; *s* of William Packer and Annabel Packer; *m* 1999, Karen Fulton; one *s*. *Educ:* Dr Challoner's Grammar Sch., Amersham; Gonville and Caius Coll., Cambridge (BA Hons English 1992); Coll. of Law (CPE 1993; Legal Practice Course 1994). Admitted solicitor 1996; Mishcon de Reya Solicitors: Trainee Solicitor, 1994–96; Asst Solicitor, 1996–98; Grade 7 Lawyer, Treasury Solicitor's Dept, 1998–2000; Office of the Parliamentary Counsel: Asst Parly Counsel, 2000–04; Sen. Asst Parly Counsel, 2004–09; Deputy Parly Counsel, 2009–14. *Recreations:* the garden, the cat, books, records, running, cooking, art. *Address:* The Legal Office, Church House, Great Smith Street, SW1P 3AZ. *T:* (020) 7898 1799. *E:* chris.packer@churchofengland.org.

PACKER, Rt Rev. John Richard; Bishop of Ripon and Leeds, 2000–14; an Honorary Assistant Bishop, Diocese of Newcastle, since 2014; *b* 10 Oct. 1946; *s* of John and Muriel Packer; *m* 1971, Barbara Jack; two *s* one *d*. *Educ:* Manchester Grammar Sch.; Keble Coll., Oxford (MA); Ripon Hall, Oxford; York Univ. (DSA). Ordained deacon, 1970, priest, 1971; Curate, St Peter, St Helier, 1970–73; Director of Pastoral Studies: Ripon Hall, 1973–75; Ripon Coll., Cuddesdon, 1975–77; Chaplain, St Nicolas, Abingdon, 1973–77; Vicar, Wath Upon Dearne with Adwick Upon Dearne, 1977–86; Rural Dean of Wath, 1983–86; Rector, Sheffield Manor, 1986–91; Rural Dean of Attercliffe, 1990–91; Archdeacon of W Cumberland, 1991–96; Priest i/c of Bridekirk, 1995–96; Bp Suffragan of Warrington, 1996–2000. Mem., Gen. Synod of C of E, 1985–91, 1992–96 and 2000–14. *Recreations:* history, walking. *Address:* Devonshire House, Alma Place, Whitley Bay NE26 2EQ. *T:* (0191) 253 4321. *E:* bppacker@googlemail.com.

PACKER, Prof. Kenneth John, PhD; FRS 1991; CChem, FRSC; Research Professor in Chemistry, Nottingham University, 1993–2001, now Emeritus; *b* 18 May 1938; *s* of late Harry James Packer and Alice Ethel Packer (*née* Purse); *m* 1962, Christine Frances Hart; one *s* one *d*. *Educ:* Harvey Grammar Sch., Folkestone; Imperial Coll., London (BSc Hons Chemistry, 1st cl., 1959); Cambridge Univ. (PhD 1962). CChem 1985, FRSC 1985. Post-doctoral Res. Fellow, Central Res. Dept, E. I. duPont de Nemours, Wilmington, USA, 1962–63; University of East Anglia: SERC Res. Fellow, 1963–64; Lectr in Chemistry, 1964–71; Sen. Lectr, 1971–78; Reader, 1978–82; Prof., 1982–84; BP Research: Sen. Res. Associate, Spectroscopy, 1984–87; Prin. Res. Associate, 1987–90; Chief Res. Associate, Analytical Res. Div., 1990–92; Chief Scientist, Gp Res. and Engrg, BP Internat., 1992–93. Visiting Professor in Chemistry: Southampton Univ.; KCL; Imperial Coll., London, 1985–92; UEA, 2004–. Science and Engineering Research Council: Member: Physical Chem. Cttee, 1976–81; Chem. Cttee, 1979–82; Sci. Bd, 1988–91; Chm., Central Services Panel, 1980–82; Cttee Mem., Chm. and Sec., British Radiofrequency Spectroscopy Gp; Mem. Council, Faraday Div., 1988–91, Mem. Scientific Affairs Bd, 1992–, RSC; Hon. Sec., Royal Instn of GB, 1993–98. Gov., Hampton Sch., Hanworth, 1990–93. Ed., Molecular Physics, 1982–88. *Publications:* NMR Spectroscopy of Solid Polymers, 1993; contrib. approx. 150 papers on topics involving develt and application of NMR spectroscopy to internat. jls. *Recreations:* fly-fishing, ski-ing, gardening, music. *Address:* The Beeches, 68 Cawston Road, Aylsham, Norwich NR11 6ED. *T:* (01263) 731728.

PACKER, Sir Richard (John), KCB 2000; consultant; Permanent Secretary, Ministry of Agriculture, Fisheries and Food, 1993–2000; *b* 18 Aug. 1944; *s* of late George Charles Packer and Dorothy May Packer (*née* Reynolds); *m* 1st, Alison Mary Sellwood; two *s* one *d*; 2nd, Lucy Jeanne Blackett-Ord (*see* Baroness Neville-Rolfe); four *s*. *Educ:* City of London School; Manchester Univ. (BSc 1965, MSc 1966). Ministry of Agriculture, Fisheries and Food, 1967–2000: on secondment as 1st Sec., Office of Perm Rep. to EEC, 1973–76; Principal Private Sec. to Minister, 1976–78; Asst Sec., 1979; Under Sec., 1985–89; Dep. Sec. (Agricl Commodities, Trade and Food Prodn), 1989–93. Non-exec. Dir, Express Dairies plc, subseq. Arla Foods (UK), 2002–07. *Publications:* The Politics of BSE, 2006. *Recreations:* ideas, sport. *Address:* 113 St George's Road, SE1 6HY.

PACKER, William John; painter and critic; art critic, Financial Times, 1974–2004; *b* 19 Aug. 1940; *o s* of Rex Packer and Evelyn Mary Packer (*née* Wornham); *m* 1965, Clare, *er d* of Thomas Winn and Cecily Philip; three *d*. *Educ:* Windsor Grammar Sch.; Wimbledon Sch. of Art (NDD 1963); Brighton Coll. of Art (ATC 1964). Teaching art full-time, 1964–67, part-time in art schs, 1967–77; external assessor, art schs and colls, 1980–2000. London corresp., Art & Artists, 1969–74. First exhibited, RA, 1963 and continues to exhibit widely; one-man exhibn, Piers Feetham Gall., 1996, 2001, 2004, 2009, 2014, jt exhibn, 2005; jt exhibn, Chapel Row Gall., Bath, 2007. Member: Fine Art Board, CNAA, 1976–83; Cttee, Contemporary Art Soc., 1977–83; Adv. Cttee, Govt Art Collection, 1977–84; Crafts Council, 1980–87; Council, Artists' Gen. Benevolent Instn, 1983–; Cttee, Nat. Trust Foundn for Art, 1986–98; Governing Council, FBA, 2006–12; Trustee, Heatherley Sch. of Art, 2007–14. Sole selector, first British Art Show, 1979–80; jt selector for exhibns and prizes, incl. Liverpool John Moores Exhibn, Hunting Prize, Discerning Eye, Lynn Painter-Stainers Prize, Threadneedle Prize. Curator, Elizabeth Blackadder Retrospective, Scottish Arts Council, 1982. Inaugural Henry Moore Lectr, Florence, 1986. Ballinglen Artist Fellow, Ballinglen Foundn, Co. Mayo, 1995. Member: NEAC, 2005–; Small Paintings Gp, 2005–. Hon. FRCA, 1988; Hon. RBA 1992; Hon. RBS; Hon. Mem., PS. *Publications:* The Art of Vogue Covers, 1980; Fashion Drawing in Vogue, 1983; Henry Moore: a pictorial biography, 1985; Carl Erickson, and René Bouët-Willaumez, 1989; John Houston, 2003; Tai-Shan Schierenberg, 2005; Sarah Raphael, 2013; contribs to magazines, newspapers and exhibn catalogues. *Recreation:* singing in a choir. *Address:* 60 Trinity Gardens, Brixton, SW9 8DR. *T:* (020) 7733 4012. *Clubs:* Garrick, Chelsea Arts, Soho Academy, London Sketch.

PACKHAM, Christopher Gary; naturalist, author, and broadcaster; *b* 4 May 1961; *s* of Colin Harold Packham and Marion Rita Packham (*née* Smith); one step *d*. *Educ:* Bitterne Park Schs; Richard Taunton Coll.; Southampton Univ. (BSc Hons Zoology 1983). Freelance camera assistant, 1983–86; freelance cameraman and photographer, 1985–89; wildlife presenter for TV, 1985–; programmes include: Really Wild Show, Go Wild,

Watchout, X-Creatures, Postcards from the Wild; Inside Out; Hands on Nature; Nature's Calendar; Springwatch; Autumnwatch; How Nature Works; The Truth About Wildlife; The Animal's Guide to Britain; Secrets of our Living Planet; Nature's Weirdest Events; Inside the Animal Mind; Wildlife Jack; Hive Alive; Chris Packham's Natural Selection. President: London Wildlife Trust, 1996–2013; Hants Ornithological Soc., 2000–; Bat Conservation Trust, 2006–; Vice-President: The Wildlife Trusts, 2005–13; Hants Wildlife Trust, 2005–13; Butterfly Conservation, 2006–; RSPB, 2007–; Trustee: Marwell Zoo Trust, 1998–2003; Herpetological Conservation Trust, 1998–2005; Wildfowl and Wetland Trust, 2000–04; Hawk Conservancy Trust, 2002–09 (Pres., 2011–). *Publications:* Chris Packham's Back Garden Nature Reserve, 2001; Chris Packham's Wild Side of Town, 2003. *Recreations:* travelling to horrible places to see beautiful things and photographing them, having no time to do anything, berating my dogs for barking. *Address:* All Electric Productions, PO Box 1805, Andover, Hants SP10 3ZN. *T:* (01305) 259605. *E:* info@allelectricproductions.co.uk.

PADDICK, Baron *cr* 2013 (Life Peer), of Brixton in the London Borough of Lambeth; **Brian Leonard Paddick;** *b* 24 April 1958; *s* of late Anthony Henry James and Evelyn Paddick; *m* 1983, Mary Stone (marr. diss. 1988); *m* 2009 (in Norway), Petter Belsvik. *Educ:* Queen's Coll., Oxford (BA PPE 1986; MA); Warwick Business Sch. (MBA 1990); Fitzwilliam Coll., Cambridge (Dip. Applied Criminology and Policing 2000). Joined Metropolitan Police Service, 1976; Borough Comdr, Lambeth, 2001–03; Dep. Asst Comr, 2003–07. Vis. Fellow, Ashridge Business Sch., 2008–13. London Mayoral candidate (Lib Dem) 2008 and 2012. *Publications:* Line of Fire (autobiog.), 2008. *Address:* House of Lords, SW1A 0PW.

PADDOCK, Very Rev. Dr John Allan Barnes; Dean of Gibraltar, since 2008; *b* Gloucester, 8 Aug. 1951; *s* of Thomas Paddock and Megan Paddock (*née* Barnes); *m* Jennifer. *Educ:* Crypt Sch., Gloucester; Liverpool Univ. (BA Hons 1974; MA); Manchester Univ. (PGCE 1975); Oxford Univ. (MA 1981); Glasgow Univ. (PhD 2005); Cardiff Univ. (LLM). Ordained deacon, 1980, priest, 1981; Curate, St Katharine, Matson, 1980–82; Chaplain: Lancaster Royal Grammar Sch., 1983–86; RAF, 1986–90; St Olave's Grammar Sch., Orpington, 1991–94; Royal Russell Sch., Croydon, 1997–2000; Vicar: St Peter's, Folkestone, 2000–03; St George's, Gloucester, 2003–08. FRSA. *Recreations:* music, literature, arts, theatre, Hispanic studies, canon and ecclesiastical law. *Address:* The Deanery, 41 Jumpers Building, Rosia Road, Gibraltar. *T:* 78377. *E:* deangib@gibraltar.gi.

PADEL, Dr Ruth Sophia, FRSL; writer; Poetry Fellow, King's College London, since 2013; *b* London, 8 May 1946; *d* of John Hunter Padel and Hilda Horatia Padel (*née* Barlow); *m* 1984, Myles Fredric Burnyeat, *qv* (marr. diss. 2000); one *d*. *Educ:* N London Collegiate Sch.; Lady Margaret Hall, Oxford (BA Lit.Hum. 1969; DPhil 1976). Lecturer in Ancient Greek: Wadham Coll. and Corpus Christi Coll., Oxford, 1973–77; King's Coll., Cambridge, 1977–78; Res. Fellow, Wolfson Coll., Oxford, 1977–80; Bowra Res. Fellow, Wadham Coll., Oxford, 1978–79; Lectr in Greek, Birkbeck Coll., Univ. of London, 1981–84. Resident Poet, Henry Wood Promenade Concerts, 2002; Writer in Residence: Somerset Hse, 2008–09; Envmt Inst., UCL, 2010–11; Royal Opera Hse, Covent Gdn, 2014; Leverhulme Artist in Residence, Christ's Coll., Cambridge, 2009–10. Inaugurated Poetry Workshop, BBC Radio 4, 2011. Chair of Judges, Forward Poetry Prize, 2010. FRSL 1998. Patron, 21st Century Tiger, 2014–. Trustee: Zool Soc. of London, 2012–; New Networks for Nature, 2015–. Writers' Award, Arts Council England, 1994; First Prize, UK Nat. Poetry Competition, 1996; Cholmondeley Award, Soc. of Authors, 2000; Res. Award, Calouste Gulbenkian Foundn, 2003; Darwin Now Award, British Council, 2009. *Publications: poetry:* Alibi, 1985; Summer Snow, 1990; Angel, 1993; Fusewire, 1996; Rembrandt Would Have Loved You, 1998; Voodoo Shop, 2002; Soho Leopard, 2004; Darwin: a life in poems, 2009; The Mara Crossing, 2010; Learning to Make an Oud in Nazareth, 2014; *fiction:* Where the Serpent Lives, 2010; *non-fiction:* In and Out of the Mind: Greek images of the tragic self, 1992; Whom Gods Destroy: elements of Greek and tragic madness, 1995; I'm a Man: sex, gods and rock 'n' roll, 2000; 52 Ways of Looking at a Poem, 2002; Tigers in Red Weather, 2005; The Poem and the Journey, 2006; (ed) Alfred Lord Tennyson, 2007; Silent Letters of the Alphabet, 2010; (ed) Walter Ralegh, Selected Poems, 2010; (ed) Gerard Manley Hopkins, 2011. *Recreations:* tiger-watching, singing 16th century music, playing chamber music (viola), watching the sea from Cretan kafeneia, conservation. *Address:* English Department, King's College London, Virginia Woolf Building, 22 Kingsway, WC2B 6LE. *E:* ruth.padel@kcl.ac.uk.

PADFIELD, Nicholas David; QC 1991; a Recorder, since 1995; a Deputy High Court Judge, Queen's Bench Division and Administrative Court, since 2008; *b* 5 Aug. 1947; *s* of David Padfield and Sushila, *d* of Sir Samuel Runganadhan; *m* 1st, 1978, Nayana Parekh (*d* 1983); one *d*; 2nd, 1986, Mary Barran, JP, *d* of Sir Edward Playfair, KCB; two *s*. *Educ:* Dragon Sch.; Charterhouse; University Coll., Oxford (Open Scholar, MA; hockey blue; England hockey internat.); Trinity Hall, Cambridge (LLM Internat. Law). FCIArb. Called to the Bar, Inner Temple, 1972, Bencher, 1995; called to various overseas Bars. Mem., Panel of Lloyd's Arbitrators, 1991–. Dep. Chm., Cons. Party Ethics and Integrity Cttee. Chairman: Commonwealth and Ethnic Barristers' Assoc., 2003–04; London br., CIArb, 2007–08. Council of Advisors: Lord Slynn Eur. Law Foundn; Internat. Council for Capital Formation, 2005–. Cttee, London Oratory Appeal, 1990–95. Freeman: City of London, 2003; Scriveners' Co., 2003. *Address:* Beauchamp House, Chapel Street, Bloxham, Oxon OX15 4NB. *T:* (01295) 720506. *E:* ndp@nicholaspadfieldqc.com. *Clubs:* Garrick, MCC; Vincent's (Oxford).

PADFIELD, Nicola Margaret; Master, Fitzwilliam College, Cambridge, since 2013 (Fellow, since 1991, and College Lecturer, since 1996); Reader in Criminal and Penal Justice, University of Cambridge, since 2012; *b* Windlesham, Surrey, 16 May 1955; *d* of late Wing Comdr James Michael Helme, DFC, AFC and Diana Wentworth Helme (*née* Howitt), JP; *m* 1979, Dr Christopher Padfield; two *s* one *d*. *Educ:* St Anne's Coll., Oxford (BA 1976); Darwin Coll., Cambridge (Dip. Criminol. 1977); Univ. of Aix-Marseille (Diplôme d'Études Supérieures 1979). Called to the Bar, Middle Temple, 1978, Bencher, 2009; Recorder, 2002–14. University of Cambridge: Alumni Affairs Officer, 1990–91; Affiliated Lectr, 1992–96; Lectr, 1998–2002, Sen. Lectr, 2002–04, Inst. of Criminology; Univ. Lectr, 2004–05; Sen. Lectr, 2005–12. Member: Advocacy Trng Council, 2007–10; Derek Wood, QC's Review of Bar Vocational Course, 2008; Res. Adv. Gp, Howard League, 2009–; Expert Advr, Council for Penological Co-operation, Council of Europe, 2010. Editor: Commonwealth Judicial Jl, 1989–2004; Archbold Review, 1996–2013. *Publications:* The Criminal Justice Process: text and materials, 1995, 4th edn 2008; (with N. Walker) Sentencing: theory, law and practice, 1996; Criminal Law, 1998, 9th edn 2014; A Guide to the Crime and Disorder Act 1998, 1998; (jtly) A Guide to the Proceeds of Crime Act 2002, 2002; Beyond the Tariff: human rights and the release of life sentence prisoners, 2002; (ed jtly) Discretion: its uses in criminal justice and beyond, 2003; (ed) Who to Release?: parole, fairness and criminal justice, 2007; (ed jtly) Release from Prison: European policy and practice, 2010; chapters in books; articles in legal and criminol. jls. *Recreations:* my granddaughter, travel (particularly on the back of a tandem), singing and playing the violin (badly). *Address:* Fitzwilliam College, Cambridge CB3 0DG. *T:* (01223) 332000, *Fax:* (01223) 332082. *E:* nmp21@cam.ac.uk.

See also P. A. Helme.

PADMORE, Elaine Marguirite, OBE 2012; opera consultant and lecturer, since 2012; Director of Opera, Royal Opera House, Covent Garden, 2000–11; *b* Haworth, Yorks, 3 Feb. 1947; *d* of Alfred and Florence Padmore. *Educ:* Newland High Sch., Hull; Arnold Sch., Blackpool; Birmingham Univ. (MA; BMus); Guildhall Sch. of Music; LTCL. Liberal Studies Lectr, Croydon and Kingston Colls of Art, 1968–70; Books Editor, OUP Music Dept, 1970–71; Producer, BBC Music Div., 1971–76; Announcer, Radio 3, 1982–90. Major BBC Radio 3 series include: Parade, Music of Tchaikovsky's Russia, England's Pleasant Land, Journal de mes Mélodies; Presenter of numerous programmes, incl. Festival Comment, Edinburgh Fest., 1973–81; Chief Producer, Opera, BBC Radio, 1976–83: series incl. complete operas of Richard Strauss and first performances of works by Delius and Havergal Brian; formerly active as professional singer (soprano), particularly of opera; Lectr in Opera, RAM, 1979–87; Artistic Director: Classical Prodns, London, 1990–92; Wexford Festival Opera, 1982–94; DGOS Opera Ireland, 1989–90 and 1991–93; Artistic Consultant, 1992 London Opera Fest.; Dir, Royal Danish Opera, Copenhagen, 1993–2000. Member: Adv. Council, Park Lane Gp, 2004–; Bd, British Youth Opera, 2013–; Trustee, Countess of Munster Musical Trust, 2008–. Hon. ARAM. Hon. FTCL; Hon. FBC. Hon. DMus Birmingham, 2008. Hungarian Radio Pro Musica Award for prog. Summertime on Bredon, 1973; Prix Musical de Radio Brno for prog. The English Renaissance, 1974; Sunday Independent Award for services to music in Ireland, 1985. Kt, Order of Dannebrog (Denmark), 1994. *Publications:* Wagner (Great Composers' Series), 1970; Music in the Modern Age: chapter on Germany, 1973; (contrib.) 100 Nights at the Opera: an anthology to celebrate the 40th anniversary of Wexford Festival Opera, 1991; contributor to: New Grove Dict. of Music, Proc. of Royal Musical Assoc., Music and Letters, The Listener. *Recreations:* gardening, travel, art exhibitions. *E:* elainepadmore@gmail.com.

PADMORE, Elizabeth Jane; Chairman, Hampshire Hospitals NHS Foundation Trust, since 2010; Board Member, Independent Parliamentary Standards Authority, since 2013; *b* Harrogate, 1 Feb. 1955; *d* of John Austen Farmar Woolley and Mary Woolley; *m* 1984, Giles Padmore (marr. diss. 2001); one *s*. *Educ:* Bar Convent, York; Brasenose Coll., Oxford (BA PPE 1977; BA Juris. 1978). Tutor in Moral and Pol Philos., 1978–79; Man. Dir, Letterstream, 1980–86; Internat. Dir, Corp. Affairs, EDS, 1987–94; Partner and Global Dir Policy and Corporate Affairs, Accenture, 1995–2006. Director: Clydesdale Bank plc, 2009–12; Nat. Australia Gp Europe, 2009–12. Member: Council and Exec. Cttee, Chatham House, 2003–09; Council of Mgt, Ditchley Foundn, 2005–13; Director and Trustee: Women for Women Internat., 2007–13; Youth Business Internat., 2008–; Dir, Global Bd, Enablis, 2010–. Barclay Fellow, Green Templeton Coll., Oxford, 2013–. *Recreations:* theatre, music, opera, fly fishing, walking, old roses, gardens, cricket, good food and wine with friends. *Address:* Hampshire Hospitals NHS Foundation Trust, Basingstoke and North Hampshire Hospital, Aldermaston Road, Basingstoke, Hants RG24 9NA. *T:* (01256) 313035, *Fax:* (01962) 825265. *E:* elizabeth.padmore@hhft.nhs.uk. *Club:* Home House.

PADMORE, Mark Joseph; tenor; *b* 8 March 1961; *s* of Peter Francis Padmore and Sheila Mary (*née* Stoyles); *m* 1996, Josette Patricia Simon (marr. diss. 2004); one *d*. *Educ:* Simon Langton Grammar Sch. for Boys; King's Coll., Cambridge (BA (Hons), MA). Has performed at major festivals, incl. Aix-en-Provence, Edinburgh, BBC Proms, Salzburg, Spoleto, Tanglewood, Glyndebourne, Mostly Mozart, NY; opera house débuts: Teatro Comunale, Florence, 1992; Opéra Comique, Paris, 1993; Théâtre du Châtelet, 1995; Royal Opera House, Covent Gdn, 1995; Scottish Opera, 1996; Opéra de Paris, 1996; ENO, 1999; has also performed with WNO and Opera de Lausanne; concert appearances include: LSO; City of Birmingham Orch.; RPO; Les Arts Florissants; English Baroque Soloists; Czech Philharmonic Orch.; Berlin Phil.; Vienna Phil.; NY Phil.; Philadelphia Orch.; Royal Concertgebouw Orchs; Freiburg Baroque; Orch. of the Age of Enlightenment; English Concert; has given recitals in Barcelona, Brussels, Copenhagen, Madrid, Milan, Moscow, NY and Paris; in Lieder has appeared at: Wigmore Hall; Cheltenham Fest.; Queen Elizabeth Hall; de Singel Hall, Antwerp; has made more than 60 recordings, incl. As Steals the Morn (Vocal Recording of the Year, BBC Music Magazine, 2008), La Clemenza di Tito, St John and St Matthew Passions, The Creation and Messiah, Winterreise (Vocal Solo Award, Gramophone Magazine, 2010). *Recreations:* cycling, theatre. *Address:* c/o Maxine Robertson Management, 14 Forge Drive, Claygate KT10 0HR. *T:* (020) 7993 2917. *E:* info@maxinerobertson.com.

PADOVAN, John Mario Faskally; Chairman, Interserve Group Pension Fund, 2003–14; *b* 7 May 1938; *s* of Umberto Mario Padovan and Mary Nina Liddon Padovan; *m* 1964, Sally Kay (*née* Anderson); three *s*. *Educ:* St George's College, Weybridge; King's College London (LLB; FKC 2003); Keble College, Oxford (BCL). FCA. County Bank, 1970–84: Dir, 1971; Dep. Chief Exec., 1974; Chief Exec., 1976; Chm., 1984; Dep. Chm., Hambros Bank and Dir, Hambros, 1984–86; Chm., Merchant Banking Div., Barclays de Zoete Wedd Gp, 1986–91; Dep. Chm., Barclays de Zoete Wedd, 1989–91; Dep. Chm., 1992, Chm., 1993–95, AAH; Dir, 1989–91, Chm., 1991–95, Mabey Hldgs. Chairman: Gardner Merchant, 1993–95; Evans of Leeds, 1997–99 (Dir, 1994–97); Furniture Village, 1998–2001; Schroder Split Fund, 2000– (Dir, 1992–); Williams Lea Gp, 2000–04 (Dir, 1992–2000); Dawnay Day Property Finance Gp, 2004–08; Director: Tesco, 1982–94; Whitbread, 1992–2002; Interserve (formerly Tilbury Douglas), 1996–2005 (Dep. Chm., 2003–05); HFC Bank, 1997–2003. Mem. Court, Drapers' Co., 1991– (Master, 1999–2000). *Recreations:* golf, walking, contemporary art. *Address:* 15 Lord North Street, SW1P 3LD. *T:* (020) 7222 3261. *Clubs:* Royal St George's Golf; St Enedoc Golf.

PAGE, Adrienne May; QC 1999; *b* 14 July 1952; *d* of late Gwythian Lloyd Page and of Betty Page (*née* Spring); *m* 1983, Anthony Crichton Waldeck (marr. diss. 2007); one step *s* one step *d*. *Educ:* Godolphin Sch., Salisbury; Univ. of Kent at Canterbury (BA Social Sci.). Called to the Bar, Middle Temple, 1974, Bencher, 2003; Asst Recorder, 1995–99; Recorder, 1999–2004; Hd of Chambers, 2003–11. *Recreation:* gardening. *Address:* 5 Gray's Inn Square, Gray's Inn, WC1R 5AH. *T:* (020) 7242 2902. *Club:* Beaulieu River Sailing.

PAGE, Andrew John Walter; HM Diplomatic Service; Senior Adviser on European Banking and Government Relations, PricewaterhouseCoopers (on secondment), 2014–March 2016; *b* Cuckfield, W Sussex, 17 Sept. 1965; *s* of late John Henry Page and of Carol Page. *Educ:* Lancing Coll., W Sussex; Jesus Coll., Cambridge (BA Classics 1987). Investment analyst, County NatWest, 1987–90; entered FCO, 1990; Desk Officer, Internat. Debt, Econ. Relns Dept, FCO, 1990–91; lang. trng (Russian and Ukrainian), FCO, 1992; Second Secretary: Kiev, 1993–96; News Dept, FCO, 1996–98; Hd, SA sect., Africa Dept (Southern), FCO, 1998–2000; First Sec., Paris, 2000–04; Dep. Dir, Russia, S Caucasus and Central Asia Directorate, FCO, 2004–08; Ambassador to Slovenia, 2009–13. *Recreations:* Real tennis, lawn tennis, squash, golf, crosswords, bridge, English, French and Russian literature, music, theatre. *Address:* c/o PricewaterhouseCoopers, 7 More London Riverside, SE1 2RT. *E:* andrew.page@uk.pwc.com. *Clubs:* Jesters, MCC, Queen's; Hawks (Cambridge); Petworth House Tennis; W Sussex Golf.

PAGE, Annette, (Mrs Ronald Hynd); Ballerina of the Royal Ballet until retirement, 1967; Ballet Mistress, Ballet of the Bayerische Staatsoper, Munich, 1984–86; *b* 18 Dec. 1932; *d* of James Lees and Margaret Page; *m* 1957, Ronald Hynd, *qv*; one *d*. *Educ:* Royal Ballet School. Audition and award of scholarship to Roy. Ballet Sch., 1944. Entry into touring company of Royal Ballet (then Sadler's Wells Theatre Ballet), 1950; promotion to major Royal Ballet Co. (Sadler's Wells Ballet), 1955. Mem., Arts Council of GB, 1976–79. *Roles included:* The Firebird, Princess Aurora in Sleeping Beauty, Odette-Odile in Swan Lake, Giselle, Lise in La Fille Mal Gardée, Juliet in Romeo and Juliet, Cinderella, Swanilda in Coppelia, Nikiya in La Bayadère, Les Sylphides, Miller's Wife in Three Cornered Hat, Terpsichore in Apollo, Blue Girl in Les Biches, Mamzelle Angot, Ballerina in Petrouchka, Symphonic Variations, Les Rendezvous, Beauty and the Beast, La Capricciosa in Lady and the Fool, Queen of Hearts in Card Game, Agon, Polka in Solitaire, Ballerina in Scènes de Ballet, Queens of Fire and Air in Homage to the Queen, Blue Girl in Les Pâtineurs, Tango and Polka in Façade, Julia and Pepè in A Wedding Bouquet, Moon and Pas de Six in Prince of the Pagodas, Danses Concertantes,

Faded Beauty and Young Lover in Noctambules, Flower Festival Pas de Deux, Ballerina in Ballet Imperial; *partners included*: Ronald Hynd, Rudolf Nureyev, Sir Anthony Dowell, Christopher Gable, Donald McLeary. *Recreations:* music, books, gardening.

PAGE, Anthony (Frederick Montague); stage, film and television director; *b* India, 21 Sept. 1935; *s* of Brig. F. G. C. Page, DSO, OBE, and P. V. M. Page. *Educ:* Oakley Hall, Cirencester; Winchester Coll. (Schol.); Magdalen Coll., Oxford (Schol., BA); Neighborhood Playhouse Sch. of the Theater, NY. Asst, Royal Court Theatre, 1958: co-directed Live Like Pigs, directed The Room; Artistic Dir, Dundee Repertory Theatre, 1962; The Caretaker, Oxford and Salisbury; Women Beware Women, and Nil Carborundum, Royal Shakespeare Co., 1963; BBC Directors' Course, then several episodes of Z-Cars, Horror of Darkness and 1st TV prodn Stephen D; Jt Artistic Dir, Royal Court, 1964–65; directed Inadmissible Evidence (later Broadway and film), A Patriot for Me, 1st revival of Waiting for Godot, Cuckoo in the Nest; Diary of a Madman, Duchess, 1966; Artistic Dir, two seasons at Royal Court: Uncle Vanya, 1970; Alpha Beta (also film); Hedda Gabler; Krapp's Last Tape; Not I; Cromwell; other plays transf. from Royal Court to West End: Time Present; Hotel in Amsterdam; revival, Look Back in Anger; West of Suez; directed Hamlet, Nottingham, 1970; Rules of the Game, Nat. Theatre; King Lear, Amer. Shakespeare Fest., 1975; Cowardice, Ambassadors, 1983; Heartbreak House, Broadway, 1984 (televised); Mrs Warren's Profession, RNT, 1985; Three Tall Women, Wyndham's, 1994; Absolute Hell, RNT, 1995; The Doll's House, Playhouse, 1996, NY, 1997 (Tony Award); A Delicate Balance, Theatre Royal, Haymarket, 1997; The Forest, Sleep With Me, 1999; Finding the Sun, Marriage Play, 2001, RNT; Cat on a Hot Tin Roof, Lyric, 2001, NY, 2003; The Master Builder, Albery, 2003; The Goat, or Who is Sylvia, Almeida, transf. Apollo, 2004; Who's Afraid of Virginia Woolf?, NY, 2005, Apollo, 2006; revival, The Night of the Iguana, Lyric, 2005; The Lady From Dubuque, Theatre Royal, Haymarket, 2007; revival, Waiting for Godot, NY, 2009; Long Day's Journey Into Night, Richmond Th., transf. Apollo, 2012; *television:* The Parachute, 1968; Emlyn; Hotel in Amsterdam; Speaking of Murder; You're Free; The Changeling; Headmaster; Sheppey; Absolute Hell, 1991; Middlemarch, 1994; My Zinc Bed, 2008; in USA: Missiles of October; Pueblo Incident; FDR, the Last Year; Bill (starring Mickey Rooney (Golden Globe Award); Johnny Belinda; Bill on His Own; The Nightmare Years; Patricia Neal Story; Murder by Reason of Insanity; Second Serve; Pack of Lies; Chernobyl: The Final Warning, 1990; Guests of the Emperor; The Human Bomb; *films:* Inadmissible Evidence; I Never Promised You a Rose Garden; Absolution; Forbidden. Directors' and Producers' Award for TV Dir of Year, 1966. *Recreations:* painting, reading, travelling.

PAGE, (Arthur) Hugo (Micklem); QC 2002; *b* 16 Sept. 1951; *s* of Sir (Arthur) John Page and of Anne Page (*née* Micklem); *m* 1992, Angélique, *d* of Marquis de Folin, Paris. *Educ:* Harrow Sch.; Magdalene Coll., Cambridge (MA). Called to the Bar, Inner Temple, 1977; in practice, specialising in commercial law. Contested (C) Pontefract and Castleford, Oct. 1978, 1979. *Publications:* (contrib.) Halsbury's Laws, 4th edn, 1991. *Recreations:* travel, book collecting. *Address:* 20 Brechin Place, SW7 4QA. *T:* (020) 7370 6826; Blackstone Chambers, Blackstone House, Temple, EC4Y 9BW. *T:* (020) 7583 1770, *Fax:* (020) 7822 7350. *E:* hugopage@blackstonechambers.com.

PAGE, Ashley, OBE 2006; freelance choreographer and director, since 2012; Artistic Director, Scottish Ballet, 2002–12; *b* 9 Aug. 1956; named Ashley Laverty; *s* of John Henry Laverty and Sheila Rachel Laverty; *m* Nicola Roberts; one *s* one *d*. *Educ:* St Andrew's Sch., Rochester; Royal Ballet Schs. Joined Royal Ballet at Covent Garden, 1976; Soloist, 1980, Principal Dancer, and choreographer, 1984–2002. Works choreographed for: Royal Ballet, incl. Fearful Symmetries (Time Out Award, 1994; Olivier Award, 1995); Ballet Rambert, subseq. Rambert Dance Co.; Dutch Nat. Ballet; Dance Umbrella Fest.; San Francisco Ballet; Polish Nat. Ballet; Vienna State Ballet; Royal Ballet of Flanders; Glyndebourne Opera and other cos in GB and abroad; for Scottish Ballet: The Nutcracker; Cinderella; The Sleeping Beauty; The Pump Room; Nightswimming into Day; Pennies from Heaven; Alice. Hon. DDra Royal Conservatoire of Scotland, 2012. Herald Archangel Award, 2011; Critics' Circle Nat. Dance Award for Outstanding Achievement, 2012. *Recreations:* interest in all the arts, travel.

PAGE, Benjamin Charles; Chief Executive, Ipsos MORI UK and Ireland, since 2009; *b* Exeter, 9 Jan. 1965; *s* of Charles Page and Elizabeth Page (*née* Barrett); *m* (marr. diss.); one *s*. *Educ:* St John's Coll., Oxford (BA Hons Modern Hist.). Researcher: MIL (NOP), 1986–87; MORI, 1988–94; Dir, Social Research, 1994–2000; Chm., Ipsos MORI Social Research Inst., 2000–09. Mem., CABE, 2003–10. Dir, Involve, 2006–09. Comr, RSA 2020 Public Services Trust, 2009–11. *Publications:* Blair's Britain, 2007; contribs to Municipal Jl, Health Service Jl, Local Govt Chronicle. *Recreations:* Italy, history, restaurants, skateboarding, insomnia. *Address:* Ipsos MORI, 3 Thomas More Square, E1W 1WY. *T:* (020) 3059 5000. *E:* ben.page@ipsos.com.

PAGE, Bruce; journalist; *b* 1 Dec. 1936; *s* of Roger and Beatrice Page; *m* 1969, Anne Louise Darnborough; one *s* one *d*. *Educ:* Melbourne High Sch.; Melbourne Univ. The Herald, Melbourne, 1956–60; Evening Standard, 1960–62; Daily Herald, 1962–64; Sunday Times, 1964–76; Daily Express, 1977; Editor, The New Statesman, 1978–82. Dir, Direct Image Systems and Communications Ltd, 1992–95. *Publications:* (jtly) Philby, 1968, 3rd edn 1977; (jtly) An American Melodrama, 1969; (jtly) Do You Sincerely Want to be Rich?, 1971, 2nd edn 2005; (jtly) Destination Disaster, 1976; contrib. Ulster, 1972; The Yom Kippur War, 1974; The British Press, 1978; The Murdoch Archipelago, 2003. *Recreations:* reading, writing. *Address:* Beach House, Shingle Street, Hollesley, Suffolk IP12 3BE.

PAGE, Prof. Christopher Howard, DPhil; FBA 2013; Senior Research Fellow, Sidney Sussex College, Cambridge, since 1985 (Vice-Master, 2008–11); Professor of Medieval Music and Literature, University of Cambridge, since 2011; Director, Gothic Voices, since 1982; *b* 8 April 1952; *s* of Ewart Lacey Page and Marie Victoria (*née* Graham); *m* 1st, 1975, Régine Fourcade (marr. diss. 2004); 2nd, 2004, Anne Dunan. *Educ:* Sir George Monoux Grammar Sch.; Balliol Coll., Oxford (BA English 1974; MA); Univ. of York (DPhil). Jun. Res. Fellow, Jesus Coll., Oxford, 1977–80; Lectr in English, New Coll., Oxford, 1980–85; Lectr in English, 1989–97, Reader in Medieval Music and Lit., 1997–2011, Univ. of Cambridge. Editor, Plainsong and Medieval Music, 1991–. Presenter, Spirit of the Age, Radio 3, 1992–97. Fellow, Fellowship of Makers and Restorers of Historical Instruments, 1982. Former Chm., Plainsong and Medieval Music Soc. FSA 2009. Dent Medal, Royal Musical Assoc., 1991. *Publications:* Voices and Instruments of the Middle Ages, 1987; The Owl and the Nightingale, 1989; the *Summa Musice*, 1991; Discarding Images, 1993; Songs of the Trouvères, 1995; Latin Poetry and Conductus Rhythm in Medieval France, 1997; The Christian West and its Singers: the first thousand years, 2010; The Guitar in Tudor England, 2015; articles in Early Music, Galpin Soc. Jl, Plainsong and Medieval Music, Musical Times, Jl of Amer. Musicological Soc. *Address:* Sidney Sussex College, Cambridge CB2 3HU. *T:* (01223) 338800.

PAGE, Prof. Clive Peter, PhD; Professor of Pharmacology, and Director, Sackler Institute of Pulmonary Pharmacology, King's College London, since 1995; *b* 14 Oct. 1958; *s* of late Peter Page and of Edna Page; *m* 2004, Clare O'Leary; two *s* one *d*. *Educ:* Grovelands Primary Sch., Hailsham; Bexhill Grammar Sch.; Chelsea Coll., Univ. of London (BSc Hons Pharmacol.); Cardiothoracic Inst., Imperial Coll., London (PhD Pharmacol. 1984). Sandoz Ltd, Basel, 1984–86; Lectr, 1986–89, Reader, 1989–95, in Pharmacol., Jt Hd, Inst. of Pharmaceutical Sci., 2010–13, KCL. Chm. Bd, Verona Pharma Ltd, 2006–14; Chm. Bd and Dir, Peptinnovate Ltd, 2015–; Director: Helperby Therapeutics plc, 2004–12; Babraham Biosciences Ltd, 2007–. Chm., Animal Scis Gp, Soc. of Biology (formerly Biosciences Fedn), 2004–12. Trustee, Babraham Inst., 2008–. *Publications:* (jtly) Integrated Pharmacology, 1997, 3rd edn 2006; over 200 scientific articles in learned jls. *Recreations:* travel, mountain walking, good food and wine. *Address:* Sackler Institute of Pulmonary Pharmacology, King's College London, Waterloo Campus, SE1 9NH. *T:* (020) 7848 4784/2, *Fax:* (020) 7848 4788. *E:* clive.page@kcl.ac.uk. *Club:* Athenæum.

PAGE, David John, FCCA; Deputy Chief Executive, Leeds City Council, 2001–09; *b* 24 Feb. 1954; *s* of Clifford Page and Evelyn Page (*née* Banks); *m* 1976, Carole Watson; one *s* one *d*. *Educ:* W Leeds Boys' High Sch.; Leeds Poly. FCCA 1976. Trainee accountant, CEGB, 1972–74; Leeds City Council, 1974–: Chief Accountant, 1985–88; Asst Dir of Finance, 1988–89; Sen. Asst Dir of Finance, 1989–92; Dir of Finance, 1992–99; Exec. Dir (Resources), 1999–2001. Chief Finance Officer, W Yorks PTA, 2000–09; non-exec. Dir, W Yorks PTE, 2000–09; Dir, Educn Leeds, 2001–09. Mem. Bd, Yorkshire CCC, 2006–09. *Recreations:* music, all sports, caravanning, quizzes. *Address:* 3 Stonegate, Ossett, Wakefield WF5 0JD. *E:* davejpage@btinternet.com.

PAGE, David Michael; Chairman, Fulham Shore plc, since 2012; *b* 20 June 1952; *s* of Edwin D. and N. M. E. Page; *m* (marr. diss. 2012); three *s* one *d*. *Educ:* by Jesuits. PizzaExpress, 1981–: Chief Exec., 1996–98, 2000–03, Chm., 1998–2002; non-exec. Dir, 2003–05; Chm., The Clapham House Group PLC, 2003–10 non-exec. Dir, Young & Co.'s Brewery plc, 2008–15. *Recreation:* none - always working. *T:* 07836 346934.

PAGE, David Norman, ARSA; RIBA; Senior Partner, Page\Park Architects, since 1981; *b* 4 Sept. 1957; *s* of Catherine and Bernard Page. *Educ:* Strathclyde Univ. (BSc; BArch). ARIAS 1982. Lectr, Dept of Architecture and Bldg Sci., Strathclyde Univ., 1982–94. Mem., Royal Fine Art Commn for Scotland, 1995. Projects include: Mus. of Scottish Country Life; Maggie's Highland Cancer Care Centre, Inverness (Best Bldg in Scotland, RIAS Award, 2006); Lighthouse Centre for Architecture and Design; Scottish NPG, 2011; Clyde Gateway, 2012. DUniv Strathclyde, 2004. *Publications:* (with Miles Glendinning) Clone City, 1999. *Recreation:* walking streets and landscapes. *Address:* Page\Park Architects, 20 James Morrison Street, Glasgow G1 5PE. *E:* d.page@pagepark.co.uk. *Club:* Adam Smith.

PAGE, Prof. Edward Charles, PhD; FBA 2001; Sidney and Beatrice Webb Professor of Public Policy, London School of Economics, since 2001; *b* London, 19 Oct. 1953; *s* of Edward Charles Page and Winifred Victoria Page; *m* 1975, Christine Mary Batty; one *s* two *d*. *Educ:* Kingston Poly. (BA (CNAA) German and Politics 1976); Univ. of Strathclyde (MSc Politics 1978; PhD Politics 1982). Lectr in Politics, Univ. of Strathclyde, 1978–81; University of Hull: Lectr, 1981–89; Sen. Lectr, 1989–92; Reader, 1992–95; Prof., 1995–2001. Vis. Associate Prof., Texas A&M Univ., 1986–87. Dir, ESRC Res. Prog. on Future Governance: Lessons from Comparative Public Policy, 1998–2003. Co-Ed., Eur. Jl Political Res., 2000–06; Associate Ed., Jl of Public Policy, 2006–11. *Publications:* (ed with R. Rose) Fiscal Stress in Cities, 1982; Political Authority and Bureaucratic Power, 1985, 2nd edn 1992; (ed with M. Goldsmith) Central and Local Government Relations: a comparative analysis of West European Unitary States, 1987; Centralism and Localism in Europe, 1992; (ed with J. Hayward) Governing the New Europe, 1995; People Who Run Europe, 1997; (ed with V. Wright) Bureaucratic Elites in Western Europe, 1999; Governing by Numbers: delegated legislation and everyday policy making, 2001; (jtly) Policy Bureaucracy: government with a cast of thousands, 2005; (ed with V. Wright) From the Active to the Enabling State, 2006; (ed with M. Goldsmith) Changing Government Relations in Europe, 2010; Policy without Politicians, 2012; contrib. to jls incl. British Jl Pol Sci., Eur. Jl Pol Res., Govt and Policy, W Eur. Politics, Jl Public Policy, Jl Theoretical Politics, Leviathan, Local Govt Studies, Pol Studies, Politique et Management Publique, Pouvoirs, Public Admin, Urban Affairs Qly. *Recreation:* jazz. *Address:* Department of Government, London School of Economics, Houghton Street, WC2A 2AE. *T:* (020) 7849 4629.

PAGE, Ewan Stafford, PhD, MA, BSc; Vice-Chancellor, University of Reading, 1979–93; *b* 17 Aug. 1928; *s* of late Joseph William Page and Lucy Quayle (*née* Stafford); *m* 1955, Sheila Margaret Smith; three *s* one *d*. *Educ:* Wyggeston Grammar Sch., Leicester; Christ's Coll., Cambridge (MA, PhD, Rayleigh Prize 1952); Univ. of London (BSc). Instr, RAF Techn. Coll., 1949–51; Lectr in Statistics, Durham Colls, 1954–57; Director: Durham Univ. Computing Lab., 1957–63; Newcastle Univ. Computing Lab., 1963–78; Visiting Prof., Univ. of N Carolina, Chapel Hill, USA, 1962–63; University of Newcastle upon Tyne: Prof. of Computing and Data Processing, 1965–78; Pro-Vice Chancellor, 1972–78 (Actg Vice-Chancellor, 1976–77). Member: Newcastle AHA, 1976–79; Berks AHA, 1980–82; Oxford RHA, 1982–84; West Berks DHA, 1984–93; Berks HA, 1993–96. Mem. Bd, Aycliffe and Peterlee Develt Corp., 1969–78. Chairman: Food Adv. Cttee, 1988–94; Univs' Authorities Panel, 1988–93. Pres., British Computer Soc., 1984–85 (Dep. Pres., 1983–84); Member: Gen. Optical Council, 1984–2001 (Vice-Chm., 1989–2001); Bd, Optical Consumer Complaints Service, 1999–2014; Vice-Pres., Assoc. of Optometrists, 2002–05; Hon. Treasurer, Royal Statistical Soc., 1983–89. CCMI (CBIM 1986); Hon. Fellow, Amer. Statistical Assoc., 1974; Hon. FBCS, 1976; Hon. Fellow, Northumbria Univ. (formerly Newcastle upon Tyne Poly.), 1979. Hon. DSc Reading, 1993. Chevalier, l'Ordre des Palmes Académiques (France), 1991. *Publications:* (jtly) Information Representation and Manipulation in a Computer, 1973, 2nd edn 1978; (jtly) Introduction to Computational Combinatorics, 1978; papers in statistical and computing jls. *Recreations:* golf, music, reading, Freemasonry. *Address:* High View, Charlcombe Lane, Bath BA1 5TT.

PAGE, Gordon Francis de Courcy, CBE 2000; DL; Chairman: Cobham plc, 2001–08; AirTanker Holdings Ltd, since 2009; *b* 17 Nov. 1943; *s* of Sir Frederick William Page, CBE, FRS and late Kathleen (*née* de Courcy); *m* 1969, Judith Cecilia Mays; two *s* two *d*. *Educ:* Moffats Prep. Sch.; Cheltenham Coll.; St Catharine's Coll., Cambridge (BA; MA 1970). With Rolls-Royce plc, 1962–89; Cobham plc, 1990–2008, Chief Exec., 1992–2001. Mem., 2000–08, Chm., 2004–08, Industrial Develt Adv. Bd, DTI. Mem., Dorset LSC, 2001–08; Pres., Dorset Chamber of Commerce and Industry, 2004–05; Mem., SW Innovation and Sci. Council, 2005–08; Chm., Dorset Local Enterprise Partnership, 2011–. Chairman: FKI plc, 2004–07; Hamworthy plc, 2004–12; PH Warr plc, 2008–. Non-exec. Dir, Bournemouth Council Trading Co. Ltd, 2014–. President: SBAC, 1997–98, 2002–03; Chartered Mgt Inst., 2003–04; Mem. Council, 2000–08, Pres., 2006–07, RAeS. Pro-Chancellor, Cranfield Univ., 2007–12. Gov., Canford Sch., 2003–12 (Dep. Chm., 2008; Chm., 2009–12). Trustee, Dorset Community Foundn, 2009–. FInstD 1990. Hon. FRAeS 2009. DL Dorset, 2006. Hon. DSc Cranfield, 2003; Hon. DBA Bournemouth, 2009. *Recreations:* theatre, travel, classic cars. *Address:* Avon Reach, The Close, Avon Castle, Ringwood, Hants BH24 2BJ. *T:* (01425) 475365, *Fax:* (01425) 425680. *E:* gordonpage@btinternet.com.

PAGE, Howard William Barrett; QC 1987; *b* 11 Feb. 1943; *s* of Leslie Herbert Barrett Page and Phyllis Elizabeth Page; *m* 1969, Helen Joanna Shotter (CVO 2011); two *s* one *d*. *Educ:* Radley Coll.; Trinity Hall, Cambridge (MA, LLB). Called to the Bar, Lincoln's Inn, 1967 (Mansfield Schol.); Bencher, 1994. Comr, Royal Ct of Jersey, 2000–15; Dep. Pres., Lloyd's Appeal Tribunal, 2000–10. *Recreations:* music, walking. *Address:* 6 New Square, Lincoln's Inn, WC2A 3QS.

PAGE, Hugo; *see* Page, A. H. M.

PAGE, Jennifer Anne, CBE 1994; Chief Executive, New Millennium Experience Company Ltd, 1997–2000; *b* 12 Nov. 1944; *d* of Edward and Olive Page; *m* 2001, Jeremy David Orme, *qv*. *Educ:* Barr's Hill Grammar School, Coventry; Royal Holloway College, Univ. of London (BA Hons). Entered Civil Service, 1968; Principal, DoE, 1974; Asst Sec., Dept of Transport,

1980; seconded BNOC, 1981; LDDC, 1983; Senior Vice-Pres., Pallas Invest SA, 1984–89; Chief Executive: English Heritage (Historic Buildings and Monuments Commn), 1989–95; Millennium Commn, 1995–97. Vice-Chair, Cathedrals Fabric Commn for England, 2006–. Member, Board: Railtrack Group, 1994–2001; Equitable Life Assurance Soc., 1994–2001. Trustee, Nat. Churches Trust, 2008–.

PAGE, Prof. John Kenneth; energy and environmental consultant; Professor of Building Science, University of Sheffield, 1960–84, now Emeritus; *b* 3 Nov. 1924; *s* of late Brig. E. K. Page, CBE, DSO, MC; *m* 1954, Anita Bell Lovell; two *s* two *d*. *Educ:* Haileybury College; Pembroke College, Cambridge. Served War of 1939–45, Royal Artillery, 1943–47. Asst Industrial Officer, Council of Industrial Design, 1950–51; taught Westminster School, 1952–53; Sen. Scientific Officer, Tropical Liaison Section, Building Research Station, 1953–56; Chief Research Officer, Nuffield Div. for Architectural Studies, 1956–57; Lecturer, Dept of Building Science, Univ. of Liverpool, 1957–60. Sen. Res. Fellow, Dept of Physics, UMIST, 2000–05; Hon. Fellow, Tyndall Centre for Climate Change, UMIST, subseq. Univ. of Manchester, 2002–08. Leverhulme Emeritus Fellow, 2006–08. Chm., Environmental Gp, and Mem., Econ. Planning Council, Yorks and Humberside Region, 1965–78; Regl Chm., Yorks and Humberside, CPRE, 2003–07. Founding Chm., UK Section, Internat. Solar Energy Soc.; Initiating Dir, Cambridge Interdisciplinary Envmtl Centre, 1990–92. Consultant author working with UN internat. agencies on energy use in Third World and on environmental health in tropical bldgs; working with WMO on revision of internat. technical note on building climatology, 2005–10. Farrington Daniels Internat. Award, for distinguished contribs to solar energy studies, 1989. *Publications:* 200 papers on Energy policy, Environmental Design and Planning, Environmental Management, Building Climatology and Solar Energy. *Address:* 15 Brincliffe Gardens, Sheffield S11 9BG. *T:* (0114) 255 1570.

PAGE, Prof. Lesley Ann, CBE 2014; PhD; President, Royal College of Midwives, since 2012; *b* High Wycombe, 18 Jan. 1944; *d* of Leslie Edwin Page and Ivy Page; *m* 1986, Mark David Starr; two *s* one *d*. *Educ:* Orchard Sch., Slough; Open Univ. (BA 1977); Univ. of Edinburgh (MSc 1978); Univ. of Technol., Sydney (PhD 2005). RN 1965; RM 1966. Staff Nurse, St Bartholomew's Hosp., London, 1966–67; Night Sister, Royal Infirmary of Edinburgh, 1967–68; Ward Sister, Western Gen. Hosp., Edinburgh, 1968–72; Relief nurse and community work, Mills Meml Hosp., Terrace, BC, 1972–77; Lectr in Nursing, N Lothian Coll. of Nursing and Midwifery, Edinburgh, 1978; Lectr, Sch. of Nursing, UBC, 1979–80; Hd, Continuing Educn and Midwife Low Risk Proj., Grace Hosp., BC, 1980–86; Clin. Instructor, UBC Sch. of Medicine, 1984–86; Dir, Midwifery, John Radcliffe Hosp., Oxford, 1986–92; Queen Charlotte's Prof. of Midwifery, Thames Valley Univ. and Queen Charlotte's Hosp., 1994–2000; Head: Dept of Midwifery, Children and Women's Health Centre, Vancouver, BC, 2000–01; Midwifery and Maternity Services, Royal Free NHS Trust, 2002–03; Midwifery and Nursing, Guy's and St Thomas' NHS Trust, 2003–06. Lectr, UBC Sch. of Nursing, 1995–98; Visiting Professor: Inst. of Obstetrics and Gynaecol., RPMS, Hammersmith Hosp., 1995–98; KCL, 2004–; Adjunct Prof., UTS, 2006–. FRSocMed 2002. Hon. Fellow, Royal Coll. of Midwives, 2007. Hon. DSc W London, 2013. *Publications:* The New Midwifery: science and sensitivity in practice, 2000, 2nd edn (with R. McCandlish) 2006; over 200 articles in midwifery jls. *Recreations:* reading novels, walking, swimming, sailing incompetent crew. *Address:* Royal College of Midwives, 15 Mansfield Street, W1G 9NH. *T:* (020) 7312 3535, *Fax:* (020) 7312 3536. *E:* president@rcm.org.uk.

PAGE, Piers John B.; *see* Burton-Page.

PAGE, Richard Lewis; *b* 22 Feb. 1941; *s* of Victor Charles and Kathleen Page; *m* 1964, Madeleine Ann Brown; one *s* one *d*. *Educ:* Hurstpierpoint Coll.; Luton Technical Coll. Apprenticeship, Vauxhall Motors, 1959–64; HNC Mech. Engineering; Chm. of family co., 1964–95, 1997–. Young Conservatives, 1964–66; Councillor, Banstead UDC, 1968–71; contested (C) Workington, Feb. and Oct. 1974; MP (C): Workington, Nov. 1976–1979; Herts SW, Dec. 1979–2005; PPS: to Sec. of State for Trade, 1981–82; to Leader of the House, 1982–87; Parly Under-Sec. of State, DTI, 1995–97; opposition front-bench spokesman on trade and industry, 2000–01. Mem., Public Accounts Cttee, 1987–95, 1997–2000; Vice-Chairman: Cons. Trade and Industry Cttee, 1988–95; All Party Engrg Gp, 1997–2005; Jt Chm., All Party Racing and Bloodstock Industries Cttee, 1998–2005; Chm., All Party Parly Scientific Cttee, 2003–05. Chm., Internat. Office, Cons. Central Office, 1999–2000. Gov., Foundn for Western Democracy, 1998–2000. Vice Chm., Chemical Industry Council, 1997–. Chm. Investment Cttee, Leukaemia Res. Fund, 2005–09 (Hon. Treas., 1987–95). Gov. and Trustee, Royal Masonic Sch., 1984–95, 1997–2014. Master, Pattenmakers' Co., 2012–13. *Recreations:* horse racing, shooting. *Address:* Marlpost, West Sussex.

PAGE, Roy Malcolm; Headmaster, Royal Grammar School, High Wycombe, 2006–15; *b* 24 June 1950; *s* of Alec John Page and Janet Selina Page; *m* 1973, Marilyn Rose Dawson; one *s* one *d*. *Educ:* Portsmouth Poly. (BSc Maths 1971); Univ. of Reading (PGCE 1972); National Coll. for Sch. Leadership (NPQH 2001). Royal Grammar School, High Wycombe: Teacher of Maths, 1972–2015; Boarding Housemaster, 1982–84; Dep. Headmaster, 1989–2001; Sen. Dep. Headmaster, 2001–06. Nat. Leader of Educn, 2011. Chm., State Boarding Schs Assoc., 2012–14. Governor: Burnham Park E-ACT Acad., 2012 (Vice Chm., 2011–15; Chm., 2015–); Bourne End Acad., 2015–. *Recreations:* Rugby, cricket, golf, keeping fit, classic cars, bird watching, foreign travel. *Clubs:* Lansdowne; Rotary (Princes Risborough); Whiteleaf Golf; Weston Turville Golf; MG Owners'.

PAGE, Simon Richard; District Judge (formerly Registrar), Guildford, Epsom and Reigate County Courts, and High Court of Justice, 1980–2000; a Recorder of the Crown Court, 1980–99; *b* 7 March 1934; *s* of Eric Rowland Page and Vera (*née* Fenton); *m* 1st, 1963 (marr. diss. 1977); three *s* one *d*; 2nd, 1984. *Educ:* Lancing; LSE (LLB External, 1956). Admitted solicitor (hons), 1957. National Service, Second Lieut RA, 1957–59. Private practice as solicitor, 1959–75; Pres., West Surrey Law Soc., 1972–73; Registrar, Croydon County Court, 1975–80; Pres., Assoc. of County Court and District Registrars, 1983–84. *Recreations:* golf, cricket, bridge. *Address:* c/o The Law Courts, Mary Road, Guildford GU1 4PS.

PAGE, Stephen Alexander; Chief Executive and Publisher, Faber & Faber Ltd, since 2001; *b* 17 Feb. 1965; *s* of James and Frances Page; *m* 1993, Caroline Hird; two *s*. *Educ:* Bristol Univ. (BA Hons History). Bookseller, 1986–88; Marketing Exec./Manager, Longman, 1988–90; variety of roles at Transworld Publishers, 1990–94; 4th Estate: Sales Dir, 1994–95; Dep. Man. Dir, 1995–2000, Man. Dir, 2000; Gp Sales and Mktg Dir, HarperCollins Publishers, 2000–01. Non-exec. Dir, Bloomsbury Publishing plc, 2013–. Member: Bd, Creative Skillset, 2011–; Govt Adv. Panel on public library service in England, 2014–; Adv. Bd, ind. review of creative industries launched by New Labour, 2014. Pres., Publishers Assoc., 2006–07. Most Inspiring Digital Publishing Person, FutureBook Awards, 2012. *Recreations:* music (listening and playing), film, reading, parenting, food. *Address:* Faber & Faber Ltd, Bloomsbury House, 74–77 Great Russell Street, WC1B 3DA. *T:* (020) 7927 3800. *E:* stephen.page@faber.co.uk.

PAGE, Stephen Dowland, DPhil; business and IT strategist; photographer; *b* Welwyn Garden City, 4 Oct. 1961; *s* of Sidney Bedford Page and (Barbara) Honeywood Page; *m* 1998, Anthea Jane Morland; one *s*. *Educ:* Ironside State Sch., Brisbane; Church of England Grammar Sch., Brisbane; Univ. of Queensland (BMus Hons 1982); New Coll., Oxford (DPhil 1986; Commonwealth Schol.). Andersen Consulting, later Accenture: Business and Technol. Strategist, 1987–99; Partner, 2000–04; Man. Dir, 2004–07; Global Man. Dir, Strategic IT Effectiveness, 2007–08; Growth and Strategy Dir, Accenture Technol. Consulting, 2008–09. Capability Strategy Advr, MoD, 2004–10; non-executive Director: GCHQ, 2009–14; Nat. Crime Agency, 2014–; BSI Gp, 2015–; Senior Advisor: PwC, 2013–: Chemring plc, 2015–. Mem. Bd, British Liby, 2011–. Associate Mem., BUPA, 2015–. Photographer, Fatkoala Images, 2009–. *Recreations:* classical music, travel, theatre. *Club:* Savile.

PAGE WOOD, Sir Anthony John, 8th Bt *cr* 1837; *b* 6 Feb. 1951; *s* of Sir David (John Hatherley) Page Wood, 7th Bt and Evelyn Hazel Rosemary, *d* of late Captain George Ernest Bellville; *S* father, 1955. *Educ:* Harrow. Dir, Société Générale, London, 1988–2001. *Heir: kinsman* Mark William Evelyn Wood [*b* 1 Aug. 1940; *m* 1962, Mary June Miller; one *s* one *d*]. *Address:* 11 Dove Mews, SW5 0LE.

PAGEL, Prof. Mark, PhD; FRS 2011; Professor of Evolutionary Biology, University of Reading, since 1998; *b* Seattle, Washington, 5 June 1954; *s* of Lloyd and Elizabeth Pagel; partner, Prof. Ruth Mace, *qv*; two *s*. *Educ:* Univ. of Washington (BA Philosophy and Maths; PhD Mathematical Stats 1981). NSF Res. Fellow, 1986–88, Res. Fellow, 1988–91, Dept of Zool., Oxford Univ.; Res. Fellow, Univ. of London, 1992–93; Res. Fellow, Dept of Zool., Oxford Univ., 1994–98. Vis. Prof., Harvard Univ., 1991–92; Ext. Prof., Santa Fe Inst., USA, 2007–. *Publications:* (with P. Harvey) The Comparative Method in Evolutionary Biology, 1991; (Ed.-in-Chief) The Oxford Encyclopedia of Evolution, 2002; (ed with A. Pomiankowski) Evolutionary Genomics and Proteomics, 2008; Wired for Culture: the natural history of human co-operation, 2012. *Recreations:* cycling, walking. *Address:* School of Biological Sciences, Reading University, Reading, Berks RG6 6BX. *T:* (0118) 378 8900, *Fax:* (0118) 378 0180. *E:* m.pagel@reading.ac.uk.

PAGET, family name of **Marquess of Anglesey**.

PAGET, His Honour David Christopher John; QC 1994; a Circuit Judge, 1997–2012; a Permanent Judge, Central Criminal Court, 1998–2012; *b* 3 Feb. 1942; *s* of late Henry Paget and Dorothy Paget (*née* Colenutt), Johannesburg, S Africa; *m* 1968, Dallas Wendy (*née* Hill); two *d*. *Educ:* St John's Coll., Johannesburg; Inns of Court Sch. of Law. Called to Bar, Inner Temple, 1967, Bencher, 2003; Jun. Prosecuting Counsel to the Crown, 1982–89, Sen. Prosecuting Counsel, 1989–94, CCC; a Recorder, 1986–97. Freeman, City of London, 1999; Liveryman, Co. of Coopers, 1999–. *Recreations:* walking, bird watching, listening to music. *Clubs:* Garrick, Dulwich.

PAGET, Lt-Col Sir Julian (Tolver), 4th Bt *cr* 1871; CVO 1984; an Extra Gentleman Usher to the Queen, since 1991 (Gentleman Usher, 1971–91); author; *b* 11 July 1921; *s* of General Sir Bernard Paget, GCB, DSO, MC (*d* 1961) (*g s* of 1st Bt), and Winifred (*d* 1986), *d* of Sir John Paget, 2nd Bt; *S* uncle, Sir James Francis Paget, 3rd Bt, 1972; *m* 1954, Diana Frances, *d* of late F. S. H. Farmer; one *s* one *d*. *Educ:* Radley College; Christ Church, Oxford (MA). Joined Coldstream Guards, 1940; served North West Europe, 1944–45; retired as Lt-Col, 1968. Ed., Guards Magazine, 1976–93. *Publications:* Counter-Insurgency Campaigning, 1967; Last Post: Aden, 1964–67, 1969; The Story of the Guards, 1976; The Pageantry of Britain, 1979; Yeomen of the Guard, 1984; Discovering London's Ceremonial and Traditions, 1989; Wellington's Peninsular War: the battles and battlefields, 1990; Hougoumont, The Key to Victory at Waterloo, 1992; No Problem Too Difficult, 1999; (ed) The Coldstream Guards 1650–2000, 2000; The Crusading General: the life of General Sir Bernard Paget, 2008. *Recreations:* fishing, shooting, travel, writing. *Heir: s* Henry James Paget [*b* 2 Feb. 1959; *m* 1993, Mrs Margrete Varvill (*née* Lynner); one *s* one *d*]. *Clubs:* Cavalry and Guards, Flyfishers'.
See also N. J. Cox.

PAGET, Sir Richard (Herbert), 4th Bt *cr* 1886, of Cranmore Hall, Co. Somerset; independent marketing consultant, since 2002; artisan food producer; *b* 17 Feb. 1957; *s* of Sir John Starr Paget, 3rd Bt and Nancy Mary, *d* of Lt-Col Francis Parish, DSO, MC; *S* father, 1992; *m* 1985, Richenda Rachel (marr. diss. 2013), *d* of Rev. Preb. J. T. C. B. Collins; three *d*. *Educ:* Eton Coll. AES, 1983–87; Nixdorf Computers, 1987–88; Inforem plc, 1988–89; Sales Manager, SAS Inst., 1989–95; Outplacement Councillor, Encos, 1995–97; Empathy Audit Manager, Harding and Yorke Ltd, 1997–99; Business Development Manager: VMTC, 1999–2001; Somersault Creative Marketing, 2001; Founder, My Apple Juice, 2010–; non-exec. Dir, SFM Technol. Ltd, 1999–2002. Mem. Ct, Russia Co. Pres., Paget Gorman Signed Speech Soc. *Recreations:* carriage driving, cricket, tennis. *Heir: b* David Vernon John Paget [*b* 26 March 1959; *m* 1990, Cluny Macpherson; one *s* two *d*]. *Address:* Warren Farm, Savernake, Marlborough, Wilts SN8 3BQ. *E:* richard@pagets.org.uk.

PAGET-WILKES, Ven. Michael Jocelyn James; Archdeacon of Warwick, 1990–2009; *b* 11 Dec. 1941; *s* of Arthur Hamilton Paget-Wilkes and Eleanor Bridget Paget-Wilkes; *m* 1969, Ruth Gillian Macnamara; one *s* two *d*. *Educ:* Harper Adams Agricultural Coll. (NDA); London Coll. of Divinity (ALCD). Agricultural Extension Officer, Tanzania, 1964–66; attended London Coll. of Divinity, 1966–69; Curate, All Saints', Wandsworth, 1969–74; Vicar: St James', Hatcham, New Cross, 1974–82; St Matthew's, Rugby, 1982–90. *Publications:* The Church and Rural Development, 1968; Poverty, Revolution and the Church, 1981. *Recreations:* squash, tennis, music, ski-ing, gardening. *Address:* 64 Tarlton, Cirencester, Glos GL7 6PA.

PAGETT, Nicola Mary; actress; *b* 15 June 1945; *d* of Barbara Scott and H. W. F. Scott; took stage name of Pagett; *m* 1977, Graham Swannell (marr. diss. 1999); one *d*. *Educ:* St Maur's Convent, Yokohama; The Beehive, Bexhill; RADA. *Stage:* Voyage Round My Father, Haymarket, 1971; Ophelia in Hamlet, Greenwich, 1974; Yahoo, Queen's, 1976; Taking Steps, Lyric, 1980; The Trojan War will not take place, NT, 1983; School for Scandal, Duke of York's, 1984; Aren't We All?, Haymarket, 1984; Old Times, Haymarket, 1985; The Light of Day, Hammersmith, 1987; The Rehearsal, Garrick, 1990; Party Time, Almeida, 1991; The Rules of the Game, Almeida, 1992; What the Butler Saw, NT, 1995; *films:* Seven Men at Daybreak, 1974; Oliver's Story, 1978; Privates on Parade, 1982; *television series:* Upstairs, Downstairs, 1972; Napoleon in Love, 1974; Anna Karenina, 1977; Scoop, 1987; A Bit of a Do, 1988–90; Ain't Misbehavin', 1994–95. *Publications:* Diamonds Behind My Eyes, 1997. *Address:* c/o Gavin Barker Associates, 2D Wimpole Street, W1G 0ED.

PAGLIARI, Paul; UK Group Human Resources Director, ISS UK Ltd, 2008–09; *b* 31 March 1960; *s* of Luigi and Giovanna Pagliari. *Educ:* Univ. of Glasgow (MA 1981). FCIPD. Director of Human Resources: Scottish Power, 1999–2001; Scottish Water, 2002–05; Immigration and Nationality Directorate, Home Office, 2005–06; Dir, Change and Corporate Services, Scottish Exec., later Scottish Govt, 2006–08. Lay Member: Employment Appeals Tribunal, 2003–; Professional Conduct Cttee, Bar Standards Bd, 2012–; Professional Standards Cttee, Asset Based Finance Assoc., 2013–. *Recreations:* ski-ing, tennis, socialising, reading, cinema. *E:* paul.pagliari@btinternet.com.

PAGNAMENTA, Peter John; television producer and writer; *b* 12 April 1941; *s* of late Charles Francis Pagnamenta, OBE and Daphne Pagnamenta; *m* 1966, Sybil Healy; one *s* one *d*. *Educ:* Shrewsbury; Trinity Hall, Cambridge (MA). Joined BBC, 1965; Prodn Asst, Tonight and 24 Hours, 1965–67; Asst Editor, 24 Hours, 1967; New York office, 1968–71 (Producer, US Election coverage and Apollo flights); Editor: 24 Hours, 1971; Midweek, 1972–75; Panorama, 1975–77; Dir of News and Current Affairs, Thames Television, 1977–80; Exec. Producer, All Our Working Lives (eleven part series), BBC2, 1984; Editor, Real Lives (documentary strand), BBC 1, 1984–85; Head of Current Affairs Gp, BBC TV, 1985–87; Exec. Producer, BBC TV Documentary Dept, 1981–85, 1987–97; Executive Producer: Nippon (eight parts), BBC 2, 1990; People's Century (26 parts), BBC 1, 1995–99; Pagnamenta Associates Ltd: Bubble Trouble (three parts), BBC 2, 2000. *Publications:* (with Richard Overy) All Our Working Lives, 1984; (ed) The Hidden Hall, 2005; (with Momoko Williams) Falling Blossom, 2006; (ed) Cambridge: an 800th anniversary portrait, 2008; Prairie

Fever, 2012. *Recreations:* walking, fishing. *Address:* 6 Hamilton House, Vicarage Gate, W8 4HL. *T:* (020) 7727 0232.

PAICE, Clifford, FCILT; Member and Group Director, Economic Regulation, Civil Aviation Authority, 1989–97; *b* 26 Feb. 1938; *s* of Owen Edward and Dorothy Paice; *m* 1968, Elisabeth Marlin (*see* E. W. Paice); one *s* two *d. Educ:* Cambridgeshire High Sch.; LSE (BSc Econ.). FCILT (FCIT 1990). Joined Civil Service, 1959: War Office, 1959–61; MoD, 1962–65; Min. of Econ. Affairs, 1965–68; Treasury, 1968–72; Head, Econ. Divs, CAA, 1972–89. FRSA 1997. *Address:* 142 Cromwell Tower, Barbican, EC2Y 8DD. *T:* (020) 7628 5228.

PAICE, Elisabeth Willemien, OBE 2011; FRCP; FAcadMed; Dean Director, London Deanery (formerly Department of Postgraduate Medical and Dental Education), University of London, 2001–10; *b* 23 April 1945; *d* of Ervin Ross, (Spike), Marlin and Hilda van Stockum, HRHA; *m* 1968, Clifford Paice, *qv*; one *s* two *d. Educ:* Trinity Coll., Dublin (MB, BCh, BAO, MA); Dundee Univ. (Dip. Med. Ed.); Inst. of Leadership and Mgt (Level 7 Dip. Exec. Coaching and Leadership Mentoring). FRCP 1989. Clinical training, Westminster Hosp.; Senior Registrar in Rheumatology: Stoke Mandeville Hosp., 1977–79; UCH, 1979–82; Consultant Rheumatologist, Whittington Hosp. NHS Trust, 1982–95; Associate Dean, N Thames E, 1992–95, Dean Dir, N Thames, 1995–2000, Postgrad. Medicine, Univ. of London. Visiting Professor: Faculty of Clinical Scis, UCL, 2002–; Imperial Coll. London, 2010–. Chairman: Conf. of Postgrad. Med. Deans, 2006–08; NW London Integrated Care Pilot, 2011–; Case Cttee, Royal Med. Benevolent Fund, 2011–13. Non-exec. Dir, Hillingdon Hosps NHS Foundn Trust, 2014–. FAcadMed 2010. Outstanding Contribn Award for Leadership of Hosp. at Night, Skills for Health, 2009; Nat. Award for Professional Excellence, British Assoc. of Physicians of Indian Origin, 2010; NHS Mentor of the Year, NHS Leadership Awards, 2010. *Publications:* Delivering the New Doctor, 1998; New Coach: reflections from a learning journey, 2012; (with Sheila Marlin) A Grandparent's Survival Guide to Childcare, 2013; contrib. res. papers, editorials and book chapters on postgrad. med. educn. *Address:* 142 Cromwell Tower, Barbican, EC2Y 8DD. *T:* (020) 7628 5228.

PAICE, Rt Hon. Sir James (Edward Thornton), Kt 2012; PC 2010; DL; *b* 24 April 1949; *s* of late Edward Paice and Winifred Paice; *m* 1973, Ava Barbara Patterson; two *s. Educ:* Framlingham College, Suffolk; Writtle Agricultural College. Farm Manager, 1970–73; farmer, 1973–79; Framlingham Management and Training Services Ltd: Training Officer, 1979–82; Training Manager, 1982–85; Gen. Manager/Exec. Dir, 1985–87; non-exec. Dir, 1987–89; non-exec. Dir, United Framlingham Farmers, 1989–94. MP (C) SE Cambridgeshire, 1987–2015. PPS to Minister of State, 1989–91, to Minister, 1991–93, MAFF, to Sec. of State for the Envmt, 1993–94; Parly Under-Sec. of State, DFE, then DFEE, 1994–97; opposition front bench spokesman on agriculture, 1997–2001, on home affairs, 2001–04; Shadow Minister for Agriculture and Rural Affairs, 2005–10 (Shadow Sec. of State, 2004–05); Minister of State, DEFRA, 2010–12. Mem., Select Cttee on Employment, 1987–89. Chm., All Party Racing and Bloodstock Cttee, 1992–94. Gov., Writtle Agricl Coll., 1991–94. DL Cambs, 2013. *Recreations:* shooting, countryside issues.

PAIGE, Deborah Penrose; freelance director of theatre, film, television and radio drama; consultant and teacher in leading UK drama schools, since 2011; *b* 7 Feb. 1950; *d* of David and Barbara Dunhill; *m* 1969, John Paige (marr. diss. 1985); two *d. Educ:* Godalming County Grammar Sch.; Dartington Hall Sch.; Bristol Old Vic Theatre Sch. Actress, 1970–84; Asst Dir, Bristol Old Vic, 1986–87; Associate Dir, Soho Theatre Co., 1988–90; Artistic Director: Salisbury Playhouse, 1990–94, productions incl. A Midsummer Night's Dream, 1991, The Tempest, 1992, States of Shock (co-production with Nat. Th.), 1993, For Services Rendered (transf. Old Vic), 1993; Sheffield Theatres, 1995–2000, productions incl. The Merchant of Venice, 1996, King Lear, 1997, South Pacific, 1997, Brassed Off (transf. NT), 1999; Founder, Paigeworks, 2005; productions incl. Afterbirth, 2005, Into the Blue, 2010, Arcola Th.; freelance productions incl. The Daughter-in-Law, 2014, The Sugar Wife, 2015, RADA. Assoc. Teacher, RADA, 2003–; Hd of Recorded Drama, LAMDA, 2009–11; Interim Hd of Performance, Mountview Acad. of Theatre Arts, 2012. Director: television: Eastenders, 2001–02; Casualty, 2003, 2005; Judge John Deed, 2004; Holby City, 2006–07; radio: (for BBC Woman's Hour) Only in London, The Farming of Bones, To The North. *Recreations:* walking, music, reading.

PAIGE, Elaine, OBE 1995; actress, singer and broadcaster; *b* 5 March 1948; *d* of Eric Bickerstaff and Irene Bickerstaff. *Educ:* Southaw Sch. for Girls, Barnet. *Theatre:* The Roar of the Greasepaint, the Smell of the Crowd, UK tour, 1964; Rock Carmen, Maybe That's Your Problem, Alexandra, Birmingham, 1966; Nuts, Stratford East, 1967; Maybe That's Your Problem, Roundhouse; West End début, Hair, Shaftesbury, 1968; Jesus Christ Superstar, Palace, 1971; Sandy in Grease, New London, 1973; Rita in Billy, Drury Lane, 1974; Eva Perón in Evita, Prince Edward, 1978 (Best Actress in a Musical, SWET, 1978); Grizabella in Cats, New London, 1981; Carabosse in Abbacadabra, Lyric Hammersmith, 1983; Florence Vassey in Chess, Prince Edward, 1986; Reno Sweeney in Anything Goes, Prince Edward, 1989 (co-producer); Edith Piaf in Piaf, Piccadilly, 1993; Norma Desmond in Sunset Boulevard, Adelphi, 1994 and 1995, NY, 1996; Célimène in The Misanthrope, Piccadilly, 1998; Anna in The King and I, London Palladium, 2000–01; Angèle in Where There's a Will, UK tour, 2003; Mrs Lovett in Sweeney Todd, NY, 2004; Beatrice Stockwell in The Drowsy Chaperone, Novello, 2007; Carlotta Campion in Follies, Washington, NY and Los Angeles, 2011–12; has appeared in four Royal Variety Performances; *film*: A Closed Book, 2009; *television:* Phyllis Dixey, Ladykillers, 1980; Ladybirds, 1980; Elaine Paige in Concert, 1985; A View of Harry Clark (play), 1988; Showstoppers: In Concert at the White House, 1988; Unexplained Laughter (play), 1989; Elaine Paige in Concert, 1991; South Bank Show: the faces of Elaine Paige, 1996; Boston Pops Opening, 1997; Dora Bunner in A Murder is Announced, 2005; Where the Heart Is, 2005; The Elaine Paige Show, 2014; *radio*: Elaine Paige on Sunday, BBC Radio 2, 2004–. Perf. at opening of Winter Olympic Games, Salt Lake City, 2002; concert tours in UK, Europe, ME, Australia, NZ and FE, 1984–2014; 40th Anniv. World Concert Tour, 2008; concert at Lincoln Center, NY, 2012, concert tour, USA and Scandinavia, 2013; 50th Anniv. World Tour, 2014–15 (filmed as I'm Still Here, 2015). Has made numerous recordings (9 gold albums, incl. 4 multi-platinum). Mem., BAFTA. Hon. LittD UEA, 2012. Variety Club Awards: Showbusiness Personality of Year, 1978; Recording Artiste of Year, 1986; Best Actress, 1995; Gold Badge of Merit, BASCA, 1993; Lifetime Achievement Award, HMV, 1996; Lifetime Achievement Award, NODA, 1999; Inspiration Award, Breakthrough Cancer, 2014. Pres., Dan Maskell Tennis Trust, 2010–. *Publications:* Memories, 2008. *Recreations:* ski-ing, tennis, clay pigeon shooting, painting. *Address:* E. P. Records Personal Management, c/o Nick Fiveash, 4 Baxendale Street, E2 7BY. *T:* 07971 240987. *E:* nickfiveash@me.com. *Clubs:* Mosimann's, Queen's, St James.

PAIN, Barry Newton, CBE 1979; QPM 1976; Commandant, Police Staff College, Bramshill, and HM Inspector of Constabulary, 1982–87, retired; *b* 25 Feb. 1931; *s* of Godfrey William Pain and Annie Newton; *m* 1st, 1952, Marguerite Agnes King (*d* 2009); one *s* one *d*; 2nd, 2010, Stella Gail Orme. *Educ:* Waverley Grammar Sch., Birmingham. Clerk to Prosecuting Solicitor, Birmingham, 1947–51; 2nd Lieut (Actg Captain) RASC, Kenya, 1949–51. Birmingham City Police, 1951–68; Staff Officer to HM Inspector of Constabulary, Birmingham, 1966–68; Asst Chief Constable, Staffordshire and Stoke-on-Trent Constabulary, 1968–74; Chief Constable of Kent, 1974–82; JSSC 1970. Adviser to Turkish Govt on Reorganization of Police, 1972. Pres., Assoc. of Chief Police Officers, 1981–82. *Recreations:* golf, shooting, boating.

PAIN, Jacqualyn Christina Mary; Headmistress, Northwood College, since 2009; *b* 31 Aug. 1957; *d* of J. K. and J. W. Pain. *Educ:* Sch. of St Helen and St Katharine, Abingdon; St David's UC, Lampeter (MA); Birkbeck Coll., London Univ. (MA); Univ. of Leicester (MBA); NPQH 2001. Teacher: Tiffin Girls' Sch., 1981–83; Old Palace Sch., 1983–84; James Allen's Girls' Sch., 1984–96 (on secondment to Inst. of Educn, Univ. of London, 1992–94); Dep. Head, Northwood Coll., 1996–2000; Head, Henrietta Barnett Sch., 2000–05; Headmistress, St Albans High Sch., 2005–08. *Recreations:* running, woodwork, philosophy, cooking. *Address:* Northwood College, Maxwell Road, Northwood, Middx HA6 2YE. *Clubs:* University Women's, International Rescue.

PAIN, Rt Rev. Richard Edward; *see* Monmouth, Bishop of.

PAINE, Sir Christopher (Hammon), Kt 1995; DM; FRCP, FRCR; Consultant in Radiotherapy and Oncology, Churchill Hospital, Oxford, 1970–95; President, British Medical Association, 2000–01; *b* 28 Aug. 1935; *s* of late Major John Hammon Paine and Hon. Mrs Joan Frances Shedden, MBE; *m* 1959, Susan Martin; two *s* two *d. Educ:* Eton Coll.; Merton Coll., Oxford (BM, BCh 1961; DM 1981); St Bartholomew's Hosp. Med. Sch. FRCP 1976; FRCR (FFR 1969). Junior med. posts, Oxford, London, Paris, 1962–70; Oxford University: Lectr in Radiotherapy and Oncology, 1972–95; Dir of Clinical Studies (clinical dean), 1982–85; Dist Gen. Manager, Oxfordshire HA, 1984–88; Chm., Oxford Med. Staff Council, 1991–92. Med. Dir, Adv. Cttee for Distinction Awards, 1994–99. Pres., British Oncological Assoc., 1989–91; Royal College of Radiologists: Dean, Faculty of Clinical Oncology, 1990–92; Vice-Pres., 1991–92; Pres., 1992–95. Pres., RSocMed, 1996–98. Mem., Adv. Bd, Weill Cornell Med. Coll., Qatar, 2001–13. Hon. Fellow: HK Coll. of Radiologists, 1995; Faculty of Radiologists, RCSI, 1995; Hon. FRCSE, 2005. *Publications:* papers on health services and cancer. *Recreation:* gardening. *Address:* The Avenue, Wotton Underwood, Aylesbury, Bucks HP18 0RP. *T:* (01296) 770742. *E:* northavenue@btinternet.com. *Club:* Farmers.

PAINE, Surg. Rear Adm. Michael Patrick William Halden, FRCS; Medical Director General (Naval), 1997–99; *b* 18 March 1939; *s* of Comdr Geoffrey W. W. H. Paine, RN and Eileen Paine (*née* Irwin); *m* 1972, Thayer Clark. *Educ:* Downside Sch.; London Hosp. Med. Coll. (MB BS 1963); Southampton Univ.; Edinburgh Univ. FRCS 1976. Joined Royal Navy, 1963; HMS Plymouth, 1965–66; HMS Repulse (SSBN), 1967–68; surgical trainee, RN Hosp. Haslar, 1969–75; PMO, HMS Bulwark, 1975–76; RN Hosp. Plymouth, 1977–79; Orthopaedic Senior Registrar: Southampton Gen. and Lord Mayor Treloar's Hosps, 1979; RN Hosp. Haslar, 1980; Cons. Orth. Surg., RN Hosp. Plymouth, 1981–82; HMS Illustrious, 1982–84; Cons. Orth. Surg., RN Hosp. Haslar, 1984–88; RAMC Sen. Officers' Course (Course Medal), 1986; Defence Med. Services Directorate, MoD, 1988–90 (Mem., Thompson Rev. of Service Hosps); Fleet MO, 1990–92; ACOS (Med. and Dental), C-in-C Fleet, 1992–97. QHS 1994–99. *Recreation:* sailing. *Address:* 513 Canaan Street, Canaan, NH 03741, USA.

PAINE, Roger Edward; management coach and consultant; Vice President, Solace Enterprises Ltd, since 2001 (Executive Director, 1996–99; Managing Director, 1999–2001); Proprietor, Gate Associates Ltd, since 2009; *b* 20 Oct. 1943; *s* of Ethel May Jones and Edward Paine. *Educ:* Stockport Sch.; Univ. of Wales (BA Hons); Univ. of Manchester (part time; Dip TP); Univ. of Birmingham (MSocSci). Town Planner: Lancs CC, 1964–66; Stockport CB, 1966–68; Lancs CC, 1968–70; Salford City, 1970; Stockport Borough: Corporate Planner, 1971–73; Head of Corporate Planning, 1973–75; Co-ordinator of Central Units, 1975–77; Dep. Chief Exec., Camden, 1977–80; Chief Executive: Wrekin Council, 1980–88; Cardiff CC, 1988–94. Pres., Solace, 1992–93. Chairman: Coll. of Traditional Acupuncture, Leamington Spa, 2006–10; Winchcombe Business Forum, 2010–14. Dir of Music, Evesham Parish Church, 2002–09; Dir, Evesham Fest. of Music, 2007–12; Chm., Winchcombe Fest. of Music and Arts, 2011–14. *Recreations:* music, travel, sport, history. *Address:* Gardens Cottage, Prideaux, St Blazey, Par, Cornwall PL24 2SS.

PAINES, Nicholas Paul Billot; QC 1997; a Law Commissioner, since 2013; *b* 29 June 1955; *s* of late Anthony John Cooper Paines and of Anne Paines; *m* 1985, Alison Jane Sargent Roberts; one *s* three *d. Educ:* Downside Sch.; New Coll., Oxford (BA 1977; MA 1984); Université Libre de Bruxelles (Licence spéciale en droit européen). Called to the Bar, Gray's Inn, 1978; in practice at the Bar, 1980–; called to the Bar, NI, 1996; Mem., Supplementary Panel of Jun. Counsel to the Crown (Common Law), 1993–97; a Recorder, 2002; a Dep. High Court Judge, 2010. A Dep. Upper Tribunal Judge (formerly a Dep. Social Security and Child Support Comr), 2001–. Mem., Bar Council, 1991–96; Treas., Bar European Gp, 2001–14 (Chm., 1996–98). Mem. Council, St Christopher's Fellowship, 1983–2002. Jt Editor, Common Market Law Reports, 1996–2010. *Publications: contributions to:* Halsbury's Laws of England, 3rd edn, 1986; Vaughan, Law of the European Communities, 1986; Bellamy and Child, Common Market Law of Competition, 4th edn, 1993; Value Added Tax: commentary and analysis, 2009. *Recreations:* family life, music, running moderate distances. *Address:* Law Commission, 1st Floor, Tower, 52 Queen Anne's Gate, SW1H 9AG.

PAINTER, Anne Elizabeth; *see* Curry, A. E.

PAINTER, Ven. David Scott; Archdeacon of Oakham, 2000–11, now Archdeacon Emeritus; Canon Residentiary of Peterborough Cathedral, 2000–11; *b* 3 Oct. 1944; *s* of Frank Painter and Winifred Ellen Painter (*née* Bibbings). *Educ:* Queen Elizabeth's Sch., Crediton; Trinity Coll. of Music (LTCL 1965); Worcester Coll., Oxford (BA 1968; MA 1972); Cuddesdon Theol Coll. Ordained deacon, 1970, priest, 1971; Curate, St Andrew, Plymouth, 1970–73; Chaplain, Plymouth Poly., 1971–73; Curate, All Saints, St Marylebone, 1973–76; Domestic Chaplain to Archbishop of Canterbury, 1976–80; Vicar, Holy Trinity, Roehampton, 1980–91; RD, Wandsworth, 1985–90; Canon Residentiary and Treas., Southwark Cathedral, and Dio. Dir of Ordinands, Southwark, 1991–2000. *Recreations:* music, country walking, crossword puzzles, bridge. *Club:* Oxford and Cambridge.

PAINTER, Sophia Mary; *see* Tickell, S. M.

PAINTER, Terence James, CB 1990; a Deputy Chairman and Director General, Board of Inland Revenue, 1986–93; *b* 28 Nov. 1935; *s* of late Edward Lawrence Painter and Ethel Violet (*née* Butler); *m* 1959, Margaret Janet Blackburn; two *s* two *d. Educ:* City of Norwich Sch.; Downing Coll., Cambridge (BA (History)). Nat. Service Commn, Royal Norfolk Regt, 1958–59. Entered Inland Revenue as Asst Principal, 1959; Principal, 1962; seconded to Civil Service Selection Bd, 1967–68; Asst Sec., 1969; seconded to HM Treasury, 1973–75; Under-Sec., 1975–86. *Recreations:* music, books, theatre, gardening. *Club:* Reform.

PAISLEY, family name of **Baroness Paisley of St George's**.

PAISLEY OF ST GEORGE'S, Baroness *cr* 2006 (Life Peer), of St George's in the County of Antrim; **Eileen Emily Paisley;** Vice-President, Democratic Unionist Party, since 1994; *m* 1956, Rev. Ian Richard Kyle Paisley (Baron Bannside, PC); twin *s* three *d.* Mem. (DemU) Belfast City Council, 1967–73. Member (DemU): East Belfast, NI Assembly, 1973–74; NI Constitutional Convention, 1975–76. *Publications:* Take a Break. *Address:* House of Lords, SW1A 0PW.

See also Hon. I. R. K. Paisley.

PAISLEY, Bishop of, (RC), since 2014; **Rt Rev. John Keenan;** *b* Glasgow, 19 Dec. 1964. *Educ:* St Gregory's Primary, Wyndford, Glasgow; Shrigley Salesian Coll., Cheshire; Univ. of Glasgow (LLB 1988); Gregorian Univ., Rome (STB 1993; PhL 1995). Ordained priest, 1995;

Asst Priest, Christ the King, Kingspark, 1995–2000; Chaplain: Holyrood, 1997–2000; Univ. of Glasgow, 2000–14; Parish Priest, St Patrick's, Anderston, 2013–14; Vocations Dir, Archdiocese of Glasgow, 2013–14. Lectr in Philosophy, Scotus Coll., 1995–2005. *Address:* Diocesan Offices, Cathedral Precincts, Incle Street, Paisley PA1 1HR.

PAISLEY, Hon. Ian Richard Kyle; MP (DemU) North Antrim, since 2010; *b* 12 Dec. 1966; *s* of Baron Bannside, PC and of Baroness Paisley of St George's, *qv*; *m* 1990, Fiona Margaret Elizabeth Currie; two *s* two *d*. *Educ:* Shaftesbury House Coll.; Methodist Coll.; Queen's Univ., Belfast (BA Hons Modern History; MSSc Irish Politics 1995). Res. Asst for Dr Ian Paisley, MP, H of C, 1989–2010. Member: NI Forum for Political Dialogue, 1996–98; NI Police Bd, 2001–10. Justice spokesman, DUP, 1992–2002. Mem. (DemU) Antrim N, NI Assembly, 1998–2010. Jun. Minister, Office of First Minister and Dep. First Minister, NI, 2007–08. Fellow, Sch. of Leadership, Maryland State Univ., 1997. Royal Humane Soc. Testimonial, 1999. *Publications:* Reasonable Doubt: the case for the UDR Four, 1991; Echoes: Protestant identity in Northern Ireland, 1994; Peace Deal?, 1998; Ian Paisley: a life in photographs, 2004; articles in jls. *Recreations:* my children, Chinese food, cinema, Rugby, motorcycling. *Address:* House of Commons, SW1A 0AA; 9–11 Church Street, Ballymena, Co. Antrim BT43 6DD.

PAISNER, Harold Michael; Senior Partner, Berwin Leighton Paisner LLP, 2001–15, now Senior Partner Emeritus; *b* 4 June 1939; *s* of Leslie and Suzanne Paisner; *m* 1967, Judith Rechtman; two *s*. *Educ:* St Paul's Sch., London; University Coll., Oxford (BA Hons); Coll. of Law, London. Investment and merchant banking, 1963; admitted Solicitor, 1971; registered with Paris Bar; former Sen. Partner, Paisner & Co. UK. Nat. Pres., Union Internat. des Avocats, 2006–11 (former Pres., Foreign Investment Cttee); Member: Internat. Issues Cttee, Law Soc. (Chm.); Internat. Bar Assoc.; British Baltic Lawyers Assoc. Hon. Mem., Lithuanian Bar. Non-executive Director: Think London, 2002–11; FIBI Bank (UK) plc, 2005–12; Interface Inc., 2007–; Puma High Income VCT plc, 2010–. Dir, Inst. of Jewish Policy Res., 1999– (Chm., 2009–). Gov., Ben Gurion Univ. of the Negev. *Recreations:* music, reading history, biography and current affairs, ski-ing. *Address:* 16 Ilchester Place, W14 8AA. *T:* (office) (020) 3400 1000. *E:* harold.paisner@blplaw.com. *Club:* Athenæum.

PAISNER, Martin David, CBE 2004; Consultant Partner, Berwin Leighton Paisner LLP, since 2003; *b* Windsor, 1 Sept. 1943; *s* of Leslie and Suzanne Paisner; *m* 1978, Susan Sarah Spence; two *s* two *d*. *Educ:* St Paul's Sch., London; Worcester Coll., Oxford (MA); Univ. of Michigan, Ann Arbor (LLM). Admitted as solicitor, 1970; Partner, Paisner & Co., subseq. Berwin Leighton Paisner LLP, 1972–2003. Chairman: Myers-JDC-Brookdale Inst., Jerusalem, 2009–; Weizmann UK, 2010–. Trustee: BL Trust; Holocaust Educnl Trust; Woolf Inst.; Oxford Centre for Hebrew and Jewish Studies; Ovarian Cancer Action; Cancerkin; Heart Cells Foundn; Stuart Young Foundn; Jerusalem Foundn; Peter Cruddas Foundn; Phillips & Rubens Charitable Trust; Wolfson Family Charitable Trust; Maurice Wohl Charitable Foundn; Maurice and Vivienne Wohl Philanthropic Foundn. *Recreations:* reading and collecting, principally 18th and 19th century English literature, travel posters, Victoriana, bronze and porcelain figures and walking sticks. *Address:* Berwin Leighton Paisner LLP, Adelaide House, London Bridge, EC4R 9HA. *T:* (020) 3400 2356, *Fax:* (020) 3400 1111. *E:* martin.paisner@blplaw.com. *Clubs:* Garrick, Reform.
See also H. M. Paisner.

PAJARES, Ramón, OBE 2000; Chairman, Savoy Educational Trust; Director and Advisor, Como Hotels and Investments Co. Ltd, 2000–05; *b* 6 July 1935; *s* of Juan Antonio Pajares Garcia and Rosario Salazar; *m* 1963, Jean Kathleen Porter; one *s* two *d*. *Educ:* Madrid Inst. of Hotel and Tourism Studies. Nat. Service, Spanish Navy, 1955–57. Hotel posts: Ritz, Barcelona, 1954–55; San Jorge, Playa de Aro, 1957; Pargue, Llavaneras, 1957–59; Mansion, Eastbourne, 1959–61; Kleiner Reisen, Koblenz, Germany, 1961; Feldbergerhof, Feldberg, 1961–62; Le Vieux Manoir, Morat, Switzerland, 1962; Reina Isabel, Canary Is, 1963–69; Food and Beverage Dir, Inn on the Park, London, 1969–71; Gen. Manager, San Antonio, Lanzarote, Canary Is, 1972–74; Gen. Manager and Vice-Pres., Inn on the Park, later Four Seasons, 1975–94; Man. Dir, Savoy Gp of Hotels and Restaurants, 1994–99. Member: Assoc. Culinaire Française, 1971; Cookery and Food Assoc., 1973. Pres., BHA, 2000–06. FIH (FHCIMA 1982). Freeman, City of London, 1988. Hon. DEd Bournemouth, 2000. Hotelier of Year Award, Brit. Hotel and Catering Ind., 1984; Personnalité de l'année for Hotel Ind., 1986; Catey Special Award, Caterer & Hotel Keeper Mag., 1997; Lifetime Achievement Award, Eur. Hotel Design and Develt Awards, 1998; British Travel Industry Hall of Fame, 1998; Hotelier of World, Hotels Mag., 1998; Spanish Govt Silver Medal, for services to tourism, 2000. Mérito Civil (Spain), 1984; Oficial de la Orden de Isabel la Católica (Spain), 1989. *Recreation:* classical music.

PAKENHAM, family name of **Earl of Longford**.

PAKENHAM, Catherine Ruth, (Kate), (Mrs Christopher Spira); Executive Producer, Donmar Warehouse, since 2012; *b* London, 4 May 1975; *d* of Hon. Kevin Pakenham and Ruth East (*née* Jackson); *m* 2006, Christopher Spira; one *s* one *d*. *Educ:* Godolphin and Latymer Sch., London; Gonville and Caius Coll., Cambridge (BA English Lit. 1996; MA). Producer and Dir for TV progs incl. Paddington Green, BBC, and What Will They Think of Next?, ITV, 1996–2001; Producer: Old Vic New Voices, 2001–07; Old Vic Th., 2007–12. *Recreations:* reading, writing, art, tennis, walking, ski-ing. *Address:* Donmar Warehouse, 41 Earlham Street, WC2H 9LX. *E:* kpakenham@donmarwarehouse.com.

PAKENHAM, Hon. Sir Michael (Aidan), KBE 2003; CMG 1993; HM Diplomatic Service, retired; Senior Adviser, Access Industries, since 2004; *b* 3 Nov. 1943; *s* of 7th Earl of Longford, KG, PC, and Elizabeth, Countess of Longford, CBE; *m* 1980, Meta (Mimi) Landreth Doak, *d* of William Conway Doak of Maryland, USA; two *d* two step *d*. *Educ:* Ampleforth College (schol.); Trinity College, Cambridge (schol.; MA Classics); Rice University, Texas (exchange fellow). Reporter, Washington Post, 1965; Foreign Office, 1965; Nairobi, 1966; Warsaw, 1967; FCO, 1970; Asst Private Sec., later Private Sec. to Chancellor of Duchy of Lancaster (European Community Affairs), on secondment to Cabinet Office, 1971–74; Geneva (CSCE), 1974; New Delhi, 1974; Washington, 1978; Head of Arms Control and Disarmament Dept, FCO, 1983–87; Counsellor (External Relations), UK Perm. Rep. to EC, Brussels, 1987–91; Ambassador and Consul-Gen., Luxembourg, 1991–94; Minister, Paris, 1994–97; Cabinet Office (on secondment): Dep. Sec. (Overseas and Defence), 1997–99; Chm., Jt Intelligence Cttee, 1997–2000 and Intelligence Co-ordinator, 1999–2000; Ambassador to Poland, 2001–03. Chm., Pakenvest International Ltd, 2004–; Consultant, Thales International, 2004–06; Sen. Advr, Droege & Co., 2005–07; Mem., European Adv. Bd, Northrop Grumman, 2008–11; Dir, Westminster Gp, 2008–. Trustee, Chevening House, 2005–. Mem. Council, 2005–13, Vice-Chm., 2009–13, KCL; FKC 2012. Freeman of City of London, 1992. *Recreations:* tennis, golf, reading history, museums, Arsenal FC. *Address:* Cope House, 15B Kensington Palace Gardens, W8 4QG. *T:* (020) 7908 9966. *Clubs:* Garrick, MCC; Sunningdale Golf, High Post Golf.

PAKENHAM, Thomas Frank Dermot; writer; *b* 14 Aug. 1933; *e s* of 7th Earl of Longford, KG, PC, and Elizabeth, Countess of Longford, CBE; *S* father, 2001, but does not use the title; *m* 1964, Valerie, *d* of Major R. G. McNair Scott; two *s* two *d*. *Educ:* Dragon School, Oxford; Belvedere Coll., Dublin; Ampleforth Coll., York; Magdalen Coll., Oxford (BA Greats 1955). Travelled, Near East and Ethiopia, 1955–56 (discovered unrecorded medieval Ethiopian church at Bethlehem, Begemdir, 1956). Free-lance writing, 1956–58. Editorial staff: Times Educational Supplement, 1958–60; Sunday Telegraph, 1961; The Observer, 1961–64. Founder Mem. 1958, and Member Cttee 1958–64, Victorian Soc.; Founder Mem., and Mem. Cttee 1968–72, Historic Irish Tourist Houses and Gardens Assoc. (HITHA); Treas., 1972–2002, Chm., 2002–05, British-Irish Assoc.; Sec. (co-founder), Christopher Ewart-Biggs Memorial Trust, 1976–; Founder and Chm., Irish Tree Soc., 1990–. Chm., Ladbroke Assoc., 1988–91. Sen. Associate Mem., St Antony's Coll., Oxford, 1979–81. Hon. DLitt: Ulster, 1992; TCD, 2000; QUB, 2004. *Publications:* The Mountains of Rasselas: an Ethiopian adventure, 1959, 1998; The Year of Liberty: the story of the Great Irish Rebellion of 1798, 1969; The Boer War, 1979 (Cheltenham Prize, 1980); (selected and introd with Valerie Pakenham) Dublin: a travellers' companion, 1988; The Scramble for Africa, 1991 (W. H. Smith Prize, 1992; Alan Paton Meml Prize, 1992); Meetings with Remarkable Trees, 1996; Remarkable Trees of the World, 2002; The Remarkable Baobab, 2004; In Search of Remarkable Trees: on safari in southern Africa, 2007. *Recreation:* water. *Address:* Tullynally, Castlepollard, Westmeath, Ireland. *T:* (44) 9661159. *Club:* Beefsteak.

PAKENHAM-WALSH, John, CB 1986; Standing Counsel to General Synod of Church of England, 1988–2000; *b* 7 Aug. 1928; *s* of late Rev. W. P. Pakenham-Walsh, formerly ICS, and Guendolen (*née* Elliott); *m* 1951, Deryn, *er d* of late Group Captain R. E. G. Fulljames, MC, and Mrs Muriel Fulljames; one *s* four *d*. *Educ:* Bradfield Coll.; University Coll., Oxford (MA). Called to the Bar, Lincoln's Inn, 1951. Crown Counsel, Hong Kong, 1953–57; Parly Counsel, Fedn of Nigeria, 1958–61; joined Legal Adviser's Br., Home Office, 1961; Under Sec. (Legal), Home Office, 1980–87. Hon. QC 1992. *Address:* 28 Brompton Court, St Stephens Road, Bournemouth BH2 6JS. *T:* (01202) 255912.

PAKER, Adam David; Chief Executive, Amateur Swimming Association, since 2014; *b* Monmouth, NJ, 19 Feb. 1971; *s* of Yakup Paker and Ruth Paker; *m* 2011, Jennifer Hepker; two *d*. *Educ:* Highgate Jun. Sch.; Westminster Sch.; Magdalen Coll., Oxford (BA Jt Hons Mod. Langs); INSEAD (MBA). Exec., Robert Fleming & Co. Ltd, 1993–99; Manager, ISL, 2000–01; Dir, FIFA, 2001–05; Hd, Global Sports, Virtual Marketing Services, 2005–07; Business Dir, Havas Sports, 2008–09; Consultant, Threshold Sports, 2009–10; Chief Exec., Commonwealth Games England, 2011–14. *Recreations:* football, running, sub-aqua, following Arsenal and England national team, supporting Team GB and Team England. *Address:* Amateur Swimming Association, Sport Park, 3 Oakwood Drive, Loughborough, Leics LE11 3QF.

PAKINGTON, family name of **Baron Hampton**.

PALACIO VALLELERSUNDI, Ana; Founding Partner, Palacio y Asociados, Madrid, 1985; Senior Strategic Counsel, Albright Stonebridge Group, Washington, DC, since 2010; *b* Madrid, 22 July 1948. *Educ:* French Lycée, Madrid; Univ. Complutense, Madrid (degrees in Law, Pol Sci., Sociol.). Lectr. MEP, 1994–2002 (Chm., Legal Affairs and Internal Market Cttee, 1999–2002); Mem. for Toledo, Congress of Deputies, Spain, 2002–06; Minister of Foreign Affairs, 2002–04; Sen. Vice-Pres. and Gen. Counsel, World Bank, 2006–08. Mem. Bd Governors, Law Soc. of Madrid; Dep. Chm. Council, European Law Socs; Pres. Exec. Council, Europäische Rechtsakademie (Acad. of European Law), Trier. Mem. Editorial Bd, Revue du Droit de l'Union Européenne. Hon. Mem., Law Soc. of England and Wales; Mem., Inner Temple. Cruz de San Raimundo de Peñafort; Banda, Orden del Aguila Azteca (Mexico), 2002; Orden de Stara Planina (Bulgaria), 2003; Gran Cruz: Orden Piana (Vatican), 2002; Placa de Plata de la Orden Nacional José Matias Delgado (El Salvador), 2003; del Sol (Brazil), 2003; Orden del Mérito de Duarte (Dominican Republic), 2003; Orden de Carlos III (Spain), 2004; Orden al Mérito (Chile), 2004.

PALCA, Julia Charlotte; Chairman: Macmillan Cancer Support, since 2010 (Trustee, since 2001); Royal Free Charity, since 2010 (Trustee, since 2005); *b* Guildford, 25 March 1956; *d* of Henry Palca and Edith, (Vicky), Palca; *m* 1985, Nicolas Stevenson; three *s*. *Educ:* Queen Anne's Sch., Caversham; Durham Univ. (BA Law and Pols 1977). Trainee and Solicitor, Oswald Hickson Collier & Co., 1978–81; Solicitor, Lovell, White & King, 1981–85; In-house Counsel, Mirror Gp Newspapers Ltd, 1985–86; Partner, 1986–2009, Consultant, 2009–12, Olswang LLP. Employment Judge (pt-time), 2001–. Dir, Inst. of Employment Studies, 2000–08. Mem. Bd, City of London Law Soc., 2005–12. Trustee: Community Self Build, 1998–2001; Cancer Link, 1999–2001; Koestler Trust, 2013–; Nuffield Trust, 2015–; Special Advr, Prison Reform Trust, 2001–; Mem., Patient Information Adv. Gp, 2001–04. *Publications:* Employment Law Checklists, 1993, 4th edn 2009; (ed jtly) Yearbook of Media and Entertainment Law, 2nd edn 1996 to 4th edn 1999; (jtly) Blackstone's Employment Law Checklists, 2006, 7th edn 2012; (jtly) Goulding on Employee Competition, 2007. *Recreations:* theatre, art, dancing. *Address:* Macmillan Cancer Support, 89 Albert Embankment, SE1 7UQ. *T:* (020) 7840 7833. *E:* jpalca@macmillan.org.uk.

PALEY, Maureen; Founder and Director, Maureen Paley (formerly Interim Art), since 1984; *b* New York, 17 Sept. 1959; *d* of Alfred and Sylvia Paley. *Educ:* Sarah Lawrence Coll., Bronxville, NY; Brown Univ. (BA); Royal Coll. of Art (MA). Worked in photography and film, 1980–84; Lecturer: Bournemouth and Poole Coll. of Art, 1981–83; AA, 1981–82; curator: Antidotes to Madness?, Riverside Studios, London, 1986; Photography as Performance, Photographer's Gall., London, 1986; Wall Works, Cornerhouse, Manchester, 1987; Symptoms of Interference, Conditions of Possibility: Ad Reinhardt, Joseph Kosuth, Felix Gonzalez-Torres, Camden Art Centre, 1994; Wall to Wall, Serpentine Gall., Southampton City Art Gall., Leeds City Art Gall., 1995; The Cauldron, Henry Moore Sculpture Trust, Halifax. Vis. Lectr, RCA, Chelsea Coll. of Art and Design. Mem., Soc. of London Art Dealers; Benefactor: Artangel; Camden Arts Centre; Chisenhale Gall.; Creative Industries Fedn; ICA; Michael Clark Co.; Open Sch. East; Serpentine Galls; South London Gall.; Studio Voltaire; Tate; The Showroom; Whitechapel Gall.; Nottingham Contemporary; Artists Space, Swiss Inst., The Kitchen, White Columns (NY). *Publications:* Technique Anglaise, 1991; Gillian Wearing—Signs…, 1997; Art London, 1999, 2nd edn 2000; Peter Hujar/Paul P.—When Ghost Meets Ghost, 2008; exhibition catalogues. *Address:* Maureen Paley, 21 Herald Street, E2 6JT. *T:* (020) 7729 4112, *Fax:* (020) 7729 4113. *E:* info@maureenpaley.com. *Clubs:* Annabel's, Groucho, Soho House.

PALIN, Michael Edward, CBE 2000; actor, writer and traveller; President, Royal Geographical Society, 2009–12; *b* 5 May 1943; *s* of late Edward and Mary Palin; *m* 1966, Helen M. Gibbins; two *s* one *d*. *Educ:* Birkdale Sch., Sheffield; Shrewsbury; Brasenose Coll., Oxford (BA 2nd Cl. Hons Mod. Hist.; Hon. Fellow, 2006). Pres., Campaign for Better Transport (formerly Transport 2000), 1987–. *Television:* actor and writer: Monty Python's Flying Circus, 1969–74; Ripping Yarns, 1976–80; actor: Three Men in a Boat, 1975; GBH, 1991; The Wipers Times, 2013; Remember Me, 2014; writer: East of Ipswich, 1987; Number 27, 1988; *stage play:* The Weekend, Strand, 1994. *Films:* actor and jt author: And Now for Something Completely Different, 1970; Monty Python and the Holy Grail, 1974; Monty Python's Life of Brian, 1978; Time Bandits, 1980; Monty Python's "The Meaning of Life", 1982; American Friends, 1991; actor, writer and co-producer: The Missionary, 1982; actor: Jabberwocky, 1976; A Private Function, 1984; Brazil, 1985; A Fish Called Wanda, 1988 (Best Supporting Film Actor, BAFTA Award, 1988); Fierce Creatures, 1997. *Television* series: contributor, Great Railway Journeys of the World, 1980, 1994; writer and presenter: Around the World in Eighty Days, 1989; Pole to Pole, 1992; Palin's Column, 1994; Full Circle, 1995–96; Michael Palin's Hemingway Adventure, 1999; Sahara With Michael Palin, 2002; Himalaya, 2004 (Best Presenter Award, RTS, 2005); Michael Palin's New Europe, 2007; Around the World in 20 Years, 2008; Brazil with Michael Palin, 2012; presenter: Palin on Redpath, 1997; The Bright Side of Life, 2000; The Ladies who Loved Matisse, 2003; Michael Palin and the Mystery of Hammershoi, 2005; Timewatch: the last day of WW1, 2008; Michael Palin in Wyeth's World, 2013; narrator, Clangers, children's series, 2015. *Live shows:*

Monty Python Live (Mostly), 02 Arena, 2014; Travelling to Work (tour), 2014; Michael Palin - Live on Stage, Australia, 2015; The Thirty Years Tour, 2015. Hon. Fellow, SOAS, 2008. Hon. DLitt: Sheffield, 1992; Edinburgh, 2007; Hon. DLit QUB, 2000. Ness Award, RGS, 1998; Lifetime Achievement Award, British Comedy Awards, 2002; Special Award, BAFTA, 2005; Fellow, BAFTA, 2013. *Publications:* Monty Python's Big Red Book, 1970; Monty Python's Brand New Bok, 1973; Dr Fegg's Encyclopeadia of *All* World Knowledge, 1984; Limericks, 1985; Around the World in Eighty Days, 1989; Pole to Pole, 1992 (Travel Writer of the Year, British Book Awards, 1993); Hemingway's Chair (novel), 1995; Full Circle, 1997; Hemingway Adventure, 1999; Sahara, 2002; (jtly) The Pythons Autobiography by The Pythons, 2003; Himalaya, 2004 (TV and Film Book of the Year, British Book Awards, 2005); Diaries: the Python years 1969–1979, 2006; New Europe, 2007; Diaries: halfway to Hollywood 1980–1988, 2009; The Truth (novel), 2012; Brazil, 2012; Diaries: travelling to work, 1988–1998, 2014; *for children:* Small Harry and the Toothache Pills, 1981; (with R. W. Seymour and Alan Lee) The Mirrorstone, 1986; The Cyril Stories, 1986. *Recreations:* reading, running, railways—preferably all three in a foreign country. *Address:* (office) Mayday Management PS Ltd, 34 Tavistock Street, WC2E 7PB. *E:* paulbird@maydaymgt.co.uk. *Club:* Athenæum.

PALIN, Air Chief Marshal Sir Roger Hewlett, KCB 1989; OBE 1978; Controller, Royal Air Force Benevolent Fund, 1993–98; *b* 8 July 1938; *m* 1967, Kathryn Elizabeth Pye; two *d*. *Educ:* Canford Sch.; St John's Coll., Cambridge (BA 1967; MA 1979; Hon. Fellow, 2007); psc. FRAeS; FIPD. Commnd KRRC, 1958; served 3 Para. Bn, 1958–59, 10 Para. Bn (TA), 1959–62; Flight Lieut, 1964; Sqn Leader, 1970; Wing Comdr, 1975; Group Captain, 1980; ADC to the Queen, 1981–82; Air Cdre, 1984; Dir of Defence Policy, MoD, 1984–85; Air Vice-Marshal, 1986; ACDS (Progs), 1986–87; AOC No 11 Gp, 1987–89; Air Marshal, 1989; C-in-C, RAF Germany and Comdr Second Allied Tactical Air Force, 1989–91; Air Chief Marshal, 1991; Air Mem. for Personnel, 1991–93; Air ADC to the Queen, 1991–93; retired 1993. Guest Schol., Woodrow Wilson Internat. Center for Scholars, Washington, 1980; Res. Associate, IISS, 1993. *Recreations:* sport, travel, international relations, defence studies.

PALING, Her Honour Helen Elizabeth, (Mrs W. J. S. Kershaw); a Circuit Judge, 1985–2000; *b* 25 April 1933; *o d* of A. Dale Paling and Mabel Eleanor Thomas; *m* 1961, William John Stanley Kershaw, PhD; one *s* three *d*. *Educ:* Prince Henry's Grammar Sch., Otley; London Sch. of Economics. LLB London 1954. Called to Bar, Lincoln's Inn, 1955; a Recorder, 1972–85. *Address:* c/o Quayside Law Courts, Newcastle upon Tyne NE1 2LA. *T:* (0191) 201 2000.

PALIOS, Markos; corporate turnaround specialist; Co-owner and Executive Chairman, Tranmere Rovers FC, since 2014; *b* 9 Nov. 1952; five *d*, and two step *s*. *Educ:* St Anselm's Coll., Birkenhead; Manchester Univ. (BSc Psychol.). FCA 1995. Professional footballer, Tranmere Rovers FC, and Crewe Alexandra FC, 1973–86; Partner, Arthur Young, 1986–89; Partner, 1989–2003, UK Leader for Business Regeneration, 1997–2003, Coopers & Lybrand, then PricewaterhouseCoopers; Chief Exec., Football Assoc., 2003–04; European Leader, FTI Palladium Partners, 2005–06. Dir, British Judo Assoc., 2012– (co-author, Elite Performance System Review, 2012; Chm., Finance, Risk and Governance); Mem., Audit Cttee, Surrey CCC, 2011–. Media commentator on football, 2010–. *Recreations:* family, sport, history, politics.

PALLEY, Dr Claire Dorothea Taylor, OBE 1998; Constitutional Adviser, 1980–94, 1999–2004 and 2005–07, Consultant to Attorney-General, since 2008, Republic of Cyprus; Principal of St Anne's College, Oxford, 1984–91, Hon. Fellow, 1992; *b* 17 Feb. 1931; *d* of Arthur Aubrey Swait, Durban; *m* 1952, Ahrn Palley (marr. diss. 1985; he *d* 1993); five *s*. *Educ:* Durban Girls' Coll.; Univs of Cape Town and London. BA 1950, LLB 1952, Cape Town; PhD London 1965; MA Oxon 1984. Called to Bar, Middle Temple. Queen's University, Belfast: Lectr, 1966–67; Reader, 1967–70; Prof. of Public Law, 1970–73; Dean of Faculty of Law, 1971–73; Prof. of Law, 1973–84, and Master of Darwin Coll., 1974–82, Univ. of Kent. Member: Council, Minority Rights Group, 1975–94; UN Sub-Commn on Prevention of Discrimination and Protection of Minorities, 1988–98. Hon. LLD: QUB, 1991; Cape Town, 2008. *Publications:* The Constitutional History and Law of Southern Rhodesia, 1966; The United Kingdom and Human Rights, 1991; An International Relations Debacle: the UN Secretary-General's Mission of Good Offices in Cyprus 1999–2004, 2005; contrib. learned jls. *Address:* 13 Nikou Sophocleous Avenue, Pachna, 4700 Limassol, Cyprus.

PALLISTER, (Rufina) Aswini; *see* Weereratne, R. A.

PALLOT, Prof. Judith, PhD; Professor of the Human Geography of Russia, University of Oxford, since 2008; Official Student of Christ Church, Oxford, since 1979; *b* Maidenhead, 25 July 1949; *d* of Arthur Keith Pallot, CB, CMG and Marjorie Pallot (*née* Smith); *m* 2003, Jeremy Charles Thomas Fairbank; one *d*. *Educ:* Lynton House Sch. for Girls; Maidenhead High Sch.; Univ. of Leeds (BA 1st Cl.); University Coll. London (PhD 1977); MA Oxon. Lectr, Univ. of Leeds, 1973–79; Lectr, 1979–, Sen. Proctor, 1996–97, Univ. of Oxford; Jun., then Sen. Censor, Christ Church, Oxford, 2001–05. *Publications:* (with D. J. B. Shaw) Planning in the Soviet Union, 1981; (with D. J. B. Shaw) Landscape and Settlement in Romanov Russia, 1990; (ed) Transforming Peasants: society, state and the peasantry, 1861–1930, 1998; Land Reform in Russia 1906–17: peasant responses to Stolypin's project of rural transformation, 1999; (with T. Nefedova) Russia's Unknown Agriculture: household production in post-socialist Russia, 2007; (with L. Piacetini) Gender, Geography and Punishment: the experience of women in Carceral Russia, 2012. *Recreations:* opera and ballet, horse riding. *Address:* Christ Church, Oxford OX1 1DP. *T:* (01865) 276222. *E:* judith.pallot@chch.ox.ac.uk.

PALMA, Kamela; High Commissioner for Belize in London, 2008–12; *b* Belize, 7 Jan. 1952; *d* of Carlton Fairweather and Isabel Palma; one *d*. *Educ:* St John's Coll., Belize; Viterbo Univ., Wisconsin; Inst. of Educn, London. Headteacher, St Peter Claver Coll., Punta Gorda, Belize; Lectr, Belize Teachers' Trng Coll.; Dir, Regl Lang. Centre, Univ. of Belize, 2000–01; CEO and Perm. Sec., Govt of Belize, 2001–03; Dep. Ambassador, Guatemala, 2004. Mem., Bd of Govs, Commonwealth Secretariat, 2009–11 (Mem., Exec. Cttee, 2008–12). Chm., Nat. Council on Ageing, 2003–08; Member, Board of Directors: Toledo Inst. for Develt and Envmt, 2001–; Belize Council for Visually Impaired, 2005–. Founder and Chair, Nurse Isabel Palma Foundn, 2013–. *Recreations:* dancing, reading, opera, travel, walking.

PALMER, family name of **Earl of Selborne** and **Barons Lucas of Crudwell, Palmer** and **Palmer of Childs Hill**.

PALMER, 4th Baron *cr* 1933, of Reading; **Adrian Bailie Nottage Palmer;** Bt 1916; *b* 8 Oct. 1951; *s* of Col the Hon. Sir Gordon Palmer, KCVO, OBE, TD, MA, FRCM and the Hon. Lady Palmer, DL; *S* uncle, 1990; *m* 1st, 1977, Cornelia Dorothy Katherine (marr. diss. 2004), *d* of R. N. Wadham, DFC, Exning, Newmarket; two *s* one *d*; 2nd, 2006, Loraine (marr. diss. 2013), *d* of Jim McMurrey, Texas, USA. *Educ:* Eton; Edinburgh Univ. Mem., Exec. Council, HHA, 1981–99; Chm., HHA for Scotland, 1994–99 (Mem., Exec. Council, 1980–99; Vice Chm., 1993). Elected Mem., H of L, 1999. Mem., Queen's Body Guard for Scotland (Royal Company of Archers), 1992–96. Scottish Rep. to European Landowning Orgn, 1986–92. Pres., British Assoc. for Biofuels and Oils, 2000–. Sec., The Royal Caledonian Hunt, 1989–2005. *Recreation:* gardening. *Heir:* *s* Hon. Hugo Bailie Rohan Palmer, *b* 5 Dec. 1980. *Address:* Manderston, Duns, Berwickshire TD11 3PP. *T:* (01361) 883450. *Clubs:* Pratt's; New (Edinburgh).

PALMER OF CHILDS HILL, Baron *cr* 2011 (Life Peer), of Childs Hill in the London Borough of Barnet; **Monroe Edward Palmer,** OBE 1982; FCA; chartered accountant; *b* 30 Nov. 1938; *s* of William and Sybil Polikoff; *m* 1962, Susette Sandra (*née* Cardash); two *s* one *d*. *Educ:* Orange Hill Grammar Sch. FCA 1963. Chm., Hendon CAB, 1981–83; Vice-Chm., Barnet CAB, 1986–88; Treasurer: Disablement Assoc., London Borough of Barnet, 1971–88; Liberal Parly Party, 1977–83; Jt Treasurer, Liberal Party, 1977–83; Chm., Lib Dem Friends of Israel, 1987–2010. Councillor (L, then Lib Dem) London Borough of Barnet, 1986–94 and 1998–2014 (Leader, Lib Dem Gp, 1999–2008). Contested: (L) Hendon South, 1979, 1983, 1987; (Lib Dem) Hastings and Rye, 1992, 1997. Lib Dem lead spokesman on Defence, H of L, 2013–. Treas., London Reg., Lib Dems, 2008–09. Dir, Barnet Homes, 1994–2009. Chm. Adv. Council, Property Redress Scheme, 2014–. *Recreations:* politics, fishing, horse riding. *Address:* 31 The Vale, NW11 8SE. *T:* (020) 8455 5140. *Club:* National Liberal.

PALMER, Adrian Oliver; QC 1992; a Recorder, since 1992; *b* 20 Aug. 1950; *s* of Richard Gilbert Palmer and Patricia Mary Palmer; *m* 1974, Rosemary Shaw; one *s* one *d*. *Educ:* Clifton Coll., Bristol; St John's Coll., Cambridge (MA); Bristol Univ. (LLM). Called to the Bar, Middle Temple, 1972, Bencher, 2003; Dep. High Court Judge, 2000–. *Recreations:* gardens, sheep, walking. *Address:* Guildhall Chambers, 23 Broad Street, Bristol BS1 2HG. *T:* (0117) 930 9000.

PALMER, Dr Andrew Charles, CMG 2014; CEng, FIMechE; Chief Executive Officer, Aston Martin, since 2014; *b* Birmingham, 30 June 1963; *s* of Brian M. Palmer and Mary C. Palmer (*née* Henshaw); *m* 2004, Hitomi Kamiomachi; one *s* three *d*. *Educ:* Coventry Univ. (Dip. Mgt 1987); Warwick Univ. (MSc Design Engrg 1990); London Business Sch. (Accelerated Develt Prog. 2002); Cranford Univ. (PhD Engrg Mgt 2004). CEng 2003; FIMechE 2003; CMgr 2004. Tech. apprentice, 1973–83, project engr, 1983–86, Automotive Products Ltd; Chief Engr, Manual Transmission, Rover Gp, 1986–91; Nissan Motor Corporation: business admin manager, 1991–2001; Dep. Man. Dir, Nissan Euro Tech. Centre, 2001–02; Prog. Dir and Corporate Vice Pres. for Light Commercial Vehicles, 2002; Pres., Motor Light Truck Co., 2003; Chm., Infiniti Co. Ltd, 2009; Senior Vice President: Global Planning and IS/IT, 2009–13; Global Mktg and Communications, 2011–13; Global Sales, 2013; Chief Planning Officer and Exec. Vice Pres., 2013–14. Vis. Prof., Tokyo Univ. of Agric. and Technol., 2009. Hon. DTech Coventry, 2010. *Recreations:* motor racing (competition licence), motor cycling, reading, listening to rock music. *Address:* Aston Martin Lagonda Ltd, Banbury Road, Gaydon, Warwicks CV35 0DB.

PALMER, Prof. Andrew Clennel, PhD; FRS 1994; FREng, FICE; Professor, Department of Civil and Environmental Engineering (formerly of Civil Engineering), National University of Singapore, 2007–15 (Keppel Professor, 2008–12); Fellow, Churchill College, Cambridge, since 1996; *b* 26 May 1938; *s* of Gerald Basil Coote Palmer and Muriel Gertrude Palmer (*née* Howes); *m* 1963, Jane Rhiannon Evans; one *d*. *Educ:* Pembroke Coll., Cambridge (BA, MA); Brown Univ. (PhD). FICE 1986; FREng (FEng 1990). Lectr, Liverpool Univ., 1965–67; Cambridge University: Sen. Asst in Res., 1967–68; Lectr, 1968–75; Fellow, Churchill Coll., 1967–75; Chief Engr, R. J. Brown and Associates, 1975–79; Prof. of Civil Engrg, UMIST, 1979–82; Vice-Pres. Engrg, R. J. Brown and Associates, 1982–85; Man. Dir, Andrew Palmer and Associates, 1985–93; Technical Dir, SAIC Ltd, 1993–96; Jafar Res. Prof. of Petroleum Engineering, Cambridge Univ., 1996–2005. Visiting Professor: Harvard Univ., 2002–03; Nat. Univ. of Singapore, 2006–07. Managing Director: Bold Is Engrg Ltd, 2005–09 (Co. Sec., 2009–15); Bold Island Engrg (Singapore) Pte Ltd, 2014–. Pres., Pipeline Industries Guild, 1998–2000. Trustee, Amer. Univ., Sharjah, 2014–. Hon. DSc Clarkson, 2007. *Publications:* Structural Mechanics, 1976; Subsea Pipeline Engineering, 2004; Dimensional Analysis, 2008; Arctic Offshore Engineering, 2012; articles and papers in scientific and engrg jls. *Recreations:* travel, glass-blowing, cooking, languages. *Address:* # 12–06 Block C, 111 Clementi Road, Singapore 129792. *E:* ceepalme@nus.edu.sg. *Club:* Athenæum.

PALMER, Andrew Eustace, CMG 1987; CVO 1981; HM Diplomatic Service, retired; an Extra Equerry to the Duke of Kent, since 1996; *b* 30 Sept. 1937; *s* of late Lt-Col Rodney Howell Palmer, MC, and of Mrs Frances Pauline Ainsworth (*née* Gordon-Duff); *m* 1962, Davina, *d* of Sir Roderick Barclay, GCVO, KCMG; two *s* one *d*. *Educ:* Winchester Coll.; Pembroke Coll., Cambridge (MA). Second Lieut, Rifle Bde, 1956–58. Joined HM Foreign (later Diplomatic) Service, 1961; American Dept, FO, 1962–63; Third, later Second, Secretary (Commercial), La Paz, 1963–65; Second Sec., Ottawa, 1965–67; Treasury Centre for Administrative Studies, 1967–68; Central Dept, FO, later Southern European Dept, FCO, 1968–72; First Sec. (Information), Paris, 1972–76; Asst Head of Defence Dept, FCO, 1976–77; RCDS 1978; Counsellor, Head of Chancery and Consul-Gen., Oslo, 1979–82; Hd, Falkland Is Dept, FCO, 1982–85; Fellow, Harvard Center for Internat. Affairs, 1985–86; Ambassador to Cuba, 1986–88; seconded as Pvte Sec. to the Duke and Duchess of Kent, 1988–90; Ambassador to the Holy See, 1991–95. Local organiser, Bilderberg Conf., Turnberry, 1998. Mem. Council, 1996–2008, Vis. Fellow, Politics and Internat. Relns, 2008–, Reading Univ.; Chm., Friends of Univ. of Reading, 2005–. Comdr, Order of St Olav (Norway), 1981. *Publications:* A Diplomat and his Birds, 2005. *Recreations:* fishing, following most sports, photography, ornithology. *Address:* Peasemore Manor, Newbury, Berks RG20 7JF. *Clubs:* Brooks's, MCC.

See also Viscount Garmoyle.

PALMER, Andrew Richard Alexander; Managing Director, Aspire Achieve Advance Ltd, since 2013; *b* Harrow, 28 Jan. 1976; *s* of Dr Neil Ingamells Palmer and Catherine Mary Palmer; *m* 2009, Sarah Meredith; two *d*. *Educ:* Nottingham High Sch.; Univ. of Leeds (BSc Hons Zoology 1998). Consultant, PSD Gp, 1998–2000; Dir, Ops, e-skills UK, 2000–07; Dir, Educn and Skills, BT, 2007–12; Man. Dir, Skillnet Ltd, 2012–13. Member: Bd, OFSTED, 2011–; Skills Commn, 2011–. Mem., Educn and Skills Cttee, CBI, 2008–12. Trustee, Dagfa Sch., Nottingham, 2011–. *Recreations:* trying to be a good dad, enjoying English countryside, Rugby Union (watching and occasionally refereeing). *Address:* Newcastle Drive, The Park, Nottingham; Aspire Achieve Advance Ltd, Sitwell House, Sitwell Street, Derby DE1 2JT. *E:* andy.r.a.palmer@me.com.

PALMER, Angela Silver, (Mrs J. D. F. Palmer); artist; *b* 27 March 1957; *m* 1988, Jeremy David Fletcher Palmer, *er s* of Maj.-Gen. Sir (Joseph) Michael Palmer, *qv*; two *s* one *d*. *Educ:* George Watson's Ladies' Coll., Edinburgh; Ruskin Sch. of Drawing and Fine Art, Oxford (BA 2005); RCA (MA 2007). Trainee, Evening News, Edinburgh, 1979–82; Peterborough Column, Daily Telegraph, 1982–84; Editor, PHS, The Times, 1984–86; News Editor, Observer, 1986–88; Editor: Observer Mag., 1988–92; Elle, 1992–93. Commissions: Wellcome Trust; Aberdeen Univ.; Pembroke Coll., Oxford; Exeter Coll., Oxford; Ashmolean Mus., Oxford; exhibtd RA Summer Exhibn, 2005; Ghost Forest, installation of African rainforest trees, Trafalgar Square, London, and Thorvaldsens Plads, Copenhagen, 2009, Oxford Univ. Mus. of Nat. Hist. and Pitt Rivers Mus., Oxford, 2010–12; solo exhibitions: Waterhouse and Dodd Gall., London, 2008, 2012; Wellcome Trust, London, 2009; Fine Art Soc., 2014; work in permanent collection: Ashmolean Mus., Oxford (Egyptian Galls); Scottish Nat. Portrait Gall.; Smithsonian Air and Space Mus. FRSA 2003. Journalist of the Year, Scotland, 1980; Waugh Scholarship and Fitzgerald Prize, Exeter Coll., Univ. of Oxford, 2003; Polly Campbell Award, Jerwood Space, 2007; RCA Soc. and Thames and Hudson Award, 2007. *Recreation:* family. *Address:* c/o Fine Art Society, 148 New Bond Street, W1S 2JT.

PALMER, Lt-Gen. Anthony Malcolm Douglas, CB 2005; CBE 1995; Chairman, Warrior Programme, since 2008; non-executive Chairman, Shoreditch Bar Group, since 2012;

Deputy Chief of Defence Staff (Personnel), 2002–05; *b* 13 March 1949; *s* of late Lt-Col A. G. D. Palmer and Joan Palmer (*née* Wintour); *m* 1972, Harriet Ann Jardine; two *s* one *d*. *Educ:* Woodcote House; Winchester Coll. Commnd RGJ, 1969; despatches, 1972, 1990; BAOR, 1969–70; NI, 1970–71; Shorncliffe, 1971–73; Catterick, 1973–74; Warminster, 1974–76; 2nd Bn RGJ, 1976, Ops Officer, 1978–80; Trng Co. Comdr, Winchester, 1980–81; Staff Coll., Pakistan, 1981; Co. Comdr, 3rd Bn RGJ, 1983–85; MoD, 1985–87; Directing Staff, Camberley, 1987–89; CO, 2nd Bn RGJ, 1989–91; Col, MoD, 1991; Comdr, 8 Inf. Bde, 1993; rcds 1995; Dir, Army Plans, 1996–99; Chief Exec., Army Trng and Recruiting Agency, 1999–2002. Chairman: Silicon CPV plc, 2008–09; Adv. Bd, Pax Mondial, 2009–14; Adv. Bd, Pyreco, 2011–; Antheda, 2011–. Chm., Pakistan Soc., 2006–12. Gov., Hazlegrove Sch. and King's Sch., Bruton, 2014– (Chm. Govs, 2015–). *Recreations:* music, bridge, golf, tennis, fishing. *Address:* c/o Army and Navy Club, 36–39 Pall Mall, SW1Y 5JN. *Clubs:* Army and Navy, Royal Green Jackets.

PALMER, Anthony Thomas Richard; *see* Palmer, Tony.

PALMER, Arnold Daniel; professional golfer, since 1954; golf course designer; *b* 10 Sept. 1929; *s* of Milfred J. and Doris Palmer; *m* 1954, Winifred Walzer (*d* 1999); two *d*; *m* 2005, Kathleen Gawthrop. *Educ:* Wake Forest Univ. Winner of numerous tournament titles, including: British Open Championship, 1961, 1962; US Open Championship, 1960; Masters Championship, 1958, 1960, 1962, 1964; Spanish Open Championship, 1975; British Professional Golfers' Assoc. Championship, 1975; Canadian PGA, 1980; USA Seniors' Championship, 1981. Hon. Dr of Laws: Wake Forest; Nat. Coll. of Educn; St Andrews; Hon. DHum: Thiel Coll.; Florida Southern College; St Vincent Coll.; Allegheny Coll.; Hon. Dr of Public Service Washington and Jefferson Coll. Hon. Member: Royal and Ancient Golf Club, 1979; Troon Golf Club, 1982; Royal Birkdale Golf Club, 1983. *Publications:* (all jointly): Arnold Palmer Golf Book, 1961; Portrait of a Professional Golfer, 1964; My Game and Yours, 1965; Situation Golf, 1970; Go for Broke, 1973; Arnold Palmer's Best 54 Golf Holes, 1977; Arnold Palmer's Complete Book of Putting, 1986; Play Great Golf, 1987; Arnold Palmer, A Personal Journey, 1994; A Golfer's Life, 1999; Playing by the Rules, 2002; Memories, Stories and Memorabilia, 2004. *Recreations:* aviation (speed record for flying round world in twin-engine jet, 1976), bridge, hunting, fishing. *Address:* PO Box 52, Youngstown, PA 15696, USA. *T:* (724) 5377751. *Clubs:* (Owner and Pres.) Latrobe Country; (Pres. and Part-Owner) Bay Hill (Orlando, Fla); (Tournament Professional) Laurel Valley Golf; (Part-Owner) Pebble Beach Co.; (Hon. Life Mem., 1992–) Carnoustie Golf; numerous other country, city, golf.

PALMER, Bernard Harold Michael, OBE 1989; MA; Editor of the Church Times, 1968–89; *b* 8 Sept. 1929; *e s* of late Christopher Harold Palmer; *m* 1954, Jane Margaret (*d* 2006), *d* of late E. L. Skinner; one *s* one *d*. *Educ:* St Edmund's School, Hindhead; Eton (King's Scholar); King's College, Cambridge. BA 1952; MA 1956. Member of editorial staff, Church Times, 1952–89; Managing Director, 1957–89; Editor-in-Chief, 1960–68; Chm., 1962–89. DLitt Lambeth, 1988. *Publications:* Gadfly for God: a history of the Church Times, 1991; High and Mitred: a study of prime ministers as bishop-makers, 1992; Reverend Rebels: five Victorian clerics and their fight against authority, 1993; Men of Habit: the Franciscan ideal in action, 1994; A Class of Their Own: six public-school headmasters who became Archbishop of Canterbury, 1997; Imperial Vineyard: the Anglican church in India under the Raj from the Mutiny to Partition, 1999; Willingly to School: a history of St Edmund's, Hindhead, 2000; Serving Two Masters: parish patronage in the Church of England since 1714, 2003; Blue Blood on the Trail: Lord Peter Wimsey and his circle, 2005; Richard Palmer: a life in letters, 2006; Service with a Smile: a memoir of Jane Palmer, 2007; Christopher Palmer: a life in letters, 2011; Pilgrim's Progress: a self-portrait, 2013. *Recreations:* cycling, penmanship. *Address:* 151 Rickstones Road, Witham, Essex CM8 2PQ. *T:* (01376) 517577.

PALMER, Caroline Ann, (Cally), CBE 2006; Chief Executive, Royal Marsden NHS Foundation Trust (formerly NHS Trust), since 1998; *d* of Christopher and Ann Palmer; *m* 2004, Phil Yeates; two *s* one *d* by a previous marriage. *Educ:* Woking Girls Grammar Sch.; Westfield Coll., London Univ. (BA 1979); London Business Sch. (MSc 1995). MHSM, DipHSM 1983. Gen. mgt trng scheme, 1980–83; Asst Unit Adminr, St Luke's Hosp., 1983–85; Royal Free Hospital, subseq. Royal Free Hampstead NHS Trust: Associate Unit Adminr, 1985–87; Dep. Manager, 1987–90; Gen. Manager, 1990–94; Dep. CEO, 1994–98. *Recreations:* history of art, ballet. *Address:* Royal Marsden NHS Trust, Fulham Road, SW3 6JJ.

PALMER, Sir (Charles) Mark, 5th Bt *cr* 1886; *b* 21 Nov. 1941; *s* of Sir Anthony Frederick Mark Palmer, 4th Bt, and Henriette Alice (later Lady Abel Smith, DCVO); *S* father, 1941; *m* 1976, Hon. Catherine Elizabeth Tennant, *y d* of 2nd Baron Glenconner; one *s* one *d*. *Heir: s* Arthur Morris Palmer, *b* 9 March 1981. *Address:* Mill Hill Farm, Sherborne, Northleach, Glos GL54 3DU. *T:* (01451) 844395.

PALMER, Cdre Christopher Laurence, CBE 2010; RN; Chief Executive, Corporation of the Church House, since 2010; Gentleman Usher to the Queen, since 2011; *b* Mablethorpe, 5 April 1954; *s* of Flt Lt Laurence George Palmer, DFC, RAF and Sheila Palmer (*née* Dingle); *m* 1979, Janet Elizabeth Hughes; one *s* one *d*. *Educ:* King Edward VI Sch.; Sudbury Grammar Sch.; Univ. of Southampton (BSc Hons 1975); BRNC. Qualified Helicopter Observer, 1977; 820 Sqn, HMS Blake, 1978; 819 Sqn, HMS Gannet, 1978–80; 815 Sqn, HMS Arrow, Falklands, 1980–82 (mentioned in despatches, 1982); 702 Sqn, HMS Osprey, 1982–84; Flying Instructor to Prince Andrew, 1983–84; HMS Battleaxe, 1984–85; RNSC, 1985; HMS Southampton, 1986–87; HMS Cumberland, 1988–90; CO 702 Sqn, 1990–91; XO HMS Fearless, 1991–93; MoD, 1993–95; Comdr BRNC, 1995–98; MoD, 1998–2002; Fleet HQ, 2002–05; CO RNAS Yeovilton, 2005–09. Trustee, Fleet Air Arm Meml Ch, 2012–. Liveryman, Hon. Co. of Air Pilots (formerly GAPAN), 2006. FCMI 2007; FRAeS 2010. *Recreations:* sailing, powerboats, motorcycling, flying, theatre, saxophone. *Address:* c/o Corporation of the Church House, 27 Great Smith Street, SW1P 3AZ. *T:* (020) 7898 1310. *E:* chris.palmer@churchofengland.org. *Clubs:* Naval and Military, Fleet Air Arm Squadron; Emsworth Sailing.

PALMER, David Erroll Prior, CBE 2003; Chairman, UK Hydrographic Office, 2005–09; *b* 20 Feb. 1941; *s* of Sir Otho Prior-Palmer, DSO, and Sheila Peers (*née* Weller-Poley), OBE; *m* 1974, Elizabeth Helen Young; two *s* one *d*. *Educ:* Eton; Christ Church, Oxford (MA PPE). Joined Financial Times, 1964: New York Correspondent, 1967; Management Editor, 1970; News Editor, 1972; Foreign Editor, 1979; Dep. Editor, 1981; Gen. Manager and Dir, 1983; Dep. Chief Exec., 1989; Chief Exec., 1990–93; Independent Newspapers (Ireland): Man. Dir, 1994–98; Chm., 1999–2002; Chairman: South-West Sussex Radio, 1995–2004; Dedalo Grupo Gráfico, 2004–06; ToxiMet, 2010–; Dir, Polestar Gp, 2003–06. Chm., Barts and E London Healthcare Merger Project, 2010–11. Dir, The Mary Rose Trust, 2004–. First British finisher, seventh over-all, Observer Singlehanded Transatlantic Race, 1976; Nat. Dragon Champion, Edinburgh Cup, 2007. *Publications:* The Atlantic Challenge, 1977. *Recreations:* sailing, travelling. *Address:* Dairy Cottage, Hunters Race, Chichester, W Sussex PO19 3BZ. *Clubs:* Garrick; Royal Yacht Squadron (Cowes); Itchenor Sailing (near Chichester); Royal St George Yacht (Dublin).

PALMER, David Vereker; DL; Chairman, 1982–88, and Chief Executive, 1978–88, Willis Faber plc; Chairman, Syndicate Capital Trust plc, 1993–96; *b* 9 Dec. 1926; *s* of late Brig. Julian W. Palmer and Lena Elizabeth (*née* Vereker); *m* 1950, Mildred Elaine O'Neal; three *d*. *Educ:* Stowe. ACII 1950. Commnd The Life Guards, 1944; served as regular officer in Europe and ME, 1944–49; joined Edward Lumley & Sons, 1949; Manager, New York office, 1953–59; joined Willis, Faber & Dumas Ltd, 1959; Dir, 1961. Mem. Lloyd's, 1953. Chm., British Insurance & Investment Brokers Assoc., 1987–90 (Dep. Chm., 1984–87); Pres., Insurance Inst. of London, 1985–86. Commissioner, Royal Hosp. Chelsea, 1982–88. Mem. Council, St George's House, Windsor, 2000–04. Pres., Henley and Dist Agricl Assoc., 2006. Trustee, Tower Hill Improvement Trust, 1978–2007. Master, Worshipful Co. of Insurers, 1982. High Sheriff, Bucks, 1993–94, DL Bucks, 1995. *Recreations:* farming, shooting. *Address:* Burrow Farm, Hambleden, near Henley-on-Thames, Oxon RG9 6LT. *T:* (01491) 571256. *Clubs:* City of London, Cavalry and Guards.

PALMER, Dame Felicity (Joan), DBE 2011 (CBE 1993); mezzo-soprano. *Educ:* Erith Grammar Sch.; Guildhall Sch. of Music and Drama. AGSM (Teacher/Performer), FGS. Kathleen Ferrier Meml Prize, 1970; major appearances at concerts in Britain, America, Belgium, France, Germany, Italy, Russia and Spain, firstly as soprano and then as mezzo-soprano; début as soprano, Dido in Dido and Aeneas, Kent Opera, 1972; début in USA, Marriage of Figaro, Houston, 1973; soprano roles included: Pamina in The Magic Flute, ENO, 1975; Cleopatra in Julius Caesar, Herrenhausen Hanover, and Frankfurt Opera, 1978; title role, Alcina, Bern Opera, 1978; Elektra in Idomeneo, Zurich Opera, 1980; the Countess in The Marriage of Figaro, ENO; Elvira in Don Giovanni, Scottish Opera and ENO; Marguerite in Damnation of Faust, ENO; mezzo-soprano roles include: ENO: Tristan und Isolde, 1981; Rienzi, 1983; Mazeppa, 1984; Herodias in Salome, and The Witch in Hansel and Gretel, 1987; Orfeo, Opera North, 1984; King Priam, Royal Opera, 1985; Albert Herring, Glyndebourne, 1985; Tamburlaine, Opera North, 1985; Katya Kabanova, Chicago Lyric Opera, 1986; début at La Scala, Milan, as Marguerita in world première of Riccardo III by Flavio Testi, 1987; Last Night of the Proms, 1987; début, Netherlands Opera, as Kabanicha in Katya Kabanova, 1988, same role, Glyndebourne, 1988; Mistress Quickly in Falstaff, 1988 and 1990, Marcellina in The Marriage of Figaro, 1989, Glyndebourne; world première of Tippett's New Year, Houston, USA, 1989; The Marriage of Figaro and The Gambler (Prokofiev), Chicago, 1991; Klytemnestra in Elektra, WNO, 1992, La Scala, Milan and Japan, 1995, Royal Opera, 1997, Netherlands Opera, 2006; Orlando, Aix-en-Provence, 1993; Dialogue des Carmélites, Geneva, 1993, Metropolitan, NY, 2002; La Fille du Régiment, San Francisco, 1993, Royal Opera, 2007; Ariodante, WNO, 1994; The Rake's Progress, Chicago, 1994; Ballo in Maschera, Catania, 1995; Countess in The Queen of Spades, Glyndebourne, 1995, ENO, 2015; Juno/Ino in Semele, Royal Opera, 1996; Mahagonny, Paris, 1997, Chicago, 1998; Fricka in The Ring, Munich, 1997 and 1999, Canaries, 1999, Met. Opera House, NY, 2000; Sweeney Todd, Royal Opera, 2003; The Yeomen of the Guard, Royal Albert Hall, 2012; Peter Grimes, ENO, 2014; recitals in Amsterdam, Paris, Vienna, 1976–77, Tokyo, 1991; concert tours with BBC SO, Europe, 1973, 1977 and 1984, Australasia, Far East and Eastern Europe, 1977–; ABC tour of Australia, 1978. Recordings include: Poèmes pour Mi, with Pierre Boulez; Holst Choral Symphony, with Sir Adrian Boult; title role in Gluck's Armide; Elektra in Idomeneo, with Nikolaus Harnoncourt; Klytemnestra in Elektra, with Semyon Bychkov, Christoph von Dohnányi, James Levine and Valery Gergiev; The Music Makers; Sea Pictures; Britten's Phaedra; recitals, with John Constable, of songs by Poulenc, Ravel and Fauré, and of Victorian ballads. *Address:* c/o Intermusica, Crystal Wharf, 36 Graham Street, N1 8GJ.

PALMER, Prof. Frank Robert, FBA 1975; Professor and Head of Department of Linguistic Science, University of Reading, 1965–87; *b* 9 April 1922; *s* of George Samuel Palmer and Gertrude Lilian (*née* Newman); *m* 1948, Jean Elisabeth Moore; three *s* two *d*. *Educ:* Bristol Grammar Sch.; New Coll., Oxford (Ella Stephens Schol., State Schol.) 1942–43 and 1945–48; Merton Coll., Oxford (Harmsworth Sen. Schol.) 1948–49; MA Oxon 1948; Craven Fellow, 1948. Served war, E Africa, 1943–45. Lectr in Linguistics, Sch. of Oriental and African Studies, Univ. of London, 1950–60 (study leave in Ethiopia, 1952–53); Prof. of Linguistics, University Coll. of N Wales, Bangor, 1960–65; Dean of Faculty of Letters and Social Sciences, Univ. of Reading, 1969–72. Linguistic Soc. of America Prof., Buffalo, 1971; Distinguished Visiting Professor: Foreign Languages Inst., Beijing, 1981; Univ. of Delaware, 1983. Professional visits to Canada, USA, Mexico, Venezuela, Peru, Chile, Argentina, Uruguay, Brazil, India, Japan, China, Indonesia, Morocco, Tunisia, Uganda, Kuwait and most countries of Europe. MAE 1991. Hon. DLitt Reading, 1996. *Publications:* The Morphology of the Tigre Noun, 1962; A Linguistic Study of the English Verb, 1965; (ed) Selected Papers of J. R. Firth, 1968; (ed) Prosodic Analysis, 1970; Grammar, 1971, 2nd edn 1984; The English Verb, 1974, 2nd edn 1987; Semantics, 1976, 2nd edn 1981; Modality and the English Modals, 1979, 2nd edn 1990; Mood and Modality, 1986, 2nd edn 2001; (ed jtly) Studies in the History of Western Linguistics, 1986; Grammatical Roles and Relations, 1994; (ed) Grammar and Meaning, 1995; (ed jtly) Modality in Contemporary English, 2003; (ed jtly) English Modality in Perspective: genre analysis and cultural studies, 2004; articles and reviews on Ethiopian langs, English and linguistic theory, in learned jls. *Recreations:* gardening, crosswords. *Address:* Whitethorns, Roundabout Lane, Winnersh, Wokingham, Berks RG41 5AD. *T:* (0118) 978 6214.

PALMER, Sir Geoff; *see* Palmer, Sir G. H. O.

PALMER, Geoffrey, OBE 2005; actor; *b* 4 June 1927; *m* 1963, Sally Green; one *s* one *d*. *Educ:* Highgate Sch. *Theatre* includes: Difference of Opinion, Garrick; West of Suez, Royal Court, 1971; Private Lives, Globe, 1973; Eden End, NT, 1974; St Joan, Old Vic, 1977; Tishoo, Wyndham's, 1979; Kafka's Dick, Royal Court, 1986; Piano, NT, 1990; *television* includes: The Fall and Rise of Reginald Perrin, 1976–78; Butterflies; The Last Song; Absurd Person Singular, 1984; Insurance Man, 1985; Fairly Secret Army, 1985; Seasons Greetings, 1986; As Time Goes By, 1992–2002; The Savages, 2001; He Knew He Was Right, 2004; Bert and Dickie, Parade's End, 2012; *films* include: O Lucky Man!, 1973; The Honorary Consul, 1982; A Zed and Two Noughts, 1985; Clockwise, 1986; A Fish Called Wanda, 1988; The Madness of King George, 1994; Mrs Brown, 1997; Tomorrow Never Dies, 1998; Anna and the King, 1999; Peter Pan, 2002; Piccadilly Jim, 2003; Pink Panther II, 2007; W. E., 2010.

PALMER, Sir Geoffrey (Christopher John), 12th Bt *cr* 1660; *b* 30 June 1936; *er s* of Lt-Col Sir Geoffrey Frederick Neill Palmer, 11th Bt, and Cicely Katherine (who *m* 1952, Robert W. B. Newton; she *d* 1989), *o d* of late Arthur Radmall, Clifton, nr Watford; *S* father, 1951; *m* 1957, Clarissa Mary, *er d* of Stephen Villiers-Smith, Knockholt, Kent; four *d*. *Educ:* Eton. Agent for Burberry, Norway, Sweden, Finland, 1971–94. *Recreations:* golf, crossword puzzles, shooting. *Heir: b* Jeremy Charles Palmer [*b* 16 May 1939; *m* 1968, Antonia (marr. diss. 2009), *d* of late Ashley Dutton; two *s*]. *Address:* Carlton Curlieu Hall, Leicestershire LE8 0PH. *T:* (0116) 259 2656. *Clubs:* MCC, I Zingari, Free Foresters, Eton Ramblers, Butterflies, Gentlemen of Leicestershire, Lincolnshire Gentlemen's Cricket, Derbyshire Friars, XL, Frogs, Old Etonian Golfing Society, Old Etonian Racquets and Tennis, Northants Amateurs' CC.

PALMER, Rt Hon. Sir Geoffrey (Winston Russell), AC 1991; KCMG 1991; PC 1986; QC (NZ) (SC 2008); barrister; Professor of Law, Victoria University of Wellington, New Zealand, 1974–79 and 1991–94, Distinguished Fellow, Faculty of Law, since 2010; *b* 21 April 1942; *s* of Leonard Russell and Jessie Patricia Palmer; *m* 1963, Margaret Eleanor Hinchcliff; one *s* one *d*. *Educ:* Nelson Coll.; Victoria Univ. of Wellington (BA; LLB); Univ. of Chicago (JD). Barrister and Solicitor, High Court of New Zealand. Prof. of Law, Univ. of Iowa, 1969–73, and 1991–95. Vis. Professor of Law, Univ. of Virginia, 1972–73. MP (Lab) Christchurch Central, NZ, 1979–90; Dep. Prime Minister, 1984–89; Attorney-Gen., 1984–89; Minister of Justice, 1984–89; Minister for the Environment, 1987–90; Prime Minister, 1989–90. Partner, Chen Palmer & Partners (formerly Chen & Palmer), barristers and solicitors, Wellington, 1995–2004; Pres., Law Commn, NZ, 2005–10; Chm., UN Sec. Gen.'s Panel on Gaza flotilla incident, 2010–11. *Publications:* Unbridled Power?—an interpretation of New Zealand's constitution and government, 1979, 2nd edn 1987; Compensation for

Incapacity—a study of law and social change in Australia and New Zealand, 1979; Environmental Politics—a greenprint for New Zealand, 1990; New Zealand's Constitution in Crisis, 1992; Environment—the international challenge, 1995; Bridled Power, 1997, 4th edn 2004; Constitutional Conversations, 2002; (with J. Carlson and B. Weston) International Environmental Law and World Order, 3rd edn 2012; Reform: a memoir, 2013. *Recreations:* cricket, golf, playing the trumpet. *Address:* 63 Roxburgh Street, Mount Victoria, Wellington, New Zealand. *T:* (4) 8015185; Harbour Chambers, 111 The Terrace, Wellington, New Zealand.

PALMER, Sir Godfrey Henry Oliver, (Sir Geoff), Kt 2014; OBE 2003; PhD, DSc; Professor of Biological Sciences, Heriot-Watt University, 1992–2005, now Emeritus; *b* St Elizabeth, Jamaica, 9 April 1940; *s* of Aubrey and Ivy Georgina Palmer; *m* 1969, Margaret Anne Wood; one *s* two *d. Educ:* North Street and Kingston Sen. Schs, Jamaica; Shelbourne Secondary Modern Sch., London; Highbury Co. Sch., London; Leicester Univ. (BSc); Univ. of Edinburgh (PhD 1968); Heriot-Watt Univ. (DSc 1985). Jun. lab. technician, Queen Elizabeth Coll., London, 1958–61; Sen. Scientist, Brewing Res. Foundn, 1968–77; Lectr, then Sen. Lectr, 1977–88, Reader, 1988–92, Heriot-Watt Univ. Hon. President: Edinburgh and Lothians Regl Equality Council, 1977; Assoc. of Jamaicans, Birmingham, 2003. Hon DSc: Abertay, 2009; Open, 2010; Heriot-Watt, 2015. *Publications:* Cereal Science and Technology, 1989; Mr White and the Ravens (novel), 2005; The Enlightenment Abolished (novel), 2007. *Recreations:* community service, Scottish-Caribbean history, TV, reading, sports. *Address:* 23 Waulkmill Drive, Penicuick, Midlothian EH26 8LA. *T:* (01968) 675148, 07906 178073.

PALMER, His Honour Henry; *see* Palmer, His Honour R. H. S.

PALMER, Horace Anthony, (Tony); Chairman, Meyer International, 1997–99 (Director, 1995–99); *b* 20 Feb. 1937; *s* of Horace Charles and Violet Victoria Palmer; *m* 1961, Beryl Eileen Freakley; two *d. Educ:* Pinner County Grammar School; Hammersmith Sch. of Building. FRICS; FCIOB. Trainee Quantity Surveyor, 1954; joined Taylor Woodrow, 1954; Contracts Manager, 1970; Subsidiary Dir, 1974; Subsidiary Man. Dir, 1987; Man. Dir, 1989; Chief Exec., 1990–97. Chairman: High Point Rendel Gp plc, 1997–2003; Monacon Hldgs Ltd, 1997–2001; Parker Plant Ltd, 1997–2001; Pilkington Tiles, 1998; Galliford, subseq. Galliford Try, 1999–2005; non-exec. Dir, Berkeley Gp, 1997–2007. *Recreations:* sports, reading biography.

PALMER, Howard William Arthur; QC 1999; a Recorder, since 2006; *b* 24 June 1954; *s* of William Alexander Palmer, CBE, DL and Cherry Anne Palmer (*née* Gibbs); *m* 1983, Catherine Margaret Jackson; one *s* three *d. Educ:* Eton Coll.; University Coll., Oxford (MA Juris). Called to the Bar, Inner Temple, 1977; Lectr, KCL, 1977–78; barrister in private practice, 1978–. Mem. Council, Univ. of Reading, 2008–. *Recreations:* cricket, golf, fieldsports, theatre, hedgelaying, enjoying the countryside. *Address:* 2 Temple Gardens, EC4Y 9AY. *T:* (020) 7822 1200. *Clubs:* MCC; Berkshire County Cricket.

PALMER, James Edwin; Senior Partner, Herbert Smith Freehills LLP, since 2015; *b* 10 Sept. 1963; *s* of late Malcolm John Frederick Palmer and of Rachel Mary Palmer; *m* 1990, Nicola Jane Lister White; three *s. Educ:* Winchester Coll.; Queens' Coll., Cambridge (BA 1985). Herbert Smith, later Herbert Smith Freehills: joined, 1986; admitted solicitor, 1988; Partner, 1994–; Mem., Partnership Council, 2002–06; Global Head: Equity Capital Mkts, 2005–10; Corporate, 2010–12. Chairman: Company Law Sub-Cttee, City of London Law Soc., 2002–06; Law Soc./City of London Law Soc. Takeovers Jt Wkg Party, 2002–; Mem., Listing Authority Adv. Cttee, FSA, 2008–13 (Chm., 2012–13); Chm., Listing Authority Adv. Panel, 2013–, Mem., Mkts Practitioner Panel, 2013–, Financial Conduct Authy. *Publications:* (contrib.) Butterworths Takeovers: law and practice, 2005, 2nd edn (ed jtly), 2014; (contrib.) Hannigan and Prentice: the Companies Act 2006—a commentary, 2007; (contrib.) Buckley on the Companies Acts, 2007–11. *Recreations:* fly fishing, reading. *Address:* Herbert Smith Freehills LLP, Exchange House, Primrose Street, EC2A 2EG. *T:* (020) 7374 8000. *E:* james.palmer@hsf.com.

PALMER, John, CB 1986; Chairman, European Passenger Services, British Rail, 1990–94; *b* 13 Nov. 1928; 2nd *s* of late William Nathaniel Palmer and Grace Dorothy May Palmer (*née* Procter); *m* 1958, Lyliane Marthe Jeanjean; two *d. Educ:* Heath Grammar Sch., Halifax; The Queen's Coll., Oxford (Lit.Hum.) (MA). Entered Min. of Housing and Local Govt, 1952; Cabinet Office, 1963–65; Asst Sec., 1965; Under Secretary: DoE, 1971; Dept of Transport, 1976–82; Dep. Sec., Dept of Transport, 1982–89. Liveryman, Carmen's Co., 1987 (Freeman, 2014). *Address:* 72 College Road, SE21 7LY. *Club:* Oxford and Cambridge.

PALMER, Sir John (Edward Somerset), 8th Bt *cr* 1791; retired; Director, W. S. Atkins Agriculture, 1979–88; *b* 27 Oct. 1926; *e s* of Sir John A. Palmer, 7th Bt; *S* father, 1963; *m* 1956, Dione Catharine Skinner; one *s* one *d. Educ:* Canford School; Cambridge Univ. (MA); Durham Univ. (MSc). Colonial Service, Northern Nigeria, 1952–61. R. A. Lister & Co. Ltd, Dursley, Glos, 1962–63; Min. Overseas Develt, 1964–68. *Recreations:* fishing, sailing. *Heir: s* Robert John Hudson Palmer [*b* 20 Dec. 1960; *m* 1990, Lucinda Margaret Barker; one *s* one *d*]. *Address:* Court Barton, Feniton, Honiton, Devon EX14 3BD. *T:* (01404) 851020.

PALMER, Maj.-Gen. Sir (Joseph) Michael, KCVO 1985; Defence Services Secretary, 1982–85; *b* 17 Oct. 1928; *s* of late Lt-Col William Robert Palmer, DSO, and late Joan Audrey Palmer (*née* Smith); *m* 1953, Jillean Monica Sherston; two *s* one *d. Educ:* Wellington College. Commissioned 14th/20th King's Hussars, 1948; Adjutant 14th/20th King's Hussars, 1953–55; Adjutant Duke of Lancaster's Own Yeomanry, 1956–59; psc 1960; jssc 1965; CO 14th/20th King's Hussars, 1969–72; Comdr RAC 1st (BR) Corps, 1974–76; Asst Chief of Staff, Allied Forces Central Europe, 1976–78; Director, Royal Armoured Corps, 1978–81. Col, 14th/20th King's Hussars, 1981–92; Hon. Col, Duke of Lancaster's Own Yeomanry, 1988–92. Chm., Copley Marshall & Co. Ltd, 1980–2004. Director: Alexanders, Laing & Cruickshank Service Co., 1986–89; Credit Lyonnais Construction Co., 1988–90. Chm. of Governors, Sandroyd Sch., 1984–99. Liveryman, Salters' Co., 1965 (Master, 1989–90). FCMI. *Recreations:* riding, shooting, music, reading. *Club:* Cavalry and Guards.

See also A. S. Palmer.

PALMER, Judith Mary; Director, Poetry Society, since 2008; *b* Epping, 14 Dec. 1965; adopted *d* of Thomas William Palmer and Mary Elizabeth Palmer (*née* Charlier). *Educ:* Brigidine Convent, Windsor; Univ. of Bristol (BA Hons English 1986). Hd, Educn Dept, W&G Foyle Booksellers, 1986–87; Mktg Asst, Macmillan Press, 1987–88; Publicity Officer, A & C Black Publishers, 1988–90; Publicity Manager, The Women's Press, 1990–91; freelance arts producer, newspaper feature writer and radio broadcaster, 1991–2008; Sen. Res. Fellow, Manchester Metropolitan Univ., 2006–07; Public Prog. Manager, The Women's Liby, London Metropolitan Univ., 2007–08. Judge, Commonwealth Writers Prize, 2002. Trustee: Poetry Soc., 1998–2001 (Chair); Poetry Sch., 2002–05 (Chair); Keats Foundn, 2010–. *Publications:* Private Views: artists working today, 2004; contributor: Oxford Companion to English Literature, 1999; Zero Gravity: a cultural user's guide, 2005; A Record of Fear, 2006; Sitting Room, 2006; Earth, Air, Sky and Water, 2006; Andrew Bracey, 2007; Lorna Graves, 2008; contribs to exhibn catalogues and jls. *Recreations:* botany, pataphysics, art, long walks. *Address:* The Poetry Society, 22 Betterton Street, WC2H 9BX. *T:* (020) 7420 9880. *E:* info@poetrysociety.org.uk.

PALMER, Keith Francis, OBE 2010; Chairman: InfraCo, since 2004; AgDevCo, since 2009; *b* Cardiff, 27 July 1947; *s* of Frank Palmer and Gwenda Palmer; *m* 1974, Penny McDonagh; four *d. Educ:* Howardian High Sch., Cardiff; Univ. of Birmingham (BSc Hons 1st Cl. 1968; PhD 1971); Churchill Coll., Cambridge (Dip. Develt Econs 1974). Asst Sec., Finance Ministry, PNG, 1974–78; Economist, Fiscal Affairs Dept, IMF, 1978–79; Sen. Economist, Energy Dept, World Bank, 1979–84; N. M. Rothschild & Sons Ltd, 1984–2008: Dir, 1987; Man. Dir, 1992; Co-Chief Exec., 1997–98; Exec. Vice-Chm., 1998–2002; non-exec. Vice-Chm., 2002–08. Non-exec. Chm., Emerging Africa Infrastructure Fund, 2002–07. *Recreations:* classical music, geology.

PALMER, Prof. Marilyn, MBE 2015; PhD; FSA 1991; Professor of Industrial Archaeology, Leicester University, 2000–08, now Emeritus; *b* 30 April 1943; *d* of Joseph Henry Allum and Mary Winifred Allum; *m* 1965, David Palmer (marr. diss. 1991). *Educ:* St Anne's Coll., Oxford (BA Hons Modern History 1965; MA 1969); Leicester Univ. (PGCE (Distinction) 1966; Postgrad. Cert. in British Archaeol. (Distinction) 1973; PhD 1976). History Teacher, Loughborough High Sch., 1966–69; Lectr, 1969–72, Sen. Lectr, 1972–77, Loughborough Coll. of Educn; Loughborough University: Lectr, 1977–80; Sen. Lectr, 1980–83; Head, History Dept, 1983–88; Leicester University: Sen. Lectr in History, 1988–98; Reader in Industrial Archaeol., and Hd, Archaeol. Div., 1998–2000; Head, Sch. of Archaeol. and Ancient Hist., 2000–06; adult educn lectr on indust. archaeology, 1973–. Gilder Lehrman Fellow, Colonial Williamsburg Foundn, 2006; Vis. Fellow, All Souls Coll., Oxford, 2007; Leverhulme Emeritus Fellow, 2009–10. Vice Pres., HA, 1986–93; Mem., Royal Commn on Historical Monuments of England, 1993–99; National Trust: Member: Industrial Archaeology Adv. Gp, 1993–99 (Chm., 1999–2001); Archaeol. Panel, 2001–14; Midlands Regl Adv. Bd (formerly E Midlands Regl Cttee), 2008–14; Mem., Industrial Archaeol. Adv. Panel, English Heritage, 2001–14 (Mem., Ancient Monuments Adv. Cttee, 1999–2001); Chm., Assoc. for Indust. Archaeology, 2004–08 (Mem. Council, 1980–2004; Pres., 1986–89, 2010–); Council for British Archaeology: Vice-Pres., 2008–; Chm., E Midlands Region, 2012–. Chm., Charnwood Br., U3A, 2012–. Jt Editor, Industrial Archaeology Review, 1984–2002. *Publications:* (with P. A. Neaverson) Industrial Landscapes of the East Midlands, 1992; Industry in the Landscape, 1994; Industrial Archaeology: principles and practice, 1998; South-West Textile Industry: a social archaeology, 2005; (with David Gwyn) Understanding the Workplace: a research framework for industrial archaeology in Britain, 2005; (with P. S. Barnwell) Post-Medieval Landscapes: landscape history after Hoskins, 2007; (with A. J. Horning) Crossing Paths or Sharing Tracks: future directions in the archaeological study of post-1550 Britain and Ireland, 2007; (with Michael Nevell and Mark Sissons) Industrial Archaeology: a practical handbook, 2012; (with P. S. Barnwell) Country House Technology, 2012; articles in jls. *Recreations:* hill walking, travelling—and industrial archaeology! *Address:* School of Archaeology and Ancient History, University of Leicester, Leicester LE1 7RH. *T:* (0116) 252 2821.

PALMER, Sir Mark; *see* Palmer, Sir C. M.

PALMER, Martin Giles; Secretary General, Alliance of Religions and Conservation, since 1995; Director, International Consultancy on Religion, Education and Culture, since 1984; *b* Bristol, 14 Oct. 1953; *s* of Rev. Canon Derek George Palmer and Cecile June Palmer (*née* Goddard); *m* 1st, 1973, Sandra Ann Fischer (marr. diss.); one *s* one *d*; 2nd, 2006, Victoria Elisabeth Strathern Finlay. *Educ:* Hartcliffe Comprehensive Sch., Bristol; Commonweal Comprehensive Sch., Swindon; Selwyn Coll., Cambridge (BA 1976; MA 1979). Regl Sec., Christian Educn Movement, NW England, 1977–79; Chair, Hong Kong Res. Gp, 1977–84; Dir, Centre for Study of Religion and Educn in Inner City, 1979–84. Religious Advr to WWF Internat., 1988–95. Fellow, Club of Rome, 2012. *Publications:* Worlds of Difference, 1985; Faith and Nature, 1987; Tao Te Ching, 1993; Living Christianity, 1993; I Ching, 1995; Travels Through Sacred China, 1996; Chuang Tzu, 1996; Sacred Britain, 1997; Kuan Yin, 1998; The Jesus Sutras, 2001; The Times Atlas of World Religions, 2002; The Sacred History of Britain, 2002; Faith in Conservation, 2003; Religions of the World, 2005; The Atlas of Religion, 2007; Sacred Land, 2012; Shangsu: the most venerable book, 2014. *Recreations:* anything old, especially churches, temples, cities, coins and brasses, cooking, all things Chinese, moderately long walks. *Address:* Alliance of Religions and Conservation, 6 Gay Street, Bath BA1 2PH. *T:* (01225) 758004, *Fax:* (01225) 442962. *E:* Martinp@arcworld.org. *Clubs:* Babington House; Foreign Correspondents' (Hong Kong).

PALMER, Maj.-Gen. Sir Michael; *see* Palmer, Maj.-Gen. Sir J. M.

PALMER, Nicholas Douglas; Director, Policy: British Union for the Abolition of Vivisection, since 2011; Cruelty Free International, since 2011; *b* 5 Feb. 1950; *s* of late Reginald Palmer and Irina Palmer (*née* Markin); *m* 2000, Fiona Hunter. *Educ:* Copenhagen Univ. (MSc equivalent); Birkbeck Coll., London (PhD Maths 1975). Computer scientist: Ciba-Geigy, Switzerland, 1977–82 and 1985–97; MRC London, 1982–85. MP (Lab) Broxtowe, 1997–2010; contested (Lab) same seat, 2010, 2015. PPS to DEFRA Ministerial team, 2003–05, to Energy Minister, DTI, 2005–07, to Sci. Minister, DTI, 2007, to Minister for Energy, BERR, 2007–08. Member: European Scrutiny Select Cttee, 1998–99; NI Select Cttee, 1999–2001; HM Treasury Select Cttee, 2001–03; Justice Select Cttee, 2008–10. Contested (Lab): Chelsea, 1983; E Sussex and S Kent, EP elecn, 1994. Dir, Internat. and Corporate Affairs, British Union for Abolition of Vivisection, 2010. *Publications:* The Comprehensive Guide to Board Wargaming, 1973; The Best of Board Wargaming, 1980; Beyond the Arcade, 1985. *Recreation:* computer games. *E:* NickMP1@aol.com.

PALMER, Prof. Nigel Fenton, DPhil; FBA 1997; Professor of German Medieval and Linguistic Studies, University of Oxford, 1992–2012, now Emeritus; Professorial Fellow, St Edmund Hall, Oxford, 1992–2012, now Emeritus; *b* 28 Oct. 1946; *s* of James Terence Palmer and Constance May Palmer (*née* Fenton); *m* 1974, Susan Patricia Aldred; one *s* one *d. Educ:* Hyde County Grammar Sch.; Worcester Coll., Oxford (MA, DPhil). Lectr in German, Durham Univ., 1970–76; University of Oxford: Univ. Lectr in Medieval German, 1976–90; Reader in German, 1990–92; Fellow, Oriel Coll., 1976–92. Corresponding Fellow: Medieval Acad. of America, 2008; Akademie der Wissenschaften zu Göttingen, 2010. Fellow, 1982, Humboldt Res. Prize, 2007, Alexander von Humboldt Foundn. *Publications:* Visio Tnugdali, 1976; Tondolus der Ritter, 1980; (with K. Speckenbach) Träume und Kräuter, 1990; Die Blockbücher der Berlin-Breslauer Sammelbandes, 1992; German Literary Culture in the Twelfth and Thirteenth Centuries, 1993; Zisterzienser und ihre Bücher, 1998; Bibelübersetzung und Heilsgeschichte, 2007. *Address:* St Edmund Hall, Oxford OX1 4AR. *T:* (01865) 510487.

PALMER, Prof. Norman Ernest, CBE 2006; barrister; Professor of the Law of Art and Cultural Property, University College London, 2001–04, now Emeritus; Visiting Professor of Law, King's College London, since 2005; Adjunct Professor of Law, University of Tasmania, since 2008; President, Foundation for International Cultural Diplomacy, 2006–11; *b* 16 Aug. 1948; *s* of Norman George Palmer and Muriel (*née* Walker); *m* 1970, Judith Ann Weeks (marr. diss.); one *d*; *m* 1994, Ruth Redmond-Cooper; one *d. Educ:* Palmer's Endowed Sch., Grays Thurrock; Magdalen Coll., Oxford (BA Jurisp. 1969; BCL 1971; MA 1974). Called to the Bar, Gray's Inn, 1973; Head of Chambers, 1992–99. Lectr and Sen. Lectr in Law, Univs of Liverpool, Tasmania and Manchester, 1971–81; Professor of Law: Univ. of Reading, 1981–84 (Head of Dept, 1982–84); Univ. of Essex, 1984–90 (Dean of Faculty, 1985–88); Prof. of English Law, Univ. of Southampton, 1990–91 (Dep. Dean of Faculty); Rowe & Maw Prof. of Commercial Law, subseq. Prof. of Commercial Law, UCL, 1991–2001. Standing Internat. Counsel, Nat. Gallery of Australia, 2001–. Sec. and a Dir, Internat. Cultural Property Soc., 1990–95 (Editor, Jl, 1991–95). Chairman: Treasure Valuation (formerly Treasure Trove Reviewing) Cttee, 2001–11 (Mem., 1996–); Ministerial Adv. Panel on Illicit Trade in

Cultural Objects, 2000–05; Wkg Gp on Human Remains in Mus. Collections, 2001–03. Member: Standing Conf. for Portable Antiquities, 1995–; Spoliation Adv. Panel, 2000–10 (Expert Advr to Panel, 2011–); Legal Sub-Cttee, Quinquennial Rev. of Reviewing Cttee on Export of Works of Art, 2001–04. Principal Academic Advr, Inst. of Art and Law, 1996–. Editor, Art, Antiquity and Law, 1996–. Hon. QC 2010. Dr *hc* Geneva, 2005. *Publications:* (ed with E. L. G. Tyler) Crossley Vaines on Personal Property, 5th edn, 1973; Bailment, 1979, 3rd edn 2009; (ed jtly) Emden's Construction Law, 1990; (with C. J. Miller) Business Law, 1992; (ed jtly) Interests in Goods, 1993, 2nd edn 1998; (with E. McKendrick) Product Liability in the Construction Industry, 1993; Art Loans, 1997; The Recovery of Stolen Art, 1998; Museums and the Holocaust, 2000; (ed jtly) Cultural Heritage Statutes, 2nd edn, 2007; Halsbury's Laws of England, 4th edn and re-issue: (ed jtly) Titles on Tort; (ed with A. Powell) Bailment; (ed with W. J. Swadling) Carriers; (ed with A. H. Hudson) Confidence and Data Protection; (ed with N. Bamforth et al) Libraries and Other Scientific and Cultural Institutions; (ed jtly) Lien; (ed jtly) Damages. *Recreations:* literature, biography, travel, antique motor cars, collecting memorial verse. *Address:* 3 Stone Buildings, Lincoln's Inn, WC2A 3XL. *T:* (020) 7242 4937.

PALMER, Penelope Jane; *see* Dash, P. J.

PALMER, Sir Reginald (Oswald), GCMG 1992; MBE 1973; Governor General, Grenada, 1992–96; *b* 15 Feb. 1923; *m* 1954, Judith Juliana Parke; two *s* five *d. Educ:* St George's RC Boys' Sch.; Govt Teachers' Trng Coll., Trinidad; Univ. of Birmingham (CertEd); Univ. of Calgary (BEd 1971). Pupil Teacher, 1939–41; pupil teacher scholarship, 1941; Asst Teacher, 1945–56; Headteacher, 1956–68; Tutor, Grenada Teachers' Coll., 1968–72; Asst Educn Officer, 1972–73; Principal, Grenada Teachers' Coll., 1973–74; Chief Educn Officer, 1974–80, retd. Manager, Grenada Teachers' Sch. Supplies Ltd, 1980–87; Pres., Grenada Employers' Fedn, 1987–89. Dir, Grenada Bank of Commerce, 1990–92. Foundn Mem., Grenada Teachers' Social Security and Welfare Assoc. (Sec. 1951–69); Pres., Grenada Union of Teachers, 1962–63. Member: Public Service Commn, 1983–87; Local Adv. Council, Sch. of Continuing Educn, 1978–98 (Pres. 1989–98). Chm., Grenada Drug Avoidance Cttee, 1988–92. Dir, Richmond Fellowship of Grenada, 1991–92. *Recreations:* reading, backyard gardening, walking, sea-bathing. *Address:* Mount Parnassus, PO Box 884, St George's, Grenada, West Indies.

PALMER, Richard William, CBE 2006 (OBE 1987); Executive Vice President, British Olympic Association, since 1997; *b* 13 April 1933; *s* of late Richard Victor Palmer and Mary Ellen Palmer (*née* Sambrook). *Educ:* Haverfordwest Grammar Sch.; Trinity Coll., Carmarthen; The College, Chester (Dip PE); Univ. of Leicester (MEd). Head, PE Dept, Windsor Grammar Sch., 1961–64; Sec., UAU, 1964–69; Gen. Sec., British Univs Sports Fedn, 1969–74; Dep. Sec. Gen., 1975–77, Sec. Gen., 1977–97, British Olympic Assoc. Vice Pres., European Olympic Cttees, 1993–97; Pres., British Inst. of Sports Administrators, 1997–2003; Chm., Confedn of British Sport, 1998–99; Mem., Sports Council of Wales, 2005–12. Gen. Sec., Commonwealth Games Council for England, 1977–86; Dep. Chef de Mission, GB, 1976, Chef de Mission, GB, 1980, 1984, 1988, 1992, 1996, Olympic Games and Olympic Winter Games; Gen. Team Manager, England, Commonwealth Games, 1978, 1982, 1986. Technical Dir, London's 2012 Olympic Bid, 2004–05; Internat. Advr, Glasgow's 2014 Commonwealth Games Bid, 2006–07. Dir, Sports Coach UK, 1998–2012. FRSA 1998. Freeman of Pembroke, 1990. Prix de Merit, Assoc. of Nat. Olympic Cttees, 1990; J. L. Manning Award, Sports Writers' Assoc., 1996; Olympic Order, IOC, 1998; Emlyn Jones Award, British Inst. of Sports Admin, 2003. *Recreations:* golf, sailing, Rugby Union, gardening, fishing. *Address:* British Olympic Association, 60 Charlotte Street, W1T 2NU. *T:* (020) 7842 5700. *Clubs:* Scribes, East India; Cardiff County; Haverfordwest and Fulwell Golf; Llangwm Boat.

PALMER, His Honour (Robert) Henry (Stephen); a Circuit Judge, 1978–93; *b* 13 Nov. 1927; *s* of Henry Alleyn Palmer and Maud (*née* Obbard); *m* 1955, Geraldine Elizabeth Anne Evens; one *s* two *d. Educ:* Charterhouse; University Coll., Oxford. Called to the Bar, 1950. Dep. Chm., Berks QS, 1970. A Recorder of the Crown Court, 1972–78. Resident Judge: Acton Crown Court, 1987–91; Harrow Crown Court, 1991–93; Pres., 1983–98, S Thames Regl Chm., 1993–99, Mental Health Rev. Tribunal. Dir of Appeals, Specialist Trng Authy, Med. Royal Colls, 1997–99. *Publications:* Harris's Criminal Law, 1960; Guide to Divorce, 1965. *Recreation:* self-sufficiency.

PALMER, Roy Newberry; HM Coroner, 2001–14, Assistant Coroner, 2014, Greater London (South District); Assistant Coroner (formerly Deputy Coroner), City of London, since 2002; Assistant Coroner (formerly Assistant Deputy Coroner), Greater London (Inner South District), since 1999; *b* Peterborough, 2 Aug. 1944; *s* of late George Joseph Palmer and Muriel Joyce Palmer (*née* Clarke); *m* 1967, Dr Celia Mountford; two *d. Educ:* St George's Coll., Salisbury, Southern Rhodesia; Mt St Mary's Coll., Spinkhill, Derbys; London Hosp. Med. Coll., Univ. of London (MB BS 1968); LLB London 1974. MRCS 1967; LRCP 1968; DObstRCOG 1970; FFFLM 2005. Called to the Bar, Middle Temple, 1977. GP, Sawbridgeworth, Herts, 1970–73; Medical Protection Society: Asst Sec., 1973–85; Dep. Sec., 1985–89; Sec. and Med. Dir, 1989–98; Dep. Coroner, Gtr London (W Dist), 2000–01. Vis. Sen. Res. Fellow, Sch. of Law (Centre of Med. Law and Ethics), 1999–2002. Gov., Expert Witness Inst., 2000–06 (Chm., Professional Bodies Adv. Gp, 1999–2006). President: Medico-Legal Soc., 2000–02; Sect. of Clin. Forensic and Legal Medicine, RSocMed, 2001–03; SE England Coroners' Soc., 2004–05 (Vice-Pres., 2003–04); British Acad. of Forensic Scis, 2009–11 (Mem., Exec. Council, 2004–06); Med. Sec., Coroners' Soc. of England and Wales, 2009–13 (Mem. Council, 2003–13); Mem. Bd, Faculty of Forensic and Legal Medicine, RCP, 2006 (Mem., Fellowship Cttee). Pres., Soc. for Relief of Widows and Orphans of Medical Men, 1997–. Medical Society of London: Hon. Sec., 2005–07; Vice-Pres., 2007–09; Pres., 2012, now Trustee and Vice-Pres. Trustee, Coroners' Courts Support Service, 2011–13 (Chm., Mgt Cttee, 2011–13). Hon. Warden, Queen's Chapel of the Savoy, 1987–2011. Freeman, City of London, 1998; Liveryman: Apothecaries' Soc., 1998 (Hon. Sec., 2003–05; Chm., Livery Cttee, 2007–09; Mem., Ct of Assts, 2009–; Master, 2015–Aug. 2016); Barbers' Co., 2012. Hon. FRCPath 2013. *Publications:* (consultant ed.) Jervis on the Office and Duties of Coroners, 13th edn 2014; contrib. chapters on medico-legal topics in textbooks. *Recreations:* classical music, opera, theatre, art galleries, food and wine. *Address:* City of London Coroner's Court, Walbrook Wharf, 78–83 Upper Thames Street, EC4R 3TD. *T:* (020) 7332 1598, *Fax:* (020) 7332 1800. *E:* LondonCoroner@aol.com. *Clubs:* Garrick, Royal Society of Medicine.

PALMER, Prof. Sarah Rosalind, (Mrs G. Williams), PhD; FRHistS; Director, Greenwich Maritime Institute, 1998–2010, and Professor of Maritime History, 1999–2010, now Emeritus, University of Greenwich; *b* 16 Sept. 1943; *d* of Arthur Montague Frank Palmer and Marian Ethel Francis, (Jill), Palmer; *m* 1st, 1969, William David Walburn (marr. diss. 1978); one *s* one *d*; 2nd, 1979, Glyndwr Williams. *Educ:* Wimbledon High Sch. (GPDST); Univ. of Durham (BA); Univ. of Indiana (MA); London Sch. of Econs and Pol Sci. (PhD 1979). FRHistS 1980. Res. Asst, LSE, 1967–68; Queen Mary College, London: Lectr, then Sen. Lectr in Econ. Hist., 1969–98; Hd, Dept of Hist., 1994–98. Chm., British Commn for Maritime Hist., 2003–09. Trustee, Nat. Mus, Liverpool, 2000–08. Member (Lab): Maidstone BC, 1970–73; Kent CC, 1985–93. Contested (Lab and Co-op): Weston-super-Mare, 1970; Bristol NW, 1983. Vice Pres., Marine Soc. and Sea Cadets, 2004–. Sen. Res. Fellow, Bahria Univ., Pakistan, 2008–10. Chair, Greenwich Forum, 2009–. Gov., Mereworth Community Primary Sch., 2010–. FRSA 1996. *Publications:* Shipping, Politics and the Repeal of the Navigation Laws, 1990; contrib. learned jls. *Recreations:* gardening, walking, cooking. *Address:* Russet Barn, 281 Broadwater Road, W Malling, Kent ME19 6HT.

PALMER, Simon Erroll P.; *see* Prior-Palmer.

PALMER, Dr Stephen Charles; Priest-in-charge, St Congan's, Turriff, Aberdeenshire, 2010–14; Chaplain to the Queen, 2008–14; *b* Lowestoft, 13 May 1947; *s* of Thomas Clement Palmer and Joanna Edith Barbara Palmer (*née* Stoy); *m* 1968, Christine, *d* of Alan Tranah and Masie Tranah (*née* Owen); one *s* one *d. Educ:* RN Weapons Electrical Sch. (HMS Collingwood); Oak Hill Theol Coll. (Dip. Pastoral Studies 1974); Portsmouth Univ. (PhD 2004). FRGS 1998; FLS 2001. Served Royal Navy, 1963–71: RN Wireless Station Suara, Singapore, 1964; HMS Whitby, 1966; HMS Blake, 1969; ordained deacon, 1974, priest, 1975; Curate, Crofton Parish, 1974; Bishop of Portsmouth's Domestic Chaplain, 1977; Rector: Brighstone, Brook and Mottistone, IoW, 1980–91; Falkland Islands, 1991–96; Vicar: Christchurch Portsdown Hill, 1996–2002; Newport Minster and Newport St John, IoW, 2002–09. Rural Dean, W Wight, 1986–91; Hon. Canon, Portsmouth Cathedral, 1991–2009, then Canon Emeritus; Bishop of Portsmouth's Advr on Envmt, 1998–2006. Chaplain: RN Reserve, 1979–91; IoW Council, 2003–09. Member: Council, Royal Nat. Mission to Deep Sea Fisherman, 1998–2007; Exec. Council, British Beekeepers Assoc., 2003–09; Exec. Cttee, Scottish Beekeepers Assoc., 2012; Trustee, S Georgia Whaling Mus., 1992–96. *Publications:* (contrib.) The Falkland Islands Dictionary of Biography, 2008; numerous articles in Falkland Islands Jl, 1995–2010. *Recreations:* beekeeping, postal history, amateur radio. *Club:* Union Jack.

PALMER, Prof. Stuart Beaumont, PhD; FREng; Professor of Experimental Physics, University of Warwick, 1987–2011, now Emeritus; Secretary-General, International Union of Pure and Applied Physics, 2012–14; *b* 6 May 1943; *s* of Frank Beaumont Palmer and Florence Beryl Palmer (*née* Wilkinson); *m* 1966, Susan Mary Clay; two *s* one *d. Educ:* Ilkeston Grammar Sch.; Sheffield Univ. (BSc 1964; PhD 1968; DSc 1986). CPhys, FInstP, 1981; FInstNDT 1989; CEng, FIET (FIEE 1992). University of Hull: Asst Lectr, 1967–70; Lectr, 1970–78; Sen. Lectr, 1978–83; Reader, 1983–87; University of Warwick: Chair, Physics Dept, 1989–2001; Pro-Vice-Chancellor, 1995–99; Sen. Pro-Vice-Chancellor, 1999–2000; Actg Vice-Chancellor, 2001; Dep. Vice-Chancellor, 2001–09; Interim Chair, Sch. of Life Scis, 2009–10; Trustee, Pension Fund, 2008–. Vis. Prof., Univ. of Grenoble, 1982–83; Vis. Scientist, Queen's Univ., Kingston, Canada, 1986; Adjunct Prof., Queensland Univ. of Technol., Brisbane, 2012–. Chm., Standing Conf. of Profs of Physics, 2001–03; chm. and mem., various SERC and EPSRC cttees and working gps. Chm., Nat. Transparent Approach to Costing Develt Gp, HEFCE, 2008–. Mem. Council, Cardiff Univ., 2014–. Hon. Sec., Inst. of Physics, 2009–; Chm. Bd, Inst. of Physics Publishing 2011–. FREng 2000. Hon. DSc Warwick, 2011. *Publications:* (with M. Rogalski) Advanced University Physics, 1995, 2nd edn 2005; (with M. Rogalski) Quantum Physics, 1999; (with M. Rogalski) Solid State Physics, 2000; over 250 contribs to learned scientific jls in magnetism, ultrasound and non destructive testing. *Recreations:* tennis, sailing, flying, ski-ing. *Address:* University of Warwick, Coventry CV4 7AL. *T:* (024) 7657 4004; Max Gate, Forrest Road, Kenilworth CV8 1LT. *Clubs:* Athenæum; Hull Sailing; Warwick Boat; Coventry Flying.

PALMER, Sue; educational writer, speaker and childhood campaigner; *b* Manchester, 25 Nov. 1948; *d* of John and Pauline Hall; *m* 1st (marr. diss.); 2nd (marr. diss.); one *d. Educ:* Moray Hse Coll., Edinburgh (Primary Teaching Dip. 1974); Univ. of Manchester (MEd 1985). Teacher, Coniston Primary Sch., 1975–82; Headteacher, Caddonfoot Primary Sch., 1982–84; writer and teacher of dyslexic children, 1986–90; Gen. Ed., Longman Book Project, 1990–94; freelance writer, travelling player (The Language Live Roadshow), consultant and speaker on literacy, 1994– (speaker on child develt in modern world, 2005–). Chair: Scottish Play Commn, 2009–13; Scottish Play Policy Forum, 2009–13; Mem., Scottish Early Years Task Force, 2011–13. Organiser: Balance campaign about literacy teaching, 1990; Time to Teach campaign, 2002; Member, Steering Group: Open EYE campaign for early years educn, 2009–; Save Childhood, 2011–14 (Dir, 2014–); Early Childhood Action, 2011–. Contribs to TV progs on literacy teaching, 1995–2005. Pres., Montessori AMI UK, 2009–13. Trustee, Play Scotland, 2010–13; Patron: English Speaking Bd, 2007–; Children's Football Alliance, 2009–; Carefree Kids, 2010–; Children's Wood, 2013–; Ringsfield Trust, 2014–. *Publications:* over 200 books on literacy, literacy teaching and child development, including: Toxic Childhood: how the modern world is damaging our children and what we can do about it, 2006; Detoxing Childhood, 2007; 21st Century Boys, 2009; 21st Century Girls, 2013; contrib. articles to educnl and nat. press and to acad. jls. *Recreations:* books, films, conversation, ranting about forward-facing pushchairs. *Address:* c/o LBA Literacy Agency, 91 Great Russell Street, WC1B 3PS. *T:* (020) 7637 1234, *Fax:* (020) 7637 2111. *E:* sue@suepalmer.co.uk.

PALMER, Prof. Timothy Noel, CBE 2015; DPhil, DSc; FRS 2003; Royal Society 2010 Anniversary Research Professor of Atmospheric Oceanic and Planetary Physics, Clarendon Laboratory, University of Oxford, since 2010; Fellow, Jesus College, Oxford, since 2010; Senior Scientist, since 2011 and Fellow, since 2014, European Centre for Medium-Range Weather Forecasts (Head, Predictability and Seasonal Forecast Division, 2002–10); *b* 31 Dec. 1952; *s* of Alfred Henry Palmer and Anne Josephine Palmer; *m* 1978, Gill Dyer; three *s. Educ:* Wimbledon Coll.; Bristol Univ. (BSc 1974); Wolfson Coll., Oxford (DPhil 1977; DSc 1999). Vis. Scientist, Univ. of Washington, 1981; PSO, Meteorological Office, 1982–2002. Lead author, Third Assessment Report, Intergovtl Panel on Climate Change, 2001. Chm., Monsoon Numerical Experimentation Gp, UN WMO, 1989–96; Co-ordinator, EU Vth Framework Project: Development of a Multi-model Ensemble System for Interannual Prediction, 1999–2003; Co-Chm., World Climate Res. Prog. Climate Variability and Predictability Scientific Steering Gp, UN WMO, 2004–. Rothschild Dist. Vis. Prof., Isaac Newton Inst. for Mathematical Scis, Univ. of Cambridge, 2010. Pres., RMetS, 2011–12. *Publications:* contrib. to learned jls. *Recreations:* golf, cycling, ski-ing, playing guitar (folk, blues, rock and roll). *Address:* Atmospheric Oceanic and Planetary Physics, Clarendon Laboratory, Oxford OX1 3PU. *T:* (01865) 272897. *E:* t.n.palmer@atm.ox.ac.uk.

PALMER, Tony; *see* Palmer, H. A.

PALMER, Tony; film, television and theatre director; author; brought up by godparents, late Bert Spencer (railway engineer) and Elsie Spencer; *m* 2001, Michela Antonello; two *s* one *d. Educ:* Lowestoft Grammar Sch. Presenter, Night Waves, R3, 1994–98 (Sony Award, 1996). FRGS 1993. *Films:* over 100, including: All My Loving, 1968; Farewell Cream, 1968 (Platinum Record); 200 Motels, 1971 (Gold Record); Rory Gallagher Irish Tour, 1974 (Platinum Record); All This & World War Two, 1976 (Gold Record); All You Need is Love, 1977; A Time There Was, 1979 (Italia Prize); The Space Movie (music by Mike Oldfield), 1979; Death in Venice (Britten opera), 1979 (Gold Medal, NY Film Fest., 1980); At the Haunted End of the Day, 1980 (Italia Prize); Once at a Border, 1981 (Special Jury Prize, San Francisco); Wagner, 1982 (Best Drama, NY Film and TV Fest.); Puccini, 1984; God Rot Tunbridge Wells, 1985 (Best Drama, NY); Callas, 1986 (Gold Medal, NY); Testimony, 1987 (Fellini Prize); The Children, 1989 (Best Director, NY); Menuhin, 1990 (Grand Award, NY); The Symphony of Sorrowful Songs, 1993 (platinum CD; Jury Prize, Chicago Film Fest.); England, My England, 1995 (Best Dir, NY); Parsifal, 1998 (1st prize, Casta Diva, Moscow; Golden Mask, Russia); The Harvest of Sorrow, 1999; Ladies and Gentlemen, Miss Renée Fleming, 2001; Hero - the Bobby Moore Story, 2002; Toward the Unknown Region - Malcolm Arnold, 2003 (Preis der Deutschen Schallplatten Kritik, 2009); John Osborne and the Gift of Friendship, 2004; Margot, 2005; The Salzburg Festival, 2006; O Thou Transcendent: the life of Ralph Vaughan Williams, 2008; O Fortuna! Carl Orff, 2009; Vangelis and the Journey to Ithaka, 2009 (Outstanding Achievement Award, Sofia Film Fest., 2010); The Wagner Family, 2010; Bird on a Wire, 2010 (filmed 1972, then lost; rediscovered 2009; Special Jury Prize, Jerusalem Film Fest., 2010; Grierson Prize, 2011; World Medal, NY Film and TV Fest., 2012); Holst - In the Bleak Midwinter, 2011; Falls The Shadow—Athol

Fugard, 2012 (Gold Medal, NY Film and TV Fest., 2013); Nocturne - Benjamin Britten, 2013 (World Medal, NY Film and TV Fest., 2014); Hindemith - A Pilgrim's Progress, 2014 (World Medal, NY Film Fest., 2014); The Pursuit of Happiness, 2015; *theatre:* Billy Connolly's Great Northern Welly Boot Show, 1972; John Osborne's Deja Vu, Comedy, 1992; dir operas, Berlin, Karlsruhe, Munich, Hamburg, Zürich, Augsburg, St Petersburg, Savonlinna, Moscow, Ravello, Helsinki, Bonn. Hon. DLitt: Winchester, 2011; West London, 2012. Numerous BAFTA and Emmy awards. *Publications:* Born Under a Bad Sign, 1970, new edn 2012; Trials of Oz, 1971, new edn 2011; Electric Revolution, 1972; Biography of Liberace, 1976, new edn 2012; All You Need is Love, 1976; Charles II, 1979; A Life on the Road (biog. of Julian Bream), 1982, 2nd edn 2010; Menuhin: a family portrait, 1991, new edn 2012. *Recreation:* walking. *Address:* Nanjizal, St Levan, Cornwall TR19 6JJ. *Club:* Garrick.

PÁLSSON, Thorsteinn; Editor-in-Chief, Fréttablaðið, 2006–09; Chairman, MP Bank, Iceland, since 2011; *b* 29 Oct. 1947; *s* of Pall Sigurdsson and Ingigerdur Thorsteinsdottir; *m* 1973, Ingibjórg Rafnar; one *s* two *d*. *Educ:* Commercial Coll., Reykjavik; Univ. of Iceland (law degree). Journalist, Morgunbladid, 1974–75; Editor-in-Chief, Visir, 1975–79; Admin. Dir, Confedn of Icelandic Employers, 1979–83; MP (Independence) Southland, Iceland, 1983–99; Minister: of Finance, 1985–87; of Industry, 1987; Prime Minister, 1987–88; Minister: of Fisheries, 1991–99; of Justice and Ecclesiastical Affairs, 1991–99; Ambassador: to UK, 1999–2002; to Denmark, 2003–05. Chm., Independence Party, 1983–91.

PALTROW, Gwyneth; actress; *b* Los Angeles, 29 Sept. 1973; *d* of late Bruce W. Paltrow and of Blythe Katharine Danner; *m* 2003, Christopher Anthony John Martin, *qv*; one *s* one *d*. *Educ:* Spence Sch., New York; Univ. of Calif, Santa Barbara. Williamstown Theater, Mass. Acting début, Picnic (with Blythe Danner); Rosalind, in As You Like It, 1999; Proof, Donmar Warehouse, 2002; other plays include: The Adventures of Huck Finn; Sweet Bye and Bye; The Seagull. Film début, Shout, 1991; films include: Moonlight and Valentino; Seven, 1995; Emma, 1996; Great Expectations, Sliding Doors (Best Actress, Golden Globe Awards, 1999), Hush, A Perfect Murder, 1998; Shakespeare in Love (Academy Award for Best Actress, 1999), The Talented Mr Ripley, 1999; Duets, 2000; Bounce, 2001; Shallow Hal, The Royal Tenenbaums, Possession, 2002; Sylvia, Sky Captain and the World of Tomorrow, 2004; Proof, Infamous, 2006; Running with Scissors, 2007; The Good Night, Iron Man, Two Lovers, 2008; Iron Man 2, 2010; Country Strong, Contagion, 2011; Iron Man 3, Thanks for Sharing, 2013; Mortdecai, 2015. Founded lifestyle website Goop, 2008. *Publications:* My Father's Daughter, 2011; (jtly) It's All Good, 2013. *Address:* c/o CAA, 2000 Avenue of the Stars, Los Angeles, CA 90067, USA.

PALUMBO, family name of **Baron Palumbo** and **Baron Palumbo of Southwark**.

PALUMBO, Baron *cr* 1991 (Life Peer), of Walbrook in the City of London; **Peter Garth Palumbo,** MA; Chairman, Arts Council of Great Britain, 1989–94; *b* 20 July 1935; *s* of late Rudolph and of Elsie Palumbo; *m* 1st, 1959, Denia (*d* 1986), *d* of late Major Lionel Wigram; one *s* two *d*; 2nd, 1986, Hayat, *er d* of late Kamel Morowa; one *s* two *d*. *Educ:* Eton College; Worcester College, Oxford. MA Hons Law. Governor, London School of Economics and Political Science, 1976–94; Chairman: Tate Gallery Foundn, 1986–87; Painshill Park Trust Appeal, 1986–96; Serpentine Gall., 1994–2014, now Chm. Emeritus; Bd Mem. and Dir, Andy Warhol Foundn for the Visual Arts, 1994–97; Trustee: Mies van der Rohe Archive, 1977–; Tate Gallery, 1978–85; Whitechapel Art Gallery Foundation, 1981–87; Natural History Mus., 1994–2004; Design Mus., 1995–2005; Trustee and Hon. Treas., Writers and Scholars Educnl Trust, 1984–99; Mem. Council, Royal Albert Hall, 1995–99. Chm., Jury, Pritzker Architecture Prize, 2004–. Chancellor, Portsmouth Univ., 1992–2007; Gov., Whitgift Sch., 2002–10 (Advr Emeritus to Bd of Govs, 2010–). Liveryman, Salters' Co., 1965–. Hon. FRIBA 1986; Hon. FFB 1994; Hon. FIStructE 1994. Hon. DLitt Portsmouth, 1993. Patronage of the Arts Award, Cranbrook Acad. of Arts, Detroit, 2002. Nat. Order of Southern Cross (Brazil), 1993. *Recreations:* music, travel, gardening, reading. *Address:* 2 Astell Street, SW3 3RU. *T:* (020) 7351 7371. *Clubs:* Athenæum, White's, Pratt's, Garrick.

PALUMBO OF SOUTHWARK, Baron *cr* 2013 (Life Peer), of Southwark in the London Borough of Southwark; **James Rudolph Palumbo;** Co-Founder, 1991, Chief Executive, 1991–2008 and Chairman, since 2008, Ministry of Sound Group Ltd (formerly Ministry of Sound); *b* London, 6 June 1963; *s* of Baron Palumbo, *qv* and Denia (*née* Wigram) (*d* 1986); one *s* by Atoosa Hariri. *Educ:* Eton; Worcester Coll., Oxford (BA Hist.). Former posts with Merrill Lynch and Morgan Grenfell & Co. *Publications:* Tomas, 2009; Tancredi, 2011. *Address:* Ministry of Sound Group Ltd, 103 Gaunt Street, Elephant & Castle, SE1 6DP.

PAMPLIN, Elizabeth Ann; human resources and corporate ethics consultant, since 1999; Chief Executive, Liberal Democrats, 1998–99; *b* 13 April 1940; *d* of Richard Thomas Webb and Hilda Ethel Webb (*née* Teague); *m* 1969, Terence Michael Pamplin (*d* 2004); twin *d*. *Educ:* Rosebery GS; St Hugh's Coll., Oxford (BA PPE 1962; DPSA 1963). FCIPD (FIPD 1991). Clarks Ltd, 1963–66; Industrial Trng Service, 1966–71; Sen. Lectr, Personnel Mgt and Trng, Slough Coll. of HE, 1973–75; human resource management and consultancy: MSC, 1975–77; Petroleum Industry Trng Bd, 1977–82; RBK&C, 1983–91; P & L Associates, 1991–93; DoT, 1993–96; Cabinet Office, 1996–97. Examr in personnel mgt, PCL, then Univ. of Westminster, 1985–98; Nat. Examr, IPD, subseq. CIPD, 1996–2004. Governor: Lord Mayor Treloar Sch., 2000–10, Treloar Sch. and Coll., 2010–12; Wavell Sch., 2006–10; Abbey Sch., 2006–. Contested (SDP), 1983, (SDP/L Alliance), 1987, Reigate. Freeman, City of London, 1997; Liveryman, Co. of Musicians, 1997–. FRGS 2000. *Publications:* reports and articles. *Recreations:* music, early dance, walking, countryside conservation. *Address:* Little Critchmere, Manor Crescent, Haslemere, Surrey GU27 1PB.

PAMUK, Orhan; writer; Robert Yik-Fong Tam Professor of Humanities, Columbia University, New York; *b* Istanbul, 7 June 1952; *m* 1982 Aylin Türegün (marr. diss. 2002); one *d*. *Educ:* private schs in Istanbul. Vis. Scholar, Columbia Univ., 1985–88. Founder, Masumiyet Müzesi (Museum of Innocence), Istanbul, 2012. Nobel Prize in Literature, 2006. *Publications:* Cevdet Bey Ve Oğulları (Cevdet Bey and His Sons), 1982; Sessiz Ev, 1983 (Silent House, 2012); Beyaz Kale, 1985 (The White Castle, 1991); Kara Kitap, 1990 (The Black Book, 1994); Gizli Yüz: Senaryo (Secret Face), 1992; Yeni Hayat, 1994 (The New Life, 1997); Benim Adım Kırmızı, 1998 (My Name is Red, 2001); Öteki Renkler: Seçme Yazılar Ve Bir Hikâye, 1999 (Other Colours: essays and a story, 2007); Kar, 2002 (Snow, 2004); İstanbul: Hatıralar Ve Şehir, 2003 (Istanbul: memories and the city, 2005); Babamin Bavulu (My Father's Suitcase), 2007; Masumiyet Müzesi, 2008 (Museum of Innocence, 2009); Manzaradan Parcalar: Hayat, Sokaklar, Edibayat (Fragments of the Landscape), 2010; Saf ve Düsüceli Romanci (The Naive and the Sentimental Novelist: understanding what happens when we write and read novels) (Norton Lectures), 2011; Kafamda Bir Tuhaflık (A Strangeness in My Mind), 2015.

PANAYI, Pavlos; QC 2014; *b* Harrow, 25 Feb. 1973; *s* of Costas Panayi and Myrophora Panayi; *m* 2004, Gabrielle Turner; three *s* one *d*. *Educ:* Whitmore High Sch. Harrow; Queen Mary Coll., Univ. of London (LLB 1994). Called to the Bar, Gray's Inn, 1995; in practice as barrister, specialising in criminal law. *Recreations:* cycling, cooking, scuba-diving, backgammon. *Address:* Carmelite Chambers, 9 Carmelite Street, EC4Y 0DR. *T:* (020) 7936 6300. *E:* ppanayi@carmelitechambers.co.uk.

PANAYIDES CHRISTOU, Tasos, Hon. GCVO 1990; Chairman, ENESEL (formerly AVRA) Shipmanagement SA, 1997–2011; *b* 9 April 1934; *s* of Christos Panayides and Efrosini Panayides; *m* 1969, Pandora Constantinides; two *s* one *d*. *Educ:* Paphos Gymnasium; Teachers' Training Coll.; Univ. of London (Diploma in Education); Univ. of Indiana, USA (MA Political Science, Diploma in Public Administration). Teacher, 1954–59; First sec. to Pres., 1960–63; Director, President's Office, 1963–69; Ambassador of Cyprus to Federal Republic of Germany, Switzerland, Austria, and Atomic Energy organisation, Vienna, 1969–78; High Comr in UK, and Ambassador to Sweden, Norway, Denmark and Iceland, 1979–90; Doyen of the Diplomatic Corps in London and Sen. High Comr, 1988–90; Permanent Sec., Min. of Foreign Affairs, Cyprus, 1990–94; Ambassador to Sweden, Finland, Norway, Denmark, Latvia, Lithuania and Estonia, 1994–96. Rep., Exec. Cttee, Union of Greek Shipowners, 1997–2003; Vice-Pres., Cypriot Union of Shipowners, 2004–08 (Cllr Mem., Exec. Steering Cttee, 2009–). Chairman: Commonwealth Foundn Grants Cttee, 1985–88; Commonwealth Fund Tech. Co-operation Bd of Reps, 1986–89; Commonwealth Steering Cttee of Sen. Officials, 1994–95. Hon. Fellow, Ealing Coll. of Higher Educn, 1983. Freeman, City of London, 1984. Hon. LLD Birmingham, 1991. 1st Cl., Grand Order and Grand Cross with Star and Sash, Federal Republic of Germany, 1978; Grand Cross in Gold with Star and Sash, Austria, 1979; Golden Cross of the Archdiocese of Thyateira and Great Britain, 1981; Grand Cross in Gold of Patriarchate of Antioch, 1984. *Publications:* articles in newspapers and magazines. *Recreations:* swimming, reading books.

PANCHO, Cassa, MBE 2013; Founder, Artistic Director, choreographer and ballet mistress, Ballet Black, since 2001; *b* London, 23 Aug. 1978; *d* of Winston and Patricia Pancho; *m* 2009, Richard Bolton. *Educ:* Acton High Sch.; Durham Univ. (BA Classical Ballet); Royal Acad. of Dance (LRAD). Estabd Ballet Black Jun. Sch., Shepherd's Bush, 2002; started BB Associate Prog., 2004. Work commnd from choreographers incl. Christopher Hampson, Will Tuckett, Richard Alston, Javier de Frutos, Arthur Pita. Patron, Central Sch. of Ballet, 2015–. *E:* balletblack@gmail.com.

PANIGUIAN, Sir Richard (Leon), Kt 2015; CBE 2007; Head of Defence and Security, UK Trade and Investment, 2008–15; *b* London, 28 July 1949; *s* of Hracia and Mary Paniguian; *m* 1991, Nil Okan Kapanci; two step *s*. *Educ:* Westminster Sch.; Durham Univ. (BA Arabic); INSEAD (MBA). Joined British Petroleum Co., 1971; BP Oman and UAE, 1972–78; BP Tehran, 1978–80; Oil Trading Dir, 1980–84; Vice-Pres., BP America, 1984–86; Gp Finance Dir, 1987–89; Pres., BP Turkey, 1989–92; Dir, BP Europe, 1992–95; CEO, BP Shipping, 1995–99; Vice-Pres., Gas and Power, Middle East, 1999–2002; Gp Vice Pres., BP plc, 2002–08. Non-executive Director: Tsakos Energy Navigation, 2008; Raytheon UK, 2015–; Chm., C5 Hldgs, 2015–. Pres., UK Chamber of Shipping, 2000–02. *Recreations:* cricket, kayaking, contemplation. *Club:* Brooks's.

PANK, Dorian Christopher L.; *see* Lovell-Pank.

PANK, Maj.-Gen. (John) David (Graham), CB 1989; Chief Executive, Newbury Racecourse plc, 1990–98; *b* 2 May 1935; *s* of late Edward Graham Pank and Margaret Sheelah Osborne Pank; *m* 1st, 1963, Julia Letitia Matheson (*d* 2002); two *s* one *d*; 2nd, 2003, Jill Sarah Bevan (*née* Murrell). *Educ:* Uppingham Sch. Commnd KSLI, 1958; served in Germany, Borneo, Singapore and Malaya; commanded: 3rd Bn The Light Infantry, 1974–76; 33rd Armoured Bde, 1979–81; Comdr Land Forces, NI, 1983–85; Dir Gen. of Personal Services, Army, 1985–88; Dir of Infantry, 1988–90. Col, The LI, 1987–90. President: Army Cricket Assoc., 1987–89; Combined Services Cricket Assoc., 1988. Dir, Racecourse Assoc., 1994–98. *Recreations:* racing, fishing, cricket. *Address:* c/o Royal Bank of Scotland, London Drummonds Branch, 49 Charing Cross, SW1A 2DX. *Clubs:* Army and Navy, Victory Services; Mounted Infantry; Free Foresters, I Zingari, Mount Cricket.

PANKHURST, Julie Kathryn; Co-founder, Friendsreunited, 2000–05; *b* 16 Jan. 1967; *d* of John Victor Hill and Patricia May Hill; *m* 1998, Stephen Pankhurst, *qv*; two *d*. *Educ:* Queen Elizabeth's Girls' Sch., Barnet; Dehavilland Coll., Borehamwood; Luton Coll. of Higher Educn (HNC); Middlesex Poly. (HND Dist.). Software engr, GEC Avionics Ltd, 1985–88; Sen. Analyst Programmer, MFI Furniture Centres Ltd, 1988–2000. Patron, Plan UK, 2005–12; Trustee, Happy Charitable Trust, 2006–. *Recreations:* philanthropy, travelling, photography, tennis, walking, swimming, jewellery making, sewing.

PANKHURST, Stephen; Director and Co-founder, Friendsreunited, 2000–05; *b* 4 Jan. 1964; *s* of Nigil Frederick Pankhurst and Irene Pankhurst; *m* 1998, Julie Kathryn Hill (*see* J. K. Pankhurst); two *d*. *Educ:* Orange Hill Sch.; Imperial Coll., London (BSc Hons Maths). Software engr, GEC Avionics Ltd, 1985–87; developer, ITL, 1987–90; Develt Manager, Bovis Construction, 1990–93; freelance software consultant, 1993–2000; Dir/Co-founder, Happygroup, 2000–05. *Recreations:* football, cinema, walking, comic collecting, playing with my children. *E:* steve@scruffybeggars.co.uk.

PANNICK, family name of **Baron Pannick**.

PANNICK, Baron *cr* 2008 (Life Peer), of Radlett in the county of Hertfordshire; **David Philip Pannick;** QC 1992; Fellow of All Souls College, Oxford, since 1978; a Recorder, 1995–2005; *b* 7 March 1956; *s* of late Maurice Pannick and Rita Pannick; *m* 1st, 1978, Denise Sloam (*d* 1999); two *s* one *d*; 2nd, 2003, Nathalie Trager-Lewis; one *s* two *d*. *Educ:* Bancroft's Sch., Woodford Green, Essex; Hertford Coll., Oxford (MA, BCL; Hon. Fellow, 2004). Called to the Bar, Gray's Inn, 1979, Bencher, 1998. Jun. Counsel to the Crown (Common Law), 1988–92; Dep. High Court Judge, 1998–2005. Mem., Select Cttee on the Constitution, H of L, 2009–13. Columnist, The Times, 1991–. Mem., Editl Bd, Public Law, 1990–2014. Hon. Fellow, Hebrew Univ., Jerusalem, 2013. Hon. LLD Hertfordshire, 1998. *Publications:* Judicial Review of the Death Penalty, 1982; Sex Discrimination Law, 1985; Judges, 1987; Advocates, 1992; (ed with Lord Lester of Herne Hill) Human Rights Law and Practice, 1999, 3rd edn 2009; I Have to Move My Car, 2008. *Recreations:* travel, supporting Arsenal FC, musicals. *Address:* Blackstone Chambers, Blackstone House, Temple, EC4Y 9BW. *T:* (020) 7583 1770.

PANNONE, Rodger John; DL; Senior Partner, Pannone & Partners (formerly Pannone March Pearson), Solicitors, 1993–2003 (Consultant, 2003–09); President of the Law Society of England and Wales, 1993–94; *b* 20 April 1943; *s* of late Cyril John Alfred Pannone and Violet Maud (*née* Weeks); *m* 1966, Patricia Jane Todd; two *s* one *d*. *Educ:* St Brendan's Coll., Bristol; Coll. of Law, London; Law Sch., Manchester. Articled to Casson & Co., Salford, 1966–69; Asst Solicitor and Partner, W. H. Thompson, 1969–73; Partner, Pannone March Pearson, subseq. Pannone & Partners, 1973–2003; Chm., Renovo PLC, 2006–11; Dir, Co-operative Legal Services Ltd, 2006–12. Member: Lord Chancellor's Adv. Cttee on Civil Justice, 1986–89; Council, Law Soc., 1979–96 (Vice-Pres., 1992–93). Gov., Univ. of Law (formerly Coll. of Law), 1990– (Chm., 1999–2005); Mem. Council, Manchester Univ., 1996– (Chm., 2000–04). Chm., Standards Cttee, Tameside MBC, 2001–11. Vice-Pres., British Acad. of Experts, 1994–. Chm., Manchester Concert Hall Ltd, 1993–2007. Regl Chm., Emmaus North West, 2005–10. FRSA 1992. DL Greater Manchester, 1999. Hon. Life Mem., Canadian Bar, 1993. Hon. Fellow: Manchester Metropolitan Univ., 1994; Birmingham Univ., 1998. Hon. DLitt Salford, 1993; Hon. LLD: Nottingham Trent, 1993; College of Law, 2009; Hon. LittD Manchester, 2004. *Publications:* numerous legal pubns. *Recreations:* the Lake District, walking slowly, food and wine. *Address:* 17 Ballbrook Avenue, Didsbury, Manchester M20 6AB. *T:* (0161) 909 3000; 123 Deansgate, Manchester M3 2BU. *Clubs:* St James's (Manchester); Wyresdale Anglers.

PANTER, Sir Howard (Hugh), Kt 2013; Joint Chief Executive and Creative Director, Ambassador Theatre Group Ltd, since 2000; *b* 25 May 1949; *s* of late Hugh Panter and Hilary Panter (*née* Robinson); *m* 1994, Rosemary Anne Squire, *qv*; one *d*, and one step *s* one step *d*.

Educ: Clayesmore Sch.; London Acad. of Music and Dramatic Art (Dip. Prodn and Stage Mgt). Producer: Knightsbridge Prodns, 1975–79; SRO Prodns, 1979–80; Man. Dir, Freedman Panter Prodns, 1980–86; Man. Dir, Turnstyle Gp Ltd, 1987–2000. Chm., Rambert Dance Company, 2009–. *Recreations:* opera, contemporary dance, visual arts, cricket. *Address:* Ambassador Theatre Group, 39–41 Charing Cross Road, WC2H 0AR. *T:* (020) 7534 6112, *Fax:* (020) 7534 6109. *E:* howardpanter@theambassadors.com. *Club:* Garrick.

PANTER, Ven. Richard James Graham, (Ricky); Archdeacon of Liverpool, since 2002; Vicar, St John and St James, Orrell Hey, Bootle, 1996–2011; *b* 18 Sept. 1948; *s* of Rev. Ernest Downes Panter and Marjorie (*née* Lea); *m* 1974, Jane Christine Wilson; two *s* two *d*. *Educ:* Monkton Combe Sch., Bath; Worcester Coll. of Educn (Cert. Ed.); Oak Hill Theol Coll. Teacher, RE, Chatham Tech. High Sch. for Boys, 1970–71; Primary Teacher, St John's Boscombe C of E Primary Sch., 1971–73. Ordained deacon, 1976, priest, 1977; Curate, Holy Trinity, Rusholme, 1976–80; Asst Vicar, St Cyprian with Christchurch, Edge Hill, 1980–85; Vicar, St Andrews, Clubmoor, 1985–96; Area Dean of Bootle, 1999–2002. *Recreations:* singing (Royal Liverpool Phil. Choir), walking, caravanning. *Address:* 115 Papillon Drive, Fazakerley, Liverpool L9 9HL. *T:* (0151) 525 7890. *E:* ricky.panter@liverpool.anglican.org.

PANTER, Rosemary Anne, (Lady Panter); *see* Squire, R. A.

PANTLING, Mary Fitzgerald; *see* Allen, M. F.

PANTON, (Elizabeth) Jane; Headmistress, Bolton School Girls' Division, 1994–2005, and Chairman of Executive Committee, Bolton School, 2002–05; *b* 20 June 1947; *d* of Richard Henry Panton and Constance Doreen Panton. *Educ:* Clayton Hall Grammar Sch., Newcastle; Merchant Taylors' Sch. for Girls, Liverpool; St Hugh's Coll., Oxford (MA Hons History); West Midlands Coll. of Educn, Walsall (PGCE). Teacher, Moreton Hall, near Oswestry, 1972–73; Third Mistress, Shrewsbury High Sch., 1973–83; Head of History and of Sixth Form, Clifton High Sch., Bristol, 1983–88; Headmistress, Merchant Taylors' Sch. for Girls, Crosby, Liverpool, 1988–94. Member: ISC (formerly HMC/GSA) Assisted Places Working Party, 1992–2000; GSA Professional Devélt Cttee, 1992–96; ISIS North Cttee, 1993–99 (Chm., 1997–99); Chm., GSA NW, 2000–02. Mem., Sefton FHSA, 1990–92. Mem. Council, Liverpool Univ., 1990–94. Member, Management Committee: Landscape Trust, 2007–12; Lake District Summer Music, 2007–13. Mem., Yealand Conyers Parish Council, 2007–. Governor: Westholme Sch., Blackburn, 2006–12; Casterton Sch., Kirkby Lonsdale, 2010–13; Sedbergh Sch., 2013–. *Recreations:* fell walking, UK and abroad, birdwatching, foreign travel, music, art, reading.

PANUFNIK, Roxanna; composer of classical music; *b* 24 April 1968; *d* of Sir Andrzej Panufnik and Camilla Panufnik (*née* Jessel); *m* 2001, Stephen Macklow-Smith; one *s* two *d*. *Educ:* Royal Acad. of Music (GRSM Hons 1989; LRAM 1989; ARAM 1998). Associate Composer, London Mozart Players, 2012–. Major *compositions:* Westminster Mass, 1998; The Music Programme (opera), 1999; Powers and Dominions (harp concerto), 2001; LEDA (ballet), 2003; Abraham (violin concerto), 2004; Love Abide (choir and orch.), 2006; Three Paths to Peace, 2008; The Audience (narrator and string quartet), 2009; Schola Missa de Angelis (choir and brass octet or strings), 2010; Dance of Life: Tallinn Mass (soprano soloist, narrator, upper voice choir, double mixed choir and orchestra), 2011; Four World Seasons, 2011; The Song of Names (Jewish oratorio), 2012; Orchestrapædia (chamber orchestra), 2013; Two Composers, Four Hands (double string orchestra), 2013; Memories of my Father (string quartet), 2013; Since We Parted, 2014; major recordings: Dance of Life: Tallinn Mass; Dreamscape; Love Abide; Westminster Mass; Angels Sing; The Upside Down Sailor; Beastly Tales; Padre Pio (Stay with Me, Prayer); Spirit of the Saints. *Recreations:* food (eating and cooking), reading, family time, cycling. *Address:* c/o Peters Edition Ltd, 2–6 Baches Street, N1 6DN. *T:* (020) 7553 4000. *E:* marc.dooley@editionpeters.com. *W:* www.roxannapanufnik.com.

PAPADEMOS, Lucas, PhD; Professor of Economics, University of Athens, since 1988; Prime Minister of Greece, 2011–12; *b* Athens, 11 Oct. 1947. *Educ:* Athens Coll.; Massachusetts Inst. of Technol. (BSc Physics 1970; MSc Electrical Engrg 1972; PhD Econs 1977). Res. Asst and Teaching Fellow, MIT, 1973–75; Lectr in Econs, 1975–77, Asst and Associate Prof. of Econs, 1977–84, Columbia Univ., NY; Sen. Economist, Federal Reserve Bank of Boston, 1980; Vis. Prof. of Econs, Athens Sch. of Econs and Business, 1984–85; Bank of Greece: Econ. Counsellor (Chief Economist), 1985–93; Dep. Gov., 1993–94; Gov., 1994–2002. Gov., IMF for Greece, 1994–2002; Member: Monetary Cttee, EC, 1985–88, 1990; Gen. Council, 1999–2010, Governing Council, 2001–10, European Central Bank (Vice Pres., 2002–10); Committee of EC Central Bank Governors, subseq. Council of EMI: Mem., 1985–93, Chm., 1989, Cttee of Alternates; Chm., Monetary Policy Sub-Cttee, 1992–94; Council Mem., 1994–98. Chm., Adv. Bd, Hellenic Observatory, Eur. Inst., LSE, 1998–. Grand Comdr, Order of Honour (Greece), 1999. *Publications:* (jtly) Efficiency, Stability and Equity: a strategy for the evolution of the economic system of the European Community, 1987; (jtly) Stabilisation and Recovery of the Greek Economy, 1990; (with P. De Grauwe) The European Monetary System in the 1990s, 1990; (jtly) External Constraints on Macroeconomic Policy: the European experience, 1991; contrib. numerous articles and essays to books and learned jls, incl. Greek Econ. Rev., Eur. Econ. Rev. and Econ. Bulletin.

PAPADOPULOS, Heather Sophia; *see* Norton, H. S.

PAPADOPULOS, Rev. Canon Nicholas Charles; Canon Treasurer, Canterbury Cathedral, since 2013; *b* Longfield, Kent, 23 July 1966; *s* of Michael and Jennifer Papadopulos; *m* 1996, Heather Sophia Norton, *qv*; one *s* one *d*. *Educ:* King's Sch., Rochester; Gonville and Caius Coll., Cambridge (BA 1988); Ripon Coll., Cuddesdon. Called to the Bar, Middle Temple, 1990. Ordained deacon, 1999, priest, 2000; Vicar, St Peter's, Eaton Square, London, 1997–2013. *Publications:* God's Transforming Work, 2011. *Address:* 15 The Precincts, Canterbury CT1 2EL. *T:* (01227) 865228. *E:* canon.treasurer@canterbury-cathedral.org.

PAPALOIZOU, Prof. John Christopher Baillie, DPhil; FRS 2003; Professor of Mathematical Physics, University of Cambridge, 2005–14, now Emeritus; *b* 4 May 1947; *s* of Michael and Sarah Papaloizou; *m* 1978, Elaine Joseph; one *s*. *Educ:* UCL (BSc 1st cl. Hons 1965); Univ. of Sussex (DPhil 1972). Research Fellow: Univ. of Sussex, 1971–73; Univ. of Oxford, 1973–74; Res. Associate, Culham Lab., 1974–76; Res. Fellow, Christ's Coll., Cambridge, 1976–80; Queen Mary College, London University: Lectr, 1980–86; Reader, 1986–88; Prof. of Mathematics and Astronomy, 1988–2004. *Publications:* monthly notices of RAS and papers in Astronomy and Astrophysics and Astrophysical Jl. *Club:* Royal Astronomical Society Dining.

PAPANDREOU, George Andreas; Prime Minister and Minister of Foreign Affairs, Greece, 2009–11; President: Panhellenic Socialist Movement, 2004–12; Socialist International, since 2006; *b* St Paul, Minn, 16 June 1952; *m* 1989, Ada Papapanou; one *s* one *d*. *Educ:* King City Secondary Sch., Toronto; Amherst Coll., Massachusetts (BA Sociol.); Stockholm Univ. (undergrad. studies Sociol.); LSE (MSc Sociol. and Devélt). Member of Parliament: Achaia (Patras) Dist, 1981–96; 1st Dist, Athens, 1996–2004; 1st Dist, Salonika, 2004–15. Under Sec. for Cultural Affairs, Ministry of Culture, 1985–87; Minister of Educn and Religious Affairs, 1988–89, 1994–96; Dep. Minister of Foreign Affairs, 1993–94; Alternate Minister of Foreign Affairs, 1996–99; Minister of Foreign Affairs, 1999–2004. Chm., Parly Cttee of Educn, 1981–85; Vice-Chm., cross-party Parly Cttee for Free Radio, 1987; in charge, Parly Cttee for Culture and Educn, 1989–93; Panhellenic Socialist Movement: Member: Central Cttee, 1984–2015; Exec. Office, 1987–88, 1996–2015; Pol Bureau, 1996–2015; Sec., Cttee on Greek Diaspora, 1990–93. Founding Member: Helsinki Citizens Assembly, Prague, 1990; Lagonisi Initiative on Co-operation in Balkans, 1994; Member Board: Foundn of Mediterranean Studies (Mem., Res. Teams); Foundn for Res. and Self-Educn. Fellow, Center for Internat. Affairs, Harvard Univ., 1992–93. Hon. Dr Law Amherst Coll., 2002. Botsis's Foundn for the Promotion of Journalism Award, 1988; SOS against Racism, and Affiliated Orgns Cttee Award, 1996; Abdi Ipekci Special Award for Peace and Friendship, 1997; (jtly) Statesman of the Year, Peace Building Awards, Eastwest Inst., 2000. Comdr, Order of Yaroslav (Ukraine), 1996; Grand Commander: Order of Polish Republic (Poland), 1996; Order of Merit (Hungary), 2003; Grand Cross: Order of the Lion (Finland), 1996; Order of Civil Merit (Spain), 1998; Order of Polar Star (Sweden), 1999; Order of White Star (Estonia), 1999; Order of Honour, first class (Austria), 1999; Order of Merit, first class (Germany), 2000; Order of Isabella the Catholic (Spain), 2001; Order of the Crown (Belgium), 2001; Order of Infante Dom Henrique (Portugal), 2002; Order of Pius IX (Vatican), 2002; Order of Merit (Italy), 2003; Order of El Sol (Peru), 2003.

PAPANDREOU, Vassiliki, (Vasso); MP (Pasok) Athens, 1985–89 and 1993–2012; *d* of Andreas and Anastasia Papandreou. *Educ:* Athens Economic Univ. (BSc 1969; Special Hon. Distinction, 1991); London Univ. (MSc 1971); Reading Univ. (PhD 1980). Economics Tutor, Exeter Univ., 1971–73; Res. Asst, Oxford Univ., 1973–74; Lectr, High Business and Econs Sch., Athens, 1981–85; Dep. Minister, 1985–86; Alternate Minister: for Industry, Energy and Technology, 1986–87; for Trade, 1988–89; Minister: of Devélt, 1996–99; of the Interior, Public Admin and Decentralisation, 1999–2001; of the Envmt, Physical Planning and Public Works, 2001–04. Mem. for Social Affairs, Employment, Industrial Relns and Educn, CEC, 1989–93. Vice President: Parly Assembly, Council of Europe, 1995–96; Parly Assembly, WEU, 1995–96. Panhellenic Socialist Movement: Mem., Central Cttee, 1974–; Mem., Exec. Bureau of Central Cttee, 1984–88, 1996–2006. Dir, Hellenic Orgn for Small and Medium Size Firms, 1981–85. Mem., Bd of Dirs, Commercial Bank of Greece, 1982–85. Hon. DEd CNAA, 1992; Hon. DLitt Sheffield, 1992; Dr *hc* Paul Sabatier Univ., Toulouse, 1993. Chevalier, Legion of Honour (France), 1993; Grand Cross, Order of Leopold II (Belgium), 1993; Great Cross, Order of North Star (Sweden), 1999; Insignia of Patriarch Cross, Order A Patriarch of Ierosolyma, 1999. *Publications:* Multinational Companies and Less Developed Countries: the case of Greece, 1981; numerous papers and articles.

PAPHIDES, Catherine Elizabeth, (Caitlin); *see* Moran, C. E.

PAPOULIAS, Dr Karolos; President of the Hellenic Republic, 2005–15; *b* 4 June 1929; *s* of Maj. Gen. Grigoris Papoulias and Vassilikh Papoulias; *m* May Panou; three *d*. *Educ:* Univ. of Athens (law degree); Univ. of Milan (Master of Law (Civil Law)); Univ. of Cologne (PhD Private Internat. Law). Sec., Socialist Democratic Union, 1967–74; Member: Central Cttee, PASOK, 1974– (Sec., Internat. Relns Cttee, 1975–85); Co-ordination Council, 1974–2004; Exec. Bureau, 1974–2004; Political Secretariat, 1974–2004; Co-ordinating Cttee, Socialist and Progressive Parties of Mediterranean, 1975–85. MP (PASOK) Ioanina, 1977–2004; Under-Sec., 1981–85; Dep. Minister of Foreign Affairs, 1981–85; Minister of Foreign Affairs, 1985–89; Dep. Minister of Defence, 1989–90; Minister of Foreign Affairs, 1993–96; Hd, Parly Delegn to OSCE, 1997–2003; Pres., Standing Cttee for Defence and Foreign Affairs, 1998–2004. Awarded numerous foreign decorations, including: Grand Cross, Order of Merit (Cyprus), 1984; Grand Cross, 1988, Grand Collar, 2005, Order of Makarios III (Cyprus); Grand Cross, Order of Redeemer (Hellenic Republic), 2005; Grand Cross, 1994, Collar, 2006, Order of Merit (Italy). *Publications:* monograph on the Greek Resistance 1941–1944; contrib. studies and articles to European newspapers and mags. *Recreations:* athletics, gardening, theatre, art, literature. *Clubs:* Athenian, Hellenic Language Heritage; Ethnicos Gymnastikos Syllogos.

PAPOUTSIS, Christos; economist; Advisor to Executive Director for Greece, World Bank Group, since 2013; *b* 11 April 1953; *m* Lia Taliouri; one *d*. *Educ:* Univ. of Athens Sch. of Law (Econs). Special Advr, Min. of Presidency, Greek Govt, 1981–84; European Parliament: Mem., 1984–95; Vice Pres., Socialist Gp, 1987–94; Mem. Cttees on Foreign Affairs, Security and Defence, Budgets and Budgetary Control, 1989–94; Mem., EC (Comr for Energy and Eurotom, Enterprise Policy, Commerce, Tourism and Social Economy), 1995–99; MP (Pasok) Athens, 2000–12; Minister of Mercantile Marine, 1999–2001, of Citizen Protection, 2010–12, Greece. *Publications:* European Destinations, 1994; The Colour of the Future, 1998; For Europe in the 21st Century, 1999. *Address:* (office) Lykavittou 5, 10672 Athens, Greece. *E:* papoutsis@otenet.gr.

PAPP, Helen Richenda; *see* Wallace, H. R.

PAPPANO, Sir Antonio, Kt 2012; conductor and pianist; Music Director, Royal Opera House, Covent Garden, since 2002; Principal Conductor, Academia Nazionale di Santa Cecilia, Rome, since 2005; *b* London, 30 Dec. 1959; *m* 1995, Pamela Bullock. *Educ:* studied under Norma Verrilli, Arnold Franchetti and Gustav Meier, USA. Has worked as pianist and assistant conductor with: NY City Opera; Gran Teatro del Liceo, Barcelona; Frankfurt Opera; Lyric Opera of Chicago; Bayreuth Fest.; Music Dir, Norwegian Opera, 1990–92; Music Dir, Th. Royal de la Monnaie, Brussels, 1992–2002. Principal Guest Conductor, Israel Philharmonic Orch., 1997–2000. Has conducted world-class orchestras in Europe and the USA, incl. Boston SO, Chicago SO, Cleveland Orch., LA Philharmonic, LSO, Berlin Philharmonic, Concertgebouw Orch., Orch. de Paris and Vienna Philharmonic Orch.; has also conducted at Metropolitan Opera and Bayreuth Fest. Recordings include: La Rondine; Il Trittico; Werther; The Turn of the Screw; Manon; Tosca; Don Carlos; Tristan und Isolde; Tchaikovsky Symphonies 4, 5, 6; Respighi's Roman Trilogy; Guillaume Tell; Aida; Verdi Requiem and Rossini Petite Messe Solennelle. Cavaliere, Gran Croce dell'Ordine al Merito (Italy), 2012. *Address:* c/o IMG Artists, The Light Box, 111Power Road, W4 5PY. *T:* (020) 7957 5800.

PAPPENHEIM, Karin; Executive Director (formerly General Manager), Association of Anaesthetists of Great Britain and Ireland, since 2011; *b* 11 Dec. 1954; *d* of Wolfgang and Joy Pappenheim; one *s* one *d*. *Educ:* St Paul's Girls' Sch.; Sussex Univ. (BA Hons Intellectual Hist.); London Coll. of Printing; Université de Toulouse; Goldsmiths' Coll. (Post grad. dip. in communicns). Weidenfeld & Nicolson, Publishers, 1977–79; Camden Social Services, 1980–82; Greater London Assoc. for Disabled People, 1982–84; Alcohol Concern, 1984–89; FPA, 1989–95; Dir, Nat. Council for One Parent Families, 1995–97; Chief Executive: Haemophilia Soc., 1998–2004; Employment Opportunities for People with Disabilities, 2004–09; Dir, Work and Independence, Shaw Trust, 2009–10; Interim Chief Exec., Vital Regeneration, 2010–11. Trustee: Terrence Higgins Trust, 1998–2003; NCVO, 1999–2005; Woman's Trust, 2010–13. *Recreations:* family and friends, travel in France.

See also M. Pappenheim.

PAPPENHEIM, Katharine; *see* Tearle, K.

PAPPENHEIM, Mark; writer and editor; *b* 25 May 1956; *s* of Wolfgang and Joy Pappenheim; *m* 1988, Katharine Tearle, *qv*; two *s*. *Educ:* St Paul's Boys' Sch.; Merton Coll., Oxford (BA Hons Lit. Hum., MA); City Univ., London (Cert. Arts Admin). Box-office manager, Buxton Fest. and Opera Hse, 1979–80; Asst Hd of Educn, WNO, 1980–81; Fest. Administrator, Vale of Glamorgan Fest., 1982; Asst Administrator, Live Music Now, 1982–83; Pubns Ed., Opera North, 1983–84; Radio Ed., Radio Times, 1984–90; with The Independent, 1990–: Arts Editor, 1996–98; Classical Music Reviews Ed., 1998–2008; Opera Critic, The Daily Express, 1998–2002. Artistic Assessor, Arts Council England, 2011. Editor: BBC Proms programmes, 1998–2005; BBC Proms Guide, 2000–06; BBC Proms interactive television notes, 2006–08; London (formerly Lufthansa) Festival of Baroque Music Programmes, 2008–; Hallé Programmes, 2011–. *Publications:* numerous articles; essays; programme notes, incl. BBC Proms, Edinburgh Internat. Fest., Royal Opera, Glyndebourne Fest. Opera, South Bank Centre, EMI Records, Decca Classics, Warner Classics; contrib. BBC Music Mag., Opera Mag. *Recreations:* beekeeping (newsletter editor, 2006–09, County Representative, 2009–10, Sussex Beekeepers' Assoc., Brighton & Lewes Div.), sourdough bread-making. *Address:* 42 Ferrers Road, Lewes, E Sussex BN7 1PZ. *T:* (01273) 483546.

See also K. Pappenheim.

PAPPS, Alastair Harkness, CB 2002; Associate Director, Centre for Management and Policy Studies, Cabinet Office (on secondment from HM Prison Service), 1999–2002; *b* 28 April 1942; *s* of Osborne Stephen Papps and Helen Papps (*née* Harkness); *m* 1963, Marian Caroline Clayton; two *s* one *d.* *Educ:* King Edward's Sch., Birmingham; St Catharine's Coll., Cambridge (MA); Univ. of Newcastle upon Tyne (Dip. in Applied Social Studies 1970). Joined HM Prison Service, 1965; Prison Service Staff Coll., Wakefield, 1965–66; Asst Gov., Huntercombe Borstal, 1966–69; Tutor, Prison Service Staff Coll., Wakefield, 1970–73; Asst Gov., 1973–75, Dep. Gov., 1975–77, Wakefield Prison; Personnel Div., Prison Service HQ, 1977–80; Governor: Acklington Prison, 1980–83; Durham Prison, 1983–87; Frankland Prison, 1987–89; Dep. Dir, subseq. Dir, North Regl Office, 1989–90; Area Manager, North East, 1990–95; Dir of Ops-North, and Mem., Prisons Bd, 1995–99. Ed., Prison Service Jl, 1987–89. Vice-Chm., Standards Cttee, Rutland CC, 2006–12. Chm., NICRO UK Trust for a Safer S Africa, 2000–09; Expert Advr, Zahid Mubarek public judicial inquiry, 2004–06. Trustee, Prisons Video Trust, 2007–. Lay Member: Professional Conduct Bd, BPsS, 2007–08; Disciplinary and Regulatory Cttees, ACCA, 2011–; Lay Rep., E Midlands Healthcare Workforce Deanery, 2009–13. *Publications:* articles in jls. *Recreations:* reading, theatre, cinema, travel, observing politics. *Address:* Wick House, 17 Well Cross, Edith Weston, Oakham, Rutland LE15 8HG. *Club:* Nottingham.

PAQUET, Dr Jean-Guy, CC 1994 (OC 1984); GOQ 2005 (OQ 1992); FRSC; Chairman of Board, National Optics Institute (President and Chief Executive Officer, 1994); *b* Montmagny, Qué, 5 Jan. 1938; *s* of Laurent W. Paquet and Louisianne Coulombe. *Educ:* Université Laval (BSc Engrg Physics, 1959; DSc Elec. Engrg, 1963); Ecole Nat. Sup. de l'Aéronautique, Paris (MSc Aeronautics, 1960). FRSC 1978; FAAAS 1981. Université Laval: Asst Prof. of Elec. Engrg, 1962; Associate Prof., 1967; Head, Elec. Engrg Dept, 1967–69; Vice-Dean (Research), Faculty of Science, 1969–72; Prof. of Elec. Engrg, 1971; Vice-Rector (Academic), 1972–77; Rector, 1977–87; Pres., La Laurentienne Vie Inc., 1987–94. Fellowships: French Govt, 1959; NATO, 1962; Nat. Science Foundn, 1964; Québec Govt, 1965. Def. Res. Bd of Canada Grant, 1965–76. National Research Council of Canada: Fellowship, 1961; Grant, 1964–77; Mem., Associate Cttee on Automatic Control, 1964–70; Special Asst to Vice-Pres. (Scientific), 1971–72. Pres., Conf. of Rectors and Principals of Univs of Prov. of Québec, 1979–81. Member: Council, Univs of Prov. of Qué, 1973–77; Bd, Assoc. of Scientific, Engrg and Technol Community of Canada, 1970–77 (Pres., 1975–76); Bd, French Canadian Assoc. for Advancement of Science, 1969–71; Canadian Assoc. of Univ. Res. Administrators; Special Task Force on Res. and Devélt, Science Council of Canada, 1976; Order of Engrs, Qué; Amer. Soc. for Engrg Educn; Amer. Management Assoc., 1980; Soc. for Res. Administrators. Member Board: Interamerican Univs Assoc., 1980–87; Assoc. des universités partiellement ou entièrement de langue française, 1981–87 (Vice-Pres., 1983); Assoc. of Commonwealth Univs, 1981–87; Founding Mem., Corporate Higher Educn Forum. Pres., Selection Cttee, Outstanding Achievement Awards, Canada, 1984 (Mem., 1983). DSc *hc* McGill Univ., 1982; DLaw *hc*, York Univ., 1983. *Publications:* (with P. A. Roy) Rapport d'études bibliographiques: l'automation dans la production et la distribution de l'énergie électrique, 1968; (with J. F. Le Maître) Méthodes pratiques d'étude des oscillations non-linéaires: application aux systèmes par plus-ou-moins, 1970; more than fifty pubns in scientific jls, on control systems engrg; articles on research, devélt and scientific policy. *Recreations:* jogging, travels, golf. *Address:* National Optics Institute, 2740 rue Einstein, Sainte-Foy, Québec, QC G1P 4S4, Canada. *T:* (418) 6577006, *Fax:* (418) 6577088. *Clubs:* Cercle de la Garnison de Québec, Golf Royal Québec (Québec).

PARASKEVA, Rt Hon. Dame Janet, DBE 2010; PC 2010; Chair: Plan UK, since 2010; Jersey Appointments Commission, since 2014; Council for Licensed Conveyancers, since 2015; *b* 28 May 1946; *d* of Antonis Paraskeva and Doris Amanda Paraskeva (*née* Fowler); *m* 1967, Alan Richard Derek Hunt (marr. diss. 1983); two *d*, and two step *s*; civil partnership 2007. *Educ:* Open Univ. (BA Social Scis 1983). HM Inspector of Schs, DES, 1983–88; Dir, Nat. Youth Bureau, 1988–91; Chief Exec., Nat. Youth Agency, 1991–95; Dir, England, Nat. Lotteries Charities Bd, 1995–2000; Chief Exec., Law Soc., 2000–06; First Civil Service Comr, 2006–10. Chair: Olympic Lottery Distributor, 2006–13; Child Maintenance and Enforcement Commn, 2008–12 (Chm. designate, 2007–08). Member: Nat. Bd for Crime Prevention, 1993–95; Youth Justice Bd, 1998–2000; Council, Competition Commn, 2012–14. Non-executive Director: Fosse Community NHS Trust, 1992–99; Serious Organised Crime Agency, 2005–13; Assets Recovery Agency, 2007–08. Ind. Mem., Consumer Council for Water, 2005–08; Mem. Panel, Detainee Inquiry, 2010–. JP City of Leicester, 1993–2000. Hon. LLD Brighton, 2006; Hon. MLitt Worcester, 2009. *Publications:* articles in youth, educn and law jls and periodicals and in TES. *Recreations:* gardening, reading.

PARAYRE, Jean-Paul Christophe; Commandeur de la Légion d'Honneur; Commandeur, l'Ordre National du Mérite, 1991; Chairman, Vallourec, 2000–13 (Member, Supervisory Board, 1989–2013); Member, Supervisory Board, Peugeot SA, 1984–2014; *b* Lorient, 5 July 1937; *s* of Louis Parayre and Jehanne Malarde; *m* 1962, Marie-Françoise Chaufour; two *s* two *d.* *Educ:* Lycées in Casablanca and Versailles; Ecole Polytechnique, Paris; Ecole Nationale des Ponts et Chaussées. Engr, Dept of Highways, 1963–67; Technical Adviser: Min. of Social Affairs, 1967; Min. of Economy and Finance, 1968; Dir of Mech. Industries, Min. of Industry and Res., 1970–74; Manager of Planning, Automobile Div. of Peugeot, 1975; Manager, Automobile Div., Peugeot-Citroën, 1976; Chm. and CEO, Peugeot SA, 1977–84; Mem., Supervisory Bd, 1977–84, Dir-Gen., 1984–88, Chm. and Chief Exec. Officer, 1988–90, Dumez SA; Vice-Chm. and Chief Operating Officer, Bolloré, 1994–99 (Dir, 1994–2000); Chm. and CEO, Saga, 1996–99. Chm., GIE Trans-Manche Construction, 1986–92; Vice-Chm., Lyonnaise des Eaux-Dumez, 1990–92; Mem., Board of Directors: Crédit National, then Natexis, 1978–97; Valeo, 1986–91; GTM, 1986–92; LVMH, 1987–89; Jean Lefebvre, 1988–92; McAlpine, 1990–92; Inchcape plc, 1991–94; Indosuez, 1991–94; Bolloré (formerly Albatros) Investissement, 1994; Coflexip, 1995–2000; Delmas, 1995–99; Stena International BV, 1995–2006; Tarmac plc, 1995–99; Sea Invest France, 1999–2004; Stena UK, 1999–2003; Carillion plc, 1999–2004; SNEF, 1999–; Stena Line, 2001–05; Stena Internat. Sarl, 2006–. *Recreations:* tennis, golf. *Address:* 203 avenue Molière, 1050 Brussels, Belgium. *Clubs:* Polo de Paris, Golf de Morfontaine; Golf de Sotogrande.

PARBO, Sir Arvi (Hillar), AC 1993; Kt 1978; non-executive Chairman, WMC (formerly Western Mining Corporation) Ltd, 1990–99 (Chairman and Managing Director, 1974–86; Executive Chairman, 1986–90); *b* 10 Feb. 1926; *s* of Aado and Hilda Parbo; *m* 1953, Saima Soots; two *s* one *d.* *Educ:* Clausthal Mining Acad., Germany; Univ. of Adelaide (BE Hons). Western Mining Corporation: Underground Surveyor, 1956; Underground Manager, Nevoria Mine, 1958–60; Techn. Asst to Man. Dir, 1960–64; Dep. Gen. Supt, WA, 1964–68; Gen. Manager, 1968–71 (Dir, 1970–); Dep. Man. Dir, 1971; Man. Dir, 1971. Director: Aluminium Co. of America, 1980–98; Hoechst Australia (formerly Hoechst Australian Investments Pty) Ltd, 1981–97; Chase AMP Bank Ltd, 1985–91; Sara Lee Corp., 1991–98; Chairman: Munich Reinsurance Company of Australia Ltd, 1984–98 (Dir, 1983–); Zurich Insurance Australian Group, 1985–98; Alcoa of Australia Ltd, 1978–96; The Broken Hill Pty Co. Ltd, 1989–92 (Dir, 1987–92). Member: Chase Internat. Adv. Bd; Degussa AG Supervisory Bd, 1988–93. Hon. DSc: Deakin, 1989; Curtin, 1989; Hon. DEng Monash, 1989; DUniv Flinders, 1991; Hon. DBus Central Qld, 1999; Hon. LLD Sydney, 2000. Australian Achiever, 1990; Centenary Medal, Australia, 2003. Comdr, Order of Merit (Germany), 1979; Grand Cordon, Order of the Sacred Treasure (Japan), 1990; Order of White Star (Estonia), 2001. *Recreations:* reading, carpentry. *Address:* 737 Highbury Road, Vermont South, Vic 3133, Australia. *T:* (3) 98028264. *Clubs:* Melbourne, Australian (Melbourne).

PARDOE, His Honour Alan Douglas William; QC 1988; a Circuit Judge, 2003–13; First-tier Tribunal Judge (formerly a Chairman), Mental Health Review Tribunals (Restricted), 2005–12; *b* 16 Aug. 1943; *s* of William Pardoe and Dr Grace Pardoe, FRSC. *Educ:* Oldbury Grammar Sch.; St Catharine's Coll., Cambridge (MA, LLB). Called to the Bar, Lincoln's Inn, 1971, Bencher, 1998. Lecturer in Law: Univ. of Exeter, 1965–70; Univ. of Auckland, NZ, 1970; Univ. of Sussex, 1970–74; in practice at the Bar, 1973–2003. A Recorder, 1990–2003. Judicial Mem., Parole Bd, 2010–. *Publications:* A Practical Guide to the Industrial Relations Act 1971, 1972; articles in legal periodicals. *Recreations:* drawing, painting and the appreciation of the work of others, travel (quite often walking in the mountains), theatre, reading. *Clubs:* Travellers, Groucho, Oxford and Cambridge.

PARDOE, John Wentworth; Chairman, Sight and Sound Education Ltd, 1979–89; *b* 27 July 1934; *s* of Cuthbert B. Pardoe and Marjorie E. W. (*née* Taylor); *m* 1958, Joyce R. Peerman; two *s* one *d.* *Educ:* Sherborne; Corpus Christi Coll., Cambridge (MA). Television Audience Measurement Ltd, 1958–60; Osborne Peacock Co. Ltd, 1960–61; Liberal News, 1961–66. MP (L) Cornwall N, 1966–79; Treasurer of the Liberal Party, 1968–69. Presenter, Look Here, LWT, 1979–81. Sen. Res. Fellow, PSI, 1979–81. Consultant to Nat. Assoc. of Schoolmasters, 1967–73. Director: William Schlackman Ltd, 1968–71; Gerald Metals, 1972–83; Mem. London Metal Exchange, 1973–83. Mem., Youth Trng Bd, 1985–89. *Recreations:* walking, reading, music, carpentry. *Address:* 18 New End Square, NW3 1LN.

PAREKH, family name of **Baron Parekh**.

PAREKH, Baron *cr* 2000 (Life Peer), of Kingston upon Hull, in the East Riding of Yorkshire; **Bhikhu Chhotalal Parekh,** FBA 2003; Professor of Political Philosophy, University of Westminster, 2001–09, now Emeritus; Professor of Political Theory, University of Hull, 1982–2001, now Emeritus; *b* 4 Jan. 1935; *s* of Chhotalal Parekh and Gajaraben Parekh; *m* 1959, Pramila (*née* Dalal); three *s.* *Educ:* Univ. of Bombay (BA 1954, MA 1956); Univ. of London (PhD 1966). Tutor, LSE, 1962–63; Asst Lectr, Univ. of Glasgow, 1963–64; Lectr, Sen. Lectr and Reader, Hull Univ., 1964–82. Vice-Chancellor, Univ. of Baroda, 1981–84. Visiting Professor: Univ. of BC, 1967–68; Concordia Univ., 1974–75; McGill Univ., 1976–77; Harvard Univ., 1996; Inst. of Advanced Study, Vienna, 1997; Univ. of Pompeu Fabra, Barcelona, 1997; Univ. of Pennsylvania, 1998; Ecole des Hautes Etudes en Sciences Sociales, Paris, 2000; Centennial Prof., LSE, 2001–03. Mem., Rampton/Swann Cttee of Inquiry into Educnl Problems of Ethnic Minority Children, 1978–82; Mem. Council, PSI, 1985–90; Vice Pres., UK Council for Overseas Students Affairs, 1989–94; Chm., British Assoc. of S Asia Scholars, 1989–91, 2004–07. Dep. Chm., CRE, 1985–90; Member: Commn on Rise of Neo-Fascism in Europe, 1992–93; Nat. Commn on Equal Opportunities, CVCP, 1994–99; Chm., Commn on Future of Multi-Ethnic Britain, 1998–2000. Trustee: Runnymede Trust, 1986–2008; Inst. for Public Policy Res., 1988–95; Gandhi Foundn, 1988– (Pres., 2012–); Anne Frank Educnl Trust, 1992–. AcSS 1999 (Pres., 2003–08); FRSA 1988; Fellow, Asiatic Soc., Bombay, 2004. Holds 16 hon. doctorates. British Asian of the Year, Asian Who's Who, 1991; Special Lifetime Achievement Award for Asians, BBC, 1999; Sir Isaiah Berlin Prize, Pol Studies Assoc., 2003. Saraswat Gaurav Award, Gujarat, 2004; Pravasi Bharatiya Samman Award, India, 2005; Pride of India Award, India Internat. Foundn, London, 2006; Distinguished Global Thinker Award, India Internat. Centre, New Delhi, 2006; Sardar Patel Vishva Pratibha Award, Ahmedabad, 2012. Padma Bhushan (India), 2007. *Publications:* Politics and Experience, 1968; Dissent and Disorder, 1971; The Morality of Politics, 1972; Knowledge and Belief in Politics, 1973; Bentham's Political Thought, 1973; Colour, Culture and Consciousness, 1974; Jeremy Bentham: ten critical essays, 1974; The Concept of Socialism, 1975; Hannah Arendt and the Search for a New Political Philosophy, 1981; Karl Marx's Theory of Ideology, 1982; Contemporary Political Thinkers, 1982; Political Discourse, 1986; Gandhi's Political Philosophy, 1989; Colonialism, Tradition and Reform, 1989; Jeremy Bentham: critical assessments (4 vols), 1993; The Decolonisation of Imagination, 1995; Crisis and Change in Contemporary India, 1995; Gandhi, 1997; Rethinking Multiculturalism, 2000; A New Politics of Identity, 2008; Talking Politics, 2011; articles in learned jls incl. Political Studies, British Jl of Political Science, Social Research, Jl of History of Ideas, Indian Jl of Social Science, Ethics, Hist. of Pol Thought, TLS, Canadian Jl of Philosophy, Radical Philosophy, THES, Transit, Les Temps Modernes, Constellations, Dialegs, Rev. of Internat. Studies, Internat. Relations. *Recreations:* reading, music, walking. *Address:* 211 Victoria Avenue, Hull HU5 3EF.

PARFIT, Derek Antony, FBA 1986; Senior Research Fellow, All Souls College, Oxford, 1984–2010, now Emeritus Fellow; *b* 11 Dec. 1942; *s* of Norman and Jessie Parfit. *Educ:* Eton; Balliol College, Oxford (BA Modern History, 1964). Fellow of All Souls Coll., Oxford, 1967–. Visiting Professor: NYU; Harvard Univ.; Rutgers Univ. *Publications:* Reasons and Persons, 1984; On What Matters (2 vols), 2011. *Recreation:* architectural photography. *Address:* All Souls College, Oxford OX1 4AL. *T:* (01865) 279282.

PARFITT, Andrew John; Chairman, National Foundation for Youth Music, since 2013; Director, Enlightened Leadership, since 2013; *b* 24 Sept. 1958; *s* of John Raymond Parfitt and Jeanne Parfitt; *m* 1996, Laura Druce; two *d.* *Educ:* Bristol Old Vic Theatre Sch.; Wharton Business Sch. Asst stage manager, Bristol Arts Centre, 1978; studio manager, BBC, 1979–84; programme presenter, British Forces Broadcasting Service, 1984; BBC: educn producer, 1985; producer, features and magazines, Radio 4, 1986–91; Breakfast Show Editor, Radio 5, 1991–93; Radio 1: Editor, 1993–95; Managing Editor, 1995–98; Controller: BBC Radio 1, 1998–2011; BBC 1Xtra, 2002–11; BBC Switch, 2006–10; BBC Asian Network, 2008–11; BBC Popular Music, 2008–11; Dir, Exec. Talent, EMEA, Saatchi & Saatchi Fallon Gp, 2011–13. Trustee, Services Sound and Vision Corp., 2013–. *Recreations:* running, painting, music, presenting radio programmes. *Address:* National Foundation for Youth Music, Suites 3–5, Swan Court, 9 Tanner Street, SE1 3LE.

PARFITT, David John; film producer; Director: Renaissance Theatre Company, since 1987; Trademark Films, since 1999; Trademark Theatre Company, since 2001; *b* 8 July 1958; *s* of late William Arnold Parfitt and Maureen Parfitt (*née* Collinson); *m* 1st, 1988, Susan Coates (marr. diss. 1993); one *s*; 2nd, 1996, Elizabeth Barron; two *s.* *Educ:* Bede Grammar Sch., Sunderland; Barbara Speake Stage Sch., London. Actor, 1970–88; producer, 1985–: productions include: *theatre:* Tell Me Honestly, 1985, John Sessions at the 11th Hour, 1986, Donmar Warehouse; Romeo and Juliet, 1986, Public Enemy, 1987, Lyric Hammersmith; Napoleon, Albery, 1987; Much Ado About Nothing, As You Like It, and Hamlet, Phoenix, 1988; Look Back in Anger, Lyric, 1989; A Midsummer Night's Dream, King Lear, Dominion, 1990; Scenes from a Marriage, Wyndhams, 1990; Travelling Tales, Haymarket, 1991; Uncle Vanya, Lyric Hammersmith, 1991; Coriolanus, Chichester Fest. Th., 1992; Les Liaisons Dangereuses, Playhouse, 2004; Elling, Bush, 2007; A Bunch of Amateurs, Watermill Newbury, 2014; *television:* Twelfth Night, 1988; Look Back in Anger, 1989; Parade's End, 2012; The Wipers Times, 2013; Glyndebourne: the untold history, 2014; *films:* Henry V,

1988; Peter's Friends, 1992; Swan Song, 1992; Much Ado About Nothing, 1993; Mary Shelley's Frankenstein, 1994; The Madness of King George, 1995; Twelfth Night, 1996; The Wings of the Dove, 1997; Shakespeare in Love, 1998; (consultant) Gangs of New York, 2002; I Capture the Castle, 2003; Chasing Liberty, 2004; (exec. prod.) Dean Spanley, 2008; A Bunch of Amateurs, 2008; My Week with Marilyn, 2011. BAFTA: Mem. Bd of Trustees, 2000–11 (Chm., 2008–10); Chm., Film Cttee, 2004–07; Chm., Film London, 2011–. Trustee, Chicken Shed Th. Co., 1997–2012; Patron, Royalty Th., Sunderland, 1999–. Hon. DA Sunderland, 1999; Hon. Dr Drama RSAMD, 2001. *Address:* Trademark Films Ltd, 14a Goodwin's Court, WC2N 4LL. *T:* (020) 3322 8900. *E:* mail@trademarkfilms.co.uk.

PARGETER, Catherine Jane; *see* Brunner, C. J.

PARGETER, Rt Rev. Philip; Auxiliary Bishop of Birmingham, (RC), and Titular Bishop of Valentiniana, 1989–2009; *b* 13 June 1933; *s* of Philip William Henry Pargeter and Ellen Pargeter. *Educ:* St Bede's Coll., Manchester; Oscott Coll., Sutton Coldfield. Priest, 1959; on staff of Cotton College, 1959–85; Administrator, St Chad's Cathedral, Birmingham, 1985–90; Canon, 1986. *Recreations:* reading, listening to music, walking.

PARHAM, Prof. Peter Robert, PhD; FRS 2008; Professor of Structural Biology, Stanford University, since 1992; scientist and immunogeneticist, since 1977; *b* Stanmore, Middx, 15 Aug. 1950; *s* of Ronald and Hilda Parham; *m* 1978, Frances Brodsky. *Educ:* Stanburn Prim. Sch., Stanmore; Haberdashers' Aske's Sch., Elstree; St John's Coll., Cambridge (BA Natural Scis 1972); Harvard Univ. (PhD Biochem. and Molecular Biol.). Jun. Fellow, Soc. of Fellows, Harvard Univ., 1977–80; Asst Prof., 1980–88, Associate Prof., 1988–92, Stanford Univ. *Publications:* The Immune System, 2000, 3rd edn 2009. *Recreations:* seaside swimming, landmarks, watching bad birds. *Address:* Department of Structural Biology, 299 Campus Drive West, Stanford University, Stanford, CA 94305–5126, USA. *T:* (650) 7237456, *Fax:* (650) 4248912. *E:* peropa@stanford.edu.

PARHAM, Philip John, CMG 2015; HM Diplomatic Service; Ambassador to the United Arab Emirates, since 2014; *b* 14 Aug. 1960; *s* of John Carey Parham and Christian Mary Parham (*née* Fitzherbert); *m* 1985, Anna Catherine Astrid Louise, (Kasia), Giedroyć; five *s* two *d*. *Educ:* Eton Coll.; Christ Church, Oxford (MA Lit.Hum.). Morgan Grenfell, 1983–89 (Sen. Asst Dir, 1988); Barclays de Zoete Wedd Ltd, 1989–93 (Dir, 1993); joined FCO, 1993; FCO, 1993–96 (Private Sec. to Parly Under-Sec. of State, 1995); First Sec. (Chancery), Washington, 1996–2000; Dir, Trade and Investment Promotion, Saudi Arabia, 2000–03; FCO, 2003–04; Hd, Counter Terrorism Policy Dept, FCO, 2004–06; High Comr to Tanzania, 2006–09; Dep. Perm. Rep., UK Mission to UN, NY, 2009–13. Liveryman, Skinners' Co. Hon. Fellow, Harris Manchester Coll., Oxford, 2014. *Recreations:* children, theology, gardening, researching the parentage of Mary Anne Smythe. *Address:* c/o Foreign and Commonwealth Office, King Charles Street, SW1A 2AH.

PARHAM, Richard David; Chairman: Dixi & Associates, 2001–10; Coventry and Warwickshire Connexions, 2001–11; *b* 17 Nov. 1944; *s* of James Parham and Lily Elizabeth Parham; *m* 1967, Janet Burton; one *s* one *d*. *Educ:* Royal Liberty Sch., Romford; Barking Coll. of Technol. Ford Motor Co., 1961–67; Rootes Motors, 1967–69; Chrysler UK, then Chrysler UK/Talbot Motor Co., 1969–81: Profit Analysis Manager, then Finance Manager, Hills Precision Ltd, 1969–72; Manager, Product and Pricing Analysis, then Pricing and Investment, 1972–76; Co. Comptroller, 1976–77; Dir of Finance, 1977–80; Asst Man. Dir, 1981–94, Man. Dir, 1994–99, Peugeot Talbot, subseq. Peugeot, Motor Co. Chairman: Coventry, Solihull and Warwicks Partnerships, 2000–08; Coventry and Warwicks Regeneration Zone, 2001–08. Mem. Council, Coventry and Warwicks LLSC. Chm. Bd of Govs, 2002–08, Pro Chancellor, 2009–11, Coventry Univ.; Mem. Ct, Warwick Univ., 1998–2009. Hon. DBA Coventry 1999. *Recreations:* Rugby, cricket, music, reading, golf.

PARIS, Archbishop of, (RC), since 2005; **His Eminence Cardinal André Armand Vingt-Trois;** Officier de la Légion d'Honneur; Officier de l'Ordre National du Mérite; *b* 7 Nov. 1942; *s* of Armand Vingt-Trois and Paulette (*née* Vuillamy). *Educ:* Lycée Henri IV, Paris; St Sulpice Seminary, Issy-les-Moulineaux; Institut Catholique, Paris (BTh 1962). Military service, Germany, 1964–65; ordained priest, 1969; Asst Pastor, St Jeanne de Chantal, Paris, 1969–74; Dir and Prof. of Sacramental and Moral Theology, St Sulpice Seminary, Issy-les-Moulineaux, 1974–81; Vicar Gen., Archdiocese of Paris, 1981–99; ordained Aux. Bishop of Paris, 1988; Metropolitan Archbishop of Tours, 1999. Cardinal, 2007. French Bishops' Conference: Member: Episcopal Cttee for Charismatic Renewal, 1988–96; Permt Cttee for Information and Communications, 1988–97; Permt Cttee for Econ. Affairs, 1997–99; Pres., Cttee for the Family, 1998–2005; Pres., 2007–13. Mem., Presidency Cttee, Pontifical Council for the Family and Congregation of Bishops, 2006–, and for the Pastoral Care of Migrants and Itinerant People, 2008–. Member: Congregation for the Clergy, 2010–; Congregation of the Oriental Churches, 2012–. Grand Cross Knight, Equestrian Order of the Holy Sepulchre, 2012. *Publications:* A Year of Blessings, 2000; To Know the Catholic Faith, 2000; Catecheses for the Jubilee Year, 2001; The Family: 15 questions to the Church, 2003; To Believe, to Hope, to Love, 2007; The Signs that God Sends Us, 2007; Freedom in Faith, 2008; Bishops, Priests and Deacons, 2009; A Mission for Liberty, 2010; Prayer: why? how?, 2010; Family Life: building happiness, 2011; What Kind of a Society Do We Want?, 2012; God Opens New Paths, 2015. *Address:* c/o Diocese de Paris, 10 rue du Cloître-Notre-Dame, 75004 Paris, France.

PARIS, Andrew Martin Ingledew, FRCS; Consultant Urological Surgeon, The Royal London Hospital, 1976–2005, and St Bartholomew's Hospital, 1994–2005, now Emeritus Consulting Urological Surgeon; *b* 27 Nov. 1940; s of Vernon Patrick Paris and Heather Constance Ingledew Paris (*née* Dear); *m* 1975, Susan Philippa, *d* of Perys Goodwin Jenkins; one *d*. *Educ:* London Hosp. Med. Coll., Univ. of London (MB BS 1964). MRCS 1964, FRCS 1971; LRCP 1964; DObstRCOG 1967. Clinical Dir of Surgery and Urology, Royal London Hosp., then Barts and the London NHS Trust, 1979–2002; Consultant Paediatric Urological Surgeon, Newham Gen. Hosp., 1995–2005. Hon. Urological Surgeon, Italian Hosp., London, 1979–90. Regl Advr on Urology, NE Thames, 1982–87. Examr in Dental Surgery, RCS, 1983–89. Founder Mem., St John Ambulance Air Wing, Hon. Surgeon, 1971–92; Trustee, St John Travelling Fellowships in Transplantation, 1992–. FRSocMed (Vice Pres., Section of Urology, 1983–84). Sen. Mem., British Assoc. of Urological Surgeons, 2005; Mem., Urological Club of GB and Ire. Trustee: Marie Celeste Samaritan Soc., 1996– (Chm., 2006–); Long Shop Mus., 2004–. Freeman, City of London, 1984; Liveryman, Soc. of Apothecaries, 1967– (Chm. Livery Cttee, 1992–93; Mem. Ct of Assts, 1994–; Master, 2007–08). OStJ 1985. *Publications:* contribs on urology and transplantation to med. jls. *Recreations:* croquet, ski-ing, sailing. *Address:* The Old Vicarage, Aldringham cum Thorpe, Suffolk IP16 4QF. *T:* (01728) 833673. *E:* andrewparis@tiscali.co.uk. *Clubs:* Athenæum; Aldeburgh Yacht; Fromus Croquet.

PARIS, Prof. Jeffrey Bruce, PhD; FBA 1999; Professor of Mathematics, Manchester University, since 1984; *b* 15 Nov. 1944; *s* of George William and Marie Eileen Paris; *m* 1st, 1967, Malvyn Loraine Blackburn (marr. diss. 1983); two *d*; 2nd, 1983, Alena Vencovská; three *s* one *d*. *Educ:* Manchester Univ. (BSc 1st Cl. Maths 1966; PhD Mathematical Logic 1969). Manchester University: Lectr, Dept of Maths, 1969–74; Reader, 1974–84. Junior Whitehead Prize, London Mathematical Soc., 1983. *Publications:* The Uncertain Reasoner's Companion, 1994; numerous research papers in learned jls. *Recreations:* football, angling, painting. *Address:* School of Mathematics, The University of Manchester, Manchester M13 9PL. *T:* (0161) 275 5880.

PARISH, Neil Quentin Gordon; MP (C) Tiverton and Honiton, since 2010; *b* 26 May 1956; *s* of Reginald Thomas Parish and Kathleen Susan Mary Parish; *m* 1981, Susan Gail; one *s* one *d*. *Educ:* Brymore Sch., Somerset. Left sch. at 16 to run farm of 100 acres; farm increased to 300 acres, dairy and arable, 1990. Member (C): Sedgemoor DC, 1983–95 (Dep. Leader, 1989–95); Somerset CC, 1989–93; Parish Council, 1985–. European Parliament: Mem. (C) SW Region, England, 1999–2009; spokesman on agriculture and on fisheries; Chairman: Agric. and Rural Develt Cttee, 1999–2009; Animal Welfare Intergroup, 2007–09; Member: Envmt Cttee, 2001–09; Fisheries Cttee, 2002–09; Chm., Select Cttee on Envmt, Food and Rural Affairs, 2015–. Mem., EU Australian and NZ delegn. Contested (C) Torfaen, 1997. *Recreations:* swimming, walking. *Address:* House of Commons, SW1A 0AA.

PARISH, Prof. Richard, CBE 2014; CBiol; FFPH, FRSPH; FRSB; Chief Executive: Royal Society for Public Health, 2008–13 (Chief Executive: Royal Society of Health, 2005–08; Royal Institute of Public Health, 2008); Institute of Healthcare Management, 2012–13; *b* 11 Oct. 1951; *s* of Leslie Thomas Parish, FCCA and Winifred Alice Parish; *m* 1976, Joan Margaret Shepherd; one *s* one *d*. *Educ:* Univ. of London (BSc ext. 1975); South Bank Poly. (PDipHEd 1978); Huddersfield Univ. (MEd). CBiol 1989; MSB (MIBiol 1989), FRSB (FSB (by distinction) 2011); Hon. MFPHM 2001; FRIPH 2006; FRSocMed 2013. Dir of Health Promotion, Stockport HA, 1980–85; Head of Progs, 'Heartbeat Wales', and Sen. Lectr, Welsh Nat. Sch. of Medicine, 1985–87; Dir of Ops, Health Promotion Authy for Wales, 1987–90; Principal and Chief Exec., Humberside Coll. of Health, 1990–96; Dir, Health and Community Studies, and Prof. of Public Health, Sheffield Hallam Univ., 1996–97; Hd, Health Studies, and Prof., Univ. of York, 1997–99; Regl Dir, Educn and Trng, NHS Eastern Reg., 1999; Chief Exec., HDA, 2000–03; Consultant, WHO, 2003–05. Chm., Pharmacy and Public Health Forum, 2011–; non-exec. Dir, Public Health England, 2013–; Mem. Bd, UK Public Health Register, 2013–. Prof. of Health Develt, Univ. of Chester, 2014–; Visiting Professor: Anglia Ruskin (formerly Anglia Poly.) Univ., 2003–; Staffordshire Univ., 2008–13; Brunel Univ., 2008–; UCL 2014–; Robert Gordon Univ., 2014–. Hon. Consultant, NE Essex PCT, 2008–13. Chm., Nat. No-Smoking Day, 2005–12. Exec. Bd Mem., Nat. Health Forum (formerly Nat. Heart Forum), 2000–13; Vice Pres. for Europe, Internat. Union for Health Promotion and Educn, 2014–15. Gov., Moggerhanger Primary Sch., 2005–09. FRSPH (FRSH 1988), Hon. FRSPH 2013; MCIPR (MIPR 1989); Foundation Fellow, Inst. of Health Visiting, 2012. Hon. Mem., APHA, 2006; Hon. FRPharmS 2013. Hon DSc Brunel, 2014. *Publications:* contribs on health promotion and health policy, incl. for WHO. *Recreations:* photography, rambling, cycling, Inland Waterways, boating. *Address:* Cop Rise, 21 Moor View, Meltham, Holmfirth, W Yorks HD9 5RT. *T:* (01484) 311783.

PARISH, Stephen William; Chairman, Norton Rose Fulbright LLP (formerly Norton Rose LLP), since 2009 (Group Chairman, Norton Rose, 2009–12); *b* Worthing, 4 Sept. 1951; *s* of Alexander Leonard Stephen Parish and Sheila Margaret Parish; *m* 1980, Joyce Smith; two *s* one *d*. *Educ:* Worthing High Sch.; Univ. of Birmingham (LLB 1973). Admitted solicitor, 1976; Norton Rose Botterell & Roche, then Norton Rose, then Norton Rose LLP, later Norton Rose Fulbright LLP, 1976–: Admin Partner, 1997–2000; Global Hd of Banking, 2006–09. *Recreations:* travel, family, theatre, ballet, opera. *Address:* Norton Rose Fulbright LLP, 3 More London Riverside, SE1 2AQ. *T:* (020) 7283 6000, *Fax:* (020) 7283 6500. *E:* stephen.parish@nortonrosefulbright.com. *Club:* MCC.

PARISOT, Pierre Louis André; Chevalier de l'Ordre du Mérite; Chevalier de la Légion d'Honneur; Chairman: Aquiris, since 2001; Transorco, since 2009; *b* Ambacourt, France, 9 Jan. 1940; *s* of Louis Parisot and Marie (*née* Boye); *m* 1963, Evelyne Treilhou; two *s* two *d*. *Educ:* Ecole Polytechnique; Ecole Nationale des Ponts et Chaussées; Institut d'Etudes Politiques de Paris. Assistant to the Director, Civil Works Department: Réunion Island, 1966–72; Morbihan, Brittany, 1973–76; Dep. Dir, Personnel Policy and Mod. Management Methods, Min. of Civil Works, Transport and Envmt, 1976–77; Technical Advr, French Home Office Cabinet, 1977–80; Internat. Dir, St Gobain subsid., SOBEA, 1980–84; Dir Gen., SOGEA (Gp Générale des Eaux), 1985–90; Chm., Supervisory Bd, Société des Tuyaux Bonna (Gp Générale des Eaux, subseq. Vivendi), 1990–; Dep. Man. Dir, Société Générale d'Entreprises, 1991–97; Vice-Pres., Strategic Sourcing and Purchasing, Veolia Environnement, 2002–08; Chm., Transmanche-Link (TML), 1991–2006; Chairman and Chief Executive: Consortium Stade de France SA, 1995–98; Omnium de Traitement et de Valorisation, 1997–2001. *Recreations:* sailing, ski-ing. *Address:* 34 rue Rieussec, 78220 Viroflay, France. *T:* (1) 30245445.

PARK, Hon. Sir Andrew (Edward Wilson), Kt 1997; a Judge of the High Court of Justice, Chancery Division, 1997–2006; *b* 27 Jan. 1939; *m* 1962, Ann Margaret Woodhead; two *s* one *d* (and one *s* decd). *Educ:* Leeds Grammar Sch.; University Coll., Oxford. Winter Williams Law Schol., 1959; BA (Jurisp.) 1960, MA 1964. FTII 1990. Various academic posts in UK and abroad, 1960–68. Called to the Bar, Lincoln's Inn, 1964, Bencher, 1986; QC 1978; QC (NI) 1992; a Recorder, 1989–94; practice at Revenue Bar, 1965–97. Chairman: Taxation and Retirement Benefits Cttee of the Bar Council, 1978–82; Revenue Bar Assoc., 1987–92; Treasurer, Senate of the Inns of Court and Bar, 1982–85. Hon. Pres., London Br., 2007–, Hon. Fellow, 2008, Chartered Inst. of Taxation. *Publications:* The Sources of Nigerian Law, 1963; various articles, notes and reviews in legal periodicals, mainly concerning taxation. *Recreations:* tennis, golf, watching Rugby League. *Address:* 10 New Road, Esher, Surrey KT10 9PG.

PARK, David; *see* Park, W. D.

PARK, Gilbert Richard, TD 1985; FRCA; Consultant in Critical Care Medicine, North Middlesex University Hospital, 2009–12; specialist photographer, podcaster and videographer in medically related areas, since 2009; Secretary General, World Federation of Societies of Intensive and Critical Care Medicine, 2001–05; *b* 17 May 1950; *s* of Whyrill Heslop and Czeslawa Park; one *s* one *d*. *Educ:* Edinburgh Univ. (BSc; MB ChB; MD); MA Cantab; Anglia Ruskin Univ. (FdA 2010). FRCA 1976. Training posts in Edinburgh, 1974–83; Associate Lectr, Univ. of Cambridge, 1984–2010; Consultant in Anaesthesia and Intensive Care, 1983–2010, Dir, Intensive Care, 1985–2000, Addenbrooke's Hosp., Cambridge; Consultant in Anaesthesia and Resuscitation, RAMC, 1985–92. Hunterian Prof., RCS, 1986; Vis. Prof., Duke Univ., 1992. Non-exec. Dir, UK Transplant, 2001–05. Hon. Mem. Bulgarian Soc. of Anaesthetists, 2001; Academician, European Acad. of Anesthesiology, 2001. Hon. Dr of Med. Sci. Pleven, 1995. Freelance journalist on sailing and power boating. *Publications: jointly:* Intensive Care: a handbook, 1988; Anaesthesia and Intensive Care Information, 1989, 2nd edn 1995; The Management of Acute Pain, 1991, 2nd edn 2001; Sedation and Analgesia in the Critically Ill Patient, 1993; A Colour Atlas of Intensive Care, 1995; Fighting for Life, 1996; A Pocket Book of Pharmacology in the Critically Ill, 1996; Algorithms for Rational Prescribing in the Critically Ill, 1997; Handbook of drugs in intensive care: an A-Z guide, 2000; Anaesthesia and Intensive Care Information: key facts in anaesthesia and intensive care, 2002; (ed) Liver Disease, 1993; *edited jointly:* Anaesthesia and Intensive Care for Patients with Liver Disease, 1995; Sedation and Analgesia in the Critically Ill, 1995; Tricks and Traps, 1997; Sepsis in the Critically Ill, 1999; Beginners Guide to Fluid and Electrolyte Balance, 2000; Pharmacology in the Critically Ill, 2001; Top Tips in Intensive Care, 2001; 150 papers in learned jls; specialised educnl calendars. *Recreations:* landscape photography, hill walking, powerboating. *Address:* 2 Harbour Way, Emsworth, Hants PO10 7BE. *E:* gilbertpark@doctors.org.uk.

PARK, Graham; *see* Park, J. G.

PARK, Ian Grahame, CBE 1995; Chairman, Northcliffe Newspapers Group Ltd, 1995–2003 (Managing Director, 1982–95); Director, Daily Mail and General Trust plc, 1994–2009; *b* 15 May 1935; *s* of William Park and Christina (*née* Scott); *m* 1965, Anne Turner; one *s*. *Educ:* Lancaster Royal Grammar Sch.; Queens' Coll., Cambridge. 1st Bn Manchester Regt, Berlin (Nat. Service Commn), 1954–56. Trainee Journalist, Press and Journal, Aberdeen, 1959; Asst Lit. Editor, Sunday Times, 1960–63; various management posts, Thomson Newspapers, 1963–65; Liverpool Daily Post and Echo, 1965–82, Man. Dir and Editor in Chief, 1972–82; Dir, Associated Newspaper Holdings Ltd, 1983–95. Mem. Council, Newspaper Soc., 1967–95 (Pres., 1980–81); Dir, Press Assoc., 1973–83 (Chm., 1978–79 and 1979–80); Dir, Reuters, 1978–82, 1988–94. Mem. Newspaper Panel, Monopolies and Mergers Commn, 1986–95. Dir, Radio City (Sound of Merseyside Ltd), 1973–82; Dir, Liverpool Playhouse, 1973–80; Trustee, Blue Coat Soc. of Arts, Liverpool, 1973–82. FRSA. Gov. and Trustee, Dr Johnson's House Trust, 1996–. *Recreations:* eighteenth-century English pottery, twentieth-century English pictures. *Address:* c/o Daily Mail and General Trust plc, 2 Derry Street, W8 5TT. *Club:* Reform.

PARK, (Ian) Michael (Scott), CBE 1982; Consultant, Paull & Williamsons, Advocates, Aberdeen, 1991–2000 (Partner, 1964–91); *b* 7 April 1938; *m* 1964, Elizabeth Mary Lamberton Struthers, MBE, BL; one *s* (and one *s* decd). *Educ:* Aberdeen Grammar Sch.; Aberdeen Univ. (MA, LLB). Admitted Mem. Soc. of Advocates, Aberdeen, 1962 (Treas., 1991–92; Pres., 1992–93). Temp. Sheriff, 1976–94; Hon. Sheriff at Aberdeen, 1997–. Law Society of Scotland: Mem. Council, 1974–85; Vice-Pres., 1979–80; Pres., 1980–81. A Chm., Med. Appeal Tribunals, 1991–96; Member: Criminal Injuries Compensation Bd, 1983–2000; Criminal Injuries Compensation Appeals Panel, 1996–2002. Chm., Aberdeen Citizens Advice Bureau, 1976–88. Frequent broadcaster on legal topics. *Recreations:* golf, gardening, cheating Parkinson's Disease. *Address:* Beechwood, 46 Rubislaw Den South, Aberdeen AB15 4AY. *T:* (01224) 313799. *Club:* New (Edinburgh).

PARK, (James) Graham, CBE 1995; Consultant, H. L. F. Berry & Co. Solicitors, 2004–07 (Senior Partner, 1983–2003); Compliance Officer, Conservative Party, 1999–2006; *b* 27 April 1941; *s* of late Alderman James Park, OBE and Joan Park (*née* Sharp); *m* 1969, Susan Don; one *s*. *Educ:* Malvern Coll., Worcs; Manchester Univ. (LLB Hons). Articled, 1965; admitted as solicitor, 1968; Partner, H. L. F. Berry & Co. Solicitors, 1969–83. Mem., Parole Bd, 1996–2002 and 2003–10 (Appraiser, 2010–); a Judge of First-tier Tribunal: Criminal Injuries Compensation (formerly Mem., Criminal Injuries Compensation Appeals Panel), 2000–11; Mental Health (formerly Mem., Mental Health Rev. Tribunal), 2003–12. Chm., Fitness to Practise Panel, NMC, 2012–. Chairman, Constituency Conservative Association: Knutsford, 1982–83; Altrincham and Sale, 1983–87; Chm., NW Area Cons. Assoc., 1992–95; Vice-Pres., 1996–98, Pres., 1998, Nat. Union of Cons. and Unionist Assocs; Pres., Nat. Cons. Convention and Mem., Bd of Mgt, 1998–99, Chm., Constitutional Cttee, 2000–06, Cons. Party; Chm., Cons. Party Conf., 1998. Contested (C): Crewe, Feb. and Oct. 1974; Middleton and Prestwich, 1979. Mem. Court, Salford Univ., 1989–97. *Recreations:* cricket, motor-racing, cycling. *Address:* (office) 758 Oldham Road, Failsworth, Manchester M35 9XB. *T:* (0161) 681 4005.

PARK, John William; Policy and Strategy Director, since 2012, and Assistant General Secretary, since 2013, Community; *b* 14 Sept. 1973; *s* of George and Elizabeth Park; two *d*. Electrical fitter, 1989–98, trade union convenor, 1998–2001, Rosyth Dockyard; Res. Officer, 2001–02, Nat. Industrial Campaigns Officer, 2002–03, AEEU, then Amicus; Hd, Employee Relns, Babcock Naval Services, 2003–04; Asst Sec., Scottish TUC, 2004–07. MSP (Lab) Mid Scotland and Fife, 2007–Dec. 2012. *Address:* Community, 465c Caledonian Road, N7 9GX. *E:* jpark@community-tu.org.

PARK, Dame Merle (Florence), (Dame Merle Bloch), DBE 1986 (CBE 1974); Principal, Royal Ballet, 1959–83; Director, Royal Ballet School, 1983–98; *b* Salisbury, S Rhodesia, 8 Oct. 1937; *d* of P. J. Park, Eastlea, Salisbury, S Rhodesia, C Africa; *m* 1st, 1965, James Monahan, CBE (marr. diss. 1970; he *d* 1985); one *s*; 2nd, 1971, Sidney Bloch (*d* 2000). *Educ:* Elmhurst Ballet Sch. Founder, Ballet Sch., St Peter's Sq., W6, 1977–83. Joined Sadler's Wells Ballet, 1955; first rôle, a Mouse (Sleeping Beauty prologue); first solo, Milkmaid (Façzce); principal soloist, 1959. First danced: Blue Bird (Act III, Sleeping Beauty), 1956; Swanhilda (Coppelia), Mamzelle Angot (Mamzelle Angot), 1958; Lise (Fille Mal Gardée), 1960; Cinderella, 1962; Juliet (Romeo and Juliet), 1965; Giselle, Celestial (Shadow Play), 1967; Clara (Nutcracker), Aurora (Sleeping Beauty), 1968; Odette (Swan Lake), 1971; A Walk to Paradise Garden, 1972; Firebird, Odette/Odile (Swan Lake), Dances at a Gathering, 1973; Manon, Emilia (The Moor's Pavane), Aureole, Terpsichore (Apollo), Elite Syncopations, 1974; Lulu, 1976; Kate (The Taming of the Shrew), La Bayadère, Tuesday's Child (Jazz Calendar), Triad, Symphonic Variations, Waltzes of Spring (in Royal Opera Fledermaus), Le Papillon, 1977; Countess Larisch (Mayerling), 1978; La Fin du Jour, 1979; Mary Vetsera (Mayerling), Natalia (A Month in the Country), Adieu, 1980; Chloë (Daphnis and Chloë), Isadora, 1981; Raymonda, 1983. Queen Elizabeth Award, Royal Acad. of Dancing, 1982. *Recreations:* gardening, coaching professionals, reading. *Address:* c/o Royal Ballet School, 46 Floral Street, Covent Garden, WC2E 9DA.

PARK, Michael; *see* Park, I. M. S.

PARK, Nicholas Wulstan, CBE 1997; RDI 2006; director and animator of 3D stop motion films; Partner, Aardman Animations Ltd, since 1995; *b* 6 Dec. 1958. *Educ:* Sheffield Poly., Faculty of Art and Design; National Film and TV Sch. Films include: A Grand Day Out, 1989 (BAFTA award for Best Animated Short, 1990); Creature Comforts, 1990 (Acad. Award for Best Animated Short, 1990); The Wrong Trousers, 1993 (Acad. Award and BAFTA award for Best Animated Short Film, 1993); A Close Shave, 1995 (Acad. Award and BAFTA award for Best Animated Film, 1995; Emmy for Best Popular Arts Programme, 1996); Chicken Run, 2000; Cracking Contraptions, 2002; Wallace and Gromit: the Curse of the Were-Rabbit, 2005 (Acad. Award and BAFTA Alexander Korda award, 2006); Wallace and Gromit: A Matter of Loaf and Death, 2008 (BAFTA award for Best Animated Short Film, 2009); (exec. prod.) Shaun the Sheep, 2015; TV series: Shaun the Sheep, BBC1, 2007–10. *Address:* Aardman Animations Ltd, 1410 Aztec West Business Park, Almondsbury, Bristol BS32 4RT. *T:* (01454) 859000.

PARK, Stephen, FCA, FCT; Managing Director, Ashley Interim Management Ltd, since 2002; *b* 7 Aug. 1952; *m* Linda Susan; three *s* one *d*. FCA 1977; FCT 1992. Articled clerk, Alliott Peirson & Co., 1972–77; Audit Sen., Arthur Andersen & Co., 1977–80; Financial Planning and Analysis Manager, Data Gen. Ltd, 1980–81; Hanson plc, 1981–92 (Associate Dir and Asst to Chm. and Chief Exec.); Gp Finance Dir, Sears plc, 1992–94; Dep. Finance Dir, Allders plc, 1995–96; Finance Dir, DERA, 1997–2001. Hon. Treasurer: Carers Bromley, 2011–; Mental Health Foundn, 2014–. Lay Mem., Finance and Audit, Guildford and Waverley CCG, 2013–. *E:* AshleyInterim@btinternet.com.

PARK, Prof. (William) David, FSA; FIIC; Director, Conservation of Wall Painting Department, since 1985, Professor, since 2008, and Director, Robert H. N. Ho Family Foundation Centre for Buddhist Art and Conservation, since 2013, Courtauld Institute of Art, London; *b* 23 May 1952; *s* of late Bill and Elizabeth Park; *m* 1984, Leslie Ross (marr. diss. 1985). *Educ:* Dorking County Grammar Sch.; Univ. of Manchester (BA 1973, MA 1974); Corpus Christi Coll., Cambridge. FSA 1986. Leverhulme Res. Fellow, Courtauld Inst., London, 1980–85. Co-ordinator, Nat. Survey of Medieval Wall Painting, 1980–; Mem. Council, British Archaeol. Assoc., 1993–96; Chm., Paintings Cttee, Council for the Care of Churches, 1996–2006. Vis. Prof., Univ. Paris 1, Panthéon-Sorbonne, 2001. FIIC 2010. *Publications:* (ed with C. Norton) Cistercian Art and Architecture in the British Isles, 1986; (with C. Norton and P. Binski) Dominican Painting in East Anglia: the Thornham Parva Retable and the Musée de Cluny Frontal, 1987; (ed with S. Cather and P. Williamson) Early Medieval Wall Painting and Painted Sculpture in England, 1990; (with S. Boldrick and P. Williamson) Wonder: painted sculpture from Medieval England, 2002; (ed with R. Griffith-Jones) The Temple Church in London: history, architecture, art, 2010; (jtly) Wall Paintings of Eton, 2012; (ed jtly) Art of Merit: studies in Buddhist art and its conservation, 2013; contrib. learned jls. *Recreation:* Paris. *Address:* Courtauld Institute of Art, Somerset House, Strand, WC2R 0RN. *T:* (020) 7848 2871.

PARKER, family name of **Earls of Macclesfield** and **Morley**.

PARKER, Sir Alan, Kt 2014; Founder and Chairman, Brunswick Group LLP, since 2004 (Senior Partner, 1987–2004); UK Business Ambassador, since 2010; *b* 3 May 1956; *s* of Sir Peter Parker, KBE, LVO; *m* 1st, 1977, Caroline Louise (marr. diss. 2006), *d* of Thaddeus Gordon; one *s* three *d*; 2nd, 2007, Jane Hardman; three *s* one *d*. Dep. Man. Dir, Broad St Associates, 1982–87. Chairman: Save the Children, 2008–; UK Now, 2011–; Duke of Edinburgh Commonwealth Study Conference, 2011–; Vice Chairman: China Now, 2008; Employment Opportunities; Trustee: Business Commitment to Envmt Leadership Awards scheme, 2007–; House of Illustration, 2007–; Queen Elizabeth Diamond Jubilee Trust, 2012–. Mem. Council, Temenos Acad.; Bd Dir, FilmClub, 2008–; Mem., Adv. Bd, Videre, 2009–. Gov., SOAS, 2007–09 (Global Ambassador, 2011–). *Recreation:* friends. *Address:* Brunswick Group LLP, 16 Lincoln's Inn Fields, WC2A 3ED. *T:* (020) 7404 5959, *Fax:* (020) 7831 2823.

PARKER, Alan Charles, CBE 2008; non-executive Chairman: Mothercare, 2011 and since 2012 (Executive Chairman, 2011–12); Darty plc, since 2012; Chairman, Park Resorts, since 2014; Chief Executive, Whitbread plc, 2004–10; *b* 25 Nov. 1946; *s* of Charles and Kathleen Parker; *m* 1974, Pauline Howell (*d* 2010); one *s* one *d*. *Educ:* West Buckland Sch.; Univ. of Surrey (BSc Hotel Mgt); Harvard Business Sch. (AMP). Sales and Mktg Dir, Thistle Hotels, 1974–82; Sales and Mktg Dir, 1982–85, Man. Dir Europe, 1985–87, Crest Hotels; Sen. Vice Pres. for Europe, ME and Africa, Holiday Inn, 1987–92; Man. Dir, Whitbread Hotel Co., 1992–2004. Non-executive Director: Jumeirah Group LLC, 2007–12; Restaurant Brands International (formerly Burger King Worldwide), 2012–. Chm., British Hospitality Assoc., 2000–05 and 2011–14 (Pres., 2014–); Dir, World Travel and Tourism Council, 2003–; Mem. Bd, VisitBritain, 2003–10. Vis. Prof., Univ. of Surrey, 2000. Trustee, West Buckland Sch., 2005–14 (Chm., Govs, 2011–14). FIH (FHCIMA 1992). Business Leader of the Year, 2003, Individual of the Year, 2009, Hotel Report Awards; inducted into British Travel Industry Hall of Fame, 2007; Lifetime Achievement Awards: Catey, 2010; Internat. Hotel Investment Forum, 2010. *Recreations:* sailing, Rugby, opera, ballet, Arsenal FC.

PARKER, Alan Frank Neil; charity trustee and education consultant; *b* 24 July 1953; *s* of Frank Parker, ISO and Joan Parker; *m* 1983, Valerie Shawcross, *qv* (marr. diss. 2002). *Educ:* Leicester Poly. (BA Hons 1977); Inst. of Education, London Univ. (MA Educn 1984). UK Council for Overseas Student Affairs, 1977–83; Sen. Adminr (Educn), ACC, 1984–85; Principal Officer (Colls), Surrey CC, 1986–89; Asst Sec. (Educn), 1990–92, Educn Officer, 1992–97, AMA; Dir of Educn, London Borough of Ealing, 1997–2002. Schools Adjudicator, 2004–11. Mem., Exam. Procedures Rev. Panel, Ofqual, 2013–. Vice-Pres., 2001, Pres., 2002, ConfEd (formerly Soc. of Educn Officers); Mem. Council, Assoc. of Dirs of Children's Services, 2007–08. Dir and Trustee, NFER, 2002–. FRSA 1996. MInstLM 2008. *Publications:* (contrib.) Visions of Post-Compulsory Education, 1992; (contrib. jtly) The Promises and Perils Facing Today's School Superintendent, 2002; Education and Inspections Act 2006: the essential guide, 2007; (contrib.) What's Next for Education?, 2015; pamphlets. *Recreations:* outdoor activities, visual and performing arts. *Address:* c/o National Foundation for Educational Research, The Mere, Upton Park, Slough, Berks SL1 2DQ. *E:* alan.parker@blueyonder.co.uk.

PARKER, Alan Philip; His Honour Judge Alan Parker; a Circuit Judge, since 2012; *b* Birmingham, 9 March 1953; adopted *s* of Harold Frederick Parker and Irene Florence Parker (*née* Gibbons); civil partnership 2012, Brendan Handley. *Educ:* Cherry Orchard Sch., Handsworth Wood, Birmingham; King Edward VI Grammar Sch., Aston, Birmingham; Univ. of Manchester (LLB Hons 1975); Coll. of Law, Chester. Articled to J. H. Duncombe at Messrs Wragge & Co., Birmingham, 1975–78; solicitor, 1978–95; called to the Bar, Gray's Inn, 1995; barrister, 1995–2012; Recorder, 2005–12; a Judge, First-tier Tribunal (Health, Educn and Social Care Chamber), Mental Health, Restricted Patients Panel, 2011–. *Recreations:* music (especially Californian folk rock), art (abstract expressionism), classic cars, Welsh springer spaniels and (more recently) Sussex spaniels, food, wine, travel. *Address:* Warwick Crown Court, Warwickshire Justice Centre, Newbold Terrace, Royal Leamington Spa CV32 4EL. *T:* (01926) 682100. *E:* hhjudgealan.parker@judiciary.gsi.gov.uk.

PARKER, Sir Alan (William), Kt 2002; CBE 1995; film director and writer; Chairman, Film Council, 1999–2004; *b* 14 Feb. 1944; *s* of William and Elsie Parker; *m* 1st, 1966, Annie Inglis (marr. diss. 1992); three *s* one *d*; 2nd, 2001, Lisa Moran; one *s*. *Educ:* Owen's Sch., Islington. Advertising Copywriter, 1965–67; Television Commercials Director, 1968–78. Wrote screenplay, Melody, 1969; wrote and directed: No Hard Feelings, 1972; Our Cissy, 1973; Footsteps, 1973; Bugsy Malone, 1975; A Turnip Head's Guide to the British Cinema, 1985; Angel Heart, 1987; Come See the Paradise, 1990; The Road to Wellville, 1995; Evita, 1996; Angela's Ashes, 2000; directed: The Evacuees, 1974; Midnight Express, 1977; Fame, 1979; Shoot the Moon, 1981; The Wall, 1982; Birdy, 1984; Mississippi Burning, 1989; The Commitments, 1991; The Life of David Gale, 2003. Vice-Chm., Directors Guild of Great Britain, 1982–86; Chm., BFI, 1998–99. Fellow, BAFTA, 2013. Hon. DLitt UEA, 1998; Hon. DArts: Sunderland, 2005; Southampton Solent, 2012. BAFTA Michael Balcon Award for Outstanding Contribution to British Film, 1985. Officier, Ordre des Arts et des Lettres (France), 2005. *Publications: novels:* Bugsy Malone, 1976; Puddles in the Lane, 1977; The Sucker's Kiss, 2003; *cartoons:* Hares in the Gate, 1983; Making Movies, 1998; Will Write and Direct For Food, 2005; *non-fiction:* The Making of Evita, 1997.

PARKER, Andrew; Director General, Security Service, since 2013. *Educ:* Univ. of Cambridge (BA Natural Scis). Security Service, 1983–: Dep. Dir Gen., 2007–13. *Address:* Security Service, PO Box 3255, SW1P 1AE.

PARKER, Ann; *see* Burdus, J. A.

PARKER, Anne Mary, CBE 1990; Chair, National Care Standards Commission, 2001–04; *b* 11 Oct. 1939; *d* of Daniel Morley and Mary Morley (*née* Waters); *m* 1968, Dr Andrew Parker (marr. diss. 2000). *Educ:* Notre Dame Grammar Sch., Blackburn; Univ. of Keele (BA Hons); Univ. of Manchester (AdvDip Social Admin; Hon. Fellow 1996). Berkshire County Council: Asst Co. Welfare Services Officer, 1967–71; Asst Dir, 1971–74, Dep. Dir, 1974–80, Dir, 1980–94, Social Services; Simon Fellow, Manchester Univ., 1994–95; freelance consultant, 1996–97; Ind. Case Examr, CSA, 1997–2001. Non-executive Director: Nestor Health Care, 1999–2001; Wirral Univ. Teaching Hosp. NHS Foundn Trust, 2005–13; Riverside English Churches Housing Gp (formerly English Churches Housing Gp), 2008–. Chairman: Complaints Panel, Audit Commn, 2004–07; Fitness to Practise Panel, NMC, 2012–13; Member: Health Educn Council, 1984–91; Criminal Injuries Compensation Appeals Panel, 2000–09; Ext. Reviewer, Office of Parly and Health Service Ombudsman, 2005–08. Board Member: Centre for Policy in Ageing, 1991–97 (Vice-Chm.); Carers Nat. Assoc., then Carers UK, 1995–2002 (Chm., 1998–2002). Hon. Sec., Assoc. of Dirs of Social Services, 1986–89.

Mem. Bd, NISW, 1990–98 (Life Fellow, 1998). Mem. Bd, Anchor Trust, 1996–99; Trustee, Lloyds TSB Foundn, 2004–10. *Address:* 50 Riverside Gardens, Romsey, Hants SO51 8HN. *T:* (01794) 518656. *E:* anne@annep1.plus.com.

PARKER, Dr Becky, MBE 2008; FInstP, FRAS; Director, Langton Star Centre, Simon Langton Grammar School for Boys, Canterbury, since 2008; *b* Hitchin, Herts, 24 Oct. 1960; *d* of John and Kathleen Parker; *m* 2000, Peter Atkin; one *d*. *Educ:* Univ. of Sussex (BSc 1st Cl. Hons 1984); Univ. of Chicago. Teacher and Hd of Educn, Inst. of Physics, 1988–90; Sen. Lectr, Sch. of Physical Scis, Univ. of Kent, 2004–05; Hd of Physics, Simon Langton Grammar Sch. for Boys, 2005–12. Acad. Visitor, Imperial Coll. London. Patrick Moore Medal, RAS, 2013. *Recreations:* playing the bassoon, swimming, walking, supporting my daughter in sailing. *Address:* Langton Star Centre, Simon Langton Grammar School for Boys, Langton Lane, Canterbury, Kent CT4 7AS. *T:* (01227) 825770. *E:* bparker@thelangton.kent.sch.uk.

PARKER, Cameron Holdsworth, CVO 2007; OBE 1993; JP; Lord-Lieutenant of Renfrewshire, 1998–2007; Vice-Chairman, Lithgows Ltd, 1991–97 (Managing Director, 1984–92); *b* 14 April 1932; *s* of George Cameron Parker and Mary Stevenson Parker; *m* 1st, 1957, Elizabeth Margaret Thomson (*d* 1985); three *s*; 2nd, 1986, Marlyne Honeyman, JP, FSI (*d* 2009). *Educ:* Morrison's Acad., Crieff; Glasgow Univ. (BSc Hons). John G. Kincaid & Co. Ltd, Greenock: Asst Manager, 1958; Asst Gen. Man., 1961; Dir, 1963; Man. Dir, 1967; Chm., 1976; Chm. and Chief Exec., Scott Lithgow Ltd, Port Glasgow, 1980–83. Bd Mem., British Shipbuilders, 1977–80, 1981–83. Director, 1984–94 (Chairman, 1984–92): Campbeltown Shipyard Ltd; J. Fleming Engrg Ltd; Glasgow Iron & Steel Co. Ltd; Landcatch Ltd; Lithgow Electronics Ltd; Malakoff & Wm Moore Ltd; McKinlay & Blair Ltd; Prosper Engrg Ltd; Director: Lithgows Pty Ltd, 1984–94; Scottish Homes, 1992–96; Clyde Shaw Ltd, 1992–94. Mem. Scottish Council, CBI, 1986–92. Mem., Argyll and Clyde Health Bd, 1991–95. Pres., SSAFA, Renfrewshire, 1998–2007. Hon. Pres., Accord Hospice, Paisley, 1998–2007. Freeman, City of London, 1981; Liveryman, Co. of Shipwrights, 1981–. DL 1993, JP 1998, Renfrewshire. DUniv Paisley, 2003. *Recreation:* golf. *Address:* Heath House, Rowantreehill Road, Kilmacolm, Renfrewshire PA13 4PE. *T:* (01505) 873197.

PARKER, Charles Herbert; Chief Executive, Baker Dearing Educational Trust, since 2012 (Director of Operations, 2010–12); *b* 26 July 1953; *e s* of late Capt. Herbert Blake Parker, RN and of Diana Katharine Parker (*née* Barnwell); *m* 1977, Victoria Kathleen Scott; two *s* one *d* (and one *d* decd). *Educ:* Winchester Coll.; Trinity Coll., Oxford (MA 1979); Insead (MBA 1982). Commercial Dir, Charter plc, 1990–96; Clerk to Mercers' Co., 1998–2008; Academies Advr, Partnerships for Schs, 2008–10. Director: Johnson Matthey plc, 1990–93; Cape plc, 1990–96; Faber Music Ltd, 2010–12. Gov., Royal Ballet Sch., 2000–09; Dir, Birmingham Royal Ballet, 2009–. Governor: Thomas Telford Sch., 2002–08; Walsall Acad., 2003–08; Sandwell Acad., 2006–08. *Recreations:* shooting, classical ballet, cycling. *Address:* Baker Dearing Educational Trust, 4 Millbank, SW1P 3JA. *Club:* Boodle's.

See also E. B. Parker, Gen. Sir N. R. Parker.

PARKER, Charles Lucian Henry; Chief Executive, Westminster City Council, since 2014; *b* Kampala, Uganda, 3 April 1961; *s* of Malcolm and Bridget Parker; *m* 2002, Ruth Christina; one *s* one *d*. *Educ:* Christ's Hosp. Sch.; Warwick Univ. (BA Hons). Dept of Employment, 1982–87; Thamesdown BC, 1987–90; Hd, Inner Cities, Manchester CC, 1990–95; Liverpool City Council: Dir, Speke-Garston Partnership, 1995–99; Exec. Dir, Regeneration, 1999–2006; Director: Enterprise plc, 2006–07; Investment, Finance and Performance, English Partnership, 2007–08; Chief Exec., Oldham MBC, 2008–14. *Recreations:* swimming, cycling, walking, sailing, music, film, watching live sport and Manchester City FC. *Address:* Westminster City Council, 64 Victoria Street, SW1E 6QP.

PARKER, Christopher James Francis; QC 2006; **His Honour Judge Christopher Parker;** a Circuit Judge, since 2012; *b* 22 June 1958; *s* of Bernard James and Peta Jocelyn Parker; *m* 1988, Stevie Jenkinson; one *s* one *d*. *Educ:* Ampleforth; Univ. of Exeter (LLB 1979). RN, 1980–88. Called to the Bar, Gray's Inn, 1986. *Address:* Chichester Crown Court, Southgate, Chichester, W Sussex PO19 1SX.

PARKER, Christopher Roy; QC 2008; *b* Leeds, 13 Oct. 1958; *s* of Roy and Margaret Parker; *m* 2000, Caroline Wilkinson; two *s*. *Educ:* Univ. of Oxford (MA, BCL); Univ. of Illinois (LLM); Harvard Univ. (LLM). Called to the Bar: Lincoln's Inn, 1984; BVI, 2006; in practice as barrister specialising in company law, insolvency, commercial fraud and trusts. *Recreations:* sailing, football, tennis. *Address:* Maitland Chambers, 7 Stone Buildings, Lincoln's Inn, WC2A 3SZ. *T:* (020) 7406 1200, *Fax:* (020) 7406 1300. *E:* cparker@maitlandchambers.com. *Clubs:* Chelsea Football; Royal Dart Yacht (Dartmouth).

PARKER, Christopher Stuart, CBE 1999; Headmaster, Nottingham High School, 1995–2007; *b* 16 Feb. 1947; *s* of late Gerald Stuart Parker and Brenda Mary Parker (*née* Briggs); *m* 1969, Margaret, *er d* of late Charles Godfrey Hannant and Frances Hannant; two *s*. *Educ:* Windsor Grammar Sch.; Bristol Univ. (BA 1968); St Catharine's Coll., Cambridge (PGCE 1969). Asst Master, Bedford Modern Sch., 1969–72; Head of Geography, Bradford Grammar Sch., 1972–78; Dep. Head, Goffs Sch., 1978–86; Headmaster, Batley Grammar Sch., 1986–95. HMC-OFSTED Lead Insp., 1995–98; Member: Admiralty Interview Bd, 1990–97; Assisted Places Cttee, ISC, 1995–2004 (Chm., 2002–04); Jt Chair, HMC/GSA/Ind. Schs Bursars' Assoc. Assisted Places Wkg Party, 1996–98; Chairman: Assisted Places Cttee, 1996–2004, Bridges and Partnerships Cttee, 1998–99, HMC; Govt Adv. Gp on Independent/State Sch. Partnerships, 1997–2002; Jt Chm., LGA/ISC Cttee, 2001–04; Mem., Permanent Forum on Independent/State Sch. Partnerships, 2002–04 (Chm., Evaluation Cttee, 2002–04). Mem., Norfolk Wildlife Trust, 2009–; Friend, Sculthorpe Moor, Hawk and Owl Trust, 2010–; Mem., Friends of Horsey Seals, 2015–. Governor: Nottingham Trent Univ., 1996–99; Bedford Modern Sch., 2007–10; Trustee, Seckford Foundn, 2007–10. FRSA 1994. *Publications:* articles in American Jl of Geography, Envmt and Planning. *Recreations:* watching sport, travel, wildlife photography. *Address:* Mill End, 19 Mill Lane, Briston, Melton Constable, Norfolk NR24 2JG. *Club:* W Norfolk Cricket Lovers' Society.

PARKER, Cornelia Ann, OBE 2010; RA 2009; sculptor and installation artist; *b* Cheshire, 1956; *m* Jeff McMillan; one *d*. *Educ:* Glos Coll. of Art and Design; Wolverhampton Poly. (BA Hons 1978); Reading Univ. (MFA 1982). Sen. Fellow in Fine Art, Cardiff Inst., 1992–95; Prof. of Conceptual Art, Eur. Grad. Sch., Saas-Fee, Switzerland. *Works* include: Cold Dark Matter: An Exploded View, 1991; The Maybe, 1995; Hanging Fire (Suspected Arson), 1999; Shirt Burnt by a meteorite, 1997; Edge of England, 1999; Blue Shift, 2001; Subconscious of a Monument, 2002; The Distance (A Kiss with String Attached), 2003; Brontëan Abstracts, 2006; Never Endings, 2007, 2008; Chomskian Abstracts, 2008; One More Time, 2015; *solo exhibitions* include: Stoke City Art Gall. and Mus., Stoke-on-Trent, 1980; Ikon Gall., Birmingham, 1988, 2007; Whitechapel Gall., 1991, 2011; Serpentine Gall., 1995, 1998; Frith Street Gall., 1999, 2002, 2008, 2013; ICA, Boston, 2000; ICA, Philadelphia, 2000; Galerie Guy Bartschi, Geneva, 2003, 2008; D'Amelio Terras, NY, 2003, 2005, 2010; Galerie Carles Tache, Barcelona, 2004, 2008, 2013; Whitworth Art Gall., Manchester, 2014; *group exhibitions* include: Ikon Gall., Birmingham, 1983; Whitechapel Gall., 1985, 1990, 1992, 2011; Kettle's Yard, Cambridge, 1990, 1991, 1998, 2001; Frith St Gall., 1995, 1997, 1999, 2001, 2002, 2006, 2010; Tate Gall., 1997; V&A Mus., 1998; Tate Modern, 2000; Tate Britain, 2003; Barbican Art Gall., 2008; Tate Liverpool, 2009; BM, 2009; MOMA, NY, 2010; RA Summer Exhibn, 2011, 2012; Wallace Collection, 2013; Guggenheim Bilbao Mus., 2014; *work in public collections* including: Arts Council of GB; British Council; BM; Fundacio La Caixa, Barcelona; Henry Moore Foundn; ICA, Boston; MOMA, NY; Musée d'Art Moderne/Centre Pompidou; Metropolitan Mus. of Art, NY; Tate Gall.; Royal Collection; V&A. Hon. Dr: Wolverhampton, 2000; Birmingham, 2005; Gloucestershire, 2008. *Address:* c/o Frith Street Gallery, 17–18 Golden Square, W1F 9JJ.

PARKER, Prof. David, DPhil; FRS 2002; CChem, FRSC; Professor of Chemistry, Durham University, since 1992; *b* 30 July 1956; 2nd *s* of late Joseph William Parker and Mary Parker (*née* Hill); *m* 1979, Fiona Mary MacEwan; one *s* two *d*. *Educ:* Durham Johnston Sch.; King Edward VI Grammar Sch., Stafford; Christ Church, Oxford (BA, MA); Hertford Coll., Oxford (DPhil 1980). CChem 1989; FRSC 1992. NATO post-doctoral Fellow, Univ. Louis Pasteur, Strasbourg, 1980–81; Durham University: Lectr, 1982–89; Sen. Lectr, 1989–92; Hd, Dept of Chemistry, 1995–98 and 2003–06. Visiting Professor: Strasbourg, 1994; Monash, 1998 and 2006; Recognising Inspiration in Sci. and Engrg Fellow, EPSRC, 2014. Lectures: Iddles, Univ. of New Hampshire, 2003; Vielberth, Regensburg, 2004; Chem. Soc. Inaugural, UCD, 2006. Royal Society of Chemistry: Hickinbottom Fellowship, 1988–89; Tilden Lectr, 2003–04; Corday-Morgan Medal, 1987; Interdisciplinary Award, 1995; Supramolecular Chem. Award, 2002; Ludwig Mond Award, 2011; ICI Prize in Organic Chem., 1991; IBC Supramolecular Sci. and Technol. Award, 2000; Wolfson Res. Merit Award, Royal Soc., 2004–08; Lecoq de Boisbaudran Award, European Rare Earth Soc., 2012. *Publications:* Macrocycle Synthesis, 1996; patents; contrib. numerous papers, res. and rev. articles to learned jls. *Recreations:* cricket, golf, hill-walking, soccer. *Address:* Department of Chemistry, University of Durham, South Road, Durham DH1 3LE. *T:* (0191) 334 2033, *Fax:* (0191) 384 4737. *E:* david.parker@dur.ac.uk. *Clubs:* Durham City Cricket; Brancepeth Castle Golf.

PARKER, Rev. Prof. David Charles, OBE 2015; DTh; FBA 2012; FSA; Edward Cadbury Professor of Theology, and Director, Institute for Textual Scholarship and Electronic Editing, University of Birmingham, since 2005; *b* Boston, Lincs, 4 July 1953; *s* of Thomas Henry Louis and Mary Parker; *m* 1976, Karen Beaumont; two *s* two *d*. *Educ:* Univ. of St Andrews (MTh 1975); Emmanuel Coll., Cambridge (DipTh 1976); Rijksuniversiteit of Leiden (DTh 1990). Curate: St Paul's Ch, Mill Hill, London, 1977–80; Bladon with Woodstock, Dio. Oxford, 1980–85; Tutor in Biblical Studies, Queens' Coll., Birmingham, 1985–93; University of Birmingham: Lectr, 1993–96; Sen. Lectr, 1996–98; Reader, 1998–2001; Professor of New Testament Textual Criticism and Palaeography, 2001–05. FSA 2009. Soc. of Royal Cumberland Youths, 2010. *Publications:* Paul's Letter to the Colossians by Philip Melanchthon, 1989; The New Testament in Greek IV, vol. 1, 1995, vol. 2, 2007; The Living Text of the Gospels, 1997; John Calvin, Commentarius in Epistolam Pauli ad Romanos, 1999; An Introduction to the New Testament Manuscripts and their Texts, 2008; Manuscripts, Texts, Theology: collected papers 1997–2007, 2009; Codex Sinaiticus: the story of the world's oldest Bible, 2010; Textual Scholarship and the Making of the New Testament, 2012. *Recreations:* bell-ringing, gardening. *Address:* Institute for Textual Scholarship and Electronic Editing, European Research Institute, University of Birmingham, Birmingham B15 2TT. *T:* (0121) 415 8341. *E:* d.c.parker@bham.ac.uk.

PARKER, Diana Clare; Partner, Withers LLP, since 1987; *b* Newcastle upon Tyne, 30 Oct. 1957; *m* 1991, Dr John Maxwell Landers, *qv*. *Educ:* Churchill Coll., Cambridge (BA 1979; MPhil 1980). Arbitrator 2012; MCIArb 2012. Admitted solicitor, 1983; Withers LLP, 1981–, specialising in family law, Chm., 1999–2007. Co-Founder, Family Mediators Assoc., 1985. *Recreation:* allotments. *Address:* Withers LLP, 16 Old Bailey, EC4M 7EG. *T:* (020) 7597 6198, *Fax:* (020) 7597 6543. *E:* diana.parker@withersworldwide.com.

PARKER, (Diana) Jean, CBE 1989; Director, Goldsborough Healthcare plc, 1994–97; *b* 7 June 1932; *d* of Lewis William Reeve Morley and Amy (*née* Southwood); *m* 1959, Dudley Frost Parker (*d* 1971); one *s* one *d*. *Educ:* Kesteven and Grantham Girls' Sch.; Birmingham Univ. (BCom). Director: Vacu-Lug Traction Tyres Ltd, 1957–; Central Independent Television Plc, 1982–97; British Steel (Industry) Ltd, 1986–90; Grantham and Dist Hosp. NHS Trust, 1995–98; Chm., Middle England Fine Food Ltd, 1995–2004. Mem. Bd, E Midlands Electricity, 1983–90; Mem., E Midlands, later Eastern Adv. Bd, National Westminster Bank, 1985–92. Chairman: Lincs Jt Devel t Cttee, 1983–97; Chm., CBI Smaller Firms Council, 1986–88. Chm., N Lincs HA, 1987–90; non-exec. Dir, Lincs Ambulance and Health Service Trust, 1991–92; Chm., Lincs Community Council, 2000–03.

PARKER, Edward Barnwell; Co-Founder and Chief Executive, Walking with the Wounded, since 2010; *b* Petersfield, Hants, 13 Oct. 1965; *s* of late Capt. Herbert Blake Parker, RN and of Diana Katharine Parker (*née* Barnwell); *m* 1992, Harriet Douglas-Bate; three *c*. *Educ:* Winchester Coll.; RMA Sandhurst. Served Army, Royal Green Jackets, 1984–92; Cazenove & Co., 1992–95; Man. Dir, Salomon Bros, then Citigroup, 1995–2003; Edward Parker Wines, 2003–12. Ambassador, SkillForce, 2011–. Mem. Adv. Bd, Endeavour Fund, 2012–. *Recreations:* theatre, walking, cinema, sailing, family holidays, Norwich City Football Club, successfully skied to North Pole in 2011 and South Pole in 2013. *Address:* Walking with the Wounded, Stody Hall Barns, Stody, Melton Constable, Norfolk NR24 2ED. *T:* (01263) 863900. *E:* edward@wwtw.org.uk.

See also C. H. Parker, Gen. Sir N. R. Parker.

PARKER, Frederick John, (Jack), FICE, FIStructE, FCIHT; Chief Highway Engineer (Under Secretary), Department of Transport, 1988–91; *b* 6 Sept. 1927; *s* of Charles Fred Parker and Eleanor Emily (*née* Wright); *m* 1955, Ann Shirley Newnham; three *d*. *Educ:* Shene Grammar School; Univ. of Liverpool (BEng 1948; MEng 1951). Engineer with Scott, Wilson, Kirkpatrick & Partners in London, Hong Kong and elsewhere, 1952–65; Sen. Engineer, then Partner, with Husband & Co., 1965–78; Director, W. S. Atkins & Partners, 1978–88. Institution of Highways and Transportation: Chm., Greater London Br., 1975–77; Vice-Pres., 1985; Pres., 1988. Vice-Chm., Brit. Nat. Cttee of Permanent Internat. Assoc. of Road Congresses, 1988–91. *Publications:* professional papers in engineering jls. *Recreations:* athletics (Olympics 1952 and 1956, European silver medallist 1954); local affairs, music. *Address:* 83A Temple Sheen Road, East Sheen, SW14 7RS. *T:* (020) 8876 1059. *Clubs:* South London Harriers; Probus (Barnes, Sheen and Mortlake) (Pres., 2011–).

PARKER, Geoffrey; *see* Parker, N. G.

PARKER, Prof. Geoffrey Alan, FRS 1989; Derby Professor of Zoology, School of Biological Sciences, University of Liverpool, 1996–2009, now Emeritus; *b* 24 May 1944; *s* of late Dr Alan Parker and G. Ethel Parker (*née* Hill); *m* 1st, 1967, Susan Mary Wallis (*d* 1994); one *s* one *d*; 2nd, 1997, Carol Elizabeth Emmett; one step *d*. *Educ:* Stockton Heath Primary Sch.; Lymm Grammar Sch.; Univ. of Bristol (BSc (1st Cl. Hons Zoology; Rose Bracher Prize for Biology); PhD); Univ. of Cambridge (MA). University of Liverpool: Asst Lectr, 1968–69; Lectr, 1969–76; Sen. Lectr, 1976–80; Reader, 1980–89; Prof. in Dept of Envmtl and Evolutionary Biol., 1989–96. Fellow of King's Coll., Cambridge, 1978–79; Nuffield Sci. Res. Fellow, 1982–83; BBSRC (formerly SERC) Sen. Res. Fellow, 1990–95. Lectures: Niko Tinbergen, Assoc. for Study of Animal Behaviour, 1995; Hamilton, Internat. Soc. for Behavioural Ecology, 2006. Hon. FRES 2012. Hon. DSc Bristol, 2011. Medal, Assoc. for Study of Animal Behaviour, 2002; Dist. Animal Behaviorist Award, Animal Behavior Soc., 2003; Spallanzani Medal, 8th Biology of Spermatozoa Conf., 2005; Frink Medal, Zool Soc. of London, 2005; Dist. Zoologist Award, Benelux Congress of Zoology, 2007; Darwin Medal, Royal Soc., 2008. *Publications:* (jtly) Evolution of Sibling Rivalry, 1997; many scientific papers in learned jls. *Recreations:* playing Dixieland and Mainstream jazz in local bands (clarinet and tenor saxophone); breeding, showing and judging exhibition bantams (Hon. Sec./Treasurer, 1987–94, Pres., 2002–, Partridge & Pencilled Wyandotte Club; Mem.

Council, 1986–90, 2004–08, Pres., 2003–06, Poultry Club; Vice-Pres., Plymouth Rock Club, 2002–05; Supreme Champion, Nat. Poultry Club GB Show, 1997; Championship Judge, Nat. Fedn Poultry Clubs Show, 2011). *Address:* Saunton, The Runnel, Neston, South Wirral, Cheshire CH64 3TG. *T:* (0151) 336 4202.

PARKER, Geoffrey John, CBE 1985; Deputy Chairman, Maritime Transport Services Ltd, 1997–98 (Chief Executive, 1989–97); Chairman, Thamesport (London) Ltd, 1997–98; *b* 20 March 1937; *s* of Stanley John Parker and Alice Ellen Parker; *m* 1957, Hazel Mary Miall; two *s* two *d. Educ:* County Grammar Sch., Hendon. Commercial Dir, Townsend Car Ferries Ltd, 1972–74; Man. Dir, Atlantic Steam Navigation Co., 1974–87; Man. Dir, 1976–87, Chm., 1983–87, Felixstowe Dock & Rly Co.; Chairman: Larne Harbour Bd, 1983–87; European Ferries PLC, 1986–87; Chief Exec., Highland Participants, 1987–89. Mem., Nat. Bus Co., 1980–87. FCIT 1982. *Recreation:* golf. *Address:* 101 Valley Road, Ipswich, Suffolk IP1 4NF. *T:* (01473) 216003. *Clubs:* Ipswich and Suffolk (Ipswich); Ipswich Golf (Purdis Heath, Ipswich).

PARKER, George William; Political Editor, Financial Times, since 2007; *b* Guildford, 19 Jan. 1966; *s* of John Parker and Margaret Parker; *m* 1992, Gabrielle O'Neill; one *s* two *d. Educ:* Tiverton Comp. Sch.; Queen Mary Coll., Univ. of London (BA Geog.); City Univ. (Dip. Newspaper Journalism). Western Morning News: North Devon reporter, 1988–89; industrial corresp., 1989–90; political corresp., 1990–95; Financial Times: political corresp., 1995–99; UK News Editor, 1999–2002; Bureau Chief, Brussels, 2002–07. Presenter, Week in Westminster, 2010–, What the Papers Say, 2010–, BBC Radio 4. *Recreations:* cycling, football, cricket. *Address:* 15 Defoe Avenue, Richmond, Surrey TW9 4DL. *T:* 07872 156468. *E:* george.parker@ft.com.

PARKER, Guy; Chief Executive, Advertising Standards Authority, since 2009; *b* London, 4 Dec. 1969; *s* of late Jonathan and of Nicola Parker; *m* 2002, Camilla Dexter; two *s* one *d. Educ:* Wellington Coll., Berks; Univ. of Kent, Canterbury (BA Politics and Internat. Relns); Watford Coll. (Dip. Advertising). Investigations Exec., ASA; Committee of Advertising Practice: Copy Advice Exec., 1994–97; Copy Advice Manager, 1997–99; Asst Sec., 1999–2001; Sec., 2001–04; Dir, Complaints and Investigations, 2004–09, Dep. Dir Gen., 2008–09, Advertising Standards Authy. Mem. Bd and Exec. Cttee, 2007–, Chm., 2013–, Eur. Advertising Standards Alliance. *Recreations:* family, history, science, walking, cricket. *Address:* Advertising Standards Authority, Mid City Place, 71 High Holborn, WC1V 6QT. *E:* guyp@asa.org.uk.

PARKER, Rear Adm. Henry Hardyman; Director (Ships Acquisition), since 2014; *b* Cheltenham, 20 Dec. 1963; *s* of William John Parker and Sidsel Annette Parker; *m* 1999, Dr Katherine Bristol; three *s* one *d. Educ:* Cheltenham Coll., Pembroke Coll., Cambridge (BA Engrg 1986); Open Univ. (PhD Evolutionary Ecol. 1995). Joined RN, 1983; Weapon Engrg Officer, HMS Invincible, 2000–01; Mil. Asst to Chief of Defence Staff, 2001–03; seconded to BAE Systems, Barrow, 2003–05; Asst Naval Attaché, Washington, DC, 2005–07; Chief Engr, Successor Prog., 2007–11; Dir (Precision Attack) and Controller of the Navy, 2012–13; Dir (Carrier Strike), 2013–14. *Publications:* three papers on landlocked Arctic Charr. *Recreations:* fishing, sailing, walking, choir, heavy duty gardening. *Address:* c/o Naval Secretary, Leech Building, Fleet Headquarters, Whale Island, Portsmouth PO2 8BY. *Club:* Leander.

PARKER, Prof. Ian, PhD; FRS 2008; Professor of Neurobiology and Behavior, since 1995, and Professor of Physiology and Biophysics, since 2006, University of California, Irvine; *b* 6 Jan. 1951. *Educ:* University Coll. London (BSc Physiol. 1972; PhD Physiol. 1984). Res. Asst, Dept of Biophysics, UCL, 1975–84; University of California, Irvine: Asst Prof., 1984–90, Associate Prof., 1990–95, Dept of Psychobiol.; Co-Dir, Imaging Core Centre for Hearing Res., 2007–. Vis. Prof., Dept of Physiol., Univ. of Maryland Sch. of Medicine, 1995–96. Member, Editorial Board: Jl Gen. Physiol., 1998–; Biophysical Jl, 2006–. Mem., Internat. Jt Projects Cttee, Royal Soc., 2009–13. FAAAS 2009. *Publications:* (contrib.) Handbook of Nonlinear Optical Microscopy, 2008; contribs to jls incl. Biophysical Jl, Jl Cell Biol., Jl Gen. Physiol., Cell Calcium, Immunol., Science. *Address:* Department of Neurobiology and Behavior, University of California, Irvine, CA 92697–4550, USA.

PARKER, Jack; *see* Parker, F. J.

PARKER, James Frederick Somerville; Vice Lord-Lieutenant, Stirling and Falkirk, since 2011; *b* Campsie Glen, Stirlingshire, 10 July 1941; *s* of George Coats Parker and Helena Bettys Adelaide Somerville (*née* Buckmaster); *m* 1968, Rosemary Janice Skelton; two *s* one *d. Educ:* Winchester Coll.; Univ. of Newcastle upon Tyne (BA Econ. Studies). Mitsubishi Heavy Industries, 1966; Elliott Automation Ltd, 1967–69; Hawker Siddeley Dynamics Ltd, 1970–72; J & J Denholm Ltd, 1972–2012. DL Stirling and Falkirk, 1991. *Recreations:* shooting, stalking, fishing, gardening. *Address:* The Moss, Killearn, Stirlingshire G63 9LJ. *T:* (01360) 550053. *E:* themoss@freeuk.com. *Club:* Western (Glasgow).

PARKER, Dr James Gordon, OBE 2002; Head of Public Lending Right, 2013–14 (Registrar, 1991–2013); *b* 1 June 1952; *s* of James Frank Taylor Parker and Mary Hutchison Gordon; *m* 1975, Catherine Ann Hyndman; one *s* one *d. Educ:* Stranraer High Sch.; Edinburgh Univ. (MA 1st Cl. Hons History 1974; PhD 1977). Vans Dunlop Res. Schol., Edinburgh Univ., 1974–77; Carnegie Travelling Schol. to India, 1976; Royal Commission on Historical Manuscripts: Res. Asst, 1977–87; Asst Keeper, resp. for Nat. Register of Archives, 1987–91. Mem., Adv. Cttee, 1991–2006, Chm., Mgt Bd, 2009–13, PLR; Co-ordinator, Internat. PLR Network, 1995–. Patron, Laser Foundn, 2001–07. FRSA 2007. Benson Medal, RSL, 2004; Medalha de Honra, Sociedade Portuguesa de Autores, 2009. *Publications:* (contrib.) The Scots Abroad, 1985; Bibliographies of British Statesmen No 5 (Lord Curzon), 1991; (contrib.) International Directory of Company Histories, vol. 4, 1991; (ed) Proceedings of the First International Conference on Authors' Lending Right, 1996; (ed) Whose Loan is it Anyway?: essays in celebration of PLR's 20th anniversary, 1999; contrib. New DNB; reviews and contribs to learned jls. *Recreations:* golf, gardening, family. *Address:* 14 Ash Grove, Kirklevington, Yarm, Stockton-on-Tees TS15 9NQ. *T:* (01642) 791445. *E:* parker-j20@sky.com.

PARKER, James Mavin, (Jim Parker); composer and conductor; *b* Hartlepool, 18 Dec. 1934; *s* of James Robertson Parker and Margaret Mavin; *m* 1969, Pauline George; two *d*; one *d* by a previous marriage. *Educ:* various grammar schools; Guildhall Sch. of Music (AGSM 1959; Silver Medal; Hon. GSM 1986). LRAM 1959. Professional oboeist, 1959; joined the Barrow Poets, 1963. Wrote musical settings of Sir John Betjeman's poems, Banana Blush, 1973 (recorded these and subsequent settings with Sir John as speaker); wrote music for Chichester Theatre, 1974–77; music for television and films, 1977–, includes: Credo; Another Six English Towns; Good Behaviour; Wynne and Penkovsky; Mapp and Lucia; Time After Time; Betjeman's Britain; Late Flowering Love; The Miser; España Viva; The Blot (silent film made in 1921); Girl Shy (Harold Lloyd silent film); Wish Me Luck; House of Cards; Parnell and the Englishwoman; The House of Eliott; Soldier Soldier; Body and Soul; To Play the King (BAFTA award for best TV music, 1993); Goggle Eyes; Late Flowering Lust; Moll Flanders (BAFTA award, 1996); Tom Jones (BAFTA award, 1997); A Rather English Marriage (BAFTA award, 1998); The Midsomer Murders; Born and Bred; Foyle's War. *Compositions* include: with William Bealby-Wright: Moonshine Rock, 1972; Mister Skillicorn Dances, 1974; with Cicely Herbert: Mayhew's London, 1978; La Comédie Humaine, 1986; (with John Betjeman) Poems (ballet), 1981; In The Gold Room (words by Oscar Wilde), 1983; (with Jeremy Lloyd) The Woodland Gospels, 1984; (with John Edmunds) Pelican Five, 1986. Recordings with Barrow Poets, Keith Michell, Peter Sellers, Harry Secombe, Twiggy, etc. *Publications:* (with Wally K. Daly) Follow the Star, 1975; (with Jeremy Lloyd) Captain Beaky, 1977; with Tom Stanier: The Shepherd King, 1979; The Burning Bush, 1980; All Aboard, 1983; Blast Off, 1986; A Londoner in New York (suite for brass), 1986; (with Tom Stanier and Chris Ellis) BabylonTimes, 1988; English Towns (for flute and piano), 1988; Mississippi Five (woodwind quintet), 1991; Lullingstone (for concert band), 1986; The Golden Section (brass quintet), 1993; Concerto for clarinet and strings, 1994; (with Alan Platt) The Happy Prince (one act opera), 1995; Light Fantastic (for string sextet or ten brass), 2002; Boulevard (for woodwind quintet), 2006; Mexican Wildlife (for brass quintet), 2006; Fat Tuesday in New Orleans (for concert wind band), 2007; Bonjour M Grappelli (string quartet), 2013; (for recorder and harpsichord) A Journey to South America, 2014. *Recreations:* literature, 20th Century art. *Address:* 16 Laurel Road, Barnes, SW13 0EE. *T:* (020) 8876 8442.

PARKER, Jean; *see* Parker, D. J.

PARKER, Sir John; *see* Parker, Sir T. J.

PARKER, Prof. John Stewart, DPhil; FLS; VMH; Director, Botanic Garden, and Professor of Plant Cytogenetics, 1996–2010, Curator, Herbarium, 2001–10, University of Cambridge; Fellow, Clare Hall, Cambridge, since 2007 (Vice-President, 2013–15); *b* 12 July 1945; *s* of George Parker and Helen Parker (*née* Teare); *m* 1970, Iris Veronica Berry (marr. diss.); two *s*; *m* 1999, Mary Elizabeth Edmunds. *Educ:* Birkenhead Sch.; Christ Church, Oxford (BA 1966; MA 1970; DPhil 1971). Lectr, 1969–90, Reader, 1990–92, QMC; Prof. of Botany, Univ. of Reading, 1992–96; Fellow, St Catharine's Coll., Cambridge, 1997–2007. Dir, NIAB, 2004–09 (Mem. Council, 1998–2001). Mem. Council, RHS, 1998–99. Trustee: Royal Botanic Gardens, Kew, 1996–2002; Brogdale Horticultural Trust, 1999–2004; Science and Plants for Schs, 1998–2008; Sci. Cttee, Mendel Mus., Brno, 2002–04 (Advr and Designer, Genetic Gdn). Reina Victoria Eugenia Chair, Complutense Univ., Madrid, 2007–08; Advr, Dean of Biol Scis, Univ. of Vienna, 2010–14. Mem. Bd, Darwin Correspondence Project Adv. Bd, 2014–. Hon. Res. Fellow, Natural History Mus., 1995–2005. FLS 1998. VMH 2012. *Publications:* (jtly) The Sainsbury Laboratory: science, architecture, art, 2012; numerous papers in scientific jls. *Recreations:* church architecture, bird watching, landscape history, gardening, apples and cheese. *Address:* Clare Hall, University of Cambridge, Herschel Road, Cambridge CB3 9AL.

PARKER, Rt Hon. Sir Jonathan (Frederic), Kt 1991; PC 2000; a Lord Justice of Appeal, 2000–07; a Justice of Appeal, Gibraltar, since 2010; *b* 8 Dec. 1937; *s* of late Sir (Walter) Edmund Parker, CBE and late Elizabeth Mary Butterfield; *m* 1967, Maria-Belen Burns; three *s* one *d. Educ:* Winchester College; Magdalene College, Cambridge (MA). Called to Bar, Inner Temple, 1962, Bencher, 1985; practising member of the Bar, 1962–91; QC 1979; a Recorder, 1989–91; Attorney Gen. of Duchy of Lancaster, 1989–91; Judge of the High Court of Justice, Chancery Div., 1991–2000; Vice Chancellor, Co. Palatine of Lancaster, 1994–98. *Recreations:* painting, reading. *Address:* The Grange, Radwinter, Saffron Walden, Essex CB10 2TF. *Club:* Garrick.

PARKER, Hon. Dame Judith Mary Frances, DBE 2008; **Hon. Mrs Justice Parker;** a Judge of the High Court, Family Division, since 2008; *b* 19 June 1950. *Educ:* Univ. of Oxford (BA Juris. 1972). Called to the Bar, Middle Temple, 1973; QC 1991; Recorder, 1998–2008. *Address:* Royal Courts of Justice, Strand, WC2A 2LL.

PARKER, Hon. Sir Kenneth (Blades), Kt 2009; **Hon. Mr Justice Kenneth Parker;** a Judge of the High Court of Justice, Queen's Bench Division, since 2009; *b* 20 Nov. 1945; *s* of Rudolph Parker, Capt., Argyll and Sutherland Highlanders and Catherine (*née* Boyd); *m* 1967, Margaretha Constance Beyerman; three *s* one *d. Educ:* Kettering Grammar Sch.; Exeter Coll., Oxford (Class. Schol.; 1st cl. Lit. Hum. 1968; 1st cl. BCL 1973; Vinerian Schol.). Lectr in Law, Univ. of Oxford and Fellow, Exeter Coll., Oxford, 1973–76; called to the Bar, Gray's Inn, 1975, Bencher, 2002; QC 1992; Recorder, 2000–09; Dep. High Ct Judge, 2006–09; a Law Comr, 2006–09. Specialist Advr, H of C Select Cttee for Trade and Ind., 1991. Mem., Information Tribunal, 2002–10. *Publications:* (Asst Ed.) Chitty on Contracts, 23rd edn, 1972; (contrib.) Common Market Law of Competition, 1987. *Recreations:* tennis, ski-ing. *Address:* Royal Courts of Justice, Strand, WC2A 2LL.

PARKER, Lyn; Chef de Cabinet, President of the International Criminal Court, since 2011; *b* 25 Nov. 1952; *s* of Ronald Arthur Parker and Tjardina Torrenga; *m* 1991, Jane Elizabeth Walker; two *d. Educ:* King's Sch., Canterbury; Magdalen Coll., Oxford (BA Jurisprudence); Manchester Univ. (MA European Community Studies). Lectr in Law, Manchester Univ., 1975–78; joined HM Diplomatic Service, 1978; Second, later First, Sec., Athens, 1980–84; FCO, 1984–88; Cabinet Office, 1989–91; Head of Chancery and Political Counsellor, New Delhi, 1992–95; Counsellor (Political), UK Perm. Repn to EU, Brussels, 1995–99; Hd, Whitehall Liaison Dept, FCO, 1999–2001; High Comr to Cyprus, 2001–05; Ambassador to the Netherlands, 2005–09. *Recreations:* music, sailing, cycling. *Address:* International Criminal Court, PO Box 19519, 2500 CM, The Hague, The Netherlands.

PARKER, (Lynda) Tanya; a Deputy Upper Tribunal Judge (formerly a Deputy Social Security and Child Support Commissioner), since 2008; *d* of Sidney Sansom and Olive May (*née* Hudson); *m* 1968, Prof. David Francis Parker; two *c. Educ:* Manchester Univ. (LLB); Univ. of Calif, Berkeley (LLM). Called to the Bar, Gray's Inn, 1966; Associate WS, 2002. Lecturer: Nottingham Univ., 1966–73; Univ. of WI, 1970–72 (on secondment). Regl Chm., Appeals Service, 1991–2000; Social Security and Child Support Comr, 2000–08; a Dep. First-tier Tribunal Judge, War Pensions and Armed Forces Compensation Chamber (formerly Chm., Pensions Appeal Tribunal), 2001–13; Dep. Social Security Comr for NI, 2006–11. *Recreations:* friends, travel, performing and visual arts. *Address:* (office) George House, 126 George Street, Edinburgh EH2 4HH. *Club:* Royal Over-Seas League.

PARKER, Margaret Lucille Jeanne, (Margot); Member (UK Ind) East Midlands Region, European Parliament, since 2014; *b* Grantham, 24 July 1943; *m*; two *s*. Gp buyer, S American lingerie co., 1989–95; Sales Dir, Itelsa Inc., 1996–2003; Sales Dir, bespoke fragrance co., 2003–08; Dir and Hd of Communications, Eur. Promotional Products Assoc., 2003–07; Dir and Eur. spokesman, British Promotional Merchandise Assoc., 1996– (Sword of Honour and Fellow, 2007). Contested (UK Ind): Sherwood, 2010; Corby and E Northants, Nov. 2012. *Address:* European Parliament, 60 Rue Wiertz, 1047 Brussels, Belgium; (office) 44b High Street, Old Village, Corby, Northants NN17 1UU.

PARKER, Ven. Matthew John; Archdeacon of Stoke-upon-Trent, since 2013; *b* Manchester, 1 June 1963; *s* of Michael and Carol Parker; *m* 1988, Sarah Pym; one *s* two *d. Educ:* Bishop Wand Sch., Sunbury-on-Thames; Univ. of Manchester (BA English Lit. 1985); Sidney Sussex Coll., Cambridge (BA 1988); Ridley Hall, Cambridge. Ordained deacon, 1988, priest, 1989; Assistant Curate: St Mary's, Twickenham, 1988–91; St George's, Stockport, 1991–94; Team Vicar, Stockport SW Team, 1993–2000; Team Rector, Leek and Meerbrook Team, 2000–13; Rural Dean, Leek, 2007–13. Hon. Canon, Lichfield Cathedral, 2013–. Chair, Moorlands Together Local Strategic Partnership, 2004–07. Chaplain, Stockport Grammar Sch., 1991–94. *Recreations:* theatre, book club, music, family, Staffordshire bull terrier. *Address:* 39 The Brackens, Newcastle under Lyme, Staffs ST5 4JL. *T:* (01782) 663066. *E:* archdeacon.stoke@lichfield.anglican.org.

PARKER, Major Sir Michael (John), KCVO 2000 (CVO 1991); CBE 1996 (MBE (mil.) 1968); Producer: Royal Tournament, 1974–99; Edinburgh Tattoo, 1991–94; 320 other events around the world, 1965–2010; *b* 21 Sept. 1941; *s* of Capt. S. J. Wilkins and V. S. M.

Wilkins (*née* Parker); name changed by Deed Poll, 1959; *m* 2005, Emma Bagwell Purefoy (*née* Gilroy). *Educ:* Dulwich Coll. Prep. Sch.; Hereford Cathedral Sch.; RMA Sandhurst. Captain, Queen's Own Hussars, 1961–71 (produced Berlin Tattoo, 1965, 1967 and 1971); Major, TA, Special List, attached QOH, 1973–. Producer of international events, 1972–2010: Berlin Tattoo, 1972–88, Bandanza, 1990; Last Tattoo, 1992; Aldershot Army Display, 1974–83; Queen's Bonfire, Windsor and others, Queen's Silver Jubilee, 1977; Wembley Musical Pageant, 1969, 1979, 1981, 1985; Great Children's Party for Internat. Year of the Child, 1979; Carols for the Queen, 1979; Royal Fireworks (Prince of Wales's wedding), 1981; Heart of the Nation, son et lumière, Horse Guards, 1983, 1985; America's Cup, Newport, 1983; Great St John Party (180,000 children), Hyde Park, 1985; King Hussein of Jordan's 50th Birthday Celebration, 1985; Finale, Christmas Horse Show, Olympia, 1986–2004; SSAFA, Queen's Shilling, Royal Albert Hall, 1987; Jordanian Royal Wedding, 1987, (of Prince Abdullah) 1993; Coronation Anniversary Celebration, Jordan, 1988; Joy to the World, Royal Albert Hall, 1988–97; Royal Equestrian Day, Oman, 1990; Fortress Fantasia, Gibraltar, 1990; Queen Mother's 90th Birthday Celebration, Horse Guards, 1990; Opening Ceremony, World Equestrian Games, 1990; Economic Summit Spectacular, Buckingham Palace, 1991; British Nat. Day Expo '92, Seville, 1992; The Queen's 40th Anniversary Celebration, 1992; Memphis in May Internat. Tattoo, 1992–94; King Hussein of Jordan's 40th Anniversary Celebrations, Unveiling of Queen Elizabeth Gate in Hyde Park, 1993; Channel Tunnel Gala Fireworks Display, D-Day Celebrations in Portsmouth, Normandy Veterans, RAH, Army Benevolent Fund, Drumhead Service, Royal Hosp. Chelsea, Pavarotti, Internat. Horse Show Modena Italy, P&O ship naming, China, 1994; P&O ship naming, Portsmouth, VE Day 50th Anniversary Celebrations in Hyde Park and Buckingham Palace, VJ 50th Anniversary Celebrations on Horse Guards, Jersey Liberation Fireworks, Horse Show in Los Angeles, 1995; Tri Service Massed Bands, Horse Guards, 1995; Oriana Gala, Sydney, 1996; Dawn Princess Naming, Fort Lauderdale, and The Countryside Rally, Hyde Park, 1997; Fireworks, Royal Windsor Horse Show, 1998–2004; re-opening of Albert Memorial, Hyde Park, 1998; Centenary Celebrations for King Abdul Aziz al Saud, Saudi Arabia, 1999; Royal Mil. Tattoo, Horse Guards, 2000; Queen Mother's 100th birthday celebrations, Horse Guards, 2000; All The Queen's Horses, Windsor, 2002; London Golden Jubilee Weekend Fest., June 2002, incl. nat. beacon, fireworks and nat. processions; Opening of Meml Gates, Constitution Hill, 2002; opening of Memphis SO, Canon Performing Arts Center, 2003; Centenary Celebration, Royal Welsh Agricl Show, 2004; Music on Fire!, RMA Sandhurst, 2004, 2006, 2008; 60th Anniv. Liberation Celebrations, Jersey, 2005; RYS Trafalgar 200th Anniv. Fireworks, 2005; Central Sch. of Speech and Drama Centenary, Old Vic, 2006; Not Forgotten Assoc. for Wounded and Disabled Service Personnel concert, Tower of London, and Christmas celebration, St James's Palace, 2006, Debt of Honour, 2007, 90th birthday celebration, Buckingham Palace, 2010. Vice-President: Morriston Orpheus Choir, 1972–; Queen Elizabeth the Queen Mother's Meml Fund, 2001–; Support for Africa, 2002–; CiB, 2002–; Patron: Chicken Shed Theatre Co., 2002–; Brooklands SLD Sch., 2002–; Trustee, ABF The Soldier's Charity, 2003–13. Evening Standard Ambassador for London, 1995; Walpole Gold Medal for Excellence, and Walpole Award for Best Cultural Achievement, 2002; CiB Communicator of the Year Award, 2002; SPAM Lifetime Achievement Award 2002; Derek Harper Technol. Award, RTS, 2003. KStJ 1985 (OStJ 1982). Grand Officer, Order of al Istiqlal (Jordan), 1987. *Publications:* The Awful Troop Leaders Gunnery Crib, 1969; It's All Going Terribly Wrong, 2012. *Recreations:* painting, antiques, giving parties. *Club:* Cavalry and Guards.

PARKER, Michael Joseph Bennett; Managing Director, 1970–80, and Chairman, 1980–98, Favor Parker Ltd; *b* 22 June 1931; *s* of Henry Gordon Parker and Alice Rose Parker; *m* 1960, Tania Henrietta Tiarks; two *s* one *d*. *Educ:* Eton; Magdalene Coll., Cambridge (BA Agric., MA). Chm., Favor Parker Gp, 1977–98. Chm., Land Settlement Assoc., 1982–85; Mem., UKAEA, 1985–88. *Recreations:* country sports, travel, lying in the sun. *Address:* Gooderstone Manor, King's Lynn, Norfolk PE33 9BP. *T:* (01366) 328255.

PARKER, (Michael) Miles, OBE 2013; PhD; FRSB; Deputy Chief Scientific Adviser and Director of Strategic Evidence and Analysis (formerly of Science, then for the Evidence Programme), Department for Environment, Food and Rural Affairs, 2002–12; Senior Research Associate, Centre for Science and Policy, University of Cambridge, since 2013 (Associate Fellow, since 2010); *b* 20 Nov. 1948; *s* of late Michael Rowton Parker and of Anne Margaret Bodkin; *m* 1991, Claire Christine Nihoul; two *s*, and two step *d*. *Educ:* Ampleforth Coll., York; Trinity Coll., Dublin Univ. (BA Mod.; PhD). FRSB (FSB 2000). Asst Inspector of Fisheries, Dept for Agric. and Fisheries, Ireland, 1975–83; Ministry of Agriculture, Fisheries and Food: PSO, Directorate of Fisheries Res., 1983–87; Principal, Food Contamination and Safety Policy, 1987–89; Sci. Liaison Officer, Chief Scientist's Gp, 1989–92; Grade 6, Cabinet Office Sci. Secretariat, 1992; Hd, Sci. Div., MAFF, 1992–98; Dir of Food Res., Central Sci. Lab., 1998; Dir, Internat., OST, 1998–2002. Non-exec. Dir, Cadbury Ltd, 1993–95. Chm., Marine Pollution Working Gp, Internat. Council for Exploration of the Sea, 1983–85. *Publications:* (ed with P. Tett) Exceptional Plankton Blooms, 1987; articles on science policy, marine ecol. and marine pollution in scientific jls. *Recreation:* omnicuriosity. *Address:* Fairhaven, Long Lane, Fowlmere, Cambs SG8 7TG. *T:* (01763) 209066.

PARKER, Michael St J.; *see* St John Parker.

PARKER, Miles; *see* Parker, Michael M.

PARKER, Gen. Sir Nicholas Ralph, (Sir Nick), KCB 2009; CBE 2002; Chairman, Step Up To Serve, since 2014; *b* 13 Oct. 1954; *s* of late Capt. Herbert Blake Parker, RN and of Diana Katharine Parker (*née* Barnwell); *m* 1979, Rebecca Clare Wellings; two *s*. *Educ:* Sherborne Sch.; RMA Sandhurst. CO, 2nd Bn Royal Green Jackets, 1994–95; Comdr, 20 Armoured Bde, 1997–2000; Comdr, Jt Task Force, Sierra Leone, 2001; GOC 2nd Div., and Gov., Edinburgh Castle, 2002–04; Comdt, Jt Services Comd and Staff Coll., 2004–05; Dep. Comdg Gen., Multinat. Corps, Iraq, 2005–06; GOC NI, 2006–07; Comdr Regl Forces, Land Forces Comd, 2007–09; Dep. Comdr ISAF—Afghanistan, and Sen. British Military Rep. (Afghanistan), later UK Nat. Contingent Comdr, 2009–10; Jt Comdr, Mil. Security Op. in Support of 2012 London Olympics, 2011–12; Comdr (formerly C-in-C) Land Forces, 2010–13; ADC Gen. to the Queen, 2010–13. Dir, Military Mutual, 2014–; Chm., Coote Capital, 2014–. Mem. Bd, Invictus Games CIC, 2014. Sen. Associate Fellow, RUSI, 2013–. Pres., Fovant Badges Soc., 2014–. Author, Independent Review of ACPO (report publd 2013). Officer, Legion of Merit (USA), 2007. *Recreations:* fishing, drawing, Coronation Street, gardening. *Club:* Army and Navy.

See also C. H. Parker, E. B. Parker.

PARKER, Prof. (Noel) Geoffrey, PhD, LittD; FBA 1984; Andreas Dorpalen Professor of European History and Associate, Mershon Center, since 1997, and Distinguished University Professor, since 2007, Ohio State University; *b* 25 Dec. 1943; *s* of late Derek Geoffrey Parker and Kathleen Betsy Symon; *m* 1st, Angela Maureen Chapman; one *s* one *d*; 2nd, Jane Helen Ohlmeyer; two *s*. *Educ:* Nottingham High Sch.; Christ's Coll., Cambridge (BA 1965; MA; PhD 1968; LittD 1981). Fellow of Christ's Coll., Cambridge, 1968–72; Lectr in Mod. Hist., 1972–78, Reader in Mod. Hist., 1978–82, and Prof. of Early Mod. Hist., 1982–86, St Andrews Univ. Charles E. Nowell Dist. Prof. of History, Univ. of Illinois at Urbana-Champaign, 1986–93 (Dept Chair, 1989–91); Robert A. Lovett Prof. of Military and Naval Hist., Yale Univ., 1993–96. British Acad. Exchange Fellow, Newberry Library, Chicago, 1981, Japan Acad., Tokyo, 2010; J. S. Guggenheim Foundn Fellow, 2001–02; H. F. Guggenheim Sen. Fellow, 2002–03; Fellow, Real Academia Hispano-Americana de Ciencias, Artes y Letras, Cádiz, 2004. Visiting Professor: Vrije Universiteit, Brussels, 1975 (Dr phil and letters *hc*, 1990); Univ. of BC, Vancouver, Canada, 1979–80; Keio Univ., Tokyo, 1984; Oxford Univ., 2004. Lees Knowles Lectr in Mil. Hist., Univ. of Cambridge, 1984. Television scripts and broadcasts. For. Mem., Royal Netherlands Acad. of Arts and Scis, 2005. Corresp. Fellow, Spanish Royal Acad. of History, 1988–. Hon. Dr Letters: Katholieke Univ., Brussels, 2005; Burgos Univ., 2010. Samuel E. Morison Prize, Soc. for Mil. Hist., 1999; Alumni Assoc. Award for Distinguished Teaching, Ohio State Univ., 2006; A. H. Heineken Foundn Prize for Hist., Royal Dutch Acad. of Scis, 2012. Order of Isabel the Catholic (Spain), Kt Grand Cross, 1992 (Encomienda, 1988); Order of Alfonso the Wise (Spain), Kt Grand Cross, 1996. *Publications:* The Army of Flanders and the Spanish Road 1567–1659, 1972, 4th edn 2004; The Dutch Revolt, 1977, 3rd edn 1985; Philip II, 1978, 4th edn 2001; Europe in Crisis 1598–1648, 1979, 2nd edn 2001; Spain and the Netherlands 1559–1659, 1979, 2nd edn 1990; The Thirty Years' War, 1984, 2nd edn 1996; (ed) The World: an illustrated history, 1986, 3rd edn 1995; The Military Revolution: military innovation and the rise of the West 1500–1800, 1988, 3rd edn 1996 (Dexter Prize, 1987–90; Soc. of Military History Dist. Book Prize for non-US Military History, 1988); (with Colin Martin) The Spanish Armada, 1988, 3rd edn 1999, rev. and expanded edn as La Gran Armada, 2011, 2nd edn 2013; (ed) Cambridge Illustrated History of Warfare, 1995, 2nd edn 2008; (ed) The Times Compact Atlas of World History, 1995, 5th edn 2008; (ed with Robert C. Cowley) The Reader's Companion to Military History, 1996; The Grand Strategy of Philip II, 1998; Success is Never Final: Empire, war and faith in early modern Europe, 2002, 2nd edn 2003; Felipe II: la biografía definitiva, 2010; Global Crisis: war, climate change and catastrophe in the seventeenth century, 2013 (Sunday Times Book of Yr, 2013; Soc. of Military History Dist. Book Prize for non-US Military History, 2013; British Acad. Medal, 2014); Imprudent King: a new life of Philip II, 2014; edited numerous other works; articles and reviews. *Recreations:* travel, archaeology. *Address:* History Department, Ohio State University, 230 West 17th Avenue, Columbus, OH 43210–1367, USA. *T:* (614) 2926721, *Fax:* (614) 2922282.

PARKER, Sir Peter; *see* Parker, Sir W. P. B.

PARKER, Peter Joseph Jacques, PhD; FMedSci; FRS 2006; Principal Scientist, Cancer Research UK (formerly Imperial Cancer Research Fund), since 1990; Head, Division of Cancer Studies, King's College London, since 2006; *b* 30 Sept. 1954; *s* of Philip Joseph Jacques Parker and late Phyllis Joyce Eileen Jacques Parker; *m* 1976, Jennifer Jean Cave; one *s*. *Educ:* Brasenose Coll., Oxford (BA 1976; PhD 1979). Gp Leader, ICRF, 1985–86; Lab. Hd, Ludwig Inst., London, 1986–90. Hon. Prof., UCL, 1997–. *Publications:* over 300 res. and review articles in learned jls. *Recreations:* tennis, walking, sculpture, theatre. *Address:* Protein Phosphorylation Laboratory, London Research Institute, Cancer Research UK, Lincoln's Inn Fields Laboratory, 44 Lincoln's Inn Fields, WC2A 3PX. *T:* (020) 7269 3513. *E:* peter.parker@cancer.org.uk; Section of Cancer Cell Biology and Imaging, 2nd Floor, New Hunt's House, Guy's Hospital, St Thomas Street, SE1 1UL. *T:* (020) 7848 6835, *Fax:* (020) 7848 6435. *E:* peter.parker@kcl.ac.uk.

PARKER, Philip Laurence; QC 2000; **His Honour Judge Parker;** a Circuit Judge, since 2008; *b* 10 Aug. 1953; *s* of late Robert Bernard Parker and Barbara Doherty Parker; *m* 1980 (marr. diss. 2002); three *d*. *Educ:* Prior Park Coll., Bath; King Edward's Sch., Birmingham; Matthew Boulton Tech. Coll., Birmingham; Univ. of Birmingham (LLB). Called to the Bar, Middle Temple, 1976. *Recreations:* golf, ski-ing. *Address:* Birmingham Crown Court, Queen Elizabeth II Law Courts, 1 Newton Street, Birmingham B4 7NA.

PARKER, Richard Jonathan, CBE 2013; FREng; Director of Research and Technology, Rolls-Royce plc, since 2001; *b* Scunthorpe, 30 Jan. 1954; *s* of Harold Colin Parker and Margaret Mavis Parker; *m* 1985, Jeanette Carol Kofler; two *d*. *Educ:* Scunthorpe Grammar Sch.; High Ridge Comprehensive Sch., Scunthorpe; John Leggott VI Form Coll., Scunthorpe; Imperial Coll. London (BSc Physics 1976); Loughborough Univ. (MBA Dist. 1992). FREng 2004. CASE Res. Student, Imperial Coll. London and Nat. Physical Lab., 1975–78; Rolls-Royce: Res. Scientist, then Sen. Res. Scientist, 1978–90, Gp Leader, Optical and Mech. Technol., 1985–90, Advanced Res. Lab.; Gp Leader, Optical Scis, Applied Sci. Lab, 1990–92; Chief of Composites and Ceramics, 1992–94; Chief of Compressor Engrg, Design and Mech. Technol., 1994–97; Gen. Manager, Compressor Engrg, 1997–98; Engrg Dir and Dep. Man. Dir, Compressor Systems, 1998–2000; Man. Dir, Compressor Systems Operating Business Unit, 2000–01; Dir, Engrg and Technol., Civil Aerospace, 2004–05. Vis. Prof., Aerospace Engrg, Loughborough Univ., 2007–; Hon. Prof., Materials Engrg, Birmingham Univ., 2010–. Hon. DEng: Pusan Nat., Korea, 2009; Sheffield, 2010; Nanyang Technol., Singapore, 2013; Loughborough, 2013; Hon. DSc Heriot Watt, 2011. *Recreations:* walking, films, music, fine dining. *Address:* Rolls-Royce plc, PO Box 31, Derby DE22 8BJ. *T:* (01332) 248380, *Fax:* (01332) 249328. *E:* richard.parker@rolls-royce.com.

PARKER, Sir Richard (William) Hyde, 12th Bt *cr* 1681; DL; *b* 5 April 1937; *o s* of Sir William Stephen Hyde Parker, 11th Bt, and Ulla Ditlef (*d* 1998), *o d* of C. Ditlef Nielsen, PhD, Copenhagen; *S* father, 1951; *m* 1972, Jean, *d* of late Sir Lindores Leslie, 9th Bt; one *s* three *d* (incl. twin *d*). *Educ:* Millfield; Royal Agricultural College. High Sheriff and DL, Suffolk, 1995. *Heir: s* William John Hyde Parker, *b* 10 June 1983. *Address:* Melford Hall, Long Melford, Suffolk CO10 9AA.

PARKER, Robert Christopher Towneley, FBA 1998; Wykeham Professor of Ancient History, and Fellow of New College, University of Oxford, since 1996; *b* 19 Oct. 1950; *s* of Geoffrey Parker and Janet Parker (*née* Chidley); *m* 1979, Joanna Hilary Martindale; one *d*. *Educ:* St Paul's Sch., London; New Coll., Oxford (MA, DPhil). CUF Lectr in Greek and Latin Languages and Literature, Oxford Univ., and Fellow of Oriel Coll., Oxford, 1976–96. Townsend Vis. Prof., Cornell Univ., 2008; Sather Prof. of Classical Lit., Univ. of Calif, Berkeley, 2013. Foreign Mem., Royal Danish Acad., 2007; MAE 2011. Officier, Ordre des Palmes Académiques (France), 2010. *Publications:* Miasma, 1983; Athenian Religion: a history, 1996; Polytheism and Society in Athens, 2005 (Criticos Prize, London Hellenic Soc.); On Greek Religion, 2011. *Recreation:* gardening. *Address:* New College, Oxford OX1 3BN.

PARKER, Dr Robert John, CSci, CChem; FRSC; Chief Executive, Royal Society of Chemistry, since 2011; *b* Palmers Green, London, 29 Oct. 1958; *s* of Claude Albert Parker and Mary Agnes Parker (*née* O'Shea); *m* 1983, Rosemary Jane Maxey; one *s* two *d*. *Educ:* St Ignatius Coll., Enfield; King's Coll. London (BSc Chem. 1981; PhD Chem. 1985). CChem 1990; FRSC 1998; CSci 2004. Royal Society of Chemistry: Asst Ed., 1985–88; Staff Ed., 1988; Editl Manager, 1988–95; Publisher, 1995–98; Gen. Manager, Journals and Reviews, 1998–2003; Editl Dir, 2003–07; Man. Dir, Publishing, 2007–11. Chm., Assoc. of Learned and Professional Soc. Publishers, 2009–10. Trustee and Mem. Bd, Sci. Council, 2011–. *Recreations:* motorcycling, art history, embarrassing my children, eating canapés for the RSC. *Address:* Royal Society of Chemistry, Burlington House, Piccadilly, W1J 0BA. *E:* parkerr@rsc.org.

PARKER, Robert Stewart, CB 1998; Parliamentary Counsel, 1992–2010; Sir Thomas Pope Fellow, Trinity College, Oxford, since 2010; *b* 13 Jan. 1949; *o s* of Robert Arnold Parker and Edna Parker (*née* Baines). *Educ:* Brentwood School; Trinity College, Oxford (Scholar; First in Mods; MA 1974). Called to the Bar, Middle Temple, 1975 (Harmsworth Exhibnr; Astbury Senior Law Scholarship); Lincoln's Inn *ad eundem*, 1977. Classics Master, Brentwood School, 1971–74; in practice at the Bar, 1975–80; Office of Parly Counsel, 1980; Law Commn, 1985–87; Dep. Parly Counsel, 1987–92. Freeman, City of London, 1984; Liveryman, Wheelwrights' Co., 1984. Member: Horatian Soc.; City of London Br., Royal Soc. of St George; Kipling Soc.; Edinburgh Walter Scott Club; Friends of Classics, 2000–; Oxford Univ. Philological Soc., 2011–; Egypt Exploration Soc., 2012–; Herculaneum Soc., 2012–; Oxford

Univ. Soc. of Bibliophiles, 2013–; U3A, Oxford Br., 2014–; Chm., Trinity Soc., 2012–. Life Friend, Bodleian Liby, 2009. MCMI (MBIM 1984); FRSA 2000. *Publications:* Cases and Statutes on General Principles of Law (with C. R. Newton), 1980; (contrib.) The Best of Days? (Brentwood School Millennium book), 2000. *Recreations:* the Livery, classical and English literature, biblical Hebrew, papyrology, palaeography, theatre, books, music. *Address:* 9 Southall Way, Brentwood CM14 5LS. *Clubs:* Athenæum, City Livery, Langbourn Ward, Civil Service.

See also E. Blackburn.

PARKER, Prof. Roger Leslie, PhD; FBA 2008; Thurston Dart Professor of Music, King's College London, since 2007; *b* 2 Aug. 1951; *m* 1972, Lynden Cranham; two *s* one *d*. *Educ:* Goldsmiths' Coll., London (BMus 1973); King's Coll., London (MMus 1975; PhD 1981). Associate Prof., Cornell Univ., 1982–93; Oxford University: Lectr in Music, 1994–97; Prof. of Music, 1997–99; Fellow, St Hugh's Coll., 1994–99; Prof. of Music, Cambridge Univ., 1999–2006; Fellow, St John's Coll., Cambridge, 1999–2006. Jt Gen. Ed., Donizetti Critical Edn, 1987–. Premio Giuseppe Verdi, Istituto nazionale di studi verdiani, 1985; Dent Medal, Royal Musical Assoc., 1991. *Publications:* (ed jtly) Reading Opera, 1988; (ed) Oxford Illustrated History of Opera, 1994; Leonora's Last Act, 1997; Remaking the Song, 2006; (with Carolyn Abbate) A History of Opera: the last 400 years, 2012. *Address:* Department of Music, King's College London, Strand, WC2R 2LS.

PARKER, Stephen, CBE 2009; Legal Adviser to HM Treasury, since 2003; *b* 3 Oct. 1957; *s* of late Fernley and Ann Parker; *m* 1987, Philippa Casimir-Mrowczynska; three *s*. *Educ:* Stockport Grammar Sch.; Emmanuel Coll., Cambridge (MA, LLB). Called to the Bar, Lincoln's Inn, 1982; Legal Asst, then Sen. Legal Asst and Lawyer, DTI, 1984–87; Law Officers' Dept, 1987–88; Lawyer: DTI, 1988–94; Home Office, 1994–2000; Dir, Legal Services A, DEFRA, 2001–03. *Recreations:* mineralogy, natural history, history. *Address:* HM Treasury, 1 Horse Guards, SW1A 2HQ. *T:* (020) 7270 5666. *E:* stephen.parker@hmtreasury.gsi.gov.uk. *Club:* Oxford and Cambridge.

PARKER, Steven Nigel; His Honour Judge Steven Parker; a Circuit Judge, since 2013; *b* Newent, Glos, 4 Dec. 1964; *s* of Brian Parker and Sylvia Parker; *m* 1988, Jane Ridgway; two *s* one *d*. *Educ:* Haberdashers' Monmouth Sch.; Lanchester Poly. (LLB Hons); Inns of Court Sch. of Law (BVC). Called to the Bar, Gray's Inn, 1987; a Dep. District Judge, 2000; a Recorder, 2008–13. *Recreations:* sport, theatre. *Address:* Liverpool Civil and Family Court, 35 Vernon Street, Liverpool L2 2BX.

PARKER, Tanya; *see* Parker, L. T.

PARKER, Sir (Thomas) John, GBE 2012; Kt 2001; DSc; FREng; Chairman: Anglo American plc, since 2009; Pennon Group plc, since 2015; Vice Chairman, DP World (Dubai), since 2006; President, Royal Academy of Engineering, 2011–14; *b* 8 April 1942; *s* of Robert Parker and Margaret Elizabeth Parker (*née* Bell); *m* 1967, Emma Elizabeth (*née* Blair); one *s* one *d*. *Educ:* Belfast Coll. of Technology; Queen's Univ. Belfast (DSc (Eng)). FREng (FEng 1983); FRINA; FIMarE. Harland & Wolff, Belfast: Student Apprentice Naval Architect, 1958–63; Ship Design Staff, 1963–69 (Nat. Physical Lab. (Ship Hydrodynamics), 1964); Numerical Applications Manager, 1969–71; Prodn Drawing Office Manager, 1971–72; Gen. Manager, Sales and Projects, 1972–74; Man. Dir, Austin-Pickersgill Ltd, Sunderland, 1974–78; British Shipbuilders: Dir of Marketing, 1977–78; Bd Mem. for Shipbuilding, 1978–83; Dep. Chief Exec., 1980–83; Chm. and Chief Exec., Harland and Wolff, 1983–93; Dep. Chm. and Chief Exec., 1993–94, Chm., 1994–2000, Babcock Internat. Gp. Mem., British Coal Corp., 1986–93; Chairman: Lattice Gp plc, 2000–02; Firth Rixson, 2001–03; RMC Gp plc, 2002–05; Nat. Grid (formerly Nat. Grid Transco) plc, 2002–12; Peninsular and Oriental Steam Navigation Co., 2005–06; Jt Chm., Mondi plc and Mondi Ltd, 2007–09; non-executive Director: GKN, 1993–2002; BG plc, 1997–2000; P&O Princess Cruises, 2000–03 (Dep. Chm., 2001–03); Brambles Industries, 2001–03; Carnival plc, 2003–; Carnival Inc., 2003–; Airbus Gp (formerly EADS), 2007–. Non-exec. Dir, 2004–09, Sen. non-exec. Dir, 2005–09, Bank of England. Chancellor, Univ. of Southampton, 2006–11. Member: Council, RINA, 1978–80, 1982– (Pres., 1996–99); Bd of Governors, Sunderland Polytechnic, 1976–81; Internat. Cttee, Bureau Veritas, Paris, 1979–83; Gen. Cttee, Lloyd's Register of Shipping, 1983– (Chm. Tech. Cttee, 1996–2001); Industrial Develt Bd of NI, 1983–87. Hon. ScD Trinity Coll. Dublin, 1986; Hon. DSc: Ulster, 1992; Abertay Dundee, 1997; Southampton, 2006; Aston, 2012; DUniv Surrey, 2001; Hon DEng Plymouth, 2011; Hon Dr Imperial Coll. London, 2013. *Publications:* papers to Trans IES, RINA, RAEng. *Recreations:* reading, ships, sailing, music. *Address:* Anglo American plc, 20 Carlton House Terrace, SW1Y 5AN.

PARKER, Timothy Charles; Chairman: Samsonite Corporation, since 2008 (Chief Executive Officer, 2008–14); National Trust, since 2014; Post Office Ltd, since 2015; Industrial Adviser, CVC Capital Partners, since 2008 (Member, Advisory Board, 2004–07); *b* 19 June 1955; *s* of Clifford and Eileen Parker; *m* 1984, Thérèse Moralis; two *s* two *d*. *Educ:* Pembroke Coll., Oxford (MA); London Business School (MSc). Chief Executive: Kenwood Appliances plc, 1986–95; C. & J. Clark Ltd, 1996–2002; CEO, 2002–04, Dep. Chm., 2004–, Kwik-Fit; Chief Exec., AA, 2004–07. Director: Kleeneze plc, 1998–2002; CDC Capital Partners, then CDC Gp plc, 2001–04; Legal & Gen. plc, 2002–04; Boots plc, 2004–07; Compass Group plc, 2007–08 and 2009–10; non-exec. Dir, Nine Entertainment Gp (formerly PBL Media), 2007–11 (Chm., 2008–11); Chairman: British Pathe Ltd, 2007–; Autobar Gp, 2010–14. Chm., Emerging Africa Infrastructure Fund, 2007–08. First Dep. Mayor of London, 2008; Chief Exec., GLA Gp, 2008. Board Member: SW Regl Develt Agency, 1998–2001; Audit Commn, 2006–07. Vis. Fellow, Oxford Univ. Centre for Corporate Reputation, 2008–11. Gov., Bedales Sch. FRSA 1990. *Address:* National Trust, 20 Grosvenor Gardens, SW1W 0DH. *Clubs:* Garrick, Travellers.

PARKER, Sir (William) Peter (Brian), 5th Bt *cr* 1844, of Shenstone Lodge, Staffordshire; FCA; Partner, Stephenson Nuttall & Co., chartered accountants, Newark, since 1988; *b* 30 Nov. 1950; *s* of Sir (William) Alan Parker, 4th Bt and Sheelagh Mary, *o d* of late Dr Sinclair Stevenson; *S* father, 1990; *m* 1976, Patricia Ann, *d* of R. Filtness and Mrs D. Filtness; one *d* (one *s* decd). *Educ:* Eton. FCA 1974. *Heir:* *cousin* Timothy John Parker, *b* 17 May 1959. *Address:* Apricot Hall, Sutton-cum-Beckingham, Lincoln LN5 0RE.

PARKER-BROWN, Hazel Christine; Executive Director for Corporate Services, Legal Services Commission, 2008–11; *m* 1978, Alexander Parker-Brown (*d* 2012); two *s* one *d*. *Educ:* Convent of the Holy Child Jesus, Combe Bank; Walthamstow Hall, Sevenoaks; Salford Univ.; Coll. of Law (Chester). Admin trainee, DoE, 1976; various posts in historic bldgs, road safety, energy and envmt, 1976–90, incl. Asst Private Sec. to Minister for Housing and Construction, 1979–81; Head, Finance Policy (formerly Public Expenditure) Div., 1990–94, Head, Finance, Strategy and Audit Div., 1994–95, PSA; Head, Office Services Div., DoE, 1995–97; Dir, Human Resource Services, Highways Agency, DETR, 1998–99; Dir, Human Resources, DETR, then DTLR, subseq. Dir of Human Resources and Corporate Services, DfT, 1999–2002; Dir, Business Delivery Services, DfT, 2002–04; Dir of Corporate Services, Commn for Social Care Inspection, 2004–08. Chm., Free Trade Wharf Residents' Assoc., 2013–. Treas., St St Anne's Limehouse PCC, 2015–.

PARKER-JERVIS, Roger; DL; Deputy Chairman, CGA plc, 1982–90; *b* 11 Sept. 1931; *s* of George Parker-Jervis and late Ruth, *d* of C. E. Farmer; *m* 1958, Diana, *d* of R. St V. Parker-Jervis; two *s* one *d*. *Educ:* Eton; Magdalene College, Cambridge. Served Rifle Brigade, 1950–51, Queen Victoria Rifles, 1951–54; ADC to Governor of Tasmania, 1954–56. Bucks County Council: Mem., 1967–93; Chm., 1981–85. Mem., Milton Keynes Develt Corp., 1975–92; Pres., Timber Growers of England and Wales, 1981–83; Vice-Chm., Forestry Cttee of GB, 1981–83. Chm., Bucks Historic Buildings Trust, 1983–98; Mem., Thames and Chiltern Regl Cttee, NT, 1987–94. High Sheriff of Bucks, 1973–74, DL Bucks, 1982. *Publications:* Down the Rhône, 1997. *Recreations:* barging and caravanning in France, painting. *Address:* The Old Schoolhouse, The Green, Brill, Bucks HP18 9RU. *T:* (01844) 238025. *Clubs:* Farmers, Rifles.

PARKER PEARSON, Prof. Michael George, PhD; FBA 2015; FSA, FSAScot; Professor of British Later Prehistory, Institute of Archaeology, University College London, since 2012; *b* Wantage, 26 June 1957; *s* of George Parker Pearson and Patricia Parker Pearson; *m* 2000, Karen Godden. *Educ:* Taunton Sch.; Univ. of Southampton (BA Archaeol. 1979); King's Coll., Cambridge (PhD Archaeol. 1985). MCIfA (MIFA 1989); FSA 1991; FSAScot 1996. Inspector of Ancient Monuments, English Heritage, 1984–90; University of Sheffield: Lectr, 1990–99, Reader, 1999–2005, in Archaeol.; Prof. of Archaeol., 2005–12. Mem. Council, 1999–2005, Vice-Pres., 2006–09, Prehistoric Soc. *Publications:* Bronze Age Britain, 1993, 2nd edn 2005; Looking at the Land, 1994; Architecture and Order, 1994; Between Land and Sea, 1999; The Archaeology of Death and Burial, 1999; Earthly Remains, 2001; In Search of the Red Slave, 2002; Food, Culture and Identity in the Neolithic and Early Bronze Age, 2003; South Uist, 2004; Fiskerton, 2004; Warfare, Violence and Slavery in Prehistory, 2005; From Stonehenge to the Baltic, 2007; Pastoralists, Warriors and Colonists, 2010; From Machair to Mountains, 2012; Stonehenge, 2012; articles in Antiquity, Jl of Material Culture, Jl of Archaeol Sci., Procs of Royal Soc., Nature, Antiquaries Jl, Procs of Prehistoric Soc. *Recreations:* cats, parties, pig roasts. *Address:* Institute of Archaeology, 31–34 Gordon Square, University College London, WC1H 0PY. *T:* (020) 7679 4767. *E:* m.parker-pearson@ucl.ac.uk.

PARKER-SMITH, Jane Caroline Rebecca; international concert organist and recording artist, since 1970; *b* 20 May 1950; *m* 1996, John Gadney (*d* 2012). *Educ:* Barton Peveril Grammar Sch., Eastleigh; Royal Coll. of Music, London (ARCM 1966); postgrad. study with Nicolas Kynaston, London, and Jean Langlais, Paris. LTCL 1969. Concerts include: Westminster Cathedral, 1970; RFH, 1975, 2003, 2014; BBC Prom. Concerts, 1972; Jyvaskyla Fest., Finland, 1977; Stockholm Concert Hall, 1980; Hong Kong Arts Fest., 1988; Roy Thomson Hall, Toronto, 1989; City of London Fest., 1992; Fest. Paris Quartier d'Été, 1995; Centennial Convention, NY, 1996, Nat. Convention, Philadelphia, 2002, American Guild of Organists; Cube Concert Hall, Shiroishi, Japan, 2000; Sejong Cultural Centre, Seoul, 2004; Westminster Abbey, 2005; Birmingham Symphony Hall, 2005; Esplanade Concert Hall, Singapore, 2005; Walt Disney Concert Hall, LA, 2006; Lahti Organ Fest., Finland, 2006; Monaco Cathedral, 2009; Verizon Hall, Philadelphia, 2009; Davies Symphony Hall, San Francisco, 2011; Mariinsky Concert Hall, St Petersburg, 2011; ZK Matthews Hall, Univ. of S Africa, Pretoria, 2011; American Guild of Organists Nat. Convention, Nashville, 2012. Mem., ISM, 1995–. Hon. FGMS 1996; Hon. FNMSM 1997. *Recreations:* cooking, antiques, travel, Daily Telegraph cryptic crossword, Formula One racing, horse racing. *Address:* 174 The Quadrangle Tower, Cambridge Square, W2 2PJ. *T:* and *Fax:* (020) 7262 9259. *E:* janeparkersmith@btconnect.com. *W:* www.janeparkersmith.com.

PARKES, Rt Rev. (Anthony) John; *see* Wangaratta, Bishop of.

PARKES, Sir Edward (Walter), Kt 1983; DL; FREng; Vice-Chancellor, University of Leeds, 1983–91; Chairman, Committee of Vice-Chancellors and Principals of the Universities of the United Kingdom, 1989–91 (Vice-Chairman, 1985–89); *b* 19 May 1926; *o s* of Walter Frederick Parkes; *m* 1950, Margaret Parr, CBE (*d* 2007); one *s* one *d*. *Educ:* King Edward's, Birmingham; St John's College, Cambridge; Scholar; 1st cl. hons Mech. Sci. Tripos, 1945; MA, PhD, ScD; FIMechE. At RAE and in the aircraft industry, 1945–48; research student and subsequently Univ. Lecturer, Cambridge, 1948–59; Fellow and Tutor of Gonville and Caius College; Vis. Prof., Stanford Univ., 1959–60; Head of the Department of Engineering, Univ. of Leicester, 1960–65; Prof. of Mechanics, Cambridge, and Professorial Fellow, Gonville and Caius Coll., 1965–74 (Mem. Gen. Bd, Dep. head of Dept of Engineering); Vice-Chancellor, City Univ., 1974–78; Chm., UGC, 1978–83. Member: Brynmor Jones Cttee, 1964–65; Adv. Bd for Res. Councils, 1974–83; University and Polytechnic Grants Cttee for Hong Kong, 1974–96; Chairman: Clinical Academic Staff Salaries Cttee, 1985–90; Academic Adv. Bd, Asian Univ. of Sci. and Technology, Thailand, 1994–98. Chm., Adv. Panel on Limestone Workings in the W Midlands, 1983–95. DL W Yorks, 1990. Hon. FIMechE 1992. Hon. DTech Loughborough, 1984; Hon. DSc: Leicester, 1984; City, 1988; Hon. LLD Wales, 1984. Silver Bauhinia Star (Hong Kong), 1999. *Publications:* Braced Frameworks, 1965, 2nd edn 1974; papers on elasticity, dynamic plasticity or thermal effects on structures in Proc. and Phil. Trans. Royal Society and other jls. *Address:* The Cottage, Headington Hill, Oxford OX3 0BT. *Club:* Athenæum.

PARKES, Rt Rev. John; *see* Parkes, Rt Rev. A. J.

PARKES, John; *see* Parkes, R. J.

PARKES, John Alan, CBE 1996; DL; Chief Executive, Humberside County Council, and Clerk to Humberside Lieutenancy, 1988–96; Director, EMIH Ltd, since 1998; *b* 18 Jan. 1939; *s* of Arthur and Alice Parkes; *m* 1963, Margaret Jill (*née* Clayton); two *d*. *Educ:* Nottingham High Sch.; Oriel Coll., Oxford (MA). IPFA 1965 (Gold Medal, 1965). Various posts from graduate traineeship, Council Finance, Derbyshire, 1961–68; Asst County Treasurer, Glos, 1968–71; Dep., then County Treasurer, Lindsey, 1971–74; Dir of Finance, Humberside, 1974–88. Member: Phildrew Ventures Adv. Cttee, 1986–96; Financial Reporting Council, 1990–95. Advr, ACC, 1976–96; Sec., 1980–86, Pres., 1987–88, Soc. of County Treasurers; Dir, Humberside TEC, 1990–96. A Public Works Loan Comr, 1996–2013 (Dep. Chm., 2002–05; Chm., 2005–13). Mem., ER and Hull HA, 2000–02. Mem. Council, Univ. of Hull, 1996–2007 (Treas. and Pro-Chancellor, 2001–07, Pro-Chancellor Emeritus, 2007). Freeman, City of London, 1988. Hon. Fellow, Univ. of Humberside, 1991. DUniv Hull, 2009. DL E Riding of Yorks, 1996. *Publications:* articles on local govt finance in prof. jls. *Recreations:* walking, cars, railways. *Address:* 2 Burton Road, Beverley HU17 7EH. *T:* (01482) 881228.

PARKES, Richard John Byerley; QC 2003; **His Honour Judge Parkes;** a Circuit Judge, since 2009; *b* 8 June 1950; *s* of Richard Byerley Parkes and Margaret Elizabeth Parkes (*née* Service); *m* 1981, Janet Oliver (marr. diss. 2006); three *s*. *Educ:* Westminster Sch. (Queen's Schol.); Peterhouse, Cambridge (Exhibnr in Classics, MA). Taught Latin and Greek, 1972–76; called to the Bar, Gray's Inn, 1977, Bencher, 2006; Asst Recorder, 1998–2000; Recorder, 2000–09; a Dep. High Court Judge, 2007–. A Pres., Restricted Patients Panel, Mental Health Review Tribunal, 2007–. A contributing editor, Civil Procedure (The White Book), 1999–; Jt Gen. Editor, Gatley on Libel and Slander, 2009–; Jt Editor, Entertainment and Media Law Reports, 2009–. *Publications:* (contrib. and ed) Gatley on Libel and Slander, 9th edn 1997 to 12th edn (Jt Gen. Ed.) 2013; (contrib.) The Law of Privacy and the Media, 2002, 2nd edn 2011. *Recreations:* country pubs, watching cricket, nursing an Austin Seven. *Address:* Winchester Combined Court Centre, Winchester SO23 9EL. *T:* (01962) 814100. *Clubs:* Garrick, MCC.

PARKES, Prof. (Ronald) John, PhD; FRS 2011; FLSW; FRSB; Professor of Geomicrobiology and Distinguished Research Professor, Cardiff University, since 2003 (Head, School of Earth and Ocean Sciences, 2009–14); *b* 21 Nov. 1950; *m* 1975, Hilary; two *s*. *Educ:* Birmingham Univ. (BEd Hons 1974); Aberdeen Univ. (PhD 1978). FRSB (FSB 2011). PDRA, UWIST, 1977–80; Sen. Scientific Officer, 1980–85, Principal Scientific

Officer, 1985–89, Scottish Marine Biol Assoc.; University of Bristol: Sen. Lectr, 1989–94; Reader 1994–96; Dir, Biogeochemistry Centre, 1995; Prof., Dept of Earth Scis, 1996–2003. FLSW 2011; Fellow, Amer. Acad. of Microbiol., 2013. *Publications:* contribs to scientific jls incl. FEMS Microbiol. Ecol., Applied and Envmtl Microbiol., Nature, Science. *Address:* School of Earth and Ocean Sciences, Cardiff University, Main Building, Park Place, Cardiff CF10 3AT.

PARKHILL, Dr Julian, FRS 2014; FMedSci; Senior Investigator, Wellcome Trust Sanger Institute, since 2003; *b* Leigh-on-Sea, 23 Sept. 1964; *s* of Gordon and Margaret Parkhill. *Educ:* Westcliff High Sch. for Boys; Univ. of Birmingham (BSc Biol Scis 1986); Univ. of Bristol (PhD 1991). Joined Sanger Centre, later Wellcome Trust Sanger Inst., 1997. Vis. Prof., Univ. of Oxford, 2003–; Hon. Professor: LSHTM, 2012–; Univ. of Cambridge, 2013–. FMedSci 2009. *Address:* Wellcome Trust Sanger Institute, Wellcome Trust Genome Campus, Hinxton, Cambridge CB10 1SA. *T:* (01223) 494975. *E:* parkhill@sanger.ac.uk.

PARKHOUSE, James, MD, FFARCS; Director, 1984–89, Hon. Assistant Director, 1989–2001, Medical Careers Research Group, Oxford; *b* 30 March 1927; *s* of Charles Frederick Parkhouse and Mary Alice Sumner; *m* 1952, Hilda Florence Rimmer; three *s* two *d*. *Educ:* Merchant Taylors' Sch., Great Crosby; Liverpool Univ. (MD 1955). MB ChB, 1950; MA Oxon 1960; MSc Manchester 1974. DA; FFARCS 1952. Anaesthetist, RAF Med. Br., 1953–55. Sen. Resident Anaesth., Mayo Clinic, 1957–58; First Asst, Nuffield Dept of Anaesths, Oxford, and Hon. Cons. Anaesth., United Oxford Hosps, 1958–66; Prof. and Head of Dept of Anaesths, Univ. of Manitoba, and Chief Anaesth., Winnipeg Gen. Hosp., 1967–68; Postgrad. Dean, Faculty of Med., Sheffield Univ., and Hon. Cons. Anaesth., United Sheffield Hosps, 1969–70; Prof. of Anaesths, Manchester Univ., and Hon. Cons. Anaesth., Manchester and Salford AHAs (Teaching), 1970–80; Prof. of Postgraduate Med. Educn, Univ. of Newcastle upon Tyne, and Postgrad. Dean and Dir, Northern Postgrad. Inst. for Medicine and Dentistry, 1980–84. Consultant, postgrad. med. trng, WHO, 1969–89; Specialist Adviser, H of C Social Services Cttee, 1980–81, 1984. Member: Sheffield Reg. Hosp. Bd, 1969–70; Bd, Faculty of Anaesthetists, 1971–82; Neurosciences Bd, MRC, 1977–80; GMC, 1979–89; Nat. Trng Council, NHS, 1981–84; North Tyneside HA, 1982–84. *Publications:* A New Look at Anaesthetics, 1965; Medical Manpower in Britain, 1979; Doctors' Careers, 1991; contrib. to The Lancet, BMJ and specialist jls. *Recreations:* music, golf. *Address:* 56 Forum Court, 80 Lord Street, Southport PR8 1JP. *T:* (01704) 545764.

PARKHOUSE, Nicholas, DM; FRCS; Consultant Plastic Surgeon, King Edward VII Hospital Sister Agnes (formerly King Edward VII Hospital for Officers), since 1998; *b* 7 Aug. 1957; *s* of late David Parkhouse and of Eileen Croxford, 'cellist; *m* 1986, Helen (*d* 2010), *d* of late Austin and of Margaret Fitzmaurice; two *s* two *d*. *Educ:* St Paul's Sch.; Oriel Coll., Oxford (Open Exhibnr; BA 1978); Middx Hosp. Med. Sch. (MB BS 1981); DM 1990, MCh 1991, Oxon. FRCS 1985. Surgical trng at John Radcliffe Hosp., Oxford, Wexham Park, Orsett and Basildon Hosp., E Grinstead, Mt Vernon and UCH, 1982–91; Consultant Plastic Surgeon: Mt Vernon Hosp., 1991–94; Queen Victoria Hosp., E Grinstead, 1994–2006. Director: Rainsford Burn Centre, 1991–94; McIndoe Burns Centre, E Grinstead, 1994–97; McIndoe Surgical Centre Ltd, 2002–. Hunterian Prof., RCS, 1989; Visiting Professor: USC, 2001; Mayo Clinic, Minn, 2001. Ed., British Jl Plastic Surgery, 1997–2002. Mem. Council, British Assoc. Plastic Surgeons, 1997–2002, 2005–. Plastic Surgery Advr to NICE, 2002–. Fellow, Amer. Assoc. of Plastic Surgeons, 2004. Freeman, City of London, 1998; Liveryman, Hon. Co. of Air Pilots (formerly GAPAN), 1998. De Havilland Trophy, 1990. *Publications:* contrib. chapters on burn injury; contrib. scientific jls on reconstructive surgery and restoration of function. *Recreations:* flying, fishing, family. *Address:* The Cadogan Clinic, 120 Sloane Street, SW1X 9BW; The McIndoe Surgical Centre, E Grinstead, W Sussex RH19 3EB. *T:* (01342) 332880; Chelworth House, Chelwood Gate, W Sussex RH17 7JZ. *T:* (01825) 740615. *Clubs:* Air Squadron, Queen's; Vincent's (Oxford); Leander (Henley); Houghton (Stockbridge).

PARKHOUSE, Peter; Chairman, Severn NHS Trust, 1992–95; *b* 22 July 1927; *s* of late William Richard Parkhouse, MBE, and Alice Vera Parkhouse (*née* Clarke); *m* 1st, 1950, Mary Alison Holland (*d* 1987); one *s* one *d*; 2nd, 1994, Sally Isabel Squires. *Educ:* Blundell's Sch.; Peterhouse, Cambridge (coll. organist, 1944–45; BA 1947; MA 1951). Instr Lieut, RN, 1947–50; Cologne Univ., 1950–51; Asst Master, Uppingham Sch., 1951–52; Asst Principal, Min. of Food, 1952; transf. to MAFF, 1955; served in private office of successive Ministers and Parly Secs, 1954–58; Principal 1958; Principal Private Sec. to Minister, 1966–67; Asst Sec. 1967; Under-Sec. 1973; Dir in Directorate-Gen. for Agriculture, Commn of European Communities, 1973–79; Under-Sec., MAFF, 1979–84. Mem., EDC for Agriculture, 1982–84. Mem., Mgt Cttee, Cheltenham Internat. Fest. of Music, 1992–95. Mem., Tetbury Hosp. Action Gp, 1989–92; Trustee, Tetbury Hosp. Trust Ltd, 1992–93 and 1996–2004; Gov., Barnwood House Trust, 1996–2004. Vice-Pres., Nat. Star Coll. (formerly Nat. Star Centre, Coll. of Further Educn), Cheltenham, 2002–07 (Dir, 1997–2002). *Recreations:* music (organist emeritus of Tetbury Parish Church), fishing. *Address:* Stafford House, 14 The Chipping, Tetbury, Glos GL8 8ET. *T:* (01666) 502540. *Club:* Oxford and Cambridge.

PARKIN, Bernard Maurice Walcroft; artist and photographer; Racing Photographer to the Queen, since 2002 (Racing Photographer to Queen Elizabeth the Queen Mother, 1961–2002) (Royal Warrant, since 1993); Official Photographer to Cheltenham Racecourse, 1972–2007; *b* 7 Jan. 1930; *s* of Horace Parkin and Dorothy Jane Parkin; *m* 1955, Pamela Edith Humphreys; one *s* one *d*. *Educ:* Cheltenham Dunalley; Cheltenham Central Boys' Sch.; Cheltenham Sch. of Art. Garrison cartographer, RA, Malta, 1948–49; estabd own business of photography, design artwork, calligraphy and cartooning, specialising in horseracing, 1953–; Spirax-Sarco Ltd: company artist, 1960–91; Ed. and Producer, Spirax News (worldwide engrg monthly), 1980–91. Press Officer, Stratford-upon-Avon Racecourse, 1968–75; Artist: to Jockeys Assoc. of GB, 1969–2007; to Stable Lads Welfare Trust, 1989–2000. Has compiled large liby of own racing photos, 1953–. Member: Royal Warrant Holders Assoc., 1993–; Horserace Writers and Photographers Assoc., 1975–. Life Mem., Royal Artillery Assoc., 2009. Hon. Life Mem., Cheltenham Racecourse, 2007. Founder Mem., Cleeve Hill Round Table, 1965. *Publications:* many books illustrated with technical drawings, cartoons, caricatures or photographs including: Steam Trapping and Air Venting, by Lionel Northcroft, 1968; The History of Royal Ascot, by Dorothy Laird, 1974; Great Horsemen of the World, by Guy Wathen, 1990; The Book of Derby Quotations, by Laurie Brannan, 2004; by Stewart Peters: Festival Gold, 2004; Grand National, 2005; The Hennessy Gold Cup, 2006. *Recreations:* travel, gardening (including landscape), hill walking, illustrated short story and letter writing, composing poetry. *Address:* Beldon House, Bushcombe Lane, Woodmancote, Cheltenham GL52 9QQ. *T:* (01242) 672784. *Club:* Stratford-upon-Avon Race (Hon. Life Mem. 1976; Chm., Entertainments Cttee, 1976–83).

PARKIN, Prof. David John, PhD; FBA 1993; Professor of Social Anthropology, Oxford University, 1996–2008, now Emeritus; Fellow of All Souls College, Oxford, 1996–2008, now Emeritus; *b* 5 Nov. 1940; *s* of Cecil Joseph Parkin and Rose May Parkin (*née* Johnson); *m* 1st, 1962, Monica Ann Lacey (marr. diss. 1998); two *s* one *d*; 2nd, 2003, Vibha Joshi; one *s*. *Educ:* London Univ. (BA 1st cl. Hons African Studies 1962); SOAS (PhD Social Anthropol. 1965). FRAI 1966. Res. Associate, E African Inst. of Social Res., Makerere Univ. Coll., Kampala, Uganda, 1962–64 and 1966–67; School of Oriental and African Studies, University of London: Asst Lectr, 1964–65; Lectr, 1965–71; Lecturer: Sussex Univ., 1971–72; SOAS, 1972–76; Reader in Anthropol., 1976–81, Prof. of Anthropology with ref. to Africa, 1981–96, SOAS (Hon. Fellow, 2009; Emeritus Life Fellow, 2009). University of Nairobi: Sen. Res. Fellow, Lang. Survey Unit, 1968–69; Sen. Res. Associate, 1977–78; Vis. Prof., Univ. of Calif, Berkeley, 1980; Directeur d'études Associé, Ecole des Hautes Etudes en Sciences Sociales, Paris, 1986, 1987 and 1993; Chercheur Associé, CNRS, Paris, 1992–93; Professorial Res. Fellow, Max Planck Inst. for Religious and Ethnic Diversity, Goettingen, 2010–11. Hon. Dir, Internat. African Inst., 1992–95. Chm., Assoc. of Social Anthropologists of GB and Commonwealth, 1989–93. MAE 1993. Rivers Meml Medal, RAI, 1985. *Publications:* Neighbours and Nationals in an African City Ward, 1969; Palms, Wine and Witnesses, 1972; (ed) Town and Country in Central and Eastern Africa, 1975; The Cultural Definition of Political Response, 1978; The Sacred Void, 1991; edited: Semantic Anthropology, 1982; The Anthropology of Evil, 1985; Swahili Language and Society, 1985; Transformations of African Marriage, 1987; Social Stratification in Swahili Society, 1989; Bush, Base, Forest, Farm, 1992; Continuity and Autonomy in Swahili Communities, 1994; The Politics of Cultural Performance, 1996; Autorité et Pouvoir chez les Swahili, 1998; Islamic Prayer Across the Indian Ocean, 2000; Anthropologists in a Wider World, 2000; Holistic Anthropology, 2007; Therapeutic Crises, 2013; Turning Therapies, 2014. *Recreations:* music, voyaging. *Address:* All Souls College, Oxford OX1 4AL.

PARKIN, Jonathan; Regional Employment Judge, South West, since 2011; *b* Buxton, 3 June 1955; *s* of Michael and Sheila Parkin; *m* 1983, Catherine Vickerman; two *d*. *Educ:* Manchester Grammar Sch.; Clare Coll., Cambridge (BA Law 1977; MA 1981). Called to the Bar, Middle Temple, 1978; barrister in private practice, 1979–2000; Chm. (pt-time), Industrial Tribunals, 1997–2000; Employment Judge, 2000–11; a Recorder, 2000–10. *Publications:* (with C. Goodier) Employment Tribunals: the complete guide to procedure, 3rd edn 2005 to 6th edn 2011. *Recreations:* walking, theatre, watching Manchester City FC. *Address:* Employment Tribunal, First Floor, The Crescent Centre, Bristol BS1 6EZ. *T:* (0117) 929 8261.

PARKIN, Sara Lamb, OBE 2001; Founder Director, since 1994, and Trustee, since 2006, Forum for the Future; *b* 9 April 1946; *d* of late Dr George Lamb McEwan and Marie Munro Rankin; *m* 1969, Dr Donald Maxwell Parkin; two *s*. *Educ:* Barr's Hill School, Coventry; Edinburgh Royal Infirmary (RGN). Ward Sister, Royal Infirmary, Edinburgh, and Res. Asst, Nursing Res. Unit, Univ. of Edinburgh, 1973–74; Council Mem., Brook Adv. Centre, 1974–76; Family Planning Nurse, Leeds AHA, 1976–80. Green Party, UK: Internat. Liaison Sec., 1983–90; Speaker, 1989–92; Chair, Executive, 1992; Co-Sec., European Green Co-ordination, 1985–90. Member: Bd, Envmt Agency, 2000–06; NERC, 2003–09; Sci. in Society Adv. Panel, Res. Councils UK, 2008–09; EU Expert, Governing Bd, European Trng Foundn, 2009–15. Founding Associate, Engrg Council (UK), 2011–. Member: Bd, Leadership Foundn for Higher Educn, 2003–09; Sci. in Soc. Adv. Gp, Living with Envmtl Change Res. Prog., 2009–12; Higher Educn Acad., 2014–; Mem., Nat. Union of Student Sustainability Direction and Oversight Bd, 2014–; Trustee, Friends of the Earth Trust, 1995–2002. Chm., Richard Sandbrook Trust, 2010–. Patron: Population Matters; Mus. of Islay Life. CompICE 1996; CompInstE 2002. Hon. FSE 2006; Hon. FIEnvSc 2011. *Publications:* Green Parties: an international guide, 1989; Green Futures: agenda for the twenty first century, 1991; Green Light on Europe, 1991; The Life and Death of Petra Kelly, 1994; The Positive Deviant: sustainability leadership in a perverse world, 2010. *Recreations:* long-distance walking, birdwatching, gardening, music, theatre, film. *Address:* Forum for the Future, 19–23 Ironmonger Row, EC1V 3QN. *T:* (020) 7324 3676.

PARKIN, Stuart Stephen Papworth, PhD; FRS 2000; FInstP; Manager, Magnetoelectronics Group, IBM Almaden Research Center, San Jose, California, since 1983, and IBM Fellow, since 1999; Director, IBM-Stanford Spintronic Science and Applications Center, since 2004; Director, Max Planck Institute of Microstructure Physics, Halle, Germany, since 2014; Alexander von Humboldt Professor, Martin Luther University Halle-Wittenberg, Germany, since 2014; *b* 9 Dec. 1955. *Educ:* Edinburgh Acad.; Trinity Coll., Cambridge (BA 1977; PhD 1980; Hon. Fellow, 2014). Res. Fellow, Trinity Coll., Cambridge, 1979. FIEEE 2003; FAAAS 2003; FInstP. Vis. Prof., Nat. Taiwan Univ., 2006–; Dist. Res. Chair Prof., Nat. Yunlin Univ. of Sci. and Technol., Taiwan, 2007–; Distinguished Visiting Professor: Nat. Univ. of Singapore, 2007–; Eindhoven Univ. of Technol., 2008–; World Class Univ. Prog., KAIST, Korea, 2008–11; Hon. Prof., UCL, 2009. Member: NAS, 2008; NAE, 2009. Fellow: APS; American Acad. of Arts and Scis, 2009; Materials Res. Soc. Hon. Fellow, Indian Acad. of Scis, 2012; Associate Fellow, World Acad. of Scis, 2012. C. V. Boys Prize, Inst. of Physics, 1991; Internat. Prize for new materials, American Physical Soc., 1994; Europhysics Prize, Hewlett Packard, 1997; IBM Master Inventor, 1997; Prize for Industrial Applications of Physics, American Inst. of Physics, 1999; Innovator of the Year, R&D Mag., 2001; Humboldt Res. Award for US Senior Scientists, 2004; Millennium Technol. Prize, Technol. Acad. Finland, 2014. *Address:* IBM Almaden Research Center, 650 Harry Road, San Jose, CA 95120–6099, USA; Weinberg 2, 06120 Halle (Saale), Germany. *E:* stuart.parkin@icloud.com.

PARKINS, Graham Charles; QC 1990; a Recorder, since 1989; *b* 11 Nov. 1942; *s* of John Charles Parkins and Nellie Elizabeth Parkins; *m* 1st, 1964, Carole Ann Rowe (marr. diss. 1977); two *s* one *d*; 2nd, 1977, Susan Ann Poole (*d* 1994); two *d*; 3rd, 1995, Linda Smith. *Educ:* Harwich County High Sch.; Mid-Essex Coll. of Law; LLB Hons London. Called to the Bar, Inner Temple, 1972; an Asst Recorder, 1986–89. Mem., FB Soc., Norwich. *Recreations:* golf, relaxing. *Address:* 41 Tollgate Drive, Stanway, Colchester CO3 0PE. *Club:* North Countryman's (Colchester).

PARKINSON, family name of **Baron Parkinson**.

PARKINSON, Baron *cr* 1992 (Life Peer), of Carnforth in the County of Lancashire; **Cecil Edward Parkinson;** PC 1981; chairman and director of companies; *b* 1 Sept. 1931; *s* of Sidney Parkinson, Carnforth, Lancs; *m* 1957, Ann Mary, *d* of F. A. Jarvis, Harpenden, Herts; three *d*. *Educ:* Royal Lancaster Grammar Sch., Lancaster; Emmanuel Coll., Cambridge (BA 1955; MA 1961). Joined Metal Box Company as a Management Trainee; joined West, Wake, Price, Chartered Accountants, 1956; qualified 1959; Partner, 1961–71; founded Parkinson Hart Securities Ltd, 1967; Director of several cos, 1965–79, 1984–87, 1992–. Constituency Chm., Hemel Hempstead Conservative Assoc.; Chm., Herts 100 Club, 1968–69; contested (C) Northampton, 1970. MP (C) Enfield West, Nov. 1970–1974, Hertfordshire South, 1974–83, Hertsmere, 1983–92. PPS to Minister for Aerospace and Shipping, DTI, 1972–74; an Asst Govt Whip, 1974; an Opposition Whip, 1974–76; Opposition Spokesman on trade, 1976–79; Minister for Trade, Dept of Trade, 1979–81; Paymaster General, 1981–83; Chancellor, Duchy of Lancaster, 1982–83; Sec. of State for Trade and Industry, June–Oct. 1983, for Energy, 1987–89, for Transport, 1989–90. Sec., Cons. Parly Finance Cttee, 1971–72; Chm., Anglo-Swiss Parly Gp, 1979–82; Pres., Anglo-Polish Cons. Soc., 1986–98. Chm., Cons. Party, 1981–83 and 1997–98. *Publications:* Right at the Centre: an autobiography, 1992. *Recreations:* reading, opera, golf, ski-ing; ran for combined Oxford and Cambridge team against Amer. Univs, 1954 and 1955; ran for Cambridge against Oxford, 1954 and 1955. *Address:* House of Lords, SW1A 0PW. *Clubs:* Beefsteak, Garrick, Pratt's; Hawks (Cambridge).

PARKINSON, Andrew David Gibson; Chief Executive, British Rowing, since 2015; *b* London, 20 May 1969; *s* of John Parkinson and Margaret Parkinson (*née* Gibson); *m* 2003, Annette Darby; one *s*. *Educ:* Highgate Sch.; Nottingham Trent Univ. (BSc Sport (Admin and Sci.)). Movt Educn Instructor, Focus 2000 Ltd, 1996–98; Nat. Co-ordinator, Sailability NZ, 1997–98; Supervisor, NZ CCS Ltd, 1998–99; Manager, Sport Services, Paralympics NZ, 1999–2003; Med. and Scientific Dir, Internat. Paralympic Cttee, 2003–06; Hd of Ops, 2006–08, Dir, 2008–09, Drug-Free Sport, UK Sport; Chief Exec., UK Anti-Doping, 2009–14. Chm., Ad-Hoc Eur. Cttee, World Anti-Doping Agency, 2012–15. Pres.,

NZ Wheelchair Rugby, 1999–2001. *Recreations:* sport, family, reading, skateboarding. *Address:* British Rowing, 6 Lower Mall, Hammersmith, W6 9DJ. *T:* (020) 8237 6700. *E:* andy.parkinson@britishrowing.org.

PARKINSON, Ewart West, OBE 2015; BSc, DPA; CEng, FICE, PPRTPI; OStJ; development adviser in urban regeneration; Director of Environment and County Engineer, County of South Glamorgan, 1973–85; *b* 9 July 1926; *s* of Thomas Edward Parkinson and Esther Lilian West (*née* Hammond); *m* 1948, Patricia Joan Wood; two *s* one *d*. *Educ:* Wyggeston Sch., Leicester; Coll. of Technology, Leicester (BSc, DPA). Miller Prize (bridge design), Instn CE, 1953. After working with Leicester, Wakefield, Bristol and Dover Councils, he became Dep. Borough Engr, Chelmsford, 1957–60; Dep. City Surveyor Plymouth, 1960–64; City Planning Officer, Cardiff, 1964–73, specialising in reconstruction of war damaged cities and urban regeneration. Mem. Council, RTPI, 1971–83 (Vice-Pres., 1973–75, Pres., 1975–76, Chm. Internat. Affairs Bd, 1975–80); Member: Sports Council for Wales, 1966–78 (Chm., Facilities Cttee); Internat. Soc. of City and Regional Planners, 1972; Govt Deleg. to UN Conf. on Human Settlements, 1976; Watt Cttee for Energy, 1977–83 (Chm., Working Gp on Energy and Envmt, 1980–83); UK mem., Internat. Wkg Party on Urban Land Policy, Internat. Fedn for Housing and Planning, 1979–85; Chairman: Internat. Wkg Party on Energy and the Environment, Internat. Fedn for Housing and Planning, 1982–85 (Life Mem. 1986); Wkg Party on Land Policy, Royal Town Planning Inst., 1983–85; Development Advisor: to Mayor of Sanya Hainan, China, 1999–2001; to cities of Nanjing and Xiamen, China, 2001; to city of Huzhou, China, 2003; to province of Fujian, 2005; led Study Tours to Soviet Union, 1977, India and Bangladesh, 1979, China, 1980, Kenya, Zimbabwe and Tanzania, 1981; lecture visits to People's Republic of China at invitation of Ministry of Construction, 1982, 1986, 1989, 1990, 1991, 1996, 1997. Chm., Ind. Commn on Councillors' Allowances, Cardiff, 1999. Director: Moving Being Theatre Co., 1986–90; W. S. Atkins (Wales), 1988–2002; Pontypridd Market Co., 1988–2010. Chairman: STAR Community Trust Ltd, 1979–95; Intervol, 1985–89; Wales Sports Centre for the Disabled Trust, 1986–2003; Norwegian Church Preservation (formerly Rebuilding) Trust, 1992–2001 (Man. Trustee, 1988; Pres., 2001); Roald Dahl Arts Project Trust, 1995–2010; Dir, Cardiff Action for the Single Homeless, 1988–2012; Vice-Pres., Wales Council for the Disabled, 1982–2000; Patron, Touch Trust and Shopmobility Wales, 2005–; Diamond Jubilee Silver Medal, Nat. Housing and Town Planning Council, 1978; many urban design awards, from Prince of Wales Cttee, Civic Trust, Concrete Soc., and Cardiff 2000; RTPI Award for outstanding contribn to planning during long and distinguished career, 2004. OStJ 1980 (S Glamorgan Council, 1975–2005). St Olav's Medal (Norway), 2004. *Publications:* The Land Question, 1974; And Who is my Neighbour?, 1976; articles in prof. jls on land policy, energy and the environment, and public participation. *Recreations:* working, travelling, being with family, talking with friends. *Address:* 42 South Rise, Llanishen, Cardiff CF14 0RH. *T:* (029) 2075 6394.

PARKINSON, Howard, CVO 1998; HM Diplomatic Service, retired; High Commissioner, Republic of Mozambique, 2003–07; *b* 29 March 1948; *s* of Ronald Parkinson and Doris (*née* Kenyon); *m* 1974, Linda Wood; one *s* one *d*. *Educ:* Openshaw Tech. High Sch., Manchester. BoT, 1967–69; joined HM Diplomatic Service, 1969; Latin American Floater, 1972–74; Vice Consul: Tegucigalpa, 1974–75; Buenos Aires, 1975–78; Second Sec., Maputo, 1978–81; Second, later First Sec., FCO, 1981–85; First Sec. (Commercial), Lisbon, 1985–89; on loan to British Gas, 1989–91; Asst Hd, Migration and Visa Dept, FCO, 1991–94; Consul Gen., Washington, 1994–96; Commercial and Econ. Counsellor, Kuala Lumpur, 1997–2000; Dep. High Comr, Mumbai (Bombay), 2001–03. *Recreations:* travel, music, reading. *E:* howardparkinson@hotmail.com.

PARKINSON, Sir Michael, Kt 2008; CBE 2000; interviewer, television presenter, writer; *b* 28 March 1935; *m* 1959, Mary Heneghan; three *s*. *Educ:* Barnsley Grammar School. Journalist on local paper; The Guardian; Daily Express; radio work; has written for Punch, The Listener, New Statesman; Columnist: Sunday Times, 1965–; Daily Mirror, 1986–90; Daily Telegraph, 1991; Radio Times, 2009–; Producer and interviewer: Granada's Scene at 6.30; Granada in the North; World in Action; What the Papers Say; reporter on 24 Hours (BBC); Exec. producer and presenter, London Weekend Television, 1968; Presenter: Cinema, 1969–70; Tea Break, Where in the World, The Movie Quiz, 1971; host of own chat show, Parkinson, 1971–82 and 1998–2007 (Most Popular Talk Show, Nat. TV Awards, 1998, 1999, 2000, 2001); TV-am, 1983–84; Parkinson in Australia, 1979–84; The Boys of '66, 1981 (documentary); Give Us a Clue, 1984–92; All Star Secrets, 1984–86; The Skag Kids, 1985; Parkinson One-to-One, 1987–88; Desert Island Discs, BBC Radio 4, 1986–88; LBC Radio, 1990; Help Squad, 1991–92; Ghostwatch, 1992; Surprise Party, 1993; A League Apart: 100 years of Rugby League, BBC2, 1995; Going for a Song, BBC1, 1995–99; Parkinson on Sport, R5, 1994–97; Parkinson's Sunday Supplement, R2, 1996–2007; Michael Parkinson's Greatest Entertainers', ITV, 2006; My Favourite Things, R2, 2011–; Parkinson: Masterclass, Sky Arts, 2012–. Founder-Director, Pavilion Books, 1980–97. Chancellor, Nottingham Trent Univ., 2008–14. Fellow, BFI, 1998. Hon. Dr: Lincs, 1999; Humberside, 1999; Huddersfield, 2008. Sports Feature Writer of the Year, British Sports Journalism Awards, 1995; Sony Radio Award, 1998; Sports Writer of the Year, British Press Awards, 1998; Media Personality of the Year, Variety Club, 1998; Best Light Entertainment, BAFTA, 1999; Media Soc. annual award, 2000. *Publications:* Football Daft, 1968; Cricket Mad, 1969; (with Clyde Jeavons) Pictorial History of Westerns, 1972; Sporting Fever, 1974; (with Willis Hall) Football Classified, 1974; George Best: an intimate biography, 1975; (with Willis Hall) A–Z of Soccer, 1975; Bats in the Pavilion, 1977; The Woofits, 1980; Parkinson's Lore, 1981; The Best of Parkinson, 1982; Sporting Lives, 1992; Sporting Profiles, 1995; Michael Parkinson on Golf, 1999; Michael Parkinson on Football, 2001; Michael Parkinson on Cricket, 2002; Parky: my autobiography, 2008; Parky's People, 2010. *Address:* c/o Parkinson Productions, Braywick House West, Windsor Road, Maidenhead, Berks SL6 1DN.

PARKINSON, Prof. Michael Henry, CBE 2007; PhD; Adviser to Vice Chancellor, University of Liverpool, since 2014; *b* 11 Aug. 1944; *s* of John Parkinson and Margaret Parkinson (*née* Corrin); *m* 1966, Fran Anderson; one *s* one *d*. *Educ:* Univ. of Liverpool (BA); Univ. of Manchester (MA (Econ) with Dist.); Liverpool John Moores Univ. (PhD 2002). Prof. of Political Sci., 1972–73, Dir, Urban Studies Prog., 1976–79, Washington Univ. in St Louis; Liverpool Univ., 1979–92; Liverpool John Moores University: Prof. of Urban Affairs and Dir, Eur. Inst. for Urban Affairs, 1992–2014; Advr on Civic Engagement to Vice Chancellor, 2012–13. Director: CITIES Prog., ESRC, 2000–03; State of English Cities Prog., ODPM, 2004–06; Neighbourhoods, Cities and Regions Panel, DCLG, 2007–. City Advr, Birmingham CC, 2006–. Dir, Merseyside Develt Corp., 1992–97. Mem. Bd, Prime Minister's Regeneration Investment Orgn, 2013–. Adviser to: EC; DCLG; ODPM; H of C Select Cttee; OECD; EUROCITIES; Core Cities; LGA. Mem., Living Landmarks Cttee, Big Lottery. Trustee: Centre for Cities, 2012–; Alternative Futures Gp, 2014–. Gov., Merseyside Further Educn Coll. and Special Sch. *Publications:* Liverpool on the Brink, 1985; Reshaping Local Government, 1987; Regenerating the Cities, 1988; Leadership and Urban Regeneration, 1990; Cultural Policy and Urban Regeneration, 1994; European Cities Towards 2000, 1994; Competitive European Cities, 2004; City Matters, 2004; State of English Cities, 2006; The Credit Crunch and Regeneration, 2009; The Credit Crunch, Recession and Regeneration in the North, 2010; Second Tier Cities: in an age of austerity why invest beyond the capital cities?, 2012; No Cities, No Civilisation, 2013; UK City Regions in Boom and Recession, 2014. *Recreations:* suffering with Liverpool FC, good wine, the cinema, exploring Crete, looking after our Joe. *E:* michael.parkinson@liverpool.ac.uk.

PARKINSON, Prof. Richard Bruce, DPhil; Professor of Egyptology, since 2013 and Director, Griffith Institute, since 2014, University of Oxford; Fellow of Queen's College, Oxford, since 2013; *b* Darlington, 25 May 1963; *o s* of Harold Parkinson and Jessie Rae Parkinson; civil partnership 2005, *m* 2014, Timothy Griffiths Reid. *Educ:* Barnard Castle Sch.; Queen's Coll., Oxford (BA 1985; DPhil 1988). Lady Wallis Budge Jun. Res. Fellow, University Coll., Oxford, 1990–91; Asst Keeper, Dept of Ancient Egypt and Sudan, BM, 1992–2013. Visiting Lecturer: Georg-August-Universität, Göttingen, 2006; Universität zu Köln, 2007–; Guest Researcher: Univ. of Copenhagen, 2009, 2013; Johannes Gutenberg-Universität, Mainz, 2011. Hon. Dr New Bulgarian, 2006. *Publications:* The Tale of the Eloquent Peasant, 1991, rev. edn 2005; Voices from Ancient Egypt: an anthology of Middle Kingdom writings, 1991; (with M. Bierbrier) Hieroglyphic Texts 12, 1993; (with S. Quirke) Papyrus, 1995 (French edn 2010); The Tale of Sinuhe and Other Ancient Egyptian Poems 1940–1640 BC, 1997, rev. edn 1999; Cracking Codes: the Rosetta Stone and decipherment, 1999; Poetry and Culture in Middle Kingdom Egypt: a dark side to perfection, 2002, rev. edn 2010; Pocket Guide to Egyptian Hieroglyphs, 2003; (with J. Nunn) The Tale of Peter Rabbit: hieroglyph edition, 2003; The Rosetta Stone, 2005; The Painted Tomb-Chapel of Nebamun, 2008; Reading Ancient Egyptian Poetry: among other histories, 2009; Hunefer and His Book of the Dead, 2010; The Book of the Dead of Hunefer: a pull-out papyrus, 2010; The Ramesseum Papyri, 2012; The Tale of the Eloquent Peasant: a reader's commentary, 2012; (with L. Baylis) Four 12th Dynasty Literary Papyri (Pap. Berlin P. 3022–5): a photographic record, 2012; A Little Gay History: desire and diversity across the world, 2013 (French edn 2013); consultant and illustrator for books by Meredith Hooper: The Tomb of Nebamun, 1997; Who Built the Pyramid?, 2000; The Tomb of Nebamun: explore an Ancient Egyptian tomb, 2008; articles in specialist jls. *Recreations:* English and French literature, music, opera, walking. *Address:* Oriental Institute, University of Oxford, Pusey Lane, Oxford OX1 2LE. *E:* richard.parkinson@orinst.ox.ac.uk.

PARKINSON, Stephen Lindsay; Partner, since 2005, and Head of Criminal and Regulatory Litigation Group (formerly Department), since 2006, Kingsley Napley LLP; *b* 15 June 1957; *s* of late Rev. Edward James Parkinson and of Dr Mary Vere Parkinson (*née* Young); *m* 1982, Penelope Jane Venvell; one *s* two *d*. *Educ:* Hampton Grammar Sch.; Chippenham Sch.; University Coll. London (LLB 1979). Called to the Bar, Lincoln's Inn, 1980; admitted to Bar, Turks and Caicos Is, 2009, 2011, 2013; admitted solicitor, 2005; pupillage, 1980–82; sub-editor, Butterworths Legal Publishers, 1982–84; Legal Asst, Dept of DPP, 1984–86; Sen. Crown Prosecutor, then Asst Br. Crown Prosecutor, CPS, 1986–88; Law Officers' Dept, 1988–91; Hd, Internat. Co-operation Unit, CPS, 1991–92; Asst Solicitor, DTI, 1992–96; Hd, Company/Chancery Litigation Gp, Treasury Solicitor's Dept, 1996–99; Dep. Legal Sec. to Law Officers, 1999–2003; barrister, seconded to Kingsley Napley, 2003–05. Member: Adv. Bd, Centre for Criminal Law, UCL, 2009–; Times Law Panel, 2009–. *Publications:* (contrib.) Blackstone's Criminal Practice, 2007–; (with David Corker) Disclosure in Criminal Proceedings, 2009; (contrib.) Fraud: criminal law and procedure, 2011; articles in national press. *Recreations:* life of Churchill, gym, walking. *Address:* Kingsley Napley LLP, Knight's Quarter, 14 St John's Lane, EC1M 4AJ.

PARKS, Timothy Harold; author; *b* 19 Dec. 1954; *s* of late Harold James Parks and of Joan Elizabeth Parks (*née* MacDowell); *m* 1979, Rita Maria Baldasarre; one *s* one *d*. *Educ:* Westminster City Sch.; Downing Coll., Cambridge (BA 1977); Harvard Univ. Mktg Exec., Tek Translation and Internat. Print, 1979–80; freelance teacher and translator, Verona, 1981–85; Lectr, Univ. of Verona, 1985–. Vis. Lectr, 1992, Assoc. Prof., 2005–, Istituto Universitario di Lingue Moderne, Milan. Mem., Soc. of Authors, 1986–. *Publications: fiction:* Tongues of Flames, 1985 (Somerset Maugham Award, Betty Trask Award); Loving Roger, 1986 (John Llewellyn Rhys Award); Home Thoughts, 1987; Family Planning, 1989; Goodness, 1991; Shear, 1993; Mimi's Ghost, 1995; Europa, 1997; Destiny, 1999; Judge Savage, 2003; Rapids, 2005; Cleaver, 2006; Dreams of Rivers and Seas, 2008; The Server, 2012; Painting Death, 2014; as John MacDowell: Cara Massimina, 1990; *essays:* Adultery and Other Diversions, 1998; Hell and Back, 2001; The Fighter, 2007; Sex is Forbidden, 2013; Where I'm Reading From: the changing world of books, 2014; non-fiction: Italian Neighbours, 1992; An Italian Education; Translating Style, 1997; A Season with Verona, 2002; Medici Money: banking, metaphysics and art in 15th-century Florence, 2005; Teach us to Sit Still: a sceptic's search for health and healing, 2010; Italian Ways: on and off the rails from Milan to Palermo, 2013; A Literary Tour of Italy, 2015; translations from Italian of books by several authors, incl. Calasso, Calvino, Machiavelli, Moravia, and Tabucchi; contribs to short story and essay collections, conf. proceedings and jls. *Address:* c/o Rogers, Coleridge & White, 20 Powis Mews, W11 1JN.

PARMINTER, Baroness *cr* 2010 (Life Peer), of Godalming in the County of Surrey; **Kathryn Jane, (Kate), Parminter;** Chief Executive, Campaign to Protect Rural England (formerly Director, Council for the Protection of Rural England), 1998–2004; *b* 24 June 1964; *d* of James Henry Parminter and June Rose Parminter; *m* 1994, Neil Roger Sherlock, *qv*; two *d*. *Educ:* Millais Sch.; Collyer's Sixth Form Coll., Horsham; Lady Margaret Hall, Oxford (MA Theol.). Graduate trainee, Nestlé Co., 1986–88; Parly researcher for Simon Hughes, MP, 1988–89; Sen. Account Exec., Juliette Hellman Public Relns, 1989–90; Royal Society for the Prevention of Cruelty to Animals: Public Relations Officer, 1990–92; Head: Campaigns and Events, 1992–95; Public Affairs, 1995–96; Press and Public Affairs, 1996–98; a Vice-Pres., 2010–. Mem., Commn into Public Services, 2003–04, Adv. Bd, 2004–10, NCC. Mem. (Lib Dem), Horsham DC, 1987–95. Member: Lib Dem Policy Review Gp, 2005–07; Lib Dem Reform Commn, 2008; Lib Dem Federal Exec., 2008–10. Trustee, IPPR, 2007–. Chm., Campaign for Protection of Hunted Animals, 1997–98. Patron, Meath Epilepsy Trust, 2010. *Publications:* (contrib.) Working For and Against Government, in Pressure Group Politics in Modern Britain, 1996; (contrib.) The Progressive Century: the future of the Centre Left in Britain, 2001. *Recreations:* pre-Raphaelite paintings, walking. *Club:* National Liberal.

PARMLEY, Dr Andrew Charles, FRCO; Principal, Harrodian School, since 2014 (Head of Senior School, 2001–14); *b* Manchester, 17 Oct. 1956; *s* of Granville and Betty Parmley; *m* 1980, Wendy Davina Calder Hodgson. *Educ:* Blackpool Grammar Sch.; Royal Acad. of Music (BMus); Manchester Univ. (MusM); Royal Holloway Coll., London (PhD 1987); Jesus Coll., Cambridge. FRCO (CHM) 1976; FTCL 1977. Director of Music: Forest Sch., 1983–92; S Hampstead High Sch., 1992–96; Grey Coat Hosp., Westminster, 1996–2001; St James' Garlickhythe, 1982–. Examr, adjudicator, composer, broadcaster, conductor, editor and writer. Chairman of Governors: City of London Sch. for Girls, 2001–03; GSMD, 2003–06. Chm., Montessori St Nicholas Charity, 2007–14; Patron: London Docklands Singers, 1992–; Marcel Sinfonia, 1995–; Thames Chamber Choir, 1999–; English Chamber Choir; Jonas Foundn (Geneva). Hon. VCM 1985; Hon. FGS (Hon. FGSM 2005). Mem., Common Council, Vintry Ward, 1992–2001, Alderman, 2001; Past Master, Parish Clerks' Co.; Master, Musicians' Co., 2011–12; Liveryman: Glass Sellers' Co., 2002– (Master, 2013–14); Vintners' Co., 2004– (Renter Warden, 2014–); Blacksmiths' Co.; Hon. Liveryman: Joiners' Co. (Ct Asst); Water Conservators' Co.; Educators' Co.; Horners' Co. (Ct Asst); Hon. Freeman, Clockmakers' Co. Sheriff, City of London, 2014–15. Comité d'Honneur, Les Editions des Abbesses. SBStJ 2014. *Recreations:* fundraising for organ restoration, Leukaemia and Lymphoma Research, etc, fundraising for 2012 Diamond Jubilee Ring of Bells for Royal Flotilla on Thames, fishing (Captain, Corp. of London Members' Fishing Team), marathons - running and walking. *Address:* 120 Marsham Court, Marsham Street, SW1P 4LB. *E:* andrew.parmley@outlook.com. *Clubs:* Reform, Guildhall.

PARMOOR, 5th Baron *cr* 1914, of Frieth, co. Bucks; **(Michael Leonard) Seddon Cripps;** a Circuit Judge, 1998–2012; Resident Judge, Aylesbury Crown Court, 2011–12; Recorder of Amersham, 2011–12; *b* 18 June 1942; *s* of (Matthew) Anthony Leonard Cripps, CBE, DSO, TD, QC and Dorothea Margaret Cripps; *S* cousin, 2008; *m* 1971, Elizabeth Anne Millward Shennan; one *s* one *d* (and one *s* decd). *Educ:* Eton Coll. Called to the Bar, Middle Temple, 1965; Member *ad eundem*, Lincoln's Inn, 1969, Inner Temple, 1984; a Recorder, 1986–98; Standing Counsel to HM Customs and Excise, 1989–98. Chairman, Disciplinary Committee: Milk Mktg Bd, 1979–90; Potato Mktg Bd, 1979–90. Legal Mem., Immigration Appeal Tribunal, 1998–2000; Pres., Immigration Services Tribunal, 2000–10; a Judge of First-tier Tribunal, and a Dep. Judge, Upper Tribunal, 2010–11. Liveryman, Fuellers' Co., 1985; Freeman, City of London, 1986; Hon. Lt Col, Alabama State Militia, 1975. *Recreations:* family, walking slowly. *Heir: s* Hon. Henry William Anthony Cripps [*b* 2 Sept. 1976; *m* 2003, Katherine Helen, *d* of Sir Michael Terence Wogan, *qv*; one *s* one *d*]. *Address:* Bessemers, Moor Wood, Lane End, High Wycombe, Bucks HP14 3HZ.

PARNELL, family name of **Baron Congleton**.

PARNELL, Rowena; *see* Arshad, Rowena.

PARR, Donald; *see* Parr, T. D.

PARR, Martin; photographer, curator, editor and film-maker; *b* 23 May 1952; *s* of Donald Parr and Joyce Parr (*née* Watts); *m* 1980, Susan P. Mitchell; one *d*. *Educ:* Manchester Poly. (1st cl. Creative Photography 1973). Freelance photographer, 1973–; Mem., Magnum, photo co-operative, 1994–; freelance TV film-maker, 1996–; Vis. Prof. of Photography, Univ. of Industrial Arts, Helsinki, 1990–92; Visiting Lecturer: Nat. Coll. of Art and Design, Dublin, and Chelsea Sch. of Art, 1975–82; Sch. of Documentary Photography, Newport, 1982–84; W Surrey Coll. of Art and Design, 1983–. Exhibitions worldwide, including: Photographer's Gall., 1977, 1981, 1982, 1987, 1995; Whitechapel Art Gall., 1978; Hayward Gall., 1979; Serpentine Gall., 1986; Nat. Centre of Photography, Paris, 1987, 1995; RA, 1989; RPS, 1989; Janet Borden Gall., NY, 1991, 1992, 1996; Nat. Mus. of Photography, Bradford, 1998; retrospective exhibn, Barbican Gall., 2002. Work in permanent collections incl. V&A Mus., MOMA, NY, Walker Art Gall., Liverpool. Arts Council of GB Photography Award, 1975, 1976, 1979. *Publications:* Bad Weather, 1982; A Fair Day, 1984; (with Ian Walker) The Last Resort: photographs of New Brighton, 1986, 2nd edn 1998; (jtly) The Actual Boot: the photographic postcard 1900–1920, 1986; The Cost of Living, 1989; Signs of the Times, 1992; Home and Abroad, 1993; From A to B, 1994; Small World, 1995; West Bay, 1997; Flowers, 1999; Common Sense, 1999; Boring Postcards, 1999; Auto Portrait, 2000; Think of England, 2000; Boring Postcards USA, 2000; Boring Postcards Germany, 2001; Martin Parr Retrospective, 2002; Phone Book, 2002; Bliss, 2003; 7 Communist Still Lives, 2003; Fashion Magazine, 2005; Mexico, 2006; Parking Spaces, 2007; Objects & Postcards, 2008; Luxury, 2009; Playas, 2009; Japan, 2010; Life's a Beach, 2012; Up and Down Peachtree, 2012; Non Conformists, 2013; Paris, 2014; We Love Britain, 2014; Hong Kong, 2014; Voewood, 2014. *Recreation:* working! *Address:* c/o Magnum, 63 Gee Street, EC1V 3RS. *T:* (020) 7490 1771. *Club:* Clifton Poker.

PARR, (Thomas) Donald, CBE 1986; Chairman, William Baird PLC, 1981–98; *b* 3 Sept. 1930; *s* of Thomas and Elizabeth Parr; *m* 1954, Gwendoline Mary Chaplin; three *s* one *d*. *Educ:* Burnage Grammar Sch. Own business, 1953–64; Chm., Thomas Marshall Investments Ltd, 1964–76; Director: William Baird PLC, 1976; Vendôme Luxury Gp (formerly Dunhill Holdings) PLC, 1986–98; Hepworth PLC, 1989–98; Kwik Save Group, 1991–98. Chm., British Clothing Industry Assoc., 1987–91; Member: NW Industrial Devalt Bd, 1975–87; Ct of Governors, UMIST, 1984–2004. *Recreation:* sailing. *Address:* Mariners, 13 Queens Road, Cowes, Isle of Wight PO31 8BQ. *Clubs:* Boodle's, Royal Ocean Racing; Royal Yacht Squadron (Cowes).

PARRIS, Matthew Francis; author, journalist and broadcaster; *b* 7 Aug. 1949; *s* of late Leslie Francis Parris and of Theresa Eunice Parris (*née* Littler); civil partnership 2006, Julian Glover. *Educ:* Waterford School, Swaziland; Clare Coll., Cambridge (BA Hons; Hon. Fellow, 2006); Yale Univ., USA (Paul Mellon Fellowship). Foreign Office, 1974–76; Conservative Research Dept, 1976–79; MP (C) West Derbyshire, 1979–86; Presenter: Weekend World, LWT, 1986–88; various series on BBC Radio 4 incl. Great Lives, 2006–. Occasional columnist, various pubns, 1986–88; Reviewer, Sunday Times, 1986–88; Parly Sketch Writer, 1988–2001, Columnist, 1988–, The Times; Columnist, The Spectator, 1996–. Mem., Broadcasting Standards Council, 1992–97. Various journalistic awards incl. Political Journalist of the Year, Press Awards, 2014. *Publications:* Inca-Kola: a traveller's tale of Peru, 1990; So Far So Good, 1991; Look Behind You!, 1993; (ed) Scorn, 1994; (jtly) Great Parliamentary Scandals, 1995, 2004; (ed) Scorn with Added Vitriol, 1995; (ed jtly) Read My Lips: a treasury of things politicians wish they hadn't said, 1996; I Couldn't Possibly Comment: parliamentary sketches, 1997; The Great Unfrocked: two thousand years of church scandal, 1998; (ed) Scorn with Extra Bile, 1999; Off-Message, 2001; Chance Witness: an outsider's life in politics (autobiog.), 2002; Castle in Spain: a mountain ruin, an impossible dream, 2005; (ed jtly) Mission Accomplished!: a treasury of things politicians wish they hadn't said, 2008; (ed) Scorn: updated for a new century, 2008; (ed) Parting Shots: undiplomatic diplomats—the ambassadors' letters you were never meant to see, 2010; (ed) The Spanish Ambassador's Suitcase, and other stories, 2012. *Address:* c/o The Times, 1 London Bridge Street, SE1 9GF.

PARRITT, Clive Anthony, FCA, CF, FIIA; Chairman: Baronsmead VCT 2 PLC, since 1998; BG Consulting Group Ltd, since 2004; Finance Director, Audiotonix Ltd, since 2014; *b* London, 11 April 1943; *s* of Allan and Peta Parritt; *m* 1st, 1968, Valerie Sears (marr. diss. 1983); two *s*; 2nd, 1985, Deborah Jones; two *s*. *Educ:* FCA 1966; FIIA 1976; CF 2006. Partner, Fuller Jenks Beecroft, later Touche Ross & Co., 1973–82; Partner, 1982–2001, Man. Partner, 1986–96, Chm., 1996–2001, Baker Tilly; Chief Exec., Business Exchange plc, 2001–03. Non-executive Director: Harvard Managed Offices Ltd, 2001–; London & Associated Properties plc, 2006–; Baronsmead Aim VCT plc, 2006–10; Jupiter US Smaller Cos plc (formerly F&C US Smaller Cos plc), 2007–; Industrial Pipefreezing Services Ltd, 2007–. Pres., London Soc. of Chartered Accountants, 1982–83; Mem. Council, ICAEW, 1983–2014 (Vice-Pres., 2009–10; Dep. Pres., 2010–11; Pres., 2011–12); Mem., Chartered Accountants' Co., 1992–. Mem., BAFTA. Gov., Arnold Hse Sch., 2003–10. *Recreations:* theatre, travel, food. *Address:* 34 Eton Avenue, NW3 3HL. *T:* (020) 7794 2443, 07713 621274. *E:* clive@parritt.com.

PARROTT, Andrew Haden; conductor and musicologist; Music Director: London Mozart Players, 2000–06; New York Collegium, 2002–09; *b* 10 March 1947. *Educ:* Merton Coll., Oxford (schol.; BA 1969). Dir of Music, Merton Coll., Oxford, 1969–71; sometime musical assistant to Sir Michael Tippett. Founded Taverner Choir, 1973, then Taverner Consort and Taverner Players, for performance of music ranging from medieval to late 18th century. Débuts: BBC Prom. concerts, 1977; EBU, 1979; La Scala, 1985; Salzburg, 1987; Guest Conductor worldwide of symphony and chamber orchs, period-instrument orchs, choirs, opera and contemporary music. Some 60 recordings. Hon. Sen. Res. Fellow, Univ. of Birmingham, 2000–. *Publications:* (ed jtly) New Oxford Book of Carols, 1992; The Essential Bach Choir, 2000, German edn 2003; contrib. learned jls. *Address:* c/o Rayfield Allied, Southbank House, Black Prince Road, SE1 7SJ.

PARROTT, Brian Robert; consultant in social care, health and local government, since 2001; Joint Chairman, Association of Directors of Adult Social Services Associates Network, since 2008; Independent Chairman: London Borough of Tower Hamlets Adults' Safeguarding Board, since 2010; London Borough of Richmond Adults' Safeguarding Board, since 2014; *b* 24 Sept. 1949; *s* of late Derek Parrott and Lilian Parrott (*née* Thoy); *m* 1974, Pamela Elizabeth Rigby; two *s*. *Educ:* Bedford Modern Sch.; Downing Coll., Cambridge (BA 1971; MA 1974); Univ. of Kent (CQSW 1973). Social Worker, Camden LBC, 1973–76; Sen. Social Worker, Notts CC, 1976–81; Area Officer, Haringey LBC, 1981–85; Asst Dir, 1985–90, First Asst Dir, 1990–95, Social Services, Suffolk CC; Dir of Social Services, Surrey CC, 1995–2001. Chm., Central Suffolk NHS PCT, 2002–05; non-exec. Dir, Norfolk and Suffolk NHS Foundn Trust, 2012–. Dir, Verita (The Inquiry Consultancy), 2002–06; Mem. Bd, Nat. Devalt Team for Inclusion, 2011–14; Chm., Suffolk Family Carers, 2006–12; Ind. Chm., London Bor. of Tower Hamlets Children's Safeguarding Bd, 2010–12. Chm., Resources Cttee, Assoc. of Dirs of Social Services, 2000–01. Trustee, In Control, 2008–11. Vis. Fellow, UEA, 2002–05, 2009–11. FRSA 1999; FRGS 2012. *Publications:* (jtly) A Unitary Approach to Social Work: application in practice, 1981; contribs to social work and local govt publications and jls. *Recreations:* world affairs, politics, travel, mountains, sport, Ipswich Town FC. *Address:* 3 Jervis Close, Holbrook, Ipswich, Suffolk IP9 2RR. *T:* (01473) 328056.

PARROTT, Eluned Siân; Member (Lib Dem) South Wales Central, National Assembly for Wales, since July 2011; *b* Abergavenny, 14 Aug. 1974; *d* of Ian Clive Jenkins and Carole Ann Jenkins; *m* 1996, Daniel David Parrott; one *s* one *d*. *Educ:* St Peter's Collegiate Sch., Wolverhampton; Cardiff Univ. (BMus Hons); Chartered Inst. of Mktg (Cert., Adv. Cert., PGDip). Press Officer, Techniquest Sci. Discovery Centre, Cardiff, 1995–97; Mkt and Devalt Officer, Nat. Youth Arts Wales, 1997–2000; Hd, Public Engagement, Cardiff Univ., 2000–11. *Recreations:* music, sport (particularly football and cricket). *Address:* National Assembly for Wales, Cardiff Bay, Cardiff CF99 1NA. *T:* 0300 200 7263. *E:* Eluned.Parrott@assembly.wales.

PARROTT, Jasper William; Director, since 1969, and Executive Chairman, since 2013, HarrisonParrott Ltd (Chairman and Managing Director, 1987–2012); *b* 8 Sept. 1944; *s* of Sir Cecil Parrott, KCMG, OBE and of Lady (Ellen) Parrott; *m* 1974, Cristina Ortiz, pianist; two *d*. *Educ:* Tonbridge Sch.; Peterhouse, Cambridge (MA). With Ibbs and Tillett, concert mgt, 1965–69. Chm., 1983–84, Pres., 1986–89, British Assoc. of Concert Agents. Dir, The Japan Festival UK, 1991; Internat. Consultant and Advr, Sakip Sabanci Mus., Istanbul, 2005–07; Consultant, Reykjavik Concert and Conf. Centre, 2007–. Hon. Trustee, Royal Botanical Gardens, Kew, 1995–. *Publications:* Beyond Frontiers, 1984 (trans. German, Japanese, French, Russian, Norwegian, Finnish and Icelandic). *Recreations:* books, tennis, languages, gardens. *Address:* c/o HarrisonParrott Ltd, 5–6 Albion Court, Albion Place, W6 0QT. *T:* (020) 7229 9166.

PARROY, Michael Picton; QC 1991; a Recorder, since 1990; *b* 22 Oct. 1946; *s* of Gerard May and Elizabeth Mary Parroy; *m* 1978, Susan Patricia Blades (*née* Winter). *Educ:* Malvern College; Brasenose College, Oxford (MA). Called to the Bar, Middle Temple, 1969, Bencher, 2001; Head of Chambers, 3 Paper Bldgs, 1995–2004. Trustee, Wincanton Recreational Trust, 2000–. *Publications:* Road Traffic, in Halsbury's Laws of England, 4th edn, vol. 40, 1983. *Recreations:* gardening, food and wine, stone carving. *Address:* 3 Paper Buildings, Temple, EC4Y 7EU.

PARRY; *see* Jones Parry and Jones-Parry.

PARRY, Alan; President, Johnson & Higgins Ltd, 1989–97 (Chairman, 1987–89); *b* 30 Oct. 1927; *s* of George Henry James Edgar Parry and Jessica Cooke; *m* 1954, Shirley Yeoman; one *s* one *d*. *Educ:* Reedham School. Leonard Hammond Ltd, 1941; Sedgwick Collins Ltd, 1948, Dir, 1960; Dir, Man. Dir, Dep. Chm. and Chm., Sedgwick companies and subsidiaries, to 1981; Chm., Carter Brito e Cunha, 1982–87. Mem., Lloyd's Insurance Brokers' Assoc., 1961–64, 1970–73, 1975–78 (Chm., 1977); Mem. Council, BIBA, and LIBA and BIBA rep. on Cttee on Invisible Exports, 1977; Mem., Cttee of Lloyd's, 1979–82, 1985–88 (Dep. Chm., 1987–88). *Recreations:* flyfishing, drama. *Address:* 2 Mayfield Grange, Little Trodgers Lane, Mayfield TN20 6BF.

PARRY, Anthony Joseph, QFSM 1990; County Fire Officer, 1985–90, and Chief Executive, County Fire Service, 1986–90, Greater Manchester; *b* 20 May 1935; *s* of Henry Joseph Parry and Mary Elizabeth McShane; *m* 1959, Elizabeth Therese Collins; three *s* one *d*. *Educ:* St Francis Xavier's Coll., Liverpool. MIFireE. Liverpool Fire Bde, 1958; Fire Service Technical Coll., 1967; Gloucestershire Fire Service, 1969; Avon Fire Service, 1974; Lancashire County Fire Service, 1975. Long Service and Good Conduct Medal, 1978. *Address:* 10 Oakenclough Drive, Bolton BL1 5QY.

PARRY, Bryn St Pierre, OBE 2010; Chief Executive and Co-Founder, Help for Heroes, since 2007; *b* Salisbury, 22 Sept. 1956; *s* of Lt Col Robin Parry, MC and Doreen Painter; *m* 1981, Emma Christina Ponsonby (*see* E. C. Parry); one *s* two *d*. *Educ:* Wellington Coll.; RMA, Sandhurst. Served Army, RGJ, 1975–85 (retd as Captain). Cartoonist, picture framer, designer, artist, 1985–2007. *Publications:* Mad Dogs and Englishmen, 2001; (with E. C. Parry) Home on the Range, 2002; (with Giles Catchpole) Shooting Types, 2003; (with Giles Catchpole) Horses for Courses, 2004; 101 Shooting Excuses, 2005; Sex in the Countryside, 2005; Dog Training with Mr Perks, 2006; Shooting Top Tips, 2007; (with Giles Catchpole) Shooting Types: second barrel, 2011. *Recreations:* shooting, walking in the hills, fly fishing, cycling, cooking, vegetable gardening. *Address:* c/o Help for Heroes, 14 Parkers Close, Downton, Wilts SP5 3RB. *E:* ceo@helpforheroes.org.uk. *Club:* Rifles.

PARRY, Rear Adm. Christopher John, CBE 2004; Managing Director (formerly Director), Merl House Ltd, since 2008; *b* 29 Nov. 1953; *s* of Comdr John Jenkyn Parry, OBE, PhD, RN and Joan Elizabeth Parry (*née* Axford); *m* 1989, Jacqueline Margaret Nicholson; one *s* one *d*. *Educ:* Portsmouth Grammar Sch.; Jesus Coll., Oxford (BA 1975, MA 1980). HMS London, 1977–78; aviation appts in FAA, 1978–88: 826 Naval Air Sqdn, HMS Antrim, incl. Falklands War (despatches); HMS Hermione and Brazen; Staff of FO Sea Trng; Exec. Officer, HMS York, 1988–89; Central Staff, MoD, 1989–92; Staff of C-in-C Fleet, 1992–93; CO, HMS Gloucester, 1994–96; Captain, Maritime Warfare Centre, 1996–98; rcds 1999; CO, HMS Fearless, 2000–01; Dir, Operational Capability, MoD, 2001–03; Comdr, UK/Netherlands Amphibious Task Gp, 2003–05; Dir-Gen., Jt Doctrine and Concepts, subseq. Developments, Concepts and Doctrine, MoD, 2005–08. Chm., Marine Mgt Orgn, 2009–10. Non-exec. Dir, SVGC Ltd, 2012–. President: Combined Services and RN Rugby Leagues, 2001–08; Portsmouth Navy Seahawks, Rugby League Club, 2009–. FCMI; FInstD; FRUSI. *Publications:* (with J. M. Parry) The Isle of Wight, 2000, 6th edn 2012; (with J. M. Parry) The Best of Hampshire, 2009; (with J. M. Parry) The Best of Sussex, 2010; Down South: a Falklands war diary, 2012; Super Highway: seapower in the 21st century, 2014; numerous anonymous and occupational contribs to successive Govt Reviews, pubns and papers; numerous strategic trends, future forecasting, defence and security articles and studies in various pubns. *Recreations:* Shakespeare, hill walking, medieval and military history, being in Wales, thinking. *Clubs:* Royal Air Force; Vincent's (Oxford).

PARRY, His Honour David Johnston; a Circuit Judge, 1995–2002; a Deputy Circuit Judge, 2002–07; *b* 26 Aug. 1941; *s* of Kenneth Johnston Parry and Joyce Isobel Cooper (formerly Parry); *m* Mary Harmer; one *s* three *d*. *Educ:* Merchant Taylors' Sch., Northwood; St Catharine's Coll., Cambridge (MA Hons). Admitted Solicitor, 1969; Partner, later Jt Sen. Partner, Dixon Ward, Richmond, 1969–95; Asst Recorder, 1986–91; Recorder, 1991–95. Co-Chm., Richmond Legal Advice Service, 1969–95; Administrator, Richmond Duty Solicitors' Scheme, 1990–95; part-time Chm., Independent Tribunal Service, 1993–96; a part-time Chm., Lord Chancellor's Adv. Cttee for SW London, 2006–12. Member: Law

Society; London Criminal Courts Solicitors' Assoc. Liveryman, Merchant Taylors' Co., 2001–. *Recreations:* family activities, reading, music, television, DIY, sport, travel, light gardening, bridge. *Address:* c/o Court Service, 2nd Floor, Rose Court, 2 Southwark Bridge, SE1 9HS. *Clubs:* Old Merchant Taylors'; Nothing (Richmond-upon-Thames).

PARRY, Sir Eldryd (Hugh Owen), KCMG 2011; OBE 1982; MD, FRCP; Joint Founder and Chairman, Tropical Health and Education Trust, 1989–2007; *b* 28 Nov. 1930; *s* of Dr Owen Parry and Dr Constance Parry (*née* Griffiths); *m* 1960, Helen Madeline, *d* of Humphry and Madeline House; one *s* three *d*. *Educ:* Shrewsbury; Emmanuel Coll., Cambridge (Hon. Fellow 2007); Welsh Nat. Sch. of Medicine (BChir 1955; MA; MD). FWACP. Junior posts, Cardiff Royal Infirmary, Nat. Heart Hosp., Hammersmith Hosp., 1956–65; seconded to UCH, Ibadan, 1960–63; Associate Prof., Haile Selassie I Univ., Addis Ababa, 1966–69; Prof. of Medicine, Ahmadu Bello Univ., 1969–77; Foundn Dean, Faculty of Health Sciences, Univ. of Ilorin, Nigeria, 1977–80; Dean and Prof. of Medicine, Sch. of Med. Scis, Kumasi, 1980–85; Dir, Wellcome Tropical Inst., 1985–90; Sen. Res. Fellow, 1990–95, Vis. Prof., 1996–, Hon. Fellow, 1997, LSHTM. Special Prof., Dept of Med., Univ. of Nottingham, 1997–. Albert Cook Meml Lectr, Kampala, 1974. Member: Med. and Dental Council, Ghana, 1980–85; Council, All Nations Christian Coll., 1986–99; Founding Mem., Amoud Univ. Med. Faculty, Somaliland, 2006. Hon. FRSTM&H 1993 (Donald Mackay Medal, 1998); Hon. FRCS 2008; Hon. Fellow: Ghana Coll. of Physicians and Surgeons, 2003; UWCM, 2004. Hon. DSc Kwame Nkrumah Univ. of Sci. and Technol., Kumasi, Ghana, 2003. Frederick Murgatroyd Prize, RCP, 1973; Centenary Lifetime Achievement Medal, RSTM&H, 2007. *Publications:* Principles of Medicine in Africa, 1976, 4th edn 2013 (RSM/Soc. of Authors prize, 2004; BMA first prize public health, 2005); papers on medicine in the tropics in med. jls. *Recreations:* allotment, Ceredigion, violin. *Address:* 21 Edenhurst Avenue, SW6 3PD.

PARRY, Emma Christina, OBE 2010; Co-Founder, Help for Heroes, 2007 and Executive Chairman, Help for Heroes Trading Ltd, since 2012 (Managing Director, 2007–12); *b* Rustington, Sussex, 29 Oct. 1959; *d* of Myles and Anne Ponsonby; *m* 1981, Bryn St Pierre Parry, *qv*; one *s* two *d*. *Educ:* New Hall Sch. Dir, Bryn Parry Studios, 1985–2009. *Publications:* (with Bryn Parry) Home on the Range, 2002. *Recreations:* walking, cycling, baking, ballet. *Address:* Help for Heroes, 14 Parkers Close, Downton Business Centre, Downton, Salisbury, Wilts SP5 3RB. *T:* (01725) 513212. *E:* emma.parry@helpforheroes.org.uk.

See also Air Vice Marshal J. M. M. Ponsonby.

PARRY, Isabel Clare; Her Honour Judge Parry; a Circuit Judge, since 2002; *b* 29 Jan. 1957; *d* of Elwyn James Griffith Parry and Joyce McLean Parry (*née* Edwards); *m* 1983, Gareth Richard Llewellyn George; one *s* one *d*. *Educ:* St Clare's Convent Grammar Sch., Porthcawl; Girton Coll., Cambridge (MA); Inns of Court Sch. of Law. Called to the Bar, Gray's Inn, 1979; Asst Recorder, 1996–2000; a Recorder, 2000–02. *Recreations:* music, theatre, cooking.

PARRY, Jann Peta Olwen; writer; *b* 12 Feb. 1942; *d* of John Hywel Parry and Evelyn Florence Upton; *m* 1994, Richard Ruegg Kershaw. *Educ:* Univ. of Cape Town (BA); Girton Coll., Cambridge (BA Hons 1965). Producer/writer, BBC World Service, 1970–89; Dance Critic: Listener, 1981; Spectator, 1982, 1995–96; writer and dance critic, The Observer, 1983–2006. Member: Dance Panel, Arts Council, 1988–90; Exec. Cttee, Dance UK, 1991–2001. Mem., Critics' Circle, 1983–. *Publications:* Different Drummer: the life of Kenneth MacMillan, 2009 (Theatre Book Prize, Soc. for Theatre Res., 2009); contrib. to Dance Now, Dance Mag. (US), Dancing Times, Dance & Dancers, About the House mag., Royal Acad. of Dance Gazette, Playbill (US). *Recreations:* research, ballet classes, volunteer at Battersea Dogs and Cats Home. *Address:* 82 Prince of Wales Mansions, Prince of Wales Drive, SW11 4BL. *T:* (020) 7738 8732.

PARRY, Johanna Elizabeth Martin; *see* Parry, J. E. M.

PARRY, Prof. Jonathan Patrick, PhD; FBA 2001; Professor of Anthropology, London School of Economics and Political Science, 1993–2009, now Emeritus; *b* 10 Sept. 1943; *s* of Dennis Arthur Parry and Kathleen Aroma Parry (*née* Forbes); *m* 1972, Margaret Dickinson; one *s* one *d*. *Educ:* King's Coll., Cambridge (BA 1965; PhD 1971). Lectr, Dept of Social Anthropol., Univ. of Edinburgh, 1971–74; Lectr, 1974–84, Sen. Lectr, 1984–86, Reader, 1986–93, Dept of Social Anthropol., subseq. Dept of Anthropol., LSE. *Publications:* Caste and Kinship in Kangra, 1979; (ed with M. Bloch) Death and the Regeneration of Life, 1982; (ed with M. Bloch) Money and the Morality of Exchange, 1989; Death in Banaras, 1994; (ed with J. Breman) The World of Indian Industrial Labour, 1999; (ed with R. Guha) Institutions and Inequalities, 1999. *Recreations:* reading novels, cinema. *Address:* Department of Anthropology, London School of Economics and Political Science, Houghton Street, WC2A 2AE.

PARRY, Rev. Canon Marilyn Marie, PhD; Canon Residentiary of Christ Church, Oxford and Diocesan Director of Ordinands, Oxford, 2001–11, now Canon Emeritus; *b* 24 Aug. 1946; *d* of Robert Warren Fortey and Jane Carolyn (*née* Turner); *m* 1969, Rev. David Thomas Newton Parry; one *s* one *d*. *Educ:* Western Coll., Oxford, Ohio (BA Maths, Theol. and Philos. 1968); Univ. of Manchester (MA Theol. 1977, PhD 2000); Gilmore Scheme (IDC 1978). Diocese of Manchester: Accredited Lay Worker, 1978; ordained deaconess, 1979, deacon, 1987, priest, 1994; Curate, St Peter, Westleigh, 1978–85 and C of E Chaplain, Leigh Infirmary, 1983–85; Chaplain's Asst, N Manchester Gen. Hosp., 1985–90 and Chaplaincy Team Leader, Booth Hall Children's Hosp., 1989–90; Northern Ordination Course: New Testament Tutor, 1990–97; Dir of Studies, 1991–97; Nat. Advr for Pre-Theol Educn and Selection Sec., Ministry Div., Archbishops' Council, 1997–2001. Select Preacher, Oxford Univ., 2003–04. *Recreations:* playing clarinet (chamber music), walking, conversation with friends. *Address:* 32 Barry Road, Pontypridd CF37 1HY.

PARRY, Prof. Martin Lewis, OBE 1998; PhD; Visiting Professor, Centre for Environmental Policy and Visiting Research Fellow, Grantham Institute, Imperial College London, since 2008; *b* 12 Dec. 1945; *s* of John Fyson Parry and Frances Joan (*née* Stewart); *m* 1968, Cynthia Jane Mueller; two *d*. *Educ:* Univ. of Durham (BA Hons); Univ. of West Indies (MSc); Univ. of Edinburgh (PhD). Lectr, Univ. of Edinburgh, 1972–73; University of Birmingham: Lectr, 1973–86; Sen. Lectr, 1986–88; Reader, 1988–89; Prof. of Envmtl Management, 1989–91; Prof. of Envmtl Management, and IBM Dir, Envmtl Change Unit, Oxford Univ., 1991–94; Prof. of Envmtl Mgt, Dept of Geography, UCL, 1996–99; Dir, Jackson Envmt Inst., UCL, subseq. at UEA, 1996–2003; Prof. of Envmtl Scis, UEA, 1999–2003. Chairman: Working Gp II, Intergovtl Panel on Climate Change, 2003–08; Scientific Steering Cttee, Prog. of Res. on Vulnerability, Impacts and Adaptation, 2010–. Ed., Global Envmtl Change, 1992–2005. Hon. FRS 1997. Peek Award, RGS, 1991; Gerbier-Mumm Internat. Award, WMO, 1993. *Publications:* Climatic Change, Agriculture and Settlement, 1976; (jtly) The Impact of Climatic Variations on Agriculture, Vol. 1 1988, Vol. 2 1989; Climate Change and World Agriculture, 1990; (jtly) Economic Implications of Climate Change in Britain, 1995; (jtly) Climate Impact and Adaptation Assessment, 1998; (ed jtly) Climate Change 2007: impacts, adaptation and vulnerability, 2007; (jtly) Assessing the Costs of Adaptation to Climate Change, 2009; (jtly) Climate Change and Hunger, 2010; (jtly) Climate Adaptation Futures, 2013; (jtly) Plant Genetic Resources and Climate Change, 2013. *Recreations:* sailing, scuba.

PARRY, Richard Hawley Grey, PhD, ScD; FICE; author; former civil engineering lecturer and consultant; Secretary General, International Society for Soil Mechanics and Geotechnical Engineering, 1981–99; *b* 27 April 1930; *s* of late Joseph Grey Parry and Ena Rachel (*née* Hawley); *m* 1954, Frances Irene McPherson; three *s* one *d*. *Educ:* Swinburne Technical Coll.; Melbourne Univ. (BCE 1951; MEngSc 1954; MEng 1963); Imperial Coll., London (PhD 1957); MA 1967, ScD 1983, Cantab. Res. Student and Sen. Demonstrator, Melbourne Univ., 1952–54; Shell Res. Student, Imperial Coll., London, 1954–56; Engr, Soil Mechanics Ltd, 1956–57; Res. Officer, CSIRO, 1957–60; Dir, Foundation Engineering (Aust.) Pty Ltd, 1960–67; Colombo Plan consultant on bridge sites, Sarawak, 1963–64; Lectr, Engrg Dept, Cambridge Univ., 1967–90; Fellow, Pembroke Coll., Cambridge, 1970–90, now Fellow Emeritus. MASCE (Life Mem.). British Geotech. Soc. Prize, 1978; Skempton Gold Medal, British Geotech. Soc., 1999. *Publications:* (ed) Stress-Strain Behaviour of Soils, 1971; Mohr Circles, Stress Paths and Geotechnics, 1995, 2nd edn 2004; Engineering the Pyramids, 2004; Engineering the Ancient World, 2005; Engineering the Pre-Industrial Age, 2013; technical papers in learned jls and proceedings. *Recreations:* archaeology, history of civil engineering, allotment, family history, reading, table tennis, golf, bridge. *Address:* 5 Farm Rise, Whittlesford, Cambridge CB22 4LZ. *T:* (01223) 832024.

PARRY, Richard James; Corporate Director (Education) and Lead Director for Children and Young People (formerly Director, then Strategic Director, of Education), City and County of Swansea, 1998–2012; *b* 4 Oct. 1953; *s* of John and Margaret Parry; *m* 1st, 1981, Barbara Parish; one *s* one *d*; 2nd, 1991, Gwyneth Selby; one *d*. *Educ:* Emmanuel Coll., Cambridge (BA, MA). Teacher, 1976–88: Head of Maths, Hatfield Sch., 1979–82; Head of Maths, Fearnhill Sch., Letchworth, 1983–88; Maths Adv. Teacher, Herts, 1985–88; Maths Advr, 1988–93, Chief Advr, 1993–96, W Glam; Asst Dir of Educn, 1996–97, acting Chief Educn Officer, 1997–98, City and County of Swansea. *Recreations:* golf, distance running, sport generally.

PARRY, Roger George, CBE 2014; Chairman: Mobile Streams plc, since 2006; YouGov plc, since 2007; MSQ Partners Ltd, since 2011; Aves Enterprises, since 2014; *b* 4 June 1953; *s* of George Parry and Margarita (*née* Mitchell); *m* 1990, Johanna Elizabeth Martin Waterous, *qv*; one *s*. *Educ:* Sutton Grammar Sch.; Bristol Univ. (BSc Hons); Jesus Coll., Oxford (MLitt). With Saatchi & Saatchi, 1976; freelance reporter: and producer, BBC, 1977–85; LBC, 1979–83; Thames TV, 1979–83; consultant, McKinsey & Co., 1985–88; Director: WCRS Gp plc, 1988–90; Aegis Gp plc, 1990–94; Advr, KPMG, 1993–95; Vice-Pres., Carat N America, 1995–98; CEO, More Gp plc, 1995–98; Chief Exec., 1998–2004, Chm., 2004–06, Clear Channel Internat. Chairman: Johnston Press plc, 2001–09; Future Network plc, subseq. Future plc, 2001–11. Director: Jazz FM plc, 1995–2002; iTouch plc, 2000–05. Chm., Local Media Alliance, 2009–10. Vis. Fellow, Oxford Univ., 2009–. Trustee: Shakespeare's Globe, 1987–2013 (Chm., 2005–13); Liver Foundn, 2004–12. *Publications:* People Businesses: managing professional service firms, 1991; Enterprise, 2003; Making Cities Work, 2003; Creating Viable Local Media Companies, 2009; The Ascent of Media: from Gilgamesh to Google via Gutenberg, 2011; Developing the Neural Nudge, 2013. *Recreations:* ski-ing, squash, sailing, tennis, croquet, backgammon, fishing, swimming, cinema, NY Times crossword. *Clubs:* Garrick, MCC; Ocean (Bahamas).

PARRY, Victor Thomas Henry, MA Oxon; FCLIP; Director of Central Library Services and Goldsmiths' Librarian, University of London, 1983–88; *b* 20 Nov. 1927; *s* of Thomas and Daisy Parry; *m* 1959, Mavis K. Russull; two *s* one *d*. *Educ:* St Julian's High Sch., Newport; St Edmund Hall, Oxford (MA); University College, London (DipLib). FCLIP (FLA 1959). Manchester Public Libraries, 1950–56; Colonial Office and CRO Library, 1956–60; Librarian, Nature Conservancy, 1960–63; British Museum (Natural History), 1963–74; Chief Librarian and Archivist, Royal Botanic Gdns, Kew, 1974–78; Librarian, SOAS, Univ. of London, 1978–83. Sen. Examiner, LA, 1959–68. Chm., Circle of State Librarians, 1966–68; Mem., Adv. Cttee, British Library Dept of Humanities and Social Scis (formerly Reference Div.), 1983–90; Council Member: Sir Anthony Panizzi Foundn, 1983–89; London Soc., 1984–88. Chm., Friends of Univ. of London Liby, 1998–2000. FRAS 1981; FRSA 1985. *Publications:* contrib. prof. books and jls. *Recreations:* ball games, books, bridge, railways. *Address:* 69 Redway Drive, Twickenham TW2 7NN. *T:* (020) 8894 0742. *Club:* Surrey CC.

PARRY, Vivienne Mary Hunt, (Mrs Tim Joss), OBE 2011; writer and broadcaster; *b* 4 June 1956; *d* of late Michael Mills and Mary Mills; *m* 1st, 1978, Paul Parry (marr. diss. 2007); two *s*; 2nd, 2012, Tim Joss. *Educ:* St Swithun's Sch., Winchester; Bedford Coll., London; University Coll. London (BSc Hons Zoology). Nat. Organiser, Birthright, 1979–94; Presenter, Tomorrow's World, 1994–97; Reporter, Panorama, How Safe is Beef?, and Test Tube Bodies, 1996; Presenter, Morning Surgery, 1997; Columnist: News of the World, 1998–2002; Guardian, 2004–05; Body & Soul supplement, The Times, 2005–09; Presenter, Radio 4: Inside the Ethics Committee (3 series), 2005, 2006, 2007; Am I Normal? (8 series), 2006–10; Just So Science, 2013, 2014. Member: MRC, 2009–; Organ Donor Taskforce, 2006–; non-exec. Bd Mem., Genomics England, 2013–. Facilitator, G8 Dementia Summit, 2013. Administrator, GUS Charitable Trust, 1997–2007; Trustee, Diana Meml Fund, 1998. Mem. Council, UCL, 2005– (Vice Chair, 2009–). Member, Advisory Board: Sci. Media Centre, 2003–12; Cheltenham Sci. Fest., 2004–. *Publications:* The Real Pregnancy Guide, 1996; The Truth About Hormones, 2005. *Recreations:* gardening, swimming, walking. *Address:* Lingermans, Burford Road, near Brize Norton, Oxon OX18 3NZ.

PARRY-EVANS, Air Chief Marshal Sir David, GCB 1991 (KCB 1985); CBE 1978; Royal Air Force, retired; *b* 19 July 1935; *s* of late Group Captain John Parry-Evans, MRCS, LRCP, DLO, and Dorothy Parry-Evans; *m* 1960, Ann, 2nd *d* of late Charles Reynolds and Gertrude Reynolds; two *s*. *Educ:* Berkhamsted School. Joined RAF, 1956; served FEAF, Coastal Command, United States Navy, RN Staff Coll., 1958–70; Headquarters Strike Command, 1970–74; OC 214 Sqn, 1974–75; OC RAF Marham, 1975–77; MoD, 1977–81 (Director of Defence Policy, 1979–81); Comdt, RAF Staff Coll., 1981–82; AOC Nos 1 and 38 Groups, RAF Strike Comd, 1982–85; C-in-C RAF Germany, and Comdr, Second ATAF, 1985–87; Dep. Chief of Defence Staff (Progs and Personnel), 1987–89; Air Mem. for Personnel, 1989–91. Gov., Royal Star and Garter Home, 1991–99 (Chm., 1996–99). Chief Comdr, St John Ambulance, 1992–98. KStJ 1992. *Address:* c/o National Westminster Bank, 26 Spring Street, W2 1JA. *Club:* Royal Air Force.

PARRY EVANS, Mary Alethea, (Lady Hallinan); a Recorder of the Crown Court, 1978–97; *b* 31 Oct. 1929; *oc* of Dr Evan Parry Evans, MD, JP, and Dr Lilian Evans; *m* 1955, Sir (Adrian) Lincoln Hallinan (*d* 1997); two *s* two *d*. *Educ:* Malvern Girls' Coll.; Somerville Coll., Oxford (BCL, MA). Called to Bar, Inner Temple, 1953; Wales and Chester Circuit. Member: Cardiff City Council, 1961–70; S Glamorgan CC, 1972–81; S Glamorgan Health Authority, 1977–81. Lady Mayoress of Cardiff, 1969–70. *Address:* Cotham Lodge, West Street, Newport, Pembrokeshire SA42 0TD.

PARRY JONES, Terence Graham; *see* Jones, Terry.

PARSLOE, Prof. Phyllida; Chairman, North Bristol NHS Trust, 1999–2003; Professor of Social Work, Bristol University, 1978–96, now Emeritus Professor; *b* 25 Dec. 1930; *d* of late Charles Guy Parsloe and Mary Zirphie (*née* Munro). *Educ:* Bristol Univ. (BA, PhD); London Univ. (Cert. in Mental Health). Probation Officer, Devon CC, 1954–59; Psychiatric Social Worker, St George's Hospital, 1959–65; Lectr, London Sch. of Economics, 1965–70; Associate Prof., Sch. of Law, Indiana Univ., 1970–73; Prof. of Social Work, Univ. of Aberdeen, 1973–78; Pro-Vice Chancellor, 1988–91, Warden of Wills Hall, 1991–97, Bristol Univ. Member: Central Council for Educn and Training in Social Work, 1986–92; Commonwealth Scholarships Commn. Mem. Bd, Ammerdown Centre, 1993–; Trustee, Winterbourne Mediaeval Barn Trust, 2009–. Mem., Thornbury Town Council, 2004–. Chair: Thornbury Community Building Trust, 2006–; Camphill Communities Thornbury, 2007–; Thornbury Arts Fest., 2007–; WEA Thornbury, 2009–; Thornbury Community

Assoc. *Publications:* The Work of the Probation and After Care Officer, 1967; Juvenile Justice in Britain and America, 1978; (with Prof. O. Stevenson) Social Service Teams: the practitioner's view, 1978; Social Service Area Teams, 1981; report to the Sec. of State for Scotland on Social Work in Prisons, 1987; (with S. Macara *et al*) Data Protection in Health and Social Services, 1988; Aiming for Partnership, 1990; (ed) Risk Assessment in Social Care and Social Work, 1999; contribs to: British Jl of Social Work, Community Care, Social Work Today, British Jl Criminology. *Recreations:* hill walking, crafts, gardening. *Address:* Lion House, 9 Castle Street, Thornbury, S Glos BS35 1HA.

PARSONS, family name of **Earl of Rosse**.

PARSONS, Adrian; *see* Parsons, C. A. H.

PARSONS, Andy; writer, actor and stand-up comedian; *b* 15 Oct. 1967. *Educ:* Helston Comp. Sch.; Churston Grammar Sch.; Christ's Coll., Cambridge (BA Hons Law 1988). *Television* includes: lead writer: Weekending; Spitting Image; writer and performer: Smith & Jones; The Lenny Henry Show; The Stand-Up Show (4 series); The Comedy Store Series; Saturday Live; Live at the Apollo; regular on Mock the Week (12 series); Live Floor Show; *radio* includes: Parsons and Naylor's Pullout Sections, Scrooby Trevithick, The PMQ Show; national tours: Citizens!, 2009; Gruntled, 2011; I've Got a Shed, 2013; also tours of Australia and New Zealand. Comedy Award, Time Out, 2002. *Recreation:* relaxing in shed. *E:* andy@andyparsons.co.uk.

PARSONS, Prof. Barry Eaton, PhD; Professor of Geodesy and Geophysics, University of Oxford, since 2003; Fellow of St Cross College, Oxford, since 1986; *b* 24 May 1948; *s* of Ernest Harold Parsons and Olive Parsons (*née* Eaton). *Educ:* Downing Coll., Cambridge (BA Natural Scis 1969; PhD 1973). Res. Asst, Principal Res. Scientist and Associate Prof., Dept of Earth and Planetary Scis, MIT, 1973–86; Reader in Geodesy, Univ. of Oxford, 1986–; Dir, Centre for Observation and Modelling of Earthquakes, Volcanoes and Tectonics (formerly Centre for Observation and Modelling of Earthquakes and Tectonics), 2002–13. Fellow, Amer. Geophys. Union, 2011. *Publications:* articles in Geophysical Jl Internat., Geophysical Res. Letters, Jl of Geophysical Res., Nature, Science, Earth and Planetary Science Letters. *Address:* Department of Earth Sciences, University of Oxford, Parks Road, Oxford OX1 3PR.

PARSONS, (Charles) Adrian (Haythorne); consultant to solicitors on charity matters; *b* 15 June 1929; *s* of Dr R. A. Parsons and Mrs W. S. Parsons (*née* Haythorne); *m* 1951, Hilary Sharpe; one *d*. *Educ:* Bembridge Sch.; Wadham Coll., Oxford. Called to Bar, Gray's Inn, 1964. Coutts & Co., Bankers, 1952–64; joined Charity Commn, 1964; Dep. Comr, 1972; Comr, 1974–89; Head of Legal Staff, 1981; Unit Trust Ombudsman, 1989–90; National Solicitors Network Ombudsman, 1989–94. Complaints Convenor, Retained Organs Commn, 2003–04. *Address:* 6 Garrick Close, The Green, Richmond, Surrey TW9 1PF. *T:* (020) 8940 3731. *Club:* Oxford and Cambridge.

See also Sir R. E. C. F. Parsons.

PARSONS, (Christopher) Nicholas, CBE 2014 (OBE 2004); actor, presenter and solo performer; *b* 10 Oct. 1923; *s* of late Dr Paul Frederick Nigel Parsons and Nell Louise Parsons (*née* Maggs); *m* 1st, 1954, Denise Pauline Rosalie Bryer (marr. diss. 1989); one *s* one *d*; 2nd, 1995, Ann Reynolds. *Educ:* St Paul's Sch.; Univ. of Glasgow. *Theatre* includes: The Hasty Heart, Aldwych, 1945; Charley's Aunt, Palace, 1947; Arsenic and Old Lace (tour); in rep., Bromley, Kent, 1949–51; cabaret incl. Quaglino's, Ciros, The Colony, Society, Café de Paris, 1951–65; comedian, Windmill Th., 1952, Watergate Revue, Lyric Revue, 1954; Swing Along with Arthur Haynes, Palladium, 1963; Boeing Boeing, Duchess, 1967; Say Who You Are, Vaudeville, 1968; Uproar in the House, Whitehall, 1968; Charlie Girl, Victoria Palace and tour, 1986–87; Into the Woods, Phoenix, 1990; Rocky Horror Show, Duke of York's, 1994 and 1995 (tours 1996, 1998–99 and 2000); numerous pantomimes and one-man shows incl. Nicholas Parsons' Happy Hour, Edinburgh Fringe, 1999–2014, Just a Laugh a Minute and Life and Work of Edward Lear, UK festivals, tours and regular cruises; *television* includes: comedy partnership with Arthur Haynes, 1956–66; Last Train to Surbiton (series), 1966; Benny Hill Show, 1968–70; host: Sale of the Century, 1971–84; The All New Alphabet Game, 1988; Laughlines, 1990; Just a Minute, 1994, 1995, 1999 and 2012; participant, Comedy World Cup, 2012; *films* include: Brothers-in-Law, Carlton-Browne at the FO, Happy is the Bride, Upstairs Downstairs, Too Many Crooks, Eyewitness, Carry on Regardless; Don't Raise the Bridge, Lower the River; *radio* includes: host, Just a Minute, 1967–; Listen to This Space, 1967–73. Rector, St Andrews Univ., 1988–91. Barker, Variety Club of GB, 1975–; Mem., Lord's Taverners, 1965– (Pres., 1998–2000); Trustee, Aspire, Deaf-Blind UK; Gov., NSPCC, 1977; Ambassador, ChildLine, 2004–. Hon. LLD St Andrews, 1991; Hon. DA Lincoln, 2007. Radio Personality of Year, Variety Club, 1967; Sony Lifetime Achievement Award, 2010. *Publications:* Egg on the Face, 1985; The Straight Man; my life in comedy, 1994; Nicholas Parsons With Just a Touch of Hesitation, Repetition and Deviation—My Life in Comedy (memoirs), 2010; Welcome to Just a Minute, 2014. *Recreations:* golf, gardening, photography. *Address:* (agent) Jean Diamond, 31 Percy Street, W1T 2DA. *T:* (020) 7631 0400, *Fax:* (020) 7631 0500. *E:* jd@diman.co.uk.

PARSONS, Colin James, FCA; Chairman, Trow Engineering (Canada), 2003–10 (Director, 1999–2003); *b* Neath, Wales, 15 Jan. 1934; *m* 1960, Alice McAuley; two *s*. *Educ:* Haverfordwest and Neath Grammar Schs. CA 1955; FCA 1991. Peat Marwick Mitchell, Toronto, 1957–59; Monarch Development Corp., 1959–99: Pres., 1977–92; Chm., 1992–99; Taylor Woodrow plc: Dir, 1987–; Gp Chm., 1992–99; Chief Exec., 1997–98. Pres. and Chm., London Chamber of Commerce and Industry, 1998–2000; Pres., Canada-UK Chamber of Commerce, 1998–99. Dir, Foundn for Canadian Studies in UK, 1997–2000. *Recreations:* tennis, golf. *Address:* 154 Valley Road, Toronto, ON M2L 1G4, Canada. *Clubs:* Brooks's; Albany, Granite, Donalda (Toronto).

PARSONS, David; *see* Parsons, J. D.

PARSONS, David Huw; a District Judge (Magistrates' Courts), since 2004; *b* 11 May 1957; *s* of Dr D. Ll. Parsons and Margaret P. G. Parsons (*née* Lumley); three *d*. *Educ:* Duffryn High Sch., Newport; University Coll. of Wales, Aberystwyth (LLB Hons); Coll. of Law, Guildford. Admitted solicitor, 1981; Sen. Partner and Founding Partner, Hodson, Parsons Solicitors, Newport, S Wales, 1983–2004; Actg Stipendiary Magistrate, 2000–01; Dep. Dist Judge (Magistrates' Courts), 2001–04; Immigration Adjudicator, 2001–04. *Recreations:* reading, Royal Navy, motorcycling, hill walking, cooking, ski-ing, Pembrokeshire, travel. *Address:* c/o Bristol Magistrates' Court, Marlborough Street, Bristol BS1 3NU. *T:* (0117) 943 5117. *Club:* Oriental.

PARSONS, David Robert, CBE 2009; Member (C), 1991–2013, and Leader, 2003–12, Leicestershire County Council; *b* Bristol, 1950; *s* of Robert Donald Probert-Parsons and Beryl Maureen Probert-Parsons (*née* Higgins); *m* 1977, Elizabeth Dolby; two *s* one *d*. *Educ:* Cotham Grammar Sch., Bristol; Salford Univ. (BSc Hons 1972); St John's Coll., Oxford (BA 1976); Bristol Poly. (Dip. Educn Mgt 1982). Pres., Students' Union, Univ. of Oxford, 1975–76. Sci. Teacher, Castle Sch., Thornbury, St Mary Redcliffe and Temple Sch., Bristol and Mangotsfield Sch., 1977–90. Mem. (C), Bristol CC, 1979–91; Leader, Blaby DC, 2001–03. Chairman: E Midlands Regl Assembly, 2002–10; E Midlands Councils, 2010–12. Mem., Cttee of the Regions, EU, 2005–13. Dep. Chm., LGA, 2008–12 (Chm., Improvement Bd, 2008–15); Mem., Regl Econ. Council, 2008–10; Chm., Local Govt Develt Agency, 2010–12. Contested (UK Ind) S Holland and The Deepings, 2015. *Recreations:* farming, cartography.

PARSONS, Sir John (Christopher), KCVO 2002 (CVO 1998; LVO 1992); Deputy Keeper of the Privy Purse and Deputy Treasurer to the Queen, 1988–2002; an Extra Equerry to the Queen, since 2002; *b* 21 May 1946; *s* of late Arthur Christopher Parsons and of Veronica Parsons; *m* 1982, Hon. Anne Manningham-Buller, *d* of 1st Viscount Dilhorne, PC; two *s* one *d*. *Educ:* Harrow; Trinity College, Cambridge (MA Mech. Scis). FCA; FIC. Dowty Group Ltd, 1968–72; Peat, Marwick, Mitchell & Co., 1972–85; Asst Treas. to the Queen, 1985–87; Dep. Dir (Finance), Royal Collection, 1992–93. Lay Mem., Chapter, 2001–14, Treas., 2004–14, Lay Canon, 2014–, Peterborough Cathedral. Trustee and Treas., Music in Country Churches, 2006–; Trustee, Country Houses Foundn, 2006–. Mem. Council and Treas., Internat. Dendrology Soc., 2009–. Gov., Elstree Sch., 1987–2014 (Vice-Chm., 2002–09; Chm., 2009–14). *Address:* The Old Rectory, Eydon, Daventry, Northants NN11 3QE. *Clubs:* Brooks's, Pratt's.

PARSONS, Prof. (John) David, DSc; FREng, FIET; independent consultant, since 1998; David Jardine Professor of Electrical Engineering, 1982–98, and Head, Department of Electrical Engineering and Electronics, 1983–86 and 1996–98, University of Liverpool; *b* 8 July 1935; *s* of Oswald Parsons and Doris Anita (*née* Roberts); *m* 1969, Mary Winifred Stella Tate (*d* 2010). *Educ:* University College of Wales, Cardiff (BSc); King's College London (MSc (Eng), DSc (Eng)). FIET (FIEE 1986); FREng (FEng 1988). GEC Applied Electronics Labs, 1959–62; Regent Street Poly., 1962–66; City of Birmingham Poly., 1966–68; Lectr, Sen. Lectr and Reader in Electronic Engrg, Univ. of Birmingham, 1969–82; University of Liverpool: Dean, Faculty of Engrg, 1986–89; Pro-Vice-Chancellor, 1990–96. Vis. Prof., Univ. of Auckland, 1982; Vis. Res. Engr, NTT, Japan, 1987. UN Expert in India, 1977; Hon. SPSO, RSRE, Malvern, 1978–82. Member Council: IERE, 1985–88; IEE, 1988–89. *Publications:* Electronic and Switching Circuits, 1975; Mobile Communication Systems, 1989; The Mobile Radio Propagation Channel, 1992, 2nd edn 2000; many papers on radio communication systems and radio propagation in learned jls. *Recreations:* golf, bridge, playing banjo and ukulele. *Address:* 5 Norcote Lodge, Old Town Lane, Formby, Merseyside L37 3HP.

PARSONS, Loretta Caroline Rose; *see* Minghella, L. C. R.

PARSONS, Luke Arthur; QC 2003; *b* 3 March 1962; *s* of John Andrew Parsons and Frances Patricia Parsons; *m* 1989, Isabelle Jane Munro; five *s*. *Educ:* John Fisher Sch., Purley; Bristol Univ. (LLB 1984). Called to the Bar, Inner Temple, 1985; practising commercial barrister, 1986–. Gov., Linacre Centre on Bioethics, 2002. *Publications:* (jtly) Admiralty and Commercial Forms and Precedents, 1991. *Recreations:* castles, classical music, theatre. *Address:* Quadrant Chambers, Quadrant House, 10 Fleet Street, EC4Y 1AU. *T:* (020) 7583 4444, *Fax:* (020) 7583 4455. *E:* luke.parsons@quadrantchambers.com.

PARSONS, Michael John; Chief Operating Officer, Home Office, since 2013; *b* St Albans, 1 Sept. 1965; *s* of John Parsons and Geraldine Parsons. *Educ:* Churston Grammar Sch.; Christ's Coll., Cambridge (BA Nat. Scis and Computer Sci. 1986). CPFA 1989. Cambridgeshire County Council, 1986–2009: various accountancy roles; Asst Dir, Resources; Dir, Resources; Dep. Chief Exec., Corp. Services; Dir, Resources and Performance, Herts CC, 2009–13; Dir, Resource and Orgnl Develt, UK Border Agency, 2013. *Recreations:* running, walking, sailing, cinema. *Address:* Home Office, 2 Marsham Street, SW1P 4DE. *T:* (020) 7035 0989. *E:* michael.parsons@homeoffice.gsi.gov.uk.

PARSONS, Nicholas; *see* Parsons, C. N.

PARSONS, Prof. Peter John, FBA 1977; Regius Professor of Greek, University of Oxford, 1989–2003; Student of Christ Church, Oxford, 1964–2003; *b* 24 Sept. 1936; *s* of Robert John Parsons and Ethel Ada (*née* Frary); *m* 2006, Barbara Montagna Macleod (*d* 2006). *Educ:* Raynes Park County Grammar Sch.; Christ Church, Oxford (MA 1961). Oxford University: Craven Scholar, 1955; 1st Cl. Hons Mods and de Paravicini Scholar, 1956; Chancellor's Prize for Latin Verse and Gaisford Prize for Greek Verse, 1st Cl. Lit. Hum., Derby Scholar, Dixon and Sen. Scholar of Christ Church, 1958; Passmore Edwards Scholar, 1959; Lectr in Documentary Papyrology, 1960–65; Lectr in Papyrology, 1965–89. J. H. Gray Lectr, Univ. of Cambridge, 1982; Heller Lectr, Univ. of Calif, Berkeley, 1988. Hon. PhD: Bern, 1985; Athens, 1995; Hon. DLitt Milan, 1994. *Publications:* (jtly) The Oxyrhynchus Papyri XXXI, 1966, XXXIII and XXXIV, 1968, LIV, 1987, LIX, 1992, LX, 1994, LXVI, 1999, LXVIII, 2003, LXXI, 2007, LXXVIII, 2012, LXXIX, 2013; The Oxyrhynchus Papyri XLII, 1973; (with H. Lloyd-Jones) Supplementum Hellenisticum, 1983; City of the Sharp-Nosed Fish: Greek lives in Roman Egypt, 2007; (jtly) The Vienna Epigrams Papyrus, 2015; articles in learned jls. *Recreations:* music, film, gardening, cooking and eating. *Address:* Christ Church, Oxford OX1 1DP. *T:* (01865) 422132.

PARSONS, Sir Richard (Edmund Clement Fownes), KCMG 1982 (CMG 1977); HM Diplomatic Service, retired; Ambassador to Sweden, 1984–87; *b* 14 March 1928; *s* of Dr R. A. Parsons; *m* 1960, Jenifer Jane Mathews (*d* 1981); three *s*. *Educ:* Bembridge Sch.; Brasenose Coll., Oxford. Served in Army, 1949–51; joined HM Foreign (subseq. Diplomatic) Service, 1951; FO, 1951–53; 3rd Sec., Washington, 1953–56; 2nd Sec., Vientiane, 1956–58; FO, 1958–60; 1st Sec., Buenos Aires, 1960–63; FO, 1963–65; 1st Sec., Ankara, 1965–67; FO, 1967–69; Counsellor, Lagos, 1969–72; Head of Personnel Ops Dept, FCO, 1972–76; Ambassador to: Hungary, 1976–79; Spain, 1980–84. Plays produced in London, Edinburgh and Brighton. Gov., Sadler's Wells Trust, 1991–98. Chm., W Norfolk Music Soc., 2004–. *Publications:* The Moon Pool, 1988; Mortmain and other plays, 1993; The Den of the Basilisk, 2012; Howling at the Moon, 2013; Rode He On Barbary?, 2014; *as John Haythorne:* None of Us Cared for Kate, 1968; The Strelsau Dimension, 1981; Mandrake in Granada, 1984; Mandrake in the Monastery, 1985. *Recreations:* reading, writing, music, travel. *Address:* Lancaster House, Old Methwold Road, Whittington, King's Lynn, Norfolk PE33 9TN. *Club:* Garrick.

See also C. A. H. Parsons.

PARSONS, Roger, PhD, DSc; FRS 1980; FRSC; Professor of Chemistry, University of Southampton, 1985–92, now Emeritus; *b* 31 Oct. 1926; *s* of Robert Harry Ashby Parsons and Ethel Fenton; *m* 1953, Ruby Millicent Turner (*d* 2008); three *s* one *d*. *Educ:* King Alfred Sch., Hampstead; Strathcona High Sch., Edmonton, Alta; Imperial Coll. of Science and Technol., (BSc, PhD). DSc Bristol 1962; ARCS 1946; FRIC 1962. Asst Lectr, Imp. Coll. of Science and Technol., 1948–50; Deedes Fellow, UC Dundee, St Andrews Univ., 1950–54; Lectr, then Reader in Electrochem., Bristol Univ., 1954–79; Dir, Lab. d'Electrochimie Interfaciale, Centre Nat. de la Recherche Scientifique, Meudon, France, 1977–84. Unesco Specialist, Buenos Aires, 1961; Vis. Prof., Calif Inst. of Technol., 1966–67. Editor, Jl of Electroanal. Chem., 1962–99. Royal Society of Chemistry: Pres., Faraday Div., 1991–93 (Vice-Pres., 1984–91, 1993–99); Liversidge Lectr, 1989–90. Hon. Fellow, Polish Chem. Soc., 1981. Palladium Medal, US Electrochem. Soc., 1979; Bruno Breyer Medal, Electrochem. Div., RACI, 1980; Prix Paul Pascal de l'Acad. des Scis, 1983; Galvani Medal, Electrochem. Div., Italian Chem. Soc., 1986; Frumkin Meml Medal, Internat. Soc. of Electrochem., 2000; Davy Medal, Royal Soc., 2003. DUniv Buenos Aires, 1997. *Publications:* Electrochemical Data, 1956; (ed with J. Lyklema) Electrical Properties of Interfaces, 1983; (ed jtly) Standard Potentials in Aqueous Solution, 1985; (ed with R. Kalvoda) Electrochemistry in Research and Development, 1985; *circa* 200 papers in scientific jls. *Recreations:* listening to music, going to the opera. *Address:* 16 Thornhill Road, Bassett, Southampton SO16 7AT.

PÄRT, Arvo; free-lance composer, since 1967; *b* Estonia, 11 Sept. 1935; *s* of August Pärt and Linda Anette Pärt (*née* Mäll); *m* 1st, 1959, Hille Aasmäe (marr. diss.); one *d*; one *d* by Marina

Nestieva; 2nd, 1972, Nora Supina; two *s*. *Educ:* composition studies with Heino Eller, Conservatory of Music, Tallinn, Estonia. Sound Engr, Estonian broadcasting station, Tallinn, 1958–67; free-lance composer, Tallinn, 1967–80; emigrated to Vienna, 1980; became Austrian citizen, 1981; Scholar, Deutscher Akademischer Austauschdienst, Berlin, 1981; in Berlin, 1981–2010, in Estonia, 2010–. Hon. Member: Amer. Acad. of Arts and Letters, 1996; Royal Sch. of Church Music, UK, 2003; Accad. Nazionale di Santa Cecilia, Rome, 2004; Associate Mem., Royal Acad. of Sci and Fine Arts, Belgium, 2001; Mem., Pontifical Council for Culture, Vatican, 2011–. Mem., Estonian Acad. of Scis, Academician for Music, 2011. Hon. PhD: Acad. of Music, Tallinn, 1990; Royal Swedish Music Acad., 1991; Hon. DMus: Sydney, 1996; Durham, 2002; Hon. Dr: Univ. of Tartu, Estonia, 1998; Univ. Nacional de Gen. San Martin Escuela de Humanidades, Argentina, 2003; Freiburg, 2007; Liège, 2009; St Andrews, 2010; Pontifical Inst. for Sacred Music, Vatican, 2011; Lugano, 2012. Triumph award, Russia, 1997; Culture Prize, Estonia, 1998; Herder Award, Germany, 2000; Composition Trophy C. A. Seghizzi, Gorizia, Italy, 2003; Borderland Award, Sejny, Poland, 2003; Composer of the Year, Musical America, 2005; Eur. Award of Sacred Music, Germany, 2005; Internat. Brückepreis, Görlitz/Zgorzelec, Germany/Poland, 2007; Baltic Star Prize, St Petersburg, 2007; Sonning Music Prize, Denmark, 2008; Lifelong Achievement Award, Republic of Estonia, 2009; Lifelong Achievement Award, Internat. Istanbul Music Fest., 2010; Hommage, Konrad Adenauer Fund, Germany, 2011; Classic Brit Award, 2011; Praemium Imperiale, Japan, 2014. Order of the Nat. Coat of Arms (Estonia), 2nd class 1998, 1st class 2006; Commandeur de l'Ordre des Arts et des Lettres (France), 2001; Cross of Honour for Sci. and Art, 1st class (Austria), 2008; Chevalier, Légion d'Honneur (France), 2011. *Compositions* include: Sinfonie No 1, 1963; Sinfonie No 2, 1966; Credo, 1968; Sinfonie No 3, 1971; Fratres (variations for ensembles, orchestra and various instruments), 1977–2009; Tabula Rasa (double violin concerto), 1977; Sarah was Ninety Years Old, 1976, 1989; Spiegel im Spiegel, 1978–2011; Passio, 1982; Stabat Mater, 1985; Te Deum, 1985; Sieben Magnificat-Antiphonen (choir a capella), 1988; Miserere, 1989; Berliner Messe (choir, soloists and organ), 1990; Berliner Messe (choir, soloists and string orch.), 1991; Litany (soloists, choir and orch.), 1994; Kanon Pokajanen (choir a cappella), 1997; Como cierva sedienta (solo soprano and orch.), 1998; Cantique des Degrés (choir and orch.), 1999; Orient & Occident (string orch.), 2000 (Classical Brit Contemp. Music Award, 2003); Cecilia, Vergine Romana (choir and orch.), 2000; My Heart's in the Highlands (voice and organ), 2000, (voice, violin, viola, violoncello and piano), 2013; Salve Regina (choir and organ), 2001; Lamentate (piano and orch.), 2002; In Principio (choir and orch.), 2003; Passacaglia (violin and piano), 2003; L'Abbé Agathon (soprano and 8 celli), 2004; Da Pacem Domine (choir and instruments), 2004–10 (Grammy Award, Best Choral Recording, 2007); Vater Unser (voice and piano), 2005, (voice and string orchestra or string quintet), 2013; La Sindone (orch.), 2005; Für Lennart (orch.), 2006; Passacaglia (violin or two violins and orch.), 2007; These Words… (string orch.), 2008; Symphony No 4 Los Angeles, 2008 (Classical Brit Award for Composer of the Yr, 2011); O-Antiphonen (cello octet), 2008; Stabat Mater (choir and string orch.), 2008; Silhouette (string orch. and percussion), 2009; Adam's Lament (choir and string orch.), 2010; In Spe (woodwind, horn and string orch.), 2010; Salve Regina (choir, celesta and string orch.), 2011; Virgencita, 2012–13; Swansong: Littlemore Tractus (orch.), 2013. *Address:* c/o Universal Edition, Bösendorferstr. 12, 1010 Vienna, Austria.

PARTASIDES, Constantine; QC 2014; Partner, Three Crowns LLP, since 2014; *b* Nicosia, Cyprus, 5 Dec. 1969; *s* of Doros and Vera Partasides; *m* 2000, Dr Patricia Cabredo Hofherr; two *d*. *Educ:* Haberdasher's Askes' Sch. for Boys, Elstree; King's Coll. London (BA Hons Modern Hist.); Peterhouse, Cambridge (MPhil Internat. Relns 1993). Admitted as Solicitor Advocate, 2008; with Freshfields, subseq. Freshfields Bruckhaus Deringer, 1994–2014, Partner, 2004–14. *Publications:* (jtly) Redfern & Hunter on International Arbitration, 2009. *Recreations:* history, politics, football. *T:* 07872 156814. *E:* constantine.partasides@threecrownsllp.com.

PARTHIER, Prof. Benno; Director, Institut für Pflanzenbiochemie, Halle, 1990–98, now Emeritus; President, Deutsche Akademie der Naturforscher Leopoldina, 1990–2003; *b* 21 Aug. 1932; *s* of Hermann and Helene Parthier; *m* 1967, Christiane Luecke; one *s* two *d*. *Educ:* Martin Luther Univ., Halle-Wittenberg (Dip. Biol. 1958; Dr rer. nat. 1961; Dr habil. 1967). Asst, Botanical Inst., Univ. Halle, 1958–65; Head, Dept of Molecular Biol., Inst. of Plant Biochemistry, Acad. of Scis, GDR, 1967–90. Mem., learned socs, Germany and overseas. Hon. Dr Würzburg, 2003. *Publications:* (with R. Wollgiehn) Von der Zelle zum Molekül, 1971 (Polish edn 1976); (with L. Nover and M. Luckner) Zell differenzierung, Molekulare Grundlagen und Probleme, 1978 (English edn 1982); numerous papers in sci. jls; Editor or co-Editor 10 sci. jls. *Recreations:* gardening, travelling. *Address:* c/o Deutsche Akademie der Naturforscher Leopoldina, Postfach 110543, 06109 Halle, Germany. *T:* (345) 4723915.

PARTINGTON, Adrian Frederick, FRCO; Director of Music, Gloucester Cathedral, since 2008; Artistic Director, BBC National Chorus of Wales, since 2000; *b* Nottingham, 1 Oct. 1958; *s* of Kendrick and Mary Partington; *m* 1981, Clare Diana Crane; four *s* one *d*. *Educ:* King's Sch., Worcester; Royal Coll. of Music; King's Coll., Cambridge (BA 1981; MA). FRCO 1978. Organ Scholar: St George's Chapel, Windsor, 1976–78; King's Coll., Cambridge, 1978–81; Asst Organist, Worcester Cathedral, 1981–91; Dir of Music, Sch. of St Mary and St Anne, Abbots Bromley, 1991–95; Lectr, RWCMD, 1995–2011. Conductor: City of Birmingham Symphony Youth Chorus, 1995–2000; Bristol Choral Soc., 2000–. Jt Artistic Dir, Three Choirs Fest., 2008–. *Address:* 7 Millers Green, Gloucester GL1 2BN. *T:* (01452) 524764. *E:* a.partington@gloucestercathedral.org.uk.

PARTINGTON, Ven. Brian Harold, OBE 2002; Archdeacon of Man, 1996–2005, now Emeritus; Vicar of St George's, Douglas, 1996–2004; *b* 31 Dec. 1936; *s* of Harold Partington and Edith (*née* Hall); *m* 1962, Valerie Nurton; two *s* one *d*. *Educ:* Burnage Grammar Sch., Manchester; St Aidan's Coll., Birkenhead. Nat. Service, RAF, 1955–57; local govt officer, Manchester Corp., 1953–59. Ordained deacon, 1963, priest, 1964; Assistant Curate: Emmanuel Church, Didsbury, Manchester, 1963–66; St Mary's, Deane, Bolton, 1966–68; Vicar: Kirk Patrick, Sodor and Man, 1968–96; Foxdale, 1977–96; St John's, 1977–96. Bishop's Youth Officer, 1968–77; Rural Dean of Peel, 1976–96; Canon of St Patrick, St German's Cathedral, 1985–96. Pres., Hospice Care, 2008– (Chm., 1988–96; Vice Pres., 1996–2008). Exec. Chm., IOM Sports Council, 1990–2002; Chm., Internat. Island Games Orgn, 2005–07 (Vice-Chm., 2001–05; Hon. Life Mem., 2007); President: IOM Hockey Assoc., 1997–2006; IOM Cricket Assoc., 1998–2006; Pres., IOM Golf Union, 2010–12. *Recreations:* cricket, golf, travel, sailing. *Address:* Brambles, Kirk Patrick, Isle of Man IM5 3AH. *T:* (01624) 844173. *Clubs:* St John's Cricket; Peel Golf (Capt., 2006); IOM Yacht (Principal, RYA Trng Centre, 2006–).

PARTINGTON, Gillian Doreen, (Mrs W. D. Partington); *see* Ruaux, Her Honour G. D.

PARTINGTON, Prof. (Thomas) Martin, CBE 2002; Professor of Law, 1987–2006, now Emeritus, and Senior Research Fellow, since 2009, Bristol University; Special Consultant to the Law Commission, 2006–07 (a Law Commissioner, 2001–05); *b* 5 March 1944; *s* of Thomas Paulett Partington and Alice Emily Mary Partington; *m* 1st, 1970, Marcia Carol Leavey (marr. diss.); one *s*; 2nd, 1978, Daphne Isobel Scharenguivel; one *s* one *d*. *Educ:* King's Sch., Canterbury; Peterhouse, Cambridge (BA 1965; LLB 1966). Called to the Bar, Middle Temple, 1984, Bencher, 2006. Asst Lectr, Bristol Univ., 1966–69; Lectr, Warwick Univ., 1969–73, LSE, 1973–80; Prof. of Law, Brunel Univ., 1980–87 (Dean, Faculty of Soc. Scis, 1985–87); Dean, Faculty of Law, 1988–92, Pro-Vice-Chancellor, 1995–99, Bristol Univ. Visiting Professor: Osgoode Hall Law Sch., Canada, 1976; Univ. of NSW, 1983; Vis. Sen. Res. Fellow, Inst. of Advanced Legal Studies, 2006–10. Academic Advr, Univ. (formerly Coll.) of Law, 2006–14. Chm., Cttee of Heads of Univ. Law Schools, 1990–92. Vice-Chm., Legal Action Gp, 1982–83; Member: Lord Chancellor's Adv. Cttee on Legal Aid, 1988–91; Law Society's Trng Cttee, 1989–92; Law Society's Academic Consultative Cttee, 1989–92; Judicial Studies Bd, 1992–95 (Mem., Tribunals Cttee, 1988–95); Trng Cttee, Ind. Tribunal Service, 1990–94; Council on Tribunals, 1994–2000; Civil Justice Council, 1998–2005; Bd, United Bristol Healthcare NHS Trust, 1998–2001; Adv. Cttee, Leverhulme Trust Res. Awards, 1999–2006; External Adviser, Educn and Trng Cttee, Inst. of Housing, 1985–89. Chm., Council, 2009–10, Bd, 2010–, Dispute Service; Specialist Advr, Public Admin Select Cttee, 2012; Consultant, Qatar Financial Centre Authy, 2012–14; External Reviewer, Hong Kong Res. Grants Council, 2012–; Chm., Review of Inst. of Advanced Legal Studies, Univ. of London, 2012. Part time Chairman: Soc. Security Appeals Tribunal, 1990–94; Med. Appeals Tribunal, 1992–94; Disability Appeals Tribunal, 1992–94. Expert Consultant: Leggatt Review of Tribunals, 2000–01; Employment Tribunals Taskforce, 2001–02. Barrister, Chambers of A. Arden, QC, 1993–2010. Chm., Socio-Legal Studies Assoc., 1993–95. Gen. Editor, Anglo-American Law, now Common Law World, Review, 1984–2003. FRSA 1999. Hon. Fellow, Soc. of Advanced Legal Studies, 2001. Hon. QC 2008. *Publications:* Landlord and Tenant, 1975; Claim in Time, 1978; (with A. Arden) Housing Law, 1983; (with P. O'Higgins) Bibliography of Social Security Law, 1986; Secretary of State's Powers of Adjudication in Social Security Law, 1990; (with J. Hill) Housing Law: cases, materials and commentary, 1991; United Kingdom: Social Security Law, 1998, 3rd edn, 2009; (with M. Harris) Administrative Justice in the 21st Century, 1999; Introduction to the English Legal System, 2000, 10th edn 2015; Consulting Ed., Halsbury's Laws of England, vol. 65, Legal Aid; articles on public law, housing law, social security law, legal educn, law reform, Legal Aid and Legal Services. *Recreations:* playing the violin, reading fiction, cooking. *Address:* First Floor Flat, 8/9 Clifton Hill, Bristol BS8 1BN. *T:* (0117) 973 6294.

PARTRIDGE, Bernard B.; *see* Brook-Partridge.

PARTRIDGE, Derek William, CMG 1987; HM Diplomatic Service, retired; *b* 15 May 1931; *o s* of late Ernest and Ethel Elizabeth Partridge (*née* Buckingham), Wembley. *Educ:* Preston Manor County Grammar Sch., Wembley. Entered Foreign Service (later Diplomatic Service), 1949. Royal Air Force, 1949–51. Served: Foreign Office, 1951–54; Oslo, 1954–56; Jedda, 1956; Khartoum, 1957–60; Sofia, 1960–62; Bangkok, 1962; Manila, 1962–65; Djakarta, 1965–67; FCO, 1967–70; Diplomatic Service Inspectorate, 1970–72; British Consul-General, Brisbane, 1972–74; First Sec. (Economic and Commercial), Colombo, 1974–77; FCO, 1977–86: Counsellor and Head of Migration and Visa Dept, 1981–83; Counsellor and Head of Nationality and Treaty Dept, 1983–86; High Comr, Sierra Leone, 1986–91. Mem. (Lib Dem) Southwark BC, 1994–2002. *Address:* 16 Wolfe Crescent, Rotherhithe, SE16 6SF. *T:* (020) 7231 2759. *Club:* National Liberal.

PARTRIDGE, Ian Harold, CBE 1992; full-time concert singer (tenor), 1963–2008; Professor, Royal Academy of Music, since 1996; *b* 12 June 1938; *s* of late Harold Partridge and Ena Stinson; *m* 1959, Ann Glover; two *s*. *Educ:* New Coll., Oxford (chorister); Clifton Coll. (music scholar); Royal Coll. of Music; Guildhall Sch. of Music (LGSM, singing and teaching). Began as piano accompanist, although sang tenor in Westminster Cath. Choir, 1958–62; performed in England and all over the world, both in recitals (with sister Jennifer) and in concerts; has worked with many leading conductors, incl. Stokowski, Boult, Giulini, Boulez and Colin Davis. Opera debut at Covent Garden as Iopas in Berlioz, Les Troyens, 1969. Title role, Britten's St Nicolas, Thames Television (Prix Italia, 1977). Over 150 records, *including:* Bach, St John Passion; Handel, Chandos Anthems, and Esther; Schubert, Die Schöne Müllerin, Die Winterreise; Schumann, Dichterliebe; Beethoven, An die ferne Geliebte; Vaughan-Williams, On Wenlock Edge; Warlock, The Curlew; Fauré and Duparc Songs; Britten, Serenade and Winter Words; Lord Berners, Complete Songs; as conductor (of Pro Cantione Antiqua), The Triumphs of Oriana. Innumerable radio broadcasts, many TV appearances. Chm., Royal Soc. of Musicians, 1999–2001 (Gov., 1995–99 and 2005–); Pres., ISM, 1996–97; Dir, Performing Artists' Media Rights Assoc., 1996–2002. Governor, Clifton Coll., 1981–. Sir Charles Santley Meml Gift, Musicians' Co., 1992. Hon. RAM 1996. Harriet Cohen Award, 1967. *Recreations:* bridge, horse racing, theatre, cricket. *Address:* 127 Pepys Road, SW20 8NP. *Club:* Garrick.

PARTRIDGE, James Richard John, OBE 2002; Founder and Chief Executive, Changing Faces, since 1992; *b* Chipping Sodbury, 30 Oct. 1952; *s* of Sir (Ernest) John Partridge, KBE and Joan Emily, (Johnnie), Partridge, MBE; *m* 1978, Caroline Judith Schofield; one *s* two *d*. *Educ:* Clifton Coll.; University Coll., Oxford (MA Hons PPE); London Sch. of Hygiene and Tropical Medicine (MSc Med. Demography). Asst Health Economist, St Thomas' Hosp., 1976–78; Res. Fellow, Unit for Study of Health Policy, Guy's Hosp., 1978–79; dairy farmer, St Andrews, Guernsey, 1979–92; econs teacher, Ladies' Coll., Guernsey, 1986–92. Dir, Dining with a Difference, 2001–. Mem., Appraisal Cttee, NICE, 1999–2004. Mem., States of Guernsey Agricl and Milk Mktg Bd, 1988–92. Associate, Business Disability Forum, 1992–. Trustee and Dir, Guernsey Community Foundn, 2010–. Hon. FRCSEd 2005. Hon. DSc: West of England, 1999; Bristol, 2005. *Publications:* Changing Faces: the challenge of facial disfigurement, 1990, 6th edn 2012. *Recreations:* family, organic vegetable growing, golf, squash, watching sport, writing and researching. *Address:* Flat 4, 134 Queen's Gate, SW7 5LE. *T:* (office) (020) 7391 9294. *E:* james.partridge@changingfaces.org.uk. *Club:* Royal Guernsey Golf.

PARTRIDGE, John Albert, CBE 1981; RA; FRIBA; architect in private practice; a Senior and Founder Partner, Howell, Killick, Partridge & Amis (HKPA), 1959–95, now Consultant; *b* 26 Aug. 1924; *s* of George and Gladys Partridge; *m* 1953, Doris (*née* Foreman); one *s* one *d*. *Educ:* Shooters Hill Grammar Sch., Woolwich; Polytechnic School of Architecture, Regent Street. FRIBA 1966 (ARIBA 1951); RA 1988 (ARA 1980). London County Council Housing Architects Dept, 1951–59; Design Tutor, Architectural Assoc., 1958–61. The work of HKPA includes universities, colleges, public buildings, housing and leisure buildings; principal commissions include: Wolfson, Rayne and Gatehouse building, St Anne's Coll., Oxford; New Hall and Common Room building, St Antony's Coll., Oxford; Wells Hall, Reading Univ.; Middlesex Polytechnic College of Art, Cat Hill; Medway Magistrates' Court; The Albany, Deptford; Hall of Justice, Trinidad and Tobago; Warrington Court House; Basildon Magistrates' Courthouse; Berlin Mineral Spa Project; Haywards Heath Magistrates' Courthouse; Japanese University Chaucer Coll., Univ. of Kent, Canterbury. RIBA: Vice-Pres., 1977–79; Hon. Librarian, 1977–81; Chm. Res. Steering Gp, 1977–84. Vice-Pres., Concrete Soc., 1979–81. External Examiner in Architecture: Bath Univ., 1975–78, 1992; Thames Polytechnic, 1978–86; Cambridge Univ., 1979–81; Manchester Univ., 1982; South Bank Polytechnic, 1982–86; Brighton Polytechnic, 1987–90; RCA, 1991–93. Governor, Building Centre Trust, 1982–96; Chm., Assoc. of Consultant Architects, 1983–85. Mem., NEDO Construction Res. Strategy Cttee, 1983–86; Architect Mem., FCO Adv. Bd on the Diplomatic Estate, 1985–92. Award for dist. services to arch., Assoc. of Consultant Architects, 2005. *Publications:* articles in technical press. *Recreations:* looking at buildings, water colours, sketching. *Address:* Cudham Court, Cudham, near Sevenoaks, Kent TN14 7QF. *T:* (01959) 571294. *Club:* Arts.

PARTRIDGE, Dame Linda, DBE 2009 (CBE 2003); FMedSci; FRS 1996; FRSE; Weldon Professor of Biometry, since 1994, and Director, Institute of Healthy Ageing, since 2007, University College London; *b* 18 March 1950; *d* of George and Ida Partridge; *m* 1st, 1983, Dr V. K. French (marr. diss. 1992); 2nd, 1996, Prof. Michael John Morgan, *qv*. *Educ:* Convent of the Sacred Heart, Tunbridge Wells; St Anne's Coll., Oxford (MA); Wolfson Coll., Oxford

(DPhil 1974). Post-doctoral Fellow, York Univ., 1974–76; Edinburgh University: Lectr, 1976–87; Reader in Zoology, 1987–92; Prof. of Evolutionary Biol., 1992–93; NERC Res. Prof., 1997–2002, BBSRC Professorial Fellow, 2002–07, UCL. Founder Dir, Max Planck Inst. for Biol. of Ageing, Cologne, 2008–. Croonian Prize Lect., Royal Soc., 2009. Mem. Council, BBSRC, 1998–2001. Trustee, Natural Hist. Mus., 2000–08. President: Internat. Soc. for Behavioural Ecology, 1990–92; Assoc. for Study of Animal Behaviour, 1995–97; Genetical Soc., 1999–2003. Member: Eur. Acad. of Scis, 2004; EMBO, 2005. FRSE 1992; FMedSci 2004. Hon. DSc: St Andrews, 2004; Oxford, 2011; Bath, 2011; Brighton, 2012. Frink Medal, Zool Soc. of London, 2000; Sewall Wright Award, Amer. Soc. of Naturalists, 2002; Fondation IPSEN Longevity Prize, 2004; Lord Cohen Medal, British Soc. for Res. on Ageing, 2004; Medal, Assoc. for Study of Animal Behaviour, 2005; Living Legend, Help the Aged, 2006; Thomassen a Thuessink Medal, Univ. of Groningen, Netherlands, 2008; Darwin-Wallace Medal, Linnean Soc., 2009; Women of Outstanding Achievement Award for Sci. Discovery, Innovation and Entrepreneurship, UK Resource Centre for Women in Sci., Engrg and Technol., 2009. *Publications:* on ageing and evolutionary biology in scientific jls. *Recreations:* birdwatching, tennis, hill walking, gardening. *Address:* Institute of Healthy Ageing, Department of Genetics, Evolution and Environment, University College London, Darwin Building, Gower Street, WC1E 6BT.

PARTRIDGE, Sir Michael (John Anthony), KCB 1990 (CB 1983); Permanent Secretary, Department of Social Security, 1988–95; *b* 29 Sept. 1935; *s* of late Dr John Henry Partridge, DSc, PhD, and Ethel Green; *m* 1968, Joan Elizabeth Hughes; two *s* one *d*. *Educ:* Merchant Taylors'; St John's Coll., Oxford (BA (1st Cl. Hons Mods and Lit Hum) 1960, MA 1963; Hon. Fellow, 1991). Entered Home Civil Service (Min. of Pensions and Nat. Insce), 1960; Private Sec. to Permanent Sec., 1962–64; Principal, 1964–71 (MPNI, Min. of Social Security and DHSS); DHSS: Asst Sec., 1971–76; Under Sec., 1976–81; Dep. Sec., 1981–83; Dep. Under-Sec. of State, Home Office, 1983–87; Second Permanent Sec., DHSS, 1987–88. Non-executive Director: Norwich Union, 1996–2000; Epworth Investment Mgt Ltd, 1996–2011; The Stationery Office, 1997–99; Aviva (formerly CGNU), 2000–03; Magdi Yacoub Inst. (formerly Harefield Res. Foundn), 2001–14 (Vice-Chm., 2003–14); Chm., The Stationery Office Pension Scheme, 2003–. Senior Treasurer, Methodist Ch Finance Div., 1980–96; Mem., Central Finance Bd and Council, Methodist Ch, 1980–2011. Trustee: Harefield Hosp. Heart Transplant Trust, 1991–2003; Methodist Ministers' Pensions Trust, 1993–2011. Member: Court, Univ. of York, 1991–95; Council, Univ. of Sheffield, 2001–03. Governor: Middlesex Univ., 1992– (Chm., 1997–2001; Pro-Chancellor, 2002–); Merchant Taylors' Sch., 1992–99; Chm. of Govs, Heathfield Sch., 2004–11. Pres., Old Merchant Taylor's Soc., 2002–03. CCMI (CBIM 1988). Liveryman, Merchant Taylors' Co., 1987. DUniv Middlesex, 2015. *Publications:* (ed jtly) Serta Scissorum, 2012. *Recreations:* Do-it-Yourself, classical sites, reading, ski-ing. *Address:* 27 High View, Pinner, Middlesex HA5 3NZ. *T:* (020) 8868 0657. *Club:* Oxford and Cambridge.

PARTRIDGE, Sir Nicholas (Wyndham), (Sir Nick), Kt 2009; OBE 1999; Chief Executive, Terrence Higgins Trust, 1991–2013; *b* Rickmansworth, 28 Aug. 1955; *s* of Miles and Patricia Partridge; civil partnership 2008, Simon Vearnals. *Educ:* W Somerset Sch., Minehead; Keele Univ. (BA Hons Internat. Relns 1978). Thorn EMI, 1978–80; Rank Xerox, 1980–82; Amsterdam, 1982–84; with Terrence Higgins Trust, 1985–2013. Chair, Involve, 1998–2011. Mem., Commn for Health Improvement, 1999–2004; Vice-Chair, Expert Adv. Gp on AIDS, 2001–12; Deputy Chair: Healthcare Commn, 2004–09; UK Clin. Res. Collaboration, 2005–; Health and Social Care Inf. Centre, 2013–; Mem., Health Honours Cttee, 2012–; Chm., Clinical Priorities Adv. Gp, NHS England, 2013–. Hon. DLitt Keele, 2008; Hon. DSc De Montfort, 2011. *Recreations:* cooking, travel, 20th century music.

PASCALE, Lorraine; television chef and cookery writer; *b* 17 Nov. *Educ:* Leith's Sch. of Food and Wine (Dip. Food and Wine); Univ. of W London (BSc 1st Cl. Culinary Arts Mgt 2011). Model, NY; worked in kitchens of hotels, restaurants, incl. Petrus, Mandarin Oriental, Gilgamesh, The Wolseley, London; opened shop, Ella's Bakehouse, Covent Gdn, 2009. Presenter, TV series: Baking Made Easy, 2011; Home Cooking Made Easy, 2011; Lorraine's Fast, Fresh and Easy Food, 2012; My Kitchen Rules, 2014; How To Be A Better Cook, 2014. Ambassador, Prince's Trust, 2012–; Govt Fostering Ambassador, 2014–. *Publications:* Home Cooking Made Easy, 2011; Baking Made Easy, 2011; Fast, Fresh and Easy Food, 2012; A Light Way To Bake, 2013; How To Be A Better Cook, 2014. *Address:* c/o James Grant Group Ltd, 94 Strand on the Green, Chiswick, W4 3NN.

PASCALL, David Lewis, CBE 1993; Managing Director, Pascall Associates, European business and financial consultancy, since 2008; *b* 5 Feb. 1949; *s* of Robert Lewis Pascall and Dorothy Pascall (*née* Smith); *m* 1980, Carolyn Judith White; one *s* two *d*. *Educ:* Queen Mary's Grammar Sch., Basingstoke; Univ. of Birmingham (BSc 1st Cl. Hons Chem. Engrg 1970); INSEAD, Fontainebleau (MBA Dist. 1979). With British Petroleum Co. plc, 1967–93: posts in oil refining, trading, finance and business management in UK and, 1974–79, Germany and France; Divl Manager, BP Finance Internat., 1986–89; Manager: BP Share Sale, 1987; Project 1990 (cultural change prog.), 1989–93; Finance Dir, 1993–94, Chief Exec., Asia Pacific, 1994–95, MAI plc; Finance Dir to Hon. Sir Rocco Forte, 1996–98; Eur. Transaction Dir, Prin. Finance Gp, Nomura Internat., 2000–02; Man. Dir, Terra Firma Capital Partners Ltd, 2002–07. On secondment to: Central Policy Rev. Staff, Cabinet Office, 1982–83; No 10 Policy Unit, 1983–84. Chairman: Bio Products Laboratory Ltd, 2010–12; DCI Biologicals Inc., 2011–12. Non-executive Director: Colt Gp Ltd, 1999–2000; Deutsche Annington Regl Supervisory Bds, 2001–11; Airports Internat., 2008–09; Royal Free NHS Trust, 2009–10. Advr, MoD Defence Costs Review, 1994. Mem., 1990–91, Chm., 1991–93, Nat. Curriculum Council; Mem. Exec. Cttee, Field Studies Council, 1993–99. Mem., Develt Adv. Council, Univ. of Birmingham, 2005–09. Chm., Newham Partnership Working Ltd, 2013–14. Foundn Gov., Sir John Cass and Redcoat Comprehensive Sch., Stepney, 1995–2001, 2008– (Chm., 2009–). Vice Chm., Trustees, Pathway, 2010–. Mem., Nat Soc., 1994–2000. FRSA 1993. *Recreations:* my family, current affairs, golf. *Address:* 31 Lanchester Road, N6 4SX. *T:* (020) 8883 8740. *E:* david@pascallassociates.co.uk. *Clubs:* Highgate Golf, Trevose Golf.

PASCO, Adam Gerhold; Managing Director, Adam Pasco Media, since 2012; Editor, BBC Gardeners' World magazine, 1991–2012; *b* 11 Jan. 1957; *s* of Cecil Filmer Pasco and Sheila Mary Pasco (*née* Gerhold); *m* 1992, Jayne Petra Fisher; one *s* one *d*. *Educ:* North East Surrey Coll. of Technol. (HND Applied Biology 1977); Univ. of Nottingham (BSc Horticulture 1982). Technical Editor, 1982–84, Editor, 1984–88, Garden Answers magazine; Editor, Garden News, 1988–90. Gardening Correspondent, Daily Telegraph, 1995–2000; Ed., then Editl Dir, BBC Easy Gardening magazine, 2002–06; Editl Dir, BBC Magazines' Gardening Gp, 2003–11; weekly blog column on gardenersworld.com, 2007–; presenter, World Radio Gardening and blogger, https://worldradiogardening.wordpress.com. *Publications:* Collins Complete Garden Manual, 1998; Greenfingers Book, 1999; Collins Gardeners' Calendar, 2000. *Recreations:* gardening, cookery, photography, writing, walking, guitar, ukelele, travel, family life.

PASCOE, Alan Peter, MBE 1975; Executive Chairman, The Partnership Consultancy, since 2014; *b* 11 Oct. 1947; *s* of late Ernest George Frank Pascoe and of Joan Rosina Pascoe; *m* 1970, Della Patricia (*née* James); one *s* one *d*. *Educ:* Portsmouth Southern Grammar Sch.; Borough Road Coll. (Cert. in Educn); London Univ. (BEd Hons). Master, Dulwich Coll., 1971–74; Lectr in Physical Educn, Borough Road Coll., Isleworth, 1974–76. Dir, 1976–83, Man. Dir, 1983, Chm., 1985–98, CEO, 1994–98, Alan Pascoe Associates Ltd, then API Gp of Cos; Chm., Carat Sponsorship, 1987–92; Dir, WCRS, then Aegis Gp, 1986–92; Chm., Fast Track, 1998–2012; Pres., CSM Sport & Entertainment (formerly Chime Sports and Events Div.), 2013–14 (Chm., 2010–13). Vice Chm., London 2012 Olympic Bid, 2003–05. Member: Sports Council, 1974–80; Minister for Sport's Working Party on Centres of Sporting Excellence; BBC Adv. Council, 1975–79. Trustee: Torch Trophy Trust, 2006–12; Young Enterprise Trust, 2008–12; Sported, 2013–. European Indoor Champion, 50m Hurdles, 1969; Eur. Games Silver Medallist, 110m Hurdles, 1971; Silver Medal, Olympic Games, Munich, 4×400m Relay, 1972; Europa Cup Gold Medallist, 400m Hurdles, 1973; Commonwealth Games Gold Medal, 400m Hurdles, and Silver Medal, 4×400m Relay, 1974; Eur. Champion and Gold Medallist in both 400m Hurdles and 4×400m Relay, 1974; Europa Cup Gold Medallist, 400m Hurdles, 1975; Olympic Finalist (injured), Montreal, 1976; Europe's Rep., World Cup, 1977. Fellow, Mktg Soc., 2014. DUniv Brunel, 1997. Hollis Sponsorship Personality of the Year, Hollis Publications, 2004; Outstanding Achievement Award, UK Sponsorship Awards, 2014; Lifetime Achievement Award, Sports Industry Awards, 2014. *Publications:* An Autobiography, 1979. *Recreations:* theatre, sport, travel. *Address:* CSM, Southside, 6th Floor, 105 Victoria Street, SW1E 6QT.

PASCOE, Martin Michael; QC 2002; *b* 1953; *s* of late Michael Raymond Pascoe and Dorothy Agnes Pascoe. *Educ:* Christ Church, Oxford (BA Juris. 1976, BCL 1977). Called to the Bar, Lincoln's Inn, 1977, Bencher, 2011; in practice, specialising in corporate and internat. insolvency law. *Address:* 3–4 South Square, Gray's Inn, WC1R 5HP. *T:* (020) 7696 9900, *Fax:* (020) 7696 9911. *E:* martinpascoe@southsquare.com.

PASCOE, Dr Michael William; Head of Science, Camberwell College of Arts (formerly Camberwell School of Arts and Crafts), 1981–90; *b* 16 June 1930; *s* of Canon W. J. T. Pascoe and Mrs D. Pascoe; *m* 1st, 1956, Janet Clark (marr. diss. 1977); three *d*; 2nd, 1977, Brenda Hale Reed; one *d*. *Educ:* St John's, Leatherhead; Selwyn Coll., Cambridge (BA, PhD). MInstP. Res. Student (Tribology), Cambridge, 1951–55; Physicist: Mount Vernon Hosp., Northwood, 1956–57; British Nylon Spinners Ltd, 1957–60; Chemist/Physicist, ICI Paints Div., 1960–67; Lectr (Polymer Science), Brunel Univ., 1967–77; Principal Scientific Officer, 1976–79, Keeper of Conservation and Technical Services, 1979–81, British Museum. Tutor and Counsellor, Open Univ., 1971–76. Occasional Lecturer: West Dean Coll., 1989–90; Camberwell Coll. of Arts; ICCROM; Vis. Lectr in Materials, Univ. of Brunel, 1995 and 1999. Consultant to: Royal Acad. of Arts (Great Japan exhibn), 1982–; Mary Rose Trust, 1978–83; Council for the Care of Churches, 1980–91; Public Record Office (Domesday exhibn), 1986; Science Museum, 1988; Crafts Council; States of Jersey; Parliament of Guyana, 1991–; Univ. of Stirling, 1991–; and advr on conservation facilities, Portsmouth CC; Govt and cultural instns of Guatemala on conservation matters, 1996–; Conservation Advr, Winchester Coll. FRSA. *Publications:* contrib. to books on polymer tribol. and technol.; articles in scientific, engrg and conservation jls on tribol., materials technol., history of adhesives and on conservation methods. *Recreations:* painting and drawing, theatre, active in University of the Third Age, lecturing in gen. sci., history and contemporary topics, *inter alia*.

PASCOE, Nigel Spencer Knight; QC 1988; a Recorder of the Crown Court, since 1979; *b* 18 Aug. 1940; *er s* of late Ernest Sydney Pascoe and of Cynthia Pascoe; *m* 1964, Elizabeth Anne Walter; two *s* four *d*. *Educ:* Epsom Coll. Called to the Bar, Inner Temple, 1966, Bencher, 1996; Leader, Western Circuit, 1995–98; a Pres., Mental Health Review Tribunal, 2002–. Chm., Bar Public Affairs Cttee, 1996–98. County Councillor for Lyndhurst, Hants, 1979–84. Founder and Editor, All England Qly Law Cassettes, 1976–85; Chm., Editl Bd, Counsel mag., 2000–07. *Publications:* The Trial of Penn and Mead, 1985; The Nearly Man, 1994; Pro Patria, 1996; Who Killed William Rufus?, 2000; Without Consent, 2004; To Encourage the Others, 2006; articles in legal jls. *Recreations:* theatre, devising and presenting with Elizabeth Pascoe legal anthologies, after-dinner speaking, cricket, play writing, broadcasting. *Address:* 3 Pump Court, Temple, EC4Y 7AJ. *T:* (020) 7353 0711. *Club:* Garrick.

PASCOE, Gen. Sir Robert (Alan), KCB 1985; MBE 1968; Adjutant General, 1988–90; Aide de Camp General to the Queen, 1989–91, retired; *b* 21 Feb. 1932; *er s* of late Clarence and Edith Mary Pascoe; *m* 1955, Pauline (*née* Myers) (*d* 2013); one *s* three *d*. *Educ:* Tavistock Grammar Sch.; RMA, Sandhurst. rcds, psc; Middle East Centre for Arab Studies, Shemlan. Commissioned Oxford and Bucks LI, 1952; served with 1 Oxf. Bucks, 1 DLI and 4 Oxf. Bucks (TA), 1953–57; Middle East Centre for Arab Studies, Lebanon, 1958–59; 1st Cl. Interpretership (Arabic); GSO2 Land Forces Persian Gulf, 1960–62; sc Camberley, 1963; Co. Comd 2RGJ, UK and Malaysia, 1964–66 (despatches (Borneo) 1966); GSO2 HQ 2 Div. BAOR, 1967–68; Co. Comd 1RGJ, UK and UNFICYP, 1968–69; Second in Comd 2RGJ, BAOR, 1969; MA to QMG, 1970–71; Comd 1RGJ, 1971–74, BAOR and NI (despatches (NI) 1974); Col General Staff HQ UKLF, 1974–76; Comd 5 Field Force BAOR, 1976–79; rcds 1979; Army Rep. on Staff of Security Co-ordinator, NI, 1979–80; Asst Chief of Gen. Staff (Operational Requirements), MoD, 1981–83; Chief of Staff, HQ, UKLF, 1983–85; GOC Northern Ireland, 1985–88. Rep. Col Comdt, RGJ, 1988–90; Colonel Commandant: 1st Bn Royal Green Jackets, 1986–91; Army Legal Corps, 1988–90. Hon. Col, Oxfordshire ACF, 1991–2002; Vice Pres., Oxfordshire ACF League, 2002–. Mem. Adv. Bd, The Rifles, 2007–12. Chm., Belautruche (UK) plc, 1997–2000; non-exec. Dir, Belautruche NV, 1997–2000. Chairman of Governors: Royal Sch., Bath, 1988–96 (Governor, 1981–96); Royal High Sch., Bath, 1996–2006. Gov., King Edward VII's Hosp., London, 2006– (Mem. of Council 1995–2006). President: Army LTA, 1986–91; Army Boxing Assoc., 1989–90; RGJ Golf Soc., 1999–2005; Reg. Forces Employment Assoc., 1997–99 (Chm., 1994–97); Potterne Br., RBL, 2006–; Veterans Charity (formerly Project 65), 2007–; Chm., Ex-Services Resettlement Gp, 1994–98. Mem. and Vice Pres., Royal Patriotic Fund Corp., 1992–2011; Patron, Retired Officers Assoc., 1991–2001. Chairman: 43rd and 52nd Club, 1992–2002; Oxford and Bucks LI Mus. Trustees, 1992–2002. Hon. Associate, Girls' Day Sch. Trust, 2007. Freeman, City of London, 1992; Hon. Liveryman, Fruiterers' Co., 1992. *Recreations:* gardening, golf, fishing, tennis, ski-ing.

PASCOE-WATSON, George William; Senior Partner, Portland Communications, (Partner, since 2009); *b* Edinburgh, 21 Aug. 1966; *s* of John and Margaret Pascoe-Watson; *m* 2011, Natalie Jane Kirby; two *s*. *Educ:* George Heriot's Sch., Edinburgh; Royal High Sch., Edinburgh; Napier Coll., Edinburgh. The Sun: reporter, 1988–94; political corresp., 1994–96; Dep. Political Ed., 1996–2006; Political Ed., 2006–010. *Recreation:* golf. *Address:* Portland, 1 Red Lion Court, EC4A 3EB. *E:* gpw@portland-communications.com. *Club:* Richmond Golf.

PASLEY, Sir Robert Killigrew Sabine, 6th Bt *cr* 1794, of Craig, Dumfriesshire; chartered accountant; Chief Financial Officer, Cell C (Pty) Ltd, South Africa; *b* 23 Oct. 1965; *s* of Sir Malcolm Pasley, 5th Bt, FBA and of Virginia Killigrew (*née* Wait); *S* father, 2004; *m* 2002, Katja Antoinette Jozefina Arnoldina Hermans; one *s* three *d*. *Educ:* Univ. of Exeter (BSc Hons Theoretical Physics 1987). ACA 1990. Formerly Strategy Dir, Vodacom Gp, SA. *Heir: s* Henry Malcolm Sabine Pasley, *b* 8 Sept. 2009.

PASSINGHAM, Prof. Richard Edward, PhD; FRS 2009; Professor of Cognitive Neuroscience, University of Oxford, 1997–2008; Fellow, Wadham College, Oxford, 1976–2008, now Emeritus; *b* London, 16 Aug. 1943; *s* of Bernard and Margaret Passingham; *m* 1971, Clare Darlington; one *s* one *d*. *Educ:* Shrewsbury Sch.; Balliol Coll., Oxford (BA 1966); Inst. of Psychiatry, Univ. of London (MSc Clin. Psychol. 1967); PhD London 1971. University of Oxford: Lectr, Dept of Exptl Psychol., 1976–93; Reader *ad hominem*, 1993–97; Hon. Sen. Lectr, MRC Cyclotron Unit, Hammersmith Hosp., 1991; Hon. Principal, Wellcome Centre for Neuroimaging, UCL, 1994. Fellow, Assoc. for Psychol Sci., 2010. *Publications:* The Human Primate, 1982; The Frontal Lobes and Voluntary Action, 1993;

What is Special About the Human Brain?, 2008; The Neurobiology of the Prefrontal Cortex, 2012. *Recreations:* playing the piano, listening to classical music, reading novels, biographies, history. *Address:* 16 Ambleside Drive, Oxford OX3 0AG. *E:* dick.passingham@psy.ox.ac.uk.

PASSLEY, Patrick Derek, LVO 2013; Founder, and Managing Director, Paralegal Charity, since 1994; *b* London, 10 Oct. 1965; *s* of Ivan Augustus Passley and Lurline Isamanda Passley; *m* 1991, Jean Francis; two *d. Educ:* Poly. of E London (LLB Hons); Middlesex Univ. (CertEd; Assessors Trainers Award Cert.). Law Lectr, Barnet Coll., 1991–2002. Commission for Racial Equality: Mem., 1999–2003; Chm., Nat. Sports Cttee, 2001; Official Observer on Disability Rights Commn, 2000–03; Special Advr to Trevor Philips, 2003–04; nominated CRE Comr for the Formal Investigation into CPS, 2000–01, and into Prison Service, 2000–03; UK Delegate, Consultative Commn on Industrial Change, Eur. and Econ. Social Cttee, Brussels, 2004–12. Member Council: Prince's Trust, 2001–12 (Mem. Adv. Bd, 2013–); King George's Jubilee Trust, 2001. Member: Equity Sub-gp, Sport England, 2000–03; Mgt Cttee, Sporting Equals, CRE/Sport England, 2005–08; Communications Cttee, FA, 2003–04; Adult Learning Cttee, Nat. LSC, 2001; London E Local LSC, 2001–03. Sec., African and Caribbean Finance Forum, 2001–03; Trustee, African Caribbean Leadership Council, 2007–. Jt Council for Anglo-Caribbean Churches, 2003. *Recreations:* amateur boxing (former Nat. Amateur Boxing Champion and Commonwealth Rep. for England at Super Heavyweight, 1989–90), movies, current affairs, sport.

PASSMORE, Colin John; Senior Partner, Simmons & Simmons LLP, since 2011; *b* Grays, Essex, 25 Jan. 1959; *s* of Roger and Dorothy Passmore; *m* 1985, Julie Braithwaite (*d* 2009); three *d. Educ:* Palmer's Endowed Sch. for Boys, Grays; Southampton Univ. (LLB 1981); Coll. of Law, Guildford. Admitted as solicitor, 1984, as solicitor-advocate (civil), 1999. Coward Chance: articled clerk, 1982–84; qualified lawyer, 1984–86; Simmons & Simmons LLP: Associate, Hong Kong, 1986–91; Partner, 1990; Sen. Litigation Partner, 2005–11. Freeman: City of London; Solicitors' Co. *Publications:* Privilege, 1998, 3rd edn 2013; (contrib.) Fraud, ed Ormerod and Montgomery, 2007. *Recreations:* the law, travel, political history, horse riding, seeking to make a small difference. *Address:* Simmons & Simmons LLP, City Point, One Ropemaker Street, EC2Y 9SS. *T:* (020) 7628 2020, *Fax:* (020) 7628 2070. *E:* colin.passmore@simmons-simmons.com.

PASSMORE, George; artist; *b* Plymouth, Devon, 1942. *Educ:* Dartington Hall Coll. of Art; Oxford Sch. of Art; St Martin's Sch. of Art. Collaboration with Gilbert Proesch, *qv*, as Gilbert and George. Gallery exhibitions include: Modern Fears, 1980, The Believing World, 1983, New Pictures, 1987, Worlds & Windows, 1990, New Democratic Pictures, 1992, Anthony d'Offay Gall.; The Rudimentary Pictures, Milton Keynes Gall., 2000; New Horny Pictures, White Cube^2, 2001; Perversive Pictures, NY, 2004; Jack Freak Pictures, White Cube, 2009, European mus. tour, 2010; museum exhibitions include: The Paintings, 1971, Photo-Pieces 1971–80, 1981, Whitechapel Art Gall.; Pictures 1982 to 85, Hayward Gall., 1987; Enclosed and Enchanted, MOMA, Oxford, 2000; The Dirty Words Pictures (retrospective), Serpentine Gall., 2002; Gilbert & George: major exhibition (retrospective), Tate Modern, 2007, US mus. tour, 2008; London Pictures, White Cube, 2012; living sculpture includes: The Red Sculpture; Underneath the Arches; The Singing Sculpture; Our New Sculpture. Work in permanent collections incl. Nat. Portrait Gall., Tate Modern and San Francisco Mus. of Modern Art. Represented GB, Venice Biennale, 2005. (Jtly) Turner Prize, 1986. *Publications:* (as George), with Gilbert Proesch: Lost Day; Oh, the Grand Old Duke of York; What Our Art Means. *Address:* c/o White Cube^2, 144–152 Bermondsey Street, SE1 3TQ.

PASSMORE, John William; QC 2015; *b* Guildford, 23 Aug. 1969; *s* of Arthur Peter Roy Passmore and Ethel Rosemarie Anne Passmore; *m* 2011, Claire Rosalind Wood; one *s* one *d. Educ:* Weydon Sch., Farnham; Univ. of Bristol (LLB Hons); Inns of Court Sch. of Law. Called to the Bar: Lincoln's Inn, 1992; NI, 2003; in practice as a barrister, specialising in commercial and Admiralty law, 1993–. Member: Equality and Diversity Cttee, Bar Council, 2012–; Bar Pro-Bono Unit. *Recreations:* running, cinema, ballet, opera, music, travelling, food and drink. *Address:* Quadrant Chambers, 10 Fleet Street, EC4Y 1AU. *T:* (020) 7583 4444. *E:* john.passmore@quadrantchambers.com.

PASTON-BEDINGFELD, Sir Henry Edgar; *see* Bedingfeld.

PATAKI, George Elmer; Principal, Pataki-Cahill Group LLC, since 2007; Of Counsel, Chadbourne and Parke LLP, since 2007; Governor, New York State, 1995–2006; *b* 24 June 1945; *s* of Louis Pataki and Margaret Pataki; *m* Elizabeth (Libby) Rowland; two *s* two *d. Educ:* Peekskill High Sch.; Yale Univ. (BA 1967); Columbia Univ. Sch. of Law (JD 1970). Associate, Dewey, Ballantine, Bushby, Palmer and Wood, 1970–74; Partner, Plunkett & Jaffe, 1974–89. Mem., State Assembly 91st AD, 1985–92; Ranking Minority Member: Assembly Envmtl Conservation Cttee, 1987–90; Assembly Educn Cttee, 1991–92; Mem., State Senate 37th SD, 1993–95; Chm., State Ethics Cttee, 1993–95. Mayor, Peekskill, Westchester City, 1982–84. Co-proprietor, Pataki Farm, Peekskill, NY. *Recreations:* hiking in the woods, skiing, basketball, working on the family farm.

PATE, Prof. John Stewart, FRS 1985; FAA 1980; FLS; Professor of Botany, University of Western Australia, 1974–2000, now Emeritus Professor and Honorary Research Fellow, since 2001; *b* 15 Jan. 1932; *s* of Henry Stewart Pate and Muriel Margaret Pate; *m* 1959, Elizabeth Lyons Sloan, BSc (*d* 2004); three *s. Educ:* Campbell College; Queen's Univ., Belfast (BSc, MSc, PhD, DSc). FLS 1990. Lectr, Sydney Univ., 1956–60; Lectr, Reader, Personal Chair in Plant Physiology, Queen's Univ. Belfast, 1960–73. Vis. Fellow, Univ. of Cape Town, 1973. Individual Excellence Award, AMEEF, 1998. Hon. DSc UWA 2006. *Publications:* (ed with J. F. Sutcliffe) Physiology of the Garden Pea, 1977; (ed with A. J. McComb) Biology of Australian Plants, 1981; (with K. W. Dixon) Tuberous, Cormous and Bulbous Plants, 1983; (ed with J. S. Beard) Kwongan: plant life of the sandplain, 1984; (ed with K. A. Meney) Australian Rushes: biology, identification and conservation of Restionaceae and allied families, 1999; (ed jtly and contrib.) Agriculture as a Mimic of Natural Ecosystems, 1999; reviews on carbon nitrogen metabolism and biology of Australian flora; reviews and articles on understanding how plants can bioengineer soil profiles (three key reviews 2001, 2006, 2012). *Recreations:* music, writing books on nature study, hobby farming, academic contact. *Address:* School of Plant Biology, University of Western Australia, 35 Stirling Highway, Crawley, WA 6009, Australia; 681 Mount Shadforth Road, Denmark, WA 6333, Australia.

PATEL, family name of **Barons Patel**, **Patel of Blackburn** and **Patel of Bradford**.

PATEL, Baron *cr* 1999 (Life Peer), of Dunkeld in Perth and Kinross; **Narendra Babubhai Patel,** KT 2009; Kt 1997; Consultant Obstetrician, Tayside Teaching Hospitals NHS Trust, Dundee, 1974–2003, now Hon. Consultant; Hon. Professor, University of Dundee, 1974–2003; *b* 11 May 1938; *m* 1970, Dr Helen Dally; twin *s* one *d. Educ:* Univ. of St Andrews (MB, ChB 1964). MRCOG 1969, FRCOG 1988; FRSE 1999; FMedSci. Chairman: Acad. of Med. Royal Colls, Scotland, 1994–95; Acad. of Med. Royal Colls, UK, 1996–98; Specialist Trng Authority, 1998–2001; Clinical Standards Bd for Scotland, 1999–2003; NHS Quality Improvement, Scotland, 2002–06; Member: Council, GMC, 1998–2003; Armed Forces Pay Review Bd, 2000–06; MRC, 2008–12. Chm., Stem Cell Steering Cttee, 2003–; Vice-Pres., All Party Parly Gp on Maternity Services, 2002–, on Infertility Services, 2003–; Mem., Sci. and Technol. Cttee, H of L, 2000, 2004, 2005–08. Pres., RCOG, 1995–98 (Hon. Sec., 1987–92; Vice-Pres., 1992–95); Vice Pres., FIGO, 2000–03. Chancellor, Dundee Univ., 2006–. Founder FMedSci 1998. Hon. Fellowships: FACOG 1996; FSOGC 1997; FSACOG 1997; FICOG 1997; FRCPE 1997; FRCSE 1997; FRCPGlas 1998; FRCS 1998; FSLCOG 1998; FRANZCOG 1998; FRCA 1998; FRCPI 2000; FFPH 2003; FRCGP 2004; FRCPsych 2005; Eur. Soc. of Perinatal Medicine, 2002. Hon. Mem., German, Finnish, Argentinian, Chilean and Italian Socs of Obstetrics and Gynaecology. Hon. DSc: Napier, 1996; Aberdeen, 2001; St Andrews, 2001; Hon. MD: Stellenbosch, 2001; Hon. Dr: Athens, 2004; London, 2008; Hon. LLD Dundee, 2004. *Publications:* books and articles on pre-term labour, foetal monitoring, birth handicap, obstetrics, etc. *Recreations:* occasional golf, walking. *Address:* University of Dundee, Nethergate, Dundee DD1 4HN.

PATEL OF BLACKBURN, Baron *cr* 2000 (Life Peer), of Langho in the co. of Lancashire; **Adam Hafejee Patel;** *b* Gujarat, India, 7 June 1940; *m* 1964, Ayesha; four *s* four *d. Educ:* Maharaja Sayajirao Univ. of Baroda, India (BCom). Accountant with chartered accountants Ivan Jacques, Blackburn and S. & R. D. Thornton, Preston, 1967–74; Chief Internal Auditor, Zamtan, Lusaka, Zambia, 1975–76; Man. Dir, Comet Cash and Carry Co. Ltd, Blackburn, 1977–97. Mem., Labour Party, 1966–. Founder Mem., Blackburn Community Relns Council, later Blackburn with Darwen Racial Equality Council (Hon. Vice Pres.; former Treas., Vice-Chm. then Chm.); Chm., Blackburn and Dist Commonwealth Friendship Soc., 1966–67; founder Gen. Sec., Blackburn Indian Workers Assoc., 1967–74 (Pres., 1977–). Mem., Home Secretary's Race Relns Adv. Forum; Chm., British Hajj Delegn, FCO, 2001–10. Founder Director: Lancs TEC; Blackburn Partnership. Jt Chm., Christian/Muslim Inter-Faith Forum; Member: Muslim Council of Britain; Lancs CC Standing Adv. Council on Religious Educn. Chm. and Trustee, W Brookhouse Community Centre, Blackburn. JP Blackburn, 1984–95. *Recreations:* community and social work, gardening, football, cricket. *Address:* Snodworth Hall, Snodworth Road, Langho, Lancs BB6 8DS.

PATEL OF BRADFORD, Baron *cr* 2006 (Life Peer), of Bradford, in the County of West Yorkshire; **Kamlesh Kumar Patel,** OBE 1999; Professor, since 2000, and Head, International School of Communities, Rights and Inclusion, since 2008, University of Central Lancashire; University Director of Strategic Partnerships, and Senior Advisor to the Vice Chancellor, University of East London, since 2010; *b* 28 Sept. 1960; *s* of Sudhindra Kumar Patel and Savita Devi Patel; *m* 1998, Yasmin Saloojee; two *s*, and two step *d. Educ:* Univ. of Huddersfield (DipSW; CQSW). Ambulance man, 1981–83; social worker, 1983–87; Specialist Case Worker, Bradford Social Services, 1987–89; Manager, The Bridge Project (voluntary orgn for substance abuse/mental health), 1987–95; University of Central Lancashire: Sen. Lectr, 1995–98, Principal Lectr in Health and Social Care Policy, 1998–2000; Hd, Centre for Ethnicity and Health, 2000–08; Prof. and Sen. Mgt Team, De Montfort Univ., 2010. Nat. Strategic Dir, Nat. Inst. for Mental Health in England, 2003–04 (on secondment); Nat. Dir, Black and Minority Ethnic Mental Health Prog., DoH, 2004–07; Expert Ministerial Advr to Sec. of State for DCLG, 2008–09. A Lord in Waiting (Govt Whip), 2008–09. Chm., All Party Parly Gp on Men's Health, 2010–. Hon. Lectr, Univs of Huddersfield, Lancaster, Salford and Northumbria, 1991–95. Chm., Mental Health Act Commn, 2002–08 (Mem., 1995–2001; Vice-Chm., 2001–02); Member: Commn for Healthcare Audit and Inspection, 2003–06; (and Trustee) UK Drug Policy Commn, 2007–09. Chm., Nat. Prison Drug Treatment Review Gp, 2008–10 (reported 2010); Member: Adv. Council on Misuse of Drugs, 1990–96; Nat. Treatment Agency, 2001–09; Global Task Force, UNICEF, 2006–; Chairman: Integrated Equality and Human Rights Cttee, Leics, Leicester and Rutland, 2010–; Internat. Deaf Foundn, 2010–; Community Innovations Enterprise and Internat. Forum for Community Innovations, 2011–; Bradford Teaching Hosps NHS Foundn Trust, 2014–. Patron: Men's Health Forum, 2006–; Sharing Voices Bradford, 2006–; Bridge Proj., Bradford, 2008–; Equality Partnerships, 2009–; Westminster Health Forum, 2009–; British Muslim Heritage Centre, 2009–; Bradford Cyrenians, 2010–; Awazz, Nottingham, 2012–; Engaged Communities, 2012–; Mental Health First Aid, 2012–. Pres., Bradford Magistrates Chaplaincy Service, 2008–. Hon. DLitt Manchester Metropolitan, 2007; Hon. DCL Huddersfield, 2008. Plaque of Recognition (India), 1999; Award of Achievements (Educn), India Internat. Foundn, 2008; Glory of India Award, 2009. *Publications:* numerous contribs to books, jls, Home Office and DoH Reports on drugs, alcohol, mental health, community engagement, research, black and minority ethnic health and social care. *Recreations:* cricket, cricket coach. *Address:* 3 Old School, 23 James Street, Thornton, Bradford BD13 3NR; House of Lords, SW1A 0PW. *E:* patelkk@parliament.uk, kkpatel@ucl.ac.uk.

PATEL, Bhikhu Chhotabhai; Co-Chairman, Waymade Plc, Atnahs Group and associated companies; *b* Kenya, 1 Aug. 1947; *s* of late Chhotabhai and of Shantaben Patel; *m* 1975, Shashikala Naranbhai Patel; one *s* two *d. Educ:* Univ. of Bristol (BA Arch.; DipArch.). RIBA 1978. (With V. C. K. Patel) co-founded: Waymade Healthcare plc, 1984; Amdipharm, 2002. CCMI 2002. Mem., Lions Clubs Internat. (Melvin Jones Fellow; Recognition of Distinguished Leadership Award, 2004). Hon. LLD Bristol, 2006; Hon. DSc Anglia Ruskin, 2008. (Jtly) UK Entrepreneur of the Year, 2001. *Recreations:* swimming, walking, travelling, reading.

See also V. C. K. Patel.

PATEL, Chaitanya, CBE 1999; FRCP; Chairman, Court Cavendish Group, since 2007; *b* 14 Sept. 1954; *s* of Bhupendra and Ashru Patel; *m* (marr. diss.); two *d. Educ:* Southampton Univ. (BM 1979). MRCP 1982, FRCP 1999. MRC Res. Fellow, Pembroke Coll., Oxford, 1985; Investment Banker, Merrill Lynch and Lehman Brothers, 1985–89; founded Court Cavendish plc, 1989, subseq. Care First plc; Chief Exec., Westminster Health Care Ltd, 1999–2002; CEO, Priory Gp, 2002–07. Chm. and Founder Partner, Elysian Capital, 2008–; Chairman: Integrated Pharmaceutical Services Ltd, 2010–; HC-One, 2011–; Dep. Chm., Care Mgt Gp, 2008–. Member: Better Regulation Task Force, 1997–2002; DoH Task Force for Older People, 1997–2002; Dir, Acute Bd, Independent Healthcare Assoc., 2003–05. Mem. Adv. Bd, Bridges Community Ventures, 2009–. Chm., The Enemy Within Appeal, Combat Stress, 2009–. Trustee: Help the Aged, 2000–02; IPPR, 2000–09 (Sec., 2000–07); Windsor Leadership Trust, 2001–11. Patron: British Olympics Team 2012 Appeal, 2009–; Policy Res. Inst. on Ageing and Ethnicity, 2004–10; The Infant Trust; Rwandan Meml Project. FRSA. DUniv Open, 2002. *Recreations:* golf, music, theatre, travelling, films, photography. *E:* chai@courtcavendish.com. *Clubs:* Royal Automobile, Mosimann's, Soho House, Arts, Harry's Bar, Eden; Queenwood Golf.

PATEL, Dame Indira, DBE 2011 (OBE 1998); National Council of Women Great Britain Representative on United Nations Non-Governmental Organisation Committee on Status of Women, New York, since 2003; *b* Kenya, 27 March 1946; *d* of Ishwerbhai Patel and Dahiben Patel; *m* 1964, Bhanu Patel; two *s* (one *d* decd). *Educ:* Bondeni Girls Primary Sch., Mombasa; Coast Girls High Sch., Mombasa; High Ridge Teachers Trng Coll., Nairobi. Primary sch. teacher, Nairobi, Kenya, 1965–75; asst, sub post office, 1976–82; Liaison Officer (pt-time), Visits Section, FCO, 1998–; newsagent retail business, 1982–87; property mgt, 1982–. Chm., UK Asian Women's Conf., 1987–93; Mem. Cttee, UN Develt Fund, 2000–03; Comr, Women's Nat. Commn, 2003–07; Mem., Organising Cttee, Commn on Status of Women, NY, 2003–10; Co-Chm., morning briefings, UN NGO Cttee on Status of Women, NY, 2003–09. Fellow, Internat. Fedn of Business and Professional Women, 1996–. Internat. speaker on human rights of women, and oppression of women in name of culture, religion and traditions, 1985–; Patron, UN Decade of Culture of Peace. *Recreations:* organising holidays and travelling, cooking, interior designing, swimming. *E:* dame.indirapatel@gmail.com.

PATEL, Dr Ketan Jayakrishna, FRS 2015; FMedSci; Senior Member of Scientific Staff, MRC Laboratory of Molecular Biology, Cambridge, since 1999; Fellow, Gonville and Caius College, Cambridge, since 1995; *b* Nairobi, Kenya, 23 Dec. 1961; *s* of Jayakrishna and Manjula Patel; partner, Dr Fanni Gergely; one *d. Educ:* Banda Sch., Nairobi; Marlborough Coll.; Royal Free Hosp., Univ. of London (MB BS); Cambridge Univ. (PhD 1995). MRCP

1988. Hse Officer, Royal Free Hosp., 1985–86; SHO, Northwick Park Hosp., 1986–88; MRC Fellow, MRC Lab. of Molecular Biol., 1989–93; Registrar in Medicine, Royal Free Hosp., 1993–95; MRC Clinician Scientist, MRC Lab. of Molecular Biol., 1994–99; Res. Fellow, GCCC, 1995–99; MRC Sen. Clin. Fellow, Cambridge Univ. Sch. of Medicine, 1999–2004. Mem., EMBO, 2013. FMedSci 2013. *Publications:* contribs to scientific jls. *Recreations:* opera, oolong teas of China, fine wine. *Address:* MRC Laboratory of Molecular Biology, Crick Avenue, Cambridge CB2 0QH. *E:* kjp@mrc-lmb.cam.ac.uk; 29 Kingfisher Gardens, Trumpington, Cambridge CB2 9AP.

PATEL, Praful Raojibhai Chaturbhai; company director; investment adviser in UK, since 1962; Chairman, Asia Fund Ltd, 1984–2011; *b* Jinja, Uganda, 7 March 1939; *s* of Raojibhai Chaturbhai Patel, Sojitra, Gujarat, India, and Maniben Jivabhai Lalaji Patel, Dharmaj, Gujarat; unmarried. *Educ:* Government Sec. Sch., Jinja, Uganda; London Inst. of World Affairs, attached to University Coll., London (Extra Mural Dept). Queen's Scout, 1956. Sec., Uganda Students Union, 1956–58; Deleg. to Internat. Youth Assembly, New Delhi, 1958; awarded two travel bursaries for visits to E, Central and S Africa, and Middle East, to study and lecture on politics and economics; arrived in Britain as student, then commenced commercial activities, 1962; increasingly involved in industrial, cultural and educational projects affecting immigrants in Britain. Spokesman for Asians in UK following restriction of immigration resulting from Commonwealth Immigrants Act 1968; Hon. Sec., All Party Parly Cttee on UK Citizenship, 1968–82; Founder and Council Mem., UK Immigration Advisory Service, 1970–82; Mem., Uganda Resettlement Bd, 1972–74; Hon. Secretary: Uganda Evacuees Resettlement Advisory Trust, 1974–2000; IBCE, 1980–82; Mem., Indian Govt Consultative Cttee on non-resident Indian investments, 1986–91; Pres., Nava Kala India Socio-Cultural Centre, London, 1962–75; Chm. Bd of Trustees, Swaminarayan Hindu Mission, UK, 1970–76 (Advr to HH Pramukh Swami Maharaj); Jt Convener, Asian Action Cttee, 1976; Director: Shree Ganesh Foundn, 1999–; Indo-British Cultural Exchange, 2002– (Hon. Sec., 1980–82); Chm. and Trustee, Manava Trust, 1979–; Trustee: Charutar Arogya Mandal Trust, 1980–; India Overseas Trust, 2002–; Kailas Manasarovar Trust, 2002–. Gen. Sec., Internat. Ayurveda Foundn, 2003–; Hon. Sec., Biomedical Foundn of India, 2010–. Contested (Lab) Brent North, 1987. Producer: ballet, Nritya Natika Ramayana, 1982; film, Kailas Manasarovar Yatra, 1997. Asian Times Award, 1986; Neasden Swaminarayan Mandir Award. *Publications:* articles in newspapers and journals regarding immigration and race relations, natural health issues, politics and business. *Recreations:* cricket, campaigning and lobbying, current affairs, promoting traditional Ayurveda medicines and inter-faith co-operation, collection of 2005 Ganesh Murtis and Hindu artefacts. *Address:* 60 Bedford Court Mansions, Bedford Avenue, WC1B 3AD. *T:* (020) 7580 0897, *Fax:* (020) 7436 2418; Praful Patel Associates, 3rd Floor, Readymoney Mansion, 43 Veer Nariman Road, Bombay 400023, India. *T:* (22) 2049248, *Fax:* (22) 2048938. *E:* prcpatel@vsnl.com.

PATEL, Rt Hon. Priti; PC 2015; MP (C) Witham, since 2010; Minister of State (Minister for Employment), Department for Work and Pensions, since 2015; *b* London, 29 March 1972; *d* of Sushil K. Patel and Anjana Patel; *m* 2004, Alex Sawyer; one *s*. *Educ:* Westfield Girls' Sch., Watford; Keele Univ. (BA Econs); Univ. of Essex (Dip. British Govt). Dep. Press Sec. to Rt Hon. William Hague, MP, 1997–2000; Associate Dir, Shandwick, 2000–03; Corporate Relns Manager, Diageo plc, 2003–07; Dir, Corporate Communications, Weber Shandwick, 2007–10. Exchequer Sec., HM Treasury, 2014–15. *Recreations:* cricket, horseracing, rock music, travel. *Address:* House of Commons, SW1A 0AA. *T:* (020) 7219 3000. *E:* priti.patel.mp@parliament.uk.

PATEL, Rashmita; *see* Shukla, R.

PATEL, Sandip; QC 2014; *b* Kampala, Uganda; *s* of Suryakant and Savita Patel; *m* 1996, Sophie Ramsay; one *s* one *d*. *Educ:* Rooks Heath Sch.; Essex Univ. (LLB Hons). Called to the Bar, Middle Temple, 1991; in practice as a barrister, 1992–. *Publications:* (contrib.) Electronic Evidence, 3rd edn. *Recreations:* cricket, walking the dog, music. *Address:* Furnival Chambers, 30–32 Furnival Street, EC4A 1JQ.

PATEL, Sarika; Partner, Zeus Caps, since 2012; *b* Bombay, 10 Aug. 1965; *d* of Jagdish Sharma and Usha Sharma; *m* 1991, Bijendra Patel; one *s*. *Educ:* Univ. of Bombay (BCom 1985; LLB 1988); Univ. of Paisley (Postgrad. Dip. Business 2002). Chartered Accountant 1988; Chartered Marketer 1996. C. M. Shah and Co. Chartered Accts, 1985–88; Audit Officer, Pricewaterhouse, 1988–89; Product Manager—Water Purifiers, and Financial Analyst and Manager Budgets, Eureka Forbes Ltd, India, 1989–94; Business Advr, North Ayrshire Council, 1996–2000; Innovation Manager, Univ. of Paisley, 2000–02; Dir, Innovation and Sectors, London Develt Agency, 2002–05; Hd, Technol., Grant Thornton UK, 2005–08; Gp Dir, MW Corp., 2008–12, and CEO, Klopman Europe, 2008–11. Non-exec. Dir, Imperial NHS Trust, 2013–. Trustee, Royal Instn of GB, 2013–. Vice Chm., Centrepoint, 2007–. Mem. Court, Univ. of Greenwich, 2010–13. *Recreations:* reading, walking, tennis, cooking, theatre, family. *Address:* 4 Thames Crescent, W4 2RU. *T:* (020) 8995 2422. *E:* sarika.sharmapatel@gmail.com.

PATEL, Vijaykumar Chhotabhai Kalidas; principal Co-founder, 1984, and Chief Executive Officer, since 1989, Waymade Healthcare plc and associated companies; *b* Kenya, 10 Nov. 1949; *s* of late Chhotabhai and of Shantaben Patel; *m* 1975, Smita Kanaiyalal Patel; two *s*. *Educ:* Leicester Sch. of Pharmacy (BSc Pharm.). MRPS 1973. Opened first pharmacy, Leigh-on-Sea, Essex, 1975, subseq. expanded to chain of pharmacies, then supplier of pharmaceuticals; (with B. C. Patel) co-founded: Waymade Healthcare plc, 1984; Amdipharm, 2002; Atnahs Pharma, 2013; Invest and Develop property co., 2013; owner, Driven Worldwide, 2013. CCMI 2002; FRSA. Mem., Lions Clubs Internat. (Melvin Jones Fellow). Mem., Bd of Govs, De Montfort Univ., 2014–. Hon. DSc: Anglia Ruskin, 2008; De Montfort, 2010. (Jtly) UK Entrepreneur of the Year, 2001; Alumnus of Yr, De Montfort Univ., 2012. *Recreations:* collector of watches and clocks, cars, keep fit, travelling, swimming, hill-walking, public speaking.

See also B. C. Patel.

PATEMAN, Prof. Carole, DPhil; FBA 2007; Professor of Political Science, University of California, Los Angeles, 1990–2011, now Distinguished Professor Emeritus; Hon. Professor, University of Cardiff, since 2008; *b* Maresfield, Sussex; *d* of Ronald and Beatrice Bennett. *Educ:* Lewes Grammar Sch.; Ruskin Coll., Oxford (Dip. Pol Sci. and Econs (Dist.) 1965); Lady Margaret Hall, Oxford (BA PPE 1967; DPhil 1971). Jun. Res. Fellow, Somerville Coll., Oxford, 1970–72; Reader in Govt, Univ. of Sydney, 1980–89. Vis. Prof. of Pol Sci., Stanford Univ., 1980; Vis. Prof. of Politics, Princeton Univ., 1985–86; Kirsten Hesselgren Prof., Swedish Council for Res. in Humanities and Social Scis, 1988–90; Adjunct Prof., Res. Sch. of Social Scis, ANU, 1993–2000; Vis. Prof., UBC, 1996; Res. Prof., Sch. of Eur. Studies, Cardiff Univ., 2006–08. President: Internat. Pol Sci. Assoc., 1991–94; Amer. Pol Sci. Assoc., 2010–11. Fellow, Univ. of Manchester, 1997. FASSA 1980; Fellow, Amer. Acad. Arts and Scis 1996; FAcSS (AcSS 2010). Hon. DLitt: ANU, 1998; NUI 2005; Hon. DSSc Helsinki, 2006. Lifetime Achievement Award, 2004, Special Recognition Award 2013, UK Pol Studies Assoc.; Johan Skytte Prize in Pol Sci., Skytte Foundn, 2012. *Publications:* Participation and Democratic Theory, 1970 (trans. Japanese, Portuguese, Chinese); The Problem of Political Obligation, 1979, 2nd edn 1985; (ed jtly) Women, Social Science and Public Policy, 1985; (ed jtly) Feminist Challenges: social and political theory, 1986, 2013; The Sexual Contract, 1988 (Victoria Schuck Award, 1989, Benjamin Lippincott Award, 2005, Amer. Pol Assoc.) (trans. French, Spanish, Portuguese, Italian, Serbian, Slovak, Croatian, Korean, Chinese); The Disorder of Women, 1989 (trans. Croatian, Japanese); (ed jtly) Feminist Interpretations and Political Theory, 1991; (ed jtly) Justice and Democracy, 2004; (with C. Mills) Contract and Domination, 2007; (ed with Matthew Murray) Basic Income Worldwide: horizons of reform, 2012. *Relevant publications:* (ed jtly) Illusions of Consent: engaging with Carole Pateman, 2008; (ed jtly) Carole Pateman: democracy, feminism and welfare, 2011. *Address:* Department of Political Science, University of California, Los Angeles, Box 951472, Los Angeles, CA 90095–1472, USA.

PATEMAN-JONES, Alan John; rare breed farmer, Poole Batten Farm; *b* Ilford, Essex, 20 Sept. 1958; *s* of Edward and Violet Jones; *m* 2006, Jacqueline; two *s*. *Educ:* Westminster City Sch.; King's Coll., London (BA Hons Geog. 1984). Joined Army 1978; Officer Cadet, RMA Sandhurst, 1978–80; Young Officers' Course, RSME, 1980; Troop Comdr, 24 Field Sqdn, 1981, 10 Field Sqdn, 1984–86; OC 4 Field Sqdn, 21 Engr Regt, 1986–88, RE; Paymasters' Course, RAPC, 1988; 29 Commando Regt, RA, 1988–89; 4th/7th Dragoon Guards, 1989–90. National Westminster Bank: Holborn Circus and City Regl Office, 1991–92; Change Mgt, NatWest Tower, 1992–93; Exec. Asst, Business Develt Dir, 1993–94; Customer Service Design Team, 1994–95; Sen. Manager, Mgt Consultancy Services, Retail Banking Team, Coopers & Lybrand, 1995–97; Exec. Consultant and Partner, Mgt Consultancy Services, Retail Banking Team, Ernst & Young, 1997–2000; Lloyds TSB: Dir, Affluent Sector, Wealth Div., 2000–01; Chief Exec., UK Wealth Mgt, 2001–02; Man. Dir, Customer and Staff Offers and Chm., UK Wealth Mgt, 2002–04; Partner, Mgt Consultancy Services and Hd, Retail Banking, 2004–06, Man. Partner, Financial Services, N Europe, Middle East, India and Africa, 2006–08, Ernst & Young; Dir Gen., Commonwealth War Graves Commn, 2010–14. Non-exec. Chm., Nolan Redsham Ltd, 2014–. Co-opted Mem., Action for Children, 2009– (Trustee, Pension Fund, 2011–14); Trustee, English Heritage Foundn, 2014–15. *Recreations:* fell walking, reading, Private Pilot's Licence (H), gardening, four border collies. *Address:* Poole Batten Farm, Burrington, Umberleigh, Devon EX37 9NG.

PATERSON, Alasdair Talbert; Librarian, 1994–2006, also Director of Information Services, 2006, University of Exeter; *b* 22 Oct. 1947; *s* of Talbert Robertson Paterson and Alys Morton Paterson (*née* Campbell); *m* 1st, 1967, Corinne Brenda Norton (marr. diss. 1975); one *s*; 2nd, 1976, Ann Mary Cecilia Mulheirn; one *s* one *d*. *Educ:* Leith Acad.; Royal High Sch., Edinburgh; Univ. of Edinburgh (MA 1st cl. Hons 1970); Univ. of Sheffield (MA 1972). ALAI 1990. Asst Librarian, Univ. of Liverpool, 1972–86; Deputy Librarian: UC Cork, 1986–89; Univ. of Sheffield, 1989–94. Mem., Devon and Exeter Instn, 1994–. Eric Gregory Award, Soc. of Authors, 1975. *Publications:* Bibliography of Studies in Regional Industrial Development, 1978; The Floating World, 1984; Brief Lives, 1987; On the Governing of Empires, 2010; Elsewhere or Thereabouts, 2014; articles in prof. jls. *Recreations:* literature, the arts, travel, gardening, walking, watching sport, boules. *Address:* Taddyforde House North, New North Road, Exeter EX4 4AT. *T:* (01392) 430498. *Club:* Isca Pétanque (Exeter).

PATERSON, Alexander Craig, (Alastair), CBE 1987; FREng; Senior Partner, Bullen and Partners, Consulting Engineers, 1969–88, retired (Partner 1960–69); *b* 15 Jan. 1924; *s* of Duncan McKellar Paterson and Lavinia (*née* Craig); *m* 1947, Betty Hannah Burley (*d* 2008); two *s* two *d*. *Educ:* Glasgow High Sch.; Royal Coll. of Science and Technol. (ARCST); Glasgow Univ. (BSc). FICE 1963; FIMechE 1964; FIStructE 1970; FREng (FEng 1983); FCIArb 1968. Commnd REME, 1944; served India and Burma, attached Indian Army, 1944–47. Engineer: with Merz and McLellan, 1947–58; with Taylor Woodrow, 1958–60. Mem., Overseas Projects Bd, 1984–87. Institution of Structural Engineers: Mem. Council, 1976–89; Vice Pres., 1981–84; Pres., 1984–85; Institution of Civil Engineers: Mem. Council, 1978–81 and 1982–91; Vice-Pres., 1985–88; Pres., 1988–89. Pres., British Section, Société des Ingénieurs et Scientifiques de France, 1980; Chm., British Consultants Bureau, 1978–80; Member: Council, British Bd of Agrément, 1982–95; Engrg Council, 1987–90. Mem. Court, Cranfield Inst. of Technol., 1970–80. Hon. DSc Strathclyde, 1989. *Publications:* professional and technical papers in engrg jls. *Recreation:* gardening. *Address:* Willows, The Byeway, West Wittering, Chichester, West Sussex PO20 8LJ. *T:* (01243) 514199. *Club:* Caledonian.

PATERSON, Bill; *see* Paterson, W. T.

PATERSON, Clare, (Mrs John Wyver); Commissioning Editor (formerly Commissioning Executive), BBC Documentaries, since 2009; *b* Kent, 14 June 1957; *d* of Peter Paterson and Beryl Paterson (*née* Johnson); *m* 1995, John Wyver; two *s* one *d*. *Educ:* Sydenham High Sch.; St Anne's Coll., Oxford (BA Classics and Modern Langs). Trainee with EU, 1978–79; Researcher/Asst Producer, BBC, 1979–83; in-house producer, Channel 4 Television, 1983–86; Dir/Exec. Producer, 1986–89, Exec. Producer, 1989–2004, BBC; Hd of Documentaries, RDF TV, 2004–09. Trustee, Horniman Mus. and Dir, Horniman Mus. Enterprises, 2002–. Gov., Graveney Sch., 2011–. *Publications:* Grow Up: 101 things your child needs to know before leaving home, 2005. *Recreations:* painting, crime fiction, my children. *E:* clarepaterson21@hotmail.com.

PATERSON, Prof. Sir Dennis (Craig), Kt 1976; MB, BS 1953, MD 1983; FRCS, FRACS; Director and Chief Orthopaedic Surgeon, Adelaide Children's Hospital, 1966–95; Consultant Orthopaedic Surgeon, Queen Victoria Hospital, 1968–95; Clinical Associate Professor, University of Adelaide, since 1988; *b* 14 Oct. 1930; *s* of Gilbert Charles Paterson and Thelma Drysdale Paterson; *m* 1st, 1955, Mary (*d* 2004), *d* of Frederick Mansell Hardy; one *s* three *d*; *m* 2nd, 2006, Katalin Clara Maria Line. *Educ:* Collegiate Sch. of St Peter; Univ. of Adelaide (MB, BS 1953; MD 1983). FRCS 1958, FRACS 1961. Res. Med. Officer: Royal Adelaide Hosp., 1954; Adelaide Children's Hosp., 1955; Registrar, Robert Jones & Agnes Hunt Orthop. Hosp., Oswestry, Shropshire, 1958–60; Royal Adelaide Hospital: Sen. Registrar, 1960–62; Cons. Orthop. Surg., 1964–86; Cons. Orthop. Surg., Repatriation Gen. Hosp., Adelaide, 1962–70; Adelaide Children's Hospital: Asst Hon. Orthop. Surg., 1964–66; Sen. Hon. Orthop. Surg., 1966–70; Mem. Bd of Management, 1976–84; Chm., Med. Adv. Cttee, 1976–84; Chm., Med. Staff Cttee, 1976–84. Amer./British/Canadian Trav. Prof., 1966. Chairman: Trauma Systems Cttee for SA, 1994–2001; SA Road Safety Consultative Council, 1994–2001; Southern Partnership, 1998–2002. Archbishop's Appeal Cttee, 1994–2002; Member: Nat. Road Trauma Adv. Council, 1990–95; Bd of Management, McLaren Vale and Fleurieu Visitors Centre, 1995–2002 (Chm., 1998–2002). Royal Australasian Coll. of Surgeons: Mem., Bd of Orthop. Surg., 1974–82, 1984–85 (Chm., 1977–82); Mem., Court of Examnrs, 1974–84; Mem., SA Cttee, 1974–78; Fellow: British Orthopaedic Assoc.; RSocMed; Member: Aust. Orthopaedic Assoc. (Censor-in-Chief, 1976–80; Dir, Continuing Educn, 1982–85); AMA; Internat. Scoliosis Res. Soc.; SICOT (Aust. Nat. Delegate, 1975–84, First Vice-Pres., 1984–87; Pres., 1987–90); Paediatric Orthopaedic Soc.; W Pacific Orthopaedic Soc.; Hon. Mem., American Acad. of Orthopaedic Surgeons, 1981. Pres., Crippled Children's Assoc. of South Australia Inc., 1970–84 (Mem. Council, 1966–84). Mem., Cook Soc., 2004–. Life Mem., S Aust. Cricket Assoc. President: Commonwealth Club of Adelaide, 2011–12 (Vice-Pres., 2009–11); Probus Club of Glen Osmond, 2011–12. Queen's Jubilee Medal, 1977. *Publications:* over 80 articles in Jl of Bone and Joint Surg., Clin. Orthopaedics and Related Res., Aust. and NZ Jl of Surg., Med. Jl of Aust., Western Pacific Jl of Orthop. Surg. *Recreations:* reading, golf, gardening. *Address:* 26 Queen Street, Glenunga, SA 5064, Australia. *T:* (8) 83792669, *Fax:* (8) 83796449. *Clubs:* Adelaide, Royal Adelaide Golf, Adelaide Oval Bowling (Adelaide).

PATERSON, Douglas McCallum, CBE 2006; Chief Executive, Aberdeen City Council, 1995–2008; *b* 20 Nov. 1949; *s* of Douglas James Paterson and Violet Joan Paterson (*née* McCallum); *m* 1971, Isobel Stewart Beaton; two *d*. *Educ:* Aberdeen Univ. (MA Hons Econs 1971; DipEd 1976; MEd Hons 1981); Aberdeen Coll. of Educn (PGCE Dist. 1976); Robert Gordon Univ. (Dip Mgt 1990, DipM 1990). Manager, John Wood Gp, 1971–75; Grampian

Regional Council: teacher, then head teacher, 1976–86; Advr in Educn, 1986–90; Depute Dir of Educn, 1990–92; Sen. Depute Dir of Educn, 1992–94; Dir of Educn, 1994–95. Hon. LLD Aberdeen, 2005. *Recreations:* walking, theatre, local history and culture, music, D-I-Y, spending time with my grandchildren.

PATERSON, Francis, (Frank), MBE 2013; FCILT; General Manager, Eastern Region, British Rail, York, 1978–85; Member, British Railways (Eastern) Board, 1978–85; Chairman, North Yorkshire Family Practitioner Committee, 1987–91; *b* 5 April 1930; *s* of Francis William Paterson and Cecilia Eliza Reid Brownie; *m* 1950, Grace Robertson (*d* 1996); two *s* two *d*. *Educ:* Robert Gordon's Coll., Aberdeen. Joined LNER as Junior Clerk, 1946; clerical and supervisory positions in NE Scotland; management training, Scotland, 1956–59; various man-management, operating and marketing posts, Scotland, Lincs and Yorks, 1960–66; Operating Supt, Glasgow North, 1967–68; Sales Manager, Edinburgh, 1968; Asst Divl Manager, S Wales, 1968–70; Dir, United Welsh Transport, 1968–70; Harbour Comr, Newport Harbour, 1968–70; Divl Manager, Central Div., Southern Region, 1970–75; Director: Southdown Motor Services Ltd, 1970–73; Brighton, Hove & District Omnibus Co., 1970–73; Dep. Gen. Man., Southern Region, 1975–77; Chief Freight Manager, British Railways Bd, 1977–78. Dir, N Yorks Moors Rly plc, 1993–2000. Vice-Chm., Nat. Railway Mus. Adv. Bd, 1984–2012 (Mem., 1978–2012); Member: CBI Southern Regional Council, 1975–77; CBI Transport Policy Cttee, 1977–78; BBC NE Adv. Council, 1987–91; Chm., BBC Local Radio Adv. Council, Radio York, 1987–91. Vice Chm., York and Selby CPRE, 2002–. President: St Andrews Soc. of York, 1989–90; Rotary Club of York, 2002–03. Trustee: Friends of Nat. Railway Museum, 1988–2012 (Chm., 2002–12); York Civic Trust, 2004–10. Mem. Court, Univ. of York, 1981–92. FCILT (FCIT 1978 (Mem. Council, CIT, 1979–84); FILT 1999). OStJ 1980. *Publications:* papers to transport societies. *Recreations:* transport, travel, hill walking, country pursuits, Scottish culture, enjoying grandchildren. *Address:* Alligin, 97 Main Street, Askham Bryan, York YO23 3QS. *T:* (01904) 708478. *E:* frankpaterson@talktalk.net.

PATERSON, Gil(bert); Member (SNP) Clydebank and Milngavie, Scottish Parliament, since 2011 (Scotland West, 2007–11); Proprietor, Gil's Motor Factors, since 1973; *b* 11 Nov. 1942; *m* (marr. diss.); one *s*. *Educ:* Possilpark Secondary Sch. Company owner and director. Mem., Strathclyde Regl Council, 1975–78. Mem. (SNP) Central Scotland, Scottish Parlt, 1999–2003; Member: Equal Opportunities Cttee, 2001–03; Procedures Cttee, 2003; Convener, Cross-Party Gp on Men's Violence against Women and Children, 1999–2003. Contested (SNP): Glasgow Central, June 1980; Strathkelvin and Bearsden, 1987; Airdrie and Shotts, Scottish Parlt, 2003. Mem. Nat. Exec., 1995–98, Vice Convenor Fundraising, 2003–, SNP. Mem. Bd, Rape Crisis, 2003–. *Recreations:* reading, climbing, motorcycling, ski-ing, snowboarding, researching oriental ceramics. *Address:* Scottish Parliament, Edinburgh EH99 1SP.

PATERSON, Prof. Ian, PhD; FRS 2005; FRSE; Professor of Organic Chemistry, University of Cambridge, since 2001; Fellow, Jesus College, Cambridge, since 1983; *b* 4 May 1954; *s* of Angus and Violet Paterson; *m* 1977, Nina Kuan. *Educ:* Kirkton High Sch., Dundee; Univ. of St Andrews (BSc 1976); Christ's Coll., Cambridge (PhD 1979). Res. Fellow, Christ's Coll., Cambridge, 1978–79; NATO/SERC Postdoctoral Res. Fellow, Columbia Univ., NY, 1979–80; Lectr in Chemistry, UCL, 1980–83; University of Cambridge: Univ. Lectr in Chemistry, 1983–97; Reader in Organic Chemistry, 1997–2001. Lectures: Organic Reactions, USA, 1992; Sandoz, Basel, 1994; Merck, McGill Univ., 2001; Wyeth-Ayerst, MIT, 2002; H. C. Brown, Purdue Univ., 2004; Novartis, Basel, 2006; Bristol-Myers Squibb, UC Irvine, 2007; Gilead Sciences, Stanford, 2008; AstraZeneca, Univ. of Alberta, 2008; Gassman, Univ. of Minnesota, 2009; Abbott, Univ. of Illinois, 2010; Wilson Baker, Univ. of Bristol, 2014; Inaugural Gilbert Stork, Univ. of Wisconsin-Madison, 2014, Univ. of Pennsylvania, 2015; Novartis Central Europe, 2014. FRSE 2010. Wilsmore Fellow, Univ. of Melbourne, 2010. Royal Society of Chemistry: Meldola Medal and Prize, 1983; Hickinbottom Res. Fellowship, 1989; Bader Prize, 1996; Synthetic Organic Chemistry Award, 2001; Robert Robinson Award, 2004; Tilden Prize, 2009; Natural Product Chemistry Award, 2014; Pfizer Award in Chemistry, 1990, 1993; ICI (AstraZeneca) Award in Organic Chemistry, 1990. *Publications:* extensive articles in jls incl. Angewandte Chemie, Organic Letters, Jl of ACS, Tetrahedron Letters, Chemical Communications. *Recreations:* gardening, travel. *Address:* Department of Chemistry, University of Cambridge, Lensfield Road, Cambridge CB2 1EW.

PATERSON, James Rupert; HM Diplomatic Service, retired; *b* 7 Aug. 1932; *s* of late Major Robert Paterson, MC, Seaforth Highlanders and Mrs Josephine Paterson; *m* 1956, Kay Dineen; two *s* two *d*. *Educ:* Nautical Coll., Pangbourne; RMA, Sandhurst. Commnd RA, 1953 (Tombs Meml Prize); Staff Coll., Camberley, 1963; retd from Army with rank of Major, 1970; joined FCO, 1970; First Sec., Pakistan, 1972; Dep. High Comr, Trinidad and Tobago, 1975; Ambassador to the Mongolian People's Republic, 1982; Consul-General, Istanbul, 1985, Geneva, 1989–92. *Recreations:* reading, travel, golf. *Address:* c/o Barclays Bank, Deal, Kent CT14 6EP.

PATERSON, Janet Lynn, MBE 2014; Chief Executive Officer, British Olympic Foundation, since 2000; Director, Olympic Relations, British Olympic Association, since 2009; *b* Lethbridge, Canada, 21 Aug. 1965; *d* of Gordon Paterson and Beverley Paterson; *m* 1999, Andrew Hibbert. Chef de Mission, Youth Olympic Games, Singapore 2010; Dep. Chef de Mission, Team GB, London 2012; Chef de Mission, Team England, Commonwealth Games, Glasgow 2014. Member, Board: Internat. Inspiration, 2009–15; Spirit of 2012, 2013–. Hon. LLD Bath, 2014. *Address:* British Olympic Association, 60 Charlotte Street, W1T 2NU. *T:* (020) 7842 5704. *E:* jan.paterson@teamgb.com.

PATERSON, Rt Rev. John Campbell; Bishop of Auckland, 1995–2010; Primate and Presiding Bishop of the Anglican Church in Aotearoa, New Zealand and Polynesia, 1998–2004; *b* 4 Jan. 1945; *s* of Thomas Paterson and Lucy Mary Paterson; *m* 1968, Marion Reid Anderson; two *d*. *Educ:* King's Coll., Auckland; Auckland Univ. (BA); St John's Coll., Auckland (LTh (Hons)); Dip. Public Speaking (NZ Speech Bd), 1969. Ordained, deacon, 1969, priest, 1970; Assistant Curate, Whangarei, 1969–71; Vicar, Waimate North Maori Pastorate, 1971–76; Co-Missioner, Auckland Maori Mission, 1976; Chaplain, Queen Victoria Sch., 1976–82; TF Chaplain, 1976–84; Sec., Te Pihopatanga o Aotearoa, 1978–86; Provincial Sec., Church of the Province of NZ, 1986–92; Gen. Sec., Anglican Church in Aotearoa, NZ and Polynesia, 1992–95. Priest in Charge: Parish of Whangarei, 2013–; Parish of Takapuna, 2014–. Chm., ACC, 2002–09 (Mem., 1990–96; Vice-Chm., 1996–2002). *Publications:* (ed) He Toenga Whatiwhatinga, 1983. *Recreations:* music, sport, literature. *Address:* c/o PO Box 87 255, Meadowbank, Auckland 1742, New Zealand.

PATERSON, Prof. Lindsay John, PhD; FBA 2013; FRSE; Professor of Education Policy, University of Edinburgh, since 1998; *b* Hamilton, Scotland, 6 June 1956; *m*; one *s*. *Educ:* Tain Royal Acad.; Univ. of Aberdeen (MA 1978); Univ. of Edinburgh (PhD 1981). Higher SO, 1981–84, Sen. SO, 1984–85, Unit of Statistics, Agricl Res. Council; Lectr in Statistics, Heriot-Watt Univ., 1985–89; Res. Fellow, Centre for Educnl Sociol., Univ. of Edinburgh, 1989–95; Prof. of Educn Policy, Heriot-Watt Univ., 1995–98. FRSE 2004. *Publications:* The Autonomy of Modern Scotland, 1994; (jtly) Politics and Society in Scotland, 1996, 2nd edn 1998; A Diverse Assembly: the debate on a Scottish Parliament, 1998; (jtly) The Scottish Electorate: the 1997 General Election and beyond, 1999; (with F. Bechhofer) Principles of Research Design in the Social Sciences, 2000; Crisis in the Classroom: the exam debacle and the way ahead for Scottish education, 2000; Education and the Scottish Parliament, 2000; (jtly) New Scotland, New Politics?, 2001; Scottish Education in the Twentieth Century, 2003; (jtly) Living in Scotland: social and economic change since 1980, 2004; chapters in scholarly books, 1991–; articles in jls incl. Biometrika, British Educnl Res. Jl, British Jl of Sociol., Internat. Statistical Rev., Jl of Royal Statistical Soc., Oxford Rev. of Educn, Political Qly, Regl and Federal Studies, Scot. Histl Rev., Sociol. of Educn, Sociol Res. Online, Sociol Rev. *Recreations:* conversation, reading, listening to music. *Address:* School of Social and Political Science, University of Edinburgh, Chrystal Macmillan Building, 15A George Square, Edinburgh EH8 9LD. *T:* (0131) 651 6380. *E:* lindsay.paterson@ed.ac.uk.

PATERSON, Prof. Michael Stewart, PhD; FRS 2001; Professor of Computer Science, University of Warwick, 1979–2009, now Emeritus; *b* 13 Sept. 1942. *Educ:* Trinity Coll., Cambridge (BA 1964; PhD 1968). Lectr, 1971–74, Reader, 1974–79, in Computer Sci., Univ. of Warwick. *Address:* Department of Computer Science, University of Warwick, Coventry CV4 7AL.

PATERSON, Rt Hon. Owen (William); PC 2010; MP (C) North Shropshire, since 1997; *b* 24 June 1956; *s* of late Alfred Paterson and Cynthia Paterson (*née* Owen); *m* 1980, Hon. Rose Emily Ridley (*see* Hon. R. E. Paterson); two *s* one *d*. *Educ:* Radley Coll.; Corpus Christi Coll., Cambridge (MA Hist.). British Leather Co.: Sales Dir, 1980; Man. Dir, 1993–97. Pres., European Tanners' Confedn, 1996–97. Contested (C) Wrexham, 1992. Opposition Whip, 2000–01; PPS to Leader of Opposition, 2001–03; Shadow Minster for DEFRA, 2003–05; Shadow Minister of State for Transport, 2005–07; Shadow Sec. of State for NI, 2007–10; Secretary of State: for NI, 2010–12; for Envmt, Food and Rural Affairs, 2012–14. *Recreations:* travel, history, trees, riding, hunting, racing, poultry. *Address:* House of Commons, SW1A 0AA.

PATERSON, Peter, WS; Sheriff of Lothian and Borders at Selkirk, since 2013; *b* 11 Oct. 1954; *s* of Dr Robert Craig Paterson and Margaret Paterson; *m* 1993, Dorothy Taylor; one step *d*. *Educ:* Cumnock Acad.; Heriot-Watt Univ. (BA); Univ. of Edinburgh (LLB); Nottingham Law Sch., Nottingham Trent Univ. (LLM). WS 1998. Partner: Skene Edwards WS, 1986–2000; Tods Murray LLP, 2000–12; pt-time Chm., Employment Tribunals, 1993–2000; temp. Sheriff, 1993–2005; pt-time Sheriff, 2005–12; All-Scotland Floating Sheriff, 2012–13. *Recreation:* running. *Address:* 448 Lanark Road, Edinburgh EH14 5BB. *T:* (0131) 441 3617. *E:* sheriffpaterson@me.com.

PATERSON, Rt Rev. Robert Mar Erskine; *see* Sodor and Man, Bishop of.

PATERSON, Hon. Rose Emily; DL; Chairman, Aintree Racecourse, since 2014 (Director, 2005–14); *b* Newcastle-upon-Tyne, 13 Aug. 1956; *d* of 4th Viscount Ridley, KG, GCVO, TD and Anne Ridley; *m* 1980, Rt Hon. Owen William Paterson, *qv*; two *s* one *d*. *Educ:* New Hall, Cambridge (BA Hist. 1978; MA 1982). With Sotheby's, 1979–2001; Hd, Paintings Dept, Sotheby's Chester, 1980–86; Paintings Specialist and Consultant, 1986–2001; Art Corresp., Daily Telegraph, 1985–95. Member: Council, Ellesmere Coll., 2012–15; Adv. Bd, University Coll., Shrewsbury, 2014–. Trustee: Develt Fund, Nat. Museums of Merseyside, 1992–95; Weston Park Foundn, 2002– (Chm., 2015–). Mem., Jockey Club, 2013–. DL Shropshire, 2014. *Recreations:* racing, hunting, gardening, medieval history. *Address:* Shellbrook Hill, Ellesmere, Shropshire SY12 9EW. *T:* (01978) 710266. *E:* rose@repaterson.co.uk.

PATERSON, Air Vice-Marshal Ross, CB 2014; OBE 2001; Air Officer Scotland, since 2014; *b* Stockton-on-Tees, 1 June 1961; *s* of late Graham Paterson and of Pauline Hope Paterson (*née* Thursz); *m* 1984, Dr Helen Mary Martindale; two *s*. *Educ:* Kimbolton Sch.; Portsmouth Poly. (BSc Biol. 1982); Univ. of Surrey (PGCE Chem. 1983). Initial officer trng, RAF, 1983; various trng and HR delivery and policy appts, 1984–98; OC Admin. Wing, RAF Leuchars, 1998–2000; Dep. Dir Defence Housing and Tri-Service Act Rev. Teams, 2000–03; CO, RAF Brampton, RAF Wyton and RAF Henlow, 2003–04; Dep. Dir, RAF Personnel Mgt Agency (Remuneration and Benefits), MoD, 2004–05; Dir Service Personnel Policy (Pay and Allowances), MoD, 2006–09; Prime Minister's Strategy Unit, Cabinet Office, 2009; Dir Personnel Policy (RAF), HQ Air Comd, 2009–11; Hd, Financial/Non-Financial Conditions of Service Rev., MoD, 2011; Chief Exec., Service Personnel and Veterans Agency, later Defence Business Services, 2011–14. Chartered FCIPD 2011. *Recreations:* family, hill walking and ski-ing (ex RAF Mountain Rescue Service), smallholding, beekeeping, reading and the arts, shooting, Scottish country life. *Address:* (office) 25 Learmonth Terrace, Edinburgh EH4 1NZ.

PATERSON, Steven; MP (SNP) Stirling, since 2015; *b* Stirling, 25 April 1975. *Educ:* Cambusbarron Prim. Sch.; Stirling High Sch.; Univ. of Stirling (BA Hons Hist. and Politics). Visitor Attraction Asst, Argyll, The Isles, Loch Lomond, Stirling and the Trossachs, Scottish Tourist Bd, then VisitScotland, 1997–2006; Media and Communications Manager for Bruce Crawford, MSP, 2006–15. Mem. (SNP), Stirling Council, 2007–15. *Address:* (office) Springfield House, Laurelhill Business Park, Stirling FK7 9JQ. *T:* (01786) 406375. *E:* steven.paterson.mp@parliament.uk.

PATERSON, Dame Vicki (Ann), DBE 2013; Executive Head, Brindishe Federation of Schools, Lewisham, since 2011; Executive Headteacher, Brindishe Manor School, since 2011; *b* Coventry, 1956; *d* of Ronald and Rose Paterson; partner, Gerlinde Achenbach; one *s* one *d*. *Educ:* Univ. of Birmingham (BEd Hons); Inst. of Educn, Univ. of london (DipEd Hons); London South Bank Univ. (MBA (Ed)). Primary sch. teacher, Bexley, 1978–85; Advr for Sci., Bexley Sch. Improvement Team, 1985–89; Headteacher, Brindishe Sch., Lewisham, 1989–2007; Exec. Headteacher, Brindishe Lee and Brindishe Green Schs, 2007–11. Nat. Leader in Educn, 2011–. *Recreation:* walking and cycling along the Thames. *Address:* Brindishe Manor School, Leahurst Road, SE13 5LS. *E:* vickipaterson@brindisheschools.org.

PATERSON, William Alexander; *see* Alexander, Bill.

PATERSON, Prof. William Edgar, OBE 1999; PhD; FRSE; Professor of German and European Politics, 1994–2008, now Emeritus, and Director, Institute for German Studies, 1994–2005 and 2006–08, now Emeritus, University of Birmingham; Honorary Professor of European and German Politics, Aston Centre for Europe, School of Languages and Social Sciences, Aston University, since 2009; *b* Blair Atholl, Perthshire, 26 Sept. 1941; *s* of late William Paterson, FRICS, FLAS, Land Agent, and Winnie Paterson (*née* McIntyre); *m* 1st, 1964, Jacqueline Cramb (*d* 1974); two *s*; 2nd, 1979, Phyllis MacDowell; one *d*, and one step *s* one step *d*. *Educ:* Morrison's Acad.; Univ. of St Andrews (MA, Class Medallist); London Sch. of Econs (S. H. Bailey Schol.; MSc, PhD 1973). FRSE 1994. Lectr in Internat. Relns, Univ. of Aberdeen, 1967–70; University of Warwick: Volkswagen Lectr in German Politics, 1970–75; Sen. Lectr, 1975–82; Reader, 1982–89; Prof. and Chm. of Dept, 1989–90; Salvesen Prof. of Eur. Insts, and Dir, Europa Inst., Univ. of Edinburgh, 1990–94. Vis. Prof., Univ., of Freiburg, 1999. Jt Ed., German Politics, 1991–2001; Member, Editorial Board: Jl Common Mkt Studies, 1991–2003 (Co-Ed., 2003–08); Internat. Affairs, 1993–; Comparative European Politics, 2000–; Perspectives on European Politics and Society, 2004–; Co-Editor: Palgrave European Union Studies, 1992–; New Perspectives in German Studies, 1998–2008; Palgrave Studies in European Union Politics, 2005–; New Perspectives in German Political Studies, 2009–. Mem., ESRC Res. Priorities Bd, 1995–99; Chm., One Europe or Several? prog. for ESRC, 2001–03. Mem., Königswinter Conf. Steering Cttee, 1994–. Chairman: Assoc. for Study of German Politics, 1974–76 (Hon. Vice Pres., 2000); Univ. Assoc. for Contemporary Eur. Studies, 1989–94; Chm., German-British Forum, 2005–13 (Vice-Chm., 1999–2005). Member: Wissenschaftliches Direktorium, Institut für Europäische Politik, Berlin, 1980–;

Lothian Lectures Cttee, 1991–94; Adv. Bd, Centre for British Studies, Humboldt Univ., Berlin, 1997–2008; Kuratorium, Allianz Kulturstiftung, 2000–04. Associate Fellow, RIIA, 1994; FAcSS (AcSS 2000). FRSA 1998. Lifetime Achievement Award: Assoc. for Study of German Politics, 2004; Univ. Assoc. for Contemporary European Studies, 2007; Special Recognition Award, Political Studies Assoc., 2011. Officer's Cross, Order of Merit (FRG), 1999. *Publications:* The SPD and European Integration, 1974; *jointly:* Social Democracy in Post-War Europe, 1974; The Federal Republic of Germany and the European Community, 1987; Government and the Chemical Industry, 1988; Governing Germany, 1991; A History of Social Democracy in Post-War Europe, 1991; The Kohl Chancellorship, 1998; The Future of the German Economy, 2000; Germany's European Diplomacy, 2000; *edited jointly:* Social and Political Movements in Western Europe, 1976; Social Democratic Parties in Western Europe, 1977; Foreign Policy Making in Western Europe, 1978; Sozialdemokratische Parteien in Europa, 1978; The West German Model, 1981; The Future of Social Democracy, 1986; Developments in West German Politics, 1989; Politics in Western Europe Today, 1990; El Futuro de la Social Democracia, 1992; Developments in German Politics, 1992; Rethinking Social Democracy in Western Europe, 1993; Developments in German Politics 2, 1996; Developments in German Politics 3, 2003; Governance in Contemporary Germany, 2005; The German Crisis, 2009; Research Agendas in European Union Studies, 2009; Developments in German Politics 4, 2013; contrib. over 100 articles to edited collections and learned jls. *Recreations:* walking, visiting galleries, collecting 20th century Scottish painting. *Address:* Aston Centre for Europe, School of Languages and Social Sciences, Aston University, Aston Triangle, Birmingham B4 7ET. *T:* (0121) 204 3173; 220 Myton Road, Warwick CV34 6PS. *T:* (01926) 492492. *E:* w.paterson@aston.ac.uk. *Club:* Royal Over-Seas League.

PATERSON, William Tulloch, (Bill); actor, since 1968; *b* 3 June 1945; *s* of late John Paris Paterson and of Ann Tulloch Paterson; *m* 1984, Hildegard Bechtler; one *s* one *d.* *Educ:* Whitehill Sen. Secondary Sch., Glasgow; RSAMD (Fellow, Royal Conservatoire of Scotland (FRSAMD 2005)). First professional engagement, Glasgow Citizens' Theatre, 1968; Asst Dir, Citizens' Theatre for Youth, 1970–72; Founder Mem., 7:84 (Scotland) Theatre Co. *Stage:* The Cheviot, the Stag and the Black Black Oil, 1973; Writer's Cramp, 1977; Whose Life is it Anyway?, Savoy, 1978; Guys and Dolls, NT, 1982; Schweyk, NT, 1983; Death and the Maiden, Royal Court, 1992; Misery, Criterion, 1993; Mongrel's Heart, Edinburgh, 1994; Ivanov, Almeida, 1997; Marriage Play, RNT, 2001; Earthquakes in London, RNT, 2010; And No More Shall We Part, Traverse, 2012; The Low Road, Jerwood, Royal Court, 2013; The Vote, Donmar, 2015; Waiting for Godot, Royal Lyceum, Edinburgh, 2015; *films:* Comfort and Joy, The Killing Fields, 1984; Defence of the Realm, 1985; A Private Function, 1986; The Adventures of Baron Munchausen, 1987; The Witches, 1989; Truly Madly Deeply, 1991; Chaplin, 1992; Richard III, 1996; Hilary and Jackie, 1998; Complicity, 2000; Crush, 2001; Bright Young Things, 2003; Rag Tale, 2005; Amazing Grace, 2006; Miss Potter, 2007; Into the Storm, 2009; Creation, 2009; *television series and serials:* Smiley's People, 1981; Auf Wiedersehen Pet, 1986; The Singing Detective, 1987; Traffik, 1989; Tell Tale Hearts, 1992; Hard Times, 1993; The Writing on the Wall, 1995; The Crow Road, 1996; Wives and Daughters, 1999; The Whistleblower, 2001; Zhivago, 2002; Danielle Cable Eye Witness, 2003; Sea of Souls, 2004–07; Criminal Justice, 2008; Little Dorrit, 2008; Law and Order UK, 2009–10; Spanish Flu: the Forgotten Fallen, 2009; Dr Who, 2010; 37 Days, 2014; Outlander, 2015. *Publications:* Tales from the Backgreen, 2008. *Address:* c/o Gordon and French, 12–13 Poland Street, W1F 8QB.

PATEY, Sir William (Charters), KCMG 2009 (CMG 2005); HM Diplomatic Service, retired; Ambassador to Afghanistan, 2010–12; *b* 11 July 1953; *s* of William Maurice Patey and Christina Kinnell Patey; *m* 1978, Vanessa Carol Morrell; two *s.* *Educ:* Trinity Acad., Edinburgh; Univ. of Dundee (MA Hons). Joined FCO, 1975; MECAS, 1977–78; Commercial Attaché, Abu Dhabi, 1978–81; Second Sec., Tripoli, 1981–84; FCO, 1984–88; First Sec. (Political), Canberra, 1988–92; Dep. Head, UN Dept, 1992–93, Inspector, 1994–95, FCO; Dep. Head of Mission and Consul-Gen., Riyadh, 1995–98; Hd, Middle East Dept, FCO, 1999–2002; Ambassador: to Sudan, 2002–05; to Iraq, 2005–06; to Saudi Arabia, 2007–10. Internat. Affairs Advr, Control Risks, 2012–; Mem. Bd, HSBC Bank Middle East, 2012–. Pres., Khartoum Cheshire Home, 2002–05. Hon. Pres., St Margaret's Film Soc., 1996. Patron: Kids for Kids Charity, 2002– (Trustee, 2002–10); Together for Sudan, 2003–; Trustee, Turquoise Mountain Foundn, 2012–. Chm., Swindon Town FC, 2012–13. Hon. Fellow: New Westminster Coll., Vancouver, 2012; Univ. of Exeter, 2013. Chevalier d'Honneur, Chaîne des Rôtisseurs, 2009. *Recreations:* tennis, theatre, golf.

PATHAK, Kirit Kumar, OBE 1997; Chairman, AB World Foods Ltd, since 2007 (Chairman and Chief Executive, Patak's Foods Ltd, 1990–2007); *b* 12 Sept. 1952; *s* of late Laxmishanker Gopalji and Shanta Gaury Pathak; *m* 1976, Meena Desai (*see* M. Pathak); two *s* one *d.* *Educ:* Banbury Technical Coll.; Lancaster Poly. Joined Patak's (family Indian food business) at age 17. Member: NW Industrial Develt Bd, 1998–; UK Trade and Investment, 1999–. Mem. Council, Food From Britain, 1998–2003; Vice-Pres., FDF, 2003. Corporate Hon. Fellow, Liverpool John Moores Univ., 2002. Hon. Dr Business Management UCE Birmingham, 1996. *Recreations:* meditation, football, tennis, ski-ing, trekking, horse riding, swimming, cooking, DIY. *Address:* AB World Foods Ltd, Kiriana House, Kiribati Way, Leigh, Lancs WN7 5RS. *T:* (01942) 267000, *Fax:* (01942) 267070. *E:* info@pataksfoods.co.uk.

PATHAK, Meena, OBE 2001; Director, 1981–2007, and Deputy Chairperson, 2000–07, Patak's Foods Ltd; *b* 12 Aug. 1956; *d* of Col Naishad Desai and Dr Hansa Desai; *m* 1976, Kirit Kumar Pathak, *qv*; two *s* one *d.* *Educ:* Bombay Internat. Sch.; hotel mgt and food technol. Bd Mem., Univ. of Central Lancashire, 2000–. Hon. Fellow, Bolton Inst., 2002. Hon. Dr Central Lancashire, 1992. *Publications:* The Flavours of India, 2002; Indian Cooking for Family and Friends, 2003; Meena Pathak Celebrates Indian Cooking, 2007. *Recreations:* meditation, music, arts, reading, sports (cricket). *Address:* Patak's Foods Ltd, AB World Foods Ltd, Kiriana House, Kiribati Way, Leigh, Lancs WN7 5RS. *T:* (01942) 267000, *Fax:* (01942) 267070. *E:* meena.pathak@pataksfoods.co.uk.

PATIENCE, Adèle; *see* Williams, J. A.

PATIENCE, His Honour Andrew; QC 1990; a Circuit Judge, 1999–2011; *b* 28 April 1941; *s* of late William Edmund John Patience and Louise Mary Patience; *m* 1975, Jean Adèle Williams, *qv*; one *s* one *d.* *Educ:* Whitgift School, Croydon; St John's College, Oxford (MA). Called to the Bar, Gray's Inn, 1966; a Recorder, 1986–99; Resident Judge, Maidstone Crown Court, 2000–10; Hon. Recorder of Dover, 2001–. Kent Ambassador, 2011–. Patron, Chatham Dockyard Historical Soc., 2012–; Ambassador, Chatham Historic Dockyard Trust, 2015–. Pres., Kent Volunteers, British Red Cross., 2012–. *Recreations:* mimicry, complaining, horse racing. *Club:* Oxford and Cambridge.

PATIL, Pratibha Devisingh; President of India, 2007–12; *b* Maharashtra, 19 Dec. 1934; *d* of Narayan Rao; *m* 1965, Dr Devisingh Ramsingh Shekhawat; one *s* one *d.* *Educ:* Mooljee Jetha Coll., Jalgaon (MA Pol Sci. and Econs); Govt Law Coll., Bombay (LLB). Formerly in practice as a lawyer, Jalgaon District Court. Mem., Maharashtra Legislative Assembly, 1962–85; Dep. Minister, Public Health, Prohibition, Tourism, Housing and Parly Affairs, 1967–72; Minister: Social Welfare, 1972–74; Public Health and Social Welfare, 1974–75; Prohibition, Rehabilitation and Cultural Affairs, 1975–76; Educn, 1977–78; Leader of the Opposition, 1979–80; Minister: Urban Develt and Housing, 1982–83; Civil Supplies and Social Welfare, 1983–85. Member: Rajya Sabha, 1985–90 (Dep. Chm., 1986–88; Chm., July–Sept. 1987); Lok Sabha, 1991–96. Gov., Rajasthan, 2004–07. Pres., Maharashtra Pradesh Congress Cttee, 1988–90. *Address:* c/o Office of the President, Rashtrapati Bhavan, New Delhi 110 004, India.

PATMORE, Prof. (John) Allan, CBE 1993; Professor of Geography, University of Hull, 1973–91, Professor Emeritus, since 1991; Vice-Chairman, Sports Council, 1988–94 (Member, 1978–94); *b* 14 Nov. 1931; *s* of John Edwin Patmore and Marjorie Patmore; *m* 1956, Barbara Janet Fraser; one *s* two *d.* *Educ:* Harrogate Grammar Sch.; Pembroke Coll., Oxford (MA, BLitt). Served RAF, Educn Br., 1952–54. Department of Geography, University of Liverpool: Tutor, 1954–55; Asst Lectr, 1955–58; Lectr, 1958–69; Sen. Lectr, 1969–73; University of Hull: Dean of Social Science, 1979–81; Pro-Vice-Chancellor, 1982–85. Visiting Professor: Univ. of Southern Illinois, 1962–63; Univ. of Canterbury, NZ, 1978. Pres. 1979–80, Trustee 1979–88, Hon. Mem., 1991, Geographical Assoc.; Pres., Sect. E, BAAS, 1987–88. Pres., N Yorks Moors Assoc., 1993–2000; Member: N York Moors National Park Cttee, 1977–92; Nat. Parks Review Panel, 1990–91; Countryside Commn, 1992–98; Inland Waterways Amenity Adv. Council, 1993–94; Bd, Nat. Lottery New Opportunities Fund, 1998–2004. Friends of National Railway Museum: Chm., 1992–2002; Vice-Chm., 2002–08; Chm., Executive, 2002–08; Pres., 2008–; Mem. Adv. Cttee, Nat. Railway Mus., 1988–2004. Methodist Local Preacher, 1959–. JP Hull, 1975–2001. Hon. DLitt Loughborough, 1993. *Publications:* Land and Leisure, 1970; People, Place and Pleasure, 1975; Recreation and Resources, 1983; Leisure and Mission, 2000. *Recreations:* pursuing railway history, enjoying the countryside.

PATNICK, Julietta, CBE 2005; Director, NHS Cancer Screening Programmes, 1995–2015; *b* 10 June 1957; *d* of Barry Freeman and Shirley (*née* Samuels); *m* 1978, Michael Patnick; one *s* one *d.* *Educ:* Univ. of Sheffield (BA Hons Ancient Hist. and Classical Civilisation 1978). FFPH 2002. Co-ordinator, Breast Screening, Trent Regl HA, 1987–90; Nat. Co-ordinator, NHS Breast Screening Prog., 1990–94. Member: Care Record Develt Bd, 2004–07; Medicines for Women's Health Expert Working Gp, 2006–13. Trustee, Cavendish Cancer Care, 2006–12. Hon. Fellow in Public Health, 2004, Vis. Prof. in Cancer Screening, 2008–, Oxford Univ. Hon. Mem., RCR, 2009. Hon. FRCSEd 2015. DUniv Sheffield Hallam, 2011; Hon. MD Sheffield, 2011; Hon. DSc Loughborough, 2012. *Recreations:* spending time with family, reading classics and history, eating good food in good company. *Address:* Cancer Epidemiology Unit, University of Oxford, Richard Doll Building, Roosevelt Drive, Oxford OX3 7LF. *E:* julietta.patnick@ceu.ox.ac.uk.

PATON, Rt Hon. Lady; Ann Paton; PC 2007; a Senator of the College of Justice in Scotland, since 2000; *d* of James McCargow and Ann Dunlop or McCargow; *m* 1974, Dr James Y. Paton; no *c.* *Educ:* Laurel Bank Sch.; Univ. of Glasgow (MA 1972; LLB 1974). Admitted to the Scottish Bar, 1977. Standing Junior Counsel: to the Queen's and Lord Treasurer's Remembrancer (excluding *Ultimus Haeres*), 1979; in Scotland to Office of Fair Trading, 1981; QC (Scot.) 1990; Advocate Depute, 1992–94. Member: Criminal Injuries Compensation Bd, 1995–2000; Parole Bd, 2003–07. Dir, Scottish Council of Law Reporting, 1995–2000. Mem. Governing Body, Queen Margaret UC, 2001–04. *Publications:* Map of Sheriffdoms and Sheriff Court Districts in Scotland, 1977, 2nd edn 1980; (Jt Asst Editor) Gloag and Henderson, Law of Scotland, 8th edn 1980, to 10th edn 1995; (with R. G. McEwan) A Casebook on Damages in Scotland, 1983, 2nd edn as Damages in Scotland (sole author), 1989, re-titled Damages for Personal Injuries in Scotland, 1997; Faculty Digest Supplement 1971–1980, 1995; contrib. Scottish Current Law Statutes, Session Cases, Scots Law Times, Green's Reparation Bulletin, and Judicial Studies in Scotland Equal Treatment Bench Bk. *Recreations:* sailing, tennis, cycling, music, art.

PATON, Alasdair Chalmers; Chief Executive, Scottish Environment Protection Agency, 1995–2000; *b* Paisley, 28 Nov. 1944; *o s* of David Paton and Margaret Elizabeth Paton (*née* Chalmers); *m* 1969, Zona Gertrude Gill; one *s* one *d.* *Educ:* John Neilson Instn, Paisley; Univ. of Glasgow (BSc). Assistant Engineer: Clyde Port Authy, 1967–71; Dept of Agric. and Fisheries for Scotland, 1971–72; Sen. Engineer, Scottish Develt Dept, 1972–77; Engineer, Public Works Dept, Hong Kong Govt, 1977–80; Scottish Development Department: Sen. Engineer, 1980–84; Principal Engineer, 1984–87; Dep. Chief Engineer, 1987–91; Dir and Chief Engineer, Water and Waste Directorate, Scottish Office Envmt Dept, 1991–95. *Recreations:* Rotary, sailing, golf. *Address:* Oriel House, Academy Square, Limekilns, Fife KY11 3HN. *Club:* Royal Scots (Edinburgh).

PATON, Alexander Charles, (Charlie), RDI 2012; Director, Seawater Greenhouse Ltd, since 2000; *b* Camberley, Surrey, 27 June 1950; *s* of Eric Giles and Joan Paton; *m* 1984, Marlene McKibbin; two *s* one *d.* *Educ:* Bryanston Sch.; Central Sch. of Art and Design. Founder and Director: Smallworks, 1974–; Light Works Ltd, 1979–. Liveryman, Gardeners' Co., 2008–. *Recreations:* forestry, gardening. *Address:* 118 Forest Road, E8 3BH.

PATON, Ann; *see* Paton, Rt Hon. Lady.

PATON, Charlie; *see* Paton, A. C.

PATON, Douglas Shaw F.; *see* Forrester-Paton.

PATON, Maj.-Gen. Douglas Stuart, CBE 1983 (MBE 1961); FFPH; Commander Medical HQ BAOR, 1983–85; retired 1986; *b* 3 March 1926; *s* of Stuart Paton and Helen Kathleen Paton (*née* Hooke); *m* 1957, Jennifer Joan Land (*d* 2014); two *d.* *Educ:* Sherborne; Bristol University. MB ChB 1951; FFPH (FFPHM 1989; FFCM 1982, MFCM 1973). Commissioned RAMC, 1952; served Middle East (Canal Zone), Malaya, Hong Kong and UK, 1952–61; 16 Para Bde, 1961–66; jssc 1966; CO Mil. Hosp., Terendak, Malaysia, 1967–70; MoD, 1970–73; CO Cambridge Mil. Hosp., Aldershot, 1973–76; rcds 1977; DDMS HQ 1 (BR) Corps, 1978–81; Dep. Dir-Gen., Army Med. Services, MoD, 1981–83. QHP 1981–86. Hon. Col 221 (Surrey) Field Amb. RAMC(V), TA, 1988–92. Chm., RAMC Assoc., 1988–98. Mem. Bd of Governors, Moorfields Eye Hosp., 1988–91. CStJ 1986. *Publications:* contribs to Jl RAMC. *Recreations:* golf, travel, opera, gardening. *Address:* Brampton, Springfield Road, Camberley, Surrey GU15 1AB.

PATON, Hon. (Frederick) Ranald N.; *see* Noel-Paton.

PATON, Ven. Michael John Macdonald; Archdeacon of Sheffield, 1978–87, Archdeacon Emeritus, since 1988; *b* 25 Nov. 1922; *s* of late Rev. William Paton, DD, and Grace Mackenzie Paton (*née* Macdonald); *m* 1952, Isobel Margaret Hogarth (*d* 2008); one *s* four *d.* *Educ:* Repton School; Magdalen Coll., Oxford (MA). Indian Army, 1942–46; HM Foreign Service, 1948–52; Lincoln Theological Coll., 1952–54; Deacon 1954, priest 1955; Curate, All Saints', Gosforth, Newcastle upon Tyne, 1954–57; Vicar, St Chad's, Sheffield, 1957–67; Chaplain, United Sheffield Hosps, 1967–70; Vicar, St Mark's, Broomhill, Sheffield, and Chaplain, Weston Park Hosp., 1970–78. *Publications:* contrib. to: Essays in Anglican Self-criticism, 1958; More Sermons from Great St Mary's, 1971; Religion and Medicine, 1976; Mud and Stars, 1991. *Recreations:* music, birdwatching.

PATON, William; Director, TÜV Süddeutschland, 2001–04; *b* 29 Nov. 1941; *s* of Matthew Paton and Elizabeth Paton (*née* Shearer); *m* 1964, Elizabeth Anne Marr; two *s.* *Educ:* Douglas Ewart Sch., Newton Stewart; Univ. of Glasgow (BSc Hons Physics). Seismologist, SSL Ltd, 1964; Mgt Trainee, Colvilles Ltd, 1965; National Engineering Laboratory: scientific posts, 1965–80; Dir of Ops, 1990–95; Dir, 1995–97; Chief Exec., TÜV Product Service Ltd, 1997–2001. Dir and Sen. Exec., Nat. Engrg Assessment Gp, 1997–. Patents relating to improvements in carbon fibre processing technol., engrg designs and sports equipment. *Publications:* various articles in technical jls. *Recreations:* golf, travel, bridge. *Address:* 2 Wester Balrymonth, St Andrews, Fife KY16 8NN. *T:* (01334) 472131.

PATON WALSH, Jill, CBE 1996; self-employed author, since 1966; *b* 29 April 1937; *d* of John Llewelyn Bliss and Patricia Paula DuBern; *m* 1st, 1961, Antony Paton Walsh (separated; he *d* 2003); one *s* two *d*; 2nd, 2004, John Rowe Townsend (*d* 2014). *Educ:* St Michael's Convent, Finchley; St Anne's Coll., Oxford (BA English; MA; DipEd). Schoolteacher, Enfield Girls' Grammar Sch., 1959–62. Arts Council Creative Writing Fellowship, Brighton Poly., 1976–77, 1977–78; Gertrude Clark Whitall Meml Lectr, Library of Congress, 1978; vis. faculty mem., Center for Children's Lit., Simmons Coll., Boston, Mass, 1978–86. A Judge, Whitbread Lit. Award, 1984; Chm., Cambridge Book Assoc., 1987–89; Mem. Council, Soc. of Authors, 1999– (Mem., Mgt Cttee, 1986–88); Member: Cttee, Children's Writers' and Illustrators' Gp; Adjunct British Bd, Children's Literature New England. FRSL 1996. *Publications: fiction:* Farewell, Great King, 1972; Lapsing, 1986; A School for Lovers, 1989; The Wyndham Case, 1993; Knowledge of Angels, 1994; A Piece of Justice, 1995; The Serpentine Cave, 1997; Thrones, Dominations (completion of novel by Dorothy L. Sayers), 1998; A Desert in Bohemia, 2000; Presumption of Death (with material by Dorothy L. Sayers), 2002; Debts of Dishonour, 2006; The Bad Quarto, 2007; The Attenbury Emeralds, 2010, The Late Scholar, 2013 (based on the characters of Dorothy L. Sayers); *for children:* The Island Sunrise: pre-historic Britain, 1975; *fiction:* Hengest's Tale, 1966; The Dolphin Crossing, 1967; (with Kevin Crossley-Holland) Wordhoard, 1969; Fireweed (Book World Fest. Award), 1970; Goldengrove, 1972; Toolmaker, 1973; The Dawnstone, 1973; The Emperor's Winding Sheet (jtly, Whitbread Prize), 1974; The Butty Boy, 1975 (US edn as The Huffler); Unleaving (Boston Globe/Horn Book Award), 1976; Crossing to Salamis, The Walls of Athens, and Persian Gold, 1977–78 (US combined edn as Children of the Fox, 1978); A Chance Child, 1978; The Green Book, 1981 (re-issued as Shine, 1988); Babylon, 1982; Lost & Found, 1984; A Parcel of Patterns (Universe Prize), 1984; Gaffer Samson's Luck, 1985 (Smarties Prize Grand Prix, 1984); Five Tides, 1986; Torch, 1987; Birdy and the Ghosties, 1989; Grace, 1991; When Grandma Came, 1992; Matthew and the Sea-Singer, 1992; Pepi and the Secret Names, 1994; When I Was Little Like You, 1997. *Recreations:* photography, gardening, reading. *Address:* c/o David Higham Associates, 7th Floor, Waverley House, 7–12 Noel Street, W1F 8GQ.

PATRIARCA, Stephen Richard; international educational leadership and management consultant for independent English-medium schools and specialised support for UK private schools seeking academy status, 2008–13; Adviser, Danube International School, Vienna, 2009–13 (Associate Director, 2008–09); *b* 3 May 1953; *s* of late Ronald and Maureen Patriarca. *Educ:* Sweyne Sch., Rayleigh; UC of Swansea (BA Hons 1975). Asst English Master, 1978–95, Hd of Sixth Form, 1988–95 (first piloted new Philosophy A Level and worked with Royal Inst. of Philosophy to encourage the subject in schs), Dep. Headmaster, 1995–2000, Hulme GS, Oldham; Headmaster, later Principal, William Hulme's GS, Manchester, 2000–08 (city acad. from 2007). Trustee, Anglo Austrian Soc., 2002–09. Advr and Consultant to Batley Grammar Sch., 2011. Mem., New Europeans. Blogger, OneEurope, 2013–. *Recreations:* Vienna coffee houses, Heurigen, lakes and mountains, music, art, cooking, wine, revaluing Habsburg Austria, Austrian Wine and campaigning for recognition of the Ukrainian Holodomor. *Address:* Siebenbrunnengaße 4/2, 1050 Vienna, Austria. *W:* www.stevepatriarca.at. *Club:* East India.

PATRICK, Andrew; HM Diplomatic Service; Ambassador to Burma, since 2013; *b* 28 Feb. 1966; *s* of Henry Patrick and Carol Patrick (*née* Biddle). *Educ:* Poltair Sch., Cornwall; Univ. of Bristol (BSc Hons Maths 1987); City Univ., London (Dip. in Law 1988). Joined FCO, 1988; Third, later Second Sec., Nicosia, 1991–95; First Sec., NATO, Brussels, 1995–96; Asst Private Sec. to Sec. of State, FCO, 1997–2000; Dep. Hd, News Dept, FCO, 2001–04; Dep. High Comr, S Africa, 2004–07; Dep. Hd of Mission, Afghanistan, 2007–09; Additional Dir S Asia, FCO, 2009–12. *Address:* c/o Foreign and Commonwealth Office, King Charles Street, SW1A 2AH.

PATRICK, Gail; *see* Patrick, L. G.

PATRICK, Graham McIntosh, CMG 1968; CVO 1981; DSC 1943; Under Secretary, Department of the Environment, 1971–81, retired; *b* 17 Oct. 1921; *m* 1945, Barbara Worboys (*d* 2013); two *s*. *Educ:* Dundee High Sch.; St Andrews Univ. RNVR (Air Branch), 1940–46. Entered Ministry of Works, 1946; Regional Director: Middle East Region, 1965–67; South West Region, DoE, 1971–75; Chm., South West Economic Planning Bd, 1971–75; Dir, Scottish Services, PSA, 1975–81. *Address:* 69 Swallows Court, Pool Close, Spalding PE11 1GZ.

PATRICK, Rev. James Harry Johnson; His Honour Judge Patrick; a Circuit Judge, since 2010; *b* Tiverton, Devon, 14 March 1967; *s* of late John Churchill Patrick and of Sally Patrick (*née* Johnson, now Mrs Peter Ward-Enticott). *Educ:* Blundell's Sch.; City of Birmingham Poly. (LLB Hons); Inns of Court Sch. of Law; Southern Theol Educn and Trng Scheme (DipHE); St Stephen's House, Oxford. Called to the Bar, Inner Temple, 1989; Recorder, 2004–10. Ordained deacon, 1999, priest, 2000; Hon. Asst Curate, All Saints with St John, Clifton, Bristol, 1999–2010; ordained deacon (RC Ordinariate of Our Lady of Walsingham), 2011; Deacon, N London Ordinariate Gp at Our Lady of Mt Carmel and St George, Enfield, 2011–13; Parish Deacon, Our Lady of the Assumption and St Gregory, Warwick St, Soho, 2013–. Wine Treas., Western Circuit, 1995–2000. Hon. Legal Advr to Bp of Ebbsfleet, 2001–10; Hon. Chaplain to High Sheriff of Bristol, 2004–05. *Recreations:* fun, friends and laughter. *Address:* Wood Green Crown Court, Woodall House, Lordship Lane, N22 5LF. *T:* (020) 8826 4100. *Club:* East India.

PATRICK, (Lilian) Gail; Sheriff of Tayside, Central and Fife at Kirkcaldy, 1991–2001; part-time Sheriff, since 2001; *b* 24 Dec. 1941; *d* of Alexander Findlay McFadzean, MA, LLB and Elizabeth Fullerton McFadzean (*née* Fenton); *m* 1967, Spencer Francis Rodger, LLB, WS, *s* of Francis and Isabel Patrick; one *s* three *d*. *Educ:* Radleigh Sch., Glasgow; Marr Coll., Troon; St Andrews Univ. (MA); Edinburgh Univ. (LLB). Enrolled as solicitor, 1966; pt-time practice, 1967–79; Lecturer and Tutor: Glasgow Univ., 1967–82; Edinburgh Univ., 1980–82, 1985–90; pt-time Procurator Fiscal Depute, 1979–80; admitted to Faculty of Advocates, 1981; Standing Jun. Counsel, Scottish Educn Dept, 1986–91; Chm., Social Security Appeal Tribunal, 1986–91; Reporter, Scottish Legal Aid Bd, 1986–91; Temp. Sheriff, 1988–91; called to the Bar, Lincoln's Inn, 1990. *Recreations:* golf, hill-walking, cycling, fishing, music. *Clubs:* Murrayfield Golf (Edinburgh), Bonar Bridge and Ardgay Golf, Elie and Earlsferry Golf.

PATRICK, Simon John; a Principal Clerk, Committee Office, House of Commons, since 2013; *b* 13 Oct. 1956; *s* of John Patrick and Mary Patrick (*née* Ansell). *Educ:* Merchant Taylors' Sch.; Pembroke Coll., Cambridge (BA Maths 1978, MA 1982). House of Commons: a clerk, 1978–: Clerk: Cttee of Public Accts, 1986–89; Employment Cttee, 1989–91; Table Office, 1991–95; Nat. Heritage Cttee, 1995–97; Treasury Cttee, 1998–2001; Jl Office, 2001–05; Eur. Scrutiny Cttee, 2005–06; Delegated Legislation, 2006–09; of Bills, 2009–13. *Publications:* (an Asst Ed) Erskine May's Parliamentary Practice, 23rd edn 2004 to 24th edn 2011. *Recreations:* classical music, typography, computing. *Address:* House of Commons, SW1A 0AA.

PATRICK, Stuart Leslie; Chief Executive, Glasgow Chamber of Commerce, since 2009; *b* Greenock, 20 May 1962; *s* of Alexander James Patrick and Jenny Irene Patrick; one *s*. *Educ:* Greenock Acad.; Univ. of Glasgow (BAcc (Hons) 1984); Univ. of Strathclyde (MBA 1992). CA 1988. Auditor and Business Advr, Ernst & Young, 1984–89; Co. Sec., Govan Initiative Ltd, 1989–92; Scottish Enterprise Glasgow: Hd, Strategy, 1992–99; Dir, Finance and Strategy, 1999–2006; Ops Dir, 2006–08; Sen. Commercial Dir, Scottish Enterprise, 2008–09. Non-exec. Chm., Wise Gp, 2013–; non-executive Director: Ashton Properties Ltd, 1996–2013; Clyde Gateway Urban Regeneration Co., 2014–; Scottish Opera, 2014–. Director: Four Acres Charitable Trust, 1985–; Arches Th. Co., 2004–; Glasgow Sci. Centre, 2006–. *Recreations:* theatre, tennis, travel, learning German. *Address:* Glasgow Chamber of Commerce, 30 George Square, Glasgow G2 1EQ. *T:* (0141) 204 2121. *E:* chamber@glasgowchamberofcommerce.com.

PATTEN, family name of **Barons Patten** and **Patten of Barnes**.

PATTEN, Baron *cr* 1997 (Life Peer), of Wincanton in the co. of Somerset; **John Haggitt Charles Patten;** PC 1990; Senior Advisor, Charterhouse Capital Partners LLP (formerly Charterhouse Development Capital Ltd), since 2001; *b* 17 July 1945; *s* of late Jack Patten and Maria Olga (*née* Sikora); *m* 1978, Louise Alexandra Virginia Charlotte Rowe (*see* Lady Patten); one *d*. *Educ:* Wimbledon Coll.; Sidney Sussex Coll., Cambridge (PhD 1972). University Lectr, 1969–79, Fellow, Hertford Coll., 1972–94, Univ. of Oxford. Oxford City Councillor, 1973–76. MP (C) City of Oxford, 1979–83; Oxford W and Abingdon, 1983–97. PPS to the Ministers of State at the Home Office, 1980–81; Parliamentary Under-Secretary of State: NI Office, 1981–83; DHSS, 1983–85; Minister of State for Housing, Urban Affairs and Construction, DoE, 1985–87; Minister of State, Home Office, 1987–92; Sec. of State for Educn, 1992–94. Advr, 1996–2000, non-exec. Dep. Chm., 2000–01, Charterhouse plc; non-executive Director: Lockheed Martin UK Ltd, 1999–2003; Lockheed Martin UK Holdings Ltd, 2003–. Advr, Lockheed Martin International (formerly Lockheed Martin Overseas Corp.), 1997–; Advr, Thomas Goode & Co. Ltd, 1997–. Hon. Fellow, Harris Manchester Coll., Oxford, 1996. *Publications:* The Conservative Opportunity (with Lord Blake), 1976; English Towns, 1500–1700, 1978; (ed) Pre-Industrial England, 1979; (ed) The Expanding City, 1983; (with Paul Coones) The Penguin Guide to the Landscape of England and Wales, 1986; Things to Come: the Tories in the 21st Century, 1995. *Recreation:* talking with my wife and daughter. *Address:* House of Lords, SW1A 0PW.

PATTEN OF BARNES, Baron *cr* 2005 (Life Peer), of Barnes in the London Borough of Richmond; **Christopher Francis Patten,** CH 1998; PC 1989; Chancellor, University of Oxford, since 2003; Chairman, BBC Trust, 2011–14; *b* 12 May 1944; *s* of late Francis Joseph Patten and Joan McCarthy; *m* 1971, Mary Lavender St Leger Thornton; three *d*. *Educ:* St Benedict's School, Ealing; Balliol College, Oxford (Hon. Fellow, 2000). Conservative Research Dept, 1966–70; Cabinet Office, 1970–72; Home Office, 1972; Personal Asst to Chairman of Conservative Party, 1972–74; Director, Conservative Research Dept, 1974–79. Governor and C-in-C, Hong Kong, 1992–97; Chm., Ind. Commn on Policing for NI, 1998–99. MP (C) Bath, 1979–92; contested (C) same seat, 1992. PPS to Chancellor of Duchy of Lancaster and Leader of House of Commons, 1979–81, to Secretary of State for Social Services, 1981; Parly Under-Sec. of State, NI Office, 1983–85; Minister of State, DES, 1985–86; Minister of State (Minister for Overseas Develt), FCO, 1986–89; Sec. of State for the Envmt, 1989–90; Chancellor of Duchy of Lancaster, 1990–92; Chm. of Cons. Party, 1990–92. Vice Chm., Cons. Parly Finance Cttee, 1981–83; Mem., Select Cttees on Defence and Procedure, 1982–83. Mem., Eur. Commn, 1999–2004. Co-Chm., Internat. Crisis Gp, 2004–11. Director: Independent Newspapers, 1998–99; Cadbury plc, 2005–10; Russell Reynolds, 2008–. Chancellor, Univ. of Newcastle, 1999–2009. Hon. FRCPE 1994. Hon. Fellow, St Antony's Coll., Oxford, 2003. Hon. DJur: Massachusetts, 1999; Birmingham, 2001; Bath, 2003; Hon. DCL: Newcastle, 1999; Oxford 2003; Hon. DLitt: Sydney, 2001; Exeter, 2002; Ulster, 2004; DUniv: Keele, 2002; Stettin, 2004; Hon. DBA Kingston, 2003; Hon. DSc SE Europe, Rep. of Macedonia, 2009. *Publications:* The Tory Case, 1983; East and West, 1998; Not Quite the Diplomat, 2005; What Next? Surviving the 21st Century, 2008. *Recreations:* reading, tennis, gardening. *Address:* House of Lords, SW1A 0PW. *Clubs:* Athenæum, Royal Automobile, Oxford and Cambridge; All England Lawn Tennis.

PATTEN, Lady; Louise Alexandra Virginia Charlotte Patten; Senior Adviser, Bain & Co. Inc., since 1997; *b* 2 Feb. 1954; *m* 1978, John Haggitt Charles Patten (*see* Baron Patten); one *d*. *Educ:* St Paul's Girls' Sch., Hammersmith; St Hugh's Coll., Oxford (MA Hons). Manager, Citibank NA, 1977–81; Resident Vice Pres., Wells Fargo Bank NA, 1981–85; Partner: PA Consulting Gp, 1985–93; Bain & Co. Inc., 1994–97. Non-executive Director: Hilton Gp plc, 1993–2003; Harveys Furnishings plc, 1993–2000; GUS (formerly Gt Universal Stores) plc, 1997–2006; Somerfield plc, 1998–2005 (Actg Chm., 1999–2000); Brixton plc, 2001–10 (Chm., 2003–10); UK Asset Resolution Ltd (formerly Bradford & Bingley plc), 2003–13; Marks & Spencer plc, 2006–11; Northern Rock (Asset Mgt) plc, 2010–14; Intu Properties plc (formerly Capital Shopping Centres), 2011–; Control Risks Gp Hldgs Ltd, 2011–14. *Publications:* Bad Money, 2009; Good As Gold, 2010. *Address:* c/o Bain & Co. Inc., 40 Strand, WC2N 5HZ. *T:* (020) 7969 6000.

PATTEN, Benedict Joseph; QC 2010; *b* Belfast, 12 March 1962; *s* of James and Patricia Patten; *m* 1998, Celia Grace; three *s*. *Educ:* Stonyhurst Coll.; New Coll., Oxford (BA); City Univ. (Dip. Law). Called to the Bar, Middle Temple, 1986. *Recreations:* tennis, reading, theatre. *Address:* 4 New Square, Lincoln's Inn, WC2A 3RJ.

PATTEN, Brian; poet; *b* 7 Feb. 1946. Regents Lectr, Univ. of Calif (San Diego), 1985. FRSL 2003. Freedom, City of Liverpool, 2001. Hon. Fellow, Liverpool John Moores Univ., 2002. Hon LittD Liverpool, 2006; DUniv Open, 2013. Cholmondeley Award for Poetry, 2002. *Publications: poetry:* Penguin Modern Poets, 1967; Little Johnny's Confession, 1967; Notes to the Hurrying Man, 1969; The Irrelevant Song, 1971; The Unreliable Nightingale, 1973; Vanishing Trick, 1976; The Shabby Angel, 1978; Grave Gossip, 1979; Love Poems, 1981; Clare's Countryside: a book on John Clare, 1982; New Volume, 1983; Storm Damage, 1988; Grinning Jack (Selected Poems), 1990; Armada, 1996; The Blue and Green Ark, 1999; New Selected Poems, 2007; Collected Love Poems, 2008; View from the Boathouse Window, 2010; *novel:* Mr Moon's Last Case, 1975 (Mystery Writers of Amer. Special Award, 1976); *for younger readers:* The Elephant and the Flower, 1969; Jumping Mouse; 1971; Emma's Doll, 1976; The Sly Cormorant and the Fish: adaptations of The Aesop Fables, 1977; (ed) Gangsters, Ghosts and Dragonflies, 1981; Gargling with Jelly, 1985; Jimmy Tag-along, 1988; Thawing Frozen Frogs, 1990; (ed) The Puffin Book of Twentieth Century Children's Verse, 1991; Grizzelda Frizzle, 1992; The Magic Bicycle, 1993; Impossible Parents, 1994; The Utter Nutters, 1994; (ed) The Puffin Book of Utterly Brilliant Poetry, 1998; Beowulf and the Monster, 1999; Juggling with Gerbils, 2000; Little Hotchpotch, 2000; Impossible Parents Go Green, 2000; The Story Giant, 2001 (and play, 2014); Ben's Magic Telescope, 2003; (with Roger McGough) The Monsters' Guide to Choosing a Pet, 2004; Puffin Book of Modern Children's Verse, 2006; The Big Snuggle-up, 2011; Can I Come Too?, 2013; *plays:* The Pig And The Junkle, 1975; (with Roger McGough) The Mouth Trap, 1982; Blind Love, 1983; Gargling with Jelly, 1989; *recordings:* Brian Patten Reading His Own Poetry, 1969; British Poets Of Our Time, 1974; Vanishing Trick, 1976; The Sly Cormorant, 1977; Grizzelda Frizzle and other stories, 1995; The Mersey Sound, 1997. *Address:* c/o Rogers, Coleridge and White, 20 Powis Mews, W11 1JN. *Club:* Chelsea Arts.

PATTEN, Louise Alexandra Virginia Charlotte; *see* Lady Patten.

PATTEN, Rt Hon. Sir Nicholas (John), Kt 2000; PC 2009; **Rt Hon. Lord Justice Patten;** a Lord Justice of Appeal, since 2009; *b* 7 Aug. 1950; *s* of late Peter Grenville Patten and Dorothy Patten (*née* Davenport); *m* 1984, Veronica Mary Schoeneich (marr. diss. 1998); two *s* one *d*. *Educ:* Tulse Hill Sch.; Christ Church, Oxford (Open Schol.; MA; BCL (1st Cl. Hons Jurisprudence)). Called to the Bar, Lincoln's Inn, 1974, Bencher, 1997; QC 1988; a Dep. High Court Judge, 1998–2000; a Judge of the High Court of Justice, Chancery Div., 2000–09. Vice-Chancellor, Co. Palatine of Lancaster, 2005–08. Chm., Chancery Bar Assoc., 1997–99. *Recreation:* gardening. *Address:* Royal Courts of Justice, Strand, WC2A 2LL.

PATTENDEN, Prof. Gerald, FRS 1991; Sir Jesse Boot Professor of Organic Chemistry, Nottingham University, 1988–2005, Emeritus Professor of Chemistry, 2009 (Pro-Vice-Chancellor, 1997–2003); *b* 4 March 1940; *s* of Albert James and Violet Eugenia Pattenden; *m* 1969, Christine Frances Doherty; three *d*. *Educ:* Brunel Univ. (BSc); Queen Mary College London (PhD, DSc; Hon. Fellow, 2000). FRSC. Lectr, UC, Cardiff, 1966–72; Nottingham University: Lectr, 1972–75; Reader, 1975–80; Prof., 1980–88; Sir Jesse Boot Prof. of Organic Chem., 1988–2005; Hd of Dept of Chem., 1988–96; Res. Prof. of Organic Chem., 2005–09. Chm., Org. Chem. Cttee, SERC, 1992–94. Mem. Council, Royal Soc., 2001–03. Royal Society of Chemistry: Pres., Perkin Div., 1995–97 (Scientific Ed., Perkin Trans); Corday-Morgan Medal and Prize, 1975; Simonsen Lect. and Medal, 1987; Tilden Lect. and Medal, 1991; Award for Synthetic Organic Chem., 1992; Pedler Lect. and Medal, 1993; Award for Heterocyclic Chem., 1994; Award for Natural Product Chemistry, 1997; Hugo Müller Lect. and Medal, 2001; Robert Robinson Lect., 2007; Merck Award Lect. and Medal, 2009. Hon. DLaws Nottingham, 2015. *Publications:* editor of several books; over 490 contribs to internat. jls of chemistry. *Recreations:* sport, DIY, gardening. *Address:* School of Chemistry, University of Nottingham, University Park, Nottingham NG7 2RD. *T:* (0115) 951 3530. *E:* gp@nottingham.ac.uk.

PATTERSON, Ben; *see* Patterson, G. B.

PATTERSON, (Constance) Marie, (Mrs Barrie Devney), CBE 1978 (OBE 1973); National Officer, Transport and General Workers' Union, 1976–84 (National Woman Officer, 1963–76); Member of General Council of TUC, 1963–84 (Chairman, 1974–75 and 1977); *b* 1 April 1934; *d* of Dr Richard Swanton Abraham; *m* 1st, 1960, Thomas Michael Valentine Patterson (marr. diss. 1976); 2nd, 1984, Barrie Devney. *Educ:* Pendleton High Sch.; Bedford Coll., Univ. of London (BA). Member: Exec., Confedn of Shipbuilding and Engrg Unions, 1966–84 (Pres., 1977–78); Hotel and Catering Trng Bd, 1966–87; Equal Opportunities Commn, 1975–84; Central Arbitration Commn, 1976–94; Legal Aid Adv. Cttee, 1988–90; Council, Office of Banking Ombudsman, 1992–2001. Dir of Remploy, 1966–87. Lay Mem., Press Council, 1964–70. Chm. Council, Queen's Coll., Harley St, 1994–2000; Mem. Court, LSE, 1984–2005 (Mem. Council, 2000–02). Chm., Galleon Trust, 1998–2005. FRSA 2000. Hon. DSc Salford, 1975. *Recreations:* sight-seeing, jig-saws.

PATTERSON, Eric, MBE 1970; HM Diplomatic Service, retired; Consul-General, 1982–88 and Counsellor (Commercial), 1986–88, Auckland; *b* 2 May 1930; *s* of Richard and Elizabeth Patterson; *m* 1st, 1953, Doris Mason (*d* 1999); two *s*; 2nd, 2001, Charlotte Pellizzaro (*née* Bathurst). *Educ:* Hookergate Grammar Sch., Co. Durham. Served Royal Signals, 1948–50. Local govt service, 1947–50; Lord Chancellor's Dept, 1950–52; BoT, 1952–62; Asst Trade Comr, Halifax, NS, 1962–67; Second Sec. (Commercial), Khartoum, 1967–70; First Sec. (Commercial), The Hague, 1970–74; FCO, 1974–76; First Sec. (Commercial), Warsaw, 1976–80; FCO, 1980–82. *Recreations:* golf, photography, bowls. *Address:* 1/35 Howe Street, Howick, Auckland 2014, New Zealand.

PATTERSON, Hon. Dame Frances (Silvia), DBE 2013; **Hon. Mrs Justice Patterson;** a Judge of the High Court, Queen's Bench Division, since 2013; *m* 1980, Dr Graham Nicholson; three *s*. *Educ:* Queen's Sch., Chester; Leicester Univ. Called to the Bar, Middle Temple, 1977, Bencher, 2005; Asst Recorder, 1997–2000; Recorder, 2000–13; QC 1998; Hd of Kings Chambers, Manchester and Leeds, 2004–09; a Dep. High Court Judge, 2008–13. A Law Comr, 2010–13. *Address:* Royal Courts of Justice, Strand, WC2A 2LL.

PATTERSON, Gavin Echlin; Chief Executive, BT Group plc, since 2013 (Executive Director, since 2008); *b* Altrincham, 6 Sept. 1967; *s* of William Echlin Patterson and Christine Anne Patterson; *m* 1997, Karen Lacovara; one *s* three *d*. *Educ:* Emmanuel Coll., Cambridge (BA 1989; MEng 1990). Procter and Gamble, 1990–99, mktg roles incl. Eur. Mktg Dir, Haircare, 1999; Man. Dir, Consumer, Telewest Communications plc, 1999–2003; BT Group plc: Man. Dir, Consumer, 2004–08; Chief Exec., BT Retail, 2008–13. Non-executive Director: Johnston Press plc, 2008–09; British Airways plc, 2010–. Pres., Advertising Assoc., 2011–14; Mem., BAFTA, 2012–. Mem., Adv. Bd, Judge Business Sch., Univ. of Cambridge, 2011–13. Trustee, BM, 2012–. *Recreations:* classic cinema, cooking, collecting movie posters, supporting Liverpool FC, live music. *Address:* BT Group plc, 81 Newgate Street, EC1A 7AJ. *T:* (020) 7356 6707. *E:* gavin.e.patterson@bt.com.

PATTERSON, George Benjamin, (Ben); Director, CJA Consultants Ltd, since 2004; *b* 21 April 1939; *s* of late Eric James Patterson and Ethel Patterson; *m* 1970, Felicity Barbara Anne Raybould; one *s* one *d*. *Educ:* Westminster Sch.; Trinity Coll., Cambridge (MA); London Sch. of Economics. Lecturer, Swinton Conservative Coll., 1961–65; Editor (at Conservative Political Centre), CPC Monthly Report, 1965–74; Dep. Head, London Office of European Parlt, 1974–79. MEP (C) Kent W, 1979–94; contested (C) Kent W, Eur. Parly elecns, 1994. Prin. Administrator, Internal Market, then Econ. and Monetary Affairs Div., DG for Res., EP, 1994–2004. Mem (C), Hammersmith LBC, 1968–71. Contested (C) Wrexham, 1970. Chm., Cons. Party, Kent Area, 2010–13. MInstD. *Publications:* The Character of Conservatism, 1973; Direct Elections to the European Parliament, 1974; Europe and Employment, 1984; Vredeling and All That, 1984; VAT: the zero rate issue, 1988; A Guide to EMU, 1990; A European Currency, 1994; Options for a Definitive VAT System, 1995; The Co-ordination of National Fiscal Policies, 1996; The Consequences of Abolishing Duty Free Within the EU, 1997; Adjusting to Asymmetric Shocks, 1998; The Feasibility of a Tobin Tax, 1999; The Determination of Interest Rates, 1999; Exchange Rates and Monetary Policy, 2000; Tax Co-ordination in the European Union, 2002; Background to the Euro, 2002; Taxation in Europe: recent developments, 2003; Understanding the EU Budget, 2011; The Conservative Party and Europe, 2011; An Exercise in Causality, 2014. *Recreations:* reading science fiction, walking. *Address:* 38 Le Village, 09300 Montségur, France. *T:* (5) 61640119, 07582 068693.

PATTERSON, Harry; novelist; *b* 27 July 1929; *s* of Henry Patterson and Rita Higgins Bell; *m* 1st, 1958, Amy Margaret Hewitt (marr. diss. 1984); one *s* three *d*; 2nd, 1985, Denise Lesley Anne Palmer. *Educ:* Roundhay Sch., Leeds; Beckett Park Coll. for Teachers; London Sch. of Economics as external student (BSc(Hons) Sociology). FRSA. NCO, The Blues, 1947–50. 1950–58: tried everything from being a clerk to a circus tent-hand; 1958–72: variously a schoolmaster, Lectr in Liberal Studies, Leeds Polytechnic, Sen. Lectr in Education, James Graham Coll. and Tutor in Sch. Practice, Leeds Univ.; since age of 41, engaged in full-time writing career. Dual citizenship, British/Irish. DUniv Leeds Metropolitan, 1995; Hon. DLitt London, 2014. *Publications:* (as Jack Higgins): Prayer for the Dying, 1973 (filmed 1985); The Eagle has Landed, 1975 (filmed 1976); Storm Warning, 1976; Day of Judgement, 1978; Solo, 1980; Luciano's Luck, 1981; Touch the Devil, 1982; Exocet, 1983; Confessional, 1985 (filmed 1985); Night of the Fox, 1986 (filmed 1989); A Season in Hell, 1989; Cold Harbour, 1990; The Eagle Has Flown, 1990; Angel of Death, 1995; Drink with the Devil, 1996; Day of Reckoning, 2000; Edge of Danger, 2001; Bad Company, 2003; Dark Justice, 2004; Wolf at the Door, 2009; The Judas Gate, 2010; (as Harry Patterson): The Valhalla Exchange, 1978; To Catch a King, 1979 (filmed 1983); Dillinger, 1983; Walking Wounded (stage play), 1987; and many others (including The Violent Enemy, filmed 1969, and The Wrath of God, filmed 1972) under pseudonyms (Martin Fallon, Hugh Marlowe, Henry Patterson); some books trans. into 60 languages. *Recreations:* tennis, old movies. *Address:* c/o Ed Victor Ltd, 6 Bayley Street, WC1B 3HB.

PATTERSON, Dr Karalyn Eve, FBA 2010; FRS 2014; Senior Scientist, MRC Cognition and Brain Sciences Unit, University of Cambridge; Emeritus Fellow, Darwin College, Cambridge. *Educ:* MA Cantab 1995. PhD. FMedSci 2003. *Publications:* (ed jtly) Memory, 1998; articles in learned jls. *Address:* MRC Cognition and Brain Sciences Unit, 15 Chaucer Road, Cambridge CB2 7EF.

PATTERSON, Prof. Laurence Hylton, PhD; CChem, FRSC; Professor of Drug Discovery, and Director, Institute of Cancer Therapeutics, University of Bradford, since 2005; *b* Ilford, 22 June 1952; *s* of George Patterson and Olive Patterson; *m* Susan Doyle; one *s* one *d*; *m* 2002, Samantha Orr; three *s*. *Educ:* West Hatch Tech. High Sch., Chigwell; Hatfield Poly. (BSc Hons 1974); King's Coll. London (PhD 1977). FRSC 2004; CChem 2004. Sen. Scientist, Fisons Pharmaceuticals, 1977–80; Prof. of Pharmacy, De Montfort Univ., 1980–99; Prof. of Medicinal Chemistry and Hd, Dept of Pharmaceutical and Biol Chem., Sch. of Pharmacy, Univ. of London, 1999–2004. Founder Dir and Shareholder, Biostatus Ltd, 2003–; Dir, PKPD Inc., 2004–; Founder Shareholder, Icanthera Ltd, 2012–. Hon. Professor: Third Military Medical Univ., Chongqing, 2008; Southwestern Univ., Beibei, 2011; Vis. Prof., Shanghai Inst. of Materia Medica, Chinese Acad. of Sci., 2008. Hon. MRPharmS 2007. *Publications:* over 200 scientific articles, patents and scientific reviews. *Recreations:* keeping up physically and mentally with three lively boys, all at primary school, learning the culture and language of China. *Address:* Institute of Cancer Therapeutics, University of Bradford, W Yorks BD7 1DP. *T:* (01274) 233226. *E:* l.h.patterson@bradford.ac.uk. *Club:* Athenæum.

PATTERSON, Dr Linda Joyce, OBE 2000; FRCP, FRCPE; Clinical Vice President, Royal College of Physicians, 2010–13; *b* Liverpool, 12 April 1951; *d* of Thomas William Matthew Patterson and Mary Frances Patterson (*née* Ollerhead); partner, Christopher Stephen Green. *Educ:* Liverpool Institute High Sch. for Girls; Middlesex Hosp. Med. Sch., Univ. of London (MB BS 1975). FRCPE 1991; FRCP 1993. Consultant physician, East Lancashire, 1986–2011. Medical Director: Burnley NHS Trust, 1995–2000; Commn for Health Improvement, 2000–04. Non-executive Director: Nat. Patient Safety Agency, 2006–12; Calderdale and Huddersfield NHS Foundn Trust, 2013–. Trustee: White Ribbon Campaign, 2008–14; Alzheimer's Soc., 2010–13. *Publications:* (jtly) Health Care for Older People: practitioner perspective in a changing society, 1998. *Recreations:* playing piano, opera, politics, feminism. *Club:* Royal Society of Medicine.

PATTERSON, Lindy Ann; QC (Scot.) 2010; WS; FCIArb; Partner, CMS Cameron McKenna (formerly Dundas & Wilson) LLP, since 2003; *b* Berwick-on-Tweed, 12 Sept. 1958. *Educ:* Univ. of Edinburgh (LLB Hons); WS 2001. FCInstCES 2011; FCIArb 2012. Admitted solicitor, Scotland, 1981, England and Wales, 2009; Partner: Bird Semple, 1988–98; MacRoberts, 1998–2003. Pt-time Lectr and Tutor, DipLP, Univ. of Edinburgh, 2008–. Accredited Adjudicator, Technol. and Construction Solicitors' Assoc., 2000; Approved Adjudicator, Internat. Fedn of Consulting Engrs, 2012–. Convener, Accreditation Cttee for Construction Law, Law Soc. of Scotland, 2009–; Mem. Cttee, Shelter (Scotland), 2011–. Mem., ARBRIX, 2009. Hon. MRICS 2008. Freeman, Arbitrators' Co., 2008. *Recreations:* hill walking, reading, singing. *E:* lindy.patterson@cms-cmck.com.

PATTERSON, Dr Margaret Florence, OBE 2014; Principal Scientific Officer, Agri-Food and Biosciences Institute, Belfast, since 1995; *b* Belfast, 26 Feb. 1959; *d* of David John and Mary Elizabeth Patterson. *Educ:* Carolan Grammar Sch., Belfast; Queen's Univ. Belfast (BSc Hons Food Sci.; MSocSc (Dist.) Orgn and Mgt; PhD Food Microbiol. 1984). CSci 2004. Res. Fellow, QUB, 1984–86; SSO, Dept of Agric. and Rural Develt, NI, 1986–95; on secondment as Food Safety Consultant, IAEA, 1995; Lectr, 1987–95, Reader, 1995–2011, Dept of Food Sci., QUB, now Hon. Prof. President: Soc. for Applied Microbiol., 2005–08; Inst. of Food Sci. and Technol., 2013–15. FIFST 1992. *Publications:* contribs to scientific pubns on food sci. and food safety. *Recreations:* travelling, gardening, walking. *Address:* Agri-Food and Biosciences Institute, Newforge Lane, Malone Upper, Belfast, Northern Ireland BT9 5PX. *T:* (028) 9025 5316. *E:* margaret.patterson@afbini.gov.uk.

PATTERSON, Marie; *see* Patterson, C. M.

PATTERSON, Dr Mark Jonathan Lister; Hon. Consultant Haematologist, Manchester Royal Infirmary, 1997–2007; Consultant Haematologist, Mid Cheshire NHS Trust, 1996–2007; *b* 2 March 1934; *s* of Alfred Patterson and Frederica Georgina Mary Lister Nicholson; *m* 1958, Jane Teresa Mary Scott Stokes; one *s* two *d*. *Educ:* privately; St Bartholomew's Hosp. Med. Coll., Univ. of London (MB 1959). MRCP. Jun. hosp. appts at St Bartholomew's Hosp., Royal Postgrad. Med. Sch., and MRC Exptl Haematol. Unit; Consultant Haematologist to Nat. Heart and Chest Hosps, 1967–84. Mem., GLC, 1970–73 and 1977–81; contested (C) Ealing N, Feb. 1974. Chm., Covent Gdn Develt Cttee, 1977–82. *Recreations:* medicine, politics, conservation and restoration of important buildings, organising concerts of all genres. *Address:* Wolverton Manor, Shorwell, Newport, Isle of Wight PO30 3JS. *T:* (01983) 740609, 07831 444149.

PATTERSON, Paul Leslie; composer; Manson Professor of Composition, Royal Academy of Music, since 1997; Artistic Director, Park Lane Group Young Composer Forum, since 1998; formed: Manson Ensemble, 1968; The Patterson Quintet, 1982; *b* 15 June 1947; *s* of Leslie and Lilian Patterson; *m* 1981, Hazel Wilson; one *s* one *d*. *Educ:* Royal Academy of Music. FRAM 1980; FRNCM 2007. Freelance composer, 1968–; Arts Council Composer in Association, English Sinfonia, 1969–70; Director, Contemporary Music, Warwick Univ., 1974–80; Prof. of Composition, and Hd of Composition and Twentieth Century Music, RAM, 1985–97; Composer in Residence: SE Arts Assoc., 1980–82; Bedford School, 1984–85; Southwark Fest., 1989–91; James Allen School, Dulwich, 1990–91; Three Spires Fest., Truro, 1992–94; NYO, 1997–; Guest Prof., Yale Univ., 1989–90; Vis. Prof. of Composition, Univ. of Canterbury, Christchurch, 2000–; Vis. Composition Tutor, RNCM, 2002–. Artistic Dir, Exeter Fest., 1991–97; Artistic Advr, N Devon Fest., 1999–. Chm., Mendelssohn Scholarship, Royal Schs of Music, 1997–. Member: Exec. Cttee, Composers Guild, 1972–75; Council, SPNM, 1975–81, 1985–; Adv. Council, BBC Radio London, 1986–; Adv. Cttee, Arts Council's Recordings Panel, 1986–94; Artistic Director of RAM Festivals: Lutosławski, 1984; Penderecki, 1986; Messiaen, 1987; Henze, 1988; Berio, 1989, 2004; Carter, 1990; Da Capo, 1993; Schnittke, 1994; Ligeti, 1995; film music, 1996; Birtwistle, 1997; Donatoni, 1998; Russian, 1999; Pärt, 2000; Kagel, 2001. Featured Composer at: Three Choirs Fest., Patterson at South Bank Fest., 1988; Cheltenham Fest., 1988, 1990; Peterborough Fest., 1989; Exeter Fest., 1991; Presteigne Fest., 2001; Sounds New, 2007; Hampstead and Highgate Fest., 2007. Performances world wide by leading orchestras and soloists and ensembles; also film and TV music. Numerous recordings. Pres., RAM Club, 1993–94. FRSA 1989. Hon. FLCM 1997. Lesley Boosey Award, Royal Philharmonic Soc., 1996. OM, 1987, Gold Medal, 2009, Polish Ministry of Culture. *Publications:* Rebecca, 1968; Trumpet Concerto, 1969; Time Piece, 1972; Kyrie, 1972; Comedy for Five Winds, 1973; Requiem, 1974; Fluorescences, 1974; Clarinet Concerto, 1976; Cracowian Counterpoints, 1977; Voices of Sleep, 1979; Concerto for Orchestra, 1981; Canterbury Psalms, 1981; Sinfonia, 1982; Mass of the Sea, 1983; Deception Pass, 1983; Duologue, 1984; Mean Time, 1984; Europhony, 1985; Missa Brevis, 1985; Stabat Mater, 1986; String Quartet, 1986; Magnificat and Nunc Dimittis, 1986; Propositions, 1987; Trombone Quartet, 1987; Suite for Cello, 1987; Sorriest Cow, 1987; Tides of Mananan, 1988; Te Deum, 1988; Tunnel of Time, 1989; White Shadows, 1989; Symphony, 1990; The End, 1990; Mighty Voice, 1991; Violin Concerto, 1992; Little Red Riding Hood, 1992; Magnificat, 1993; Music for Opening Channel Tunnel, 1994; Overture: Songs of the West, 1995; Soliloquy, 1996; Rustic Sketches, 1997; Hell Angels, 1998; Gloria, 1999; Western Winds, 1999; Millennium Mass, 2000; Deviations, 2001; Cello Concerto, 2002; Jubilee Dances, 2002; Three Little Pigs, 2003; Bug for Solo Harp, 2003; Harpo Maniac, 2004; Fifth Continent, 2005; Orchestra on Parade, 2005; Allusions, 2007; Viola Concerto, 2008; Phoenix

Concerto, 2009; Two Grooves, 2009; Avians Harp Quartet, 2010; Lizards for Solo Harp, 2012; Serenade for Violin and Orchestra, 2013; Spirals for Solo Harp, 2013; Fantasia for Harp and Orchestra, 2014; Spiders Web, Harp and String Quartet, 2014. *Recreations:* sailing, croquet, swimming, computing. *Address:* 31 Cromwell Avenue, Highgate, N6 5HN. *T:* (020) 8348 3711.

PATTERSON, Most Hon. Percival (Noel James), ON 2002; PC 1992; QC 1983; Prime Minister of Jamaica, 1992–2006; *b* 10 April 1935; *s* of Henry Patterson and Ina James; *m* (marr. diss.); one *s* one *d*. *Educ:* Somerton Primary, St James; Calabar High Sch., Kingston; Univ. of the West Indies (BA Hons English 1958); LSE (LLB 1963). Called to the Bar, Middle Temple, 1963; admitted to Jamaican Bar, 1963; private legal practice, Kingston. Senator, Leader of Opposition Business, 1969–70; MP (PNP) SE, then Eastern, Westmoreland, Jamaica, 1972–80 and 1989–2006; Minister of Industry, Trade and Tourism, 1972–77; Dep. Prime Minister, 1978–80, 1989–91; Minister: of Foreign Affairs and Foreign Trade, 1978–80; of Develt Planning and Production, 1989–90; of Finance and Planning, 1990–91; of Defence, 1992–2006. People's National Party: Mem. Exec. Council, 1964; Vice-Pres., 1969; Chm., 1983–92; Pres. and Leader, 1992–2006. Agricola Medal, FAO, 2001; Golden Star Award, Caribbean and Latin Amer. Action Gp, 2002; Chancellor's Medal, Univ. of W Indies, 2006. Order of Francisco Morazán, Gran Cruz Placa de Oro (Honduras), 1990; Order of Águila Azteca (Mexico), 1990; Order of Liberator Simon Bolivar (Venezuela), 1st Class, 1992; Order of San Martin (Argentina), 1992; Order of Gran Cruz Gonzalo Jiménez de Quesada (Colombia), 1994; Order of Jose Marti (Cuba), 1997; Order of the Volta (Ghana), 1999; Gran Cruz Placa de Orode Juan Mora Fernández (Costa Rica), 2001; Grand Cross, Nat. Order of Civil Merit (Spain), 2006; Order of Belize, 2006; Grand Cross, Order of Southern Cross (Brazil), 2006; Order of Excellence (Guyana), 2006; OCC 2009; Supreme Companion, Order of the Companions of O. R. Tambo (Gold) (South Africa), 2013. *Recreations:* music (jazz/ Jamaican), sports (cricket, boxing, track and field, tennis). *Address:* Heisconsults, Sagicor Building, 10th Floor, 28–48 Barbados Avenue, Kingston 5, Jamaica.

PATTERSON, Simon Iain; a Managing Director, Silver Lake, since 2012; *b* Birmingham, 4 May 1973; *s* of Timothy John Patterson and Cherry Patterson; *m* 2002, Harriet Jo Bell; two *s* one *d*. *Educ:* King's Coll., Cambridge (BA 1995); Stanford Univ. (MBA 2005). Business Analyst, McKinsey, 1995–97; Dir, Financial Times, 1997–99; Sen. Vice Pres., GF-X, 1999–2003; Silver Lake, 2005–. Non-exec. Dir, N Brown Gp plc, 2013–. Mem., Adv. Bd, Prince's Trust, 2013– (Chm., Internet and Media Leadership Gp, 2010–13); Trustee, Natural History Mus., 2015–. *Recreations:* sailing, golf. *Clubs:* Lansdowne; Itchenor Sailing.

PATTERSON, Vilma Hazel Ann, MBE 2004; Chairman, Probation Board for Northern Ireland, since 2012 (Member, 2009–12); *b* Belfast, 5 Feb. 1957; *d* of John G. Duff and Hazel Duff; *m* 1981, Geoffrey Patterson; one *s* one *d*. *Educ:* Victoria Coll., Belfast; St Godric's Coll., Hampstead. Sportsground and Landscape Mgt Analyst, 1976–2005, Dir, 1985–2005, John G. Duff (Annadale) Ltd. Mem., Independent Monitoring Bd, 1996–2008 (Chm., 1998–2001); Chm., Assoc. of Independent Monitoring Bd Members, 2003–08. Member: Parades Commn for NI, 2005–10; Prison Service Pay Rev. Body, 2011–13; a Civil Service Comr for NI, 2009–15; non-exec. Mem., Audit Cttee, Office of Police Ombudsman, 2010–15. Chm., Women in Business Network, 2001–04; Dir, Women on the Move, 2009–15. *Recreations:* striving for peace and harmony, gardening, craft, art, theatre, museums. *Address:* Probation Board for Northern Ireland, 80–90 North Street, Belfast BT1 1LD. *T:* (028) 9026 2439. *E:* vilma.patterson@pbni.gsi.gov.uk. *Club:* Belvoir Park Golf.

PATTIE, Rt Hon. Sir Geoffrey (Edwin), Kt 1987; PC 1987; Senior Partner, Terrington Management LLP, since 1999; Chairman, GEC-Marconi, 1996–99 (Joint Chairman, 1991–96); *b* 17 Jan. 1936; *s* of late Alfred Edwin Pattie, LDS, and Ada Olive (*née* Carr); *m* 1960, Tuëma Caroline (*née* Eyre-Maunsell); one *s* (one *d* decd). *Educ:* Durham Sch.; St Catharine's Coll., Cambridge (BA 1959, MA; Fellow Commoner, 2005; Hon. Fellow, 2007). Called to Bar, Gray's Inn, 1964. Served: Queen Victoria's Rifles (TA), 1959–61; (on amalgamation) Queen's Royal Rifles (TA), then 4th Royal Green Jackets, later 7th (TA) Battalion, The Rifles, 1961–65; Captain, 1964, Hon. Col, 1996–99, Dep. Col Comdt (TA and Cadets), 1999–2007. Mem. GLC, Lambeth, 1967–70; Chm. ILEA Finance Cttee, 1968–70. Marketing Dir, 1997–98, Dir of Communications, 1998–99, GEC. Contested (C) Barking, 1966 and 1970. MP (C) Chertsey and Walton, Feb. 1974–1997. Parly Under Sec. of State for Defence for the RAF, 1979–81, for Defence Procurement, 1981–83; Minister of State: for Defence Procurement, 1983–84; DTI (Minister for IT), 1984–87; Vice-Chm., Cons. Party, 1990–97. Sec., Cons. Parly Aviation Cttee, 1974–75, 1975–76, Vice Chm., 1976–77, 1977–78; Jt Sec., Cons. Parly Defence Cttee, 1975–76, 1976–77, 1977–78, Vice Chm., 1978–79; Mem., Cttee of Public Accounts, 1976–79; Vice-Chm., All Party Cttee on Mental Health, 1977–79. Mem. General Synod of Church of England, 1970–75. Chm., Intellectual Property Inst., 1994–99. Chm. of Governors, London Coll. of Printing, 1968–69. Trustee, Excalibur Scholarship Scheme, 1992–. FRSA 1990. Hon. LLD Sheffield, 1996. *Publications:* Towards a New Defence Policy, 1976; (with James Bellini) A New World Role for the Medium Power: the British Opportunity, 1977; One of our Delegations is Missing, 2002. *Recreations:* opera, theatre, following Middlesbrough Football Club. *Address:* Terrington Management, 45 Great Peter Street, SW1P 3LT. *Club:* Reform.

PATTINSON, Kristina; *see* Harrison, K.

PATTINSON, Timothy John Hull; a District Judge (Magistrates' Courts), since 2009; *b* Winchester, 15 March 1956; *s* of John Pattinson and Mary Grace Pattinson (*née* Hull); *m* 2003, Juliet Elizabeth Winsor. *Educ:* Winchester Coll.; University Coll. London (BA Hons English Lit.). Trainee solicitor, Lawrence Graham, London, 1980–83; admitted as solicitor, 1983; English Teacher, 1984; Assistant Solicitor: Thomas Coombs, Dorchester, 1985–86; Dutton Gregory, Winchester, 1987–89; sole practitioner, Winchester, 1989–2001; Consultant, Talbot Walker, Andover, 2001–09; Dep. Dist Judge (Magistrates' Courts), 1999–2009. *Recreations:* walking, books, visiting old churches and country houses. *Address:* Oxford Magistrates' Court, Speedwell Street, Oxford OX1 1RZ.

PATTISON, David Arnold, PhD; Best Value Inspector, Audit Commission, 2000–06; *b* 9 Feb. 1941; *s* of David Pattison and Christina Russell Bone; *m* 1967, Anne Ross Wilson; two *s* one *d*. *Educ:* Glasgow Univ. (BSc 1st Cl. Hons, PhD). Planning Assistant, Dunbarton County Council, 1966–67; Lecturer, Strathclyde Univ., 1967–70; Head of Tourism Division, Highlands and Islands Development Board, 1970–81; Chief Exec., Scottish Tourist Board, 1981–85; Dir of Leisure and Tourism Consulting, Arthur Young Group, 1985–90; Principal Associate: Cobham Resource Consultants, 1990–96; Scott Wilson Resource Consultants, 1996–98; Dir, David A. Pattison Associates, 1998–2000. Hon. Pres., Scottish YHA, 1995–. *Publications:* Tourism Development Plans for: Argyll, Bute, Ayrshire, Burgh of Ayr, Ulster. *Recreations:* reading, watching soccer and Rugby, golf, gardening. *Address:* 4 Braefoot Grove, Dalgety Bay, Fife KY11 9YS.

PATTISON, Rev. Prof. George Linsley, DD; 1640 Professor of Divinity, University of Glasgow, since 2013; *b* 25 May 1950; *s* of George William Pattison and Jean Pattison; *m* 1971, Hilary Christine Cochrane; one *s* two *d*. *Educ:* Perse Sch., Cambridge; Edinburgh Univ. (MA, BD); Durham Univ. (PhD 1983, DD 2004). Ordained deacon, 1977, priest, 1978; Curate, St James' Church, Benwell, Newcastle upon Tyne, 1977–80; Priest-in-charge, St Philip and St James' Church, Kimblesworth, Co. Durham, 1980–83; Res. Student, Durham Univ., 1980–83; Rector, Badwell Ash, Great Ashfield, Hunston and Stowlangtoft with Langham, Suffolk, 1983–91; Dean of Chapel, King's Coll., Cambridge, 1991–2001; Associate Prof. of Theol., 2002–03, Vis. Prof. of Theol., 2005–11, Univ. of Aarhus, Denmark; Lady Margaret Prof. of Divinity, Univ. of Oxford 2004–13; Canon of Christ Church, Oxford, 2004–13. Vis. Res. Prof., 1997, 2000, Vis. Prof. of Theol., 2011–, Univ. of Copenhagen. Vice-Pres., Modern Churchpeople's Union, 1999–2008. Has broadcast on BBC Radio 3, Radio 4 and World Service on subjects of art and religion. Editor, Modern Believing, 1994–98. *Publications:* Art, Modernity and Faith, 1991, 2nd edn 1998; Kierkegaard: the aesthetic and the religious, 1992, 2nd edn 1999; (ed) Kierkegaard on Art and Communication, 1993; (with Sister Wendy Beckett) Pains of Glass, 1995; (with S. Platten) Spirit and Tradition, 1996; Agnosis: theology in the void, 1996; Kierkegaard and the Crisis of Faith, 1997; (ed with S. Shakespeare) Kierkegaard: the self in society, 1998; The End of Theology and the Task of Thinking About God, 1998; Poor Paris!, 1998; Anxious Angels, 1999; The Later Heidegger, 2000; A Short Course in the Philosophy of Religion, 2001; Kierkegaard's Upbuilding Discourses, 2002; Kierkegaard, Religion and the Nineteenth Century Crisis of Culture, 2002; A Short Course in Christian Doctrine, 2005; The Philosophy of Kierkegaard, 2005; Thinking About God in an Age of Technology, 2005; Crucifixions and Resurrections of the Image, 2009; God and Being, 2011; Kierkegaard and the Theology of the Nineteenth Century, 2012; Kierkegaard and the Quest for Unambiguous Life, 2013; Heidegger and Death, 2013; The Heart Cold Never Speak, 2013; (ed with J. Lippitt) The Oxford Handbook of Kierkegaard, 2013; (ed jtly) The Oxford Handbook of Theology and Modern European Thought, 2013; Paul Tillich's Philosophical Theology: a fifty year reappraisal, 2015; Eternal God/Saving Time, 2015; articles on theology, philosophy of religion and the arts in specialist and non-specialist jls. *Recreations:* family life, music, films, theatre, visiting cities, walking, riding. *Address:* Theology and Religious Studies, University of Glasgow, Glasgow G12 8QQ.

PATTISON, Sir John (Ridley), Kt 1998; DM; FRCPath, FMedSci; Professor of Medical Microbiology, University College London, 1984–2004, now Emeritus; *b* 1 Aug. 1942; *s* of Tom Frederick and Elizabeth Pattison; *m* 1965, Pauline Evans; one *s* two *d*. *Educ:* Barnard Castle Sch.; University Coll., Oxford (BSc, MA; BM, BCh 1968; DM 1975); Middlesex Hosp. Med. Sch. FRCPath 1985. Asst Lectr in Pathology, then Lectr in Virology, Middx Hosp. Med. Sch., 1970–75; Lectr, then Sen. Lectr in Virology, St Bartholomew's and London Hosp. Med. Colls, 1976–77; Prof. of Medical Microbiol., KCH Med. Sch., 1977–84; Dean, UCL Med. Sch., 1990–98; Vice-Provost, UCL, 1994–99; Dir of R&D, DoH and NHS, 1999–2004 (on secondment). Hon. NHS Consultant, UCH, subseq. UCL Hosps NHS Trust, 1984–2004; Hon. Consultant, PHLS, 1980–2003 (Board Mem., 1989–95); Sen. Med. Advr, MRC, 1996–99. Mem., MRC, 1992–95, 1999–2004 (Mem., Grants Cttee, 1985–87, Systems Bd, 1988–92; Chm., Physiol Medicine and Infection Bd, 1992–95); Chm., Spongiform Encephalopathy Adv. Cttee, 1995–99 (Mem., 1994–95). Mem. Council, Soc. of Gen. Microbiol., 1981–87. Member of Board: LSHTM, 1989–92; Inst. of Child Health, 1992–96; Inst. of Neurology, 1995–97. Member: Mgt Cttee, King's Fund, 1993–99 (Dep. Chm., 1994–99); King's Fund London Commn, 1994–95. Editor-in-Chief, Epidemiology & Infection, 1980–94; Mem. Council, Internat. Jl Exptl Pathology, 1979–. Founder FMedSci 1998. *Publications:* (ed jtly) Principles & Practice of Clinical Virology, 1987, 5th edn 2004; (ed jtly) Practical Guide to Clinical Virology, 1989; (ed jtly) Practical Guide to Clinical Bacteriology, 1995; papers and reviews on aspects of medical virology, esp. rubella virus and parvovirus infections. *Recreations:* family, windsurfing, books. *Address:* 17 Broadwater Lane, Towcester, Northants NN12 6YF. *T:* (01327) 352116. *E:* portsea200@btopenworld.com.

PATTISON, Lindsay; Worldwide Chief Executive Officer, Maxus, since 2014; *b* Chipping Norton, 17 April 1973; *d* of late Desmond James and of Christine James (*née* Houlton); *m* 2011, David Pattison. *Educ:* Univ. of Stirling (BA Hons Eng. Lit.). Media Manager, Team Y&R, 1998–2001; Brand Manager, Sony Ericsson, 1998–2001; Man. Partner, PHD, 2003–09; UK CEO and Global Chief Strategy Officer, Maxus, 2009–14. Vice Chair, WEF Global Agenda Council, 2014–. Mem., WACL, 2008–. *Publications:* blogs and articles. *Recreations:* music, theatre, swimming, tennis, fashion. *Address:* Maxus, 11–33 St John Street, EC1M 4AA. *T:* (020) 7025 3934. *E:* lindsay.pattison@maxusglobal.com.

PATTISON, Michael Ambrose, CBE 1996; Director, Sainsbury Family Charitable Trusts, 1995–2006; *b* 14 July 1946; *s* of late Osmond John Pattison and Eileen Susanna Pattison (*née* Cullen); *m* 1975, Beverley Jean, *d* of Dr Genevieve Rhines (*née* Downes) and late Hugh E. Webber, II, Florida, USA; one *d*. *Educ:* Sedbergh School; University of Sussex (BA Hons 1968). Min. of Overseas Develt, 1968; Asst Private Sec. to Minister, 1970; seconded to HM Diplomatic Service as First Sec., Perm. Mission to UN, New York, 1974; ODA, 1977; Private Sec. to successive Prime Ministers, 1979–82; ODA, 1982, Establishment Officer, 1983–85; Chief Exec. and Sec. Gen., RICS, 1985–95; Dir, Surveyors Holdings Ltd, 1985–95. Mem. Council, British Consultants Bureau, 1985–95. Non-exec. Dir, Ordnance Survey, 1997–2001. Trustee: Battersea Arts Centre Trust, 1988–94; Sedbergh Sch. Foundn, 2007–14; Cedars Castle Hill, Shaftesbury, 2007–. Member: Cambridge Univ. Careers Service Syndicate, 1989–93; HEFCE Appeals Panel, 1999–; Gov., Thames Poly., subseq. Greenwich Univ., 1989–97 (Pro-Chancellor, 1994–97). Vis. Fellow, City Univ., 1990–. FRSA 1990. *Recreations:* tennis, golf, cricket, Real tennis, local history in UK and USA, countryside. *Address:* 8 Bimport, Shaftesbury, Dorset SP7 8AX. *T:* (01747) 852017. *Clubs:* Athenæum; Warwickshire CC.

PATTISON, Scott; Floating Sheriff of South Strathclyde, Dumfries and Galloway at Ayr, since 2012; *b* Motherwell, 18 Sept. 1969; *s* of Samuel Pattison and Jean Pattison (*née* Campbell); *m* 1992, Aileen Beggan; one *d*. *Educ:* Dalziel High Sch., Motherwell; Univ. of Glasgow (MA; LLB; DipLP). Trainee solicitor, Crown Office and Procurator Fiscal Service, 1993–94; Procurator Fiscal Depute, Hamilton, 1994–98; Principal Procurator Fiscal Depute: specialising in human rights, 1998–99; Crown Office Appeals Unit, 1999–2001; Race Equality and Diversity, Crown Office Policy Gp, 2001–02; Divl Procurator Fiscal, Glasgow, 2002–04; Hd, Policy Gp, Crown Office, 2005–06; Procurator Fiscal, Paisley, 2006–08; Dir of Ops, Crown Office, 2008–11; Floating Sheriff, Grampian, Highlands and Islands at Aberdeen, 2011–12. *Recreations:* music, songwriting, running. *Address:* Sheriff Court House, Wellington Square, Ayr KA7 1EE. *E:* sheriffspattison@scotcourts.gov.uk.

PATTISON, Rev. Prof. Stephen Bewley, DLitt; H. G. Wood Professor of Theology, University of Birmingham, since 2010 (Professor of Religion, Ethics and Practice, 2007–10); *b* 14 Sept. 1953; *s* of Theodore Pattison and Rosamund Audrey Pattison (*née* Greening); *m* 2003, Charmian Beer. *Educ:* Bootham Sch., York; Selwyn Coll., Cambridge (BA 1976); Edinburgh Theol Coll. (Dip. in Pastoral Studies 1978); Univ. of Edinburgh (PhD 1982; DLitt 2001); Univ. of Birmingham (MSocSc 1991). Ordained deacon, 1978, priest, 1980; Asst Curate, All Saints' Ch, Gosforth, 1978–79; Chaplain, Edinburgh Theol Coll., 1982–83; Lectr, Dept of Theol., Univ. of Birmingham, 1983–88; Chief Officer, Central Birmingham CHC, 1988–90; Lectr, then Sen. Lectr, Sch. of Health and Social Welfare, Open Univ., 1990–98; Dist. Sen. Res. Fellow, 1998–2000, Prof. and Head, 2000–07, Sch. of Religious and Theol Studies, Cardiff Univ. Vis. Sen. Res. Fellow, Jesus Coll., Oxford, 2004–05; Hon. Prof., Sch. of Medicine and Health, Durham Univ., 2011–. Gifford Lectr, Aberdeen Univ., 2007. Hon. FRCGP 2013. *Publications:* A Critique of Pastoral Care, 1987, 3rd edn 2000; Alive and Kicking: towards a practical theology of healing and illness, 1988; Pastoral Care and Liberation Theology, 1994; The Faith of the Managers, 1997; Shame: theory, therapy, theology, 2000; (ed jtly) The Blackwell Reader in Pastoral and Practical Theology, 2000; (ed jtly) Values in Professional Practice, 2004; The Challenge of Practical Theology, 2007; Seeing Things: deepening relations with visual artefacts, 2007; (ed jtly) Emerging Values in Health Care, 2010; Saving Face, 2013. *Recreation:* growing things. *Address:* 11A Salisbury Road, Moseley, Birmingham B13 8JS. *T:* 07951 145989. *E:* sbpattison@hotmail.com.

PATTISON, Stephen Dexter, CMG 2003; DPhil; HM Diplomatic Service, retired; Vice President, Public Affairs, ARM Holdings, since 2012; *b* 24 Dec. 1953; *s* of George Stanley and May Elizabeth Pattison; *m* 1987, Helen Chaoushis; one *d*. *Educ:* Sir George Monoux Sch.; Queens' Coll., Cambridge (BA 1976); Wadham Coll., Oxford (DPhil 1980). Joined FCO, 1981: Second Sec., Nicosia, 1983–86; FCO, 1986–89; First Sec., Washington, 1989–94; Dep. Hd, Non-Proliferation Dept, FCO, 1994–96; Dir of Trade Promotion and Consul-Gen., Warsaw, 1997–2000; Hd, UN Dept, FCO, 2000–03; Fellow, Harvard Univ., 2003–04; Dir, Internat. Security, FCO, 2004–07; Head, Internat. Business Develt, Dyson, 2008–11; CEO, Internat. Chamber of Commerce (UK), 2011–12. *Recreations:* the arts, cricket. *Address:* c/o ARM Holdings, 110 Fulbourn Road, Cambridge CB1 9NJ.

PATTRICK, Prof. Richard Annandale Douglas, PhD; Professor of Earth Science, University of Manchester, since 2001; *b* 31 March 1953; *s* of Dr Francis Gilson Pattrick and Hope Annandale Pattrick; *m* 1979, Sheila Margaret Murdoch; two *s* one *d*. *Educ:* Univ. of St Andrews (BSc Hons Geol.); Univ. of Strathclyde (PhD Applied Geol. 1980). University of Manchester: Lectr in Geol., 1979–98; Reader in Mineralogy, 1998–2001; Hd, Grad. Sch., 2001–03; Hd, Sch. of Earth, Atmospheric and Envmtl Sci., 2003–07; Associate Dean, Grad. Educn, 2007–08. Chm., Diamond Light Source Sci. Adv. Cttee, 2015– (Mem., 2011–13; Vice Chm., 2013–15). Vice Pres., 1988–92, Pres., 2010–11, Mineralogical Soc. of GB and Ireland. *Publications:* (with D. A. Polya) Mineralisation in the British Isles, 1993; (ed with D. J. Vaughan) Mineral Surfaces, 1995; 135 contribs on metallogenesis, applied mineralogy and envmtl geosci. in peer reviewed jls. *Recreations:* sport: tennis (county level, student international), hockey (student international), supporter of Macclesfield Town FC, live internet commentator. *Address:* University of Manchester, Manchester M13 9PL. *E:* richard.pattrick@manchester.ac.uk. *Clubs:* Macclesfield Town Football (Vice-Pres.); Buxton High Peak Golf.

PATTULLO, Sir (David) Bruce, Kt 1995; CBE 1989; Governor, Bank of Scotland, 1991–98 (Group Chief Executive, 1988–96); *b* 2 Jan. 1938; *s* of late Colin Arthur Pattullo and Elizabeth Mary Bruce; *m* 1962, Fiona Jane Nicholson; three *s* one *d*. *Educ:* Rugby Sch.; Hertford Coll., Oxford (BA). FCIBS. Commnd Royal Scots and seconded to Queen's Own Nigeria Regt. Gen. Man., Bank of Scotland Finance Co. Ltd, 1973–77; Chief Exec., British Linen Bank Ltd, 1977–78 (Dir, 1977–98); Bank of Scotland: Dep. Treas., 1978; Treas. and Gen. Manager (Chief Exec.), 1979–88; Dir, 1980–98; Dep. Governor, 1988–91. Director: Melville Street Investments, 1973–90; Bank of Wales, 1986–98; NWS Bank plc, 1986–98; Standard Life Assurance Co., 1985–96. Chm., Cttee, Scottish Clearing Bankers, 1981–83, 1987–89; Pres., Inst. of Bankers in Scotland, 1990–92 (a Vice-Pres., 1977–90). First Prizeman (Bilsland Prize), Inst. of Bankers in Scotland, 1964. FRSE 1990. Hon. LLD Aberdeen, 1995; DUniv Stirling, 1996; Hon. DBA Strathclyde, 1998. *Recreations:* tennis, hill walking. *Address:* 6 Cammo Road, Edinburgh EH4 8EB. *Club:* New (Edinburgh).

PAUFFLEY, Hon. Dame Anna (Evelyn Hamilton), DBE 2003; **Hon. Mrs Justice Pauffley;** a Judge of the High Court of Justice, Family Division, since 2003; *b* 13 Jan. 1956; *d* of late Donald Eric Hamilton Pauffley and Josephine Sybil Pauffley; *m* 2001, Frank Harris; one step *s* two step *d*. *Educ:* Godolphin Sch., Salisbury; London Univ. (BA Hons). Called to the Bar, Middle Temple, 1979, Bencher 2003; QC 1995; a Recorder, 1998–2003. Hon. LLD City, 2005. Family Div. Liaison Judge, London and Thames Valley, 2004–; Sen. Family Liaison Judge, 2013–. *Address:* Royal Courts of Justice, Strand, WC2A 2LL.

PAUK, György; Order of the Hungarian Republic, 1998; international concert violinist; Professor at Guildhall School of Music and Drama; Professor, Royal Academy of Music, since 1987; Professor Emeritus, Franz Liszt Academy, Budapest, since 2007; *b* 26 Oct. 1936; *s* of Imre and Magda Pauk; *m* 1959, Susanne Mautner; one *s* one *d*. *Educ:* Franz Liszt Acad. of Music, Budapest. Toured E Europe while still a student; won three internat. violin competitions, Genoa 1956, Munich 1957, Paris 1959; soon after leaving Hungary, settled in London, 1961, and became a British citizen. London début, 1961; seasonal appearances there and in the provinces, with orchestra, in recital and chamber music; also plays at Bath, Cheltenham and Edinburgh Fests and London Promenade Concerts; performs in major European music venues; US début, under Sir George Solti, with Chicago Symph. Orch., 1970, followed by further visits to USA and Canada to appear with major orchs; holds master classes in many US univs, major music schs in Japan and Internat. Mozart Acad., Prague; Vis. Prof., Winterthur Conservatorium, Switzerland, 1996; plays regularly in Hungary following return in 1973; overseas tours to Australia, NZ, S America, S Africa, Middle and Far East; many performances for BBC, incl. Berg and Bartók concertos, with Boulez. As conductor/ soloist, has worked with the English, Scottish and Franz Liszt chamber orchs and London Mozart Players; guest dir, Acad. of St Martin-in-the-Fields; with Peter Frankl and Ralph Kirshbaum, formed chamber music trio, 1973; performances at major fests; public concerts in GB have incl. complete Brahms and Beethoven Cycles; the trio has also made many broadcasts for the BBC. First performances: Penderecki's Violin Concerto, Japan, 1979, UK, 1980; Tippett's Triple Concerto, London, 1980; Lutosawski's Chain 2, with composer conducting, Britain, The Netherlands and Hungary, 1986–87; Sir Peter Maxwell Davies' Violin Concerto, Switzerland, 1988; William Mathias' Violin Concerto, Manchester, 1991. Has made many recordings including: Bartok Sonatas (among top records in US, 1982), and Bartok's music for solo violin, with piano, for two violins and violin concertos; Tippett Concerto (Best Gramophone Record Award, 1983); Berg Concerto (Caecilia Prize, Belgium, 1983); complete sonatas for violin and harpsichord by Handel; all violin concertos and orch. works by Mozart; Brahms Sonatas. Hon. GSM 1980. Hon. RAM 1990. Bartók Pásztory Prize, Hungary, 2008.

PAUL, family name of **Baron Paul**.

PAUL, Baron *cr* 1996 (Life Peer), of Marylebone in the City of Westminster; **Swraj Paul;** PC 2009; Padma Bhushan; Chairman, Caparo Group Ltd, since 1978; *b* 18 Feb. 1931; *s* of Payare and Mongwati Paul; *m* 1956, Aruna Vij; three *s* one *d* (and one *d* decd). *Educ:* Punjab Univ. (BSc); Mass Inst. of Technol. (BSc, MSc (Mech. Engrg)). Began work as Partner in family-owned Apeejay Surrendra Gp, India, 1953; came to UK in 1966 and estabd first business, Natural Gas Tubes Ltd; Caparo Group Ltd formed in 1978 as holding co. for UK businesses involved in engrg, hotel and property develt, investment; Caparo Industries Plc (engrg, metals) formed in 1981. Founder Chm., Indo-British Assoc., 1975–2000. Chancellor: Univ. of Wolverhampton, 1999–; Univ. of Westminster, 2006–14; Pro-Chancellor, 1997–2000, Chancellor, 2000–01, Thames Valley Univ. FRSA. Padma Bhushan (equivalent to British Peerage), 1983. Hon. PhD Amer. Coll. of Switzerland, Leysin, 1986; Hon. DSc (Econ) Hull, 1992; Buckingham, 1999; DUniv: Bradford, 1997; Central England, 1999; Hon. DLitt Westminster, 1997. Corporate Leadership Award, MIT, 1987. Freeman, City of London, 1998. *Publications:* Indira Gandhi, 1984, 2nd edn 1985; Beyond Boundaries, 1998. *Address:* Caparo House, 103 Baker Street, W1U 6LN. *T:* (020) 7486 1417. *Clubs:* MCC; Royal Calcutta Turf, Royal Calcutta Golf (Calcutta); Cricket of India (Bombay).

PAUL, Alan Roderick, CMG 1997; Founder and Managing Director, Alan Paul Partners Ltd (formerly Sirius Search Ltd), Hong Kong, since 2010; Chairman, Glasford International, since 2014; *b* 13 May 1950; *s* of late Roderick Ernest Paul and Hilda May Paul (*née* Choules); *m* 1979, Rosana Yuen-Ling Tam; one *s* one *d*. *Educ:* Wallington High Sch. for Boys; Christ Church, Oxford (Scholar; MA Modern Langs, 1st class Hons). HM Diplomatic Service, 1972–2001: FCO, 1972–73; language training, Univs of Cambridge and Hong Kong, 1973–75; FCO, 1975–77; Peking, 1977–80; FCO, 1980–84; Head of Chancery, The Hague, 1984–87; Asst Head, 1987–89, Head, 1989–91, Hong Kong Dept, FCO; Counsellor and Dep. Sen. Rep., 1991–97, Sen. Rep. (with personal rank of Ambassador), 1997–2000, Sino-British Jt Liaison Gp, Hong Kong; FCO, 2000–01. Dir, 2001–04, Partner, 2004–10, Executive Access Ltd, Hong Kong. *Recreations:* reading, music, chess, gym. *Address:* Alan Paul Partners, Level 8, Two Exchange Square, 8 Connaught Place, Central, Hong Kong.

PAUL, Prof. Douglas John, PhD; Professor of Semiconductor Devices, Department of Electronics and Electrical Engineering, since 2007 and Director, James Watt Nanofabrication Centre, since 2010, University of Glasgow; *b* Greenock, 25 Feb. 1969; *s* of John Stuart Paul and Margaret Paul; *m* 2011, Amy Jane Lloyd. *Educ:* Greenock Acad.; Churchill Coll., Cambridge (BA Phys and Theoretical Phys 1990; PhD 1994). CPhys 1999; FInstP 2007. Cavendish Laboratory, University of Cambridge: Res. Associate, 1994–98; EPSRC Advanced Res. Fellow, 1998–2003; Sen. Res. Associate, 2003–07; Res. Fellow, 1994–98, Fellow, 1998–2007, St Edmund's Coll., Cambridge. Member: Chem., Biol Physics Panel, NATO Sci. Cttee, 2004–08; Chem., Biol, Radiol and Nuclear Scientific Adv. Cttee, Home Office, 2004–; DSAC, 2010–13; High Impact Threats Expert Adv. Gp, 2013, Scientific Adv. Gp for Emergencies, 2014, Cabinet Office. Mem., Sci. Bd, Inst. of Phys, 2004–10. Mem., Enhancing Value: getting the most out of UK res. Task Force, Nat. Centre for Univs and Business (formerly Council for Industry and Higher Educn), 2011–. SMIEEE 2003; FHEA 2009; FRSE 2011. President's Medal, Inst. of Phys, 2014. *Publications:* (ed with L. W. Molenkamp) Technology Roadmap for European Nanoelectronics, 1999, 2nd edn 2000; (with E. Kasper) Silicon Quantum Information Circuits, 2005; articles in Applied Phys Letters, Phys. Rev. and IEEE jls. *Recreations:* wine tasting, cooking, cycling, singing, piano. *Address:* Rankine Building, School of Engineering, University of Glasgow, Oakfield Avenue, Glasgow G12 8LT. *T:* (0141) 330 5219. *E:* Douglas.Paul@glasgow.ac.uk.

PAUL, Geoffrey David, OBE 1991; freelance editorial consultant; *b* 26 March 1929; *s* of Reuben Goldstein and Anne Goldstein; *m* 1st, 1952, Joy Stirling (marr. diss. 1972); one *d*; 2nd, 1974, Rachel Mann; one *s*. *Educ:* Liverpool, Kendal, Dublin. Weekly newspaper and news agency reporter, 1947–57; asst editor, Jewish Observer and Middle East Review, 1957–62; Jewish Chronicle, 1962–96: successively sub-editor, foreign editor, Israel corresp., deputy editor; Editor, 1977–90; US Affairs Editor, 1991–96; Consultant, Sternberg Foundn, 1996–2012. Dir, Anglo-Israel Assoc., 2001–03. FRSA 1993. *Publications:* Living in Jerusalem, 1981. *Address:* 1 Carlton Close, West Heath Road, NW3 7UA.

PAUL, George William; DL; Secretary, Suffolk Horse Society, since 2015 (Chairman, 2012–15); *b* 25 Feb. 1940; *s* of William Stuart Hamilton Paul and Diana Violet Anne Martin; *m* 1st, 1963, Mary Annette Mitchell (*d* 1989); two *s* one *d*; 2nd, Margaret J. Kilgour (*née* Hedges). *Educ:* Harrow; Wye Coll., Univ. of London (BSc Agric. Hons). Pauls & Whites Foods: Marketing Dir, 1968; Managing Dir, 1972; Pauls & Whites: Dir, 1972; Group Managing Dir, 1982; Chm., Pauls, 1985; Harrisons & Crosfield: Dir, 1985; Jt Chief Exec., 1986; Chief Exec., 1987–94; Chm., 1994–97; Norwich Union: Dir, 1990–2000; Vice-Chm., 1992–94; Chm., 1994–2000; Dep. Chm., CGNU, then Aviva, 2000–05. Chairman: Agricola Holdings Ltd, 1998–2000; Agricola Gp Ltd, 2000–12; J. P. Morgan Fleming Overseas Investment Trust, 2001–10; Notcutts Ltd, 2006–10 (Dir, 1998–2010). Mem., Jockey Club; Chm., Jockey Club Estates Ltd, 1991–2005. Chm. Trustees, Nat. Horseracing Mus., 2008–12. Pres., Suffolk Agricultural Assoc., 1984, 2010. Chm., Essex and Suffolk Foxhounds, 1974–77, 1993–2013 (Jt Master and Huntsman, 1977–85). High Sheriff, 1990, DL, 1991, Suffolk. *Recreations:* theatre, the arts, country sports, sailing. *Clubs:* Boodle's, Farmers.

PAUL, Air Marshal Sir Ronald Ian S.; *see* Stuart-Paul.

PAUL, Wesley Irwin; Chairman, Firsthaven Partners LLP, since 2010; *b* Georgetown, Guyana, 1957. JP Morgan & Co., 1975–2000: a Man. Dir; Global Hd of Fixed Income, Foreign Exchange, Emerging Mkts, Econ. Res.; Global Hd of Investments; Mem., Global Mgt Cttee, London and NY; former Chief Exec., Edgeworth Capital, Lehman Brothers JV Hedge Fund. Chm., Bd of Trustees, Royal Armouries, 2012–15. Non-exec. Dir, Harbour Capital LLP, Hong Kong, 2010–. Member: Adv. Bd, Durham Univ. Global Security Inst., 2012–; Adv. Council, RUSI, 2013–. *Recreations:* human development, international security and geopolitics, arms and armour, history, museums, fishing, shooting, theatre, books, arts. *E:* wesleyipaul@gmail.com.

PAUL-CHOUDHURY, Sumit; Editor, New Scientist, since 2011; *b* London; *s* of Sukhendu Paul-Choudhury and Mandira Paul-Choudhury; *m* 1st, 2001, Kathryn Oates (*d* 2005); 2nd, 2009, Lucia Graves. *Educ:* Imperial Coll. London (BSc Hons Physics 1992); Queen Mary and Westfield Coll., Univ. of London (MSc Maths 1994). ARCS 1992. Technical Editor, Risk Magazine, 1994–99; Vice Pres., ERisk, 2000–02; Man. Dir, Risk Communications, 2003–05; Online Editor, New Scientist, 2008–11; Editor-in-Chief, Arc, 2012–. *Recreations:* electronic music, dancing, writing fiction, London, psychogeography, archaeology, travel, theatre, ranting. *Address:* c/o New Scientist, 110 High Holborn, WC1V 6EU. *T:* (020) 7611 1202. *E:* sumit@paulchoudhury.com. *Club:* Adam Street.

PAULET, family name of **Marquess of Winchester**.

PAULIN, Oswyn George, CB 2013; Head, Government Legal Service for Northern Ireland, and Departmental Solicitor, since 2007; *b* Leeds, 16 July 1951; *s* of Douglas Paulin and Mary Paulin (*née* Robertson); *m* 1987, Romaine Gail Hamilton; four *s* one *d*. *Educ:* Rosetta Primary Sch., Belfast; Annadale Grammar Sch., Belfast; Queen's Univ., Belfast (LLB). Articled clerk, Elliott Duffy Garrett, 1973–76; admitted as solicitor, 1976; Professional Asst, Crown Solicitor's Office, 1976–85; Sen. Legal Asst, NI Office, 1985–89; Crown Solicitor's Office: Sen. Legal Asst, 1989–92; Asst Crown Solicitor, 1992–2002; Crown Solicitor, 2002–07. Pres., Belfast Literary Soc., 2010–11. Mem., Gen. Synod, C of I, 2012–. Gov., Wellington Coll. Belfast. *Address:* (office) Victoria Hall, 12 May Street, Belfast BT1 4NL.
See also T. N. Paulin.

PAULIN, Prof. Roger Cole, DrPhil, LittD; Schröder Professor of German, University of Cambridge, 1989–2005, now Emeritus; Fellow, Trinity College, Cambridge since 1989; *b* 18 Dec. 1937; *s* of Thomas Gerald Paulin and Paulina (*née* Duff); *m* 1966, Traute Fielitz; one *s* one *d*. *Educ:* Otago Boys' High Sch., Dunedin, NZ; Univ. of Otago (MA); Heidelberg Univ. (DrPhil); MA, LittD (Cantab). Asst Lectr, Univ. of Birmingham, 1963–64; Lectr, Univ. of Bristol, 1965–73; Fellow and Coll. Lectr in German, Trinity Coll., Cambridge, 1974–87; Univ. Lectr, Univ. of Cambridge, 1975–87; Henry Simon Prof. of German, Univ. of Manchester, 1987–89. Mem., Editl Bd, Literatur-Lexikon, 1988–93. Bundesverdienstkreuz, 2011. *Publications:* Ludwig Tieck: a literary biography, 1985, 2nd edn 1986 (trans. German 1988); The Brief Compass, 1985; Ludwig Tieck, 1987; Theodor Storm, 1991; Wilhelm Jerusalem, 1999; Shakespeare in Germany, 2003. *Recreation:* gardening. *Address:* 45 Fulbrooke Road, Cambridge CB3 9EE. *T:* (01223) 322564.

PAULIN, Thomas Neilson; poet and critic; G. M. Young Lecturer in English, University of Oxford, 1994–2010; Fellow, Hertford College, Oxford, 1994–2010, now Emeritus; *b* 25 Jan. 1949; *s* of Douglas and Mary Paulin (*née* Robinson); *m* 1973, Munjiet Kaur Khosa; two *s*. *Educ:* Hull Univ. (BA); Lincoln Coll., Oxford (BLitt). English Department, University of Nottingham: Lectr, 1972–89; Reader in Poetry, 1989–94; Prof. of Poetry, 1994. NESTA Fellow, 2000–03. Hon. DLitt: Saskatchewan, 1987; Stafford, 1995; Hull, 2000. *Publications:* Thomas Hardy: the poetry of perception, 1975; A State of Justice, 1977 (Eric Gregory Award, 1976, Somerset Maugham Award, 1978); The Strange Museum, 1980 (Geoffrey Faber Meml Award, 1982); Liberty Tree, 1983; The Riot Act, 1985; Ireland and the English Crisis, 1985; (ed) The Faber Book of Political Verse, 1986; The Hillsborough Script, 1987; Fivemiletown,

1987; Seize the Fire, 1989; (ed) The Faber Book of Vernacular Verse, 1990; Minotaur: poetry and the nation state, 1992; Walking a Line, 1994; Writing to the Moment: selected critical essays, 1996; The Day-Star of Liberty: William Hazlitt's radical style, 1998; The Wind Dog, 1999; The Invasion Handbook, 2002; The Road to Inver, 2004; Crusoe's Secret: the aesthetics of dissent (essays), 2005; The Secret Life of Poems, 2008; Euripides' Medea, 2010; Love's Bonfire, 2012. *Address:* c/o Faber & Faber, Bloomsbury House, 74–77 Great Russell Street, WC1B 3DA.

PAUNCEFORT-DUNCOMBE, Sir David (Philip Henry), 5th Bt *cr* 1859, of Great Brickhill, Bucks; *b* Aldershot, Hants, 21 May 1956; *s* of Sir Philip Digby Pauncefort-Duncombe, 4th Bt and of Rachel Moyra Pauncefort-Duncombe (*née* Aylmer); *S* father, 2011; *m* 1987, Sarah Ann Battrum; one *s* one *d*. *Educ:* Gordonstoun; RAC Cirencester. Estate manager. *Recreation:* fly fishing. *Heir: s* Henry Digby Pauncefort-Duncombe, *b* 16 Dec. 1988. *Address:* Great Brickhill Manor, Milton Keynes, Bucks MK17 9BE.

PAVEY, Martin Christopher; Headmaster, Cranbrook School, 1981–88; *b* 2 Dec. 1940; *s* of Archibald Lindsay Pavey and Margaret Alice Pavey (*née* Salsbury); *m* 1969, Louise Margaret (*née* Bird); two *s*. *Educ:* Magdalen College Sch., Oxford; University Coll., London (Hons English); Nottingham Univ. (MA English); Univ. of Cambridge (Dip. Educn). Wigglesworth & Co., London and E. Africa (Shipping and Finance), 1956–62; Assistant Master: King's Sch., Ely, 1962–64; Lancing Coll., 1968–71; Fairham Comprehensive School, Nottingham: Head of English, 1971–75; Dep. Headmaster, 1975–76; Headmaster, 1976–81; Headmaster, Latymer Upper School, Hammersmith, 1988–91. Chm., AgeCare, RSAS, 2002–08. *Recreations:* art, architecture, cinema. *Address:* 5 Vineyards, Bath BA1 5NA.

PAVLOPOULOS, Prof. Prokopis, PhD; President of the Hellenic Republic, since 2015; *b* Kalamata, 10 July 1950; *s* of Vasilis and Maria Pavlopoulou; *m* Viassia Peltsemi; one *s* two *d*. *Educ:* 4th Elementary Sch., Kalamata; Paralia High Sch., Kalamata; Law Sch., Univ. of Athens (degree with dist. 1973); Univ. of Paris II (Master of Advanced Studies in Public Law 1974; PhD 1977). University of Athens Law School: Asst Prof., 1983–85; Associate Prof., 1985–89; Prof. of Public Law, 1989, now Prof. Emeritus. Vis. Prof., Univ. of Paris II, 1986. Sec. to first (interim) Pres. of Greece, 1974–75; Dep. Minister of Presidency responsible for Media, and Govt Spokesman, Nat. Unity Govt, 1989–90; Dir, Presidency Legal Office, 1990–95; Spokesman, New Democracy pol party, 1995–96; State MP (New Democracy), 1996–2000; Hd, Public Admin, Public Order and Justice Dept, 1996–2000; MP (New Democracy) Athens, 2000–14; Parly Spokesman for New Democracy Party, 2000–04; Minister: of Interior, Public Admin and Decentralization, 2004–07; of Interior, 2007–09. Member: Standing Cttees on Public Admin, Public Order and Justice; special Standing Cttee on Instns and Transparency; Cttee for Revision of Constitution. Officier, Légion d'Honneur (France), 2010; Grand Cross, Order of Redeemer, 2015, Grand Collar, Order of Makarios III, 2015 (Hellenic Republic). *Publications:* La directive en droit administrative, 1978; (with Dr G. Timagenis) The Law and Practice Relating to Pollution Control in Greece, 1982; The Constitutional Guarantee of the Writ of Annulment: a contemporary viewpoint of the rule of law, 1982; Courses in Administrative Science, 1983; The Civil Liability of the State, vol. I, 1986, vol. II, 1989; Guarantees of the Right to Judicial Protection in European Community Law, 1993; The Public Works Contract, 1997; Articles, 1987–2003, 2003; Constitutional Reform, Looked at from the Parliamentary Experience, 2010; The Twilight of Political Leaderships: cause or effect of the economic crisis?, 2011; Public Law at the Time of Economic Crisis, vol. I, 2nd edn 2014; (jtly) Public Law, 3rd edn 2015. *Address:* Presidential Mansion, Vassileos Georgiou B' 2 Avenue, 10028 Athens, Greece. *T:* 2107283211, 2107283251, *Fax:* 2108821165. *E:* secretariat@presidency.gr.

PAVORD, Anna, (Mrs T. D. O. Ware); Gardening Correspondent, The Independent, since 1986; *b* 20 Sept. 1940; *d* of Arthur Vincent Pavord and Christabel Frances (*née* Lewis); *m* 1966, Trevor David Oliver Ware; three *d*. *Educ:* Univ. of Leicester (BA Hons English). PA/ Dir, Line Up, BBC2, 1963–70; contributor, Observer Mag., 1970–92; writer and presenter, Flowering Passions, Channel 4 TV, 1991–92. Associate Editor, Gardens Illustrated, 1993–2008. Member: NT Gardens Panel, 1996–2006 (Chm., 2002–06); English Heritage Parks and Gardens Panel, 2001–10. Hon. DLitt Leicester, 2005. Veitch Meml Gold Medal, 2001. *Publications:* Foliage, 1990; The Flowering Year, 1991; Gardening Companion, 1992; Hidcote, 1993; The Border Book, 1994; The New Kitchen Garden, 1996; The Tulip, 1999; Plant Partners, 2001; The Naming of Names, 2005; Bulb, 2009; The Curious Gardener, 2010. *Recreations:* sailing, walking, gardening, visiting Sikkim. *Address:* c/o The Independent, Northcliffe House, 2 Derry Street, W8 5HF. *T:* (020) 7938 6000.

PAVORD, Prof. Ian Douglas, DM; FRCP; FMedSci; Professor of Respiratory Medicine, University of Oxford, since 2013; Hon. Consultant Physician, Oxford University Hospitals NHS Trust, since 2013; NIHR Senior Investigator, since 2011; *b* Abergavenny, 3 July 1961; *s* of Antony and Jenny Pavord; *m* 1989, Sue Harris; two *s* one *d* (incl. twin *s* and *d*). *Educ:* King Henry VIII Comprehensive Sch.; University Coll. London and Westminster Hosp. (MB BS 1984); Univ. of Nottingham (DM 1992); Univ. of Oxford (MA 2013). MRCP 1987, FRCP 2000. House Officer, Westminster and Rochford Hosps, 1984–85; SHO in Medicine, Taunton and Somerset Hosps, 1985–87; Registrar in Gen. Medicine, Peterborough and Leicester Hosps, 1987–90; Res. Fellow in Respiratory Medicine, 1990–92, Lectr in Respiratory Medicine, 1992–95, Nottingham City Hosp.; Consultant Physician, Glenfield Hosp., Leicester, 1995–2013. Vis. Fellow, St Joseph's Hosp.-McMaster Univ., Canada, 1995; Hon. Prof., Inst. for Lung Health, 2005–13. Med. Dir, Asthma UK, 2008–14. British Thoracic Society: Co-Chm., cough guidelines gp, 2004–06; Chm., BTS/SIGN asthma diagnosis and monitoring guidelines gp, 2007–14; Mem., scientific meetings cttee, 2004–07. Mem., MRC Coll. of Experts. FERS 2014; FMedSci 2015. Associate Ed., Amer. Jl Respiratory and Critical Care Medicine, 2005–10; Jt Ed., Thorax, 2010–15. *Publications:* contributor: Current Diagnosis and Therapy, 1995; Handbook of Respiratory Medicine, 2001; Clinical Respiratory Medicine, 2004; Allergy and Allergic Diseases, 2nd edn, 2008; Handbook of Experimental Pharmacology, 2009; contribs to scientific jls incl. Lancet, BMJ, Thorax, Chest, Cough, Internat. Jl Cardiol., Eur. Respiratory Jl, Jl RCP, Clin. Exptl Allergy, New England Jl of Medicine. *Recreation:* golf. *Address:* Nuffield Department of Medicine Research Building, University of Oxford, Roosevelt Drive, Oxford OX3 7FZ.

PAWLAK, Witold Expedyt; His Honour Judge Pawlak; a Circuit Judge, since 2004; *b* 1947; *s* of Felicjan and Jolanta Pawlak; *m* 1971, Susan Dimsdale; one *s* one *d*. *Educ:* Trinity Coll., Cambridge (BA 1969; MA). Called to the Bar, Inner Temple, 1970; in practice, 1970–2004; a Recorder, 1995–2004. *Address:* Woodhall House, Lordship Lane, Wood Green, N22 5LF.

PAWLE, Oliver John Woodforde; Chairman: FTI Consulting (formerly Financial Dynamics), since 2005; Board Services, Korn/Ferry Whitehead Mann, since 2009; Founder and Chairman of Trustees, New Entrepreneurs Foundation, since 2011; *b* Ndola, Northern Rhodesia, 24 June 1950; *s* of Roger and Nan Pawle; *m* 1983, Emma Mary Frances Birtwistle; one *s* two *d*. *Educ:* Downside Sch.; Nottingham Univ. (BA Industrial Econs). Accountant, Price Waterhouse, 1971–76; Baring Brothers, 1976–84, Dir, 1980–84; Dir, County NatWest, 1984–97; Vice Chm., UBS Investment Bank, 1997–2007. Dir, Adv. Bd, Delancey plc, 2007–. Director: Reform, 2004–; Develt Bd, CAFOD, 2010–; Adv. Bd, Nat. Theatre, 2005–; Gov., Goodenough Trust, 1998–. *Recreations:* theatre, politics, opera, golf, cricket, horse-racing. *Address:* 33 Blenkarne Road, SW11 6HZ. *T:* 07836 337179. *E:* oliver.pawle@kornferry.com. *Clubs:* Boodles, Hurlingham, MCC; Berkshire; St Enodoc Golf.

PAWLEY, Prof. (Godfrey) Stuart, PhD; FRS 1992; FRSE; Professor of Computational Physics, University of Edinburgh, 1985–2002, now Emeritus; *b* 22 June 1937; *s* of George Charles Pawley and Winifred Mary (*née* Wardle); *m* 1961, Anthea Jean Miller; two *s* one *d*. *Educ:* Bolton Sch.; Corpus Christi Coll., Cambridge (MA, PhD 1962). FRSE 1975. Chem. Dept, Harvard Univ., 1962–64; University of Edinburgh: Lect, 1964–69; Reader, 1970–85. Guest Prof., Chem. Dept, Århus Univ., Denmark, 1969–70. *Publications:* (contrib.) An Introduction to OCCAM 2 programming, 2nd edn, 1989; numerous scientific papers. *Recreations:* choral singing, mountain walking, rock gardening (seed reception manager, Scottish Rock Gdn Club). *Address:* Acres of Keillour, Methven, Perth PH1 3RA. *T:* (01738) 840874.

PAWLEY, (Robert) John; Director of Professional Services, Valuation Office Agency, 1995–99; *b* 10 Sept. 1939; *s* of Frederick Clifford and Marjorie Pawley; *m* 1965, Simone Elizabeth Tayar; two *s*. *Educ:* Plymouth Coll.; Exeter Univ. (BA). Private practice, Plymouth, 1962–71; joined Valuation Office, 1972; Dist Valuer, Waltham Forest, 1977, Haringey, 1978–81; Suptg Valuer, Chief Valuer's Office, London, 1981–84, Cambridge, 1984–87; Asst Chief Valuer, 1987–88; Dep. Chief Valuer, Inland Revenue Valuation Office, later Dep. Chief Exec. (Technical), Valuation Office Agency, 1989–95. *Recreations:* 18th century English naval history and exploration, period model boats, antiques.

PAWLEY, Stuart; *see* Pawley, G. S.

PAWSEY, James Francis; Director: Shilton Consultants LLP, 2006–09; Alavan Consulting Ltd 2003–05; *b* 21 Aug. 1933; *s* of William Pawsey and Mary Mumford; *m* 1956, Cynthia Margaret Francis; six *s* (including twins twice). *Educ:* Coventry Tech. School; Coventry Tech. Coll. Chief Exec., Autobar Machine Div., 1970–80; Dir, Autobar Gp, 1980–2006; non-exec. Dir, St Martins Hosps, 1989–2004; Director: Love Lane Investments, 1995–2008; Keyturn Solutions, 1997–2004. MP (C) Rugby, 1979–83, Rugby and Kenilworth, 1983–97; contested (C) Rugby and Kenilworth, 1997. Parliamentary Private Secretary: DES, 1982–83; DHSS, 1983–84; to Minister of State for NI, 1984–86. Member: Parly Scientific Cttee, 1982–97; Select Cttee of Parly Comr for Admin, 1983–97 (Chm., 1993); Select Cttee on Standing Orders, 1987–97; Exec., 1922 Cttee, 1989–97; Liaison Cttee, 1993–97; Ct of Referees, 1993–97; Chm., Cons Parly Educn Cttee, 1985–97; Mem. Exec., IPU, 1984–97 (Vice-Chm., 1994–96); Chm., W Midlands Gp of Cons. MPs, 1993–97; Pres., Rugby Constituency Cons. Assoc., 2013–. Member: Rugby RDC, 1965–73; Rugby Borough Council, 1973–75; Warwickshire CC, 1974–79; former Chm. and Pres., Warwickshire Assoc. of Parish Councils. Founder Mem., Snakes and Ladders Dining Club, H of C. KLJ. *Publications:* The Tringo Phenomenon, 1983. *Address:* 38 Shilton Lane, Bulkington, Warwickshire CV12 9JP.
See also M. Pawsey.

PAWSEY, Mark; MP (C) Rugby, since 2010; *b* Meriden, 16 Jan. 1957; *s* of James Francis Pawsey, *qv*; *m* 1984, Tracy Harris; two *s* two *d*. *Educ:* Reading Univ. (BSc Estate Mgt 1978). Trainee Surveyor, Strutt & Parker, 1978–79; Account Manager, Autobar Vending Supplied Ltd, 1979–82; Founder and Man. Dir, Central Catering Supplies, 1982–2008. Mem., Communities and Local Govt Select Cttee, 2010–15. Contested (C) Nuneaton, 2005. *Recreations:* Rugby football, planting woodland, cooking. *Address:* House of Commons, SW1A 0AA. *E:* mark.pawsey.mp@parliament.uk.

PAWSON, Anthony John Dalby; Head of Defence Export Services, Ministry of Defence, 2007–09; *b* 14 Oct. 1946; *s* of Donald Pawson and Kathleen (*née* Goodwin); *m* 1969, Kathleen Chisholm (*d* 2004); one *s* one *d*. *Educ:* Kent Coll., Canterbury; City Univ. (BSc 1st Class Hons Computer Science). MoD 1967; Private Sec. to Chief of Air Staff, 1978–80; First Sec., UK Delegn to NATO, Brussels, 1981–83; Private Sec. to Sec. of State for NI, 1990–92; RCDS 1992; Asst Under-Sec. of State (Fleet Support), MoD, 1993–95; Under-Sec. (Overseas and Defence), Cabinet Office, 1995–97; Ministry of Defence: Dir Gen. Marketing, 1997–98; Dir Gen. Defence Export Services, 1998–2003; Dir Gen. of Corp. Communication, 2003–04; Dep. Chief of Defence Intelligence, 2004–07. *Recreations:* Rugby, cricket. *Clubs:* Civil Service; Tunbridge Wells Rugby Football; Borderers' Cricket.

PAWSON, John Ward, RDI 2005; architectural designer; *b* 6 May 1949; *s* of James Stoddart Pawson and Winifred Mary Pawson (*née* Ward); *m* 1989, Catherine Mary Clare Berning; one *s*; one *s* by Hester van Roijen. *Educ:* Eton; Architectural Assoc. Sch. Dir, W. L. Pawson and Son Ltd, Halifax, 1967–73; Lectr, Nagoya Univ. of Commerce, 1974–77. *Architectural projects include:* van Roijen Apt, London, 1981; Bruce Chatwin Apt, London, 1982; Waddington Galls, London, 1983; Neuendorf House, Mallorca, 1989; Calvin Klein Store, NY, 1995; Cathay Pacific Lounges, Hong Kong, 1998; Pawson House, London, 1999; Monastery of Our Lady of Novy Dvur, Bohemia, 2004; Sackler Crossing, Royal Botanic Gardens, Kew, 2006; 50 Gramercy Park North, NY, 2006; Montemaggio Estate, Tuscany, 2007; Martyrs Pavilion, St Edward's Sch., Oxford, 2009; Schrager Apartment, NY, 2009; Bel Air House, LA, 2009; Casa delle Bottere, Treviso, 2011; Syukou Fujisawa Gall. and Café, Okinawa, 2012; St Tropez Houses, Provence, 2012; Palmgren House, Stockholm, 2013; Picornell House, Mallorca, 2013; Montauk House, Long Island, NY, 2013; Christopher Kane Store, London, 2015; *set design:* Chroma, Royal Opera House, 2006; L'Anatomie de la Sensation, Opéra Bastille, Paris, 2011; *interiors:* B60 Sloop, Kiel, 2007; Baracuda Ketch, Viareggio, 2008; *interior renovations:* Basilica, Archabbey of Pannonhalma, 2012; St Moritz Ch, Augsburg, 2013; (installation) Perspectives, St Paul's Cathedral, 2011, Basilica di San Giorgio Maggiore, Venice, 2013. *Publications:* Minimum, 1996; Mini-Minimum, 1998; Barn (photography by Fi McGhee), 1999; (ed) Architecture of Truth, by Lucien Hervé, 2000; (with Annie Bell) Living and Eating, 2001; Themes and Projects, 2002; Leçons du Thoronet, 2006; A Visual Inventory, John Pawson, 2012; *relevant publications:* John Pawson, 1992; Critic, 1995; John Pawson Works, by Deyan Sudjic, 2000, rev. edn 2005; John Pawson Plain Space, by Alison Morris, 2010; John Pawson Katalog, by Winifred Nerdinger, Alison Morris, 2012. *Address:* Unit B, 70–78 York Way, N1 9AG. *T:* (020) 7837 2929, *Fax:* (020) 7837 4949. *E:* email@johnpawson.com.

PAXMAN, Giles; *see* Paxman, T. G.

PAXMAN, Jeremy Dickson; journalist, author and broadcaster; *b* 11 May 1950; *s* of late Arthur Keith Paxman and Joan McKay Dickson; partner, Elizabeth Ann Clough; one *s* two *d* (of whom one *s* one *d* are twins). *Educ:* Malvern College; St Catharine's College, Cambridge (Exhibnr; Hon. Fellow, 2000). Reporter: N Ireland, 1974–77; BBC TV Tonight, 1977–79; Panorama, 1979–85; The Bear Next Door; presenter: Breakfast Time, 1986–89; Newsnight, 1989–2014; Did You See?, 1991–93; You Decide—with Paxman, 1995–96; Start The Week, R4, 1998–2002; Britain's Great War (series), 2014; Chairman: University Challenge, 1994–; Times Past, Times Present, R4, 1996; writer and presenter: The Victorians, 2009; Empire, 2012. Hon. Fellow, St Edmund Hall, Oxford, 2000. Hon. LLD Leeds, 1999; Hon. DLitt Bradford, 1999; DUniv Open, 2006. Award for Internat. Current Affairs, RTS, 1985; Award for best personal contribution to television, Voice of Viewer and Listener, 1993, 1998, 2006; Richard Dimbleby Award, BAFTA, 1996, 2000; Interview of the Year, RTS, 1997 and 1998; BPG Award, 1998; Variety Club Media Personality of the Year, 1999; Presenter of the Year, RTS, 2001, 2007. *Publications:* (jtly) A Higher Form of Killing: the secret story of gas and germ warfare, 1982; Through the Volcanoes: a Central American journey, 1985; Friends in High Places: who runs Britain?, 1990; Fish, Fishing and the Meaning of Life, 1994; The Compleat Angler, 1996; The English: a portrait of a people, 1998; The Political Animal, 2002; On Royalty, 2006; The Victorians: Britain through the paintings of the age, 2009; Empire: what ruling the world did to the British, 2011; Great Britain's Great War, 2013. *Recreations:* food, books, fishing. *Address:* c/o Anita Land Ltd, 10 Wyndham Place, W1H 2PU. *Clubs:* Garrick, Chelsea Arts; Piscatorial Society.

See also T. G. Paxman.

PAXMAN, (Timothy) Giles, CMG 2013; LVO 1989; HM Diplomatic Service, retired; government and international relations consultant, since 2014; Partner, Ambassador Partnership, since 2014; *b* 15 Nov. 1951; *s* of late Arthur Keith Paxman and Joan McKay Paxman (*née* Dickson); *m* 1980, Segolene Claude Marie Cayol; three *d.* *Educ:* Malvern Coll.; New Coll., Oxford; Ecole Nat. d'Admin, Paris. DoE, 1974–76; Dept of Transport, 1976–78; joined FCO, 1980: 1st Secretary: UK Perm. Rep. to EC, 1980–84; FCO, 1984–88; Head of Chancery, Singapore, 1988–92; on secondment to Cabinet Office, 1992–94; Counsellor (Econ. and Commercial), Rome, 1994–98; Counsellor (Pol Affairs), UK Perm. Repn to EU, Brussels, 1999–2002; Minister and Dep. Hd of Mission, Paris, 2002–05; Ambassador to Mexico, 2005–09; Ambassador to Spain and concurrently (non-resident) to Andorra, 2009–13. *Recreations:* sailing, ski-ing, jazz and blues music, cinema, golf.

See also J. D. Paxman.

PAXTON, John; author; Editor, The Statesman's Year-Book, 1969–90; *b* 23 Aug. 1923; *m* 1950, Joan Thorne; one *s* one *d.* Head of Economics department, Millfield, 1952–63. Joined The Statesman's Year-Book, 1963, Dep. Ed., 1968; Consultant Editor, The New Illustrated Everyman's Encyclopaedia, 1981–84. Jt Treas., English Centre, Internat. PEN, 1973–78; Chm., West Country Writers' Assoc., 1993–95. *Publications:* (with A. E. Walsh) Trade in the Common Market Countries, 1965; (with A. E. Walsh) The Structure and Development of the Common Market, 1968; (with A. E. Walsh) Trade and Industrial Resources of the Common Market and Efta Countries, 1970; (with John Wroughton) Smuggling, 1971; (with A. E. Walsh) Into Europe, 1972; (ed) Everyman's Dictionary of Abbreviations, 1974, 2nd edn 1986, as Penguin Dictionary of Abbreviations, 1989; World Legislatures, 1974; (with C. Cook) European Political Facts 1789–1999, 3 vols, 1975–2000; The Statesman's Year-Book World Gazetteer, 1975, 4th edn, 1991; (with A. E. Walsh) Competition Policy: European and International Trends and Practices, 1975; The Developing Common Market, 1976; A Dictionary of the European Economic Community, 1977, 2nd edn, A Dictionary of the European Communities, 1982; (with C. Cook) Commonwealth Political Facts, 1979; (with S. Fairfield) Calendar of Creative Man, 1980; Companion to Russian History, 1984, 2nd edn as Encyclopedia of Russian History, 1993; Companion to the French Revolution, 1988; The Statesman's Year-Book Historical Companion, 1988; (with G. Payton) Penguin Dictionary of Proper Names, 1991; European Communities (a bibliography), 1992; Calendar of World History, 1999; (with W. G. Moore) Penguin Encyclopedia of Places, 1999; Imperial Russia: a reference handbook, 2000; Dictionary of Financial Abbreviations, 2002; Leaders of Russia and the Soviet Union: from the Romanov dynasty to Vladimir Putin, 2004; contrib. to Keesing's Contemporary Archives, Children's Britannica, TLS. *Recreation:* music (listening). *Address:* Moss Cottage, Hardway, Bruton, Somerset BA10 0LN. *T:* (01749) 813423.

PAXTON, (Peter) Robin; Director, Nimbus Communications Limited, since 2007; Associate Director, Criticaleye, since 2008; *b* 14 April 1951; *s* of late Richard Gordon Paxton and of Marion Paxton; *m* 1987, Linda Jane French; two *s.* *Educ:* Leighton Park Sch.; Sussex Univ. (BA Hons); LSE (MScEcon); Nuffield Coll., Oxford. Joined London Weekend Television, 1977; Managing Director: LWT Broadcasting Ltd, 1993–94; Carlton Television (India), 1995–97; Walt Disney TV Internat. (Asia-Pacific), 1997–2001; Discovery Networks, EMEA, 2002–07. Chm., YoYo Media Ltd, 2008–11. Chairman: Tourette Syndrome Assoc., 2009–; Headlong Theatre Company, 2009–.

PAY, Jill Patricia; Serjeant at Arms, House of Commons, 2008–12; management consultant, since 2013; *b* Anerley, London, 16 Jan. 1946; *d* of late William and Joan Arnold; *m* 1967, John Pay; two *d.* *Educ:* Croydon High Sch. for Girls; Croydon Coll. (Business Studies). Exec. Asst to Creative Dir, Ogilvy & Mather, 1963–72; Business Manager, private med. practice, 1978–87; Croydon TVEI Project, Dept of Employment, 1987–94; House of Commons, 1994–2012: Hd Office Keeper, 1994; Accommodation Rationalisation Manager, 1999–2001; Exec. Officer to Serjeant at Arms, 2001–04; Asst Serjeant at Arms, 2004–08. Chm. Govs, Edenham High Sch., 1987–94. Trustee, Beanstalk, literacy charity, 2013–. Chm., Senate, Pink Shoe Club, 2013–. *Recreations:* performing arts, travel, food (eating and cooking), reading, family and friends. *E:* jillypay@gmail.com.

PAYE, Jean-Claude; Chevalier de la Légion d'Honneur; Commandeur de l'Ordre National du Mérite; Chevalier de l'Ordre National du Mérite agricole; Croix de la Valeur militaire; Attorney at Law, Cabinet Gide Loyrette Nouel, Paris, 2001–09; *b* 26 Aug. 1934; *s* of late Lucien Paye and of Suzanne Paye (*née* Guignard); *m* 1963, Laurence Hélène Marianne Jeanneney; two *s* two *d.* *Educ:* Lycée Bugeaud, Algiers; Lycée Carnot, Tunis; Faculté de droit, Tunis; Institut d'Etudes Politiques, Paris; Ecole Nationale d'Administration. Government service, 1961–64; Technical Adviser to Sec. of State for Scientific Research, 1965; Advisor to Minister of Social Affairs, 1966; Chief Adviser to Vice-Pres., EEC, 1967–73; Adviser, Embassy, Bonn, 1973; Asst Principal Private Sec. to Minister of Foreign Affairs, 1974–76; Diplomatic Advr to Prime Minister, 1976–79; Head of Economic and Financial Affairs, Ministry of Foreign Affairs, 1979–84; Sec.-Gen., OECD, 1984–96 (Pres., Exec. Cttee in special Session, 1980–84); Mem., Conseil d'Etat, France, 1996–2000. Bd Mem., Renault SA, 1997–2009. Board Member: Transparence International—France, 1996–; Fondation Nationale des Sciences Politiques, 1998–; Fondation pour l'innovation politique, 2005–. *Address:* 1 Place A. Deville, 75006 Paris, France.

PAYKEL, Prof. Eugene Stern, MD; FRCP, FRCPsych; FMedSci; Professor of Psychiatry, University of Cambridge, 1985–2001, now Emeritus Professor (Head of Department, 1985–2000); Professorial Fellow, Gonville and Caius College, Cambridge, 1985–2001, now Emeritus Fellow; *b* 9 Sept. 1934; *s* of late Joshua Paykel and Eva Paykel; *m* 1969, Margaret, *d* of late John Melrose and Joan Melrose; two *s.* *Educ:* Auckland Grammar Sch.; Univ. of Otago (MB ChB, MD; Stuart Prize, Joseph Pullar Schol., 1956); DPM London. Maudsley Hosp., 1962–65; Asst Prof. of Psychiatry and Co-Dir/Dir, Depression Res. Unit, Yale Univ., 1966–71; Consultant and Sen. Lectr, 1971–75, Reader, 1975–77, Prof. of Psychiatry, 1977–85, St George's Hosp. Med. Sch., Univ. of London. Chief Scientist's Adviser and Mem., Mental Illness Res. Liaison Gp, DHSS, 1984–88; Chm., Jt Cttee on Higher Psychiatric Trng, 1990–95. Previously examiner Univs of Edinburgh, Nottingham, Manchester, London, and RCPsych. Mem., Neurosciences Bd, MRC, 1981–85, 1995–99. Mem., Bethlem Royal and Maudsley Hosp. SHA, 1990–94. Vice Pres., RCPsych, 1994–96 (Chm., Social and Community Psych. Sect., 1984–88); Zonal Rep., World Psychiatric Assoc., 1993–99 (Chm., Pharmaco-psychiatry Sect., 1993–98); Hon. Mem., British Assoc. for Psychopharmacology, 1991 (Pres., 1982–84); President: Marcé Soc., 1992–94; Collegium Internat. Neuropsychopharmacologicum, 2000–02. Trustee, Mental Health Foundn, 1988–95. Founder FMedSci 1998; Hon. FRCPsych 2001 (MRCPsych 1971, FRCPsych 1977). Hon. Mem., Assoc. of Eur. Psychiatrists, 2007. Foundations Fund Prize for Res. in Psychiatry, 1978; BMA Film Competition Bronze Award, 1981; Anna Monika Stiftung 2nd Prize, 1985; Eur. Coll. of Neuropsychopharmacol.-Lilly Award for Clin. Neurosci., 2001. Jt Editor, Jl of Affective Disorders, 1979–93; Editor, Psychological Medicine, 1994–2006; Mem., Editl Bd, Jl of Affective Disorders, etc. *Publications:* The Depressed Woman, 1974; Psychopharmacology of Affective Disorders, 1979; Monoamine Oxidase Inhibitors: the state of the art, 1981; Handbook of Affective Disorders, 1982, 2nd edn 1992; Community Psychiatric Nursing for Neurotic Patients, 1983; papers on depression, psychopharmacology, social psychiatry, life events, evaluation of treatment. *Recreations:* opera, music, theatre. *Address:* Department of Psychiatry, University of Cambridge, Douglas House, 18B Trumpington Road, Cambridge CB2 8AH.

PAYNE, Alan Jeffrey, CMG 1988; HM Diplomatic Service, retired; *b* 11 May 1933; *s* of Sydney Ellis Payne and Lydia Payne; *m* 1959, Letitia Freeman; three *s.* *Educ:* Enfield Grammar Sch.; Queens' Coll., Cambridge (Exhibnr). FIL 1962. RN, 1955–57. EMI, London, later Paris, 1957–62; Secretariat, NATO, Paris, 1962–64; joined Diplomatic Service, 1965; Commonwealth Relations Office (later FCO), 1965–67; British High Commn, Kuala Lumpur, 1967–70; FCO, 1970–72; British Embassy, Budapest, 1972–75; Counsellor, Mexico City, 1975–79; FCO, 1979–82; Consul-General, Lyons, 1982–87; High Comr, Jamaica, and Ambassador (non-resident) to Haiti, 1987–89. Sec. Gen., Internat. Primary Aluminium Inst., 1989–97. *Recreations:* music, theatre, growing trees, restoring old cars. *Club:* Royal Automobile.

PAYNE, (Andrew John) Sebastian, MW; Buyer, International Exhibition Co-operative Wine Society, since 2012 (Chief Buyer, 1985–2012); *b* 3 April 1947; *s* of John Laurence Payne and Dorothy Gwendoline Payne (*née* Attenborough); *m* 1973, Frances Elizabeth Harrison; two *d.* *Educ:* Tonbridge Sch. (Schol.); Trinity Coll., Oxford (BA Lit. Hum. and Med. and Mod. Greek 1970; MA 1973). MW 1977. F. & E. May, wine shippers, 1970–73; IEC Wine Soc., 1973–. Mem., Govt Wine Adv. Cttee, 1993–. Chm., Inst. of Masters of Wine, 1995–96. Chevalier, Ordre Nat. du Mérite Agricole (France), 1999. *Address:* International Exhibition Co-operative Wine Society, Gunnelswood Road, Stevenage SG1 2BT. *T:* (01438) 761283. *Club:* Travellers.

See also G. J. N. Payne.

PAYNE, Anthony Edward; freelance composer and writer; *b* 2 Aug. 1936; *s* of Edward Alexander Payne and Muriel Margaret Elsie Payne (*née* Stroud); *m* 1966, Jane Marian Manning, *qv.* *Educ:* Dulwich Coll.; Durham Univ. (BA Hons Music 1961). Composition Tutor: London Coll. of Music, 1983–85; Sydney Conservatorium, 1986; Univ. of W Australia, 1996; Vis. Milhaud Prof., Mills Coll., Calif, 1983; Vis. Professorial Fellow in composition, UEA, 2012–13. Contributor: Daily Telegraph, 1964–; Times, 1964–; Independent, 1986–; Country Life, 1995–. FRCM 2005. Hon. DMus: Birmingham, 2001; Kingston, 2002; Durham, 2007. Elgar Medal, Elgar Soc., 2011. *Compositions:* principal works include: Paraphrases and Cadenzas, 1969; Paean, 1971; Phoenix Mass, 1972; Concerto for Orchestra, 1974; The World's Winter, 1976; String Quartet, 1978; The Stones and Lonely Places Sing, 1979; Song of the Clouds, 1980; Springs Shining Wake, 1981; A Day in the Life of a Mayfly, 1981; Evening Land, 1981; The Spirit's Harvest, 1985; The Song Streams in the Firmament, 1986; Half Heard in the Stillness, 1987; Sea Change, 1988; Time's Arrow, 1990; Symphonies of Wind and Rain, 1991; A Hidden Music, 1992; Orchestral Variations, 1994; Empty Landscape, 1995; completion of Elgar's Third Symphony, 1997; Piano Trio, 1998; Scenes from the Woodlanders, 1999; Of Knots and Skeins, 2000; Visions and Journeys, 2002; Poems of Edward Thomas, 2003; Storm Chorale for Solo Violin, 2004; Horn Trio, 2004; completion of Elgar's Sixth Pomp and Circumstance March, 2005; Windows on Eternity, 2006; Piano Quintet, 2007; Out of the Depths Comes Song, 2008; From a Mouthful of Air, 2008; The Period of Cosmographie, 2009; Second String Quartet, 2010; arrangement for chamber ensemble of Bruckner's Second Symphony, 2011; The Unknown Country, 2012; arrangement for orchestra of Vaughan Williams' Four Last Songs, 2013; Piano Quartet, 2013; arrangement for orchestra of Vaughan Williams' Two Nocturnes, 2014; Of Land and Sea, and of the Sky, 2015. *Publications:* Schoenberg, 1968; Frank Bridge—Radical and Conservative, 1976, 2nd edn 1984; Elgar's Third Symphony: the story of the reconstruction, 1998; articles in learned jls, incl. Musical Times, Tempo, Listener, etc, 1962–. *Recreations:* cinema, English countryside. *Address:* 2 Wilton Square, N1 3DL. *T:* (020) 7359 1593. *E:* paynecomp@googlemail.com.

PAYNE, Christine Grace; General Secretary, Equity, since 2005; *b* 30 Dec. 1956; *d* of Jeffrey and Shirley Brass; *m* 1981, Terry Payne; one *d.* *Educ:* Loughborough Univ. (BSc Hons Psychol.); Middlesex Poly. (Dip. Industrial Relns and Trade Union Studies). Joined Equity, 1979: TV Commercials Orgnr, 1981–91; Asst Sec., recorded perfs, 1991–99; Asst Gen. Sec., live perfs, 1999–2005. *Address:* c/o Equity, Guild House, Upper St Martin's Lane, WC2H 9EG. *T:* (020) 7379 6000. *E:* cpayne@equity.org.uk.

PAYNE, Dr Christopher Charles, OBE 1997; researcher and writer, since 2011; *b* 15 May 1946; *s* of Rupert George Payne and Evelyn Violet (*née* Abbott); *m* 1969, Margaret Susan Street; one *s* one *d.* *Educ:* Wadham Coll., Oxford (MA, DPhil). Post-Doctoral Fellow, Univ. of Otago, NZ, 1972; SSO, NERC, Oxford, 1973–77; PSO, 1977–83, Head, Entomology Dept, 1983–86, Glasshouse Crops Res. Inst., Littlehampton; Head, Crop Protection Div., Inst. of Horticultural Res., E Malling, 1987–90; Chief Exec., Horticulture Research Internat., 1990–99; Prof. of Horticulture and Landscape, Univ. of Reading, 1999–2003; self-employed consultant in biol sci., 2003–11. Vis. Prof. of Plant Scis, Univ. of Reading, 2003–07. Hon. Professor: Univ. of Warwick, 1991–99; Univ. of Birmingham, 1995–99. President: Soc. for Invertebrate Pathology, 1993–94; Assoc. of Applied Biologists, 1995–96. Chm., Assured Produce Scheme, 2001–06; Dir, Assured Food Standards, 2003–06; Sen. Exec., Nat. Horticultural Forum, 2004–05; Chm., Tech. Cttee, Horticultural Trades Assoc., 2007–11. Trustee, Royal Botanic Gdns, Kew, 1997–2003. Member: Western Front Assoc., 2009– (Chm., Cumbria Br., 2015–); Police Hist. Soc., 2010–; CWA, 2011–. Editor in Chief, Biocontrol Science and Technology, 1991–2000. *Publications:* (with R. Hull and F. Brown) Virology: directory and dictionary of animal, bacterial and plant viruses, 1989; The Chieftain: Victorian true crime through the eyes of a Scotland Yard detective, 2011; numerous contribs to books and learned jls. *Recreations:* gardening, walking, cycling, history of the London Metropolitan Police (1840–78) and of the First World War. *Address:* The Outlook, Back Lane, Arnside, Cumbria LA5 0BS. *T:* (01524) 761418. *E:* oldthatch@btinternet.com. *W:* chrispaynebooks.com.

PAYNE, Christopher Frederick, CBE 1987; QPM 1975; DL; Chief Constable of Cleveland Constabulary, 1976–90; *b* 15 Feb. 1930; *o s* of late Gerald Frederick Payne, OBE, BEM, QPM, and Amy Florence Elizabeth Payne (*née* Parker); *m* 1952, Barbara Janet Saxby; one *s* three *d.* *Educ:* Christ's Coll., Finchley; Hendon Technical Coll. Joined Metropolitan Police, 1950; Sen. Comd course, 1965; Home Office R&D Br., 1968–70; Comdr 'X' Div., 1971–74; Comdr Airport Div., 1974–76. Pres., Chief Constables' Club, 1989–90. Sen. Vis. Res. Fellow, Univ. of Bradford, 1991–2001. County Dir, St John Ambulance, 1978–85, Comdr, SJAB, 1985–89, Chm., St John Council, 1986–89, Cleveland. Vice Chm., Royal Jubilee and Prince's Trusts Cttee for Durham and Cleveland, 1984–90. Chm., Castlegate Quay Trust, 1991–2005. Chm. Mgt Develt Cttee and Mem. Exec. Bd, Inst. of Mgt, 1998–2001. Freeman, City of London, 1988. DL Cleveland, 1983, N Yorks, 1996. CStJ 1985 (OStJ 1980). *Publications:* various articles on contingency planning and management. *Recreations:* painting, philately, gardening. *Address:* c/o The Chief Constable's Office, PO Box 70, Ladgate Lane, Middlesbrough TS8 9EH.

PAYNE, Sir David Neil, Kt 2013; CBE 2004; FRS 1992; FREng; Director, Optoelectronics Research Centre, since 1995 (Deputy Director, 1989–95), and Professor of Photonics, since 1991, University of Southampton; *b* 13 Aug. 1944; *s* of Raymond and Maisie Payne. *Educ:* Univ. of Southampton (BSc, PhD). FREng 2005; FIET (FIEE 2005). Commissioning Engineer, English Electric Co., 1962; University of Southampton: Research Asst, 1969; Jun. Res. Fellow, 1971; Pirelli Res. Fellow, 1972, Sen. Res. Fellow, 1978, Principal Res. Fellow, 1981; Pirelli Reader, 1984. Chm., SPI Optics Inc., 2000–05 (Dir, 2005–). Fellow, Optical

Soc. of America, 1995; Foreign Member: Norwegian Acad. of Scis, 2004; Russian Acad. of Scis, 2006. Awards include: Rank Prize for Optoelectronics, 1991; IEEE/OSA John Tyndall Award, 1991; Computers and Communications Prize, Foundn for Computer and Communications Promotion in Japan, 1993; Franklin Medal, Franklin Inst., 1998; Edward Rhein Foundn Basic Res. Award, Germany, 2000; Mountbatten Medal, IEE, 2001; Kelvin Medal (jt award of 8 engrg socs), 2004; Microptics Award, Optical Soc. of Japan, 2005. *Publications:* numerous contribs to learned jls. *Recreations:* cooking, motorcycling, gardening. *Address:* Optoelectronics Research Centre, University of Southampton, Highfield, Southampton SO17 1BJ. *T:* (023) 8059 3583.

PAYNE, (Geoffrey John) Nicholas; Director, Opera Europa, since 2003; *b* 4 Jan. 1945; *s* of John Laurence Payne and Dorothy Gwendoline Payne (*née* Attenborough); *m* 1986, Linda Jane Adamson; two *s*. *Educ:* Eton Coll. (King's Schol.); Trinity Coll., Cambridge (BA Eng Lit). Finance Assistant, Royal Opera House, 1968–70; Subsidy Officer, Arts Council, 1970–76; Financial Controller, Welsh National Opera, 1976–82; Gen. Adminr, Opera North, 1982–93; Dir, Royal Opera, Covent Garden, 1993–98; Gen. Dir, ENO, 1998–2002. *E:* nicholas.payne@opera-europa.org.
See also A. J. S. Payne.

PAYNE, Henry Salusbury Legh D.; *see* Dalzell Payne.

PAYNE, Jane Marian, (Mrs A. E. Payne); *see* Manning, J. M.

PAYNE, Keith, VC 1969; OAM 2006; *b* 30 Aug. 1933; *s* of Henry Thomas Payne and Remilda Payne (*née* Hussey); *m* 1954, Florence Catherine Payne (*née* Plaw); five *s*. *Educ:* State School, Ingham, North Queensland. Soldier, Department of Army, Aug. 1951–75; 1 RAR, Korea, 1952–53; 3 RAR, Malaya, 1963–65; Aust. Army Trng Team, Vietnam, 1969 (Warrant Officer; awarded VC after deliberately exposing himself to enemy fire while trying to cover his outnumbered men); WO Instructor: RMC, Duntroon, ACT, 1970–72; 42 Bn, Royal Qld Regt, Mackay, 1973–75; Captain, Oman Army, 1975–76. Member: VC and GC Assoc.; Legion of Valour, USA; Aust. Army Training Team Vietnam Assoc.; Life Member: and Qld State Patron, Totally and Permanently Disabled Soldiers' Assoc. (Mackay Centre); Korea & SE Asia Forces Assoc.; Special Operations Assoc., USA; RSL (also Sarina Sub Br.). Patron: TRY-Sponsored Aust. Cadet Corps Units (Victoria); Mackay Legacy; Nat. Vice Patron, Australian Bravery Assoc. Life Gov., TRY and Community Services, Vic. Mem. Cttee (overseas), Victoria Cross and George Cross Assoc. Freeman City of Brisbane and of Shire of Hinchinbrook. Vietnamese Cross of Gallantry, with bronze star, 1969; US Meritorious Unit Citation; Vietnamese Unit Citation Cross of Gallantry with Palm; DSC (US); SSM (US). *Recreations:* football, fishing, hunting. *Address:* 1 Forest Court, Andergrove, Mackay, Qld 4740, Australia. *T:* (7) 49552794.

PAYNE, Leonard Sidney, CBE 1983; Director, J. Sainsbury Ltd, 1974–86; Adviser on Distribution and Retailing, Coopers & Lybrand, since 1986; *b* 16 Dec. 1925; *s* of Leonard Sydney Payne and Lillian May Leggatt; *m* 1944, Marjorie Vincent; two *s*. *Educ:* Woodhouse Grammar School. FCCA, FCILT. Asst Accountant, Peek Frean & Co. Ltd, 1949–52; Chief Accountant, Administrator of various factory units, head office appts, Philips Electrical Industries, 1952–62; Dep. Gp Comptroller, Morgan Crucible Co. Ltd, 1962–64; British Road Services Ltd: Finance Dir, 1964–67; Asst Man. Dir, 1967–69; Man. Dir, 1969–71; Dir of Techn. Services and Develt, Nat. Freight Corp., 1971–74, Vice-Chm. Executive 1974. President: Freight Transport Assoc., 1980–82; Chartered Inst. of Transport, 1983–84. Chm., CBI Transport Policy Cttee, 1980–86. CCMI. *Recreations:* gardening, swimming, squash, chess. *Address:* Apartment 5, Evenholme, Green Walk, Bowdon, Altrincham, Cheshire WA14 2SL.

PAYNE, Prof. Michael Christopher, PhD; FRS 2008; Professor of Computational Physics, University of Cambridge, since 2000; Fellow, Pembroke College, Cambridge, since 1984; *b* 1960. *Educ:* Pembroke Coll., Cambridge (BA 1981; PhD 1985). Lectr in Physics, until 1998, Reader in Computational Physics, 1998–2000, Univ. of Cambridge. Institute of Physics: Hon. Fellow; Maxwell Medal and Prize, 1996; Mott Lect., 1998. Swan Medal, Inst. of Physics, 2014. *Address:* Theory of Condensed Matter Group, Cavendish Laboratory, University of Cambridge, JJ Thomson Avenue, Cambridge CB3 0HE.

PAYNE, Michael Robert; international strategic advisor to sports and business industry; board member to various groups, including Formula One, WPP, media companies, sports federations and governments, since 2004; *b* 25 March 1958; *s* of Robert Gilmore Payne and Sheila Brennan Savory; *m* Marta Salsas; two *s* one *d*. *Educ:* St Anthony's Prep. Sch., London; Highgate Sch., London. Mem., British Ski Team, 1974–78; British Professional Freestyle Ski Champion, 1977, 1978. West Nally Sports Mktg Agency, London, 1979–83; ISL Agency, Switzerland and Korea, 1983–88; Dir of Mktg and Broadcast Rights, IOC, 1983–2004, later Advr. Dir, Montreux Jazz Fest. Mem. Adv. Bd, Imperial Coll., London. Contributor on sports business issues, FT, BBC, CNN, Fortune, Japan Yomiuri Shimbun. *Publications:* Olympic Turnaround, 2005 (trans. Chinese, Japanese, Korean, Spanish, German, Greek, Italian, Russian, Bulgarian, Portuguese, Turkish, Slovak). *Recreation:* ski-ing. *Address:* 74 Boulevard d'Italie, MC 98000, Monaco. *T:* (6) 80867976. *E:* michael@michaelrpayne.com. *W:* www.michaelrpayne.com, www.twitter.com/michaelrpayne1.

PAYNE, Nicholas; *see* Payne, G. J. N.

PAYNE, Nicholas Kevin, FCCA; Finance and Operations Director, Government Legal Department (formerly Treasury Solicitor's Department), since 2014; *b* Isleworth, 21 Jan. 1966; *s* of Michael Charles and Kay Payne; *m* 2011, Carolyn Marie Mackay. *Educ:* Teddington Boys' Sch.; Richmond upon Thames Coll. of Further Educn; Open Univ. (BSc Hons; MBA). FCCA 1999. Customer Accounting Asst, 1984–85, Customer Accounting Supervisor, 1985–86, SE Electricity Bd; London Electricity Board, then London Electricity plc: Systems Accounting Asst, 1986–87; Bought Ledger Supervisor, 1987–88; Internal Auditor, 1988–89; Sen. Internal Auditor, 1989–90; Area Accounting Unit Manager (Western), 1990–91; Finance Officer (Engrg Resource Mgt System), 1991–93; Budgets and Forecast Officer (Engrg), 1993–94; Financial Planning Manager (Network Services), 1994–97; Chief Accountant, RAF Logistics Comd, 1997–2000; Financial Controller, Defence Logistics Orgn (Air), 2000–01; Director of Finance: Cambs Constabulary, 2001–05; Centre Top Level Budget, MoD, 2006–07; Financial Controller, 2007–09, Dir, Commercial and Financial Control, 2009–10, BERR; Hd, Commercial Scrutiny, 2010–12, Commercial Strategy and Industrial Policy Dir, 2012–14, MoD; rcds 2011–12. MCIPS 2011. FCMA 2000. *Recreations:* ballet, cinema, theatre, walking, member of MENSA; UK, European and world championship medallist for Team GB in Tang Soo Do. *Address:* Government Legal Department, Zone 7.07, One Kemble Street, WC2B 4TS. *T:* (020) 7210 1327, 07825 420772, *Fax:* (020) 7210 3104.

PAYNE, Nicholas Milne, OBE 2012; Vice President, National Gardens Scheme, since 2009 (Chairman, 2002–08); *b* 14 May 1937; *s* of Robert Orlando Payne and Frances Elisabeth Payne; *m* 1st, 1985, Mona Helen de Ferranti (*née* Cunningham) (*d* 2008); one step *s* two step *d*; 2nd, 2012, Anne Frances Builder; one step *d*. *Educ:* St Edward's Sch., Oxford; Trinity Hall, Cambridge (MA). Commercial Dir, Caradon Rolinx, 1964–87. Chm., NW Reg., NACF, 1993–2004; Chm., Friends of Manchester City Galls, 1984–2009; Trustee: Clonter Opera, 1984–2002; Tabley House Collection Trust, 1993–2011; Manchester City Galls Trust, 2001–11 (Vice Pres., 2009–11). *Recreations:* gardening, music, the arts. *Address:* Wingstone, Manaton, Devon TQ13 9UL. *T:* and *Fax:* (01647) 221660. *E:* ngs@themount1.freeserve.co.uk.

PAYNE, Peter Charles John, PhD; MSc(AgrEng); farmer, 1975–2000; *b* 8 Feb. 1928; *s* of late C. J. Payne, China Clay Merchant, and Mrs F. M. Payne; *m* 1961, Margaret Grover; two *s* one *d*. *Educ:* Plymouth Coll.; Teignmouth Grammar School; Reading University. BSc Reading 1948; Min. of Agriculture Scholar, Durham Univ., MSc(AgrEng) 1950; Scientific Officer, Nat. Institute of Agricultural Engineering, 1950–55; PhD Reading 1954; Lecturer in Farm Mechanisation, Wye College, London Univ., 1955–60; Lecturer in Agricultural Engineering, Durham Univ., 1960–61; Principal, Nat. Coll. of Agricultural Engineering, Silsoe, 1962–75 (Hon. Fellow, 1980); Visiting Professor: Univ. of Reading, 1969–75; Cranfield Inst. of Technology, 1975–80. Chm., Agricl Panel, Intermed. Technol. Develt Gp, 1979–86. Vice-Pres., Section III, Commn Internationale du Génie Rural, 1969. FIAgrE 1968; FRAgS 1971; CEng 1980. *Publications:* various papers in agricultural and engineering journals. *Recreation:* sailing. *Address:* 5 Mulberry Quay, Market Strand, Falmouth TR11 3HD. *T:* (01326) 318880.

PAYNE, Sebastian; *see* Payne, A. J. S.

PAYNE, Most Rev. (Sidney) Stewart; Metropolitan of the Ecclesiastical Province of Canada and Archbishop of Western Newfoundland, 1990–97, retired; *b* 6 June 1932; *s* of Albert and Hilda Payne; *m* 1962, Selma Carlson Penney, St Anthony, Newfoundland; two *s* two *d*. *Educ:* Elementary and High School, Fogo, Newfoundland; Memorial Univ. of Newfoundland (BA); Queen's Coll., Newfoundland (LTh); BD (General Synod). Incumbent of Mission of Happy Valley, 1957–65; Rector, Parish of Bay Roberts, 1965–70; Rector, Parish of St Anthony, 1970–78; Bishop of Western Newfoundland, 1978–97. DD *hc*: Univ. of King's Coll., Halifax, NS, 1981; Queen's Coll., St John's, NL, 2006. *Address:* 101A East Valley Road, Corner Brook, NL A2H 2L4, Canada.

PAYNE, Stephen Michael, OBE 2004; RDI 2006; CEng; FRINA; FREng; independent consultant, since 2011; President, Royal Institution of Naval Architects, 2007–10; *b* 28 Jan. 1960; *s* of Michael John Robert Payne and Pauline Patricia Payne. *Educ:* Univ. of Southampton (BSc Eng (Hons) Ship Sci. 1984). CEng 2002; FRINA 2002; FREng 2008. Naval architect, Marconi Radar Systems, Chelmsford, 1984–85; Jun. Naval Architect, 1985–87, Naval Architect, 1987–92, Sen. Naval Architect, 1992–95, Technical Marine Planning Ltd, London; Carnival Corporation, 1995–: Sen. Naval Architect, 1995; Project Manager: MS Rotterdam (VI), 1995–97; MS Costa Atlantica, 1997–98; Chief Designer, then Proj. Manager, RMS Queen Mary 2, 1998; Dir, Proj. Mgt, 2000–04, Vice Pres. and Chief Naval Architect, 2004–10, Carnival Corporate Shipbuilding. Mem. Council, 2005–, Exec. Cttee, 2006–, RINA. Co-founder, Future Engineers 2008, in assoc. with RAEng; Awards Cttee, RAEng, 2009–11. Dir/Trustee, Southampton Cultural Develt Trust, 2010–15; Trustee, Webb Inst., Glen Cove, NY, 2011–. Gov., Quilley Sch. of Engrg, Eastleigh, 2009–15. Freeman, City of London, 2004; Liveryman, Co. of Shipwrights, 2005– (Freeman, 2004). Hon. FIED 2009. Hon. DSc Southampton, 2007. Bronze Medal, RINA, 1988; Special Achievement Award, RAEng, 2006; MN Medal, 2006; Admiral Land Medal, SNAME, 2011. *Publications:* Grande Dame: Holland America Line and the SS Rotterdam, 1990; MS Statendam, 1993; contribs to Naval Architect, Ships Monthly, Steamboat Bill, Designs, Cruise Industry News. *Recreations:* public speaking, model-ship making, writing, cooking, airships, history of passenger ships. *Address:* c/o Royal Institution of Naval Architects, 8–9 Northumberland Street, WC2N 5DA.

PAYNE, Most Rev. Stewart; *see* Payne, Most Rev. S. S.

PAYNTER, Alan Guy Hadley; Commissioner, 1997–2000, and Director, Corporate Services, 1999–2000, HM Customs and Excise; *b* 5 Nov. 1941; *s* of Leslie Alan Paynter and Dorothy Victoria Paynter (*née* Voak); *m* 1964, Mary Teresa Houghton; two *d*. *Educ:* East Ham Grammar Sch.; Central London Poly. (Post-grad. DMS 1972). EO, then HEO, MPBW, 1960–72 (Asst Private Sec. to Minister of Public Bldg and Works, 1968–71); HM Customs and Excise: Sen. Exec. Officer, 1972; Principal, 1978; on secondment to Overseas Containers Ltd, 1981–83; Sen. Principal, Computer Services, 1983–87; Asst Sec., 1987; Head, 1989–93, Dir, 1993–99, Information Systems; Mem. of Board, 1993–2000. Hon. Treas., Thorpe Bay Bowling Club, 2006–10. Trustee, 2007–, Chm. of Trustees, 2007–11, Havens Hospices. *Recreations:* golf, bowling, theatre, gardening.

PAYNTER, John Gregor Hugh; Chairman, Standard Life Investments Holdings, 2012–15 (non-executive Director, 2010–15); non-executive Director, Standard Chartered plc, 2008–14; Senior Independent Director, Standard Life plc, 2012–15; *b* London, 7 July 1954; *s* of Rex Paynter and Muriel Paynter (*née* McGregor); *m* 1983, Kym Elizabeth Sheldon; one *s* two *d*. *Educ:* Merchant Taylors' Sch., Northwood; University Coll., Oxford (BA Hons). Called to the Bar, Gray's Inn, 1976; in practice as barrister, 1976–78; Cazenove & Co., then Cazenove Group, later JP Morgan Cazenove, 1979–2008: Partner, 1986–2001; Dep. Chm., 2001–05; Vice Chm., 2005–08. Non-exec. Dir, Jardine Lloyd Thompson Gp plc, 2008–12. Sen. Advr, Greenhill Internat., 2008–. *Recreations:* music, gardening, countryside, history, arts. *T:* 07770 746758. *E:* John.paynter@btinternet.com.

PAYTON, Michael Andrew Hartland; Chairman, Clyde & Co., Solicitors, since 2013 (Senior Partner, 1984–2013); *b* Llandrindod Wells, 8 June 1944; *oc* of late Geoffrey Hartland Payton and of Pamela Payton (*née* Miller Kerr); *m* 1978, Sally Ann, *d* of late Dick and Pamela Farmer; two *d* and two step *s*. *Educ:* Felsted Sch. (Schol.). Articled, Hunt & Wrigley, Northallerton, 1962–66; admitted solicitor, 1966; Asst Solicitor, 1967–71, Partner, 1971–, Clyde & Co., specialising in shipping, then insurance. Chairman: Solicitors' Indemnity Mutual Insce Assoc., 1984–2000; Exec., British Maritime Law Assoc., 1986–; Novae Insce Co. Ltd, 2005–09; Internat. Dispute Resolution Centre, 2011–; Dir, London Authorities Mutual Ltd, 2007–09. Freeman, City of London, 2007–; Liveryman: Solicitors' Co., 2002– (Additl Asst to Ct, 2014–); Shipwrights' Co., 2010–. Hon. QC 2012; Hon. Bencher, Inner Temple, 2012. *Publications:* contribs to learned jls on insce, arbitration and mediation. *Recreations:* horse racing, my wife, Normandy. *Address:* 30 Bisham Gardens, N6 6DD. *T:* (020) 8340 8986. *E:* michael.payton@clydeco.com. *Clubs:* Garrick, MCC.

PEACE, Elizabeth Ann, CBE 2008; Chief Executive, British Property Federation, 2002–14; Chairman, LandAid Charitable Trust, since 2015; *b* Birmingham, 5 Dec. 1952; *d* of Herbert Powers and Gwendoline Powers (*née* Burbridge); *m* 1978, Nigel David Peace; two *s*. *Educ:* King Edward VI Camp Hill Grammar Sch. for Girls, Birmingham; Royal Holloway Coll., Univ. of London (BA Hons Hist.). Admin. trainee, then Grade 7, MoD, 1974–91; Dir, Corporate Affairs and Co. Sec., QinetiQ plc (formerly DERA), 1991–2002. Pres., Farnborough Aerospace Consortium, 1996–2002. Non-executive Director: Planning Inspectorate, 2005–08; Turley Assocs, 2008–; Redrow plc, 2014–; Howard de Walden Estates, 2014–; Member, Board: Peabody Housing Assoc., 2009–; Morgan Sindall plc, 2012–. Chm., Eur. Property Fedn, 2004–11. Comr, CABE, 2008–11. Mem., Standards Cttee, Westminster CC, 2008–11. Trustee: Inst. for Sustainability, 2009–12; Churches Conservation Trust, 2013–; Architectural Heritage Fund, 2014–. Hon. Vice Pres., Cambridge Univ. Land Soc., 2011–. Hon. Fellow, Coll. of Estate Mgt, 2008; Hon. FRIBA, 2010. Liveryman, Chartered Surveyors' Co., 2007. Hon. DLitt Westminster, 2011. *Recreations:* opera, reading, gardening and conservation, keeping age at bay, hounding offspring – and shopping. *Address:* c/o LandAid Charitable Trust, St Albans House, 57–59 Haymarket, SW1Y 4QX. *E:* liz@lizpeace.co.uk.

PEACE, Sir John (Wilfred), Kt 2011; Chairman: Burberry, since 2002; Standard Chartered plc (formerly Standard Chartered Bank), 2009–16 (Deputy Chairman, 2007–09); Lord-Lieutenant for Nottinghamshire, since 2012; *b* 2 March 1949; *m* 1971, Christine Blakemore; three *d*. *Educ:* Sandhurst. Experian (formerly CCN): Founding Dir, 1980; Man. Dir, 1991–96; Chief Exec., 1996–2000; Chm., 2006–14; Chief Exec., Great Universal Stores, later GUS, plc, 2000–06. High Sheriff, Notts, 2011–12. *Recreations:* horse riding, golf.

PEACH, Prof. (Guthlac) Ceri (Klaus), DPhil; FRGS; Professor of Social Geography, Oxford University, 1992–2007, now Emeritus; Fellow, St Catherine's College, Oxford, 1969–2007, now Emeritus; Professor of Social Geography, Institute for Social Change, University of Manchester, 2007–12; *b* 26 Oct. 1939; *s* of Wystan Adams Peach and Charlotte Marianne (*née* Klaus); *m* 1964, Susan Lesley Godfrey; two *s* one *d*. *Educ:* Howardian High Sch., Cardiff; Merton Coll., Oxford (MA, DPhil). Oxford University: Demonstrator, 1964–66; Faculty Lectr in Geography, 1966–92; Strakosch Fellow, 1969; Hd of Dept, Sch. of Geography, 1995–98; St Catherine's College: Dean, 1971–73; Sen. Tutor, 1973–77; Finance Bursar, 1981–84; Domestic Bursar, 1986–89; Vice-Master, 1990–92; Pro-Master, 1993–94. Mem., Hebdomadal Council, Oxford Univ., 1996–2001. Visiting Fellow: Dept of Demography, ANU, 1972; Dept of Sociology, Yale Univ., 1977; Visiting Professor: Dept of Geog., Univ. of BC, 1998; Dept of Sociology, Harvard Univ., 1998; Office of Population Res., Princeton Univ., 2006–07; Fulbright Vis. Prof., Dept of Geog., Univ. of Calif, Berkeley, 1985. FRGS 1965. Ethnic Geography Dist. Schol. Award, Assoc. of Amer. Geographers, 2008. *Publications:* West Indian Migration to Britain: a social geography, 1968; Urban Social Segregation, 1975; (ed jtly) Ethnic Segregation in Cities, 1981; (ed jtly) Geography and Ethnic Pluralism, 1984; (ed jtly) South Asians Overseas, 1990, repr. 2009; The Caribbean in Europe, 1991; The Ethnic Minority Populations of Great Britain, 1996; (ed jtly) Islam in Europe, 1997; (ed jtly) Global Japan, 2003. *Recreations:* travelling, reading, computing. *Address:* St Catherine's College, Oxford OX1 3UJ. *Club:* Leander (Henley).

PEACH, Sir Leonard (Harry), Kt 1989; a Civil Service Commissioner, 1995–2000; *b* 17 Dec. 1932; *s* of late Harry and Beatrice Peach; *m* 1958, Doreen Lilian (*née* Barker); two *s*. *Educ:* Queen Mary's Grammar Sch., Walsall; Pembroke Coll., Oxford (MA; Hon. Fellow, 1996); LSE (Dip. Personnel Management). Research Asst to Randolph S. Churchill, 1956; personnel management posts, 1956–62; IBM UK Ltd: personnel management posts, 1962–71; Dir of Personnel, 1971–72; Gp Dir, Personnel, IBM Europe, Africa, Middle East (based Paris), 1972–75; Dir, Personnel and Corporate Affairs, 1975–85 and 1989–92; seconded to DHSS, 1985–89: Dir, Personnel, NHS Management Bd, 1985; Chief Exec., NHS Management Bd, 1986–89 (in rank of 2nd Perm. Sec.); Chairman: NHS Training Authy, 1986–91; Skillbase Ltd, 1990–94; Standards Develt Cttee, Management Charter Initiative, 1989–97; Development Partnership Consultancy, 1993–2006; Mgt Verification Consortium Bd, 1995–99; UKCC Commn on Educn and Trng of Nurses, Midwives and Health Visitors, 1998–99 (report Fitness for Practice, 1999); Dep. Chm., Regulatory Decisions Cttee, FSA, 2001–05; Member: Data Protection Tribunal, 1985–99; Civilian Trng Bd and Personnel Bd, MoD, 1992–2000; Forensic Science Service Remuneration Cttee, 1999–2005; non-exec. Dir, Appeals Service, 2004–06 (Chm., Audit Cttee, 2004–06); Mem., Audit Cttee, DWP, 2004–06. Chm., Police Complaints Authy, 1992–95; Comr for Public Appts, 1995–99; Comr for Public Appts in NI, 1995–99. Non-exec. Dir, Royal London Hosp., 1991–94. Chm., PSI, 1991–2001. Chm., Nationwide Pension Fund, 2002–03 (Dep. Chm., 1992–2002); Director: IBM UK Rentals, 1971–76; IBM UK Holdings, 1976–85, and 1989–92; IBM UK Pensions Trust, 1989–92; IBM UK Trust, 1989–92; PIA, 1993–97 (Dep. Chm., Memship and Discipline Cttee, 1996–2001); non-executive Director: Nationwide Anglia Bldg Soc., 1990–93; Coutts Consulting plc, 1993–99; Affinity Internet Hldgs plc, 2001–03. Pres., IPM, and Chm., IPM Services Ltd, 1983–85 and 1991–98 (President's Gold Medal, 1988); Chairman: Inst. of Continuing Professional Develt, 1998–2006; Selection Bd, RICS Disciplinary Panels and Bds, 2001–06; President: Manpower Soc., 1991–97; Assoc. of Business Schs, 1993–99. Vice-President: British Sports Assoc. for Disabled, 1988–; Industrial Participation Soc., 1989–2004. Chm., Remuneration and Succession Cttee, SCOPE, 1996–2003. Chairman: Quentin Hogg Trust, 1999–2009; Regent Street Poly. Trust, 1999–2009. Chm., Univ. of Westminster, 1993–99; Vice-Chm., Morley Coll., 1993–99; Gov., Portsmouth Grammar Sch., 1976–2001. CCIPD. Hon. FFOM, RCP, 1994. Hon. Fellow, Thames Polytechnic, 1990. Hon. DSc: Aston, 1991; UWE, 2000; Hon. DLitt Westminster, 1998; Hon. DCL Huddersfield, 2000. *Publications:* report on appt processes of judges and QCs in England and Wales, 1999; articles on personnel management and social responsibility. *Recreations:* opera, theatre, cricket, gardening. *Address:* Santhari, Heath Close, Wentworth, Virginia Water, Surrey GU25 4AY. *T:* (01344) 842258. *Club:* Oxford & Cambridge University.

PEACH, Air Chief Marshal Sir Stuart (William), KCB 2009; CBE 2001; DL; Vice Chief of the Defence Staff, since 2013; *b* Staffordshire, 22 Feb. 1956; *s* of Clifford Peach and Jean Mary Peach; *m* 1986, Brigitte Ender; one *s* one *d*. *Educ:* Sheffield Univ. (BA 1977); Downing Coll., Cambridge (MPhil 1997). Joined RAF, 1974; 13 Sqdn, 1979–81; IX (B) Sqdn, 1982–84; 31 Sqdn, 1984–89; RAF Staff Coll., 1990; HQ RAF Germany, 1991–93; OC IX (Bomber) Sqdn, 1993–96; Dir, Defence Studies, 1997–99; Comdr British Forces (Air) Italy, 1999–2000; Air Comdr (Forward) Kosovo, 2000; Comdt, Air Warfare Centre, 2000–03; Dir Gen., Intelligence Collection, 2003–06; Chief, Defence Intelligence, 2006–09; Chief of Jt Ops, 2009–11; Comdr Jt Forces Comd, 2011–13. Hon. Col, Intelligence Corps (Army). Trustee, Imperial War Mus., 2012–. Hon. DTech Kingston, 2003; Hon. DLitt Sheffield, 2007. DL Lincs, 2014. *Publications:* Perspectives on Air Power, 1998; service manuals; articles in defence jls on air power and ops. *Recreations:* military history, cooking, sport. *Club:* Royal Air Force.

PEACOCK, Dame Alison (Margaret), DBE 2014; DL; Headteacher, Wroxham School, Potters Bar, since 2003; *b* London, 17 Oct. 1959; *d* of Leslie and Patricia Mann; *m* 1983, Jonathan Peacock; two *d*. *Educ:* Univ. of London (BA Hons); Univ. of Warwick (PGCE); Queens' Coll., Cambridge (MEd 1997). Hon. DLitt Brighton, 2014. DL Herts, 2015. *Publications:* (jtly) Creating Learning Without Limits, 2012. *Address:* Wroxham School, Wroxham Gardens, Potters Bar, Herts EN6 3DJ. *E:* alison.peacock@thewroxham.net.

PEACOCK, Hon. Andrew (Sharp), AC 1997; Chairman, Amadeus Energy Ltd, 2007–09; *b* 13 Feb. 1939; *s* of late A. S. Peacock and Iris Peacock. *Educ:* Scotch Coll., Melbourne, Vic; Melbourne Univ. (LLB). Former Partner, Rigby & Fielding, Solicitors; Chm., Peacock and Smith Pty Ltd, 1962–69. Army Reserve (Captain), 1966–94. Pres., Victorian Liberal Party, 1965–66; MP (L) Kooyong, Australia, 1966–94; Minister for Army and Minister assisting Prime Minister, 1969–71; Minister for Army and Minister asstg Treasurer, 1971–72; Minister for External Territories, Feb.–Dec. 1972; Mem., Opposition Exec., 1973–75; Oppos. Shadow Minister for For. Affairs, 1973–75, 1985–87; Minister for: the Envmt, 1975; Foreign Affairs, 1975–80; Industrial Relns, 1980–81; Industry and Commerce, 1982–83; Leader of the Parly Liberal Party, and of the Opposition, 1983–85; Dep. Leader, Liberal Party and Dep. Leader, Opposition, 1987–89; Leader, Parly Liberal Party, and of the Opposition, 1989–90; Shadow Attorney-Gen. and Shadow Minister for Justice, 1990–92; Shadow Minister: for Trade, 1992–93; for Foreign Affairs, 1993–94; Australian Ambassador to the USA, 1997–2000. Pres., Boeing Australia, 2002–07; Chm., MFS Ltd, 2007–08. Chm., Internat. Democrat Union, 1989–92. Mem., Business Council of Australia, 2003–07. Mem., Internat. Adv. Panel, Graduate Sch. of Govt, Univ. of Sydney, 2003–. *Recreations:* horse racing, sailboarding, Australian Rules football. *Clubs:* Australian (Sydney); Melbourne, Melbourne Cricket, Victoria Racing, Melbourne Racing (Melbourne); Moonee Valley Racing.

PEACOCK, Dr Christabel Phyllis, CBE 2014; FRSB; FRAgS; Chairman and Founder, Sidai Africa Ltd, since 2011; *b* Bristol, 27 Feb. 1958; *d* of late Prof. Joseph Henry Peacock and of Dr Gillian Frances Peacock. *Educ:* St Mary's Calne; Univ. of Reading (BSc Hons 1980; PhD 1984). FRSB (FSB 2009). Vis. Scientist, Internat. Livestock Centre of Africa, 1980–84; CSIRO Advr to Govt of Indonesia, 1985–86; Agricl Systems Specialist, UNFAO and Asst Prof., Asian Inst. of Technol., Bangkok, 1986–88; Project Co-ordinator, Ethiopia, 1988–96; Farm Africa: Regl Goat Develt Dir, 1995–96; Dep. Dir, 1996–99; CEO, 1999–2010. Mem., Editl Bd, World Agric. Mem., Global Develt website Adv. Panel, Guardian. Founding Mem., All Party Parly Gp for Agric. and Food for Develt; Mem., Ind. Adv. Gp on Zoonoses and Emerging Livestock Systems, BBSRC. Mem. Bd, Internat. Goat Assoc., until 2012. FRAgS 2009. Hon. DSc Reading, 2011. Charity Principal of Year, UK Charity Awards, 2003; Ashoka Fellow, 2011; Outstanding Social Entrepreneur of Year, Schwab Foundn, 2015. *Publications:* Improving Goat Production in the Tropics: a manual for development workers, 1996; Goat Types of Ethiopia and Eritrea, 1996; contrib. scientific papers and book chapters. *Recreations:* scuba diving, watching the England cricket team beat Australia, walking, gardening, travelling. *Address:* Glebe Cottage, Bryants Bottom, Great Missenden, Bucks HP16 0JS. *T:* (01494) 488399. *E:* christie.peacock@sidai.com. *Club:* MCC.

PEACOCK, Elizabeth Joan; JP; DL; *b* 4 Sept. 1937; *d* of late John and Dorothy Gates; *m* 1963, Brian David Peacock; two *s*. *Educ:* St Monica's Convent, Skipton. Asst to Exec. Dir, York Community Council, 1979–83; Administrator, four charitable trusts, York, 1979–83. County Councillor, N Yorks, 1981–84. MP (C) Batley and Spen, 1983–97; contested (C) same seat, 1997, 2001. PPS to Minister of State, Home Office, 1991–92, to Minister for Social Security and disabled people, 1992. Mem., Select Cttee on Employment, 1983–87. Chairman: All Party Trans Pennine Gp, 1988–94; All Party Wool Textile Gp, 1989–97. Hon. Sec., Yorks Cons. MPs, 1983–88; Vice Chm., Cons. Back-bench Party Organisation Cttee, 1985–87; Mem. Exec. Cttee, 1922 Cttee, 1987–91; Mem. Exec., CPA, 1987–92. Mem., BBC Gen. Adv. Council, 1987–93; Chm., BBC Yorkshire Regl Audience Council (formerly Local Regl Cttee, Yorks), 2006–10. Vice Pres., Yorks Area Young Conservatives, 1984–87; Pres., Yorks Area Cons. Trade Unionists, 1991–98 (Vice Pres., 1987–91). FRSA 1990–2010 (Chm., Yorks Reg., 2003–06). JP Macclesfield, 1975–79, Bulmer East 1983; DL W Yorks, 1998. Spectator Campaigner of Year, 1992; Yorkshire Woman of Year, 1993; Yorkshire Woman of Achievement, 1993. *Recreations:* reading, motoring. *Address:* Spen House, George Lane, Notton, Wakefield, W Yorks WF4 2NQ.

See also J. D. Peacock, N. C. Peacock.

PEACOCK, Eric; *see* Peacock, W. E.

PEACOCK, Geraldine, CBE 2001; Chair, Charity Commission for England and Wales, 2004–06; freelance facilitator, since 2007; *b* 26 Jan. 1948; *d* of late Peter Davies and of Joyce Davies (*née* Pullin); *m* 1971, Harry Peacock (marr. diss. 1988); three *s*. *Educ:* Redland High Sch., Bristol; Durham Univ. (BA Hons Sociology 1969); Univ. of California; Univ. of Newcastle upon Tyne (CQSW 1981; post-grad. dip. in Applied Social Work Studies 1981). Teaching Asst, Univ. of California, and Heroin Addiction Counsellor, San Bernardino State Prison, 1969–70; Med. Social Worker, Durham Hosp. Bd, 1970–72; Lectr in Criminology, Teesside Poly., 1972–75; Social Worker: Thalidomide Children's Trust, 1975–85; Lady Hoare Trust for Handicapped Children, 1975–79; Course Co-ordinator, Open Univ., 1975–82; Lectr in Social Work, Queen's Coll., Glasgow, 1982–86; Dep. Dir, London Boroughs Training Cttee, 1986–89; Chief Executive: Nat. Autistic Soc., 1989–97; Guide Dogs for the Blind Assoc., 1997–2003. Associate Fellow, Skoll Centre for Social Entrepreneurship, Saïd Business Sch., Oxford Univ., 2006–; Vis. Fellow, Centre for Charity Effectiveness, Cass Business Sch., London, 2007–. A Civil Service Comr, 2001–04; Comr and Bd Mem., Commn on Unclaimed Assets, 2006–. HM Treasury: Mem., Social Investment Taskforces, 2000–06; Chm., Futurebuilders Taskforce, 2003–04; Member: Strategy Unit Adv. Panel on Charity Law and Regulation, Cabinet Office, 2002–06; Action Community Unit Adv. Panel, Home Office, 2002–06. Columnist: Third Sector mag., 1999–, and other charity mags. Lectr, Stanford and Berkeley Univs, 2009–. Member: Exec. Cttee, ACEVO (formerly ACENVO), 1994–2006 (Chm., 1996–2000); Council, Industrial Soc., 1996–2001; Exec. Cttee, NCVO, 2000–03 (Trustee, 1999–2006). Vice-Chm., Internat. Fedn of Guide Dog Schs for the Blind, 2001–03; Vice Pres., Parkinson's Disease Soc., 2006–. Member: Social Enterprise Initiative Adv. Bd, Harvard Business Sch., 2003–; Business Adv. Forum, Saïd Business Sch., Oxford Univ., 2006–; Trustee, Rainbow Trust, 2007–; Patron: Movers and Shakers, 2005–; CDFA, 2004–. Hon. LLD Teesside, 2005. *Publications:* (jtly) Social Work and Received Ideas, 1988; (ed jtly) The Haunt of Misery: essays in helping and caring, 1989; Appraising the Chief Executive, 1996; The Magic Roundabout: a guide to social investment for charities, 2004. *Recreations:* theatre, cinema, art, literature, family. *Address:* White Lion House, 5 New Street, Wells, Somerset BA5 2LA. *T:* (01749) 672926. *E:* gerpea@gmail.com.

PEACOCK, Ian Douglas, OBE 1998; Chief Executive, Lawn Tennis Association, 1986–96; *b* 9 April 1934; *s* of Andrew Inglis Peacock and Minnie Maria (*née* King); *m* 1st, 1962, Joanna Hepburn MacGregor (marr. diss. 2007); one *s* one *d*; 2nd, 2008, Philippa Katharine Bland. *Educ:* Sevenoaks Sch. Pilot Officer, RAF, 1953–54. Slazengers Ltd, 1955–83, Man. Dir 1976–83; Sports Marketing Surveys Ltd, 1984–85. President: British Sports & Allied Industry Fedn, 1984–85; UK Tennis Industry Assoc., 2008–. Director: Golf Foundn, 1982– (Chm., 1996–2003; Vice Pres., 2003–; Chm., Golf Ball Cttee, 1976–96); LTA Trust, 1988–96; Queen's Club Ltd, 1993–96; Wembley Nat. Stadium Ltd, 1998–2002; Tennis Foundn (formerly British Tennis Foundn), 1998–2010. Trustee: Torch Trophy Trust, 1993– (Chm., 1998–2006; Vice Pres., 2006–); Dan Maskell Tennis Trust, 1997–; English Nat. Stadium Trust, 1998–2009. *Recreations:* golf, ski-ing, painting. *Address:* 135 More Close, St Paul's Court, West Kensington, W14 9BW. *Clubs:* Royal Air Force, All England Lawn Tennis and Croquet, Queen's; Royal Ashdown Forest Golf (Forest Row).

PEACOCK, (Ian) Michael, OBE 2005; Chairman: UBC Media Group plc (formerly Unique Broadcasting Co. Ltd), 1989–95; The Michael Peacock Charitable Foundation, 1990–2010; *b* 14 Sept. 1929; *e s* of Norman Henry and Sara Barbara Peacock; *m* 1956, Daphne Lee; two *s* one *d*. *Educ:* Kimball Union Academy, USA; Welwyn Garden City Grammar School; London School of Economics (BSc Econ.). BBC Television: Producer, 1952–56; Producer Panorama, 1955–58; Asst Head of Television Outside Broadcasts, 1958–59; Editor, Panorama, 1959–61; Editor, BBC Television News, 1961–63; Chief of Programmes, BBC 2, 1963–65; Controller, BBC 1, BBC Television Service, 1965–67; Managing Dir, London Weekend Television Ltd, 1967–69; Chm., Monitor Enterprises Ltd, 1970–89; Man. Dir, Warner Bros TV Ltd, 1972–74; Exec. Vice-Pres., Warner Bros Television Inc., 1974–76. Dir, Video Arts Ltd, 1972–89; Pres., Video Arts Inc., 1976–78; Man. Dir, Dumbarton Films Ltd (formerly Video Arts Television), 1978–87; Chairman: Video Answers, 1989–90; Publishing Projects plc, 1990–92. Dep. Chm., Piccadilly Radio, 1988–89; Man. Dir, Truly Classic Yachts Ltd, 1994–2002. IPPA: First Chm., 1981–82; Mem. Council, 1983–88. Mem., Ct of Governors, LSE, 1982–2009, now Emeritus Gov. (Chm., Campaign for the LSE, 2001–04). Hon. FTCL 2003; Hon. Fellow, LSE 2004. *Address:* 21 Woodlands Road, Barnes, SW13 0JZ. *T:* (020) 8876 2025. *Club:* Savile.

PEACOCK, Ian Rex; Chairman: Mothercare plc, 2002–11; MFI Furniture Group plc, 2000–06; Housing Finance Corporation, since 2013 (non-executive Director, since 2013); *b* 5 July 1947; *s* of late Mervyn (George) and Evelyn (Joyce) Peacock; *m* 1973, Alyanee Chya-Rochana; one *s*. *Educ:* Kingswood Grammar Sch.; Trinity Coll., Cambridge (MA); Open Univ. (MA). Economist: Unilever Plc, 1968–73; Cripps Warburg Ltd, 1973–75; Kleinwort Benson Gp, 1975–94 (Gp Dir, 1990–94); Co-Hd, Merchant Banking Div., USA, 1994–97,

Chief Operating Officer, Investment Banking, 1997–98, BZW Ltd; Special Advr, Bank of England, 1998–2000. Non-executive Director: Norwich & Peterborough Bldg Soc., 1997–2005; C. Hoare & Co., 2010– (Consultant to Bd, 2008–10); Director: Lombard Risk Mgt, 2000–10 (Dep. Chm., 2004–10); i-documentsystems, 2000–03. Chm., Family Mosaic Housing Assoc., 2007–13. Trustee: WRVS, 2001–07; PHG Foundn, 2007–; Chiswick House and Gardens Trust, 2011–. Quondam Fellow, Hughes Hall, Cambridge, 2012– (City Fellow, 2009–12). *Recreations:* music, particularly opera, squash, gardening, travel. *E:* ianrpeacock@hotmail.com. *Club:* Athenæum.

PEACOCK, James; *see* Peacock, W. J.

PEACOCK, Prof. John Andrew, PhD; FRS 2007; FRSE; Professor of Cosmology, University of Edinburgh, since 1998; *b* 27 March 1956; *s* of Arthur John Peacock and Isobel Watson Peacock (*née* Moir); *m* 1982, Catherine Heather Lewis; one *s* two *d. Educ:* Jesus Coll., Cambridge (BA 1977; PhD 1981). Res. astronomer, 1983–92, Hd of Res., 1992–98, Royal Observatory, Edinburgh. FRSE 2006. Shaw Prize in Astronomy, 2014. *Publications:* Cosmological Physics, 1999. *Recreations:* playing classical clarinet, hill walking. *Address:* Institute for Astronomy, University of Edinburgh, Royal Observatory, Blackford Hill, Edinburgh EH9 3HJ. *T:* (0131) 668 8100, *Fax:* (0131) 668 8416. *E:* jap@roe.ac.uk.

PEACOCK, Jonathan David; QC 2001; *b* 21 April 1964; *s* of Brian David Peacock and Elizabeth Joan Peacock, *qv*; *m* 1997, Charlotte Ann Cole; one *s* one *d. Educ:* King's Sch., Macclesfield; Nunthorpe Grammar Sch., York; Corpus Christi Coll., Oxford (MA Juris 1st Cl.). Called to the Bar, Middle Temple, 1987 (Sen. Schol.). *Recreations:* cricket, sailing. *Address:* 11 New Square, Lincoln's Inn, WC2A 3QB. *T:* (020) 7242 4017. *Clubs:* United and Cecil; Itchenor Sailing.

See also N. C. Peacock.

PEACOCK, Michael; *see* Peacock, I. M.

PEACOCK, Nicholas Christopher; QC 2009; *b* Keighley, W Yorks; *s* of Brian David Peacock and Elizabeth Joan Peacock, *qv*; *m* 1995, Susan; two *d. Educ:* Nunthorpe Grammar Sch., York; St Edmund Hall, Oxford (BA Juris.). Called to the Bar, Middle Temple, 1989. *Recreations:* cycling, Land Rovers. *Address:* Maitland Chambers, 7 Stone Buildings, Lincoln's Inn, WC2A 3SZ. *T:* (020) 7406 1200, *Fax:* (020) 7406 1300. *E:* npeacock@maitlandchambers.com.

PEACOCK, Peter James, CBE 1998; Member (Lab) Highland and Islands, Scottish Parliament, 1999–2011; *b* 27 Feb. 1952; *s* of James and Doreen Peacock; *m* 1973, Shona Pearson; two *s. Educ:* Hawick High Sch.; Jordanhill Coll. of Educn (Dip. Youth Work and Community Studies 1973). Community Educn Officer, Orkney CC, 1973–75; Area Officer for Highland, Grampian, Tayside, Orkney, Shetland and Western Isles, and Central Policy Advr, Scottish Assoc. of CABx, 1975–87; Partner, The Apt Partnership, 1987–96. Member: Highland Regl Council (Dep. Leader; Chm. Finance Cttee), 1982–96; (Lab) Highland Council, 1995–99 (Leader/Convenor; Chm., Policy and Resources Cttee). Scottish Executive: Dep. Minister for Children and Educn, 1999–2000, for Finance and Local Govt, then for Finance and Public Services, 2000–03; Minister for Educn and Young People, 2003–06. Vice Pres., COSLA. Chm., Customer Forum for Water in Scotland, 2011–; Policy Dir, Community Land Scotland, 2011–. Mem., Ofcom Adv. Cttee for Scotland, 2012–. Former Member: Bd, Scottish Natural Heritage; European Cttee of Regions; Scottish Economic Council; Bd, Scottish Post Office; Bd, Cairngorm Partnership. Chm., Scottish Library and Information Council, 1991–94; former Chairman: Moray Firth Community Radio; Community Work North; former Member: Scottish Valuation Adv. Council; Centres for Highlands and Islands Policy Studies. *E:* peter.peacock@btinternet.com.

PEACOCK, Prof. Sharon Jayne, CBE 2015; PhD; Professor of Clinical Microbiology, Department of Medicine, University of Cambridge, since 2009; *b* Margate, Kent, 24 March 1959; *d* of Francis and Mary Hardstaffe; *m* 1983, Peter Peacock; one *s* two *d. Educ:* Southampton Univ. (BM 1988); Open Univ. (PhD 2003). MRCP 1991; MRCPath 1997. Postgrad. med. trng, Southampton, Brighton and Oxford, 1988–95; Wellcome Trust Res. Trng Fellow in Microbiol., Univ. of Oxford and Trinity Coll. Dublin, 1995–98; Sen. Lectr in Microbiol., Univ. of Oxford, 1998–2002; Hd, Bacterial Diseases Res., Mahidol-Oxford Tropical Medicine Res. Unit, Mahidol Univ., Bangkok, 2002–09. FMedSci 2013; Fellow, American Acad. of Microbiol., 2014. *Publications:* contrib. book chapters and scientific articles to peer-reviewed jls. *Recreations:* red wine, cycling. *Address:* Department of Medicine, University of Cambridge, Box 157, Addenbrooke's Hospital, Cambridge CB2 0QQ. *T:* (01223) 336808. *E:* sjp97@medschl.cam.ac.uk.

PEACOCK, (William) Eric, CMG 2003; DBA; DL; non-executive Director, Exemplas Holdings Ltd (Chief Executive, 1996); Chief Executive, Business Link Hertfordshire, 1996–2006; *b* 22 Sept. 1944; *s* of Robert and Violet Peacock; *m* 1988, Carole Nicholls; one *s. Educ:* Bellahouston Acad.; Queen's Univ. Belfast (MBA 1974, DBA 1976). Barbour Ltd, 1960–79, Man. Dir, 1974–79; Managing Director: Hollis Gp plc, 1979–83; Hartsford Dales Ltd, 1983–93; Chm. and CEO, Babygro plc, 1983–88; Man. Dir, Missenden Abbey Management Develt Centre, 1993–96. Chairman: Cafe Slim Ltd, 2002–; What If, 2002–; Stevenage Packaging Ltd, 2003–; Eupac Ltd, 2003–06; 4 Less Finance Plc, 2004–; Silent Edge Ltd, 2004–06; Rialto Gp Ltd, 2004–. Non-executive Director: Hertfordshire Univ. Business Sch., 2002–; FCO, 2003; DTI, later BERR; ECGD, 2011–. Gp Chm., Acad. for Chief Execs Ltd, 1997–. Chm., Peacock Foundn, 1987–. DL Herts 2003. *Recreation:* enthusiast and alchemist. *Address:* Green Fallow House, Bury Rise, Bovingdon, Herts HP3 0DN. *T:* (01442) 832154.

PEACOCK, Dr (William) James, AC 1994; BSc, PhD; FRS 1982; FAA; Chief, Division of Plant Industry, 1978–2003, Fellow, since 2004, Commonwealth Scientific and Industrial Research Organization; Chief Scientist, Australian Government, 2006–08; *b* 14 Dec. 1937; *m* 1961, Margaret Woodward; one *s* two *d. Educ:* Katoomba High Sch.; Univ. of Sydney (BSc, PhD). FAA 1976. CSIRO Postdoctoral Fellow, 1963 and Vis. Associate Prof. of Biology, 1964–65, Univ. of Oregon; Res. Consultant, Oak Ridge National Lab., USA, 1965; res. staff, Div. of Plant Industry, CSIRO, 1965–. Adjunct Prof. of Biology, Univ. of Calif, San Diego, 1969; Vis. Prof. of Biochem., Stanford Univ., 1970; Vis. Distinguished Prof. of Molecular Biol., Univ. of Calif, LA, 1977; Distinguished Prof., UTS, 2011–. Pres., Aust. Academy of Sci., 2002–06. For. Associate, US Nat. Acad. of Scis, 1990; For. Fellow, Indian Nat. Science Acad., 1990. FTSE (FTS 1988); FAIAST (FAIAS 1989). Hon. DSc: Charles Sturt, 1996; Ghent, 2004; NSW, 2008; Univ. of Technol., Sydney, 2014; Hon. DAgrSc Sydney, 2002. Edgeworth David Medal, Royal Soc. of NSW, 1967; Lemberg Medal, Aust. Biochem. Soc., 1978; BHP Bicentennial Prize for Pursuit of Excellence in Science and Technol., 1988; CSIRO Medal for Leadership of Div. of Plant Industry, 1989; Burnet Medal, Aust. Acad. of Sci., 1989; (jtly) Prime Minister's Prize for Science (inaugural winner), 2000; CSIRO Lifetime Achievement Award, 2005; Radobank Leadership Award, 2012; ACT Sen. Australian of the Yr, 2013. *Publications:* editor of 5 books on genetics and molecular biology; approx. 350 papers. *Recreations:* cultivation of native plants, bush-walking. *Address:* 16 Brassey Street, Deakin, ACT 2600, Australia. *T:* (home) (2) 62814485.

PEACOCKE, Prof. Christopher Arthur Bruce, FBA 1990; Professor of Philosophy, since 2004, Johnsonian Professor of Philosophy, since 2013, and Chair, Department of Philosophy, since 2013, Columbia University; Richard Wollheim Professor of Philosophy, University College London, since 2007; *b* 22 May 1950; *s* of late Rev. Dr Arthur Robert Peacocke, MBE; *m* 1980, Teresa Anne Rosen; one *s* one *d. Educ:* Magdalen College Sch., Oxford; Exeter Coll., Oxford (MA, BPhil, DPhil). Kennedy Schol., Harvard Univ., 1971; Sen. Schol., Merton Coll., Oxford, 1972; Jun. Res. Fellow, Queen's Coll., Oxford, 1973; Prize Fellow, All Souls Coll., Oxford, 1975; Fellow and Tutor, New Coll., Oxford, and CUF Lectr in Philosophy, 1979–85; Susan Stebbing Prof. of Philosophy, KCL, 1985–88; Waynflete Prof. of Metaphysical Philosophy, Univ. of Oxford and Fellow of Magdalen Coll., Oxford, 1989–2000; Prof. of Philosophy, New York Univ., 2000–04; Chm., Promotions and Tenure Cttee, Faculty of Arts and Scis, Columbia Univ., 2011–13. Visiting Professor: Berkeley, 1975; Ann Arbor, 1978; UCLA, 1981; Maryland, 1987; NY Univ., 1996–99; Vis. Fellow, ANU, 1981; Fellow, Center for Advanced Study in the Behavioral Sciences, Stanford, 1983; Vis. Res. Associate, Center for Study of Language and Information, Stanford, 1984; Leverhulme Personal Res. Professorship, 1996–2000. Whitehead Lectr, Harvard, 2001; Immanuel Kant Lectr, Stanford, 2003; Content and Context Lectr, Institut Jean Nicod, Paris, 2010; Gareth Evans Meml Lectr, Oxford, 2010; Kohut Lectr, Chicago, 2011. Pres., Mind Assoc., 1986; Mem., Steering Cttee, European Soc. for Philosophy and Psychology, 1991–95. Fellow, Amer. Acad. of Arts and Scis, 2010. Hon. DLitt Warwick, 2007. *Publications:* Holistic Explanation: action, space, interpretation, 1979; Sense and Content, 1983; Thoughts: an essay on content, 1986; A Study of Concepts, 1992; Being Known, 1999; The Realm of Reason, 2004; Truly Understood, 2008; The Mirror of the World: subjects, consciousness, and self-consciousness, 2014; papers on philosophy of mind and language, metaphysics and epistemology, and the perception of music, in Jl of Philosophy, Philosophical Rev., etc. *Recreations:* music, visual arts. *Address:* Department of Philosophy, Columbia University, 1150 Amsterdam Avenue, 708 Philosophy Hall, MC 4971, New York, NY 10027, USA. *T:* (212) 8543384.

PEAKE, John Fordyce; consultant; Associate Director (Scientific Development), Natural History Museum, 1989–92; *b* 4 June 1933; *s* of late William Joseph Peake and of Helena (*née* Fordyce); *m* 1963, Pamela Joyce Hollis; two *d. Educ:* City of Norwich Grammar Sch.; University Coll. London (BSc). National Trust, 1955–56; Norwich Technical Coll., 1956–58; Nature Conservancy Studentship, 1958–59; British Museum (Natural History): Research Fellow, 1959–61; Sen. Scientific Officer, 1961–69; PSO, 1969–71; Dep. Keeper, 1971–85; Keeper of Zoology, 1985–89. Hon. Research Associate, Bernice P. Bishop Mus., Honolulu, 1972. Royal Society: Member: Aldabra Research Cttee, 1972–77; Southern Zones Cttee, 1982–86; Unitas Malacologica: Treas. 1962–63, Mem. Council, 1963–75; Vice Pres., Malacological Soc. of London, 1976–78; Council Mem., Zoological Soc. of London, 1985–88. *Publications:* (editor and contributor with Dr V. Fretter) Pulmonates, 3 vols, 1975–79; papers on taxonomy, biogeography and ecology of terrestrial molluscs in sci. jls. *Recreations:* gardening, local history. *Address:* Crows Nest, Back Lane, Blakeney, Holt, Norfolk NR25 7NP. *T:* (01263) 740388.

PEAKE, John Morris, CBE 1986; Chairman: Cambridgeshire Careers Guidance Ltd, 1995–98; Careers Services National Association, 1997–98; *b* 26 Aug. 1924; *s* of late Albert Edward Peake and Ruby Peake (*née* Morris); *m* 1953, Elizabeth Rought; one *s* one *d. Educ:* Repton School; Clare College, Cambridge (Mech. Scis Tripos; MA 1949); Royal Naval College, Greenwich (Dip. Naval Arch.). CEng, FIMechE; CMath, FIMA. Royal Corps of Naval Constructors, 1944–50; Personnel Administration Ltd, 1950–51; Baker Perkins (BP): joined 1951; Dir, parent co., 1956; Jt Man. Dir, BP Ltd, 1963–66; Man. Dir, BP Pty, 1969–74, in Australia; Pres., BP Inc., 1975–77, in USA; Dep. Man. Dir, BP Holdings, 1978–79, Man. Dir, 1980–85; Chm., Baker Perkins plc, 1984–87. Member: Council, CBI, 1980–89 (Chairman: Overseas Schols Bd, 1981–87; Educn and Trng Cttee, 1986–88); Council, BTEC, 1986–89 (Chm., Bd for Engineering, 1985–91); MSC, subseq. Trng Commn, 1986–88; RSA Examinations Bd, 1987–93 (Chm., 1989–93); RSA Council, 1989–93; Design Council, 1991–93 (Chm. Educn Cttee, 1990–94); Chm., Greater Peterborough Partnership, 1994–95; Vice Chm., Gtr Peterborough TEC, 1990–94. Chm., Nene Park Trust, 1988–93. Hockey Silver Medal, London Olympics, 1948. CCMI. Hon. DTech CNAA, 1986. *Recreations:* sport, travel. *Address:* 14 Beech Court, 33B Arterberry Road, Wimbledon, SW20 8AG. *T:* (020) 3105 6256. *Clubs:* East India, MCC; Hawks (Cambridge).

PEAKE, Joseph Anthony; Headmaster, St George's College, Weybridge, 1995–Aug. 2016; *b* Manchester, 13 March 1954; *s* of Patrick and Margaret Peake; *m* 1981, Julie Foster; two *s* one *d. Educ:* St Cuthbert's RC Sch., Bolton; Queen's Coll., Oxford (MA Chem.; PGCE). VSO, Ghana, 1976–78; Asst Master, Manchester GS, 1979–84; Hd of Chemistry and Dir of Curriculum, Millfield Sch., 1984–94. Chief Examr, A-Level Chem., 1990–95. Mem., Ind. Schs Inspectorate Cttee, 1999–2003. Chm., Soc. of Heads, 2005 (Chm., Educn Cttee, 1998–2003). Mem., Ind. Schs Governing Council, 2006–09. Chm., Catholic Ind. Schs Conf., 2009–15. Gov., St Teresa's Sch., Effingham, 2013–. *Publications:* Chemistry for Senior Secondary Schools, 1990. *Recreations:* music, walking, Bolton Wanderers. *Address:* St George's College, Woburn Park, Weybridge, Surrey KT15 2QS. *E:* jpeake@stgeorgesweybridge.com. *Club:* East India.

PEAKE, Timothy Nigel, FRAeS; astronaut, European Space Agency, since 2009; *b* Chichester, 7 April 1972. *Educ:* Chichester High Sch. for Boys; RMA, Sandhurst; Portsmouth Univ. (BSc Hons Flight Dynamics 2005). Commnd AAC, 1992; qualified as helicopter pilot, 1994; Instructor, 1998; Test Pilot, 2005–09; Sen. Test Pilot, AugustaWestland Helicopters, 2009. FBIS. Mem., Soc. of Exptl Test Pilots. *Recreations:* diving, ski-ing, flying, family. *Address:* European Astronaut Centre, Linder Höhe, 51147 Cologne, Germany. *T:* 22036001224. *E:* astrocom@esa.int.

PEAKER, Prof. Malcolm, DSc, PhD; FRS 1996; FZS, FRSB, FRSE; Director, Hannah Research Institute, Ayr, 1981–2003; Hannah Professor, University of Glasgow, 1981–2003; *b* 21 Aug. 1943; *s* of Ronald Smith Peaker and Marian (*née* Tomasin); *m* 1965, Stephanie Jane Large; three *s. Educ:* Henry Mellish Grammar Sch., Nottingham; Univ. of Sheffield (BSc Zoology; DSc); Univ. of Hong Kong (SRC NATO Scholar; PhD). FZS 1969; FRSB (FIBiol 1979); FRSE 1983. Inst. of Animal Physiology, ARC, 1968–78; Head, Dept of Physiol., Hannah Res. Inst., 1978–81. Chm. Bd, London Zoo, 1992–93; Vice-Pres., Council, Zoological Soc. of London, 1992–94; Mem. Council, RSE, 1999–2002. Mem., Rank Prize Funds Adv. Cttee on Nutrition, 1997–. Scientific Governor, British Nutrition Foundn, 1997– (Chm., 2002–04). Non-exec. Dir, Edinburgh Instruments Ltd, 2004–11. Raine Distinguished Visitor, Univ. of WA, 1998. Munro Kerr Lecture, Munro Kerr Soc., 1997; Annual Lecture, Edinburgh Centre for Rural Res./RSE/Inst. of Biol., 2000; Dist. Lectr, Univ. of Hong Kong, 2000. Hon. DSc Hong Kong, 2000. Mem. Editorial Board: Jl of Dairy Science, 1975–78; Internat. Zoo Yearbook, 1978–82; Jl of Endocrinology, 1981–91; Procs of RSE, 1989–92; Mammary Gland Biology and Neoplasia, 1993–2000; Editor, British Jl of Herpetology, 1977–81. *Publications:* Salt Glands in Birds and Reptiles, 1975; (ed) Avian Physiology, 1975; (ed) Comparative Aspects of Lactation, 1977; (ed jtly) Physiological Strategies in Lactation, 1984; (ed jtly) Intercellular Signalling in the Mammary Gland, 1995; (ed jtly) Biological Signalling and the Mammary Gland, 1997; papers in physiol, endocrinol, zool, biochem., vet. and agricl science jls. *Recreations:* vertebrate zoology, natural history, golf, grumbling about bureaucrats. *Address:* Rushmere, 13 Upper Crofts, Alloway, Ayr KA7 4QX. *Club:* Royal Troon Golf.

PEARCE, Prof. Alastair Tom Parslow, PhD; President, LASALLE College of Arts, Singapore, 2008–12, Advisor, 2012; *b* 9 Dec. 1953; *s* of Tom and Florence Pearce; *m* Dr Maureen Cleary. *Educ:* Royal Acad. of Music (LRAM); King's Coll., London (BMus, MMus; PhD). Nat. Advr for Computing in the Arts, Univ. of Oxford, 1979–82; University of Central

England: Vice-Principal, Birmingham Conservatoire, 1994–98; Dean, Fac. of Educn, 1998–2001; Principal, Rose Bruford Coll., 2001–08. *Publications:* contribs to music jls and articles on managing performing arts higher educn. *Recreations:* fine wine, cooking, writing.

PEARCE, Andrew; Deputy Head of Distributive Trades Unit, European Commission, Brussels, 1994–2002; *b* 1 Dec. 1937; *s* of late Henry Pearce, Liverpool cotton broker, and Evelyn Pearce; *m* 1966, Myra Whelan (*d* 2006); three *s* one *d*. *Educ:* Rydal School, Colwyn Bay; University of Durham (BA). Formerly in construction industry; in Customs Dept, EEC, Brussels, 1974–79. Contested (C) Islington North, 1969 and 1970; Mem. (C) Cheshire W, Eur. Parlt, 1979–89; contested: (C) Cheshire W, EP elecn, 1989; (C) Ellesmere Port and Neston, 1992; (Pro Euro C) NW Reg., EP elecn, 1999. Founder and Vice-Pres., British Cons. Assoc. in Belgium; Vice-Pres., Consultative Assembly of Lomé Convention, 1980–89. Chm., Internat. Trade Cttee, British Retail Consortium, 1990–93; Vice Chm., European Business Develt Gp, 1991–93, Mem. Council, 2004–10, Liverpool Chamber of Commerce. Chm., Liverpool Cultural Heritage Forum (formerly Liverpool Heritage Forum), 2005–10; Mem. Council, Merseyside Civic Soc., 2004–. Governor: Archway Comprehensive School, 1967–70; Woodchurch High Sch., Birkenhead, 1985–90; Nugent Sch., Liverpool, 1992–94. FRSA 2004–09. *Address:* 3 St John's Court, Byron Close, Freshfield, Liverpool L37 3QL. *Club:* Athenæum (Liverpool).

PEARCE, Andrew John, OBE 2013; HM Diplomatic Service; Head of Security, Foreign and Commonwealth Office, since 2009; *b* 7 Oct. 1960; *s* of Edward Peter Pearce and Renee Joyce Pearce; *m* 1986, Pornpun Pathumvivatana; one *s* one *d*. *Educ:* St Catherine's Coll., Oxford (MA 1st Cl. Hons Chemistry 1983). Joined FCO, 1983; Third Sec., Nr East and N Africa Dept, FCO, 1983–84; lang. trng, SOAS, London, 1984–85; Second Sec. (Pol), Bangkok, 1985–88; Head: Chemical Weapons Sect., Arms Control and Disarmament Dept, FCO, 1988–90; Iberian Sec., S European Dept, FCO, 1990–92; First Secretary: Pol and Public Affairs, Tel Aviv, 1992–96; Econ. Affairs, Pretoria, 1996–2000; Counsellor and Deputy Head of Mission: Bucharest, 2001–03; Bangkok, 2004–08. *Recreations:* tennis, long-distance walking, exploring, cat rearing. *Address:* c/o Foreign and Commonwealth Office, King Charles Street, SW1A 2AH. *E:* andy.pearce@fco.gov.uk.

PEARCE, Brian; *see* Pearce, J. B.

PEARCE, Christopher Donovan James; Chief Executive Officer, Proteome Sciences (formerly Electrophoretics International) plc, since 1991; *b* 1 March 1953; *m* 1981, Sandra Lynette Jenkins; two *s* one *d* (and one *d* decd). *Educ:* St John's Coll., Hurstpierpoint. CFA (AIIMR 1977). Partner, Scott Goff Hancock & Co., 1971, acquired by Smith New Court Securities plc, 1986, Dir, 1986–90; Exec. Chm. and Jt Founder, Fitness First, 1992–2003; non-exec. Dir, Fitness First Hldgs Ltd, 2003–05. Mem., London Stock Exchange, 1978–90; MSI (Dip) 1990. *Recreations:* theatre, ballet, opera, Rugby, golf, tennis. *Address:* Proteome Sciences plc, Coveham House, Downside Bridge Road, Cobham, Surrey KT11 3EP. *Club:* Burhill Golf.

PEARCE, Sir (Daniel Norton) Idris, Kt 1990; CBE 1982; TD 1972; DL; Deputy Chairman, English Partnerships, 1993–2001; *b* 28 Nov. 1933; *s* of late Lemuel George Douglas Pearce and Evelyn Mary Pearce; *m* 1963, Ursula Helene Langley (marr. diss. 1997); two *d*. *Educ:* West Buckland Sch.; College of Estate Management. FRICS. Commnd RE, 1958; comd 135 Field Survey Sqdn, RE(TA), 1970–73. Joined Richard Ellis, 1959: Partner, 1961–92; Man. Partner, 1981–87; Consultant, 1992–2000. Chairman: English Estates, 1989–94; Flexit Cos, 1993–98; Varsity Funding, 1995–2000; Redburgh Ltd, 1996–2000; Director: The Phoenix Initiative, 1991; ITC, 1992–94; Nat. Mortgage Bank, 1992–97; Swan Hill (formerly Higgs & Hill), 1993–2002; Dusco UK Ltd, 1993–2002; Innisfree, 1996–2006; Millennium & Copthorne Hotels, 1996–2006; Regalian, 1998–2001; Resolution, 1998–2002. Royal Instn of Chartered Surveyors: Member: Gen. Council, 1980–94; Management Bd, 1984–91; Chm., Parly and Public Affairs Cttee, 1984–89; Vice Pres., 1986–90; Pres., 1990–91. Chm., Internat. Assets Valuation Standards Cttee, 1981–86. Member: Adv. Panel for Instnl Finance in New Towns, 1974–80; Sec. of State for Health and Social Security Inquiry into Surplus Land in the NHS, 1982; PSA Adv. Bd, 1981–86; FCO Adv. Panel on Diplomatic Estate, 1985–97; Financial Reporting Review Panel, 1991–93; Bd, London Forum, 1993–2001; Property Advr, NHS Management Bd, 1985–90; Dep. Chm., Urban Regeneration Agency, 1993–2001; Dir, London First Centre, 1995–2001. Chm., Higher Educn Funding Council for Wales, 1992–96; Member: UFC, 1991–93; HEFCE, 1992–96. Vice Chm., Greater London TA&VRA, 1991–94 (Mem., 1970–98; Chm., Works and Bldgs Sub-Cttee, 1983–90). Chm. Develt Bd, Nat. Art-Collections Fund, 1988–92. Dir, English Courtyard Assoc., 2007–09. Member: Court, City Univ., 1987–2000; Council, Univ. of Surrey, 1993–2004 (Pro-Chancellor, 1994–2004, now Emeritus; Chm., 1998–2001); Council, Reading Univ., 1997–2000; Comr, Royal Hosp., 1995–2001. Chairman: Governors, Stanway Sch., Dorking, 1982–85; W Buckland Sch. Foundn, 2002–07. Trustee, Rochester Bridge Trust, 1991–94. Governor: Peabody Trust, 1992–2003; RCA, 1997–2012 (Sen. Fellow 2012). Contested (C) Neath, 1959. DL Greater London, 1986. Hon. Fellow: Coll. of Estate Management, 1987; Univ. of Wales Cardiff, 1997; Centenary Fellow, Thames Poly., 1991; Companion, De Montfort Univ., 1992. Hon. Col, 135 Ind. Topographic Sqn, RE(V), TA, 1989–94. FRSA 1989. Hon. DSc: City, 1990; Oxford Poly., 1991; Salford Univ., 1991; Hon. DEng West of England, 1994; Hon. DTech E London, 1999; DUniv: Surrey, 2004; Glamorgan, 2010. Royal Engineers Gold Medal, 2011. *Publications:* A Call to Talent, 1993; various articles on valuation and property matters. *Recreations:* reading, opera, ballet, travel. *Club:* Brooks's.

PEARCE, Edward Robin; historian and political commentator; *b* 28 March 1939; *s* of late Frank Pearce and Olive Pearce (*née* Johnson); *m* 1966, Deanna Maria Stanwell (*née* Singer); one *d*. *Educ:* Queen Elizabeth Grammar Sch., Darlington; St Peter's Coll., Oxford (MA); Univ. of Stockholm. Res. Asst, Labour Party, Transport Hse, 1964–66; Res. Officer, Police Fedn, 1966–68; with Douglas Mann & Co., solicitors, 1968–70; teacher, S Shields, 1970–75; contributor, Sunday Express, 1975–77; Leader-writer, Daily Express, 1977–79; Parliamentary sketch-writer: Daily Telegraph, 1979–87; freelance career, 1987–: columnist: Sunday Times, 1987–90; The Guardian, 1990–95; The Scotsman, 1998–2000; Commissioning Editor, Punch, 2000–02; regular contributor, later lead reviewer, Tribune, 2005–; regular contributor: Political Quarterly, 2009–12; London Rev. blog, 2010–; contrib. Punch, Sunday Telegraph, Daily Mail, The Herald (Glasgow), Evening Standard, Wall St Jl, Sunday Tribune (Dublin), New Statesman, Spectator, History Today, Encounter, Tatler, New Republic (Washington), London Rev. of Books, Lit. Rev., TLS, Prospect, Yorkshire Post, Guardian Online, etc. Panel Member: The Moral Maze, Radio 4, 1991–95; Dateline, BBC World Service TV, 1997–2002; contrib. News Talk, LBC, 1989–92. Columnist of Year Award, What the Papers Say, 1987; Peter Wilson Award, League Against Cruel Sports, 1993. *Publications:* The Senate of Lilliput, 1983; Hummingbirds and Hyenas, 1985; Looking Down on Mrs Thatcher (collected Commons sketches), 1987; The Shooting Gallery, 1989; The Quiet Rise of John Major, 1990; Election Rides, 1992; Machiavelli's Children, 1993; The Lost Leaders, 1997; Lines of Most Resistance: the Lords, the Tories and Ireland 1886–1914, 1999; Denis Healey: a life in our times, 2002; Reform! the fight for the 1832 Reform Act, 2003; The Diaries of Charles Greville, 2005; The Great Man: a life of Sir Robert Walpole, 2007; Man of War: a life of William Pitt, the Elder, 2010; plays include: Mr Wilkinson of York, 2004; Mr Hudson's Excursion, 2006; Ladies Night, 2007. *Recreations:* listening to classical music, esp. Schubert, watching cricket, esp. Lancashire, and football, esp. Oldham Athletic, reading history, esp. 18th Century, travel, esp. Italy, wandering around old towns, esp. ones with bookshops. *Address:* Ryedale House, Thormanby, York YO61 4NN. *Club:* Easingwold Cricket.

PEARCE, Gareth David, FCA; Chairman, Smith & Williamson, 2000–13; *b* 13 Aug. 1953; *s* of late Howard Spencer Pearce and Enid Norma Pearce (*née* Richards); *m* 1984, Virginia Louise Miller; four *d*. *Educ:* Abingdon Sch.; Balliol Coll., Oxford (MA). FCA 1997 (ACA 1979). Peat Marwick Mitchell & Co., 1975–81; Electra Investment Trust plc, 1982–86, Dir, Electra Mgt plc, 1984–86; Smith & Williamson, Chartered Accountants: Dir, 1986–2013; Hd, Corporate Finance Dept, 1986–95; Man. Dir, 1995–2000. Chm., Nexia Internat., 2000–08. Dir, Nat. Mutual Life Assce Soc., 1997–2002 (Dep. Chm., 1999–2002). *Recreations:* chess, fishing, reading, travelling. *Address:* Bewley Court, Lacock, Wilts SN15 2PG. *T:* (01249) 730573. *Club:* Hurlingham.

PEARCE, Geoffrey John; Director of Finance and Resources, London Borough of Redbridge, 1999–2015; *b* Edgware, 7 Oct. 1951; *s* of Ridley and Peggy Pearce; *m* 1982, Janet McIntyre; one *s* one *d*. *Educ:* Wembley Co. Grammar Sch.; Nottingham Univ. (BA Hons Philosophy 1973). CIPFA 1977. Accountancy Asst, London Borough of Barnet, 1973–74; Sen. Accountancy Asst, Royal Borough of Kensington and Chelsea, 1974–76; Senior Accountant: London Borough of Brent, 1976–80; City of London, 1980–83; Gp Accountant, London Borough of Brent, 1983–85; London Borough of Redbridge: Chief Accountant, 1985–88; Chief Payments and Benefits Officer, 1988–99; Finance Dir, E London Waste Authy, 1999–2015. Advr to govt and professional wkg gps on London finance, schools funding, housing finance and public sector auditing. Pres., 2006, Sec., 2008–15, Soc. of London Treasurers. Freeman, City of London, 1981. *Publications:* contrib. articles to local govt and IT/computer jls. *Recreations:* music, gym, hoping Spurs win a trophy. *E:* Geoff.PearceServices@gmail.com.

PEARCE, Most Rev. George Hamilton, SM; Archbishop Emeritus of Suva (RC); *b* 9 Jan. 1921; *s* of George H. Pearce and Marie Louise Duval. *Educ:* Marist Coll. and Seminary, Framingham Center, Mass, USA. Entered Seminary, 1940; Priest, 1947; taught in secondary sch. in New England, USA, 1948–49; assigned as missionary to Samoa, 1949; consecrated Vicar Apostolic of Samoa, 1956; first Bishop of Apia, 1966; Archbishop of Suva, 1967–76, retired 1976. *Address:* Cathedral Rectory, 30 Fenner Street, Providence, RI 02903, USA. *T:* (401) 3312434.

PEARCE, Howard John Stredder, CVO 1993; HM Diplomatic Service, retired; Governor of the Falkland Islands and Commissioner, South Georgia and the South Sandwich Islands, 2002–06; *b* 13 April 1949; *s* of late Ernest Victor Pearce and Ida (*née* Booth); *m* 2004, Caroline Thomée; one *d*. *Educ:* City of London Sch.; Pembroke Coll., Cambridge (MA, LLB). Joined HM Diplomatic Service, 1972; FCO, 1972–74; Third Sec., Buenos Aires, 1975–78; FCO, 1978–83; First Sec. and Hd of Chancery, Nairobi, 1983–87; FCO, 1987–90; Sen. Associate Mem., St Antony's Coll., Oxford, 1990–91; Dep. Hd of Mission, Budapest, 1991–94; Fellow, Center for Internat. Affairs, Harvard Univ., 1994–95; Hd, Central European Dept, FCO, 1996–99; High Comr, Malta, 1999–2002. Mem., Exec. Cttee, VSO, 1988–90. Chairman: S Georgia Heritage Trust, 2006–; Exhibiting Socs of Scottish Artists, 2008–; Fortingall Art, 2012–; Scottish Trust for Underwater Archaeol., 2013–; Dep. Chm., Greenspace Scotland, 2009–. Trustee, New Island Conservation Trust, 2008–. Officer's Cross (Republic of Hungary), 1999. *Recreations:* classical music, opera, reading, travel.

PEARCE, Sir Idris; *see* Pearce, Sir D. N. I.

PEARCE, Jessica Mary; *see* Hand, J. M.

PEARCE, (John) Brian, OBE 2000; Director, The Inter Faith Network for the United Kingdom, 1987–2007; *b* 25 Sept. 1935; *s* of late George Frederic Pearce and Constance Josephine Pearce; *m* 1960, Michelle Etcheverry; four *s*. *Educ:* Queen Elizabeth Grammar Sch., Wakefield; Brasenose Coll., Oxford (BA). Asst Principal: Min. of Power, 1959; Colonial Office, 1960; Private Sec. to Parly Under-Sec. of State, 1963; Principal: Colonial Office, 1964; Dept of Economic Affairs, 1967; Principal Private Sec. to Sec. of State for Economic Affairs, 1968–69; Asst Sec., Civil Service Dept, 1969, Under-Sec., 1976; Under-Sec., HM Treasury, 1981–86, retd. MLitt Lambeth, 1993; Hon. DLaws Warwick, 2009. *Recreations:* comparative theology, music, architecture. *Address:* 124 Court Lane, SE21 7EA.

PEARCE, Prof. John Martindale, DPhil; FRS 2006; FLSW; Professor of Psychology, Cardiff University, since 1992; *b* 6 Dec. 1947; *s* of Jack and Mavis Pearce; *m* 1976, Victoria Anne Bradley; one *s* two *d*. *Educ:* Univ. of Leeds (BSc Hons); Univ. of Sussex (DPhil). Lectr, Sch. of Psychol., Cardiff Univ., 1980–92. Vis. Prof., Dept of Psychol., Duke Univ., 1987–88; Vis. Fellow, Inst. of Advanced Study, Indiana Univ., Bloomington, 1999; Vis. Erskine Fellow, Univ. of Canterbury, Christchurch, 2001; Humboldt Res. Fellow, Philipps Univ., Marburg, 2010–11. Ed., Qly Jl of Experimental Psychology: Comparative and Physiological Psychology, 1997–2000. Pres., Exptl Psychol. Soc., 2012–14. FLSW 2010. *Publications:* Introduction to Animal Cognition, 1987, 3rd edn as Animal Learning and Cognition: an introduction, 2008. *Recreations:* music, travelling in remote places. *Address:* School of Psychology, Cardiff University, Cardiff CF10 3YG. *T:* (029) 2087 4483, *Fax:* (029) 2087 4848. *E:* pearcejm@cf.ac.uk.

PEARCE, Rev. Neville John Lewis; Priest-in-charge, Swainswick/Woolley, Diocese of Bath and Wells, 1993–98; Chief Executive, Avon County Council, 1982–89; *b* 27 Feb. 1933; *s* of John and Ethel Pearce; *m* 1958, Eileen Frances Potter (*d* 2014); two *d*. *Educ:* Queen Elizabeth's Hosp., Bristol; Silcoates Sch., Wakefield; Univ. of Leeds (LLB Hons 1953, LLM 1954); Trinity Theol Coll., Bristol. Asst Solicitor: Wakefield CBC, 1957–59; Darlington CBC, 1959–61; Chief Asst Solicitor, Grimsby CBC, 1961–63, Dep. Town Clerk, 1963–65; Dep. Town Clerk, Blackpool CBC, 1965–66; Town Clerk, Bath CBC, 1967–73; Dir of Admin and County Solicitor, Avon CC, 1973–82. Ordained (C of E), 1991; Asst Curate, St Swithin, Walcot, Bath, 1991–93. *Recreations:* family and friends, ministering to local churches. *Address:* Penshurst, Weston Lane, Bath BA1 4AB. *T:* (01225) 426925.

PEARCE, Prof. Nicholas John, FSA; Sir John Richmond Professor of Fine Art, University of Glasgow, since 2012; *b* 7 Nov. 1956; *s* of late Dennis William Pearce and of Audrey Joyce Pearce (*née* Bray); partner, Sarah Louise Foskett; two *d*. *Educ:* Huddersfield Poly. (BA Politics and Oriental Studies); Sch. of Oriental and African Studies, Univ. of London (MA Chinese Art and Archaeol.). Curatorial Asst, V&A Mus., 1983–87; Curator, Eastern Art and Design, Burrell Collection, Glasgow Mus, 1987–96 (Hon. Curator, 1998–); Dep. Keeper (pt-time), Oriental Mus., Univ. of Durham, 1994–96; University of Glasgow: Lectr, then Sen. Lectr, 1997–2006; Hd, Hist. of Art, 1998–2003 and 2008–10; Prof., 2007–12; Hd, Sch. of Culture and Creative Arts, 2010–14. Exchange Prof., Hist. of Decorative Arts Prog., 2012–15, Fellow, Smithsonian Provenance Res. Initiative, 2014–15, Smithsonian Instn, Washington. Hon. Res. Associate, Dept of Hist. and Applied Art, Nat. Mus of Scotland, 1998–2005. Trustee: Textile Conservation Foundn, 2012–; Nat. Galls of Scotland, 2014–; Sir William Burrell Trust, 2014–. FSA 2011; FRSA 2002. Hon. Fellow, Faculty of Arts, Univ. of Edinburgh, 1991–93. *Publications:* (jtly) Chinese Export Art and Design, 1987; (jtly) Mingei - The Living Tradition in Japanese Arts, 1991; (with J. Wilkinson) Harmony and Contrast: a journey through East Asian art, 1996; Photographs of Peking, China 1861–1908: through Peking with a camera, 2005; (with J. Steuber) Original Intentions: essays on production, reproduction and interpretation in the arts of China, 2012; (ed jtly) William Hunter's World: William Hunter and the art and science of eighteenth century collecting, 2015; contrib. to books and jls.

Recreations: music, painting and decorating, an attempt at gardening. *Address:* School of Culture and Creative Arts, University of Glasgow, 8 University Gardens, Glasgow G12 8QH. *T:* (0141) 330 3826. *E:* nick.pearce@glasgow.ac.uk.

PEARCE, Nicholas Robin; Director, Institute for Public Policy Research, 2004–07 and since 2010; *b* 24 May 1968; *s* of late Peter Bailes Pearce and of Lynda Margaret Pearce; *m* 2000, Rebecca Asher; one *s* one *d*. *Educ:* Univ. of Manchester (BA Hons); Balliol Coll., Oxford (MPhil Politics). Res. Asst to Bryan Davies, MP, 1993–97; Res. Fellow in Educn, IPPR, 1997; Special Advr to Leader of H of C, 1998; Sen. Res. Fellow in Educn, IPPR, 1998–99; Advr (pt-time), Social Exclusion Unit, 1998–99; Special Adviser: to Sec. of State for Educn and Employment, 1999–2001; to Home Sec., 2001–03; Hd, Strategic Policy, Prime Minister's Office, 2007–08; Hd, Prime Minister's Policy Unit, 2008–10. Mem., UK/India Roundtable, 2006–. Chm., Council of Trustees, Tavistock Inst. of Med. Psychol., 2014–; Member, Board: British Archtl Trust Bd (formerly RIBA Trust), 2008–14; RIBA, 2014–. Hon. FRIBA 2014. *Publications:* (with J. Hillman) Wasted Youth, 1998; (ed with J. Hallgarten) Tomorrow's Citizens, 2000; (ed with W. Paxton) Social Justice: building a fairer Britain, 2005; (jtly) Freedom's Orphans, 2006; (ed with J. Margo) Politics for a New Generation, 2007; (jtly) The Condition of Britain, 2014. *Recreations:* twentieth century architecture, travel in South America. *Address:* Institute for Public Policy Research, 4th Floor, 13–14 Buckingham Street, WC2N 6DF. *E:* nicholasrpearce@googlemail.com.

PEARCE, Peter Huxley; Chief Executive, Edward James Foundation, since 2012; *b* 16 May 1956; *s* of Dr Alan John Pearce and Marion Joyce (*née* Wright); *m* 1983, Christina Zalichi; two *s*. *Educ:* Reading Univ. (BSc Hons Rural Estate Mgt). FRICS 1981. National Trust: Man. Land Agent, E Midlands Reg., 1982–87, Southern Reg., 1988–95; Dir, Uppark Repair Project, 1989–95; Dir, Landmark Trust, 1995–2012. Trustee, Edward James Foundn, 2008–11. *Recreations:* historic buildings, music, fishing, landscape and conservation, family life. *Address:* Edward James Foundation, West Dean, Chichester, W Sussex PO18 0QZ.

PEARCE, Prof. Robert Alasdair; Professor in Law, University of Buckingham, since 2010; *b* 28 Nov. 1951; *s* of Walter Charles Pearce and Dorothy Kate Pearce. *Educ:* George Dixon's Grammar Sch.; Cotham Grammar Sch.; Sir Thomas Rich's Sch.; Pembroke Coll., Oxford (BA Hons (Jurisprudence) 1973; BCL 1974; MA 1978). Lectr in Law: Univ. of Newcastle upon Tyne, 1974–79; Univ. of Lancaster, 1979–80; Lectr, then Statutory Lectr, UC, Cork, NUI, 1981–89; University of Buckingham: Sen. Lectr in Law, 1989–90; Prof. of Law of Property and Equity, 1990–2003; Dean, Acad. Affairs, 1993–94; Pro-Vice-Chancellor, 1994–2002; Actg Vice-Chancellor, 2000–01; Vice-Chancellor, Univ. of Wales, Lampeter, 2003–08. Welsh Supernumerary Fellow, Jesus Coll., Oxford, 2007–08. Vis. Prof., Univ. of Glos, 2010–. Auditor, HEQC, then QAA, 1993–2003; Mem., Adv. Cttee on Degree Awarding Powers, QAA, 2003–08; Chm., Postgrad. Internat. Assessment Bd, Irish Res. Council for Humanities and Social Scis, 2006–07 (Bd Mem., 2004–05). Chairman: Oxford Univ. Law Course Adv. Cttee, 1971–72; Univs Assoc. for Lifelong Learning Cymru, 2004–08. Mem., Future Skills Wales, 2003–06. Parkside Housing Group, Windsor: Dir, 1998–2003; Vice-Chm., 2000–02; Chm., 2002–03. Mem., Cttee of Mgt, Rockboro Sch. Assoc., 1983–87; Governor: Pebble Brook Sch., Aylesbury, 1997–2000; Rycotewood Coll., Thame, 2000–03 (Vice-Chm., 2001–03). Hon. LLD Buckingham, 2007. *Publications:* A Commentary on the Succession Act 1965, 2nd revd edn 1986; (with I. J. Dawson) Licences Relating to the Occupation or Use of Land, 1979; Land Law (of the Republic of Ireland and Northern Ireland), 1985, 3rd edn (with Dr John Mee) 2011; (with A. J. Stevens) The Law of Trusts and Equitable Obligations, 1995, 6th edn (with W. Barr) 2014; (with A. J. Stevens) Land Law, 1997, 5th edn 2013. *Recreation:* gardening. *Address:* Villiers Court, 37 Graham Road, Great Malvern, Worcs WR14 2HU.

PEARCE, Robert Edgar; QC 2006; *b* 22 June 1953; *s* of Edgar Pearce and Stella Mary Louise Pearce (*née* Dimock); *m* 1984, Janice Linscott; two *d*. *Educ:* Whitgift Sch.; Christ Church, Oxford (BA 1st Cl. Jurisprudence 1975; BCL 1976). Called to the Bar, Middle Temple, 1977; in practice at Chancery bar, 1978–; Bencher, Lincoln's Inn, 2013. Standing Counsel to the Charity Commn, 2001–06. *Publications:* (contrib. ed.) Butterworths Civil Court Practice, annually 1997–; various articles. *Recreation:* music. *Address:* Radcliffe Chambers, 11 New Square, Lincoln's Inn, WC2A 3QB. *T:* (020) 7831 0081, *Fax:* (020) 7405 2560. *E:* rpearce@radcliffechambers.com.

PEARCE, Prof. Robert Penrose, FRSE; Professor of Meteorology and Head of Department of Meteorology, University of Reading, 1970–90, now Emeritus Professor; *b* 21 Nov. 1924; *s* of Arthur Penrose Pearce and Ada Pearce; *m* 1951, Patricia Frances Maureen Curling; one *s* two *d*. *Educ:* Bishop Wordsworth Sch., Salisbury; Imperial Coll., London (BSc, ARCS, DIC, PhD). Asst, Meteorological Office, 1941–43. Served RAF, 1943–47 (commnd 1945). Lectr, then Sen. Lectr in Mathematics, University Coll. Dundee, Univ. of St Andrews, later at Univ. of Dundee, 1952–66; Reader in Phys. Climatology, Imperial Coll., 1966–70. Pres., Royal Meteorological Soc., 1972–74 (Hon. Fellow (Hon. Mem., 1998)); Chm., World Meteorol Org. Working Gp in Trop. Meteorology, 1978–90. *Publications:* Observer's Book of Weather, 1980; (co-ed) Monsoon Dynamics, 1981; (ed) Meteorology at the Millennium, 2002; sci. papers in meteorol jls. *Recreations:* walking, gardening, bridge, music. *Address:* Schiehallion, 27 Copped Hall Way, Camberley, Surrey GU15 1PB. *T:* (01276) 501523.

PEARCE, Teresa; MP (Lab) Erith and Thamesmead, since 2010; *b* Southport, 1 Feb. 1955; *d* of Arthur and Josephine Farrington; two *d*. *Educ:* St Thomas More RC Sch., Eltham. Inland Revenue, 1975–79; Knox Cropper, 1989–99; Sen. Manager, PricewaterhouseCoopers, 1999–2009. Mem. (Lab) Bexley LBC, 1998–2002. Mem., Erith Slopes Socialist Book Club. *Recreations:* cinema, reading, travel. *Address:* House of Commons, SW1A 0AA. *T:* (020) 7210 6936. *E:* teresa.pearce.mp@parliament.uk. *W:* www.teresapearce.org.uk.

PEARCE-HIGGINS, Daniel John; QC 1998; **His Honour Judge Pearce-Higgins;** a Circuit Judge, since 2004; Designated Civil Judge, Worcester Combined Court, since 2009; *b* 26 Dec. 1949; *m*. *Educ:* St Paul's Sch., London; Univ. of Bristol (BSc Philosophy and Politics). Called to the Bar, Middle Temple, 1973, Bencher, 2009; an Asst Recorder, 1995–99; a Recorder, 1999–2004. Mem., Mental Health Review Tribunal, 2000–. CEDR accredited mediator, 1999–2004. FCIArb 1999–2004. Mem., Prog. Adv. Cttee, Cumberland Lodge, 2007–; Gov., Hereford Cathedral Perpetual Trust, 2014–. *Address:* c/o Worcester Combined Court Centre, Shirehall, Foregate Street, Worcester WR1 1EQ.

PEARCEY, Oliver Henry James; historic environment consultant, since 2006; Special Projects Director, English Heritage, 2004–06; *b* 13 June 1951; *s* of late Lawrence Henry Victor Pearcey and Gladys Winifred Pearcey (*née* Bond); *m* 1979, Elizabeth Platts; two *d*. *Educ:* Westminster Sch.; Univ. of Sussex (BSc Biochem). Department of the Environment: Admin. trainee, 1972–78; Principal, 1978–85; on secondment to GLC, 1981–83; English Heritage: Team Leader, 1985–88, Head, 1988–91, Historic Bldgs Div.; Dir, Conservation, Midlands Reg., 1991–94; Dep. Dir, 1994–97, Dir, 1997–2002, Conservation; Designation Dir, 2002–04. Mem., IHBC, 1998. *Recreations:* industrial archaeology, English salt-glaze stoneware, reading voraciously. *Address:* 125B Dalling Road, W6 0ET. *T:* (020) 8222 8468.

PEAREY, David Dacre; HM Diplomatic Service, retired; Governor, British Virgin Islands, 2006–10; *b* 15 July 1948; *s* of William Pearey and Dorothy Pearey; *m* 1996, Susan Anne (*née* Knowles); one *d*. *Educ:* Oundle Sch.; Bristol Univ. (BSc Hons Econs). Joined MoD as trainee, 1971; Pvte Sec. to Parly Under Sec. of State for Defence (RAF), 1974–76; joined FCO, 1979; First Secretary: Ankara, 1979–82; Energy and Policy Planning Depts, FCO, 1983–87; Dep. High Comr, Kampala, 1987–90; Southern European and Inspectorate Depts, FCO, 1990–95; Counsellor, Lagos, 1995–99; Dep. High Comr, Karachi, 2000–04; High Comr, Malaŵi, 2004–06. Mem., Glyndebourne Fest. Soc., 1998–. FRGS 1993. *Recreations:* travel, mountains, opera, walking, reading. *E:* dandspearey@aol.com. *Clubs:* Travellers, Hurlingham.

PEARL, His Honour David Stephen, PhD; a Circuit Judge, 1994–2012; a Deputy High Court Judge, 2008–12; an Upper Tribunal Judge (Administrative Appeals Chamber), since 2008; Chair, Medical Practitioners Tribunal Service, since 2012; *b* 11 Aug. 1944; *s* of late Chaim Pearl and Anita Pearl (*née* Newman); *m* 1st, 1967, Susan Roer (marr. diss.); three *s*; 2nd, 1985, Gillian Furr (*née* Maciejewska); one step *s* one step *d*. *Educ:* George Dixon Grammar Sch., Birmingham; Westminster City Sch.; Birmingham Univ. (LLB); Queens' Coll., Cambridge (Sen. Scholar; LLM, MA, PhD). Called to the Bar, Gray's Inn, 1968, Bencher, 2002; Cambridge University: Asst Lectr in Law, 1967–72; Lectr, 1972–89; Res. Fellow, Queens' Coll., 1967–69; Fellow and Dir of Studies in Law, Fitzwilliam Coll., Cambridge, 1969–89 (Life Fellow, 1989); Prof. of Law and Dean, Sch. of Law, UEA, 1989–94, Hon. Prof., 1995–; a Recorder, 1992–94. Immigration Appeals Adjudicator, 1980–92; Chm., 1992–97, Pres., 1998–99, Immigration Appeal Tribunal; Chief Immigration Adjudicator, 1994–98; Pres., Care Standards Tribunal, 2002–08; Chm., Restricted Patients Panel, 2009–15. Mem., Judicial Appts Commn, 2006–12. Judicial Studies Board: Member: Civil and Family Cttee, 1994–96; Tribunals Cttee, 1996–99, 2004–11; Dir of Studies, 1999–2001. Vice-Pres., Internat. Soc. for Family Law, 1991–97. Ind. Mem., Standards Cttee, Uttlesford DC, 2015–. Yorke Prize, Cambridge, 1972; Shaw Prize, Boston Coll. Law Sch., 1985; Van Heyden de Lancy Prize, Cambridge, 1991. *Publications:* A Textbook on Muslim Law, 1979, 3rd edn as Muslim Family Law (with W. Menski), 1998; Interpersonal Conflict of Laws in India, Pakistan and Bangladesh, 1980; (with K. Gray) Social Welfare Law, 1980; (jtly) Family Law and Society, 1983, 6th edn 2008; Family Law and Immigrant Communities, 1986; (with A. Grubb) Blood Testing AIDS and DNA Profiling, 1990; (jtly) Butterworth's Immigration Law Service, 1991–2007; (ed jtly) Clarke, Hall and Morrison on Children, 2004–14. *Recreation:* very amateur dramatics. *Address:* Medical Practitioners Tribunal Service, 7th Floor, St James Building, 79 Oxford Road, Manchester M1 6FQ. *T:* (0161) 240 7297.

PEARL, Prof. Laurence Harris, PhD; FRS 2008; Professor of Structural Biology, Genome Damage and Stability Centre, and Head, School of Life Sciences, University of Sussex, since 2009; *b* Manchester, 18 June 1956; *s* of Monty and Carole Pearl; *m* 1994, Frances M. G.; two *s* one *d*. Prof. of Structural Biol., UCL, 1996–99; Prof. of Protein Crystallography and Section Chm., Inst. of Cancer Res., 1999–2009. Wellcome Trust Sen. Investigator, 2011–. Mem., EMBO, 2005; MAE 2012. FMedSci 2007. Translational Cancer Res. Prize, Cancer Res. UK, 2013. *Publications:* contrib. scientific jls. *Recreations:* feeding my family, juggling, computer animation. *Address:* Genome Damage and Stability Centre, Science Park Road, University of Sussex, Falmer, Brighton, E Sussex BN1 9RQ. *E:* Laurence.Pearl@sussex.ac.uk.

PEARL, Patricia; Her Honour Judge Pearl; a Circuit Judge, since 2006; *b* Derby, 5 June 1953; *d* of Thomas Andrew Smallwood and Eva May Smallwood; *m* 1975; one *d*; partner, Ian S. Hilton. *Educ:* Parkfield Cedars Grammar Sch., Derby; Rugby High Sch. for Girls; Lady Margaret Hall, Oxford (BA Hons Geog. 1974). Admitted solicitor, 1977; a District Judge, 1998–2006. Chm., Restricted Patients Panel, Tribunals Service Mental Health, 2009–15. *Publications:* Small Claims Procedure: a practical guide, 1999, 6th edn 2014; (contrib. ed) Civil Procedure (The White Book), 2001–. *Recreations:* photography, walking the long-distance footpaths of Britain. *Address:* Central Family Court, First Avenue House, 42–49 High Holborn, WC1V 6NP. *T:* (020) 7947 7004.

PEARL, Valerie Louise, DPhil; FRHistS; President, New Hall, Cambridge, 1981–95; *b* 31 Dec. 1926; *d* of late Cyril Raymond Bence, sometime MP and Florence Bence; *m* 1949, Morris Leonard Pearl (*d* 2000); one *d*. *Educ:* King Edward VI High Sch., Birmingham; St Anne's Coll., Oxford (Exhibnr; Hon. Fellow, 1994); BA Hons Mod. History; MA, DPhil (Oxon). Allen Research Studentship, St Hugh's Coll., Oxford, 1951; Eileen Power Studentship, 1952; Sen. Research Studentship, Westfield Coll., London, 1962; Leverhulme Research Award, 1962; Graham Res. Fellow and Lectr in History, Somerville Coll., Oxford, 1965; Reader in History of London, 1968–76, Prof. of History of London, 1976–81, University College London. Convenor of confs to found The London Journal, Chm. of Editorial Bd, Editor-in-Chief, 1973–77; McBride Vis. Prof., Cities Program, Bryn Mawr Coll., Pennsylvania, 1974; Lectures: Woodward, Yale Univ., New Haven, 1974; Indian Council for Soc. Sci., Calcutta, New Delhi, 1977; John Stow Commem., City of London, 1979; James Ford Special, Oxford, 1980; Sir Lionel Denny, Barber Surgeons' Co., 1981. Literary Dir, Royal Historical Soc., 1975–77; Pres., London and Middx Archaeol. Soc., 1980–82; Governor, Museum of London, 1978; Comr, Royal Commn on Historical MSS, 1983; Syndic: Cambridge Univ. Library, 1982; Cambridge Univ. Press, 1984. Trustee, Henry and Procter Fellowships, 1985. FSA 1976. *Publications:* London and the Outbreak of the Puritan Revolution, 1625–43, 1961; Change and Stability in 17th Century London (inaugural lecture, Univ. of London), 1978; (ed jtly) History and Imagination: essays for Hugh Trevor-Roper, 1981; (ed) J. Stow, The Survey of London, 1987; Studies in Social Change in Puritan London, Parts 1, 2 (trans. Japanese, ed S. Sugawara), 1994; contributor to: Studies in London History (ed W. Kellaway, A. Hollaender), 1969; The Interregnum (ed G. Aylmer), 1972; Puritans and Revolutionaries (ed K. Thomas, D. Pennington), 1978; The Tudor and Stuart Town (ed J. Barry), 1990; also to learned jls and other works, including Trans Royal Hist. Soc., Eng. Historical Rev., History of English Speaking Peoples, Past and Present, Archives, Economic Hist. Rev., History, Jl of Eccles. History, Times Literary Supplement, The London Journal, London Rev. of Books, Albion, Listener, BBC, Rev. of English Studies, (jtly) Proc. Mass. Hist. Soc., DNB Missing Persons, Urban History, Encyclopedia Americana. *Recreation:* walking and swimming.

PEARLMAN, Her Honour Valerie Anne, CBE 2008; a Circuit Judge, 1985–2008; Designated Family Circuit Judge, 1991–2008 (a Senior Circuit Judge, 2003–08); *b* 6 Aug. 1936; *d* of late Sidney and Marjorie Pearlman; *m* 1972; one *s* one *d*. *Educ:* Wycombe Abbey Sch. Called to the Bar, Lincoln's Inn, 1958, Bencher, 2002; a Recorder, 1982–85. Member: Parole Bd, 1989–94; Civil and Family Cttee, Judicial Studies Bd, 1992–97; Chm., Home Sec's Adv. Bd on Restricted Patients, 1991–98; Mem., Cttee on Mentally Disordered Offenders, Mental Health Foundn, 1992–95. Mem., Council of Circuit Judges, 1998–2001; Vice-Pres., Inner London Magistrates' Assoc., 1999–. Patron, Children UK (formerly British Juvenile and Family Courts Soc.), 2000–. Member: Council, Marlborough Coll., 1989–97; Governing Body, Godolphin and and Latymer Sch., 1998–2003. Patron, Suzy Lamplugh Trust, 1987–. *Recreations:* gardening, reading.

PEARMAN, Hugh Geoffrey; architecture and design critic, Sunday Times, since 1986; Editor, RIBA Journal, since 2006; *b* 29 May 1955; *s* of late Douglas Pearman and Tegwyn Pearman (*née* Jones); *m* 2005, Kate Hobson; two *s* two *d*. *Educ:* Skinners' Sch., Tunbridge Wells; St Chad's Coll., Durham Univ. (BA Hons Eng. Lang. and Lit.). Asst Editor, Building Design Magazine, 1978–82; Communications Editor, BDP, 1982–86. Member: Envmtl and Arts Panel, South Bank Employers' Gp, 1990–2000; Architectl Adv. Panel, Arts Council of GB, then of England, 1992–95; Council, RSA, 2004–06 (Chm., Art for Architecture Adv. Panel, 2000–04). Curator, British Council internat. touring exhibn, 12 for 2000: Building for the Millennium, 1998–2000. Vis. teacher in architecture, Univ. of Greenwich, 1999–2000; Vis. Prof. in Architecture, RCA, 2015. Trustee and Dir, 2012–, Vice Pres., 2014–, AA. Founder and Juror, Stirling Prize for Architecture, 1996–98; judge, various architecture competitions; Mem. Nat. Panel, Civic Trust Awards, 2014–. FRSA 1990. Hon. FRBS 1996; Hon. FRIBA 2001. Contributor to television and radio. *Publications:* Excellent Accommodation, 1984; Rick Mather: urban approaches, 1992; The Ark, London, 1993;

Contemporary World Architecture, 1998; Equilibrium: the work of Nicholas Grimshaw and Partners, 2000; (introd.) Ten Years, Ten Cities: Terry Farrell and Partners 1991–2001, 2002; (introd.) 30 Bridges, 2002; The Deep, 2002; The Architecture of Eden, 2003; Airports: a century of architecture, 2004; (contrib.) The Brits Who Built the Modern World, 2014; articles in newspapers, magazines and periodicals. *Recreations:* walking, looking, photographing. *Address:* 29 Nelson Road, N8 9RX. *T:* (020) 8374 5454. *E:* hughpearman@blueyonder.co.uk.

PEARS, Dr Iain George; author; *b* 8 Aug. 1955; *s* of George Derrick Pears and Betty Mitchell Pears (*née* Proudfoot); *m* 1985, Prof. Ruth Harris, *qv*; two *s*. *Educ:* Wadham Coll., Oxford (BA, MA); Wolfson Coll., Oxford (DPhil). Correspondent for Reuters: Italy, 1983–84; London, 1984–87; USA, 1987–89; France, 1989–90. *Publications:* The Discovery of Painting, 1988; The Raphael Affair, 1990; The Titian Committee, 1991; The Bernini Bust, 1992; The Last Judgement, 1993; Giotto's Hand, 1994; Death and Restoration, 1995; An Instance of the Fingerpost, 1997; The Immaculate Deception, 1999; The Dream of Scipio, 2002; The Portrait, 2005; Stone's Fall, 2009; Arcadia, 2015. *Recreation:* print collecting. *E:* iainpears@hotmail.com.

PEARS, Mary Madeline; *see* Chapman, M. M.

PEARS, Ruth; *see* Harris, R.

PEARS, Tim(othy); novelist; *b* 15 Nov. 1956; *s* of William Steuart Pears and Jill (*née* Charles-Edwards); *m* 1998, Hania Porucznik; one *s* one *d*. *Educ:* Exeter Sch.; National Film and Television Sch. (Directing course 1993). Various jobs, including building labourer, farm worker, night porter, teacher, museum gall. manager, etc. *Publications:* In the Place of Fallen Leaves, 1993 (Ruth Hadden Meml Award, 1993; Hawthornden Prize, 1994); In a Land of Plenty, 1997 (televised, 2001); A Revolution of the Sun, 2000; Wake Up, 2002; Blenheim Orchard, 2007; Landed, 2010; Disputed Land, 2011; In the Light of Morning, 2014. *Recreations:* football coaching, urban exploring, rural wandering. *Address:* 462 Banbury Road, Oxford OX2 7RG. *T:* (01865) 552605. *E:* pearznik@yahoo.co.uk.

PEARS, Trevor Steven, CMG 2011; Executive Chairman, Pears Foundation, since 2000; Director, William Pears Group, since 1986; *b* London, 18 June 1964; *s* of Clive and Clarice Pears; *m* 1993, Daniela; one *s* two *d*. *Educ:* City of London Sch.; City of London Poly. (BA Hons Business Law). *Recreations:* golf, swimming, salsa dancing.

PEARSE, Barbara Mary Frances, (Mrs M. S. Bretscher), PhD; FRS 1988; Staff Scientist, Medical Research Council Laboratory of Molecular Biology, Cambridge, 1981–2005; *b* 24 March 1948; *d* of Reginald William Blake Pearse and Enid Alice (*née* Mitchell); *m* 1978, Mark Steven Bretscher, *qv*; one *s* one *d*. *Educ:* The Lady Eleanor Holles Sch., Hampton, Middx; University Coll. London (BSc Biochemistry, PhD; Fellow, 1996). MRC Res. Fellowship, 1972–74; Beit Meml Fellowship, 1974–77; SRC Advanced Fellowship, 1977–82; CRC Internat. Fellowship Vis. Prof., Stanford Med. Centre, USA, 1984–85. Mem., EMBO, 1982–. EMBO Medal, 1987. *Publications:* contribs to sci. jls. *Recreations:* wild flowers, planting trees, fresh landscapes. *Address:* Ram Cottage, 63 Commercial End, Swaffham Bulbeck, Cambridge CB25 0ND. *T:* (01223) 811276.

PEARSE, Sir Brian (Gerald), Kt 1994; FCIB; Deputy Chairman, Britannic Assurance Plc, 1997–2002; Chief Executive, Midland Bank, 1991–94; *b* 23 Aug. 1933; *s* of Francis and Eileen Pearse; *m* 1959, Patricia M. Callaghan; one *s* two *d*. *Educ:* St Edward's Coll., Liverpool. Martin's Bank Ltd, 1950; Barclays Bank, 1969–91: Local Dir, Birmingham, 1972; Gen. Man., 1977; Chief Exec. Officer, N America, 1983; Finance Dir, 1987–91; Dir, Midland Bank, 1994–95. Chm., Lucas Industries, later LucasVarity, PLC, 1994–98; non-executive Director: Smith & Nephew, 1993–2002; HSBC plc, 1992–94. Chm., Assoc. for Payments Clearing Services, 1987–91. Director: British American Chamber of Commerce, 1987–98; Private Finance Panel, 1993–95; BOTB, 1994–97; Charities Aid Foundn Bank, 1998–92. Chairman: Young Enterprise, 1992–95; British Invisibles, 1994–97; Housing Corp., 1994–97; Dep. Chm., Tor Homes, 1998–2003. Chm. Council, Centre for Study of Financial Innovation, 1998–2013. Member: Council for Industry of Higher Educn, 1994–98; City Promotion Panel, 1995–97; Bd of Banking Supervision, 1998–2001. Treas., KCL, 1992–99 (FKC 1996). Pres., CIB, 1993–94. Trustee, Charities Aid Foundn, 1995–99. Gov., Univ. of Plymouth, 1997–2006 (Chm. Govs, 2002–06). Trustee, 2007–, Chm., Trustees, 2013–, Dio. of Plymouth (Chm., Finance Cttee, 2006–12); Chm., Plymouth Catholic and Anglican Acad. Trust, 2013–. Hon. DLaws Plymouth, 2006. *Recreations:* Rugby football, opera. *Address:* Coach House, Modbury, Ivybridge PL21 0TE. *Club:* Royal Automobile.

PEARSE, Charlotte Louisa; *see* May, C. L.

PEARSE, Rear-Adm. John Roger Southey G.; *see* Gerard-Pearse.

PEARSON, family name of **Viscount Cowdray** and **Baron Pearson of Rannoch**.

PEARSON OF RANNOCH, Baron *cr* 1990 (Life Peer), of Bridge of Gaur in the district of Perth and Kinross; **Malcolm Everard MacLaren Pearson;** *b* 20 July 1942; *s* of Col John MacLaren Pearson; *m* 1st, 1965, Francesca Frua De Angeli (marr. diss. 1970); one *d*; 2nd, 1977, Hon. Mary (marr. diss. 1995), *d* of Baron Charteris of Amisfield, GCB, GCVO, QSO, OBE, PC; two *d*; 3rd, 1998, Caroline, *d* of Major Hugh Launcelot St Vincent Rose. *Educ:* Eton. Founded Pearson Webb Springbett, later PWS gp of reinsurance brokers, 1964, Chm., 1970–2008. Member: H of L Select Cttee on Eur. Communities, 1992–96; Sub-cttee C on Envmt and Social Affairs, 1992–95. Founded Rannoch Trust, 1984 (Exec. Trustee). Mem., Council for Nat. Academic Awards, 1983–93 (Hon. Treas., 1986–93). Patron: Nat. Soc. for Mentally Handicapped People in Residential Care (Rescare), 1994–; British Register of Chinese Herbal Medicine, 1998–. *Recreations:* stalking, fishing, golf. *Address:* House of Lords, SW1A 0PW. *Clubs:* White's; Swinley Forest Golf.

PEARSON, Prof. Andrew David John, MD; FRCP, FRCPCH; Cancer Research UK Professor of Paediatric Oncology and Head, Paediatric Section, Institute of Cancer Research, University of London, since 2005; Head, Children's Unit, and Hon. Consultant Paediatric Oncologist, Royal Marsden Hospital Foundation NHS Trust, since 2005; *b* 2 March 1955; *s* of John and Jean Pearson; *m*; two *s* three *d*; *m* 2006, Gaby Charlton; one *d*. *Educ:* Univ. of Newcastle upon Tyne (MB BS 1st Cl. Hons 1977); DCH 1980; MD 1989. MRCP 1979, FRCP 1992; FRCPCH 1996. MRC Lilly Internat. Travelling Fellow, Dept of Paediatrics, Univ. of Minnesota, 1983–84; Sen. Registrar in Paediatric Oncology, 1984, Hon. Sen. Registrar, 1985–89, Royal Victoria Inf., Newcastle upon Tyne; Hon. Consultant Paediatrician, Newcastle HA, 1989–94; Hd, Dept of Paediatric Oncology, Children's Services Directorate, 1992–2005, and Hon. Consultant Paediatric Oncologist, 1994–2005, Newcastle upon Tyne Hosps NHS Trust; University of Newcastle upon Tyne: Lectr, 1985–89, Sen. Lectr, 1989–94, in Paediatric Oncology, Dept of Child Health; Prof. of Paediatric Oncology, Sch. of Clinical Med. Scis, 1994–2005; Postgrad. Sub-Dean, 1998–2002, Dean of Postgrad. Studies, 2002–05, Fac. of Med. Scis. Trustee, Inst. of Cancer Res., 2005–11. United Kingdom Cancer Study Group: Chm., Neuroblastoma Wkg Gp, 1991–95; Chm., Biol Studies Cttee, 1996–2002; Hd, Div. of Therapeutics, 1999–; Co-Chm., UKCCSG/Childhood Leukaemia Wkg Party Clin. Res. Governance Gp, 2003–06; Chm., 2003–06. Chairman: Eur. Neuroblastoma Study Gp, 1994–99; Europe Neuroblastoma (SIOPEN), Internat. Soc. of Paediatric Oncology, 1998–2001 (Founding Chm.), 2005–07; Co-Chm., Internat. Neuroblastoma Risk Gp Strategy Cttee, 2004–. *Publications:* over 2000 articles on children's cancer res., particularly neuroblastoma, drug develt and pharmacol. *Recreation:* walking. *Address:* Institute of Cancer Research, 15 Cotswold Road, Sutton, Surrey SM2 5NG. *T:* (020) 8661 3453, *Fax:* (020) 8661 3617. *E:* andrew.pearson@icr.ac.uk.

PEARSON, Anthony James, CBE 2002; Director of Security, Prison Service, 1993–99; *b* 2 Nov. 1939; 2nd *s* of Leslie Pearson and Winifred Pearson (*née* Busby); *m* 1964, Sandra Lowe; two *d*. *Educ:* Saltley Grammar Sch., Birmingham; Exeter Univ. (BA Hons 1961); Oxford Univ. (Dip. Soc. and Public Admin 1962). Assistant Prison Governor: Maidstone, 1963–67; Albany, 1967–69; Parkhurst, 1970–72; Dep. Governor, Wandsworth Prison, 1972–73; Prison Service HQ, 1973–77; Prison Governor: Gartree, 1977–81; Brixton, 1981–85; HM Dep. Chief Inspector of Prisons, 1985–87; Prison Service Headquarters: Hd of Div., 1987–89; Hd, Directorate of Telecommunications, 1989–91; Area Manager, 1991–93. Trustee: Centre for Crime & Justice Studies, 1998–2010 (Chm., 2002–10); Butler Trust, 1999–2014 (Dep. Chm., 2001–10; Chm., 2010–14); Langley House Trust, 2001–12. *Recreations:* Rugby, cricket (armchair expert).

PEARSON, Rev. Canon Brian William; Associate Director of Vocations, Diocese of Bath and Wells, since 2011; *b* 18 Aug. 1949; *s* of Victor William Charles Pearson and Florence Irene (*née* Webster); *m* 1974, Althea Mary Stride; two *s*. *Educ:* Roan Sch. for Boys, Blackheath; Brighton Polytechnic (BSc Hons); City Univ. (MSc); Ordination Training (Southwark Ordination Course); MTh Oxford 1994. Systems Engineer: IBM UK, 1967–71; Rohm and Haas UK, 1971–72; Lectr, Thames Polytechnic, 1972–81; College Head of Dept, Northbrook Coll., W Sussex, 1981–88; Bishop's Research Officer and Communications Officer, Bath and Wells, 1988–91; Archbishop's Officer for Mission and Evangelism and Tait Missioner, dio. of Canterbury, 1991–97; Hon. Canon, Canterbury Cathedral, 1992; Gen. Dir, CPAS, 1997–2000; Dir of Studies for Ordained Local Ministry, and Priest i/c, Leek Wootton, diocese of Coventry, 2000–06. Ministerial Trng Advr, Bath and Wells Dio., 2007–11; Assisting Minister, Langport Team Ministry, 2008–; Lectr (pt-time), Strode Coll., 2006–09; Archdeacon's Visitor to St Andrew's, Compton Dundon, Bath and Wells, 2010–13. Trustee, Christians in Sport, 1996–2001. Partner, Woodspring Psychological Services, 2006–14. Non-executive Director: Trinity Coll., Bristol, 1997–2000; Christian Research, 2000–03; 2K Plus Internat. Sports Media, 2004–09, 2011–13. Regl Rep., Over The Wall Orgn, 2002–06. Hon. Chaplain: Warwicks Police HQ, 2000–06; Centrex Police Trng Centre, Ryton, 2002–06; Avon and Somerset Police, 2007–. Fellow, Coll. of Preachers, 1995. *Publications:* Yes Manager: Management in the local church, 1986; (with George Carey) My Journey, Your Journey, 1996; How to Guide: managing change, 1996; (contrib.) A Preacher's Companion, 2004; A Sporting Month with 2K Plus, 2012. *Recreations:* cricket player (Som Over-60s), ECB umpire and coach, theatre, learning more about life through the experiences of highly perceptive sons, biblical history and applied theology, travel associated with family history research. *Address:* London House, New Street, Somerton, Som TA11 7NU.

PEARSON, Daniel John, RDI 2012; landscape designer, journalist and writer; Principal, Dan Pearson Studio, since 1987; *b* Windsor, 9 April 1964; *s* of Raymond and Sheila Pearson; partner, Dafydd Huw Morgan. *Educ:* RHS Wisley (Cert. Hons); Royal Botanic Garden, Kew (Dip. Hons). Columnist: Sunday Times, 1994–2003; Daily Telegraph, 2003–06; Observer Magazine, 2006–. Projects include: Althorp House, 1997; Millennium Dome, 1999; Tokachi Millennium Forest, Hokkaido, 2002; Maggie's Cancer Caring Centre, London, 2005. Mem., Soc. of Garden Designers, 2006–. Tree Ambassador, Tree Council, 2006–. Hon. FRIBA 2011. Grand Award, 2012, Historic Garden Award, 2014, Soc. of Garden Designers; Gold Medal, Chelsea Flower Show, 2015. *Publications:* (with Steve Bradley) Garden Doctors, 1996; (with Terence Conran) The Essential Garden Book, 1998; The Garden: a year at Home Farm, 2001; Spirit: garden inspiration, 2009; Home Ground: sanctuary in the city, 2011. *Recreations:* gardening, listening to music, natural landscapes (travel). *Address:* The Nursery, The Chandlery, 50 Westminster Bridge Road, SE1 7QY. *T:* (020) 7928 3800, *Fax:* (020) 7928 3854. *E:* dan@danpearsonstudio.com.

PEARSON, David Compton Froome; Deputy Chairman, Robert Fleming Holdings Ltd, 1986–90 (Director, 1974–90); *b* 28 July 1931; *s* of late Compton Edwin Pearson, OBE and of Marjorie (*née* Froome); *m* 1st, 1966, Venetia Jane Lynn (marr. diss. 1994); two *d*; 2nd, 1997, Mrs Bridget Thomson. *Educ:* Haileybury; Downing Coll., Cambridge (MA). Linklaters & Paines, Solicitors, 1957–69 (Partner, 1961–69); Dir, Robert Fleming & Co. Ltd, 1969–90; Chairman: The Fleming Property Unit Trust, 1971–90; Gill & Duffus Group Plc, 1982–85 (Dir, 1973–85); Robert Fleming Securities, 1985–90; River & Mercantile Investment Management Ltd, 1994–96; Dep. Chm., Austin Reed Group Plc, 1977–96 (Dir, 1971–96); Director: Blue Circle Industries Plc, 1972–87; Lane Fox and Partners Ltd, 1987–91; Fleming Income & Growth Investment Trust plc (formerly River & Mercantile Trust Plc), 1994–2001; Chesterton International Plc, 1994–98. Mem., Finance Act 1960 Tribunal, 1978–84. Mem., Wessex Regl Cttee, NT, 1995–2004. *Recreations:* gardening, walking. *Address:* The Manor, Berwick St John, Shaftesbury, Dorset SP7 0EX. *T:* (01747) 828363. *Clubs:* Brooks's, Army and Navy.

PEARSON, David Robert Stanley, FSA; FCLIP; Director, Culture, Heritage and Libraries (formerly Libraries, Archives and Guildhall Art Gallery), City of London, since 2009; *b* 7 May 1955; *s* of Robert Edward Orlando Pearson and Gladys Pearson (*née* Goldsworthy); *m* 1987, Lynne Wallace; one *s*. *Educ:* St Bees Sch., Cumbria; Sidney Sussex Coll., Cambridge (BA 1977; PhD 2009); Loughborough Univ. (DipLib). FCLIP 2001; FSA 2005. Curator, Eighteenth-century Short Title Catalogue, BL, 1986–92; Hd, Collection Develt, Nat. Art Liby, 1992–96; Librarian, Wellcome Trust, 1996–2004; Dir, Res. Liby Services, Univ. of London, 2004–09. Pres., Bibliographical Soc., 2010–12 (Hon. Sec., 1994–2002; Vice-Pres., 1995–2010). Freeman of the City of London, 2010; Liveryman, Stationers' and Newspaper Makers' Co., 2010–. *Publications:* Provenance Research in Book History, 1994; Oxford Bookbinding 1500–1640, 2000; (ed) For the Love of the Binding: studies in bookbinding history, 2000; English Bookbinding Styles 1450–1800, 2005; Books as History, 2008; (ed) London 1000 Years, 2011. *Recreations:* bibliography, walking by the sea. *Address:* The Old Vicarage, 10 Copperfields, Royston, Herts SG8 5BH. *T:* (01763) 241379. *E:* drspearson@dsl.pipex.com.

PEARSON, (Edward) John (David); Hon. Director General, European Commission, since 2001; *b* 1 March 1938; *s* of Sydney Pearson and Hilda Beaumont; *m* 1963, Hilary Stuttard; three *s* two *d*. *Educ:* Huddersfield Coll.; Emmanuel Coll., Cambridge (MA). Admin. Trainee, London Transport Exec., 1959; Asst Principal, MoT, 1960, Principal 1965; Sen. Principal, 1971, Asst Sec., 1973, DoE; European Commission: Head of Div., Transport Directorate-Gen., 1973–81; Dir, Fisheries Directorate-Gen., 1981–91; Dir, Regl Policy and Cohesion Directorate-Gen., 1991–98; Dep. Financial Controller, EC, 1999–2001 (Acting Financial Controller, July–Aug. 2000). *Recreations:* orienteering (Pres., Belgian Orienteering Assoc., 1982–87; Chm., Develt and Promotion Cttee, 1986–88, Mem. Council, 1988–94, Pin of Honour, 1994, Internat. Orienteering Fedn), hill-walking (Pyrenees High Level Route from Atlantic to Mediterranean in 43 days, 2006; climbed the 283 Scottish Munros between 1964 and 2011; completed Annapurna Circuit, Nepal, 2011), writing (magazine articles published on ornithology, Hungarian language and history, mountaineering, Arthur Ransome). *Address:* Mas d'en Clarimon, Route de Paloll à la Selva, 66400 Céret, France. *T:* (4) 68833458. *E:* hilaryandjohnpearson@hotmail.com.

PEARSON, Sir (Francis) Nicholas (Fraser), 2nd Bt *cr* 1964, of Gressingham, Co. Palatine of Lancaster; *b* 28 Aug. 1943; *s* of Sir Francis Fenwick Pearson, 1st Bt, MBE and of Katharine Mary, *d* of Rev. D. Denholm Fraser; *S* father, 1991; *m* 1978, Henrietta Elizabeth, *d* of Comdr Henry Pasley-Tyler, CBE and Haroldine Lucas. *Educ:* Radley Coll. Commnd The Rifle

Brigade, 1961; ADC to: Army Comdr, Far East, 1967; C-in-C, Far East, 1968. Dir, Hill & Delamain Ltd, 1970–75; Dep. Chm., Claughton Manor Brickworks, 1978; Chm., Turner Gp Ltd, 1979; Director: Intercontinental Hotel Group Ltd, 1989–92; Virgin Atlantic Airlines, 1989–92; Saison Hldgs BV, 1990–93. Chm., Pure Gym Ltd. Trustee: Ruskin Foundn; Temenos Foundn. Prospective Parly Cand. (C), Oldham West, 1976–79. *Recreations:* shooting, fishing. *Heir:* none. *Address:* c/o HSBC Private Bank, 69 Pall Mall, SW1Y 5EY.

PEARSON, Rt Rev. Geoffrey Seagrave; *see* Lancaster, Bishop Suffragan of.

PEARSON, Dr Graham Scott, CB 1990; CChem, FRSC; Hon. Visiting Professor of International Security, Division of Peace Studies, University of Bradford, since 1996; Director General, Chemical and Biological Defence Establishment (formerly Director, Chemical Defence Establishment), Porton Down, 1984–95; *b* 20 July 1935; *s* of Ernest Reginald Pearson and Alice (*née* Maclachlan); *m* 1960, Susan Elizabeth Meriton Benn; two *s. Educ:* Woodhouse Grove Sch., Bradford; St Salvator's Coll., Univ. of St Andrews (BSc 1st Cl. Hons Chemistry, 1957; PhD 1960). Postdoctoral Fellow, Univ. of Rochester, NY, USA, 1960–62; joined Scientific Civil Service, 1962; Rocket Propulsion Estab., 1962–69; Def. Res. and Develt Staff, Washington, DC, 1969–72; PSO to Dir Gen. Res. Weapons, 1972–73; Asst Dir, Naval Ordnance Services/Scientific, 1973–76; Technical Adviser/Explosives, Materials and Safety (Polaris), 1976–79; Principal Supt, Propellants Explosives and Rocket Motor Estab., Westcott, 1979–80; Dep. Dir 1, 1980–82 and Dep. Dir 2, 1982–83, RARDE, Fort Halstead; Dir Gen., ROF (Res. and Develt), 1983–84; Asst Chief Scientific Advr (Non-Proliferation), MoD, 1995. Archivist, Hidcote Manor Garden, 2002–. Fellow, IUPAC, 2004. *Publications:* (ed jtly) Key Points for the Fourth Review Conference, 1996; The UNSCOM Saga: chemical and biological weapons non-proliferation, 1999; (ed jtly) Key Points for the Fifth Review Conference, 2001; (ed jtly) Scientific and Technical Means of Distinguishing Between Natural and Other Outbreaks of Disease, 2001; (ed jtly) Maximizing the Security and Development Benefits from the Biological and Toxin Weapons Convention, 2002; (ed jtly) The Implementation of Legally Binding Measures to Strengthen the Biological and Toxin Weapons Convention, 2004; The Search for Iraq's Weapons of Mass Destruction: inspection, verification and non-proliferation, 2005; (ed jtly) Key Points for the Sixth Review Conference, 2006; Hidcote: the garden and Lawrence Johnston, 2007, 3rd edn 2013; Lawrence Johnston: the creator of Hidcote, 2010, 2nd edn 2013; (ed jtly) Key Points for the Seventh Review Conference, 2011; (ed jtly) BioWeapons Monitor, 2014; contributor to: Advances in Photochemistry, vol. 3, 1964; Advances in Inorganic and Radio Chemistry, vol. 8, 1966; Oxidation and Combustion Reviews, vol. 3, 1968 and vol. 4, 1969; Biological Weapons: Weapons of the Future?, 1993; Non-Conventional Weapons Proliferation in the Middle East, 1993; Verification after the Cold War, 1994; Weapons Proliferation in the 1990s, 1995; Verification 1997, 1997; Biological Weapons: limiting the threat, 1999; Biological Warfare: modern offense and defense, 2000; Encyclopedia of Bioterrorism Defense, 2005; Deadly Cultures: biological weapons since 1945, 2006; Terrorism, War or Disease? Unraveling the Use of Biological Weapons, 2008; Encyclopedia of Bioterrorism Defense, 2nd edn 2011; Turning International Obligations into Effective National Action: the 2007–2010 Intersessional Process of the Biological Weapons Convention, 2011; articles on combustion, and on chemical and biological defence and arms control, in scientific jls, and on Hidcote and Lawrence Johnston in horticultural jls; official reports. *Recreations:* walking, photography, reading, archival research, gardening. *Address:* Division of Peace Studies, University of Bradford, Bradford, W Yorks BD7 1DP. *T:* (01274) 234188.

PEARSON, Ian Howard; His Honour Judge Pearson; a Circuit Judge, since 2004; *b* 30 May 1949; *s* of Harry Seabourn and Elsie Margaret Pearson; *m* 1971, Sian Williams; two *d. Educ:* Farnham Grammar Sch.; Univ. of Leicester (LLB Hons); Coll. of Law, Guildford. Admitted as solicitor, 1973; Partner, Tanner & Taylor, Solicitors, Hants and Surrey, 1975–94; a Judge Advocate (pt time), 1992; Dep. Judge Advocate, 1994–95; Asst JAG, 1995–2004; Vice JAG, 2004; Asst Recorder, 1999–2000; a Recorder, 2000–04. Mem. (Lab), Rushmoor BC, 1986–94. Contested (Lab) Aldershot, 1987. *Recreations:* travel, literature, visual arts, food and wine, sport, avoiding watching opera. *Address:* Portsmouth Crown Court, Winston Churchill Way, Portsmouth, Hants PO1 2EB. *T:* (023) 9289 3000.

PEARSON, Ian Phares, PhD; Chief Executive, IPP Associates, since 2010; Chairman: Octopus VCT2 plc, since 2011; CrowdBnk Ltd, since 2013; *b* 5 April 1959; *m* 1988, Annette Pearson (marr. diss. 2009); one *s* two *d. Educ:* Brierley Hill GS; Balliol Coll., Oxford (BA Hons PPE); Warwick Univ. (MA, PhD). Mem. (Lab) Dudley MBC, 1984–87. Local Govt Policy Res. Officer, Lab. Party, 1985–87; Dep. Dir, Urban Trust, 1987–88; business and economic develt consultant, 1988–91; Jt Chief Exec., W Midlands Enterprise Bd, 1991–94. MP (Lab) Dudley W, Dec. 1994–1997, Dudley S, 1997–2010. An Asst Govt Whip, 2001–02; a Lord Comr of HM Treasury (Govt Whip), 2002–03; Parly Under-Sec. of State, NI Office, 2002–05; Minister of State (Minister for Trade), FCO and DTI, 2005–06; Minister of State, DEFRA, 2006–07; Minister of State (Minister for Sci. and Innovation), DIUS, 2007–08; Econ. Sec., BERR, 2008–09; Econ. Sec. to HM Treasury, 2008–10. Non-exec. Dir, Thames Water Utilities Ltd, 2014–.

PEARSON, Prof. Jeremy David, PhD; FMedSci; Professor of Vascular Biology, King's College London, 1991–2010, now Emeritus; Associate Medical Director (Research), British Heart Foundation, since 2002; *b* Upminster, Essex, 24 Dec. 1947; *s* of Kenneth and Margot Pearson; *m* 1974, Jane McCarthy; two *s. Educ:* Hertford Grammar Sch.; Queens' Coll., Cambridge (BA Natural Scis 1968; MA 1972; PhD 1975); St Cross Coll., Oxford (MA 1974). IBM Res. Fellow, Univ. of Oxford, 1974–76; SSO, then PSO, Babraham Inst., 1976–83; Sen. Scientist, then Hd, Section of Vascular Biol., MRC Clin. Res. Centre, Harrow, 1983–91. President: British Soc. for Haemostasis and Thrombosis, 1997–98; British Microcirculation Soc., 2002–05; Secretary: British Atherosclerosis Soc., 1998–2003; Eur. Vascular Biol. Orgn, 2000–10; Chm., Strategy Cttee, Eur. Soc. for Microcirculation, 1998–2004; Mem., Basic Sci. Council, Eur. Soc. Cardiol., 2004– (Chm., 2016–). Trustee: William Harvey Res. Foundn, 2003–14 (Chm. Bd, 2005–14); Raynaud's and Scleroderma Assoc., 2007– (Chm. Bd, 2014–). FMedSci 2004; Fellow, Eur. Soc. Cardiol. 2013. Hon. FRCP 2006. *Publications:* contrib. scientific papers and reviews in field of endothelial cell biol. *Recreations:* walking, fine wine, good food, modern classical music. *Address:* British Heart Foundation, Greater London House, 180 Hampstead Road, NW1 7AW. *T:* (020) 7554 0344. *E:* pearsonj@bhf.org.uk.

PEARSON, John; *see* Pearson, E. J. D.

PEARSON, Prof. John Richard Anthony, PhD, ScD; FRS 2005; Scientific Consultant, Schlumberger Cambridge Research, since 1996 (Scientific Adviser, 1982–95); Chairman, Pearson Publishing Group, since 1993; *b* Cairo, 18 Sept. 1930; *s* of Charles Robert Pearson and Olive Pearson (*née* Nock); *m* 1954, Emma Margaret Anderson; three *s* one *d. Educ:* English Sch., Cairo; Bedford Modern Sch.; Trinity Coll., Cambridge (BA 1953; PhD 1958; ScD 1975); Harvard Univ. (AM 1954). CEng 1970; FIMMM; MIChemE 1970. Nat. Service, 2nd Lieut, Royal Signals, 1948–50; Tech. Officer, ICI Ltd, 1957–59; Res. Scientist, Metal Box Co., 1959–60; Asst Dir Res., Dept of Chemical Engrg, Univ. of Cambridge, 1960–73; Dir of Studies in Maths and Fellow, Trinity Hall, Cambridge, 1961–73; Prof. of Chemical Engrg, Imperial Coll., London Univ., 1973–82. Visiting Professor: Princeton Univ., 1967; Univ. of Wisconsin, 1967; Rice Univ., 1969; MIT, 1973–76; Univ. of Sydney, 1982; Univ. of Louvain, 1994–95; D. A. Katz Lectr, Univ. of Michigan, 1975; Fairchild Schol., CIT, 1978–79, 1981; MTS Prof., Univ. of Minnesota, 2004. Hon. Professorial Fellow: Univ. of Wales, 1984–2012; Univ. of Birmingham, 1995–2013. Member and Chairman: UNIDO Tech. Assistance Cttee, Planta Piloto de Ingenieria Quimica, Argentina, 1973–79; Yucca Mountain Peer Rev. Cttee, US Dept of Energy, 2002–03; Mem., Internat. Geomechanics Commn, Govt of France, 1996–99. Pres., British Soc. of Rheology, 1980–82 (Gold Medal, 1986). Foreign Mem., NAE, 1980. Hon. DSc Minnesota, 2002. *Publications:* Mechanical Principles of Polymer Melt Processing, 1966; Polymer Melt Processing, 1985; papers on engrg sci. in scientific jls. *Recreations:* travel, opera, wine. *Address:* Pearson Publishing Group, Chesterton Mill, French's Road, Cambridge CB4 3NP. *E:* jrap@pearson.co.uk. *Clubs:* MCC; Cambridge University Real Tennis.

PEARSON, Keith Philip, MA; FRSE; Headmaster, George Heriot's School, Edinburgh, 1983–97; *b* 5 Aug. 1941; *s* of Fred G. and Phyllis Pearson; *m* 1965, Dorothy (*née* Atkinson); two *d. Educ:* Madrid Univ. (Dip. de Estudios Hispánicos); Univ. of Cambridge (MA; Cert. of Educn). FRSE 1995. Teacher, Rossall Sch., 1964–72 (Head of Mod. Langs, 1968–72); George Watson's College: Head of Mod. Langs, 1972–79; Dep. Principal, 1979–83. *Recreations:* sport, mountains, music, DIY.

PEARSON, Sir Keith (Samuel), Kt 2010; JP; DL; Chair, Health Education England, since 2012; *b* Fulwood, Lancs, 6 April 1947. Gen. mgt, BUPA UK, 1976–89; Chief Executive Officer: BUPA Hong Kong, 1989–93; AON Thailand and Singapore, 1993–97; Summerlands Consultants Ltd, 1997–2004; Chair: NHS S Somerset PCG and PCT, 1998–2004; Norfolk, Suffolk and Cambs SHA, 2004–06; E of England SHA, 2006–10; NHS Confederation, 2010–12. Chm., Nat. Adv. Gp on Health in Criminal Justice, DoH and MoJ, 2009–; former Co-Chair, NHS State of Readiness Gp. Chm., Med. Revalidation Prog., GMC, 2009–. Chm., Tallaght Hosp., 2011–. JP Peterborough, 1999; DL Cambs, 2011. *Publications:* Children in Her Shadow (novel), 2011; Reflections from Her Shadow (novel), 2014. *Address:* Health Education England, Level 16, Portland House, Bressenden Place, SW1E 5RS.

PEARSON, Rt Rev. Kevin; *see* Argyll and the Isles, Bishop of.

PEARSON, Prof. Margaret Anne, PhD; Pro-Vice-Chancellor (Public Benefit) and Executive Dean, College of Health and Social Care, University of Salford, since 2013; *b* 13 Oct. 1952; *d* of late Charles Yorke and of Betty Yorke; one *s* one *d*; *m* 2012, Matthew Maisey. *Educ:* Newnham Coll., Cambridge (BA Hons Geog. 1975; MA 1977); RGN 1978; Liverpool Univ. (PhD Geog. 1985). Student Nurse, 1975–78, Staff Nurse, 1978–79, Sheffield AHA; Res. Officer, then Dir, Centre for Ethnic Minorities Health, Bradford Univ., 1982–84; Lectr in Health Policy, Nuffield Inst. for Health Services Studies, Leeds Univ., 1983–85; University of Liverpool: Lectr, then Sen. Lectr, in Med. Sociology, 1985–93; Prof. of Health and Community Care, 1993–96; Regl Dir of R&D, DoH/NHS Exec. NW, 1996–2001; Dep. Dir, NHS Human Resources, DoH, 2001–04; Dep. Vice-Chancellor, Keele Univ., 2004–07; Dir, Maggie Pearson Solutions, 2007–10; Academic Dir, Office of CSO, DoH, 2008–13. Member: UK Commn on Human Medicines, 2005–; Bd, UK Sector Skills Develt Agency, 2006–08. Chm., Main Panel C (Nursing and Midwifery, Dentistry, Pharmacy and Allied Health Professions and Subjects), 2008 RAE. Hon. MFPH 1995. *Recreations:* family, music (flute player), reading, textile art. *E:* m.a.pearson@salford.ac.uk.

PEARSON, Michael; *see* Pearson, T. M.

PEARSON, Prof. Michael George, FRCP; Professor of Clinical Evaluation, University of Liverpool, 2007–12, now Hon. Professor (Professor of Medicine, 2003–07); Consultant Physician, University Hospital, Aintree, Liverpool, since 1984; *b* 11 Jan. 1950; *s* of Dr C. Andrew Pearson, OBE and Jean M. Pearson; *m* 1973, Diane Kay Park; three *d. Educ:* Culford Sch., Bury St Edmunds; Gonville and Caius Coll., Cambridge (MA; MB BChir 1975); Liverpool Univ. Med. Sch. FRCP 1991. Royal College of Physicians: Associate Dir, 1997–98, Dir, 1998–2006, Clinical Effectiveness and Evaluation Unit; Dir, Clinical Standards, 2005–07. Trustee Dir, Respiratory Educn Training (formerly Resource) Centres, 1998–; Dir, Nat. Collaborating Centre for Chronic Conditions, 2000–04. Hon. Prof., Dept of Biol Scis, Salford Univ., 1991–. Theme Lead, NW Coast Collaboration for Leadership in Applied Health Res. and Care, 2013–. Non-exec. Dir, Health and Social Care Inf. Centre, 2005–14. Mem. Exec., British Thoracic Soc., 1995–99. *Publications:* Questions in Respiratory Medicine, 1994; Controversies in Chronic Obstructive Pulmonary Diseases, 2003; contrib. numerous papers to scientific jls. *Recreations:* gardening, music. *Address:* 12 Willow Hey, Maghull, Liverpool L31 3DL. *E:* michael.pearson@liverpool.ac.uk.

PEARSON, Michael George P.; *see* Parker Pearson.

PEARSON, Sir Nicholas; *see* Pearson, Sir F. N. F.

PEARSON, Lt Gen. Peter Thomas Clayton, CB 2010; CBE 2000; Executive Director, British Exploring Society (formerly British Schools Exploring Society), 2010–14; *b* Hong Kong, 22 Oct. 1954; *s* of Robert Pearson and Irene Pearson; *m* 1979, Francesca Beill; two *s* one *d. Educ:* St Edward's, Oxford; Royal Military Acad. Sandhurst; Army Staff Coll. Platoon Commander: 10th Princess Mary's Own Gurkha Rifles, Hong Kong, 1976–77; 1st Bn, Argyll and Sutherland Highlanders, 1977–78; Intelligence Officer, 10th PMO Gurkha Rifles, Brunei, 1978–79; Instructor, Platoon Comdrs Div., Sch. of Infantry, Warminster, 1979–81; Adjutant, 10th PMO Gurkha Rifles, Hong Kong, 1981–83; OC Support Co., 10th PMO Gurkha Rifles, 5 Airborne Bde, Aldershot, 1983–85; Staff Coll., Camberley, 1986; COS 20 Armoured Bde, 1986–88; OC D Co., 10th PMO Gurkha Rifles, Brunei, 1989–90; Mil. Asst to C-in-C, 1990–93; Commanding Officer: 10th PMO Gurkha Rifles, 1993–94; 3rd Bn The Royal Gurkha Rifles, 1994–95; HCSC, 1996; Comdr 19 Mechanized Bde, 1997–2000; COS to Comdr Field Army, 2000–02; Dep. Comdr Ops, Stabilisation Force Bosnia, 2002–03; Comdr British Forces and Adminr Sovereign Base Areas Cyprus, 2003–06; Comdt, RMA Sandhurst, 2006–07; Dep. Comdr Allied Jt Force Comd, Naples, 2007–09. Col of Regt, The Royal Gurkha Rifles, 1999–2009. Lieut, Tower of London, 2010–15. Governor: Corps of Commissionaires, 2010–15; Mil. Knights of Windsor, 2012–. Trustee, British Forces Foundn, 2006–. *Publications:* Bugle and Kukri, vol. 3: the story of the 10th Princess Mary's Own Gurkha Rifles, 2000. *Recreations:* fly fishing, Rugby Union (watching).

PEARSON, Rebecca Astley; *see* Clarke, R. A.

PEARSON, Prof. Roger Anthony George, DPhil; FBA 2009; Professor of French, University of Oxford, since 1997; Fellow and Praelector in French, Queen's College, Oxford, since 1977; *b* Belfast, 7 April 1949; *s* of Philip Arnold Pearson and Barbara Mary Pearson (*née* McKee); *m* 1981, Vivienne Gregory; one *s* one *d. Educ:* Harrow Sch.; Exeter Coll., Oxford (BA Hons 1971; DPhil 1976). Lectr in French, Queen's Coll., Oxford, 1973–77; Lectr, Univ. of Oxford, 1977–. Leverhulme Maj. Res. Fellow, 2009–11. Officier, Ordre des Palmes Académiques (France), 2005. *Publications:* Stendhal's Violin: a novelist and his reader, 1988; The Fables of Reason: a study of Voltaire's contes philosophiques, 1993; Unfolding Mallarmé: the development of a poetic art, 1996; Mallarmé and Circumstance: the translation of silence, 2004; Voltaire Almighty: a life in pursuit of freedom, 2005; Stéphane Mallarmé, 2010; *literary translations:* Voltaire, Candide and Other Stories, 1990, rev. edn 2006; Zola, La Bête humaine, 1996; Maupassant, A Life, 1999; Zola, Germinal, 2004. *Address:* Queen's College, Oxford OX1 4AW. *T:* (01865) 279120, *Fax:* (01865) 790819. *E:* roger.pearson@queens.ox.ac.uk.

PEARSON, Siobhan Mary; *see* Kenny, S. M.

PEARSON, Sybil Angela Margaret, (Mrs Michael Pearson); *see* Jones, S. A. M.

PEARSON, Gen. Sir Thomas (Cecil Hook), KCB 1967 (CB 1964); CBE 1959 (OBE 1953); DSO 1940, and Bar, 1943; DL; retired 1974; *b* 1 July 1914; *s* of late Vice-Admiral J.

L. Pearson, CMG; *m* 1947, Aud (*d* 2013), *d* of late Alf Skjelkvale, Oslo; two *s*. *Educ:* Charterhouse; Sandhurst. 2nd Lieutenant Rifle Bde, 1934. Served War of 1939–45, M East and Europe; CO 2nd Bn The Rifle Bde, 1942; Dep. Comdr 2nd Independent Parachute Bde Gp 1944; Dep. Comdr 1st Air-landing Bde 1945; GSO1 1st Airborne Div. 1945; CO 1st Bn The Parachute Regt 1946; CO 7th Bn The Parachute Regt 1947; GSO1 (Land Air Warfare), WO, 1948; JSSC, GSO1, HQ Malaya, 1950; GSO1 (Plans), FARELF, 1951; Directing Staff, JSSC, 1953; Comdr 45 Parachute Bde TA 1955; Nat. Defence Coll., Canada, 1956; Comdr 16 Ind. Parachute Bde 1957; Chief of Staff to Dir of Ops Cyprus, 1960; Head of Brit. Mil. Mission to Soviet Zone of Germany, 1960; Major-General Commanding 1st Division, BAOR, 1961–63; Chief of Staff, Northern Army Group, 1963–67; Comdr, FARELF, 1967–68; Military Sec., MoD, 1968–72; C-in-C, Allied Forces, Northern Europe, 1972–74; psc 1942; jssc 1950; ndc Canada 1957. ADC Gen. to the Queen, 1974. Col Comdt, the Royal Green Jackets, 1973–77. Fisheries Mem., Welsh Water Authy, 1980–83. DL Hereford and Worcester, 1983. Haakon VII Liberty Cross, 1948; Medal of Honour, Norwegian Defence Assoc., 1973. *Recreations:* field sports, yachting. *Clubs:* Naval and Military; Kongelig Norsk Seilforenning.

PEARSON, (Thomas) Michael, MBE 2007; Trustee and Member Council, Cruse Bereavement Care, since 1986 (Hon. Officer, since 1987; Chair, 1992–2005); human resources adviser in private and charity/voluntary sectors, since 2001; *b* 23 Dec. 1941; *s* of Harold Hird Pearson and Mary Anderson Pearson (*née* Preston); *m* 1967, Margaret Green; one *s* one *d*. *Educ:* Lancaster Royal Grammar Sch.; Univ. of Liverpool (BA Hons Soc. Studies 1966); Univ. of Kent (BA Hons Archaeol Studies 2007). Chartered CCIPD (CIPM 1990). Career in personnel mgt/human resources: Glaxo Gp, 1966–85; Smiths Industries Group, 1985–2000: Dir of Personnel, Healthcare Gp, 1987–94, Personnel Dir, then Human Resources Dir, Portex Ltd, 1994–2000. Mem., Employment Tribunals, 1995–2011. Vice-Pres., IPM, 1990–92. Governor, Chichester Coll., W Sussex, 1986–2004 (Vice-Chm., Governing Body, 1992–2003). *Recreations:* archaeology, visiting historic places and gardens. *Address:* Rose Cottage, Belcaire Close, Lympne, Hythe, Kent CT21 4JR. *T:* and *Fax:* (01303) 269557. *E:* margaretandmike.pearson@gmail.com.

PEART, Brian; Under-Secretary, Ministry of Agriculture, Fisheries and Food, 1976–85; *b* 17 Aug. 1925; *s* of late Joseph Garfield Peart and Frances Hannah Peart (*née* English); *m* 1952, Dorothy (*née* Thompson); one *s* one *d*. *Educ:* Wolsingham Grammar Sch.; Durham Univ. (BA). Served War, RAF, 1943–47. Agricultural Economist, Edinburgh Sch. of Agric., 1950–57; Sen. Agricultural Economist, 1957–64; Regional Farm Management Adviser, MAFF, West Midlands Region, 1964–67; Chief Farm Management Adviser, MAFF, 1967–71; Regional Manager, MAFF, Yorks/Lancs Region, 1971–74; Head of Intelligence and Trng Div., 1974–76; Chief Administrator, ADAS, 1976–80; Under Sec., Lands Gp, MAFF, 1980–85. Kellogg Fellow, USA, 1960. *Recreations:* golf, genealogy, bridge, The Times crossword. *Address:* 18 Derwent Close, Claygate, Surrey KT10 0RF. *Club:* Farmers.

PEART, Icah Delano Everard; QC 2002; a Recorder, since 2000; *b* 19 Jan. 1956; *s* of Everard Leopold Peart and Doreen Mildred Peart; partner, Linda Torpey; two *s* one *d*. *Educ:* Ashmead Boys' Secondary Sch., Reading; London Sch. of Econs (LLB Hons); Coll. of Law. Called to the Bar, Middle Temple, 1978, Bencher, 2005; in practice specialising in criminal law; Asst Recorder, 1997–2000. Volunteer, Internat. Sen. Lawyers Project, 2010–. Appeal Steward, British Boxing Bd of Control, 2012–. *Recreations:* reading, cinema, watching Reading FC (Mem. Supporters' Club), my children, gym, cycling. *Address:* Garden Court Chambers, 57–60 Lincoln's Inn Fields, WC2A 3LS. *T:* (020) 7993 7600, *Fax:* (020) 7993 7700. *E:* icahp@gclaw.co.uk.

PEART, Michael John, CMG 1995; LVO 1983; HM Diplomatic Service, retired; *b* 15 Dec. 1943; *s* of Joseph Albert William Peart and Thelma Theresa Peart (*née* Rasmussen); *m* 1968, Helena Mary Stuttle; one *s* (one *d* decd). *Educ:* Gillingham County Grammar Sch., Kent. Prison Dept, Home Office, 1960–65; FCO 1966–69; served Blantyre, 1969–71; Warsaw, 1972–75; Mexico City, 1975–80; FCO, 1980–83; Dhaka, 1983–86; FCO, 1987–91; Ambassador, Lithuania, 1991–94; Ambassador, later High Comr, Fiji, and High Comr, Kiribati, Nauru and Tuvalu, 1995–97. Chm., Tiltas Trust, 2007–; Dep. Chm., Sherborne Community Arts Centre Trust, 2009–. Mem., Rotary Club of Sherborne Castles. Grand Cross of Commander, Order for Merits (Lithuania), 2006; Diplomacy Star (Lithuania), 2011. *Recreations:* music, reading, walking. *Address:* Amberleigh Cottage, 2 Dunstan Street, Sherborne, Dorset DT9 3SE.

PEART, Prof. Sir (William) Stanley, Kt 1985; MD; FRS 1969; Professor of Medicine, University of London, at St Mary's Hospital Medical School, 1956–87, now Emeritus; *b* 31 March 1922; *s* of J. G. and M. Peart; *m* 1947, Peggy Parkes (*d* 2002); one *s* one *d*. *Educ:* King's College School, Wimbledon; St Mary's Hospital Medical Sch. (MB, BS (Hons) 1945; MD 1949). FRCP 1959. Lecturer in Medicine, St Mary's Hospital, 1950–56. Master, Hunterian Inst., RCS, 1988–92. Wellcome Trust: Trustee, 1975–94; Dep. Chm., 1991–94; Consultant, 1994–98; Beit Trustee, 1986–2003. Goulstonian Lectr, 1959, Croonian Lectr, 1979, RCP. Founder FMedSci 1998. Hon. For. Mem., Académie Royale de Médecine de Belgique, 1984. Hon. FIC 1988; Hon. FRCA 1991; Hon. FRCS 1995; Hon. Fellow, UCL, 1997. Hon. DSc Edinburgh, 1993. Stouffer Prize, Amer. Heart Assoc., 1968; Nuffield Medal, RSM, 1990; Buchanan Medal, Royal Soc., 2000. *Publications:* chapters in: Cecil-Loeb, Textbook of Medicine; Renal Disease; Biochemical Disorders in Human Disease; articles in Biochemical Journal, Journal of Physiology, Lancet. *Recreations:* ski-ing, reading, tennis. *Address:* 17 Highgate Close, N6 4SD.

PEASE, family name of **Barons Gainford** and **Wardington**.

PEASE, George; *S* brother, 2013 as 4th Baron Gainford, but does not use the title.

PEASE, Sir (Joseph) Gurney, 5th Bt *cr* 1882, of Hutton Lowcross and Pinchinthorpe, co. York; hotelier; *b* Guisborough, N Yorkshire, 16 Nov. 1927; *s* of Sir Alfred Edward Pease, 2nd Bt, and his 3rd wife, Emily Elizabeth Pease; *S* brother, 2008; *m* 1953, Shelagh Munro, *d* of Cyril Gounod Bulman; one *s* one *d*. *Educ:* Bootham Sch., York. Mem., Guisborough UDC, 1950–53. Contested (L): Bishop Auckland, 1959; Darlington, 1964; Westmorland, 1970; Penrith and the Border, 1974. Council Mem., Liberal Party, 1969; President: NE Young Liberal Fedn, 1961; NW Regl Liberal Party, 1970, 1971. *Publications:* A Wealth of Happiness and Many Bitter Trials, 1992. *Recreations:* fell-walking, writing, reading, family. *Heir: s* Charles Edward Gurney Pease, *b* 17 July 1955. *E:* gurneypease@btinternet.com.

See also C. C. Bright.

PEASE, Sir Richard Thorn, 3rd Bt *cr* 1920; Chairman, Yorkshire Bank, 1986–90 (Director, 1977; Deputy Chairman, 1981–86); *b* 20 May 1922; *s* of Sir Richard Arthur Pease, 2nd Bt, and Jeannette Thorn (*d* 1957), *d* of late Gustav Edward Kissel, New York; *S* father, 1969; *m* 1956, Anne, *d* of late Lt-Col Reginald Francis Heyworth; one *s* two *d*. *Educ:* Eton. Served with 60th Rifles, Middle East, Italy and Greece, 1941–46 (Captain). Director: Owners of the Middlesbrough Estate Ltd, 1954–86; Barclays Bank, 1964–89; Bank of Scotland, 1977–85; Grainger Trust PLC, 1986–94; Vice-Chairman: Barclays Bank Ltd, 1970–82; Barclays Bank UK Management, 1971–82; Chm., Foreign and Colonial High Income Trust, 1990–92. DL Northumberland, 1990. *Heir: s* Richard Peter Pease [*b* 4 Sept. 1958; *m* T. C. C., (Cecilie), (marr. diss. 1999), *d* of P. H. Tholstrup; one *s* by Kate Chubb].

PEASE, Rosamund Dorothy Benson; Under Secretary, Department of Health, 1989–95; *b* 20 March 1935; *d* of Helen Bowen (*née* Wedgwood) and Michael Stewart Pease; one *s*. *Educ:* Chester Sch., Nova Scotia; Perse Sch., Cambridge; Mount Sch., York; Newnham Coll., Cambridge (BA Classical Tripos). Asst Principal, Min. of Health, 1958; Principal, 1965; Asst Sec., Pay Board, 1973; Office of Manpower Economics, 1974; Cabinet Office, 1975–76; DHSS, 1976; Office of Population Censuses and Surveys, 1983; Under Sec., NI Office, 1985. *Recreations:* music, gardening, family.

PEAT, Adam Erskine, OBE 2009; Public Services Ombudsman for Wales, 2006–08; Chairman, Magna Housing Group, since 2013; *b* 30 Nov. 1948; *s* of late Raymond Basil Peat and Cynthia Elisabeth Peat; *m* 1973, Christine Janet Champion; one *s* one *d*. *Educ:* Stowmarket Co. Grammar Sch.; Pembroke Coll., Oxford (MA). Joined Welsh Office, 1972: Principal, 1977; Private Sec. to Sec. of State for Wales, 1983–84; Asst Sec., 1984–89; Chief Exec., Tai Cymru, 1989–98; Gp Dir, Welsh Office, 1998–99; Dir, Local Govt Gp, subseq. Local Govt, Housing & Culture Dept, then Local Govt, Communities & Culture Dept, Nat. Assembly for Wales, 1999–2003; Local Govt Ombudsman and Health Service Ombudsman for Wales, 2003–06, and Welsh Admin Ombudsman, 2004–06. *Recreations:* music, walking, ski-ing.

PEAT, Sir Gerrard (Charles), KCVO 1988; FCA; Partner, Peat Marwick Mitchell & Co., Chartered Accountants, 1956–87; Auditor to the Queen's Privy Purse, 1980–88 (Assistant Auditor, 1969–80); *b* 14 June 1920; *s* of Charles Urie Peat, MC, FCA, sometime MP and Ruth (*née* Pulley); *m* 1949, Margaret Josephine Collingwood; one *s* one *d*. *Educ:* Sedbergh Sch. FCA 1961. Served War, RAF and ATA (pilot), 1940–45 (Service Medals; Badge of Honour for services in ATA in WWII, 2008); Pilot, 600 City of London Auxiliary Sqdn, 1948–51. Underwriting Mem. of Lloyd's, 1973–; Member: Cttee, Assoc. of Lloyd's Members, 1983–89; Council of Lloyd's, 1989–92. Member: Corp. of City of London, 1973–78; Worshipful Co. of Turners, 1970–. Hon. Treasurer, Assoc. of Conservative Clubs, 1971–78. Jubilee Medal, 1977. *Recreations:* travel, fishing, golf. *Address:* Flat 10, 35 Pont Street, SW1X 0BB. *T:* (020) 7245 9736. *Clubs:* Boodle's, MCC.

PEAT, Jeremy Alastair, OBE 2012; Member, Competition and Markets Authority, since 2014; *b* 20 March 1945; *s* of John Scott Grainger Peat and Pamela Mary Peat (*née* Stephany); *m* 1972, Philippa Ann Jones; two *d*. *Educ:* Univ. of Bristol (BA Hons 1968); University College London (MSc 1977). Govt Econ. Service, 1969–80; Hd, Employment Policy Unit, Govt of Botswana, 1980–84; HM Treasury, 1984–85; Sen. Econ. Advr, Scottish Office, 1985–93; Gp Chief Economist, Royal Bank of Scotland, 1993–2005. Mem., Competition Commn, 2005–14. Dir, David Hume Inst., 2005–14. Board Member: Signet Accreditation Co. Ltd, 2007–; Scottish Enterprise, 2011–. Hon. Prof., Heriot-Watt Univ., 1994; Vis. Prof., Internat. Public Policy Inst., Univ. of Strathclyde, 2014–. Vice Chm., SHEFC, 1999–2005. Mem., Lay Cttee, RCPE, 2012 (Hon. Fellow, 2015). Trustee: BBC, 2006–10 (a Gov., 2005–06; Chm., BBC Pension Trust, 2005–11); RZSScot, 2010– (Vice Chm., 2011–12; Chm., 2012–). FCIBS 1999; FRSE 2005; FRSA. Hon. LLD Aberdeen, 1997; Hon. DLitt Heriot-Watt, 2010. *Publications:* (with Stephen Boyle) An Illustrated Guide to the Scottish Economy, 1999; (ed jtly) Scotland in a Global Economy: the 20:20 vision, 2002. *Recreations:* golf, reading, films, watching TV, walking dogs. *Address:* Croft Dyke, Roslin Glen, Midlothian EH25 9PX. *T:* (0131) 440 2247.

PEAT, Ven. Lawrence Joseph; Archdeacon of Westmorland and Furness, 1989–95, now Emeritus; *b* 29 Aug. 1928; *s* of Joseph Edward and Lilian Edith Peat; *m* 1953, Sheila Shipway; three *s* three *d*. *Educ:* Lincoln Theological College. Curate of Bramley, Leeds, 1958–61; Rector of All Saints', Heaton Norris, Stockport, 1961–65; Vicar of Bramley, Leeds, 1965–73; Team Rector of Southend-on-Sea, 1973–79; Vicar of Skelmsmergh, Selside and Longsleddale, Cumbria, 1979–86; RD of Kendal, 1984–88; Team Vicar of Kirkby Lonsdale, 1986–88. Canon of Carlisle Cathedral, 1988–95, now Emeritus. *Recreations:* walking, music, reading, theatre. *Address:* 56 Primrose Court, Primley Park View, Leeds LP17 7UY. *E:* lawrie.peat@fsmail.net.

PEAT, Sir Michael (Charles Gerrard), GCVO 2011 (KCVO 1998; CVO 1994); FCA; Principal Private Secretary to the Prince of Wales and the Duchess of Cornwall, 2005–11 (Private Secretary to the Prince of Wales, 2002–05); *b* 16 Nov. 1949; *m* 1976, Deborah Sage (*née* Wood); one *s* two *d* (and one *s* decd). *Educ:* Eton; Trinity Coll., Oxford (MA; Hon. Fellow, 2004); INSEAD, Fontainebleau (MBA). FCA 1975. KPMG Peat Marwick, 1972–93; Dir, Finance and Property Services, HM Household, 1990–96; Keeper of the Privy Purse, Treas. to the Queen, and Receiver-Gen., Duchy of Lancaster, 1996–2002. Sen. Advr, CQS Gp, and Dir, CQS Mgt Ltd, 2011–; non-executive Director: Arbuthnot Banking Gp, 2007–10; Tamar Energy Ltd, 2012– (Chm., 2015–); Arbuthnot Latham Ltd, 2015–; Sen. Ind. non-exec. Dir, Evraz plc, 2011–; Ind. Bd Mem., Deloitte LLP, 2011–; Advr to Mr Wafic Rida Saïd, 2011–; Mem., UK Adv. Bd, Barclays Wealth and Investment Mgt, 2011–13; Chairman of Advisory Board: GEMS UK, 2013–15 (Chm., GEMS MENASA Hldgs Ltd, 2015–); Bellaziz Hldgs Ltd, 2013–.

PEATTIE, Catherine; Member (Lab) Falkirk East, Scottish Parliament, 1999–2011; *b* 24 Nov. 1951; *d* of late Ian Roxburgh and Catherine Cheape (*née* Menzies); *m* 1969, Ian Peattie; two *d*. *Educ:* Moray Secondary Sch., Grangemouth. Shop worker, 1966–68; factory worker, 1968–69; Trng Supervisor, 1970–75; Field Worker and Trng Officer, SPPA, 1980–86; Develt worker, Volunteer Network, Falkirk, 1986–90; Community Develt worker, Langlees Community Flat, Falkirk, 1990–91; Manager, Community Outreach, 1991–93; Dir, Falkirk Voluntary Action Resource Centre, 1993–99. Scottish Parliament: Convener, Equal Opportunities Cttee, 2003–07; Dep. Convener, Transport, Infrastructure and Climate Change Cttee, 2007–11; Mem., Scottish Commn for Public Audit, 2003–07. Contested (Lab) Falkirk E, Scottish Parlt, 2011. *E:* CathyPeattie@gmail.com.

See also C. L. Hilton.

PEATTIE, Charles William Davidson, MBE 2003; freelance cartoonist, since 1985; *b* 3 April 1958; *s* of Richard Peattie and Frances Peattie; *m* 1st, 1988, Siobhan Clark (marr. diss.); two *d*; 2nd, 2005, Claudia Granados; two *s*. *Educ:* Charterhouse; St Martin's Sch. of Art (BA Fine Art). Portrait painter, 1980–85; artist: Alex cartoon (written with Russell Taylor) in: London Daily News, 1987; The Independent, 1987–91; Daily Telegraph, 1992–; Celeb cartoon (written with Mark Warren and Russell Taylor) in Private Eye, 1987–. *Television:* co-writer: Lenny Henry in Pieces (series), 1991; Passion Killers, 1999; Celeb (series), 2002; *radio:* Alex Presents, 2012. Writer, producer, animator, Alex (stage play), Arts Th., 2007, toured UK and abroad, 2008. *Publications:* (with Mark Warren) Dick, 1987; Celeb, 1991; (co-designed with Phil Healey) Incredible Model Dinosaurs, 1994; The Original Celeb Gary Bloke, 2002; with Russell Taylor, Alex Year Books, 1987–: Alex, 1987; The Unabashed Alex, 1988; Alex II: Magnum Force, 1989; Alex III: Son of Alex, 1990; Alex IV: The Man with the Golden Handshake, 1991; Alex V: For the Love of Alex, 1992; Alex Calls the Shots, 1993; Alex Plays the Game, 1994; Alex Knows the Score, 1995; Alex Sweeps the Board, 1996; Alex Feels the Pinch, 1997; The Full Alex, 1998; The Alex Technique, 1999; The Best of Alex 1998–2001, 2001; The Best of Alex, annually 2002–14. *Address:* 29A Queens Avenue, Muswell Hill, N10 3PE. *T:* (020) 8374 1225. *Clubs:* Groucho, Soho House, Every House.

PEAY, Prof. Jill Valerie, PhD; Professor of Law, London School of Economics, since 2005; *b* Kingston-upon-Thames, 11 June 1955; *d* of Kenneth Ernest Peay and Audrey Jean Peay (*née* Udall); partner, Alastair Partington. *Educ:* Tiffin Girls' Sch.; Birmingham Univ. (BSc; PhD 1980); Oxford Brookes Univ. (CPE (exemptions)); Inns of Court Sch. of Law. Called to the Bar, Gray's Inn, 1991. Res. Officer, 1980–82, Fellow, 1982–88, Centre for Criminological Res., Univ. of Oxford; Lectr, 1988–95, Sen. Lectr, 1995–96, Brunel Univ.; Sen. Lectr, 1996–2000, Reader, 2000–05, Law Dept, LSE; Associate Tenant, Doughty St Chambers,

1994–. Member: Richardson Cttee (Expert Adv. Cttee on mental health law reform), 1998–99; Res. Ethics Cttee, MoD, 2002–13. Mem., Wkg Party on Dementia: Ethical Issues, Nuffield Council on Bioethics, 2007–09. *Publications:* (with G. Mansfield) The Director of Public Prosecutions: principles and practices for the Crown Prosecutor, 1987; Tribunals on Trial: a study of decision-making under the Mental Health Act 1983, 1989; Inquiries after Homicide, 1996; Criminal Justice and the Mentally Disordered, 1998; (with N. Eastman) Law without Enforcement: integrating mental health and justice, 1999; Decisions and Dilemmas: working with mental health law, 2003; Seminal Issues in Mental Health Law, 2005; Mental Health and Crime, 2010; (with T. Newburn) Policing: politics, culture and control, 2012. *Recreations:* friends, Scilly, paddling in the back seat of a kayak. *Address:* Department of Law, London School of Economics, Houghton Street, WC2A 2AE. *T:* (020) 7955 6391. *E:* j.peay@lse.ac.uk.

PÉBEREAU, Michel, Grand Officier de la Légion d'honneur, 2008 (Commandeur, 2004); Commandeur de l'Ordre National du Mérite; Chairman, BNP Paribas, 2000–12, now Honorary Chairman (Chief Executive Officer, 2000–03); *b* 23 Jan. 1942; *m* 1962, Agnès Faure; two *s* two *d. Educ:* Ecole Polytechnique; Ecole Nationale d'Administration. Inspecteur Général des Finances honoraire. Inspecteur des Finances, 1967–70; Rep., later Tech. Advr, Cabinet of Minister of Econ. and Finance, 1970–74; Rep., Sub-Dir, Asst Dir and Hd of Service, Treasury Directorate, Ministry of Econ. and Finances, 1971–82; Dir, then Rep., Cabinet of Minister of Econ., 1978–81; Crédit Commercial de France: Man. Dir, 1982–87; Chm. and Chief Exec. Officer, 1987–93; Chm. and CEO, Banque Nationale de Paris, 1993–2000; Chm., Banque Paribas, 1999–2000. Chairman: French Banking Fedn, 2002–03 (Chm., Mkt and Investment Banking Commn, 2000–); French Banking Assoc., 2002–04; European Banking Fedn, 2004; Bd, Institut de l'Entreprise, 2005; Supervisory Bd, French Aspen Inst., 2005; IIEB, 2006. Director: BNP Paribas UK Ltd; Lafarge; Saint-Gobain; Total; Société Anonyme des Galeries Lafayette; Mem., Supervisory Bd, AXA. Institute of Political Studies, Paris: Sen. Lectr, 1967–78; Prof., 1980–2000; Mem., 1984, Chm., 1988, Mgt Cttee; Sen. Lectr, Nat. Sch. of Statistics and Econ. Admin, 1968–79. Mem., Acad. des Scis Morales et Politiques. Dep. Chm., Commn of Control for Film Industry, 1981–85; Chm., Commn for Selective Assistance for Film Distribn, 1987–89. *Publications:* La Politique Economique de France, 3 Vols; science fiction book reviews for La Recherche, 1983–2002, for Le Journal du Dimanche, 2003–. *Address:* c/o BNP Paribas, 3 rue d'Antin, 75002 Paris, France.

PECK, David Arthur; Clerk to Merchant Taylors' Company, 1995–2006; *b* 3 May 1940; *s* of late Frank Archibald Peck and Molly Peck (*née* Eyels); *m* 1968, Jennifer Mary Still; one *s* two *d. Educ:* Wellingborough Sch.; St John's Coll., Cambridge (MA). Admitted Solicitor, 1966; Partner, Birkbeck Julius Coburn & Broad, 1967; Sen. Partner, Birkbeck Montagu's, 1985–91; Partner, Penningtons, 1991–95. Mem. Council, Radley Coll., 1993–2013. *Recreations:* golf, walking, cinema. *Address:* 45 Homefeld Road, W4 2LW. *Clubs:* MCC (Cttee, 1998–2001; Foundn Trustee, 2010–); Hawks (Cambridge).

See also Maj.-Gen. R. L. Peck.

PECK, Donald MacInnes, DPhil; social investor; Co-Founder, Lok Capital, Gurgaon, India, since 2006; Treasurer, Institute for Public Policy Research, since 2008; *b* Pembury, Kent, 28 May 1952; *s* of Sir Edward Heywood Peck, GCMG and Alison Mary Peck (*née* MacInnes); *m* 1979, Lucy Veronica Macnair; two *s. Educ:* Winchester Coll.; Wadham Coll., Oxford (BA Mod. Hist. 1973); St Antony's Coll., Oxford (DPhil Latin Amer. Studies 1977). Asst Dir, Morgan Grenfell & Co., 1978–81; Dir, Lloyds Merchant Bank, 1981–87; Sen. Investment Officer, Internat. Finance Corp., Washington, DC, 1988–91; Commonwealth Development Corporation, later Actis LLP, 1991–2008: Dir, 1999–2004; Partner, New Delhi, 2004–08. Advr, India Prog. Cttee, Paul Hamlyn Foundn, 2009–. Trustee, Foundn Rachel and Pamela Schiele, 1994– (Chm., 2010–); Chm., Health Poverty Action, 2013–. *Recreations:* walking amid mountains, music, tennis, agrarian history. *Address:* The Old Post Office, Combe, Hungerford, W Berks RG17 9EH. *T:* (01488) 668518.

PECK, Prof. Edward William, PhD; Vice-Chancellor, Nottingham Trent University, since 2014; *b* Ormskirk, 10 May 1959; *s* of Edward and Vera Peck; *m* 1989, Ingrid Barker; two *d. Educ:* Ormskirk Grammar Sch.; Univ. of Bristol (BA Philosophy 1981); Univ. of Nottingham (MA Social Policy and Admin 1986); Univ. of Newcastle upon Tyne (PhD 1996). NHS Mgt Trainee, Wessex RHA, 1982–84; Community Mental Health Team Manager, Nottingham HA, 1984–86; Gen. Manager, Mental Health Services, Newcastle HA, 1986–92; Sen. Consultant, 1992–94, Dir, 1994–2002, Centre for Mental Health Services Develt, KCL; University of Birmingham: Dir, Health Services Mgt Centre, 2002–08; Pro-Vice-Chancellor and Hd, Coll. of Social Sci., 2008–14. Non-exec. Dir, Heart of England Foundn NHS Trust, 2012–14. *Publications:* (jtly) Managing Networks of Twenty-first Century Organisations, 2006; (with Perri 6) Beyond Delivery: policy implementation as sense-making and settlement, 2006; (with H. Dickinson) Leading and Managing in Inter-Agency Settings, 2008; (with H. Dickinson) Performing Leadership, 2009; book chapters; contribs to peer-reviewed jls. *Recreations:* playing hockey, watching Everton, funding horses, music, history, horticulture. *Address:* Nottingham Trent University, Burton Street, Nottingham NG1 4BU. *T:* (0115) 848 6561. *E:* edward.peck@ntu.ac.uk.

PECK, Maj.-Gen. Richard Leslie, CB 1991; FRGS; CEng, FICE; Director, The Churches Conservation Trust (formerly Redundant Churches Fund), 1992–97; *b* 27 May 1937; *s* of late Frank Archibald Peck and Molly Peck (*née* Eyels); *m* 1962, Elizabeth Ann, *d* of late Major Denis James Bradley and Barbara Edith Amy Bradley (*née* Metcalfe); two *s* one *d. Educ:* Wellingborough Sch.; Royal Mil. Acad., Sandhurst; Royal Mil. Coll. of Science, Shrivenham. BScEng. Commnd RE, 1957; served Cyprus, Libya, Germany, UK; psc 1969; Bde Major 5 Inf. Bde, 1969–71; Sqn Comd BAOR, 1972–73; Directing Staff, Staff Coll., 1973–77; CO 21 Engr Regt, 1977–79; Asst Mil. Sec., 1979–81; Comd 19 Inf. Bde, 1981–83; RCDS 1984; Dir Army Service Conditions, MoD, 1985; Dir Personnel, Staff of CDS, 1985–87; Engr-in-Chief (Army), 1988–91. Trustee and Mem. Council, 1992–2013, Treas., 1999–2013, Vice-Pres., 2014–, Lord Kitchener Nat. Meml Fund. Col Comdt, RE, 1991–97; Col, Queen's Gurkha Engineers, 1991–96. Pres., London South-West Br., SSAFA (formerly SSAFA Forces Help), 2008–. Freeman, City of London, 1991; Mem., Engineers' Co., 1990–. *Recreations:* Association football, cricket, golf, shooting, ski-ing, Rugby football. *Clubs:* MCC; I Zingari, Free Foresters, Band of Brothers, Cryptics; Royal Mid-Surrey Golf.

See also D. A. Peck.

PECKFORD, Hon. (Alfred) Brian; PC (Can.) 1982; Premier of the Province of Newfoundland and Labrador, 1979–89; *b* Whitbourne, Newfoundland, 27 Aug. 1942; *s* of Ewart Peckford and Allison (*née* Young), St John's; *m* 1st, 1969, Marina Dicks; three *d;* 2nd, 1986, Carol Ellsworth; one *s. Educ:* Lewisporte High Sch.; Memorial Univ. of Newfoundland (BAEd). Schoolmaster, 1962–63 and 1966–72. MHA (Progressive C) Green Bay, 1972–89; Special Asst to Premier, 1973; Minister: of Dept of Municipal Affairs and Housing, 1974; of Mines and Energy, 1976, also of Rural Development, 1978. Leader of Progressive Cons. Party, Newfoundland and Labrador, 1979–89. Pres., Peckford Consulting Ltd (formerly Peckford Inc.), 1989–. Conducted inquiries for Govts of Canada and British Columbia. Served on boards of Canadian Broadcasting Corp., and several Canadian junior mining cos. Chancellor, Acsenda Sch. of Mgt (formerly Sprott Shaw Degree Coll.), 2007–. Hon. LLD Meml Univ. of Newfoundland, 1986. Vanier Award, 1982; Outstanding Service Award, Newfoundland and Labrador Oil and Gas Industries Assoc., 2001. *Publications:* The Past in the Present, 1982; Some Day the Sun Will Shine and Have Not Will Be No More, 2012. *Recreations:* swimming, bicycling and reading. *Address:* 441 West Crescent Road, Qualicum Beach, BC V9K 1J5, Canada.

PECKHAM, Arthur John; UK Permanent Representative, Food and Agriculture Organisation, Rome, 1977–80; *b* 22 Sept. 1920; *s* of Richard William Peckham and Agnes Mercy (*née* Parker); *m* 1949, Margaret Enid Quirk (*d* 2011); two *s* one *d. Educ:* The Judd Sch., Tonbridge. RAF (Pilot), 1942–46, 59 Sqdn Coastal Command. Cadet, Min. of Labour and Nat. Service, 1948; Colonial Office: Asst Principal, 1950; Private Sec. to Perm. Under-Sec., 1952; Principal, 1954; Counsellor (Technical Assistance), Lagos, 1964; Asst Sec., Min. of Overseas Develt, 1966; Minister, FAO, Rome, 1977. *Recreation:* gardening. *Address:* 147A Newmarket Road, Norwich NR4 6SY.

PECKHAM, Prof. Catherine Stevenson, CBE 1998; MD, FRCP, FRCOG, FRCPath, FFPH, FMedSci; Professor of Paediatric Epidemiology, since 1985, and former Head, Centre for Paediatric Epidemiology and Biostatistics, Institute of Child Health, University of London; Hon. Consultant, Hospital for Sick Children, Great Ormond Street, 1985–2002; *b* 7 March 1937; *d* of late Alexander King, CMG, CBE; *m* 1958, Sir Michael John Peckham, *qv*; three *s. Educ:* St Paul's Girls' Sch.; University Coll., London (MB BS, MD). FFPH (FFPM 1980); FRCP 1988; FRCPath 1991; FRCOG 1994. Reader in Community Medicine and Head of Dept, Charing Cross Hosp. Med. Sch., 1980–85. Dir, Infections in Pregnancy Screening Prog. in England, 2008–. Member: Standing Med. Adv. Cttee, DoH, 1992–2001; Health Adv. Cttee, British Council, 1992–95; Bd, PHLS, 1989–92; Children Nationwide, Scientific Adv. Cttee, 1994–; Chairman: Steering Cttee on Epidemiol Res., Surveillance and Forecasting, WHO Global Prog. on AIDS, 1991–93; Exec. Cttee, British Paediatric Surveillance Unit, 1993–2002; Adv. Cttee on Dangerous Pathogens, DoH, 1999–2002; London Children's Taskforce, 2001–03; Military Health Res. Adv. Gp, 2001–; Confidential Enquiries Adv. Cttee, NICE, 2002–; Medical Foundn for AIDS Res. & Sexual Health, 2002–. Member: Fulbright Commn, 1987–95; Bd of Govs, St Paul's Sch., 1992– (Dep. Chm., 2001–06); Nuffield Council of Bioethics, 2000–06 (Vice-Chm., 2003–06); Council, Inst. of Educn, 2001–05; ASA, 1993–99. Chair, Positive Action for Children Fund, 2010–. Founder FMedSci 1998; Founder FRCPCH. Harding Award, Action Research, 1993; James Spence Medal, RCPCH, 2003. *Publications:* The Peckham Report: national immunization study, 1989; chapters and papers on infections in pregnancy and early childhood, national cohort studies and epidemiology of common childhood conditions. *Recreation:* flute.

PECKHAM, Sir Michael (John), Kt 1995; FRCP, FRCS, FRCR, FRCPath; artist; Founder, and Director, School of Public Policy, University College London, 1996–2000; *b* 2 Aug. 1935; *s* of William Stuart Peckham and Gladys Mary Peckham; *m* 1958, Catherine Stevenson King (*see* Prof. C. S. Peckham); three *s. Educ:* St Catharine's Coll., Cambridge (MA; Hon. Fellow, 1998); University College Hosp. Med. Sch., London (MD). MRC Clin. Res. Schol., Inst. Gustav Roussy, Paris, 1965–67; Institute of Cancer Research, London: Lectr, 1967–71; Sen. Lectr, 1971–74; Prof. of Radiotherapy, 1974–86; Dean, 1984–86; Dir, BPMF, 1986–90; Dir, R&D, DoH, 1991–95. Consultant: Royal Marsden Hosp., 1971–86; to Royal Navy, 1974–86. Mem., MRC, 1991–95; Mem., MRC Cell Biology and Disorders Bd, 1977–81. Member, Special Health Authority: Gt Ormond St Hosp., 1988–90; Brompton Nat. Heart and London Chest Hosps, 1986–90; Hammersmith and Queen Charlotte's Hosps, 1989–90. President: European Soc. of Therapeutic Radiology and Oncology, 1983–85; British Oncological Assoc., 1986–88; Fedn of European Cancer Socs, 1989–91; Mem., British Council Scientific Adv. Cttee, 1988–92. Vice-Chm., Council, ICRF, 1988–91. Chairman: BUPA Foundn, 1996–2004; Nat. Educn Res. Forum, 1999–2006; OST Foresight, Future of Healthcare, 1999–2000; Develt Forum, 2000–05; MS Soc. Sci. and Develt Bd, 2001–06; Macmillan Cancer Support Observatory, 2003–07. Founder: Bob Champion Cancer Trust, 1983; British Oncological Assoc., 1985; Co-founder, European Soc. of Therapeutic Radiology and Oncology, 1988. Mem., Inst. of Medicine, Nat. Acad. of Scis, Washington, 1995. Pres., Internat. Adv. Cttee, Canadian Inst. of Health Res., 2000–05. Trustee: Louise Buchanan Meml Trust, 1973–99; Guy's and St Thomas' Charitable Foundn, 1996–2000. Editor-in-Chief, European Jl of Cancer, 1989–95. Artist: first show, Bangor Univ., 1962; solo exhibitions: Bear Lane Gall., Oxford, 1964; Woodstock Gall., London, 1970; Upper Street Gall., London, 1976; Consort Gall., London, 1982; Christopher Hull Gall., London, 1983, 1989, 1992, 1997; Richard Demarco Gall., Edinburgh, 1989; Millinery Works Gall., London, 2001; ICH Gall., London, 2004; Tryon Street Gall., London, 2013; group exhibition: Treatments, RA Summer Exhibn, 2004 (drawings in clin. notes of his patients). Fellow: UCL, 1995; UCL Hosps, 1998; Inst. of Cancer Res., 1999. Founder FMedSci 1998. Dr *hc*: Univ. de Franche-Comté at Besançon, 1991; Catholic Univ. of Louvain, 1993; Hon. DSc: Loughborough, 1992; Exeter, 1996; London, 2007. *Publications:* Management of Testicular Tumours, 1981; (jtly) The Biological Basis of Radiotherapy, 1983; (jtly) Primary Management of Early Breast Cancer, 1985; (jt sen. editor) Oxford Textbook of Oncology, 1995; (with M. Marinker) Clinical Futures, 1998; A Model for Health: innovation and the future of health services, 1999.

PEDDER, William Arthur; Director, Corporate Affairs, Hutchison Whampoa (Europe) Ltd, 2006–11; *b* 20 Sept. 1950; *s* of Vice Adm. Sir Arthur Reid Pedder, KBE, CB, and Dulcie, *d* of O. L. Bickford; *m* 1983, Rosemarie Ghazaros; one *s* one *d. Educ:* Winchester Coll.; Merton Coll., Oxford (BA). Lieut, RN, 1972–79. Hogg Robinson Insce Gp, 1979–82; Manager, Lazard Bros, 1982–85; Dir, Dresdner Kleinwort Wasserstein, 1987–2001; Chief Exec., Invest·UK, subseq. Inward Investment, UK Trade & Investment, 2001–06. *Recreations:* sailing, theatre, ski-ing, tennis, shooting.

PEDDIE, Hon. Ian James Crofton; QC 1992; a Recorder, since 1997; *b* 17 Dec. 1945; *s* of Baron Peddie, MBE, JP, LLD and Hilda Mary Alice (*née* Bull), (Lady Peddie); *m* 1976, Susan Renée Howes; two *s* two *d. Educ:* Gordonstoun Sch.; University Coll. London (LLB Hons). Called to the Bar, Inner Temple, 1971; Asst Recorder, 1992–97. Member: SE Circuit, 1971–; Family Law Bar Assoc., 1980–; Exec. Cttee, Assoc. Lawyers for Children, 2010–. *Recreations:* family life, classic cars. *Address:* Garden Court Chambers, 57–60 Lincoln's Inn Fields, WC2A 3LS. *T:* (020) 7993 7600, *Fax:* (020) 7993 7700.

PEDERSEN, Prof. (Knud) George, OC 1993; OOnt 1994; OBC 2002; PhD; FCCT; FRSA; Professor, The University of Western Ontario, 1985–96 (President and Vice-Chancellor, 1985–94); Chancellor, University of Northern British Columbia, 1998–2004; *b* 13 June 1931; *s* of Hjalmar Nielsen Pedersen and Anna (*née* Jensen); *m* 1st, 1953, Joan Elaine Vanderwarker (*d* 1988); one *s* one *d;* 2nd, 1988, Penny Ann Jones. *Educ:* Vancouver Normal Sch. (Dip. in Teaching 1952); Univ. of BC (BA History and Geography, 1959); Univ. of Washington (MA 1964); Univ. of Chicago (PhD 1969). FCCT 1977; FRSA 1983. Schools in North Vancouver: Teacher, Highlands Elem. Sch., 1952–56; Vice-Principal, North Star Elem. Sch., 1956–59; Principal, Carisbrooke Elem. Sch., 1959–61; Vice-Principal, Handsworth Sec. Sch., 1961–63; Principal, Balmoral Sec. Sch., 1963–65; Univ. of Chicago: Teaching Intern, 1966; Staff Associate, Midwest Admin Center, 1965–66, Res. Associate (Asst Prof.), 1966–68; Asst Prof., Ontario Inst. for Studies in Educn and Univ. of Toronto, 1968–70; Asst Prof. and Associate Dir, Midwest Admin Center, Div. of Social Sciences, Univ. of Chicago, 1970–72; Faculty of Educn, Univ. of Victoria: Associate Prof., 1972–75; Dean, 1972–75; Vice-Pres. (Academic), and Prof., Univ. of Victoria, 1975–79; President and Professor: Simon Fraser Univ., 1979–83; Univ. of British Columbia, 1983–85; Interim Pres., Univ. of Northern BC, 1995; Pres., Royal Roads Univ., 1995–96. Universities Council of British Columbia: Mem., Prog. Co-ordinating Cttee, 1975–78; Mem., Business Affairs Cttee, 1975–78; Mem., Long-range Planning Cttee, 1979–85; Mem. Council, Ontario Univ., 1985–94 (Chm.). Chm., Adv. Cttee on Educnl Planning, Min. of Educn (Prov. of BC), 1977–78; Member: Jt Bd of Teacher Educn, Prov. of BC, 1972–75; BC Council for Leadership in Educn, 1973–80; Interior Univ. Progs Bd, Min. of Educn, 1977–78. Member,

Board of Directors: Assoc. of Univs and Colls of Canada, 1979–84 (Mem., Adv. Cttee, Office of Internat. Develt, 1979–83; Chm., 1989–91); Public Employers' Council of BC, 1979–84; Vancouver Bd of Trade, 1983–85; Pulp and Paper Res. Inst. of Canada, 1983–85; Corporate and Higher Educn Forum, 1988–94; President: N Vancouver Teachers' Assoc., 1962–63; N Vancouver Principals' and Vice-Principals' Assoc., 1963–64; Vice-Pres., Inter-American Orgn for Higher Educn, 1991–93 (Mem. Bd of Dirs, 1979–85; Vice-Pres., N America, 1985–89); Sec.-Treasurer, Canadian Assoc. of Deans and Directors of Educn, 1972–73 and 1973–74; Mem., Exec. Bd, ACU, 1991–94. Member: BoT, Vancouver, 1983–85; Nat. Council, Canadian Human Rights Foundn, 1984–94. Mem., Bd of Dirs, MacMillan Bloedel Ltd, 1984–86. Member, Board of Governors: Arts, Sciences and Technol. Centre, 1980–85; Leon and Thea Koerner Foundn, 1981–85; Member: Bd of Trustees, Discovery Foundn, 1980–85; Bd, Bill Reid Foundn, 2000–07 (Pres., 2000–02). Consultant, Salzburg Seminar, Austria, 1987–99. Hon. LLD: McMaster, 1996; Simon Fraser 2003; Northern BC, 2005; Hon. DLitt: Emily Carr Inst. of Art and Design, 2003; Fraser Valley Univ. Coll., 2007. Confedn of Canada 125th Anniversary Medal 1992; Golden Jubilee Medal, 2003; Diamond Jubilee Medal, 2012. *Publications:* The Itinerant Schoolmaster: a socio-economic analysis of teacher turnover, 1973; chapters in books on educn; articles in Administrator's Notebook (Univ. of Chicago), selected articles for Elem. Sch. Principals, Res. in Educn, Educn and Urban Soc., Educn Canada, Teacher Educn, Resources in Educn, Elem. Sch. Jl, Jl of Educnl Admin, Canadian Jl of Univ. Continuing Educn, and Book of the States; book reviews; proc. of confs and symposia; governmental and institutional studies and reports. *Address:* 2232 Spruce Street, Vancouver, BC V6H 2P3, Canada. *T:* (604) 7332400. *E:* pgpedersen@telus.net. *Club:* University Golf (Vancouver).

PEDERSEN, Prof. Roger Arnold, PhD; FRSB; Professor of Regenerative Medicine, 2002–11, now Emeritus, and Director of Research, Laboratory for Regenerative Medicine and Department of Surgery, School of Clinical Medicine, 2011, University of Cambridge; *b* 1 Aug. 1944; *s* of Viggo Bernhardt Pedersen and Emily Anita Pedersen. *Educ:* Stanford Univ. (AB with Dist. 1965); Yale Univ. (PhD 1970). FRSB (FSB 2011). Postdoctoral Fellow, Johns Hopkins Univ., 1970–71; University of California, San Francisco: Asst Prof., 1971–79; Associate Prof., 1980–84; Prof., 1985–2001; University of Cambridge, 2001–: Dir, Anne McLaren Lab. for Regenerative Medicine, 2008–11. Mem., Internat. Soc. for Stem Cell Res. *Publications:* (ed jtly) Experimental Approaches to Mammalian Embryonic Development, 1986; (ed jtly) Animal Applications of Research in Mammalian Development, 1991; (ed jtly) Current Topics in Developmental Biology, Vols 30–48, 1995–2000; (ed jtly) Handbook of Stem Cells, Vol. 1, Embryonic Stem Cells, 2004; (ed jtly) Human Embryonic Stem Cells, 2005; (ed jtly) Essentials of Stem Cell Biology, 2006; over 100 peer-reviewed articles in scientific jls, 1971–. *Recreations:* violin playing and making, flying (single engine airplanes). *Address:* Anne McLaren Laboratory for Regenerative Medicine, Wellcome Trust/MRC Cambridge Stem Cell Institute, West Forvie Building, Forvie Site, Robinson Way, Cambridge CB2 0SZ. *T:* (01223) 763236. *E:* roger@stemcells.cam.ac.uk.

PEDLEY, Rt Rev. (Geoffrey) Stephen; Bishop Suffragan of Lancaster, 1998–2005; an Honorary Assistant Bishop, Diocese of Newcastle, since 2005; *b* 13 Sept. 1940; *s* of Geoffrey Heber Knight and Muriel Pedley; *m* 1970, Mary Frances Macdonald; two *s* one *d*. *Educ:* Marlborough College; Queens' College, Cambridge (MA); Cuddesdon Theological College. Curate: Liverpool Parish Church, 1966; Holy Trinity, Coventry, 1969; Rector of Kitwe, Zambia, 1971–77; Vicar of St Peter's, Stockton, 1977–88; Rector, Whickham, 1988–93; Residentiary Canon, Durham Cathedral, 1993–98. Chaplain to the Queen, 1984–98. *Recreations:* architecture, English literature, travel. *Address:* The Blue House, Newbrough, Northumberland NE47 5AN.

PEDLEY, Prof. Timothy John, PhD, ScD; FRS 1995; G. I. Taylor Professor of Fluid Mechanics, 1996–2009, now Emeritus, and Head of Department of Applied Mathematics and Theoretical Physics, 2000–05, University of Cambridge; Fellow of Gonville and Caius College, Cambridge, 1973–89 and since 1996; *b* 23 March 1942; *s* of Richard Rodman Pedley and Jean Mary Mudie Pedley (*née* Evans); *m* 1965, Avril Jennifer Martin Uden; two *s*. *Educ:* Rugby Sch.; Trinity Coll., Cambridge (BA 1963; MA, PhD 1967; ScD 1982). Post-doctoral Fellow, Johns Hopkins Univ., 1966–68; Res. Associate, then Lectr, Physiol. Flow Studies Unit and Dept of Maths, Imperial Coll. London, 1968–73; Department of Applied Mathematics and Theoretical Physics, University of Cambridge: Asst Dir of Res., 1973–77; Lectr, 1977–89; Reader in Biolog. Fluid Dynamics, 1989; Prof. of Applied Maths, Univ. of Leeds, 1990–96. EPSRC Sen. Res. Fellow, 1995–2000. Chairman: Math. Scis Section, BAAS, 1996–97; World Council for Biomechanics, 2002–06; RAE Applied Maths sub-panel 2007, 2005–08; President: IMA, 2004–05; Cambridge Philosophical Soc., 2006–07; IUTAM, 2008–12; Member, Council: EPSRC, 2009–13; Royal Soc., 2012–14; Mem., Royal Soc./RAEng Adv. Cttee for NPL, 2012–14. Lectures: G. I. Taylor, Univ. of Cambridge, 1998; Clifford, Tulane Univ., 2003; Rutherford Meml, NZ, 2003; Talbot, Univ. of Illinois, 2004; Ludwig Prandtl Meml, Zurich, 2007; Ascher H. Shapiro, MIT, 2010. MAE 2011. Foreign Associate, US NAE, 1999; Fellow: Amer. Inst. of Med. and Biol Engrg, 2001; Amer. Phys. Soc., 2005; Foreign Fellow, Nat. Acad. of Sci., India, 2007. Editor, Jl of Fluid Mechanics, 2000–06. Hon. DSc Imperial Coll. London, 2013. Adams Prize, Faculty of Maths, Cambridge Univ., 1977. Gold Medal, IMA, 2008. *Publications:* (ed) Scale Effects in Animal Locomotion, 1977; (jtly) The Mechanics of the Circulation, 1978; The Fluid Mechanics of Large Blood Vessels, 1980; (ed with C. P. Ellington) Biological Fluid Dynamics, 1995; (ed with P. W. Carpenter) Flow in collapsible tubes and past other highly compliant boundaries, 2003; numerous articles in fluid mechanics and biomechanics jls. *Recreations:* bird-watching, running, reading, crosswords. *Address:* Oakhurst Farm, 375 Shadwell Lane, Leeds LS17 8AH; Department of Applied Mathematics and Theoretical Physics, Centre for Mathematical Sciences, Wilberforce Road, Cambridge CB3 0WA. *T:* (01223) 339842.

PEEBLES, Iain Alexander Scott; *see* Bannatyne, Hon. Lord.

PEEBLES, Prof. Phillip James Edwin, FRS 1982; Professor of Physics, 1965, and Albert Einstein Professor of Science, 1984, Princeton University, now Professor Emeritus; *b* Winnipeg, 25 April 1935; *s* of Andrew Charles Peebles and Ada Marian (*née* Green); *m* 1958, Jean Alison Peebles; three *d*. *Educ:* Univ. of Manitoba (BSc 1958); Princeton Univ. (MA 1959; PhD 1962). Member: Amer. Phys. Soc.; Amer. Astron. Soc.; AAAS; Internat. Astron. Union; Fellow: Amer. Physical Soc.; Amer. Acad. of Arts and Scis; Royal Soc. of Canada. Hon. DSc: Univ. of Toronto, 1986; Univ. of Chicago, 1986; McMaster Univ., 1989; Univ. of Manitoba, 1989. *Publications:* Physical Cosmology, 1971; The Large Scale Structure of the Universe, 1979; (ed jtly) Objects of High Redshift, 1980; Quantum Mechanics, 1992; Principles of Physical Cosmology, 1993. *Address:* 24 Markham Road, Princeton, NJ 08540, USA; Joseph Henry Laboratory, Princeton University, Princeton, NJ 08544, USA.

PEEK, Bruno Mark, LVO 2012 (MVO 2002); OBE 2000; Pageantmaster, organiser and co-ordinator, national and international events, since 1981; Chairman, Beacon Millennium Ltd; *b* 12 Sept. 1951; adopted *s* of George and Mildred Peek; one *d*; *m* 1st (marr. diss.); 2nd (marr. diss. 1999); one step *d*. *Educ:* Alderman Leach Secondary Sch., Gorleston, Great Yarmouth. Event organiser and consultant, English Tourist Bd (Mem., England Entertains Exec. Cttee, 1984); Develt Dir, Sparks Creative Services, 1989–92. Major nat. and internat. events include: Operation Sea Fire (chain of beacon fires), 1981; Great Armada Pageant, 1987–88; Fire over England (beacon signal fires), 1988; Beacon Europe (beacon signal fires), 1992; 50th Anniv. Celebrations, VE Day, 1995; Great British Poppy Chain for 75th Anniv. of RBL, 1996; Beacon Millennium, Millennium Flame, 1999–2000; Nelson Returns to England for Great Yarmouth Pageant, 2000; Golden Jubilee Summer Party, Golden Jubilee Summer Party Torch Relay, Golden Jubilee Dinner, 2002; Nelson's Farewell to Norfolk, Royal Norfolk Show, 2005; VC and GC Dinner for 60th Anniv. Celebrations, end of World War II, 2005; Trafalgar Weekend, 2005; Rededication of Nelson's Monument, Great Yarmouth, 2007; Grand Tour of 50 English cities of the Loving Cup of England, 2007; Nat. St George's Day Banquet, Banqueting House, Whitehall, 2007; Service of Commemoration of Falkland Islands conflict and Heroes' Dinner, Old Royal Naval Coll., Greenwich, 2007; Celebration Dinner and Ball, Diamond Wedding Anniversary of the Queen and Duke of Edinburgh, 2007; official visit of Loving Cup of England to Malta, 2008; St George's Day Reception, Westminster Hall, 2008; Millennium Flame handover to Variety Club GB, 2008; Queen's Birthday Dinner, 2009; Trafalgar Night Dinner, 2009; Royal Wedding Dinner, 2011; Great Poppy Party Weekend (England, Wales and NI) for 90th Anniv. of RBL, 2011; Queen's Diamond Jubilee Beacons, 2012; Olympic Games Dinner at Ritz Hotel, London, 2012; Fly a Flag for the Commonwealth, 2014–15. Coordinator: Enjoy England Celebrate St George's Day campaign, 2008; Fly the Flag, 2008; Fly a Flag for Our Armed Forces, 2009. Trustee, 1998–, and Internat. Co-ordinator, 2000–, Covenant Home Ministries (Kisumu) Kenya. Freedom of the City of London, 1989. Order of Polonia Restituta, 1988. *Recreations:* walking, gardening. *Address:* Pageantmasters House, 110 Lowestoft Road, Gorleston-on-Sea, Great Yarmouth, Norfolk NR31 6NB. *T:* 07737 262913.

PEEK, Sir Richard Grenville, 6th Bt *cr* 1874, of Rousdon, Devon; *b* 3 Feb. 1955; *s* of Sir William Grenville Peek, 5th Bt and of Lucy Jane Peek (*née* Dorrien-Smith); *S* father, 2004; *m* 1983, Melanie Jane Waterson; three *s*. *Educ:* Eton. *Heir: s* Timothy Grenville Peek, *b* 21 Nov. 1989.

PEEL, family name of **Earl Peel**.

PEEL, 3rd Earl *cr* 1929; **William James Robert Peel,** GCVO 2006; PC 2006; DL; Bt 1800; Viscount Peel, 1895; Viscount Clanfield, 1929; Lord Chamberlain of HM Household, since 2006; *b* 3 Oct. 1947; *s* of 2nd Earl Peel and Kathleen (*d* 1972), *d* of Michael McGrath; *S* father, 1969; *m* 1st, 1973, Veronica Naomi Livingston (marr. diss. 1987), *d* of Alastair Timpson; one *s* one *d*; 2nd, 1989, Hon. Mrs Charlotte Hambro, *yr d* of Baron Soames, PC, GCMG, GCVO, CH, CBE and Lady Soames, LG, DBE; one *d*. *Educ:* Ampleforth; University of Tours; Cirencester Agric. Coll. Duchy of Cornwall: Mem., Prince's Council, 1993–96; Lord Warden of the Stannaries and Keeper of the Privy Seal, 1994–2006. Mem., Nature Conservancy Council for England, then English Nature, 1991–96; Chm., 1994–2000, Pres., 2000–08, Game and Wildlife Conservation Trust (formerly Game Conservancy Trust); former Mem. Cttee, Yorkshire Dales Nat. Park. President: Yorks Wildlife Trust, 1989–96; Gun Trade Assoc., 1993–99; Chm., Standing Conf. on Country Sports, 2001–06. Elected Mem., H of L, 1999–; Mem., Sub-Cttee D, H of L Select Cttee on EU (Envmt and Agric.), 2004–. DL N Yorks, 1998. *Heir: s* Viscount Clanfield, *qv*. *Address:* Eelmire, Masham, Ripon, N Yorks HG4 4PF.

PEEL, Catherine Anne; *see* Mackintosh, C. A.

PEEL, David Alexander Robert; Inquiry Manager (formerly Reference Secretary, then Inquiry Secretary), Competition (formerly Monopolies and Mergers) Commission, 1996–2011; *b* 12 Nov. 1940; *s* of late Maj. Robert Edmund Peel and Sheila Mary (*née* Slattery); *m* 1971, Patricia Muriel Essery; two *s*. *Educ:* St Edmund's Coll., Ware; University Coll., Oxford. Building labourer, New Scotland Yard develt, 1963; joined MoT, 1964; Private Sec. to Minister of State, 1967; Principal, 1968; DoE, 1970; First Sec., UK Perm. Repn to EC, Brussels, 1972; Private Sec. to Minister for Transport, 1975; Asst Sec., Depts of Transport and the Environment, 1976–90: Nat. Roads Prog. and Highway Policy, 1982; Okehampton Bypass (Confirmation of Orders) Act, 1985; Interdeptl Review on Using Private Enterprise in Govt, 1986; Office Services, 1987–90; Under Sec., Dir of Admin. Resources, DoE, 1990–96. *Recreations:* allotment gardening, ballet, baroque architecture.

PEEL, Prof. John David Yeadon, FBA 1991; Professor of Anthropology and Sociology, with reference to Africa, School of Oriental and African Studies, University of London, 1989–2007, now Professor Emeritus; *b* 13 Nov. 1941; *e s* of late Prof. Edwin Arthur Peel and Nora Kathleen Yeadon; *m* 1st, 1969, Jennifer Christine Ferial (marr. diss. 2000), *d* of K. N. Pare, Leicester; three *s*; 2nd, 2014, Anne Ogbigbo. *Educ:* King Edward's Sch., Birmingham; Balliol Coll., Oxford (Scholar; BA 1963, MA 1966); LSE (PhD 1966); DLit London 1985. Asst Lectr, then Lectr in Sociology, Nottingham Univ., 1965–70; Lectr in Sociology, LSE, 1970–73; Charles Booth Prof. of Sociology, 1975–89, Dean, Faculty of Social and Envmtl Studies, 1985–88, Univ. of Liverpool; Dean of Undergraduate Studies, SOAS, 1990–94. Vis. Reader in Sociology and Anthropology, Univ. of Ife, Nigeria, 1973–75; Vis. Prof. in Anthropology and Sociology, Univ. of Chicago, 1982–83; Marett Lectr, 1993, Associate, Inst. of Develt Studies, 1973–94. Pres., African Studies Assoc. of UK, 1996–98; Vice-Pres., British Acad., 1999–2000. Chm. Trustees, Internat. African Inst., 2006– (Editor, Africa, and Officer, 1979–86); Gen. Editor, Internat. African Library, 1986–. Frazer Lectr, Univ. of Oxford, 2000; Galton Lectr, 2003; Roy H. Rappaport Lectr, 2003; Birkbeck Lectr in Ecclesiastical History, Univ. of Cambridge, 2009; Winchester Lectr in World Religions, Univ. of Oxford, 2011. Hon. DLitt Birmingham, 2012. Amaury Talbot Prize, RAI, 1983, 2000; Herskovits Award, African Studies Assoc., USA, 1984, 2001. *Publications:* Aladura: a religious movement among the Yoruba, 1968; Herbert Spencer: the evolution of a sociologist, 1971; (ed) Herbert Spencer on Social Evolution, 1972; Ijeshas and Nigerians, 1983; Religious Encounter and the Making of the Yoruba, 2000; articles in anthropological, sociological and Africanist jls; *Festschrift:* Christianity and Social Change in Africa: essays in honour of J. D. Y. Peel, ed Toyin Falola, 2005. *Recreations:* gardening, fell-walking, French church architecture. *Address:* 80 Archway Road, N19 3TT. *T:* (020) 7272 9487.

PEEL, Robert Edmund Guy, FIH; Chairman, Peel Hotels plc, since 1998; *b* 13 March 1947; *s* of John and Joanna Peel. *Educ:* Eton Coll. FIH (FHCIMA 1985). Various hotel appts, Europe, 1964–66; Queen Anne's Hotels & Properties, then Trust Houses Ltd, later Trust House Forte plc, 1966–76; Dir, 1976–98, Chief Exec., 1977–97, Mount Charlotte Investments, later Thistle Hotels plc. Director: Brierley Investments Ltd, 1992–96; Ivory & Sime Discovery Trust, 1994–2005. Dir, London Tourist Bd, 1994–98. *Recreations:* deep sea fishing, marine biology, tennis, gardening. *Address:* (office) 19 Warwick Avenue, Maida Vale, W9 2PS. *Club:* White's.

PEEL, Robert Roger; QC 2010; a Recorder, since 2011; *b* Singapore, 29 Jan. 1966; *s* of Geoffrey Peel and Joan Peel; *m* 1993, Victoria Williams; two *s* one *d*. *Educ:* Eton Coll.; Brasenose Coll., Oxford (BA Mod. Langs); City Univ. (DipLaw). Called to the Bar, Middle Temple, 1990. *Recreations:* Real tennis, cricket, National Hunt. *Address:* 29 Bedford Row, WC1R 4HE. *Clubs:* MCC; Strollers Cricket; Holyport Real Tennis.

PEERS, Most Rev. Michael Geoffrey; Primate of the Anglican Church of Canada, 1986–2004; *b* 31 July 1934; *s* of Geoffrey Hugh Peers and Dorothy Enid Mantle; *m* 1963, Dorothy Elizabeth Bradley; two *s* one *d*. *Educ:* University of British Columbia (BA Hons); Universität Heidelberg (Zert. Dolm.-Interpreter's Certificate); Trinity Coll., Toronto (LTh). Deacon 1959, priest 1960; Curate: St Thomas', Ottawa, 1959–61; Trinity, Ottawa, 1961–65; University Chaplain, Diocese of Ottawa, 1961–66; Rector: St Bede's, Winnipeg, 1966–72; St Martin's, Winnipeg, with St Paul's Middlechurch, 1972–74; Archdeacon of Winnipeg, 1969–74; Rector, St Paul's Cathedral, Regina, 1974–77; Dean of Qu'Appelle, 1974–77; Bishop of Qu'Appelle, 1977–82; Archbishop of Qu'Appelle and Metropolitan of Rupert's Land, 1982–86. Ecumenist-in-Residence, Toronto Sch. of Theol., Univ. of Toronto, 2004–06. Sen. Res. Associate, Trinity Coll., Toronto, 2008–. Hon. DD: Trinity Coll.,

Toronto, 1978; St John's Coll., Winnipeg, 1981; Wycliffe Coll., Toronto, 1987; Univ. of Kent, 1988; Montreal Dio. Coll., 1989; Coll. of Emmanuel and St Chad, Saskatoon, 1990; Thorneloe Univ., 1991; Univ. of Huron Coll., 1998; Lutheran Theol Seminary, Saskatoon, 2001; Vancouver Sch. of Theol., 2003; Episcopal Divinity Sch., Cambridge, Mass, 2004; Gen. Theol Seminary, NY, 2007; Hon. DCL Bishop's Univ., Lennoxville, 1993. *Publications:* Grace Notes: journeying with the Primate 1995–2004, 2005; The Anglican Episcopate in Canada, vol. 4, 2009.

PEET, Ronald Hugh, CBE 1974; Chief Executive, Legal & General Group plc, 1972–84; *b* 12 July 1925; *s* of Henry Leonard and Stella Peet; *m* 1st, 1949, Winifred Joy Adamson (*d* 1979); two *s* two *d*; 2nd, 1981, Lynette Judy Burgess Kinsella. *Educ:* Doncaster Grammar Sch.; Queen's Coll., Oxford (MA). Served in HM Forces, Captain RA, 1944–47. Legal and General Assurance Society Limited: joined 1952; emigrated to Australia, 1955; Sec., Australian Branch, 1955–59; Asst Life Manager, 1959–65; Manager and Actuary for Australia, 1965–69; returned to UK as General Manager (Ops), 1969; Dir, 1969–84; Chm., 1980–84. Chairman: Aviation & General Insurance Co. Ltd, 1978–80; Stockley Plc, 1984–87; PWS Holdings plc, 1987–88; Director: AMEC Plc, 1984–96; Howard Gp plc, 1985–86; Independent Insurance Group plc, 1988–99. Director: City Arts Trust Ltd, 1976–90 (Chm., 1980–87); Royal Philharmonic Orchestra Ltd, 1977–88; English National Opera, 1978–84, 1985–95. Chm., British Insurance Assoc., 1978–79. FIA. *Recreations:* music, opera. *Address:* 9 Marlowe Court, Petyward, SW3 3PD. *Clubs:* Hurlingham, City of London.

PEET, Sara Elizabeth; *see* Staite, S. E.

PEGDEN, Jeffrey Vincent; QC 1996; **His Honour Judge Pegden;** a Circuit Judge, since 2007; a Circuit Judge, Court of Appeal Criminal Division, since 2015; *b* 24 June 1950; *s* of late George Vincent Pegden and Stella Blanche Kathleen Pegden; *m* 1981, Delia Mary Coonan; one *s* one *d. Educ:* Univ. of Hull (LLB Hons 1972). Called to the Bar, Inner Temple, 1973, Bencher, 2002; a Recorder, 1996–2007. Mem., Crown Court Rules Cttee, 2001–07. Judicial Coll. Course Dir, Criminal Seminars, 2010–. FRSA. *Recreations:* reading, music, gardening, walking, films, theatre, travel.

PEGGIE, Robert Galloway Emslie, CBE 1986; Commissioner for Local Administration (Ombudsman) in Scotland, 1986–94; Chairman, Scottish Local Government Staff Commission, 1994–97; *b* 5 Jan. 1929; *s* of John and Euphemia Peggie; *m* 1st, 1955, Christine Jeanette Simpson (*d* 2000); one *s* one *d*; 2nd, 2001, Janice Helen Renton. *Educ:* Lasswade High Sch. Certified accountant; Accountancy apprenticeship, 1946–52; Accountant in industry, 1952–57; Public Service, Edinburgh City, 1957–74; Chief Exec., Lothian Regl Council, 1974–86. Trustee, Lloyds TSB Foundn, 1995–98. Mem., Gen. Convocation and Court, Heriot-Watt Univ., 1988–97 (Convener, Finance Cttee, 1989–97); Governor, Edinburgh Coll. of Art, 1989–99 (Vice-Chm., 1995–97; Chm., 1998–99). DUniv Heriot-Watt, 1998. *Recreation:* golf. *Address:* 9A Napier Road, Edinburgh EH10 5AZ. *T:* (0131) 229 6775.

PEI, Ieoh Ming, FAIA, RIBA; architect; Founding Partner, Pei Cobb Freed & Partners (formerly I. M. Pei & Partners), Architects, New York, 1955–96; *b* Canton, China, 26 April 1917; naturalized citizen of USA, 1954; *m* 1942, Eileen Loo (*d* 2014); three *s* one *d. Educ:* St John's Middle Sch., Shanghai; MIT (BArch 1940); Harvard Grad. Sch. of Design (MArch 1946). FAIA 1964. Nat. Defense Res. Cttee, 1943–45; Asst Prof., Harvard Grad. Sch. of Design, 1945–48; Dir Architecture, Webb & Knapp Inc., 1948–55; Wheelwright Travelling Fellow, Harvard, 1951. Designed Nat. Center for Atmospheric Res., Boulder, Colo, 1961–67; other projects include: John F. Kennedy Library, Boston, 1965–79; E Building, Nat. Gall. of Art, Washington, 1968–78; Morton H. Myerson Symphony Center, Dallas, 1982–89; Four Seasons Hotel, NY, 1989–93; Rock and Roll Hall of Fame and Mus., Cleveland, 1990–95; also church, hosp., municipal and corporate bldgs, schs, libraries and museums in US; numerous projects worldwide include: Fragrant Hill Hotel, Beijing, 1979–82; Bank of China, Hong Kong, 1982–89, Head Office, Beijing, 1994–2001; expansion and renovation, The Louvre, Paris, 1983–93; Mus. of Modern Art, Luxembourg, 1995–2006; Mus. of Islamic Art, Qatar, 2000–08; Suzhou Mus., China, 2006. Member: Nat. Council on Humanities, 1966–70; Urban Design Council, NYC, 1967–72; AIA Nat. Urban Policy Task Force, 1970–74; Nat. Council on Arts, 1981–84. Member: Nat. Acad. Design, 1965; Amer. Acad. Arts and Scis, 1967; AAIL, 1975 (Chancellor, 1978–80); Institut de France, 1983. Hon. RA 1993. Hon. Degrees include: Pennsylvania, Columbia, NY, Brown, Colorado, Chinese Univ. of Hong Kong, Amer. Univ. of Paris. Numerous awards including: Arnold Brunner Award, Nat. Inst. Arts and Letters, 1961; Medal of Honour, NY Chapter, AIA, 1963; Thomas Jefferson Meml Medal for Architecture, 1976; Gold Medal, AAAL, 1979; Gold Medal, AIA, 1979; La Grande Médaille d'Or L'Académie d'Architecture, France, 1981; Architectural Firm Award, AIA, 1968; Praemium Imperiale, US, 1989; Ambassador for the Arts Award, 1994; Gold Medal, Architectural Soc. of China, Beijing, 1994; Jerusalem Prize for Arts and Letters, 1994; Jacqueline Kennedy Onassis Medal, Municipal Arts Soc., NY, 1996; Royal Gold Medal for Architecture, RIBA, 2010; Gold Medal, IUA, 2014. Medal of Liberty, US, 1986; Officier de La Légion d'Honneur, 1993; US Medal of Freedom, 1993.

PEIRCE, Rev. Canon (John) Martin; Canon Residentiary of Christ Church, Oxford, 1987–2001, now Canon Emeritus, and Oxford Diocesan Director of Ordinands, 1985–2001; *b* 9 July 1936; *s* of Martin Westley and Winifred Mary Peirce; *m* 1968, Rosemary Susan Milne; two *s. Educ:* Brentwood Sch.; Jesus Coll., Cambridge (MA); Westcott House, Cambridge. Served Royal Air Force, 1954–56. Teacher, St Stephen's Coll., Hong Kong, 1960–64; Curate, St John Baptist, Croydon, 1966–70; Team Vicar, St Columba, Fareham, 1970–76; Team Rector, Langley, Slough, 1976–85. *Recreations:* walking, gardening. *Address:* 8 Burwell Meadow, Witney, Oxon OX28 5JQ. *T:* (01993) 200103.

PEIRCE, Robert Nigel; HM Diplomatic Service, retired; Chairman, Britweek Inc., since 2007; Director, Beverly Hills Wealth Management, since 2010; Co-founder, Voice Technology Solutions, since 2014; *b* 18 March 1955; *s* of Kenneth Frank Peirce and Margaret Peirce. *Educ:* Taunton Sch.; St Catherine's Coll., Oxford (MA); Faculty of Oriental Studies, Univ. of Cambridge. Joined FCO, 1977; Hong Kong, 1979–80; Peking, 1980–83; FCO, 1983–85; Cabinet Office, 1985–86; Dep. Political Advr, Hong Kong, 1986–88; Private Sec. to Sec. of State for Foreign and Commonwealth Affairs, 1988–90; UK Mission to UN, 1990–93; Political Advr to Governor, Hong Kong, 1993–97; RCDS, 1998; Sec., Ind. Commn on Policing for NI, 1998–99; Counsellor, Washington, 1999–2004; Consul-Gen., Los Angeles, 2005–09. Senior Vice President: Abraxis Bioscience Inc., 2009–10; All About Advanced Health Proj., 2010–11; NantWorks LLC, 2011–12. Trustee, Education Develt Center, 2012–. *Recreations:* family, friends, speculation. *Address:* 223 S Plymouth Boulevard, Los Angeles, CA 90004, USA. *Club:* Hong Kong (Hong Kong).

PEIRIS, Prof. (Joseph Sriyal) Malik, DPhil; FRCPath; FRS 2006; Professor of Virology, Tam Wah-Ching Professor in Medical Science, and Director, School of Public Health, University of Hong Kong; Scientific Director, HKU-Pasteur Research Centre, since 2007; *b* Sri Lanka. *Educ:* Univ. of Ceylon (MB BS 1972); Univ. of Oxford (DPhil 1981). Dept of Microbiol., Univ. of Peradeniya, 1982–88; virologist, Royal Victoria Infirmary, Newcastle upon Tyne, 1988–95; Univ. of Hong Kong, 1995–; former Prof., Dept of Microbiol. Pres., Asia Pacific Soc. of Medical Virology. Chevalier, Légion d'Honneur (France), 2007. *Publications:* articles in jls and chapters in books. *Address:* School of Public Health, University of Hong Kong, 5–6/F Laboratory Block, 21 Sassoon Road, Hong Kong.

PEIRSE, Sir Henry Njerš de la Poer B.; *see* Beresford-Peirse.

PELHAM, family name of **Earls of Chichester** and **Yarborough**.

PELHAM, Clare Elizabeth; Chief Executive, Leonard Cheshire Disability, since 2010; *m* 1983, Prof. David Barr (marr. diss.); one *s* one *d. Educ:* London Sch. of Econs (BSc Econ). Home Office: Principal, 1987–93; Hd, Efficiency and Consultancy, 1993–95; Hd, Police Strategy, 1995–97; Customer Satisfaction Mgr, IBM, 1997–98; Dir of Corporate Affairs, HM Prison Service, 1998–2001; Dir, Cabinet Office, 2001–02; Dir, Coca-Cola Co., GB and Ire., 2002–03; Sen. Dir, Rev. of Immigration Enforcement, Home Office, 2004; Dir, DCA, 2004–06; Chief Exec., Judicial Appts Commn, 2006–10. Chm., Voluntary Organisations Disability Gp, 2013–. *Recreations:* cake, conversation, changing the world. *Address:* Leonard Cheshire Disability, 66 South Lambeth Road, SW8 1RL. *T:* (020) 3242 0202. *E:* clare.pelham@leonardcheshire.org.

PELHAM, Sir Hugh (Reginald Brentnall), Kt 2011; PhD; FRS 1988; Director, Medical Research Council Laboratory of Molecular Biology, Cambridge, since 2006 (Deputy Director, 1996–2006); *b* 26 Aug. 1954; *s* of late Reginald A. and Pauline M. Pelham; *m* 1st, 1976, Alison Slowe (marr. diss. 1989); 2nd, 1996, Mariann Bienz, *qv*; one *s* one *d. Educ:* Marlborough Coll., Wiltshire; Christ's Coll., Cambridge (MA, PhD). Research Fellow, Christ's Coll., 1978–84; Dept of Embryology, Carnegie Instn of Washington Baltimore, Md, 1979–81; Mem., Scientific Staff, MRC Lab. of Molecular Biol., Cambridge, 1981–, Hd, Cell Biol. Div., 1992–2006. Visitor, Univ. of Zürich, 1987–88. Mem., EMBO, 1985. Founder FMedSci 1998. Colworth Medal, Biochemical Soc., 1988; EMBO medal, 1989; Louis Jeantet Prize for Medicine, 1991; King Faisal Internat. Prize for Sci., 1996; Croonian Lecture and Medal, Royal Soc., 1999. *Publications:* papers in sci. jls on molecular and cell biology. *Address:* MRC Laboratory of Molecular Biology, Francis Crick Avenue, Cambridge Biomedical Campus, Cambridge CB2 0QH. *T:* (01223) 267000.

PELHAM, Mariann, (Lady Pelham); *see* Bienz, M.

PELHAM BURN, Angus Maitland; DL; Vice Lord-Lieutenant for Kincardineshire, 1978–2000; Director, Bank of Scotland, 1977–2000 (Director, 1973–2001, Chairman, 1977–2001, North Local Board); *b* 13 Dec. 1931; *s* of late Brig. Gen. H. Pelham Burn, CMG, DSO, and late Mrs K. E. S. Pelham Burn; *m* 1959, Anne R. Pelham Burn (*née* Forbes-Leith); four *d. Educ:* Harrow; N of Scotland Coll. of Agriculture. Hudson's Bay Co., 1951–58. Director: Aberdeen and Northern Marts Ltd, 1970–86 (Chm., 1974–86); Jessfield Ltd, 1970–88; Aberdeen Meat Marketing Co. Ltd, 1973–86 (Chm., 1974–86); Prime Space Design (Scotland) Ltd, 1981–87; Status Timber Systems, 1986–90; Skeendale Ltd, 1987–88; Abtrust Scotland Investment Co., 1989–96; Dana Petroleum plc, 1999–2008; Chairman and Director: MacRobert Farms (Douneside) Ltd, 1970–87; Pelett Administration Ltd, 1973–94; Taw Meat Co., 1984–86; Oilcats Ltd, 2006–07; Chairman: Aberdeen Asset Mgt (formerly Aberdeen Trust) plc, 1993–2000; Scottish Provident Instn, 1995–98 (Dir, 1975–98; Dep. Chm., 1991–95). Chm., Aberdeen Airport Consultative Cttee, 1986–2006; Mem., Accounts Commn, 1980–94 (Dep. Chm., 1992–94). Chm., Global Philanthropic Internat. Ltd, 2002–; Dir, Global Philanthropic Ops Pty Ltd, 2004–11. Mem. Council, Winston Churchill Meml Trust, 1984–93; Dir, Aberdeen Assoc. for Prevention of Cruelty to Animals, 1975–95 (Chm., 1984–89). Pres., Aberdeen Br., Inst. of Marketing, 1987–90. Member: Kincardine CC, 1967–75 (Vice Convener, 1973–75); Grampian Regional Council, 1974–94. Patron, Knockando Woolmill Trust, 2012–. Member, Queen's Body Guard for Scotland (Royal Co. of Archers), 1968–2010. Hon. FInstM. JP Kincardine and Deeside, 1984–2005; DL Kincardineshire 1978. LlD Robert Gordon Univ., 1996. CStJ 1995 (OStJ 1978). *Recreations:* photography esp. wildlife, vegetable gardening. *Address:* Kennels Cottage, Dess, Aboyne, Aberdeenshire AB34 5AY. *T:* (013398) 84445, *Fax:* (013398) 84430. *E:* snow.bunting2@gmail.com. *Clubs:* Sloane; Royal Northern (Aberdeen).

PELL, His Eminence Cardinal George, AC 2005; DD, DPhil; Prefect, Secretariat for the Economy, Vatican, since 2014; *b* 8 June 1941; *s* of G. A. and M. L. Pell. *Educ:* St Patrick's Coll., Vic; Corpus Christi Coll., Vic; Urban Univ., Rome (STB, STL); Campion Hall, Oxford Univ. (DPhil); Monash Univ. (MEd). FACE. Episcopal Vicar for Educn, Dio. of Ballarat, 1973–84; Principal, Inst. for Catholic Educn, 1981–84; Rector, Corpus Christi Coll., Clayton, 1985–87; Auxiliary Bishop, Archdio. of Melbourne, 1987–96; Archbishop of Melbourne, 1996–2001; Archbishop of Sydney, 2001–14. Cardinal, 2003. Nat. Chaplain, Order of St Lazarus, 2001–07; Grand Prior, NSW Lieutenancy of the Equestrian Order of the Holy Sepulchre of Jerusalem, 2001–14; Conventual Chaplain ad honorem, SMO Malta, 2007–. Member: Vatican Council for Justice and Peace, 1990–95, 2002–; Vatican Congregation for the Doctrine of the Faith, 1990–2000; Vatican Council, Synod of Bishops, 2001–08, 2012–; Presidential Cttee, Vatican Council for the Family, 2003–; Vatican Congregation for Divine Worship, 2005–; Vatican Supreme Cttee, Pontifical Missions Socs, 2005–; Vatican Council of Cardinals on Orgnl and Econ. Problems of the Holy See, 2007–14; Pontifical Council for Pastoral Assistance to Healthcare Workers, 2010, for Promoting the New Evangelisation, 2010; Vatican Congregation for Bishops, 2012–; Adv. Gp of Cardinals to Pope Francis, 2013–; Pres., Vatican *Vox Clara* Cttee, 2001–. Cardinal Elector in Papal Conclave, 2005 and 2013. Chm., Australian Catholic Relief, 1989–97; Mem., Gov. Cttee, Internat. Catholic Migration Commn, 2008–14. Foundn Pres., John Paul II Institute for Marriage and the Family, Melbourne, 2000–01. Foundn Pro-Chancellor, Australian Catholic Univ., 1990–95 (Pres., 1996–2014). Apostolic Visitor, Seminaries of NZ, 1994, PNG, and Solomon Is, 1995, Pacific, 1996, Irian Jaya, and Sulawesi, 1998. Hon. Fellow, St Edmund's Coll., Cambridge, 2003. LHD *hc* Christendom Coll., Va, 2006; Hon. DLaws: Notre Dame, Australia, 2010; Australian Catholic Univ., 2014. Honour of the Pallium, Rome, 1997, 2001; GCLJ 1998; KGCHS 2002; Bailiff Grand Cross: of Honour and Devotion, SMO Malta, 2008; of Justice, Sacred Mil. Constantinian Order of St George, 2009. *Publications:* The Sisters of St Joseph in Swan Hill 1922–72, 1972; Catholicism in Australia, 1988; Rerum Novarum: one hundred years later, 1992; Issues of Faith and Morals, 1996; Catholicism and the Architecture of Freedom, 1999; Be Not Afraid, 2004; God and Caesar, 2007; Freedom for All: negotiating freedom in a world of individuals, 2009; Test Everything: hold fast to what is good, 2010; One Christian Perspective on Climate Change, 2011; Contemplating Christ with Luke, 2012. *Address:* Secretariat for the Economy, Vatican City State. *Clubs:* Melbourne, Australian (Sydney); Richmond Football (Vic).

PELLEW, family name of **Viscount Exmouth**.

PELLEW, Dr Jill Hosford; Senior Research Fellow, Institute of Historical Research, University of London, since 2009; *b* 29 April 1942; *d* of late Prof. Frank Thistlethwaite, CBE and Jane (*née* Hosford); *m* 1965, Mark Edward Pellew, *qv*; two *s. Educ:* Cambs High Sch. for Girls; St Hilda's Coll., Oxford (BA 1964; MA 1968); Queen Mary Coll., London (MA 1970); PhD London 1976. MoD, 1964–66; part-time univ. teaching, Univ. of Saigon, Univ. of Sussex, Hollins Coll., Va, American Univ., Washington, DC, 1967–89; Exec. Sec., Chatham Hse Foundn, Washington, DC, 1984–89; Develt Officer, St Hilda's Coll., Oxford, 1989–90; Dir of Develt, Imperial Coll. of Science, Technology and Medicine, London, 1991–94; Dir, Develt Office, Univ. of Oxford, 1994–99; Fellow, Trinity Coll., Oxford, 1995–99; Vice-Pres., Grenzebach Glier Europe, 2000–07. Mem., Council, British Sch. at Rome, 2003–09; Trustee: Council for Advancement and Support of Educn (Europe), 1996–99; Estorick Foundn, 1999–2009; Schola Cantorum of Oxford, 2003–; Inst. of Historical Res., Univ. of London, 2005– (Mem., Adv. Council, 2005–12); Victoria Co. History of Oxon, 2005–; Young Classical Artists Trust, 2012–. FRHistS 2015. *Publications:* The Home Office 1848–1914: from clerks to bureaucrats, 1982; (ed with S. Cassese) The Comparative History of Public Administration: the merit system, 1987; (ed with D. Cannadine) History and

Philanthropy: past, present, future, 2008; articles in learned jls on admin. hist. and hist. of universities and philanthropy. *Recreations:* reading, listening to music, entertaining family and friends. *Address:* 51 St George's Square, SW1V 3QN. *Club:* Reform.

PELLEW, Mark Edward, CVO 2000 (LVO 1980); HM Diplomatic Service, retired; Chief Executive to the Secretary General, Anglican Communion, 2002–05; *b* 28 Aug. 1942; *e s* of late Comdr Anthony Pownoll Pellew, RN retd, and Margaret Julia Critchley (*née* Cookson); *m* 1965, Jill Hosford Thistlethwaite (*see* J. H. Pellew); two *s*. *Educ:* Winchester; Trinity Coll., Oxford (BA). Entered HM Diplomatic Service, 1965; FO, 1965–67; Third Sec., Singapore, 1967–69; Second Sec., Saigon, 1969–70; FCO, 1970–76; First Sec., Rome, 1976–80; Asst Head of Personnel Ops Dept, FCO, 1981–83; Counsellor: Washington, 1983–89; on secondment to Hambros Bank, 1989–91; Head of N America Dept, FCO, 1991–96; Ambassador to the Holy See, 1998–2002. Chairman: Hosting for Overseas Students, 2005–; Friends of Diocese in Europe, 2010–. *Recreations:* singing, playing the horn. *Address:* 51 St George's Square, SW1V 3QN. *Club:* Hurlingham.
See also R. A. Pellew.

PELLEW, Robin Anthony, OBE 2006; PhD; Chief Executive, National Trust for Scotland, 2001–07; *b* 27 Sept. 1945; *s* of late Comdr Anthony Pownoll Pellew, RN and Margaret Julia Critchley (*née* Cookson); *m* 1974, Pamela Daphne Gibson MacLellan; one *s* one *d*. *Educ:* Marlborough Coll.; Edinburgh Univ. (BSc 1968); University College London (MSc 1972; PhD 1981). Sen. Res. Scientist, Serengeti Res. Inst., Tanzania, 1973–78; BBC Natural History Unit, 1978–79; Res. Fellow, Physiology Lab., Cambridge, 1979–82; Cambridge University Press: Sen. Editor, 1982–86; Editorial Manager, 1986–87; Dir, Conservation Monitoring Centre, IUCN, 1987–88; Dir, World Conservation Monitoring Centre, Cambridge, 1988–93; Dir and Chief Exec., WWF-World Wide Fund for Nature, 1994–99; Chief Exec., Animal Health Trust, 1999–2001. Non-exec. Dir, Nat. Forest Co., 2007–14. Member: Envmt Cttee, RSA, 1993–98; UK Round Table on Sustainable Develt, 1995–99; Conservation and Science Cttee, 1997–2001, Inst. of Zool. Cttee, 1997–2001, Zool. Soc. of London. Chm., Cambridge Past, Present & Future, 2008–. *Publications:* numerous scientific papers on wild life management and conservation in professional jls. *Recreations:* travel, watching wild life. *Address:* 32 Selwyn Gardens, Cambridge CB3 9AY.
See also M. E. Pellew.

PELLING, Andrew John; Contributing Editor, insidecroydon.com, since 2011; Member (Lab), Croydon Borough Council, since 2014; *b* 1959; *s* of Anthony Adair Pelling, *qv*; *m* Sanae (marr. diss.); one *s* two *d*; *m* 2006, Lucy (marr. diss.); one *d*. *Educ:* Trinity Sch., Croydon; New Coll., Oxford (MA PPE; Sec. and Librarian, Oxford Union Soc., 1979–80; Pres., Cons. Assoc., 1980). Head of Debt Syndicate: Samuel Montagu & Co. Ltd, 1981–82; Nikko Europe, 1982–84; Citicorp, 1984–86; Namura Internat. plc, 1986–94; NatWest Markets, 1994–97; Hd of Debt Capital Markets, UFJ Internat. plc, 1997–2005; Hd of Origination, Tokai Tokyo Securities Europe Ltd, 2007–12. Croydon Borough Council: Mem. (C), 1982–2006; Chm., Educn, 1988–94; Dep. Opposition Leader, 1996–2002, Opposition Leader, 2002–05, Cons. Gp. Greater London Authority: Mem. (C) Croydon and Sutton, London Assembly, 2000–08; Cons. spokesman on London business, 2000–04; Bd Mem., LDA, 2000–04 (Chm., Audit Panel, 2001–04); Mem., Private Investment Commn, 2002–04; London Assembly: Chairman: Graffiti Investigative Cttee, 2001–02; Public Services Cttee, 2002–04; Budget Cttee, 2004–05, 2007; Audit Panel, 2004–07. MP Croydon Central, 2005–10 (C, 2005–07, Ind, 2007–10); contested (Ind) same seat, 2010. Member: Croydon Police Consultative Cttee, 2000–10; LSC, London S, 2001–04; Educn Select Cttee, 2006–08; Children, Schools and Families Select Cttee, 2008–10. Chm., London Road Safety Panel Exec., 2015–. Mem., CATE, 1990–94. Mem., S Wandle Valley Partnership, 2001–05. Presenter, Croydon Radio, 2012–14. Dir, Croydon Carers Centre, 2008–11; Vice Chm., Croydon FC, 2011–13. Treas., Croydon Co-op. Party, 2013–. *E:* puttingcroydonfirst@gmail.com.

PELLING, Anthony Adair; Lecturer, Osher Institute, University of Richmond, since 2015; *b* 3 May 1934; *s* of Brian and Alice Pelling; *m* 1st, 1958, Margaret Lightfoot (*d* 1986); one *s* one *d*; 2nd, 1989, Virginia Glen-Calvert. *Educ:* Purley Grammar Sch.; London Sch. of Economics (BSc (Econ); Gen. Sec., Students' Union); Wolverhampton Coll. of Technol. MIPM. Nat. Service, RAOC, Sgt, 1955–57. National Coal Board, 1957–67; entered MPBW as Principal, 1967; Asst Sec., 1970, Under Sec., 1981, DoE; seconded as Dep. Dir, Business in the Community, 1981–83; Dept of Transport, 1983–85; Dir, Construction Industry, and Dir, Sports and Recreation Div., DoE, 1985–87; London Regional Dir, DoE, 1987–91; Dir, Construction Policy, DoE, 1991–93. Dir, GJW Government Relations Ltd, London and Washington, 1993–95. President: ESU, Richmond, 1998–2000; Byrd Theatre Foundn, Richmond, 2002–08; Chm., Region IV, and Mem. Nat. Bd, US ESU, 2000–02, 2007–09; Mem. Bd, Guardian Foundn, United Methodist Family Services, VA, 2006–08. *Recreations:* theatre, Torch Club. *Address:* 70 West Square Drive, Richmond, VA 23238–6158, USA. *E:* gjw1995pel@aol.com. *Clubs:* Reform; Kiwanis (Richmond, VA) (Mem. Bd, 2014–).
See also A. J. Pelling.

PELLING, Prof. Christopher Brendan Reginald, DPhil; FBA 2009; FLSW; Regius Professor of Greek, University of Oxford, 2003–15, now Emeritus; Student of Christ Church, Oxford, 2003–15; *b* 14 Dec. 1947; *s* of Reginald Charles Pelling and (Frances Lilian) Brenda Pelling; *m* 1973, Margaret Ann Giddy; one *s* one *d* (and one *s* decd). *Educ:* Balliol Coll., Oxford (BA 1970); Christ Church, Oxford (DPhil 1975). Res. Fellow, Peterhouse, Cambridge, 1972–74; Lectr, 1974–75, McConnell Laing Fellow and Praelector in Classics, 1975–2003, University Coll., Oxford. Adjunct Prof. of Hist., Utah State Univ., 1998–; Visiting Professor: Washington and Lee Univ., Lexington, Va, 1986, 1989, 1997, 2000; Univ. of N Carolina, Chapel Hill, 2002. FLSW 2011. Hon. Fellow, University Coll., Oxford, 2012. *Publications:* Plutarch: life of Antony, 1988; (ed) Characterization and Individuality in Greek Literature, 1990; (ed) Greek Tragedy and the Historian, 1997; Literary Texts and the Greek Historian, 2000; Plutarch and History, 2002; Rome in Crisis, 2010; Plutarch: life of Caesar, 2011; (with Maria Wyke) Twelve Voices from Greece and Rome: ancient ideas for modern times, 2014; articles in learned jls. *Recreations:* cricket, golf, music, conviviality. *Address:* Christ Church, Oxford OX1 1DP. *T:* (01865) 276204, *Fax:* (01865) 276150. *E:* chris.pelling@chch.ox.ac.uk. *Club:* MCC.

PELLING, (Philip) Mark; QC 2003; **His Honour Judge Pelling;** a Specialist Chancery Senior Circuit Judge, since 2006; *b* 27 June 1956; *s* of Philip Clive and Jean Rosemary Pelling; *m* 1986, Charlotte Jones; one *s* one *d*. *Educ:* Bancroft's Sch., Woodford Green; King's Coll., London (LLB; AKC). Called to the Bar, Middle Temple, 1979, Bencher, 2011; Accredited Mediator, CEDR, 2000; a Recorder, 2004–06. Board of Governors, Ravensbourne College of Design and Communication, London: Mem., 1992–2000; Chm., Audit Cttee, 1994–95; Chm., Standing Cttee, 1995–97; Chm., 1997–2000. *Publications:* (with R. A. Purdie) Matrimonial and Domestic Injunctions, 1982, 2nd edn 1987. *Recreations:* sailing, flying, shooting. *Address:* Manchester Civil Justice Centre, 1 Bridge Street West, Manchester M60 9DJ. *Clubs:* Royal Western Yacht; Royal Plymouth Corinthian Yacht.

PELLING, Rowan Dorothy; Founding Editor, Erotic Review, 1996–2004; *b* 17 Jan. 1968; *d* of Ronald and Hazel Pelling; *m* 1995, Angus MacKinnon; two *s*. *Educ:* Walthamstow Hall, Sevenoaks; St Hugh's Coll., Oxford. Columnist: Independent on Sunday, 2000–08; Daily Telegraph, 2008–; Daily Mail, 2009–. Consultant, Dedalus Ltd. Judge, Man Booker Prize, 2004. Fellow, British American Project, 2004. *Publications:* The Erotic Review Bedside Companion, 2000; (ed) The Decadent Handbook, 2006; Debrett's: a modern Royal marriage, 2011. *Recreations:* racy novels, red wine, TV detective dramas, Maine Coon cats, Vivienne Westwood frocks, skinny-dipping at Newnham Riverbank club. *E:* rowan@pelling.demon.co.uk. *Clubs:* Chelsea Arts, Academy, Blacks.

PELLY, Deborah Susan; *see* Mattinson, D. S.

PELLY, Laurent; freelance opera and theatre director; Co-Director, National Theatre of Toulouse, since 2008; *b* Fontenay sous Bois, France, 14 Jan. 1962; *s* of Jacques Pelly and Jeanine Pelly (*née* Loiseau). Founder and Artistic Dir, Compagnie Théâtre du Pélican, 1980; Dir, Centre Dramatique National des Alpes, Grenoble, 1997–2007. Freelance opera and theatre projects at opera houses including: Royal Opera Hse, Covent Garden; Metropolitan Opera, NY; Vienna State Opera; San Francisco Opera; Santa Fe Opera; Opera Nat. de Paris; Opera de Lyons; La Scala, Milan; Teatro Regio, Turin; Th. Royal de la Monnaie, Brussels; Teatro del Liceu, Barcelona; Teatro Royal, Madrid; *productions include:* La fille du régiment, 2007; Manon, 2010; Cendrillon, 2011; L'heure espagnole/L'enfant et les sortilèges, 2012; L'étoile, 2014; Don Pasquale, 2014. *Address:* c/o Maestro Arts, 1 Eastfields Avenue, SW18 1FQ. *T:* (020) 3637 2789. *E:* sally@maestroarts.com.

PELLY, Sir Richard (John), 7th Bt *cr* 1840, of Upton, Essex; farmer, since 1991; *b* 10 April 1951; *s* of Richard Heywood Pelly, 2nd *s* of Sir Alwyne Pelly, 5th Bt, MC and of Mary Elizabeth Pelly (*née* Luscombe); *S* uncle, 1993; *m* 1983, Clare Gemma Dove; three *s*. *Educ:* Wellington Coll., Berks; Wadham Coll., Oxford (BA Agriculture and Forestry Science). ACA 1978–82. Price Waterhouse, London, 1974–78; Birds Eye Foods Ltd, 1978–81; New Century Software Ltd, 1981–99. *Heir:* *s* Anthony Alwyne Pelly, *b* 30 Oct. 1984. *Address:* The Manor House, Preshaw, Upham, Southampton SO32 1HP. *T:* (01962) 771757.

PEMBER, Susan Alison, OBE 2000; Director, Further Education and Skills Investment, Department for Business, Innovation and Skills, 2010–13; *b* 23 Dec. 1954; *d* of Bernard Pember and Muriel Pember; one *s*; *m* 1996, Brian Hudgell. *Educ:* Glamorgan Coll. of Educn (Cert Ed); Poly. of Wales, Pontypridd (BEd Univ. of Wales). Lectr, Redbridge Coll., 1977–83; Sen. Lectr, Southgate Coll., 1983–86; Educn Officer, 1986–87, Sen. Educn Officer, 1987–91, London Bor. of Enfield; Principal, Canterbury Coll., 1991–2000; Dir, Adult Basic Skills Strategy Gp, then Apprenticeships and Skills for Life, later Further Educn and Learning and Skills Perf. Gp, DFES, later DIUS, 2000–09; Dir, Learning and Skills Council Transition to Skills Funding Agency, DIUS, later BIS, 2009–10. *Recreations:* textiles, ski-ing, gardening.

PEMBERTON, (Christopher) Mark, OBE 2012; Director of National Collections, English Heritage, 2010–15; *b* Much Wenlock, Shropshire, 24 Oct. 1952; *s* of Frank and Freda May Pemberton. *Educ:* Abraham Darby Sch., Telford; Fitzwilliam Coll., Cambridge (BA 1975). Ironbridge Gorge Museum Trust: mus. asst, 1975–80; Gen. Manager, 1980–85; Dep. Dir, 1985–87; Science Museum, London: Mktg Dir, 1987–91; Asst Dir and Hd, Public Affairs, 1991–2000; English Heritage: Business Dir, 2000–05; Dir, Properties and Educn, 2005–10. Chm., RCGP Enterprises Ltd, 2014–. Chm., Waltham Abbey Royal Gunpowder Mills Charitable Foundn, 2011–. FMA 1987. *Address:* 117B Dartmouth Road, NW2 4ES. *T:* (020) 8450 4613. *Club:* Athenæum.

PEMBERTON, Gary Milton, AC 1999; Chairman, Racing NSW, 2004–08; *s* of Eric Pemberton; *m* Margaret Whitford; four *c*. *Educ:* Fort Street High Sch. Australian Wool Bd, 1961–72; joined Brambles Industries Ltd, 1972: Chief Exec., 1982–93; Dep. Chm., 1994–96; Chairman: Qantas Airways Ltd, 1993–2000; TAB Ltd, 1997–2002; Billabong International, 2002–06; Director: Commonwealth Bank, 1989–93; John Fairfax Hldgs Ltd, 1992–93; CSR Ltd, 1993–94. Chief Exec. Officer, 1994–95, Pres., 1995–96, Sydney Organising Cttee of the Olympic Games.

PEMBERTON, Jessica Louise Chantall; Her Honour Judge Pemberton; a Circuit Judge, since 2014; *b* Sheffield, 10 Aug. 1968; *d* of Adam and Brigitte Pemberton; *m* 1991, David; two *s*. *Educ:* Keele Univ. (BA Jt Hons Law and Sociol. 1991); Coll. of Law, Guildford. Admitted Solicitor, 1992; in practice as solicitor, 1994–2007; called to the Bar, Inner Temple, 2007; a Recorder, 2012–14. *Recreations:* singing, travel, theatre. *Address:* Kingston-upon-Hull Combined Court, Lowgate, Humberside HU1 2EZ.

PEMBERTON, Mark; *see* Pemberton, C. M.

PEMBROKE, 18th Earl of, *cr* 1551, **AND MONTGOMERY,** 15th Earl of, *cr* 1605; **William Alexander Sidney Herbert;** Baron Herbert of Cardiff, 1551; Baron Herbert of Shurland, 1605; Baron Herbert of Lea (UK); *b* 18 May 1978; *s* of 17th Earl of Pembroke and Montgomery, and Claire Rose Herbert (*née* Pelly); *S* father, 2003; *m* 2010, Victoria, *d* of Michael Bullough, Perth; one *s* one *d*. *Educ:* Bryanston Sch.; Sheffield Hallam Univ. (1st cl. Hons Industrial Design). Two years as product designer, Conran & Partners. Runs Wilton Estate. *Recreations:* scuba diving, ski-ing. *Heir:* *s* Lord Herbert, *qv*.

PEMSEL, David Skipwith; Chief Executive Officer, Guardian Media Group, since 2015; *b* London, 31 March 1968; *s* of Christopher John Pemsel and Heather Sonia Pemsel (*née* Leslie); *m* 2001, Katharine Stanners; one *s*. *Educ:* East Shene Sch. Gp Account Dir, Ogilvy & Mather, 1994–96; Man. Partner, St Lukes Communications, 1996–2000; Partner, Shine, 2000–02; Gp Mktg Dir, ITV, 2005–10; Guardian News and Media: Chief Mktg Officer, 2011–12; Chief Commercial Officer, 2012–13; Dep. CEO, 2013–15. Member: Council, Mktg Gp of GB, 2009–; Client Council, IPA, 2013–. Mem., BAFTA, 2006–. *Recreations:* tennis, cycling. *Address:* Guardian Media Group, Kings Place, 40 York Way, N1 9GU. *T:* (020) 3353 3969. *E:* david.pemsel@theguardian.com. *Clubs:* Soho House, Ivy.

PEÑA, Paco; musician; flamenco guitar player, since 1954; Professor of Flamenco, Rotterdam Conservatory, since 1985; *b* 1 June 1942; *s* of Antonio Peña and Rosario Perez; *m* 1982, Karin Vaessen; two *d*. *Educ:* Córdoba, Spain. London début, 1968; New York début, 1983; founded: Paco Peña Flamenco Co., 1970; Centro Flamenco Paco Peña, Córdoba, 1981; composed Misa Flamenca, 1991, Requiem for the Earth, 2004; Quimeras, 2010; produced: Musa Gitana, 1999; Voces y Ecos, 2002; A Compás, 2006; Flamenco sin Fronteras, 2010; Flamencura, 2015. Ramón Montoya Prize, 1983; Gold Medal in Arts, John F. Kennedy Center for Performing Arts, 2012. Officer, Order of Merit (Spain), 1997. *Address:* c/o MPM London, Suite 20, 1 Prince of Wales Road, NW5 3LW. *T:* (020) 7681 7475, (020) 7681 7476; c/o Karin Vaessen, 4 Boscastle Road, NW5 1EG. *Fax:* (020) 7485 2320.

PENDER, 3rd Baron *cr* 1937; **John Willoughby Denison-Pender;** Joint Chairman, Bremar Trust Ltd, 1977–83; Chairman, J. J. L. D. Frost plc, 1983–84; *b* 6 May 1933; *s* of 2nd Baron Pender, CBE and Camilla Lethbridge (*d* 1988), *o d* of late Willoughby Arthur Pemberton; *S* father, 1965; *m* 1962, Julia (*d* 2013), *yr d* of Richard Nevill Cannon; one *s* two *d*. *Educ:* Eton. Formerly Lieut, 10th Royal Hussars and Captain, City of London Yeomanry (TA). Dir, Globe Investment Trust Ltd. Vice Pres., Royal Sch. for Deaf Children, 1992– (Treas., 1999–2004). Steward: Folkestone Racecourse, 1985–2003; Lingfield Park, 1989–2003. *Heir:* *s* Hon. Henry John Richard Denison-Pender [*b* 19 March 1968; *m* 1994, Vanessa (marr. diss. 2012), *d* of John Eley, NSW, Australia; one *s* one *d*]. *Address:* 3 St George's Place, Sandwich, Kent CT13 9LW. *T:* (01304) 611726. *Clubs:* White's, Pratt's.
See also Viscount Esher.

PENDER, David James; Sheriff of North Strathclyde, since 1995; *b* 7 Sept. 1949; *s* of James and Isa Pender; *m* 1974, Elizabeth Jean McKillop; two *s* two *d*. *Educ:* Queen's Park Sen. Secondary Sch., Glasgow; Edinburgh Univ. (LLB Hons). Qualified as Solicitor, 1973; Partner, MacArthur Stewart, Solicitors, Oban, 1977–95. Sec., Oban Faculty of Solicitors, 1977–95.

Recreations: travel, bridge, reading. *Address:* Sheriff's Chambers, Paisley Sheriff Court, St James Street, Paisley PA3 2HW. *T:* (0141) 887 5291.

PENDER, Prof. Gareth, PhD; FREng; FRSE; Professor of Environmental Engineering, since 2000, and Head, School of Energy, Geoscience, Infrastructure and Society (formerly School of the Built Environment), since 2008, Heriot-Watt University; *b* Helensburgh, 24 Jan. 1960; *s* of Blair and Gweneth Pender; *m* 1984, Isobel McNaught Connell; one *s* two *d*. *Educ:* Strathclyde Univ. (BSc Civil Engrg 1981; PhD 1985). FREng 2013. Engr, Crouch & Hogg, 1984–89; Lectr, Univ. of Glasgow, 1989–2000. FRSE 2007. *Recreations:* golf, ski-ing, walking. *Address:* School of Energy, Geoscience, Infrastructure and Society, Heriot-Watt University, Edinburgh EH14 4AS. *T:* (0131) 451 3312. *E:* g.pender@hw.ac.uk.

PENDER, Simon Charles; Sheriff of North Strathclyde at Dumbarton, since 2004; *b* 23 June 1953; *s* of Robert R. E. Pender and Jean Elisabeth (*née* Haddow); *m* 1984, Linda Jeanne Miller; two *s* two *d*. *Educ:* Trinity Coll., Glenalmond; Univ. of Heidelberg; Univ. of Edinburgh (LLB). Solicitor, 1976–99: Partner: Breeze Paterson & Chapman, 1980–95; Dundas & Wilson, CS, 1995–99; Temp. Sheriff, 1995–99; Sheriff of S Strathclyde, Dumfries and Galloway at Hamilton, 1999–2004. Mem., Royal Scottish Pipers' Soc. *Recreations:* sailing, playing the great Highland bagpipe, ski-ing and various other sports, including golf, shooting and cycling. *Address:* Sheriff Court House, Church Street, Dumbarton G82 1QR. *T:* (01389) 763266. *E:* sheriff.scpender@scotcourts.gov.uk. *Clubs:* Glasgow Highland; Royal Northern and Clyde Yacht, Mudhook Yacht.

PENDERECKI, Krzysztof; Rector, State Academy of Music, Kraków, 1972–87; Professor of Composition, School of Music, Yale University, New Haven, Conn, 1973–78; *b* Debica, Poland, 23 Nov. 1933; *s* of Tadeusz Penderecki and Zofia Penderecki; *m* 1965, Elzbieta Solecka; one *s* one *d*. *Educ:* State Acad. of Music, Kraków, Poland (Graduate 1958). Compositions include: Threnody to the Victims of Hiroshima, 1960 (52 strings); Passion According to St Luke, 1965–66 (oratorio); Dies irae, 1967; Utrenja, 1969–71 (oratorio); Devils of Loudon, 1969 (opera); Cello Concerto No 1, 1971–72; First Symphony, 1972; Magnificat, 1974 (oratorio); Awakening of Jacob, 1974 (orchestra); Paradise Lost, 1976–78 (rappresentazione for Chicago Lyric Opera; Milton libretto, Christopher Fry); Violin Concerto, 1977; Te Deum, 1979–80; (Christmas) Symphony No 2, 1980; Lacrimosa, 1980; Agnus Dei (for chorus a cappella), 1981; Cello Concerto No 2, 1982 (Grammy Award, Nat. Acad. of Recording Arts and Scis, 1988); Viola Concerto, 1983; Polish Requiem, 1983–84; Die schwarze Maske, 1986 (opera); Veni creator and Song of Cherubin (for chorus a cappella), 1987; Das unterbrochene Gedanke (for string quartet), 1988; Symphony No 3, 1988–95; Symphony No 4, 1989; Ubu Rex, 1991 (opera); Symphony No 5, 1991–92; Sinfonietta per archi, 1992; Flute Concerto, 1992–93; Quartet for clarinet and string trio, 1993; Violin Concerto No 2, 1995 (Grammy Award, 1999); Seven Gates of Jerusalem (oratorio), 1997; Credo (oratorio), 1998 (Grammy Award, 2001); Sextett, 2000; Concerto grosso per tre violocelli, 2000; Concerto per pianoforte e orch., 2001; Largo per violoncello ed orchestra, 2003; Concerto grosso No 2 per 5 clarinetti, 2004; Symphony No 8, Lieder der Vergänglichkeit, 2005–07; Katyn (film score), 2007 (Best Film Score, Polish Film Awards, 2008). Hon. Professor: Moscow Tchaikovsky Conservatory, 1997; Beijing Conservatory, 1998; Komitas State Conservatory, Yerevan, 2008. Hon. Dr: Univ. of Rochester, NY; St Olaf Coll., Northfield, Minn; Katholieke Univ., Leuven; Univ. of Bordeaux; Georgetown Univ., Washington; Univ. of Belgrade; Universidad Autónoma, Madrid; Adam Mickiewicz Univ.; Warsaw Univ.; Acad. of Music, Cracow and Warsaw; Univ. of Glasgow; Duquesne Univ., Pittsburgh. Member: RAM (Hon.); Akad. der Künste, Berlin (Extraordinary); Akad. der Künste der DDR, Berlin (Corresp.); Kungl. Musikaliska Akad., Stockholm; Accad. Nazionale di Santa Cecilia, Rome (Hon.); Acad. Nacional de Bellas Artes, Buenos Aires (Corresp.); Royal Acad. of Music, Dublin; Akad. der schönen Künste, Munich (Corresp.); Composers Union of Armenia (Hon.); Musikverein Graz (Hon.); Hon. Foreign Mem., Amer. Acad. Arts and Letters. Grosser Kunstpreis, 1966, Staatspreis, 2002, des Landes Nordrhein-Westfalen; Prix Italia, 1967/68; Gottfried von Herder Preis der Stiftung FvS zu Hamburg, 1977; Prix Arthur Honegger, 1977; Sibelius Prize, Wihouri Foundn, 1983; Premio Lorenzo Magnifico, 1985; Wolf Prize, 1987; Manuel de Falla Gold Medal, Accademia de Bellas Artes, Granada, 1989; Grawemeyer Award, Univ. of Louisville, 1992; Internat. Music Council/UNESCO Prize for Music, 1993; Prime Time Emmy Award, Acad. of Television Arts and Scis, 1995 and 1996; Crystall Award, Econ. Forum, Davos, 1997; Music Award, City of Duisburg, 1999; Cannes Classical Award, 2000; Prince of Asturios Award, 2001; Eduardo Martínez Torner Medal, Conservatorio Superior de Música, Oviedo, 2003; Romano Guardini Prize, Catholic Acad., Bavaria, 2002; Praemium Imperiale, 2004; Super Wiktor Award, Polish Wiktory TV Acad., 2011; Lifetime Achievement Award, Internat. Classical Music Awards, 2014; Viadrina Prize, Europa-Universität, Frankfurt an der Oder, 2012. Das Grosse Verdienstkreuz des Verdienstordens (Germany), 1990; Order of White Eagle, 2005; Commander, Three Star Order, Riga, 2006; Order of Cross, Terra Mariana, Estonia, 2014. *Publications:* all works published. *Recreations:* dendrology, gardening. *Address:* Schott Musik International, Concert Opera Media Division, Weihergarten 5, 55116 Mainz, Germany. *T:* (6131) 2460, *Fax:* (6131) 246250.

PENDLEBURY, Edward; Assistant Under Secretary of State (Sales Administration), Ministry of Defence, 1983–85, retired; *b* 5 March 1925; *s* of Thomas Cecil Pendlebury and Alice (*née* Sumner); *m* 1957, Joan Elizabeth Bell; one *s*. *Educ:* King George V Sch., Southport; Magdalen Coll., Oxford (MA). Served War, RNVR, 1943–46. Asst Principal, Min. of Food, 1949–53; Principal: MAFF, 1953–56; MoD (British Defence Staff, Washington), 1956–60; MAFF, 1960–66; Asst Secretary: DEA, 1966–70; MoD, 1970–80; Exec. Dir (Civilian Management), MoD, 1980–83. *Recreations:* gramophone, gazing. *Address:* 9 Farnley Close, Menston, Ilkley, W Yorks LS29 6JJ.

PENDLEBURY, Graham; Director, Local Transport, Department for Transport, since 2013; *b* 7 Oct. 1958; *s* of Alan Pendlebury and late Margaret Elizabeth Pendlebury (*née* Moore); *m* 1991, Jill Amanda Thatcher; one *s*. *Educ:* Bolton Sch. (Boys' Div.); Sidney Sussex Coll., Cambridge (MA Hons Hist. 1981). Entered Civil Service, 1984; grad. trainee, 1986–90; Grade 7, Cabinet Office, then Dept of Transport, then DETR, 1990–99; Hd, Policy Strategy Integration Div., DETR, then DTLR, 1999–2001; Hd, Aviation Envmtl Div., DTLR, then DfT, 2001–04; Dir, Road and Vehicle Safety and Standards, 2004–07, Dir, Envmt and Internat., 2007–10, Dir, Greener Transport and Internat., 2010–13, DfT. Policy Fellow, Centre for Sci. and Policy, Univ. of Cambridge, 2011–13. *Publications:* Aspects of the English Civil War in Bolton and its Neighbourhood 1640–1660, 1983. *Recreations:* history, reading, walking, family, Bolton Wanderers FC. *Address:* Department for Transport, Great Minster House, 33 Horseferry Road, SW1P 4DR. *T:* (020) 7944 6425. *E:* graham.pendlebury@dft.gsi.gov.uk.

PENDOWER, John Edward Hicks, FRCS; Dean, Charing Cross and Westminster Medical School, 1989–93; *b* 6 Aug. 1927; *s* of Thomas Curtis Hicks Pendower and Muriel May Pendower (*née* Newbury); *m* 1st, 1960, Kate Tuohy (*d* 1987); one *s* two *d*; 2nd, 1989, Mrs Paulette Gleave. *Educ:* Dulwich College; King's College London; Charing Cross Hosp. Med. Sch. (MB BS (Hons Med.) 1950). FRCS 1955. Called to the Bar, Inner Temple, 1972. Served RAMC. Charing Cross Hosp. and St Mark's Hosp., 1950–62; Harvey Cushing Fellow, Harvard Med. Sch., 1959–60; Consultant Surgeon: Mayday Hosp., Croydon, 1964–89; Charing Cross Hosp., 1965–87 (Vice Dean, 1979–84; Sub Dean, Charing Cross and Westminster Med. Sch., 1984–87); former examr in surgery, London Univ. Mem., Hammersmith and Fulham, subseq. Riverside, HA, 1983–90. Special Trustee, Charing Cross Hosp.; Chm. Trustees, Sargent Cancer Care for Children (formerly Malcolm Sargent Cancer Fund for Children), 1992–2001 (Trustee, 1988–92). *Recreations:* formerly squash rackets, now walking; collecting campaign medals. *Address:* 2 Brockham Warren, Boxhill Road, Tadworth, Surrey KT20 7JX. *T:* (01737) 843108.

PENDRED, Piers Loughnan; Director General, International Psychoanalytical Association, 2000–07; *b* 24 Aug. 1943; *s* of Loughnan Wildig Pendred and Dulcie Treen Hall; *m* 1973, Carol Ann Haslam; one *s* one *d*. *Educ:* Ardingly College; Trinity Hall, Cambridge (MA Fine Arts and Architecture). VSO teacher, S India, 1965–67; British Council, 1967–99: Television Officer, Sudan, 1967–69, Ethiopia, 1969–71; TV Training Officer, London, 1972–76; Head of Production, 1976–81; Dir, Design, Production and Publishing, 1981–84; Dir, Press and Inf., 1984–87; Controller, later Dir of Finance, 1987–94; Special Asst to Dir-Gen., 1994–95; Asst Dir-Gen., 1996–99. Sen. Exec. Programme, London Business Sch., 1987. Trustee, Centre for Internat. Briefing, 1996–99.

PENDRY, family name of **Baron Pendry**.

PENDRY, Baron *cr* 2001 (Life Peer), of Stalybridge in the County of Greater Manchester; **Thomas Pendry;** PC 2000; *b* 10 June 1934; *m* 1966, Moira Anne Smith (separated 1983); one *s* one *d*. *Educ:* St Augustine's, Ramsgate; Oxford Univ. RAF, 1955–57. Full time official, Nat. Union of Public Employees, 1960–70; Mem., Paddington Borough Council, 1962–65; Chm., Derby Labour Party, 1966. MP (Lab) Stalybridge and Hyde, 1970–2001. An Opposition Whip, 1971–74; a Lord Comr of the Treasury and Govt Whip, 1974, resigned 1977; Parly Under-Sec. of State, NI Office, 1978–79; Opposition spokesman on NI, 1979–81, on overseas development, 1981–82, on regional affairs and devolution, 1982–84, on sport and tourism, 1992–97. Member: Select Cttee on Envmt, 1987–92; Select Cttee on Members' Interests, 1987–92. Founder Mem., and Chm., 1980–92, All Party Football Gp. Member: Speaker's Conf., 1973; UK delegn to WEU and Council of Europe, 1973–75. Pres., Football Foundn, 2003– (Chm., 1999–2003); Chm., Football Trust, 1997–99. Steward, British Boxing Bd of Control, 1987–98. President: Stalybridge Public Band; Stalybridge Labour Club; Patron, Nat. Fedn of Football Supporters, 1998–. Freeman, Bor. of Tameside and Lordship of Mottram in Longendale, 1995. *Recreations:* sport; football, cricket, boxing (sometime Middleweight Champion, Hong Kong; boxed for Oxford Univ.). *Address:* House of Lords, SW1A 0PW. *Clubs:* Garrick, Royal Air Force, MCC, Lord's Taverners; Vincent's (Oxford).

PENDRY, Sir John (Brian), Kt 2004; PhD; FRS 1984; Professor of Theoretical Solid State Physics, Department of Physics, Imperial College of Science, Technology and Medicine, University of London, since 1981 (Head, Department of Physics, 1998–2001); Dean, Royal College of Science, 1993–96; *b* 4 July 1943; *s* of Frank Johnson Pendry and Kathleen (*née* Shaw); *m* 1977, Patricia Gard. *Educ:* Downing Coll., Cambridge (MA; PhD 1969; Hon. Fellow, 2005). Res. Fellow in Physics, Downing Coll., Cambridge, 1969–72; Mem. of Technical Staff, Bell Labs, USA, 1972–73; Sen. Asst in Res., Cavendish Lab., Cambridge Univ., and Fellow in Physics and Praelector, Downing Coll., 1973–75; SPSO and Head of Theory Gp, Daresbury Lab., 1975–81. Mem., PPARC, 1998–2002. Foreign Associate, US NAS, 2013; Foreign Mem., Norwegian Acad. of Sci. and Letters, 2014. *Publications:* Low Energy Electron Diffraction, 1974; Surface Crystallographic Information Service, 1987; scientific papers. *Recreations:* music, gardening, photography. *Address:* The Blackett Laboratory, Imperial College of Science, Technology and Medicine, SW7 2AZ. *T:* (020) 7594 7606. *Clubs:* Athenæum, Oxford and Cambridge.

PENFOLD, Peter Alfred, CMG 1995; OBE 1986; international consultant; formerly HM Diplomatic Service; *b* 27 Feb. 1944; *s* of Alfred Penfold and Florence (*née* Green); *m* 1st, 1972, Margaret Quigley (marr. diss. 1983); 2nd, 1992, Celia Dolores Koenig. *Educ:* Sutton Co. Grammar Sch. Joined Foreign Service, 1963; Bonn, 1965–68; Kaduna, 1968–70; Latin American Floater, 1970–72; Canberra, 1972; FCO, 1972–75; Second Secretary: Addis Ababa, 1975–78; Port of Spain, 1978–81; First Sec., FCO, 1981–84; Dep. High Comr, Kampala, 1984–87; First Sec., FCO, 1987–91; Gov., BVI, 1991–95; Special Advr on Drugs in the Caribbean, 1995–96; High Comr, Sierra Leone, 1997–2000; Sen. Conflict Advr, DFID, 2001. Pres., UK Assoc. for Schs for the Blind, Sierra Leone, 2010–; Patron: Dorothy Springer Trust, 2010–; Hastings Sierra Leone Link, 2010–. *Publications:* Atrocities, Diamonds and Diplomacy, 2012. *Recreations:* travel, reading. *Address:* Fisherman's Wharf, Abingdon, Oxfordshire OX14 5RX.

PENGELLY, Richard Anthony; Under Secretary, Welsh Office, 1977–85; *b* 18 Aug. 1925; *s* of Richard Francis Pengelly and Ivy Mildred Pengelly; *m* 1st, 1952, Phyllis Mary Rippon; one *s*; 2nd, 1972, Margaret Ruth Crossley; two *s* one *d*. *Educ:* Plymouth Coll.; School of Oriental and African Studies; London Sch. of Economics and Political Science (BScEcon). Served War: Monmouthshire Regt and Intell. Corps, 1943–47. Joined Min. of Supply as Asst Principal, 1950, Principal, 1954; NATO Defence Coll., 1960–61; Asst Sec., Min. of Aviation, 1964; RCDS 1971; Min. of Defence, 1972. *Recreations:* ski-ing, golf. *Address:* Byways, 8 Wern Goch Road, Cyncoed, Cardiff, S Wales CF23 6SD. *T:* (029) 2076 4418.

PENHALIGON, Dame Annette, DBE 1993; Member (Lib Dem): Restormel Borough Council, Cornwall, 2003–09; Cornwall County Council, 2005–09; *b* 9 Feb. 1946; *d* of late Owen Bennett Lidgey and Mabel Lidgey; *m* 1968, David Charles Penhaligon, MP (*d* 1986); one *s* one *d*; *m* 1994, Robert William Egerton. *Educ:* Truro Girls' Grammar Sch. Subpostmistress, Chacewater PO, 1967–79; Sec. to husband, David Penhaligon, MP (L) Truro, 1974–86. Mem. (L, then Lib Dem), Carrick DC, Cornwall, 1987–94. Non-exec. Dir, Cornwall Independent Radio, 1992–2002. Patron, Penhaligon's Friends. *Publications:* Penhaligon, 1989. *Recreation:* supporting charities helping people with learning disabilities. *Address:* Trevillick House, Fore Street, Grampound, Truro, Cornwall TR2 4RS. *T:* (01726) 884451.

PENLEY, William Henry, CB 1967; CBE 1961; PhD; FREng; Controller, R&D Establishments, and Research, Ministry of Defence, and Professional Head of Science Group of the Civil Service, 1976–77; engineering consultant, 1985–2000; *b* 22 March 1917; *s* of late William Edward Penley and late Clara (*née* Dodgson), Wallasey, Cheshire; *m* 1st, 1943, Raymonde Evelyn (*d* 1975), *d* of late Frederick Richard Gough, Swanage, Dorset; two *s* one *d*; 2nd, 1977, Marion Claytor (*d* 2004), *d* of late Joseph Enoch Airey, MBE, Swanage, Dorset; 3rd, 2006, Joanna Anderson-Doig, *d* of late Richard Barnett, Hedge End, Hants. *Educ:* Wallasey Grammar Sch.; Liverpool Univ.; BEng, 1937; PhD, 1940. FIET (MIEE 1964); FRAeS 1967; FRSA 1975; FREng (FEng 1978). Head of Guided Weapons Department, Royal Radar Establishment, 1953–61; Director, Royal Radar Establishment, 1961–62; Director-General of Electronics Research and Development, Ministry of Aviation, 1962–64; Deputy Controller of Electronics, Ministry of Aviation, then Ministry of Technology, 1964–67; Dir, Royal Armament R&D Establishment, 1967–70; Chief Scientist (Army), 1970–75, Dep. Controller, Establishments and Res. B, 1971–75, MoD; Chm., Appleton Lab. Establishment Cttee, 1977–79; Dep. Dir, Under Water Weapons, Marconi Space and Defence Systems Ltd, Stanmore, 1979–82; Engrg Dir, Marconi Underwater Systems Ltd, 1982–85. Vis. Res. Fellow, Bournemouth Univ., 1996–2002. Sec., Swanage Choral and Operatic Soc., 1986–2000; Pres., Defence Electronics History Soc., 2003–08. Vice-Chm., Purbeck Radar Mus. Trust, 1998–. Silver Jubilee Medal, 1977. *Address:* 28 Walrond Road, Swanage, Dorset BH19 1PD. *T:* (01929) 425042.

PENMAN, Ian Dalgleish, CB 1987; Deputy Secretary, Central Services, Scottish Office, 1984–91; *b* 1 Aug. 1931; *s* of late John B. Penman and Dorothy Dalgleish; *m* 1963, Elisabeth Stewart Strachan; three *s*. *Educ:* High Sch., Glasgow; Glasgow Univ. (MA Classics); Balliol

Coll., Oxford (MA Lit. Hum.; Snell Exhibnr and Ferguson Scholar). National Service, RAF, 1955–57 (Educn Br.). Asst Principal, HM Treasury, 1957–58; Scottish Office, 1958–91; Private Sec. to Parly Under-Sec. of State, 1960–62; Principal, Scottish Develt Dept, 1962–69; Asst Sec., Estab. Div., 1970–72; Asst Sec., Scottish Home and Health Dept, 1972–78; Under-Sec., Scottish Develt Dept, 1978–84. Member: Chm.'s Panel, CSSB, 1991–95; Sec. of State's Panel of Inquiry Reporters, 1992–94; Council on Tribunals, 1994–2001 (Mem., Scottish Cttee, 1994–2001); Church of Scotland Cttee on Probationers, 1994–97; C of S Bd of Ministry, 1997–2003. Chm., Viewpoint Housing Assoc., 1991–95; Chief Exec., Scottish Homes, April–Oct. 1991. *Recreations:* walking, music, travel. *Address:* 1/3 Fettes Rise, Edinburgh EH4 1QH. *T:* (0131) 552 2180.

PENN, Charles Richard, TD 1990; PhD; Coordinator for Antimicrobial Resistance and Chairman, Guidelines Review Committee, World Health Organization, since 2011; *b* 12 June 1957; *s* of Lt Col Charles Edward Penn and Mary Elizabeth Penn; *m* 1980, Elizabeth Jane Dawson; two *d. Educ:* Christ Church, Oxford (MA 1979); Wolfson Coll., Cambridge (PhD 1982). Res. Fellow, Wolfson Coll., Cambridge, 1982–84; SSO, Inst. for Animal Health, 1984–88; Sen. Res. Associate, Glaxo R&D, 1988–95; Sen. Med. Strategy Hd, Glaxo Wellcome, 1995–98; Dir for R&D, Centre for Applied Microbiol. and Res., subseq. HPA Porton Down, 1998–2005; Founder and Chief Develt Officer, Syntaxin, 2005–08; Scientist, WHO, 2009–11. Vis. Professorial Fellow, Univ. of Bath, 1999–2005. TAVR (RE), 1975–92. Co-inventor on patent, oxathiolane nucleoside analogues (treatment for AIDS/HIV). *Publications:* papers in professional jls, inc. Nature. *Recreations:* marine biology (inc. rearing cephalopods), fishing, walking, ski-ing.

PENN, Jeremy John Harley; Chief Executive, Baltic Exchange, since 2004; *b* 11 March 1959; *s* of Comdr Geoffrey Briscoe Penn and Barbara Penn (*née* Beverley Robinson); marr. diss.; one *s* one *d. Educ:* Warwick Sch., Warwick; Corpus Christi Coll., Oxford (MA 1981); Harvard Business Sch. (AMP 1999). Reuters Gp plc, 1981–2001: Man. Dir, Reuters Asia, 1997–99; Dep. CEO, Reuterspace Div., 1999–2001; ind. consultant, 2002–03; Baltic Exchange, 2003–. Director: Maritime London, 2004–; Maritime UK, 2010–14. Trustee, Royal Museums Greenwich, 2015–. *Recreations:* theatre, running, ski-ing, golf, joinery. *Address:* The Baltic Exchange, 38 St Mary Axe, EC3A 8BH. *E:* JPenn@Balticexchange.com. *Club:* Tanglin (Singapore).

PENN, Richard; General Manager, Caldicot and Wentlooge Levels Internal Drainage Board, 2011–15; Chair, Independent Remuneration Panel for Wales, 2008–15; *b* 4 Oct. 1945; *s* of George Stanley Penn; *m* 1968, Jillian Mary Elias; three *s* one *d. Educ:* Canton High Sch., Cardiff; University Coll., Cardiff (BSc Econs Jt Hons); University Coll., Swansea (DipEd). MBPS. Lectr, University Coll., Cardiff, 1968–70; Glamorgan, then W Glamorgan, CC, 1970–76; Asst Chief Exec., Cleveland CC, 1976–78; Dep. Chief Exec., W Midlands CC, 1978–81; Chief Executive: Knowsley Metropolitan Council, 1981–89; City of Bradford Metropolitan Council, 1989–98. Comr for Standards, Nat. Assembly for Wales, 2000–10; Chm., S Wales Probation Bd, 2001–07; Member: EOC, 1997–2002; Legal Services Commn, 2000–03. FCMI; FRSA. *Recreations:* family, Rugby Union, theatre, good food.

PENN, Sean Justin; actor, director and writer; *b* Burbank, Calif, 17 Aug. 1960; *s* of Leo Penn and Eileen Penn (*née* Ryan); *m* 1st, 1985, Madonna Louise Veronica Ciccone, *qv* (marr. diss. 1989); 2nd, 1996, Robin Wright (marr. diss. 2010); one *s* one *d. Educ:* Santa Monica High Sch.; studied acting with Peggy Feury. Joined LA Gp Repertory Theater (backstage work; dir, Terrible Jim Fitch (one-act play)); moved to NYC, 1980; *theatre includes:* Earthworms, 1980; Heartland, 1981; Slab Boys, 1983; Hurlyburly, 1988; The Late Henry Moss, 2000. *Films include:* Taps, 1981; Fast Times at Ridgemont High, 1982; Summerspell, Bad Boys, 1983; Crackers, Racing with the Moon, 1984; The Falcon and the Snowman, 1985; At Close Range, Shanghai Surprise, 1986; Colors, Judgement in Berlin, Cool Blue, 1988; Casualties of War, We're No Angels, 1989; State of Grace, 1990; The Last Party, Carlito's Way, 1993; Dead Man Walking, 1996; U-Turn, She's So Lovely (also prod.), The Game, Hugo Pool, 1997; As I Lay Dying (also prod.), Loved (also prod.), The Thin Red Line, Hurlyburly, Sweet and Lowdown, Being John Malkovich, 1999; Up at the Villa, The Weight of Water, 2000; Before Night Falls, 2001; I Am Sam, 2002; Mystic River (Academy Award for best actor), 2003; It's All About Love, 21 Grams, 2004; The Interpreter, The Assassination of Richard Nixon, 2005; All the King's Men, 2006; Milk (Academy Award for best actor), 2009; Fair Game, 2010; The Tree of Life, 2011; This Must be the Place, 2012; Gangster Squad, The Secret Life of Walter Mitty, 2013; The Gunman, 2015; *director:* The Pledge, 2001; *director and writer:* The Indian Runner, 1991; The Crossing Guard, 1995; Autumn of the Patriarch, 1999; Into the Wild, 2007. *Address:* Suite 2500, 2049 Century Park East, Los Angeles, CA 90067–3101, USA.

PENNA, Jai; Her Honour Judge Penna; a Circuit Judge, since 2010; *b* Glasgow, 16 Jan. 1961; *née* Jacqueline Anne; *d* of Jeffery Warne Penna and Vivienne Aldcroft Penna (*née* Carrier); partner, Paula Margot Tyler, *qv. Educ:* Redland High Sch., Bristol; Trinity Coll., Cambridge (BA Hons Classics 1983); Manchester Poly. (CPE). Admitted as solicitor, 1989; a Recorder, 2002–10. *Publications:* (contrib.) Civil Court Practice, 2006; (contrib.) Child Case Management Practice, 2009; (contrib.) Children and Same Sex Families, 2012. *Recreations:* ski-ing, Italian language, travel.

PENNANT; *see* Douglas-Pennant.

PENNANT-REA, Rupert Lascelles; Chairman: The Economist Group, since 2009 (non-executive Director, since 2006); Royal London Group, since 2013; *b* 23 Jan. 1948; *s* of late Peter Athelwold Pennant-Rea and Pauline Elizabeth Pennant-Rea; two *s* one *d*; *m* 2011, Cinzia De Santis; one step *d. Educ:* Peterhouse, Zimbabwe; Trinity Coll., Dublin (BA); Manchester Univ. (MA). Confedn of Irish Industry, 1970–71; Gen. and Municipal Workers Union, 1972–73; Bank of England, 1973–77; The Economist, 1977–93, Editor, 1986–93; Dep. Gov., Bank of England, 1993–95; Chairman: The Stationery Office, 1996–2005; PGI plc (formerly Plantation & Gen. Investments), 1997–; Security Printing and Systems, 1999–2006; Acuity Growth VCT (formerly Electra Kingsway VCT), 2002–11; Henderson Gp, 2005–13. Non-executive Director: British American Tobacco, 1995–2007; Sherritt Internat. Inc., 1995–2007; First Quantum Minerals, 2001–11; Gold Fields, 2002–13; Go Ahead Gp, 2002–13; Times Newspapers, 2003–; Hochschild Mining plc, 2012–13. Trustee: Action Med. Res., 2000–07; Wincott Foundn, 2000–; Marjorie Deane Financial Journalism Foundn, 1998–. Chm., Shakespeare Schs Fest., 2001–. Gov., Peterhouse, Zimbabwe, 1994–. *Publications:* Gold Foil, 1979; (jtly) Who Runs the Economy?, 1980; (jtly) The Pocket Economist, 1983; (jtly) The Economist Economics, 1986. *Recreations:* music, tennis, golf, fishing, family. *Address:* Royal London Group, 55 Gracechurch Street, EC3V 0RL. *Clubs:* MCC, Reform; Harare (Zimbabwe).

PENNECK, Stephen John, CStat, FSS; Director General, Office for National Statistics, 2009–12; *b* 25 June 1951; *s* of Norman James Penneck and Rose Esther Penneck; *m* 1979, Pauline Ann Tunnell; two *d. Educ:* Southampton Univ. (BSc Social Sc 1972); Birmingham Univ. (MSocSc 1973). Cadet statistician, CSO, 1972–73; Asst and Sen. Asst Statistician, 1973–78, Statistician, 1978–85, DTI; OFT, 1985–91; CSO, 1991–93; Chief Statistician, Hd of Profession, DTI, 1993–96; Office for National Statistics: Director: Nat. Accounts Div., 1997–2000; Nat. Stats and Policy Div., 2000–03; Statistical Outputs Gp, 2003–05; Exec. Dir, Surveys and Admin. Sources, 2005–08; Exec. Dir, Methodology, 2008–09. Pres., Internat. Assoc. for Official Statistics, 2011–13; Mem. Council and Exec. Cttee, Royal Statistical Soc., 2014–. Mem., ISI (Chm., Adv. Bd on Ethics; Vice Pres., 2014–). Mem. (Lib Dem), Sutton LBC, 1983–94 and 2014– (Chm., Educn Cttee, 1986–91; Dep. Leader, 1988–94). Governor: Greenshaw High Sch., 1983–2004; All Saints (Benhilton) Primary Sch., 1986–2006. *Publications:* contrib. articles to Econ. Trends, Statistical News, Jl of Official Statistics, Statistical Jl of IAOS and conf. proceedings. *Recreations:* gardening, walking, travel, music. *Address:* 13 Worcester Road, Sutton, Surrey SM2 6PQ. *E:* stephen.penneck@gmail.com.

PENNEFATHER, Maj.-Gen. David Anthony Somerset, CB 1996; OBE 1991; Commandant General, Royal Marines, 1996–98; *b* 17 May 1945; *s* of late Capt. R. R. S. Pennefather, RN and Rachael Ann Pennefather (*née* Fawcitt); *m* 1972, Sheila Elizabeth Blacklee (*d* 2002); one *s* one *d. Educ:* Wellington Coll. Entered RM, 1963; commando service incl. US Marine Corps exchange, 1965–76; Army Staff Coll., 1977 (psc(m)); commando service and MoD, 1978–85; DS, Army Staff Coll., 1986–88; CO, 42 Commando, 1988–90; rcds 1991; hcsc 1992; Comdr, 3rd Commando Bde, 1992–94; Dir of Operations for Bosnia, JHQ Wilton, 1994; COS to CGRM, 1995; Comdr, Rapid Reaction Force Ops Staff, Bosnia, 1995; Sen. DS (Navy), RCDS, 2000 and 2002. Chm. Trustees, Royal Marines Mus., 2007–12. Sec., Royal Humane Soc., 2004–07. Liveryman, Co. of Clockmakers, 1973– (Mem., Ct of Assts, 1998–; Master, 2006–07). Comdr, Legion of Merit (USA), 1997. *Recreations:* fell-walking, fishing. *Club:* Army and Navy.

PENNEY, Most Rev. Alphonsus Liguori; Archbishop (RC) of St John's (Newfoundland), 1979–91, now Emeritus; *b* 17 Sept. 1924; *s* of Alphonsus Penney and Catherine Penney (*née* Mullaly). *Educ:* St Bonaventure's Coll., St John's, Newfoundland; University Seminary, Ottawa (LPh, LTh). Assistant Priest: St Joseph's Parish, St John's, 1950–56; St Patrick's Parish, St John's, 1956; Parish Priest: Marystown, Placentia Bay, Newfoundland, 1957; Basilica Parish, St John's, 1969. Prelate of Honour, 1971. Bishop of Grand Falls, Newfoundland, 1972. Hon. LLD, Memorial Univ. of Newfoundland, 1980. Confederation Medal, 1967. *Recreation:* walking.

PENNEY, Jennifer Beverly; Senior Principal, Royal Ballet, retired 1988; *b* 5 April 1946; *d* of Beverley Guy Penney and Gwen Penney. *Educ:* in Canada (grades 1–12). Entered Royal Ballet Sch., 1962; joined Royal Ballet, 1963; became soloist during 1967, principal dancer during 1970, and senior principal dancer during 1974. Evening Standard Award, 1980. *Recreation:* painting (water-colours). *Address:* 2.258 Lower Ganges Road, Saltspring Island, BC V8K 1S7, Canada.

PENNEY, John Anthony, CMG 2000; translator and lecturer, since 2000; *b* 30 Oct. 1940; *s* of late William Welch Penney and of Lily Penney; *m* 1st, 1968, Mary Hurley; 2nd, 1995, Miriam Franchini. *Educ:* Madrid Univ. (Dip. of Hispanic Studies 1960); St Catharine's Coll., Cambridge (BA (Hons) Mod. Langs, 1963; MA 1966); Nat. Autonomous Univ. of Mexico; Univ. of Paris IX, Ecole Supérieure d'Interpretation et de Traducteurs. HM Diplomatic Service, 1966–99: Jt Res./Analysis Dept, FCO, 1966–68; Lima, 1968–72; Hd, Americas Unit, FCO Res. & Analysis Dept, 1973–95; 1st Sec., Political Cttee, CSCE, UKMIS to UN, Geneva, 1974–75; Central Amer. and Caribbean Dept, FCO, 1977–78; Havana, 1978; Mexico and Central Amer. Dept, FCO, 1981–82; Paris, 1984–86; Santiago de Chile, 1988; Chief FCO Interpreter (Spanish), 1986–99; Antarctic Treaty UK Inspection Team, 1989; Minister-Counsellor, Consul-Gen., Dep. Hd of Mission and Commercial Manager, Brasilia, 1995–99. *Recreation:* music. *Address:* SMDB, Conj 4, Lote 3, Casa A, Lago Sul, Brasilia 71680–040, Brazil. *T:* (61) 33665344. *E:* penneyjohn@gmail.com.

PENNEY, Penelope Anne; Headmistress, Surval Montreux International Boarding School for Girls, since 2012; education consultant, since 2005; *b* 30 Sept. 1942; *d* of late Richard Chamberlain, TD and (Lydia) Joan (*née* Kay); *m* 1963, Rev. William Affleck Penney; one *s* two *d. Educ:* Chatelard Sch., Switzerland; Bristol Univ. (BA Hons 1964). Head of Langs and Communications, Astor of Hever Sch., Maidstone, 1974–79; Headmistress: Prendergast Sch., Catford, 1980–86; Putney High Sch. (GPDST), 1987–91; Haberdashers' Aske's Sch. for Girls, Elstree, 1991–2005. Educn Advr, London Diocesan Bd for Schools, 2005–10. Pres., GSA, 1994–95 (Chm., Inspections Cttee, 2001–03); Mem., Teacher Induction Panel, ISC, 1999–2003. Trustee, Villiers Park Educnl Trust, 2008–12. Freeman, City of London, 1993; Liveryman, Haberdashers' Co., 2005. MInstD 1995. FCMI (FIMgt 1995); FZS 2007. FRSA. *Publications:* Hearing the Squirrel's Heartbeat, 2006; Go and Open the Door, 2008. *Recreations:* education, fast cars, grandparental duties. *Address:* Surval Montreux, Route de Glion 56, 1820 Montreux, Switzerland. *E:* head@surval.ch; 2 Harbord Road, Oxford OX2 8LQ. *T:* (01865) 557198. *E:* p.a.penney@btinternet.com.

PENNEY, Robert Charles H.; *see* Hughes-Penney.

PENNICOTT, Maj.-Gen. Brian Thomas, CVO 1994; Extra Gentleman Usher to the Queen, since 2008 (Gentleman Usher, 1995–2007); management consultant, 1998–2001; *b* 15 Feb. 1938; *s* of Thomas Edward Pennicott and Vera Ethel (*née* Gale); *m* 1962, Patricia Anne Chilcott (*d* 2010); two *s* three *d. Educ:* Portsmouth Northern Grammar Sch.; RMA, Sandhurst. Commnd, RA, 1957; RMCS, Shrivenham, 1969–70; Staff Coll., Camberley, 1971; GSO2 (W), Project Management Team 155mm Systems, 1972–73; NDC, Latimer, 1976–77; CO 29 Commando Regt, RA, 1977–80; SO1 Mil. Sec.'s Br. 6, MoD, 1980–82; Comdr Artillery, Falkland Is, 1982; Asst Mil. Attaché, Washington, 1982–83; Comdr Artillery, 1 Armd Div., 1983–86; NDC, Canada, 1986–87; Dep. Mil. Sec. (A), 1987–89; Dir, RA, 1989–91; Defence Services Sec., 1991–94 and ACDS (Personnel and Reserves), 1992–94. Gp Security Advr, 1994–95, Gp Personnel Manager, later Gp Human Resources Manager, 1995–96, Sun Alliance Gp; Gp Human Resources Manager, Royal & Sun Alliance Insurance Gp, 1996–98. Chm., Inksane (formerly BrandGuardian) Ltd (Hong Kong), 1999–2002. Chm., Simplyhealth Gp Ltd (formerly Hospital Saving Assoc., subseq. HSA Gp Ltd), 1999–2008. Col Comdt, RA, 1991–96; Hon. Col, 289 Commando Battery, RA(V), 1991–99. Chm., Army FA, 1991–94. *Recreations:* golf, bridge. *Address:* c/o Lloyds, Cox's & King's Branch, PO Box 1190, 7 Pall Mall, SW1Y 5NA.

PENNICOTT, Ian; QC 2003; SC (Hong Kong) 2014; *b* 5 Sept. 1958; *s* of Roy Stephen Pennicott and Patricia Dorothy Pennicott; *m* 1991, Andrea Clare (*née* Whitlock); two *d. Educ:* Kingston Poly. (BA Hons); Corpus Christi Coll., Cambridge (LLM). Called to the Bar: Middle Temple, 1982; Hong Kong, 1984; in practice, specialising in building and engineering law, and construction related professional negligence. MCIArb. *Publications:* (contrib.) Keating on Building Contracts, 5th edn 1991 to 8th edn 2006; (contrib.) Halsbury's Laws of England, Vol. 4 (3), Building Contractors, Architects, Engineers, Valuers and Surveyors, reissue 2002; consultant editor: Halsbury's Laws of England, Vols 19 (1) and (2), Fuel and Energy, reissue 2007, Vol. 39 (14), Cross-Country Pipelines, reissue 2008; Halsbury's Laws of England, Vol. 6, Building Contracts, 5th edn 2011; Halsbury's Laws of England, Vols 19 (1) and (2), Energy and Climate Change, 5th edn 2011. *Recreations:* golf, Southampton Football Club. *Address:* Keating Chambers, 15 Essex Street, WC2R 3AU. *T:* (020) 7544 2600, *Fax:* (020) 7240 7722. *E:* ipennicott@keatingchambers.com; Des Voeux Chambers, 38/F Gloucester Tower, The Landmark, Central, Hong Kong. *E:* ianpennicott@dvc.com.hk. *Clubs:* Royal Automobile; Frilford Heath Golf (Oxon); Foreign Correspondents' (Hong Kong).

PENNING, Rt Hon. Michael (Allan); PC 2014; MP (C) Hemel Hempstead, since 2005; Minister of State, Home Office and Ministry of Justice, since 2014; *b* 28 Sept. 1957; *s* of Brian and Freda Penning; *m* 1988, Angela Louden; two *d. Educ:* Appleton Comp. Sch., Benfleet; King Edmund Comp. Sch., Rochford. Served Grenadier Guards, 1974–79; RAMC, 1979–81; Essex Fire and Rescue Service, 1981–88; freelance media consultant, 1999–2000; Dep. Hd, News and Media, Conservative Party, 2000–04. Parly Under-Sec. of State, DfT, 2010–12; Minister of State: NI Office, 2012–13; DWP, 2013–14. Contested (C) Thurrock,

2001. GSM 1976. *Recreations:* keen angler, passionate Rugby Union supporter. *Address:* House of Commons, SW1A 0AA. *T:* (020) 7219 3000. *E:* penningm@parliament.uk.

PENNING-ROWSELL, Prof. Edmund Charles, OBE 2006; FRGS; Professor of Geography, since 1984, and Pro Vice-Chancellor (Research), since 1997, Middlesex University (formerly Middlesex Polytechnic) (Head, Flood Hazard Research Centre, 1970–2010); *b* 1 May 1946; *s* of late Edmund Lionel Penning-Rowsell and Margaret Penning-Rowsell; *m* 1968, Jacqueline Pritchett; two *d. Educ:* Chipping Norton Grammar Sch.; Sidcot Friends Sch.; University Coll. London (BSc 1967; PhD 1970; MA 1986). Lectr, Enfield Coll. of Technol., 1970–84; Dean of Social Sci., Middx Poly., then Middx Univ., 1984–97. FRGS 2000. Back Award, RGS, 2011. *Publications:* (with J. Chatterton) The Benefits of Flood Alleviation: a manual of assessment techniques, 1977; (with D. J. Parker) Water Planning in Britain, 1980; (jtly) Floods and Drainage: British policies for hazard reduction, agricultural improvement and wetland conservation, 1986; (jtly) The Economics of Coastal Management: a manual of benefit assessment techniques, 1992; (jtly) The Benefits of Flood and Coastal Risk Management: a manual of assessment techniques, 2005; (jtly) Flood and Coastal Erosion Risk Management: a manual for economic appraisal, 2013. *Recreations:* wine, gardening. *E:* Edmund@Penningrowsell.com.

PENNINGTON, Hugh; *see* Pennington, T. H.

PENNINGTON, Michael Vivian Fyfe; freelance actor and writer; *b* 7 June 1943; *s* of late Vivian Maynard Cecil Pennington and Euphemia Willock (*née* Fyfe); *m* Katharine Ann Letitia Barker (marr. diss.); one *s. Educ:* Marlborough Coll.; Trinity Coll., Cambridge (BA English). RSC, 1964–65; BBC, ITV, Woodfall Films Ltd, West End Theatre, Royal Court Theatre, etc, 1966–74; RSC, 1974–81: roles included Berowne, Angelo and Hamlet; Crime and Punishment, Lyric Hammersmith, 1983; National Theatre: Strider, 1984; Venice Preserv'd, 1984; Anton Chekhov, 1984; The Real Thing, Strand, 1985; Jt Artistic Dir, English Shakespeare Co., 1986–93: three world tours playing Henry V, Richard II, Coriolanus, Leontes, Macbeth, and Dir, Twelfth Night; Playing with Trains, RSC, 1989; Vershinin, The Three Sisters, Gate, Dublin, 1990; The Gift of the Gorgon, Barbican, 1992, Wyndhams, 1993; Dir, Twelfth Night, Tokyo, 1993; Hamlet, Gielgud, 1994; Taking Sides, Chichester, transf. Criterion, 1995; Dir, Twelfth Night, Chicago, 1996; The Entertainer, Hampstead, 1996; Waste, The Seagull, The Provok'd Wife, Anton Chekhov, Old Vic, 1997; The Misanthrope, Filumena, Major Barbara, Piccadilly, 1998; Gross Indecency, Gielgud, 1999; Timon of Athens, RSC, 1999; The Guardsman, Albery, 2000; What the Butler Saw, nat. tour, 2001; The Shawl, Sheffield Crucible, 2001; The Front Page, Chichester, 2002; John Gabriel Borkman, English Touring Th., 2003; Dir, A Midsummer Night's Dream, Regent's Park, 2003; The Seagull, Edinburgh Fest., 2003; The Madness of George III, W Yorks Playhouse, 2003; When the Night Begins, Hampstead, 2004; Colder Than Here, Soho, 2005; The Cosmonaut's Last Message, Donmar, 2005; Nathan the Wise, Hampstead, 2005; The Best of Friends, Hampstead and nat. tour, 2006; The Bargain, nat. tour, 2007; Little Nell, Th. Royal, Bath, 2007; Sweet William (solo Shakespeare show), NT, nat. and internat. tour and W End, 2007–09; Taking Sides, Collaboration, Chichester and W End, 2008–09; Love is My Sin, US and Eur. Tour, 2009–10; A Jubilee for Anton Chekhov, Hampstead, 2010; The Master Builder, Chichester, 2010; The Syndicate, Chichester, 2011; Judgement Day, Print Room, 2011; Antony and Cleopatra, Chichester, 2012; Dances of Death, Gate, 2013; Richard II, RSC, 2013; King Lear, NY, 2014; Single Spies, Rose Th., Kingston, 2014; She Stoops to Conquer, Th. Royal Bath, 2015; *film:* The Iron Lady, 2011; *television* includes: Oedipus the King, 1985; Return of Sherlock Holmes, 1986; Dr Terrible's House of Horrible, 2001; Trial and Retribution, 2007. *Publications:* Rossya—A Journey Through Siberia, 1977; The English Shakespeare Company, 1990; Hamlet: a user's guide, 1995; Twelfth Night: a user's guide, 1999; Are You There, Crocodile: inventing Anton Chekhov, 2002; A Midsummer Night's Dream: a user's guide, 2005; Sweet William: twenty thousand hours with Shakespeare, 2012; Let Me Play the Lion Too, 2015. *Recreations:* music, literature. *Address:* c/o Diamond Management, 31 Percy Street, W1T 2DD.

PENNINGTON, Prof. (Thomas) Hugh, CBE 2013; PhD; FRCPath, FRCPE, FMedSci; FRSE; Professor of Bacteriology, University of Aberdeen, 1979–2003, now Emeritus (Dean, Faculty of Medicine, 1987–92); *b* 19 April 1938; *s* of Thomas Wearing Pennington and Dorothy Pennington; *m* 1965, Carolyn Ingram Beattie; two *d. Educ:* Lancaster Royal Grammar Sch.; St Thomas's Hosp. Med. Sch. (MB BS (Hons), Clutton Medal, Bristowe Medal, Beaney Scholarship; PhD). FRCPath 1990. House appts, St Thomas's Hosp., 1962–63; Asst Lectr, 1963–66, Lectr, 1966–67, Dept of Med. Microbiology, St Thomas's Hosp. Med. Sch.; Postdoctoral Fellow, Univ. of Wisconsin, 1967–69; Mem. Scientific Staff, 1969–70, Lectr, 1970–75, Sen. Lectr, 1975–79, MRC Virology Unit and Dept of Virology, Univ. of Glasgow. Chairman: Expert Gp on 1996 E.coli O157 outbreak in Central Scotland, 1996–97; Public Inquiry into 2005 Welsh E.coli O157 outbreak, 2006–09; Member: Scottish Food Adv. Cttee, Food Standards Agency, Scotland, 2000–05; Broadcasting Council for Scotland, 2000–05 (Vice Chair, 2003–05); BBC Rural Affairs Adv. Cttee, 2000–09; World Food Prog. Tech. Adv. Gp, 2002–07. Gov., Rowett Res. Inst., 1980–88, 1995–2004; Mem., Bd of Dirs, Moredun Res. Inst., 2003–06. Pres., Soc. for Gen. Microbiology, 2003–07. Lectures: Pumphandle, John Snow Soc., 1997; Appleyard, BVA, 1997; Col Stock, APHA, 1999; Frank May, Leicester Univ., 2001; Victor Horsley, BMA, 2003; Sampson Gamgee, Birmingham Med. Inst., 2004; Al-Hammadi, RCPE, 2007; Haldane Tait, Scottish Soc. of History of Medicine, 2010. Hon. Vice-Pres., Inst. of Food Sci. and Technol., 2010. Founder FMedSci 1998; FRES 1957; FRSA 1997; FRSE 1997; FRCPE 1998. Hon. DSc: Lancaster, 1999; Strathclyde, 2001; Aberdeen, 2003; Hull, 2004. Caroline Walker Award, 1997; John Kershaw Meml Prize, RIPH&H, 1998; Silver Medal, Royal Scottish Soc. of Arts, 1999; Thomas Graham Medal, Royal Glasgow Philosophical Soc., 2001; 25th Anniv. Award for Achievement, Soc. of Food Hygiene Technol., 2004; Joseph Lister Medal, Soc. of Chemical Industry, 2009; Award for Meritorious Endeavours in Envmtl Health, Royal Envmtl Health Inst. of Scotland, 2010. *Publications:* (with D. A. Ritchie) Molecular Virology, 1975; When Food Kills, 2003; papers on molecular virology, molecular epidemiology and systematics of pathogenic bacteria; contrib. London Review of Books. *Recreations:* collecting books, dipterology. *Address:* 13 Carlton Place, Aberdeen AB15 4BR. *T:* (01224) 645136.

PENNY, family name of **Viscount Marchwood**.

PENNY, Gareth Peter Herbert; Executive Chairman, New World Resources plc, since 2012; Chairman, MMC Norilsk Nickel, since 2013; *b* Cape Town, SA, 24 Dec. 1962; *s* of Peter Penny and Shirley Penny; *m* 1994, Kate Halsted; one *s* one *d. Educ:* Bishops Diocesan Coll., Cape Town; Eton Coll.; Univ. of Oxford (Rhodes Schol.; BA PPE). Various positions, Anglo American Corp., Johannesburg, 1988–91; De Beers: various positions, 1991–2001; Exec. Dir, Sales and Mktg, 2001–04, Man. Dir, 2004–06, Diamond Trading Co.; Gp CEO, De Beers, 2006–10; CEO, AMG Mining, 2011–12. *Recreations:* walking, cycling, sailing, reading. *Address:* New World Resources plc, 115 Park Street, W1K 7AP. *T:* (020) 7317 5990. *E:* jcollins@nwrgroup.eu. *Club:* Royal Automobile.

PENNY, Sir Nicholas (Beaver), Kt 2015; MA, PhD; FBA 2010; FSA; Director, National Gallery, 2008–15; *b* 21 Dec. 1949; *s* of Joseph Noel Bailey Penny, QC; *m* 1st, 1971, Anne Philomel Udy (marr. diss.); two *d*; 2nd, 1994, Mary Agnes Wall, now Crettier (*née* Crettier). *Educ:* Shrewsbury Sch.; St Catharine's Coll., Cambridge (BA, MA; Hon. Fellow, 2009); Courtauld Inst., Univ. of London (MA, PhD). Leverhulme Fellow in the History of Western Art, Clare Hall, Cambridge, 1973–75; Lectr, History of Art Dept, Univ. of Manchester, 1975–82; Sen. Res. Fellow, History of Western Art, King's Coll., Cambridge, 1982–84; Keeper of Western Art, Ashmolean Mus., Oxford, and Professorial Fellow, Balliol Coll., Oxford, 1984–89; Clore Curator of Renaissance Painting, 1990–2002, Keeper, 1998–2002, Nat. Gall.; Sen. Curator of Sculpture and Decorative Arts, Nat. Gall. of Art, Washington, 2002–08. Slade Prof. of Fine Art, Univ. of Oxford, 1980–81; Mellon Prof. at Center for Advanced Study in the Visual Arts, Nat. Gall. of Art, Washington, 2000–02. Mem., Amer. Acad. Arts and Scis, 2007. FSA 2003. Hon. FKC 2013; Hon. Fellow, Balliol Coll., Oxford, 2014. DUniv St Andrews, 2014. Cavaliere nell'Ordine al merito della Repubblica Italiana, 1990. *Publications:* Church Monuments in Romantic England, 1977; Piranesi, 1978; (with Francis Haskell) Taste and the Antique, 1981; Mourning, 1981; (ed jtly) The Arrogant Connoisseur, 1982; (with Roger Jones) Raphael, 1983; (ed) Reynolds, 1986; Alfred and Winifred Turner, 1988; (with Robert Flynn Johnson) Lucian Freud, Works on Paper, 1988; Ruskin's Drawings, 1988; (jtly) From Giotto to Dürer, 1991; Catalogue of European Sculpture in the Ashmolean Museum: 1540 to the present day, 3 vols, 1992; The Materials of Sculpture, 1993; Picture Frames, 1997; (jtly) From Dürer to Veronese, 1999; The Sixteenth Century Italian Paintings in the National Gallery, vol. 1, 2004, vol. 2, 2008; (with A. Radcliffe) Art of the Renaissance Bronze, 2004; Director's Choice, 2011; (jtly) The Sansovino Frame, 2015; reviews for London Review of Books; articles in Apollo, Burlington Magazine, Connoisseur, Jl of Warburg and Courtauld Insts, Past and Present, and elsewhere.

PENNY, Patricia Joyce; *see* Longdon, P. J.

PENNYCOOK, Matthew Thomas; MP (Lab) Greenwich and Woolwich, since 2015; *b* 29 Oct. 1982; partner, Joanna. *Educ:* London Sch. of Econs and Pol Sci. (BA 1st Cl. Hons Internat. Relns and Hist.); Balliol Coll., Oxford (Schol.; MPhil Internat. Relns (Dist.)). Volunteer, Child Poverty Action Gp; sen. roles in charity and voluntary sectors, incl. Fair Pay Network; Sen. Res. and Policy Analyst, Resolution Foundn. Mem., Energy and Climate Change Select Cttee, 2015–. Mem. (Lab) Greenwich LBC, 2010–15. *Address:* House of Commons, SW1A 0AA.

PENNYCOOK, Richard John; Chief Executive Officer, Co-operative Group, since 2014 (Chief Financial Officer, 2013–14); *b* Salisbury, 26 Feb. 1964; *s* of late Gerald Douglas Pennycook and of Margaret Gladys Pennycook; *m* 1995, Suzanne Beal; two *d. Educ:* Univ. of Bristol (BSc 1985). ACA 1987, FCA 1997. Arthur Andersen, 1985–90; Allders plc, 1990–95; Finance Dir, JD Wetherspoon plc, 1995–98; Chief Exec., Welcome Break Hldgs plc, 1998–2002; Finance Director: RAC plc, 2003–05; Wm Morrison Supermarkets plc, 2005–13. Non-executive Director: Persimmon plc, 2008–; Hut Gp Ltd, 2012–; Howden Joinery Gp plc, 2013–. *Address:* Co-operative Group, 1 Angel Square, Manchester M60 0AG. *E:* patricia.chapman@co-operative.coop.

PENNYCUICK, Prof. Colin James, FRS 1990; Senior Research Fellow, University of Bristol, since 1997 (Research Professor in Zoology, 1993); *b* 11 June 1933; *s* of Brig. James Alexander Charles Pennycuick, DSO and Marjorie Pennycuick; *m* Sandy; one *s. Educ:* Wellington College; Merton College, Oxford (MA); Peterhouse, Cambridge (PhD). Lectr in Zoology, 1964–75, Reader, 1975–83, Bristol Univ.; seconded as Lectr in Zoology, Univ. of Nairobi, 1968–71, as Dep. Dir, Serengeti Res. Inst., 1971–73; Maytag Prof. of Ornithology, Univ. of Miami, 1983–92. *Publications:* Animal Flight, 1972; Bird Flight Performance, 1989; Newton Rules Biology, 1992; Modelling the Flying Bird, 2008. *Recreation:* astronomy. *Address:* School of Biological Sciences, University of Bristol, Woodland Road, Bristol BS8 1TQ.

PENRHYN, 7th Baron *cr* 1866; **Simon Douglas-Pennant;** *b* 28 June 1938; *s* of late Hon. Nigel Douglas-Pennant and Margaret Dorothy Douglas-Pennant (*née* Kirkham); *S* uncle, 2003; *m* 1963, Josephine Maxwell, *yr d* of Robert Upcott; two *s* two *d. Educ:* Eton Coll.; Clare Coll., Cambridge (BA Hons). Dir, Brintons Ltd, Kidderminster, 1990–98. *Recreations:* sport (golf, tennis), music, travelling. *Heir: s* Hon. Edward Sholto Douglas-Pennant, *b* 6 June 1966. *Address:* The Old Vicarage, Church Road, Castlemorton, Malvern, Worcs WR13 6BQ. *T:* (01684) 833513. *E:* simon.penrhyn@gmail.com. *Club:* MCC.

PENRITH, Bishop Suffragan of, since 2011; **Rt Rev. Robert John Freeman;** *b* 26 Oct. 1952; *s* of Ralph and Constance Freeman; *m* 1974, Christine Weight; three *d. Educ:* Durham Univ. (BSc Psychol. 1974); Fitzwilliam Coll., Cambridge (MA Theol. 1976). Ordained deacon, 1977, priest, 1978; Asst Curate, Blackpool Parish Ch, 1977–81; Team Vicar, Chigwell (St Winifred), 1981–85; Vicar, Ch of the Martyrs, Leicester, 1985–99; Nat. Evangelism Advr, Archbishops' Council, 1999–2003; Archdeacon of Halifax, 2003–11. RD, Christianity South (Leicester), 1994–98; Hon. Canon, Leicester Cathedral, 1994–2003. Dir and Chm., rejesus.co.uk, 2001–; Chm. and Trustee, Christian Enquiry Agency, 2006–11; Trustee, Simeon's and Hyndman's Trustees, 2007–10; Dir, Active Faith Communities, 2005–10. Mem., Churches Regional Commn Yorks and Humberside, 2004–10. *Publications:* (jtly) 20 from 10: insights from the Decade of Evangelism, 2000; (ed) Mission-shaped Church, 2004. *Recreations:* Motown, electric blues and rock, puddings, computer games, walking, adventure and detective novels. *Address:* Holm Croft, 13 Castle Road, Kendal LA9 7AU. *T:* (01539) 727836. *E:* frmn@frmn.com.

PENROSE, family name of **Baroness Harding of Winscombe**.

PENROSE, Rt Hon. Lord; George William Penrose; PC 2001; a Senator of the College of Justice in Scotland, 1990–2005; *b* 2 June 1938; *s* of late George W. Penrose and Janet L. Penrose; *m* 1964, Wendy Margaret Cooper; one *s* two *d. Educ:* Glasgow Univ. (MA, LLB). CA. Advocate, 1964; QC 1978; Advocate Depute, 1986; Home Advocate Depute, 1988. Procurator to Gen. Assembly of Ch of Scotland, 1984–90. Pres., Scottish procs of Aircraft and Shipbuilding Industries Arbitration Tribunal, 1977–83; Mem., panel of Chairmen, Financial Services Tribunal, 1988–90. Leader, Equitable Life Inquiry, 2001–04. Reporter, Penrose Inquiry, 2009–. Chm. Court, Heriot-Watt Univ., 2008–. FRSE 2010. Hon. LLD Glasgow, 2000; DUniv Stirling, 2001. *Recreation:* walking. *Address:* c/o Court of Session, Parliament House, Edinburgh EH1 1RQ.

PENROSE, Anne Josephine, (Mrs J. Penrose); *see* Robinson, A. J.

PENROSE, George William; *see* Penrose, Rt Hon. Lord.

PENROSE, John David; MP (C) Weston-super-Mare, since 2005; a Lord Commissioner of HM Treasury (Government Whip), since 2014; Parliamentary Secretary, Cabinet Office, since 2015; *b* 22 June 1964; *s* of late David Goronwe Penrose and of Anna Jill Penrose (who *m* 1995, Tom Lawrie); *m* 1995, Hon. Diana Mary Harding (*see* Baroness Harding of Winscombe); two *d. Educ:* Ipswich Sch.; Downing Coll., Cambridge (BA Hons 1986); Columbia Univ., NY (MBA 1991). J. P. Morgan, 1986–90; McKinsey & Co., 1992–94; Commercial Dir, Academic Books Div., Thomson Publishing, 1995–96; Man. Dir, Longman sch. textbooks for UK and Africa, Pearson plc, 1996–2000; Chm., Logotron, 2001–08. Contested (C): Ealing Southall, 1997; Weston-super-Mare, 2001. PPS to Chm., Cons. Policy Rev., 2006–08; Shadow Minister for Business, 2009–10; Parly Under-Sec. of State, DCMS, 2010–12; an Asst Govt Whip, 2013–14. Mem., Amnesty Internat. Mem., Blagdon and Dist Beekeeping Club. *Recreations:* fishing, beekeeping, listening to other people's opinions. *Address:* House of Commons, SW1A 0AA. *Clubs:* Weston-super-Mare Conservative; Weston-super-Mare Constitutional.

PENROSE, Prof. Oliver, FRS 1987; FRSE; Professor of Mathematics, Heriot-Watt University, 1986–94, now Professor Emeritus; *b* 6 June 1929; *s* of Lionel S. Penrose, FRS, and Margaret Penrose, *d* of John Beresford Leathes, FRS; *m* 1953, Joan Lomas Dilley; two *s* one *d* (and one *s* decd). *Educ:* Central Collegiate Inst., London, Ont; University Coll. London (BSc 1949); Cambridge Univ. (PhD 1953). FRSE 1989. Mathematical Physicist, English Electric Co., Luton, 1952–55; Res. Asst, Yale Univ., 1955–56; Lectr, then Reader, in Mathematics, Imperial Coll., London 1956–69; Prof. of Mathematics, Open Univ., 1969–86. *Publications:* Foundations of Statistical Mechanics, 1970, repr. 2005; about 90 papers in physics and maths jls; various book reviews and book chapters. *Recreations:* making music, chess. *Address:* Fir Trees, Doctors Commons Road, Berkhamsted, Herts HP4 3DW. *T:* (01442) 862427. *W:* www.macs.hw.ac.uk/~oliver.

See also Sir R. Penrose.

PENROSE, Sir Roger, OM 2000; Kt 1994; FRS 1972; Rouse Ball Professor of Mathematics, University of Oxford, 1973–98, now Emeritus; Fellow of Wadham College, Oxford, 1973–98, now Emeritus; *b* Colchester, Essex, 8 Aug. 1931; *s* of Lionel Sharples Penrose, FRS; *m* 1959, Joan Isabel Wedge (marr. diss. 1981); three *s*; *m* 1988, Vanessa Dee Thomas; one *s*. *Educ:* University Coll. Sch.; University Coll., Univ. of London (BSc spec. 1st cl. Mathematics), Fellow 1975; St John's Coll., Cambridge (PhD; Hon. Fellow, 1987). NRDC (temp. post, Feb.–Aug. 1956); Asst Lectr (Pure Mathematics), Bedford Coll., London, 1956–57; Research Fellow, St John's Coll., Cambridge, 1957–60; NATO Research Fellow, Princeton Univ. and Syracuse Univ., 1959–61; Research Associate King's Coll., London, 1961–63; Visiting Associate Prof., Univ. of Texas, Austin, Texas, 1963–64; Reader, 1964–66, Prof. of Applied Mathematics, 1966–73, Birkbeck Coll., London. Visiting Prof., Yeshiva, Princeton, Cornell, 1966–67 and 1969; Lovett Prof., Rice Univ., Houston, 1983–87; Distinguished Prof. of Physics and Maths, Syracuse Univ., NY, 1987–. Member: London Mathematical Soc.; Cambridge Philosophical Soc.; Inst. for Mathematics and its Applications; International Soc. for General Relativity and Gravitation. Adams Prize (Cambridge Univ.), 1966–67; Dannie Heineman Prize (Amer. Phys. Soc. and Amer. Inst. Physics), 1971; Eddington Medal (with S. W. Hawking), RAS, 1975; Royal Medal, Royal Soc., 1985; Wolf Foundn Prize for Physics (with S. W. Hawking), 1988; Dirac Medal and Prize, Inst. of Physics, 1989; Einstein Medal, 1990; Copley Medal, Royal Soc., 2008. *Publications:* Techniques of Differential Topology in Relativity, 1973; (with W. Rindler) Spinors and Space-time, Vol. 1, 1984, Vol. 2, 1986; The Emperor's New Mind, 1989 (Science Book Prize, 1990); Shadows of the Mind, 1994; (jtly) The Large, the Small and the Human Mind, 1997; The Road to Reality, 2004; many articles in scientific jls. *Recreations:* 3 dimensional puzzles, doodling at the piano. *Address:* Mathematical Institute, University of Oxford, Andrew Wiles Building, Radcliffe Observatory Quarter, Woodstock Road, Oxford OX2 6GG. *T:* (01865) 273538.

PENRY-DAVEY, Hon. Sir David (Herbert), Kt 1997; a Judge of the High Court of Justice, Queen's Bench Division, 1997–2010; *b* 16 May 1942; *s* of late Watson and Lorna Penry-Davey; *m* 1970, Judy Walter; two *s* one *d*. *Educ:* Hastings Grammar Sch.; King's Coll., London (LLB Hons; FKC 1998). British Univs debating tour of Canada, 1964. Called to the Bar, Inner Temple, 1965, Bencher, 1993; a Recorder, 1986–97; QC 1988; Leader, S Eastern Circuit, 1992–95; a Dep. High Court Judge, 1994–97; Presiding Judge, Northern Circuit, 2000–03. Dep. Chm., Security Vetting Appeals Panel, 2004–13. Chm., Gen. Council of the Bar, 1996 (Vice-Chm., 1995). *Recreations:* music, golf, cycling, hill-walking.

PENSLAR, Prof. Derek Jonathan, PhD; FRSC 2011; Stanley Lewis Professor of Israel Studies, University of Oxford, since 2012; Fellow, St Anne's College, Oxford, since 2012; *b* Los Angeles, 12 Aug. 1958; *s* of Bruce David Penslar and Alice Natalie Penslar (now Krone Harnell); *m* 1983, Robin Levin; one *s* one *d*. *Educ:* Stanford Univ. (BA with Dist. Hist. 1979); Univ. of Calif, Berkeley (MA Hist. 1980; PhD Hist. 1987). Asst Prof. of Hist. and Jewish Studies, 1987–93, Associate Prof., 1993–98, Indiana Univ., Bloomington; Associate Prof. of Jewish Hist., 1998–2001, Samuel Zacks Prof. of Jewish History, 2001–12, Dir, Centre for Jewish Studies, 2002–08, Univ. of Toronto. Nachshon Vis. Prof. of Israel Studies, Harvard Univ., 2006; Vis. Prof. of Israel Studies, Columbia Univ., 2009. *Publications:* Zionism and Technocracy: the engineering of Jewish settlement in Palestine, 1870–1918, 1991 (trans. Hebrew, 2001); (ed with M. Brenner) In Search of Jewish Community: Jewish identity in Germany and Austria, 1918–1933, 1998; Shylock's Children: economics and Jewish identity in modern Europe, 2001; (ed with A. Shapira) Israeli Historical Revisionism: from left to right, 2002; (ed with I. Kalmar) Orientalism and the Jews, 2004; (ed jtly) Contemporary Antisemitism: Canada and the World, 2005; Israel in History: the Jewish State in comparative perspective, 2007; (ed jtly) A New Jewish Time: Jewish culture in an era of secularization, 5 vols in Hebrew, 2007; (with E. Kaplan) The Origins of Modern Israel: a documentary history, 2011; Jews and the Military: a history, 2013; contribs to Annales, Cathedra, German Hist., Hist. & Memory, Israel Studies, Jewish Social Studies, Jewish Hist., Jl Contemp. Hist., Jl Israel Hist., Jl Modern Jewish Studies, Leo Baeck Inst. Year Book, Tsiyon, Yisra'el. *Recreations:* travel, hiking, music, literature, cinema. *Address:* School of Interdisciplinary Area Studies, University of Oxford, 12 Bevington Road, Oxford OX2 6LH; Department of Politics and International Relations, University of Oxford, Manor Road, Oxford OX1 3UQ; St Anne's College, Oxford OX2 6HS.

PENTLAND, Hon. Lord; Paul Benedict Cullen; a Senator of the College of Justice in Scotland, since 2008; Chairman, Scottish Law Commission, since 2014; *b* 11 March 1957; *s* of James Finbarr Cullen and Ann Evaline Black or Cullen; *m* 1983, Joyce Nicol; two *s* one *d*. *Educ:* St Augustine's High Sch., Edinburgh; Edinburgh Univ. (LLB Hons). Admitted to Faculty of Advocates, 1982 (Clerk of Faculty, 1986–90); Standing Jun. Counsel to DoE in Scotland, 1988–91; Advocate Depute, 1992–95; QC (Scot.) 1995; Solicitor Gen. for Scotland, 1995–97. Chairman: Police Appeals Tribunal, 2003–08; Chm., Appeal Cttee, ICAS, 2005–08; a Judge of Upper Tax Tribunal, 2010–14; an Intellectual Property Judge of Court of Session, 2011–14. Scottish Cons. spokesman on home and legal affairs, 1997–98; Chm. Disciplinary Panel, Scottish Cons. Party, 2000–08. Cons. rep. on Scottish Office consultative steering gp on Scottish Parlt, 1998–99. Chm., Gilmerton Limestone Emergency inquiry, 2001–02. Vice Pres., Edinburgh S Cons. & Unionist Assoc., 1997–2008. Contested (C) Eastwood, 1997. *Recreations:* tennis, bridge, the Turf. *Address:* Court of Session, Parliament House, Edinburgh EH1 1RQ. *T:* (0131) 225 2595. *Clubs:* New (Edinburgh); Braid Lawn Tennis.

PENTLAND, Ven. Raymond Jackson, CB 2013; Archdeacon, 2006–14, and Director General Chaplaincy Services Headquarters Air Command and Chaplain-in-Chief, 2009–14, Royal Air Force; *b* 14 July 1957; *s* of Adam Jackson Pentland and Edith Henderson Pentland; *m* 1979, Christine Ann Lyth; one *s* one *d*. *Educ:* Cowdenknowes High Sch.; William Booth Meml Coll.; St John's Coll., Nottingham (DPS 1988); Open Univ. (BA 1990); Westminster Coll., Oxford (MTh 2002; Farmington Fellow, 2004). Salvation Army Officer, 1979–86; ordained deacon, 1988, priest, 1989; Asst Curate, St Jude's, Nottingham, 1988–90; Chaplain, 1990–2005, Comd Chaplain, 2005–06, RAF. QHC 2006–14. Mem., Gen. Synod, 2005–14. Hon. Canon, Lincoln Cathedral, 2006–14, now Canon Emeritus; Hon. Asst Curate, St Andrew by the Wardrobe and St James Garlickhythe, 2015–. Permission to officiate, Oxford and London, 2015. Hon. Chaplain: Coachmakers' and Coach Harness Makers' Co., 2010–; Battle of Britain Fighter Assoc., 2011–; Hon. Co. of Air Pilots, 2014–; Hon. Vice Pres., 101 Sqn Assoc., 2014–. Officer, RAuxAF, 2014– (Mem., Defence Bd Service Complaints Panel, 2014–). Pres., Friends of St Clement Danes Church, 2013–; Patron, RAF Widows Assoc., 2014–; Trustee, Battle of Britain Meml Trust, 2015–. *Publications:* contrib. Political Theol. *Recreations:* gourmet cuisine, travel, modern military history. *Address:* 16 Nicholas Charles Crescent, Aylesbury HP18 0GU. *T:* (01296) 323213. *E:* r.pentland@btopenworld.com. *Club:* Royal Air Force.

PENTREATH, Prof. Richard John, (Jan), DSc, PhD; CBiol, FRSB; CRadP; FSRP; Research Professor, Environmental Systems Science Centre, University of Reading, 2000–07, now Professor Emeritus; *b* 28 Dec. 1943; *s* of John Alistair Dudley Pentreath and Mary Lena (*née* Gendall); *m* 1965, Elisabeth Amanda Leach; two *d*. *Educ:* Humphry Davy Grammar Sch.; QMC, London (BSc (Special)); DSc London; Univ. of Auckland (PhD). FRSB (FIBiol 1980); CBiol 1984; FSRP 1989; CRadP 2008. Commonwealth Schol., 1966–68; SRC Fellow, 1969; Fisheries Radiobiol Lab., MAFF, 1969–89: Hd, Aquatic Envmtl Protection Div. and Dep. Dir, Fisheries Res., 1988–89; Chief Scientist, and Dir Water Quality, NRA, 1989–95; Chief Scientist, and Dir, Envmtl Strategy, EA, 1995–2000. Member: NERC, 1992–98; Adv. Bd, Centre for Social and Econ. Res. on Global Envmt, 1994–2005; Res. Assessment Panel, HEFC, 1995–96, 1999–2001; Council, Marine Biol Assoc. of UK, 1997–2000; Council, Assoc. for Schs Science Engrg and Technol., 1998–2000; Internat. Commn on Radiol Protection, 2003–13, now Emeritus Mem. (Chm., Cttee 5, Envmtl Protection, 2005–13); Trustee, SAHFOS, 2001–; Ind. Mem., JNCC, 2000–06. Res. Fellow, Plymouth Marine Lab., 2009–. Pres., Cornwall Sustainable Bldg Trust, 2005–11. Non-exec. Dir, Research Sites Restoration Ltd, 2009–. Hon. Prof., UEA, 1996–2008; Vis. Prof., ICSTM, 1997–2003. Pres., Cornwall Wildlife Trust, 2003–. Hon. DSc: Hertfordshire, 1998; UWE, 1999; Plymouth, 2002. *Publications:* Nuclear Power, Man and the Environment, 1980; contrib. numerous scientific papers. *Recreations:* Cornish history, crewing tall ships, visual arts. *Address:* Camelot House, Ropewalk, Penpol, Truro, Cornwall TR3 6NA. *T:* (01872) 862838.

PENTY, Prof. Richard Vincent, PhD; FREng; Professor of Photonics, Department of Engineering, University of Cambridge, since 2002; Fellow, since 2002, and Master, since 2013, Sidney Sussex College, Cambridge; *b* Nottingham, 9 Sept. 1964; *s* of Peter Richard Penty and (Patricia) Janet Penty; *m* 1992, Victoria Frances Mary Eve; two *s* one *d*. *Educ:* Repton Sch.; Sidney Sussex Coll., Cambridge (BA Engrg and Electrical Sci. 1986; PhD Engrg 1990). SMIEE 2010; FIET 2012; FREng 2012. SERC IT Res. Fellow, Dept of Engrg, Univ. of Cambridge, 1989–90; Maudslay Res. Fellow, Pembroke Coll., Cambridge, 1989–90; Lectr, Sch. of Phys, Univ. of Bath, 1990–95; University of Bristol: Lectr in Electronic Engrg, 1995–98; Reader in Optical Communications, 1998–2001; Prof. of Photonics, 2001; Asst Dir of Res., Dept of Engrg, Univ. of Cambridge, 2001–02; Vice Master, 2008, 2011–12, Actg Master, 2012–13, Sidney Sussex Coll., Cambridge. Founder and Dir, 2003–05, Mem., Technical Adv. Bd, 2005–11, Zinwave Ltd; Founder and Dir, PervasID Ltd, 2011–. Editor-in-Chief, IET Optoelectronics Jl, 2006–. *Recreations:* reading, running, sleeping. *Address:* The Master's Lodge, Sidney Sussex College, Cambridge CB2 3HU. *T:* (01223) 330868. *E:* master@sid.cam.ac.uk.

PENZER, Dr Geoffrey Ronald, FRSC; Partner, Penzer Allen, since 1992; *b* 15 Nov. 1943; *s* of Ronald and Dora Penzer; *m* 1966, Sylvia Elaine (*née* Smith); one *s* one *d*. *Educ:* Merchant Taylors' Sch.; St John's Coll., Oxford (MA; DPhil 1969). CChem, FRSC 1979. Jun. Res. Fellow, Merton Coll., Oxford, 1967–69; Res. Chemist, Univ. of Calif, 1969–70; Lectr in Biol Chem., Univ. of York, 1970–75; British Council: Science Officer, Cairo, 1975–80; Science Officer, Mexico, 1980–84; Dir, Technical Co-operation Training Dept, 1984–87; Dir, Management Div., and Manager, HQ Location Project, 1987–91. Dir, Penzer Allen Ltd, 1993–. Mem., Ind. Monitoring Bd, HMP Belmarsh, 2009–12; Chm., Ind. Monitoring Bd, HMP Thameside, 2012–; Mem. for Gtr London, Nat. Council for Ind. Monitoring Bds, 2015–; Mem., Professional Conduct Panel, Nat. Coll. for Teaching and Leadership (formerly Teaching Agency), 2012–. Trustee: Outset, 1994–2002; bss Ltd, 2001–09. *Publications:* contrib. scientific books and jls. *Recreations:* music, landscapes, walking. *Address:* c/o Penzer Allen, Windward Lodge, West Kingsdown, Sevenoaks, Kent TN15 6AH.

PENZIAS, Dr Arno Allan; Venture Partner, New Enterprise Associates, since 1998; *b* 26 April 1933; *s* of Karl and Justine Penzias; *m*; one *s* two *d*; *m* 1996, Sherry Levit Penzias. *Educ:* City Coll. of New York (BS Physics, 1954); Columbia Univ. (MA Physics, 1958; PhD Physics, 1962). Bell Laboratories: Mem., Technical Staff, 1961–72; Head, Radio Physics Res., 1972–76; Dir, Radio Res. Lab., 1976–79; Exec. Dir, Research, Communications Sciences, 1979–81; Vice-Pres., Research, 1981–95; Vice-Pres. and Chief Scientist, AT&T Bell Laboratories, 1995–96; Lucent Technologies, Bell Labs Innovations: Vice-Pres. and Chief Scientist, 1996–98; Sen. Tech. Advr, 1998–2000. Lectr, Princeton Univ., 1967–72, Vis. Prof., Astrophysical Scis Dept, 1972–85; Res. Associate, Harvard Univ., 1968–80; Adjunct Prof., State Univ. of NY, Stony Brook, 1974–84; Lee Kuan Yew Dist. Vis., Nat. Univ. of Singapore, 1991. Lectures: Kompfner, Stanford Univ., 1979; Gamow, Colorado Univ., 1980; Jansky, NRAO, 1983; Michelson Meml, Dept US Navy, 1985; Tanner, Southern Utah State Coll., 1987; Klopsteg, Northwestern Univ., 1987; NSF Distinguished, 1987; Regent's, Univ. of Calif., Berkeley, 1990; Einstein, Princeton, 1996. Member: Sch. of Engrg and Applied Science (Bd Overseers), Univ. Pennsylvania, 1983–86; Union Councils for Soviet Jews Adv. Bd, 1983–95; NSF Industrial Panel on Science and Technology, 1982–92; CIT Vis. Cttee, 1977–79; NSF Astronomy Adv. Panel, 1978–79; MNAS, 1975–; Wissenschaftliche Fachbeirat, Max-Planck Inst., Bonn, 1978–85 (Chm., 1981–83); Technology Adv. Council, EarthLink Network Inc., 1996–98; Board of Directors: IMNET, 1986–92; A. D. Little, 1992–2001; Duracell, 1995–96; LCC, 1996–2001; Warpspeed, 1996–2001. Vice-Chm., Cttee of Concerned Scientists, 1976– (Mem., 1975–). Mem., National Acad. of Engrg, 1990. Hon. MIEEE, 1990. Trustee, Trenton State Coll., 1977–79. Hon. degrees: Paris Observatory, 1976; Wilkes Coll., City Coll. of NY, Yeshiva Univ., and Rutgers Univ., 1979; Bar Ilan Univ., 1983; Monmouth Coll., 1984; Technion-Israel Inst. of Technology, Pittsburgh Univ., Ball State Univ., Kean Coll., 1986; Ohio State Univ., Iona Coll., 1988; Drew Univ., 1989; Lafayette Coll., 1990; Columbia Univ., 1990; George Washington Univ., 1992; Rensselaer Polytechnic Inst., 1992; Pennsylvania Univ., 1992; Bloomfield Coll., 1994; Ranken Tech. Coll., 1997; Hebrew Union Coll., 1997; Oxford, 2002. Henry Draper Medal, National Acad. of Sciences, 1977; Herschel Medal, RAS, 1977; (jtly) Nobel Prize for Physics, 1978; Townsend Harris Medal, City Coll. NY, 1979; Newman Award, City Coll. NY, 1983; Joseph Handleman Prize in the Scis, 1983; Grad. Faculties Alumni Award, 1984; Big Brothers Inc. of NY, City Achievement in Science Award, 1985; Priestly Award, Dickinson Coll., 1989; Pake Prize, APS, 1990; NJ Literary Hall of Fame, 1991; Pender Award, Pennsylvania Univ., 1992; NJ Science/Technology Medal, R&D Council of NJ, 1996; Industrial Res. Inst. Medalist, 1998. Mem. Editorial Bd, Annual Revs of Astronomy and Astrophysics, 1974–78; Associate Editor, Astrophysical Jl Letters, 1978–82. *Publications:* Ideas and Information: managing in a high-tech world, 1989; Harmony: business, technology & life after paperwork, 1995; 100 published articles, principally in Astrophysical Jl. *Address:* 2855 Sand Hill Road, Menlo Park, CA 94025, USA.

PEPINSTER, Catherine; Editor, The Tablet, since 2004; *b* 7 June 1959; *d* of late Michel Joseph Pepinster and of Winifred Pepinster (*née* Jones); *m* 2003, Kevin Charles Morley. *Educ:* Manchester Univ. (BA (Econ. and Soc. Sci.) 1980); City Univ., London (Postgrad. Dip. Journalism 1981); Heythrop Coll., Univ. of London (MA (Philos. and Religion) 2002). Local newspaper reporter, Manchester and London, 1981–85; Property Correspondent, Sheffield Morning Telegraph, 1985–86; Chief Reporter, Estates Times, 1986; News Ed., Building, 1987–89; reporter, The Observer, 1989–90; News Ed., Time Out, 1990–94; Asst News Ed., The Independent, 1994–95; Dep. News Ed., 1995–97, News Ed., 1997–98, Independent on Sunday; Features Ed., The Independent, 1998; Asst Ed., 1999–2002, Exec. Ed., 2002–04, Independent on Sunday. Regular contributor, Thought for the Day, BBC Radio 4; contribs to other radio and TV. Vis. Scholar, St Benet's Hall, Oxford, 2014–15. Dir, Kaleidoscope, 2010–. Trustee, Bible Soc., 2014–. *Publications:* (ed) John Paul II: reflections from The Tablet, 2005; (contrib.) Religion and the News, 2012; (contrib.) Religion, Society and God: public theology in action, 2013. *Recreations:* walking, reading, architecture, Belgian culture. *Address:*

The Tablet, 1 King Street Cloisters, Clifton Walk, W6 0GY. *T:* (020) 8748 8484, *Fax:* (020) 8748 1550. *E:* cpepinster@thetablet.co.uk. *Club:* Reform.

PEPPÉ, Comdr William Lawrence Tosco, OBE 1987; Vice Lord-Lieutenant of Ross and Cromarty, 2005–12; *b* 25 Nov. 1937; *s* of Lt-Col William Tosco Hill Peppé, DSO, OBE, MC and Alison Mary (*née* Johnson); *m* 1966, Deirdre Eva Preston Wakefield; three *s*. *Educ:* Wellington Coll.; King's Coll., Cambridge. Joined RN, 1955; Commanding Officer: 892 Naval Air Sqn, 1974–76; HMS Diomede, 1980–81; retd 1991. Chm., Skye and Lochalsh Access Forum, 2007–10. JP Skye and Lochalsh, 1992–2007; DL Ross and Cromarty, Skye and Lochalsh, 1996–2012. Hon. Sheriff, Portree and Lochmaddy, 2007. *Recreation:* country. *Address:* Glendrynoch Lodge, Carbost, Isle of Skye IV47 8SX.

PEPPER, Sir David (Edwin), KCMG 2005; DPhil; Chairman, Defence Science and Technology Laboratory, since 2014; *b* 8 Feb. 1948; *s* of Samuel Edwin Pepper and Rose Pepper (*née* Pell); *m* 1970, Margaret Meehan; two *s*. *Educ:* Chigwell Sch.; St John's Coll., Oxford (MA, DPhil 1972). Joined Government Communications Headquarters, 1972: Principal, 1979; Grade 5, 1984; RCDS 1991; Dir of Admin, 1995–98; on loan to Home Office as Dir, Corporate Develt, 1998–2000; Dir, Policy and Resources, 2000–03; Dir, GCHQ, 2003–08. Mem., UK Adv. Bd, Thales, 2009–13; Advr, Deloitte, 2011–14. *Recreations:* walking, music, reading, cooking, family history.

PEPPER, Prof. Gordon Terry, CBE 1990; Hon. Visiting Professor, Sir John Cass Business School, City of London (formerly City University Business School), 1987–90 and 1998–2011 (Director, Centre for Financial Markets, 1988–97 and Professor, 1991–97); Director, Lombard Street Research Ltd, since 1998 (Chairman, 2000–09); *b* 2 June 1934; *s* of Harold Terry Pepper and Jean Margaret Gordon Pepper (*née* Furness); *m* 1958, Gillian Clare Huelin; three *s* one *d*. *Educ:* Repton; Trinity College, Cambridge (MA); FIA, FSIP. Equity & Law Life Assurance Soc., 1957–60; W. Greenwell & Co.: Partner, 1962; Joint Senior Partner, 1980–86; Chairman, Greenwell Montagu & Co., 1986–87; Dir and Sen. Advr, Midland Montagu, 1985–90; Chm., Payton Pepper & Sons Ltd, 1987–97. Member: Cttee on Industry and Finance, NEDC, 1988–90; ESRC, 1989–93; Adv. Cttee, Dept of Applied Econs, Cambridge Univ., 1992–97; Shadow Monetary Policy Cttee, 1997–2011; Council of Econ. Advrs to Opposition front bench, 1999–2006. *Publications:* Money, Credit and Inflation, 1990; Money, Credit and Asset Prices, 1994; Inside Thatcher's Monetarist Revolution, 1998; (with M. Oliver) Monetarism under Thatcher - Lessons for the Future, 2001; Liquidity Theory of Asset Prices, 2006; papers to Jl of Inst. of Actuaries. *Recreations:* sailing, family. *Address:* Durnsford Mill, Mildenhall, Marlborough, Wilts SN8 2NG. *T:* (01672) 511073, *Fax:* (01672) 513715. *E:* gordonpepper@btopenworld.com. *Clubs:* Reform, Royal Ocean Racing.

PEPPER, Prof. John Robert, OBE 2015; FRCS; Professor of Cardiothoracic Surgery, National Heart and Lung Institute, Imperial College London, since 1999; Consultant Cardiothoracic Surgeon, Royal Brompton Hospital, since 1990; *b* Plymouth, 8 March 1948; *s* of Donald and Maureen Pepper; *m* 1973, Hilary; two *s*. *Educ:* Clare Coll., Cambridge (BA 1968; MB BChir 1971; MChir); Guy's Hosp. Med. Sch. Hse surgeon, 1971–72, SHO, Cardiothoracic Unit, 1972–73, Guy's Hosp.; Registrar: Gen. Surgery, St James' Hosp., Leeds, 1973–75; Cardiothoracic Surgery, Nat. Heart Hosp., London Chest Hosp. and Guy's Hosp., 1975–79; Consultant Cardiothoracic Surgeon: London Chest Hosp. and Southend Hosp., 1980–82; St George's Hosp. and St Helier Hosp., 1982–90. Mem., Soc. of Apothecaries. *Publications:* chapters to med. textbooks and contribs to scientific jls. *Recreations:* sailing, photography. *Address:* Royal Brompton Hospital, Sydney Street, SW3 6NP. *T:* (020) 7351 8530. *E:* j.pepper@rbht.nhs.uk.

PEPPER, Sir Michael, Kt 2006; FRS 1983; FREng; Pender Professor of Nanoelectronics, University College London, since 2009 (Hon. Professor of Physics, since 2009); Fellow of Trinity College, Cambridge, since 1982 (Senior Research Fellow, 1982–87; Professorial Fellow, 1987–2009); *b* 10 Aug. 1942; *s* of Morris and Ruby Pepper; *m* 1973, Jeannette Denise Josse, MB, BS, FRCPsych; two *d*. *Educ:* St Marylebone Grammar Sch.; Reading Univ. (BSc Physics, 1963; PhD Physics, 1967); MA 1987, ScD 1989, Cantab. FInstP 1991, Hon. FInstP 2012; FREng 2009. Res. Physicist, Mullard Ltd, 1967–69; res. in solid state physics, The Plessey Co., Allen Clark Res. Centre, 1969–73; Cavendish Lab., 1973–2009 (in association with The Plessey Co., 1973–82); Warren Res. Fellow of Royal Soc., Cavendish Lab., 1978–86; Principal Res. Fellow, GEC plc, Hirst Res. Centre, 1982–87; Prof. of Physics, Univ. of Cambridge, 1987–2009, now Emeritus. Jt Man. Dir, 1991–2007, Sen. Adviser, 2007–, Toshiba Res. Europe Ltd (formerly Toshiba Cambridge Res. Centre Ltd); Jt Founder and Dir, TeraView Ltd, 2001–. Mem., Univ. Council, 1993–97, 2000, Gen. Bd of Faculties, 1995–99, and various cttees of Council and Bd, 1993–99, Cambridge. Visiting Professor: Bar-Ilan Univ., Israel, 1984; in Physical Scis and Engrg, Univ. of Oxford, 2010–; Hon. Prof. of Pharmaceutical Sci., Univ. of Otago, NZ, 2005–. Lectures: Inaugural Mott, Inst. of Physics, 1985; Royal Soc. Review, 1987; Rankin, Liverpool Univ., 1987; G. I. Taylor, Cambridge Philosophical Soc., 1988; Resnick, Bar-Ilan Univ., 1995; Mountbatten Meml, IEE, 2003; Bakerian, Royal Soc., 2004; Saha Meml, Kolkata, 2008; Cherwell-Simon Meml, Oxford, 2010; C. V. Raman Meml, Indian Inst. of Sci., Bangalore, 2010; Inst. of Physics Prestige Speaker, Hereford and Worcester, 2010; Waterloo Inst. of Nanotechnol. Dist. Lectr, 2010; Inst. of Physics Cockroft-Walton Lectr, India, 2013; Srinivasan Meml Lectr, Indian Inst. of Sci., Bangalore, 2013; Fr Verstraeten Meml, St Xavier, Kolkata, 2013; Dirac, Univ. of NSW, 2013; Gustave Eiffel, ICE, 2014; Kelvin, IET, 2015. Past and present mem. of various cttees and panels of Inst. of Physics (Editl Bd, Jl of Physics, Condensed Matter, 1991–96; Sci. Adv. Cttee, Inst. of Physics Publishing, 2005–), Royal Soc. (Associate Editor, 1983–89; Mem. Council, 1999–2001; Editor, Phil. Trans A, 2008–10), Rutherford Meml Cttee, 1987–91, DTI and SERC (Cttees on Solid State Devices, Semiconductors, 1984–89); Mem., Council for Industry and Higher Educn, 2005–08. Trustee, Wolfson Foundn, 2011–. Fellow, Amer. Physical Soc., 1992; MAE 2012. Hon. DSc: Bar-Ilan, 1993; Linköping, 1997; Hon. DSc NSW, 2013. Guthrie Prize and Medal, 1985, Mott Prize and Medal, 2000, Business and Innovation Medal (Gold), 2010, Inst. of Physics; Hewlett-Packard Prize, European Physical Soc., 1985; Hughes Medal, 1987, Royal Medal, 2005, Royal Soc.; Faraday Medal, IET, 2013; Silver Dirac Medal, Australian Inst. of Physics, 2013. *Publications:* papers on semiconductors and solid state physics in jls. *Recreations:* whisky tasting, reading, travel. *Address:* Department of Electronic and Electrical Engineering, University College London, Torrington Place, WC1E 7JE. *E:* michael.pepper@ucl.ac.uk, mp10000@cam.ac.uk. *Clubs:* Athenæum; Arsenal Football.

PEPPER, Michael Peter Gregory, PhD; independent international statistical consultant, since 2004; *b* 2 June 1945; *s* of Arthur Pepper and Anne (*née* Panian); *m* 1st; two *s*; 2nd; one step *d*; 3rd, 2013, Ruth Lewis; two step *d*. *Educ:* Dr Challoner's Grammar Sch., Amersham; London Univ. (BSc Maths (Ext.)); Essex Univ. (MSc); PhD Bath. Res. Fellow, Univ. of Bath, 1970–74; Statistician, Dept of Energy, 1974–79; Sen. Statistician, Govt of Botswana, 1979–81; Statistician, Dept of Energy, 1981–86; Chief Statistician and Dir of Stats, Welsh Office, 1986–93; Hd of Price and Business Statistics Gp, CSO, subseq. ONS, 1993–2002; Exec. Dir, Business Transformation, ONS, 2002–04. *Recreations:* travel, gardening, choral music. *Address:* 2 Wetherell Place, Bristol BS8 1AR.

PEPPER, Simon Richard, OBE 2000; independent adviser on environment and sustainability; *b* Worthing, 1947; *s* of Dr Richard Pepper and Patricia Pepper; *m* 1973, Morag Mackenzie; one *s* one *d* and one step *s* two step *d*. *Educ:* Univ. of Aberdeen (BSc Zool.); University Coll. London (MSc Conservation). Dir, WWF Scotland, 1985–2005; Rector, Univ. of St Andrews, 2005–08. Member: Nat. Cttee, Forestry Commn Scotland, 2003–09; Cabinet Sub-cttee on Sustainable Scotland, Scottish Exec., 2004–07; Deer Commn Scotland, 2005–10; Bd, Scottish Natural Heritage, 2010–. Mem., Scottish Cttee, HLF, 2011–. Chm., Awards Panel, Scottish Govt's Climate Challenge Fund, 2008–12. Hon. LLD St Andrews, 2008. *Recreations:* enjoying the wild, stewardship of 100 acres in Perthshire Hills.

PEPPER, Terence, OBE 2002; Curator of Photographs and Exhibitions Organiser, 1978–2014, Senior Special Adviser on Photographs, since 2014, National Portrait Gallery; *b* 2 Jan. 1949; *s* of (Herbert Walter) Trevor Pepper and (Catherine) Rosemary (*née* Earle); partner, Rosalind Crowe. *Educ:* Epsom Coll.; Queen Mary Coll., Univ. of London (LLB); Council of Legal Educn; Sch. of Librarianship, Ealing Tech. Coll. ALA 1977. Asst Librarian, 1975, Librarian, 1976–78, NPG. Mem. Council, John Kobal Foundn, 1992–. Hon. FRPS 2002. *Publications:* exhibition catalogues: Monday's Children: fair and famous of the 1920s and 1930s, 1977; Camera Portraits by E. O. Hoppe, 1978; Photographs by Norman Parkinson: fifty years of portraits and fashion, 1981; Howard Coster's Celebrity Portraits, 1985; (contrib. with D. Mellor) Cecil Beaton, 1986; Portraits Helmut Newton, 1988; Lewis Morley: photographer of the sixties, 1989; (with J. Kobal) The Man Who Shot Garbo: the photographs of Clarence Sinclair Bull, 1989; Dorothy Wilding: the pursuit of perfection, 1991; The Lure of the Limelight: James Abbe, photographer of cinema and stage, 1995; High Society: photographs 1897–1914, 1998; (curated with P. Hoare) Icons of Pop, 1999; Horst Portraits, 2001; Cecil Beaton: Portraits, 2004 (German edn 2005); Angus McBean: Portraits, 2006; (curated with D. Friend) Vanity Fair Portraits: photographs 1913–2008, 2008 (Curator/Exhibn of the Year (jtly), Lucie Awards, 2008); Beatles to Bowie: the 60s exposed, 2009 (German edn 2009); Twiggy: a life in photographs, 2009; (with P. Prodger) Hoppe Portraits: society, studio and street, 2011; Man Ray Portraits, 2013. *Recreations:* swimming, cinema, reading Sunday newspapers, pop music. *Address:* c/o National Portrait Gallery, 2 St Martin's Place, WC2H 0HE. *T:* (020) 7306 0055, *Fax:* (020) 7306 0056. *E:* tpepper@npg.org.uk.

PEPPERALL, Edward Brian; QC 2013; a Recorder, since 2009; *b* Bristol, 27 Dec. 1966; *s* of Brian Robert Pepperall and Marcia Louise Pepperall; *m* 2003, Sarah Josephine Fardell; one *s* two *d*. *Educ:* Queen Elizabeth's Hospital, Bristol; Univ. of Birmingham (LLB Law Hons 1988); Inns of Court Sch. of Law. Called to the Bar, Lincoln's Inn, 1989; in practice as a barrister, specialising in commercial and employment law; 2 Fountain Court, Birmingham, 1989–98, St Philips Chambers, Birmingham and London, 1998–, 2 Temple Gardens, London, 2011–13. Mem., Civil Procedure Rule Cttee, 2010–. *Publications:* contrib. to legal jls. *Recreations:* tennis, theatre. *Address:* St Philips Chambers, 55 Temple Row, Birmingham B2 5LS. *T:* (0121) 246 7000, *Fax:* (0121) 246 7001; St Philips Chambers, 9 Gower Street, WC1E 6HB. *E:* ep@st-philips.com.

PEPPIATT, Hugh Stephen Kenneth; Chairman, Moorfields Eye Hospital, 1991–98 (Special Trustee, 1991–2000); *b* 18 Aug. 1930; *s* of late Sir Leslie Peppiatt, MC and Lady (Cicely) Peppiatt; *m* 1960, Claire, *e d* of late Ian Douglas Davidson, CBE and Claire Davidson; three *s* two *d*. *Educ:* Winchester College; Trinity College, Oxford (schol.; MA); Univ. of Wisconsin. 2nd Lt, Coldstream Guards, 1948–50. Partner, Freshfields, Solicitors, 1960–90: Resident Partner, New York, 1977–81; Sen. Partner, 1982–90. Director: Greig Fester Gp, 1990–97; Hardy Oil & Gas, 1992–98; Benfield Greig Gp plc, 1997–99. Dir, St John Eye Hosp., Jerusalem, 1998–2005. Trustee, Help the Aged, 1991–97. CStJ 2003. *Recreations:* hillwalking, fly fishing, birdwatching. *Address:* 28 Bathgate Road, Wimbledon, SW19 5PN. *T:* (020) 8947 2709. *Clubs:* City of London; Royal Wimbledon Golf; Larchmont Yacht (New York).

PEPPITT, His Honour John Raymond; QC 1976; a Circuit Judge, 1991–2000; *b* 22 Sept. 1931; *s* of late Reginald Peppitt and Phyllis Claire Peppitt; *m* 1960, Judith Penelope James; three *s*. *Educ:* St Paul's Sch.; Jesus Coll., Cambridge (BA Classical Tripos). Called to the Bar, Gray's Inn, 1958, Bencher, 1982; a Recorder, 1976–91. *Recreation:* collecting water-colours. *Address:* The Old Rectory, Snargate, Romney Marsh, Kent TN29 0EW. *Club:* Farmers.

PEPYS, family name of **Earl of Cottenham**.

PEPYS, Sir Mark (Brian), Kt 2012; MD, PhD; FRS 1998; FRCP, FRCPath, FMedSci; Director, Wolfson Drug Discovery Unit, University College London, since 2011; Hon. Consultant Physician, Royal Free Hospital, since 1999; *b* 18 Sept. 1944; *s* of Prof. Jack Pepys, MD, FRCP, FRCPE, FRCPath, and Rhoda Gertrude Pepys (*née* Kussel); *m* 1971, Dr Elizabeth Olga Winternitz; one *s* one *d*. *Educ:* Trinity Coll., Cambridge (BA, MA; MD 1982; PhD 1973; Hon. Fellow, 2014); UCH Med. Sch., London. FRCP 1981; FRCPath 1991. Sen. Schol., 1964–65, Res. Schol., 1970–73, Fellow, 1973–79, Trinity Coll., Cambridge; MRC Trng Fellow, Dept of Pathology, Univ. of Cambridge, 1970–73; Registrar, then Sen. Registrar and Asst Lectr in Medicine, Hammersmith Hosp., 1973–75; Sen. Lectr, Hd of Immunology and Hon. Consultant Physician, Royal Free Hosp. Sch. of Medicine, 1975–77; Sen. Lectr in Medicine, 1977–80, Hon. Consultant Physician, 1977–99, Reader, 1980–84, Prof. of Immunol Medicine, 1984–99, RPMS, then ICSM, Hammersmith Hosp.; Prof. of Medicine and Hd, Div. of Medicine, Royal Free Campus, UCL Med. Sch. (formerly Royal Free and University Coll. Med. Sch.), 1999–2011, now Emeritus Prof.; Founder and Hd, NHS Nat. Amyloidosis Centre, 1999–2011. Mem., Scientific Council, Cardiothoracic Centre of Monaco, 2008–. Goulstonian Lectr, 1982, Lumleian Lectr, 1998, Harveian Orator, 2007, RCP; Sir Arthur Sims Travelling Prof., RCS, 1991; Kohn Lectr, RCPath, 1991; Chandos Lectr, Renal Assoc., 2000; Heberden Orator and Medallist, British Soc. for Rheumatology, 2002; Richard Kovacs Lectr, RSM, 2009; Michael Feiwel Meml Lectr, RSM, 2010; Gordon Cumming Meml Lectr, Med. Res. Soc., 2010; Adam Neville Lectr, Univ. of Dundee, 2010; Enno Mandema Meml Lectr, Internat. Soc. for Amyloidosis, 2012. Member Council: Royal Soc., 2003–05; Acad. of Med. Scis, 2003–06. Hon. Mem., Assoc. of Physicians of GB and Ireland, 1998. Founder FMedSci 1998. Fellow: UCL, 2003; Faculty of Medicine, Imperial Coll. London, 2004. Moxon Trust Medal, RCP, 1999; Glaxo Smith Kline Prize and Lect., Royal Soc., 2007; Ernst Chain Prize, Imperial Coll. London, 2008. *Publications:* international patents on drug design and novel therapies; contrib. articles on immunology, acute phase proteins and amyloidosis in learned jls. *Recreations:* ski-ing, wine. *Address:* 22 Wildwood Road, NW11 6TE. *T:* (020) 8455 9387. *Club:* Hurlingham.

PERAHIA, Murray, Hon. KBE 2004; FRCM; pianist and conductor; Principal Guest Conductor, Academy of St Martin-in-the-Fields, since 2001; *b* New York, 19 April 1947; *s* of David and Flora Perahia; *m* 1980, Naomi Shohet (Ninette); two *s*. *Educ:* High Sch. of Performing Arts; Mannes College (MS); studied piano with Jeanette Haien, M. Horszowski, Arthur Balsam. FRCM 1987; FRAM 1994. Co-Artistic Dir, Aldeburgh Fest., 1981–89; Hon. Dir, Britten-Pears Sch. for Advanced Musical Studies, 1981–. Won Kosciuszko Chopin Prize, 1965; début Carnegie Recital Hall, 1966; won Leeds Internat. Piano Festival, 1972; Avery Fisher Award, 1975; regular tours of Europe, Asia, USA; numerous recordings include complete Mozart Piano Concertos (as dir and soloist with English Chamber Orch.), complete Beethoven Piano Concertos (with Bernard Haitink and Royal Concertgebouw), Bartók Sonata for Two Pianos and Percussion (Grammy Award, 1989); Gramophone award for Handel and Scarlatti recording, 1997; Gramophone award for Bach English Suites recording, 1999; Chopin Études (Grammy Award, 2002). Hon. Fellow, Jesus Coll., Cambridge, 2007. *Address:* c/o IMG Artists-Europe, The Light Box, 111 Power Road, W4 5PY.

PERCEVAL, Michael; HM Diplomatic Service, retired; Consul-General, Barcelona, 1992–96; *b* 27 April 1936; *o s* of late Hugh Perceval and Guida Brind; *m* 1968, Alessandra Grandis; one *s* one *d*. *Educ:* Downside Sch.; Christ Church, Oxford (Schol.; 2nd Cl. Hons English Lit.). Served Royal Air Force, Nicosia, 1956–60; film production asst, Athens, 1960; freelance correspondent, Madrid, 1961–69; joined FCO, 1970; First Sec. (Press), UK Rep. to

EC, Brussels, 1972–74; First Sec. and subseq. Head of Chancery, British High Commission, Nicosia, 1974–78; Asst Head of Mexico and Caribbean Dept, FCO, 1978–79; Counsellor, Havana, 1980–82; Counsellor (Political and Economic) and Consul-Gen., Brasilia, 1982–85; Counsellor (Commercial), Rome, 1985–89; Consul-General, São Paulo, 1990–92. *Publications:* The Spaniards, 1969, 2nd edn 1972; Sonatas and Variations, 2008. *Recreations:* music, walking, the Mediterranean.

PERCHARD, Colin William, CVO 1997; OBE 1984; Minister (Cultural Affairs), India, British Council, 1993–2000; *b* 19 Oct. 1940; *m* 1970, Elisabeth Penelope Glynis, *d* of Sir Glyn Jones, GCMG, MBE; three *s*. *Educ:* Victoria Coll., Jersey; Liverpool Univ. (BA Hons History); Internat. Inst. for Educnl Planning, UNESCO, Paris (DipEd Planning and Admin). British Council: Asst Rep., Blantyre, Malawi, 1964–68; Regional Officer, Africa S of the Sahara, 1968–71: Asst Rep., Calcutta, 1971–72; Officer i/c Dhaka, 1972; Rep., Seoul, 1973–76; Dir, Technical Co-operation Trng Dept, 1976–79; Internat. Inst. for Educnl Planning, Paris, 1979–80; Rep., Harare, 1980–86; Controller, Africa Div., 1986–90; Dir and Cultural Counsellor, Turkey, 1990–93. Chm., Jersey Arts Trust, 2001–10; Vice-Pres., Société Jersiaise, 2013–. Patron, Jersey Architects Assoc., 2003–. *Recreations:* theatre, music, cooking. *Address:* La Source, Rue de la Vignette, St Martin, Jersey JE3 6HY.

PERCHE, Neisha; *see* Crosland, N.

PERCIVAL, Allan Arthur, LVO 1996; consultant, since 2010; *b* 28 Oct. 1950; *s* of Arthur Percival and Rita Margaret Percival. *Educ:* Grimsby Wintringham Grammar Sch. Press Officer, MoD, 1973–82; Chief Inf. Officer, HQ NI, 1982–86; DDPR (Army), 1986–89; NI Office, 1989–93; Press Sec. to Prince of Wales, 1993–96; Dep. Press Sec., Prime Minister's Office, 1996–98; Dir of Communications, LCD, subseq. DCA, 1998–2004; consultant: Kathmandu, Nepal, 2004–07; London, 2004–07; UK Embassy, Kabul, Afghanistan, 2007–10. *Recreations:* friends, military history, reading. *Address:* 47 Kindersley Way, Abbots Langley, Herts WD5 0DG. *T:* (01923) 260882.

PERCIVAL, Prof. Ian Colin, PhD; FRS 1985; Professor of Theoretical Physics, 1991–96, Research Professor in Physics, since 2000, Queen Mary University of London (formerly Queen Mary College, then Queen Mary and Westfield College, University of London); *b* 27 July 1931; *m* 1955, Jill Cuff (*née* Herbert) (*d* 1999); two *s* one *d*. *Educ:* Ealing County Grammar Sch.; UCL (BSc, PhD; Fellow, 1986). FRAS. Lectr in Physics, UCL, 1957–61; Reader in Applied Maths, QMC, 1961–67; Prof. of Theoret. Physics, Univ. of Stirling, 1967–74; Prof. of Applied Maths, QMC, 1974–91. Naylor Prize, London Mathematical Soc., 1985; Alexander von Humboldt Foundn Award, 1993; Dirac Medal and Prize, Inst. of Physics, 1999. *Publications:* (with Derek Richards) Introduction to Dynamics, 1983; (with Owen Greene and Irene Ridge) Nuclear Winter, 1985; Quantum State Diffusion, 1998; papers in learned jls on scattering theory, atomic and molecular theory, statistical mechanics, classical dynamics and theory of chaos and foundations of quantum theory. *Address:* Queen Mary University of London, Mile End Road, E1 4NS. *T:* (020) 7882 5555. *E:* i.c.percival@qmul.ac.uk.

PERCY, family name of **Duke of Northumberland**.

PERCY, Earl; George Dominic Percy; *b* 4 May 1984; *e s* and *heir* of Duke of Northumberland, *qv*. *Educ:* Eton. A Page of Honour to the Queen, 1996–98. *Address:* Alnwick Castle, Alnwick, Northumberland NE66 1NG.

PERCY, Algernon Eustace Hugh H.; *see* Heber-Percy.

PERCY, Andrew; MP (C) Brigg and Goole, since 2010; *b* Hull, 1977. *Educ:* York Univ. (BA Hons); Leeds Univ. (PGCE). History teacher in schs in E Yorks and N Lincs; MP's researcher; pt-time primary sch. teacher. Mem. (C) Hull CC, 2000–10. Contested (C) Normanton, 2005. Member, Select Committee: on Procedure, 2010–11; on Regulatory Reform, 2010–15; on Standing Orders, 2011–; on Health, 2012–; on NI Affairs, 2012–15; Panel of Chairs, 2015–. *Address:* House of Commons, SW1A 0AA.

PERCY, John Pitkeathly, (Ian), CBE 1997; CA; Chairman, John Menzies plc Pension Fund, since 2007; Trustee, National Trust for Scotland, since 2011 (Deputy Chairman, 2013–15); *b* 16 Jan. 1942; *s* of John Percy and Helen Glass Percy (*née* Pitkeathly); *m* 1965, Sheila Isobel Horn; two *d*. *Educ:* Edinburgh Acad. Qualified as a Chartered Accountant with Graham Smart & Annan, Edinburgh, 1967; Grant Thornton: Partner, Edinburgh, 1970–78; London, 1978–91; Managing Partner, 1981–88; Sen. Partner, 1988–93; Chairman: Accounts Commn for Scotland, 1992–2000; Audit Scotland, 1998–2000; Companies House, 2002–06. Director: William Wilson (Holdings), 1993–2005; Weir Gp plc, 1996–2010 (Dep. Chm., 2005–10); Kiln plc, 1998–2005 (Chm., 2002–05); Ricardo plc, 2000–08 (Dep. Chm., 2005–08); Cala Gp Ltd, 2000–12 (Chm., 2009–11); Chairman: Cala Pension Fund, 2001–14; Wolseley Gp Pension Fund, 2005–; Romanes Media Pension Fund, 2007–. Dir, Scottish Legal Aid Bd, 2000–06; Member: Auditing Practices Bd, 1992–2002; Internat. Auditing Practices Cttee, 1995–2000. Hon. Prof. of Accounting and Auditing, Aberdeen Univ., 1988–. Pres., Inst. of Chartered Accountants of Scotland, 1990–91 (Sen. Vice-Pres., 1989–91). Chm. Court, Queen Margaret Univ., Edinburgh, 2004–10. Freeman, City of London, 1983; Liveryman, Painter Stainers' Co., 1983. FRSA 1989. Hon. LLD Aberdeen, 1999; DUniv Queen Margaret, Edinburgh, 2012. *Recreations:* golf, fishing. *Address:* 4 Westbank, Easter Park Drive, Edinburgh EH4 6SL. *T:* (0131) 312 6446. *Clubs:* Royal Automobile; New (Edinburgh); Royal & Ancient (St Andrews), Hon. Company of Edinburgh Golfers; Luffness New Golf; Gairloch Golf.

PERCY, Rev. Canon Prof. Martyn William, PhD; Dean of Christ Church, Oxford, since 2014; Professor of Theological Education, King's College London, since 2004; Professorial Research Fellow, Heythrop College, University of London, since 2010; *b* 31 July 1962; *s* of Roy Percy and Sylvia Percy (*née* Owens); *m* 1989, Emma Bray; two *s*. *Educ:* Merchant Taylors' Sch., Northwood; Univ. of Bristol (BA Hons 1984); Univ. of Durham (Cert. Counselling 1990); KCL (PhD 1993); Univ. of Sheffield (MEd 2003); Univ. of Oxford (MA 2004). Publisher, 1984–88; ordained deacon, 1990, priest, 1991; Curate, St Andrew's, Bedford, 1990–94; Chaplain and Dir of Theol. and Religious Studies, Christ's Coll., Cambridge, 1994–97; Dir of Studies, Sidney Sussex Coll., Cambridge, 1995–97; Dir, Lincoln Theol Inst. for Study of Religion and Society, 1997–2004; Sen. Lectr, 1997–2000, Reader, 2000–03, Univ. of Sheffield; Reader, Univ. of Manchester, 2003–04; Principal, Ripon Coll. Cuddesdon, 2004–14, and Oxford Ministry Course, Oxford, 2006–14. Prof. of Theol. and Ministry, Hartford Seminary, Conn, USA, 2002–08. Vis. Fellow, Regent's Park Coll., Oxford, 2006–. Hon. Canon, 1997–2004, Canon Theologian, 2004–10, Sheffield Cathedral; Hon. Canon, Salisbury Cathedral, 2009–14, now Emeritus. Mem. Council and Dir, ASA, 2000–06; Member: Faith and Order Adv. Gp, 1998–2006; HEFCE RAE Panel (Humanities), 2005–08; Ind. Complaints Panel, Portman Gp, 2006–11; BBC Standing Cttee on Religion and Belief, 2009–14. Comr, Direct Mktg Authy, 2008–14; Advr, BBFC, 2010–. Founder and Co-Chair, Soc. for Study of Anglicanism, 2003–. Chair, Cliff Coll. Council, 2002–06. Trustee: William Temple Foundn, 2002–14; Gladstone's Library, Hawarden, 2014–; Grubb Inst., 2015–. Patron, St Francis Children's Soc., 1997. Ed., Modern Believing, 1997–2005. Freeman: City of London, 1989; Merchant Taylors' Co., 1989; Barbers' Co., 2015. *Publications:* Words, Wonders and Power: understanding contemporary Christian fundamentalism and revivalism, 1996; (ed) Intimate Affairs: spirituality and sexuality in perspective, 1997; Power and the Church: ecclesiology in an age of transition, 1998; Richard Hooker: an introduction, 1999; (ed) Previous Convictions: studies in religious conversion, 2000; (ed with G. R. Evans) Managing the Church?: order and organisation in a secular age, 2000; (ed) Calling Time: religion, society and change at the turn of the millennium, 2000; (ed with A. Walker) Restoring the Image: essays in honour of David Martin, 2001; (ed jtly) Darkness Yielding, 2001, 3rd edn 2009; Salt of the Earth: religious resilience in a secular age, 2002; (ed with I. Jones) Fundamentalism, Church and Society, 2002; (ed with S. Lowe) The Character of Wisdom: essays in honour of Wesley Carr, 2004; Engaging Theology: Christianity and contemporary culture, 2005; Clergy: the origin of species, 2006; (ed with I. Markham) Why Liberal Churches are Growing, 2006; (with L. Nelstrop) Evaluating Fresh Expressions, 2008; (jtly) Christ and Culture: essays after Lambeth, 2010; (ed with Christina Rees) Transfiguring Episcope: women and Church leadership, 2010; Shaping the Church: the promise of implicit theology, 2010; (ed jtly) Worship-Shaped Life: liturgical formation and the people of God, 2010; The Ecclesial Canopy: Faith, Hope, Charity, 2012; (ed with Robert Slocum) A Point of Balance, 2012; Anglicanism: confidence, commitment and communion, 2013; Thirty-Nine New Articles: preaching and proclaiming Anglican faith, 2013; (ed with Pete Ward) The Wisdom of the Spirit, 2014; (ed jtly) The Bright Field, 2014; (ed jtly) The Oxford Handbook of Anglican Studies, 2016. *Recreations:* reading, cinema, listening to jazz. *Address:* The Deanery, Christ Church, Oxford OX1 1DP. *T:* (01865) 276150. *E:* dean@chch.ox.ac.uk. *Clubs:* Athenæum, Oxford and Cambridge; Cowley Workers Social.

PERCY, Tulip; *see* Siddiq, T.

PEREIRA, Margaret, CBE 1985; BSc; FRSB; Controller, Home Office Forensic Science Service, 1982–88; *b* 22 April 1928. *Educ:* La Sainte Union Convent, Bexley Heath; Dartford County Grammar School for Girls; Chelsea Coll. of Science and Technol. BSc 1953. Joined Metropolitan Police Forensic Science Lab., New Scotland Yard, 1947; Dep. Dir, Home Office Forensic Science Central Res. Estab., 1976; Director, Home Office Forensic Science Laboratory: Aldermaston, 1977; Chepstow, 1979.

PEREIRA GRAY, Prof. Sir Denis (John), Kt 1999; OBE 1981; FRCP, FRCGP, FMedSci; General Medical Practitioner, 1962–2000; Professor of General Practice, University of Exeter, 1986–2001, now Emeritus (Director of Postgraduate Medical School, 1987–97); President, Royal College of General Practitioners, 1997–2000; *b* 2 Oct. 1935; *s* of late Dr Sydney Joseph Pereira Gray and Alice Evelyn Gray; forename Pereira changed to surname by deed poll; *m* 1962, Jill Margaret Hoyte; one *s* three *d*. *Educ:* Exeter Sch.; St John's Coll., Cambridge (MA); St Bartholomew's Hosp. Med. Sch. MB BChir. FRCGP 1973; FRCP 1999. Sen. Lectr in Charge, Univ. of Exeter, 1973–86. Regional Adviser in Gen. Practice, 1975–2000; Consultant Adviser in Gen. Practice to Chief MO, DHSS, 1984–87. Mem., GMC, 1994–2003; Chm., Jt Cttee on Postgrad. Trng for Gen. Practice, 1994–97. Trustee, The Nuffield Trust (formerly Nuffield Provincial Hosps Trust), 1994–2006 (Chm., 2003–06). Chm. Council, RCGP, 1987–90 (Hon. Editor, Journal, 1972–80, Publications, 1976–2000); Vice-Chm., 1998–2000, Chm., 2000–02, Acad. of Medical Royal Colls. Vice-Chm., Ethics and Confidentiality Cttee, Nat. Information Governance Bd, 2009–11. Editor, Medical Annual, 1983–87. Pres., What About the Children?, 2007–; Patron, Nat. Assoc. for Patient Participation, 2003–. Honorary Professor: Peninsula Coll. of Medicine and Dentistry, 2010; Univ. of Exeter Med. Sch., 2013–. Lectures: James Mackenzie, RCGP, 1977; Pfizer, N England Faculty, RCGP, Gale Meml, SW England Faculty, RCGP, 1979; Eli Lilly, Haliburton Hume Meml, Newcastle upon Tyne and Northern Counties Med. Soc., Northcott Meml, Barnstaple, Harvard Davis, Denbigh, McConaghey Meml, Lifton, 1988; Murray Scott Meml, Aberdeen, 1990; Harben Meml, London, 1994; Sally Irvine, Ashridge Mgt Coll., 1995; Albert Wander, RSocMed, 1998; Andrew Smith, Durham, 1998; David Bruce, London, 1999; Frans Huygen, Nijmegen, Netherlands, 2001; Lung Fox, Bristol, 2002; Deakin, Australia, 2005; Goodman, What About the Children?, 2013. Founder FMedSci 1998. Hon. FRSPH (Hon. FRSH 1997); Hon. FFPH 1997; Hon. FIHM 2000 (FHSM 1997); Hon. FRCPI 2001; Hon. FFGDP 2003; Hon. Fellow, QMC, Univ. of London, 2000. Hon. DSc: De Montfort, 1997; Exeter, 2009; Hon. DM Nottingham, 2003. Gold Medal, Hunterian Soc., 1966, 1969; Sir Charles Hastings Prize, BMA, 1967, 1970; George Abercrombie Award, RCGP, 1978; Foundn Council Award, RCGP, 1980; Sir Harry Platt Prize, Modern Medicine Jl, 1981; Silver Medal, SIMG, 1989; Gold Medal, RIPH&H, 1999. *Publications:* Running a Practice (jtly), 1978, 3rd edn 1981; Training for General Practice, 1981; Forty Years On: the story of the first forty years of the RCGP, 1992; articles in Lancet, BMJ, Jl RCGP, British Jl Gen. Pract. *Recreation:* reading. *Address:* Alford House, 9 Marlborough Road, Exeter EX2 4TJ. *T:* (01392) 218080.

PERES, Shimon, Hon. GCMG 2008; President of Israel, 2007–14; Member of Knesset, 1959–2007; *b* 1923; *s* of Yitzhak and Sarah Persky; *m* 1945, Sonia Gelman; two *s* one *d*. *Educ:* New York Univ.; Harvard Univ. Head of Naval Services, 1948–49; Head of Israel Defense Min. delegn to US, 1949–52; Dir-Gen., Defense Min., 1953–59; Dep. Defense Minister, 1959–65; Sec. Gen., Rafi Party, 1965–68; Minister: of Immigrant Absorption, 1969–70; of Transport and Communications, 1970–74; of Information, 1974; of Defense, 1974–77; Acting Prime Minister, 1977; Prime Minister, 1984–86 and 1995–96; Vice Premier, 1986–90; Minister of Foreign Affairs, 1986–88 and 1992–95; Minister of Finance, 1988–90. Chm., Israel Labour Party, 1977–92 and 1995–97; Vice-Pres., Socialist Internat., 1978. (Jtly) Nobel Peace Prize, 1994; Presidential Medal of Freedom (USA), 2012; Congressional Gold Medal (USA), 2014. *Publications:* The Next Phase, 1965; David's Sling, 1970; Tomorrow is Now, 1978; From These Men, 1980; Entebbe Diary, 1991; The New Middle East, 1993; Battling for Peace: memoirs, 1995. *Recreation:* reading. *Address:* c/o Office of the President, 3 Hanassi Street, Jerusalem 92188, Israel.

PERETZ, David Lindsay Corbett, CB 1996; independent consultant on international financial issues, since 1999; *b* 29 May 1943; *s* of Michael and April Peretz; *m* 1966, Jane Wildman; one *s* one *d*. *Educ:* The Leys Sch., Cambridge; Exeter Coll., Oxford (MA). Asst Principal, Min. of Technol., 1965–69; Head of Public Policy and Institutional Studies, IBRO, 1969–76; HM Treasury: Principal, 1976–80; Asst Sec., External Finance, 1980–84; Principal Pvte Sec. to Chancellor of Exchequer, 1984–85; Under-Secretary: Home Finance, 1985–86; Monetary Gp, Public Finance, 1986–90; UK Exec. Dir, IMF and World Bank, and Economic Minister, Washington, 1990–94; Dep. Dir, Internat. Finance, HM Treasury, 1994–99. Chair, Ind. Adv. Cttee on Develt Impact, DFID, 2007–10. *Recreations:* walking, gardening, listening to music, sailing. *E:* dlcperetz@yahoo.co.uk.

See also G. M. J. Peretz.

PERETZ, George Michael John; QC 2015; *b* London, 1967; *s* of David Lindsay Corbett Peretz, *qv*; *m* 1995, Mandy Brown; one *d*. *Educ:* William Ellis Sch., Highgate; Exeter Coll., Oxford (BA Hons PPE); City Univ. (DipLaw). Called to the Bar, Middle Temple, 1990; Legal Advr, OFT, 1992–97; Judge (pt-time), First-tier Tribunal (Social Entitlement Chamber), 2011–. Dir, Advocates for Internat. Develt, 2012–. Co-Chair, UK State Aid Law Assoc., 2012–. *Recreations:* music (clarinet and piano), opera, France, walking, cycling, ancient Greece and Rome, history. *Address:* Monckton Chambers, 1–2 Raymond Buildings, Gray's Inn, WC1R 5NR. *T:* (020) 7405 7211. *E:* gperetz@monckton.com.

PÉREZ DE CUÉLLAR, Javier, Hon. GCMG 1992; Ambassador of Peru to France, 2001–04; holds personal rank of Ambassador; *b* 19 Jan. 1920; *m* Marcela (*née* Temple); one *s* one *d*. *Educ:* Law Faculty, Catholic Univ., Lima, Peru. Joined Peruvian Foreign Ministry, 1940; Diplomatic Service, 1944; Sec., Peruvian Embassies in France, UK, Bolivia and Brazil and Counsellor, Embassy, Brazil, 1944–60; Mem., Peruvian Delegn to First Session of Gen. Assembly, UN, 1946; Dir, Legal, Personnel, Admin, Protocol and Political Affairs Depts, Min. of Foreign Affairs, Peru, 1961–63; Peruvian Ambassador to Switzerland, 1964–66; Perm.

Under-Sec. and Sec.-Gen. of Foreign Office, 1966–69; Ambassador of Peru to USSR and to Poland, 1969–71; Perm. Rep. of Peru to UN, 1971–75 (Rep. to UN Security Council, 1973–74); Special Rep. of UN Sec.-Gen. in Cyprus, 1975–77; Ambassador of Peru to Venezuela, 1978; UN Under-Sec.-Gen. for Special Political Affairs, 1979–81; Sec.-Gen., UN, 1982–91. Prime Minister and Foreign Minister, Peru, 2000–01. Pres., World Commn on Culture and Develt, UN/UNESCO, 1992–; Chm. Emeritus, Inter-Amer. Dialogue, 1992–. Former Professor: of Diplomatic Law, Academia Diplomática del Perú; of Internat. Relations, Academia de Guerra Aérea del Perú. LLD *hc:* Univ. of Nice, France, 1983; Carleton Univ., Ottawa, 1985; Osnabruck Univ., 1986; Coimbra Univ., 1986; Oxford, 1993; other hon. degrees include: Jagiellonian Univ., Poland, 1984; Charles Univ. Czechoslovakia, 1984; Sofia Univ., Bulgaria, 1984; Universidad Nacional Mayor de San Marcos, Perú, 1984; Vrije Universiteit Brussel, Belgium, 1984; Sorbonne Univ., Paris, 1985; Cambridge Univ., 1989; Univ. of Salamanca, 1991; Oxford Univ., 1993. Various internat. awards including: Prince of Asturias Prize, 1987; Olof Palme Prize, 1989; Jawaharlal Nehru Award, 1989. Grand Cross, Order of El Sol (Peru); foreign decorations include: US Medal of Freedom; Grand Cross, Legion of Honour (France). *Publications:* Manual de Derecho Diplomático, 1964; Anarchy or Order, 1992; Pilgrimage for Peace, 1997. *Address:* Avenida Aurelio Miró Quesada 1071, Lima 27, Perú. *Clubs:* Travellers (Paris); Nacional, Ecuestre Huachipa, Jockey (Lima, Peru).

PÉREZ ESQUIVEL, Adolfo; sculptor; Hon. President: Servicio Paz y Justicia en América Latina, since 1986; Servicio Paz y Justicia Argentina, since 1973; President, International League for the Rights and Liberation of Peoples, since 1987; *b* 26 Nov. 1931; *m* 1956, Amanda Guerreño; three *s*. *Educ:* Nat. Sch. of Fine Arts, Buenos Aires. Prof. of Art, Manuel Belgrano Nat. Sch. of Fine Arts, Buenos Aires, 1956–76; Prof., Faculty of Architecture and Urban Studies, Univ. Nacional de la Plata, 1969–73; Gen. Co-ordinator, Servicio Paz y Justicia en América Latina, 1974–86. Work in permanent collections: Buenos Aires Mus. of Modern Art; Mus. of Fine Arts, Córdoba; Fine Arts Mus., Rosario. Joined group dedicated to principles of militant non-violence, and engaged in projects to promote self-sufficiency in urban areas, 1971; founded Paz y Justicia magazine, 1973. Co-founder, Ecumenical Movement for Human Rights, Argentina; Pres., Permanent Assembly for Human Rights. Premio la Nación de Escultura; Pope John XXIII prize, Pax Christi Orgn, 1977; Nobel Peace Prize, 1980. *Publications:* Resistir en la Esperanza, 2011. *Address:* Servicio Paz y Justicia, Piedras 730, CP 1070, Buenos Aires, Argentina.

PERFECT, Fiona Elizabeth; *see* Rae, F. E.

PERFECT, Henry George, FICE; Chairman: Babtie Group Ltd, 1996–2002; British Water, 2000–02; *b* 31 March 1944; *s* of George Hunter Perfect and Constance Mary Perfect (*née* Holland); *m* 1971, Kathleen Margaret Lilian Bain; two *s* one *d*. *Educ:* West Bridgford Grammar Sch., Nottingham; Birmingham Univ. (BSc Civil Engrg); Glasgow Univ. (MEng Foundn Engrg). FICE 1987. Asst Engr, C. H. Dobbie & Partners, 1965–69; Babtie Shaw & Morton, subseq. Babtie Group: Engr (projects incl. Kielder Water Scheme, and numerous reservoir, water and sewerage projects), 1969–83; Associate, 1983–86; Partner, 1987–93; Man. Dir, Water Business, 1994–95. *Publications:* several papers on civil and water engrg. *Recreations:* hill walking, cycling and tennis. *Address:* 15 Thorn Road, Bearsden, Glasgow G61 4BS.

PERHAM, Linda; JP; Chair, Thames Water Trust Fund, since 2009; Director and Trustee, Vision Redbridge Culture and Leisure, since 2011; *b* 29 June 1947; *d* of late George Sidney Conroy and of Edith Louisa Conroy (*née* Overton); *m* 1972, Raymond John Perham; two *d*. *Educ:* Mary Datchelor Girls' Sch.; Univ. of Leicester (BA Special Hons Classics); Ealing Tech. Coll. Postgrad. Dip. Liby Assoc.; MCLIP (ALA 1972). Library Asst, London Borough of Southwark, 1966; Inf. Officer, GLC Research Liby, 1970–72; City of London Polytechnic: Archives and Publications Librarian, 1972–76; Staff Develt Librarian, 1976–78; Cataloguer, Fawcett Liby, 1981–92; Bibliographical Librarian, Epping Forest Coll., 1992–97. MP (Lab) Ilford N, 1997–2005; contested (Lab) same seat, 2005. Mem., Select Cttee on Trade and Industry, 1998–2005; Chairman: All Party Gp on Libraries, 1998–2005; All Party Gp on Crossrail, 2003–05; Vice Chairman: All Party Gp on Male Cancers, 1998–2005; All Party Gp on Men's Health, 2001–05; Labour Friends of Israel, 2001–05; Hon. Secretary: All Party Gp on Ageing and Older People, 1998–2005; British-Israel Parly Gp, 1998–2005; All Party Parly Gp on Corporate Social Responsibility, 2001–05; All Party Gp on Patient and Public Involvement in Health, 2004–05. London Borough of Redbridge: Councillor, 1989–97; Mayor, 1994–95; Chm., Highways Cttee, 1995–96, Leisure Cttee, 1996–97. Mem., Consumer Council for Water, London & SE (formerly Thames), 2005–11; Consumer Dir, TrustMark, 2006–11. Chair, East Living housing assoc., 2006–11; Vice Chair, London Voluntary Service Council, 2005–08; Board Member: East Thames Gp, 2006–11; Housing and Community Assoc., 2006–08. Mem. Ct, Univ. of Leicester, 2010–. Trustee, Friends of the Women's Library, 2005–09. Patron, Anxiety Care, Ilford, 1998–. Pres., Hainault Forest Community Assoc., 1997–. Lay Visitor, Eur. Care Gp, 2011–12. FRSA 2005. Hon. FCLIP 2003. JP: Redbridge, 1990; Newham, 2006; Redbridge, 2007. *Publications:* Directory of GLC Library Resources, 1970, 2nd edn 1971; Greater London Council Publications 1965–71, 1972; Libraries of London, 1973; How to Find Out in French, 1977. *Recreations:* travel, arts, cinema, theatre, sudoku, watching tennis and cricket. *E:* lindaperham@hotmail.com.

PERHAM, Rt Rev. Michael Francis; Bishop of Gloucester, 2004–14; *b* 8 Nov. 1947; *s* of Raymond Maxwell Perham and Marcelle Winifred Perham; *m* 1982, Alison Jane Grove; four *d*. *Educ:* Hardye's Sch., Dorchester; Keble Coll., Oxford (BA 1974; MA 1978); Cuddesdon Theol Coll. Curate, St Mary, Addington, 1976–81; Sec., C of E Doctrine Commn, 1979–84; Chaplain to Bp of Winchester, 1981–84; Team Rector, Oakdale Team Ministry, Poole, 1984–92; Canon Residentiary and Precentor, 1992–98, Vice Dean, 1995–98, Norwich Cathedral; Provost, subseq. Dean, of Derby, 1998–2004. Bishop Protector, Soc. of St Francis, 2005–14. Member: Liturgical Commn of C of E, 1986–2001; Archbishops' Commn on Church Music, 1988–92; Gen. Synod of C of E, 1989–92 and 1993– (Chm., Business Cttee, 2001–04); Cathedrals' Fabric Commn for England, 1996–2001; Archbishops' Council, 1999–2004; Governing Body, SPCK, 2002–11 (Vice Chm., 2005–06; Chm., 2006–11); Chairman: Praxis, 1990–97; Cathedrals' Liturgy Gp, 1994–2001; Hosp. Chaplaincies' Council, 2007–10; Governing Body, Ripon Coll., 2009–; Vice Chm., C of E Mission and Public Affairs Council, 2007–10. Mem., Church Heritage Forum, 1999–2001. President: Retired Clergy Assoc., 2007–14; Affirming Catholicism, 2010–14; Vice Pres., WATCH (Women and the Church), 2011–. Pro-Chancellor, 2007–, Vice-Chair, Council, 2012–, Univ. of Gloucestershire. Fellow, Woodard Corp., 2000–04. FRSCM 2002. Freeman, City of Gloucester, 2014. Hon. DPhil Gloucestershire, 2007. *Publications:* The Eucharist, 1978, 2nd edn 1981; The Communion of Saints, 1980; Liturgy Pastoral and Parochial, 1984; (with Kenneth Stevenson) Waiting for the Risen Christ, 1986; (ed) Towards Liturgy 2000, 1989; (ed) Liturgy for a New Century, 1991; (with Kenneth Stevenson) Welcoming the Light of Christ, 1991; Lively Sacrifice, 1992; (ed) The Renewal of Common Prayer, 1993; (ed) Model and Inspiration, 1993; (compiled) Enriching the Christian Year, 1993; Celebrate the Christian Story, 1997; The Sorrowful Way, 1998; A New Handbook of Pastoral Liturgy, 2000; Signs of Your Kingdom, 2002; Glory in our Midst, 2005; To Tell Afresh, 2010; (with Mary Gray-Reeves) The Hospitality of God, 2011; Jesus and Peter: growing in friendship with God, 2012; (with Paula Gooder) Echoing the Word, 2013. *Recreations:* reading, writing, creating liturgical texts, walking in the Yorkshire dales. *Address:* The Old Mill, Bleadney, Wells, Som BA5 1PF. *T:* (01749) 670239, 07837 815605. *E:* michaelperham47@gmail.com.

PERHAM, Nancy Jane; *see* Lane, N. J.

PERKINS, Alice Elizabeth, CB 2002; Partner and Executive Coach, JCA Group, since 2006; *b* 24 May 1949; *d* of Derrick Leslie John Perkins and Elsa Rose Perkins, CBE (*née* Rink); *m* 1978, John Whitaker Straw, *qv*; one *s* one *d*. *Educ:* North London Collegiate Sch. for Girls; St Anne's Coll., Oxford (BA Hons Modern Hist. 1971; Hon. Fellow 2008). Joined CS, DHSS, 1971; Principal, 1976–84; Asst Sec., DHSS, then DSS, 1984–90; Dir of Personnel, DSS, 1990–93; Under Sec., Defence Policy and Materiel Gp, HM Treasury, 1993–95; Dep. Dir, Public Spending, HM Treasury, 1995–98; Dir, Corporate Mgt, DoH, 1998–2000; Hd of Civil Service Corporate Mgt, then Dir Gen., Corporate Develt Gp, Cabinet Office, 2000–05. Chm., Post Office Ltd, 2011–15. Non-executive Director: Littlewoods Orgn, 1997–2000; Taylor Nelson Sofres, 2005–08; BAA, 2006; BBC, 2014–. Ext. Mem. Council, Oxford Univ., 2006–14; Faculty Mem., Meyler Campbell, 2009–. *Recreations:* gardening, looking at paintings.

PERKINS, Brian Temple; newsreader, BBC Radio 4, 1965–69 and 1978–2003; freelance broadcaster, since 2003; *b* 11 Sept. 1943; *s* of Ray and Laurel Perkins; *m* 1964, Joan Russell; one *s* two *d*. *Educ:* Wanganui and Wellington, NZ. Broadcaster: NZ Broadcasting Co., 1962–64; BBC, 1965–69; double bass player, NZBC SO, 1970–75; broadcaster: Radio NZ, 1975–78; BBC, 1978–2003. *Recreations:* music, fell-walking, France. *T:* (01483) 233919.

PERKINS, Crispian G. S.; *see* Steele-Perkins.

PERKINS, Prof. Donald Hill, CBE 1991; FRS 1966; Professor of Elementary Particle Physics, 1965–93, and Fellow of St Catherine's College, since 1965, Oxford University; *b* 15 Oct. 1925; *s* of George W. and Gertrude Perkins; *m* 1955, Dorothy Mary (*née* Maloney); two *d*. *Educ:* Malet Lambert High School, Hull. BSc London 1945; PhD London 1948; 1851 Senior Scholar, 1948–51. G. A. Wills Research Associate in Physics, Univ. of Bristol, 1951–55; Lawrence Radiation Lab., Univ. of California, 1955–56; Lectr in Physics, 1956–60, Reader in Physics, 1960–65, Univ. of Bristol. Mem., SERC, 1985–89. Hon. DSc: Sheffield, 1982; Bristol, 1995. Guthrie Medal, Inst. of Physics, 1979; Holweck Medal and Prize, Société Française de Physique, 1992; Royal Medal, Royal Soc., 1997; High Energy Physics Prize, Eur. Physical Soc., 2001. *Publications:* The Study of Elementary Particles by the Photographic Method (with C. F. Powell and P. H. Fowler), 1959; Introduction to High Energy Physics, 1972, 4th edn 2000; Particle Astrophysics, 2003; about 50 papers and review articles in Nature, Physical Review, Philosophical Magazine, Physics Letters, Proc. Royal Soc., Nuovo Cimento, etc. *Recreations:* squash, tennis. *Address:* 4A Brookside, Oxford OX3 7PJ. *T:* (01865) 741449.

PERKINS, Douglas John David; Co-founder, Co-owner and Managing Director, Specsavers Optical Group Ltd, since 1984; *b* Llanelli, 2 April 1943; *s* of Philip Denzil Perkins and Muriel Ester Perkins (*née* Thomas); *m* 1967, Mary Lesley Bebbington (*see* Dame M. L. Perkins); one *s* two *d*. *Educ:* Advanced Technology Coll. of Wales, Cardiff; British Optical Assoc. (Dip. Contact Lens Practice). FCOptom. Co-owner and optometrist, Bebbington and Perkins Gp, 1966–80. Liveryman, Spectacle Makers' Co. Hon. Fellow: Cardiff Univ., 2005; Swansea Inst., 2006. Hon. Dr Anglia Ruskin, 2006; Hon. Dr Plymouth, 2012. *Recreations:* walking, yoga, grandchildren, watching Rugby and cricket. *Address:* Hautes Falaises, Fort George, St Peter Port, Guernsey GY1 2SR. *T:* (01481) 725901, *Fax:* (01481) 725968. *E:* doug.perkins@specsavers.com.

PERKINS, Prof. Edwin Arend, PhD; FRS 2007; FRSC; Professor of Mathematics, since 1989, and Canada Research Chair in Probability, since 2001, University of British Columbia; *b* 31 Aug. 1953; *s* of John Albert Perkins and Karin Brita (*née* Kunst); *m* 1974, Karen Marie Woitak; one *s* two *d*. *Educ:* Univ. of Toronto (BSc 1975); Univ. of Illinois (PhD 1979). University of British Columbia: Postdoctoral Fellow, 1979–80; NSERC Univ. Res. Fellow, 1980–81; Asst Prof. of Maths, 1982–85; Associate Prof. of Maths, 1985–89. Prof. Associé, Univ. of Strasbourg, 1984; SERC Res. Fellow, Cambridge Univ., 1986–87; Vis. Prof., Univ. of Wisconsin, 2000–01. FRSC 1988. *Publications:* Dawson-Watanabe Superprocesses and Measure-valued Diffusions, 1999; contribs to Memoirs Amer. Maths Soc. *Recreations:* hiking, cross-country ski-ing, canoeing. *Address:* Department of Mathematics, University of British Columbia, Vancouver, BC V6T 1Z2, Canada. *T:* (604) 8226670, *Fax:* (604) 8226074. *E:* perkins@math.ubc.ca.

PERKINS, Prof. John Douglas, CBE 2007; PhD; FIChemE, FIMA; CEng, FREng; Chief Scientific Adviser, Department for Business, Innovation and Skills, 2012–15; Director, JP2 Consulting Ltd, since 2015; *b* 18 March 1950; *s* of late Douglas Herbert and of Isobel Mary Perkins; *m* 1st, 1975, Chantal Marie Lestavel (marr. diss. 1992); one *s*; 2nd, 2009, Jennifer Anne Chambers. *Educ:* Imperial Coll., London (BSc Eng; PhD 1976; DIC). ACGI 1971, FCGI 1996; FIChemE 1986; CEng 1986; CMath 1992; FIMA 1992; FREng 1993; CSci 2004. Demonstrator in Chem. Engrg, Univ. of Cambridge, 1973–77; Lectr in Chem. Engrg, 1977–83, Sen. Lectr, 1983–85, Imperial Coll., London; ICI Prof. of Process Systems Engrg, Univ. of Sydney, Aust., 1985–88; Imperial College, University of London: Prof. of Chem. Engrg, 1988–99; Dir, Centre for Process Systems Engrg, 1992–98; Hd, Dept of Chem. Engrg and Chem. Technol., 1996–2001; Courtaulds Prof. of Chem. Engrg, 2000–04; Principal, Faculty of Engrg, 2001–04; Vice Pres. and Dean of Engrg and Phys. Scis, Univ. of Manchester, 2004–09; Provost, MASDAR Inst. of Sci. and Technol., Abu Dhabi, 2009–10. Vis. Prof., Imperial Coll. London, 2004–07, 2012–; Hon. Prof., Univ. of Manchester, 2009–. Member: EPSRC, 2012–15; Council, IMA, 2015–. UK Delegate, Governing Bd, EU Jt Res. Centre, 2012–. Pres., IChemE, 2000–01 (Dep. Pres., 1999–2000; Mem. Council, 1997–2002); Vice Pres., RAEng, 2007–10 (Mem. Council, 2004–10). FRSA 2004. *Recreations:* cinema, theatre, gastronomy, reading.

PERKINS, John Vernon; District Judge (Magistrates' Courts) (formerly Metropolitan Stipendiary Magistrate), 1999–2015; *b* 13 June 1950; *s* of late Sidney and Lilian Florence Perkins; *m* 1975, Margaret Craig; one *s* one *d*. *Educ:* Tottenham Grammar Sch. Admitted Solicitor, 1975; Articled Clerk, 1970–75, Asst Solicitor, 1975–80, Partner, 1980–99 (Sen. Partner, 1988–99), J. B. Wheatley & Co. Mem., London Criminal Courts Solicitors' Assoc., 1975–99 (Hon. Mem. 1999). *Recreations:* walking, swimming, gardening.

PERKINS, Jonathan David; a Judge of the Upper Tribunal (Immigration and Asylum Chamber) (formerly a Vice President, Immigration Appeal Tribunal, later a Senior Immigration Judge, Asylum and Immigration Tribunal), since 2003; *b* 15 Feb. 1958; *s* of Thomas Edward Perkins and Constance Perkins; *m* 1991, Margaret Anne Jackson; one *s* one *d*. *Educ:* Brierley Hill Grammar Sch.; University Coll. Cardiff (LLB Wales). Called to the Bar, Middle Temple, 1980; barrister, Midland and Oxford Circuit, 1981–99; Immigration Appeals Adjudicator, pt-time, 1993–99, full-time, 1999–2003. Methodist local preacher, 1988–. *Recreations:* church work, model making. *Address:* Upper Tribunal (Immigration and Asylum Chamber), Field House, Breams Building, Chancery Lane, EC4A 1DZ. *T:* (020) 7073 4200. *E:* perkins.family@btinternet.com.

PERKINS, Dame Mary (Lesley), DBE 2007; Co-founder, Co-owner and Public Relations Director, Specsavers Optical Group Ltd, 1984; *b* 14 Feb. 1944; *d* of late (George) Leslie Bebbington and of Eileen Hilda Constance Bebbington (*née* Mawditt); *m* 1967, Douglas John David Perkins, *qv*; one *s* two *d*. *Educ:* Fairfield Grammar Sch., Bristol; Advanced Technol. Coll. of Wales, Cardiff. FBOA 1965. Co-owner and optometrist, Bebbington and Perkins, 1966–80. Freeman, City of London, 2001; Liveryman, Spectacle Makers' Co., 2008. Dir, Women's Refuge Guernsey, 1999–; Pres., Age Concern Guernsey, 1999–; Patron,

Everywoman Ltd, 2006–. Gov., Ladies Coll. Guernsey, 2004–. Hon. Fellow, Cardiff Univ., 2005. Hon. Dr: Plymouth, 2012; Sterling, 2014. *Address:* Specsavers Optical Group Ltd, La Villiaze, St Andrews, Guernsey GY6 8YP.

PERKINS, (Matthew) Toby; MP (Lab) Chesterfield, since 2010; *b* 12 Aug. 1970; *s* of Victor F. Perkins and late Teresa Perkins; *m* 1996, Susan Beverley Francis; one *s* one *d*. *Educ:* Trinity Sch., Leamington Spa; Silverdale Sch., Sheffield. Telephone sales, CCS Media, 1991–95; Prime Time Recruitment: Recruitment Consultant, 1995–97; Branch Manager, 1997–99; Area Manager, 2000–02; estabd Club Rugby, 2005–10; Dir, Birdholme Children's Centre Nursery, 2007–10. Mem. (Lab) Chesterfield BC, 2003–11. Shadow Educn Minister, 2010–11; Shadow Business Minister, 2011–. Member: Communities and Local Govt Select Cttee, 2010; Jt Cttee on Statutory Instruments, 2010–15. Former player, Chesterfield, Sheffield Tigers and Derbys Rugby Union; qualified Rugby coach, 2006. *Address:* House of Commons, SW1A 0AA.

PERKS, David Michael; Principal, East London Science School, since 2013; *b* Hemel Hempstead, 2 Sept. 1962; *s* of Brian Perks and Audrey Perks; *m* 2004, Jennifer Davey; one *s* one *d*. *Educ:* Robert Smythe Sch., Market Harborough; Magdalen Coll., Oxford (BA Hons Physics; PGCE). Teacher of Physics: Benfield Community Coll., Newcastle upon Tyne, 1986–91; Rossett High Sch., Harrogate, 1991–97; Hd of Physics, Graveney Sch., 1997–2012. Dir, Physics Factory, 2008–. Founder, 2003, and Advr, Debating Matters, sixth form debating competition, 2004–. *Publications:* (contrib.) The Routledge Falmer Guide to Key Debates in Education, 2004; What is Science Education For?, 2006; The Corruption of the Curriculum, 2007. *Recreations:* theatre, cricket, politics, technology. *Address:* East London Science School, The Clock Mill, Three Mill Lane, E3 3DU. *T:* 07795 323862. *E:* mail@davidperks.com.

PERL, Alfredo; pianist; Music Director, Detmold Chamber Orchestra, since 2009; *b* Chile, 25 June 1965. *Educ:* German Sch., Santiago; Univ. de Chile, Santiago; Cologne Conservatoire; with Maria Curcio in London. First performance at age of 9; début in Internat. Piano Series, Queen Elizabeth Hall, 1992; first recital at Wigmore Hall, 1994, and performed complete Beethoven Sonata cycle, 1996–97; UK recital appearances include: BBC Manchester and Scotland; Bridgewater Hall; St John's Smith Sq. Concert Series; has performed worldwide, including: Vienna Musikverein; London Barbican; Rudolfinum, Prague; Munich Herkulessaal; Izumi Hall, Osaka; Teatro Colón, Buenos Aires; Sydney Town Hall; Nat. Arts Centre, Ottawa; Great Hall, Moscow Conservatoire; orchestral appearances include: LSO; BBC SO; RPO; Hague Residentie; Florida Philharmonic; Leipzig Radio; Adelaide SO; Melbourne SO; Mozarteum Orch.; Orch. de la Suisse Romande; MDR Leipzig; début at BBC Prom. Concerts, with BBC Philharmonic Orch., 1997. Has made numerous recordings, incl. complete Beethoven Sonatas.

PERLMAN, Itzhak; violinist and conductor; *b* Tel Aviv, 31 Aug. 1945; *s* of Chaim and Shoshana Perlman; *m* 1967, Toby Lynn Friedlander; two *s* three *d*. *Educ:* Studied at Tel Aviv Acad. of Music with Ryvka Goldgart, and at Juilliard Sch., NY, under Dorothy Delay and Ivan Galamian. First solo recital at age of 10 in Israel; New York début, 1958. Leventritt Meml Award, NY, 1964. Tours extensively in USA and plays with all major American symphony orchestras; has conducted major orchestras worldwide incl. NY, Chicago, LA, Boston and Berlin Philharmonic Orchestras, LPO, Amsterdam Concertgebouw; recital tours of Canada, South America, Europe, Israel, Far East and Australia; Principal Guest Conductor, Detroit SO, 2001–; Music Advr, St Louis SO, 2003–05. Has recorded numerous works for violin. Teacher, Juilliard Sch. and Perlman Music Prog. Has received many Grammy Awards. Hon. degrees: Harvard; Yale; Brandeis. *Recreation:* cooking. *Address:* c/o IMG Artists, Carnegie Hall Tower, 152 West 57th Street, 5th Floor, New York, NY 10019, USA.

PERLMUTTER, Prof. Saul, PhD; Franklin W. and Karen Weber Dabby Professor, Physics Department, University of California, Berkeley; astrophysicist, Lawrence Berkeley National Laboratory; *b* 1959; *s* of Prof. Daniel D. Perlmutter and Prof. Felice Perlmutter (*née* Davidson); *m* Laura Nelson; one *d*. *Educ:* Germantown Friends Sch.; Harvard Univ. (AB Physics *magna cum laude* 1981); Univ. of Calif, Berkeley (PhD Physics 1986). University of California, Berkeley: postdoctoral res., 1986; Prof. of Physics, 2004–. Co-founder, 1988, Leader, 1992–, Internat. Supernova Cosmology Project. Mem., NAS. FAAAS 2003. Henri Chrétien Award, Amer. Astronomical Soc., 1996; (jtly) Shaw Prize in Astronomy, Shaw Foundn, 2006; (jtly) Gruber Prize in Cosmol., Gruber Foundn, 2007; (jtly) Einstein Medal, Albert Einstein Soc., 2011; (jtly) Nobel Prize in Physics, 2011. *Address:* Lawrence Berkeley National Laboratory, University of California, Berkeley, CA 94720, USA.

PERMAN, Raymond John; Director, David Hume Institute, since 2014; Chairman, James Hutton Institute, since 2011; *b* 22 Aug. 1947; *s* of late Leonard Perman and Gladys Perman (*née* Rockingham); *m* 1974, Fay Young, writer and editor; three *s*. *Educ:* Univ. of St Andrews; BA Hons Open Univ.; Univ. of Edinburgh (MBA 1987). Journalist: Westminster Press, 1969–71; The Times, 1971–75; Financial Times, 1976–81; Dep. Editor, Sunday Standard, 1981–83; Man. Dir, Insider Publications Ltd, 1983–94; Director: Caledonian Publishing plc, 1994–96; GJWS, 1997–98; Chief Exec., Scottish Financial Enterprise, 1999–2003. Chairman: Social Investment Scotland, 2002–09; Good Practice Ltd, 2005–11; Small Business Investment Taskforce, then Access to Finance Expert Gp, DTI, then BERR, later BIS, 2005–13; Mem. Bd, Scottish Enterprise, 2004–09. Chm., Scottish Adv. Council, WWF, 2000–04; Trustee, WWF UK, 2001–04. Mem. Court, Heriot-Watt Univ., 2003–09. *Publications:* The Man Who Gave Away His Island: a biography of John Lorne Campbell of Canna, 2010; HUBRIS: how HBOS wrecked the best bank in Britain, 2012; numerous newspaper and magazine articles. *Recreations:* forestry, painting. *Address:* David Hume Institute, 26 Forth Street, Edinburgh EH1 3LH. *T:* (0131) 550 3746.

PERMANAND, Rabindranath; High Commissioner in London for Trinidad and Tobago, 1993–96; *b* 17 July 1935; *s* of late Ram Narais Permanand and of Kalawatee Permanand (*née* Capildeo); *m* 1969, Ursel Edda Schmid; one *s* one *d*. *Educ:* Queen's Royal Coll., Trinidad; Univ. of Calcutta (BA Hons); Univ. of Delhi (MA); Univ. of West Indies (Dip. Internat. Relations). History Teacher, Queen's Royal Coll., 1959–66; joined Min. of Foreign Affairs, 1966; Dep. High Comr, Georgetown, Guyana, 1966–69; First Sec., Ottawa, 1969–72; Chief of Protocol, 1973–77; Counsellor and Minister Counsellor, Brussels, 1977–81; Consul-Gen., Toronto, 1981–84; Head, Political Div., 1984–88; Ambassador and Perm. Rep. to UN, Geneva, 1988–93. *Recreations:* reading, music, cricket.

PEROLLS, Graham Keith, CMG 2014; OBE 1999; Founder and Executive Director, Hospices of Hope, since 2000; *b* Dartford, 21 Sept. 1950; *s* of late Norman Grahame Perolls and Ellen Clara Perolls; *m* 1982, Carolyn Angela Eames; one *s* four *d*. *Educ:* Dartford Grammar Sch.; North West Kent Coll.; Univ. of Lund (Associate Inst. of Linguists). Dir, K.T. Coachworks Ltd, 1972–2008. Founder, Ellenor Foundn, 1985–2004; Pres., Hospice Casa Sperantei Romania, 1992–. *Recreations:* music, gardening, church. *Address:* Hospices of Hope, 11 High Street, Otford, Kent TN14 5PG. *T:* (01959) 525110. *E:* graham@hospicesofhope.co.uk.

PEROWNE, Rear-Adm. (Benjamin) Brian, CB 2001; DL; Chief Executive, Hft (formerly Home Farm Trust), 2001–11; *b* 24 July 1947; *s* of Rear-Adm. Benjamin Cubitt Perowne, CB and Phyllis Marjorie Perowne (*née* Peel); *m* 1975, Honora Rose Mary Wykes-Sneyd; two *s*. *Educ:* Gresham's Sch., Holt; BRNC, Dartmouth. FCIPD; CDipAF. Joined RN, 1965; RN Staff Coll., 1977; HM Yacht Britannia, 1980–82; CO, HMS Alacrity, 1982–83; Staff, CBNS Washington, 1986–88; CO, HMS Brazen, 1988–89; Asst Dir (Strategic Systems), MoD, 1989–90; Chief Naval Signals Officer, MoD, 1990–92; rcds 1993; Commodore Clyde and Naval Base Comdr, 1994–96; Dir Gen., Fleet Support (Ops and Plans), 1996–99; Chief Exec., Naval Bases and Supply Agency, 1999–2001, and Chief of Fleet Support, 2000–01. ADC to the Queen, 1994–96. Non-exec. Dir, Musgrove Park Hosp., 2013–. Trustee: Bletchley Park Trust, 2000–08; Assoc. for Real Change, 2001–09; Voluntary Orgn Disability Gp, 2008–11; Greenwich Foundn, 2010–; Somerset Sight, 2011–. DL Somerset, 2012. *Recreations:* family, people, country and maritime, most sports. *Address:* Sticklynch Manor, West Pennard, Glastonbury, Som BA6 8NA. *Club:* Army and Navy.

PEROWNE, Adm. Sir James (Francis), KBE 2000 (OBE 1983); Constable and Governor, Windsor Castle, since 2014; *b* 29 July 1947; *s* of late Lt Comdr John Herbert Francis Perowne and Mary Joy Perowne (*née* Dibb); *m* 1st, 1971, Susan Anne Holloway (marr. diss. 1990); four *s*; 2nd, 1992, Caroline Nicola Grimson. *Educ:* Sherborne Sch.; BRNC Dartmouth. CO, HMS Opportune, 1976–77; CO, HMS Superb, 1981–83; Staff of CBNS Washington, 1983–86; CO, HMS Boxer, 1986–88; Asst Dir, Naval Warfare, 1988–90; Captain, Second Submarine Sqdn, 1990–92; Captain, Sixth Frigate Sqdn and CO, HMS Norfolk, 1992–94; Sen. Naval Member, RCDS, 1995–96; Flag Officer Submarines, 1996–98; Comdr Submarines (NATO), Eastern Atlantic and Northwest Europe, 1996–98; COS (Ops) to C-in-C Fleet, 1996–98; Dep. SACLANT, 1998–2002. Chm., Central and Eastern (formerly Central, subseq. Midland) Region Cttee, Consumer Council for Water (formerly Watervoice), 2002–10. Non-executive Director: S Staffs Water plc, 2011–; Cambridge Water Co., 2012–13. Member: MoJ (formerly DCA) Judiciary Review Bd, 2006–12; GMC Fitness to Practise Panel, 2006–08; GMC Interim Orders Panel, 2008–12; MPTS Interim Orders Panel, 2012–14. Pres., Submarines Assoc., 2002–; Chairman: Submarine Officers' Life Members Assoc., 2002–; Leics and Rutland Br., SSAFA (formerly SSAFA Forces Help), 2011–14. Pres., Assoc. of RN Officers and Royal Naval Benevolent Soc. for Officers, 2003–14; Chairman: British Red Cross Queen Mother Meml Fund, 2003–06; The James Caird Soc., 2006–; Trustee, British Forces Foundn, 2002–. Patron, HMS Protector Assoc., 2007–. *Recreations:* golf, gardening, family. *Address:* c/o ARNO, 70 Porchester Terrace, W2 3TP. *E:* jamesperowne@aol.com. *Club:* Royal Navy of 1765 and 1785.

PERRETT, Prof. David Ian, DPhil; FBA 2005; FRSE; Professor of Psychology and Wardlaw Professor, University of St Andrews; *b* 11 April 1954. *Educ:* Univ. of St Andrews (BSc 1976); Univ. of Oxford (DPhil 1981). FRSE 1999. Lectr, then Reader in Psychol., Univ. of St Andrews. British Acad. Wolfson Res. Prof., 2009–12. President's Award, BPsS, 2000; Golden Brain Award, Minerva Foundn, 2002. *Publications:* In Your Face: the new science of human attraction, 2010; articles in learned jls. *Address:* School of Psychology and Neuroscience, University of St Andrews, Westburn Lane, St Andrews, Fife KY16 9JP.

PERRIN, Charles John, CBE 2004; Deputy Chairman, Hambros Bank Ltd, 1986–98 (Chief Executive, 1995–98); *b* 1 May 1940; *s* of late Sir Michael Perrin, CBE, and Nancy May, *d* of late Rt Rev. C. E. Curzon; *m* 1966, Gillian Margaret, *d* of late Rev. M. Hughes-Thomas; two *d*. *Educ:* Winchester; New Coll., Oxford (Schol.; MA; Hon. Fellow, 1999). Called to the Bar, Inner Temple, 1965. Joined Hambros Bank, 1963, Dir, 1973–98; Chm., Hambro Pacific, Hong Kong, 1983–94; Dir, Hambros PLC, 1985–98. Non-exec. Dir, Harland and Wolff, 1984–89. Chairman: Retroscreen Virology, 1993–2011; MRC Pension Trust, 2004–10. Mem., Royal Brompton Nat. Heart and Lung Hosps SHA, 1993–94; non-exec. Dir, Royal Brompton Hosp. NHS Trust, 1994–98; Vice Chm., Royal Brompton & Harefield NHS Trust, 1998–2007. Mem. Council, 1994–2008, Trustee, 2008–10, Univ. of London; Mem. Council 1997, Treas., 1999–2009, QMUL (formerly QMW) (Hon. Fellow, 2010); Gov., Royal Central Sch. of Speech and Drama (formerly Central Sch. of Speech and Drama), 2006–. Hon. Treas., RVC, 2010–. Vice-Chm., UK Cttee for UNICEF, 1972–91. Governor: Queen Anne's Sch., Caversham, 1981–2006; London Hosp. Med. Coll., 1991–95. Trustee: Med. Res. Foundn, 2006 (Chm., 2008–15); Nuffield Trust, 2006–14; RCP, 2007–11; Hampstead Wells and Campden Trust, 2011–. Liveryman, Shipwrights' Co., 1991. Hon. FRCP 2009 (Hon. MRCP 1999). *Recreation:* sailing. *Address:* 4 Holford Road, Hampstead, NW3 1AD. *T:* (020) 7435 8103. *Club:* Athenæum.

PERRIN, Air Vice-Marshal Norman Arthur; Secretary General, ECTEL (European Conference of Telecommunications Industry Associations), 1991–97; *b* 30 Sept. 1930; *s* of late Albert Arthur and Mona Victoria (*née* Stacey); *m* 1956, Marie (*née* Bannon) (*d* 2014), *d* of late Peter and Lucy Bannon; one *s*. *Educ:* Liverpool Collegiate School; Hertford College, Oxford; RAF Technical College. BA. Nat. Service commn, Airfield Construction Branch, RAF, Suez Canal Zone, 1951–53; perm. commn, Tech. Branch, 1953; Advanced GW course, 1956–57; Air Ministry, 1958–61; HQ 11 Group, 1961–62; Staff Coll., 1963; 390 Maintenance Unit, FEAF, 1964–65; OC Eng Wing, RAF Seletar, 1966–67; JSSC 1967; Op. Requirements, SAGW, 1967–70; Chief Instructor, Systems Engineering, RAF Coll., 1970–72; Group Captain Plans, HQ Maintenance Comd, 1972–75; C. Mech. Eng., HQ Strike Comd, 1975–78; RCDS 1979; Dir Air GW MoD (PE), 1980–83; Vice-Pres. (Air), Ordnance Board, 1983: Pres., Ordnance Board, 1984–86. Dir, TEMA, 1987–91. *Recreations:* bridge, crosswords, Liverpool FC watching, choral singing. *Address:* c/o Barclays Bank, 10 High Street, Marlow, Bucks SL7 1AR. *Club:* Royal Air Force.

PERRING, Sir John (Raymond), 2nd Bt *cr* 1963, of Frensham Manor, Surrey; TD 1965; Chairman, Perrings Finance Ltd, 1987–2008; *b* 7 July 1931; *e s* of Sir Ralph Perring, 1st Bt and Ethel Mary (*d* 1991); *S* father, 1998; *m* 1961, Ella Christine, *e d* of late Tony and Ann Pelham; two *s* two *d*. *Educ:* Stowe School. Nat. Service, then TA, RA, 1949–60; Royal Fusiliers (City of London), 1960–65. Joined family business, Perring Furnishings, 1951, Dir 1957, Jt Man. Dir 1964, Vice-Chm., 1972, Chm., 1981–88. Nat. Pres., Nat. Assoc. of Retail Furnishers, 1971–73; Mem. Council, Retail Consortium, 1972–91 (Chm., non-food policy cttee, 1987–91); Mem. EDC (Distributive Trades), 1974–78. City of London: Sheriff, 1991–92; One of HM Lieutenants, 1963–; Assistant, Merchant Taylors' Co., 1980, Master, 1988, 1994; Master, Furniture Makers' Co., 1978. Trustee, Ranyard Meml Charitable Trust, 1983–2004 (Chm., 1990–2001); Chm., Wimbledon DFAS, 1998–2002. Gov., Bishopsgate Foundn, 1993–2002. President: Bishopsgate Ward Club, 1997–98; Old Stoic Soc., 2002–03. OStJ 1986. *Recreations:* outdoor pursuits, Masia in Madremanya, Gerona. *Heir:* *s* John Simon Pelham Perring, *b* 20 July 1962. *Clubs:* Royal Automobile; Royal Wimbledon Golf; Bembridge Sailing.

PERRINGS, Prof. Charles Aubrey, PhD; Professor of Environmental Economics, Arizona State University, since 2005; *b* 7 July 1949; *s* of Aubrey and Noelle Perrings; *m* 2005, Ann Kinzig. *Educ:* SOAS, Univ. of London (BA Hons 1973, PhD 1976). Lectr in Econs, Nat. Univ. of Lesotho, 1976–78; Lectr, Sen. Lectr, then Associate Prof. of Econs, Univ. of Auckland, 1979–90; Prof. of Econs, Univ. of Calif, Riverside, 1991–92; Prof. of Envmtl Economics, Univ. of York, 1992–2005. Vis. Prof. of Econs, Univ. of Botswana, 1987–89. Ed., Envmt and Develt Econs, 1995–2005. Fellow, Beijer Inst., Royal Swedish Acad. of Scis, 1996–. *Publications:* Economy and Environment: a theoretical essay on the interdependence of economic and environmental systems, 1987 (trans. Italian 1992); (ed jtly) Biodiversity Conservation: problems and policies, 1994; (ed jtly) Biological Diversity: economic and ecological issues, 1995; Sustainable Development and Poverty Alleviation in Sub-Saharan Africa: the case of Botswana, 1996; (ed jtly) The Development of Ecological Economics, 1997; Economics of Ecological Resources: selected essays, 1997; (ed) The Economics of Biodiversity Conservation in Sub-Saharan Africa: mending the Ark, 2000; (ed jtly) The Economics of Biological Invasions, 2000; (ed jtly) Natural Resource Accounting and Economic Development, 2003; (ed) Ecological Economics: origins and development, 2008; (ed jtly) Bioinvasions and Globalization: ecology, economics, management and policy, 2009; (ed jtly) Biodiversity, Ecosystem Functioning and Human Wellbeing: an ecological and economic perspective, 2009; (ed jtly) Bioinvasions and Globalization: ecology, economics, management, and policy, 2010; numerous papers in jls. *Recreations:* music, reading, walking. *Address:* School of Life Sciences, Arizona State University, Box 874501, Tempe, AZ 85287–4501, USA.

PERRINS, Prof. Christopher Miles, LVO 1987; DPhil; FRS 1997; Director, Edward Grey Institute of Field Ornithology, 1974–2002, Professor of Ornithology, 1992–2002, Leverhulme Emeritus Fellow, 2002–04, Oxford University; Fellow, Wolfson College, Oxford, 1970–2002, now Emeritus; *b* 11 May 1935; *s* of Leslie Howard Perrins and Violet Amy (*née* Moore); *m* 1963, Mary Ceresole Carslake; two *s*. *Educ:* Charterhouse; QMC (BSc Hons Zool.; Hon. Fellow, QMW, 1996); Oxford Univ. (DPhil). Edward Grey Institute of Field Ornithology, University of Oxford: Research Officer, 1963–66; Sen. Res. Officer, 1966–84; Reader, 1984–92. Mem., General Bd of Faculties, Oxford Univ., 1983–91, 1995–99 (Chm., Bldgs Cttee, 1995–99); Delegate, OUP, 1994–2002. The Queen's Swan Warden, 1993–. President: Internat. Ornithol Congress, 1990–94; European Ornithologists' Union, 1997–99; BOU, 2003–07; Hon. Corresp. Mem. 1976–83, Hon. Fellow 1983–, Amer. Ornithologists' Union; Hon. Corresp. Mem. 1991–2002, Hon. Fellow 2002, German Ornithologists' Union; Hon. Fellow: Netherlands Ornithologists' Union, 1992; Spanish Ornithologists' Union, 2004. Godman-Salvin Medal, British Ornithologists Union, 1988; Conservation Medal, RSPB, 1992. *Publications:* (ed with B. Stonehouse) Evolutionary Ecology, 1977; British Tits, 1979; (with T. R. Birkhead) Avian Ecology, 1983; (ed with A. L. A. Middleton) The Encyclopaedia of Birds, 1985; (with M. E. Birkhead) The Mute Swan, 1986; New Generation Guide: Birds, 1987; (ed with J. D. Lebreton and G. J. M. Hirons) Bird Population Studies, 1991; (Senior Ed.) Birds of the Western Palearctic, vol. VII, 1993, vols VIII and IX, 1994; (ed with D. W. Snow) The Birds of the Western Palearctic, concise edn, 2 vols, 1998; (ed) The New Encyclopedia of Birds, 2003; (ed jtly) Wytham Woods, 2010. *Recreations:* photography, walking. *Address:* Edward Grey Institute of Field Ornithology, Department of Zoology, University of Oxford, South Parks Road, Oxford OX1 3PS. *T:* (01865) 271169.

PERRIS, Sir David (Arthur), Kt 1977; MBE 1970; JP; Secretary, Trades Union Congress West Midlands Regional Council, 1974–94; Vice President, Birmingham Hospital Saturday Fund, since 2000 (Vice-Chairman, 1975–85; Chairman, 1985–2000); *b* 25 May 1929; *s* of Arthur Perris; *m* 1955, Constance Parkes, BPharm, FRPharmS; one *s* one *d*. *Educ:* Sparkhill Commercial Sch., Birmingham. Film distribution industry, 1944–61; Reed Paper Group, 1961–65; Vice-Chm., ATV Midlands Ltd, 1980–81; Dir, Central Independent Television plc, 1982–83 (Vice Chm., W Midlands Bd). Sec., Birmingham Trades Council, 1966–83; a Chm., Greater Birmingham Supplementary Benefits Appeal Tribunal, 1982–89. Chairman: Birmingham Regional Hosp. Bd, 1970–74; West Midlands RHA, 1974–82; NHS National Trng Council, 1975–82; Mem. Bd of Governors, United Birmingham Hosps, 1965–74; Mem., Birmingham Children's Hosp. House Cttee, 1958–71 (Chm. 1967–71). Member: W Mids Econ. Planning Council, 1968–70; W Midlands Rent Assessment Panel, 1969–99; Midlands Postal Bd, 1974–81. Chairman: Central Telethon Trust, 1987–96; W Midlands Charitable Trust Gp, 1991–93; Pres., W Midlands Charity Trustees' Forum, 1999– (Chm., 1995–99). Life Governor, Univ. of Birmingham, 1972; Elective Gov., Birmingham & Midland Inst., 1989– (Vice Pres., 2009–). Mem. Council, Magistrates' Assoc., 1995–98 (Chm., 1975–86, Pres., 1986–98, Birmingham Br.); Pres., Public Service Announcements Assoc., subseq. Community Media Assoc., 1983–98; Pres., British Health Care Assoc., 1995–98 (Vice-Pres., 1994). Patron, Birmingham Rathbone Soc., 1998–. Fellow, Birmingham Med. Inst., 2010; Life Fellow, British Fluoridation Soc., 1987. Hon. LLD Birmingham, 1981. JP Birmingham, 1961. *Recreation:* reading. *Address:* Broadway, 21 Highfield Road, Moseley, Birmingham B13 9HL. *T:* (0121) 449 3652.

PERRIS, John Douglas; HM Diplomatic Service, retired; *b* 28 March 1928; *s* of Frank William Perris and Alice Perris; *m* 1954, Kathleen Mary Lewington; one *s* two *d*. *Educ:* St Paul's, Knightsbridge; Westminster City Sch. Entered FO, 1945; Bahrain, 1951; Bucharest, 1953; Hamburg, 1955; FO, 1957; Tehran, 1960; Second Sec. (Admin), Caracas, 1963; Second Sec. (Econ.), Berlin, 1966; First Sec. (Admin), Baghdad, 1969; FCO (Inspectorate), 1972; First Sec./Head of Chancery/Consul, Tegucigalpa, 1974; First Sec. (Consular and Immigration), New Delhi, 1976; FCO, 1979; Counsellor (Admin), Bonn, 1982–86. *Recreations:* sport (non-active), reading (thrillers). *Address:* 3 Suffolk Villas, Longfield Street, SW18 5RG. *T:* (020) 8871 3495.

PERROTT, John Gayford; HM Diplomatic Service, retired; British High Commissioner, The Gambia, 2000–02; *b* 5 July 1943; *s* of Dr Charles Hardy Perrott and Dr Phylis Perrott (*née* Dearns); *m* 1964, (Joan) Wendy Lewis; one *s* one *d*. *Educ:* Newport High Sch. Joined CRO, later FCO, 1962; Karachi, 1966–69; Ankara, 1970–72; Calcutta, 1973–76; Kathmandu, 1979–84; Istanbul, 1984–88; St Helena, 1993–97. *Recreations:* walking, golf.

PERROW, (Joseph) Howard; Chairman, Co-operative Union Ltd, 1975–83; Chief Executive Officer and Secretary, Greater Lancastria Co-operative Society Ltd, 1976–83; *b* 18 Nov. 1923; *s* of Joseph and Mary Elizabeth Perrow; *m* 1947, Lorraine Strick (*d* 2007); two *s*. *Educ:* St Just, Penzance, Cornwall; Co-operative Coll., Stanford Hall, Leics (CSD). Joined Penzance Co-operative Soc., 1940. Served RAF, 1943–47. Various managerial positions in Co-operative Movement: in W Cornwall, with CRS N Devon, Carmarthen Soc., Silverdale (Staffs) and Burslem Socs; Mem., Co-operative Union Central Exec., 1966–83, Vice-Chm., 1973–75; Vice-Chm., NW Sectional Bd, 1970–75; Director: CWS, 1970–83; Nat. Co-operative Chemists, 1973–83; Greater Manchester Independent Radio, 1973–83; Mem., Central Cttee, Internat. Co-operative Alliance, 1975–83; Mem. Council (rep. Co-operative Union), Retail Consortium, 1976–83. President, Co-operative Congress, 1979. *Recreations:* football, cricket. *Address:* Blue Seas, Cliff Road, Mousehole, Penzance, Cornwall TR19 6QT. *T:* (01736) 731330.

PERRY, family name of **Baroness Perry of Southwark**.

PERRY OF SOUTHWARK, Baroness *cr* 1991 (Life Peer), of Charlbury in the County of Oxfordshire; **Pauline Perry;** President, Lucy Cavendish College, Cambridge University, 1994–2001; a Conservative Party Whip, House of Lords, since 2011; *b* 15 Oct. 1931; *d* of John George Embleton Welch and Elizabeth Welch; *m* 1952, George Walter Perry (*d* 2008); three *s* one *d*. *Educ:* Girton Coll., Cambridge (MA; Hon. Fellow 1995). Teacher in English Secondary Sch., Canadian and American High Schs, 1953–54 and 1959–61; High School Evaluator, New England, USA, 1959–61; Research Fellow, Univ. of Manitoba, 1956–57; Lecturer in Philosophy: Univ. of Manitoba, 1957–59; Univ. of Massachusetts at Salem, 1960–62; Lectr in Education (part-time), Univ. of Exeter, 1962–66; Tutor for In-Service Trng, Berks, 1966–70; Part-time Lectr in Educn, Dept of Educational Studies, Oxford Univ., 1966–70; HM Inspector of Schools, 1970–86; Staff Inspector, 1975; Chief Inspector, 1981. Dir, S Bank Poly., 1987–92; Vice-Chancellor, S Bank Univ., 1992–93. Alexander Stone Lectr in Rhetoric, Glasgow, 1999. Member: Cttee on Internat. Co-operation in Higher Educn, British Council, 1987–97; ESRC, 1988–91; Governing Body, Institute of Develt Studies, Sussex Univ., 1987–94; Bd, South Bank Centre, 1992–94; NI Higher Educn Council, 1992–94; Nat. Adv. Council on Educn and Training Targets, 1992–95; Prime Minister's Adv. Panel on Citizen's Charter, 1993–97; Overseas Project Bd, 1993–98; Royal Soc. Project Sci. Bd of Patrons, 1995–2003. Member, H of L Select Committee: on Science and Technol., 1992–95, 1997–2005, 2008–10, 2010–14 (Chair, Inquiry into Energy Efficiency, 2004–05); on Scrutiny of Delegated Powers, 1994–98; on relationships between local and central govt, 1995–96; on Stem Cell Research, 2001–02; on Religious Offences, 2002–03; Jt Select Cttee of Commons and Lords on Human Rights, 2000–03; Ecclesiastical Cttee, 2002–; Chm., All-Party Parly Univs Gp, 1996–2009. Chairman: DTI Export Gp for Educn and Trng Sector, 1993–98; Judges Panel on Citizen's Charter, 1997–2004; C of E Rev. Gp on Operation of Crown Appts Commn, 1999–2001; Inquiry into Animals in Scientific Experiments, Nuffield Council on Bio-Ethics, 2003–05; Cttee on Quality and Standards, C&G, 2005–10; Advr on Police Trng to Home Office, 1991–93. Co-Chm., Policy Gp on Public Services, Cons Party, 2006–07. President: Westminster & City Br., Chartered Mgt Inst. (formerly Inst. of Mgt), 2000–14; Higher Educn Foundn, 2002–06. Rector's Warden, Southwark Cath., 1990–94; Chair, Friends of Southwark Cath., 1994–2002. MInstD; CCMI (CIMgt 1993). Mem. Court, Univ. of Bath, 1991–99; Trustee: Bacon's City Technol. Coll., 1991–2009; Cambridge Univ. Foundn, 1997–2006; Pro-Chancellor, Univ. of Surrey, 2001–06; Vice-Pres., C&G, 1994–99; Pres., CIFE, 2000–13; Chm., Council, Roehampton Univ. (formerly Roehampton Inst.), 2001–06; Chair, Governing Body, Kaplan Coll., 2014–. Governor: Gresham's Sch., 2000–06; Abbey Schs, 2012–14. Patron: British Friends of Neve Shalom-Wahat al Salaam, 2005–; St Mark's Coll., Limpopo, SA, 1991–; British Youth Opera, 1992–. Freeman, City of London, 1992; Liveryman, Bakers' Co., 1992–; Hon. Freeman, Fishmongers' Co., 2006. Hon. FCollP 1987; Hon. FRSA 1988; Hon. FCGI 2000. Hon. Fellow: Sunderland Polytechnic, 1990; Lucy Cavendish Coll., 2001; Roehampton Univ., 2005. Hon. LLD: Bath, 1991; Aberdeen, 1994; Hon. DLitt: Sussex, 1992; South Bank, 1994; City, 2000; DUniv Surrey, 1995; Hon. DEd Wolverhampton, 1994; Hon. Dr, Mercy Coll., NY, 2014. Mem., Pedagogical Acad., Swedish Acad. of Sci., 1992. *Publications:* Case Studies in Teaching, 1969; Case Studies in Adolescence, 1970; Your Guide to the Opposite Sex, 1970; The Womb in Which I Lay, 2003; *contributions to:* Advances in Teacher Education, 1989; Women in Education Management, 1992; Public Accountability and Quality Control in Higher Education, 1990; The Future of Higher Education, 1991; Technology: the challenge to education, 1992; What is Quality in Higher Education?, 1993; Education in the Age of Information, 1993; School Inspection, 1995; Women and Higher Education, 1996; Against the Tide: women leaders in American and British higher education, 1996; Higher Education Reform, 2000; Diversity and Excellence, 2001; Creative Church Leadership, 2004; articles in various educnl jls; freelance journalism for radio and TV. *Recreations:* music, walking, cooking. *Address:* House of Lords, SW1A 0PW.

PERRY, Alan Joseph; Director, Whitehall Strategic Management Consultants Ltd, 1992–95; *b* 17 Jan. 1930; *s* of late Joseph and Elsie Perry; *m* 1961, Vivien Anne Ball; two *s*. *Educ:* John Bright Grammar Sch., Llandudno; Dartford Grammar Sch. Served RE, 1948–50. HM Treasury, 1951–68 and 1970–78; CSD, 1968–70; Principal 1968, Asst Sec. 1976; Counsellor (Economic), Washington, 1978–80; HM Treasury, 1980–86; Advr on Govt Affairs, Ernst & Whinney, 1986–88; Dir, Public Sector Services, Ernst & Young, 1989–92. Chm., Review of BBC External Services, 1984.

PERRY, (Christopher) Grenville; His Honour Judge Perry; a Circuit Judge, since 2012; Designated Family Judge for Staffordshire, since 2014; *b* Plymouth, 17 Oct. 1953; *s* of Gerald Perry and Gaynor Perry; *m* 1987, Carolynne Holland; two *s*. *Educ:* Nantwich and Acton Grammar Sch.; Univ. of Nottingham (LLB Hons 1975). Admitted solicitor, 1978; solicitor, private practice, 1980–82; Lectr, 1982–84, Sen. Lectr, 1984–89, Principal Lectr, 1989–94, Coll. of Law, Chester; a District Judge, 1994–2012; a Recorder, 2001–12. Course Dir, Dep. District Judge Trng, Judicial Coll., 2009–12. Trustee: Nantwich Parish Church Preservation Fund, 2000–; Greyhound Rescue West of England, 2002–08. *Recreations:* spending time in North Norfolk, walking three retired greyhounds, pub quizzes, watching Crewe Alexandra FC. *Address:* Stoke-on-Trent Combined Court, Bethesda Street, Hanley, Stoke-on-Trent ST1 3BP. *T:* (01782) 854000. *Club:* Royal Over-Seas League.

PERRY, Claire Louise; MP (C) Devizes, since 2010; Parliamentary Under-Secretary of State, Department for Transport, since 2014; *b* Bromsgrove, 3 April 1964; *d* of David Richens and Joanna Richens; *m* 1996, Clayton Perry (marr. diss. 2014); one *s* two *d*. *Educ:* Brasenose Coll., Oxford (BA Hons Geog. 1985); Harvard Business Sch. (MBA 1990). Vice Pres., Bank of America, 1985–88; Engagement Manager, McKinsey & Co., 1990–94; Dir and Hd of Equities E-commerce, Credit Suisse, 1994–2000. PPS to Sec. of State for Defence, 2011–12; an Asst Govt Whip, 2013–14. Adviser to Prime Minister on preventing the commercialisation and sexualisation of childhood, 2012–. *Recreations:* gardening, cycling, reading. *Address:* House of Commons, SW1A 0AA. *T:* (020) 7219 7050. *E:* claire.perry.mp@parliament.uk.

PERRY, David Gordon; Chairman: Anglian Group, 1996–2001; John Waddington, later Waddington, plc, 1993–97; *b* 26 Dec. 1937; *s* of late Elliott Gordon Perry and Lois Evelyn Perry; *m* 1961, Dorne Mary Busby; four *d*. *Educ:* Clifton Coll.; Christ's Coll., Cambridge. Management Trainee and Sales Exec., ES&A Robinson Ltd, 1960–66; Sales Dir 1966–69, Man. Dir 1969–78, Fell & Briant Ltd (subsid. of British Printing Corp.); British Printing Corporation: Chm. and Chief Exec., Packaging Div., 1978–80; Dir, 1980–81; John Waddington plc: Dep. Man. Dir, 1981–82; Man. Dir, 1982–88; Chief Exec., 1988–92. Non-executive Director: Whitecroft plc, 1991–95; Dewhirst Gp plc, 1992–2001; National & Provincial Building Soc., 1993–96; Kelda Gp plc (formerly Yorkshire Water plc), 1996–2000; Minorplanet Systems plc, 1997–2007 (Chm., 2004–07); Euler Hermes UK (formerly Euler Hldgs UK, then Euler Trade Indemnity) plc, 1998–2008; Bellway plc, 1999–2010. CCMI (CBIM 1985). FRSA 1990. *Recreation:* Rugby football (Cambridge Blue 1958, England XV 1963–66, Captain 1965). *Clubs:* Oxford and Cambridge, MCC.

PERRY, Sir David (Howard), KCB 1986; Chief of Defence Equipment Collaboration, Ministry of Defence, 1985–87, retired; *b* 13 April 1931; *s* of Howard Dace Perry and Annie Evelyn Perry; *m* 1961, Rosemary Grigg; one *s* two *d*. *Educ:* Berkhamsted Sch.; Pembroke Coll., Cambridge (MA). CEng, FRAeS. Joined Aero Dept, RAE, 1954; Aero Flt Div., 1954–66; Aero Projs Div., 1966–71; Head of Dynamics Div., 1971–73; RCDS, 1974; Head of Systems Assessment Dept, RAE, 1975–77; Ministry of Defence (Procurement Executive): Dir-Gen. Future Projects, 1978–80; Dir-Gen. Aircraft 1, 1980–81; Dep. Controller of Aircraft, 1981–82, Controller of Aircraft 1982; Chief of Defence Procurement, 1983–85. *Recreations:* gardening, painting. *Address:* 23 Rectory Road, Farnborough, Hants GU14 7BU.

PERRY, Grayson, CBE 2013; RA 2011; artist in ceramics, print and textiles; occasional broadcaster and journalist; *b* 24 March 1960; *m* 1992, Philippa Fairclough; one *d*. *Educ:* King Edward VI Grammar Sch., Chelmsford; Braintree Coll. of Further Educn; Portsmouth Poly. (BA Fine Art). Chancellor, Univ. of the Arts, London, 2015–. Trustee, British Mus., 2015–. Patron: Grierson Trust; Art Room. *Solo exhibitions* include: James Birch Gall., London, 1984, 1985; The Minories, Colchester, 1986; Birch & Conran, London, 1987, 1988, 1990; Garth Clark Gall., NY, 1991; David Gill Gall., London, 1991–92; Clara Scremini Gall., Paris, 1994; Anthony d'Offay Gall., London, 1994, 1996–97; Laurent Delaye Gall., London, 2000; fig-1, London, 2000; Guerilla Tactics, Stedelijk Mus., Amsterdam and Barbican Art Gall., 2002; Tate St Ives, 2004; Victoria Miro Gall., London, 2004, 2006, 2012; Gall. Il Capricorno, Venice, 2005; Andy Warhol Mus., Pittsburgh, 2006; The Collection, Lincoln, 2006; Mus. of 21st Century Contemp. Art, Kanazawa, Japan; The Tomb of the Unknown Craftsman, British Mus., 2011–12; Who are You?, NPG, 2014–15; Provincial Punk (retrospective), Turner Contemporary, Margate, 2015; *group exhibitions* include: ICA, 1981–82; Garth Clark Gall., NY, 1990, 1999; Whitechapel Gall., 1996, 2000; Crafts Council and Amer. Crafts Mus., NY, 1997–98; Richard Salmon Gall., London and Kettle's Yard, Cambridge, 1997–98; Stedelijk Mus., Amsterdam, Hydra Foundn, Greece, 1999; Laurent Delaye Gall., Saatchi Gall., 2001; Courtauld Inst., 2001–03; Blue Gall., London, Vancouver Art Gall., 2003; Tate Liverpool, 2004; Auckland Art Gall., NZ, 2005; MOMA, NY, 2006; British Mus., 2011; *work in public collections* including British Council, Crafts Council, Saatchi Collection, Pottery Mus.,

Stoke-on-Trent, MOMA, Glasgow, Stedelijk Mus., Amsterdam and Hydra Foundn, Greece; A House for Essex, Wrabness, 2015. *Television:* All in the Best Possible Taste, Channel 4, 2012; Who are You?, Channel 4, 2014. Reith Lectr, BBC Radio 4, 2013. Turner Prize, 2003. *Publications:* Cycle of Violence, 1992; (with W. Jones) Portrait of the Artist as a Young Girl, 2006; Playing to the Gallery, 2014. *Address:* c/o Victoria Miro Gallery, 16 Wharf Road, N1 7RW.

PERRY, Grenville; *see* Perry, C. G.

PERRY, Hugh; *see* Perry, V. H.

PERRY, Jacqueline Anne, (Mrs V. Levene); QC 2006; barrister; attorney at law; *b* 7 March 1952; *d* of late Clarence and Diana Perry; *m* 1980, Victor Levene; one *s*. *Educ:* Copthall Co. Grammar Sch. for Girls; Lady Margaret Hall, Oxford (BA 1973, MA 1977). Called to the Bar, Gray's Inn, 1975, Bencher, 2005; practising as barrister, 1975–, specialising in personal injury, and clinical and professional negligence; admitted to Bar, California, 2001; Associate: Schuler & Brown, Van Nuys, Calif, 2006–10; Rufus-Isaacs, Acland & Grantham, Beverly Hills, Calif, 2010–. Mediator and Mem., ADR (UK) Ltd, 2000. Grade A Advocacy Teacher, Master of Students, 2010–, Gray's Inn. Mem., UK Editl Cttee, Medicine, Sci. and Law, 2011–. Fellow, Internat. Acad. of Trial Lawyers, 2008. Broadcaster, as Nicola Charles: Granada TV, 1989–94; BBC Radio, 1990–96. *Publications:* (as Nicola Charles) with Janice James: Rights of Woman, 1990; Know Your Law, 1995. *Recreations:* cinema, theatre, motor cruising, cooking, reading (both high and low brow). *Address:* 2 Temple Gardens, Temple, EC4Y 9AY. *T:* (020) 7822 1200, *Fax:* (020) 7822 1300. *E:* jperry@2tg.co.uk.

PERRY, John; *see* Perry, R. J.

PERRY, Rt Rev. John Freeman; Bishop of Chelmsford, 1996–2003; an Assistant Bishop, Diocese of Bath and Wells, since 2011; *b* 15 June 1935; *s* of Richard and Elsie Perry; *m* 1st, 1959, Gay Valerie Brown (*d* 2009); three *s* two *d*; 2nd, 2011, Marilyn Eve Sertin; two step *s* two step *d*. *Educ:* Mill Hill School; London College of Divinity (ALCD); LTh St John's Coll., Nottingham, 1974; MPhil Westminster Coll., Oxford, 1986. Royal Signals, 1953–55; Assistant Curate: Christ Church, Woking, 1959–62; Christ Church, Chorleywood, 1962–63; Vicar, St Andrew's, Chorleywood, 1963–77; RD of Rickmansworth, 1972–77; Warden, Lee Abbey, Lynton, Devon, 1977–89; RD of Shirwell, 1980–84; Suffragan Bishop of Southampton, 1989–96. Hon. Canon, Winchester Cathedral, 1989–96. Took seat in H of L, 2000. Member: C of E Bd of Ministry, 1989–2002; Bd, Christian Solidarity Worldwide, 2004–13 (Chm., 2010–13); Chm., Cttee for Ministry of and among Deaf and Disabled, 1989–2001. Chm., Burrswood, 1989–2003; Pres., Fellowship of Christ the Healer, 2000–; Vice-Pres., Lee Abbey Movt, 2010– (Chm., 2004–10). Vice-Pres., Univ. of Glos, 2004–. Gov., Monkton Combe Sch., Bath, 2004–10. Hon. Dr Anglia Poly. Univ., 2000. *Publications:* Effective Christian Leadership, 1983; (contrib.) Celebrating Community, 2006. *Recreations:* a large family, walking, sport, travel, classical music, films. *Address:* 8 The Firs, Combe Down, Bath BA2 5ED.

PERRY, Rev. John Neville; *b* 29 March 1920; *s* of Robert and Enid Perry; *m* 1946, Rita Dyson Rooke; four *s* four *d*. *Educ:* The Crypt Gram. Sch., Gloucester; Univ. of Leeds (BA 1941), College of the Resurrection, Mirfield. Asst Curate, All Saints', Poplar, 1943–50; Vicar, St Peter De Beauvoir Town, Hackney, 1950–63; Vicar, St Dunstan with St Catherine, Feltham, Middx, 1963–75; Rural Dean of Hounslow, 1967–75; Archdeacon of Middlesex, 1975–82; Rector of Orlestone with Ruckinge and Warehorne, Kent, 1982–86. Mem. Latey Cttee on the Age of Majority, 1966–67. *Recreation:* enjoying life to the full and socialising. *Address:* 73 Elizabeth Crescent, East Grinstead, West Sussex RH19 3JG.

PERRY, John Scott, (Jack), CBE 2010; DL; Chief Executive, Scottish Enterprise, 2004–09; Chairman: Hospice Developments Ltd, since 2012; ICG-Longbow Senior Secured UK Property Debt Investments Ltd, since 2012; European Assets Trust NV, since 2015; *b* 23 Nov. 1954; *s* of George Michael Perry, CBE and Madalynn Heber; *m* 1977, Lydia; one *s* two *d*. *Educ:* Glasgow Univ. (BSc (Pure Sci.) 1975); Strathclyde Univ. (Postgrad. Dip. Accountancy 1976). CA (ICAS) 1979; Certified Public Accountant (USA) 1985; CCIM 2004. Ernst & Young, 1976–2003: Managing Partner, Glasgow, 1995–2003; Regl Industry Leader, Technol. Communications and Entertainment, Scotland and NI, 1999–2003. Non-executive Director: Robert Wiseman Dairies plc, 2010–12; Capital for Enterprise Ltd, 2013–14; Silent Herdsman Hldgs Ltd, 2013–; Mem., Adv. Cttee, Barclays UK and Ireland Private Bank, Barclays Wealth, 2010–13. Chm., CBI Scotland, 2001–03 (Mem. Council, 1996–2004, 2011–); Chm., Regl Chairmen, Mem., President's Cttee, CBI. Chm., TMRI Ltd, 2007–09. Chm., Scottish Aquaculture Innovation Centre, 2014–. Former Mem., Ministerial Task Force on Econ. Forums. Member: Financial Services Adv. Bd, 2005–09; Adv. Bd, Asia Scotland Inst., 2013–14. Former Chm. Bd of Dirs, Craigholme Sch.; Vis. Tutor, Leadership Trust. FInstD 2010. Mem. Court, 2010–, Treas., 2011–, Univ. of Strathclyde; Mem., Adv. Bd, Univ. of Edinburgh Business Sch., 2010–. DL Renfrewshire, 2011. Hon. DBA: Edinburgh Napier, 2010; Abertay Dundee, 2011. *Recreations:* golf, ski-ing, reading, current affairs. *Address:* c/o European Assets Trust NV, F&C Asset Management plc, 80 George Street, Edinburgh EH2 3BU. *Clubs:* Glasgow Academical; Royal and Ancient Golf, Western Gailes Golf (Captain, 2011).

PERRY, John William; Chairman, Trace Computers, 1996–2001 (non-executive Director, 1994–96 and 2001–04); *b* 23 Sept. 1938; *s* of John and Cecilia Perry; *m* 1961, Gillian Margaret (*d* 2007); two *d*. *Educ:* Wallington Grammar Sch.; Brasenose Coll., Oxford (MA). Burroughs: Dir of Marketing, UK, 1967–71, Europe Africa Div., 1977–78; Group Dir, Internat. Marketing, 1978–80; Vice-President: Strategic Planning, 1981; Financial Systems Gp, 1983; Central USA, 1985–86; Man. Dir, Burroughs UK, 1986; Chm. and Man. Dir, Unisys, 1987–94; Corporate Officer, 1990, Pres., Financial Services, 1993–94, Unisys Corp.; Director, 1987–94: Sperry; Burroughs Machines; BMX Information Systems; BMX Holdings; Unisys Holdings; Convergent Technologies (UK). Mem., Nat. Task Force, Business in the Community, 1988–94. Trustee, Information Age Project, 1989. Mem., Bd of Governors, Polytechnic of East London, 1989. *Recreations:* gardening, reading, music. *Address:* The Great Barn, Sandpit Lane, Bledlow, Bucks HP27 9QQ.

PERRY, Jonathan Peter Langman; Chairman, Paragon Group of Companies PLC (formerly National Home Loans Holdings), 1992–2007; *b* 6 Sept. 1939; *s* of Thomas Charles Perry and Kathleen Mary Perry; *m* 1965, Sheila Johnson; two *s* one *d*. *Educ:* Peter Symonds Sch., Winchester. FCA. Butler Viney Childs, 1956–62; Cooper Brothers, 1962–66; Morgan Grenfell & Co., 1966–88 (Dir, 1973–88); Principal, Perry Associates, 1988–90; Chm. and Chief Exec., Ogilvie Adams & Rinehart, 1990–92; Vice-Chm., HSBC Investment Banking, 1997–99. *Recreations:* sailboat racing, golf, music. *Clubs:* Brooks's; Royal Yacht Squadron, Itchenor Sailing; West Sussex Golf.

PERRY, Prof. Malcolm John, PhD, ScD; Professor of Theoretical Physics, University of Cambridge, since 2005; Fellow and Lecturer in Mathematics, Trinity College, Cambridge, since 1986; *b* Birmingham, 13 Nov. 1951; *s* of John and Joan Perry; partner, Anna Nikola Żytkow. *Educ:* King Edward's Sch., Birmingham; St John's Coll., Oxford (BA Phys 1973); King's Coll., Cambridge (MA 1977; PhD 1978; ScD 1999). Res. Fellow, King's Coll., Cambridge, 1977–81; Mem., Inst. for Advanced Study, Princeton, 1978–79; Asst Prof., Princeton Univ., 1979–86; University of Cambridge: Royal Soc. Univ. Res. Fellow, Dept of Applied Maths and Theoretical Phys, 1986–93; Newton Lectr, 1994–98; Asst Dir of Res., 1999–2000; Reader in Theoretical Phys, 2000–05. Distinguished Res. Prof., Perimeter Inst., Waterloo, Ont, 2009–12. *Publications:* articles in professional jls. *Recreations:* early and classical music, mountaineering. *Address:* Trinity College, Cambridge CB2 1TQ. *T:* (01223) 338400. *E:* mjp1@cam.ac.uk.

PERRY, Sir Michael (Sydney), GBE 2002 (CBE 1990; OBE 1978); Kt 1994; Chairman, Centrica plc, 1997–2004; *b* 26 Feb. 1934; *s* of Sydney Albert Perry and Jessie Kate (*née* Brooker); *m* 1958, Joan Mary Stallard; one *s* two *d*. *Educ:* King William's Coll., IoM; St John's Coll., Oxford (MA). Unilever, 1957–96: Chm., Lever Brothers (Thailand) Ltd, 1973–77; Pres., Lever y Asociados SACIF, Argentina, 1977–81; Chm., Nippon Lever KK, 1981–83; Jt Man. Dir, UAC Internat., 1983–85, Chm., 1985–87; Dir, Unilever plc and Unilever NV, 1985–96; Personal Products Co-ordinator, 1987–91; Vice-Chm., 1991–92, Chm., 1992–96, Unilever plc; Vice Chm., Unilever NV, 1992–96. Non-executive Director: Bass plc, 1991–2001 (Dep. Chm., 1996–2001); British Gas plc, 1994–97; Marks and Spencer plc, 1996–2001; Royal Ahold BV, 1997–2004; non-exec. Chm., Dunlop Slazenger Gp Ltd, 1996–2001; Chm., Chairmen's Counsel Ltd, 2006–12. Mem., BOTB, 1986–92; Jt Chm., Netherlands British Chamber of Commerce, 1989–93; Chairman: Japan Trade Gp, 1991–99; Sen. Salaries Rev. Body, 1995–2002; Marketing Council, 1996–99. Pres., Advertising Assoc., 1993–96. Pres., Liverpool Sch. of Trop. Med., 1997–2002 (Vice-Pres., 1991–97, 2002–); Trustee, IPPR, 2004–08; Member Council: Cheltenham Coll., 1995–2000; Alice Ottley Sch., Worcester, 2001–08. Chairman: Shakespeare Globe Trust, 1993–2006; Three Choirs Foundn, 2014–; Trustee: Leverhulme Trust, 1991–2008 (Chm., 2008–13); Glyndebourne Arts Trust, 1996–2004; Dyson Perrins Mus. Trust, 2000–; Daiwa Foundn, 2008–15; Three Choirs Fest. Assoc., 2007–. CCMI (CBIM 1992). FRSA 1992. Hon. LLD South Bank, 1995; DUniv Brunel, 1995; Hon. DSc Cranfield, 1995; Hon. DLit Worcester, 2013. *Recreations:* music (choral), walking. *Clubs:* Oriental, Sloane; Worcestershire Golf.

PERRY, Nicholas Proctor; Permanent Secretary, Department of Justice, Northern Ireland, since 2010; *b* 24 May 1958; *s* of Very Rev. Thomas Perry and Joyce Perry (*née* Proctor); *m* 1988, Belinda Jane Neill (marr. diss. 1998); one *s* one *d*. *Educ:* St Columba's Coll., Dublin; Trinity Coll., Dublin (BA Hons 1980). Joined HM Customs and Excise, 1981; MoD, 1984–91 (Private Sec. to Parly Under-Sec., Defence Procurement, 1987–89); Northern Ireland Office, 1991–: Asst Sec., 1994; Principal Private Sec. to Sec. of State for NI, 1998–2000; Associate Dir, 2003–04, Dir Gen., 2004–08, Policing and Security; Dir Gen., Criminal Justice and Policing, 2008–10. *Publications:* (ed) Major General Oliver Nugent and the Ulster Division 1915–1918, 2007; (contrib.) Oxford DNB; contrib. books and jls on military history. *Recreations:* cricket, military history. *Address:* c/o Department of Justice, Castle Buildings, Stormont Estate, Belfast BT4 3SG.

PERRY, Norman Henry, PhD; Chairman, Public Services Group, HBJ Gateley Wareing LLP, 2007–12; *b* 5 March 1944; *s* of late Charles and Josephine Perry; *m* 1970, Barbara Ann Marsden; two *s*. *Educ:* Quintin Sch., NW8; University Coll. London (BA 1965; PhD 1969). Lectr in Geography, UCL, 1965–69; Sen. Res. Officer, GLC, 1969–73; Sen. Res. Fellow, SSRC Survey Unit, 1973–75; joined DoE, 1975; Principal, London and Birmingham, 1975–80; Asst Sec., W Midlands Regl Office, 1980–86; Head of Inner Cities Unit (G4), Dept of Employment, then DTI, 1986–88; Under Sec., and Dir W Midlands, DTI, 1988–90; Chief Exec. and Policy Co-ordinator, Wolverhampton MBC, 1990–95; Chief Executive: Solihull MBC, 1995–2000; Housing Corp., 2000–04. Non-executive Director: English Partnerships, 2002–04; THFC plc, 2003–04; Merlion Gp plc, 2004–07. Dir, Wolverhampton TEC, 1990–95; Gov., Univ. of Wolverhampton, 1993–95; Mem., Adv. Bd, Inst. of Public Mgt, Warwick Univ., 2005–. Company Sec., Solihull Business Partnership Ltd, 1996–2000; Dir, Central Careers Ltd, 1996–99. Sec., Soc. of Metropolitan Chief Execs, 1998–2000; Chm., Assoc. of Local Authority Chief Execs, 1995–96. Mem., Adv. Body, Almshouse Assoc., 2005–. FCMI (FIMgt 1983); FRSA 1996. Hon. CIPFA 2003. *Publications:* (contrib.) European Glossary of Legal and Administrative Terminology, 1974, 1979, 1988; contribs to books and learned jls in fields of geography, planning, organisational sociology and urban policy. *Address:* The Beeches, Howe Road, Watlington, Oxon OX49 5EL.

PERRY, Roy James; Member (C) South East Region, England, European Parliament, 1999–2004 (Wight and Hampshire South, 1994–99); *b* 12 Feb. 1943; *s* of George and Dora Perry; *m* 1968, Veronica Haswell; two *d*. *Educ:* Tottenham County Grammar Sch.; Exeter Univ. Marks & Spencer, 1964–66; Lectr in Govt and Politics, 1966–75, Sen. Lectr, 1975–94, Southampton Tech. Coll. Leader, Test Valley Borough Council, 1985–94. Cons. spokesman on educn, culture and media, EP, 1994–2004; EPP co-ordinator, Petitions Cttee, 1999–2004 (Vice-Pres., 1999–2004). Mem. (C), Hants CC, 2005– (Dep. Leader, 2008–13; Leader, 2013–; Exec. Lead Mem. for Children's Services; Exec. Mem., Ext. Affairs). Chairman: Test Valley Arts Foundn, 2004 (Trustee); Hampshire Strategic Crime and Disorder Partnership, 2007. Trustee: Hampshire Museums Trust, 1998–2004; Hampshire Cultural Trust. *Recreations:* bridge, French travel and food. *Address:* Tarrants Farmhouse, Maurys Lane, West Wellow, Romsey, Hants SO51 6DA.

See also C. Nokes.

PERRY, (Rudolph) John; QC 1989; *b* 20 Feb. 1936; *s* of late Rudolph Perry and Beatrice (*née* Tingling, subseq. Robertson); *m*; two *s* (one *d* decd). *Educ:* Ruseas High Sch., Lucea, Jamaica; Southgate Technical Coll.; London Sch. of Economics (LLB (Hons), LLM); Univ. of Warwick (MA (Industrial Relations)). Lectr (part-time), LSE, 1970–78; Lectr, 1971, Sen. Lectr, 1974–78, City of London Poly. Called to the Bar, Middle Temple, 1975; in practice, 1976; an Asst Recorder, 1988, Recorder, 1992–2002. Mem. Panel of Chairmen, Police Disciplinary Appeals Tribunals, 1997–2011. *Recreations:* watching cricket, travel, cinema. *Address:* 58c Mill Street, Old Kidlington, Oxon OX5 2EF.

PERRY, Rev. Dr Simon; Chaplain, Robinson College, University of Cambridge, since 2011; *b* 10 Sept. 1969; *s* of Bill and Joan Perry; *m* 1994, Rachel Olyott (marr. diss. 2008); three *s* one *d*. *Educ:* Regent's Park Coll., Oxford (BTh 1998); Bristol Univ. (PhD 2005). Data Analyst, Special Reaction Force, RAF, 1987–94; Minister, Fivehead Baptist Church, Somerset, 1998–2003; Chaplain, Fitzwilliam Coll., Cambridge, 2003–06; Jt Minister, Bloomsbury Central Baptist Ch, 2006–11. *Publications:* All Who Came Before, 2011; Resurrecting Interpretation, 2012; Atheism After Christendom, 2015. *Recreations:* rowing, running, guitar, conning clever people into thinking I'm one of them. *Address:* Robinson College, Grange Road, Cambridge CB3 9AN. *E:* revslammer@googlemail.com.

PERRY, Prof. (Victor) Hugh, DPhil; Professor of Experimental Neuropathology, University of Southampton, since 1998; *b* 18 April 1952; *s* of Eric and Marie Perry; *m* 1992, Jessica Duxbury; one *s* two *d*. *Educ:* Magdalen Coll., Oxford (BA Hons 1974; MA; DPhil 1977). University of Oxford: Royal Soc. Locke Res. Fellow, 1982–86; Wellcome Trust Sen. Res. Fellow, 1986–95; Prof. of Exptl Neuropathology, 1996–98; Dir, Southampton Neurosci. Gp, 2001–08. Vis. Prof., Coll. of Medicine and Veterinary Medicine, Univ. of Edinburgh, 2011–. Mem., Nuffield Council on Bioethics, 2006–12. FMedSci 2005. Corresp. Mem., Brazilian Acad. of Scis, 2014. *Publications:* Macrophages and the Nervous System, 1994; over 300 papers and 55 reviews in scientific jls. *Recreations:* reading, walking, sailing, gardening. *Address:* Centre for Biological Sciences, University of Southampton, Mailpoint 840, LD80B, Southampton General Hospital, Hants SO16 6YD. *T:* (023) 8125 6103, *Fax:* (023) 8079 5332. *E:* vhp@soton.ac.uk.

PERRY, William Arthur; Command Secretary (Adjutant General, Personnel and Training Command), Ministry of Defence, 1994–97; *b* 5 Aug. 1937; *s* of Arthur Perry and Elizabeth Grace (*née* Geller); *m* 1962, Anne Rosemary Dight; two *d*. *Educ:* St Dunstan's Coll.; Kellogg Coll., Oxford (MSc 2004). Min. of Aviation, 1960–61; Second Sec. (Defence Supply), Bonn,

1964–66; Min. of Technology, then MoD, 1966–74; First Sec., UK Delegn to NATO, 1974–77; Head, Defence Secretariat 8, MoD, 1978–80; Counsellor (Defence Supply), Bonn, 1980–84; Regl Marketing Dir, Defence Exports Services Orgn, 1984–88; Asst Sec., MoD (PE), 1988–92; Dir (Finance and Secretariat), Air 1, MoD (PE), 1992–94. Mem., Royal Patriotic Fund Corp., 1994–97. Trustee, Wilts Archaeological and Natural History Soc. and Wilts Mus. (formerly Wilts Heritage Mus.), 2001– (Chm., 2004–10). *Recreations:* opera, gardening, genealogy.

PERRY, Dr William James, Hon. KBE 1998; Michael and Barbara Berberian Professor, Freeman Spogli Institute for International Studies and School of Engineering, Stanford University, 1997, now Emeritus; Secretary of Defense, United States of America, 1994–97; *b* Pa, 11 Oct. 1927; *m* Lee; three *s* two *d.* *Educ:* Butler High Sch., Butler, Pa; Carnegie Tech.; Stanford Univ. (BS Maths, MS); Penn State Univ. (PhD Maths). Served US Army: Fort Belvoir, Japan and Okinawa, 1946–47; Army Reserves, 1950–55. Dir, Electronic Defense Labs, Sylvania/General Telephone; Exec. Vice Pres., Hambrecht and Quist Inc.; Founder, ESL Inc., 1964, Pres., 1964–77; Under-Sec. of Defense for Res. and Engrg, 1977–81; Stanford University: Co-Dir, Center for Internat. Security and Arms Control, 1988–93; Chm., Technol. Strategies & Alliances, 1985–93; Dep. Sec. of Defense, 1993–94. Mem., Nat. Acad. Engrg; Fellow, Amer. Acad. Arts and Scis. Distinguished Public Service Medal, Dept of Defense, 1980 and 1981; Distinguished Service Medal, NASA, 1981; Medal of Achievement, Amer. Electronics Assoc., 1980; US Presidential Medal of Freedom, 1997. *Address:* Stanford University, CA 94305, USA.

PERSAUD, Dr Rajendra Dhwarka, FRCPsych; consultant psychiatrist in private practice, Harley Street, since 2008; *b* 13 May 1963; *s* of Prof. Bishnudat Persaud and Dr Lakshmi Seeteram; *m* 1994, Maria Francesca Cordeiro; one *s* one *d.* *Educ:* Haberdashers' Aske's Sch., Elstree; University Coll. London (BSc 1st Cl. Hons Psychol.; MB BS Medicine; MSc; Fellow 2002); Birkbeck Coll., London (Dip Phil); Inst. of Psychiatry, London (MPhil). MRCPsych 1991, FRCPsych 2005; DHMSA 1992. HO, UCH, 1986–87; SHO, Maudsley Hosp., 1987–90; Research Fellow: Johns Hopkins Med. Sch., Baltimore, 1990–91; Inst. of Neurol., 1991–93; Lectr, 1993–2000, Sen. Lectr, 2000, Inst. of Psychiatry; Consultant Psychiatrist: Maudsley Hosp., 1994–2008; Surrey and Borders NHS Partnership Trust, 2008–10; practising privileges: Wellington Hosp.; Capio Hosp. Vis. Gresham Prof. of Psychiatry, 2004–07, now Emeritus. Presenter, All in the Mind, BBC Radio 4; writer and presenter of TV series, incl. Psychology of Hostage Negotiation. Jt Podcast Ed., RCPsych., 2014–. Member: Med. Soc. of London, 2003; Ind. Doctor's Fedn. Denis Hill Prize, Royal Maudsley Hosp., 1990; Res. Prize and Medal, 1994, Morris Markowe Prize, 2005, RCPsych. *Publications:* Staying Sane: how to make your mind work for you, 1999; From the Edge of the Couch: bizarre psychiatric cases and what they teach us about ourselves, 2003; The Motivated Mind, 2005; Simply Irresistible, 2007; The Mind: a user's guide, 2008; contrib. papers to BMJ, The Lancet, British Jl Psychiatry, New England Jl Medicine; contrib. Huffington Post. *Recreations:* poker, tennis, golf, theatre, shooting. *Address:* 10 Harley Street, W1G 6AT. *Clubs:* Athenæum, Royal Automobile, Reform, Queen's.

PERSEY, Lionel Edward; QC 1997; a Recorder, since 2002; a Deputy High Court Judge, since 2010; *b* 19 Jan. 1958; *s* of Dr Paul Ronald Persey and Irene Persey; *m* 1984, Lynn Mear; one *s.* *Educ:* Haberdashers' Aske's Sch., Elstree; Birmingham Univ. (LLB Hons 1980). Called to the Bar, Gray's Inn, 1981; in practice as commercial and maritime barrister, 1982–; Jt Hd, Quadrant Chambers, 2006–12. Mem., Supplementary Panel, Jun. Treasury Counsel, 1992–97. Lloyd's Arbitrator, 2009–. *Recreations:* classical music, opera, reading, gardening. *Address:* Quadrant Chambers, Quadrant House, 10 Fleet Street, EC4Y 1AU. *T:* (020) 7583 4444, *Fax:* (020) 7583 4455. *E:* lionel.persey@quadrantchambers.com. *Club:* Reform.

PERSSON, Göran; Senior Advisor, JKL Group, Stockholm, since 2007; Chairman, Sveaskog Förvaltning AB, since 2008; Prime Minister of Sweden, 1996–2006; *b* 20 Jan. 1949; *m* Annika Persson (marr. diss. 2002); *m* 2003, Anitra Steen; two *d* from a previous marriage. *Educ:* Orebro Univ. Organising Sec., 1971, Mem. of Bd, 1972–75, Swedish Social Democratic Youth League; mil. service, 1973–74; Sec., Workers' Educn Assoc., Sörmland, 1974–76; Chairman: Katrineholm Educn Authy, 1977–79; Bd of Educn, Södermanland Co., 1982–89. Mem., Riksdag (MP), 1979–84, 1991–94; Municipal Comr, Katrineholm, 1985–89; Minister for Schs and Educn, 1989–91; Minister of Finance, 1994–96. Chm., Swedish Social Democratic Party, 1996–2007. Vice-Chm., Oppunda Savings Bank, 1976–89; Chm., Södermanland Co-op. Soc., 1976–89; Nat. Auditor, Swedish Co-op. Wholesale Soc., 1988–89. Vice-Chm., Nordic Mus., 1983–89. *Address:* JKL Group, Box 1405, Sveavägen 24–26, 111 84 Stockholm, Sweden.

PERSSON, Rt Rev. William Michael Dermot; Suffragan Bishop of Doncaster, 1982–92; an Assistant Bishop, Diocese of Bath and Wells, since 1994; *b* 27 Sept. 1927; *s* of Leslie Charles Grenville Alan and Elizabeth Mercer Persson; *m* 1957, Ann Davey; two *s* one *d.* *Educ:* Monkton Combe School; Oriel Coll., Oxford (MA); Wycliffe Hall Theological Coll. National service, Army, 1945–48; commissioned, Royal Signals. Deacon 1953, priest 1954; Curate: Emmanuel, South Croydon, 1953–55; St John, Tunbridge Wells, 1955–58; Vicar, Christ Church, Barnet, 1958–67; Rector, Bebington, Cheshire, 1967–79; Vicar, Knutsford with Toft, 1979–82. General Synod: Mem., House of Clergy, 1975–82, House of Bishops, 1985–92; Chm., Council for Christian Unity, 1991–92. *Recreations:* gardening, writing poetry. *Address:* Ryall's Cottage, Burton Street, Marnhull, Sturminster Newton, Dorset DT10 1PS.

PERT, Prof. Geoffrey James, PhD; FRS 1995; FInstP; Professor of Computational Physics, University of York, 1987–2007, now Emeritus Professor of Physics; *b* 15 Aug. 1941; *s* of Norman James Pert and Grace Winifred Pert (*née* Barnes); *m* 1967, Janice Ann Alexander; one *d.* *Educ:* Norwich Sch.; Imperial Coll., Univ. of London (BSc; PhD 1966). FInstP 1979. University of Alberta: Fellow, 1967–68; Asst Prof., 1968–70; University of Hull: Lectr, 1970–74; Sen. Lectr, 1974–78; Reader, 1978–82; Prof., 1982–87. *Publications:* papers in learned scientific jls. *Recreations:* hill-walking, gardening. *Address:* Department of Physics, University of York, Heslington, York YO10 5DD. *T:* (01904) 432250.

PERT, His Honour Michael; QC 1992; a Circuit Judge, 2004–15; Resident Judge for Leicester, 2006–14; *b* 17 May 1947; *s* of Lieut Henry McKay Pert (RN, retd) and Noreen (*née* Murphy); *m* 1971, Vivien Victoria Braithwaite (marr. diss. 1993); one *s* two *d.* *Educ:* St Boniface's Coll., Plymouth; Manchester Univ. (LLB Hons). Called to the Bar, Gray's Inn, 1970. A Recorder, 1988–2004. *Recreations:* beekeeping, sailing.

PERTH, 18th Earl of, *cr* 1605; **John Eric Drummond;** Baron Drummond of Cargill, 1488; Baron Maderty, 1609; Baron Drummond, 1686; Lord Drummond of Gilston, 1685; Lord Drummond of Rickertoun and Castlemaine, 1686; Viscount Strathallan, 1686; Hereditary Thane of Lennox and Hereditary Steward of Menteith and Strathearn; *b* 7 July 1935; *e s* of 17th Earl of Perth, PC and Nancy Seymour, *d* of Reginald Fincke, NYC; *S* father, 2002; *m* 1963, Margaret Ann (marr. diss. 1972), *o d* of Robin Gordon; two *s*; *m* 1988, Mrs Marion Elliot. *Educ:* Trinity Coll., Cambridge; Harvard Univ. (MBA). *Heir: s* Viscount Strathallan, *qv.*

PERTH (Australia), Archbishop of, since 2005; **Most Rev. Roger Adrian Herft,** AM 2012; Metropolitan of the Province of Western Australia, since 2005; *b* 11 July 1948; *s* of Richard Clarence and Esmie Marie Herft; *m* 1976, Cheryl Oranee Jayasekera; two *s.* *Educ:* Royal College, Colombo; Theological Coll. of Lanka. BTh, BD (Serampore). Employed at Carson Cumberbatch & Co. Ltd, 1966–69; theol coll., 1969–73; deacon 1972, priest 1973; Assistant Curate: Holy Emmanuel Church, Moratuwa, 1972; St Luke's Church, Borella, with chaplaincy to Colombo Prison, 1973; Vicar: Holy Emmanuel, Moratuwa, 1976; SS Mary and John Nugegoda, 1979; Parish Consultant, Diocese of Waikato, NZ, 1983; Bishop of Waikato, 1986–93; Bishop of Newcastle, NSW, 1993–2005. Chaplain, Lambeth Conf. of Bishops, 1998; Archbishop of Canterbury's rep. on L'Arche Internat. Church Leaders' Commn, 1998–2013; Anglican Co-Chair, Internat. Anglican-Orthodox Theol Dialogue Commn, 2008–. Sub-Prelate, WA Commandery, Order of St John of Jerusalem, Australia, 2005–. *Publications:* (co-ed) Encounter with Reality, 1971; Christ's Battlers, 1997. *Recreations:* reading, avid follower of cricket. *Address:* Anglican Church of Australia, Diocese of Perth, GPO Box W2067, Perth, WA 6846, Australia. *T:* (8) 93257455, *Fax:* (8) 93256741.

PERTH, (St Ninian's Cathedral), Provost of; *see* Farquharson, Very Rev. H. B.

PERU, Bishop of, since 1998; **Rt Rev. (Harold) William Godfrey;** *b* 21 April 1948; *s* of Charles Robert Godfrey and Irene Eva Godfrey (*née* Kirk); *m* 1968, Judith Moya (*née* Fenton); one *s* two *d.* *Educ:* Chesterfield School; King's Coll., Univ. of London (AKC; Jelf Medal); St Augustine's Coll., Canterbury. VSO, Isfahan, Iran, 1966–67; Asst Curate, Warsop with Sookholme, Diocese of Southwell, 1972–75; Team Vicar of St Peter and St Paul, Hucknall Torkard, 1975–86; Bishop of Southwell's Ecumenical Officer, 1981–82; Rector of Montevideo, 1986–87, Archdeacon of Montevideo, 1986–87; Asst Bishop of Argentina and Uruguay, 1987–88; Bishop of Uruguay, 1988–98; Asst Presiding Bishop, Prov. of Southern Cone of America, 1989–95, 2010–. Oblate, Elmore Abbey, 2008–. Consultant for Confessional Affairs, Min. of Justice, Peru, 2004–; Dir, Sociedad Bíblica del Perú, 2003–; Pres., Interconfessional Cttee of Peru, 2004–09; Pres. (formerly Co-Pres.), Interreligious Cttee of Peru, 2009–. Member: Anglican Consultative Council, 2009–; Anglican Witness (formerly Core Gp), Evangelism and Ch Growth Initiative, Anglican Communion, 2009–. Founder: Instituto Teológico Anglicano del Uruguay, 1990; Seminario Diocesano Santos Agustín, 2000; Founder and Pres., Comunión-Perú NGO, 2005. Member: Jesus Caritas Fraternity, 1974–86; Us (formerly USPG) Mission, 1986–. Hon. DD Nashotah Hse, USA, 2008. *Publications:* Santa Eucaristía, Rito Anglicano. *Address:* Calle Alcalá 336, Urbanización La Castellana, Santiago de Surco, Lima 33, Peru. *T:* and *Fax:* (1) 4480024. *E:* hwgodfrey@gmail.com.

PERUMBALATH, Ven. Dr John; Archdeacon of Barking, since 2013; *b* 1966. *Educ:* Calicut Univ. (BA 1986); Union Bible Seminary, Pune (BD 1990); Osmania Univ., Hyderabad (MA 1993); Serampore Theol Coll. (MTh 1993); NW Univ., S Africa (PhD 2007). Ordained deacon, 1994, priest, 1995; Curate, St John's, Calcutta, 1994–95; Vicar, St James', Calcutta, 1995–2001; Curate, St George's, Beckenham, 2002–05; Team Vicar, Northfleet and Rosherville, 2005–08; Vicar, All Saints, Northfleet, 2008–13; Diocesan Link Officer, Church Urban Fund, 2008–13. *Address:* 11 Bridgefields Close, Hornchurch, Essex RM11 1GQ. *T:* (01708) 474951.

PERUTZ, Prof. Robin Noel, PhD; FRS 2010; Professor of Chemistry, University of York, since 1991; *b* Dec. 1949; *s* of Max Ferdinand Perutz, OM, CH, CBE, FRS. *Educ:* Pembroke Coll., Cambridge (BA 1968); Univ. of Newcastle upon Tyne (PhD 1974). Posts in Muelheim, Edinburgh and Oxford; University of York: Lectr, 1983–89; Reader, 1989–91; Hd, Dept of Chem., 2000–04. Pres., Dalton Div., RSC, 2007–10. Nyholm Medal and Lect., RSC, 2005; Luigi Sacconi Medal, Italian Chemical Soc., 2008. *Address:* Department of Chemistry, University of York, Heslington, York YO10 5DD.

PERVEZ, Sir (Mohammed) Anwar, Kt 1999; OBE 1992; HPk 2000; Chairman, Bestway Group, since 2004 (Managing Director, 1975–2004); *b* 15 March 1935. *Educ:* Jhelum, Pakistan. Chairman: Batleys Ltd, 2005–; Well Pharmacy, 2014–. Founder, Bestway Foundn Charitable Trust. Hon. DLaws: Forman Christian Coll., Lahore, 2011; Bradford, 2012. *Address:* Bestway Group, 2 Abbey Road, Park Royal, NW10 7BW. *T:* (020) 8453 1234.

PERY, family name of **Earl of Limerick**.

PERY, Viscount; Felix Edmund Pery; *b* 16 Nov. 1991; *s* and *heir* of Earl of Limerick, *qv.* *Educ:* Latymer Upper Sch.; Ardingly Coll.

PESARAN, Prof. (Mohammad) Hashem, FBA 1998; PhD; Professor of Economics, Cambridge University, 1988–2012, now Emeritus; Fellow of Trinity College, Cambridge, since 1988; John Elliot Professor of Economics, since 2003, Distinguished Professor, since 2013, Director, Centre for Applied Financial Economics, since 2012, and Director, Dornsife Institute of New Economic Thinking, since 2014, University of Southern California; *b* 30 March 1946; *s* of Jamal and Effat Pesaran; *m* 1969, Marion Fay Swainston; three *s* two *d.* *Educ:* Salford Univ. (BSc 1968); Cambridge Univ. (PhD 1972; MA 2003). Jun. Res. Officer, Dept of Applied Econs, Cambridge Univ., and Lektor, Trinity Coll., Cambridge, 1971–73; Asst to Vice-Governor, 1973–74, and Head of Econ. Res. Dept, 1974–76, Central Bank of Iran; Under-Sec., Min. of Educn, Iran, 1977–78; Teaching Fellow, and Dir of Studies in Econs, Trinity Coll., Cambridge, 1979–88; Lectr in Econs, 1979–85, and Reader in Econs, 1985–88, Cambridge Univ. Prof. of Econs, and Dir, Program in Applied Econometrics, UCLA, 1989–93; Research Fellow: Inst. for Study of Labour, Bonn, 1999–; CESifo (Center for Economic Studies and Ifo Institute for Econ. Res.) Res. Network, Munich, 2000–. Visiting Lecturer: Harvard Univ., 1982; Dutch Network for Quantitative Econs, Groningen, 1985; Vis. Fellow, ANU, 1984 and 1988; Visiting Professor: Univ. of Rome, 1986; Univ. of Calif, LA, 1987–88; Univ. of Pennsylvania, 1993; Univ. of S Calif, 1995, 1997, 1999 and 2003. Director: Camfit Data Ltd, 1986–2009; Acorn Investment Trust, 1987–89 and 1991–93; Cambridge Econometrics, 1985, 1988–89 and 1992–96 (Hon. Pres., 1996–2005); (non-exec.), Chiltern Gp plc, 1999–2003; Vice Pres., Tudor Investment Corp., 2000–02. Member: HM Treasury Academic Panel, 1993–; Academic Econometric Panel, ONS, 1997–2002; Outside Mem., Meteorol Office, 1994–97. Member: Bd of Trustees, Econ. Res. Forum of Arab Countries, Iran and Turkey, 1996–2001 (Mem. Adv. Bd and Res. Fellow, 1993–96); World Bank Council for the Middle East and N Africa region, 1996–2000; Bd of Trustees, British Iranian Trust, 1997–; Charter Mem., Oliver Wyman Inst., 1997–2000. Mem. Council, Royal Econ. Soc., 2007–. Fellow, Econometric Soc., 1989; Life Fellow, Econ. Res. Forum, Middle East, 2009. Founding Ed., Jl of Applied Econometrics, 1985–2014. Hon. Fellow, Grad. Sch. of Business and Econs, Maastricht Univ., 2013. Hon. DLitt Salford, 1993; Hon. Dr rer. pol. Goethe, Frankfurt, 2008; Hon. Dr Maastricht, 2013. Royal Econ. Soc. Prize, 1992. *Publications:* World Economic Prospects and the Iranian Economy—a short term view, 1974 (also Persian); (with L. J. Slater) Dynamic Regression: theory and algorithms, 1980 (trans. Russian 1984); (ed with T. Lawson) Keynes' Economics: methodological issues, 1985; The Limits to Rational Expectations, 1987; (with B. Pesaran) Data-FIT: an interactive software econometric package, 1987 (paperback edn, as Microfit, 1989); (ed with T. Barker) Disaggregation in Economic Modelling, 1990; (with B. Pesaran) Microfit 3.0, 1991, Microfit 4.0, 1997, Microfit 4.1, 2001, Time Series Econometrics using Microfit 5, 2009; (ed with S. Potter) Non-Linear Dynamics, Chaos and Econometrics, 1993; Handbook of Applied Econometrics, Vol. I (ed with M. Wickens), 1995, Vol. II (ed with P. Schmidt), 1997; (jtly) Energy Demand in Asian Developing Economies, 1998; (ed jtly) Analysis of Panels and Limited Dependent Variables, 1999; (jtly) Global and National Macroeconometric Modelling: a long-run structural approach, 2006; (ed with J. Nugent) Explaining Growth in the Middle East, 2007; (ed with F. di Mauro) The GVAR Handbook, 2013; scientific papers in econ. and econometric jls (Best Paper award 2002–04, Econometric Reviews; Best Paper Award 2004–05, Internat. Jl of Forecasting; Multa Scripsit Award, Jl of Econometric Theory, 2008). *Recreations:* basketball (half-blue, Cambridge University), squash, swimming. *Address:* Trinity College, Cambridge CB2 1TQ. *T:* (01223) 335216. *E:* mhp1@cam.ac.uk.

PESCOD, Prof. Mainwaring Bainbridge, OBE 1977; CEng, FICE, FCIWEM, FCIWM; Senior Environmental Consultant, Cundall, Johnston and Partners LLP, 2008–10; Tyne and Wear Professor of Environmental Control Engineering, 1976–98, now Emeritus, and Head of Department of Civil Engineering, 1983–98, University of Newcastle upon Tyne; *b* 6 Jan. 1933; *s* of Bainbridge and Elizabeth Pescod; *m* 1957, Mary Lorenza (*née* Coyle); two *s*. *Educ:* Stanley Grammar Sch., Co. Durham; King's Coll., Univ. of Durham (BSc); MIT (SM). CEng 1973, FICE 1980; FCIWEM (FIPHE 1971; FIWES 1983; FIWEM 1987; MIWPC 1967); FCIWM (FIWM 1997; MInstWM 1985). Lectr in Engrg, Fourah Bay Coll., Freetown, Sierra Leone, 1957–61; Asst Engr, Babtie, Shaw & Morton, CCE, Glasgow, 1961–64; Asst and Associate Prof. of Environmental Engrg, 1964–72, Prof. and Head of Div. of Environmental Engrg, 1972–76, Asian Inst. of Technol., Bangkok, Thailand. Chm. and Man. Dir, Envmtl Technology Consultants, 1988–2003; Corporate Fellow, SEC Ltd, 2003–08. Mem., Northumbrian Water Authority, 1986–89; Director: Northumbrian Water Group, 1989–97; Motherwell Bridge Envirotec, 1991–95; Chm., MB Technology (Malaysia) Sdn Bhd, 1996–2002. *Publications:* (ed with D. A. Okun) Water Supply and Wastewater Disposal in Developing Countries, 1971; (ed. with A. Arar) Treatment and Use of Sewage Effluent for Irrigation, 1988; (ed) Urban Solid Waste Management, 1991; pubns on water supply, wastewater treatment, environmental pollution control and management in learned jls and conf. proc. *Recreations:* golf, reading. *Address:* Tall Trees, High Horse Close Wood, Rowlands Gill, Tyne and Wear NE39 1AN. *T:* (01207) 542104. *Clubs:* British, Royal Bangkok Sports (Bangkok, Thailand).

PEŠEK, Libor, Hon. KBE 1996; Music Director, 1987–97, Conductor Laureate, since 1997, Royal Liverpool Philharmonic Society and Orchestra; Principal Guest Conductor, Prague Symphony Orchestra; *b* 22 June 1933. *Educ:* Academy of Musical Arts, Prague (studied conducting, piano, 'cello, trombone). Worked at Pilsen and Prague Opera Houses; Founder Director, Prague Chamber Harmony, 1958–64; Chief Conductor, Slovak Philharmonic, 1980–81; Conductor in residence, Czech Philharmonic, 1982– (tours and fests, Europe, Russia, Far East); guest conductor: Los Angeles Philharmonic, St Louis Symphony and other US orchestras; The Philharmonia, LSO, Orchestre Nat. de France, and other European orchestras; numerous recordings incl. much Czech repertoire. Pres., Prague Spring Fest., 1994. Hon. DMus Liverpool Polytechnic, 1989. *Recreations:* physics, Eastern philosophy and literature, particularly Kafka, Dostoyevsky and Tolstoy. *Address:* c/o IMG Artists (Europe), The Light Box, 111 Power Road, Chiswick, W4 5PY.

PESHAWAR, Bishop of; *see* Rumalshah, Rt Rev. M. K.

PESKIN, Richard Martin; Chairman, Great Portland Estates plc, 1986–2009; *b* 21 May 1944; *s* of Leslie and Hazel Peskin; *m* 1979, Penelope Howard Triebner; one *s* two *d*. *Educ:* Charterhouse; Queens' Coll., Cambridge (MA, LLM). Great Portland Estates, 1967–2009: Dir, 1968; Asst Man. Dir, 1972–78; Jt Man. Dir, 1978–84; Man. Dir, 1984–2000. Chm., Internos Global Investors (formerly Internos Real Investors LLP), 2009–; Mem., London Bd, Royal & Sun Alliance, 1990–2009. Consultant, Farrer & Co., 2010–13. FRSA 1989; FRICS 2010. CCMI (CBIM 1989). *Recreations:* crosswords, composing limericks. *Address:* 41 Circus Road, NW8 9JH. *T:* (020) 7289 0492. *Clubs:* MCC (Mem., Estates Cttee, 1999–2005), Royal Automobile; Wentworth Golf.

PESSINA, Stefano; Executive Vice Chairman and Chief Executive Officer, Walgreens Boots Alliance, since 2015; *b* 4 June 1941; *s* of Oreste Pessina and Elena Fusco Pessina; separated; one *s* one *d*. Various academic posts; independent business consultant; work in pharmaceutical wholesaling, 1976–; Founder, Alliance Santé Gp, merged with UniChem plc, 1997, to form Alliance UniChem Gp; Chief Exec., 2001–04, Exec. Dep. Chm., 2004–06, Alliance UniChem plc; merged with Boots Gp, 2006, to form Alliance Boots; Exec. Dep. Chm., 2006–07, Exec. Chm., 2007–15, Alliance Boots; merged with Walgreens, 2015, to form Walgreens Boots Alliance. Exec. Dir, Walgreens, 2012–15. *Recreations:* yachting, art. *Address:* Walgreens Boots Alliance, Sedley Place, 4th Floor, 361 Oxford Street, W1C 2JL. *E:* stefano.pessina@wba.com.

PESTELL, John Edmund; Partnership Secretary, Linklaters & Paines, 1990–94; *b* 8 Dec. 1930; *s* of late Edmund Pestell and Isabella (*née* Sangster); *m* 1958, Muriel Ada (*née* Whitby) (*d* 2015); three *s*. *Educ:* Roundhay Sch.; New Coll., Oxford (State Scholar; MA). National Service, 1949–50. Jt Intell. Bureau, 1953–57; Asst Principal, WO, 1957–60; Private Sec. to Parly Under Sec. of State for War, 1958–60; Principal, WO and MoD, 1960–70; Admin. Staff Coll., Henley, 1963; Private Sec. to Minister of Defence (Equipment), 1969–70; Asst Sec., MoD, 1970–72; Press Sec. (Co-ordination), Prime Minister's Office, 1972–74; Asst Sec., CSD, 1974–76, Under Sec., 1976–81; Under Sec., HM Treasury, 1981–84; Asst Under-Sec. of State, MoD, 1984–88; Resident Chm., CSSB, 1988–90. Mem., CS Pay Res. Unit Bd, 1978–80. Governor, Cranleigh Sch., 1975–95. *Address:* 42 Oatley House, Cote Lane, Bristol BS9 3TN. *T:* (0117) 962 5768. *Club:* Athenæum.

PESTON, family name of **Baron Peston**.

PESTON, Baron *cr* 1987 (Life Peer), of Mile End in Greater London; **Maurice Harry Peston;** Professor of Economics at Queen Mary College, University of London, 1965–88, now Emeritus; *b* 19 March 1931; *s* of Abraham and Yetta Peston; *m* 1958, Helen Conroy; two *s* one *d*. *Educ:* Belle Vue School, Bradford; Hackney Downs School; London School of Economics (BSc Econ; Hon. Fellow, 1995); Princeton Univ., NJ, USA. Scientific Officer, then Sen. Scientific Officer, Army Operational Research Group, 1954–57; Asst Lecturer, Lectr, Reader in Economics, LSE, 1957–65. Economic Adviser: HM Treasury, 1962–64; Min. of Defence, 1964–66; H of C Select Cttee on Nationalised Industries, 1966–70, 1972–73; Special Adviser to Sec. of State for Education, 1974–75, to Sec. of State for Prices, 1976–79. Chairman: H of L Cttee on Monetary Policy, 1998–2001; H of L Econ. Affairs Cttee, 2001–. Chairman: Pools Panel, 1991–95; NFER, 1991–97; Office of Health Econs, 1991–2000; Member: CNAA (and Chm. of Econs Bd), 1967–73; SSRC (Chm. of Econs Bd), 1976–79; Council of Royal Pharmaceutical Soc. of GB, 1986–96; Hon. Mem., RPSGB, 1996. Fellow: Portsmouth Poly., 1987; QMW, 1992; LSE 1995. Hon. FInstAM 1998. Hon. DEd E London, 1994; Hon. DPhil Guildhall, 1999. *Publications:* Elementary Matrices for Economics, 1969; Public Goods and the Public Sector, 1972; Theory of Macroeconomic Policy, 1974, 2nd edn 1982; Whatever Happened to Macroeconomics?, 1980; The British Economy, 1982, 2nd edn 1984; ed and contrib. to many other books; articles in economic jls. *Address:* House of Lords, SW1A 0PW. *T:* (020) 7219 3000.

See also R. J. K. Peston.

PESTON, Robert James Kenneth; Economics Editor, BBC News, since 2014 (Business Editor, 2006–14); *b* 25 April 1960; *s* of Baron Peston, *qv*; *m* 1998, Siân E. Busby (*d* 2012); one *s*, and one step *s*. *Educ:* Highgate Wood Comp. Sch.; Balliol Coll., Oxford (BA PPE 1982). City Editor, Independent on Sunday, 1991–92; Financial Times: Banking Editor, 1992–93; Hd of Investigations, 1993–95; Political Editor, 1995–2000; Financial Editor and Asst Editor, 2000; Editl Dir, CSQuest.com, 2000–02; Associate Editor, Spectator, 2000–01; City Ed. and Asst Ed., Sunday Telegraph, 2002–06. Columnist: New Statesman, 2001–02; Sunday Times, 2001–02. Writer and Presenter: TV documentaries: Super-Rich: the greed game, 2008; Britain's Banks: too big to save?, 2011; How China Fooled the World, 2014; Scotland: for richer or poorer?, 2014; Quelle Catastrophe! France, with Robert Peston, 2015; TV series: On the Money with Robert Peston, 2010; The Party's Over - How the West Went Bust, 2011; Robert Peston Goes Shopping, 2013; film, The Great Euro Crash, BBC2, 2012; radio, The Robert Peston Interview Show (with Eddie Mair), 2015. Member: Bd, Media Standards Trust, 2006–11; Council, ICA, 2012–13. Trustee, Educn and Employers Taskforce, 2011–. Founder and Trustee, Speakers for Schools, 2011–. Patron, Pro Bono Econs, 2009–. Hon. Fellow, Aberystwyth Univ., 2011. Hon. DLit Heriot-Watt, 2010. Investigative Journalist of the Year, What the Papers Say awards, 1993; Sen. Financial Journalist of the Year, 2005, Online Media Award and Broadcaster of the Year, 2008, Harold Wincott awards; Scoop of the Year, 2005, Business Journalist of the Year, 2009, London Press Club; Scoop of the Year, 2007, 2008, Television Journalist of the Year and Specialist Journalist of the Year, 2008, RTS TV Journalism Awards; Business News/Current Affairs Prog. of the Year, Wincott Foundn, 2007; Journalist of the Year, 2007, 2008, Scoop of the Year, 2007, 2008, 2009, Business Journalist of Year Awards; Documentary of the Year, 2007, Broadcast News Journalist of the Year, 2007, 2008, Online Journalist Award, 2008, Work Foundn Workworld Media Awards; Private Equity and Venture Capital Digital Journalist of the Year, 2007; Best Performer in Non-acting Role, Broadcasting Press Guild, 2009; Broadcaster of the Year, Headline Money Awards, 2009; Political Journalist of the Year, Political Studies Assoc., 2009; Business and Finance Journalist of the Year, Press Gazette, 2009; Mainstream Media Blogger Award, Editl Intelligence Comment Awards, 2011; Financial/Econ. Story of Year Award, Foreign Press Assoc., 2012; Lung Cancer Journalism Award, Global Lung Cancer Coalition, 2014. *Publications:* Brown's Britain, 2005; Who Runs Britain?, 2008; How Do We Fix This Mess?, 2012. *Recreations:* Arsenal, dance/ballet. *Address:* BBC Broadcasting House, Portland Place, W1A 1AA. *T:* (020) 3614 0823; 125 Dukes Avenue, N10 2QD. *E:* peston@gmail.com.

PETCH, Barry Irvine, FCA; General Manager, IBM Financing International Ltd, 1989–93; *b* 12 Oct. 1933; *s* of Charles Reginald Petch and Anne (*née* Fryer); *m* 1966, Anne Elisabeth (*née* Johannessen); two *s* one *d*. *Educ:* Doncaster Grammar Sch.; Kingston Univ. (MA 1998). FCA 1967. IBM United Kingdom Ltd, 1959–80; Controller, IBM Europe, 1981–83; Vice-Pres., Finance, IBM Europe, 1983–89. Part-time Mem., Price Commn, 1973–77. Director: Pathfinder NHS Trust, 1995–99; IBM UK Pensions Trust Ltd, 1997–2000. Hon. Treas., RNID, 1998–2001. *Recreations:* tennis, golf, sailing. *Club:* Reform.

PETCHEY, Philip Neil; barrister; Chancellor, Diocese of Southwark, since 2010; *b* Barking, 2 Sept. 1953; *s* of Joyce and Ronald Petchey; *m* 1995, Helen Lawford. *Educ:* Barking Abbey School; Oriel Coll., Oxford (BA 1975). Called to the Bar, Middle Temple, 1976; barrister in private practice, 1977–. Chm., London Br., Elgar Soc., 2014–. *Publications:* articles in legal jls. *Recreations:* walking, bell-ringing, reading, listening to music. *Address:* Francis Taylor Building, Inner Temple, EC4Y 7BY. *T:* (020) 7353 8415, *Fax:* (020) 7353 7622. *E:* philip.petchey@ftb.eu.com. *Club:* Oxford and Cambridge.

PETERBOROUGH, Bishop of, since 2010; **Rt Rev. Donald Spargo Allister;** Assistant Bishop, Diocese of Ely, since 2011; *b* 27 Aug. 1952; *s* of Charles and Barbara Allister; *m* 1976, Janice Reynolds; one *s* two *d*. *Educ:* Birkenhead Sch.; Peterhouse, Cambridge (BA 1974, MA 1977); Trinity Coll., Bristol. Ordained deacon, 1976, priest, 1977; Curate: St George's, Hyde, 1976–79; St Nicholas', Sevenoaks, 1979–83; Vicar, Christ Church, Birkenhead, 1983–89; Rector, St Mary's, Cheadle, 1989–2002; Archdeacon of Chester, 2002–10. Took seat in H of L, 2014. Chaplain, Arrowe Park Hosp., 1983–86; RD, Cheadle, 1999–2002. Chm., Church Soc., 1995–2000; Member: Gen. Synod, 2005–; Council for Christian Unity, 2006– (Chm., 2013–). Hon. DTh Chester, 2011. Consultant Ed., C of E Newspaper, 1981–83. *Publications:* numerous articles in church and theol jls. *Recreations:* hill-walking, science fiction, medical ethics. *Address:* Bishop's Lodging, The Palace, Minster Precincts, Peterborough PE1 1YA. *E:* bishop@peterborough-diocese.org.uk. *Club:* Farmers.

PETERBOROUGH, Dean of; *see* Taylor, Very Rev. C. W.

PETERKEN, Dr Alexander Laurence Raynal; Headmaster, Cheltenham College, since 2010; *b* Guildford, 4 June 1974; *s* of Laurence Edwin Peterken, *qv*; *m* 1st, 2000, Clare Sophia Guthrie (*d* 2011); one *s* two *d*; 2nd, 2012, Henrietta Ruth Ford; one *s* one *d*. *Educ:* Eton Coll. (Music Exhibnr); Univ. of Durham (Choral Schol.; BA Theol. 1996); Inst. of Educn, Univ. of London (MA Educnl Mgt 2002); Univ. of Surrey (EdD 2008). Charterhouse School: Asst Master, 1997–99; Hd, Higher Educn and Careers, 1999–2001; Housemaster, Saunderites, 2002–08; Dep. Headmaster, Cheltenham Coll., 2008–10. Vice Chm., Ind. Schs Exam Bd, 2011–. Governor: St Mark's Sch., Godalming, 2006–08; Pinewood Prep. Sch., Shrivenham, 2010–. *Recreations:* family, singing, Cornish walks, church architecture. *Address:* Cheltenham College, Bath Road, Cheltenham, Glos GL53 7LD. *T:* (01242) 265600. *E:* headmaster@cheltenhamcollege.org. *Clubs:* Lansdowne, East India.

PETERKEN, Laurence Edwin, CBE 1990; consultant, since 1996; Special Projects Director, NHS in Scotland, 1993–96; *b* 2 Oct. 1931; *s* of Edwin James Peterken and Constance Fanny (*née* Giffin); *m* 1st, 1955, Hanne Birgithe Von Der Recke (decd); one *s* one *d*; 2nd, 1970, Margaret Raynal Blair; one *s* one *d*. *Educ:* Harrow Sch. (Scholar); Peterhouse, Cambridge (Scholar); MA. Pilot Officer, RAF Regt, Adjt No 20 LAA Sqdn, 1950–52. Service Div. Manager, Hotpoint Ltd, 1961–63, Commercial Dir, 1963–66; Man. Dir, British Domestic Appliances Ltd, 1966–68; Dir, British Printing Corporation Ltd, 1969–73; Debenhams Ltd: Man. Dir, Fashion Multiple Div., 1974–76; Management Auditor, 1976–77; Controller, Operational Services, GLC, 1977–85; Acting Dir, Royal Festival Hall, 1983–85, to implement open foyer policy; Gen. Man., 1986–93, Dir, 1989–93, Gtr Glasgow Health Bd. Chairman: Working Party on Disposal of Clinical Waste in London, 1982–83; GLC Chief Officers' Guild, 1983–85; Member: Scottish Health Management Efficiency Gp, 1986–95; Scottish Health Clinical Resources and Audit Gp, 1989–93; Scottish Health Service Adv. Council, 1989–93; Criminal Injuries Compensation Appeal Panel, 1997–2006; Lay Member, Professional Conduct Committee: NMC, 2004–08; CIMA, 2005–08. Lay Chm., Conduct and Competence Cttee, NMC, 2008–13. Vice Chm., RIPA, W of Scotland, 1991–93. Trustee: Rodolfus Choir, 1998–2008; Council for Music in Hosps, 2004–08 (Mem., Scottish Cttee, 1997–2008). Churchwarden, Haslemere Parish Church, 1985–86. *Recreations:* music, memoirs. *Address:* Daltons, Hinton St Mary, Sturminster Newton, Dorset DT10 1NA. *Club:* Athenæum.

See also A. L. R. Peterken.

PETERKIN, Maj. Gen. (Anthony) Peter G.; *see* Grant Peterkin.

PETERS, Prof. (Adrien) Michael, MD, DSc; FRCR, FRCP, FMedSci; Professor of Applied Physiology, Brighton and Sussex Medical School, and Hon. Consultant in Nuclear Medicine, Royal Sussex County Hospital, Brighton, since 2004; *b* 17 May 1945; *s* of Adrien John Peters and Barbara Muriel Peters; *m* 1st; one *s*; 2nd, 1980, Rosemary Cox; two *s* one *d*. *Educ:* St Mary's Hosp. Med. Sch., Univ. of London (BSc, MSc); Univ. of Liverpool (MB ChB, MD 1970; DSc 2009). FRCR 1995; FRCPath 1996; FRCP 1997. GP, NSW, Australia, 1974–78, Liverpool, 1978–79; Res. Fellow, RPMS, 1979–82; Res. Physician, Glaxo Gp Res. Ltd, 1982–84; Sen. Lectr in Diagnostic Radiol., 1984–89, Reader in Nuclear Medicine, 1989–95, RPMS; Prof. of Diagnostic Radiol., RPMS, then ICSM, 1995–99; Prof. of Nuclear Medicine, Univ. of Cambridge, 1999–2004. Consultant in Paediatric Radiol., 1984–88, Hon. Consultant, 1988–93 and 1996–2001, Hosp. for Sick Children, Gt Ormond St; Hon. Consultant: Hammersmith Hosp., 1984–99; Addenbrooke's Hosp., 1999–2004. Sen. Vis. Res. Fellow, Univ. of Cambridge, 2004–. FMedSci 2002. *Publications:* Physiological Measurement with Radionuclides in Clinical Practice, 1998; (ed) Nuclear Medicine in Radiological Diagnosis, 2003; numerous contribs to learned jls. *Address:* Brighton and Sussex Medical School, Eastern Road, Brighton BN2 5BE. *T:* (01273) 523360.

PETERS, Most Rev. Arthur Gordon; Archbishop of Nova Scotia and Metropolitan of the Ecclesiastical Province of Canada, 1997–2002 (Bishop of Nova Scotia, 1984–2002); *b* 21 Dec. 1935; *s* of William Peters and Charlotte Peters (*née* Symes); *m* 1962, Elizabeth Baert; one *s* two *d. Educ:* High School, North Sydney, NS; Univ. of King's College, Halifax, NS (BA 1960, BST 1963, BD 1973). Student, Parish of Waverley, 1961–63; deacon 1962, priest 1963, Nova Scotia; Morris Scholar, 1963, at Canterbury (Eng.), Geneva, Jerusalem, Norton (dio. Durham, Eng.); Rector: Weymouth, NS, 1964–68; Annapolis-Granville, NS, 1968–73; Christ Church, Sydney, NS, 1973–82; Bishop Coadjutor of Nova Scotia, 1982–84. Hon. DD Univ. of King's College, 1982. *Recreations:* swimming, ski-ing, reading, skating, photography. *Address:* 113–5 Ramsgate Lane, Halifax, NS B3P 2S6, Canada.

PETERS, (Boris) Kai (Georg); Chief Executive, Ashridge, since 2003; Chief Academic Officer, Hult International Business School, since 2015; *b* 26 Sept. 1962; *s* of late Gerhard Peters and Hilla Westerhold Peters. *Educ:* Glendon Coll.; York Univ., Toronto; Univ. of Quebec at Chicoutimi; Erasmus Univ., Rotterdam. Man. Dir, Westerhold, 1989–; Rotterdam School of Management: Dir, MBA Progs, 1994–99; Dean, 2000–03. Member, Board: Graduate Mgt Admissions Council, USA, 2002–04, 2006–11 (Chm., 2009–10); Assoc. of Business Schs, 2008–. Mem., Supervisory Bd, GAIA AG, Germany, 2002–. Mem. Bd, Centrepoint, 2007–. *Publications:* books and articles about strategy, leadership and mgt educn. *Recreations:* food, travel, commuting against the flow from London. *Address:* Ashridge Business School, Berkhamsted, Herts HP4 1NS. *T:* (01442) 841041, *Fax:* (01442) 841002.

PETERS, Sir (David) Keith, Kt 1993; FRCP; FRS 1995; FMedSci; Regius Professor of Physic, University of Cambridge, 1987–2005, now Emeritus; Fellow, Christ's College, Cambridge, 1987–2005, now Hon. Fellow; *b* 26 July 1938; *s* of Herbert Lionel and Olive Peters; *m* 1st, 1961, Jean Mair Garfield (marr. diss. 1978); one *s* one *d*; 2nd, 1979, Pamela Wilson Ewan, *qv*; two *s* one *d*; one *d* by Dr Elizabeth Warburton. *Educ:* Welsh National Sch. of Medicine (MB BCh 1961). MRCP 1964, FRCP 1975; FRCPath 1991; FRCPE 1995. Junior posts in United Cardiff Hosps, 1961–65; Med. Research Council, Clinical Res. Fellowship, 1965–68; Lectr in Med., Welsh Nat. Sch. of Med., 1968–69; Royal Postgraduate Medical School: Lectr, 1969; Sen. Lectr, 1974; Reader in Med., 1975; Prof. of Medicine and Dir, Dept of Medicine, 1977–87; Consultant Physician, Hammersmith Hosp., 1969–87. Interim Dir, MRC NIMR, 2006–08. Member: MRC, 1984–88 (Chm., MRC Physiological Systems Bd, 1986–88); ACOST, 1987–90; Council for Sci. and Technol., 2004–09 (Jt Chm., 2004–07); Chairman: NRPB, 1994–98; Council of Hds of Med. Schs and Deans of UK Faculties of Medicine, 1996–97; Global Med. Excellence Cluster, 2009–12. Chairman: Nat. Kidney Res. Fund, 1980–86 (Trustee, 2000–01); BHF, 1998–2002. Gov. and Mem., PPP Foundation, 1998–2002 (Chm., 2002). Member: Bd, Amersham Plc, 2000–04 (Mem., Sci. Adv. Bd, 1998– (Chm., 2001–04)); Chm., Sci. Adv. Bd, GE Healthcare Technologies, 2005–07; Sen. Advr in R & D, GlaxoSmithKline, 2005–. Mem. Council, Royal Soc., 1999–2001. Chm. Council, Cardiff Univ., 2004–11. Foreign Mem., Amer. Philos. Soc., 1999. Founder FMedSci 1998 (Pres., 2002–06). Friend of Singapore, 2011. Hon. Fellow: Univ. of Wales Coll. of Medicine, 1997; ICSM, 1999; Cardiff Univ., 2001; Univ. of Wales, Swansea, 2001; Clare Hall, Cambridge, 2004. Hon. MD: Wales, 1987; Nottingham, 1996; Paris, 1996; Birmingham, 1998; Bristol, 2005; St Andrews, 2006; Edinburgh, 2007; Warwick, 2012; Hon. DSc: Aberdeen, 1994; Leicester, 1999; Glasgow, 2001; Sussex, 2004; Keele, 2006; KCL, 2010; UCL, 2011; Imperial Coll. London, 2014; Hon. Dr Cardiff, 2012. *Publications:* (ed jtly) Clinical Aspects of Immunology, 4th edn 1982, 5th edn 1993; in various jls on immunology of renal and vascular disease. *Recreations:* tennis, chess. *Club:* Garrick.

PETERS, Kai; *see* Peters, B. K. G.

PETERS, Sir Keith; *see* Peters, Sir D. K.

PETERS, Martin Trevor, CB 1991; CEng, FRAeS; Technical Planning Director, British Aerospace plc, 1992–94; *b* 23 Dec. 1936; *s* of Reginald Thomas Peters and Catherine Mary Peters (*née* Ings); *m* 1958, Vera Joan Horton (*d* 2004); one *s*. *Educ:* Aylesbury Grammar Sch.; Watford Tech. Coll.; High Wycombe Coll. of Further Educn. MIMechE, CEng 1968; FRAeS 1988. Airtech, 1953–55; RAF, 1955–57; Airtech, 1957–59; RPE Westcott, 1959–64; NGTE Pyestock, 1964–71; MoD, 1971–77; Supt of Engineering, A&AEE Boscombe Down, 1977–79; NAMMA, Munich, 1979–81; Dir, Aircraft Post Design Services, MoD (PE), 1981–83; RCDS, 1984; Dir-Gen. Aircraft, 1984–87; Dep. Controller Aircraft, 1987–89; Dir, RAE, 1989–91; Tech. Dir, BAe Commercial Aircraft Ltd, 1991–92. *Recreations:* walking, music, 18th century ship modelling. *Address:* 96 East Avenue, Talbot Woods, Bournemouth BH3 7DD.

PETERS, Dame Mary (Elizabeth), CH 2015; DBE 2000 (CBE 1990; MBE 1973); Lord-Lieutenant, County Borough of Belfast, 2009–14; Managing Director, Mary Peters Sports Ltd, 1977; *b* 6 July 1939; *d* of Arthur Henry Peters and Hilda Mary Peters. *Educ:* Portadown Coll., Co. Armagh; Belfast Coll. of Domestic Science (DipDomSc). Represented Great Britain: Olympic Games: 4th place, Pentathlon, 1964; 1st, Pentathlon (world record), 1972; Commonwealth Games: 2nd, Shot, 1966; 1st, Shot, 1st Pentathlon, 1970; 1st, Pentathlon, 1974. Member: Sports Council, 1974–80, 1987–94; NI Sports Council, 1974–93 (Vice-Chm., 1977–81); Ulster Games Foundn, 1984–93; NI BBC Broadcasting Council, 1981–84; NI Tourist Bd, 1993–2002. Dir, Churchill Foundn Fellowship Scholarship, Calif, 1972. Asst Sec., Multiple Sclerosis Soc., 1974–78. President: NI WAAA, 1985–87; British Athletic Fedn, 1996–98; Mary Peters Trust (formerly Ulster Sports and Recreation Trust), 1996– (Trustee, 1972); Mem., Women's Cttee, IAAF, 1995–97. Hon. Senior Athletic Coach, 1975–; BAAB Pentathlon Coach, 1976; Team Manager: GB women's athletic team, European Cup, 1979; GB women's athletic team, Moscow, 1980 and Los Angeles, 1984. President: OAPs' Coal and Grocery Fund; Lady Taverners, NI; Vice-President: Assoc. of Youth Clubs; NI Assoc. of Youth Clubs; Riding for the Disabled; Driving for the Disabled; Action Cancer; Patron: NIAAA, 1981–; Friends of Royal Victoria Hosp., Belfast, 1988–96. Freeman: Lisburn, 1998; Belfast, 2012. Awards: BBC Sports personality, 1972; Athletic Writers', 1972; Sports Writers', 1972; Elizabeth Arden Visible Difference, 1976; Athletics, Dublin (Texaco), 1970 and 1972; British Airways Tourist Endeavour, 1981; Living Action, 1985; Evian Health, 1985. Hon. DSc New Univ. of Ulster, 1974; DUniv QUB, 1998; Hon. DLitt Loughborough, 1999. *Publications:* Mary P., an autobiography, 1974. *Address:* Willowtree Cottage, River Road, Dunmurry, Belfast, N Ireland BT17 9DP.

PETERS, Michael; *see* Peters, A. M.

PETERS, Nigel Melvin; QC 1997; **His Honour Judge Peters;** a Circuit Judge, since 2012; *b* 14 Nov. 1952; *s* of Sidney Peters and Maisie Peters (*née* Pepper). *Educ:* Hasmonean GS; Leicester Univ. (LLB 1975). Called to the Bar, Lincoln's Inn, 1976 (Mansfield Schol.; Bencher, 2006); Asst Recorder, 1994–98; Recorder, 1998–2012. *Recreations:* cricket, Real tennis, travel, food, wine. *Address:* Snaresbrook Crown Court, 75 Hollybush Hill, E11 1QW. *Club:* MCC (Mem. Cttee, 1999–).

PETERS, Air Vice-Marshal Robert Geoffrey, CB 1992; Clerk to the Guild of Air Pilots and Air Navigators, 1998–2000; *b* 22 Aug. 1940; *s* of Geoffrey Ridgway Peters and Henriette Catharine Peters; *m* 1966, Mary Elizabeth (*née* Fletcher) (*d* 2013); one *d* three *s*. *Educ:* St Paul's Sch., London; RAF Coll., Cranwell (Gen. Duties/Pilot). Beverley C Mk1 Pilot Nos 34 and 47 Sqdns, Singapore and UK, 1961–66; Flt Comdr, No 46 Sqdn (Andovers), RAF Abingdon, 1967–68; MoD Central Staffs (Asst MA to Chief Adviser Personnel and Logistics), 1968–69; OC Flying Trng Sqdn, Air Electronics and Air Engr Trng Sch., RAF Topcliffe, 1970–72; RAF Staff Coll., Bracknell, 1973; Air Sec.'s Dept, MoD, 1974–76; OC 10 Sqdn (VC10), RAF Brize Norton, 1977–78; Directorate of Forward Policy (RAF), MoD, 1979–81; PSO to Dep. SACEUR(UK), SHAPE, Belgium, 1981–83; OC RAF St Mawgan, 1984–85; RCDS 1986; Comdr, RAF Staff and Air Attaché, Washington, 1987–90; Comdt, RAF Staff Coll., Bracknell, 1990–93; Dir of Welfare, RAF Benevolent Fund, 1993–97. President: RAF Fencing Union, 1986–93; Combined Services Fencing Assoc., 1988–97. Freeman, City of London, 1977; Liveryman, Co. of Coachmakers and Coach Harness Makers, 1977; Upper Freeman, GAPAN, 1997–2000. QCVSA 1973. *Recreations:* golf, sailing. *Club:* Naunton Downs Golf.

PETERS, Roger; Regional Employment Judge (formerly Regional Chairman of Employment Tribunals), Southampton, 2004–11, fee-paid Judge, 2011–14; *b* 25 April 1945; *s* of Frederick James and Lilian Ivy Peters; *m* 1973, Isobel Susan Bell Briggs; three *s*. *Educ:* Reading Blue Coat Sch.; Coll. of Law. Admitted solicitor, 1968; Solicitor, Blandy & Blandy, Reading, 1968–71; Asst Chief Legal Officer, Redditch Develt Corp., 1971–76; Principal Legal Officer, S Yorks CC, 1976–81; Chief Solicitor, Leeds Perm. Bldg Soc., 1981–87; Partner, Staffurth & Bray, Bognor Regis, 1987–94; Chairman, Employment Tribunals: Manchester, 1995–96; London, 1997–2003; Chm., Reinstatement Cttee and Reserve Forces Tribunal, 2010–11. Legal corresp., Hospitality mag., 1987–95. *Publications:* Essential Law for Catering Students, 1992, 2nd edn 1995; (jt author and ed.) Health and Safety: liability and litigation, 1995; articles in Solicitors' Jl. *Recreations:* listening to classical music, motor boating.

PETERS, Siobhan, CMG 2007; Director, Strategy and Change, Home Office, since 2010; *b* Welwyn Garden City, 27 June 1970; *d* of Susan Peters; one *s* one *d*. *Educ:* Wadham Coll., Oxford (BA Hons Oriental Studies 1991); Open Univ. (MA Envmt Policy 2004). Auditor, Touche Ross, 1992–96; Desk Officer, FCO, London and Beijing, 1997–2004; Hd, G8 Climate Change Unit, DEFRA, 2004–05; Hd, Review Team, Stern Review of the Econs of Climate Change, HM Treasury, 2005–07; Team Leader, Energy, Envmt and Agriculture, HM Treasury, 2007–10. *Recreation:* family life. *Address:* Home Office, 2 Marsham Street, SW1P 4DF.

PETERS, Prof. Timothy James, PhD; FSS; FMedSci; Professor of Primary Care Health Services Research, since 2002, and Head, School of Clinical Sciences, since 2010, University of Bristol; *b* London, 8 June 1958; *s* of Eric and Pauline Peters; *m* 1984, Janet Mary Taylor. *Educ:* Bognor Regis Comprehensive Sch.; Univ. of Exeter (BSc Hons Math. Stats and Operational Res. 1979; PhD Stats 1985); Univ. of Oxford (MSc Applied Stats 1980). FSS 1986; CStat 1993. Res. Asst, Univ. of Bristol, 1982–86; Lectr in Med. Stats, UWCM, 1986–92; University of Bristol: Sen. Lectr, then Reader in Med. Stats, 1999–2001; Res. Dir, Faculty of Medicine and Dentistry, 2006–09; Hd, Dept of Community Based Medicine, 2008–10; Associate Dean, Faculty of Medicine and Dentistry, 2012–15. Sen. Investigator, NIHR, 2008. Co-Ed., Paediatric and Perinatal Epidemiol., 1987–2012. Chair or mem., strategic res. grants cttees for MRC, NIHR, Health and Care Res., Wales, Health Res. Bd in Ireland, HEFCE, HEFCW, Marie Curie and Dimbleby Cancer Care. Gov., University Hosps Bristol, 2011–. FHEA 2002; FFPH 2002; FMedSci 2014. Hon. FRCSLT 2003; Hon. FRCGP 2007. *Publications:* (ed jtly) When to Screen in Obstetrics and Gynaecology, 1996, 2nd edn 2006; (ed with W. Hamilton) Cancer Diagnosis in Primary Care, 2007; contribs to internat. peer-reviewed jls. *Recreations:* horse riding and ownership, care of horses and ponies, cryptic crosswords. *Address:* School of Clinical Sciences, University of Bristol, 69 St Michael's Hill, Bristol BS2 8DZ. *T:* (0117) 331 1698. *E:* tim.peters@bristol.ac.uk. *Club:* Wye Valley Riding.

PETERS, Prof. Timothy John, PhD, DSc; FRCP; Professor of Clinical Biochemistry, King's College, London, 1988–2004; Hon. Consultant Physician and Chemical Pathologist, King's College Hospital, 1988–2004; Hon. Senior Research Fellow, Institute of Archaeology and Antiquity, University of Birmingham, since 2007; *b* 10 May 1939; *s* of Stanley and Paula Peters; *m* 1965, Judith Mary Bacon; one *s* two *d*. *Educ:* King Edward VI Sch., Macclesfield; Univ. of St Andrews (MB ChB (Hons) 1964; MSc 1966; DSc 1986); RPMS, Univ. of London (PhD 1970); Univ. of Birmingham (MA 2006). MRCPE 1969, FRCPE 1986; MRCP 1970, FRCP 1976; MRCPath 1983, FRCPath 1988. MRC Trng Fellow, RPMS, 1967–70; MRC Travelling Fellow, Rockefeller Univ., NY, 1970–72; Lectr, Sen. Lectr, then Reader, RPMS, and Hon. Cons. Physician, Hammersmith Hosp., 1972–79; Head, Div. of Clin. Cell Biology, MRC Clin. Res. Centre, and Hon. Cons. Physician, Northwick Park Hosp., 1979–88; Head, Dept of Clin. Biochemistry, 1988–2004, Sub-Dean for Postgrads and Higher Degree, Sch. of Medicine, 1988–2000, KCL; Associate Dean, London and SE Region, London Univ., 2000–04. Foundation Ed., Addiction Biology, 1995–2003. *Publications:* (ed) Alcohol Misuse: a European perspective, 1996; (ed jtly) International Handbook of Alcohol Dependence and Problems, 2001; (ed jtly) Skeletal Muscle: pathology, diagnosis and management of disease, 2002; over 500 articles on subcellular fractionation, alcohol misuse and toxicology, porphyria and iron metabolism, absorption and toxicology. *Recreations:* industrial archaeology and medical history, esp. of Stuart and Hanoverian monarchs and their relatives; contribs to Hist. of Psychiatry on nature of madness of King George III and related topics; use of computer diagnostics and handwriting analysis on historical figures. *Address:* Iron Lock Cottage, Beeston Brook, Tiverton, Tarporley, Cheshire CW6 9NH.

PETERS, Prof. Wallace, MD, DSc; FRCP; Director, 1999–2003, Consultant, 2004, Centre for Tropical Antiprotozoal Chemotherapy (formerly Tropical Parasitic Diseases Unit), Northwick Park Institute for Medical Research; Professor of Medical Protozoology, London School of Hygiene and Tropical Medicine, University of London, 1979–89, now Emeritus; *b* 1 April 1924; *s* of Henry and Fanny Peters; *m* 1954, Ruth (*née* Scheidegger). *Educ:* Tollington Boys' Sch.; Haberdashers' Aske's Sch.; St Bartholomew's Hosp., London. MB BS, 1947; MRCS, DTM&H. Served in RAMC, 1947–49; practised tropical medicine in West and East Africa, 1950–52; Staff Mem., WHO, Liberia and Nepal, 1952–55; Asst Dir (Malariology), Health Dept, Territory of Papua and New Guinea, 1956–61; Research Associate, CIBA, Basle, Switzerland, 1961–66; Walter Myers Prof. of Parasitology, Univ. of Liverpool, 1966–79; Dean, Liverpool Sch. of Tropical Medicine, 1975–78; Jt Dir, Malaria Reference Lab., PHLS, 1979–89; Hon. Res. Fellow, Internat. Inst. of Parasitology, then CABI Bioscience, 1992–99; Hon. Prof. Res. Fellow, Imperial Coll., 2000–. Vice-Pres. and Pres., Brit. Soc. Parasit., 1972–76; President: Brit. Sect., Soc. Protozool., 1972–75; Royal Soc. of Trop. Medicine and Hygiene, 1987–89 (Vice-Pres., 1982–83, 1985–87; Hon. Fellow, 1997). Chm., WHO Steering Cttee on Chemotherapy of Malaria, 1975–83; Member: Expert Adv. Panel, WHO, 1967–2005; WHO Steering Cttees on Leishmaniasis, 1979; Editorial Bd, Ann. Trop. Med. Parasit., 1966–79; Trop. Med. Research Bd, MRC, 1973–77; Scientific Council, Inst. of Cellular and Molecular Path., 1981–84; Parasitol. Bd, Institut Pasteur, 1979–87; Sec., European Fedn Parasit., 1979–84 (Vice-Pres., 1975–79). Hon. Consultant on malariology to the Army, 1986–89. Hon. Fellow, Amer. Soc. of Tropical Medicine and Hygiene, 1995. Dr *hc*, Univ. René Descartes, Paris, 1992. Rudolf Leuckart Medal, German Soc. of Parasitol., 1980; King Faisal Internat. Prize in Medicine, 1983; Le Prince Medal, Amer. Soc. of Tropical Medicine and Hygiene, 1994; Emile Brumpt Medal and Prize, Soc. de Pathologie Exotique, Paris, 1999; Manson Medal, RSTM&H, 2004; Dist. Parasitologist Award, World Fedn of Parasitologists, 2010. *Publications:* A Provisional Checklist of Butterflies of the Ethiopian Region, 1952; Chemotherapy and Drug Resistance in Malaria, 1970, 2nd edn 1987; (with H. M. Gilles) A Colour Atlas of Tropical Medicine and Parasitology, 1977, 6th edn (with G. Pasvol), as Atlas of Tropical Medicine and Parasitology, 2007; (ed with R. Killick-Kendrick) Rodent Malaria, 1978; (ed with W. H. G. Richards) Antimalarial Drugs, 2 vols, 1984; (ed with R. Killick-Kendrick) The Leishmaniases in Biology and Medicine, 1987; A Colour Atlas of Arthropods in Clinical Medicine, 1992; Four Passions: conversations with myself, 2012;

numerous papers in jls, on trop. med. and parasitology. *Recreation:* photography. *Address:* Department of Infectious and Tropical Disease, London School of Hygiene and Tropical Medicine, Keppel Street, WC1E 7HT. *E:* wallacepeters2@aol.com.

PETERS, Rt Hon. Winston (Raymond); PC 1998; Leader, New Zealand First Party, since 1993; *b* 11 April 1945; *s* of Len Peters and Joan (*née* McInnes); *m* 1973; one *s* one *d*. *Educ:* Auckland Univ. (BA 1969; LLB 1973). With Russell, McVeagh, lawyers, 1974–75, Davenports, 1976–78; estabd own legal practice, Howick, 1982. MP: (Nat.) Hunua, 1979–81; Tauranga, 1984–2005 (Nat., 1984–93, NZ First, 1993–2005); (NZ First), 2005–08, 2011–; Minister of Maori Affairs and i/c of Iwi Transition Agency, 1990–93; Dep. Prime Minister and Treasurer, NZ, 1996–98; Minister of Foreign Affairs and Trade, 2005–08.

PETERSEN, Niels Helveg; MP (Social Liberal) Denmark, 1966–74, and 1977–2011; *b* 17 Jan. 1939; *s* of Lilly and Kresten Helveg Petersen; *m* 1984, Kirsten Lee, MD; two *s*. *Educ:* Univ. of Copenhagen (LLB 1965); Univ. of Stanford, Calif. Chief of Cabinet, Danish EU Comr, 1974–77; Chm., Parly Group, 1978–88; Minister for Economic Affairs, 1988–90; Minister for Foreign Affairs, 1993–2000. *Recreations:* chess, tennis, soccer football.

PETERSEN, Prof. Ole Holger, CBE 2008; MD; FRCP; FRS 2000; Chair and Director, Cardiff School of Biosciences, since 2010, and Medical Research Council Professor, since 2012, Cardiff University; *b* 3 March 1943; *s* of Rear Adm. Joergen Petersen, Royal Danish Navy, and Elisabeth Klein, pianist; *m* 1st, 1968, Nina Bratting Jensen (marr. diss. 1995); two *s*; 2nd, 1995, Nina Burdakova. *Educ:* Univ. of Copenhagen Med. Sch. (MB ChB 1969; MD 1972). FRCP 2001. Lectr, 1969–73, Sen. Lectr, 1973–75, Inst. of Med. Physiology, Univ. of Copenhagen; Wellcome-Carlsberg Travelling Res. Fellow, Dept of Pharmacology, Univ. of Cambridge, 1971–72; Symers Prof. of Physiology, Univ. of Dundee, 1975–81; George Holt Prof. of Physiology, 1981–2009, and MRC Res. Prof., 1998–2009, Univ. of Liverpool. Vis. Prof., Stellenbosch Univ., 2000; Hon. Prof., Coll. of Medicine, Jinan Nat. Univ., Guangzhou, 2011–. Morton Grossman Meml Lectr, UCLA, 1985; Halliburton Lectr, KCL, 1986; Jacobaeus Prize Lectr, Nordic Insulin Foundn, 1994; Keynote Lectr, Gordon Res. Conf. on Calcium Signaling, Mass, USA, 2003, on Salivary Glands and Exocrine Secretion, Calif, USA, 2005; IUPS Lectr, FEPS Congress, Bratislava, 2007; State-of-the-Art Lectr, Amer. Gastroenterol. Assoc., Chicago, 2009; Horace W. Davenport Dist. Lectr, Exptl Biology, Amer. Physiological Soc., Boston, 2013; Hon. Pres. and Keynote Lectr, 37th Internat. Congress of Physiol Scis, Birmingham, 2013; Plenary Lect., Annual Congress, Brazilian Soc. of Physiol., 2013. Chairman: Starting Grant Panel for Physiol., Pathophysiol. and Endocrinol., Eur. Res. Council, 2009–11; Biol Scis Panel, HEFCE REF, 2010–14; Member: Sci. Adv. Council for Wales, 2010–; Bioscis Steering Panel, Eur. Academies Sci. Adv. Council, 2013–; Champion for Wales, Acad. of Med. Sci., 2014–. President: FEPS, 2001–03; Physiological Soc. (UK), 2006–08; Sec.-Gen., IUPS, 2001–10; Member Council: Bioscis Fedn, 2004–08; Royal Soc., 2004–06 (Vice-Pres., 2005–06); Mem. Exec. Bd, Academia Europaea, 2009– (Chm., Biomed. and Life Scis Class, 2014–); Vice Pres. (Sci., Technol. and Medicine), Learned Soc. of Wales, 2014–. Chm., Eur. Editl Bd, Physiological Reviews, 2003–11. MAE 1988; Mem., German Nat. Acad. of Scis Leopoldina, 2010; Foreign Mem., Royal Danish Acad. of Scis and Letters, 1988; Hon. Member: Polish Physiological Soc., 1993 (Czubalski Medal, 1993); Hungarian Physiological Soc., 2002; Hungarian Acad. of Scis, 2004. FMedSci 1998; FLSW 2011. Jubilee Medal, Charles Univ., Prague, 1998; Purkyne Medal, Czech Acad. of Scis, 2003; Lifetime Achievement Award, Eur. Pancreatic Club, 2010. *Publications:* The Electrophysiology of Gland Cells, 1980; (jtly) Landmarks in Intracellular Signalling, 1997; Measuring Calcium and Calmodulin Inside and Outside Cells, 2001; Human Physiology, 2007; more than 200 articles in scientific jls on intracellular signalling mechanisms, including many articles in Cell, Nature and PNAS. *Recreation:* classical music. *Address:* Cardiff School of Biosciences, Cardiff University, Sir Martin Evans Building, Museum Avenue, Cardiff CF10 3AX. *T:* (029) 2087 4120, *Fax:* (029) 2087 4116. *E:* PetersenOH@cardiff.ac.uk.

PETERSHAM, Viscount; William Henry Leicester Stanhope; *b* 14 Oct. 1967; *s* and *heir* of Earl of Harrington, *qv*; *m* 2001, Candida Sophia, *e d* of Ian Bond; one *s* one *d*. *Educ:* Aysgarth; Aiglon Coll. Patron, Save the Rhino Internat. Mem., RGS. *Recreations:* mountaineering, wildlife conservation, shooting, diggers. *Heir: s* Hon. Augustus Henry Leicester Stanhope, *b* 26 Sept. 2005. *Address:* Crimonmogate, Lonmay, Fraserburgh, Aberdeenshire AB43 8SE. *Club:* Central Buchan Rotary.

PETERSON, Colin Vyvyan, CVO 1982; Lay Assistant to Bishop of Winchester, 1985–94; *b* 24 Oct. 1932; *s* of late Sir Maurice Drummond Peterson, GCMG; *m* 1966, Pamela Rosemary Barry; two *s* two *d*. *Educ:* Winchester Coll.; Magdalen Coll., Oxford. Joined HM Treasury, 1959; Sec. for Appointments to PM and Ecclesiastical Sec. to the Lord Chancellor, 1974–82; Under Sec., Cabinet Office (MPO), 1982–85. *Recreation:* fishing. *Address:* Easter Cottage, 62 Edgar Road, Winchester, Hants SO23 9TN. *T:* (01962) 890258.

PETERSON, Rev. David Gilbert, PhD; Research Fellow, Moore Theological College, Sydney, 2007–12, now Emeritus Faculty Member; Principal, Oak Hill Theological College, 1996–2007; *b* 29 Oct. 1944; *s* of Gilbert Samuel and Marie Jean Peterson; *m* 1970, Lesley Victoria (*née* Stock); three *s*. *Educ:* Univ. of Sydney (MA); Moore Theol Coll., Sydney (BD (Lond.)); Univ. of Manchester (PhD 1978). Ordained deacon, 1968, priest, 1969; St Matthew's, Manly, dio. of Sydney, 1968–71; Lectr, Moore Theol Coll., 1971–75, 1978–79, 1984–96; Post-grad. study, Univ. of Manchester and Sunday Asst, St Mary's, Cheadle, dio. of Chester, 1975–78; Rector and Sen. Canon, St Michael's, Provisional Cathedral, Wollongong, dio. of Sydney, 1980–83. Hon. Vis. Prof., Middlesex Univ., 2004–09. *Publications:* Hebrews and Perfection, 1982; Engaging with God, 1992; Possessed by God, 1995; The Book of Acts and its Theology, 1996; Where Wrath and Mercy Meet: proclaiming the atonement today, 2001; The Word Made Flesh: evangelicals and the incarnation, 2003; Christ and His People in the Book of Isaiah, 2003; Holiness and Sexuality, 2004; The Acts of the Apostles, 2009; Transformed by God: new covenant life and ministry, 2012; Encountering God Together: biblical patterns for ministry and worship, 2013. *Recreations:* golf, swimming, music. *Address:* 1 Vista Street, Belrose, NSW 2085, Australia.

PETERSON, Hon. David Robert; PC (Can.) 1992; QC (Can.) 1980; Senior Partner, since 1991, and Chairman, since 1998, Cassels Brock & Blackwell LLP; *b* 28 Dec. 1943; *s* of Clarence Marwin Peterson and Laura Marie (*née* Scott); *m* 1974, Shelley Christine Matthews; two *s* one *d*. *Educ:* Univ. of Western Ontario (BA Phil./PolSci); Univ. of Toronto (LLB). Called to Bar, Ontario, 1969. Chm. and Pres., C. M. Peterson Co. Ltd, 1969–75; MLA for London Centre, Ontario, 1975–90; Leader, Liberal Party of Ontario, 1982–90; Leader of the Opposition, 1982–85; Premier of Ontario, 1985–90. Chm. and Dir of public cos. CStJ 1987. Chevalier, Légion d'Honneur (France), 1994. *Recreations:* theatre, riding, jogging, ski-ing, tennis, scuba diving, golf, reading, gardening. *Address:* Cassels Brock & Blackwell LLP, Suite 2100, Scotia Plaza, 40 King Street W, Toronto, ON M5H 3C2, Canada. *Club:* London (Ontario) Hunt.

PETERSON, Gilles, MBE 2004; broadcaster, producer and DJ; *b* Caen, France, 28 Sept. 1964; *s* of Armin and Michelle Moehrle; *m* Atsuko Hirai; two *s*. *Educ:* John Fisher Sch., Purley; Greenshaw Sch., Sutton. Work on pirate radio stations: Radio Invicta; K Jazz; Solar Radio; Horizon Radio; presenter: Radio London, 1986–87; Jazz FM, 1990–91; Kiss FM, 1991–98; Radio 1, 1998–2012; BBC 6Music, 2012–; Founder: record labels: Hardback; BGP; Acid Jazz, 1988; Talkin' Loud, 1989; Brownswood Recordings, 2006; publishing co., Omakase Music. *Publications:* Freedom Rhythm and Sound, 2009. *Address:* Brownswood Recordings, 29A Brownswood Road, N4 2HP. *T:* (020) 8802 4981. *E:* simon@brownswoodrecordings.com. *W:* www.gillespetersonworldwide.com.

PETERSON, Rev. Canon John Louis, ThD; Canon for Global Justice and Reconciliation, Diocese of Washington, since 2005; *b* 17 Dec. 1942; *s* of J. Harold Peterson and Edythe V. Peterson; *m* 1966, Kirsten Ruth Bratlie; two *d*. *Educ:* Concordia Coll. (BA 1965); Harvard Divinity Sch. (STB 1968); Chicago Inst. for Advanced Theol Studies (ThD 1976). Instr, OT and Syro-Palestinian Archaeol., Seabury-Western Theol Seminary, Evanston, 1968–76; Canon Theologian and Admin. Asst to Bishop, dio. of Western Michigan, 1976–82; Vicar, St Stephen's Plainwell, Mich, 1976–82; Dean of St George's Coll., and Canon Residentiary, St George's Cathedral, Jerusalem, 1982–94, Hon. Canon, 1995–; Sec. Gen., Anglican Consultative Council, 1995–2004. Hon. Canon: Cathedral Ch of Christ the King, Kalamazoo, Mich, 1982–; Cathedral Church of Christ, Canterbury, 1995–2004; St Michael's Cathedral, Kaduna, Nigeria, 1999–; St Paul's Cathedral, 2000–05; All Saints Cathedral, Mpwapwa, Tanzania, 2002–; St Dunstan's Cathedral, Benoni, SA, 2004–; Cathedral of St Peter and St Paul, Washington DC, 2005–; St Stephen's Cathedral, Harrisburg, Pennsylvania, 2008–. Special Asst for Internat. Affairs, Anglican Bishop in Jerusalem, 2009–. Board Member: Spafford Children Center, Jerusalem, 1994– (Chair, 1994–2009); Anglican Communion Compass Rose Soc., 2010– (Pres., 2013–15; Vice Pres., 2015–). Hon. DD: Virginia Theol Seminary, 1993; Univ. of South (Sewanee), 1996; Seabury-Western Theol Seminary, 1997; Seminary of the SW, 2015. *Publications:* A Walk in Jerusalem, 1998; contrib. Anchor Bible Dictionary, 1992. *Address:* 1001 Red Oak Drive, Hendersonville, NC 28791, USA.

PETERSON, Will; *see* Billingham, M. P. D.

PETFORD, Prof. Nicholas, PhD, DSc; FGS; Vice Chancellor and Chief Executive Officer, University of Northampton, since 2010; *b* London, 27 May 1961; *s* of Brian Petford and Shirley Petford; *m* 1998, Gina Cherrett; one *s* two *d*. *Educ:* Mountbatten Sch., Southampton; Eastleigh Tech. Coll. (City and Guilds); Southwark Coll. (Access Course); Goldsmiths Coll. (BSc Geology 1987); Univ. of Liverpool (PhD 1991; DSc 2009); Harvard Business Sch. (Gen. Mgt Program 17). FGS 1986. Royal Soc. Res. Fellow, Univ. of Liverpool, 1990–93; Res. Fellow, Churchill Coll., Cambridge, 1991–94; Kingston University: Sen. Lectr, then Reader, 1995–2003, e-HR/Mktg, BP, 2001 (on sabbatical); Prof., 2003–06; Pro-Vice Chancellor, Bournemouth Univ., 2006–10. Vis. Researcher, Univ. of Michigan, 1991; Visiting Professor: Univ. of Vermont, 2004; Macquarie Univ., 2005, 2010–12; Open Univ., 2010–13. Vice Pres., Mineralogical Soc. of GB and Ireland, 2002–04. FRSA. *Publications:* (ed jtly) Hydrocarbons in Crystalline Rocks, 2003; (ed jtly) Physical Geology of High-Level Magmatic Systems, 2004; (ed jtly) Structure and Emplacement of High-Level Magmatic Systems, 2008; (jtly) The Field Description of Igneous Rocks, 2nd edn, 2011. *Recreations:* astronomy, sailing, Chelsea FC, crowdsurfing. *Address:* University of Northampton, Park Campus, Boughton Green Road, Northampton NN2 7AL. *T:* (01604) 892001. *E:* nick.petford@northampton.ac.uk. *Club:* Athenæum.

PETHERBRIDGE, Edward; actor and director; *b* 3 Aug. 1936; *s* of late William and Hannah Petherbridge; *m* 1st, 1957, Louise Harris (marr. diss. 1980); one *s*; 2nd, 1981, Emily Richard, actress; one *s* one *d*. *Educ:* Grange Grammar Sch., Bradford; Northern Theatre Sch. Early experience in repertory and on tour; London début, Dumain in Love's Labours Lost and Demetrius in A Midsummer Night's Dream, Regent's Park Open Air Theatre, 1962; All in Good Time, Mermaid, and Phoenix, 1963; with Nat. Theatre Co. at Old Vic, 1964–70, chief appearances in: Trelawny of the Wells, Rosencrantz and Guildenstern are Dead, A Flea in her Ear, Love for Love, Volpone, The Advertisement, The Way of the World, The White Devil; Alceste in The Misanthrope, Nottingham, Lulu, Royal Court, and Apollo, 1970; John Bull's Other Island, Mermaid, Swansong, opening of Crucible, Sheffield, 1971; Founder Mem., Actors' Co., 1972; chief appearances at Edinburgh Fests, NY, and on tour, 1972–75: 'Tis Pity she's a Whore, Rooling the Roost, The Way of the World, Tartuffe, King Lear; also devised, dir. and appeared in Knots (from R. D. Laing's book), The Beanstalk, a wordless pantomime, and dir. The Bacchae; RSC tour of Australia and NZ, 1976; dir. Uncle Vanya, Cambridge Theatre Co., 1977; Chasuble in The Importance of Being Earnest, and dir., devised and appeared in Do You Love Me (from R. D. Laing's book), Actors' Co. tour and Round House, 1977; Crucifer of Blood, Haymarket, 1979; Royal Shakespeare Company: tour, 1978, Twelfth Night; Three Sisters, 1979; Suicide, Newman Noggs in Nicholas Nickleby (Best Supporting Actor, London Drama Critics' Award, 1981), No Limits to Love, 1980; Nicholas Nickleby, Broadway, 1981; Twelfth Night, British Council tour (Philippines, Singapore, Malaysia, China and Japan), followed by season at Warehouse, London, 1982; Peter Pan, Barbican, 1983; The Rivals, NT, 1983; Strange Interlude, Duke of York's, 1984, Broadway, 1985 (Olivier Award, 1984); Love's Labours Lost, Stratford, 1984; Co-Dir, McKellen Petherbridge Co. at NT, 1984–86, acting in Duchess of Malfi, The Cherry Orchard, The Real Inspector Hound, and The Critic, 1985, company appeared at Internat. Theatre Fests, Paris and Chicago, 1986; Busman's Honeymoon, Lyric, Hammersmith, 1988; The Eight O'Clock Muse, one-man show, Riverside Studios, 1989; Alceste in The Misanthrope, co-prodn with Bristol Old Vic, 1989; The Power and the Glory, Chichester, 1990; Cyrano de Bergerac (title rôle), Greenwich, 1990; Point Valaine, and Valentine's Day (musical, from Shaw's You Never Can Tell), Chichester, 1991; Noël & Gertie, Duke of York's, 1991; The Seagull, RNT, 1994; Twelfth Night, Barbican, 1996; The Merry Wives of Windsor, Stratford, 1996; Cymbeline, Hamlet, Krapp's Last Tape, Stratford, 1997, transf. Barbican, NY, Washington and Edinburgh, 1997–98, Arts Th., 1999; The Accused, Haymarket Theatre Royal, 2000; The Relapse, RNT, 2001; The Woman in White, Palace Th., 2004; Donkeys' Years, Comedy, 2006; Office Suite, Chichester, 2007; The Importance of Being Earnest (musical), Riverside Studios, 2011; (and co-writer) My Perfect Mind, Plymouth Th. Royal, transf. Young Vic, 2013, Birmingham Repertory Th., Birmingham, 2014. Numerous television appearances include: Vershinin in Three Sisters (from RSC prod.); Lytton Strachey in No Need to Lie; Newman Noggs in Nicholas Nickleby (from RSC prod.); Gower in Pericles; Lord Peter Wimsey; Marsden in Strange Interlude; Uncle in Journey's End; No Strings. Hon. DLitt Bradford, 1989. *Publications:* Slim Chances and Unscheduled Appearances, 2011. *Recreations:* listening to music, photography, theatre history. *Address:* c/o United Agents, 12–26 Lexington Street, W1F 0LE.

PETHICA, Sir John Bernard, Kt 2014; PhD; FRS 1999; FREng; SFI Research Professor, since 2001, and Professor of Physics, Trinity College, Dublin; Chief Scientific Adviser, National Physical Laboratory, Teddington, since 2007; Fellow of St Cross College, Oxford, since 1986. *Educ:* Trinity Hall, Cambridge (BA 1974; PhD 1978); MA Oxon. Lectr, Dept of Materials, 1987, Prof. of Materials Sci., 1996–2001, Vis. Prof., 2001–, Univ. of Oxford; Sony Corp. R&D Prof. (on leave of absence), Japan, 1993–94; Founding Dir, Centre for Res. on Adaptive Nanostructures and Nanodevices, Trinity Coll., Dublin, 2002–05. Dir, Nano Instruments Inc., Knoxville, Tenn, 1985–98. Physical Scis Sec. and Vice Pres., Royal Soc., 2009–14. Mem. Council, Royal Soc., 2004–06. FREng 2013. Rosenhain Medal and Prize, Inst. of Materials, 1997; Hughes Medal, Royal Soc., 2001; Holweck Medal, Soc. Française de Physique, 2002. *Publications:* contribs to jls. *Address:* Department of Physics, Trinity College, Dublin 2, Ireland.

PETIT, Sir Dinshaw Manockjee, 5th Bt *cr* 1890, of Petit Hall, Bombay; *b* 21 Jan. 1965; *er s* of Sir Dinshaw Manockjee Petit, 4th Bt and of his 1st wife, Nirmala Nanavatty; *S* father, 1998; *m* 1994, Laila, *d* of Homi Commissariat; one *s* one *d*. President: N. M. Petit Charities, 1998–; Sir D. M. Petit Charities, 1998–; F. D. Petit Sanatorium, 1998–; Persian Zoroastrian Amelioration Fund, 1998–; Petit Girls' Orphanage, 1998–; D. M. Petit Gymnasium, 1998–; Native Gen. Dispensary, 1998–; Bai Avabai F. Petit Residuary Estate Trust, 1998–; Two

Account Trust, 1998; J. N. Petit Inst., 2004–. Trustee: Soc. for Prevention of Cruelty to Animals, 1998–; Concern India, 2005–; J. B. Petit High Sch. for Girls, 2007–. Member: Exec. Cttee, B. D. Petit Parsi Gen. Hospital, 1998–; Mgt Cttee, Garib Zarthostiona Rehethan Fund, 2003–; Governing Body, K. R. Cama Oriental Inst., 2008–. Gov., Veermata Jijabai Tech. Inst., 2004–11. Founder Mem., Nat. Centre for Performing Arts, 2008–. Chevalier, Ordre National du Mérite (France), 2005. *Heir:* s Rehan Jehangir Petit, *b* 4 May 1995. *Address:* Petit Hall, 66 Nepean Sea Road, Bombay 400006, India.

PETITGAS, Franck R.; Global Co-Head, Investment Banking, Morgan Stanley & Co., since 2005; *b* Nantes, 25 Feb. 1961; *s* of Victor and Denise Petitgas; *m* 1985, Catherine Gex; one *s*. *Educ:* Ecole Supérieure de Commerce, Paris. With S. G. Warburg & Co. Ltd, London and NY, 1986–93; Morgan Stanley & Co., NY, 1993; Man. Dir and Hd, Global Capital Markets, Europe, Morgan Stanley & Co., until 2005. Trustee: Tate, 2008–; Chichester Harbour Trust; Member Council: Serpentine Gall.; Artangel. Conseiller du Commerce Extérieur, UK. *Recreations:* yachting, ski-ing, arts, history. *E:* franck.petitgas@ms.com. *Clubs:* Royal Ocean Racing; Bosham Sailing.

PETLEY, Vanessa Jane; *see* Ward, V. J.

PETO, Anthony Nicholas George; QC 2009; *b* Salisbury, 21 Sept. 1960; *s* of Stefan and Johanna Peto; *m* 1991, Gloria Davenport; three *s* one *d*. *Educ:* Bishop Wordsworth's Sch., Salisbury; Brasenose Coll., Oxford (BA, BCL). Called to the Bar, Middle Temple, 1985; in private practice, Blackstone Chambers, Temple, specialising in commercial law, public law, civil fraud and asset recovery, 1985–; Co-Hd, Blackstone Chambers, 2012–. Counsel to Crown on Attorney Gen.'s A-Panel, 2008–09. *Recreations:* chamber music, keen amateur pianist. *Address:* Blackstone Chambers, Temple, EC4Y 9BW. *T:* (020) 7583 1770, *Fax:* (020) 7822 7350. *E:* tonypeto@blackstonechambers.com.

PETO, Sir Francis (Michael Morton), 5th Bt *cr* 1855, of Somerleyton Hall, Suffolk; *b* 11 Jan. 1949; *er s* of Sir Henry George Morton Peto, 4th Bt, and Frances Jacqueline, *d* of Ralph Haldane Evers; *S* father, 2010; *m* 1974, Felicity Margaret, *d* of late Lt-Col John Alan Burns; two *s*. *Educ:* Sherborne; Leeds Univ. *Heir:* *s* David James Morton Peto [*b* 25 Aug. 1978; *m* 2008, Aika Yukino, *d* of Karl Engels; one *s* one *d*].

PETO, Sir Henry (Christopher Morton Bampfylde), 5th Bt *cr* 1927, of Barnstaple, co. Devon; *b* 8 April 1967; *s* of Sir Michael Henry Basil Peto, 4th Bt and Sarah Susan, *y d* of Major Sir Dennis Stucley, 5th Bt; *S* father, 2008; *m* 1998, Louise Imogen, *y d* of Christopher Balck-Foote; one *s* two *d*. *Educ:* Eton; Oxford Brookes Univ. MRICS. *Heir:* *s* Jake Christopher Bampfylde Peto, *b* 11 Oct. 2004.

PETO, Sir Richard, Kt 1999; FRS 1989; Professor of Medical Statistics and Epidemiology, University of Oxford, since 1992; Fellow of Green Templeton College (formerly Green College), Oxford, since 1979; *b* 14 May 1943; *s* of Leonard Huntley Peto and Carrie Clarinda Peto; *m* 1970, Sallie Messum (marr. diss.); two *s*, and two *s* by Gale Mead (*d* 2001). *Educ:* Trinity Coll., Cambridge (MA Natural Sci.); Imperial Coll., London (MSc Statistics). Research Officer: MRC, 1967–69; Univ. of Oxford, 1969–72; Lectr, Dept of Regius Prof. of Medicine, 1972–75, Reader in Cancer Studies, 1975–92, Univ. of Oxford. Founder FMedSci 1998. *Publications:* Natural History of Chronic Bronchitis and Emphysema, 1976; Quantification of Occupational Cancer, 1981; The Causes of Cancer, 1983; Diet, Lifestyle and Mortality in China, 1990, 2nd edn 2006; (jtly) Mortality from Smoking in Developed Countries 1950–2000, 1994, 2nd edn 2006. *Recreations:* science, children. *Address:* Richard Doll Building, Old Road Campus, Roosevelt Drive, Oxford OX3 7LF. *T:* (01865) 552830/743801.

PETO, Prof. Timothy Edward Alexander, DPhil; FRCP, FRCPath; Professor of Medicine, University of Oxford, since 1999; Consultant Physician in Infectious Diseases and General Medicine, John Radcliffe Hospital, since 1988; *b* London, 10 March 1950; *s* of late Stephen Peto and Johanna, (Hanni), Peto (*née* Stadlen); *m* 1974, Verity Robertson Cottrill; three *d* (and one *d* decd). *Educ:* Bishop Wordsworth's Sch., Salisbury; Brasenose Coll., Oxford (Hulme Schol.; BA 1st Cl. Animal Physiol. 1971; DPhil Neurophysiol. 1974); Oxford Med. Sch. (Hobson Meml Schol.; BM BCh 1977). MRCP 1979, FRCP 1992; FRCPath 2000. MRC Trng Fellow, 1979–82; Wellcome Res. Fellow, 1982–83; Clin. Lectr, 1982–88, Reader in Medicine, 1996–99, Univ. of Oxford. Co-Dir, Infection Theme, Oxford Biomed. Centre, 2007–; NIHR Sen. Investigator, 2009–. Scientific Sec., MRC AIDS Therapeutic Trials Cttee, 1987–2003. Hon. Scientist, MRC Clin. Trials Unit, 2000–. *Publications:* contrib. articles to scientific jls on clin. trials and epidemiol. of HIV and tropical medicine, and characterization of transmission of bacterial infections using whole genome sequencing. *Recreations:* family, talking, thinking about mathematics. *Address:* Nuffield Department of Medicine, John Radcliffe Hospital, Oxford OX3 9DU. *T:* (01865) 741166. *E:* tim.peto@ndm.ox.ac.uk.

PETRAEUS, Gen. David Howell; Chairman, KKR Global Institute, since 2013; *b* Cornwall-on-Hudson, NY, 7 Nov. 1952; *s* of Sixtus Petraeus and Miriam Petraeus (*née* Howell); *m* 1974, Hollister Knowlton; one *s* one *d*. *Educ:* US Military Acad., West Point (BS 1974); US Army Command and General Staff Coll., Fort Leavenworth; Princeton Univ. (MPA 1985; PhD Internat. Relns 1987). Mil. Asst to Gen. John Galvin, SACEUR, 1987–89; Aide and Asst Exec. Officer to US Army Chief of Staff, 1989–91; Comdr, 3rd Bn, 187th Infantry Regt, 101st Airborne Div., 1991–93; ACOS for Plans, Ops and Trng, 101st Airborne Div., 1993–94; Chief of Ops, UN Force, Haiti, 1995; Comdr, 1st Bde, 82nd Airborne Div., 1995–97; Exec. Asst to Chm., Jt Chiefs, 1997–99; Asst Div. Comdr, 82nd Airborne Div., 1999–2000; COS, XVIII Airborne Corps, 2000–01; ACOS for Ops and Dep. Comdr, US Jt Interagency Counter-Terrorism Task Force, Bosnia, 2001–02; Commanding Gen., 101st Airborne Div., 2002–04 (incl. Operation Iraqi Freedom, 2003–04); Comdr, Multi-National Security Transition Command Iraq and NATO Trng Mission Iraq, 2004–05; Commanding General: Combined Arms Center, Fort Leavenworth, 2005–07; Multi-National Force—Iraq, 2007–08; Commander: US Central Command, 2008–10; NATO Internat. Security Assistance Force, and US Forces—Afghanistan, 2010–11; Dir, CIA, USA, 2011–12. Member: 82nd Airborne Div. Assoc.; 101st Airborne Div. Assoc. Defense Distinguished Service Medal (4 awards); Army Distinguished Service Medal (3 awards); Defense Superior Service Medal (2 awards); Bronze Star Medal with 'V'; State Dept Sec.'s Distinguished Service Award; NATO Meritorious Service Medal (2 awards). Officer, Order of Australia; Meritorious Service Cross (Canada); Cross of Merit of Minister of Defense (Czech Republic); Comdr, Légion d'Honneur (France); Comdr, Order of Merit (Poland); Knight Comdr's Cross (Germany); Knight Grand Cross, Order of Orange-Nassau (Netherlands); Gold Cross of Merit of the Carabinieri (Italy); Gold Award, Order of the Date Palm, (Iraq); Tong-il Security Medal (Korea); Chief of Defense Honor Emblem (Romania); Mil. Merit Order, First Cl. (UAE). *Publications:* Lessons of History and Lessons of Vietnam, 1987; (jtly) The US Army/Marine Corps Counterinsurgency Manual, 2007; articles in Washington Institute for Near East Policy, insights, Amer. Interest Mag., Parameters, Global Policy, Army Mag., Policy Options, Military Rev., Military Affairs, Army Jl, Armed Forces Jl Internat., Armed Forces and Soc., Infantry Mag., Field Artillery. *Recreations:* running, cycling, reading. *Clubs:* Cosmos (Washington, DC); Army Navy Country (Va).

PETRE, family name of **Baron Petre**.

PETRE, 18th Baron *cr* 1603; **John Patrick Lionel Petre;** Lord-Lieutenant of Essex, since 2002; *b* 4 Aug. 1942; *s* of 17th Baron Petre and Marguerite Eileen, *d* of late Ion Wentworth Hamilton; *S* father, 1989; *m* 1965, Marcia Gwendolyn, *d* of Alfred Plumpton; two *s* one *d*. *Educ:* Eton; Trinity College, Oxford (MA). DL Essex, 1991. KStJ 2003. *Heir:* *s* Hon. Dominic William Petre [*b* 9 Aug. 1966; *m* 1998, Marisa Verna, *o d* of Anthony J. Perry; one *s* one *d*]. *Address:* Writtle Park, Highwood, Chelmsford, Essex CM1 3QF.

PETRIDES, Prof. Michael, PhD; FRS 2012; FRSC 2011; Professor, Department of Neurology and Neurosurgery and Department of Psychology, Director, Cognitive Neuroscience Unit, Montreal Neurological Institute and Hospital, since 1990, and James McGill Professor, since 2001, McGill University. *Educ:* Univ. of London; Christ's Coll., Cambridge (PhD). McGill University: Postdoctoral Fellow, 1977–79; Montreal Neurol Inst. and Hosp., 1979–. Killam Schol., 2002–07. James S. McDonnell 21st Century Scientist Award, 2001. *Publications:* (contrib.) Neuroscience of Rule-Guided Behavior, 2008; (contrib.) Neuropsychological Research: a review, 2008; contribs to Jl Neurosurgery, Neurosci. *Address:* Montreal Neurological Institute and Hospital, 3801 University Street, Montreal, QC H3A 2B4, Canada.

PETRIE, Sir Peter (Charles), 5th Bt *cr* 1918, of Carrowcarden; CMG 1980; Adviser on European and Parliamentary Affairs to Governor of Bank of England, 1989–2003; HM Diplomatic Service, retired; *b* 7 March 1932; *s* of Sir Charles Petrie, 3rd Bt, CBE, FRHistS and Jessie Cecilia (*d* 1987), *d* of Frederick James George Mason; *S* half-brother, 1988; *m* 1958, Countess Lydwine Maria Fortunata v. Oberndorff, *d* of Count v. Oberndorff, The Hague and Paris; two *s* one *d*. *Educ:* Westminster; Christ Church, Oxford. BA Lit. Hum., MA. 2nd Lieut Grenadier Guards, 1954–56. Entered HM Foreign Service, 1956; served in UK Delegn to NATO, Paris 1958–61; UK High Commn, New Delhi (seconded CRO), 1961–64; Chargé d'Affaires, Katmandu, 1963; Cabinet Office, 1965–67; UK Mission to UN, NY, 1969–73; Counsellor (Head of Chancery), Bonn, 1973–76; Head of European Integration Dept (Internal), FCO, 1976–79; Minister, Paris, 1979–85; Ambassador to Belgium, 1985–89. Member: Franco-British Council, 1994–2002 (Chm., British section, 1997–2002); Inst de l'Euro, Lyon, 1995–99; Acad. de Comptabilité, 1997–. Mem. Council, City Univ., 1997–2002. Chevalier, Légion d'Honneur (France), 2006. *Recreation:* country pursuits. *Heir:* *s* Charles James Petrie (OBE 2014) [*b* 16 Sept. 1959; *m* 1981, France de Hauteclocque; three *s* (one *d* decd)]. *Address:* 16A Cambridge Street, SW1V 4QH; 40 rue Lauriston, 75116 Paris, France; Le Hameau du Jardin, Lestre, 50310 Montebourg, France. *E:* lydwinepo@aol.fr. *Clubs:* Brooks's, Beefsteak; Jockey (Paris).

PETROW, Judith Caroline; *see* Bingham, J. C.

PETT, Maj.-Gen. Raymond Austin, CB 1995; MBE 1976; DL; Chairman: Coventry and Rugby Hospital Co. plc, 2002–11; Walsall Hospital Co. plc, 2007–11; *b* 23 Sept. 1941; *s* of late Richard John Austin Pett and Jessie Lyle Pett (*née* Adamson); *m* 1965, (Joan) Marie McGrath Price, *d* of FO Bernard Christopher McGrath, RAF (killed in action 1943) and of Mrs Robert Henry Benbow Price; one *s* one *d*. *Educ:* Christ's Coll.; RMA Sandhurst; rcds, psc. Commnd Lancashire Regt (Prince of Wales's Vols), 1961; regtl service in GB, BAOR, Swaziland and Cyprus; seconded 2nd Bn 6th QEO Gurkha Rifles, Malaysia and Hong Kong, 1967–69; Instr, RMA Sandhurst, 1969–72; Staff Coll., 1972–73; DAA&QMG, HQ 48 Gurkha Inf. Bde, 1974–75; 1st Bn, Queen's Lancashire Regt, 1976–78; GSO2 ASD 3, MoD, 1978–80; CO, 1st Bn King's Own Royal Border Regt, 1980–82; Staff Coll. (HQ and Directing Staff), 1983–84; Col ASD 2, MoD, 1984; Col Army Plans, MoD, 1985; Comd Gurkha Field Force, 1985–86, and Comd 48 Gurkha Inf. Bde, 1986–87, Hong Kong; RCDS 1988; Dir, Army Staff Duties, MoD, 1989–91; DCS and Sen. British Officer, HQ AFNORTH, 1991–94; Dir of Infantry, 1994–96. Dir of Capital Develts, Royal Hosps NHS Trust, 1996–97; Chief Exec., Barts and the London NHS Trust, 1997–2000; Chairman: Derby Healthcare plc, 2005–07; Central Notts Hosps plc, 2006–07; Managing Director: HCP (Bidding) Ltd, 2004–06; HCP Defence Projects Ltd, 2001–04; Director: HCP (Holdings) Ltd, 2001–06; Healthcare Projects Ltd, 2001–06. Col, 6th QEO Gurkha Rifles, 1988–94; Col Comdt, King's Div., 1994–97. Trustee: Gurkha Welfare Trust, 1988–2007 (Chm., 1995–2011, Pres., 2012–, Western Br.); Somerset ACF Trust, 2008– (Chm., 2010–). Chm., Army Mountaineering Assoc., 1994–96. President: Mid-Somerset Agricl Soc., 1996 (Vice-Pres., 1997–); Shepton Mallet Br., RBL, 1996–; League of Friends, Shepton Mallet Community Hosp., 2011–. FRSA 1997. Freeman, City of London, 2000; Liveryman, Painter Stainers' Co., 2000–. DL Somerset, 2007. *Recreations:* the arts, house restoration, cross-country ski-ing, shooting. *Clubs:* Army and Navy, Ronnie Scott's.

PETTEGREE, Prof. Andrew David Mark, DPhil; Professor of Modern History, University of St Andrews, since 1998; *b* 16 Sept. 1957; *s* of Kenneth William Pettegree and Jean Dorcas Pettegree; *m* 1995, Jane Karen Ryan; two *d*. *Educ:* Oundle Sch.; Merton Coll., Oxford (BA 1979; MA, DPhil 1983). Hanseatic Schol., Hamburg, 1982–84; Res. Fellow, Peterhouse, Cambridge, 1984–86; University of St Andrews: Lectr, 1986–94; Reader, 1994–98; Founding Dir, St Andrews Reformation Studies Inst., 1993–2004. Dir, Universal Short Title Catalogue, 2011–. FRHistS 1986 (Literary Dir, 1998–2003; Vice-Pres., 2012–14). *Publications:* Foreign Protestant Communities in Sixteenth Century London, 1986; Emden and the Dutch Revolt, 1992; The Early Reformation in Europe, 1992; Marian Protestantism, 1996; Reformation World, 2000; Europe in the Sixteenth Century, 2002; Reformation and the Culture of Persuasion, 2005; The Book in the Renaissance, 2010 (Phyllis Goodhart Gordon Prize, Renaissance Soc. of America, 2011); The Invention of News, 2014. *Recreations:* golf, tennis. *Address:* School of History, University of St Andrews, St Andrews, Fife KY16 9AL. *E:* admp@St-And.ac.uk. *Club:* MCC.

PETTIFER, Julian, OBE 2010; freelance writer and broadcaster; *b* 21 July 1935; *s* of Stephen Henry Pettifer and Diana Mary (*née* Burton); unmarried. *Educ:* Marlborough; St John's Coll., Cambridge. Television reporter, writer and presenter: Southern TV, 1958–62; Tonight, BBC, 1962–64; 24 Hours, BBC, 1964–69; Panorama, BBC, 1969–75; Presenter, Cuba—25 years of revolution (series), ITV, 1984; Host, Busman's Holiday, ITV, 1985–86. Numerous television documentaries, including: Vietnam, War without End, 1970; The World About Us, 1976; The Spirit of '76, 1976; Diamonds in the Sky, 1979; Nature Watch, 1981–82, 1985–86, 1988, 1990, 1992; Automania, 1984; The Living Isles, 1986; Missionaries, 1990; See for Yourself, 1991; Assignment, 1991; Nature, 1992; The Culling Fields, 1999; Warnings from the Wild, 2000, 2001; radio broadcasts include: Asia File, 1995–, and Crossing Continents, 1999–, BBC Radio 4; The Sixties, BBC Radio 2, 2000. Trustee, Royal Botanic Gdns, Kew, 1993–96. President: Berks, Bucks and Oxfordshire Naturalists Trust, 1990–2009; RSPB, 1995–2001 and 2004–09; Vice-Pres., RSNC, 1992–. Reporter of the Year Award, Guild of Television Directors and Producers, 1968; Cherry Kearton Award for Contribution to Wildlife Films, RGS, 1990; Mungo Park Medal, RSGS, 1998. *Publications:* (jtly) Diamonds in the Sky: a social history of air travel, 1979; (jtly) Nature Watch, 1981; (jtly) Automania, 1984; (jtly) Missionaries, 1990; (jtly) Nature Watch, 1994. *Recreations:* gardening, sport, cinema. *Address:* c/o Bryony Kinnear, Apartment 1, 72 Courtfield Gardens, SW5 0NL.

PETTIFER, Dr Richard Edward William, MBE 2008; meteorological consultant, since 1998; General Secretary, PRIMET, since 2007; Executive Director, Royal Meteorological Society, 1998–2006; *b* 19 Sept. 1941; *s* of Reginald Charles Edward Pettifer and Irene May Pettifer (*née* Bradley); *m* 1st, 1965, Colleen Rosemary Adams (*d* 1984); one *s* two *d*; 2nd, 1986, Maureen Eileen Macartney (*née* McCullough); one step *d*. *Educ:* Ealing County Grammar Sch. for Boys; London Polytechnic; Queen's Univ., Belfast (BSc 1st cl. Physics 1969; PhD Laser and Atmos. Physics 1975). FRMetS 1979; CMet 1994. Asst Dir, Meteorological Office, 1980–85; Managing Director: Vaisala (UK) Ltd, 1985–98; Scientific and Technical Mgt Ltd, 1998–2005. Chairman: COST Project 43, 1978–84; LINK/Seasense, 1994–2001. Vice Pres.,

CIMO, 1980–84. *Publications:* over 100 papers, book contribs, public reports, etc on meteorological/oceanographic instrumentation and measurements, commercial meteorological mkt in Europe and the case for open data in meteorology. *Recreations:* gardening, golf, bee keeping, cricket, community support projects. *Address:* West Oaks, 4 Cranes Road, Sherborne St John, Hants RG24 9JD. *T:* 07739 212227. *E:* pettifer190@btinternet.com. *Clubs:* Meteorological; Weybrook Park Golf; Eversley Cricket.

PETTIFOR, Prof. David Godfrey, CBE 2005; PhD; FRS 1994; Isaac Wolfson Professor of Metallurgy, Oxford University, 1992–2010, now Emeritus; Fellow, St Edmund Hall, Oxford, 1992–2010; *b* 9 March 1945; *s* of late Percy Hayward Pettifor and Margaret Cotterill; *m* 1st, 1969, Lynda Ann Potgieter (marr. diss. 1989); two *s*; 2nd, 2004, Diane Gold. *Educ:* Univ. of Witwatersrand (BSc Hons 1967); PhD Cantab 1970. Lectr, Dept of Physics, Univ. of Dar es Salaam, 1971; Res. Asst, Cavendish Lab., Cambridge, 1974; Vis. Res. Scientist, Bell Labs, USA, 1978; Imperial College, London: Lectr and Reader, Dept of Mathematics, 1978–88; Prof. of Theoretical Solid State Physics, 1988–92. Lectures: Mott, Inst. of Physics, 1993; Maddin, Univ. of Pa, 1995. Hume-Rothery Award, Minerals, Metals and Materials Soc., USA, 1995; Armourers' and Brasiers' Award, Royal Soc., 1999. *Publications:* Bonding and Structure of Molecules and Solids, 1995; papers incl. Structures maps for pseudo-binary and ternary phases (Inst. of Metals Prize, 1989). *Recreation:* walking. *Address:* Department of Materials, University of Oxford, Parks Road, Oxford OX1 3PH. *T:* (01865) 273751.

PETTIGREW, Prof. Andrew Marshall, OBE 2009; PhD; FBA 2003; Professor of Strategy and Organisation, Saïd Business School, University of Oxford, since 2008; *b* 11 June 1944; *s* of late George Pettigrew and Martha (*née* Marshall); *m* 1967, Mary Ethna Veronica Moores (marr. diss. 2009); three *s* (one *d* decd). *Educ:* Corby Grammar Sch.; Liverpool Univ. (BA 1965; Dip. Ind. Admin 1967); Manchester Univ. (PhD Bus. Admin 1970). Res. Associate, Manchester Business Sch., 1966–69; Vis. Asst Prof., Yale Univ., 1969–71; Lectr, London Business Sch., 1971–76; Warwick Business School, University of Warwick: Prof. of Organisational Behaviour, 1976–85; Dir, Centre for Corporate Strategy and Change, 1985–95; Prof. of Strategy and Orgn, 1995–2003; Associate Dean of Res., 2002–03; Dean of Mgt Sch. and Prof. of Strategy and Orgn, Univ. of Bath, 2003–08. Sen. Golding Fellow, Brasenose Coll., Oxford, 2009–. Vis. Schol., 1981, Vis. Prof., 2001, Harvard Business Sch.; Vis. Schol., Stanford Univ., 1982. Member: Industry and Employment Cttee, ESRC, 1984–87; Jt Cttee, ESRC and SERC, 1988–91; Council, ESRC, 2005–10; Bd, Eur. Foundn for Mgt Develt, 2006–09 (Vice Pres., 2008–09; Chm., R & D Cttee, 2010–); Dep. Chm., Mgt Studies Panel, RAE, UFC, 1992. Fellow: British Acad. of Mgt, 1996 (Chm., 1986–90; Pres., 1990–93); Acad. of Mgt, 1997; SMS, 2005; AcSS 1999. Hon. Dr Linköping, 1989; Hon. LLD Liverpool, 2010; Dr *hc* Copenhagen Business Sch., 2010. *Publications:* The Politics of Organisational Decision Making, 1973; (with E. Mumford) Implementing Strategic Decisions, 1975; The Awakening Giant: continuity and change in ICI, 1985; The Management of Strategic Change, 1987; (with R. Whipp) Managing Change for Competitive Success, 1991; (jtly) Shaping Strategic Change: making change in the NHS, 1992; (jtly) The New Public Management in Action, 1996; (with E. Fenton) The Innovating Organisation, 2000; (jtly) The Handbook of Strategy and Management, 2002; (jtly) Innovative Forms of Organising, 2003; articles in professional jls. *Recreations:* antiquarian horology, military history, Herefordshire. *Address:* Saïd Business School, University of Oxford, Park End Street, Oxford OX1 1HP. *E:* andrew.pettigrew@sbs.ox.ac.uk.

PETTIGREW, Colin William; Sheriff of North Strathclyde at Paisley, since 2010 (Floating Sheriff, 2002–10); *b* 19 June 1957; *s* of Thomas Whitelaw Pettigrew and Mary Macrae Pettigrew (*née* Muir); *m* 1981, Linda McGill; one *s* one *d*. *Educ:* High Sch. of Glasgow; Glasgow Univ. (LLB Hons 1978). Admitted as solicitor, 1980. Trainee solicitor, 1978–80, Asst Solicitor, 1980–82, McClure Naismith Brodie & Co., Glasgow; Asst Solicitor, 1982–83, Partner, 1983–2002, Borland Johnson & Orr, subseq. Borland Montgomerie Keyden, Glasgow and T. J. & W. A. Dykes, Hamilton. Pres., Sheriffs' Assoc., 2015– (Vice Pres., 2013–15). Elder and Clerk to Congregational Bd, Uddington Old Parish Ch, Church of Scotland, 2013–. *Recreations:* Rugby, golf, gardening, travel. *Address:* Paisley Sheriff Court House, St James Street, Paisley PA3 2HW. *T:* (0141) 887 5291.

PETTIGREW, James Nellson; Chairman: Clydesdale Bank plc, since 2014; Edinburgh Investment Trust plc, since 2011; President, Institute of Chartered Accountants of Scotland, 2015–April 2016 (Deputy President, 2014–15); *b* Dundee; *s* of James Pettigrew and Sheila Pettigrew; *m* Dr Joanna Lawson. *Educ:* Aberdeen Univ. (LLB); Univ. of Glasgow (Dip. Accountancy). CA trainee, Arthur Young McCleland Moores & Co., 1980–84; Chief Accountant, J. Fleming & Co. Ltd, 1985–87; Divl Financial Dir, 1988–92, Gp Treas., 1993–98, Sedgwick Gp plc; Chief Finance Officer, ICAP plc, 1999–2006; Chief Operating Officer and Chief Finance Officer, Ashmore Gp plc, 2006–07; CEO, CMC Markets plc, 2007–09. Non-executive Director: Aberdeen Asset Mgt plc, 2010–; Crest Nicholson plc, 2013–. *Recreations:* golf, gardening. *Club:* Caledonian.

PETTIGREW, Prof. John Douglas, FRS 1987; FAA 1987; Professor of Physiology, 1983, now Emeritus, and Director, Vision, Touch and Hearing Research Centre, 1988–2006, University of Queensland; *b* 2 Oct. 1943; *s* of John James Pettigrew and Enid Dellmere Holt; *m* 1968, Rona Butler (marr. diss. 1996); one *s* two *d*. *Educ:* Katoomba High Sch.; Univ. of Sydney (BSc Med., MSc, MB BS). Jun. Resident MO, Royal Prince Alfred Hosp., 1969; Miller Fellow 1970–72, Res. Associate 1973, Univ. of California, Berkeley; Asst Prof. of Biology 1974, Associate Prof. of Biology 1978, CIT; Actg Dir, National Vision Res. Inst. of Aust., 1981. H. B. Collin Medal, 2011. *Publications:* Visual Neuroscience, 1986; numerous pubns in Nature, Science, Jl of Physiol., Jl of Comp. Neurol., Exp. Brain Res., etc. *Recreations:* bird watching, mountaineering. *Address:* 207/180 Swann Road, Taringa, Qld 4068, Australia. *T:* (7) 38711062.

PETTIGREW, Hon. Pierre Stewart; PC (Canada) 1996; Executive Advisor, International, Deloitte & Touche, Toronto, since 2006; Member, Advisory Board, Forbes Manhattan, Toronto, since 2006; *b* 18 April 1951. *Educ:* Univ. du Québec à Trois Rivières (BA Philos.); Balliol Coll., Oxford (MPhil Internat. Relns 1976). Dir, Pol Cttee, NATO Assembly, Brussels, 1976–78; Exec. Asst to Leader of Quebec Liberal Party, 1978–81; Foreign Policy Advr to Prime Minister, 1981–84; Vice Pres., Samson Bélair Deloitte & Touche Internat. (Montreal), 1985–95. MP (L) Papineau, Quebec, 1996–2006. Minister: for Internat. Co-operation, 1996; responsible for La Francophonie, 1996; of Human Resources Develt, 1996–99; for Internat. Trade, 1999–2003; of Health, of Intergovtl Affairs, and responsible for Official Langs, 2003–04; of Foreign Affairs, 2004–06. Bd Mem., Inter Amer. Dialogue, Washington, 2010–. Hon. LLD Warwick, 2008. *Publications:* Pour une politique de la confiance, 1999. *E:* ppettigrew@deloitte.ca.

PETTINI, Prof. Max, PhD; FRS 2010; Professor of Observational Astronomy, University of Cambridge, since 2002; *b* 15 June 1949. *Educ:* University Coll. London (PhD Astrophysics 1978; Hon. Fellow 2011). Royal Greenwich Observatory; Anglo-Australian Observatory; UWA. *Publications:* articles in jls. *Address:* Institute of Astronomy, University of Cambridge, Madingley Road, Cambridge CB3 0HA.

PETTITT, Adam Sven, MA; Head Master, Highgate School, since 2006; *b* 5 Feb. 1966; *s* of Robin Garth Pettitt and Elizabeth Margaret Pettitt (*née* Jenkins); *m* 1997, Barbara Sauron; two *s* one *d*. *Educ:* Hailsham Sch.; Eastbourne Sixth Form Coll.; New Coll., Oxford (BA Mod and Medieval Langs 1988; MA 1995). Eton Coll., 1988–92; Hd of German, Oundle Sch., 1992–94; Hd of Mod. Langs, Abingdon Sch., 1994–98; Second Master, Norwich Sch., 1998–2006. Governor: Havelock Acad., Grimsby, 2006–11; Brighton Coll., 2007–; The Hall, Hampstead, 2008–; London Acad. of Excellence, 2012–. *Recreations:* cross-country running, reading, old buildings. *Address:* Highgate School, North Road, N6 4AY. *T:* (020) 8340 1524, *Fax:* (020) 8340 7674. *Club:* Athenæum.

PETTITT, Gordon Charles, OBE 1991; transport management consultant, 1993–2000; Managing Director, Regional Railways, British Rail, 1991–92; *b* 12 April 1934; *s* of Charles and Annie Pettitt; *m* 1956, Ursula Margareta Agnes Hokamp; three *d*. *Educ:* St Columba's Coll., St Albans; Pitman's Coll., London. FCILT. British Rail, 1950–92: Freight Sales Manager, Eastern Reg., 1976; Chief Passenger Manager, Western Reg., 1978; Divl Manager, Liverpool Street, Eastern Reg., 1979; Dep. Gen. Manager, 1983, Gen. Manager, 1985, Southern Reg.; Dir, Provincial, 1990–91. Director: Connex Rail Ltd, 1997–98; Heathrow Express Operating Co. Ltd, 1997–99; Network Rail Property Adv. Bd, 2003–06. Pres., Instn of Railway Operators, 2000–02 (Fellow, 2002). Governor, Middlesex Univ. (formerly Polytechnic), 1989–95. Pres., Bluebell Railway Preservation Soc., 2014–. *Recreations:* walking, foreign travel, Victorian art. *Address:* Beeches Green, Woodham Lane, Woking, Surrey GU21 5SP.

PETTS, Prof. Geoffrey Eric, PhD; Vice Chancellor and Rector, University of Westminster, since 2007; *b* 28 March 1953; *s* of Horace and Eva Petts; *m* 1977, Judith Irene Armitt (*see* Prof. J. I. Petts). *Educ:* St Michael's Primary Sch., Tenterden; Ashford Grammar Sch.; Univ. of Liverpool (BSc Hons Geol and Phys. Geog. 1974); Univ. of Exeter; Univ. of Southampton (PhD 1978). Lectr, Dorset Inst. of Higher Educn, 1977–79; Loughborough University: Lectr, 1979–86; Sen. Lectr, 1986–89; Prof. of Phys. Geog., 1989–94; Hd, Dept of Geog., 1991–94; University of Birmingham: Prof. of Phys. Geog., 1994–2007; Dir, Centre for Envmtl Res. and Trng, 1997–2007; Hd, Sch. of Geog., 1998–2001; Pro Vice Chancellor, 2001–07. Visiting Professor: KCL, 2003–09; Univ. of Birmingham, 2007–13; Hon. Prof., Beijing Normal Univ., 2011. Founding Editor-in-Chief, Regulated Rivers: Research and Management, subseq. River Research and Applications, 1986–. Member Scientific Advisory Board: Prep. Gp for Internat. Lake Envmts Cttee, UNEP, 1985; Mgt of Land-Water Ecotones, UNESCO Man and Biosphere prog., 1989–97; Long-term Monitoring Upper Mississippi River, Fish and Wildlife Service, US Dept of Interior, 1989–99; Water Res., ICSU, 1996–2003; Eco-Hydrology, UNESCO Internat. Hydrol. Prog., 1998–2000. Co-Chm., Eur. Network for Scientific and Tech. Co-operation, Large Alluvial Rivers, 1986–89; Dir, Internat. Water Resources Assoc., 1992–95. Member: British Soc. of Geomorphol. (formerly British Geomorphol Res. Gp) (Chm., Pubns Sub-cttee, 1986–89); British Hydrol Soc. (Sec., 1988–90; Pres., 2015–); Freshwater Biol Assoc. (Mem. Council, 1999–2003). Chm., Podium, 2010–; Mem. Bd, London Higher, 2007– (Chm., 2014–Sept. 2016). FRGS; FRSA 2003. Busk Medal, RGS, 2006; Lifetime Achievement Award, Internat. Soc. for River Sci., 2009. *Publications:* Rivers, 1983; Impounded Rivers: perspectives for ecological management, 1984; (with I. D. L. Foster) Rivers and Landscapes, 1985; (ed jtly) Alternatives in River Regulation, 1989; (ed jtly) Historical Analysis of Large Alluvial Rivers in Western Europe, 1989; (ed jtly) Water, Engineering and Landscape, 1990; (ed jtly) Lowland Floodplain Rivers: geomorphological perspectives, 1992; (ed jtly) River Conservation and Management, 1992; (ed jtly) Rivers Handbook, vol 1, 1992, vol 2, 1994; (ed jtly) Hydrosystèmes Fluviaux, 1993 (Hydrosystems, 1996); (ed jtly) Changing River Channels, 1995; (ed) Man's Influence on Freshwater Ecosystems and Water Use, 1995; (ed jtly) River Restoration, 1996; (ed jtly) River Flows and Channel Forms, 1996; (ed jtly) River Biota, 1996; (ed jtly) Global Perspectives on River Conservation, 2000; (with J. Heathcote and D. Martin) Urban Rivers: our inheritance and future, 2002; (ed jtly) Braided Rivers, 2006. *Recreations:* walking, gardening, cricket, hockey, golf, the Arctic, painting and sketching. *Address:* University of Westminster, 309 Regent Street, W1B 2UW. *T:* (020) 7911 5115, *Fax:* (020) 7911 5103. *E:* G.Petts@westminster.ac.uk. *Club:* East India.

PETTS, Prof. Judith Irene, CBE 2012; PhD; Professor of Environmental Risk Management, since 2010, and Pro-Vice-Chancellor (Research and Enterprise), since 2014, University of Southampton; *b* 7 Jan. 1954; *d* of Alexander and Rene Armitt; *m* 1977, Prof. Geoffrey Eric Petts, *qv*. *Educ:* Univ. of Exeter (BA Hons (Geog.) 1975); Loughborough Univ. (PhD 1996). MCIWM 2002. Loughborough University: Lectr, Centre for Extension Studies, 1987–95; Sen. Lectr, 1995–97, Dir, 1997–99, Centre for Hazard and Risk Mgt; Prof. of Envmtl Risk Mgt, 1999–2010, Hd, Sch. of Geog., Earth and Envmtl Scis, 2001–07, Pro-Vice-Chancellor (Res. and Knowledge Transfer), 2007–10, Univ. of Birmingham; Dean, Faculty of Social and Human Scis, Univ. of Southampton, 2010–13. Member: Council, NERC, 2000–06; Royal Commn on Envmtl Pollution, 2005–11; EPSRC Societal Issues Panel, 2006–11; EPSRC Strategic Adv. Network, 2011–13; Science Adv. Council, DEFRA, 2011–; Council, BBSRC, 2014–; Innovation Adv. Panel, NERC, 2015–. FRGS 1999; FRSA 2003; FAcSS (AcSS 2007). *Publications:* (with G. Eduljee) Environmental Impact Assessment for Waste Treatment and Disposal Facilities, 1994; (jtly) Risk-based Contaminated Land Investigation and Assessment, 1997; (ed) Handbook of Environmental Impact Assessment, 1999. *Recreations:* travelling to remote places (particularly the Arctic), walking. *Address:* University of Southampton, University Road, Southampton SO17 1BJ.

PETTY, Very Rev. John Fitzmaurice; Chaplain, Mount House Residential Home for the Elderly, Shrewsbury, 2001–07; *b* 9 March 1935; *m* 1963, Susan Shakerley; three *s* one *d*. *Educ:* RMA Sandhurst; Trinity Hall, Cambridge (BA 1959, MA 1965); Cuddesdon College. Commnd RE, 1955; seconded Gurkha Engineers, 1959–62; resigned commission as Captain, 1964. Deacon 1966, priest 1967; Curate: St Cuthbert, Sheffield, 1966–69; St Helier, Southwark Dio., 1969–75; Vicar of St John's, Hurst, Ashton-under-Lyne, 1975–87; Area Dean of Ashton-under-Lyne, 1983–87; Provost, then Dean, Coventry Cathedral, 1988–2000. Hon. Canon of Manchester Cathedral, 1986. Trustee, Simeon Trust, 2003–. Hon. DLitt Coventry, 1996. *Recreations:* cycling, ski-ing. *Address:* 4 Granville Street, Copthorne, Shrewsbury SY3 8NE. *T:* (01743) 231513.

PETTY, Prof. Michael Charles, PhD, DSc; Professor of Engineering, University of Durham, since 1994; Co-Director, Durham Centre for Molecular and Nanoscale Electronics (formerly for Molecular Electronics), 1987–2013; *b* 30 Dec. 1950; *s* of John Leonard Petty and Doreen Rosemary Petty (*née* Bellarby); *m* 1998, Anne Mathers Brawley; one step *d*. *Educ:* Sussex Univ. (BSc 1st Cl. Hons Electronics 1972; DSc 1994); Imperial Coll., London (PhD 1976). University of Durham: Lectr in Applied Physics, 1976–88; Sen. Lectr, Sch. of Engrg, 1988–94; Chm., Sch. of Engrg, 1997–2000; Sir James Knott Res. Fellow, 2000–01; Chm. Council, St Mary's Coll., 2002–09. Non-exec. Dir, Centre of Excellence for Nanotechnol., Micro and Photonic Systems, 2004–06. *Publications:* Langmuir-Blodgett Films, 1995; Introduction to Molecular Electronics, 1996; Molecular Electronics, 2007; numerous contribs on molecular electronics and nanoelectronics to scientific jls. *Recreations:* Yorkshire Dales, supporter of Crystal Palace FC. *Address:* School of Engineering, University of Durham, South Road, Durham DH1 3LE. *T:* (0191) 334 2419.

PETTY-FITZMAURICE, family name of **Marquess of Lansdowne**.

PEYTON, Kathleen Wendy, MBE 2014; writer (as K. M. Peyton); *b* 2 Aug. 1929; *d* of William Joseph Herald and Ivy Kathleen Herald; *m* 1950, Michael Peyton; two *d*. *Educ:* Wimbledon High Sch.; Manchester Sch. of Art (ATD). Taught art at Northampton High Sch., 1953–55; started writing seriously after birth of first child, although had already had 4 books published. *Publications: as Kathleen Herald:* Sabre, the Horse from the Sea, 1947, USA 1963; The Mandrake, 1949; Crab the Roan, 1953; *as K. M. Peyton:* North to Adventure, 1959, USA 1965; Stormcock Meets Trouble, 1961; The Hard Way Home, 1962; Windfall, 1963, USA (as Sea Fever), 1963; Brownsea Silver, 1964; The Maplin Bird, 1964, USA 1965

(New York Herald Tribune Award, 1965); The Plan for Birdsmarsh, 1965, USA 1966; Thunder in the Sky, 1966, USA 1967; Flambards Trilogy (Guardian Award, 1970; televised, 1977): Flambards, 1967, USA 1968; The Edge of the Cloud, 1969, USA 1969 (Carnegie Medal, 1969); Flambards in Summer, 1969, USA 1970; Fly-by-Night, 1968, USA 1969; Pennington's Seventeenth Summer, 1970, USA (as Pennington's Last Term), 1971; The Beethoven Medal, 1971, USA 1972; The Pattern of Roses, 1972, USA 1973 (televised); Pennington's Heir, 1973, USA 1974; The Team, 1975; The Right-Hand Man, 1977; Prove Yourself a Hero, 1977, USA 1978; A Midsummer Night's Death, 1978, USA 1979; Marion's Angels, 1979, USA 1979; Flambards Divided, 1981; Dear Fred, 1981, USA 1981; Going Home, 1983, USA 1983; Who, Sir? Me, Sir?, 1983 (televised); The Last Ditch, 1984, USA (as Free Rein), 1983; Froggett's Revenge, 1985; The Sound of Distant Cheering, 1986; Downhill All the Way, 1988; Darkling, 1989, USA 1990; Skylark, 1989; No Roses Round the Door, 1990; Poor Badger, 1991, USA 1991; Late to Smile, 1992; The Boy Who Wasn't There, 1992, USA 1992; The Wild Boy, 1993; Snowfall, 1994, USA 1998; The Swallow Tale, 1995; Swallow Summer, 1996; Swallow the Star, 1997; Unquiet Spirits, 1997; Firehead, 1998; Blind Beauty, 1999; Small Gains, 2003; Greater Gains, 2005; Blue Skies and Gunfire, 2006; Minna's Quest, 2007; No Turning Back, 2008; A Long Way from Home, 2009; Paradise House, 2011; When the Siren Sounded, 2013; All that Glitters, 2014; Wild Lily, 2015. *Recreations:* walking, gardening, sailing. *Address:* Rookery Cottage, North Fambridge, Chelmsford, Essex CM3 6LP.

PEYTON, Rt Rev. Dr Nigel; *see* Brechin, Bishop of.

PEYTON, Oliver, Hon. OBE 2012; Founder and Chairman, Peyton and Byrne (formerly Gruppo Ltd); *b* 26 Sept. 1961; *s* of Patrick Peyton; *m* 1999, Charlotte Polizzi; two *s* one *d*. *Educ:* Leicester Poly. (Textiles course 1979). Founder, The Can night club, Brighton, 1981; owner, import business, 1985–92; owner, Gruppo Ltd, 1993; proprietor of restaurants: Atlantic Bar and Grill, Regent Palace Hotel, London, 1994–2005; Coast, Mayfair, 1995–2000 (Best Restaurant, The Times; Restaurant of Year, Time Out, 1998); Mash, Oxford Circus, 1998; Isola, subseq. Iso-bar, Knightsbridge, 1999–2004; The Admiralty, Somerset House, 2000–02 (Best New Restaurant, Time Out); Inn the Park, St James's Park, 2004–; National Dining Rooms and National Café, Nat. Gall., 2006–; Wallace Restaurant, Wallace Collection, 2006–; Meals Café and Bakery, Heal's, Tottenham Ct Rd, 2006–; Food From Kew, Royal Botanic Gardens; Restaurant at the Royal Academy, 2011–; Peyton & Byrne bakeries. *Address:* Peyton Events, Sunley Tower, National Gallery, Trafalgar Square, WC2N 5DN.

PEYTON-JONES, Julia, OBE 2003; Director, Serpentine Gallery, since 1991, and Co-Director, Exhibitions and Programmes; Professor, University of the Arts, London, since 2008; *b* 18 Feb. 1952; *d* of late Jeremy Norman Peyton-Jones and Rhona Gertrude Jean (*née* Wood); *m* 1975, Prosper Riley-Smith (marr. diss. 1985). *Educ:* Tudor Hall; Byam Shaw Sch. of Drawing and Painting (Dip BSD; LCAD); Royal Coll. of Art (MA; Sen. Fellow, 2008). LWT/Byam Shaw Bursary, 1973–74, 1974–75; John Minton Travelling Schol., 1978. Started 20th century Picture Dept, Phillips, auctioneers, 1974–75; Lectr, Painting and Humanities Depts, Edinburgh Sch. of Art, 1978–79; Organiser: Atlantis Gall., London, 1980–81; Wapping Artists' Open Studios Exhibn, 1981–82; Tolly Cobbold Eastern Arts 4th Nat. Exhibn, Cambridge and tour, 1982–84; Raoul Dufy 1877–1953 exhibn, Hayward Gall., 1983–84; Linbury Prize for Stage Design (selection and exhibn), 1986–87 (Mem., Exec. Cttee, 1988–96); Sponsorship Officer, Arts Council and S Bank Bd, 1984–87; Curator, Hayward Gall., 1988–91. Arts Council: Collection Purchaser, 1989–90; Mem., Visual Arts Projects Cttee, 1991–93; Mem., Visual Arts, Photography and Architecture Panel, 1994–96. Member: Westminster Public Art Adv. Panel, 1996–; Artists' Film and Video Adv. Panel, 1997–99. Jury Member: Citibank Private Banking Photography Prize, 1997; BP Portrait Award, NPG, 1997–99; Turner Prize, 2000. Trustee: Public Art Develt Trust, 1987–88; Chisenhale Trust, 1987–89; New Contemporaries Exhibn, 1988–90; The Place, 2002. Painter, 1974–87; exhibitions include: Riverside Studios (individual), 1978; ICA, 1973; John Moores, Liverpool, 1978; Royal Scottish Acad., 1979. Mem. Ct of Govs, London Inst., 1998–2002. Hon. FRIBA 2003; Hon. FRCA 1997. *Recreations:* contemporary arts in general, visual arts in particular. *Address:* Serpentine Gallery, Kensington Gardens, W2 3XA.

PFEIFFER, Michelle; actress; *b* Santa Ana, Calif, 29 April 1958; *d* of late Dick Pfeiffer and of Donna Pfeiffer; *m* 1st, 1981, Peter Horton (marr. diss.); 2nd, 1993, David E. Kelley; one *s*; one adopted *d*. *Educ:* Fountain High Valley Sch., Calif. Co-owner, Via Rosa (production co.), 1989–2001. *Theatre:* Playground in the Fall, LA, 1981; Twelfth Night, NY 1989. *Films include:* Falling in Love Again, 1980; Grease 2, 1982; Scarface, 1983; Into the Night, Ladyhawke, 1985; Sweet Liberty, 1986; Amazon Women on the Moon, The Witches of Eastwick, 1987; Married to the Mob, 1988; Tequila Sunrise, Dangerous Liaisons, The Fabulous Baker Boys (Best Actress, Golden Globe Awards, 1990), 1989; The Russia House, 1990; Frankie and Johnny, 1991; Batman Returns, 1992; Love Field, 1993; The Age of Innocence, Wolf, My Posse Don't Do Homework, 1994; Dangerous Minds, Up Close and Personal, To Gillian on her 37th Birthday, 1996; One Fine Day (also exec. prod.), Privacy, 1997; A Thousand Acres (also prod.), 1998; The Deep End of the Ocean, A Midsummer Night's Dream, 1999; The Story of Us, What Lies Beneath, 2000; I Am Sam, 2002; White Oleander, 2003; Hairspray, Stardust, 2007; Chéri, Personal Effects, 2009; Dark Shadows, 2012; The Family, 2013. *Television includes:* Delta House, The Solitary Man, 1979; B. A. D. Cats, 1980; Collie and Son, Splendour in the Grass, The Children Nobody Wanted, 1981; One Too Many, 1983; Power, Passion and Murder, Natica Jackson, 1987. *Address:* c/o CAA, 2000 Avenue of the Stars, Los Angeles, CA 90067, USA.

PFIRTER, Rogelio (Francisco Emilio); Director-General, Technical Secretariat, Organization for the Prohibition of Chemical Weapons, 2002–10; *b* 25 Aug. 1948; *s* of Rogelio and Amanda Pfirter von Mayenfisch; *m* 1980, Isabel Serantes Braun. *Educ:* Colegio Inmaculada SJ, Argentina; Universidad de Litoral (grad as lawyer); Inst. of Foreign Service, Argentina. Third Sec., S America Dept, 1974; Second, then First Sec., Perm. Mission to UN, 1975–80; Counsellor: Undersecretariat of Foreign Affairs, 1980–81; London, 1982; Minister Counsellor, then Minister Plenipotentiary, Perm. Mission to UN, 1982–90; Alternate Perm. Rep. to UN, 1989; Dep. Hd, Foreign Minister's Cabinet, 1990–91; Dir, Internat. Security, Nuclear and Space Affairs, 1991; Under-Sec., Foreign Policy, 1992; Mem., Posting and Promotion Bd, 1993–95; Argentine Ambassador to UK, 1995–2000; Pres., Argentine Delegn, River Plate Commn, 2000–02; Under-Sec., Foreign Policy, 2002. Mem., Bd of Dirs, Argentine Nat. Commn for Space Activities, 1994–95. Pres., General Assembly, IMO, 1993–97; Member: UN Adv. Bd on Disarmament Matters, 1993–96; Consulting Bd, G8 Global Partnership's Internat. Working Gp, 2011–12; IISS, 2012–; Vice Chm., Global Agenda Council on Nuclear, Biol and Chemical Weapons, World Econ. Forum, 2010–12. Laurea ad hon. in Industrial Chem., Bologna, 2010. Interfaith Award, Internat. Council of Christians and Jews, 1998; City Council Medal, City of Ieper, Belgium. Order of Merit, Cavaliere di Gran Croce (Italy), 1992; Order of Isabel la Católica (Spain), 1994; Nat. Order of Merit in the Great Cross (Colombia), 2005; Sigillum of the Alma Mater Studiorum (Bologna), 2006; Medal of Honour of Pope Benedict XVI, 2006; Order of Duke Branimira (Croatia), 2006; Grand Cross: Order of Merit (Chile), 2010; Order of Merit (Germany), 2010; Officier, Légion d'Honneur (France), 2010; Commander, Order of Orange-Nassau (Netherlands), 2010. *Publications:* (jtly) Cuentos Originales, 1965; articles on policy. *Address:* Montevideo 1790, 6th Floor, 1021 Buenos Aires, Argentina. *Clubs:* White's; Círculo de Armas (Buenos Aires).

PHAROAH, Prof. Peter Oswald Derrick, MD; FRCP, FRCPCH, FFPHM; Professor of Public Health (formerly of Community Health), University of Liverpool, 1979–97, now Professor Emeritus; *b* 19 May 1934; *s* of Oswald Higgins Pharoah and Phyllis Christine Gahan; *m* 1960, Margaret Rose McMinn; three *s* one *d*. *Educ:* Lawrence Memorial Royal Military School, Lovedale, India; Palmers School, Grays, Essex; St Mary's Hospital Medical School. MD, MSc. Graduated, 1958; Med. House Officer and Med. Registrar appointments at various London Hosps, 1958–63; MO and Research MO, Dept of Public Health, Papua New Guinea, 1963–74; Sen. Lectr in Community Health, London School of Hygiene and Tropical Medicine, 1974–79. *Publications:* Endemic Cretinism, 1971. *Recreations:* walking, philately. *Address:* 11 Fawley Road, Liverpool L18 9TE. *T:* (0151) 724 4896.

PHELAN, Sean Patrick; Founder, 1995, and Chairman, 1995–2007, Multimap.com (sold to Microsoft, 2007); *b* 8 April 1958; *s* of Anthony Michael Phelan and Gwendoline Theresa Phelan (*née* Stock); partner, Audrey Mandela. *Educ:* St Ignatius Coll., Enfield; Univ. of Sussex (BSc Electronic Engrg); Institute Theseus, Sophia Antipolis, France (MBA). With Geac Computers, 1982–89; Principal Analyst, Yankee Gp Europe, 1991–95; Principal Consultant, Telecommunications and Media Convergence Practice, KPMG, 1995. Active early-stage investor through two angel networks, Cambridge Angels and London Business Sch.'s E100. *Recreations:* sailing, travel. *Address:* 2 Hampstead Hill Gardens, NW3 2PL.

PHELOUNG, Barrington Somers James; composer, conductor and classical guitarist; *b* Manley, Sydney, NSW; *s* of John Syrell Pheloung and Adel Monica Pheloung; *m* Heather Kate; three *s* one *d*. *Educ:* St Aloysius' Coll., Milsons Point, Sydney; Royal Coll. of Music, London. Musical Dir/Advr and Principal Conductor, London Contemporary Dance Theatre, 1979–95. Conducting début, Royal Gala Performance, Covent Garden, 1988. Vis. Prof. of Composition, RCM. Freelance composer of ballet and contemporary dance scores, string quartets, concertos, film and television scores, 1984–; *television scores* include: Boon, 1985; Inspector Morse, 1987–2000; Cinder Path, 1994; Dalziel and Pascoe, 1995–98; Lewis, 2007–12; Red Riding Trilogy, 2009; *film scores* include: Truly Madly Deeply, 1991; Nostradamus, 1994; Hilary and Jackie, 1998; Shopgirl, 2005; And When Did You Last See Your Father?, 2007; *theatre* includes: Made in Bangkok, Aldwych, 1986; Sweet Bird of Youth, NY, 1986; After the Fall, NT, 1990; The Graduate, Gielgud, 2000, transf. NY. *Recreations:* parenting, cricket, surfing. *Address:* Andrews, High Roding, Dunmow, Essex CM6 1NQ. *E:* barrington@pheloung.co.uk. *Clubs:* MCC, Groucho.

PHELPS, Annamarie; Chairman, British Rowing, since 2013; Vice Chairman, British Paralympic Association, since 2013; *b* London, 24 May 1966; *d* of Vincent Stapleton and Ethna Stapleton; *m* 1997, Richard Charles Phelps; two *s* one *d*. *Educ:* Watford Grammar Sch. for Girls; Loreto Coll., St Albans; St John's Coll., Cambridge (BA Geog. 1987). Rowing: World Championships: Silver Medal, lightweight coxless four, Vienna 1991, Montreal 1992, Indianapolis 1994; Gold Medal, lightweight coxless four, Prague 1993; Bronze, lightweight coxless 4, Commonwealth Regatta, London Ont 1994; Indoor Rowing World Championships: World Champion, lightweight women, 1992–94; world record holder, lightweight women, 1992–95. Fine Art Society, London: Decorative Arts Dir, 1994–2002; non-exec. Dir, 2002–; independent decorative arts specialist, 2002–. Editor, Decorative Art Soc. Jl, 2007–12. Dir, British Rowing (formerly Amateur Rowing Assoc.), 1996–; Trustee, British Paralympic Assoc., 2008–. Chm., Cambridge Univ. Women's Boat Club, 2010–14; Dir, Boat Race Co. Ltd, 2012–14. Steward, Henley Royal Regatta, 2002–. Freeman: City of London, 2006; Watermen and Lightermen's Co., 2012; Goldsmiths' Co., 2006 (Liveryman, 2012). *Publications:* as Annamarie Stapleton: (jtly) Austerity to Affluence: British art and design 1945–1962, 1997; John Moyr Smith, 1839–1912: a Victorian designer, 2002; (jtly) Artists' Textiles 1945–1970, 2002; (jtly) Jacqueline Groag: Wiener Werkstatte to American Modern, 2009; (jtly) Artists' Textiles in Britain and America 1940–1976, 2012; (contrib.) The Ambassador Magazine, 2012; (jtly) Pop!: design culture fashion, 2012; contrib. articles to Country Life, Decorative Art Soc. Jl, Rowing and Regatta Mag. *Address:* British Rowing, 6 Lower Mall, W6 9DJ. *T:* (020) 8237 6700. *Clubs:* Chelsea Arts; Thames Rowing; Cambridge Univ. Women's Boat.

PHELPS, Prof. Edmund Strother, PhD; McVickar Professor of Political Economy, since 1982, and Director, Center on Capitalism and Society, since 2001, Columbia University, New York; Dean, New Huadu Business School, Minjiang University, since 2010; *b* 26 July 1933; *s* of Edmund Strother Phelps and Florence Esther Phelps (*née* Stone); *m* 1974, Viviana Regina Montdor. *Educ:* Amherst Coll., (BA 1955); Yale Univ. (PhD 1959). Economist, RAND Corp., 1959–60; Asst Prof., 1960–62, Associate Prof., 1963–66, Yale Univ.; Professor of Economics: Univ. of Pennsylvania, 1966–71; Columbia Univ., 1971–78, 1979–82; New York Univ., 1978–79. Nobel Prize in Economics, 2006. *Publications:* Fiscal Neutrality Toward Economic Growth, 1965; Golden Rules of Economic Growth, 1966; (jtly) Microeconomic Foundations of Employment and Inflation Theory, 1970; Inflation Policy and Unemployment Theory, 1972; Studies in Macroeconomic Theory, vol. 1, 1979, vol. 2, 1980; Political Economy, 1985; (jtly) The Slump in Europe, 1988; Structural Slumps, 1994 (trans. Chinese, 2003); Rewarding Work, 1997; Enterprise and Inclusion in the Italian Economy, 2002; Mass Flourishing, 2013; articles in learned jls. *Address:* Department of Economics, Columbia University, 1004 International Affairs Building, 420 West 118th Street, New York, NY 10027, USA; (home) 45 East 89th Street, New York, NY 10128–1251, USA.

PHELPS, Maurice Arthur; human resource consultant, since 1989; Managing Director, Maurice Phelps Associates, since 1989; Managing Partner, E. P. First, since 2001 (Managing Partner, Emslie Phelps Consultancy Group, 1990–2001); *b* 17 May 1935; *s* of H. T. Phelps; *m* 1960, Elizabeth Anne Hurley; two *s* one *d*. *Educ:* Wandsworth School; Corpus Christi College, Oxford Univ. BA Hons Modern History. Shell Chemical Co. Ltd, 1959–68; Group Personnel Planning Adviser, Pilkington Bros Ltd, 1968–70; Group Personnel Dir, Unicorn Industries Ltd, 1970–72; Dir of Labour and Staff Relations, W Midland Passenger Transport Exec., 1973–77; Dir of Personnel, Heavy Vehicle Div., Leyland Vehicles Ltd, 1977–80; Bd Mem. for Personnel and Industrial Relations, 1980–87, non-exec. Bd Mem., 1987–90, British Shipbuilders; Dir, British Ferries, and Dep. Chm. and HR Dir, Sealink UK Ltd, 1987–89. Jt Founding Partner, Emslie Phelps Associates, subseq. Emslie Phelps First, 1989–2003; Human Resource Consultant: Value Through People Ltd, 1991–; Saratoga (Europe), 1993–. Freeman: City of London, 1995; Co. of Watermen and Lightermen, 1995. *Publications:* The People Policy Audit, 1999; Human Resources Benchmarking, 2002; A Thameside Family, 2007; The Adventures of Mr Golly, 2007; The Phelps Dynasty, 2012. *Address:* Abbotsfield, Goring Heath, S Oxon RG8 7SA.

PHILIP, Rt Hon. Lord; Alexander Morrison Philip; PC 2005; a Senator of the College of Justice in Scotland, 1996–2007; *b* 3 Aug. 1942; *s* of late Alexander Philip, OBE and Isobel Thomson Morrison; *m* 1971, Shona Mary Macrae (marr. diss.); three *s*. *Educ:* High School of Glasgow; St Andrews University (MA 1963); Glasgow University (LLB 1965). Solicitor, 1967–72; Advocate 1973; Advocate-Depute, 1982–85; QC (Scotland), 1984; Chm., Scottish Land Court, 1993–96; Pres., Lands Tribunal for Scotland, 1993–96. Chm., Medical Appeal Tribunals, 1988–92. Chm., Mull of Kintyre Rev., 2010–11. *Publications:* contrib. Oxford DNB. *Recreations:* golf, piping (Hon. Pipe-Major, Royal Scottish Pipers Soc., 2011–13). *Clubs:* Royal Scottish Pipers' Society (Edinburgh); Hon. Co. of Edinburgh Golfers, Prestwick Golf.

PHILIP, Alexander Morrison; *see* Philip, Rt Hon. Lord.

PHILIPPE, André J., Hon. GCVO 1972; Dr-en-Droit; Luxembourg Ambassador to the United States of America, 1987–91; *b* Luxembourg City, 28 June 1926. Barrister-at-Law,

Luxembourg, 1951–52. Joined Luxembourg Diplomatic Service, 1952; Dep. to Dir of Pol Affairs, Min. of Foreign Affairs, 1952–54; Dep. Perm. Rep. to NATO, 1954–61 and to OECD, 1959–61; Dir of Protocol and Legal Adviser, Min. of For. Affairs, 1961–68; Ambassador and Perm. Rep. to UN and Consul-Gen., New York, 1968–72 (Vice-Pres., 24th Session of Gen. Assembly of UN, 1969); Ambassador to UK, Perm. Rep. to Council of WEU, and concurrently Ambassador to Ireland and Iceland, 1972–78; Ambassador to France, 1978–84; Ambassador to UN, NY, 1984–87. Commander: Order of Adolphe Nassau (Luxembourg); Légion d'Honneur (France); Grand Officer: Order of Merit (Luxembourg), 1983; Order of Oaken Crown (Luxembourg), 1988.

PHILIPPS, family name of **Viscount St Davids** and **Baron Milford**.

PHILIPPS, Charles Edward Laurence; Chief Executive, Amlin plc, since 1999; *b* 20 Jan. 1959; *s* of Peter Anthony Philipps and Suzannah Margaret Philipps; *m* 1984, Fiona Land (marr. diss. 2011); one *s* two *d*. *Educ:* Eton Coll. Chartered Accountant, 1983. Binder Hamlyn, 1979–83; County Bank, subseq. NatWest Markets Corporate Finance, 1983–97 (Dir, 1993–97); Finance Dir, Angerstein Underwriting Trust plc, 1997–99. Non-exec. Dir, Great Portland Estates plc, 2014–. Pres., Insce Inst. of London, 2009–10. Trustee, Outward Bound Trust, 2011–. *Recreations:* country pursuits, golf. *Address:* c/o Amlin plc, St Helen's, 1 Undershaft, EC3A 8ND. *T:* (020) 7746 1000, *Fax:* (020) 7746 1696. *Clubs:* Boodle's; Jockey Club Rooms (Newmarket); Royal St George's Golf, Royal Worlington and Newmarket Golf.

PHILIPPS, Nicola Jane; artist, predominantly portraiture, since 1988; *b* London, 27 Aug. 1964; *d* of Jeremy and Susan Philipps. *Educ:* St Mary's Sch., Wantage; Queensgate Sch., London; City & Guilds Art Sch.; Studio Cecil Graves, Florence. *Solo exhibitions:* Malcolm Innes Gall., Bury St James's, 1997; Arndean Gall., 2001, 2003, 2007; *group exhibitions* include: Malcolm Innes Gall., Knightsbridge, 1994, Bury St James's, 1995; Fine Art Commns, Art London, 2002–08, Internat. Art Fair, Palm Beach, 2008, Duke St, 2013; BP Portrait Exhibn, NPG, 2005, 2009. Commissions include: Judge Michael Boudin, commnd by US Court of Appeals for First Circuit, Boston, 2009; Hugh Bonneville, 2009; Princes William and Henry of Wales, commnd by NPG, 2010; Princes William and Henry of Wales, commnd by Eton Coll., 2010; Duke and Duchess of Northumberland, 2011; Duchess of Cambridge, commnd by the Prince of Wales, 2012; Hon. Louis B. Susman, commnd by American Embassy, London, 2012; The Queen, commnd by Royal Mail, 2013; Dean of Westminster, 2014; Fiona Bruce, 2014; Simon Weston, commnd by NPG, 2014; Baron George; Baron Richardson of Duntisbourne. *Publications:* Philipps: a family of artists at Picton, 2010. *Recreations:* riding, ski-ing, bridge. *Address:* c/o Fine Art Commissions Ltd, 34 Duke Street, St James's, SW1Y 6DF. *E:* nicky@nickyphilipps.com. *Club:* Chelsea Arts.

PHILIPS, Dalton; *see* Philips, T. D. D.

PHILIPS, Justin Robin Drew; District Judge (Magistrates' Courts) (formerly Metropolitan Stipendiary Magistrate), 1989–2012; Lead Judge, Dedicated Drug Court, London, 2005–12; *b* 18 July 1948; *s* of late Albert Lewis Philips, Solicitor and Henrietta Philips (*née* Woolfson). *Educ:* John Lyon School, Harrow; College of Law, London. Called to the Bar, Gray's Inn, 1969; practised criminal bar, 1970–89; Chm., Youth Court, 1993–98; an Asst Recorder, 1994–99; a Recorder, 1999–2006. Mem., Adv. Council on Misuse of Drugs, 2008–12; Seminar Leader, MSc Adolescent Addiction, Keele Univ., 2009. Hon. Sec., Hendon Reform Synagogue, 1990–94 (Mem. Council, 1979–90). Trustee, Tzedek Charity, 1993–2008; Patron: DrugFam, 2008–; Kids Count, 2010–; Drugsline, 2011–12. *Recreations:* music, Judaic studies, attempting to keep fit. *Address:* Lev Yerushalayim, PO Box 71156, Jerusalem 9426201, Israel.

PHILIPS, (Timothy David) Dalton; Chief Executive Officer, Wm Morrison Supermarkets plc, 2010–15; *b* Dublin; *s* of Tim Philips and Susan Philips; *m* 1998, Penny; two *s* one *d*. *Educ:* St Gerard's Sch., Bray; St Columba's Sch., Dublin; Stowe Sch.; University Coll., Dublin (BA Hons 1991); Harvard Business Sch. (MBA 1998). Jardine Matheson, Hong Kong, 1993–96; Wal-Mart, 1998–2005; CEO, Brown Thomas Gp, Ire., 2005–07; Chief Operating Officer, Loblaw Cos Ltd, Canada, 2007–10. *Recreations:* marathon running, church affairs, wine and food. *Address:* Ballinacoola, Glenealy, Wicklow, Ireland.

PHILIPSON-STOW, Sir (Robert) Matthew, 6th Bt *cr* 1907, of Cape Town, Colony of Cape of Good Hope, and Blackdown House, Lodsworth, Co. Sussex; professional engineer with MacViro Consultants Inc., 1989–2006; *b* 29 Aug. 1953; *s* of Sir Christopher Philipson-Stow, 5th Bt, DFC and Elizabeth Nairn Philipson-Stow (*née* Trees); *S* father 2005, but his name does not appear on the Official Roll of the Baronetage; *m* 2001, Wendy Bracken (*née* Harrel); one step *d*. *Educ:* Univ. of Waterloo (BASc 1978). PEng. MacLaren Engineers Inc., 1978–89. *Recreations:* cabinetry, sailing, reading, lawn bowling, walking. *Heir:* *b* Rowland Frederick Philipson-Stow [*b* 2 Sept. 1954; *m* 1979, Mary Susan (*née* Stroud); one *s* one *d*]. *Address:* 3760 Crestview Road, Victoria, BC V8P 5C6, Canada. *E:* stowmatthew@gmail.com.

PHILIPSZ, Susan Mary, OBE 2014; artist; *b* Glasgow, 21 Nov. 1965; *d* of John Philipsz and Susan Philipsz; *m* 2009, Eoghan McTigue. *Educ:* Duncan of Jordanstone Coll., Dundee (BA Fine Art); Univ. of Ulster, Belfast (MA Fine Art 1995). Mem., Mgt Cttee, Catalyst Arts, Belfast, 1996–98; Founder, Grassy Knoll Prodns, Belfast, 1998–. Artist in residence: Internat. Studio Prog., MoMA PS1, NY, 2000–01; Residency Prog., Kunst Werke eV, Berlin, 2001–02. *Solo exhibitions* include: Day is Done (perm. sound installation), Governor's Island, NY, 2013; K21 Ständehaus, Kunstsammlung Nordrhein-Westfalen, Dusseldorf, 2013; Susan Philipsz, Hamburger Bahnhof, Berlin, 2014; *group exhibitions* include: Skulptur Projekte Münster 07, Münster, 2007; Solomon R. Guggenheim Mus., NY, 2010; dOCUMENTA (13), Kassel, 2012; Mus. of Modern Art, NY, 2013. Turner Prize, 2010. *Publications: relevant publication:* Susan Philipsz: projects 2007–12 (ed J. Lingwood and B. Franzen), 2013. *Address:* Starnberger Strasse 2, 10781 Berlin, Germany.

PHILLIMORE, family name of **Baron Phillimore**.

PHILLIMORE, 5th Baron *cr* 1918, of Shiplake, Oxfordshire; **Francis Stephen Phillimore;** Bt 1881; land manager; *b* 25 Nov. 1944; *o s* of 4th Baron Phillimore and Anne Elizabeth Phillimore (*d* 1995), *e d* of Major Arthur Algernon Dorrien Smith, DSO; *S* father, 1994; *m* 1971, Nathalie Berthe Louisa Pequin; two *s* one *d*. *Educ:* Eton Coll.; Trinity Coll., Cambridge (BA). Called to the Bar, Middle Temple, 1972; in practice as barrister, 1972–2002. Member: Shiplake Parish Council, 1995–2011 (Chm., 1998–2003); Eye and Dunsden Parish Council, 2003–15. Mem., Ct of Assistants, Fishmongers' Co., 2001–. Trustee, Venice in Peril Fund, 1996–2013. Steward, Hurlingham Polo Assoc., 1998–. *Recreations:* polo, sailing, the arts, shooting, Venetian rowing, travel. *Heir:* *er s* Hon. Tristan Anthony Stephen Phillimore [*b* 18 Aug. 1977; *m* 2013, Jemma Tuomey; one *d*]. *Address:* Coppid Hall, Binfield Heath, Henley-on-Thames, Oxon RG9 4JR. *T:* (01491) 573174. *Clubs:* Brooks's, Pratt's, City Barge; Royal Yacht Squadron.

PHILLIMORE, (John) Roger (Broughton); Chairman, Lonmin plc, 2009–14; *b* Johannesburg, 21 June 1949; *s* of Michael and Felicity Phillimore; *m* 1981, Virginia Anne Crookshank. *Educ:* St Aidan's Coll., Grahamstown, SA; Univ. of Witwatersrand (BA Hons Applied Econs). Joined Anglo American, 1972; Divl Manager, Gold Div., 1978; Sec. to Exec. Cttee, 1978–81; Jt Man. Dir, Minorco, 1981–92. Dir, Harry Winston Diamond Corp., 1994–2012. *Recreations:* music, golf, equestrian. *Address:* Little Bentley Farm, Mottisfont, Romsey, Hants SO51 0LT. *Clubs:* Boodle's; Rand; Gassin Golf.

PHILLIPS, family name of **Barons Phillips of Sudbury** and **Phillips of Worth Matravers**.

PHILLIPS OF SUDBURY, Baron *cr* 1998 (Life Peer), of Sudbury in the co. of Suffolk; **Andrew Wyndham Phillips,** OBE 1996; founding Partner, Bates, Wells & Braithwaite, solicitors, London, 1970; freelance journalist; *b* 15 March 1939; *s* of late Alan Clifford Phillips and Dorothy Alice Phillips (*née* Wyndham); *m* 1968, Penelope Ann Bennett; one *s* two *d*. *Educ:* Uppingham; Trinity Hall, Cambridge (BA 1962). Qualified solicitor, 1964. Co-founder, 1971 and first Chm., Legal Action Gp; founder and first Chm., 1989–2000, first Pres., 2000–, Citizenship Foundn; Initiator and First Pres., Solicitors' Pro Bono Gp (Law Works), 1997–; Mem., Nat. Lottery Charities Bd, 1994–96. Mem., H of L, 1998–2015. Trustee, Scott Trust (Guardian/Observer), 1994–2004. Pres., British-Iranian Chamber of Commerce, 2002–. Trustee and Patron of various charities. Vice-Pres., Gainsborough's House. Presenter, London Programme, LWT, 1980–81; regular broadcaster, incl. Legal Eagle, Jimmy Young Show, BBC Radio Two, 1976–2001. Chancellor, Univ. of Essex, 2003–13. Contested: (Lab) Harwich, 1970; (L) Saffron Walden, July 1977 and 1979; (L/Alliance) Gainsborough and Horncastle, 1983; (L) NE Essex, European Parlt, 1979. *Publications:* The Living Law; Charitable Status: a practical handbook, 1980, 6th edn 2008; (jtly) Charity Investment: law and practice. *Recreations:* the arts, local history, architecture, golf, cricket, walking. *Address:* River House, The Croft, Sudbury, Suffolk CO10 1HW. *T:* (01787) 882151.

PHILLIPS OF WORTH MATRAVERS, Baron *cr* 1999 (Life Peer), of Belsize Park in the London Borough of Camden; **Nicholas Addison Phillips,** KG 2011; Kt 1987; PC 1995; President: of the Supreme Court of the United Kingdom, 2009–12 (Senior Lord of Appeal in Ordinary, 2008–09); Qatar International Court and Dispute Resolution Centre, since 2012; non-permanent Judge, Court of Final Appeal, Hong Kong, since 2013; *b* 21 Jan. 1938; *m* 1972, Christylle Marie-Thérèse Rouffiac (*née* Doreau); two *d*, and one step *s* one step *d*. *Educ:* Bryanston Sch.; King's Coll., Cambridge (MA; Hon. Fellow, 2004). Nat. Service with RN; commnd RNVR, 1956–58. Called to Bar, Middle Temple (Harmsworth Scholar), 1962, Bencher, 1984. In practice at Bar, 1962–87; Jun. Counsel to Minister of Defence and to Treasury in Admiralty matters, 1973–78; QC 1978; a Recorder, 1982–87; a Judge of High Court of Justice, QBD, 1987–95; a Lord Justice of Appeal, 1995–98; a Lord of Appeal in Ordinary, 1999–2000; Master of the Rolls, 2000–05; Hd of Civil Justice, 2000–05; Lord Chief Justice, 2005–08. Mem., Panel of Wreck Comrs, 1979–87. Chairman: Law Adv. Cttee, British Council, 1991–97; Council of Legal Educn, 1992–97; BSE Inquiry, 1998–2000; Lord Chancellor's Adv. Cttee on Public Records, 2000–05; European Maritime Law Orgn, 2012–; Member: Adv. Council, Inst. of Eur. and Comparative Law, 1999–2007; Council of Mgt, British Inst. of Internat. and Comparative Law, 1999–; Adv. Council, Inst. of Global Law, 2000–; President: British Maritime Law Assoc., 2005– (Vice Pres., 1993–2005); Network of Presidents of Supreme Cts of EC, 2006–08. Patron, CIArb, 2011–14. Trustee, Magna Carta Trust, 2000–05. Governor, Bryanston Sch., 1975–2008 (Chm. of Governors, 1981–2008); Visitor: Nuffield Coll., Oxford, 2000–05; UCL, 2000–05; Darwin Coll., Cambridge, 2005–08; Chancellor, Bournemouth Univ., 2009–; Visiting Fellow: Dixon Poon Sch. of Law, KCL, 2013–; Oxford Inst. of Islamic Studies and Mansfield Coll., Oxford, 2013–; Vis. Prof., Law Faculty, Univ. of Oxford, 2014–Dec. 2016. Liveryman: Drapers' Co., 2005–; Shipwrights' Co., 2007–. Hon. Fellow: Soc. of Advanced Legal Studies, 1999–; UCL, 2006; Hughes Hall, Cambridge, 2012. Hon. Bencher, Gray's Inn, 2009. Hon. LLD: Exeter, 1998; Birmingham, 2003; London, 2004; Wolverhampton, 2009; Washington and Lee, Lexington, Va, 2009; Wake Forest, 2010; Hon. DCL City, 2003; Hon. LLD: Internat. Inst. of Maritime Law, 2007; BPP Univ., 2014. *Recreations:* sea, mountains, Mauzac. *Address:* House of Lords, SW1A 0PW. *Clubs:* Brooks's, Garrick.

PHILLIPS, Adam; psychoanalyst in private practice; writer; *b* 19 Sept. 1954; *s* of Eric and Jacqueline Phillips; partner, Judith Clark; two *d* one *s*. *Educ:* Clifton Coll., Bristol; St John's Coll., Oxford. Principal Child Psychotherapist, Charing Cross Hosp., 1990–97. Vis. Prof., English Dept, Univ. of York, 2006–09. Gen. Ed., New Penguin Freud, 2003–. *Publications:* Winnicott, 1988; On Kissing, Tickling and Being Bored, 1992; On Flirtation, 1994; Terrors and Experts, 1995; Monogamy, 1996; The Beast in the Nursery, 1997; Darwin's Worms, 1999; Promises, Promises, 2000; Houdini's Box, 2001; Equals, 2002; Going Sane, 2005; Side-Effects, 2007; (with L. Bersani) Intimacies, 2008; (with B. Taylor) On Kindness, 2009; (with J. Clark) The Concise Dictionary of Dress, 2010; On Balance, 2010; Missing Out: in praise of the unlived life, 2012; Becoming Freud: the making of a psychoanalyst, 2014.

PHILLIPS, Adrian Alexander Christian, CBE 1998; freelance environmental consultant; *b* 11 Jan. 1940; *s* of Eric Lawrance Phillips, CMG and Phyllis Phillips (*née* Bray); *m* 1963, Cassandra Frances Elaïs Hubback, MA Oxon, *d* of D. F. Hubback, CB; two *s*. *Educ:* The Hall, Hampstead; Westminster Sch.; Christ Church, Oxford (1st Cl. Hons MA Geography); University Coll. London (DipT&CP). MRTPI 1966; FRGS 1984. Planning Services, Min. of Housing and Local Govt, 1962–68; Sen. Research Officer and Asst Director, Countryside Commission, 1968–74; Special Asst, Executive Director, United Nations Environment Programme (UNEP), Nairobi, Kenya, 1974–75; Head, Programme Coordination Unit, UNEP, Nairobi, 1975–78; Director of Programmes, IUCN, Switzerland, 1978–81; Dir, then Dir Gen., Countryside Commn, 1981–92; Prof. of Countryside and Envmtl Planning, City and Regl Planning Dept, UWCC, 1992–2001. Chairman: Commn on Nat. Parks and Protected Areas, IUCN, 1994–96 (Dep. Chm., 1988–94); World Commn on Protected Areas, IUCN, 1996–2000; Sen. Advr on World Heritage, IUCN, 2000–04; Chm., Policy Cttee, CPRE, 2001–06. Chm., Cttee for Wales, RSPB, 1992–98. Trustee: WWF UK, 1997–2003; Woodland Trust, 2004–08; National Trust, 2005–12 (Mem., SW Regl Adv. Bd, 2013–); Chm., Glos Envmtl Trust, 2001–09; Sec. of State Appointee, Cotswold Conservation Bd, 2005–15. FRSA 1983. Hon. FLI. *Publications:* (ed jtly) Countryside Planning, 2004; articles and chapters on envmtl and conservation topics. *Recreations:* walking, stroking the cat. *Address:* 30 Painswick Road, Cheltenham, Glos GL50 2HA. *T:* (01386) 576147.

PHILLIPS, Alan; *see* Phillips, His Honour D. A.

PHILLIPS, Alan David John, CMG 1999; international adviser on human and minority rights; Executive Director, Minority Rights Group, 1989–2000; *b* 4 April 1947; *s* of Reginald and Irene Phillips; *m* 1970, Hilary Siddell; one *s* two *d*. *Educ:* Brighton Coll.; Warwick Univ. (BSc Hons 1st class Physics; Pres., Students' Union, 1968–69). Systems Auditor, Rank Xerox, 1970–73; Gen. Sec., World Univ. Service (UK), 1973–81; Dep. Dir, British Refugee Council, 1982–89. NGO Expert to UK and EC delegns at intergovtl Human Rights fora, 1991–; UK nominated ind. expert, 1998–, Vice Pres., 1999–2002, Pres., 2006–10, Council of Europe Adv. Cttee, Framework Convention on Nat. Minorities (contrib., Review, 2012). Internat. Lectr on Minority Rights, 2011–. Advr to Prime Minister of Kosovo, 2004–06. Mem., Cttee, Council for Assisting Refugee Academics, 1998–2005. Advr on Roma integration to EU, OSCE and Council of Europe, 2003–. Chairman: Brighton and Hove Organic Gardening, 2001–; Seedy Sunday, 2011–; Brighton and Hove Allotment Fedn, 2013–. Hon. LLD Warwick, 2005. Caballero Comandante, Orden B. O'Higgins (Chile), 2010. *Publications:* British Aid for Overseas Students, 1980; UN Minority Rights Declaration, 1993; Universal Minority Rights, 1995; (contrib.) World Directory of Minorities, 1997; Ethnicity, Pluralism and Human Rights, 2003; (contrib.) Mechanisms for the Implementation of Minority Rights, 2004. *Recreations:* family, organic gardening, swimming, education. *E:* alan@alanphillips.org. *Club:* Brighton and Hove Allotment Soc.

PHILLIPS, Alice Mary; Headteacher, St Catherine's School, Bramley, since 2000; *b* 1 Aug. 1960; *d* of David and Lesley Alban; *m* 1986, Simon John Phillips; one *d*. *Educ:* Kendal High

Sch.; Newnham Coll., Cambridge (BA 1982). Teacher of English, 1983–93, Hd, Dept of English, 1989–93, Royal Masonic Sch., Rickmansworth; Dep. Hd, Tormead Sch., 1993–99. Mem. Council, GSA, 2008– (Pres., 2014). MInstD 2004. *Recreations:* gardening, singing, cooking, music, ballet. *Address:* St Catherine's School, Bramley, Surrey GU5 0DF. *T:* (01483) 899605, *Fax:* (01483) 899608. *E:* headmistress@stcatherines.info. *Clubs:* Lansdowne, University Women's.

PHILLIPS, Andrew Bassett; Head, Legal Deposit Review, British Library, 1996–99; *b* 26 Sept. 1945; *s* of William Phillips and Doreen (*née* Harris); *m* 1976, Valerie Cuthbert; two *s* one *d. Educ:* Newport High Sch.; Reading Univ. (BA). MCLIP. British Nat. Bibliography Ltd, 1969–70; Research Officer, Nat. Libraries ADP Study, 1970–71; Admin. Officer, Nat. Council for Educnl Technol., 1971–73; British Library: various posts in Bibliographic Servs and Ref. (subseq. Humanities and Social Scis) Divs, 1973–86; Dir, Public Services and Planning and Admin, 1987–90; Dir, Humanities and Social Scis, 1990–96. Part-time Lectr, West London Coll., 1972–75. Director: Cedar Audio Ltd, 1992–94; Saga Continuation Ltd, 1993–99. Advr, British Univs Film and Video Council, 2000–06. Mem., Mgt Cttee, Hoxton Health, 2011–14. Member: Governing Body, City Lit. Inst., 1982–87; Archives Cttee, Barts Health (formerly Barts & The London) NHS Trust (formerly St Bartholomew's Hosp.), 2000–; Works of Art Cttee, Homerton Univ. Hosp., 2008–; Sec., Friends of the British Liby, 2004–06 (Mem. Council, 1990–2002); Trustee: Black Country Mus. Develt Trust, 2004–12; Guild of Royal Hosp. of St Bartholomew, 2010–12 (Chm., 2012–); Age UK E London, 2012–. Hon. Fellow, Shakespeare's Birthplace, 2003– (Trustee, 1991–2003). *Publications:* (ed) The People's Heritage, 2000; (contrib.) Inventing the 20th Century, 2000; various reviews, articles. *Address:* 23 Meynell Road, E9 7AP. *T:* (020) 8985 7413. *Club:* London Press.

PHILLIPS, Anne, (Mrs Basil Phillips); *see* Dickinson, V. A.

PHILLIPS, Prof. Anne, PhD; FBA 2003; FAcSS; Graham Wallas Professor of Political Science (formerly Professor of Gender Theory, then of Political and Gender Theory), London School of Economics, since 1999; *b* 2 June 1950; *d* of Frederick Phillips and Margaret Hill; *m* 1982, Ciaran Driver; two *s. Educ:* Univ. of Bristol (BSc Philos. and Pols 1971); Sch. of Oriental and African Studies, London (MSc W African Pols 1972); City Univ., London (PhD 1982). FAcSS (AcSS 2012). Lectr, 1975–88, Reader, 1988–90, in Politics, City of London Poly.; Prof. of Politics, London Guildhall Univ., 1990–99. Adjunct Prof., ANU, 2002–05. Hon. Dr phil Aalborg, 1999; Hon. LLD Bristol, 2013. *Publications:* Hidden Hands: women and economic policies, 1983; Divided Loyalties: dilemmas of sex and class, 1987; The Enigma of Colonialism, 1989; Engendering Democracy, 1991, 2nd edn 1997; Democracy and Difference, 1993; The Politics of Presence, 1995, 2nd edn 1998; Which Equalities Matter?, 1999; Multiculturalism without Culture, 2007; Gender and Culture, 2010; Our Bodies: whose property?, 2013; The Politics of the Human, 2015. *Recreations:* swimming, reading novels, gardening. *Address:* Government Department, London School of Economics, Houghton Street, WC2A 2AE. *T:* (020) 7955 6979, *Fax:* (020) 7955 6408. *E:* a.phillips@lse.ac.uk.

PHILLIPS, Anne Fyfe; *see* Pringle, Dame A. F.

PHILLIPS, Rev. Canon Anthony Charles Julian; Headmaster, King's School, Canterbury, 1986–96; *b* 2 June 1936; *s* of Arthur Reginald Phillips and Esmée Mary Phillips; *m* 1970, Victoria Ann Stainton; two *s* one *d. Educ:* Kelly Coll., Tavistock (schol.); King's Coll., London (BD, 1st cl.; AKC, 1st cl.; Archibald Robertson Prize, 1962; Jun. McCaul Hebrew Prize, 1963); Gonville and Caius Coll., Cambridge (PhD 1967); College of the Resurrection, Mirfield. Solicitor, 1958; ordained priest, 1967; Curate, Good Shepherd, Cambridge, 1966–69; Dean, Chaplain and Fellow, Trinity Hall, Cambridge, 1969–74; Chaplain and Fellow, 1975–86, Domestic Bursar, 1982–84, St John's Coll., Oxford; Lecturer in Theology: Jesus Coll., Oxford, 1975–86; Hertford Coll., Oxford, 1984–86; S. A. Cook Bye Fellow, Gonville and Caius Coll., 1984; Canon Theologian, Dio. of Truro, 1986–2002; Chapter Canon, Truro Cath., 2001–02, now Canon Emeritus. Hon. Chaplain to Bishop of Norwich, 1970–71; Examining Chaplain to: Bp of Oxford, 1979–86; Bp of Manchester, 1980–86; Bp of Wakefield, 1984–86; Hon. Canon, Canterbury Cathedral, 1987–96. Archbps of Canterbury and York Interfaith Cons. for Judaism, 1984–86. Rep., Art Fund Cornwall, 2014–15. Hon. Vice-Pres., Royal Cornwall Poly. Soc., 2011– (Dir, 2003–08; Chm., 2004–08; Pres., 2008–11). Governor: Sherborne Sch., 1997–2001; Sherborne Sch. for Girls, 1997–2001; Cornwall Coll., 1997–2001, 2004–05; SPCK, 1998–2006 (Chair of Publishing, 2000–05). SBStJ 2003. Freeman, City of London, 2004; Liveryman, Broderers' Co., 2005. *Publications:* Ancient Israel's Criminal Law, 1970; Deuteronomy (Cambridge Bible Commentary), 1973; God BC, 1977; (ed) Israel's Prophetic Tradition, 1982; Lower Than the Angels, 1983, 2nd edn 1996; Preaching from the Psalter, 1987; The Passion of God, 1995; Essays on Biblical Law, 2002; Entering into the Mind of God, 2002; Standing up to God, 2005; David: a story of passion and tragedy, 2008; contrib. to: Words and Meanings (ed P. R. Ackroyd and B. Lindars), 1968; Witness to the Spirit (ed W. Harrington), 1979; The Ministry of the Word (ed G. Cuming), 1979; Heaven and Earth (ed A. Linzey and P. Wexler), 1986; Tradition and Unity (ed Dan Cohn-Sherbok), 1991; Glimpses of God (ed Dan Cohn-Sherbok), 1993; Splashes of God Light (ed T. Copley and others), 1997; Intelligent Faith (ed J. Quenby and J. MacDonald Smith), 2009; articles in theol jls, The Times, Expository Times, etc. *Recreations:* gardening, beachcombing. *Address:* The Old Vicarage, 10 St Peter's Road, Flushing, Falmouth, Cornwall TR11 5TP. *T:* (01326) 377217. *E:* a.phillips920@btinternet.com. *Club:* Sloane.

PHILLIPS, Arlene, CBE 2013 (OBE 2002); Choreographer, Creative Director and Producer, Arlene Phillips Hot Gossip Ltd, since 1978; *b* Manchester, 22 May 1943; *d* of Emanuel Phillips and Rita Phillips; two *d. Educ:* Manchester Central High Sch. for Girls; Muriel Tweedy's Sch. of Dance. Dance teacher: Muriel Tweedy's Sch. of Dance, 1962–66; Dance Centre, Floral St, 1968; Pineapple, 1979–84; creator and choreographer, Hot Gossip, dance gp, 1974; *choreographer:* films: Can't Stop The Music, 1980; Annie, 1982; Monty Python's The Meaning of Life, 1983; The Wind in the Willows, 1996; stage: Starlight Express, 1984, internat. tour, 2013; Grease, London, 1993, internat. tour, 1997; (and dir) Saturday Night Fever, London, NY and internat. tour, 1998; We Will Rock You, London and world tour, 2002; (and dir) The Music of Andrew Lloyd Webber, US tour, 2005; The Sound of Music, London, 2006; The Wizard of Oz, London, 2011, Canada, 2012, US tour, 2013; Monty Python Live, 2014; (and dir) Brazouka, 2014; Whelan/Watson: Other Stories, London, 2015; Creative Dir, Judy - The Songbook of Judy Garland, 2015; Dir of Choreography, Manchester Commonwealth Games, 2002; judge of television shows: Strictly Come Dancing, 2004–08; Strictly Dance Fever, 2005–06; So You Think You Can Dance?, 2010–11; Over the Rainbow, 2012; creator, television shows: (and appeared in) DanceX, 2007; Britannia High, 2008; Dir, Strictly Come Dancing Live Tour, 2008, 2009; Co-Producer, Midnight Tango (dance show), London and tours, 2011. Mem. Bd, 2009–11, Ambassador, 2011–, Sadler's Wells Th. Ambassador: Prince's Trust; Alzheimer's Soc.; Youth Dance England; Patron: Midlands Acad. of Dance and Drama; Laine Theatre Arts; Dance UK; Dance Umbrella; Urdan Acad.; Stella Mann Coll.; Liberatus Sch. of Dance and Drama; Candoco Dance Co.; Dance Proms 2014. Companion, Liverpool Inst. for Performing Arts, 2004. Hon. Mem., Internat. Dance Teachers' Assoc., 2006. Carl Alan Award for Stage/Theatre Outstanding Services to Dance, Internat. Dance Teachers' Assoc., 2007; Gold Badge Award, BASCA, 2011. *Publications:* Alana Dancing Star (children's book series), 2010; Dance to the Musicals, 2011. *Recreations:* theatre, dance, art, charity, family, cooking. *Address:* c/o Alex Segal, Cole Kitchenn, Roar House, 46 Charlotte Street, W1T 2GS. *T:* (020) 7427 5681. *E:* alex@colekitchenn.com.

PHILLIPS, Prof. Calbert Inglis, FRCS, FRCSE; Professor of Ophthalmology, University of Edinburgh and Ophthalmic Surgeon, Royal Infirmary, Edinburgh, 1972–90, now Professor Emeritus; *b* 20 March 1925; *o s* of Rev. David Horner Phillips and Margaret Calbert Phillips; *m* 1962, Christina Anne Fulton, MB, FRCSE; one *s. Educ:* Glasgow High Sch.; Robert Gordon's Coll., Aberdeen; Aberdeen Univ. MB, ChB Aberdeen 1946; DPH Edinburgh 1950; FRCS 1955; MD Aberdeen 1957; PhD Bristol 1961; MSc Manchester 1969; FRCSE 1973. Lieut and Captain, RAMC, 1947–49. House Surgeon: Aberdeen Royal Infirmary, 1946–47 (House Phys., 1951); Aberdeen Maternity Hosp., 1949; Glasgow Eye Infirmary, 1950–51; Asst, Anatomy Dept, Glasgow Univ., 1951–52; Resident Registrar, Moorfields Eye Hosp., 1953–55; Sen. Registrar, St Thomas' Hosp. and Moorfields Eye Hosp., and Res. Asst, Inst. of Ophthalmology, 1955–58; Consultant Surg., Bristol Eye Hosp., 1958–63; Alexander Piggott Wernher Trav. Fellow, Dept of Ophthalmol., Harvard Univ., 1960–61; Consultant Ophthalmic Surg., St George's Hosp., 1963–65; Prof. of Ophthal., Manchester Univ., and Hon. Consultant Ophthalmic Surg. to United Manchester Hosps, 1965–72. Hon. FBOA 1975. *Publications:* (ed jtly) Clinical Practice and Economics, 1977; Basic Clinical Ophthalmology, 1984; Logic in Medicine, 1988, 2nd edn 1995; (jtly) Ophthalmology: a primer for medical students and practitioners, 1994; papers in Eur., Amer., and Japanese Jls of Ophthal., Nature, Brain, BMJ, etc, mainly on intra-ocular pressure and glaucoma, retinal detachments, ocular surgery and hereditary diseases. *Address:* 5 Braid Mount Crest, Edinburgh EH10 6JN.

PHILLIPS, Caryl, FRSL; writer; Professor of English, Yale University, since 2005; *b* 13 March 1958. *Educ:* Queen's Coll., Oxford (BA English 1979; Hon. Fellow, 2006). Writer in Residence: Literary Criterion Centre, Mysore, India, 1987; Univ. of Stockholm, Sweden, 1989; Nat. Inst. of Educn, Singapore, 1994; Amherst College, Massachusetts: Vis. Writer, 1990–92; Writer in Residence, 1992–94; Prof. of English and Writer in Residence, 1994–98; Barnard College, Columbia University: Prof. of English and Henry R. Luce Prof. of Migration and Social Order, 1998–2005; Dir, Initiatives in the Humanities, 2003–05. Visiting Professor: NY Univ., 1993; Univ. of WI, Barbados, 1999–2000; Dartmouth Coll., NH, 2008; Oxford Univ., 2009. British Council Fiftieth Anniversary Fellow, 1984; Guggenheim Fellow, 1992; Rockefeller Foundn (Bellagio) Residency, 1993; Fellow, Centre for Scholars and Writers, NY Public Liby, 2002–03; Montgomery Fellow, Dartmouth Coll., NH, 2008. Ed., Faber Caribbean series, 1998–2001. FRSL 2000. Humanities Schol. of the Year, Univ. of WI, 1999. Hon. AM Amherst, 1995; DUniv: Leeds Metropolitan, 1997; York, 2003; Hon. LittD Leeds, 2003; Hon. MA Yale, 2006; Hon. DLitt: West Indies, 2010; Edinburgh, 2012. Giles Cooper Award, BBC, 1984; Bursary in Drama, Arts Council of GB, 1984; Martin Luther King Meml Prize, 1987; James Tait Black Meml Prize, 1994; Lannan Foundn Literary Award, 1994. *Publications: plays:* Strange Fruit, 1981; Where There is Darkness, 1982; The Shelter, 1984; Rough Crossings, 2007; *novels:* The Final Passage, 1985; A State of Independence, 1986; Higher Ground, 1989; Cambridge, 1991; Crossing the River, 1993; The Nature of Blood, 1997; A Distant Shore, 2003 (Commonwealth Writers Prize, 2004); Dancing in the Dark, 2005; In the Falling Snow, 2009; The Lost Child, 2015; *screenplays:* Playing Away, 1987; The Mystic Masseur (Silver Ombu award for best screenplay, Mar del Plata Film Fest.), 2002; *non-fiction:* The European Tribe, 1987; The Atlantic Sound, 2000; A New World Order, 2001; Foreigners, 2007; Colour Me English, 2011; *anthology:* (ed) Extravagant Strangers, 1997; (ed) The Right Set: the Faber Book of Tennis, 1999. *Recreations:* running, golf. *Address:* c/o Georgia Garrett, Rogers Coleridge and White, 20 Powis Mews, W11 1JN.

PHILLIPS, Sir David; *see* Phillips, Sir J. D.

PHILLIPS, Prof. David, CBE 2012 (OBE 1999); FRS 2015; Professor of Physical Chemistry, 1989–2006, Hofmann Professor of Chemistry, 1999–2006, now Professor Emeritus, and Dean, Faculties of Life Sciences and Physical Sciences, 2002–06, Imperial College London; *b* 3 Dec. 1939; *s* of Stanley and Daphne Ivy Phillips; *m* 1970, Caroline Lucy Scoble; one *d. Educ:* South Shields Grammar-Technical Sch.; Univ. of Birmingham (BSc, PhD). Post doctoral Fellow, Univ. of Texas, 1964–66; Vis. Scientist, Inst. of Chemical Physics, Acad. of Scis of USSR, Moscow, 1966–67; Lectr 1967–73, Sen. Lectr 1973–76, Reader 1976–80, in Phys. Chem., Univ. of Southampton; Royal Institution of Great Britain: Wolfson Prof. of Natural Philosophy, 1980–89; Actg Dir, Jan.–Oct. 1986; Dep. Dir, 1986–89; Head, Dept of Chemistry, Imperial Coll., London, 1992–2002. Vice-Pres. and Gen. Officer, BAAS, 1988–89. Mem., Faraday Council, 1990–93, Pres., 2010–12, RSC. Nyholm Lectr, RSC, 1994. Chm., London Gifted and Talented, 2003–08. FRSC 1973; Fellow, Imperial Coll. London, 2008; Hon. FCGI 2004; Honorary Life Fellow: Royal Inst., 2005; BAAS, 2006. Hon. DSc: Birmingham, 2011; Southampton, 2012; Durham, 2013; Leicester, 2014; Westminster, 2014; Hon. LLD Bath, 2013. Michael Faraday Award, Royal Soc., 1997; Porter Medal, Eur. Photochemistry Assoc., Inter-American Photochem. Soc. and Oceanic Photochem. Assoc., 2010. *Publications:* (jtly) Time-Correlated Single-Photon Counting, 1984; Polymer Photophysics, 1985; (jtly) Jet Spectroscopy and Dynamics, 1995; over 593 res. papers and revs in sci. lit. on photochem., photophys. and lasers. *Recreations:* music, travel, tennis, theatre. *Address:* 195 Barnett Wood Lane, Ashtead, Surrey KT21 2LP. *T:* (01372) 274385. *Club:* Athenæum.

PHILLIPS, His Honour (David) Alan; a Circuit Judge, 1983–95; Chancellor, diocese of Bangor, 1988–95; *b* 21 July 1926; *s* of Stephen Thomas Phillips, MC and Elizabeth Mary Phillips; *m* 1960, Jean Louise (*née* Godsell); two *s. Educ:* Llanelli Grammar Sch.; University Coll., Oxford (MA). Left school, 1944. Served War, Army, 1944; commnd, 1946, RWF; Captain (GS), 1947; demobilised, 1948. Oxford, 1948–51. Lectr, 1952–59. Called to Bar, Gray's Inn, 1960. Stipendiary Magistrate for Mid-Glamorgan, 1975–83; a Recorder of the Crown Court, 1974–83. *Recreations:* music, chess, swimming.

See also Hon. Sir S. E. Phillips.

PHILLIPS, Prof. David George, DPhil; FRHistS, FAcSS; Professor of Comparative Education, University of Oxford, 2000–12, now Emeritus; Fellow of St Edmund Hall, Oxford, 1984–2012, now Emeritus; *b* 15 Dec. 1944; *s* of late George and Doris Phillips; *m* 1968, Valerie Mary Bache; two *d. Educ:* Sir Walter St John's Sch., Battersea; BA London 1966; St Edmund Hall, Oxford (DipEd 1967; MA; DPhil 1984). Assistant teacher: Huntingdon Grammar Sch., 1967–69; Chipping Norton Sch., 1969–75; University of Oxford: Tutor, then Univ. Lectr, Dept of Educnl Studies, 1975–96; Reader in Comparative Educn, 1996–2000; Professorial Sen. Res. Fellow in Comparative Educn, 2012–13. Member: Teacher Educn Commn of Wissenschaftsrat, 1990–91; Council, 1992–94, Scientific Cttee, 1992–98, German Inst. for Internat. Educnl Res., Frankfurt-am-Main; Educnl Sci. Commn, Ministry of Sci., Res. and the Arts, Baden-Württemberg, 2003–04; Chm., British Assoc. for Internat. and Comparative Educn, 1998–2000; Emeritus Res. Fellow, Leverhulme Trust, 2012. FAcSS (AcSS 2002); FRHistS 2002. FRSA 1987. Editor, Oxford Review of Education, 1984–2003; Series Editor, Oxford Studies in Comparative Educn, 1991–; Ed., Res. in Comparative and Internat. Educn, 2006–; Editor, Comparative Educn, 2015– (Chm. Editl Bd, 2009–15). *Publications include:* Zur Universitätsreform in der Britischen Besatzungszone 1945–48, 1983; (ed) German Universities After the Surrender, 1983; (with Veronica Stencel) The Second Foreign Language, 1983; (ed) Which Language?, 1989; (with Caroline Filmer-Sankey) Diversification in Modern Language Teaching, 1993; Pragmatismus und Idealismus: das Blaue Gutachten und die Britische Hochschulpolitik in Deutschland 1948, 1995; (ed) Education in Germany: tradition and reform in historical context, 1995; (ed jtly) Learning from Comparing, vol. 1, 1999, vol. 2, 2000; (ed) Education in Eastern Germany since Unification, 2000; Reflections on British Interest in Education in Germany in the Nineteenth Century, 2002; (jtly) Towards a Structural Typology of Cross-National Attraction in Education, 2002; (ed jtly) Can the Japanese Change Their Education System?, 2003; (ed jtly) Implementing European Union Education and Training Policy: a comparative study of issues in four member states, 2003; (ed jtly) Educational Policy Borrowing: historical perspectives, 2005; (jtly) Comparative and International Education: an introduction to theory, method and practice, 2006; The German Example: English interest in educational provision in Germany since 1800, 2011; Investigating Education in Germany: historical studies from a British perspective, 2015; *festschrift:* (ed Hubert Ertl) Cross-National Attraction in Education: accounts from England and Germany, 2006; numerous articles in jls. *Recreations:* art history, antiquarian books. *Address:* Department of Education, 15 Norham Gardens, Oxford OX2 6PY; St Edmund Hall, Oxford OX1 4AR.

PHILLIPS, David John; QC 1997; a Recorder, since 1998; a Deputy High Court Judge, since 2001; *b* 4 May 1953; *s* of Hon. Sir (John) Raymond Phillips MC, and of Hazel Bradbury Phillips; *m* 1981, Ann Nicola Beckett, *d* of late Ronald Beckett; one *s* one *d*. *Educ:* Rugby Sch.; Aix-en-Provence Univ.; Balliol Coll., Oxford (BA (Jurisprudence) 1977; MA 1996). Called to the Bar, Gray's Inn, 1976 (Arden, Atkin, Mould & Reid Prize, 1977), Bencher, 2004; admitted Bar of Gibraltar, 2004; Mem., Bar of Eastern Caribbean, 2005; Mem., Wales and Chester Circuit, 1983; Asst Recorder, 1994–98; Hd of Chambers, 199 Strand, 2000–06. Chairman: FA Premier League Tribunal, 2003–; Sports Dispute Resolution Panel, 2003–; Judicial Chm., Nat. Greyhound Racing Club's Appeal Tribunal, 2006–. Dir, Disability Law Service, 1999–. Mem. Cttee, Barristers' Benevolent Assoc., 1993– (Jt Hon. Treas., 1999–). *Recreations:* hill walking, cinema. *Address:* Wilberforce Chambers, 8 New Square, Lincoln's Inn, WC2A 3QP. *T:* (020) 7306 0102. *E:* dphillips@wilberforce.co.uk.

PHILLIPS, Diane Susan, CB 2000; Director, Transport Strategy, Department for Transport (formerly of the Environment, Transport and the Regions, then Department for Transport, Local Government and the Regions), 2000–02; *b* 29 Aug. 1942; *d* of Michael Keogh and Jessie (*née* Tite); *m* 1967, John Phillips; two *d*. *Educ:* Univ. of Wales. NEDO, 1967–72; Civil Service, 1972–2002: Principal, DoE, 1972–77, Cabinet Office, 1977–78; Asst Sec., Dept of Transport, 1978–80; Department of the Environment, then Department of the Environment, Transport and the Regions, now Department for Transport, Local Government and the Regions, 1981–2002: Grade 4, Local Govt Finance, 1988–90; Under Sec. (Grade 3) and Principal Finance Officer, Property Hldgs, 1990–94; Dir, Social Housing Policy and Resources, 1994–98; Dir, Roads and Traffic, 1998–2000; Dep. Hd, Integrated Transport Taskforce, 2000. Mem. Bd, London & Quadrant Housing Trust, 1998–2013 (Dep. Chm., 2010–13). Gov., St George's Coll., Weybridge, 1995–2004. *Address:* 60 Portmore Park Road, Weybridge, Surrey KT13 8EU.

PHILLIPS, Rt Rev. Donald David; *see* Rupert's Land, Bishop of.

PHILLIPS, Sir (Gerald) Hayden, GCB 2002 (KCB 1998; CB 1989); DL; Director, St Just Farms Ltd, since 1997; Chairman: IPSO Appointments Panel, since 2014; Reviewing Committee on the Export of Works of Art and Cultural Objects, since 2014; Independent Reviewer of Rulings of Advertising Standards Authority Council, since 2010; *b* 9 Feb. 1943; *s* of Gerald Phillips and Dorothy Phillips; *m* 1st, 1967, Dr Ann Watkins (marr. diss.); one *s* one *d*; 2nd, 1980, Hon. Laura Grenfell; one *s* two *d*. *Educ:* Cambridgeshire High Sch.; Clare Coll., Cambridge (MA); Yale Univ., USA (MA). Home Office: Asst Principal, 1967; Economic Adviser, 1970–72; Principal, 1972–74; Asst Sec., and Principal Private Sec. to Sec. of State for Home Dept, 1974–76; Dep. Chef de Cabinet to Pres., Commn of European Communities, 1977–79; Asst Sec., Home Office, 1979–81, Asst Under-Sec. of State, 1981–86; Dep. Sec., Cabinet Office (MPO, subseq. Office of the Minister for the Civil Service), 1986–88; Dep. Sec., HM Treasury, 1988–92; Permanent Secretary: DNH, later Dept for Culture, Media and Sport, 1992–98; LCD, 1998–2003; Dept for Constitutional Affairs, 2003–04; Clerk of the Crown in Chancery, 1998–2004. Reviewer: the Honours System, 2004; the Funding of Political Parties, 2006–07; Chm., Inter-Party Talks on Political Funding, 2007. Charities Consultant to HRH the Prince of Wales, 2004–09. Chm., NT, 2004–10. Chm., Digital Cinema Funding Partnership, 2010–14. Director: Global Solutions Ltd, 2005–08; Hanson Family Hldgs, 2007–13; Westhouse Hldgs, 2009–14; Chm., Hanson Westhouse Ltd, 2007–09. Adviser: Hanson Capital, 2004–06; Englefield Capital, 2004–11. Dir, Energy Saving Trust, 2011–. Member: Council, KCL, 1993–99; Ct of Govs, Henley Mgt Coll., 1993–2002; Council, Marlborough Coll., 1997–2013 (Chm., 2006–13); Bd, Inst. of Advanced Legal Studies, 1998–2004; Fitzwilliam Mus. Trust, 1999–2005; Salisbury Cathedral Council, 2002–14; Chm., Salisbury Cathedral Fabric Adv. Cttee, 2006–. Lay Canon, Salisbury Cathedral, 2008–. Chm. Cttee, Apsley Hse, 2010–; Gov., Wilts Historic Buildings Trust, 2006– (Dep. Chm., 2007–). Patron, Southern Spinal Injuries Trust, 2007–. Hon. Bencher, Inner Temple, 1998. DL Wilts, 2007. Actor in film, Jane Eyre, 2011. *Publications:* Review of the Honours System, 2004; Strengthening Democracy: fair and sustainable funding of political parties, 2007. *Recreations:* theatre, other arts, shooting and fishing, India. *Address:* Homington Farm, Homington, Salisbury, Wilts SP5 4NG. *Clubs:* Brooks's, Pratt's.

PHILLIPS, Dr Helen Mary; Chair, Chesterfield Royal Hospital NHS Foundation Trust, since 2015; *b* Dublin, 29 May 1966; *d* of James Phillips and Anne Phillips (*née* Duggan); *m* 1st, 1991, Desmond Ryan (marr. diss. 2008); one *s* one *d*; 2nd, 2009, Adrian Belton, *qv*; one step *s* two step *d*. *Educ:* University Coll., Dublin (BSc Hons 1987; PhD 1993). Environment Agency: Regl Tech. Planning Manager, 1996–97, Regl Planning Manager, 1997–98, Midlands Reg.; Area Manager, Thames Reg., 1998–2001; Head of Strategic Develt, 2001; Dir, Wales, 2002–06; Chief Exec., Natural England, 2006–12; Dir of Customer Services and Networks, Yorkshire Water, 2012–14; Chm., Loop Customer Mgt Ltd, Kelda Gp, 2012–14. Lead Accounting Officer, Jt Nature Conservation Cttee, 2006–11. Mem., Legal Services Bd, 2015–. FRSB. *Recreations:* walking, shoes, handbags, chocolate. *Address:* Chesterfield Royal Hospital NHS Foundation Trust, Calow, Chesterfield, Derbys S44 5BL. *Club:* Farmers.

PHILLIPS, Prof. Ian, MD; FRCP, FRCPath, FFPH; Professor of Medical Microbiology, 1974–96 (at St Thomas' Hospital, 1974–82), and Clinical Dean, 1992–96, United Medical and Dental Schools of Guy's and St Thomas's Hospitals, now Emeritus Professor; *b* 10 April 1936; *s* of late Stanley Phillips and Emma (*née* Price). *Educ:* St John's Coll., Cambridge (MA, MD); St Thomas's Hosp. Med. Sch. (MB BChir). FRCPath 1981; FRCP 1983; FFPH (FFPHM 1996). House Officer, St Thomas' Hosp., 1961–62; Lecturer in Microbiology: St Thomas's Hosp. Med. Sch., 1962–66; Makerere UC, 1966–69; Sen. Lectr, 1969–72, Reader, 1972–74, St Thomas's Hosp. Med. Sch.; Chm., Dist Mgt Team, St Thomas' Hosp., 1978–79; Hon. Cons. Microbiologist, St Thomas' Hosp., subseq. Guy's and St Thomas's Hosp. NHS Trust, 1969–96, now Emeritus Consultant; Chm., Pathology, Guy's and St Thomas's Hosp. NHS Trust, 1990–96. Civil Consultant, RAF, 1979–2000. Mem., Veterinary Products Cttee, 1981–85. An editor, Clinical Microbiology and Infection, 1997–2005. Mem. Council, RCPath, 1974–76 and 1987–90; Chairman: Brit. Soc. for Antimicrobial Chemotherapy, 1979–82; Assoc. of Med. Microbiologists, 1989–93; Pres., European Soc. for Clinical Microbiol. and Infectious Diseases, 1995–96. Member: S London Botanical Inst.; BSBI. Hon. Mem., Croatian Acad. of Med. Sci., 1997. Freeman, City of London, 1975; Liveryman, Soc. of Apothecaries, 1975. *Publications:* (ed jtly) Laboratory Methods in Antimicrobial Chemotherapy, 1978; (jtly) Microbial Disease, 1979; contrib. chapters and papers. *Recreations:* botany, music. *Clubs:* Athenæum, Royal Society of Medicine.

PHILLIPS, (Ian) Peter, OBE 2004; JP; Director, Kroll Buchler Phillips Ltd, 1999–2005; Chairman, Kroll (formerly Buchler Phillips) Lindquist Avey, 1997–2005; *b* 13 Oct. 1944; *s* of Bernard Phillips and Constance Mary Clayton; *m* 1970, Wendy Berne; one *s* one *d*. *Educ:* Highgate Sch.; Sorbonne, Paris. FCA, FIPA. Partner, Bernard Phillips & Co., 1968; UK Head of Corporate Recovery Services, Arthur Andersen & Co., 1982–88; Chm., Buchler Phillips Gp, 1988–99. Jt Administrator, British and Commonwealth Holdings, 1990; Court Receiver, Estate of Robert Maxwell, 1991. Dir, Jt Insolvency Monitoring Unit, 1997–98; Mem., Insolvency Tribunal, 1997–. Pres., Insolvency Practitioners Assoc., 1988–89. Member: Lord Chancellor's Adv. Cttee on JPs for Inner London, City and Westminster, 1999–2009; 2nd and 3rd Selection Panels, Gtr London Magistrates' Cts Authy, 2002–04. Mem., Global Adv. Bd, Centre for Internat. Business and Mgt, Judge Inst. of Mgt, Cambridge Univ., 1999–. Trustee: Israel-Palestine Centre for Res. and Inf., 1991–96; Papyrus (Prevention of Suicide) Co. Ltd, 2000–04; Restorative Justice Consortium, 2006–07. Treas., N Kensington Neighbourhood Law Centre, 1970–76. Chm., Hampstead Theatre, 1997–2001 (Dir, 1991–2004; Mem., Adv. Council, 2004–); Chair, Develt Gp (formerly Major Donors Cttee), Anna Freud Centre, 2012–. Mem., British Acad. of Experts, 1991–. Accredited Relate Counsellor, 2006. JP Inner London, 1979 (Dep. Chm., Highbury Corner Bench, 2004–08). Mem., Magic Circle, 2003–. *Publications:* Life After Debt, 2010. *Recreations:* theatre, baroque and modern jazz music, horse riding, coastal path walking, close-up magic. *Address:* The Fourth House, 5 Turner Drive, NW11 6TX. *T:* 07836 572277.

PHILLIPS, Jeremy Patrick Manfred; QC 1980; *b* 27 Feb. 1941; *s* of late Manfred Henry Phillips, CA, and late Irene Margaret (*née* Symondson); *m* 1962, Margaret Ann (*née* Adams) (marr. diss. 1968); *m* 1968, Virginia Gwendoline (*née* Dwyer) (marr. diss. 1974); one *s* (and one *s* decd); *m* 1976, Judith Gaskell (*née* Hetherington); two *s* two *d*. *Educ:* St Edmund's Sch., Hindhead, Surrey; Charterhouse. Apprentice Accountant, Thomson McLintock & Co., 1957–61. Called to Bar, Gray's Inn, 1964; in practice, accountancy and commercial law, 1964–2003 (won case in HK that resulted in first modern mobile tel. system); Head of Chambers: 2 Temple Gdns, 1990–98; New Ct Chambers, 2000–03; DTI Inspector, affairs of Queens Moat Houses plc, 1993. Owner and Dir of Ops, Kentwell Hall, Long Melford, Suffolk, 1971–; originator of domestic living history events in UK with Kentwell's Annual Historical Re-Creations of Tudor Domestic Life, 1978–, World War II domestic events, 1995–, Halloween event, Scaresville, 2007–. Founding Dir, CARE Britain. *Publications:* contrib. early edns of Cooper's Students' Manual of Auditing, Cooper's Manual of Auditing and various pamphlets, papers, guides, etc, on Kentwell Hall and Tudor period, on democracy and educn issues. *Recreations:* historic buildings, Tudor history, constitutional and educational issues, cricket, conversation. *Address:* Kentwell Hall, Long Melford, Suffolk CO10 9BA.

PHILLIPS, Jessica Rose; MP (Lab) Birmingham Yardley, since 2015; *b* Yardley, 9 Oct. 1981; *m* Tom Phillips; two *s*. *Educ:* Univ. of Leeds (BA Jt Hons Econ. and Social Hist. and Social Policy 2003); Univ. of Birmingham (Postgrad. Dip. Public Sector Mgt 2013). Project and Event Manager, Health Links, 2008–10; Business Develt Manager, Sandwell Women's Aid, 2010–15. Mem. (Lab), Birmingham CC, 2012–. Mem., Women and Equalities Select Cttee, 2015–. Victims' Champion, Birmingham, 2011. *Address:* House of Commons, SW1A 0AA.

PHILLIPS, John Andrew, CBE 2006; **His Honour Judge Phillips;** a Circuit Judge, since 1998; Director of Training (Courts), Judicial College, since 2012; *b* 26 May 1950; *s* of Jack and Mary Nolan Phillips; *m* 1993, Moira Margaret Kynnersley (*d* 2012); two *d*. *Educ:* Fitzwilliam Coll., Cambridge (MA). Mem., Fitzwilliam String Quartet, Quartet in Residence, York Univ., 1971–74; called to the Bar, Gray's Inn, 1976, Bencher, 2008; in practice at the Bar, 1977–98. Dir of Studies, Judicial Studies Bd of England and Wales, 2007–11. Hon. DLaws BPP Univ. Coll. of Professional Studies, 2012. *Recreation:* playing the violin. *Address:* Judicial College, 3A Red Zone, 102 Petty France, SW1H 9AJ.

PHILLIPS, Sir (John) David, Kt 2000; QPM 1994; lecturer and writer; *b* 22 April 1944; *s* of late Percy Phillips and Alfreda Phillips; *m* 1970, Nancy Wynn Rothwell; one *s*. *Educ:* Leigh Grammar Sch.; Manchester Univ. (BA 1st Cl. Hons Econs). Served: Lancs Constabulary, 1963–84; Gtr Manchester Constabulary, 1984–89; Dep. Chief Constable, Devon and Cornwall, 1989–93; Chief Constable of Kent, 1993–2003; Dir, Nat. Centre of Policing Excellence, 2003–05. Chm., Nat. Crime Faculty; Pres., ACPO, 2001–03. CCMI 2002. Hon. Fellow, Christchurch Coll., Canterbury, 1998. Hon. LLD Coventry, 2010. *Recreations:* history, golf.

PHILLIPS, John Randall; Member, 1995–99, Chairman, 1995–96, then Lord Mayor, 1996–97, Cardiff City and County Council; *b* 22 April 1940; *s* of James Phillips and Charlotte Phillips (*née* Phelps); *m* 1967, Margaret Ray Davies; one *s* one *d*. *Educ:* Cardiff High Sch.; University Coll., Cardiff (BA Econ. 1961). Dip. Soc. Studies 1967. Cardiff City Council, 1963–66; Glam CC, 1967–74; Mid Glam CC, 1974–96: Principal Trng Officer, 1974–82; Principal Asst (Child Abuse), 1982–89; Dist Social Services Officer, Cynon Valley, 1989–94; Principal Officer, 1994–96. Cardiff City Council: Member (Lab), 1972–96; Chm. of Personnel, 1974–76 and 1979–83; Dep. Leader, Labour Gp, 1986, Ldr, 1990–94; Vice Chm., 1987, Chm., 1990, Policy; Leader, 1990–94; Dep. Lord Mayor, 1994–95. Mem., Cardiff Bay Develt Corp., 1990–99. First Pres., UWIC, 1996–97. *Recreations:* politics, listening to music. *Address:* 15 Kyle Crescent, Whitchurch, Cardiff CF14 1ST. *T:* (029) 2062 4878.

PHILLIPS, Sir Jonathan, KCB 2009; Warden, Keble College, Oxford, since 2010; *b* 21 May 1952; *s* of Gilbert Reginald Phillips and Ruby May Phillips (*née* Hughes); *m* 1974, Amanda Rosemary Broomhead; two *s*. *Educ:* Queen Mary's Grammar Sch., Walsall; St John's Coll., Cambridge (BA 1973; PhD 1978); London Univ. Inst. of Educn (PGCE 1974). Department of Trade, later Department of Trade and Industry, 1977–93: seconded: to CBI econs directorate, 1982–83; as Sec., Cttee of Inquiry into regulatory arrangements at Lloyd's, 1986–87; Asst Sec., 1987–93; Under-Sec., 1993; Dir, Exec. Agencies, Dept of Transport, 1993–96; Department of Trade and Industry: Dir, Investigations and Enforcement, 1996–98; Dir, Finance and Resource Mgt, 1998–2000; Dir Gen., Resources and Services, 2000–02; Operating Strategy Dir, Sea Systems, BAE Systems, 2002 (on secondment); Pol Dir, 2002–05, Perm. Sec., 2005–10, NI Office. Non-executive Director: Forward Trust Gp, 1995–96; Charlie Goldsmith Associates, 2011–. Mem. Bd, Cooperation Ireland, 2010–. Gov., St Saviour's and St Olave's Sch., Southwark, 1998–2005. Trustee, Esmée Fairbairn Foundn, 2011–. Pres., Friends of the Oxford Bach Choir, 2012–; Chm. Trustees, Schola Cantorum, Oxford, 2013–. *Address:* Keble College, Oxford OX1 3PG. *Clubs:* Athenæum, Oxford and Cambridge.

PHILLIPS, Prof. Judith Eleri, OBE 2013; PhD; Professor of Gerontology and Social Work, since 2004, Scientific Director, Centre for Innovative Ageing, since 2009, Director, Research Institute for Applied Social Science, since 2009, and Deputy Pro Vice Chancellor, since 2011, Swansea University (formerly University of Wales, Swansea); *b* Cardiff, 7 Feb. 1959; *d* of Thomas William Pugh Phillips and Bridget Phillips; *m* 1991, Peter Harbottell. *Educ:* Pontypridd Girls' Grammar Sch.; University Coll. of Wales, Aberystwyth (BA Hons 1980); Stockholm Univ. (Dip. Social Sci. 1981); Jesus Coll., Oxford (MSc, CQSW 1983); Univ. of E Anglia (PhD 1989). Social worker, Wilts CC, 1983–85; Researcher, 1988–89, Lectr in Social Work, 1989–93, UEA; Keele University: Lectr in Social Work and Gerontol., 1993–98; Sen. Lectr, 1998–2001; Prof. of Social Gerontol., 2001–04. Dir, Older People and Ageing R&D Network in Wales, 2006–. Chair, Res. Cttee, Guide Dogs, 2015. Guest Professor: Umeå Univ., Sweden, 2011–13; Lund Univ., Sweden, 2012; Vis. Fellow, New Coll., Oxford, 2011; Vis. Sen. Res. Fellow, LSE, 2011–13. AcSS 2009; Fellow, British Soc. Gerontol., 2011; FLSW 2012. FRSA 2014. *Publications:* Social Work with Older People, 2006, 5th edn 2011; Care: key concepts, 2007; Ageing at the Intersection of Work and Home Life: blurring the boundaries, 2008; Critical Issues in Social Work with Older People, 2008; Key Concepts in Social Gerontology, 2010. *Recreations:* hill walking, history of tea shops, international public speaking. *Address:* Centre for Innovative Ageing, Swansea University, Singleton Park, Swansea SA2 8PP. *T:* (01792) 602341. *E:* Judith.E.Phillips@swansea.ac.uk.

PHILLIPS, Leslie Samuel, CBE 2008 (OBE 1998); actor, director, producer; *b* 20 April 1924; *s* of late Frederick and Cecelia Phillips; *m* 1st, 1948, Penelope Bartley (marr. diss. 1965; she *d* 1981); two *s* two *d*; 2nd, 1982, Angela Scoular (*d* 2011); one step *s*; 3rd, 2013, Zara Carr. *Educ:* Chingford Sch.; Italia Conti Stage Sch. Army, 1942–45 (Lieut, DLI; invalided out). *Theatre* includes: début, Peter Pan, London Palladium, 1937; Zeal of Thy House, Garrick, 1938; Otello, and Turandot, Covent Garden, 1939; Dear Octopus, Queen's, 1939–40; Nutmeg Tree, Lyric, 1941–42; The Doctor's Dilemma, Haymarket, 1942; Daddy Long-Legs, Comedy, 1947–48; Charley's Aunt, Saville, 1948; On Monday Next, Comedy, 1949; For Better, For Worse, Comedy, 1952–54; Diary of a Nobody, Arts, 1954; Lost Generation, Garrick, 1955; The Whole Truth, Aldwych, 1955–56; The Big Killing, Shaftesbury, 1961–62; Boeing-Boeing, Apollo, 1963–65; The Deadly Game (also dir), Savoy, 1967; The Man Most Likely To… (also dir), Vaudeville, 1968–69, tour, S Africa, 1970–71, Duke of York's, 1972, tour of Australia, 1974; Sextet, Criterion, 1977–78; Canaries Sometimes Sing, tour, 1978; Not Now Darling, Savoy, 1979, world tour, 1980; Pygmalion, tour, 1980; The Cherry Orchard, Haymarket, 1983; Chapter 17, tour, 1983; Passion Play, Wyndham's, 1984–85; Pride and Prejudice, tour, 1988; Taking Steps, world tour, 1989; Painting Churches, Playhouse, 1992; August, tour of Wales, 1994; Love for Love, Chichester, 1996; Merry Wives of Windsor, RSC, 1997; Camino Real, 1998; On The Whole It's Been Jolly Good, Edin. Fest., 1999, Hampstead, 2000; Naked Justice, W Yorks Playhouse, 2001, 2002; The Play What I Wrote, Wyndhams, 2003; more than 100 *films*, including: A Lassie from Lancashire, 1938; The Citadel, 1938; Four Feathers, 1938; Mikado, 1938; Climbing High, 1939; Proud Valley, 1939; Thief of Baghdad, 1939; Train of Events, 1949; Sound Barrier, 1949; Pool of London, 1950; Gamma People, 1955; The Smallest Show on Earth, 1956; Brothers in Law, 1956; High Flight, 1957; Les Girls, 1957; Carry on Nurse, 1958; I Was Monty's Double, 1958; Carry on Constable, 1959; This Other Eden, 1959; Ferdinando, 1959; Doctor in Love, 1960; Very Important Person, 1961; In the Doghouse, 1961; Raising the Wind, 1961; Crooks Anonymous, 1962; Fast Lady, 1962; The Longest Day, 1963; Doctor in Clover, 1965; You Must Be Joking, 1965; Maroc 7 (also prod.), 1966; Some Will Some Won't, 1969; Doctor in Trouble, 1970; Magnificent Seven Deadly Sins, 1971; Don't Just Lie There, 1973; Spanish Fly, 1975; Out of Africa, 1986; Empire of the Sun, 1987; Scandal, 1988; Mountains of the Moon, 1989; King Ralph, 1990; August, 1995; Day of the Jackal, 1997; Cinderella, 1999; Saving Grace, 2000; Lara Croft: Tomb Raider, 2001; Thunderpants, 2001; Harry Potter and the Philosopher's Stone, 2001; Collusion, 2002; Harry Potter and the Chamber of Secrets, 2002; Carry On Columbus, 2002; Churchill: the Hollywood years, 2002; Colour Me Kubrick, 2004; Walking With Shadows, 2004; Millions, 2005; Venus, 2007; Is Anybody There?, 2009; Harry Potter and the Deathly Hallows, Pt 2, 2011; *television* includes: Morning Departure (first TV from Alexandra Palace), 1948; My Wife Jacqueline, 1952; Our Man at St Mark's, 1963; Impasse, 1963; The Reluctant Debutante, 1965; The Gong Game, 1965; Foreign Affairs, 1966; Blandings Castle, 1967; Very Fine Line, 1968; The Suit, 1969; Casanova, 1973; Redundant and the Wife's Revenge, 1983; You'll Never See Me Again, 1983; Mr Palfrey of Westminster, 1985; Monte Carlo, 1986; Rumpole, 1988; Summer's Lease, 1989; Comic Strip, 1989, 1990, 1991; Chancer, 1989–90; Who Bombed Birmingham, 1990; Life After Life, 1990; Thacker, 1991; The Trials of Oz, 1991; Boon, 1992; Lovejoy, 1992; Bermuda Grace, 1993; The Changeling, 1993; Vanity Dies Hard, 1993; Love on a Branch Line, 1993; House of Windsor, 1994; Two Golden Balls, 1994; Honey for Tea, 1994; The Canterville Ghost, 1995; L for Liverpool, 1998; Dalziel & Pascoe, 1998; The Best of British, 2000; Sword of Honour, 2000; Take a Girl Like You, 2000; Into the Void, 2001; Legends, 2002; Monarch of the Glen, 2002; Holby City, 2002; Midsomer Murders, 2002; Unto the Wicked, 2002; Where The Heart Is, 2003; The Last Detective, 2007; Miss Marple, 2007; Harley Street, 2008; Edgar Wallace series: The Pale Horse, 1996; Tales from the Crypt, 1996; *radio* includes: The Navy Lark, 1959–76; Three Men in a Boat, 1962; Vera Lynn Story, 1973; Would the Last Businessman to Leave England Please Turn out the Light, 1977–78; Round the World in 80 Days, 1991–92; Red Riding Hood and the Wolf's Story, 1994; England Their England, 1994; Wind in the Willows, 1994; Truth in Dark Places, 1994–95; Falling Heads, 1995; Philip and Rowena, 1995; Envious Casca, 1996; Half a Sixpence, 1996; Me and Little Boots, 2000; Maclean the Memorex Years, 2000; Cousin Bette, 2000; Tales from the Backbench, 2001; Democracy and Language, 2001; Les Miserables, 2002; Hitchhiker's Guide to the Galaxy, 2003; Cads, 2004; Dr Who, 2004; presenter, Carry on Forever!, 2010. Vice Pres., Royal Theatrical Fund; Founder Mem., Theatre of Comedy; Vice Pres., Disabled Living Foundn, 2002–. Award for lifetime achievement in films, Evening Standard, 1997; Comic Icon Award, 2003, Greatest Living Englishman Award, 2006, Loaded mag.; Dilys Powell Award for Lifetime Achievement in Film, London Critics Circle, 2007; Best Supporting Actor, BIFA, 2007; Best Trouper Award, Oldie mag., 2007. *Publications:* Hello: the autobiography, 2006. *Recreations:* cats, restoration, racing, collecting, gardening, classical music, weaving, chess, all sport. *Address:* c/o Independent Talent Group Ltd, 40 Whitfield Street, W1T 2RH. *T:* (020) 7636 6565.

PHILLIPS, Malcolm Edward, MD; FRCP; Consultant Physician and Nephrologist, Imperial College Healthcare NHS Trust (formerly Charing Cross Hospital, then Hammersmith Hospitals NHS Trust), 1981–2005, now Honorary Consulting Physician and Nephrologist (Director of Renal Services, 1994–2001); *b* 24 March 1940; *s* of Albert H. Phillips and Kathleen M. Phillips; *m* 1st, 1967, Rona Lendon (marr. diss. 2012); one *s* one *d*; 2nd, 2013, Shu-Ching Cheng. *Educ:* Charing Cross Hosp. Med. Sch., London (MB BS 1964; MD 1979). MRCS 1964; FRCP 1986. Jun. hosp. med. posts, Fulham Hosp. and Charing Cross Hosp., 1964–81; Wellcome Trust Fellow, Univ. of Naples, 1970–72; Gen. Manager, 1989, Med. Dir, 1995–97, Charing Cross Hosp. Panellist, Fitness to Practise Panel, GMC, 2006–12; Chm., Fitness to Practise Panels, MPTS, 2012–14. Canterbury Trustbank Vis. Prof., Christchurch, NZ, 1997. Pres., W London Medico-Chirurgical Soc., 2005–06. *Publications:* articles in jls. *Recreations:* cricket, philately.

PHILLIPS, Margaret Corinna, (Mrs D. R. Hunt), FRCO; Professor of Organ, Royal College of Music, since 1996; concert organist; *b* 16 Nov. 1950; *d* of John George Phillips and Cora Frances (*née* Hurford); *m* 1983, Dr David Richard Hunt, MA, ARCO. *Educ:* Sittingbourne Grammar Sch. for Girls; Maidstone Grammar Sch. for Girls; Royal Coll. of Music (ARCM). GRSM 1971; FRCO 1971. Director of Music, St Lawrence Jewry next Guildhall, London, 1976–85; Prof. of Organ and Harpsichord, London Coll. of Music, 1985–91; Tutor in Organ Studies, RNCM, 1993–97 (Vis. Tutor, 1997–2005). Co-founder with Dr D. R. Hunt, and Chm., English Organ Sch. and Museum, Milborne Port, Som, 1996–. Pres., IAO, 1997–99; Mem. Council, RCO, 1982–2003. Recitals throughout Europe, USA, Mexico and Australia; radio broadcasts, UK, Scandinavia, Netherlands, Australia, USA; numerous recordings incl. complete organ works of J. S. Bach. *Publications:* articles on style and performance of organ music. *Recreations:* reading, tennis, playing the violin. *Address:* The Manse, Chapel Lane, Milborne Port, Sherborne DT9 5DL. *T:* (01963) 250011. *W:* www.margaretphillips.org.uk.

PHILLIPS, Marisa, DLitt; President, Mental Health Review Tribunal, 1990–2007; *b* 14 April 1932; *d* of Dr and Mrs J. Fargion; *m* 1956, Philip Harold Phillips; one *s* one *d*. *Educ:* Henrietta Barnett Sch., London; Univ. of Redlands, California (Fulbright Schol.; BA Hons); Rome Univ. (DLitt). Called to Bar, Lincoln's Inn, 1963. On return from Redlands Univ., worked for US Inf. Service, Rome, 1954–56; spent one year in Berlin, as husband then in Army; period of work with Penguin Books; read for the Bar, joining DPP as Legal Asst, 1964; Legal Adviser, Police Complaints Bd, 1977; returned to DPP, 1979; Asst Dir, DPP, 1981; Principal Asst DPP, 1985; Asst Hd of Legal Services, 1986–87, Dir of Legal Casework, 1987–90, Crown Prosecution Service. Sen. Legal Advr, Banking Ombudsman, 1990–94. Comr, Mental Health Act Commn, 1991–96; Chm., Rent Assessment Panel, 1992–2003. Trustee, Camden Victim Support, 2006–10. *Recreations:* music, theatre, foreign travel.

PHILLIPS, Captain Mark Anthony Peter, CVO 1974; ADC(P); Chef d'Equipe and Coach, US Three Day Event Team, 1993–2012; Consultant, Gleneagles Mark Phillips Equestrian Centre, 1992–97 (Director, 1988–92); *b* 22 Sept. 1948; *s* of late P. W. G. Phillips, MC, and Anne Patricia (*née* Tiarks); *m* 1st, 1973, HRH The Princess Anne (marr. diss. 1992); one *s* one *d*; 2nd, 1997, Sandy Pflueger; one *d*. *Educ:* Marlborough Coll.; RMA Sandhurst. Joined 1st The Queen's Dragoon Guards, July 1969; Regimental duty, 1969–74; Company Instructor, RMA Sandhurst, 1974–77; Army Trng Directorate, MoD, 1977–78, retired. Personal ADC to HM the Queen, 1974–. Student, RAC Cirencester, 1978. Chm., British Olympic Equestrian Fund, subseq. British Equestrian Fedn Fund, 1989–2000. In Three Day Equestrian Event, GB winning teams: Team Championships: World, 1970; European, 1971; Olympic Gold Medallists (Team), Olympic Games, Munich, 1972; Olympic Silver Medallists (Team), Olympic Games, Seoul, 1988; Mem., Equestrian Team (Reserve), Olympic Games, Mexico, 1968 and Montreal, 1976. Winner, Badminton Three Day Event, 1971, 1972, 1974, 1981. Dir, Glos TEC, 1991–98. Hon. FBHS 2005. Liveryman: Farriers' Co.; Farmers' Co.; Carmen's Co.; Loriners' Co.; Freeman: City of London; Yeoman, Saddlers' Co. *Recreations:* riding, Rugby football, athletics. *Address:* Aston Farm, Cherington, Tetbury, Glos GL8 8SW. *Club:* (Hon. Mem.) Buck's.

See also under Royal Family.

PHILLIPS, Mark Paul; QC 1999; a Recorder, 2000–07; *b* 28 Dec. 1959; *s* of Norman John Phillips and Wendy Sharron Phillips; *m* 1984, Deborah Elizabeth Fisher (*d* 2010); one *s* two *d*; *m* 2011, Samantha Jayne Wilding; one *s* two step *d*. *Educ:* John Hampden Sch., High Wycombe; Univ. of Bristol (LLB 1982; LLM 1983). Called to the Bar, Inner Temple, 1984; in practice, 1986–; Asst Recorder, 1998–2000. Pres., Insolvency Lawyers' Assoc., 2002–03; Member: Council, Assoc. of Business Recovery Professionals, 2004–10 (Fellow, 2004); Internat. Insolvency Inst., 2007–. Founder and Mem. Bd, Debbie Fund, 2010–12. Gov., John Hampden Grammar Sch., 2014–. *Publications:* (ed jtly) Butterworths Insolvency Law Handbook, 1987, 13th edn 2011; contrib. chapter on Insolvency in: Byles on Bills of Exchange, 26th edn 1983; Paget's Law of Banking, 10th edn 1989 to 13th edn 2007; chap. on insolvency procedures in Insolvency of Banks: managing the risks, 1996. *Recreations:* dating my wife, family, watching football, motor sport. *Address:* 3–4 South Square, Gray's Inn, WC1R 5HP. *T:* (020) 7696 9900, *Fax:* (020) 7696 9911. *E:* markphillips@southsquare.com.

PHILLIPS, (Mark) Trevor, OBE 1999; broadcaster and journalist; Chair, Equality and Human Rights Commission, 2006–12; *b* 31 Dec. 1953; *s* of George Milton Phillips and Marjorie Eileen Phillips (*née* Canzius); *m* 1st, 1981, Asha Bhownagary (marr. diss. 2009); two *d*; 2nd, 2013, Helen Veale. *Educ:* Queen's Coll., Georgetown, Guyana; Imperial Coll., London (BSc; ARCS). Pres., NUS, 1978–80; London Weekend Television: researcher, 1980–81; producer, Black on Black, The Making of Britain, 1981–86; reporter, This Week, Thames TV, 1986–87; London Weekend Television: Editor, London Prog., 1987–92; Hd, Current Affairs, 1992–94; Presenter: London Prog., 1987–2000; Crosstalk, 1994–2000; The Material World, 1998–2000. Man. Dir, Pepper Prodns, 1994–. Mem. (Lab), 2000–03, Chm., 2000–01 and 2002–03, Dep. Chm., 2001–02, London Assembly, GLA. Chairman: Runnymede Trust, 1993–98; Hampstead Theatre, 1993–97; London Arts Bd, 1997–2000; CRE, 2003–06. Mem., Social Integration Commn, 2014–. Pres., John Lewis Partnership Council, 2015–. FRSA 1995. Hon. MA N London, 1995; Hon. DLitt: Westminster, 1999; South Bank, 2001; City, 2002. Journalism Award, RTS, 1988 and 1993; Best Documentary Series (for Windrush), RTS, 1998. Chevalier, Légion d'Honneur (France), 2007. *Publications:* Windrush: the irresistible rise of multi-racial Britain, 1998; Britain's Slave Trade, 1999. *Recreations:* music, running, crosswords. *Clubs:* Groucho, Home House.

PHILLIPS, Max; Assistant Under Secretary of State, Ministry of Defence, 1977–84; *b* 31 March 1924; *m* 1953, Patricia Moore; two *s* one *d* (and one *d* decd). *Educ:* Colston's Sch., Bristol; Christ's Hospital; Magdalene Coll., Cambridge (Schol.; 1st cl. Hist. Tripos, pts I and II; MA). Served War, RA, 1943–46. Appointed to Home Civil Service, 1949; Colonial Office, 1949–59; Sec., Nigeria Fiscal Commn, 1957–58; UKAEA, 1959–73; Procurement Exec., MoD, 1973–74; HM Treasury, 1974–77; retired 1984, re-employed as Asst Sec., MoD, 1984–87. Chm., Guildford Evening DFAS, 2003–06. Gov., Christ's Hospital, 1979– (Almoner, 1981–92). *Recreations:* modern myths, exploring the imagination and the countryside. *Address:* 2 Wilderness Farmhouse, Onslow Village, Guildford, Surrey GU2 7QP. *T:* (01483) 561308.

PHILLIPS, Melanie; columnist, The Times, since 2014; *b* 4 June 1951; *d* of late Alfred and Mabel Phillips; *m* 1974, Joshua Rufus Rozenberg, *qv*; one *s* one *d*. *Educ:* Putney High Sch. for Girls; St Anne's Coll., Oxford (BA 1973). Grad. trainee, Evening Echo, Hemel Hempstead, 1974–76; staff writer, New Society, 1976–77; Guardian: reporter, 1977; social services corresp., 1978–80; leader writer, 1980–84; news ed., 1984–87; Asst Ed. and columnist, 1987–93; columnist: Observer, 1993–98; Sunday Times, 1998–2001; Daily Mail, 2001–14. Panellist, The Moral Maze, BBC Radio 4. *Publications:* The Divided House, 1980; (with J. Dawson) Doctors' Dilemmas, 1984; All Must Have Prizes, 1996, 3rd edn 1998; The Sex-Change Society: feminised Britain and the neutered male, 1999; The Ascent of Woman, 2003, 2nd edn 2004; Londonistan, 2006; The World Turned Upside Down: the global battle over God, truth and power, 2010; Guardian Angel, 2013. *Recreations:* family, friends, theatre, cinema. *Address:* BCM Rozenberg, WC1N 3XX. *E:* melanie@melaniephillips.com. *W:* www.melaniephillips.com.

PHILLIPS, Prof. Nelson William, PhD; Professor of Strategy and Organizational Behaviour, Imperial College Business School (formerly Tanaka Business School), Imperial College London, since 2005; *b* 7 Nov. 1962; *s* of Murray and Lucille Phillips. *Educ:* Univ. of Calgary (BSc, MBA); Univ. of Alberta (PhD 1995). Asst Prof., 1993–98, Associate Prof., 1998–2002, Faculty of Mgt, McGill Univ.; Beckwith Prof. of Mgt Studies and MBA Dir, Judge Inst. of Mgt, and Fellow, Hughes Hall, Cambridge Univ., 2002–05. *Publications:* (with C. Hardy) Discourse Analysis, 2002; contribs to Acad. of Mgt Jl, Organization Science, Organization Studies, Jl Mgt Studies. *Address:* Imperial College Business School, Imperial College London, S Kensington Campus, SW7 2AZ. *T:* (020) 7589 5111, *Fax:* (020) 7823 7685. *E:* n.phillips@imperial.ac.uk.

PHILLIPS, Prof. Paddy Andrew, FRACP, FACP, FRCP; Chief Medical Officer, Department of Health, South Australia, since 2008; Chief Public Health Officer, Department of Health, Australia, since 2015; Professor of Medicine, Flinders University, Adelaide, since 1997; Consultant, Flinders Medical Centre and Repatriation Hospitals, Adelaide, since 1997 (Head of Medicine, 1997–2008); *b* 26 Oct. 1956; *s* of Walter Alfred Peter Phillips and Lilian Phillips (*née* Watt); one *s* one *d*. *Educ:* Univ. of Adelaide (MB, BS); Univ. of Oxford (DPhil 1983; MA 1997). Intern, Royal Adelaide Hosp., 1980; Hon. Sen. House Officer, John Radcliffe Hosp., Oxford, 1981–83; Resident MO and Registrar, Prince Henry's Hosp., Melbourne, 1984–86; Fellow in Clinical Pharmacology, 1987, Res. Fellow, 1988–90, Consultant, 1988–96, Austin Hosp., Melbourne; Sen. Lectr, 1990–94, Associate Prof., 1994–96, Dept of Medicine, Melbourne Univ.; May Reader in Medicine, Nuffield Dept of Clinical Medicine, Univ. of Oxford, and Professorial Fellow, New Coll., Oxford, 1996–97; Consultant, Oxford Radcliffe NHS Trust, 1996–97. Public Service Medal for Health Services, 2011. *Publications:* scientific papers in physiol., pharmacol., cardiovascular disease, health services research. *Recreations:* mountain and road cycling, wine, fly fishing, ski-ing, music. *Address:* South Australia Department of Health, Citicentre Building, Hindmarsh Square, Adelaide, SA 5000, Australia. *T:* (8) 82266000.

PHILLIPS, Patricia Ruth; HM Diplomatic Service, retired; Counsellor, Foreign and Commonwealth Office, 2010–14; *b* 11 March 1962; *d* of Alan and Diana Phillips. *Educ:* N London Collegiate Sch.; Newnham Coll., Cambridge (BA Hist. 1984); Open Univ. (MBA 2011). MAFF, 1984–91; Fulbright Fellow, Univ. of Minnesota, 1991–92; First Secretary: Washington, 1992–97; FCO, 1997–2002; Counsellor (Econ.), The Hague, 2002–04; Dep. Hd of Mission, Amman, 2004–07; Ambassador to Angola and concurrently to São Tomé and Príncipe, 2007–09. *Recreations:* music, history.

PHILLIPS, Peter; *see* Phillips, I. P.

PHILLIPS, Peter Andrew Jestyn; Chief Executive, Secretary of the Press Syndicate, and University Printer, Cambridge University Press, since 2012; Fellow, Wolfson College, Cambridge, since 2012; *b* Cardiff, 1 May 1962; *s* of late Dr Ernest Phillips and of Barbara Phillips; *m* 1988, Clare Higgins; two *s* one *d*. *Educ:* Culford Sch.; Merton Coll., Oxford (BA 1st Cl. Maths); Harvard Business Sch. (AMP 2002); Univ. of Cambridge (MA). Associate Consultant, 1984–86, Consultant, 1986–89, Manager, 1989–91, Bain & Co.; Sen. Manager, Corporate Finance, S G Warburg, 1991–93; BBC: Hd, Corporate Planning, 1993–96; Finance Dir, 1997–2000, Chief Operating Officer, 2001–04, News; Dir, Business Develt, 2005–06; Bd Mem. and Partner, Strategy and Market Develts, Ofcom, 2006–10; Chief Operating Officer, CUP, 2010–12. Dir, Parly Broadcasting Ltd, 1998–2006. Advr, RCP, 2004–11. Chm., Sabre Trust, 1990–93; Trustee: John Schofield Trust, 1995–2011; Article 19, 2001–05; Crafts Council, 2004–11; Nuffield Trust, 2008–14. Mem. Council, Publishers' Assoc., 2015–. *Recreations:* walking, small islands, chamber music, motorbikes, Arsenal FC, contemporary crafts. *Address:* Cambridge University Press, University Printing House, Shaftesbury Road, Cambridge CB2 8BS. *T:* (01223) 312393. *E:* pphillips@cambridge.org.

PHILLIPS, Sir Peter (John), Kt 1990; OBE 1983; Chairman, Principality Building Society, 1991–2000 (Deputy Chairman, 1988–91); *b* 18 June 1930; *s* of Walter Alfred Phillips and Victoria Mary Phillips; *m* 1956, Jean Gwendoline Williams; one *s* one *d*. *Educ:* Radley College; Pembroke College, Oxford (MA). Joined Aberthaw and Bristol Channel Portland Cement Co., 1956, Jt Man. Dir, 1964–83; Western Area Dir, Blue Circle Industries, 1983–84; Dep. Chm., 1985, Chm., 1987–93, A. B. Electronic Products Gp. Dep. Chm. Bd of Governors, Univ. of Glam., 1996–98; Chm. Council, Univ. of Wales, Cardiff, 1998–2004 (Vice-Chm., 1997–98). *Recreations:* walking, fishing, reading. *Address:* Fromheulog, Church Road, Llanbethian, Cowbridge CF71 7JF. *Club:* Cardiff and County.

PHILLIPS, Peter Sayer; Founder and Musical Director, The Tallis Scholars, since 1973; Music Critic, The Spectator, since 1983; Director of Music, since 2008, and Bodley Fellow, since 2010, Merton College, Oxford; *b* 15 Oct. 1953; *s* of Nigel Sayer Phillips and Patricia Ann Witchell (*née* Wyatt); *m* 1st, 1987, Clio (marr. diss. 1993), *d* of late David Oliver Lloyd-Jacob, CBE; 2nd, 1997, Caroline Trevor; one *s*. *Educ:* Winchester Coll.; St John's Coll., Oxford (Organ Scholar). Teacher: Oxford Univ., 1976–81; Trinity Coll. of Music, 1980–84; RCM, 1981–88. Co-founder and Artistic Director: Gimell Records, 1980–; Tallis Scholars Summer Schs, Oakham, 2000–11 and Uppingham, 2012–14 (teacher, 2000–14), Seattle, 2005–13, Sydney, 2007–12; Founder, Winchester Consort Course, 2015–. Has conducted Dutch Chamber Choir, Collegium Vocale Gent, BBC Singers, Finnish Radio Choir, Tudor Choir of Seattle, Markell's Voices of Novosibirsk, Taipei Chamber Singers, Intrada of Moscow, Musica Reservata Barcelona, El Leon de Oro. Mem., Early Music Cttee, Arts Council, 1987–88. Chm., Judges, London A Cappella Choir Competition, 2014–. Ed., Early Music Gazette, 1980–82; cricket correspondent, Spectator, 1989; Prop. and Adv. Ed., Musical Times, 1995–. Many awards for recordings made by Tallis Scholars, incl. Gramophone Record of the Year, 1987, and Early Music Record of the Year, 1987, 1991, 1994 and 2005, Gramophone magazine. Chevalier de l'Ordre des Arts et des Lettres (France), 2005. *Publications:* English Sacred Music 1549–1649, 1991; (contrib.) Companion to Medieval and Renaissance Music, 1992; What We Really Do, 2003, 2nd edn 2013; contrib. Spectator, Guardian, Times, Musical Times, New Republic, Listener, Early Music, Music and Letters, Royal Acad. magazine, Evening Standard, BBC Music Magazine, TLS, Sunday Telegraph. *Recreations:* black and white photography, cricket, cooking, Arabia. *Address:* 22 Gibson Square, N1 0RD. *T:* (020) 7226 8047; 48 rue des Francs Bourgeois, 75003 Paris, France. *T:* 42724461; Merton College, Merton Street, Oxford OX1 4JD. *Clubs:* Chelsea Arts, MCC.

PHILLIPS, (Rachel) Sarah, OBE 2005; DL; Chairman, Demelza Hospice Care for Children, since 2012; *b* 8 Feb. 1943; *d* of late Air Cdre John Lawrance Kirby, CB, CBE, JP, DL and Rachel Kirby; *m* 1966, Peter, *s* of Maj.-Gen. Sir Farndale Phillips, KBE, CB, DSO, and Lady (Lovering Catherine) Phillips; one *s* one *d*. *Educ:* Benenden Sch.; Heidelberg. Qualified as: LTA coach, 1978; remedial tutor, Kingsbury Centre, Washington, 1983; diagnosed with MS, 1981. Trustee, 1992–2005, Chm., 1998–2005, Multiple Sclerosis Society of GB and NI; Chm., Colchester Br., MS Soc., 1989–98; Chm., Homes Cttee, MS Soc., 1993–98; Trustee, Internat. Fedn of MS Socs, now MS Internat. Fedn, 1997 (Pres. and Chm., 2004–11; Chm., Nominating Cttee, 2002–03, Hon. Sec., 2003–04). Chm., Disability Adv. Gp, NHS Appts Commn, 2003–07. Chm., Victim Support, 2005–11. Non-executive Director: Mid Essex Community and Mental Health Trust, 2000–01; N Essex Partnership NHS Foundn Trust (formerly N Essex Mental Health Partnership NHS Trust), 2001–13. Mem., Registration and Conduct Cttees, Gen. Social Care Council, 2003–12. Comr, Royal Hosp. Chelsea, 2007–12. Trustee, Leonard Cheshire, 1999–2002. DL Essex, 2005. *Recreations:* bridge, choral singing. *Address:* Wistaria House, Coggeshall, Essex CO6 1UF.

PHILLIPS, Raymond Mark; Policy Adviser to European Union, Department for International Development and World Bank and author of National Employment Plans for Central and East European Governments, since 1998; *b* 15 April 1944; *s* of Vernon Phillips and Claudia Phillips; *m* 1968, Janet Harris; four *s*. *Educ:* Cowbridge Grammar Sch.; UC Cardiff. Department of Employment: Operational Planning and Res., 1976–78; Pay Policy Advr, 1978–79; Asst Sec., Standing Commn on Pay Comparability, 1979–80; Regl Gen. Manager, Trng Services Agency, 1980–82; Exec. Dir, Employment Service, 1982–83; Regional Director: MSC, 1983–86; Employment and Enterprise Gp, 1986–87; Regl Dir, 1987–93, Dir of Inf. and Systems, 1993–95, Employment Service, Dept of Employment; Dir, Policy and Process Design, Employment Service, DfEE, 1995–97. *Recreations:* gardening, cosmology, running, tennis (Chairman: Bramhall Queensgate Sports Club; Bramhall Queensgate Tennis Club). *Address:* Stockport, Cheshire.

PHILLIPS, Richard Charles Jonathan; QC 1990; *b* 8 Aug. 1947; *yr s* of Air Commodore M. N. Phillips, MD, ChB, DMRD and Dorothy E. Phillips; *m* 1978, Alison Jane Francis (OBE 1991); one *d*. *Educ:* King's School, Ely; Sidney Sussex College, Cambridge (Exhibnr). Called to the Bar, Inner Temple, 1970. Asst Parly Boundary Comr, 1992–. *Recreations:* travel, natural history, photography, walking. *Address:* Francis Taylor Building, Temple, EC4Y 7BY. *T:* (020) 7353 8415.

PHILLIPS, Dr Richard Peter, CMG 2006; Director, Global Shared Services, British Council, 2009–10; *b* 2 May 1950; *s* of William Leslie Phillips and Dorothy May Phillips; *m* 1st, 1976, Alice Detoya (*d* 2003); one *s* one *d*; 2nd, 2006, Adele Sinclair (*née* McNaughton). *Educ:* Univ. of Bristol (BSc Hons Chem. 1971; PhD Inorganic Chem. 1975); Huddersfield Poly. (PGCE 1981). Pt-time Tutor of Chem., Univ. of Bristol, 1971–74; Vis. Prof. of Chem., Mindanao State Univ., Philippines, 1974–76; Field Officer, Philippines, 1976–77, Field Dir, Indonesia, 1978–80, VSO; HM Diplomatic Service, 1981–82; joined British Council, 1982: Sci. Officer, Yugoslavia, 1983–85; Sen. Sci. Officer, London, 1985–89; Educn Officer/Dep. Dir, Indonesia, 1989–93; Hd, Mgt Services, London, 1993–95; Contract Ops Dir, Manchester, 1995–2000; Dir, Indonesia, 2000–03; Prog. Dir, Finance and Business Systems, 2003–06; Dir, Customer Services and Innovation, 2007–08; Dep. Dir, Resources, 2008–09. *Publications:* contrib. various papers to Chemical Communications and Jl Inorganic Chemistry. *Recreations:* tennis, sailing, reading, classical studies. *Address:* 107 Sussex Road, Petersfield, Hants GU31 4LB. *E:* rpphillips01@gmail.com.

PHILLIPS, Rear Adm. Richard Thomas Ryder, CB 1998; FNI; Chief Executive Officer/Clerk, Worshipful Company of Haberdashers, 2005–13; Vice Chairman, JMW Energy Ventures (Bahrain), since 2013; *b* 1 Feb. 1947; *s* of late Thomas Hall Phillips and Arabella Sadie Phillips; *m* 1st, 1969, Susan Elizabeth Groves (*d* 1996); one *d*; 2nd, 1999, Belinda Susan Kelway Round Turner; one step *s* one step *d*. *Educ:* Kingsland Grange, Shrewsbury; Wrekin Coll. BRNC Dartmouth, 1965; Commanding Officer: HMS Scimitar, 1974; HMS Hubberston, 1978; ndc Canberra, 1981; Directorate of Naval Plans, 1982; Commanding Officer: HMS Charybdis, 1985; HMS Scylla, 1986; Asst Dir, Defence Op. Requirements (Maritime), 1987; CO, HMS Cornwall, and Capt., 8 Frigate Sqn, 1988; Capt., RN Presentation Team, 1991; Cabinet Office Top Mgt Prog., 1992; COS, Flag Officer Surface Flotilla, 1992; CO, HMS Illustrious, 1993–96; ACDS Op. Requirements (Sea Systems), 1996–99. ADC to the Queen, 1993. Director: Marconi Naval Systems, 1999–2000; BAE SYSTEMS, 2000–04; East Africa Oil Co., 2013–. Special Adviser: Internat. Energy Adv. Council, 2004–07; Oil and Gas Adv. Bd, Renaissance Capital, 2011–12; Mem., Exec. Adv. Bd, XSMG Defence, 2011–. Younger Brother, Trinity Hse, 1984. FNI 1999; Associate Fellow, RUSI, 2004. *Recreations:* shooting, gardening, sailing, ski-ing. *Club:* Royal Yacht Squadron.

PHILLIPS, Sir Robin Francis, 3rd Bt *cr* 1912; Owner and Principal, Ravenscourt Theatre School, London, 1989–2007; *b* 29 July 1940; *s* of Sir Lionel Francis Phillips, 2nd Bt, and Camilla Mary, *er d* of late Hugh Parker, 22 Chapel Street, Belgrave Square, SW1; *S* father, 1944. *Educ:* Aiglon Coll., Switzerland. Chief Air Traffic Control Officer, Biggin Hill, 1970–78; Hazel Malone Management, 1978–81; Devonair Radio, 1981–83; Radio Luxembourg, 1984; Hd of Casting, Corona Stage School, 1985–89. *Heir:* none. *Address:* 12 Manson Mews, Queens Gate, SW7 5AF.

PHILLIPS, Prof. Robin Kenneth Stewart, FRCS, FRCSE, FRCPSGlas; Consultant Surgeon, since 1987, and Clinical Director, Gastroenterology, Upper Gastrointestinal Surgery and Emergency Surgery, since 2006, St Mark's Hospital, Harrow; *b* 18 Nov. 1952; *s* of John Fleetwood Stewart Phillips and Mary Gordon Phillips (*née* Shaw); *m* 1975, Janina Fairley Nowak; one *s* one *d*. *Educ:* Sherborne Sch. for Boys; Royal Free Hosp. Med. Sch. (MB BS 1975); MS London 1984. FRCS 1979; FRCSE 2002; FRCPSGlas *ad eundem*, 2004. Higher surgical trng with St Mary's Gp of Hosps, 1980–85; St Mark's Hospital: Resident Surgical Officer, 1986; Chm., Surgery, 1993–97; Dean, Acad. Inst., 1999–2002; Sen. Lectr in Surgery, St Bartholomew's Hosp., London, 1987–90; Consultant Surgeon, Homerton Hosp., London, 1990–93; Civilian Consultant in Colorectal Surgery to the RN, 2001–. Dir, CRUK (formerly ICRF) Polyposis Registry, 1993–2013. President: British Colostomy Assoc., 2001–05; Sect. of Coloproctology, RSocMed, 2006–07. Prof. of Colorectal Surgery, Imperial Coll., London, 2000–. *Publications:* edited: Familial adenomatous polyposis and other polyposis syndromes, 1994; Fistula-in-ano, 1996; A Companion to Specialist Surgical Practice: colorectal surgery, 1997, 5th edn 2014; Frontiers in Coloproctology, 2005; contrib. numerous peer-reviewed res. articles, mainly in familial adenomatous polyposis (an inherited form of bowel cancer), anal fistula and other painful conditions. *Recreations:* fly-fishing, being walked by the dog. *Address:* St Mark's Hospital, Harrow, Middx HA1 3UJ. *T:* (020) 8235 4251, *Fax:* (020) 8235 4277. *E:* robin.phillips@nhs.net. *Club:* Royal Society of Medicine.

PHILLIPS, (Ronald) William; fruit grower, 2002–06; Director: NB Selection Ltd, 1991–2002; Norman Broadbent International, 1998–2002; *b* 21 April 1949; *s* of late Ronald Phillips and Phoebe Nora Haynes; *m* 1979, Dorothy Parsons. *Educ:* Steyning Grammar Sch.; University College of Wales, Aberystwyth (BScEcon). Joined CS, 1971; served in Dept of Transport, PSA, DoE, Develt Commn (Private Sec. to Lord Northfield); Asst County Sec., Kent CC, 1979–80; UK Expert to EC Council of Ministers Wkg Party on Environmental Impact Assessment, 1980–83; Greater London Reg. Office, DoE (Local Govt Reorganisation), 1983–86; Head of Policy Unit, 1986–87, Man. Dir, 1987–91, Westminster CC. FRSA 1990; FCMI (FBIM 1990). JP Maidstone, 1992–96. *Recreation:* travel. *Address:* Livesey Cottage, Livesey Street, Teston, Kent ME18 5AY.

PHILLIPS, Rory Andrew Livingstone; QC 2002; *b* 30 May 1961; *s* of Peter and Jean Phillips; *m* 1987, Claire Imogen Haggard; two *s* one *d*. *Educ:* Eton; King's Coll., Cambridge (MA). Called to the Bar, Inner Temple, 1984, Bencher, 2013. *Address:* 3 Verulam Buildings, Gray's Inn, WC1R 5NT.

PHILLIPS, Sarah; *see* Phillips, R. S.

PHILLIPS, Sharon Katherine, (Mrs Charles Cowling); Principal, King Edward VI College, Stourbridge, 2008–15; *b* Bristol, 17 Feb. 1957; *d* of Gordon and Gloria Damsell; *m* 1st, 1979, Paul Phillips (marr. diss. 1995); one *s* one *d*; 2nd, 2008, Charles Cowling. *Educ:* Churchill Coll., Cambridge (BA Hons English 1979; PGCE 1981; MA 1982); Open Univ. (BA Hons 1988); Reading Univ. (MA Lit. and Visual Arts 1995). Hd of English, Newbury Coll., 1990–95; North East Worcestershire College: Curriculum Manager, Humanities, 1995–97; Associate Dir, 1997–99; Dir of Quality, 1999–2001; Dep. Principal, Halesowen Coll., 2001–08. *Publications:* English Language and Literature A Level, 1994, 2nd edn 2000; English Literature Resource Bank, 1995. *Recreations:* reading, visiting art galleries, looking, walking, spending time with husband, children and dogs.

PHILLIPS, Siân, CBE 2000; actress; *d* of D. Phillips and Sally Phillips; *m* 1st, 1954, Dr D. H. Roy (marr. diss. 1960); 2nd, 1960, (Seamus) Peter O'Toole (marr. diss. 1979; he *d* 2013); two *d*; 3rd, 1979, Robin Sachs (marr. diss. 1992). *Educ:* Pontardawe Grammar Sch.; Univ. of Wales (Cardiff Coll.) (BA Hons English; Fellow, 1982); RADA (Maggie Albanesi Scholarship, 1956; Bancroft Gold Medal, 1958). BBC Radio Wales, mid 1940s–, and BBC TV Wales, early 1950s–; Newsreader and Announcer, and Mem. Rep. Co., BBC, 1953–55; toured for Welsh Arts Council with National Theatre Co., 1953–55; Arts Council Bursary to study drama outside Wales, 1955. Mem., Arts Council Drama Cttee, 1970–75. Governor: St David's Trust, 1970–73; Welsh Coll. of Music and Drama, 1992–. *Theatre:* London: Hedda Gabler, 1959; Ondine, and the Duchess of Malfi, 1960–61 (1st RSC season at Aldwych); The Lizard on the Rock, 1961; Gentle Jack, Maxibules, and The Night of the Iguana, 1964; Ride a Cock Horse, 1965; Man and Superman, and Man of Destiny, 1966; The Burglar, 1967; Epitaph for George Dillon, 1972; A Nightingale in Bloomsbury Square, 1973; The Gay Lord Quex, 1975; Spinechiller, 1978; You Never Can Tell, Lyric, Hammersmith, 1979; Pal Joey, Half Moon, 1980 and Albery, 1981; Dear Liar, Mermaid, 1982; Major Barbara, NT, 1982; Peg, Phoenix, 1984; Gigi, Lyric, Shaftesbury Ave., 1985; Thursday's Ladies, Apollo, 1987; Brel, Donmar, 1987; Paris Match, Garrick, 1989; Vanilla, Lyric, 1990; The Manchurian Candidate, Lyric, Hammersmith, and nat. tour, 1991; Painting Churches, Playhouse, 1992; The Glass Menagerie, Cambridge Theatre Co. nat. tour, 1989; Ghosts, Welsh Arts Council tour, and Sherman Theatre, Wales, 1993; The Lion in Winter, UK nat. tour, 1994; An Inspector Calls, NY, 1995; A Little Night Music, RNT, 1995; Marlene, nat. tour, 1996, Lyric, 1997, S Africa, Paris, 1998, NY, 1999; Lettice and Lovage, tour, 2001; My Old Lady, LA, 2001, NY, 2002; The Old Ladies, UK tour, 2003; The Dark, Donmar Th., 2004; The

Play What I Wrote, UK tour, The Unexpected Man, UK tour, 2005; Great Expectations, RSC, 2005–06; Rockaby, Barbican and Gate, Dublin, 2006; Quartet, USA, 2006; Regrets Only, NY, 2007; Les Liaisons Dangereuses, NY, 2008; Calendar Girls, UK tour, 2008–09, Noel Coward Th., 2009; Juliet and Her Romeo, Th. Royal, Bristol, 2010; A Little Night Music, St Louis Opera, 2010; Siân Phillips Crossing Borders (solo show), Wiltons Music Hall, London, 2011, Pheasantry, London, 2012; Bittersweet (operetta), NY, 2011; Lovesong, tour for Frantic Assembly, 2011, then Lyric Hammersmith, 2012; Little Dogs, Nat. Th. of Wales, 2012; My Fair Lady, Royal Albert Hall, 2012; Cabaret, Savoy and tour, 2012 (Best Actress in a Vis. Prodn, Manchester Th. Awards, 2013); This is My Family, Crucible Studio, Sheffield, 2013 (Best Supporting Perf., UK Th. Awards, 2013); People, RNT UK tour, 2013; The Importance of Being Earnest, Shakespeare Th., Washington, 2013, Harold Pinter Th. and UK tour, 2014; Playing For Time, Crucible Th., Sheffield, 2015; concert tours, UK and US, 2000, UK 2001; *cabaret*: NY, 2000, RNT and tour, 2001; Divas at the Donmar, Donmar Th., 2001; UK concert tour, 2003; Both Sides Now, touring UK and overseas, 2007–; solo cabaret in Welsh, S4C, 2013. *TV drama series* include: Shoulder to Shoulder, 1974; How Green was my Valley, 1975; I, Claudius, 1976; Boudicca, and Off to Philadelphia in the Morning, 1977; The Oresteia of Aeschylus, 1978; Crime and Punishment, 1979; Sean O'Casey (RTE), 1980; Winston Churchill, The Wilderness Years, 1981; Language and Landscape (6 bilingual films, Welsh and English), 1985; The Snow Spider, 1988; Shadow of the Noose, 1989; Emlyn's Moon, 1990; Perfect Scoundrels, 1990; Tonight at 8.30: Hands Across the Sea; The Astonished Heart; Ways and Means, 1991; The Borrowers, 1992, 1993; The Aristocrats, 1999; Nikita, The Magician's House, 2000; The Last Detective, 2002; Midsomer Murders, 2006; Canu Grwndi, 2006; *TV films* include: A Painful Case (RTE), 1985; While Reason Sleeps; Return to Endor, 1986 (USA); Siân (biographical), 1987, 2002; Heidi, 1993; Mind to Kill (also in Welsh), 1995; Summer Silence (musical, also in Welsh), 1995. *Films* include: Becket, 1963; Goodbye Mr Chips, and Laughter in the Dark, 1968; Murphy's War, 1970; Under Milk Wood, 1971; The Clash of the Titans, 1979; Dune, 1984; Ewocks Again, and The Doctor and the Devils, 1985; Valmont, 1989; Age of Innocence, 1994; House of America, 1996; Alice Through the Looking Glass, 1999; Coming and Going, 2000; The Gigolos, 2007. Has made recordings, incl. Peg, Gigi, I remember Mama, Pal Joey, Bewitched, Bothered and Bewildered, A Little Night Music, Marlene. RTS Annual Lecture (Eng. and Welsh transmissions), 1993. FRSA. FWNCMD, 1991; Fellow, Cardiff Coll., Univ. of Wales, 1983; Hon. Fellow: Polytechnic of Wales, 1988; Trinity Coll., Carms, 1998; Univ. of Wales Swansea, 1998. Hon. DLitt Wales, 1984. Critics Circle Award, New York Critics Award, and Famous 7 Critics Award, for Goodbye Mr Chips, 1969; BAFTA Award for How Green was my Valley and I, Claudius, 1978; Royal Television Soc. Award for I, Claudius (Best Performer), 1978; Lifetime Achievement Award, BAFTA Wales, 2000; St David Award for Culture, Welsh Govt, 2015. Mem., Gorsedd of Bards, 1960 (for services to drama in Wales). *Publications:* Siân Phillips' Needlepoint, 1987; autobiography: Private Faces, 1999; Public Places, 2001; gen. journalism (Vogue, Cosmopolitan, Daily Mail, 3 years for Radio Times, Country Living, Options). *Recreations:* walking, gardening, needlepoint, drawing. *Address:* c/o Dalzell Beresford, Paddock Suite, The Courtyard, 55 Charterhouse Street, EC1M 6HA. *W:* www.sian-phillips-cabaret.com.

PHILLIPS, Simon Benjamin; QC 2010; a Recorder, since 2002; *b* Watford, 24 Sept. 1961; *s* of late Peter John Phillips and Josephine Beryl Phillips (*née* Isaacs); *m* 1986, Hon. Sophia Rosalind Vane, *d* of Baron Barnard, *qv*; two *s* one *d*. *Educ:* Harrow Sch.; Sussex Univ. (BA Law 1983); Trinity Hall, Cambridge (LLM 1984); Inns of Court Sch. of Law. Called to the Bar, Inner Temple, 1985 (Basil Nield Schol.); in practice as barrister specialising in serious crime law and regulatory law; Fee Paid Immigration Judge, 2006–. *Recreations:* family, rural life, travel, squash, lawn tennis, golf, ski-ing. *Address:* New Park Court Chambers, 16 Park Place, Leeds LS1 2SJ. *T:* (0113) 243 3277, *Fax:* (0113) 242 1285. *E:* simon.phillips@npc-l.co.uk. *Clubs:* Royal Automobile, Farmers; Jesters; Alwoodley Golf.

PHILLIPS, Prof. Simon Edward Victor, PhD; FRSC; Director, Research Complex at Harwell, since 2008; Adjunct Fellow, Linacre College, Oxford, since 2015; *b* Cirencester, 14 March 1950; *s* of Edward and Norah Mary Phillips; *m* 1974, Deborah Anne Cowell; two *s*. *Educ:* Cirencester Grammar Sch.; University Coll. London (BSc Chem. 1971; PhD Chem. 1974). FRSC 2002. Post-doctoral Fellow in Chem., Univ. of BC, Vancouver, 1974–76; scientist, MRC Lab. of Molecular Biol., Cambridge, 1976–82; Chargé de Recherche, Immunologie, Inst. Pasteur, Paris, 1982–85; University of Leeds: Lectr in Biophysics, 1985–89; Reader in Biophysics, 1989–92; SERC Sen. Fellow, 1989–94; Prof. of Molecular Biophysics, 1992–96; Astbury Prof. of Biophysics, 1996–2008; Dir, Astbury Centre for Structural Molecular Biol., 1999–2001; Dean for Res., Faculty of Biol Scis, 2001–04. Visiting Professor: of Biophysics, Univ. of Leeds, 2008–; of Molecular Biophysics, Univ. of Oxford, 2008–; Vis. Scientist, Brookhaven Nat. Lab., NY, 1980; EMBO Fellow, Inst. Pasteur, Paris, 1985; Internat. Res. Schol., Howard Hughes Med. Inst., USA, 1993–97. *Publications:* contribs to scientific pubns. *Recreations:* music, gardening, theatre, wine, finding out how things work. *Address:* Research Complex at Harwell, Rutherford Appleton Laboratory, Harwell, Didcot OX11 0FA. *T:* (01235) 567700. *E:* simon.phillips@re-harwell.ac.uk.

PHILLIPS, Hon. Sir Stephen (Edmund), Kt 2013; **Hon. Mr Justice Phillips;** a Judge of the High Court of Justice, Queen's Bench Division, since 2013; *b* 10 Oct. 1961; *s* of His Honour (David) Alan Phillips, *qv*; *m* 1998, Sonia (*née* Tolaney). *Educ:* King's Sch., Chester; University Coll., Oxford (MA Oxon; Martin Wronker Prize, 1983). Called to the Bar, Gray's Inn, 1984 (Birkenhead Award, 1984; Reid Scholarship; David Karmel Prize, 1985; Bencher, 2006); an Asst Recorder, 1999–2000; a Recorder, 2000–13; QC 2002; a Dep. High Ct Judge, 2008–13. *Recreations:* hill walking, football, tennis. *Address:* Royal Courts of Justice, Strand, WC2A 2LL.

PHILLIPS, Stephen James; freelance writer, producer and broadcaster; *b* 28 May 1947; *s* of James Ronald Phillips and Diana Betty Phillips (*née* Bradshaw); *m* 1988, Simone Lila Lopez; two *d*. *Educ:* Univ. of London (ext. BA Hons Ancient Hist.); St John's Coll., Cambridge (Dip. Classical Archaeol.). Reporter and critic, Yorks Evening Post, 1965–69; critic and feature writer, Daily Express, 1969–72; Manager, Holiday Village, Thasos, Greece, 1973; BBC reporter and presenter, 1973–76; Gen. Administrator, Prospect Theatre Co., Old Vic, 1976–78; presenter, Kaleidoscope and other BBC programmes, 1978–81; Arts Corresp., ITN and Channel Four, 1982–89; Series Ed., Signals, 1989–91; exec. producer, Antelope Films, 1992–2000; Hd of Arts, 1991–95, Arts consultant, 1996–2000, Meridian Broadcasting; Culture/communications consultant: Arts Sponsorship Panel, J. Sainsbury plc, 1990–2003; RIBA, 2000–; Theatre Mgt Assoc., 2011–; Director and Executive Producer: Jazz Music Ltd, 2012–; Aarya Ltd, 2012–. Lectr, Dramatic Writing MA, 1997–2007, Vis. Res. Fellow, 1999–2007, Sussex Univ. Member: Arts Council of England, 1994–98 (Chm., Touring Adv. Panel, 1994–98); SE Arts Bd, 1999–2002; SE England Regl Assembly and Exec. Cttee, 2000–02; Vice Chm., SE Regl Cultural Consortium, 2000–03. Chairman: Isaac Newton Arts Trust, 2002–09; Anglo Chinese Creative Industries Assoc., 2010–; British Architectural Trust, 2011–13. Board Member: Tricycle Theatre, Kilburn, 1982–2002 (Chm., 1984–94); English Nat. Ballet, 1996–2005; Chichester Fest. Theatre, 1999–2003; Chm., Arts for Everyone Lottery Panel, 1996–98. Chm., Friends of Herstmonceux Castle, 1995–2002; Trustee: Brighton's West Pier, 1997–2007; RIBA Cultural Trust, 2003–10 (Vice Chair, 2007–10; Chair, 2010–); Patron, Brighton Dome Appeal. Hon. FRIBA 2003. *Recreations:* theatre, art, history, Mediterranean travel, family.

PHILLIPS, Stephen James; QC 2009; MP (C) Sleaford and North Hykeham, since 2010; a Recorder, since 2009; *b* London, 9 March 1970; *s* of late Stewart Charles Phillips and of Janice Frances Phillips (*née* Woodall, now Pavey); *m* 1998, Fiona Jane Parkin (marr. diss. 2013); one *s* two *d*. *Educ:* Canford Sch.; Oriel Coll., Oxford (BA Juris 1991; BCL 1992). Late 14/20 King's Hussars and Welsh Guards. Called to the Bar, Lincoln's Inn, 1993; in practice specialising in commercial litigation. Chm. of Govs, Frank Barnes Sch. for Deaf Children, 2006–10. Member: European Scrutiny Cttee, 2010–15; Public Accounts Cttee, 2014–. *Recreation:* getting muddy with my kids. *Address:* 7 King's Bench Walk, Temple, EC4Y 7DS. *T:* (020) 7910 8300, *Fax:* (020) 7910 8400. *E:* clerks@7kbw.com; House of Commons, SW1A 0AA. *Club:* Cavalry and Guards.

PHILLIPS, Timothy Dewe, CBE 2007; Chairman: All England Lawn Tennis and Croquet Club, 1999–2010; Committee of Management, Wimbledon Championships, 1999–2010; *b* 22 April 1942; *s* of late Warren Phillips and Marjorie Phillips (*née* Thornton); *m* 1969, Elizabeth Wheeldon; two *s* one *d*. *Educ:* Mill Hill Sch.; Merton Coll., Oxford (MA; Hon. Fellow 2008); Harvard Business Sch. (AMP). British Airways, 1966–2001: worked overseas in various mgt posts based in Hong Kong, Zambia, Brunei, Lebanon, The Gulf, Australia and Italy, 1969–83; Head Office, London, 1983–2001: General Manager: Africa, 1983–84; UK, 1984–86; Hd, Logistics and Dep. Ops Dir, 1986–88; Dep. Mktg Dir, 1989–91; Regl Gen. Manager, Europe, 1992–94; Hd, Regs, 1994–96; Hd, Community Relns, 1996–2001. Played in 3 of the 4 Grand Slam tennis events incl. Wimbledon; semi-finalist, Men's Doubles, US Nationals, 1964. Chm., Fields in Trust (NPFA), 2013–. Mem., Internat. Tennis Clubs of GB, France, US, Australia, Czech Republic and Hong Kong (Capt. Internat. Club of GB, 2012). Chm., Wimbledon Lawn Tennis Mus., 2011–. *Recreations:* tennis, squash, hockey (Triple Blue at Oxford). *Clubs:* All England Lawn Tennis, Queen's, Roehampton; Vincent's (Oxford).

PHILLIPS, Tom, CBE 2002; RA 1989 (ARA 1984); RE 1987; RP 1999; painter, writer and composer; *b* 25 May 1937; *s* of David John Phillips and Margaret Agnes (*née* Arnold); *m* 1961, Jill Purdy (marr. diss. 1988); one *s* one *d*; *m* 1995, Fiona Maddocks, *qv*. *Educ:* St Catherine's College, Oxford (MA; Hon. Fellow, 1992); Camberwell School of Art. NDD. One man shows: AIA Galleries, 1965; Angela Flowers Gall., 1970–71; Marlborough Fine Art, 1973–75; Dante Works, Waddington Galleries, 1983; retrospective exhibitions: Gemeente Museum, The Hague, 1975; Kunsthalle, Basel, 1975; Serpentine, 1975; 50 years of Tom Phillips, Angela Flowers Gall., 1987; Mappin Art Gall., Sheffield, 1987; Nat. Gall., Jamaica, 1987; Bass Mus., Miami, 1988; Nat. Gall., Australia, 1988; City Art Inst., Sydney, 1988; Nat. Portrait Gall., 1989; N Carolina Mus., 1990; Royal Acad., 1992; V&A, 1992; Ulster Mus., 1993; Yale Center, USA, 1993; S London Art Gall., 1998; Dulwich Picture Gall., 1998; Modern Art Mus., Fort Worth, 2001; Flowers Gall., London, 2004, 2012; Flowers Gall., NY, 2005; Massachusetts Mus. of Contemp. Art, 2013; work in collections: British Museum, Tate Gall., V&A, Nat. Portrait Gall., Imperial War Mus., Ashmolean Mus., Oxford, Mus. Fine Arts, Budapest, MOMA NY, Philadelphia Museum, Bibliothèque Nationale, Paris, Gemeente Museum, Boymans Museum, Rotterdam, Nat. Museum, Stockholm, Nat. Gall. of Australia; designed tapestries for St Catherine's, Oxford; music: first perf. opera Irma, 1973; York, 1974; ICA, 1983; librettist, Heart of Darkness chamber opera, Linbury Th., Royal Opera Hse, 2011, Cadogan Hall, 2013; recordings incl. Irma, 1980 (new version, 1988); Intervalles/Music of Tom Phillips 1982; Six of Hearts, 1997; television: co-dir, Dante series, 1984–89 (1st prize Montreal Fest., 1990; Prix Italia, 1991); film scripts: Tom Phillips (Grierson Award, BFI, 1976; Golden Palm Award, Chicago, 1976); The Artist's Eye (TV film), 1988; Twenty Sites (TV film), 1989; designer, The Winter's Tale, Globe Theatre, 1997; designer and translator, Otello, ENO, 1998; designer, The Entertainer, Derby Playhouse, 2003, The Magic Flute, Opera Holland Park, 2008. Curator: Africa: the art of a continent, RA, 1995, Berlin and NY, 1996; We Are The People, NPG, 2004. Slade Prof. of Fine Art, Univ. of Oxford, 2005–06; Visitor, IAS, Princeton, 2005–11. Chairman: RA Library, 1987–95; RA Exhibns Cttee, 1995; Vice-Chm., British Copyright Council, 1984–88. Trustee: Ruskin House, 1996–2002; Nat. Portrait Gall., 1998–2006; BM, 1999–2007. Pres., Heatherley's Sch. of Art, 2003–. Hon. Pres., S London Artists, 1987–. Hon. Fellow, London Inst., 1999. Francis Williams Prize, V&A 1983; First Prize, Hunting Gp of Cos, 1988. *Publications:* Trailer, 1971; A Humument, 1980, 5th rev. edn 2012; illustr. trans. Dante's Inferno, 1982; Works/Texts to 1974, 1975; Heart of a Humument, 1985; The Class of Forty-Seven, 1990; Works/Texts vol. II, 1992; Humument Supplement, 1992; Plato's Symposium, 1992; (with Salman Rushdie) Merely Connect, 1994; (ed) Africa: the art of a continent, 1995; Music in Art, 1997; Aspects of Art, 1997; (illustrator) Waiting for Godot, 2000; The Postcard Century, 2000; We Are The People, 2004; Merry Meetings, 2005; Goldweights: miniature sculptures from Ghana 1400–1900, 2010; Ashanti Weights, 2010; Vintage People on Photo Postcards: women and hats, 2010, Readers, 2010, Bicycles, 2011, Weddings, 2011; Menswear, 2012; Fantasy Transport, 2012; (illustrator) Cicero Orations, 2011; Humument Images to Accompany James Joyce's Ulysses, 2014; The Sound in My Life, 2015. *Recreations:* ping pong, cricket, postcards. *Address:* 57 Talfourd Road, SE15 5NN. *T:* (020) 7701 3978, *Fax:* (020) 7703 2800. *E:* tom@tomphillips.co.uk. *Clubs:* Chelsea Arts, Groucho; Surrey County Cricket.

PHILLIPS, Sir Tom (Richard Vaughan), KCMG 2010 (CMG 1998); HM Diplomatic Service, retired; Commandant, Royal College of Defence Studies, since 2014; *b* 21 June 1950; *s* of late Comdr Tom Vaughan Gerald Phillips, DSC, OBE, RN and of Margaret Sproull (*née* Gameson); *m* 1986, Anne de la Motte; two *s*. *Educ:* Harlow Technical Coll.; Exeter Univ.; Jesus Coll., Oxford; Wolfson Coll., Oxford (MLitt). Journalist, West Herts and Watford Observer, 1969–72; DHSS, 1977–83; FCO, 1983–85; First Sec., Harare, 1985–88; FCO, 1988–90; Dep. Head of Mission and Consul-Gen., Tel Aviv, 1990–93; Counsellor, Washington, 1993–97; Hd, Eastern Adriatic Dept, FCO, 1997–99; High Comr to Uganda, 2000–02; UK Special Rep. for Afghanistan, 2002–06; Dir, S Asia and Afghanistan, FCO, 2003–06; Ambassador: to Israel, 2006–10; to Saudi Arabia, 2010–12. Internat. Advr, Internat. Sustainability Unit, Prince's Charities, 2013–14; Sen. Advr, GPW Ltd, 2013–14. Associate Fellow, Middle East Prog., RIIA, Chatham House, 2012–. Mem., Adv. Council, Wilton Park, 2012–. Hon. Fellow, St Edmund's Coll., Cambridge, 2014. *Publications:* (as Tom Vaughan): No Second Prize, 1993; Sampler (poems), 2010; Envoy (poems), 2013.

PHILLIPS, Trevor; *see* Phillips, M. T.

PHILLIPS, Trevor Thomas; *see* Phillips, Tom.

PHILLIPS, Vernon Francis, CPFA; FCA; Chief Executive, Bedfordshire County Council, 1989–92; *b* 7 July 1930; *s* of Charles and May Phillips; *m* 1955, Valerie P. Jones; two *s* one *d*. *Educ:* Wilson Sch., Reading. CIPFA (Hons) 1954; ASAA 1958; FCA 1970. Berkshire CC, 1946–53; Swindon BC, 1953–55; Bristol City Council, 1955–58; Coventry City Council, 1958–61; Dep. Borough Treas., Luton CB, 1962–73; County Treas., Bedfordshire CC, 1973–89. Adviser to ACC, 1985–92. Member: Soc. of County Treas., 1973–; Assoc. of County Chief Execs, 1989–95; SOLACE, 1989–95. Chm., Bedford Citizens Housing Assoc., 1999–2004. Mem., Bedford Rotary Club. *Recreations:* reading, music (listening), dancing, walking, paperweights, stained glass windows, photography. *Address:* 55 Wentworth Drive, Bedford MK41 8QB. *T:* (01234) 345628.

PHILLIPS, William; *see* Phillips, R. W.

PHILLIPS, Prof. William Daniel, PhD; physicist; National Institute of Standards and Technology Fellow, since 1995; Distinguished University Professor, since 2001, and College Park Professor, since 2006, University of Maryland (Adjunct Professor, 1992–2001); Fellow, Joint Quantum Institute, Maryland, since 2006; *b* 5 Nov. 1948; *s* of William Cornelius Phillips and Mary Catherine Savine Phillips; *m* 1970, Jane Van Wynen; two *d*. *Educ:* Juniata Coll. (BS Physics 1970); Massachusetts Inst. of Technol. (PhD Physics 1976). Chaim Weizmann Fellow, MIT, 1976–78; physicist, Nat. Bureau of Standards, later Nat. Inst. of Standards and Technol.,

1978–95. Eastman Vis. Prof., Oxford Univ., 2002–03. Fellow: Amer. Physical Soc., 1986; Optical Soc. of America, 1994 (Hon. Mem., 2004); Amer. Acad. of Arts and Scis, 1995. Member: NAS, 1997; Pontifical Acad. of Scis, 2004. Gold Medal, Dept of Commerce, 1993; Michelson Medal, Franklin Inst., 1996; Nobel Prize in Physics, 1997; Schawlow Prize, Amer. Physical Soc., 1998; Richtmeyer Award, Amer. Assoc. Physics Teachers, 2000; Archie Mahan Prize, Optical Soc., 2002; Samuel J. Heyman Service to America Medal, Career Achievement Award, 2006; Moyal Medal, Macquarie Univ., 2010; Pioneer in Photonics Award, Duke Univ., 2013. *Publications:* contrib. numerous articles in Physical Rev. Letters and other professional jls, and in proc. nat. and internat. confs. *Recreations:* photography, tennis, gospel music, Bible study. *Address:* 100 Bureau Drive, Stop 8424, National Institute of Standards and Technology, Gaithersburg, MD 20899–8424, USA.

PHILLIPS GRIFFITHS, Allen; *see* Griffiths, Allen P.

PHILLIPSON, Antony John; HM Diplomatic Service; High Commissioner to Singapore, 2011–15; *b* Johannesburg, 13 Jan. 1971; *s* of Nicolas Guy Phillipson and Veronica Phillipson; *m* 2000, Julie Elizabeth Pilley; three *s*. *Educ:* Marlborough Coll.; Keble Coll., Oxford (BA Hons Mod. Hist. 1992). Department of Trade and Industry: Policy Officer, 1993–96; Private Sec., 1996–98, Prin. Private Sec., 1998–2000, to Sec. of State; First Sec., 2000–02, Counsellor, 2002–04, Washington; Private Sec. for Foreign Affairs to the Prime Minister, 2004–07; Hd, Iran Coordination Gp, FCO, 2007–10. *Recreations:* travel, current affairs, family. *Address:* c/o Foreign and Commonwealth Office, King Charles Street, SW1A 2AH. *E:* antony.phillipson@fco.gov.uk. *Clubs:* British, Tanglin (Singapore); Singapore Cricket.

PHILLIPSON, Bridget Maeve; MP (Lab) Houghton and Sunderland South, since 2010; *b* Gateshead, 19 Dec. 1983; *d* of Clare Phillipson; *m* 2009, Lawrence Dimery; one *d*. *Educ:* St Robert of Newminster Catholic Sch., Washington; Hertford Coll., Oxford (BA Hons Modern Hist. 2005). Sunderland CC, 2005–07; Manager, Wearside Women in Need refuge, 2007–10. Mem., Lab Party Nat. Policy Forum, 2002–04. Chm., Oxford Univ. Labour Club, 2003. *Recreations:* reading, music, dog-walking. *Address:* House of Commons, SW1A 0AA. *T:* (020) 7219 7087. *E:* bridget.phillipson.mp@parliament.uk.

PHILLIPSON, Prof. David Walter, LittD; FBA 2002; FSA; Director, Cambridge University Museum of Archaeology and Anthropology, 1981–2006 and Professor of African Archaeology, University of Cambridge, 2001–06; Fellow, Gonville and Caius College, Cambridge, 1988–2006, now Emeritus; *b* 17 Oct. 1942; *s* of late Herbert Phillipson and Mildred Phillipson (*née* Atkinson); *m* 1967, Laurel Lofgren; one *s* one *d*. *Educ:* Merchant Taylors' Sch., Northwood; Gonville and Caius Coll., Cambridge (BA 1964; MA 1968; PhD 1978; LittD 2003). Sec. and Inspector, Nat. Monuments Commn, N Rhodesia, then Zambia, 1964–73; Asst Dir, British Inst. in Eastern Africa, 1973–78; Keeper of Archaeol., Ethnography and Hist., Glasgow Mus., 1979–81; Reader in African Prehistory, Univ. of Cambridge, 1991–2001. Ed., African Archaeol Rev., 1987–94. Reckitt Archaeol Lectr, British Acad., 2000; Dist. Lectr in African Archaeol., Univ. of Florida, 2006. Hon. Vis. Prof., Addis Ababa Univ., 2006. FSA 1979 (Frend Medal, 2005); Associate Fellow, Ethiopian Acad. of Scis, 2014. *Publications:* (ed) Mosi-oa-Tunya: a handbook to the Victoria Falls Region, 1975; Prehistory of Eastern Zambia, 1976; Later Prehistory of Eastern and Southern Africa, 1977; African Archaeology, 1985, 3rd edn 2005; The Monuments of Aksum, 1997; Ancient Ethiopia, 1998; Archaeology at Aksum, Ethiopia, 1993–97, 2000; Archaeology in Africa and in Museums, 2003; Ancient Churches of Ethiopia, 2009; Foundations of an African Civilisation, 2012; numerous contribs to ed vols and learned jls. *Recreation:* bibliomania. *Address:* 11 Brooklyn Terrace, Threshfield, Skipton, N Yorks BD23 5ER. *T:* (01756) 753965. *Club:* Oxford and Cambridge.

PHILLPOT, Hereward Lindon; QC 2015; *b* Hagworthingham, Lincs, 26 March 1973; *s* of Vernon and Meryl Phillpot; *m* 2001, Antonia Johnson; two *s* one *d*. *Educ:* Queen Elizabeth I Grammar Sch., Alford; Univ. of York (BA 1st Cl. Hons Hist.); City Univ. (Postgrad. DipLaw). Called to the Bar, Gray's Inn, 1997; in practice as barrister, specialising in planning and envmtl law, 1997–. Mem., Attorney Gen.'s A Panel of Jun. Counsel, 2010–. *Publications:* National Infrastructure Planning Handbook, 2015. *Recreations:* fishing, cycling, ski-ing. *Address:* Francis Taylor Building, Inner Temple, EC4Y 7BY.

PHILP, Chris; MP (C) Croydon South, since 2015; *b* Bromley, 6 July 1976; *s* of Brian Philp and Edna Philp; *m* 2009, Elizabeth Purves; one *s* one *d* (twins). *Educ:* St Olave's Grammar Sch., Orpington; University Coll., Oxford (MPhys 1st Cl.). Analyst, McKinsey & Co., 1998–2000; Co-Founder and Dir, Blueheath, 2000–04; Co-Founder and Chief Executive Officer: Pluto Capital, 2004–15; Pluto Finance. Contested (C) Hampstead and Kilburn, 2010. *Publications:* (ed) Conservative Revival, 2006. *Recreations:* football, ski-ing, riding. *Address:* House of Commons, SW1A 0AA. *T:* (020) 7219 3000. *E:* chris.philp.mp@parliament.uk.

PHILP, Prof. Ian, CBE 2008; MD; FRCP, FRCPE; Hon. Professor of Health Care for Older People, University of Warwick, since 2011; Chief Medical Officer, Hull and East Yorkshire NHS Hospitals Trust, since 2013; *b* 14 Nov. 1958; *s* of Thomas Philp and Nancy Philp (*née* Yule); *m* 1984, Elizabeth Anne Boyd; one *s* two *d*. *Educ:* Univ. of Edinburgh (MB ChB, MD 1990). FRCPE 1993; FRCP 1994. Trained in geriatric medicine, general medicine, rehabilitation and public health in UK and USA, 1981–90; Hon. Consultant and Sen. Lectr in Geriatric Medicine, Univ. of Southampton, 1990–94; Hon. Consultant and Marjorie Coote Prof. of Health Care for Older People, Univ. of Sheffield, 1994–2011; Med. Dir, NHS Warwickshire, 2009–11; Med. Dir and Consultant in Old Age Medicine, S Warwicks NHS Trust, 2011–13. Nat. Dir for Older People (formerly Older People's Services and Neurol Conditions), Dept of Health, 2000–08. Founder, and Mem., Core Academic Gp, Sheffield Inst. for Studies on Ageing, 1999–. Developed EASY-Care and COPE Index, instruments for assessing needs of older people and family carers, used worldwide. Team Leader, UK Hosp. Doctor Team of the Year, 1999. Co-presenter, BBC TV series, How To Live Longer, 2006. Hon. FFPH 2008. Queen's Anniv. Prize for Higher Educn, 2000. *Publications:* (ed) Assessing Elderly People, 1994; (ed) Outcomes Assessment, 1998; (ed) Carers of Older People in Europe, 2001; numerous contribs to acad. and med. press on care of older people. *Recreations:* cinema, travelling with family. *Address:* Hull and East Yorkshire NHS Hospitals Trust, Hull Royal Infirmary, Anlaby Road, Hull HU3 2JZ.

PHILPOT, His Honour Nicholas Anthony John; a Circuit Judge, 1992–2010; a Deputy Circuit Judge, 2010–12; *b* 19 Dec. 1944; *s* of late Oliver Lawrence Spurling Philpot, MC, DFC, and Margaret Nathalie Forsyth (*née* Owen); *m* 2008, Bahia Naïdji; two *s* and one step *d*. *Educ:* Winchester Coll.; New Coll., Oxford (BA PPE 1966). VSO, Bolivia, 1966–67. Called to the Bar, Lincoln's Inn, 1970; Asst Recorder, 1987–90; Recorder, 1990–92.

PHILPOT, Robert Terence Samuel; Director, Progress, 2001–06, 2007–08 and since 2010; *b* Chelmsford, Essex, 28 Dec. 1972; *s* of Terence Philpot and Mary Philpot; partner, Paul Lantsbury. *Educ:* Trinity Sch., Croydon; Univ. of Durham (BA 1st Cl. Hons Politics); Inst. of United States Studies, Univ. of London (MA (Dist.) Area Studies). Graduate Teaching Asst, Brunel Univ., 1996–99; Progress: Dep. Editor, 1998–99; Publications Editor, 2000–01; Special Adviser: to Sec. of State for NI, 2006–07; to Minister for the Olympics and for the Cabinet Office, 2009–10. *Publications:* (ed) The Purple Book, 2011. *Recreations:* travel, gym, reading, cinema. *Address:* Progress, Waterloo House, 207 Waterloo Road, SE1 8XD. *T:* (020) 3435 6490. *E:* robert@progressonline.org.uk.

PHILPOTT, Hugh Stanley; HM Diplomatic Service; Ambassador to Tajikistan, since 2015; *b* 24 Jan. 1961; *s* of Gordon Cecil Haig Philpott and Janet Philpott (*née* Guy, now Downer); *m* 1984, Janine Frederica Rule; one *d*. *Educ:* Brockenhurst Coll.; Open Univ. Barclays Bank Internat., 1979; FCO, 1980; Oslo, 1982–84; Third Secretary: Budapest, 1985–86; Arabic lang. trng, 1987–88; Baghdad, 1988–90; Second Secretary: FCO, 1990–93; Washington, 1993–97; First Secretary: DFID, 1997–99; FCO, 1999–2001; Counsellor and Dep. Hd of Mission, Muscat, 2001–04; Dep. Hd, Overseas Territories Dept, FCO, and Dep. Comr, British Indian Ocean Territory, 2005–07; Dep. Hd, Internat. Sci. and Innovation Gp, FCO, 2007–08; Hd, UK Sci. and Innovation Network, FCO and BIS, 2008–12; Russian Lang. Trng, 2012–13; Country Dir, UK Trade and Investment, 2013–14; Charge D'Affaires Astana, Kazakhstan, 2014; Tajiki Lang. Trng, 2014–15. *Recreations:* computers, growing walnuts, opera, learning foreign languages. *Address:* c/o Foreign and Commonwealth Office, King Charles Street, SW1A 2AH; Crouttes, Orne, France.

PHINBOW, Sandra Anne; Dermatology Product Specialist UK, Athrodax Healthcare Ltd, since 2015; *b* Welwyn Garden City, 6 July 1973; *d* of Gerald Edward Head and Joan Sandra Charlotte Head; *m* 2015, Matthew John Phinbow; two *s*. *Educ:* Thanet Coll. (Access to Sci. 2000); Univ. of Westminster (Cert. Higher Educn Biomed. Scis 2004); Univ. of Greenwich (BSc Hons Biomed. Sci. 2006); Univ. of Kent (MSc Sci., Communication and Society 2009). CBiol 2012–14, CSci 2012; FSB 2012–14. Jun. retained fire fighter, Kent Fire Service, 1989–91; served Army as soldier and HGV driver, NI, 1991–94 (Mil. Campaign Service Medal 1993). Biomed. scientist and specialist team leader, William Harvey Hosp., Ashford, Kent, 2002–07; Sales Account Manager, Leica Microsystems, 2008; Regl Manager, Schulke & Mayr, 2010–11; Biomed. Scientist, Cellular Pathology, John Radcliffe Hosp., 2011–15. Mem., Inst. of Biomed. Sci., 2005– (Member: Nat. Council, 2013–; Mktg Cttee, 2013–). Founder, Witney Astro Telescopes Soc., 2010. Contributor, NHS Employers' Blog, 2013–. *Publications:* contrib. articles to Biomed. Scientist, Oxford Univ. Hosp. NHS Trust mag., STEMNET. *Recreations:* amateur astronomy, prog rock, general awesomeness.

PHIPPARD, Sonia Clare, CBE 2015; Director-General, Policy Delivery, Department for Environment, Food and Rural Affairs, since 2015; *b* 8 Jan. 1960; *d* of Brig. Roy Phippard and Gillian Phippard (*née* Menzies); *m* 2001, Michael Hartley. *Educ:* Wadhurst Coll.; Somerville Coll., Oxford (BA Physics 1981). Joined Civil Service Department, later Cabinet Office (MPO), 1981: on secondment to DES, 1987–89; Private Sec. to Sec. of Cabinet, 1989–92; Asst Sec., Next Steps Project Dir, 1992–94; on secondment to Coopers and Lybrand, 1995–97; Dep. Dir, 1997–99, Head, 2000–01, Central Secretariat, Cabinet Office; Dir, Sustainable Agriculture and Livestock Products, 2001–06, Dir, Analysis and Common Agricl Policy Strategy, then Food and Farming (EU, Internat. and Evidence), 2006–10, Dir, Water and Flood Risk Mgt (formerly Water, Floods, Envmtl Risk and Regulation), 2010–15, DEFRA. *Recreations:* amateur dramatics, food, time with friends. *Address:* Department for Environment, Food and Rural Affairs, Nobel House, 17 Smith Square, SW1P 3JR.

PHIPPEN, (Conway) Paul; Partner, Macfarlanes, Solicitors, 1989–2009; *b* 30 Jan. 1957; *s* of late Rev. Charles Dennis Phippen and of Margaret Helen Phippen; *m* 1981, Jennifer Caroline Nash; two *s* one *d*. *Educ:* Kingswood Sch., Bath; Exeter Univ. (LLB). Admitted solicitor, 1982; Man. Partner, Macfarlanes, 1999–2008.

PHIPPS, family name of **Marquess of Normanby**.

PHIPPS, Belinda Clare; Chair, Fawcett Society, since 2013; *b* 11 April 1958; *d* of Leonie May Kerslake; partner, Nigel John Simmons; three *d*. *Educ:* The Holt Grammar Sch., Wokingham; Bath Univ. (BSc Hons Microbiol. 1980); Ashridge Management Coll. (MBA 1992). Glaxo Pharmaceuticals, 1980–90; Man. Dir, NHS Blood Transfusion Service, 1991–94; co-ordinating Wells report on London Ambulance Service, 1995; CEO, East Berks Community Trust, 1996–99; Chief Exec., National Childbirth Trust (NCT), 1999–2014. *Recreation:* ballroom dancing. *E:* chair@fawcettsociety.org.uk.

PHIPPS, Maj. Gen. Jeremy Julian Joseph, CB 1997; Director: Saladin Security Ltd, 2007–12; Bibury Club, Salisbury Racecourse, 2004–10; *b* 30 June 1942; *s* of Lt Alan Phipps, RN (killed in action, 1943), 2nd *s* of Rt Hon. Sir Eric Phipps, GCB, GCMG, GCVO, and Hon. Veronica Phipps, 2nd *d* of 16th Lord Lovat, KT, GCVO, KCMG, CB, DSO; *m* 1974, Susan Louise, *d* of late Comdr Wilfrid and Patricia Crawford; one *s* one *d*. *Educ:* Ampleforth Coll.; RMA, Sandhurst. Commnd Queen's Own Hussars, 1962; served in Germany, Middle East, Far East; student, US Armed Forces Staff Coll., Norfolk, Va, 1980; commanded Queen's Own Hussars, 1981–83; COS, RMA, Sandhurst, 1983–85; Comdr 11th Armoured Bde, 1985–89; Dir Special Forces, 1989–93; Sen. British Loan Service Officer, Sultanate of Oman, 1993–96; retd 1997. Man. Dir, Network Internat., 1997–2000; Dir of Special Accounts, Control Risks Gp, 2000–02; Dir of Security, Jockey Club, 2002–03; Dir, Derby House Stabling, 2003–05; Dir of Global Risks, Group 4 Security, 2005–07. Order of Achievement (1st cl.), (Sultanate of Oman), 1995. *Recreations:* shooting, trout fishing, sailing, ski-ing. *Address:* Royal Bank of Scotland, 28 High Street, Jedburgh TD8 6DQ. *Clubs:* White's; Houghton.

See also Sir C. E. Maclean of Dunconnel, Bt.

PHIPPS, His Honour John Christopher; a Circuit Judge, 1996–2012; *b* 29 Aug. 1946; *s* of Thomas Phipps and Jane Bridget Phipps; *m* 1969, Elizabeth Bower; one *s* three *d*. *Educ:* Liskeard GS, Cornwall; Univ. of Liverpool (LLB Hons 1967). Called to the Bar, Middle Temple, 1970; practised on Northern Circuit, 1971–96; Asst Recorder, 1989–93; Recorder, 1993–96. *Recreations:* theatre, opera.

PHIPPS, Air Vice-Marshal Leslie William, CB 1983; AFC 1959; *b* 17 April 1930; *s* of late Frank Walter Phipps and Beatrice Kate (*née* Bearman). *Educ:* SS Philip and James Sch., Oxford. Commnd RAF, 1950; served, 1951–69: Fighter Sqdns; Stn Comdr, RAF Aqaba, Jordan; OC No 19 (F) Sqdn; Central Fighter Estab.; RN Staff Coll.; HQ 1 (British) Corps; Stn Comdr, RAF Labuan, Borneo; OC No 29 (F) Sqdn; Jt Services Staff Coll.; Dir, RAF Staff Coll., 1970–72; Comdr, Sultan of Oman's Air Force, 1973–74; RCDS, 1975; Comdr, UK Team to Kingdom of Saudi Arabia, 1976–78; Dir of Air Def. and Overseas Ops, 1978–79; Air Sec., (RAF), 1980–82; Sen. Directing Staff, RCDS, 1983; retired. BAe (Mil. Aircraft Div.), 1984–91. Service with nat. and local charities, schs and armed forces cadet orgns, 1991–. *Publications:* contribs to military aviation pubns and archives. *Recreations:* sailing, squash, music. *Address:* 33 Knole Wood, Devenish Road, Sunningdale, Berks SL5 9QR. *Clubs:* Royal Air Force; Royal Air Force Yacht.

PHIZACKERLEY, Ven. Gerald Robert; Archdeacon of Chesterfield, 1978–96, now Emeritus; *b* 3 Oct. 1929; *s* of John Dawson and Lilian Mabel Ruthven Phizackerley; *m* 1959, Annette Catherine, *d* of Cecil Frank and Inez Florence Margaret Baker; one *s* one *d*. *Educ:* Queen Elizabeth Grammar School, Penrith; University Coll., Oxford (Open Exhibnr; MA); Wells Theological Coll. Curate of St Barnabas Church, Carlisle, 1954–57; Chaplain of Abingdon School, 1957–64; Rector of Gaywood, Bawsey and Mintlyn, Norfolk, 1964–78; Rural Dean of Lynn, 1968–78; Hon. Canon of Norwich Cathedral, 1975, of Derby Cathedral, 1978; Priest-in-charge, Ashford-in-the-Water with Sheldon, 1978–90. Fellow, Woodard Corporation, 1981. JP Norfolk, 1972. *Publications:* (ed) The Diaries of Maria Gyte of Sheldon, Derbyshire, 1913–1920, 1999. *Recreations:* books, theatre, Border collies. *Address:* Archway Cottage, Hall Road, Leamington Spa, Warwickshire CV32 5RA. *T:* (01926) 332740.

PHOENIX, Prof. David Andrew, OBE 2010; PhD, DSc; FRCPE, FRSocMed; FRSB, FRSC, FIMA; AcSS, SFHEA; DL; Vice Chancellor and Chief Executive, London South Bank University, since 2014; *b* Davyhulme, Gtr Manchester, 26 Feb. 1966; *s* of Derek

Phoenix and Edna Marion Phoenix (*née* Tate); *m* 1994, Stephanie Jayne Bailey; one *s* two *d*. *Educ:* Univ. of Liverpool (BSc Biochem. 1987; PhD Biochem. 1991; DSc Biochem. 2009); Open Univ. (BA Maths 1993; MA Educn 1999; MBA Business 2005); London Business Sch. (Exec. Prog. 2008). CChem 1991; CBiol 1991; CMath 1999. Postdoctoral Res. Asst, Univ. of Liverpool, 1990; Postdoctoral Res. Fellow, Utrecht Univ., 1991–92; University of Central Lancashire: Lectr, 1992–94; Sen. Lectr, 1994–96; Reader, 1996–2000; Prof. of Biochem., 2000–13; Inaugural Hd, Forensic Sci., 2000–02; Dean, Sci. and Technol., 2002–08; Dep. Vice Chancellor and Vice Pres., 2008–13; Vis. Prof., 2013–. Director: Environmental Ltd, 2002–04; UCLan Biomedical Technology (Shenzhen) Ltd, 2010–13 (Chm., 2010–13); UCLan Cyprus Ltd, 2011–13 (Chm., 2011–13); Consultant, SmithKline Beecham, 1993–95. Vis. Specialist in Clin. Biochem., Preston HA, 1993–96; Vis. Consultant in Clin. Biochem., Royal Preston Hosp., 1996–2014; Hon. Consultant in Clin. Biochem., Lancs Teaching Hosps NHS Trust, 2014–. Fellow, EMBO, 1990, 1991; Vis. Fellow, Univ. of Liverpool, 1996–99; Vis. Prof. in Bioinformatics, Moscow Inst. of Physical Engrg, 1996–2000; Dist. Vis. Prof., Univ. of Ontario Inst. of Technol., 2004; Visiting Professor: Sichuan Univ., 2013–; KCL, 2014–. Trustee: Inst. of Biol., 1997–2000; Mus. of Sci. and Industry, Manchester, 2009–11; Darwin Community Acad., 2009–11. Member: Preston and Chorley NHS Trusts Res. Directorate, 2001–03; Daresbury Lab. Facility Access Panel, 2006–10; Lord Chancellor's Adv. Sub-cttee for JPs, Lancs, 2005–08. Bioscis Discipline Consultant, Learning and Teaching Support Network, 2001–03; Nat. Teaching Fellowship Projs Bd, Higher Educn Acad., 2008–10; Ambassador, Diversity in Public Appts, Govt Equalities Office, 2009–; Mem., Teaching, Quality and Student Experience Strategic Cttee, HEFCE, 2013–. European Committee of Biology Associations: Comr for Biotechnol., 2000–02; UK Rep., 2003–07; Chm., Membership and Professional Recognition Panel, 2003–07. Internat. Advr, Sci. and HE, Univ. of Guyana, 2012–. Trustee, Sci. Mus. Gp, 2015–. FSS 1993–95; FRSB (FSB 2001); FRSC 2001; FHEA 2007, SFHEA 2008; FRSocMed 2007; FIMA 2008; AcSS 2012; FRCPE 2013. DL Greater London, 2015. DUniv Bolton, 2013. Individual Excellence Award, Vice-Premier Liu Yandong (China), 2014. *Publications:* Introductory Mathematics for Life Scientists, 1997; (ed) Protein Targeting and Translocation, 1998; (ed) Transcription, 2001; (jtly) Antimicrobial Peptides, 2013; (jtly) Proliposomes: a manufacturing technology for pulmonary delivery via nebulization, 2014; (ed jtly) Novel Antimicrobial Agents and Strategies, 2014; 23 book chapters; approx. 125 conf. procs and 200 articles. *Recreations:* theatre, music, walking, travelling, science. *Address:* London South Bank University, 103 Borough Road, SE1 0AA. *T:* (020) 7815 6001, *Fax:* (020) 7815 6099. *E:* phoenixd@lsbu.ac.uk.

PIACHAUD, Prof. David François James; Professor of Social Policy (formerly Social Administration), London School of Economics, since 1987; *b* 2 Oct. 1945; *s* of late Rev. Preb. François A. Piachaud and Mary R. Piachaud; *m* 1988, Louise K. Carpenter, *d* of late Rev. Dr E. F. Carpenter, KCVO; one *s* one *d*. *Educ:* Westminster Sch.; Christ Church, Oxford (MA); Univ. of Michigan (MPA). Economic Asst, DHSS, 1968–70; Lectr, 1970–83, Reader, 1983–87, LSE. Policy Advr, Prime Minister's Policy Unit, 1974–79. Associate: Centre for Analysis of Social Exclusion, 1997–; Asia Res. Centre, 2012–. Consultant: EU, 1976–79; OECD, 1982–84; World Bank, 1983–84, 2012; ILO, 1986. Mem., Commn on Life Chances and Child Poverty, Fabian Soc., 2004–06. *Publications:* The Causes of Poverty (jtly), 1978; The Cost of a Child, 1979; (jtly) Child Support in the European Community, 1980; The Distribution and Redistribution of Incomes, 1982; (jtly) The Fields and Methods of Social Planning, 1984; (jtly) The Goals of Social Policy, 1989; (jtly) The Price of Food, 1997; (jtly) Understanding Social Exclusion, 2002; (jtly) Making Social Policy Work, 2007; (jtly) Colonialism and Welfare, 2011; (jtly) Social Protection, Economic Growth and Social Change, 2013; contribs to learned jls and periodicals. *Recreations:* walking with Tiger, metal sculpture, travelling. *Address:* London School of Economics, Houghton Street, WC2A 2AE. *T:* (020) 7405 7686.

PIANO, Renzo; architect; founder, Renzo Piano Building Workshop, 1992; *b* 14 Sept. 1937; *m* 1st, 1962, Magda Ardnino; two *s* one *d*; 2nd, 1992, Milly Rossato. *Educ:* Milan Poly. Sch. of Architecture. Founded with Peter Rice, Atelier Piano & Rice, 1977–92. Works include: Pompidou Centre, Paris (with Sir Richard Rogers), and IRCAM, 1977; Schlumberger research labs, Paris, 1984; Menil Collection Mus., Houston, 1986; S Nicola Football Stadium, Bari, Italy, 1990; Kansai Internat. Airport, Osaka, 1994; Concert Hall, hotel and shopping mall, Lingotto, Turin, 1994–96; Contemp. Art Mus. and Congress Centre, Lyon, 1996; Mus. of Sci. and Technol., Amsterdam, and Beyeler Foundn Mus., Basle, 1997; Daimler Benz projects for redevelopment of Potsdamer Platz, Berlin, 1997–98; KPN Telecom office tower, Rotterdam, 2000; Aurora Place high rise office block, Sydney, 2000; Central St Giles, London, 2010; Shard, London, 2012; Astrup Fearnley Mus. of Modern Art, Oslo, 2012; Whitney Mus. of American Art, New York, 2015; numerous exhibitions worldwide. Hon. FAIA, 1981; Hon. FRIBA, 1985; Hon. Fellow: Amer. Acad. of Arts and Scis, 1993; Amer. Acad. of Arts and Letters, 1994. RIBA Gold Medal, 1989; Kyoto Prize, Inamori Foundn, 1990; Erasmus Prize, Amsterdam, 1995; Pritzker Architect Prize, USA, 1998. Cavaliere di Gran Croce (Italy), 1989; Officier, Ordre Nat. du Mérite (France), 1994; Officier, Légion d'Honneur (France), 2000. *Publications:* (jtly) Antico è bello, il recupero della città, 1980; Chantier ouvert au public, 1985; Progetti e Architetture 1984–1986, 1986; Renzo Piano, 1987; (with R. Rogers) Du Plateau Beaubourg au Centre G. Pompidou, 1987; (jtly) Le Isole del tesoro, 1989; Renzo Piano Building Workshop 1964–1988, 1989; Renzo Piano Building and Projects 1971–1989, 1989; Renzo Piano Building Workshop 1964–1991: in search of a balance, 1992; The Making of Kansai International Airport Terminal, 1994; Giornale di Bordo, 1997; Fondation Beyeler: une maison de l'art, 1998. *Address:* Via Rubens 29, 16158 Genoa, Italy; 34 rue des Archives, 75004 Paris, France.

PIATKUS, Judy; strategic consultant, investor, coach, mentor and keynote speaker on entrepreneurship, future trends and conscious leadership, since 2008; Founder, ConsciousCafe, personal development network, since 2011; *b* 16 Oct. 1949; *d* of Ralph and Estelle Assersohn; *m* 1st, 1971, Brian Piatkus; one *s* two *d*; 2nd, 1990, Cyril Ashberg. *Educ:* S Hampstead High Sch. for Girls; Dip. Psychodynamic Psychotherapy 2001; Regent's Univ. London (MA Creative Leadership 2014). Founder, Man. Dir and Publisher, Piatkus Books, 1979–2007. *Publications:* (as Judy Ashberg): Little Book of Women's Wisdom, 2001; Lovers' Wisdom, 2004. *Recreation:* enjoying stimulating conversations with interesting people and constantly learning new things. *W:* www.judypiatkus.com.

PIATT, Wendy Louisa, DPhil; Director General, Russell Group, since 2007; *b* Heswall, Wirral, 17 Nov. 1970; *d* of Barrie Piatt and Ann Piatt. *Educ:* King's Coll. London (BA 1992); Lincoln Coll., Oxford (MPhil 1995; DPhil 1998). Hd of Academic Studies, Centre for Internat. Educn, Oxford, 1996–2000; Sen. Res. Fellow and Hd of Educn, IPPR, 2000–02; Sen. Policy Advr, DFES, 2002–04; Dep. Dir and Sen. Civil Servant, Prime Minister's Strategy Unit, 2004–07. *Publications:* (with Tony Millns) Paying for Learning: the future of individual learning accounts, 2000; (with Peter Robinson) Opportunity for Whom?: options for the funding and structure of post-16 education, 2001; Diverse Missions: achieving excellence and equity in post-16 education, 2004; The UK Government's Approach to Public Service Reform, 2006. *Recreations:* reading, music, football, walking. *T:* (office) (020) 3816 1300. *E:* piatt.pa@russellgroup.ac.uk.

PICARDA, Hubert Alistair Paul; QC 1992; *b* 4 March 1936; *s* of late Pierre Adrien Picarda, Docteur en Droit (Paris), Avocat à la Cour d'Appel de Paris, Barrister, Middle Temple, and Winifred Laura (*née* Kemp); *m* 1976, Ann Hulse (marr. diss. 1995); one *s* one *d*; *m* 2000, Sarah Elizabeth, *d* of His Honour Judge William Alan Belcher Goss. *Educ:* Westminster Sch.; Magdalen Coll., Oxford (Open Exhibnr in Classics; BA Jurisprudence 1961; MA; BCL 1963); University Coll. London (Bunnell Lewis Prize for Latin Verse, 1962). Called to the Bar, Inner Temple, 1962, *ad eundem* Lincoln's Inn and Gray's Inn, 1965; in practice at Chancery Bar, 1964–; Night Lawyer, Daily Express, 1964–72; Lectr, Holborn Coll. Law, Langs and Commerce, 1965–68. Visiting Lecturer: Malaysian Bar Council, 1994, 1995, 1996; Law Soc. of Singapore, 1994, 1996; Hong Kong, 1994; Sarawak, 1995; Singapore Legal Acad., 1999; Cayman Islands Law Sch., 2003; WA Lee Equity Lectr, Brisbane, 2001; Max Planck Inst., Heidelberg Univ., 2006; Univ. of Melbourne, 2013; Univ. of Montréal, 2015. Mem., Senate and Bar Council, 1978–81. Pres., Charity Law Assoc., 1992–2005; Mem., Trust Law Cttee, 1995–. Pres., Inst. Conveyancers, 2000. Pres., Hardwicke Soc., 1968–72; Member: Classical Assoc.; Horatian Soc.; London Roman Law Gp. Managing Editor: Charity Law and Practice Rev., 1992–2004; Receivers, Administrators and Liquidators Qly, 1994–99 (Consulting Editor, 1999–); Member, Editorial Board: Butterworths Jl of Internat. Banking and Financial Law, 1995–; Trust Law Internat., 1992–. *Publications:* Study Guide to Law of Evidence, 1965; Law and Practice Relating to Charities, 1977, 4th edn 2010, suppl. 2014; Law Relating to Receivers, Managers and Administrators, 1984, 4th edn 2006; (ed) Receivers, in Halsbury's Laws of England, 4th edn, reissue, 1998; (ed) Charities, in Halsbury's Laws of England, 4th edn, reissue, 2001; (contrib.) Dictionary of British Classicists, 2004; contrib. legal periodicals and The Spectator. *Recreations:* Spain in World War II, Andalusian baroque churches, Latin, music, conversation. *Address:* Third Floor North, 9 Old Square, Lincoln's Inn, WC2A 3SR. *T:* (020) 7242 3566. *E:* hubert@hpicarda.com. *Clubs:* White's, Turf, Pratt's, Beefsteak.

PICARDO, Hon. Fabian; MP (Gibraltar Socialist Labour), since 2003; Chief Minister of Gibraltar, since 2011; *b* Gibraltar, 18 Feb. 1972; *m* 2011, Justine Olivero; one *s*. *Educ:* Bayside Comprehensive Sch., Gibraltar; Oriel Coll., Oxford (BA Juris. 1993); Inns of Court Sch. of Law. Called to the Bar, Middle Temple, 1994; Associate, 1994–2000, Partner, 2000–, Hassans Internal Law Firm. Leader, Gibraltar Socialist Lab. Party, 2011– (Mem., 2002–). *Address:* Office of the Chief Minister, No 6 Convent Place, Gibraltar.

PICK, Geoffrey Michael Boyd; Director, London Metropolitan Archives, since 2013; *b* Wigan, Lancs, 15 May 1956; *s* of Rev. William Harry Pick and Audrey Joan Pick (*née* Boyd); *m* 1983, Jacqueline Andrews. *Educ:* Liverpool Coll., Liverpool; Bristol Univ. (BA Classics); Liverpool Univ. (Postgrad. Dip. Archive Admin). Archivist: Worcester Cathedral Liby, 1978–79; Lambeth Palace Liby, 1979–86; City of London: Dep. Record Keeper, Gtr London Record Office, 1986–95; Hd, Public Services, London Metropolitan Archives, 1995–2007; Hd, Learning and Access, London Metropolitan Archives, Keats Hse and Guildhall Art Gall., 2007–10; Hd, Guildhall Art Gall. and Keats Hse, 2010–13. Consultant in Ghana on govtl records mgt, Internat. Records Mgt Trust, 1996–97. Lectr, liby and archive postgrad. course, UCL, 2008–11. National Council on Archives: Chair: Nat. Surveys Wkg Party, 2001–; Public Services Quality Gp, 2004–; Vice Chair, 2006–08; Chair, 2008–10. Museums, Libraries and Archives Council: Member: Inspiring Learning for All Think Tank, 2003–06; Comprehensive Performance Assessment Bd, 2005–07; Adult Learners Bd, 2009–10; Adv. Panel, NHMF, 2015–. Vice Chair, London Mus. Gp, 2005–12. Mem. Bd, 2010–14, Vice Chair, 2014–, Archives and Records Assoc. of UK and Ireland. Co-founder and Mem. Cttee, 2003–12, LitHouses (Literary Homes and Mus of GB). Freeman, City of London, 2006. *Publications:* contrib. articles to professional archival jls. *Recreations:* ski-ing, ballroom dancing, allotment tending, guest lyricist/triangle player with the Saggy Bottom Boys. *Address:* London Metropolitan Archives, 40 Northampton Road, EC1R 0HB. *T:* (020) 7332 3833, 07950 157226. *E:* Geoff.Pick@cityoflondon.gov.uk.

PICK, Hella Henrietta, CBE 2000; writer and journalist; Director, Art and Culture Programme, Institute (formerly Weidenfeld Institute) for Strategic Dialogue, since 2005; *b* 24 April 1929; *d* of Ernst Pick and Johanna Marie Pick (*née* Spitz). *Educ:* Fairfield PNEU Sch., Ambleside; London Sch. of Econs (BSc Econ). Commercial Ed., West Africa mag., 1958–60; The Guardian: UN Corresp., 1960–67; Europe Corresp., 1967–72; Washington Corresp., 1972–75; East-West Affairs Corresp., 1975–82; Diplomatic Ed., 1983–94; Associate Foreign Affairs Ed., 1994–96. Consultant and Ameurus Conference Organiser, Club of Three, Weidenfeld Inst. for Strategic Dialogue, 1997–2005. Mem., RIIA. Goldenes Ehrenzeichen (Austria), 1980; Grosses Verdienstkreuz (Germany), 2002. *Publications:* Simon Wiesenthal: a life in search of justice, 1996, 2nd edn 2000; Guilty Victim: Austria from the Holocaust to Haider, 2000. *Recreations:* walking, swimming, travel, opera. *Address:* Flat 11, 115 Haverstock Hill, NW3 4RY. *T:* (020) 7586 3072. *E:* hpick@aol.com. *Clubs:* University Women's, PEN (also Austria).

PICK, Prof. Otto, CMG 2002; Ambassador at Large, Czech Ministry of Foreign Affairs, 2000–13; *b* 4 March 1925; *m* 1948, Zdenka Hajek; one *s* two *d*. *Educ:* Prague English Grammar Sch.; Appleby Grammar Sch.; Faculty of Laws, Charles Univ., Prague (grad. 1948); Queen's Coll., Oxford (BA 1950). Military service, UK, 1943–45. BBC, 1950–58; Rockefeller Res. Student, LSE, 1958–61; Ext. Dir, Council of African-British Relns, 1963–66; Dir, Atlantic Inf. Centre for Teachers, 1966–76; University of Surrey: Prof. of Internat. Relns, 1973–83, now Prof. Emeritus; Dean, Human Studies, 1976–79; Pro-Vice-Chancellor, 1981–83; Dir, Czechoslovak Service Radio Free Europe, 1983–85; Prof., Munich Univ., and Professorial Lectr, Johns Hopkins Bologna, 1986–91; Prof. of Political Sci., Charles Univ., Prague, 1991–2000; Dir, Inst. of Internat. Relns, Prague, 1993–98; Dep. Minister of Foreign Affairs, Czech Republic, 1998–2000. Chm. Council, Diplomatic Acad., Prague, 2007–13. DUniv Surrey, 2003. Grand Cross of Merit (Germany), 2002. *Publications:* (with J. Critchley) Collective Security, 1974; (ed with H. Maull) The Gulf War, 1989; (ed) The Cold War Legacy in Europe, 1991; numerous contribs to edited collections and articles in relevant jls in UK, US, Germany, Italy, etc. *Recreations:* theatre, especially opera.

PICKARD, Prof. Christopher James, PhD; FInstP; Sir Alan Cottrell Professor of Materials Science, University of Cambridge, since 2015; *b* Huntingdon, 1 July 1973; *s* of Robert and Daphne Claire Pickard; *m* 2007, Sylvie Marie Pauline Delacroix; one *s*. *Educ:* Oakham Sch.; Christ's Coll., Cambridge (BA 1994; PhD 1997). FInstP 2007. Res. Fellow, Darwin Coll., Cambridge, 2001–04; Fellow, Corpus Christi Coll., Cambridge, 2004–06; Reader in Physics, Univ. of St Andrews, 2006–08; Prof. of Physics, UCL, 2009–15. EPSRC Advanced Fellow, 2002–07; EPSRC Leadership Fellow, 2008–14. Rayleigh Medal and Prize, Inst. of Physics, 2015. *Publications:* contribs to learned jls incl. Nature Physics, Nature Materials, Nature Chem., Jl Amer. Chem. Soc., Proc. NAS, Physical Rev. Letters. *Recreation:* fishing. *Address:* Department of Materials Science and Metallurgy, University of Cambridge, 27 Charles Babbage Road, Cambridge CB3 0FS.

PICKARD, David Keith; Director, BBC Proms, since 2015; *b* 8 April 1960; *s* of Roger Willows Pickard and June Mary Pickard; *m* 1991, Annette Elizabeth Finney; two *s*. *Educ:* King's Sch., Ely (Choir Sch.); St Albans Sch.; Corpus Christi Coll., Cambridge (Choral Schol.; MA Music). Co. Manager, Royal Opera, 1984–87; Administrator, New Shakespeare Co., 1987–89; Man. Dir, Kent Opera, 1989–90; Asst Dir, Japan Fest. 1991, 1990–92; Artistic Administrator, Eur. Arts Fest., 1992–93; Chief Exec., Orch. of Age of Enlightenment, 1993–2001; Gen. Dir, Glyndebourne, 2001–15. Trustee: Nat. Opera Studio, 2001–; Shakespeare Globe Trust, 2005–14; Cambridge Univ. Music Soc., 2013–. *Recreations:* playing piano duets, cooking.

PICKARD, (James) Nigel; Director, Dial Square 86, since 2014; *b* Worthing, 10 March 1952; *m* 1974, Hazel; two *s* one *d*. Film ed., floor manager, trainee dir, then Asst Dir, Southern TV, 1972–82; TVS: Sen. Dir, 1982–85, Exec. Prod., 1985–86, Children's Dept; Controller, Children's and Family Programming, 1986–92; Controller of Entertainment and Drama

Features, Scottish TV, 1992–93; Dir of Progs, 1993–96, Gen. Manager, 1996–97, Family Channel; Vice-Pres. of Prodn, and Gen. Manager, Challenge TV, Flextech TV, 1997–98; Controller: Children's and Youth Progs, ITV Network Ltd, 1998–2000; Children's Progs, BBC, 2000–02; Dir of Progs, ITV, 2003–06; Dir of Family & Children's Programming, later Gp Dir, Family Entertainment and Drama, RDF Media Gp, 2006–10; Chief Exec., Zodiak MEAA/UK Family and Kids, 2010–14. Chm., The Foundn, 2006–14. FRTS 2006. *Address:* Peasridge Farmhouse, Bubhurst Lane, Frittenden, Cranbrook TN17 2BD.

PICKARD, John Anthony, (Tony); professional tennis coach; *b* 13 Sept. 1934; *s* of John William Pickard and Harriet Haywood Pickard; *m* 1958, Janet Sisson; one *s* twin *d*. *Educ:* Ripley Sch.; Diocesan Sch., Derby; Derby Tech. Coll. Worked under Harry Hopman, Australia (LTA), 1953–54; Sherwood Foresters, 1954–56; Mem., British Davis Cup team, 1958–63; Dir, Chellaston Brick Co., Derby, 1965; Dir, 1967, Man. Dir, 1971, F. Sisson & Sons and subsidiaries, Langley Mill; Captain, under-21 tennis team, winning Galea Cup, 1972; non-playing Captain, British Davis Cup team, 1973–76, 1991–94. Professional tennis coach to Stefan Edberg, 1985–94, to Greg Rusedski, 1997–98. Pres., Notts LTA, 2002–. GB Coach of the Year, 1988. *Recreations:* golf, walking, cars, spending time at home, football. *Clubs:* All England Lawn Tennis; International Tennis Clubs of GB, America, Germany, Sweden; Ripley Tennis; Lindrick Golf.

PICKARD, Prof. John Douglas, FRCS, FRCSE, FMedSci; Professor of Neurosurgery, University of Cambridge, 1991–2013, now Emeritus; Consultant Neurosurgeon, Addenbrooke's Hospital, Cambridge, 1991–2013; Chairman, Wolfson Brain Imaging Centre, 1995–2013; Professorial Fellow, St Catharine's College, Cambridge, 1991–2013, now Emeritus; *b* 21 March 1946; *s* of late Reginald James Pickard and Eileen Muriel Pickard (*née* Alexander); *m* 1971, Charlotte Mary, *d* of late Robert Stuart Townshend and Maureen Charlotte Townshend (*née* Moran); one *s* two *d* (and one *s* decd). *Educ:* King George V Grammar Sch., Southport; St Catharine's Coll., Cambridge (BA 1st Class 1967; MA); King's Coll. Hosp. Med. Sch., London (MB BChir 1970; MChir 1981 (distinction)). KCH, 1970–72; Inst. of Neurol Sci., Glasgow, 1972–73; Falkirk Hosp., 1973–74; Univ. of Pennsylvania Hosp., 1974–75; Registrar, Sen. Registrar, Lectr in Neurosurgery, Inst. of Neurol Sci., Glasgow, 1976–79; Consultant Neurosurgeon, Wessex Neurol Centre, Southampton, 1979–91; Sen. Lectr, 1979, Reader, 1984, Prof. of Clin. Neurol Scis, 1987–91, Univ. of Southampton. Dir, NIHR Brain Injury Healthcare Technol. Co-operative, 2012–16. Pres., Soc. of British Neurological Surgeons, 2006–08; Chm., Jt Neuroscis Council, 2007–10; Pres., Academia Eurasiana Neurochirurgica, 2011–. Hon. Consultant Advr (Neurosurgery) to Army, 2009–. Founder Trustee, Brain and Spine Foundn, 1992; Trustee, Brain Res. Trust. Founder FMedSci 1998. Dr *hc* Liege, 2008. Robert H. Pudenz Award for Excellence in Cerebro-Spinal Fluid Physiology Res., 2000; Guthrie Meml Prize, AMS, 2009. *Publications:* numerous articles in med. and sci. jls. *Recreation:* family life. *Address:* Academic Neurosurgical Unit, Addenbrooke's Hospital, Cambridge CB2 0QQ. *T:* (01223) 336946. *Club:* Athenæum.

PICKARD, Sir (John) Michael, Kt 1997; FCA; Chairman: National House-Building Council, 1998–2002; London Docklands Development Corporation, 1992–98 (Deputy Chairman, 1991–92); Deputy Chairman, Epsom Downs Racecourses Ltd, 2003–06; *b* 29 July 1932; *s* of John Stanley Pickard and Winifred Joan Pickard; *m* 1959, Penelope Jane (*née* Catterall); three *s* one *d*. *Educ:* Oundle School. Finance Dir, British Printing Corp., 1965–68; Man. Dir, Trust Houses Ltd/Trusthouse Forte Ltd, 1968–71; Founder Chm., Happy Eater Ltd, 1972–86; Dep. Chief Exec., 1986–88, Chief Exec., 1988–92, Sears plc; Chairman: Grattan plc, 1978–84; Courage Ltd and Imperial Brewing & Leisure Ltd, 1981–86; Dep. Chief Exec., Imperial Gp plc, 1985–86; Chm., Freemans, 1988–92. Director: Brown Shipley Hlgs, 1986–93; Electra Investment Trust plc, 1989–2002; Nationwide Building Soc., 1991–94; Pinnacle Leisure Gp Ltd (formerly Wates Leisure), 1992–99; London First, 1992–2002 (Dep. Chm., 1998–2002); Bentalls plc, 1993–2001; Racecourse Leisure Corp., 1993–96; United Racecourses (Holdings) Ltd, 1995–2003; Chairman: Bullough plc, 1996–2002; Servus (formerly Opus) Hldgs, 1997–2001; London First Centre, 1998–2001; The Housing Forum, 1999–2002; Freeport, 2001–03. Dir, Surrey Cricket Bd Ltd, 2009–14; Dep. Pres., 2011–12, Pres., 2012–13, Surrey CCC. Chm. Council, Roedean Sch., 1980–91; Chm. of Govs, Oundle Sch., 2004–07 (Gov., 1988–2000). Member: Bd, BTA, 1968–71; Cttee, AA, 1994–99. Mem., Court of Assistants, Co. of Grocers, 1990– (Master, 1996). Hon. LLD E London, 1997. *Recreations:* cricket, golf, bridge. *Clubs:* Boodle's, Pilgrims, MCC; Walton Heath Golf; Headley Cricket, Surrey County Cricket; Dorking Rugby Football.

PICKARD, Nigel; *see* Pickard, J. N.

PICKARD, Tony; *see* Pickard, J. A.

PICKEN, Ven. David Anthony; Archdeacon of Newark, since 2012; *b* Hednesford, Staffs, 5 June 1963; *s* of Norman Anthony Picken and late Valerie Picken; *m* 1985, Catherine Ann Edwards. *Educ:* Kingsmead Comprehensive Sch.; Univ. of London (BA Hons 1984); Christ Church, Canterbury (PGCE 1985); Univ. of Nottingham (MA 1996). Teacher of Religious Studies: Seaford Head, 1985–86; Elizabethan High Sch., Retford, 1986–87; ordained deacon, 1990, priest, 1991; Asst Curate, Worth Team Ministry, 1990–93; Team Vicar and Hospital Chaplain, Wordsley Team Ministry, 1993–97; Team Rector: Wordsley, 1997–2004; High Wycombe, 2004–11; Area Dean, Wycombe, 2007–11. Hon. Canon: Christ Church, Oxford, 2011; Southwell, 2012. *Recreations:* theatre, sport, literature. *Address:* Jubilee House, Westgate, Southwell, Notts NG25 0JH. *E:* archdeacon-newark@southwell.anglican.org.

PICKEN, Hon. Sir Simon Derek, Kt 2015; **Hon. Mr Justice Picken;** a Judge of the High Court, Queen's Bench Division, since 2015; *b* 23 April 1966; *s* of Keith and Ann Picken; *m* 1992, Sophie Victoria Seddon; one *s* three *d*. *Educ:* Cardiff High Sch.; University Coll., Cardiff (LLB Hons 1987); Magdalene Coll., Cambridge (LLM 1988). Called to the Bar, Middle Temple, 1989; in practice as a barrister, specialising in commercial law, 1989–2015; QC 2006; a Recorder, 2005–15; a Dep. High Court Judge, 2010–15; a Church Comr, 2013–15. *Publications:* Good Faith and Insurance Contracts, 3rd edn 2010. *Recreations:* Rugby Union, Italy.

PICKERING, Prof. Alan Durward, PhD, DSc; CBiol, FRSB; Director, CEH Windermere (formerly Institute of Freshwater Ecology), 1995–2001 (acting Director, 1993–95); Independent Advisor, Department for Environment, Food and Rural Affairs, 2002–13; *b* 7 Sept. 1944; *s* of Frank Hadfield Pickering and Olive Pickering (*née* Page); *m* 1969, Christine Mary Pott; two *s* one *d*. *Educ:* Ecclesfield Grammar Sch.; Univ. of Nottingham (BSc 1st cl. Zoology 1966; PhD 1970; DSc 1986). CBiol, FRSB (FIBiol 1995). Res. Physiologist, Freshwater Biological Assoc., 1969–89; Head, Windermere Lab., 1989–93. Associate Prof., Dept of Biology and Biochemistry, Brunel Univ., 1991–2002. *Publications:* (ed) Stress and Fish, 1981; numerous articles in scientific jls. *Recreations:* gardening, woodwork, golf, sailing, travel.

PICKERING, Alan Michael, CBE 2004; Chairman, BESTrustees plc, since 2008; *b* 4 Dec. 1948; *s* of Frank and Betty Pickering; *m* 1982, Christine Tull. *Educ:* Exhall Grange Sch., Coventry; Univ. of Newcastle upon Tyne (BA Hons Politics and Social Admin). APMI 1981. With BR, 1967–69; Hd, Membership Services Dept, EETPU, 1972–92; Partner, then Sen. Consultant, Watson Wyatt, 1992–2008. Member: Occupational Pensions Bd, 1992–97; Bd, Pensions Regulator, 2005–13; Chairman: Nat. Assoc. of Pension Funds, 1999–2001; Plumbing Ind. Pension Scheme, 2001–; Eur. Fedn of Retirement Provision, 2001–04; Royal Mail Statutory Pension Scheme, 2012–. Mem., Rules Cttee, British Horseracing Authy, 2009–; Mem. Council, Racehorse Owners Assoc., 2011– (Vice Pres., 2015–). Trustee: Life Academy (Pre-Retirement Assoc.), 2005–13 (Chm., 2006–13); Kosovan Pensions Savings Trust, 2012–. Pres., Blackheath Harriers, 1992. *Publications:* A Simpler Way to Better Pensions, 2002. *Recreations:* running, gardening, horse racing, travel. *Club:* Blackheath and Bromley Harriers Athletic.

PICKERING, Prof. Brian Thomas; Deputy Vice-Chancellor, University of Bristol, 1992–2001, now Emeritus Professor (Hon. Fellow, 2002); *b* 24 May 1936; *s* of Thomas Pickering and Dorothy May Pickering; *m* 1965, Joan Perry (*d* 2005); two *d*. *Educ:* Haberdashers' Aske's Hatcham Boys' Sch.; Univ. of Bristol (BSc 1958; PhD 1961; DSc 1974). Research Biochemist, Hormone Res. Lab., Univ. of California, 1961–62; Scientific Staff, NIMR, MRC, 1963–65; University of Bristol: Lectr in Biochem. and Pharmacol., 1965–70 (Mem., MRC Gp for Res. in Neurosecretion); Lectr in Anatomy and Biochem., 1970–72; Reader in Anatomy and Biochem., 1972–78; Prof. of Anatomy and Head of Dept, 1978–92; Dean, Faculty of Medicine, 1985–87. Vis. Prof., Univ. of Geneva, 1977; Anatomical Soc. Review Lectr, 1984. Mem., Bristol & Weston HA, 1988–90; non-exec. Dir, United Bristol Healthcare NHS Trust, 1990–98. Mem., Animal Grants Bd, AFRC, 1988–94 (Chm., 1991–94). Associate Editor, Jl of Endocrinology, 1972–77. Sec. and Treasurer, 1971–77, Vice-Pres., 1986–90, Pres., 1990–94, European Soc. for Comparative Endocrinology; Sec., British Neuroendocrine Gp, 1986–92; mem., other learned bodies. Hon. Fellow, Romanian Acad. of Med. Sci., 1991. Hon. MD Carol Davila, Bucharest, 1994; Hon. LLD Bristol, 2001. Medal, Soc. for Endocrinology, 1977. *Publications:* contribs to professional jls. *Address:* 243 Canford Lane, Bristol BS9 3PD.

PICKERING, Errol Neil, PhD; Director General, International Hospital Federation, 1987–98; *b* 5 May 1938; *s* of Russell Gordon and Sylvia Mary Pickering. *Educ:* York Univ., Canada (BA Hons); Univ. of Toronto (DipHA); Univ. of New South Wales (PhD). Asst Administrator, St Michael's Hosp., Toronto, 1971–73; Executive Director: Aust. Council on Hosp. Standards, 1973–80; Aust. Hosp. Assoc., 1980–87. Dir, Health Care Risk Solutions Ltd, 1994–98. Pres., UNICEF Australia, 1984–86. Vice Pres., RSPCA, Gold Coast, 2006–. Chm., Internat. Assoc. Forum, 1990–92. Bd Mem., European Soc. of Assoc. Execs, 1995–98. *Publications:* many articles on hosp. and health policy issues. *Recreations:* classical music, bridge. *Address:* 13 Firestone Court, Robina Woods, Qld 4226, Australia.

PICKERING, Janet Dolton; Headmistress, Withington Girls' School, 2000–10; *b* 21 June 1949; *d* of George Browning and Marjorie Dolton Haywood; *m* 1971, William Ronald Pickering; two *s*. *Educ:* Bridlington High Sch.; Malton Grammar Sch.; Univ. of Sheffield (BSc 1st Cl. Biochem.). SRC res. student, Univ. of Sheffield, 1970–73; Scientific Officer, Hallamshire Hosp. Med. Sch., 1973–75; Teaching Fellow, Univ. of Leeds, 1975–79; freelance proof-reader, editor, indexer (sch. sci. texts and scientific jls), 1980–88; part-time teacher and tutor, Gordonstoun Sch., 1983–85; King's School, Canterbury, 1986–97: teacher, tutor, housemistress, 1990–94; Dep. Hd, 1994–97; Hd, St Bees Sch., Cumbria, 1998–2000. HMC/ISI Inspector, 1994–, Reporting Inspector, 2011–. Chm., Sen. Mistresses Gp, 1995–96, Mem., Inspections Cttee, 2004–10 (Chm., 2007–10), Mem. Council, 2007–10, GSA; Co-Chm., Sports Sub-Cttee, GSA/HMC, 2004–05; Bd Mem., ISI, 2007–10. Consultant, Ogden Trust, 2012–. University of Manchester: Lay Mem., Assembly, 2007–; Mem., Nominations Cttee, 2009–. Governor: Copthorne Prep. Sch., 1995–97; Windlesham House Sch., 1996–98; Branwood Prep. Sch., 2001–08; Colfe's Sch., 2005–08; Chetham's Sch. of Music, 2005–15; Bury Grammar Schs, 2008–15. Hon. Fellow, Rank Foundn, 2010. *Publications:* (jtly) Nucleic Acid Biochemistry, 1982; (contrib.) Children's Britannica, 4th edn 1988; contrib. articles to Jl Gen. Micro., Inserm, Hum. Hered. *Recreations:* reading, theatre, cinema, natural history, travel, running. *Address:* 119 Dane Road, Sale, Cheshire M33 2BY. *T:* (0161) 962 0764. *Club:* University Women's.

PICKERING, Prof. John Frederick; business management and economic consultant; Professor of Business Strategy, Bath University, 1997–2000; *b* 26 Dec. 1939; *er s* of late William Frederick and Jean Mary Pickering; *m* 1967, Jane Rosamund Day; two *d*. *Educ:* Slough Grammar Sch.; University Coll. London (BSc Econ; PhD; DSc Econ); MSc Manchester. In indust. market res., 1961–62; Lectr, Univ. of Durham, 1964–66, Univ. of Sussex, 1966–73; Sen. Directing Staff, Admin. Staff Coll., Henley, 1974–75; UMIST: Prof. of Industrial Economics, 1975–88; Vice-Principal, 1983–85; Dep. Principal, 1984–85; Dean, 1985–87; Vice-Pres. (Business and Finance), 1988–90, actg Pres., 1990–91, Dep. Pres., 1991–92, Portsmouth Poly.; Dep. Vice Chancellor, Portsmouth Univ., 1992–94. Visiting Professor: Durham Univ. Business Sch., 1995–98; Sch. of Mgt, Univ. of Southampton, 2001–04. Mem., UGC Business and Management Studies sub-cttee, 1985–88. Dir, Staniland Hall Ltd, 1988–94; Dir and Chm., Univ. of Portsmouth (formerly Portsmouth Polytechnic) Enterprise Ltd, 1989–94. Consultant, NIESR, 1994–97. Mem., Gen. Synod of Church of England, 1980–90; Church Comr for England, 1983–90; Mem., Archbishop's Commn on Urban Priority Areas, 1983–85; Pres., BCMS-Crosslinks (formerly BCMS), 1986–92. Member: Council of Management, Consumers' Assoc., 1969–73, 1980–83; Retail Prices Index Adv. Cttee, 1974–95; Monopolies and Mergers Commn, 1990–99; Competition Appeal Tribunal (formerly Appeals Panel, Competition Commn), 2000–11; Strategic Adv. Bd for Intellectual Property Policy, 2008–10. Chm. Trustees, Vocational Training Charitable Trust, 2004–06 (Trustee, 2004–06). Chm., Rowlands Castle Parish Council, 2011–. MInstD 1996. *Publications:* Resale Price Maintenance in Practice, 1966; (jtly) The Small Firm in the Hotel and Catering Industry, 1971; Industrial Structure and Market Conduct, 1974; The Acquisition of Consumer Durables, 1977; (jtly) The Economic Management of the Firm, 1984; papers and articles in learned jls in economics and management. *Recreations:* music, cricket, theatre, family. *Address:* 1 The Fairway, Rowlands Castle, Hants PO9 6AQ. *T:* (023) 9241 2007, *Fax:* (023) 9241 3385. *Club:* Sussex County Cricket.

PICKERING, His Honour Richard Edward Ingram; a Circuit Judge, 1981–98; *b* 16 Aug. 1929; *s* of late Richard and Dorothy Pickering; *m* 1962, Jean Margaret Eley; two *s*. *Educ:* Birkenhead Sch.; Magdalene Coll., Cambridge (MA). Called to the Bar, Lincoln's Inn, 1953; has practised on Northern Circuit, 1955–81 (Junior, 1960–61); a Recorder of the Crown Court, 1977–81. Admitted as advocate in Manx Courts (Summerland Fire Inquiry), 1973–74. Councillor, Hoylake UDC, 1961–64; Legal Chm., Min. of Pensions and Nat. Insurance Tribunal, Liverpool, 1967–77; pt-time Chm., Liverpool Industrial Tribunal, 1977–79; Nominated Judge, NW Reg. (formerly Judicial Mem., Merseyside), Mental Health Rev. Tribunal, 1984–2001 (Legal Mem., 1967–79; Regional Chm., 1979–81); Northern Circuit Rep., Cttee, Council of Circuit Judges, 1984–89. Pres., League of Friends, Clatterbridge Hosp., 2001–11. *Recreations:* walking, bowls, gardening, study of military history. *Address:* Trelyon, Croft Drive, Caldy, Wirral CH48 2JN. *Clubs:* Athenæum (Liverpool) (Hon. Proprietor, 2012); Union (Cambridge).

PICKERING, Robert Mark; Chief Executive, JPMorgan Cazenove (formerly Cazenove Group plc), 2001–08; *b* 30 Nov. 1959; *s* of Richard Pickering and Lorna Pickering (*née* Browne); *m* 1st, 1983, Harriet Jump (marr. diss. 2005); two *s* one *d*; 2nd, 2006, Miho Umino; two *d*. *Educ:* Westminster Sch.; Lincoln Coll., Oxford (MA Law). Admitted solicitor, 1982; Solicitor: Allen & Overy, 1982–85; Cazenove & Co., 1985–2001 (Partner, 1993). Non-executive Director: Neptune Investment Mgt Ltd, 2009–; Hikma Pharmaceuticals plc, 2011–; Itau BBA Internat. plc, 2012–; CLSA UK, 2014–. *Recreations:* fishing, drinking wine, art. *Clubs:* Garrick; Flyfishers'; Vincent's (Oxford); Links (New York).

PICKERING, Thomas Reeve; Vice Chairman, Hills & Company, since 2006; Co-Chairman and Board Member, International Crisis Group, since 2006; *b* Orange, NJ, 5 Nov.

1931; *s* of Hamilton R. Pickering and Sarah C. (*née* Chasteney); *m* 1955, Alice J. Stover (*d* 2011); one *s* one *d*. *Educ:* Bowdoin Coll. (AB); Fletcher Sch. of Law and Diplomacy (MA); Univ. of Melbourne (MA). Served to Lt-Comdr, USNR, 1956–59. Joined US For. Service, 1959; For. Affairs Officer, Arms Control and Disarmament Agency, 1961; Political Advr, US Delegn to 18 Nation Disarmament Conf., Geneva, 1962–64; Consul, Zanzibar, 1965–67; Counselor, Dep. Chief of Mission, Amer. Embassy, Dar-es-Salaam, 1967–69; Dep. Dir Bureau, Politico-Mil. Affairs, State Dept, 1969–73; Special Asst to Sec. of State and Exec. Sec., Dept of State, 1973–74; Amb. to Jordan, 1974–78; Asst Sec. for Bureau of Oceans, Internat. Environmental and Sci. Affairs, Washington, 1978–81; Ambassador: to Nigeria, 1981–83; to El Salvador, 1983–85; to Israel, 1986–88; Ambassador and US Perm. Rep. to UN, 1989–92; Ambassador: to India, 1992–93; to Russia, 1993–96; Under Sec. for Political Affairs, US Dept of State, 1997–2000. Sen. Vice Pres., Internat. Relations, Boeing Co., 2001–06. Member: Council, For. Relns, IISS, 1973–; Global Leadership Foundn, 2008–. Phi Beta Kappa. Hon. LLD: Bowdoin Coll., 1984; Atlantic Union Coll., 1990; Tufts Univ., 1990; Hebrew Union Coll., 1991; Willamette Univ., 1991; Drew Univ., 1991; Franklin Pierce Coll., 1991; Hofstra, 1992; Lafayette Coll., 1992. *Address:* Hills & Co., 1120 20th Street NW, Washington, DC 20036, USA. *Club:* Cosmos (Washington).

PICKETT, Prof. George Richard, DPhil; FRS 1997; Professor of Low Temperature Physics, University of Lancaster, since 1988. *Educ:* Magdalen Coll., Oxford (BA 1962; DPhil). Lectr, then Sen. Lectr, later Reader, Dept of Physics, Univ. of Lancaster. *Address:* Department of Physics, University of Lancaster LA1 4YB.

PICKETT, Prof. John Anthony, CBE 2004; PhD, DSc; FRS 1996; Michael Elliott Distinguished Research Fellow, Rothamsted Research, since 2010; *b* 21 April 1945; *s* of Samuel Victor Pickett and Lilian Frances Pickett (*née* Hoar); *m* 1970, Ulla Birgitta Skålèn; one *s* one *d*. *Educ:* King Edward VII Grammar Sch., Coalville; Univ. of Surrey (BSc Hons Chem. 1967; PhD Organic Chem. 1971); DSc Nottingham 1993. CChem 1975, FRSC 1982; CSci 2004. Postdoctoral Fellow, UMIST, 1970–72; Chem. Dept, Brewing Res. Foundn (flavour active components of hops and malt), 1972–76; Dept of Insecticides and Fungicides, Rothamsted Exptl Stn (semiochem. aspects of insect chem. ecology), 1976–83; Hd, Dept of Insecticides and Fungicides, subseq. Biol and Ecol Chem. Dept, then Biol Chem. Dept, IACR-Rothamsted, then Rothamsted Res., 1984–2010; Scientific Dir, Rothamsted Centre for Sustainable Pest and Disease Mgt, 2007–10. Special Prof., later Vis. Prof., then Hon. Prof., Sch. of Biol., Univ. of Nottingham, 1991–. Lectures: Boyce Thompson Inst. for Plant Res., Cornell Univ., 1991; Alfred M. Boyce, Univ. of California, Riverside, 1993; Woolhouse, Soc. for Experimental Biology, York Univ., 1998; Barrington Meml, Univ. of Nottingham, 1999; Cameron-Gifford, Univ. of Newcastle, 2000; Andersonian Chem. Soc. Centenary, Univ. of Strathclyde, 2006; H. R. MacCarthy Pest Mgt, Univ. of BC, 2007; Croonian, Royal Soc., 2008; Cornell Univ., Ithaca, 2009; Wilson Baker, Univ. of Bristol, 2010. Mem. Council, Royal Soc., 2000–02. Pres., Royal Entomological Soc., 2014–16. Hon. FRES 2010. Hon. Mem., Chem. Soc. of Ethiopia, 2010. Foreign Associate, Nat. Acad. of Scis, USA, 2014. Hon. DSc Aberdeen, 2008. Rank Prize for Nutrition and Crop Husbandry, 1995; Silver Medal, Internat. Soc. of Chem. Ecology, 2002; Wolf Foundn Prize in Agriculture, 2008; Millennium Award, Associated Chambers of Commerce and Industry of India, 2011; Cert. of Distinction, Internat. Congress of Entomol., Daegu, Korea, 2012. *Publications:* over 490 papers and patents. *Recreation:* jazz trumpet playing. *Address:* Biological Chemistry and Crop Protection Department, Rothamsted Research, Harpenden, Herts AL5 2JQ. *T:* (01582) 763133.

PICKETT, Philip; Director, New London Consort, since 1978. *Educ:* Guildhall Sch. of Music and Drama (Maisie Lewis Foundn Award; Wedgewood Award). Prof. of Recorder and Historical Performance Practice, GSMD, 1972–97. Began career as trumpet player; subseq. took up recorder, crumhorn, shawm, rackett, etc; as soloist, has performed with many leading ensembles, incl. Acad. of St Martin-in-the-Fields, London Chamber Orch., Polish Chamber Orch., English Chamber Orch., London Mozart Players; with New London Consort, performs a wide repertoire of medieval, Renaissance and Baroque music; resident early music ensemble, S Bank Centre; nat. and internat. concerts, operas and recitals, incl. BBC Proms, and regular performances at art fests. Dir of Early Music, Globe Theatre, 1993–; Artistic Director: Purcell Room Early Music Series, 1993–; Aldeburgh Early Music Fest., 1994–97 (also Founder); Early Music Fest., S Bank Centre, 1996–2003; Associate Artist, Bridgewater Hall, Manchester, 2010–. Appearances on radio and television; film soundtracks. Solo recordings incl. Handel recorder concertos and trio concertos, and Vivaldi and Telemann concertos. *Publications:* articles in books and jls.

PICKETT-HEAPS, Prof. Jeremy David, PhD; FRS 1995; FAA; Professor, 1988–2002, now Professorial Fellow, School of Botany, University of Melbourne; *b* 5 June 1940; *s* of Harold Arthur Pickett-Heaps and Edna Azura (*née* May); *m* 1st, 1965, Daphne Charmian Scott (*d* 1970); one *s* one *d*; 2nd, 1977, Julianne Francis Jack; two *s*. *Educ:* Clare Coll., Cambridge (BA; PhD 1965). Fellow, Research Sch. of Biol Sci., ANU, 1965–70; Prof., Dept of Molecular, Cellular and Developmental Biol., Univ. of Colorado, 1970–88. FAA 1992. *Publications:* Green Algae, 1972; numerous scientific res. papers. *Recreation:* various. *Address:* PO Box 247, Mallacoota, Vic 3892, Australia. *T:* (3) 51580123.

PICKFORD, Meredith William; QC 2015; *b* 13 April 1972; *s* of Nigel Pickford and Rosamund Pickford; *m* 2003, Helen Louise Jones; two *s* one *d*. *Educ:* Chesterton Community Coll., Cambridge; Hills Road Sixth Form Coll., Cambridge; Clare Coll., Cambridge (BA Econs 1994); City Univ. (DipLaw 1998). Corporate Strategy Consultant, L/E/K Partnership, 1994–96; Econ. Consultant, Smithers & Co. Ltd, 1996–98; called to the Bar, Middle Temple, 1999; barrister specialising in competition law and economic regulation. *Address:* Monckton Chambers, 1–2 Raymond Buildings, Gray's Inn, WC1R 5NR. *T:* (020) 7405 7211, *Fax:* (020) 7405 2084.

PICKFORD, Stephen John, CB 2004; Senior Research Fellow, Royal Institute of International Affairs, Chatham House, since 2012; Managing Director, International and Finance Directorate, HM Treasury, 2007–09; *b* 26 Aug. 1950; *s* of Frank and May Pickford; *m* 1978, Carolyn M. Ruffle; two *s*. *Educ:* St John's Coll., Cambridge (BA Hons 1971; MA 1974); Univ. of British Columbia (MA 1984). Economist, Dept of Employment, 1971–79; HM Treasury: Economist, 1979–85; Dep. Press Sec., 1985–87; Sen. Economic Advr, 1987–89, 1993–98; Manager, Macroeconomics, New Zealand Treasury, 1989–93; UK Exec. Dir, IMF and World Bank, 1998–2001; Minister (Econ.), British Embassy, Washington, 1998–2001; Dir, Internat. Finance, 2001–06, Europe, 2006–07, HM Treasury. Associate Fellow, RIIA, 2011–12. *Publications:* (contrib.) Government Economic Statistics, 1989; Chatham Hse pubns. *Recreations:* cycling, film.

PICKING, Anne; *see* Moffat, A.

PICKLES, Rt Hon. Sir Eric (Jack), Kt 2015; PC 2010; MP (C) Brentwood and Ongar, since 1992; *b* 20 April 1952; *m* 1976, Irene. *Educ:* Greenhead Grammar Sch.; Leeds Polytechnic. Joined Conservative Party, 1968; Young Conservatives: Area Chm., 1976–78; Nat. Vice-Chm., 1978–80; Nat. Chm., 1980–81; Conservative Party: Member: Nat. Union Exec. Cttee, 1975–91; One Nation Forum, 1987–91; Nat. Local Govt Adv. Cttee, 1985– (Chm., 1992–93); Lectr, Cons. Agents Examination Courses, 1988–; Local Govt Editor, Newsline, 1990–92; a Vice-Chm., 1993–97; Dep. Chm., 2005–07. Bradford Council: Councillor, 1979–91; Chm., Social Services, 1982–84; Chm., Educn, 1984–86; Leader, Cons. Gp, 1987–91; Leader of Council, 1988–90. Dep. Leader, Cons. Gp, AMA, 1989–91. PPS to Minister for Industry, 1993; Opposition frontbench spokesman on social security, 1998–2001; Shadow Transport Minister, 2001–02; Shadow Sec. of State for Local Govt and the Regions, 2002–07, for Communities and Local Govt, 2007–09; Sec. of State for Communities and Local Govt, 2010–15. Chm., All Party Film Gp, 1997–2004; Vice-Chm., Cons. Envmt, Transport and Regions Cttee, 1997–98. Chm., Conservative Party, 2009–10. UK Envoy on post-Holocaust Issues, 2015–. Mem., Council of Europe, 1997–. Mem., Yorks Area RHA, 1982–90. *Recreations:* film buff, opera, serious walking. *Address:* House of Commons, SW1A 0AA.

PICKTHALL, Colin; Chairman of Trustees, Ford Park Community Trust, since 2007; *b* 13 Sept. 1944; *s* of Frank Pickthall and Edith (*née* Bonser), Dalton-in-Furness; *m* 1973, Judith Ann Tranter; two *d*. *Educ:* Univ. of Wales (BA); Univ. of Lancaster (MA). Teacher, Ruffwood Comprehensive Sch., Kirkby, 1967–70; Edge Hill College of Higher Education: Sen. Lectr in English Lit., 1970–83; Head, European Studies, 1983–92. County Councillor, Ormskirk, Lancs CC, 1989–93. Contested (Lab) Lancashire West, 1987; MP (Lab) Lancs W, 1992–2005; PPS to Sec. of State for Home Office, 1998–2001, for Foreign and Commonwealth Affairs, 2001–05. Mem., Ulverston Town Council, 2012–. Chm., Keep Ulverston Special (anti-supermarket campaign), 2011–14. Founder and Sec., Friends of Coronation Hall, Ulverston, 2013–. *Recreations:* fell-walking, gardening, cricket, theatre. *Address:* 25 Fountain Street, Ulverston, Cumbria LA12 7EQ.

PICKTHORN, Sir James (Francis Mann), 3rd Bt *cr* 1959, of Orford, Suffolk; Partner, Pickthorn, estate agents and chartered surveyors, since 1994; *b* 18 Feb. 1955; *o s* of Sir Charles William Richards Pickthorn, 2nd Bt and of Helen Antonia, *o d* of Sir James Gow Mann, KCVO; *S* father, 1995; *m* 1998, Clare, *yr d* of Brian Craig-McFeely; two *s*. *Educ:* Eton; Reading Univ. (BSc Estate Management). With Healey & Baker, 1977–82; Debenham Tewson & Chinnocks, 1982–86; Kinney & Green, 1986–94 (Partner, 1991–94); founded Pickthorn, 1994. TA (HAC), 1978–98. *Recreation:* sailing. *Heir:* *s* William Edward Craig Pickthorn, *b* 2 Dec. 1998. *Address:* 45 Ringmer Avenue, SW6 5LP. *T:* (020) 7621 1380; (office) 8 Laurence Pountney Hill, EC4R 0BE.

PICKUP, David Cunliffe; Chief Executive, Sports Council Trust Company, 1993–94; Director General, Sports Council, 1988–93; *b* 17 Sept. 1936; *s* of Robert and Florence Pickup; *m* 1960, Patricia Moira Aileen (*née* Neill); three *s*. *Educ:* Bacup and Rawtenstall Grammar Sch. Min. of Education, 1955–63; MPBW, 1964–71 (incl. periods as Pvte Sec. to four Ministers); Department of the Environment: Prin. Pvte Sec. to Minister for Housing and Construction, 1971–72; Asst Sec., 1972; Housing, 1972–75; Personnel, 1975–77; Under Sec., 1977; Regl Dir, Northern Reg., 1977–80; Housing, 1980–84; Local Govt, 1984–85; Dep. Sec., Assoc. of Dist Councils, 1986–88. Dir, Bromley Mytime, 2004–; Vice-Chm., Proactive S London (formerly S London Sport and Physical Activity Partnership), 2010–13; Chm., ProActive Bromley, 2013–. FRSA 1992. *Publications:* Not Another Messiah, 1996; Bracken Point, 2002; Legacy, 2005; Robbed of Air, 2008; Short Measures, 2012. *Recreations:* reading, music, sport, walking. *Address:* 15 Sandford Road, Bromley, Kent BR2 9AL. *T:* (020) 8402 2354.

PICKUP, David Francis William, CB 2002; Attorney General of the Falkland Islands, 2007–11; *b* 28 May 1953; *s* of Joseph and Muriel Pickup; *m* 1975, Anne Elizabeth Round. *Educ:* Poole Grammar Sch.; Polytechnic of Central London (Univ. of London External LLB Hons). Called to the Bar, Lincoln's Inn, 1976, Gibraltar, 1988. Joined Treasury Solicitor's Dept as Legal Asst, 1978, Sen. Legal Asst, 1981; Grade 5 1987; Estabt Finance and Security Officer, 1988–90; Grade 3, Chancery Litigation Div., 1990; Legal Advr, MoD, 1991–95; Solicitor (Grade 2), HM Customs and Excise, subseq. HM Revenue and Customs, 1995–2005; Dir Gen., HMRC, 2006–07. *Recreations:* playing and watching cricket, ski-ing, listening to music, food and wine, travel. *Address:* Post House, Marston, Pembridge, Leominster HR6 9JA. *T:* (01544) 388264. *E:* dfwp.aep@icloud.com. *Club:* Kington Golf.

PICKUP, Ronald Alfred; actor; *b* 7 June 1940; *s* of Eric and Daisy Pickup; *m* 1964, Lans Traverse, USA; one *s* one *d*. *Educ:* King's Sch., Chester; Leeds Univ. (BA); Royal Academy of Dramatic Art. Repertory, Leicester, 1964; Royal Court, 1964 and 1965–66; National Theatre, 1965, 1966–73, 1977: appearances include: Rosalind, in all-male As You Like It, 1967; Richard II, 1972; Edmund, in Long Day's Journey into Night, 1971; Cassius, in Julius Caesar, 1977; Philip Madras, in The Madras House, 1977; Norman, in Norman Conquests, Globe, 1974; Play, Royal Court, 1976; Hobson's Choice, Lyric, Hammersmith, 1981; Astrov, in Uncle Vanya, Haymarket, 1982; Allmers in Little Eyolf, Lyric, Hammersmith, 1985; Gayev, in The Cherry Orchard, Aldwych, 1989; Amy's View, RNT, 1997, NY, 1999; Peer Gynt, Romeo and Juliet, RNT, 2000; Proof, Donmar Warehouse, 2002; Col Redfern in Look Back in Anger, Th. Royal, Bath, 2006; Uncle Vanya, Rose Th., Kingston, 2008; Waiting for Godot, tour then Th. Royal, Haymarket, 2010; Heartbreak House, Chichester, 2012; *films:* Three Sisters, 1969; Day of the Jackal, 1972; Joseph Andrews, 1976; 39 Steps, Zulu Dawn, 1978; Nijinsky, 1979; Never Say Never Again, John Paul II, 1983; Eleni, Camille (remake), 1984; The Mission, 1985; The Fourth Protocol, 1986; Bring Me the Head of Mavis Davis, 1996; Breathtaking, 1999; Evilenko, 2004; Greyfriars Bobby, 2006; Dark Floors, 2008; Prince of Persia, 2010; The Best Exotic Marigold Hotel, 2012; The Second Best Exotic Marigold Hotel, 2015; *television:* series and serials: Dragon's Opponent, 1973; Jennie, Fight Against Slavery, 1974; Tropic, 1979; Life of Giuseppe Verdi, 1982; Wagner, 1982; Life of Einstein, 1983; Moving, 1984; The Fortunes of War, 1987; Behaving Badly, 1988; A Time to Dance, 1992; My Friend Walter, 1992; The Riff Raff Element, 1993, 1994; Ivanhoe, 1996; Hornblower, 1998; Dalziel and Pascoe, 1999; The Worst Week of my Life, 2003–05; Feather Boy, 2004; Holby City, 2006–07; The Jury, 2011; Atlantis, 2014; other: The Philanthropist, Ghost Trio, The Discretion of Dominic Ayres, 1977; Memories, Henry VIII, 1978; England's Green and Pleasant Land, Christ Hero, 1979; The Letter, Ivanhoe, 1981; Orwell on Jura, 1983; The Rivals, 1986; The Attic, Chekhov in Yalta, 1988; A Murder of Quality, 1990; Absolute Hell, 1991; The War that Never Ends, 1991; The Golden Years, 1992; In the Cold Light of Day, 1994; Milner, 1994; A Case of Coincidence, 1994; A Very Open Prison, 1995; The Dying Day, Henry IV (title rôle), 1995; Cherished, 2003. Hon. DLitt Chester, 2012. *Recreations:* listening to music, walking, reading.

PICKUP, Sarah Jane, OBE 2014; Deputy Chief Executive, Hertfordshire County Council, since 2013; *b* Ramsgate, Kent, 29 Dec. 1962; *d* of Patrick and Anne Malone; *m* 1989, Michael Pickup; two *s* two *d*. *Educ:* Holy Trinity Convent, Bromley, Kent; Univ. of Sussex (BA Hons Econs 1984); W London Inst. of Higher Educn. CIPFA 1989. Trainee Acct, Richmond LBC, 1984–88; Hertfordshire County Council: Principal Tech. Asst, 1988–91; Principal Acct, 1991–93; Educn Finance Manager, 1993–95; Asst Dir, Adult Care Service, 1995–2003; Dir, Health and Community Services, 2003–13. Pres., Assoc. of Dirs of Adult Social Services, 2012–13. FRSA. *Recreations:* reading, family, theatre, yoga, swimming, ski-ing, music. *Address:* Hertfordshire County Council, County Hall, Pegs Lane, Hertford SG13 8DQ. *E:* sarah.pickup@hertfordshire.gov.uk.

PICTET, François-Charles; Ambassador of Switzerland to Austria, 1990–94, and Ambassador on Special Mission to the Holy See, 1993–97; *b* Geneva, 21 July 1929; *e s* of Charles Pictet, Geneva, and Elisabeth (*née* Decazes), France; *m* 1st, 1954, Elisabeth Choisy (*d* 1980), Geneva; three *s*; 2nd, 1983, Countess Marie-Thérèse Althann, Austria. *Educ:* College Calvin, Geneva; Univ. of Geneva (Faculty of Law). Called to the Swiss Bar, 1954. Joined Swiss Federal Dept of Foreign Affairs, 1956; Attaché, Vienna, 1957; Sec., Moscow, 1958–60; 1st Sec., Ankara, 1961–66; Dep. Dir, Internat. Orgns, Dept of For. Affairs, Berne, 1966–75; Minister Plenipotentiary, 1975; Ambassador to Canada and (non-resident) to the Bahamas,

1975–79; Ambassador, Perm. Rep. to Internat. Orgns in Geneva, 1980–84; Ambassador to UK, 1984–89, to the Netherlands, 1989–90; Hd of Swiss Delegn to CSCE, Vienna, 1991–93. *Address:* 6 rue Robert-de-Traz, 1206 Geneva, Switzerland. *T:* (22) 7890086.

PICTON, Julian Mark; QC 2010; *b* Kingston-upon-Thames, 25 April 1964; *s* of Prof. Denis Charles Alec Picton and Jane Picton. *Educ:* Reigate Grammar Sch.; Oriel Coll., Oxford (BA Law). Called to the Bar, Middle Temple, 1988. Chair, Disability Gp, Bar Council, 2009–. Vice Chm., Essex Yeomanry Assoc., 2008–. *Publications:* (contrib.) McGregor on Damages, 17th edn 2003, 18th edn 2009. *Recreations:* buildings, English furniture, English porcelain. *Address:* The Manor House, Wisbech St Mary, Cambs PE13 4RY. *T:* (020) 7643 5000, *Fax:* (020) 7353 5778. *E:* julian.picton@hailshamchambers.com.

PICTON, Martin Thomas; His Honour Judge Picton; a Circuit Judge, since 2005; *b* 20 Jan. 1958; *s* of Gerald and Daphne Picton; *m* 1992, Dr Susan Wensley; three *s* one *d. Educ:* Haberdashers' Aske's Sch., New Cross; King's Coll. London (LLB). Called to the Bar, Middle Temple, 1981; tenant, Albion Chambers, Bristol, 1982–2005; a Recorder, 1998–2005. *Recreations:* running, ski-ing, bringing up four children. *Address:* Gloucester Crown Court, PO Box 9051 GL1 2XG. *T:* (01452) 420100, *Fax:* (01452) 833599.

PIDD, Prof. Michael, PhD; Professor of Management Science, Lancaster University, 1992–2014, now Emeritus; *b* Sheffield, 1948; *s* of Ernest Pidd and Marion Pidd; *m* 1971, Sally Anne Nutt; two *d. Educ:* High Storrs Grammar Sch., Sheffield; Brunel Univ. (BTech 1970); Univ. of Birmingham (MSc 1971); Lancaster Univ. (PhD 2006). Operational Res. Analyst, Cadbury Schweppes, 1971–74; Lectr in Operational Res., Aston Univ., 1974–79; Lectr, 1979–89, Sen. Lectr, 1989–92, in Operational Res., Lancaster Univ. Pres., Operational Res. Soc., 2000–01. Chair, Business and Mgt Studies Panel, RAE 2008 and REF 2014. Mem. Bd, Centre for Workforce Intelligence, 2012–14. Companion of Operational Res. 2011; FBAM 2009; FAcSS (AcSS 2012). *Publications:* Computer Simulation in Management Science, 1984, 5th edn 2004; (ed) Computer Modelling for Discrete Simulation, 1989; Tools for Thinking: modelling in management science, 1996, 3rd edn 2009; (ed) Systems Modelling: theory and practice, 2004; Measuring the Performance of Public Services: principles and practice, 2012; articles in jls relating to operational res. and computer simulation. *Recreations:* walking, family, church work, local charitable work. *Address:* Department of Management Science, Lancaster University, Lancaster LA1 4YX. *T:* (01524) 593870, *Fax:* (01524) 844885. *E:* m.pidd@lancaster.ac.uk.

PIDDING, Baroness *cr* 2015 (Life Peer), of Amersham in the County of Buckinghamshire; **Emma Samantha Pidding,** CBE 2014; Chairman, National Conservative Convention, 2012–15; partner, Tim Butcher. *Educ:* Brudenell Co. Secondary Sch.; Dr Challoner's High Sch. Work in retail, then private banking; Mktg and Events Manager, IT consultancy, Bucks; Consultant, ESP Consultancy, 2009–12. Conservative Party: joined 1986; Chm., Chesham and Amersham Young Conservatives, 1991–94; Dep. Chm., 1997–2000, Chm., 2000–03, Chesham and Amersham Cons. Assoc.; Area Dep. Chm., 2002–04, Area Chm., 2004–06, Oxon and Bucks; Vice Pres., 2006–08, Pres., 2009–10, Nat. Convention; Jt Performance Improvement Co-ordinator, 2010–12; Nat. Volunteer Parly By-election Co-ordinator, 2010–12. Pres., NI Conservatives, 2007–. Mem. (C), Chiltern DC, 1991–99. *Address:* House of Lords, SW1A 0PW.

PIDDINGTON, Philip Michael, CBE 1988; HM Diplomatic Service, retired; Counsellor, Foreign and Commonwealth Office, 1987–90; *b* 27 March 1931; *s* of Percy Howard Piddington and Florence Emma (*née* Pearson); *m* 1955, Sylvia Mary Price; one *s* one *d. Educ:* Waverley Grammar Sch., Birmingham. Served HM Forces, 1949–51. Entered Min. of Works, 1947; FO, 1952; Jedda, 1956; Tokyo, 1962–66; First Sec., Lagos, 1969–71; Consul: NY, 1971–73; Istanbul, 1973–77; First Sec., FCO, 1978–83; Counsellor and Consul-Gen., Brussels, 1983–87. *Recreations:* riding, walking, photography. *Address:* Hammond Lodge, Breakspear Road North, Harefield, Uxbridge UB9 6NA. *T:* (01895) 825004.

PIDGEON, Caroline Valerie, MBE 2013; Member (Lib Dem), London Assembly, Greater London Authority, since 2008; *b* Eastleigh, Hants, 29 Sept. 1972; *d* of Eric and Valerie Pidgeon; *m* 2006, Paul Miles; one *s. Educ:* Univ. of Wales, Aberystwyth (BSc Econ Hons). Political Researcher: Cllr Rose Colley, Southwark BC, 1994–96; Brent Council, 1996–99; Communications Manager: Croydon HA, 1999–2002; Guy's and St Thomas' NHS Foundn Trust, 2002–06. Mem. (Lib Dem), Southwark BC, 1998–2010 (Dep. Leader, 2002–04; Exec. Mem., for Educn, 2004–06, for Children's Services, 2006–08). Contested (Lib Dem) Vauxhall, 2010. *Recreations:* cinema, modern art. *Address:* Greater London Authority, City Hall, The Queen's Walk, SE1 2AA. *T:* (020) 7983 4362. *E:* caroline.pidgeon@london.gov.uk.

PIDGEON, Sir John (Allan Stewart), Kt 1989; Chairman, since 1980, and Managing Director, since 1960, F. A. Pidgeon & Son and associated companies; *b* 15 July 1926; *s* of Frederick Allan Pidgeon and Margaret Ellen Pidgeon, MBE; *m* 1st, 1952, Sylvia Dawn (*d* 1991); one *s* four *d*; 2nd, 1993, Mrs Pamela Barbara Howell (*d* 2011). *Educ:* Church of England Grammar Sch., Brisbane. Fellow, Aust. Inst. of Building; FIDA. Served 2nd AIF, 1944–45. Joined F. A. Pidgeon & Son Pty, 1946. Director: Suncorp Building Soc., 1976–91; Folkestone Ltd, 1985–95. Chm., Builders' Registration Bd of Qld, 1985–93. Pres., Qld Master Builders' Assoc., 1970–72 (Trustee, 1978–95). Chm., Salvation Army Adv. Bd, 1988–93. FAICD. *Recreations:* ski-ing, tennis, swimming. *Address:* 14 Otway Street, Holland Park, Brisbane, Qld 4121, Australia. *T:* (7) 38971137. *Clubs:* Brisbane, Queensland, Tattersalls, Polo, Brisbane Amateur Turf (Brisbane); Brisbane Yacht.

PIEBALGS, Andris; Member, European Commission, 2004–14; *b* 17 Sept. 1957; *m* Anda; one *s* two *d. Educ:* Univ. of Latvia (degree in physics). Teacher, then Headmaster, Secondary Sch. No 1, Valmiera, 1980–88; Desk Officer, then Hd of Dept, Min. of Educn, Latvia, 1988–90; Minister of Educn, 1990–93; MP, 1993–94; Minister of Finance, 1994–95; Ambassador to Estonia, 1995–97; Perm. Rep. of Latvia to EU, 1998–2003; Dep. Sec. of State, Min. of Foreign Affairs, 2003–04; Hd of Cabinet, Latvian Mem. of EC, 2004.

PIËCH, Ferdinand; Chairman, Supervisory Board: Volkswagen AG, 2002–15 (Member, 1992–2002, Chairman, 1993–2002, Board of Management); Man AG, 2007; *b* Vienna, 17 April 1937; *s* of Dr jur Anton Piëch and Louise (*née* Porsche). *Educ:* in Switzerland; Tech. Univ. of Zurich. Mem., Management Bd i/c R and D, Audi NSU Auto Union AG/Audi AG, 1975–88; Chm., Bd of Management, Audi AG, 1988–92. Dr *hc* Vienna Technical Univ., 1984.

PIENAAR, John Adrian; Chief Political Correspondent, since 2002, and Presenter, Pienaar's Politics, since 2010, BBC Radio Five-Live; *b* 2 Nov. 1956; *s* of Eric and Johanna Pienaar; *m* 1st, 1980, Denise Walsh (marr. diss.); one *s* one *d*; 2nd, Penny Davies; two *d. Educ:* Ravenswood Sch., Bromley. Political staff, Press Assoc., 1980–86; Political Correspondent: Independent, 1986–92; BBC News, 1992–; Presenter, The Weekend News, Radio Five-Live, 2006–10. *Recreations:* reading, history, novels, almost anything, watching films, near-obsessive fan of Crystal Palace FC. *Address:* BBC Westminster, 4 Millbank, SW1P 3JQ. *E:* john.pienaar@bbc.co.uk.

PIEŃKOWSKI, Jan Michał; author and illustrator, since 1958; *b* 8 Aug. 1936; *s* of late Jerzy Dominik Pieńkowski and Wanda Maria Pieńkowska. *Educ:* Cardinal Vaughan Sch., London; King's Coll., Cambridge (MA Classics and English). Art Dir, J. Walter Thompson, William Collins, and Time and Tide, London, 1958–61. Work includes graphics and murals, posters and greeting cards, children's TV, and book illustration. *Stage designs:* Meg and Mog Show, 1981–88; Beauty and the Beast, Royal Opera House, 1986; Théâtre de Complicité, 1988; Sleeping Beauty, Euro Disney, 1992; Beauty and the Beast, Kremlin Palace Th., 2013; Captain Blood's Revenge, Glyndebourne, 2013. Kate Greenaway Medal, Library Assoc., 1972 and 1979. *Publications:* illustrator: A Necklace of Raindrops, by Joan Aiken, 1968, new edn 2009; The Kingdom under the Sea, 1971, new edn 2011; Tale of a One Way Street, 1978; Past Eight O'Clock, 1986; A Foot in the Grave, 1989 (new format edn with addnl artwork, 2013); M.O.L.E., 1993, etc; (co-author with Helen Nicoll and illustrator) Meg and Mog series, 1973–90 (televised, 2004); The Glass Mountain, by David Walser, 2014; illustrator/author: Nursery series, 1973–91; Haunted House, 1979; Robot, 1981; Dinner Time, 1981 (new large-format edn 2007); Christmas, 1984; Little Monsters, 1986 (new large-format edn 2007); Small Talk, 1988; Easter, 1989; Fancy That, 1990; Phone Book, 1991; Christmas Kingdom, 1991; Door Bell, 1992; Road Hog, 1993; ABC Dinosaurs, 1993; Toilet Book, 1994; 1001 Words, 1994; Furrytails series, 1994; Nursery Cloth Books series, 1994; Botticelli's Bed and Breakfast, 1996; Nursery Pop-Up series, 1996–97; Tickle-me Books, 1997; Good Night, 1998; Bel and Bub series, 2000; The Monster Pet, 2000; Pizza!, 2001; The Cat with Nine Lives, 2001; The Animals went in Two by Two, 2001; Meg, Mog and Og, 2003; Meg's Mummy, 2004; The First Noël, 2004; The Fairy Tales, 2005; Mog's Missing, 2005; Haunted House, 25th anniversary edn, 2005; The First Christmas, 2006; Meg & Mog Touch and Feel Counting Book, 2006; The Thousand Nights and One Night, 2007; Meg and Mog, 35th anniversary edn, 2007, 40th birthday edn, 2012; Nut Cracker, 2008; In the Beginning, 2010; Meg Goes to Bed, 2010; A River of Stories: tales and poems from across the Commonwealth, 2011; (co-author with David Walsher and illustrator) Meg and the Pirate, 2014. *Recreations:* keeping bantams, Latin, drawing from life on computer. *Address:* Oakgates, Barnes. *Club:* Polish Hearth.

PIEPER, Philippa; *see* Whitford, P.

PIERCE, Rt Rev. Anthony Edward; Bishop of Swansea and Brecon, 1999–2008; *b* 16 Jan. 1941; *s* of Gwynfor Pierce and Martha Jane Pierce (*née* Owen). *Educ:* Dynevor Sch., Swansea; University Coll., Swansea (BA Hons Hist. 1963); Linacre Coll., Oxford (BA Hons Theol 1965; MA 1971); Ripon Hall, Oxford. Deacon 1965, priest 1966; Curate: St Peter, Swansea, 1965–67; St Mary and Holy Trinity, Swansea, 1967–74; Vicar of Llwynderw, 1974–92; Priest-in-charge, St Barnabas, Swansea, 1992–96; Canon Res., Brecon Cathedral, 1993; Archdeacon of Gower, 1995–99; Vicar, St Mary, Swansea, 1996–99. Sec., Dio. Conf. and Dio. Patronage Bd, 1991–95; Dio. Dir of Educn, 1992–96. Mem., Prov. Selection Panel, 1984–97; Chm., Social Action Sect., 1985–90, Chm. Div. Social Responsibility, 1990–92, Prov. Bd of Mission. Chm., Ecumenical Aids Monitoring Gp (Wales), 1988–95. University College, Swansea: Bp's Chaplain to Anglican Students, 1971–74; Mem. Ct of Govs, 1981–2010 (Life Mem., 2010); Chaplain, 1984–88. Mem. Council, Univ. of Wales, Swansea, 1995–2010. Chaplain, Singleton Hosp., 1980–95; Co-ordinator, Hosp. Chaplains, 1982–95. Chair, Gwalia Housing Gp, 2009–. Pres., Friends of Swansea Music Fest., 2002–. Hon. Fellow, Swansea Univ., 2011. Hon. Ed., Welsh Churchman, 1972–75. KStJ 2010 (Sub-Prelate, Order of St John, Priory of Wales, 2002–10). *Recreations:* reading, theatre, music. *Address:* 2 Coed Ceirios, Swansea Vale, Swansea SA7 0NU.

PIERCE, Karen Elizabeth, (Mrs C. F. Roxburgh), CMG 2008; HM Diplomatic Service; Ambassador to Afghanistan, since 2015; *b* 23 Sept. 1959; *d* of late Derek Robert Pierce and of Barbara Florence Pierce; *m* 1987, Charles Fergusson Roxburgh, *qv*; two *s. Educ:* Penwortham Girls' High Sch.; Girton Coll., Cambridge (BA Hons English 1981; MA 1991); London Sch. of Econs and Pol Sci. (MSc Internat. Strategy and Diplomacy 2012). Joined FCO, 1981; Tokyo, 1984–87; Security Policy Dept, FCO, 1987–91; Washington, 1991–96; Eastern Dept, then Eastern Adriatic Dept, FCO, 1996–99; Head: Newsroom, FCO, 1999–2000; EU Dept (Bilateral), FCO, 2001–02; Eastern Adriatic Dept, FCO, 2002–06; Dep. Permanent Rep., UK Mission to UN, New York and Pres., UN Trusteeship Council, 2006–09; Dir, South Asia and Afghanistan, 2009–11; UK Perm. Rep. to UN and WTO, Geneva, 2012–15. *Recreations:* collecting ceramics, baskets, fridge magnets. *Address:* c/o Foreign and Commonwealth Office, King Charles Street, SW1A 2AH.

PIERCY, family name of **Baron Piercy**.

PIERCY, 3rd Baron *cr* 1945, of Burford; **James William Piercy;** *b* 19 Jan. 1946; *s* of 2nd Baron Piercy and Oonagh Lavinia (*d* 1990), *d* of late Major Edward John Lake Baylay, DSO; *S* father, 1981. *Educ:* Shrewsbury; Edinburgh Univ. (BSc 1968). AMIEE; FCCA. *Heir: b* Hon. Mark Edward Pelham Piercy [*b* 30 June 1953; *m* 1979, Vivien Angela, *d* of His Honour Evelyn Faithfull Monier-Williams; one *s* three *d*]. *Address:* 36 Richford Street, W6 7HP.

PIERCY, Prof. Nigel Francis, PhD, DLitt; Professor of Marketing and Strategy, and Dean, School of Management, Swansea University, since 2013; *b* Hounslow, Middx; *s* of Gilbert Piercy and Helena Piercy (*née* Sargent); *m* 1996, Nikala Lane; one *s. Educ:* Heriot-Watt Univ. (BA 1972; DLitt 2006); Durham Univ. (MA 1980); Univ. of Wales (PhD 1985). Cardiff Business Sch., Cardiff Univ., 1981–2001, latterly as Sir Julian Hodge Prof. of Mktg and Strategy, 1996–2001; Prof. of Strategic Mktg, Cranfield Sch. of Mgt, Cranfield Univ., 2002–03; Prof. of Mktg and Strategy, 2003–13, Associate Dean, 2009–13, Warwick Business Sch., Univ. of Warwick. Visiting Professor: M. J. Neeley Sch. of Business, Texas Christian Univ., 1993–94; Grad. Sch. of Business Admin, Columbia Univ., 1998, 2002; Fuqua Sch. of Business, Duke Univ., 1999; Sch. of Business, Vienna Univ. of Business and Econs, 2003–07; Aalto Exec. Programs, Finland, 2011; Cyprus Inst. of Mktg, 2012; Vis. Scholar, W. Haas Sch. of Business, Univ. of Calif, Berkeley, 1994. *Publications:* Export Strategy, 1982; (with M. J. Evans) Managing Marketing Information, 1983; Marketing Organisation, 1985; Marketing Budgeting, 1986; Market-Led Strategic Change: making marketing happen in your organization, 1991, 4th edn as Market-Led Strategic Change: transforming the process of going to market, 2009 (trans. Chinese 2005); (jtly) Marketing Strategy and Competitive Positioning, 2nd edn 1998 to 5th edn 2012 (trans. Portuguese 2001, 2005, Russian 2005, Chinese 2007); Strategic Management, 1999; Tales from the Marketplace, 1999; (with D. W. Dravens) Strategic Marketing, 7th edn 2002 to 10th edn 2012 (trans. Chinese 2003, 2004); (jtly) Total Integrated Marketing, 2005; (jtly) Marketing Bundle, 2006; (with N. Lane) Strategic Customer Management, 2009; (ed jtly) Oxford Handbook in Strategic Sales and Sales Management, 2011; (jtly) Principles of Marketing, 6th edn 2013; approx. 300 articles. *Address:* School of Management, Swansea University, Swansea SA2 8PP. *T:* (01792) 295296. *E:* nigel.piercy@swansea.ac.uk.

PIERI, Frank; Sheriff of South Strathclyde, Dumfries and Galloway at Airdrie, since 2009 (at Hamilton, 2005–09); *b* 10 Aug. 1954; *s* of Ralph Pieri and Teresa Pieri; *m* 1977, Dorothy Telfer; two *d. Educ:* St Aloysius Coll., Glasgow; Univ. of Glasgow (LLB 1974). Solicitor, 1976–93; called to the Scottish Bar, 1994; in practice as Advocate, 1994–2000; Immigration Adjudicator (full time), 2000–04. Member: Council, Scottish Law Agents Soc., 1991–93; Council of Immigration Judges, 2003. *Recreations:* ambling, crime fiction, opera, Partick Thistle FC. *Address:* Airdrie Sheriff Court, Graham Street, Airdrie ML6 6EE. *T:* (01236) 751121. *E:* sherifffpieri@scotcourts.gov.uk. *Club:* Glasgow Art.

PIERS, Sir James (Desmond), 11th Bt *cr* 1661, of Tristernagh Abbey, Westmeath; Partner, Fasken Martineau DuMoulin (formerly Russell & DuMoulin), lawyers, since 1982; *b* 24 July 1947; *s* of Sir Charles Robert Fitzmaurice Piers, 10th Bt and Ann Blanche Scott (*d* 1975); *S* father, 1996; *m* 1975, Sandra Mae Dixon; one *s* one *d. Educ:* Univ. of Victoria (BA 1969); Univ. of British Columbia (LLB 1973). Called to the Bar, British Columbia, 1974, Yukon Territory, 1975. *Heir: s* Stephen James Piers, *b* 14 Sept. 1979. *Address:* Fasken Martineau DuMoulin, 2900–550 Burrard Street, Vancouver, BC V6C 0A3, Canada.

PIETRONI, Prof. Patrick Claude, FRCP, FRCGP; Director, Centre for Psychological Therapies in Primary Care, University of Chester, since 2012; Public Health Associate Director, Mental Health Shropshire, since 2013; *b* 8 Nov. 1942; *s* of Michael and Jeannette Pietroni; *m* 1st, 1963, Theresa Wilkinson (marr. diss.); two *s* one *d*; 2nd, 1977, Marilyn Miller. *Educ:* Guy's Hosp. Med. Sch. (MB BS 1966). MRCP 1973, FRCP 2000; FRCGP 1985; MFPH (MFPHM 2000). MO, RAMC, 1967–69; Principal, Gen. Practice, 1971–; Associate Prof., Family Medicine, Univ. of Cincinnati, 1978–80; Sen. Lectr in Gen. Practice, St Mary's Hosp. Med. Sch., 1981–93; Prof. and Dir, Centre for Community Care and Primary Health, Univ. of Westminster, 1993–97; Dean, Postgrad. Gen. Practice, N Thames (West) Dept of Postgrad. Med. and Dental Educn, London Univ., 1996–2001; Dir, Educnl Support Unit, London Region, NHS Exec., 2001–04. Founder and Advr, Internat. Inst. for Study of Cuba, London Metropolitan Univ., 2008–. Dir, 4Ps Res. and Develt Unit, 2001–04. Hon. DSc Westminster, 2001. *Publications:* Holistic Living, 1986; The Greening of Medicine, 1990; Innovation in Community Care and Primary Health, 1995. *Recreations:* tennis, riding, bridge, opera.

PIGEON, Michel, PhD; Member (Québec Liberal) Charlesbourg, National Assembly of Québec, 2008–11; *b* 1945; *s* of Louis-Philippe Pigeon and Madeleine Gaudry; *m* 1968, Marie-José des Rivières; two *d*. *Educ:* Laval Univ. (BA 1963, BScA 1967); ICSTM (MPhil 1969); Univ. Pierre et Marie Curie, Paris (PhD 1984). Laval University: Department of Civil Engineering: Asst Prof., 1972–77; Associate Prof., 1977–87; Tenured Prof., 1987–2009; Dir, 1999–2001; Dir, Interuniv. Res. Centre on Concrete, 1992–98, 2000–01; Vice Dean, Res., Sci. and Engrg Faculty, 2001; Dean, Sci. and Engrg Faculty, 2002; Rector, 2002–07. *Publications:* (with R. Pleau) Durability of Concrete in Cold Climates, 1995; book chapters and articles in learned jls.

PIGGOTT, Ven. Andrew John; Archdeacon of Bath, since 2005; *b* 27 Sept. 1951; *s* of David Geoffrey John and late Joyce Vera Piggott; *m* 1979, Ruth Elizabeth Morris; two *d*. *Educ:* Queen Mary Coll., London (BScEcon 1972); Leeds Univ. (PGCE 1973); Nottingham Univ. (DipTh 1984). Various teaching posts, 1973–83; ordained deacon, 1986, priest, 1987; Curate, St Philip with St James, Dorridge, 1986–89; Team Vicar, St Chad's, Kidderminster, 1989–94; Incumbent, St Lawrence, Biddulph, 1994–99; Church Pastoral Aid Society: Ministry and Vocations Advr, 1999–2001; Acting Gen. Dir, 2000–01; Patronage Sec., 2001–05. Mem., Gen. Synod, 2009–. *Address:* 56 Grange Road, Saltford, Bristol BS31 3AG. *T:* (01225) 873609, *Fax:* (01225) 874110. *E:* adbath@bathwells.anglican.org.

PIGGOTT, Donald James; Director-General, British Red Cross Society, 1980–85; *b* 1 Sept. 1920; *s* of late James Piggott and Edith Piggott (*née* Tempest); *m* 1974, Kathryn Courtenay-Evans (*d* 2010), *e d* of late William and Gwendoline Eckford. *Educ:* Bradford Grammar School; Christ's College, Cambridge (MA); London School of Economics. Served Army in NW Europe and India, 1941–46. PA to Finance and Supply Director, London Transport, 1947–50; Shell-Mex and BP Ltd, 1951–58; Manager Development Div., Marketing Dept, British Petroleum Co. Ltd, 1958–73; BRCS: Dir, Internat. Affairs, 1973; Head of Internat. Div., 1975; Asst Dir-Gen. International, 1980. Member: Central Appeals Adv. Cttee, BBC and IBA, 1980–83; Jt Cttee, St John and Red Cross, 1980–91; Dep. Pres., Suffolk Br., BRCS, 1987–93. Liveryman, Co. of Carmen, 1988–2012. FRSocMed 1993. OStJ 1983. *Recreations:* music, theatre. *Address:* Beech Tree House, The Green, Tostock, Bury St Edmunds, Suffolk IP30 9NY. *T:* (01359) 270589. *Clubs:* Hawks (Cambridge); Achilles.

PIGGOTT, Lester Keith; jockey, 1948–85 and 1990–95; trainer, 1985–87; *b* 5 Nov. 1935; *s* of late Keith Piggott and Iris Rickaby; *m* 1960, Susan Armstrong; two *d*. Selection of races won: the Derby (9 times): 1954 (on Never Say Die); 1957 (on Crepello); 1960 (on St Paddy); 1968 (on Sir Ivor); 1970 (on Nijinsky); 1972 (on Roberto); 1976 (on Empery); 1977 (on The Minstrel); 1983 (on Teenoso); St Leger (8 times); The Oaks (6 times); 2,000 guineas (5 times); 1,000 guineas (twice). In many seasons 1955–85 he rode well over 100 winners a year, in this country alone; rode 4,000th winner in Britain, 14 Aug. 1982; record 30th classic win, 1 May 1992; Champion Jockey 11 times, 1960, 1964–71, 1981, 1982; rode frequently in France; won Prix de l'Arc de Triomphe on Rheingold, 1973, on Alleged, 1977 and 1978; won Washington, DC, International on Sir Ivor, 1968 (first time since 1922 an English Derby winner raced in USA), on Karabas, 1969, on Argument, 1980. *Publications:* (with Sean Magee) Lester's Derbys, 2004; *relevant publication:* Lester, the Official Biography, by Dick Francis, 1986. *Recreations:* swimming, water ski-ing, golf.

PIGNATELLI, Frank, CBE 2005; pro bono adviser and mentor to individuals and charitable, voluntary and not-for-profit organisations, since 2006; Chief Executive, University for Industry, Scotland, 1999–2006; *b* 22 Dec. 1946; *s* of Frank and Elizabeth Pignatelli; *m* 1969, Rosetta Anne McFadyen; one *s* one *d*. *Educ:* Univ. of Glasgow (MA; DipEd, MEd); Jordanhill Coll. of Educn (Secondary Teachers Cert.). Teacher, St Mungo's Acad., Glasgow, 1970; Hd of Dept, St Gregory's Secondary Sch., Glasgow, 1974; Asst Headteacher, St Margaret Mary's Secondary Sch., Glasgow, 1977; Strathclyde Region: Educn Officer, Renfrew Div., 1978; Asst Dir of Educn, 1983; Depute Dir of Educn, 1985; Dir of Educn, 1988–96; Gp Dir, Human Resources, Associated Newspapers, London, 1996–97; Chm. and Man. Dir, Exec. Support and Develt Consultancy, 1997–2000; Chief Exec., ScotBIC, 1998–99. Hon. Lectr in Educn, 1988–90, Vis. Prof., 1990–, Univ. of Glasgow Sch. of Educn; Vis. Prof. of Mgt Educn, Univ. of Glasgow Business Sch., 1997–. Chairman: RIPA (West of Scotland), 1990–93; Scottish Mgt and Enterprise Council, 1999–; Scottish Skills and Employability Network, 1999–; Member: Adv. Scottish Council for Educn and Trng Targets, 1993–96; Bd, SCOTVEC, 1993–96 (Fellow, 1996); UK Nuffield Langs Inquiry, 1998–2000; Ministerial Trade Union Wkg Pty on Lifelong Learning, 2000–. Chairman: Technol. Review Gp, 1993–; Nat. Cttee for Review of Post 16 educn and trng, 1993–; Assoc. for Mgt Educn and Trng in Scotland, 1998–; Scottish Parlt Futures Forum Project Bd, 2007–08. Pres., Glasgow and West of Scotland Inst. of Mgt, 2001–; Hon. Pres., Scottish Assoc. for Language Teaching, 1998–2000. CCMI (CIMgt 2000; FBIM 1989; Pres., Renfrewshire, 1991–93). FRSA 1992; FSQA 1997; FICPD 1998; Fellow, Scotland's Colls, 2006. DUniv Paisley, 1993; Hon. DEd Abertay, 2003. *Publications:* Basic Knowledge 'O' French, 1974; Higher French Past Papers, 1975; Scottish Education Policy Review, 1994; contrib., World Year Book in Education, TES, Mgt of Educnl Policy - Scottish Perspectives. *Recreations:* swimming, genealogy, do-it-yourself, reading and all things French. *T:* 07867 862945. *E:* frank@pignatelli.co.uk.

PIGOT, Sir George (Hugh), 8th Bt *cr* 1764, of Patshull, Staffs; Managing Director, Custom Metalcraft Ltd, 1998–2012; *b* 28 Nov. 1946; *s* of Maj.-Gen. Sir Robert Pigot, 7th Bt, CB, OBE, DL, and Honor (*d* 1966), *d* of Captain Wilfred St Martin Gibbon; *S* father, 1986; *m* 1st, 1967, Judith Sandeman-Allen (marr. diss. 1973); one *d*; 2nd, 1980, Lucinda Jane (marr. diss. 1993), *d* of D. C. Spandler; two *s*; 3rd, 2006, Odette (marr. diss. 2008), *yr d* of Walter Stanley, Port Elizabeth, SA. *Educ:* Stowe. Man. Dir, Padworth Fisheries Ltd, 1981–95; Dir, Southern Trout Ltd, 1993–95 (Man. Dir, 1994–95); business consultant, Positive Response, 1995–; Sec.-Gen., 1998–2003, Administrator, 2007–, Residential Sprinkler Assoc.; Chief Exec., Fire Sprinkler Assoc., 2003–07; Dir, Integrated Fire Protection Ltd, 2008–. Member: Council, British Trout Assoc., 1986–93 (Hon. Treas., 1990–92); Fish Farming Exec. Cttee, NFU, 1987–90 (Chm. Health and Technical Sub-Cttee, 1989–90). *Recreations:* classic cars, golf. *Heir:* s George Douglas Hugh Pigot, *b* 17 Sept. 1982. *Address:* Mill House, Mill Lane, Padworth, near Reading, Berks RG7 4JX.

PIGOTT, Sir (Berkeley) Henry (Sebastian), 5th Bt *cr* 1808; farmer; *b* 24 June 1925; *s* of Sir Berkeley Pigott, 4th Bt, and Christabel (*d* 1974), *d* of late Rev. F. H. Bowden-Smith; *S* father, 1982; *m* 1954, (Olive) Jean, *d* of John William Balls; two *s* one *d*. *Educ:* Ampleforth College. Served War with Royal Marines, 1944–45. *Recreation:* sailing (blue water). *Heir:* *er s* David John Berkeley Pigott [*b* 16 Aug. 1955; *m* 1st, 1981 (marr. diss.); 2nd, 1986, Julie Wiffen (marr. diss.); one *d*]. *Address:* Brook Farm, Shobley, Ringwood, Hants BH24 3HT. *T:* (01425) 474423.

PIGOTT, Prof. Christopher Donald, PhD; Director, University Botanic Garden, Cambridge, 1984–95; *b* 7 April 1928; *s* of John Richards Pigott and Helen Constance Pigott (*née* Lee); *m* 1st, 1954, Margaret Elsie Beatson (*d* 1981); one *d*; 2nd, 1986, Sheila Lloyd (*née* Megaw). *Educ:* Mill Hill School; University of Cambridge. MA, PhD. Asst Lectr, and Lectr, Univ. of Sheffield, 1951–60; Univ. Lectr, Cambridge, 1960–64; Fellow of Emmanuel Coll., Cambridge, 1962–64; Prof. of Biology, Univ. of Lancaster, 1964–84, Prof. Emeritus, 1995–; Professorial Fellow, Emmanuel Coll., Cambridge, 1984–95, Emeritus Fellow, 2010. Member: Scientific Policy Cttee, Nature Conservancy Council, 1964–82; Scientific Adv. Cttee, Field Studies Council, 1964–68; Internat. Biol Prog., UK/Uganda Proj., Royal Soc. Cttee, 1965–74; Nature Conservancy, 1971–73; Council, 1980–92, Properties Cttee, 1990–2002, Nat. Trust; Home Grown Timber Adv. Cttee, 1987–94, Res. Users Adv. Gp, 1993–96, Forestry Commn. Vis. Prof., Botany and Microbiol., Univ. of Witwatersrand, 1975; Consultant, Nilsvlei Proj., CSRI Pretoria, 1975–81; Advr on univ. curricula for applied plant ecology, Min. of Sci. and Res., Algeria, 1980. Foreign Correspondent, Acad. d'Agriculture de France (Silviculture), 1982–. *Publications:* Lime-trees and Basswoods: a biological monograph of the genus Tilia, 2012; contribs to sci. jls, books and symposia (ecology and physiology of plants). *Recreations:* walking, gardening, drawing. *Address:* Greenbank, Cartmel, Grange-over-Sands LA11 7ST.

PIGOTT, Sir Henry; *see* Pigott, Sir B. H. S.

PIGOTT, Ronald Wellesley, FRCS, FRCSI; Consultant Plastic Surgeon, Frenchay Hospital, Bristol, 1969–93, Hon. Consultant, since 1993; *b* 16 Sept. 1932; *s* of Thomas Ian Wellesley Pigott and Kathleen Muriel (*née* Parsons); *m* 1958, Sheila King; four *s*. *Educ:* Oakham Sch., Rutland; Univ. of Dublin (BA, MB, BCh, BAO). FRCSI 1960; FRCS 1962. Short service commn, Parachute Field Ambulance, 1960–62. Sen. Registrar, Plastic Surgery, Stoke Mandeville Hosp., 1962–68; Robert Johnson Fellow, Univ. of Miami, 1967. Pioneered endoscopy of velopharyngeal isthmus in the condition of velopharyngeal incompetence; developed split screen recording of endoscopic and radiological examn of velopharyngeal isthmus with A. P. W. Makepeace; pioneered computer-based assessment of symmetry for application to cleft lip and nose deformity with B. Coghlan and D. Matthews. President: Eur. Assoc. of Plastic Surgeons, 1992–93; British Assoc. of Aesthetic Plastic Surgeons, 1993. James Halloran Bennet Medal in Surgery, 1956; James Berry Prize 1979, Jacksonian Prize 1979, RCS; Mowlem Award, Brit. Assoc. Plastic Surgeons, 1982. *Publications:* chapters regarding investigation and treatment of cleft lip and palate in: Advances in the Management of Cleft Lip and Palate, 1980; Clinics in Plastic Surgery, 1985; Scott Brown's Paediatric Otolaryngology, 5th edn 1987; Current Therapy in Plastic and Reconstructive Surgery, 1989; article on develt of endoscopy of palatopharyngeal isthmus, Proc. Royal Soc., 1977; articles in Lancet, Brit. Jl Plastic Surgery, Plastic Reconstructive Surgery, Annals Plastic Surgery, Scandinavian Jl Plastic Reconstructive Surgery. *Recreations:* formerly hockey (represented Ireland, University of Dublin and Army and Combined Services), tennis (represented Univ. of Dublin), painting, sculpture, gardening.

PIGOTT-BROWN, Sir William Brian, 3rd Bt *cr* 1902; *b* 20 Jan. 1941; *s* of Sir John Pigott-Brown, 2nd Bt (killed in action, 1942) and of Helen (who *m* 1948, Capt. Charles Raymond Radclyffe), *o d* of Major Gilbert Egerton Cotton, Priestland, Tarporley, Cheshire; *S* father, 1942. *Heir:* none.

PIGOTT-SMITH, Timothy Peter; actor, director and writer; *b* 13 May 1946; *s* of late Harry Thomas Pigott-Smith and of Margaret Muriel (*née* Goodman); *m* 1972, Pamela Miles; one *s*. *Educ:* Bristol Univ. (BA Hons 1967); Bristol Old Vic Theatre Sch. Appeared with: Bristol Old Vic, 1967–69; Prospect Th. Co., 1970–71; RSC, 1972–75; Birmingham, Cambridge, Nottingham and Royal Court Th., 1975–77; *stage appearances include:* Benefactors, Vaudeville, 1984; Bengal Lancer (one-man show), Leicester, transf. Lyric, Hammersmith, 1985; Coming in to Land, Antony and Cleopatra, Entertaining Strangers, Winter's Tale, Cymbeline, and Tempest, NT, 1986–88; dir, Samuel Beckett's Company, Donmar Warehouse (Edinburgh Fest. Fringe award), 1987; Artistic Dir, Compass Th., 1989–92; Brutus in Julius Caesar, 1990; Salieri in Amadeus, 1991; Saki—an anthology, 1991; Mr Rochester in Jane Eyre, Playhouse, 1993; The Picture of Dorian Gray, Lyric, 1994; Retreat, Orange Tree, Richmond, 1995; The Letter, Lyric, 1995; Mary Stuart, The Alchemist, RNT, 1996; Heritage, Hampstead, 1997; The Iceman Cometh, Almeida, 1998, transf. Old Vic, then NY, 1999; Five Kinds of Silence, Lyric, 2000; Cassius in Julius Caesar, RSC, 2001; Scrooge in A Christmas Carol, Lyric Hammersmith, 2002; Ezra Mannon in Mourning Becomes Electra, NT, 2003; Agamemnon in Hecuba, Donmar Warehouse, 2004; Women Beware Women, RSC, 2006; The Exonerated, Riverside, 2006; See How They Run, Duchess, 2006; Pygmalion, Th. Royal Bath and tour, 2007, transf. Old Vic, 2008; Little Nell, Th. Royal Bath, 2007; Enron, Chichester, transf. Royal Court, 2009, then Noël Coward, 2010; Educating Rita, Trafalgar Studios, 2010; Delicate Balance, Almeida, 2011; King Lear, West Yorks Playhouse, 2011; The Tempest, Th. Royal Bath, 2012; Stroke of Luck, Park Th., 2014; King Charles III, Almeida Th., trans. Wyndham's Th., 2014, adapted for radio, 2015; Who's Afraid of Virginia Woolf, Theatre Royal. Bath, 2014; director: Royal Hunt of the Sun, 1989; Playing the Wife, 1992; Hamlet, Regent's Park, 1994; The Real Thing, UK tour, 2005. *Films:* Aces High, 1975; Joseph Andrews, 1977; Sweet William, 1978; The Day Christ Died, 1979; Richard's Things, 1981; Clash of the Titans, 1981; Escape to Victory, 1981; Hunchback of Notre Dame, 1982; State of Emergency, 1985; Life Story (Best TV Film, BAFTA), 1987; The True Adventures of Christopher Columbus, 1992; The Remains of the Day, 1993; The Bullion Boys, 1993; The Shadowy Third, 1994; Four Feathers, Laissez Passer, Bloody Sunday, Gangs of New York, 2002; Johnny English, 2003; Alexander, 2004; Entente Cordiale, V for Vendetta, Flyboys, 2005; Quantum of Solace, 2008; Alice in Wonderland, 2010; Ma Part du Gâteau, 2011; *television: series and serials:* Dr Who, 1970; Glittering Prizes, 1975; North and South, 1975; Wings, 1976; Eustace and Hilda, 1977; The Lost Boys, 1978; The Wilderness Years, 1978; Fame is the Spur, 1982; The Jewel in the Crown (Best TV Actor, BAFTA; TV Times Best Actor; BPG Best Actor), 1984; The Chief, 1989–91; The Vice, 2001; Dr Terrible's House of Horrible, 2001; North and South, 2004; Holby Blue, 2007; The Little House, 2010; Money, 2010; The Hour, 2011; Downton Abbey, 2012; 37 Days, 2014; *films for television:* On Expenses, 2010; The Suspicions of Mr Whicher, 2011; Strike Back 3, Silent Witness, 2012; Wodehouse in Exile, 2013; *plays:* No Mama No, 1976; Measure for Measure, 1978; School Play, 1979; Henry IV part 1, 1980; Eroica, 2003; *documentaries:* Calcutta Chronicles (presenter and writer), 1996; Innocents, 2001; Pompeii: the last day, 2003; Peter Ackroyd's London, 2004. Hon. DLitt: Leicester, 2002; Bristol, 2007. *Publications:* Out of India, 1987; The Dragon Tattoo, 2008; The Rose of Africa, 2009; The Shadow of Evil, 2009. *Recreations:* music, sport.

PIKE, Prof. (Edward) Roy, PhD; FRS 1981; Clerk Maxwell Professor of Theoretical Physics, University of London at King's College, 1986–2010, now Professor Emeritus (Head of School of Physical Sciences and Engineering, 1991–94); *b* 4 Dec. 1929; *s* of Anthony Pike and Rosalind Irene Pike (*née* Davies); *m* 1955, Pamela Sawtell; one *s* two *d*. *Educ:* Southfield Grammar Sch., Oxford; University Coll., Cardiff (BSc, PhD; Fellow, 1981). CPhys, FInstP, CMath, FIMA, FRMS. Served Royal Corps of Signals, 1948–50. Fulbright Schol., Physics Dept, MIT, 1958–60; Royal Signals and Radar Estabt Physics Group, 1960: theoretical and experimental research condensed matter physics and optics; Individual Merit: SPSO 1967; DCSO 1973; CSO, 1984–90. Vis. Prof. of Maths, Imperial Coll., London, 1985–86.

Chairman: Adam Hilger Ltd, 1981–85; Oval (114) Ltd, 1984–85; non-executive Director: Richard Clay plc, 1985–86; Stilo Technology Ltd, 1995–2004 (Chm., 1995–2002); Stilo Internat. plc, 2000–04 (Chm., 2000–02); Phonologica Ltd, 2004–06. Govt assessor, SRC Physics Cttee, 1973–76. Mem. Council: Inst. of Physics, 1976–85 (Vice-Pres. for Publications, 1981–85); European Physical Soc., 1981–83; Director: NATO Advanced Study Insts, 1973, 1976; NATO Advanced Res. Workshops, 1987–88, 1991 and 1996. Hon. Editor: Journal of Physics A, 1973–78; Optica Acta, 1978–83; Quantum Optics, 1989–94. Nat. Science Foundn Vis. Lectr, USA, 1959; Lectures: Univ. of Rome, 1976; Univ. of Bordeaux, 1977; Simon Fraser Univ., 1978; Univ. of Genoa, 1980. FKC 1993. Charles Parsons medal and lecture, Royal Society, 1975; MacRobert award (jtly) and lecture, Council of Engrg Instns, 1977; Worshipful Co. of Scientific Instrument Makers Annual Achievement award (jtly), 1978; Committee on Awards to Inventors award, 1980; Guthrie Medal and Prize, Inst. of Physics, 1996. Confrérie St-Etienne, 1980–. *Publications:* (jtly) The Quantum Theory of Radiation, 1995; (ed) High Power Gas Lasers, 1975; edited jointly: Photon Correlation and Light Beating Spectroscopy, 1974; Photon Correlation Spectroscopy and Velocimetry, 1977; Frontiers in Quantum Optics, 1986; Fractals, Noise and Chaos, 1987; Quantum Measurement and Chaos, 1987; Squeezed and Non-classical Light, 1988; Photons and Quantum Fluctuations, 1988; Inverse Problems in Scattering and Imaging, 1991; Photon Correlation and Light Scattering Spectroscopy, 1997; Scattering, 2002; numerous papers in scientific jls. *Recreations:* music, languages, woodwork. *Address:* 22 Matthew Close, North Kensington, W10 5YJ; 8 Bredon Grove, Malvern, Worcs WR14 3JR.

PIKE, Rt Rev. Eric; Bishop of Port Elizabeth, 1993–2001; *b* 11 Nov. 1936; *s* of Eric and Elizabeth Pike; *m* 1st, 1963, Wendy Anne Walker; one *s* one *d*; 2nd, 1977, Joyce Davidson; two step *s* three step *d*. *Educ:* Graaff Reinet Teachers' Training Coll. (Primary Teachers Cert. 1957); St Paul's Theol Coll., Grahamstown (DipTh 1968). Worked in Govt Service, Transkei, SA, 1955; taught at Queen's Coll. Boys' High Sch., 1958–65; ordained deacon, 1968, priest, 1969; Asst Priest, St John's, E London, 1969–71; Rector: St Paul's, Komga, 1971–72; St Mark's, E London, 1972–77; Archdeacon of E London and Operation Outreach, 1978–87; Rector, St Alban's, E London, 1987–89; Suffragan Bishop of Grahamstown, 1989–93. *Recreations:* walking, gardening. *Address:* Farne, 11 Barling Crescent, Fish Hoek 7975, South Africa.

PIKE, Helen Laura; Headmistress, South Hampstead High School GDST, since 2013; *b* Birkenhead, 28 March 1973; *d* of Barry and Margaret Pike; partner, Prof. George Garnett; two step *s* one step *d*. *Educ:* All Hallows RC High Sch., Penwortham; Cardinal Newman Coll., Preston; Christ Church, Oxford (MA Modern Hist.); Univ. of Michigan, Ann Arbor (MA Modern Hist.); Birkbeck, Univ. of London (MA Creative Writing); Open Univ. (PGCE). Teacher of Hist., Westminster Sch., 1998; teacher of Hist. and Politics, 1998–2003, Dep. Hd of Sixth Form, 2000–03, City of London Sch. for Boys; Teacher of Hist., 2003–05, Hd of Politics, 2005–09, St Paul's Sch.; Dir of Studies, Royal GS, Guildford, 2009–13. Ed., acad. hist. textbooks for Anthem Press, 2009–14. *Publications:* The Harlot's Press, 2011. *Recreations:* long-distance running, YMCA qualified instructor in Exercise to Music, writing fiction. *Address:* South Hampstead High School, 3 Maresfield Gardens, NW3 5SS. *T:* (020) 7309 6218. *E:* h.pike@shhs.gdst.net. *Club:* Lansdowne.

PIKE, Lt-Gen. Sir Hew (William Royston), KCB 1997; DSO 1982; MBE 1977; General Officer Commanding and Director of Military Operations, Northern Ireland, 1998–2001; *b* 24 April 1943; *s* of Lt-Gen. Sir William Pike, KCB, CBE, DSO; *m* 1966, Jean, *d* of Col Donald Matheson, RAMC; one *s* two *d*. *Educ:* Winchester Coll.; RMA Sandhurst. Commissioned Parachute Regt, 1962; 3 Para, Middle East, British Guiana, UK, 1963–66; ADC, UK and Norway, 1966–67; 1 Para, Middle East, UK, 1967–70; Sch. of Infantry, 44 Para Bde (V), 1970–74; Staff College, 1975; Brigade Major, 16 Para Bde, 1976–77; Co. Comdr, 3 Para Germany and NI, 1978–79; CO, 3 Para, UK and Falkland Is Campaign, 1980–83 (despatches NI 1981); Comd 22 Armd Bde, Bergen-Hohne, 1987–90; RCDS 1990; GOC 3rd (UK) Div., 1992–94; Comdt, RMA, Sandhurst, 1994–95; Dep. C-in-C, and Inspector Gen. TA, HQ Land Comd, 1995–97; Dep. Comdr, SFOR, Bosnia, 1997–98. Lieut, HM Tower of London, 2004–07. Pres., Airborne Assault Normandy Trust, 2011–. Dir, GAP Activity Projects, 2001–06. Chm. Govs, Treloar Sch., 2001–08, Trustee, Treloar Trust, 2001–08. Pres., Army Ornithological Soc., 2012–. Freeman, City of London, 1982. *Publications:* From the Front Line—Family Letters and Diaries: 1900 to the Falklands and Afghanistan, 2008. *Recreation:* country pursuits. *Address:* c/o Lloyds Bank, Castle Street, Farnham, Surrey.

PIKE, Sir Michael (Edmund), KCVO 1989; CMG 1984; HM Diplomatic Service, retired; *b* 4 Oct. 1931; *s* of Henry Pike and Eleanor Pike; *m* 1962, Catherine (*née* Lim); one *s* two *d*. *Educ:* Wimbledon Coll.; London Sch. of Econs and Pol Science; Brasenose Coll., Oxford (MA 1956). Service in HM Armed Forces, 1950–52. Editor, Cherwell, Oxford Univ., 1954; part-time News Reporter, Sunday Express, 1954–55; Feature Writer and Film Critic, Surrey Comet, 1955–56; joined HM Foreign (now Diplomatic) Service, 1956; Third Secretary: FO, 1956–57; Seoul, 1957–59; Second Secretary: Office of Comr Gen. for Singapore and SE Asia, 1960–62; Seoul, 1962–64; FO, 1964–68; First Sec., Warsaw, 1968–70; FCO, 1970–73; First Sec., Washington, 1973–75; Counsellor: Washington, 1975–78; Tel Aviv, 1978–82; RCDS, 1982; Ambassador to Vietnam, 1982–85; Minister and Dep. UK Perm. Rep. to NATO, Brussels, 1985–87; High Comr, Singapore, 1987–90. Political Affairs Advr, Sun Internat. Exploration and Production Co., 1991–93; Dir, AIB Govett Asian Smaller Cos Investment Trust, 1993–2001. Member: Bid Cttee, British Olympic Bid: Manchester 2000, 1991–93; Bid Cttee, English Commonwealth Games Bid, Manchester 2002, 1994–95; Sensitivity Review Unit, FCO, 1992–2001. Special Rep. of Sec. of State for Foreign and Commonwealth Affairs, 1992–99; HM Govt Co-ordinator, Conf., Britain in the World, 1995. Dir, Greenwich Millennium Trust, 1995–2000; Co-Chm., Greenwich Town Centre Management Agency, 1993–2001; Vice-Chm., Greenwich Develt Agency, 1998–2003 (Mem., 1997–2003); Member: Greenwich Tourism Partnership, 1998–2001; Cutty Sark Wkg Gp, Maritime Greenwich - World Heritage Site Partnership, 2002–04; Standards Cttee (formerly Probity and Conduct Panel), Greenwich London Bor., subseq. Royal Bor. Council, 2002– (Chm., 2009–12). Pres., Union of Catholic Students of GB, 1955–56; Director: Housing Justice (formerly Catholic Housing Aid Soc.), 1995–2004; Catholic Housing Aid Soc. (Central London), 2003–10; Nat. New Infant and Parent Network, 1995–99. Chm., Editorial Bd, Asian Affairs, 2002–14. *Recreations:* reading, running, contemplating London. *Address:* 5 Crooms Hill, SE10 8ER.

PIKE, Peter Leslie; *b* 26 June 1937; *s* of Leslie Henry Pike and Gladys (*née* Cunliffe); *m* 1962, Sheila Lillian Bull; two *d*. *Educ:* Hinchley Wood County Secondary Sch. (Commercial Dept); Kingston Technical Coll. Pt 1 Exam., Inst. of Bankers. National Service, RM, 1956–58. Midland Bank, 1954–62; Twinings Tea, 1962–63; Organiser/Agent, Labour Party, 1963–73; Mullard (Simonstone) Ltd, 1973–83. Mem., GMBATU (Shop Steward, 1976–83). Member (Lab): Merton and Morden UDC, 1962–63; Burnley BC, 1976–84 (Leader, Labour Gp, 1980–83; Gp Sec., 1976–80). MP (Lab) Burnley, 1983–2005. Opposition front bench spokesperson: on Rural Affairs, 1990–92; on Housing, 1992–94. Member: Envmt Select Cttee, 1984–90; Procedural Select Cttee, 1995–97; Regulatory Reform Cttee (formerly Deregulation Select Cttee), 1995–2005 (Chm., 1997–2005); Modernisation Select Cttee, 1997–2005; Liaison Cttee, 1997–2005; Speakers Panel of Chairmen, 2001–05; Chm., Rights of Way Rev. Cttee, 1997–2005. All-Party Groups: Chairman: Romania Gp, 1994–2005; Southern Africa Gp; Mongolia Gp; Joint Chairman: Road Passenger Transport Gp, 1995–2005; Kidney Gp, 2001–05; Associate Parly Transport Forum, 1997–2001; Vice Chairman: Paper Industry Gp; Homelessness Gp; (Jt), Manufacturing Gp; Kashmir Gp, 2005; Secretary: Pakistan Gp, 1997–2005; Building Socs Gp, 1997–2005; Jt Sec., Overseas Develt Gp; Treas., Road Transport Study Gp, 1997–2000. Chm., PLP Envmt Cttee, 1987–90. Chairman: Clarets Trust, 2005–; E Lancs (formerly Burnley, Pendle and Rossendale) Learning Difficulties Partnership, 2005–12; Emmaus Burnley, 2005–; Burnley Area Community Credit Union, 2007–; Burnley Labour Party, 2008–; Member Board: Burnley Youth Th., until 2012; Burnley Area Self Help Agency, 2005–; Pendle CAB, 2005–11; SW Burnley Enterprise, 2005–12 (Chm., 2007–12); Burnley Homestart, 2006–08; Mem. Cttee, Burnley Civic Soc., 2005–; President: Burnley WEA, 2005–10; Friends of Freshfields, 2005–08; Hon. Pres., Burnley Municipal Choir and Orch., 2005–; Treas., Friends of St Peters, 2006–. Member: Nat. Trust, 1974–2011; CND; Anti-Apartheid. Hon. Fellow, Univ. of Central Lancs, 2011. *Recreation:* Burnley Football Club supporter. *Address:* 30 Deerpark Road, Burnley, Lancs BB10 4SD. *T:* (01282) 434719, 07976 891801. *E:* peterl.pike@btinternet.com. *Club:* Byerden House Socialist.

PIKE, Roy; *see* Pike, E. R.

PIKE, Roy Ernest; Chief Executive, Torquay Boys' Grammar School Multi Academy Trust, since 2014; Headmaster, Torquay Boys' Grammar School, 1987–2013; *b* Taunton, 1 May 1948; *s* of Ernest and Nora Pike; *m* 1971, Philippa Gordon; two *s* four *d*. *Educ:* Ilminster Grammar Sch.; St Luke's Coll., Exeter (BEd 1970); University Coll. London (BA Hons 1977 ext.). Torquay Boys' Grammar School: History Teacher, 1970; Hd of Dept, 1975–83; Pastoral Hd, 1977–83; Dep. Headmaster, 1983–87. Mem. Cttee, Freedom and Autonomy for Schs - Nat. Assoc. (formerly Grant Maintained Schs Adv. Cttee, later Foundn and Voluntary Aided Schs Assoc., then Foundn and Aided Schs Nat. Assoc., subseq. Foundn, Aided Schs and Academies Nat. Assoc.), 1993–; Chm., Nat. Grammar Schs' Assoc., 2011–13; Mem., Boys' Academic Selective Schs. Trustee, Torbay Coast and Countryside Trust, 2002– (Vice Chm.). FRSA. Hon. LLD Exeter, 2014. *Publications:* (contrib.) The Beacon School Experience: case studies in excellence, vol. 1, 2000, developing the curriculum, vol. 2, 2002. *Recreations:* family, tennis, country pursuits, conservation of natural and built environment.

PIKE, Air Vice-Marshal Warwick John; Director General, RAF Medical Services, 2002–04; *b* 31 Dec. 1944; *s* of late Captain Thomas Pike and Molly (*née* Buckley); *m* 1st, 1968, Susan Margaret Davies-Johns (*d* 2007); two *s* two *d*; 2nd, 2011, Shirley Jacqueline Cotterill. *Educ:* Sir John Port Sch.; Guy's Hosp., London (MB BS 1968); London Sch. of Hygiene and Tropical Medicine (MSc 1988). MRCS, LRCP 1968; DObstRCOG 1975; MRCGP 1975; DAvMed 1979; MFOM 1993. Joined RAF, 1970; served in UK, Singapore, Hong Kong and Germany; CO, Princess Mary's Hosp., Akrotiri, Cyprus, 1990–92; Dir, Med. Personnel, 1992–94; Asst Dir of Med. Co-ordination, Surgeon Gen.'s Dept, MoD, 1994–96; Dir, Primary Health Services, 1996–99; QHP 1997–2004; COS, later Chief Exec., Defence Secondary Care Agency, 1999–2002. *Recreations:* walking, theatre, history. *Address:* 7 Prebendal Green, Yarwell, Peterborough PE8 6PJ. *E:* wjpike@gmail.com. *Club:* Royal Air Force.

PILA, Dr Jonathan Solomon, FRS 2015; Reader in Mathematical Logic, University of Oxford, since 2010; Fellow, Wolfson College, Oxford, since 2010; *b* Melbourne, 28 July 1962; *s* of Joshua Pila and Mary Joan Pila (*née* Lloyd); *m* 1999, Justine FitzGerald; two *d*. *Educ:* Univ. of Melbourne (BSc Hons 1984); Stanford Univ. (PhD 1988). Asst Prof., Columbia Univ., 1989–92; Associate, 1993–94 and 1996–99, Sen. Fellow, 2000–04, Univ. of Melbourne; Asst Prof., McGill Univ., 2003–05; Lectr, 2005–07, Sen. Lectr, 2007–10, Univ. of Bristol. Mem., Inst. for Advanced Study, Princeton, 1988–89 and 2002–03. Dir and Manager, James Nelson Textile Gp, 1992–2002. Clay Res. Award, 2011; Sen. Whitehead Prize, LMS, 2011; (jtly) Karp Prize, Assoc. for Symbolic Logic, 2013. *Publications:* articles in learned jls. *Address:* Mathematical Institute, University of Oxford, Andrew Wiles Building, Radcliffe Observatory Quarter, Woodstock Road, Oxford OX2 6GG.

PILBROW, Richard Hugh; Founder and Chairman, Theatre Projects Consultants, 1957–2006; *b* 28 April 1933; *s* of Arthur Gordon Pilbrow and Marjorie Pilbrow; *m* 1st, 1958, Viki Brinton; one *s* one *d*; 2nd, 1974, Molly Friedel; one *d*. *Educ:* Cranbrook Sch.; Central Sch. of Speech and Drama. Stage Manager, Teahouse of the August Moon, 1954; Lighting Designer for over 200 prodns in London, New York, Paris and Moscow, incl.: Brand, 1959; Blitz, 1962; Zorba, 1968; Annie, 1978; The Little Foxes, Windy City, 1982; Singin' In the Rain, 1983; Heliotrope Bouquet, 1991; Four Baboons Adoring the Sun, 1992; The Magic Flute, LA, 1993; Showboat, 1993; The Life, 1997; Our Town, 2003; The Boy Friend, 2005; The Sleeping Beauty, Amer. Ballet Th., 2007; A Tale of Two Cities, 2008; Candida, 2010; Molly Sweeney, 2011; Dancing at Lughnasa, 2011; Transport, 2014; for Nat. Theatre Co., 1963–, incl. Hamlet, 1963, Love for Love, 1965, 1985, Rosencrantz and Guildenstern are Dead, 1966, Heartbreak House, 1975. Theatrical Producer in London of prodns incl.: A Funny Thing Happened on the Way to the Forum, 1963, 1986; Cabaret, 1968; Company, 1972; A Little Night Music, 1975; West Side Story, 1984; The Mysteries, Lyceum, 1985; I'm Not Rappaport, 1986. Film Prod., Swallows and Amazons, 1973; TV Productions: All You Need is Love—the story of popular music, 1975; Swallows and Amazons for Ever, 1984; Dir, Mister, 1971. Theatre Projects Consultants have been consultants on over 800 theatres and arts centres, incl. Disney Concert Hall, LA, Kimmel Performing Arts Centre, Philadelphia, New Amsterdam Theatre, NY, Nat. Theatre of GB, Barbican Theatre, and theatres and arts centres in Canada, Iran, Hong Kong, Saudi Arabia, Mexico, Iceland, Nigeria, Singapore, USA, etc. Co-founder, Soc. of British Theatre Designers, 1975; Fellow, Assoc. of British Theatre Technicians, 2003–; Pres., Assoc. of Lighting Designers, 2008– (Chm., 1982–85; Jt Pres., 2003–08); Member: Drama Panel, Arts Council of GB, 1968–70; Soc. of West End Theatre; Council, London Acad. of Music and Drama. Fellow, US Inst. of Theatre Tech., 2001. Hon. Fellow: Hong Kong Acad. for Performing Arts, 2010; Royal Central Sch. of Speech and Drama, 2012. FRSA. *Publications:* Stage Lighting, 1970, 3rd edn 1991; Stage Lighting Design, 1997; (with Patricia Mackay) The Walt Disney Concert Hall—The Backstage Story, 2003; A Theatre Project, 2011, 2nd edn 2015. *Recreations:* The Hebrides, cooking, dogs. *Address:* 78 Barrack Hill Road, Ridgefield, CT 06877, USA. *Club:* Garrick.

PILCHER, Rosamunde, OBE 2002; writing and publishing short stories and novels, since 1944; *b* 22 Sept. 1924; *d* of Charles Montagu Lawrence Scott and Helen Scott; *m* 1946, Graham Pilcher (*d* 2009); two *s* two *d*. *Educ:* St Clare's, Polwithen, Penzance; Howell's Sch., Llandaff, Cardiff. Hon. LLD Dundee, 2010. Author of Year, Bertelsmann Book Club, Germany, 1991; Berliner Zeitung Kulturpreis, 1993; Deutscher Videopreis, 1996; Bambi Award, Bunte magazine, 1997; Goldene Kamera Award, Hörzu, 1998. *Publications:* Sleeping Tiger; Another View; End of Summer; Snow in April; Empty House; Day of the Storm; Under Gemini; Wild Mountain Thyme; Carousel; Blue Bedroom; The Shell Seekers (Amer. Booksellers' Assoc. award, 1991; televised); September, 1990; Voices in Summer; Flowers in Rain; Coming Home, 1995 (Romantic Novelist of the Year, RNA, 1996; televised, 1998); The World of Rosamunde Pilcher; Winter Solstice, 2000. *Recreations:* walking, gardening, reading, travel. *Address:* Penrowan, Longforgan, Dundee DD2 5ET.

PILDITCH, Sir John (Richard), 5th Bt *cr* 1929, of Bartropps, Weybridge, Surrey; *b* London, 24 Sept. 1955; *o s* of Sir Richard Edward Pilditch, 4th Bt and of (Pauline) Elizabeth Pilditch (*née* Smith); *S* father, 2012. *Educ:* privately. *Recreation:* sailing.

PILE, Sir Anthony (John Devereux), 4th Bt *cr* 1900, of Kenilworth House, Rathgar, co. Dublin; Chairman, Blue Skies Holdings, since 1997; *b* Bristol, 7 June 1947; *s* of Sir John Devereux Pile (*d* 1982), *yr s* of 2nd Bt, and Katharine Mary (*d* 2010), *d* of late Austin George Shafe; *S* uncle, 2010; *m* 1977, Jenny Clare Youngman; two *s* one *d*. *Educ:* Durham Sch.

Durham LI, then LI; Major, 1980. JP Northants, 1994–96. Hon. DSc Cranfield, 2011. *Recreations:* entrepreneurial activity in Africa and S America, reading, walking. *Heir: s* Thomas Charles Devereux Pile, *b* 6 April 1978. *Address:* The Manor House, Pitsford, Northants NN6 9AZ. *E:* anthony.pile@blueskies.com.

PILGER, John Richard; journalist, author and film-maker; *s* of Claude Pilger and Elsie (*née* Marheine); one *s* one *d*. *Educ:* Sydney High Sch. Cadet journalist, Sydney Daily Telegraph, Australia, qualified, 1961; freelance journalist, Italy, 1962; Reuter, London, 1962; feature writer, chief foreign correspondent, Daily Mirror, London, 1962–86 (reporter, Vietnam War, 1966–75, Cambodia, 1979–91, etc); columnist, New Statesman, 1991–; contributor: The Guardian, The Independent, NY Times, Sydney Morning Herald, The Age, Melbourne, Aftonbladet, Sweden; Mail and Guardian, SA, Il Manifesto, Italy. Campaigns incl. Thalidomide 'X list' victims, and Australian Aboriginal land rights. Documentary film-maker, 1970–, films include: The Quiet Mutiny, 1970; A Faraway Country (Czechoslovakia), 1977; Year Zero: the silent death of Cambodia, 1979; Nicaragua, 1983; Japan Behind the Mask, 1986; The Last Dream, 1988; Death of a Nation: the Timor conspiracy, 1994; Vietnam: the last battle, 1995; Inside Burma: land of fear, 1996; Breaking the Mirror: the Murdoch Effect, 1997; Apartheid Did Not Die, 1998; Paying the Price: killing the children of Iraq, 2000; The New Rulers of the World, 2001; Palestine is Still the Issue, 2002; Breaking the Silence, 2003; Stealing a Nation, 2004; The War on Democracy, 2007; The War You Don't See, 2010; Utopia, 2013. Edward Wilson Fellow, Deakin Univ., Aust., 1995; Vis. Prof., Cornell Univ., USA, 2004–. Hon. DLitt: Staffordshire, 1994; Kingston, 1999; Rhodes Univ., SA, 2008; Lincoln, 2009; DPhil *hc* Dublin City, 1995; Hon. DArts Oxford Brookes, 1997; Hon. LLD St Andrews, 1999; DUniv Open, 2001. Awards include: Descriptive Writer of the Year, 1966; Reporter of the Year, 1967; Journalist of the Year, 1967, 1979; Internat. Reporter of the Year, 1970; News Reporter of the Year, 1974; Campaigning Journalist of the Year, 1977; UN Media Peace Prize and Gold Medal, 1979–80; George Foster Peabody Award, USA, 1990; Reporters Sans Frontiers Award, France, 1990; Richard Dimbleby Award, 1991; US TV Academy Award (Emmy), 1991; Premis Actual Award, Spain, 1996; Sophie Prize for Human Rights, 2003; RTS Award, 2005; Sydney Peace Prize, 2009; Grierson Trustees Award for Documentary Film-making, 2011. *Publications:* The Last Day, 1975; Aftermath: the struggle of Cambodia and Vietnam, 1981; The Outsiders, 1984; Heroes, 1986; A Secret Country, 1989; Distant Voices, 1992; Hidden Agendas, 1998; The New Rulers of the World, 2002; (ed) Tell Me No Lies: investigative journalism and its triumphs, 2004; Freedom Next Time, 2006. *Recreations:* swimming, sunning, mulling, reading. *Address:* 57 Hambalt Road, SW4 9EQ. *T:* (020) 8673 2848. *E:* jpilger2003@yahoo.co.uk. *W:* www.johnpilger.com.

PILGRIM, Martin George; non-executive director, since 2007; Chief Executive, Association of London Government, subseq. London Councils, 1997–2007; *b* 10 Feb. 1950; *s* of late George and Audrey Pilgrim; *m* 1974, Angela Muriel Staples; two *d*. *Educ:* Arden St Co. Primary Sch., Gillingham; Gillingham Grammar Sch.; Univ. of Kent at Canterbury (MA Mgt). CIPFA. Various posts, Kent CC, 1968–81; Association of Metropolitan Authorities: Under Sec. (Finance), 1981–96; Dep. Sec., 1996–97. Dir, Film London, 2005–11; Associate, Criticaleye, 2007–. Prince's Trust: Chm., London Regl Council, 2007–13; Chm., England Council, 2009–13; Trustee, 2009–10; Mem., Nat. Adv. Bd, 2010–13. Chair, London Sustainability Exchange, 2007–15. Trustee: Family and Childcare (formerly Daycare) Trust, 2007–; Family Rights Gp, 2011–; Young Women's Trust, 2013–; Swanswell, 2014–; Diana Award, 2014–. *Publications:* articles in acad. jls and local govt press. *Recreations:* keeping fit, hill-walking, moderate ski-ing, France and French. *Address:* Hoades Court, Hoath Road, Hoath, Canterbury, Kent CT3 4JL. *T:* (01227) 710625.

PILKINGTON, Muriel Norma, MA; Headteacher, Wycombe High School, 1986–98; *b* 1 Jan. 1941; *d* of Norman Herbert Fosbury and Lilian Alice Fosbury; *m* 1st, 1962, Anthony Leonard Andrews; one *s*; 2nd, 1983, Derek Brogden Pilkington; one step *s* one step *d*. *Educ:* Woking County Grammar Sch.; Helene Lange Hochschule, Hamburg; Lady Margaret Hall, Oxford (BA 1962; MA 1970). Asst Teacher, Shephalbury Sch., Stevenage, 1962–64; 2nd in Dept, Hatfield Girls' Grammar Sch., 1964–66; Head of Dept/Faculty, Sir James Altham Sch., Watford, 1970–81; Dep. Head, Francis Bacon Sch., St Albans, 1981–86. Chm., Area 6 SHA, 1993–95. Consultant, Centre for Educnl Mgt, 1999–. Trustee: Whitmore Vale Housing Assoc., 1970–; London Arts Schs, 1994– (Mem. Council, 2000–08). Governor: Bucks Chilterns UC (formerly Bucks Coll., Brunel Univ.), 1993–2006 (consultant/guest lectr, 1999; Vice Chm., Council, 2001–06); Dr Challoner's High Sch., 2003–13; Wimbledon High Sch., 2004–08. Contributor, Inf. for Sch. and Coll. Govs, 2003–07. Regular lectr, Oxfordshire Probus Clubs and U3As on local history. FRSA 1990. Hon. PhD Bucks Chilterns UC, 2006. *Publications:* A History of the Wycombe High School Guild 1910–2010, 2010; Past, Present and Future: a history of the Buckinghamshire New University, 2010; contribs to Educn Update pubns for Centre for Educn and Finance Mgt. *Recreations:* music, jogging, gastronomy, travel, theatre, ballet. *Address:* 1 Bishops Farm Mill, Witan Way, Witney, Oxon OX28 4DG; (summer) 304A Residence Tinssimo Parc, Boulevard Simon Batlle, 66400 Ceret, France.

PILKINGTON, Stephen Charles, CBE 2005; QPM 1998; DL; PhD; Chief Constable, Avon and Somerset Constabulary, 1998–2005; *b* 4 June 1948; *s* of Charles Leonard Pilkington and Joan Pilkington; *m* 1974, Anne Bernadette Brett; three *s*. *Educ:* Queen Elizabeth Coll., Univ. of London (BSc 1st cl. Hons Biology, 1969; PhD Plant Physiology, 1973). Joined Metropolitan Police, 1972; Constable, Battersea; seconded to American Police Force, 1984; Dep. Asst Comr, Central London, 1996–97. DL Somerset, 2005. *Recreations:* walking, ornithology, Rugby (spectator), cycling, conservation volunteer (holidays).

PILKINGTON, Sir Thomas Henry Milborne-Swinnerton-, 14th Bt *cr* 1635; *b* 10 March 1934; *s* of Sir Arthur W. Milborne-Swinnerton-Pilkington, 13th Bt and Elizabeth Mary (she *m* 1950, A. Burke), *d* of late Major J. F. Harrison, King's Walden Bury, Hitchin; *S* father, 1952; *m* 1961, Susan, *e d* of N. S. R. Adamson, Durban, South Africa; one *s* two *d*. *Educ:* Eton College. Sen. Steward, Jockey Club, 1994–98. *Recreations:* golf, racing. *Heir: s* Richard Arthur Milborne-Swinnerton-Pilkington [*b* 4 Sept. 1964; *m* 1994, Katya (marr. diss. 2000), *d* of T. J. Clemence; one *d*; *m* 2001, Henrietta Kirk; two *d*]. *Address:* Parsonage Farm, King's Walden, Hitchin, Herts SG4 8LF. *Clubs:* White's, City of London.

PILKINGTON, Victoria Lucy Annabel; *see* Stapleton, V. L. A.

PILL, Rt Hon. Sir Malcolm (Thomas), Kt 1988; PC 1995; a Lord Justice of Appeal, 1995–2013; *b* 11 March 1938; *s* of late Reginald Thomas Pill, MBE and Anne Pill (*née* Wright); *m* 1966, Roisin Pill (*née* Riordan), DL; two *s* one *d*. *Educ:* Whitchurch Grammar Sch.; Trinity Coll., Cambridge (MA, LLM); Dip. Hague Acad. of Internat. Law; Univ. of Buckingham (MA 2015). Served RA, 1956–58; Capt., Glamorgan Yeomanry (TA), 1958–67. Called to Bar, Gray's Inn, 1962, Bencher, 1987; Wales and Chester Circuit, 1963 (Treas., 1985–87; Presiding Judge, 1989–93); a Recorder, 1976–87; QC 1978; a Judge of the High Court, QBD, 1988–95; a Judge, Employment Appeal Tribunal, 1992–95. 3rd Sec., Foreign Office, 1963–64 (delegns to UN Gen. Assembly, ECOSOC, Human Rights Commn). Dep. Chm., Parly Boundary Commn for Wales, 1993–95. Chm., Assoc. of Judges of Wales, 2008–12. Chairman: UNA (Welsh Centre) Trust, 1969–77, 1980–87; Welsh Centre for Internat. Affairs, 1973–76; Eur. Parly Boundary Cttee for Wales, 1993. Chm., UK Cttee, Freedom from Hunger Campaign, 1978–87. Trustee, Dominic Barker Trust, 1997–2007. Hon. Fellow, Univ. of Wales Cardiff, subseq. Cardiff Univ., 1998; Fellow, Aberystwyth Univ., 2011. Hon. LLD Glamorgan, 1998. *Publications:* A Cardiff Family in the Forties, 1999. *Address:* 9 Westbourne Crescent, Whitchurch, Cardiff CF14 2BL. *Clubs:* Army and Navy; Cardiff and County.

PILLAY, Prof. Gerald John; DL; DTheol, PhD; Vice-Chancellor and Rector, Liverpool Hope University, since 2005 (Rector and Chief Executive, Liverpool Hope University College, 2003–05); *b* 21 Dec. 1953; *s* of Jimmy and Theena Pillay; *m* 1983, Nirmala Pillay; two *s*. *Educ:* Univ. of Durban-Westville (BA 1975; BD 1978; DTheol 1985); Rhodes Univ. (PhD 1984). Lectr, then Sen. Lectr in Church Hist., Univ. of Durban-Westville, 1979–87; Prof. of Church Hist., Univ. of SA, 1988–97; Foundn Prof. of Theology and Dean of Liberal Arts, Otago Univ., NZ, 1997–2003. DL Merseyside, 2009. *Publications:* Voices of Liberation, vol. 1, Albert Lutuli, 1993; Religion at the Limits?: Pentecostalism among Indian South Africans, 1994; (ed) A History of Christianity in South Africa, vol. 1, 1994; contribs to books and learned jls. *Recreations:* squash, gardening. *Address:* Liverpool Hope University, Hope Park, Liverpool L16 9JD. *T:* (0151) 291 3403, *Fax:* (0151) 291 3100. *E:* pillayg@hope.ac.uk.

PILLING, Benjamin; QC 2015; *b* Cambridge, Mass, 18 Dec. 1972; *s* of Sir Joseph (Grant) Pilling, *qv*; *m* 2000, Naomi Ruth Hillman; two *s* one *d*. *Educ:* Abingdon Sch.; Lincoln Coll., Oxford (BA Eng. Lit.); City Univ., London (DipLaw). Called to the Bar, Inner Temple, 1997; in practice as barrister in independent practice, 1998–. Trustee, Campden Charities, 2007–. *Publications:* (contrib.) Halsbury's Laws, 2003. *Recreations:* cooking, wine, music, friends. *Address:* 4 Pump Court, Temple, EC4Y 7AN. *T:* (020) 7842 5555. *E:* bpilling@4pumpcourt.com. *Club:* Athenæum.

PILLING, Sir Joseph (Grant), KCB 2001 (CB 1995); Permanent Under-Secretary of State, Northern Ireland Office, 1997–2005; *b* 8 July 1945; *s* of late Fred and Eva Pilling; *m* 1968, Ann Cheetham; two *s*. *Educ:* Rochdale Grammar Sch.; King's Coll., London; Harvard. Asst Principal, 1966, Pvte Sec. to Minister of State, 1970, Home Office; Asst Pvte Sec. to Home Sec., 1970–71; NI Office, 1972; Harkness Fellow, Harvard Univ. and Univ. of Calif at Berkeley, 1972–74; Home Office, 1974–78; Pvte Sec. to Sec. of State for NI, 1978–79; Home Office, 1979–84; Under Sec., DHSS, 1984–87; Dir of Personnel and Finance, HM Prison Service, Home Office, 1987–90; Dep. Under Sec. of State, NI Office, 1990–91; Dir-Gen., HM Prison Service, Home Office, 1991–92; Prin. Estabt and Finance Officer, DoH, 1993–97. Strategic Reviewer of CAA, 2007–08; Mem., Rev. of 30 Year Rule, 2007–09; Reviewer, Govt's Official History Prog. 2009; Identity Comr, 2009–10; Chairman: Rev. Gp on Sen. Appts in C of E, 2005–07; Koestler Trust, 2006–13; Adv. Bd, Relationships Foundn, 2006–10; House of Bishops Wkg Gp on Human Sexuality, 2012–14; Pres., New Bridge Foundn, 2006–; Member: Adv. Council, Mgt Sch., Imperial Coll., London, 1989–97; Bd of Trustees, Macmillan Cancer Support, 2005–15; Council, Univ. of London, 2006–08; Dio. Bd of Finance, Oxford, 2006–09. *Club:* Athenæum.

See also B. Pilling.

PILLING, Prof. Michael John, CBE 2008; PhD; CChem, FRSC; Research Professor, University of Leeds, 2008–10, now Emeritus Professor; *b* 25 Sept. 1942; *s* of John and Joan Pilling; *m* 1966, Gwenda Madeline Harrison; one *s* one *d*. *Educ:* Bacup and Rawtenstall Grammar Sch.; Churchill Coll., Cambridge (MA, PhD). CChem, FRSC 1991. Cambridge University: SRC Fellow, 1967–68; Jun. Res. Fellow, Churchill Coll., 1967–70; ICI Fellow, 1969–70; Vis. Scientist, Nat. Bureau of Standards, USA, 1968–69; Lectr in Physical Chemistry, and Fellow and Tutor of Jesus Coll., Oxford Univ., 1970–89; Leeds University: Prof. of Physical Chem., 1989–2007; Pro-Vice-Chancellor, 1992–94; Hd of Sch. of Chem., 1995–98; Dean for Res., Faculty of Maths and Phys. Scis, 2000–02; Dir, NERC Distributed Inst. for Atmospheric Composition, 2002–07. Visiting Professor: Univ. of Oregon, 1975; Univ. of Maryland, 1980; Univ. of Rome, 1984; Stanford Univ., 1987. Pres., Faraday Div., RSC, 2003–06 (Vice Pres., 1991–98; Sec., 1992–98); Mem. Council, NERC, 1995–2000 (Chm., Atmospheric Science and Tech. Bd, 1995–2000); Chm., Air Quality Expert Gp, DEFRA, 2001–09. Hon. Dr rer. nat. 2007 and Hon. Prof., 2007, Eötvös Loránd Univ., Budapest. Lectures: John Jeyes, RSC, 2001; Dist. Guest, Envmtl Chm. Gp, RSC, 2006. Award in Reaction Kinetics, 1991, Michael Polanyi Medal, Gas Kinetics Gp, 1994, Award for Combustion and Hydrocarbon Oxidation Chem., 2001, RSC; Sugden Award, Combustion Inst., 1993; Haagen-Smit Prize, Atmospheric Envmt, 2010. *Publications:* Reaction Kinetics, 1975; (ed jtly) Modern Gas Kinetics, 1985; (jtly) Reaction Kinetics, 1995; (jtly) Unimolecular Reactions, 1996; (ed) Low Temperature Combustion and Autoignition, 1997; (jtly) The Mechanisms of Atmospheric Oxidation of the Oxygenates, 2011; res. papers in learned jls. *Recreations:* hill-walking, running, music. *Address:* School of Chemistry, University of Leeds, Leeds LS2 9JT. *T:* (0113) 343 6451. *E:* m.j.pilling@leeds.ac.uk.

PILLING, Simon Richard, QFSM 2014; Chief Fire Officer and Chief Executive, West Yorkshire Fire and Rescue Service, since 2008; *b* Leeds, 1965; *s* of Ian Pilling and Yvonne Pilling; *m* 1997, Kathryn Scott; one *s*. *Educ:* Ossett Comp. Sch.; Univ. of Central Lancashire (MSc Fire Comd and Mgt 2002); Coventry Univ. (MA Mgt Studies 2003). West Yorkshire Fire and Rescue Service: Dir, Fire Safety and Tech. Services, 2004–06; Dir, Ops, 2006–08; Dep. Chief Fire Officer, 2006–08. Queen's Golden Jubilee Medal, 2002; Fire Service Long Service and Good Conduct Medal, 2005; Queen's Diamond Jubilee Medal, 2012. *Recreation:* sporting activities. *Address:* West Yorkshire Fire and Rescue Service, Oakroyd Hall, Birkenshaw, West Yorks BD11 2DY. *T:* (01274) 655701, *Fax:* (01274) 655766. *E:* simon.pilling@westyorksfire.gov.uk.

PILLMAN, (Annabel) Clare, OBE 2000; Director, Department for Culture, Media and Sport, since 2011; *b* Liverpool, 20 Feb. 1965; *d* of late Joseph Robert Pillman and Joan Meirion Pillman (*née* Evans). *Educ:* Wycombe Abbey Sch.; St Andrews Univ. (MA); Courtauld Inst. of Art (MA). Joined Department for National Heritage, 1992: Private Sec., 1994–96; Head: Millennium Celebrations Team, 1996–2000; Architecture and Historic Envmt, 2001–03; Hd of Strategy, DCA, 2003–04; Area Dir, N Wales, 2004–07, Dir, Wales, 2007–11, HM Courts Service. Trustee: Inst. of Cancer Res., 2003–; Nat. Th. of Wales, 2013–. *Recreations:* medieval history, opera, walking the dog. *Address:* Department for Culture, Media and Sport, 100 Parliament Street, SW1A 2BQ. *T:* (020) 7211 2368. *E:* clare.pillman@culture.gsi.gov.uk. *Club:* Oriental.

PILLOW, Nathan Charles; QC 2015; *b* Ilkeston, Derbyshire, 9 Aug. 1974; *s* of Christopher Pillow and Susan Pillow; *m* 2002, Aleksandra; two *d*. *Educ:* Nottingham High Sch.; Magdalen Coll., Oxford (BA Hons Law and French Law 1996); Univ. of Paris II, Panthéon-Assas (Dip. French Law 1995). Called to the Bar, Gray's Inn, 1997; in practice as a barrister, specialising in commercial litigation and civil fraud, Essex Court Chambers, 1998–. Bar Professional Trng Course Chief Examnr for Civil Litigation, Bar Standards Bd, 2011–14. *Address:* Essex Court Chambers, 24 Lincoln's Inn Fields, WC2A 3EG. *T:* (020) 7813 8000, *Fax:* (020) 7813 8080. *E:* npillow@essexcourt.com.

PINCHAM, Roger James, CBE 1982; Chairman, Venture Consultants Ltd, 1980–2014; Consultant: Gerrard, 2000–06; J. M. Finn & Co., 2006–10; *b* 19 Oct. 1935; *y s* of late Sam and Bessie Pincham; *m* 1965, Gisela von Ulardt (*d* 1974); one *s* two *d*. *Educ:* Wimbledon Park Primary Sch.; Kingston Grammar School. National Service, RAF, 1954–56. With Phillips & Drew, 1956–88, Partner, 1967–76, consultant, 1976–88. Mem., London Stock Exchange, 1963–91; MCSI (MSI 1992). Director: Market Access Internat., then Eur. Political Consultancy Gp, 1985–94; Gerrard Vivian Gray, subseq. Greig Middleton, 1988–2000; UKRD Ltd, 1991–2006; Cornwall Independent Radio Ltd, 1991–99; ICOR(LPG) Internat. Ltd, 1992–; County Sound Radio Network Ltd, 1998–2003. Contested (L) Leominster, 1970, Feb. and Oct. 1974, 1979, 1983. Liberal Party: Nat. Exec., 1974–75 and 1978–87; Assembly Cttee, 1974–87; Standing Cttee, 1975–83; Chm. of Liberal Party, 1979–82; Jt Negotiating Cttee with SDP, and signatory to A Fresh Start for Britain, 1981. Mem., Agenda Cttee, Congress for Democracy, 2001–. Pres., St John Ambulance, St Pancras Div.,

1996–2000. Founder Chm., Gladstone Club, 1973–; First Chairman: Ind. Educnl Assoc., 1974–2007; St James and St Vedast Schools, 1974–2007; Mem. Council, City Appeal for Eng. Coll. in Prague, 1991–; Gov., Sidney Perry Foundn, 1993–; Founder Trustee, John Stuart Mill Inst., 1992–. Trustee: Princess Margarita of Romania Trust, 1994–2004; Nat. Benevolent Fund for the Aged, 2001–12. Pres., Lloyd George Soc., 1996–2012. Pres., Kington Eisteddfod, 1978. FRSA 1994. Fellow, Churchill Meml, Fulton, Mo, 1997–. Freeman, City of London. Liveryman: Barbers' Co. (Master, 1993–94); Founders' Co.; Freeman, Co. of Watermen and Lightermen. *Publications:* (jtly) New Deal for Rural Britain, 1977; (ed) New Deal for British Farmers, 1978; (contrib.) Dictionary of Liberal Biography, 1998; (contrib.) Standing for Justice, 2001; (contrib.) Sheila Rosenberg: a Renaissance lady, 2004. *Recreations:* gardening, cricket, visiting Aldeburgh and Kullu. *Address:* Babbacombe, Snape Bridge, Saxmundham, Suffolk IP17 1ST. *T:* (01728) 688010. *Clubs:* Beefsteak, Reform, National Liberal, City of London, Royal Automobile; Woolhope Naturalists' Field.

PINCHER, Christopher John; MP (C) Tamworth, since 2010; *b* Walsall, 24 Sept. 1969; *s* of John and Sandra Pincher. *Educ:* Ounsdale Sch., Wombourne, Staffs; London Sch. of Econs and Pol Sci. (BSc (Econ) Govt and Hist. 1991). Exec., outsourcing practice, Accenture, 1993–2010. PPS to Foreign Sec., 2015–; Mem., Energy and Climate Change Select Cttee, 2010–15. *Recreations:* horse racing, motor sports, history. *Address:* House of Commons, SW1A 0AA. *T:* (020) 7219 7169. *E:* christopher.pincher.mp@parliament.uk. *Club:* Travellers.

PINCHERA, Albert Anthony; Principal, BP Con LLP, since 2009; *b* 2 Sept. 1947; *s* of Albert Storre Pinchera and Edith Pinchera (*née* DeLuca); *m* 1971, Linda Avril Garrad; one *d*. *Educ:* Upton House Sch.; University Coll. London (BSc Hons Geol.). Exploration Geologist, 1969–72; Boots Company plc: Buyer, 1972–74; Sen. Buyer, 1974–77; Asst Merchandise Controller, 1977–81; Mktg Controller, 1981–86; Business Gen. Manager, 1986–90; Man. Dir, Boots Opticians, 1990–95; Hd, Internat. Retail Develt, 1995–97; Chief Exec., Nat. Kidney Res. Fund, 1998–2003; Dir, Greater London Magistrates' Courts Authy, 2003–05; Dir, HM Courts Service, 2005–07; Chief Operating Officer, HMRC (Prosecutions), 2007–08. Non-exec. Dir, Queen's Univ. Hosp. Trust, 2001–06; Mem., NHS Postgrad. Medical Bd, 2007–11. Chair, League of Friends, Queen's Med. Centre, Nottingham, 2012–. *Recreations:* military history, art restoration. *Address:* The Old School House, Elston, Notts NG23 5NP.

PINCHING, Prof. Anthony John, DPhil; FRCP; Associate Dean for Cornwall, Peninsula Medical School, 2003–11; *b* 10 March 1947; *s* of John Pinching and Wilhelmina Hermina Pinching (*née* Jonkers); *m* 1971, Katherine Susan Sloper; two *s* two *d*. *Educ:* Sherborne Sch., Dorset; St John's Coll., Oxford (BA 1968); St Edmund Hall, Oxford; Oxford Univ. Med. Sch. (DPhil 1972; BM BCh, MA 1973). MRCP 1976; FRCP 1986. Royal Postgraduate Medical School, London: Registrar and Sen. Registrar, Medicine and Immunology, 1976–79; Res. Fellow (Immunology), 1979–82; St Mary's Hospital Medical School, London: Sen. Lectr in Clinical Immunology, 1982–89; Reader, 1989–92; Louis Freedman Prof. of Immunology, 1992–2003, and Hd, Div. of Molecular Pathology Infection and Immunity, 1998–2003, St Bartholomew's and the Royal London Sch. of Medicine and Dentistry, subseq. Bart's and The London Sch. of Medicine and Dentistry, QMW, London Univ.; Clinical Dir, Infection and Immunity, St Bartholomew's Hosp. and Royal Hosps NHS Trust, 1992–99. Vis. Prof., Univ. of Malta, 1986. Dep. Chm., CMO's Wkg Gp on CFS/ME, 2000–02; Principal Med. Advr, Action for ME, 2002–11; Chm., CFS/ME Service Investment Steering Gp, DoH, 2003–06. Terrence Higgins Trust Award, 1986; Evian Health Award, 1990. *Publications:* (ed) AIDS and HIV Infection, 1986; (ed jtly) AIDS and HIV Infection: the wider perspective, 1988; (ed jtly) New Dictionary of Medical Ethics, 1997; res. papers on neuroanatomy, autoimmune disease, HIV and AIDS and other immuno-deficiency. *Recreations:* music, especially opera, playing clarinet, literature, especially 20th Century, writing poetry, walking, librettist for composer, Russell Pascoe, in choral works and song.

PINDER, (John) Andrew, CBE 2004; Chairman: Finnergy Ltd, since 2010; PhonePay Plus Ltd, 2012–15; Digital Mobile Spectrum Ltd, since 2012; Managing Director, Andrew Pinder Consultancy Ltd, since 2004; *b* 5 May 1947; *s* of Norah Joan Pinder and William Gordon Pinder; *m* 1st, 1970, Patricia Munyard (marr. diss. 1980); one *d*; 2nd, 1981, Susan Ellen Tyrrell; one *d* and one step *s*. *Educ:* De La Salle Coll., Sheffield; Coleshill Grammar Sch., Warwicks; Univ. of Liverpool (BA Hons Social Studies). Inspector of Taxes, 1972–76; Board of Inland Revenue: Policy Div., 1976–79; Management Div., 1979–90, Under Sec., Dir of IT, 1989; Prudential Corporation: Dir of Systems, 1990–92; Dir, Gp Management Services, 1991–92; Dir, Systems and Business Ops, 1992–94; Citibank, 1995–99: Hd of Eur. Ops and Technol., 1995; Hd of Ops and Technol., Global Transaction Services, 1995–97; Hd of Eur. Br. Ops, Global Corp. Bank, 1998–99; ind. consultant on corporate and info. technol. strategy, 1999–2000; Prime Minister's e-envoy, Cabinet Office, 2000–04. Chm., BECTA (formerly British Educnl Communications and Technol. Agency), 2006–09. Chairman: Dovetail Sabrina Ltd, 1998–2002; Dovetail of Shrewsbury Ltd, 1999–2002; Will Network Ltd, 2000–05; Ind. Nat. Will Register, 2000–04; Elexon Ltd, 2010–13; non-executive Director: United Utilities plc, 2001–10; Entrust Inc., 2004–06; Vertex Data Sciences, 2004–06; Spring Gp plc, 2005–09; Nominet Ltd, 2015–. Mem., Intel Global Adv. Bd, 2005–; Critical Friend, UK Digital TV Switchover Prog., 2006–. Chm., Electricity Industry Balancing and Settlement Panel, 2010–13. Chm., Shropshire Learning & Skills Council, 2000–01. Trustee, Box of Tricks Th. Co., 2012–. FRSA 1995. Freeman, City of London, 1994; Liveryman, Co. of Information Technologists, 1995. *Recreations:* music, walking, gardening, reading, fly-fishing. *Address:* c/o Digital Mobile Spectrum Ltd, 83 Baker Street, W1U 6AG. *Clubs:* Institute of Directors, Century.

PINDLING, Dame Marguerite (Matilda), GCMG 2014 (DCMG 2007); Governor General of the Bahamas, since 2014 (Deputy to Governor General of the Bahamas, 2006–07 and 2012–14); *b* 26 June 1932; *d* of Ruebin and Viola McKenzie; *m* 1956, Rt Hon. Sir Lynden Oscar Pindling, KCMG, OM, PC (*d* 2000); two *s* two *d*. *Educ:* South Andros All Age Sch., Andros Is., Bahamas. Businesswoman. *Publications:* The Life and Times of Dame Marguerite Pindling, 2007. *Recreations:* charitable work, Bahamas Red Cross Society. *Address:* Lynmar, Skyline Drive, Nassau, NP, Bahamas.

PINE, Courtney, CBE 2009 (OBE 2000); jazz saxophonist; *b* 18 March 1964; *m* 1997, June Guishard; one *s* three *d*. Founder Mem., Jazz Warriors, 1985. *Albums* include: Journey to the Urge Within, 1987; Destiny's Song, 1988; The Vision's Tale, 1989; Closer to Home, 1990; Within the Realms of Our Dreams; To the Eyes of Creation; Modern Day Jazz Stories, 1995; Underground, 1997; Back in the Day, 2000; Devotion, 2003; Resistance, 2005; Transition in Tradition, 2009; Courtney Pine Band Live, 2010; Europa, 2011; House of Legends, 2012; has also produced and arranged albums; contrib. to albums by other artists, incl. Mick Jagger, and to Larry Adler tribute album; has toured internationally. Presenter, Jazz Crusade, Radio 2, 2001–08 (12 series). Jt producer, Jazzdaze (film), 2005. Hon. Prof., Thames Univ., 2005. Hon. DMus Westminster, 2005.

PINE, Prof. Cynthia Margaret, CBE 2006; PhD; Professor of Dental Public Health, Institute of Dentistry, Barts and The London, since 2013, and Academic Lead and Head, Unit of Dental Public Health, since 2014, Queen Mary University of London; Consultant in Dental Public Health, Salford Royal NHS Foundation Trust, since 2013; Managing Director, Kippax Design Ltd, since 2013; *b* 2 Oct. 1953; *d* of Frederick and Nora Freeman; *m* 1992, Geoffrey Pine; two *d*, and one step *s*. *Educ:* Swanshurst Grammar Sch., Birmingham; Univ. of Manchester (BDS 1976; PhD 1982); Univ. of Dundee (MBA Dist. 2001). FDSRCSE 1997; FDSRCS 2004. Lectr, in Child Dental Health, 1982–85, in Dental Public Health, 1985–92, Univ. of Manchester; Dental Epidemiologist, NW RHA, 1985–92; University of Dundee: Sen. Lectr, 1992–99, Reader, 1999–2001, in Dental Public Health; Prof. of Dental Public Health, 2001–02; Prof. of Dental Public Health and Primary Dental Care, 2002–08, Dean of Dental Studies, 2003–08, Univ. of Liverpool; Exec. Dean, Coll. (formerly Faculty) of Health and Social Care, 2008–12, Pro Vice-Chancellor Internat., 2010–12, Univ. of Salford. Hon. Consultant in Dental Public Health: Dundee Hosp., 1992–2001; Royal Liverpool Hosp., 2002–08; NHS Salford PCT, 2008–13. Dir, WHO Collaborating Centre in Res. in Oral Health of Deprived Communities, 2003–13. Non-exec. Dir, Aintree Univ. Hosp. NHS Foundn Trust, 2006–08; Mem., Health is Wealth Commn, 2007–08; Chm., NW Cttee of Res. for Patient Benefit, NIHR, 2011–. Chair, Fiveways Trust, 2007–09. Gov., Birkenhead Sixth Form Coll., 2005–08. FRSA 2007. Hon. FCGI 2014. *Publications:* Community Oral Health, 1997, 2nd edn 2007; over 100 articles in learned jls. *Recreations:* enjoying holidays with my family, reading, collecting porcelain, going to the Royal Ballet, being a grandmother. *Clubs:* Royal Society of Medicine, International Women's Forum.

PINI, John Peter Julian; QC 2006; **His Honour Judge Pini;** a Circuit Judge, since 2014; Resident Judge, Lincoln Crown Court, since 2014; *b* 27 Nov. 1954; *s* of Pierino and Roberta Pini; *m* 1991, Yvonne Anne Coen, *qv*; one *s* one *d*, and one *d* from a previous marriage. *Educ:* Queen's Univ., Belfast (BA 1st Cl. Hons Philos. 1977); City Univ. (Dip. Law 1979). Called to the Bar, Gray's Inn, 1981 (Lord Justice Holker Exhibnr); criminal practitioner, SE Circuit, 1981–91, Midland Circuit, 1991–2014; Asst Recorder, 1999–2000; Recorder, 2000–14. *Recreations:* jazz guitar, cookery, family. *Address:* Lincoln Crown Court, The Castle, Castle Hill, Lincoln LN1 3GA.

PINI, Yvonne Anne; *see* Coen, Y. A.

PINKER, Prof. Robert Arthur, CBE 2005; independent reviewer, Press Complaints Commission, 2012–14 (international consultant, 2004–12); Professor of Social Administration, London School of Economics and Political Science, 1993–96, now Emeritus; *b* 27 May 1931; *s* of Dora Elizabeth and Joseph Pinker; *m* 1955, Jennifer Farrington Boulton (*d* 1994); two *d*. *Educ:* Holloway County Sch.; LSE (Cert. in Social Sci. and Admin 1959; BSc Sociology 1962; MSc Econ 1965). University of London: Head of Sociology Dept, Goldsmiths' Coll., 1964–72; Lewisham Prof. of Social Admin, Goldsmiths' Coll. and Bedford Coll., 1972–74; Prof. of Social Studies, Chelsea Coll., 1974–78; Prof. of Social Work Studies, LSE, 1978–93; Pro-Director, LSE, 1985–88; Pro-Vice-Chancellor for Social Scis, London Univ., 1989–90. Vis. Prof., Univ. of Ulster, 2012–. Press Complaints Commission: Mem., 1991–2004; Privacy Comr, 1994–2004; Acting Chm., 2002–03; Chm., Bosnia-Hercegovina Press Council, 2003–05. Chm., British Library Project on Family and Social Research, 1983–86; Mem., Council, Advertising Standards Authority, 1988–95. Chm., Deptford Challenge Trust, 2005–14. Chm. Governors, Centre for Policy on Ageing, 1988–94; Gov., BPMF, 1990–94; Mem. Council, Goldsmiths Coll., Univ. of London, 2001–07 (Hon. Fellow, 1999). Fellow, Soc. of Editors, 2004–. Chm., Editl Bd, Jl of Social Policy, 1981–86. *Publications:* English Hospital Statistics 1861–1938, 1964; Social Theory and Social Policy, 1971; The Idea of Welfare, 1979; Social Work in an Enterprise Society, 1990; (with R. Deacon and N. Lipton) Privacy and Personality Rights, 2010. *Recreations:* reading, writing, travel, unskilled gardening. *Address:* 76 Coleraine Road, Blackheath, SE3 7PE.

PINKER, Prof. Steven (Arthur), PhD; Johnstone Family Professor, Department of Psychology, Harvard University, since 2003; *b* Montreal, 18 Sept. 1954; *s* of Harry and Roslyn Pinker; US citizen; *m* 1st, 1980, Nancy Etcoff (marr. diss. 1992); 2nd, 1995, Ilavenil Subbiah (marr. diss.); 3rd, 2007, Rebecca Goldstein. *Educ:* McGill Univ. (BA Psychol. 1976); Harvard Univ. (PhD Exptl Psychol. 1979). Postdoctoral Fellow, Center for Cognitive Sci., MIT, 1979–80; Assistant Professor, Department of Psychology: Harvard Univ., 1980–81; Stanford Univ., 1981–82; Massachusetts Institute of Technology: Asst Prof., Dept of Psychol., 1982–85; Associate Prof., 1985–89, Prof., 1989–2003, Dept of Brain and Cognitive Scis; Co-Dir, Center for Cognitive Scis, 1985–94; Dir, McDonnell-Pew Center for Cognitive Neurosci., 1994–99; Margaret MacVicar Faculty Fellow, 2000; Peter de Florez Prof., 2000–03. Hon. DSc: McGill, 1999; Newcastle, 2005; Hon. PhD: Tel Aviv, 2003; Surrey, 2003; Tromso, 2008; Hon. DHL Albion Coll., 2007. Dist. Scientific Award, 1984, Boyd R. McCandless Young Scientist Award, 1986, Amer. Psychol Assoc.; Troland Res. Award, NAS, 1993; Golden Plate Award, Amer. Acad. Achievement, 1999; Henry Dale Prize, Royal Instn of GB, 2004; George Miller Prize, Cognitive Neurosci. Soc., 2010. *Publications:* Language Learnability and Language Development, 1984; (ed) Visual Cognition, 1985; (ed with J. Mehler) Connections and Symbols, 1988; Learnability and Cognition: the acquisition of argument structure, 1989; (ed with B. Levin) Lexical and Conceptual Semantics, 1992; The Language Instinct, 1994 (Wm James Bk Prize, Amer. Psychol Assoc., 1995; Public Interest Award, Linguistics Soc., of America, 1997); How the Mind Works, 1997 (LA Times Bk Prize, 1998; Wm James Bk Prize, Amer. Psychol Assoc., 1999); Words and Rules: the ingredients of language, 1999; The Blank Slate: the modern denial of human nature, 2002 (Eleanor Maccoby Book Prize, 2003, William James Book Prize, Amer. Psychol Assoc., 2003; Kistler Book Prize, Foundn for the Future, 2005); The Stuff of Thought: language as a window into human nature, 2007; The Better Angels of our Nature: the decline of violence in history and its causes, 2011; The Sense of Style: the thinking person's guide to writing in the 21st Century, 2014; contrib. articles to Science, Cognition, Cognitive Sci., Proc. Nat. Acad. of Scis and other jls. *Recreations:* bicycling, photography. *Address:* Department of Psychology, Harvard University, William James Hall, 33 Kirkland Street, Cambridge, MA 02138, USA. *E:* pinker@wjh.harvard.edu.

PINKERTON, Anthony James Moxon L.; *see* Lowther-Pinkerton.

PINKERTON, Prof. (Charles) Ross, MD; Professor of Oncology, University of Queensland, since 2003; Director, Oncology Unit, Children's Health Queensland (formerly Director of Paediatric Oncology, Royal Children's Hospital and Mater Children's Hospital), since 2007; *b* 6 Oct. 1950; *s* of late Prof. John Henry McKnight Pinkerton, CBE; *m* 1989, Janet Hardy; three *d*. *Educ:* Campbell Coll.; Queen's Univ., Belfast (MD 1981). Postgrad. trng in paediatrics, Dublin and London, 1976–80; trng in children's cancer, London and France, 1980–86. Consultant Paediatric Oncologist and Hd, Children's Unit, Royal Marsden Hosp., 1989–2003 (Sen. Res. Fellow, 1986–89); Prof. of Paediatric Oncology, Inst. of Cancer Res., London, 1995–2003; Dir of Cancer Services, Mater Hosps, Brisbane, 2003–07. Chm., UK Children's Cancer Study Gp, 2000–02. *Publications:* editor: Paediatric Oncology: clinical practice and controversies, 1991, 2nd edn 1997; Childhood Cancer Management, 1995; Clinical Challenges in Paediatric Oncology, 1998; over 200 papers on children's cancer management. *Recreation:* tennis. *Address:* 107 Ironbark Road, Chapel Hill, Qld 4069, Australia.

PINKERTON, Francis Trevor Woodman; a Judge of the Upper Tribunal (Immigration and Asylum Chamber), since 2010; Resident Judge, Taylor House Hearing Centre, London, since 2011; *b* Hitchin, Herts, 5 March 1946; *s* of Dr George Eustace Pinkerton, MC and Doreen Patricia Pinkerton (*née* Tooley); *m* 1974, Hilary Claire Youldon (marr. diss. 1994; she *m* 2003, Sir (Frederick Douglas) David Thomson, *qv*); one *s* one *d* (and one *d* decd); *m* 2015, Jacqueline Margaret Martin (*née* Carter). *Educ:* Gadebridge Park Sch., Hemel Hempstead; Tonbridge Sch., Kent; Coll. of Law, Lancaster Gate; Coll. of Law, Guildford. Admitted as solicitor, 1970; Legal Asst, Anglo American Corp., Johannesburg, 1971–72; Solicitor: Needham & Grant, Clements Inn, 1973–74; John Duncombe & Co., Cheltenham, 1974–75; Partner, Pinkerton Leeke & Co., 1976–99; Immigration Adjudicator (pt-time), 1996–99, salaried, 1999–2002; on secondment to S African Refugee Appeal Bd, 2002; Dep. Dist Judge

(Civil), 2000–08; Resident Senior Immigration Judge: Central London, Asylum and Immigration Tribunal, 2002–10; First-tier Tribunal (Immigration and Asylum Chamber), Central London, 2010–. *Recreations:* rowing, opera, ballet, singing, motorcycling, classic cars, ski-ing. *Address:* Taylor House, 88 Rosebery Avenue, Islington, EC1R 4QU. *T:* (020) 7862 4322, *Fax:* (020) 7862 4323. *E:* francis.pinkerton@judiciary.gsi.gov.uk. *Clubs:* Remenham, London Rowing, Tideway Scullers School.

PINKERTON, Ross; *see* Pinkerton, C. R.

PINKERTON, William Ross, CBE 1977; JP; HM Nominee for Northern Ireland on General Medical Council, 1979–83, retired; a director of companies; *b* 10 April 1913; *s* of William Ross Pinkerton and Eva Pinkerton; *m* 1943, Anna Isobel Lyness; two *d.* Managing Director, H. Stevenson & Co. Ltd, Londonderry, 1941–76. Mem., Baking Wages Council (NI), 1957–74. Mem. later Chm., Londonderry/Gransha Psychiatric HMC, 1951–69; Vice-Chm., then Chm., North West HMC, 1969–72; Chm., Western Health and Social Services Board, 1972–79; Member: Central Services Agency (NI), 1972–79; NI Health and Social Services Council, 1975–79; Lay Mem., Health and Personal Social Services Tribunal, NI, 1978–. Member, New Ulster Univ. Court, 1973–85, Council, 1979–85. Hon. Life Governor: Altnagelvin, Gransha, Waterside, St Columb's, Roe Valley, Strabane, Foyle and Stradreagh Hosps. JP Co. Londonderry, 1965–84, Div. of Ards, 1984–91, Div. of Craigavon, 1991. *Recreations:* yachting, fishing. *Address:* 9 Harwich Mews, Culcavey Road, Hillsborough, Co. Down, Northern Ireland BT26 6RH. *T:* (028) 9268 2421. *Club:* Royal Highland Yacht (Oban).

PINNER, Ruth Margaret, (Mrs M. J. Pinner); *see* Kempson, R. M.

PINNINGTON, Roger Adrian, TD 1967; consultant; *b* 27 Aug. 1932; *s* of William Austin Pinnington and Elsie Amy Pinnington; *m* 1st, 1961, Jean Heather Goodall (marr. diss. 1977); 2nd, 1978, Marjorie Ann Pearson; one *s* three *d.* *Educ:* Rydal Sch., Colwyn Bay; Lincoln Coll., Oxford (MA Law). Nat. Service, 1951–53. Marketing Dir, Jonas Woodhead & Sons, 1963–74; 1975–82: Vice Pres., TRW Europe Inc.; Man. Dir, CAM Gears Ltd; Pres., TRW Italia SpA; Dir Gen., Gemmer France; Pres., Torfinasa; Dep. Chm. and Chief Exec., UBM Gp, 1982–85; Dir, Norcros, 1985–86; Dir and Chief Exec., Royal Ordnance PLC, 1986–87; Dir and Gp Chief Exec., RHP, subseq. Pilgrim House Gp, 1987–89. Chairman: Telfos Hldgs, subseq. Jenbacher Hldgs (UK), 1991–95; Lynx Holdings PLC, 1992–98; Cortworth PLC, 1994–97; British World Aviation Ltd, later BWA Gp plc, 1994–2000; Huntingdon Internat. Hldgs plc, 1994–98 (Dep. Chm., 1998–99); Montanaro Hldgs Ltd, 1995–2001; Armour Gp plc, 1996–2001; SEA Gp, 2001–07. *Recreations:* gardening, arguing with Sally, collecting silver and porcelain sauce bottle labels, staying alive! *Address:* Whitelands Cottage, Pickhurst Road, Chiddingfold, Surrey GU8 4TS. *E:* pinnington@hotmail.com. *Clubs:* Royal Automobile; Vincent's (Oxford).

PINNOCK, family name of **Baroness Pinnock**.

PINNOCK, Baroness *cr* 2014 (Life Peer), of Cleckheaton in the County of West Yorkshire; **Kathryn Mary Pinnock;** *m* Andrew Pinnock, MA; three *c.* *Educ:* Univ. of Keele. History teacher. Mem. (Lib Dem) Kirklees Council, 1987– (Leader, 2000–06). Mem. Bd, Yorkshire Forward RDA, 2001–11. Non-exec. Dir, Yorkshire Water, 2008–. Chm., Assoc. of Lib Dem Cllrs, 2008–12. Chm. Govs, Whitcliffe Mount Sch., 1998–2014. Contested (Lib Dem) Batley and Spen, 1997, 2001.

PINNOCK, Comdr Harry James, RN retd; Director, Cement Makers' Federation, 1979–87; *b* 6 April 1927; *s* of Frederick Walter Pinnock and Kate Ada (*née* Shepherd); *m* 1st, 1962, Fru Inger Connie Åhgren (*d* 1978); one *d*; 2nd, 2002, Deborah Olivares, USA. *Educ:* Sutton Valence Sch. Joined RN, 1945; Midshipman, HMS Nelson, 1945–47; Sub-Lieut/ Lieut, HMS Belfast, Far East, 1948–50; RN Rhine Flotilla, 1951–52; Staff of First Sea Lord, 1952–55; Lt-Comdr, Mediterranean Minesweepers, 1955–57; HMS Ceylon, E of Suez, 1957–59; Staff of C-in-C Plymouth, 1960–61; HQ Allied Naval Forces, Northern Europe, Oslo, 1961–63; Comdr, MoD, 1964–67, retd. Cement Makers' Fedn, 1970–87. Chm., Gala Day Services, 2007–09. *Recreations:* walking, travel. *Address:* Flat 7, Halyard Place, Trinity Way, Minehead TA24 6GL.

PINNOCK, Trevor, CBE 1992; ARCM; harpsichordist; conductor; Director, The English Concert, 1973–2003; *b* Canterbury, 16 Dec. 1946. *Educ:* Canterbury Cathedral Choir Sch.; Simon Langton Grammar Sch., Canterbury; Royal Coll. of Music, London (Foundn Scholar; Harpsichord and Organ Prizes). ARCM Hons (organ) 1965, FRCM 1996. London début with Galliard Harpsichord Trio (Jt Founder with Stephen Preston, flute and Anthony Pleeth, 'cello), 1966; solo début, Purcell Room, London, 1968. Formed The English Concert for purpose of performing music of baroque period on instruments in original condition or good modern copies, 1972, making its London début in English Bach Festival, Purcell Room, 1973. NY début at Metropolitan Opera, conducting Handel Giulio Cesare, 1988. Artistic Dir and Principal Conductor, 1991–96, Artistic Advr, 1996–98, Nat. Arts Centre Orch., Ottawa. Recordings of complete keyboard works of Rameau; Bach Toccatas, Partitas, Goldberg Variations, Concerti, Handel Messiah and Suites, Purcell Dido and Aeneas, orchestral and choral works of Bach, Handel, Vivaldi, complete symphonies of Mozart, etc. Hon. RAM 1988. Hon. DMus: Ottawa, 1993; Kent, 1995; Sheffield, 2005. Officier, Ordre des Arts et des Lettres (France), 1998. *Address:* c/o Ms Melanie Moult, Askonas Holt, Lincoln House, 300 High Holborn, WC1V 7JH. *T:* (020) 7400 1700.

PINSENT, Sir Matthew (Clive), Kt 2005; CBE 2001 (MBE 1992); oarsman; International Rowing Umpire, since 2012; *b* 10 Oct. 1970; *s* of Rev. Ewen and Jean Pinsent; *m* 2002, Demetra Ekaterina Koutsoukos; twin *s* one *d.* *Educ:* Eton College; St Catherine's College, Oxford (BA Hons Geography 1993). Winner: coxless pairs: (with Tim Foster) Junior World Championship, 1988; (with Steven Redgrave): World Championship, 1991, 1993, 1994 and 1995; Olympic Gold Medal, 1992 and 1996; (with James Cracknell) coxed and coxless pairs, 2001, coxless pairs, 2002, World Championship; coxless fours: World Championship, 1997, 1998, 1999; Olympic Gold Medal, 2000 and 2004; Mem., Oxford Boat Race winning crew, 1990, 1991. Sports presenter, BBC, 2006–. Dir, JJB Sports plc, 2010–12. Mem., IOC, 2002–04. *Publications:* A Lifetime in a Race, 2004. *Recreations:* golf, flying. *Club:* Leander (Henley-on-Thames).

PINSENT, Sir Thomas Benjamin Roy, 4th Bt *cr* 1938, of Selly Hill, City of Birmingham; *b* 21 July 1967; *s* of Sir Christopher Roy Pinsent, 3rd Bt and of Susan Mary Pinsent (*née* Scorer); *S* father, 2015, but his name does not appear on the Official Roll of the Baronetage; *m* 2007, Angelika Waltraud Heinkel. *Heir: uncle* Michael Roy Pinsent [*b* 4 Feb. 1927; *m* 1952, Stella Marie Priestman (marr. diss.); one *s* two *d*].

PINSON, Barry; QC 1973; *b* 18 Dec. 1925; *s* of Thomas Alfred Pinson and Alice Cicily Pinson; *m* 1950, Miriam Mary; one *s* one *d*; *m* 1977, Anne Kathleen Golby. *Educ:* King Edward's Sch., Birmingham; Univ. of Birmingham. LLB Hons 1945. Fellow Inst. Taxation. Mil. Service, 1944–47. Called to Bar, Gray's Inn, 1949, Bencher 1981. Trustee, RAF Museum, 1980–98; Chm., Addington Soc., 1987–90. *Publications:* Revenue Law, 17 edns. *Recreations:* music, theatre, photography. *T:* (020) 7798 8450.

PINTER, Rabbi Abraham, (Avraham); Principal, Yesodey Hatorah Schools, since 1994; Dean, Beer Miriam Seminary, since 2008; *b* London, 21 Jan. 1949; *s* of Rabbi Samuel Pinter and Gertrude Pinter; *m* 1971, Rachel, OBE (*d* 2014); two *s* five *d.* Mem. (Lab) Hackney BC, 1982–90. Chm., Chizuk, 1996–; Trustee, Union of Orthodox Hebrew Congregations, 1990– (Chm., Social Services, 1990–); Vice Chm., Ezer Lyoldos (Children and Families). Founder Member: Jewish-Christian Forum of Stamford Hill; Muslim Jewish Forum. *Address:* 6 Northdene Gardens, N15 6LX. *T:* (020) 8826 5500, *Fax:* (020) 8826 5505. *E:* yeshatorah@ aol.com.

PINTER, Lady Antonia; *see* Fraser, Antonia.

PINTER, Rabbi Avraham; *see* Pinter, Rabbi Abraham.

PINTO, Amanda Eve; QC 2006; a Recorder, since 2003; *b* 28 July 1960; *d* of John and Marigold Pinto; *m* 1987, Charles Spencer Porter; one *s* two *d.* *Educ:* St Paul's Girls' Sch., London; Gonville and Caius Coll., Cambridge (exhibnr; BA Law 1982; MA); Birkbeck Coll., London (Dip. Hist. of Art 1991). Called to the Bar, Middle Temple, 1983, Bencher, 2012; in practice as barrister, specialising in internat. corruption, fraud, corporate and art crime. Dir, Internat. Affairs, Criminal Bar Assoc., 2007–13; Mem., Bar Council (Co-Chm., Internat. Rule of Law Panel, 2013–14; Chair, Internat. Cttee); UK Rep., Internat. Criminal Bar Council, 2008–. Trustee: Tate Members Council, 2013–; Slynn Foundn, 2014–. *Publications:* (with M. Evans) Corporate Criminal Liability, 2003, 3rd edn 2013; (contrib. on corporate crime) Blackstone's Criminal Practice, 2011–; contribs to The Times, FT. *Recreations:* art, theatre and music, baking cakes, ski-ing, travelling, walking my dog. *Address:* 33 Chancery Lane, WC2A 1EN. *T:* (020) 74409950. *E:* ap@33cllaw.com. *Club:* Hurlingham.

PIOT, Baron Prof. Peter, Hon. CMG 2010; MD, PhD; FRCP, FMedSci; Professor of Global Health, and Director, London School of Hygiene and Tropical Medicine, since 2010; *b* Leuven, 17 Feb. 1949; *s* of René Piot and Joanna Pardon; *cr* Baron (Belgium) 1995; *m* 2012, Heidi Larson; two *s* one *d.* *Educ:* Koninklijk Atheneum Keerbergen; Univ. of Ghent (MD 1974); Univ. of Antwerp (PhD Microbiol. 1980). FRCP 2001. Asst Prof., Inst. of Tropical Medicine, Antwerp, 1974–92; Associate Prof., Univ. of Nairobi, 1986–87; Asst Dir, Global Prog. on AIDS, WHO, Geneva, 1992–94; Exec. Dir, UNAIDS and Under Sec. Gen., UN, Geneva, 1995–2008; Prof. of Global Health, Imperial Coll. London, 2009–10. Senior Fellow: Univ. of Washington, 1978–79; Gates Foundn, 2009. FMedSci 2011. Mem., Royal Acad. of Medicine, Belgium, 1989; For. Mem., Inst. of Medicine, NAS, 2000. Pres., King Baudouin Foundn, Brussels, 2007–11. Hideyo Noguchi Africa Prize for Med. Res., Japan, 2013; Prince Mahidol Award, 2014; Canada Gairdner Global Health Award, 2015. Commandeur: Ordre du Lion (Senegal), 2005; Nat. Order (Mali), 2008; Grand Official, Order of Henrique the Navigator (Portugal), 2007. *Publications:* Basic Laboratory Procedures in Clinical Bacteriology, 1991; Reproductive Tract Infections in Women, 1992; Aids in Africa: a handbook for physicians, 1992; L'Épidémie du Sida et la Mondialisation des Risques, 2005; Sexually Transmitted Diseases, 2008; Over AIDS, 2009; Le Sida dans le Monde, 2011; No Time to Lose, 2012 (trans. Dutch, French, Japanese); AIDS: between science and politics, 2015; over 500 scientific papers. *Address:* London School of Hygiene and Tropical Medicine, Keppel Street, WC1E 7HT. *E:* director@lshtm.ac.uk. *Club:* Athenæum.

PIPE, Martin Charles, CBE 2000; racehorse trainer, National Hunt and flat racing, 1977–2006; *b* 29 May 1945; *m* 1971, Mary Caroline; one *s.* First trainer's licence, 1977; first British trainer to saddle 200 winners in a season, 1989; trained more than 200 winners in a season 8 times, 1989–2006; fifteen times champion trainer, National Hunt, to 2005; holder of British record for jump winners trained with 3929 winners, 2014; trained 6 winners, Royal Ascot, 34 winners, Cheltenham Fest.; major wins include: Champion Hurdles, Granville Again, 1993, Make a Stand, 1997; Grand National, Miinnehoma, 1994; Welsh Grand National, five times; Hennessy Gold Cup, twice; Irish Hennessy Gold Cup; Mackeson Gold Cup, eight times. Hon. DSc Liverpool, 2007. *Publications:* (with Richard Pitman) Martin Pipe: the champion trainer's story, 1992. *Address:* Pond House, Nicholashayne, near Wellington, Somerset TA21 9QY.

PIPER, Rev. Canon Clifford John; Rector, St John the Evangelist, Forres, since 2009 (Priest-in-charge, 2003–09); Dean of Moray, Ross and Caithness, 2009–14; *b* Tintagel, Cornwall, 8 April 1953; *s* of John Henry Piper and Lilian Mary Piper (*née* Knight); *m* 1974, Susan Ruth Greaves; one *s* one *d.* *Educ:* Aberdeen Univ. (Cert. Social Services); Theol Inst. of the Scottish Episcopal Church; Robert Gordon Univ. (Postgrad. Dip. Community Care). Principal Officer Social Work, then Area Social Work Manager Sutherland, Highland Council, 1983–98; ordained deacon, 1993, priest, 1994; Asst Curate, St Ninians, Invergordon, 1993–96; NSM, 1996–98, Priest-in-charge, 1998–2003, St Andrew's, Tain; Priest-in-charge, St Ninians, Invergordon, 2000–03; Canon, 2000–09, Hon. Canon, 2014–, St Andrew's Cathedral, Inverness. Provincial Child Protection Officer, Scottish Episcopal Church, 1998–2000. *Recreations:* golf, walking, reading, information technology, horology, cooking, motorcycling. *Address:* The Rectory, Victoria Road, Forres, Moray IV36 3BN. *T:* (01309) 672856. *E:* stjohnsforres@btinternet.com.

PIPER, Rt Rev. Dr Reginald John; Assistant Minister, St Michael's Anglican Cathedral, Wollongong, since 2010; Bishop of Wollongong, and an Assistant Bishop, Diocese of Sydney, 1993–2007; *b* 25 Feb. 1942; *s* of Leslie and Myra Elaine Piper; *m* 1967, Dorothy Patricia Lock; one *s* two *d* (and one *s* decd). *Educ:* Australian Nat. Univ. (BSc 1963); Moore Coll., Sydney (Theol. Schol. 1970); Melbourne Coll. of Divinity (BD 1975); Fuller Theol Seminary, LA (DMin 1992). Ordained deacon, 1966, priest, 1967; Curate: St Stephen's, Willoughby, 1966–69; St Clement's, Lalor Park, 1970–71; Rector: St Aidan's, Hurstville Grove, 1972–75; Christ Church, Kiama, 1975–79; Holy Trinity, Adelaide, 1980–93; St Paul's Anglican Ch, Gymea, 2007–10. *Publications:* The Ephesus Plan, 1998; Forty Days with the Risen Lord, 2005; The Ephesus Code, 2006; Ephesus and the New Humanity, 2010; From Rome with Love, 2013. *Address:* 111/201 Pioneer Road, Fairy Meadow, NSW 2519, Australia.

PIPER, Thomas Stephen Towry, MBE 2015; freelance theatre designer, since 1990; *b* London, 24 Nov. 1964; *s* of Sir David Towry Piper, CBE and Anne Horatia Piper (*née* Richmond); *m* 1992, Caroline Rohais Millar; five *d.* *Educ:* Magdalen Coll. Sch., Oxford; Trinity Coll., Cambridge (Schol.; BA Art Hist.); Slade Sch. of Art (MA Th. Design). Associate Designer, RSC, 2004–14; designer, Histories Cycle, RSC, 2008 ((jtly) Olivier Award for Best Costume Design). Designer: (with A. Farlie) BM exhibn, Shakespeare, staging the world, 2012; (with P. Cummins) Blood Swept Lands and Seas of Red installation, Tower of London, 2014. Hon. Fellow, RWCMD. *Recreations:* cycling, theatre, photography, exhibitions, family. *Address:* 17 Lordship Park, N16 5UN. *T:* (020) 8802 2833. *E:* tom@tompiperdesign.co.uk.

PIRIE, Madsen (Duncan), PhD; President, Adam Smith Institute, since 1978; *b* 24 Aug. 1940; *s* of Douglas Gordon Pirie and Eva (*née* Madsen). *Educ:* Univ. of Edinburgh (MA Hons 1970); Univ. of St Andrews (PhD 1974); MPhil Cantab 1997. Distinguished Vis. Prof. of Philosophy, Hillsdale Coll., Michigan, 1975–78; Sen. Vis. Fellow in Land Economy, Univ. of Cambridge, 2010–. Mem., Adv. Panel on Citizen's Charter, 1991–95. (Jtly) Nat. Free Enterprise Award, 2010. *Publications:* Trial and Error and the Idea of Progress, 1978; The Book of the Fallacy, 1985; Privatization, 1988; Micropolitics, 1988; (with Eamonn Butler) The Sherlock Holmes IQ Book, 1995; How to Win Every Argument, 2006; Children of the Night, 2007; Dark Visitor, 2007; The Waters of Andros, 2007; Freedom 101, 2008; Zero Base Policy, 2009; 101 Great Philosophers, 2009; The Emerald Warriors, 2011; Economics Made Simple, 2012; Think Tank: the story of the Adam Smith Institute, 2012; Tree Boy, 2012; Team Games, 2013; Why Liberty Works, 2014; Silver Dawn, 2014. *Recreations:* calligraphy, cooking, motion pictures, science fiction. *Address:* Adam Smith Institute, 23 Great Smith Street, SW1P 3BL. *W:* www.madsen-pirie.com.

PIRMOHAMED, Sir Munir, Kt 2015; PhD; FRCP, FRCPE; FBPhS; FMedSci; NHS Chair of Pharmacogenetics, since 2007, Director, Wolfson Centre for Personalised Medicine, since 2009, David Weatherall Professor of Medicine, since 2013, and Director, MRC Centre for Drug Safety Science, since 2014, University of Liverpool; Hon. Consultant Physician, Royal Liverpool University Hospital, since 1996; *b* Ngora, Uganda, 29 Aug. 1962; *s* of Mohamedali and Malek Pirmohamed; *m* 1989, Jacqueline Anne Clark; two *s*. *Educ:* Univ. of Liverpool (MB ChB Hons 1985; PhD 1993). MRCP 1988, FRCP 2000; FRCPE 1999; FBPhS (FBPharmacolS 2004). University of Liverpool: MRC Trng Fellow, 1989–92; Sen. Clin. Res. Fellow, 1992–94; Lectr, 1994–95, Sen. Lectr, 1996–2000, Reader, 2000–01, Dept of Pharmacol.; Prof. of Clin. Pharmacol., 2001–13; Associate Exec. Pro Vice Chancellor (Clin. Res.), 2013–. Sir Desmond Pond Fellow, Epilepsy Res. Foundn, 1992–95. Rand Lectr, British Pharmacol Soc., 2007. Dir, Mersey Yellow Card Centre for Adverse Drug Reaction Monitoring, 1995–. Mem., Commn on Human Medicines, 2005–. Chair, Pharmacovigilance Expert Adv. Gp, 2006–. Mem., Cttee on Safety of Medicines, 2002–05 (Mem., Sub-cttee on Pharmacovigilance, 1996–2005). Chair, Clin. Section Cttee, British Pharmacol Soc., 2012–. FMedSci 2013. British Assoc. of Pharmaceutical Physicians Prize, 1994, GSK Clin. Travelling Prize, 2002, British Pharmacol Soc.; Inaugural NIHR Sen. Investigator Award, 2008; William Withering Medal, RCP, 2010; IPIT Award for Public Service, Univ. of N Carolina, 2011. *Publications:* (ed) Textbook of Pharmacogenetics, 2006; contrib. articles on clin. pharmacol., drug safety and genetics to med. and scientific jls. *Recreations:* fast cars, Arsenal Football Club, movies. *Address:* Department of Molecular and Clinical Pharmacology, University of Liverpool, Liverpool L69 3GL. *T:* (0151) 794 5549. *E:* munirp@liverpool.ac.uk.

PIRNIE, Graham John Campbell; HM Diplomatic Service, retired; Counsellor and Deputy Head of Mission, Abu Dhabi, 1998–2001; *b* 9 Aug. 1941; *s* of late Ian Campbell Pirnie and of Emily Elizabeth Pirnie; *m* 1st, 1967, Kathleen Gunstone (marr. diss. 2001); two *s* one *d*; 2nd, 2001, Dora Ines Guerrero Velez. *Educ:* Surbiton Grammar Sch.; Birmingham Univ. (BSocSc). Graduate VSO, 1963–64; joined Foreign and Commonwealth Office, 1965: Information Res. Dept, 1965; FCO, 1966–68; Third Sec. and Vice Consul, Phnom Penh, 1968–70; Commercial Officer, Paris, 1970–74; Second Sec. (Commercial), The Hague, 1974–77; FCO, 1977–82; First Sec. and Consul, Geneva, 1982–86; JSDC 1986; FCO, 1986–89; Dep. Head of Mission and Consul, Quito, 1989–93; FCO, 1993–95; Ambassador to Paraguay, 1995–98. *Recreations:* town and country walking, natural history, antique/vintage clock restoration, reading, current affairs, ski-ing. *E:* graham.pirnie@btinternet.com.

PIRNIE, Rear Adm. Ian Hugh, CB 1992; DL; Chairman, Morecambe Bay Health Authority, 1994–2002; *b* 17 June 1935; *s* of late Hugh Pirnie, KPM and Linda Pirnie; *m* 1958, Sally Patricia (*née* Duckworth); three *d*. *Educ:* Christ's Hosp., Horsham; Pembroke Coll., Cambridge (MA). CEng 1986; FIEE 1986. Qualified in submarines, 1964; post-graduate educn, RMCS, Shrivenham, 1964–65, US Guided Missile Sch., Dam Neck, VA, 1966; sea service in aircraft carrier HMS Bulwark, destroyers HMS Finistere and HMS Antrim, and submarines HMS Resolution and HMS Repulse; Dir, Naval Officer Appts (Engrs), 1984–86; commanded RNEC, Manadon, Plymouth as ADC, 1986–88; Chief, Strategic Systems Exec., MoD (in overall charge of Trident procurement prog.), 1988–93, RN retd, 1993. Chairman: Furness Enterprise Ltd, 1993–2000; Ashworth High Security Hosp., 1999; non-executive Director: Cumbria Ambulance Service, 1992–94; Cumbria and Lancs Strategic Health Authy, 2002–06. Trustee, Francis C. Scott Charitable Trust, 1993–2011. DL Cumbria, 2000. *Recreations:* family, fell walking, opera, classical music, topiary. *Club:* Army and Navy.

PIRRIE, David Blair, FCIB; Director of International and Private Banking, Lloyds Bank Plc, 1992–97; *b* 15 Dec. 1938; *s* of John and Sylvia Pirrie; *m* 1966, Angela Sellos; three *s* one *d*. *Educ:* Strathallan Sch., Perthshire; Harvard Business Sch. (Management Develt). FCIB 1987. Lloyds Bank: Gen. Man., Brazil, 1975–81; Dir, Lloyds Bank International, 1981–83; Gen. Man., Gp HQ, 1983–85; Sen. Dir, Internat. Banking, 1985–87; Sen. Gen. Man., UK Retail Banking, 1987–89; Dir, UK Retail Banking, 1989–92. *Recreations:* golf, theatre, music.

PIRZADA, Syed Sharif Uddin, SPk 1964; Hon. Senior Adviser to Chief Executive on Foreign Affairs, Law, Justice and Human Rights, Pakistan, 2000–08; Member, National Security Council, 1999–2008; Ambassador-at-Large, since 1999; Attorney-General of Pakistan, 1965–66, 1968–71 and 1977–89; *b* 12 June 1923; *s* of Syed Vilayat Ali Pirzada; *m* 1960; two *s* two *d*. *Educ:* University of Bombay. LLB 1945; barrister-at-law. Secretary, Provincial Muslim League, 1945–47; Managing Editor, Morning Herald, 1947; Prof., Sind Muslim Law Coll., 1947–55; Advocate: Bombay High Court, 1946; Sind Chief Court, 1947; West Pakistan High Court, 1955; Supreme Court of Pakistan, 1961; Senior Advocate Supreme Court of Pakistan; Foreign Minister of Pakistan, 1966–68; Minister for Law and Parly Affairs, 1979–85; Advr to Chief Martial Law Administrator and Federal Minister, 1978. Ambassador-at-Large with status of Federal Minister, 1989–93; Chm., Heritage Council, 1989–93. Sec.-Gen., Orgn of the Islamic Conf., 1984–88 (Chm. Cttee of Experts for drafting statute of Islamic Internat. Ct of Justice, 1980). Represented Pakistan: before International Tribunal on Rann of Kutch, 1965; before Internat. Ct of Justice regarding Namibia, SW Africa, 1971; Pakistan Chief Counsel before ICAO Montreal in complaint concerning overflights over Indian territory; Leader of Pakistan delegations to Commonwealth Conf. and General Assembly of UN, 1966; Mem., UN Sub-Commn on Prevention of Discrimination and Protection of Minorities, 1972–82 (Chm., 1968). Hon. Advisor, Constitutional Commn, 1961; Chm., Pakistan Company Law Commn, 1962; Mem., Internat. River Cttee, 1961–68; President: Pakistan Br., Internat. Law Assoc., 1964–67; Karachi Bar Assoc., 1964; Pakistan Bar Council, 1966; Inst. of Internat. Affairs. Led Pakistan Delegn to Law of the Sea Conferences, NY, 1978 and 1979, and Geneva, 1980. Member: Pakistan Nat. Gp, Panel of the Permanent Ct of Arbitration; Panel of Arbitrators and Umpires, Council of Internat. Civil Aviation Organisation; Panel of Arbitrators, Internat. Centre for Settlement of Investment Disputes, Washington; Internat. Law Commn, 1981–86. Chm., Nat. Cttee for Quaid-I-Azam Year, 2001. *Publications:* Pakistan at a Glance, 1941; Jinnah on Pakistan, 1943; Leaders Correspondence with Jinnah, 1944, 3rd edn 1978; Evolution of Pakistan, 1962 (also published in Urdu and Arabic); Fundamental Rights and Constitutional Remedies in Pakistan, 1966; The Pakistan Resolution and the Historic Lahore Session, 1970; Foundations of Pakistan, vol. I, 1969, vol. II, 1970; Some Aspects of Quaid-i-Azam's Life, 1978; Collected Works of Quaid-i-Azam Mohammad Ali Jinnah, vol. I, 1985, vol. II, 1986. *Recreation:* bridge. *Clubs:* Sind (Karachi); Karachi Boat, Karachi Gymkhana.

PISANI, Edgard (Edouard Marie Victor); Chevalier de la Légion d'honneur; *b* Tunis, 9 Oct. 1918; *s* of François and Zoë Pisani. *Educ:* Lycée Carnot, Tunis; Lycée Louis-le-Grand, Paris. LèsL. War of 1939–45 (Croix de Guerre; Médaille de la Résistance). Chef du Cabinet, later Dir, Office of Prefect of Police, Paris, 1944; Dir, Office of Minister of Interior, 1946; Prefect: of Haute-Loire, 1946; of Haute-Marne, 1947; Senator (democratic left) from Haute-Marne, 1954–61; Minister of Agriculture, 1961–66; (first) Minister of Equipment, 1966–67; Deputy, Maine et Loire, 1967–68; Minister of Equipment and Housing, 1967; Conseiller Général, Maine et Loire, 1964–73; Mayor of Montreuil Bellay, 1965–75; Senator (socialist) from Haute-Marne, 1974–81; Mem., European Parlt, 1978–79 (Pres., Econ. and Monetary Affairs Cttee); Mem. for France, EEC, 1981–84; High Comr and Special Envoy to New Caledonia, 1984–85; Minister for New Caledonia, 1985–86. Member: Commn on Develt Issues (Brandt Commn), 1978–80; Economic and Social Cttee. Mem., Club of Rome, 1975. President: Inst. du Monde Arabe, 1988–95; Centre Internat. des Hautes Etudes Agronomiques Méditerranéennes, 1991–95. Dir, L'Evénement Européen, 1988–94. *Publications:* Principes, 1946; La région: pourquoi faire?, 1969; Le général indivis, 1974; Utopie foncière, 1977; Socialiste de raison, 1978; Défi du monde, campagne d'Europe, 1979; (contrib.) Pour la science, 1980; La main et l'outil, 1984; Pour l'Afrique, 1988; Persiste et Signe, 1992; Pour une agriculture marchande et ménagère, 1994; La passion de l'Etat, 1997; Une certaine idée du Monde, 2001; Un vieil homme et la terre, 2004; Le monde pourra-t-il nourrir le monde, 2004; Vive la Révolte, 2006; Une politique mondiale pour nourrir le monde, 2007; Le sens de l'Etat, 2008; Mes mots: pistes à réflexion, 2013; Croire pour Vivre: meditations politiques, 2015.

PISSARIDES, Sir Christopher (Antoniou), Kt 2013; PhD; FBA 2002; Regius Professor of Economics, and School Professor of Economics and Political Science, London School of Economics and Political Science, since 2012 (Professor of Economics, since 1986; Norman Sosnow Professor of Economics, 2006–12); *b* 20 Feb. 1948; *s* of Antonios and Evdokia Pissarides; *m* 1986, Francesca Michela Cassano (marr. diss. 2009); one *s* one *d*; *m* 2011, Liwa (Rachel) Ngai; one *s*. *Educ:* Essex Univ. (BA Econs 1970, MA Econs 1971); London Sch. of Econs and Pol Sci. (PhD 1974). Central Bank of Cyprus, 1974; Lectr, Univ. of Southampton, 1974–76; London School of Economics: Lectr, 1976–82; Reader, 1982–86; Prog. Dir, Centre for Econ. Performance, 1999–2007. Prof. of Eur. Studies, Univ. of Cyprus, 2013–; Helmut and Anna Pao Sohmen Prof. at Large, Inst. of Advanced Study, Univ. of Sci. and Technol., Hong Kong, 2013–; Pres., Growth Lab., St Petersburg State Univ., 2013–. Mem., Employment Taskforce, EC, 2003–04. Research Fellow: Centre for Economic Policy Res., London, 1994–; Inst. for Study of Labor (IZA), Bonn, 2001– (Prize in Labor Econs (jtly), 2005). Associate Ed., Economica, 1996– (Chm. Bd, 2007–); Mem., Editl Bd, AEJ Macroeconomics, 2007–. Specialist Advr, Treasury Cttee, H of C, 2001–05. Chm., Council of Nat. Economy, Cyprus, 2013–; Mem., Monetary Policy Cttee, Central Bank of Cyprus, 2000–07. Member Council: REconS, 1996–2003; Econometric Soc., 2005–; Eur. Econ. Assoc., 2005– (Pres., 2011). Mem., Interim Governing Bd, Univ. of Cyprus, 1989–95. Fellow: Econometric Soc., 1997; Soc. of Labor Economists, 2008; Academia Europaea; Acad. of Athens. For. Hon. Mem., AEA, 2011. Hon. Dr: Cyprus, 2009; Athens Univ. of Econs, 2011; Essex, 2012. Aristeion Award, Republic of Cyprus, 2008; (jtly) Nobel Prize in Economics, 2010. Grand Cross of Republic of Cyprus, 2011. *Publications:* Labour Market Adjustment, 1976; Equilibrium Unemployment Theory, 1990, 2nd edn 2000; (jtly) After the Crisis: the way ahead, 2010; (with Dale T. Mortensen) Job Matching, Wage Dispersion and Unemployment, 2011; contribs to professional jls, conf. proc. and ed books. *Recreations:* cooking, gardening, walking. *Address:* London School of Economics and Political Science, Houghton Street, WC2A 2AE. *T:* (020) 7955 7513, *Fax:* (020) 7955 6092. *E:* c.pissarides@lse.ac.uk.

PISTORIUS, Prof. Carl Wilhelm Irene, (Calie), CEng, FIET; Vice-Chancellor, University of Hull, since 2009; *b* Pretoria, S Africa, 9 Aug. 1958; *s* of Carl Wilhelm Irene Pistorius and Iolanthé Pistorius (*née* Tancred); *m* 2005, Michèle Emily Olivier; two *d* by a previous marriage. *Educ:* High Sch., Menlo Park, Pretoria; Univ. of Pretoria (BSc(Eng) cum laude 1979; BEng Hons cum laude 1981); Ohio State Univ. (MS 1984; PhD 1986); Massachusetts Inst. of Technol. (SM 1994); Harvard Business Sch. (AMP 2003). CEng 2010; FIET 2010. University of Pretoria: Hd, Dept of Electrical and Electronic Engrg, 1989–94; Dir, Inst. for Technol Innovation, 1994–98; Dir, Inf. Technol., 1998–99; Dean, Faculty of Engrg, Built Envmt and Inf. Technol., 2000–01; Vice-Chancellor and Principal, 2001–09. *Publications:* (jtly) Introduction to the Uniform Geometrical Theory of Diffraction, 1990; articles in IEEE Trans on antennas and propagation research policy, technol forecasting and social change. *Address:* University of Hull, Hull HU6 7RX. *T:* (01482) 465131, *Fax:* (01482) 466557. *E:* calie.pistorius@hull.ac.uk.

PITA, Arthur; choreographer; Artistic Director, Arthur Pita Productions, since 2003; *b* Johannesburg, SA, 21 Feb. 1972; *s* of Francisco Alberto Pita and Teresinha Delgado Pita; partner, Matthew Christopher Bourne, *qv*. *Educ:* Johannesburg Art, Ballet, Drama and Music Sch. (matriculation); London Contemporary Dance Sch. (MA Dance and Choreography). Associate Artist: The Place, 2003–05; Jerwood DanceHouse DanceEast, 2013–15. *Choreographic works* include: Snow White in Black, Phoenix Dance Th., 2006; Mischief, in collaboration with Theatre Rites, 2007 (TMA Th. Award for Achievement in Dance, 2008); The Metamorphosis, Linbury Studio Th., Royal Opera House, 2011 (Critics' Circle Nat. Dance Award for Best Modern Choreography, 2012; South Bank Sky Arts Award, 2012). *Recreations:* travel, music, film, dog lover, nature. *Address:* Church Cottage, St Marys Path, N1 2RR. *T:* 07940 548201. *E:* arthurpita@mac.com. *W:* www.arthurpita.com.

PITCHER, Sir Desmond (Henry), Kt 1992; CEng, FIET, FBCS; Chairman, United Utilities (formerly North West Water Group), 1993–98 (Director, 1990–98; Deputy Chairman, 1991–93); *b* 23 March 1935; *s* of George Charles and Alice Marion Pitcher; *m* 1st, 1961 (marr. diss.); twin *d*; 2nd, 1978 (marr. diss.); two *s*; 3rd, 1991, Norma Barbara Niven. *Educ:* Liverpool Coll. of Technology. MIEEE (USA). A. V. Roe & Co., Develt Engr, 1955; Automatic Telephone and Elec. Co. (now Plessey), Systems Engr, 1958; Univac Remington Rand (now Sperry Rand Ltd), Systems Engr, 1961; Sperry Univac: Dir, Systems, 1966; Managing Dir, 1971; Vice-Pres., 1974; Dir, Sperry Rand, 1971–76, Dep. Chm., 1974–76; Man. Dir, Leyland Truck and Bus Ltd, 1976–78; Dir, British Leyland, 1976–78; Man. Dir, Plessey Telecommunications and Office Systems, 1978–83; Dir, Plessey Co., 1979–83; Director: The Littlewoods Orgn, 1983–95 (Gp Chief Exec., 1983–93; Vice-Chm., 1993–95); National Westminster Bank, 1994–98; (Mem., Northern Adv. Bd, 1989–92). Chm. & Dir, Signbrick Ltd, 2001–12; Dir, Steeltower Ltd, 2001–05. Chairman: Mersey Barrage Co., 1986–96; Merseyside Develt Corp., 1991–98; Westminster Green Management Co. Ltd, 2010–. Pres., NW Chambers of Commerce, 1994–98. Vis. Prof. of Business Policy, Univ. of Manchester, 1993–98. Faraday Lectures, The Social Computer, IEE, 1974–75. Dir, CEI, 1979; Pres., TEMA, 1981–83. Dep. Chm., Everton Football Club, 1990–98 (Dir, 1987–98); Chm., Royal Liverpool Philharmonic Soc. Develt Trust, 1992–2005. Mem., Twickenham Regeneration Adv. Panel, Richmond upon Thames LBC, 2011–. Chm. and Trustee, Rocking Horse Appeal, Royal Liverpool Children's NHS Trust, 1996–2005; Trustee, Outward Bound, 2005–07. DL Merseyside, 1992–99. Freeman, City of London, 1987; Liveryman, Co. of Information Technologists, 1992–. CCMI; FRIAS; FRSA 1987; Hon. FIDE; Hon. Fellow, Liverpool John Moores Univ., 1993. Knight, Order of St Hubert (Austria), 1991. *Publications:* Institution of Electrical Engineers Faraday Lectures, 1974–75; Water Under the Bridge: 30 years in industrial management (autobiog.), 2003; various lectures on social implications of computers and micro-electronics. *Recreations:* golf, music. *Address:* Pill Heath Place, Pill Heath, Andover, Hants SP11 0JG. *E:* desmondpitcher@aol.com. *Clubs:* Brooks's, Royal Automobile, Carlton; Royal Birkdale Golf; Royal Liverpool; Lancs CC.

PITCHER, Rev. George Martell; Editor-in-Chief, International Business Times UK, since 2014; non-executive Chairman and co-founder, Jericho Chambers, since 2013; *b* Sherborne, Dorset, 30 May 1955; *s* of George Thomas Pitcher and Mary Pitcher (*née* Brownscombe); *m* 1985, Lynda Caire Silvana Mobbs; three *s* one *d*. *Educ:* Blundell's Sch., Devon; Birmingham Univ. (BA Hons Drama and Th. Arts); N Thames Ministerial Trng Course, Middx Univ. (BA Hons Theol.). Journalist, Haymarket Publishing Ltd, 1980–83; Man. Dir, BH Pubns Ltd, 1983–85; financial journalist, 1985–88, Industrial Ed., 1988–91, The Observer; Contributing Ed. and columnist, Mktg Week, 1988–2005; Luther Pendragon: Co-founder and Dir, 1992–95; Chief Exec., 1995–2000; Partner, 2000–05; Religion Ed. and columnist, Daily Telegraph, 2008–10; Sec. for Public Affairs to Archbp of Canterbury, 2010–11. Contrib., Daily Mail, 2011–13; Associate Ed., Newsweek Europe, 2015– (Contrib. Ed., 2014–15); Hd, Editl Panel, IBT Media, 2014–15. Ordained deacon, 2005, priest, 2006; Curate, Dio. of London, 2005–08; Associate Priest, St Bride's, Fleet St, 2008–12; Chaplain, Guild of St Bride's, 2013–; non-stipendiary Priest-in-charge, Waldron, E Sussex, 2013–. Ext. Examiner,

Univ. of Westminster, 2013–. Governor: Battle Abbey Sch., 2011–; Cross in Hand C of E Primary Sch., 2013–. Nat. Newspaper Industrial Journalist of Year, Industrial Soc., 1991. *Publications:* The Death of Spin, 2002; A Time to Live: the case against euthanasia and assisted suicide, 2010. *Recreations:* Sussex, donkeys, woods, writing, theology. *Address:* International Business Times UK, 25 Canada Square, E14 5LQ. *Clubs:* Garrick, Lansdowne.

PITCHERS, Hon. Sir Christopher (John), Kt 2002; a Judge of the High Court, Queen's Bench Division, 2002–08; Commissioner, Royal Court of Jersey, since 2008; *b* 2 Oct. 1942; *s* of late Thomas Pitchers and Melissa Pitchers; *m* 1965, Judith Stevenson, MBE (*d* 2006); two *s*. *Educ:* Uppingham Sch.; Worcester Coll., Oxford. MA. Called to the Bar, Inner Temple, 1965, Bencher, 1996; a Recorder, 1981–86; a Circuit Judge, 1986–2002. Dir of Studies, Judicial Studies Bd, 1996–97 (Mem., Criminal Cttee, 1991–95; Jt Dir, 1995–96). Hon. Sec., Council of HM Circuit Judges, 1992–95 (Pres., 1999). Vice-Pres., NACRO, 1994–2002. Hon. Vis. Prof., Nottingham Law Sch., 2008. Hon. LLD De Montfort, 2002.

PITCHFORD, Rt Hon. Sir Christopher (John), Kt 2000; PC 2010; **Rt Hon. Lord Justice Pitchford;** DL; a Lord Justice of Appeal, since 2010; *b* 28 March 1947; *s* of His Honour Charles Neville Pitchford; *m* 1st, 1970, Rosalind (*née* Eaton) (marr. diss. 1991); two *d*; 2nd, 1991, Denise (*née* James); two *s*. *Educ:* Duffryn Comprehensive Sch., Newport, Gwent; Queen's Coll., Taunton, Somerset; Queen Mary Coll., London (LLB). Called to the Bar, Middle Temple, 1969, Bencher, 1996; QC 1987; a Recorder, 1987–2000; a Dep. High Ct Judge, 1996–2000; a Judge of the High Court, Queen's Bench Div., 2000–10. Leader, 1999–2000, a Presiding Judge, 2002–05, Wales and Chester Circuit. Arbitrator, Motor Insurers Bureau, 1994–2000. Pres. Council of Inns of Court, 2012–. Dir of Trng, Criminal Gp, Judicial Studies Bd, 2006–10; Mem., Sentencing Guidelines Council, 2006–10. Pres., Bedlinog RFC, 2002–12 (Patron, 2012–). DL Mid Glamorgan, 2004. *Recreation:* fishing. *Address:* Royal Courts of Justice, Strand, WC2A 2LL.

PITFIELD, Hon. (Peter) Michael, OC 2012; CVO 1982; PC (Can.) 1984; QC (Can.) 1972; Senator, Canada, Dec. 1982–2010; *b* Montreal, 18 June 1937; *s* of Ward Chipman Pitfield and Grace Edith (*née* MacDougall); *m* 1971, Nancy Snow (decd); one *s* two *d*. *Educ:* Lower Canada Coll., Montreal; Sedbergh Sch., Montebello; St Lawrence Univ. (BASc; Hon. DLitt 1979); McGill Univ. (BCL); Univ. of Ottawa (DESD). Lieut, RCNR. Read Law with Mathewson Lafleur & Brown, Montreal (associated with firm, 1958–59); called to Quebec Bar, 1962; QC (Fed.) 1972; Admin. Asst to Minister of Justice and Attorney-Gen. of Canada, 1959–61; Sec. and Exec. Dir, Royal Commn on Pubns, Ottawa, 1961–62; Attaché to Gov.-Gen. of Canada, 1962–65; Sec. and Res. Supervisor of Royal Commn on Taxation, 1963–66; entered Privy Council Office and Cabinet Secretariat of Govt of Canada, 1965; Asst Sec. to Cabinet, 1966; Dep. Sec. to Cabinet (Plans), and Dep. Clerk to Council, 1969; Dep. Minister, Consumer and Corporate Affairs, 1973; Clerk of Privy Council and Sec. to Cabinet, 1975–79 and 1980–Nov. 1982; Sen. Adviser to Privy Council Office, Nov.–Dec. 1982. Rep., UN Gen. Assembly, 1983; Chm., Senate Cttee on Security and Intelligence, 1983. Director: Power Corp., Montreal; Trust Co., LaPresse; Great West Life Assurance Co.; Investor's Gp Ltd, Winnipeg; Fellow, Harvard Univ., 1974; Mackenzie King Vis. Prof., Kennedy Sch. of Govt, Harvard, 1979–80. Member: Canadian, Quebec and Montreal Bar Assocs; Can. Inst. of Public Admin; Can. Hist. Assoc.; Can. Pol Sci. Assoc.; Amer. Soc. Pol and Social Sci.; Internat. Commn of Jurists; Beta Theta Pi. Trustee, Twentieth Century Fund, NY; Member Council: Canadian Inst. for Advanced Res., Toronto; IISS. *Recreations:* squash, ski-ing, reading. *Address:* c/o The Senate, 111 Wellington Street, Ottawa, ON K1A 0A4, Canada. *Clubs:* University, Mount Royal, Racket (Montreal).

PITKEATHLEY, family name of **Baroness Pitkeathley**.

PITKEATHLEY, Baroness *cr* 1997 (Life Peer), of Caversham in the Royal co. of Berkshire; **Jill Elizabeth Pitkeathley,** OBE 1993; Chair: Professional Standards Authority for Health and Social Care (formerly Council for Healthcare Regulatory Excellence), since 2009; *b* 4 Jan. 1940; *d* of Roland Wilfred Bisson and Edith May Bisson (*née* Muston); *m* 1st, 1961, W. Pitkeathley (marr. diss. 1978); one *s* one *d*; 2nd, 2008, (John) David Emerson, *qv*. *Educ:* Ladies' Coll., Guernsey; Bristol Univ. (BA Econ). Social worker, 1961–64; Voluntary Service Co-ordinator, Manchester and Essex, 1970–83; Nat. Consumer Council, 1983–86; Dir, Nat. Council for Carers, 1986 until merger with Assoc. of Carers, 1988; Chief Exec., Carers Nat. Assoc., 1988–98; Chm., New Opportunities Fund, 1998–2004. Advr to Griffiths' Rev. of Community Care, 1986–88; Mem., Health Adv. Service, 1993–97; Chm. Adv. Gp, 1999–2000, Interim Chair, 2001–02, Gen. Social Care Council; Chair: Children and Families Court Adv. and Support Service, 2004–08; Adv. Panel on Futurebuilders, 2005–08; Adv. Body, Office of the Third Sector, Cabinet Office, 2008–11. Dir, Big Society Trust, 2011– (Chm., 2015–). President: Community Council for Berks, 1998–2013 (Vice-Pres., 1990–98); Volunteering England (formerly Nat. Centre for Volunteering), 2002–; Vice Pres., Carers UK, 2003–; Pres., Eurocarers, 2007–11. Patron, Bracknell CVS. Mem. Bd of Governors, Nat. Inst. of Social Work, 1995–98. Trustee, Cumberland Lodge, 2011–. Hon. LLD: Bristol, 2002; London Metropolitan, 2002. *Publications:* When I Went Home, 1978; Mobilising Voluntary Resources, 1982; Volunteers in Hospitals, 1984; Supporting Volunteers, 1985; It's my duty, isn't it?, 1989; (with David Emerson) The Only Child, 1992; (with David Emerson) Age Gap Relationships, 1994; Cassandra and Jane: a personal journey through the lives of the Austen sisters, 2004; Dearest Cousin Jane: the story of Jane Austen's cousin, 2010. *Recreations:* gardening, grand-children, writing. *T:* (office) (020) 7389 8041.

See also C. M. Wilson.

PITMAN, Rt Rev. Cyrus Clement James; Bishop of Newfoundland, Eastern, and Labrador, 2004–13; *b* 24 March 1944; *s* of John and Ella Pitman; *m* 1968, Mary (*née* Lee); three *s* one *d*. *Educ:* Newfoundland Meml Univ. (BA); Queen's Coll., Newfoundland (LTh). Ordained deacon, 1967, priest, 1968; Curate, Channel, 1967–70; Incumbent, Flower's Cove, 1970–75; Rector, Meadows, 1975–80; Dir of Prog., Dio. W Newfoundland, 1980–82; Curate, St Mary the Virgin, St John's, 1982–87; Rector: Petty Harbour, 1987–90; St Paul, Goulds, Kilbride, 1990–93; All Saints, Conception Bay S, 1993–2000; St Mary the Virgin, St John's, 2000–03; Archdeacon, Avalon E and W, 2002–03; Exec. Archdeacon and Admin. Asst to Bishop of Eastern Newfoundland and Labrador, 2003–04. Regl Dean, Avalon W, 1990; Canon, Stall of St Columba, 1997. *Address:* c/o Synod Office, 19 King's Bridge Road, St John's, NL A1C 3K4, Canada. *T:* (709) 5766697, *Fax:* (709) 5767122. *E:* cpitman@anglicanenl.net.

PITMAN, His Honour David Christian; a Circuit Judge, 1986–2006; a Deputy Circuit Judge, 2006–08; *b* 1 Dec. 1936; 3rd *s* of Sir (Isaac) James Pitman, KBE, and Hon. Margaret Beaufort Pitman (*née* Lawson Johnston); *m* 1971, Christina Mary Malone-Lee; one *s* two *d*. *Educ:* Eton Coll.; Christ Church, Oxford (BA (PPE) 1961, MA 1964). Editorial role in publishing books in Initial Teaching Alphabet, 1960–63; called to Bar, Middle Temple, 1963; commenced practice, 1964; a Recorder, 1986. National Service: 2nd Lieut, 60th Rifles, 1955–57; Territorial Army: Lieut Queen's Westminsters, KRRC, 1957–61; Captain, then Major, Queen's Royal Rifles (TA), 1961–67; Major, 5th (T) Bn RGJ, 1967–69. *Recreations:* music, the open air. *Address:* c/o The Crown Court, Snaresbrook, Hollybush Hill, E11 1QW.

PITMAN, Jennifer Susan, OBE 1998; professional racehorse trainer (National Hunt), 1975–99; Partner, DJS Racing, 1996; *b* 11 June 1946; *d* of George and Mary Harvey; *m* 1st, 1965, Richard Pitman (marr. diss.); two *s*; 2nd, 1997, David Stait. *Educ:* Sarson Secondary Girls' School. Dir, Jenny Pitman Racing Ltd, 1975–99. Training of major race winners includes: Midlands National, 1977 (Watafella), 1990 (Willsford); Massey Ferguson Gold Cup, Cheltenham, 1980 (Bueche Giorod); Welsh National, 1982 (Corbiere), 1983 (Burrough Hill Lad), 1986 (Stearsby); Grand National, 1983 (Corbiere), 1995 (Royal Athlete); Mildmay/Cazalet Gold Cup, 1983 (Burrough Hill Lad), 1986 (Stearsby), 1993 (Superior Finish); Cheltenham Gold Cup, 1984 (Burrough Hill Lad), 1991 (Garrison Savannah); King George VI Gold Cup, 1984 (Burrough Hill Lad); Hennessy Gold Cup, Newbury, 1984 (Burrough Hill Lad); Whitbread Trophy, 1985 (Smith's Man); Ritz Club Chase, Cheltenham, 1987 (Gainsay); Philip Cornes Saddle of Gold Final, Newbury, 1988 (Crumpet Delite); Welsh Champion Hurdle, 1991 (Wonderman), 1992 (Don Valentino); Scottish National, 1995 (Willsford). Piper Heidsieck Trainer of the Year, 1983/84, 1989/90. *Publications:* Glorious Uncertainty (autobiog.), 1984; Jenny Pitman: the autobiography, 1998; *novels:* On the Edge, 2002; Double Deal, 2002; The Dilemma, 2003; The Vendetta, 2004; The Inheritance, 2005. *Address:* Owl's Barn, Kintbury, Hungerford, Berks RG17 9SX. *Club:* International Sporting.

PITMAN, Joanna Beaufort; author and journalist; consultant on Japanese affairs; *b* London, 29 Sept. 1963; *d* of Peter Pitman and Jenny Pitman; *m* 1st, 1996, Giles Worsley (*d* 2006); three *d*; 2nd, 2011, (Anthony) Patrick (Mycroft) Beeley. *Educ:* Westminster Sch.; St John's Coll., Cambridge (BA Japanese Studies 1986). Staff writer: Euromoney mag., 1987–88; Internat. Financing Review mag., 1988–89; The Times: Tokyo Bureau Chief, 1989–93; columnist and feature writer, London, 1993–2010; Exec., Hakluyt & Co., 2010–12. Trustee: Somerset House, 2009–; Great Britain Sasakawa Foundn, 2010–; John Kobal Foundn, 2009–. *Publications:* On Blondes, 2003; The Raphael Trail, 2006. *Recreations:* family, art, architecture, cooking. *Address:* c/o A. P. Watt, 12–26 Lexington Street, W1F 0LE.

PITT, Brad; *see* Pitt, W. B.

PITT, Joanna; *see* Read, J.

PITT, Sir Michael (Edward), Kt 2005; DL; CEng, FICE; Chairman, Legal Services Board, since 2014; *b* 2 Feb. 1949; *s* of Albert and Doris Joan Pitt; *m* 1969, Anna Maria Di Claudio; two *d*. *Educ:* University College London (first class Hons BSc Engrg). CEng 1974; FICE 1989. Civil Servant, 1970–72; motorway design and construction, 1972–75; transportation planner in private sector and local govt, 1975–80; Asst County Surveyor, Northumberland CC, 1980–84; Dir of Property Services and Dir of Tech. Services, Humberside CC, 1984–90; Chief Executive: Cheshire CC, 1990–97; Kent CC, 1997–2005; Swindon BC, 2005–06; Chairman: South West Strategic HA, 2006–09; Infrastructure Planning Commn, 2009–12; Chair and Chief Exec., Planning Inspectorate, 2011–14. DL Wilts, 2009. *Publications:* papers in technical jls. *Recreations:* family life, walking, cycling, the voluntary sector.

PITT, William Bradley, (Brad); actor; *b* Shawnee, Oklahoma, 18 Dec. 1963; *s* of Bill Pitt and Jane Pitt (*née* Hillhouse); *m* 2000, Jennifer Aniston (marr. diss. 2005); *m* 2014, Angelina Jolie; one *s* two *d* (incl. twin *s* and *d*) and two adopted *s* one adopted *d*. *Educ:* Univ. of Missouri. *Films* include: as actor: Cutting Class, Happy Together, 1989; Across the Tracks, Thelma & Louise, Johnny Suede, 1991; Contact, Cool World, A River Runs Through It, 1992; Kalifornia, True Romance, 1993; The Favor, Interview with the Vampire, Legends of the Fall, 1994; Se7en, 1995; Twelve Monkeys, Sleepers, 1996; The Devil's Own, Seven Years in Tibet, The Dark Side of the Sun, 1997; Meet Joe Black, Fight Club, 1999; Snatch, 2000; The Mexican, Spy Game, 2001; Ocean's Eleven, 2002; Confessions of a Dangerous Mind, Full Frontal, 2003; Troy, 2004; Ocean's Twelve, Mr & Mrs Smith, 2005; Babel, 2006; Ocean's Thirteen, The Assassination of Jesse James by the Coward Robert Ford (also prod.) (Best Actor, Venice Film Fest.), 2007; Burn After Reading, 2008; The Curious Case of Benjamin Button, Inglourious Basterds, 2009; The Tree of Life, Moneyball, 2011 (also prod.); Killing Them Softly, 2012; World War Z (also prod.), The Counsellor, 2013; Fury, 2014; as producer: God Grew Tired of Us, The Departed, Running with Scissors, 2006; Year of the Dog, The Tehuacan Project, A Mighty Heart, 2007; Pretty/Handsome, 2008; The Private Lives of Pippa Lee, 2009; 12 Years a Slave, 2013; *television* includes: as actor: Dallas, 1987–88; The Image, 1990; Glory Days (series), 1990; Freedom: a history of Us (series), 2003; Rx for Survival: a global health challenge (series), 2005. *Address:* c/o Creative Artists Agency, 2000 Avenue of the Stars, Los Angeles, CA 90067, USA.

PITT, William F.; *see* Fox-Pitt.

PITT, William Henry; Independent Learning and Development Consultant; *b* 17 July 1937; *m* 1961, Janet Pitt (*née* Wearn); one *d*. *Educ:* Heath Clark Sch., Croydon; London Nautical Sch.; Polytechnic of N London (BA Philos./Classics). Lighting Engineer, 1955–75; Housing Officer, Lambeth Borough Council, 1975–81. Gp Training Manager, Canary Wharf Gp plc, 1999–2004. Chm., Lambeth Br., NALGO, 1979–81. Joined Liberal Party, 1959; contested: (L) Croydon NW, Feb. and Oct. 1974, 1979, 1983; Thanet South (L/Alliance), 1987, (Lib Dem), 1992. MP (L) Croydon NW, Oct. 1981–1983; joined Labour Party, 1996. Chm., Industrial Trng Bd Pensioners' Assoc., 2009–. Chairman: Broadstairs Music Recital Soc., 2011–; Churches Together in Broadstairs and St Peter's, 2012–14. Mem., Assoc. of Former MPs, 2011–. Volunteer newsreader, Academy FM Thanet. *Recreations:* photography, choral singing, listening to music, reading, walking, going to France, travelling around the world, making pots and ceramics. *Address:* 10 Inverness Terrace, Broadstairs, Kent CT10 1QZ.

PITT-BROOKE, John Stephen, CB 2009; General Secretary, Forces Pension Society, since 2015; *b* 9 Sept. 1950; *s* of late Reginald Pitt-Brooke and of Hilda (*née* Wright); *m* 1st, 1986, Rosalind (*d* 1996), *d* of Prof. William Mulligan, *qv*; two *s*; 2nd, 1999, Frances Way, *d* of B. T. McDade. *Educ:* Salford Grammar Sch.; Queens' Coll., Cambridge (MA). MoD, 1971–74; NI Office, 1974–77; Private Sec. to Minister of State for NI, 1975–77; MoD, 1978; NATO Defence Coll., 1980; Private Sec. to Permanent Under Sec., MoD, 1984–87; Cabinet Office, 1988–89; Ministry of Defence, 1989–2011: Head of Industrial Relns Div., 1989–92; Private Sec. to Sec. of State for Defence, 1992–94; Comd Sec., Land Comd, 1995–98; Fellow, Center for Internat. Affairs, Harvard Univ., 1998–99; Director General: Corporate Communications, 1999–2001; Civilian Personnel, 2001–04; Media and Communications, 2005–06; Secretariat, 2006–10; Hd, Civilian Review Team, 2010–11; Project Dir, Standard Life Charitable Trust, 2011–13. *Recreations:* family life, literature, Salisbury Cathedral, Manchester City Football Club. *Club:* MCC.

PITT-RIVERS, Valerie, CVO 2014; Lord-Lieutenant of Dorset, 2006–14 (Vice Lord-Lieutenant, 1999–2006); *b* 23 Jan. 1939; *d* of Derek and Eva Scott; *m* 1964, George Anthony Lane-Fox Pitt-Rivers, OBE, DL. *Educ:* Prior's Field, Godalming. Advertising and public relns, 1957–63; worked for NHS, charities and the arts in Dorset, 1970–. Non-exec. Dir and Vice Chm., W Dorset Gen. Hosps NHS Trust, 1991–98. Founder, 1987, Chm., 1987–98, Arts in Hospital Project for NHS, Dorchester; Patron or Pres., numerous charitable orgns in Dorset. Pro Chancellor, Bournemouth Univ., 2014–. DL Dorset, 1995. CStJ 2007. *Recreations:* gardens, opera. *Address:* Manor House, Hinton St Mary, Sturminster Newton, Dorset DT10 1NA.

PITT-WATSON, David James; Executive Fellow, London Business School, since 2013; *b* Aberdeen, 23 Sept. 1956; *s* of Ian Robertson Pitt-Watson and Helen Maud Pitt-Watson (*née* McCall); *m* 1989, Ursula Barnes; one *s* two *d*. *Educ:* Bearsden Acad.; Aberdeen Grammar Sch.; Queen's Coll., Oxford (BA PPE 1977); Stanford Univ. (MA 1980; MBA 1980). Investment Controller, 3i, 1977–78; Man. Dir, Braxton Associates, 1980–97; Asst Gen. Sec., Labour Party, 1997–99; Chief Exec., Hermes Focus Asset Mgt, 1999–2006; Sen. Advr, Hermes Fund Managers, 2008–09; Chair, Hermes Focus Asset Mgt, 2009–12. Dir, Oxford Analytica, 2006–. Non-exec. Dir, KPMG, 2013–. Vis. Prof., Cranfield Univ., 1990–96. Chair, Finance Initiative, UNEP, 2013–15. Trustee: IPPR, 2004–; Oxfam (UK), 2011–; NESTA, 2013–.

FRSA. *Publications:* The New Capitalists, 2006; Privatisation and Transition in Russia in the Early 1990s, 2013. *Recreations:* history, politics, singing, jogging. *Address:* London Business School, Regents Park, NW1 4SA. *E:* dpittwatson@london.edu.

PITTAM, Jonathan Charles; County Treasurer, Hampshire County Council, 1997–2010; *b* 9 June 1950; *s* of Brian and Sheila Pittam; *m* 1972, Mary Catherine Davey; two *s* one *d*. *Educ:* Tavistock Sch.; King's Coll., Univ. of London (BSc Hons). CPFA 1975. London Borough of Croydon: grad. trainee, 1971–73; Sen. Audit Asst, 1973; Accountant, 1973–75; Gp Accountant, 1975–76; Asst Prin. Accountant, 1976–78; Chief Accountant, 1979–80, Asst Dir, Finance and Admin, 1980–83, Cambs CC; Dep. Co. Treas., Hants CC, 1983–97; Treasurer: Hants Police Authy, 1997–2010; Hants Fire and Rescue Authy, 1997–2010. Expenditure Co-ordinator, LGA, 2005–10. Non-exec. Dir, Solent NHS Trust, 2011– (Chm., Finance Cttee, 2011–). Mem. Council, CIPFA, 2008–10; President: Soc. of County Treasurers, 2002–03; Assoc. of Local Authority Treasurers' Societies, 2004–10. *Address:* 25 Shepherds Down, Alresford, Hants SO24 9PP.

PITTAWAY, David Michael; QC 2000; a Recorder, since 2000; a Deputy High Court Judge (Queen's Bench Division), since 2008, and (Administration Court), since 2012; *b* 29 June 1955; *s* of Michael Pittaway, JP, MRCVS, and Heather Yvette Pittaway (*née* Scott); *m* 1983, Jill Suzanne Newsam, *d* of Dr Ian Douglas Newsam, MRCVS; two *s*. *Educ:* Uppingham Sch.; Sidney Sussex Coll., Cambridge (Exhibnr; MA). Called to the Bar: Inner Temple, 1977 (Bencher, 1998; Reader, 2016); Gibraltar (Temp.), 2007; NI, 2011; Asst Recorder, 1998; Midland and Oxford Circuit. Bar Council: Mem., 1999–2005, 2008–11; Mem., Gen. Mgt Cttee, 2008–11; Chairman: Trng for Bar Cttee, 2008–11; Neuberger Monitoring Implementation Gp, 2010–11; Mem., Exec. Cttee, 1994–98 and 2004–09, 2012–, Chm., Educn Cttee, 2004–09, Inner Temple; Mem., Council of Inns of Court, 2008–11 and 2013–. Actg Chancellor, Birmingham Dio., 2001–04; Chancellor, Peterborough Dio., 2006–. Legal Mem., Mental Health Review Tribunal, 2002–; Legal Assessor: GMC, 2002–04; RCVS, 2004–; Gen. Social Care Council, 2008–10. Course Dir, Clinical Negligence Seminars, 1998–2003, Chm., 2005–07, Professional Negligence Bar Assoc. Trustee: Nat. Educn Trust, 2011–14; Council of Inns of Court, 2013–. Gov., Compton Verney Hse Trust, 2010–12 (Chm., Develt Bd, 2010–12). Mem. Council, Cheltenham Ladies Coll., 2012–. FCIArb 1992. *Publications:* (contrib.) Atkin's Court Forms, vol. 8, Carriers, 1990, rev. edn 2010, vol. 29(2), Personal Injury, 1996, rev. edn 2014; Professional Negligence, 1996, rev. edn 2013, vol. 28, National Health Service, 2003, rev. edn 2014, vol. 27(2); (Gen. Ed.) Pittaway & Hammerton, Professional Negligence Cases, 1998. *Recreations:* gardening, travel, music. *Address:* Hailsham Chambers, 4 Paper Buildings, Temple, EC4Y 7EX. *T:* (020) 7643 5000. *Clubs:* Garrick, Royal Automobile; Redclyffe Yacht (Wareham).

PITTS, Anthony Brian; His Honour Judge Pitts; a Circuit Judge, since 2002; *b* 18 May 1946; *s* of Sir Cyril Alfred Pitts and of Barbara Pitts; *m* 1980, Sally-Jane Spencer; one *s* one *d*. *Educ:* Pembroke Coll., Oxford (BA Law). Called to the Bar, Gray's Inn, 1975; a Recorder, 1997–2002. *Recreations:* motor sport, guitar, France.

PITTS, Antony Philip David; Composer and Artistic Director, Tonus Peregrinus, since 1990; *b* Farnborough, Kent, 24 March 1969; *s* of David and Rosemary Pitts; *m* 1989, Karen Jonckheere; three *s* two *d*. *Educ:* Tiffin Boys' Sch., Kingston-upon-Thames; New Coll., Oxford (MA 1st Cl. Hons Music). BBC, 1992–2005: Producer, 1994–98 (Facing the Radio, Radio Acad. BT Award, 1996); Sen. Producer, Radio 3, 1999–2005 (A Pebble in the Pond, Prix Italia, 2004); Sen. Lectr in Creative Technol., RAM, 2006–09. Res. Leader, MusicDNA Ltd, 2010–. Founder, 1equalmusic, 2011. Hon. FFCM, Central Sch. of Religion, Indiana, 2008. With Tonus Peregrinus: perf. at meml for Alexander Litvinenko, 2006; composer, oratorio, Jerusalem-Yerushalayim, 2008. Numerous recordings, incl. Passio, 2003 (Cannes Classical Award, 2004). *Publications:* The Naxos Book of Carols, 2004; published music scores. *Address:* The Welcome Stranger, High Street, Flimwell, E Sussex TN5 7PB. *T:* 07595 223000. *E:* antony@1equalmusic.com.

PITTS, John Kennedy; Chairman, Legal Aid Board, 1988–95; *b* 6 Oct. 1925; *s* of Thomas Alwyn Pitts and Kathleen Margaret Pitts (*née* Kennedy); *m* 1st, 1957, Joan Iris Light (*d* 1986); 2nd, 1990, Julia Bentall. *Educ:* Bristol Univ. (BSc). Res. Officer, British Cotton Industry Res. Assoc., 1948–53; ICI, 1953–78; Dir, ICI Mond Div., 1969–71; Dep. Chm., ICI Agricl Div., 1972–77; Chairman: Richardsons Fertilizers, 1972–76; Hargreaves Fertilizers, 1975–77; Vice-Pres., Cie Neerlandaise de l'Azote, 1975–77. Chm. and Chief Exec., Tioxide Group, 1978–87. Mem., Tees and Hartlepool Port Authy, 1976–78; Chm., SASDA (formerly Shildon & Sedgefield Develt Agency), 1991–94. Pres., Chem. Industries Assoc., 1984–86. *Address:* Hall Garth House, Carthorpe, Bedale, N Yorks DL8 2LD.

PITTSBURGH, Assistant Bishop of; *see* Scriven, Rt Rev. H. W.

PIZARRO, Artur; pianist; *b* Portugal. Performances with orchs incl. Philadelphia, LA Philharmonic, Baltimore Symphony, NHK Symphony (Tokyo), Montreal Symphony, Toronto Symphony, Hong Kong Philharmonic, Leipzig Chamber, Rotterdam Philharmonic, Vienna Symphony, Royal Philharmonic, BBC Symphony. Recitals worldwide. Numerous recordings. Winner, Leeds Internat. Piano Competition, 1990. *Address:* Tom Croxon Management Ltd, 22 Hurst Road, Buckhurst Hill, Essex IG9 6AB. *T:* (020) 8279 2516. *E:* tom@tomcroxonmanagement.co.uk.

PIZZEY, Erin Patria Margaret; international founder of refuges for victims of domestic violence; *b* 19 Feb. 1939; *d* of late Cyril Edward Antony Carney, MBE and of Ruth Patricia Balfour-Last; *m* 1961, John Leo Pizzey (marr. diss. 1979); one *s* one *d*. *Educ:* St Antony's; Leweston Manor, Sherborne, Dorset. Somewhat chequered career as pioneering attracts frequent clashes with the law; appearances at such places as Acton Magistrates Court and the House of Lords could be considered milestones in the fulfilment of a career dedicated to defending women and children; Founder of first Shelter for Battered Wives (subseq. Women) and their children, 1971; helped fund and open Health Care Centre, Wandsworth Prison, 2001. Patron: Mankind Charity, 2004–; Derwentside Domestic Violence Forum, 2005–; Compassion in Care, 2005–. Presenter, Domestic Violence is not a Gender Issue, Internat. Conf., Sacramento, 2008 (Lifetime Achievement Award); held lectures about domestic violence and child advocacy for Slovenia Ombudsman, 2008; contribs to: New Statesman, Sunday Times, Cosmopolitan. Member: Soc. of Authors; AFI; Smithsonian Instn; Royal Soc. of Literature. Patron, Care and Comfort Romania, 1998–. Attended Women of Achievement Lunch, Buckingham Palace, 2004. Diploma of Honour, Internat. order of volunteers for peace, 1981; Nancy Astor Award for Journalism, 1983; Distinguished Leadership Award, World Congress of Victimology, 1987; San Valentino d'Oro prize for lit., 1994. *Publications:* (as Erin Pizzey) Scream Quietly or the Neighbours Will Hear, 1974, 2nd edn 1978; Infernal Child (autobiog.), 1978; The Slut's Cookbook, 1981; Prone to Violence, 1982; Erin Pizzey Collects, 1983; Wild Child (autobiog.), 1996; (jtly) Grandmothers of the Revolution, 2000; (jtly) Women or Men - Who Are the Victims?, 2000; This Way to the Revolution (autobiog.), 2011; *novels:* The Watershed, 1983; In the Shadow of the Castle, 1984; The Pleasure Palace, 1986; First Lady, 1987; The Consul General's Daughter, 1988; The Snow Leopard of Shanghai, 1989; Other Lovers, 1991; Morning Star, 1991; Swimming with Dolphins, 1992; For the Love of a Stranger, 1993; Kisses, 1995; The Wicked World of Women, 1996; The Fame Game, 1999; poems and short stories. *Recreations:* reading, writing, cooking, antiques, violin, gardening, wine, travel. *Address:* Flat 5, 29 Lebanon Park, Twickenham TW1 3DH. *T:* (020) 8241 6541, 07967 136453. *E:* erin.pizzey@blueyonder.co.uk. *W:* www.erinpizzey.com.

PLACE, Joanna Ruth; Executive Director, Human Resources, Bank of England, since 2014; *b* Derby, 21 June 1962; *d* of Frank Place and Stella Place; *m* 1999, Graeme Danton; one *s* two *d*. *Educ:* Fitzwilliam Coll., Cambridge (BSc Econ; PGCE Maths and PE). Teacher of Maths, Rainham Mark GS, 1984–86; Bank of England: Banking Supervisor, 1986–90; Internat. Div., 1990–92; Governor's Office, 1992–94; various managerial roles, 1994–2000; Hd, Monetary and Financial Statistics Div., 2000–04; Dir, Change, UK Border Agency, Home Office, 2004–07; Bank of England: Hd, Customer Banking, 2007–12; Dir, Regulatory Ops, 2012–14. Gov., Woking High Sch. *Recreations:* running, swimming, walking, family. *Address:* Bank of England, Threadneedle Street, EC2R 8AH. *T:* (020) 7601 4284. *E:* joanna.place@bankofengland.co.uk.

PLAISTOWE, (William) Ian (David), FCA; Managing Practice Director of Audit and Business Advisory Practice for Europe, Middle East, Africa and India, Arthur Andersen, 1993–2002; *b* 18 Nov. 1942; *s* of late David William Plaistowe and Julia (*née* Ross Smith); *m* 1968, Carolyn Anne Noble Wilson; two *s* one *d*. *Educ:* Marlborough Coll.; Queens' Coll., Cambridge. Joined Arthur Andersen & Co., 1964; Partner, 1976; Head of Accounting and Audit practice, London, 1984–87; Dir of Acctg and Audit for UK and Ireland, 1987–93. Chm., Auditing Practices Bd of UK and Ireland, 1994–2002; Mem., Internat. Audit and Assurance Standards Bd, 2002–04. Institute of Chartered Accountants in England and Wales: Chairman: London Soc. of Chartered Accountants, 1981–82; Mem. Council, 1985–99; Vice-Pres., 1990–91; Dep. Pres., 1991–92; Pres., 1992–93. Chm., FPA, 2006–12; Dir, Abbeyfield Soc., 2009– (Chm., 2015–). Mem. Council, Univ. of Buckingham, 2003–. Chm., Beacon Sch., 1999–2012. Master, Co. of Chartered Accountants in England and Wales, 2002–03. *Publications:* articles in learned jls. *Recreations:* golf, tennis, squash, ski-ing, gardening. *Address:* Heybote, Ellesborough, Aylesbury, Bucks HP17 0XF. *T:* (01296) 622758. *Clubs:* Carlton; Moor Park Golf, Huntercombe Golf.

PLANE, Robert Edward, FRAM; solo and chamber clarinettist; Principal Clarinet, BBC National Orchestra of Wales, since 1999; *b* Great Yarmouth, 13 April 1969; *s* of Nathaniel and Kathleen Plane; *m* 1997, Lucy Gould; one *s* two *d*. *Educ:* Chetham's Sch. of Music; Univ. of Bristol (BA Hons); Royal Acad. of Music (MMus; Dip. RAM). LRAM 1991; ARAM; FRAM 2014. Principal Clarinet: Northern Sinfonia, 1992–99; City of Birmingham SO, 2010–11. Winner, Royal Over-Seas League Music Competition, 1992. *Recreation:* marathon running. *Address:* 16 Teilo Street, Cardiff CF11 9JN. *T:* 07966 206634. *E:* rob.e.plane@googlemail.com. *W:* www.robertplane.com. *Club:* Royal Over-Seas League.

PLANT, family name of **Baron Plant of Highfield**.

PLANT OF HIGHFIELD, Baron *cr* 1992 (Life Peer), of Weelsby in the County of Humberside; **Raymond Plant,** PhD; DLitt; Professor of Jurisprudence and Legal Philosophy, King's College London, since 2001; *b* 19 March 1945; *s* of Stanley and Marjorie Plant; *m* 1967, Katherine Sylvia Dixon; three *s*. *Educ:* Havelock Sch., Grimsby; King's Coll. London (BA); Hull Univ. (PhD 1971). Lectr, then Sen. Lectr in Philosophy, Univ. of Manchester, 1967–79; Prof. of Politics, 1979–94, Pro-Chancellor, 1996–99, Res. Prof., 1999–2001, Univ. of Southampton; Master, St Catherine's Coll., Oxford, 1994–99. Vincent Wright Prof., Inst. d'Etudes Politiques de Paris, Sciences Po, 2008; Gresham Prof. of Divinity, 2012. Lectures: Stevenson, Univ. of Glasgow, 1981; Agnes Cumming, UC Dublin, 1987; Stanton, 1989–90 and 1990–91, Boutwood, 2006, Univ. of Cambridge; Sarum, 1991, Bampton, 2007, Univ. of Oxford; Ferguson, Manchester Univ., 1994; Scott Holland, Manchester Cathedral, 1995; Charles Gore, Westminster Abbey, 1995; J. P. MacIntosh Meml, Edinburgh Univ., 1995; Eleanor Rathbone, Bristol Univ., 1997; G. Ganz, Southampton Univ., 2005; A. J. Milne, Durham, 2006; Zutshi-Smith, Bristol, 2010. Chair: Labour Party Commn on Electoral Systems, 1991–93; Fabian Soc. Commn on Taxation and Citizenship, 1999–2000. President: Acad. of Learned Socs in Social Scis, 2000–01; NCVO, 1997–2002. Times columnist, 1988–92. Chm., Centrepoint, 2002–04. Lay Canon, Winchester Cathedral, 2008–. FKC 2008. Hon. Fellow: Cardiff Univ., 2000; St Catherine's Coll., Oxford, 2000; Harris Manchester Coll., Oxford, 2001. Hon. DLitt: London Guildhall Univ., 1993; Hull, 1994; DUniv: York, 2007; Winchester, 2008; Tallinn, 2012; Hon. LLD Southampton, 2012. *Publications:* Hegel, 1974, 2nd edn 1984; Community and Ideology, 1974; Political Philosophy and Social Welfare, 1981; Philosophy, Politics and Citizenship, 1984; Conservative Capitalism in Britain and the United States: a critical appraisal, 1988; Modern Political Thought, 1991; Politics, Theology and History, 2001; The Neo-Liberal State, 2009. *Recreations:* music, opera, thinking about the garden, listening to my wife playing the piano, reading. *Address:* 6 Woodview Close, Bassett, Southampton SO16 3PZ. *T:* (023) 8076 9529, (020) 7928 1330. *Club:* Athenæum.

PLANT, Dr Gordon Terence, FRCP, FRCOphth; Consultant Neurologist, National Hospital for Neurology and Neurosurgery, Moorfields Eye Hospital and St Thomas' Hospital, since 1991; *b* 4 July 1952; *s* of Thomas Edmund Plant and Sheila May Plant (*née* Atkinson); *m* 1978, Marilyn Jane Dirkin; three *d*. *Educ:* Downing Coll., Cambridge (BA 1974, MA 1977; MB BChir 1978; MD 1987). FRCP 1993; FRCOphth 2005. Hse Physician, St Thomas' Hosp., 1977; Hse Surgeon, Kingston Gen. Hosp., 1978; SHO, Westminster Hosp., 1978, Nat. Hosp., Queen Sq., 1979; Registrar in Neurol., Addenbrooke's Hosp., 1980–82. Wellcome Trust Res. Associate, Physiol Lab., Cambridge, 1982–85; Registrar, Nat. Hosp., Queen Sq., 1985–91; MRC Travelling Fellow, Smith-Kettlewell Res. Inst., San Francisco, 1989. Visiting Professor: City Univ., 2005–; Wills Eye Inst., Philadelphia, 2011. Pres., Clin. Neuroscis Section, RSocMed, 2011–12. Founder, UK Neuro-Ophthalmol. Special Interest Gp, 2008–. Member: British Is Neuro-ophthalmology Club, 1992–; Ophthalmic Club, 1996– (Sec., 2012–). Hon. Fellow, Neurological Soc. of Thailand, 2014. Editor-in-Chief, Neuro-ophthalmology, 2008–. Allvat Gulstrand Medal, Swedish Ophthalmol Soc., 2009; Claffey Medal, Sydney Eye Hosp., 2009; Lang Medal, RSocMed, 2010; Mooney Medal, Irish Ophthalmol Soc., 2013; Lettsonian Medal, Med. Soc. of London, 2016. *Publications:* Optic Neuritis, 1986; contribs to med., neurol, ophthalmol and visual sci. jls. *Recreations:* music, painting, book collecting. *Address:* 246 Sheen Lane, SW14 8RL. *T:* (020) 3448 3388, *Fax:* (020) 3448 8994. *E:* gordon@plant.globalnet.co.uk.

PLANT, Prof. Jane Ann, (Mrs P. R. Simpson), CBE 1997; PhD; CEng, CGeol; FRSE, FIMMM; FREng; Professor of Geochemistry, Imperial College London, since 2001; *b* 1 Feb. 1945; *d* of Ralph Lunn and Marjorie Lunn (*née* Langton); *m* 1st, 1967, Dr I. D. Plant (marr. diss. 1974); one *s*; 2nd, 1974, Prof. P. R. Simpson; one *s* one *d*. *Educ:* Liverpool Univ. (BSc 1966 with Dist.; BSc Hons 1967); Leicester Univ. (PhD 1977). CEng 1986; CGeol 1990; FRSE 2002; FREng 2012. British Geological Survey: SO to Atomic Energy Div. (subseq. Geochem. Div.), 1967–71; SO, 1971; PSO, 1977; sabbatical year to work in N America, 1988; Hd, Applied Geochem. Gp, 1989–91; Asst Dir and Chief Geochemist, 1991–97; Chief Scientist and a Dir, 2000–05. Vis. Prof., Liverpool Univ., 1992; Special Prof., Nottingham Univ., 1996. Mem., Royal Commn on Envmtl Pollution, 1999–2006; Chair, Adv. Cttee on Hazardous Substances, 2001–06 (Chm., UK Chemicals Stakeholders Forum, 2001–06); Mem. Council, All-Party Parly and Scientific Cttee, 2003–. Mem., Scientific Adv. Cttee, Coll. of Medicine, 2010–. Freeman, City of London, 1999; Mem., Water Conservators' Co., 1999. FRGS 1998; FRSA 2000; FRSocMed 2005. DUniv Open, 1997; Hon. DSc: Exeter, 2001; Kingston, 2003; Keele, 2005; Åbo/Turku, 2005; Leicester, 2005. Lord Lloyd of Kilgerran Award, 1999; Coke Medal, Geological Soc., 2009. *Publications:* Your Life in Your Hands, 2000; (with G. Tidey) The Plant Programme, 2001; (with G. Tidey) Understanding, Preventing and Overcoming Osteoporosis, 2003; (with G. Tidey) Prostate Cancer, 2004; Eating for Better Health, 2005; Beating Stress, Anxiety and Depression, 2008; (ed jtly) Pollutants, Human Health and the Environment: a risk-based approach, 2012; Beat Cancer,

2014; numerous peer-reviewed papers and contrib. books on econ. and envmtl geochem. *Recreations:* gardening, theatre. *Address:* Earth Science and Engineering, Royal School of Mines, Imperial College London, SW7 2AZ.

PLANT, Patrick Gerard; Partner, Linklaters LLP, since 1994; *b* Manchester, 11 April 1962; *s* of Walter Patrick Plant and Margaret Mary Plant. *Educ:* Univ. of Manchester (LLB Hons Law 1983). Articled clerk, Wilsons, Salisbury, 1984–86; admitted as solicitor, 1986; Assistant Solicitor: Linklaters and Paines, London, 1986–89; Mallesons Stephen Jaques, Sydney, 1989–90; Linklaters LLP, London, 1990–: Asst Solicitor, 1990–94; Global Hd, Real Estate, 2003–11. Non-exec. Dir, Falcon Property Trust, 2012–14. Mem. Bd, British Liby, 2012–. Hon. Lectr in Law, Faculty of Humanities, Univ. of Manchester, 2013–. Trustee, Royal London Soc. for Blind People, 2014–. *Recreations:* 20th century British art, family. *Address:* Linklaters LLP, One Silk Street, EC2Y 8HQ. *T:* (020) 7456 4718, *Fax:* (020) 7456 2222. *E:* patrick.plant@linklaters.com.

PLANT, Robert Anthony, CBE 2009; singer and songwriter; solo singer, since 1980; *b* W Bromwich, Staffs, 20 Aug. 1948; *m* 1968, Maureen; one *s* one *d* (and one *s* decd). Lead singer, New Yardbirds, later Led Zeppelin, 1968–80; albums: Led Zeppelin, 1969; Led Zeppelin II, 1969; Led Zeppelin III, 1970; Untitled, 1971; Houses of the Holy, 1973; Physical Graffiti, 1975; Presence, 1976; In Through the Out Door, 1979; Coda, 1982; solo albums: Pictures at Eleven, 1982; The Principle of Moments, 1983; Shaken 'n' Stirred, 1985; Now and Zen, 1988; Manic Nirvana, 1989; Fate of Nations, 1993; Dreamland, 2002; Sixty Six to Timbuktu, 2003; with The Honeydrippers, The Honeydrippers Volume I, 1984; with Jimmy Page: No Quarter—Unledded, 1994; Walking into Clarksdale, 1998; with The Strange Sensation, Mighty ReArranger, 2005; with Alison Krauss, Raising Sand, 2007 (Grammy Award, 2009); with Band of Joy, Band of Joy, 2010; with Sensational Space Shifters, Lullaby and… The Ceaseless Roar, 2014. *Address:* c/o Trinifold Management, 12 Oval Road, NW1 7DH.

PLANTIN, Marcus; healer and tutor, Ham Healing Centre, since 2005; *b* 23 Oct. 1945. Producer/director, BBC TV, 1970–84; London Weekend Television: Head of Light Entertainment, 1985–87; Controller of Entertainment, 1987–90; Dir of Progs, 1990–92; ITV Network Dir, 1992–97; Dir of Progs, LWT, 1997–2001; Dir of Entertainment, Granada, 2001–02; CEO, September Films, 2003–05. FRTS. *Address:* 4 Morgans House, Ham Common, Richmond TW10 7JU.

PLASCHKES, Sarah Georgina; QC 2011; a Recorder, since 2004; *b* Bournemouth, 15 July 1965; *d* of Eric and Sheila Plaschkes; two *d*. *Educ:* Bournemouth Sch. for Girls; Southampton Univ. (LLB). Called to the Bar, Inner Temple, 1988; in practice as barrister, specialising in professional discipline and criminal law. *Recreations:* swimming, cycling, running, theatre, films, miniature long-haired dachshunds. *Address:* QEB Hollis Whiteman, 1–2 Laurence Pountney Hill, EC4R 0EU. *E:* barristers@qebhw.co.uk.

PLASKETT, Maj.-Gen. Frederick Joseph, CB 1980; MBE 1966; FCILT; Director General and Chief Executive, Road Haulage Association, 1981–88; *b* 23 Oct. 1926; *s* of Frederick Joseph Plaskett and Grace Mary Plaskett; *m* 1st, 1950, Heather (*née* Kington) (*d* 1982); four *d*; 2nd, 1984, Mrs Patricia Joan Healy. *Educ:* Wallasey Grammar Sch.; Chelsea Polytechnic. RN (trainee pilot, FAA), 1944–45; transf. to Army, 1945; commnd infantry (Green Howards), 1946; RASC, 1951; RCT, 1965; regimental and staff appts, India, Korea, Nigeria, Malaya, Germany and UK; Student, Staff Coll., Camberley, 1958; Jt Services Staff Coll., 1964; Instr, Staff Coll., Camberley, 1966–68; Management Coll., Henley, 1969; RCDS, 1975; Dir of Movements (Army), 1975–78; Dir Gen., Transport and Movements (Army), 1978–81, retired. Col Comdt, RCT, 1981–91 (Rep. Col Comdt, 1989). Chm., British Railways Bd, London Midland Region, 1989–92 (Mem., 1986–88). Director: Foden Trucks (Paccar UK) (formerly Sandbach Engrg Co.), 1981–97; RHA Insce Services Ltd, 1982–88; British Road Federation, 1982–88. Comr, Royal Hosp., Chelsea, 1985–88. Freeman, City of London, 1979; Liveryman, Co. of Carmen, 1979–. *Publications:* Shoot Like a Gentleman! (memoir), 2005; numerous articles in mil. and commercial jls on defence and transport related subjects. *Recreations:* fishing, sailing, gardening. *Address:* c/o National Westminster Bank, The Commons, Shaftesbury, Dorset SP7 8JY.

See also J. F. G. Logan.

PLASKITT, James Andrew; Senior Counsel, Cicero Group, since 2014; *b* 23 June 1954; *s* of late Ronald Plaskitt and Phyllis Irene Plaskitt. *Educ:* Pilgrim Sch., Bedford; University Coll., Oxford (MPhil 1979; MA 1980). Lecturer in Politics: University Coll., Oxford, 1977–79; Christ Church, Oxford, 1984–86; Lectr in Govt, Brunel Univ., 1979–84; Oxford Analytica Ltd: Western European Editor, 1986–90; Dir of Consultancy, 1993–96. Mem. (Lab) Oxfordshire CC, 1985–97 (Leader, Labour Gp, 1990–96). Contested (Lab) Witney, 1992. MP (Lab) Warwick and Leamington, 1997–2010; contested (Lab) same seat, 2010. Parly Under-Sec. of State, DWP, 2005–08.

PLASSNIK, Ursula, DIur; Ambassador of Austria to France, since 2011; *b* 23 May 1956. *Educ:* elementary and grammar schs, Klagenfurt; High Sch., Foxcroft, Va; Vienna Univ. (DIur 1978); Coll. of Europe, Bruges (Postgrad. Dip.). Federal Ministry for Foreign Affairs, 1981–2008: COS of Vice Chancellor, 1997–2000, Federal Chancellor, 2000–04, Dr Wolfgang Schüssel, Federal Chancellery; Ambassador to Switzerland, 2004; Minister: for Foreign Affairs, 2004–07; for European and Internat. Affairs, 2007–08. MP (People's Party) Austria, 2006–07, 2008–11. *Address:* Austrian Embassy, 6 rue Fabert, 75007 Paris, France.

PLASTOW, Sir David (Arnold Stuart), Kt 1986; Chairman, Medical Research Council, 1990–98; *b* Grimsby, 9 May 1932; *s* of late James Stuart Plastow and Marie Plastow; *m* 1954, Barbara Ann May; one *s* one *d*. *Educ:* Culford Sch., Bury St Edmunds. Apprentice, Vauxhall Motors Ltd, 1950; joined Rolls-Royce Ltd, Motor Car Div., Crewe, Sept. 1958; apptd Marketing Dir, Motor Car Div., 1967; Managing Director: Motor Car Div., 1971; Rolls-Royce Motors Ltd, 1972; Vickers Plc: Dir, 1975–92; Man. Dir, 1980–86; Chief Exec., 1980–92; Chm., 1987–92. Dep. Chm., 1987–89, Jt Dep. Chm., 1989–94, Guinness PLC; Dep. Chm., TSB Gp, 1991–95; Chm., Inchcape plc, 1992–95; Regional Dir, Lloyds Bank, 1974–76; non-executive Director: GKN, 1978–84; Legal & General Gp Plc, 1985–87; Cable & Wireless, 1991–93; F. T. Everard & Sons, 1991–2001; Lloyds TSB, 1996–99. Trustee, Royal Opera House Trust, 1992–93 (Chm., 1992–93). Mem., European Adv. Council, Tenneco, 1984–86 and 1992–96; Bd Mem., Tenneco Inc., 1985–92, 1996–2004. Vice-Pres., Inst. of Motor Industry, 1974–82; Pres., SMMT, 1976–77, 1977–78 (Dep. Pres., 1978–79, 1979–80); Pres., Motor Industry Res. Assoc., 1978–81; Chm., Grand Council, Motor and Cycle Trades Benevolent Fund, 1976–82. Chm., Industrial Soc., 1983–87 (Mem., 1981); Dep. Chm., Listed Cos Adv. Cttee, 1987–90; Member: Council, CBI, 1983–92; BOTB, 1980–83; Engineering Council, 1980–83; Offshore Energy Technology Bd, 1985–86; Bd of Companions, BIM; Council, Regular Forces Employment Assoc. Patron, The Samaritans, 1987–99; Chm., 40th Anniversary Appeal Cttee, Mental Health Foundn, 1988–91; Gov., BUPA, 1990–95 (Dep. Chm., 1992–95). Chancellor, Univ. of Luton, 1993–2000 (Hon. Fellow, 1991). Chm. Governors, Culford Sch., 1979–2002. Pres., Crewe Alexandra FC, 1975–82. Liveryman, Worshipful Co. of Coachmakers & Coach Harness Makers. FRSA. Young Business Man of the Year Award, The Guardian, 1976. Hon. DSc Cranfield, 1978. *Recreations:* golf, music. *Clubs:* Royal and Ancient (St Andrews); Royal St George's (Sandwich); Senior Golfers' Society (Pres., 2011–13).

PLATELL, Amanda Jane; writer and broadcaster; columnist, Daily Mail, since 2007; *b* 12 Nov. 1957; *d* of Francis Ernest Platell and Norma June Platell. *Educ:* Univ. of Western Australia (BA Hons Philosophy and Politics). Dep. Ed., Today newspaper, 1987–92; Man. Ed., Mirror Gp, 1993; Mktg Dir, 1993–95, Man. Dir, 1995–96, The Independent; Acting Ed., Sunday Mirror, 1996–97; Ed., Sunday Express, 1998–99; Hd of Media, Cons. Party, 1999–2001. *Publications:* Scandal, 1999. *Recreations:* travelling, cooking, cars, writing.

PLATT, Alison; *see* Platt, E. A.

PLATT, Anthony Michael Westlake, CBE 1991; Chief Executive, London Chamber of Commerce and Industry, 1984–91; *b* 28 Sept. 1928; *s* of late James Westlake Platt, CBE and Veronica Norma Hope Platt (*née* Arnold); *m* 1st, 1952, Jennifer Susan Scott-Fox; three *s*; 2nd, 1984, Heather Mary Stubbs; one step *s* one step *d*; 3rd, 1987, Sarah Elizabeth Russell. *Educ:* Stowe School; Balliol College, Oxford (PPE 1951). Foreign Office, 1951, served Prague, 1953–54, NY, 1955–56; Shell Group of Cos: Switzerland, 1957; Guatemala, 1959; S Africa, 1961; Venezuela, 1963; London, 1969; The Hague, 1972; London, 1975–77 (Billiton UK); The Hague, 1977–78 (Billiton Internat.); Man. Dir, Consolidated Petroleum, London, 1979–84. Advr, Council of British Chambers in Europe, 1992–95. Freeman, City of London, 1991. *Publications:* (ed) Parallel 40 North to Eureka, 2000; Belovedest—A Marriage of Opposites, 2006. *Recreations:* walking, music, languages. *Address:* 17 Westgate Street, Bury St Edmunds, Suffolk IP33 1QG.

PLATT, David Wallace; QC 2011; *b* Northern Ireland, 1964; *s* of Christopher Platt and Susan Harriette La Nauze; *m* 2007, Jessica Perks; one *s*. *Educ:* Campbell Coll., Belfast; Trinity Hall, Cambridge (BA 1986; MA). Called to the Bar, Middle Temple, 1987; in practice as a barrister, specialising in personal injury, envmtl and insurance law. Presenter, BBC TV progs, The Stand and Dilemma, 1991–95. Contested (C) Cambridge, 1997. Governor: Churchill Gardens, 2003–11; Pimlico Sch., 2005–07. *Publications:* contrib. to various political and cultural jls. *Recreations:* walking, conservation, theatre, opera, J. R. R. Tolkien. *Address:* Crown Office Chambers, Temple, EC4Y 7HJ. *T:* (020) 7797 8100. *E:* platt@crownofficechambers.com. *Club:* Brooks's.

PLATT, Dame Denise, DBE 2004 (CBE 1996); Chair: Local Innovation Award Scheme, 2009–10; Commission for Social Care Inspection, 2004–09; *b* 21 Feb. 1945; *d* of Victor Platt and May Platt (*née* Keeling). *Educ:* UCW, Cardiff (BSc Econ 1967); AIMSW 1968. Social Worker, then Sen. Social Worker, Middx Hosp., 1968–73; Sen. Social Worker, Guy's Hosp., 1973–76; Gp Leader, Southwark Social Services, 1976–78; Prin. Social Worker, Hammersmith Hosp., 1978–83; London Borough of Hammersmith and Fulham: Asst Dir, Social Services, 1983–86; Dir, 1986–95 (on leave of absence, 1994–95); Under Sec., Social Services, AMA, 1994–97; Hd of Social Services, LGA, 1997–98; Jt Hd, Social Care Gp, DoH, 1998–2001; Chief Inspector, Social Services Inspectorate, 1998–2004 and Dir of Children, Older People and Social Care Services, DoH, 2001–04. Pres., Assoc. Dirs of Social Services, 1993–94. Chm., Nat. AIDS Trust, 2006– (Trustee, 1987–98; Vice Chm., 1994–98); Trustee and Dir, FPA, 2005–10; Trustee: NSPCC, 2007–; Adventure Capital Fund, 2008–11. Member: Central Council Educn and Trng in Social Work, 1994–98; Youth Justice Task Force, 1997–98; Disability Rights Task Force, 1997–98; Ind. Reference Gp on Mental Health, 1997–98; Review Team, Strategic Review of London's Health Services, 1997–98; Ind. Review Bd, Cheshire CC Fire and Rescue Service, 2007–; Audit Commn, 2007–10; Cttee on Standards in Public Life, 2008–14; Commn on Assisted Dying, 2010–12; GMC, 2013–. Mem., Adv. Bd, Sch. of Social Care Res., NIHR, LSE, 2008–. Patron, Advocacy Plus, 2009–12. Trustee, Lloyds (formerly Lloyds TSB) Foundn for England and Wales, 2011–. Governor: Nat. Inst. for Social Work, 1995–98 (Chm., 1997–99); Univ. of Bedfordshire, 2006–12. Hon. Fellow, Univ. of Bedfordshire, 2014. Hon. DSocSc Brunel, 1998; Hon. LLD Brighton, 2008. *Publications:* various articles in social services press. *Recreations:* music, watercolours, walking, travel. *Club:* Reform.

PLATT, Eleanor Frances; QC 1982; a Recorder of the Crown Court, 1982–2004; a Deputy High Court Judge, Family Division, 1987–2004; *b* 6 May 1938; *er d* of late Dr Maurice Leon Platt and Sara Platt (*née* Stein), Hove, Sussex; *m* 1963; two *c*. *Educ:* Hove County School for Girls; University College London. LLB 1959. Called to the Bar, Gray's Inn, 1960; Jt Head of Specialist Family Law Chambers, 1990–2007. Mem., Matrimonial Causes Rule Cttee, 1986–90. Dep. Chm., NHS Tribunal, 1995–2001; Legal Assessor: GMC, 1995–; GDC, 2009–; Mem., Gene Therapy Adv. Cttee, 1993–98. Treas., Family Law Bar Assoc., 1990–95 (Acting Chm., 1995); Pres., Jewish Family Mediation Register, 1998–. Chm., Law, Parly and Gen. Purposes Cttee, 1988–94, Dep. Chm. Defence Bd, 1997–2003, Vice Pres., 2003–06, Chm. Family Law Gp, 2006–, Bd of Deputies of British Jews; Chm., New London Synagogue, 1994–99. Pres., Medico-Legal Soc., 2002–04 (Mem. Council, 1995–). Mem., Ethics and Jewish Genealogy Panel, Internat. Inst. for Jewish Genealogy, 2012–. *Recreations:* the arts, travel, grandchildren. *Address:* One Garden Court, Temple, EC4Y 9BJ. *T:* (020) 7797 7900. *E:* platt@1gc.com.

PLATT, (Elizabeth) Alison, (Mrs William Ward), CMG 2011; Group Chief Executive, Countrywide plc, since 2014; *b* Oldham, 25 Feb. 1962; *d* of Gerard and Elizabeth Platt; *m* 2001, William Ward; one *s*. *Educ:* Adelphi House Grammar Sch., Salford. Mgt Prog., British Airways plc, 1980–93; Bupa Health and Wellbeing: Dir, Customer Service, 1993–95; Dir, Ops, 1995–98; Dep. Man. Dir, 1998–2004; Chief Operating Officer, Bupa Hosps, 2004–07; Bupa: Gp Develt Dir, 2007–09; Man. Dir, Europe, 2009–10; Divl Man. Dir, Europe and N America, 2010–12; Man. Dir, Internat. Develt Markets, 2012–14. Chair, Opportunity Now, 2009–13. Non-executive Director: FCO, 2005–10; Cable & Wireless Communications, 2012–. *Recreations:* reading, running, football (watching). *Address:* Countrywide plc, County House, 100 New London Road, Chelmsford CM2 0RG.

PLATT, Prof. Frances Mary, PhD; FMedSci; Professor of Biochemistry and Pharmacology, University of Oxford, since 2008; Fellow, Merton College, Oxford, since 2007; *b* Shipley, W Yorks, 12 April 1961; *d* of David Judson and Helen Judson; *m* 1985, Nicholas Platt; one *s* one *d* (twins). *Educ:* Bradford Girls' Grammar Sch.; Imperial Coll. London (BSc Zool. 1982); Univ. of Bath (PhD Animal Physiol. 1986). Postdoctoral Res. Fellow, Washington Univ. Med. Sch., St Louis, 1986–87; Res. Scientist, Monsanto Co., St Louis, 1987–89; University of Oxford: Glycobiology Institute, Department of Biochemistry: Sen. Res. Scientist, Searle Res. Gp, 1989–93; Sen. Res. Fellow, 1993–96; Lister Institute Sen. Res. Fellow, 1996–2002; Reader in Glycobiol., 1999–2006; Reader, Dept of Pharmacol., 2006–08. FMedSci 2011. *Recreations:* horse riding, gardening, keeping chickens. *Address:* Department of Pharmacology, University of Oxford, Mansfield Road, Oxford OX1 3QT. *E:* frances.platt@pharm.ox.ac.uk.

PLATT, Jane Christine, CBE 2013; Chief Executive, National Savings and Investments, since 2006; *b* 8 Jan. 1957; *d* of George Platt and Miriam Platt (*née* Knowles); *m* 1980, David Bill. *Educ:* St Catherine's Coll., Oxford (MA). Sen. Pension Fund Manager, Mercury Asset Mgt, 1982–88; Dir, Business Develt, 1988–94, Man. Dir, 1994–95, BZW Investment Management; Chief Operating Officer, Barclays Asset Mgt, 1995–96; CEO, Barclays Stockbrokers and Barclays Bank Trust Co., 1996–2001; Chief Operating Officer, (Business Divs) Reuters, 2001–04. Non-executive Director: Edinburgh UK Investment Trust Plc, 2004–06; Witan Plc, 2005–06; Financial Conduct Authy, 2013–. Chartered Fellow, CISI, 2010. Mem., Cornhill Club. *Recreation:* performing arts. *Address:* National Savings and Investments, 1 Drummond Gate, SW1V 2QX. *T:* (020) 7932 6600. *E:* jane.platt@nsandi.com.

PLATT, His Honour John Richard; a Circuit Judge, 1992–2012; *b* 21 Nov. 1942; *s* of Arthur James Platt and Joan Platt; *m* 1986, Jayne Mary Webb; two *d*. *Educ:* Sherborne Sch.; Trinity Hall, Cambridge. Partner, Lee Davies & Co., Solicitors, 1969–82; Registrar and District Judge, Bow County Court, 1982–92. *Publications:* A Guide to Judicial Pensions for

Circuit Judges, 1995; A Guide to Judicial Pensions for District Judges, 1996; A Guide to Judicial Pensions for Stipendiary Magistrates, 1996; A Guide to the Judicial Pensions and Retirement Act, 1997; contribs to Jordans Civil Court Service, New Law Jl, Liverpool Law Review, Family Law. *Recreations:* wine and food, music, travel.

PLATT, Margaret; *see* Wright, Margaret.

PLATT, Sir Martin Philip, 3rd Bt *cr* 1959, of Grindleford, co. Derby; *b* 9 March 1952; *o s* of Hon. Sir Peter Platt, 2nd Bt, AM and of Jean Halliday Platt (*née* Brentnall); *S* father, 2000; *m* 1971, Francis Corinne Moana, *d* of Trevor Samuel Conley; two *s* two *d. Heir: s* Philip Stephen Platt, *b* 17 Oct. 1972.

PLATT, Michael Edward Horsfall; Pensions Ombudsman, 1991–94; *b* 24 Aug. 1934; *s* of Fred Horsfall Platt and Alice Martha Taylor Platt (*née* Wilde). *Educ:* Taunton Sch.; The Queen's Coll., Oxford. Nat. Service, RAF, 1952–54. Min. of Labour, 1959; Min. of Pensions and Nat. Insurance, 1960; Min. of Social Security, 1966; Private Sec. to Minister of State, DHSS, 1968–70; Cabinet Office, 1970–71; DHSS, 1971–86; Chief Adjudication Officer, 1986–90. *Recreations:* theatre, music. *Address:* c/o Office of the Pensions Ombudsman, 11 Belgrave Road, SW1V 1RB. *T:* (020) 7834 9144.

PLATT, Stephen, (Steve); writer and journalist; *b* 29 Sept. 1954; *s* of Kenneth Norman Platt and Joyce (*née* Pritchard); one *d. Educ:* Longton High Sch., Stoke-on-Trent; Wade Deacon Sch., Widnes; LSE (BSc (Econ)). Teacher, Moss Brook Special Sch., Widnes, 1972–73; Dir, Self Help Housing Resource Library, Poly. of N London, 1977–80; Co-ordinator, Islington Community Housing, 1980–83; News Editor, subseq. Acting Editor, New Society, 1985–88; Editor: Roof, 1988; Midweek, 1988–89; columnist and writer, 1988–91; Editor, New Statesman and Society, 1991–96; freelance writer, 1996–. Editor, Enjoying the Countryside, 1988–93; Editl Consultant, Channel 4, 1996–; Website Editor: Time Team, 1999–2010; Dispatches, 1999–2005. Hon. Chm., Medical Aid for Iraq, 1991–. *Publications:* various. *Recreations:* archaeology, amphibians, bears (real and fictional), countryside, football, growing things, mountains, music, poetry, running, long-distance walking. *Address:* 46 Tufnell Park Road, N7 0DT. *T:* (020) 7263 4185. *E:* mail@steveplatt.net. *Clubs:* Red Rose; Port Vale.

PLATT, Terence Charles, CB 1996; Deputy Under-Secretary of State and Principal Establishment Officer, Home Office, 1992–96; *b* 22 Sept. 1936; *yr s* of Bertram Reginald Platt, QPM and Nina Platt; *m* 1959, Margaret Anne Cotmore; two *s. Educ:* St Olave's and St Saviour's Grammar School; Joint Services School for Linguists; Russian Interpreter. HM Immigration Officer, 1957; Asst Principal, Home Office, 1962; Principal, 1966; Cabinet Office, 1970; Principal Private Sec. to Sec. of State for NI (Rt Hon. William Whitelaw), 1972–73; Asst Sec., Home Office, 1973–81; Asst Under-Sec. of State and Princ. Estabt and Finance Officer, NI Office, 1981–82; Asst Under-Sec. of State and Dir of Regimes and Services, Prison Dept, Home Office, 1982–86; Asst Under-Sec. of State (Ops and Resources), Immigration and Nationality Dept, Home Office, 1986–92; Chief Inspector, Immigration Service, 1991–92. Mem., Civil Service Appeal Bd, 1997–2001. *Publications:* New Directions in Prison Design (Wkg Party Report), 1985. *Recreations:* photography, butterflies, water-colour painting.

PLATT, Prof. Trevor, PhD; FRS 1998; FRSC 1990; Executive Director, Partnership for Observation of the Global Oceans, Plymouth Marine Laboratory, 2008–14, now Professorial Fellow; Head of Biological Oceanography, Bedford Institute of Oceanography, Nova Scotia, 1972–2002, Emeritus Scientist, since 2009; Adjunct Professor, Dalhousie University, Canada, since 1980; *b* 12 Aug. 1942; *s* of John Platt and Lily Platt (*née* Hibbert); *m* 1988, Shuba Sathyendranath. *Educ:* Univ. of Nottingham (BSc); Univ. of Toronto (MA); Dalhousie Univ. (PhD 1970). Res. Scientist in Marine Ecology, Bedford Inst. of Oceanography, Nova Scotia, 1965–72. Chairman: Jt Global Ocean Flux Study, 1991–93; Internat. Ocean-colour Co-ordinating Gp, 1996–2005. Pres., Amer. Soc. Limnology and Oceanography, 1990–92. *Publications:* numerous res. papers in scholarly jls. *Recreations:* cycling, fly-fishing, languages, music. *Address:* Bedford Institute of Oceanography, Dartmouth, NS B2Y 4A2, Canada. *T:* (902) 4263793; Plymouth Marine Laboratory, Prospect Place, The Hoe, Plymouth, Devon PL1 3DH. *T:* (01752) 633100.

PLATTEN, Rt Rev. Stephen George; Rector, St Michael's, Cornhill, City of London, since 2014; an Honorary Assistant Bishop: Diocese of London, since 2014; Diocese of Newcastle, since 2014; Diocese of Southwark, since 2015; *b* 17 May 1947; *s* of George Henry and Marjory Platten; *m* 1972, Rosslie Thompson; two *s. Educ:* Stationers' Company's Sch.; Univ. of London (BEd Hons 1972); Trinity Coll., Oxford (Dip. Theol. 1974; BD 2003); Cuddesdon Theol Coll. Shell Internat. Petroleum Co., 1966–68. Deacon 1975, Priest 1976; Asst Curate, St Andrew, Headington, Oxford, 1975–78; Chaplain and Tutor, Lincoln Theol Coll., 1978–82; Diocesan Dir of Ordinands and Canon Residentiary, Portsmouth Cathedral, 1983–89; Dir, post-ordination trng and continuing ministerial educn, Dio. Portsmouth, 1984–89; Archbishop of Canterbury's Sec. for Ecumenical Affairs, 1990–95; Dean of Norwich, 1995–2003; Bishop of Wakefield, 2003–14; Chaplain, Order of St John, S and W Yorks Priory, 2003–14. Hon. Canon: Canterbury Cathedral, 1990–95; St John's Cathedral, Musoma, Tanzania, 2008–. Anglican Sec., ARCIC (II), 1990–95; Chm., Liturgical Commn, 2005–. Chairman: Soc. for Study of Christian Ethics, 1983–88; Govs, Anglican Centre in Rome, 2001–; Council, Coll. of the Resurrection, 2004–14. Minister Provincial, European Province, Third Order, SSF, 1991–96. Dir, SCM Press, 1990– (Chm., 2001–); Member: Council, Hymns Ancient and Modern, 1997– (Chm., 2014–); Faith and Order Commn (formerly Adv. Gp), C of E, 2000–10, Faith and Order Commn, 2010–12; Cathedrals Fabric Commn for England, 2005–. Entered H of L, 2009. Member: Exec., Georgian Gp, 2014–; Council, RSCM, 2014–; Council, Guild of Church Musicians, 2014–. Trustee: Hepworth Wakefield, 2007–14; Media Standards Trust, 2008–. Lectures: Cheney, Yale, 1998; Warburton, Lincoln's Inn, 2004. Guestmaster, Nikaean Club, 1990–95. Liveryman, Stationers' Co., 2004 (Mem., Ct of Assts, 2011–). Hon. FGCM 2012. Hon. DLitt East Anglia, 2003; DUniv Huddersfield, 2012. *Publications:* (series editor) Ethics and Our Choices, 1990–; (jtly) Spirit and Tradition: an essay on Change, 1996; Pilgrims, 1996; (ed jtly) New Soundings, 1997; Augustine's Legacy: authority and leadership in the Anglican Communion, 1997; (ed jtly) Flagships of the Spirit: cathedrals in society, 1998; Pilgrim Guide to Norwich, 1998; Cathedrals and Abbeys of England, 1999, 2nd edn 2011; Ink and Spirit, 2000; Rebuilding Jerusalem: the Church's hold on hearts and minds, 2007; Vocation: singing the Lord's song, 2007; contributor: Deacons in the Ministry of the Church, 1987; Spirituality and Psychology, 1990; Say One for Me, 1991; (and ed) Seeing Ourselves: who are the interpreters of contemporary society?, 1998; (and ed) The Retreat of the State, 1999; (and ed) Open Government, 2002; A New Dictionary of Liturgy and Worship, 2002; (and ed) Runcie: on reflection, 2002; (and ed) Anglicanism and the Western Tradition, 2003; Jesus in History, Thought and Culture, 2003, 2nd edn as Jesus: the complete guide, 2005; (and ed jtly) Dreaming Spires: cathedrals in a new age, 2006; In Search of Humanity and Deity: a celebration of John Macquarrie's theology, 2006; (and ed jtly) Reinhold Niebuhr and Contemporary Politics: God and power, 2010; Unity in Process: reflections on ecumenical activity, 2012; (and ed) Comfortable Words: polity, piety and the Book of Common Prayer, 2012; (contrib.) Liturgical Spirituality: Anglican reflections on the Church's prayer; contribs to theol and educnl jls. *Recreations:* walking, music, literature, Land Rovers, Northumberland. *Address:* 73a Gloucester Place, W1U 8JW. *T:* (020) 7283 3121. *E:* stephen.platten@icloud.com. *Clubs:* Athenæum, City University.

PLATTS, (Charles) Graham (Gregory); His Honour Judge Platts; a Circuit Judge, since 2005; *b* 25 Aug. 1956; *s* of Arthur Platts and Georgina Platts; *m* 1985, Hazel Carty; one *s* one *d. Educ:* Fitzwilliam Coll., Cambridge (BA 1977). Called to the Bar, Gray's Inn, 1978; in practice as barrister specialising in clinical negligence and personal injury, 1978–2005; Asst Recorder, 1999–2000; a Recorder, 2000–05. Pt-time Legal Mem., 2002–05, Mem., Restricted Patients' Panel, 2007–, Mental Health Rev. Tribunal. *Recreations:* piano, walking, ski-ing, Manchester City FC.

PLATTS-MILLS, Mark Fortescue; QC 1995; *b* 17 Jan. 1951; *s* of John Faithful Fortescue Platts-Mills, QC; *m* 1982, Dr Juliet Anne Britton; one *s. Educ:* Bryanston Sch.; Balliol Coll., Oxford (BA Eng. Sci. and Econ.). Called to the Bar, Inner Temple, 1974; Bencher, Lincoln's Inn, 2006. *Recreations:* gardening, hockey, cricket. *Address:* 8 New Square, Lincoln's Inn, WC2A 3QP.

PLATTS-MILLS, Prof. Thomas Alexander, FRS 2010; Professor of Medicine, Head of Division of Allergy and Clinical Immunology, and Head of Asthma and Allergic Diseases, University of Virginia, since 1982; *b* Colchester, 22 Nov. 1941; *s* of John Faithful Fortescue Platts-Mills, QC, and Janet Katherine Platts-Mills (*née* Cree); *m* 1970, Roberta Rosenstock; three *s* one *d. Educ:* University College Sch., Hampstead; Balliol Coll., Oxford (BA 1963; BM BCh 1967); St Thomas' Hospital, London. Fellow, Johns Hopkins Univ., 1971–74; Perm. Mem., Clinical Res. Centre, MRC, 1974–82. Pres., Amer. Acad. of Allergy, Asthma and Immunology, 2006–07. *Publications:* over 330 articles in scientific jls. *Recreations:* hiking, sailing. *Address:* University of Virginia School of Medicine, Box 801355, Charlottesville, VA 22908, USA. *T:* (434) 9245917. *E:* tap2z@virginia.edu.

See also M. F. Platts-Mills.

PLAYER, Dr David Arnott, FRCPE, FRCPsych, FFCM; District Medical Officer, South Birmingham Health Authority, 1987–91; *b* 2 April 1927; *s* of John Player and Agnes Gray; *m* 1955, Anne Darragh; two *s. Educ:* Calder Street Sch.; Bellahouston Acad., Glasgow; Glasgow Univ. (MB, ChB 1949; DPH 1960); DPM RCSI 1964; St Andrews Univ. (MA Hons 1995). House Surgeon, Dumfries and Galloway Royal Infirmary, 1950; Consultant in Dermatology and VD, RAMC (Far East), 1950–52; House Surgeon, Western Infirmary, Glasgow, 1952; House Physician, Bridge of Earn Hosp., 1952–53; House Surgeon (Obst., Gyn. and Paed.), Halifax Royal Infirmary, 1953–54; GP, W Cumberland and Dumfriesshire, 1954–59; Registrar (Infectious Diseases), Paisley Infectious Diseases Hosp., 1959–60; Asst MOH, Dumfriesshire, 1960–62; Registrar (Psychiatry), Crichton Royal Hosp., Dumfries, 1962–64; MOH, Dumfries Burgh, 1964–70; MO (Mental Health Div.), SHHD and Med. and Psych. Adviser to Sec. of State for Scotland on Scottish Prison and Borstal Service, 1970–73; Dir, Scottish Health Educn Group, 1973–82; Dir Gen., Health Educn Council, 1982–87. Hon. Vis. Prof., Dept of Clinical Epidemiology and Gen. Practice, Royal Free Hosp. Sch. of Medicine, 1983–. *Publications:* articles in Health Bulletin, Internat. Jl of Health Educn, Scottish Trade Union Review. *Recreations:* golf, cycling. *Address:* 57 Learmonth Court, Edinburgh EH4 1PD.

PLAYER, Gary James; professional golfer, since 1953; *b* Johannesburg, 1 Nov. 1935; *s* of Francis Harry Audley Player and late Muriel Marie Ferguson; *m* 1957, Vivienne, *d* of Jacob Wynand Verwey; two *s* four *d. Educ:* King Edward Sch., Johannesburg. Won first, Dunlop tournament, 1956; major championship wins include: British Open, 1959, 1968, 1974; US Masters, 1961, 1974, 1978; US PGA, 1962, 1972; US Open, 1965; S African Open, thirteen times, 1956–81; S African PGA, 1959, 1960, 1969, 1979, 1982; Australian Open, seven times, 1958–74; Johnnie Walker Trophy, Spain, 1984; World Match Play Tournament, 1965, 1966, 1968, 1971, 1973. *Publications:* Golf Begins at 50 (with Desmond Tolhurst), 1988; To Be the Best, 1991; The Meaning of Life, 2000.

PLAYFORD, His Honour Jonathan Richard; QC 1982; a Circuit Judge, 1998–2006; *b* 6 Aug. 1940; *s* of late Cecil R. B. Playford and Euphrasia J. Playford; *m* 1978, Jill Margaret Dunlop; one *s* one *d. Educ:* Eton Coll.; London Univ. (LLB). Called to the Bar, Inner Temple, 1962, Bencher, 1991; a Recorder, 1985–98. Mem., CICB, 1995–98. Freeman, Clockmakers' Co., 2004. *Recreations:* music, horology, golf. *Address:* c/o Reading Crown Court, Old Shire Hall, Forbury, Reading RG1 3EH. *Clubs:* Garrick; Huntercombe Golf (Henley); New Zealand Golf.

PLAYLE, Colin; Managing Director, Cicero, The Talking Company, 1995–2012; *b* 13 May 1933; *s* of James and Florence Playle; *m* 1st, 1957, Reena Mary Cuppleditch (marr. diss. 1975); two *d*; 2nd, 1976, Patricia Margaret Golds (*d* 1998); 3rd, 2007, Rosemary Margaret Henderson. *Educ:* University College London (BA Hons). CompIGasE. British Gas: Marketing and Customer Service, E Midlands Gas Bd, 1957–75; Regl Marketing Manager, E Midlands, 1975–78; Dir of Marketing, British Gas NE, 1978–86; Sen. Mem., British Gas Privatisation Team, 1986; HQ Dir, Industrial and Commercial Gas, London, 1988–91; Regl Chm., British Gas Scotland, 1991–94; Project Dir, Retail, 1994–95. Chm., Combined Heat and Power Assoc., 1991–93. Vis. Prof. in Business Studies, Liverpool Business Sch., 1997–2012. Co-ordinator, Azerbaijan, TAM programme, EBRD, 1999–2000. *Recreations:* ski-ing, ornithology, modern literature, theatrical productions. *Address:* Upton Barn, 83 Main Street, Upton, Newark, Notts NG23 5SY.

PLEASENCE, Prof. Pascoe Thomas; Professor of Empirical Legal Studies, University College London, since 2007; *b* London, 24 May 1965; *s* of Michael Cadman and Angela Pleasence; partner, Sophie Weeks; one *d. Educ:* Hampton Sch.; University Coll. London (BA Philosophy); St Edmund's Coll., Cambridge (MPhil Criminol. 1989); City Univ. (DipLaw); Inns of Court Sch. of Law. Called to the Bar, Middle Temple, 1991; Hd, Legal Services Res. Centre, London, 1995–2009; Sen. Res. Fellow, Law and Justice Foundn of NSW, Sydney, 2012–14; Man. Dir, Pascoe Pleasence Ltd, 2011–. *Publications:* Profiling Civil Litigation, 1996; Personal Injury Litigation in Practice, 1998; Local Legal Need, 2001; Causes of Action: civil law and social justice, 2004, 2nd edn 2006; Transforming Lives, 2007; Reaching Further, 2009; In Need of Advice?: findings of a small business legal needs benchmarking survey, 2013; Paths to Justice: a past, present and future road map, 2013; Reshaping Legal Services, 2014; How People Resolve Legal problems, 2014; contrib. articles to jls. *Recreations:* travel, music, swimming; formerly surf life saver, Queenscliff Beach, Sydney. *Address:* UCL Laws, Bentham House, Endsleigh Gardens, WC1H 0EG. *E:* p.pleasence@ucl.ac.uk.

PLEDGER, Air Chief Marshal Sir Malcolm (David), KCB 2001; OBE 1988; AFC 1981; *b* 24 July 1948; *m* 1969, Betty Barker Kershaw; two *s. Educ:* Newcastle Univ. (BSc 1st Cl. Chemistry 1970). Commnd RAF, 1970; served RAF Stations at Akrotiri, Shawbury, Sek Kong, Upavon, RAF Staff Coll., and MoD, 1972–85; OC 240 Operational Conversion Unit, RAF Odiham, 1985–88, incl. tour as OC 78 Sqdn, RAF Mount Pleasant, Falkland Is; Air Sec.'s Dept, 1988–90; Station Comdr, RAF Shawbury, 1990–92; rcds 1993; Air Officer Plans, HQ RAF Strike Command, 1993–97; COS, Dep. C-in-C and AOC, Directly Administered Units, HQ RAF Logistics Comd, 1997–99; Air Mem. for Logistics and AOC-in-C, RAF Logistics Comd, 1999; DCDS (Personnel), 1999–2002; Chief of Defence Logistics, MoD, 2002–04. *Recreation:* golf. *Club:* Royal Air Force.

PLEMING, Nigel Peter; QC 1992; a Judge of the Courts of Appeal of Jersey and Guernsey, since 2007; *b* 13 March 1946; *s* of late Rev. Percy Francis Pleming and Cynthia Myra Pleming (later Mrs Leslie Tuxworth); *m* 1979, Evelyn Carol Joan Hoffmann; one *s* two *d. Educ:* King Edward VI Grammar Sch., Spilsby; Kingston Polytechnic (LLB); University Coll. London (LLM). Lectr, Kingston Poly., 1969–73; called to the Bar, Inner Temple, 1971, Bencher, 2001; in practice at the Bar, 1974–; Junior Counsel to the Crown (Common Law), 1987–92; Member: Belize Bar, 2010–; BVI Bar, 2013–; occasional Mem., Bars of Hong Kong, Cayman Is, and Trinidad and Tobago. Vice-Chm., Mental Health Act Commn, 1994–97; Mem., Govt working party on mental health reform, 1998–99. Mem., UK Res. Integrity Office, 2009–. Hon. LLD Kingston, 1999. *Recreations:* theatre, guitar, watching cricket. *Address:* 39 Essex Street, WC2R 3AT. *T:* (020) 7832 1111. *Club:* Garrick.

PLEMING, Richard Thomas Francis; Headmaster, Charterhouse, since 2014; *b* Cuckfield, Sussex, 20 May 1962; *s* of late Peter Pleming and of Morag Pleming; *m* 1989, Rachel Crowther; one *s* four *d*. *Educ:* Pembroke Coll., Cambridge (BA 1st Cl. Hons Eng. 1984). Mktg Exec., Scottish Opera, 1984–85; Corporate Finance Exec., Schroders, 1985–88; Investment Controller, Investors in Industry, 1988–90; Teacher of English: St Paul's Sch., Barnes, 1990–91; Eton Coll., 1991–97; Hd of English, 1997–2007, Housemaster, 2006–11, St Edward's, Oxford; Headmaster, Wrekin Coll., 2011–13. *Recreations:* hill walking, reading, opera, dogs, fatherhood, singing, church visiting, five-a-side football. *Address:* Charterhouse, Godalming, Surrey GU7 2DX. *T:* (01483) 291600.

PLENDER, John; *see* Plender, W. J. T.

PLENDER, Hon. Sir Richard (Owen), Kt 2008; a Judge of the High Court of Justice, Queen's Bench Division, 2008–10; Professor of Economic and Commercial Law, University of Groningen, Netherlands, 2010–14; *b* 9 Oct. 1945; *s* of George Plender and Louise Mary (*née* Savage); *m* 1978, Patricia Clare (*née* Ward); two *d*. *Educ:* Dulwich Coll.; Queens' Coll., Cambridge (MA, LLB; LLD 1993); Univ. of Illinois (LLM; JSD 1972); Univ. of Sheffield (PhD 1973). Called to the Bar, Inner Temple, 1972, Bencher, 1996; in practice at the Bar, 1974–2008; QC 1989; Recorder, 1998–2008. Consultant, UN Law and Population Programme, 1972–74; Legal Adviser, UN High Comr for Refugees, 1974–78; Legal Sec., Court of Justice of European Communities, 1980–83; Dir of Studies, 1987, Dir of Res., 1988, and Lectr, 1998, Hague Acad. of Internat. Law; Dir, Centre of European Law, KCL, 1988–91; Special Legal Advr to States of Jersey, 1988–2008. Leverhulme Fellow, Yale Law Sch., 1980; British Acad. Fellow, Soviet Acad. of Sciences, 1985; Sen. Mem., Robinson Coll., Cambridge, 1983–; Associate Prof., Univ. de Paris II (Univ. de Droit, d'Economie et des Sciences Sociales), 1989–90; Hon. Vis. Prof., City Univ., 1991–. *Publications:* International Migration Law, 1972, 2nd edn 1988; (ed and contrib.) Fundamental Rights, 1973; Cases and Materials on the Law of the European Communities, 1980 (with J. Usher), 3rd edn 1993; A Practical Introduction to European Community Law, 1980; (with J. Peres Santos) Introducción al Derecho Comunitario Europeo, 1984; Basic Documents on International Migration Law, 1988, 3rd edn 2006; (ed and contrib.) Legal History and Comparative Law: essays in honour of Albert Kiralfy, 1990; The European Contracts Convention: the Rome Convention on the Choice of Law for Contracts, 1991, 3rd edn (with M. Wilderspin) as The European Private International Law of Obligations, 2009; (ed and contrib.) The European Courts Practice and Precedents, 1996, supplement 1997, as European Courts Procedure, 2000–; contribs in English, French, German and Spanish to jls and encyclopedias. *Recreations:* writing light verse, classical music (especially sacred choral). *Address:* The Old Rectory, Sundridge, Kent TN14 6EA.

PLENDER, (William) John (Turner), FCA; writer and columnist, Financial Times, since 1981; *b* Cardiff, 9 May 1945; *s* of William Plender and late Averil Maud Plender (*née* Turnbull); *m* 1st, 1972, Sophia Mary, *e d* of late Alistair and Nancy Crombie (marr. diss. 1989); one *s* two *d*; 2nd, 1997, Stephanie Julia Michell, *d* of late David and Joan Harris; two *s*. *Educ:* Downside Sch.; Oriel Coll., Oxford (BA). FCA 1970. Chartered Accountant, Deloitte, Plender, Griffiths & Co., 1967–70; Staff writer: Investors Chronicle, 1970–71; The Times, 1972–74; Financial Ed., Economist, 1974–79; Mem., Planning Staff, FCO, 1980–81; freelance journalist, publisher, author and broadcaster, 1982–. Chm., Pensions and Investment Res. Consultants, 1992–2002. Non-executive Director: Quintain Estates and Development plc, 2002–10 (Chm., 2007–09); OMFIF, 2012– (Chm., 2014–). Member: Co. Law Rev. Steering Gp, DTI, 1998–2001; Private Sector Adv. Gp on Corporate Governance, World Bank/OECD, 2002–. Mem., Quality of Mkts Adv. Cttee, London Stock Exchange, 1992–95; Chm., Adv. Council, Centre for Study of Financial Innovation, 1997–. Mem., Adv. Bd, Assoc. of Corporate Treasurers, 2002–. Trustee, Pearson Gp Pension Fund, 2010–. Sen. Wincott Award for Financial Journalism, 1994. *Publications:* That's The Way The Money Goes, 1981; (with P. Wallace) The Square Mile, 1985; A Stake in the Future, 1997; Going Off the Rails, 2003; (with A. Persaud) Ethics and Finance, 2007; Capitalism: money, morals and markets, 2015. *Recreation:* piano. *Address:* c/o The Financial Times, Number One, Southwark Bridge, SE1 9HL. *T:* (020) 7873 3000, *Fax:* (020) 7478 9438. *E:* john.plender@ft.com. *Club:* Travellers.

PLENDERLEITH, Ian, CBE 2002; Deputy Governor and Member, Monetary Policy Committee, South African Reserve Bank, 2003–05; Executive Director, 1994–2002, Member, Monetary Policy Committee, 1997–2002, Bank of England; Chairman: BH Macro Ltd, since 2007; Morgan Stanley International Ltd, since 2014 (non-executive Director, since 2011); *b* 27 Sept. 1943; *s* of late Raymond William Plenderleith and Louise Helen Plenderleith (*née* Martin); *m* 1st, 1967, Kristina Mary Bentley (marr. diss. 2007); one *s* two *d*; 2nd, 2007, Elizabeth Ann Campbell Barrell. *Educ:* King Edward's Sch., Birmingham; Christ Church, Oxford (MA); Columbia Business Sch., NY (MBA; Beta Gamma Sigma Medal, 1971). Joined Bank of England, 1965; seconded to IMF, Washington DC, 1972–74; Private Sec. to Governor, 1976–79; Alternate Dir, EIB, 1980–86; Hd of Gilt-Edged Div., 1982–90; Asst Dir, 1986–90; Associate Dir, 1990–94. Dir, Bank of England Nominees Ltd, 1994–2002; Alternate Dir, BIS, 1994–2002; Sen. Broker to Comrs for Reduction of Nat. Debt, 1989–2002. Dir, London Stock Exchange (formerly Mem., Stock Exchange Council), 1989–2001 (Dep. Chm., 1996). Internat. Consultant, Invoice Clearing Bureau SA (Pty) Ltd, 2006–. Non-executive Director: Sanlam Ltd, 2006–13; BMCE Bank Internat. (formerly Medicapital Bank plc), 2006–; Bond Exchange of S Africa, 2007–09; Europe Arab Bank plc, 2009–12; Sanlam UK Ltd, 2010–; Sanlam Private Investments (UK) Hldgs Ltd, 2013–; Sanlam Life & Pensions Ltd, 2013–. Sen. Advr, Anthem Corp. Finance, 2009–. Chairman: Stock Borrowing and Lending Cttee, 1990–95; G-10 Gold and Foreign Exchange Cttee, 1995–2001; Sterling Money Mkts Liaison Gp, 1999–2002; Corporation for Public Deposits, 2003–05; SA Money Mkts Liaison Gp, 2004–05; Co-Chm., Govt Borrowers Forum, 1991–94; Mem., G-10 Cttee on Global Financial System, 1994–2002. Member: Editl Cttee, OECD Study on Debt Management, 1990–93; Legal Risk Rev. Cttee, 1991–92; Financial Law Panel, 1992–94; Global Borrowers and Investors Forum Adv. Bd, 2003–05; Sen. Adv. Council, Internat. Capital Mkts Assoc., 2006–; Adv. Bd, Central Banking Pubns, 2006–. Member: Adv. Bd, Inst. of Archaeology Develt Trust, UCL, 1987–96; Bd of Overseers, Columbia Business Sch., 1991–2009 (Mem., Adv. Bd, London Alumni Club, 2002, 2006–09); London Old Edwardians Assoc. Cttee, 1996–2004 (Vice-Pres., 2004–); Ext. Adv. Panel, Oxford Math. Inst., 2000–03; Oxford Business Alumni Adv. Bd, 2002–03; Adv. Bd, Witwatersrand Business Sch., 2007–. Member: Fund-raising Planning Gp, St Bartholomew's Hosp., 1992–94; Fund-raising Planning Cttee, St Bartholomew's and The London Hosps, 1998–2003; Council, British Museum Soc., subseq. BM Friends, 1993–99, 2000–03 and 2005–12; BM Townley Steering Gp, 2002–03; Adv. Bd, Actors Centre, 2002–; Council (formerly Develt Council), Shakespeare's Globe, 2002–; Christ Church Develt Bd, 2008– (Mem. Bd, 2002–08, Mem., Finance Cttee, 1998–2003, Christ Church Campaign); Chm., Reed's Sch. Foundn Appeal, 2006–07; Gov., Reed's Sch., 2007– (Chm., 2008–). Dir, City Arts Trust, 1997–2003. FCSI (FSI 2006, MSI 1991); Mem., Assoc. of Black Securities and Investment Professionals, 2005–06. Fellow, ACT, 1989 (Mem. Adv. Bd, 2007–). Liveryman, Innholders' Co., 1977 (Mem., Investment Cttee, 2007–). *Recreations:* archaeology, theatre, cricket, travel. *Address:* Goldneys, River, Petworth, W Sussex GU28 9AU. *Clubs:* Athenæum (Mem., 2007–, Chm., 2008–14, Investment Cttee), London Capital (Mem. Adv. Bd, 2002–), MCC; Tillington Cricket (Hon. Sec., 1983–2003).

PLETNEV, Mikhail Vasilievich; pianist, conductor and composer; *b* Archangel, Russia, 14 April 1957. *Educ:* Central Sch. of Music; Moscow State Conservatory (under Yakov Flier and Lev Vlasenko (piano), and Albert Leman (composition)). Founder and Principal Conductor, Russian Nat. Orch., 1990–99, now Conductor Laureate; Guest Conductor of orchs incl. Philharmonia, LSO, CBSO and Los Angeles Philharmonic. Piano recitals and tours with orchs worldwide; numerous recordings. Teacher, Moscow State Conservatory, 1981–. Works composed include: Classical Symphony; Triptych for Symphony Orch.; Fantasy on Kazakh Themes for Violin and Orch.; Capriccio for Piano and Orch.; Concerto for Viola and Orch. Gold Medal, Tchaikovsky Internat. Piano Competition, 1978; State Prize of Russia, 1995, 2002. *Address:* c/o Salpeter Artists Management, 4 Denman Drive, NW11 6RG.

PLEWS, Derek Alexander; Policy Lead, Private Sector Employer Engagement, Ministry of Defence, since 2014; *b* 14 Dec. 1960; *s* of Albert Alexander Plews and Doris Plews; *m* 1984, Sandra Elizabeth Joyce Ming; two *s*. *Educ:* Clondermott Sec. Sch., Londonderry; Open Univ. (BA Hons Hist. 2012); Univ. of Birmingham (MA 2014). Reporter, Belfast Telegraph, 1979–82; Actg Ed., Londonderry Sentinel, 1982–85; Press Officer, MoD, 1985–91; Chief Press Officer, Employment Dept, 1991–94; Dep. Hd of Inf., Dept of Transport, 1994–97; Hd of News, DETR, 1997–98; Press Sec. to Dep. Prime Minister, 1998–2001; Dir of Communications, Assoc. of Train Operating Cos, 2001; Dir of News, MoD, 2001–02; Dir of Communication, ODPM, then DCLG, 2002–06; Principal Consultant, Media Outcomes, 2006–07; Lt Col, Royal Irish Regt, attached to Defence Media Ops Centre, mobilized mil. service, SO1 Media Ops, HQ MND (SE), Basra, Iraq, 2007; full-time Reserve Service (Army), SO1 Jt Media Ops Team, Defence Media Ops Centre, RAF Uxbridge, then RAF Halton, 2008–11; Dir of Communications, Reading BC, 2011–14. *Recreations:* hill-walking, angling. *Address:* 6.D.28 Main Building, Ministry of Defence, Horseguards Avenue, SW1A 2HB.

PLEYDELL-BOUVERIE, family name of **Earl of Radnor**.

PLOMIN, Judith Frances; *see* Dunn, J. F.

PLOMIN, Prof. Robert, PhD; FBA 2005; Research Professor in Behavioural Genetics, and Deputy Director, MRC Research Centre on Social, Genetic, and Developmental Psychiatry, Institute of Psychiatry, Psychology and Neuroscience (formerly Institute of Psychiatry), King's College, London, since 1994; *b* 20 Feb. 1948; *m* 1987, Judith Frances Dunn, *qv*. *Educ:* DePaul Univ., Chicago (BA Psychology 1970); Univ. of Texas, Austin (PhD Psychology 1974). University of Colorado: Faculty Fellow, Inst. for Behavioral Genetics, 1974–86; Asst Prof., 1974–78; Associate Prof., 1978–82; Prof., 1982–86; Dist. Prof. and Dir, Center for Develtl and Health Genetics, Pennsylvania State Univ., 1986–94. Pres., Behavior Genetics Assoc., 1989–90. Ed., Sage Series on Individual Differences and Development, 1990–. *Publications:* (with A. H. Buss) Temperament: early developing personality traits, 1984; (with J. C. DeFries) Origins of Individual Differences in Infancy: the Colorado Adoption Project, 1985; Development, Genetics and Psychology, 1986; (ed with J. Dunn) The Study of Temperament: changes, continuities, and challenges, 1986; (jtly) Nature and Nurture in Infancy and Early Childhood, 1988; (with J. Dunn) Separate Lives: why siblings are so different, 1990; (jtly) Behavioral Genetics: a primer, 2nd edn 1990 to 6th edn 2014; (ed jtly) Nature and Nurture during Middle Childhood, 1994; (ed jtly) Separate Social Worlds of Siblings: impact of nonshared environment on development, 1994; Genetics and Experience: the interplay between nature and nurture, 1994; (jtly) The Relationship Code, 2000; numerous articles in learned jls. *Address:* MRC Centre for Social, Genetic and Developmental Psychiatry, Institute of Psychiatry, Psychology and Neuroscience, King's College London, De Crespigny Park, Denmark Hill, SE5 8AF.

PLOTKIN, Prof. Gordon David, PhD; FRS 1992; FRSE; Professor of Computation Theory, Edinburgh University, since 1986; *b* 9 Sept. 1946; *s* of Manuel Plotkin and Mary (*née* Levin); *m* 1st, 1984, Lynda (*née* Stephenson) (marr. diss.); one *s*; 2nd, 1994, Hephzibah (*née* Kolban). *Educ:* Univ. of Glasgow (BSc 1967); Univ. of Edinburgh (PhD 1972). University of Edinburgh: Res. Associate and Res. Fellow, 1971–72; Lectr, 1975; Reader, 1982–86. BP Venture Res. Fellow, 1981–87; SERC Sen. Res. Fellow, 1992–97. MAE 1989. FRSE 1993. Royal Soc.-Wolfson Res. Merit Award, 2005–11. (Jtly) Test of Time Award, Logic in Computer Sci., 2007; Programming Langs Achievement Award, ACM Special Interest Gp on Programming Langs, 2010; Blaise Pascal Medal in Computational Scis and Information, Eur. Acad. of Scis, 2011; Milner Award, Royal Soc., 2012; Eur. Assoc. of Theoretical Computer Sci. Award, 2014. *Publications:* (ed with G. Kahn) Semantics of Data Types, 1984; (ed with G. Huet) Logical Frameworks, 1991; (ed with J.-L. Lassez) Computational Logic: essays in honour of Alan Robinson, 1991; (ed jtly) Situation Theory and its Applications, 1991; (ed with G. Huet) Logical Environments, 1993; (ed with M. Dezani-Ciancaglini) Typed Lambda Calculi and Applications, 1995; (ed jtly) Proof, Language and Interaction: essays in honour of Robin Milner, 2000; contribs to jls of computer science and logic. *Recreations:* hill-walking, chess. *Address:* School of Informatics, University of Edinburgh, 10 Crichton Street, Edinburgh EH8 9AB.

PLOTKIN, Prof. Henry Charles, PhD; Professor of Psychobiology, University College London, 1993–2005, now Emeritus; *b* Johannesburg, 11 Dec. 1940; *s* of Bernard Solomon Plotkin and Edythe Plotkin (*née* Poplak); *m* 1st, 1965, Patricia Ruehl (marr. diss. 1970); 2nd, 1975, Victoria Mary Welch; one *s* one *d*. *Educ:* Univ. of Witwatersrand (BSc 1st cl. Hons 1964); University College London (PhD 1968). Res. Asst, Univ. of Witwatersrand, 1964; Res. Scientist, MRC Unit on Neural Mechanisms of Behaviour, 1965–72; MRC Travelling Fellowship, Stanford Univ., Calif, 1970–71; Department of Psychology, University College London: Lectr, 1972–88; Reader, 1988–93; Head of Dept, 1993–98. *Publications:* Darwin Machines and the Nature of Knowledge, 1994; Evolution in Mind, 1997; The Imagined World Made Real, 2002; Evolutionary Thought in Psychology, 2004; Necessary Knowledge, 2007; Evolutionary Worlds Without End, 2010; *edited:* (with D. A. Oakley) Brain, Behaviour and Evolution, 1979; Essays in Evolutionary Epistemology, 1982; The Role of Behaviour in Evolution, 1988; articles in learned jls. *Recreations:* family, Dorset cottage, books, music. *Address:* Department of Psychology, University College London, WC1E 6BT.

PLOUVIEZ, Peter William; Chairman, Equity Trust Fund, 1992–2006; *b* 30 July 1931; *s* of C. A. W. and E. A. Plouviez; *m* 1978, Alison Dorothy Macrae; two *d* by previous marr. Gen. Sec., British Actors' Equity Assoc., 1974–91. FRSA 1992. *Address:* c/o Equity Charitable Trust, Plouviez House, 19–20 Hatton Place, EC1N 8RU.

PLOWDEN, Hon. Francis John; Member, Judicial Appointments Commission, 2006–12; Chairman, Child Exploitation and On-line Protection Centre, 2010–13; Board Member, Serious Organised Crime Agency, 2009–13; *b* 25 June 1945; *s* of Lord Plowden, GBE, KCB, and Lady Plowden, DBE; *m* 1984, Geraldine Wickman; one *s*. *Educ:* Eton; Trinity Coll., Cambridge (BA 1966). FCA 1969. Cooper Brothers, then Coopers & Lybrand, subseq. PricewaterhouseCoopers: consulting and acctg experience, UK, Ghana, the Gambia and Zaire, 1966–76; Partner, Nigeria, 1976–79; on secondment to HM Treasury/Cabinet Office Financial Mgt Unit, 1982–85; Partner, 1985; Hd, Govt Consulting, 1987–95; Man. Partner Internat. Affairs, and Mem. Internat. Exec. Cttee, 1995–98; Global Govt Leader, 1998–2001. Chm., Nat. Council for Palliative Care, 2001–08. Director: ITNET plc, 2001–05; Hedra plc, 2007–08; Draxmont Ltd, 2010–. Member: Audit Cttee, BM, 2009–13; Bd, Children and

Family Court Adv. and Support Services, 2012–; Asst Boundary Comr, Boundary Commn for England, 2011–13. Chm., Greenwich Foundn for Old Royal Naval Coll., 2003–11. Treas., Family Housing Assoc., 1979–84. Trustee: Royal Armouries, 1989–97; Royal Ballet Sch., 1989–2003; Anna Plowden Trust, 2000–; Edward James Foundn (W Dean Coll.), 2014–; CARE Internat. (UK), 2014–. *Publications:* (with Sir Christopher Foster) The State Under Stress, 1996; Review of Court Fees in Child Care Proceedings, 2009. *Recreations:* walking, ballet, theatre, built and natural environment. *Address:* 4 Highbury Road, SW19 7PR. *T:* (020) 8879 9841. *E:* f.plowden@btopenworld.com. *Clubs:* Royal Automobile, MCC.

PLOWDEN ROBERTS, Hugh Martin; Director, Argyll Group plc, 1983–95; *b* 6 Aug. 1932; *s* of Stanley and Joan Plowden Roberts; *m* 1st, 1956, Susan Jane Patrick (*d* 1996); two *d*; 2nd, 2000, Mrs Jane Hall (*d* 2007). *Educ:* St Edward's School, Oxford; St Edmund Hall, Oxford. BA 1954, MA 1956. FIGD 1980. Payne & Son Meat Group, 1954–60 (Dir, 1958); Asst Gen. Manager (Meat Group), Co-operative Wholesale Society, 1960–67; Allied Suppliers Ltd, 1967–82: Dir, 1971; Dep. Man. Dir, 1974; Man. Dir, 1978; Chm., 1980–82; Dir, Cavenham Ltd, 1979, Chm., 1981–82; Dir, Argyll Stores Ltd, subseq. Safeway Stores, 1982–97 (Dep. Chm., 1983–85); Chm., Dairy Crest Foods, subseq. Dairy Crest Ltd, 1985–88; Dir, Lawson Mardon Gp Ltd, 1987–91. Comr, Meat and Livestock Commn, 1975–79; Mem., MMB, 1983–89. *Recreation:* country pursuits. *Address:* Barn Cottage, Fulking, Henfield, W Sussex BN5 9NB. *T:* (01273) 857622. *Club:* Farmers.

PLOWMAN, John Patrick; consultant; Chairman, London Sustainable Development Commission, 2009–14; *b* 20 March 1944; *s* of late Robert and Ruth Plowman, Lane End, Bucks; *m* 1973, Daphne Margaret Brock Kennett; two *s* one *d*. *Educ:* St Edward's Sch., Oxford; Grenoble Univ.; University Coll., Univ. of Durham (BA). MoD, 1967–75: Private Office, Minister of State for Defence, 1969–71; Resident Observer, CSSB, 1975; Cabinet Office, 1976–78; MoD and UK Delegn to UN Law of Sea Conf., 1979–81; Asst Sec., DoE, 1982–86; Counsellor, UK Repn to EC, 1986–90; Head, Envmtl Protection (Europe), 1990–93; Regl Dir for NW, DoE and Dept of Transport, 1993–94; Dir, Wildlife and Countryside, DoE, then DETR, 1994–98; Dir, Road Safety and Envmt, DETR, 1998–2001; Chm., Driver and Vehicle Operator Gp, DETR, subseq. DTLR, then DfT, 2001–02; Gp Modernisation Dir, Driver and Vehicle Operator Gp, DfT, 2003. Dir, John Plowman Associates (governance, strategy and policy analysis), 2003–. Served Royal Marines Reserve, 1968–71. Director and Trustee: Parly Adv. Council for Transport Safety, 2004–; Road Safety Foundn, 2009–; Dir, RoadSafe, 2006–. Gov., Charlotte Sharman Sch., Southwark, 2002– (Chm., 2008–). Freeman, City of London, 2010; Liveryman, Coachmakers' Co., 2010–. *Recreations:* music, fishing, gardening (English Gardening Sch., 2004), book collecting. *Club:* Royal Over-Seas League.

PLOWMAN, (Phillip) Jon, OBE 2013; freelance executive TV producer, since 2006; *b* Hatfield, Herts, 4 July 1953; *s* of Charles Edward Plowman and Florence Joan Plowman (*née* Bentley); civil partnership 2007, Francis Matthews. *Educ:* Stanborough Sch., Welwyn Garden City; University Coll., Oxford (BA Hons). Asst Dir, Royal Court Th., 1971–75; Arts Council Drama Officer, 1978–79; Entertainment Producer, Granada TV, 1980–81; BBC TV: producer, 1981–94; Hd of Comedy Entertainment, 1994–2001; Hd of Comedy, 2001–06. Production credits include: Comic Relief, 1989 and 1991; French and Saunders, 1990–2004; Smith and Jones, 1990–92; Murder Most Horrid, 1991–94; Absolutely Fabulous, 1992–2014; The Vicar of Dibley, 1994–2007; Bottom, 1994; A Bit of Fry and Laurie, 1995; Executive Producer: Goodness Gracious Me, 1998–2001; Gimme, Gimme, Gimme, 1999–2001; The League of Gentlemen, 1999–2002; The Office, 2001–03; Little Britain, 2003–06; Beautiful People, 2008–09; Psychoville, 2009–11; Roger and Val Have Just Got In, 2011–12; Twenty Twelve, 2011–12; Inside No 9, 2014; W1A, 2014. FRTS 2003; FRSA. Judges' Award for Outstanding Achievement in Broadcasting, RTS, 2006; Lifetime Achievement Award, Banff World TV Fest., 2007. *Recreations:* music, walking in the French Pyrenees, reading, Somerset. *Address:* c/o Comedy Department, BBC Television, Grafton House, 379–381 Euston Road, NW1 3AU. *T:* (020) 8743 8000. *E:* jon.plowman@bbc.co.uk. *Club:* Soho House.

PLOWRIGHT, Dame Joan (Ann), (The Lady Olivier), DBE 2004 (CBE 1970); leading actress with the National Theatre, 1963–74; Member of the RADA Council; Honorary President, English Stage Company, since 2009; *b* 28 Oct. 1929; *d* of late William Ernest Plowright and of Daisy Margaret (*née* Burton); *m* 1st, 1953, Roger Gage (marr. diss.); 2nd, 1961, (as Sir Laurence Olivier) Baron Olivier, OM (*d* 1989); one *s* two *d*. *Educ:* Scunthorpe Grammar School; Laban Art of Movement Studio; Old Vic Theatre School. First stage appearance in If Four Walls Told, Croydon Rep. Theatre, 1948; Bristol Old Vic and Mem. Old Vic Co., S Africa tour, 1952; first London appearance in The Duenna, Westminster, 1954; Moby Dick, Duke of York's, 1955; season of leading parts, Nottingham Playhouse, 1955–56; English Stage Co., Royal Court, 1956; The Crucible, Don Juan, The Death of Satan, Cards of Identity, The Good Woman of Setzuan, The Country Wife (transferred to Adelphi, 1957); The Chairs, The Making of Moo, Royal Court, 1957; The Entertainer, Palace, 1957; The Chairs, The Lesson, Phoenix, NY, 1958; The Entertainer, Royale, NY, 1958; The Chairs, The Lesson, Major Barbara, Royal Court, 1958; Hook, Line and Sinker, Piccadilly, 1958; Roots, Royal Court, Duke of York's, 1959; Rhinoceros, Royal Court, 1960; A Taste of Honey, Lyceum, NY, 1960 (Best Actress Tony Award); Rosmersholm, Greenwich, 1973; Saturday, Sunday, Monday, Queen's, 1974–75; The Sea Gull, Lyric, 1975; The Bed Before Yesterday, Lyric, 1975 (Variety Club of GB Award, 1977); Filumena, Lyric, 1977 (Soc. of West End Theatre Award, 1978); Enjoy, Vaudeville, 1980; The Cherry Orchard, Haymarket, 1983; The House of Bernada Alba, Globe, 1986; Time and the Conways, Old Vic, 1990; If We are Women, Greenwich, 1995; Absolutely! (perhaps), Wyndham's, 2003; Chichester Festival: Uncle Vanya, The Chances, 1962; St Joan (Best Actress Evening Standard Award), Uncle Vanya, 1963; The Doctor's Dilemma, The Taming of the Shrew, 1972; Cavell, 1982; The Way of the World, 1984; National Theatre: St Joan, Uncle Vanya, Hobson's Choice, opening season, 1963; The Master Builder, 1964; Much Ado About Nothing, 1967, 1968; Three Sisters, 1967, 1968; Tartuffe, 1967, 1968; The Advertisement, 1968; Love's Labour's Lost, 1968; The Merchant of Venice, 1970; A Woman Killed With Kindness, 1971; The Rules of the Game, 1971; Eden End, 1974; Mrs Warren's Profession, 1985. Produced The Travails of Sancho Panza, 1969; directed: Rites, 1969; A Prayer for Wings, 1985; Married Love, 1988. *Films include:* The Entertainer, 1960; Three Sisters, 1970; Equus; Britannia Hospital, 1982; Wagner, Revolution, 1985; Drowning by Numbers, The Dressmaker, 1988; I Love You to Death, Avalon, 1989; Stalin, 1992 (Golden Globe Award, 1993); Enchanted April, 1993 (Golden Globe Award, 1993); Denis the Menace, A Place for Annie, A Pin for the Butterfly, Widow's Peak, Last Action Hero, 1993; On Promised Land, Hotel Sorrento, A Pyromaniac's Love Story, The Scarlett Letter, 1994; Mr Wrong, 1995; Jane Eyre, 101 Dalmatians, Surviving Picasso, 1996; The Assistant, 1996; Dance with Me, 1998; America Betrayed, 1998; Tea with Mussolini, 1999; Return to the Secret Garden, Frankie and Hazel, Global Heresy, 2000; Callas Forever, 2001; George and the Dragon, I Am David, 2002; Bringing Down the House, 2003; Mrs Palfrey at the Claremont, 2006; The Spiderwick Chronicles, 2007; *films for TV:* The Merchant of Venice; Brimstone and Treacle, 1982; A Dedicated Man; Return of the Natives, 1994; Tom's Midnight Garden, 1998; This Could Be the Last Time, 1998; other *television* appearances include: Daphne Laureola, 1976; The Birthday Party, 1987; The Importance of Being Earnest, 1988; And a Nightingale Sang, 1989; House of Bernada Alba, 1991; Clothes in the Wardrobe, 1992. 18th annual Crystal Award, Women in Film, USA, 1994. Hon. DLitt Hull, 2001. *Publications:* And That's Not All (memoirs), 2001. *Recreations:* reading, music, entertaining. *Address:* c/o 7 Newham Lane, Steyning, W Sussex BN44 3LR.

PLOWRIGHT, Jonathan Daniel, FRAM; concert pianist, since 1985; Head of Keyboard, University of Chichester, since 2007; Member of Keyboard Faculty, Royal Conservatoire of Scotland, since 2007; *b* Doncaster, 1959; *s* of Cyril James and Molly Plowright; *m* 1990, Diane Shaw. *Educ:* Stonyhurst Coll., Lancs; Royal Acad. of Music, London (Macfarren Gold Medal 1983); Peabody Conservatory of Music, Johns Hopkins Univ. FRAM 2013. Fulbright Schol., 1983. Débuts: Carnegie Recital Hall, NY, 1984; Southbank, London, 1985; winner, Eur. Piano Competition, 1989. World première perf. of Constant Lambert Piano Concerto, 1988; world première recordings of piano works by Sigismund Stojowski, 2003–04; has performed with leading orchestras and chamber ensembles and at major concert halls and music fests. *Publications:* contribs to magazines, incl. Musical Opinion, Klassisk Musikkmagasin (Norway), Internat. Piano Mag., Limelight (Australia). *Recreations:* watching cricket and Rugby, fishing, cooking. *E:* jonathan@jonathan.plowright.com. *W:* www.jonathanplowright.com. *Club:* Royal Over-Seas League (Hon. Mem.).

PLOWRIGHT, Rosalind Anne, (Mrs J. A. Kaye), OBE 2007; mezzo-soprano; *b* 21 May 1949; *d* of Robert Arthur Plowright and Celia Adelaide Plowright; *m* 1984, J(ames) Anthony Kaye; one *s* one *d*. *Educ:* Notre Dame High Sch., Wigan; Royal Northern Coll. of Music, Manchester. LRAM. London Opera Centre, 1974–75; Glyndebourne Chorus and Touring Co., début as soprano, Agathe in Der Freischutz, 1975; WNO, ENO, Kent Opera, 1975–78; Miss Jessel in Turn of the Screw, ENO, 1979 (SWET award); début at Covent Garden as Ortlinde in Die Walküre, 1980; with Bern Opera, 1980–81, Frankfurt Opera and Munich Opera, 1981; débuts: in USA (Philadelphia and San Diego), Paris, Madrid and Hamburg, 1982; at La Scala, Milan, Edinburgh Fest., San Francisco and New York (Carnegie Hall), 1983; at Deutsche Oper, Berlin, 1984; in Houston, Pittsburgh, Verona, Montpellier and Venice, 1985; in Rome, Florence and Holland, 1986; in Tulsa, Buenos Aires, Santiago di Chile, Israel and Bonn, 1987; with NY Phil. and Paris Opera, 1987; in Lausanne, Geneva, Oviedo and Bilbao, 1988; in Zurich, Copenhagen, Lisbon and Torre del Lago, 1989; with Vienna State Opera, 1990; in Nice, 1991; in Wiesbaden, 1992; in Leeds, 1993; in Athens and Bregenz, 1994; BBC Prom. Concerts; with Berlin Deutsche Staatsoper, 1996; with Scottish Opera, 1999; with Opera New Zealand, 2000; with Opera Holland Park, 2002; with NY Metropolitan Opera; Paris Châtelet, 2003; with Florence Maggio Musicale, 2004; Tokyo, 2006; Seattle, 2008; Lisbon, 2009; Stuttgart and Madrid, 2011; Portland, 2013. Principal rôles as soprano include: Ariadne; Aida; Amelia in Un Ballo in Maschera; Leonora in Il Trovatore; Leonora in La Forza del Destino; Desdemona in Otello; Violetta in La Traviata; Medora in Il Corsaro; Elena in I Vespri Siciliani; Abigaille in Nabucco; Elisabetta in Don Carlos; Lady Macbeth; Manon Lescaut; Giorgetta in Il Tabarro; Suor Angelica; Norma; Alceste; Médée; Maddalena in Andrea Chénier; La Gioconda; Tatyana in Eugene Onegin; Tosca; principal rôles as mezzo-soprano include: Amneris in Aida; Kostelnicka in Jenufa; Fricka in Das Rheingold and Die Walküre; Ortrud in Lohengrin; Marfa in Khovanshchina; Gertrude in Hansel and Gretel; Klytämnestra in Elektra. Has given recitals and concerts in UK, USA and Europe, made opera and concert recordings, and opera telecasts; acting début, House of Elliott, TV serial, 1993; The Man Who Made Husbands Jealous, TV, 1997; Two's a Crowd, UK th. tour, 2002. Teacher of singing; masterclasses at Royal Acad. of Music, Guildhall Sch. of Music, RNCM and Trinity Coll. First prize, 7th Internat. Comp. for Opera Singers, Sofia, 1979; Prix Fondation Fanny Heldy, Acad. Nat. du Disque Lyrique, 1985. *Recreation:* fell walking. *Address:* c/o James Black Management, 9 Burnhams, Rye, E Sussex TN31 7LW. *W:* www.rosalindplowright.com, www.ros-sing.co.uk.

PLUMB, family name of **Baron Plumb**.

PLUMB, Baron *cr* 1987 (Life Peer), of Coleshill in the County of Warwickshire; **Charles Henry Plumb,** Kt 1973; DL; Member (C) The Cotswolds, European Parliament, 1979–99; *b* 27 March 1925; *s* of Charles and Louise Plumb; *m* 1947, Marjorie Dorothy Dunn; one *s* two *d*. *Educ:* King Edward VI School, Nuneaton. National Farmers Union: Member Council, 1959; Vice-President, 1964, 1965; Deputy-President, 1966, 1967, 1968, 1969; President, 1970–79. European Parliament: Chm., Agricl Cttee, 1979–82; Leader, EDG, 1982–87; Pres., 1987–89; Co-Chm., EU/ACP Jt Assembly, 1994; Vice-Pres., EPP, 1994–97; Leader, British Conservatives, 1994–97. Non-executive Director: Lloyds Bank, 1970–81; United Biscuits, 1970–80; Fisons, 1970–78. Chm., British Agricl Council, 1975–79. Chm., Agricultural Mortgage Corp., 1994–95. Mem., Duke of Northumberland's Cttee of Enquiry on Foot and Mouth Disease, 1967–68; Member Council: CBI; Animal Health Trust. Chm., Internat. Agricl Trng Programme, 1987–. Pres., Royal Agric. Soc. of England, 1977, Dep. Pres. 1978; President: Internat. Fedn of Agricl Producers, 1979–82; Comité des Organisations Professionnels Agricoles de la CEE (COPA), 1975–77. Pres., Nat. Fedn of Young Farmers' Clubs, 1976–; Patron, Warwicks Co. Fedn of YFC, 1974–; Hon. Pres., Ayrshire Cattle Soc. Pres., Nat. Sleep Assoc., 2000–. Chancellor, Coventry Univ., 1995–; Gov., RAU (formerly RAC), Cirencester, 1995–. Liveryman, Farmers' Co. (Master, 2005–06). FRSA 1970; FRAgS 1974. DL Warwick 1977. Hon. Fellow, Wye Coll., London Univ., 1988. Hon. DSc: Cranfield, 1983; Silsoe Coll. of Technol., 1987; De Montfort, 1995; Hon. LLD Warwick, 1990; Hon. Dr: Cheltenham & Gloucester Coll. of HE, 1999; Public Service Ohio State, 2010. Gold Medal, RASE, 1983; Robert Schuman Gold Medal, France, 1989; Lifetime Achievement Award, Farmers Weekly. Ordén de Merito (Portugal), 1987; Order of Merit (Luxembourg), 1988; Grand Cross, Order of Civil Merit (Spain), 1989; Knight Comdr's Cross, Order of Merit (FRG), 1990 (Order of Merit, 1979); Grand Order of the Phoenix (Greece), 1997. *Recreations:* country pursuits, fishing. *Address:* The Dairy Farm, Maxstoke, Coleshill, Warwicks B46 2QJ. *T:* (01675) 463133, *Fax:* (01675) 464156; House of Lords, SW1A 0PW. *T:* (020) 7219 1233, *Fax:* (020) 7219 1649. *E:* plumbh@parliament.uk. *Club:* Farmers.

PLUMB, Alan; *see* Plumb, R. A.

PLUMB, Paula Maria H.; *see* Hay-Plumb.

PLUMB, Prof. (Raymond) Alan, PhD; FRS 1998; Professor of Meteorology, since 1988, and Director, Program in Atmospheres, Oceans and Climate, 2003–08, Massachusetts Institute of Technology; *b* 30 March 1948; *s* of Tom and Dorothy Plumb; *m* 1st, 1981, Janet Gormly (marr. diss. 2007); one *s* one *d*; 2nd, 2010, Donna Jane Bulpett. *Educ:* Manchester Univ. (BSc Physics 1969; PhD Astronomy 1972). SO, then SSO, Met. Office, Bracknell, 1972–76; Res. Scientist, then Principal Res. Scientist, CSIRO Div. of Atmospheric Res., Aspendale, Vic, 1976–88. Haurwitz Meml Lectr, Amer. Meteorol Soc., 2001. Fellow: Amer. Geophysical Union, 2000; Amer. Meteorol Soc., 2002. Jule G. Charney Award, Amer. Meteorol Soc., 2013. *Publications:* (ed with R. A. Vincent) Middle Atmosphere, 1989; (with J. C. Marshall) Atmosphere, Ocean, and Climate Dynamics, 2007; (with P. D. Clift) The Asian Monsoon, 2008; numerous papers in refereed scientific jls, incl. Jl Atmospheric Scis, Jl Geophysical Res. *Recreations:* angling, hiking. *Address:* 76 Westford Street, Chelmsford, MA 01824, USA. *T:* (978) 2561402.

PLUMBLY, Sir Derek (John), KCMG 2001 (CMG 1991); HM Diplomatic Service, retired; Under Secretary General and Special Coordinator for Lebanon, United Nations, 2012–15; *b* 15 May 1948; *s* of late John C. Plumbly and Jean Elizabeth (*née* Baker); *m* 1979, Nadia Gohar; two *s* one *d*. *Educ:* Brockenhurst Grammar Sch.; Magdalen Coll., Oxford (BA PPE). VSO, Pakistan, 1970; Third Sec., FCO, 1972; MECAS, 1973; Second Sec., Jedda, 1975; First Sec., Cairo, 1977; FCO, 1980; First Sec., Washington, 1984; Dep. Head of Mission, Riyadh, 1988; Head of Chancery, UK Mission to UN, NY, 1992–96; Internat. Drugs Co-ordinator, and Dir, Drugs and Internat. Crime, FCO, 1996–97; Dir, Middle East and N Africa, FCO, 1997–2000; Ambassador: to Saudi Arabia, 2000–03; to Egypt, 2003–07. Chm., Assessment and Evaluation Commn, Comprehensive Peace Agreement, Sudan, 2008–11. Pres., Levantine Foundn, 2009–. Trustee, British Univ. in Egypt, 2007–. DUniv Loughborough, 2008. *Club:* Travellers.

PLUME, John Trevor; Regional Chairman, Industrial Tribunals (London North), 1984–87; *b* 5 Oct. 1914; *s* of William Thomas and Gertrude Plume; *m* 1948, Christine Mary Wells; one *d*. *Educ:* City of London School; Inns of Court School of Law. Called to the Bar, Gray's Inn, 1936, Bencher, 1969. Legal Associate Mem., Town Planning Inst., 1939; served Royal Artillery, 1940–46 (Captain). Practised at Bar, specialising in property law, 1936–76; Chm., Industrial Tribunals, 1976–87. Liveryman, Clockmakers' Co. *Recreations:* beekeeping, carpentry, gardening, fishing. *Address:* Mulberry Cottage, Forest Side, Epping, Essex CM16 4ED. *T:* (01992) 572389.

PLUMMER, (Arthur) Christopher (Orme), CC (Canada) 1968; actor; *b* Toronto, 13 Dec. 1929; *m* 1st, 1956, Tammy Lee Grimes; one *d*; 2nd, 1962, Patricia Audrey Lewis (marr. diss. 1966); 3rd, 1970, Elaine Regina Taylor. *Educ:* public and private schs, Montreal. French and English radio, Canada, 1949–52; Ottawa Rep. Theatre; Broadway: Starcross Story, 1951–52; Home is the Hero, 1953; The Dark is Light Enough, 1954 (Theatre World Award); The Lark, 1955; J. B., 1958 (Tony nomination); Arturo Ui, 1963; Royal Hunt of the Sun, 1965–66; Stratford, Conn, 1955: Mark Antony, Ferdinand; leading actor, Stratford Festival, Canada, 1956–67: Henry V, The Bastard, Hamlet, Leontes, Mercutio, Macbeth, Cyrano de Bergerac, Benedick, Aguecheek, Antony; Royal Shakespeare Co., Stratford-on-Avon, 1961–62: Benedick, Richard III; London debut as Henry II in Becket, Aldwych and Globe, 1961 (Evening Standard Best Actor Award, 1961); National Theatre, 1971–72: Amphytrion 38, Danton's Death; Broadway musical, Cyrano, 1973 (Outer Critics Circle Award and Tony Award for Best Actor in a Musical, NY Drama Desk Award); The Good Doctor, NY, 1974; Iago in Othello, NY, 1982 (Drama Desk Award); Macbeth, NY, 1988; No Man's Land, NY, 1994; Barrymore (one-man show), 1997 (Tony Award for Best Actor); King Lear, Stratford Fest., 2002, NY, 2004. *Films:* Stage-Struck, 1956; Across the Everglades, 1957; The Fall of the Roman Empire, 1963; The Sound of Music (Golden Badge of Honour, Austria), Daisy Clover, 1964; Triple Cross, 1966; Oedipus Rex, 1967; The Battle of Britain, 1968; Royal Hunt of the Sun, 1969; The Pyx, 1973; The Man Who Would Be King, 1975; Aces High, The Moneychangers (Emmy Award), 1976; International Velvet, The Silent Partner, 1978; Hanover Street, 1979; Murder by Decree, 1980 (Genie Award, Canada); The Disappearance, The Janitor, 1981; The Amateur, 1982; Dreamscape, 1984; Playing for Keeps, Lily in Love, 1985; Souvenir, 1989; Where The Heart Is, 1990; Twelve Monkeys, 1996; The Insider, 2000; Dracula 2001, Lucky Break, A Beautiful Mind, 2001; Ararat, Nicholas Nickleby, 2002; Blizzard, Gospel of John, 2003; National Treasure, 2004; Alexander, 2005; Inside Man, Syriana, 2006; Closing the Ring, 2007; Man in the Chair, 2008; The Imaginarium of Doctor Parnassus, 2009; The Last Station, 2010; Priest, The Girl with the Dragon Tattoo, Beginners, 2011 (Academy, Golden Globe and BAFTA Awards for Best Supporting Actor, 2012); Muhammad Ali's Greatest Fight (TV film), 2013; Danny Collins, Remember, 2015, and others. TV appearances, Britain, Denmark, and major N American networks, incl. Hamlet at Elsinore, BBC and Danish TV, 1964 (4 Emmy Award nominations). First entertainer to win Maple Leaf Award (Arts and Letters), 1982. *Publications:* In Spite of Myself: a memoir, (USA), 2008. *Recreations:* tennis, ski-ing, piano. *Clubs:* Players, River (New York).

PLUMMER, Maj.-Gen. Brian Peter, CBE 2002; Clerk to Worshipful Company of Skinners, since 2003; *b* 30 Aug. 1948. *Educ:* Univ. of Durham (BA). Commnd RWF, 1970; Regt and Staff Duty, 1974–85; jsdc, 1986; ASC, 1986–88; CO 1 RWF, 1989–91; HCSC, 1995; Comd, 1st Mechanised Bde, 1995–96; rcds, 1997; Comd, Combined Arms Trng Centre, 1998–99; Dir Gen. Trng Support, HQ Land Comd, 1999–2002. Col, RWF, 2001–05. *Address:* c/o RHQ RWF, Hightown Barracks, Wrexham, Clwyd LL13 8RD.

PLUMMER, Christopher; *see* Plummer, A. C. O.

PLUMPTON, Alan, CBE 1980; BSc; FREng, FIET; Chairman, Schlumberger plc, 1992–2001; Chairman, 1992–99, Director, 1999–2001, Beaufort Group PLC (formerly Beaufort Management Consultants); *b* 24 Nov. 1926; *s* of late John Plumpton and Doris Plumpton; *m* 1950, Audrey Smith; one *s* one *d*. *Educ:* Sunderland Technical Sch.; Durham Univ. (BSc Elec. Eng). FREng (FEng 1991). Pupil Engr, Sunderland Corp. Elec. Undertaking, 1942; various engrg and commercial appts, NEEB, 1948–61; Dist Manager, E Monmouthshire Dist, S Wales Electricity Bd, 1961–64. Admin. Staff Coll., Henley, 1963; Dep. Chief Commercial Engr, S Wales Elec. Bd, 1964–67; Chief Commercial Engr, S Wales Elec. Bd, 1967–72; Dep. Chm., London Elec. Bd, 1972–76, Chm., 1976–81; Dep. Chm., Electricity Council, 1981–86. Chairman: Ewbank Preece Group, 1986–92; Manx Electricity Authority, 1986–97; Schlumberger Measurement and Systems, 1988–92; Dir, Eleco Holdings, 1993–97. MInstD 1986; CCMI. Liveryman, Gardeners' Co. JP Mon, 1971–72. *Recreations:* golf, gardening. *Address:* Lockhill, Stubbs Wood, Amersham, Bucks HP6 6EX. *T:* (01494) 433791. *Club:* Harewood Downs Golf (Chm., 1996–98).

PLUMPTON, Denise Kathryn; Director of Information, Highways Agency, Department for Transport, 2005–10; *b* 31 Oct. 1954; *d* of late Dennis Plumpton and Mabel Jenny Plumpton; *m* 2015, Peter John Finney. *Educ:* Univ. of Sheffield (BSc 1st Cl. Hons Maths 1976). Cert. IoD 2010. Rover Gp, 1976–82; ISTEL, 1983–89; Powergen: Commercial Manager, 1989–96; IT Dir, 1996–99; Information Technology Director: TNT UK Ltd, 1999–2004; Sendo, 2004. Non-executive Director: Heart of Birmingham Teaching PCT, 2007–11; Centro, 2009–15; Reed Exhibns 360°IT - The Infrastructure Event, 2010; Dir, Process Doctor, 2010–. Vice Chair, Birmingham S Central CCG, 2011–. MInstD 1997. *Recreations:* Judge for British Racing and Sports Car Club, MG Car Club and Classic Sports Car Club. *Address:* Knowle, Solihull. *T:* 07713 780110. *E:* deniseplumpton@btinternet.com.

PLUMPTRE, family name of **Baron FitzWalter**.

PLUMPTRE, Hon. (Wyndham) George; Chief Executive, National Gardens Scheme, since 2011 (Deputy Chairman, 2009–10); *b* 24 April 1956; 3rd *s* of 21st Baron FitzWalter; *m* 1st, 1984 (marr. diss. 2008); two *s* one *d*; 2nd, 2010, Annabel Louise Williams. *Educ:* Radley Coll.; Jesus Coll., Cambridge (BA Mod. Hist.). Author, journalist and lecturer, 1978–; contributor, Country Life, 1979–; Gardens Correspondent, 1993–95, columnist, 1995–97, The Times; Ed., Sotheby's Preview Mag., 1995–97; Dir, S Africa, Sotheby's, 1997–99; Founder and Editl Dir, greenfingers.com, 1999–2002; Publisher, Bonhams Mag., 2004–09. Trustee: Kent Gardens Trust, 1992–99; Nat. Gardens Scheme, 2005–10; Member: SE Regl Cttee, Nat. Trust, 1993–96; Arts and Library Sub Cttee, MCC, 2000–10. *Publications:* Royal Gardens, 1981; Collins Book of British Gardens, 1985; The Fast Set, 1985; The Latest Country Gardens, 1988; Homes of Cricket, 1988; Garden Ornament, 1989; Cricket Cartoons and Caricatures, 1989; Back Page Racing, 1989; The Golden Age of Cricket, 1990; The Water Garden, 1993; The Garden Makers, 1993; Great Gardens, Great Designers, 1994; Edward VII, 1995; The Country House Guide, 1996; Classic Planting, 1998; Royal Gardens of Europe, 2005; Heritage Gardens, 2007; (ed) The Gardens of England, 2013; The English Country House Garden, 2014. *T:* (01483) 213906. *E:* gplumptre@ngs.org.uk.

PLUMSTEAD, Her Honour Isobel Mary, (Mrs N. J. Coleman); a Circuit Judge, 2001–14; authorised to sit as Judge of High Court, Family Division, 2002; Designated Family Judge: Cambridge, 2003–09; Peterborough and Cambridge, 2007–09; *b* 19 July 1947; *d* of John Archibald Plumstead, DFM, MA and Nancy Plumstead (*née* Drummond); *m* 1971, Nicholas John Coleman, *qv*; one *s* two *d*. *Educ:* Norwich High Sch. for Girls (GPDST); St Hugh's College, Oxford (BA 1969; MA 1985); Inns of Court Sch. of Law. Blackstone Entrance Scholar, 1967, Colombos Prize for Internat. Law, 1970, Harmsworth Scholar, 1970–73, Middle Temple. Called to the Bar, Middle Temple, 1970, Bencher 2006; Registrar, Principal Registry, Family Div. of High Court, 1990; District Judge, Principal Registry, Family Div. of the High Ct, 1990–2001; Asst Recorder, 1994–98; a Recorder, 1998–2001. Member: Independent Schs Tribunal, 1992–2000; Family Cttee (formerly Civil and Family Cttee), 1993–99, Main Bd, 1997–99, Judicial Studies Bd; Hon. Sec., Council of HM Circuit Judges, 2009–11 (Sen. Vice Pres., 2012; Pres., 2013). Trustee: New Parents' Infant Network (Newpin), 1989–96; Hackney and E London Family Mediation Service, 1993–96; Vice Pres., Family Mediators Assoc., 1999–. Gov., St Margaret's Sch., Hampstead, 1993–98. *Publications:* (contrib.) Emergency Remedies in the Family Courts, 1997; (contrib.) Rayden and Jackson on Divorce and Family Matters, 1997. *Recreation:* when time permits, spending the kids' inheritance. *Clubs:* Anmer Social; Hunstanton Golf.

See also J. C. Plumstead.

PLUMSTEAD, John Charles; His Honour Judge John Plumstead; a Circuit Judge, since 2006; *b* 7 Feb. 1953; *s* of John Archibald Plumstead, DFM, MA, and Nancy Plumstead (*née* Drummond); *m* 1984, Leonora Woollam (*d* 2004); one *d*. *Educ:* King Edward VI Norwich Sch.; Univ. of Liverpool (LLB 1974). Called to the Bar, Middle Temple, 1975 (Winston Churchill pupillage award); in practice as a barrister, 1975–2006; a Recorder, 2000–06. *Recreations:* life, liberty and the pursuit of happiness. *Address:* St Albans Crown Court, Bricket Road, St Albans, Herts AL1 3JW.

See also I. M. Plumstead.

PLUNKET, family name of **Baron Plunket**.

PLUNKET, 9th Baron *cr* 1827; **Tyrone Shaun Terence Plunket;** *b* 5 Feb. 1966; *s* of Hon. Shaun Albert Frederick Sheridan Plunket and of Judith Ann Plunket (*née* Power); *S* uncle 2013; *m* 2000, Lucy Marguerite, *d* of late James Currie, MC; twin *s*. *Heir: s* Hon. Rory Peter Robin Plunket, *b* 11 March 2001.

PLUNKET GREENE, Dame Mary; *see* Quant, Dame M.

PLUNKETT, family name of **Barons Dunsany** and **Louth**.

PLUNKETT, (Andrew) Christopher; His Honour Judge Plunkett; a Circuit Judge, since 2005; *b* 31 March 1961; *s* of Anthony Penson Plunkett and Anne Malkin Plunkett; *m* 2001, Rachel Anne Stewart; two *s*. *Educ:* Warwick Univ. (LLB); Inns of Court Sch. of Law, London. Called to the Bar, Gray's Inn, 1983; a Recorder, 2002–05. *Recreations:* cycling, on and off road. *Address:* Birmingham Civil Justice Centre, Priory Courts, 33 Bull Street, Birmingham B4 6DS. *T:* (0121) 681 4441, *Fax:* (0121) 681 3001. *Clubs:* Cyclists' Touring, Rugged Meanderers.

PLUTHERO, John; Chairman: Essensys, since 2011; MyAppConverter Ltd, since 2013; *b* 10 Feb. 1964; *m*; three *c*. *Educ:* Colchester Royal Grammar Sch.; London Sch. of Econs (BSc 1st Cl. Hons Econs). ACA 1989. Dir, Chelsea Harbour, P&O Develts, 1990–94; Strategy and Planning, Bass plc, 1994–95; Business Review Dir, Dixons Gp, 1995–98; Man. Dir, Mastercare DSG, 1998–99; Founder, Freeserve plc, subseq. Freeserve.com plc, CEO, 1998–2002; Chief Exec., Energis plc, 2002–05; Cable & Wireless plc: Dir, UK Business, 2005–06; Gp Man. Dir and Exec. Chm., Worldwide, 2006–10; Exec. Chm., Internat., 2007–08; Exec. Chm., 2010–11; Chief Exec., 2010–11. MInstD. *Recreation:* modern art.

PLYMOUTH, 3rd Earl of, *cr* 1905; **Other Robert Ivor Windsor-Clive;** DL; FRSA 1953; Viscount Windsor (UK 1905); 15th Baron Windsor (England, *cr* 1529); *b* 9 Oct. 1923; *e s* of 2nd Earl of Plymouth, PC and Lady Irene Charteris (*d* 1989), *d* of 11th Earl of Wemyss; *S* father, 1943; *m* 1950, Caroline Helen, *o d* of Edward Rice, Dane Court, Eastry, Kent; three *s* one *d*. *Educ:* Eton. Mem., Museums and Galls Commn (formerly Standing Commn on Museums and Galls), 1972–82; Chm., Reviewing Cttee on Export of Works of Art, 1982–85. DL County of Salop, 1961. *Heir: s* Viscount Windsor, *qv*. *Address:* The Stables, Oakly Park, Ludlow, Shropshire SY8 2JW.

PLYMOUTH, Bishop Suffragan of, since 2015; **Rt Rev. Nicholas Howard Paul McKinnel;** *b* Liverpool, 19 Aug. 1954; *s* of Hugh McKinnel and Hazel McKinnel; *m* 1981, Jacqueline Shipley; one *s* three *d*. *Educ:* Marlborough Coll.; Queens' Coll., Cambridge (BA 1975; MA 1979); Wycliffe Hall, Oxford (BA 1979; MA 1986). Ordained deacon, 1980, priest, 1981; Curate, St Mary's Church, W Kensington, 1980–83; Anglican Chaplain, Liverpool Univ., 1983–87; Rector: Hatherleigh, Meeth, Exbourne and Jacobstowe, 1987–94; Minster Church of St Andrew, Plymouth, 1994–2012; Bishop Suffragan of Crediton, 2012–15. Hon. DD Plymouth, 2013. *Address:* 108 Molesworth Road, Plymouth PL3 4AQ. *T:* (01752) 500059. *E:* bishop.of.plymouth@exeter.anglican.org.

PLYMOUTH, Bishop of, (RC), since 2014; **Rt Rev. Mark Anthony O'Toole;** *b* London, 22 June 1963; *s* of Marcus and Maura O'Toole. *Educ:* St Ignatius Primary Sch., Stamford Hill; St Thomas More Secondary Sch., Wood Green; Univ. of Leicester (BSc Geog. 1984); Allen Hall Seminary (BD 1989); Univ. of Oxford (MPhil 1992); Pontifical Univ., Leuven (STL 2000). Pastoral work, St Joan of Arc Parish, Highbury, 1989–90; ordained priest, 1990; Asst Priest, St Mary Magdalene Parish, Willesden Green, and part-time Lectr in Catechesis, 1992–97; Allen Hall Seminary: Lectr in Theology and Formation Advr to seminarians, 1997–2002; Dean of Studies, 1999–2002; Private Sec. to Cardinal Murphy-O'Connor, Archbishop of Westminster, 2002–08; Rector, Allen Hall Seminary, 2008–13; Ecumenical Canon, Truro Cathedral, 2014–. *Recreations:* reading, swimming, film. *Address:* Bishop's House, 45 Cecil Street, Plymouth, Devon PL1 5RZ. *T:* (01752) 224414. *E:* bishopmark@prcdtr.org.uk.

PLYMOUTH, Archdeacon of; *see* Chandler, Ven. I. N.

POCKLINGTON, Jeremy Mark; Director General, Markets and Infrastructure, Department of Energy and Climate Change, since 2015; *b* Manchester, 13 Oct. 1973; *s* of David Pocklington and Valerie Pocklington; *m* 2005, Katy Jane Wigley. *Educ:* Manchester Grammar Sch.; Exeter Coll., Oxford (BA Mod. Hist. 1995; MPhil Econ. and Social Hist. (Distinction) 1997); INSEAD (MBA (Distinction) 2004). HM Treasury: joined, 1997; Head: Property Tax, 2004–06; Corporate and Private Finance, 2006–09; Cabinet Office: Director: Nat. Econ. Council Secretariat, 2009–10; Econ. and Domestic Affairs Secretariat, 2010–12; Enterprise and Growth Unit, HM Treasury, 2012–15. *Recreation:* hillwalking. *Address:* Department of Energy and Climate Change, 3 Whitehall Place, SW1A 2AW. *T:* 0300 068 5668. *E:* jeremy.pocklington@decc.gsi.gov.uk.

POCOCK, Sir Andrew (John), KCMG 2015 (CMG 2008); PhD; HM Diplomatic Service, retired; High Commissioner to Nigeria, 2012–15; *b* 23 Aug. 1955; *s* of John Francis Pocock and Vida Erica Pocock (*née* Duruty); *m* 1995, Julie Mason. *Educ:* St Mary's Coll., Trinidad; Queen Mary Coll., London (BA, MA); Peterhouse, Cambridge (PhD 1987). Joined HM Diplomatic Service, 1981; Second, later First Sec., Lagos, 1983–86; First Secretary: Southern African Dept, FCO, 1986–87; Washington, 1988–92; Personnel Mgt Dept, FCO, 1992–94; Asst, S Asia Dept, FCO, 1994–95; Counsellor, on loan to RCDS, 1996; Dep. High Comr, Canberra, 1997–2001; Hd of African Dept (Southern), FCO, 2001–03; High Comr to Tanzania, 2003–06; Ambassador to Zimbabwe, 2006–09; Africa Dir, FCO, 2010; High Comr to Canada, 2011–12. Liveryman, Cutlers' Co., 1979–. *Recreations:* tennis, cricket, walking.

POCOCK, Christopher James; QC 2009; *b* Chatham, 3 Nov. 1960; *s* of Roy Allan Pocock and Shirley Ann Rose Pocock; *m* Karen Anne (marr. diss. 2013); two *d*. *Educ:* St Dunstan's

Coll., Catford; Pembroke Coll., Oxford (BA Hons Juris.). Called to the Bar, Inner Temple, 1984; in practice as barrister specialising in family law. *Recreations:* fishing, scuba diving, amateur astronomy. *Address:* 1 King's Bench Walk, Temple, EC4Y 7DB. *T:* (020) 7936 1500, *Fax:* (020) 7936 1590. *E:* cpocockqc@1kbw.co.uk.

POCOCK, Gordon James; Director, Communications Educational Services Ltd, 1983–87; *b* 27 March 1933; *s* of late Leslie and Elizabeth Maud Pocock; *m* 1959, Audrey Singleton (*d* 1990). *Educ:* Royal Liberty Sch., Romford; Keble Coll., Oxford. Joined PO, 1954; Private Sec. to Dir Gen., 1958–59; Principal, 1960–68; Asst Sec., 1968–72; Dep. Dir, 1972–76; Dir, Ext. Telecommns, 1976–79; Dir, Telecommns Marketing, 1979, Sen. Dir, 1979–81; Chief Exec., Merlin Business Systems, BT, 1981–84. Fellow, Nolan Norton & Co., 1985–87. *Publications:* Corneille and Racine, 1973; Boileau and the Nature of Neo-Classicism, 1980; article on Nation, Community, Devolution and Sovereignty. *Recreations:* travel, theatre, local history. *Address:* 131 Lichfield Court, Sheen Road, Richmond, Surrey TW9 1AY. *T:* (020) 8940 7118.

POCOCK, Leslie Frederick, CBE 1985; Chairman, Liverpool Health Authority, 1982–86; *b* 22 June 1918; *s* of Frederick Pocock and Alice Helena Pocock; *m* 1946, Eileen Horton; two *s*. *Educ:* Emanuel School. FCCA. Observer Lieut, ROC, 1941–62. Chief Accountant: London & Lancashire Insurance Co. Ltd, 1959; Royal Insurance Co. Ltd, 1966; Chief Accountant and Taxation Manager, 1971, Dep. Gp Comptroller, 1974, Royal Insurance Gp; retired 1981. Gen. Comr of Income Tax, 1982–93. Dir, Federated Pension Services (Guarantee) Ltd, 1995–98. Pres., Assoc. of Certified Accountants, 1977–78. Mem., UK Central Council for Nursing, Midwifery and Health Visiting, 1983–87; Chm., Merseyside Residuary Body, 1985; Hon. Treas., 1986–96, Vice Chm., 1996–98, Merseyside Improved Houses, subseq. Riverside Housing Assoc. Chm. Governors, Sandown Coll., Liverpool, 1989–91. *Recreations:* bridge, crosswords. *Address:* Barn Lee, Tithebarn Close, Lower Heswall, Wirral, Merseyside CH60 0EY. *T:* (0151) 342 2917.

POCOCK, Margaret A.; *see* Aderin-Pocock.

PODGER, Geoffrey John Freeman, CB 2003; Chief Executive, Health and Safety Executive, 2005–13; Acting Chief Executive, WorkSafe New Zealand, 2013–14; *b* 3 Aug. 1952; *s* of late Leonard and Beryl Podger. *Educ:* Worthing High Sch. for Boys; Pembroke Coll., Oxford (Open Scholar; BA Medieval and Modern Langs 1974; MA 1977). MoD, 1974–82; Internat. Staff, NATO HQ, Brussels, 1977–79; Department of Health and Social Security, subseq. Department of Health, 1982–96; loaned to Falkland Islands Govt as Sec. to Port Stanley Hosp. Fire Inquiry, 1985; Private Sec. to Chm. (subseq. Chief Exec.), NHS Management Bd and Sec. to Bd, 1985–87; Principal Private Sec. to Sec. of State for Social Services, 1987–88; Head, Internat. Relations Unit, 1992–93; Under Sec. for Health Promotion, 1993–96; Hd of Food Safety and Sci. Gp, MAFF, 1996–97; Hd, Jt Food Safety and Standards Gp, MAFF and DoH, 1997–2000; Chief Exec., Food Standards Agency, 2000–03; Exec. Dir, European Food Safety Authy, 2003–05. Mem. Council, Inst. for Employment Studies, 2006– (Mem. Bd, 2007–). Chm., Occupational Safety and Health Consultants Register, 2011–. Hon. Vice Pres., IOSH, 2007. Hon. Fellow, IIRSM, 2007; CCMI 2009. MInstD. *Club:* Athenæum.

PODMORE, Dr Colin John; Director, Forward in Faith, since 2013; *b* Redruth, 22 Feb. 1960; *s* of late Raymond Podmore and of (Averil) Iris Podmore (*née* Collins). *Educ:* Bodmin Grammar Sch.; Bodmin Sch.; Keble Coll., Oxford (MA 1985; DPhil 1995); Selwyn Coll., Cambridge (PGCE 1983). Teacher, St Michael's C of E High Sch., Chorley, 1983–85; Asst Sec., Bd for Mission and Unity, Gen. Synod, 1988–91; Asst Sec., 1991–97, Dep. Sec., 1997–98, Council for Christian Unity; Secretary: Liturgical Publishing Gp, 1999–2002; CAC Rev. Gp, 1999–2001; House of Clergy of the Gen. Synod, 2002–11; Liturgical Commn, 2002–09; Dioceses Commn, 2002–11; Sen. Appts Rev. Gp, 2005–07; Clerk to the Gen. Synod, C of E, 2011–13. Parish Clerk, St Michael, Crooked Lane, London, 2004–. Mem. Council, Roehampton Univ., 2003–06. FRHistS 2002. *Publications:* The German Evangelical Churches: an introduction, 1992; (contrib.) Blackwell Dictionary of Evangelical Biography 1730–1860, 1995; (ed jtly) Leuenberg, Meissen and Porvoo, 1996; The Moravian Church in England 1728–1760, 1998; (ed and contrib.) Community-Unity-Communion: essays in honour of Mary Tanner, 1998; Prayers to Remember, 2001; (contrib.) New SCM Press Dictionary of Liturgy and Worship, 2002; (contrib.) Oxford Dictionary of National Biography, 2004; Aspects of Anglican Identity, 2005; (ed and contrib.) Maiden, Mother and Queen: Mary in the Anglican tradition, 2013; (ed and contrib.) Part of the One Church? The ordination of women and Anglican identity, 2014; articles in various jls incl. Anglican and Episcopal History, Ecclesiastical Law Jl, Ecclesiology, Internat. Jl for Study of the Christian Church, Jl of Anglican Studies, Jl of Ecclesiastical History, Jl of Moravian History, Theology, Unitas Fratrum. *Recreations:* church history, travel, dining with friends, gardening. *Address:* Forward in Faith, 2A The Cloisters, Gordon Square, WC1H 0AG. *T:* (020) 7388 3588. *E:* colin.podmore@forwardinfaith.com. *Club:* Savile.

PODMORE, Ian Laing; Chief Executive, Sheffield City Council, 1974–89; *b* 6 Oct. 1933; *s* of Harry Samuel Podmore and Annie Marion (*née* Laing); *m* 1961, Kathleen Margaret (*née* Langton); one *s* one *d*. *Educ:* Birkenhead School; Open Univ. (BA Hons 2010). Admitted Solicitor 1960. Asst Solicitor, Wallasey County Borough, 1960–63; Sen. Asst Solicitor, Southport Co. Borough, 1963–66; Deputy Town Clerk: Southport, 1966–70; Sheffield, 1970–74. *Recreations:* golf, gardening, classics. *Club:* Abbeydale Golf.

POET, Bruno; freelance lighting designer, since 1994; *b* Wimbledon, 1972; *s* of Robert Poet and Margarete Poet; *m* 2004, Annabel Ingram; one *d*. *Educ:* Oundle Sch.; Mansfield Coll., Oxford (BA Hons Geog.). Lighting designs include: *theatre:* Midnight's Children, 2003, Romeo and Juliet, 2008, RSC; Major Barbara, Volpone, Royal Exchange, Manchester, 2004; National Theatre: Aristocrats, 2005; The Enchantment, 2007; Every Good Boy Deserves Favour, 2009; Season's Greetings, 2010; Frankenstein, 2011 (Olivier Award for Lighting Design, 2012); London Road, 2012; Travelling Light, 2012; A Midsummer Night's Dream, Dundee Rep., 2006 ((jtly) Best Design Award, Critics' Awards for Scotland, 2006–07); Phaedra, Donmar, 2006; Tobias and the Angel, 2006, A Prayer for My Daughter, 2008, The Human Comedy, Young Vic; All About My Mother, 2007, Cause Célèbre, 2011, Old Vic; The Horse Marines, 2008, Grand Guignol, 2009, Chekhov in Hell, 2010, Th. Royal, Plymouth; Breakfast at Tiffany's, Th. Royal, Haymarket, 2009; Coram Boy, Bristol Old Vic, Colston Hall, 2011; Being Shakespeare, Trafalgar Studies, 2011; South Downs, The Browning Version, Minerva Th., Chichester, 2011; *opera:* Al Gran Sole Carico d'Amore, Staatsoper Berlin, Salzburg Fest.; L'Arbore di Diana, Barcelona, Madrid; Pelléas et Mélisande, Buenos Aires; Rusalka, Sydney Opera House; Rinaldo, Lyric Opera Chicago; Cavalleria Rusticana, I Pagliacci, Partenope, Royal Danish Opera; I Puritani, De Nederlandse, Grand Théâtre de Genève; The Enchanted Pig, Royal Opera House, Young Vic; Aida, The Marriage of Figaro, ENO; Il Trovatore, Den Jyske Opera; Carousel, Makropulos Case, Macbeth, NZ Opera; From the House of the Dead, A Midsummer Night's Dream, Romeo et Juliette, Dido and Aeneas, Les Noces, Opera North; A Midsummer Night's Dream, Linbury Studio; Das Portrait, Bregenzer Festspiele; Peter Grimes, Grand Théâtre de Genève; Una Cosa Rara, La Corte del Faraon, Valencia; Eine Florentinische Tragödie, Gianni Schicchi, Greek Nat. Opera; Varjak Paw, Opera Gp at Linbury Studio and UK tour; La Clemenza di Tito, Liceu, Barcelona, Oper Leipzig; Il Trovatore, Abao-Olbe, Bilbao; Rigoletto, Aarhus; Macbeth, Scottish Opera-Go-Round; *ballet:* Connectome, Royal Opera Hse, 2014. Lighting designer, Garsington Opera, 1998–. *Recreations:* sailing, travel. *Address:* Dodbrook Cottage, Millbrook, Torpoint, Cornwall PL10 1AN. *E:* brunopoet@mac.com.

POGGIO, Albert Andrew, GMH 2014; OBE 2006 (MBE 1995); United Kingdom Representative of HM Government of Gibraltar, since 1988; *b* 18 Aug. 1946; *s* of late Joseph Ernest and Sally Poggio; *m* 1966, Sally Sofaer (marr. diss. 1987); one *d*; partner, Doreen Isobel Mellor. *Educ:* Christian Brothers Coll., Gibraltar; Robert Montefiore Sch., London; City of London Coll. Chairman: Westex Go of Cos, 1980–88; Vital Health Gp, 1990–2003; Dir, 1996–, Sen. Vice Pres., 2003–09, Medcruise, Assoc. of Mediterranean Ports. Vice Pres., UK Overseas Territories Assoc., 1993–2000 (Chm., 2004 and 2014–15). Vice Chairman: Calpe House Charitable Trust, 1989–; Friends of Gibraltar Heritage Trust, 2013–. *Recreations:* sports, military memorabilia, travelling. *Address:* (office) 150 Strand, WC2R 1JA. *T:* (020) 7836 0777. *E:* albert.poggio@gmail.com. *Clubs:* Royal Automobile, Caledonian; Casino Calpe (Gibraltar); Royal Gibraltar Yacht.

POGSON, Kevin Edward, CBE 2006; Regional Director for London, HM Courts Service, 2006–10; *b* 5 Sept. 1950; *s* of Edward Pogson and Ivy (*née* Hubble); *m* (marr. diss.); two *s*. *Educ:* state schools in London. Joined Lord Chancellor's Department, 1967; various positions at HQ, 1967–79; Knightsbridge Crown Court, 1979–86; Personnel Dept, 1987–92; Dir of Finance, 1992–99, of Change, 1999–2001, Court Service; Circuit Adminr, SE Circuit, LCD, 2001–02; Dir of Field Services, Court Service, 2003–04; SE Circuit Adminr, Court Service, subseq. Regl Dir for SE, HM Courts Service, 2004–06. *Recreations:* chess, music, cooking. *Club:* UNATS Chess.

POINTER, Martin John; QC 1996; barrister; *b* 17 July 1953; *s* of late Michael Edward Pointer and of Mary Isabel Pointer (*née* Simms); *m* 1st, 1985 (marr. diss. 1997); two *s* one *d*; 2nd, 2001, Janet Bridal. *Educ:* King's Sch., Grantham; Univ. of Leicester (LLB Hons). Called to the Bar, Gray's Inn, 1976 (Reid Schol., 1977). Fellow, Internat. Acad. of Matrimonial Lawyers, 1994. *Address:* 1 Hare Court, Temple, EC4Y 7BE. *T:* (020) 7797 7070. *Club:* Travellers.

POITIER, Sidney, KBE (Hon.) 1974; actor, film and stage; director; *b* Miami, Florida, 20 Feb. 1927; *s* of Reginald Poitier and Evelyn (*née* Outten); *m* 1950, Juanita Hardy (marr. diss.); four *d*; *m* 1975, Joanna Shimkus; two *d*. *Educ:* private tutors; Western Senior High Sch., Nassau; Governor's High Sch., Nassau. Served War of 1941–45 with 1267th Medical Detachment, United States Army. Started acting with American Negro Theatre, 1946. *Plays include:* Anna Lucasta, Broadway, 1948; A Raisin in the Sun, Broadway, 1959; *films include:* Cry, the Beloved Country, 1952; Red Ball Express, 1952; Go, Man, Go, 1954; Blackboard Jungle, 1955; Goodbye, My Lady, 1956; Edge of the City, 1957; Band of Angels, 1957; Something of Value, 1957; The Mark of the Hawk, 1958; The Defiant Ones, 1958 (Silver Bear Award, Berlin Film Festival, and New York Critics Award, 1958); Porgy and Bess, 1959; A Raisin in the Sun, 1960; Paris Blues, 1960; Lilies of the Field, 1963 (award for Best Actor of 1963, Motion Picture Academy of Arts and Sciences); The Bedford Incident, 1965; The Slender Thread, 1966; A Patch of Blue, 1966; Duel at Diablo, 1966; To Sir With Love, 1967; In the Heat of the Night, 1967; Guess Who's Coming to Dinner, 1968; For Love of Ivy, 1968; They Call Me Mister Tibbs, 1971; The Organization, 1971; The Wilby Conspiracy, 1975; Deadly Pursuit, 1988; Sneakers, 1991; Separate But Equal, 1990; Children of the Dust, 1995; To Sir With Love II, 1996; Mandela and De Klerk, One Man, One Vote, 1997; The Jackal, 1998; David and Lisa, 1998; Free of Eden, 1999; The Simple Life of Noah Dearborn, 1999; director and actor: Buck and the Preacher, 1972; A Warm December, 1973; Uptown Saturday Night, 1974; Let's Do It Again, 1975; A Piece of the Action, 1977; *director:* Stir Crazy, 1981; Hanky Panky, 1982. Non-resident Ambassador of the Bahamas to Japan, 1997–, to UNESCO, 2003–. Hon. Acad. Award for Lifetime Achievement, 2002. Presidential Medal of Freedom (USA), 2009. *Publications:* This Life (autobiography), 1980; The Measure of a Man: a spiritual autobiography, 2000; Life Beyond Measure: letters to my great-grandaughter, 2009. *Address:* c/o CAA, 2000 Avenue of the Stars, Los Angeles, CA 90067, USA.

POLAK, Stuart, Baron *cr* 2015 (Life Peer), of Hertsmere in the County of Hertfordshire; **Stuart Polak,** CBE 2015; Chairman, TWC Associates; Senior Consultant, Jardine Lloyd Thompson. Youth and community worker, United Synagogue, Edgware; Officer, Bd of Deputies of British Jews, until 1989; Dir, Cons. Friends of Israel, 1989–2015 (Hon. Pres., 2015). *Address:* House of Lords, SW1A 0PW.

POLANYI, Prof. Hon. John Charles; PC (Can.) 1992; CC (Canada) 1979 (OC 1974); FRS 1971; FRSC 1966 (Hon. FRSC 1991); University Professor, since 1974 and Professor of Chemistry, since 1962, University of Toronto; *b* 23 Jan. 1929; *m* 1958, Anne Ferrar Davidson; one *s* one *d*; *m* 2004, Brenda Mary Bury. *Educ:* Manchester Grammar Sch.; Victoria Univ., Manchester (BSc, PhD, DSc). Research Fellow: Nat. Research Council, Ottawa, 1952–54; Princeton Univ., 1954–56; Univ. of Toronto: Lectr, 1956; Asst Prof., 1957–60; Assoc. Prof., 1960–62. Mem., Scientific Adv. Bd, Max Planck Inst. for Quantum Optics, Garching, Germany, 1982–92. Sloan Foundn Fellow, 1959–63; Guggenheim Meml Fellow, 1970–71, 1979–80; Sherman Fairchild Distinguished Scholar, CIT, 1982; Vis. Prof. of Chem., Texas A & M Univ., 1986; John W. Cowper Dist. Vis. Lectr, SUNY at Buffalo, 1986; Consolidated Bathurst Vis. Lectr, Concordia Univ., 1988; Beam Dist. Vis. Prof., Iowa Univ., 1992; Hitchcock Prof., Calif Univ., Berkeley, 1994; Lectures include: Centennial, Chem. Soc., 1965; Ohio State Univ., 1969 (and Mack Award); Reilly, Univ. of Notre Dame, 1970; Harkins Meml, Univ. of Chicago, 1971; Killam Meml Schol., 1974, 1975; F. J. Toole, Univ. of New Brunswick, 1974; Kistiakowsky, Harvard Univ., 1975; Camille and Henry Dreyfus, Kansas, 1975; Jacob Bronowski Meml, Toronto Univ., 1978; Hutchison, Rochester Univ., 1979; Priestley, Penn State Univ., 1980; Barré, Univ. of Montreal, 1982; Wiegand, Toronto Univ., 1984; Walker-Ames, Univ. of Washington, 1986; Morino, Japan, J. T. Wilson, Ont Sci. Centre, and Spiers Meml, Faraday Div., RSChem., 1987; Polanyi, IUPAC, W. B. Lewis, Atomic Energy of Canada Ltd, Killam, Univ. of Windsor, and Herzberg, Carleton Univ., 1988; C. R. Mueller, Purdue Univ., 1989; Phillips, Pittsburgh, 1991; Dove Meml, Toronto, 1992; Fritz London, Duke Univ., 1993; Linus Pauling, CIT, 1994; Hagey, Waterloo Univ., 1995. Hon. FRSE 1988; Hon. For. Mem., Amer. Acad. of Arts and Sciences, 1976; For. Associate, Nat. Acad. of Sciences, USA, 1978; Mem., Pontifical Acad. of Scis, 1986. Hon. DSc: Waterloo, 1970; Memorial, 1976; McMaster, 1977; Carleton, 1981; Harvard, 1982; Rensselaer, Brock, 1984; Lethbridge, Victoria, Ottawa, Sherbrooke, Laval, 1987; Manchester, York, 1988; Acadia, Univ. de Montréal, and Weizmann Inst. of Science, Israel, 1989; Univ. of Bari, Italy, Univ. of BC, and McGill Univ., 1990; Queen's, 1992; Free Univ., Berlin, 1993; Laurentian, Toronto, Liverpool, 1995; Hon. LLD: Trent, 1977; Dalhousie, 1983; St Francis Xavier, 1984; Concordia Univ., 1990; Calgary, 1994. Marlow Medal, Faraday Soc., 1963; Steacie Prize for Natural Scis, 1965; Chem. Inst. Canada Medal, 1976 (Noranda Award, 1967); Chem. Soc. Award, 1970; Henry Marshall Tory Medal, 1977, Michael Polanyi Medal, 1989, RSC; Remsen Award, Amer. Chem. Soc., 1978; (jtly) Wolf Prize in Chemistry, Wolf Foundn, Israel, 1982; (jtly) Nobel Prize for Chemistry, 1986; Killam Meml Prize, Canada Council, 1988; Royal Medal, 1989, Bakerian Prize, 1994, Royal Soc.; eponymous award, Canadian Soc. for Chem., 1992; Herzberg Canada Gold Medal, NSERC, 2008. KStJ 1987. *Film:* Concept in Reaction Dynamics, 1970. *Publications:* (with F. G. Griffiths) The Dangers of Nuclear War, 1979; papers in scientific jls, articles on science policy and on control of armaments. *Address:* Department of Chemistry, University of Toronto, 80 St George Street, Toronto, ON M5S 3H6, Canada; 1 Sullivan Street, Toronto, ON M5T 1B8, Canada.

POLDEN, Martin Alan, OBE 2006; Joint Founder, 1987, and Vice President, since 2011, Environmental Law Foundation (ELF) (Chairman, 1987–95); *b* 23 June 1928; *s* of Ralph Polden and Deborah Polden (*née* Tree); *m* 1956, Margaret Fry (*d* 1998); one *s* three *d*. *Educ:* Royal Grammar Sch., High Wycombe; LSE (LLB); Law Soc. Sch. of Law. Admitted solicitor, 1953; estabd Polden & Co., 1958, subseq. Polden Bishop & Gale, 1964; merged with

Rubinstein Callingham, 1987, Sen. Partner, 1990–94; Consultant, Ross & Craig, 1994–2001. Member: All-Party Envmt Gp, 1993–; Planning and Envmtl Law Cttee, Law Soc., 1994–2002. Member: Green Alliance, 1990–; The Maccabaeans, 1993–; BAFTA, 1999–; Justice, 2000–. Founding Trustee, 1983–2003, Patron, 2003–, Gandhi Trust; Founding Trustee, Hugo Gryn Meml Trust, 1997–2011. Mem., Bd of Visitors, Wormwood Scrubs Prison, 1986–91. Fellow, Soc. for Advanced Legal Studies, 1998. FRSA 2000. *Publications:* The Law, the Environment and the Mosquito, 1990; The Environment and the Law: earth, air, fire and water, 1994; articles in legal and envmtl jls, and newspapers. *Recreations:* reading, writing, theatre, cinema, boating, walking, grandchildering and philosophying with them. *Address:* London and Christchurch, Dorset. *Clubs:* MCC, City University.

POLDEN, Richard; His Honour Judge Polden; a Circuit Judge, since 2006; *b* 13 Nov. 1953; *s* of Stanley Richard Edward Polden and Gladys Mary Polden; *m* 1975, Susan James; one *s* one *d*. *Educ:* Knockhall Primary Sch.; Dartford Technical High Sch. for Boys; Coll. of Law, Guildford. Admitted Solicitor, 1978; joined Church Bruce Hawkes Brasington & Phillips Solicitors, Gravesend, 1978, Partner, 1980; a Dep. District Judge, 1993–95; District Judge, 1995; a Recorder, 2001–06; Designated Family Judge for Kent, 2008–14. *Recreations:* football, dog walking, foreign travel, trying to play golf. *Address:* Maidstone Combined Court, Barker Road, Maidstone, Kent ME16 8EQ. *T:* (01622) 202000. *E:* hhjudge.polden@judiciary.gsi.gov.uk. *Clubs:* Gravesend and Meopham Rotary; Gravesend 41; Mid Kent Golf.

POLE, Sir John (Chandos), 6th Bt *cr* 1791, of Wolverton, Hampshire; company director; *b* 27 April 1952; *o s* of Sir Peter Van Notten Pole, 5th Bt and of Jean Emily, *d* of late Charles Douglas Stone, Borden, WA; *S* father, 2010; *m* 1973, Suzanne Norah, BAppSc(MT), *d* of late Harold Raymond Hughes, Nedlands, WA; two *s* one *d*. *Educ:* Hale Sch.; Curtin Univ., Perth. *Heir: s* Michael Van Notten Pole [*b* 12 May 1980; *m* 2007, Susan Lila, *d* of David William Kay; one *s* one *d*]. *Address:* 41 Webster Street, Nedlands, WA 6009, Australia.

POLIAKOFF, Prof. Sir Martyn, Kt 2015; CBE 2008; PhD; FRS 2002; Research Professor in Chemistry, University of Nottingham, since 1991; *b* 16 Dec. 1947; *s* of late Alexander Poliakoff, OBE and Ina Miriam Poliakoff (*née* Montagu); *m* 1969, Dr Janet Frances Keene; one *s* one *d*. *Educ:* Westminster Sch.; King's Coll., Cambridge (BA 1969, PhD 1973). CChem, FRSC 2002, Hon. FRSC 2015; CEng, FIChemE 2004. Sen. Res. Officer, Dept of Inorganic Chem., Univ. of Newcastle upon Tyne, 1972–79; Lectr in Inorganic Chem., 1979–85, Reader, 1985–91, Univ. of Nottingham. Rutherford Lect., Royal Soc., 2012. Mem. Council, IChemE, 2009–13. Hon. Prof. of Chem., Moscow State Univ., 1999–. Foreign Sec. and Vice-Pres., Royal Soc., 2011–. MAE 2013. Hon. Mem., Chem. Soc. of Ethiopia, 2008; Associate Member: Third World Acad. Sci., 2013; Ethiopian Acad. of Scis, 2014; Foreign Mem., Russian Acad. of Scis, 2012. Hon. ScD E Anglia, 2008; Hon. DSc Heriot-Watt, 2011. Hansen Medal, IChemE, 2009; Leverhulme Medal, Royal Soc., 2010; Nyholm Prize for Education, RSC, 2011. *Publications:* contrib. scientific papers to chem. jls. *Recreations:* hill-walking, second-hand books, architecture. *Address:* School of Chemistry, University of Nottingham, Nottingham NG7 2RD. *T:* (0115) 951 3520, *Fax:* (0115) 951 3058. *E:* martyn.poliakoff@nottingham.ac.uk.

See also E. S. Coen, S. Poliakoff.

POLIAKOFF, Stephen, CBE 2007; playwright and film director; *b* 1 Dec. 1952; *s* of late Alexander Poliakoff, OBE and Ina Miriam Poliakoff (*née* Montagu); *m* 1983, Sandy Welch; one *s* one *d*. *Educ:* Westminster Sch.; King's Coll., Cambridge. *Plays:* writer: Clever Soldiers, 1974; The Carnation Gang, 1974; Hitting Town, 1975; City Sugar (Evening Standard Most Promising Playwright Award), 1976; Strawberry Fields, NT, Shout Across the River, RSC, 1978; The Summer Party, 1980; Favourite Nights, 1981; Breaking the Silence, RSC, 1984; Coming in to Land, NT, 1987; Playing With Trains, RSC, 1989; Sienna Red, nat. tour, 1992; Blinded by the Sun, RNT (Critics' Circle Best Play Award), 1996; Remember This, RNT, 1999; writer and director: Sweet Panic, Hampstead, 1996, Duke of York's, 2003; Talk of the City, RSC, 1998; My City, Almeida, 2011; *films:* writer: Bloody Kids, 1980; Runners, 1982; Soft Targets, 1982; writer and director: Hidden City; Close My Eyes (Evening Standard Best British Film Award), 1992; Century, 1995; The Tribe, 1998; Food of Love, 1998; Glorious 39, 2009; *TV plays include:* writer: Caught on a Train (BAFTA Award), 1980; She's Been Away (Venice Film Festival Prize); writer and director: Shooting the Past (serial) (PrixItalia), 1999; Perfect Strangers (serial), 2001 (Dennis Potter BAFTA Award, 2002); The Lost Prince (Emmy Award), 2003; Friends and Crocodiles, 2005; Gideon's Daughter, 2005; Joe's Palace, Capturing Mary, A Real Summer, 2007; Dancing on the Edge, 2013. *Publications:* all plays; Plays One, 1989; Plays Two, 1994; Plays Three, 1998. *Recreations:* watching cricket, going to the cinema. *Address:* 33 Devonia Road, N1 8JQ. *T:* (020) 7354 2695.

See also E. S. Coen, Sir M. Poliakoff.

POLITO, Simon William; Inquiry Chair, Competition and Markets Authority, since 2014 (a Deputy Chairman, Competition Commission, 2012–14); *b* Leics, 11 March 1949; *s* of John and Dodo Polito; *m* 1992, Helen Cormack; two *s*. *Educ:* Lancing Coll., Sussex; Liverpool Univ. (LLB Hons). Called to the Bar, Middle Temple, 1972; admitted as solicitor, 1976; Solicitor, 1976–82, Partner, 1982–2009, Consultant, 2009–11, Lovells. Mem., Jt Wkg Party on Competition Laws of UK and Irish Bars and Law Societies, 1991–2006 (Chm., 2006–11). Mem. Court, Leathersellers' Co., 2007–. Gov., Colfe's Sch., Lewisham, 1999–. *Recreations:* sport, now mainly as a spectator, gardening, architecture, food and wine. *Address:* Competition and Markets Authority, Victoria House, Southampton Row, WC1B 4AD. *T:* (020) 7271 0146, *Fax:* (020) 7271 0203. *E:* simon.polito@cma.gsi.gov.uk. *Club:* Hurlingham.

POLITZER, Prof. (Hugh) David, PhD; Richard Chace Tolman Professor of Theoretical Astrophysics, California Institute of Technology, since 2004; *b* 31 Aug. 1949; *s* of Alan A. Politzer and Valerie T. Politzer (*née* Diamant). *Educ:* Michigan Univ. (BS 1969); Harvard Univ. (PhD 1974). Visiting Associate, 1975–76, Associate Prof., 1976–79, Prof. of Theoretical Physics, 1979–2004, Calif Inst. of Technol. (Jtly) Nobel Prize in Physics, 2004. *Address:* Particle Theory Group, California Institute of Technology, 1200 East California Boulevard, Pasadena, CA 91125, USA.

POLIZZI, Hon. Olga, (Hon. Mrs William Shawcross), CBE 1990; Director, Rocco Forte Hotels (formerly RF Hotels), since 1996; Director: Tresanton Hotel Ltd, since 1996; Hotel Endsleigh Ltd, since 2004; Millers Bespoke Bakery Ltd, since 1996; Forte plc, 1983–96 (Managing Director, Building and Design Department, 1980–96); *d* of Baron Forte; *m* 1st, 1966, Alessandro Polizzi di Sorrentino (*d* 1980); two *d*; 2nd, 1993, Hon. William Hartley Hume Shawcross, *qv*. *Educ:* St Mary's Sch., Ascot. Westminster City Councillor, 1989–94. Trustee: Italian Hosp. Fund, 1992–; Trusthouse Charitable Foundn, 1997– (Chm.); St Mary's Sch., Ascot, 1997– (Gov., 1988–97); Trustee and Gov., Landau Forte Acads; Vice Chm., King Edward VII's Hosp., 2007–. *Recreations:* walking, opera. *Address:* (office) 70 Jermyn Street, SW1Y 6NY.

See also Hon. Sir R. J. V. Forte, O. Peyton.

POLKINGHORNE, Rev. Canon John Charlton, KBE 1997; PhD, ScD; FRS 1974; Fellow, Queens' College, Cambridge, since 1996 (President, 1989–96; Hon. Fellow, 1996); *b* 16 Oct. 1930; *s* of George Baulkwill Polkinghorne and Dorothy Evelyn Polkinghorne (*née* Charlton); *m* 1955, Ruth Isobel Martin (*d* 2006); two *s* one *d*. *Educ:* Elmhurst Grammar Sch.; Perse Sch.; Trinity Coll., Cambridge (MA 1956; PhD 1955; ScD 1974; Hon. Fellow 2014); Westcott House, Cambridge, 1979–81. Commonwealth Fund Fellow, California Institute of Technology, 1955–56; Lecturer in Mathematical Physics, Univ. of Edinburgh, 1956–58; Cambridge University: Fellow, Trinity Coll., 1954–86; Lecturer in Applied Mathematics, 1958–65; Reader in Theoretical Physics, 1965–68; Prof. of Mathematical Physics, 1968–79; Fellow, Dean and Chaplain of Trinity Hall, Cambridge, 1986–89 (Hon. Fellow, 1989). Hon. Prof. of Theoretical Physics, Univ. of Kent at Canterbury, 1985. Ordained deacon 1981, priest 1982; Curate: St Andrew's, Chesterton, 1981–82; St Michael's, Bedminster, 1982–84; Vicar of St Cosmus and St Damian in the Blean, 1984–86; Canon Theologian, Liverpool Cathedral, 1994–2005; Six Preacher, Canterbury Cathedral, 1996–2006. Member: SRC, 1975–79; Human Genetics Adv. Commn, 1996–99; Human Genetics Commn, 2000–02; Chairman: Nuclear Phys Bd, 1978–79; Cttee to Review the Research Use of Fetuses and Fetal Material, 1988–89; Task Force to Review Services for Drugs Misusers, 1994–96; Adv. Cttee on Genetic Testing, 1996–99. Member: C of E Doctrine Commn, 1989–95; Gen. Synod of C of E, 1990–2000. Chm. of Governors, Perse Sch., 1972–81; Governor, SPCK, 1984–2002. Licensed Reader, Diocese of Ely, 1975. Hon. DD: Kent, 1994; Durham, 1999; Gen. Theol. Seminary, NY, 2010; Wycliffe Coll., 2011; Hon. DSc: Exeter, 1994; Leicester, 1995; Marquette, 2003; Hon. DHum Hong Kong Baptist, 2006. Templeton Prize, 2002. *Publications:* (jtly) The Analytic S-Matrix, 1966; The Particle Play, 1979; Models of High Energy Processes, 1980; The Way the World Is, 1983; The Quantum World, 1984; One World, 1986; Science and Creation, 1988; Science and Providence, 1989; Rochester Roundabout, 1989; Reason and Reality, 1991; Science and Christian Belief, 1994; Quarks, Chaos and Christianity, 1994; Serious Talk, 1995; Scientists as Theologians, 1996; Beyond Science, 1996; Searching for Truth, 1996; Belief in God in an Age of Science, 1998; Science and Theology, 1998; Faith, Science and Understanding, 2000; (jtly) The End of the World and the Ends of Gods, 2000; (jtly) Faith in the Living God, 2001; (ed) The Work of Love, 2001; The God of Hope and the End of the World, 2002; Quantum Theory: a very short introduction, 2002; Living with Hope, 2003; Science and the Trinity, 2004; Exploring Reality, 2005; Quantum Physics and Theology, 2007; From Physicist to Priest: an autobiography, 2007; Theology in the Context of Science, 2008; (with N. Beale) Questions of Truth: fifty-one responses to questions about God, science, and belief, 2009; Encountering Scripture: a scientist explores the Bible, 2010; (ed) The Trinity and an Entangled World: relationality in physical science and theology, 2010; Science and Religion in Quest of Truth, 2011; many articles on elementary particle physics in learned journals. *Recreation:* gardening. *Address:* Queens' College, Cambridge CB3 9ET.

POLL, Prof. (David) Ian (Alistair), OBE 2002; FREng, FRAeS, FCGI; Professor of Aerospace Engineering (formerly Professor of Aerodynamics), 1995–2012, now Professor Emeritus; Managing Director, Poll AeroSciences Ltd, since 2012; *b* 1 Oct. 1950; *s* of Ralph Angus Poll and Mary Poll (*née* Hall); *m* 1975, Elizabeth Mary Read; two *s* one *d*. *Educ:* Heckmondwike Grammar Sch.; Imperial Coll. London (BSc Hons); Cranfield Inst. of Technol. (PhD). FRAeS 1987; FREng (FEng 1996). Engineer, Future Projects, Hawker Siddeley Aviation, 1972–75; Res. Asst, 1975–78, Lectr, 1978–85, Sen. Lectr, 1985–87, Cranfield Inst. of Tech.; University of Manchester: Prof. of Aeronautical Engineering, and Dir of Goldstein Aeronaut. Engrg Lab., 1987–95; Man. Dir, Flow Science Ltd, 1990–95; Head, Dept of Engineering, 1991–94; Hd, Coll. of Aeronautics, subseq. Dir, Cranfield Coll. of Aeronautics, 1995–2004, Cranfield Univ. Cranfield Aerospace Ltd: Man. Dir, 1995–99; Tech. Dir, 1999–2004; Business Develt and Tech. Dir, 2004–12; non-exec. Dir, 2012–. Mem., NERC, 2014–. Royal Aeronautical Society: Mem. Council, 1996–2010; Vice Pres., 1998–2000; Pres., 2001; Chairman: Learned Soc. Bd, 1996–2000; Strategic Review Bd, 2000–01; Uninhabited Air Vehicle Cttee, 2005–; Cranfield Univ. Br., 1997–. Member: Fluid Dynamics Panel, AGARD, 1990–97; Council, Air League, 1997–2012; Gen. Assembly, Internat. Council of the Aeronautical Scis, 1997–2012 (Chm., Programme Cttee, 2006–; Pres., 2008–10; Past Pres., 2011–12); Foresight Action Steering Cttee, SBAC, 1997–99; Aerospace Cttee, DTI, 1999–2004; Aerospace Technol. Steering Gp, DTI, 2004–; Council, Royal Acad. Engrg, 2004–07; Uninhabited Air Vehicle Steering Cttee, CAA, 2006–; Chm., Defence Sci. Adv. Council, MoD, 2011–14; Founder Mem., Greener-By-Design, 2000– (Mem., Steering Cttee, 2000–); Mem., Ind. Sci. and Technol. Advrs Register, MoD, 2014–. Vice-Pres., Confedn of European Aerospace Socs, 2001–04. FAIAA 2000, Hon. FAIAA 2012; ACGI 1972, FCGI 2004 (Vice Pres., City and Guilds Coll. Assoc., 2004–06). Hon. Fellow, Internat. Council Aeronautical Scis, 2012. Mem., RUSI, 2005. Liveryman, Co. of Coachmakers and Coach Harness Makers, 2001. Mem., British Model Flying Assoc. (A Cert. 2015). Wilbur and Orville Wright Lectr, 2002, Lanchester Lectr, 2008, RAeS; Dryden Lectr, AIAA, 2010. Hodgson Prize, RAeS, 2001. *Publications:* more than 100 papers on fluid mechanics in learned jls and for tech. conferences. *Recreations:* golf, aviation, wine and conversation. *Address:* Cranfield Aerospace Ltd, Cranfield, Beds MK43 0AL. *T:* (01234) 754743. *E:* d.i.a.poll@cranfield.ac.uk. *Clubs:* Athenæum, Royal Air Force.

POLL, Ven. Martin George; Canon of Windsor, Chaplain in the Great Park and Chaplain, Cumberland Lodge, since 2012; Canon Chaplain, St George's Chapel, Windsor, since 2012; Domestic Chaplain to HM the Queen, Royal Chapel, Windsor Great Park, since 2014; *b* Enfield, Middx, 10 Dec. 1961; *s* of Maurice and Violet Poll; *m* 1984, Diana Hudson; one *s* one *d*. *Educ:* Edmonton Co. Sch.; Christchurch Coll., Canterbury (BA Hons); Ripon Coll., Cuddesdon (CTh). Ordained deacon 1987, priest 1988; Curate, John Keble Ch, Mill Hill, 1987–90; Chaplain: HMS Raleigh, 1990–92; Commando Helicopters, 1992–94; BRNC, Dartmouth, 1994–97; HMS Invincible, 1997–99; HM Naval Base, Faslane, 1999–2002; RNAS Yeovilton, 2002–04; Staff Chaplain, 2004–06; Fleet Staff Chaplain, 2006–07; Chaplain: HMS Illustrious, 2007; HM Naval Base, Portsmouth, 2007–10; Principal Anglican Chaplain, Archdeacon for RN and Dep. Chaplain of the Fleet (formerly Dir, Naval Chaplaincy Service), 2010–12. QHC 2010–12. Mem., Gen. Synod, C of E, 2010–. Governor: Royal Sch. Windsor Great Park, 2012–; St George's Sch., Windsor Castle, 2012–. Trustee: Assoc. of RN Officers, 2009–; Windsor Fest., 2012–. *Recreations:* amateur dramatics, choral singing, history, theatre. *Address:* Chaplain's Lodge, The Great Park, Windsor SL4 2HP.

POLLACK, Anita Jean; writer and European consultant, since 2006; *b* NSW, Australia, 3 June 1946; *d* of late John and Kathleen Pollack; *m* 1986, Philip Bradbury; one *d*. *Educ:* City of London Polytechnic (BA 1979); Birkbeck Coll., Univ. of London (MSc Polit. Sociology 1981). Advertising copy writer, Australia, 1963–69; book editor, 1970–75; student, 1976–79; Research Asst to Rt Hon. Barbara Castle, MEP, 1981–89. MEP (Lab) London SW, 1989–99; Hd of Eur. Liaison, later Eur. Policy, English Heritage, 2000–06. Contested (Lab), EP elections: SE Region, 1999; London, 2004. *Publications:* Wreckers or Builders?: a history of Labour MEPs 1979–99, 2009; New Labour in Europe, 2015. *Recreation:* family. *Address:* 139 Windsor Road, E7 0RA. *W:* www.anitapollack.eu.

POLLARD, Prof. (Alan) Mark, DPhil; Edward Hall Professor of Archaeological Science, and Director, Research Laboratory for Archaeology and the History of Art, University of Oxford, 2004–14; Fellow, Linacre College, Oxford, since 2004; *b* Takapuna, Auckland, NZ, 5 July 1954; *s* of Alan and Elizabeth Pollard; *m* 1993, Dr Rebecca Nicholson; two *d*. *Educ:* Univ. of York (BA Physics; DPhil Physics). Res. Fellow, Res. Lab. for Archaeol. and the Hist. of Art, Univ. of Oxford, 1978–84; New Blood Lectr in Chem. and Archaeol., UC Cardiff, 1984–90; University of Bradford: Prof. of Archaeol Scis, 1990–2004; Hd of Dept, 1990–99; Pro-Vice Chancellor, 1999–2004. Nat. Co-ordinator for Science-based Archaeol., 1997–2000. *Publications:* (jtly) Archaeological Chemistry, 1996, 2nd edn 2008; (jtly) Handbook of Archaeological Science, 2001; (jtly) Analytical Chemistry in Archaeology, 2007; numerous articles. *Recreations:* Morris dancing, fishing. *Address:* Research Laboratory for Archaeology and the History of Art, Dyson Perrins Building, South Parks Road, Oxford OX1 3QY. *T:* (01865) 285228. *E:* mark.pollard@rlaha.ox.ac.uk.

POLLARD, Prof. Andrew John, PhD; Professor of Education: Institute of Education, University College London (formerly Institute of Education, University of London), since 2006; Graduate School of Education, University of Bristol, 2011–15 (Visiting Professor, since 2015); Fellow of Wolfson College, Cambridge, since 2000; *b* 13 Nov. 1949; *s* of Michael and Anne Pollard; *m* 1971, Rosalind Croft; one *s* one *d*. *Educ:* Univ. of Leeds (BA 1971); Univ. of Lancaster (PGCE 1972); Univ. of Sheffield (MEd 1976; PhD 1981). Teaching in primary schools, 1972–81; Sen. Lectr, 1981–84, Principal Lectr, 1984–85, Oxford Poly.; Reader, 1985–90, Associate Dean, 1990–95, UWE; Prof. of Educn, Univ. of Bristol, 1996–2000; Prof. of Educn, Univ. of Cambridge, 2000–05; Dir, ESRC Teaching and Learning Res. Prog., 2002–09. Chm., Educn Panel, REF 2014, HEFCE, 2011–14; Mem., Expert Panel on Review of National Curriculum, Dept for Educn, 2011. Chm., UK Strategic Forum for Res. in Educn, 2008–11; Dir, ESCalate, HEA, 2011. Chm., William Pollard & Co. Ltd, 1997–2014. Hon. DEd Edinburgh, 2010. *Publications:* The Social World of the Primary School, 1985; Reflective Teaching, 1987, 4th edn (as Reflective Teaching in Schools), 2014; (jtly) Changing English Primary Schools, 1994; The Social World of Children's Learning, 1996; (with A. Filer) The Social World of Pupil Career, 1999; (with P. Triggs) What Pupils Say: changing policy and practice in primary education, 2000; (with A. Filer) The Social World of Pupil Assessment, 2000; Professionalism and Pedagogy: a contemporary opportunity, 2010; (with M. James) Principles for Effective Pedagogy, 2011. *Recreations:* sailing, gardening, bird watching. *Address:* UCL Institute of Education, 20 Bedford Way, WC1H 0AL.

POLLARD, Maj.-Gen. Anthony John Griffin, CB 1992; CBE 1985; DL; General Officer Commanding, South West District, 1990–92, retired; *b* 8 April 1937; *s* of William Pollard and Anne Irene Griffin; *m* Marie-Luise; four *s*. *Educ:* Oakham Sch.; Jesus Coll., Cambridge. Commnd Royal Leics Regt, 1956; served Cyprus, Germany, Hong Kong, Borneo, Malta; Staff Coll., 1969; Staff 7 Armd Bde, 1970–72; Instr, Staff Coll., 1975–77; CO 1st Bn Royal Anglian Regt, 1977–79; (Norway, NI, Germany); QMG's Secretariat, 1980; Col, Tactical Doctrine, BAOR, 1981; Col, Ops and Tactical Doctrine, 1(BR) Corps, 1982; Comdr, British Forces, Belize, 1983–84; Comdt, Sch. of Infantry, 1984–87; Comdr, British Mil. Mission to Uganda, 1985–86; Dir Gen., Trng and Doctrine (Army), 1987–90. Dep. Col, Royal Anglian Regt, 1986–92; Colonel Commandant: Small Arms Sch. Corps, 1987–92; Queen's Div., 1990–92; Hon. Col Suffolk ACF, 1992–2000. Pres., Royal Tigers Assoc., 1996–2010. DL Suffolk, 1999. OStJ 2004 (Chm., St John Council, Suffolk, 2004–10). *Recreations:* family, fishing, gardening, archaeology, ancient buildings. *Club:* Victory Services (Vice Chm., 2003–08; Vice Pres., 2010–).

POLLARD, Sir Charles, Kt 2001; QPM 1990; Chairman, Restorative Solutions Community Interest Company, since 2006; *b* 4 Feb. 1945; *s* of Humphrey Charles Pollard and Margaret Isobel Pollard (*née* Philpott); *m* 1972, Erica Jane Allison Jack; two *s* one *d*. *Educ:* Oundle Sch.; Bristol Univ. (LLB). Metropolitan Police, 1964; Sussex Police, 1980; Asst Chief Constable, Thames Valley Police, 1985–88; Dep. Asst Comr, i/c No 5 (SW) Area of London, Metropolitan Police, 1988–91; Chief Constable, Thames Valley Police, 1991–2002. Chm., Quality of Service Cttee, ACPO, 1993–94; Vice-Chm., Thames Valley Partnership (working for safer communities), 1992–2002; Mem., Youth Justice Bd for England and Wales, 1998–2006 (actg Chm., 2003–04). Chairman: Winchester Restorative Justice Gp, 1999–2008; Justice Res. Consortium, 2002–05. Mem. Bd, Centre for Mgt and Policy Studies, 2000–02. Chm., Oxford Common Purpose, 1996–98; Vice Chm., Why Me?, Victims for Restorative Justice, 2009–. Vis. Fellow, Nuffield Coll., Oxford, 1993–2001. Hon. LLD: Buckingham, 2001; Bristol, 2003. *Publications:* contribs to nat. media and learned jls on policing, criminal justice and restorative justice. *Recreations:* tennis, walking, family pursuits. *Address:* Restorative Solutions Community Interest Company, Unit 5, Albert House, The Pavilions, Ashton-on-Ribble, Preston PR2 2YD. *Club:* Royal Over-Seas League.

POLLARD, Christopher Charles; *b* 30 April 1957; s of Anthony Cecil and Margaret Noelle Pollard; *m* 1984, Margaret Ann Langlois; three *d*. *Educ:* Merchant Taylors' Sch., Northwood; Newland Park Coll. Gramophone, 1981–99; Editor, 1986–90; Man. Editor, 1990–93; Editl Dir, 1993–99. Director: Jethou, 1995–; Out of the Blue Productions, 2001–07; Songlines Publications, 2002–15; Kryotrans Internat., 2006–10; TOWER Cold Chain Solutions, 2009–; Themis Analytics, 2011–. *Recreations:* Rugby football, cricket, cars, music. *Address:* Beechcroft, Hotley Bottom, Great Missenden, Bucks HP16 9PL.

POLLARD, Eve, (Lady Lloyd), OBE 2008; Chief Executive Officer, Eve Pollard Designs Ltd; *d* of late Ivor and Mimi Pollard; *m* 1st, 1968, Barry Winkleman (marr. diss. 1979); one *d*; 2nd, 1979, Sir Nicholas Lloyd, *qv*; one *s*. Fashion Editor: Honey, 1967–68; Daily Mirror Magazine, 1968–69; Women's Editor: Observer Magazine, 1970–71; Sunday Mirror, 1971–81; Asst Ed., Sunday People, 1981–83; Features Ed. and presenter, TV-am, 1983–85; Editor: Elle USA (launched magazine in NY), 1985–86; Sunday magazine, News of the World, 1986; You magazine, Mail on Sunday, 1986–87; Sunday Mirror and Sunday Mirror Magazine, 1987–91; Sunday Express and Sunday Express Magazine, 1991–94. Founder, Wedding Day magazine, 1999. Formerly contributor to Sunday Times. Member: English Tourism Council (formerly English Tourist Bd), 1993–2000; Competition Commn, 1999–2007; Mem., Newspaper Takeover Panel, Competition Commn, 1999–2007. Chair and Founder Mem., Women in Journalism, 1995–. Vice-Chm., Wellbeing of Women. Vis. Fellow, Bournemouth Univ., 2001–. *Publications:* Jackie: biography of Mrs J. K. Onassis, 1971; (jtly) Splash, 1995; (jtly) Best of Enemies, 1996; (jtly) Double Trouble, 1997; Unfinished Business, 1998; Jack's Widow, 2006. *Address:* c/o Jackie Gill Management Ltd, 3 Warren Mews, W1T 6AN. *T:* (020) 7383 5550.

See also C. Winkleman.

POLLARD, (George) Nicholas; Chief Executive, Services Sound and Vision Corporation, since 2009; *b* 15 Nov. 1950; *s* of Thomas Bewcastle Pollard and Helen Pollard; *m* 1981, Sally Jane Behenna; two *s*. *Educ:* Birkenhead Sch. Television journalist, BBC, 1977–80; ITN: television journalist, 1980–92; Exec. Producer, News at Ten, 1987–92; Producer, Election coverage, 1987, 1992; ind. producer, current affairs progs, 1992–94; Dir of Progs, Channel One TV, 1994–96; Hd of News, British Sky Broadcasting, 1996–2006. Mem., Adv. Panel, DCMS Free-to-Air Events Listing Review, 2009. *Recreations:* family, walking, reading.

POLLARD, Prof. Jeffrey William, PhD; FRSB; FRSE; Professor of Resilience Biology and Director, MRC Centre for Reproductive Health, University of Edinburgh, since 2012; *b* Rochford, Essex, 23 Jan. 1950; *s* of Clifford Pollard and Marjorie Althea Pollard; *m* 1981, Ooi-Thye Chong. *Educ:* Westcliff High Sch.; Univ. of Sheffield (BSc Special Hons 1971); Imperial Cancer Res. Fund/King's Coll. London (PhD 1974). FRSB (FSB 2013). Lectr, Queen Elizabeth Coll., subseq. King's Coll. London, 1980–88; Albert Einstein College of Medicine, New York: Associate Prof., 1988–93; Prof., 1993–; Louis Goldstein Swan Chair, 2008–. Wellcome Sen. Investigator, 2013–. FAAAS 2011; FRSE 2015. Medal of Honor, Amer. Cancer Soc., 2010. *Publications:* (ed) Evolutionary Theory: paths into the future, 1984; (ed) Methods in Molecular Biology: Animal Cell Culture, vol. 5 1990, 2nd edn (vol. 75) 1997, Plant Cell Culture, vol. 6 1990; over 200 articles in Nature, Sci., Cell, Immunity, Nature Reviews, etc. *Recreations:* Japanese art, music, wine and food, travel. *Address:* University of Edinburgh, Room C1.17, Queen's Medical Research Institute, 47 Little France Crescent, Edinburgh EH16 4TJ. *T:* (0131) 242 6231, *Fax:* (0131) 242 6441. *E:* jeff.pollard@ed.ac.uk.

POLLARD, Joy Kerr; *see* Larkcom, J. K.

POLLARD, Kerry Patrick; JP; *b* 27 April 1944; *s* of late Patrick Joseph Pollard and of Iris Betty Pollard; *m* 1966, Maralyn Murphy; five *s* two *d*. *Educ:* St Joseph's Primary Sch., Heywood, Lancs; Thornleigh Coll., Bolton. Engr, British Gas, 1960–92; Co-ordinator, Homes for Homeless People, 1992; Dir and Co. Sec., Cherry Tree Housing Assoc., 1992–97; Chair, NACRO Housing, 2011–. Chair, Labour Housing Gp, 2010–. Member (Lab): St Albans DC, 1982–98; Herts CC, 1989–97. MP (Lab) St Albans, 1997–2005; contested (Lab) same seat, 1992, 2005, 2015. Hon. Fellow, Royal Coll. of Midwives, 2003. JP St Albans, 1984. *Recreations:* swimming, theatre, country walking.

POLLARD, L. Edwin, OBE 2003; High Commissioner for Barbados in the United Kingdom, 2003–08; *b* 21 May 1942; *m* 1968, Deanna Winifred Warner; one *s* one *d*. *Educ:* Combermere Sch., Barbados. CDipAF. Joined Barclays Bank plc, 1961: Staff and Industrial Relns Manager, Barclays, Caribbean; Asst Caribbean Dir (Mem., Barclays UK Exec. Cttee); Personal Sector and Offshore Dir; Product Develt and Mktg Dir, until 2000. Member Board: Barbados Inst. Banking and Finance; Securities Exchange of Barbados. FCIB. *Recreations:* golf, cricket, hockey, football. *Address:* c/o Barbados High Commission, 1 Great Russell Street, WC1B 3ND. *T:* (020) 7631 4975, *Fax:* (020) 7323 6872. *Club:* London Golf.

POLLARD, Linda, CBE 2013 (OBE 2004); JP; DL; Chairman, Leeds Teaching Hospitals NHS Trust, since 2013; Founding Chairman, An Inspirational Journey, since 2009; *b* Shipley, W Yorks, 13 Sept. 1945; *d* of William Edward Bannister and Ada Bannister; *m* 1973, David Ernest Pollard; one *s*, and one step *s* one step *d*. *Educ:* Bingley Grammar Sch. Regl Manager, Deal Marketing, London, 1967–70; Co-Founder and Man. Dir, Quorum Ltd, fashion retail, 1972–84; Founder and Man. Dir, Concept Marketing Ltd, 1985–95. Director: Andrews of Bradford (BMW) Ltd, 1980–96; Oak Lane Hldgs Ltd, 1991–2008; Mem. Bd, Real Radio Yorkshire, 2000–04; Regl Chm., Coutts Bank plc, 2007– (Nat. Women's Ambassador, 2008–10). Chairman: Bradford Property Forum, 2007–09; Two Percent Club, 2013– (Chm., Yorks, 2000–13). Non-exec. Dir, Bradford HA, 1994–96; Chairman: Bradford NHS Teaching Hosps Trust, 1996–2000; Bradford Dist Care Trust, 2002–04; West Yorks Strategic HA, 2004–06; Airedale, Bradford, Leeds NHS Cluster PCT, 2009–13; Adv. Bd, Leeds Inst. for Quality Healthcare. Associate Mem., Fitness to Practise Cttee, GMC, 2001–05. Regl Chm., Learning and Skills Council, 2002–06; Mem., Strategy Cttee, HEFCE, 2007–09; non-exec. Mem. Bd, UCEA, 2010–12. Dep. Chm., Yorkshire Forward, 2004–12; Member, Board: Fair Cities Bradford, 2004–06; Northern Way, 2004–06; Welcome to Yorkshire, 2009–11. Chairman: Bradford Can Appeal, 2001–03; Born in Bradford Res. Appeal, 2005–07; Breast Cancer Haven Yorks, 2008–10; Trustee, Leeds Teaching Hosps Foundn Charity, 2013–. Pro Chancellor and Chm. Council, Univ. of Leeds, 2007–13. JP Bradford, 1979; DL West Yorks, 2006. Hon. LLD Leeds, 2013. *Recreations:* keen gardener, travel, work. *T:* 07802 325532. *E:* linda@lindapollard.org. *Club:* Sloane.

POLLARD, Mark; *see* Pollard, A. M.

POLLARD, Nicholas; *see* Pollard, G. N.

POLLARD, His Honour Richard Frederick David; a Circuit Judge, 1990–2006; Senior Circuit Judge, Nottingham Crown Court, 2002–06; *b* 26 April 1941; *s* of William Pollard and Anne Irene Pollard (*née* Griffin), CBE; *m* 1964, Angela Susan Hardy; one *s* two *d*. *Educ:* Oakham School; Trinity College Dublin (BA); Univ. of Cambridge (Dip. Crim.). Called to the Bar, Gray's Inn, 1967, Bencher, 2001. *Recreations:* walking, art nouveau, looking out of the window.

POLLARD, Stephen Bernard; Partner, WilmerHale, solicitors, since 2012; *b* London, 5 Sept. 1958; *s* of David Pollard and Pauline Pollard; *m* 1990, Margaret Ainscough; two *s* two *d*. *Educ:* Manchester Grammar Sch.; Pembroke Coll., Oxford (BA Hons Juris.). Admitted solicitor, 1985; Partner, Kingsley Napley, 1990–2011. *Recreations:* family, sport (especially running and cycling), walking, theatre, Fulham FC. *Address:* WilmerHale, 49 Park Lane, W1K 1PS. *T:* (020) 7872 1006. *E:* stephen.pollard@wilmerhale.com.

POLLARD, Stephen Ian; Editor, Jewish Chronicle, since 2008; *b* London, 18 Dec. 1964; *s* of Bernard Pollard, CB and of Regina Pollard; *m* 2007, Samantha Benjamin; one *s* one *d*. *Educ:* St Martin's Sch., Northwood; John Lyon Sch., Harrow; Mansfield Coll., Oxford (MA Modern Hist.). Res. asst to Rt Hon. Peter Shore, MP, 1989–92; Res. Dir, Fabian Soc., 1992–95; Hd of Res., Social Mkt Foundn, 1995–97; freelance writer, various newspapers, 1997–99; Chief Leader Writer and columnist, Daily Express, 1999–2001; Sen. Fellow, 2001–05, Pres., 2005–08, Centre for New Europe. Chm., Eur. Inst. for Study of Contemporary Antisemitism, 2007–08. Mem., Adv. Council, Reform, 2001–. Fellow, Civitas, 2001–06. *Publications:* (with A. Adonis) A Class Act: the myth of Britain's classless society, 1997; David Blunkett, 2004; Ten Days that Changed the Nation: the making of modern Britain, 2009. *Recreations:* National Hunt racing, Tottenham Hotspur FC, classical music, opera, wine, good food, obscure public policy books. *Address:* Jewish Chronicle, 28 St Albans Lane, NW11 7QE. *T:* (020) 7415 1500. *E:* stephen@stephenpollard.net.

POLLEN, Peregrine Michael Hungerford; Executive Deputy Chairman, 1975–77, Deputy Chairman, 1977–82, Sotheby Parke Bernet and Co.; *b* 24 Jan. 1931; *s* of late Sir Walter Michael Hungerford Pollen, MC, JP, and Lady Pollen; *m* 1958, Patricia Helen Barry; one *s* two *d*. *Educ:* Eton Coll.; Christ Church, Oxford. National Service, KRRC, 1949–51. ADC to Sir Evelyn Baring, Governor of Kenya, 1955–57; Sotheby's, 1957–82: Dir, 1961; Pres., Sotheby Parke Bernet, New York, 1965–72. *Address:* The Farmhouse, Norton Hall, Mickleton, Glos GL55 6PU. *Clubs:* Brooks's, Beefsteak.

POLLEN, Sir Richard (John Hungerford), 8th Bt *cr* 1795, of Redenham, Hampshire; Independent Corporate Communications Consultant; Director, Pollen Organics Ltd, since 2000; *b* 3 Nov. 1946; *o s* of Sir John Michael Hungerford Pollen, 7th Bt and Angela Pollen (*née* Russi, later Henderson); *S* father, 2003; *m* 1971, Christianne Mary, *d* of Sir Godfrey Agnew, KCVO, CB; four *s* three *d* (and one *s* decd). *Educ:* Worth Sch. Capel-Cure Myers, 1964–68; Financial Times, 1970–71; Charles Barker, 1971–79; Valin Pollen, 1979–91; Richard Pollen & Co., 1990–94; Ludgate Pollen, 1994–96; Communication Consultant, Pollen Associates, 1996–2000. Dir, Hampshire Fare, 2004–12. FCIPR. *Publications:* (contrib.) The Management Audit, 1993; (contrib.) Maw on Corporate Governance, 1994. *Recreations:* riding, running, ski-ing, walking. *Heir:* *s* William Richard Hungerford Pollen [*b* 28 June 1976; *m* 2007, Jennifer, *d* of Vance Kyte; one *s* two *d*]. *Club:* Royal Automobile.

POLLINGTON, Viscount; John Andrew Bruce Savile; *b* 30 Nov. 1959; *s* and *heir* of 8th Earl of Mexborough, *qv*.

POLLINI, Maurizio; pianist; *b* Milan, 5 Jan. 1942; *s* of Gino Pollini and Renata Melotti; *m* 1968, Maria Elisabetta Marzotto; one *s*. Has performed with all major orchestras, including: Chicago Symphony; Cleveland; Berlin Philharmonic; Boston Symphony; LPO; LSO; New York Philharmonic; Vienna Philharmonic; has played at Berlin, Prague, Salzburg and Vienna Fests. First Prize, Internat. Chopin Competition, Warsaw, 1960; Ernst von Siemens Music Prize, Munich, 1996. Has made numerous recordings. *Address:* c/o HarrisonParrott Ltd, 5–6 Albion Court, Albion Place, W6 0QT.

POLLOCK, family name of **Viscount Hanworth**.

POLLOCK, Alexander; Sheriff of Grampian, Highland and Islands at Inverness, 2005–09 (at Inverness and Portree, 2001–05); *b* 21 July 1944; *s* of late Robert Faulds Pollock, OBE, and Margaret Findlay Pollock; *m* 1975, Verena Francesca Gertraud Alice Ursula Critchley; one *s* one *d*. *Educ:* Rutherglen Academy; Glasgow Academy; Brasenose Coll., Oxford (Domus Exhibnr; MA); Edinburgh Univ. (LLB); Univ. for Foreigners, Perugia. Solicitor, Bonar Mackenzie & Kermack, WS, 1970–73; passed advocate, 1973; Advocate Depute, 1990–91;

Sheriff (floating) of Tayside, Central and Fife at Stirling, 1991–93; Sheriff of Grampian, Highland and Is at Aberdeen and Stonehaven, 1993–2001. Contested (C) Moray, 1987. MP (C): Moray and Nairn, 1979–83; Moray, 1983–87. PPS to Sec. of State for Scotland, 1982–86, to Sec. of State for Defence, 1986–87. Mem., Commons Select Cttee on Scottish Affairs, 1979–82, 1986–87. Sec., British-Austrian Parly Gp, 1979–87. Mem., Queen's Body Guard for Scotland, Royal Co. of Archers, 1984–. *Publications:* (contrib.) Stair Memorial Encyclopaedia of Scots Law. *Recreations:* music, cycling, dogs. *Address:* Drumdarrach, Forres, Moray, Scotland IV36 1DW. *Clubs:* New (Edinburgh); Highland (Inverness).

POLLOCK, Prof. Allyson Mary; Professor of Public Health Research and Policy, and Co-Director, Global Health, Policy and Innovation Unit, Centre for Primary Care and Public Health, Queen Mary University of London, since 2011. *Educ:* Univ. of Dundee (BA Hons Physiol. 1979; MB ChB 1983); London Sch. of Hygiene and Tropical Medicine (MSc Community Medicine 1989). MFPH (MFPHM 1991), FFPH 1993; FRCGP 2012. Prof. of Health Policy and Health Services Res., Sch. of Public Policy, UCL, 1998–2005, Hon. Prof., 2005–; Dir, R&D, UCL Hosps NHS Trust, 1998–2005; Prof. of Internat. Public Health Policy, 2005–11, Dir, Centre for Internat. Public Health Policy, 2006–11, Univ. of Edinburgh. *Publications:* NHS plc: the privatisation of our health care, 2004; The New NHS Explained, 2006; Tackling Rugby: what every parent should know about injuries, 2014; contrib. BMJ, British Jl of Gen. Practice, Lancet, Jl of PHM, Public Law, Public Money and Mgt. *Address:* Centre for Primary Care and Public Health, Queen Mary University of London, 58 Turner Street, E1 2AB. *T:* (020) 7882 5637. *E:* a.pollock@qmul.ac.uk, allyson.pollock@gmail.com.

POLLOCK, Brian; *see* Pollock, His Honour P. B.

POLLOCK, Prof. Christopher John, CBE 2002; PhD, DSc; Hon. Professor, Institute of Biological, Environmental and Rural Sciences (formerly of Rural Sciences), Aberystwyth University (formerly University of Wales, Aberystwyth), since 2007; Director, Institute of Grassland and Environmental Research, 1993–2007; *b* 28 March 1947; *s* of Neil Cunningham Pollock and Margaret Pollock (*née* Charlton); *m* 1970, Elizabeth Anne Bates; one *s* one *d*. *Educ:* Trinity Hall, Cambridge (BA 1968, MA 1972); Birmingham Univ. (PhD 1972; DSc 1993). Post-Doctoral Fellow, Botany Sch., Cambridge, 1971–74; joined Welsh Plant Breeding Station, later Inst. of Grassland and Envmtl Res., then Inst. of Biol, Envmtl and Rural Scis, 1974; Head, Res. Gp, 1985; Head, Envmtl Biology Dept, 1989. Fulbright Fellow, Univ. of California, Davis, 1978–79; NATO Sen. Res. Fellow, Purdue Univ., 1987–92; Hon. Professor: Univ. of Wales, Aberystwyth, 1993; Nottingham Univ., 1994–2006. Chairman: Scientific Steering Cttee for Farm-scale Trials of GM Crops, 1999–2005; Res. Priorities Gp for Sustainable Farming and Food, 2003–06; Adv. Cttee for Releases into the Envmt, 2003–13; Chief Scientific Advr to First Minister of Wales, 2007–08; Mem., BBSRC, 2008–14. FRSB (FIBiol 1997); FRAgS 2000; FLSW 2013. DUniv Birmingham, 2011. *Publications:* (jtly) Carbon Partitioning Within and Between Organisms, 1992; (with J. F. Farrar) The Biology of Fructans, 1993; approx. 100 reviews; papers in sci. jls. *Recreations:* golf, walking, woodwork. *Address:* Institute of Biological, Environmental and Rural Sciences, Aberystwyth University, Aberystwyth SY23 3AL. *T:* (01970) 624471. *Club:* St David's (Aberystwyth).

POLLOCK, David John Frederick; President, European Humanist Federation, 2006–12; *b* 3 Feb. 1942; *s* of late Leslie William Pollock and Dorothy Emily (*née* Holt); *m* 1976, Lois Jaques (marr. diss. 1991); one *s*. *Educ:* Beckenham and Penge Grammar Sch.; Keble Coll., Oxford (BA Lit. Hum. 1964; MA); London Business Sch. British Coal Corporation, 1964–90: Head of Central Secretariat, 1972–78; Head of Staff Planning and Orgn, 1980–90; Dir, ASH, 1991–94; Dir, Continence Foundn, 1996–2001. Mem., Hackney BC, 1974–78. Sec., Charity Law Reform Cttee, 1972–77. Trustee (formerly Mem., Exec. Cttee), British Humanist Assoc., 1965–75 and 1997– (Chm., 1970–72); Mem. Bd, Rationalist Assoc. (formerly Rationalist Press Assoc.), 1979– (Chm., 1989–91). Hd, Internat. Humanist and Ethical Union delegn to Council of Europe, 2013–. Treasurer, Hackney North Labour Party, 1989–92. *Publications:* Denial & Delay: the political history of smoking and health 1950–64, 1999; Article 17: reasons for concern, 2013; (contrib.) Belief, Law and Politics, 2014; articles in humanist, health and other jls. *Recreations:* theatre, gardening. *Address:* 13 Dunsmure Road, N16 5PU. *T:* (020) 8800 3542, 07866 806932, *Fax:* (020) 7502 0283. *E:* david.pollock@virgin.net. *W:* www.david-pollock.org.uk.

POLLOCK, Sir George F(rederick), 5th Bt *cr* 1866; artist-photographer, since 1963; *b* 13 Aug. 1928; *s* of Sir (Frederick) John Pollock, 4th Bt and Alix l'Estom (*née* Soubiran); *S* father, 1963; *m* 1951, Doreen Mumford (*d* 2012), *o d* of N. E. K. Nash, CMG; one *s* two *d*. *Educ:* Eton; Trinity Coll., Cambridge. BA 1953, MA 1957. 2nd Lieut, 17/21 Lancers, 1948–49. Admitted Solicitor, 1956, retd. Hon. FRPS (Past Pres.); Hon. MPAGB (J. S. Lancaster Medal for exceptional services to photography, 2003); EFIAP. FRSA. *Heir:* *s* David Frederick Pollock [*b* 13 April 1959; *m* 1985, Helena, *o d* of late L. J. Tompsett, OBE; one *d*]. *Address:* 83 Minster Way, Bath BA2 6RL. *T:* (01225) 464692. *W:* www.georgepollock.co.uk. *Club:* Downhill Only (Wengen).

POLLOCK, Sir Giles (Hampden) Montagu-, 5th Bt *cr* 1872; management consultant, 1974–2002; *b* 19 Oct. 1928; *s* of Sir George Seymour Montagu-Pollock, 4th Bt, and Karen-Sofie (*d* 1991), *d* of Hans Ludwig Dedekam, Oslo; *S* father, 1985; *m* 1963, Caroline Veronica, *d* of Richard F. Russell; one *s* one *d*. *Educ:* Eton; de Havilland Aeronautical Technical School. With de Havilland Enterprise, 1949–56; Bristol Aeroplane Co. Ltd, 1956–59; Bristol Siddeley Engines Ltd, 1959–61; Associate Dir, J. Walter Thompson Co. Ltd, 1961–69; Director: C. Vernon & Sons Ltd, 1969–71; Acumen Marketing Group Ltd, 1971–74; 119 Pall Mall Ltd, 1972–78; Associate, John Stork & Partners, subseq. John Stork Internat., then Korn/Ferry Internat., 1980–2002. *Recreations:* bicycling, water ski-ing, walking. *Heir:* *s* Guy Maximilian Montagu-Pollock, *b* 27 Aug. 1966. *Address:* The White House, 7 Washington Road, SW13 9BG. *T:* (020) 8748 8491.

POLLOCK, Isobel Anne, OBE 2014; CEng, FIMechE; Royal Academy of Engineering Visiting Professor in Engineering and Design, University of Leeds, since 2006; *b* Ballymoney, NI, 10 Nov. 1954; *d* of late Charles Wilson Pollock and Elisabeth Margaret Pollock (*née* Watson); *m* 1980, Graham Ramsden (*d* 1997); *m* 2015, Robin Hulf. *Educ:* Dalriada, Ballymoney; Imperial Coll., London (BScEng 1976). CEng 1981; FIMechE 1991. ICI, 1976–87; DuPont, 1987–96; Beatson Clark, 1997–99; Dir, Benbane Engrg Consultants, 1999–. Engineering Council UK: Chm., Quality Assce Cttee, 2005–12; Mem., Trustee Bd, 2005–13; Associate, 2013–; Chairman: BIS (formerly DTI, then DIUS) Pathfinder Measurement Wkg Gp, subseq. Electromagnetics and Time Prog., 2006–; Steering Bd, Nat. Measurement Office, 2013–. Pres., IMechE, 2012–13 (Vice Pres., 2000–06; Dep. Pres., 2010–12). Trustee, Audi Design Foundn, 1999–2010. Liveryman, Engineers' Co., 2003– (Sen. Warden, 2015–). FCGI. Hon. DSc Huddersfield, 2004. *Recreations:* engineering heritage, history of measurement, family history research, bridge, golf. *Address:* School of Mechanical Engineering, University of Leeds, Woodhouse Lane, Leeds LS2 9JT. *Club:* Woodsome Hall Golf.

POLLOCK, His Honour (Peter) Brian; a Circuit Judge, 1987–2003; *b* 27 April 1936; *s* of late Brian Treherne Pollock and Helen Evelyn Pollock (*née* Holt-Wilson); *m* 1st, 1966, Joan Maryon Leggett (marr. diss. 1981); two *s* (and one *s* decd); 2nd, 1988, Jeannette Mary Nightingale; two step *s* one step *d*. *Educ:* St Lawrence College. Called to the Bar, Middle Temple, 1958. A Recorder of the Crown Court, 1986–87. *Recreations:* croquet, watching cricket, travel, walking, reading. *Address:* 18 Sanditon, Sidmouth, Devon EX10 8NU. *T:* (01395) 514425. *Clubs:* MCC; Sidmouth Cricket, Tennis and Croquet.

POLTIMORE, 7th Baron *cr* 1831; **Mark Coplestone Bampfylde;** Bt 1641; Chairman, Sotheby's Russia and Deputy Chairman, Sotheby's Europe, since 2007; *b* 8 June 1957; *s* of Captain the Hon. Anthony Gerard Hugh Bampfylde (*d* 1969) (*er s* of 6th Baron) and of Brita Yvonne (who *m* 2nd, 1975, Guy Elmes), *o d* of late Baron Rudolph Cederström; *S* grandfather, 1978; *m* 1982, Sally Anne, *d* of late Dr Norman Miles; two *s* one *d*. Christie's: Associate Dir, 1984–87; Dir, 1987–2000; Dep. Chm., 1998–2000; Man. Dir, Eauctionroom.com, 2000–02; Sen. Dir, Sotheby's, 2002–06; Chm., Sotheby's UK, 2006–07. *Publications:* (with Philip Hook) Popular Nineteenth Century Painting: a dictionary of European genre painters, 1986. *Heir:* *s* Hon. Henry Anthony Warwick Bampfylde, *b* 3 June 1985. *Address:* North Hidden Farm, Hungerford, Berks RG17 0PY. *Club:* White's.

POLWARTH, 11th Lord *cr* 1690 (Scot.); **Andrew Walter Hepburne Scott;** *b* 30 Nov. 1947; *s* of 10th Lord Polwarth, TD and Caroline Margaret (*née* Hay); *S* father, 2005; *m* 1971, Anna, *e d* of late Maj. J. F. H. Surtees, OBE, MC; two *s* two *d*. *Educ:* Eton; Trinity Hall, Cambridge. JP Roxburgh Div., Scottish Borders, 1997–2005. *Heir:* *s* Master of Polwarth, *qv*. *Club:* Knickerbocker (New York).

POLWARTH; Master of; Hon. William Henry Hepburne Scott; Director, Investment Management Division, Brewin Dolphin Ltd; *b* 21 March 1973; *s* and *heir* of Lord Polwarth, *qv*; *m* 2008, Donna Louise, *d* of Maj. Gen. Anthony Neil Carlier, *qv*; one *s* one *d*. *Educ:* Charterhouse; Newcastle Univ. With Brewin Dolphin Ltd, 1996–. *Heir:* *s* Harry Walter Hepburne Scott, *b* 21 March 2010.

POLYCHRONAKIS, John; Chief Executive, Dudley Metropolitan Borough Council, 2008–15; *b* Liverpool, 22 Nov. 1952; *s* of George and Ann Polychronakis; *m* 1980, Jacqueline Greaves; one *s* one *d*. *Educ:* St Francis Xavier's Coll., Liverpool; Liverpool Univ. (LLB). Admitted as solicitor, 1977; Solicitor, Liverpool CC, 1977–83; Asst Dir, Sefton MBC, 1983–87; Sen. Asst Chief Legal Officer, 1987–92, Dir, Law and Property, 1992–2008, Dudley MBC. Company Secretary: Black Country Living Mus. Ltd, 1994–2015; Black Country Consortium Ltd, 2008–15. Pres., Assoc. of Council Secretaries and Solicitors, 2004. *Recreations:* running, cycling, walking.

POMEROY, family name of **Viscount Harberton**.

POMEROY, Sir Brian (Walter), Kt 2012; CBE 2006; *b* 26 June 1944; *m* 1974, Hilary Susan Price; two *d*. *Educ:* King's Sch., Canterbury; Magdalene Coll., Cambridge (MA). FCA (ACA 1968). Partner, Touche Ross Mgt Consultants, subseq. Deloitte Consulting, 1975–99: on secondment as Under Sec., DTI, 1981–83; Man. Dir, 1987–95; Sen. Partner, 1995–99. Non-executive Director: Rover Gp plc, 1985–88; QBE Insurance Gp Ltd, 2014–. Member: Nat. Lottery Commn, 1999–2007 (Chm., 1999–2000, 2002–03); Audit Commn, 2003–09; Gambling Commn, 2007–11 (Chm., 2008–11). Mem., Cttee of Enquiry into Regulatory Arrangements at Lloyd's, 1986; Ind. Mem. Council, Lloyd's, 1996–2004; Dep. Chm., Lloyd's Regulatory Bd, 1996–2002. Chairman: Telecommunications Interconnection Cttee, 1988–91; Financial Inclusion Task Force, HM Treasury, 2005–11; Payments Council, 2007–09; Ind. Commn on Equitable Life Payments, 2010–11; Responsible Gambling Strategy Bd, 2012–13. Member: Disability Rights Task Force, 1997–99; Pensions Protection Investments Accreditation Bd, 2000–05; Bd, Social Market Foundn, 2000–; Ind. Inquiry into Drug Testing at Work, Joseph Rowntree Foundn, 2003–04; Financial Reporting Rev. Panel, 2004–13. Non-executive Director: FSA, 2009–13; Financial Conduct Authy, 2013–March 2016. Mem. Council, Mgt Consultants Assoc., 1996–99. Chairman: AIDS Awareness Trust, 1993–96; Centrepoint, 1993–2001; Eur. Public Health Foundn, 1997–2002; Homeless Link, 2001–05; Raleigh Internat., 2005–07. Trustee: Money Advice Trust, 1999–2009 (Ambassador, 2010–); Children's Express, 2004–07; SPACE Studios, 2004–05; Lloyd's Charitable Trust, 2004–10; Photographers' Gall., 2006–13 (Chm. of Trustees, 2008–13); Chm. of Trustees, The King's Consort, 2000–05. Master, Mgt Consultants' Co., 2000–01. FRSA 1994. *Publications:* contrib. articles on public finance and regulation. *Recreations:* photography (ARPS 2004; MA 2006), listening to music, theatre, cycling. *Address:* 7 Ferncroft Avenue, NW3 7PG. *T:* 07785 304368. *E:* pomeroybw@aol.com.

POMERY, (Susannah) Victoria (Louise), OBE 2012; Director, Turner Contemporary, since 2002; *b* Wirksworth, Derbys, 30 Aug. 1964; *d* of Peter Pomery and Briar Pomery. *Educ:* Norton Hill Sch., Midsomer Norton; North Staffordshire Poly. (BA Hons Hist. of Design and Visual Arts); Birmingham Poly. (MA (Dist.) Hist. of Art and Design). Pt-time Lectr in Hist. of Art and Design, Stourbridge Coll. of Art and Design, 1989; Asst Curator, Mead Gall., Univ. of Warwick, Coventry, 1989–95; Exhibns Officer, Angel Row Gall., Nottingham, 1995–97; Sen. Curator, Tate Liverpool, 1997–2002. Hon. MA Univ. for the Creative Arts, 2013. *Publications:* (ed with Dr Christoph Grunenberg) Marc Quinn, 2002. *Recreations:* arts, walking, gardening. *Address:* Turner Contemporary, Rendezvous, Margate, Kent CT9 1HG. *T:* (01843) 233001. *E:* vpomery@turnercontemporary.org.

POND, Christopher; Partner and Head, Public Affairs, Kreab Worldwide, since 2013; *b* 25 Sept. 1952; *s* of Charles Richard Pond and Doris Violet Pond; *m* 1990, Carole Tongue, *qv* (marr. diss. 1999); one *d*; *m* 2003, Lorraine Melvin; one *s* one *d*. *Educ:* Univ. of Sussex (BA Hons Econs). Research Asst in Econs, Birkbeck Coll., Univ. of London, 1974–75; Res. Officer, Low Pay Unit, 1975–78; Lectr in Econs, CS Coll., 1978–79; Dir, Low Pay Unit, 1980–97. Contested (Lab) Welwyn Hatfield, 1987; MP (Lab) Gravesham, 1997–2005; contested (Lab) same seat, 2005; Parly Under-Sec. of State, DWP, 2003–05. Chief Exec., Nat. Council for One Parent Families, subseq. One Parent Families|Gingerbread, 2005–08; Financial Services Authority: Dir, Financial Capability, 2007–10; Sen. Advr, 2010–11; Hd, Consumer Affairs, 2011–12; Vice Chm., Financial Inclusion Commn, 2014–. Chm., Capacitybuilders UK Ltd, 2005–09. Chm., Standards Bd, Safe Home Income Plans, later Equity Release Council, 2012–. Chm., Wkg Gp on debt, Centre for Social Justice, 2012–14. Ind. Mem., Ethics and Responsibility Bd Sub-Cttee, HMRC, 2009–13. Vis. Lectr in Econs, Univ. of Kent, 1983–84; Hon. Vis. Prof. and Res. Fellow, Univ. of Surrey, 1984–86; Hon. Vis. Prof., Univ. of Middlesex, 1995–. Consultant, Open Univ., 1987–88 and 1991–92. Chm., Credit Action, Money Charity, 2011–. Vice Chm., End Child Poverty, 2007–09; Mem. Council, IFS, 2005–14; Trustee: Nat. Family and Parenting Inst., 2009–13; Family and Childcare Trust, 2013–. FRSA 1992. *Publications:* (jtly) To Him Who Hath, 1977; (jtly) Taxation and Social Policy, 1981; (contrib.) Old and New Poverty, 1995; Out of Poverty: towards prosperity, 1996; (contrib.) Working for Full Employment, 1997; (contrib.) Beyond 2002, 1999. *Recreations:* running, reading, family. *Address:* Kreab, 90 Long Acre, WC2E 9RA.

PONDER, Sir Bruce (Anthony John), Kt 2008; PhD; FRCP, FMedSci; FRS 2001; Li Ka Shing Professor of Oncology, University of Cambridge, 2006–11, now Emeritus; Director: Cancer Research UK Cambridge Institute, 2005–13, now Emeritus; Cambridge Cancer Centre, 2010–15; Fellow, Jesus College, Cambridge, 1993–2011, now Emeritus; *b* 25 April 1944; *s* of late Anthony West Ponder and Dorothy Mary Ponder (*née* Peachey); *m* 1969, Margaret Ann Hickinbotham; one *s* three *d*. *Educ:* Charterhouse Sch.; Jesus Coll., Cambridge (MA, MB BChir); St Thomas's Hosp. Med. Sch.; PhD London. FRCP 1987; FRCPath 2001–10. NHS hosp. appts, 1968–73; Clinical Research Fellow, ICRF, 1973–76; first Hamilton Fairley Fellow, CRC, at Harvard Med. Sch., 1977–78; Clinical Scientific Officer, ICRF, St Bartholomew's Hosp., 1978–80; Institute of Cancer Research: CRC Fellow and Sen. Lectr in Med., Royal Marsden Hosp., 1980–87; Reader in Human Cancer Genetics and Head, Section of Cancer Genetics, 1987–89; University of Cambridge: Dir, Cancer Res. UK (formerly CRC) Human Cancer Genetics Gp, 1989–2008; CRC Prof. of Human Cancer Genetics, 1992–96; CRUK (formerly CRC) Prof. of Oncology, 1996–2006. Mem., Bd of Dirs, Amer. Assoc. for Cancer Res., 2008–11 (Founding Mem., Academy, 2013); Pres., British Assoc. for Cancer Res., 2010–14. Hon. Consultant Physician: Royal Marsden Hosp., 1980–2003; Addenbrooke's Hosp., Cambridge, 1989–. Croonian Lectr, RCP, 1998. Gibb Fellow, CRC, 1990, CRUK, 2013. Founder FMedSci 1998; Founding Fellow, European Acad. of Cancer Scis, 2011–. Internat. Public Service Award, Nat. Neurofibromatosis Foundn, USA, 1992; Merck Prize, European Thyroid Assoc., 1996; Hamilton Fairley Award, European Soc. of Med. Oncology, 2004; Bertner Award, M. D. Anderson Hosp., 2007; Alfred Knudson Award for Cancer Genetics, Nat. Cancer Inst., USA, 2008; Ambuj Nath Bose Prize, RCP, 2008; Donald Ware Waddell Award for Cancer Res., Univ. of Arizona, 2010; Lifetime Achievement Award, CRUK, 2013. *Publications:* papers on genetics, cancer, developmental biology. *Recreations:* gardening, travel, golf, wine, photography. *Address:* Hutchison/MRC Research Centre, Box 197, Hills Road, Cambridge CB2 0XZ. *T:* (01223) 761860; Sutton Fields, Bircham Road, Snettisham, Norfolk PE31 7NF. *Club:* Royal West Norfolk Golf (Brancaster).

PONSOLLE, Patrick Henry Jean; Chairman and Chief Executive Officer, Pajoma SA; *b* 20 July 1944; *s* of Jean Ponsolle and Marie-Rose Ponsolle (*née* Courthaliac); *m* 2nd, 1983, Nathalie Elie-Lefebvre; two *d*, and two step *s* two step *d*. *Educ:* Lycée Janson-de-Sailly, Paris; Lycée Henri IV, Paris; Ecole Normale Supérieure; Institut d'Etudes Politiques, Paris; Ecole Nationale d'Administration. Adminr, Min. of Econ. and Finance, 1973–77; Financial Attaché, French Embassy, Washington, 1977–79; Ministry of Economy and Finance: Chargé de Mission to Dir of Forecasting, 1980; Dep. Chief of Staff of Laurent Fabius, Minister responsible for the budget, 1981–83; Gen. Sec., Nat. Accounts and Budget Commn, France, 1980–81; Compagnie de Suez: Asst Dir Gen., 1983–87; Dir Gen., 1988–93; Adminr, 1991–93; Jt Chm., 1994–96, Exec. Chm., 1996–2001, Eurotunnel Gp; Chm., Eurotunnel SA, 1994–2001; Man. Dir and Vice Chm., Morgan Stanley Internat. Ltd, and Pres., Morgan Stanley SA, 2001–09; Vice Chm., Rothschild Europe, 2009–14.

PONSONBY, family name of **Earl of Bessborough,** and of **Barons de Mauley** and **Ponsonby of Shulbrede.**

PONSONBY OF SHULBREDE, 4th Baron *cr* 1930, of Shulbrede; **Frederick Matthew Thomas Ponsonby;** Baron Ponsonby of Roehampton (Life Peer), 2000; JP; *b* 27 Oct. 1958; *o s* of 3rd Baron and of Ursula Mary, *yr d* of Comdr Thomas Stanley Lane Fox-Pitt, OBE, RN; *S* father, 1990; *m* 1995, Sarah Catriona Pilkington Jackson; one *s* one *d*. *Educ:* Holland Park Comprehensive Sch.; University Coll., Cardiff; Imperial Coll., London. FIMMM (FIMM 1996); CEng 1997. Councillor (Lab), London Borough of Wandsworth, 1990–94. Opposition frontbench spokesman on educn, H of L, 1992–97. Member: Sub-cttee C, European Select Cttee, H of L, 1997–98; Select Cttee on Sci. and Technol., H of L, 1998–99; Select Cttee on Constitution, 2001–02. Delegate: Council of Europe and WEU, 1997–2001; OSCE, 2001–10. JP Westminster, 2006, Inner London Youth Panel, 2008, Gtr London Family Panel, 2012. *Heir: s* Hon. Cameron John Jackson Ponsonby, *b* 4 Aug. 1995. *Address:* House of Lords, SW1A 0PW.

PONSONBY, Sir Charles (Ashley), 3rd Bt *cr* 1956, of Wootton, co. Oxfordshire; DL; *b* 10 June 1951; *e s* of Sir Ashley Ponsonby, 2nd Bt, KCVO, MC and Lady Martha Butler, *yr d* of 6th Marquess of Ormonde, CVO, MC; *S* father, 2010; *m* 1983, Mary Priscilla Bromley Davenport; two *s* one *d*. *Educ:* Eton; Christ Church, Oxford (BA 1973; MA). FCA 1977. DL Oxon, 2014. *Heir: s* Arthur Ashley Ponsonby, *b* 15 Sept. 1984. *Address:* Woodleys, Woodstock, Oxon OX20 1HJ. *T:* (01993) 811717. *E:* cponsonby88@gmail.com. *Clubs:* Pratt's, White's.

PONSONBY, Air Vice Marshal John Maurice Maynard, OBE 1999; Senior Vice President, Training, AgustaWestland, since 2007; Chairman, Aviation Training International Ltd, since 2011 (Director, since 2007); Director, Rotorsim Srl, since 2008; *b* 8 Aug. 1955; *s* of Myles and Anne Ponsonby; *m* 1980, Marie-José Van Huizen; one *s* two *d*. *Educ:* Ampleforth Coll. Commn Royal Green Jackets, 1975–83; commnd RAF, 1983; qualified helicopter instructor, Hong Kong, Germany and UK, 1983–88; Flight Comdr, Germany, NI and Falkland Is, 1988–91; Staff HQ RAF Germany, 1991; Staff Coll., 1992; Staff, HQ No 1 Gp, MoD, 1993–95; Comd 27 Sqdn RAF, 1995–98; PSO to CDS, MoD, 1998–2000; HCSC, 2000; Station Comdr, RAF Aldergrove and Comdr Jt Helicopter Force, NI, 2000–02; AO Plans HQ Strike Comd, 2002–04; AOC Trng Gp and Chief Exec., Trng Gp Defence Agency, 2005–07; COS Ops, HQ Air Comd, 2007. Founder Patron, Help for Heroes, 2011– (Trustee, 2007–11). QCVS 2002. *Recreations:* flying, golf, tennis, cricket, military history. *Address:* c/o Lloyds Bank, 38 Blue Boar Road, Salisbury, Wilts SP1 1DB. *E:* cepon@waitrose.com. *Clubs:* Royal Air Force, Royal Automobile.

PONSONBY, Robert Noel, CBE 1985; Controller of Music, BBC, 1972–85; *b* 19 Dec. 1926; *o s* of late Noel Ponsonby, BMus, Organist Christ Church Cathedral, Oxford, and Mary White-Thomson; *m* 1st, 1957, Una Mary (marr. diss.), *er d* of late W. J. Kenny; 2nd, 1977, Lesley Margaret Black (marr. diss.), *o d* of late G. T. Black. *Educ:* Eton; Trinity Coll., Oxford. MA Oxon, Eng. Litt. Commissioned Scots Guards, 1945–47. Organ Scholar, Trinity Coll., Oxford, 1948–50; staff of Glyndebourne Opera, 1951–55; Artistic Director of the Edinburgh International Festival, 1955–60; with Independent Television Authority, 1962–64; Gen. Administrator, Scottish Nat. Orchestra, 1964–72. Director: Commonwealth Arts Festival, Glasgow, 1965; Henry Wood Promenade Concerts, 1974–86; Artistic Dir, Canterbury Fest., 1987–88. Adminr, Friends of the Musicians Benevolent Fund, 1987–93. Artistic Adviser to Internat. Arts Guild of Bahamas, 1960–72. Chm., London Choral Soc., 1990–94; Programme Consultant, RPO, 1993–96. Mem., Music Adv. Panel, Arts Council of GB, 1986–89; Music Advr, Wingate Scholarships, 1988–2008. Trustee: Young Concert Artists Trust, 1984–89; Nash Concert Soc., 1988–2004; Michael Tippett Musical Foundn, 1989–2013. Governor, Purcell Sch., 1985–88. Originator, Choirbook for the Queen, 2012. Hon. RAM 1975; Hon. Mem., ISM, 1992. FRSA 1979. *Publications:* Short History of Oxford University Opera Club, 1950; Musical Heroes, 2009. *Recreations:* bird-watching, English and Scottish painting, music. *Address:* 11 St Cuthbert's Road, NW2 3QJ.

PONTEFRACT, Archdeacon of; *see* Townley, Ven. P. K.

PONTI, Signora Carlo; *see* Loren, Sophia.

PONTIN, John Graham, OBE 2004; Chairman, JT Group Ltd, since 1961; Founder Trustee, Converging World, since 2007; *b* 2 June 1937; *s* of Charles Cyril Pontin and Phyllis (*née* Frieze); *m* 1st, 1966, Gillian Margaret Harris (marr. diss. 1971); one *s* one *d*; 2nd, 1977, Sylviane Marie-Louise Aubel (*d* 1998). *Educ:* Bristol Tech. Sch. (Building). Founder, JT Group, 1961. Chm., Dartington Hall Trust, 1984–97 (Trustee, 1980–97); Trustee, Quartet Community Foundn (formerly Gtr Bristol Community Trust, then Gtr Bristol Foundn), 1987–. FRSA. *Recreations:* gardening, walking. *Club:* Reform.

PONTIUS, Timothy Gordon; His Honour Judge Pontius; a Circuit Judge, since 1995; a Specialist Circuit Judge, Central Criminal Court, since 2008; *b* 5 Sept. 1948; *s* of Gordon Stuart Malzard Pontius and Elizabeth Mary (*née* Donaldson). *Educ:* Boroughmuir Sen. Secondary Sch., Edinburgh; London Univ. (external, LLB Hons). Called to the Bar, Middle Temple, 1972, Bencher, 2008; in practice at the Bar, 1972–88; Dep. Judge-Advocate, 1988–91; AJAG, 1991–95; a Recorder, 1993–95. *Recreations:* music, travel, swimming. *Address:* Central Criminal Court, Old Bailey, EC4M 7EH.

POOBALAN, Very Rev. Dr Isaac Munuswamy; Provost, St Andrew's Cathedral, Aberdeen, since 2015; *b* Vellore, S India, 14 July 1962; *s* of Subramani and Devasitham Poobalan; *m* 1995, Amudha Sujatha; one *s* one *d*. *Educ:* Don Bosco Higher, Vellore, India; Christian Medical Coll., Vellore, India (RGN 1984); Univ. of Edinburgh (BD 1994; MTh 1997); Pittsburgh Theol Seminary (DMin). RGN, Christian Medical Coll., Vellore, 1984–87; RGN (Psych.), DMS, Abu Dhabi, 1987–91; CGFNS, Philadelphia; ordained deacon, 1994, priest, 1995; Curate, St Peter's, Edinburgh, 1994–97; Priest-in-charge, St Clement's, Aberdeen, 1997–2001; Rector, St John's, Aberdeen, 2001–15. Chm., Friends of Vellore, Scotland, 2008–. Mem., Grampian Theol Club. Spiritual Dir, 2012–. *Publications:* Pain - a blessed suffering: reflections on Prof. Paul Brand, 2014. *Recreations:* music (fusion percussion), cricket (bowling), graphic design, liturgy. *Address:* 15 Ashley Road, Aberdeen AB10 6RU. *T:* (01224) 591527. *E:* provost@aberdeen.anglican.org.

POOK, Jocelyn, (Mrs Dragan Aleksic); musician and composer; *b* Birmingham, 14 Feb. 1960; *d* of Mary and Wilfred Pook; *m* 2003, Dragan Aleksic; one *d*. *Educ:* King Edward VI Upper Sch., Bury St Edmunds; Guildhall Sch. of Music and Drama (viola and piano 1983). AGSM 1982. Performer (viola) with The Communards, 1985–89; string arrangements and collaborations with artists incl. Peter Gabriel, Massive Attack, PJ Harvey, Mark Knopfler and Laurie Anderson. Composer of *film scores:* Eyes Wide Shut, 1999 (ASCAP Award, Chicago Film Award, 2000); L'Emploi du Temps, 2001; Gangs of New York, 2002; Wild Side, 2004; Merchant of Venice, 2005; Heidi, 2006; Caotica Ana, 2007; Brick Lane, 2008 (ASCAP Award); Room in Rome, 2010; *opera:* Ingerland for Royal Opera Hse Linbury Studio, 2010; *theatre scores:* Speaking in Tunes, UK tour, incl. ICA and Tron Th., Glasgow, 2003–04 (British Composer Award (multi-media), BASCA, 2003); St Joan, NT, 2007 (Olivier Award for Best Music and Sound Design, 2008); DESH, worldwide tour, incl. Sadlers Wells, 2011–14 (British Composer Award (stage works), BASCA, 2012); King Charles III, Wyndhams and Music Box, NY, 2014; *commissions* include: Mobile for BBC Proms/Kings Singers in collaboration with Andrew Motion, Royal Albert Hall, 2002; Hearing Voices for BBC Concert Orchestra, 2012; iTMOi for Sadlers Wells, 2013; Anxiety Fanfare for Mental Health Foundn, 2014; Dust, 2014, Lest We Forget, 2015, for English Nat. Ballet. Albums: Deluge, 1998; Flood, 2000; Untold Things 2001, 2013. *Address:* c/o Nicky Thomas Media, 101 Bell Street, NW1 6TL. *T:* (020) 3714 7594, (020) 7258 0909. *E:* info@nickythomasmedia.com; c/o Chester Music Publishing, Music Sales Group, 14–15 Berners Street, W1T 3LJ. *T:* (020) 7612 7400. *E:* promotion@musicsales.co.uk.

POOLE, family name of **Baron Poole.**

POOLE, 2nd Baron *cr* 1958, of Aldgate; **David Charles Poole;** Director, RGA (UK) Ltd, since 2002; *b* 6 Jan. 1945; *s* of 1st Baron Poole, PC, CBE, TD and Betty Margaret Gilkison (*d* 1988); *S* father, 1993; *m* 1967; one *s*; *m* 2004, Kate Watts. *Educ:* Dragon Sch., Oxford; Gordonstoun; Christ Church, Oxford (MA); INSEAD, Fontainebleau (MBA). Samuel Montagu & Co. Ltd, 1967–74; Bland Payne & Co. Ltd, 1974–78; Capel-Cure Myers, 1978–87; Bonomi Group, 1987–90; James Capel, 1990–92; Mem., Prime Minister's Policy Unit (on secondment), 1992–94; Gp Chief Exec., Sturge, subseq. Ockham, Hldgs plc, 1994–2002; Chm. Govs, West Hill Park Sch., Titchfield, 2009–. *Recreations:* sailing, ballet. *Heir: s* Hon. Oliver John Poole [*b* 30 May 1972; two *d* by Kate White]. *E:* davidpoole300@hotmail.com. *Clubs:* Brooks's, City of London, Beefsteak; Island Sailing.

POOLE, Anna Isabel; QC (Scot.) 2012; *b* Craigtoun, 11 Aug. 1970; *d* of David Poole and Julie Poole; *m* 2000, Richard Sweet; one *s* one *d*. *Educ:* Madras Coll., St Andrews; Somerville Coll., Oxford (BA Juris. 1991); Magdalen Coll., Oxford (MSt 1993). Admitted solicitor, England and Wales, 1996, Scotland, 1997; Advocate, 1998; First Standing Jun. Counsel to Scottish Govt, 2010–12; pt-time fee-paid Judge, First-tier Tribunal (Social Entitlement Chamber), 2014–. *Publications:* (contrib.) Court of Session Practice, 2004–; articles in Juridical Rev., Scots Law Times, Scottish Law and Practice Qly, Judicial Rev., Internat. Insurance Law Rev., IJPICL, Jl of Law Soc. of Scotland. *Recreations:* music, walking, travel. *Address:* Advocates Library, Parliament House, Edinburgh EH1 1RF.

POOLE, Dame Anne; *see* Poole, Dame Avril A. B.

POOLE, Anthony Cecil James; Head of Administration Department, House of Commons, 1985–88, retired; *b* 9 Oct. 1927; *s* of Walter James Poole and Daisy Poole (*née* Voyle); *m* 1951, Amelia Keziah (*née* Pracy); one *d*. *Educ:* Headlands Grammar School, Swindon. Served RN, 1945–47; Department of Employment, 1947–76; Principal Establishments Officer, Manpower Services Commn, 1976–80; House of Commons, 1980, Head of Establishments Office, 1981. *Recreations:* golf, gardening.

POOLE, Dame (Avril) Anne (Barker), DBE 1992; Chief Nursing Officer, Department of Health (formerly of Health and Social Security), 1982–92; *b* 11 April 1934; *d* of Arthur George and Norah Heritage; *m* 1959, John Percy Poole. *Educ:* High Sch., Southampton. SRN 1955, SCM 1957, Health Visitors Cert., 1958. Asst Chief Nursing Officer, City of Westminster, 1967–69; Chief Nursing Officer, London Borough of Merton, 1969–73; Area Nursing Officer, Surrey AHA, 1974–81; Dep. Chief Nursing Officer, DHSS, 1981–82. Non-exec. Dir, SW Surrey HA, 1993–96; Mem., Criminal Injuries Compensation Panel, 1996–2006. Trustee, Marie Curie Cancer Care (formerly Marie Curie Meml Foundn), 1992–2001. FRSocMed 1993; CCMI (CBIM 1984).

POOLE, David Arthur Ramsay; Managing Director, Blue Circle Industries, 1987–89; *b* 30 Sept. 1935; *s* of late Arthur Poole and Viola Isbol (*née* Ramsay); *m* 1961, Jean Mary Male; three *d*. *Educ:* King's Sch., Canterbury; St Edmund Hall, Oxford (MA Jurisprudence). Nat. service, 2nd Lieut, RA, 1955–57. Baring Bros & Co., 1960–65; APCM Ltd (now BCI), 1965–70; Wm Brandts & Co., 1970–73; British Caledonian Gp, 1973–75; Blue Circle Industries, 1976–89. *Recreation:* travel. *Address:* Dalwood Cottage, Long Reach, Ockham, Surrey GU23 6PF. *T:* (01483) 284986. *Clubs:* East India, Royal Automobile.

POOLE, David James, PPRP (RP 1969); ARCA; artist; *b* 5 June 1931; *s* of Thomas Herbert Poole and Catherine Poole; *m* 1958, Iris Mary Toomer; three *s*. *Educ:* Stoneleigh Secondary Sch.; Wimbledon Sch. of Art; Royal Coll. of Art. National Service, RE, 1949–51. Sen. Lectr in Painting and Drawing, Wimbledon Sch. of Art, 1962–77. Pres., Royal Soc. of Portrait Painters, 1983–91. One-man exhibns, Zurich and London; exhibn of non-portrait work, Curwen and New Acad. Gall., London, 2008. Portraits include: the Queen, The Duke of Edinburgh, The Queen Mother, Prince Charles, Princess Anne, Princess Margaret, Earl Mountbatten of Burma and The Duke of Kent; Private Secretaries to the Queen: Sir Alan Lascelles, Sir Michael Adeane, Sir Martin Charteris, Sir Philip Moore, Sir William Heseltine, Sir Robert Fellowes, Sir Robin Janvrin; also distinguished members of govt, industry, commerce, medicine, the academic and legal professions. Work in private collections of the Queen and the Duke of Edinburgh, and in Australia, S Africa, Bermuda, France, W Germany, Switzerland, Saudi Arabia and USA. *Recreations:* French travel, food and drink. *Address:* Trinity Flint Barn, Weston Lane, Weston, Petersfield, Hants GU32 3NN. *T:* (01730) 265075.

POOLE, Isobel Anne, OBE 2013; Sheriff of the Lothian and Borders, 1979–2007, at Edinburgh, 1986–2007; part-time Sheriff, all Scotland, since 2007; *b* 9 Dec. 1941; *d* of late John Cecil Findlay Poole, DM Oxon, and Constance Mary (*née* Gilkes), SRN. *Educ:* Oxford High Sch. for Girls; Edinburgh Univ. (LLB). Admitted to Faculty of Advocates, 1964. Formerly Standing Jun. Counsel to Registrar Gen. for Scotland. Ext. Examr in Comparative Criminal Procedure, Edinburgh Univ., 2001, 2002. Member: Sheriffs' Council, 1980–85; Scottish Lawyers European Gp, 1977–; Franco-British Lawyers Assoc. Chm., Edinburgh Sir

Walter Scott Club, 2004–07. *Publications:* contrib. to Oxford DNB. *Recreations:* country, arts, houses, gardens, friends. *Address:* Sheriff's Chambers, Sheriff Court House, Chambers Street, Edinburgh EH1 1LB. *Clubs:* New, Scottish Arts (Edinburgh).

POOLE, Jennifer Nancy; *see* Willott, J. N.

POOLE, Nigel David; QC 2012; a Recorder, since 2009; *b* Shipley, W Yorks, 10 Nov. 1965; *s* of Michael and Susan Poole; *m* 1999, Annmarie Danson; one *s* one *d*. *Educ:* Bradford Grammar Sch.; Queen's Coll., Oxford (BA Hons); City Univ., London (DipLaw); Inns of Court Sch. of Law. Called to the Bar, Middle Temple, 1989; in practice as barrister, specialising in clinical negligence and personal injury, 1989–. Legal Assessor, GMC, 2002–09. Panel Chair, Bar Tribunals and Adjudication Service. *Recreations:* singing in a Gospel choir, open water swimming, fell walking. *Address:* Kings Chambers, 36 Young Street, Manchester M3 3FT. *T:* (0161) 832 9082. *E:* npoole@kingschambers.com.

POOLE, Nigel Robert; a Judge of the Upper Tribunal (Immigration and Asylum Chamber) (formerly a Senior Immigration Judge, Asylum and Immigration Tribunal), since 2005; *b* Southampton, 22 March 1949; *s* of Alfred Poole and Phyllis Harley Poole (*née* Anstey); *m* 1971, Gloria Durkin (*d* 2007); one *s* one *d*. *Educ:* Regents Park Boys Sch., Southampton; Cardiff Jt Law Sch. (LLB Hons); Coll. of Law, Guildford. Admitted solicitor, 1975; Partner, Blatch & Co., 1978–99. Chm. (fee paid), Appeals Service, 1984–2002; Immigration Adjudicator (fee paid), 1995–2000; Immigration Judge, 2000. Dep. District Chm., Social Entitlement Chamber, 2010–. *Recreations:* enjoying time with my children and grandchildren, spending time with friends and family, growing tomatoes. *Address:* Columbus House, Langstone, Gwent NP18 2LX. *T:* (01633) 416791. *E:* poole_nigel@hotmail.com.

POOLE, Col Peter Michael, CBE 1992; TD 1964; Vice Lord-Lieutenant, County of Merseyside, 1994–2004; Consultant, Denton Clark & Co., 1995–2000; *b* 29 Sept. 1929; *s* of Reginald and Madeline Isobel Poole; *m* 1956, Diana Rosemary Hiam Wilson; three *s* one *d*. *Educ:* Sedbergh Sch.; Gonville and Caius Coll., Cambridge. FRICS (Ryde Meml Prizewinner, 1955); Fellow, CAAV. Univ. Officer, Cambridge, 1954–60; Chartered Surveyor and Land Agent; Principal, Poole & Partners, Liverpool, 1960–91; Partner, Denton Clark & Co., 1991–95. Mem., Lord Chancellor's Panel of Arbitrators, 1977–95; Chm., Merseyside Adv. Cttee on Gen. Comrs of Income Tax, 1993–2004. Dir, Merseyside Youth Assoc., 1973–2004. Liveryman and Mem., Chartered Surveyors' Co., 1980–2008. JP Liverpool 1976–96; DL Merseyside 1975. CO, 107 Corps Engr Regt, RE (TA), 1965–67; Brevet Col, 1967; Hon. Col, 75 Engr Regt, RE (V), 1972–80; Chm., North West TA&VRA, 1990–92; Hon. Mem., NW RFCA, 2003. *Publications:* The Valuation of Pipeline Easements and Wayleaves, 1962. *Recreations:* ornithology, golf, travel, photography. *Address:* Shelford, 3 Heron Court, Parkgate, Neston, Cheshire CH64 6TB. *T:* (0151) 336 2529.

POOLES, Michael Philip Holmes; QC 1999; a Recorder, 2000–12; *b* 14 Dec. 1955; *s* of late Dennis John Pooles and of Joan Ellen Pooles; *m* 1982, Fiona Grant Chalmers; two *s*. *Educ:* Perse Sch., Cambridge; Queen Mary Coll., Univ. of London (LLB). Called to the Bar, Inner Temple, 1978, Bencher, 2011; in practice at the Bar, 1980–; Asst Recorder, 2000. Hd, Hailsham Chambers, 2004–09. Mem., Bar Standards Bd, 2006–10. Gov., Perse Sch. *Publications:* (contrib.) Professional Negligence and Liability, 2001. *Recreations:* reading, gardening. *Address:* Hailsham Chambers, 4 Paper Buildings, Temple, EC4Y 7EX. *T:* (020) 7643 5000. *Club:* Royal Automobile.

POOLEY, Dr Derek, CBE 1995; Chief Executive, UK Atomic Energy Authority, 1996–97; *b* 28 Oct. 1937; *s* of Richard Pike Pooley and Evelyn Pooley; *m* 1961, Jennifer Mary Davey; two *s* one *d*. *Educ:* Sir James Smith's Sch., Camelford, Cornwall; Birmingham Univ. (BSc 1958; PhD 1961). FInstP 1979. A. A. Noyes Res. Fellow, Calif Inst. of Technol., Pasadena, 1961–62; UKAEA, Harwell: Res. Scientist, 1962–68; Leader of Defects Gp, later of Physics Applications Gp, 1968–76; Head of Materials Develt Div., 1976–81; Dir of Non-nuclear Energy Res., 1981–83; Chief Scientist, Dept of Energy, 1983–86; Dep. Dir, 1986–89, Dir, 1989–90, Atomic Energy Estabt, Winfrith, later AEA Technol.; Dir, AEA Thermal Reactor Services, 1990–91; Man. Dir, Nuclear Business Gp, AEA Technol., 1991–94; Chief Exec., UKAEA Govt Div., 1994–96. Consultant, Derek Pooley Associates, 1998–2011. Non-exec. Dir, UK Nirex Ltd, 1995–97; Dir, BNES Ltd, 1997–2000. Chm., Waste Management Technology Ltd, 2006–08. Pres., British Nuclear Energy Soc., 1992–94; Chm., Scientific and Technical Cttee, Euratom, 1994–99. Mem., EU Adv. Gp on Energy, 2002–08. *Publications:* Real Solids and Radiation, 1975; (contrib.) Radiation Damage Processes in Materials, 1975; (contrib.) Energy and Feedstocks in the Chemical Industry, 1983; A Radical Approach to Nuclear Decommissioning, 1995; (contrib.) Key Tasks for Future European Energy R&D, 2005. *Recreations:* history, astronomy, walking. *Address:* 11 Halls Close, Drayton, Abingdon, Oxon OX14 4LU. *T:* (01235) 559454.

POOLEY, Peter, CMG 1996; a Deputy Director General, European Commission, 1983–95, now an Hon. Director-General; *b* 19 June 1936; *er* (twin) *s* of late W. M. Pooley, OBE, and Grace Lidbury, Truro; *m* 1966, Janet Mary, *er d* of Jack Pearson, Banbury; one *s* one *d*. *Educ:* Brentwood Sch.; Clare Coll., Cambridge (BA). Joined MAFF as Asst Principal, 1959; seconded to: Diplomatic Service, 1961–63 and 1979–82 (Minister (Agric.), Office of UK Perm. Rep. to EEC, Brussels); CSD, 1977–79; Under-Sec., 1979, Fisheries Sec., 1982, MAFF; Dep. Dir Gen., for Agric., 1983–89, for Develt, 1989–95 (Actg DG, 1992–95), EC. Interim Sec.-Gen., COPA/COGECA, 1995–96. Chm., British African Business Assoc., 1996–2001; with Business Council Europe-Africa, 1996–2002 (Pres., 1998). Chm., UK Br., 2002–05, Vice Pres., 2005–09, AIACE. Lay Mem., Winchester Diocesan Synod, 2009–. Chm., Alresford Soc., 2008–12. *Address:* The Lodge, 25 Rosebery Road, Alresford, Hampshire SO24 9HQ. *T:* (01962) 732779. *Club:* Oxford and Cambridge.

See also R. Pooley.

POOLEY, Robin, OBE 1997; Chairman, English Apples and Pears Ltd, 2000–07; *b* 19 June 1936; *yr* (twin) *s* of late W. Melville Pooley, OBE and of Grace M. Pooley (*née* Lidbury); *m* 1972, Margaret Anne, *yr d* of Jack Pearson, Banbury; one *d*. *Educ:* Brentwood School. Various posts, Towers & Co. Ltd, 1954–71; Gen. Manager, CWS Gp, 1971–76; Man. Dir, Buxted Poultry Ltd, 1976–81; Chief Exec., Potato Marketing Bd, 1981–88; Managing Director: Anglian Produce Ltd, 1988–97; Anglian Potato Services Ltd, 1988–97; Chairman: Pseedco Ltd, 1995–98; Abbey Gp Ltd, 1997–2002; United Pig Marketing Ltd, 1999–2003. Director: North Country Primestock Ltd, 1996–2003; Smith and Holbourne, then Garden Isle, Ltd, 1997–2006. Chm., NFU Corporate, 1998–2003; Mem. Council, NFU, 1996–2003. Chm., MAFF Enquiry into meat hygiene, 1999; Mem., Scientific and Economic Co-ordinating Cttee, Min. of Agriculture for Italy, 1998–2007. Special Lectr in Mgt, Univ. of Nottingham, 1996–2008. Pres., CUPGRA, 1999–2006, now Pres. Emeritus. Master, Co. of Butchers, 1987. *Recreations:* fly fishing, freemasonry. *Address:* Barn Hill House, Strumpshaw, Norfolk NR13 4NS. *T:* (01603) 715992. *Club:* Farmers.

See also P. Pooley.

POORE, Dr (Martin Edward) Duncan, MA, PhD; FRSB, FRGS; consultant in conservation and land use, since 1983; *b* 25 May 1925; *s* of T. E. D. Poore and Elizabeth McMartin; *m* 1949, Judith Ursula, *d* of Lt-Gen. Sir Treffry Thompson, KCSI, CB, CBE, and late Mary Emily, *d* of Rev. Canon Medd; two *s*. *Educ:* Trinity Coll., Glenalmond; Edinburgh Univ.; Clare Coll., Cambridge. MA, PhD Cantab.; MA Oxon. MCIEEM. GCCS, Bletchley Park and HMS Anderson, Colombo, 1943–45. Nature Conservancy, 1953–56; Consultant Ecologist, Hunting Technical Services, 1956–59; Prof. of Botany, Univ. of Malaya, Kuala Lumpur, 1959–65; Dean of Science, Univ. of Malaya, 1964–65; Lectr, Forestry Dept, Oxford, 1965–66; Dir, Nature Conservancy, 1966–73; Scientific Dir, Internat. Union for Conservation of Nature and Natural Resources, Switzerland, 1974–78; Prof. of Forest Science and Dir, Commonwealth Forestry Inst., Oxford Univ., 1980–83; Fellow of St John's Coll., Oxford, 1980–83; Dir, 1983–86, Sen. Conslt, 1986–90, Forestry and Land Use Prog., Internat. Inst. for Envmt and Develt. Member: Thames Water Authority, 1981–83; Nature Conservancy Council, 1981–84. Pres., British Assoc. of Nature Conservationists, 1984–92 (Vice Pres., 1993–); Vice-Pres., Commonwealth Forestry Assoc., 1989–; Mem. Council, Scottish Wildlife Trust, 2001–04; Hon. Member: Botanical Soc. of Scotland, 1992; IUCN (World Conservation Union), 1978 (Hon. Mem., and Fred M. Packard Award, 1990, Commn for Nat. Parks and Protected Areas). FRSA. *Publications:* The Vanishing Forest, 1986; No Timber without Trees, 1990; (with Jeffrey Sayer) The Management of Tropical Moist Forest Lands, 1991; Guidelines for Mountain Protected Areas, 1992; (with Judy Poore) Protected Landscapes in the United Kingdom, 1992; Where Next?: reflections on the human future, 2000; Changing Landscapes: the development of the international tropical timber organisation and its influence on tropical forest management, 2003; (jtly) State of Tropical Forest Management, 2006; papers on ecology and land use in various jls and scientific periodicals. *Recreations:* hill walking, natural history, music, gardening, photography. *Address:* Balnacarn, Glenmoriston, Inverness-shire IV63 7YJ. *T:* (01320) 340261. *Club:* Royal Over-Seas League.

POORE, Sir Roger Ricardo, 7th Bt *cr* 1795, of Rushall, Wiltshire; *b* 21 Oct. 1930; *e s* of Nasionceno Poore, *b* of 5th Bt; *S* cousin, Sir Herbert Edward Poore, 6th Bt, but his name does not appear on the Official Roll of the Baronetage; *m* Norma Naso Poore (decd), *widow* of Roberto Poore. *Heir: nephew* Fernando Nasionceno Poore [*b* 1964; *m* Maria del Carmen; one *s*].

POORTA, Amanda Felicity; *see* Mackenzie, A. F.

POOTS, Edwin; Member (DemU) Lagan Valley, Northern Ireland Assembly, since 1998; *b* 1965; *m*; four *c*. *Educ:* Wallace High Sch., Lisburn; Greenmount Agricl Coll. Farmer, Lagan Valley. Mem., NI Forum, 1996–98. Mem. (DemU) Lisburn CC, 1997–2010 (Dep. Mayor, 2008–10). Minister for Culture, Arts and Leisure, 2007–08, for the Envmt, 2009–11, of Health, Social Services and Public Safety, 2011–14, NI. *Address:* Northern Ireland Assembly, Parliament Buildings, Belfast BT4 3XX; (office) Old Town Hall, 29 Castle Street, Lisburn, Co. Antrim BT27 4DH.

POPAT, family name of **Baron Popat**.

POPAT, Baron *cr* 2010 (Life Peer), of Harrow in the London Borough of Harrow; **Dolar Amarshi Popat;** *b* Uganda, 14 June 1953; *m* Sandhya; three *s*. ACMA 1977. Arrived in UK, 1971; worked as waiter to fund studies. Business and corporate finance specialist. Mem., Small and Medium Enterprises Exports Cttee, 2012–13. Cons. Party Whip, 2012–13; a Lord in Waiting (Govt Whip), 2013–15. Pres., Harrow E Cons. Assoc. Founding Chm., Cons. Friends of India; former Chm., One Nation Forum; Sec., Anglo-Asian Cons. Assoc.; Mem., Cons. Ethnic Diversity Council. Founding Dir, St Luke's Hospice, Kenton. *Address:* House of Lords, SW1A 0PW. *T:* (020) 7219 5353.

POPAT, Prashant; QC 2008; barrister, since 1992; *b* Saroti, Uganda, 24 Sept. 1968; *s* of Shantilal and late Saroj Popat; *m* 1991, Pritti Lakhani; one *s* one *d*. *Educ:* Mansfield Coll., Oxford (MA Jurisprudence 1990). Called to the Bar, Gray's Inn, 1992, Bencher. Judicial Asst to Master of the Rolls, 1997. *Publications:* (jtly) Civil Advocacy: a practical guide, 1997, 2nd edn 2001; (contrib. ed.) Halsbury's Laws: practice and procedure, 2001; (ed jtly) International Product Law Manual, 2012. *Recreation:* as much as possible. *Address:* Henderson Chambers, 2 Harcourt Buildings, Temple, EC4Y 9DB. *T:* (020) 7583 9020, *Fax:* (020) 7583 2686. *E:* ppopat@hendersonchambers.co.uk.

POPAT, Prof. Sita Helen, PhD; Professor of Performance and Technology, University of Leeds, since 2011 (Head, School of Performance and Cultural Industries, 2010–15); *b* Lusaka, Zambia, 18 May 1967; *d* of Ratilal and Clare Chiba; *m* 1st, 1989, Kris Popat (marr. diss. 2010); two *s*; 2nd, 2011, Calvin Taylor. *Educ:* Univ. of Leeds (BA Hons Dance 1998; PhD 2002). Sec., Royal Opera Hse, 1988–89; Lectr in Dance, Univ. of Leeds, 2002–11. Mem., Adv. Bd, AHRC, 2014–. Trustee, DV8 Physical Th., 2010–. *Publications:* Invisible Connections: dance, choreography and internet communities, 2006; (ed with J. Pitches) Performance Perspectives: a critical introduction, 2011; (ed with N. Salazar Sutil) Digital Movement: essays in motion technology and performance, 2015; contribs to scholarly jls on performance, the body and new media. *Recreations:* performance arts, family, walking, playing a gnome healer in World of Warcraft. *Address:* School of Performance and Cultural Industries, University of Leeds, Woodhouse Lane, Leeds LS2 9JT. *T:* (0113) 343 8716. *E:* s.popat@leeds.ac.uk.

POPAT, (Surendra) Andrew, CBE 1997; a Recorder, since 1998; *b* 31 Dec. 1943; *s* of late Dhirajlal Kurji Popat and Kashiben Popat (*née* Chitalia); *m* 1995, Suzanne Joy, *d* of late Edward James Wayman and Beatrice Joyce Wayman; one *s*. *Educ:* Univ. of London (LLB); Univ. of Calif, Berkeley (LLM). Called to the Bar, Lincoln's Inn, 1969; Mem., Inner Temple, 1985; Associate Attorney, Willkie Farr & Gallaghar (NY), 1970–74; practising Barrister, specialising in criminal law, 1975–; Asst Recorder, 1992–98; Tribunal Judge, First-tier Chamber (Criminal Injuries Compensation Tribunal), 2009–. Legal Mem., Criminal Injuries Compensation Appeals Panel, 2000; Mem., Professional Performance Cttee, 2002, Chm., Fitness to Practise Panel, 2006–, GMC; Co-Chm., Professional Conduct Cttee, Gen. Osteopathic Council, 2003–07; Chm., Hearings of Appeals, Postgrad. Med. Educn and Trng Appeals Panel, 2004–; Mem., Fitness to Practise Panel, GDC, 2007–. Contested (C): Durham NE, 1983; Bradford S, 1992; London Reg., EP, 1999. Dir, John Patten's election campaign, 1987. Treas., Surbiton Cons. Assoc., 1985. Chm., Disraeli Club, 1993–. Trustee, Brooke Hosp. for Animals, 1998–2000. Freeman, City of London, 1987; Liveryman, Plaisterers' Co., 1987 (Mem. Ct of Assts, 2001, now Asst Emeritus). *Recreations:* travel, theatre, cricket, tennis. *Club:* MCC.

POPE, His Holiness the; *see* Francis, His Holiness.

POPE EMERITUS, His Holiness Benedict XVI, (Joseph Alois Ratzinger); *see* Benedict XVI, His Holiness.

POPE, Cathryn Mary; soprano; *b* 6 July 1957; *m* 1st, 1982, Stuart Petersen (marr. diss. 1998); 2nd, 2003, Martin Barrell. *Educ:* Royal College of Music (ARCM); National Opera Studio. Début, ENO: Sophie, in Werther, 1983; Anna, in Moses, 1986; Susanna, in Marriage of Figaro, 1987; Gretel, in Hansel and Gretel, 1987; Oksana, in Christmas Eve, 1988; Despina, in Così fan tutte, 1988; Pamina, in Die Zauberflöte, 1989; Micaëla, in Carmen, 1993; Tatyana, in Eugene Onegin, 1994; Amsterdam: début, Gretel, 1990; Mélisande, in Pelléas et Mélisande, 1991; Elvira, in Don Giovanni, and Susanna, 1991; Opera Europa: Nedda, in Pagliacci, 1995; Giorgetta, in Il Tabarro; Nantes: Le Prostitué, in La Ronde. Numerous recordings.

POPE, Col Christopher Michael, OBE 2003; Director, Chabe Ltd, since 2014; *b* Wargrave, 31 Aug. 1960; *s* of Michael Pope and Marion Audrey Pope; *m* 1997, Deborah Jane Searle; two *s* two *d*. *Educ:* Maidenhead Grammar Sch.; Cranfield Univ. (BScEng Hons Civil Engrg 1985; MSc Defence Technol. 1992). Army officer, 1978–2005; retired in rank of Col. Gp Projects Dir, Tribal Gp plc, 2005–07; Hd, Operational Engrg Services, Laing O'Rourke, 2008–09; Dir of Transformation, London Bor. of Merton, 2009–11; Exec. Dir, Resources and Commercial Develt, London Bor. of Newham, 2011–14. Mem. Bd, Local Space Ltd,

2011–14. *Recreations:* amateur dramatics, hockey, fishing. *Address:* Orchard Cottage, The Street, Assington, Sudbury, Suffolk CO10 5LW. *T:* 07502 088536. *E:* chabe@btinternet.com.

POPE, Geoffrey Robert; Member (Lib Dem), London Assembly, Greater London Authority, 2005–08; *b* 9 April 1944; *s* of late George Pope and Stella Pope (*née* Edwards); *m* 1968, Margaret Victoria Thompson; one *s* one *d*. *Educ:* Kingsbury County Grammar Sch.; Hendon Coll. (HNC Applied Physics 1965). Mgt, SmithKline Beecham, 1969–98. Chm., Teddington Meml Hosp. and Community NHS Trust, 1998–2001; Dir, Kingston Hosp. NHS Trust, 2001–04. Chm., Addiction Care and Support Agency, 2000–. Mem. (Lib Dem) Richmond upon Thames LBC, 1982–98 (Mayor, 1989–90; Chm., Social Services, 1994–98). Chm., Transport Cttee, London Assembly, 2006–07. Chm., Twickenham and Richmond Lib Dems, 2009–12. *E:* geoff.pope1@gmail.com.

POPE, George Maurice, FRICS; independent surveyor, since 1999; *b* 12 Jan. 1943; *s* of Maj. John Pope; *m* 1968, Tessa Roselle Norman; one *s* two *d*. *Educ:* Eton. Capt., Coldstream Guards, 1962–69. With John D. Wood & Co., 1970–99, Chm., 1982–99. *Recreations:* racing, hunting, shooting, golf. *Address:* (office) 2nd Floor, 48 Elizabeth Street, SW1W 9PA. *T:* (020) 7730 6615; Grounds Farm House, Fernham Road, Uffington, near Faringdon, Oxon SN7 7RD. *T:* (01367) 820234. *Clubs:* White's; Royal St George's Golf, Sunningdale Golf.

POPE, Gregory James; Deputy Director, Catholic Education Service for England and Wales, since 2010; Head of Parliamentary Relations, Catholic Bishops' Conference of England and Wales, since 2013; *b* 29 Aug. 1960; *s* of Samuel J. Pope and Sheila M. (*née* Day); *m* 1985, Catherine M. Fallon; two *s* one *d*. *Educ:* St Mary's Coll., Blackburn; Univ. of Hull (BA Hons). Local govt officer, 1987–92. MP (Lab) Hyndburn, 1992–2010. An Asst Govt Whip, 1997–99; a Lord Comr of HM Treasury (Govt Whip), 1999–2001. *Recreations:* walking, football, chess, music. *Address:* Catholic Bishops' Conference of England and Wales, 39 Eccleston Square, SW1V 1BX.

POPE, Jeffrey Charles; Head, Factual Drama, ITV Studios (formerly Granada Productions, then ITV Productions), since 1998; *b* Cowley, Middx, 2 Oct. 1961; *s* of David Pope and Patricia Pope; *m* 1992, Tina Jane Phillips; three *s*. *Educ:* Hayes Co. Grammar Sch. NCTJ Qualified Journalist 1981 (Distinction). Journalist, Ealing Gazette, 1980–83; ITV: Researcher, Factual Progs, LWT, 1983–86; Producer, 1986–89; Editor, 1989–92 (progs incl. Friday Now, 1988–90, Crime Monthly, 1990–93); Exec. Producer, Factual Progs, 1992–98. *Television:* Exec Producer, See No Evil: the Moors Murders, 2006 (Drama Serial award (jtly), BAFTA, 2007); writer: Mrs Biggs, 2013; Lucan, 2013; co-writer and producer, The Widower, 2014; writer and producer, Cilla, 2014; *film:* co-writer, screenplay, Philomena, 2014. Mem., BAFTA, 1996–. Guild of British Newspaper Editors' Award, 1981; BAFTA Special Award, 2015. *Publications:* (with Simon Shaps) Michael Winner's True Crimes, 1992. *Recreations:* Laurel and Hardy films, travel/holidays, golf with my sons—they beat me but I enjoy their company. *Address:* c/o ITV Studios, London TV Centre, Upper Ground, SE1 9LT.

POPE, Jeremy James Richard, OBE 1985; DL; Member of Board, English Farming and Food Partnership, 2008–10 (Chairman, 2003–08); *b* 15 July 1943; *s* of late Philip William Rolph Pope and Joyce Winifred Harcourt Pope (*née* Slade); *m* 1969, Hon. Jacqueline Best; three *s*. *Educ:* Charterhouse; Trinity Coll., Cambridge. Law tripos, MA. Solicitor. Eldridge, Pope & Co., 1969–99: Finance and Planning Dir, 1972–82; Jt Man. Dir, 1982–88; Man. Dir, 1988–99; Chairman: Eldridge, Pope Fine Wines Ltd, 1999–2000; Milk Link Ltd, 2000–05; Chilworth Science Park Ltd, 2001–04; Exeter Investment Gp plc, 2003–04 (non-exec. Dir, 1999–2003). Chm., Smaller Firms Council, CBI, 1981–83; Member: NEDC, 1981–85; Top Salaries Review Body, 1986–93; Exec. Cttee, Food and Drinks Fedn, 1986–89 (Dep. Pres., 1987–89). Member: Royal Commn on Environmental Pollution, 1984–92; Wessex Regl Rivers Adv. Cttee, NRA, 1994–95; Bd, Bournemouth, Dorset and Poole LSC, 2001–04; Sustainable Farming and Food Strategy Implementation Gp, DEFRA, 2002–05. Chairman: Winterbourne Hosp. plc, 1981–89; Trustees, Wessex Medical Trust, 1993–97 (Trustee, 1991–97); Dorset Private Sector Forum, 1997–2000; Bournemouth, Dorset & Poole Economic Partnership, 1997–99; SW Chamber of Rural Enterprise, 2001–04; Deputy Chairman: SW of England RDA, 1999–2004 (Bd Mem., 1998–2004); Dorset Olympic Bd, 2010–. Mem., Wessex Regl Cttee, NT, 2008–10. Chm., Spirit of the Sea Ltd, 2010–13; Dir, Expia CIC Ltd, 2013–. Dir, Weymouth and Portland Nat. Sailing Acad., 2004–13. Gov., Forres Sch., Swanage, 1984–92; Mem. Council, Southampton Univ., 1999–2004. Trustee: Devonshire and Dorset Regtl Charity, 1994–2000; Tank Mus., 2000–; Jurassic Coast Trust (formerly World Heritage Coast Trust), 2004–; Chesil Trust, 2004–13; Springboard, 2009–12; Dorset Shrieval Charitable Trust, 2012–14; SafeWise, 2013; Friends of Portland Prison, 2014–. Chm. Mgt Cttee, Mus. of Regts of Devon and Dorset, 1994–2000. DL 2008, High Sheriff, 2012–13, Dorset. Liveryman: Gunmakers' Co., 1988; Innholders' Co., 1991 (Master, 2008–09). FRAgS. Hon. DLitt Bournemouth, 1999. *Recreations:* shooting, fishing, gardening, beekeeping, cooking the resultant produce. *Address:* Field Cottage, West Compton, Dorchester, Dorset DT2 0EY. *T:* (01300) 320469.

POPE, Prof. Stephen Bailey, PhD, DSc (Eng); FRS 2007; FInstP; Sibley College Professor of Mechanical Engineering, Cornell University, since 1998; *b* 26 Nov. 1949; *s* of Sir Joseph Albert Pope; *m* 1979, Linda Ann Syatt; one *s* one *d*. *Educ:* Rydal Sch., Colwyn Bay; Imperial Coll., London (BSc (Eng.); MSc; PhD 1976; DIC); DSc (Eng) London 1986. ACGI; FInstP 2004. Mech. Engrg, Imperial Coll., London, 1972–77; Res. Fellow, Applied Maths, CIT, 1977–78; Asst Prof., then Associate Prof., of Mech. Engrg, MIT, 1978–81; Associate Prof., then Prof. of Mech. and Aerospace Engrg, Cornell Univ., 1982–. Dir, TQ Gp Ltd, 1995–2011. Fellow: APS, 1991; Amer. Acad. Arts and Scis, 2007; Soc. for Industrial and Applied Maths, 2009; Amer. Soc. of Mech. Engrs, 2014; Mem., NAE, 2010. Zeldovich Gold Medal, Combustion Inst., 2008; Fluid Dynamics Prize, APS, 2009; Propellants and Combustion Award, AIAA, 2012. *Publications:* Turbulent Flows, 2000; scientific articles in combustion and fluid dynamics. *Address:* Sibley School of Mechanical and Aerospace Engineering, Upson Hall, Cornell University, Ithaca, NY 14853, USA. *T:* (607) 2554314. *E:* s.b.pope@cornell.edu.

POPHAM, Stuart Godfrey; Vice-Chairman of Banking for Europe, Middle East and Africa, Citigroup, since 2011; *b* 20 July 1954; *s* of late George Godfrey Popham and Ena Majorie Popham; *m* 1978, Carolyn Dawe; one *s* two *d*. *Educ:* Southampton Univ. (LLB 1975). Admitted solicitor, 1978; joined Clifford-Turner, subseq. Clifford Chance, 1976: Partner, 1984; Hd of Finance, 2000–03; Sen. Partner, 2003–10. Non-exec. Dir, Legal & General Gp plc, 2011–. Confederation of British Industry: Chm., 2008–10, Vice Chm., 2011, London Bd (Mem., 2005–11); Mem., Internat. Adv. Bd, 2005–10. Chm., TheCityUK, 2009–12. Member: Council, RIIA, 2005– (Chm., 2012–); Adv. Forum, Saïd Business Sch., Oxford, 2005–13; Council, Birkbeck, Univ. of London, 2012–; Bd of Advrs, Business Sch. Faculty, Univ. of Southampton, 2012–. Trustee, RNLI, 2013–. Hon. QC 2011. DUniv: Middx, 2008; Southampton, 2013; Glamorgan, 2013. *Recreations:* sailing, theatre, ballet, water sports. *Address:* c/o Citi, Citigroup Centre, 33 Canada Square, Canary Wharf, E14 5LB.

POPLE, Alison Ruth; QC 2015; *b* Ulverston, 8 Nov. 1968; *d* of John Ravenhill Pople and Elizabeth Allan Pople; *m* 2001, Denis Fintan Barry; two *d*. *Educ:* Ulverston Victoria High Sch.; Huddersfield Poly. (LLB Hons Business Law). Called to the Bar, Middle Temple, 1993. *Address:* Cloth Fair Chambers, 39–40 Cloth Fair, EC1A 7NT. *T:* (020) 7710 6444. *E:* alisonpople@clothfairchambers.com.

POPLI, Dame Nicola Anne; *see* Cullum, Dame N. A.

POPPLEWELL, Lady; *see* Gloster, Hon. Dame Elizabeth.

POPPLEWELL, Hon. Sir Andrew John, Kt 2011; **Hon. Mr Justice Popplewell;** a Judge of the High Court of Justice, Queen's Bench Division, since 2011; *b* 14 Jan. 1959; *s* of Sir Oliver Popplewell, *qv* and late (Catharine) Margaret Popplewell; *m* 1984, Debra Ellen Lomas; one *s* two *d*. *Educ:* Radley Coll.; Downing Coll., Cambridge (MA 1st cl. Law). Called to the Bar, Inner Temple, 1981; QC 1997; Recorder, 2002–11. *Address:* Royal Courts of Justice, Strand, WC2A 2LL. *Club:* Hawks (Cambridge).

POPPLEWELL, Sir Oliver (Bury), Kt 1983; Judge of the High Court of Justice, Queen's Bench Division, 1983–99; *b* 15 Aug. 1927; *s* of late Frank and Nina Popplewell; *m* 1st, 1954, Catharine Margaret Storey (*d* 2001); four *s* (and one *s* decd); 2nd, 2008, Hon. Dame Elizabeth Gloster, *qv*. *Educ:* Charterhouse (Schol.); Queens' Coll., Cambridge (Class. exhibnr; BA 1950; LLB 1951; MA); Harris Manchester Coll., Oxford (BA 2006; Hon. Fellow, 2006); London Sch. of Economics (MA 2008); Univ. of Buckingham (MA 2015). FCIArb 1996. CUCC, 1949–51. Called to the Bar, Inner Temple, 1951, Bencher, 1978; QC 1969; Chartered Arbitrator; Accredited Mediator, 2000. Recorder, Burton-on-Trent, 1970–71; Dep. Chm., Oxon QS, 1970–71; a Recorder of the Crown Court, 1972–82. Ind. Mem., Wages Councils, 1962–82, Chm. 1973–82; Mem., Home Office Adv. Bd on Restricted Patients, 1981–82; Vice-Chm., Parole Bd, 1986–87 (Mem., 1985–87); Mem., Parole Review Cttee, 1987–88; Pres., Employment Appeal Tribunal, 1986–88 (Mem., 1984–85); Mem., London Court of Internat. Arbitration, 2000–. Chairman: Inquiry into Crowd Safety and Control at sports grounds, 1985–86; Sports Dispute Panel, 2000–; English Rep., ICC Commn into Corruption, 1999; Mem., Ct of Arbitration for Sport, 2000–. MCC: Mem. Cttee, 1971–74, 1976–79, 1980–97; Trustee, 1983–94; Pres., 1994–96; Hon. Life Vice Pres., 2010. Gov., Sutton's Hosp. in Charterhouse, 1986–88. Trustee, Bletchley Park Trust, 1999–2008. Hon. LLD Buckingham, 2015. *Publications:* Benchmark: life, laughter and the law, 2003; Hallmark: a judge at Oxford, 2008; The Prime Minister and His Mistress, 2014. *Recreations:* sailing, cricket, tennis. *Address:* Brick Court Chambers, 7 Essex Street, WC2R 3LD. *T:* (020) 7379 3550. *E:* oliver.popplewell@virgin.net. *Clubs:* Garrick, MCC; Hawks (Cambridge); Vincent's (Oxford); XL; Blakeney Sailing.

See also Hon. Sir A. J. Popplewell.

POPPY, Prof. Guy Matthew, DPhil; FRSB; Professor of Ecology, University of Southampton, since 2004; Chief Scientific Adviser, Food Standards Agency, since 2014; *b* Kettering, Northants, 14 Sept. 1965; *s* of Victor and Pam Poppy; *m* 1990, Jenny Baverstock; one *s* one *d*. *Educ:* Tideway Sch.; Brighton, Hove and Sussex VIth Form Coll.; Imperial Coll. London (BSc ARCS 1987); Wolfson Coll., Oxford (DPhil 1990). FRSB (FSB 2002). Rothamsted Research: HSO, 1991–95; SSO, 1995–98; PSO, 1998–2001; University of Southampton: Sen. Lectr, 2001–03; Reader, 2003–04; Hd, Sch. of Biol Scis, 2009–11; Dir, Interdisciplinary Strategy, 2011–14. Visiting Professor: Oregon State Univ., 2008; Imperial Coll. London, 2009–. Trustee, Marwell Wildlife, 2004–14. *Publications:* (with M. J. Wilkinson) Geneflow from GM PLants, 2005; contrib. articles to jls incl. Nature. *Recreations:* cycling, fine wine, travelling, natural history. *Address:* Centre for Biological Sciences, Faculty of Natural and Environmental Sciences, Life Sciences Building 85, University of Southampton, Highfield Campus, Southampton SO17 1BJ. *T:* (023) 8059 3217. *E:* gmp@soton.ac.uk. *Club:* Farmers.

PORCHESTER, Lord; George Kenneth Oliver Molyneux Herbert; *b* 13 Oct. 1992; *s* and *heir* of Earl of Carnarvon, *qv*.

PORRITT, Hon. Sir Jonathon (Espie), 2nd Bt *cr* 1963, of Hampstead, co. London; CBE 2000; freelance writer and broadcaster; Chairman, Sustainable Development Commission, 2000–09; *b* 6 July 1950; *s* of Baron Porritt, GCMG, GCVO, CBE and Kathleen Mary (*d* 1998), 2nd *d* of A. S. Peck; *S* to Btcy of father, 1994; *m* 1986, Sarah Elizabeth Staniforth, *qv*; two *d*. *Educ:* Eton; Magdalen Coll., Oxford (BA (First Cl.) Modern Languages). ILEA Teacher, 1975–84: Head of English and Drama, Burlington Danes School, W12, 1980–84; Director: Friends of The Earth, 1984–90; Forum for the Future, 1996–. Co-Founder, Prince of Wales's Business and Envmtl Prog., 1994–. Non-exec. Dir, Willmott-Dixon Hldgs, 2009–. Chancellor, Keele Univ., 2012–. Pres., Conservation Volunteers, 2014–. Presenter, Where on earth are we going?, BBC TV, 1990. Ecology Party: candidate: General Elections, 1979 and 1983; European Elections, 1979 and 1984; Local Elections, 1977, 1978, 1982; Party Council Member, 1978–80, 1982–84; Chairman, 1979–80, 1982–84. *Publications:* Seeing Green—the Politics of Ecology, 1984; Friends of the Earth Handbook, 1987; The Coming of the Greens, 1988; Where on Earth are We Going?, 1991; (ed) Save the Earth, 1991; Captain Eco (for children), 1991; Playing Safe: science and the environment, 2000; Capitalism as if the World Matters, 2005; The World We Made, 2013. *Recreation:* walking. *Heir:* *b* Hon. Jeremy Charles Porritt [*b* 19 Jan. 1953; *m* 1980, Penny, *d* of J. H. Moore; two *s*]. *Address:* 9 Lypiatt Terrace, Cheltenham, Glos GL50 2SX.

PORRITT, Sarah Elizabeth, (Hon. Lady Porritt); *see* Staniforth, S. E.

PORTAL, Sir Jonathan (Francis), 6th Bt *cr* 1901; FCA; freelance accountant, since 1993; *b* 13 Jan. 1953; *s* of Sir Francis Spencer Portal, 5th Bt, and of Jane Mary, *d* of late Albert Henry Williams, OBE; *S* father, 1984; *m* 1982, Louisa Caroline, *er d* of Sir (Frederick) John (Charles Gordon) Hervey-Bathurst, 7th Bt; three *s*. *Educ:* Marlborough; Univ. of Edinburgh (BCom). FCA (ACA 1977). Gp Financial Controller, Henderson Admin, 1989–91; Finance Dir, Grosvenor Ventures Ltd, 1992–93. Trustee, Friends of Winchester Cathedral, 2010–14. Mem., Clothworkers' Co. *Heir:* *s* William Jonathan Francis Portal, *b* 1 Jan. 1987. *Address:* Burley Wood, Ashe, Basingstoke, Hants RG25 3AG.

PORTARLINGTON, 7th Earl of, *cr* 1785; **George Lionel Yuill Seymour Dawson-Damer;** Baron Dawson 1770; Viscount Carlow 1776; *b* 10 Aug. 1938; *er s* of Air Commodore Viscount Carlow (killed on active service, 1944) and Peggy (who *m* 2nd, 1945, Peter Nugent; she *d* 1963), *yr d* of late Charles Cambie; *S* grandfather, 1959; *m* 1961, Davina, *e d* of Sir Edward Windley, KCMG, KCVO; three *s* one *d*. *Educ:* Eton. Page of Honour to the Queen, 1953–55. Director: G. S. Yuill & Co. Ltd, Sydney, 1964–; Australian Stock Breeders Co. Ltd, Brisbane, 1966–94. *Recreations:* fishing, ski-ing, books. *Heir:* *s* Viscount Carlow, *qv*. *Address:* Gledswood, Melrose, Roxburghshire TD6 9DN. *T:* (01896) 822558; 118 Wolseley Road, Point Piper, NSW 2027, Australia. *T:* (2) 93639725. *Clubs:* Australian (Sydney); Royal Sydney Golf.

PORTEN, Anthony Ralph; QC 1988; *b* 1 March 1947; *s* of late Ralph Charles Porten and Joan Porten (*née* Edden); *m* 1970, Kathryn Mary (*née* Edwards); two *d*. *Educ:* Epsom Coll.; Emmanuel Coll., Cambridge (BA; Athletics Blue, 1967). Called to the Bar, Inner Temple, 1969, Bencher, 2002; joined Lincoln's Inn (*ad eund.*), 1973; Hd of Chambers, 2001–06; practising mainly in town and country planning and local government work. A Recorder, 1993–2001; Asst Boundary Comr, 2001–. Fellow, Soc. for Advanced Legal Studies, 1999. *Address:* Claremont Cottage, The Reeds Road, Frensham, Surrey GU10 3DQ. *T:* (01252) 793062. *Clubs:* Hawks (Cambridge); Claremont Park Golf; Blacknest Golf.

PORTEOUS, Christopher Selwyn, CBE 1993; Solicitor to Commissioner of Police for the Metropolis, 1987–95; *b* 8 Nov. 1935; *s* of Selwyn Berkeley Porteous (*né* Potous) and Marjorie Irene Porteous; *m* 1st, 1960, Brenda Jacqueline Wallis (marr. diss. 2005); four *d*; 2nd, 2007, Kathleen Patricia Horton. *Educ:* Dulwich Coll.; Law Society Sch. of Law. Articled to Clerk to Malling RDC, 1954–60; qual. as solicitor, 1960; LCC, 1960–62; Legal Asst with Scotland Yard, 1962–68; Sen. Legal Asst, 1968–76; Asst Solicitor, 1976–87. Pres., Assoc. of Police

Lawyers, 1995–98; Mem., Solicitors European Gp, 1991–96. Anglican Reader, 1958–2002; Mem., Pastoral Cttee, Rochester Dio., 1984–88. Hon. Mem., ACPO, 1995. *Recreations:* reading, poetry, hymn writing, walking, local history. *Address:* c/o Boys and Maughan, 83 Station Road, Birchington, Kent CT7 9RB.

PORTEOUS, Prof. David John, OBE 2013; PhD; FRCPE, FMedSci; FRSE; Professor of Human Molecular Genetics and Medicine, University of Edinburgh, since 1996; *b* 3 July 1954; *s* of John and Jean Porteous; *m* 1976, Rosemary Braid; three *d. Educ:* Aberdeen Grammar Sch.; Univ. of Edinburgh (BSc Biol Scis 1975; PhD Genetics 1978). FRCPE 2004. Res. Fellow, Univ. of Oxford, 1978–81; Jun. Res. Fellow, Wolfson Coll., Oxford, 1980–81; MRC Recombinant DNA Res. Fellow, MRC Mammalian Genome Unit, Edinburgh, 1981–84; MRC Human Genetics Unit, Edinburgh: Staff Scientist, 1984–86; scientific non-clinical career appt to MRC, Grade 1, 1986–93; Hd of Molecular Genetics, 1993–96. Scientific Advr, H of C Select Cttee on Sci. and Technol., 1994–96. Founder, Generation Scotland, 2001. Pioneered Cystic Fibrosis Gene Therapy, 1995; discovered DISC1, 2000. FMedSci 1999; FRSE 2001; Mem., EMBO, 2010. *Recreations:* walking, cycling, windsurfing, ski-ing, reading, cinema, travelling, family, France. *Address:* Medical Genetics Section, Centre for Genomic and Experimental Medicine, MRC IGMM, University of Edinburgh, Crewe Road South, Edinburgh EH4 2XU. *T:* (0131) 651 1040, *Fax:* (0131) 651 1059. *E:* david.porteous@ed.ac.uk.

PORTER, Alan Fraser; Group Company Secretary, Prudential plc, since 2012; *b* UK, 22 Sept. 1963; *s* of Air Vice-Marshal John Alan Porter, *qv*; *m* 1994, Manuela Lozano; one *s* one *d. Educ:* Warwick Sch.; City of London Poly. (LLB); London Sch. of Econs (LLM). Admitted solicitor, 1988; Attorney, State Bar of Calif, 1997; Solicitor, Simmons & Simmons, 1986–93; Asst Solicitor, BAT Industries plc, 1993–96; Co. Sec., Farmers Gp Inc., 1996–98; Business Develt Counsel, British American Tobacco plc, 1998–2000; Sen. Counsel, Brown & Williamson Tobacco Inc., 2000–02; Co. Sec., 2002–06, Hd of Mktg Legal, 2006–08, British American Tobacco plc; Gp Gen. Counsel, Tesco plc, 2008–12. Mem., Takeover Panel, 2006–. Vice-Chm., GC100 Gp, 2010–. Chm., Companies Cttee, CBI, 2006–. FRSA. *Recreations:* opera, shooting, football, literature, art. *Address:* Prudential plc, 12 Arthur Street, EC4R 9AQ. *T:* (020) 7220 7588. *Club:* East India.

PORTER, Alastair Robert Wilson, CBE 1985; Secretary and Registrar, Royal College of Veterinary Surgeons, 1966–91, retired; barrister; *b* 28 Sept. 1928; *s* of late James and Olivia Porter (*née* Duncan); *m* 1954, Jennifer Mary Priaulx Forman; two *s* one *d. Educ:* Irvine Royal Academy; Glasgow Academy; Merton Coll., Oxford (MA). Called to Bar, Gray's Inn, 1952. Resident Magistrate, N Rhodesia, 1954; Registrar of High Court of N Rhodesia, 1961; Permanent Secretary: Min. of Justice, N Rhodesia, 1964; Min. of Justice, Govt of Republic of Zambia, Oct. 1964. Mem., Fedn (formerly Liaison Cttee) of Veterinarians of the EEC, 1966–86, Sec.-Gen., 1973–79; Chm., EEC's Adv. Cttee on Veterinary Trng, 1986–87 (Vice-Chm., 1981–86). Lectures: Wooldridge Meml, BVA Congress, 1976; MacKellar Meml, Western Counties Veterinary Assoc., Tavistock, 1978; Weipers, Glasgow Univ., 1985; Keith Entwhistle Meml, Cambridge Univ., 1987. Vice-Chm., Haywards Heath Police Community Forum, 2000–02; Chm., Univ. of the Third Age, Haywards Heath, 2007–08. Hon. Member: BVA, 1978; British Small Animals Vet. Assoc., 1991; Australian Vet. Assoc., 1991; Latvian Vet. Assoc., 1997; Fedn of Veterinarians of Europe, 2002; Hon. Associate, RCVS, 1979. Vice-Pres., Blue Cross, 2006–12 (Gov., 1991–2000; Chm., Bd of Govs, 1995–98; Pres., 2000–05). Hon. DVMS Glasgow, 1994. Centenary Prize, 1981, and Victory Medal, 1991, Central Vet. Soc.; Akademische Ehrenbürger, Hannover Veterinary Sch., 1988. *Publications:* (jtly) An Anatomy of Veterinary Europe, 1972. *Address:* 4 Savill Road, Lindfield, West Sussex RH16 2NX. *T:* (01444) 482001.

See also Dr A. J. Porter.

PORTER, Amanda Eve; *see* Pinto, A. E.

PORTER, Sir Andrew Alexander Marshall H.; *see* Horsbrugh-Porter.

PORTER, Andrew James; Partner, Brunswick Group, since 2014 (Director, 2012–14); *b* Welwyn Garden City, 28 Sept. 1972; *s* of Arthur George Porter and Eileen Porter (*née* Nickolls). *Educ:* Dame Alice Owen's Sch.; Warwick Univ. (BA Hons Hist. and Pols); Cardiff Univ. (Postgrad. Dip. Journalism). Reporter, 1997–98, London Ed., 1998–2000, Western Morning News; Political Ed., Sunday Business, 2000–03; Business Corresp., 2003–04, Dep. Political Ed., 2004–06, Sunday Times; Dep. Political Ed., The Sun, 2006–07; Political Ed., Daily Telegraph, 2007–11. *Recreations:* golf, football. *Clubs:* Royal Automobile; Old Fold Manor Golf.

PORTER, Prof. Andrew Neil, PhD; Rhodes Professor of Imperial History, King's College, London, 1993–2008, now Emeritus; *b* 12 Oct. 1945; *s* of Peter Tozer Porter and Muriel Betty Porter (*née* Luer); *m* 1972, Mary Faulkner; two *s. Educ:* Chester Cathedral Choir Sch.; Christ's Hosp., Horsham; St John's Coll., Cambridge (MA, PhD). LRAM. Lectr in History, Univ. of Manchester, 1970–71; King's College, London: Lectr in History, 1971–85; Reader, 1985–90; Head of History Dept, 1988–94 and 2000–01; Prof. of History, 1990–93; FKC 2005. Hon. Sec., RHistS, 1986–90 (FRHistS 1980); Convenor, History at Univs Defence Gp, 1992–96 (Mem., Steering Cttee, 1990–99); Chm., Adv. Council (formerly Bd of Mgt), Inst. of Commonwealth Studies, 1994–2001. Trustee, FCO Library, 2008–. Life Mem., Friends of the Inst. of Commonwealth Studies, 1980; Mem. Council, Friends of PRO, 1991–99. FRSA 1998. Editor, Jl of Imperial and Commonwealth History, 1979–90. *Publications:* The Origins of the South African War, 1980; Victorian Shipping, Business and Imperial Policy, 1986; (jtly) British Imperial Policy and Decolonization 1938–64, vol. 1, 1987, vol. 2, 1989; (ed jtly) Money, Finance and Empire 1790–1860, 1985; (ed jtly) Theory and Practice in the History of European Expansion Overseas, 1988; (ed) Atlas of British Overseas Expansion, 1991 (Japanese edn 1996); European Imperialism 1860–1914, 1994 (Korean edn 2001, Japanese edn 2006); (ed and contrib.) The Oxford History of the British Empire, Vol. III, The Nineteenth Century, 1999; (ed) Bibliography of Imperial, Colonial and Commonwealth History since 1600, 2002; (ed) The Imperial Horizons of British Protestant Missions, 1880–1914, 2003; Religion versus Empire? British Protestant Missionaries and Overseas Expansion 1700–1914 (Trevor Reese Meml Prize, Inst. of Commonwealth Studies), 2004. *Recreations:* playing chamber music, mountain walking, travel. *Address:* 5 Farm Close, High Street, Clun, Shropshire SY7 8LJ; Department of History, King's College London, Strand, WC2R 2LS. *T:* (020) 7848 1078. *Club:* Clun Bowling.

PORTER, Dr Angus James; Chief Executive, Professional Cricketers' Association, since 2010; *b* Kitwe, Northern Rhodesia, 9 June 1957; *s* of Alastair Robert Wilson Porter, *qv*; *m* 1989, Kate Francis; two *s* one *d. Educ:* Jesus Coll., Cambridge (BA 1978; MA 1979; PhD 1982). Mars Confectionery: Product Manager, 1985–86; Sen. Product Manager, 1987–91; New Business Develt Manager, 1992–93; Impulse Sales Dir, 1994–95; Mktg Dir, 1995–98; Eur. Gen. Manager (Sugar Confectionery), 1998–99; Man. Dir, Consumer Div., BT, 1999–2003; Customer Dir, Abbey National, 2003–05; Chief Exec., Added Value, 2005–08; Gp Strategy Dir, Thomas Cook, 2008–09. Non-executive Director: Direct Wines Ltd, 2010–; Tele Danmark Communications, 2011–; Punch Taverns plc, 2012–. *Recreations:* cricket, golf, cooking, photography. *Address:* 1 Beechwood Drive, Marlow, Bucks SL7 2DH. *T:* (01628) 471280; Professional Cricketers' Association, Laker Stand, The Kia Oval, SE11 5SS. *E:* aporter@thepca.co.uk. *Club:* MCC.

PORTER, Rt Rev. Anthony; *see* Sherwood, Bishop Suffragan of.

PORTER, Arthur Thomas, MRSL 1979; MA, PhD; Pro-Chancellor and Chairman of Court, University of Sierra Leone, Freetown, Sierra Leone, 1992–99 (Vice-Chancellor, 1974–84); *b* 26 Jan. 1924; *m* 1953, Rigmor Sondergaard (*née* Rasmussen) (*d* 2005); one *s* one *d. Educ:* Fourah Bay Coll. (BA Dunelm); Cambridge Univ. (BA (Hist Tripos), MA); Boston Univ. (PhD). Asst, Dept of Social Anthropology, Edinburgh Univ., UK, 1951–52. Prof. of History and Head of Dept of Hist., also Dir of Inst. of African Studies, Fourah Bay Coll., 1963–64; Principal, University Coll., Nairobi, Univ. of E Africa, 1964–70; UNESCO Field Staff Officer; Educnl Planning Advr, Min. of Educn, Kenya, 1970–74. Mem. Exec. Bd, UNESCO, 1976–80. Africanus Horton Meml Lectr, Edinburgh Univ., 1983; Fulbright Schol.-in-Residence, Bethany Coll., Kansas, 1986–87. Chm., Bd of Dirs, Sierra Leone Nat. Diamond Mining Co., 1976–85. Hon. LHD Boston 1969; Hon. LLD Royal Univ. of Malta, 1969; Hon. DLitt: Sierra Leone, 1988; Nairobi, 1994. Phi Beta Kappa 1972. Symonds Medal, ACU, 1985. *Publications:* Creoledom, a Study of the Development of Freetown Society, 1963; contribs to The Times, Africa, African Affairs. *Recreation:* photography. *Address:* 85 Marlborough Avenue, Ottawa, ON K1N 8E8, Canada; 81 Fitzjohn Avenue, Barnet, Herts EN5 2HN; 26b Spur Road, Wilberforce, PO Box 1363, Freetown, Sierra Leone. *T:* (22) 231736.

PORTER, Sister Bernadette Mary, CBE 2005; PhD; Treasurer General, Society of the Sacred Heart, since 2010 (Provincial Treasurer, 2007–10); Vice-Chancellor, Roehampton University (formerly Rector and Chief Executive, Roehampton Institute, then University of Surrey Roehampton), 1999–2004 (Hon. Fellow, 2006); *b* 21 July 1952; *d* of Owen and Teresa Porter. *Educ:* Merrow Grange, Guildford; Digby Stuart Coll. (Cert Ed); King's Coll. London (BEd 1979; PhD 1989); Kingston Univ. (DMS). Mem., Soc. of the Sacred Heart, 1973–. Teacher: Woldingham Sch., 1973–75; Sacred Heart, Newcastle, 1975–78; Our Lady's Convent, 1980–82; Kalunga Girls' Sch., Masaka, Uganda, 1982–83; Roehampton Institute, London: Lectr, 1983–89; Coll. Principal, 1989–99; Sen. Pro-Rector, 1995–99. Member: Council of Church Colls, 1989–2004; Council, Univ. of Surrey, 1999–2004; UUK, 1999–2004; Southwark Cathedral Council, 2001–; Cumberlege Commn, 2006–07; Chm., Educn Cttee, RC dio. of Southwark, 2006–09. Mem., Internat. Women's Forum, 2000–07. Hon. Treas., Solidarity with S Sudan, 2010–12. Pres., English/French Speaking Treasurers Gen., 2011–12. Trustee: St Mary's Sch., Shaftesbury, 1999–2007; Higher Educn Foundn, 2002–05; Regent, Marymount Internat. Sch., 2002–05; Villiers Park Educnl Trust, 2004–07. Chm. Trustees, Regenerate.com, 2005–09; Mem., Neuro-disability Res. Trust, 2005–09. Patron, Coll., of Teachers, 2005–. Governor: Wimbledon Sch. of Art, 2003–07; Heythrop Coll., 2007–09. MInstD 1999. FRSA 1997. DUniv Middlesex, 2004; Hon. DLitt Leicester, 2012. *Publications:* contrib. various articles. *Recreations:* gardening, walking, travel, music. *Address:* 9 Bute Gardens, W6 7DR. *Club:* Reform.

PORTER, David John; Director, David Porter Communications with Human Touch, since 2010; Head of Drama, 1998–2002 and Co-ordinator of Performance Studies, 2002–10, Kirkley High School, Lowestoft; *b* 16 April 1948; *s* of late George Porter and of Margaret Porter; *m* 1978, Sarah Jane Shaw; two *s* two *d. Educ:* Lowestoft Grammar School; New College of Speech and Drama, London. Teacher, London, 1970–72; Dir and Co-Founder, Vivid Children's Theatre, 1972–78; Head of Drama, Benjamin Britten High School, Lowestoft, 1978–81; Conservative Party Agent: Eltham, 1982–83; Norwich North, 1983–84; Waveney, 1985–87. MP (C) Waveney, 1987–97; contested (C) same seat, 1997. Member, Select Committee: on Social Security, 1991–92; for Educn, 1992–96; for Educn and Employment, 1996–97. Dir, David Porter Freelance Communications, 1997–99. Examr in A-Level Perf. Studies and Drama, OCR, IGCSE Drama, First Lang. English, Directed Writing, Edexcel Drama, 1999–. *Recreations:* family of 4 children and 6 grandchildren, Waveney area—past, present and future. *Address:* 11 Irex Road, Pakefield, Lowestoft, Suffolk NR33 7BU. *W:* www.davidporter.co.uk.

PORTER, Prof. Dorothy Elizabeth, (Mrs B. P. Dolan), PhD; FRHistS; Professor in History of the Health Sciences, since 2002 and Chair, 2004–09, Department of Anthropology, History and Social Medicine, University of California, San Francisco; *b* 8 June 1953; *d* of John Dudley Mayne Watkins and Eileen Catherine Watkins (*née* Justice); *m* 1st, 1987, Roy Sydney Porter, FBA (marr. diss. 1997; he *d* 2002); 2nd, 2000, Brian Patrick Dolan. *Educ:* Univ. of Sussex (BA Sociol. 1976; MA Urban and Regl Studies 1977); University Coll. London (PhD 1984). FRHistS 1991. Fellow, Wellcome Inst. for Hist. of Medicine, 1985–88; Res. Associate, UCLA, 1988–89; Res. Fellow, Univ. of Calif., San Francisco, 1989–90; Vis. Asst Prof., Harvard Univ., 1990–91; Birkbeck College, University of London: Lectr, 1991–94, Sen. Lectr, 1994–97; Wellcome Reader in Hist. of Medicine, 1997–98; Prof. in the Hist. of Sci. and Medicine, 1998–2002; Pro-Vice Master for Internat. and Res. Students, 2001–02. Mem., Soc. for Social Hist. of Medicine, 1981. Founding Mem., Internat. Network for Hist. of Public Health, 1991; Member: Amer. Assoc. for Hist. of Medicine, 1990; Eur. Assoc. for Hist. of Medicine and Health, 1994. *Publications:* (with R. Porter) In Sickness and In Health: the British experience 1650–1850, 1988; (with R. Porter) Patient's Progress: doctors and doctoring in Eighteenth Century England, 1989; (ed jtly) The Codification of Medical Ethics, vol. 1, The Eighteenth Century, 1992; (ed with R. Porter) Doctors, Politics and Society: historical essays, 1993; (Introd.) John Ryle, Changing Disciplines, 1994; (ed) The History of Health and the Modern State, 1994, 2nd edn 2006; (ed) Social Medicine and Medical Sociology in the Twentieth Century, 1997; Health, Civilisation and the State: a history of public health from ancient to modern times, 1999, 2nd edn 2005; Health Citizenship: essays on social medicine and bio-medical politics, 2012. *Address:* Department of Anthropology, History and Social Medicine, University of California, 3333 California Street, Suite 485, San Francisco, CA 94143–0850, USA. *T:* (415) 4768826, *Fax:* (415) 4769453. *E:* porterd@dahsm.ucsf.edu.

PORTER, Gary Andrew, CBE 2013; Chairman, Local Government Association, since 2015 (Vice Chairman, 2011–15); *m* Karen. *Educ:* De Montfort Univ. (BA Hons 2000); Canterbury Christ Church Univ. (Postgrad. Cert. 2011). Mem. (C), S Holland DC, 2001– (Leader, 2003–). Chm., Cons. Councillors' Association, 2013–. *Address:* House of Lords, SW1A 0PW.

[Created a Baron (Life Peer) 2015 but title not yet gazetted at time of going to press.]

PORTER, Henry Christopher Mansel; writer and journalist; London Editor, Vanity Fair, since 1992; *b* 23 March 1953; *s* of Major H. R. M. Porter, MBE and Anne Victoria Porter (*née* Seymour); *m* 1990, Elizabeth Mary Elliot; two *d. Educ:* Wellington Coll.; Manchester Univ. (BA Hons). Columnist, Sunday Times, 1982–87; Editor: Illustrated London News, 1987–89; Correspondent Mag., 1989–90; Exec. Ed., Independent on Sunday, 1990–91; contributor, 1991–, to London Evening Standard, Guardian, Observer, Daily Telegraph, Independent on Sunday. Co-Dir, Convention on Modern Liberty, 2009–. *Publications:* Lies, Damned Lies, 1984; *novels:* Remembrance Day, 1999; A Spy's Life, 2001; Empire State, 2003; Brandenburg (CWA Ian Fleming Steel Dagger), 2005; The Master of the Fallen Chairs, 2008; The Dying Light, 2009. *Recreations:* painting, walking, gardening, reading. *Address:* c/o Lloyds Private Banking, PO Box 1060 Heathside, 131 Pembroke Road, Clifton, Bristol BS99 1UX.

PORTER, Janet S.; *see* Street-Porter.

PORTER, Air Vice-Marshal John Alan, OBE 1973; CEng, FRAeS, FIET; Deputy Vice-Chancellor and Professor, University of Glamorgan, 1994–99, now Professor Emeritus, University of South Wales (formerly University of Glamorgan); *b* 29 Sept. 1934; *s* of late Alan and Etta Porter; *m* 1961, Sandra Rose (marr. diss.); two *s*; *m* 2002, Veronica Kennedy. *Educ:* Lawrence Sheriff School, Rugby; Bristol Univ. (BSc); Southampton Univ. (Dip Soton). Commissioned in Engineer Branch, RAF, 1953; appts in UK, USA and Cyprus, 1953–79;

Royal College of Defence Studies, 1980; Dep. Gen. Manager, NATO MRCA Develt and Production Agency (NAMMA), Munich, 1981–84; Dir-Gen. Aircraft 2, MoD(PE), 1984–88; Dir-Gen., Communications, Inf. Systems and Orgn (RAF), 1988–89; RAF retd, 1989. Dir, Communications-Electronics Security Gp, 1989–91; Dir, Sci. and Technol., GCHQ, 1991–94. Public and Lead Gov., Guy's and St Thomas' Foundn Trust, 2013–. Vis. Fellow, Cranfield Univ., 1994–97. Chm. Council, University Coll. Plymouth St Mark and St John, 2008–12. Hon. DSc Glamorgan, 2005. *Recreations:* music, horology. *Address:* University of South Wales, Pontypridd, Mid Glam CF37 1DC. *Club:* Royal Air Force.

See also A. F. Porter.

PORTER, (Jonathan) Mark, FRCA; Consultant Anaesthetist, University Hospitals Coventry and Warwickshire NHS Trust, since 1998; *b* Newcastle-under-Lyme, 18 April 1962; *s* of John and Jean Porter; *m* 1989, Linda Barrow; one *s* one *d*. *Educ:* Univ. of Leicester (BSc Med. Sci. 1983; MB ChB 1989). FRCA 1994. Hse Officer, 1989–90; SHO (anaesthesia), Peterborough Dist Hosp., Leicester Royal Infirmary, Leicester Gen. Hosp. and Glenfield Gen. Hosp., Leicester, 1990–92; SHO (Intensive Care Unit and Emergency Dept), Derbys Royal Infirmary, Derby, 1992–93; Specialist Registrar (anaesthesia), Coventry, Nuneaton and Birmingham, 1993–98. Chm. Council, British Med. Assoc., 2012– (Mem. Council, 1992–98 and 2004–; Chair: Jun. Doctors Cttee, 1997–98; Consultants Cttee, 2009–12). Hon. Col, 202 (Midlands) Field Hosp., 2014–. *Recreations:* family, visiting Roman ruins. *Address:* British Medical Association, BMA House, Tavistock Square, WC1H 9JP. *E:* MPorter@bma.org.uk.

PORTER, Prof. Sir Keith (Macdonald), Kt 2011; FRCS, FRCSE; Professor of Clinical Traumatology, University Hospitals Birmingham NHS Foundation Trust, University of Birmingham and Royal Centre for Defence Medicine, since 2005; *b* Swindon, 31 Dec. 1948; *s* of Albert Porter and Hilda Porter; *m* 2008, Shamim Donnelly; two *s* one *d* by a previous marriage. *Educ:* Marlborough Coll.; St Thomas's Hosp. Med. Sch., London (MB BS 1974). FRCS 1978; FRCSE 1998; FIMCRCSE 2001. Surgical Hse Officer, St Thomas's Hosp., London, 1974; Hse Physician, St Helier's Hosp., Carshalton, 1975; Surgical Hse Officer, Gen. and Thoracic Surgery, St Mary's Hosp., Portsmouth, 1975–76; gen. surgical rotation, Wolverhampton, 1977–79; higher surgical trng, Birmingham, 1979–86. Consultant Trauma Surgeon: Birmingham Accident Hosp., 1986–93; Selly Oak Hosp., 1986–2010; Birmingham Gen. Hosp., 1993–95; Queen Elizabeth Hosp., Birmingham, 2010–; Dir, NIHR Surgical Reconstruction and Microbiol. Centre, 2010–; Clinical Lead for Military Trauma, Queen Elizabeth Hosp., Birmingham, 2003. OStJ 2012. Queen's Jubilee Medal, 2002; College Medal, RCSE, 2011. *Publications:* 15 books; 150 articles in learned jls. *Recreations:* my family, walking. *Address:* Longfield Cottage, Rowney Green, Alvechurch, Birmingham B48 7RB. *T:* 07989 408752. *E:* Keith.Porter@uhb.nhs.uk. *Club:* Royal Society of Medicine.

PORTER, Leonard Keith; Chairman, eAsset Management, since 2014; *b* 17 March 1952; *s* of Leonard Oram Porter and Irene Anne Porter (*née* Whitfield); *m* 1983, Victoria Louise Wigham; one *s* two *d*. *Educ:* Grangefield Grammar Sch. for Boys, Stockton-on-Tees; Univ. of Leeds (BSc Hons Metallurgy). Commercial saturation diver, Subsea Offshore, 1977–81; Founder/Dir, MOM Gp, 1981–94; Dep. Chm. and Chief Exec., Marine Offshore Mgt, 1994–96; Dir, Global Transportation Business, Lloyds Register of Shipping, 1996–2003; Chief Exec., Rail Safety and Standards Bd, 2003–14. Non-executive Director: LPA Gp plc, 2014–; Jetwing Symphony Ltd (Sri Lanka), 2014–; Angel Trains Gp Ltd, 2015–. *Publications:* A Handbook for Underwater Inspectors, 1992. *Recreations:* golf, Rugby (now spectating), scuba diving, interest in Sri Lanka, sustainable development, Boxer dogs. *Address:* 13 Silver Lane, Purley, Surrey CR8 3HJ. *T:* (office) (020) 8660 1883. *E:* (home) dovecote13@aol.com, (office) len.porter13@gmail.com. *Club:* Woodcote Park Golf.

PORTER, Margaret Jane; *see* Dallman, M. J.

PORTER, Marguerite Ann, (Mrs Nicky Henson), MBE 2015; Guest Artist, Royal Ballet Co., since 1986 (Senior Principal Dancer, 1976–85); *b* 30 Nov. 1948; *d* of William Albert and Mary Porter; *m* (marr. diss.); *m* 1986, Nicky Henson, *qv*; one *s*. *Educ:* Doncaster. Joined Royal Ballet School, 1964; graduated to Royal Ballet Co., 1966; soloist, 1972; Principal, 1976; favourite roles include: Juliet in Romeo and Juliet, Manon, Natalia in A Month in the Country; The Queen in Matthew Bourne's Swan Lake, NY, 1999. *Film:* Comrade Lady. Dir, Yorkshire Ballet Seminars, 2005–; Gov., Royal Ballet, 2006–. *Publications:* Ballerina: a dancer's life, 1989. *Recreations:* my family, friends. *Address:* c/o Richard Stone Partnership, Suite 3, De Walden Court, 85 New Cavendish Street, W1W 6XD.

PORTER, Mark; *see* Porter, J. M.

PORTER, Mark Christopher Milsom, MBE 2005; General Practitioner, Culverhay Surgery, Wotton-under-Edge, Gloucestershire, since 2006; Medical Correspondent, The Times, since 2009; Presenter, Inside Health, BBC Radio 4, since 2011; *b* Ross-on-Wye, Herefordshire, 12 Nov. 1962; *s* of Alan and Lesley Porter; *m* 1987, Ros Lovell; two *d*. *Educ:* Wycliffe Coll., Stonehouse, Glos; University Coll. London and Westminster Med. Sch. (MB BS 1986). DA 1989; DCH 1990; GP VTS 1990. Trng posts in medicine and surgery, A&E, anaesthetics, paediatrics, age care, psychiatry and obstetrics and gynaecol., 1986–91; Registrar, 1991, NHS GP Asst, 1992–2001, Locking Hill Surgery, Stroud; NHS GP Principal, Stroud, 2002–05. Presenter: BBC1, 1993–; BBC Radio 4, 2003–. Team Doctor, Ford World Rally Team, 1990–96. *Recreations:* fine wines, good food, trying to start classic cars. *E:* drmarkp@aol.com. *W:* drmarkporter.co.uk.

PORTER, Mark Edward; editorial design consultant, since 2010; Principal, Mark Porter Associates, since 2010; *b* 15 March 1960; *s* of Robert George Porter and Sybil Elizabeth Porter; *m* 2001, Elizabeth Hubbard; two *s*. *Educ:* Trinity Sch. of John Whitgift, Surrey; Trinity Coll., Oxford (BA Hons, MA 1985). Art Dir of several mags, 1986–93; freelance art dir and design consultant, 1993–95; The Guardian: Associate Art Dir, 1995–98; Art Dir, 1998–2000; Creative Ed., then Creative Dir, 2000–10. Mem., AGI, 2004. *Publications:* contrib. to many books and jls on mag. and newspaper design. *Recreations:* family, food and cooking, Hispanophilia. *Address:* Studio 6, The Lux Building, 2–4 Hoxton Square, N1 6NU. *E:* info@markporter.com.

PORTER, Martin Hugh Ninnis; QC 2006; *b* 3 Nov. 1962; *s* of late William Hugh Lancelot Porter and of Elizabeth Hilary Porter (*née* Oddie); *m* 1989, Dr Kelly Jean Stanhope; two *d*. *Educ:* St John's Coll., Cambridge (BA 1984; LLM 1985). Called to the Bar, Inner Temple, 1986. *Recreations:* cycling, ski-ing, flying and drinking at moderate speed. *Address:* 2 Temple Gardens, EC4Y 9AY. *T:* (020) 7822 1200, *Fax:* (020) 7822 1300. *E:* mporter@2tg.co.uk. *Club:* Thames Velo.

PORTER, Richard Bruce; Chairman, Fred Hollows Foundation (UK), since 2009; *b* 20 Jan. 1942; *s* of Maynard Eustace Prettyman Porter and Irene Marjorie Porter; *m* 1965, Susan Mary Early; two *d*. *Educ:* St Joseph's Coll., Ipswich; City of London Coll. (BSc Econ). Account Supervisor, A. C. Nielsen Co., 1965–70; Divl Manager, Brooke Bond Oxo Ltd, 1970–74; Market Develt Manager, Mackenzie Hill Hldgs, 1974–75; Management Consultant, 1975–79, Sen. Manager and Partner, 1984–94, KPMG Management Consulting; Project Economist, Engineering Science Inc., 1979–84; Exec. Dir, Sight Savers Internat., 1994–2005; Dir of Ops, Internat. Agency for the Prevention of Blindness, 2005–08. *Publications:* (jtly) Science Parks and the Growth of High Technology, 1988. *Recreations:* tennis, hockey, reading, bridge, gardening. *Address:* 15 Park Road, Burgess Hill, W Sussex RH15 8EU. *T:* (01444) 232602. *Club:* Royal Over-Seas League.

PORTER, Prof. Robert, AC 2001; DM; FRACMA, FRACP, FAA; Director, Research Development, Faculty of Medicine, Health and Molecular Sciences, James Cook University, Queensland, 1999–2008 (Planning Dean (Medicine), 1998–99), now Honorary Adjunct Professor, Division of Tropical Health and Medicine; *b* 10 Sept. 1932; *s* of late William John Porter and Amy Porter (*née* Tottman); *m* 1961, Anne Dorothy Steell; two *s* two *d*. *Educ:* Univ. of Adelaide (BMedSc, DSc); Univ. of Oxford (MA, BM BCh, DM). Rhodes Scholarship, South Australia, 1954; Radcliffe Travelling Fellowship in Med. Sci., University Coll., Oxford, 1962; Lectr, Univ. Lab. of Physiology, Oxford, 1960–67; Fellow, St Catherine's Coll., and Medical Tutor, Oxford, 1963–67; Prof. of Physiology and Chm., Dept of Physiology, Monash Univ., 1967–79; Howard Florey Prof. of Med. Res., and Dir, John Curtin Sch. of Med. Res., ANU, 1980–89; Dean, Faculty of Medicine, 1989–98, Dep. Vice Chancellor (Res.), 1992–93, Monash Univ. Sen. Fulbright Travelling Fellow and Vis. Prof., Washington Univ. Sch. of Medicine, St Louis, Mo, 1973; Fogarty Scholar-in-Residence, NIH, 1986–87. Member: Bd of Dirs, Alfred Gp of Hosps and Monash Med. Centre, 1989–99; Bd of Govs, Menzies Sch. of Health Res., Darwin, 1985–92; Bd of Management, Baker Med. Res. Inst., 1980–99. Hon. DSc: Sydney, 2001; James Cook, 2009. Centenary Medal, Australia, 2003. *Publications:* (with C. G. Phillips) Corticospinal Neurones: their role in movement, 1977; (with R. N. Lemon) Corticospinal function and voluntary movement, 1993; articles on neurophysiology and control of movement by the brain. *Recreation:* reading. *Address:* Apt 140/21 Baywater Drive, Twin Waters, Qld 4564, Australia. *T:* (7) 54570905.

PORTER, Maj. Gen. Roderick John Murray, MBE 1994; Director-General, Royal Over-Seas League, since 2011; *b* Tamerton Foliot, Devon, 29 June 1960; *s* of John William Porter and Jane Elisabeth Porter (*née* Langdon); *m* 1987, Martina Marianne Heslam; three *s*. *Educ:* Lipsom Vale Primary Sch., Plymouth; Mount House Sch., Tavistock; Sherborne Sch.; RMA Sandhurst; Univ. of Newcastle upon Tyne (BA Hons Combined Studies (German and Hist.)); US Army War Coll. (Combined/Jt Force Land Component Commander's Course). Platoon Comd, 1981–82, Regtl Signals Officer, 1985–87, Adjt, 1987–89, 1 RWF; SO3 G3 (Ops), HQ 4th Armd Bde (Germany and Gulf), 1989–91; Army Staff Course Div. II, 1991–92 (psc†); COS, HQ 4th Armd Bde (Germany and Bosnia), 1992–94; Co. Comd, 1 RWF (UK and Bosnia), 1994–96; SO1 Policy ACDS Operational Requirements (Land), 1997–99; CO, 1 RWF (NI), 1999–2001; Dep. Dir, Equipt Capability (Direct Battlefield Engagement), MoD, 2001–03; HCSC, Shrivenham, 2003; Bde Comd, 3 Inf. Bde (NI), 2003–04, 8 Inf. Bde (NI), 2004–05; Dir, Equipt Plans, MoD, 2006–08; Dir, Force Strategic Engagement Cell, Multinat. Force HQ, Iraq, 2008–09; COS (Jt Warfare Develt), Permanent Joint HQ, Northwood, 2009–11. Col, Royal Welsh, 2006–11; Col Comdt, Prince of Wales's Div., 2009–13. Pres., Armed Forces Christian Union, 2008–14. Army Rugby Union: Chm., 2005–11, Vice Pres., 2012–, Referees' Soc.; Life Vice Pres., 2012–; Chm., Combined Services Rugby Referees' Fedn, 2006–11. *Recreations:* most sports, especially cricket, golf, dinghy sailing and Rugby (Rugby referee); hill walking, reading, military and ancient history, music (especially classical, blues and rock; playing guitar, violin, saxophone). *Address:* Royal Over-Seas League, Over-Seas House, Park Place, St James's Street, SW1A 1LR. *E:* roddyporter@googlemail.com.

PORTER, Sally Curtis; *see* Keeble, S. C.

PORTER, Dame Shirley, (Lady Porter), DBE 1991; Councillor, Hyde Park Ward, 1974–93, Leader, 1983–91, Westminster City Council; Lord Mayor of Westminster, 1991–92; *b* 29 Nov. 1930; *d* of late Sir John (Edward) Cohen and Lady (Sarah) Cohen; *m* 1949, Sir Leslie Porter (*d* 2005); one *s* one *d*. *Educ:* Warren Sch., Worthing, Sussex; La Ramée, Lausanne, Switzerland. Founded Designers' Guild, 1970; Chairman: Neurotech Medical Systems, 1992–94; LBC, 1992–93; Dir, Capital Radio, 1982–88. Westminster City Council: Conservative Whip, 1974–77; Road Safety Cttee, 1974–82; Member: Co-ordinating Cttee, 1981–82; Chairman: Highways and Works Cttee, 1978–82 (Vice-Chm., 1977–78); Gen. Purposes Cttee, 1982–83; Policy Review Cttee, 1982–83; Policy and Resources Cttee, 1983–91. Chairman: (also Founder), WARS Campaign (Westminster Against Reckless Spending), 1981–84; Cleaner City Campaign, 1979–81; Pres., Eur. Conf. on Tourism and the Envmt, 1992; Vice-Pres., Cleaner London Campaign, 1979–81; Mem. Exec., Keep Britain Tidy Gp, 1977–81. Pres., British Inst. of Cleaning Science, 1991; Mem. Ct, Guild of Cleaners, 1976–2002. Former Dep. Chm., Bd, London Festival Ballet. Trustee, London Philharmonic Trust, 1991–93. Hon. Mem., London Community Cricket Assoc., 1989–. Governor, Tel Aviv Univ., 1982–; Internat. Fellow, Porter Sch. of Envmtl Studies, Tel Aviv Univ., 2001–. JP Inner London, 1972–84; DL Greater London, 1988–94. FRSA 1989. Hon. PhD Tel Aviv, 1991. *Recreations:* golf, tennis, ballet. *Club:* Dyrham Park Golf.

PORTER, Stanley Leonard, CB 2005; Director, Winterbourne Consultancy Ltd, since 2006; *b* 16 March 1945; *s* of Leonard James and Lilian Elizabeth Porter; *m* 1966, Mary Roche; two *s* one *d*. *Educ:* King Edward VI Grammar Sch., Chelmsford. MCIPS 1994; FRAeS 1996. Ministry of Defence, 1963–2006: Asst Private Sec. to Minister of State for Defence Procurement, 1971–73; Principal, Tornado Finance, 1979–81; Asst Dir, Commercial, 1981–87; Director: Commercial Policy, 1987–89; Finance and Secretariat, 1989–92; Principal Dir, Commercial, 1992–98; Dir Gen., Commercial, 1998–2006 and Exec. Dir, Defence Procurement Agency, 1999–2006. *Recreations:* my family, travel, gardening. *T:* (01454) 775384. *E:* stanporter@tiscali.co.uk.

PORTES, Hélène; *see* Rey, H.

PORTES, Jonathan; Principal Research Fellow, National Institute of Economic and Social Research, 2015–April 2016 (Director, 2011–15); *b* 18 April 1966; *s* of Prof. Richard David Portes, *qv*. *Educ:* Balliol Coll., Oxford (BA Hons 1987); Princeton Univ. (MPA 1994). HM Treasury: various posts, 1987–91; Private Sec. and Speechwriter to the Chancellor of the Exchequer, 1991–92; Project Leader, Debt Mgt Review, 1994–95; Sen. Consultant, Nat. Economic Research Associates, 1995–98; Special Consultant, IMF, 1998–99; Project Leader, Performance and Innovation Unit, Cabinet Office, 1999–2000; Partner, Develt Strategies, 2000–02; Dir, Work, Welfare and Poverty, 2002–06, Chief Economist (Work), 2002–08, Dir, Children and Poverty, 2006–08, DWP; Chief Economist, Cabinet Office, 2008–11. FRSA. *Publications:* govt policy papers, econs jls and press articles. *Recreations:* walking, cooking. *Address:* National Institute of Economic and Social Research, 2 Dean Trench Street, Smith Square, SW1P 3HE. *E:* j.portes@niesr.ac.uk.

PORTES, Prof. Richard David, CBE 2003; DPhil; FBA 2004; Tommaso Padoa-Schioppa Professor of European Economic and Monetary Integration, European University Institute, since 2014; Professor of Economics, London Business School, since 1995; President (formerly Director), Centre for Economic Policy Research, since 1983; *b* 10 Dec. 1941; *s* of Herbert Portes and Abra Halperin Portes; *m* 1st, 1963, Bobbi Frank (marr. diss. 2005); one *s* one *d*; 2nd, 2006, Prof. Hélène Rey, *qv*; one *d*. *Educ:* Yale Univ. (BA 1962 *summa cum laude* maths and philosophy); Balliol and Nuffield Colls, Oxford (Rhodes Schol., Woodrow Wilson Fellow, Danforth Fellow; MA 1965; DPhil 1969; Hon. Fellow, Balliol Coll., 2014). Official Fellow and Tutor in Econs, Balliol Coll., Oxford, 1965–69; Asst Prof. of Econs and Internat. Affairs, Princeton Univ., 1969–72; Prof. of Econs, Birkbeck Coll., Univ. of London, 1972–94 (Head, Dept of Econs, 1975–77 and 1980–83). Dir d'Etudes, Ecole des Hautes Etudes en Sciences Sociales, Paris, 1978–2011. Guggenheim Fellow, 1977–78; British Acad. Overseas Vis. Fellow, 1977–78; Res. Associate, Nat. Bureau of Econ. Res., Cambridge, Mass, 1980–; Vis. Prof., Harvard Univ., 1977–78; Dist. Global Vis. Prof., Haas Business Sch., Univ. of Calif at Berkeley, 1999–2000; Joel Stern Vis. Prof. of Internat. Finance, Columbia Business Sch., 2003–04. Vice-Chm., Econs Cttee, SSRC, 1981–84. Member: Bd of Dirs, Soc. for Econ. Analysis (Rev. of Econ. Studies), 1967–69, 1972–80 (Sec. 1974–77); Council on Foreign

Relations, 1978–; Hon. Degrees Cttee, Univ. of London, 1984–89; Bellagio Gp on the Internat. Econ., 1990–; Franco-British Council, 1997–2002; Commn Economique de la Nation, France, 1999–2005; Conseil d'Admin, Fondation Banque de France, 1999–; ALSSS Commn on Social Scis, 2000–02; Gp of Econ. Policy Advrs, Presidency of EC, 2001–10; Euro-area Business Cycle Dating Cttee, CEPR, 2003–; Bd of Dirs, CEPREMAP, 2006–; Comité d'Honneur, Centre des Professions Financières, France, 2008–; Adv. Scientific Cttee, European Systemic Risk Bd, 2014–; Chm., Collegio di Probiviri, Società per il Mercato dei Titoli di Stato, 2001–. Fellow, Econometric Soc., 1983–; Sec.-Gen., Royal Econ. Soc., 1992–2008 (Mem. Council, 1986–92; Exec. Cttee, 1987–2008; Vice-Pres., 2009–); Council, European Econ. Assoc., 1992–96 (Fellow, 2004). Co-Chm., Bd of Governors, 1985–, and Sen. Editor, 1985–2014, Economic Policy. Pres., Richard and Margaret Merrell Foundn, 1996–. Hon. DSc Univ. Libre de Bruxelles, 2000; Hon. PhD: London Guildhall, 2000; Paris IX (Dauphine), 2013. *Publications:* (ed) Planning and Market Relations, 1971; The Polish Crisis, 1981; Deficits and Détente, 1983; (ed) Threats to International Financial Stability, 1987; (ed) Global Macroeconomics: policy conflict and cooperation, 1987; (ed) Blueprints for Exchange Rate Management, 1989; (ed) Macroeconomic Policies in an Interdependent World, 1989; (ed) Economic Transformation in Hungary and Poland, 1990; (ed) External Constraints on Macroeconomic Policy: the experience of Europe, 1991; (ed) The Path of Reform in Central and Eastern Europe, 1991; (ed) Economic Transformation in Central Europe, 1993; (ed) European Union Trade with Eastern Europe, 1995; Crisis? What Crisis? Orderly Workouts for Sovereign Debtors, 1995; Crises de la Dette, 2003; International Financial Stability, 2007; Macroeconomic Stability and Financial Regulation, 2009; (ed) the Social Value of the Financial Sector, 2013; contribs to many learned jls. *Recreation:* living beyond my means. *Address:* London Business School, Regent's Park, NW1 4SA. *T:* (020) 7000 8424. *E:* rportes@london.edu.

See also J. Portes.

PORTILLO, Rt Hon. Michael (Denzil Xavier); PC 1992; broadcaster and journalist; *b* 26 May 1953; *s* of late Luis Gabriel Portillo and Cora Waldegrave Blyth; *m* 1982, Carolyn Claire Eadie. *Educ:* Harrow County Boys' School; Peterhouse, Cambridge (1st cl. Hons MA History). Ocean Transport & Trading Co., 1975–76; Conservative Res. Dept, 1976–79; Special Advr, Sec. of State for Energy, 1979–81; Kerr McGee Oil (UK) Ltd, 1981–83; Special Adviser: to Sec. of State for Trade and Industry, 1983; to Chancellor of the Exchequer, 1983–84. MP (C) Enfield, Southgate, Dec. 1984–1997; contested (C) same seat, 1997; MP (C) Kensington and Chelsea, Nov. 1999–2005. An Asst Govt Whip, 1986–87; Parly Under Sec. of State, DHSS, 1987–88; Minister of State, Dept of Transport, 1988–90; Minister of State for Local Govt, DoE, 1990–92; Chief Sec. to HM Treasury, 1992–94; Sec. of State for Employment, 1994–95, for Defence, 1995–97; Shadow Chancellor, 2000–01. Chm. Judges, Man Booker Prize, 2008. BBC TV: regular contributor to This Week, 2003–; writer and presenter: Great British Railway Journeys, 2010–12, 2015; Great Continental Railway Journeys, 2012–; Railways of the Great War with Michael Portillo, 2014; Portillo's State Secrets, 2015. Columnist, The Sunday Times, 2004–. *W:* www.michaelportillo.co.uk. *Club:* Chelsea Arts.

PORTLAND, 12th Earl of, *cr* 1689; **Timothy Charles Robert Noel Bentinck;** Viscount Woodstock, Baron Cirencester, 1689; Count of the Holy Roman Empire; actor (as Timothy Bentinck); *b* 1 June 1953; *s* of 11th Earl of Portland and Pauline (*d* 1967), *y d* of late Frederick William Mellowes; *S* father, 1997; *m* 1979, Judith Ann, *d* of John Robert Emerson; two *s*. *Educ:* Harrow; Univ. of East Anglia (BA Hons). Trained Bristol Old Vic Theatre Sch. Winner BBC Drama Schs Radio Competition, 1978. London theatre appearances include: Pirates of Penzance, Theatre Royal, Drury Lane, 1982; Reluctant Heroes, Theatre of Comedy, 1984; Hedda Gabler, King's Head Theatre, 1990; A Doll's House, Bridge Lane Theatre, London, 1992; Arcadia, Haymarket, 1994; Night Must Fall, Haymarket, 1996; Educating Rita, Watermill, 2010; Love Your Chocolates (one-man show), tour, 2013; *radio:* David Archer in The Archers, 1982–; over 75 plays; *films:* North Sea Hijack, 1979; Pirates of Penzance, 1981; Winter Flight, 1985; Year of the Comet, 1992; Twelfth Night, 1995; Enigma, 2000; Fast Girls, 2012; *television* includes: By the Sword Divided, 1983; Square Deal, 1989; Made in Heaven, 1990; Sharpe, 1993; Grange Hill, 1994; Strike Force, 1995; Prince Among Men, 1997; The Gathering Storm, 2002; Born and Bred, 2003; D-Day, Murder in Suburbia, 2004; Silent Witness, Frances Tuesday, The Thick of It, Broken News, Absolute Power, 2005; Heartbeat, 2006; Doctors, 2006, 2012; Kingdom, 2009; The Pride of Wade Ellison, 2011; The Royal Bodyguard, 2011–12; Twenty Twelve, 2012; Eastenders, 2013; The Politician's Husband, Lucan, Gangsta Granny, 2013; The Game, 2015; winner: University Challenge - The Professionals, 2004; Celebrity Mastermind 2011; Celebrity Eggheads, 2012; Pointless Celebrities, 2012; composer of theme music for Easy Money, BBC TV, 1984; voice artist, radio and TV commercials, narrations, audio books, computer games and dubbing on films and TV progs. Travel journalist, Mail on Sunday. Computer programmer. Inventor of The Hippo (child-carrying device). HGV licence. *Publications:* Colin the Camper Van (for children), 2015. *Recreations:* guitar, banjo, writing comedy songs, scuba diving, house renovation, website design, computer advice, Mongolian archery. *Heir:* *s* Viscount Woodstock, *qv*.

PORTMAN, family name of **Viscount Portman**.

PORTMAN, 10th Viscount *cr* 1873; **Christopher Edward Berkeley Portman;** Baron 1837; Chairman, Portman Settled Estates Ltd, since 1998; *b* 30 July 1958; *s* of 9th Viscount Portman and of Rosemary Joy Portman (*née* Farris); *S* father, 1999; *m* 1st, 1983, Caroline Steenson (marr. diss.); one *s*; 2nd, 1987, Patricia Martins Pim; two *s*. *Educ:* Marlborough Coll. Director: Bioquiddity Inc., San Francisco, 2006–; Natural Bioscis SA, Switzerland, 2006–. *Recreations:* molecular nanotechnology, computer science, reading. *Heir:* *e s* Hon. Luke Oliver Berkeley Portman, *b* 31 Aug. 1984. *Address:* Ground Floor, 40 Portman Square, W1H 6LT. *T:* (020) 7563 1400. *Clubs:* Whites, Home House.

PORTMAN, Rachel Mary Berkeley, OBE 2010; composer; *b* Haslemere, 11 Dec. 1960; *m*; three *d*. *Educ:* Worcester Coll., Oxford (BA Music). *Compositions: for film and television include:* Experience Preferred… But Not Essential, 1982; The Storyteller (TV series), 1986–88, 1990; Life is Sweet, 1990; Oranges are Not the Only Fruit (TV series), 1990; Antonia & Jane, 1991; Where Angels Fear to Tread, 1991; Used People, 1992; The Joy Luck Club, 1993; Benny & Joon, 1993; Friends, 1993; Sirens, 1994; Only You, 1994; War of the Buttons, 1994; To Wong Foo, Thanks for Everything!, 1995; A Pyromaniac's Love Story, 1995; Smoke, 1995; The Adventures of Pinocchio, 1996; Marvin's Room, 1996; Emma, 1996 (Acad. Award for best orig. score, 1997); Addicted to Love, 1997; The Cider House Rules, 1999; Chocolat, 2000; The Emperor's New Clothes, 2001; Hart's War, 2002; The Truth About Charlie, 2002; Nicholas Nickleby, 2002; The Human Stain, 2003; Mona Lisa Smile, 2003; Lard, 2004; The Manchurian Candidate, 2004; Because of Winn-Dixie, 2005; Oliver Twist, 2005; The Lake House, 2006; Miss Potter, 2006; Infamous, 2006; The Duchess, 2008; Grey Gardens (TV), 2009; Never Let Me Go, 2010; The Snowflower of the Secret Fan, 2011; One Day, 2011; *for theatre:* The Little Prince (opera), 2003; Little House on the Prairie (musical), 2009; London Assurance, National Theatre Live, 2010; A Tale of Two Cities, Royal & Derngate, Northampton, 2014; The Water Diviner's Tale, BBC Proms, 2009. *W:* www.rachelportman.co.uk.

PORTO, Sue; Chief Executive Officer, St John's Hospital, Bath, since 2015; *b* Weymouth, 8 Nov. 1969; *d* of Colin and Sylvia Iliffe; two *s* one *d*. *Educ:* Weymouth Grammar Sch.; Open Univ. Sen. Manager, HM Prison Service, incl. Hd, Nat. Trng and Clinical Support, Offending Behaviour Progs, 1992–2007; Dir, SW of England, Prince's Trust, 2007–10; Chief Exec., Beanstalk charity (formerly Volunteer Reading Help), 2010–15. *Recreations:* horses, running, mountain biking. *Address:* 6 Stone Close, Corsham, Wilts SN13 0QU. *T:* 07590 069334.

PORTSDOWN, Archdeacon of; *see* Grenfell, Ven. J. W.

PORTSMOUTH, 10th Earl of, *cr* 1743; **Quentin Gerard Carew Wallop;** DL; Viscount Lymington, Baron Wallop, 1720; Hereditary Bailiff of Burley, New Forest; *b* 25 July 1954; *s* of Oliver Kintzing Wallop (Viscount Lymington) (*d* 1984) and Ruth Violet (*d* 1978), *yr d* of Brig.-Gen. G. C. Sladen, CB, CMG, DSO, MC; *S* grandfather, 1984; *m* 1st, 1981, Candia (*née* McWilliam) (marr. diss. 1984); one *s* one *d*; 2nd, 1990, Annabel, *d* of Dr and Mrs Ian Fergusson; one *d*. *Educ:* Eton; Millfield. Non-exec. Dir, Grainger Trust plc, 1987–2002. Patron, Hants Br., BRCS, 1995–. Warden, St Andrew's Ch, Farleigh Wallop. Mem., Fishmongers' Co., 1997– (Mem., Court of Assts, 2006–). DL Hants, 2004. *Heir:* *s* Viscount Lymington, *qv*. *Address:* Farleigh House, Farleigh Wallop, Basingstoke, Hants RG25 2HT. *Clubs:* White's, Buck's, Pilgrims; International Association of Cape Horners; Hampshire Hunt.

PORTSMOUTH, Bishop of, since 2010; **Rt Rev. Christopher Richard James Foster;** *b* Wednesbury, Staffs, 7 Nov. 1953; *s* of Joseph James Frederick Foster and Elizabeth Foster (*née* Gibbs); *m* 1st, 1982, Julia Marie Jones (*d* 2001); one *s* one *d*; 2nd, 2006, Rev. Sally Elizabeth Davenport. *Educ:* University Coll., Univ. of Durham (BA 1975); Univ. of Manchester (MA (Econ.) 1977); Trinity Hall, Cambridge (BA 1979, MA 1983); Westcott House, Cambridge. Lectr in Economics, Univ. of Durham, 1976–77; ordained deacon, 1980, priest, 1981; Asst Curate, Tettenhall Regis, Wolverhampton, 1980–82; Chaplain, Wadham Coll., Oxford and Asst Priest, Univ. Church of St Mary, with St Cross and St Peter in the East, Oxford, 1982–86; Vicar, Christ Church, Southgate, London, 1986–94; CME Dir, Edmonton Episcopal Area, 1988–94; Sub Dean and Canon Residentiary, Cathedral and Abbey Church of St Alban, 1994–2001; Bishop Suffragan of Hertford, 2001–10. Took seat in H of L, 2014. Member: Church Comrs Pastoral Cttee, 2013–14; Dioceses Commn, 2014–. Member, Council: Westcott House, Cambridge, 2004–12; Ripon Coll., Cuddesdon, 2014– (Chm., 2015–). Chm. Trustees and Convenor, Enabling Gp, Churches Together in England, 2012–. Governor: Univ. of Herts, 2002–10 (Chm., F and GP Cttee, 2007–10); Univ. of Portsmouth, 2014–. Hon. DLitt Herts, 2011. *Address:* Bishopsgrove, 26 Osborn Road, Fareham, Hants PO16 7DQ. *T:* (01329) 280247. *E:* bishop@portsmouth.anglican.org.

PORTSMOUTH, Bishop of, (RC), since 2012; **Rt Rev. Philip Egan;** *b* Altrincham, 14 Nov. 1955; *s* of Bill and Rosalie Egan. *Educ:* St Vincent's Primary Sch.; St Ambrose Coll.; King's Coll. London (BA); Allen Hall Seminary; Venerable English Coll., Rome (STL); Boston Coll. (MA); Univ. of Birmingham (PhD 2004). Ordained priest, 1984; Asst Priest, St Anthony's Woodhouse Park, 1985–88; Asst Chaplain, Fisher House, Chaplaincy to Univ. of Cambridge, 1988–91; Chaplain, Arrowe Park Hosp., Wirral, 1991–94; Dean of Studies and Prof. of Fundamental Theol., St Mary's Coll., Oscott, 1996–2007; Parish Priest, Our Lady and St Christopher's, Romiley, 2008–12. *Publications:* Philosophy and Catholic Theology: a primer, 2009. *Address:* Bishop's House, Bishop Crispian Way, Portsmouth PO1 3HG. *T:* (023) 9282 0894. *E:* bishop@portsmouthdiocese.org.uk.

PORTSMOUTH, Dean of; *see* Brindley, Very Rev. D. C.

PORTWOOD, Nigel David; Secretary to the Delegates, and Chief Executive, Oxford University Press, since 2009; Fellow of Exeter College, Oxford, since 2009; *b* Plymouth, 6 Dec. 1965; *s* of Leslie and Ruth Portwood; *m* 1995, Hayley Frances Morse; one *s* two *d*. *Educ:* Queens' Coll., Cambridge (BA Engrg 1988; MA 1991); INSEAD (MBA 1994). Mgt Consultant, OC&C Strategy Consultants, 1990–95; Strategy and Develt Exec., 1995–96, Dir of Strategy, 1997–99, Pearson plc; CEO, Pearson Educn EMEA, 1999–2002; Chief Financial Officer, 2003–08, Exec. Vice-Pres., Global Ops, 2008–09, Penguin Gp. Mem., Governing Council, Nat. Coll. for Sch. Leadership, 2000–03. Mem. Council, Publishers Assoc., 2000–02 and 2009–. Mem., Mgt Bd, Blavatnik Sch. of Govt, Oxford Univ., 2014–. *Address:* Oxford University Press, Great Clarendon Street, Oxford OX2 6DP.

POSEN, Adam Simon, Hon. CBE 2013; PhD; Senior Fellow, since 1997, and President, since 2013, Peterson Institute for International Economics (Deputy Director, 2007–09); *b* Boston, Mass, Dec. 1966; *s* of Harold Posen and Annette Posen; *m* 2000, Jennifer Sosin. *Educ:* Harvard Coll. (AB Govt 1988); Harvard Graduate Sch. of Arts and Scis (PhD Pol Econ. and Govt 1997). Nat. Sci. Foundn Graduate Fellow, Harvard Univ., 1988–92; Bosch Foundn Fellow, Germany, 1992–93; Okun Meml Fellow, Brookings Instn, 1993–94; Economist, Federal Reserve Bank of New York, 1994–97. Mem., Panel of Advrs, US Congressional Budget Office, 2007–11; External Mem., Monetary Policy Cttee, Bank of England, 2009–12. Mem., Bd of Dirs, Bruegel, 2007–. Co-Founder and Chm., Editl Bd, International Finance, 1997–; columnist: International Economy, 2007–09; Welt am Sonntag, 2007–; Eurointelligence syndicate, 2009–. *Publications:* Restoring Japan's Economic Growth, 1998 (trans. Japanese 1999); (jtly) Inflation Targeting: lessons from the international experience, 1999; (ed jtly and contrib.) Japan's Financial Crisis and its Parallels to US Experience, 2000; (ed and contrib.) The Euro at Five: ready for a global role?, 2005; (ed jtly and contrib.) The Euro at Ten: the next global currency?, 2009; contrib. articles in jls incl. Brookings Papers on Econ. Activity, NBER Macroecons Annual, Oxford Econ. Papers and numerous Central Bank conf. vols. *Recreations:* cooking, urban walking, European travel. *Address:* Peterson Institute for International Economics, Washington, DC 20036–1903, USA.

POSNANSKY, Jeremy Ross Leon; QC 1994; a Deputy High Court Judge, since 1997; *b* 8 March 1951; *s* of Anthony Posnansky and late Evelyn Davis (formerly Posnansky), JP; *m* 1974, Julia Sadler, *d* of late Richard Sadler, MBE; two *d*. *Educ:* St Paul's Sch.; Coll. of Law. Called to the Bar, Gray's Inn, 1972 (Bencher, 2003), Antigua and Barbuda, 1995; in ind. practice at the Bar, 1972–2007; Asst Recorder, 1993–98; a Recorder, 1998–2002; admitted solicitor, 2007; Partner, Farrer & Co. LLP, 2007–. Mem., Family Courts Business and Service Cttees, Inner London, 1991–94. Fellow, Internat. Acad. of Matrimonial Lawyers, 1996–2015. *Publications:* contrib. Internat. Family Law, Family Law. *Recreations:* travel, scuba diving, photography, gardening. *Address:* Farrer & Co., 66 Lincoln's Inn Fields, WC2A 3LH. *T:* (020) 3375 7000.

POSNER, Lindsay Steven; theatre director; *b* 6 June 1959; *s* of Dennis and Pauline Posner; *m* 2000, Megan Wheldon; one *s* two *d*. *Educ:* Exeter Univ. (BA Eng. Lit.); Royal Acad. Dramatic Art. Associate Dir, Royal Court Th., 1987–92; productions include: The Treatment; No One Sees the Video; Built on Sand; Blood; Downfall; Ambulance; Colquhoun and McBryde; Death and the Maiden, 1991 (Olivier Award for Best Play); Royal Shakespeare Co. productions include: Volpone, Taming of the Shrew, 1999; The Rivals, 2000; Twelfth Night, 2001; National Theatre: Tartuffe, 2002; Power, 2003; Almeida Theatre productions include: The Hypochondriac, Romance, Tom and Viv, Man and Boy, Dada, Love Counts, 2005–06; House of Games, 2010; The Turn of the Screw, 2013; other productions include: American Buffalo, Young Vic, 1997; After Darwin, Hampstead Th., 1998; Sexual Perversity in Chicago, Comedy, 2003; A Life in the Theatre, Apollo, 2004; Oleanna, Garrick, 2004; Fool for Love, Apollo, 2005; The Birthday Party, Duchess, 2005; Fiddler on the Roof, Crucible, Sheffield, 2006, transf. Savoy, 2007; 3 Sisters on Hope Street, Everyman, Liverpool, 2008; Carousel, Savoy, 2008; A View from the Bridge, Duke of York's, 2009; An Ideal Husband, Vaudeville, 2010; Butley, Duchess, 2011; Noises Off, Old Vic, 2011; Abigail's Party, Menier, 2012; Uncle Vanya, Vaudeville, 2012; The Winslow Boy, Old Vic, 2013; Relatively Speaking, Wyndham's, 2013; A Little Hotel on the Side, Th. Royal,

Bath, 2013; Other Desert Cities, Old Vic, 2014; Hay Fever, Theatre Royal, Bath, 2014, transf. Duke of York's Th., 2015; Speed-the-Plow, Playhouse Th., 2014; Harvey, Birmingham Repertory Th., transf. Theatre Royal, 2015; Communicating Doors, Menier Chocolate Factory, 2015; She Stoops to Conquer, Theatre Royal, Bath, 2015; Dinner with Saddam, Menier Chocolate Factory, 2015; *opera*: Giulio Cesare, Royal Opera Hse, 1997; Roberto Devereux, Holland Park, 2009; Tosca, The Grange, 2010; Rigoletto, Holland Park, 2011; *television* includes: The Maitlands, 1993; Two Oranges and a Mango, 1994. *Recreations:* Italian white wine, family, reading, a multiplicity of obsessions. *Address:* 58 Chaucer Road, W3 6DP. *T:* (020) 8993 5575. *E:* posner.lindsay50@googlemail.com.

POSNER, Prof. Rebecca; Professor of the Romance Languages, University of Oxford, 1978–96, now Emeritus; Fellow, St Hugh's College, Oxford, 1978–96, Hon. Fellow, 1996; Research Associate, Oxford University Centre for Linguistics and Philology, since 1996; *b* 17 Aug. 1929; *d* of William and Rebecca Reynolds; *m* 1953, Michael Vivian Posner, CBE (*d* 2006), one *s* one *d*. *Educ:* Somerville Coll., Oxford. MA, DPhil (Oxon); PhD (Cantab). Fellow, Girton Coll., Cambridge, 1960–63; Prof. of French Studies, Univ. of Ghana, 1963–65; Reader in Language, Univ. of York, 1965–78. Vis. Prof. of Romance Philology, Columbia Univ., NY, 1971–72; Vis. Senior Fellow, Princeton Univ., 1983; Emeritus Leverhulme Fellow, 1997. Vice-Pres., Philological Soc., 2000– (Pres., 1996–2000). *Publications:* Consonantal Dissimilation in the Romance Languages, 1961; The Romance Languages: a linguistic introduction, 1966 (trans. Japanese); (with J. Orr and I. Iordan) Introduction to Romance Linguistics, 1970; (ed with J. N. Green) Trends in Romance Linguistics and Philology: vol. 1, Romance Comparative and Historical Linguistics, 1980; vol. 2, Synchronic Romance Linguistics, 1981; vol. 3, Language and Philology in Romance, 1982; vol. 4, National and Regional Trends in Romance Linguistics and Philology, 1982; vol. 5, Bilingualism and Conflict in Romance, 1993; (contrib.) Legacy of Latin, ed R. Jenkyns, 1992; The Romance Languages, 1996 (trans. Spanish 1998); Linguistic Change in French, 1997; (contrib.) The History of the University of Oxford, vol. vii: Nineteenth Century Oxford, Part 2, 2000; (contrib.) Lexikon der Romanistischen Linguistik, vol. I, 1: Geschichte des Faches Romanistik, 2001; numerous articles. *Recreations:* walking, gardening, theatre, music. *Address:* St Hugh's College, Oxford OX2 6LE; Rushwood, Jack Straw's Lane, Oxford OX3 0DN. *T:* (01865) 763578.

POSNETT, David Wilson, OBE 2012; *b* Runcorn, 6 May 1942; *s* of Charles Christopher Posnett and Coralie Howard Posnett (*née* Wilson); *m* 2007, Sarah Anne Clare Addington; two *s* one *d*. *Educ:* Leys Sch., Cambridge; Trinity Coll., Cambridge (BA 1964; MA 1967). Chm. and Man. Dir, Leger Galls, fine art dealers, 1966–96. Trustee and Chm., Holburne Mus., 1999–2012. Chm., Soc. of London Art Dealers, 1991–93. Freeman, City of London, 1963; Liveryman, Leathersellers' Co., 1967.

POST, Andrew John; QC 2012; *b* London, 12 May 1962; *s* of Jack Post and Valerie Post; *m* 1995, Mary Aylmer. *Educ:* Radley Coll.; Trinity Coll., Cambridge (BA Hist. 1984); City Univ. (DipLaw). Called to the Bar, Middle Temple, 1988; in practice as a barrister, 1988–, specialising in medical law, incl. clinical negligence, healthcare and disciplinary cases, and in the law of costs; High Court legal assessor for costs appeals. Co-founder, Chadwell Award, 2010. *Recreations:* contemporary art, travel. *Address:* Hailsham Chambers, 4 Paper Buildings, Temple, EC4Y 7EX. *T:* (020) 7643 5000. *E:* clerks@hailshamchambers.com.

POST, Herschel, MBE 2006; International Managing Director, Business Development, 2000–05, and Director, 2003–05, Christie's International plc; *b* 9 Oct. 1939; *s* of Herschel E. and Marie C. Post; adopted British citizenship, 1992; *m* 1963, Peggy Mayne; one *s* three *d*. *Educ:* Yale Univ. (AB); Oxford Univ. (BA, MA); Harvard Law Sch. (LLB). Associate, Davis Polk & Wardwell, attorneys, 1966–69; Exec. Dir, Parks Council of NY, 1969–72; Dep. Adminr and Comr, Parks, Recreation and Cultural Affairs Admin, NYC, 1973; Vice-Pres., Morgan Guaranty Trust Co., 1974–83; Mem., Bd of Dirs, 1988–95, Dep. Chm., 1989–95, Internat. Stock Exchange, subseq. London Stock Exchange; Chief Operating Officer, Lehman Brothers Internat. (Europe) and Lehman Brothers Securities Ltd, 1990–94; Chief Operating Officer, 1994–95, Chief Exec. and Dep. Chm., 1995–2000, Coutts & Co. President: Shearson Lehman Global Asset Management, 1984–90; Posthorn Global Asset Management, 1984–90; Director: Euro-clear Clearance Systems plc, 1992–; Investors Capital Trust plc, 1999– (Sen. Ind. Dir, 2007–); Ahli United Bank (UK) plc, 2001–; Ahli United Bank BSC, 2002–; Euroclear (formerly CrestCo) UK and Ireland, 2002–12; Ahli United Bank (Egypt) BSE, 2006–; Euroclear SA/NV, 2006–12; Ahli United Bank Kuwait (formerly Bank of Kuwait and Middle East), 2009–; Threadneedle Asset Mgt, 2006–; Dep. Chm., EFG Private Bank Ltd, 2002–05. Pres., Woodcock Foundn (US), 2000–11; Dir, Notting Hill Housing Gp, 2002–06; Trustee: Earthwatch Inst. (Europe) (formerly Earthwatch Europe), 1988– (Chm., 1997–2010); You Can Do I.T., 2001–14; Royal Opera House Benevolent Fund, 2002–. *Address:* 3 Kensington Park Gardens, W11 3HB. *T:* (020) 7792 9337, *Fax:* (020) 7912 0352. *Clubs:* Athenæum, Queen's.

POST, Martin Richard, MA; Regional Schools Commissioner for North West London and South Central Region, Department for Education, since 2014; *b* 3 Sept. 1958; *s* of Kenneth and Barbara Post; *m* 1999, Kate Watts; one *s*. *Educ:* Univ. of York (BA Eng. and Related Lit.); MA Educnl Mgt Open Univ. King's Sch., Rochester, 1982–84; Darwin Coll., Cambridge, 1984–85; Mill Hill Co. High Sch., 1985–89; Richard Hale Sch., 1989–95; Dep. Head (Pastoral and Finance), 1995–2000, Headmaster, 2000–14, Watford GS for Boys. FRSA 2004. *Recreations:* sports, reading, theatre.

POSTE, Dr George (Henry), CBE 1999; FRCPath, FMedSci; FRS 1997; FRCVS; Chief Executive Officer, Health Technology Networks, since 2000; Chief Scientist, Complex Adaptive Systems Initiative, and Regents' Professor, Arizona State University, since 2009; *b* 30 April 1944; *s* of late John H. Poste and of Kathleen B. Poste; *m* 1992, Linda Suhler; one *s* two *d*. *Educ:* Bristol Univ. (BVSc 1st. cl. hons 1966; DVM 1966; PhD Virology 1969). FRCVS 1987; FRCPath 1989; FRSB (FIBiol 1998). Lectr, RPMS, Univ. of London, 1969–72; Prof. of Experimental Pathology, SUNY, 1972–80; SmithKline Beckman, then SmithKline Beecham: Vice Pres., R&D, 1980–88; Pres., R&D Technologies, 1989–90; Vice Chm. and Exec. Vice Pres., R&D, 1990–91; Dir, 1992–99; Pres., R&D, 1992–97; Chief Sci. and Technol. Officer, 1997–99. Dir, Arizona Biodesign Institute, Arizona State Univ., 2003–09. Partner, Care Capital, Princeton, 2000–03; non-executive Chairman: diaDexus, 1997–2003; Structural Genomi X, 2000–01. Director: Illumina, 2000–; Monsanto, 2004–; Exelixis, 2005–; Caris Diagnostics, 2007–. Pitt Fellow, Pembroke Coll., Cambridge, 1995–2001; Fellow, Hoover Inst., Stanford Univ., 2000–. Member: Human Genetics Adv. Cttee, 1996–99; US Defense Sci. Bd, 2000–. Governor, Center for Molecular Medicine and Genetics, Stanford Univ., 1992–96. Founder FMedSci 1998. Hon. FRCP 1993; Hon. FRVC 2000. Hon. Fellow, UCL, 1999. Hon. DSc 1987, Hon. LLD 1995, Bristol; Hon. LLD Dundee, 1998; Hon. DSc Sussex, 1999. *Publications:* joint ed. of fifteen books; numerous reviews and papers in learned jls; column in FT. *Recreations:* automobile racing, military history, photography, helicopter piloting, exploring the deserts of American Southwest. *Address:* Health Technology Networks, 2338 Casmar Way, Gilbertsville, PA 19525, USA. *T:* (610) 7050828, *Fax:* (610) 7050810. *E:* gposte@healthtechnetwork.com; Complex Adaptive Systems Initiative, Arizona State University - SkySong, 1475 N Scottsdale Road, Suite 300, Scottsdale, AZ 85257–3538, USA. *T:* (480) 7278662, *Fax:* (480) 9652765. *Club:* Athenæum.

POSTGATE, Prof. (John) Nicholas, FBA 1993; Professor of Assyriology, University of Cambridge, 1994–2013; Fellow, Trinity College, Cambridge, since 1982; *b* 5 Nov. 1945; *s* of Ormond Oliver Postgate and Patricia Mary Postgate (*née* Peet); *m* 1st, 1968, Carolyn June Prater (marr. diss. 1999); one *s* one *d*; 2nd, 1999, Sarah Helen Blakeney; one *s* two *d*. *Educ:* Winchester Coll.; Trinity Coll., Cambridge (BA Oriental Studies 1967; MA 1970). Lectr in Akkadian, SOAS, 1967–71; Fellow, Trinity Coll., Cambridge, 1970–74; Asst Dir, British Sch. of Archaeology, Iraq, 1971–75; Dir, British Archaeol. Expedn to Iraq, 1975–81; Lectr in Hist. and Archaeol. of Ancient Near East, 1981–85, Reader in Mesopotamian Studies, 1985–94, Univ. of Cambridge. Director of excavations: Abu Salabikh, S Iraq, 1975–89; Kilise Tepe, S Turkey, 1994–99, 2007–13. *Publications:* Neo-Assyrian Royal Grants and Decrees, 1969; The Governor's Palace Archive, 1973; Taxation and Conscription in the Assyrian Empire, 1974; Fifty Neo-Assyrian Legal Documents, 1976; The First Empires, 1977; (ed) Abu Salabikh Excavations, vols 1–4, 1983–93; (with S. M. Dalley) Tablets from Fort Shalmaneser, 1984; The archive of Urad-Šerua and his family, 1988; Early Mesopotamia: society and economy at the dawn of history, 1992; (with F. M. Fales) Imperial administrative records, pt I 1992, pt II 1995; (with B. K. Ismail) Texts from Nineveh, 1993; (ed jtly) Concise Dictionary of Akkadian, 1999; (ed jtly) Excavations at Kilise Tepe 1994–98, 2007; The Land of Assur and the Yoke of Assur, 2007; (ed) Languages of Iraq, Ancient and Modern, 2007; (with A. Y. Ahmad) Archives from the domestic wing of the North-West Palace at Kalhu/Nimrud, 2007; Bronze Age Bureaucracy: writing and the practice of government in Assyria, 2013; articles in Iraq and other learned jls. *Address:* Trinity College, Cambridge CB2 1TQ. *T:* (01223) 338443.

POSTON, Prof. Graeme John, FRCS, FRCSE; Professor of Surgery, University of Liverpool, since 2011; Consultant Surgeon, Aintree University Hospital, Liverpool, since 2004; *b* Oldham, 6 Aug. 1955; *s* of Richard George Poston and Christine Poston; *m* 1981, June Henry. *Educ:* Hulme Grammar Sch., Oldham; St George's Hosp. Med. Sch., London (MB BS 1979; MS 1988). FRCS 1984; FRCSE 1984. Instructor in Surgery, Univ. of Texas, 1986–87; Lectr in Surgery, Univ. of London, 1988–91; Consultant Surgeon, Royal Liverpool University Hosp., 1991–2004. Chm., NHS Specialised Commng Internal Medicine Prog. of Care Bd, 2012–April 2016. President: British Assoc. of Surgical Oncol., 2005–07; Assoc. of Upper Gastrointestinal Surgeons of GB and Ire., 2010–12; Eur. Soc. of Surgical Oncol., 2012–14. *Publications:* Surgical Management of Hepatobiliary and Pancreatic Disorders, 2002, 2nd edn 2010; Textbook of Surgical Oncology, 2004, 2nd edn 2015; Liver Metastases, 2009; over 200 scientific papers. *Recreation:* trekking in high places (Kilimanjaro, Kalar Pattar, Annapurna Base Camp, Lakya La). *Address:* Department of Surgery, Aintree University Hospital, Longmoor Lane, Liverpool L9 7AL. *T:* (0151) 525 5980, *Fax:* (0151) 525 8547. *E:* graeme.poston@aintree.nhs.uk.

POTOČNIK, Janez, PhD; Co-Chairman, International Resource Panel, United Nations Environment Programme, since 2014; *b* 22 March 1958; *m*; two *s*. *Educ:* Univ. of Ljubljana (BEc, MEc; PhD 1993). Econ. Analyst, SDK (APP) Agency, Kranj, 1983–84; Asst Dir, Inst. of Macroecon. Analysis and Develt, Ljubljana, 1984–87; Sen. Researcher, Inst. for Econ. Res., Ljubljana, 1988–93; Dir, Inst. of Macroecon. Analysis and Develt, Ljubljana, 1993–2001; Minister Councillor, Office of the Prime Minister, Slovenia, 2001–02; Minister for European Affairs, 2002–04. Asst Prof., Faculty of Law, Univ. of Ljubljana, 1991–2004. Mem., Eur. Commn, 2004–14.

POTTER, Christopher Frank Rendall, OBE 2001; MA; Headmaster, Old Swinford Hospital, Stourbridge, 1978–2001; *b* 9 Sept. 1939; *s* of late Cedric Hardcastle Potter and Phyllis Potter (*née* Rendall); *m* 1971, Charlotte Ann Millis, San Francisco; two *s* three *d*. *Educ:* March Grammar Sch.; Trinity Coll., Cambridge (MA Classics). Ardingly College, Sussex: Asst Master, 1961–78; Head of Classics, 1964–78; Housemaster, 1966–78. Chief Examr in Archaeol., London Exam Bd, 1976–80. Chm., State Boarding Inf. Service, 1996–98. Schoolmaster Studentship, Christ Church, Oxford, 1989. Pres., Stourbridge Archaeol and Historical Soc., 1988; Chm., Ludlow Historical Res. Gp, 2005–. Chm., Trustees, Knoll Sch., Kidderminster, 1989–2009; Gov., The Elms Sch., Colwall, 1984– (Vice Chm., 1985–2004; Chm., 2004–12). Churchwarden, St Laurence's, Ludlow, 2003–07. *Publications:* (with T. W. Potter) Romano-British Village at Grandford, Cambridgeshire, 1980; (ed) Parish Register Transcripts: Romsley, Worcs, 1988; Stone, Worcs, 1989; (jtly) St Laurence's Church, Ludlow 1199–2009: the Parish Church and people, 2010. *Recreations:* Italian opera, genealogy, red wine, the poetry of Horace, Bean Club. *Address:* St Leonard's House, Upper Linney, Ludlow SY8 1EF. *T:* (01584) 878770.

POTTER, Ven. Christopher Nicholas Lynden; Archdeacon of St Asaph, 2011–14; *b* 4 Oct. 1949; *s* of Sir (Joseph) Raymond (Lynden) Potter and of (Daphne) Marguerite Potter; *m* 1973, Jenny Lees; three *s* one *d*. *Educ:* Haileybury Coll.; Univ. of Leeds (BA (Hons) English/Fine Art 1971); St Asaph Diocesan Ordination Trng Course. Lectr, Tutor and Librarian, Bradford Art Coll., 1971–73; self-employed furniture designer and cabinet maker, 1975–90; ordained deacon, 1993, priest, 1994; Curate, Flint, 1993–96; Vicar of grouped parishes of Llanfair DC, Llanelidan, Efenechtyd and Derwen, 1996–2001; Dean of St Asaph, 2001–11. *Recreations:* pilgrimage, hill walking, reading, mending things.

POTTER, Dr David Edwin, CBE 1997; FREng; Founder, and Chairman, Psion plc, 1980–2009 (Chief Executive, 1980–99); a Director, Bank of England, 2003–09; *b* 4 July 1943; *s* of Paul James Potter and Mary Agnes (*née* Snape); *m* 1969, Elaine Goldberg; three *s*. *Educ:* Trinity Coll., Cambridge (Exhibnr; MA); Imperial Coll., London (PhD 1970). Lectr, Blackett Lab., Imperial Coll., London, 1970–80. Commonwealth Schol., 1966–69; Asst Prof., UCLA, 1974. Director: Charterhouse Venture Fund Management Ltd, 1985–94; Press Assoc. Ltd, 1994–97 (Vice-Chm., 1995–97); London First Centre, 1994–2002; Finsbury Technology Trust, 1995–; Chairman: Symbian Ltd, 1998–2004; Knowledge=Power, 2000–02. Member: Nat. Cttee of Inquiry into Higher Educn (Dearing Cttee), 1996–97; HEFCE, 1997–2003; Council for Sci. and Technol., Cabinet Office, 1998–2004. Mem., London Regl Council, CBI, 1993–99. Vis. Fellow, Nuffield Coll., Oxford, 1998–2006. Gov., London Business Sch., 1998–2009. Founder and Trustee, Bureau of Investigative Journalism, 2009–. Lectures: Stockton, London Business Sch., 1998; Millennium, 10 Downing St, 1999; Tacitus, World Traders' Co., 2000. FRSA 1989; FREng 2001. Hon. Fellow: Imperial Coll., 1998; London Business Sch., 1998. Hon. DTech: Kingston, 1998; Oxford Brookes, 1999; Hon. DSc: Brunel, 1998; Westminster, 1998; Warwick, 1999; Sheffield, 1999; York, 2002; Edinburgh, 2002; Cape Town, 2012; Open, 2012. Mountbatten Medal for Outstanding Services to Electronics Industry, Nat. Electronics Council, 1994. *Publications:* Computational Physics, 1972; contribs to various physics jls. *Recreations:* tennis, golf, flute, bridge, reading, ideas. *Address:* (office) 6 Hamilton Close, NW8 8QY. *Club:* Portland.

POTTER, David Roger William; Chairman: Spark Ventures (formerly New Media Spark), since 2009 (Director, since 2002); Quercus Publishing, 2009–14 (Director, 2006–14); Ortus VCT, 2011–13; *b* 27 July 1944; *s* of late William Edward Potter and Joan Louise (*née* Frost); *m* 1966, Joanna Trollope, *qv* (marr. diss. 1983); two *d*; *m* 1991, Teresa Jill Benson; one *d*. *Educ:* Bryanston Sch.; University Coll., Oxford (MA). Nat. Discount Co., 1965–69; Managing Director: Credit Suisse First Boston and Credit Suisse White Weld, 1969–81; Samuel Montagu & Co. Ltd, 1981–89; Midland Montagu Corporate Banking, 1986–89; Gp Chief Exec., Guinness Mahon Holdings, 1990–98; Chm. and Chief Exec., Guinness Mahon & Co. Ltd, Merchant Bankers, 1990–98; Dep. Chm., Investec Bank (UK) Ltd, 1998–99. Chairman: EON Lifestyle, 2001–06; DictaScribe, 2001–03; Deltron Electronics, 2005–06; Camco Internat., 2006–10; non-executive Director: Maybox plc, 1987–90; Thomas Cook, 1989–91; Tyndal plc, 1989–91; Execution Noble (formerly Noble Gp), 2000–10; Rose Partnership, 2000; WMC Communications, 2001–03; Numerica Gp plc, 2003–05; Solar Integrated Technologies, 2004–09 (Chm., 2004–06); Ortus plc (formerly Guinness Flight VCT), 2006–; Vycon Inc., 2007–09; Vantis plc, 2009–10; Maven Income and Growth VCT 4, 2013–15; Illustrated London News, 2013–; Fundsmith Emerging Equities Trust, 2014–. Chm., London

Film Commn, 1996–2000. Gov., Bryanston Sch., 1982–2007; Mem. Council, KCL, 1997–2007 (Treas., 1998–2007; FKC 2006); Mem. Adv. Council, Centre for the Study of Financial Innovation, 1990–. Chm., Nat. Film and Television Sch. Foundn, 2004– (Mem., 1997–2004); Trustee: Worldwide Volunteering (formerly Youth for Britain, then Worldwide Volunteering for Young People), 1994–; Nelson Mandela Children Foundn, 1998–2015. Mem., Adv. Bd, London Capital Club, 1995–. Gov., Godolphin and Latymer Sch., 2009–11. FRSA. *Recreations:* shooting, gardening, golf. *Address:* (office) Brook House, Donnington, Newbury, Berks RG14 2JT. *E:* david@davidpotter.org. *Clubs:* Garrick, Capital (Mem., Adv. Bd, 1990–); Vincent's (Oxford).

POTTER, Jeremy Patrick L.; *see* Lee-Potter.

POTTER, Rt Hon. Sir Mark (Howard), Kt 1988; PC 1996; arbitrator, since 2010; President of the Family Division and Head of Family Justice, 2005–10; President, Court of Protection, 2007–10; *b* 27 Aug. 1937; *s* of Prof. Harold Potter, LLD, PhD, and Beatrice Spencer Potter (*née* Crowder); *m* 1962, Undine Amanda Fay, *d* of Major James Miller, 5/6th Rajputana Rifles, and Bunty Miller, painter; two *s*. *Educ:* Perse Sch., Cambridge; Gonville and Caius Coll., Cambridge (Schol.; BA (Law Tripos) 1960; MA 1963; Hon. Fellow 1998). National Service, 15 Med. Regt RA, 1955–57 (commnd 1956); 289 Lt Parachute Regt RHA(TA), 1958–64. Asst Supervisor, Legal Studies, Girton, Gonville and Caius, Queens' and Sidney Sussex Colls, 1961–68; called to Bar, Gray's Inn, 1961, Bencher, 1987, Treasurer, 2004; in practice, 1962–88; QC 1980; a Recorder, 1986–88; a Judge of the High Court of Justice, QBD (Commercial Court), 1988–96; a Presiding Judge, Northern Circuit, 1991–94; a Lord Justice of Appeal, 1996–2005. Member: Supreme Ct Rule Cttee, 1980–84; Lord Chancellor's Civil Justice Review Cttee, 1985–88; Chm., Bar Public Affairs Cttee, 1987; Vice-Chm., Council of Legal Educn, 1989–91; Chairman: Lord Chancellor's Adv. Cttee on Legal Educn and Conduct, 1998–99; Legal Services Adv. Panel, subseq. Consultancy Panel, 2000–05; Co-Chm., Legal Educn and Trng Review Consultancy Panel, 2011–. Mem. Council, Nottingham Univ., 1996–99. Trustee: Somerset House Trust, 1997–; Gt Ormond St Charity, 2010–. Hon. FKC 2005. Hon. LLD London Guildhall, 2000. *Recreations:* family and sporting. *Address:* Fountain Court Chambers, Fountain Court, Temple, EC4Y 9DH. *Clubs:* Garrick, Saintsbury; St Enodoc Golf; Denham Golf.

POTTER, Michael Nicholas; co-founder and non-executive Chairman, Seven Publishing, 2008–10 (publishers of Sainsbury's Magazine) (Executive Chairman, 2003–08); *b* 17 Oct. 1949; *s* of Alan Edward and Evelyn Mabel Potter; *m* 1973, Janet Nyasa Griffiths; one *s* two *d*. *Educ:* Royal Grammar Sch., Guildford; London Univ. (BSc Econ. (ext.)). DipM, MCIM 1974. Joined Haymarket Publishing, 1971 (Publishing Dir, Campaign and Marketing, 1979–83); founded Redwood Publishing, 1983, Chm., 2001–03: launched over 50 mags, incl. BBC Top Gear, M & S Mag., Sky TV Guide. Dir, Prince's Trust Trading, 1999–2007; non-exec. Dir, 4 imprint plc, 2001–03. Mem. Council, Mktg Gp of GB, 1993–2011 (Chm., 1995–97); Dir, PPA, 1995–2003; Mem., Assoc. of Publishing Agencies, 1993– (Chm., 1994–95). Member, Development Board: Nat. Portrait Gall., 1999–2007; Royal Court Th., 1999–2007. Mem., Nat. Fundraising and Marketing Cttee, Cancer Research UK, 2009–11. FRSA 1998. Marcus Morris Award for contrib. to magazine ind., PPA, 1998. *Recreations:* cars, motor-racing, theatre, opera, cinema, cricket. *Address:* Greentails Residence One, Sion Hill, St James 24025, Barbados.

POTTER, Raymond, CB 1990; Deputy Secretary, 1986–93 (Courts and Legal Services, 1986–91), Head of the Court Service and Deputy Clerk of the Crown in Chancery, 1989–93, Lord Chancellor's Department; *b* 26 March 1933; *s* of William Thomas Potter and Elsie May Potter; *m* 1959, Jennifer Mary Quicke; one *s*. *Educ:* Henry Thornton Grammar School. Called to the Bar, Inner Temple, 1971, Bencher, 1989. Central Office, Royal Courts of Justice, 1950; Western Circuit, 1963; Chief Clerk, Bristol Crown Court, 1972; Dep. Circuit Administrator, Western Circuit, 1976; Circuit Administrator, Northern Circuit, 1982–86. Vice-Pres., Southern Rent Assessment Panel, 2001–03 (Pres., SW Panel, 1995–2001); Standing Chm., Strategic Health Authy Review Panel, 2003–09. *Recreation:* painting. *Address:* 8 Robinson Way, Backwell, Bristol BS48 3BP. *Club:* Athenæum.

POTTER, Roderick John Conwy; His Honour Judge Potter; a Circuit Judge, since 2010; Resident Judge, Manchester Crown Court, since 2014; *b* Shrewsbury, 8 June 1962; *s* of Robert Michael Conwy Potter and Christobel Ann Potter; *m* 1993, Ann Marie O'Brien; three *s*. *Educ:* Wandsworth Sch.; Trent Poly. (BA Hons Law). Admitted solicitor, 1987; Solicitor, Messrs Dunderdale Wignall, Manchester, 1987–92; Partner, Messrs Platt Halpern, 1992–2010; Higher Court Advocate, 1997; Recorder, 2004–10. Mem., Solicitors Disciplinary Tribunal, 1997–2010. *Recreations:* going on the match, Weller. *Address:* Manchester Crown Court, Minshull Street, Manchester M1 3FS.

PÖTTERING, Hans-Gert; Member, 1979–2014 and President, 2007–09, European Parliament; Chairman, Konrad Adenauer Foundation, since 2010; *b* Bersenbrück, 15 Sept. 1945; two *s*. *Educ:* Univ. of Bonn; Univ. of Geneva; Institut des Hautes Études Internationales, Geneva. Res. Asst, 1976–79; Lectr, Univ. of Osnabrück, 1989; Hon. Prof., 1995. European Parliament: Chm., Subcttee on Security and Disarmament, 1984–94; Vice-Chm., EPP Gp, 1994–99; Chm., EPP-ED Gp, 1999–2007; Head, EPP's and EPP-ED Gp's Working Party: on 1996 Intergovtl Conf., 1994–96; on EU Enlargement, 1996–99. Land Chm., Europa-Union in Lower Saxony, 1981–91; Chm., Europa-Union Deutschland, 1997–99. Chairman: Osnabrück Dist, Junge Union, CDU, 1974–76; Bersenbrück Br., CDU, 1974–80; Osnabrück Dist, CDU, 1990–2010; Mem. Exec. Cttee, 1999–2009, and Federal Exec., 1999–2009, CDU; Mem., Bureau, EPP, 1999–2009. Hon. Dr: Babeş-Bolyai; Opole; Warmia and Mazury; Korea; Miguel de Cervantes; Bahçeşehir. Robert Schuman Medal, EPP, 1995; Walter Hallstein Prize, Frankfurt, 2007; René Cassin Medaille for Human Rights, Consultative Council Jewish Orgns, 2010; Polish-German Prize, 2011. Grand Cross of Merit (Germany), 2010; Grand Golden Medal of Merit (Austria), 2002; Mérite Européen en or (Luxembourg), 2002; Grand Cross, Order of St Gregory the Great, 2007; Great Cross of Merit of Queen Jelena with Sash and Star (Croatia), 2007; Grand Cross (Italy), 2008; Three-Star Medal (Latvia), 2009; Medal of Jaroslaw the Wise (Ukraine), 2009; Grand Cross of Civil Merit (Spain), 2011; Comdr, Legion of Honour (France), 2011; Cross of Terra Mariana 1st cl., 2013; Knight Comdr's Cross (Poland), 2013; Grand Cross (Hungary), 2013; Grand Cross, Order of Star (Romania), 2014. *Publications:* Adenauers Sicherheitspolitik 1955–63, 1975; (with F. Wiehler) Die vergessenen Regionen, 1983; (with L. Kühnhardt) Europas vereinigte Staaten: Annäherungen an Werte und Ziele, 1993; (with L. Kühnhardt) Kontinent Europa: Kern, Übergänge, Grenzen, 1998; (with L. Kühnhardt) Weltpartner Europäische Union, 2001; Von der Vision zur Wirklichkeit: auf dem Weg zur Einigung Europas, 2004; Im Dienste Europas, 2009; Mein Europäischer Weg, 2014.

POTTERTON, Homan; art historian and writer; Editor, 1993–2002, and publisher, 2000–02, Irish Arts Review; Director, National Gallery of Ireland, 1980–88; *b* 9 May 1946; sixth *s* of late Thomas Edward Potterton and Eileen Potterton (*née* Tong). *Educ:* Kilkenny Coll.; Trinity Coll., Dublin (BA 1968, MA 1973); Edinburgh Univ. (Dip. Hist. Art 1971). FSA 1981. Cataloguer, National Gall. of Ireland, 1971–73; Asst Keeper, National Gall., London, 1974–80. Mem. Bd, GPA Dublin Internat. Piano Competition, 1987–92. HRHA 1982. *Publications:* Irish Church Monuments 1570–1880, 1975; A Guide to the National Gallery, 1976, rev. edn 1980 (German, French, Italian and Japanese edns 1977); The National Gallery, London, 1977; Reynolds and Gainsborough: themes and painters in the National Gallery, 1976; Pageant and Panorama: the elegant world of Canaletto, 1978; (jtly) Irish Art and Architecture, 1978; Venetian Seventeenth Century Painting (National Gallery Exhibn Catalogue), 1979; introd. to National Gallery of Ireland Illustrated Summary Catalogue of Paintings, 1981; (jtly) National Gallery of Ireland, 50 Pictures, 1981; Dutch 17th and 18th Century Paintings in the National Gallery of Ireland: a complete catalogue, 1986; Rathcormick: a childhood recalled, 2001; Potterton People and Places: three centuries of an Irish family, 2006; contrib. Burlington Mag., Apollo, Connoisseur, FT and Country Life. *Recreation:* genealogy. *Address:* Colombel Bas, 81140 Castelnau-de-Montmiral, France. *T:* and *Fax:* (5) 63405352. *E:* hpotterton@orange.fr. *W:* www.potterton.ie.

POTTINGER, Frank Vernon Hunter, RSA 1991; sculptor; *b* 1 Oct. 1932; *s* of William Pottinger and Veronica (*née* Irvine); *m* 1991, Evelyn Norah Smith (marr. diss. 2007); one step *s* two step *d*. *Educ:* Boroughmuir Secondary Sch.; Edinburgh Coll. of Art (DA 1963). Apprentice fitter engineer, 1948–53; nat. service, 1953–55; teacher: Portobello Secondary Sch., 1965–73; Aberdeen Coll. of Educn, 1973–85; vis. lectr, colls of art in Scotland, 1980–91; full-time artist, 1985–. *Address:* 30/5 Elbe Street, Edinburgh EH6 7HW. *T:* (0131) 553 5082.

POTTINGER, Graham Robert; Chief Executive, Scottish Mutual Assurance plc, 1997–2002 (Finance Director, 1992–96); Managing Director, Abbey National Financial Investment Services plc, 1997–2002; *b* 14 June 1949; *s* of Arthur and Mary Pottinger; *m* 1970, Dorothy McLean; one *s* one *d*. *Educ:* Jordanhill Coll. Sch., Glasgow; Glasgow Univ. (LLB). CA 1992; ACMA 1993. Peat Marwick Mitchell & Co., 1969–72; Partner, Deloitte Haskins & Sells, 1972–79; Controller, UK and Africa, Cargill Plc, 1980–92. Mem. Council, ICAS, 1995–2001.

POTTINGER, Piers Julian Dominic; Chairman, Bell Pottinger (formerly Pelham Bell Pottinger) Asia (Singapore), since 2013; Deputy Chairman, Bell Pottinger Private, since 2012; *b* 3 March 1954; *s* of late W. G. Pottinger; *m* 1979, Carolyn Ann Rhodes; one *s* three *d*. *Educ:* Edinburgh Acad.; Winchester Coll. Trainee, J. Henry Schroder Wagg, 1972–74; Res. Analyst, Laurence Prust and Co., 1974–78; Exec., Charles Barker, 1978–80; Dir, Media Relations Manufacturers, Hanover, NY, 1980–82; Man. Dir, Sterling Financial Public Relations, 1982–85; Man. Dir, then Chm., Bell Pottinger (formerly Lowe Bell) Financial, 1985–2009; Gp Man. Dir, then Dep. Chm., Chime Communications plc, 1993–2012. Director: Newmarket Investments plc (formerly British Bloodstock Agency plc), 2001–06 (Chm., 2001–06); Northern Racing Ltd, 2002–05; Chairman: Sportech plc, 2006–10; KAI Square Pte Ltd (Singapore), 2014–. Former Member: Bd, Scottish Ballet; Gen. Council, Poetry Soc. Trustee: Racing Welfare, 2009–12; Foundn for Liver Res. (formerly Liver Res. Trust), 2010–; Vice-Pres., Nat. Soc. for Epilepsy, 2004–. *Recreations:* horse racing, golf. *Address:* #04–01 Nassim Regency, 37 Nassim Road, Singapore 258423. *T:* 94507996. *Clubs:* Garrick, Turf; New Zealand Golf; China (Singapore).

POTTS, Archibold; Director, Bewick Press, since 1989; *b* 27 Jan. 1932; *s* of late Ernest W. Potts and Ellen Potts; *m* 1957, Marguerite Elsie (*née* Elliott) (*d* 1983); one *s* one *d*. *Educ:* Monkwearmouth Central Sch., Sunderland; Ruskin and Oriel Colls, Oxford (Dip. Econ. and Pol Sci., 1958; BA PPE 2nd cl. hons, 1960); ext. postgrad. student, London Univ. (Postgrad. CertEd 1964) and Durham Univ. (MEd 1969). Nat. Service, RAF, 1950–53. Railway Clerk, 1947–50 and 1953–56. Lecturer: N Oxfordshire Tech. Coll., 1961; York Tech. Coll., 1962–65; Rutherford Coll. of Technology and Newcastle upon Tyne Polytechnic, 1965–80; Head of Sch. of Business Admin, 1980–87, Associate Dean, Faculty of Business and Professional Studies, 1988, Newcastle upon Tyne Polytechnic. Moderator, history courses, Tyneside Open Coll. Network, 1992–2005. Tyne and Wear County Council: Councillor, 1979–86; Vice-Chm., Planning Cttee, 1981–86; Vice-Chm., Council, 1983–84; Chm., Council, 1984–85. Contested (Lab) Westmorland, 1979. Chm., NE Labour History Soc., 1990–96 (Vice Pres., 1997–2011; Pres., 2012–); Mem., Exec. Cttee, Soc. for Study of Labour History, 1987–96. *Publications:* Stand True, 1976; Bibliography of Northern Labour History, 1982–; (ed) Shipbuilders and Engineers, 1987; Jack Casey, the Sunderland Assassin, 1991; The Wearside Champions, 1993; Jack London, the forgotten champion, 1997; Zilliacus, a life for peace and socialism, 2002; Headlocks and Handbags, 2005; contributions to: Dictionary of Labour Biography, vol. 2 1974, vol. 4 1977, vol. 5 1979, vol. 9 1993, vol. 11 2003, vol. 12 2005; Oxford DNB, 2004; articles on economics and history. *Recreations:* local history, watching old films. *Address:* 47 Graham Park Road, Gosforth, Newcastle upon Tyne NE3 4BJ. *T:* (0191) 284 5132. *Club:* Victory Service.

POTTS, Prof. David Malcolm, PhD, DSc; FREng, FICE; GCG Professor of Geotechnical Engineering, and Head, Department of Geotechnics, Imperial College London; *b* 26 April 1952; *s* of Leonard Francis Potts and Doris Florence Potts; *m* 1974, Deborah Margot Peel; two *d*. *Educ:* King's Coll., London (BSc Eng); Churchill Coll., Cambridge (PhD 1976); Imperial Coll., London (DSc 1996). FICE 1997; FREng 2001. Res. Engr, Shell, Netherlands, 1976–79; Imperial College of Science, Technology and Medicine, later Imperial College London: Lectr, 1979–89; Reader, 1989–94; Prof. of Analytical Soil Mechanics, 1994; Dep. Hd, Dept of Civil and Envmtl Engrg, 2001. *Publications:* Finite Element Analysis in Geotechnical Engineering: theory, 1999; Finite Element Analysis in Geotechnical Engineering: application, 2001; numerous contribs to learned jls incl. Geotechnique, Internat. Jl Num. Anal. Meth. in Geomech., Internat. Jl Num. Meth. Engrg, Engrg Computations, Computers and Geotechnics, Canadian Geotechnical Jl, Computational Methods, Appl. Mech. Engrg, Geotechnical Engrg, Jl Geotechnical and Geoenvmtl Engrg. *Recreations:* fly fishing, swimming. *Address:* Geotechnics Section, Department of Civil and Environmental Engineering, Skempton Building, Imperial College London, South Kensington Campus, SW7 2AZ. *T:* (020) 7594 6084, *Fax:* (020) 7594 6150. *E:* d.potts@imperial.ac.uk.

POTTS, Vice Adm. Duncan Laurence, CB 2014; Director General Joint Force Development and Defence Academy, since 2014; *b* Malta, 10 March 1961; *s* of Major Gordon Potts and Jane Potts; *m* 1987, Pamela Sleigh; one *s* one *d*. *Educ:* Wellington Sch.; City Univ., London (BSc Hons Systems and Mgt 1983). Joined Royal Navy, 1979; commanded: HMS Brilliant, 1996; HMS Southampton, 1996–98; HMS Marlborough, 2000–02; Navy Plans and Asst to VCDS, MoD, 2002–06; rcds 2007; Comdr UK Task Gp, 2007–09, Coalition Maritime Comdr, N Gulf and Iraq, 2008; Hd of Planning, UK Jt Operational HQ, 2009–11; Commander: UK Maritime Forces, 2011–12; EU Counter Piracy Ops in Indian Ocean, 2011–12; Rear Adm. Surface Ships, 2011–12; Asst Chief of Naval Staff (Capability), 2013–14; Controller of the Navy, 2013–14. Younger Brother, Trinity House, 2006–. *Recreations:* fly fishing, shooting, walking, keeping fit, reading, ski-ing.

POTTS, James Rupert; QC 2013; *b* London, 28 June 1970; *s* of Robin Potts and Rebeca Potts; *m* 2000, Diana; two *s* one *d*. *Educ:* Charterhouse Sch.; Magdalen Coll., Oxford (BA 1st Cl. Hons Mod. Hist.). Called to the Bar, Gray's Inn, 1994. *Publications:* contributions to: Practice and Procedure of the Companies Court, 1997; Company Directors: law and liability; Buckley on the Companies Acts. *Recreations:* history, walking, family. *E:* clerks@erskinechambers.com.

POTTS, Paul John, CBE 2009; Group Chief Executive, 2000–10, and a Director, 1995–2010, PA Group (Chairman, 2008–09); Editor-in-Chief, The Press Association, 1996–2006; *b* 21 Jan. 1950; *s* of late Michael Henry Potts and of Sylvia Brenda Potts; *m* 1st, 1976, Gabrielle Jane Fagan (marr. diss. 1994); one *s* two *d*; 2nd, 1994, Judith Anne Fielding. *Educ:* Worksop Coll. Gen. Reporter, Sheffield Star, 1968–74; Lobby Corresp., Yorkshire Post, 1974–78; General Reporter: Daily Telegraph, 1978–81; Mail on Sunday, 1981–82; Political Ed., News of the World, 1982–86; Political Ed., then Asst Ed., later Dep. Ed., Daily Express, 1986–95. Chm., CNW Gp (formerly Canada NewsWire), 2003–10 (Dir, 2000–09); Mem., Nomination Cttee, Reuters Founders Share Co. Ltd, 2002–07. Non-exec. Dir, Channel 4, 2012–. Mem., Code of Practice Cttee, 1996–2007. Vis. Prof. of Journalism, Univ.

of Sheffield, 2010–. Patron, Sheffield Wednesday Supporters Trust, 2001. Gov., St Anselm's Sch., Bakewell, 2010–14. Hon. DLitt Sheffield, 2002. *Recreations:* history, horse racing, travel. *Club:* Garrick.

POTTS, Timothy Faulkner, DPhil; FSA; Director, J. Paul Getty Museum, Los Angeles, since 2012; *b* 17 June 1958; *s* of Ian Faulkner Potts and Judy Potts; one *s* one *d*. *Educ:* Univ. of Sydney (BA Hons 1980); DPhil Oxon 1987. Res. Lectr, 1985–87, British Acad. Postdoctoral Res. Fellow, 1987–90, Christ Church, Oxford; Associate and Dir, Lehman Bros, NY and London, 1990–94; Director: Nat. Gall. of Victoria, Melbourne, 1994–98; Kimbell Art Mus., Texas, 1998–2007; Fitzwilliam Mus., Cambridge, 2008–12; Fellow, Clare Coll., Cambridge, 2010–12. FSA 2010. *Publications:* Civilization: ancient treasures from the British Museum, 1990, 1997; Mesopotamia and the East: an archaeological and historical study of foreign relations *c* 3400–2000 BC, 1994; (ed jtly) Culture Through Objects: ancient Near Eastern studies in honour of P. R. S. Moorey, 2003; (ed) Kimbell Art Museum: handbook of the collection, 2003. *Address:* J. Paul Getty Museum, 1200 Getty Center Drive, Los Angeles, CA 90049–1687, USA.

POULSEN, Ole Lønsmann, Hon. GCVO 2000; Kt Comdr, Order of Dannebrog, 2005 (Comdr 1999); member of commercial boards of directors; *b* 14 May 1945; *s* of Aage Lønsmann Poulsen, head teacher, and Tove Alice (*née* Gyldenstein); *m* 1973, Zareen Mehta; two *s*. *Educ:* Copenhagen Univ. (LLM 1971). Hd of Dept, Danchurchaid, 1969–73; joined Danish Diplomatic Service, 1973; Hd of Section, Min. of Foreign Affairs, Denmark, 1973–76; Advr, Asian Develt Bank, Manila, 1976–77; First Sec., New Delhi and Trade Comr, Bombay, 1977–80; Alternate Exec. Dir, World Bank, Washington, 1980–83; Dep. Head, 1983–85, Head, 1985–88, Dept of Internat. Develt Co-operation, then Under-Sec. for Multilateral Affairs (Ambassador), 1988–92, Min. of Foreign Affairs; Ambassador to Austria and Perm. Rep. to IAEA, UNIDO and UN, Vienna, also accredited to Slovenia and Bosnia Hercegovina, 1992–93; State Sec., Min. of Foreign Affairs, 1993–96; Ambassador: to UK, 1996–2001; to China, 2001–04; to Sweden, 2004–06; to India, 2006–10. Chm., Industrial Develt Bd, UNIDO, 1990–91. Alternate Gov., World Bank and Gov. for Asian, African and Interamerican Develt Banks, 1989–92 and 1993–96. Chairman: Scandinavian Seminar Coll., 1975–76; Nordic Develt Fund, 1990–91. Grand Decoration of Honour with Sash (Austria), 1993; Grand Cross of Northern Star (Sweden), 2006. *Recreations:* music, literature, sport. *Address:* Sollerodlund 17, 2840 Holte, Denmark.

POULTER, Brian Henry; Secretary, Northern Ireland Audit Office, 1989–2000; *b* 1 Sept. 1941; *s* of William Henry Poulter, PhC, MPS, and Marjorie Elizabeth Everett McBride; *m* 1968, Margaret Ann Dodds; one *s* twin *d*. *Educ:* Regent House Grammar Sch., Newtownards. Qual. as certified accountant, 1966. Hill, Vellacott and Bailey, Chartered Accountants, 1959–62; entered NICS, 1962; Min. of Health and Local Govt, 1962–65; Min. of Health and Social Services, 1965–71; Deputy Principal: Local Enterprise Develt Unit, 1971–74; Dept of Commerce, 1974–75; Chief Auditor 1975–81, Dep. Dir 1981–82, Dir 1982–87, Exchequer and Audit Dept; Dir, NI Audit Office, 1987–88. *Recreations:* reading, walking, cricket. *Address:* 20 Manse Road, Newtownards, Co. Down BT23 4TP.

POULTER, Dr Daniel Leonard James; MP (C) Central Suffolk and North Ipswich, since 2010; *b* Beckenham, 30 Oct. 1978. *Educ:* Univ. of Bristol (LLB Hons); Univ. of London (MB BS); King's Coll., London (AKC). Medical doctor specialising in obstetrics and gynaecol. Mem. (C) Hastings BC, 2006–07; Dep. Leader, Reigate and Banstead BC, 2008–10. Parly Under-Sec. of State, DoH, 2012–15. Member: Health Select Cttee, 2011–12; House of Lords Reform Cttee, 2011–12. *Publications:* articles in field of women's health. *Recreations:* Rugby, cricket, golf. *Address:* House of Commons, SW1A 0AA. *E:* daniel.poulter.mp@parliament.uk.

POULTER, Jane Anne Marie; *see* Bonvin, Her Honour J. A. M.

POULTER, John William; Chairman: 4imprint plc, since 2010; RM plc, since 2013; *b* 22 Nov. 1942; *m* 1968, Margaret Winifred Thorn; one *s* one *d*. *Educ:* Berkhamsted Sch.; Queen's Coll., Oxford (MA). Cambridge Instruments Gp, 1968, Marketing Dir, 1972–77; Dir and Gen. Manager, Robinsons Carton Packaging, 1977–81; Man. Dir, Vokes Ltd, and other BTR subsids, 1981–88; Spectris plc, 1988–2008: Gp Man. Dir, 1988–91; Chief Exec., 1991–2001. Chairman: Kymata Ltd, 1999–2001; Wyko Gp, 2001–04; Spectris plc, 2001–08; Snell & Wilcox Ltd, 2002–09; Filtronic plc, 2006–09; Zenergy Power plc, 2010–11; Hampson Gp plc, 2011–12; non-executive Director: Lloyds Smaller Cos Investment Trust plc, 1992–2002; Crest Packaging plc, 1993–96; BTP plc, 1997–2000; Kidde plc, 2000–05; RAC plc, 2002–05; Smaller Cos Value Trust plc, 2002–09; London Metal Exchange Ltd, 2003–05; MacQuarie European Infrastructure plc, 2003–05; Suffolk Life plc, 2006–09. Gov., Ipswich Sch., 2000–. *Recreations:* sailing, walking, opera. *Club:* Oxford and Cambridge.

POULTON, Denise; *see* Lewis, Denise.

POULTON, Michael Graham; playwright and adapter of classic and contemporary plays and novels; *b* 6 April 1947; *yr s* of late John William Lines Poulton and Ella Poulton (*née* Clayton). Asst Ed., Pergamon Press, Oxford, 1973–74; Ed., then Dep. Chief Ed., Religious Educn Press, A. Wheaton & Co., Exeter, 1974–77; Oxford University Press, Oxford: Sen. Ed., Educn Div. and Religious Educn, 1977–78; Man. Ed., Primary Educn and Children's Information Books, 1978–90; Creator, Oxford Reading Tree, 1979–90; Consultant, John Murray, Publisher, London, 1990–92; Advr, Northern Broadsides Th. Co., 1992–94. *Plays and adaptations*, 1994–: Chekhov's Uncle Vanya, Turgenev's Fortune's Fool, Chichester, 1996; Chekhov's Three Sisters, Birmingham Rep., 1998; Ibsen's Ghosts, Plymouth, 1999; Uncle Vanya, 1999, Strindberg's Dance of Death, 2001, Three Sisters, 2003, Euripides' Ion, 2004, Chekhov's The Seagull, 2005, Colchester; Uncle Vanya, NY, 2000; The York Mysteries, York Minster, 2000; Fortune's Fool, NY, 2002; Schiller's Don Carlos, Sheffield Crucible, transf. Gielgud, 2004; Ibsen's Hedda Gabler, W Yorks Playhouse and Liverpool Playhouse, 2006; Aeschylus' Myrmidons, Dublin, 2006; Chaucer's Canterbury Tales, Parts One and Two, RSC, Stratford, London, Washington and Spain, 2006; Strindberg's The Father, Chichester, 2006; Chekhov's The Cherry Orchard, Schiller's Mary Stuart, Clwyd Th. Cymru, 2007; Don Carlos, Dublin, 2007, Göteborgs Stadsteater, 2007–08, Copenhagen, 2008–09; Ibsen's Rosmersholm, Almeida, 2008; Ibsen's The Lady from The Sea, Birmingham Rep., 2008; The Cherry Orchard, 2008, Schiller's Wallenstein, 2009, Chichester; Malory's Morte d'Arthur, RSC, Stratford, 2010; Schiller's Luise Miller, Donmar Warehouse, 2011; Uncle Vanya, The Print Room, London, 2012; Anjin: The English Samurai, Horipro/RSC, Tokyo, Osaka, Yokohama, Sadler's Wells, 2013; Fortune's Fool, Old Vic, 2013; Wolf Hall and Bring Up the Bodies, RSC, Stratford, transf. Aldwych, 2014; A Tale of Two Cities, Northampton, 2014. *Publications:* books for children; (contrib.) My First Play, 2013; *adaptations*: The York Mysteries, 2000; Uncle Vanya, 2001, rev. trans. 2012; Fortune's Fool, 2002, rev. trans. 2013; The Seagull, 2004; Don Carlos, 2005; The Canterbury Tales, 2005; The Father, 2006; The Cherry Orchard, 2008; Rosmersholm, 2008; Mary Stuart, 2009; Wallenstein, 2009; Morte d'Arthur, 2010; Bacchae, 2010; Luise Miller, 2011; Judgement Day, 2011; Anjin: the shogun and the English samurai, 2013; Wolf Hall and Bring up the Bodies, 2013; A Tale of Two Cities, 2014; Ghosts, 2014. *Recreations:* Norfolk, dogs. *Address:* c/o Alan Brodie Representation Ltd, Paddock Suite, The Courtyard at 55 Charterhouse Street, EC1M 6HA. *Club:* Royal Over-Seas League.

POULTON, Richard Christopher, MA; Director of Development, Round Square International Association of Schools, 2003–05; *b* 21 June 1938; *e s* of Rev. Christopher Poulton and Aileen (*née* Sparrow); *m* 1965, Zara, *o d* of late Prof. P. Crossley-Holland and Mrs J. Crossley-Holland; two *s* one *d*. *Educ:* King's Coll., Taunton; Wesleyan Univ., Middletown, Conn, USA; Pembroke Coll., Cambridge (BA 1961, CertEd 1962, MA 1965). Asst Master: Bedford Sch., 1962–63; Beckenham and Penge Grammar Sch., 1963–66; Bryanston School: Asst Master, 1966–80; Head of History Dept, 1971–76; Housemaster, 1972–80; Headmaster, Wycliffe Coll., 1980–86; Head Master, Christ's Hospital, Horsham, 1987–96; Founder Head Master, Internat. Sch. of the Regents, Pattaya, Thailand, 1996–97; Develt Officer, Inner Cities Young People's Project, 1998–2000; Clerk, All Saints Educnl Trust, 2001–04. Chm. Govs, 2010–13, Chm. Trustees, 2011–13, Sir Robert Geffery's Acad. (formerly Sir Robert Geffery's Sch.), Cornwall; Governor: Oxford and Cambridge Examinations Bd, 1987–90; Aiglon Coll., Switzerland, 1998–2000; Royal Bridewell Hosp., 1999–2004 and 2006–08; Beausoleil Internat. Coll., Switzerland, 2003–12; Box Hill Sch., 2004–08; Presentation Gov., Christ's Hosp., 1999–. JP S Glos, 1985–86. Freeman, City of London, 1987; Liveryman, Ironmongers' Co., 1993– (Yeoman, 1990; Mem. Court, 1999–; Jun. Warden, 2006–07; Sen. Warden, 2007–08; Master, 2008–09). FRSA 1994. *Publications:* Victoria, Queen of a Changing Land, 1975; Kings and Commoners, 1977; A History of the Modern World, 1980. *Recreations:* writing, choral music. *Address:* 2 Hill Cottages, Hoyle Lane, Heyshott GU29 0DU.

POUND, Sir John David, 5th Bt *cr* 1905; *b* 1 Nov. 1946; *s* of Sir Derek Allen Pound, 4th Bt; *S* father, 1980; *m* 1st, 1968 (marr. diss.); one *s*; 2nd, 1978, Penelope Ann, *er d* of late Grahame Arthur Rayden, Bramhall, Cheshire; two *s*. Liveryman, Leathersellers' Co. *Heir: s* Robert John Pound [*b* 12 Feb. 1973; *m* 2005, Tessa, *o d* of Michael Froggatt]. *Address:* 6 Summerfield Place, Kenmore, Qld 4069, Australia.

POUND, Rev. Canon Keith Salisbury; a Chaplain to the Queen, 1988–2003; *b* 3 April 1933; *s* of Percy Salisbury Pound and Annie Florence Pound. *Educ:* Roan School, Blackheath; St Catharine's Coll., Cambridge (BA 1954, MA 1958); Cuddesdon Coll., Oxford. Curate, St Peter, St Helier, Dio. Southwark, 1957–61; Training Officer, Hollowford Training and Conference Centre, Sheffield, 1961–64, Warden 1964–67; Rector of Holy Trinity, Southwark, with St Matthew, Newington, 1968–78; RD, Southwark and Newington, 1973–78; Rector of Thamesmead, 1978–86; Sub-Dean of Woolwich, 1984–86; Dean of Greenwich, 1985–86; Chaplain-Gen. and Archdeacon to Prison Service, 1986–93; Chaplain to HM Prison, Grendon and Spring Hill, 1993–98. Hon. Canon of Southwark Cathedral, 1985–. *Publications:* Creeds and Controversies, 1976; Previous Convictions, 2012. *Recreations:* theatre, music, books, crosswords. *Address:* 1 Sinnock Square, High Street, Hastings, East Sussex TN34 3HQ. *T:* (01424) 428330. *Club:* Civil Service.

POUND, Stephen Pelham; MP (Lab) Ealing North, since 1997; *b* 3 July 1948; *s* of late Pelham Pound and Dominica James; *m* 1976, Marilyn Anne Griffiths; one *s* two *d*. *Educ:* London Sch. of Economics (BSc Econ., Dip. Indust. Relations). Seaman, 1967–69; Bus Conductor, 1969–70; Hosp. Porter, 1970–79; student, 1980–84; Housing Officer, Camden Council, 1984–88; Homeless Persons Officer, Hammersmith and Fulham Council, 1988–90; Housing Officer, Paddington Churches HA, 1990–97. Councillor, London Borough of Ealing, 1982–98; Mayor of Ealing, 1995–96. Opposition Whip, 2010; Shadow Minister of State for NI, 2011–15. *Recreations:* Fulham FC, cricket, walking, collecting comics. *Address:* House of Commons, SW1A 0AA. *T:* (020) 7219 6238; 115 Milton Road, Hanwell, W7 1LG. *Clubs:* St Joseph's Catholic Social; Fulham Football Club Supporters'.

POUNDER, Prof. Robert Edward, (Roy), MD, DSc; FRCP; Professor of Medicine, Royal Free and University College Medical School, 1992–2005, now Professor Emeritus, University of London; Hon. Consultant Physician and Gastroenterologist, Royal Free Hospital, since 1980; *b* 31 May 1944; *s* of Edward Pounder and Annie Pounder (*née* Langdale); *m* 1972, Christine Lee; two *s*. *Educ:* Eltham Coll.; Peterhouse, Cambridge (BA 1st Cl. Hons Nat. Sci. 1966; BChir 1969; MB, MA 1970; MD 1977); Guy's Hosp. Med. Sch.; DSc (Med.) London 1992. MRCP 1971, FRCP 1984. Registrar, Central Middlesex Hosp., 1972–76; Sen. Registrar, St Thomas' Hosp., 1976–80; Royal Free Hospital School of Medicine: Sen. Lectr, 1980–85, Reader, 1985–92, in Medicine; Clin. Sub-Dean, 1986–88; Admissions Sub-Dean, 1992–95; Chm., Collegiate Cttee of Examrs, 1996–2003. Co-Founder and Chm., RotaGeek Ltd, 2010–. Non-exec. Dir, Camden and Islington HA, 1996–2002 (Vice-Chm., 2001–02). Royal College of Physicians: Mem. Council, 1987–89 and 1997–2000; Vice-Pres., 2002–04; Associate Internat. Dir, Australasia and FE, 2004–08. Member Council: British Digestive Foundn, 1987–98; British Soc. of Gastroenterology, 1996–2000 (Sec., 1982–86). Trustee, Alimentary Pharmacology and Therapeutics Trust, 1988–99. Chm., Friends of Peterhouse, 1999–2002 (Mem. Council, 1982–2002). Gov., St Paul's Sch., London, 2001–10 (Dep. Chm., 2007–09). Founding Co-Editor, Alimentary Pharmacology and Therapeutics, 1987–; Ed.-in-Chief, GastroHep.com, 2000–. Hon. FRACP 2007; Hon. FRCPI 2009. *Publications:* (ed) Long Cases in General Medicine, 1983, 2nd edn 1988; (ed) Doctor, There's Something Wrong with my Guts, 1983; (ed) Recent Advances in Gastroenterology, 6th edn 1986 to 10th edn 1994; (ed jtly) Diseases of the Gut and Pancreas, 1987, 2nd edn 1994 (trans. Italian and Greek); (ed jtly) Advanced Medicine, 1987; (ed jtly) A Colour Atlas of the Digestive System, 1989 (trans. Japanese); (ed) Landmark Papers: the histamine H_2-receptor antagonists, 1990; (ed jtly) Current Diagnosis and Treatment, 1996; (ed jtly) Inflammatory Bowel Disease, 1998; papers on pharmacological control of acid secretion, inflammatory bowel disease and med. workforce. *Recreations:* gardening, family life, travelling. *Address:* High Tun Cottages, Itlay, Daglingworth, Glos GL7 7JA. *Club:* Garrick.

POUNDS, Prof. Kenneth Alwyne, CBE 1984; FRS 1981; Professor of Space Physics, 1973–2002, now Emeritus, and Leverhulme Fellow, 2003–05, University of Leicester; *b* 17 Nov. 1934; *s* of Harry and Dorothy Pounds; *m* 1st, 1961, Margaret Mary (*née* Connell); two *s* one *d*; 2nd, 1982, Joan Mary (*née* Millit); one *s* one *d*. *Educ:* Salt Sch., Shipley, Yorkshire; University Coll. London (BSc, PhD; Fellow, 1993). Department of Physics, University of Leicester: Asst Lectr, 1960; Lectr, 1961; Sen. Lectr, 1969; Prof., 1973; Hd, Dept of Physics and Astronomy, 1986–2002; Chief Exec., PPARC (on leave of absence from Univ. of Leicester), 1994–98. Member: SERC, 1980–84 (Chm., Astronomy, Space and Radio Bd); Management Bd, British Nat. Space Centre, 1986–88; Pres., RAS, 1990–92. Dist. Hon. Fellow, Univ. of Leicester, 2013. DUniv York, 1984; Hon. DSc: Loughborough, 1992; Sheffield Hallam, 1997; Warwick, 2001; Leicester, 2005. Gold Medal, RAS, 1989; Planetary Scientist of the Year, 2007; COSPAR Space Science Medal, 2008. *Publications:* many, in Monthly Notices, Nature, Astrophysical Jl, etc. *Recreations:* sport, music. *Address:* 12 Swale Close, Oadby, Leicester LE2 4GF. *T:* (0116) 271 9370.

POUNTNEY, David Willoughby, CBE 1994; freelance director; Chief Executive and Artistic Director, Welsh National Opera, since 2011; *b* 10 Sept. 1947; *s* of late Dorothy and Willoughby Pountney; *m* 1st, 1980, Jane Henderson (marr. diss. 2001); one *s* one *d*; 2nd, 2007, Nicola Raab. *Educ:* St John's College Choir School, Cambridge; Radley College; St John's College, Cambridge (MA; Hon. Fellow, 2007). Joined Scottish Opera, 1970; 1st major production Katya Kabanova (Janácek), Wexford Fest., 1972; Dir of Productions, Scottish Opera, 1976–80; individual guest productions for all British Opera companies, also USA (Metropolitan Opera début, world première of The Voyage by Philip Glass, 1992), Aust., Italy, Germany, The Netherlands; Dir of Prodns, ENO, 1982–93; Intendant, Bregenzer Festspiele, 2003–. Productions for ENO include: Rusalka (Dvorak); Osud (Janácek); Dr Faust (Busoni); Lady Macbeth of Mtsensk (Shostakovich); Wozzeck (Berg); Pelléas and Mélisande (Debussy); Don Carlos (Verdi); Falstaff (Verdi); The Adventures of Mr Broucek (Janácek); The Fairy Queen (Purcell); Nabucco (Verdi), 2000; for WNO: The Doctor of Myddfai (and libretto) (Peter Maxwell Davies), 1996; Khovanshchina, 2007; Lulu, 2013; The Cunning Little Vixen, 2013; Usher House/La chute de la maison Usher, 2014; Pelléas and Mélisande

(Debussy), 2015; other major productions include: Julietta (Martinu), Opera North, 1997; Dalibor (Smetana), Scottish Opera, 1998; Guillaume Tell (Rossini), Vienna State Opera, 1998; Greek Passion, Bregenz, 1999, Royal Opera House, 2000; Faust (Gounod), Munich, 2000; Mr Emmet Takes a Walk (Peter Maxwell Davies), première, Orkney Fest., 2000; Jenufa, Vienna State Opera, 2002; Turandot, Salzburg Fest., 2002; Euryanthe, Netherlands Opera, 2003; La Juive, Zurich, 2007; Carmen, Bolshoi, Moscow, 2008; Die Soldaten, Lincoln Center Fest., NY, 2008; Paradise Moscow, Opera North, 2009; Chorus!, Houston Grand Opera, 2009; Die Frau Ohne Schatten, Zürich, 2009; The Passenger (Weinberg), world première, Bregenz Fest., 2010; Kommilitonen (Peter Maxwell Davies), world première, RAM, 2011, US première, Juilliard Sch., 2011; Portrait (Weinberg), Opera North and Nancy, 2011; Prince Igor, Zurich, 2012; (libretto) The Wasp Factory, world première, Bregenz Fest., 2013; Spuren der Verirrten (Philip Glass), world première, Linz, 2013; Die Zauberflöte (Mozart), Bregenz Fest. Seebühne, 2014. Martinu Medal, Prague, 2000. Hon. RAM 2012. Chevalier de l'Ordre des Arts et des Lettres (France), 1993; Cavalier, Order of Merit (Poland), 2013. *Publications:* (with Mark Elder and Peter Jonas) Power House, 1992; numerous trans. of opera, esp. Czech and Russian repertoire. *Recreations:* croquet, gardening, cooking. *Address:* Château d'Azu, 71230 St Romain sous Gourdon, France. *Club:* Garrick.

POUYANNÉ, Patrick Jean; Chevalier de la Légion d'Honneur, 2012; Chief Executive Officer, since 2014, and Member of Board, since 2015, Total SA; *b* Petit Quenlly, France, 24 June 1963; *s* of Bernard and Renée Pouyanné; *m* 1989, Anne Le Calvet; three *s* one *d*. *Educ:* École Polytechnique (Engr 1986); Corps des Mines (Chief Engr 1989). Tech. Advr to Prime Minister's office, 1993–95; COS, Telecommunication Minister, 1995–99; Man. Dir, Total Qatar, 1999–2002; Total SA: Senior Vice President: Finance, Exploration and Prodn, 2002–06; Strategy, Business Develt, R&D, Exploration and Prodn, 2006–12; Pres., Refining and Chemicals, 2012–14. *Recreations:* tennis, ski-ing, trips around the world. *Address:* Total SA, 2 place Jean Miller, 92078 Paris La Défense Cedex 6, France. *T:* 147443883. *E:* patrick.pouyanne@total.com.

POVER, Alan John, CMG 1990; HM Diplomatic Service, retired; High Commissioner to the Republic of Gambia, 1990–93; *b* 16 Dec. 1933; *s* of John Pover and Anne (*née* Hession); *m* 1964, Doreen Elizabeth Dawson; one *s* two *d*. *Educ:* Salesian College, Thornleigh, Bolton. Served HM Forces, 1953–55; Min. of Pensions and Nat. Insce, 1955–61; Commonwealth Relations Office, 1961; Second Secretary: Lagos, 1962–66; Tel Aviv, 1966–69; Second, later First, Sec., Karachi/Islamabad, 1969–73; First Sec., FCO, 1973–76; Consul, Cape Town, 1976–80; Counsellor, Diplomatic Service Inspector, 1983–86; Counsellor and Consul-Gen., Washington, 1986–90. *Recreations:* cricket, golf, gardening. *Club:* West Berkshire Golf.

POVEY, Sir Keith, Kt 2001; QPM 1991; HM Chief Inspector of Constabulary, 2002–05; *b* 30 April 1943; *s* of late Trevor Roberts Povey and Dorothy (*née* Parsonnage); *m* 1964, Carol Ann Harvey; two *d*. *Educ:* Abbeydale Grammar Sch., Sheffield; Sheffield Univ. (BA Law). Joined Sheffield City Police, 1962; Chief Superintendent, S Yorks, seconded as Staff Officer to Sir Lawrence Byford, HMCIC, 1984–86; Asst Chief Constable, Humberside, 1986–90; Dep. Chief Constable, Northants, 1990–93; Chief Constable, Leics, 1993–97; HM Inspector of Constabulary, 1997–2001. Hon. Secretary: ACPO General Purposes Cttee, 1994–96 (Chm., 1996–97); ACPO Crime Prevention Sub-cttee, 1994–96 (Chm., 1996–97). Hon. LLD Sheffield, 2004; Hon. DCL Northumbria, 2005. *Recreations:* jogging, flying (private pilot's licence).

POW, Rebecca Faye; MP (C) Taunton Deane, since 2015; *b* Somerset, 10 Oct. 1960; *m* Charles Clark; three *c*. *Educ:* Wye Coll., Univ. of London (BSc Hons Rural Envmt Studies 1982). Presenter, producer and dir, HTV, ITV West and Channel 4, 1989–2005, incl. Envmt Corresp., HTV; producer and presenter, Farming Today, BBC Radio 4; work for NFU; Dir, Pow Prodns, PR co., 1988–. Member: Envmtl Audit Cttee, 2015–; Envmt Food and Rural Affairs Select Cttee, 2015–. Trustee, Somerset Wildlife Trust. *Address:* House of Commons, SW1A 0AA.

POWELL; *see* Baden-Powell.

POWELL, family name of **Baron Powell of Bayswater**.

POWELL OF BAYSWATER, Baron *cr* 2000 (Life Peer), of Canterbury in the County of Kent; **Charles David Powell,** KCMG 1990; Chairman, LVMH (UK), since 2000; *b* 6 July 1941; *s* of Air Vice-Marshal John Frederick Powell, OBE and Geraldine Ysolda Powell (*née* Moylan); *m* 1964, Carla Bonardi; two *s*. *Educ:* King's Sch., Canterbury; New Coll., Oxford (BA). Diplomatic Service, 1963–83: served Helsinki, Washington, Bonn, Brussels (UK Perm. Repn to EU); Counsellor, 1979; Special Counsellor for Rhodesia negotiations, 1979–80; Private Sec. and Advr on For. Affairs to the Prime Minister, 1983–91. Director: National Westminster Bank, 1991–2000; Jardine Matheson Hldgs, 1991–2000; Matheson & Co., 1991–; Mandarin Oriental Hotel Gp, 1992–; Hong Kong Land Holdings, 1991–2000, 2008–; J. Rothschild Name Co., 1993–2003; Said Holdings, 1994–2000; LVMH Moët-Hennessy-Louis Vuitton, 1995–; British-Mediterranean Airways, 1998–2007 (Dep. Chm.); Caterpillar Inc., 2001–13; Textron Inc., 2001–; Schindler Holdings, 2003–13; Northern Trust Corp., 2015–; Sen. Ind. Dir, Yell Gp, 2003–09; Chairman: Phillips, 1999–2001; Sagitta Asset Mgt Ltd, 2000–05; Safinvest, later Capital Generation Partners, 2006–13; Magna Hldgs Internat., 2007–13. Chairman: Internat. Adv. Bd, Rolls Royce, 2006–; Adv. Bd, Bowmark, 2008–; Member: Eur. Adv. Bd, Hicks Muse Tate & Furst, 2001–05; Internat. Adv. Council, Textron Corp., 1995–2007; International Advisory Board: Barrick Gold, 2000–; Magna Corp., 2002–05; Alfa Capital Partners, 2004–10; ACE Insce, 2006–; Adv. Bd, Diligence, 2000–10; Adv. Bd, Thales UK, 2005–; Strategist Advr, BAe Systems, 2006–. Mem., Global Bd of Advrs, Council on Foreign Relns, NY, 2011–. Chairman: Singapore British Business Council, 1994–2001; Atlantic Partnership, 2004–; Co-Chm., UK Govt Asia Task Force, 2006–14; Pres., China-Britain Business Council, 1998–2007. Mem., Select Cttee on the Constitution, H of L, 2010–; Chm., All Party Parly Gp on Entrepreneurship, 2005–09. Trustee: Aspen Inst., 1995–; British Mus., 2001–10; British Mus. Trust, 2011–; IISS, 2010–; Chm., Trustees, Oxford Business Sch. Foundn, 1998–. Public Service Medal (Singapore), 1998. *Recreation:* walking. *Address:* House of Lords, SW1A 0PW.

See also Hon. H. E. Powell, Sir J. C. Powell, J. N. Powell.

POWELL, Sir Christopher; *see* Powell, Sir J. C.

POWELL, Gen. Colin Luther, Hon. KCB 1993; Legion of Merit, Bronze Star, Air Medal, Purple Heart; Secretary of State, USA, 2001–05; Strategic Limited Partner, Kleiner, Perkins, Caufield & Byers, since 2005; *b* 5 April 1937; *s* of late Luther Powell and Maud Ariel Powell (*née* McKoy); *m* 1962, Alma V. Johnson; one *s* two *d*. *Educ:* City Coll. of New York (BS Geology); George Washington Univ. (MBA). Commissioned 2nd Lieut, US Army, 1958; White House Fellow, 1972–73; Comdr, 2nd Brigade, 101st Airborne Div., 1976–77; exec. asst to Sec. of Energy, 1979; sen. mil. asst to Dep. Sec. of Defense, 1979–81; Asst Div. Comdr, 4th Inf. Div., Fort Carson, 1981–83; sen. mil. asst to Sec. of Defense, 1983–86; US V Corps, Europe, 1986–87; dep. asst to President 1987, asst 1987–89, for Nat. Security Affairs; General 1989; C-in-C, US Forces Command, Fort McPherson, April–Sept. 1989; Chm., Jt Chiefs of Staff, 1989–93. *Publications:* My American Journey (autobiog.), 1995 (UK title, A Soldier's Way); It Worked For Me: in life and leadership, 2012. *Recreations:* racquetball, restoring old Volvos. *Address:* (office) Suite 700, 909 North Washington Street, Alexandria, VA 22314, USA.

POWELL, David Hebbert; HM Diplomatic Service, retired; Ambassador to Norway, 2006–10; Policy Adviser, University of Kent, since 2014; *b* 29 April 1952; *s* of John Laycock Powell and Barbara Myrrha Powell (*née* Hebbert); *m* 1st, 1984, Gillian Mary Croft (marr. diss. 2010; she *d* 2010); one *d*; 2nd, 2010, Katerina Sternbergova; two *s* one *d*. *Educ:* Fitzwilliam Coll., Cambridge (BA 1974). MoD, 1974–85; FCO, 1985–88; First Sec., Tokyo, 1988–92; FCO, 1992–95; Counsellor: Cabinet Office, 1995–97; UK Delegn to NATO, 1997–2001; Asst Dir, Human Resources, FCO, 2002–06. Mem., London Library. *Recreations:* reading, chess, Victorian crime. *E:* david.h.powell@hotmail.com.

POWELL, His Honour (Dewi) Watkin; JP; a Circuit Judge, and Official Referee for Wales, 1972–92; *b* Aberdare, 29 July 1920; *o s* of W. H. Powell, AMICE and of M. A. Powell, Radyr, Glam; *m* 1951, Alice, *e d* of William and Mary Williams, Nantmor, Caerns; one *d*. *Educ:* Penarth Grammar Sch.; Jesus Coll., Oxford (MA). Called to Bar, Inner Temple, 1949. Dep. Chm., Merioneth and Cardigan QS, 1966–71; Dep. Recorder of Cardiff, Birkenhead, Merthyr Tydfil and Swansea, 1965–71; Junior, Wales and Chester Circuit, 1968; Liaison Judge for Dyfed, 1974–84, for Mid Glamorgan, 1984–91. Vice-Pres., South and Mid Glamorgan and Gwynedd branches of Magistrates' Assoc. Mem. Exec. Cttee, Plaid Cymru, 1943–55. Chairman: Constitutional Cttee, 1967–70; Govt of Wales Bill Drafting Gp, 1994–97; Constitutional Wkg Party, Parlt for Wales Campaign, 1994–; Member Council: Hon. Soc. of Cymmrodorion, 1965–93 (Chm., 1978–84; Vice Pres., 1984–); Cytun, 1993–98. Member, Court and Council: Univ. of Wales; Univ. of Wales Coll. of Cardiff (Vice Pres. and Vice Chm. of Council, 1987–98; Hon. Fellow). Hon. Mem., Gorsedd of Bards. President: Cymdeithas Theatr Cymru, 1984–89; Baptist Union of Wales, 1993–94; Pres., Free Church Council of Wales, 1994–98 (Vice-Pres., 1993–94). JP Mid Glamorgan. Hon. LLD Wales, 1997. *Publications:* Ymadroddion Llys Barn (Forensic Phraseology), 1974; (contrib.) Y Gair a'r Genedl, 1986; (contrib.) Lawyers and Laymen, 1986; (contrib.) Challenges to a Challenging Faith, 1995; (with John Osmond) Power to the People of Wales (Grym i Bobl Cymru), 1997; Cynulliad i Genedl, 1999. *Recreations:* gardening, reading theology, Welsh history and literature. *Address:* Nanmor, Morannedd, Cricieth, Gwynedd LL52 0PP.

POWELL, Earl Alexander, III, PhD; Director, National Gallery of Art, Washington, since 1992; *b* 24 Oct. 1943; *s* of Earl Alexander Powell and Elizabeth Powell; *m* 1971, Nancy Landry; three *d*. *Educ:* A. B. Williams Coll.; Harvard Univ. (PhD 1974). A. M. Fogg Art Mus. Teaching Fellow in Fine Arts, Harvard Univ., 1970–74 (Travelling Fellowship, 1973–74); Curator, Michener Collection and Asst Prof. of Art History, Univ. of Texas at Austin, 1974–76; National Gallery of Art, Washington: Mus. Curator, Sen. Staff Asst to Asst Director and Chief Curator, 1976–78; Exec. Curator, 1979–80; Dir, LA County Mus. of Art, 1980–92. Chm., US Commn of Fine Arts, 2005–; Member: Amer. Acad. of Arts and Scis; Amer. Acad. Commn on the Humanities and Social Scis; Amer. Philos. Soc.; Cttee for Preservation of the White House; Fed. Council on Arts and Humanities; Friends of Art and Preservation in Embassies; Nat. Portrait Gall. Commn; President's Cttee on Arts and Humanities. Trustee: American Fedn of the Arts; Assoc. of Art Museum Dirs; John F. Kennedy Center for Performing Arts; Morris and Gwendolyn Cafritz Foundn; Nat. Trust for Historic Preservation; Norton Simon Mus.; White House Historical Assoc. Hon. DFA: Otis Parsons, 1987; Williams, 1993. Williams Bicentennial Medal, 1995; Centennial Medal, Harvard Grad. Sch. of Arts and Scis, 2008. King Olav Medal (Norway), 1978; Grand Official, Order of Infante D. Henrique (Portugal), 1995; Commendatore, Ordine al Merito (Italy), 1998; Chevalier, Légion d'Honneur (France), 2000; Officier, Ordre des Arts et des Lettres (France), 2004; Order of the Aztec Eagle (Mexico), 2007; Officer's Cross, Order of Merit (Hungary), 2009. *Publications:* Thomas Cole, 1990. *Address:* National Gallery of Art, 2000B South Club Drive, Landover, MD 20785, USA. *T:* (202) 8426001. *Clubs:* Metropolitan (Washington); Knickerbocker (New York).

POWELL, Very Rev. Frances Elizabeth Fearn; *see* Ward, Very Rev. F. E. F.

POWELL, Rev. Gareth John; Secretary, Methodist Conference of the Methodist Church of Great Britain, since 2015; *b* Neath, 10 Dec. 1970; *s* of Cyril Powell and Eirlys M. Powell; *m* 2002, Suzanne N. Thomas; two *d*. *Educ:* Westminster Coll., Oxford (BA 1992); Univ. of Birmingham (MA 1995); Queen's Coll., Birmingham. Minister, Coventry Circuit and Chaplain, Coventry Univ., 1997–99; Minister, Cardiff Circuit and Chaplain, Cardiff Univ., 1999–2009; Methodist Church: President's Asst, 2009–10; Hd of Governance Support, 2010–12; Asst Sec. of Methodist Conf., 2012–14. *Publications:* Christian Community Now: ecclesiological investigations, 2008. *Recreations:* gardening, poetry, theatre, reading. *Address:* Methodist Church House, 25 Marylebone Road, NW1 5JR. *T:* (020) 7486 5502. *E:* soc@methodistchurch.org.uk. *Club:* Athenæum.

POWELL, Geoffrey Colin, CBE 2005 (OBE 1995); Chairman, Jersey Financial Services Commission, 1999–2009; *b* 17 Sept. 1937; *s* of late Eric and Kate Powell; *m* 1962, Jennifer Mary Catt; three *d*. *Educ:* Wallington Co. Grammar Sch.; Jesus Coll., Cambridge (BA 1st Cl. Econs 1961). Econ. advr to NI Govt, 1963–68; States of Jersey: Econ. Advr, 1969–92; Chief Advr, 1992–98; Advr on Internat. Affairs, Chief Minister's Dept, 1999–. Chm., Offshore Gp of Banking Supervisors, 1981–2011. Chm., Jersey Child Care Trust, 2001–12; Hon. Mem. Council, NSPCC. Paul Harris Fellow, Rotary Club. *Publications:* Economic Survey of Jersey, 1971; Annual Reports on the Jersey Economy/Budget, 1969–1998; articles on Jersey econ., Jersey's role as an internat. finance centre, Jersey's relationship with the EU and role of offshore centres generally. *Recreations:* historical research, swimming, gardening, golf, grandchildren. *Address:* (office) Cyril Le Marquand House, St Helier, Jersey JE4 8QT. *T:* (01534) 440414. *E:* c.powell@gov.je. *Clubs:* United, Rotary (Jersey); Royal Jersey Golf.

POWELL, (Geoffrey) Mark; Chairman, Rathbone Brothers plc, 2003–11 (non-executive Chairman, 2008–11); *b* Streatham, London, 14 Jan. 1946; *s* of late Francis Turner Powell, MBE and Joan Audrey Powell (*née* Bartlett); *m* 1st, 1971, Veronica Joan Rowland (marr. diss. 2009); two *d*; 2nd, 2011, Margaret Elizabeth Victoria, (Alva), Patton (*née* Smyth). *Educ:* Tonbridge Sch.; Univ. of Durham (BA 1968). FCSI 1971. Powell Popham Dawes & Co., 1968–77, Partner, 1972–77; Laing & Cruickshank: Dir, 1977–89; Hd, Private Client Investment Mgt, 1980–86; CL-Alexanders Laing & Cruickshank Hldgs Ltd: Hd, Investment Mgt Div., 1986–87; Gp Chief Exec., 1987–89; Laurence Keen Ltd, later Rathbone Brothers plc: Chief Exec., 1989–97; Gp Man. Dir, 1995–2003; Dep. Chm., 1997–2003. Chm., SVM UK Active Fund plc, 2006–10; Dir, HgCapital Trust plc, 2010–. Chm., Assoc. of Private Client Investment Managers and Stockbrokers, 2000–06. Mem., Takeover Panel, 2001–07 (Chm., Remuneration Cttee, 2004–07). Chm., Chichester Cathedral Restoration and Develt Trust, 2015–; Member: Investment Cttee, C of E Pensions Fund, 2007–15; Westminster Abbey Finance Adv. Cttee, 2012–. Mem. Council, REACH, 1996–2001. Trustee, Fight for Sight, 1999–2014. Chm. Govs, Haberdashers' Aske's Schs, Elstree, 2008–12 (Gov., 2001–13). Liveryman, Haberdashers' Co., 1968 (Master, 2008–09 and 2012–13). FRSA. *Recreations:* National Hunt racing, golf, theatre, opera, wine (Maître Emérite, La Commanderie de Vin de Bordeaux à Londres). *Address:* Rumbolds Farmhouse, Plaistow, W Sussex RH14 0PZ. *T:* (01403) 871514, 07774 842329. *E:* mark@gm-powell.com. *Clubs:* Boodle's, City of London, MCC; W Sussex Golf.

POWELL, Greg; Managing and Senior Partner, Powell Spencer & Partners Solicitors, since 1977; *b* London, 21 Jan. 1948; *s* of Victor Harold and Barbara Powell. *Educ:* London Sch. of Econs and Pol Sci. (LLB); Birkbeck Coll., Univ. of London (BSc). Admitted Solicitor, 1973. Pres., London Criminal Courts Solicitors' Assoc., 2007. Criminal Aid Lawyer of Year, 2004. *Publications:* (jtly) A Practical Guide to the Police and Criminal Evidence Act, 1984; In Love's

Shawl (poetry), 2014. *Recreation:* gardening. *Address:* Powell Spencer & Partners Solicitors, 290 Kilburn High Road, NW6 2DD. *T:* (020) 7604 5600, *Fax:* (020) 7328 1221. *E:* gregpowell@psplaw.co.uk.

POWELL, Hope Patricia, CBE 2010 (OBE 2002); coach education instructor; Consultant, FIFA; UEFA Technical Observer; *b* London; *d* of Vernon Powell and Lynn Francis; partner, 1994, Michelle Pryce. *Educ:* Abbeywood Sch.; West London Inst. of Higher Educn. Football player: Millwall Lionesses, 1978–86, 1988–90; Friends of Fulham, 1986–88; Bromley, 1990–92; Croydon, 1992–98; 66 caps for England (35 goals; Vice Capt.). Football Develt Officer, Crystal Palace FC, 1993–96; Team Leader, Prince's Trust, 1996–98; Football Develt Officer, Lewisham LBC, 1998; Nat. Coach, England Women's Football, 1998–2013. Hon. LLD Roehampton, 2011; Hon. DA E London, 2012; DUniv Loughborough, 2009; Hon. MSc: Leeds Metropolitan, 2008; St Mark and St John, Plymouth, 2014; Hon. MA Nottingham, 2012. *Recreations:* family, friends, theatre, reading, walking, photography.

POWELL, Hon. Hugh Eric, CMG 2010; HM Diplomatic Service; Division Director, Macquarie Bank, Sydney, since 2015; *b* 16 Feb. 1967; *s* of Baron Powell of Bayswater, *qv*; *m* 1993, Catherine Young; three *s*. *Educ:* Eton; Balliol Coll., Oxford (BA Hons 1988); Kennedy Sch. of Govt, Harvard (MPA 1990). Audit Commn, 1990–91; joined FCO, 1991; Second Sec., Paris, 1993–97; FCO, 1997–2000; First Sec., Berlin, 2000–03; Dir, Policy on Internat. Orgns, MoD, 2004; Hd, Security Policy Gp, FCO, 2005–08; UK Senior Rep. in Southern Afghanistan, 2008–09; Dir, 2010–13, Dep. Nat. Security Advr, 2013–14, Nat. Security Secretariat, Cabinet Office. *Recreation:* Left Back. *Address:* 5 Milton Avenue, Mosman, NSW 2008, Australia. *E:* hugh.powell@macquarie.com.

POWELL, Ian Clifford; Chairman and Senior Partner, PricewaterhouseCoopers, since 2008; *b* Coseley, W Midlands, 16 March 1956; *s* of Clifford Powell and Jean Powell; *m* 1977, June Morris; two *s* two *d*. *Educ:* High Arcal Grammar Sch., Sedgley; Wolverhampton Poly. (BA Hons Econ. 1977). FCA 1981. Price Waterhouse, later PricewaterhouseCoopers: Assurance, 1977–86; Business Recovery Services, 1986–2006; Partner, 1991; Member: UK Mgt Bd, 2006–08; Internat. Bd, 2008–. Member: World Business Council for Sustainable Develt, 2009; Adv. Council, City UK, 2010–. Mem., Develt Cttee, Nat. Gall., 2013–. Hon. DBA Wolverhampton, 2010. Freedom, City of London, 2010; Mem., Co. of Chartered Accountants in England and Wales, 2010. *Recreations:* music, motor sport, football. *Address:* PricewaterhouseCoopers, 1 Embankment Place, WC2N 6RH. *T:* (020) 7583 5000, *Fax:* (020) 7804 2444. *E:* ian.powell@uk.pwc.com.

POWELL, Prof. James Alfred, OBE 1996; PhD, DSc; CEng; Eur Ing; FIOA, FCIOB, FASI; Professor of Academic Enterprise, Salford University, 2001–10, now Emeritus (Pro Vice Chancellor for Enterprise and Regional Affairs, 2001–10); Academic Director, PASCAL Universities for Modern Renaissance, since 2010; *b* Sutton, 30 Oct. 1945; *s* of James Herbert Powell and Eileen Powell (*née* Newell); *m* 1969, Jennifer Elizabeth Morton; one *s*. *Educ:* De Burgh Sch., Tadworth; UMIST (BSc, MSc; AUMIST); Salford Univ. (PhD 1984; DSc 2000). FIOA 1984; CEng 1996; FASI 1999. ICI Schol., Salford Univ., 1970–71; Lectr, then Sen. Res. Associate, Sch. of Architecture, Dundee Univ., 1971–74; School of Architecture, Portsmouth Polytechnic: Reader in Building Utilisation, 1975–84; Prof. of Design Studies, 1984–91; Hd of Dept, 1990–91; Dep. Dean of Technol., Hd of Dept of Engrg and Mfg Systems and Lucas Prof. of Design Systems, Brunel Univ., 1991–94; Lucas Prof. of Informing Design Technol., 1994–2001, Dir of Acad. Enterprise, 1999–2001, Salford Univ. Hon. Prof., Sch. of Educn, Glasgow Univ., 2011–. Science and Engineering Research Council: IT Applications Co-ordinator, 1988–93; Mem., Engrg Bd, 1988–93; Chm., Educn and Trng Cttee, 1988–93; IT Awareness in Engrg Co-ordinator, EPSRC, 1994. Mem., Learning Foresight Panel, OST, 1996–. Internat. Speaker, Nat. IT Council of Malaysia, 1998–. Sen. Advr, Aalto Camp for Societal Innovation, 2009–. UK Ambassador, Leonardo European Corporate Learning Awards, 2009–; UK Ambassador of Social Entrepreneurship in HE, 2010–. Designer, Menuhin Auditorium for Portsmouth String Quartet Fest., 1980. FRSA; FIMgt; MInstD. Mem., New Club, Paris, 2010–. Taylor Woodrow Prize, 1967; British Interactive Multi Media Award, 1978; European Multi Media Award, 1979; Artificial Intelligence in Learning Award, 1983; Award for Interactive Audio in Multi Media, European Multi Media Assoc., 1992; Queen's Award for Higher and Further Education, 1999; Shell LIVEWire North West Enterprise Award, 2001; North West Excellence Award for Innovative Excellence, 2002. *Publications:* Design: Science: Methods, 1981; Changing Design, 1982; Designing for Building Utilisation, 1984; Noise at Work Regulations, 1990, 2nd edn 1994; Intelligent Command and Control Acquisition and Review using Simulation, 1992; The Powell Report: review of SERC engineering education and training, 1993; Informing Technologies for Construction, Civil Engineering and Transport, 1993; Neural Computing, 1994; Engineering Decision Support, 1995; Virtual Reality and Rapid Prototyping, 1995; (jtly) Universities for a Modern Renaissance, 2009; Smart City Futures, 2009; (contrib.) Handbook of Engaged Scholarship: contemporary landscapes, future directions, vol. 1: institutional change, 2010; (contrib.) Building Prosperous Knowledge Cities: policies, plans and metrics, 2012; (contrib.) European Higher Education at a Crossroads, 2012. *Recreations:* meditation, Tai Chi, cycling, squash, yoga, boating, painting. *Address:* UPBEAT, 127 Hale Road, Hale, Lancs WA15 9HQ.

POWELL, Prof. Janet Tinka, PhD, MD; FRCPath; Professor of Vascular Medicine, University of Warwick, 2000–04; Medical Director, University Hospitals of Coventry and Warwickshire NHS Trust, 2000–04; Professor (part time), running clinical trials in vascular surgery and medicine, Imperial College, London, since 2004; *b* 1 Aug. 1945; *d* of Reginald Y. Powell and Mina Powell; partner, Douglas W. Ribbons (*d* 2002); one *s* one *d*. *Educ:* Lady Margaret Hall, Oxford (BA); King's Coll. London (PhD 1972); Univ. of Miami (MD 1981). FRCPath 2001. Asst Prof. of Medicine (Pulmonary), Univ. of Miami Sch. of Medicine, 1978–79; Hse Surgeon, Ysbyty Glan Clywd, 1982; Hse Physician, Bristol Royal Infirmary, 1982–83; SHO in Dermatol., Geriatrics and Medicine, St David's Hosp., Bangor, 1983; Charing Cross and Westminster Medical School: Lectr in Biochem. and Surgery, 1983–89; Sen. Lectr, 1989–91; Reader in Cardiovascular Biol., 1991–94; Prof. of Vascular Biol., 1994–97; Registrar in Chem. Pathol., Charing Cross Hosp., 1985–87; Imperial College School of Medicine: Chm., Vascular Scis and Diseases Gp, 1997–2000; Dean, 2000. Vis. Prof., ICSTM, subseq. Res. Prof., Imperial Coll. London, 2001–04. Member: BMA, 1982; British Matrix Biol. Soc., 1984; Biochem. Soc., 1985; Vascular Surgical Soc., 1990; Surgical Res. Soc., 1990; British Atherosclerosis Soc., 1999. Member: Amer. Soc. Biochem. & Molecular Biol., 1975; Eur. Soc. for Vascular Surgery, 1992. Ed., Eur. Jl of Vascular and Endovascular Surgery, 2004–; Associate Ed., Arteriosclerosis Thrombosis and Vascular Biol., 2012–. Lifetime Achievement Award, Vascular Soc. of GB and Ireland, 2012. *Publications:* numerous contribs to learned jls incl. New England Jl of Medicine, Lancet, BMJ and Nature. *Recreations:* hiking, cycling, theatre, film. *Address:* 8 The Square, Long Itchington, Warwickshire CV47 9PE. *E:* Jtp700@aol.com.

POWELL, Sir (John) Christopher, Kt 2009; Chairman, Advertising Standards Board of Finance, since 2010; *b* 4 Oct. 1943; *s* of Air Vice-Marshal John Frederick Powell, OBE and Geraldine Ysolda Powell (*née* Moylan); *m* 1973, Rosemary Jeanne Symmons; two *s* one *d*. *Educ:* St Peter's Sch., York; London Sch. of Econs (BSc Econ.). Worked in advertising agencies, in London, 1965–69; BMP, subseq. BMP DDB: Partner, 1969–82; Jt Man. Dir, 1975–85; Chief Exec., 1986–98; Chm., 1999–2003. Non-executive Director: Riverside Studios, 1989– (Chm., 2010–); United Business Media (formerly United News & Media) plc, 1995–2006; Dr Foster LLP, 2006– (Chm., 2009–); Member: Adv. Bd (formerly Corporate Finance Adv. Panel), PricewaterhouseCoopers, 2005–; Adv. Bd, Portland PR, 2009–; Chm., Parcel Genie, 2010–. Dep. Chm., Riverside Community NHS Trust, 1994–2000; Chm., Ealing, Hammersmith & Hounslow HA, 2000–02. Chairman: British Council Creative Industries Adv. Panel, 2002–08; NESTA, 2003–09; Advertising Bd, Royal Mail, 2013–; Dep. Chm., Public Diplomacy Bd, 2006–09; Mem. Bd, Britain in Europe, 2005–. Pres., Inst. Practitioners in Advertising, 1993–95. Trustee: IPPR, 1999– (Chm., 2001–08); Alzheimer's Soc., 2012–. *Recreations:* tennis, gardening, theatre. *Address:* DDBLondon Ltd, 12 Bishop's Bridge Road, W2 6AA. *T:* (020) 7258 3979.

See also Baron Powell of Bayswater, J. N. Powell.

POWELL, John Lewis; QC 1990; a Recorder, since 2000; a Deputy High Court Judge; *b* 14 Sept. 1950; *s* of Gwyn Powell and Lilian Mary Powell (*née* Griffiths); *m* 1973, Eva Zofia Lomnicka; one *s* two *d*. *Educ:* Christ Coll., Brecon; Amman Valley Grammar Sch.; Trinity Hall, Cambridge (MA, LLB). Called to the Bar, Middle Temple, 1974 (Harmsworth Schol.), Bencher 1998. In practice, 1974–. Pres., Soc. of Construction Law, 1991–93; Member: Bar Council, 1997–2004 (Chm., Law Reform Cttee, 1997–98); Exec. Cttee, Commercial Bar Assoc., 2002–04. Contested (Lab) Cardigan, 1979. *Publications:* (with R. Jackson, QC) Professional Negligence, 1982, 5th edn; (with Eva Lomnicka) Encyclopedia of Financial Services Law, 1987; Palmer's Company Law, 24th edn 1987, 25th edn 1992; Issues and Offers of Company Securities: the new regimes, 1988; various articles. *Recreations:* travel, walking, sheep farming. *Address:* 4 New Square, Lincoln's Inn, WC2A 3RJ. *T:* (020) 7822 2000.

POWELL, John Mark Heywood; QC 2006; a Recorder, since 1997; a Deputy High Court Judge, since 2008; a President, Mental Health Tribunal for Wales, and Judge of the First-tier Tribunal, since 2012; *b* 18 July 1952; *s* of John Harford Powell, OBE, MC, and Lucinda Joan Eve Powell; *m* 1998, Carole Mary Symons-Jones; two *s* one *d*. *Educ:* Rugby Sch.; University Coll. London (BA Hons Hist. 1974). Solicitor, then Partner, Hugh James, solicitors, 1977–; barrister and solicitor, High Court of NZ, 1990–; HM Coroner, Monmouthshire, 1983–. Chancellor, Dio. of Birmingham, 2012–. Chm., Assoc. of Lawyers for Children, 1999–2001. Trustee: Triangle Trust, 2000–; Tros Gynnal, 2005–14. *Recreations:* boating in Pembrokeshire, French history and French living, watching Ebbw Vale play Rugby. *Address:* Garden Cottage, Pantygelli, Abergavenny NP7 7HR. *T:* (01813) 850647. *E:* jmhp@hotmail.co.uk. *Clubs:* MCC; Dale Yacht; Ebbw Vale Rugby Football (Pres., 2002–); Club Athletic (Riberac).

POWELL, Jonathan Charles Boyd; JP; Chief Executive, Queen Elizabeth's Foundation for Disabled People, since 2010; *b* 21 Jan. 1960; *s* of late Jeremy Boyd Powell and of Evangeline Anne Powell (*née* Simons); *m* 1993, Sarah Rhiannon Morgan; one *s* one *d*. *Educ:* Wellington Coll.; Southampton Univ. (BA Hons French and German); Thames Valley Univ. (Grad. Dip. in Law). RN, 1983–89. RBL, 1990–2001 (Hd, Ops and Develt, 1997–2001); Chief Exec., IndependentAge, RUKBA, 2001–06; Chief Exec., Vitalise, 2007–09. Director: Crossways Trust Ltd, 2002–06; IndependentAge Enterprises Ltd, 2003–06; Careways Ltd, 2007–09; Vitalise Enterprises Ltd, 2007–09; Surrey Care Assoc., 2010– (Vice Chm., 2013–). JP Ealing, 1995. *Address:* 22 Albany Road, W13 8PG. *E:* jonathan.powell@qef.org.uk.

POWELL, Jonathan Leslie; Professor of Media, Royal Holloway, University of London, since 2007; *b* 25 April 1947; *s* of James Dawson Powell and Phyllis Nora Sylvester (*née* Doubleday); *m* 1990, Sally Jane Brampton, *qv* (marr. diss.); one *d*. *Educ:* Sherborne; University of East Anglia. BA Hons (English and American Studies). Script editor and producer of drama, Granada TV, 1970–77; BBC TV: Producer, drama serials, 1977–83; Hd of Drama Series and Serials, 1983–87; Hd of Drama, 1987; Controller, BBC1, 1988–92; Dir of Drama and Co-prodn, Carlton TV, 1993–2004. *TV serials include:* Testament of Youth, 1979 (BAFTA award); Tinker Tailor Soldier Spy, 1979; Pride and Prejudice, 1980; Thérèse Raquin, 1980; The Bell, 1982; Smiley's People, 1982 (Peabody Medal, USA); The Old Men at the Zoo, 1983; Bleak House, 1985; Tender is the Night, 1985; A Perfect Spy, 1987. Royal Television Soc. Silver Award for outstanding achievement, 1979–80. *Address:* 1 First Avenue, W3 7JP.

POWELL, Jonathan Nicholas; Founder and Chief Executive, Inter Mediate, since 2011; Prime Minister's Envoy to Libya, since 2014; *b* 14 Aug. 1956; *s* of Air Vice-Marshal John Frederick Powell, OBE and Geraldine Ysolda Powell (*née* Moylan); *m* 1st, 1980, Karen Elizabeth Drayne (marr. diss. 1997); two *s*; 2nd, 2007, Sarah Helm; two *d*. *Educ:* University Coll., Oxford (MA Hist.); Univ. of Pennsylvania (MA Hist.). With BBC, 1978; Granada TV, 1978–79; joined FCO, 1979; Lisbon, 1980–83; FCO, 1983–85; Member, British Delegation to: CDE, Stockholm, 1985; CSCE, Vienna, 1985–89; FCO, 1989–91; Washington, 1991–95; COS to Leader of the Opposition, 1995–97, to the Prime Minister, 1997–2007. Senior Adviser: Centre for Humanitarian Dialogue, Geneva, 2008–13; Save the Children, 2008–; Morgan Stanley, 2008–13; Electrum Gp (UK) LLP (formerly Tigris Financial), 2009–13. *Publications:* Great Hatred, Little Room, 2008; The New Machiavelli: how to wield power in the modern world, 2010; Talking to Terrorists: how to end armed conflicts, 2014. *Recreations:* sailing, tennis.

See also Baron Powell of Bayswater, Sir J. C. Powell.

POWELL, Kenneth George; architectural critic, consultant and journalist; Consultant Director, Twentieth Century Society, 1995–2002; *b* 17 March 1947; *s* of Alan Powell and Winifred Alice Powell (*née* Hill); *m* 1969, Susan Harris-Smith. *Educ:* Canton High Sch. for Boys, Cardiff; London Sch. of Econs (BA 1968); Univ. of Manchester (MA Arch 1979). Research Assistant: Inst. of Historical Res., London, 1971–74; History of Univ. of Oxford, 1974–77; Temp. Lectr in Hist., UCL, 1977–78; worked in museums and as freelance researcher, 1978–84; Sec., SAVE Britain's Heritage, 1984–87; Architectural Corresp., Daily Telegraph, 1987–94; freelance writer. Member: Art and Architecture Cttee, Westminster Cathedral, 1994–2003; London DAC, 1996–2007, 2011–; Historic Churches Cttee, Dio. of Leeds, 1996–; Fabric Cttee, Guildford Cathedral, 2006–12; Hon. Sec., Architectural Assoc., 2006–07 (Mem. Council, 2002–12). Hon. FRIBA 2000. *Publications:* Stansted: Norman Foster and the architecture of flight, 1991; Vauxhall Cross, 1992; (with R. Moore) Structures, Space and Skin, 1993; World Cities: London, 1993; Richard Rogers, 1994; Edward Cullinan Architects, 1995; Grand Central Terminal, 1996; Richard Rogers: complete works (I), 1999, (II), 2001, (III), 2006; Architecture Transformed, 1999; Jubilee Line Architecture, 2000; The City Transformed, 2000; (jtly) The National Portrait Gallery: an architectural history, 2000; New London Architecture, 2001, 2nd edn (with Cathy Strongman) as New London Architecture 2, 2007; The Modern House Today, 2001; Will Alsop: book 1, 2001, book 2, 2002; New Architecture in Britain, 2003; KPF: process and vision, 2003; Nottingham Transformed, 2006; 30 St Mary Axe: a tower for London, 2006; (with P. Barclay) Wembley Stadium: venue of legends, 2007; Powell and Moya: twentieth century architects, 2009; 21st Century London: the new architecture, 2011; (with N. Foster) Sainsbury Centre for the Visual Arts, 2011; (ed) Great Builders, 2011; Ahrends, Burton and Koralek: twentieth century architects, 2012; Wills Building: Foster + Partners, 2012; (ed) the Great Builders, 2012; London Buildings: David Walker Architects, 2014; contrib. many articles in Country Life, Architects Jl, etc. *Recreations:* architecture, food, wine and places, preferably Mediterranean or Celtic, music, book collecting. *Address:* Flat 1, 78 Nightingale Lane, SW12 8NR. *T:* (020) 8673 3383.

POWELL, Prof. Kenneth Leslie, PhD; Chairman, ReViral Ltd, since 2012; Hon. Professor, University College London, since 2000; *b* 23 July 1949; *s* of Alec and Ada Powell; *m* 1st, 1968, Anne (marr. diss. 1974); 2nd, 1975, Dorothy J. M. Purifoy; two *d*, and one step *s* one step *d*. *Educ:* Apsley Grammar Sch.; Univ. of Reading (BSc Microbiology 1970); Univ. of Birmingham (PhD 1973). Post-doctoral Fellow, 1973–75, Asst Prof., 1975–77, Baylor Coll. of Medicine, Houston; Lectr, 1978–85, Sen. Lectr, 1985–86, Univ. of Leeds; Wellcome Foundation: Head of: Biochemical Virology, 1986–88; Antiviral Res., 1988–90; Cell Biology,

1990–93; Biology, 1993–95; Dep. Dir, Cruciform Project, subseq. Wolfson Inst. for Biomed. Res., and Prof., UCL, 1995–2000. Vis. Prof., Univ. of Michigan, 1985. CEO, Inpharmatica Ltd, 1998–2000; Chief Exec., 1998–2007, Head, 2007–08, Arrow Therapeutics; Chairman: ITS Ltd, 2009–11; Pharmidex Ltd, 2009–11; Exec. Chm., Q-Chip Ltd, 2009–14. *Publications:* more than 50 articles in learned jls. *Address:* Flat 12, 20 New Globe Walk, SE1 9DX.

POWELL, Prof. Lawrie William, AC 1990; MD, PhD; FRACP, FRCP; Professor of Medicine, University of Queensland, since 1975; Director of Research (formerly Research Co-ordinator), Royal Brisbane and Women's Hospital, since 2000; *s* of Victor Alexander Powell and Ellen Evelyn (*née* Davidson); *m* 1958, Margaret Emily Ingram; two *s* three *d*. *Educ:* Univ. of Queensland (MB BS 1958; MD 1965; PhD 1973); Univ. of London; Harvard Medical Sch. FRACP 1975; FRCP 1991. Dir, Qld Inst. of Med. Res., 1990–2000. Hon. Lectr, Royal Free Hosp. and Univ. of London, 1963–65; Vis. Prof., Harvard Medical Sch., 1972–73. Mem. Bd, Australian Stem Cell Centre, 2007–08. FTSE 1995–2008. Hon. FRCP Thailand, 1997. DUniv Griffith, 1996. *Publications:* Metals and the Liver, 1978; Fundamentals of Gastroenterology, 1975, 6th edn 1995; over 400 articles on liver disease and iron metabolism. *Recreations:* music, reading, chess, bushwalking. *Address:* Royal Brisbane and Women's Hospital, Brisbane, Qld 4029, Australia.

POWELL, Lucy Maria; MP (Lab) Manchester Central, since Nov. 2012; *b* Manchester, 10 Oct. 1974; *d* of John Lloyd Powell and Mary Powell; *m* 2009, James Williamson; one *s* one *d* and one step *s*. *Educ:* Parrs Wood High Sch.; Somerville Coll., Oxford; King's Coll. London (BSc Chem.). Parly asst to Glenda Jackson, MP, 1997–98, to Beverley Hughes, MP, 1998–99; PR rôle, later Hd, Regl Campaigning, then Campaign Dir, Britain in Europe, 1999–2005; Gov. relns, 2006–07, Leader, Manchester Innovation Fund project, 2007–10, NESTA; Manager, Labour Party leadership campaign for Rt Hon. Edward Miliband, 2010; Actg COS, then Dep. COS to Leader of Opposition, 2010–12; Shadow Minister for Childcare and Children, 2013–14, for Cabinet Office, 2014–15; Shadow Sec. of State for Educn, 2015–. Mem., Transport Select Cttee, 2012–13. *Address:* House of Commons, SW1A 0AA.

POWELL, Mark; *see* Powell, G. M.

POWELL, Sir Nicholas (Folliott Douglas), 4th Bt *cr* 1897; Company Director; *b* 17 July 1935; *s* of Sir Richard George Douglas Powell, 3rd Bt, MC, and Elizabeth Josephine (*d* 1979), *d* of late Lt-Col O. R. McMullen, CMG; *S* father, 1980; *m* 1st, 1960, Daphne Jean (marr. diss. 1987), 2nd *d* of G. H. Errington, MC; one *s* one *d*; 2nd, 1987, Davina Allsopp (marr. diss. 2003); two *s* one *d*. *Educ:* Gordonstoun. Lieut Welsh Guards, 1953–57. *Heir: s* James Richard Douglas Powell [*b* 17 Oct. 1962; *m* 1991, Susanna, *e d* of David Murray Threipland; two *s* one *d*].

POWELL, Nikolas Mark; Director, National Film and Television School, since 2003; *b* 4 Nov. 1950; *s* of A. B. Powell and Jane Powell (*née* Weir); one *s* one *d*. *Educ:* Ampleforth Coll. Co-founder and Dir, Virgin Records, 1967–81; Co-Chm., Palace Gp of Cos Ltd, 1982–91; Chm., Scala Prodns Ltd, 1991–. Chm., 1995–2003, Vice Chm., 2004–, European Film Acad. Board Director: Film Consortium, 1996–2003; Northern Irish Film and TV Commn, 2001–. Mem., Bd of Trustees, 2007–, Chm., Film Cttee, BAFTA. *Address:* National Film and Television School, Station Road, Beaconsfield, Bucks HP9 1LG. *Clubs:* Groucho, Soho House; European Producers.

POWELL, Peter James Barnard; Vice-Chairman, James Grant Group, since 2009 (Co-Founder and Executive Chairman, James Grant Management Ltd, 1984–2009); *b* Stourbridge, 24 March 1951; *s* of James and Margaret Powell. *Educ:* Uppingham. Radio disc jockey: launched first show on BBC Radio Birmingham, 1970; Radio 1, 1972; Radio Luxembourg, 1972–77; Radio 1, 1977–88; TV presenter: Top of the Pops, Montreux Rock Fest. (annually), Saturday Night Seaside Special, Oxford Roadshow, 1977–88. Dir, Formation Gp plc, 2008–09. Mem., RYA. *Recreations:* sailing, world travel, politics, music. *Address:* James Grant Group, 94 Strand on the Green, Chiswick, W4 3NN. *T:* (020) 8742 4950, *Fax:* (020) 8742 4951. *Clubs:* Royal Automobile; Royal Ocean Racing.

POWELL, Richard Stephen; HM Diplomatic Service, retired; Deputy High Commissioner, Lagos, 2007–10; *b* 19 Oct. 1959; *s* of late David Ronald Powell and Audrey Grace Powell. *Educ:* Pwll Co. Primary Sch.; Llanelli Grammar Sch.; Emmanuel Coll., Cambridge (BA Natural Scis 1981); Imperial Coll., London (MBA 1997). Entered HM Diplomatic Service, 1981; FCO, 1981–82; Attaché, UK Mission to UN, NY, 1982; Third, later Second, Sec., Helsinki, 1983–88; FCO, 1988–92; First Secretary: Tokyo, 1992–96; FCO, 1997–2003; Dep. Hd of Mission, Helsinki, 2003–07; Dep. High Comr, Accra, 2007. *Recreations:* pottering, pubs. *E:* Richard.Pwll@yahoo.co.uk.

POWELL, Dame Sally (Ann Vickers), DBE 2001; *b* 2 Oct. 1955; *d* of Alan Vickers Powell and Ena Esther Powell (*née* Crewe); *m* 1996, Iain Coleman, *qv*; one *s*. *Educ:* Royal Ballet Sch.; Univ. of Southampton (LLB 1984); Coll. of Law (Law Soc. Finals). Sadler's Wells Royal Ballet, 1974–80; joined Lewis Silkin, Solicitors, 1985; with Glazer Delmar, Solicitors, until 1997. Mem. (Lab) Hammersmith and Fulham London BC, 1986–2014 (formerly Cabinet Mem. for Regeneration). Dep. Leader, Assoc. of London Govt; Chm., Gtr London Enterprise; Dep. Chm., Business Link for London; Mem. Bd, London Develt Agency; Dep. Leader, Labour Gp, LGA. Mem. Bd, W London Mental Health Trust, 2008–11. *Recreations:* theatre, opera, football.

POWELL, Sandy, OBE 2011; RDI 2013; costume designer for film and theatre; *b* London, 7 April 1960; *d* of Sydney and Maureen Powell. *Educ:* Sydenham High Sch. for Girls; St Martin's Sch. of Art; Central Sch. of Art. Costume design for films including: Caravaggio, 1986; The Last of England, Stormy Monday, For Queen and Country, 1988; Venus Peter, 1989; Shadow of China, Killing Dad or How to Love Your Mother, 1990; The Miracle, The Pope Must Die, Edward II, 1991; Orlando, The Crying Game, 1992; Wittgenstein, 1993; Being Human, Interview with the Vampire: The Vampire Chronicles, 1994; Rob Roy, 1995; Michael Collins, 1996; The Butcher Boy, The Wings of the Dove, 1997; Velvet Goldmine (BAFTA Award, 1998), Hilary and Jackie, Shakespeare in Love (Acad. Award, 1999), 1998; Felicia's Journey, Miss Julie, The End of the Affair, 1999; Far from Heaven, Gangs of New York, 2002; Sylvia, 2003; The Aviator, 2004 (Acad. Award, 2005); Mrs Henderson Presents, 2005; The Departed, 2006; The Other Boleyn Girl, 2008; The Young Victoria, 2009 (BAFTA Award, 2009, Acad. Award, 2010); Shutter Island, 2010; The Tempest, Hugo, 2011; The Wolf of Wall Street, 2014; Cinderella, 2015. *Address:* c/o Independent Talent Group, 40 Whitfield Street, W1T 2RH. *T:* (020) 7636 6565.

POWELL, Watkin; *see* Powell, His Honour D. W.

POWELL, William Rhys; barrister, arbitrator; *b* 3 Aug. 1948; *s* of late Rev. Canon Edward Powell and Anne Powell; *m* 1973, Elizabeth Vaudin; three *d*. *Educ:* Lancing College; Emmanuel College, Cambridge (BA 1970; MA 1973); DipArb Reading Univ. 2000. FCIArb 2001. Called to the Bar, Lincoln's Inn, 1971. MP (C) Corby, 1983–97; contested (C) same seat, 1997. PPS to Minister for Overseas Develt, 1985–86, to Sec. of State for the Envmt, 1990–92. Member, Select Committee: on Procedure, 1987–90; on Foreign Affairs, 1990–91; on Sci. and Technol., 1992–95; on Agriculture, 1995–97; Mem., Jt Parly Ecclesiastical Cttee, 1987–97; Joint Secretary: Cons. Back-bench For. Affairs Cttee, 1985 and 1987–90; Cons. Back-bench Defence Cttee, 1988–90; Chairman: All-Party Parly Gp for the Gulf, 1993–97; British-Italian Parly Gp, 1992–96; British-Taiwan Parly Gp, 1992–97; British-Mongolia Parly Gp, 1993–97; British-Tunisia Parly Gp, 1995–97. Jt Chm., CAABU, 1992–95; Mem. Council, British Atlantic Cttee, 1985–90. Fellow, Industry and Parlt Trust, 1991. As Private Mem. piloted Copyright (Computer Software) Amendment Act, 1985. Vis. Scholar, Academia Sinaca, Taiwan, 1999. *Address:* Regency Chambers, 45 Priestgate, Peterborough PE1 1LB. *Clubs:* Dinosaurs; Corby Conservative.

POWELL-SMITH, Christopher Brian, TD 1985; Chairman, Black & Decker Group Inc., since 1995 (Director, since 1980); *b* 3 Oct. 1936; *s* of Edgar and Theodora Powell-Smith; *m* 1964, Jennifer Goslett; two *s* two *d*. *Educ:* City of London Sch. Asst Solicitor, McKenna & Co., 1959; Nat. Service, 4th Regt, RHA, 1959–61; McKenna & Co.: Partner, 1964–97; Finance Partner, 1975–84; Managing Partner, 1984–87; Head, Corporate Dept, 1987–92; Sen. Partner, 1992–97; Partner, Cameron McKenna, 1997–99. Non-exec. Chm., KBC Advanced Technology plc, 2004–08 (Dir, 1997–2008); non-exec. Dir, MPG Gp Ltd, 1998–2006. Chm., Richmond Parish Lands Charity, 2000–05. CO and Regimental Col, HAC, 1975–79. *Recreations:* golf, choral singing. *Address:* 23 Clarence Road, Kew, Richmond, Surrey TW9 3NL. *T:* (020) 8940 3949. *E:* chrispowellsmith@gmail.com. *Club:* Royal Mid-Surrey Golf.

POWER, Sir Alastair John Cecil, 4th Bt *cr* 1924, of Newlands Manor; *b* 15 Aug. 1958; *s* of Sir John Patrick McLannahan Power, 3rd Bt and of Melanie, *d* of Hon. Alastair Erskine; *S* father, 1984; *m* 1981, Virginia Newton; one *s* two *d*. *Heir: s* Mark Alastair John Power, *b* 15 Oct. 1989.

POWER, Prof. Anne Elizabeth, CBE 2000 (MBE 1983); PhD; Professor of Social Policy and Director, LSE Housing and Communities (formerly Postgraduate MSc/Diploma in Housing), London School of Economics, since 1997. *Educ:* Univ. of Manchester (BA Mod. Langs); London Sch. of Econs (Dip. Social Admin 1964); Univ. of Wisconsin (MA Sociol. 1966); PhD London 1985. Teacher, Tanzania, 1966; with Martin Luther King's End Slums Campaign, Chicago, 1966; Warden, Africa Centre, London, 1966–67; Co-ordinator: Friends Neighbourhood House, Islington, 1967–72; N Islington Housing Rights Project, 1972–79; Nat. Consultant, Priority Estates Project, DoE, 1979–89; Advr, Welsh Office and Rhondda BC, 1989–93. Co-ordinator and Res. Dir, prog. with Brookings Instn on Weak Mkt Cities, funded by Joseph Rowntree Foundn and DCLG, 2005–. Vis. Res. Associate, Dept of Social Policy, LSE, 1981–88. Founding Dir, Nat. Communities (formerly Tenants') Resource Centre, 1991– (Chm., 2010–); Dep. Dir, Centre for Analysis of Social Exclusion, 1997–2009. Adv. Mem., Panel of Experts to EC on urban problems; Member: Govt Sounding Bds, Housing, 1997, Urban, 2000; Urban Task Force, 1998; Sustainable Develt Commn, 2000–09. *Publications:* Property Before People: the management of Twentieth Century council housing, 1987; Housing Management: a guide to quality and creativity, 1991; Hovels to High-rise, 1993; (with R. Tunstall) Swimming Against the Tide, 1995; (with R. Tunstall) Dangerous Disorder, 1997; Estates on the Edge, 1997; (with K. Mumford) The Slow Death of Great Cities?, 1999; (with R. Rogers) Cities for a Small Country, 2000; (with K. Mumford) East Enders: family and community in East London, 2003; (with K. Mumford) Boom or Abandonment, 2003; Census Briefs: (with R. Lupton) Minority Ethnic Groups in Britain, 2004; (with R. Lupton) The Growth and Decline of Cities and Regions, 2005; (with J. Houghton) Jigsaw City, 2007; City Survivors, 2007; (jtly) the Built Environment and Health Inequalities, 2009; (with Laura Lane) Soup Runs in Central London: the right help in the right place at the right time?, 2009; Phoenix Cities: the fall and rise of great industrial cities, 2010; (jtly) Family Futures: childhood and poverty in urban neighbourhoods, 2011; numerous governmental reports; contrib. articles in press on social policy and housing issues. *Address:* CASE - LSE Housing and Communities, London School of Economics, Houghton Street, WC2A 2AE. *E:* anne.power@lse.ac.uk.

POWER, Benjamin James; Associate Director, Royal National Theatre, since 2010; *b* Macclesfield, Cheshire, 18 Aug. 1981; *s* of Jonathan and Carolyn Power; *m* 2007, Dione Miller; one *s*. *Educ:* Poynton Co. High Sch.; Clare Coll., Cambridge (BA 1st Cl. English 2007). Freelance writer and dramaturg, BBC, NBC, RSC and Complicité, 2004–; Associate Dir, Headlong Th., 2006–10. *Publications:* Faustus, 2007; A Tender Thing, 2010; *adaptations:* Paradise Lost, 2006; Six Characters in Search of an Author, 2008; Emperor and Galilean, 2011; Medea, 2014. *Recreations:* cooking, music, Shakespeare. *Address:* c/o Royal National Theatre, Upper Ground, SE1 9PX. *T:* (020) 7452 3000.

POWER, Jonathan; syndicated columnist and author, since 1973; film maker; *b* N Mimms, Herts, 4 June 1941; *s* of Patrick and Dorothy Power; four *d*. *Educ:* Liverpool Inst. High Sch.; Manchester Univ. (BA); Univ. of Wisconsin (MSc). Chm., Manchester Univ. Campaign for Nuclear Disarmament. Advr to peasant farmers in Tanzania; on staff of Martin Luther King in Chicago, 1966–67; maker of BBC Third Prog. radio documentaries, 1968–70; documentary films for BBC TV, incl. for World in Action and This Week, and ITV, 1969–76; foreign affairs feature writer, Guardian, NY Times, Observer and Economist, 1970–75; foreign affairs columnist, 1975–90, foreign affairs commentator, 2003–06, Internat. Herald Tribune; regular contribs to Encounter and Prospect mags, 1972–2009; regular guest columnist, New York Times, Washington Post and Los Angeles Times; 56 full length interviews with world leaders for Internat. Herald Tribune, Washington Post, Times and Prospect mag. Prod., BBC TV documentary, It's Ours Whatever They Say, 1972 (Silver Medal, Venice Film Fest.). Former consultant: Internat. Red Cross; WCC; IFAD; UNICEF; Catholic Ch Commn for Justice and Peace in England and Wales. Editl Advr to Ind. Commn on Nuclear Disarmament and Common Security. Mem., Transnat. Foundn for Peace and Future Res., Sweden. Mem., Anti-Apartheid Soc., London Univ., 1962–63. *Publications:* Economic Development, 1971; World of Hunger, 1976; Migrant Workers in Europe and the USA, 1979; Against Oblivion, 1981; Vision of Hope: fiftieth anniversary of the United Nations, 1995; Like Water on Stone: the story of Amnesty International, 2002; Conundrums of Humanity: the big foreign questions of our age, 2013; Ending War Crimes, Chasing the War Criminals, 2015. *Recreations:* walking, cycling, opera, ballet, history. *Address:* Adelgatan 6, Lund 22350, Sweden. *T:* 706510879. *E:* jonathanpower95@gmail.com.

POWER, Lewis Niall; QC 2011; *b* Belfast, 16 July 1965; *s* of Gerard and Rose Noel Power; *m* 1993, Anne McQuillan; one *s* two *d*. *Educ:* Our Lady and St Patrick's Coll., Knock, Belfast; Wolverhampton Univ. (LLB Hons). Called to the Bar, Gray's Inn, 1990; in practice as barrister specialising in criminal and internat. law. Lectr and Ext. Examr in Internat. Law, Birkbeck Coll., London, 1990–97. Member: Northern Irish Bar; Criminal Bar Assoc.; Internat. Bar Assoc.; Sussex Bar Mess. FA approved lawyer, 2011. *Recreations:* American law, laughter, golf, Irish sports, football, architecture, travel, international law, family. *Address:* Lamb Building, Temple, EC4Y 7AS. *T:* (020) 7797 7788, *Fax:* (020) 7353 0535. *E:* clerks@lambbuilding.co.uk.

POWER, Nigel John; QC 2010; barrister; *b* Oswestry, Shropshire, 30 Jan. 1968; *s* of John Power and Olive Power; *m* 1997, Kate Symms; one *s* one *d*. *Educ:* Our Lady and St Oswald's Catholic Prim. Sch., Oswestry; Fitzalan Comp. Sch., Oswestry; Oswestry Sch.; Univ. of Reading (LLB 1990). Called to the Bar, Inner Temple, 1992; in practice as barrister, specialising in crime. *Recreation:* playing and watching cricket and football (Liverpool FC). *Address:* 7 Harrington Street Chambers, 7 Harrington Street, Liverpool L2 9YH. *T:* (0151) 242 0707. *Club:* Liverpool Ramblers Association Football (Hon. Secretary).

POWER, Prof. Philip Patrick, PhD; FRS 2005; Professor of Chemistry, University of California, Davis. *Educ:* Trinity Coll., Dublin (BA 1974); PhD Sussex 1977. Joined Univ. of Calif, Davis, 1981. Alexander von Humboldt Award, 1992; Mond Medal, RSC, 2004. *Publications:* articles in learned jls. *Address:* Department of Chemistry, University of California, Davis, CA 95616, USA.

POWER, Vince, Hon. CBE 2006; Chief Executive, Music Festivals plc, 2011; *b* Co. Waterford, Ireland, 29 April 1947; *s* of late John Power and Brigid Power; *m* 1967 (marr. diss. 1979); three *c*; five *c* with former partners. *Educ:* Dungarvan Vocational Coll. Owner, chain of furniture shops, N London, 1964–82; Founder and Chm., Mean Fiddler Orgn, subseq. Mean Fiddler Music Gp plc, 1982–2005; founder, Vince Power Music Group, 2005–10; opened club, Mean Fiddler, Harlesden, 1982; founder of clubs and bars: Powerhaus, Islington, 1988, moved to Finsbury Park, 1996; Subterania, 1988; The Grand, 1991; Jazz Cafe, 1992; The Forum, 1993; The Garage, 1993; Upstairs at the Garage, 1994; Crossbar, 1995; Mean Fiddler, Dublin, 1995; The Palace, Luton, 1995; The Complex, 1996; The Cube, 1996; Power's Bar, 1996; Zd, 1996; Bartok, 1998; Ion Bar and Restaurant, 1998; Point 101, 1998; The Rex, 1999; One Seven Nine, 2001; G-A-Y, 2002; Union-Undeb, Cardiff, 2003; Berkeley Square Cafe, 2003; acquired nightclubs: London Astoria, 2000; LA2, renamed Mean Fiddler, 2000; Media, 2002; Tunnel, 2002; Universe, 2002; promoter of events: Reading Fest., 1989–2005; Fleadh, London, 1990–2005; Fleadh, Glasgow, 1992; Madstock, 1992, 1994, 1996, 1998; Fleadh Mor, Ireland, 1993; Neil Young, 1993; Phoenix Fest., 1993–97; Tribal Gathering, 1995–97; Paul Weller, 1996; The Sex Pistols, 1996; Big Love, 1996; Mount Universe, 1996; Jamiroquai, 1997; Fleadh New York, 1997–2005; Fleadh Chicago, 1998–2005; Fleadh San Francisco, 1998–2005; Creamfields, 1998; Pulp, 1998; Temptation, 1998; Fleadh Boston, 1999–2005; We Love…Homelands (formerly Homelands), 1999–2005; Homelands Scotland, 1999–2005; Homelands Ireland, 1999–2005; Leeds Fest., 1999–2005; Glasgow Green, 2000–05; Nat. Adventure Sports Weekender, 2001–; Dr Music Fest., Spain, 2003–; Benicassim Fest., 2006–; Hop Farm Fest., 2008–; Costa de Fuego Fest., 2012–; operational manager, Glastonbury Fest., 2002–05; co-owner, Tramore racecourse.

POWERS, Dr Alan Adrian Robelou, FSA; art historian, critic, teacher and curator; *b* 5 Feb. 1955; *s* of Michael Powers and Frances Powers (*née* Wilson); *m* 1982, Susanna Curtis; one *s* one *d*. *Educ:* Bryanston Sch.; Clare Coll., Cambridge (BA 1977; PhD 1983). Dir, Judd Street Gall., 1985–91; Librarian and Tutor, Prince of Wales's Inst. of Architecture, 1992–2000; Sen. Lectr, 1999–2004, Reader, 2004–07, Prof. of Architecture and Cultural Hist., 2007–12, Univ. of Greenwich. Curator: Modern Britain 1929–39, Design Mus., 1999; Serge Chermayeff, Kettle's Yard, Cambridge, 2001; Eric Ravilious, Imagined Realities, Imperial War Mus., 2003; Mind into Matter, De La Warr Pavilion, Bexhill on Sea, 2009. Chairman: Twentieth Century Soc., 2007–12 (Vice-Chm., 1996–99); Pollock's Toy Mus. Trust, 1999–. Mem., Art Workers' Guild. FSA 2009. Hon. FRIBA 2008. *Publications:* (jtly) The National Trust Book of the English House, 1985; Seaside Lithographs, 1986; The English Tivoli, 1988; Shop Fronts, 1989; Oliver Hill, 1989; Modern Block-Printed Textiles, 1992; Living with Books, 1999; Nature in Design, 1999; Francis Pollen, 1999; Living with Pictures, 2000; Serge Chermayeff, 2001; Front Cover, 2001; Children's Book Covers, 2003; The Twentieth Century House in Britain, 2004; Modern: the Modern movement in Britain, 2005; Modern Architectures in History: Britain, 2007; Art and Print: the Curwen story, 2008; Adlington, Craig and Collinge, 2009; Robin Hood Gardens Re-Visions, 2010; (jtly) British Murals and Decorative Painting 1920–1960, 2013; Eric Ravilious, 2013. *Recreations:* painting, printmaking. *Address:* 99 Judd Street, WC1H 9NE. *T:* (020) 7387 3154. *E:* alanpowers@btinternet.com. *Club:* Double Crown.

POWERS, Dr Michael John; QC 1995; *b* 9 Feb. 1947; *o s* of late Reginald Frederick and of Kathleen Powers; *m* 1st, 1968, Meryl Hall (marr. diss. 2001); one *s* one *d*; 2nd, 2001, Pamela Barnes. *Educ:* Poole Grammar Sch.; Middlesex Hosp. Med. Sch., London Univ. (BSc, MB BS, DA). House Surgeon, Middlesex Hosp., 1972; House Physician, Royal S Hants Hosp., 1973; Sen. House Officer, Anaesthetics, Royal United Hosp., Bath, 1974; GP, Parson Drove, Cambs, 1975; Registrar in Anaesthetics, Northwick Park Hosp., Harrow, 1975–77; called to the Bar: Lincoln's Inn, 1979, Bencher, 1998; Trinidad and Tobago, 2012; HM Asst Dep. Coroner, Westminster, 1981–87. Pres., S of England Coroners' Soc., 1987–88. FFFLM 2007. Hon. LLD Plymouth, 2010. *Publications:* Thurston's Coronership: the law and practice on coroners, 1985; Medical Negligence, 1990, 5th edn (ed jtly), as Clinical Negligence, 2015; chapters in medical and legal texts on medico-legal subjects. *Recreations:* music, hill-walking, flying (former helicopter pilot). *Address:* Clerksroom, Equity House, Blackbrook Park Avenue, Taunton TA1 2PX. *T:* 0845 083 3000. *E:* powersqc@medneg.co.uk. *Club:* Royal Society of Medicine.

POWERS-FREELING, Laurel Claire; non-executive director and senior banking advisor; *b* 16 May 1957; *d* of Lloyd M. Powers and Catharine Berry Powers; *m* 1989, Dr Anthony Nigel Stanley Freeling, *qv*; two *d*. *Educ:* Columbia Univ., NY (AB *cum laude*): Massachusetts Inst. of Technol. (Sloan Schol.); Univ. de Reims Champagne-Ardenne (Dip. Haute études du Goût). Sen. Consultant, Price Waterhouse, 1981–85; manager, McKinsey & Co., 1985–89; Corporate Finance, Morgan Stanley Internat., 1989–91; Dir, Corporate Strategy, Prudential Gp plc, 1991–94; Gp Finance Dir, Lloyds Abbey Life Gp plc, 1994–97; Lloyds TSB Group plc: Finance and Develt Dir, Retail, 1997–99; Man. Dir, Wealth Mgt, 1999–2001; Exec. Dir, Marks & Spencer Gp plc, 2001–04; CEO, Marks & Spencer Financial Services plc, 2001–04; Sen. Vice-Pres., UK Country Manager and Chm., American Express Insce Services Europe, 2005–07; Gp Chief Exec., Dubai First International, 2007–09. Non-exec. Dir, 2002–05, Sen. Advr, 2010–11, Bank of England; Sen. Gp Advr, Erste Bank Gp, 2008–10; non-executive Director: Bank of Ireland UK plc, 2010–; BBA-LIBOR Ltd, 2010–13; C. Hoare & Co., 2010–; Findel plc, 2010–14; ACE Europe Gp, 2012–; Premium Credit Ltd, 2012–; Callcredit Information Gp, 2014–. Chm., Nat. Joint Registry, 2011–. Chairman: Piccola Accademia di Montisi Music (formerly Montisi Harpsichord Performance Centre), Siena, 2005–12; Amer. Soc. for Royal Acad. of Music, 2011–; Gov., RAM, 2007–; Dir, English Concert, 2008–12. *Recreations:* interior design, sewing, music, restoring ancient buildings, gastronomy and wines. *Address:* Bank of Ireland UK plc, 1 Bread Street, EC4M 9BE. *T:* (020) 3201 6244. *E:* laurel@powers-freeling.com.

POWERSCOURT, 11th Viscount *cr* 1743 (Ire.); **Mervyn Anthony Wingfield;** Baron Wingfield 1743; Baron Powerscourt (UK) 1885; *b* 21 Aug. 1963; *s* of 10th Viscount Powerscourt and Wendy Ann Pauline Wingfield (*née* Slazenger); *S* father, 2015; *m* 2010, Sarah Ann Hall. *Heir: uncle* Hon. Guy Claude Patrick Wingfield, *b* 5 Oct. 1940.

POWIS, 8th Earl of, *cr* 1804; **John George Herbert;** Baron Clive (Ire.), 1762; Baron Clive (GB), 1794; Viscount Clive, Baron Herbert of Chirbury, Baron Powis, 1804; *b* 19 May 1952; *s* of 7th Earl of Powis and of Hon. Katharine Odeyne de Grey, *d* of 8th Baron Walsingham, DSO, OBE; *S* father, 1993; *m* 1977, Marijke Sophia, *d* of Maarten Nanne Guther, Ancaster, Canada; two *s* two *d*. *Educ:* Wellington; McMaster Univ., Ontario, Canada (MA; PhD 1994). Formerly Lectr, McMaster Univ.; Asst Prof., Redeemer Coll., Ont, Canada, 1990–92. *Heir: s* Viscount Clive, *qv*. *Address:* Powis Castle Estate Office, Welshpool, Powys SY21 8RG.

POWLES, Prof. Raymond Leonard, CBE 2003; MD; FRCP; FRCPath; Professor of Haemato-Oncology, University of London, at Institute of Cancer Research, 1997–2004, now Emeritus; Head, Leukaemia, Myeloma and Bone Marrow Transplant Units, Cancer Centre London, Wimbledon, since 2004; Director, London Haemato-oncology Ltd, since 2010; *b* 9 March 1938; *s* of late Leonard William David Powles and Florence Irene Powles (*née* Conolly); *m* 1980, Louise Jane Richmond; three *s* one *d*. *Educ:* Eltham Coll.; St Bartholomew's Hosp. Med. Coll. (BSc 1961; MB BS 1964; MD 1976). MRCP 1968, FRCP 1980; FRCPath 1993. House Physician and Surgeon, St Bartholomew's Hosp., 1965–66; RMO, Royal Marsden Hosp., 1967–68; Leukaemia Res. Fund Fellow, Ville Juif, Paris, 1968; Tata Meml Fund Fellow, Royal Marsden Hosp. and Inst. of Cancer Res., Sutton, 1969–72; SSO, ICRF, St Bartholomew's Hosp. and Royal Marsden Hosp., 1972–74; Physician in Charge, 1974–2003, and Gp Hd, Haemato-Oncology, 1993–2003, Leukaemia and Myeloma Units, Royal Marsden Hosp. Clin. Tutor, RCP, 1990; internat. lectures on leukaemia, myeloma and bone marrow transplantation. Member: MRC Wkg Party on Leukaemia, 1974–2003; Royal Marsden SHA, 1989–92; Standing Med. Adv. Sub-Cttee on Cancer, DoH, 1991–93; WHO Cttee on Internat. Programme Chernobyl Accident, 1990–92; Ind. Reconfiguration Panel, 2002–13; Healthcare Inspections Adv. Panel, Cabinet Office Public Sector Team, 2002–. Chm., Nuclear Accidents Sub-Cttee, European Gp for Blood and Marrow Transplantation, 2001–. Bd Mem., European Soc. Med. Oncology, 1985–90; Scientific Advr, Internat. Myeloma Foundn, 1995–; American Society of Hematology: Mem., Scientific Cttee on hemopoetic growth factors, 2004– (Chm., 2006–08); Chm., Ad-Hoc Scientific Cttee on plasma cell biol., 2008–10. Mem. Bd, BioPartners GmbH, 2000–07. Trustee, and Bd Mem., New Health Network, 2002–. Board Member: Bone Marrow Transplantation, 1986–; Experimental Haematology, 1992–. Founding Patron, New India Cancer Care Initiative, 2010–. Lifetime Achievement Award, Cancer Patients Aid Assoc., India, 1999; Outstanding Contribn Award, Ind. Healthcare Awards, 2009; Pride of Britain Lifetime Achievement Award, 2013. *Publications:* more than 1200 sci. papers, articles, and chapters in books on leukaemia, myeloma and bone marrow transplantation. *Recreations:* sport, travel, cinema, theatre. *Address:* Little Garratts, 19 Garratts Lane, Banstead, Surrey SM7 2EA. *T:* 07768 165882, *Fax:* (office) (020) 8605 9103. *E:* myeloma@clara.co.uk.

See also T. J. Powles.

POWLES, His Honour Stephen Robert; QC 1995; a Circuit Judge, 2005–14; *b* 7 June 1948; *s* of late Andrew Frederick Arthur Powles and Nora (*née* Bristol); *m* 1975, Geraldine Patricia Hilda Adamson; one *s* one *d*. *Educ:* Westminster Sch.; University Coll., Oxford (MA). Called to the Bar: Middle Temple, 1972 (Harmsworth Maj. Exhibnr, 1971; Astbury Law Schol., 1972); Lincoln's Inn (*ad eundem*), 1977; a Recorder, 1994–2005. CEDR registered mediator, 2001–. Member: Civil Mediation Council, 2002–; Tribunal Panel, Financial Reporting Council (formerly Accountancy Investigation and Discipline Bd, then Accountancy and Actuarial Discipline Bd), 2004–; Parole Bd, 2006–. Hon. CIMechE 2001. *Recreations:* hill-walking, sailing, my border terrier.

POWLES, Prof. Trevor James, CBE 2003; PhD; FRCP; Consultant Breast Oncologist: St Anthony's Hospital, since 1978; Lister Hospital, 2002–14; Cancer Centre London, Parkside Hospital, since 2013 (Medical Director, since 2010); Consultant Physician in Breast Cancer, 1978–2003, Head of Breast Cancer Unit, 1993–2003, and Medical Director, Common Tumours Division, 2000–03, Royal Marsden Hospital; Professor of Breast Oncology, Institute of Cancer Research, London University, 1998–2003, now Emeritus; *b* 8 March 1938; *s* of late Leonard William David Powles and Florence Irene Powles (*née* Conolly); *m* 1968, Penelope Margaret Meyers; two *s* one *d*. *Educ:* Eltham Coll.; St Bartholomew's Hosp. Med. Coll. (MB BS 1964); Inst. of Cancer Res. (PhD 1975). FRCP 1983. House Physician and Registrar, Hammersmith Hosp., 1967–68; Med. Registrar, St Bartholomew's Hosp., 1965–70; MRC Clin. Res. Fellow, Inst. of Cancer Res., 1971–73; Sen. Registrar and Sen. Lectr, Royal Marsden Hosp., 1974–78; Consultant Breast Oncologist, Parkside Oncology Clinic, 2003–10. Visiting Professor: M. D. Anderson Cancer Center, Houston, 1993; Dana Farber Cancer Center, Harvard, Boston, 1996; Tom Baker Cancer Centre, Calgary, 1998. Director: Oncotech Inc., Calif, 1996–2008; Intact Medical Inc. (formerly Neothermia Inc.), Ohio, 2000–. Vice Pres., Internat. Soc. for Prevention of Cancer, 1996–2010. Patron, Breast Cancer Care, 2003–. Trustee: Breakthrough Breast Cancer; Breast Cancer Res. Trust. All Party Parly Gp Award for lifetime achievement in breast cancer, 2003; Brinker Award for Scientific Distinction, Komen Foundn, 2005; Ind. Healthcare Award, Laing & Buisson, 2009; Pride of Britain Lifetime Achievement Award, 2013. *Publications:* Breast Cancer Management, 1981; Prostaglandins and Cancer, 1982; Medical Management of Breast Cancer, 1991; scientific papers on diagnosis, prevention and treatment of breast cancer. *Recreations:* horse riding, ski-ing, reading, golf, fishing. *Address:* Green Hedges, Coulsdon Lane, Chipstead, Surrey CR5 3QL; Cancer Center London, 49 Parkside, Wimbledon, SW19 5NB. *T:* (020) 8247 3384, *Fax:* (020) 8247 3385. *Club:* Royal Automobile.

See also R. L. Powles.

POWLETT; *see* Orde-Powlett.

POWLEY, John Albert; Enquiry Officer, Post Office, 1991–96; *b* 3 Aug. 1936; *s* of Albert and Evelyn Powley; *m* 1957, Jill (*née* Palmer); two *s* one *d*. *Educ:* Cambridge Grammar Sch.; Cambridgeshire Coll. of Arts and Technology. Apprenticeship, Pye Ltd, 1952–57; RAF, 1957–59; retail shop selling and servicing radio, television and electrical goods, 1960–84. Member (C): Cambs CC, 1967–77, 1997–2013 (Chm., Social Services Cttee, 1998–2005; Cabinet Mem. for finance and corp. services, 2005–07; Vice Chm., 2009–11; Chm., 2011–13); Cambridge City Council, 1967–79 (Leader, Cons. Group, 1973–79; Chm., Housing Cttee, 1972–74, 1976–79; Leader of Council, 1976–79). Contested (C): Harlow, 1979; Norwich S, 1987. MP (C) Norwich S, 1983–87. Chm., Soham Cons. Assoc., 1991–2001. Sec./Manager, Wensum Valley Golf Club, Taverham, Norfolk, 1989–90. Hon. Alderman for Cambs, 2014–. *Recreations:* golf, cricket, football. *Address:* Kyte End, 70A Brook Street, Soham, Ely, Cambs CB7 5AE. *T:* (01353) 624552. *E:* johnjill.powley@gmail.com.

POWNALL, David; novelist and playwright, since 1970; *b* 19 May 1938; *s* of John Charles Pownall and Elsie Pownall (*née* Russell); *m* 1962, Glenys Elsie Jones (marr. diss. 1973; she *d* 1995); one *s*; partner 1972–89, Mary Ellen Ray; one *s*; *m* 1993, Jean Alexander Sutton; one *s*. *Educ:* Greasby Primary Sch., Wirral; Lord Wandsworth Coll., Long Sutton; Keele Univ. (BA Hons 1960). Grad. Trainee, then Personnel Officer, Ford Motor Co., 1960–63; Personnel Manager, Anglo-American Corp., Zambian Copperbelt, 1963–69. FRSL 1976. Hon. DLitt Keele, 2000. John Whiting Award, 1981; Giles Cooper Award, 1981, 1985; Sony Silver Award, 1993, 1994, Sony Gold Award, 1995; Writers Guild Award, 2013. *Publications: novels:* The Raining Tree War, 1974; African Horse, 1975; God Perkins, 1977; Light on a Honeycomb, 1978; Beloved Latitudes, 1981; The White Cutter, 1987; The Gardener, 1988; Stagg and his Mother, 1990; The Sphinx and the Sybarites, 1993; The Catalogue of Men, 1999; The Ruling Passion, 2008; The Archivist, 2010; *plays:* The Dream of Chief Crazy Horse (for children), 1975; Music to Murder By, 1976; Motocar/Richard III Part Two, 1979; An Audience Called Edouard, 1979; Master Class, 1983; The Composer Plays, 1993; Elgar's Rondo, 1993; Death of a Faun, 1996; Radio Plays, 1998; Getting the Picture, 1998; Collected Plays, 2000; *short stories:* My Organic Uncle and other stories, 1976; The Bunch from Bananas (for children), 1980; *poetry:* Another Country, 1978; Poems, 2007; *non-fiction:* Between Ribble and Lune, 1980; Sound Theatre, 2011; Writing Master Class, 2014. *Recreations:* fishing, fell-walking, gardening, music, reading. *Address:* c/o Johnson & Alcock Ltd, Clerkenwell House, 45/47 Clerkenwell Green, EC1R 0HT. *T:* (020) 7251 0125.

POWNALL, Brig. John Lionel, OBE 1972; Deputy Chairman, Police Complaints Authority, 1986–93 (Member, 1985–86); *b* 10 May 1929; *yr s* of late John Cecil Glossop Pownall, CB and Margaret Nina Pownall (*née* Jesson); *m* 1962, Sylvia Joan Cameron Conn (*d* 2011), *d* of late J. Cameron Conn, WS and Florence Conn (*née* Lennox); two *s*. *Educ:* Rugby School; RMA Sandhurst. Commissioned 16th/5th Lancers, 1949; served Egypt, Cyrenaica, Tripolitania, BAOR, Hong Kong, Cyprus; psc, jssc; Comd 16th/5th The Queen's Royal Lancers, 1969–71; Adjutant-Gen.'s Secretariat, 1971–72; Officer i/c RAC Manning and Records, 1973–75; Col, GS Near East Land Forces/Land Forces Cyprus, 1975–78; Asst Dir, Defence Policy Staff, MoD, 1978–79; Brig. RAC, UKLF, 1979–82; Brig. GS, MoD, 1982–84; retired 1984. Col, 16th/5th The Queen's Royal Lancers, 1985–90. *Recreations:* country pursuits, arts. *Address:* 5 Park Way, Easebourne, Midhurst, W Sussex GU29 0AW. *Clubs:* Cavalry and Guards, Army and Navy.

POWNALL, Sir Michael (Graham), KCB 2011; Clerk of the Parliaments, House of Lords, 2007–11; *b* 11 Oct. 1949; *s* of Raymond Pownall and Elisabeth Mary Pownall (*née* Robinson); *m* 1974, Deborah Ann (*d* 2013), *e d* of T. H. McQueen; two *d*. *Educ:* Repton Sch.; Exeter Univ. Joined Parliament Office, House of Lords, 1971: seconded to CSD as Private Sec. to Leader of House and Govt Chief Whip, 1980–83; Estabt Officer and Sec. to Chm. of Cttees, 1983–88; Principal Clerk of Private Bills, 1988–90; Principal Clerk, Overseas Office, 1988–95; Clerk of Cttees, 1991–95; Clerk of the Journals, 1995–96; Reading Clerk and Principal Finance Officer, 1997–2003; Clerk Asst, 2003–07. Trustee, History of Parliament Trust, 2007–11. Hon. LLD Exeter, 2012. *Recreations:* bird-watching, squash, house in Italy. *T:* (020) 8994 0797. *Club:* Brooks's.

POWNALL, (Stephen) Orlando (Fletcher); QC 2002; *b* 13 Nov. 1952; *s* of Alan Pownall and Carola Pownall (*née* Thielker); *m* 1978, Catherine Higgins; one *s* two *d*. *Educ:* Oundle Sch.; Faculté de Droit, Paris. Called to the Bar, Inner Temple, 1975, Bencher, 2007; Jun. Treasury Counsel, 1991–95; Sen. Treasury Counsel, CCC, 1995–2002; Hd of Chambers, 2 Hare Court, 2009–13. *Recreations:* Rugby, golf, painting, gardening, Liverpool FC. *Address:* 2 Hare Court, Temple, EC4Y 7BH. *T:* (020) 7353 5324.

POWRIE, Prof. Fiona Margaret, DPhil; FRS 2011; Director, Kennedy Institute of Rheumatology and Professor, Nuffield Department of Orthopaedics, Rheumatology and Muskuloskeletal Sciences, University of Oxford, since 2014; Fellow of Green Templeton College, since 2009; *b* Luton, 1963. *Educ:* Univ. of Bath (BSc Biochem. 1985); Univ. of Oxford (DPhil). University of Oxford: Wellcome Trust Sen. Res. Fellow, 1996–2009; Prof. of Immunol., until 2009; Sidney Truelove Prof. of Gastroenterology, 2009–14; former Hd, Experimental Med. Div., Nuffield Dept of Clinical Med. (Jtly) Louis-Jeantet Prize for Medicine, 2012. *Address:* Kennedy Institute of Rheumatology, University of Oxford, Roosevelt Drive, Headington, Oxford OX3 7FY.

POWRIE, Prof. William, PhD; CEng, FREng, FICE; Professor of Geotechnical Engineering, since 1995, and Dean, Faculty of Engineering and the Environment, since 2010, University of Southampton; *b* 25 Sept. 1959; *s* of William Powrie and Jean (*née* Darby); *m* 1988, Dr Christine Lorraine Solomon; three *s* one *d*. *Educ:* St Catharine's Coll., Cambridge (BA Engrg 1982; MA 1986; PhD Soil Mechanics 1986); King's Coll., London (MSc Construction Law and Arbitration 1991). CEng 1991; FICE 1997; FREng 2009. Civil Engrg Trainee, British Rail (Eastern Reg.), 1978–82; Lectr in Civil Engrg, KCL, 1985–88; Queen Mary and Westfield College, London: Lectr in Civil Engrg, 1988–93; Reader in Civil Engrg, 1993–94; Hd, Sch. of Civil Engrg and the Envmt (formerly Dept of Civil and Envmtl Engrg), Univ. of Southampton, 1999–2008. Chm., Southampton Univ. Res. into Sustainability and Envmt, 1998–2007. Geotechnical Cons. to W. J. Groundwater Ltd, Bushey, 1987–; Director: WJ Associates Ltd (geotechnical consultants), 1992–2003; Envmtl Services Assoc. Res. Trust, 1998–2002. Sponsor, Scientists for Global Responsibility (formerly Architects and Engrs for Social Responsibility), 2000–; Trustee, Inst. for Sustainability, 2010–. Chm., DEFRA Technologies Adv. Cttee for Biodegradable Municipal Waste, 2005–10. Hon. Editor and Chm. Editl Adv. Panel, ICE Procs (Geotech. Engrg), 1997–99, (Waste and Resource Mgt), 2005–09. *Publications:* Soil Mechanics: concepts and applications, 1997, 3rd edn 2014; *c* 100 papers in acad. and professional jls incl. Geotechnique, ICE Procs, Procs ASCE, Canadian Geotech. Jl, Jl of Petroleum Sci. and Engrg, Waste Mgt, Jl of Rail and Rapid Transit, Internat. Jl of Rock Mechanics and Mining Scis. *Recreations:* music (playing and listening, mainly classical and jazz, piano, church organ and alto saxophone), cycling, walking, DIY. *Address:* Faculty of Engineering and the Environment, University of Southampton, Highfield, Southampton SO17 1BJ. *T:* (023) 8059 3214, *Fax:* (023) 8067 7519. *E:* wp@soton.ac.uk.

POWYS, family name of **Baron Lilford**.

POYNTER, Kieran Charles, FCA; Chairman, Nomura International, since 2011; *b* 20 Aug. 1950; *s* of Kenneth and Betty Poynter; *m* 1977, Marylyn Melvin; three *s* one *d*. *Educ:* Salesian Coll.; Imperial Coll., London (BSc, ARCS). FCA 1977. Price Waterhouse, 1971–98, PricewaterhouseCoopers, 1998–2008: articled clerk, 1971; Partner, 1982; Dir, Insce Services, 1982–95; Member: Supervisory Bd, 1993–95; Mgt Bd, 1995–2008; Man. Partner, 1996–2000; Chm. and Sen. Partner, 2000–08. Chm., F & C Asset Mgt plc, 2013–; non-executive Director: F&C Asset Mgt plc, 2009–; Nomura European Hldgs plc, Nomura Internat. plc and Nomura Bank Internat. plc, 2009–; British American Tobacco plc, 2010–; Internat. Consolidated Airlines Gp SA, 2010–. Member: Insce Cttee, ICAEW, 1982–95; Life Accounting Cttee, ABI, 1992; Govt Task Force on Deregulation of Financial Services, 1993. Lloyd's Committees: Member: Accounting and Auditing Standards, 1988–90; Solvency and Reporting, 1994–95; Disputes Resolution Panel, 1996–97; Chm., Gooda Walker Loss Review, 1991–92. Member: Council for Industry and Higher Educn, 1997–2008; Council, NIESR, 2000–14; President's Cttee, CBI, 2001–08; Council, Prince of Wales' Internat. Business Leaders Forum, 2001–13 (Chm., Audit Cttee, 2007–11); Transatlantic Council, British American Business Inc., 2001–08; Steering Cttee, Heart of the City, 2003–11; Task Force on Ethnic Diversity, IPPR, 2005–06; President's Cttee, Employers Forum on Disability, 2006–11; Council, British Olympic Appeal, 2008–13. Trustee: Industry in Educn, 1999–2008; Royal Anniversary Trust, 2007– (Chm., 2010–). Director: Royal Automobile Club Ltd, 2007–13; Digital Theatre Ltd (formerly Digital Theatre TV Ltd), 2009–12. KHS 1999. *Publications:* contrib. various insurance articles to professional jls. *Recreations:* golf, watching sport, shooting. *Address:* 15 Montpelier Mews, SW7 1HB. *T:* (020) 7581 5812, 07715 376784. *Clubs:* Royal Automobile, Brooks's.

POYNTZ, Rt Rev. Samuel Greenfield; Bishop of Connor, 1987–95; *b* 4 March 1926; *s* of James and Katharine Jane Poyntz; *m* 1952, Noreen Henrietta Armstrong; one *s* two *d*. *Educ:* Portora Royal School, Enniskillen; Univ. of Dublin. Mod., Mental and Moral Sci. and Oriental Langs, 1948; 1st cl. Div. Test., 1950; MA 1951; BD 1953; PhD 1960. Deacon 1950, priest 1951; Curate Assistant: St George's, Dublin, 1950–52; Bray, 1952–55; St Michan and St Paul, Dublin, 1955–59; Rector of St Stephen's, Dublin, 1959–67; Vicar of St Ann's, Dublin, 1967–78; Archdeacon of Dublin, 1974–78; Exam. Chaplain to Archbishop of Dublin, 1974–78; Bishop of Cork, Cloyne and Ross, 1978–87. Chairman: Youth Dept, British Council of Churches, 1965–69; Irish Council of Churches, 1986–88; Jt Chm., Irish Inter-Church Meeting, 1986–88; Vice-Pres., BCC, 1987–90. Member: Governing Body, UC Cork, 1978–87; Ct, Ulster Univ., 1987–2006. Hon. Chaplain, Boys' Brigade, Ireland, 1978–. Hon. DLitt Ulster, 1995. *Publications:* The Exaltation of the Blessed Virgin Mary, 1953; St Stephen's—One Hundred and Fifty Years of Worship and Witness, 1974; Journey towards Unity, 1975; St Ann's—the Church in the heart of the City, 1976; (ed) Christ the Way, the Truth, and Your Life, 1955; Our Church—Praying with our Church Family, 1983; (contrib.) Mary for Earth and Heaven: essays on Mary and ecumenism, 2002; (contrib.) Inter-Church Relations: developments and perspectives - a tribute to Bishop Anthony Farquhar, 2008. *Recreations:* interest in Rugby football, travel, stamp collecting. *Address:* 3 The Gables, Ballinteer Road, Dundrum, Dublin 16, Ireland. *T:* (1) 2966748.

POYSER, Crispin John; Clerk, Overseas Office, House of Commons, since 2011; *b* Nottingham, 9 Nov. 1957; *s* of Eric and Pamela Poyser; *m* 1994, Kristine Williams; one *s* one *d*. *Educ:* Ampleforth Coll.; Merton Coll., Oxford (BA 1978). House of Commons: Clerk: Cttee, Journal, Public Bill and Table Offices, 1978–2002; Treasury Select Cttee, 2002–05; Parly Advr, Cabinet Office, 2005–08; Principal Clerk, Cttee Office, 2008–11. Jt Sec., Assoc. of Secretaries Gen. of Parlts, 1991–96. *Recreations:* classical ballet, history, reading, armchair sport. *Address:* Department of Chamber and Committee Services, House of Commons, SW1A 0AA. *T:* (020) 7219 3000.

POZNANSKY, Dulcie Vivien; *see* Coleman, D. V.

PRACY, Robert, FRCS; Dean of the Institute of Laryngology and Otology, University of London, 1981–85, retired; a Medical Chairman, Pensions Appeal Tribunals, since 1984 (Medical Member, since 1982); *b* 19 Sept. 1921; *s* of Douglas Sherrin Pracy and Gwendoline Blanche Power; *m* 1946, Elizabeth Patricia Spicer (*d* 2008); one *s* two *d* (and one *s* decd). *Educ:* Berkhamsted Sch.; St Bartholomew's Hosp. Med. Coll. (MB BS 1945); MPhil (Lond.) 1984. LRCP 1944; MRCS, FRCS 1953. Former Captain, RAMC. House Surgeon appts, St Bartholomew's Hosp.; formerly: Registrar, Royal Nat. Throat, Nose and Ear Hosp.; Consultant Surgeon: Liverpool Regional Board, 1954; United Liverpool Hosps, 1959; Alder Hey Children's Hosp., 1960; Royal Nat. Throat, Nose and Ear Hosp.; Hosp. for Sick Children, Gt Ormond St; Dir, Dept of Otolaryngology, Liverpool Univ. Mem. Ct of Examnrs, RCS and RCSI. Lectures: Yearsley, 1976; Joshi, 1978; Wilde, 1979; Semon, London Univ., 1980. Pres., British Assoc. of Otolaryngologists; FRSocMed (Pres., Sect. of Laryngology, 1982–83). Hon. FRCSI 1982; Hon. Fellow: Irish Otolaryngol Assoc.; Assoc. of Otolaryngologists of India; Polish Otolaryngological Assoc. *Publications:* (jtly) Short Textbook: Ear, Nose and Throat, 1970, 2nd edn 1974 (trans. Italian, Portuguese, Spanish); (jtly) Ear, Nose and Throat Surgery and Nursing, 1977; contribs to learned jls. *Recreations:* painting, engraving, theatre. *Address:* Ginkgo House, New Road, Moreton-in-Marsh, Glos GL56 0AS. *T:* (01608) 650740.

PRADA, Miuccia, PhD; Head of Prada SpA, since 1978; *b* 1949; *d* of late Luisa Prada; *m* 1987, Patrizio Bertelli; two *s*. Mime artist, Teatro Piccolo, Milan. Joined Prada, 1970; launched: women's clothing collection, 1988; Miu Miu, 1992; men's collection, 1994. Internat. Award, Council of Fashion Designers of America, 2004. *Address:* Prada SpA, Via Andrea Maffei 2, 20135 Milan, Italy.

PRAG, Prof. (Andrew) John (Nicholas Warburg), MA, DPhil; FSA; Keeper of Archaeology, Manchester Museum, 1969–2004, now Hon. Professor; Professor of Archaeological Studies, University of Manchester, 2004–05, Professor Emeritus of Classics, since 2005; *b* 28 Aug. 1941; *s* of late Adolf Prag and Frede Charlotte (*née* Warburg); *m* 1969, Kay (*née* Wright); one *s* one *d*. *Educ:* Westminster Sch. (Queen's Scholar); Brasenose Coll., Oxford (Domus Exhibnr 1960; Hon. Scholar 1962; BA 1964; Dip. Classical Archaeol. 1966; Sen. Hulme Scholar, 1967; MA 1967; DPhil 1975). FSA 1977. Temp. Asst Keeper, Ashmolean Museum, Oxford, 1966–67; University of Manchester: Hon. Lectr, Dept of History, 1977–83, Dept of Archaeology, 1984–2005. Vis. Prof. of Classics, McMaster Univ., 1978; Vis. Fellow, British Sch. at Athens, 1994. Editor, Archaeological Reports, 1975–87. *Publications:* The Oresteia: iconographic and narrative tradition, 1985; (with Richard Neave) Making Faces Using the Forensic and Archaeological Evidence, 1997; (ed jtly) Periplous: papers on classical art and archaeology, 2000; (with J. Swaddling) Seianti Hanunia Tlesnasa: the story of an Etruscan noblewoman, 2002; (with Simon Timberlake) The Archaeology of Alderley Edge, 2005; Living with the Edge: Alderley's story, 2015; articles on Greek art and archaeology in learned jls. *Recreations:* travel, cooking, music. *Address:* Manchester Museum, The University, Manchester M13 9PL. *T:* (0161) 275 2665. *E:* john.prag@manchester.ac.uk.
See also T. G. A. Prag.

PRAG, Thomas Gregory Andrew; Chairman, Media Support Partnership, since 2001; Director, iMedia Associates, since 2012; *b* 2 Jan. 1947; *s* of late Adolf Prag and Frede Charlotte Prag (*née* Warburg); *m* 1970, Angela Hughes; three *s*. *Educ:* Westminster Sch.; Brasenose Coll., Oxford (MA PPE). Producer/presenter, BBC Radio Oxford, 1970–78; Prog. Organiser, BBC Highland, 1978–81; Man. Dir, 1981–2000, Chm., 2000–01, Moray Firth Radio; Mem. for Scotland, Radio Authority, 2001–03; Mem., Scottish Adv. Cttee, Ofcom, 2004–12 (Chm., 2006–08). Pres., Inverness Chamber of Commerce, 1996–98; Member, Board: Inverness Harbour Trust, 2003–13 (Vice-Chm. 2009–13); Inverness Airport Business Park, 2012–. Mem. Bd, Assoc. of Ind. Radio Contractors, subseq. Commercial Radio Cos Assoc., 1993–2000. Dir, 1993–2004, Chm., 2002–04, Highland Fest. Mem. Court (formerly Bd Governors), UHI (formerly UHI Millennium Inst.), 2002–13; Chm., UHI Millennium Inst. Develt Trust, 2004–07; Vice-Chairman: Highland Opportunity Ltd, 2012–; Highlands and Islands Transport Partnership, 2014–. Mem. (Lib Dem), Highland Council, 2007– (Chm., Planning Envmt and Develt, later Planning, Develt and Infrastructure, 2012–). Gov., Eden Court Theatre, 2007–. FCMI (FBIM 1978); FRA 1998. Hon Fellow, UHI, 2014. *Recreations:* wife and family, acquiring old things - clocks, radios, etc, 1950 Convertible Daimler, casual gardener, sculler and cox, music, travel, Founder member of Truly Terrible Orchestra. *Address:* Windrush, Easter Muckovie, Inverness IV2 5BN. *E:* thomas@prags.co.uk. *Club:* Inverness Rotary (Pres., 2004–05).
See also A. J. N. W. Prag.

PRAGNELL, Michael Patrick; Chairman and Trustee, Cancer Research UK, since 2010; *b* Hindhead, Surrey, 19 Dec. 1946; *s* of George Pragnell and Margaret Pragnell (*née* Lowry); *m* 1983, Susan Williams; two *s*. *Educ:* Douai Sch.; St John's Coll., Oxford (MA); INSEAD (MBA). Courtaulds plc, 1975–95: CEO, Coatings, 1986–92; Dir, 1990–95; Chief Financial Officer, 1992–94; CEO, Zeneca Agrochemicals, 1995–2000, Dir, 1997–2000, Zeneca, later AstraZeneca plc; Founder CEO and Dir, Syngenta AG, Switzerland, 2000–07. Mem., Supervisory Bd, Advanta BV, 1996–2000; non-executive Director: D. S. Smith plc, 1996–2000; VINCI SA, Paris, 2009–. Pres., CropLife Internat., 2002–05. Mem., Swiss-American Bd, Chamber of Commerce, 2005–07. Mem. Bd, INSEAD, 2009–. *Recreations:* skiing, walking, shooting, theatre, opera, music, modern art, travel. *Address:* Cancer Research UK, Angel Building, 407 St John Street, EC1V 4AD. *T:* (020) 3469 8177. *E:* michael.pragnell@cancer.org.uk.

PRANCE, Sir Ghillean (Tolmie), Kt 1995; DPhil; FRS 1993; FLS, FRSB; FRGS; VMH; Scientific Director, Eden Project, Cornwall, 1999–2013; *b* 13 July 1937; *s* of Basil Camden Prance, CIE, OBE and Margaret Hope Prance (*née* Tolmie); *m* 1961, Anne Elizabeth Hay; two *d*. *Educ:* Malvern Coll.; Keble Coll., Oxford (BA, MA, DPhil). FLS 1961; FRSB (FIBiol 1988). New York Botanical Garden: Res. Asst, 1963–66; Associate Curator, 1966–68; B. A. Krukoff Curator of Amazonian Botany, 1968–75; Dir of Research, 1975–81; Vice-Pres., 1977–81; Senior Vice-Pres., 1981–88; Dir, Royal Botanic Gdns, Kew, 1988–99. Adjunct Prof., City Univ. of NY, 1968–99; Vis. Prof. in Tropical Studies, Yale, 1983–89; Vis. Prof., Reading Univ., 1988–; McBryde Prof., 2000–02, McBryde Sen. Res. Fellow, 2006–, Nat. Tropical Botanical Gdn, Kalaheo, Hawaii; Dir of Graduate Studies, Instituto Nacional de Pesquisas da Amazônia, Manaus, Brazil, 1973–75; 29 botanical expedns to Amazonia. President: Assoc. of Tropical Biol., 1979–80 (Hon. Fellow, 2007); Amer. Assoc. of Plant Taxonomists, 1984–85; Systematics Assoc., 1989–91; Econ. Botany Soc., 1996–97; Linnean Soc., 1997–2000; Internat. Assoc. for Plant Taxonomy, 1999–2005; Inst. of Biology, 2000–02; Internat. Tree Foundn, 2005–; Chm., MEMO Project, 2006–. Mem. Council, RHS, 1990–2000. Chm., A Rocha Internat., 2008–12; Trustee, Eden Project, 2009–. FRGS 1989; Fellow: AAAS, 1990; Perak Acad., 2006; Corresponding Member: Brazilian Acad. of Scis, 1976; Botanical Soc. of America, 1994; Foreign Member: Royal Danish Acad. of Scis and Letters, 1988; Royal Swedish Acad. of Scis, 1989; Associate Mem., Third World Acad. of Scis, 1993; Hon. Mem., British Ecol Soc., 1996. Hon. Freeman, Gardeners' Co., 1997. Fil Dr *hc* Univ. Göteborgs, Sweden, 1983; Hon. DSc: Kent, Portsmouth, Kingston, 1994; St Andrews, 1995; Bergen Univ., Norway, 1996; Florida Internat. Univ., Herbert H. Lehman Coll., NY, and Sheffield Univ., 1997; Liverpool, 1998; Glasgow, Plymouth, 1999; Keele, Exeter, 2000; Gloucestershire, 2009. Henry Shaw Medal, Missouri Botanical Garden, St Louis, 1988; Linnean Medal, 1990; Internat. Cosmos Prize, Japan, 1993; Patron's Medal, RGS, 1994; Janaki Ammal Medal, Soc. of Ethnobotany, 1996; Internat. Award of Excellence,

Botanical Res. Inst., Texas, 1998; Medalho do Mérito, Jardim Botânico, Rio de Janeiro, 1998; VMH 1999; Lifetime of Discovery Award, Discovery Channel and RGS, 1999; Fairchild Medal for Plant Exploration, Nat. Tropical Botanical Gdn, 2000; Dist. Econ. Botanist Award, Soc. of Econ. Botany, 2002; Graziela Maciel Barroso Prize, Botanical Soc. of Brazil, 2004; Allerton Award, Nat. Tropical Botanical Gdn, 2005; Gold Medal, New York Botanical Gdn, 2008. Ordem Nacional do Mérito Científico-Grã-Cruz (Brazil), 1995; Comendador da Ordem Nacional do Cruzeiro do Sul (Brazil), 2000; Order of the Rising Sun (Japan), 2012. *Publications:* Arvores de Manaus, 1975; Algumas Flores da Amazonia, 1976; Extinction is Forever, 1977; Biological Diversification in the Tropics, 1981; Amazonia: key environments, 1985; Leaves, 1986; Manual de Botânica Econômica do Maranhão, 1988; Flowers for all Seasons, 1989; Out of the Amazon, 1992; Bark, 1993; The Earth Under Threat: a Christian perspective, 1996; Rainforests: water, fire, earth and air, 1997; Chrysobalanaceae of the World, 2003; Rainforest: light and spirit, 2008; Go to the Ant, 2013; That Glorious Forest, 2014. *Recreations:* flower stamp collecting, bird watching. *Address:* The Old Vicarage, Silver Street, Lyme Regis, Dorset DT7 3HS. *T:* (01297) 444991. *E:* siriain01@yahoo.co.uk. *Club:* Explorers (New York) (Fellow).

PRANKERD, Thomas Arthur John, FRCP; Professor of Clinical Haematology, 1965–79 and Dean, 1972–77, University College Hospital Medical School; Hon. Consultant Physician: University College Hospital; Whittington Hospital; *b* 11 Sept. 1924; *s* of late H. A. Prankerd, Barrister-at-Law, and J. D. Shorthose; *m* 1950, Margaret Vera Harrison Cripps (decd); two *s* (and one *s* one *d* decd). *Educ:* Charterhouse Sch.; St Bartholomew's Hospital Med. Sch. MD (London) Gold Medal 1949; FRCP 1962. Jr med. appts, St Bart's and University Coll. Hosp., 1947–60. Major, RAMC, 1948–50. Univ. Travelling Fellow, USA, 1953–54; Consultant Physician, University Coll. Hosp., 1960–65. Examr, RCP, and various univs. Goulstonian Lectr, RCP, 1963; Visiting Professor: Univ. of Perth, WA, 1972; Univ. of Cape Town, 1973. Mem., NE Thames RHA, 1976–79. Mem. Bd of Governors, UCH, 1972–74. Mem., Assoc. of Physicians, 1965. *Publications:* The Red Cell, 1961; Haematology in Medical Practice, 1968; articles in med. jls. *Recreations:* fishing, gardening, music. *Address:* 6 Stinsford House, Stinsford, Dorchester DT2 8PT. *T:* (01305) 751521.

PRASAD, Dr Sunand, RIBA; Senior Partner, Penoyre & Prasad Architects, since 1988; President, Royal Institute of British Architects, 2007–09 (Member, Council, 2004–10); *b* 22 May 1950; *s* of Devi and Janaki Prasad; *m* 1982, Susan Francis; three *s*. *Educ:* Univ. of Cambridge Sch. of Architecture (MA); Architectural Assoc. (AA Dip.); PhD RCA 1988. RIBA 1987. Partner, Edward Cullinan Architects, 1978–84; Leverhulme Res. Fellow, RCA, 1985–88. Comr, Commn for Architecture and the Built Envmt, 1999–2006; Mem., Green Construction Bd, 2011–. Member: Awards Gp, 1995–2000, Practice Cttee, 1999–2002, RIBA; Council, AA, 1997–2001; London Mayor's Design Adv. Panel, 2008–. Presenter, The Essay: Architecture, The Fourth R, BBC Radio 3, 2010. Trustee: Article 25, 2008–12; Centre for Cities, 2010–; Cape Farewell, 2011–. FRSA. Hon. Member: AIA 2008; RTPI 2009. Hon. FRIAS 2008; Hon. FRAIC 2010. Hon. DA UEL. *Publications:* contributor to: Le Corbusier: architect of the century, 1987; Paradigms of Indian Architecture, 1998; Macmillan Dictionary of Art, 1997; Design Quality, 2002; London: postcolonial city, 2002; Transformations: the architecture of Penoyre & Prasad, 2007; Changing Hospital Architecture, 2008; Retrofit for Purpose, 2014. *Recreations:* music, sailboarding. *Address:* Penoyre & Prasad Architects, 28–42 Banner Street, EC1Y 8QE. *T:* (020) 7250 3477, *Fax:* (020) 7250 0844. *E:* mail@penoyreprasad.com.

PRASHAR, Baroness *cr* 1999 (Life Peer), of Runnymede in the county of Surrey; **Usha Kumari Prashar,** CBE 1995; PC 2009; Chairman, Judicial Appointments Commission, 2006–10; Deputy Chairman, British Council, since 2012; Member, Iraq Inquiry, since 2009; *b* 29 June 1948; *d* of Nauhria Lal Prashar and Durga Devi Prashar; *m* 1973, Vijay Kumar Sharma. *Educ:* Duchess of Gloucester Sch., Nairobi; Wakefield Girls' High Sch. (Head Girl, 1966–67); Univ. of Leeds (BA Hons Pol Studies); Univ. of Glasgow (postgrad. Dip. Social Admin). Race Relations Bd, 1971–76; Asst Dir, Runnymede Trust, 1976–77, Dir, 1976–84; Res. Fellow, PSI, 1984–86; Dir, NCVO, 1986–91; Dep. Chm., 1992–2000, Chm., 2000–05, Nat. Literacy Trust. CS Comr (part-time), 1990–96; Chm., Parole Bd, 1997–2000; First CS Comr, 2000–05. Non-executive Director: Channel 4, 1992–99; Unite plc, 2001–04; ITV, 2005–10. Vice-Chm., British Refugee Council, 1987–89. Member: Arts Council of GB, 1979–81, Arts Council of England, 1994–97; Study Commn on the Family, 1980–83; Social Security Adv. Cttee, 1980–83; Exec. Cttee, Child Poverty Action Gp, 1984–85; GLAA, 1984–86; London Food Commn, 1984–90; BBC Educnl Broadcasting Council, 1987–89; Adv. Council, Open College, 1987–89; Solicitors' Complaints Bureau, 1989–90; Royal Commn on Criminal Justice, 1991–93; Lord Chancellor's Adv. Cttee on Legal Educn and Conduct, 1991–97; Council, PSI, 1992–97; Bd, Energy Saving Trust, 1992–98; King's Fund, 1998–2002. President: UK Council for Internat. Student Affairs, 2006–; Community Foundn Network, 2007–; Hon. Vice-Pres., Council for Overseas Student Affairs, 1986–98. Trustee: Thames Help Trust, 1984–86; Charities Aid Foundn, 1986–91; Independent Broadcasting Telethon Trust, 1987–92; Acad. of Indian Dance, 1987–91; Camelot Foundn, 1996–2001; Ethnic Minority Foundn, 1997–2002; BBC World Service Trust, 2001–05; Miriam Rothschild and John Foster Trust, 2007–10; Cumberland Lodge, 2007–; Chm., English Adv. Cttee, Nat. AIDS Trust, 1988–89; Gov., Ditchley Foundn, 2003–; Patron, Runnymede Trust, 2008–. Chancellor, De Montfort Univ., 2000–06 (Gov., 1996–2006). Trustee, 2001–11, Chm., 2001–08, Pres., 2008–11, Royal Commonwealth Soc. FRSA. Hon. Fellow, Goldsmiths' Coll., Univ. of London, 1992; Hon. Bencher, Inner Temple, 2012. Hon. LLD: De Montfort, 1994; South Bank Univ., 1994; Greenwich, 1999; Leeds Metropolitan, 1999; Ulster, 2000; Oxford Brookes, 2000; Hon. Dr: Leeds; Glasgow; Exeter; Aston. *Publications: contributed to:* Britain's Black Population, 1980; The System: a study of Lambeth Borough Council's race relations unit, 1981; Scarman and After, 1984; Sickle Cell Anaemia, Who Cares? a survey of screening, counselling, training and educational facilities in England, 1985; Routes or Road Blocks, a study of consultation arrangements between local authorities and local communities, 1985; Acheson and After: primary health care in the inner city, 1986. *Recreations:* reading, country walks, music, golf, international affairs. *Address:* House of Lords, SW1A 0PW.

PRAT, Prof. Andrea, PhD; FBA 2011; Richard Paul Richman Professor of Business, Columbia Business School, and Professor of Economics, Columbia University, New York, since 2012. *Educ:* Turin Univ. (Laurea in Economia e Commercio 1992); Stanford Univ. (PhD 1997). Fellow, Compagnia di San Paolo, Italy, 1992–94; Res. Asst, Stanford Univ., 1995–96; Marie Curie Fellow, EC, 1997–99; Asst Prof., Tilburg Univ., 1997–2000; Lectr, 2000–02, Reader, 2002–04, Prof. of Econs, 2004–13, Dept of Econs, LSE; Co-Dir, Prog. for Study of Econ. Orgn and Public Policy, Suntory and Toyota Internat. Centres for Econs and Related Disciplines, 2004–12. Man. Ed., 2005–09, Chair, 2010–13, Rev. of Econ. Studies; Associate Ed., Theoretical Econs, 2007–. Mem. Council, REconS. *Publications:* (contrib.) Oxford Handbook of Political Economy, 2006; (ed jtly) The Ruling Class: management and politics in modern Italy, 2010; contribs to Jl Finance, Rev. of Financial Studies, Jl Econ. Theory, Qly Jl Pol Sci., Econometrica, Jl Public Econs. *Address:* Graduate School of Business, Columbia University, 3022 Broadway, Uris 624, New York, NY 10027–6902, USA.

PRATLEY, Alan Sawyer; Deputy Financial Controller, Commission of the European Communities, 1990–98 (Director, Financial Control, 1986–90); *b* 25 Nov. 1933; *s* of Frederick Pratley and Hannah Pratley (*née* Sawyer); *m* 1st, 1960, Dorothea Rohland (marr. diss. 1979); two *d*; 2nd, 1979, Josette Kairis (marr. diss. 1994); one *d*; 3rd, 1996, Marie-Hélène Ledivelec. *Educ:* Latymer Upper School; Sidney Sussex Coll., Cambridge (BA Modern Languages (German, Russian)). Head, German Dept, Stratford Grammar Sch., West Ham, 1958–60; Asst Dir, Examinations, Civil Service Commn, 1960–68; Home Office, 1968–73; Commission of the European Communities: Head, Individual Rights Div., 1973–79; Dep. Chef de Cabinet to Christopher Tugendhat, 1979–80; Adviser to Michael O'Kennedy, 1980–81; Dir of Admin, 1981–86. *Recreations:* tennis, gardening. *Address:* 18 Avenue de l'Armée, 1040 Brussels, Belgium. *T:* and *Fax:* (2) 7352483. *E:* alan.pratley@skynet.be.

PRATLEY, David Illingworth; Principal, David Pratley Associates, 1996; *b* 24 Dec. 1948; *s* of Arthur George Pratley and Olive Constance Illingworth; *m* 1st, 1996, Caryn Faure Walker (*née* Becker) (*d* 2004); 2nd, 2008, Diane Linda Fredericks (*née* Cane). *Educ:* Westminster Abbey Choir Sch.; Westminster Sch.; Univ. of Bristol (LLB). PRO, Thorndike Theatre, Leatherhead, 1970–71; Gen. Asst, Queen's Univ. Festival, Belfast, 1971–73; Dep. Dir, Merseyside Arts Assoc., 1973–76; Dir, Greater London Arts Assoc., 1976–81; Regl Dir, Arts Council of GB, 1981–86; Chief Exec., Royal Liverpool Philharmonic Soc., 1987–88; Man. Dir, Trinity Coll. of Music, 1988–91; Dir of Leisure, Tourism and Econ. Develt, Bath CC, 1992–96. Chm., Alliance Arts Panel, 1987–88; Council Mem., Nat. Campaign for the Arts, 1986–92 (Chm., 1988–92); Dir, Dance Umbrella Ltd, 1986– (Chm., 1990–92). Lottery Policy Advr, Arts Council England (formerly Arts Council of England), 1996–. Trustee, Sainsbury Internat. Arts Festival, 2009–. Chairman: Poole Arts Trust, 2009–; Poole Lighthouse, 2009–; Wilts Music Centre, 2009–15. FRSA. *Recreations:* music, theatre and film, art, design and architecture, photography, gardens, sailing, walking, travel. *Address:* 5 Little Burn, Sway, Hampshire SO41 6DZ.

PRATT, family name of **Marquess Camden**.

PRATT, (Richard) Camden; QC 1992; a Recorder, 1993–2013; a Deputy High Court Judge (Family Division), 1995–2013; *b* 14 Dec. 1947; *s* of late Richard Sheldon Pratt, MA Oxon, and Irene Gladys Pratt; *m* 1973, (Dorothy Jane) Marchia, *d* of late Capt. W. P. and Aphrodite Allsebrook. *Educ:* Boston Grammar Sch.; Westcliff High Sch.; Lincoln Coll., Oxford (Hanbury Law Scholar; MA Jurisp). Called to the Bar, Gray's Inn, 1970, Bencher, 2002. Chairman: Sussex Courts Liaison Cttee, 1993–2009; Sussex Sessions Bar Mess, 1994–2006; Mem., Area Criminal Justice Liaison Cttee, 1994–2002. *Recreations:* walking, sailing, travel, people. *E:* camdenprattqc@btinternet.com.

PRATT, Richard Charles; JP; regulatory consultant; *b* 3 Nov. 1949; *s* of Charles Pratt and Rosemary Pratt (*née* Robson); *m* 1974, Christine Whiteman; one *s*. *Educ:* Eltham Coll.; Bristol Univ. (BSc Politics and Econs 1972); Sch. of Oriental and African Studies, London Univ. (MA 1973). Joined Civil Service, 1973; Press Officer, Prime Minister's Office, 1975–76; Asst Private Sec., Lord Privy Seal's Office, 1976; Head of Pay Negotiations Br., CSD, 1977–80; Head of Special Employment Measures Br., Dept of Employment, 1980–82; HM Treasury: Head of NI Public Expenditure Br., 1982–84; Mem., Central Unit for UK Budget, 1984–86; Head of Gen. Expenditure Div., 1986–87; Economic Counsellor, Washington, 1987–90 (on secondment); Head, EC Div. (EMU and Trade Policy), 1990–93; Advr to Sec. of State for Social Services on Expenditure Review, DSS, 1993; Head of Securities and Mkts Div., HM Treasury, 1993–95; Dir of External Affairs, LIFFE, 1995–98; Dir Gen., Jersey Financial Services Commn, 1999–2003. Ombudsman for KPMG, 2004–; Special Advr, RSM Robson Rhodes, 2004–06; Director: UK Financial Services Compensation Scheme, 2004–09; Look Ahead Care and Support (formerly Look Ahead Housing), 2008–14. Chm., Friends of Urambo and Mwanhala, 2014–. JP Stratford, 2009. *Publications:* (ed) How to Combat Money Laundering and Terrorist Financing, 2005; (ed) Working Together: international cooperation between financial services regulators, 2007. *Recreations:* flying, travelling. *Address:* Redwoods, Ridgeway, Horsell, Surrey GU21 4QR.

PRATT, Ven. Dr Richard David; Archdeacon of West Cumberland, since 2009; *b* Cheltenham, 25 Dec. 1955; *s* of Kenneth Pratt and Margaret Pratt; *m* 1983, Diane Tomlinson; three *s*. *Educ:* Ranelagh Sch., Bracknell; Lincoln Coll., Oxford (Exhibnr; MA 1980); Lincoln Theol Coll. and Univ. of Nottingham (BCS 1984); Univ. of Birmingham (PhD 2001). Pt-time Porter, Broadmoor Hosp., 1972–74; VSO, Ghana Secondary Sch., Tamale, Ghana, 1977–79; Systems Analyst, Perkins Engines, Peterborough, 1979–81; ordained deacon, 1984, priest, 1985; Asst Curate, All Hallows, Wellingborough, 1984–87; Team Vicar, St Mark's, Kingsthorpe, 1987–92; Vicar, St Benedict's, Hunsbury, 1992–97; Priest-in-charge, St Cuthbert's, Carlisle, 1997–2008; Communications Officer, Dio. of Carlisle, 1997–2008. *Publications:* contribs to jls incl. Christian Community, Theology. *Recreations:* walking the Lakeland Fells, growing vegetables, the music of Bach. *Address:* 50 Stainburn Road, Workington, Cumbria CA14 1SN. *T:* (01900) 66190. *E:* richard.pratt@lincoln.oxon.org. *W:* www.pratt.org.

PRATT, Richard James; QC 2006; a Recorder, since 2000; *b* 22 June 1956; *s* of Gordon Francis Pratt and Audrey Pratt (*née* Upton-Prowse); *m* 1987, Kim Lorraine Emmerson; two *d*. *Educ:* St Mary's Coll., Crosby, Liverpool; Lanchester Poly., Coventry (BA Hons 1978). Called to the Bar, Gray's Inn, 1980, Bencher, 2010; in practice as barrister, 7 Harrington Street, Liverpool; Asst Recorder, 1997–2000; Leader, Northern Circuit, 2011–13. *Recreations:* watching Everton Football Club and old films, listening to music, practising ventriloquism. *Address:* 7 Harrington Street, Liverpool L2 9YH. *T:* (0151) 242 0707, *Fax:* (0151) 236 1120. *E:* Rickpratt2@aol.com. *Club:* John Mc's (Liverpool).

PRATT, Prof. Robert John, CBE 2003; FRCN; Professor of Nursing and Director, Richard Wells Research Centre, Thames Valley University, 1994–2010, now Emeritus Professor; *b* 27 June 1941; *s* of Loren Delbert Pratt and Mary Jane Stubbs, and step *s* of Leonard William Paulson. *Educ:* Univ. of London (DN 1974); New Coll. of Calif, San Francisco (BA (Humanities) 1981); Chelsea Coll., London (MSc (Health Educn) 1984). Served US Navy, Hospital Corpsman, Fleet Marine Force, 1959–63. Various nursing appts, USA and UK, 1964–71; Charge Nurse, Charing Cross Hosp., 1971–76; Hd, Dept of Professional and Vocational Studies, Charing Cross Hosp. Sch. of Nursing, 1978–86; Vice Principal, Riverside Coll. of Health Studies, London, 1986–94. Pres., Infection Control Nurses Assoc. of British Isles, 2000–06; Patron, UK Nat. HIV Nurses Assoc., 1999–. FRCN 1999; FHEA 2007; FRSA 2006. *Publications:* HIV & AIDS: a foundation for nursing and healthcare practice, 1986, 5th edn 2003; (jtly) Tuberculosis: a foundation for nursing and healthcare practice, 2005; frequent articles in a variety of nursing and med. peer-reviewed jls. *Recreations:* theatre, cinema, travel, reading. *Address:* Richard Wells Research Centre, University of West London, Paragon House, Boston Manor Road, Brentford, Middx TW8 9GA. *E:* robert.pratt5@btopenworld.com.

PRATT, Roger Allan, CBE 1996; Director, Welsh Conservative Party, since 2012; *b* 28 Dec. 1950; *s* of late Allan Pratt and Joyce Isobel Pratt (*née* Dodds); *m* 1st, 1975, Ann Heaton (marr. diss. 1993; she *d* 2010); one *s* one *d*; 2nd, 1993, Lynn Mary Tomlinson (marr. diss. 2011); one step *s* one step *d*; 3rd, 2014, Jane Thomas; two step *s* one step *d*. *Educ:* King Edward's Fiveways Sch., Birmingham. Organiser, E Midlands Area YC, 1971–72; NW Area Youth Develt Officer, 1972–74; Agent, Liverpool Wavertree Cons. Assoc., 1975–76; Nat. YC Organiser, 1976–79; Agent, Pendle, Burnley and Hyndburn Cons. Assocs, 1980–84; North West Area, then NW Region: Dep. Central Office Agent, 1984–89; Central Office Agent, 1989–93; Regl Dir, 1993; Dir, Cons. Pty in Scotland, 1993–97; Conservative Central Office: Dep. Dir, Campaigning Dept, 1997–98; Area Campaign Dir, London Western, and Regl Eur. Campaign Dir for London, 1998–2000; Dep. Dir of Ops, 2004; Boundary Rev. Project Dir, 2000–05, Dep. Dir of Campaigning, 2005–07, Cons. Campaign HQ; Acting Sec., Nat. Cons. Convention, 2005–07; Regl Dir, SW Conservatives, 2008–10; Boundary Rev. Manager,

2010–12. *Recreation:* cricket. *Address:* Welsh Conservative Party, Ground Floor, Rhymney House, Copse Walk, Cardiff Gate Business Park, Cardiff CF23 8RB.

PRATT, His Honour Simon; a Circuit Judge, 1995–2012; *b* 23 June 1949; *s* of Harry James Roffey Pratt and Ann Loveday Pratt (*née* Peter); *m* 1974, Sheena Maynard; one *s* one *d.* Called to the Bar, Inner Temple, 1971; a Recorder, SE Circuit, 1989–95. Freeman, City of London, 1984. *Recreation:* dwindling. *Address:* 3 Temple Gardens, Temple, EC4Y 9AU. *T:* (020) 7353 3102.

PREBBLE, David Lawrence; Master, Queen's Bench Division, Supreme Court of Justice, 1981–2001; *b* 21 Aug. 1932; *s* of late George Wilson Prebble and Margaret Jessie Prebble (*née* Cuthbertson); *m* 1959, Fiona W. Melville; three *d. Educ:* Cranleigh; Christ Church, Oxford. MA. National Service, 1950–52; commissioned in 3rd Carabiniers (Prince of Wales's Dragoon Guards); served TA, 1952–61, City of London Yeomanry (Rough Riders) TA (Captain). Called to the Bar, Middle Temple, 1957; practised at Bar, 1957–81. *Recreations:* reading; operetta; hounds and dogs; friends' horses; own wife and family; (not necessarily in foregoing order as to precedence). *Address:* Clunie Beag, Taybridge Road, Aberfeldy, Perthshire PH15 2BH. *T:* (01887) 820060.

PREBBLE, Stuart Colin; Director, StoryVault Ltd and Chairman, StoryVault Films, since 2010; *b* 15 April 1951; *s* of Dennis Stanley Prebble and Jean Margaret Prebble; *m* 1978, Marilyn Anne Charlton; one *d* (and one *d* decd). *Educ:* Univ. of Newcastle upon Tyne (BA Hons English Lang. and Lit.). Reporter, BBC TV News, 1975–80; Presenter, Granada TV, 1981; Producer, 1983–88, Editor, 1988–89, World in Action; Head of Regl Progs, Granada, 1989–90; Man. Dir, North East TV, 1990–91; Head of Factual Progs, Granada, 1992; Controller, ITV Network Factual Progs, 1993–96; Chief Exec., Granada Sky Broadcasting, 1996–98; Man. Dir, Channels and Interactive Media, Granada Media Gp, 1999; Chief Executive: ONdigital, subseq. ITV Digital, 1999–2002; ITV Network, 2001–02; Man. Dir, Liberty Bell Ltd, 2002–10 (Jt Man. Dir, 2002–05). *Publications:* A Power in the Land, 1988; The Lazarus File, 1989; The Official Grumpy Old Men Handbook, 2004; Grumpy Old Men: the secret diary, 2005; Grumpy Old Christmas, 2006; Grumpy Old Workers, 2007; Grumpy Old Drivers, 2008; Secrets of the Conqueror, 2011; The Insect Farm, 2015. *Recreations:* walking, cinema, music.

PREBENSEN, Preben; Chief Executive, Close Brothers Group plc, since 2009; *b* London, 19 Nov. 1956; *s* of Peter and Else Prebensen; *m* 1983, Annie Whitehead; three *s* one *d. Educ:* St Paul's Sch., London; Magdalene Coll., Cambridge (BA Hist. 1978). J. P. Morgan, later JP Morgan Chase: UK Corporate Finance, 1978–84; US Capital Mkts, 1984–91; Head, UK, Scandinavia and Holland, 1991–2001; Co-Head, Eur. Investment Banking, Chm., London Mgt Cttee and Mem., Global Investment Banking Cttee, 1996–2000; investment consultant, 2001–04; Chief Exec., Wellington Underwriting plc, 2004–06; Chief Investment Officer, Catlin Gp Ltd, 2006–09. *Recreations:* theatre, forestry, farming. *Address:* Close Brothers Group plc, 10 Crown Place, EC2A 4FT. *T:* (020) 7655 3100.

PREECE, Prof. Michael Andrew, MD; FRCP, FRCPCH; Professor of Child Health and Growth, Institute of Child Health, University College London, 1985–2007, now Emeritus; Medical Director, Great Ormond Street Hospital for Children, 2005–07; *b* 11 May 1944; *s* of Roy and Norah Preece; *m* 1977, Jan Baines; one *s. Educ:* Guy's Hosp. Med. Sch., Univ. of London (MB BS 1967; MD 1976; MSc 1977). FRCP 1982; FRCPCH 1997. Institute of Child Health, London University: Lectr In Growth and Develt, 1974–77; Sen. Lectr, 1977–83; Reader in Child Health and Growth, 1983–85. Visiting Professor: RPMS, later ICSM, 1994–2005; Hosp. for Sick Children, Univ. of Toronto, 2003; Lectures: Teale, RCP, 1990; Gaisford, Manchester Med. Soc., 1994. Mem., Selection Panel, Snowdon Trust. Guthrie Medal, British Paediatric Assoc., 1980. *Publications:* (with J. M. Tanner) The Physiology of Human Growth, 1989; (jtly) The Cambridge Encyclopaedia of Human Growth and Development, 1998; (jtly) Neoplasia: growth and growth hormone treatment, 2004. *Recreations:* nature photography, theatre, sport (mostly watching nowadays). *E:* m.preece@ucl.ac.uk.

PREISS, Prof. David, FRS 2004; Professor of Mathematics, University of Warwick, since 2006; *b* 21 Jan. 1947; *s* of Alfred and Marta Preiss; *m* 1977, Irena; one *d. Educ:* Charles Univ., Prague (RNDr (Dr of Natural Sci.) 1970; Candidate of Sci. 1979). Various posts, Charles Univ., Prague, 1970–89; Astor Prof. of Maths, UCL, 1990–2006. Vis. posts at univs in Jerusalem, Palermo, Santa Barbara and Vancouver. (Jtly) Ostrowski Prize, 2011. *Publications:* Fréchet Differentiability of Lipschitz Functions and Porous Sets in Banach Spaces (jtly), 2012; res. papers, chiefly in mathematical analysis, in scientific jls. *Address:* Mathematics Institute, University of Warwick, Coventry CV4 7AL. *E:* d.preiss@warwick.ac.uk.

PRENDERGAST, Prof. Christopher Alan Joseph, PhD; FBA 1996; Fellow, King's College, Cambridge, since 1970; Professor of Modern French Literature, Cambridge University, 1997–2003, now Professor Emeritus; *b* 27 Sept. 1942; *s* of James Prendergast and Celia (*née* Sevitt); *m* 1st, 1965, Shirley Busbridge (marr. diss. 1979); two *d*; 2nd, 1997, Inge Birgitte Siegumfeldt (marr. diss. 2008); one *d. Educ:* Keble Coll., Oxford (BA 1965; BPhil 1967); MA 1968, PhD 1989, Cantab. Lectr, Pembroke Coll., Oxford, 1967–68; Fellow, Downing Coll., Cambridge, 1968–70; Univ. Lectr, Cambridge Univ., 1968–89; Distinguished Prof. in French and Comparative Lit., Grad. Sch., CUNY, 1989–92; Reader in Modern French Lit., Cambridge Univ., 1992–97. Vis. Prof., 1998–2000, Hon. Prof., 2004, Univ. of Copenhagen, Denmark. *Publications:* Balzac: fiction and melodrama, 1978; The Order of Mimesis, 1986; (ed) Nineteenth-Century French Poetry, 1990; Paris and the Nineteenth Century, 1992; (ed jtly) Anthology of World Literature, 1994; (ed) Cultural Materialism, 1996; Napoleon and History Painting, 1997; The Triangle of Representation, 2000; (ed) Proust, In Search of Lost Time, 6 vols, 2002; (ed) Debating World Literature, 2004; The Classic: Sainte-Beuve and the nineteenth-century culture wars, 2007; The Fourteenth of July: and the taking of the Bastille, 2008. *Recreations:* gardening, cooking, opera. *Address:* 26 Bermuda Road, Cambridge CB4 3JX.

PRENDERGAST, Sir Kieran; *see* Prendergast, Sir W. K.

PRENDERGAST, His Honour Robert James Christie; a Circuit Judge, 1989–2006; *b* 21 Oct. 1941; *s* of Richard Henry Prendergast and Jean (*née* Christie); *m* 1971, Berit, (Bibi), Thauland; one *d. Educ:* Downside; Trinity Coll., Cambridge (BA (Hons) Law; MA); Cert. of Higher Educn (Hist. of Architecture), London Univ., 2010. Called to the Bar, Middle Temple, 1964; Harmsworth Law Schol.; S Eastern Circuit, 1964–89; an Asst Recorder, 1984–87; a Recorder, 1987–89. Pres., St Gregory's Soc., 1999–2002. *Recreations:* most gentle pursuits. *Address:* c/o 5 King's Bench Walk, Temple, EC4Y 7DN.

PRENDERGAST, Sir (Walter) Kieran, KCVO 1991; CMG 1990; HM Diplomatic Service, retired; Under-Secretary-General for Political Affairs, United Nations, New York, 1997–2005; *b* 2 July 1942; *s* of late Lt-Comdr J. H. Prendergast and Mai Hennessy; *m* 1967, Joan Reynolds; two *s* two *d. Educ:* St Patrick's College, Strathfield, Sydney, NSW; Salesian College, Chertsey; St Edmund Hall, Oxford. Turkish language student Istanbul, 1964; Ankara, 1965; FO (later FCO), 1967; 2nd Sec. Nicosia, 1969; 1st Sec. FCO, 1972; The Hague, 1973; Asst Private Sec. to Foreign and Commonwealth Sec. (Rt Hon. Anthony Crosland, Rt Hon. Dr David Owen), 1976; UK Mission to UN, NY, 1979 (detached for duty Jan.–March 1980 at Govt House, Salisbury); Counsellor, Tel Aviv, 1982–86; Head of Southern African Dept, FCO, 1986–89; High Comr to Zimbabwe, 1989–92; High Comr to Kenya, 1992–95; Ambassador to Turkey, 1995–97. Sen. Advr, Centre for Humanitarian Dialogue, Geneva, 2006–. Member: Internat. Adv. Bd, Independent Diplomat, 2007–; Adv. Bd, Albany Associates, 2012–; Counsellor, Dragoman Global, 2013–. Chm., Anglo-Turkish Soc., 2009–; Counsellor, ESU. Trustee, Beit Trust, 2009–. Rhodesia Medal, 1980; Zimbabwe Independence Medal, 1980. *Recreations:* family, wine, walking, reading. *Address:* Swallow Brook Barn, Weston, Pembridge HR6 9JE; 333 Milkwood Road, SE24 0HA; Bonneval, La Chapelle-aux-Saints, Beaulieu-sur-Dordogne 19120, France. *T:* (555) 912960. *E:* prendergast@hdcentre.org. *Clubs:* Beefsteak, Garrick.

PRENN, Helen Gillian; *see* Robinson, H. G.

PRENTER, Patrick Robert, CBE 1995; Chairman, Mactaggart Scott Holdings, Loanhead, Midlothian, since 1991; Lord-Lieutenant for Midlothian, 2003–13; *b* 9 Sept. 1939; *s* of Robert Gibson Prenter, OBE and Katherine Emily Prenter (*née* Scott); *m* 1962, Susan, *d* of Francis Patrick, OBE and Isabel Patrick (*née* Spencer); two *s* two *d. Educ:* Loretto Sch., Musselburgh; Trinity Hall, Cambridge (BA Mech. Scis 1962). Man. Dir, 1967–99, Chm., 1991–2004, Mactaggart Scott & Co. Ltd. Tax Comr, 1985–2003. Dir, 1984–91, Vice Chm., 1990–91, Forth Ports Authy. Mem. Bd, Castle Rock Housing Assoc., 1975–2005 (Chm., 1995–2000). Pres., Scottish Engrg Employers' Assoc., 1985–86. Dir, Scottish Chamber Orch., 1995–2009. JP Midlothian, 1980–2003. Gov., Loretto Sch., 1982–89. *Recreations:* music, opera, reading, golf, tennis, ski-ing. *Address:* Carlyle House, 5/2 East Suffolk Park, Edinburgh EH16 5PL. *T:* (0131) 667 4635. *E:* patrick.prenter@mactag.com; 41 Ocean Quay, Harbour Island, Gordons Bay, Western Cape, 7150, South Africa. *Clubs:* New (Edinburgh); Hon. Company of Edinburgh Golfers; Free Foresters.

PRENTICE, Dr Ann, OBE 2006; Director, MRC Human Nutrition Research (formerly MRC Resource, then MRC Collaborative Centre for Human Nutrition Research), since 1998; *b* 8 April 1952; *d* of Alexander Rubach and Beryl Ann Rubach; *m* 1976, Andrew Major Prentice (marr. diss. 2009); two *d. Educ:* Somerville Coll., Oxford (BA Hons Chemistry; MA 1977); Univ. of Surrey (MSc Med. Physics); Darwin Coll., Cambridge (PhD Natural Scis, 1978). Scientist, MRC Dunn Nutrition Gp, Keneba, Gambia, 1978–83; Scientist, 1984–91, Sen. Scientist, 1991–98, MRC Dunn Nutrition Unit, Cambridge. Hon. Prof., Shenyang Med. Coll., People's Republic of China, 1995–; Vis. Prof. KCL, 2003–09. Pres., Nutrition Soc., 2004–07. Chm., Sci. Adv. Cttee on Nutrition, 2010–. FRSB (FSB 2010); FMedSci 2012; FAfN 2011, Hon. FafN 2012; Hon. FRCPCH 2015. Hon. Dr Surrey, 2014. *Publications:* book chapters and reviews; numerous contribs to peer-reviewed scientific jls. *Recreations:* music, theatre, literature, foreign travel. *Address:* MRC Human Nutrition Research, Elsie Widdowson Laboratory, Fulbourn Road, Cambridge CB1 9NL. *T:* (01223) 426356.

PRENTICE, Bridget Theresa; JP; Director, Bridget Prentice Associates, since 2010; Independent Consultant, The Pampered Chef, since 2012; Electoral Commissioner, since 2014; *b* 28 Dec. 1952; *d* of James and Bridget Corr; *m* 1975, Gordon Prentice, *qv* (marr. diss. 2000). *Educ:* Glasgow Univ. (MA English Lit. and Mod. Hist.); London University: Avery Hill Coll. (PGCE); Southlands Coll. (Adv. Dip. in Careers Educn and Guidance); South Bank Univ. (LLB 1992). Teacher, ILEA, 1974–88. Councillor, Hammersmith and Fulham London BC, 1986–92. MP (Lab) Lewisham E, 1992–2010. An Asst Govt Whip, 1997–98 and 2003–05; Parly Under-Sec. of State, DCA, later MoJ, 2005–10. Chair, Blackheath Historic Bldgs Trust, 2011–14; Trustee: Jimmy Mizen Foundn, 2012–; Age Exchange, 2012–; Patron, Grove Park Community Gp, 2012–. JP Inner London, 1985. *Recreations:* music, reading, crosswords, knitting, my three cats, football.

PRENTICE, Christopher Norman Russell, CMG 2009; HM Diplomatic Service; Ambassador to Italy, since 2011; *b* 5 Sept. 1954; *s* of Ronald Prentice and Sonia Prentice (*née* Bowring); *m* 1978, Marie-Josephine, (Nina), King; two *s* two *d. Educ:* Christ Church, Oxford (BA Lit.Hum., MA). Entered FCO, 1977; Arabic lang. student, MECAS, 1978; Third, later Second, Sec., Kuwait, 1980–83; First Secretary: on loan to Cabinet Office, 1983–85; Washington, 1985–89; FCO, 1989–94; Counsellor and Dep. Hd of Mission, Budapest, 1994–98; Counsellor, FCO, 1998–2002; Ambassador to Jordan, 2002–06; UK Special Rep., later FCO co-ordinator, Sudan Peace Process, 2006–07; Ambassador to Iraq, 2007–09; Special Envoy for Libya, March–May 2011. *Recreations:* music, sport, reading, mountains. *Address:* c/o Foreign and Commonwealth Office, King Charles Street, SW1A 2AH. *Clubs:* Athenæum, Beefsteak, MCC.

PRENTICE, Prof. Daniel David; Allen & Overy Professor of Corporate Law, Oxford University, 1991–2008, now Emeritus; Fellow of Pembroke College, Oxford, 1973–2008; *b* 7 Aug. 1941; *s* of Thomas James Prentice and Agnes Prentice (*née* Fox); *m* 1965, Judith Mary Keane; one *s* one *d. Educ:* St Malachy's Coll., Belfast; Queen's Univ., Belfast (LLB); Univ. of Chicago (JD); MA Oxford (by special resolution). Called to the Bar, Lincoln's Inn, 1982; Mem., Erskine Chambers. Associate Prof., Univ. of Ontario, 1966–68; Lectr, UCL, 1968–73; Lectr, 1973–90, Reader, 1991, Univ. of Oxford. Vis. Prof., various univs incl. UCL, 2008–. Asst Editor, Law Qly Rev., 1988–2008. *Publications:* (ed) Chitty, Law of Contracts, 25th edn 1983 to 29th edn 2004. *Address:* Erskine Chambers, 33 Chancery Lane, WC2A 1EN.

PRENTICE, Gordon; *b* 28 Jan. 1951; *s* of Esther and William Prentice; *m* 1975, Bridget Theresa Corr (*see* B. T. Prentice) (marr. diss. 2000); *m* 2011, Heather J. A. Halliday. *Educ:* Univ. of Glasgow (MA; Pres., Glasgow Univ. Union, 1972–73). Mercury House Publications, 1974–78; Local Govt Officer, 1978–81; Labour Party Policy Directorate, 1982–92. Mem. Council, London Borough of Hammersmith and Fulham, 1982–90 (Leader of Council, 1986–88). MP (Lab) Pendle, 1992–2010; contested (Lab) same seat, 2010. *Recreations:* cooking, hill walking, gardening.

PRENTIS, David; General Secretary, UNISON, since 2001 (Deputy General Secretary, 1993–2000); President, Trades Union Congress, 2007–08; *b* Leeds. *Educ:* QMC, Univ. of London (BA Hist.); Univ. of Warwick (MA Industrial Relns). Member: TUC Gen. Council (Mem. Exec. Cttee); Trade Union Labour Party Liaison Cttee; Econ. Commn and Jt Policy Cttee, Labour Party; Bd, ACAS, 2004–10. Comr, UK Commn for Employment and Skills. Director: IPPR; Catalyst. Pres., Unity Trust Bank plc; non-exec. Dir, Bank of England, 2012–. Advr, Warwick Inst. of Governance and Public Mgt. Vis. Fellow, Nuffield Coll., Oxford. *Address:* UNISON Centre, 130 Euston Road, NW1 2AY.

PRENTIS, Hon. Victoria Mary Boswell; MP (C) Banbury, since 2015; *b* Banbury, 24 March 1971; *d* of Baron Boswell of Aynho, *qv*; *m* 1996, Sebastian Hugh Runton Prentis; two *d* (one *s* decd). *Educ:* Royal Holloway and Bedford New Coll., London (BA Hons English Lit.); Downing Coll., Cambridge (MA Law). Called to the Bar, Middle Temple, 1995; with Govt Legal Service, latterly Sen. CS, 1997–2014. *Recreations:* the countryside, detective fiction, cider making, fundraising. *Address:* House of Commons, SW1A 0AA. *T:* (020) 7219 8756. *E:* victoria.prentis.mp@parliament.uk. *Clubs:* Carlton, Farmers.

PRESCOTT, family name of **Baron Prescott**.

PRESCOTT, Baron *cr* 2010 (Life Peer), of Kingston upon Hull in the County of East Yorkshire; **John Leslie Prescott;** *b* 31 May 1938; *s* of late John Herbert Prescott, JP and Phyllis Prescott; *m* 1961, Pauline Tilston; two *s. Educ:* Ellesmere Port Secondary Modern Sch.; WEA; correspondence courses; Ruskin Coll., Oxford (DipEcon/Pol Oxon); Hull Univ. (BSc Econ). Trainee Chef, 1953–55; Steward, Passenger Lines, Merchant Navy, 1955–63; Ruskin Coll., Oxford, 1963–65; Recruitment Officer, General and Municipal Workers Union (temp.), 1965; Hull Univ., 1965–68. Full-time Official, National Union of Seamen, 1968–70. Contested (Lab) Southport, 1966. MP (Lab) Kingston upon Hull (East), 1970–83, Hull East,

1983–97, Kingston upon Hull East, 1997–2010. PPS to Sec. of State for Trade, 1974–76; opposition spokesman on Transport, 1979–81; opposition front bench spokesman on Regional Affairs and Devolution, 1981–83, on Transport, 1983–84 and 1988–93, on Employment, 1984–87 and 1993–94, on Energy, 1987–89; Mem., Shadow Cabinet, 1983–97; PC 1994–2013; Sec. of State for the Envmt, Transport and the Regions, 1997–2001; Dep. Prime Minister, 1997–2007; First Sec. of State, 2001–07. Dep. Leader, Labour Party, 1994–2007. Member: Select Cttee Nationalized Industries, 1973–79; Council of Europe, 1972–75; European Parlt, 1975–79 (Leader, Labour Party Delegn, 1976–79); Leader, British Labour Delegn, Council of Europe and WEU, 2007–. Mem., NEC, Labour Party, 1989–. *Publications:* Not Wanted on Voyage, 1966; (jtly) Prezza: my story - pulling no punches, 2008. *Address:* House of Lords, SW1A 0PW.

PRESCOTT, David Julian Brian; Chief Executive, Blackwell's, since 2013; *b* Nottingham, 25 Oct. 1971; *s* of Brian and Christine Prescott; *m* 2003, Claire Sheehan; two *d*. *Educ:* Huddersfield Univ. (BA Histl and Pol Studies). Blackwell's: Goods-in Supervisor, Nottingham Trent, 1995–97; Manager, Univ. of Glamorgan, 1997–2000; Manager, Univ. of Cardiff, 2000–03; SW Regl Manager, 2001–03; Hd, Retail Ops, 2003–09; Hd of Sales, 2009–11, Man. Dir, 2011–13, Blackwell Ltd. Booksellers' Association: Chair, Acad. Professional and Specialist Booksellers' Gp, 2009–11; Vice Pres., 2011–. Mem., Book Soc. *Recreations:* guitar, sport, reading. *Address:* Blackwell's, 50 Broad Street, Oxford OX1 3BQ. *E:* david.prescott@blackwell.co.uk.

PRESCOTT, Prof. Edward C., PhD; W. P. Carey Professor of Economics, Arizona State University, since 2003; Senior Monetary Adviser, Federal Reserve Bank of Minneapolis, since 2003 (Senior Adviser, Research Department, 1981–2003); *b* 26 Dec. 1940; *s* of William Clyde Prescott and Mathilde Helwig Prescott; *m* 1965, Janet Dale Simpson; two *s* one *d*. *Educ:* Swarthmore Coll., Penn (BA 1962); Case Inst. of Technol. (MS 1963); Carnegie Mellon Univ. (PhD 1967). Lectr, 1966–67, Asst Prof., 1967–71, Econs Dept, Univ. of Pennsylvania; Asst Prof., 1971–72, Associate Prof., 1972–75, Prof. of Econs, 1975–80, Carnegie-Mellon Univ.; Prof. of Econs, 1980–98, 1999–2003, Univ. of Minnesota; Prof. of Econs, Univ. of Chicago, 1998–99. Irwin Plein Nemmers Prize, 2002; (jtly) Nobel Prize in Economics, 2004. *Publications:* (with S. L. Parente) Barriers to Riches, 2000; contrib. learned jls. *Address:* Department of Economics, W. P. Carey School of Business, Arizona State University, Tempe, AZ 85287–3806, USA; Research Department, Federal Reserve Bank of Minneapolis, 90 Hennepin Avenue, Minneapolis, MN 55401–1804, USA.

PRESCOTT, John Barry, AC 1996; Chairman, Aurizon Holdings Ltd (formerly Queensland Rail, then QR National Ltd), since 2006; Member, Commonwealth Remuneration Tribunal, since 2010; *b* 22 Oct. 1940; *s* of late John Norman Prescott and Margaret Ellen (*née* Brownie); *m* 1985, Jennifer Cahill; one *s* two *d* (and one *d* decd). *Educ:* N Sydney Boys' High Sch.; Univ. of NSW (BComm Industrial Relns). Joined The Broken Hill Pty Co. Ltd as Industrial Relns Trainee, 1958: various industrial relns positions, 1958–69; Superintendent, Industrial Relns, Shipping and Stevedoring, Newcastle and Sydney, 1969–74; Asst Fleet Manager, Ops, Newcastle, 1974–79; Exec. Asst to Gen. Manager, Transport, 1979–80; Manager Ops, Transport, 1980–82; Gen. Manager, Transport, 1982–87; Exec. Gen. Manager and Chief Exec. Officer, BHP Steel, 1987–91; Dir, 1988–98; Man. Dir and CEO, 1991–98. Chairman: Horizon Private Equity Pty Ltd, 1998–2005; ASC Pty Ltd (formerly Australian Submarine Corp.), 2000–09; Dir, Tubemakers of Aust. Ltd, 1988–92; non-executive Director: Normandy Mining Ltd, 1999–2002; Newmont Mining Corp., 2002–; Member: Adv. Bd, Booz, Allen & Hamilton Inc., 1991–2003; Internat. Council, J. P. Morgan, 1994–2003; Asia Pacific Adv. Cttee, New York Stock Exchange Inc., 1995–2005. Chm., 2004–07, Patron, 2007–09, Sunshine Coast Business Council; Member Board: Business Council of Aust., 1995–97; Walter and Eliza Hall Inst. of Med. Res., 1994–98; Global Counsellor, Conference Bd, 2001– (Mem., Bd of Trustees, 1995–2001; Mem., Global Adv. Council, 2013–). Mem. Internat. Council, 1991–2003, Mem., President's Circle, AustralAsiaCentre, 1999–, Asia Soc. Hon. LLD Monash, 1994; Hon. DSc NSW, 1995. *Recreations:* tennis, golf. *Address:* (office) Level 39, 140 William Street, Melbourne, Vic 3000, Australia. *Clubs:* Australian, Melbourne (Melbourne); Newcastle (Newcastle); Huntingdale Golf, National Golf (Vic).

PRESCOTT, Prof. John Herbert Dudley, PhD; FRSB; FRAgS; Principal, Wye College, and Professor of Animal Production, University of London, 1988–2000, now Professor Emeritus; *b* 21 Feb. 1937; *s* of Herbert Prescott and Edith Vera Prescott; *m* 1960, Diana Margaret Mullock; two *s* two *d*. *Educ:* Haileybury; Univ. of Nottingham (BSc (Agric), PhD). FRSB (FIBiol 1983); FRAgS 1986. Lectr in Animal Prodn, Univ. of Newcastle upon Tyne, 1963–72; Animal Prodn Officer in Argentina, FAO, UN, 1972–74; Head of Animal Prodn Advisory and Develt, E of Scotland Coll. of Agric., 1974–78; Prof. of Animal Prodn, Univ. of Edinburgh, 1978–84, and Head of Animal Div., Edinburgh Sch. of Agric., 1978–84; Dir, Grassland, later Animal and Grassland, Res. Inst., 1984–86; Dir, Grassland and Animal Prodn Res., AFRC, 1986–88. Visiting Professor: Univ. of Reading, 1985–88; UCW, Aberystwyth, 1988. Non-exec. Dir, Natural Resources Internat. Ltd, 1997–2000 (Actg Chm., 1996). Chm., Tech. Cttee on Response to Nutrients, AFRC, 1988–94. British Council: Member: Cttee for Internat. Co-operation in Higher Educn, 1989–2000; Agric. and Vet. Adv. Cttee, 1988–96; Vice-Chm., Sci., Engrg and Envmt Adv. Cttee, 1997–2001. Member: Adv. Bd, Centre for Tropical Vet. Medicine, 1978–84; Board of Directors: Hill Farming Res. Orgn, 1980–84; Hannah Res. Inst., 1981–84; Scientific Adv. Cttee, 1990–92, Governing Body, 1992–97, Macaulay Land Use Res. Inst.; various cttees on cattle and beef, MLC, 1969–90. President: British Soc. of Animal Prodn, 1988; Agricl and Forestry Sect., BAAS, 1994–95; Mem. Council, British Grassland Soc., 1984–87. Chairman: Stapledon Meml Trust, 1992–2004; Natural Resources Internat. Foundn, 1997–2004; Trustee, E Malling Trust for Horticl Res., 1998–2010. Member: Gov. Body and Corp., Hadlow Coll., 1988–98; Council: RVC, 1988–98, 2001–04; Univ. of Kent, 1988–2000. Liveryman, Farmers' Co., 2000–. FRSA 2000. Hon. Fellow: Inst. for Grassland and Envmtl Res., 1989; Wye Coll., 2000; ICSTM, 2001. *Publications:* scientific papers in Animal Prodn and Agricultural Science; technical articles. *Recreations:* farming, walking, wildlife, the countryside. *Club:* Farmers.

PRESCOTT, Lisa Ellen Buch; *see* Christensen, L. E. B.

PRESCOTT, Sir Mark, 3rd Bt *cr* 1938, of Godmanchester; racehorse trainer, in Newmarket; *b* 3 March 1948; *s* of late Major W. R. Stanley Prescott (MP for Darwen Div., 1943–51; 2nd *s* of Colonel Sir William Prescott, 1st Bt) and Gwendolen (who *m* 2nd, 1952, Daniel Orme (*d* 1972); she *d* 1992), *oc* of late Leonard Aldridge, CBE; *S* uncle, Sir Richard Stanley Prescott, 2nd Bt, 1965. *Educ:* Harrow. *Address:* Heath House, Moulton Road, Newmarket, Suffolk CB8 8DU. *T:* (01638) 662117.

PRESCOTT, Peter Richard Kyle; QC 1990; *b* 23 Jan. 1943; *s* of Richard Stanley Prescott and Sarah Aitchison Shand; *m* 1st, 1967, Frances Rosemary Bland; two *s* one *d*; 2nd, 2014, Gillian Luciana Leddy. *Educ:* St Andrew's Scots' Sch., Argentina; St George's Coll., Argentina; Dulwich Coll.; University Coll. London (BSc); Queen Mary Coll., London (MSc Eng). Pres., Univ. of London Union. Called to the Bar, Lincoln's Inn, 1970, Bencher, 2001; in practice as a barrister, 1970–2012; a Dep. High Court Judge, 1997–2011. *Publications:* The Modern Law of Copyright (with Hugh Laddie, QC, and Mary Vitoria), 1980, 4th edn 2011; various articles. *Recreations:* music, reading, cooking. *Address:* Limehouse Marina, London.

PRESCOTT, Dr Robert George Whitelock, FSAScot; Chairman, Department for Culture Media and Sport Advisory Committee on National Historic Ships, University of St Andrews, since 2006; *b* 9 Dec. 1938; *y s* of Edward Frank Whitelock Prescott and Ethel Prescott (*née* Shrubb); *m* 1st, 1964, Julia Margaret Palmer (marr. diss. 1982); two *d*; 2nd, 2005, Lloyd Carson. *Educ:* Latymer Upper Sch.; Peterhouse, Cambridge (BA 1961; PhD 1965). NATO Res. Fellow and Sen. Student, Royal Commn for Exhibn of 1851, Yale Univ., 1964–66; Sen. Asst in Res., Univ. of Cambridge, 1966–74; University of St Andrews: Lectr, then Sen. Lectr, 1974–2002; Co-founder, Scottish Inst. for Maritime Studies (Dir, 1984–2002); Caird Sen. Fellow, Nat. Maritime Mus., 2002–04. National Historic Ships Committee: Dir, Nat. Historic Ships Project, 1995–2001; Mem., 2003–06; Chm., 2005–06. Council Member: Royal Archaeol Inst., 1990–94; Soc. for Nautical Res., 1994–97, 1999–2002 and 2008–12; Scottish Executive/Scottish Museums Council: Scotland's Nat. Cultural Audit (Mem. Bd, 2000–02); Mem., RRS Discovery Conservation Cttee, 2004–06; Fife Mus Forum (Chm., 2004–07). Trustee: Nat. Mus. of Antiquities of Scotland, 1980–85; Scottish Fisheries Mus., 1977–2006 (Hon. Vice-Pres., 2007); frigate Unicorn, 1984–98; World Ship Trust, 1996–2001. Writer and presenter of radio and TV documentaries. FSAScot 1981. *Publications:* (with Ann V. Gunn) Lifting the Veil: research and scholarship in United Kingdom museums and galleries, 1999; articles and reviews in learned periodicals. *Recreations:* restoring and sailing historic ships, collecting books and things, watching birds, conversation, exploring the world of Samuel Pepys. *Address:* School of History, University of St Andrews, St Andrews, Fife KY16 9AL. *T:* (01334) 463017. *E:* rgwp@st-andrews.ac.uk.

PRESCOTT-DECIE, Elizabeth Anne Scott, MA; Head Mistress, Godolphin School, Salisbury, 1980–89; *b* 28 Dec. 1942; *d* of Thomas Scott Hannay and Doreen Hewitt Hannay; *m* 2000, John Prescott-Decie. *Educ:* Heathfield Sch., Ascot; St Hugh's Coll., Oxford (MA). Assistant Mistress: St Mary's Sch., Calne, 1966–70; Moreton Hall Sch., Shropshire, 1970–72; St Michael's, Burton Park, Petworth, 1973–75; Dep. Headmistress, St George's Sch., Ascot, 1975–80. Governor: Norman Ct Sch., W Tytherley, 1982–2012; Prior's Field Sch., Godalming, 1991–2013.

PRESLAND, Frank George; Chairman: Rocket Music Entertainment Group, 2010–12; William A. Bong Ltd, and other companies in Elton John Group, 2012–14 (Chief Executive, 1999–2012); *b* 27 Feb. 1944; *s* of Reginald Charles Presland and Elsie Presland; *m*; one *s* one *d*. *Educ:* London Sch. of Economics (BSc Econ); University Coll. of Rhodesia and Nyasaland (Fairbridge Schol.). Admitted solicitor, 1973; Partner, Frere Cholmeley, 1976–92; Chm., Frere Cholmeley Bischoff, 1992–98, when co. merged with Eversheds; Jt Chm., Eversheds, 1998–99. Chief Executive: Twentyfirst Artists Ltd, 2001–10; Sanctuary Gp plc, 2006–08. Dir, Edge VCT, 2005–. Dir, Elstree UTC Ltd, 2012–. Dir, Elton John AIDS Foundn, UK and USA, 1999–2014. Hon. FRAM 2010. *Recreation:* yachting.

PRESS, Dr Frank; Principal, Washington Advisory Group, 1996–2013; Consultant, Huron Consulting Group, since 2011; *b* 4 Dec. 1924; *m* 1946, Billie Kallick (*d* 2009); one *s* one *d*. *Educ:* City Coll., NY (BS 1944); Columbia Univ. (MA 1946; PhD 1949). Columbia University: Res. Associate, 1946–49; Instr in Geology, 1949–51; Asst Prof. of Geology, 1951–52; Associate Prof., 1952–55; Prof. of Geophysics, 1955–65 and Dir, Seismol. Lab., 1957–65, CIT; Prof. of Geophysics and Chm., Dept of Earth and Planetary Scis, MIT, 1965–77; Sci. Advisor to Pres. and Dir, Office of Sci. and Tech. Policy, 1977–80; Prof., MIT, 1981; Pres., NAS, 1981–93; Cecil and Ida Green Sen. Fellow, Carnegie Instn of Washington, 1993–97. Member: President's Sci. Adv. Commn, 1961–64; Nat. Sci. Bd, 1970–; Lunar and Planetary Missions Bd, NASA; participant, bilateral scis agreement with People's Republic of China and USSR; US Deleg. to Nuclear Test Ban Negotiations, Geneva and Moscow. Mem., Acad. of Arts and Scis, and other US and internat. bodies. Life Mem., MIT Bd, 1985. Numerous awards, incl. Japan Prize, Sci. and Technol. Foundn of Japan, 1993, US Nat. Medal of Science, 1994, Lomonosov Gold Medal, Russian Acad. of Sci., 1998, and hon. degrees. Officer, Legion of Honour, 1989. *Publications:* (jtly) Propagation of Elastic Waves in Layered Media, 1957; (ed jtly) Physics and Chemistry of the Earth, 1957; (jtly) Earth, 1986; Understanding Earth, 1994, 4th edn 2005; numerous papers. *Address:* Building 5, Apt 306, Carolina Meadows, Chapel Hill, NC 27517, USA.

PRESS, Prof. Malcolm Colin, PhD; Vice-Chancellor and Chief Executive, Manchester Metropolitan University, since 2015; *b* 18 Sept. 1958; *s* of Kenneth and Sylvia Press. *Educ:* Kingsbury High Sch., London; Westfield Coll., Univ. of London (BSc (Envmtl Sci.) 1980); Univ. of Manchester (PhD (Botany) 1984). Res. Associate, UCL, 1985–89; Lectr, then Sen. Lectr, Univ. of Manchester, 1989–94; University of Sheffield: Reader, 1994–98; Prof. of Physiol Ecol., 1998–2008; Dir, Res. in the Envmt, 2001–08; Hd, Animal and Plant Scis, 2002–08; University of Birmingham: Prof. of Ecol. and Hd, Coll. of Life and Envmtl Scis, 2008–13; Pro-Vice-Chancellor, 2009–15; Dir, Inst. of Advanced Studies, 2012–15. Mem., Sci. and Innovation Strategy Bd, NERC, 2007–10; Dep. Chair, REF sub-panel for Biol Scis, 2011–14. Pres., British Ecol Soc., 2007–09 (Mem. Council, 1992–2001); Mem. Council, Soc. of Biol., 2009–10. Mem. Council, Nat. Trust, 2009–12; Trustee: Royal Botanic Gdns, Kew, 2012– (Mem., Kew Audit Cttee, 2013–; Chm., Kew Sci. Cttee, 2014–); WWF UK, 2014–. Ed., Jl Ecol., 2004–06. *Publications:* scientific papers and contribs to books on ecol., agric. and forests. *Recreations:* Spanish language and culture, travel, walking the dog, gardening. *Address:* Manchester Metropolitan University, All Saints, Manchester M15 6BH. *T:* (0161) 247 1560. *E:* malcolm.press@mmu.ac.uk.

PRESSDEE, Piers Charles William; QC 2010; *b* London, 29 Dec. 1968; *s* of Comdr William Pressdee and Hilda Pressdee; *m* 1997, Sally Max; four *d*. *Educ:* St Paul's Sch., London; St John's Coll., Cambridge (BA Hons 1989); Inns of Court Sch. of Law. Called to the Bar, Middle Temple, 1991; in practice as barrister, specialising in children law, 1992–. Co-Chm., Assoc. of Lawyers for Children, 2008–10. *Publications:* Contact: the new deal, 2006; The Public Law Outline: the Court companion, 2008; (Contrib. Ed.) Halsbury's Laws of England, children vols, 2012. *Recreations:* my children, football (Chelsea season ticket holder), writing. *Address:* 29 Bedford Row, WC1R 4HE. *T:* (020) 7404 1044. *E:* ppressdee@29br.co.uk.

PRESSLER, Christopher Carson; Director of Library Services and University Librarian, Dublin City University, since 2014; *b* Belfast, 12 Aug. 1972; *s* of John Evans and Ruth Miller (*née* Pressler); partner, Brett Tryner. *Educ:* Grosvenor Grammar Sch., Belfast; Queen's Univ. Belfast (BA Hons); Nottingham Trent Univ. (MA); Univ. of Sheffield (MSc). IT Services Librarian, UCL, 1998–2000; JISC Prog. Manager, KCL, 2000–02; Hd of Arts Collections, Univ. of London, 2002–04; Dean, Information and Learning, Dartington Coll. of Arts, 2004–07; Director: Libraries and Archives, Univ. of Nottingham, 2007–10; Senate House Libraries, Univ. of London, 2010–13. FRSA 2004. *Publications:* Canning Circus, 2001; Director's Choice, Senate House Library, 2012; (ed) Senate House Library: historic collections, 2012; 94 Degrees in the Shade, 2015. *Recreations:* playing the violin, listening to and writing about music, attending concerts.

PREST, Nicholas Martin, CBE 2001; Chairman: Cohort plc, since 2006; Shephard Group Ltd, since 2007; *b* 3 April 1953; *s* of late Alan Richmond Prest and Pauline Chasey Prest (*née* Noble); *m* 1985, Anthea Joy Elisabeth Neal; one *s* two *d*. *Educ:* Manchester Grammar Sch.; Christ Church, Oxford (MA Hist. and Econs). Admin. trainee, 1974, Principal, 1980–82, MoD; joined United Scientific Hldgs Plc, later Alvis Plc, 1982; Gp Mktg Dir, 1985–89; Chief Exec., 1989–2004; Chm., 1996–2004. Chm., Aveva Gp plc, 2006–12. Chm., 2001–04, Mem. Council, 2006–09, Defence Manufrs Assoc.; Mem. Council, ADS, 2009–10; Mem., Nat. Defence Industries Council, 2001–04. *Recreations:* music, walking, shooting, watching cricket and Rugby. *Address:* Pilstone House, Llandogo, Monmouth NP25 4TH. *T:* (01594) 531007. *Clubs:* Cavalry and Guards, MCC.

PRESTON, family name of **Viscount Gormanston**.

PRESTON; *see* Campbell-Preston.

PRESTON, Ben James; Editor, Radio Times, since 2009; *b* Crosby, 24 Sept. 1963; *s* of Peter John Preston, *qv*; *m* 1995, Janice Turner; two *s*. *Educ:* Alleyn's Sch., London; Bristol Univ. (BSSc Pols 1986); City Univ. (Dip. Journalism 1987). Reporter, Bristol Evening Post, 1987–89; Reporter, 1990–91, Educn Corresp., 1991–93, Press Assoc.; The Times: Educn Corresp., 1993–96; News Ed., 1997–99; Dep. Ed., 2000–08; Actg Ed., 2001; Exec. Ed., The Independent, 2008–09. *Recreations:* film, football, family. *Address:* Radio Times, Immediate Media, Vineyard House, 44 Brook Green, W6 7BT. *T:* 0870 608 4455. *E:* Ben.preston@radiotimes.com. *Club:* Millwall Football.

PRESTON, David Michael; mediator and law consultant; Partner, Hosack & Sutherland, Solicitors, Oban, 1978–2005; Chairman: Mental Health Tribunal for Scotland, since 2005; Private Rented Housing Panel, since 2011; Home Owners Housing Panel, since 2012; *b* 26 Aug. 1952; *s* of Robert Matthew Preston and Lily Stewart Preston; *m* 1975, Sheila Elizabeth McMeekin; two *s*. *Educ:* Hillhead High Sch., Glasgow; Univ. of Dundee (LLB 1974). Depute Procurator Fiscal (pt-time), 1976–79; Clerk to Gen. Comrs of Income Tax, 1976–. Legal Assessor, Gen. Teaching Council for Scotland, 2011–. Registrar, Episcopal Dio. Argyll and the Isles, 1977–2007. Mem. Council, 1990–2007, 2012–, Pres., 2002–03, Law Soc. of Scotland. Chm., Oban Youth and Community Assoc., 1980–2013. Sec., Atlantis Leisure, Oban, 1991–2000. *Recreations:* sailing, ski-ing, golf, reading, family. *Address:* Westbank, Duncraggan Road, Oban PA34 5DU. *Clubs:* Royal Highland Yacht, Oban Sailing (Cdre, 1992–93); Taynuilt and Hilton Park Golf.

PRESTON, Hugh Geoffrey; QC 2012; *b* Westow, N Yorks, 21 Oct. 1970; *s* of Brig. Roger Preston, CBE and Polly Preston; *m* 1998, the Noble Mary Louisa; two *s* two *d*. *Educ:* Eton Coll.; Durham Univ. (BA Hons Theol. 1992; DipLaw 1993). Called to the Bar, Middle Temple, 1994; in practice as a barrister, East Anglian Chambers, 1994–2000, 7 Bedford Row, 2000–. *Publications:* regular contrib. to legal jls. *Recreations:* shooting, gardening, cycling with my children, driving my Morris Traveller. *Address:* 7 Bedford Row, WC1R 4BS. *T:* (020) 7242 3555. *E:* hpreston@7br.co.uk.

PRESTON, Dr Ian Mathieson Hamilton, CBE 1993; FREng, FIET; Chairman, Motherwell Bridge Holdings, 1996–2001; *b* 18 July 1932; *s* of John Hamilton Preston and Edna Irene Paul; *m* 1958, Sheila Hope Pringle; two *s*. *Educ:* Univ. of Glasgow (BSc 1st cl. Hons; PhD). MInstP 1959; FIET (FIEE 1974); FREng (FEng 1982). Asst Lectr, Univ. of Glasgow, 1954–59; joined SSEB, 1959, Chief Engineer, Generation Design and Construction, 1972–77; Dir Gen., Generation Develt and Construction Div., CEGB, 1977–83; Dep. Chm., SSEB, 1983–90; Chief Exec., Scottish Power, 1990–95. Director: Deutsche (Scotland) (formerly Morgan Grenfell (Scotland)), 1994–2002; Clydeport plc, 1994–2000. Chairman: Mining Scotland, 1995–98; East of Scotland Water Authy, 1995–98. Pres., Scottish Council Develt and Industry, 1997–99 (Chm., 1992–97). Hon. FCIWEM 1995. *Recreations:* fishing, gardening. *Address:* 10 Cameron Crescent, Carmunnock, Glasgow G76 9DX.

PRESTON, Jeffrey William, CB 1989; Director General, Energy, Department of Trade and Industry, 1996–98; *b* 28 Jan. 1940; *s* of William and Sybil Grace Preston. *Educ:* Liverpool Collegiate Sch.; Hertford Coll., Oxford (MA Lit. Hum. 1966). Asst Principal, Min. of Aviation, 1963; Private Sec. to Permanent Sec., BoT, 1966; Principal: BoT, 1967; HM Treasury, 1970; DTI, 1973; Asst Sec., Dept of Trade, 1975–82; Under Sec. and Regional Dir, Yorks and Humberside Region, DTI, 1982–85; Dep. Sec., Industrial and Economic Affairs, Welsh Office, 1985–90; Dep. Dir Gen., OFT, 1990–96 (Acting Dir Gen., 1995). Vice-Pres., Hertford Soc., 2004– (Chm., 1987–95). *Recreations:* travel, opera, wine. *T:* (020) 8940 7166. *Club:* Oxford and Cambridge (Chm., 1999–2001; Trustee, 2007–15).

PRESTON, Kieran Thomas, OBE 2006; FCIT, FCIPD; Director General, West Yorkshire Passenger Transport Executive, 1993–2014; *b* 30 Nov. 1950; *s* of Charles Edward Preston and Mary Kate Preston; *m* 1974, Denise Marie Gregory (*d* 2010); two *s*. *Educ:* Leeds Poly. (BA Hons Mgt and Admin). FCIT 1994. Local Govt Officer, various appts, 1972–89; Leeds City Council: Projects Dir, 1989–91; Actg Dir of Admin, 1991–92; Chief Services Officer, 1992–93. Chm., PTE Gp, 2001–05. FCIPD (FIPM 1992). *Recreations:* keeping fit, horse riding, football, cricket, judo. *Address:* 15 Morritt Avenue, Leeds LS15 7EP.

PRESTON, Mark Robin; Group Chief Executive, Grosvenor, since 2008; *b* Westow, 20 Jan. 1968; *s* of Roger St Clair Preston and Polly Mary Preston (*née* Marriot); *m* 1997, Kate Whittaker; one *s* two *d*. *Educ:* Eton Coll.; Reading Univ. (BSc Land Mgt). MRICS 1992. Joined Grosvenor, 1989; seconded to Hong Kong, 1995–97; Gp Fund Mgt Dir, 1997–2002; Pres., Grosvenor USA, San Francisco, 2002–06; Chief Exec., Grosvenor Britain and Ireland, 2006–08. Non-exec. Dir, London Bd, Royal & Sun Alliance, 2006–08. Non-exec. Dir, Sonae Sierra SGPS, 2008–. Mem. Bd, Assoc. of Foreign Investors in Real Estate, 2001– (Chm., 2007). Mem., North West Business Leadership Team, 2006–. *Recreation:* field sports. *Address:* Grosvenor, 70 Grosvenor Street, W1K 3JP. *T:* (020) 7408 0988. *Club:* Lansdowne.

PRESTON, Michael Richard, ATD; FCSD; consultant designer; *b* 15 Oct. 1927; *s* of Major Frederick Allan Preston, MC and Winifred Gertrude (*née* Archer); *m* 1st, 1955, Anne Gillespie Smith; 2nd, 1980, Judith Gaye James. *Educ:* Whitgift Sch.; Guildford Sch. of Art; Goldsmiths' Coll., London Univ. (NDD 1953; ATD 1954); Dip. in Humanities (London) 1964. FCSD (FSIAD 1972; MSIAD 1953). Served HM Forces, Queen's Royal Regt, 1944–48, Queen's Royal Regt, TA & HAC, 1948–61. Asst Art Master, Whitgift Sch., 1954–55; Drawing Master, Dulwich Coll., 1955–64; Science Mus., 1964–87; Head of Design, 1964–86; Keeper, Dept of Museum Services, 1987; designed exhibitions, including: Centenary of Charles Babbage, 1971; A Word to the Mermaids, 1973; Tower Bridge Observed, 1974; The Breath of Life, 1974; Nat. Rly Mus., York, 1975; Sci. and Technol. of Islam, 1976; Nat. Mus. of Photography, Bradford, 1977–83; Stanley Spencer in the Shipyard, 1979; Wellcome Mus. of Hist. of Medicine, 1980; Sci. and Technol. of India, 1982; The Great Cover-up Show, 1982; Beads of Glass, 1983; Louis Pasteur and Rabies, 1985. Advisory Assignments on Museum Projects: Iran, 1976–79; Spain, 1977–80; Germany, 1978–79; Canada, 1979–82, 1984–86; Trinidad, 1982–83; Turkey, 1984–94; Hong Kong, 1985; consultant to: Dean and Chapter of Canterbury, 1987–96; Wellcome Foundn, 1987–95; TAVRA Greater London, 1988–94; Mus. of East Asian Art, Bath, 1988–93; Design Expo '89, Nagoya; Bank of England Museum, 1989; Norwich Tourism Agency, 1989–91; Tricycle Theatre, 1989–90; Nat. Theatre, 1989–90; Scottish Office, 1990; English Heritage, 1990; Richmond Theatre, 1990; Accademia Italiana, 1990–94; Société Générale, 1992–95; Castrol Internat., 1994–95; Dean and Chapter of Westminster Abbey, 1997–98; Westminster CC, 1997–99. Mem., BTEC Validation Panel, 1986–92. Chm., Greenwich Soc., 1961–64. Society of Industrial Artists and Designers (now Chartered Society of Designers): Mem., 1953–; Vice-Pres., 1976, 1979–81; Chm., Membership Bd, 1976–79; Chm., Design Management Panel, 1976–80. Mem., ICOM, 1964–. Trustee, Vivat Trust, 1989–92. Hon. Keeper of Pictures, Arts Club, 1992–2009. Vis. Prof., NID, Ahmedabad, 1989–2000. Monthly lectures in Hist. of Art, U3A, 2007–. Guild of Glass Engravers: Hon. FGGE 1980; Pres., 1986–92. FRSA 1955–68, 2001. *Recreations:* travel, food, conversation, jazz. *Clubs:* Arts; Australasian Pioneers', Union (Sydney).

PRESTON, Prof. Paul, CBE 2000; FRHistS; FBA 1994; Professor of International History, London School of Economics, since 1991; *b* 21 July 1946; *s* of Charles Ronald Preston and Alice Hoskisson; *m* 1983, Gabrielle Patricia Ashford-Hodges; two *s*. *Educ:* St Edward's Coll., Liverpool; Oriel Coll., Oxford. Lectr in Modern History, Univ. of Reading, 1974–75; Queen Mary College, University of London: Lectr and Reader in Modern History, 1975–85; Prof. of History, 1985–91. Marcel Proust Chair, Academia Europea de Yuste, 2006. Mem., Institut d'Estudis Catalans, 2008. Ramon Llull Internat. Prize, Catalonia, 2005; Pompeu Fabra Prize, Catalonia, 2012; Lluís Carulla Prize, Catalonia, 2013. Comendador de la Orden de Mérito Civil (Spain), 1986; Gran Cruz, Orden de Isabel la Católica (Spain), 2007. *Publications:* (ed) Spain in Crisis, 1976; The Coming of the Spanish Civil War, 1978, 2nd edn 1994; (ed) Revolution and War in Spain 1931–1939, 1984; (with Denis Smyth) Spain, the EEC and NATO, 1984; The Triumph of Democracy in Spain, 1986; The Spanish Civil War 1936–1939, 1986; The Politics of Revenge, 1990; Franco, 1993 (Yorkshire Post Book of the Year, 1993); Las tres Españas del 36, 1998 (Así fue, 1998); Comrades! Portraits from the Spanish Civil War, 1999; Doves of War: four women of Spain, 2002; Juan Carlos: a people's king, 2004; We Saw Spain Die, 2008; The Spanish Holocaust, 2011; The Last Stalinist: the life of Santiago Carrillo, 2014. *Recreations:* classical music, opera, modern fiction, wine, supporting Everton Football Club. *Address:* Department of International History, London School of Economics, Houghton Street, WC2A 2AE. *T:* (020) 7955 7107.

PRESTON, Peter John; journalist and writer; Co-Director, Guardian Foundation, since 1997; *b* 23 May 1938; *s* of John Whittle Preston and Kathlyn (*née* Chell); *m* 1962, Jean Mary Burrell; two *s* two *d*. *Educ:* Loughborough Grammar Sch.; St John's Coll., Oxford (MA EngLit; Hon. Fellow, 2003). Editorial trainee, Liverpool Daily Post, 1960–63; Guardian: Political Reporter, 1963–64; Education Correspondent, 1965–66; Diary Editor, 1966–68; Features Editor, 1968–72; Production Editor, 1972–75; Editor, 1975–95; Ed.-in-chief and Chm., Guardian and Observer, 1995–96; Editl Dir, Guardian Media Gp, 1996–98. Mem., Scott Trust, 1976–2004. British Exec. Chm., IPI, 1988– (World Chm., 1995–97); Chm., Assoc. of British Editors, 1996–99. Mem., UNESCO Adv. Gp on Press Freedom, 2000–03. Gov., British Assoc. for Central and Eastern Europe, 2000–08. Hon. DLitt: Loughborough, 1982; City, 2000; Leicester, 2003; Roehampton, 2010; DU Essex, 1994. *Publications:* Dunblane: reflecting tragedy, 1996; The Fifty-First State (novel), 1998; Bess (novel), 1999. *Recreations:* football, films; four children, eight grandchildren. *Address:* The Guardian, Kings Place, 90 York Way, N1 9AG.

See also B. J. Preston.

PRESTON, Sir Philip (Charles Henry Hulton), 8th Bt *cr* 1815, of Beeston St Lawrence, Norfolk; Partner, Bumphrey Preston Associates, architects, 1989–2011; *b* 30 Aug. 1946; *s* of Lt-Col Philip Henry Herbert Hulton Preston, OBE, MC and Katherine Janet Preston (*née* Broomhall); *S* cousin, 1999; *m* 1980, Kirsi Sylvi Annikki, *d* of Eino Yrjö Pullinen; one *s* two *d*. *Educ:* Nautical Coll., Pangbourne; Architectural Assoc. Sch. of Architecture. *Publications:* (ed jtly) The Battle of Crécy 1346, 2005. *Heir: s* Philip Thomas Henry Hulton Preston, *b* 15 Aug. 1990. *Address:* 32 rue Pierre Brossolette, 76680 Saint-Saëns, Normandie, France.

PRESTON, Roberta Lynn; *see* Gilchrist, R. L.

PRESTON, Rosalind, OBE 1993; Co-Chairman, Inter Faith Network for UK, 2000–04 (Co-Vice-Chairman, 1994–2000); Vice President, Board of Deputies of British Jews, 1991–94; *b* 29 Dec. 1935; *d* of Benjamin and Marie Morris; *m* 1958, Ronald Preston; one *s* one *d*. *Educ:* Talbot Heath Sch., Bournemouth. Voluntary sector activity, 1960–; Nat. Pres., Nat. Council of Women, 1988–90; Hon. Vice Pres., British Section, Women's Internat. Zionist Orgn, 1999– (Vice Pres., 1993–99); Jt Hon. Sec., CCJ, 1996–2005. Dir (non-exec.), Harrow and Hillingdon Healthcare NHS Trust, 1994–96; Mental Health Manager, Central and NW London (formerly Brent, Kensington & Chelsea and Westminster) Mental Health NHS Trust, 2002–10. Chm., Nightingale Home, 2001–07. Trustee: Jewish Chronicle, 2000–11; Olive Tree Trust, 2004–08; Jewish Volunteering Network, 2008– (Pres., 2009–); WIZO UK, 2014–; Co-Chair, Jewish Human Rights Coalition UK, 2008–13. FRSA 1990. Paul Harris Fellow, Rotary Internat., 1992. *Recreations:* walking, volunteering, international/national news, family and friends. *Address:* 7 Woodside Close, Stanmore, Middx HA7 3AJ.

PRESTON, Simon John, CBE 2009 (OBE 2000); Organist and Master of the Choristers, Westminster Abbey, 1981–87; concert organist, since 1987; *b* 4 Aug. 1938; *m* Elizabeth Hays. *Educ:* Canford Sch.; King's Coll., Cambridge (Dr Mann Organ Student; BA 1961; MusB 1962; MA 1964). ARCM, FRAM. Sub Organist, Westminster Abbey, 1962–67; Acting Organist, St Albans Abbey, 1968–69; Organist and Tutor in Music, Christ Church, Oxford, 1970–81. Conductor, Oxford Bach Choir, 1971–74. Artistic Dir, Calgary Internat. Organ Comp., 1990–2002. Has performed with major orchestras incl. Berlin Philharmonic, LA Philharmonic and Boston SO, as well as British orchestras; soloist, Last Night of the Proms, 2005. Tours to USA and performance in Far East, Australia and major Eur. countries, incl. Russia. FRSA. Hon. FRCO 1975; Hon. FRCCO 1986; Hon. FRCM 1986. Hon. Student, Christ Church, Oxford, 2010. Edison Award, 1971; Grand Prix du Disque, 1979; Performer of the Year Award, NY Chapter, Amer. Guild of Organists, 1987. *Recreations:* croquet, crosswords.

PRESTON, Susanna; *see* Gross, S.

PRESTON, Walter James, FRICS; Partner, Jones Lang Wootton, 1957–87, Consultant, 1987–99; *b* 20 March 1925; *s* of Walter Ronald and Agnes Ann McNeil Preston; *m* 1956, Joy Dorothea Ashton; two *s* one *d*. *Educ:* Dollar Academy, Perthshire. Served Royal Engineers, 1943–47. Jones Lang Wootton, 1948–99, Staff, 1948–57. Dir (non-exec.), Lynton Property and Reversionary plc, 1985–88. Liveryman: Chartered Surveyors' Co., 1977–; Vintners' Co., 1990–. *Recreation:* golf. *Clubs:* Phyllis Court (Henley); Woking Golf; Trevose Golf and Country.

PRESTWICH, Prof. Michael Charles, OBE 2010; FRHistS; FSA; Professor of History, University of Durham, 1986–2008, now Emeritus; *b* 30 Jan. 1943; *s* of late John Oswald Prestwich and Menna Prestwich; *m* 1973, Margaret Joan Daniel; two *s* one *d*. *Educ:* Charterhouse; Magdalen Coll., Oxford (MA); Christ Church, Oxford (DPhil). FSA 1980. Res. Lectr, Christ Church, Oxford, 1965–69; Lectr in Mediaeval History, Univ. of St Andrews, 1969–79; University of Durham: Reader in Medieval History, 1979–86; Pro-Vice-Chancellor, 1992–99; Sub-Warden, 1997–99. *Publications:* War, Politics and Finance under Edward I, 1972; The Three Edwards: war and state in England 1272–1377, 1980; Documents illustrating the Crisis of 1297–98 in England, 1980; Edward I, 1988; English Politics in the Thirteenth Century, 1990; Armies and Warfare in the Middle Ages, 1996; Plantagenet England, 1225–1360, 2005; Knight, 2010; Medieval People, 2014; articles in learned jls. *Recreation:* ski-ing. *Address:* Langdale, Hillrise Lane, Longframlington, Morpeth, Northumberland NE65 8BN. *T:* (01665) 570684.

PRETORIA, Bishop of, since 1998; **Rt Rev. Dr Johannes Thomas Seoka;** *b* 29 Aug. 1948; *s* of Isaac and Margaret Seoka; *m* 1980, Sybil Elizabeth Nomathonya; two *s*. *Educ:* school in Stanger; Eshowe Coll. of Educn, Zululand (grad. as teacher, 1971); St Bede's Coll., Umtata; Chicago Theol Seminary, Ill, USA (MTh); Univ. of Chicago (DMin); studies in industrial mgt, W Germany and USA. Deacon 1974, priest 1975, Natal; Curate, St Augustine, Umlazi, Natal, 1976–78; Rector, St Peter's, Greytown, 1978–80; Rector, St Hilda's, Senaoane, Soweto, 1980; seconded as Dir of Industrial Mission, 1981; Priest-in-Charge: Trinity Episcopal Church, Chicago, Ill, 1986; St James's, Diepkloof, Soweto, 1993–95; Church of the Good Shepherd, Tladi, Soweto, 1995–96; Dean of Pretoria and Rector, St Alban's Cathedral, 1996–98. Pres., SA Council of Churches, 2010–. Continuing urban and industrial work, including: Dir, Agency for Industrial Mission; Dir, Urban and Industrial Mission, 1994. CPSA Rep., Faith and Order Commn, WCC; Mem., WCC Adv. Gp on Urban and Rural Mission, 1983–. Hon. DD Gen. Theol Seminary, NY, 2006. *Publications:* contribs to books and magazines. *Address:* PO Box 1032, Pretoria 0001, S Africa. *T:* (12) 3222218; 237 Schoeman Street, Pretoria 0002, S Africa.

PRETTEJOHN, Nicholas Edward Tucker; Chairman, Scottish Widows Group, since 2014; *b* 22 July 1960; *s* of Dr Edward Joseph Tucker Prettejohn and Diana Sally Prettejohn; *m* 1997, Claire Helen McKenna; two *d*. *Educ:* Balliol Coll., Oxford (BA 1st Cl. Hons PPE 1981; Pres., Oxford Union, 1980). Mgt Consultant, Bain & Co., 1982–91; Dir, Apax Partners, 1991–94; Dir of Corporate Strategy, NFC plc, 1994–95; Lloyd's of London: Head of Strategy, 1995–97; Man. Dir, Business Develt Unit, 1997–99, and N America Business Unit, 1998–99; Chief Exec., 1999–2005; Chief Exec., Prudential UK and Europe, and Dir, Prudential plc, 2006–09. Non-executive Director: Legal and General plc, 2010–13; Lloyds Banking Gp, 2014–; Chm., Brit Insurance, 2011–13. Chm., Financial Services Practitioner Panel, 2007–09; Mem. Bd, Prudential Regulation Authy, Bank of England, 2013–14. Trustee, Royal Opera House, 2005–13; Mem., BBC Trust, 2014–. Chairman: Britten-Pears Foundn, 2009–; Bd of Govs, RNCM, 2012–. *Recreations:* opera, music, theatre, horse racing, golf, cricket, Rugby.

PRETTY, Prof. Jules Nicholas, OBE 2006; Professor of Environment and Society, since 2000 and Deputy Vice-Chancellor, since 2011, University of Essex; *b* Jos, Nigeria, 5 Oct. 1958; *s* of John and Susan Pretty; partner, Gill Boardman; one *s* one *d*. *Educ:* Denes High Sch., Lowestoft; Univ. of York (BA Hons Biol. 1979); Imperial Coll., London (MSc Envmtl Technol. 1981). Res. Officer, Imperial Coll., London, 1985–86; Res. Associate and Associate Dir, 1986–91, Dir, 1991–97, Sustainable Agric. Prog., Internat. Inst. for Envmt and Develt; University of Essex: Vis. Prof., 1997; Dir, Centre for Envmt and Society, 1997–99, 2000–04; Hd, Dept of Biol Scis, 2004–08; Pro-Vice-Chancellor, 2010–. A. D. White Prof.-at-Large, Cornell Univ., 2001–07; Nat C. Robertson Vis. Prof., Emory Univ., Atlanta, 2007. Dep. Chm., UK Adv. Cttee on Releases to the Envmt, 1999–2009; Member: Strategy Bd, 2009–11, Food Security Strategy Adv. Panel, 2011–15, BBSRC; Lead Expert Gp, Foresight Food and Farming Futures Project, 2009–11; Expert Panel, UK Nat. Ecosystem Assessment, 2009–11; Expert Panel, Greening the Economies, Switzerland, 2014–; Wkg Gp, Health of the Public 2040, Acad. of Med. Scis, 2014–; Chair, Sustainable Intensification Innovation Lab., Kansas State Univ., 2014–. Member, Royal Society commn on Biological Approaches to Improving Crop Prodn, 2008–09, on People and the Planet, 2010–12. Chm., Essex Rural Commn, 2008–; Vice-President: Suffolk ACRE, 2009–; Rural Community Council of Essex, 2010–; Essex Wildlife Trust, 2010– (Trustee, 2005–09). Presenter: Ploughing Eden (also writer), BBC Radio 4, 1999; The Magic Bean (also co-writer), BBC TV, 2001; Silent Spring (also writer), BBC Radio 3 essay, 2012. Mem., Judges Panel, New Angle Prize for Literature, 2015. FRSB (FIBiol 2003); FRSA 2004. Chief Ed., Internat. Jl of Agricl Sustainability, 2002–. Hon. Dr Ohio State, 2009. *Publications:* Unwelcome Harvest: agriculture and pollution (with G. R. Conway), 1991; Regenerating Agriculture: policies and practice for sustainability and self-reliance, 1995; (jtly) A Trainers' Guide to Participatory Learning and Action, 1995; The Living Land, 1998; (ed jtly) Fertile Ground: the impact of participatory watershed management, 1999; Agri-Culture: reconnecting people, land and nature, 2002; (ed) Guide to a Green Planet, 2002; (ed jtly) Waste Management, 2003; (ed) The Pesticide Detox: towards a more sustainable agriculture, 2005; (ed) The Earthscan Reader in Sustainable Agriculture, 2005; (ed) The Sage Major Work on the Environment, 2006; (jtly) Biological Approaches for Sustainable Soil Systems, 2006; (jtly) Guide to a Healthy Planet, 2006; (ed jtly) Sage Handbook on Environment and Society, 2007; The Earth Only Endures: on reconnecting with nature and our place in it, 2007; (ed) Sustainable Agriculture and Food, 4 vols, 2008; (jtly) Nature and Culture, 2010; This Luminous Coast (East Anglian nature book of the year, East Anglian Book Awards, 2011; New Angle Prize for Literature, 2013); (jtly) Eco-Cultures, 2014; The Edge of Extinction: travels with enduring people in vanishing lands, 2014; over 300 papers and articles. *Recreations:* walking, cycling, gardening, watching real football (Colchester United). *Address:* University of Essex, Wivenhoe Park, Colchester, Essex CO4 3SQ. *T:* (01206) 874889. *E:* jpretty@essex.ac.uk. *W:* www.julespretty.com.

PRETTY, Dr Katharine Bridget, CBE 2009; FSA, FSA (Scot.); Principal, Homerton College, Cambridge, 1991–2013 (Hon. Fellow, 2013); Deputy Vice-Chancellor, University of Cambridge, 2010–13 (Pro-Vice-Chancellor, 2004–10); *b* 18 Oct. 1945; *d* of M. W. and B. E. W. Hughes; *m* 1988, Prof. Tjeerd Hendrik van Andel (*d* 2010). *Educ:* King Edward VI High Sch. for Girls, Birmingham; New Hall, Cambridge (MA, PhD). New Hall, Cambridge: College Lectr and Fellow in Archaeology, 1972–91; Admissions Tutor, 1979–85; Sen. Tutor, 1985–91; Emeritus Fellow, 1995–; University of Cambridge: Member: Council of Senate, 1981–89; Financial Bd, 1986–96; Gen. Bd, 1997–2004; Chm. Council, Sch. of Humanities and Social Scis, 1997–2004; Sen. Fellow, McDonald Inst. for Archaeol Res., 2013–. Chairman: Rescue, 1978–83; OCR Examng Bd, 1998–2013. Pres., Council for British Archaeol., 2008–13. Trustee, Prince's Teaching Inst., 2007–15. Mem., Council, Durham Univ., 2014–. Vice-Pres., RSA, 1998–2004. FSA 2000 (Mem. Council, 2011–15); FSA (Scot.) 2013. Hon. Fellow, Harris Manchester Coll., Oxford, 2011. *Recreations:* archaeology, botany.

PREVEZER, Susan Rachel; QC 2000; a Recorder, since 2000; *b* 25 March 1959; *d* of late Prof. Sydney Prevezer and of Enid Margaret Prevezer (*née* Austin); *m* 1994, Benjamin Freedman; two *d*. *Educ:* St Paul's Girls' Sch.; Girton Coll., Cambridge (MA). Called to the Bar, Inner Temple, 1983. *Address:* Quinn Emanuel Urquhart & Sullivan LLP, 1 Fleet Place, EC4M 7RA.

PREVIN, André (George), Hon. KBE 1996; conductor, pianist and composer; Conductor Laureate, London Symphony Orchestra, since 1992; Music Director, Oslo Philharmonic, 2002–06; *b* Berlin, Germany, 6 April 1929; *s* of Jack Previn and Charlotte Epstein; *m* 1970; three *s* (incl. twin *s*), three *d*; *m* 1982, Heather (marr. diss.), *d* of Robert Sneddon; one *s*; *m* 2002, Anne-Sophie Mutter, *qv* (marr. diss. 2006). *Educ:* Berlin and Paris Conservatoires; private study with Pierre Monteux, Castelnuovo-Tedesco. Composer of film scores, 1950–62 (four Academy Awards). Music Dir, Houston Symphony Orchestra, 1967–69; Principal Conductor, London Symphony Orchestra, 1968–79, Conductor Emeritus, 1979; Music Director: Pittsburgh Symphony Orchestra, 1976–84; Los Angeles Phil. Orch., 1986–89; Music Dir, 1985–86, Prin. Conductor, 1987–91, RPO; Prin. Guest Conductor, NHK SO, Tokyo, 2009–; Guest Conductor, most major orchestras, US and Europe, Covent Garden Opera, Salzburg Festival, Edinburgh Festival, Osaka Festival; Music Dir, London South Bank Summer Festival, 1972–74. Formed André Previn Jazz Trio, 1990. Member: Composers Guild of GB; Amer. Composers League; Dramatists League. Recording artist. Principal *compositions*: Cello Sonata; Violin Sonata, 1994; Bassoon Sonata; Guitar Concerto; Wind Quintet; Serenades for Violin; piano preludes; Piano Concerto, 1984; Trio for piano, oboe and bassoon, 1994; Principals, Reflections (for orchestra); Every Good Boy Deserves Favour (text by Tom Stoppard); Six Songs Mezzo-Soprano (text by Philip Larkin); Honey and Rue (text by Toni Morrison); Sally Chisum Remembers Billy the Kid (text by Michael Ondaatje); Four Songs for soprano, cello and piano (text by Toni Morrison), 1994; The Magic Number (for soprano and orch.), 1997; A Streetcar Named Desire (opera), 1998; Violin Concerto, 2002; Brief Encounter (opera), 2009. Annual TV series: specials for BBC; PBS (USA). *Publications:* Music Face to Face, 1971; (ed) Orchestra, 1979; André Previn's Guide to Music, 1983; No Minor Chords (autobiog.), 1992; *relevant publications:* André Previn, by Edward Greenfield, 1973; Previn, by H. Ruttencutter, 1985.

PREVITE, His Honour John Edward; QC 1989; a Circuit Judge, 1992–2001; *b* 11 May 1934; *s* of late Lt Col K. E. Previte, OBE and Edith Frances (*née* Capper); *m* 1959, Hon. Phyllida Browne, *d* of 6th Baron Kilmaine, CBE; two *s*. *Educ:* Wellington Coll.; Christ Church, Oxford (MA). Called to the Bar, Inner Temple, 1959, Bencher, 1986; a Recorder, Western Circuit, 1987–92. *Recreations:* sailing, skiffing, Real tennis, gardening.

PREVOST, Sir Christopher (Gerald), 6th Bt *cr* 1805; *b* 25 July 1935; *s* of Sir George James Augustine Prevost, 5th Bt and Muriel Emily (*d* 1939), *d* of late Lewis William Oram; *S* father, 1985; *m* 1964, Dolores Nelly, *o d* of Dezo Hoffmann; one *s* one *d*. *Educ:* Cranleigh School. Served 60th Regt (formed by Prevost family) and Rifle Bde; Kenya Service Medal, 1955. IBM, 1955–61; Pitney-Bowes, 1963–76; founder of Mailtronic Ltd, manufacturers and suppliers of mailroom equipment, 1977, Chm. and Man. Dir, 1977–91; owner of water sports business, Algarve, Portugal, 1991–98. Mem., Huguenot Soc. *Heir:* *s* Nicholas Marc Prevost, *b* 13 March 1971.

PRIAULX, Andrew Graham, MBE 2008; racing driver; *b* 10 Aug. 1973; *s* of Graham Ernold Priaulx and Judith Anne Priaulx; *m* 1997, Joanne Le Tocq; one *s* one *d*. *Educ:* Elizabeth Coll., Guernsey. Winner, British Hillclimb Championship, 1995; competed Formula Renault and British Formula 3, 1996; winner, British Renault Spider Cup Championship, 1999–2002; competed British Formula 3, 2000–02; joined BMW UK team, 2003; winner: European Touring Car Championship, 2004; World Touring Car Championship, 2005, 2006, 2007. BMW Ambassador competing in DTM series, 2012, 2013, and in USCC with BMW Motorsport, USA, 2014; Awards include: Lifetime Ambassador, States of Guernsey, 2005; BBC SW Sports Personality of Year, 2005. Gold Medal, British Racing Drivers Club, 2007; Gold Medal, BARC, 2006, 2007. *Recreations:* running, boating, family. *Address:* Andy Priaulx Racing, 2/37 York Place, Harrogate HG1 5RH. *Clubs:* British Racing Drivers', Midland Automobile, British Automobile Racing.

PRICE, Adam; Public Innovation Lead, National Endowment for Science, Technology and the Arts, since 2012; *b* 23 Sept. 1968. *Educ:* Amman Valley Comprehensive Sch.; Saarland Univ.; Univ. of Wales Coll. of Cardiff (BA 1991). Res. Associate, Dept of City and Regl Planning, UWCC, 1991–93; Project Manager, 1993–95, Exec. Manager, 1995–96, Exec. Dir, 1996–98, Menter an Busnes; Man. Dir, Newidiem Econ. Develt Consultancy, 1998–2001. Contested (Plaid Cymru) Gower, 1992. MP (Plaid Cymru) Carmarthen E and Dinefwr, 2001–10. *Publications:* The Collective Entrepreneur; (jtly) The Welsh Renaissance: innovation and inward investment in Wales, 1992; Rebuilding Our Communities: a new agenda for the valleys, 1993; Quiet Revolution? language, culture and economy in the nineties, 1994; The Diversity Dividend, 1996; (jtly) The Other Wales: the case for objective 1 funding post 1999, 1998. *Recreations:* contemporary culture, good friends, good food, travel.

PRICE, (Alan) Anthony; author and journalist; Editor, The Oxford Times, 1972–88; *b* 16 Aug. 1928; *s* of Walter Longsdon Price and Kathleen Price (*née* Lawrence); *m* 1953, Yvonne Ann Stone; two *s* one *d*. *Educ:* King's Sch., Canterbury; Merton Coll., Oxford (Exhibnr; MA). Oxford & County Newspapers, 1952–88. *Publications:* The Labyrinth Makers, 1970 (CWA Silver Dagger); The Alamut Ambush, 1971; Colonel Butler's Wolf, 1972; October Men, 1973; Other Paths to Glory, 1974 (CWA Gold Dagger, 1974; Swedish Acad. of Detection Prize, 1978); Our Man in Camelot, 1975; War Game, 1976; The '44 Vintage, 1978; Tomorrow's Ghost, 1979; The Hour of the Donkey, 1980; Soldier No More, 1981; The Old Vengeful, 1982; Gunner Kelly, 1983; Sion Crossing, 1984; Here Be Monsters, 1985; For the Good of the State, 1986; A New Kind of War, 1987; A Prospect of Vengeance, 1988; The Memory Trap, 1989; Eyes of the Fleet, 1990. *Recreation:* history. *Address:* Flat 2, 53 Blackheath Park, Blackheath, SE3 9SQ. *T:* (020) 8852 2642.

PRICE, (Albert) John; QC 2009; a Recorder, since 2007; *b* Bradford, Yorks, 29 April 1960; *s* of Albert and Eileen Price; *m* 1996, Ruth Caroline Sainsbury; four *d*. *Educ:* Jesus Coll., Oxford (BA Hons Juris.). Called to the Bar, Inner Temple, 1982. *Recreations:* golf, gardening. *Address:* 23 Essex Street, WC2R 3AA. *T:* (020) 7413 0353, *Fax:* (020) 7413 0374. *E:* JohnPrice@23es.com.

PRICE, Bernard Albert, CBE 1997; DL; County Clerk and Chief Executive, Staffordshire County Council, and Clerk to the Lieutenancy, 1983–2003; Clerk to the Staffordshire Police Authority, 1995–2003; *b* 6 Jan. 1944; *s* of Albert and Doris Price; *m* 1966, Christine Mary, *d* of Roy William Henry Combes; two *s* one *d*. *Educ:* Whitchurch Grammar Sch., Salop; King's Sch., Rochester, Kent; Merton Coll., Oxford (BA 1965, MA 1970). DMS, Wolverhampton Polytechnic, 1972. Articled, later Asst Solicitor, Worcs CC, 1966–70; Asst Solicitor, subseq. Dep. Dir of Admin, Staffs CC, 1970–80; Sen. Dep. Clerk, Staffs CC, 1980–83. Mem. Council, 2004–, Hon. Sec., 2012–, Staffs Wildlife Trust; Mem., W Midlands Regl Cttee, 2004–10, Dep. Chm., Midlands Adv. Bd, 2010–12, National Trust. Lay Mem., Chapter, 2004–09, Mem. Council, 2009–13, Lichfield Cathedral. Trustee, Abbots Bromley Hosp., 2011–. DL Stafford, 2003. Hon. LLD Keele, 2002. *Recreations:* walking, Spain. *Address:* The Cottage, Yeatsall Lane, Abbots Bromley, Rugeley, Staffs WS15 3DY. *T:* (01283) 840269.

PRICE, Prof. Christopher Philip, PhD; CSci; FRCPath; CChem, FRSC; FACB; Visiting Professor in Clinical Biochemistry, University of Oxford, since 2002; *b* 28 Feb. 1945; *s* of Philip Bright Price and Frances Gwendoline Price; *m* 1968, Elizabeth Ann Dix; two *d*. *Educ:* Cirencester Grammar Sch.; Lanchester Poly. (BSc); Univ. of Birmingham (PhD 1973); MA Cantab 1983. CChem 1977; FRSC 1982; FRCPath 1989; FACB 2000; CSci 2005. Basic Grade Clin. Biochemist, Coventry and Warwickshire Hosp., 1967–72; Principal Grade Clin. Biochemist, E Birmingham Hosp., 1972–76; Consultant Clinical Biochemist: Southampton Gen. Hosp., 1976–80; Addenbrooke's Hosp., Cambridge, 1980–88; Prof. of Clin. Biochem., London Hosp. Med. Coll., then QMW, 1988–2001; Dir of Pathol., The Royal Hosps, then Barts and the London, NHS Trust, 1995–2001; Vice-Pres., Outcomes Res., Diagnostics Div., Bayer HealthCare, Tarrytown, NY, 2002–05; Emeritus Prof. in Clinical Biochemistry, QMUL, 2006. Vis. Prof. in Med. Diagnostics, Cranfield Univ., 2005–08. Mem., Ind. Rev. of Pathology Services in England, 2006–08. Pres., Assoc. for Clinical Biochem., 2003–06. Hon. DSc: De Montfort, 1998; Coventry, 2011. *Publications:* Centrifugal Analysers in Clinical Chemistry, 1980; Recent Advances in Clinical Biochemistry, Vol. 2, 1981, Vol. 3, 1985; Principles and Practice of Immunoassay, 1991, 2nd edn 1997; Point-of-Care Testing, 1999, 3rd edn 2010; Evidence-Based Laboratory Medicine, 2003, 2nd edn 2007; Point-of-Care Testing for Managers and Policymakers, 2006; Applying Evidence Based Laboratory Medicine: a step-by-step guide, 2008; Point-of-Care Testing: making innovation work for patient centred care, 2012. *Recreations:* walking, concerts, dry stone walling.

PRICE, Sir Curtis (Alexander), KBE 2005; PhD; Warden, New College, Oxford, 2009–Sept. 2016; *b* 7 Sept. 1945; *s* of Dalias Price and Lillian Price (*née* Alexander); adopted British nationality, 2006; *m* 1981, Rhian Samuel; one step *s*. *Educ:* Southern Illinois Univ. (BA 1967); Harvard Univ. (AM 1970; PhD 1974). Washington University, St Louis: Asst Prof., 1974–79; Associate Prof., 1979–82; King's College London: Lectr, 1982–85; Reader in Historical Musicology, 1985–88; King Edward Prof. and Head of Dept of Music, 1988–95; FKC 1994; Principal, Royal Acad. of Music, 1995–2008. Guggenheim Fellow, 1982–83. Pres., Royal Musical Assoc., 1999–2002. Hon. RAM 1993; Hon. FRNCM 2001; Hon. FRCM 2002. Einstein Award, Amer. Musicol. Soc., 1979; Dent Medal, Royal Musical Assoc., 1985. *Publications:* Music in the Restoration Theatre, 1979; Henry Purcell and the London Stage, 1984; Dido and Aeneas: a critical score, 1986; The Impresario's Ten Commandments, 1992. *Address:* New College, Oxford OX1 3BN. *E:* curtis.price@btinternet.com. *Club:* Garrick.

PRICE, His Honour David; a Circuit Judge, 2004–10; *b* 27 Sept. 1943; *s* of Bevan Glyn Price and Nora Price; *m* 1971, Jennifer Newton; two *s*. *Educ:* King Edward VI Sch., Stratford upon Avon; Univ. of Leeds (LLB). Called to the Bar, Inner Temple, 1968; in practice on Midland Circuit, 1968–93; a Recorder, 1992–2004. Asst Parly Boundary Comr, 1992; Chairman: Employment Tribunals, 1993–2004; Reinstatement Cttee, Reserve Forces, 1996–2004. *Recreations:* golf, music, theatre. *Club:* Luffenham Heath Golf.

PRICE, David; *see* Price, Geoffrey D.

PRICE, David Jack; QC 2011; Principal, David Price Solicitors & Advocates, since 1993; *b* London, 16 Oct. 1963; *s* of Lionel and Judith Price; *m* 1992, Nicole Cohen; two *s* one *d*. *Educ:* Haberdashers' Aske's Sch., Elstree; Harvard High Sch., LA (ESU Schol.); Manchester Univ. (LLB 1986); Coll. of Law, Lancaster Gate. Admitted as solicitor, 1990; barrister, 1991; re-admitted as solicitor, 1992; Solicitor-Advocate, 1995. *Publications:* Defamation: law procedure and practice, 1995, 4th edn 2009. *Recreations:* balls (hitting, bowling and kicking), snow, sea and sand. *Address:* David Price Solicitors & Advocates, 21 Fleet Street, EC4Y 1AA. *T:* (020) 7353 9999, *Fax:* (020) 7353 9990. *E:* enquiries@lawyers-media.com. *Clubs:* MCC; Arsenal Football.

PRICE, Dr David John, CBE 2010; CEng, CSci; Chairman: Telesoft Technologies Ltd, since 2013; RTL Materials Ltd, since 2014; Optitune plc, since 2014; Symetrica Ltd, since 2015; *b* Hawkhurst, Kent, 27 March 1955; *s* of Ifan and Margaret Price; *m* 1979, Rosalynd Fiona Davidson; two *d*. *Educ:* Maidstone Grammar Sch.; University Coll. London (BSc 1977; PhD 1982). CEng 1984; CSci 2003. Thorn EMI: Prog. Manager, 1980–87, Chief Scientist, 1987–90, Defence Systems Div.; Systems Dir, 1990–93, Prog. Dir, 1993–95, Defence Gp; Chief Exec., Thomson-Thorn Missile Electronics, 1995–98; Managing Director: Thomson (UK) Hldgs Ltd, 1998–2000; Rolls-Royce Naval Marine, 2000–05; Chief Exec., Chemring Gp plc, 2005–12. Non-exec. Dir, AZ Electronic Materials plc, 2011–. Mem. Adv. Bd, DK Group BV, 2013–. Public Mem., Network Rail, 2013–. Member: Defence Scientific Adv. Council, 1998–2005; Nat. Defence Industries Council, 2008–. Member: Adv. Bd, Loughborough Univ. Business Sch., 2005–10; Council, Univ. of Southampton, 2010–. Hon. DSc Cranfield, 2011. *Recreations:* opera, cinema, tennis, horse riding, reading, travel. *Address:* Ashe Hill, Ashe, Basingstoke, Hants RG25 3AE. *T:* (01256) 771228. *E:* dprice2703@aol.com.

PRICE, David William James; investment director and farmer; Chairman, F and C (formerly Foreign and Colonial) Management Ltd, 1999–2004; *b* 11 June 1947; *s* of Richard James Emlyn Price and Miriam Joan Dunsford; *m* 1971, Shervie Ann Lander Whitaker, *d* of Sir James Whitaker, 3rd Bt, OBE; one *s* one *d*. *Educ:* Ampleforth Coll.; Corpus Christi Coll., Oxford (MA). Director: Mercury Asset Management Gp, 1978–97 (Dep. Chm., 1985–97); S. G. Warburg and Co. Ltd, 1982–86; London Bd, Halifax Building Soc., 1993–96; Merrill Lynch European Investment (formerly Mercury Privatisation, then Mercury European Investment) Trust, 1994–2004; Scottish American Investment Co., 1997–; Booker plc, 1998–2000; Big Food Gp, 2000–04; Melchior Japan Investment Trust, 2006–11; Chairman: Aberdeen All Asia Investment (formerly Govett Asian Recovery, later Gartmore Asia Pacific) Trust, 1998–2009; Gartmore Absolute Growth & Income Trust, 2000–04; Iceland Group, 2001–04. Dir, Heritage Trust of Lincs, 1997–2012; Trustee, Orders of St John Care Trust, 2001–10. Councillor (C), London Borough of Lambeth, 1979–82. Mem. Council, KCL, 2001–08. *Recreations:* history, gardening. *Address:* Harrington Hall, Spilsby, Lincs PE23 4NH. *T:* (01790) 753764. *Clubs:* Brooks's; Lincolnshire.

PRICE, Elizabeth, PhD; artist; Lecturer in Fine Art, Ruskin School of Drawing and Fine Art, University of Oxford, since 2012; Fellow, Lady Margaret Hall, Oxford, since 2012; *b* Bradford, 1966. *Educ:* Ruskin Sch. of Art, Univ. of Oxford (BA Fine Art 1988); Royal Coll. of Art (MA Fine Art 1991); Univ. of Leeds (PhD Fine Art 1998). Principal Lectr, then Reader, Kingston Univ., until 2010; Arts Council England Helen Chadwick Fellow, Univ. of Oxford and British Sch. at Rome, 2010–11. Works include video installations: At the House of Mr X, 2007; Welcome (The Atrium), 2008; User Group Disco, 2009; The Tent, 2010; The Woolworths Choir of 1979, 2012; West Hinder, 2012; *solo exhibitions and screenings* include: Help, 2001, Denness, 2003, Mobile Home, London; Jerwood Artists Platform, Jerwood Space, London, 2004; Cry, 2006, O Fontana, 2008, The Woolworths Choir of 1979, 2012, MOT International; At the House of Mr X, Stanley Picker Gall., London, 2007, BFI, 2008; User Group Disco, Spike Island, Bristol, 2009, Whitechapel Gall., London, 2010, Contemp. Art Soc., London, 2013; Choir, New Mus., NY, Chisenhale Gall., London, 2011, Bielefelder Kunstverein, 2012; Here, Baltic, Gateshead, 2012; The Tent, Bloomberg SPACE, London, 2012; Sleep, MOT Internat., Brussels, 2014; Tate Britain, 2012. Jarman Award, FLAMIN, 2011; Paul Hamlyn Award, 2012; Turner Prize, 2012. *Address:* MOT International, First Floor, 72 New Bond Street, W1S 1RR. *T:* (020) 7491 7208. *E:* info@motinternational.com.

PRICE, Eric Hardiman Mockford; Director, Robinson Brothers (Ryders Green) Ltd, since 1985; Partner, Batchworth Heath Farm and Stud, since 2000; *b* 14 Nov. 1931; *s* of Frederick H. Price and Florence N. H. Price (*née* Mockford); *m* 1963, Diana M. S. Robinson; one *s* three *d*. *Educ:* St Marylebone Grammar Sch.; Christ's Coll., Cambridge. Econs Tripos, 1955; MA 1958. FREconS, 1956; FSS 1958; MInstPet 1992. Army service, 1950–52; HAC, 1952–57. Supply Dept, Esso Petroleum Co. Ltd, 1955–56; Economist: Central Electricity Authority, 1956–57; Electricity Council, 1957–58; British Iron & Steel Fedn, 1958–62; Chief Economist, Port of London Authority, 1962–67; Sen. Econ. Adviser, Min. of Transport, 1966–69; Chief Econ. Adviser, Min. of Transport, 1969–71; Dir of Econs, 1971–75, Under Sec., 1972–76, Dir of Econs and Stats, 1975–76, DoE; Under Sec., Econs and Stats Div., Depts of Industry, Trade and Consumer Protection, 1977–80; Head of Econs and Stats Div., Dept of Energy, 1980–92; Chief Econ. Advr, Dept of Energy, later DTI, 1980–93. Proprietor, Energy Economics Consultancy, 1995–99; Special Consultant, Nat. Econ. Res. Associates, 1993–98. Member: Soc. of Business Economists, 1961; Expert Adv. Gp on Entry into Freight Transport Market, EEC, 1973–75; Northern Regional Strategy Steering Gp, 1976–77; Expert Gp on Venture Capital for Industrial Innovation, EEC, 1978–79; Soc. of Strategic and Long-range Planning, 1980–; Council, Internat. Assoc. of Energy Economists, 1981–85; Energy Panel, SSRC, 1980–83; Council, British Inst. of Energy Economics, 1986–2006 (Mem., 1980–2005; Hon. Fellow, 2006; Vice-Chm., 1981–82 and 1988–89; Chm., 1982–85); Steering Cttee, Jt Energy Programme, RIIA, 1981–89, Steering Cttee, Energy and Envmtl Prog., 1989–; Adv. Council, Energy Econs Centre, Univ. of Surrey, 1989–93. UK rep., Econ. Res. Cttee, European Council of Ministers of Transport, 1968–76; UK rep. on Six Nations' Prog. on Govt Policies towards Technological Innovation in Industry, 1977–80; Mem., World Bank's Groupe des Sages on Econs of Global Warming, 1990–93. Member, Advisory Board: Transport Studies Unit, Oxford Univ., 1973–75; Centre for Res. in Industrial, Business and Admin Studies, Univ. of Warwick, 1977–80. FInstD 1990. *Publications:* various articles in learned jls on transport and industrial economics, energy and energy efficiency, investment, utilities, technological innovation in industry, regional planning, environmental abatement policies, and East European energy issues. *Recreations:* racehorse breeding, local history, horse racing. *Address:* Batchworth Heath Farm and Stud, London Road, Rickmansworth, Herts WD3 1QB. *Clubs:* Moor Park Golf (Hon. Mem.); Riverside Health and Leisure (Northwood, Middx).

PRICE, Sir Francis (Caradoc Rose), 7th Bt *cr* 1815; QC (Can.) 1992; barrister and solicitor; *b* 9 Sept. 1950; *s* of Sir Rose Francis Price, 6th Bt and Kathleen June, *d* of late Norman W. Hutchinson, Melbourne; *S* father, 1979; *m* 1975, Marguerite Jean Trussler, retired Justice, Court of Queen's Bench, Alberta, *d* of late Roy S. Trussler, Victoria, BC; three *d*. *Educ:* Eton; Trinity College, Melbourne Univ. (Sen. Student 1971–72, LLB Hons 1973); Univ. of Alberta (LLM 1975); Canadian Petroleum Law Foundn Fellow, 1974–75. Admitted barrister and solicitor, Province of Alberta 1976, Northwest Territories 1978, Canada; Bencher, Law Soc. of Alberta, 1990–94. Lectr, 1979–89, and Course Head, 1983–89, Alberta Bar Admission Course. Chartered Arbitrator, Arbitration and Mediation Inst. of Canada, 1994. CLJ 2000. *Publications:* Pipelines in Western Canada, 1975; Mortgage Actions in Alberta, 1985; Conducting a Foreclosure Action, 1996; contribs to Alberta and Melbourne Univ. Law Revs, etc. *Recreations:* opera, cricket, theatre. *Heir:* *b* Norman William Rose Price [*b* 17 March 1953; *m* 1987, Charlotte Louise, *yr d* of late R. R. B. Baker]. *Address:* 9626 95th Avenue, Edmonton, AB T6C 2A4, Canada. *Club:* Faculty (Edmonton).

PRICE, Sir Frank (Leslie), Kt 1966; Chairman, Price-Brown Partnership (formerly Sir Frank Price Associates), 1985–2006; *b* 26 July 1922; *s* of G. F. Price. *Educ:* St Matthias Church Sch., Birmingham; Vittoria Street Arts Sch. FRICS (FSVA 1960); FCIT 1969. Dir, 1958–68, Man. Dir, 1965–68, Murrayfield Real Estate Co.; Chairman: Birmingham Midland Investments, 1967–74; Alexander Stevens Real Estate, 1968–80; Wharf Holdings, 1968–72; Beagle Shipping, 1968–72; Butlers & Colonial Wharfs, 1971–76. Elected to Birmingham City Council, 1949; Alderman, 1958–74; Lord Mayor, 1964–65. Member: Council, Town and Country Planning Assoc., 1958–74; W Midlands Economic Planning Council, 1965–72; Nat. Water Council, 1975–79; Chm., British Waterways Bd, 1968–84. Founder/Chm., Midlands Art Centre for Young People, 1960–71; Chairman: W Midlands Sports Council, 1965–69; Telford Development Corporation, 1968–71; Comprehensive Develt Assoc., 1968–80; Dir, National Exhibn Centre, 1968–74. Member: Minister of Transport's Cttee of Inquiry into Major Ports, 1961; English Tourist Board, 1976–83; President: BAIE, 1979–83; Mojacar Assoc. of Commerce, 1994–2009. Mem., Fédn Internat. des Professions Immobilières. DL: Warwicks, 1970–77; West Midlands, 1974–77; Herefordshire and Worcestershire, 1977–84. Freeman, City of London; Liveryman, Basketmakers' Co., 1966–. Hon. Citizen, New Orleans, 1980. *Publications:* Being There (autobiog.), 2002; various pamphlets and articles on town planning, transport and public affairs. *Recreations:* painting, cruising. *Address:* Casa Noel, Limoneros - Huerta Nueva 42, 04280 Los Gallardos, Almeria, Spain. *Club:* Reform.

PRICE, Gareth; broadcast management consultant, since 2005; *b* 30 Aug. 1939; *s* of Rowena and Morgan Price; *m* 1962, Mari Griffiths; two *s* one *d*. *Educ:* Aberaeron Grammar School and Ardwyn Grammar School, Aberystwyth; University College of Wales, Aberystwyth (BA Econ). Asst Lectr in Economics, Queen's Univ., Belfast, 1962–64; BBC Wales: Radio Producer, Current Affairs, 1964–66; Television Producer, Features and Documentaries, 1966–74; Dep. Head of Programmes, 1974–81; Head of Programmes, 1981–85; Controller, 1986–90; Thomson Foundation: Controller of Broadcasting, 1990–93; Dir, 1993–2005. Vice-Pres., Welsh Centre for Internat. Affairs, 2012– (Chm., 2003–12). Consultant, Asia-Pacific Broadcasting Union, 2010–. Vice-Chm., Communication and Inf. Cttee, UNESCO UK, 2006–10. Hon. Sec., Elizabeth R. Fund, 2006–. Hon. Prof. of Communication, Univ. of Wales, Cardiff, 1994–99; Hon. Fellow, Univ. of Wales, Aberystwyth, 2000–. Elizabeth R Lifetime Achievement Award for Promoting Public Broadcasting, Commonwealth Broadcasting Assoc., 2006. *Publications:* David Lloyd George (with Emyr Price and Bryn Parry), 1981; Broadcast Management for Asians, 2006. *Address:* 98 Pencisely Road, Cardiff CF5 1DQ.

PRICE, Prof. (Geoffrey) David, PhD; FGS; Professor of Mineral Physics, since 2006, and Vice Provost (Research), since 2007, University College London; *b* 12 Jan. 1956; *s* of Prof. Neville J. Price and Joan J. Price; *m* 1978, Prof. Sarah L. Price (*née* Millar); one *s* one *d*. *Educ:* Latymer Upper Sch.; Clare Coll., Cambridge (MA; PhD 1980). Royal Soc. Res. Fellow, 1983–88; Reader in Mineral Physics, 1988–91, Prof. of Mineral Physics, 1991–2006, UCL and Birkbeck Coll., London Univ.; Hd, Dept of Earth Scis, 1992–2002 and 2004–05, Vice Dean (Res.), 2003–06, Exec. Dean, 2006–07, Math. and Physical Scis, UCL. Ed., Earth and Planetary Sci. Letters, 2005–07. Chairman: HEFCE REF 2014 sub-panel for Earth and Envmtl Scis, 2011–14; Policy Cttee, League of Eur. Res. Univs, 2014–; Mem., STFC, 2012–. Pres., Mineralogical Soc. of GB, 2004–06 (Mem., 1977–; Schlumberger Medal, 1999); FGS 1992 (Murchison Medal, 2002); FMSA 1997; Fellow, Amer. Geophysical Union, 2005. MAE 2000. Non-exec. Dir, North Middlesex Univ. Hosp. NHS Trust, 2012–15. Chm. Govs, UCL Academy Sch., Camden, 2011–. Mem., Editl Bd, The Conversation, 2014–. Louis Néel Medal, Eur. Geoscis Union, 2006. *Publications:* over 270 papers in learned jls on mineralogy, geophysics and micropalaeontology. *Recreations:* philately, family history. *Address:* Office of Vice Provost (Research), University College London, 2 Taviton Street, WC1H 0BT. *T:* (020) 7679 8581. *E:* d.price@ucl.ac.uk.

PRICE, Geraint; *see* Price, William G.

PRICE, His Honour Gerald Alexander Lewin; QC 1992; a Circuit Judge, 2000–10; *b* 13 Sept. 1948; *s* of Denis Lewin Price and Patricia Rosemary (*née* Metcalfe); *m* 1974, Theresa Elisabeth Iremonger-Watts; two *s*. *Educ:* Haileybury Coll.; College of Law; Inns of Court Law Sch. Called to the Bar, Middle Temple, 1969; in private practice, Cardiff, 1970–77; Bermuda: Resident Stipendiary Magistrate, 1977–81; Chief Stipendiary Magistrate and Sen. Coroner, 1981–84; in private practice, Cardiff, 1984–2000; a Recorder, 1990–2000. Chairman: Liquor Licence Authority, Land Valuation Appeals Tribunal, Price Control Commn and Jury Revising Tribunal, 1981–84. Mem., Commonwealth Magistrates and Judges Assoc., 1984–. Mem., RYA. *Recreations:* travel, classical music, sunshine, motorboating in Menorca. *Clubs:* Glamorgan Lawn Tennis and Croquet (Merthyr Mawr); Menorca Cricket.

PRICE, Prof. Huw, PhD; FBA 2012; Bertrand Russell Professor of Philosophy, University of Cambridge, since 2011; Fellow, Trinity College, Cambridge, since 2011; *b* 1953. *Educ:* Australian Nat. Univ. (BA 1976); Univ. of Oxford (MSc 1977); PhD Cantab 1981. Sydney Univ., 1989–2000, Prof. of Natural Metaphysics, 1997–2000; Prof. of Logic and Metaphysics, Univ. of Edinburgh, 2000–03; ARC Fedn Fellow, 2002–11, and Challis Prof. of Philosophy and Founding Dir, Centre for Time, 2002–12, Univ. of Sydney. Consulting Ed., Stanford Encyclopedia of Philosophy, 1995–2006; Associate Ed., Australasian Jl Philosophy; Member, Editorial Advisory Board: Contemp. Pragmatism; Logic and Philosophy of Sci.; Eur. Jl for Philosophy of Sci. Past Pres., Australasian Assoc. Philosophy. FAHA 1994. *Publications:* Facts and the Function of Truth, 1988; Time's Arrow and Archimedes' Point, 1996; (ed with R. Corry) Naturalism Without Mirrors, 2011; Expressivism, Pragmatism and Representationalism, 2013; contribs to Jl Philosophy, Mind, British jl for Philosophy of Sci., Nature. *Address:* Faculty of Philosophy, University of Cambridge, Sidgwick Avenue, Cambridge CB3 9DA.

PRICE, Isobel Clare M.; *see* McKenzie-Price.

PRICE, Jackie D.; *see* Doyle-Price.

PRICE, Sir James Keith Peter Rugge-, 10th Bt *cr* 1804, of Spring Grove, Richmond, Surrey; *b* 8 April 1967; *er s* of Sir Keith Rugge-Price, 9th Bt and of Jacqueline Mary Rugge-Price (*née* Loranger); *S* father, 2000, but his name does not appear on the Official Roll of the Baronetage. *Heir:* *b* Andrew Philip Richard Rugge-Price, *b* 6 Jan. 1970.

PRICE, James Richard Kenrick; QC 1995; *b* 14 Sept. 1948; *s* of Lt-Col Kenrick Jack Price, DSO, MC, 9th Lancers and Juliet Hermione, *d* of Marshal of the Royal Air Force Sir John Cotesworth Slessor, GCB, DSO, MC; *m* 1983, Hon. Virginia Yvonne, *d* of 5th Baron Mostyn, MC. *Educ:* Eton College; St Edmund Hall, Oxford. Called to the Bar, Inner Temple, 1974. Dir, Mostyn Estates Ltd, 1994–. *Recreations:* fine and decorative arts, gardening, mountains, ski-ing, Corfu. *Address:* 5 Gray's Inn Square, Gray's Inn, WC1R 5AH. *T:* (020) 7242 2902. *Clubs:* Brooks's, Beefsteak.

PRICE, John; *see* Price, A. J.

PRICE, His Honour John Charles; a Circuit Judge, 2003–15; *b* 8 March 1945; *s* of Hubert and Betty Price. *Educ:* Wrekin Coll., Wellington, Shropshire; The Hill Sch., Pottstown, Pa,

USA; Univ. of Birmingham (LLB Hons). Called to the Bar, Gray's Inn, 1969, Bencher, 2009; in practice, 1969–2003; a Recorder of the Crown Court, 1990–2003. *Recreations:* tennis, sailing, ski-ing, maintaining friendships. *Club:* Garrick.

PRICE, Prof. John Frederick, MD; FRCP, FRCPCH; Consultant Paediatrician, King's College Hospital, 1978–2010; Professor of Paediatric Respiratory Medicine, University of London, since 1992; Clinical Director of Paediatrics, King's NHS Healthcare Trust, 1993–96 and 1999–2010; *b* 26 April 1944; *s* of Drs Cyril Frederick Price and Dora Elizabeth Price; *m* 1971, Dr Valerie Pickup; two *d. Educ:* Dulwich Coll.; St John's Coll., Cambridge (MB BCh; MA; MD 1986); Guy's Hosp., London. DCH 1973; FRCP 1985; FRCPCH 1997. MRC Trng Fellowship, Inst. of Child Health and Gt Ormond St Hosp., 1975–78; Hd, Acad. Dept of Child Health, 1995–98, and Chm., Div. of Child Health and Reproductive Medicine, 1995–98, GKT Med. and Dental Sch., KCL (formerly King's Coll. Sch. of Medicine and Dentistry), Univ. of London. Vis. Prof. and Ext. Examr, Hong Kong Univ. and Univ. of Malaya, 1997. Altounyan Address, Brit. Thoracic Soc., 1989; C. Elaine Field Lecture, Hong Kong Paediatric Soc., 1997, 2000. Sec., Paediatric Section, Royal Soc. Medicine, 1988–90; Chm., Brit. Paediatric Respiratory Soc., 1992–94; Council Member: Brit. Thoracic Soc., 1990–; European Respiratory Soc., 1990–95. Chm., Nat. Asthma Campaign, subseq. Asthma UK, 2003–09 (Trustee, 1990–2009; Vice Pres., 2010); Trustee: Brit. Lung Foundn, 1990–95; Demelza Hospice Care for Children, 2015; Member: Med. Adv. Panel, Nat. Eczema Soc., 1987–91; Res. and Med. Adv. Cttee, Cystic Fibrosis Trust, 1993–98 (Trustee, 2010–). Master, Fruiterers' Co., 2013. Associate Editor: Respiratory Medicine, 1987–93; European Respiratory Jl, 1990–93. *Publications:* (with J. Rees) ABC of Asthma, 1984, 3rd edn 1995; contrib. chapters in books; numerous articles in learned jls related to respiratory disease in childhood. *Recreations:* theatre, music, Austen, Trollope, conversations with family and friends. *Address:* Wychling Hall, Wichling, Kent ME9 0DJ. *Clubs:* Athenæum, Walbrook Ward; Hawks (Cambridge).

PRICE, Air Vice-Marshal John Walter, CBE 1979 (OBE 1973); UK Manager, Courage Energy Corporation (UK Manager, Altaquest Energy Corporation, 1997); *b* Birmingham, 26 Jan. 1930; *s* of late Henry Walter Price, MM, and Myrza Price (*née* Griffiths); *m* 1st, 1956, Margaret Sinclair McIntyre (*d* 1989), Sydney, Aust.; 2nd, 2004, Ilse Gertrud Burrows (*née* Koepke). *Educ:* Solihull Sch.; RAF Coll., Cranwell. Joined RAF, 1948; commnd 1950; Adjutant, No 11 (Vampires and Venoms) Sqn, 1950–52; No 77 (Meteor) Sqn, RAAF, Korea, 1952–53 (mentioned in despatches, 1953; Air Medal, US); Flt Comdr, No 98 Sqn (Venoms and Vampires), 1953–54; Tactics and Gunnery Instructor, No 2 (F) Op. Trng Unit (Vampires) and Flt Comdr, No 75 (F) Sqn (Meteors), RAAF, 1954–56; Cadet Wing Adjutant, RAF Tech. Coll., Henlow, 1956–60; RAF Staff Coll., 1960; Air Ministry (Ops Overseas), 1961–64; Comd No 110 Sqn (Sycamore and Whirlwind), Malaya and Borneo, 1964–66; Directing Staff, RAF Staff Coll., 1966–68; PSO to Chief of Air Staff, 1968–70; Comd No 72 (Wessex) Sqn, NATO and NI, 1970–72; student, Coll. of Air Warfare, 1972; Dep. Dir Ops (Offensive Support and Jt Warfare), MoD (Air), 1973–75; sowc, RNC, Greenwich 1975–76; Comd RAF Laarbruch (Buccaneers and Jaguars), 1976–78; Gp Capt. Ops, HQ Strike Comd, 1979; Dir of Ops (Strike), MoD (Air), 1980–82; ACAS (Ops), 1982–84, retd. Clyde Petroleum plc, 1984–95 (Manager, External Affairs and Exploration Admin, 1986–95). MRAeS 1971; CCMI (FBIM 1979, CIMgt 1997; Mem. Council, 1994–2000); MEI. Gov., Solihull Sch., 1979–2005 (Chm., 1983–2005). Pres., 98 Sqn Assoc., 2010–. Freeman, City of London, 2001; Liveryman, Co. of Fuellers, 2001– (Mem. Court, 2003–; Jun. Warden, 2005; Mem. Hon. Court, 2009). DL Hereford and Worcester, 1995–2005. *Recreations:* studying political and economic current questions, European history 1815–1945, enjoying company of my wife and my friends, travel. *Address:* 2 Palace Yard, Hereford HR4 9BJ. *Clubs:* Army and Navy; Colonels.

PRICE, Leontyne; Opera Prima Donna (Soprano), United States; *b* 10 Feb. 1927. *Educ:* Public Schools, Laurel, Mississippi; Central State College, Wilberforce, Ohio (BA); Juilliard Sch. of Music, NY. Four Saints, 1952; Porgy and Bess, 1952–54. Operatic Debut on TV, 1955, as Tosca; Concerts in America, England, Australia, Europe. Operatic debut as Madame Lidouine in Dialogues of Carmelites, San Francisco, 1957; Covent Garden, Verona Arena, Vienna Staatsoper, 1958; five roles, inc. Leonora in Il Trovatore, Madame Butterfly, Donna Anna in Don Giovanni, Metropolitan, 1960–61; Salzburg debut singing soprano lead in Missa Solemnis, 1959; Aida in Aida, Liu in Turandot, La Scala, 1960; opened season at Metropolitan in 1961 as Minnie in Fanciulla del West; opened new Metropolitan Opera House, 1966, as Cleopatra in world premiere of Samuel Barber's Antony and Cleopatra; debut Teatro Dell'Opera, Rome, in Aida, 1967; debut Paris Opera, in Aida, 1968; debut Teatro Colon, Buenos Aires, as Leonora in Il Trovatore, 1969; opened season at Metropolitan Opera, in Aida, 1969. Numerous recordings. Vice-Chm., Nat. Inst. for Music Theatre. Member: Metropolitan Opera Assoc.; Bd of Dirs, Dance Theatre of Harlem; Bd of Trustees, NY Univ. Life Mem., NAACP. Fellow, Amer. Acad. of Arts and Sciences. Hon. Dr of Music: Howard Univ., Washington, DC, 1962; Central State Coll., Wilberforce, Ohio, 1968; Hon. DHL, Dartmouth Univ., 1962; Hon. Dr of Humanities, Rust Coll., Holly Springs, Miss, 1968; Hon. Dr of Humane Letters, Fordham Univ., New York, 1969. Hon. Mem. Bd of Dirs, Campfire Girls, 1966. Presidential Medal of Freedom, 1965; Spingarn Medal, NAACP, 1965; Nat. Medal of Arts, 1985; 18 Grammy Awards, Nat. Acad. Recording Arts and Scis. Order of Merit (Italy), 1966; Commandeur, Ordre des Arts et des Lettres (France), 1986. *Recreations:* cooking, dancing, shopping for clothes, etc, antiques for homes in Rome and New York.

PRICE, Mark Ian, CVO 2014; Managing Director, Waitrose Ltd, since 2007; Deputy Chairman, John Lewis Partnership, since 2013; *b* 2 March 1961; *s* of Graham and Marjorie Price; *m* 1991, Judith Caroline Bolt; two *d. Educ:* Lancaster Univ. (BA Archaeol.). Managing Director: John Lewis, High Wycombe, 1992–95; John Lewis, Cheadle, 1995–98; Mktg Dir, 1998–2000, Dir of Selling and Mktg, 2000–05, Waitrose Ltd; Man. Dir, Partnership Develt, John Lewis, 2005–07; Dir, John Lewis Partnership, 2005–. Chairman: Prince's Countryside Fund, 2010–; Business in the Community, 2011–15. Mem. Bd, Channel 4, 2010– (Dep. Chair, 2013–). *Publications:* The Great British Picnic Guide, 2008; Modern Manner, 2014. *Recreations:* picnics, gardening, shooting, fishing, golf. *Address:* Waitrose Ltd, Doncastle Road, Bracknell RG12 8YA. *T:* (01344) 824286, *Fax:* (01344) 824488. *E:* mark_price@waitrose.co.uk.

PRICE, His Honour Nicholas Peter Lees; QC 1992; a Circuit Judge, 2006–14; Senior Circuit Judge and Resident Judge, Kingston-upon-Thames Crown Court Centre, 2011–14; *b* 29 Sept. 1944; *s* of Frank Henry Edmund Price, MBE (mil.) and Agnes Lees Price; *m* 1969, Wilma Ann Alison (*née* Steel); one *s* one *d. Educ:* Prince of Wales Sch., Nairobi; Edinburgh Univ. (LLB). Called to the Bar, Gray's Inn, 1968, Bencher, 2000; *ad eundem* Mem., Middle Temple; Asst Recorder, 1983–87; a Recorder, 1987–2006. Member: Gen. Council of the Bar, 1993–95 (Jt Vice Chm., Legal Services Cttee, 1994; Vice Chm., Public Affairs Cttee, 1995; Professional Standards Cttee, 2002–05; Vice Chm., Professional Conduct & Complaints Cttee, 2005–06); Gray's Inn Continuing Educn Cttee, 1998–2003 (Vice Chm., 1999–2000; Chm., 2001–03); Associate Mem., Criminal Bar Assoc., 1993–95. Hon. Recorder, Richmond on Thames, 2013–14. *Recreations:* watching Rugby, crosswords, destructive gardening, cinema.

PRICE, Nick; golfer; founded Nick Price Golf Course Design, 2001; *b* Durban, 28 Jan. 1957; *m* Sue Price; one *s* two *d.* Wins include: US PGA, 1992, 1994; Open, Turnberry, 1994; Vardon Trophy, 1993; record for PGA Tournament lowest score (269), 1994. *Publications:* The Swing, 1997. *Address:* c/o Professional Golfers' Association Tour, 112 PGA Tour Boulevard, Ponte Vedra Beach, FL 32082, USA.

PRICE, Nigel Stewart; Master of the Senior (formerly Supreme) Court, Chancery Division, since 1999; *b* 18 May 1954; *s* of late Ernest Henry Price and Diana Price (*née* Lane). *Educ:* Billesley Infant and Jun. Schs; Moseley Grammar Sch., Birmingham; Christ's Coll., Cambridge (MA); Coll. of Law; City of Birmingham Poly; Open Univ. (BA Hons Classics, French and Spanish 2010). Admitted solicitor, 1978; articled clerk and Asst Solicitor, Clifford Turner, 1976–80; Asst Solicitor, Pinsent & Co., 1980–82; Lectr in Law, Univ. of Buckingham, 1983–86; Partner, Kimbell & Co., 1986–99; Dep. Master, Chancery Div., 1992–99; Immigration Adjudicator, 1996–98. Consulting Ed., Atkin's Court Forms, 2014–; Ed., Civil Procedure, 2015–. Alfred Syrett 2nd Prize, City of London Solicitors' Co., 1976. *Publications:* (ed and contrib.) Jowitt's Dictionary of English Law, 3rd edn 2010; contribs to legal jls. *Recreations:* languages, music, literature, ski-ing, dog walking. *Address:* Chancery and Commercial Courts, Rolls Building, 110 Fetter Lane, EC4A 1BR.

PRICE, Rt Rev. Peter Bryan; Bishop of Bath and Wells, 2002–13; *b* 17 May 1944; *s* of Alec Henry Price and Phyllis Evelyn Mary Price; *m* 1967, Edith Margaret Burns (MBE 2010); four *s. Educ:* Redland Coll., Bristol (Cert Ed 1966); Oak Hill Theol Coll. (Dip. in Pastoral Studies, 1974). Asst Master, Ashton Park Sch., Bristol, 1966–70; Tutor, Lindley Lodge, Nuneaton, 1970; Head of Religious Studies, Cordeaux Sch., Louth, 1970–72; ordained, 1974; Community Chaplain, Crookhorn, Portsmouth and Asst Curate, Christ Church, Portsdown, 1974–78; Chaplain, Scargill House, Kettlewell, 1978–80; Vicar, St Mary Magdalene, Addiscombe, Croydon, 1980–88; Canon Residentiary and Chancellor, Southwark Cathedral, 1988–91, Canon Emeritus, 1992–97; Gen. Sec., USPG, 1992–97; Area Bp, Kingston-upon-Thames, 1997–2002. Chairman: Anglican Communion Pastoral Visitors, 2008–13; Conciliation Resources, 2013–. Mem., Inst. for Policy Develt, Univ. of Bath, 2014. Founding Trustee, Burns Price Foundn, 2015. Vice Pres., Royal Bath and West Soc., 2014– (Pres. 2012–13). Visitor, Wadham Coll., Oxford, 2002–13. Entered House of Lords, 2008. Hon. LLD Bath, 2013. *Publications:* The Church as Kingdom, 1987; Seeds of the Word, 1996; Telling it as it is, 1998; Living Faith in the World through Word and Action, 1998; To Each their Place, 1999; Mark Today, 1999; Jesus Manifesto: reflections on St Luke's gospel, 2000; Undersong: listening to the soul, 2001; Playing the Blue Note, 2002; (with Jeanne Hinton) Changing Communities, 2003. *Recreations:* painting, swimming, walking, conversation. *Address:* 4 Longways, Shaftesbury Road, Gillingham, Dorset SP8 4ED.

PRICE, Peter Nicholas; European Strategy Counsel, since 1994; *b* 19 Feb. 1942; *s* of Rev. Dewi Emlyn Price and Kate Mary Price; *m* 1988, Joy Bhola; one *d. Educ:* Worcester Royal Grammar Sch.; Aberdare Boys' Grammar Sch.; Univ. of Southampton (BA (Law)); Coll. of Law, Guildford; KCL (Postgrad. Dip. in EC Law). Solicitor. Freelance broadcaster, 1962–67; Asst Solicitor, Glamorgan CC, 1967–68; solicitor in private practice, 1966–67 and 1968–85; part-time EC consultant: Payne Hicks Beach, 1990–93; Howard Kennedy, 1993–2001; pt-time Employment Judge (formerly Chm., Employment Tribunal), 2000–12. Contested (C) Gen. Elecns: Aberdare 1964, 1966; Caerphilly 1970; Nat. Vice-Chm., Young Conservatives, 1971–72; Mem., Nat. Union Exec. Cttee, 1969–72 and 1978–79; Vice-Chm., Cons. Pol Centre Nat. Cttee, 1978–79; Hon. Sec., For. Affairs Forum, 1977–79; Vice-Chm., Cons. Gp for Europe, 1979–81; Mem. Council, Eur. Movement, 1971–81. MEP (C): Lancashire W, 1979–84; London SE, 1984–94; Hon. MEP, 1994; European Parliament: Chm., Budgetary Control Cttee, 1989–92 (Vice-Chm., 1979–84, and its Rapporteur for series of 4 major reports on Community finances, 1985–86); spokesman for EDG, Legal Affairs Cttee, 1984–87, Budgets Cttee, 1986–89; Member: ACP/EEC Jt Assembly, 1981–94; Ext. Econ. Relns Cttee, 1992–94; delegns for relns with Japan, 1989–92, US Congress, 1992–94. Member: Lib Dem Federal Policy Cttee, 1998–; Alliance of Liberals and Democrats for Europe Party Council (formerly European Lib Dem and Reformist (Party) Council), 1999–; Lib Dem Federal Finance Cttee, 2001–06; Lib Dem Internat. Affairs Cttee, 2010–. Contested (Lib Dem) Wales, EP elecn, 1999. Standing Orders Comr, 1998–99, Mem., Commn on Powers of Nat. Assembly, 2002–04, Nat. Assembly for Wales. Non-executive Director: Bureau Veritas Quality Internat. Ltd, 1991–2001; Ravensbourne NHS Trust, 1998–99; Welsh Ambulance Services NHS Trust, 2005–13 (Vice Chm., 2010–12); Wales Audit Office, 2013–. Mem. Bd (formerly Exec. Cttee), Cymru Yfory/Tomorrow's Wales, 2004– (Chm., 2012–). Mem., NEC, FPA, 1973–77 (Mem., then Chm., Long-term Planning Gp, 1973–76). Fellow, Industry and Parlt Trust, 1981–82; Vice-Pres., UK Cttee, Eur. Year of Small and Med.-sized Enterprises, 1983. Mem., RIIA. Vice-Pres., Llangollen Internat. Eisteddfod, 1981–. Gov., Thames Valley Univ., 1996–2005. *Publications:* misc. pol pamphlets and newspaper articles. *Recreations:* theatre, music, photography. *Address:* 37 Heol St Denys, Lisvane, Cardiff CF14 0RU. *T:* (029) 2076 1792; 60 Marlings Park Avenue, Chislehurst, Kent BR7 6RD. *T:* (01689) 820681. *E:* peterprice@btinternet.com.

PRICE, Rev. Peter Owen, CBE 1983; BA; FPhS; RN retired; Minister of Blantyre Old Parish Church, Glasgow, 1985–96; *b* Swansea, 18 April 1930; *e s* of late Idwal Price and Florence Price; *m* 1957, Margaret Trevan (*d* 1977); three *d*; *m* 1996, Mary Hamill Robertson (*d* 2008). *Educ:* Hutchesons' Grammar Sch., Glasgow; King Edward's Grammar Sch., Camp Hill, Birmingham; Wyggeston Sch., Leicester; Didsbury Theol Coll., Bristol. BA Open Univ. Ordained, 1960, Methodist Minister, Birmingham; commnd RN as Chaplain, 1960; served: HMS Collingwood, 1960; HQ 3 Cdo Bde, RM, 1962–64; Staff of C-in-C Med., 1964–68; RNAS Brawdy, 1968–69; HQ 3 Cdo Bde, 1969–70, HQ Cdo Forces, 1970–73, RM; HMS Raleigh, 1973; HMS Drake, 1974–78; BRNC Dartmouth, 1978–80; Principal Chaplain, Church of Scotland and Free Churches (Naval), MoD, 1981–84. Hon. Chaplain to the Queen, 1981. *Recreations:* freemasonry (Past Grand Chaplain, Grand Lodge of Scotland), warm water sailing, music. *Address:* Duncraigan, 22 Old Bothwell Road, Bothwell, Glasgow G71 8AW.

PRICE, His Honour Philip John; QC 1989; a Circuit Judge, 1993–2008; Designated Family Judge, Cardiff, 1998–2006; *b* 16 May 1943; *s* of late Ernest and Eunice Price; *m* 1967, Mari Josephine Davies; one *s* two *d. Educ:* Cardiff High Sch.; Pembroke Coll., Oxford (MA). Lectr in Law, Univ. of Leeds, 1966–70; called to the Bar, Gray's Inn, 1969; in practice on Wales and Chester Circuit and Temple, 1971–93; a Recorder, 1985–93. Chancellor, Dio. Monmouth, 1992–; Pres., Disciplinary Tribunal, Church in Wales, 2001–05. Member: Mental Health Rev. Tribunal, 1995–; Cttee, Council of Circuit Judges, 1998–2007 (Sen. Vice Pres., 2007). Mem., 1993–, Chm., Standing Cttee, 2005–, Governing Body, Church in Wales. Trustee, LATCH-Welsh Children's Cancer Charity, 1996– (Chm., 2006–). *Recreations:* architecture, books, cricket. *Address:* HMCS Wales, Churchill House, Churchill Way, Cardiff CF10 2HH. *Club:* Cardiff and County.

PRICE, Richard Alexander David; Chief Executive, Office of Rail and Road (formerly Office of Rail Regulation), since 2011; Chair, UK Regulators' Network, since 2013; *b* 18 Aug. 1967; *s* of Prof. Roger David Price and Heather Lynne Price; *m* 1999, Dr Luisa Affuso; one *s* one *d. Educ:* Hewett Sch., Norwich; Univ. of York (BA Econs 1987, MSc Econs 1989). Economist, HM Treasury, 1989–93; Nat. Econ. Res. Associates, 1993–97; Home and Legal Team, HM Treasury, 1997–99; Chief Economist, Home Office, 1999–2001; Performance and Innovation Unit, Cabinet Office, 2001; Strategy Advr to the Permanent Sec., Home Office, 2001–02; Hd of Enterprise Policy, HM Treasury, 2002–05; Chief Economist, 2005–11, and Dir of Corporate Performance, 2008–11, DEFRA. Mem., Govt Economic Service Bd, 1999–2001, 2005–11. Non-exec. Dir, ETC Venues Ltd, 2005–06; alternate non-exec. Dir, Capital for Enterprise Bd, 2005. Sec., Highbury Railway Allotments and Gardens Soc., 2009–. FRSA. *Publications:* various policy and res. papers and articles on econ. regulation, entrepreneurship, migration, crime reduction, envmtl econs, globalisation and social impacts of policy. *Recreations:* modern and contemporary art, exploring Italy, food. *Address:* Office of Rail and Road, 1 Kemble Street, WC2B 4AN. *T:* (020) 7282 2000. *E:* richard.price@orr.gsi.gov.uk.

PRICE, Richard Mervyn, OBE 1995; QC 1996; a Recorder, since 2004; *b* 15 May 1948; *s* of late William James Price and Josephine May Price; *m* 1971, Caroline Sarah (marr. diss. 2007), *d* of Geoffrey and Mary Ball; one *s* two *d. Educ:* King Edward VII Sch., Sheffield; King's Coll., London (LLB Hons). Called to the Bar, Gray's Inn, 1969, Bencher, 2002; Accredited Mediator, 1997. Standing Counsel on Election Law to Conservative Central Office, 1986–. Mem., Bar Council, 1998–2002 (Vice-Chm., 2002–04, Chm., 2005, Professional Conduct and Complaints Cttee); Mem., Bar Standards Bd, 2006–07 (Chm., Conduct Cttee, 2006–07). Legal Assessor: to Disciplinary Cttee, RCVS, 2007–; to GMC, 2010–. *Publications:* (ed) Parker's Law and Conduct of Elections, 2003–; (cons. ed.) Halsbury's Laws of England, Elections and Referendums, 5th edn 2014. *Recreations:* politics, theatre, films, music, walking, cycling. *Address:* Littleton Chambers, 3 King's Bench Walk North, Temple, EC4Y 7HR. *T:* (020) 7797 8600; New Park Court Chambers, 16 Park Place, Leeds LS1 2SJ. *T:* (0113) 243 3277. *Clubs:* Garrick, Royal Automobile.

PRICE, His Honour Richard Neville Meredith; a Circuit Judge, 1996–2014; *b* 30 May 1945; *s* of Christopher Llewelyn Price and Valerie Ruby Price (*née* Greenham); *m* 1971, Avril Judith Lancaster; three *s. Educ:* Marsh Court, Stockbridge, Hants; Sutton Valence, Kent. Admitted solicitor, 1970; Asst Recorder, 1985–90; called to the Bar, Middle Temple, 1990; Recorder, 1990–96; Resident Judge, Portsmouth and Newport Crown Courts, 2004–11; Hon. Recorder, City of Portsmouth, 2006–11. *Recreations:* choral singing, sailing, reading, listening to music, appreciating Dr Who. *Clubs:* Bar Yacht; Seaview Yacht (IoW).

PRICE, Richard Ralph, FCA; Chairman, British Association for Performing Arts Medicine, since 2007; Director, Pearson Education Ltd, since 2014; *b* London, 1 Aug. 1944; *s* of Llewelyn Ralph Price and Vera Patricia Price; *m* 1967, Susan Jennifer Mary Smellie; one *s* one *d. Educ:* Glasgow Acad.; Watford Boys Grammar Sch.; Univ. Coll. of S Wales and Monmouthshire (BSc (Econ)). FCA 1969. Co-founder, BPP Hldgs plc, 1976, Chm., 1976–2002; Chm., EDI plc, 2004–12. Vice Pres., Action Med. Res. (Chm., 2008–14). Mem. Council, RCM, 2004–14 (Hon. FRCM 2015). Mem., Bach Choir (Chm., 2000–08). Hon. DLaws BPP. *Recreations:* golf, tennis, music, walking. *Clubs:* Brooks's; Denham Golf, Campden Hill Tennis; Royal Solent Yacht.

PRICE, Air Vice-Marshal Robert George, CB 1983; *b* 18 July 1928; *s* of Charles and Agnes Price, Hale, Cheshire; *m* 1st, 1958, Celia Anne Mary Talamo (*d* 1987); one *s* four *d*; 2nd, 1989, Edith Barbara Dye. *Educ:* Oundle Sch.; RAF Coll., Cranwell. 74 Sqn, 1950; Central Flying Sch., 1952; 60 Sqn, 1956; Guided Weapons Trials Sqn, 1958; Staff Coll., 1960; Bomber Comd, 1961; JSSC 1964; CO 31 Sqn, 1965; PSO to Dep. SACEUR, 1968; CO RAF Linton-on-Ouse, 1970; RCDS 1973; Dep. Dir Operations, 1974; Group Captain Flying Trng, Support Comd, 1978; Dep. Chief of Staff, Support HQ, 2nd Allied Tactical Air Force, 1979; AOA, RAF Germany, 1980; AOA, HQ Strike Comd, 1981–83.

PRICE, Sir Robert (John) G.; *see* Green-Price.

PRICE, Samantha Anna; Headmistress, Benenden School, since 2014; *b* London, 13 Jan. 1974; *d* of Graham Rangeley Mitchell and Valerie Joy Mitchell, *qv*; *m* 2000, Rev. Iorwerth Price; one *s* one *d. Educ:* Malvern Girls' Coll.; Univ. of Edinburgh (MA Hons Hist. of Art 1997). Direct Mktg Officer, Tate Gall., 1997–99; Hd of History of Art and Hd of Year, Reading Blue Coat Sch., 1999–2003; teacher and housemistress, King's Sch., Canterbury, 2003–07; Dep. Head, Hereford Cathedral Sch., 2007–10; Head, Godolphin Sch., Salisbury, 2010–13. Governor: Brambletye Prep. Sch., 2014–; Tonbridge Sch., 2014–. *Recreations:* cycling, horseriding, opera appreciation. *Address:* Benenden School, Cranbrook Road, Benenden, Kent TN17 4ES. *T:* (01580) 240592. *E:* saprice@benenden.kent.sch.uk.

PRICE, Sarah Helena; HM Diplomatic Service; Ambassador to Finland, since 2014; *b* 4 June 1966; *d* of John Michael Anthony Price and Mary Price; *m* 2006, Simon McGrath; two *s. Educ:* Holy Child Sch., Edgbaston; Somerville Coll., Oxford (BA Hons Classics and Mod. Langs 1989). Joined FCO, 1990: Third Sec., FCO, 1990–92; Second Secretary: UK Delegn to CSCE, Helsinki, 1992; Prague, 1993–96; First Sec., FCO, 1996–99; on secondment to Finnish Foreign Ministry, 1999–2000; Dep. Hd of Mission, Belgrade, 2000–04; Dep. Hd, Counter-Proliferation Dept, 2004–07, Hd, Drugs and Internat. Crime Dept, 2008, Counsellor, Strategic Finance Directorate, 2009–10, Hd, Arabian Peninsula and Iraq Dept, 2011–13, FCO. *Address:* c/o Foreign and Commonwealth Office, King Charles Street, SW1A 2AH.

PRICE, Prof. Shirley Christine, (Mrs P. L. Lane), PhD; FRSB, FBTS, FHEA; Head of Academic Appeals and Academic Quality, since 2014, and Professor of Toxicology, since 2010, University of Surrey; *b* London, 3 March 1956; *d* of Cecil Price and Irene Price; *m* 1984, Peter Leslie Lane; one *s* one *d. Educ:* Honor Oak Grammar Sch., London; Chelsea Coll., Univ. of London (BSc (Hons) Biochem.); Univ. of Surrey (MSc Toxicol.; PhD Toxicopathology 1985). University of Surrey: Robens Institute of Industrial and Environmental Health and Safety: Res. Asst, 1980–83; Res. Fellow, 1983–85; Res. Fellow in Electron Microscopy, 1985–87; Manager of Histopathology, 1987–88; Manager, In Vivo Toxicol. Gp, 1988–98; School of Biomedical and Molecular Sciences: Tutor, 1998–2001; Sen. Tutor, 2001–04; Sen. Lectr and Dir of Postgrad. Studies, 2004–10; Associate Dean (Learning and Teaching), 2009–14. Chm., UK Register of Toxicologists, 2007–12. Expert Toxicologist: Special Prog. of Res. Devel and Trng in Human Reproduction, WHO, 2000–04; Expert Adv. Gp on Veterinary Residues, 2005–; Expert Adv. Gp on Paediatric Medicines, 2009–; Mem., Commn on Human Medicines, 2014–. Mem., Kent, Surrey and Sussex Deanery Adv. Bd, 2011–. Gov., Royal Grammar Sch., Guildford, 2008–. Eur. Registered Toxicologist, 2000. FHEA 2008; FBTS 2009; FRSB (FSB 2012). *Publications:* Principles and Practice of Skin Toxicology, 2008; contrib. Eur. Jl of Pharmaceutical Scis. *Recreations:* theatre, singing in local choir, family, walking. *Address:* Office of the Deputy Vice-Chancellor (Academic Affairs), Directorate of Quality Enhancement and Standards, Senate House, University of Surrey, Guildford, Surrey GU2 7XH. *T:* (01483) 689215. *E:* s.price@surrey.ac.uk.

PRICE, Prof. Susan Ann, PhD; FCIL, FCMI, FHEA; Vice Chancellor, Leeds Beckett (formerly Leeds Metropolitan) University, since 2010; *b* South Shields, 11 Sept. 1956; *d* of Michael and Dorothea Price; *m* 1982, Dr Uwe Zemke. *Educ:* Salford Univ. (BSc 1st Cl. Hons Modern Langs); Salford Univ. and University Coll. London (PhD Linguistics 1982); Bradford Univ. (MBA). FCIL 2004. Lectr in Spanish, Bradford Univ., 1983–89; ESRC Fellow in Internat. Business, Manchester Univ., 1992–93; Dir of Academic Affairs, Dept of Modern Langs, Bradford Univ., 1993–97; Associate Dean, Faculty of Langs and Eur. Studies, UWE, 1998–2002; Pro Vice Chancellor (Academic), 2002–07, Dep. Vice Chancellor, 2007–08, Acting Vice Chancellor, 2008–09, Univ. of E London. MCIM 1993; FCMI 2003; FHEA 2008; FRSA. *Publications:* Comparative Constructions in Spanish and French Syntax, 1990. *Recreations:* travel, reading, food and wine. *Address:* Vice Chancellor's Office, The Rose Bowl, Portland Crescent, Leeds LS1 3HB. *T:* (0113) 812 3100, *Fax:* (0113) 812 6125. *E:* s.a.price@leedsbeckett.ac.uk.

PRICE, Thomas; QC 2010; *b* Burton on Trent, 23 March 1963; *s* of John Price and Josephine Maguire; partner, Claire Sugrue. *Educ:* Univ. of Southampton (LLB Hons). Called to the Bar, Inner Temple, 1985. *Recreations:* art, theatre, cooking, angling. *Address:* 25 Bedford Row, WC1R 4HD. *T:* (020) 7067 1500. *E:* tprice@25bedfordrow.com.

PRICE, Tristan Robert Julian; Group Finance Director, M. P. Evans Group PLC, since 2010 (Group Finance Controller, 2007–09); *b* 24 Nov. 1966; *s* of Julian Price and Isolde (*née* Buchloh); *m* 1988, Judith Ann Torrance; three *s* one *d. Educ:* Tonbridge Sch.; Corpus Christi Coll., Cambridge (BA Hons Econs 1988); University Coll. London (MSc Econs 1993). FCA 2007 (ACA 1992). Coopers & Lybrand, 1988–91; Treuhandanstalt, Berlin, 1992; joined FCO, 1993, Econ. Advr, 1993–98; OECD, 1999–2002; rejoined FCO, 2003; Dep. Hd, Econ. Policy Dept, 2003; Hd, Financial Planning and Perf. Dept, 2003–06. Chair, Faculty of Finance and Mgt, ICAEW, 2014–. *Publications:* (jtly) OECD Economic Surveys: Baltic States, 1999, Brazil, 2000, Yugoslavia, 2002. *Recreations:* my children, ski-ing, cycling, eating good cheese. *Address:* M. P. Evans Group PLC, 3 Clanricarde Gardens, Tunbridge Wells, Kent TN1 1HQ.

PRICE, Prof. (William) Geraint, FRS 1988; FREng, FIMechE, FRINA; Professor of Ship Science, 1990–2009, now Emeritus, and Head of School of Engineering Sciences, 1998, University of Southampton; *b* 1 Aug. 1943; *s* of Thomas Price and Ursula Maude Price (*née* Roberts); *m* 1967, Jennifer Mary Whitten; two *d. Educ:* Merthyr Tydfil County Grammar Sch.; University Coll. Cardiff (Univ. of Wales) (G. H. Latham Open Sci. Scholar; BSc, PhD); Univ. of London (DSc(Eng)). FRINA 1980; FREng (FEng 1986); FIMechE 1989. Res. Asst, later Lectr, UCL, 1969–81; Reader in Applied Mechanics, Univ. of London, 1981–82; Prof. of Applied Mechanics, Brunel Univ., 1982–90. Fellow: Japan Soc. for Promotion of Science, 1987; Y. S. Hui Foundn, 2004. Pres., RINA, 2001–04. Foreign Mem., Chinese Acad. of Engrg, 2000. *Publications:* Probabilistic Theory of Ship Dynamics, 1974; Hydroelasticity of Ships, 1979. *Recreations:* walking, Rugby, golf, barbecueing. *Address:* Tŷ Gwyn, 45 Palmerston Way, Alverstoke, Gosport, Hants PO12 2LY. *T:* (023) 9235 1719.

PRICE, William John R.; *see* Rea Price.

PRICE, Winford Hugh Protheroe, OBE 1983; FCA; City Treasurer, Cardiff City Council, 1975–83; *b* 5 Feb. 1926; *s* of Martin Price and Doris Blanche Price. *Educ:* Cardiff High Sch. IPFA 1952; FCA 1954. Served War, RAFVR, 1944–48. City Treasurer's and Controller's Dept, Cardiff, 1942; Dep. City Treasurer, Cardiff, 1973–75. Public Works Loan Comr, 1979–83. Treasurer and Financial Adviser, Council for the Principality, 1975–83; Financial Adviser, Assoc. of Dist Councils Cttee for Wales, 1975–83; Treasurer: The Queen's Silver Jubilee Trust (S Glam), 1976–83; Royal National Eisteddfod of Wales (Cardiff), 1978. Occasional lectr on local govt topics. *Publications:* contrib. to jls. *Recreation:* chess.

PRICE EVANS, David Alan; *see* Evans, David A. P.

PRICHARD, David Colville Mostyn, MBE 2002; Headmaster, Wycliffe College, 1994–98; *b* 26 May 1934; *s* of Rev. George Mostyn Prichard and Joan Mary Mostyn Prichard; *m* 1992, Catherine Elizabeth Major (formerly Headmistress, Warwick Prep. Sch.). *Educ:* Radley Coll.; Pembroke Coll., Oxford (Captain of Boats; MA; Mem., Society Cttee, 1956–2005). FCollP. Asst Master, Monkton Combe Sch., 1955–68 (Dir, Centenary Appeal, 1962; Founder, GB 1st Vol. Police Cadets, 1964; CO, CCF, 1964–68); Headmaster, Port Regis, Motcombe Park, 1969–93. Founder, Nat. Conf. for Govs, Bursars and Heads, 1981–93; Chm., IAPS, 1989–90. Mem. Develt Cttee, SW Arts, 1998–2006. Trustee, Smallpeice Trust, 1980–2003; Chm., Smallpeice Enterprises, 1986–95; Co-Chm., Operation New World, 1992–99 (Trustee, 1992–); Vice President: Glos Pied Piper Appeal, 1995; Wycliffe Watermen, 1998–. Governor: Swanbourne House Sch., 1985–2000; Holmewood House Sch., 1987–98; Orwell Park Sch., 1995–98; St John's Sch., Chepstow, 1995–99; West Hill Park Sch., 1998–2002; Sherborne Prep. Sch., 1999–2006 (Chm., 2002–06); Mem., Govs' Adv. Body, Wycliffe Coll., 2006–11. Vice-Chm., Sherborne and District Soc., 2009–15. Trustee, Sherborne House Trust, 1998–2006. Mem. Cttee, Friends of Yeatman Hosp., 2000–03. Church Warden, Castleton Church, 1999–2005. Freeman, City of London, 1990; Liveryman, Loriners' Co., 1990–. FRSA. *Publications:* Training for Service, 1967. *Recreations:* education, travel, rowing (OUBC Isis VIII). *Address:* Thornhill Lodge, North Road, Sherborne, Dorset DT9 3JW. *T:* (01935) 816539. *Clubs:* National, Carlton; Leander.

PRICHARD, Jonathan Layton, CEng, FICE; Chief Executive Officer, Engineering Council, since 2010; *b* Llanelli, 12 Feb. 1964; *s* of David Layton Prichard and Veronica Kay Prichard (*née* Evans); *m* 1989, Gillian Sarah Owen; two *s* one *d. Educ:* Shrewsbury Sch.; RMA Sandhurst; RMCS Shrivenham (BEng 1988). CEng 1998; CEnv 2004; FICE 2005. Served RE, 1983–2001. Dir, Membership, 2001–05, Dir, Engrg, 2005–07, ICE; Dir, Resources, High-Point Rendel, 2007–10. Served TA, 2003– (Col, 2007–); Actg Adjt, Engr and Logistic Staff Corps RE (V), 2004–. FInstRE 2009. Hon. FSE 2008. *Recreations:* sailing, ski-ing, DIY. *Address:* Engineering Council, Aldgate House, 33 Aldgate High Street, EC3N 1EN. *E:* info@engc.org.uk. *Clubs:* Royal Air Force; Royal Engineer Yacht.

PRICHARD, Mathew Caradoc Thomas, CBE 1992; DL; Chairman, Agatha Christie Ltd, since 1976; *b* 21 Sept. 1943; *s* of late Major H. de B. Prichard and Rosalind Hicks; *m* 1st, 1967, Angela Caroline Maples (*d* 2004); one *s* two *d*; 2nd, 2007, Lucinda Mary Oliver. *Educ:* Eton College; New College, Oxford. BA (PPE). Penguin Books, 1965–69. Pres., Nat. Mus. of Wales, 1996–2002 (Mem. Court of Governors and Council, 1975–2007); Member: Welsh Arts Council, 1980–94 (Chm., 1988–94); Arts Council of GB, 1983–94. High Sheriff, Glamorgan, 1972–73; DL S Glam, 1994. Prince of Wales Medal for Philanthropy, 2012. *Publications:* (ed) The Grand Tour: letters and photographs from the British Empire Expedition 1922, 2012. *Recreations:* golf, cricket, bridge. *Address:* Bettws Lodge, Bettws Newydd, Usk, Monmouthshire NP15 1JN. *T:* (01873) 881127. *Clubs:* Boodle's, MCC; Cardiff and County; Royal & Ancient Golf (St Andrews); Royal Porthcawl Golf.

PRICHARD, Air Vice-Marshal Richard Augustin R.; *see* Riseley-Prichard.

PRICHARD-JONES, Sir David John Walter, 3rd Bt *cr* 1910, of Bron Menai, Anglesey; *b* 14 March 1943; *s* of Sir John Prichard-Jones, 2nd Bt and Heather, *er d* of Sir Walter Nugent, 4th Bt; *S* father, 2007. *Educ:* Ampleforth; Christ Church, Oxford (BA). *Heir: cousin* Richard Stephen Prichard-Jones [*b* 23 Nov. 1952; *m* 2000, Jane Emma Lewsley; one *s* two *d* (of whom one *s* one *d* are twins)]. *Address:* 17 Tresco House, 2 Sancroft Street, Kennington, SE11 5UQ.

PRICKETT, Prof. (Alexander Thomas) Stephen, PhD; FEA; Honorary Professor of English, University of Kent at Canterbury, since 2008; *b* 4 June 1939; *s* of Rev. William Ewart Prickett and Barbara Browning (*née* Lyne); *m* 1st, 1967, Diana Joan Mabbutt; one *s* one *d*; 2nd, 1983, Maria Angelica Alvarez (marr. diss. 2001); 3rd, 2001, Patricia Erskine-Hill. *Educ:* Kent Coll., Canterbury; Trinity Hall, Cambridge (BA 1961; PhD 1968); University Coll., Oxford (DipEd). English teacher, Uzuakoli, E Nigeria, 1962–64; Asst Lectr, Lectr, and Reader, Univ. of Sussex, 1967–82; Prof. of English, ANU, Canberra, 1983–89; Regius Prof. of English Lang. and Lit., Univ. of Glasgow, 1990–2001; Margaret Root Brown Prof. of English and Dir, Armstrong Browning Liby, Baylor Univ., Texas, 2003–08. Vis. Lectr, Smith Coll., Mass, USA, 1970–71; Vis. Fulbright Prof., Univ. of Minnesota, 1979–80; Vis. Prof. of English, Duke Univ., USA, 2001–03. Trustee, Higher Educn Foundn, 1976–2004. President: Soc. for Study of Literature and Theology, 1991–2000; George MacDonald Soc., 1994–. FAHA 1986; Fellow, Soc. for Values in Higher Educn, USA, 1992; FRSA 1993; FEA 2004. Dr *hc*: Artois, France, 2002; Bucharest, 2015. Lifetime Achievement Award, Conf. on Christianity and Literature, 2015. *Publications:* Do It Yourself Doom, 1962; Coleridge and Wordsworth: the poetry of growth, 1970, 2nd edn 1980; Romanticism and Religion, 1976; Victorian Fantasy, 1979, 2nd edn 2005; Words and the Word: language poetics and biblical interpretation, 1986,

2nd edn 1988; England and the French Revolution, 1988; Reading the Text: biblical criticism and literary theory, 1991; (jtly) The Bible, 1991; Origins of Narrative: the romantic appropriation of the Bible, 1996; (ed) World's Classics Bible, 1997; (jtly) The Bible and Literature: a reader, 1999; Narrative, Religion and Science, 2002; (ed) Education! Education! Education!: managerial ethics and the law of unintended consequences, 2002; Modernity and the Reinvention of Tradition, 2009; (ed) European Romanticism: a reader, 2010; (ed) The Edinburgh Companion to the Bible and the Arts, 2014. *Recreations:* walking, ski-ing, drama.

PRIDDIS, Rt Rev. Anthony Martin; Bishop of Hereford, 2004–13; *b* 15 March 1948; *s* of Ted and Joan Priddis; *m* 1973, Kathy Armstrong; two *s* one *d*. *Educ:* Corpus Christi Coll., Cambridge (BA 1969; MA 1973); New Coll., Oxford (DipTh 1971; MA 1975); Cuddesdon Coll., Oxford. Ordained deacon, 1972, priest, 1973; Asst Curate, New Addington, 1972–75; Chaplain, Christ Church, Oxford, 1975–80; Team Vicar, High Wycombe, 1980–86; Priest-in-charge, 1986–90, Rector, 1990–96, Amersham; RD of Amersham, 1992–96; Suffragan Bp of Warwick, 1996–2004. Chair and Mem., Central Safeguarding Liaison Gp, C of E, 2002–10; Chm., Rural Bishops' Panel, 2006–09; Mem., Rural Strategy Gp, 2009–. Entered H of L, 2009. Lay Mem. Bd, CEM (formerly FAEM), 2002–08; Mem., W Midlands Cultural Consortium, 2002–05. Co-Chm., Family Life and Marriage Educn Network, 2001–06. Hon. FRCEM (Hon. FFAEM 2005). *Publications:* (contrib.) Study of Spirituality, 1986; various articles for mags, local and nat. radio and television. *Recreations:* walking the dogs, music, golf, gardening, watching sport, fly-fishing. *Address:* Round Oak Cottage, Bridstow, Ross-on-Wye HR9 6QJ. *E:* anthony@priddis.me.

PRIDDLE, Robert John, CB 1994; energy consultant: Endless Energy, since 2002; Plexus Energy, since 2002; Editor, World Energy Outlook, International Energy Agency, since 2003; *b* 9 Sept. 1938; *s* of late Albert Leslie Priddle and Alberta Edith Priddle; *m* 1962, Janice Elizabeth Gorham; two *s*. *Educ:* King's Coll. Sch., Wimbledon; Peterhouse, Cambridge (MA). Asst Principal, Min. of Aviation, 1960, Principal 1965; Private Sec. to Minister for Aerospace, 1971–73; Asst Sec., DTI, 1973, and Dept of Energy, 1974; Under Sec., Dept of Energy, 1977–85; Under Sec., DTI, 1985–89; Dep. Sec. and Dir Gen. of Energy Resources, Dept of Energy, subseq. DTI, 1989–92; Dep. Sec., Corporate and Consumer Affairs, DTI, 1992–94; Exec. Dir, Internat. Energy Agency, 1994–2002 (Chm., Governing Bd, 1991–92). Pres., Conf. of European Posts and Telecommunications Administrations, 1987–89. Mem., Financial Reporting Council, 1992–94. Chevalier de la Légion d'Honneur (France), 2001. *Publications:* Victoriana, 1959, 2nd edn 1963. *Address:* 1 Stable Court, Stodham Park, Liss, Hants GU33 7QX.

PRIDEAUX, John Denys Charles Anstice, CBE 1994; PhD; Chairman: Festiniog Railway Company, since 2006; Ffestiniog and Welsh Highland Railways Trust (formerly Festiniog Railway Trust), since 1998; Danube Eastern Railway Company, since 2013; *b* 8 Aug. 1944; *s* of Denys Robert Anstice-Prideaux and Frances Hester Dorothy Anstice-Prideaux (*née* Glaze); *m* 1972, Philippa Mary (*née* Morgan); one *s* one *d*. *Educ:* St Paul's; Univ. of Nottingham (BSc, PhD). British Railways: Operational Research, 1965; Area Manager, Newton Abbot, 1972; Strategic Planning Officer, 1974; Divl Manager, Birmingham, 1980; Dir, Policy Unit, 1983–86; Dir, 1986–91, Man. Dir, 1991, InterCity; Man. Dir, New Ventures, 1992–94; Chm., Union Railways, 1992–93; Director: Green Arrow, 1994–95; Docklands Light Railway, 1994–98; Chairman: Prideaux and Associates, 1994–99; Angel Train Contracts, 1996–98 (Dir, 1996–2008); Image Scan Hldgs Plc, 1998–2000; Altram (Manchester) Ltd, 1999–2003; Superlink Ltd, 2004–10. Member: Adv. Cttee on Trunk Road Assessment, 1977; Transport Cttee, SERC and ESRC, 1982; Planning and Envmt Cttee, ESRC, 1985; Special Advr on Railways, FIPRA Internat., 2005–. Mem., Council, Manchester Business School, 1987. *Publications:* railway histories, papers on management and transport. *Recreations:* rural affairs, farming, conservation, history, sailing, ski-ing, design. *Address:* Ffestiniog Railway Company, Harbour Station, Porthmadog, Gwynedd LL49 9NF.

PRIDEAUX, Julian Humphrey, OBE 1995; Deputy Director-General and Secretary, National Trust, 1997–2002; *b* 19 June 1942; 2nd *s* of Sir Humphrey Povah Treverbian Prideaux, OBE; *m* 1967, Jill, 3rd *d* of R. P. Roney-Dougal; two *s*. *Educ:* St Aubyn's, Rottingdean; Eton; Royal Agricultural Coll. (Dip. Estate Management). ARICS 1966, FRICS 1974. Land Agent with Burd & Evans, Shrewsbury, 1964–67; Agent to Col Hon. C. G. Cubitt and others, 1967–69; National Trust: Land Agent, Cornwall Region, 1969–77; Dir, Thames and Chilterns Region, 1978–86; Chief Agent, 1987–96. Mem. Council, 1987–2005, Trustee, 2003–05, Nat. Gardens Scheme; Trustee: Rural Housing Trust, 2001–14; Chelsea Physic Gdn, 2003–12; Goldsmiths Centre, 2007–12. *Recreation:* walking. *Address:* Bellbrook, Donhead St Mary, Shaftesbury, Dorset SP7 9DL. *Club:* Farmers.

PRIDHAM, Brian Robert; HM Diplomatic Service, retired; Hon. Research Fellow, Centre for Arab Gulf Studies, University of Exeter, 1995–2000 (Research Fellow, 1983–95; Director, 1985–86, 1987–95); *b* 22 Feb. 1934; *s* of Reginald Buller Pridham and Emily Pridham (*née* Winser); *m* 1st, 1954, Fay Coles (marr. diss. 1996); three *s*; 2nd, Lorraine Patricia Waitt (*née* Moore). *Educ:* Hele's Sch., Exeter. MA Exon, 1984. RWAFF (Nigeria Regt), 1952–54; Foreign Office, 1954–57; MECAS, 1957–59; Bahrain, 1959; Vice-Consul, Muscat, 1959–62; Foreign Office, 1962–64; 2nd Sec., Algiers, 1964–66, 1st Sec., 1966–67; Foreign Office, 1967–70; Head of Chancery: La Paz, 1970–73; Abu Dhabi, 1973–75; Dir of MECAS, Shemlan, Lebanon, 1975–76; Counsellor, Khartoum, 1976–79; Head of Communications Ops Dept, FCO, 1979–81. University of Exeter: Lectr in Arabic, Dept of Arabic and Islamic Studies, 1984–87; Dep. Dir, Centre for Arab Gulf Studies, 1984–85. Dep. Hd, EU Observer Mission to Palestinian Elections, 1995–96; Hd, OSCE Observer Mission to Albanian Elections, 1997; Hd, EU Observer Mission to Tanzanian Elections, 2000. Jt Ed., New Arabian Studies series, 1994–2007. *Publications:* (ed) Contemporary Yemen: politics and historical background, 1984; (ed) Economy, Society and Culture in Contemporary Yemen, 1984; (ed) The Arab Gulf and the West, 1985; (ed) Oman: economic, social and strategic developments, 1986; The Arab Gulf and the Arab World, 1987; (trans.) Omani-French Relations 1715–1905, 1996; (trans.) A Permissible Narrative, 2010; (ed) My Early Life, 2010. *Recreations:* shrubs, photography.

PRIDHAM, Kenneth Robert Comyn, CMG 1976; HM Diplomatic Service, retired; *b* 28 July 1922; *s* of late Colonel G. R. Pridham, CBE, DSO, and Mignonne, *d* of late Charles Cumming, ICS; *m* 1965, Ann Rosalind, *d* of late E. Gilbert Woodward, Metropolitan Magistrate, and of Mrs Woodward. *Educ:* Winchester; Oriel Coll., Oxford. Lieut, 60th Rifles, 1942–46; served North Africa, Italy, Middle East (despatches). Entered Foreign (subseq. Diplomatic) Service, 1946; served at Berlin, Washington, Belgrade and Khartoum, and at the Foreign Office; Counsellor: Copenhagen, 1968–72; FCO, 1972–74; Asst Under Sec. of State, FCO, 1974–78; Ambassador to Poland, 1978–81. Vis. Res. Fellow, RIIA, 1981–82. *Address:* c/o Lloyds Bank, 8/10 Waterloo Place, SW1Y 4BE. *Club:* Travellers.

PRIDHAM, Brig. Robert, OBE 1991; Clerk to the Grocers' Company, since 2006; *b* 9 Dec. 1949; *s* of late Kenneth Reginald Pridham, Grenadier Guards, and Theresia Pridham (*née* Berkemeier); *m* 1979, Jane Elizabeth Stibbon; four *d*. *Educ:* Hele's Sch., Exeter; RMCS Shrivenham (BSc Applied Sci. 1975); Univ. of Westminster (MA Internat. Liaison and Commns 2007). CEng 1998; FICE 1998. Enlisted Grenadier Guards, 1968; RMA Sandhurst, 1969–70; commnd RE, 1970; Troop Comd, Berlin and Cyprus, 1971; RMCS Shrivenham; Aide/Speechwriter, US Congress, Washington, 1972–75; Troop Comd, BAOR and NI, 1975–77; 3 Field Sqn, NI and Oman, 1977–79; Instructor, RMA Sandhurst, 1980; Army Comd and Staff Coll., Shrivenham and Camberley, 1981–82; Defence Operational Analysis Estabt, UK and Berlin, 1983–85; OC 39 Field Sqn BAOR, Canada and Australia, 1985–87; SO2 Mil Sec., MoD, 1987–88; SO1 Defence (Budget) Prog., MoD, 1988–90; CO 39 Engr Regt, UK, RAF Germany and Gulf, 1990–91; CRE 3rd UK Div., UK and France, 1991–94; Comdt RSME, 1995–97; RCDS, London and E Asia, 1998; Dir Staff Ops SHAPE, Mons, 1999–2000; lang. trng, Germany, 2001–02; Defence Attaché, Berlin, 2002–06. Member: British-German Assoc.; British-German Officers Assoc. FCIL 2006; FCMI 2006; FInstRE 2009. *Recreations:* family, house-building, sports cars, opera, choral music, France, Germany, travel, biographies, rowing, langlauf. *Address:* Grocers' Hall, Princes Street, EC2R 8AD. *T:* (020) 7606 3113, *Fax:* (020) 7600 3082. *E:* clerk@grocershall.co.uk.

PRIEST, Christopher McKenzie; author (novelist and dramatist), since 1968; *b* Cheadle, Cheshire, 14 July 1943; *s* of Walter Mackenzie Priest and Millicent Alice Priest; *m* 1988, Leigh Kennedy (marr. diss. 2011); one *s* one *d* (twins). *Educ:* Cheadle Hulme Sch. Jun. clerical posts, 1959–68. Mem., Mgt Cttee, Soc. of Authors, 1985–88. Vice Pres., H. G. Wells Soc., 2003–. Patron, Hastings and Rother CAB, 1999–2005. JP E Sussex, 1996–2013. Lifetime Achievement Award, Prix Utopia, 2001. *Publications:* Indoctrinaire, 1970; Fugue for a Darkening Island, 1972; Inverted World, 1974; Real-Time World, 1974, rev. edn 2008; The Space Machine, 1976; A Dream of Wessex, 1977; (ed) Anticipations, 1978; An Infinite Summer, 1979; (ed with R. P. Holdstock) Stars of Albion, 1979; The Affirmation, 1981; The Glamour, 1984; The Quiet Woman, 1990; The Book on the Edge of Forever, 1994; The Prestige, 1995 (James Tait Black Meml Prize, 1995; World Fantasy Award, 1996); The Extremes, 1999; The Dream Archipelago, 1999; The Separation, 2002 (Arthur C. Clarke Award, 2002); Ersatz Wines, 2008; The Magic, 2008; 'It' Came from Outer Space, 2008; The Islanders, 2011 (John W. Campbell Jr Meml Award, 2012); The Adjacent, 2013. *Recreations:* reading, photography, cinema, aviation. *Address:* c/o United Agents, 12–26 Lexington Street, W1F 0LE. *T:* (020) 3214 0800. *E:* cp@christopher-priest.co.uk.

PRIEST, Rear-Adm. Colin Herbert Dickinson C.; *see* Cooke-Priest.

PRIEST, Prof. Eric Ronald, PhD; FRS 2002; FRSE; James Gregory Professor of Mathematics, 1997–2010 and Wardlaw Professor, 2002–10, University of St Andrews, now Professor Emeritus; *b* 7 Nov. 1943; *s* of Ronald Priest and Olive Vera Priest (*née* Dolan); *m* 1970, Clare Margaret Wilson; three *s* one *d*. *Educ:* Nottingham Univ. (BSc 1965); Leeds Univ. (MSc 1966; PhD 1969). FRSE 1985. St Andrews University: Lectr, 1968–77; Reader, 1977–83; Prof. of Theoretical Solar Physics, 1983–97. Marlar Lectr, Rice Univ., 1991; Lindsay Meml Lectr, Washington, 1998. Mem., Norwegian Acad. Scis and Letters, 1994. Leverhulme Emeritus Fellow, 2011. Hon. DSc St Andrews, 2013. Hale Prize, AAS, 2002; Gold Medal, RAS, 2009; Payne-Gaposchkin Medal and Prize, Inst. of Physics, 2009. *Publications:* Solar Magnetohydrodynamics, 1982 (trans. Russian 1985); (jtly) Plasma Astrophysics, 1994; (jtly) Magnetic Reconnection: MHD Theory and Applications, 2000; Magnetohydrodynamics of the Sun, 2014; *edited:* Solar Flare Magnetohydrodynamics, 1981; Solar System Magnetic Fields, 1985; Dynamics and Structure of Quiescent Solar Prominences, 1989; (jtly) Magnetic Flux Ropes, 1990; (jtly) Mechanisms of Chromospheric and Coronal Heating, 1991; (jtly) Advances in Solar System Magnetohydrodynamics, 1991 (trans. Russian 1995); (jtly) Reconnection in the Solar Corona and Magnetospheric Substorms, 1997; (jtly) A Crossroads for European Solar and Heliospheric Physics, 1998; over 400 res. papers and articles. *Recreations:* bridge, hill walking, aerobics, singing, having fun with my family. *Address:* Mathematical Institute, St Andrews University, St Andrews, Fife KY16 9SS. *T:* (01334) 463709.

PRIEST, Prof. Robert George, MD, FRCPsych; Professor of Psychiatry, University of London and Head of Department of Psychiatry at St Mary's Hospital Medical School, Imperial College of Science, Technology and Medicine, 1973–96, now Emeritus Professor; Hon. Consultant Psychiatrist, St Mary's Hospital, London, since 1973; *b* 28 Sept. 1933; *er s* of late James Priest and of Phoebe Priest; *m* 1955, Marilyn, *er d* of late Baden Roberts Baker and of Evelyn Baker; two *s*. *Educ:* University Coll., London and University Coll. Hosp. Med. Sch. MB, BS 1956; DPM 1963; MRCPE 1964; MD 1970; MRCPsych 1971 (Foundn Mem.); FRCPE 1974; FRCPsych 1974. Lectr in Psychiatry, Univ. of Edinburgh, 1964–67; Exchange Lectr, Univ. of Chicago, 1966; Consultant, Illinois State Psychiatric Inst., Chicago, 1966; Sen. Lectr, St George's Hosp. Med. Sch., London, 1967–73; Hon. Consultant: St George's Hosp., London, 1967–73; Springfield Hosp., London, 1967–73. University of London: Mem., Bd of Studies in Medicine, 1968–93 (Chm., 1987–89); Mem., Academic Adv. Bd in Medicine, 1987–90; Mem. Senate, 1989–93; Mem., Academic Council, 1989–93. Examiner in Psychiatry, NUI, 1975–78, 1980–83. Chm., Psychiatric Adv. Sub-Cttee, NW Thames RHA, 1976–79 (Vice-Chm., Reg. Manpower Cttee, 1980–83). Member: Council (Chm. Membership Cttee), British Assoc. for Psychopharmacology, 1977–81; World Psychiatric Assoc., 1980–93 (Mem. Cttee, 1985–93, Mem. Council, 1989–93); Central Cttee for Hosp. Med. Services, 1983–89 (Chm., Psych. Sub-Cttee, 1983–87); Pres., Soc. for Psychosomatic Res., 1980–81 (Vice-Pres., 1978–80); Chm., Mental Health Gp Cttee, BMA, 1982–85 (Mem., 1978–85, 1990–); Internat. Coll. of Psychosomatic Medicine: Fellow, 1977; Mem. Gov. Body and UK Delegate, 1978–81; Treasurer, 1981–83; Secretary, 1981–85; Vice-Pres., 1985–87; Royal College of Psychiatrists: Mem., Public Policy Cttee, 1972–80, 1983–89 (Chm., 1983–88); Mem. Council, 1982–88; Registrar, 1983–88; Chm., Gen. Psych. Cttee, 1985–89; Mem., Court of Electors, 1983–88 (Chm., Fellowship Sub-Cttee, 1984–88). A. E. Bennett Award, Soc. for Biol Psychiatry, USA (jtly), 1965; Doris Odlum Prize (BMA), 1968; Gutheil Von Domarus Award, Assoc. for Advancement of Psychotherapy and Amer. Jl of Psychotherapy, NY, 1970. *Publications:* Insanity: A Study of Major Psychiatric Disorders, 1977; (ed jtly) Sleep Research, 1979; (ed jtly) Benzodiazepines Today and Tomorrow, 1980; (ed) Psychiatry in Medical Practice, 1982; Anxiety and Depression, 1983, 3rd edn 1996; (ed) Sleep, 1984; (ed) Psychological Disorders in Obstetrics and Gynaecology, 1985 (Spanish edn 1987); (jtly) Minski's Handbook of Psychiatry, 7th edn, 1978, 8th edn as Handbook of Psychiatry, 1986; (jtly) Sleepless Nights, 1990; (jtly) Depression and Anxiety, 1992 (Spanish edn 1992); (jtly) Depression in General Practice, 1996; chapters in: Current Themes in Psychiatry, 1978; Mental Illness in Pregnancy and the Puerperium, 1978; Psychiatry in General Practice, 1981; Modern Emergency Department Practice, 1983; The Scientific Basis of Psychiatry, 1983, 2nd edn 1992; The Psychosomatic Approach: contemporary practice of wholeperson care, 1986; articles in BMJ, Brit. Jl of Psychiatry, Amer. Jl of Psychotherapy and other learned jls. *Recreations:* swimming, foreign languages, nature study. *Address:* Woodeaves, 29 Old Slade Lane, Richings Park, Iver, Bucks SL0 9DY.

PRIESTLEY, Christopher; writer, illustrator, painter; *b* Hull, 25 Aug. 1958; *s* of Thomas Victor and Rosina Priestley; *m* Sally May; one *s*. *Educ:* Manchester Poly. (BA Hons Graphic Design/Illustration 1980). Freelance illustrator and cartoonist, 1980–; cartoonist: Economist, 1990–96; Independent, 1996–98; strip cartoonist, Observer, New Statesman, Independent and Independent on Sunday; writer for children and teenagers, 2000–. *Publications:* Dog Magic!, 2000; Jail-Breaker Jack, 2001; My Story: Battle of Britain, 2002; Battle of Hastings, 2003; Witch Hunt, 2003; Death and the Arrow, 2004; The White Rider, 2004; Redwulf's Curse, 2005; New World, 2007; Uncle Montague's Tales of Terror, 2007; Tales of Terror from the Black Ship, 2008; Tales of Terror from the Tunnel's Mouth, 2009; The Dead of Winter, 2010; Blood Oath, 2011; Mister Screecher, 2011; Through Dead Eyes, 2013; The Dead Men Stoop Together, 2013; The Last of the Spirits, 2014; The Wickford Doom, 2015; Anything That Isn't This, 2015. *Recreations:* hill-walking, nature, art, music, reading, cinema, talking, history, looking round old buildings and ancient sites, thinking. *Address:* c/o Philippa Milnes-Smith, Lucas Alexander Whitley, 14 Vernon Street, W14 0RJ. *T:* (020) 7471 7900. *E:* admin@lawagency.co.uk.

PRIESTLEY, Sir Julian (Gordon), KCMG 2007; Secretary-General, European Parliament, 1997–2007; *b* 26 May 1950; *s* of Arthur David Noel Priestley and Patricia (*née* Maynard). *Educ:* St Boniface's Coll., Plymouth; Balliol Coll., Oxford (BA Hons PPE). European Parliament, 1973–2007: Head of Div., Secretariat of Cttee on Energy, Res. and Technology, 1983–87; Dir, Parly Cttees, 1987–89; Sec.-Gen., Socialist Gp, 1989–94; Head, Private Office of the Pres., 1994–97. Chm. Bd, European Public Policy Advisers, 2009–; Member, Board: Notre Europe/Jacques Delors Inst. (formerly Notre Europe), 2009–; votewatch.eu, 2011–; Scientific Council, Foundn for Eur. Progressive Studies, 2013–; Co-Founder and former Chair, Pro Europa. Advr, European University Inst., 2010–11. Eur. Campaign Co-ordinator for Martin Schulz, candidate for Presidency of EC, 2014. Vis. Prof., Coll. of Europe, Bruges, 2015. *Publications:* Six Battles that Shaped Europe's Parliament, 2008; European Political Parties: the missing link, 2010; (with Stephen Clark) Europe's Parliament: people, places, politics, 2012; (ed) Our Europe, Not Theirs (essays), 2013; (with Nereo Penalver Garcia) The Making of a European President, 2014. *Recreations:* golf, cinema, reading. *Address:* 4 Clos du Quebec, 1410 Waterloo, Belgium.

PRIESTLEY, Kathleen, (Kate), (Mrs Alan Humphreys); portfolio director; *b* 25 Aug. 1949; *d* of late John Fletcher Taylor and Joan Taylor (*née* Hannon); *m* 1st, 1967 (marr. diss. 1983); one *s*; 2nd, 1985, Alan Humphreys. *Educ:* Notre Dame, Manchester; Manchester Univ. (CQSW); Edinburgh Univ. (MBA). Psychiatric social worker and Sen. Social Worker, Oldham, 1972–79; Manager, Mental Health Service, Salford, 1979–84; Chief Exec., Family Care, Edinburgh, 1984–89; Asst Dir, Social Services, Newcastle upon Tyne, 1989–92; Exec. Dir, Northern RHA, 1992–94; Department of Health: Dir, Purchase Performance Mgt, Northern and Yorkshire Reg., NHS Exec., 1994–97; Chief Exec., NHS Estates, 1998–2004; Chief Exec., Inventures, 2001–04; Chm., Leadership Centre for Local Govt, 2004–10. Non-exec. Dir, Scarborough Bldg Soc., 2001– (Vice-Chm., 2005–09); Chairman: Island Healthcare, 2003–10; Inspired Spaces, 2008–13; Shared Interest, 2010–15; Northumberland Tourism, 2012–14. Non-executive Director: Nat. Property Bd, Dept of Constitutional Affairs, 2003–07; Living Independently, EU, 2006–07; Govt Office NE, 2008–11. Chairman: Standing Cttee on Structural Safety, 2002–09; Mental Health NE, 2010–11; Scene CIC, 2010–12; Mem., Govt Skills Council, 2005–. Trustee, BRE Trust (formerly Foundn for the Built Envmt), 2003–08. FRSA 1999. Mem., Council, Univ. of Newcastle, 2005–13. Hon. Fellow: Univ. of Manchester, 1993; Univ. of York, 1995; Inst. Healthcare Engrg and Estate Mgt, 2000. CompICE 2003; MInstD. *Recreations:* graphology, cooking and entertaining, opera. *Address:* Kitty Frisk House, Corbridge Road, Hexham, Northumberland NE46 1UN. *T:* (01434) 601533.

PRIESTLEY, Leslie William, TD 1974; FCIB; FCIM; Chairman, Tenax Capital Ltd, 2005–13; *b* 22 Sept. 1933; *s* of Winifred and George Priestley; *m* 1960, Audrey Elizabeth (*née* Humber); one *s* one *d*. *Educ:* Shooters Hill Grammar School. Head of Marketing, Barclaycard, 1966–73; Asst Gen. Manager, Barclays Bank, 1974–77, Local Dir, 1978–79; Sec. Gen., Cttee of London Clearing Bankers, 1979–83; Dir, Bankers' Automated Clearing Services, 1979–83; Man. Dir, Barclays Insurance Services Co., 1983–84; Regional Gen. Manager, Barclays Bank, 1984–85; Dir and Chief Exec., TSB England & Wales plc (formerly TSB England and Wales and Central Trustee Savings Bank), 1985–89; Director: TSB Gp plc, 1986–89; Hill Samuel Bank, 1988–89; Pearce Signs Gp (formerly Pearce Gp Hldgs), 1989–2003. Chairman: CAA Pension Scheme Trustees, 1993–2003; Caviapen Investments Ltd, 1993–2003; Generali Pan Europe Ltd, 2006–; Vice-Chm., Guernsey Financial Services Commn, 2003–05 (Mem., 1999–2005); Director: London Electricity plc (formerly London Electricity Board), 1984–97; Pinnacle Insurance, 1990–2003; Omnia/ICL, 1991–94; London Chamber of Commerce and Industry, 1993–96; Expatriate Management Ltd, 1994–99; Prudential Banking plc, 1996–2006; Egg plc, 2000–06; Currencies Direct Ltd, 2006–. Banking Advr, Touche Ross & Co., 1990–96; Financial Services Advisor: ICL, 1991–97; Satyam Computer Services Ltd, 2005–08. Member: Monopolies and Mergers Commn, 1990–96; Bd, CAA, 1990–96. Member of Council: Chartered Inst. of Bankers, 1988–89; Assoc. for Payment Clearing Services, 1988–89. Vis. Fellow, UCNW, 1989–95. Consultant Editor, Bankers' Magazine, 1972–81. FCIM (FInstM 1987); CCMI; FRSA. *Publications:* (ed) Bank Lending with Management Accounts, 1981. *Recreations:* reading, gardening, swimming, golf. *Clubs:* Royal Automobile; Sundridge Park Golf, Chislehurst Golf.

PRIESTLEY, Philip John, CBE 1996; HM Diplomatic Service, retired; High Commissioner to Belize, 2001–04; *b* 29 Aug. 1946; *s* of late Frederick Priestley and Caroline (*née* Rolfe); *m* 1972, Christine Rainforth; one *s* one *d*. *Educ:* Boston Grammar Sch.; Univ. of East Anglia (BA Hons). FCO 1969; served Sofia and Kinshasa; First Sec., FCO, 1976; Wellington, 1979–83; FCO, 1984–87; Commercial Counsellor and Dep. Head of Mission, Manila, 1987–90; Ambassador to Gabon, 1990–91; Fellow, Center for Internat. Affairs, Harvard Univ., 1991–92; Consul-Gen., Geneva, 1992–95; Hd, N America Dept, FCO, 1996–2000. Blue Diamond Ventures, 2006–08; Dir, BCB Hldgs Ltd, 2009–. Mem., Adv. Bd, Friends of Belize, 2011–. Trustee, West India Cttee, 2012–. FRSA 1999. *Recreations:* walking, watching Rugby.

PRIESTLEY, Dr Robert Henry; owner, Ro-Po Publishing, since 2007; *b* 19 March 1946; *s* of late Henry Benjamin Priestley, MA, BSc and Margaret Alice (*née* Lambert); *m* 1970, Penelope Ann Fox, BSc; two *d*. *Educ:* Brunts Grammar Sch., Mansfield; Univ. of Southampton (BSc 1967); Univ. of Exeter (PhD 1972); CS Coll. (Dip. in Consultancy Practice, 1999). FRSB (FIBiol 1988). Plant Pathologist, Lord Rank Res. Centre, Rank Hovis McDougall, 1970–73; National Institute of Agricultural Botany: Cereal Pathologist, 1973–78; Head of Cereal Path. Section, 1978–82; Head of Plant Path. Dept, 1982–88; Gen. Sec., Inst. of Biol., 1989–97. Mgt consultant, HQ Strike Comd, RAF High Wycombe, 1998–2002; Principal Consultant and Lectr, Centre for Mgt and Policy Studies, Sunningdale Park, 2002–06. Sec., UK Cereal Pathogen Virulence Survey, 1974–82; Member: Council Fedn of British Plant Pathologists, 1980–81; Internat. Soc. for Plant Path., 1988–92; Treasurer, British Soc. for Plant Path., 1981–87; Member: British Nat. Cttee for Microbiology, 1982–89; Cttee of Management, Biol. Council, 1989–91; Bd, CSTI, 1989–97; Parly and Sci. Cttee, 1989–97; Chairman: European Communities Biol. Assoc., 1992–96; Eur. Biologist Registration Cttee, 1994–97. FCMI (FIMgt 1997). *Publications:* Football League Programmes of the late 1940s, 2007; consultancy reports; papers on diseases of crops; popular articles. *Recreations:* music, art, architecture, football.

PRIESTLY, Paul Graham; Permanent Secretary, Department for Regional Development, Northern Ireland, 2007–10; project finance and business development consultant, 2011–12; Strategic Adviser, Strategic Investment Board Ltd, since 2012; *b* Belfast, 30 March 1958; *s* of Samuel Robert and Clara Priestly; *m* 1984, Pamela Ann Hawkins; one *s* two *d*. *Educ:* Grosvenor Grammar Sch., Belfast; Queen's Univ., Belfast (BA Hons 1st Cl. Geog.). Joined NI Office, 1985; Hd, Policing Reforms Div., NI Office, 1998–2000; Principal Private Sec. to Sec. of State for NI, 2000–02; Hd, Criminal Justice Reform Div., 2002–03, Dir of Resources, 2003–07, NI Office; Dir of Policy and Strategy, Office of the First Minister and Dep. First Minister, NI, 2007. *Recreations:* hill-walking, reading natural and military history, sailing, playing guitar (badly).

PRIESTMAN, Jane, OBE 1991; FCSD; design management consultant; *b* 7 April 1930; *d* of late Reuben Stanley Herbert and Mary Elizabeth Herbert (*née* Ramply); *m* 1954, Arthur Martin Priestman (marr. diss. 1986); two *s*. *Educ:* Northwood College; Liverpool Coll. of Art (NDD, ATD). Design practice, 1954–75; Design Manager, Gen. Manager, Architecture and Design, BAA, 1975–86; Dir, Architecture and Design, BRB, 1986–91. Member: LRT Design Panel, 1985–88; Jaguar Styling Panel, 1988–91; Percentage for Art Steering Gp, Arts Council, 1989–91; Council, Design Council, 1996–99; Design Panel, SE England Region, 2000–; Design Review Panel, Home Office, 2003–. Vis. Prof. of Internat. Design, De Montfort Univ., 1997–2001. Enabler, CABE, 2001–11. Trustee, London Open House, 1995– (Chair of Trustees, 1998–2009). Governor: Commonwealth Inst., 1987–99; Kingston Univ. (formerly Kingston Polytechnic), 1988–96. Hon. FRIBA; FRSA. Hon. DDes: De Montfort, 1994; Sheffield Hallam, 1998. Ada Louise Huxtable Award, 2015. *Recreations:* textiles, city architecture, opera, travel. *Address:* 30 Duncan Terrace, N1 8BS. *T:* (020) 7837 4525. *Club:* Architecture.

See also P. D. Priestman.

PRIESTMAN, Paul Dominic; designer; Co-founding Director, PriestmanGoode, since 1989; Global Creative Director, CSR Sifang, since 2013; *b* UK, 8 June 1961; *s* of Arthur Martin Priestman and Jane Priestman, *qv*; *m* 1990, Hon. Tessa Mitford, *d* of 5th Baron Redesdale. *Educ:* St Christopher's Sch., Letchworth; Central St Martin's Coll. of Arts and Design (BA); Royal Coll. of Art (MA; MDes). Member: Design Council, 2004–06 (Chair, Design Skills Adv. Panel, 2004–06); Exec., D&AD, 2005–07; Council, RCA, 2010–16. Pres., Design Business Assoc., 2001–03. Student Design Award, RSA; Melchett Meml Award, Design and Industries Assoc.; Award, 2nd Internat. Design Awards, Osaka. *Address:* PriestmanGoode, 150 Great Portland Street, W1W 6QD. *T:* (020) 7580 3444. *E:* studio@priestmangoode.com.

PRIMAROLO, Rt Hon. Dame Dawn, DBE 2014; PC 2002; *b* 2 May 1954; *m* 1972 (marr. diss.); one *s*; *m* 1990, Thomas Ian Ducat. *Educ:* Thomas Bennett Comprehensive Sch., Crawley; Bristol Poly.; Bristol Univ. Mem., Avon CC, 1985–87. MP (Lab) Bristol S, 1987–2015. Opposition front bench spokesman on health, 1992–94, on Treasury affairs, 1994–97; Financial Sec., HM Treasury, 1997–99; HM Paymaster Gen., 1999–2007; Minister of State: DoH, 2007–09; DCSF, 2009–10; Shadow Minister for Children, 2010; Second Dep. Chm. of Ways and Means and a Dep. Speaker, H of C, 2010–15. Mem., Select Cttee on Members' Interests, 1988–92.

[Created a Baroness (Life Peer) 2015 but title not yet gazetted at time of going to press.]

PRIMROSE, family name of **Earl of Rosebery**.

PRIMROSE, Prof. John Neil, MD; Professor of Surgery, University of Southampton, since 1993; Clinical Director, NIHR Clinical Research Network (Wessex), since 2007; *s* of late William Murray Primrose and of Evelyn Primrose; partner, Ursula Ward, two *s* one *d*. *Educ:* Clydebank High Sch., Clydebank; Univ. of Glasgow (MB ChB Hons 1977; MD 1984). Lectr, then Sen. Lectr in Surgery, Univ. of Leeds, 1984–93; Hon. Consultant Surgeon, University Hosps Southampton NHS Foundn Trust (formerly Southampton Univ. Hosps NHS Trust), 1993–. Pres., Assoc. of Surgeons of GB and Ireland, 2013–15. *Publications:* contrib. papers and book chapters on surgery and cancer. *Recreations:* travel, ski-ing. *Address:* University Surgery (816), C Level, South Academic Block, Southampton General Hospital, Southampton, Hants SO16 6YD. *T:* (023) 8120 6143, *Fax:* (023) 8120 4020. *E:* j.n.primrose@soton.ac.uk.

PRIMROSE, Sir John Ure, 5th Bt *cr* 1903, of Redholme, Dumbreck, Govan; *b* 28 May 1960; *s* of Sir Alasdair Neil Primrose, 4th Bt and of Elaine Noreen, *d* of Edmund Cecil Lowndes, Buenos Aires; *S* father, 1986; *m* 1st, 1983, Marion Cecilia (marr. diss. 1987), *d* of Hans Otto Altgelt; two *d*; 2nd, Claudia Ines Schwarz. *Heir:* *b* Andrew Richard Primrose [*b* 19 Jan. 1966. *Educ:* St Peter's School and Military Acad. BA].

PRIMUS, The; *see* Chillingworth, Most Rev. D. R., Bishop of St Andrews, Dunkeld and Dunblane.

PRINCE, David, CBE 2009; Chief Executive, The Standards Board for England, 2004–08; *b* 31 May 1948; *s* of late Charles and Phyllis Grace Prince; *m* 1973, Davina Ann Pugh. *Educ:* Exeter Univ. (BA Hons English). CPFA. Hants CC Grad. Trainee, 1969–71; finance posts, Berks CC, 1971–76; Chief Accountant, Cambs CC, 1976–81, and Asst Co. Treasurer; Dep. Co. Treasurer, Herts CC, 1981–86; Dir, Finance and Admin, Cambs CC, 1986–91; Chief Exec., Leics CC, 1991–94; Audit Commission: Chief Exec., Dist Audit Service, then Dist Audit, 1994–2000; Dir of Ops, 2000–01; Dir of Strategy and Resources, 2001–03; Managing Dir, 2003–04. Mem., Cttee on Standards in Public Life, 2009–15; Lay Member: Gen. Social Care Council, 2007–12; Gen. Pharmaceutical Council, 2013–; Independent Member: Leicestershire Police Authy, 2008–12; Governance, Risk and Audit Cttee, Bar Standards Bd, 2008–13; Audit and Corporate Governance Cttee (formerly Audit, Risk and Assurance Cttee, Care Quality Commn), 2012–15. Vis. Prof., Bath Spa Univ., 2015–. FRSA. *Recreations:* theatre, music, gardening.

PRINCE, Harold; theatrical director/producer; *b* NYC, 30 Jan. 1928; *s* of Milton A. Prince and Blanche (*née* Stern); *m* 1962, Judith Chaplin; one *s* one *d*. *Educ:* Univ. of Pennsylvania (AB 1948). Co-Producer: The Pajama Game, 1954–56 (co-prod film, 1957); Damn Yankees, 1955–57 (co-prod film, 1958); New Girl in Town, 1957–58; West Side Story, 1957–59; Fiorello!, 1959–61 (Pulitzer Prize); Tenderloin, 1960–61; A Call on Kuprin, 1961; They Might Be Giants, London 1961; Side By Side By Sondheim, 1977–78. Producer: Take Her She's Mine, 1961–62; A Funny Thing Happened on the Way to the Forum, 1962–64; Fiddler on the Roof, 1964–72; Poor Bitos, 1964; Flora the Red Menace, 1965. Director-Producer: She Loves Me, 1963–64, London 1964; Superman, 1966; Cabaret, 1966–69, London 1968, tour and NY, 1987; Zorba, 1968–69; Company, 1970–72, London 1972; A Little Night Music, 1973–74, London 1975 (dir. film, 1977); Pacific Overtures, 1976. Director: A Family Affair, 1962; Baker Street, 1965; Something For Everyone (film), 1970; New Phoenix Rep. prodns of Great God Brown, 1972–73, The Visit, 1973–74, and Love for Love, 1974–75; Some of my Best Friends, 1977; On the Twentieth Century, 1978; Evita, London 1978, USA 1979–83, Australia, Vienna, 1980, Mexico City, 1981; Sweeney Todd, 1979, London 1980; Girl of the Golden West, San Francisco Op., 1979; world première, Willie Stark, Houston Grand Opera, 1981; Merrily We Roll Along (musical) 1981; A Doll's Life (musical), 1982; Madama Butterfly, Chicago Lyric Op., 1982; Turandot, Vienna State Op., 1983; Play Memory, 1984; End of the World, 1984; Diamonds, 1985; The Phantom of the Opera, London, 1986, NY, 1988, Los Angeles, 1989, Canada, 1989; Roza, USA, 1987; Cabaret (20th anniversary revival), tour and Broadway, 1987; Kiss of the Spider Woman, 1990, Toronto, London, Broadway, 1993; (also adapted) Grandchild of Kings, 1992; Showboat, Toronto, 1993, NY, 1994; Parade (musical), NY, 1999; 3HREE, Philadelphia, 2000, LA, 2001; Hollywood Arms, Chicago, 2002; Paradise Found (musical), London, 2010. Directed for NY City Opera: Ashmedai, 1976; Kurt Weill's Silverlake, 1980; Candide, 1982, 1997; Don Giovanni, 1989; Faust, Metropolitan Opera, 1990; co-Director-Producer, Follies, 1971–72; co-Producer-Director: Candide, 1974–75; Merrily We Roll Along, 1981; A Doll's Life, 1982; Grind (musical), 1985. Antoinette Perry Awards for: The Pajama Game; Damn Yankees; Fiorello!; A Funny Thing Happened on the Way to the Forum; Fiddler on the Roof; Cabaret; Company; A Little Night Music; Candide; Sweeney Todd; Evita; The Phantom of the Opera; Show Boat, etc (total of 20); SWET award: Evita, 1977–78. Member: League of New York Theatres (Pres., 1964–65); Council for National Endowment for the Arts. Hon. DLit, Emerson College, 1971; Hon. Dr of Fine Arts, Univ. of Pennsylvania, 1971. Drama Critics' Circle Awards; Best Musical Award, London Evening Standard, 1955–58, 1972 and 1992; Tony Award for lifetime achievement, 2006. Kennedy Center Honoree, 1994. *Publications:* Contradictions: notes on twenty-six years in the theatre, 1974. *Recreation:* tennis. *Address:* Suite 1009, 10 Rockefeller Plaza, New York, NY 10020, USA. *T:* (212) 3990960.

PRINCE, Rose Amanda; food writer and columnist, Daily Telegraph, since 2002; *b* 4 Dec. 1962; *d* of 2nd Baron Jeffreys and of Sarah Clarke; *m* 1993, Dominic Prince; one *s* one *d*. *Educ:*

Hatherop Castle Sch., Glos; St Mary's Wantage, Berks. Food columnist: Daily Express, 1998–2001; Evening Standard, 2007; cook, Spectator mag., 1998–2005; columnist: The Tablet, 2004–; Resurgence, 2006–08; Telegraph Mag., 2008–10; contributor, 1998–: Spectator, New Statesman, Saveur (USA), Daily Mail, Sunday Telegraph, The Times. Reporter, Food Prog., BBC Radio 4. Prod., TV series, In the Foot Steps of Elizabeth David, 1999. Mem., H of L Cttee of Inquiry into misregulation of meat industry, 2000. Founder, The Pocket Bakery, 2010. Glenfiddich Food Writer of the Year, 2001; Fortnum & Mason Food Writer of the Year, 2014. *Publications:* The New English Kitchen: changing the way you shop, cook and eat, 2005; The Savvy Shopper, 2006; The New English Table, 2008; The Good Produce Guide (annually), 2009–12; Kitchenella, 2010; The Pocket Bakery, 2013. *Recreations:* lunch, wine, sunbathing, children, reading, racing. *Address:* 177 Battersea Bridge Road, SW11 3AS. *T:* 07968 359376. *E:* rose@roseprince.co.uk. *Clubs:* Bluebird, Blacks; Sixpenny Handley Tennis.

PRINCE, Susanne, OBE 2004; DL; artist, since 1983; tourism provider, since 1985; organic farmer, since 1997; eco-tourism consultant, since 2001; *b* London, Aug. 1956; *d* of Brian and Breege Norrie; *m* 1976, Terence Prince; two *d*. *Educ:* Graham Balfour High Sch., Stafford. Artist in Swedish folk art, teaching in Sweden, 2005–. Food project Consultant, Univ. of Derby, 2001–08; Eco-tourism Consultant: for Belmont Mgt Consultants, in Transylvania, 2006–09; for Renewal of Peak Dist Envmtl Quality Mark, 2010–11. Member: Peak Dist Nat. Park Authy, 2000–09; Bd, Advantage W Midlands RDA, 2004–11; Rural Enterprise Panel (formerly Land Use and Access Panel), NT, 2005–14; Commn for Rural Communities, 2009–11; Bd, Staffs Local Enterprise Partnership, 2011. Chm., Sustainable Tourism Action Gp for Staffs, 2007–; Vice-Chm., Peak Dist Leader Action Gp, 2007–. Mem., Governing Council, Keele Univ., 2008–11. Trustee, Ilam Cross, 2005–. A West Midlands Greenleader, 2010. DL Staffs 2011. *Recreations:* avid reader, social media, walking, painting, cinema, friends and family, throwing balls for small dog and grandchildren. *Address:* Beechenhill Farm, Ilam, Ashbourne, Derbys DE6 2BD. *E:* info@beechenhill.co.uk.

PRINDL, Dr Andreas Robert, Hon. CBE 2001; Chairman, Nomura Bank International, 1990–97 (Managing Director, 1986–90); Deputy Chairman, Lloyd's, 2009–12 (Member of Council, since 2003); *b* 25 Nov. 1939; *s* of Frank Joseph Prindl and Vivian Prindl (*née* Mitchell); *m* 1st, 1963, Veronica Maria Koerber (marr. diss. 2004); one *s* one *d*; 2nd, 2009, Patricia Norland (*d* 2014). *Educ:* Princeton Univ. (BA); Univ. of Kentucky (MA, PhD). Morgan Guaranty Trust Company: NY and Frankfurt, 1964–70; Vice-Pres., IMM, London, 1970–76; Gen. Manager, Tokyo, 1976–80; CEO Saudi Internat. Bank, London, 1980–82; Vice-Pres., Mergers and Acquisitions, Morgan Guaranty, 1982–84; Man. Dir, Nomura Internat., 1984–86. Chm., Banking Industry Trng and Develt Council, 1994–96; Provost, Gresham Coll., 1996–99. President: Chartered Inst. of Bankers, 1994–95; Assoc. of Corporate Treasurers, 1996. Vis. Prof., People's Univ. of China, Beijing, 2000–. Chm., Good Vibrations, charity, 2009–14. Non-exec. Dir, ACE European Gp, 2012–. Freeman, City of London, 1999; Liveryman: Musicians' Co., 1999– (Mem., Ct of Assts, 2001–; Master, 2006–07); World Traders' Co., 2000–11. Hon. Treas., C&G, 1998–2000. Hon. Fellow, Acad. of Moral Sci., Beijing, 1998. Hon. DSc City, 1996. *Publications:* (jtly) International Money Management, 1972 (trans. Italian as La Gestione Aziendale Plurimonetaria, 1975); Foreign Exchange Risk, 1976 (trans. Japanese as Kawase Risuku, 1978; Spanish as El Riesgo de Cambio, 1980); Japanese Finance, 1981; Money in the Far East, 1986; (ed) Banking and Finance in Eastern Europe, 1992; (ed jtly) Ethical Conflicts in Finance, 1994; The First XV, 1995; A Companion to Lucca, 2000; A Companion to Angoulême, 2005 (trans. French as Du haut des remparts d'Angoulême, 2007); A Companion to Fauquier County, Virginia, 2008; A Companion to Rye and Winchelsea, 2015. *Recreations:* classical music, Asian art and history. *Club:* Reform.

PRING, Prof. Richard Anthony; Professor and Director of Department of Educational Studies, University of Oxford, 1989–2003; Fellow of Green College, Oxford, 1989–2003, now Emeritus; *b* 20 April 1938; *s* of Joseph Edwin and Anne-Marie Pring; *m* 1970, Helen Faye Evans; three *d*. *Educ:* Gregorian Univ. and English College, Rome (PhL); University Coll. London (BA Hons Philosophy); Univ. of London Inst. of Education (PhD); College of St Mark and St John (PGCE). Asst Principal, Dept of Educn and Science, 1962–64; teacher in London comprehensive schools, 1965–67; Lectr in Education: Goldsmiths' Coll., 1967–70; Univ. of London Inst. of Educn, 1972–78; Prof. of Educn, Univ. of Exeter, 1978–89. Lead Dir, Nuffield Rev. of 14–19 Educn and Trng, 2003–09 (report, Education for All: the future of educn and trng for 14–19 year olds, 2009). Pres., Socialist Educn Assoc., 2008–. Hon. DLitt: Kent, 1995; Inst. of Educn, Univ. of London, 2015. Editor, British Jl of Educational Studies, 1986–2001. Bene Merenti Medal (Pius XII), 1958. Annual Award of Distinction, Aga Khan Univ., Karachi, 2007. *Publications:* Knowledge and Schooling, 1976; Personal and Social Education, 1984; The New Curriculum, 1989; Closing the Gap: liberal education and vocational preparation, 1995; (ed with Geoffrey Walford) Affirming the Comprehensive Ideal, 1997; Philosophy of Educational Research, 2000, 3rd edn 2014; Philosophy of Education: aims, theory, common sense and research, 2004; (ed with G. Thomas) Evidence Based Practice in Education, 2004; John Dewey: a philosopher of education for our time?, 2007; (jtly) Education for All: the future of education and training for 14–19 year olds, 2009; The Life and Death of Secondary Education for All: dream or reality?, 2012. *Recreations:* running marathons, cycling, writing, campaigning for comprehensive schools. *Address:* Green Templeton College, Woodstock Road, Oxford OX2 6HG.

PRINGLE, Maj. Gen. Andrew Robert Douglas, CB 2000; CBE 1992 (MBE 1980); President, Infrastructure Government and Power (Europe, Middle East and Africa), Kellogg Brown and Root, since 2014; *b* 9 Oct. 1946; *s* of late Douglas Alexander Pringle and Wendy Pringle (*née* Gordon); *m* 1975, Jane Carolyn Mitchison; one *s* two *d*. *Educ:* Wellington Coll.; RMA, Sandhurst; RMCS, Shrivenham (BSc Hons). Commnd RGJ, 1966: served in UK, Cyprus, NI, Germany, 1967–77; Staff Coll., Camberley, 1977–78; Staff and Regtl appts, NI, 1979–82; Directing Staff, Staff Coll., Camberley, 1983–85; CO, 3rd Bn, RGJ, 1985–88; MoD, 1988–91; Higher Comd and Staff Course, 1990; rcds, 1991; Cabinet Office, 1992–94; Commander: 20 Armoured Bde, 1994–96; UN Sector SW, Bosnia, 1995; Dir, Land Warfare, 1996–97; Comdr, Multi-Nat. Div. (SW), Bosnia, 1997–98; COS, Perm. Jt HQ, 1998–2001. Regtl (formerly Rep.) Col Comdt, Royal Green Jackets, 1999–2002; Col Comdt, 2nd Bn Royal Green Jackets, 1999–2001. Defence consultant, 2002–08; Dir, AP JOINTSOLUTIONS Ltd, 2003–08; Vice Pres., Govt and Defence, EMEA, 2008–09, Pres., Internat. Govt, Defence and Support Services (formerly Internat. Govt and Defence), Kellogg Brown and Root, 2010–14. Non-exec. Dir, Allocate (formerly Manpower) Software plc, 2004–. QCVS 1996 and 1998. *Recreations:* reading, ski-ing, Cresta Run, a little light farming. *Clubs:* Army and Navy; St Moritz Tobogganing.

PRINGLE, Dame Anne Fyfe, DCMG 2010 (CMG 2004); HM Diplomatic Service, retired; Ambassador to Russia, 2008–11; *b* 13 Jan. 1955; *d* of late George Grant Pringle and Margaret Fyfe Pringle (*née* Cameron); *m* 1987, Bleddyn Glynne Leyshon Phillips. *Educ:* Glasgow High Sch. for Girls; St Andrews Univ. (MA Hons French and German). Joined FCO, 1977: Third Sec., Moscow, 1980–83; Vice Consul, San Francisco, 1983–85; Second Sec., UK Rep., Brussels, 1986–87; FCO, 1988–91; First Sec., Eur. Political Co-operation Secretariat, Brussels, 1991–93; Dep. Hd, Security Co-ordination Dept, then African Dept (Equatorial), FCO, 1994–96; Head, Common Foreign and Security Policy Dept, FCO, and European Correspondent, 1996–98; Head, Eastern Dept, FCO, 1998–2001; Ambassador to the Czech Republic, 2001–04; Dir, Strategy and Information, FCO, 2004–07. Public Appts Assessor, 2012–. Non-exec. Dir, Ashmore plc, 2013–. Mem. Court, St Andrews Univ., 2012–. FRSA 2001. *Recreations:* sport, gardening, walking.

PRINGLE, Derek Raymond; Cricket Correspondent, The Daily Telegraph, 2002–14; *b* Nairobi, 18 Sept. 1958; *s* of late Donald James Pringle and of Doris May Pringle (*née* Newton). *Educ:* St Mary's Sch., Nairobi; Felsted Sch., Essex; Fitzwilliam Coll., Cambridge (MA). Professional cricketer, Essex and England, 1978–93; Cricket Correspondent: Independent on Sunday, 1993–95; Independent, 1995–2002. *Publications:* England's Ashes, 2005. *Recreations:* photography, music, conchology.

PRINGLE, Hamish Patrick, FIPA; Partner, Pringle and Pringle LLP, since 2011; *b* Chiswick Mall, London, 1951; *s* of Robert Henry and Pamela Ann Pringle; *m* 1977, Vivienne Elizabeth Lloyd; three *s* one *d*. *Educ:* Trinity Coll., Glenalmond (Captain of Sch., 1968–69); Trinity Coll., Oxford (BA PPE 1973). Account Exec., Ogilvy & Mather, 1973–75; Account Manager, McCormick Richards, 1975–76; Account Manager, 1976–77, Account Dir, 1978–79, Boase Massimi Pollitt; New Business Dir, McCormick Intermarco-Farner, 1980–82; Bd Dir, Abbott Mead Vickers SMS, 1982–86; Man. Dir, Madell Wilmot Pringle, 1986–90; Bd Dir, Leagas Delaney, 1990–92; CME KHHB: New Business Dir, 1992–94; Jt Man. Dir, 1994–95; Chm. and CEO, 1995–96; Chm. and CEO, K Advertising, 1996–97; Vice-Chm. and Dir of Mktg, Saatchi & Saatchi, 1997–99; Dir, Brand Beliefs, 1999–2001; Dir Gen., Inst. of Practitioners in Advertising, 2001–11. Strategic Advr, 23red, 2011–. Member: Bd, Advertising Assoc., 2001–11; Advertising Standards Bd of Finance, 2001–11; Broadcasters' Audience Res. Bd, 2001–11; Bd, Eur. Assoc. of Communication Agencies, 2001–11; Broadcast Advertising Standards Bd of Finance, 2006–11; Council, ASA, 2011–. Institute of Practitioners in Advertising: Society Chm., 1984–85; Mem. Council, 1985–86 and 1989–98; Member: Advertising Effectiveness Cttee, 1986–96 (Chm., 1993–96); President's Cttee, 1994–96. Mem., 1993–96, Chm., 1996–98, Gen. Mgt Cttee, Nat. Advertising Benevolent Soc.; Jt Chm., Fund-raising Cttee, Cinema and Television Benevolent Fund, 1994–95. FIPA 1992; Fellow, Mktg Soc., 2009. Mem., Mktg Gp of GB. Ron Miller Award, Nat. Advertising Benevolent Soc., 1998. *Publications:* (with M. Thompson) Brand Spirit: how cause related marketing builds brands, 1999; (with W. Gordon) Brand Manners: how to create the self-confident organisation to live the brand, 2001; Celebrity Sells, 2004; (with P. Field) Brand Immortality: how brands can live long and prosper, 2008; (with J. Marshall) Spending Advertising Money in the Digital Age: how to navigate the media flow, 2012. *Recreation:* art. *E:* hamish@pringleandpringle.co.uk. *T:* 07977 269778. *Club:* Soho House.

PRINGLE, Ian Derek; QC 2003; **His Honour Judge Pringle;** a Circuit Judge, since 2012; Resident Judge, Oxford Crown Court, since 2014; *b* 19 Jan. 1957; *s* of late Dr Derek Hair Pringle and of Anne Collier Pringle (*née* Caw); *m* 1980, Mary Seeney; one *s* one *d*. *Educ:* Edinburgh Acad.; St Catharine's Coll., Cambridge (MA). Called to the Bar, Gray's Inn, 1979, Bencher, 2009; in practice, specialising in criminal law; Mem., Guildhall Chambers, Bristol, 1981–2012; a Recorder, 1998–2012. Hon. Recorder, Oxford, 2014–. Mem. Council, Burden Neurol Inst., Bristol, 1996–. *Recreations:* history, sport, particularly football, Rugby, golf and athletics. *Address:* Oxford Crown Court, St Aldates, Oxford OX1 1TL. *Club:* Hibernian Football.

PRINGLE, Jack Brown, PPRIBA; Principal and Managing Director, Pringle Brandon Perkins+Will (formerly Pringle Brandon), since 2012; President, Royal Institute of British Architects, 2005–07; Chairman, Construction Industry Council, 2012–14; *b* 13 March 1952; *s* of John and Grace Mason Pringle; *m* 2010 Holly Anne Porter; one *d*, and two *d* from a previous marriage. *Educ:* Bristol Univ. (BA Hons 1973; DipArch 1975). RIBA 1977. Architect: Powell and Moya, 1973–81; Jack Pringle Architects, 1981–86; Partner, Pringle Brandon, 1986–2012. Royal Institute of British Architects: Mem. Council, 1979–89 and 2003–; Vice-Pres. for Educn, 2003–; Chm., Professional Services Co., 2003–05. Chair: Article 25, 2007–14; Editl Bd, Jl of Architecture, 2012–. FRSA. Commandeur de l'Ordre des Arts et des Lettres (France), 2007. *Recreations:* flying (Private Pilot's Licence), racing offshore yachts, exhibitions, travelling with wife and daughters. *Address:* Pringle Brandon Perkins+Will, 10 Bonhill Street, EC2A 4QJ. *T:* (020) 7466 1000, *Fax:* (020) 7466 1050. *E:* Jack.Pringle@PringleBrandonpw.com.

PRINGLE, Sir John (Kenneth), Kt 1993; Justice of the High Court of Northern Ireland, 1993–99; *b* 23 June 1929; *s* of late Kenneth Pringle and Katie (*née* Batchen); *m* 1960, Ruth Henry; two *s* one *d*. *Educ:* Campbell Coll., Belfast; Queen's Univ., Belfast (BSc 1st Cl. Hons 1950; LLB 1st Cl. Hons 1953). Called to the Bar, NI, 1953, Bencher, 1973; QC (NI), 1970; Recorder of Belfast, 1984–93. Chm., Bar Council of NI, 1975–80. Member: Parades Commn for NI, 2000–05; Investigatory Powers Tribunal, 2001–06. *Recreations:* gardening, being outdoors.

PRINGLE, Jonathan Helier W.; *see* Watt-Pringle.

PRINGLE, Margaret Ann; Associate Director, Centre for the Study of Comprehensive Schools, since 1995; *b* 28 Sept. 1946. *Educ:* Holton Park Girls' Grammar Sch.; Somerville College, Oxford (MA, BLitt English Lang. and Lit.). English Teacher, Selhurst High School, Croydon, 1972–76; Head of English, Thomas Calton School, Peckham, 1976–81; Dep. Head, George Green's School, Isle of Dogs, 1981–86; Head, Holland Park Sch., 1986–95. *Recreations:* all food, all music, most dancing, and occasionally not thinking about education. *Address:* Flat 3, 64 Pembridge Villas, W11 3ET.

PRINGLE, Prof. Michael Alexander Leary, CBE 2001; FRCGP; Professor of General Practice, University of Nottingham, 1993–2010; President, Royal College of General Practitioners, 2012–15; *b* 14 May 1950; *s* of Alexander and Yvonne Pringle; *m* 1974, Nicola Mary Wood; three *d*. *Educ:* St Edward's Sch., Oxford; Guy's Hosp. Med. Sch. (MB BS 1973). FRCGP 1989. Vocational Trng Scheme for Gen. Practice, Reading, 1975–78. Principal in gen. practice, Collingham, Notts, 1979–2004; Lectr and Sen. Lectr, Dept of Gen. Practice, Univ. of Nottingham, 1983–93. GP Clinical Hd, NHS Connecting for Health, 2004–07. Chm. Council, RCGP, 1998–2001. Co-Chm., Expert Ref. Gp for Diabetes Nat. Service Framework, 1999–2002. FMedSci 1999. Hon. FRCP 2000. *Publications:* (jtly) Managing Change in Primary Care, 1991; (ed) Change and Teamwork in Primary Care, 1993; (ed) Fellowship by Assessment, 1995; (jtly) A Guide for New Principals, 1996; (ed) Primary Care: core values, 1998; contrib. numerous chapters in books, res. articles and editorials in jls. *Recreations:* chess, reading, Italy, walking. *E:* mikepringle@btinternet.com.

PRINGLE, Michael Stanley Robert; Member (Lib Dem) Edinburgh South, Scottish Parliament, 2003–11; *b* 25 Dec. 1945; *s* of Robert Stanley Valdemar Pringle and Pauline Olga Pringle (*née* Brian); *m* 1971, Margaret Isobel Gilfillan Birkett; two *s*. *Educ:* Edinburgh Acad. Bank teller, Inst. of Bankers of Scotland, Royal Bank of Scotland, 1965–71; Trainee Hotel Manager, North British Trust Hotels, 1971–74; Man. Dir, TMM Ltd, 1974–92. Member: Edinburgh DC, 1992–96; Lothian Regl Council, 1994–96; Edinburgh CC, 1995–2003. Contested (Lib Dem) Edinburgh S, Scottish Parlt, 2011. *Recreations:* fishing, wine tasting, sport, cooking.

PRINGLE, Sir Simon Robert, 11th Bt *cr* 1683 (NS), of Stichill, Roxburghshire; *b* 6 Jan. 1959; *s* of Lt-Gen. Sir Steuart Robert Pringle, 10th Bt, KCB and Jacqueline Marie Pringle (*née* Gladwell); *S* father, 2013, but his name does not appear on the Official Roll of the

Baronetage; *m* 1992, Pamela Margaret, *d* of George Hunter; one *s* one *d*. *Educ:* Worth Abbey; Trinity Coll. Oxford (BA). *Heir: s* Ruairi George Robert Pringle, *b* 21 Oct. 2002.

PRIOR, family name of **Barons Prior** and **Prior of Brampton**.

PRIOR, Baron *cr* 1987 (Life Peer), of Brampton in the County of Suffolk; **James Michael Leathes Prior;** PC 1970; Chairman, The General Electric Company plc, 1984–98; *b* 11 Oct. 1927; 2nd *s* of late C. B. L. and A. S. M. Prior, Norwich; *m* 1954, Jane Primrose Gifford, 2nd *d* of late Air Vice-Marshal O. G. Lywood, CB, CBE; three *s* one *d*. *Educ:* Charterhouse; Pembroke College, Cambridge (1st class degree in Estate Management, 1950; Hon. Fellow, 1992). Commissioned in Royal Norfolk Regt, 1946; served in India and Germany; farmer and land agent in Norfolk and Suffolk. MP (C): Lowestoft, Suffolk, 1959–83; Waveney, 1983–87. PPS to Pres. of Bd of Trade, 1963, to Minister of Power, 1963–64, to Mr Edward Heath, Leader of the Opposition, 1965–70; Minister of Agriculture, Fisheries and Food, 1970–72; Lord Pres. of Council and Leader of House of Commons, 1972–74; Opposition front bench spokesman on Employment, 1974–79; Sec. of State for Employment, 1979–81; Sec. of State for NI, 1981–84. A Dep. Chm., Cons. Party, 1972–74 (Vice-Chm., 1965). Chairman: Allders, 1989–94; East Anglian Radio PLC, 1992–96; African Cargo Handling Ltd, 1998–2001; Ispat Energy Hldgs Ltd, 1998–2000; Ascot Underwriting Ltd, 2001–06; Dep. Chm., MSI Cellular Investments BV, 2000–04; Director: United Biscuits (Holdings), 1984–94; Barclays Bank, 1984–89; Barclays International, 1984–89; J. Sainsbury, 1984–92; Celtel, 2000–05; Member: Tenneco European Adv. Bd, 1986–97; Internat. Adv. Bd, Amer. Internat. Gp, 1988–2006. Chancellor, Anglia Poly. Univ., 1992–99 (Hon. PhD 1992). Chairman: Council for Industry and Higher Educn, 1986–91; Archbishops' Commn on Rural Areas, 1988–91; Great Ormond Street Wishing Well Appeal, 1985–89; Special Trustees, Great Ormond Street, 1989–94; Industry and Parliament Trust, 1990–94; Rural Housing Trust, 1990–99; Royal Veterinary Coll., 1990–99; Arab-British Chamber of Commerce, 1996–2004. *Publications:* (jtly) The Right Approach to the Economy, 1977; A Balance of Power, 1986. *Recreations:* cricket, tennis, golf, gardening. *Address:* House of Lords, SW1A 0PW. *Clubs:* MCC; Butterflies Cricket.

See also Baron Prior of Brampton.

PRIOR OF BRAMPTON, Baron *cr* 2015 (Life Peer), of Swannington in the County of Norfolk; **David Gifford Leathes Prior;** Parliamentary Under-Secretary of State, Department of Health, since 2015; chairman and director of various private companies; *b* 3 Dec. 1954; *s* of Baron Prior, *qv*; *m* 1987, Caroline Henrietta Holmes; twin *s* and *d*. *Educ:* Charterhouse; Pembroke Coll., Cambridge (Exhibnr; MA Law 1976). Called to the Bar, Gray's Inn, 1977; Commercial Dir, British Steel, 1980–87. MP (C) N Norfolk, 1997–2001; contested (C) same seat, 2001. Vice Chm., 1998–99, Dep. Chm. and Chief Exec., 1999–2001, Conservative Party. Chm., Norfolk and Norwich University Hospital Trust, 2002–06 and 2007–13; Chm., Care Quality Commn, 2013–15. *Recreations:* gardening, farming, most sports. *Address:* Swannington Manor, Swannington, Norwich NR9 5NR. *T:* (01603) 861560. *Club:* Royal Automobile.

PRIOR, (Alice) Mary, MBE 1999; Lord-Lieutenant of the County of Bristol, since 2007; Pro-Chancellor, University of Bristol, since 2014; *b* 22 April 1942; *d* of Harry Forty and Kathleen Louise Forty; *m* 1982, John Michael Prior; one *s* one *d*. *Educ:* Kingswood Grammar Sch. Bowater Paper Corp., 1959–65; Gen. Sales Manager, Sales Dir, then Sales and Mktg Dir, Alexandra plc, 1973–97. Trustee: St Monica Trust, 1999–2008; Quartet Community Foundn, 2004–10; Patron, Bristol Cathedral Trust, 2005– (Trustee, 1988–2005). Patron or Pres., numerous charitable orgns in Bristol. Mem., Soc. of Merchant Venturers, 2008–. DL County of Bristol, 1996. DStJ 2011. *Recreations:* reading, gardening, music. *Address:* Youngwood Farm, Youngwood Lane, Nailsea, Bristol BS48 4NR. *T:* (01275) 852374, *Fax:* (01275) 810031. *E:* mary@youngwoodfarm.co.uk.

PRIOR, Anthony Basil, FRICS; Consultant Valuer to Institute of Revenues Rating & Valuation, since 2001; Advisor to European Group of Valuers' Associations, since 2005; *b* 23 March 1941; *s* of Rev. Christopher Prior and May Prior (*née* Theobald); *m* 1967, Susan Margaret Parry; two *s*. *Educ:* Commonweal Grammar Sch., Swindon. FRICS 1977; IRRV (Hons) 1988. Joined Valuation Office, 1967: Dist Valuer, Southampton, 1979–84; Superintending Valuer, Chief Valuer's Office, 1984–91; Regl Dir, Western Reg., later London Reg., 1991–98; Dir, Professional and Customer Services, and Mem., Mgt Bd, Valuation Office Agency, 1999–2001; Consultant Valuer to IOM Govt, 2001–07. Mem., Adv. Panel on Standards for the Planning Inspectorate, 2001–11. Member: Rating Valuers' Assoc., 1984; Council, IRRV, 1988–2001. Hon. Recognised European Valuer, 2009. *Publications:* (jtly) Encyclopedia on Contractors Basis of Valuation, 1990. *Recreations:* bee-keeping, fly fishing, Greek and Roman history. *Address:* c/o Institute of Revenues Rating & Valuation, Northumberland House, 303–306 High Holborn, WC1V 7JZ.

PRIOR, Clifford James, CBE 2002; Chief Executive, UnLtd, since 2006; *b* 14 Feb. 1957; *s* of Colin Prior and Beatrice (*née* Maber). *Educ:* Alleyn's Sch., Dulwich; St Catherine's Coll., Oxford (BA Biochem. 1978). Counsellor: Andover Crisis Support Centre, 1978–80; Social Services, Tower Hamlets LBC, 1980–82; Housing Asst, 1982–84, Area Manager, 1984–85, Special Projects Co-ordinator, 1985–88, New Islington and Hackney Housing Assoc.; Housing Services Manager, 1988–90, Asst Dir of Policy and Inf., 1990–92, Dir of Policy and Planning, 1992–94, Stonham Housing Assoc.; Progs Dir, Mental Health Foundn, 1994–98; Chief Exec., Nat. Schizophrenia Fellowship, subseq. Rethink, 1998–2006. Vice Chairman: Homeless Network, 1996–99; Long Term Med. Conditions Alliance, 2000–06; Member: NHS Mental Health Task Force, 2000–06; NHS Modernisation Bd, 2000–04; Nat. Leadership Gp, 2005–06; Medicines Commn, 2004–05; Third Sector Commissioning Task Force, 2005–06; Healthcare Commn, 2007–09; Civil Society Adv. Body to Cabinet Office, 2008–11; Adv. Bd, Big Society Capital, 2011–; Cabinet Office Skills Social Action Rev., 2012–13. Chm., Health and Social Care Gp, ACEVO, 2005–06; Mem., Comic Relief UK Grants Cttee, 2007–. Chm., FSE Trading Ltd, 2008–11; non-exec. Dir, UCL Partners, 2013–. Trustee: Clore Social Leadership Prog., 2010–; Empower Community Foundn, 2015–; Founder Trustee, Local Trust, 2012–14; Chair, Mission Alignment Gp to G8 Social Impact Investment Taskforce, 2014–. Founder Member and Treasurer: Stonewall Housing Assoc., 1983–87; Strutton Housing Assoc., 1987–90; Chm. Supported Housing, Circle 33 Housing Trust, 1992–98. *Recreations:* scuba diving, travel, film, music, friends. *Address:* UnLtd, 123 Whitecross Street, EC1Y 8JJ. *T:* (020) 7566 1100, *Fax:* (020) 7566 1101. *E:* cliffprior@unltd.org.uk. *W:* www.twitter.com/cliffprior.

PRIOR, Mary; *see* Prior, A. M.

PRIOR-PALMER, Simon Erroll; non-executive director, public, private and not-for-profit sectors, since 2005; Head, UK Investment Banking, Credit Suisse First Boston, 1987–98; *b* London, 5 Feb. 1951; *s* of Maj.-Gen. George Erroll Prior-Palmer, CB, DSO and Lady Doreen Hersey Winifred Prior-Palmer (*née* Hope); *m* 1984, Lady Julia Margaret Violet Lloyd George, *d* of 3rd Earl Lloyd George of Dwyfor; three *s* one *d*. *Educ:* Eton; Christ Church, Oxford (BA PPE 1973; MA). JP Morgan, London and NY, 1973–82; Credit Suisse First Boston, 1982–2005, Sen. Advr, 2003–05. Mem., Postal Services Commn, 2006–10; Sen. Advr, FSA, 2010–11. Non-executive Director: Inter Lotto (UK) Ltd, 2006–07; Gabriel Resources Ltd, 2006–12; Burani Designer Hldgs NV, 2007–09; Chm., DJI Hldgs plc, 2013–. Trustee, Macmillan Cancer Support, 2001–13. FRSA 1989. *Recreations:* tennis, golf, ski-ing, unusual travel. *Club:* Whites.

See also L. J. Green, Earl Lloyd George of Dwyfor.

PRISK, (Michael) Mark; MP (C) Hertford and Stortford, since 2001; Prime Minister's Investment Envoy to the Nordic and Baltic Nations, since 2014; *b* 12 June 1962; *s* of Michael Raymond Prisk and June Irene Prisk; *m* 1989, Lesley Jane Titcomb, *qv*. *Educ:* Truro Sch., Cornwall; Univ. of Reading (BSc (Hons) Land Mgt). Knight Frank & Rutley, 1983–85; Chartered Surveyor, 1985–; Dir, Derrick, Wade & Waters, 1989–91; Principal: Mark Prisk Connection, 1991–97; mp2, 1997–2001. Shadow Financial Sec., 2002–03; Shadow Paymaster Gen., 2003–04; Opposition Whip, 2004–05; Shadow Minister, Small Business and Enterprise, 2005–08, Business, 2008–10; Minister of State, BIS, 2010–12; Minister of State (Minister for Housing), DCLG, 2012–13. Contested (C): Newham NW, 1992; Wansdyke, 1997. Nat. Vice Chm., FCS, 1981–82; Trustee: Industry and Parliament Trust, 2007–; Parliament Choir, 2014–. Dir, Edward Stanfords Ltd, 2014–. Chm., Youth for Peace through NATO, 1983–85. Chm. Governors, Stratford GM Sch., 1992–93. *Recreations:* piano, choral music, Rugby and cricket supporter. *Address:* House of Commons, SW1A 0AA. *T:* (020) 7219 3000.

PRITCHARD, Alison Alexis; Director, Government Equalities Office, since 2014; *b* London, 29 June 1965; *d* of Terence Graham Pritchard and Sylvia Marion Pritchard; one *s* one *d*. *Educ:* Alleyn's Sch., Dulwich; Univ. of Bath (BSc Hons Econs and Politics 1987). Ministry of Defence: Desk Officer, Air Armaments (Finance and Secretariat), 1987–89, Secretariat Overseas (Commitments), 1989–91; Systems Analyst and Programmer, Army Staff Duties (IT), 1991–93; Project Manager, Dir Gen. IT Services, 1993–95; Implementation Officer, Service Personnel (Policy), 1995–96; Hd of Section, Naval Support Command (Secretariat), 1996; Hd of Finance, MoD Team Riyadh, 1996–2001; Dir, Chief Exec.'s Office, Office of Govt Commerce, HM Treasury, 2001–04; Cabinet Office: Dir, Ind. Air Travel Review, 2004–06; Hd of Business Strategy, Corporate Develt Gp, 2004–07; Dir of Progs, Lokahi Foundn (on secondment), 2006–07; Hd of Strategy, 2007–10, Hd of Delivery, 2010–12, Govt Equalities Office, Home Office; Hd of Gambling and Nat. Lottery, DCMS, 2012–14. Dir and CEO, Kirrin Prodns Ltd, 2014–. Chair: Ind. Monitoring Bd, Harmondsworth Immigration Removal Centre, 2004–06; Nat. Forum for Immigration Removal Centres, 2006–07. *Recreation:* comedy writer and producer for radio. *Address:* Government Equalities Office, 100 Parliament Street, SW1A 2BQ. *T:* (020) 7211 6050. *E:* Alison.Pritchard@geo.gov.uk.

PRITCHARD, David Alan, CB 2006; Consultant Adviser to Vice Chancellor, Cardiff Metropolitan University, since 2012; *b* 23 March 1946; *s* of John Merfyn Pritchard and Anne Louise Pritchard; *m* 1970, Kathryn Henton; two *s*. *Educ:* UCNW, Bangor (BA Hons Econs). Welsh Office: Head: Industry Policy Div., 1989; Health Strategy and Rev. Div., 1990–97; Local Govt Policy and Finance Div., 1997–99; Welsh Assembly Government: Corporate Planning Unit, 1999–2000; Gp Dir, Econ. Develt, then Econ. Develt and Transport, Dept, 2000–06; Dean, Cardiff Sch. of Mgt, Univ. of Wales Inst., Cardiff, later Cardiff Metropolitan Univ., 2006–12. Non-exec. Dir, Carbon Trust, 2001–08. Hon. Fellow, Cardiff Metropolitan Univ., 2012. Mem., Ordre des Chevaliers Bretvins, Bailliage du Pays de Galles, 2013. *Recreations:* walking, gardening, Liverpool and Cardiff FCs, theatre, politics, wine, just being with my grandchildren. *Address:* Ty'r Ardd, Cardiff Road, Creigiau CF15 9NL. *T:* (029) 2089 0932.

PRITCHARD, David Edward; independent consultant (international conservation policy and environmental arts), since 2008; *b* Jarrow, 7 Oct. 1958; *s* of David Lloyd Pritchard and Elizabeth Buchanan Young Pritchard (*née* Livingston). *Educ:* S Shields Grammar-Tech. Sch. for Boys; Durham Univ. (BSc Hons Zool. 1980); University Coll. London (MSc Conservation 1981). Royal Society for the Protection of Birds: res. ecologist/conservation planner, 1981–86; Casework Officer, 1986–90; Manager, Planning and Local Govt Unit, 1990–97; Hd, Site Protection and Wetlands Policy, 1997–99; Internat. Treaties Advr, 1999–2009. Non-executive Director: Wetlands Internat., 2001–07 (Chm., Prog. and Sci. Cttee, 2006–07; Associate Expert, 2014–); Jt Nature Conservation Cttee, 2006–12 (Chm., Audit and Risk Mgt Cttee, 2007–12). Assessor, Arts Council England, 2011–12. Ramsar Convention: Mem., Scientific and Tech. Rev. Panel, 1999–; Chm., Thematic Area 3, 2003–12; Jt Coordinator, Culture Network (formerly Co-Chm., Culture Wkg Gp), 2006–; Member: IUCN Specialist Gp on Cultural and Spiritual Values of Protected Areas, 2005–; Ind. Rev., Northumberland Nat. Park Authy, 2013–14. Chm., UK Arts and Envmt Network, 2008–; Mem., Expert Network, UNESCO UK Commn, 2014–. Vis. Lectr, Durham Univ., 2013–. Trustee: Bedford Creative Arts, 2006–10 (Vice Chm., 2007–10); Centre for Contemp. Art and the Natural World, 2009–13. Hon. FCIWEM 2011. Wetland Conservation Award and Evian Special Prize, Ramsar, 2008. *Publications:* (ed jtly) Important Bird Areas in the UK, 1992; (ed) Strategic Environmental Assessment, 1992; (ed) Conservation Policy Directions, 1996; Dendros: horizons of change, 2006; (series ed.) Ramsar Handbooks for the Wise Use of Wetlands, 4th edn 2010; (with T. Papayannis) Culture and Wetlands in the Mediterranean: an evolving story, 2011; contrib. chapters in books; contrib. tech. papers. *Recreations:* hill-walking, tree art, photographing shadows, staring at the sea. *Address:* 20 Burswell Avenue, Hexham NE46 3JL.

PRITCHARD, David Peter; Chairman, AIB Group (UK) plc, since 2007; *b* 20 July 1944; *s* of Norman and Peggy Pritchard; *m* 1993, Elizabeth Cresswell; one *s* one *d*. *Educ:* Read Sch., Drax, Yorks; Southampton Univ. (BScEng 1966). Hawker Siddeley Aviation, 1966–71; Wm Brandt's Sons & Co., 1971–73; Edward Bates & Sons Ltd, 1973–78; Man. Dir, Citicorp Investment Bank, 1978–87; Vice Chm., Orion Royal Bank, 1987–88; Gen. Manager, Europe, Royal Bank of Canada, 1988–95; Treas., TSB Gp plc, 1995–96; on secondment to FSA, 1996–98; Gp Dir, Wholesale and Internat. Banking, 1998–2003, Dep. Chm., 2003–05, Lloyds TSB Gp plc. Chairman: Cheltenham & Gloucester, 2004–05; Songbird Estates plc, 2005–15; non-executive Director: LCH.Clearnet Gp Ltd (formerly London Clearing House), 2001–07; Scottish Widows plc, 2003–07; Allied Irish Banks plc, 2007–11; Euromoney Institutional Investor plc, 2008–. *Recreations:* cycling, Nordic ski-ing, photography. *Address:* 17 Thorney Crescent, SW11 3TT. *T:* (020) 7585 2253. *Club:* London Capital.

PRITCHARD, Frances Jean; *see* Judd, F. J.

PRITCHARD, (Iorwerth) Gwynn; broadcasting consultant and television producer; Secretary General, International Public Television (INPUT) (formerly International Public Television Screening Conference), 2001–06; *b* 1 Feb. 1946; *s* of late Rev. Islwyn Pritchard and Megan Mair Pritchard; *m* 1st, 1970, Marilyn Bartholomew (*d* 1994); two *s* one *d*; 2nd, 1998, Althea Sharp. *Educ:* Bolton Sch.; King's Coll., Cambridge (MA). Producer and Director: BBC Television, London, 1969–78; BBC Wales, 1979–82; HTV Wales, 1982–85; Commissioning Editor, 1985–88, Sen. Commissioning Editor for Educn, 1989–92, Channel 4; Hd of Welsh Progs, then of Welsh Broadcasting, BBC Cymru/Wales, 1992–2001. Pres., INPUT Internat. Bd, 1988–93. Trustee, Welsh Writers Trust, 1990–; Chm., Menter Iaith Bro Morgannwg/Vale of Glamorgan Lang. Initiative, 2011–13. Chm., Cardiff Unitarian Congregation, 2011–; Mem., Exec. Cttee, Gen. Assembly of Unitarian and Free Christian Chs, 2015–. Mem. Council, Coleg Harlech, 1992–2000; Gov., Ysgol Gynradd Pencae, 1992–2002. Winston Churchill Fellow, Winston Churchill Meml Trust, 1973; Huw Weldon Fellow, UCNW, Bangor, 1990–91. Chevalier de l'Ordre des Arts et des Lettres (France), 1990. *Recreations:* swimming, walking, cinema, reading. *Address:* 25 Westbourne Road, Penarth, Vale of Glamorgan CF64 3HA. *T:* (029) 2070 3608.

PRITCHARD, Rt Rev. John Lawrence; Bishop of Oxford, 2007–14; *b* 22 April 1948; *s* of late Rev. Canon Neil Lawrence Pritchard and Winifred Mary Coverdale (*née* Savill); *m* 1972, Susan Wendy Claridge; two *d*. *Educ:* St Peter's Coll., Oxford (MA (Law) 1973; Hon. Fellow,

2007); St John's Coll., Durham (MLitt (Theol.) 1993). Ordained deacon, 1972, priest, 1973; Asst Curate, St Martin in the Bull Ring, Birmingham, 1972–76; Diocesan Youth Chaplain and Asst Dir of Educn, dio. of Bath and Wells, 1976–80; Vicar, St George's, Wilton, Taunton, 1980–88; Dir of Pastoral Studies, 1989–93, Warden, 1993–96, Cranmer Hall, St John's Coll., Durham; Archdeacon of Canterbury, 1996–2001; Bishop Suffragan of Jarrow, 2002–07. Took seat in H of L, 2011. Member: Gen. Synod of C of E, 1999–2001, 2007–; Bd, Church Army, 2003–11; Min. Council, 2008–11; Chm., C of E Bd of Educn, 2011–14. Bishops' Inspector, 1999–2004. Pres., St John's Coll., Durham, 2008–11. Pres., Guild of Health, 2003–. *Publications:* Practical Theology in Action, 1996; The Intercessions Handbook, 1997; Beginning Again, 2000; Living the Gospel Stories Today, 2001; How to Pray, 2002; The Second Intercessions Handbook, 2004; Living Easter through the Year, 2005; Leading Intercessions, 2005; How to Explain your Faith, 2006; The Life and Work of a Priest, 2007; Going to Church: a user's guide, 2009; Pocket Prayers for Troubled Times, 2010; Living Jesus, 2010; God Lost and Found, 2011; Pocket Prayers for Pilgrims, 2011; Living Faithfully, 2013; Ten: why Christianity makes sense, 2014; The Journey: with Jesus to Jerusalem and the cross, 2014. *Recreations:* photography, walking, travel, music, cricket, reading. *E:* johnpritchard@btinternet.com.

PRITCHARD, John Michael; Founder and Chairman, Legalease Ltd, Publishers, since 1988; *b* 18 June 1949; *s* of Arthur Glyn Pritchard and Sybil Roderick Pritchard; *m* 1st, 1976, Mary Margaret Freeman (marr. diss. 1998); two *s* one *d*; 2nd, 1999, Hilary Baker. *Educ:* Penarth Grammar Sch.; Bristol Univ. Admitted solicitor, 1974; articled with Thompsons, solicitors, London; in practice with Powell Spencer, Kilburn, 1974–88. Editor: The Practical Lawyer, 1988–; Legal Business mag., 1990–; In House Lawyer mag., 1992–; Editor in Chief: Property Law Jl, 1997–; Employment Law Jl; Commercial Law Jl, Trusts and Estates Law Jl; Personal Injury Law Jl; Family Law Jl; Procurement and Outsourcing Law Jl. *Publications:* (ed) Penguin Guide to the Law, 1982, 5th edn, as New Penguin Guide to the Law: your rights and the law explained, 2001; (ed) Legal 500, annually 1988–; Young Solicitors' Handbook, 1990, rev. edn 1991; (ed) Who's Who in the Law: eminent practising lawyers in the UK, 1991; (ed) European Legal 500, annually 1991–; Which Firm of Solicitors?, 1993; Legal Experts, annually 1994–; (ed) Commercial Client Directory: guide to legal service buyers at the UK's top 15,000 companies, 1996; (ed) Asia Pacific Legal 500, annually 1996–; Kanzleien in Deutschland, annually 1997–; (ed) Cabinets d'Avocats en France, annually, 1999–. *Recreation:* anything that does not involve lawyers. *Address:* c/o 12–14 Ansdell Street, W8 5BN. *T:* (020) 7396 9292, *Fax:* (020) 7396 9300.

PRITCHARD, Kenneth John, CB 1982; Director, Greenwich Hospital, 1987–92; *b* 18 March 1926; *s* of William Edward Pritchard and Ethel Mary Pritchard (*née* Cornfield); *m* 1st, 1949, Elizabeth Margaret Bradshaw (*d* 1978); two *d*; 2nd, 1979, Angela Madeleine Palmer; one *s* two *d*. *Educ:* Newport High Sch.; St Catherine's Coll., Oxford (MA 1951). Served Army, 1944–48; Indian Mil. Acad., Dehra Dun, 1945; served with 8th/12th Frontier Force Regt and 2nd Royal W Kent Regt. Asst Principal, Admiralty, 1951; Private Sec. to Sec. of State for Wales, 1964; Asst Sec., Min. of Aviation, 1966; RCDS, 1972; Principal Supply and Transport Officer (Naval), Portsmouth, 1978, Exec. Dir 1980; Dir Gen. of Supplies and Transport (Naval), MoD, 1981–86, retd. Vice Patron, Royal Naval Benevolent Trust, 1992–. Chairman: Beckington Music Hall, 1985–2012; Frome Tourist Information Ltd, 1996–2010. Almoner, Christ's Hosp. Sch., 1988–92. Freeman, City of London, 1988; Liveryman, Coopers' Co., 1988. Mem., Cousinerie de Bourgogne, 1997 (Ambassadeur, 2009–). FCIPS (FInstPS 1986). *Recreations:* tennis, music hall, good wine. *Address:* Pickford House, Beckington, Som BA11 6SJ. *T:* (01373) 830329.

PRITCHARD, Kenneth William, OBE 1992; WS; part-time Sheriff, 2000–03 (Temporary Sheriff, 1995–99); Secretary of the Law Society of Scotland, 1976–97; *b* 14 Nov. 1933; *s* of Dr Kenneth Pritchard, MB, BS, DPH, and Isobel Pritchard, LDS (*née* Broom); *m* 1962, Gretta (*née* Murray), BL, MBA, WS; two *s* one *d*. *Educ:* Dundee High Sch.; Fettes Coll.; St Andrews Univ. (BL). National Service, Argyll and Sutherland Highlanders, 1955–57; commnd 2nd Lieut, 1956; TA 1957–62 (Captain). Joined J. & J. Scrimgeour, Solicitors, Dundee, 1957, Sen. Partner, 1970–76; WS 1984. Hon. Sheriff, Dundee, 1978. Member: Sheriff Court Rules Council, 1973–76; Lord Dunpark's Cttee Considering Reparation upon Criminal Conviction, 1973–77; Secretary, Scottish Council of Law Reporting, 1976–97. Governor, Moray House Coll. of Educn, 1982–84; Mem. Ct, Univ. of Dundee, 1990–93. Mem., National Trust for Scotland Jubilee Appeal Cttee, 1980–82. Pres., Dundee High Sch. Old Boys Club, 1975–76; Captain of the Former Pupil RFC, Dundee High Sch., 1959–62. Hon. Prof. of Law, Strathclyde Univ., 1986–94. *Recreation:* golf. *Address:* 22/4 Kinellan Road, Edinburgh EH12 6ES. *T:* (0131) 337 4294. *Clubs:* New, Bruntsfield Links Golfing Society (Edinburgh); Hon. Company of Edinburgh Golfers (Muirfield).

PRITCHARD, Mark Andrew; MP (C) The Wrekin, since 2005; *b* 22 Nov. 1966; *s* of late Francis Pritchard and of Romona Pritchard; *m* 1997, Sondra Janae Spaeth (marr. diss. 2013). *Educ:* London Guildhall Univ. (MA Mktg Mgt); CIM Postgrad. Dip. Mktg; Elim Coll. (Cert. Theol. and Pastoral Studies); Univ. of Buckingham (MA Internat. Diplomacy, 2013). Parly researcher, 1994–95; founder and owner: Pritchard Communications Ltd, 1999–2007; Next Steps Mkt Res. Ltd, 2002–06. Member: Harrow BC, 1993–94; Woking BC, 2000–03. Contested (C) Warley, 2001. Member: Envmtl Audit Select Cttee, 2005–07; DWP Select Cttee, 2006–08; Welsh Affairs Select Cttee, 2007–10; Transport Select Cttee, 2008–10; Jt Nat. Security Strategy Cttee, 2010–; DFID Select Cttee, 2012–; Speaker's Panel, 2013–; Vice Chairman: All Party Parly Gp on Social Care, 2005; ASEAN Parly Gp, 2010–; Parly Gp for Abolition of Death Penalty, 2012–; Secretary: Cons. Parly Defence Cttee, 2006; Cons. Parly Foreign Affairs Gp, 2006; 1922 Cttee, 2010–12; Vice Chm., Cons. Parly Foreign Affairs and Defence Cttee; Mem., Cons. Homeland Security Team, 2006–; Founding Mem. and Comr, Cons. Human Rights Commn, 2006–; Mem. Bd, Parliamentarians for Global Action, 2007–. Member: Parly Delegn to NATO, 2010–14; British Irish Parly Assembly, 2013–. Dep. Chm., Internat. Office, Cons. Party, 2010–12. Member: Council, Bow Gp, 1993–94; Bd, Cons. Councillors Assoc., 2002–05. *Recreations:* writing comedy, trainee bird watcher, jazz, ski-ing, animal welfare. *Address:* c/o House of Commons, SW1A 0AA. *T:* (020) 7219 3000. *E:* pritchardm@parliament.uk.

PRITCHARD, Mehmuda Nighat Mian; Associate Director and Clerk to Trustees, Lokahi Foundation; *b* 30 July 1962; *d* of Manzoor Alam and Naziran Mian; *m* 2003, Khalid Pritchard. *Educ:* Teesside High Sch. for Girls; Univ. of Birmingham (LLB Hons Law with French 1994); Coll. of Law, Chester. Admitted solicitor, 1989; articled clerk, then solicitor, Edge & Ellison, 1985–91; solicitor, Wansbroughs Willey Hargrave, 1991–94; Office for the Supervision of Solicitors, Law Soc., 1994–98. Member: Police Complaints Authy, 1998–2004; Ind. Police Complaints Commn, 2004–09; Ind. Safeguarding Authy, 2008–12. Trustee, BBC Trust, 2006–12. *Recreations:* reading, trekking, travelling, charity fund raising, spending time with family and friends, trying to keep fit.

PRITCHARD, Prof. Thomas Owen, OBE 2005; JP; Chairman, Cynefin Environmental Ltd, consultants in sustainable development, since 1991; Deputy Chairman, National Heritage Memorial Fund, 1999–2005; Professorial Fellow, University of Wales; *b* 13 May 1932; *s* of late Owen and Mary Pritchard; *m* 1957, Enyd Ashton; one *s* one *d*. *Educ:* Botwnnog Grammar Sch.; Univ. of Wales (BSc Hons Botany and Agric. Botany); Univ. of Leeds (PhD Genetics). Midlands Regl Officer and Head of Educn, Nature Conservancy, 1957–67; Dep. Dir for Wales, Nature Conservancy—NERC, 1967–73; Dir for Wales, NCC, 1973–91. Consultant, Council of Europe, 1968. Vis. Prof., Dept of Forestry and Resource Management, Univ. of California, Berkeley, 1981–. Dir, CTF Training Ltd, 1982–91; Chairman: Coed Cymru Ltd, 1983–92; Slate Ecology Co. Ltd, 1995–. Chairman: Bardsey Island Trust, 1987–93; Welsh Historic Gdns Trust, 1994–98 (Pres., 2001); Exec., POW Cttee, 1971–73; Country Cttee for Wales, Heritage Lottery Fund, 1999–2005; Envmt Protection Adv. Cttee for Wales, Envmt Agency, Wales, 2005–; Vice Chm. (Educn), IUCN, 1966–73; former Chm. and Mem., conservation and envmtl bodies, nat. and internat. Member: Genetical Soc.; British Ecological Soc. Member: Ct of Govs and Council: Univ. of Wales, Bangor (formerly UC, Bangor), 1981–2002; Nat. Museum of Wales, 1981–91. Member: Gorsedd of Bards, Royal Nat. Eisteddfod; Hon. Soc. of Cymmrodorion. FRSA. JP Bangor, 1978. *Publications:* Cynefin y Cymro, 1989; numerous contribs to sci. and educn jls. *Recreation:* sailing. *Address:* Graig Lwyd, 134 Ffordd Penrhos, Bangor, Gwynedd LL57 2BX. *T:* (01248) 370401.

PRITCHARD-JONES, Prof. Kathryn, PhD; FRCPCH, FRCPE; Chief Medical Officer, London Cancer, UCLPartners, since 2011; Professor of Paediatric Oncology, University College London, since 2010; Honorary Consultant Oncologist, Great Ormond Street NHS Foundation Trust, since 2010; *b* Coventry, 1958; *d* of John Pritchard-Jones and Marianne Pritchard-Jones; one *s* one *d*. *Educ:* John Port Comp. Sch., Etwall; St Hugh's Coll., Oxford (BA Physiol Sci. 1980; BM BCh 1983); MRC Human Genetics Unit, Univ. of Edinburgh (PhD 1992). FRCPCH 1997; FRCPE 1998. Jun. dr trng posts, paediatrics and paediatric oncology, Oxford, Newcastle and Adelaide, 1984–87; MRC Recombinant DNA trng fellowship, MRC Human Genetics Unit, Univ. of Edinburgh, 1987–92; Team Leader, 1993–2010, Prof. of Childhood Cancer Biol., 2004–10, Inst. of Cancer Res., Univ. of London; Consultant Paediatric Oncologist, Royal Marsden Hosp., 1994–2010. FMedSci 2012. *Publications:* approx. 200 articles in scientific jls on childhood cancer, particularly Wilms tumour and rhabdomyosarcoma. *Recreations:* ski-ing, sailing, fine wines, mountain walking, foreign travel, Boris biking around London's sights. *Address:* UCLPartners, 170 Tottenham Court Road, W1T 7HA. *T:* (020) 7679 6393; UCL Institute of Child Health, 30 Guilford Street, WC1N 1EH. *T:* (020) 7905 2774. *E:* k.pritchard-jones@ucl.ac.uk.

PRITCHETT, Matthew, (Matt), MBE 2002; front page cartoonist for Daily Telegraph, since 1988; *b* 14 July 1964; *s* of Oliver Pritchett and Joan Pritchett (*née* Hill); *m* 1992, Pascale Charlotte Marie Smets; one *s* three *d*. *Educ:* Addey and Stanhope Sch.; St Martin's Sch. of Art. Freelance cartoonist for New Statesman, Punch and Spectator, 1986–88. Awards from: What the Papers Say, 1992, 2004, 2006; Cartoon Arts Trust, 1995, 1996, 1999, 2005, 2006, 2009, 2013; UK Press Gazette, 1996, 1998; British Press Awards, 2000, 2008, 2009; Sports Cartoonist of the Year, Sports Journalism Awards, 2013; Journalists' Charity Award, 2014. *Publications:* Best of Matt, annually, 1991–; 10 Years of Matt, 2001. *Address:* c/o The Daily Telegraph, 111 Buckingham Palace Road, SW1W 0DT.

PRITTIE, family name of **Baron Dunalley**.

PROBERT, (William) Ronald; Managing Director, Business Development, 1992–93, Member of the Board, 1985–93, Group Executive Member, 1989–93, British Gas plc (formerly British Gas Corporation), retired; *b* 11 Aug. 1934; *s* of William and Florence Probert; *m* 1957, Jean (*née* Howard); three *s*. *Educ:* Grammar Sch., Ashton-under-Lyne; Univ. of Leeds (BA). FIGEM. Entered gas industry, 1957; various marketing appts in E Midlands Gas Bd, 1957–67; Conversion Manager, 1967, Service Manager, 1971, Marketing Dir, 1973, E Midlands Gas Bd; Asst Dir of Marketing, 1975, Dir of Sales, 1977, British Gas Corp.; Man. Dir Marketing, British Gas, 1982–89; Man. Dir, Gas Supply and Strategy, 1989–92. Dir, E Berks NHS Trust, 1991. CCMI. *Recreations:* narrowboats, music, winemaking. *Address:* Paddock End, 1 Ambrose Crescent, Diggle, Saddleworth, Lancs OL3 5XG. *T:* (01457) 239873.

PROBY, Sir William Henry, 3rd Bt *cr* 1952, of Elton Hall, co. Huntingdon; CBE 2009; DL; farmer; *b* 13 June 1949; *s* of Sir Peter Proby, 2nd Bt and Blanche Harrison (*née* Cripps); *S* father, 2002; *m* 1974, Meredyth Anne, *d* of Timothy David Brentnall; four *d*. *Educ:* Eton; Lincoln Coll., Oxford (MA); Brooksby Coll. of Agric. FCA. Price Waterhouse & Co., 1971–76; Morgan Grenfell & Co., 1976–80; Chief Exec., MWP Ltd, 1980–82; Chm., Elton Estates Co. Ltd, 1982–. Chairman: Marine and Gen. Mutual Life Assce Soc. (formerly MGM Assce Ltd), 2007– (non-exec. Dir, 2006–); Direct Building Gp, 2010–12. Pres., Historic Houses Assoc., 1994–99; Chm., Nat. Trust, 2003–08. Mem. Adv. Council, Tate Britain, 1999–2010. Trustee, Nat. Portrait Gall., 2009– (Vice Chm., 2011–12; Chm., 2012–). DL Cambs, 1995; High Sheriff, Cambs, 2001–02. *Address:* Elton Hall, Elton, Peterborough PE8 6SH. *T:* (01832) 280223, *Fax:* (01832) 280584. *E:* whp@eltonhall.com. *Clubs:* Brooks's, Boodle's, Dilettanti, Roxburghe.

PROBYN, Calista Jane, (Mrs N. C. Dinnage); Her Honour Judge Probyn; a Circuit Judge, since 2013; *b* Calgary, Canada, 23 July 1960; *d* of late Alfred John Probyn and Calista Helen Probyn; *m* 1995, Nicholas Charles Dinnage; one *s*. *Educ:* Llandrindod Wells High Sch.; Univ. of Westminster (LLB Hons); Inns of Court Sch. of Law. Called to the Bar, Middle Temple, 1988; in practice as a barrister, specialising in family law, 1988–2013; a Recorder, 2003–13. *Recreations:* family life, walking, reading, theatre.

PROCHASKA, Dr Alice Marjorie Sheila, FRHistS; Principal, Somerville College, Oxford, since 2010; Pro-Vice-Chancellor, University of Oxford, since 2014; *b* 12 July 1947; *d* of John Harold Barwell and Hon. Sheila McNair; *m* 1971, Dr Franklyn Kimmel Prochaska; one *s* one *d*. *Educ:* Perse Sch. for Girls, Cambridge; Somerville Coll., Oxford (BA 1968; MA 1973; DPhil 1975). Assistant Keeper: London Museum, 1971–73; Public Record Office, 1975–84; Sec. and Librarian, Inst. of Historical Res., 1984–92; Dir of Special Collections, BL, 1992–2001; University Librarian, Yale Univ., 2001–10. Chm., Nat. Council on Archives, 1991–95; Mem., Royal Commn on Historical MSS, 1998–2001. Member: History Working Gp on Nat. Curriculum, DES, 1989–90; Council, RHistS, 1991–95 (Vice Pres., 1995–99); Heritage Educn Trust, 1992–2001; Hereford Mappa Mundi Trust, 1992–95; Adv. Council, Inst. of Historical Res., 1992–2001; Library Panel, Wellcome Inst., 1993–97; Adv. Panel, Qualidata, Univ. of Essex, 1995–98; Sir Winston Churchill Archive Trust, 1995–2001 (Chm., 2010–); Steering Cttee, Digital Library Fedn, 2001–05 (Trustee, 2005–09); Adv. Council, Yale Center for British Art, 2002–10; Bd, Yale Univ. Press, 2005–10; Main Panel D, REF 2014, HEFCE, 2011–; Steering Cttee, Conference of Colls, 2011–, Supervisory Cttee, Recognised Ind. Centres, 2012–, Oxford Univ.; Adv. Gp, Re-Imagine, India-UK Cultural Relns in the 21st Century, British Council, 2012–. Chairman: Section Panel, Rare Books and Manuscripts, IFLA, 1999–2003; Trustees of Lewis Walpole Library, 2001–10; Chm., Collections and Access Cttee, 2003–05, Mem., Res., Trng and Learning Cttee, 2005–06, Chair, Special Collections Wkg Gp, 2007–09, Assoc. of Res. Libraries; Bd Mem., Center for Res. Libraries, 2003–10 (Vice-Chair, 2005–07; Chair, 2007–09). Gov., London Guildhall Univ., 1995–2001. Hon. Fellow: Inst. of Histl Res., London Univ., 2001; RHUL, 2002. Blog, http://principal2010.wordpress.com. *Publications:* London in the Thirties, 1973; History of the General Federation of Trade Unions 1899–1980, 1982; Irish History from 1700: a guide to sources in the Public Record Office, 1986; (ed jtly with F. K. Prochaska) Margaretta Acworth's Georgian Cookery Book, 1987; contribs to books, learned jls and collections of conf. papers. *Recreations:* family life, collecting watercolours, walking, museums. *Address:* Somerville College, Oxford OX2 6HD. *E:* alice.prochaska@some.ox.ac.uk.

PROCTER, Jane Hilary; artist; media consultant, since 2002; *m* 1985, Thomas Charles Goldstaub; one *s* one *d*. *Educ:* Queen's Coll., Harley St. Fashion Asst, Vogue, 1974–75; Asst Fashion Editor, Good Housekeeping, 1975–77; Actg Fashion Editor, Woman's Jl, 1977–78; Fashion Writer, Country Life, 1978–80; Freelance Fashion Editor, The Times, Sunday Times and Daily Express, 1980–87; Editor: British W, 1987–88; Tatler, 1990–99; Editl Dir, PeopleNews Network, 1999–2002. *Publications:* Dress Your Best, 1983. *Recreations:* sailing, ski-ing. *E:* jane@janeprocter.net.

PROCTER, (Mary) Norma; contralto; international concert singer; *b* Cleethorpes, Lincolnshire, 15 Feb. 1928. *Educ:* Wintringham Secondary Sch. Vocal studies with Roy Henderson, musicianship with Alec Redshaw, lieder with Hans Oppenheim and Paul Hamburger. London début, Southwark Cathedral, 1948; operatic début, Lucretia, in Britten's Rape of Lucretia, Aldeburgh Festival, 1959; Covent Garden début, Gluck's Orpheus, 1961. Specialist in concert works, oratorios and recitals; appeared with all major conductors and orchestras, and in all major festivals, UK and Europe; performed in Germany, France, Spain, Italy, Portugal, Holland, Belgium, Norway, Denmark, Sweden, Finland, Austria, Luxembourg, Israel, S America; BBC Last Night of the Proms, 1974. Many recordings. Hon. RAM 1974. *Address:* 194 Clee Road, Grimsby, NE Lincs DN32 8NG.

PROCTER, Robert John Dudley; Chief Executive, Lincolnshire County Council, 1983–95; *b* 19 Oct. 1935; *s* of Luther Donald Procter and Edith Muriel Procter; *m* 1962, Adrienne Allen; one *s* one *d. Educ:* Cheltenham Grammar School. Admitted Solicitor, 1961. Articled Clerk, Glos CC, 1956–61; Assistant Solicitor: Bath City, 1961–63; Cumberland CC, 1963–65; Lindsey County Council: Sen. Asst Solicitor, 1965–69; Asst Clerk, 1969–71; Dep. Clerk, Kesteven CC, 1971–73; Dir of Personnel, 1973–77, Dir of Admin, 1977–83, Lincolnshire CC. Chm., Assoc. of County Chief Execs, 1994–95. Mem., Warner Cttee of Inquiry into recruitment and selection of staff in children's homes, 1992. Vice Chm., Linkage Community Trust, 2001–04; Treas., Lincoln Cathedral Community Assoc., 2001–06. Chm. Govs, Lincoln Christ's Hosp. Sch. and Foundn, 2001–05. Chm., Eastgate Lincoln Bowls Club, 2007–08. *Recreations:* horse racing, swimming, family history, bowls. *Address:* Flat 3, The Lodge, 38B Nettleham Road, Lincoln LN2 1RE. *T:* (01522) 532105.

PROCTER, Sidney, CBE 1986; Commissioner, Building Societies Commission, 1986–93; company director; *b* 10 March 1925; *s* of Robert and Georgina Margaret Procter; *m* 1952, Isabel (*née* Simmons); one *d. Educ:* Ormskirk Grammar School. Served RAF, 1943–47. Entered former Williams Deacon's Bank, 1941; Asst General Manager, 1969; Dep. Dir, Williams & Glyn's Bank, 1970; Divl Dir, 1975; Exec. Dir, 1976–85; Asst Chief Executive, 1976; Dep. Chief Executive, 1977; Chief Exec., 1978–82; Dep. Gp Man. Dir, Royal Bank of Scotland Gp, 1979–82; Gp Chief Exec., 1982–85; Vice Chm., 1986; Director: Royal Bank of Scotland, 1978–86 (Vice Chm., 1986); Provincial Insurance Co., 1985–86; Dep. Chm., Provincial Group, 1991–94 (Dir, 1986–94); Chairman: Exeter Bank, 1991–97; Provincial Group Holdings, 1994–96. Adviser to Governor, Bank of England, 1985–87. Chm., Exeter Trust, 1986–97 (Dir, 1985–97).

PROCTOR, His Honour Anthony James; a Circuit Judge, 1988–2001; *b* 18 Sept. 1931; *s* of James Proctor and Savina Maud (*née* Horsfield); *m* 1964, Patricia Mary Bryan; one *d. Educ:* Mexborough Grammar Sch., Yorkshire; St Catharine's Coll., Cambridge (MA, LLM). Flying Officer, RAF, 1953–55. Articled to Sir Bernard Kenyon, County Hall, Wakefield, 1955–58; admitted Solicitor 1958. Sen. Prosecuting Solicitor, Sheffield Corp., 1959–64; Partner, Broomhead & Neals, Solicitors, Sheffield, 1964–74; Dist Registrar and County Court Registrar, Barrow in Furness, Lancaster, Preston, 1974–88; a Recorder, 1985–88; Hon. Recorder of Lancaster, 2000–05. Pres., Assoc. of Dist and Court Registrars, 1985–86. *Recreations:* photography, travel, genealogy.

PROCTOR, Rev. John; General Secretary, United Reformed Church, since 2014; *b* Stirling, 22 Dec. 1952; *s* of Lawrence Proctor and Marion Proctor (*née* Davis); *m* 1977, Elaine Patricia Low; one *s* one *d. Educ:* Queen Mary's Grammar Sch., Walsall; St John's Coll., Cambridge (MA); Univ. of Glasgow (MSc; BD). Lectr in Statistics, Univ. of Glasgow, 1975–77; Church of Scotland Minister, Colston Milton, Glasgow, 1981–86; Dir of New Testament Studies, 1986–2014, Vice-Principal, 1997–2014, Westminster Coll., Cambridge. *Publications:* The People's Bible Commentary: Matthew, 2001; Westminster Bible Companion: first and second Corinthians, 2015. *Recreations:* following football and cricket, bird-watching. *Address:* United Reformed Church House, 86 Tavistock Place, WC1H 9RT. *T:* (020) 7916 2020.

PROCTOR, (Keith) Harvey; Private Secretary to the Duke and Duchess of Rutland, 2002–15; *b* 16 Jan. 1947; *s* of late Albert Proctor and Hilda Tegerdine. *Educ:* High School for Boys, Scarborough; Univ. of York (BA History Hons, 1969). Asst Director, Monday Club, 1969–71; Research Officer, Conservative 1970s Parliamentary Gp, 1971–72; Exec. Director, Parliamentary Digest Ltd, 1972–74; British Paper & Board Industry Federation: Asst Sec., 1974–78; Secretary, 1978–79; Consultant, 1979–87. Dir, Proctor's Shirts and Ties, 1992–2000. MP (C): Basildon, 1979–83; Billericay, 1983–87. Mem., Exec. Council, Monday Club, 1983–87. Chief Exec., Richmond Bor. Chamber of Commerce, 1996–98 (Vice-Pres., 1990–92; Pres., 1992–94). Trustee, SW London Community Foundn, 1993–94; Chairman: Richmond Town Centre Cttee, 1995–97; Parkview Court Residents' Assoc., 1996–97 (Sec., 1994–96); Co-Chm., Richmond Victorian Evening Cttee, 1999. Clerk, Earl of Rutland and Dr Fleming's Hosp. Trust, 2013–15. Editor, News and Views, 1991–98. *Publications:* Billericay in Old Picture Postcards, 1985. *Recreations:* collecting British contemporary art, walking boxer dogs, travelling.

PROCTOR, Prof. Michael Richard Edward, PhD, ScD; FRS 2006; FRAS, FIMA; Professor of Astrophysical Fluid Dynamics, University of Cambridge, since 2000; Provost of King's College, Cambridge, since 2013; *b* 19 Sept. 1950; *s* of Edward Francis Proctor and Stella Mary Major Proctor (*née* Jones); *m* 1st, 1973, Linda Irene Powell (marr. diss. 1998); two *s* one *d*; 2nd, 1999, Elizabeth Julia Colgate (*née* Nuttall); two step *s. Educ:* Stoke House Prep. Sch., Seaford; Shrewsbury Sch.; Trinity Coll., Cambridge (Entrance Scholar 1968; BA 1971, MA; PhD 1975; ScD 1994). FRAS 1977; FIMA 2007. University of Cambridge: Asst Lectr, 1977–81; Lectr, 1981–94; Reader, 1994–2000; Trinity College: Res. Fellow, 1974–77; Teaching Fellow, 1977–2013; Tutor, 1980–90, 1991–94; Dean, 1994–2006; Vice-Master, 2006–12. Instructor and Asst Prof., MIT, 1975–77. *Publications:* (with N. O. Weiss) Magnetoconvection, 2014; over 185 articles in learned jls. *Recreations:* gardening, rowing, foreign travel, theatre, concerts. *Address:* The Provost's Lodge, King's College, Cambridge CB2 1ST. *T:* (01223) 331253, *Fax:* (01223) 331195. *E:* mrep@cam.ac.uk. *Club:* Oxford and Cambridge.

PROCTOR, Prof. Stephen John, FRCP, FRCPath; Professor of Haematological Oncology, University of Newcastle upon Tyne, 1991, now Emeritus; *b* 21 Nov. 1945; *s* of Jack and Betty Proctor; *m* 1971, Susan; one *s* two *d. Educ:* Morley Grammar Sch.; Univ. of Newcastle upon Tyne (MB BS 1970). FRCP 1985; FRCPath 1989. Sen. Lectr in Medicine and Haematology, Univ. of Newcastle upon Tyne, 1982–91. *Publications:* over 200 peer reviewed articles in scientific jls and med. jls. *Recreations:* gardening, horticulture, enjoying Northumberland, motoring, travel. *Address:* Academic Haematology Department, Medical School, Framlington Place, Newcastle upon Tyne NE2 4HH. *T:* (0191) 222 7791. *E:* s.j.proctor@ncl.ac.uk.

PROCTOR, William Angus; Clerk of the Journals, House of Commons, 2003–04; *b* 1 May 1945; 3rd *s* of late George Longmate Proctor and Anne Ines Louie Proctor (*née* Angus); *m* 1969, Susan Irene Mottram; two *s* one *d. Educ:* Bristol Cathedral Sch. (chorister); Keele Univ. (BA Hons English and Political Instns; Pres., Students Union, 1965–66). A Clerk, H of C, 1968–70 and 1972–2004; Res. Associate, Manchester Univ., 1970–72; Delegn Sec., H of C Overseas Office, 1972–74; Clerk, Select Committees on: Sci. and Technol., 1974–77; Procedure, 1977–79; Transport, 1979–82; Foreign Affairs, 1982–87; Sec., H of C Commn, 1987–92; Principal Clerk: of Financial Cttees and Clerk, Treasury and CS Cttee, 1992–95; of Standing Cttees, 1995–97; of Bills, 1997–99; of Delegated Legislation, 1999–2003. Procedural Advr to Pres., Council of Europe Assembly, 1989–92. Occasional advr to overseas parliaments, 2004–. *Publications:* (jtly) The European Parliament, 1973; (ed) The Parliamentary Assembly of the Council of Europe: procedure and practice, 9th edn (with J. Sweetman) 1990; (Asst Ed. and contrib.) Erskine May's Parliamentary Practice, 22nd edn, 1997; contrib. articles and reviews to parly jls. *Recreations:* music, family, completing Keele Foundation Year reading course from 1963–64. *E:* billproctor2012@hotmail.co.uk.

PROCTOR-BEAUCHAMP, Sir Christopher Radstock; *see* Beauchamp.

PRODI, Romano; Prime Minister of Italy, 1996–98 and 2006–08; Professor-at-Large, Watson Institute for International Studies, Brown University, since 2009; Special Envoy for the Sahel, United Nations, since 2012; *b* Scandiano, Italy, 9 Aug. 1939; *m* Flavia Franzoni; two *s. Educ:* Catholic Univ. of Milan (degree in law); LSE (post-grad. studies; Hon. Fellow). Asst in Political Econs, 1963–71, Prof. of Industrial Organisation and Industrial Policy, 1971–99, Univ. of Bologna; Researcher: Lombard Inst. of Economic and Social Studies, 1963–64; Stanford Res. Inst., 1968. Prof. of Econs and Indust. Politics, Free Univ. of Trento, 1973–74; Vis. Prof., Harvard Univ., 1974. Minister of Industry, 1978–79; Chm., Inst. for Industrial Reconstruction, 1982–89, 1993–94. Chm., Ulivo (centre-left coalition gp), 1995–2007; Pres., Democratic Party, 2007–08. MP (Ulivo), Italy, 1996–99; Pres., Eur. Commn, 1999–2004; MP (Union), Italy, 2006–08. Hon. Mem., Real Academia de Ciencias Morales y Políticas, Madrid. Hon. Dr: Madras; Sofia; Brown; Barcelona; Pisa; Ottawa; Seoul; Modena-Reggio; Hon. DCL Oxon, 2002. Premio Schumpeter, 1999.

PROESCH, Gilbert; artist; *b* Dolomites, Italy, 1943. *Educ:* Wolkenstein Sch. of Art; Hallein Sch. of Art; Munich Acad. of Art; St Martin's Sch. of Art. Collaboration with George Passmore, *qv*, as Gilbert and George. Gallery exhibitions include: Modern Fears, 1980, The Believing World, 1983, New Pictures, 1987, Worlds & Windows, 1990, New Democratic Pictures, 1992, Anthony d'Offay Gall.; The Rudimentary Pictures, Milton Keynes Gall., 2000; New Horny Pictures, White Cube^2, 2001; Perversive Pictures, NY, 2004; Jack Freak Pictures, White Cube, 2009, and European mus. tour, 2010; museum exhibitions include: The Paintings, 1971, Photo-Pieces 1971–80, 1981, Whitechapel Art Gall.; Pictures 1982 to 85, Hayward Gall., 1987; Enclosed and Enchanted, MOMA, Oxford, 2000; The Dirty Words Pictures (retrospective), Serpentine Gall., 2002; Gilbert & George: major exhibition (retrospective), Tate Modern, 2007, and US mus. tour, 2008; London Pictures, White Cube, 2012; living sculpture includes: The Red Sculpture; Underneath the Arches; The Singing Sculpture; Our New Sculpture. Work in permanent collections incl. Nat. Portrait Gall., Tate Modern and San Francisco Mus. of Modern Art. Represented GB, Venice Biennale, 2005. (Jtly) Turner Prize, 1986. *Publications:* (as Gilbert), with George Passmore: Lost Day; Oh, the Grand Old Duke of York; What Our Art Means. *Address:* c/o White Cube^2, 144–152 Bermondsey Street, SE1 3TQ.

PROFFITT, Stuart Graham; Publishing Director, Penguin Press, since 1998; *b* Bolton, 24 Aug. 1961; *s* of late Geoffrey Arnold Proffitt and of Sheila Patricia (*née* Whitehurst); *m* 2003, Anya Catherine Suschitzky; two *d. Educ:* Uppingham Sch., Rutland; Worcester Coll., Oxford (BA Modern Hist. 1982). Various posts, Collins, later HarperCollins, Publishers, 1983–92; Publisher, Trade Div., HarperCollins Publishers, 1992–98. Chair, Samuel Johnson Prize for Non-fiction, 1999–. London Library/Christie's Life in Literature Award, 2014. *Recreations:* reading, music, hill-walking. *Address:* c/o Penguin Books, 80 Strand, WC2R 0RL. *T:* (020) 7010 3000. *Club:* Brooks's.

PROFIT, (George) Richard, CBE 2003 (OBE 1980); AFC 1974; Board Member, and Group Director, Safety Regulation, Civil Aviation Authority, 1997–2003; *b* 31 Oct. 1940; *s* of Richard George Profit and Lillian Cotterill Profit; *m* 1965, Pamela Shepherd; one *d. Educ:* Oldershaw Grammar Sch.; Army Staff Coll., Camberley; RCDS. Commissioned Royal Air Force, 1961: operational pilot, UK, Singapore, Germany, 1963–77; Officer Commanding: No 3 (F) Sqdn, 1977–80; RAF Coltishall, 1982–85; Inspector of Flight Safety, 1987–90; retd in rank of Air Cdre, 1990; Dir, Safety, Security and Quality Assurance, NATS Ltd, 1990–97; Hd, Aerodrome and Air Traffic Services, Safety Regulation Gp, CAA, 1997. Non-exec. Dir, Railway Safety Bd, 2001–03; Ind. non-exec. Dir, Rail and Safety Standards Bd, 2003–10. *Publications:* Systematic Safety Management in the Air Traffic Services, 1995. *Recreations:* trout fishing, photography. *Club:* Royal Air Force.

PROKHOROVA, Violetta; *see* Elvin, V.

PROPHET, His Honour John; a Circuit Judge, 1997–2006; a Judge of the Employment Appeal Tribunal, 2002–06; *b* 19 Nov. 1931; *s* of Benjamin and Elsie Prophet; *m* 1961, Pauline Newby; three *d. Educ:* Trinity Coll., Cambridge (MA). Called to the Bar, Lincoln's Inn, 1956; Shell International, 1956–60; private practice at the Bar, 1960–63; Sen. Lectr, Law Faculty, Leeds Univ., 1968–76; full-time Chm. of Industrial Tribunals, 1976–88; Regl Chm. of Industrial Tribunals, Yorkshire and Humberside, 1988–97; Pres., Industrial, subseq. Employment, Tribunals for England and Wales, 1997–2002. Consultant, Nat. Assoc. of Local Councils, 1968–89. *Publications:* The Structure of Government, 1968; The Parish Councillor's Guide, 1974, 17th edn 2000; Fair Rents, 1976; The Councillor, 1979, 11th edn 1997. *Recreations:* tennis, chess, gardening, eight grandchildren!

PROPHIT, Penny Pauline; Member, Board of Directors, Trustee and Chair, College Board of Trustees, Our Lady of the Lake Regional Medical Center, Baton Rouge, Louisiana, since 2004; *b* 7 Feb. 1939; *d* of C. Alston Prophit and Hortense Callahan. *Educ:* Marillac Coll., St Louis Univ., USA (BSN); Catholic Univ. of America (MSN, DNSc, PhD). Asst Prof., Catholic Univ. of America, 1975; Associate Professor: Univ. of Southern Mississippi, 1975; Louisiana State Univ. Med. Center, 1975; Cons., WHO, Eur. Office, Copenhagen, 1977; Prof., Katholieke Univ., Leuven, Belgium, 1977; Prof. of Nursing Studies, 1983–92, Hd of Dept, 1983–88, Univ. of Edinburgh. Mental Welfare Comr for Scotland, 1985; Mem., UK Central Council for Nursing, Midwifery and Health Visiting, 1988. Delta Epsilon Sigma, Nat. Catholic Scholastic Honor Soc., 1966; Sigma Theta Tau, Internat. Nursing Scholastic Honor Soc., 1970; Sigma Epsilon Phi, Catholic Univ. of Amer. Honor Soc., 1975. *Publications:* (with Lynette Long) Understanding and Responding, 1982; res. articles on nursing care of the elderly, stress in nursing, interdisciplinary collaboration, etc. *Recreations:* jogging, reading and writing poetry and short stories, playing piano and listening to music of all kinds.

PROSOR, Ron; Permanent Representative of Israel to the United Nations, since 2011; *m* Hadas; two *s* one *d. Educ:* Hebrew Univ. of Jerusalem (MA *cum laude* Pol Sci.). Joined Min. of Foreign Affairs of Israel, 1980; Spokesman, Israeli Embassy, Bonn, 1988–92; Dep. Dir, Eur. Div., 1992–93, Dir, Ops Centre, 1993–95, Min. of Foreign Affairs; Spokesman, Israeli Embassy, London, 1995–98; Minister-Counsellor, Pol Affairs, Washington, 1998–2002; Foreign Min. Spokesman, 2002–03; Dep. Dir Gen. for Strategic Affairs, Counter-Terrorism and Nuclear Disarmament, 2003; COS to Foreign Minister, 2003–04; Sen. Dep. Dir Gen., 2004, Dir Gen., 2004–07, Min. of Foreign Affairs; Ambassador of Israel to Court of St James's, 2007–11. Dist. Service Award, Min. of Foreign Affairs, Israel, 2002. *Address:* c/o Permanent Mission of Israel to the United Nations, 800 Second Avenue, New York, NY 10017, USA.

PROSSER, family name of **Baroness Prosser**.

PROSSER, Baroness *cr* 2004 (Life Peer), of Battersea in the London Borough of Wandsworth; **Margaret Theresa Prosser,** OBE 1997; *b* 22 Aug. 1937; *d* of Frederick James and Lillian (*née* Barry); *m* (marr. diss.); one *s* two *d. Educ:* St Philomena's Convent, Carshalton; North

East London Polytechnic (Post Grad. Dip. in Advice and Inf. Studies, 1977). Associate Mem., Inst. of Legal Execs, 1982. Advice Centre Organiser, Southwark Community Develt Project, 1974–76; Advr, Southwark Law Project, 1976–83; Transport and General Workers' Union: official, 1983–2002; Nat. Sec., 1984–92; Nat. Organiser, 1992–99; Dep. Gen. Sec., 1999–2002. Pres., TUC, 1995–96. Non-exec. Dir, Royal Mail, 2004–10. Member: Equal Opportunities Commn, 1987–93; Employment Appeal Tribunal, 1995–2007; Central Arbitration Cttee, 2000–03; Low Pay Commn, 2000–05; Chair, Women's Nat. Commn, 2002–07; Dep. Chair, Commn for Equality and Human Rights, 2006–12. Treas., Labour Party, 1996–2001. *Recreations:* walking, gardening, reading. *Address:* 281 Limpsfield Road, Warlingham, Surrey CR6 9RL.

PROSSER, Benjamin Charles W.; *see* Wegg-Prosser.

PROSSER, Charles; *see* Prosser, L. C.

PROSSER, Sir David (John), Kt 2005; Chief Executive, Legal & General Group, 1991–2006; Joint Chairman, Investec plc, 2011–14 (Director, since 2006); *b* 26 March 1944; *s* of Ronald and Dorothy Prosser; *m* 1971, Rosemary Margaret Snuggs; two *d. Educ:* Univ. of Wales (BSc). FIA. Sun Alliance Group, 1965–69; Hoare Govett, 1969–73; CIN Management, 1973–88; Legal & General, 1988–2006. Director: SWALEC, 1991–96; InterContinental Hotels Gp, 2003–08; Epsom Downs Racecourse, 2006–13. Chm., Financial Services Skills Council, 2004–06. Mem. of Bd, ABI, 1994–97, 1999–2006. *Recreation:* family life. *Club:* Royal Automobile (Chm., 2007–12).

PROSSER, His Honour (Elvet) John; QC 1978; a Circuit Judge, 1988–2001; a Deputy High Court Judge, 1984–2001; Resident Judge, Newport (Gwent) Crown Court, 1993–2001; *b* 10 July 1932; *s* of David and Hannah Prosser; *m* 1957, Mary Louise Cowdry; two *d. Educ:* Pontypridd Grammar Sch.; King's Coll., London Univ. LLB. Flt Lt, RAF, 1957–59. Called to the Bar, Gray's Inn, 1956, Bencher, 1986; Mem., Senate of Inns of Court and the Bar, 1980–87; a Recorder, 1972–88; Leader, Wales and Chester Circuit, 1984–87. Part-time Chm. of Industrial Tribunals, 1975–81. An Asst Boundary Comr for Wales, 1977–2001. *Recreations:* watching cricket and television. *Address:* 15 Redwood Court, Llanishen, Cardiff CF14 5RD. *Clubs:* East India, Devonshire, Sports and Public Schools; Cardiff and County (Cardiff).

PROSSER, Gwynfor Mathews, (Gwyn); *b* 27 April 1943; *s* of late Glyndwr Jenkin Prosser and of Edith Doreen Prosser; *m* 1972, Rodina Beaton MacLeod; one *s* two *d. Educ:* Dunvant Sch., Swansea; Swansea Secondary Tech. Sch. Nat. Dip. Mech. Engrg; First Cl. Cert. Steam and Motor Engrg; CEng, MIMarEST. Merchant Navy Engr Cadet, 1960–65; sea-going Marine Engr, 1965–72; shore-based Marine Engr, Greenock and Saudi Arabia, 1972–79; Chief Engr, Sealink, 1979–92; OPCS, 1992–96. MP (Lab) Dover, 1997–2010; contested (Lab) same seat, 2010. Mem., Select Cttee on Home Affairs, H of C, 2001–10. Chm., Associated Parly Ports and Merchant Navy Gp, 2002–10. Mem. (Lab), Kent CC, 1989–97 (Chm., Economic Develt Cttee, 1993–97). *Recreations:* hill walking, family outings, awaiting the revival of Welsh Rugby. *Club:* Marine Officers' (Dover).

PROSSER, Sir Ian (Maurice Gray), Kt 1995; FCA; Chairman, InterContinental Hotels Group, 2003; Chairman and Chief Executive, 1987–2000, Executive Chairman, 2000–03, Bass PLC, later Six Continents PLC; *b* 5 July 1943; *s* of late Maurice and Freda Prosser; *m* 1st, 1964, Elizabeth Herman (marr. diss. 2003); two *d*; 2nd, 2003, Hilary Prewer. *Educ:* King Edward's School, Bath; Watford Grammar School; Birmingham Univ. (BComm). Coopers & Lybrand, 1964–69; Bass Charrington Ltd, later Bass PLC, subseq. Six Continents PLC, 1969–2003: Financial Dir, 1978–84; Vice Chm., 1982–87; Gp Man. Dir, 1984–87. Director: Boots Co., 1984–96; Lloyds TSB Gp (formerly Lloyds Bank), 1988–99; BP, 1997–2010 (Dep. Chm., 1999–2010); Glaxo SmithKline plc (formerly SmithKline Beecham PLC), 1999–2009; Hillshire Brands Co. (formerly Sara Lee Corp.), 2004–14; Chairman: NAAFI, 2008–; BP Pension Fund Trustees, 2010–; Aviva Staff Pension Fund, 2013–. Chm., Stock Exchange Listed Cos Adv. Cttee, 1992–98 (Mem., 1990–98). Chm., World Travel and Tourism Council, 2001–03. Chm., Brewers and Licensed Retailers Assoc. (formerly Brewers' Soc.), 1992–94 (Dir, 1983–2000). DUniv Birmingham, 2001. *Recreations:* golf, theatre, music. *Clubs:* Home House; Leander.

PROSSER, Prof. James Anthony William, (Tony), FBA 2014; Professor of Public Law, University of Bristol, since 2002; *b* Ludlow, 3 May 1954; *s* of James Prosser and Flora Prosser; *m* 1998, Charlotte Villiers; one *s* one *d. Educ:* Ludlow Grammar Sch.; Univ. of Liverpool (LLB 1974). Res. Asst, Univ. of Southampton, 1974–76; Lectr in Law, Univ. of Hull, 1976–80; Lectr, 1980–89, Sen. Lectr, 1989–92, Univ. of Sheffield; John Millar Prof. of Law, Univ. of Glasgow, 1992–2002. Jean Monnet Fellow, European University Inst., Florence, 1987–88; Vis. Prof., Coll. of Europe, Bruges, 2009–. *Publications:* Nationalised Industries and Public Control, 1986; (with C. Graham) Privatizing Public Enterprises, 1991; Law and the Regulators, 1997; The Limits of Competition Law, 2005; The Regulatory Enterprise, 2010; The Economic Constitution, 2014. *Recreations:* hillwalking, cycling, travel, cinema, listening to modern jazz. *Address:* University of Bristol Law School, Wills Memorial Building, Queens Road, Bristol BS8 1RJ. *T:* (0117) 954 5302, *Fax:* (0117) 925 1870. *E:* t.prosser@bristol.ac.uk.

PROSSER, Jeffrey; Chairman, Queen Elizabeth Hospital King's Lynn (formerly King's Lynn and Wisbech Hospitals) NHS Trust, 2000–05; *b* 13 June 1942; *s* of Trevor and Beryl Prosser; *m* 1st, 1968, Margaret Sumpter (marr. diss. 1988); three *s*; 2nd, 1989, Sandra Walmsley. *Educ:* University Coll., Cardiff (Dip. Social Services); Leicester Univ. (Dip. Social Work); UEA (BA 2004; MA 2006). Social worker, Herts CC, 1968–72; Principal Social Worker, Northwick Park Hosp., 1972–74; Divl Manager, Cambs CC, 1974–79; Asst Dir, Haringey LBC, 1979–82; Area Dir, Devon CC, 1982–84; Dep. Dir of Social Services, Enfield LBC, 1984–86; Gen. Manager, Tower Hamlets HA, 1986–89; Dir of Community Care, Court Cavendish plc, 1989–92; Controller of Community Services, 1993–95, Dir of Community Services, 1995–99, Dir of Social Affairs, 1999, London Bor. of Barnet. Chm., Flagship Hsg Gp, 1999–2006; Vice Chm., Peddars Way Housing Assoc., 1998–99. Chm., Red2Green, 2004–07; Dir, impressionsprints ltd, 2007–10. Chm., Bd of Govs, Methvold High Sch., 2008–12. Mem., Weeting Parish Council, 2008– (Chm., 1999–2000). *Recreations:* gardening, cycling, photography, St Edmundsbury Male Voice Choir. *Address:* The Old Rectory, Rectory Lane, Weeting, Brandon, Suffolk IP27 0PX. *T:* (01842) 812672.

PROSSER, His Honour John; *see* Prosser, His Honour E. J.

PROSSER, Kevin John; QC 1996; tax barrister; a Recorder, since 2000; a Deputy High Court Judge (Chancery Division), since 2008; *b* 26 Aug. 1957; *s* of Sidney Ronald Prosser and Rita Lillian Prosser; *m* 1st, 1994, Mary Elizabeth Stokes (marr. diss. 2010); one *s* one *d*; 2nd, 2011, Rebecca Louise Murray. *Educ:* Broxbourne Sch.; UCL (LLB); St Edmund Hall, Oxford (BCL). Called to the Bar, Lincoln's Inn, 1982, Bencher, 2005; Asst Recorder, 2000. Chm., Revenue Bar Assoc., 2008–13. *Publications:* (with D. C. Potter) Tax Appeals, 1990. *Recreations:* opera, squash, reading. *Address:* 16 Bedford Row, WC1R 4EF. *T:* (020) 7414 8080. *Club:* Garrick.

PROSSER, (Leslie) Charles, DFA; Secretary, Royal Fine Art Commission for Scotland, 1976–2005; *b* 27 Oct. 1939; *s* of Dr Leslie John Prosser and Eleanor Alice May (*née* Chapman); *m* 1960, Coral Williams; one *s* two *d. Educ:* Sedbergh Sch.; Bath Acad. of Art, Corsham; Slade Sch. of Fine Art (DFA); Kungl. Akademien Konsthögskolan, Stockholm; Inst. of Educn, Leeds Univ. (DAEd). Asst Lectr in Fine Art, Blackpool Sch. of Art, 1962–64; Leverhulme European Arts Research Award, Stockholm, 1964–65; Lectr in Fine Art, Leeds Coll. of Art, later Jacob Kramer Coll. of Art, 1965–76; research in art educn, 1974–75. Ed., Royal Fine Art Commn for Scotland pubns, 1976–2005. Mem. UK Cttee, Hong Kong Architecture Exhibn, Edinburgh, 1996–97. Mem., Scotch Malt Whisky Soc., Leith, 1991–. FRSA 1997; Hon. FRIAS 1997; Hon. MRTPI 2002. *Publications:* contrib. to environmental design jls. *Recreations:* appreciating the art of planning our surroundings, unneeded walking, opining. *Address:* 28 Mayfield Terrace, Edinburgh EH9 1RZ. *T:* (0131) 668 1141.

PROSSER, Tony; *see* Prosser, J. A. W.

PROUD, Rt Rev. Andrew John; *see* Reading, Area Bishop of.

PROUDFOOT, Bruce; *see* Proudfoot, V. B.

PROUDFOOT, Prof. Nicholas Jarvis, PhD; FRS 2005; Brownlee-Abraham Professor of Molecular Biology, University of Oxford, since 2003; Fellow of Brasenose College, Oxford, since 1982; *b* Chicago, 6 June 1951; *s* of Malcolm Jarvis Proudfoot and Mary Proudfoot (*née* MacDonald); *m* 1975, Anne Semple; two *s. Educ:* Bedford Coll., London (BSc Biochem. 1972); King's Coll., Cambridge (PhD Molecular Biol. 1975). MRC Laboratory of Molecular Biology, Cambridge: MRC Res. Student, 1972–75; Jun. Beit Meml Res. Fellow, 1975–78; MRC Scientific Staff, 1978–79; Jun. Res. Fellow, St John's Coll., Cambridge, 1976–79; Sen. Res. Fellow, CIT, 1979–80; Res. Associate, Harvard Univ., 1980–81; University of Oxford: Lectr in Chemical Pathology, Sir William Dunn Sch. of Pathology, 1981–96; Prof. of Experimental Pathology, 1996–2003; Tutor in Biochem., Brasenose Coll., 1982–2003. Mem. EMBO, 1982. Royal Soc./Wolfson Res. Merit Award, 2002–07. *Publications:* contrib. molecular biology/genetics jls. *Recreations:* amateur musician (horn player and baritone), walking, cycling. *Address:* 14 Northmoor Road, Oxford OX2 6UP. *T:* (01865) 275566. *E:* nicholas.proudfoot@path.ox.ac.uk.

PROUDFOOT, Prof. (Vincent) Bruce, OBE 1997; FSA 1963; FRSE 1979; FRSGS; Professor of Geography, University of St Andrews, 1974–93, Emeritus 1993; *b* 24 Sept. 1930; *s* of late Bruce Falconer Proudfoot; *m* 1961, Edwina Valmai Windram Field; two *s. Educ:* Royal Belfast Academical Instn; Queen's Univ., Belfast (BA, PhD). Research Officer, Nuffield Quaternary Research Unit, QUB, 1954–58; Lectr in Geography, QUB, 1958–59, Durham Univ., 1959–67; Tutor, 1960–63, Librarian, 1963–65, Hatfield Coll., Durham; Visiting Fellow, Univ. of Auckland, NZ, and Commonwealth Vis. Fellow, Australia, 1966; Associate Prof., 1967–70, Prof., 1970–74, Univ. of Alberta, Edmonton, Canada; Acting Chm., Dept of Geography, Univ. of Alberta, 1970–71; Co-ordinator, Socio-Economic Opportunity Studies, and Staff Consultant, Alberta Human Resources Research Council, 1971–72. Trustee, Nat. Mus. of Antiquities of Scotland, 1982–85. Chairman: Rural Geog. Study Gp, Inst. of British Geographers, 1980–84; Soc. for Landscape Studies, 1979–83. Royal Society of Edinburgh: Mem. Council, 1982–85 and 1990–91; Vice-Pres., 1985–88; Gen. Sec., 1991–96; Bicentenary Medal, 1997. Vice-Pres., Soc. of Antiquaries of Scotland, 1982–85; Pres., Section H (Anthrop. and Archaeol.), BAAS, 1985; Hon. Pres., Scottish Assoc. of Geography Teachers, 1982–84; Royal Scottish Geographical Society: Mem. Council, 1975–78, 1992–93; Chm. Council, 1993–99; Vice-Pres., 1993–; Hon. Editor, 1978–92; Fellow, 1991; Chm., Dundee Centre, 1993–99 (Mem., Cttee, 1976–93, 1999–2003); Treas., Scottish Church Heritage Research, 2010–. Lectures: Lister, BAAS, 1964; Annual, Soc. for Landscape Studies, 1983; Estyn Evans, QUB, 1985. *Publications:* The Downpatrick Gold Find, 1955; (with R. G. Ironside *et al*) Frontier Settlement Studies, 1974; (ed) Site, Environment and Economy, 1983; numerous papers in geographical, archaeological and soils jls. *Recreation:* gardening. *Address:* Westgate, Wardlaw Gardens, St Andrews, Scotland KY16 9DW. *T:* (01334) 473293. *Club:* Royal Scots (Edinburgh).

PROUDMAN, Hon. Dame Sonia Rosemary Susan, (Dame Sonia Cartwright), DBE 2008; **Hon. Mrs Justice Proudman;** a Judge of the High Court of Justice, Chancery Division, since 2008; *b* 30 July 1949; *d* of late Kenneth Oliphant Proudman and Sati Proudman (*née* Hekimian); *m* 1987, Crispian Cartwright; one *d. Educ:* St Paul's Girls' Sch. (Foundn Schol.); Lady Margaret Hall, Oxford (Open Schol.; BA 1st Cl. Hons Jurisprudence 1971; MA 1973; Hon. Fellow 2009). Called to the Bar, Lincoln's Inn, 1972 (Kennedy Schol., Buchanan Prize), Bencher, 1996; Oxford Univ. Eldon Law Schol., 1973; in practice at Chancery Bar, 1974–2008; QC 1994; Asst Recorder, 1996–2000; Recorder, 2000–08; Dep. High Court Judge, 2001–08. Mem., Panel of Chairmen, Competition Appeal Tribunal, 2008–. Member: Oxford Law Faculty Adv. Bd, 2000; QC Selection Panel, 2005. *Recreation:* taking enormous notice of hats and backchat. *Address:* Royal Courts of Justice, 7 Rolls Building, Fetter Lane, EC4A 1NL. *Clubs:* Hurlingham, CWIL.

PROUT, David Michael, PhD; Director General, High Speed Two, Department for Transport, since 2013; *b* 14 March 1963; *s* of late Prof. Charles Keith Prout and of Lesley Craven Prout; *m* 1992, Penelope Sarah Gibbs; two *d. Educ:* Magdalen Coll. Sch., Oxford; Wadham Coll., Oxford (BA Hons (Mod. Hist.) 1985); Courtauld Inst. of Art, London (PhD 1991). Joined Civil Service, 1993; various posts, DoE, 1993–95; UK Perm. Repn to EU, 1995–98; Private Sec., 1999–2001, Principal Private Sec., 2001–04, to Dep. Prime Minister; Dir of Local Govt Policy, ODPM, subseq. DCLG, 2004–07; Exec. Dir, Planning and Bor. Develt, Royal Bor. of Kensington and Chelsea, 2007–09; Dir Gen., Localism (formerly Communities), DCLG, 2009–12. *Recreations:* cycling, tennis, cinema, family, travel. *Address:* Department for Transport, Great Minster House, 33 Horseferry Road, SW1P 4DR. *E:* David.Prout@dft.gsi.gov.uk.

PROVAN, James Lyal Clark; politician, farmer, businessman; *b* 19 Dec. 1936; *s* of John Provan and Jean (*née* Clark); *m* 1960, Roweena Adele Lewis; twin *s* one *d. Educ:* Ardvreck Sch., Crieff; Oundle Sch., Northants; Royal Agricultural Coll., Cirencester. Member: Tayside Regional Council, 1978–82; Tay River Purification Bd, 1978–82. Chairman: McIntosh Donald Ltd, 1989–94; James McIntosh & Co., 1990–94. MEP (C): NE Scotland, 1979–89; S Downs W, 1994–99; SE Reg., England, 1999–2004; European Parliament: Quaestor, 1987–89; Cons. Chief Whip, 1994–96; Vice Pres. and Chief Whip, EPP, 1996–99; Vice Pres., 1999–2004; Member: Agriculture and Fisheries Cttee, 1979–89 (EDG spokesman on agricl and fisheries affairs, 1982–87); Environment, Consumer Affairs and Public Health Cttee, 1979–89; Chairman: Cross-Party Tourism Gp, 1996–2004; Conciliation Cttee to Council of Ministers, 1999–2002. Exec. Dir, Scottish Financial Enterprise, 1990–91; non-exec. Dir, CNH Global NV, 1999–2006 (Director: New Holland Holdings NV, 1995–99; New Holland NV, 1996–99). Mem. Bd, Rowett Res. Inst., 1990–2004 (Chm., 1992–98); Mem., AFRC, 1990–94. Area President, Scottish NFU, 1965 and 1971; Treasurer, Perth and E Perthshire Conservative Assoc., 1975–77; Member, Lord Lieutenant's Queen's Jubilee Appeal Cttee, 1977. FRAgS 2000. FRSA 1987. *Publications:* The European Community: an ever closer union?, 1989; Europe's Freedom to Farm, 1996, 1998; Europe's Fishing Blues, 1997. *Recreations:* country pursuits, sailing, flying, musical appreciation, travel. *Address:* Summerfield, Glenfarg, Perth PH2 9QD. *Clubs:* Farmers; Royal Perth Golfing Society.

PROVAN, Marie; *see* Staunton, M.

PROVERA, Marco T.; *see* Tronchetti Provera.

PROWSE, Most Rev. Christopher Charles; *see* Canberra and Goulburn, Archbishop of, (RC).

PROWSE, Philip (John); theatre director and designer; Professor of Theatre Design, Slade School of Fine Art, University College London, 1999–2003 (Head of Theatre Design Department, 1995–2003), now Professor Emeritus; *b* 29 Dec. 1937; *s* of late Alan William

Auger Prowse and Violet Beatrice (*née* Williamson). *Educ:* King's Sch., Worcester; Malvern Coll. of Art; Slade Sch. of Fine Art. Professional début: Diversions for Royal Ballet, Royal Opera House, 1961; subsequent prodns and designs for opera, ballet and drama including: Glasgow Citizens' Theatre; rep. theatres; West End theatres; Royal Nat. Theatre; RSC, Barbican; Old Vic Theatre; Royal Opera; Royal Ballet; ENO; Sadler's Wells Royal Ballet; Birmingham Royal Ballet; WNO; Scottish Opera; Opera North; English Nat. Ballet (Festival Ballet); Scottish Ballet; Chichester Fest. Theatre; prodns in Europe and US; festival appearances: Rome, Wiesbaden, Holland, Warsaw, Zurich, Belgrade, Edinburgh, Cologne, Hamburg, Venice, Parma, E Berlin, Halle, Caracas. Co-Dir, Glasgow Citizens' Theatre, 1970–2004. *Address:* c/o Cruickshank Cazenove, 97 Old South Lambeth Road, SW8 1XU.

PRUSINER, Prof. Stanley Ben, MD; Professor of Neurology, University of California, San Francisco, since 1984; *b* 28 May 1942; *s* of Lawrence Albert Prusiner and Miriam Prusiner (*née* Spigel); two *d*. *Educ:* Univ. of Pennsylvania (AB 1964; MD 1968). University of California, San Francisco: Med. Intern, 1968–69; Resident in Neurology, 1972–74; Asst Prof. of Neurology, 1974–80; Associate Prof., 1980–84; Prof., 1984–; Prof. of Virology, Univ. of Calif, Berkeley, 1984–. FAAAS 1998. Foreign Mem., Royal Soc., 1997. Max Planck Res. Award, Alexander von Humboldt Foundn and Max Planck Soc., 1992; Gairdner Foundn Award, 1994; Wolf Prize for Medicine, 1996; Nobel Prize in Physiology or Medicine, 1997. *Publications:* (ed) The Enzymes of Glutamine Metabolism, 1973; Slow Transmissible Diseases of the Nervous System, 2 vols, 1979; Prions, 1987; Prion Diseases of Humans and Animals, 1992; Molecular and Genetic Basis of Neurologic Disease, 1993, 3rd edn 2003; Prions, Prions, Prions, 1996, 2nd edn as Prion Biology and Diseases, 2004; more than 300 articles in learned jls. *Address:* University of California, 675 Nelson Rising Lane, San Francisco, CA 94143, USA.

PRYCE, (George) Terry, CBE 1994; Chairman, G. T. Pryce (Farms) Ltd, since 1996; *b* 26 March 1934; *s* of Edwin Pryce and Hilda Florence (*née* Price); *m* 1957, Thurza Elizabeth Tatham, JP; two *s* one *d*. *Educ:* Welshpool Grammar Sch.; National Coll. of Food Technol. MFC, FIFST. Dir, various food cos in THF Gp, 1965–70; Asst Man. Dir, Dalgety (UK) Ltd, 1970–72; Man. Dir, Dalgety (UK) and Dir, DPLC, 1972–78; Man. Dir, 1978–81, Chief Exec., 1981–89, Dalgety PLC. Chairman: Solway Foods Ltd, 1990–94; York House Group Ltd, 1996–2003; Jas Bowman and Sons Ltd, 1999– (Dir, 1991–); Dir, H. P. Bulmer Holdings PLC, 1984–94. Chm., British Soc. for Horticultural Res., later Horticulture Res. Internat., 1990–97; Council Member: AFRC, 1986–94; UK Food and Drink Fedn, 1987–89; Mem. Adv. Bd, Inst. of Food Res., 1988–94. Chm., UK Food Assoc., 1986–88. CCMI. *Recreation:* sport. *Address:* 89 Brookmans Avenue, Brookmans Park, Hatfield, Herts AL9 7QG. *T:* (01707) 642039. *Clubs:* Athenæum, MCC.

See also S. C. C. Pryce, T. J. R. Pryce.

PRYCE, Jonathan, CBE 2009; actor; *b* 1 June 1947; *m* 2014, Kate Fahy; two *s* one *d*. *Educ:* RADA. FRWCMD (FWCMD 1995). Patron: Friendship Works (formerly Friends United Network), 1992–; Facial Surgery Res. Foundn, Saving Faces, 2001–. *Theatre includes:* Comedians, Nottingham Playhouse, Old Vic, 1975, NY 1976 (Tony Award); title rôle, Hamlet, Royal Court, 1980 (Olivier Award); The Caretaker, Nat. Th., 1981; Accidental Death of an Anarchist, Broadway, 1984; The Seagull, Queen's, 1985; title rôle, Macbeth, RSC, 1986; Uncle Vanya, Vaudeville, 1988; Miss Saigon, Drury Lane, 1989 (Olivier Award and Variety Club Award), NY, 1991 (Tony Award for Best Actor in Musical, 1991); Oliver!, Palladium, 1994; My Fair Lady, RNT, transf. Theatre Royal, Drury Lane, 2001, Kennedy Centre, Washington, 2013; The Reckoning, Soho Th., 2003; The Goat, or Who is Sylvia, Almeida, 2004, transf. Apollo, 2004; Dirty Rotten Scoundrels, NY, 2006; Glengarry Glen Ross, Apollo, 2007; Dimetos, Donmar, The Caretaker, Liverpool Everyman, 2009, transf. Trafalgar Studios, 2010, world tour, 2012; King Lear, Almeida, 2012; The Merchant of Venice, Shakespeare's Globe, 2015; *television includes:* Roger Doesn't Live Here Anymore (series), 1981; Timon of Athens, 1981; Martin Luther, 1983; Praying Mantis, 1983; Whose Line Is It Anyway?, 1988; The Man from the Pru, 1990; Selling Hitler, 1991; Mr Wroe's Virgins, 1993; Thicker Than Water, 1993; David, 1997; HR, 2007; The Baker Street Irregulars, 2007; My Zinc Bed, 2008; Clone, 2008; Cranford, 2009; Wolf Hall, 2015; Game of Thrones, 2015; *films include:* Something wicked this way comes, 1982; The Ploughman's Lunch, 1983; Brazil, 1985; The Doctor and the Devils, 1986; Haunted Honeymoon, 1986; Jumpin' Jack Flash, 1987; Consuming Passions, 1988; The Adventures of Baron Munchausen, 1988; The Rachel Papers, 1989; Glengarry Glen Ross, 1992; The Age of Innocence, 1992; Barbarians at the Gate, 1992; Great Moments in Aviation, 1993; A Business Affair, 1993; Shopping, 1994; Carrington, 1995 (Best Actor Award: Cannes, 1995; Evening Standard, 1996); Evita, 1996; Regeneration, 1997; Tomorrow Never Dies, 1997; Ronin, 1998; Stigmata, 1999; Very Annie Mary, 2001; Bride of the Wind, 2001; The Affair of the Necklace, 2002; Unconditional Love, 2002; Pirates of the Caribbean: The Curse of the Black Pearl, 2003; What a Girl Wants, 2003; De-Lovely, 2004; The Brothers Grimm, 2005; Pirates of the Caribbean: Dead Man's Chest, 2006; Pirates of the Caribbean: At World's End, 2007; Leatherheads, 2007; Bedtime Stories, 2008; GI Joe: The Rise of the Cobra, 2009; Hysteria, Borgriki, 2011; Dark Blood, 2012; GI Joe: Retaliation, 2013; Listen Up Philip, 2014; Under Milk Wood, 2014; The Salvation, 2014; Woman in Gold, 2015; *recordings include:* Miss Saigon; Nine—the Concert; Under Milk Wood; Cabaret; Oliver!; Evita; Hey Mr Producer; My Fair Lady. Hon. Patron, Northern Lights Symphony Orchestra, 2010–. Hon. DLitt Liverpool, 2006. Special BAFTA Cymru, 2001; Cymru for the World Award, 2009. *Address:* c/o Julian Belfrage Associates, 3rd Floor, 9 Argyll Street, W1F 7TG.

PRYCE, Prof. Roy; Director, 1973–78, Senior Advisor for Direct Elections, 1978–79, Chief Advisor, 1979–81, Directorate General for Information, Commission of the European Communities; *b* 4 Oct. 1928; *s* of Thomas and Madeline Pryce; *m* 1954, Sheila Rose, *d* of Rt Hon. James Griffiths, CH; three *d*. *Educ:* Grammar Sch., Burton-on-Trent; Emmanuel Coll., Cambridge (MA, PhD). MA Oxon. Research Fellow: Emmanuel Coll., Cambridge, 1953–55; St Antony's Coll., Oxford, 1955–57; Head of London Information Office of High Authority of European Coal and Steel Community, 1957–60; Head of London Inf. Office, Jt Inf. Service of European Communities, 1960–64; Rockefeller Foundn Res. Fellow, 1964–65; Dir, Centre for Contemp. European Studies, Univ. of Sussex, 1965–73. Dir, 1983–90, Sen. Res. Fellow, 1990–99, Federal Trust for Educn and Res. Vis. Professorial Fellow, Centre for Contemporary European Studies, Univ. of Sussex, 1973–81; Visiting Professor: Coll. of Europe, Bruges, 1965–72; Eur. Univ. Inst., Florence, 1981–83; Eur. Inst. for Public Admin, Maastricht, 1983–88. *Publications:* The Italian Local Elections 1956, 1957; The Political Future of the European Community, 1962; (with John Pinder) Europe After de Gaulle, 1969, German and Ital. edns 1970; The Politics of the European Community, 1973; (ed) The Dynamics of European Union, 1987; (ed jtly) Maastricht and Beyond, 1994; Heathfield Park: a private estate and a Wealden town, 1996; Heathfield and Waldron: an illustrated history, 2000; Rotherfield Hall, 2002; Battle Abbey and the Websters, 2005; (jtly) Old Heathfield and Cade Street in the 19th Century, 2008. *Recreations:* gardening, local history.

PRYCE, Simon Charles Conrad; Chief Executive, BBA Aviation plc, since 2007; *b* 8 Dec. 1961; *s* of (George) Terry Pryce, *qv* and Thurza Elizabeth Pryce (*née* Tatham); *m* 1997, Katharine Mary Childs; two *s*. *Educ:* Haberdashers' Aske's Sch., Elstree; Reading Univ. (BSc Food Scis). Chartered Accountant. Dir, Lazard, 1987–96; Sen. Vice Pres., JPMorgan, 1996–97; GKN plc: Dir, Corporate Finance, 1997–2001; Chief Financial Officer, Automotive, 2001–04; Chief Exec., Diversified Businesses Gp, 2004–07. Director: SMMT, 2005–07; General Aviation Manufacturers Assoc., 2010–. Mem. Council and Mem. Inv. Cttee, Reading Univ., 2013–. MCSI (MSI 1997). FRAeS 2010. *Recreations:* sports, travel, performing arts, reading. *Address:* c/o BBA Aviation plc, 105 Wigmore Street, W1U 1QY. *T:* (020) 7514 3999, *Fax:* (020) 7408 2318. *Clubs:* Athenaeum, MCC.

See also T. J. R. Pryce.

PRYCE, Terry; *see* Pryce, G. T.

PRYCE, Tim John Robert; Chief Executive Officer, Terra Firma Capital Partners, since 2009; *b* Cleethorpes, 1 July 1965; *s* of (George) Terry Pryce, *qv*; civil partnership 2007, Jonathan Kemp. *Educ:* King's Coll. London and Pantheon Sorbonne, Paris (LLB English Law 1988; Maîtrise French Law 1988; AKC 1988). Admitted as solicitor, 1991. Solicitor, Slaughter and May, 1989–96; General Counsel: GE Capital AFS Europe, 1996–98; Transamerica TDF Europe, 1998–2000; Team Hd, Nomura TMD-PFG, 2000–02; Gen. Counsel, Terra Firma Capital Partners, 2002–09. *Recreations:* theatre, ballet, opera, travel. *Address:* Terra Firma Capital Partners, 2 More London Riverside, SE1 2AP. *T:* (020) 7015 9690.

See also S. C. C. Pryce.

PRYCE, Vicky; Chief Economic Adviser, Centre for Economics and Business Research, since 2014; *b* Athens; *d* of late Nicolas Courmouzis and of Voula Courmouzis; *m* 1st, 1972, G. Pryce (marr. diss. 1981); two *d*; 2nd, 1984, Christopher Murray Paul Huhne (*see* Rt Hon. C. M. P. Huhne) (marr. diss. 2011); two *s* one *d*. *Educ:* London Sch. of Econs and Pol Sci. (BSc Econs, MSc Monetary Econs). Economist, then Chief Economist, Williams & Glyn's Bank, 1973–83; Corporate Economist, Esso Europe, 1983–86; Chief Economist, then Partner, KPMG, 1986–2001; Chm., Good Corp., 2001–02; Partner, London Economics, 2001–02; Chief Economic Advr and Dir Gen., Econs, DTI, then BERR, later BIS, 2002–10; Dep. Hd, 2004–07, Jt Hd, 2007–10, Govt Economic Service; Sen. Man. Dir, FTI Consulting, 2010–13. Hon. Vis. Prof., Cass Business Sch., City Univ., 2002–06, 2008–11; Vis. Fellow, Nuffield Coll., Oxford, 2008–13; Adjunct Prof., Imperial Coll. Business Sch., Imperial Coll. London, 2010–13; Visiting Professor: Sch. of Econs and Finance, QMUL, 2011–; Birmingham City Univ., 2014–; Aston Univ., 2015–; Hon. Prof., Guildhall Faculty of Business and Law, London Metropolitan Univ., 2014–. Mem. Internat. Adv. Bd, British Amer. Business Inc., 2003–13. Member: Standing Adv. Gp to Financial Reporting Rev. Panel, Financial Reporting Council, 2006–12; Exec. Cttee, 2010–12, Council, 2010–, IFS; Panel on Monitoring the Economy, BIS, 2010–; Adv. Bd, OMFIF, 2013–; non-exec. Mem. Cttee, NESTA, 2011–13. Fellow, Soc. of Business Economists, 2005–. Mem. Court, Co. of Mgt Consultants, 2001– (Master, 2010–11). Member: Council, REconS, 2002–07; Council, Univ. of Kent, 2005–11; Adv. Bd, Centre for Internat. Business and Mgt, Univ. of Bath Business Sch., 2013– (Judge Inst., Cambridge, 1999–2013); Res. Adv. Bd, ABI, 2006–11; Court, LSE, 2011–13; Bd of Trustees: RSA, 2006–08; Centre for Economic Policy Res., 2010–. Patron: Pro-Bono Economics, 2011–; Working Chance, 2014–. FAcSS (AcSS 2011). *Publications:* (ed jtly) Green Business, Green Values and Sustainability, 2011; Prisonomics: behind bars in Britain's failing prisons, 2013; Greekonomics: the Euro crisis and why politicians don't get it, 2013; (jtly) It's the Economy, Stupid, 2015; Why Women Need Quotas, 2015; (jtly) Redesigning Manufacturing, 2015. *Recreations:* theatre, cinema, Chelsea football supporter. *Club:* Reform.

PRYDE, Roderick Stokes, OBE 1999; Director, Spain, British Council, 2009–15; Director, Roderick Pryde Consulting Ltd, since 2015; *b* 26 Jan. 1953; *s* of William Gerard Pryde and Patricia Mary Pryde; *m* 1989, Susanne Mona Graham Hamilton; one *s* three *d*. *Educ:* George Watson's Coll., Edinburgh; Univ. of Sussex (BA Hons); UCNW, Bangor (PGCE, TESL). Lectr, Univ. of Dijon, 1975–76; English Teaching Co-ordinator, Cie Française des Pneumatiques, Michelin, 1979–81; British Council, 1981–2015: Asst Regl Lang. Officer, London, 1981–83; Dir of Studies, Milan, 1983–87; Regional Director: Andalucia, 1987–88; Bilbao, 1988–89; Director: Kyoto and Western Japan, 1990–94; English Lang. Centre, Hong Kong, 1994–98; Portugal, 1998–2000; Dir, Educnl Enterprises, 2000–02; Asst Dir-Gen., 2002–05; Regl Dir, India and Sri Lanka, 2005–09. *Recreations:* walking, family, reading. *Club:* Watsonian (Edinburgh).

PRYKE, Sir Christopher Dudley, 4th Bt *cr* 1926, of Wanstead, co. Essex; *b* 17 April 1946; *s* of William Dudley Pryke and Lucy Irene Pryke (*née* Madgett); *S* uncle, 1998; *m* 1st, 1973, Angela Gay Meek (marr. diss. 1986); one *s*; 2nd, 1999, Marilyn Wright, *d* of late Gerald William Henry Williamson. *Educ:* Hurstpierpoint. MRICS. *Heir:* *s* James Dudley Pryke, *b* 29 Dec. 1977. *Address:* 43 Bramble Rise, Cobham, Surrey KT11 2HP.

PRYKE, Paula Shane, (Mrs P. Romaniuk), OBE 2014; floral artist and author; *b* 29 April 1960; *d* of Ralph and Gladys Pryke; *m* 1987, Peter Romaniuk. *Educ:* Culford Sch.; Univ. of Leeds (BEd Hons Hist.). LRAM (Speech and Drama) 1985. Founder, Paula Pryke Flowers, London, 1998. Lectr and demonstrator on floral art around the world. Ambassador for Floral Industry Award, NFU, 2000. *Publications:* The New Floral Artist, 1993; Flower Innovations, 1995; Flower Celebrations, 1995; Simple Flowers, 1999; Candles, 1999; Wreaths and Garlands, 1999; Living Colour, 2001; Wedding Flowers, 2004; Classic Paula Pryke, 2004; The Flower School, 2006; Table Flowers, 2007; Seasonal Wreaths and Bouquets, 2008; Simply Pink, 2009; The Ultimate Floral Collection, 2010; Paula Pryke Wedding Flowers, 2015. *Recreations:* gardening, cooking, the arts. *Address:* The Old Post Office, Dalham, Suffolk CB8 8TG. *T:* 07802 784166. *E:* paula@paulapryke.com.

PRYKE, Roy Thomas; Director of the Virtual Staff College, University of Exeter, 2000–06; *b* 30 Nov. 1940; *s* of Thomas George and Nellie Matilda Pryke; *m* 1962, Susan Pauline Andrew; one *s* three *d*. *Educ:* Univ. of Wales (BA Hons); Univ. of Manchester (PGCE). Teacher, Manchester, 1963–71; Education Officer, Devon, 1971–79; Deputy Chief Education Officer: Somerset, 1980–82; Devon, 1983–87; Dep. Chief Educn Officer and Head of Operations, Cambridgeshire, 1987–89; Dir, Educn Services, Kent CC, 1989–98. Adviser to: Council of Local Educn Authorities, 1992–98; ACC, 1994–97; LGA, 1997–98; Chm., Assoc. of Chief Educn Officers, 1996–97. Chm., DFEE Adv. Gp, Schs Improvement Internat., 1999–2002; Mem., President of Zimbabwe's Commn on Educn and Trng, 1998–99. Chm., Rolle Exmouth Ltd, 2010–. Vis. Prof. of Educn, 1998–2000, Hon. Fellow, 2006, Univ. of Exeter. Chm., Exmouth Community Assoc., 2007–. FRSA 1988; Hon. FCP 1991. Chevalier, Ordre des Palmes Académiques (France), 1994. *Publications:* contributor to: Open Plan Schools, 1978; The Head's Legal Guide, 1984; The Revolution in Education and Training, 1986; articles in Education Jl on curriculum and on education management. *Recreations:* foreign travel and languages, sailing, golf. *Address:* 1 West Checkstone, 2 Douglas Avenue, Exmouth, Devon EX8 2AU. *T:* (01395) 277173.

PRYN, Maj.-Gen. William John, OBE 1973; MB, BS; FRCS, FRCSEd; Director of Army Surgery, and Consulting Surgeon to the Army, 1982–86, retired; *b* 25 Jan. 1928; *s* of late Col Richard Harold Cotter Pryn, FRCS, late RAMC and Una St George Ormsby (*née* Roe); *m* 1st, 1952, Alison Lynette (marr. diss.), 2nd *d* of Captain Norman Arthur Cyril Hardy, RN; two *s* one *d*; 2nd, 1982, June de Medina, *d* of Surg. Comdr Norman Bernard de Medina Greenstreet, RN; one step *s* one step *d*. *Educ:* Malvern Coll.; Guy's Hosp. Med. Sch., London Univ. (MB, BS 1951). MRCS, LRCP 1951; FRCS 1958; FRCSEd 1984. Trooper, 21st SAS Regt (Artists Rifles), TA, 1948–50. House appts, Gen. Hosp., Ramsgate and Royal Berks Hosp., Reading, 1951–52; commnd into RAMC, 1952; Regtl MO to No 9 Training Regt RE, 1952–53; surg. appts in mil. hosps in UK, Cyprus and N Africa, 1953–58; seconded as Surg. Registrar, Royal Postgrad. Med. Sch., Hammersmith Hosp., 1958–59; Officer i/c Surg. Div. and Consultant Surgeon to mil. hosps, Malaya, Singapore, N Borneo and UK, 1959–69; CO BMH Dhekelia, 1969–72; Sen. Consultant Surgeon in mil. hosps, UK and NI, 1972–77; Consulting Surgeon to BAOR, 1977–82; Consultant in Surgery to Royal Hosp., Chelsea, 1982–86; Hon. Consultant to S Dist, Kensington and Chelsea and Westminster AHA (T),

1981. Member: EUROMED Gp on Emergency Medicine, 1980–86; Specialty Bd in Surgery, and Reg. Trng Cttee in Gen. Surgery, Defence Medical Services, 1982–86; Med. Cttee, Defence Scientific Adv. Council, 1982–86; BMA, 1950–; Wessex Surgeons Club, 1976–. Member Council: RAMC, 1982–86; Mil. Surgical Soc., 1982–. Fellow, Assoc. of Surgeons of GB and Ireland, 1960 (Mem., Educn Adv. Cttee, 1982–86). QHS 1981–86. OStJ 1984. Mem., Editorial Bd, Injury, 1982–86. *Publications:* (contrib.) Field Surgery Pocket Book, 1981; original articles in the Lancet and British Jl of Surgery. *Recreations:* fishing, shooting and other country pursuits, golf, tennis, sailing, gardening, joinery, house maintenance.

PRYNNE, Andrew Geoffrey Lockyer; QC 1995; *b* 28 May 1953; *s* of late Maj.-Gen. Michael Whitworth Prynne, CB, CBE and Jean Violet Prynne; *m* 1977, Catriona Mary Brougham; three *d*. *Educ:* Marlborough Coll.; Univ. of Southampton (LLB Hons). Called to the Bar, Middle Temple, 1975. Mem., Lord Chancellor's Multi-Party Actions Wkg Gp, 1997–. Asst Boundary Comr, 2000–. Legal Assessor, NMC, 2012–. CEDR Accredited Mediator, 2000. *Recreations:* sailing, shooting, ski-ing. *Address:* Temple Garden Chambers, 1 Harcourt Buildings, Temple, EC4Y 9DA. *T:* (020) 7583 1315. *Clubs:* Royal Yacht Squadron, Royal Solent Yacht, Island Sailing (IoW), Royal Southampton Yacht; Bar Yacht.

PRYOR, Arthur John, CB 1997; PhD; competition consultant, since 1996; Head, Competition Policy Division, Department of Trade and Industry, 1993–96; *b* 7 March 1939; *s* of late Quinton Arthur Pryor, FRICS and Elsie Margaret (*née* Luscombe); *m* 1964, Marilyn Kay Petley; one *s* one *d*. *Educ:* Harrow County Grammar Sch.; Downing Coll., Cambridge (MA; PhD). Asst Lectr, then Lectr, in Spanish and Portuguese, UC Cardiff, 1963–66; Asst Principal, BoT and ECGD, 1966–69; Principal, DTI, 1970–73; First Sec., British Embassy, Washington, 1973–75; Principal, Dept of Trade, 1975–77; Assistant Secretary: Shipping Policy Div., Dept of Trade, 1977–80; Air Div., DoI, 1980–83; Department of Trade and Industry: Asst Sec., Internat. Trade Policy Div., 1984–85; Under Sec. and Regional Dir, W Midlands Region, 1985–88; Dir Gen., BNSC, 1988–93. Mem., Competition (formerly Monopolies and Mergers) Commn, 1998–2003; Competition Commn Appeal Panel, subseq. Competition Appeal Tribunal, 2000–11. *Publications:* contribs to modern lang., space and competition jls. *Recreations:* tennis, golf, book collecting. *Address:* c/o Competition Appeal Tribunal, Victoria House, Bloomsbury Place, WC1A 2EB. *T:* (020) 7979 7979.

PRYOR, Dr Francis Manning Marlborough, MBE 1999; archaeologist; Director of Archaeology, Flag Fen Bronze Age Centre, Peterborough, since 1987; *b* 13 Jan. 1945; *s* of late Robert Matthew Marlborough Pryor, MBE and Barbara Helen Pryor (*née* Robertson); *m* 1st, 1969, Sylvia Jean Page (marr. diss. 1977); one *d*; 2nd, 1988, Maisie Taylor. *Educ:* Eton; Trinity Coll., Cambridge (MA Archaeol. and Anthropol.; PhD 1985). Asst Curator, Royal Ontario Mus., Toronto, 1969–78; Welland Valley Field Officer, Cambs CC, 1978–82; Dir, Etton and Flag Fen Excavations, 1982–87. Vis. Prof. of Archaeol., Leicester Univ., 2007–. Pres., Council for British Archaeol., 1998–2005. Presenter, TV series: Britain BC, 2003; Britain AD, 2004. *Publications:* Excavations at Fengate, Peterborough, 4 vols, 1974–1984; Flag Fen, 1992; Prehistoric Farmers, 1998; Excavations at Etton, 1998; Sea Henge, 2001; The Flag Fen Basin, 2001; Britain BC, 2003; Britain AD, 2004; Britain in the Middle Ages, 2006; The Making of the British Landscape, 2010; The Birth of Modern Britain: a journey into Britain's archaeological past: 1550 to the present, 2011; The Lifers' Club (novel), 2014; Home: a time traveller's tales from Britain's prehistory, 2014. *Recreations:* gardening, eating my own vegetables (it's about ingredients, not sauces). *Address:* Flag Fen Bronze Age Centre, The Droveway, Northey Road, Peterborough PE6 7QF. *T:* (01733) 313414, *Fax:* (01733) 349957. *E:* office@flagfen.freeserve.co.uk.

PRYOR, John Pembro, MS; FRCS; consultant uroandrologist, retired; *b* 25 Aug. 1937; *s* of William Benjamin Pryor and Kathleen Pryor; *m* 1959, Marion Hopkins; four *s*. *Educ:* Reading Sch.; King's Coll. and King's Coll. Hosp. Med. Sch. (MB, BS). AKC 1961; FRCS 1967; MS London 1971. Training appointments: Doncaster Royal Infirm., 1965–66; Univ. of Calif, San Francisco, 1968–69; KCH and St Paul's Hosp., 1971–72; Consultant Urol Surgeon to KCH and St Peter's Hosp., 1975–94; Dean, Inst. of Urology, London Univ., 1978–85; Reader, Inst. of Urology, UCL and Hon. Cons. Urol Surgeon, St Peter's Hosp., 1994–99. Hunterian Prof., RCS, 1971 and 1995. Chairman: (first), British Andrology Soc., 1979–84; European Assoc. of Genital Microsurgeons, 1992–95; Impotence Assoc., 1999–2001; Eur. Sexual Alliance, 1999–2004; Trustees, Eur. Acad. for Sexual Medicine, 2004–07; Pres., Eur. Soc. for Impotence Research, 1999–2001. Treas., British Jl of Urology, 1991–99. St Peter's Medal, British Assoc. of Urol Surgeons, 1995. *Publications:* (ed jtly) Andrology, 1987; (ed) Urological prostheses, appliances and catheters, 1992; (jtly) Impotence: an integrated approach to clinical practice, 1992; articles on urology and andrology in scientific jls. *Address:* The Beacon, Channel Way, Fairlight, E Sussex TN35 4BP. *T:* (01424) 814949.

PRYOR, His Honour Robert Charles; QC 1983; a Circuit Judge, 1991–2004; *b* 10 Dec. 1938; *s* of Charles Selwyn Pryor and Olive Woodall Pryor; *m* 1969, Virginia Sykes; one *s* one *d*. *Educ:* Eton; Trinity Coll., Cambridge (BA). National Service, KRRC, 2nd Lieut 1958. Called to the Bar, Inner Temple, 1963; a Recorder, 1989–91. Director, Sun Life Corp. (formerly Sun Life Assurance) plc, 1977–91.

See also Viscount Hampden.

PRYS-DAVIES, family name of **Baron Prys-Davies**.

PRYS-DAVIES, Baron *cr* 1982 (Life Peer), of Llanegryn in the County of Gwynedd; **Gwilym Prys Prys-Davies;** Partner, Morgan Bruce (formerly Morgan Bruce & Nicholas), Solicitors, Cardiff, Pontypridd, 1957–87, retired; *b* 8 Dec. 1923; *s* of William and Mary Matilda Davies; *m* 1951, Llinos Evans (*d* 2010); three *d*. *Educ:* Towyn Sch., Towyn, Merioneth; University College of Wales, Aberystwyth. Served RN, 1942–46. Faculty of Law, UCW, Aberystwyth, 1946–52; President of Debates, Union UCW, 1949; President Students' Rep. Council, 1950; LLB 1949; LLM 1952. Admitted Solicitor, 1956. Contested (Lab) Carmarthen, 1966. Special Adviser to Sec. of State for Wales, 1974–78. Mem., H of L, 1982–2015. Official opposition spokesman: on health, 1983–89; on N Ireland, 1982–93; on Welsh Office, 1987–95. Member, H of L Select Committee: on Parochial Charities Bill and Small Charities Bill, 1983–84; on murder and life imprisonment, 1988–89; on Central and Local Govt, 1995–96; Member: British-Irish Inter-Parly Body, 1990–96; Jt Cttee on Statutory Instruments, 1990–98; Delegated Powers and Deregulation Cttee, 1998–2002. Chm., Welsh Hosps Bd, 1968–74; Member: Welsh Council, 1967–69; Welsh Adv. Cttee, ITA, 1966–69; Working Party on 4th TV Service in Wales, Home Office and Welsh Office, 1975–76; Adv. Gp, Use of Fetuses and Fetal Material for Res., DHSS and Welsh Office, 1972; Econ. and Social Cttee, EEC, 1978–82. Chm., NPFA (Cymru), 1998–2001. A Vice-Pres., Hon. Soc. of Cymmrodorion, 1993–. Pres., Univ. of Wales Swansea, 1997–2001; Vice-Pres., Coleg Harlech, 1989–95. Hon. Fellow: UCW, Aberystwyth, 1992; Trinity Coll., Carmarthen, 1995; Univ. of Wales Inst., Cardiff, 1995. Hon. LLD: Wales, 1996; Glamorgan, 2009. OStJ 1968. *Publications:* A Central Welsh Council, 1963; Y Ffermwr a'r Gyfraith, 1967; Llafur y Blynyddaedd, 1993; Cynhaeaf Hanner Canrif, 2008; Ysgol Llanegryn, 2009. *Address:* Hafod Wen, 7 Fountain Drive, SE19 1UW. *T:* (020) 8670 7208.

PRYS-ROBERTS, Prof. Cedric, DM; FRCA; Professor of Anaesthesia, University of Bristol, 1976–99, Emeritus since 2000; President, Royal College of Anaesthetists, 1994–97; *b* 8 Aug. 1935; *s* of late William Prys Roberts and Winifred Prys Roberts (*née* Osborne Jones); *m* 1961, Linda Joyce Bickerstaff; two *s* two *d*. *Educ:* Dulwich Coll.; St Bartholomew's Hosp. Med. Sch. (MB BS London); MA, DM Oxon; PhD Leeds. FANZCA; FCA. Research Fellow, Univ. of Leeds, 1964–67; Clinical Reader in Anaesthetics, Oxford Univ., 1967–76; Fellow, Worcester Coll., Oxford, 1970–76; Hon. Cons. Anaesthetist, Radcliffe Infirmary, 1967–76; Prof. of Anaesthesia, Univ. of California, San Diego, 1974; Hon. Consultant Anaesthetist, Bristol Royal Infirmary and Bristol Royal Hosp. for Sick Children, 1976–99. Hunterian Prof., RCS, 1978. Hon. FCMSA 1996; Hon. FCAI (FFARCSI 1998). *Publications:* (ed) The Circulation in Anaesthesia, 1980; (ed) Pharmacokinetics of Anaesthesia, 1984; (ed) Monitoring in Anaesthesia and Intensive Care, 1994; (ed) International Practice of Anaesthesia, 2 vols, 1996; contribs to learned jls. *Recreations:* mountaineering, ski-ing, philately and postal history, music (playing trumpet), videography of birds. *Address:* Foxes Mead, Cleeve Hill Road, Cleeve, Bristol BS49 4PG.

PRZYBORSKI, Prof. Stefan Alexander, PhD; Professor of Cell Technology, Durham University, since 2000; *b* Norwich, 26 Oct. 1966; *s* of Stefan and Kathleen Przyborski; *m* 1996, Jane; two *d*. *Educ:* Univ. of Sheffield (BSc Anatomy and Cell Biol. 1989; PhD 1992); Durham Univ. (PGCHE 2005). Wellcome Trust Postdoctoral Fellow, Univ. of Sheffield, 1992–95; MRC Postdoctoral Travelling Fellow, Jackson Lab., USA, 1995–97; Res. Scientist, Wyeth Neurosci., Princeton, NJ, 1997–98; J. G. Graves Sen. Med. Res. Fellow, Univ. of Sheffield, 1998–99. Dir and CSO, Reinnervate Ltd, 2002–14. *Publications:* Technology Platforms for 3D Cell Culture, 2015; contribs to peer-reviewed pubns. *Recreations:* running, football, hiking, cycling, carpentry, DIY, music, cinema. *Address:* School of Biological and Biomedical Science, Durham University, South Road, Durham DH1 3LE. *T:* (0191) 334 3988. *E:* stefan.przyborski@durham.ac.uk.

PTASZYNSKI, André Jan; theatre producer, trading as Pola Jones Ltd, since 1980; Head of Theatres, Really Useful Group, since 2011; *b* 7 May 1953; *s* of Wladyslaw Ptaszynski and Joan Ptaszynski (*née* Holmes); *m* 1985, Judith Terry; two *s* two *d*. *Educ:* Ipswich Sch.; Jesus Coll., Oxford (BA 1975, MA 1978). Associate Dir, Crucible Th., Sheffield, 1978–80; ind. theatre and television producer trading as Pola Jones Ltd, 1980–: produced over 50 West End and touring shows including: Return to the Forbidden Planet, West Side Story, Fosse, Chicago, Spend, Spend, Spend, Tommy, Show Boat and (with RSC, West End and NY) Matilda the Musical; produced sitcoms for BBC including Joking Apart (Bronze Rose, Montreux TV Fest., 1995); promoted live work of comedians including: Rowan Atkinson, Dave Allen, Victoria Wood, Eddie Izzard and League of Gentlemen; Chief Executive: Really Useful Th., 2000–05; Really Useful Gp, 2005–11. Member, Board: Oxford Stage Co., 1990–97; RNT, 2001–10. Pres., Soc. of London Th., 1996–99. *Recreations:* mountain trekking, fell-walking, cycling around London, reading, yoga, drinking wine on sunny terraces. *Address:* Hill Farm, Chiselhampton, Oxford OX44 7XH. *T:* (office) (020) 7928 1589. *E:* andre@polajones.com.

PUAPUA, Rt Hon. Sir Tomasi, GCMG 2002; KBE 1998; PC 1982; Governor General of Tuvalu, 1998–2003; *b* 10 Sept. 1938; *s* of Fitilau and Olive Puapua; *m* 1971, Riana Tabokai; two *s* two *d*. *Educ:* King George V Secondary Sch.; Fiji Sch. of Medicine; Otago Med. Sch., NZ (DPH). Gilbert and Ellice Islands Colony Government: gen. med. practitioner, 1964–70; MO, Public Health, 1971–76; Tuvalu: MP Vaitupu, 1977–98; Prime Minister, 1981–89; Speaker of Parliament, 1993–98. *Recreations:* cricket, fishing, gardening, reading. *Address:* c/o Government House, Funafuti, Tuvalu.

PUBLICOVER, Ralph Martin; HM Diplomatic Service, retired; *b* 2 May 1952; *s* of John Publicover and Nora (*née* Bates); *m* 1973, Rosemary Sheward; one *s* two *d*. *Educ:* Haberdashers' Aske's Sch., Elstree; Univ. of Manchester (BA Econ 1973); Sch. of Oriental and African Studies, London. Joined HM Diplomatic Service, 1976; Second, then First Sec., Dubai, 1979–81; First Sec. (Econ.), Ottawa, 1981–85; Assessments Staff, Cabinet Office, 1985–87; First Sec., Washington, 1989–92; Dep. Hd, Central Eur. Dept, FCO, 1992–94; Deputy Head of Mission: Bucharest, 1994–97; Lisbon, 1998–2003; Hd, Consular Crisis Gp, FCO, 2003–04; Ambassador to Angola, 2005–07; Clerk, Cttee Office, H of L, 2008–10. Sensitivity Reviewer, FCO, 2012–. *Recreations:* music, cricket, ancient monuments, ducks and geese. *Address:* 87 Great Brownings, College Road, SE21 7HR. *E:* ralphpublicover@ntlworld.com.

PUDDEPHATT, Andrew Charles, OBE 2003; Managing Director, Global Partners Digital (formerly Global Partners and Associates), since 2005; *b* 2 April 1950; *s* of Andrew Ross Puddephatt and Margaret McGuire; two *d*. *Educ:* Sidney Sussex College, Cambridge (BA 1971). Worked as teacher in 1970s; computer programmer, 1978–81. Councillor, Hackney Council, 1982–90 (Leader, 1986–89). Gen. Sec., NCCL, subseq. Liberty, 1989–95; Dir, Charter 88, 1995–99; Exec. Dir, Article 19, Internat. Centre Against Censorship, 1999–2005. Vis. Fellow, LSE, 2005–08. Chm., Internat. Media Support (Denmark) (Dep. Chm., 2001). Trustee, Sigfrid Rausing Trust, 2008–. *Recreations:* literature, music. *Address:* c/o Global Partners, Development House, 56–64 Leonard Street, EC2A 4LT.

PUDDEPHATT, Prof. Richard John, OC 2007; PhD; FRS 1998; FRS (Can) 1991; Distinguished University Professor of Chemistry, University of Western Ontario, since 2005 (Professor of Chemistry, 1978–2005); *b* 12 Oct. 1943; *s* of late Harry and Ena Puddephatt; *m* 1979, Alice Ruth Poulton; one *s* one *d*. *Educ:* University Coll. London (BSc 1965; PhD 1968). Teaching Fellow, Univ. of Western Ont, 1968–70; Lectr, 1970–77, Sen. Lectr, 1977–78, Univ. of Liverpool. Canada Res. Chair, Univ. of Western Ont., 2001–. Sen. Editor, Canadian Jl Chem., 1998–. Royal Society of Chemistry: Noble Metals Award, 1991; Nyholm Award, 1997; Chemical Society of Canada: Alcan Award, 1985; Steacie Award, 1996; CIC Medal, 1998; Hellmuth Prize, 2000. *Publications:* The Periodic Table of the Elements, 1972, 2nd edn 1986; The Chemistry of Gold, 1978; contrib. numerous papers to learned jls, mostly on organometallic chemistry. *Recreations:* gardening, golf. *Address:* Department of Chemistry, University of Western Ontario, London, ON N6A 5B7, Canada. *T:* (519) 6792111.

PUGH, Alastair Tarrant, CBE 1986; Chairman, Alastair Pugh and Associates, 1988–2008; *b* 16 Sept. 1928; *s* of Sqdn Leader Rev. Herbert Cecil Pugh, GC, MA, and Amy Lilian Pugh; *m* 1957, Sylvia Victoria Marlow (marr. diss. 2001); two *s* one *d*. *Educ:* Tettenhall Coll., Staffs; De Havilland Aeronautical Tech. Sch.; Harvard Business Sch. FRAeS; FCILT. Design Dept, De Havilland Aircraft Co., 1949–52; Sen. Designer, H. M. Hobson, 1952–55; journalist, Flight, 1955–61; Channel Air Bridge, 1961–63; British United Airways, 1963–70: Planning Dir, 1968; British Caledonian Airways: Dir, R&D, 1970; Production Dir, 1973–74; Corporate Planning Dir, 1974–77; Dep. Chief Exec., 1977–78; Man. Dir, 1978–85; Exec. Vice-Chm./Dir of Strategy, British Caledonian Gp, 1985–88; Consultant, Goldman Sachs Internat. Ltd, 1988–2007. Dir, Gambia Airways, 1985–87; International Board: Royal Jordanian Airways, 1988–89; Air France, 1990–92. President: Inst. of Freight Forwarders, 1981–82; CIT, 1988–89. Trustee, Brooklands Mus. Trust, 1988–. *Recreation:* the chain-driven Frazer Nash. *Address:* England's Cottage, Sidlow Bridge, Reigate, Surrey RH2 8PN. *T:* (01737) 243456.

PUGH, Alun John; writer and consultant specialising in public services and public consultations; *b* 9 June 1955; *s* of late Maurice Thomas Pugh, coal miner, and Violet Jane Pugh, nurse; *m* 1st, 1978, Janet Hughes (marr. diss. 2002); one *s* one *d*; 2nd, 2006, Mary Juliet Chaffé. *Educ:* Tonypandy Grammar Sch.; Poly. of Wales; UC, Cardiff. Lectr in Accounting, Bridgend Coll., 1983–87; Sen. Lectr, Newcastle Coll., 1987–92; Head of Sch., Llandrillo Coll., 1992–96; Asst Principal, W Cheshire Coll., 1996–99. Dir, Snowdonia Soc., 2008–10; Columnist, Daily Post, 2010–12. Mem. (Lab) Clwyd W, Nat. Assembly for Wales, 1999–2007; Dep. Health and Social Services Sec., 2000–01; Dep. Educn Minister, 2001–03; Minister for Culture, the Welsh Lang. and Sports, 2003–07. Contested (Lab): Clwyd West, Nat. Assembly for Wales, 2007; Arfon, 2010, 2015. Mem., British Mountaineering Council, 2009–. *Recreations:* mountaineering, cycling. *E:* alunpugh@hotmail.com.

PUGH, Brett, PhD; Director, School Standards and Workforce Group, Welsh Government, since 2013; *b* Abertysswg, Caerphilly, 19 Feb. 1956; *s* of Gomer Pugh and Beatrice Rose Pugh; civil partnership 2006, Eric Serebro. *Educ:* Univ. of Warwick (BA Hons 1977; PGCE 1978; MEd 1983); Univ. of Glamorgan (MSc 1997); Univ. of Cardiff (PhD 2002). Secondary sch. teacher of English and Music, Warks, 1978–83, Caerphilly, 1983–89; primary sch. teacher, Redbridge, 1989, Tower Hamlets, 1989–91; Dep. Headteacher, St Mary's RC Primary Sch., Bridgend, 1991–94; Headteacher, Phillipstown Primary Sch., Caerphilly, 1995–98; Advr, Caerphilly CBC, 1998–2003; Chief Educn Officer, 2003–05, Dir of Educn, 2005–07, Blaenau Gwent BC; Chief Educn Officer, Newport, 2007–11; Hd, Sch. Standards Unit, Welsh Govt, 2011–13. Chm., SE Wales Educn Consortium, 2007–11. Vice Chm., 2008–10, Chm., 2010–11, Assoc. of Dirs of Educn in Wales. *Publications:* contribs to inspection reports, govt reports and plans. *Recreations:* church organist and music co-ordinator, theatre, ballet, opera, music, biblical studies, archaeology. *Address:* Welsh Government, Cathays Park, Cardiff CF10 3NQ. *T:* (029) 2082 3915. *E:* brett.pugh@wales.gsi.gov.uk, brett.pugh@talktalk.net.

PUGH, Edward Clevely; Director, British Council, Poland, 1994–97; *b* 14 Sept. 1937; *s* of late Edgar Pallister Pugh and Dora Lois Pugh (*née* Clevely); *m* 1962, Thirza Carolyn Browning; one *s* one *d*. *Educ:* Exeter Univ. (BA Econs and Govt 1962); SOAS, Univ. of London. Nat. Service, RN, 1955–57. Robinson Waxed Paper Co. Ltd, 1955 and 1962; British Council, 1963–97: Lectr, Tehran, 1963–67; Asst Rep., Tripoli, 1967–71; Regl Dir, Ndola, Zambia, 1971–74; Dep. Rep., 1974–75, Rep., 1975–77, Ethiopia; seconded to ODM, 1977–79; Dir, FE and Pacific Dept, London, 1979–80; Rep., Tanzania, 1980–83; Dep. Rep., Delhi, 1983–86; Rep., Thailand, 1986–90; Americas, Pacific and Asia Division: Asst Dir, 1990–91; Dep. Dir, 1991–92; Dir, 1992–93; Regl Dir, S Asia and Oceania, 1993–94. *Recreations:* reading, music, theatre, art, walking, swimming. *Address:* 43 Offham Road, W Malling, Maidstone, Kent ME19 6RB. *T:* (01732) 843317.

PUGH, Dame Gillian (Mary), DBE 2005 (OBE 1998); Chief Executive, Coram Family (formerly Thomas Coram Foundation for Children), 1997–2005; Chair, National Children's Bureau, 2006–12; *b* 13 May 1944; *d* of late Robert Quested Drayson, DSC and of Rachel Drayson; *m* 1975, Gareth Nigel Pugh (*d* 1981); one *d*; *m* 1989, Martin Waldron; one step *s* two step *d*. *Educ:* Ashford Sch. for Girls; Univ. of Exeter (BA Hons). Editor: Careers Res. and Adv. Centre, Cambridge, 1966–67; Humanities Curriculum Project, Schs Council/Nuffield Foundn, 1967–70; Asst Dir of Information, Schs Council for Curriculum and Examinations, 1970–74; National Children's Bureau: Sen. Information Officer, 1974–77; Sen. Develt Officer, 1980–86; Dir, Early Childhood Unit, 1986–97; Develt Officer, Voluntary Council for Handicapped Children, 1978–80. Jt Editor, Children & Society, 1992–2003. Vis. Prof., London Univ. Inst. of Educn, 2000–11. Member: Effective Preschool Educn Project Adv. Gp, DfEE, 1997–2006; Bd, Children's Workforce Develt Council, 2005–08; Bd, Trng and Develt Agency, 2006–11; Family Justice Rev. Panel, 2010–11; Chair, Cambridge Primary Rev. (formerly Primary Educn Rev.), 2006–09. President: Child Develt Soc., 1994–96; Nat. Childminding Assoc., 2009–12; Chm., Parenting Educn and Support Forum, 1999–2006; Vice President: Preschool Learning Alliance, 1998–2003; British Assoc. of Early Childhood Educn, 1998–2012; Chair of Governors: Thomas Coram Early Childhood Centre, 1998–2005; Christ Church Chorleywood C of E Sch., 2015– (Gov., 2013–). Trustee: Nat. Family and Parenting Inst., 1999–2006; Friends Provident Charitable Foundn, 2005–09. FRSA 1993. Hon. DEd: Manchester Metropolitan, 1994; West of England, 1998; DUniv Open, 1995; Hon. DLitt Sheffield, 2013. *Publications* include: (jtly) The Needs of Parents, 1984; Contemporary Issues in the Early Years, 1992, 6th edn 2013; Confident Parents, Confident Children, 1994; (jtly) Learning to Be a Parent, 1996; (jtly) Training to Work in the Early Years, 1998; London's Forgotten Children: Thomas Coram and the Foundling Hospital, 2007; (contrib.) Children, Their World, Their Education, 2009. *Recreations:* gardening, choral singing, walking, golf. *Address:* Weathervane, Old Shire Lane, Chorleywood, Herts WD3 5PW. *T:* (01923) 285505.

PUGH, Jeanette Mary, CB 2008; PhD; Director, Gambling Commission, 2013–14; *b* Bognor Regis, 4 June 1959; *d* of William and Eileen Pugh. *Educ:* St Francis of Assisi Prim. Sch., Liverpool; La Sagesse High Sch., Liverpool; Univ. of Bradford (BA Hons 1st Cl. Mod. Langs); Univ. of Manchester Inst. of Sci. and Technol. (PhD Linguistics 1984). Res. Associate, then Proj. Officer, UMIST, 1985–91; Department for Education, then Department for Education and Employment, later Department for Education and Skills: various team leader posts, 1991–98; Divl Manager, Lifelong Learning and Technologies Div., 1998–2001; Divl Manager, Funding Directorate, 2001–02; Divl Manager, Strategy and Communications and Dep. Chief Exec., Connexions Service Nat. Unit, 2002–03; Transition Manager, Children and Families Directorate, 2003; Dir, Children's Workforce Unit, 2003–06; Dir, Safeguarding Gp, DfES, later DCSF, then DFE, 2006–13. *Recreations:* going to the theatre, reading.

PUGH, Dr John David; MP (Lib Dem) Southport, since 2001; *b* 28 June 1948; *s* of James and Patricia Pugh; *m* 1971, Annette; one *s* three *d*. *Educ:* Maidstone Grammar Sch.; Durham Univ.; PhD Manchester; MPhil Nottingham; MA Liverpool. Head: Social Studies, Salesian High Sch., Bootle, 1972–83; Philosophy and Religious Studies, Merchant Taylors' Sch., Crosby, 1983–2001. Mem. (Lib Dem) Sefton MBC, 1987–2002 (Leader, Lib Dem Gp, 1992–2001; Leader of Council, 2000–01). *Publications:* The Christian Understanding of God, 1990. *Recreation:* cycling. *Address:* House of Commons, SW1A 0AA; 27 The Walk, Birkdale, Southport, Lancs PR8 4BG. *T:* (01704) 569025. *Club:* National Liberal.

PUGH, Paul William; Registrar General (formerly Chief Executive), HM Passport Office, 2013–14; *b* Liverpool, 5 Aug. 1960; *s* of James Pugh and Patricia Pugh; *m* 1982, Kathryn Burton; two *s* one *d*. *Educ:* Nottingham High Sch.; Jesus Coll., Cambridge (BA Hons Mod. Langs 1982). Home Office, 1984–2003: Pte Sec. to Home Sec., 1990–92; Hd, Operational Policing Policy Unit, 1996–99; Hd, Police Leadership and Powers Unit, 2000–03; Chief Exec., Central Police Trng and Develt Authy, 2003–04; Exec. Dir, NW London Strategic HA, 2005–07; Regl Dir, Govt Office for E of England, 2008–10; Exec. Dir of Ops, Identity and Passport Service, 2010–13. *Recreations:* spending time with family and friends, shopping in John Lewis. *E:* paul.pugh@homeoffice.gsi.gov.uk.

PUGSLEY, His Honour David Philip; a Circuit Judge, 1992–2014; *b* 11 Dec. 1944; *s* of Rev. Clement Pugsley and Edith (*née* Schofield); *m* 1966, Judith Mary Mappin; two *d*. *Educ:* Shebbear College; St Catharine's College, Cambridge (MA); MPhil Birmingham, 1995. Called to the Bar, Middle Temple, 1968; practised Midland and Oxford Circuit until 1985; Chm. of Industrial Tribunals, Birmingham Reg., 1985–92; a Recorder, 1991–92. Pres., Council of Industrial Tribunal Chairmen, 1991–92; Mem., Parole Bd, 1999–2005, 2010–12. Mem., Editl Bd, Civil Court Procedure, 1999–. Freeman, City of London, 2006. *Publications:* (jtly) Industrial Tribunals Compensation for Loss of Pension Rights, 1990; (jtly) The Contract of Employment, 1997; (jtly) Butterworths Employment Compensation Calculator, 1999. *Recreations:* fly fishing, theatre. *Address:* Cruck Barn Cottage, The Green, Brailsford, Derbyshire DE6 3BX.

PUIG de la BELLACASA, José Joaquín, Hon. GCVO 1986; Knight of Calatrava; Counsellor of State, Spain, since 1997 (Chairman, Council for Foreign Affairs, 1995–97); *b* 5 June 1931; *s* of José Maria Puig de la Bellacasa and Consuelo de Urdampilleta; *m* 1960, Paz de Aznar Ybarra; four *s* two *d*. *Educ:* Areneros Jesuit Coll., Madrid; Madrid Univ. Barrister-at-law. Entered Diplomatic Service, 1959; Dirección General Politica Exterior, 1961–62; Minister's Cabinet, 1962–69; Counsellor, Spanish Embassy, London, 1971–74; Private Sec. to Prince of Spain, 1974–75, to HM King Juan Carlos, 1975–76; Director-General: Co-op. Tecnica Internacional, 1976; Servicio Exterior, 1977–78; Under-Sec. of State for Foreign Affairs, 1978–80; Ambassador to Holy See, 1980–83; Ambassador to UK, 1983–90; Sec.-Gen., Spanish Royal Household, 1990–91; Ambassador to Portugal, 1991–95. Hon. Fellow, QMC, 1987. Grand Cross of Isabel la Católica; Grand Cross of Merito Naval; Encomienda de Numero de Carlos III; holds several foreign decorations. *Address:* Felipe IV 7, Madrid 28014, Spain. *Clubs:* Beefsteak, White's; Nuevo, Golf de Puerta de Hierro (Madrid).

PULAY, Jessica Mary; Co-Head of Policy and Markets, United Kingdom Debt Management Office, since 2015; *b* London, 19 July 1966; *d* of late George Pulay and Katharine Frances Goddard Pulay (*née* Sachs, later Harman). *Educ:* Wycombe Abbey Sch.; Christ Church, Oxford (Open Schol.; BA Hons 1987; MA; Pres., Oxford Union, 1987). Coverage Officer, Credit Suisse First Boston Ltd, 1987–90; Staff Reporter, Economist, 1990; Exec. Dir, Goldman Sachs Internat. Ltd, 1991–97; Man. Dir, Deutsche Morgan Grenfell, 1997; Exec. Dir, Morgan Stanley Internat. Ltd, 1997–98; Manager, Funding, European Bank for Reconstruction and Develt, 1999–2004; Dep. Hd, Funding, EBRD, 2004–15. Mem., Council, Queen's Coll. London, 1998– (Vice Chm., 2010–; Chm., Finance Cttee, 2006–08). Trustee: Nat. Centre for Languages, CILT, 2007–08; Wallace Collection, 2013– (Mem., Audit Cttee, 2013–); Arts Foundn, 2014–. MCIL 2004. *Address:* United Kingdom Debt Management Office, Eastcheap Court, 11 Philpot Lane, EC3M 8UD.

PULFORD, Air Chief Marshal Sir Andrew (Douglas), KCB 2013; CBE 2004; Chief of the Air Staff, since 2013; Air Aide-de-Camp to the Queen, since 2013; *b* 22 March 1958; *s* of Douglas and Jean Pulford; *m* 1982, Nicola Jane Pearse; one *s* one *d*. *Educ:* Magnus Grammar Sch., Newark. Support helicopter pilot, 1978–92; Fleet Air Arm Exchange, 1980–82; RAAF Exchange, 1985–87; OC 18 Sqn, 1996–99; PSO to CAS, 1999–2000; HCSC, 2001; OC RAF Odiham and Chinook Wing, 2002–03; Dir Air Resources and Plans, MoD, 2004–06; AOC No 2 Gp, 2007–08; ACDS (Ops), 2008–10; Dep. C-in-C (Personnel) Air Comd, and Air Mem. for Personnel, 2010–13. *Recreations:* military history, motorcycling, old cars, sailing. *Address:* Air Command, RAF High Wycombe, Bucks HP14 4UE. *Club:* Royal Air Force.

PULHAM, Mary Helen; *see* Creagh, M. H.

PULLAN, Prof. Brian Sebastian, PhD; FBA 1985; Professor of Modern History, University of Manchester, 1973–98; *b* 10 Dec. 1935; *s* of late Horace William Virgo Pullan and Ella Lister Pullan; *m* 1962, Janet Elizabeth Maltby; two *s*. *Educ:* Epsom Coll.; Trinity Coll., Cambridge (MA, PhD); MA Manchester. Nat. Service, RA, 1954–56. Cambridge University: Res. Fellow, Trinity Coll., 1961–63; Official Fellow, Queens' Coll., 1963–72; Univ. Asst Lectr in History, 1964–67; Lectr, 1967–72; Dean, Faculty of Arts, Manchester Univ., 1982–84. Feoffee of Chetham's Hosp. and Library, Manchester, 1981–2004. Corresp. Fellow, Ateneo Veneto, 1986. Serena Medal, British Academy, 1991. *Publications:* (ed) Sources for the History of Medieval Europe, 1966; (ed) Crisis and Change in the Venetian Economy in the Sixteenth and Seventeenth Centuries, 1968; Rich and Poor in Renaissance Venice, 1971; A History of Early Renaissance Italy, 1973; The Jews of Europe and the Inquisition of Venice, 1983; (ed with Susan Reynolds) Towns and Townspeople in Medieval and Renaissance Europe: essays in memory of Kenneth Hyde, 1990; (ed with David Chambers) Venice: a documentary history 1450–1630, 1992; Poverty and Charity: Europe, Italy, Venice, 1400–1700, 1994; (with Michele Abendstern) A History of the University of Manchester 1951–73, 2000; (ed with Maureen Mulholland and Anne Pullan) Judicial Tribunals in England and Europe 1200–1700, 2003; (with Michele Abendstern) A History of the University of Manchester 1973–90, 2004; (ed) A Portrait of the University of Manchester, 2007; articles and reviews in learned jls and collections. *Recreations:* dogs, theatre. *Address:* 33 Green Pastures, Heaton Mersey, Stockport SK4 3RB.

PULLEN, Dr Roderick Allen; HM Diplomatic Service, retired; Fellow, Trinity College, Cambridge, since 2006; *b* 11 April 1949; *s* of late Derrick and Celia Pullen; *m* 1971, Karen Lesley Sketchley; four *s* one *d*. *Educ:* Maidstone Grammar Sch.; Mansfield Coll., Oxford (MA); Sussex Univ. (DPhil). MoD, 1975–78; Second Sec., UK Delegn to NATO, 1978–80; MoD, 1980–81; First Sec., UK Delegn to CSCE, 1981–82; FCO, 1982–84; Dep. High Comr, Suva, 1984–88; FCO, 1988–90; Counsellor, Paris, 1990–94; Dep. High Comr, Nairobi, 1994–97; Dep. High Comr, Lagos, 1997–2000; High Comr, Ghana, 2000–04; Ambassador to Zimbabwe, 2004–06; UK Special Rep. to Sudan/Darfur Peace Process, 2006. Gov., Thomas Alleyne Acad. (formerly Thomas Alleyne Sch.), Stevenage, 2009–. Trustee, Cambridge and Peterborough Probation Trust, 2010–14. *Address:* Trinity College, Cambridge CB2 1TQ.

PULLINGER, John James, CB 2014; Chief Executive, UK Statistics Authority, National Statistician and Permanent Secretary, since 2014; *b* 1 June 1959; *s* of Desmond and Kathleen Pullinger; *m* 1981, Alison Taylor; two *s* one *d*. *Educ:* Alleyn's Sch., Dulwich; Univ. of Exeter (BA 1st Cl. Hons Geog. and Stats 1980); Harvard Business Sch. (AMP 2003). Asst Statistician, then Sen. Asst Statistician, DTI, 1980–85; Section Hd, DoE, 1985–91; Hd of Pay Res., Office of Manpower Econs, 1991–92; Central Statistical Office, subseq. Office for National Statistics: Dir, Policy and Planning, 1992–96; Dir, Social and Regl Statistics, 1996–98; Exec. Dir, 1999–2004; Librarian, H of C, 2004–14. Pres., Royal Statistical Soc., 2013–14. *Recreations:* family, church, gardening, politics, current affairs. *Address:* UK Statistics Authority, 1 Drummond Gate, SW1V 2QQ.

PULLMAN, Philip Nicholas Outram, CBE 2004; FRSL; author and playwright; *b* 19 Oct. 1946; *s* of late Alfred and Audrey Pullman (*née* Merrifield); *m* 1970, Judith Speller; two *s*. *Educ:* Ysgol Ardudwy, Harlech; Exeter Coll., Oxford (BA English Lang. and Lit. 1968; Hon. Fellow, 2004). Teacher, Oxford Middle Schools, 1973–86; Lectr (part-time), Westminster Coll., Oxford, 1986–96. Patron, Centre for the Children's Book, 2000. Pres., Soc. of Authors, 2013–. Mem., Guild of Rocking Horse Makers, 2007–. Hon. Freeman, City of Oxford, 2007. Hon. Prof., Bangor Univ., 2008. Hon. Fellow: Westminster Inst. of Educn, 1999; Univ. of Wales, Bangor, 2003. Hon. DLitt: Oxford Brookes, 2002; UEA, 2003; Oxford, 2009; Exeter, 2010; Bath, 2013; Anglia Ruskin, 2013; DUniv: UCE, 2003; Surrey, 2003; Open, 2008; Hon. LLD Dundee, 2007. Booksellers Assoc. Author of the Year, 2000, 2001; Author of the Year, Br. Bk Awards, 2002; Eleanor Farjeon Award, 2003; Astrid Lindgren Memorial Award, 2005. *Plays:* Sherlock Holmes and the Adventure of the Limehouse Horror, 1984; The Three Musketeers, 1985; Frankenstein, 1986; Puss in Boots, 1997. *Publications: novels and stories:* Galatea, 1978; Count Karlstein, 1982, illustrated edn 1991; The Ruby in the Smoke, 1985 (Children's Book Award, Internat. Reading Assoc., 1988; televised 2006); The Shadow in the North, 1987; How To Be Cool, 1987; Spring-Heeled Jack, 1989; The Broken Bridge, 1990; The Tiger in the Well, 1991; The White Mercedes, 1992, re-issued as The Butterfly Tattoo, 1998; The Wonderful Story of Aladdin and the Enchanted Lamp, 1993; The Tin Princess, 1994; Thunderbolt's Waxwork, 1994; The Gas-Fitters' Ball, 1995; The Firework-Maker's Daughter, 1995 (Smarties Gold Award, 1996); His Dark Materials: Book One: Northern Lights, 1995 (US title: The Golden Compass) (Guardian Children's Fiction Award, 1996; Carnegie Medal, 1996; British Book Award: Children's Book of the Year, 1996; filmed, 2007); Book Two: The Subtle Knife, 1997; Book Three: The Amber Spyglass, 2000 (British Book Award: Children's Book of the Year, 2001; Whitbread Book of the Year, 2002; trilogy adapted for stage by Nicholas Wright, NT, 2003); Clockwork, or All Wound Up, 1996 (Smarties Silver Award, 1997); I Was a Rat!, 1999 (televised 2001); Mossycoat, 1999; Puss in Boots, 2000; Lyra's Oxford, 2003; The Scarecrow and His Servant, 2004; Aladdin, 2004; Once Upon a Time in the North, 2008; The Good Man Jesus and the Scoundrel Christ, 2010; The Adventures of the New Cut Gang, 2011; Grimm Tales for Young and Old, 2012; *plays:*

Sherlock Holmes and the Adventure of the Limehouse Horror, 1993; Frankenstein, 1992. *Recreations:* drawing, music. *Address:* c/o A. P. Watt Ltd, United Agents, 12–26 Lexington Street, W1F 0LE.

PULLUM, Prof. Geoffrey Keith, PhD; FBA 2009; Professor of General Linguistics, University of Edinburgh, since 2007; *b* Irvine, 8 March 1945; *s* of Keith Francis and Marjorie Joan Pullum; *m* 1994, Barbara Caroline Scholz (*d* 2011); one *s* from former marriage; *m* 2014, Patricia Catherine Shannon. *Educ:* Eltham Coll.; Univ. of York (BA Hons Lang.); King's Coll., Cambridge; Univ. of London (PhD Gen. Linguistics 1976). Lectr, UCL, 1974–81; Prof. of Linguistics, 1981–2007, Dean of Grad. Studies and Res., 1987–93, Univ. of Calif, Santa Cruz; Fellow: Center for Advanced Study in Behavioral Scis, Stanford Univ., 1990–91; Radcliffe Inst. for Advanced Study, Harvard Univ., 2005–06. Gerard Vis. Prof. of Cognitive, Linguistic and Psychol Scis, Brown Univ., 2012–13. Fellow, Amer. Acad. of Arts and Scis, 2003. *Publications:* (ed with D. L. Goyvaerts) Essays on the Sound Pattern of English, 1975; (with G. Gazdar and E. H. Klein) A Bibliography of Contemporary Linguistic Research, 1978; Rule Interaction and the Organization of a Grammar, 1979; (ed with P. Jacobson) The Nature of Syntactic Representation, 1982; (ed with G. Gazdar and E. H. Klein) Order, Concord, and Constituency, 1983; (with G. Gazdar, E. H. Klein and I. A. Sag) Generalized Phrase Structure Grammar, 1985; (ed with D. C. Derbyshire) Handbook of Amazonian Languages, vol. 1, 1986, vol. 2, 1990, vol. 3, 1991, vol. 4, 1998; The Great Eskimo Vocabulary Hoax, 1991; (with W. A. Ladusaw) Phonetic Symbol Guide, 1986, 2nd edn 1996; (jtly) The Cambridge Grammar of the English Language, 2002; (with R. Huddleston) A Student's Introduction to English Grammar, 2005; (with M. Liberman) Far from the Madding Gerund and Other Dispatches from Language Log, 2006; over 200 articles. *Recreations:* walking, swimming, blogging (www.languagelog.org and chronicle.com/blogs/linguafranca). *Address:* 11 Gordon Terrace, Edinburgh EH16 5QW. *T:* (0131) 650 3603, *Fax:* (0131) 651 3190. *E:* pullum@gmail.com.

PULLUM, Megan Michelle Elaine; QC (Guernsey) 2012; HM Comptroller and Deputy Receiver General, Guernsey, since 2012; *b* UK, 1971; *d* of Dr Geoffrey Pullum and Anne Pullum (*née* Steer); *m* 2009, Simon Guest; two *c*. *Educ:* Herts and Essex High Sch. for Girls; Univ. de Nantes, France (Dip. d'études universitaires générales 1, 1992); Univ. of Wales Coll. of Cardiff (LLB Jt Hons Law and French 1993); Coll. of Law, York 1994; Univ. of Glamorgan (LLM Eur. Law 2000); Univ. de Caen, France (Certificat d'études juridiques françaises et normandes 2005). Admitted as solicitor, 1996; called to the Guernsey Bar, 2006; Accredited Workplace and Employment Mediator, 2011. *Address:* c/o Law Offices of the Crown, St James Chambers, St Peter Port, Guernsey, Channel Islands GY1 2PA. *T:* (01481) 723355. *E:* law@gov.gg.

PULMAN, Prof. Stephen Guy, PhD; FBA 2001; Professor of Computational Linguistics, University of Oxford, since 2006; Fellow, Somerville College, Oxford, since 2000; *b* 1 Oct. 1949; *s* of Raymond Pulman and Celia Margaret Pulman; *m* 1989, Nicola Jane Verney; one *s* two *d*. *Educ:* Bedford Coll., London (BA Hons English 1972); Univ. of Essex (MA Theoretical Linguistics 1974; PhD Linguistics 1977). Lecturer: Dept of Lang. and Linguistics, Univ. of Essex, 1977–78; Sch. of English and American Studies, UEA, 1978–84; University of Cambridge Computer Laboratory: Lectr, 1984–97; Reader in Computational Linguistics, 1997–2000; Dep. Hd, 1999–2000; Dir, 1988–97, Principal Scientist, 1998–2001, SRI Internat. (formerly Stanford Res. Inst.) Cambridge Computer Sci. Res. Centre; University of Oxford: Prof. of Gen. Linguistics, 2000–06; Dep. Hd, 2007–08, Hd, 2008–09, Computing Lab; Dep. Hd, Dept of Computer Sci., 2010–13. *Publications:* Word Meaning and Belief, 1983; (jtly) Computational Morphology: practical mechanisms for the English lexicon, 1992; contrib. papers to Computational Linguistics, Artificial Intelligence, Linguistics and Philosophy, Philosophical Trans of Royal Soc., etc. *Recreations:* gardening, bird-watching, walking. *Address:* Somerville College, Oxford OX2 6HD.

PULVERTAFT, Rear-Adm. David Martin, CB 1990; Secretary, Defence, Press and Broadcasting Advisory Committee, 1992–99; *b* 26 March 1938; *s* of late Captain William Godfrey Pulvertaft, OBE, RN and Annie Joan Pulvertaft (*née* Martin); *m* 1961, Mary Rose Jeacock; one *s* two *d*. *Educ:* Canford Sch., Dorset; Britannia RN Coll., Dartmouth; RN Engineering Coll., Manadon. BSc (Eng) 1962. FIMechE 1989 (MIMechE 1974). HMS Ceylon, 1958–59; HMS Anchorite, Singapore, 1963–66; HMS Dreadnought, 1967–71; 10th Submarine Sqdn, 1971–72; HM Dockyard, Devonport, 1973–75; Nat. Defence Coll., Latimer, 1975–76; MoD 1976–78; HM Dockyard, Devonport, 1979–82; RCDS, 1983; MoD, 1984–87; Dir Gen. Aircraft (Navy), 1987–90; Dir Gen., Procurement and Support Orgn (Navy), 1990–92. Chm. of Trustees, Plymouth Naval Base Mus., 2001–05; Chm., SW Maritime Hist. Soc., 2000–03; Mem. Council, Soc. for Nautical Res., 2002–11, 2012–. *Publications:* The Warship Figureheads of Portsmouth, 2009; Figureheads of the Royal Navy, 2011. *Recreations:* genealogy, printing, bookbinding, British warship figureheads. *Address:* Staffords, 3 Paternoster Row, Ottery St Mary, Devon EX11 1DP. *Club:* Army and Navy.

PULZER, Prof. Peter George Julius, PhD; FRHistS; Professorial Fellow, Institute for German Studies, University of Birmingham, 1996–99; Gladstone Professor of Government and Public Administration, University of Oxford, 1985–96, now Emeritus; Fellow of All Souls College, 1985–96, now Emeritus; *b* 20 May 1929; *s* of Felix and Margaret Pulzer; *m* 1962, Gillian Mary Marshall; two *s*. *Educ:* Surbiton County Grammar Sch.; King's Coll., Cambridge (1st Cl. Hons Historical Tripos 1950; PhD 1960); London Univ. (1st Cl. Hons BSc Econ 1954). FRHistS 1971. Lectr in Politics, Magdalen Coll. and Christ Church, Oxford, 1957–62; University Lectr in Politics, Oxford, 1960–84; Official Student and Tutor in Politics, Christ Church, 1962–84. Visiting Professor: Univ. of Wisconsin, 1965; Sch. of Advanced Internat. Studies, Johns Hopkins Univ., 1972; Univ. of Calif, LA, 1972; Eric Voegelin, Munich Univ., 1988; Potsdam Univ., 1993; Technical Univ., Dresden, 1997; Humboldt Univ., Berlin, 2000; Leipzig Univ., 2003; Max Kade, Lafayette Coll., Easton, Pennsylvania, 2004. Chairman: Academic Adv. Cttee, Centre for German-Jewish Studies, Univ. of Sussex, 1997–2009; Leo Baeck Inst., London, 1998–2013; Mem. Governing Body, Historisches Kolleg, Munich, 1993–97. Hon. Vice-Pres., Internat. Assoc. for the Study of Germany Politics, 1997–. Hon. Dr rer. soc. oec. Innsbruck, 2007; Hon. DPhil Vienna, 2012. Bundesverdienstkreuz (Germany), 2004; Grand Silver Medal of Honour for Meritorious Service to the Republic of Austria, 2008; Leo Baeck Medal of Recognition, 2015. *Publications:* The Rise of Political Anti-Semitism in Germany and Austria, 1964, 2nd edn 1988 (German edn 1966); Political Representation and Elections in Britain, 1967, 3rd edn 1975; Jews and the German State, 1992, 2nd edn 2003; German Politics 1945–1995, 1995; Germany 1870–1945: politics, state formation and war, 1997; (ed with K. R. Luther) Austria 1945–1995: fifty years of the Second Republic, 1998; (ed with Wolfgang Benz) Jews in the Weimer Republic, 1998; (contrib.) German-Jewish History in Modern Times, 1998; contrib. to jls, year books and symposia. *Recreations:* opera, walking. *Address:* All Souls College, Oxford OX1 4AL.

PUNTER, Prof. David Godfrey, PhD; DLitt; FSAScot; FEA; Professor of English, University of Bristol, since 2000; *b* 19 Nov. 1949; *s* of Douglas Herbert and Hilda Mary Punter; *m* 1988, Caroline Mary Case; one *s* two *d*. *Educ:* Fitzwilliam Coll., Cambridge (BA 1970; PhD 1984); DLitt Stirling, 1999. FSAScot; FEA. Lectr, 1973–84, Sen. Lectr, 1984–86, in English, UEA; Prof. of English and Hd of Dept, Chinese Univ. of Hong Kong, 1986–88; Prof. of English, 1988–2000, and Hd of Dept, 1988–94 and 1996, Univ. of Stirling; Dean, Grad. Studies, 2002–03, Res. Dean, 2003–09, Faculty of Arts, Univ. of Bristol. Vis. Prof. of Modern English, Fudan Univ., Shanghai, 1983. Dir, Develt of Univ. English Teaching Project, 1985–86. Chair, W Reg., RSA, 2012–; Mem. Bd, Poetry Can, 2013–. Dir, Bristol Poetry Inst., 2014–. Fellow, Inst. Contemp. Scotland; FRSA; FHEA. *Publications:* The Literature of Terror: a history of Gothic fictions from 1765 to the present day, 1980, 2nd edn 1996; (jtly) Romanticism and Ideology: studies in English writing 1765–1830, 1981; Blake, Hegel and Dialectic, 1982; The Hidden Script: writing and the unconscious, 1985; (ed) Introduction to Contemporary Cultural Studies, 1986; William Blake: selected poetry and prose, 1988; The Romantic Unconscious: a study in narcissism and patriarchy, 1989; Selected Poems of Philip Larkin: notes, 1991; (ed) William Blake: new casebook, 1996; Romanticism, 1997; William Blake's Songs of Innocence and of Experience: notes, 1998; Gothic Pathologies: the text, the body and the law, 1998; (ed with G. Byron) Spectral Readings: towards a Gothic geography, 1999; (ed) A Companion to the Gothic, 2000; Writing the Passions, 2000; Postcolonial Imaginings: fictions of a new world order, 2000; Philip Larkin's The Whitsun Weddings and Selected Poems: advanced notes, 2003; William Blake's Songs of Innocence and of Experience: advanced notes, 2003; (with G. Byron) The Gothic, 2004; The Influence of Postmodernism on Contemporary Writing, 2005; (ed) Francis Latham, The Midnight Bell, 2007; Metaphor, 2007; Modernity, 2007; Rapture: literature, addiction, secrecy, 2009; (ed) A New Companion to the Gothic, 2012; (ed jtly) The Encyclopaedia of the Gothic, 2013; The Literature of Pity, 2014; *poetry:* China and Glass, 1985; Lost in the Supermarket, 1987; Asleep at the Wheel, 1996, Foreign Ministry, 2011; Selected Short Stories, 1999; Flashes in the Dark, 2015; contrib. numerous articles and book chapters. *Recreations:* gardening, walking, collecting maps. *Address:* Department of English, University of Bristol, Bristol BS8 1TB. *T:* (0117) 928 8082, *Fax:* (0117) 928 8860. *E:* david.punter@bristol.ac.uk. *Clubs:* Oxford and Cambridge, Arts.

PURCELL, Prof. Nicholas, FBA 2007; Camden Professor of Ancient History, University of Oxford, since 2011; Fellow, Brasenose College, Oxford, since 2011. *Educ:* Worcester Coll., Oxford (BA 1977). Prize Fellow, All Souls Coll., Oxford, 1977–79; Lectr in Ancient Hist., Univ. of Oxford and Fellow, St John's Coll., Oxford, 1979–2011. Vis. Sather Prof. of Classical Lit., Univ. of Calif, Berkeley, 2012. *Publications:* (with P. Horden) The Corrupting Sea: a study of Mediterranean history, 2000; (contrib.) The Cambridge Companion to the Age of Augustus, 2005; (contrib.) Mediterranean Urbanization 800–600 BC, 2005; (contrib.) Ancient Colonizations: analogies, similarity and differences, 2005; contribs to Amer. Jl Philol., Amer. Histl Rev. *Address:* Brasenose College, Oxford OX1 4AJ.

PURCELL, Philip James; President, Continental Investors LLC, since 2006; *b* 5 Sept. 1943; *m* 1964, Anne Marie McNamara; seven *s*. *Educ:* Univ. of Notre Dame (BBA 1964); LSE (MSc 1966); Univ. of Chicago (MBA 1967). Man. Dir, McKinsey & Co., 1967–78; Vice Pres. of Planning and Admin, Sears, Roebuck & Co., 1978–82; CEO, and Pres., subseq. Chm., Dean Witter Discover & Co., 1982–97; Chm. and CEO, Morgan Stanley Dean Witter & Co., subseq. Morgan Stanley, 1997–2005. Dir, NY Stock Exchange, 1991–96. Dir, AMR Corp., 2000–. *Address:* Continental Investors LLC, 227 West Monroe Street, Suite 5045, Chicago, IL 60606, USA.

PURCELL, Prof. Wendy Maria, PhD; President, University of Plymouth, since 2015 (Chief Executive, later Vice-Chancellor, President and Chief Executive, 2007–14); *b* Kingsbury, 21 June 1961; *m* 1987, Geoff Hendron. *Educ:* Univ. of Plymouth (BSc Hons Biol Scis 1985); Hatfield Poly. and University Coll. London (PhD Immunopharmacology 1989). CBiol 1989, MRSB (MIBiol 1989). Lectr in Health Studies and Related Biosci. Progs, Roehampton Inst., 1990–92; University of Hertfordshire: Sen. Lectr in Physiol. and Pharmacol., 1992–93; Hd, Div. of Physiol., Pharmacol. and Toxicol., 1993–97; University of West of England: Associate Dean and Hd, Dept of Biol and Biomed. Scis, 1997–2000; Exec. Dean, Faculty of Applied Scis, 2000–05; Pro Vice-Chancellor (Res.), 2003–05; Dep. Vice-Chancellor, Univ. of Herts, 2005–07. Fellow, Top Mgt Programme, 2001. *Publications:* (jtly) Approaches to High Throughput Toxicity Screening, 1999; contribs to jls incl. Cellular Biochem., NeuroReport, Chem. Res. Toxicol., Pediatric Transplant, Neurotoxicol., Neurochem. Res. *Recreations:* swimming, theatre, modern art. *Address:* Office of the President, Plymouth University, Drake Circus, Plymouth PL4 8AA. *T:* (01752) 582000, *Fax:* (01752) 582011. *E:* wendympurcell@gmail.com.

PURCHAS, Christopher Patrick Brooks; QC 1990; a Recorder, since 1986; *b* 20 June 1943; *s* of Rt Hon. Sir Francis Purchas, PC and Patricia Mona Kathleen Purchas; *m* 1st, 1974, Bronwen Mary Vaughan (marr. diss. 1995); two *d*; 2nd, 1998, Diana, *widow* of Dr Ian Hatrick. *Educ:* Summerfield Sch.; Marlborough Coll.; Trinity Coll., Cambridge (MA). Called to the Bar, Inner Temple, 1966, Bencher, 1995. *Recreations:* golf, tennis, shooting, ski-ing. *Address:* Crown Office Chambers, Temple, EC4Y 7HJ. *T:* (020) 7797 8100.

See also R. M. Purchas.

PURCHAS, Robin Michael; QC 1987; a Recorder, since 1989; Deputy High Court Judge, since 1994; *b* 12 June 1946; *s* of Rt Hon. Sir Francis Brooks Purchas, PC and Patricia Mona Kathleen Purchas; *m* 1970, Denise Anne Kerr Finlay; one *s* one *d*. *Educ:* Summerfields; Marlborough College; Trinity College, Cambridge (MA). Called to the Bar, Inner Temple, 1968, Bencher, 1996. Mem., Bar Council, 1999–2002 (Chm., Educn and Trng Cttee, 2000–02). *Recreations:* opera, music, fishing, tennis, ski-ing, sailing, shooting, golf. *Address:* (chambers) Francis Taylor Building, Temple, EC4Y 7BY. *T:* (020) 7353 8415. *Clubs:* Boodle's, Lansdowne, Queen's; Royal West Norfolk Golf; Royal Worlington and Newmarket Golf; Brancaster Staithe Sailing.

See also C. P. B. Purchas.

PURCHASE, Kenneth; *b* 8 Jan. 1939; *m* 1960, Brenda Sanders; two *d*. *Educ:* Springfield Secondary Modern Sch.; Wolverhampton Polytechnic (BA). Toolmaker: Lucas, 1960–68; Ever Ready, 1968–76; with Telford Development Corp., 1977–80; with Walsall MBC, 1981–82; Business Development Advr and Company Sec., Black Country CDA Ltd, 1982–92. Mem., Wolverhampton HA, 1972–87. Mem. (Lab) Wolverhampton CBC, subseq. MBC, 1970–90. Contested (Lab) Wolverhampton NE, 1987. MP (Lab and Co-op) Wolverhampton NE, 1992–2010. PPS to Sec. of State for Foreign Affairs, 1997–2001, to Pres. of the Council and Ldr of the H of C, 2001–03. Mem., Select Cttee on Trade and Industry, 1993–97, on Foreign Affairs, 2005–10; Jt Chm., All Party Exports Gp, 1993–10; Chm., PLP Trade and Industry Cttee, 1992–97; Secretary: All Party Jazz Appreciation Soc., 1996–98; All-Party UK Bahrain Gp, 1997–10; All-Party UK Egypt Gp, 1999–10.

PURDEN, Roma Laurette, (Laurie), (Mrs J. K. Kotch), MBE 1973; journalist and writer; *b* 30 Sept. 1928; *d* of George Cecil Arnold Purden and Constance Mary Sheppard; *m* 1957, John Keith Kotch (*d* 1979); two *d*. *Educ:* Harecroft Sch., Tunbridge Wells. Fiction Editor, Home Notes, 1948–51; Asst Editor, Home Notes, 1951–52; Asst Editor, Woman's Own, 1952; Sen. Asst Editor, Girl, 1952–54; Editor of: Housewife, 1954–57; Home, 1957–62; House Beautiful, 1963–65; Good Housekeeping, 1965–73; Editor-in-Chief: Good Housekeeping, and Womancraft, 1973–77; Woman's Journal, 1978–88; Woman & Home, 1982–83. Dir, Brickfield Publications Ltd, 1978–80. Magazine Editor of the Year, 1979, British Soc. of Magazine Editors; Consumer Magazine of the Year awarded by Periodical Publishers Assoc. to Woman's Journal, 1985. *Address:* 30 Elizabeth Court, Milmans Street, SW10 0DA. *T:* (020) 7352 4166.

PURDEW, Stephen James; Director, and Co-owner, Champneys Health Resorts; *b* 25 May 1959; *s* of late Robert and of Dorothy Purdew; one *s*; *m* 2009, Isabelle Cave; one *s* one *d*. *Educ:* Midhurst Grammar Sch. Dir, Henlow Grange Health Farm, 1981– (Manager, 1981–90); acquisition of: Springs Health Hydro (Dir), 1990; Forest Mere Health Farm, 1997; Champneys, 2001, when all resorts rebranded under that name. *Address:* Champneys Health Resort, Henlow, Beds SG16 6DB. *T:* (01462) 811111, *Fax:* (01462) 815310.

PURDON, Maj.-Gen. Corran William Brooke, CBE 1970; MC 1945; CPM 1982; *b* 4 May 1921; *s* of Maj.-Gen. William Brooke Purdon, DSO, OBE, MC, KHS, and Dorothy Myrtle Coates; *m* 1st, 1945, Maureen Patricia (*d* 2008), *d* of Major J. F. Petrie, Guides Infantry, IA; one *s* one *d* (and one *s* decd); 2nd, 2009, Jean Otway (*née* Walker), *widow* of Lt Col Terence Otway, DSO. *Educ:* Rokeby, Wimbledon; Campbell Coll., Belfast; RMC Sandhurst. MBIM. Commnd into Royal Ulster Rifles, 1939; service with Army Commandos, France and Germany, 1940–45 (wounded; MC); 1st Bn RU Rifles, Palestine, 1945–46; GHQ MELF, 1949–51; psc 1955; Staff, Malayan Emergency, 1956–58; Co. Comdr, 1 RU Rifles, Cyprus Emergency, 1958; CO, 1st Bn RU Rifles, BAOR and Borneo Confrontation, 1962–64; GSO1 and Chief Instructor, Sch. of Infantry, Warminster, 1965–67; Comdr, Sultan's Armed Forces, Oman, and Dir of Ops, Dhofar War, 1967–70 (Sultan's Bravery Medal, 1968 and Distinguished Service Medal for Gallantry, 1969, Oman; CBE); Commandant: Sch. of Infantry, Warminster, 1970–72; Small Arms Sch. Corps, 1970–72; GOC, NW Dist, 1972–74; GOC Near East Land Forces, 1974–76, retired. Dep. Comr, Royal Hong Kong Police Force, 1978–81; St John Ambulance: Comdr, Wilts, 1981–84; Mem. Council, 1981–86; Pres., Devizes Div., 1993–2000. President: London Irish Rifles Assoc., 1993–; RUR Regtl Assoc., 1994–; Hon. Colonel: Queen's Univ. Belfast OTC, 1975–78; D (London Irish Rifles), 4th Bn Royal Irish Rangers, 1986–93. Pres. Army Gymnastic Union, 1973–76; Patron, Small Arms Sch. Corps Assoc., 1985–90; Life Pres., St Nazaire Soc., 2011. KStJ 1983 (Service Medal, 1999). Commendation Medal (Oman), 1970; Médaille d'Honneur de St Nazaire, 2000; Chevalier de la Légion d'Honneur (France), 2005; Pingat Jasa Malaysia, 2006. *Publications:* List the Bugle: reminiscences of an Irish soldier, 1993; articles in military jls. *Recreations:* physical training, dogs (English bull terriers, German shepherds). *Address:* Old Park House, Devizes, Wilts SN10 5JR. *Clubs:* Army and Navy; Hong Kong.

PURDUE, Marie Theresa; *see* Conte-Helm, M. T.

PURDY, George; *see* Purdy, W. G.

PURDY, Quentin Alexander; a District Judge (Magistrates' Courts), since 2003; *b* 23 Aug. 1960; *s* of late Gordon Purdy, OBE, FRCS and of Margaret Purdy; *m* 1988, Elizabeth Audrey Hazelwood; two *d*. *Educ:* Gresham's Sch., Holt; Leicester Poly. (BA Hons 1982); Inns of Court Sch. of Law; University Coll. London (LLM 1985). Called to the Bar, Gray's Inn, 1983; barrister, Common Law Chambers, London, 1983–2003; Actg Metropolitan Stipendiary Magistrate, 1998–2000; Dep. Dist Judge (Magistrates' Courts), 2000–03. Deacon, Dormansland Baptist Church, 2001–08. Band Trust Award, 1983. *Publications:* (contrib. ed.) Archbold Magistrates' Courts Criminal Practice, 2012–. *Recreations:* badminton, sailing, cycling, dog walking, foreign travel. *Address:* Westminster Magistrates' Court, 181 Marylebone Road, NW1 5BR; Goldsmith Chambers, Goldsmith Building, Temple, EC4Y 7BL.

PURDY, (William) George, CBE 2002; Vice President, Scout Association, since 2007 (Chief Scout, 1996–2004); President, County Down Scouts, since 2008; Vice President, Northern Ireland Scouts, since 2012; *b* 16 April 1942; *s* of George Purdy and Amelia Jane Purdy (*née* McConnell); *m* 1969, Judith Sara Isabell Kerr; two *s*. *Educ:* Annadale Grammar Sch. NICS, 1960–91, 1993–96; Chief Exec., NI Software Industry Fedn, 1991–93. Scout Leader, 1962–94, Chief Comr, NI, 1994–96, Scout Assoc. *Recreations:* golf, Rugby, tennis, bowls, Probus, photography, music. *Address:* 16 Carshaulton Road, Donaghadee, Co. Down BT21 0QB.

PURKIS, Dr Andrew James, OBE 2002; Member, International Board, ActionAid, since 2013; Executive Director, Samworth Foundation, since 2013; *b* 24 Jan. 1949; *s* of late Clifford Henry Purkis and Mildred Jeannie Purkis; *m* 1980, Jennifer Harwood Smith; one *s* one *d*. *Educ:* Highgate Sch.; Corpus Christi Coll., Oxford; St Antony's Coll., Oxford. 1st class Hons MA Mod. Hist. 1970; DPhil 1978. Home Civil Service, N Ireland Office, 1974; Private Sec. to Perm. Under-Sec. of State, NI Office, 1976–77; Head of Policy Unit, 1980, Asst Dir, 1986, NCVO; Dir, CPRE, 1987–91; Public Affairs Advr to the Archbishop of Canterbury, 1992–98; Chief Executive: Diana, Princess of Wales Meml Fund, 1998–2005; Tropical Health and Educn Trust, 2005–09. Member, Board: Contact a Family (charity), 1986–93; Green Alliance, 1992–2004; Charity Commn, 2007–10; Office of Ind. Adjudicator for Higher Educn, 2010– (Dep. Chair, 2014–); Ind. Mem., Parole Bd, 2010–14; Chair: Living Streets (formerly Pedestrians' Assoc.), 1999–2007; Empty Homes Agency, 2004–07; ActionAid UK, 2009–14. *Publications:* (with Paul Hodson) Housing and Community Care, 1982; (with Rosemary Allen) Health in the Round, 1983; (contrib.) The Big Society Challenge, 2011. *Recreations:* walking, surf-riding, bird-watching, music, theatre. *Address:* 38 Endlesham Road, Balham, SW12 8JL. *T:* (020) 8675 2439.

PURKISS, Cathleen, (Kate); Her Honour Judge Purkiss; a Circuit Judge, since 2013; *b* Surrey, 7 Sept. 1962; *d* of Norman Charles Purkiss and Rena Purkiss (*née* Greensmythe); *m* 1992, Michael Alexander Curtis, *qv*; one *s* two *d*. *Educ:* University Coll. London (BA Hons Eng.); Poly. of Central London (DipLaw); Inns of Court Sch. of Law. Called to the Bar, Lincoln's Inn, 1988; a Recorder, 2009–13. *Recreations:* opera, theatre, cinema, watching football. *Club:* Arsenal Football.

PURKISS, Robert Ivan, MBE 2000; independent consultant on diversity and change management; *b* 11 Nov. 1945; *s* of Howard Flanagan and Betty Purkiss; *m* 1971, Monica Dell Richardson; two *d*. *Educ:* Toynbee Rd Boys' Sch.; Southampton Inst. of Higher Educn; Southampton Univ. (Dip. Industrial Relns). Chief Petty Officer, MN, 1961–72; Advr, Industrial Soc., 1972–74; Nat. Officer, Nat. Workers' Union of Jamaica, 1974–76; TGWU, 1976–2000 (Nat. Sec., 1989–2000); Chm., Eur. Monitoring Centre on Racism and Xenophobia, 2001–04. Member: CRE, 1993–2001; Central Arbitration Cttee, 2002–. Ind. Assessor for Public Appts, DTI, 2001–; Ind. Mem., Hampshire Police Authy, 2003–12 (Chm., Personal and Professional Standards); Mem., Employment Tribunals, 2010–; Ind. Mem., Hampshire Police and Crime Panel, 2012– (Chair, Complaints Panel, 2012–); Chair: Black & Ethnic Minorities Network, 2004–10; Race and Diversity Policy, Assoc. of Police Authorities, 2005–08; Panel, Discrimination Discipline Cttee, FA, 2014–. Man. Dir, Different Realities Partnership, 2004–08. *Publications:* contrib. numerous articles on anti-racism, industrial relns and diversity. *Recreations:* football referee (Mem., Southampton Referees Soc.; Develt Officer, Wessex League, 2012– (Chm., 2009–12)), athletics (Vice-Chm., Team Solent Athletics Club), AAA starter/marksman, grandchildren. *Address:* Penderyn, Norlands Drive, Otterbourne, Winchester SO21 2DT.

PURLE, Charles Lambert; QC 1989; **His Honour Judge Purle;** a Circuit Judge, since 2007; *b* 9 Feb. 1947; *s* of Robert Herbert Purle and Doreen Florence (*née* Button); *m* 1st, 1969, Lorna Barbara Brown (marr. diss. 1990); one *s* one *d*; 2nd, 1991, Virginia Dabney Hopkins Rylatt; two *s* two *d*. *Educ:* Nottingham Univ. (LLB 1969); Worcester Coll., Oxford (BCL 1971). Called to the Bar, Gray's Inn, 1970; in practice, 1972–2007. *Recreations:* opera, music, theatre, my children and grandchildren. *Address:* Priory Courts, 33 Bull Street, Birmingham B4 6DS.

PURNELL, Rt Hon. James; PC 2007; Director, Strategy and Digital, BBC, since 2013; *b* 2 March 1970; *s* of John and Janet Purnell. *Educ:* Balliol Coll., Oxford (BA PPE). Researcher for Tony Blair, MP, 1990–92; Strategy Consultant, Hydra Associates, 1992–94; Res. Fellow, Media and Communications, IPPR, 1994–95; Hd, Corporate Planning, BBC, 1995–97; Special Advr to Prime Minister on culture, media, sport and the knowledge econ., 1997–2001. Mem. (Lab) Islington BC, 1994–95 (Chairman: Early Years Cttee; Housing Cttee). MP (Lab) Stalybridge and Hyde, 2001–10. Asst Govt Whip, 2004–05; Parly Under-Sec. of State, DCMS, 2005–06; Minister of State, DWP, 2006–07; Sec. of State for Culture, Media and Sport, 2007–08, for Work and Pensions, 2008–09. Sen. Producer, Rare Day, 2010–13. Sen. Advr, Boston Consulting Gp, 2011–13. Mem. Bd, Nat. Theatre, 2010–; Gov., BFI, 2011–13. Chm., Trustees, IPPR, 2010–12; Trustee, Citizens UK, 2010–13. *Publications:* contrib. various publications for IPPR. *Recreations:* football, film, theatre, music.

PURNELL, Nicholas Robert; QC 1985; *b* 29 Jan. 1944; *s* of late Oliver Cuthbert Purnell and Pauline Purnell; *m* 1970, Melanie Stanway; four *s*. *Educ:* Oratory Sch.; King's Coll. Cambridge (Open Exhibnr; MA). Called to the Bar, Middle Temple, 1968 (Astbury Schol.), Bencher 1990; Junior of Central Criminal Court Bar Mess, 1972–75; Prosecuting Counsel to Inland Revenue, 1977–79; Jun. Treasury Counsel, 1979–85; Recorder, 1986–2010. Mem., Bar Council and Senate, 1973–77, 1982–85, 1989–91 (Chm., Legal Aid Fees Cttee, 1989–90); Member: Lord Chancellor's and Home Secretary's Working Party on the Training of the Judiciary, 1975–78; Crown Court Rules Cttee, 1982–88; Lord Chancellor's Adv. Cttee on Educn and Conduct, 1991–97; Criminal Cttee, Judicial Studies Bd, 1991–96. Chm., Criminal Bar Assoc., 1990–91. Governor, The Oratory Sch., 1994–. *Recreations:* living in France as much as possible, supporting Wimbledon AFC. *Address:* Cloth Fair Chambers, 39–40 Cloth Fair, EC1A 7NT.

See also P. O. Purnell.

PURNELL, Paul Oliver; QC 1982; a Recorder, since 1985; *s* of late Oliver Cuthbert and Pauline Purnell; *m* 1966, Celia Consuelo Ocampo; one *s* two *d*. *Educ:* The Oratory Sch.; Jesus Coll., Oxford (MA). Served 4th/7th Royal Dragoon Guards, 1958–62. Called to the Bar, Inner Temple, 1962, Bencher, 1991; Head of Chambers, 2007–. Jun. Treasury Counsel at Central Criminal Court, 1976–82. *Recreation:* motorcycling. *Address:* Farringdon Chambers, Gemini House, 180 Bermondsey Street, SE1 3TQ. *T:* (020) 7089 5700. *Clubs:* Cavalry and Guards, Hurlingham.

See also N. R. Purnell.

PURSE, Hugh Robert Leslie; barrister; part-time Chairman of Employment (formerly Industrial) Tribunals, 1996–2003; *b* 22 Oct. 1940; *s* of Robert Purse and Elsie Purse (*née* Kemp). *Educ:* St Peter's School, York; King's College London (LLB). Called to the Bar, Gray's Inn, 1964 (Atkin Scholar). Legal Asst, Dept of Employment, 1969; Legal Adviser to Price Commission, 1978–79; Govt legal service, 1979–96: Legal Advr, Dept of Employment, and Principal Asst Treasury Solicitor, 1988–96.

PURSEY, Nigel Thomas; Chief Executive, Staffordshire County Council, 2003–07; *b* 4 Aug. 1949. *Educ:* Manchester Univ. (MusB). CPFA 1975. Trainee Accountant, Cheshire CC, 1971–75; Accountant, Mid Glamorgan CC, 1975–78; Wiltshire County Council: Group Accountant, 1978–81; Chief Admin. Assistant (Finance), 1981–83; Chief Accountant, 1983–86; Asst County Treasurer, 1986–92; Shropshire County Council: County Treas., 1992–97; Chief Exec., 1997–2003. Clerk to: Shropshire Lieutenancy, 1997–2003; Staffs Lieutenancy, 2003–07; Staffs Police Authy, 2003–07. Dep. Chm., Shropshire Learning and Skills Council, 2001–03; Mem. Bd and Chair of Audit Cttee, Children's Workforce Develt Council, 2008–12. Associate Master of the Music, Shrewsbury Abbey, 2001–. Treas., Pontesbury-Muheza Link Charity, 2008– (Trustee, 2012–); Trustee, Lingen Davies Appeal, 2010– (Chm., Trustees, 2012–). Gov., Staffs Univ., 2003–07. *Recreations:* music, walking, bridge, family activities.

PURSGLOVE, Thomas Christopher John; MP (C) Corby, since 2015; *b* 5 Nov. 1988. *Educ:* Sir Christopher Hatton Sch., Wellingborough; Queen Mary Coll., Univ. of London (BA Politics). Pt-time work for Rt Hon. Douglas Hogg, MP, 2008–10; Parly Asst to Christopher Heaton-Harris, MP, 2010–15; Dir, Together Against Wind, 2014–. Mem. (C), Wellingborough BC, 2007–15. *Recreations:* cricket, swimming, golf. *Address:* House of Commons, SW1A 0AA.

PURSHOUSE, Michael, PhD; CEng, FIMechE, FIET, FREng, FInstP, FIMA; independent technical and management consultant, since 2012; *b* Rotherham, 19 Sept. 1951; *s* of Edwin Purshouse and Rita Purshouse (*née* Bryars); *m* 1981, Sabine Gabriele Rohrssen; two *d*. *Educ:* St John's C of E Sch., Mexborough; Mexborough Grammar Sch.; Rolls-Royce Tech. Coll., Bristol; Sidney Sussex Coll., Cambridge (BAC Industrial Scholar; Coll. Scholar; BA 1973; Robert Angus Engrg Student; RAeS Geoffrey de Havilland Scholar; PhD 1978). CEng 1980; FIMechE 1994; FIET (FIEE 1996); FREng 2007; FInstP 2008; FIMA 2010. Undergrad. apprentice, BAC, Bristol, 1969–74; Acoustics Consultant, YARD Ltd, Glasgow, 1978–81; Res. Scientist, Fraunhofer-Gesellschaft, Stuttgart, Germany, 1981–83; Principal Consultant, YARD Ltd, 1984–92; Business Gp Manager, Naval Engrg, BAeSEMA Ltd, 1992–2000; Chief Engr, Thales Aircraft Carrier Team, 2000–03; Sen. Systems Engineer, Thales UK plc, 2000–12; Hd, Systems Engrg, Aircraft Carrier Alliance, 2003–06; Proj. Dir and Chief Engr, Thales-Boeing FRES System of Systems Integrator, 2007–10; Technical Dir, Thales UK Land Systems, 2010–12. Hon. Prof., Dept of Physics and Astronomy, Univ. of Glasgow, 1997–2010; Hon. Fellow, Sidney Sussex Coll., Cambridge, 2014– (Fellow Commoner, 2004–14). Pres., Cambridge Univ. Engrs' Assoc., 2012– (Mem. Exec. Cttee, 2007–12); Educn, Training and Careers Cttee, STFC, 2009–12. Chm., Glasgow Panel, IMechE, 1992–95. Vice-Pres., Stephenson Soc., Sidney Sussex Coll., 1996–2006; 1st Cl. Mem., Smeatonian Soc. of Civil Engrs, 2014–. Trustee Dir and Company Sec., Mt Pleasant Community Centre Ltd, 2007–10; Dir, Avonbrook Glade Ltd, 2012–; Hon. Treas., Christ Church Friends, Bradford-on-Avon, 2014–. Freeman: Engineers' Co., 2011 (Liveryman, 2012–); City of London, 2012. *Recreations:* visiting country estates, reading, music (play piano), dining out with friends and family, foreign travel. *Address:* c/o Sidney Sussex College, Cambridge CB2 3HU. *E:* mpurshouse@theiet.org. *Club:* Bath and County.

PURSSELL, Anthony John Richard; Vice-President, National Society for Epilepsy, since 2010 (Trustee, 1993–2008; Chairman, 1995–98); *b* 5 July 1926; *m* 1952, Ann Margaret Batchelor; two *s* one *d*. *Educ:* Oriel Coll., Oxford (MA Hons Chemistry). Managing Director: Arthur Guinness Son & Co. (Park Royal) Ltd, 1968; Arthur Guinness Son & Co. (Dublin) Ltd, 1973; Arthur Guinness & Sons plc, 1975–81; Jt Dep. Chm., 1981–83. Thames Valley and S Midlands Regl Bd, Lloyds Bank plc: Regl Dir, 1982–91; Chm., 1989–91. Member: IBA, 1976–81; Bd, CAA, 1984–90. Trustee and Hon. Treas., Oxfam, 1985–92. *Recreations:* travel, golf, books. *Address:* Allendale, 53 Bulstrode Way, Gerrards Cross, Bucks SL9 7QT. *Club:* Leander (Henley).

PURVES, Elizabeth Mary, (Libby), (Mrs Paul Heiney), OBE 1999; writer, broadcaster and theatre critic; *b* 2 Feb. 1950; *d* of late James Grant Purves, CMG; *m* 1980, Paul Heiney, *qv*; one *d* (one *s* decd). *Educ:* Convent of the Sacred Heart, Tunbridge Wells; St Anne's Coll., Oxford (1st Cl. Hons Eng. Lang. and Lit.). BBC Local Radio (Oxford), 1972–76; Radio 4: Reporter, 1976–79, Presenter, 1979–81, Today; Presenter, Midweek, 1984–. Editor, Tatler, March–Oct. 1983, resigned; columnist, 1990–, chief theatre critic, 2010–13, The Times. Pres., Council for Nat. Parks, 2000–01. Founder, Theatrecat.com, 2014. *Publications:* (ed) The Happy Unicorns, 1971; (ed) Adventures Under Sail, H. W. Tilman, 1982; Britain At Play, 1982; Sailing Weekend Book, 1985; How Not to be a Perfect Mother, 1986; Where Did You Leave the Admiral, 1987; (jtly) The English and their Horses, 1988; The Hurricane Tree, 1988; One Summer's Grace, 1989; How Not to Raise a Perfect Child, 1991; Getting the Story, 1993; Working Times, 1993; How Not to be a Perfect Family, 1994; (with Paul Heiney) Grumpers' Farm, 1996; Holy Smoke, 1998; Nature's Masterpiece: a family survival book, 2000; Radio - a True Love Story, 2002; *novels:* Casting Off, 1995; A Long Walk in Wintertime, 1996; Home Leave, 1997; More Lives Than One, 1998; Regatta, 1999; Passing

Go, 2000; A Free Woman, 2001; Mother Country, 2002; Continental Drift, 2003; Acting Up, 2004; Love Songs and Lies, 2007; Shadow Child, 2009. *Recreations:* sailing, walking, theatre, radio. *Address:* c/o The Times, 1 London Bridge Street, SE1 9GF. *Clubs:* Groucho; Royal Cruising.

PURVES, Sir William, Kt 1993; CBE 1988; DSO 1951; Chairman, 1990–98, Chief Executive, 1990–92, HSBC Holdings plc; *b* 27 Dec. 1931; *s* of Andrew and Ida Purves; *m* 1st, 1958, Diana Troutbeck Richardson (marr. diss. 1988); two *s* two *d*; 2nd, 1989, Rebecca Jane Lewellen. *Educ:* Kelso High School. FIBScot; FCIB. National Service, with Commonwealth Div. in Korea (Subaltern; DSO). National Bank of Scotland, 1948–54; Hongkong and Shanghai Banking Corporation: Germany, Hong Kong, Malaysia, Singapore, Sri Lanka, Japan, 1954–70; Chief Accountant, Hong Kong, 1970; Manager, Tokyo, 1974; Sen. Manager Overseas Operations, 1976; Asst General Manager, Overseas Operations, 1978; General Manager, 1979–82; Executive Director, 1982–84; Dep. Chm., 1984–86; Chm. and Chief Exec., 1986–92; Chm., Midland Bank Plc, 1994–97 (Dir, 1987–98); Dir, Marine Midland Banks Inc., 1982–98. Chairman: British Bank of ME, 1979–98; Hakluyt & Co., Ltd, 2000–08; non-executive Director: Shell Transport and Trading, 1993–2002; Reuters Founders Share Co. Ltd, 1995–2009; Trident Safeguards Ltd, 1999–2003; BW Gp Ltd, 2003–12; Aquarius Platinum, 2004–12; Dep. Chm., Alstom, 1998–2003. Pres., Internat. Monetary Conf., 1992. Trustee and Dep. Chm., Imperial War Mus., 1996–2004. Hon. LLD: Sheffield, 1993; Hong Kong, 1994; Hon. DBA: Stirling, 1987; Hong Kong Poly., 1993; Napier, 1998; Hon. MBA Strathclyde, 1996; UMIST, 2001. GBM 1999. *Address:* Flat 1, Ebury House, 39 Elizabeth Street, SW1W 9RP. *Clubs:* Royal Automobile, Caledonian; Hong Kong Jockey, Hong Kong.

PURVIS OF TWEED, Baron *cr* 2013 (Life Peer), of East March in the Scottish Borders; **Jeremy Purvis;** Member (Lib Dem) Tweeddale, Ettrick and Lauderdale, Scottish Parliament, 2003–11; *b* 15 Jan. 1974; *s* of George Purvis and Eileen Purvis. *Educ:* Brunel Univ. (BSc Hons Politics and Mod. Hist.). Personal Asst to Sir David Steel, later Lord Steel of Aikwood, 1995–98. Director: GJW Scotland, 1998–2001; McEwan Purvis, 2001–03. Contested (Lib Dem) Midlothian S, Tweeddale and Lauderdale, 2011. Leader, Devo Plus Gp, 2012–13; Campaigns Dir, Keep Scotland Beautiful, 2013. *Recreations:* classic cars, painting, reading.

PURVIS, Bryan John; Head Master, William Hulme's Grammar School, Manchester, 1997–99; Founder, Hale Educational Consultancy, 2000; *b* 6 Aug. 1947; *s* of Robert Hunt Purvis and Eleanor Liddle Purvis; *m* 1969, Irene Anne Griffiths (*d* 2008); one *s* two *d*. *Educ:* Tynemouth High Sch.; Bedford Coll., London (BSc); Durham Univ. (MSc). Biology Master, St Joseph's Grammar Tech. Sch., Hebburn on Tyne, 1969–74; Dep. Headmaster and Head of Biology, King's Sch., Tynemouth, 1974–93; Head Master, Altrincham GS for Boys, 1993–97. Sen. Consultant, Nat. Coll. for Sch. Leadership, 2007–. *Recreations:* gardening, hill-walking, watching football (Manchester City) and Rugby. *Address:* Grange End, 219 Hale Road, Hale, Cheshire WA15 8DL. *T:* (0161) 980 4506. *E:* BPrvs@aol.com. *Club:* St James' (Manchester).

PURVIS, Dawn; Programme Director, Marie Stopes Northern Ireland, since 2011; Chair, Healing Through Remembering, since 2011; *b* 22 Oct. 1966; two *s*. *Educ:* Queen's Univ. Belfast (BA Hons 1st cl. Sociol. and Social Policy 2003). Researcher: Sch. of Envmtl Scis, Univ. of Ulster, Coleraine, 2004–06; Sch. of Sociology, Huddersfield Univ., 2006–07. Mem. for Belfast E, NI Assembly, Jan. 2007–2011 (PUP, 2007–10, Ind, 2010–11); contested (Ind) same seat, 2011. Leader, PUP, 2007–10. Mem., NI Policing Bd, 2006–07.

PURVIS, Air Vice-Marshal Henry R.; *see* Reed-Purvis.

PURVIS, Iain Younie; QC 2006; a Recorder, since 2010; a Deputy High Court Judge, since 2012; *b* 23 Aug. 1963; *s* of John Younie Purvis and Juliet Purvis (*née* Parker); *m* 1993, Beverley Jane Myers; two *s* one *d*. *Educ:* Royal Grammar Sch., High Wycombe; Clare Coll., Cambridge (BA Law 1984, MA); St Edmund Hall, Oxford (BCL). Called to the Bar, Gray's Inn, 1986. *Publications:* Working with Technology, 2001. *Recreations:* neolithic monuments, ski-ing, running. *Address:* 11 South Square, Gray's Inn, WC1R 5EY. *E:* ipurvis@11southsquare.com.

PURVIS, John Robert, CBE 1990; Partner, Purvis & Co., since 1986; *b* 6 July 1938; *s* of Lt-Col R. W. B. Purvis, MC, JP, and Mrs R. W. B. Purvis, JP; *m* 1962, Louise S. Durham; one *s* two *d*. *Educ:* Cargilfield, Barnton, Edinburgh; Trinity Coll., Glenalmond, Perthshire; St Salvator's Coll., Univ. of St Andrews (MA Hons). National Service, Lieut Scots Guards, 1956–58. First National City Bank, New York, 1962–69: London, 1962–63; New York, 1963–65; Milan, 1965–69; Treasurer, Noble Grossart Ltd, Edinburgh, 1969–73; Man. Dir, Gilmerton Management Services Ltd, 1973–92. MEP (C): Mid-Scotland and Fife, 1979–84, contested same seat, 1984; Scotland, 1999–2009. European Democratic Group, European Parliament: whip, 1980–82; spokesman on energy, research and technology, 1982–84; Vice-Pres., Economic and Monetary Affairs Cttee, EPP Gp, 2001–09. Vice Pres., Scottish Cons. and Unionist Assoc., 1987–89 (Chm., Industry Cttee, 1986–97); Mem., IBA, 1985–89 (Chm., Scottish Adv. Cttee, 1985–89); Mem., Scottish Adv. Cttee on Telecommunications, 1990–98. Chm., Financial Future Forum, Brussels, 2009–. Director: James River Fine Papers Ltd, 1984–95; Edgar Astaire & Co. Ltd, 1993–94; Jamont NV, 1994–95; European Utilities Trust plc, 1994–2007; Curtis Fine Papers Ltd, 1995–2001; Crown Vantage Ltd, 1995–2001; Chairman: Kingdom FM Radio Ltd, 1998–2008 (Dir, 2008–13); Belgrave Capital Management Ltd, 1999–. *Publications:* (section 'Money') in Power and Manoeuvrability, 1978. *Address:* PO Box 29222, St Andrews, Fife KY16 8WL. *T:* (01334) 475830. *E:* purvisco@jpurvis.co.uk. *Clubs:* Cavalry and Guards, Farmers; New (Edinburgh); Royal and Ancient (St Andrews).

PURVIS, Sir Neville, KCB 1992; Vice Admiral, retired; Chairman, Grays International of Cambridge, 2001–07; *b* 8 May 1936; *s* of Charles Geoffrey and Sylvia Rose Purvis; *m* 2nd, 1970, Alice Margaret (*née* Hill) (marr. diss. 1998); two *s*; 3rd, 2008, Susan Legh Bancroft. *Educ:* Charterhouse; Selwyn College, Cambridge (MA). BRNC Dartmouth, 1953; reading engineering at Cambridge, 1954–57; joined submarine service, 1959; served in HM Ships Turpin, 1960, Dreadnought, 1963, Repulse, 1967; Naval Staff, 1970; Sqdn Engineer Officer, 3rd Submarine Sqdn, 1973; Staff of Flag Officer, Submarines, 1975; RCDS 1980; in Command, HMS Collingwood, 1985–87; Dir Gen., Future Material Projects (Naval), 1987–88; Dir Gen., Naval Manpower and Trng, 1988–90; Mem., Admiralty Bd, and Chief of Fleet Support, 1991–94; Chief Exec., BSI, 1994–96; Dir Gen., British Safety Council, 1997–2001; Chm., Reliance Secure Task Mgt, 2001–05. Chm., Council, Friends of Nat. Maritime Mus., 2002–05; Chm. and Trustee, Marine Soc. and Sea Cadets, 2005–07 (Trustee, Sea Cadets Assoc., 2003–05). President: Westminster Br., Royal Soc. of St George, 2007–; London Br., Submariners Assoc., 2007–. FRSA 1992. *Recreation:* wining and dining. *Address:* 11 Kingswood Terrace, Chiswick, W4 5BN.

PURVIS, Prof. Stewart Peter, CBE 2000; Professor of Television Journalism, City University, since 2003; *b* 28 Oct. 1947; *s* of late Peter and Lydia Purvis; *m* 1st, 1972 (marr. diss. 1993); one *d*; 2nd, 2004, Jacqui Marson; two *s*. *Educ:* Dulwich Coll.; Univ. of Exeter (BA). Presenter, Harlech TV, 1968–69; BBC News trainee, 1969; ITN journalist, 1972; Programme Editor, News At Ten, 1980; Editor, Channel Four News, 1983; Independent Television News: Dep. Editor, 1986; Editor, 1989; Editor-in-Chief, 1991–95; Chief Exec., 1995–2003. Dir, ITN Ltd, 1989–2003; Pres., Euronews, 1998–2002. News Internat. Prof. of Broadcast Media, Univ. of Oxford, 2004–05. Partner, Content and Standards, Ofcom, 2007–10; Chairman: Digital Britain Media Literacy Wkg Gp, 2009; Consortium for Digital Participation, 2009–10. Non-exec. Dir, Royal Marsden NHS Trust, 1999–2004. FRTS 1991. Hon. LLD Exeter, 2005. BAFTA Award for Best News or Outside Broadcast, 1986, 1987; BPG Award for Best News or Current Affairs Prog., 1988; Gold Medal, RTS, 2009. *Address:* Department of Journalism, City University, Northampton Square, EC1V 0HB.

PUSEY, Prof. Charles Dickson, DSc; FRCP, FRCPath, FMedSci, FRSB; Professor of Medicine, since 2003, Head of Renal Section, Division of Medicine, since 1997, and Head of Postgraduate Medicine, since 2006, Imperial College, London; Hon. Consultant Physician, since 1984, and Lead Clinician, since 2001, Directorate of Renal Medicine and Transplantation, Imperial College Healthcare NHS Trust (formerly Hammersmith Hospitals NHS Trust). *Educ:* Corpus Christi Coll., Cambridge (BA 1969; MB BChir 1972; MA 1973); Guy's Hosp. Med. Sch., London Univ. (MSc 1983; DSc 2002). FRCP 1989; FRCPath 1997. House Officer and Jun. Med. Registrar, Guy's Hosp., 1972–74; Unit Med. Officer, Specialist then Sen. Specialist, in Medicine, RAF, 1974–79; Sen. Registrar, MRC Trng Fellow and Wellcome Trust Sen. Fellow in Clin. Sci., RPMS and Hammersmith Hosp., 1980–89; Sen. Lectr, Reader and then Prof. in Renal Medicine, RPMS and Imperial Coll., London, 1989–2002; Dir of Res. and Develt, 2005–08, Dir of Educn, 2008–11, Hammersmith Hosps NHS Trust, subseq. Imperial Coll. Healthcare NHS Trust. Acad. Registrar, RCP, 2001–05. Chm., Kidney Research UK, 2002–07. FMedSci 2002; Fellow, American Soc. of Nephrology, 2009; FRSB (FSB 2011). *Publications:* Fast Facts: Renal Disorders, 2006; over 400 articles, reviews, and book chapters in field of renal medicine. *Recreations:* tennis, walking, music. *Address:* Renal Section, Division of Medicine, Imperial College London, Hammersmith Campus, Du Cane Road, W12 0NN. *T:* (020) 8383 3152, *Fax:* (020) 8383 2062. *E:* c.pusey@imperial.ac.uk.

PUSEY, Prof. Peter Nicholas, PhD; FRS 1996; FRSE; FInstP; Professor of Physics, University of Edinburgh, 1991–2008, now Emeritus (Head, Department of Physics and Astronomy, 1994–97 and 2000–03); *b* 30 Dec. 1942; *s* of late Harold Kenneth Pusey and Edith Joan Pusey (*née* Sparks); *m* 1966, Elizabeth Ann Nind; two *d*. *Educ:* St Edward's Sch., Oxford; Clare Coll., Cambridge (MA); Univ. of Pittsburgh (PhD 1969). FInstP 1981; FRSE 1996. Postdoctoral Fellow, IBM T. J. Watson Res. Center, Yorktown Heights, NY, 1969–72; SPSO, later Grade 6, RSRE, Malvern, 1972–91. *Publications:* numerous contribs in scientific literature. *Address:* School of Physics and Astronomy, University of Edinburgh, Peter Guthrie Tait Road, Edinburgh EH9 3FD. *E:* p.n.pusey@ed.ac.uk.

PUTIN, Vladimir Vladimirovich; President of Russia, 2000–08 and since 2012; Leader, People's Front for Russia, since 2013; *b* Leningrad, 7 Oct. 1952; *s* of late Vladimir Putin and Maria Putin; *m* 1983, Lyudmila Shkrebneva (marr. diss. 2014); two *d*. *Educ:* Leningrad State Univ. (law degree 1975); St Petersburg Mining Univ. (PhD Econs 1997). With KGB, in USSR and Germany, 1975–90; Adviser: to Rector, Leningrad State Univ., 1990; to Mayor of Leningrad, 1990–91; Chm., Cttee on Foreign Relations, Office of the Mayor, St Petersburg, 1991–94; first Dep. Mayor, and Chm. Cttee on Foreign Relations, St Petersburg, 1994–96; first Dep. Hd, Gen. Mgt Dept of Presidential Admin, 1996–97; Hd of Control Dept, 1997–98, first Dep. Hd of Admin, 1998, Kremlin; Dir, Fed. Security Service, Russia, 1998–99; Sec., Security Council, Russia, 1999; Prime Minister of Russia, 1999, 2008–12; Chm., United Russia Party, 2008–12. Chm., Bd of Trustees, Russian Geographical Soc., 2009–. *Publications:* First Person (autobiog.), 2000. *Recreations:* mountain ski-ing, judo. *Address:* Office of the President, The Kremlin, Kremlevskaya Naberezhnaya, Moscow 103073, Russia.

PUTNAM, Roger George, CBE 2007; Visiting Professor of Automotive Business, City University, since 2006; Chairman, Ford Motor Co. Ltd, 2002–05; *b* 17 Aug. 1945; *s* of George William Putnam and Peggy May Putnam (*née* Morgan); *m* 1969, Patricia Elizabeth Williams; one *s* one *d*. *Educ:* Haberdashers' Aske's Sch., Elstree. Public Relations Officer, 1966–68, Gen. Manager, Sales and Marketing, 1968–74, Lotus Cars Ltd; Director, Sales and Marketing: JCL Marine Ltd, 1974–76; Lotus Cars Ltd, 1976–82; Jaguar Cars Ltd, 1982–2002. Trustee, Jaguar Trust (formerly Jaguar Daimler Heritage Trust), 1985–2010; Chairman: Retail Motor Strategy Gp, BERR, later BIS, 2005–10; The Learning Grid, 2007–09. Non-exec. Director: Halcyon Days Ltd, 2002–11; ITM Power plc, 2006– (Chm., 2010–); Autologic Gp plc, 2007–08; Chm., Suila Ltd, 2008–. Dir, SMMT, 2002–08 (Pres., 2005–06). Pres., CIM (Midland), 2002. FIMI 1984. *Recreations:* walking, cameras, photography, theatre, reading. *Address:* Further Hill Grange, Ullenhall, Henley-in-Arden, Warwicks B95 5PN. *Club:* Royal Automobile.

PUTTNAM, family name of **Baron Puttnam**.

PUTTNAM, Baron *cr* 1997 (Life Peer), of Queensgate in the Royal Borough of Kensington and Chelsea; **David Terence Puttnam,** Kt 1995; CBE 1983; Chairman: Enigma Productions Ltd, since 1978; National Endowment for Science, Technology and the Arts, 1998–2003; Deputy Chairman, Channel Four, 2006–12; Chairman: Advisory Board, Prime Hotels (UK) Ltd, since 2011; Atticus Education, since 2012; *b* 25 Feb. 1941; *s* of Leonard Arthur Puttnam and Marie Beatrice Puttnam; *m* 1961, Patricia Mary (*née* Jones); one *s* one *d*. *Educ:* Minchenden Grammar Sch., London. Advertising, 1958–66; photography, 1966–68; film prodn, 1968–2000. Producer of feature films including: Bugsy Malone, 1976 (four BAFTA awards); The Duellists, 1977 (Jury Prize, Cannes); Midnight Express, 1978 (two Acad. Awards, three BAFTA Awards); Chariots of Fire, 1981 (four Acad. Awards, three BAFTA Awards, incl. awards for best film); Local Hero, 1982 (two BAFTA Awards); The Killing Fields, 1985 (three Acad. Awards, eight BAFTA Awards incl. Best Film); The Mission, 1986 (Palme d'Or, Cannes, 1986, one Acad. Award, three BAFTA awards, 1987). Chm. and Chief Exec. Officer, Columbia Pictures, 1986–88. Visiting Professor: Drama Dept, Bristol Univ., 1986–98; Inst. of Educn, London Univ., 2008–; Adjunct Prof., University Coll. Cork, 2012–. Digital Champion, Republic of Ireland, 2012–. Prime Minister's Trade Envoy to Vietnam, Laos and Cambodia, 2012–. Director: National Film Finance Corp., 1980–85; Anglia Television Gp, 1982–99; Claridge's Hotel, 1984–99; Village Roadshow Corp., 1989–99; Chrysalis Group, 1993–96; Promethean World plc (formerly Chalkfree), 2006–; Huntsworth plc, 2007–12; EMPGI (Ireland), 2012–; Chairman: Internat. Television Enterprises Ltd, 1988–99; Spectrum Strategy Consultants, 1999–2006; Futurelab, 2006–11; Dep. Chm., Profero, 2010–14 (Chm., 2007–10). Governor: National Film and Television Sch., 1974–96 (Chm., 1988–96); Central Sch. of Speech and Drama, 1993–96; LSE, 1997–2002 (Vis. Prof.); London Inst., 1998–2002; Member: Governing Council, Nat. Coll. for Sch. Leadership; Academic Adv. Bd, Inst. for Advanced Studies, Univ. of Bristol; Co-founder, European Media Business Sch., Madrid 1991. President: UNICEF UK, 2002–09 (Ambassador, 2010–); Film Distributors' Assoc., 2009–; Vice President: BAFTA, 1993–2004; CPRE, 1997–2007 (Pres., 1985–92). Member: British Screen Adv. Council, 1988–98; Arts Council Lottery Panel, 1995–98; Educn Standards Task Force, 1997–2002; Creative Industries Task Force, 1997–99; British Educnl Communications and Technol. Agency; Arts and Humanities Res. Bd; Senate, Engrg Council; Council, Hansard Soc., 2007–; Accenture Adv. Council, Ireland, 2013–; Nat. Forum for Enhancement of Teaching and Learning, Ireland, 2013–. Chairman: Arts Adv. Cttee, British Council, 1991–2003; Gen. Teaching Council, 1998–2001; Jt Scrutiny Cttee for Communications Bill, 2002; Media and Culture Sector Adv. Gp, QCA, 2000–03; TSL Adv. Bd, 2010–; Ateliers du cinéma européen 1991–94; Nat. Meml Arboretum, 1993–2003; Nat. Mus. of Photography, Film and Television, 1994–2003; Jt Cttee on Draft Climate Change Bill, 2007; Academic Bd, Pearson Coll., 2014. Trustee: Tate Gall., 1986–93; Science Museum, 1996–2004; Royal Acad. of Arts, 2000–03; Thomson Foundn, 2003–; Forum for the Future, 1996–2004 (Chm., 1996–99); Eden Project, 2009–13; Transformation Trust, 2009–11; Mohamed S. Farsi Foundn, 2011–;

Chm. Trustees, Nat. Teaching Awards, 1998–2008; Chm., North Music Trust, Sage Gateshead, 2007. Patron, Schools North East, 2014–. Hon. Mem., British Business Gp Vietnam, 2014–. Hon. Chancellor: Univ. of Sunderland, 1998–2007; Open Univ., 2007–14. Lay Canon, Durham Cathedral, 2002–08. FRGS; FRSA; FRPS; Fellow: BFI, 1997; BAFTA, 2006; FCGI 1999. Freedom, City of Sunderland, 2007. Charter Fellow, Coll. of Teachers, 2001. Hon. Fellow: Manchester Polytechnic, 1990; Inst. of Educn, London Univ., 2007; IPA, 2013. Hon. FCSD 1990; Hon. FLI 1994. Hon. LLD Bristol, 1983; Hon. DLitt: Leicester, 1986; Sunderland, 1992; Bradford, 1993; Humberside, 1996; Westminster, 1997; Kent, 1998; London Guildhall, 1999; City, 2000; Nottingham, 2000; Heriot-Watt, 2001; Birmingham, 2002; Southampton, 2002; Keele, 2002; Abertay, 2003; Hon. LittD: Leeds, 1992; N London, 2001; Hon. DLit QUB, 2001; Hon. Dr of Drama RSAMD, 1998; Hon. DPhil Cheltenham and Gloucester Coll. of Higher Educn, 1998; Hon. DSc (Med.) Imperial Coll., London, 1999; Hon. DFA American Univ. in London, 2000; Hon. Dr: Navarra, Spain, 1999; Sheffield Hallam, 2000; King Alfred's Coll., Winchester, 2002; Herzen Univ., St Petersburg, 2003; Surrey, 2003; Thames Valley, 2004; Queen Margaret Univ. Coll., 2004; Brunel, 2004; Middx, 2004; Greenwich, 2004; Nottingham Trent, 2007; Open, 2007; Edinburgh, 2013; Hon. DEd Sunderland, 2007. Michael Balcon Award for outstanding contribn to British Film Industry, 1982, Fellowship, 2006, BAFTA; Benjamin Franklin Medal, RSA, 1996; Crystal Award, World Economic Forum, 1997; President's Medal, RPS, 2003; Akiro Kurasawa Award, 2007; Bicentennial Medal, RSA, 2008; New Media Consortium Fellows Award (USA), 2012. Commandeur de l'Ordre des Arts et des Lettres (France), 2006 (Officier, 1992). *Publications:* (with Brian Wenham) The Third Age of Broadcasting, 1982; (jtly) Rural England, 1988; What Needs to Change?, 1996; Undeclared War, 1997. *Recreations:* reading, watching movies. *Address:* House of Lords, SW1A 0PW. *Clubs:* Athenæum, Chelsea Arts, MCC.

PUXLEY, James Henry Lavallin; Lord-Lieutenant of Berkshire, since 2015 (Vice Lord-Lieutenant, 2011–15); *b* London, 23 Oct. 1948; *s* of John Philip Lavallin Puxley and Aline Carlos Puxley; *m* 1991, Deborah Ferguson; one *s* one *d*. *Educ:* Eton; Univ. of Bristol (BA); Royal Agricl Coll., Cirencester (Dip.). ARICS. Partner, Britton Poole and Burns, chartered surveyors, 1978–81; Dir, Welford Farms Ltd, 1981–; Partner: Elton Farm Partners, 1981–2011; Welford Estate Partners, 2012–. Chm., W Berks Anglo-American Community Relns Cttee, 1984–92. Hon. Comdr, RAF Welford, 2007–. DL Berks, 2005. *Recreations:* travel, theatre, walking. *Address:* Welford Park, Welford, Newbury, Berks RG20 8HU. *T:* (01488) 608691. *E:* jpuxley@welfordpark.co.uk. *Club:* Travellers.

PWAISIHO, Rt Rev. William Alaha, OBE 2004; Rector of Gawsworth, since 1999; an Hon. Assistant Bishop, Diocese of Chester, since 1997; *b* Solomon Is, 14 May 1948; *s* of Stephen Honiuhi and Esther Makatoro; *m* 1976, Sister Kate Kome Oikada; one *s* three *d* and one adopted *s*. *Educ:* C of E primary, sen. and secondary schs in Solomon Is; Bp Patterson Theol Coll., Kohimarama (Dip. in Theol. and Biblical Studies). Ordained deacon, 1974, priest, 1975; Chaplain to Archbp of Melanesia and to Central Police HQ, Honiara, 1976; Curate, Mission Bay, Auckland, NZ (first missionary priest from Melanesia), 1977–78; Chaplain and Tutor, Bp Patterson Theol Coll., 1979–80; Dean, St Barnabas Provincial Cathedral, Honiara, 1980–81; Diocesan Bishop, Malaita, 1981–89; Tutor, Melanesian Brotherhood HQ, Tabalia, 1989–90; (first) Gen. Sec., Melanesian Bd of Mission, Honiara, 1990–95; Parish Priest, E of Honiara, 1995–97; Curate, St Anne and St Francis, Sale, UK, 1997–99. Chaplain to High Sheriff of Cheshire, 2002–03. Hon. Chaplain, Crimebeat in England and Wales, 2004–; Mem., Ethnic Minority Ind. Adv. Gp, Cheshire Constabulary. Member: Melanesian Mission UK; UK and NI Churches Together Pacific Forum. *Recreations:* football, Rugby, fishing, volleyball. *Address:* The Rectory, Church Lane, Gawsworth, Macclesfield, Cheshire SK11 9RJ. *T:* and *Fax:* (01260) 223201. *E:* bishop.gawsworth@virgin.net. *Club:* Macclesfield Rotary (Pres., 2011–12).

PYANT, Paul; lighting designer, since 1980; *b* 22 July 1953; *s* of late Leonard Vincent Pyant and of Jean Phoebe Pyant (*née* Frampton); partner, Stephen Lawless. *Educ:* Royal Acad. of Dramatic Art (Hons Dip.). Lighting designs for: Glyndebourne Opera, 1974–, including: Death in Venice, Falstaff, 1990; Le Nozze di Figaro, 1991; Die Fledermaus, 2003; A Midsummer Night's Dream, 2006; English National Opera, 1985–, including: Xerxes, 1985; Lady Macbeth of Mtsensk, 1987; Street Scene (Scottish Opera/ENO), 1989; Royal National Theatre, 1988–, including: Wind in the Willows, 1990; The Madness of George III, 1991; Carousel, 1992 (NY, 1994, Japan, 1995); Candide, 1999; Streetcar Named Desire, 2003; Othello, 1997 (and Salzburg); 2000 Years, 2005; King Lear, 2014; Houston Grand Opera, 1989–, incl. New Year, 1989; Royal Opera House, 1991–; Royal Shakespeare Co., 1991–, including: Richard III, 1992; The Tempest, 1993; Northern Ballet Theatre, 1991–, including: Romeo and Juliet, 1991; Cinderella, 1993; Dracula, 1996; Donmar Warehouse, 1992–, including: Assassins, 1992; Cabaret, 1993; Company, 1995; English National Ballet, 1993–, incl. Cinderella, 1996; LA Opera, 1995–, incl. The Elixir of Love, 1996; *theatre* includes: Orpheus Descending, Th. Royal, Haymarket, 1988 (NY, 1989); Hamlet, Old Vic, 2004; The Woman in White, Palace Th., 2004 (NY, 2005); Lord of the Rings, Toronto, 2006, Th. Royal, Drury Lane, 2007; Aristo, Chichester, 2008; The Secret Garden, W Yorks Playhouse, 2009; Richard III, Old Vic, 2011; Charlie and the Chocolate Factory, Th. Royal, Drury Lane, 2013 (Olivier Award for Best Lighting Design, 2014); Oh What a Lovely War, Th. Royal, Stratford E, 2014; opera work includes: productions in USA: for Metropolitan Opera, Seattle Opera, San Francisco Opera and Chicago Opera; in Australia and NZ; in Europe, incl. La Scala, Milan; ballet productions for: Royal NZ Ballet, Norwegian Nat. Ballet, Boston Ballet, Atlanta Ballet, Colorado Ballet and Asami Maki Ballet, Tokyo. *Recreations:* steam locomotives, gardening. *Address:* c/o Jeffrey Cambell Management, 7 Homelatch House, St Leonards Road, Eastbourne, E Sussex BN21 3UW. *T:* (01323) 730526. *E:* cambell@theatricaldesigners.co.uk.

PYATT, David John; Principal Horn, London Philharmonic Orchestra, since 2013; *b* 26 Sept. 1973; *s* of John Douglas Pyatt and Frances Margaret Pyatt; *m* 1997, Catherine Anne Whiteside; one *s* one *d*. *Educ:* Watford Boys' Grammar Sch.; Selwyn Coll., Cambridge. Guest Principal Horn, Scottish Opera, 1994–96; Co-Principal Horn, BBC Nat. Orch. of Wales, 1996–98; Principal Horn, LSO, 1998–2012. Professor of Horn, GSMD, 2012–. Young Musician of the Year, BBC, 1988; Gramophone Young Artist of the Year, 1996. *Recreations:* cooking, eating and drinking enough to keep up with the Wine Society brochures. *Address:* c/o Clarion/Seven Muses, 47 Whitehall Park, N19 3TW. *T:* (020) 7272 4413, 5125, *Fax:* (020) 7281 9687. *E:* caroline@c7m.co.uk.

PYCROFT, Stephen Gerard; Executive Chairman, Mace, since 2013; *b* Bradford, 18 Oct. 1958; *s* of Arnold and Joyce Pycroft; *m* 1992, Joanne Camilleri (*d* 2006); one *s* one *d*. *Educ:* Nottingham Poly. (BSc Hons). ARICS 1982. With Bovis, 1985–93; Mace, 1993–: Bd Dir, 1995–; Chief Operating Officer, 2001–04; CEO, 2004–08; CEO and Chm., 2008–13. *Recreation:* golf. *Address:* Mace, 155 Moorgate, EC2M 6XB. *T:* (020) 3522 3055.

PYE, Prof. (John) David, FLS; Professor of Zoology, Queen Mary and Westfield College (formerly Queen Mary College), University of London, 1973–91, now Emeritus Professor, Queen Mary, University of London; *b* 14 May 1932; *s* of Wilfred Frank Pye and Gwenllian Pye (*née* Davies); *m* 1958, Dr Ade Pye (*née* Kuku), Sen. Lectr, UCL, retd. *Educ:* Queen Elizabeth's Grammar School for Boys, Mansfield; University Coll. of Wales, Aberystwyth (BSc 1954, Hons 1955); Bedford Coll., London Univ. (PhD 1961). FZS 1956; FLS 1980; MInstP 2001, FInstP 2003. Research Asst, Inst. of Laryngology and Otology, London Univ., 1958–64; Lectr in Zoology, 1964–70, Reader, 1970–73, King's Coll. London; Head of Dept of Zoology and Comparative Physiology, Queen Mary Coll., 1977–82. A founder Dir, QMC Instruments Ltd, 1976–89. Linnean Society: Editor, Zoological Jl, 1981–85; Editl Sec. and Mem. Council, 1985–91; Vice-Pres., 1987–90; Mem., IEE Professional Gp Cttee E15, Radar, Sonar, Navigation and Avionics, 1983–86. Member Editorial Boards: Zool Soc., 1972–77, 1978–83, 1985–90; Jl of Exper. Biol., 1974–78; Jl of Comp. Physiol. A, 1978–96; Bioacoustics, 1987–. Royal Institution: Associate Mem., 1979–92; Mem., 1992–2002; delivered Friday discourses 1979, 1983, and televised Christmas Lects for Children, 1985–86; co-organizer, discussion evenings, 1994–2002; Mem. Council, 1999–2002; Vice Pres., 2001–02; Hon. FRI 2002. *Publications:* Bats, 1968; (with G. D. Sales) Ultrasonic Communication by Animals, 1974; (ed with R. J. Bench and A. Pye) Sound Reception in Mammals, 1975; Polarised Light in Science and Nature, 2001; articles and research papers. *Recreations:* baking and brewing, travel, arts. *Address:* Woodside, 24 St Mary's Avenue, Finchley, N3 1SN. *T:* (020) 8346 6869.

PYE, Prof. Kenneth, ScD, PhD; CGeol, FGS; Managing Director, Kenneth Pye Associates Ltd, since 2004 (Founder Director, since 2002); *b* 24 Aug. 1956; *s* of Leonard Pye and Joyce Pye; *m* 1st, 1979, Diane Cadman (marr. diss. 2007); one *s* one *d*; 2nd, 2014, Samantha Jayne Witton. *Educ:* Upholland Grammar Sch., Lancs; Hertford Coll., Oxford (Scholar; BA 1977; MA 1981); St John's Coll., Cambridge (PhD 1981; ScD 1992). CGeol 1995; FGS 1980. Cambridge University: NERC Postdoctoral Res. Fellow, 1980–82; Sarah Woodhead Res. Fellow, 1980–83, Non-stipendiary Fellow, 1983–89, Girton Coll.; Royal Society 1983 Univ. Res. Fellow, 1983–88; Reading University: Lectr in Quaternary Sedimentology, 1989–92; Reader in Sedimentology, 1992–94; Prof. of Envmtl Sedimentology, 1994–98; Royal Holloway, University of London: Prof. of Envmtl Geology, 1999–2004; Vis. Prof., 2004–07. Visiting Professor: Earth and Ocean Sci., Nat. Oceanography Centre, Southampton, 2011–; Sch. of Engrg and Envmt, Univ. of Southampton, 2013–. Founder Director: Cambridge Envmtl Research Consultants Ltd, 1986–95; K. Pye Associates, 1998–. Expert Witness, forensic geology (criminal and civil investigations). Leverhulme Trust Fellowship, 1991; Leverhulme Trust Sen. Res. Fellowship, 1996. Sedgwick Prize, Univ. of Cambridge, 1984; British Geomorphological Research Group: Wiley Award, 1989; Gordon Warwick Award, 1991. *Publications:* Chemical Sediments and Geomorphology, 1983; Aeolian Dust and Dust Deposits, 1987; Aeolian Sand and Sand Dunes, 1990, 2nd edn, 2009; Saltmarshes, 1992; The Dynamics and Environmental Context of Aeolian Sedimentary Systems, 1993; Aeolian Sediments Ancient and Modern, 1993; Sediment Transport and Depositional Processes, 1994; Environmental Change in Drylands, 1994; Backscattered Scanning Electron Microscopy and Image Analysis of Sediments and Sedimentary Rocks, 1998; Coastal and Estuarine Environments: sedimentology, geomorphology and geoarchaeology, 2000; Forensic Geoscience: principles, techniques and applications, 2004; Geological and Soil Evidence: forensic applications, 2007; The Measurement of Coastal Change, 2009; contribs to learned jls. *Recreations:* world travel, visiting historic sites and houses, collecting rocks and minerals, reading. *Address:* Kenneth Pye Associates Ltd, Blythe Valley Innovation Centre, Central Boulevard, Blythe Valley Park, Solihull, W Midlands B90 8AJ. *T:* (0121) 506 9067.

PYE, Dame Wendy (Edith), DNZM 2013; MBE 1994; Owner and Director, Wendy Pye Publishing Ltd, since 1985; *b* Yarloop, WA; *d* of Thomas Jackson and Marie Louise Jackson; *m* 1965, Donald Norman Pye. *Educ:* Auckland Univ. of Technol. (mgt degree). With NZ Newspapers Ltd, from jun. journalist to manager of eight cos in publishing div. With Wendy Pye Publishing, publisher of early learning reading series (2700 titles), television series and online digital books and activities. NZ Rep., Apec Business Adv. Council, 2001–07. Co-Chairman: Capacity Building Wkg Gp, 2004; Technol. and Information Wkg Gp, 2007; Chm., Technol. Wkg Gp, 2005–06. Dir, NZ Trade and Enterprise, 2005–07. FInstD, NZ. *Address:* Private Bag 17.905, Greenlane, Auckland 1546, New Zealand. *T:* (9) 5253575. *E:* wendy@sunshine.co.nz. *Club:* Northern (Auckland).

PYE, William Burns, FRBS 1992; sculptor; *b* 16 July 1938; *m* 1963, Susan Marsh; one *s* two *d*. *Educ:* Charterhouse; Wimbledon Sch. of Art; Royal Coll. of Art (ARCA). Vis. Prof., Calif. State Univ., 1975–76. Pres., Hampshire Sculpture Trust, 2002–. Directed film, Reflections, 1971. *Solo exhibitions:* Winchester Great Hall, 1979; Hong Kong (retrospective), 1987; RBS Gall., 2008; *public sculpture:* Zemran, South Bank, London, 1971; Curlicue, Greenland Dock, London, 1989; Cader Idris, Cardiff, 1998; *public water sculpture:* Slipstream and Jetstream, Gatwick Airport, 1988; Chalice, Fountain Sq., London, 1990; Water Wall and Portico, Expo '92, Seville, 1992; Orchid, the Peacocks, Woking, 1992; Cristos, St Christopher's Place, London, 1993; Confluence, Hertford, 1994; Downpour, British Embassy, Oman, 1995; Derby Cascade, Derby, 1995; Antony House, Cornwall, 1996; Archimedes Screw feature, West India Quay, London, 1997; Aquarena, Millennium Square, Bristol, 2000; Scaladaqua Tonda, Nat. Botanical Gardens, Wales, 2000; Tureen, St John's Coll., Cambridge, 2001; Monolith, Sunderland Winter Garden, 2001; Cornucopia, Millfield Sch., 2001; Scala Aquae Pembrochiana, Wilton House, 2001; Charybdis, Seaham Hall, Sunderland, 2001; Haberdashers' Co. new hall, 2002; Argosy, Lloyd's Register of Shipping, 2002; Divine Influx in Bath, Cross Bath, 2003; Jubilee Fountain, New Square, Lincoln's Inn, 2003; eight features for new gardens at Alnwick Castle, 2005; Sunken Garden, Aberglasney Gardens, Wales, 2005; font, Salisbury Cathedral, 2008; Hypanthium water piece, Univ. of BC Botanical Gdns, Vancouver, 2010; Water Pavilion, Drammen, Norway, 2011; Starburst, Sainsbury Lab., Cambridge, 2011; Cedra, Woolbeding House (Nat. Trust), Midhurst, 2012; Vortex CPFL, Campinas, Brazil, 2012; Vortex Bank Muscat, Brazil, 2012; Hydrodendron, Chateau La Trapperie, Belgium, 2013; Arroyo, Maggie's, Cheltenham, 2013; Thistle and Pergola fountains, Dumfries House, Scotland, 2014; *portrait bust of* Rt Hon. Douglas Hurd, Nat. Portrait Gall., 1996. Hon. FRIBA 1993. Prix de Sculpture, Vth Internat. Sculpture Exhibn, Budapest; Peace Sculpture Prize, W Midlands CC, 1984; ABSA Awards for Best Sculpture in UK (Gatwick Airport), 1988, and in Scotland (Glasgow), 1989; UENO Royal Museum Award, Japan, 1989. *Recreation:* playing the flute. *Address:* 43 Hambalt Road, Clapham, SW4 9EQ. *T:* (home) (020) 8673 2318, (studio) (020) 8682 2727. *W:* www.williampye.com.

PYE-JEARY, Anthony John; Founder, Dewynters Ltd, since 1998 (Partner, since 1975); *b* London, 19 May 1949; *s* of Thomas Pye-Jeary and Peggy Pye-Jeary (*née* Banks); *m* 1985, Katharine Phillips; one *s*. *Educ:* Dulwich Coll. Advertising and promotions trainee, Rediffusion Television, 1966–68; ind. theatrical PR, 1969–75. *Recreations:* theatre, horse racing, Jumby Bay. *Address:* Dewynters Ltd, Wellington House, 125 Strand, WC2R 0AP. *T:* (020) 7321 0488. *E:* anthony@dewynters.com.

PYKE, Elaine; Executive Producer, New Pictures Ltd, since 2014; *b* Aberdare, Wales, 8 Feb. 1971; *d* of George Pyke and Margaret Pyke (*née* Hayter); partner, Richard George Dawson; two *d*. *Educ:* Howells Sch., LLandaff; Marlborough Coll.; Exeter Coll., Oxford; Rose Bruford Coll. of Drama. Actress, RSC, 1990–2000; Script Editor: Carlton TV, 2001–02; Thames Talkback, 2002; producer, Mediae Kenya, 2002–03; Sky One: Exec. Producer, 2003–04; Drama Comr, 2004–05; Controller of Drama, Sky TV, 2005–11; Controller, Sky Atlantic, 2011–14. Mem., BAFTA, 2009–. *T:* 07841 220871. *E:* Pyke.Elaine@googlemail.com.

PYLE, Derek Colin Wilson; Sheriff Principal of Grampian, Highland and Islands, since 2012; *b* 15 Oct. 1952; *s* of Colin Lawson Pyle and Mary Best Johnston Pyle; *m* 1980, Jean Blackwood Baillie May; six *s* one *d*. *Educ:* Royal High Sch., Edinburgh; Univ. of Edinburgh (LLB Hons). Law Apprentice, Lindsays, WS, Edinburgh, 1974–76; Partner, Dove Lockhart, WS, Solicitors, Edinburgh, 1977–80; Sole Partner, Wilson Pyle & Co., WS, Solicitors, Edinburgh, 1980–88; Partner, Henderson Boyd Jackson, WS, Solicitors, Edinburgh, 1989–99; Sheriff: of Tayside, Central and Fife, 2000–05; of Grampian, Highland and Islands at Inverness, 2005–08; of Tayside, Central and Fife at Dundee, 2008–12. *Recreations:* golf, hill-walking, writing unpublished best-sellers. *Address:* The Old Manor, Grange, Errol, Perthshire PH2 7SZ. *T:* (01821) 642198. *Club:* Craigielaw Golf.

PYLE, Prof. John Adrian, DPhil, ScD; FRS 2004; Director, Centre for Atmospheric Science, since 1992, and 1920 Professor of Physical Chemistry, since 2007, University of Cambridge; Fellow, St Catharine's College, Cambridge, since 1986; *b* 4 April 1951; *s* of Harold Pyle and Agnes Pyle (*née* Rimmer); *m* 1979, Elizabeth Caroline Lynnell Davies; one *s* two *d*. *Educ:* De La Salle Coll., Salford; Univ. of Durham (BSc Physics); Jesus Coll., Oxford (DPhil 1976); ScD Cantab 2012. Res. asst, Dept of Atmospheric Physics, Univ. of Oxford, 1976–82; Rutherford Appleton Lab., 1982–85; University of Cambridge: Lectr in Physical Chem., 1985–95; Reader in Atmospheric Chem., 1995–2000; Prof. of Atmospheric Sci., 2000–07; Head: Eur. Ozone Res. Co-ordinating Res. Unit, 1990–95; Atmospheric Chem. Modelling Support Unit, 1992–2005; Co-Dir, 2005–13, Chief Scientist, 2013–, NCAS. Member: Stratospheric Ozone Rev. Gp, DoE, later DEFRA, 1986– (Chm., 1988–); EC DG Res. Panel on Stratospheric Ozone, 1990–; Subcttee on Envmtl Sci., ACOST, 1990–92; NERC Sci. and Technol. Bd, then Sci. and Implementation Strategy Bd, 2000–02. Co-Chm., UNEP-WMO Ozone Scientific Adv. Panel, 2007–. Member, Council: Eur. Geophysical Soc., 1986–89; Royal Soc., 2009–11. MAE 1993. Sec. II, RMetS, 1979–84. John Jeyes Lect., RSC, 2009. Fellow, Amer. Geophysical Union, 2011. (Jtly) Eurotrac Award, Remote Sensing Soc., 1985; Interdisciplinary Award, RSC, 1991; (jtly) Körber Eur. Sci. Foundn Award, 1999; Adrian Gill Prize, RMetS, 2003; (jtly) NERC Internat. Impact Award and overall Impact Award, 2015. *Publications:* (ed jtly) Encyclopedia of Atmospheric Science, 2002, 2nd edn 2014; contrib. numerous papers to scientific jls. *Recreations:* hill walking, sport, supporting Bolton Wanderers. *Address:* Centre for Atmospheric Science, Department of Chemistry, Lensfield Road, Cambridge CB2 1EW. *T:* (01223) 336473, *Fax:* (01223) 763818. *E:* john.pyle@atm.ch.cam.ac.uk.

PYLE, Leo Michael Peter; a Recorder, since 2009; a District Judge (Magistrates' Courts), since 2011; *b* Beaconsfield, 30 Aug. 1961; *s* of Anthony Joseph and Mary Patricia Pyle; *m* 1987, Angela Claire Darke; one *s* two *d*. *Educ:* Slough Grammar Sch.; Liverpool Poly. (LLB Hons); Coll. of Law, Chester. Higher Courts (Criminal Proc.) Qualif. 2005. Admitted solicitor 1986; Partner: Page Nelson (formerly Page & Co.), Lincoln, 1992–2005; McKinnells, Lincoln, 2005–11. Dep. Dist Judge (Magistrates' Courts), 2000–11. *Recreations:* trying to stay on the backs of fast horses, playing all other sports badly. *Address:* c/o Nottingham Magistrates' Court, Wilford Street, Nottingham NG2 1EE. *Club:* Primary Cricket.

PYLE, Nicholas John, OBE 2010 (MBE 1999); HM Diplomatic Service; High Commissioner to Botswana, and UK Representative to Southern African Development Community, since 2013; *b* 9 Dec. 1960; *m* 1993, Rosamund Day, MBE; two *s* one *d*. *Educ:* Bearwood Coll. Entered FCO, 1981; UKMIS, Geneva, 1984–86; Kabul, 1986–88; Jeddah, 1989–93; Second Sec. (Immigration) and Consul, Sri Lanka, 1996–99; Second Sec. (Pol), 2000–03, Dep. Hd of Mission, 2003–04, Barbados; Political Counsellor (Somalia), Nairobi, 2005–08; Special Advr to UN Sec.-Gen.'s Special Rep. to Somalia (on secondment), 2008–09; Deputy Head: E Africa and Gt Lakes Dept, FCO, 2010–12; Africa Dept Central and Southern, FCO, 2012–13. *Address:* c/o Foreign and Commonwealth Office, King Charles Street, SW1A 2AH.

PYLKKÄNEN, Juha, (Jussi); Global President, Christie's, since 2015; *b* Helsinki, 27 May 1963; *m* 1986, Alison Green; one *s* one *d*. *Educ:* Lady Margaret Hall, Oxford (MA English Lit.). Christie's: Specialist, Old Master and Modern Prints, 1986–90; Associate Dir, Impressionist and Modern Art, 1990–95; Dir, Impressionist Dept, 1995–2000; Dep. Chm., Christie's, UK, 2000–06; Pres., Christie's Europe, Middle East and Russia (formerly Europe), 2005–14; Chm., Impressionist and Modern Art Dept, 2006–14. *Address:* Christie's, 8 King Street, St James's, SW1Y 6QT. *E:* jpylkkanen@christies.com.

PYM, Richard Alan, CBE 2015; FCA; Chairman: Bradford & Bingley plc, since 2009 (Chief Executive, 2008; Executive Chairman, 2008–09); Northern Rock (Asset Management) plc, since 2010; UK Asset Resolution Ltd, since 2010; Allied Irish Banks, since 2014. *Educ:* Univ. of Warwick (BSc 1971). FCA 1974. Thomson McLintock & Co., 1971–75; British Gas plc, 1975–77; BAT Industries plc, 1978–82; The Burton Gp plc, 1983–92; Alliance & Leicester plc: Gp Finance Dir, 1993–2001; Man. Dir, Retail Banking, 2001–02; Gp Chief Exec., 2002–07; Chm., Co-operative Bank plc, 2013–14. Director: Selfridges plc, 1998–2003; Halfords plc, 2004–08 (Chm., 2006–08); Old Mutual, 2007–10. Vice-Pres., BBA, 2004–07.

PYMAN, Avril; *see* Sokolov, A.

PYMONT, Christopher Howard; QC 1996; a Recorder, since 2004; a Deputy High Court Judge, since 2008; *b* 16 March 1956; *s* of John and Joan Pymont; *m* 1996, Meriel Rosalind, *d* of Roger and late Ann Lester; two *s* one *d*. *Educ:* Marlborough Coll.; Christ Church, Oxford (BA Hons 1977; MA 1979). Called to the Bar, Gray's Inn, 1979; in practice at the Bar, 1980–. *Address:* Maitland Chambers, 7 Stone Buildings, Lincoln's Inn, WC2A 3SZ. *T:* (020) 7406 1200.

PYNE, Kenneth John, (Ken); cartoonist, since 1970; *b* London, 30 April 1951; *s* of John Ernest Pyne and Dorothy Maud Pyne; partner, Pamela Todd. *Educ:* Holloway Co. Sch., London. First cartoon published in Punch, 1967; contributed to: The Times, TES, Daily Mirror, Mail on Sunday, Private Eye, Punch, Independent, Evening Standard, Daily Telegraph, The People, Observer, Guardian, Manchester Evening News, Hampstead & Highgate Express, Sunday Times, The Oldie, Reader's Digest, Which, Stern (Germany), Today, Sunday Express, Marketing Week, Spectator, New Statesman, The Listener, Radio Times, Esquire, House Beautiful, Fedn of Small Businesses, MoneyMarketing, FM World, The Pavement, Cambridge Univ. Press, Literary Review, etc. *Exhibitions:* Cartoonist Gall., London, 1991 and 1996; Barbican Centre, 1992; Burgh House, Hampstead, 2001; *work in collections:* V&A Mus.; Cartoon Art Trust Mus.; Salon Internat. du Pressin et d'Humour, Switzerland. Member: British Cartoonist Assoc., 1979–; Professional Cartoonists' Orgn, 2008–; Burgh House (Hon. Friend, 2009); Professional Cartoonist Orgn. Cartoonist of Year, Cartoonist Club of GB, 1981; Strip Cartoonist of Year, 2001, Cartoonist of Year and Caricaturist of the Year, 2006, Cartoon Art Trust; Hampstead Cartoonist of The Year, Hampstead Village Voice, 2010. *Publications:* The Relationship, 1981; Martin Minton, 1982; Silly Mid-off, 1985; This Sporting Life, 1986; In the Bleak Mid-winter, 1987; (with Craig Brown) 1966 and All That, 2005; illustrated numerous book; work reproduced in numerous books. *Recreations:* walking, drawing, drinking, reading. *Address:* 15 Well Walk, Hampstead, NW3 1BY. *T:* (020) 7431 3480. *E:* pyne9@hotmail.com.

PYOTT, David Edmund Ian, CBE 2006; Chairman and Chief Executive Officer, Allergan Inc., California, 1998–2015; *b* London, 13 Oct. 1953; *s* of Robert Macgregor Pyott and Margaret Pyott (*née* Martin); *m* 1990, Julianna Racz; three *s* one *d*. *Educ:* Glasgow Acad.; Univ. of Edinburgh (MA); Univ. of Amsterdam (Dip. Eur. and Internat. Law); London Business Sch. (MBA). Sandoz AG, Basel: Hd, Strategic Planning, Nutrition Div., 1980–83; Marketing Manager, Nutrition Div., Malaysia, Singapore, 1984–86; Gen. Manager, Nutrition Div., Austria, 1986–89; Gen. Manager, Nutrition Div., Spain, 1990–92; Chief Exec., Nutrition Div., USA, 1993–95; Mem., Exec. Bd, 1995–; Mem., Exec. Bd, Novartis Internat. AG, Basel, 1995–97; Director: Avery Dennison Inc., Pasadena, Calif, 1999–; Edward Life Scis Corp., Irvine, Calif, 2000–. Director: California Healthcare Inst., 1998–; Biotechnol. Industry Orgn, 2005–. *Recreations:* ski-ing, mountaineering, cycling, travel, gardening, history.

PYPER, Mark Christopher Spring-Rice, OBE 2011; Principal (formerly Headmaster), Gordonstoun School, 1990–2011; *b* 13 Aug. 1947; *s* of late Arthur Spring-Rice Pyper and of Rosemary Isabel Pyper; *m* 1979, Jennifer Lindsay Gilderson; one *s* two *d*. *Educ:* Winchester College; Balliol College, Oxford; London Univ. (BA Mod. Hist. ext.). Asst Master, Stoke Brunswick Sch., East Grinstead, 1966–69; Asst Master, then Joint Headmaster, St Wilfrid's Sch., Seaford, 1969–79; Registrar, Housemaster, then Dep. Headmaster, Sevenoaks Sch., 1979–90. Dir, Sevenoaks Summer Festival, 1981–90. Member: SE Arts Cttee, 1984–90; HMC Community Service Cttee, 1995–2000; Council, Round Square Internat., 1995–2001 (Chm., Strategy Cttee, 1999–2001); Oxfordshire Deanery Synod, 2013–. Governor: Rosebrae Nursery Sch., Elgin, 1998–2002; Bellhaven Hill Sch., Dunbar, 2000–04; Ardvreck Sch., Crieff, 2004–07; Bedales Sch., Petersfield, 2012– (Chair, Educn Cttee, 2015–); Westonbirt Sch., 2013–; Governor and Chair Education Committee: Samworth Ch. Acad., 2011–13; Beaudesert Park Sch., 2011– (Chair, Bd, 2015–); Bloxham Sch., 2012–. Educn Advr, Alexandria Trust, 2012–. Fellow, Woodard Corp., 2012. Hon. Fellow, Rank Foundn, 2011. *Address:* 16 Osberton Road, Oxford OX2 7NU. *Club:* MCC.

PYPER, Susan Elizabeth; Lord-Lieutenant of West Sussex, since 2008; *b* London, 12 Dec. 1951; *d* of Ronald Harrison and Joan Harrison; *m* 1987, Jonathan Pyper; one *s* one *d*. *Educ:* Prendergast Grammar Sch.; Univ. of Durham (BSc Hons); Chelsea Coll., London Univ. (Postgrad. Dip.). Forensic scientist, Metropolitan Police, 1973–76; Officer, RAF, 1976–87; Scientific Exec., Milupa (UK) Ltd, 1990–92; Chairman: Merton and Sutton Community NHS Trust, 1992–99; Sussex Weald and Downs NHS Trust, 1999–2002; Western Sussex NHS PCT, 2002–05; Royal W Sussex NHS Trust, 2005–09. Chm., Regl Envmt Protection Adv. Cttee, 2002–10; Mem., Regl Flood Defence Cttee, 2002–10. Lay Mem., Preliminary Investigation Cttee, RCVS, 1999–2006. Joint President: Sussex Community Foundn, 2008–; Action in Rural Sussex, 2009–; Sussex Historic Churches Trust, 2009–; Vice President: SSAFA (formerly SSAFA Forces Help), Sussex; SE RFCA; Army Benevolent Fund, W Sussex; Weald and Downland Mus.; Mem. Council, Chichester Cathedral; Patron: Chichester Harbour Trust; Pallant House Gall.; Chichester Cathedral Restoration Trust; Lodge Hill Trust; St Barnabas Hospice, Chichester, 2011; St Wilfrid's Hospice, Worthing, 2013; Jt Pres., Sussex Council, Order of St John. DStJ (CStJ 2009). *Recreations:* family, classical music, walking, ski-ing, outdoor pursuits, travel. *Address:* Fair Oaks, Monkmead Lane, W Chiltington, W Sussex RH20 2PF. *E:* jandspyper@btinternet.com.

PYTCHES, Rt Rev. (George Edward) David; Vicar of St Andrew's, Chorleywood, Rickmansworth, 1977–96; *b* 9 Jan. 1931; 9th *c* and 6th *s* of late Rev. Thomas Arthur Pytches and late Eirene Mildred Pytches (*née* Welldon); *m* 1958, Mary Trevisick; four *d*. *Educ:* Old Buckenham Hall, Norfolk; Framlingham Coll., Suffolk; Univ. of Bristol (BA); Trinity Coll., Bristol; MPhil Nottingham, 1984. Deacon 1955, priest 1956; Asst Curate, St Ebbe's, Oxford, 1955–58; Asst Curate, Holy Trinity, Wallington, 1958–59; Missionary Priest in Chol Chol, Chile, 1959–62; in Valparaiso, Chile, 1962–68; Rural Dean, Valparaiso, 1966–70; Asst Bishop, 1970–72, Vicar General, 1971–72, Bishop, 1972–77, Dio. of Chile, Bolivia and Peru. Co-ordinator, Fellowship of Ind. Anglican Churches, 1992–; Founding Director, New Wine Family Conf., 1989–2000 (Trustee, 1999–); Founding Sponsor, and Trustee, Soul Survivor Youth Confs, 1993–2004; Co-ordinating Dir, Lakeside Family Conf., 1994–99. Dir, Kingdom Power Trust, 1987–2007. *Publications:* (contrib.) Bishop's Move, 1977; Come Holy Spirit, 1985; (contrib.) Riding the Third Wave, 1987; Does God Speak Today?, 1989; Some Said It Thundered, 1990; (jtly) New Wineskins, 1991; (contrib.) Planting New Churches, 1992; Prophecy in the Local Church, 1993; (contrib.) Recovering the Ground, 1995; (contrib.) Meeting John Wimber, 1996; (ed) John Wimber: his influence and legacy, 1998; Leadership for New Life, 1998; (ed) Burying the Bishop, 1999; (ed) Four Funerals and a Wedding, 1999; (ed) Out of the Mouths of Babes, 1999; Family Matters, 2002; Church Matters, 2002; Living at the Edge, 2002; (contrib.) Setting the Church of England Free, 2003; Can Anyone Be a Leader?, 2004; Upside Down Kingdom, 2007; If You Think My Preaching's Bad, Try My Jokes, 2008; What They Say About Prayer, 2011; The Way They Pray, 2015. *Recreations:* reading, travelling, enjoying twelve grandchildren. *Address:* 5 Churleswood Court, Shire Lane, Chorleywood, Rickmansworth, Herts WD3 5NH. *T:* (01923) 283763. *E:* pytches@btinternet.com.

Q

QADIR, Catherine Anne; *see* Stephens, C. A.

QESKU, Pavli; Ambassador of the Republic of Albania to the Court of St James's, 1993–97; writer of English-Albanian and Albanian-English dictionaries, since 1999; *b* 16 June 1943; *s* of Mihal and Vasilika Qesku; *m* 1973, Lidia Daka; one *s* one *d*. *Educ:* Tirana State Univ. (English Language). Translator at State publishing house, 1968; English teaching, 1975; translator and editor at publishing house, 1978; Ministry of Foreign Affairs, 1993. *Recreations:* reading, writing, music.

QUADEN, Prof. Guy, PhD; Governor, National Bank of Belgium, 1999–2011 (Director, 1988–99); Member, Governing Council and General Council, European Central Bank, 1999–2011; *b* 5 Aug. 1945; *m* Brigitte Tilman; two *s*. *Educ:* Univ. of Liège (grad. Econ 1967; PhD Econ 1973); La Sorbonne (grad. Econ and Soc. Scis 1972). University of Liège: First Asst, 1974–76; Lectr, 1977; Prof. in Economic Policy, 1978–88; Special Prof., 1988–. Mem. Bd Dirs, BIS, 1994–; Alternate Governor: IDA, 1994–2011; IBRD, 1999–2011; IFC, 1999–2011; Governor, IMF, 1999–2011. Member: Conseil supérieur des Finances; Institut des Comptes nationaux. Officier: Ordre de Léopold (Belgium), 1987; Légion d'Honneur (France), 2001. *Publications:* Le budget de l'Etat belge, 1980; La crise de finances publiques, 1984; L'économie belge dans la crise, 1987; Politique économique, 1985, 2nd edn 1991. *Recreations:* football, music, literature. *Address:* c/o National Bank of Belgium, Boulevard de Berlaimont 14, 1000 Brussels, Belgium.

QUAH, Prof. Danny, PhD; Professor of Economics, since 1996, Kuwait Professor, since 2012, Director, Kuwait Research Programme, since 2013, and Professor of Economics and International Development, since 2013, London School of Economics and Political Science (Co-Director, Global Governance, 2010–11); *b* Penang, Malaysia, 1958; *s* of Chong-eng Quah and Phaik-im Goh; two *s*. *Educ:* Princeton Univ. (AB 1980); Harvard Univ. (PhD Econs 1986). Asst Prof., Econs Dept, MIT, 1986–91; Lectr, then Reader in Econs, LSE, 1991–95. *Publications:* (ed) Oxford Handbook of Information and Communication Technologies, 2007; articles in Amer. Econ. Rev., Econometrica, Jl of Pol Economy, Econ. Jl, European Econ. Rev., Jl of Econ. Growth, Scandinavian Jl of Econs, Jl of Monetary Econs, etc. *Recreations:* Taekwon-do, running, videogaming. *Address:* Economics Department, London School of Economics and Political Science, Houghton Street, WC2A 2AE. *T:* (020) 7955 7535, *Fax:* (020) 7955 6592. *E:* d.quah@lse.ac.uk.

QUANT, Dame Mary, (Dame Mary Plunket Greene), DBE 2015 (OBE 1966); RDI 1969; Director, 1955–2000, Co-Chairman, 1991–2000, Mary Quant Group of companies; *b* 11 Feb. 1934; *d* of Jack and Mildred Quant; *m* 1957, Alexander Plunket Greene (*d* 1990); one *s*. *Educ:* Goldsmiths' College of Art (Hon. Fellow, 1993). Fashion designer. Founded Mary Quant Cosmetics, 1966. Mem., Design Council, 1971–74. Member: British/USA Bicentennial Liaison Cttee, 1973; Adv. Council, V&A Museum, 1976–78. Non-exec. Dir, House of Fraser, 1997–. Exhibition, Mary Quant's London, London Museum, 1973–74. FCSD (FSIA 1967); Sen. FRCA 1991; FRSA 1996. Hon. Dr Wales; hon. degree, Winchester Sch. of Art, 2000. Maison Blanche Rex Award (US), 1964; Sunday Times Internat. Award, 1964; Piavola d'Oro Award (Italy), 1966; Annual Design Medal, Inst. of Industrial Artists and Designers, 1966; Hall of Fame Award, British Fashion Council, 1990. *Publications:* Quant by Quant, 1966; Colour by Quant, 1984; Quant on Make-up, 1986; Classic Make-up and Beauty Book, 1996; Mary Quant: my autobiography, 2012.

QUANTRILL, William Ernest; HM Diplomatic Service, retired; Ambassador to the Republic of Cameroon, and concurrently to the Central African Republic, Equatorial Guinea and the Republic of Chad, 1991–95; *b* 4 May 1939; *s* of late Ronald Frederick Quantrill and Norah Elsie Quantrill (*née* Matthews); *m* 1964, Rowena Mary Collins; three *s* one *d*. *Educ:* Colston's Sch., Bristol; Hatfield Coll., Univ. of Durham (BA Hons French). Entered FO, 1962; served Brussels, Havana, Manila, Lagos, 1964–80; Head of Training Dept, FCO, 1980–81; Dep. Head of Personnel Ops Dept, FCO, 1981–84; Counsellor and Hd of Chancery, Caracas, 1984–88; Dep. Gov., Gibraltar, 1988–90. *Recreations:* wild life, travel. *Address:* Tor House, 36 Newtown, Bradford-on-Avon, Wilts BA15 1NF. *T:* (01225) 866245.

QUARMBY, David Anthony, CBE 2003; MA, PhD; FCILT, FCIHT; consultant in transport, planning, tourism and economics, since 2006; Chairman: RAC Foundation, 2009–13; Strategic Rail Authority, 2004–06 (Deputy Chairman, 2002–04); *b* 22 July 1941; *s* of Frank Reginald and Dorothy Margaret Quarmby; *m* 1968, Hilmary Hunter; four *d*. *Educ:* Shrewsbury Sch.; King's Coll., Cambridge (MA); Leeds Univ. (PhD, Dip. Industrial Management). Asst Lectr, then Lectr, Dept of Management Studies, Leeds Univ., 1963; Economic Adviser, Economic Planning Directorate, Min. of Transport, 1966; London Transport Executive: Dir of Operational Research, 1970; Chief Commercial and Planning Officer, 1974; Mem., 1975–84; Man. Dir (Buses), 1978–84; Mem., London Regional Transport, 1984; Director: Homebase Ltd, 1987–89; Shaw's Supermarkets Inc., 1987–92; Jt Man. Dir, J. Sainsbury plc, 1988–96 (Dir, 1984–96). Chairman: English Tourist Bd, 1996–99; S London Business Leadership Ltd, 1996–99; British Tourist Authy, 1996–2003; Docklands Light Railway Ltd, 1999–2001 (Dir, 1998–2001); SeaBritain 2005 Steering Gp, Nat. Maritime Mus., 2003–05; English Tourism Intelligence Partnership, 2008–11; Winter Resilience Rev., DfT, 2010; Motorists' Forum, DfT, 2011–12; Transport Adv. Gp, Royal Borough of Greenwich, 2013–; Freight Adv. Gp, Canal and River Trust, 2012–; Dep. Chm., S London Econ. Develt Alliance, 1999–2003; Director: New Millennium Experience Co. Ltd, 1997–2001 (Chm., May–Sept. 2000; Dep. Chm., 2000–01); London First, 1998–2002; BRB (Shadow Strategic Rail Authy), 1999–2001; Abellio Gp (formerly Ned Railways Ltd), 2007–11; Colin Buchanan & Partners Ltd, 2007–08; Member: RAC Public Policy Cttee, 1996–; Panel 2000, 1999–2002; London Sustainable Develt Commn, 2002–03; Ind. Transport Commn, 2007–10 (Chm., 2007–10); Greenwich Waterfront Regeneration Agency, 2008–11; Woolwich Regeneration Agency, 2011–14; Expert Adv. Panel, Airports Commn, 2013–; Project Dir, Major Roads for the Future, Rees Jeffreys Road Fund, 2014–. Chm., Retail Action Gp for Crime Prevention, Home Office, 1995–96; Mem., Crime Prevention Agency Bd, Home Office, 1995–97; non-exec. Dir, Dept of Transport Central Mgt Bd, 1996–97, DETR Bd, 1997–98; Mem. Bd, Transport for London, 2000–04 (Ministerial Advr, 1999–2000). Mem. Bd, Elderhostel Inc., 2006–09. Vice-President: Bus and Coach Council, 1981–84; CIT, 1987–91; Mem., Nat. Council, Freight Transport Assoc., 1985–88; Pres., Commercial Boat Operators Assoc., 2015–. Chm., Transport Res. Inst., Edinburgh Napier (formerly Napier) Univ., 2006–11. Member: London Educn Business Partnership, 1988–92; Sch. Curriculum and Assessment Authy, 1993–95; Southwark Diocesan Bd of Finance, 1982–85; London Adv. Bd, Salvation Army, 1982–87; Mem., Friends' Council, 2004–07, Trustee, 2005–13, Nat. Maritime Mus.; Trustee, St Paul's Cathedral Foundn, 2005–07; Mem., A12 Commn of Inquiry, 2008. Dir, and Chm. Develt Cttee, Blackheath Concert Halls, 1990–94. Gov., 1987–98 (Chm., 1995–98), Chm., Finance Cttee, 1991–95, James Allen's Girls' Sch., London; Mem. Ct, Greenwich Univ., 2000–08. Pres., Inst. of Logistics, 1996–99. CompOR; FTS 1997; FRSA 2006. Hon. DSc Huddersfield, 1999; Hon. DEng Napier, 2008. *Publications:* Factors Affecting Commuter Travel Behaviour (PhD Thesis, Leeds), 1967; contribs to Jl of Transport Economics and Policy, Regional Studies, Enterprise Management, Transport Times, and to other journals and books on transport, distribution, tourism, economics and operational research. *Recreations:* music, singing, walking, photography, family life. *Address:* 13 Shooters Hill Road, Blackheath, SE3 7AR.

QUARME, Giles Thomas, RIBA; Principal, Giles Quarme & Associates, since 1989; *b* Chelsea, London, 19 June 1951; *s* of Philip Anthony Thomas and Wendy Kathlene Quarme; *m* 1986, Margaret Henrietta Augusta Casely-Hayford, *qv*; one *d*. *Educ:* Marlborough Coll.; Univ. of East Anglia (BA Hons Art Hist. 1973); Univ. of Westminster (BA Hons Architecture 1976; DipArch 1979); Architectural Association (DipCons 1984). RIBA 1980. Sole practitioner in association with John Dickinson, RIBA, 1979–82; Co-Founder, Dickinson, Quarme & Associates, 1982–89. Surveyor of the Fabric, RNC, Greenwich, 1996–2009; Historic Bldg Advr to Foster & Partners on British Mus. Millennium proj., 1997. Projects include: restoration of Royal Victoria Patriotic Bldg Complex, Wandsworth, 1988 (Europa Nostra Award, 1988); restoration of High Comr of India's residence, London, 1995; restoration of 14 & 18 St Leonards Terrace, London, 1995; restoration of 49 Thames Street, Sunbury-on-Thames, 1996 (Spelthorne Design Award, 1996); Princess Diana Mus., Althorp Park, 1997; Queen Anne Court, RNC, Greenwich, 2000 (Civic Trust Award); Althorp House (RICS Award); Bentley Priory Battle of Britain Mus. Chm. Trustees, Ancient Monuments Soc., 2000– (Mem. Council, 1993–); Member: Adv. Cttee, 1991–92, Cttee, 1992, Save Britain's Heritage; British Acad. of Experts, 1993–; Exec. Council, ICOMOS UK, 1993–99; London Adv. Cttee, English Heritage, 1999–2014; Exec. Council, Georgian Gp, 1999–. FRSA 1986; Fellow, Royal Asiatic Soc., 1996. Freeman, Co. of Chartered Architects, 1994–. *Publications:* articles in ASCHB Transactions. *Recreations:* trying to understand historic events, analysing old buildings, walking on Exmoor. *Address:* 36 Smith Street, Chelsea, SW3 4EP. *T:* (020) 7582 0748; Giles Quarme & Associates, 7 Bishops Terrace, SE11 4UE. *E:* mail@quarme.com.

QUARME, Margaret Henrietta Augusta; *see* Casely-Hayford, M. H. A.

QUARREN EVANS, His Honour (John) Kerry; a Circuit Judge, on South Eastern circuit, 1980–95; *b* 4 July 1926; *s* of Hubert Royston Quarren Evans, MC and Violet Soule Quarren Evans (*née* George); *m* 1958, Janet Shaw Lawson; one *s* one *d*. *Educ:* King Henry VIII Sch., Coventry; Cardiff High Sch.; Trinity Hall, Cambridge, 1948–51 (MA, LLM). 21st Glam. (Cardiff) Bn Home Guard, 1943–44; enlisted, Grenadier Gds, 1944; commnd Royal Welch Fusiliers, 1946, from OTS Bangalore; attd 2nd Bn The Welch Regt, Burma, 1946–47; Captain 1947. Admitted solicitor, 1953; Partner: Lyndon Moore & Co., Newport, 1954–71; T. S. Edwards & Son, Newport, 1971–80; Recorder, Wales and Chester Circuit, 1974–80. Clerk to Gen. Comrs of Income Tax, Dinas Powis Div., 1960–80; Chm., Newport Nat. Insurance Local Tribunal, 1968–71. *Recreations:* golf, Rugby football, oenology, staurologosophy, old things. *Address:* Coddleston, 8 Russett Hill, Gerrards Cross, Bucks SL9 8JY. *T:* (01753) 880819. *Clubs:* Arkaves (Cardiff); Woodpeckers, Denham Golf, Royal Porthcawl Golf, Crawshay's Welsh Rugby Football.

QUARTA, Roberto; Partner, Clayton, Dubilier & Rice, since 2001; Chairman: Smith & Nephew plc, since 2014; WPP Group, since 2015; *b* 10 May 1949; *m*; one *s* one *d*. *Educ:* Italy and USA; Coll. of the Holy Cross, Mass, USA (BA 1971). Management Trainee, David Gessner, 1971–73; Worcester Controls Corp., 1973–78: Manager, Purchasing and Production Control; Vice-Pres., Internat. Procurement; BTR plc, 1979–85: Manufacturing Dir, Worcester Controls Corp.; Man. Dir, Worcester Controls UK; Group Man. Dir, Valves Group; Chief Exec., Hitchiner Manufacturing Corp., 1985–89; a Chief Divl Exec., BTR, 1989–93 (Dir, Main Bd, 1993); BBA Group plc: Dir, 1993–2007; Chief Exec., 1993–2000; Chm., 2000–07. Non-executive Director: PowerGen, 1996–2001; Equant NV, 2000–05; Azure Dynamics Corp., 2004–07; BAE Systems plc, 2005–11; Foster Wheeler AG, 2011–; Spie SA, 2011–; Smith & Nephew plc, 2013–; Chm., IMI plc, 2011–15; Chm., Supervisory Bd, Rexel SA, 2007–. Former Trustee, Coll. of the Holy Cross. *Recreations:* aviation, music. *Address:* CD&R LLP, Cleveland House, 33 King Street, SW1Y 6RJ.

QUARTANO, Ralph Nicholas, CBE 1987; Chairman, PosTel Investment Management Ltd, 1987–91 (Chief Executive, 1983–87); *b* 3 Aug. 1927; *s* of late Charles and Vivienne Mary Quartano; *m* 1st, 1954, Cornelia Johanna de Gunst (*d* 1996); two *d*; 2nd, 2006, Kathryn Margaret Brown. *Educ:* Sherborne Sch.; Pembroke Coll., Cambridge (MA). Bataafsche Petroleum Mij, 1952–58; The Lummus Co., 1958–59; Temple Press, 1959–65; Man. Director: Heywood Temple Industrial Publications, 1965–68; Engineering Chemical and Marine Press, 1968–70. The Post Office, 1971–74; Sen. Dir, Central Finance, 1973–74; Chief Exec., Post Office Staff Superannuation Fund, 1974–83. Dir, 1985–93, Dep. Chm., 1987–93, SIB. Director: London American Energy NV, 1981–88; Britoil plc, 1982–88; 3i Group plc (formerly Investors in Industry), 1986–97; John Lewis Partnership Pensions Trust, 1986–89; Clerical Medical Investment Group, 1987–98; Booker plc, 1988–98; British Maritime Technology Ltd, 1988–97 (Chm., 1995–97); Heitman Financial LLC, 1991–2000; Laird Group, 1991–98; Enterprise Oil, 1991–97; Lyonnaise Pension Trustees Ltd, 1994–2005; Chm., Murray Emerging Economies Trust plc, 1994–98. Member: Engrg Council, 1981–83; City Capital Markets Cttee, 1985–93; Investment Cttee, Pensioen Fonds PGGM, Netherlands, 1986–98; Investment Cttee, KPN (formerly PTT) Pensioen, Netherlands, 1988–98; Financial Reporting Council, 1990–93. City Advr to Dir-Gen., CBI, 1985–93. Sloan Fellow of London Business School. Gov., BUPA, 1987–98. Mem.

Council, 1993–99, and Treas., 1994–99, RSA. Trustee, Monteverdi Trust, 1986–93. *Address:* 20 Oakcroft Road, SE13 7ED. *T:* (020) 8852 1607. *Clubs:* Athenæum; Anagnostiki Etairia (Corfu).

QUAYLE, James Danforth, (Dan), JD; Chairman, Cerberus Global Investments, LLC, New York, since 2000; Vice-President of the United States of America, 1989–93; *b* 4 Feb. 1947; *m* 1972, Marilyn Tucker; two *s* one *d.* *Educ:* DePauw Univ. (BS 1969); Indiana Univ. (JD 1974). Admitted to Indiana Bar, 1974. Journalist, 1965–69, Associate Publisher and Gen. Manager, 1974–76, Huntington Herald Press; Investigator, Consumer Protection Div., Office of the Attorney General, Indiana, 1970–71; Admin. Assistant to Gov. of Indiana, 1971–73; Dir, Inheritance Tax Div., Indiana, 1973–74; Professor of Business Law, Huntington Coll., 1975. Mem. of Congress, 1976–80; Mem. for Indiana, US Senate, 1981–88. Chm., Circle Investors, Inc., 1993–. Vis. Prof., Thunderbird Internat. Business Sch., 1997–99. *Publications:* Standing Firm, 1994; The American Family, 1996; Worth Fighting For, 1999. *Address:* 7001 North Scottsdale Road, Suite 2010, Scottsdale, AZ 85253, USA.

QUAYLE, Quinton Mark; HM Diplomatic Service, retired; Hon. Chairman, International Beverages Holdings Ltd, since 2011; *b* 5 June 1955; *s* of Eric Stanley Quayle and late Elizabeth Jean (*née* Thorne); *m* 1979, Alison Marshall; two *s.* *Educ:* Humphry Davy GS; Bristol Univ. (BA). Entered HM Diplomatic Service, 1977; Third, later Second Sec., Bangkok, 1979–82; FCO, 1983–86; Ecole Nat. d'Admin, Paris, 1986–87; First Sec., Paris, 1987–91; FCO, 1991–93; on secondment to Price Waterhouse Management Consultants, 1993–94; Dir, Jt Export Promotion Directorate, FCO, 1994–96; Counsellor, Consul-Gen. and Dep. Hd of Mission, Jakarta, 1996–99; Internat. Gp Dir, Trade Partners UK, British Trade Internat., 1999–2002; Ambassador: to Romania, 2002–06; to Thailand, 2007–10. *Recreation:* book collecting.

QUEBEC, Bishop of, since 2009; **Rt Rev. Dennis Paul Drainville;** *b* Joliette, Quebec, 20 Feb. 1954; *s* of Gabriel Joseph Drainville and Dorothy May Drainville (*née* Griffin); *m* 1995, Cynthia Ann Patterson; one *d.* *Educ:* E York Collegiate Inst., Toronto; Trinity Coll., Univ. of Toronto (BA 1978; MDiv 1982). Ordained deacon, 1982, priest, 1983; Parish Priest, Land O' Lakes, Ontario, 1982–84; Exec. Dir, STOP 103 Ministry to the Poor, Toronto, 1984; Associate Priest, Christ Church Cathedral, Montreal, 1986; Incumbent, Fenelon Falls and Coboconk, Toronto, 1987–90; Regl Dean, Victoria-Haliburton, 1989; elected to Provincial Parlt, 1990–93; Teacher, CEGEP de la Gaspésie et des Isles, Gaspé, 1994–2006; Archdeacon of Gaspé and Incumbent, Greater Parish of Gaspé, 2002–06; Missioner to Dio. of Quebec, 2006–07; Coadjutor Bishop, 2007. Hon. DD: Montreal Diocesan Theol Coll., 2010; Trinity Coll., Univ. of Toronto, 2015. 125th Anniv. of Confedn of Canada Medal, 1992. *Publications:* Poverty in Canada, 1985. *Recreations:* medieval studies, music. *Address:* 31 rue des Jardins, Quebec City, QC G1R 4L6, Canada. *T:* (418) 6923858, *Fax:* (418) 6923876. *E:* bishopqc@quebec.anglican.ca.

QUEENSBERRY, 12th Marquess of, *cr* 1682; **David Harrington Angus Douglas;** Viscount Drumlanrig and Baron Douglas, 1628; Earl of Queensberry, 1633; Bt (Nova Scotia), 1668; late Royal Horse Guards; Professor of Ceramics, Royal College of Art, 1959–83; Partner, Queensberry Hunt design group; *b* 19 Dec. 1929; *s* of 11th Marquess of Queensberry and late Cathleen Mann; *S* father, 1954; *m* 1st, 1956, Mrs Ann Radford; two *d*; 2nd, 1969, Alexandra (marr. diss. 1986), *d* of Guy Wyndham Sich; two *s* one *d* (and one *s* decd); 3rd, 2000, Hsueh-Chun Liao; one *d.* *Educ:* Eton. Dir, Highland Stoneware. Pres., Design and Industries Assoc., 1976–78. Trustee, Paolozzi Foundn. Sen. FRCA, 1990. Hon. DDes Staffordshire, 1993. *Heir:* *s* Viscount Drumlanrig, *qv.*

QUEENSLAND, Metropolitan of; *see* Brisbane, Archbishop of.

QUEENSLAND, NORTH, Bishop of, since 2007; **Rt Rev. William James Ray;** *b* Yarram, Vic, 19 Oct. 1950; *s* of Vernon Henry Ray and Violet June Colbert; *m* 1978, Robin Adele, *d* of Rees William Llewellyn and Beryl Allison Koeteveld; one *s* one *d.* *Educ:* Yarram High Sch.; Frankston Teachers' Coll. (Teaching Dip.); Western Australian Coll. of Educn (BEd); Australian Coll. of Theology (ThL); Duke Univ., USA (MRE). Teacher, Stradbroke Primary Sch., 1973–75; Headteacher, Seaspray Primary Sch., 1976–77; Youth Officer, Dio. of Brisbane, 1978–81; Youth and Children's Officer, St Luke's, Toowoomba, 1981–83, 1986–87; Educn Officer, Dio. of Gippsland, 1987–91; Ministry Trng Officer, Dio. of Rockhampton, 1991–96; ordained priest, 1992; Rector, St Luke's, Wandal, 1996–99; Dir Gen., Bd of Religious Educn, 2000–01 (Mem., 1974–97); Vicar: St George's, E Ivanhoe, 2001–03; St John the Divine, Croydon, 2003–07; Archdeacon of Maroondah, Melbourne, 2004–07. Chair, Diocesan Catechumenate Working Gp, 2002–; Mem., Archbishop in CI Exec., 2004–. CI Crescent Lagoon Sch., 1980–; Mem., Australian Coll. of Educn; Founding Mem., Academic Bd, Inst. of Theol. Educn, 1993–97; Trainer, Australian Educn for Ministry, 2005–07. Chaplain, Scouting Assoc., 1977–99. *Recreations:* walking, bushwalking, reading biographies and newspapers, cycling, movies, cooking. *Address:* PO Box 1244, Townsville, Qld 4810, Australia.

QUELCH, Prof. John Anthony, CBE 2011; DBA; Charles Edward Wilson Professor of Business Administration, Harvard Business School, and Professor in Health Policy and Management, Harvard School of Public Health, since 2013; *b* 8 Aug. 1951; *s* of late Norman Quelch and Laura Sally (*née* Jones); *m* 1978, Joyce Ann Huntley. *Educ:* Norwich Sch.; Exeter Coll., Oxford (BA 1972; Hon. Fellow, 2002); Wharton Sch., Univ. of Pennsylvania (MBA 1974); Harvard Univ. (DBA 1977; SM 1978). Asst Prof. of Business Admin, Univ. of Western Ontario, 1977–79; Harvard Business School: Asst Prof. of Business Admin, 1979–84, Associate Prof., 1984–88, Prof., 1988–93; Sebastian S. Kresge Prof. of Marketing, 1993–98; Dean and Prof. of Mktg, London Business Sch., 1998–2001; Sen. Associate Dean and Lincoln Filene Prof. of Business Admin, Harvard Business Sch., 2001–11; Dean, Vice Pres. and Distinguished Prof. of Internat. Mgt, China Europe Internat. Business Sch., Shanghai, 2011–13. La Caixa Vis. Prof. of Internat. Mgt and Chm., Academic Adv. Council, China Europe Internat. Business Sch., 2009. Chm., Massachusetts Port Authy, 2002–11. Non-executive Director: Reebok Internat. Ltd, 1985–97; European Communication Mgt Ltd, 1988–97; WPP Gp plc, 1988–2013; US Office Products Co., 1995–97; Pentland Gp plc, 1997–99; Blue Circle Industries plc, 2000–01; easyJet plc, 2000–03; Loyalty Management UK Ltd, 2003–06; Alere Inc., 2003–; Pepsi Bottling Gp, 2005–09; Gentiva Health Services, 2006–09; Epiphany Biosciences, 2007–09; BBC Worldwide Americas, 2007–10; Datalogix, 2014–15; Luvo, 2015–. Mem. Adv. Bd, PricewaterhouseCoopers Corporate Finance, 2002–03. Director: Council of Better Business Bureaux, 1995–97; Graduate Mgt Admissions Council, 1999–2001; Accion Internat., 2003–06; Member: Council on Foreign Relns, 2009–; Trilateral Commn, 2012–. Mem., Internat. Adv. Bd, British Amer. Business Council (formerly British Amer. Business Inc.), 2001–; Mem., Adv. Bd, AT Kearney Global Policy Council, 2002–06; Dir, Americans For Oxford, 2006–11. Hon. Chm., British Amer. Business Council of New England, 2008–11. Hon. Consul Gen. of Morocco in New England, 2004–. CCMI (CIMgt 1998). FRSA 1998; FRGS 2009. Hon. Fellow, London Business Sch., 2008; Hon. PhD Vietnam National, 2011. *Publications:* (jtly) Advertising and Promotion Management, 1983; (jtly) Cases in Advertising and Promotion Management, 1983, 4th edn 1996; (jtly) Marketing Management, 1985, 2nd edn 1993; (jtly) Global Marketing Management, 1988, 5th edn 2005; How to Market to Consumers, 1989; Sales Promotion Management, 1989; (jtly) The Marketing Challenge of Europe 1992, 1990, 2nd edn 1991; (jtly) Ethics in Marketing, 1992; (jtly) Cases in Product Management, 1995; (jtly) Cases in Marketing Management and Strategy, 1996; (jtly) Cases in European Marketing Management, 1997; (jtly) Cases in Strategic Marketing Management: business strategies in Latin America, 2001; Business Strategies in Muslim Countries, 2001; (jtly) Marketing Management, 2004; (jtly) Problems and Cases in Health Care Marketing, 2004; (jtly) The Global Market, 2005; (jtly) The New Global Brands, 2006; (jtly) Business Solutions for the Global Poor, 2007; Readings in Modern Marketing, 2007; (jtly) Greater Good: how good marketing makes for better democracy, 2008; (jtly) All Business Is Local: why place matters more than ever in a global, virtual world, 2011; contribs to learned and professional jls. *Recreations:* squash, tennis. *Address:* Harvard Business School, Bloomberg 355, Soldiers Field, Boston, MA 02163, USA. *T:* (617) 4956325, *Fax:* (617) 4963564. *Clubs:* Brooks's, Harvard (Boston).

QUENTIN, Caroline; actress; *b* 11 July 1960; *d* of Frederick and Katie Emily Jones; adopted stage name of Quentin; *m* 1991, Paul James Martin, *qv* (marr. diss. 1999); *m* 2006, Sam Farmer; one *s* one *d.* *Educ:* Arts Educnl, Tring Park. *Theatre includes:* The Seagull, tour; Roots, RNT; Our Country's Good, Garrick; Low Level Panic, Sugar and Spice, Royal Court; Les Miserables, Barbican, transf. Palace; An Evening with Gary Lineker; A Game of Love and Chance, RNT; Les Enfants du Paradis, tour; Lysistrata; Mirandolina, Lyric, Hammersmith; The Live Bed Show, Garrick, 1994; The London Cuckolds, RNT, 1998; Life After Scandal, Hampstead, 2007; Pippin, Menier Chocolate Factory, 2012; Relative Values, Th. Royal, Bath, 2013, transf. Harold Pinter Th., 2014; Oh What a Lovely War, Th. Royal, Stratford E, 2014; The Life and Times of Fanny Hill, Bristol Old Vic, 2015; dir, Dead Funny, Palace, Watford, 1998. *Television includes:* series: Don't Tell Father, 1992; Men Behaving Badly, 1992–97; Jonathan Creek, 1997–2002; Kiss Me Kate, 1998–2002; The Innocent, 2001; Blue Murder, 2003–09; Life Begins, 2004–06; Von Trapped, 2004; Life of Riley, 2009; *film:* An Evening with Gary Lineker, 1994. *Recreation:* bird-watching. *Address:* c/o Amanda Howard Associates, 74 Clerkenwell Road, EC1M 5QA.

QUEST, David Charles; QC 2013; *b* Manchester, 1 June 1971; *s* of Barry Quest and Janet Quest; *m* 2004, Paula; two *s* one *d.* *Educ:* Manchester Grammar Sch.; Trinity Coll., Cambridge (BA 1991). Called to the Bar, Gray's Inn, 1993. *Address:* 3 Verulam Buildings, Gray's Inn, WC1R 5NT.

QUICK, Dorothy, (Mrs Charles Denis Scanlan); a District Judge (Magistrates' Courts) (formerly Metropolitan Stipendiary Magistrate), 1986–2010; *b* 10 Dec. 1944; *d* of Frederick and Doris Quick; *m* 1971, Charles Denis Scanlan; two *s.* *Educ:* Glanafan Grammar Sch., Port Talbot; University Coll. London (LLB). Called to the Bar, Inner Temple, 1969; barrister-at-law, 1969–86. Mem., British Acad. of Forensic Sciences, 1987–2010. *Recreations:* gardening, theatre, books. *Club:* Reform.

QUICK, Robert Frederick, QPM 2003; Chief Executive, BlueLight Global Solutions Ltd, since 2010; *b* London, 25 April 1959; *s* of Robert Edward Quick and Patricia Quick; *m* 2001, Judith Jane Clark; one *s* four *d.* *Educ:* Exeter Univ. (MBA with Dist.); Civil Service Coll. Top Managers Prog.; Police Staff Coll., Bramshill (Police Strategic Comd Course 2001); Univ. of Cambridge (Dip. Applied Criminol. 2001). Metropolitan Police Service: Constable, Lambeth, 1978–82; Detective Constable, Brixton, Lambeth, 1982–84; Sergeant, 1984–87, Detective Sergeant, 1987–90, Catford, Lewisham; Detective Inspector, Lambeth, 1990–92, Greenwich, 1994–95; Detective Chief Inspector, SE London Crime Squad, 1995–96, Croydon, 1996–97; SO to Asst Comr, 1997–98; Superintendent, Southwark, 1998–99; Detective Chief Superintendent, Anti-Corruption Comd, New Scotland Yard, 1999–2001; Comdr, New Scotland Yard, 2001–03; Dep. Chief Constable, 2003–04, Chief Constable, 2004–08, Surrey Police; Asst Comr, Specialist Ops, Metropolitan Police Service, 2008–09. Partner, RQC Solutions—Policing and Justice. MInstD 2001. *Recreations:* ski-ing, walking, motorcycling, collector of classic motorcycles and motorcars.

QUICKE, Rev. Michael John; C. W. Koller Professor of Preaching and Communication, Northern Seminary (formerly Northern Baptist Theological Seminary), Chicago, 2000–14, now Emeritus Professor of Preaching; *b* 30 July 1945; *s* of George and Joan Quicke; *m* 1968, Carol Bentall; two *s.* *Educ:* Jesus Coll., Cambridge (MA); Regent's Park Coll., Oxford (MA). Nat. Sec. for Student Work, Baptist Union, 1967–69; Minister: Leamington Road Baptist Church, Blackburn, 1972–80; St Andrew's Street Baptist Church, Cambridge, 1980–93; Principal, Spurgeon's Coll., 1993–2000. Interim Preacher, First Baptist Ch, Wheaton, Ill., 2000–02. Religious Advr, ITV, 1987–88. Mem. Council, Baptist Union of GB, 1976–2000; Vice Chm., Doctrine Commn, 1990–95, Mem., Worship Commn, 1995–2005, Mem., Church Leadership Commn, 2006–10, Baptist World Alliance. Member: Council of Mgt, Open Theol Coll., 1993–2000; Council, Evangelical Alliance, 1997–2000. Mem., Acad. of Homiletics, 1995–. Fellow, Coll. of Preachers, 1996 (Mem., Exec., 1996–2000). Hon. DD William Jewell Coll., Liberty, USA, 1994. *Publications:* Christian Apologetics, 1976; Something to Declare, 1996; On the Way of Trust, 1997; Doing Theology in a Baptist Way, 2000; 360 Degree Preaching, 2003; 360 Degree Leadership, 2006; Preaching as Worship, 2011. *Recreations:* listening to sermons, music, travel. *Address:* 14 Brierley Walk, Cambridge CB4 3NH.

QUIGLEY, Anthony Leslie Coupland, CEng, FIET; Tony Quigley Consulting, since 2001; *b* 14 July 1946; *s* of late Leslie Quigley and Vera Barbara Rodaway (*née* Martin); *m* 1968, Monica Dean; one *s* two *d.* *Educ:* Apsley Grammar Sch.; Queen Mary Coll., Univ. of London (BSc Eng). Command Control and Computer Divs, ASWE, 1967–81 (Exchange Scientist, US Naval Surface Weapons Center, 1976–79); Supt, Command and Control Div., 1981–84, Hd, Command, Control and Assessment Gp, 1984–87, RARDE; Dep. Head, Science and Technology Assessment Office, Cabinet Office, 1987–90; Dir, SDI Participation Office, 1990–93, Asst Chief Scientific Advr (Nuclear), 1993–95, MoD; Under Sec., OST, 1995–99 (on secondment); Dir Gen., Scrutiny and Analysis, MoD, 1999–2001. Member, Council: Foundn for Sci. and Technol., 2001–; Kent Univ., 2003– (Dep. Chm., 2012–). MInstD. *Publications:* technical papers on radar tracking and command and control. *Address:* 21 Yew Tree Road, Tunbridge Wells, Kent TN4 0BD.

QUIGLEY, Conor; QC 2003; *b* 21 Feb. 1958; *s* of Edmond Gerard Quigley and Kathleen Theresa Quigley (*née* Murphy). *Educ:* King's Coll. London (LLB); MA Oxon. Called to the Bar, Gray's Inn, 1985; in practice as barrister specialising in EU law, 1985–. Fellow, LMH, Oxford Univ., 1991–96. Chm., Bar European Gp, 1992–94. *Publications:* European Community Contract Law, 1997; EC State Aid Law and Policy, 2002, 2nd edn 2009. *Recreations:* history, wine, Europe. *Address:* Serle Court, 6 New Square, Lincoln's Inn, WC2A 3QS. *T:* (020) 7242 6105, *Fax:* (020) 7400 4005. *E:* cquigley@serlecourt.co.uk.

QUIGLEY, Rebecca; Chief Executive Officer, Stage Entertainment UK, since 2011; *b* London, 1 July 1969; *d* of Gerry Quigley and Diane Quigley; partner, 2001, Elliott Rae. *Educ:* Old Palace Sch., Croydon; Wimbledon Sch. of Art and Design, London; Guildhall Sch. of Music and Drama, London. Various positions, Pola Jones Assoc., 1995–2000; General Manager: Clear Channel, 2000–01; Tiger Aspect, 2001–03; Working Title Films, 2003–08; Exec. Producer, Stage Entertainment UK, 2008–11. *Recreations:* safari holidays, wildlife adventures, walking, film, socialising. *Address:* Stage Entertainment UK, Wellington House, 125 Strand, W2R 0AP. *T:* (020) 7632 4700. *E:* rebeccaquigley@seuk.uk.com.

QUILTER, Sir Guy Raymond Cuthbert, 5th Bt *cr* 1897, of Bawdsey Manor, Suffolk; *b* 13 April 1967; *o s* of Sir Anthony Raymond Leopold Cuthbert Quilter, 4th Bt and Mary Elise (*d* 2013), *er d* of late Colonel Brian (Sherlock) Gooch, DSO, TD; *S* father, 2014; *m* 1992, Jenifer Redvers-Cox; three *s.* *Heir:* *s* William Raymond Cuthbert Quilter, *b* 29 Nov. 1995.

QUIN, Baroness *cr* 2006 (Life Peer), of Gateshead in the County of Tyne and Wear; **Joyce Gwendolen Quin;** PC 1998; *b* 26 Nov. 1944; *d* of late Basil Godfrey Quin, MC and Ida (*née* Ritson); *m* 2010, Guy MacMullen. *Educ:* Univ. of Newcastle upon Tyne (BA French, 1st Cl. Hons); Univ. of London (MSc Internat. Relns). Research Asst, Internat. Dept, Labour Party Headquarters, Transport House, 1969–72; Lecturer in French, Univ. of Bath, 1972–76; Resident Tutor, St Mary's Coll., and Lectr in French and Politics, Univ. of Durham, 1977–79. Mem. (Lab) European Parliament, S Tyne and Wear, 1979–84, Tyne and Wear, 1984–89. MP (Lab) Gateshead E, 1987–97, Gateshead E and Washington W, 1997–2005. Opposition front bench spokesman on trade and industry, 1989–92, on employment, 1992–93, on European affairs, 1993–97; Minister of State: Home Office, 1997–98; (Minister for Europe), FCO, 1998–99, MAFF, 1999–2001; opposition spokesman on envmt, food and rural affairs, 2010–11. Member: Select Cttee on Treasury and Civil Service, 1987–89; EU Select Cttee, H of L, 2014– (Chm., EU Justice, Instns and Consumer Protection Sub-Cttee, 2014–); Chairman: Franco-British Parly Relns Cttee, 2001–05; Regl Govt Gp, PLP, 2001–05; Mem., Franco-British Council, 2001–13 (Chm., 2007–13). Vice Chairman: NE Constit. Convention, 2001–05; Franco-British Soc., 2013–. Vis. Prof., Centre for Urban and Regl Develt Studies, Newcastle upon Tyne Univ., 2001–; Vis. Parly Fellow, St Antony's Coll., Oxford, 2007–08. Pres., Northumbrian Pipers Soc., 2009–. Hon. Fellow: Sunderland Polytechnic, subseq. Univ. of Sunderland, 1986; St Mary's Coll., Durham Univ., 1994. Hon. Freeman, Bor. of Gateshead, 2006. Officier de la Légion d'Honneur (France), 2010. *Publications:* The British Constitution: continuity and change—an inside view, 2010; various articles in newspapers and journals. *Recreations:* North-East local history (Newcastle upon Tyne City Guide), music, theatre, walking, cycling. *Address:* House of Lords, SW1A 0PW.

QUIN, Jeremy Mark; MP (C) Horsham, since 2015; *b* Aylesbury, 24 Sept. 1968; *s* of Rev. David Quin and late Elizabeth Quin; *m* 2003, Joanna Healey. *Educ:* St Albans Sch.; Hertford Coll., Oxford (BA Hons Mod. Hist. 1990). Natwest Wood Mackenzie & Co. Ltd, 1990–99; BT Alex Brown, 1999–2000; a Man. Dir, Deutsche Bank, 2000–15. Mem., Work and Pensions Select Cttee, 2015–. Contested (C) Meirionnydd Nant Conwy, 1997. *Address:* House of Commons, SW1A 0AA. *E:* jeremy.quin.mp@parliament.uk.

QUINAN, Lloyd; Member (SNP) West Scotland, Scottish Parliament, 1999–2003; *b* 29 April 1957; *s* of Andrew and Ann Quinan. *Educ:* Queen Margaret Coll., Edinburgh. Actor, 1978–83; theatre dir, 1983–89; television presenter, producer and dir, 1989–99. Contested (SNP) Motherwell & Wishaw, Scottish Parlt, 2003. *Recreations:* reading, travel, music, football.

QUINCE, Will; MP (C) Colchester, since 2015; *b* Ascot; *s* of Nigel Anthony Quince and Jane Frances Quince; *m* 2009, Elinor Ann; one *d* (one *s* decd). *Educ:* Windsor Boys' Sch.; Univ. of Wales, Aberystwyth (LLB Hons Law); Univ. of West of England (DipLP 2012). Mkt Develt Exec., Concur Technologies Ltd, 2005–06; Customer Develt Manager, Britvic Soft Drinks plc, 2006–10; trainee solicitor, Asher Prior Bates, 2010–13; Solicitor, Thompson Smith and Puxon, 2013–15. Member (C): E Herts DC, 2007–08; Colchester BC, 2011–. *Address:* 66 Prettygate Road, Colchester, Essex CO3 4ED. *T:* 07944 098398. *E:* will.quince.mp@parliament.uk.

QUINEY, Charles Benedictus Alexander, (Ben); QC 2014; *b* London; *s* of Adrian Quiney and Indira Quiney; two *s*. *Educ:* Birkdale Sch., Sheffield; University Coll., Oxford (BA, BCL). Called to the Bar, Gray's Inn, 1998. *Address:* Crown Office Chambers, 2 Crown Office Row, Temple, EC4Y 7HJ.

QUINLAN, Rt Rev. (Alan) Geoffrey; a Bishop Suffragan, Diocese of Cape Town, 1988–98; now involved in spiritual direction, teaching, training and the conduct of retreats, quiet days, confirmations and preaching; *b* 20 Aug. 1933; *s* of late Robert Quinlan and Eileen Beatrice Quinlan; *m* 1963, Rosalind Arlen Sallie (*née* Reed); three *s* one *d*. *Educ:* Kelham Theological College. RAF, 1952–54. Deacon 1958, priest 1959; Asst Curate, St Thomas's, Leigh, Lancs, 1958–61; Rector: St Margaret's, Bloemfontein, 1962–68; St Michael and All Angels, Sasolburg, OFS, 1968–72; Warden, Community of Resurrection of Our Lord, Grahamstown and Chaplain, Grahamstown Training Coll., 1972–76; Priest-in-Charge of Training in Ministries and Discipleship, Cape Town Diocese, 1976–80; Rector, All Saints, Plumstead, Cape Town, 1980–88. Canon, St George's Cathedral, Cape Town, 1980–88. *Publications:* A Manual for Worship Leaders; Discipleship and the Alternative Society; Churchwardens' Handbook; My Personal Prayer Book, 2006. *Recreations:* chess, reading, computers, music, painting. *Address:* 132 Woodley Road, Plumstead, Cape Town, 7800, South Africa.

QUINLAN, Christopher John; QC 2011; a Recorder, since 2009; *b* Bristol, 1 Oct. 1968; *s* of Margaret Rew (formerly Quinlan, *née* Broe); *m* 1996, Julia Donaldson; one *s* one *d*. *Educ:* Henbury Sch., Bristol; Manchester Poly. (LLB Hons). Called to the Bar, Inner Temple, 1992, Bencher, 2015. Judicial Officer: RFU, 2004–; European Rugby Cup, 2007–; World Rugby (formerly Internat. Rugby Bd), 2007–; Legal Member: Nat. Anti-Doping Panel, 2008–; Nat. Safeguarding Panel, 2012–; Specialist Mem., FA Judicial Panel, 2008–; Legal Arbitrator, Sport Resolutions (UK) Panel of Arbitrators, 2006–. *Recreations:* Eloise and Thomas, Bristol RFC, Liverpool FC, sailing and gin. *Address:* Guildhall Chambers, 23 Broad Street, Bristol BS1 2HG. *T:* (0117) 930 9000, *Fax:* (0117) 930 3824. *E:* christopher.quinlan@guildhallchambers.co.uk; Farrar's Building, Temple, EC4Y 7BD.

QUINLAN, Rt Rev. Geoffrey; *see* Quinlan, Rt Rev. A. G.

QUINN, Aiden O'Brien; *see* Quinn, J. A. O'B.

QUINN, Andrea Helen, (Mrs R. Champ); conductor; Music Director and Chief Conductor, Symphony Orchestra of Norrlands Opera, Umeå, Sweden, 2005–09; *b* 22 Dec. 1964; *d* of Desmond Bone and Theresa Bone (*née* MacLaren) (who *m* 1971, John Quinn); *m* 1991, Dr Roderick Champ; one *s* two *d*. *Educ:* Nottingham Univ. (BA Hons); Royal Acad. of Music (Adv. Cert. in Conducting; ARAM 1999). Music Director: London Philharmonic Youth Orch., 1993–96; Royal Ballet, 1998–2001; NY City Ballet, 2001–06. Hon. FTCL 2000. *Recreations:* literature, endurance horse riding (member of Endurance GB and Arab Horse Soc.), animal husbandry, fine art. *Address:* Urishay Barn, Michaelchurch Escley, Herefordshire HR2 0LR. *T:* (01981) 510686. *E:* quinnchamp@gmail.com. *W:* www.andreaquinn.com.

QUINN, Brian, CBE 1996; Managing Director, Brian Quinn Consulting (formerly Brian Quinn Consultancy plc), since 1996; *b* 18 Nov. 1936; *s* of Thomas Quinn and Margaret (*née* Cairns); *m* 1961, Mary Bradley; two *s* one *d*. *Educ:* Glasgow Univ. (MA Hons); Manchester Univ. (MA Econs); Cornell Univ. (PhD). FCIBS 1995. Economist, African Dept, IMF, 1964–70, Rep., Sierra Leone, 1966–68; joined Bank of England, 1970: Economic Div., 1970–74; Chief Cashier's Dept, 1974–77; Head of Information Div., 1977–82; Asst Dir, 1982–88; Head of Banking Supervision, 1986–88; Exec. Dir, 1988–96; Acting Dep. Gov., 1995. Chairman: Nomura Bank Internat., 1996–99; Celtic plc, 2000–07 (non-exec. Dir, 1996–2000); Bvalco Ltd, 2011–. Non-executive Director: Bank Gesellschaft Berlin UK Ltd, 1996–2002; Britannic (formerly Britannia) Asset Mgt, 1998–2004; Sumitomo-Mitsui Banking Corp., 2000–02; Genworth Mortgage Insce Europe, 2005–10; Qatar Finance Centre Regulatory Authy, 2006–11. Chm., Financial Markets Gp, LSE, 1996–2000. Advr, Singapore Govt, 1997–2002; Consultant: World Bank, 1997–; IMF, 1997–; McKinsey and Co., 1998–; Mem. Bd of Dirs, Toronto Centre, 2008–10 (Mem. Adv. Bd, 1998–2010; Chm., Banking Adv. Bd, 2008–10). Mem., City Disputes Panel, 2003–. Mem., Investigatory Chamber, UEFA Club Financial Control Body (formerly Vice Pres., UEFA Club Financial Control Panel), 2009–. Glasgow University: Hon. Prof. of Econs and Finance, 2006–; Mem., Strategic Adv. Bd, Business Sch., 2011–. *Publications:* (contrib.) Surveys of African Economies, vol. 4, 1971; (contrib.) The New Inflation, 1976; articles in learned jls. *Recreations:* fishing, football, pilates. *Address:* 14 Homewood Road, St Albans, Herts AL1 4BH. *Club:* Reform.

QUINN, Brian; *see* Quinn, J. S. B.

QUINN, Carolyn; Presenter: PM programme, BBC Radio 4, since 2000; Westminster Hour, BBC Radio 4, since 2007; *b* 22 July 1961; *d* of late Edward James Quinn and of Maureen Quinn; *m* 2003, Nigel Paul Morris. *Educ:* St Joseph's RC Primary Sch., Crayford; Dartford Grammar Sch. for Girls; Kent Univ. (BA Hons French 1983); Inst. of Educn, Univ. of London (PGCE). Clerical worker, Charing Cross Hosp., London, 1984–85; Irish Post newspaper, London, 1985–86; trainee, BBC Radio, Local Radio Reporter Scheme, 1986–87; reporter/producer, BBC Radio Solent, 1987–89; BBC Westminster, covering Parlt and politics, 1989–; political corresp., BBC, 1994–2006; Presenter, Today prog., BBC Radio 4, 2004–08. *Recreations:* cycling, cinema, walking, jazz. *Address:* c/o BBC News Centre, Broadcasting House, Portland Place, W1A 1AA.

QUINN, Geoffrey; Chief Executive, T. M. Lewin, since 1993 (Director, since 1980); *b* Margate, 10 March 1959; *s* of Francis and Jennifer Quinn; *m* 1981, Janine Willis; one *s* two *d*. *Educ:* Hartsdown Comprehensive Sch., Westbrook, Kent. Salesman, Turnbull & Asser, 1976–80. *Recreations:* theatre, family, travel, Prince's Trust. *Address:* T. M. Lewin, 6–7 St Cross Street Courtyard, EC1N 8UA. *T:* (020) 7877 3500.

QUINN, Gregory; *see* Quinn, J. G.

QUINN, (James) Aiden O'Brien; QC (Seychelles) 1973; Vice-President, Immigration Appeal Tribunal, 1996–2004 (Adjudicator, 1990–93; Special Adjudicator, 1993–96); Member, Special Immigration Appeals Commission, 1998–2002; *b* 3 Jan. 1932; *s* of late William Patrick Quinn (Comr, Gárda Siochána) and Helen Mary (*née* Walshe); *m* 1960, Christel Tyner; two *s* one *d*. *Educ:* Presentation Coll., Bray, Co. Wicklow, Ireland; University Coll., Dublin, NUI (BA, LLB Hons). Called to the Bar: Kings' Inns, Dublin, 1957; Inner Temple, 1967. National City Bank, Dublin, 1949–53; in practice at the Bar, under Colonial Office Scheme, 1958–60; Crown Counsel and Actg Sen. Crown Counsel, Nyasaland, 1960–64; Asst Attorney Gen. and Actg Attorney Gen., West Cameroon, 1964–66; Procureur Général, West Cameroon, and Avocat Général, Fed. Republic of Cameroon, 1966–68; Fed. Republic of Cameroon, 1968–72: Conseiller, Cour Fédérale de Justice; Judge, W Cameroon Supreme Court; Conseiller Technique (Harmonisation des Lois), Ministère de la Justice, Yaoundé; Président, Tribunal Administratif, Cameroun Occidental; Chargé de Cours, Ecole Nationale de l'Administration et de la Magistrature, Yaoundé; Republic of Seychelles: Attorney Gen., also of British Indian Ocean Territory, 1972–76; MLC, MEC and Mem. Parlt, 1972–76; Chief Justice, 1976–77; Actg Dep. Governor, 1974; Mem., Official Delegn on Self-Govt, 1975, and on Independence Constitutions, 1976; collab. with Prof. A. G. Chloros on translation and up-dating of Code Napoleon, 1975–76; Chm., Judicial Service Commn, 1976–77; Gilbert Islands (Kiribati): Chief Justice, 1977–81; Chm., Judicial Service Commn, 1977–81; set up new Courts' system, 1978; Mem., Council of State, 1979–81; Judge, High Court of Solomon Is, 1977–79; Special Prosecutor, Falkland Is, 1981; Botswana: Chief Justice, 1981–87; Chm., Judicial Service Commn, 1981–87; retired, 1987–89; Investment Advr, 1989–90. Mem., Panel of Experts of UN on Prevention of Crime and Treatment of Offenders, 1985–87. Chevalier, Ordre de la Valeur, Republic of Cameroon, 1967; Kiribati Independence Medal, 1979. *Publications:* Magistrates' Courts Handbook: West Cameroon, 1968; Kiribati, 1979; compiled and edited: West Cameroon Law Reports, 1961–68; Gilbert Islands Law Reports, 1977–79; Kiribati Law Reports, 1977–80; articles in Commonwealth Law Jl, The Magistrate, etc. *Recreations:* languages, travel, reading, swimming. *Address:* 24 Deer Park Drive, Newport, Shropshire TF10 7HB. *Club:* Lansdowne.

QUINN, (James) Gregory; HM Diplomatic Service; High Commissioner to Guyana, and non-resident Ambassador to Suriname, since 2015; *b* Lurgan, NI, 16 June 1971; *s* of James Eric Quinn and Gwendoline Audrey Quinn; *m* 1995, Wendy Ann Dackombe. *Educ:* Univ. of Wales, Aberystwyth (BSc (Econ) Hons Internat. Politics and Internat. Hist. 1992); Open Univ. (MA Hist. 2008). Joined FCO, 1995; Res. Asst, then Asst Editor, Documents on British Policy Overseas, FCO Historians, 1995–98; Desk Officer for Estonia, Latvia and Lithuania, FCO, 1998–2000; Dep. Hd of Mission (temp. duty), Tallinn, 2000; Political, Press and Public Affairs Officer, Accra, 2000–03; Dep. Hd of Mission, Minsk, 2004–07; Iraq/Middle East Liaison Officer, Washington, seconded to State Dept, 2007–09; Hd, UN Political Team, FCO, 2009–12; Dep. Hd of Mission, Astana, 2012–14. *Recreations:* golf, Rugby, cricket, walking, avid reader of non-fiction (especially on World War 2 and aviation). *Address:* Foreign and Commonwealth Office, King Charles Street, SW1A 2AH. *T:* (020) 7008 1500. *E:* greg.quinn@fco.gov.uk.

QUINN, (James Steven) Brian; Director General, International Institute of Communications, 2003–09; Honorary Irish Consul for the Bahamas, 2011–14; *b* 16 June 1936; *s* of James and Elizabeth Quinn; *m* 1st, 1962, Blanche Cecilia James (marr. diss. 1987); two *s* one *d*; 2nd, 2004, Catherine Mann. *Educ:* St Mary's Coll., Crosby; Waterpark Coll., Ireland; University Coll., Dublin (BCL, LLB). Barrister-at-law, Kings Inn, Dublin. Director: Johnson Radley, 1966–68; United Glass Containers, 1968–69; Head of Industrial Activities, Prices and Incomes Board, 1969–71; Dir, M. L. H. Consultants, 1971–79; Corporate Develt Advr, Midland Bank Internat., 1977–80; Chief Industrial Advr, Price Commn, 1977–78; Man. Dir, Visnews, 1980–86; Digital Computer Services: Dir, 1985–96; Chief Exec., 1989–92; Chm., 1992–96. Chairman: BrightStar Communications, 1983–85; BAJ Holdings, 1985–87; Harmer Holbrook, 1987–88; Signet Online, 1996–99; Loan Line Ltd, 1997–2000; Central Equipment Hldgs Ltd, 2003–04; Director: Telematique Services, 1985–90; QM Security Ltd; IP Solutions Internat., Bahamas, 2009–13 (Dep. Chm., 2010–13). Telecom res. into cross border transmissions, TCD, 1995–97. Institute of Management (formerly British Institute of Management): CCMI (CBIM 1985; FBIM 1978); Mem. Council, 1981–87, 1990–98; Mem. Finance Cttee, 1981–84; Chm., City of London Branch, 1981–83; Vice Pres., 1983–90; Chm., Gtr London Regl Council, 1990–94. International Institute of Communications: Trustee, 1982–88, 1992–97; Chm., Exec. Cttee, 1984–88; Pres., 1988–91; Life Trustee, 2009. Mem., Exec. Cttee, Inst. of European Trade and Technology, 1983–96. Trustee: Internat. Center of Communications, San Diego State Univ., 1990–2006. Chm., Finance Cttee, Great Japan Exhibn, 1979–82. Chm., Editl Bd, Professional Manager, 1993–98. *Recreations:* golf, reading, veteran vehicles. *Address:* Hicks Grove House, Halls Green, Weston, Herts SG4 7DX. *Clubs:* Athenæum, Lansdowne; Royal Nassau Sailing.

QUINN, Jane Elisabeth, OBE 2014; Founding Partner, Public Relations Consultant and Director, Bolton & Quinn Ltd, since 1981; *b* 2 March 1949; *d* of Dr Francis Prime and Barbara Prime; *m* 1st, 1971, Stephen Quinn (marr. diss. 1998); three *s*; 2nd, 2000, Martin Duignan. *Educ:* Convent of the Sacred Heart, Tunbridge Wells; Queen's Coll., London. Media buyer, Ogilvy & Mather, 1969–70; PR Exec., Prime Associates, 1970–72; Publicity Exec., Riverside Studios, 1978–81. Dir, Michael Clark Co., 2005–. Director: Art Baby, 2003–; London Children's Mus., 2010–. *Address:* Bolton & Quinn Ltd, 6 Addison Avenue, W11 4QR.

QUINN, Lawrence William; Rail Projects Delivery Manager, Bechtel, since 2005; *b* 25 Dec. 1956; *s* of late Jimmy Quinn and Sheila Quinn; *m* 1982, Ann Eames. *Educ:* Pennine Way Schs, Carlisle; Harraby Sch., Carlisle; Hatfield Poly. (BSc). CEng; FICE. Formerly Planning Develt Engr, London NE, Railtrack. MP (Lab) Scarborough and Whitby, 1997–2005; contested (Lab) same seat, 2005. PPS to Minister of State, DTI, 2001–02, Cabinet Office, 2002–05.

Chm., All Party Railways (formerly Rail Freight) Gp, 1997–2005; Secretary: Labour backbench Agriculture Cttee, 1997–2001; All Party Brazil Gp, 2000–05; Chairman: All Party Saudi Arabia Gp, 1998–2005; All Party Underground Space Gp, 2003–05. Sec., PLP Yorks and Humber Gp, 2001–05; PLP Rep., Nat. Policy Forum, 2001–05; Labour Party Policy Comr, 2001–. Sec., Railway Civil Engineers' Assoc., 2008–; Chm., Railway Engrg Forum, 2013–15. Mem., Regl Bd, ICE London, 2013–; Founder Mem., High Speed Rail Leaders Gp, 2013–. *Address:* 11 Bramble Dene, Woodthorpe, York YO24 2RL.

QUINN, Leo; Group Chief Executive, Balfour Beatty plc, since 2015; *b* 13 Dec. 1956; *s* of Kevin and Mary Quinn; *m* 1993, Elaine Fitzpatrick; two *s*. *Educ:* Portsmouth Poly. (BSc Hons Civil Engrg 1979); Imperial Coll., London (DIC Mgt Sci. 1982). Civil Engr, Balfour Beatty Construction, 1979–81; Planning Manager, Texas Instruments, UK and Portugal, 1982–84; Honeywell, 1984–2000: various posts in UK, Europe and USA; Pres., Honeywell H&BC Enterprise Solutions Worldwide, 2000; Pres. Europe, ME and Africa, Tridium Inc., 2000–01; Chief Operating Officer, Prodn Mgt Div., Invensys plc (USA), 2001–04; CEO, De La Rue, 2004–09; Chief Exec., QinetiQ Gp plc, 2009–14. Non-exec. Dir, Betfair, 2014–. *Recreations:* ski-ing, theatre, water sports, shooting, horse racing. *Address:* Balfour Beatty plc, 130 Wilton Road, SW1V 1LQ. *E:* leo.quinn@balfourbeatty.com.

QUINN, Lisa Dawn; Director, Capita Asset Services, Treasury Solutions, since 2013; *b* Salford, 3 Oct. 1967; *d* of Joseph Watson Quinn and Betty Joyce Quinn. *Educ:* Salford Coll. of Technol.; Liverpool John Moores Univ. MAAT 1990; CPFA 1996. Macclesfield Borough Council: Clerical Asst, 1986–90; Accountancy Technician, 1990–94; Sen. Accountant, 1994–2002; Gp Accountant, 2002–03; Financial Gp Manager, 2003–06; Service Manager, Financial Services, 2006; Corporate Manager, Finance and Asset Mgt, 2006–09; Interim Chief Finance Officer, Cheshire East Shadow Authy, 2008–09; Cheshire East Council: Borough Treas. and Hd of Assets, 2009–11; Dir of Finance and Business Services, 2011–13; Dir of Local Authy Treasury and Capital Finance, Sector Gp, 2013. *Recreations:* travel, walking, reading, archaeology, ancient history, Arthurian legends, oh yes, and work. *Address:* Capita Asset Services, 1st Floor, 40 Dukes Place, EC3A 7NH. *T:* 0871 664 6800. *E:* lisa.quinn@capita.co.uk.

QUINN, Matthew John; Director, Environment and Sustainable Development (formerly Environment, Sustainability and Housing), Welsh Government (formerly Welsh Assembly Government), since 2007; *b* Leicester, 21 July 1963; *s* of John and June Quinn; partner, Dr Rhian Davies. *Educ:* Gateway Sch., Leicester; Hertford Coll., Oxford (BA Lit.Hum. 1986; MA). Admin. trainee, DoE and Dept of Transport, 1986–89; Private Sec. to Perm. Sec., Dept of Transport, 1989–90; Hd of Branch, Envmt White Paper Div., DoE, 1990–92; Nuffield and Leverhulme Travelling Fellow, 1992–93; Hd of Br., Planning Policy Div., DoE, 1993–95; Dir, Envmt and Transport, Govt Office for SW, 1995–98; Dir, Policy Unit, Nat. Assembly for Wales, 1998–2003; Hd, of Strategy, 2003–06, of Envmtl Protection and Quality, 2006–07, Welsh Assembly Govt. Non-exec. Dir, Carbon Trust, 2008–11. Dir and Trustee, Gregynog Festival, 2008–. *Publications:* (contrib.) British Planning Policy in Transition, 1996; (contrib.) Introduction to Planning Practice, 2000. *Recreations:* classical music, gadgets. *Address:* Welsh Government, Cathays Park, Cardiff CF10 3NQ. *T:* (029) 2082 3256. *E:* matthew.quinn@wales.gsi.gov.uk.

QUINN, Richard; *see* Quinn, T. R.

QUINN, Ruairi; TD (Lab) Dublin South-East, 1977–81 and since 1982; Minister for Education and Skills, Ireland, 2011–14; *b* 2 April 1946; *s* of Malachi Quinn and Julia Quinn; *m* 1st, 1969, Nicola Underwood; one *s* one *d*; 2nd, 1990, Liz Allman; one *s*. *Educ:* University Coll., Dublin (BArch, Higher Dip. in Ekistics). Dublin City Council: Mem., 1974–77; Leader, Lab Gp and Civic Alliance, 1991–93. Mem., Seanad Eireann, 1976–77 and 1981–82; Minister of State, Envmt, 1982–83; Minister: for Labour, 1984–87, and for Public Service, 1986–87; for Enterprise and Employment, 1993–94; for Finance, 1995–97. Leader, Irish Labour Party, 1997–2002. *Publications:* Straight Left: a journey in politics, 2006; contrib. to Architects Jl, Irish Architect, Ekistics, Tilt. *Recreations:* reading, cooking, walking, music, gardening, cycling. *Address:* Dáil Eireann, Kildare Street, Dublin 2, Republic of Ireland.

QUINN, Dame Sheila (Margaret Imelda), DBE 1987 (CBE 1978); FRCN; President, Royal College of Nursing, 1982–86, now Life Vice President; *b* 16 Sept. 1920; *d* of late Wilfred Amos Quinn and Ada Mazella (*née* Bottomley). *Educ:* Convent of Holy Child, Blackpool; London Univ. (BScEcon Hons); Royal Lancaster Infirmary (SRN 1947); Birmingham (SCM); Royal Coll. of Nursing, London (RNT). FRCN 1978. Admin. Sister, then Principal Sister Tutor, Prince of Wales' Gen. Hosp., London, 1950–61; Internat. Council of Nurses, Geneva: Dir, Social and Econ. Welfare Div., 1961–66; Exec. Dir, 1967–70; Chief Nursing Officer, Southampton Univ. Hosps, 1970–74; Area Nursing Officer, Hampshire AHA (Teaching), 1974–78; Regional Nursing Officer, Wessex RHA, 1978–83. Member: E Dorset DHA, 1987–90; Dorset FHSA, 1990–96. Nursing Advr, BRCS, 1983–88. Pres., Standing Cttee of Nurses of EEC, 1983–91; Member: Council, Royal Coll. of Nursing, 1971–79 (Chm. Council, 1974–79; Dep. Pres., 1980–82); Bd of Dirs, Internat. Council of Nurses, 1977–85 (first Vice-Pres., 1981–85); Mem., EEC Adv. Cttee on Trng in Nursing, 1978–90. Consultant, Dreyfus Health Foundn, NY, 1999–2005. Hon. DSc (Social Sciences) Southampton, 1986. *Publications:* Nursing in The European Community, 1980; Caring for the Carers, 1981; ICN Past and Present, 1989; Nursing, the EC Dimension, 1993; A Dame Abroad (memoir), 2004; articles, mainly on internat. nursing and EEC, in national and internat. jls. *Recreations:* travel, gardening. *Clubs:* St John's House, Royal Society of Medicine.

QUINN, Stephen, CB 2008; Permanent Secretary, Department of Enterprise, Trade and Investment, Northern Ireland, 2006–09; *b* 22 Aug. 1950; *s* of Thomas Charles Quinn and Jane Quinn (*née* Kirkpatrick); *m* 1983, Deirdre Mary Brady. *Educ:* Portora Royal Sch., Enniskillen; Trinity Coll., Dublin (BA Hons Hist. and Pol Sci.). Northern Ireland Civil Service: Dept of Finance, 1974–86 (Sec., Kincora Inquiry, 1984–85); Assistant Secretary: Dept of Health and Social Services, 1986–87; Dept of Finance and Personnel, 1987–90; Dept of Educn, 1990–92; Central Secretariat, 1992–94; Under Secretary: Dept of Finance and Personnel, 1994–98; DoE, 1998–99; Permanent Secretary: DoE, 1999–2002; Dept for Regl Develt, 2002–06.

QUINN, Terence James; Editor-in-Chief, APN Regional Newspapers, Australia and New Zealand, 2004–10; *b* 17 Nov. 1951; *s* of Thomas Quinn and Shirley (*née* Anderson); *m* 1973, Patricia Anna-Maria Gillespie; one *s* one *d* (and one *s* decd). *Educ:* St Aloysius Coll., Glasgow. Editor: Telegraph & Argus, Bradford, 1984–89; Evening News, Edinburgh, 1989–92; Dep. Editl Dir, 1992–94, Editl Dir, 1994, Thomson Regl Newspapers; Editor, Daily Record, 1994–98; Sen. Vice Pres., Readership, Thomson Newspapers (US), 1998–2000; Pres., Reader Inc. (US), 2000–02; Publisher, Fairfax Sundays, NZ, 2002–04. *Recreations:* tennis, sailing, golf.

QUINN, Dr Terence John, CBE 2004; FRS 2002; Emeritus Director, Bureau International des Poids et Mesures, Sèvres, France, since 2004 (Deputy Director, 1977–88; Director, 1988–2003); *b* 19 March 1938; *s* of John Henry and Olive Hilda Quinn; *m* 1962, Renée Marie Goujard; two *s*. *Educ:* Univ. of Southampton (BSc 1959); Univ. of Oxford (DPhil 1963). National Physical Laboratory, Teddington: Jun. Res. Fellow, 1962–64; Staff Mem., 1964–77. Vis. Scientist, Nat. Bureau of Standards, Washington, DC, 1967–68; Royal Soc. Vis. Fellow, Cavendish Lab., and Dist. Vis. Fellow, Christ's Coll., Cambridge, 1984–85. Corresp. Mem., Bureau des Longitudes, Paris, 2011. Chm., Paris Decorative and Fine Arts Soc., 2014–. FInstP 1975; Fellow, APS, 1995; FAAAS 2001. Hon. Prof., Birmingham Univ., 2000. Hon. Dr Conservatoire Nat. des Arts et Métiers, Paris, 2000. Editor, Notes & Records of the Royal Soc., 2004–07. *Publications:* Temperature, 1983, 2nd edn 1990; From Artefacts to Atoms: the BIPM and the search for ultimate measurement standards, 2011; papers in sci. press on thermometry, radiometry, mass standards, lab. gravitational experiments, fundamental phys. constants and gen. metrology. *Recreations:* photography, bee keeping, violin playing. *Address:* 92 rue Brancas, 92310 Sèvres, France. *T:* (1) 46230656. *E:* tjqfrs@gmail.com. *Club:* Athenæum.

QUINN, (Thomas) Richard; flat jockey, 1978–2006 and since 2007; *b* 2 Dec. 1961; *s* of late Thomas Quinn and of Helen Quinn (*née* McDonald); *m* 1990, Fiona Christine Johnson (marr. diss. 1993); one *s* one *d*; *m* 2007, Alex. *Educ:* Bannockburn High Sch. First winner, Kempton, 1981; Champion Apprentice, Europe, 1983, GB, 1984; 2nd in Jockey's Championship, 1996, 1999. Winning races include: Irish Oaks, 1986, 1990; French 1,000 Guineas, 1986; St Leger, 1990, 2001; Irish St Leger, 1990, 1995; Dewhurst Stakes, 1990; Prix Royal Oak, 1992; Italian Derby, 1994; Juddmonte Lockinge Stakes, 1996; Prix Vermeille, 1998; Oaks, 2000; has ridden winners in 25 countries worldwide. Vice-Pres., Jockeys Assoc., 1992. *Address:* c/o Jockey Club, 42 Portman Square, W1H 0EN.

QUIRK, family name of **Baron Quirk**.

QUIRK, Baron *cr* 1994 (Life Peer), of Bloomsbury in the London Borough of Camden; **(Charles) Randolph Quirk,** Kt 1985; CBE 1976; FBA 1975; President, British Academy, 1985–89; Fellow of University College London; *b* 12 July 1920; *s* of late Thomas and Amy Randolph Quirk, Lambfell, Isle of Man; *m* 1st, 1946, Jean (marr. diss. 1979; she *d* 1995), *d* of Ellis Gauntlett Williams; two *s*; 2nd, 1984, Gabriele, *d* of Judge Helmut Stein. *Educ:* Cronk y Voddy Sch.; Douglas High Sch., IOM; University College London. MA, PhD, DLit London. Served RAF, 1940–45. Lecturer in English, University College London, 1947–54; Commonwealth Fund Fellow, Yale Univ. and University of Michigan, 1951–52; Reader in English Language and Literature, University of Durham, 1954–58; Professor of English Language in the University of Durham, 1958–60, in the University of London, 1960–68; Quain Prof. of English Language and Literature, University Coll. London, 1968–81; Vice-Chancellor, Univ. of London, 1981–85. Dir, Survey of English Usage, 1959–83. Member: Senate, Univ. of London, 1970–85 (Chm., Acad. Council, 1972–75); Ct, Univ. of London, 1972–85; Bd, British Council, 1983–91; BBC Archives Cttee, 1975–81; RADA Council, 1985–2004; Select Cttee on Sci., H of L, 1998–2003. President: Inst. of Linguists, 1982–85; Coll. of Speech Therapists, 1987–91; North of England Educn Conf., 1989; Vice-Pres., Foundn for Science and Technology, 1986–90; Governor: British Inst. of Recorded Sound, 1975–80; E-SU, 1980–85; Richmond Coll., London, 1981–2006; City Technology Colls, 1986–95. Chairman: Cttee of Enquiry into Speech Therapy Services, 1969–72; Hornby Educnl Trust, 1979–93; Anglo-Spanish Foundn, 1983–85; British Library Adv. Cttee, 1984–97; Vice-Chm., English Language Council, E-SU, 1985–2007. Trustee: Wolfson Foundn, 1987–2012; American Sch. in London, 1987–89; Royal Comr, 1851 Exhibn, 1987–95. Mem., Academia Europaea, 1988. Foreign Fellow: Royal Belgian Acad. of Scis, 1975; Royal Swedish Acad., 1987; Finnish Acad. of Scis, 1991; American Acad. of Arts and Scis, 1994. Hon. FCST; Hon. FCIL; Hon. Fellow: Imperial Coll., 1985; QMC, 1986; Goldsmiths' Coll., 1987; King's Coll., 1990; RHBNC, 1990. Hon. Bencher, Gray's Inn, 1982. Hon. Fil. Dr: Lund; Uppsala; Helsinki; Copenhagen; Hon. DU: Essex; Bar Ilan; Brunel; DUniv Open; Hon. DHC: Liège; Paris; Prague; Bucharest; Hon. DLitt: Reading; Newcastle upon Tyne; Durham; Bath; Salford; Queen Margaret; Southern California; Sheffield; Glasgow; Poznan; Nijmegen; Richmond Coll.; Hon. DCL Westminster; Hon. LLD: Leicester; London; Hon. DSc Aston. Jubilee Medal, Inst. of Linguists, 1973. *Publications:* The Concessive Relation in Old English Poetry, 1954; Studies in Communication (with A. J. Ayer and others), 1955; An Old English Grammar (with C. L. Wrenn), 1955, enlarged edn (with S. E. Deskis), 1994; Charles Dickens and Appropriate Language, 1959; The Teaching of English (with A. H. Smith), 1959, revised edn, 1964; The Study of the Mother-Tongue, 1961; The Use of English (with Supplements by A. C. Gimson and J. Warburg), 1962, enlarged edn, 1968; Prosodic and Paralinguistic Features in English (with D. Crystal), 1964; A Common Language (with A. H. Marckwardt), 1964; Investigating Linguistic Acceptability (with J. Svartvik), 1966; Essays on the English Language—Mediaeval and Modern, 1968; (with S. Greenbaum) Elicitation Experiments in English, 1970; (with S. Greenbaum, G. Leech, J. Svartvik) A Grammar of Contemporary English, 1972; The English Language and Images of Matter, 1972; (with S. Greenbaum) A University Grammar of English, 1973; The Linguist and the English Language, 1974; (with V. Adams, D. Davy) Old English Literature: a practical introduction, 1975; (with J. Svartvik) A Corpus of English Conversation, 1980; Style and Communication in the English Language, 1982; (with S. Greenbaum, G. Leech, J. Svartvik) A Comprehensive Grammar of the English Language, 1985; (with H. Widdowson) English in the World, 1985; Words at Work: lectures on textual structure, 1986; (with G. Stein) English in Use, 1990; (with S. Greenbaum) A Student's Grammar of the English Language, 1990; (with G. Stein) An Introduction to Standard English, 1993; Grammatical and Lexical Variance in English, 1995; (with K. Brown and others) Linguistics in Britain: personal histories, 2002; (with V. Cottle) Memories of Cronk y Voddy, 2010; contrib. to: conf. proceedings and volumes of studies; papers in linguistic and literary journals. *Address:* University College London, Gower Street, WC1E 6BT. *T:* (020) 7219 2226, *Fax:* (020) 7219 5979. *Club:* Athenæum.

QUIRK, Barry John, CBE 2001; PhD; Chief Executive, London Borough of Lewisham, since 1994; *b* 20 Nov. 1953; *s* of John Quirk and Iris (*née* Cope; now Aldridge); *m* 2009, Katherine Kerswell; three *s* one *d* by former marriage. *Educ:* London Univ. (ext. BSc Hons 1975); Portsmouth Poly. (PhD 1984). Head of Corporate Policy, London Borough of Newham, 1987; Asst Chief Exec., London Borough of Lewisham, 1987–94. Non-exec. Dir, HM Customs and Excise, subseq. Revenue and Customs, 2002–06. Pres., 2005–06, Chm., 2006–08, SOLACE. Vis. Fellow of Social Policy and Politics, Goldsmiths Coll., Univ. of London, 1998–. Associate, Inst. for Govt, 2010–.

QUIRKE, Pauline; actress; *b* 8 July 1959; *m* Steve; one *s* one *d*. *Educ:* Anna Scher Theatre Sch., London. Appeared in Dixon of Dock Green, BBC TV, 1968; *television series include:* Angels, 1976; Shine on Harvey Moon, 1982; Rockliffe's Babies, 1987; Birds of a Feather (10 series), 1989–98, 2014; Jobs for the Girls, 1993; First Sign of Madness, 1996; Double Nougat, 1996; Real Women, 1997–99; Maisie Raine, 1998–99; Down to Earth, 2000–03; Office Gossip, 2001; Being April, 2002; North and South, 2004; Missing, 2009; Emmerdale, 2010–12; Broadchurch, 2013; You, Me and the Apocalypse, 2015; *television drama includes:* The Sculptress, 1996; Our Boy, 1997; Deadly Summer, 1997; David Copperfield, 1999; The Flint Street Nativity, 1999; Carrie's War, 2003. *Films include:* Little Dorrit, 1986; Getting it Right, 1988; The Return of the Soldiers, 1988; Still Lives—Distant Voices, 1989; The Canterville Ghost, 1997; Check-out Girl, 1998; Arthur's Dyke, 2000; Redemption Road, 2001. *Theatre includes:* A Tale of Two Cities, Royal Court Theatre, 1979; Birds of a Feather, New Victoria, Woking, 2012, tour, 2012–13. Opened The Pauline Quirke Academy of Performing Arts, 2007. *Address:* Quirky Media Stuff, Custodia House, Queensmead Road, Loudwater, High Wycombe, Bucks HP10 9XA.

QUIRKE, Prof. Philip, PhD; FRCPath, FMedSci; Professor of Pathology, Head, Pathology and Tumour Biology, since 1997, and Sub Dean, Academic Training, since 2007, University of Leeds; Honorary Consultant, Leeds Teaching Hospitals NHS Trust, since 1990; *b* Romford, Essex, 14 Dec. 1955; *s* of Daniel Quirke and Barbara Quirke; *m* 1984, Judith Wyatt; one *s* one *d*. *Educ:* Coopers Company Grammar Sch., Mile End, subseq. Coopers' Company and Coborn Comp. Sch., Upminster; Univ. of Southampton (BM 1980); Univ. of Leeds (PhD 1987). MRCPath 1983, FRCPath 1997. University of Leeds: Lectr, 1982–90; Sen. Lectr, 1990–95; Reader, 1995–97. Hd, Histopathol. and Molecular Pathol., Leeds Teaching

Hosps NHS Trust, 1991–2004. Lead Pathology NHS England Bowel Cancer Screening Prog., 2007–. NIHR Sen. Investigator, 2015. Pres., Pathol Soc. of GB and Ire., 2015–. FMedSci 2014. *Publications:* (ed jtly) PCR: a practical approach, 1991; (with M. F. Dixon) Aids to Pathology, 3rd edn 1993. *Recreations:* travel, films, photography, dining. *Address:* Pathology and Tumour Biology, Wellcome Trust Brenner Building, Saint James's University Hospital, Beckett Street, Leeds, W Yorks LS9 7TF.

QURESHI, Bashir Ahmad, FRCGP, FRCPCH, FFSRH; medical journalist, since 1964; general practitioner, Hounslow, since 1969; *b* 25 Sept. 1935; four *d* (one *s* decd). *Educ:* Nishtar Medical Coll., Multan, Pakistan (MB BS); DHMSA 1974; DCH 1976; DPMSA 1980. AFOM 1978; MRCGP 1976, FRCGP 1984; MICGP 1984; MFFP 1993; MRCPCH 1998, FRCPCH 2006; FFSRH (FFFP 2006). MO Paediatrics, Nishtar Hosp., Multan, Pakistan, 1961–64; med. doctor, UK hosps, 1964–69; MO (pt-time), British Army and HM Prisons, 1998–; Expert Witness in cultural, religious and ethnic issues in litigation, UK, 1992–; Expert Witness in GP clinical negligence, 1992–. Mem. Council, RCGP, 1990–; Chm. Council, 1997–98, Emeritus Vice Pres., 2005–, RSPH (formerly RSH); Dep. Chm. and Sec., Nat. Assoc. of Sessional GPs, 2007–11 (Mem., BMA Subcttee, 1998–May 2016); Chm., NHS Trusts Assoc., 2006–10. Dep. Chm., Local Med. Cttee, Hounslow, 2003–12; Med. Advr, London Area, British Red Cross, 2006–. Life Mem., BMA, 2014. Vice Pres., Hounslow Conservative Assoc., 2005–. Mem. Council, Conservative Med. Soc., 1988–; Vice Pres., Conservative Health, 2009–. Member: Ct of Govs, LSHTM, 2004–; Trustees Bd, English PEN, 2008–12; Life Mem., Coll. of St George, Windsor Castle, 1986. Mem., Med. Music Soc. of London. Hon. FRSPH (Hon. FRSH 1998); Hon. Mem. APHA, 1998. Badge of Honour, British Red Cross, 1999; Plaque of Recognition, H of L, 2001. *Publications:* Transcultural Medicine, 1989, 2nd edn 1994; contrib. 12 chapters in med. books; over 214 articles in med. jls; handouts and 385 lects to med. meetings, mainly UK, USA, India and Tanzania. *Recreations:* cinema, writing short stories, music, dancing, travel, reading, theatre, dining out, holidays, public speaking, guest broadcasting on British TV and radio. *T:* 07710 402276, *T:* and *Fax:* (020) 8570 4008. *E:* drbashirqureshi@hotmail.com. *W:* www.drbashirqureshi.com. *Clubs:* Royal Society of Medicine; Society of Authors; English PEN.

QURESHI, Murad; Member (Lab) London Assembly, Greater London Authority, since 2004; *b* 27 May 1965. *Educ:* Univ. of E Anglia (BA 1987); University Coll. London (MSc 1993). Mem. (Lab) Westminster CC, 1998–2006. Member: Metropolitan Police Authy, 2004–06; London Fire and Emergency Planning Authy, 2004–12. *Recreations:* football and cricket (playing and watching). *Address:* Greater London Authority, City Hall, Queen's Walk, SE1 2AA. *T:* (020) 7983 4400, *Fax:* (020) 7983 5679. *E:* murad.qureshi@london.gov.uk.

QURESHI, Shamim Ahmed; a District Judge (Magistrates' Courts), since 2004; a Recorder of the Crown Court, since 2005; Director of Programmes, Commonwealth Magistrates' and Judges' Association, since 2009; *b* 28 Feb. 1960; *s* of late Mohammed Aslam Qureshi and of Sara Begum; *m* 1987; three *s* one *d*. *Educ:* Bristol Poly. (BA Law). Called to the Bar, Gray's Inn, 1982; pupillage in London, 1982–83; Sen. Crown Prosecutor, CPS, 1984–89; in practice at the Bar, Bristol, 1989–2002; Immigration Adjudicator, 2002–04; Judge Advocate at Courts Martial (pt-time), later Dep. Judge Advocate of the Armed Forces, 2001–. Served TA, 1986–2001 (Capt. 1998). TEM 1998. *Recreations:* travelling around the world, lounging around the swimming pool, sailing a catamaran, golf once a year but hoping to increase to twice this year, member of local gym but still not been once yet. *Address:* Victoria Law Courts, Corporation Street, Birmingham B4 6QA.

QURESHI, Yasmin; MP (Lab) Bolton South East, since 2010; *b* Pakistan, 5 July 1963; *d* of Mohammad Qureshi and Sakina Beg; *m* 2008, Nadeem Ashraf Butt. *Educ:* Westfield Sch.; South Bank Poly. (BA Law 1984); Council of Legal Educn; University Coll. London (LLM 1987). Called to the Bar, Lincoln's Inn, 1985; in practice as barrister, 1987–; Crown Prosecutor, CPS, 1987–2000; Hd, Criminal Legal Section, UN Mission, Kosovo, 2000–01; Dir, Dept of Judicial Admin, Kosovo, 2001–02; Policy Adviser, CPS, 2002–04; Human Rights Advr to Mayor of London, 2004–08; barrister: 2 King's Bench Walk Chambers, 2004–08; Kenworthy's Chambers, Manchester, 2008–10. Contested (Lab) Brent E, 2005. Mem., Justice Select Cttee, 2010–15. *Address:* House of Commons, SW1A 0AA.

QUYSNER, David William, CBE 2008; Chairman, Abingworth Management Ltd, 2002–14; *b* Westhoughton, Lancs, 26 Dec. 1946; *s* of late Charles William Quysner and Marjorie Alice Quysner; *m* 1971, Lindsay Jean Parris (*née* Biggs); one *s* two *d*. *Educ:* Bolton Sch.; Selwyn Coll., Cambridge (BA 1969; MA); London Business Sch. (London Exec. Prog. 27). Investment Exec., 1968–76, Local Dir, 1976–82, Industrial and Commercial Finance Corp. Ltd; Dir, 1982–94, Man. Dir, 1994–2002, Abingworth Mgt Ltd. Chairman: RCM Technology Trust plc, 2004–14; Capital for Enterprise Ltd, 2008–12; Director: ANGLE plc, 2004–14; Foresight 2 VCT plc, 2004–; MRC Technology Ltd, 2004–14; Private Equity Investor plc, 2004–14. Dir, British Venture Capital Assoc., 1992–98 (Chm., 1996–97). *Recreations:* travel, opera, cricket. *Address:* The Old Vicarage, Selmeston, Polegate, E Sussex BN26 6TY. *T:* (01323) 811898. *E:* quysner@abingworth.com. *Club:* MCC.

R

RA JONG-YIL, Dr; University Distinguished Professor, Hangyang University, Republic of Korea, since 2011; *b* 5 Dec. 1940; *s* of Ra Iong-Gwyn and Ra Gwi-Nye; *m* 1968, Ra Jae-Ja; one *s* three *d*. *Educ:* Seoul Nat. Univ. (BA Pol Sci., MA Pol Sci.); Trinity Coll., Cambridge (PhD Internat. Relns, 1972). Kyung Hee University, Korea: Prof. of Pol Sci., 1972–; Dean: Coll. of Econs and Pol Sci., 1980–81; Grad. Sch., 1988–92. Fellow Commoner, Churchill Coll., Cambridge, 1981; Fulbright Sen. Fellow, Univ. of Southern Calif, 1985. Vice-Chm., Forum of Democratic Leaders in Asia-Pacific, 1994; Mem., Exec. Cttee and Special Asst to Pres., Nat. Congress for New Politics, 1996–97; Hd, Admin. Office, Presidential Transition Cttee, 1997; 2nd and 1st Dir, Nat. Security Planning Bd, 1998; 1st Dir, Nat. Intelligence Service, 1998–99; Director-General: Res. Inst. of Peace Studies, 1999–2000; Circle Millennium Korea, 1999–2000; Special Assistant: to Pres., Foreign and Security Affairs, Millennium Democratic Party, 1999–2000; to Dir-Gen., Foreign Affairs, Nat. Intelligence Service, 2000–01; Ambassador of Republic of Korea to UK, 2001–03; Nat. Security Advr to Pres., 2003–04; Ambassador to Japan, 2004–07. Chm., Cttee on Ideological Conflict, Presidential Commn on Social Cohesion, 2008–; Mem., Presidential Cttee of Preparation for Unification, 2014–. National Commission for Human Rights: Member: Policy Adv. Cttee, 2012–14; Special Cttee on Internat. Human Rights, 2013–15; Internat. Human Rights Cttee, 2015–; Chm., Special Cttee on Human Rights in N Korea, 2013–15. Mem., Special Adv. Cttee to Pres., Korean Red Cross, 2015–. Pres., Woosuk Univ., Korea, 2007–11. *Publications:* Co-operation and Conflict, 1986; Points of Departure, 1992; Human Beings and Politics, 1995; Preparing for the New Millennium, 1998; Fairy Stories of Ra, Jong-Yil, 2006; Bibimbap Story, 2008; The Discovery of the World, 2008 (Korean edn 2009); The Wizard of River Nakdong, 2010; (trans.) Fiction and Politics in the Modern World, 2012; (trans.) Aristotle's Politics, 2012. *Recreations:* tennis, golf, Kendo, Aikido. *Address:* Division of International Studies, Hanyang University, 222 Wangsimni-ro, Seongdong-gu, Seoul 133–791, Republic of Korea; Songpa-gu, Joongdae-ro 24, Olympic Family Apts #211–204, Republic of Korea. *Club:* Seoul.

RAAB, Dominic Rennie; MP (C) Esher and Walton, since 2010; Parliamentary Under-Secretary of State, Ministry of Justice, since 2015; *b* Bucks, 25 Feb. 1974; *m* 2005, Erika Rey. *Educ:* Dr Challoner's Grammar Sch., Amersham; Lady Margaret Hall, Oxford (BA Law); Jesus Coll., Cambridge (LLM). Internat. lawyer; Linklaters, incl. secondments to Liberty and in Brussels advising on EU and WTO law, 1998–2000; entered FCO, 2000; advr on legal issues, 2000–03; First Sec. (Legal), The Hague, 2003–06; COS to Shadow Home Sec., 2006–08, to Shadow Justice Sec., 2008–10. Member: Jt Cttee on Human Rights, 2010–13; Educn Select Cttee, 2013–15. *Publications:* The Assault on Liberty: what went wrong with rights, 2009. *Recreations:* sport (karate black belt 3rd dan, boxing), theatre, travel. *Address:* House of Commons, SW1A 0AA.

RABAN, Antony John; Conseiller, Relations Internationales, Association Bernard Gregory, 2003–07 (Committee Member, 1996–2002; Membre d'Honneur, since 2005); *s* of Rev. Harry Priaulx Raban and Freda Mary Raban (*née* Probert); *m* 1965, Sandra Gilham Brown. *Educ:* St John's Sch., Leatherhead; Corpus Christi Coll., Cambridge (MA Hist.). Asst Master, Doncaster GS, 1964–67; Careers Officer, 1967–69, Professional Asst, 1969–71, Cambs & Isle of Ely CC; Asst Sec. (Careers Advr), Oxford Univ. Careers Service, 1971–74; Careers Advr, 1974–92, Dir, 1992–2002, Cambridge Univ. Careers Service. Chm., Assoc. of Grad. Careers Adv. Services, 1979–81; Pres., Eur. Forum on Student Guidance, 1988–92; Mem. Council, CRAC, 1998–2002. *Publications:* Working in the European Union: a guide for graduate recruiters and job-seekers, 1985, 4th edn 1995; The Entry of New Graduates into the European Labour Market, 1991; From PhD to Employment, 2000, 2nd edn 2003; numerous reports and contribs to professional jls. *Recreations:* art history, France.

RABAN, Jonathan, FRSL; essayist, travel writer, novelist; *b* 14 June 1942; *s* of late Rev. Canon J. Peter C. P. Raban and Monica Raban (*née* Sandison); *m* 1992, Jean Lenihan (marr. diss.); one *d*. *Educ:* Univ. of Hull (BA Hons English). Lecturer in English and American Literature: UCW, Aberystwyth, 1965–67; Univ. of E Anglia, 1967–69; professional writer, 1969–. FRSL 1975. Hon. DLitt Hull, 2005. *Publications:* The Technique of Modern Fiction, 1969; Mark Twain: Huckleberry Finn, 1969; The Society of the Poem, 1971; Soft City, 1973; Arabia Through the Looking Glass, 1979; Old Glory, 1981 (Heinemann Award, RSL, 1982; Thomas Cook Award, 1982); Foreign Land, 1985; Coasting, 1986; For Love and Money, 1987; God, Man & Mrs Thatcher, 1989; Hunting Mister Heartbreak, 1990 (Thomas Cook Award, 1991); (ed) The Oxford Book of the Sea, 1992; Bad Land, 1996 (National Book Critics Circle Award, 1997; PEN Award for creative non-fiction, 1997); Passage to Juneau, 1999; Waxwings, 2003; My Holy War, 2005; Surveillance, 2006; Driving Home: an American scrapbook, 2010. *Recreation:* sailing. *Address:* c/o Aitken Alexander Associates Ltd, 291 Gray's Inn Road, WC1X 8EB. *Clubs:* Groucho; Rainier (Seattle).

RABBATTS, Heather Victoria, CBE 2000; Managing Director, Smuggler Entertainment LLP, since 2013; *b* 6 Dec. 1955; *d* of Thomas Rabbatts and Hyacinth Rabbatts; one *s* by Edmund Gerard O'Sullivan; *m* 2001, Michael Lee. *Educ:* London Sch. of Econs (BA Hons Hist.; MSc). Called to the Bar, Lincoln's Inn, 1981. Equalities Officer, then Parly Liaison Officer, Local Govt Inf. Unit, 1983–86; London Borough of Hammersmith and Fulham: Hd, Women's Dept, 1987–89; Dir of Personnel, 1989–91; Dep. Chief Exec. and Dir, Strategic Services, 1991–93; Chief Executive: Merton LBC, 1993–95; Lambeth LBC, 1995–2000; Man. Dir, 4Learning, Channel 4, 2002–06; Chief Exec., 2006–09, non-exec. Dir, 2009–10, Millwall Hldgs; Exec. Dep. Chm., Millwall FC, 2006–09; Chm., Shed Media plc, 2009–10. A Gov., BBC, 1999–2002. Non-executive Director: Bank of England, 2003–07; Crossrail, 2008–; Grosvenor (Britain and Ireland), 2009–; Malaria No More, 2010–; FA, 2011– (Chm., Inclusion Adv. Bd, 2014–); Supervisory Bd, FCO, 2012–. Member: Bd, Qualifications and Curriculum Authority, 1997–99; Bd, British Council, 1998–2004; ESRC, 1998–2000; Bd, UK Film Council, 2003–11; Bd, Royal Opera House, 2009–. Trustee, Runnymede Trust, 1997–99. Gov., LSE, 1997–2004. *Recreations:* opera, literature, shopping, champagne. *Address:* Smuggler Entertainment LLP, 6–10 Great Portland Street, W1W 8QL.

RABBI, The Chief; *see* Mirvis, E.

RABBITT, Prof. Patrick Michael Anthony, PhD; Research Professor in Gerontology and Cognitive Psychology, and Director, Age and Cognitive Research Centre, University of Manchester, 1983–2004, now Emeritus Professor; *b* 23 Sept. 1934; *s* of Joseph Bernard Rabbitt and Edna Maude Smith; *m* 1st, 1955, Adriana Habers (marr. diss. 1976); one *s* two *d*; 2nd, 1976, Dorothy Vera Bishop, *qv*. *Educ:* Queens' Coll., Cambridge (MA, PhD); MA Oxon; Manchester Univ. (MSc). Scientific Staff, MRC Applied Psychology Unit, Cambridge, 1962–68; Univ. Lectr in Psychology, and Official Fellow, Queen's Coll., Univ. of Oxford, 1968–82; Prof. of Psychology, Univ. of Durham, 1982–83. University of Western Australia: Adjunct Prof. of Psychology, 1991–2003; Hon. Res. Fellow, then Sen. Res. Fellow, 2003–; Hon. Res. Fellow, then Sen. Res. Fellow, Dept of Exptl Psychol., Univ. of Oxford, 2004–. FRSA 1997; Founding Fellow, British Gerontological Soc., 2009. Mem., Eur. Acad., 2013. Hon. Mem., Experimental Psychol. Soc., 1999; Hon. FBPsS 1995. Hon. DSc Western Australia, 2001. *Publications:* (ed) Cognitive Gerontology, 1990; Methodology of Frontal and Executive Function, 1997; Inside Psychology, 2009; Cognitive Gerontology, 2009; The Aging Mind: an owner's manual, 2015; 374 papers in learned jls. *Recreations:* whisky, nostalgia. *Address:* Department of Experimental Psychology, University of Oxford, South Parks Road, Oxford OX1 3UD; Department of Psychology, University of Western Australia, Crawley, Perth, WA 6009, Australia; 10 North Parade Avenue, Oxford OX2 6LX.

RABBITTS, Prof. Terence Howard, PhD; FRS 1987; FMedSci; Professor of Molecular Biology, University of Oxford, since 2012; *b* 17 June 1946; *s* of Joan and Frederick Rabbitts; *m* 1984, Pamela Gage; one *d*, and one step *s* one step *d*. *Educ:* John Ruskin Grammar School; Univ. of East Anglia (BSc); Nat. Inst. for Medical Research (PhD). Research Fellow, Dept of Genetics, Univ. of Edinburgh, 1971–73; Mem., Scientific Staff, 1973–2006, Jt Hd of Protein and Nucleic Acid Div., 1988–2002, MRC Lab. of Molecular Biology, Cambridge; Dir, Leeds Inst. of Molecular Medicine, Univ. of Leeds, 2006–11. Non-executive Director: Aptuscan, 2010–11; Abeterno, 2014–. Chair, Scientific Advisory Board: Cambridge Antibody Tech., 1990–97; Quadrant Healthcare, 1992–2000; Kymab, 2010–; Member: Sci. Adv. Bd, Domantis, 2001–08; Oakes Lyman Consolidated Hldgs Ltd, 2002–07; Med. Adv. Bd, OLK Investments, 2007–; Oryzon Genomics, 2009–; DiThera, 2009–12; Biosceptre, 2010–; Avacta, 2012–. Member: CRUK Drug Discovery Cttee, 2012–15; Hooke Cttee, Royal Soc., 2012–15. Mem., EMBO, 1981–. FMedSci 1998 (Mem. Council, 2009–11); FRSocMed 2005. Associate Mem., Amer. Assoc. for Cancer Res., 1991. Colworth Medal, 1981, Ciba Medal and Prize, 1993, Biochemical Soc.; Clotten Foundn Prize, 2015. *Publications:* papers in scientific jls. *Address:* Weatherall Institute of Molecular Medicine, MRC Molecular Haematology Unit, University of Oxford, John Radcliffe Hospital, Headington, Oxford OX3 9DS.

RABENIRINA, Rt Rev. Remi Joseph; Archbishop of the Indian Ocean, 1995–2005, Archbishop Emeritus, 2013; Bishop of Antananarivo, 1984–2008; *b* 6 March 1938; *s* of Joseph Razafindrabe and Josephine Ramanantenasoa; *m* 1971, Elisabeth Razaizanany; two *s* four *d*. *Educ:* Protestant Church schs; St Paul's Theol Coll., Ambatoharanana, Madagascar; Univ. of Madagascar; St Chad's Theol Coll., Lichfield; Ecumenical Inst. of Bossey, Switzerland. School teacher, 1958–61; Parish Priest: St James', Toamasina, 1967–68; St Matthew's, Antsiranana, 1968–73; St John's, Ambohimangakely (Antananarivo), 1973–84; Diocesan Chancellor, Antananarivo, 1982–84. Chevalier, Officier, Commandeur et Grand Officier de l'Ordre National (Malagasy). *Publications:* (in Malagasy) An Open Door: a short history of the beginning of the Anglican Church in Northern Madagascar, 1969; (trans.) J. C. Fenton, Preaching the Cross, 1990; Some of the Saints (biogs of Saints remembered in the Anglican Church Calendar, Madagascar), 1998. *Recreations:* reading, writing. *Address:* Fonenana Nirina I, Andranomahery, Anosiala, 105 Ambohidratrimo, Madagascar. *T:* (20) 2474852.

RABINOWITZ, Harry, MBE 1977; freelance conductor and composer; *b* 26 March 1916; *s* of Israel and Eva Rabinowitz; *m* 1st, 1944, Lorna Thurlow Anderson (marr. diss. 2000); one *s* two *d*; 2nd, 2001, Mitzi Scott. *Educ:* Athlone High Sch., S Africa; Witwatersrand Univ.; Guildhall Sch. of Music. Conductor, BBC Radio, 1953–60; Musical Dir, BBC TV Light Entertainment, 1960–68; Head of Music, LWT, 1968–77; freelance film, TV, radio and disc activities, 1977–. Conductor, world premieres of: Cats, New London Th., 1981; Song and Dance, Palace Th., 1982; Hollywood Bowl Concerts, 1983 and 1984; Boston "Pops" concerts, 1985, 1986, 1988–92; concerts with RPO, LSO (incl. LSO: A Life in Film, Barbican, 2009) and London Concert Orch.; *films:* conductor: Funeral in Berlin, 1966; Please Sir!, 1971; Inside Out, 1975; Seven Nights in Japan (conductor, string ensemble), 1977; La Dentellière, 1977; The Greek Tycoon (also music supervisor), 1978; Hanover Street, 1979; Goldengirl, 1979; La mort en direct, 1980; Mon Oncle d'Amérique, 1980; Time Bandits, 1980; music coordinator, Chariots of Fire, 1981; conductor: Heat and Dust, 1982; The Missionary, 1983; additional music adaptor/classical music coordinator, Electric Dreams, 1984; conductor: Nemo, 1984; The Bostonians, 1984; Return to Oz, Lady Jane Grey, and Revolution—1776, 1985; F/X, and Manhattan Project, 1986; Masters of the Universe, Maurice, 1987; Simon Wiesenthal, Camille Claudel, 1988; Shirley Valentine (jt composer/conductor), Queen of Hearts, 1989; Music Box, Lord of the Flies, La Fille des Collines, 1990; Jalousie, La Tribu, Jesuit Joe, Iran Day of Crisis, Ballad of the Sad Café, J'embrasse pas, Pour Sascha, 1991; Howards End, The Ark and the Flood, 1992; The Remains of the Day, Taxi de Nuit, Moonfish, Petite Apocalypse, 1993; Grosse Fatigue, The Flemish Board, Mantegna & Sons, 1994; Jefferson in Paris, Jenny et Mr Arnaud, The Stupids, 1995; The Proprietor, Secret Agent, Star Command, Surviving Picasso, The English Patient, 1996; Tonka, Wings of the Dove, My Story So Far, 1997; City of Angels, Soldiers' Daughters Don't Cry, Place Vendôme, 1998; Message in a Bottle, Cotton Mary, The Talented Mr Ripley, 1999; The Golden Bowl, 2000; Obsession, 2001; Le Divorce, 2002; Bon Voyage, 2003; Cold Mountain, 2003; Donkey Xote, 2008; *television:* composer-conductor: Top of the Pops, BBC theme, 1964; Thomas and Sarah, 1978; Agatha Christie Hour, 1982; Reilly Ace of Spies, 1983; Love for Lydia, 1984; conductor, The Ewok Adventure, 1984; Glorious Day, 1985; Land of the Eagle, 1990; D. W. Griffiths Father of Film, Memento Mori, 1993; Project Ayrton Senna, 1995; Alien Empire, 1996; Battle of the Sexes, Impossible Journeys, 1998. Freeman, City of London, 1995. Gold Badge of Merit, British Acad. of Songwriters, Composers and Authors, 1985; Award for lifetime contribution, Wavendon Allmusic, 1990. *Recreations:* listening to others making music, gathering edible fungi, wine tasting. *Address:* Yellow Cottage, Walking Bottom, Peaslake, Surrey GU5 9RR. *T:* (01306) 730674. *E:* mitziscott@aol.com.

RABINOWITZ, Laurence Anton; QC 2002; *b* 3 May 1960; *s* of Joseph and Mary Rabinowitz; *m* 1989, Suzanne Benster; two *s* one *d. Educ:* Univ. of Witwatersrand (BA, LLB); Merton Coll., Oxford (BA, BCL). Called to the Bar, Middle Temple, 1987, Bencher, 2008; in practice specialising in commercial law; Jun. Counsel to Crown, Chancery, 1995–2002. Gov., N London Collegiate Sch., 2008–. *Publications:* (ed) Weinberg and Blank on Take-overs and Mergers, 5th edn, 1989. *Recreations:* sport, music, reading. *Address:* (chambers) One Essex Court, Temple, EC4Y 9AR. *T:* (020) 7583 2000, *Fax:* (020) 7583 0118. *E:* lrabinowitz@oeclaw.co.uk.

RACE, (Denys Alan) Reg; management and policy consultant; Managing Director, Quality Health management consultants, since 1993; *b* 23 June 1947; *s* of Denys and Elsie Race. *Educ:* Sale Grammar School; Univ. of Kent (BA (Politics and Sociology), PhD (Politics)). Senior Research Officer, National Union of Public Employees, 1972. MP (Lab) Haringey, Wood Green, 1979–83. Contested (Lab) Chesterfield, 2001. Head of Programme Office, GLC, 1983–86; Special Res. Officer, ACTT, 1986; County Dir, Derbys County Council, 1988. Advr, Health Policy Adv. Unit, 1989–93.

RACE, John William B.; *see* Burton-Race.

RACE, Reg; *see* Race, D. A. R.

RACEY, Prof. Paul Adrian, FRSE; FRSB; Regius Professor of Natural History, University of Aberdeen, 1993–2009, now Emeritus; Visiting Professor, University of Exeter, Cornwall Campus, since 2007; *b* 7 May 1944; *s* of Albert and Esme Racey; *m* 1968, Anna Priscilla Notcutt; three *s. Educ:* Ratcliffe Coll.; Downing Coll., Cambridge (MA); London Univ. (PhD); Univ. of Aberdeen (DSc). FRSB (FIBiol 1987); FRSE 1992. Rothamsted Experimental Station, 1965–66; Zoological Soc. of London, 1966–71; Res. Fellow, Univ. of Liverpool, 1971–73; University of Aberdeen: Lectr and Sen. Lectr in Zoology, 1973–85; Prof. of Zoology, 1985–93. Chairman: Bat (formerly Chiroptera) Specialist Gp, IUCN Species Survival Commn, 1986–2014; Bat Conservation Trust, 1990–96 (Hon. Sci. and Conservation Advr, 1996–); Member: Scottish Exam. Bd, 1985–90; Management Cttee, Scottish Univs Res. and Reactor Centre, 1991–95 (Mem. Sci. Adv. Bd, 1986–90); Council, Fauna & Flora International (formerly Fauna & Flora Preservation Soc.), 1990–2012 (Chm., Conservation Cttee, 1993–2012; Vice-Pres., 2006–12); Bd of Govs, Macaulay Land Use Res. Inst., 1990–2001; NCC for Scotland, 1991–92; Terrestrial and Freshwater Sci. Cttee, NERC, 1991–94; Exec. Cttee, Mammal Soc., 1991–98; Res. Bd, 1992–94, Scientific Adv. Cttee, 1994–2001 (Chm., 1996–2001), SE Regl Bd, 1996–97, Scottish Natural Heritage; Council, Zool Soc. of London, 1999–2003 (Vice Pres., 2001–03; Member: Adv. Cttee for Sci. and Conservation, 1996–2000 (Chm., 1999–2000); Awards Cttee, 2003–07); Council for Scotland, WWF, 1997–2000. *Publications:* numerous res. papers in professional jls. *Recreations:* riding, sailing, walking. *Address:* Chapel Cottage, Prazegooth Lane, Cadgwith, Ruan Minor, Helston, Cornwall TR12 7LA. *T:* (01326) 291255.

RADAELLI, Prof. Paolo Giuseppe, PhD; FInstP; Dr Lee's Professor of Experimental Philosophy, since 2008, and Associate Head, Oxford Physics and Head, Oxford Condensed Matter Physics, since 2011, University of Oxford; Fellow of Wadham College, Oxford, since 2008; *b* Milan, 11 Oct. 1961; *s* of Bruno Radaelli and Annamaria Trovato Radaelli; *m* 1988, Anna Raimondi; one *s* one *d. Educ:* Liceo G. Garducci, Milan (Maturità Classica 1980); Università degli Studi, Milan (Laurea Physics 1986); Illinois Inst. of Technol. (PhD Physics 1992). FInstP 2012. Res. Associate, Inst. for Technol. of Non-conventional Metals, CNR, Milan, 1988–89; Res. Associate and Lectr, Illinois Inst. of Technol., 1989–90; Grad. Res. Asst, 1990–92, Post-doctoral Res. Asst, 1992–93, Materials Sci. Div., Argonne Nat. Lab.; Post-doctoral Res. Asst, Lab. de Cristallographie-CNRS, Grenoble, 1993–94; Scientist, Institut Laue-Langevin, Grenoble, 1994–98; Scientist, 1998–2003, STFC Fellow, 2003–08, ISIS, STFC. Vis. Prof., UCL, 2002–. *Publications:* Symmetry in Crystallography, 2011; articles in Nature, Science, Physical Rev. Letters, Physical Rev. *Recreations:* piano, sailing. *Address:* Clarendon Laboratory, Department of Physics, University of Oxford, Parks Road, Oxford OX1 3PU.

RADAKIN, Rear Adm. Antony David; Rear Admiral Surface Ships, since 2014; Commander, UK Maritime Forces, since 2014; *b* Oldham, 10 Nov. 1965; *s* of Brian John Radakin and Dorothy Radakin (*née* Sanderson); *m* 1995, Louise Sarah Carron; four *s. Educ:* St Brendan's Coll.; Southampton Univ. (LLB Hons 1989); King's Coll. London (MA Internat. Defence Relns 2000). Commnd 1990; watchkeeping, HMS Leeds Castle, 1990–91; Navigating Officer, HMS Charybdis and HMS Andromeda, 1991–92; CO, HMS Blazer, 1993–95; PWO, HMS Beaver, 1996; called to the Bar, Middle Temple, 1996; Mem. Staff, BRNC, 1998–99; acsc 1999–2000; MA to Under Sec. of State for Defence, 2000–02; CO, HMS Norfolk, 2002–04; Captain i/c Operation Telic, Iraq, 2006–07; PJHQ Plans, 2007–08; MA to VCDS, 2008–09; hcsc 2010; Cdre i/c Operation Telic, Iraq, 2010–11; Comdr, Portsmouth Naval Base, 2011–12; Hd of Strategy Mgt, MoD, 2012–14. Chm., Surface Warfare Officer Assoc., 2014–. Pres., RN Squash Assoc., 2014–. *Recreations:* follows most sports and active participant in squash, sailing, ski-ing and mountain biking. *Address:* COMUKMARFOR Office, Fieldhouse Building, HMS Excellent, Whale Island, Portsmouth PO2 8ER. *Club:* Royal Navy of 1765 and 1785.

RADCLIFFE, Andrew Allen; QC 2000; *b* 21 Jan. 1952; *s* of Reginald Allen Radcliffe and Sheila Radcliffe (*née* McNeil); *m* 1977 (marr. diss. 1990); two *s* one *d. Educ:* Birkenhead Sch.; St Edmund Hall, Oxford (BA Hons 1974). Called to the Bar, Middle Temple, 1975; Asst Recorder, 1998–2000; Recorder, 2000–11. Mem. Cttee, Criminal Bar Assoc., 1998–2001. *Address:* 2 Hare Court, Temple, EC4Y 7BH. *T:* (020) 7353 5324. *Club:* Radlett Cricket.

RADCLIFFE, Francis Charles Joseph; *b* 23 Oct. 1939; *s* of Charles Joseph Basil Nicholas Radcliffe and Norah Radcliffe (*née* Percy); *m* 1968, Nicolette, *e d* of Eugene Randag; one *s* two *d. Educ:* Ampleforth Coll.; Gonville and Caius Coll., Cambridge (MA). Called to the Bar, Gray's Inn, 1962; a Recorder of the Crown Court, 1979, until submitted 'Lawful marriage is good, just and indissoluble' (1540 Henry VIII c. 38). Contested (Christian: stop abortion candidate) York, 1979; founded York Christian Party, 1981. Chm., Life, York. *Recreations:* shooting, beagling, gardening, etc.

RADCLIFFE, Nora; Member (Lib Dem) Gordon, Scottish Parliament, 1999–2007; *b* 4 March 1946; *d* of late James Stuart MacPherson and Doreen MacPherson (*née* McRobb); *m* 1972, Michael Anthony Radcliffe; one *s* one *d. Educ:* Bowmore Primary Sch.; Peterculter Primary Sch.; High Sch. for Girls, Aberdeen; Aberdeen Univ. Hotel mgt, 1968–72; Grampian Health Board: Community Liaison Team, 1993–96; Primary Care Develt Team, 1996–99. Mem. (Lib Dem), Gordon DC, 1988–92. Contested (Lib Dem) Gordon, Scottish Parlt, 2007. *Recreations:* reading, walking, good food. *Address:* 3 King Street, Inverurie, Aberdeenshire AB51 4SY. *T:* (01467) 622575.

RADCLIFFE, Paula Jane, MBE 2002; professional athlete; Great Britain Women's Team Captain, 1998; *b* 17 Dec. 1973; *d* of Peter Radcliffe and Patricia Radcliffe; *m* 2000, Gary Lough; one *s* one *d. Educ:* Loughborough Univ. (1st cl. Hons Mod. European Studies 1996). World Junior Champion, cross-country, 1992; European Champion: cross-country, 1998, 2003; 10,000m, 2002; Silver Medal for 10,000m, World Championships, 1999; World Champion: half marathon, 2000, 2001, 2003; cross-country, 2001, 2002; marathon, 2005; Commonwealth Champion, 5000m, 2002; winner of London Marathon, 2002, 2003 (World Record, 2 hours 15 mins 25 secs), 2005; winner of Chicago Marathon, 2002; winner of New York Marathon, 2004, 2007, 2008; European Record Holder: 10,000m (30 mins 1.09 secs, 2002), half marathon (1 hour 6 mins 47 secs, 2001), marathon; GB Record Holder: 3000m (8 mins 22.20 secs, 2002), 5000m (14 mins 29.11 secs, 2004), 10,000m (30 mins 1.10 secs, 2002), half marathon, marathon. DUniv: De Montfort, 2001; Loughborough, 2002. London Marathon Lifetime Achievement Award, 2015. *Publications:* Paula: my story so far, 2004. *Recreations:* athletics!, travel, reading. *Club:* Bedford and County Athletic.

RADCLIFFE, Sir Sebastian Everard, 7th Bt *cr* 1813; *b* 8 June 1972; *s* of Sir Joseph Benedict Everard Henry Radcliffe, 6th Bt, MC and of Marcia Anne Helen (who *m* 1988, H. M. S. Tanner), *y d* of Major David Turville Constable Maxwell, Bosworth Hall, Husbands Bosworth, Rugby; *S* father, 1975; *m* 2005, Jacinta (*née* Lynch); one *s* two *d. Heir: s* Hugh Everard Benedict Radcliffe, *b* 8 Jan. 2013. *Address:* Le Château de Cheseaux, 1033 Cheseaux, Vaud, Switzerland.

RADCLIFFE, Fr Timothy Peter Joseph, OP; Master of the Order of Preachers (Dominicans), 1992–2001; Sarum Canon of Salisbury Cathedral, since 2007; *b* 22 Aug. 1945; 3rd *s* of late Hugh John Reginald Joseph Radcliffe, MBE, and Marie-Therese, *d* of Maj.-Gen. Sir Cecil Pereira, KCB, CMG; *g s* of Sir Everard Radcliffe, 5th Bt. *Educ:* Downside; St John's College, Oxford (MA; Hon. Fellow, 1993). Entered Dominican Order, 1965; Chaplain to Imperial Coll., 1976–78; taught theology at Blackfriars, Oxford, 1978–88; Prior of Blackfriars, 1982–88; Faculty of Theology, Oxford Univ., 1985–88; Provincial of the English Province, OP, 1988–92. John Toohey Schol. in Residence, Sydney Univ., 1984. Grand Chancellor: Pontifical Univ. of St Thomas (Angelicum), Rome, 1992–2001; Univ. of Santo Tomas, Manila, 1992–2001; Theol. Faculty, Fribourg, 1992–2001; Ecole Biblique, Jerusalem, 1992–2001. Dir, Las Casas Inst., Blackfriars, Oxford, 2014–. Trustee (formerly Mem. Bd), 2002–, and Mem. Develt Bd, 2010–, CAFOD. Pres., Conf. of Major Religious Superiors, 1991–92. Mem. Bd, New Blackfriars, 2003 (Chm., Editl Bd, 1983–88). Mem., Theol Commn, Caritas Internationalis, 2008–. Patron: Margaret Beaufort Inst., Cambridge, 1992–; Eckhart Soc., 1999–. Freedom, City of London, 2013. Hon. STD Providence Coll., RI, 1993; Hon. LLD: Barry Univ., Florida, 1996; Molloy Coll., NY, 2005; Hon. DHumLit: Ohio Dominican Coll., 1996; Dominican Univ., Chicago, 2002; Aquinas Inst., St Louis Univ., 2007; Siena Heights Univ., 2007; Felician Coll., New Jersey, 2010; Hon. DD Oxford, 2003; Hon. Dr Univ. Catholique de l'Ouest, 2006. Prix de littérature religieuse, Le syndicat des libraires de littérature religieuse de France, 2001; Spiritualités d'aujourd'hui, Le Centre Méditerranéen de Littérature, 2001. Hon. Citizen: Augusta (Italy); Sepahua (Peru). *Publications:* El Manantial de la Esperanza Salamanca, 1998; Sing a New Song: the Christian vocation, 2000; I Call You Friends, 2001; Seven Last Words, 2004; What is the Point of Being a Christian?, 2005 (trans. French; Prix des Lecteurs de la Procure, 2006; Michael Ramsey Prize, 2007); (ed) Just One Year, 2006; Why Go to Church?: the drama of the Eucharist, 2008; Essere Cristiani nel XXI Secolo: una spiritualità per il nostro tempo, 2011; Take the Plunge: living baptism and confirmation, 2012; (jtly) Le livre noir de la condition des chrétiens dans le monde, 2014; Parole di Oggi, 2014; Stations of the Cross, 2015; articles in books and periodicals. *Recreations:* walking and talking with friends, reading Dickens and Patrick O'Brian. *Address:* Blackfriars, St Giles, Oxford OX1 3LY. *T:* (01865) 278422. *E:* timothy.radcliffe@english.op.org.

RADCLYFFE, Sarah; Managing Director, Sarah Radclyffe Productions Ltd, since 1993; *b* 14 Nov. 1950; *d* of Charles Raymond Radclyffe, LVO and late Helen Egerton Radclyffe; one *s* by Graham Bradstreet; *m* 1996, William Godfrey; one *s. Educ:* Heathfield Sch., Ascot. Jt Founder, 1984, Jt Man. Dir, 1984–93, Working Title; *films* produced include: My Beautiful Laundrette, 1984; Caravaggio, 1985; Wish You Were Here, 1985; Paperhouse, 1987; Sammy and Rosie Get Laid, 1988; A World Apart, 1988; Fools of Fortune, 1989; Robin Hood, 1990; Edward II, 1991; Sirens, 1993; Second Best, 1993; Bent, 1997; Cousin Bette, 1997; Les Misérables, 1997; The War Zone, 1998; There's Only One Jimmy Grimble, 1999; Love's Brother, 2003; Tara Road, 2004; Free Jimmy, 2006; How About You, 2007; Cirque du Freak: The Vampire's Assistant, 2009; The Edge of Love, 2008; Good Morning Karachi, 2011. Non-exec. Dir, Channel Four TV, 1995–99; Gov., BFI, 1996–99; Dir, Film Council, 2000–04. Simon Olswang Business Woman of the Year Award, 1993. *Recreations:* travel, ski-ing. *Address:* Sarah Radclyffe Productions Ltd, 10/11 St George's Mews, NW1 8XE. *E:* sarah@srpltd.co.uk.

RADDA, Prof. Sir George (Karoly), Kt 2000; CBE 1993; MA, DPhil; FRS 1980; Chairman, Biomedical Research Council, Agency for Science, Technology and Research, Singapore, since 2009; *b* 9 June 1936; *s* of Dr Gyula Radda and Dr Anna Bernolak; *m* 1st, 1961, Mary O'Brien (marr. diss. 1995); two *s* one *d*; 2nd, 1995, Sue Bailey. *Educ:* Pannonhalma, Hungary; Eötvös Univ., Budapest, Hungary; Merton Coll., Oxford (BA Cl. 1, Chem., 1960; DPhil 1962). Res. Associate, Univ. of California, 1962–63; University of Oxford: Lectr in Organic Chemistry, St John's Coll., 1963–64; Fellow and Tutor in Organic Chem., Merton Coll., 1964–84; Lectr in Biochem., 1966–84, Hd of Dept of Biochem., 1991–96; British Heart Foundn Prof. of Molecular Cardiol., 1984–2003 (on leave of absence, 1996–2003); Chief Exec., MRC, 1996–2003; Prof. and Hd, Dept of Physiol., Anatomy and Genetics, Univ. of Oxford, 2005–08, now Emeritus Prof. of Molecular Cardiol.; Professorial Fellow, Merton Coll., Oxford, 1984–2003 and 2005–08, now Emeritus Fellow; Chm., Singapore Bioimaging Consortium, 2005–10. Vis. Prof., Cleveland Clinic, 1987. Medical Research Council: Mem. Council, 1988–92; Chm., Cell Biology and Disorders Bd, 1988–92; Chm., Human Genome Directed Programme Cttee, 1992–96; Hon. Dir, Unit of Biochemical and Clin. Magnetic Resonance, 1988–96. Member of Council: Royal Soc., 1990–92; ICRF, 1991–96 (Chm., Scientific Adv. Cttee, 1994–96). Res. Dir, Lab. of Metabolic Medicine, Singapore, 2005–; Sen. Advr, Dean's Office, Nat. Univ. Health System, Singapore, 2009–. Non-exec. Dir, BTG plc, 1999–2005. Mem., various Editorial Bds of scientific jls including: Editor, Biochemical and Biophysical Research Communications, 1977–85; Man. Editor, Biochimica et Biophysica Acta, 1977–94 (Chm. Editl Bd, 1989–94); Mem. Editorial Bd, Interface, 2004–09. Founder Mem., Oxford Enzyme Gp, 1970–86; Pres., Soc. for Magnetic Resonance in Medicine, 1985–86. Mem., Fachbeirat, Max Planck Inst. für Systemphysiologie, Dortmund, 1987–93; Internat. Adv. Council Mem., Biomed. Res. Council, Singapore, 2003–06 (Bd Mem., 2005–). Trustee, Cancer Res. UK, 2003–06 (Dep. Chm., 2005–06). Mem., EMBO, 1997; MAE 1999; Fellow: Soc. of Magnetic Resonance, 1994; Internat. Acad. Cardiovascular Scis, 2001; ISMAR, 2008; Founding Fellow, Internat. Soc. Heart Res., 2000. Founder FMedSci 1998. Hon. Member: Eur. Soc. of Magnetic Resonance and Biol., 2007; Hungarian Acad. of Scis, 2010. Hon. FRCR 1985; Hon. MRCP 1987, Hon. FRCP 1997; Hon. Fellow, Amer. Heart Assoc., 1988. Hon. DM Bern, 1985; Hon. DSc (Med) London, 1991; Hon. DSc: Stirling, 1998; Sheffield, 1999; Debrecen, Hungary, 2001; Birmingham, 2003; Univ. de la Méditerranée, 2003; Aberdeen, 2004; Düsseldorf, 2004; Semmelweis Univ., Budapest, 2004; Hull, 2005; Leicester, 2006. Colworth Medal, Biochem. Soc., 1969; Feldberg Prize, Feldberg Foundn, 1982; British Heart Foundn Prize and Gold Medal for cardiovascular research, 1982; CIBA Medal and Prize, Biochem. Soc., 1983; Gold Medal, Soc. for Magnetic Resonance in Medicine, 1984; Buchanan Medal, Royal Soc., 1987; Internat. Lectr and Citation, Amer. Heart Assoc., 1987; Skinner Lecture and Medal, RCR, 1989; Rank Prize in Nutrition, 1991; Medal of Merit, Internat. Acad. of Cardiovascular Res., 2006; Public Service Medal, Friends of Singapore, 2008; Semmelweis Budapest Award, 2011; Biospectrum Asia Pacific Lifetime Award, 2013. Hon. Citizen of Republic of Singapore, 2015. *Publications:* articles in books and in jls of biochemistry and medicine. *Recreations:* opera, swimming, jazz. *Address:* Merton College, Oxford OX1 4JD.

RADER, Gen. Paul Alexander; General of the Salvation Army, 1994–99; *b* 14 March 1934; *s* of Lt-Col Lyell Rader and Gladys (*née* Damon); *m* 1956, (Frances) Kay Fuller; one *s* two *d*. *Educ:* Asbury Coll. and Seminary, USA (BA, BD); Southern Baptist Seminary (MTh); Fuller Theol Seminary (DMiss). Salvation Army: trng work in Korea, 1962–73; Trng Principal, 1973; Educn Sec., 1974–76; Asst Chief Sec., 1976, Chief Sec., 1977–84, Korea; Trng Principal, USA Eastern Territory, 1984–87; Divl Comdr, 1987–89; Chief Sec., 1989; Territorial Comdr, USA Western, 1989–94. Pres., Asbury Coll., Wilmore, Ky, 2000–06. Hon. LLD Asbury Coll., USA, 1984; Hon. DD: Asbury Theol Seminary, USA, 1995; Roberts Wesleyan Coll., USA, 1998; Hon. LHD Greenville Coll., USA, 1997. *Recreations:* jogging, reading, music. *Address:* 3953 Rock Ledge Lane, Lexington, KY 40513, USA.

RADFORD, Dr David; Chairman, NHS Devon, Plymouth and Torbay, 2011–13 (Chairman, Devon Primary Care Trust, later NHS Devon, 2006–11); *b* 22 April 1949; *s* of Ken and Dorothy Radford; *m* 1st, 1970, Josephine Mogridge; one *d*; 2nd, 1976, Madeleine Margaret Simms; two *d*. *Educ:* RN Sch., Malta; St John's Sch., Singapore; Manchester Univ. (BSc Hons Chem., MSc Organisation of Technology, PhD). Consumer Services Manager, CWS, 1974–75; Res. Dir, Welsh Consumer Council, 1975–77; Head of Res., Inst. of Housing, 1977–81; Asst Dir of Housing, Wolverhampton MBC, 1981–86; Asst Chief Exec., Wolverhampton MBC, 1986–90; Asst Chief Exec., Northants CC, 1990–97; Chief Exec., Somerset CC, 1997–2002; Lead Govt Official, Plymouth CC, 2003–06. Chm., SW Constitutional Convention, 2003–. *Recreations:* hill and coast walking, concert-going, sailing.

RADFORD, David Wyn; His Honour Judge Radford; Circuit Judge, since 1996, Senior Circuit Judge, since 2002; *b* 3 Jan. 1947; *s* of late Robert Edwin Radford, CB and Eleanor Margaret Radford (*née* Jones); *m* 1972, Nadine Radford, *qv*; two *s* two *d*. *Educ:* Cranleigh Sch.; Selwyn Coll., Cambridge (MA, LLM). Called to the Bar, Gray's Inn, 1969, Bencher, 2008; Asst Recorder, 1988; Recorder, 1993. Hon. Recorder of Redbridge, 2009–. *Recreations:* supporting Manchester City FC, theatre, walking, spending time with family. *Address:* Snaresbrook Crown Court, 75 Hollybush Hill, E11 1QW.

RADFORD, Georgina Margaret, (Gina), FRCP, FFPH; Deputy Chief Medical Officer, since 2015; *b* 25 April 1955; *d* of Edward Arthur Radford and Elsie (*née* Burdon). *Educ:* Guildford Co. Grammar Sch. for Girls; Royal Free Hosp. Sch. of Medicine (MB BS 1979). DCH 1982; DRCOG 1983; MFPHM 1989, FFPH (FFPHM 1997); FRCP 2002. Consultant in Public Health Medicine, S and W Surrey DHA, 1988–94; Dir of Public Health, S and W Devon HA, 1994–97; Hd, Public Health Develt Unit, NHS Exec., DoH, 1997–99; Regl Dir of Public Health, E of England, DoH, 2000–06; Dir of Public Health, NHS Fife, 2006–08; former Consultant in Public Health, Cambridgeshire PCT; Public Health Adviser: Anglia Cancer Network, 2009–13; Anglia Heart and Stroke Network, 2009–13; Centre Dir, Norfolk, Suffolk, Cambridge and Essex, PHE, 2013–14. *Recreations:* riding, singing/music, reading, travel, church warden and village duck warden, licensed Lay Minister in the Church of England.

RADFORD, Nadine Poggioli; QC 1995; *m* 1972, David Wyn Radford, *qv*; two *s* two *d*. Called to the Bar, Lincoln's Inn, 1974, Bencher, 1999; formerly an Assistant Recorder. *Address:* 3 Temple Gardens, EC4Y 9AU.

RADFORD, Prof. Peter Frank, PhD; Professor, Department of Sport Sciences, Brunel University, 1997–2005 (Hon. Professor Associate, School of Sport and Education, 2007; Visiting Professor, 2012–14); *b* 20 Sept. 1939; *s* of Frank Radford and Lillian E. Radford (*née* Marks); *m* 1961, Margaret M. (*née* Beard); one *d*. *Educ:* Tettenhall Coll.; Cardiff Coll. of Educn (Dip. of Physical Educn); Purdue Univ., USA (MSc); Univ. of Glasgow (PhD 1978). Mem., GB Athletics Teams, 1958–64: held British 100m record, 1958–78; World Records: Jun. 100m and Jun. 200m, 1958; Indoor 50m, 1959; 200m and 220 yards, 1960; 4 × 110 yards Relay, 1963; Bronze Medals, 100m and 4 × 100m Relay, Olympic Games, Rome, 1960. Lectr and Asst Prof., Sch. of Physical Educn and Athletics, McMaster Univ., 1967–75; University of Glasgow: Professor and Head of Departments of: Physical Educn and Recreation, 1976–87; Physical Educn and Sports Sci., 1987–94; Head of Dept, 1997–2000, Dir of Res., 2000–05, Dept of Sport Scis, Brunel Univ. Non-exec. Dir, Performance Brunel Ltd, 2004–. Vice-Chm., 1992–93, Chm., 1993–94, Exec. Chm., 1994–97, British Athletic Fedn. Scottish Sports Council: Mem., 1983–90; Mem., 1988–91, Chm., 1991–96, Drug Adv. Gp; Chm., Rev. of Coaching in Sport, 1991–93. Mem., Internat. Wkg Gp on Anti-Doping in Sport, 1991–93; Vice-Chm., 1992–94, Chm., 1994–98, Internat. Doping Convention, Council of Europe; Member: Saudi/British Memorandum of Understanding for Sport and Youth Welfare, 1990–2007; Compliance with Commitments Project, Council of Europe, 1998–99. Pres., Nat. Union of Track Statisticians, 2009–. Hon. DSc Wolverhampton, 2006. *Publications:* The Celebrated Captain Barclay, 2001; contrib. to various jls, conf. proc. and books on topics of sport, educn, sports science, sports history and doping control. *Recreations:* sports history 1650–1850, 18th and 19th century sporting art, gardening. *Address:* Bank House, 8 Sheep Street, Burford, Oxon OX18 4LT. *T:* (01993) 824836.

RADFORD, Lt Gen. Timothy Buchan, DSO 2010; OBE 2006 (MBE 1994); Deputy Commander Resolute Support, since 2015; *b* Dalton, Lancs, 23 Feb. 1963; *s* of Colin and Inge Radford; *m* 2001, Tracey Mary Titterington; two *s* one *d*. *Educ:* Methodist Coll. Belfast; Rugby Sch.; Durham Univ. (BA Hons Politics); King's Coll. London (MA War Studies). Joined Army, 1984; regtl duty and command, NI, Sierra Leone, Balkans, Iraq, 1984–2006; i/c 19 Lt Bde (Comd Task Force Helmand, Afghanistan), 2009; Hd, Overseas Ops, MoD, 2010–11; COS HQ ISAF Jt Comd, Kabul, Afghanistan, 2012; GOC Force Troops Comd, 2013–15; COS Land Forces, Army HQ, 2015. Pres., Army Lawn Tennis Assoc., 2012–. QCVS 2013. *Recreations:* family, tennis, gardening, art history. *Address:* c/o Military Secretary, Army Personnel Centre, Kentigern House, 65 Brown Street, Glasgow G2 8EX.

RADFORD, Timothy Robin; Science Editor, The Guardian, 1992–2005; *b* NZ, 9 Oct. 1940; *s* of Keith Ballantyne Radford and Agnes Radford; *m* 1964, Maureen Grace Coveney; one *s* one *d*. *Educ:* Sacred Heart Coll., Auckland. Reporter, NZ Herald, 1957–60; sub-ed., Fishing News, London, 1961–62; reporter, Hull Daily Mail, 1963–65; sub-ed., Dover Express, 1965–68; COI, 1968–73; joined The Guardian, 1973: Letters Ed., 1975–77; Arts Ed., 1977–80; Dep. Features Ed., 1980–88; Literary Ed., 1989–91. FRGS 1990. *Publications:* The Crisis of Life on Earth, 1990; (ed) Frontiers 01: science and technology 2001–02, 2002; (ed) Frontiers 03: new writing on cutting edge science by leading scientists, 2003; The Address Book: our place in the scheme of things, 2011. *Recreations:* reading, walking, travel. *Address:* 41 Downside Close, Eastbourne, E Sussex BN20 8EL.

RADICE, Baron *cr* 2001 (Life Peer), of Chester-le-Street in the County of Durham; **Giles Heneage Radice;** PC 1999; *b* 4 Oct. 1936. *Educ:* Winchester; Magdalen Coll., Oxford. Head of Research Dept, General and Municipal Workers' Union (GMWU), 1966–73. MP (Lab) Chester-le-Street, March 1973–1983, Durham North, 1983–2001. Opposition front bench spokesman on foreign affairs, 1981, on employment, 1981–83, on education, 1983–87; Mem., Treasury and Civil Service Select Cttee, 1987–96; Chairman: Public Service Select Cttee, 1996–97; Treasury Select Cttee, 1997–2001. Chm., EU Economic and Financial Affairs Sub-cttee, H of L, 2002–06; Mem., EU External Affairs Sub-cttee, H of L, 2011. Mem., Council, Policy Studies Inst., 1978–83. Chairman: European Movt, 1995–2001; British Assoc. for Central and Eastern Europe, 1997–2008 (Vice Chm., 1991–97); Franco British Council, 2002–07; Policy Network, 2007–09. Parly Fellow, St Antony's Coll., Oxford, 1994–95. Order of Merit (Germany), 1996; Légion d'Honneur (France), 2004. *Publications:* Democratic Socialism, 1965; (ed jointly) More Power to People, 1968; (co-author) Will Thorne, 1974; The Industrial Democrats, 1978; (co-author) Socialists in Recession, 1986; Labour's Path to Power: the new revisionism, 1989; Offshore: Britain and the European idea, 1992; The New Germans, 1995; (ed) What Needs to Change, 1996; Friends & Rivals, 2002; Diaries 1980–2001: the political diaries of Giles Radice, 2004; The Tortoise and the Hares, 2008; Trio, 2010; Odd Couples: the great political pairings of modern Britain, 2015. *Recreations:* reading, tennis. *Address:* The Longhouse, 3 Gelston, near Grantham, Lincs NG32 2AE.

RADICE, Elizabeth Joy; Headmistress, Haberdashers' Aske's School for Girls, Elstree, 2005–11; *b* 5 Feb. 1951; *d* of Donald and Joy Stephenson; *m* 1973, William Radice; two *d*. *Educ:* Wycombe Abbey Sch., High Wycombe; Somerville Coll., Oxford (BA Hons 1972). Hd of English, Sch. of St Helen and St Katharine, Abingdon, 1985–92; Dir of Studies, Royal Grammar Sch., Newcastle-upon-Tyne, 1996–98; Headmistress, Channing Sch., Highgate, London, 1999–2005. *Recreations:* books, theatre, film, cooking.

RADICE, Vittorio; Chief Executive, La Rinascente, since 2005; *b* Como, Italy, 2 April 1957; *m* Gemma; two *s*. *Educ:* Univ. of Milan. Head of Worldwide Sourcing, Home Furnishings Dept, Associated Merchandising Corp.; Buying Dir, Habitat Internat., 1990–92; Man. Dir, Habitat UK, 1992–96; Man. Dir, 1996–98, Chief Exec., 1998–2003, Selfridges plc; Exec. Dir, Home, Marks and Spencer plc, 2003–04. Non-executive Director: Abbey (formerly Abbey National) plc, 2001–04; Shoppers Stop India, 2001–06; McArthurGlen, 2005–; Ishaan Real Estate plc, 2006–; Conran Hldgs, 2011–.

RADNOR, 9th Earl of, *cr* 1765; **William Pleydell-Bouverie;** Bt 1714; Viscount Folkestone, Baron Longford, 1747; Baron Pleydell-Bouverie, 1765; *b* 5 Jan. 1955; *s* of 8th Earl of Radnor and of Anne (who later *m* Vice-Adm. Sir John Cox, KCB), *d* of Donald Seth-Smith, MC; *S* father, 2008; *m* 1996, Melissa, *d* of James Stanford, *qv*; four *s* two *d*. *Educ:* Harrow; Royal Agricultural Coll., Cirencester. Landowner and farmer, 1980s; with Christie's, 2008–. Gov., French Hosp., 'La Providence', Rochester. Trustee, Creative Foundn, Folkestone. Patron of two livings. *Recreations:* photography, looking at art, ski-ing. *Heir: s* Viscount Folkestone, *qv*. *Address:* Estate Office, Longford Castle, Salisbury, Wilts SP5 4ED.

RADOMSKY, Rabbi David; educational consultant; *b* 4 Sept. 1956; *s* of Benjamin and Rachel Radomsky; *m* 1981, Naomi; three *s* one *d*. *Educ:* BA Hons, MA (Dist.); Teaching Dip. NPQH. Ordained rabbi; rabbi/teacher, Mid Rashiat Noam Yeshiva High Sch., Israel, 1982–85; Communal Rabbi, Dublin, 1985–88; Rabbi, Wembley Synagogue, 1988–93; pt-time Lectr, Jews' Coll., 1991–93; Dep. Headteacher, Immanuel Coll., 1993–2000; Headteacher, Hasmonean High Sch., 2000–06. *E:* david@radomsky.co.uk.

RADWAY, Jonathan Mark; a District Judge (Magistrates' Courts), since 2011; *b* London, 6 Feb. 1955; *s* of John and Patricia Radway; *m* 1981, Margaret Rimmer (marr. diss. 2011); one *s* one *d*. *Educ:* Ardingly Coll.; Mid-Essex Tech. Coll. (LLB Hons London ext.); Inns of Court Sch. of Law. CEDR Accredited Mediator 2007. Called to the Bar, Middle Temple, 1977; Justices' Clerk, Huntingdon, Peterborough and Fenland Divs and Clerk to Cambs Magistrates' Courts Cttee, 1987–96; Justices' Chief Exec., Herts, 1996–2004; Actg Metropolitan Stipendiary Magistrate, subseq. Dep. Dist Judge (Magistrates' Courts), 1999–2011; Performance Dir, Courts Service, 2004–05. Internat. Consultancy with Agencia Consulting and British Embassies in Zagreb, Kyiv and Belgrade, undertaking Judicial Reform progs in Croatia, Ukraine and Serbia, 2006–11. Dir, Confugium Film Ltd, 2006–11; non-exec. Dir, Peterborough and Stamford Hosps NHS Foundn Trust, 2005–11 (Dep. Chm., 2006–11). Lay Mem., Chapter of Peterborough Cathedral, 2002–05. *Recreations:* travel, heritage railways, horology, playing the piano. *Address:* Stratford Magistrates' Court, 389–397 High Street, E15 4SB.

RAE, Hon. Lady; Rita Emilia Anna Rae; a Senator of the College of Justice in Scotland, since 2014; *b* 20 June 1950; *d* of Alexander Smith Cowie Rae and Bianca Bruno. *Educ:* Univ. of Edinburgh (LLB Hons). Apprentice, 1972–74, Asst Solicitor, 1974–76, Biggart Baillie & Gifford, Glasgow; Asst Solicitor and Partner, Ross Harper & Murphy, Glasgow, 1976–81; admitted Advocate, 1982; Temporary Sheriff, 1988–97; QC (Scot.) 1992; Sheriff of Glasgow and Strathkelvin, 1997–2014; Temporary Judge of High Ct, 2004–14. Tutor in Advocacy and Pleading, Strathclyde Univ., 1979–82; Mem., Legal 40, Univ. of Glasgow, 2010–. Vice-Chm., Parole Bd for Scotland, 2005–07 (Mem., 2001–07); Member: Sentencing Commn for Scotland, 2003–06; SACRO, 1998–; Nat. Strategic Adv. Gp on Violence Reduction, 2011–. Chm., Glasgow Br., Scottish Assoc. for Study of Offending (formerly Scottish Assoc. for Study of Delinquency), 2003–14 (Life Mem.). Mem. Bd, Conforti Inst., Coatbridge, 2011–. *Recreations:* classical music, opera, theatre, walking, gardening, learning piano. *Address:* Supreme Courts, Parliament House, 11 Parliament Square, Edinburgh EH1 1RQ. *T:* (0131) 225 2595.

RAE, Barbara Davis, CBE 1999; RA 1996, RSA 1992; RSW 1975; RGI; FRCA; FRSE; painter and printmaker; *d* of James Rae and Mary (*née* Young); *m*; one *s*. *Educ:* Morrison's Acad., Crieff; Edinburgh Coll. of Art (Dip.; Postgrad. Travelling Schol.); Moray House Coll. of Education. Art Teacher: Ainsley Park Comprehensive, Edinburgh, 1968–69; Portobello Secondary Sch., Edinburgh, 1969–72; Lectr in Drawing, Painting and Printmaking, Aberdeen Coll. of Educn, 1972–75; Lectr in Drawing and Painting, Glasgow Sch. of Art, 1975–96. Mem., Royal Fine Art Commn for Scotland, 1995–2005. Solo exhibitions include: New '57 Gall., Edinburgh, 1967, 1971; Univ. of York, 1969; Univ. of Aberdeen and Aberdeen Art Gall., 1974; Peterloo Gall., Manchester, 1975; Stirling Gall. and Greenock Arts Guild, 1976; Univ. of Edinburgh, 1978, 1979; Gilbert Parr Gall., London, 1977; Scottish Gall., Edinburgh, 1979, 1983, 1987, 1988, 1990, 1995, 1998, 2000, 2002, 2003, 2005, 2006; Festival Exhibn, Edinburgh, 2006, 2012; Wright Gall., Dallas, 1988; Leinster Fine Art, London, 1986; Glasgow Print Studio, 1987, 1992, 1997, 2003, 2013; Scottish Gall., London, 1989, 1990; Wm Jackson Gall., London, 1990, 1992; Perth Mus. and Art Gall., 1991; Clive Jennings Gall., London, 1992; Jorgensen Fine Art, Dublin, 1993, 1995, 2005; Waxlander Gall., Santa Fe, 1996; Bohun Gall., Henley on Thames, 1996; Art First, London, 1996, 1997, 1999, 2001, 2002; Graphic Studio Gall., Dublin, 1997, 2003, 2007, 2011; Printmakers Workshop, Edinburgh, 1997; Gall. Galtung, Oslo, 1998; Castlegate House Gall., Cumbria, 2003; North House Gall., Essex, 2004, New Prints, 2006; Tom Caldwell Gall., Belfast, 2004, 2006, 2011; Adam Gall., Bath, 2005; Sierra, Edinburgh Fest., 2006; Arizona, Richmond Hill Gall., Richmond, 2006, 2012; Adam Gall., London, 2008, 2012; Belfast Print Studio, 2008; RA, 2008, 2009, 2010, 2011, 2012, 2014; Stoney Road Print Studio, Dublin, 2012; Open Eye Gall., Edinburgh, 2013; Royal Scottish Acad. of Art, 2013, 2014; Dundas Gall., Edinburgh, 2013; Edinburgh Art Fest., 2013; Chris Caldwell Gall., Belfast, 2013; Pallant Gall., Chichester, 2014; touring exhibn, Scotland and Leeds, 1993–94; numerous gp exhibitions in Britain, Europe, USA, S America and Australia; art works in private and commercial collections worldwide, and museums in Scotland, England, Ire. and USA; commissions include: tapestry for Festival Theatre, Edinburgh, 1994; rug for Royal Mus. of Scotland, 1999; portraits. Hon. FRCA 2005 (FRCA 2003); Hon. RE 2009. Hon. DArts Napier, 1999; Hon. DLitt: Aberdeen, 2003; St Andrew's, 2008. Awards: Arts Council, 1968; Major Arts Council, 1975–81; Guthrie Medal, RSA, 1977; May Marshall Brown, RSW Centenary Exhibn, 1979; RSA Sir Wm Gillies Travel, 1983; Calouste Gulbenkian Printmaking, 1983; Alexander Graham Munro, RSW, 1989; Hunting Gp Prizewinner, 1990; Scottish PO Bd, RSA, 1990; Scottish Amicable, RGI, 1990; W. J. Burness, Royal Scottish Acad., 1990. *Relevant publications:* Barbara Rae, by B. Hare *et al*, 2008; Barbara Rae Prints, by A. Lambirth *et al*, 2010; Barbara Rae: sketchbooks, by Gareth Wardell *et al*, 2011. *Recreation:* travelling.

RAE, Fiona Elizabeth, RA 2002; artist; Professor of Painting, Royal Academy Schools, since 2011; *b* 10 Oct. 1963; *d* of Alexander Edward Ian Rae and Pamela Christine Rae; *m* 2002, Daniel Jonathan Perfect. *Educ:* Croydon Coll. of Art (Foundn Course Fine Art 1984); Goldsmiths Coll., London Univ. (BA 1st Cl. Hons Fine Art 1987). Artist Trustee, Tate, 2005–09. Selected *solo exhibitions:* Kunsthalle Basel, 1992; ICA, London, 1993–94; Galerie Nathalie Obadia, Paris, 1994, 2000, 2004, 2009, 2013; Buchmann Galerie, Cologne, 2000, 2005; Carré d'Art - Musée d'art contemporain de Nîmes, 2002–03; Tate Modern Restaurant commn, 2002–05; Timothy Taylor Gall., London, 2003, 2008, 2013; commn for Art Site, BBC Broadcasting House Public Art Prog., London, 2003; PaceWildenstein, NY, 2006, The Pace Gall., 2010; selected *group exhibitions:* Freeze, Surrey Docks, London, 1988; Aperto, La Biennale di Venezia XLIV, 1990; Turner Prize Exhibn, Tate Gall., London, 1991; Unbound: Possibilities in Painting, Hayward Gall., London, 1994; Sensation: Young British Artists from the Saatchi Collection, RA, London, Hamburger Bahnhof - Mus. für Gegenwart, Berlin and Brooklyn Mus. of Art, NY, 1997–2000; Painting Pictures: Painting and Media in the Digital Age, Kunstmus. Wolfsburg, 2003; Pictograms: the Loneliness of Signs, Kunstmus. Stuttgart, 2006–07; Reset: Werke aus der Sammlung Marx, Hamburger Bahnhof - Mus. für Gegenwart, Berlin, 2007–08; Classified: Contemporary British Art from Tate Collection, Tate Britain, 2009; Leeds Art Gall., 2012; New Art Gall., Walsall, 2012; Towner, Eastbourne, 2013. *Relevant publication:* Fiona Rae, by S. Wallis and J.-P. Criqui, 2002. *Address:* c/o Timothy Taylor Gallery, 15 Carlos Place, W1K 2EX. *T:* (020) 7409 3344. *E:* mail@timothytaylorgallery.com.

RAE, Gordon Hamilton; Director General, Royal Horticultural Society, 1993–99; *b* 12 Sept. 1938; *s* of Peter and Gwendoline Elizabeth Rae; *m* 1965, Judith Elizabeth Pickup; one *s* two *d*. *Educ:* Bablake Sch., Coventry; Wye Coll., Univ. of London (BSc Agric. Hons); Clare Coll., Cambridge (Dip. Agric.); Imperial Coll. of Tropical Agric., Trinidad (DTA). Agricl and Dist Agricl Officer, HM Colonial Service, Kenya, 1962–65; ICI, 1965–93: Gen. Manager, Agricl Chemicals Div., ICI do Brasil, São Paulo, 1980–84; Gen. Manager, ICI Garden and Professional Products, 1989–92. Non-exec. Dir, D. J. Squire & Co. Ltd, 1999–2007. LRPS 2012. Jt Patron, Garden Media Guild, 2007–; Patron, Grayshott Gardening, 2015–. FCIHort (FIHort 1996). VMH 1999. *Recreations:* gardening, family, travel, photography. *Address:* New House, Church Lane, Grayshott, Hindhead, Surrey GU26 6LY. *T:* (01428) 606025. *Club:* Farmers.

RAE, Dr John; Vice-Chairman, AWE plc, 2001–02 (Chief Executive, 2000–01); *b* 29 Sept. 1942; *s* of late John Rae and of Marion Rae (*née* Dow); *m* 1968, Irene (*née* Cassells); one *s* one *d*. *Educ:* Rutherglen Academy; University of Glasgow (BSc 1964, PhD 1967). FInstE 1987; FInstP 1996. Lecturing and research in physics: Univ. of Glasgow, 1967–68; Univ. of Texas, 1968–70; Univ. Libre, Brussels, 1970–72; Queen Mary College London, 1972–74; Theoretical Physics Div., Harwell: Industrial Fellow, 1974–76; Leader, Theory of Fluids Group, 1976–85; Acting Div. Head, 1985; Chief Scientist, Dept of Energy, 1986–89; Chief Exec., AEA Envmt & Energy, 1990–93; Business Develt Dir, 1993–95, Dir, Nat. Envmtl Technology Centre, 1994–95, AEA Technology; Man. Dir, NPL Mgt Ltd, 1995–2000. Member: SERC, 1986–89; NERC, 1986–89. Pres., NPL Sports Club, 1996–2000. Freeman, City of London, 1997; Liveryman, Scientific Instrument Makers' Co., 1997–. *Publications:* scientific papers in professional jls. *Recreations:* music, especially singing; gardening, astronomy.

RAE, Rita Emilia Ann; *see* Rae, Hon. Lady.

RAE, Hon. Robert Keith; PC (Can.) 1998; OC 2000; OOnt 2004; QC (Can.) 1984; Senior Partner, Olthius Kleer Townshend LLP, Toronto, since 2014; MP (Liberal) Toronto Centre, Canada, 2008–June 2013; interim Leader, Liberal Party, 2011–13; *b* 2 Aug. 1948; *s* of Saul Rae and Lois (*née* George); *m* 1980, Arlene Perly; three *d*. *Educ:* Ecole Internationale, Geneva; Univ. of Toronto (BA Hons 1969; LLB 1977); Balliol Coll., Oxford (BPhil 1971). MP for Broadview-Greenwood, Ontario, 1978–82; Finance Critic, New Democratic Party, 1979–82; MPP (NDP) York South, Ontario, 1982–95; Leader, Ontario New Democrats, 1982–96; Leader, Official Opposition, Ontario legislature, 1987–90; Premier of Ontario, 1990–95. Partner, Goodmans LLP (formerly Goodmans Phillips & Vineberg), 1996–2007. Director: Tembec Ltd, 1997–2006; Trojan Technologies, 2001–06. Adjunct Prof., Univ. of Toronto, 1997–; Sen. Fellow, Massey Coll., 1997–; Sen. Dist. Fellow, Sch. of Public Policy and Governance, Univ. of Toronto, 2013–. Dir, Canadian Ditchley Foundn, 1997–2006. Chairman: Forum of Fedns, 1999–2006; Royal Conservatory of Music, 2000; Toronto SO, 2002; Canadian Unity Council, 2002–06. Trustee, University Health Network, 1999–2006. Gov., Univ. of Toronto, 1999–2006; Nat. spokesperson, Leukemia Res. Fund of Canada, 1996–. Hon. LLD: Law Soc. of Upper Canada, 1998; Toronto, 1999; Assumption, 2001; Huntington, 2002. *Publications:* From Protest to Power, 1996; The Three Questions, 1998; Canada in the Balance, 2006; Exporting Democracy: the risks and rewards of pursuing a good idea, 2010. *Recreations:* tennis, golf, ski-ing, fishing, reading. *Address:* Olthius Kleer Townshend LLP, 8th Floor, 250 University Avenue, Toronto, ON M5H 3E5, Canada.

RAE, Air Vice-Marshal William McCulloch, CB 1993; Director, United Services Trustees (formerly United Services Trustee), 1996–2015; *b* 22 June 1940; *s* of William Brewster Rae and Margaret Rae; *m* 1964, Helen, *d* of Thomas and Eileen Reading; two *d*. *Educ:* Aberdeen Grammar School; psc, ndc, rcds. RAF 1958; Nos 213, 10, 55 Sqns, 1960–64; CFS (helicopter element), 1965–67; Radar Res. Flying Unit, Pershore, 1968–70; Sqn Comdr, 6 FTS, 1970–72; Inspectorate of Recruiting, 1973; RAF Staff Coll., 1974; Air Sec's Dept, 1975–77; NDC, 1978; OC 360 Sqn, 1979–81; CDS Staff, 1981–82; Central Policy Staff, MoD, 1982–85; Station Comdr, RAF Finningley, 1985–87; RCDS, 1988; Branch Chief, Policy, SHAPE, 1989–91; Sen. DS (Air), RCDS, 1992–95; Sen. Assessor, Charter Mark, Cabinet Office, 1996–97. Dealer in early English barometers, 1997–2007. *Recreations:* antiques, fly-fishing, wine, golf. *Club:* Royal Air Force.

RAEBURN, David Antony; College Lecturer, since 2000, and Rodewald Lector in Classical Languages, since 2003, New College, Oxford; Grammatikos (tutor in Ancient Greek Language), Faculty of Literae Humaniores, 1991–96, Grocyn Lecturer, 1992–96, University of Oxford; *b* 22 May 1927; *e s* of late Walter Augustus Leopold Raeburn, QC; *m* 1961, Mary Faith, *d* of Arthur Hubbard, Salisbury, Rhodesia (*d* 2013); two *s* one *d*. *Educ:* Charterhouse; Christ Church, Oxford (Schol., MA). 1st cl. hons Hon. Mods, 2nd in Greats. Nat. Service, 1949–51: Temp. Captain, RAEC. Asst Master: Bristol Grammar Sch., 1951–54; Bradfield Coll., 1955–58 (prod. Greek Play, 1955 and 1958); Senior Classics Master, Alleyn's Sch., Dulwich, 1958–62; Headmaster: Beckenham and Penge Grammar Sch., 1963–70 (school's name changed to Langley Park School for Boys, Beckenham in 1969); Whitgift Sch., Croydon, 1970–91. Schoolteacher Fellow-Commoner, Jesus Coll., Cambridge, 1980. Vis. Fellow, New Coll., Oxford, 1997. Chm. Classics Cttee, Schs Council, 1974–80; Pres., Jt Assoc. of Classical Teachers, 1983–85; Treas., HMC, 1984–89. FRSA 1969. *Publications:* trans. Ovid, Metamorphoses, 2004; trans. Sophocles, Electra and Other Plays, 2008; (jtly) The Agamemnon of Aeschylus: a commentary for students, 2011; essays on education; articles on Greek tragedy and Greek play production. *Recreation:* play production (produced Cambridge Greek Play, 1980, 1983). *Address:* 41 Ritchie Court, 380 Banbury Road, Oxford OX2 7PW. *T:* (01865) 553075.

RAEBURN, Michael Edward Norman; (4th Bt, *cr* 1923, but does not use the title); *b* 12 Nov. 1954; *s* of Sir Edward Alfred Raeburn, 3rd Bt, and Joan, *d* of Frederick Hill; *S* father, 1977; *m* 1979, Penelope Henrietta Theodora (marr. diss. 1997), *d* of Alfred Louis Penn; two *s* three *d*. *Heir: s* Christopher Edward Alfred Raeburn, *b* 4 Dec. 1981.

RAEBURN, Susan Adiel Ogilvie; QC (Scot.) 1991; Sheriff of Grampian, Highlands and Islands at Elgin, 2011–15; *b* 23 April 1954; *d* of George Ferguson Raeburn and Rose Anne Bainbridge (*née* Morison). *Educ:* St Margaret's Sch. for Girls, Aberdeen; Edinburgh Univ. (LLB). Admitted to Faculty of Advocates, 1977; temp. Sheriff, 1988–93; Sheriff of Glasgow and Strathkelvin, 1993–2011. Part-time Chairman: Social Security Appeal Tribunals, 1986–92; Med. Appeal Tribunals, 1992–93. *Recreations:* travel, the arts.

RAESIDE, Alison Louise; Her Honour Judge Raeside; a Circuit Judge, since 2011; *b* London, 3 Dec. 1958; *d* of Major John Powell and Gertrude Powell; *m* 1985, Mark Andrew Raeside, *qv*; three *s* one *d*. *Educ:* Godolphin and Latymer Sch., Hammersmith; Univ. of Manchester. Called to the Bar, Inner Temple, 1982; a District Judge, 2000–11. *Address:* Guildford County Court, Mary Road, Guildford GU1 4PS.

RAESIDE, Mark Andrew; QC 2002; **His Honour Judge Mark Raeside;** a Specialist Senior Circuit Judge, since 2013; *b* 27 Nov. 1955; *s* of Dr John Robertson Raeside and Annelie Raeside; *m* 1985, Alison Louise (*see* A. L. Raeside); three *s* one *d*. *Educ:* Univ. of Kent; Wolfson Coll., Cambridge (BA; MPhil). FCIArb 2001. Called to the Bar, Middle Temple, 1982, Bencher, 2011. Accredited Mediator, 2003; domestic and internat. commercial lawyer specialising in construction and engineering disputes. Military Cross (2nd class) (Estonia), 2004. *Recreations:* country and community life at West Sussex and Wester Ross estates, family life. *Address:* Leeds Combined Court Centre, The Courthouse, 1 Oxford Row, Leeds LS1 3BG. *Club:* Garrick.

RAFF, Prof. Jordan, PhD; César Milstein Professor of Cancer Cell Biology, University of Oxford, since 2009; Fellow, Lincoln College, Oxford, since 2009; *b* Montreal, 2 Nov. 1964; *s* of Prof. Martin Charles Raff, *qv* and Edith Dorsey Raff; *m* 1990, Rachel Crook; two *s* one *d*. *Educ:* Bristol Univ. (BSc); Imperial Coll. London (PhD 1989). Post-doctoral Fellow, Univ. of Calif, San Francisco, 1990–94; Gp Leader, 1994–2004, Sen. Gp Leader, 2004–08, Wellcome Trust/CRC, then CRUK Inst., later Gurdon Inst., Univ. of Cambridge. Member: British Soc. of Cell Biol., 1988– (Pres., 2011–); Amer. Soc. of Cell Biol., 1988–. Mem., EMBO, 2011. Editor-in-Chief, Biology Open, 2011–. *Publications:* Why Don't People Like Me?, 1999; contrib. Cell. *Recreation:* have you met my family? *Address:* Sir William Dunn School of Pathology, University of Oxford, South Parks Road, Oxford OX1 3RE. *E:* jordan.raff@path.ox.ac.uk.

RAFF, Prof. Martin Charles, CBE 2009; FRS 1985; Professor of Biology, 1979–2002, now Emeritus, and Hon. Fellow, since 2004, University College London; Member, MRC Laboratory for Molecular Cell Biology, since 1995; *b* 15 Jan. 1938; *s* of David and Reba Raff; *m* 1979, Carol Winter; two *s* one *d* by a previous marriage. *Educ:* McGill Univ. (BSc; MD; CM). House Officer, Royal Victoria Hosp., Montreal, 1963–65; Resident in Neurology, Massachusetts General Hosp., 1965–68; Postdoctoral Fellow, Nat. Inst. for Med. Res., 1968–71; Sen. Res. Fellow, UCL, 1971–79; Dir, MRC Develtl Neurobiology Programme, 1971–2002. Chm., UK Life Scis Cttee, 1997–2001. Pres., British Soc. of Cell Biology, 1991–95. Founder FMedSci 1998. Foreign Hon. Mem., American Acad. of Arts and Scis, 1999; For. Associate Mem., NAS, US, 2003. Hon. DSc McGill, 2005; Vrije Univ. Brussel, 2007. *Publications:* (jtly) T and B Lymphocytes, 1973; (jtly) Molecular Biology of the Cell, 1983, 6th edn 2015; (jtly) Essential Cell Biology, 1997, 4th edn 2014.
See also J. Raff.

RAFFAELLI, Surgeon Vice Adm. Philip Iain, CB 2012; FFOM, FRCP; Surgeon General, Ministry of Defence, 2009–12; *b* Kirkcaldy, Fife, 24 Nov. 1955; *s* of Nello and Margaret Raffaelli; *m* 2006, Fiona Ivy Buchanan; one *s* two *d*. *Educ:* St Andrew's High Sch., Kirkcaldy; Edinburgh Univ. (BSc Med. Sci. 1976; MB ChB 1979); London Sch. of Hygiene and Tropical Medicine (MSc 1987). MRCGP 1984; AFOM 1987, FFOM 1997; FRCP 1989. MO, HMS Renown, 1981–82; GP Trng, RN Hosp. Haslar and RM Deal, 1982–85; Dep. Sqn MO, Faslane, 1985–87; Sen. MO (Submarine Medicine), Inst. of Naval Medicine, 1988–89; Principal MO, HMS Neptune, 1990–92; Naval MO Health (Portsmouth), 1992–94; Submarine Flotilla MO, 1994–95; jsdc 1995; Med Op 2 (NATO) 1996–97. Prof. of Naval Occupational Medicine, 1997–99; Dir, Health (Navy), 1999–2002; MO i/c, Inst. of Naval Medicine, 2003–04; Chief Exec., Defence Med. Educn and Trng Agency, 2004–06; Dir, Med. Ops Capability, 2006–08; Dir Gen., Strategic Change and Inspector Gen., 2008–09. QHP, 2006–. Mem., Mgt Bd, 1999–2002, Chief Examr, 2002–05, Faculty of Occupational Medicine. Mem., Ct of Govs, LSHTM, 2007–; Gov., Univ. Hosp. of Birmingham Foundn Trust, 2009–12. Mem., Adv. Bd, Tickets for Troops, 2012–. Assoc. Officer, Gosport Conservatives. Hon. Fellow, Assoc. Surgeons of GB and Ireland, 2011. CStJ 2012. Order of Mil. Med. Merit (USA), 2011. *Recreations:* music, reading, gardening, travel, family. *Address:* Chadwick House, 14 St Mark's Road, Alverstoke, Gosport, Hants PO12 2DA. *T:* (023) 9236 2415. *E:* philip.raffaelli@gmail.com. *Club:* Royal Society of Medicine.

RAFFAN, Keith William Twort; Member (Lib Dem) Scotland Mid and Fife, Scottish Parliament, 1999–Jan. 2005; *b* 21 June 1949; *s* of A. W. Raffan, TD, MB, ChB, FFARCS and late Jean Crampton Raffan (*née* Twort), MB, ChB. *Educ:* Robert Gordon's Coll., Aberdeen; Trinity Coll., Glenalmond; Corpus Christi Coll., Cambridge (BA 1971; MA 1977). Parly Correspondent and sketch writer, Daily Express, 1981–83; internat. public relns consultant, NY, 1992–94; presenter, Welsh Agenda, HTV, 1994–98. Contested (C) Dulwich, Feb. 1974, and East Aberdeenshire, Oct. 1974; MP (C) Delyn, 1983–92. Mem., Select Cttee on Welsh Affairs, 1983–92. Introduced: Controlled Drugs (Penalties) Act (Private Member's Bill, 1985); Tourism (Overseas Promotion) (Wales) Act, 1991. Chief spokesman on home affairs, Scottish Lib Dem Party, 1998. Nat. Chm., PEST, 1970–74. *Clubs:* Chelsea Arts, Royal Automobile.

RAFFARIN, Jean-Pierre; Grand Officier de la Légion d'Honneur; Grand Croix, Ordre National du Mérite; Member for Vienne (UMP), French Senate, since 2005 (Vice President, 2011–14); Prime Minister of France, 2002–05; *b* 3 Aug. 1948; *s* of Jean Raffarin and Renée (*née* Michaud); *m* 1980, Anne-Marie Perrier; one *d*. *Educ:* Lycée Henri IV, Poitiers; Faculté de Droit, Paris-Assas; Ecole Supérieure de Commerce, Paris. Mktg Dept, Cafés Jacques Vabre, 1973–76; Advr, Office of Minister of Labour, 1976–81; Lectr, Inst. d'Etudes Politiques, Paris, 1979–88; Dir-Gen., Bernard Krief Communications, 1981–88; Gen. delegate, Inst. Euro-92, 1988–89. MEP (RPR-UDF), Poitou-Charentes, 1989–95; elected Mem. of Senate, for Vienne, 1995, 1997, 2004; Minister of Small and Medium Sized Businesses, Trade and Small Scale Industry, 1995–97. City Councillor, Poitiers, 1977–95; Regl Councillor, 1986–88, Chm., Regl Council, 1988–2002, Poitou-Charentes; Dep. Mayor, Chasseneuil-du-Poitou, 1995–2001. Nat. Delegate, Dep. Sec.-Gen. and Mem., Pol Bureau, 1977, Nat. Sec., 1989–95, PR; Dep. Sec.-Gen. and Spokesman, 1993–95, Sec.-Gen., 1995–97, UDF; Vice-Chm., Démocratie Libérale, 1997–2002. Pres., Assoc. of the Regions of France, 1998–2002. *Publications:* La vie en jaune, 1977; La publicité, nerf de la communication, 1983; L'avenir a ses racines, 1986; Nous sommes tous les régionaux, 1988; Pour une morale de l'action, 1992; Le livre de l'Atlantique, 1994; Pour une nouvelle gouvernance, 2002. *Recreations:* contemporary painting, regional literature.

RAFFE, Prof. David James; Professor of Sociology of Education, University of Edinburgh, since 1992; *b* Felixstowe, Suffolk, 5 May 1951; *s* of Jock and Elizabeth Raffe; *m* 1979, Shirley Paine; one *s* one *d*. *Educ:* Leys Sch., Cambridge; New Coll., Oxford (BA PPE 1972); Nuffield Coll., Oxford (BPhil Sociol. 1974). University of Edinburgh: Res. Fellow, Centre for Educnl Sociol., 1975–79; Lectr in Educn, 1979–84; Reader in Educn, 1984–92; Dir, Centre for Educnl Sociol., 1987–2001 and 2010–12. *Publications:* Reconstructions of Secondary Education, 1983, reissued 2012; Fourteen to Eighteen, 1984; Education and the Youth Labour Market, 1988; Part-time Higher Education, 1999; Policy-making and Policy Learning in 14–19 Education, 2007; contrib. articles to educnl and other social sci. jls. *Recreations:* walking in the diverse landscapes of Scotland and occasionally elsewhere, concerts, family, various educational committees, informal participatory research into the NHS. *Address:* Centre for Educational Sociology, University of Edinburgh, St John's Land, Holyrood Road, Edinburgh EH8 8AQ. *T:* (0131) 651 6237. *E:* David.Raffe@ed.ac.uk.

RAFFERTY, Rt Hon. Dame Anne (Judith), (Dame Anne Barker), DBE 2000; PC 2011; **Rt Hon. Lady Justice Rafferty;** a Lord Justice of Appeal, since 2011; *m* 1977, Brian John Barker, *qv*; three *d* (and one *d* decd). *Educ:* Univ. of Sheffield (LLB; Hon. LLD 2005). Called to the Bar, Gray's Inn, 1973, Inner Temple *ad eundem*, 1996; Bencher, Gray's Inn, 1998; QC 1990; a Recorder, 1991–2000; Head of Chambers, 1994–2000; a Dep. High Court Judge, 1996–2000; a Judge of the High Court of Justice, Queen's Bench Div., 2000–11; Presiding Judge, SE Circuit, 2003–06. Criminal Bar Association: Mem. Cttee, 1986–89; Sec., 1989–91; Vice-Chm., 1993–95; Chm., 1995–97; Chm., Bar Conf., 1992. Chm., Judicial Coll., 2014–; Vice Chm., Criminal Procedure Rule Cttee, 2012–. Mem., Royal Commn on Criminal Justice, 1991–93. Member: SE Circuit Cttee, 1987–90; Pigot Cttee, 1988–89; Circuit Cttee, SE Circuit, 1991–94; Criminal Cttee, Judicial Studies Bd, 1998–2000; Sentencing Council, 2010–12. Gov., Expert Witness Inst., 1997–99. Chancellor, Univ. of Sheffield, 2015–. Mem., Appeal Ct, Oxford Univ., 2003–. Mem. Council, Eastbourne Coll., 1993–2006. *Recreation:* Apostrophe Chambers. *Address:* Royal Courts of Justice, Strand, WC2A 2LL.

See also P. A. Darling.

RAFFERTY, Kevin Robert; Professor, Institute for Academic Initiatives, Osaka University, since 2013; Editor in Chief, PlainWords Media, London, Hong Kong and Osaka, since 2003; Editor/Publisher, HandaiGlobal, since 2014; Columnist, South China Morning Post, Hong Kong, The Japan Times, Tokyo, since 2006, and Dainik Bhaskar, India, since 2010; *b* 5 Nov. 1944; *s* of Leo and Thérèse Rafferty; *m* 2009, Prof. Mikako Hayashi. *Educ:* Marist Coll., Kingston upon Hull; Queen's Coll., Oxford (MA). Journalistic training, The Guardian, Sun, 1966–69; Financial Times, 1970–76; Founder Editor, Business Times Malaysia, 1976–77; Consultant Editor, Indian Express Gp, 1978–79; Foreign Correspondent, Financial Times, 1980; Asia Pacific Editor, Institutional Investor, 1981–87; Ed., The Universe, 1987–88. Founder Editor, then Associate Editor, Asia and Pacific Review, Saffron Walden, 1980–93; Managing Editor: Internat. Media Partners, NY, 1989–96; World Bank, Washington, 1997–99; Business Editor, then Actg Editor, Hong Kong Standard, 1999–2001; Editor in Chief, Business Day, Thailand, 2001–05. *Publications:* City on the Rocks: Hong Kong's uncertain future, 1989; Inside Japan's Power Houses, 1995; India: briefing book, 2007; Faces of the Bank's World (calendars), 1998, 1999. *Recreations:* travelling, meeting ordinary people, reading, taking photographs. *E:* editor@handaiglobal.org, plainwordseditor@gmail.com. *Clubs:* Oxford and Cambridge; Foreign Correspondents (Hong Kong).

RAFFERTY, Stuart; QC 2009; **His Honour Judge Rafferty;** a Circuit Judge, since 2012; *b* Mexborough, Yorks, 22 Sept. 1952; *s* of Ronald Stuart and Nellie Rafferty; *m* 1983, Ann Saxby; two *s*. *Educ:* Long Eaton Grammar Sch.; Lanchester Poly., Coventry (BA Hons Business Law); Inns of Court Sch. of Law. Called to the Bar, Gray's Inn, 1975; in practice as barrister specialising in crime; a Recorder (Crime), 2001–12, (Civil), 2004–12. *Recreations:* family life, gardening, music, the theatre, walking, convivial company. *Address:* Nottingham Crown Court, 60 Canal Street, Nottingham NG1 7EL. *Club:* Reform.

RAGGATT, Timothy Walter Harold; QC 1993; a Recorder, since 1994; *b* 13 April 1950; *s* of late Walter George and Norah Margaret Raggatt. *Educ:* Redditch County High Sch.; King's Coll. London (LLB 1971). Called to the Bar, Inner Temple, 1972, Bencher, 1999; Tutor, Inns of Court Sch. of Law, 1972–73; in practice on Midland and Oxford Circuit, 1974–; an Asst Recorder, 1991–94. Mem., Professional Assoc. of Diving Instructors, 1992–. *Recreations:* golf, scuba diving, bridge and snooker. *Address:* 4 King's Bench Walk, Temple, EC4Y 7DL; St Philips Chambers, 55 Temple Row, Birmingham B2 5LS. *Clubs:* Athenæum, Royal Automobile; Blackwell Golf (Birmingham).

RAGHUNATHAN, Prof. Madabusi Santanam, Padma Bhushan, 2012 (Padma Shri, 2001); PhD; FRS 2000; FIASc, FNA; Distinguished Guest Professor and Head, National Mathematics Center, India Institute of Technology Bombay, since 2011; *b* 11 Aug. 1941; *s* of Madabusi Sudarsanam Iyengar Santanam and Ambuja Santanam; *m* 1968, Ramaa Rangarajan; one *s*. *Educ:* Vivekananda Coll., Univ. of Madras (BA Hons 1960); Bombay Univ. (PhD 1966). Tata Institute of Fundamental Research: Associate Prof., 1966–70; Prof., 1970–80; Sen. Prof., 1980–90; Distinguished Prof., 1990–97; Prof. of Eminence, 1997–2006; Homi Bhabha Prof., 2006–11. FIASc 1974; FNA 1975; Fellow, Third World Acad. of Scis, 1994. Bhatnagar Award, Council of Scientific and Industrial Res., India, 1977; Third World Acad. Award, Trieste, 1991. *Publications:* Discrete Subgroups of Lie Groups, 1972; contrib. papers to Annals of Maths, Inventiones Mathematicae, etc. *Address:* Department of Mathematics, IIT Bombay, Powai, Mumbai 400 076, India. *T:* (office) (22) 25769453; (home) (22) 25504766.

RAGLAN, 6th Baron *cr* 1852; **Geoffrey Somerset;** *b* Usk, Monmouthshire, 29 Aug. 1932; *yr s* of 4th Baron Raglan and Hon. Julia Hamilton, CStJ (*d* 1971), *d* of 11th Baron Belhaven and Stenton, CIE; *S* brother, 2010; *m* 1956, Caroline Rachel (*d* 2014), *d* of late Col E. R. Hill, DSO; two *d* (one *s* decd). *Educ:* Dragon Sch.; Westminster; Royal Agricultural Coll., Cirencester. Nat. Service, Grenadier Guards, 1952–54. Sales Promoter, Standard Motor Co., 1957–60; Gp Mktg Manager, Lambourn Engrg Gp, 1960–71; wine shipper, 1971–94. Member: Berks CC, 1966–75; Newbury DC, 1978–83; Oxon CC, 1988–93. Mem., Thames Valley Valuation Tribunals, 1987–2004 (a Chm., 1996–2004). Chm., Vale of White Horse Dist, CPRE, 2000–04. *Recreations:* shooting, conservation. *Heir:* *g s* Inigo Arthur Fitzroy Somerset, *b* 6 July 2004. *Address:* Manor Farm Cottage, Sutton-in-the-Vale, Faringdon, Oxon SN7 8NN. *T:* (01367) 710558. *E:* geoffrey.somerset@btinternet.com.

RAHMAN, Prof. Atta-ur-, Nishan-i-Imtiaz, 2002; PhD, ScD; FRS 2006; Director, H. E. J. Research Institute of Chemistry, 1990–2008, Patron in Chief, International Center for Chemical and Biological Sciences, since 2008, and Professor Emeritus, 2010, University of Karachi; Coordinator General, Organization of Islamic Conference Standing Committee on Scientific and Technological Cooperation, 1996–2012; President: Pakistan Academy of Sciences, 2003–06 and since 2011 (Vice President, 1997–2001); Network of Academies of Science of Islamic Countries, since 2004; *b* Delhi, 22 Sept. 1942; *s* of Jameel-Ur-Rahman and Amtul Subhan Begum; *m* Nargis Jamal; four *s*. *Educ:* Karachi Univ. (BSc 1963; MSc 1964); King's Coll., Cambridge (PhD 1968; ScD 1987; Hon. Life Fellow, 2007). Karachi University: Lectr, 1964–69; Asst Prof., 1969–74; Associate Prof., 1974–76; Prof. 1981–90; Co-Director, H. E. J. Research Inst. of Chem., 1977–80 and 1981–90. D. A. A. D. Fellow, Univ. of Tübingen, 1979; Einstein Prof., Chinese Acad. of Scis, 2013. Government of Pakistan: Minister: for Sci. and Technol., 2000–02; Min. of Educn, 2002; Min. of Sci. and Technol., 2003–04; Chm., Higher Educn Commn, 2002–08; Advr to Prime Minister for Sci. and Technol., 2005–07. Higher Educn Commn Dist. Nat. Prof., 2011. Pres., Chem. Soc. of Pakistan, 1992; Vice-Pres. (Central and S Asia), Acad. of Scis for the Developing World, 2007–. Editor: Studies in Natural Products Chemistry series, vols 1–35, 1986–; Current Medicinal Chem., Organic Synthesis, Organic Chem., Pharmaceutical Analysis, Nanosci., Analytical Chem., Bioactive Compounds, Chemical Biol.; Medicinal Chem.; Nanosci. and Nanotechnol.—Asia; Natural Products Jl. FRSC 1981; Fellow: Pakistan Acad. of Scis, 1982; Islamic Acad. of Scis, 1988; Third World Acad. of Scis; Inst. of Chemistry, Colombo, 2014. Hon. DEd Coventry, 2007; Hon. DSc: Sir Syed Engrg Univ., Karachi, 2003; Gomal Univ., 2004; Univ. of Karachi, 2005; Bradford, 2010; Hon. PhD: Asian Inst. of Technol., Thailand, 2010; Univ. of Technol., Mara, Malaysia, 2011. Islamic Gold Medal, 1977, Open Gold Medal, 1984, Pakistan Acad. Scis; Fedn of Pakistan Chambers of Commerce and Industry Prize for Technol Innovation, 1985; Scientist of the Yr Award, Pakistan, 1987; Islamic Orgn Prize, Kuwait Foundn for Advancement of Scis, 1988; Babai Urdu Award, 1994; Pakistan Acad. Scis-Infaq Foundn Prize, Gold Medal, 1996; UNESCO Sci. Prize, 1999; Award for Chem. Scis, 1999, Prize for Instn Bldg (Italy), 2009, Third World Acad. Scis; Econ. Cooperation Orgn Prize, 2000; Chem. Award, Islamic Educnl, Scientific and Cultural Orgn, 2001; Engro Excellence Award, 2010. Nishan-i-Imtiaz (Pakistan), 2002 (Tamgha-i-Imtiaz, 1983; Sitara-i-Imtiaz, 1991; Hilal-i-Imtiaz, 1998); Gold Medal (Kuwait), 1980; Order of Golden Sash (Austria), 2007; Friendship Award (China), 2014. *Publications:* Biosynthesis of Indole Alkaloids (with A. Basha), 1983; Nuclear Magnetic Resonance, 1986; One and Two Dimensional Nuclear Magnetic Resonance Spectroscopy, 1989; (with Zahir Shah) Stereoselective Synthesis in Organic Chemistry, 1993; (with M. I. Choudhary) Solving Problems with Nuclear Magnetic Resonance Spectroscopy, 1996; contrib. over 155 books and jls; over 900 res. articles; 37 patents. *Address:* H. E. J. Research Institute of Chemistry, International Centre for Chemical and Biological Sciences, University of Karachi, Karachi 75270, Pakistan.

RAILTON, David; QC 1996; a Recorder, since 2000; *b* 5 June 1957; *s* of late Andrew Scott Railton, MC and of Margaret Elizabeth Railton (*née* Armit); *m* 1996, Sinéad Major; one *s* one *d*. *Educ:* Balliol Coll., Oxford (BA). Called to the Bar, Gray's Inn, 1979, Bencher, 2005. *Recreations:* cricket, golf. *Address:* Fountain Court, Temple, EC4Y 9DH.

RAILTON, Elizabeth Jane, CBE 2006; Director for Children's Services Self-Improvement, Children's Improvement Board, Local Government Association, 2011–12; *b* 21 Nov. 1952; *d* of John and Jill Nisbet; *m* 1974, James Lancelot Railton (*d* 2012); two *s*. *Educ:* Somerville Coll., Oxford (MA, MSc). CQSW 1978. Social worker, 1974–86; Hertfordshire County Council: Social Services Manager, 1986–91; Asst Dir of Social Services, 1991–95; Dep. Dir, Social Services, 1995–96; Dir, Social Services, Cambs CC, 1998–2002; Essex County Council: Dep. Chief Exec., Learning and Social Care, 2003–05; Dir, Children's Services, 2005–06; Nat. Programmes Dir, Serco Ltd, 2007–11 (Together for Children, 2007–08; Together for Children and Together for Disabled Children, 2008–11; Together for Children and Learners, 2009–11). Hon. Sec., Assoc. of Dirs of Social Services, 2002–06. Trustee: British Assoc. Adoption and Fostering, 2001–06; Nat. Children's Bureau, 2015. *Recreations:* shopping, travel.

RAINBOW, Prof. Philip Stephen, DSc, PhD; CBiol, FRSB, FLS, FMBA; Keeper of Zoology, 1997–2013 and Head, Department of Life Sciences, 2012–13, Natural History Museum (Director of Science, 2011); *b* 21 Oct. 1950; *s* of Frank Evelyn Rainbow, OBE and Joyce May Victoria Rainbow (*née* Turner); *m* 1973, Mary Meaken; two *s*. *Educ:* Bedford Sch., Bedford; Clare Coll., Cambridge (MA); UCNW, Bangor (PhD 1975; DSc 1994). CBiol 1998, FRSB (FIBiol 1998). Queen Mary College, later Queen Mary and Westfield College, University of London: Lectr, 1975–89; Reader in Marine Biology, 1989–94; Prof. of Marine Biology, 1994–97; Head, Sch. of Biol Scis, 1995–97; Vis. Prof., 1997–2013. Mem., Darwin Initiative Adv. Cttee, DEFRA, 2003–09. Gov. and Mem. Council, Marine Biol Assoc. UK, 2008–; Mem., Bd of Trustees, Nat. Biodiversity Network, 2008–13. FLS 1985; FMBA 2014. *Publications:* (ed jtly) Aspects of Decapod Crustacean Biology, 1988; (ed jtly) Heavy Metals in the Marine Environment, 1990; (ed jtly) Ecotoxicology of Metals in Invertebrates, 1993; (jtly) Biomonitoring of Trace Aquatic Contaminants, 1993, 2nd edn 1994; (ed jtly) Forecasting the Environmental Fate and Effects of Chemicals, 2001; (jtly) Metal Contamination in Aquatic Environments: science and lateral management, 2008; (ed jtly) Environmental Assessment of Estuarine Ecosystems, 2009; (ed jtly) Tolerance to Environmental Contaminants, 2011; (ed jtly) Ecological Biomarkers: indicators of ecotoxicological effects, 2012; numerous papers in scientific jls. *Recreations:* cricket, Rugby, natural history. *E:* philipstephenrainbow@gmail.com. *Club:* Tetrapods.

RAINE, Craig Anthony; poet; Fellow of New College, Oxford, 1991–2010, now Emeritus; Editor, Areté, since 1999; *b* 3 Dec. 1944; *s* of Norman Edward Raine and Olive Marie Raine; *m* 1972, Ann Pasternak Slater; one *d* three *s*. *Educ:* Barnard Castle Sch.; Exeter Coll., Oxford (BA Hons in English; BPhil). College Lecturer, Oxford University: Exeter Coll., 1971–72; Lincoln Coll., 1974–75; Exeter Coll., 1975–76; Christ Church, 1976–79. Books Editor, New Review, 1977–78; Editor, Quarto, 1979–80; Poetry Editor: New Statesman, 1981; Faber & Faber, 1981–91. Cholmondeley Poetry Award, 1983; Sunday Times Writer of the Year, 1998. *Publications:* The Onion, Memory, 1978, 5th edn 1986; A Martian Sends a Postcard Home, 1979, 8th edn 1990; A Free Translation, 1981, 2nd edn 1981; Rich, 1984, 3rd edn 1985; The Electrification of the Soviet Union, 1986; (ed) A Choice of Kipling's Prose, 1987; The Prophetic Book, 1988; '1953', 1990; Haydn and the Valve Trumpet (essays), 1990; (ed) Rudyard Kipling: Selected Poetry, 1992; History: The Home Movie, 1994; Clay. Whereabouts Unknown, 1996; (ed jtly) New Writing 7, 1998; A la recherche du temps perdu, 2000; In Defence of T. S. Eliot (essays), 2000; Collected Poems 1978–1999, 2000; (ed) Rudyard Kipling: The Wish House and other stories, 2002; T. S. Eliot, 2006; Heartbreak (novel), 2010; How Snow Falls (poetry), 2010; The Divine Comedy (novel), 2012; More Dynamite (essays), 2013; My Grandmother's Glass Eye: a look at poetry, 2015. *Recreations:* music, ski-ing. *Address:* c/o New College, Oxford OX1 3BN.

RAINE, John Stephen; County Director, then Chief Executive, Derbyshire County Council, 1989–97; *b* 13 April 1941; *s* of Alan and Ruby Raine; *m* 1961, Josephine Elizabeth Marlow; two *s*. *Educ:* Sir Joseph Williamson's Mathematical School, Rochester. MCIPR. Journalist; Kent Messenger, Sheffield Morning Telegraph, Sheffield Star, Raymond's News Agency, 1957–70; Press Officer, East Midlands Gas, 1970–73; Derbyshire County Council: County Public Relations Officer, 1973–79; Asst to Clerk and Chief Exec., 1979–81; Asst Chief Exec., 1981–88; Dep. County Dir, 1988–89. Chairman: Derbys Probation Bd, 2001–07; Nat. Assoc. of Probation Bds for England and Wales, 2004–07. Chairman: Hearing Aid Council, 1997–2003; Derbys Assoc. for the Blind, 1997–2007. Non-exec. Dir, Chesterfield and N Derbys Royal Hosp. NHS Trust, 1998–2006; Chairman: Derbys County NHS PCT, 2006–09; Scottish Borders NHS Bd, 2011–; Ind. Chm., Child Protection Cttee, Scottish Borders, 2010–12. *Recreations:* gardening, walking, travel. *Address:* Prieston House, Melrose, Roxburghshire TD6 9HQ. *T:* (01835) 870219.

RAINE, June Munro, CBE 2009; FRCP, FRCPE; Director, Vigilance and Risk Management of Medicines Division (formerly Post Licensing Division), Medicines and Healthcare products Regulatory Agency, since 2003 (Director, Post-Licensing Division, Medicines Control Agency, 1998–2003), Department of Health; *b* 20 June 1952; *d* of David Harris and Isobel Harris (*née* Munro); *m* 1975, Prof. Anthony Evan Gerald Raine (*d* 1995); one *s* one *d*. *Educ:* Herts & Essex High Sch.; Somerville Coll., Oxford (BA Hons 1st Cl. 1974; MSc 1976; BM BCh 1978). MRCP 1980, FRCP 2003; MRCGP 1982; FRCPE 1995. Department of Health: SMO, Medicines Div., 1985–89; Gp Manager, Medicines Control Agency, 1989–98; Principal Assessor to Medicines Commn, 1992–2005. Mem., wkg gps on aspects of pharmaceutical regulation, EC; Chm., Pharmacovigilance Risk Assessment Cttee, Eur. Medicines Agency, 2010–. FRSocMed 2000. Hon. FBPhS (Hon. FBPharmacolS 2015). *Publications:* papers on pharmacology, adverse drug effects and regulation of medicines. *Recreations:* music, opera, travel. *Address:* Medicines and Healthcare products Regulatory Agency, 151 Buckingham Palace Road, SW1W 9SZ.

RAINE, Sandra Margaret; company secretary, until 2014; *b* 7 March 1958; *d* of Charles Kitchener Lovell and Mary Rosaline Lovell (*née* O'Hare); *m* 1980, Ian Henry Raine. *Educ:* Univ. of Newcastle upon Tyne (BA Hons Sociol. and Social Admin). ACIS 1986. Pensions Asst, Dunlop Ltd, 1980; Admin. Officer, NE Council on Alcoholism, 1980–82; Sen. Admin. Asst, Newcastle upon Tyne Poly., 1982–85; Asst Co-ordinator, Urban Programmes, Gateshead MBC, 1985–86; Asst Divl Dir, Berks Social Services, 1986–90; Asst Co. Sec., AA, 1990–91; Ben Fund Sec., Chartered Inst. Building, 1992–94; Sec. and Chief Exec., IGasE, 1994–99; Co. Sec., Paddington Churches Housing Assoc., subseq. Gp Co. Sec., Genesis Housing Gp Ltd, 1999–2003; Exec. Dir, Internat. Headache Soc., 2003–05. Trustee, subseq. Chm., Inst. of Plumbing and Heating Engrg, 2005–11. Liveryman, Plumbers' Co., 2007. *Recreations:* keep fit, reading, genealogy. *Club:* Nirvana (Berkshire).

RAINEY, Mary Teresa, OBE 2015; Chairman, Think Ltd, since 2008; Founder and Director, horsesmouth.co.uk, since 2005; *d* of Peter and Margaret Rainey. *Educ:* Glasgow Univ. (MA Hons); Aston Univ. Corporate Hd of Planning, Chiat/Day, US, 1983–89; CEO, Chiat/Day, London, 1989–93; Founding Partner, Rainey Kelly Campbell Roalfe, 1993–99; Jt CEO, 1999–2003, Chm., 2003–05, Rainey Kelly Campbell Roalfe/Y&R. Non-executive Director: WH Smith, 2003–08; SMG, 2005–07; Channel 4, 2012–; Pinewood Gp, 2015–. Chm., Marketing Gp of GB, 2005–06. Mem., Women's Advertising Club of London, 1991–; Pres., Thirty Club, 2012–13. Mem., Nat. Skills Forum, 2007–12; Vice Chm., Creative Skillset, 2009–. *Publications:* numerous contribs to jls of advertising and mkt res. industries incl. ADMAP and Market Leader. *Recreations:* reading, music, hill-walking. *E:* mt@mtrainey.com.

RAINEY, Philip Carslake; QC 2010; *b* Tyneside, 25 Oct. 1968; *s* of George Rainey and Mavis Storey; *m* 1995, Helen Staples; two *s* one *d*. *Educ:* King's Sch., Tynemouth; Univ. of Leicester (LLB 1989). Called to the Bar, Middle Temple, 1990; in practice as barrister, 1991–; Hd of Chambers, 2013–. Mem., Civil Procedure Rule Cttee, 2001–08. Member: Property Bar Assoc., 2000–; Chancery Bar Assoc., 2007–. MCIArb 1999. *Publications:* (jtly) Service Charges and Management, 2006, 3rd edn 2013; (jtly) Rent Review, 2008; (contrib.) Smith and Monckcom: The Law of Gambling, 3rd edn 2009; (jtly) Megarry's Manual of the Law of Real Property, 9th edn 2014. *Recreations:* family, sailing (fairweather), history. *Address:* Tanfield Chambers, 2–5 Warwick Court, WC1R 5DJ. *T:* (020) 7421 5300, *Fax:* (020) 7421 5333. *E:* clerks@tanfieldchambers.co.uk.

RAINEY, Simon Piers Nicholas, FCIArb; QC 2000; a Recorder, since 2001; a Deputy High Court Judge, since 2008; *b* 14 Feb. 1958; *s* of Peter Michael Rainey and Theresa Cora Rainey (*née* Heffernan); *m* 1st, 1986, Pia Witlox (marr. diss. 1999); twin *s* one *d*; 2nd, 2000, Charlotte Rice. *Educ:* Cranbrook Sch.; Corpus Christi Coll., Cambridge (BA 1st Cl. Hons Law 1980; MA 1984); Univ. Libre de Bruxelles (Licence en Droit Européen (Dist) 1981). FCIArb 2013. Called to the Bar, Lincoln's Inn, 1982; Western Circuit. *Publications:* Maritime Laws of West Africa, 1985; Ship Sale and Purchase, 1993; Law of Tug and Tow, 1996, 3rd edn 2011; Law and Practice of Voyage Charterparties, 2009; Cargo Claims: from The Hague to the Rotterdam Rules, 2010; Pollution at Sea: law and liability, 2012; Carriage of Goods by Land, Sea and Air, 2014. *Recreations:* classical music, print-collecting, ski-ing. *Address:* Quadrant Chambers, 10 Fleet Street, EC4Y 1AU. *T:* (020) 7583 4444. *E:* simon.rainey@quadrantchambers.com.

RAINFORD, Rev. (Robert) Graham; Associate Priest, Holy Trinity Church, Sloane Street, since 2012 (Priest Administrator, 2005–08; Assistant Priest, 2008–12); Head of Religious Studies, Sussex House School, Cadogan Square, since 2011; *b* 23 April 1955; *s* of late Robert Rainford and Mary Madeline Victory Rainford (*née* Saunders); *m* 1979 (marr. diss. 2006); two *s* one *d*; *m* 2006, Anne Barrett. *Educ:* Bootle Grammar Sch. for Boys; St Martin's Coll. of Educn, Lancaster (Cert Ed; BEd); St Stephen's House, Oxford (Cert. Theol. 1983). Schoolmaster, Seedfield Sch., Bury, 1977–81. Ordained deacon, 1983, priest, 1984; Curate, St Catherine with St Alban and St Paul, Burnley, 1983–86; Priest-in-charge, 1986–89, Vicar, 1989–2003, St Christopher, Hawes Side, Blackpool; Priest-in-charge, St Nicholas, Marton Moss, Blackpool, 2001–03; Area Dean of Blackpool, 2000–03; Sen. Chaplain to the Bishop of Dover and Canterbury Chaplain to the Archbishop of Canterbury, 2003–05. Industrial Chaplain, Blackpool Pleasure Beach, 1987–2003; Chaplain, 1988–2012, Mem. Council, 2011–12, Actors' Church Union; Asst Theatre Chaplain, Marlowe Th., Canterbury, 2004–05; Theatre Chaplin, Garrick Th., London, 2011–12; Chaplain, Peter Jones, Sloane Sq., 2012–. Chm., House of Clergy, Blackburn Diocesan Synod, 2000–03; Hon. Canon, Blackburn Cathedral, 2001–03. Hon. Chaplain, Garden House Sch., Chelsea; Hon. Asst Chaplain, Lister Hosp., Chelsea, 2008–12. Member: London Diocesan Synod, 2012–; Bishop of London's Council, 2012–. Chairman of Governors: Marton Primary Sch., 1991–2003; Holy Trinity C of E Primary Sch., Chelsea, 2006–; Vice Chm. Govs, Hawes Side Primary Sch., Blackpool; Gov., St George's C of E High Sch., Blackpool, 2002–03. Non-magisterial Mem., Lord-Lieut of Lancs Adv. Cttee. *Recreations:* travel (pilgrimage), theatre, opera, music, art, architecture, reading, cooking, gardening, photography, walking. *Address:* Holy Trinity Church, Sloane Street, SW1X 9BZ. *T:* (020) 7730 7270. *E:* priest@holytrinitysloanesquare.co.uk.

RAINGER, Peter, CBE 1978; FRS 1982; FREng; Deputy Director of Engineering, British Broadcasting Corporation, 1978–84, retired; *b* 17 May 1924; *s* of Cyril and Ethel Rainger; *m* 1st, 1953, Josephine Campbell (decd); two *s*; 2nd, 1972, Barbara Gibson. *Educ:* Northampton Engrg Coll.; London Univ. (BSc(Eng)). CEng, FIET; FREng (FEng 1979). British Broadcasting Corporation: Head of Designs Dept, 1968–71; Head of Research Dept, 1971–76; Asst Dir of Engrg, 1976–78. Chairman: Professional Gp E14, IEE, 1973–76; various working parties, EBU, 1971–84. Fellow, Royal Television Soc., 1969. Geoffrey Parr Award, Royal TV Soc., 1964; J. J. Thompson Premium, IEE, 1966; TV Acad. Award, Nat. Acad. of Arts and Scis, 1968; David Sarnoff Gold Medal, SMPTE, 1972. *Publications:* Satellite Broadcasting, 1985; technical papers in IEE, Royal TV Soc. and SMPTE jls. *Recreations:* painting, model engineering. *Address:* 22 Mill Meadow, Milford on Sea, Hants SO41 0UG.

RAINHAM, Tina Jeanette; *see* Landale, T. J.

RAINSFORD, (David) Mark; QC 2006; *b* 3 May 1962; *s* of David and June Rainsford; *m* 1991, Fiona Caroline Munro; one *s* four *d*. *Educ:* London Sch. of Econs (LLB Hons). Called to the Bar, Lincoln's Inn, 1985; in practice as a barrister, 33 Chancery Lane, specialising in corporate wrongdoing. *Recreation:* tennis. *Address:* The Old House, 27 Leyton Road, Harpenden, Herts AL5 2JB. *E:* mr@33cllaw.com.

RAISER, Rev. Dr Konrad; General Secretary, World Council of Churches, 1993–2003; *b* Magdeburg, 25 Jan. 1938; *m* 1967, Elisabeth von Weizsäcker; four *s*. *Educ:* Univ. of Tübingen (DTheol 1970). Ordained into German Evangelical Ch, 1964; Asst Pastor, Württemberg, 1963–65; Lectr, Protestant Theol. Faculty, Tübingen, 1967–69; World Council of Churches: Study Sec., Commn on Faith and Order, 1969–73; Dep. Gen. Sec., 1973–83; Prof. of Systematic Theol. and Ecumenics, and Dir, Ecumenical Inst., Protestant Theol. Faculty, Univ. of Ruhr, 1983–93. *Publications:* Identität und Sozialität, 1971; Ökumene im Übergang, 1989 (Ecumenism in Transition, 1991); (contrib.) Dictionary of the Ecumenical Movement, 1991; Wir stehen noch am Anfang, 1994; To Be the Church, 1997; For a Culture of Life, 2002; Hoffen auf Gerechtigkeit und Versöhnung, 2002; Schritte auf dem Weg der Ökumene, 2005; Religion-Macht-Politik, 2010 (Religion, Power, Politics, 2013); Ökumene zwischen Kirche und Welt, 2013; many essays and articles. *Address:* Zikadenweg 14, 14055 Berlin, Germany.

RAISMAN, Prof. Geoffrey, DPhil, DM; FMedSci; FRS 2001; Founder Director, Spinal Repair Unit, Institute of Neurology, 2005–12, Professor of Neural Regeneration, since 2005, and Chair, Neural Regeneration, Department of Cell and Developmental Biology, since 2012, University College London; *b* 28 June 1939; *s* of Harry Raisman and Celia Raisman (*née* Newton); *m* 1958, Vivien Margolin; one *d*. *Educ:* Roundhay Sch., Leeds; Pembroke Coll., Oxford (Theodore Williams Open Schol. in Medicine; BA 1st Cl. Hons Animal Physiol. 1960); Christ Church, Oxford (MA, DPhil 1964; BM BCh 1965); DM Oxon 1974. Demonstrator, 1965–66, Schorstein Res. Fellow, 1965–67, Univ. Lectr, 1966–74, Dept of Human Anatomy, Oxford Univ. Med. Sch.; Res. Fellow, Dept of Anatomy, Harvard Univ., 1968–69; Fellow, 1970–74, Med. Tutor, 1973–74, Oriel Coll., Oxford; Head, Div. of Neurobiology, NIMR, 1974–2004. Scientific Director: Norman and Sadie Lee Res. Centre, Mill Hill, 1987–2004; Teijin Biomed. Centre, MRC Collaborative Centre, Mill Hill, 1992–97. Visiting Professor: in Neuroscis, KCL, 1977–82; of Anatomy and Develtl Biol., UCL, 1989–2004; St George's Univ., London, 2014–; Royal Soc. Exchange Prog. with China at Shanghai Physiol. Inst., Chinese Acad. of Scis, 1982; Norman and Sadie Lee Vis. Scientist, City of Hope Med. Center, Duarte, Calif, 1983. Member: MRC Co-ordinating Gp on Rehabilitation after Acute Brain Damage, 1977–85; MRC Neurobiol. and Mental Health Bd, 1980–83; Scientific Cttee, Internat. Spinal Res. Trust, 1986–. Trustee: British Neurol Res. Trust, 1987–95; American Friends of BNRT, 1995–. Life Pres., Internat. Soc. for Neurorestoratology, 2010. Mem., Editl Bds, incl. Brain Res., Anatomy and Embryol., Exptl Brain Res., Exptl Neurol. FMedSci 1999; FRSA 2002; FRSB (FSB 2012). Wakeman Award for Res. in Neuroscis, Duke Univ., N Carolina, 1980; Outstanding Contrib. to Neurosci. Award, British Neurosci. Assoc., 2004; Reeve-Irvine Res. Medal, UC Irvine, Calif, 2005. *Publications:* The Undark Sky: a story of four poor brothers, 2002; contrib. articles on brain structure and plasticity, sexual dimorphism in the brain and repair of spinal cord injury to scientific jls. *Recreations:* writing, photography, travel, ancient civilisations, Chinese, Japanese, Buddhist art, Arabic. *Address:* Spinal Repair Unit, Institute of Neurology, University College London, Queen Square, WC1N 3BG. *T:* (020) 7676 2172, *Fax:* (020) 7676 2174. *E:* G.Raisman@ucl.ac.uk. *Club:* Oxford and Cambridge.

RAISMAN, Jeremy Philip; Senior Partner, Eversheds, London (formerly Jaques & Lewis), 1993–99; *b* 6 March 1935; *s* of Sir (Abraham) Jeremy Raisman, GCMG, GCIE, KCSI, and late Renee Mary (*née* Kelly); *m* 1963, Diana Rosamund Clifford, *d* of late Maj.-Gen. Cedric Rhys Price, CB, CBE; one *s* two *d*. *Educ:* Dragon Sch., Oxford; Rugby Sch. Articled, Norton Rose, 1953–59; admitted solicitor, 1959; Asst Solicitor, Clifford-Turner & Co., 1960–62; Asst Solicitor, then Partner, Nabarro Nathanson & Co., 1962–67; Partner, Jaques & Co., 1967, subseq. Jaques & Lewis, 1982, then Eversheds, London, 1995. *Recreations:* beagling (Jt Master, W Surrey & Horsell Beagles 1959–71), sailing, riding, trekking. *Address:* Winterdown, Holmbury St Mary, Dorking, Surrey RH5 6NL. *Club:* Rock Sailing (Wadebridge, Cornwall).
See also *J. M. Raisman.*

RAISMAN, John Michael, CBE 1983; Chairman, Shell UK Ltd, 1979–85; *b* 12 Feb. 1929; *er s* of Sir Jeremy Raisman, GCMG, GCIE, KCSI, and late Renee Mary Raisman; *m* 1953, Evelyn Anne, *d* of Brig. J. I. Muirhead, CIE, MC; one *s* two *d* (and one *d* decd). *Educ:* Dragon Sch., Oxford; Rugby Sch.; The Queen's Coll., Oxford (Jodrell Schol., MA Lit Hum). Joined Royal Dutch/Shell Group, 1953; served in Brazil, 1954–60; General Manager, Shell Panama, 1961–62; Asst to Exploration and Production Co-ordinator, The Hague, 1963–65; Gen. Man., Shell Co. of Turkey, 1966–69; President, Shell Sekiyu K. K. Japan, 1970–73; Head, European Supply and Marketing, 1974–77; Man. Dir, Shell UK Oil, 1977–78; Regional Co-ordinator, UK and Eire, Shell Internat. Pet. Co. Ltd, 1978–85; Shell UK Ltd: Dep. Chm., 1978–79; Chief Exec., 1978–85; Govt Dir, 1984–87, Dep. Chm., 1987–91, British Telecom. Chm., British Biotech plc, 1995–98 (Dir, 1993–98); Director: Vickers PLC, 1981–90; Glaxo Hldgs PLC, 1982–90; Lloyds Bank Plc, 1985–95; Lloyds Merchant Bank Hldgs Ltd, 1985–87; Candover Investments PLC, 1990–98; Tandem Computers Ltd, 1991–97; Lloyds TSB plc, 1996–98. Chairman: Adv. Council, London Enterprise Agency, 1979–85; UK Oil Industry Emergency Cttee, 1980–85; Council of Industry for Management Educn, 1981–85; Investment Bd, Electra-Candover Partners, 1985–95. Member: Council, CBI, 1979–90 (Chm., CBI Europe Cttee, 1980–88; Mem., President's Cttee, 1980–88); Council, Inst. of Petroleum, 1979–81; Council, Inst. for Fiscal Studies, 1982–; Governing Council, Business in the Community, 1982–85; Council, UK Centre for Econ. and Environmental Develt, 1985–89; Royal Commn on Environmental Pollution, 1986–87; Chm., Electronics Industry EDC, 1986–87. Chairman: Langs Lead Body, 1990–95; Council for Industry and Higher Educn, 1991–98 (Mem., 1988–98); Dep. Chm., Nat. Commn on Educn, 1991–2000; Pres., Council for Educn in World Citizenship, 1992–2003. Mem., Council for Charitable Support, 1986–91; Chairman: RA Trust, 1987–96 (Emeritus Trustee, RA, 1996–); Trustees, British Empire and Commonwealth Mus., 2003–06. Governor, NIESR, 1983–; Pro-Chancellor, Aston Univ., 1987–93. CCMI (CBIM 1980). DUniv Stirling, 1983; Hon. LLD: Aberdeen, 1985; Manchester, 1986; UWE, 1998; Hon. DSc Aston, 1992. *Recreations:* reading, music, theatre, travel. *Address:* Netheravon House, Netheravon Road South, W4 2PY. *T:* (020) 8994 3731. *Club:* Brooks's.
See also *J. P. Raisman.*

RAJAH, Eason Thurai; QC 2011; *b* Ipoh, Malaysia, 18 Jan. 1967; *s* of N. T. Rajah and Gnanambigai Rajah; *m* 1993, Ann Collier; one *s* one *d*. *Educ:* Epsom Coll.; Univ. of Nottingham (LLB Hons). Called to the Bar, Gray's Inn, 1989; in practice as a barrister specialising in Chancery law; Advocate and Solicitor, High Court of Malaya, 1991. An Editor, Court of Protection Law Reports, 2012–. *Publications:* (ed) Mellows Taxation of Executors of Trustees (looseleaf), 2006–. *Address:* 10 Old Square, Lincoln's Inn, WC2A 3SU. *T:* (020) 7405 0758. *E:* clerks@tenoldsquare.com.

RAJAN, Amol; Editor, The Independent, since 2013; *b* Calcutta, 4 July 1983; *s* of P. Varadarajan and Sunanda Joshi Rajan; *m* 2013, Charlotte Rosemary Faircloth. *Educ:* Graveney Sch.; Downing Coll., Cambridge (BA Hons English Lit. 2005). Asst Desk Officer, Eastern Adriatic Dept, FCO, 2001–02; on-screen audience researcher, The Wright Stuff, Channel 5, 2005–07; news reporter, sports news corresp., 2007–09, Dep. Comment Ed., 2009–10, The Independent; Media Advr to Evgeny Lebedev, owner of The Independent and London Evening Standard, 2010–13. *Publications:* Twirlymen: the unlikely history of cricket's greatest spin bowlers, 2011. *Recreations:* cricket, reggae, avoiding lifts. *Address:* The Independent, 2 Derry Street, W8 5HF.

RAJOY BREY, Mariano; Prime Minister of Spain, since 2011; *b* Santiago de Compostela, 27 March 1955; *m* 1996, Elvira Fernández Balboa; two *s*. *Educ:* Univ. of Santiago de Compostela (LLB). Registrar of Deeds; Pres., Local and Provincial Press, Pontevedra. Mem. (People's Alliance), Galician Regl Parlt, 1981; Gen. Dir, Instnl Relns, Xunta de Galicia; Pres., Provincial de Pontevedra, 1983–86; Vice Pres., Xunta de Galicia, 1986–87; Minister: of Public Admin, 1996–99; of Educn and Culture, 1999–2000; First Dep. Prime Minister and Minister of Interior, 2001–02; First Dep. Prime Minister and Speaker, and Minister of the Presidency, 2002–03. Popular Party: Mem., Nat. Exec. Cttee, 1989–; Dep. Sec. Gen., 1990–2003; Gen. Sec., 2003–04; Pres., 2004–. *Publications:* In Confidence (autobiog.), 2011. *Address:* Presidencia del Gobierno, Complejo de la Moncloa, 28071, Spain.

RAKE, Sir Michael Derek Vaughan, Kt 2007; FCA; Chairman: British Telecommunications plc, since 2007; RAC, since 2014; Worldpay, since 2015; William Pitt Fellow, Pembroke College, Cambridge, since 2010; *b* 17 Jan. 1948; *s* of Derek Shannon Vaughan Rake and Rosamund Rake (*née* Barrett); *m* 1st, 1970, Julia (*née* Cook); three *s*; 2nd, 1986, Caroline (*née* Thomas); one *s*. *Educ:* Wellington Coll. FCA 1970. Turquands Barton

Mayhew, London and Brussels, 1968–74; KPMG: Brussels, 1974; Partner, 1979–; Partner i/c of Audit, Belgium and Luxembourg, 1983–86; Sen. Resident Partner, ME, 1986–89; Partner, London office, 1989–; Mem., UK Bd, 1991– (Chm., 1998–); Regl Man. Partner, SE Reg., 1992–94; Chief Exec., London and SE Reg., 1994–96; Chief Operating Officer, UK, 1996–98; Sen. Partner, KPMG UK, 1998–2006; Chairman: KPMG Europe, 1999–2002; KPMG Internat., 2002–07; easyJet plc, 2010–13 (Dep. Chm., 2009–10). Director: Barclays Gp plc, 2008– (Dep. Chm., 2012–); FRC, 2008–11; McGraw Hill Inc., 2008–. Mem., Task Force on US/UK Regulation, DTI, 2006; Chm., UK Commn for Employment and Skills, 2007–10; BVCA Guidelines Monitoring Gp, 2008–13. Chm., BITC, 2004–07; Pres., CBI, 2013–15; Member: Bd, Prince of Wales Internat. Business Leaders Forum, 1999–2007; Bd, Transatlantic Business Dialogue, 2004–; Bd, Business for New Europe, 2006–; Internat. Business Council, World Econ. Forum, 2006–12; Global Adv. Bd, Oxford Univ. Centre for Corporate Reputation, 2008–; Sen. Advr, Chatham House, 2008–. Trustee, Prince of Wales Charitable Foundn, 2011–. Gov., Wellington Coll., 2007– (Chm. and Vice Pres., 2010–). Vice Pres., RNIB, 2003–. *Recreations:* tennis, ski-ing. *Address:* BT Group plc, BT Centre, 81 Newgate Street, EC1A 7AJ. *Club:* Guards Polo Club (Mem. Bd, 2005–).

RALEIGH, Dr Jean Margaret Macdonald C.; *see* Curtis-Raleigh.

RALLI, Sir David (Charles), 4th Bt *cr* 1912, of Park Street, City of Westminster; farmer; *b* London, 5 April 1946; *o s* of Sir Godfrey Victor Ralli, 3rd Bt, TD and Nora Margaret Forman (*d* 1990); *S* father, 2010; *m* 1975, Jacqueline Cecilia, *d* of late David Smith; one *s* one *d*. *Educ:* Eton; Harper Adams Agricultural Coll. Chm., Dereham Farm Services, 1985–87; Dir, Mid Norfolk Farmers, 1985–93; Chm., Norfolk Gp, Game Conservancy, 1993–97. Founder, Guineafowl Trust Safaris, 1996. Mem. (C), Breckland DC, 1987–95 (Chm., Envmtl Health Cttee, 1990–95). Chm. of Govs, St Andrews First Sch., N Pickenham, 1992–94. Area Pres., St John Ambulance, SW Norfolk, 2005–; Pres., Mid Norfolk Cons. Assoc., 2014–. Liveryman, Farmers' Co., 1985. OStJ 2014. *Recreations:* golf, fishing, shooting. *Heir: s* Philip Neil David Ralli, *b* 31 March 1983. *Address:* Panworth Hall, Ashill, Thetford, Norfolk IP25 7BB. *T:* (01760) 440852. *E:* davidralli62@gmail.com. *Clubs:* White's, Farmers.
See also Sir A. R. Milburn, Bt.

RALLING, (Antony) Christopher, OBE 1992; FRGS; freelance writer/director; *b* 12 April 1929; *s* of Harold St George Ralling and Dorothy Blanche Ralling; *m* 1963, Angela Norma (*née* Gardner); one *d*. *Educ:* Charterhouse; Wadham Coll., Oxford (BA 2nd Cl. Hons English). Joined BBC External Services, Scriptwriter, 1955; British Meml Foundn Fellowship to Australia, 1959; Dep. Editor, Panorama, BBC TV, 1964; joined BBC TV Documentaries, 1966; directed The Search for the Nile, 1972 (Amer. Acad. Award, 1972; Peabody Award, 1972); Mem., British Everest Expedn, 1975; produced The Voyage of Charles Darwin, 1978 (British Acad. Award, 1978; Desmond Davies British Acad. Award, 1978; RTS Silver Medal, 1979); Hd of Documentaries, BBC TV, 1980; left BBC to start Dolphin Productions, 1982; directed: The History of Africa, 1984; Chasing a Rainbow (Josephine Baker), 1986 (Amer. Acad. Award, 1986); Prince Charles at Forty, LWT, 1988; The Kon-Tiki Man, BBC, 1989; The Buried Mirror, BBC, 1992; A Diplomat in Japan, BBC, 1992; Return to Everest, Channel 4, 1993. FRGS 1978. *Publications:* Muggeridge Through the Microphone, 1967; The Voyage of Charles Darwin, 1978; Shackleton, 1983; The Kon-Tiki Man, 1990. *Recreations:* tennis, ski-ing. *Address:* Tankerville Cottage, Kingston Hill, Surrey KT2 7JH. *Club:* Alpine.

RALLS, Peter John Henry; QC 1997; **His Honour Judge Ralls;** a Circuit Judge, since 2008; *b* 18 July 1947; *s* of Ivan Jack Douglas Ralls and Sybil Gladys Child; *m* 1st, 1979, Anne Elizabeth Marriott (marr. diss. 1986); 2nd, 1997, Tonia Anne Clark; two *s* one *d*. *Educ:* Royal Russell Sch., Surrey; UCL (LLB Hons). Called to the Bar, Middle Temple, 1972; admitted Solicitor, 1981; returned to the Bar, 1982; an Asst Recorder, 1998–2000; a Recorder, 2000–08. Chm., Cowes Combined Clubs, 2001–. *Recreations:* yacht racing, cricket. *Address:* Southampton Crown Court, Courts of Justice, London Road, Southampton SO15 2XQ. *Clubs:* Brooks's, MCC; Royal London Yacht; Royal Yacht Squadron.

RALPH, Richard Peter, CMG 1997; CVO 1991; HM Diplomatic Service, retired; *b* 27 April 1946; *s* of Peter and Marion Ralph; *m* 1st, 1970 (marr. diss. 2001); one *s* one *d*; 2nd, 2002, Jemma Victoria Elizabeth Marlor; one *d*. *Educ:* King's Sch., Canterbury; Edinburgh Univ. (MSc). Third Sec., FCO, 1969–70; Third, later Second, Sec., Vientiane, Laos, 1970–73; Second, later First, Sec., Lisbon, 1974–77; FCO, 1977–81; Head of Chancery, Harare, Zimbabwe, 1981–85; Counsellor, FCO, 1985–89; Head of Chancery and Congressional Counsellor, Washington, 1989–93; Ambassador to Latvia, 1993–95; Gov., Falkland Is, and Comr for S Georgia and S Sandwich Is, 1996–99; Ambassador: to Romania and to Moldova, 1999–2002; to Peru, 2003–06. Chairman: Anglo-Peruvian Soc., 2006–09; S Georgia Soc., 2006–09. *Recreations:* tennis, reading, travelling. *Address:* 51 High Street, Sandwich, Kent CT13 9EG.

RALSTON, Gen. Joseph W., DFC 1967; DSM 1990; Vice Chairman, The Cohen Group, since 2003; *b* 4 Nov. 1943; *m* 1989, Diana Dougherty; one *s* one *d*, and one step *s* one step *d*. *Educ:* Miami Univ. (BA Chemistry 1965); Central Michigan Univ. (MA Personnel Mgt 1976); John F. Kennedy Sch. of Govt, Harvard Univ. Commissioned USAF, Reserve Officer Trng Corps Program, 1965; F-105 Pilot, Laos and N Vietnam; US Army Comd and Gen. Staff Coll., 1976; Nat. War Coll., Washington, 1984; Asst Dep. COS (Ops), and Dep. COS (Requirements), HQ Tactical Air Comd, 1987–90; Dir, Tactical Progs, 1990–91, Opnl Requirements, 1991–92, HQ USAF; Comdr, Alaskan Comd, 11 Air Force, Alaskan N Amer. Aerospace Defense Comd Reg., and Jt Task Force Alaska, 1992–94; Dep. COS (Plans and Ops), HQ USAF, 1994–95; Comdr, Air Combat Comd, 1995–96; Vice Chm., Jt Chiefs of Staff, 1996–2000; SACEUR, NATO, and C-in-C, US European Comd, 2000–03. US Legion of Merit, DDSM, MSM, Air Medal, Air Force Commendation Medal. Highest degree, Mil. Order of Merit (Morocco), 1996; Officer, Legion of Honour (France), 1997; Kt Comdr's Cross, Order of Merit (Germany), 1999; Grand Cross, Royal Norwegian Order of Merit (Norway), 2000. *Recreations:* hunting, fishing, gardening. *Address:* The Cohen Group, 500 8th Street NW, Suite 200, Washington, DC 20004, USA.

RAMADAN, Prof. Tariq, PhD; His Highness Sheikh Hamad Bin Khalifa Al-Thani Professor of Contemporary Islamic Studies, University of Oxford, since 2009; Fellow, St Antony's College, since 2009 (Visiting Fellow, 2005–06; Research Fellow, 2006–09); Executive Director, Centre for Islamic Legislation and Ethics, Qatar Faculty of Islamic Studies, since 2012; *b* Geneva, 26 Aug. 1962. *Educ:* Univ. of Geneva (MA Phil. and French Lit.; PhD Phil. and Islamic Studies). Dean, Collège de Saussure, Geneva, 1988–92; Prof. of Islamology, Fribourg Univ., 1997–2003; Prof. of Islamic Studies, Notre Dame Univ., 2004; Senior Research Fellow: Lokahi Foundn, 2005–; Doshisha Univ., Kyoto, 2007–; Vis. Prof., Erasmus Univ., Rotterdam, 2007–09. European of the Year, European Voice/The Economist, 2006. *Publications:* To Be a European Muslim, 1999; Muslims in France: the way towards coexistence, 1999; Western Muslims and the Future of Islam, 2003; Islam, the West, and Challenges of Modernity, 2003; The Messenger: the meanings of the life of Muhammad, 2007; In the Footsteps of the Prophet: lessons from the life of Muhammad, 2007; Radical Reform: Islamic ethics and liberation, 2009; What I believe, 2009; The Quest for Meaning, 2010; The Arab Awakening: Islam and the new Middle East, 2012. *Address:* St Antony's College,62 Woodstock Road OX2 6JF. *T:* (01865) 284780.

RAMADHANI, Rt Rev. John Acland; Bishop of Zanzibar and Tanga, 1980–2000, Bishop of Zanzibar, 2000–02; *b* 1 Aug. 1932. *Educ:* Univ. of Birmingham (DipTh 1975); Univ. of Dar-es-Salaam (BA 1967); Queen's Coll., Birmingham. Deacon 1975, Birmingham; priest 1976, Dar-es-Salaam; Asst Chaplain, Queen's Coll., Birmingham, 1975–76; Warden, St Mark's Theol Coll., Dar-es-Salaam, 1976–80; Archbishop of Tanzania, 1984–98. *Address:* PO Box 5, Mkunazini, Zanzibar, Tanzania.

RAMAGE, Dr James Cumming, CPhys, FInstP; CEng, FREng; Chairman: Tesla Engineering Ltd, since 1995; Storrington Industries Ltd, since 2005; *b* Kilmarnock, 28 March 1951; *s* of James T. Ramage and Eva B. Ramage; *m* 1975, Jane C. Freer; two *d*. *Educ:* Univ. of Glasgow (BSc Maths and Natural Philosophy 1973); Balliol Coll., Oxford (DPhil Semiconductor Physics 1976). CPhys 1994; FInstP 1994; CEng 2010; FREng 2014. Lecturer in Physics: Balliol Coll., Oxford, 1976–77; Open Univ., 1977–80; Man. Dir, VG Gas Analysis Ltd, 1981–85; Chief Exec., VG Instruments Inc., 1985–88; Man. Dir, VG Scientific Ltd, 1988–90; Exec. Dir, VG Instruments plc, 1986–90; Divl Man. Dir (Inorganic Instrumentation), Fisons Instruments, 1990–94. Non-exec. Dir, Microsaic Systems plc, 2010–. *Recreations:* family, gardening, dinghy sailing. *Address:* Tesla Engineering Ltd, Water Lane, Storrington, W Sussex RH20 3EA. *E:* ramage@tesla.co.uk.

RAMAGE, Prof. Robert, DSc; FRS 1992; CChem, FRSC; FRSE; Forbes Professor of Organic Chemistry, University of Edinburgh, 1984–2001; *b* 4 Oct. 1935; *s* of Robert Bain Ramage and Jessie Boag Ramage; *m* 1961, Joan Fraser Paterson; three *d*. *Educ:* Whitehill Sen. Secondary Sch., Glasgow; Univ. of Glasgow (BSc Hons 1958; PhD 1961; DSc 1982). Fulbright Fellow and Fellow of Harvard Coll., 1961–63; Research at Woodward Res. Inst., 1963–64; Lectr then Sen. Lectr, Univ. of Liverpool, 1964–77; Prof., 1977–84, Head of Dept, 1979–84, UMIST; Head, Dept of Chem., Univ. of Edinburgh, 1987–90, 1997–2000; Dir, Edinburgh Centre for Protein Technology, 1996–2000; Scientific Dir, 2002–07 and Vice Pres., 2004–07, Almac Scis (Scotland) Ltd (formerly Albachem Ltd, then CSS Albachem). FRSE 1986. Dr (*hc*) Lille. *Recreations:* sport, gardening, current affairs.

RAMAKRISHNAN, Prof. Tiruppattur Venkatachalamurti, FRS 2000; DST Year of Science Professor; DAE Homi Bhabha Professor, Department of Physics, Banaras Hindu University, 2003–08, now Emeritus; Distinguished Associate, Centre for Condensed Matter Theory, Department of Physics, Indian Institute of Science, Bangalore, since 2003; *b* 14 Aug. 1941; *s* of Tiruppattur Ramaseshayyar Venkatachala-Murti and Jayalakshmi Murti; *m* 1970, Meera Rao; one *s* one *d*. *Educ:* Banaras Hindu Univ., Varanasi (BSc 1959; MSc 1961); Columbia Univ., NY (PhD 1966). Lectr, 1966, Asst Prof., 1967, Indian Inst. of Technol., Kanpur; Asst Res. Physicist, UCSD, 1968–70; Asst Prof., 1970–77, Prof. of Physics, 1977–80, Indian Inst. of Technol., Kanpur; Prof. of Physics, 1981–84 and 1986–2003, INSA Srinivasa Ramanujan Res. Prof., 1997–2002, Indian Inst. of Sci., Bangalore; Prof. of Physics, Banaras Hindu Univ., 1984–86. Vis. Res. Physicist, 1978–81, Vis. Prof., 1990–91, Princeton Univ. Consultant, Bell Labs, 1979–81. Pres., Indian Acad. of Scis, 2004–06. Fellow: INSA, 1984; APS, 1984; Third World Acad. of Scis, 1990. Padma Sri, 2001. *Publications:* (jtly) Physics, 1988, 2nd edn 1994; (with C. N. R. Rao) Superconductivity Today, 1990, 2nd edn 1997; about 120 research papers and 6 review articles. *Recreation:* trekking. *Address:* Centre for Condensed Matter Theory, Department of Physics, Indian Institute of Science, Bangalore 560012, India. *T:* (80) 23600591, (94) 48363379.

RAMAKRISHNAN, Sir Venkatraman, Kt 2012; PhD; FRS 2003; Senior Scientist and Group Leader, Structural Studies Division, MRC Laboratory of Molecular Biology, Cambridge, since 1999. *Educ:* Baroda Univ., India (BSc 1971); Ohio Univ. (PhD 1976); Univ. of Calif, San Diego. Postdoctoral Fellow, Dept of Chem., Yale Univ., 1978–82; Res. Staff, Oak Ridge Nat. Lab., 1982–83; Brookhaven National Laboratory: Asst Biophysicist, 1983–85; Associate Biophysicist, 1985–88; Biophysicist, 1988–94; Sen. Biophysicist, 1994–95; Prof., Biochem. Dept, Univ. of Utah, 1995–99. (Jtly) Nobel Prize in Chemistry, 2009. *Address:* Structural Studies Division, MRC Laboratory of Molecular Biology, Francis Crick Avenue, Cambridge CB2 0QH.

RAMAPHOSA, (Matamela) Cyril; Deputy President, African National Congress, since 2012; Deputy President of the Republic of South Africa, since 2014; *b* 17 Nov. 1952; *s* of late Samuel Ramaphosa and of Erdmuth Ramaphosa; *m* 1996, Tshepo Motsepe; two *s* two *d*. *Educ:* Sekano-Ntoane High Sch., Soweto; Univ. of North, Turfloop (BProc 1981). Detained under Terrorism Act for 11 months, 1974, and 6 months, 1976; active in Black People's Convention, 1975; articled clerk, Attorney Henry Dolovitz, 1977; Legal Advr, Council of Unions of SA, 1981–82; First Gen. Sec., NUM, SA, 1982–91; arrested and detained under Riotous Assemblies Act, 1984; organised first legal one day strike by black mineworkers, 1984; African National Congress: Mem., Nat. Exec. Cttee, 1991–; Sec.-Gen., 1991–96; Leader, ANC Delegn to Multi-Party Negotiations, 1992–94; Chm., Constitutional Assembly, Govt of Nat. Unity, 1994–96. Exec. Dep. Chm., New Africa Investments Ltd, 1996–99; Chm. and Chief Exec., Molope Gp, 1999–2000; Chairman: Rebhold Services (Pty), 2000–03; Shanduka Gp, 2000–13; non-executive Chairman: MCI Gp, 2003; MTN Gp; Bidvest Gp Ltd; Standard Bank Ltd; former joint non-executive Chairman: Mondi plc; Mondi Ltd. Mem., Adv. Council, SAB Miller plc. Former Dep. Chm., Commonwealth Business Council. Vis. Prof. of Law, Stanford Univ., USA, 1991. Hon. Dr: Massachusetts, 1992; Univ. of the North, 2002; Hon. PhD Port Elizabeth, 1995; Hon. LLD: Natal, 1997; Cape Town, 1997; Lesotho, 2002. *Recreation:* fly-fishing. *Address:* (office) Union Buildings, Private Bag X1000, Pretoria, 0001, South Africa. *Club:* River (Johannesburg).

RAMBAHADUR LIMBU, Captain, VC 1966; MVO 1984; HM the Queen's Gurkha Orderly Officer, 1983–84; employed in Sultanate of Negara Brunei Darussalam, 1985–92; *b* Nov. 1939; *s* of late Tekbir Limbu; *m* 1st, 1960, Tikamaya Limbuni (*d* 1966); two *s*; 2nd, 1967, Punimaya Limbuni; three *s*. Army Cert. of Educn 1st cl. Enlisted 10th Princess Mary's Own Gurkha Rifles, 1957; served on ops in Borneo (VC); promoted Sergeant, 1971; WO II, 1976; commissioned, 1977. Hon. Captain (Gurkha Commnd Officer), 1985. *Publications:* My Life Story, 1978. *Recreations:* football, volley-ball, badminton, basketball. *Address:* Ward No 13 Damak, Nagar Palika, PO Box Damak, District Jhapa, Mechi Zone, East Nepal. *Clubs:* VC and GC Association, Royal Society of St George (England).

RAMGOOLAM, Dr the Hon. Navinchandra, GCSK 2008; FRCP; Member, National Assembly, Mauritius, 1991–2014; Prime Minister of Republic of Mauritius, 1995–2000 and 2005–14; *b* 14 July 1947; *s* of Rt Hon. Sir Seewoosagur Ramgoolam, GCMG, PC (First Prime Minister of Mauritius) and Lady Sushil Ramgoolam; *m* 1979, Veena Brizmohun. *Educ:* Royal Coll. of Surgeons, Dublin; London Sch. of Econs (LLB Hons 1990; Hon. Fellow, 1998); Inns of Court Sch. of Law. LRCP, LRCSI 1975; FRCP 2009. Called to the Bar, Inner Temple, 1993, Overseas Bencher, 2011. Mauritius Labour Party: Leader, 1991–; Pres., 1991–92. Leader of the Opposition, 1991–95 and 2000–05. Hon. Freeman, Rodrigues, 2007. Dr *hc*: Mauritius, 1998; Aligarh Muslim, India, 1998; Jawaharlal Nehru, India, 2005; Hon. DSc Padmashree Dr D. Y. Patil Univ., India, 2009; Hon. Dr Staffordshire, 2010; Hon. DLaws, Kurukshetra Univ., Haryana, India, 2012. Wilberforce Medal, Wilberforce Lect. Trust, 2007; Rajiv Gandhi Award, India, 2007; Pravasi Bharatiya Samman Award, India, 2008; Prix Louise Michel, CEPS, Paris, 2008; Order of Rule of Law, World Jurist Assoc., USA, 2011. Grand Officier, Légion d'Honneur (France), 2006. *Recreation:* reading.

RAMIN, Ileana, (Mme Manfred Ramin); *see* Cotrubas, I.

RAMMELL, William Ernest; Vice-Chancellor and Chief Executive, University of Bedfordshire, since 2012; *b* 10 Oct. 1959; *s* of William Ernest Rammell and Joan Elizabeth Rammell; *m* 1983, Beryl Jarhall; one *s* one *d*. *Educ:* University Coll., Cardiff (BA French). Pres., Cardiff Students' Union, 1982–83; mgt trainee, BR, 1983–84; NUS Regl Official, 1984–87; Hd of Youth Services, Basildon Council, 1987–89; General Manager: Students'

Union, KCL, 1989–94; Univ. of London Union, 1994–97. MP (Lab) Harlow, 1997–2010; contested (Lab) same seat, 2010. PPS to Sec. of State for Culture, Media and Sport, 2001–02; Parly Under-Sec. of State, FCO, 2002–05; Minister of State: (Minister for Univs), DfES, 2005–07; DIUS, 2007–08; FCO, 2008–09; (Minister for Armed Forces), MoD, 2009–10. Dep. Vice-Chancellor, Univ. of Plymouth, 2011–12. Chm., Lab Movt for Europe. *Recreations:* football, cricket, socialising. *Address:* 9 Orchard Croft, Harlow, Essex CM20 3BA. *T:* (01279) 439706.

RAMOS, Gen. Fidel Valdez; Founder and Chairman, Ramos Peace and Development Foundation; President of the Philippines, 1992–98; *b* 18 March 1928; *s* of Narciso Ramos and Angela (*née* Valdez); *m* Amelita Martinez; five *d. Educ:* Nat. Univ. of Manila; USMA W Point; Univ. of Illinois. Active service in Korea and Vietnam; Dep. Chief of Staff, 1981, Chief of Staff, 1986, Philippines Armed Forces; Sec. of Nat. Defence, 1988. Leader, People's Power Party. Légion d'Honneur (France), 1987. *Address:* Ramos Peace and Development Foundation, 26th Floor, Export Bank Plaza, Corner Senator Gil Puyat and Chino Roces Avenues, 1200 Makati City, Philippines; 120 Maria Cristina Street, Ayala Alabang Village, Muntinlupa City, Philippines.

RAMOS-HORTA, José; President of Timor-Leste, 2007–12; Chairman, United Nations High-Level Independent Panel on Peace Operations, since 2014; *b* Dili, E Timor, 26 Dec. 1949; *s* of late Francisco Horta and of Natalina Ramos Filipe Horta; *m* 1978, Ana Pessoa (marr. diss.); one *s*. *Educ:* Hague Acad. of Internat. Law; Internat. Inst. of Human Rights, Strasbourg; Columbia Univ., NY; Antioch Univ. (MA 1984). Journalist, radio and TV correspondent, 1969–74; Minister for Ext. Affairs and Inf., E Timor, Dec. 1975; Perm. Rep. for Fretilin to UN, NY, 1976–89; Public Affairs and Media Dir, Embassy of Mozambique, Washington, 1987–88; Special Rep. of Nat. Council of Maubere Resistance, 1991; Foreign Minister, 2002–06, Prime Minister, 2006–07, E Timor; Special Rep. and Hd, UN Integrated Peacebuilding Office in Guinea-Bissau, 2013–14. Founder Dir and Lectr, Diplomacy Trng Prog., 1990, and Vis. Prof., 1996, Law Faculty, Univ. of NSW. Member: Peace Action Council, Unrepresented Nations and Peoples Orgn, The Hague (UNPO Award, 1996); Exec. Council, Internat. Service for Human Rights, Geneva; Bd, E Timor Human Rights Centre, Melbourne. Sen. Associate Mem., St Antony's Coll., Oxford, 1987. Nobel Peace Prize (jtly), 1996. Order of Freedom (Portugal), 1996. *Publications:* Funu: the unfinished saga of East Timor, 1987; contrib. to newspapers and periodicals in Portugal, France, USA and Australia. *Recreation:* tennis. *Address:* (office) Rua São Lazaro 16, 1°, 1150 Lisbon, Portugal. *T:* (1) 8863727, *Fax:* (1) 8863791.

RAMOTAR, Donald; President, Republic of Guyana, 2011–15; General Secretary, People's Progressive Party, Guyana, 1997–2013; *b* Caria-Caria, Essequibo River, 22 Oct. 1950; *s* of Sam Ramotar and Olive Constantine; *m* 1974, Deolatchmee; two *s* one *d*. *Educ:* Univ. of Guyana (Econs degree); Technical Inst. (electronics). Worked as a journalist. People's Progressive Party: joined, 1967; party representative in Czechoslovakia, 1983–88; represented the party and Progressive Youth Orgn at many internat. fora. *Publications:* contrib. to People's Progressive Party Mirror newspaper and Thunder mag. *Recreations:* reading, long walks. *E:* donald.ramotar@gmail.com.

RAMPEN, Prof. William Hugh Salvin, (Win), PhD; FREng; CEng, FIMechE; Professor of Energy Storage, University of Edinburgh, since 2014; Founder, 1994, and Chairman, Artemis Intelligent Power Ltd, since 2014 (Managing Director, 1994–2013); *b* Oakville, Ont, 1956; *s* of Leonardus Rampen and Sybil Rampen (*née* Calverley); *m* 1988, Dr Rosemary Dixon; one *s* two *d*. *Educ:* Ryerson Univ., Toronto (BTech 1977); Univ. of New Brunswick (MScE 1986); Univ. of Edinburgh (PhD 1993). CEng 2011; FIMechE 2011; FREng 2012. Res. Associate, Univ. of Edinburgh, 1978–81; Lectr, Ryerson Univ., Toronto, 1981–86; Res. Fellow, Univ. of Edinburgh, 1987–93. FRSA. *Publications:* many papers and patents in subject area of Digital Displacement® Hydraulics. *Recreations:* hill running, old machinery, farming. *Address:* Artemis Intelligent Power Ltd, Unit 3, Edgefield Industrial Estate, Loanhead, Midlothian EH20 9TB. *T:* (0131) 440 6262. *E:* w.rampen@artemisip.com.

RAMPHAL, Sir Shridath Surendranath, OE 1983; GCMG 1990 (CMG 1966); OM (Jamaica) 1990; OCC 1991; Kt 1970; QC (Guyana) 1965, SC 1966; Secretary-General of the Commonwealth, 1975–90; *b* 3 Oct. 1928; *s* of James and Grace Ramphal; *m* 1951, Lois Winifred King; two *s* two *d*. *Educ:* King's Coll., London (LLM 1952; FKC 1975). Called to the Bar, Gray's Inn, 1951 (Hon. Bencher 1981). Colonial Legal Probationer, 1951; Arden and Atkin Prize, 1952; John Simon Guggenheim Fellow, Harvard Law Sch., 1962. Crown Counsel, British Guiana, 1953–54; Asst to Attorney-Gen., 1954–56; Legal Draftsman, 1956–58; First Legal Draftsman, West Indies, 1958–59; Solicitor-Gen., British Guiana, 1959–61; Asst Attorney-Gen., West Indies, 1961–62, Attorney-Gen., Guyana, 1965–73; Minister of State for External Affairs, Guyana, 1967–72; Foreign Minister and Attorney General, Guyana, 1972–73; Minister, Foreign Affairs and Justice, 1973–75; Mem., Nat. Assembly, Guyana, 1965–75. Member: Ind. (Brandt) Commn on Internat. Develt Issues, 1977–83; Ind. (Palme) Commn on Disarmament and Security Issues, 1980–89; Ind. Commn on Internat. Humanitarian Issues, 1983–88; World (Brundtland) Commn on Environment and Develt, 1984–87; South Commn, 1987–90; Carnegie Commn on Preventing Deadly Conflict, 1994–98; Chm., W Indian Commn, 1990–92; Co-Chm., Commn on Global Governance, 1992–2000. Special Advr, Sec. Gen., UN Conf. on Envmt and Develt, 1992; Chm., UN Cttee on Develt Planning, 1984–87; Chief Negotiator on Ext. Economic Relations in Caribbean Reg., 1997–2001; Facilitator, Belize-Guatemala Dispute, 2002–02; Counsel, Guyana-Suriname UN Convention on the Law of the Sea Arbitration, 2004–07. Chairman: Internat. Adv. Cttee, Future Generations Alliance Foundn, Kyoto, 1994–97; Bd, Internat. Inst. for Democracy and Electoral Assistance, Stockholm, 1995–2001; Pres., Internat. Steering Cttee, Leadership in Envmt and Develt, 1991–98; Member: Bd, Internat. Develt Res. Centre, Ottawa, 1994–98; Council, Internat. Negotiating Network, Carter Centre, Atlanta, 1991–97. Mem., Internat. Commn of Jurists, 1970–. Chancellor: Univ. of Guyana, 1988–92; Univ. of Warwick, 1989–2002; Univ. of WI, 1989–2003. Visiting Professor: Exeter Univ., 1988; Faculty of Laws, KCL, 1988. Toronto Univ., 1995; Osgoode Hall Law Sch., Univ. of York, Toronto, 1995. FRSA 1981; CCMI (CBIM 1986). Fellow, LSE, 1979; Hon. Fellow, Magdalen Coll., Oxford, 1982; Companion, Leicester Poly., 1991. Hon. LLD: Panjab, 1975; Southampton, 1976; St Francis Xavier, NS, 1978; Univ. of WI, 1978; Aberdeen, 1979; Cape Coast, Ghana, 1980; London, 1981; Benin, Nigeria, 1982; Hull, 1983; Yale, 1985; Cambridge, 1985; Warwick, 1988; York, Ont, 1988; Malta, 1989; Otago, 1990; DUniv: Surrey, 1979; Essex, 1980; Hon. DHL: Simmons Coll., Boston, 1982; Duke Univ., 1985; Hon. DCL: Oxon, 1982; E Anglia, 1983; Durham, 1985; Hon. DLitt: Bradford, 1985; Indira Gandhi Nat. Open Univ., New Delhi, 1989; Hon. DSc Cranfield Inst. of Technology, 1987. Albert Medal, RSA, 1988; Internat. Educn Award, Richmond Coll., 1988; Rene Dubos Human Envmt Award, 1993. AC 1982; ONZ 1990; Comdr, Order of Golden Ark (Netherlands), 1994. *Publications:* One World to Share: selected speeches of the Commonwealth Secretary-General 1975–79, 1979; Nkrumah and the Eighties: Kwame Nkrumah Memorial Lectures, 1980; Sovereignty and Solidarity: Callander Memorial Lectures, 1981; Some in Light and Some in Darkness: the long shadow of slavery (Wilberforce Lecture), 1983; The Message not the Messenger (STC Communication Lecture), 1985; The Trampling of the Grass (Economic Commn for Africa Silver Jubilee Lecture), 1985; Inseparable Humanity: an anthology of reflections of Shridath Ramphal (ed Ron Sanders), 1988; An End to Otherness (eight speeches by the Commonwealth Secretary-General), 1990; Our Country, The Planet, 1992; Glimpses of a Global Life (memoirs), 2014; contrib. various political, legal and other jls incl. International and Comparative Law Qly, Caribbean Qly, Public Law, Guyana Jl, Round Table, Foreign Policy, Third World Qly, RSA Jl Internat. Affairs. *Address:* The Garden House, Pleasant Hall Drive, Dayrells Road, Christchurch BB14030, Barbados, West Indies. *T:* 435 7531. *Clubs:* Athenæum, Royal Automobile, Travellers.

RAMPHUL, Sir Indurduth, Kt 1991; Governor, Bank of Mauritius, 1982–96; *b* 10 Oct. 1931; *m* 1962, Taramatee Seedoyal; one *s* one *d*. *Educ:* Univ. of Exeter (Dip. Public Admin). Asst Sec., Min. of Finance, 1966–67; Bank of Mauritius: Manager, 1967; Chief Manager, 1970; Man. Dir, 1973. Alternate Governor, IMF for Mauritius, 1982–96. *Recreations:* reading, swimming. *Address:* 9 Buswell Avenue, Quatre Bornes, Mauritius. *T:* 4541643, *Fax:* 4540559. *E:* sir.indur@intnet.mu. *Clubs:* Mauritius Turf; Cadets.

RAMSAY, family name of **Earl of Dalhousie**.

RAMSAY, Lord; Simon David Ramsay; Captain, 1st Battalion, Scots Guards; *b* 18 April 1981; *s* and *heir* of Earl of Dalhousie, *qv*. *Educ:* Harrow. *Recreations:* history of art, sculpture, country sports. *Address:* Brechin Castle, Brechin, Angus DD9 6SG.

RAMSAY OF CARTVALE, Baroness *cr* 1996 (Life Peer), of Langside in the City of Glasgow; **Meta Ramsay;** international affairs consultant; a Deputy Speaker, House of Lords, 2002–06; *b* 12 July 1936; *d* of Alexander Ramsay and Sheila Ramsay (*née* Jackson). *Educ:* Hutchesons' Girls' Grammar Sch.; Univ. of Glasgow (MA; MEd); Graduate Inst. of Internat. Studies, Geneva. President: Students' Rep. Council, Univ. of Glasgow, 1958–59; Scottish Union of Students, 1959–60; Associate Sec. for Europe, Co-ordinating Secretariat, Nat. Unions of Students, Leiden, Netherlands, 1960–63; Manager, Fund for Internat. Student Co-operation, 1963–67; HM Diplomatic Service, 1969–91: Stockholm, 1970–73; Helsinki, 1981–85; Counsellor, FCO, 1987–91. Foreign Policy Advr to Leader of Opposition, 1992–94; Special Advr to Shadow Sec. of State for Trade and Industry, 1994–95; a Baroness in Waiting (Govt Whip), 1997–2001. Member: Intelligence and Security Cttee, 1997, 2005–07; Jt Cttee on Nat. Security Strategy, 2010–. Mem., Labour Finance and Industry Gp, 1997–. Mem., UK Parly delegn to NATO Parly Assembly, 2003–. Chm., Atlantic Council of the UK, 2001–10. Co-Chair, Scottish Constitutional Convention, 1997–99; Chm., Scotland in Europe, 2004–. Hon. Vis. Res. Fellow in Peace Studies, Univ. of Bradford, 1996. Mem., Lewisham CHC, 1992–94. Chm., Bd of Governors, Fairlawn Primary Sch., Lewisham, 1991–97. Member: RIIA; Inst. of Jewish Policy Res.; Fabian Soc.; Labour Movement in Europe; Co-operative Party. FRSA 1995. Hon. DLitt Bradford, 1997; DUniv: Glasgow, 2004; Stirling, 2009. *Recreations:* theatre, opera, ballet. *Address:* House of Lords, SW1A 0PW. *T:* (020) 7219 5353. *Clubs:* Reform, University Women's.

RAMSAY, Sir Alexander William Burnett, 7th Bt *cr* 1806, of Balmain (also *heir-pres.* to Btcy of Burnett, *cr* 1626 (Nova Scotia), of Leys, Kincardineshire, which became dormant, 1959, on death of Sir Alexander Edwin Burnett of Leys, and was not claimed by Sir Alexander Burnett Ramsay, 6th Bt, of Balmain); *b* 4 Aug. 1938; *s* of Sir Alexander Burnett Ramsay, 6th Bt and Isabel Ellice, *e d* of late William Whitney, Woodstock, New South Wales; *S* father, 1965; *m* 1963, Neryl Eileen, *d* of J. C. Smith Thornton, Trangie, NSW; three *s*. *Heir: s* Alexander David Ramsay [*b* 20 Aug. 1966; *m* 1990, Annette Yvonne, *d* of H. M. Plummer; three *d*]. *Address:* Bulbah, Warren, NSW 2824, Australia.

RAMSAY, Sir Allan (John Heppel Ramsay), KBE 1992; CMG 1989; HM Diplomatic Service, retired; Ambassador to the Kingdom of Morocco, 1992–96; *b* 19 Oct. 1937; *s* of Norman Ramsay Ramsay and Evelyn Faith Sorel-Cameron; *m* 1966, Pauline Therèse Lescher; two *s* one *d*. *Educ:* Bedford Sch.; RMA Sandhurst; Durham Univ. Served Army, 1957–70: Somerset Light Infantry, 1957–64; Trucial Oman Scouts, 1964–66; DLI, 1966–68. MECAS, 1968–69; entered FCO, 1970; First Sec. (Commercial), Cairo, 1973–76; First Sec. and Hd of Chancery, Kabul, 1976–78; Counsellor and Head of Chancery: Baghdad, 1980–83; Mexico City, 1983–85; Ambassador: to Lebanon, 1988–90; to Sudan, 1990–91. *Address:* Le Genest, 53190 Landivy, France.

RAMSAY, Andrew Charles Bruce, CB 2007; Director General, Partnerships and Programmes, Department for Culture, Media and Sport, 2008–11; *b* 30 May 1951; *s* of Norman Bruce Ramsay and Marysha Octavia Ramsay; *m* 1983, Katharine Celia Marsh; two *d*. *Educ:* Winchester Coll.; Bedford Coll., London Univ. (BA). Joined DoE, 1974; Private Sec. to Parly Sec., Dept of Transport, 1978–80; Principal, DoE and Dept of Transport, 1980–85; Asst Sec., DoE, 1986–93; Under Sec. and Head of Arts, Sport and Lottery Gp, DNH, 1993–96; Under Sec. and Hd of Finance, Lottery and Personnel, then Corporate Services, Gp, DNH then DCMS, 1996–2000; Dir Gen., Creative Industries, Broadcasting, Gambling and Lottery Gp, 2000–04, Econ. Impact, 2004–06, Culture, Creativity and Economy, 2006–08, DCMS. *Recreations:* gardening, opera, birds, moths. *Address:* West Hall, Sedgeford, Hunstanton, Norfolk PE36 5NX.

RAMSAY, Andrew Vernon, CEng, FIET; FCIS; Chief Executive Officer (formerly Executive Director), Engineering Council, 2002–10 (Acting Director, 2001–02); *b* 7 July 1948; *s* of Douglas Charles Ramsay and Dorothy Isobel Ramsay (*née* Shankland); *m* 1971, Ruth Irene Mullen; one *s* one *d*. *Educ:* Churchill Coll., Cambridge (MA). CEng 1979; FIET (FIEE 2000). Student apprentice, AEI, 1966–70; Project Engr, GEC, 1970–72; various posts, CEGB, 1973–79; Dep. Sec., 1979–84, Sec. and CEO, 1985–97, CIBSE; Dir for Engrs Regulation, Engrg Council, 1997–2001; Construction Industry Council: Sec., 1988–90; Mem., 1990–97. Member, Board: QAA, 2006–10; Mathematics in Educn and Industry, 2011–; Chm., Adv. Cttee on Degree Awarding Powers, 2015–. Gov., Univ. for the Creative Arts, 2011–. FCIS 1982. *Recreations:* cycling, S London Swimming Club. *Club:* Rumford.

RAMSAY, Maj.-Gen. Charles Alexander, CB 1989; OBE 1979; *b* 12 Oct. 1936; *s* of Adm. Sir Bertram Home Ramsay, KCB, KBE, MVO, Allied Naval C-in-C, Invasion of Europe, 1944 (killed on active service, 1945), and Helen Margaret Menzies; *m* 1967, Hon. Mary MacAndrew, *d* of 1st Baron MacAndrew, PC, TD; two *s* two *d*. *Educ:* Eton; Sandhurst. Commissioned Royal Scots Greys, 1956; attended Canadian Army Staff Coll., 1967–68; served abroad in Germany, Middle East and Far East; Mil. Asst to VCDS, 1974–77; commanded Royal Scots Dragoon Guards, 1977–79; Colonel General Staff, MoD, 1979–80; Comdr 12th Armoured Bde, BAOR and Osnabrück Garrison, 1980–82; Dep. Dir of Mil. Ops, MoD, 1983–84; GOC Eastern District, 1984–87; Dir Gen., Army Orgn and TA, 1987–89; resigned from Army. Col, Royal Scots Dragoon Guards, 1992–98. Director: John Menzies plc, 1990–2004; Morningside Mgt LLC USA, 1990–2004, and other cos; Chairman: Eagle Enterprises Ltd, Bermuda, 1991–95; Cockburns of Leith Ltd, 1992–2004. Member, Queen's Body Guard for Scotland, Royal Company of Archers. *Recreations:* field sports, horse racing, travel, country affairs. *Address:* Pittlesheugh, Greenlaw, Berwickshire TD10 6UL. *Clubs:* Boodle's, Cavalry and Guards, Pratt's; New (Edinburgh).

RAMSAY, Douglas John; Parliamentary Counsel, 2004–11; *b* 29 Nov. 1959; *s* of Douglas Ramsay and Susan McFadyen Ramsay; *m* 1999, Gillian Platt; one *s* one *d*. *Educ:* Northgate Grammar Sch., Ipswich; Univ. of Leeds (LLB 1981); Chester Coll. of Law. Articled clerk, then solicitor, Titmuss, Sainer & Webb, 1982–87; Office of the Parliamentary Counsel: Asst Parly Counsel, 1987–91; Sen. Asst Parly Counsel, 1991–94; Principal Asst Parly Counsel, 1994–98; Dep. Parly Counsel, 1998–2004, seconded: to Law Commn, 1999–2002; to Tax Law Rewrite, 2006–09. *Recreations:* Rugby, football, my family. *Address:* c/o Office of the Parliamentary Counsel, 1 Horse Guards Road, SW1A 2HQ.

RAMSAY, Gordon James, OBE 2006; chef, restaurateur and television personality; *b* 8 Nov. 1966; *s* of late Gordon Scott Ramsay and Helen Ramsay (*née* Mitchell); *m* 1996, Cayetana Elizabeth Hutcheson; one *s* three *d* (of whom one *s* one *d* are twins). *Educ:* Stratford-upon-Avon High Sch.; North Oxon Tech. Coll., Banbury (HND Hotel Mgt 1987). Professional footballer, Glasgow Rangers FC, 1982–85; worked: with Marco Pierre White at Harvey's, 1989–91; with Albert Roux at La Gavroche, 1992–93; in Paris kitchens of Guy Savoy and Joël Robuchon, 1993–94; chef/proprietor: Aubergine restaurant, 1994–98 (Michelin Star, 1995, 1997); Gordon Ramsay Restaurant, Royal Hospital Road, Chelsea, 1998– (Michelin Star, 2001); Pétrus, Mayfair, 1999–2003, at The Berkeley, 2003–08 (Michelin Star, 2000); Amaryllis, Glasgow, 2001–04 (Michelin Star, 2002); Gordon Ramsay at Claridge's, 2001–13 (Michelin Star, 2003); Gordon Ramsay at The Connaught, 2002–07 (Michelin Star, 2003); The Savoy Grill, 2003–07 (Michelin Star, 2004), 2010–; Boxwood at The Berkeley, 2003–10; Maze, Grosvenor Square, 2005–; Gordon Ramsay at The London, NY, 2006–09; Gordon Ramsay at The Trianon Palace Hotel, Versailles, 2008– (2 Michelin Stars, 2009); York & Albany, 2008–; Foxtrot Oscar, 2008–; Maze Grill, 2008–; Bread Street Kitchen, One New Change, 2011–; GR Steak, Las Vegas, 2012–; Opal by Gordon Ramsay, Doha, 2012–; Gordon Ramsay Doha, 2012–; Fat Cow, LA, 2012–; Gordon Ramsay Pub & Grill, Las Vegas, 2012–; Gordon Ramsay BurGR, Las Vegas, 2012–; Union Street Café, 2013–; Bread Street Kitchen & Bar, Hong Kong, 2014–; Heddon Street Kitchen, 2014–; Pressoir d'Argent, Bordeaux, 2015–. Television series include: Hell's Kitchen, 2004; Ramsay's Kitchen Nightmares, 2004– (BAFTA Award, 2005); The F Word, 2005–; Ramsay's Kitchen Nightmares USA, 2007–; Cookalong Live, 2008; Gordon's Great Escape, 2010–; Ramsay's Best Restaurant, 2010; Christmas with Gordon, 2010; Gordon's Christmas Cookalong Live, 2011, 2012; Hotel Hell, USA, 2012, 2014; Gordon Behind Bars, 2012; Gordon Ramsay's Ultimate Cookery Course, 2012; Ramsay's Hotel Hell, 2013; Ramsay's Costa del Nightmares, 2014. *Publications:* Passion for Flavour, 1996; Passion for Seafood, 1999; A Chef for All Seasons, 2000; Just Desserts, 2001; Gordon Ramsay's Secrets, 2003; Gordon Ramsay's Kitchen Heaven, 2004; Gordon Ramsay makes it Easy, 2005; Gordon Ramsay's Sunday Dinners, 2006; The F Word, 2006; Humble Pie (autobiog.), 2006; Gordon Ramsay's Fast Food, 2007; Cooking for Friends, 2008; Gordon Ramsay's Healthy Appetite, 2008; Gordon Ramsay's Great British Pub Food, 2009; Gordon Ramsay's World Kitchen: recipes from The F Word, 2009; Gordon Ramsay's Great Escape: 100 of my favourite Indian recipes, 2010; Ramsay's Best Menus, 2010; Christmas with Gordon, 2010; Gordon's Great Escape: Southeast Asia, 2011; Gordon Ramsay's Ultimate Cookery Course, 2012. *Recreations:* salmon fishing, scuba diving, long distance running. *Address:* Gordon Ramsay Group, 539–547 Wandsworth Road, SW8 3JD. *T:* (020) 7592 1370.

RAMSAY, Prof. John Graham, CBE 1992; FRS 1973; Professor of Geology, Eidgenössische Technische Hochschule and University of Zürich, 1977–92, now Professor Emeritus; *b* 17 June 1931; *s* of Robert William Ramsay and Kathleen May Ramsay; *m* 1st, 1952, Sylvia Hiorns (marr. diss. 1957); 2nd, 1960, Christine Marden (marr. diss. 1987); three *d* (and one *d* decd); 3rd, 1990, Dorothee Dietrich. *Educ:* Edmonton County Grammar Sch.; Imperial Coll., London. DSc, PhD, DIC, BSc, ARCS, FGS. Musician, Corps of Royal Engineers, 1955–57; academic staff Imperial Coll., London, 1957–73: Prof. of Geology, 1966–73; Prof. of Earth Sciences, Leeds Univ., 1973–76. Mem., NERC, 1989–92. Vice-Pres., Société Géologique de France, 1973. Hon. Prof. of Earth Sci., Univ. of Cardiff, 2002; Hon. Prof. of Geology, Ben-Gurion Univ., 2008. For. Associate, US Nat. Acad. of Scis, 1985. Dr *hc* Rennes, 1978. *Publications:* Folding and Fracturing of Rocks, 1967; The Techniques of Modern Structural Geology, vol. 1, 1983, vol. 2, 1987, vol. 3, 2000. *Recreations:* music composition, chamber music, ski-ing, writing poetry. *Address:* Cratoule, Issirac, 30760 St Julien de Peyrolas, France.

RAMSAY, Jonathan William Alexander, FRCS; Consultant Urologist: Charing Cross Hospital, since 1988; West Middlesex Hospital, since 1988; *b* 27 Oct. 1953; *s* of late Raymond Ramsay, MBE, FRCS and Lillian Jane Ramsay, MBE (*née* Bateman); *m* 1983, Priscilla Jaqueline Russell Webster; two *s* one *d*. *Educ:* Bradfield Coll.; St Bartholomew's Hosp. Med. Coll. (MB BS, MS). FRCS 1981. Qualified, St Bartholomew's Hosp. (Brackenbury Schol.), 1977; Chief Asst (Urology), St Bartholomew's, 1985–88; Hon. Consultant Urologist, St Luke's Hosp. for Clergy, 1989–. Examr, Intercollegiate Speciality Bd in Urology, 2008–. Mem., Clinical Senate, NHS London, 2012–. Royal College of Surgeons: Regl Specialty Advr, 1995–2000; Mem., Court of Examrs, 1997–2005; Regl Advr, 1999–2006; Dir, Professional Affairs, 2010–; RCS Mem., NW London Clinical Bd, 2011–. Sec., Sect. Urology, RSocMed, 2006. President: W London Medico-Chirurgical Soc., 1999; Eur. Intrarenal Surgery Soc., 1999–. Fellow, Eur. Bd of Urology, 1991. *Publications:* contribs on treatment of stones by minimally invasive means and investigations of male fertility. *Recreations:* fishing, sailing. *Address:* Yew Trees House, Southlea Road, Datchet SL3 9BY; 149 Harley Street, W1N 1HG. *Clubs:* Flyfishers'; Royal Society of Medicine.

RAMSAY, Nicholas Harvey; Member (C) Monmouth, National Assembly for Wales, since 2007; *b* 10 June 1975; *s* of Graham George Ramsay and Carole Ann Mann, and step *s* of Andrew John Mann. *Educ:* Univ. of Durham (BA Jt Hons English and Philosophy); Cardiff Univ. (Postgrad. Dip. Applied Linguistics). Driving instructor, 2000–01; press officer/researcher, Nat. Assembly for Wales, 2001–07. Mem. (C) Monmouthshire CC, 2004–08. Mem., Lions Club Internat. *Recreations:* tennis, reading, keen pub quizzer. *Address:* National Assembly for Wales, Cardiff Bay, Cardiff CF99 1NA. *T:* 0300 200 7211. *E:* Nicholas.Ramsay@assembly.wales.

RAMSAY, Patrick George Alexander; Controller, BBC Scotland, 1979–83; retired; *b* 14 April 1926; *yr s* of late Rt Rev. Ronald Erskine Ramsay, sometime Bishop of Malmesbury, and Winifred Constance Ramsay (*née* Partridge); *m* 1948, Hope Seymour Dorothy, *y d* of late Rt Rev. Algernon Markham, sometime Bishop of Grantham, and Winifred Edith Markham (*née* Barne) (*d* 2013); two *s*. *Educ:* Marlborough Coll.; Jesus Coll., Cambridge (MA). Served War, Royal Navy (Fleet Air Arm), 1944–46. Joined BBC as Report Writer, Eastern European Desk, Monitoring Service, 1949; Liaison Officer, US Foreign Broadcasts Information Service, Cyprus, 1951–52; Asst, Appts Dept, 1953–56; Sen. Admin. Asst, External Broadcasting, 1956–58; Admin. Officer News and Head of News Administration, 1958–64; Planning Manager, Television Programme Planning, 1964–66; Asst Controller: Programme Services, 1966–69; Programme Planning, 1969–72; Controller, Programme Services, 1972–79. General Managerial Advr, Oman Broadcasting Service, 1984–85. A Dir, Windsor Festival Soc., 1973–76. Councillor and Alderman, Royal Borough of New Windsor, 1962–67; Chm., Windsor and Eton Soc., 1971–76. Chm., Windsor Liberal Assoc., 1961–66. *Recreations:* fellwalking, gardening, foreign travel, history, looking in junk shops, thwarting bureaucrats. *Address:* Abcott Manor, Clungunford, Shropshire SY7 0PX.

RAMSAY, Richard Alexander McGregor; Director, The Shareholder Executive, 2007–11; *b* 27 Dec. 1949; *s* of Alexander John McGregor Ramsay and Beatrice Kent La Nauze; *m* 1975, Elizabeth Catherine Margaret Blackwood; one *s* one *d*. *Educ:* Dalhousie Sch.; Trinity Coll., Glenalmond; Aberdeen Univ. (MA Hons in Politics and Sociology). ACA 1975; FCA. Price Waterhouse & Co., 1972–75; Grindlay Brandts, 1976–78; Hill Samuel & Co. Ltd, 1979–87 (Dir, 1984–87); on secondment as Dir, Industrial Develt Unit, DTI, 1984–86; Dir, 1988–91, Man. Dir, Corporate Finance Div., 1991–93, Barclays De Zoete Wedd; Director: Ivory & Sime, 1993–94; Ivory & Sime Investment Mgt, 1994–96; Finance Dir, Aberdeen FC, 1997–2000; Man. Dir for Regulation and Financial Affairs, Ofgem, 2001–03; Dir, Intelli Corporate Finance Ltd, 2003–09 (Vice Chm., 2003–05). Non-executive Director: Artemis AiM VCT plc, 2001–09 (Chm., 2001–03); Xploite plc, 2007–09; Castleton Tech. (formerly Redstone) plc, 2010–14 (Chm., 2011–13); Castle Trust plc, 2011– (Chm., 2015); Seneca Global Income and Growth (formerly Midas Income and Growth) Trust, 2013–; John Laing Envmtl Assets Gp Ltd, 2014–; Chairman: Wolsey Group Ltd, 2008–; Northcourt Ltd, 2011–; URICA Finance Ltd, 2012–; Redcentric plc, 2013–14. Consultant, Armstrong Bonham Carter, 2007–. *Recreations:* hill walking, ski-ing, classic cars, gardening. *Address:* The Little Priory, Sandy Lane, South Nutfield, Surrey RH1 4EJ. *T:* (01737) 822329.

RAMSAY, Robert, CMG 2000; DPhil; Director General for Research, European Parliament, 1989–99; *b* 11 Sept. 1940; *s* of Robert and Mabel Hamilton Ramsay; *m* 1963, Patricia Buckley (*d* 2009); four *s* (and one *s* decd). *Educ:* Royal Belfast Academical Instn; Queen's Univ., Belfast (BA Hons); Univ. of Ulster (DPhil 1979). Commonwealth Fellow, Victoria Univ. of Wellington, 1963–65; entered NICS, 1965; Principal Private Sec. to Prime Minister, 1971–72; European Dir, Inward Investment, Brussels, 1972–74; Sec. to Economic Council, 1974–76; Principal Private Sec. to Sec. of State for NI, 1976–78; Under Sec., DoE, 1978–83; Sec. Gen., EDG, EP, 1983–87; Dir, President's Office, EP, 1987–89. Sen. Policy Advr on EU affairs, PRM European Lobbyists, Brussels, 1999–. Leverhulme Fellow, 1978. *Publications:* The Corsican Time Bomb, 1983; Ringside Seats, 2009. *Recreations:* sailing, European literature. *E:* ramsayrobert@hotmail.com. *Club:* Carlton.

RAMSAY-FAIRFAX-LUCY, Sir Edmund John William Hugh Cameron; *see* Fairfax-Lucy.

RAMSBOTHAM, family name of **Baron Ramsbotham.**

RAMSBOTHAM, Baron *cr* 2005 (Life Peer), of Kensington, in the Royal Borough of Kensington and Chelsea; **Gen. David John Ramsbotham,** GCB 1993 (KCB 1987); CBE 1980 (OBE 1974); HM Chief Inspector of Prisons for England and Wales, 1995–2001; *b* 6 Nov. 1934; *s* of Rt Rev. J. A. Ramsbotham; *m* 1958, Susan Caroline (*née* Dickinson); two *s*. *Educ:* Haileybury Coll.; Corpus Christi Coll., Cambridge (BA 1957, MA 1973; Hon. Fellow, 2001). Nat. Service, 1952–54; Rifle Bde, UK and BAOR, 1958–62; seconded to KAR, 1962–63; Staff Coll., 1964; Rifle Bde, Far East, 1965; Staff, 7 Armoured Bde, 1966–68; 3 and 2 Green Jackets (BAOR), 1968–71; MA to CGS (Lt-Col), 1971–73; CO, 2 RGJ, 1974–76; Staff, 4 Armd Div., BAOR, 1976–78; Comd, 39 Infantry Bde, 1978–80; RCDS, 1981; Dir of Public Relns (Army), 1982–84; Comdr, 3 Armd Div., 1984–87; Comdr, UK Field Army and Inspector Gen., TA, 1987–90; Adjt Gen., 1990–93; ADC Gen. to the Queen, 1990–93. Dir of Internat. Affairs, DSL Ltd, 1994–99. Chm., Hillingdon Hosp. NHS Trust, 1995. Mem. Council, IISS, 1996–2002. Col Comdt, 2nd Battalion, The Royal Green Jackets, 1987–92; Hon. Col, Cambridge Univ. OTC, 1987–93; Hon. Bencher, Gray's Inn, 2002. FRSA 1999; FCGI 2000. Hon. FRCSLT 2012. Hon. DCL: Huddersfield, 1999; E London, 2002; Nottingham Trent, 2002; Birmingham, 2002; Keele, 2004; Portsmouth, 2004; Kent, 2004. *Publications:* Prisongate (memoirs), 2003. *Recreations:* sailing, gardening, art and art history. *Club:* Beefsteak.

RAMSBOTTOM, Paul Benjamin; Chief Executive (formerly Executive Secretary), Wolfson Foundation, since 2007; Chief Executive (formerly Secretary), Wolfson Family Charitable Trust, since 2007; *b* 27 May 1976; *s* of Benjamin Ashworth Ramsbottom and Jean Margaret Ramsbottom (*née* Kelsall); *m* 2002, Karen Rachel Taylor; four *d*. *Educ:* St Albans Sch.; Corpus Christi Coll., Oxford (BA 1st Cl. Hons Modern Hist. 1997; MSt 1998). With Wolfson Foundation, 1998–: Grants Adminr, 1998–2000; Asst Exec. Sec., 2000–01; Dep. Exec. Sec., 2001–06. CCB Fellow, Univ. of Oxford, 2009–. Chm., Savannah Educn Trust, 2004–; Chair, Foundns Forum, 2013–. Mem. Ct, LSHTM, 2009–14. FRSocMed 2007. Trustee, Mercy Ships UK, 2015–. Hon. DLitt Bedfordshire, 2013. *Recreations:* exotic travel and food, theology, various sports. *Address:* The Wolfson Foundation, 8 Queen Anne Street, W1G 9LD. *T:* (020) 7323 5730, *Fax:* (020) 7323 3241.

RAMSBURY, Bishop Suffragan of, since 2012; **Rt Rev. Dr Edward Francis Condry;** *b* 25 April 1953; *s* of Roy and Muriel Condry; *m* 1977, Sarah Louise Long; two *s* two *d*. *Educ:* Latymer Upper Sch.; Univ. of E Anglia (BA 1974); Exeter Coll., Oxford (BLitt 1977); DPhil Oxon 1980; Lincoln Theol Coll.; Univ. of Nottingham (DipTh 1981); MBA Open Univ. 2002. Ordained deacon, 1982, priest, 1983; Asst Curate, Weston Favell, Northampton, 1982–85; Vicar, Bloxham with Milcombe and S Newington, 1985–93; Rector, Rugby Team Ministry, 1993–2002; Canon Treas., Canterbury Cathedral, 2002–12. *Recreations:* running, cycling, canoeing, rowing, walking, laughing at my own jokes, planning adventures. *Address:* c/o Ramsbury Office, Church House, Crane Street, Salisbury, Wilts SP1 2QB. *T:* (01722) 438662. *E:* edward.condry@salisbury.anglican.org. *Clubs:* Canterbury Velo, Warminster Running.

RAMSDEN, Sir David Edward John, Kt 2015; CBE 2004; Chief Economic Adviser, since 2008 and a Director General (formerly Managing Director), since 2007, HM Treasury; *b* 9 Feb. 1964; *s* of late William Ramsden, OBE and of Elizabeth Ramsden (now Thompson); *m* 1993, Niccola Shearman; one *s* one *d*. *Educ:* Brasenose Coll., Oxford; London Sch. of Econs. Economist posts in DHSS and HM Treasury, 1986–98; HM Treasury: Head: EMU Policy Team, 1999–2003; O'Donnell Rev. Team, 2003; Dir, Tax and Budget, 2004–05; Dir, Macroeconomics and Fiscal Policy Gp, 2006–07; Hd, Govt Economic Service, 2010. Vice Chair, Economic Policy Cttee, OECD, 2014–. Pres., Soc. of Business Economists, 2012–. Trustee, Pro Bono Economics, 2010–. *Recreations:* cycling, climbing, walking, reading, wine. *Address:* HM Treasury, 1 Horse Guards Road, SW1A 2HQ. *T:* (020) 7270 4318, *Fax:* (020) 7451 7610. *E:* dave.ramsden@hmtreasury.gsi.gov.uk.

RAMSDEN, Rt Hon. James Edward; PC 1963; *b* 1 Nov. 1923; *s* of late Capt. Edward Ramsden, MC, and Geraldine Ramsden, OBE; *m* 1949, Juliet Barbara Anna, *y d* of late Col Sir Charles Ponsonby, 1st Bt, TD, and Hon. Lady Ponsonby, *d* of 1st Baron Hunsdon; three *s* two *d*. *Educ:* Eton; Trinity College, Oxford (MA). Commnd KRRC, 1942; served North-West Europe with Rifle Brigade, 1944–45. MP (C) Harrogate, WR Yorks, March 1954–Feb. 1974; PPS to Home Secretary, Nov. 1959–Oct. 1960; Under-Sec. and Financial Sec., War Office, Oct. 1960–Oct. 1963; Sec. of State for War, 1963–64; Minister of Defence for the Army, April–Oct. 1964. Director: UK Board, Colonial Mutual Life Assurance Society, 1966–72; Standard Telephones and Cables, 1971–81; Prudential Assurance Co. Ltd, 1972–91 (Dep. Chm., 1976–82); Prudential Corp. Ltd, 1979–91 (Dep. Chm., 1979–82). Dir, London Clinic, 1973–96 (Chm., 1984–96). Chm., The Hackfall Trust, 1988–. Mem., Historic Buildings Council for England, 1971–72. Pres., Northern Horticultural Soc., 1996–2001. *Address:* 14 High Agnesgate, Ripon, North Yorks HG4 1QR. *T:* (01765) 692229. *Club:* Pratt's.

RAMSDEN, Sir John (Charles Josslyn), 9th Bt *cr* 1689, of Byram, Yorks; HM Diplomatic Service, retired; Ambassador to Croatia, 2004–08; *b* 19 Aug. 1950; *s* of Sir Caryl Oliver Imbert Ramsden, 8th Bt, CMG, CVO, and Anne, *d* of Sir Charles Wickham, KCMG, KBE, DSO; *S* father, 1987; *m* 1985, (Jennifer) Jane Bevan; two *d*. *Educ:* Eton; Trinity Coll., Cambridge (MA). With merchant bank, Dawnay, Day & Co. Ltd, 1972–74. Entered FCO, 1975; 2nd Sec., Dakar, 1976; 1st Sec., MBFR, Vienna, 1978; 1st Sec., Head of Chancery and Consul, Hanoi, 1980; FCO, 1982–90; Counsellor, E Berlin, 1990; Counsellor and Dep. Hd of Mission, Berlin, 1991–93; Hd, Information Dept, FCO, 1993–96; UK Dep. Perm. Rep. to UN, Geneva, 1996–99; Hd, Central and NW Europe Dept, FCO, 1999–2003. Accredited Mediator, 2009; Partner, Ambassador Partnership (formerly ADRg Ambassadors) LLP, 2009–. Mem., Lord Chancellor's Adv. Council on Nat. Records and Archives, 2014–. Trustee, Mus. of E Asian Art, Bath, 2010–. Patron, British Croatian Soc.

RAMSDEN, (John) Michael; Editor of Publications, Royal Aeronautical Society, 1989–93; *b* 2 Oct. 1928; *s* of John Leonard Ramsden and Edith Alexandra Ramsden; *m* 1953, Angela Mary Mortimer; one *s* one *d*. *Educ:* Bedford Sch.; de Havilland Aeronautical Tech. Sch. CEng, FRAeS. With de Havilland Aircraft Co. Ltd, 1946–55; Flight, 1955–89: Air Transport Editor, 1961–64; Editor, 1964–81; Editor-in-Chief, Flight International, 1981–89. Chm., Press and Broadcasting Side, Defence Press and Broadcasting Cttee, 1983–89. Dir, de Havilland Aircraft Mus., 1970–2011 (Vice Pres., 2012–). Trustee, Geoffrey de Havilland Flying Foundn, 1992–. Pres., RAeS Hatfield Br., 2001–. Cumberbatch Trophy, GAPAN, 1981; Wakefield Gold Medal, RAeS, 1987; Douglas Weightman Award, Flight Safety Cttee, 1988. Silver Jubilee Medal, 1977. *Publications:* The Safe Airline, 1976, 2nd edn 1978 (Publications Award, Flight Safety Foundn, 1976); Caring for the Mature Jet, 1981; Chinook Justice, 2002; Sir Geoffrey de Havilland, 2015. *Recreations:* light-aircraft flying (now retired), water-colour painting. *Club:* de Havilland Moth.

RAMSDEN, Prof. Richard Thomas, MBE 2015; FRCS; Consultant Otolaryngologist, Manchester Royal Infirmary, 1977–2009; Professor of Otolaryngology, University of Manchester, 1994–2009; *b* 30 Dec. 1944; *s* of late Thomas William Ramsden and Elaine Napier Ramsden (*née* Meikle); *m* 1st, 1968, Wendy Margaret Johnson (marr. diss. 1984); one *s* two *d*; 2nd, 1987, Eileen Gillian Richardson (*née* Whitehurst); two step *s*. *Educ:* Madras Coll., St Andrews; St Andrews Univ. (MB ChB 1968). FRCS 1972. Registrar in Otolaryngol., 1972–74, Sen. Registrar, 1974–75, RNTNEH; Sen. Registrar, Otolaryngol., London Hosp., 1975–77. TWJ Travelling Fellow to N America, 1978. Lectures: Subramaniam, Indian Soc. of Otolaryngol., McBride, Univ. of Edinburgh, 1987; Dalby, Otology Section, RSocMed, 1992; Younis, Pakistan Soc. of Otolaryngol., 1993; Wilde, Irish Otolaryngol Soc., Graham Fraser, Otology Section, RSocMed, 1994; Goldman, Groote Schuur Hosp., Univ. of Cape Town, 1998; Yearsley, RCS, 2001; Gordon Smyth, BAO-HNS, 2004; Susan Bellman, British Assoc. of Audiol Physicians, 2004; William F. House, American Neurol. Soc., 2005; Philip Stell, N of Eng. Otolaryngol. Soc., 2006; Block Jacobson, Univ. of Dundee, 2008; Hunterian Oration, Hunterian Soc., 2008; Thomas Simm Littler, British Soc. of Audiology, 2009; Stirk Adams, Midland Inst. of Otology, 2012; Brinkmann, Univ. of Nijmegen, 2013; Toynbee, RCS, 2013. Pres., British Assoc. of Otolaryngologists-Head and Neck Surgeons, 2006–09. Trustee, Dowager Countess Eleanor Peel Trust, 2009–; Patron, Nat. Assoc. for Deafened People. FRCSE (*ad hominem*) 2000. Hon. Member: German ENT Soc.; Irish ENT Soc.; Danish ENT Soc.; Amer. Otological Soc. (Corresp. Mem., 2006); Slovak Soc. of Otolaryngol. and Head and Neck Surgery; German Skull Base Soc. Dalby Prize, W. J. Harrison Prize, RSocMed; Jobson Horne Prize, BMA. *Publications:* chapters on aspects of otology and neuro-otology; contrib. learned jls of otology and neuro-otology. *Recreations:* playing the bassoon, trying to resuscitate the golf, observing the maturation of the grandchildren. *Address:* Church House, 28 High Street, Thame, Oxon OX9 2AA. *T:* (01844) 212421. *Clubs:* Royal Society of Medicine; St Andrews New Golf; Middlesex County Cricket.

RAMSEY, Basil Albert Rowland; Editor, Music & Vision, 1999; *b* 26 April 1929; *s* of Florence Lily Ramsey (*née* Childs) and Alfred John Rowland Ramsey; *m* 1953, Violet Mary Simpson; one *s* two *d*. *Educ:* State schools. ARCO. Novello & Co.: Music Editor, 1949; Head of Publishing, 1963; established own publishing Co., 1976; Serious Music Publishing Consultant, Filmtrax plc, 1987–90. Editor: Organists' Review, 1972–84; Music & Musicians, 1989–90; The Musical Times, 1990–92; Choir & Organ, 1993–98. *Publications:* The Music of Charles Camilleri, 1996; articles and reviews in Musical Times, 1955–93; regular contributor to weekly and daily press on musical matters. *Recreations:* reading, calligraphy.

RAMSEY, Brig. Gael Kathleen, CBE 1992 (MBE 1976); Chief Executive, British Executive Service Overseas, 1997–2004; *b* 8 June 1942; *d* of Lt Col William Hammond, MBE and Kathleen Hammond; *m* 1977 (marr. diss. 1996). *Educ:* Convent of Good Shepherd, Singapore; High Sch. for Girls, Worcester, Gloucester and Dover. Commissioned, WRAC, 1968; Dir, WRAC, 1989–92; ADC to the Queen, 1989–92; Dir Women (Army), 1992; Comdr, Aldershot Bde Area, 1992–95, retd. Dep. Col Comdt, AGC, 1998–2002. Chm., Arnhem Wharf Residential Mgt Co. Ltd, 2011–. Freeman, City of London, 1991; Member: Guild of Freemen of City of London, 1992–; WRAC Assoc., 1989– (Life Mem.). FInstD 1995. *Recreations:* golf, tennis, reading, needlework, travel, messing about with plants. *Clubs:* Army and Navy; Royal Cinque Ports Yacht.

RAMSEY, Hon. Sir Vivian (Arthur), Kt 2005; FREng; a Judge of the High Court, Queen's Bench Division, 2005–14; Judge in charge, Technology and Construction Court, 2007–10; *b* 24 May 1950; *s* of Rt Rev. Ian Thomas Ramsey and late Margretta Ramsey (*née* McKay); *m* 1974, Barbara Walker; two *s* two *d*. *Educ:* Harley Sch., Rochester, NY; Abingdon Sch., Oxon; Oriel Coll., Oxford (MA); City Univ. (Dip. Law). CEng, MICE 1977; FREng 2013. Civil and Structural Engineer, Ove Arup & Partners, 1972–77, 1979–80; called to the Bar, Middle Temple, 1979, Bencher, 2002. Barrister and Arbitrator, 1981–2005; QC 1992; Head of Keating Chambers, 2002–05; Asst Recorder, 1998–2000; a Recorder, 2000–05. Special Prof., Dept of Civil Engineering, Nottingham Univ., 1990–; Vis. Prof., Centre of Construction Law, KCL, 2007–. Chm., Swanley Action Gp, 1989–2005. Fellow, American Coll. of Construction Lawyers, 2005– (Co-Chm., Internat. Cttee, 2008–11). Liveryman, Constructors' Co., 2009 (Freeman, 1995); Hon. Freeman, Paviors' Co., 2011. President's Medal, Soc. of Construction Law, 2010; Clare Edwards Award, Technol. and Construction Solicitors' Assoc., 2010. Editor, 1984–2005, Consultant Ed., 2005–, Construction Law Jl. *Publications:* (ed) Keating on Building Contracts, 7th edn, 2000, 8th edn, 2006. *Recreations:* building renovation, vineyards.

RAMSEY, Waldo Emerson W.; *see* Waldron-Ramsey.

RAMSHAW, Wendy Anne Jopling, (Mrs D. J. Watkins), CBE 2003 (OBE 1993); RDI 2000; freelance artist and designer, since 1960; *b* 26 May 1939; *d* of Angus Ramshaw and Flora (*née* Hollingshead); *m* 1962, Prof. David John Watkins, *qv*; one *s* one *d*. *Educ:* Sunderland Girls' High Sch.; Saint Mary's Convent, Berwick-upon-Tweed; Coll. of Art and Industrial Design, Newcastle upon Tyne (NDD); Univ. of Reading (ATD); Central Sch. of Art and Design, London (postgrad. studies). Artist in Residence: Western Australian Inst. of Technol., 1978–79; Printmakers Workshop, Inverness, 1996; Pallant House, Chichester; St John's Coll., Oxford, 2005; Pilchuck Glass Sch., Seattle, 2006; Somerset House, 2010; Visiting Artist: in collaboration with Wedgwood, 1981–82; Glass Dept, RCA, 1985–86; Visiting Professor: San Diego State Univ., 1984; Bezalel Acad., Jerusalem, 1984; Dept of Goldsmithing, Silversmithing, Metalwork and Jewellery, RCA, 1998–2001; St John's Coll., Oxford, 2005; Pilchuck Glass Sch., Seattle, 2006. Patron, Contemporary Applied Arts, London. Lady Liveryman, Co. of Goldsmiths, 1986–. FCSD 1972; FRSA 1972. Hon. Fellow London Inst., 1999 (Governor, 2000–06); Sen. Fellow RCA, 2006. *Exhibitions include:* Wendy Ramshaw - David Watkins: Goldsmiths Hall, London, 1973; Nat. Gall. of Victoria, 1978; Schmuckmuseum, Pforzheim, 1987; Wendy Ramshaw: V&A Mus., 1982; Retrospective, Bristol City Mus. & Art Gall., 1983; Jewellery Strategies/Jewellery Variations, Mikimoto, Tokyo, 1993; Picasso's Ladies: V&A Mus. and American Crafts Mus., NY, 1998; Institute Mathildenhohe, Darmstadt, 2001; Millennium Exhibn, Contemporary Applied Arts, London, 2000; Room of Dreams, Scottish Gall., Edinburgh, 2002; Prospero's Table, SOFA, Chicago, 2004; Collect, V&A, 2005; A Journey through Glass, Scottish Gall., 2007; Rooms of Dreams, Somerset House, London, Ruthin Craft Centre and tour, 2012–14; Inspired, Electrum Gall., London, 2012; Inventor, Scottish Gall., Edinburgh, 2013; *major commissions:* Bird of Paradise Gift from British Govt to Papua New Guinea, 1976; Garden Gate, St John's Coll., Oxford, 1993; Double Screen EH 9681, V&A Mus., 1996; semi-circular entrance gate, Mowbray Pk, Sunderland, 1998; Columbus screen, Canary Wharf, 1999; Queen's Millennium Medal, BM, 2000; glass door panels and bronze handles, Southwark Cathedral, 2000; aluminium park gates, Sculpture at Goodwood, 2001; garden gate, Clare Coll., Cambridge, 2007; New Edinburgh gate, One Hyde Park, 2010; two pairs of gates, Kendrew Quadrangle, St John's Coll., Oxford, 2010; *work in public collections:* Australian Nat. Gall., Canberra; BM; Kunstindustrimuseet, Oslo; Musée des Art Décoratifs, Paris; Mus. of Mod. Art, Kyoto; Philadelphia Mus. of Art; Royal Mus. of Scotland, Edinburgh; Schmuckmuseum, Pforzheim; Science Mus., London; Smithsonian Inst., Cooper-Hewitt Nat. Design Mus., NY; Stedelijk Mus., Amsterdam; V&A Mus.; Powerhouse, Sydney; Corning Mus. of Glass, Corning, USA; Nat. Mus. of Wales; Metropolitan Mus., NY; Mus. of Fine Art, Houston. Council of Industrial Design award, 1972; De Beers Diamond Internat. Award, 1975; Art in Architecture award, RSA, 1993. *Relevant publications:* Wendy Ramshaw (exhibn catalogue), 1982; From Paper to Gold (exhibn catalogue), 1990; Jewel Drawings and Projects: contemporary jewellery issues, 1998; Picasso's Ladies: jewellery by Wendy Ramshaw, 1998; Wendy Ramshaw: jewellery (Blackwell exhibn catalogue); The Big Works: Wendy Ramshaw, 2004; Drawings in Gold, 2008; David Watkins, Wendy Ramshaw: a life's partnership, by Graham Hughes, 2009; Rooms of Dreams, 2012. *Recreations:* visiting museums and art galleries, travelling. *Address:* c/o Faculty of Royal Designers for Industry, Royal Society of Arts, 8 John Adams Street, WC2N 6EZ.

RAMZAN GOLANT, Farah, CBE 2011; Chief Executive, All3Media, since 2012; *b* Kenya, 11 May 1964; *d* of Fateh and Gulshan Ramzan; *m* 1990, Dr Benjamin Golant; one *s* one *d*. *Educ:* Emmanuel Coll., Cambridge (BA Hons Mod. and Medieval Langs 1987). Abbott Mead Vickers BBDO (formerly Abbott Mead Vickers), 1990–2012: Man. Dir, 2003–05; CEO, 2005–10; Exec. Chm., 2010–12; Mem., Worldwide Bd, BBDO, 2007–12. Member: Bd, National Theatre, 2008–; Adv. Gp, Cancer Research UK, 2009–; Prime Minister's Business Adv. Gp, 2013–. *Recreations:* tennis, dance, family, cinema, theatre, holidays. *Address:* All3Media, Berkshire House, 168–173 High Holborn, WC1V 7AA. *Clubs:* Thirty, Women in Advertising and Communications London.

RANA, Baron *cr* 2004 (Life Peer), of Malone in the County of Antrim; **Diljit Singh Rana,** MBE 1996; JP; Founder and Managing Director, Andras House Ltd, since 1981; *b* 20 Sept. 1938; *s* of Paras Ram Rana; *m* 1966, Uma Passi; two *s*. *Educ:* Punjab Univ. (BA (Econs) 1958). Founder and Chm., Indian Business Forum, 1985. Founder, Rana Charitable Trust, 1996; Chm., Thanksgiving Square, Belfast, 2002–. Vice Pres., UNICEF, 2004–08. Chm., Sanghol Educn Complex, India, 2004–. Pres., Global Orgn of People of Indian Origin, 2009–. Hon. Indian Consul in NI, 2004–. President: S Belfast Safer Towns Assoc., 1991–93; Belfast Chamber of Trade, 1991–92; NI Chamber of Commerce and Industry, 2004–05; NI Hon. Consular Assoc., 2008–. Gov., Lagan Coll., 1990–94. Hon. Dr: Ulster, 1999; QUB, 2003. JP Belfast, 1986. Pravasi Bharatiya Samman Award (India), 2007. *Address:* 13 Malone Park, Belfast BT9 6NH. *Clubs:* Ulster Reform, Dunmurry Golf (Belfast).

RANASINGHE, (Kulatilaka Arthanayake) Parinda; Chief Justice of Sri Lanka, 1988–91; *b* 20 Aug. 1926; *s* of Solomon Ranasinghe and Somawathie Ranasinghe; *m* 1956, Chitra (*née* Mapaguneratne); one *s* three *d*. *Educ:* Royal Coll., Colombo. Advocate of the Supreme Court; appointed Magistrate, 1958; District Judge, 1966–74; High Court Judge, 1974–78; Judge, Court of Appeal, 1978–82, Pres. 1982; Judge, Supreme Court, 1982–88. *Recreation:* walking. *Address:* 18/48 Muhandiram E. D. Dabare Mawatha, Colombo 5, Sri Lanka. *T:* (1) 508310.

RANDALL, Rt Hon. Sir (Alexander) John, Kt 2013; PC 2010; *b* 5 Aug. 1955; *s* of late Alec Albert Randall and Joyce Margaret (*née* Gore); *m* 1986, Katherine Frances Gray; two *s* one *d*. *Educ:* Rutland House Sch., Hillingdon; Merchant Taylors' Sch., Herts; SSEES, Univ. of London (BA Hons Serbo-Croat Lang. and Lit. 1979). Dir, Randalls of Uxbridge Ltd, 1981– (Man. Dir, 1986–97). MP (C) Uxbridge, Aug. 1997–2010, Uxbridge and S Ruislip, 2010–15. An Opposition Whip, 2000–March 2003, July 2003–05; Opposition Asst Chief Whip, 2005–10; Treasurer of HM Household (Dep. Chief Whip), 2010–13. *Recreations:* ornithology, theatre, opera, travel, sport. *Clubs:* Uxbridge Conservative; Saracens Rugby Football, Middlesex County Cricket.

See also P. A. Gore-Randall.

RANDALL, Jeff William; Editor-at-Large, The Daily Telegraph, 2005–13; Presenter, Jeff Randall Live, Sky Television, 2007–14; *b* 3 Oct. 1954; *s* of late Jeffrey Charles Randall and Grace Annie (*née* Hawkridge); *m* 1986, Susan Diane Fidler; one *d*. *Educ:* Royal Liberty Grammar Sch., Romford; Univ. of Nottingham (BA Hons Econs); Univ. of Florida. Hawkins Publishers, 1982–85; Asst Editor, Financial Weekly, 1985–86; City Corresp., Sunday Telegraph, 1986–88; The Sunday Times: Dep. City Editor, 1988–89; City Editor, 1989–94; City and Business Editor, 1994–95; Asst Editor and Sports Editor, 1996–97; Editor, Sunday Business, 1997–2001; Business Ed., BBC, 2001–05. Dir, Times Newspapers, 1994–95; Dep. Chm., Financial Dynamics Ltd, 1995–96. Columnist, Sunday Telegraph, 2002–04. Non-executive Director: Babcock Internat. plc, 2014–; Sandown Park Racecourse, 2014–. Vis. Fellow, Univ. of Oxford Business Sch., 2008. Hon. Prof., Nottingham Univ. Business Sch., 2011. Mem. Council, Nottingham Univ., 2013–. Hon. DLit: Anglia Poly. Univ., 2001; Univ. of Nottingham, 2006; Hon. DBA BPP Univ. Coll., 2011. Financial Journalist of the Year, FT-Analysis, 1991; Business Journalist of the Year, London Press Club, 2001; Sony Gold Award for best radio sports prog., The Bankrupt Game, BBC 5 Live, 2002; Broadcast Journalist of the Year and Decade of Excellence Award, Business Journalist of the Year Awards, 2003; Harold Wincott Award for Best Business Broadcaster, 2004; Communicator of the Year Award, PR Week, 2004; Best Broadcast Feature, Where's My Pension Gone?, Business Journalist of the Year Awards, 2007. *Publications:* (contrib.) The Day that Shook the World, 2001. *Recreations:* golf, horseracing. *Address:* c/o Babcock International, 33 Wigmore Street, W1U 1QX. *Clubs:* Brooks's; Thorndon Park Golf.

RANDALL, Rt Hon. Sir John; *see* Randall, Rt Hon. Sir A. J.

RANDALL, John Norman; Registrar General for Scotland, 1999–2003; *b* 1 Aug. 1945; *s* of Frederick William Randall and Daphne Constance Randall (*née* Gawn); *m* 1st, 1967, Sandra Philpott (marr. diss. 1991); one *s* one *d*; 2nd, 1997, Eileen Wilson (marr. diss. 2014). *Educ:* Bromley Grammar Sch.; Bristol Univ. (BA Hons Geography); Glasgow Univ. (MPhil Town and Regl Planning 1968; MPhil Econs 1979). Economist: Dept of Economic Affairs, 1968–70; Scottish Office, 1970–85; Dep. Registrar Gen. for Scotland, 1985–89; Asst Sec., Scottish Office, 1989–99. Trustee, Islands Book Trust, 2002–; Mem. Council, Butterfly Conservation, 2002–06. Chm., Co-Chomunn na Pairc, 2007–13; Dir, Pairc Trust, 2008–. *Recreations:* hill walking, natural history, island history, Gaelic. *Address:* 31 Lemreway, South Lochs, Isle of Lewis HS2 9RD.

RANDALL, John Paul, CBE 2015; international consultant on higher education and professional training, since 2001; Chairman: Police Negotiating Board, 2004–15; Police Advisory Board for Northern Ireland, 2007–14; Scottish Police Consultative Forum, since 2013; *b* 23 Nov. 1947; *s* of late E. T. (Ted) Randall and Mollie Randall (*née* Macrae); *m* (marr. diss.); one *s* one *d*; 2nd, 1993, Marie Catherine Hague. *Educ:* Wallington County Grammar Sch. for Boys; Univ. of York (BA Hons Biol and Educn 1971). National Union of Students: Dep. Pres., 1971–73; Pres., 1973–75; Civil Service Union: Asst Sec., 1975–77; Asst Gen. Sec., 1977–81; Dep. Gen. Sec., 1981–87; Dir, Professional Standards and Develt, Law Soc., 1987–97; Chief Exec., QAA, 1997–2001. Chm., Skills for Justice (Justice Sector Skills Council), 2003–10. Mem. Council, NCVQ, 1992–97 (Chm., Accreditation Cttee, 1993–96; Chm., NVQ Policy Cttee, 1996–97; Mem. Jt Cttee, NCVQ and Schools Curriculum and Assessment Authy, 1996–97); Mem. Bd, Internat. Network of QAAs, 1999–2001. Member:

Information Tribunal, 2003–10; Legal Services Consultative Panel, 2004–09; Gen. Regulatory Chamber (Information Rights and Estate Agents' jurisdictions), Tribunals Service, 2010– (Consumer Credit, 2010–14). Independent Chair, Police Adv. Bd for Eng. and Wales, 2004–14; Consultative Gp, Coll. of Policing, 2014–. Lay Assessor: Nat. Clin. Assessment Service (formerly Authy), 2003–11; PMETB, 2006–10; Lay Trng Partner, GMC, 2010–13. Quality Assurance Dir, Internat. Compliance Assoc., 2002–13. Vis. Academic Advr, Univ. of HK, 2002; Tech. Sec., UGC (Hong Kong), 2003–04, 2010–11, 2014–15; Specialist Consultant, Asia Develt Bank Tech. Assistance Project, Commn on Higher Educn, Philippines, 2004; Consultant, Hong Kong Council on Academic Accreditation, 2005–08. Sen. Res. Fellow, Legal Services Inst. (formerly Legal Services Policy Inst.), Univ. (formerly Coll.) of Law, 2008–13. Mem. Council, C&G, 1999–2015 (Mem., Trustee Bd (formerly Exec. Cttee), 2004–13). Mem. Bd of Mgt, Focus Housing Assoc., 1996–99. FRSA 1998. FCGI 2007. Hon. LLD Nottingham Trent, 1998. *Publications:* (contrib.) Higher Education Re-formed, 2000; Collective Bargaining for a Modernised Workforce, 2006; articles in educnl and legal jls. *Recreations:* walking, music, wine, travel, jogging. *Address:* Orchard Cottage, The Rampings, Longdon, Worcs GL20 6AL. *E:* john.randall23@btopenworld.com. *Clubs:* South London Harriers, Orion Harriers.

RANDALL, John Yeoman; QC 1995; a Recorder, since 1999; a Deputy High Court Judge, since 2000; *b* 26 April 1956; *s* of Richard and Jean Randall; *m* 1982, Christine Robinson; one *s* one *d*. *Educ:* Rugby Sch.; Loomis Inst., USA; Jesus Coll., Cambridge (MA). Called to the Bar: Lincoln's Inn, 1978, Bencher, 2003; NSW, 1979; WA, 2001; in practice at English Bar, 1980–; an Asst Recorder, 1995–99. Hd of Chambers, 2001–04. Mem., Legal Services Consultative Panel, 2000–09. Vis. Fellow, 2004–13, Adjunct Prof., 2013–, Univ. of NSW; Sen. Fellow, Melbourne Law Sch., 2014–. *Publications:* (with Sarah Green) The Tort of Conversion, 2009. *Recreations:* travel, sports, music. *Address:* St Philip's Chambers, 55 Temple Row, Birmingham B2 5LS. *T:* (0121) 246 7000, *Fax:* (0121) 246 7001. *E:* civil@st-philips.com.

RANDALL, Philip Allan G.; *see* Gore-Randall.

RANDELL, Charles; Partner, Corporate Department, Slaughter and May, 1989–2013; External Member, Prudential Regulation Authority, Bank of England, since 2013; *b* Rheindahlen, 6 June 1958; *s* of Keith and Annette Randell; *m* 1983, Celia Van Oss; three *s*. *Educ:* Streete Court Prep. Sch.; Bradfield Coll.; Trinity Coll., Oxford (BA Juris. 1979); College of Law, Guildford. Slaughter and May: Articled Clerk, 1980–82; Solicitor, 1982–89. Non-exec. Dir, DECC, 2013–. Vis. Fellow, Centre for Commercial Law Studies, QMUL, 2011–12. Member, Editorial Board: PLC Corporate Law, 1990–2013; Law and Financial Markets Review, 2012–. *Publications:* (jtly) Public Company Takeovers in Germany, 2002; various articles relating to financial regulation, corporate law and corporate governance. *Recreations:* sailing, theatre, travel.

RANDENIYA, Vijith, OBE 2007; Chief Fire Officer, West Midlands Fire Service, 2009–13; *b* Croydon, 21 July 1960; *s* of Sarath Randeniya and Kamala Randeniya; *m* 2005, Shindo Barquer. *Educ:* Selhurst High Sch.; Univ. of Wales, Bangor (BA Hons Mod. Hist. 1981); Coventry Univ. (MA Mgt 2002). Firefighter, latterly Gp Comdr, London Fire Bde, 1983–98; Hd, Ops, Nottinghamshire Fire and Rescue Service, 1998–2000; West Midlands Fire Service: Asst Chief Fire Officer, 2000–03; Dep. Chief Fire Officer, 2003–09. Chm., Bd of Trustees, Birmingham St Mary's Hospice, 2014–. FRSA. Mem., Lunar Soc. Hon. DSc Aston, 2010. *Recreations:* Victorian house refurbishments, military history, JFK memorabilia, cooking, shopping. *Club:* Royal Air Force.

RANDEREE, Shabir Ahmed, CBE 2013; Executive Chairman, DCD London and Mutual plc, since 1990; *b* Durban, 12 March 1962; *s* of Ahmed Randeree and Fareda Randeree; *m* 1989, Ruwaida; three *s*. *Educ:* Kingston Poly. (BA Hons Accounting and Finance 1984); Schiller Internat. Univ., London (MBA 1986). Various posts within DCD Gp Divisions, 1986–90; Dep. Chm., Al Baraka Bank Ltd, South Africa, 2002–; Chm., European Islamic Investment Bank plc, 2005–12; Director: Islamic Bank of Britain plc, 2003–08; BankIslami Ltd, 2005–. Mem., Young Presidents' Orgn, 2003–. *Address:* DCD London and Mutual plc, 90 Long Acre, WC2E 9RA. *T:* (020) 7324 2000. *E:* sr@dcdgroup.com.

RANDERSON, family name of **Baroness Randerson**.

RANDERSON, Baroness *cr* 2011 (Life Peer), of Roath Park in the City of Cardiff; **Jennifer Elizabeth Randerson;** JP; *b* 26 May 1948; *m* 1970, Dr Peter Frederick Randerson; one *s* one *d*. *Educ:* Bedford Coll., London Univ. (BA Hons History); Inst. of Educn, London Univ. (PGCE 1970). Teacher: Sydenham High Sch., 1970–72; Spalding High Sch., 1972–74; Llanishen High Sch., 1974–76; Lectr, Coleg Glan Hafren, Cardiff, 1976–99. Member (L, then Lib Dem): Cardiff City Council, 1983–96; Cardiff County Council, 1995–2000 (Leader of Opposition, 1995–99). Mem. (Lib Dem) Cardiff Central, Nat. Assembly for Wales, 1999–2011. National Assembly for Wales: Sec., then Minister, for Culture, Sports and the Welsh Lang., 2000–03; Lib Dem spokesperson on economic develt and finance, 2003–05, on health, finance and equal opportunities, 2005–07, on health, social services, local govt and finance, 2007–09, on educn, economy and transport, 2009–11. Parly Under-Sec. of State, Wales Office, 2012–15; spokesperson on NI, H of L, 2012–. Chair of Exec., Welsh Lib Dems, 1988–90. Contested: (L) Cardiff S and Penarth, 1987; (Lib Dem) Cardiff Central, 1992, 1997. JP Cardiff 1982. *Recreations:* travel, theatre and concert going, gardening. *Address:* House of Lords, SW1A 0PW.

RANDLE, James Neville, FREng; RDI 1994; Chief Executive Officer, Lea Francis Ltd, 2000–10 (Director, 1997–2010); *b* Birmingham, 24 April 1938; *s* of James Randle and Florence (*née* Wilkins); *m* 1963, Jean Violet Allen (*d* 2006); one *s* one *d*. *Educ:* Waverley Grammar Sch., Birmingham. MIMechE 1969, FIMechE 1980; FREng (FEng 1988). Rover Car Company: apprentice, 1954–59; design and develt engr, 1959–63; Project Manager, 1963–65; Jaguar: R&D Engr, 1965–72; Chief Res. Engr, 1972–78; Vehicle Engrg Dir, 1978–80; Product Engrg Dir, 1980–91. Hon. Prof., 1992–2006, Dir, Automotive Engrg Centre, 1993–2006, Univ. of Birmingham. Chm., Randle Engrg and Design, 1994–; Dir, Volvo Aero Turbines, 1992–98. Institution of Mechanical Engineers: Mem. Bd, 1979–88, Chm., 1986–87, Automobile Div.; Mem. Council, 1986–93. Member: Prince Philip Design Prize Cttee, 1992–95 and 1997–2002; Misha Black Awards Cttee for Design Educn, 1992–. Pres., Engrg Div., BAAS, 1995–96. Chm., Coventry Aeroplane Club, 2007–11. FInstD 1986. FRSA 1989. Hon. FCSD 2000. James Clayton Prize, 1986, Crompton Lanchester Medal, 1986, IMechE. *Publications:* technical papers and presentations on automobile engrg and Jaguar and Lea Francis histories. *Recreations:* flying powered aircraft (private pilot's licence and owner), sailing (yacht master's certificate), ski-ing, hill walking, designing automobiles. *Address:* Pear Tree House, High Street, Welford on Avon, Warwickshire CV37 8EF.

RANDLE, Prof. Valerie, PhD, DSc; Professor of Materials Engineering, Swansea University (formerly University of Wales Swansea), 1999–2013, now Emeritus (Head of Materials Research Centre, 2007–09); *b* 8 May 1953; *d* of Bertram and Edith Brushfield; *m* 1st, 1971, Michael Randle (decd); one *s* one *d*; 2nd, 2006, Victor Pinheiro (decd). *Educ:* Univ. of Wales, Cardiff (BSc 1983; PhD 1986; DSc 1996). FIMMM 1993; CEng 1998. Royal Soc. Univ. Res. Fellow, Bristol Univ., 1987–92, UC of Swansea, 1992–95; Sen. Lectr, 1995–97, Reader, 1997–99, UC of Swansea, then Univ. of Wales Swansea. Volunteer, Cruse Bereavement Care. Welsh Woman of the Year, 1998. *Publications:* Microtexture Determination and its Applications, 1992, 2nd edn 2003; Grain Boundary Geometry in Polycrystals, 1993; (jtly) An Atlas of Backscatter Kikuchi Diffraction Patterns, 1994; The Role of the Coincidence Site Lattice in Grain Boundary Engineering, 1996; (with Olaf Engler) Introduction to Texture Analysis: macrotexture, microtexture and orientation mapping, 2000, 2nd edn 2009; 350 scientific papers in learned jls. *Recreations:* walking, swimming, yoga, meditation, singing. *T:* 07732 357348. *E:* valeriepinheiro@gmail.com.

RANDOLPH, Fergus Mark Harry, QC 2009; *b* London, 6 Oct. 1961; *s* of late Peter and Rippy Randolph; *m* 1991, Criet Descheemaeker; three *s*. *Educ:* Harrow Sch.; Buckingham Univ. (LLB); Univ. of Aix-en-Provence (Licence en Droit). Called to the Bar, Middle Temple, 1985, Bencher, 2011; in practice as barrister specialising in EU and competition law, Brick Court Chambers, London and Brussels, 1991–. Liveryman, Cutlers' Co., 1992–. *Publications:* Commercial Agency and Distribution Agreements, 1987; Shipping and EC Competition Law, 1991; Banking Secrecy, 1993; (jtly) Guide to the Commercial Agents Regulations, 1994, 3rd edn 2010. *Recreations:* running, fishing, stalking, opera. *Address:* Brick Court Chambers, 7–8 Essex Street, WC2R 3LD. *T:* (020) 7379 3550, *Fax:* (020) 7379 3558. *E:* fergus.randolph@brickcourt.co.uk. *Club:* Royal Automobile.

RANDOLPH, Prof. Mark Felton, PhD; FRS 2011; FREng; FAA; Professor of Civil Engineering, Centre for Offshore Foundation Systems, University of Western Australia, since 1990; Director, Advanced Geomechanics, since 1994; *b* 3 July 1951; *s* of late Lt-Col John Hervey Randolph and Dorothy Elizabeth Randolph (*née* Eyre). *Educ:* Sherborne Sch.; Queen's Coll., Oxford (BA 1973; MA 1978); St John's Coll., Cambridge (PhD 1978). CPEng 1987; FIEAust 1994; FREng 2002. Scientific Officer, 1973–75, Higher Scientific Officer, 1975–77, BRE; Fellow, St John's Coll., Cambridge, 1977–86; Asst Lectr, 1978–83, Lectr, 1983–86, Engrg Dept, Univ. of Cambridge; University of Western Australia: Sen. Lectr, 1986–89; Associate Prof., 1989–90; Dir, Centre for Offshore Foundn Systems, 1997–2005. Fedn Fellow, Australian Res. Council, 2005–10. FTSE 1993; FAA 2000. *Publications:* (jtly) Piling Engineering, 1985, 3rd edn 2009; (jtly) Offshore Geotechnical Engineering, 2011; contrib. articles to geotech. engrg jls. *Recreations:* hiking, tennis, theatre, bridge. *Address:* Centre for Offshore Foundation Systems (MO53), University of Western Australia, 35 Stirling Highway, Crawley, WA 6009, Australia. *T:* (61) 864883075, *Fax:* (61) 864881044. *E:* mark.randolph@uwa.edu.au.

RANDS, Dr Michael Russell Wheldon; Executive Director, Cambridge Conservation Initiative, since 2009; *b* 2 Aug. 1956; *s* of late Russell Fuller Rands and Freda Millicent Rands; *m* 1984, Dr Gillian Frances Porter Goff; one *s* one *d*. *Educ:* Univ. of E Anglia (BSc Hons Envmtl Sci. 1978); Wolfson Coll., Oxford (DPhil 1982). Res. Biologist, Game Conservancy, 1982–86; Programme Dir, ICBP, 1986–94; Dir, Strategic Planning and Policy, 1994–96, Dir and Chief Exec., 1996–2009, BirdLife Internat. *Publications:* (with P. J. Hudson) Ecology and Management of Gamebirds, 1988; contrib. numerous papers to learned jls. *Recreations:* bird-watching, travelling with family, music. *Address:* Judge Business School, University of Cambridge, Trumpington Street, Cambridge CB2 1AG.

RANELAGH, John O'B.; *see* O'Beirne Ranelagh.

RANFURLY, 7th Earl of, *cr* 1831 (Ire.); **Gerald François Needham Knox;** Baron Welles 1781; Viscount Northland 1791; Baron Ranfurly (UK) 1826; *b* 4 Jan. 1929; *s* of Captain John Needham Knox, RN (*d* 1967) (*gggs* of 1st Earl) and Monica B. H. (*d* 1975), *d* of Maj.-Gen. Sir Gerald Kitson, KCVO, CB, CMG; *S* cousin, 1988; *m* 1955, Rosemary, *o d* of Air Vice-Marshal Felton Vesey Holt, CMG, DSO; two *s* two *d*. *Educ:* Wellington College. Served RN, 1947–60; retired as Lieut Comdr. Member of Stock Exchange, 1964; Partner in Brewin & Co., 1965; Senior Partner, 1982, Chm., 1987–95, Brewin Dolphin & Co. *Recreation:* foxhunting. *Heir:* *s* Edward John Knox [*b* 21 May 1957; *m* 1st, 1980, Rachel Sarah (marr. diss. 1984), *d* of F. H. Lee; 2nd, 1994, Johanna Humphrey, *d* of Sqdn Leader H. R. Walton, MBE; one *s* one *d*]. *Address:* Chase Cottage, Nayland, Colchester, Essex CO6 4LZ.

RANG, Prof. Humphrey Peter, DPhil; FRS 1980; Director, Sandoz, later Novartis, 1983–97, Institute for Medical Research, and Professor of Pharmacology, 1979–83 and 1995–2001, now Emeritus, University College London; President, British Pharmacological Society, from Jan. 2014; *b* 13 June 1936; *s* of Charles Rang and Sybil Rang; *m* 1992, Isobel Heyman. *Educ:* University Coll. Sch.; University Coll. London (MSc 1960); UCH Med. Sch. (MB, BS 1961); Balliol Coll., Oxford (DPhil 1965). J. H. Burn Res. Fellow, Dept of Pharmacol., Oxford, 1961–65; Vis. Res. Associate, Albert Einstein Coll. of Medicine, NY, 1966–67; Univ. Lectr in Pharmacol., Oxford, 1966–72; Fellow and Tutor in Physiol., Lincoln Coll., Oxford, 1967–72; Prof. of Pharmacology: Univ. of Southampton, 1972–74; St George's Hosp. Med. Sch., London, 1974–79; Fellow, 1983, and Vis. Prof., 1983–95, UCL. Founder FMedSci 1998. *Publications:* Drug Receptors, 1973; Pharmacology, 1987; Drug Discovery and Development, 2006. *Recreations:* sailing, music, painting. *Address:* 1 Willow Road, NW3 1TH.

RANGARAJAN, (Francis) Vijay (Narasimhan), CMG 2015; PhD; Europe Director, Foreign and Commonwealth Office, since 2013; *b* New Delhi, 22 Sept. 1969; *s* of Lakshmi Narasimhan Rangarajan and Joyce Rangarajan; *m* 2000, Rosie Frances Cox; two *s*. *Educ:* Cranbrook Sch.; Selwyn Coll., Cambridge (BA Hons 1990, Pt III Maths; PhD Astrophysics 1995). Joined FCO, 1995; Second, later First Sec., UK Perm. Repn, Brussels, 1997–99; Pte Sec. to Perm. Under-Sec., FCO, 1999–2001; Hd of Eur. Defence, FCO, 2001–03; Dep. Hd of Mission, Mexico, 2003–06; Hd of Justice and Home Affairs, UK Repn, Brussels, 2006–09; Constitution Dir, MoJ and Cabinet Office, 2009–11; Multilateral Policy Dir, FCO, 2011–13. *Publications:* papers in Monthly Notices of RAS and Astrophysical Jl. *Recreations:* singing (Chair, City Chamber Choir), cycling, technology, family. *Address:* Foreign and Commonwealth Office, King Charles Street, SW1A 2AH. *T:* (020) 7008 2311. *E:* vijay.rangarajan@fco.gov.uk.

RANK-BROADLEY, Ian, FRBS; sculptor, since 1976; *b* 4 Sept. 1952; *s* of late John Kenneth Broadley and Barbara Anne Broadley (*née* Barker); *m* 1980, Hazel G. Rank; one *s* one *d*. *Educ:* Epsom Sch. of Art; Slade Sch. of Fine Art; University Coll. London (Boise Travelling Schol., Italy). FRBS 1994. Effigy of: HM Queen Elizabeth II, for use on UK and Commonwealth coinage, 1998, and Golden Jubilee hallmark, 2002; HM Queen Elizabeth the Queen Mother, for Centenary Crown, 2000; the Queen for Golden Jubilee Crown and Medal, 2002; HRH Prince of Wales for 60th Birthday Crown, 2008; the Queen for Diamond Jubilee Crown and Kilo Coin, 2012; King George VI and Queen Elizabeth Diamond Stakes Trophy, 2005; Armed Forces Meml, Nat. Meml Arboretum, 2007; Portrait of HM Queen Elizabeth II, for Supreme Court, 2009; St Matthew, for St Matthew's Church, Northampton, 2009; Colet Meml, St Paul's Cathedral, 2010; Royal Anglian Regt Meml, Imperial War Mus., Duxford, 2010; Lord Lovat, Sword Beach, Ouistreham, Normandy, 2014. *Works in public collections:* British Mus.; Nat. Portrait Gall.; Imperial War Mus.; Royal Mus. of Scotland; Fitzwilliam Mus.; Goldsmiths' Hall; London Library; Staatliche Mus., Berlin; Rijksmus., Leiden; Nat. Collection of Finland; Royal Swedish Coin Cabinet; All England Lawn Tennis & Croquet Club. Trustee, Prince's Sch. of Traditional Arts, 2010–14. Brother, Art Workers' Guild, 1995 (Mem. Cttee, 1999–2002; Trustee, 2002–05); Freeman, City of London, 1996; Liveryman, Goldsmiths' Co., 2009 (Mem., Modern Collection Cttee, 2004–10). Prizewinner, XI Biennale Dantesca, Ravenna, Italy, 1996; first prize, Goldsmiths' Craft and Design Council Awards, 2000, 2002; Olin-Stones Prize, Soc. of Portrait Sculptors, 2002, 2010; Marsh Award for Public Sculpture, Public Monument and Sculpture Assoc., 2008; Lifetime Achievement Award, Vicenza Numismatica, 2012. *Recreations:* yoga, gardening, swimming. *Address:* Green Farm, Nastend, Stonehouse, Glos GL10 3RS. *T:* (01453) 791424. *E:* irb@ianrank-broadley.co.uk.

RANKEILLOUR, 5th Baron *cr* 1932, of Buxted, co. Sussex; **Michael Richard Hope;** *b* 21 Oct. 1940; *s* of Hon. Richard Frederick Hope, OBE, *y s* of 1st Baron and Helen Hope (*née* Lambart); *S* cousin, 2005; *m* 1964, Elizabeth Rosemary, *e d* of Col F. H. Fuller; one *s* two *d.* *Educ:* Downside Sch.; Loughborough Coll. (Engrg Dip.). Prodn engr then mgt trainee, Pye Gp, Cambridge, 1961; IBM UK: tech. sales, 1965; Original Equipment Manufr Gp, 1969; marketing mgt, 1974; new business mgt, computer sales, 1979; retired 1997. Trustee: Norwich Open Christmas; All Saints Centre; Songbird Survival; St John's Catholic Cathedral. *Recreations:* fishing, wildlife. *Heir: s* Hon. James Francis Richard Hope [*b* 5 Aug. 1968; *m* 2000, Felicity Gallimore; one *s*]. *Address:* The Old Vicarage, Thurton, Norwich NR14 6AG. *T:* (01508) 480300. *E:* mandrhope@btinternet.com.

RANKIN, Ian James, OBE 2002; DL; novelist; *b* 28 April 1960; *s* of James Hill Rankin and Isobel Rankin (*née* Vickers); *m* 1986, Anna Miranda Harvey; two *s.* *Educ:* Beath Sen. High Sch.; Univ. of Edinburgh (MA Hons). Tax Collector, then punk musician, then alcohol researcher, then swineherd, then music journalist, 1986–90. Fulbright/Chandler Fellow, USA, 1991–92. Chm., Crime Writers Assoc., 1999–2000 (Short Story Dagger, 1994, 1996); Mem., Detection Club, 1998–. Co-writer, stage play, Dark Road, Royal Lyceum, Edinburgh, 2013. Book and culture reviewer, radio and newspapers. FRSE 2015. DL City of Edinburgh, 2007. Hon. DLitt: Abertay Dundee, 1999; St Andrews, 2000; Edinburgh, 2003; Open, 2005; Hull, 2006. Cartier Diamond Dagger Award for Lifetime Achievement, 2005. *Publications:* The Flood, 1986; Watchman, 1988; Westwind, 1989; Beggars Banquet, 2002; Doors Open, 2008 (adapted for TV, 2012); The Complaints, 2009; Dark Entries (graphic novel), 2009; The Impossible Dead, 2011; *Inspector Rebus series:* Knots and Crosses, 1987; Hide and Seek, 1990; Tooth and Nail, 1992; A Good Hanging and other stories, 1992; Strip Jack, 1992; The Black Book, 1993; Mortal Causes, 1994; Let it Bleed, 1995; Black and Blue (CWA Gold Dagger award), 1997; The Hanging Garden (Grand Prix du Roman Noir), 1998; Death is not the End (novella), 1998; Dead Souls, 1999; Set in Darkness, 2000; The Falls, 2001; Resurrection Men (MWA Edgar award), 2001; Question of Blood, 2003; Fleshmarket Close, 2004 (Best Crime Novel, British Book Awards, 2005); The Naming of the Dead, 2006 (Best Crime Novel, British Book Awards, 2007); Exit Music, 2007; Standing in Another Man's Grave, 2012; Saints of the Shadow Bible, 2013; The Beat Goes On (short stories), 2014; *as Jack Harvey:* Witch Hunt, 1993; Bleeding Hearts, 1994; Blood Hunt, 1995. *Recreations:* couch potato, regular visitor to Edinburgh pubs, '70s rock music. *Address:* c/o Rogers, Coleridge & White, 20 Powis Mews, W11 1JN. *Club:* Oyster (Edinburgh).

RANKIN, Sir Ian (Niall), 4th Bt *cr* 1898, of Bryngwyn, Much Dewchurch, Co. Hereford; Chairman, I. N. Rankin Oil Ltd, since 1981; *b* 19 Dec. 1932; *s* of Lt-Col Arthur Niall Rankin (*d* 1965) (*yr s* of 2nd Bt) and Lady Jean Rankin, DCVO; *S* uncle, 1988; *m* 1st, 1959, Alexandra (marr. diss.), *d* of Adm. Sir Laurence Durlacher, KCB, OBE, DSC; one *s* one *d*; 2nd, 1980, Mrs June Norman (marr. diss. 1998), *d* of late Captain Thomas Marsham-Townshend; one *s*; 3rd, 2013, Mrs Prudence Lane Fox (*née* Sporborg). *Educ:* Eton College; Christ Church, Oxford (MA). Lieut, Scots Guards. Chm., Slumberfleece Ltd, 1979–; Director: Lindsay and Williams Ltd, 1973; Bayfine Ltd and subsidiaries, 1974–85 (Jt Chm., 1974–81); Highgate Optical and Industrial Co. Ltd and subsidiary, 1976–84 (Jt Chm., 1976–81); New Arcadia Explorations Ltd, 1987–; Bristol Scotts, 1993–2001. Patron, Samaritans, 1991–; Mem. Council, Alexandra Rose Day, 1970–. Gov., Moorfields Eye Hosp., 2005–. *Publications:* Doomsday Just Ahead, 2004. *Recreations:* shooting, ski-ing, chess. *Heir: s* Gavin Niall Rankin, *b* 19 May 1962. *Address:* 97 Elgin Avenue, W9 2DA. *T:* (office) (020) 7286 0251, (home) (020) 7286 5117. *Clubs:* White's, Beefsteak, Pratt's; Royal Yacht Squadron.

RANKIN, James Deans, FREng, FIChemE; Senior Science and Technology Associate, ICI, 1995–2000; Technology Transfer Director, Molecular Materials Centre, University of Manchester, 2002–08; *b* 17 Feb. 1943; *s* of Dr James Deans Rankin and Florence Elizabeth (*née* Wight); *m* 1973, Susan Margaret Adams; one *s* one *d.* *Educ:* Merchiston Castle Sch., Edinburgh; Gonville and Caius Coll., Cambridge (MA). FREng (FEng 1987); FIChemE 1987. Joined ICI, 1965: Agricl Div., 1965–83; Process Technology Gp Manager, New Sci. Gp, 1983–88; Melinex R&D Manager, 1988–93; Technology, 1993–2000. Royal Acad. of Engrg Vis. Prof. of Engrg Design, Univ. of Oxford, 1997–2000; Vis. Prof., Univ. of Manchester (formerly UMIST), 2000–14. *Recreations:* steam boats, motoring.

RANKIN, John James; HM Diplomatic Service; High Commissioner to Sri Lanka and (non-resident) to the Maldives, 2011–15; *b* 12 March 1957; *s* of late James Rankin, CBE, and Agnes Rankin (*née* Stobie); *m* 1987, Lesley Marshall; one *s* two *d.* *Educ:* Hutchesons' Boys' Grammar Sch.; Univ. of Glasgow (LLB 1st Cl. Hons); McGill Univ., Montreal (LLM with distinction). Solicitor and Mem., Law Soc. of Scotland. Lectr in Public Law, Univ. of Aberdeen, 1984–88; Asst, then Sen. Asst Legal Advr, FCO, 1988–90; Legal Advr, UKMIS and UKDIS, Geneva, 1991–94; Legal Counsellor, FCO, 1995; Dep. Head, OSCE Dept, 1996–98; Counsellor and Dep. Head of Mission, Dublin, 1999–2003; Consul Gen., Boston, 2003–07; Dir, Americas, FCO, 2008–10. *Publications:* articles on Scots law and international law. *Recreations:* tennis, golf, gardening, food, Scottish literature. *Address:* c/o Foreign and Commonwealth Office, King Charles Street, SW1A 2AH.

RANKIN, Maggie Mary; *see* Gee, M. M.

RANKIN, Rear-Adm. Neil Erskine, CB 1995; CBE 1988; Chairman, Scottish Environment LINK, 2000–03; *b* 24 Dec. 1940; *s* of late James Hall Rankin and of Jean Laura Rankin (*née* Honeyman); *m* 1969, Jillian Mary Cobb; one *s* one *d.* *Educ:* HMS Conway; BRNC Dartmouth. Joined RN 1958; pilot's wings, 1963; CO HMS Achilles, 1977; CO HMS Bacchante, 1978; Comdr (Air), RNAS Yeovilton, 1979, HMS Invincible, 1981; Naval Air Warfare, MoD, 1982; COS, Flag Officer Third Flotilla, 1984; CO, Captain F8, HMS Andromeda, 1985; Sen. Naval Officer, Middle East, 1985; Dep. Dir, Naval Warfare, MoD, 1987; CO HMS Ark Royal, 1990; Comdr, British Forces Falkland Is, 1992–93; FO, Portsmouth, 1993–96. Chm., Caledonian MacBrayne Ltd, 1996–99. Director: Portsmouth Naval Base Property Trust, 1997–; Former Royal Yacht Britannia Trust, 1999–. Chm., Scottish Seabird Centre, 1997–2012; Mem., Central Council, King George's Fund for Sailors, 1997. Trustee, RZSScot, 2000. Mem., RNSA, 1995–. Comr, Queen Victoria Sch., Dunblane, 1999–. Liveryman, Shipwrights' Co., 1992; Younger Brother, Trinity House, 1993–; Mem., Incorporation of Hammermen, Glasgow, 1998–. *Recreations:* Rugby (former Pres., Combined Services RFU, and RNRU, Pres., United Services Portsmouth RFC, 1994–96), sailing, golf. *Address:* c/o Lloyds, Cox's & King's Branch, Pall Mall, SW1Y 5NA. *Clubs:* Royal Navy of 1765 and 1785, Naval; Royal Naval Golfing; North Berwick Golf; Gullane Golf; Royal Yacht Squadron; Royal Naval and Royal Albert Yacht; East Lothian Yacht.

RANKIN, Robert Craig McPherson, CompICE; Chairman, BKR Financial Ltd, 1988–2004; Director, British Shipbuilders, 1985–91; *b* 15 Aug. 1937; *s* of Robert Craig Rankin and Julia Rankin (*née* Duff); *m* 1963, Alison Barbara Black Douglas; one *s* one *d.* *Educ:* The Academy, Ayr; Royal College of Science and Technology, Glasgow. CompICE 1987. Dir, Balfour Beatty Construction (Scotland) Ltd, 1973–74; Dir 1974–83, Exec. Dir 1983–85, Balfour Beatty Construction Ltd; Balfour Beatty Ltd: Dir, 1983–88; Dep. Man. Dir, 1985–86; Man. Dir, 1986–87; Chief Exec., 1986–88; Dir, BICC PLC, 1987–88; Non-executive Director: London & Edinburgh Trust PLC, 1988–91; LDDC, 1989–93. CCMI (CBIM 1987). *Recreations:* opera, music.

RANKIN, Prof. Susan Kathleen, PhD; FBA 2009; FSA; Professor of Medieval Music, University of Cambridge, since 2006; Fellow of Emmanuel College, Cambridge, since 1984; *b* Belfast; *d* of (James) Frederick Rankin and Dr Kathleen Rankin; *m* 1999, Prof. David Michael Ganz. *Educ:* Victoria Coll., Belfast; Newnham Coll., Cambridge (BA 1975; PhD 1982); King's Coll., London (MMus 1976). Res. Fellow, Emmanuel Coll., Cambridge, 1981–84; Asst Lectr, 1990–93, Lectr, 1993–99, Reader in Medieval Music, 1999–2006, Univ. of Cambridge. Vis. Helen Waddell Prof., QUB, 2000–05. Member: Council, Plainsong and Mediæval Music Soc., 1984–; Council, Henry Bradshaw Soc., 1993– (Chm., 2013–); Cttee, Early English Church Music, 2005–. Gov., Forest Sch., London, 2000–12. FSA 2006; MAE 2007. Dent Medal, Royal Musical Assoc., 1995. *Publications:* The Music of the Medieval Liturgical Drama in France and England, 2 vols, 1989; (ed with D. Hiley) Music in the Medieval English Liturgy: Plainsong and Mediæval Music Society centennial essays, 1993; (ed with W. Arlt) Stiftsbibliothek St Gallen Codices 484 & 381, 3 vols, 1996; The Winchester Troper, Introduction and Facsimile, 2007; numerous book chapters and articles in jls incl. Early Music, Early Music History, Jl of Amer. Musicological Soc., Anglo-Saxon England and Revue bénédictine. *Recreations:* music, European art, Irish sea. *Address:* Emmanuel College, Cambridge CB2 3AP. *T:* (01223) 334206. *E:* skr1000@cam.ac.uk.

RANKINE, Fiona Grace; *see* McLeod, F. G.

RANKINE, Jean Morag, (Mrs N. A. Hall); Deputy Director of the British Museum, 1983–97; *b* 5 Sept. 1941; *d* of late Alan Rankine and Margaret Mary Sloan Rankine (*née* Reid); *m* 1992, Norman Anthony Hall. *Educ:* Central Newcastle High Sch.; University College London (BA, MPhil; Fellow, 1990); Univ. of Copenhagen. Grad. Assistant, Durham Univ. Library, 1966–67; British Museum: Res. Assistant, Dept of Printed Books, 1967–73; Asst Keeper, Director's Office, 1973–78; Head of Public Services, 1978–83. *Recreations:* sculling, ski-ing, fell-walking, opera, motorcycling. *Address:* 49 Hartington Road, W4 3TS. *Clubs:* Thames Rowing; Clydesdale Amateur Rowing (Glasgow).

RANN, Hon. Michael David, CNZM 2009; Ambassador of Australia to Italy, Libya, Albania and San Marino, since 2014; *b* Sidcup, Kent, 5 Jan. 1953; *s* of Frederick George and Winifred Hetty Rann; *m* 1st, 1982, Jennifer Russell (marr. diss.); one *s* one *d*; 2nd, 2006, Sasha Carruozzo. *Educ:* Northcote Coll., NZ; Auckland Univ. (MA). Political Journalist, Radio NZ, 1976–77; Press Secretary: to Premier of SA, 1977–79, 1982–85; to Leader of the Opposition, 1979–82. MHA (ALP) Briggs, 1985–93, Ramsay, 1993–2012, SA. South Australia Government: Minister: for Employment and Further Educn, of Youth Affairs, of Aboriginal Affairs, and Assisting Minister of Ethnic Affairs, 1989–92; for Business and Regl Develt, of Tourism and of State Services, 1992–93; Dep. Leader of the Opposition, and Shadow Minister for Regl Develt, Employment, Training and Further Educn, 1993–94; Leader of the Opposition, 1994–2002; Shadow Minister: for Industry, Manufacturing and Small Business, 1994–95; for Economic Develt, 1994–2002; for Jobs, 1998 and 2000–02; for Industry, 1999–2000; Premier of SA, 2002–11; Minister: for Volunteers, 2002–06; for the Arts and for Econ. Develt, 2002–11; for Social Inclusion, 2004–11; for Sustainability and Climate Change, 2006–11. Mem., Parly Public Works Standing Cttee, 1986–89. Nat. Pres., 2008, Nat. Vice Pres., 2009, ALP. High Comr for Australia in the UK, 2012–14. Member: Australian Aboriginal Affairs Council, 1989–92; Australian Educn Council, 1990–92; SA Manuf. Council (Dep. Chm., 1992–93); Dep. Chm., Automotive Industry Task Force; Chair, Internat. States and Regions Network, 2008–11, Mem., Internat. Leadership Council, 2012–, Climate Gp. Chm., Low Carbon Australia Ltd, 2012. Mem. Bd, Techsearch, 1986–89; Member Council: SA Inst. of Technol., 1986–89; Univ. of SA, 1994–97. Mem., Commonwealth War Graves Commn, 2012–; Trustee, Imperial War Mus., 2012–. Professorial Fellow, Flinders Univ., 2012–; Adjunct Prof., Carnegie Mellon Univ., 2012–; Vis. Sen. Res. Fellow, Univ. of Auckland, 2012–. Sen. Fellow, Center for National Policy, Washington, DC, 2012–. Philip of Macedonia Award, Fed. Pan Macedonian Assoc., Australia, 1996; Nikki (Victory) Award, Aust. Hellenic Council, 1997. *Recreations:* reading, films, travel, soccer, arts, writing. *Address:* Australian Embassy, Via Antonio Bosio 5, Rome 00161, Italy. *Clubs:* Northern (NZ); South Adelaide Football, Port Adelaide Football.

RANNARD, Prof. Steven Paul, DPhil; FRSC; Professor of Chemistry, University of Liverpool, since 2007; *b* Orpington; *s* of Alfred James Rannard and Patricia Mary Bruce Rannard (*née* Ta'Bois); *m* 1992, Amanda Jane Bates; one *s* one *d.* *Educ:* Holyhead Secondary Sch.; Univ. of Sussex (BSc Hons 1988; DPhil 1992). FRSC 2007. Res. Associate, Cookson Technol. Centre, 1992–93; Principal Scientist: Courtaulds Strategic and Corporate Res., 1993–96; Courtaulds Coatings and Sealants, 1996–98; Unilever Research and Development - Port Sunlight Laboratory: Molecular Sci. Unit Leader, 1998–2001; Functional Ingredients Sci. Area Leader, 2001–05; Molecular and Nano Technols Discovery Platform Dir, 2005–07. Vis. Prof., Univ. of Liverpool, 2003–07; Vis. Lectr, Univ. of Sussex, 1999–2001; RSC Industrial Lecturer: Strathclyde Univ., 2001; Univ. of Sussex, 2002; Royal Soc. Industry Fellow, 2005–09. Co-Founder and CSO, IOTA NanoSolutions Ltd, 2005–13 (IOTA NanoSolutions Industrial Sen. Res. Fellow, 2007–10); Co-Founder and non-exec. Dir, Hydra Polymers Ltd, 2007–12; Co-Founder, Tandem Nano Ltd, 2014–. Mem., Welsh Govt Sêr Cymru (Rising Stars) Delivery Bd, 2012–. Member: Applied Polymer Sci. Cttee, Inst. of Materials, 1997–2000; UK Cttee, RSC/SCI Macro Gp, 1998–2002; Co-Founder and Mem. Cttee, Recent Appointees in Polymer Sci. Gp, 1999–2004. Mem., Mgt Team, Manchester Organic Materials Innovation Centre, 2002–06. Vice-Chair and Co-Founder, British Soc. for Nanomedicine, 2012–. Trustee, High Polymer Res. Gp, 2001–06. Co-Founder and Co-Ed. in Chief, Jl Interdisciplinary Nanomedicine, 2015–. *Publications:* contrib. chapters to scientific text books; contribs to peer-reviewed scientific jls; co-inventor for 59 patent families. *Recreations:* theatre, cinema, reading, music, walking, photography, travel. *Address:* Department of Chemistry, University of Liverpool, Crown Street, Liverpool L69 7ZD. *T:* (0151) 794 3501. *E:* srannard@liv.ac.uk.

RANSFORD, John Anthony, CBE 1997; Chief Executive, Local Government Association, 2009–11 (Deputy Chief Executive, 2005–08); *b* 19 Sept. 1948; *s* of Sydney George Ransford and Ethel Alice Ransford (*née* Peters); *m* 1971, Liz Hainsworth; one *s* one *d.* *Educ:* Letchworth Grammar Sch.; Univ. of Sussex (BA Hons Sociol.; MSocWork). CQSW 1972. Probation Officer, SE London Probation and After-Care Service, 1972–74; Kirklees Metropolitan Council: Trng Officer, Social Services Dept, 1974–77; Health Liaison Officer, 1977–79; Asst Dir, Social Services, 1979–82, Dir, 1982–87; Actg Chief Exec., 1987; Dir, Social Services, 1988–94, Chief Exec., 1994–99, N Yorks CC; Hd, Social Affairs, Health and Housing, subseq. Dir, Educn and Social Policy, LGA, 1999–2005. Chm., Spurriergate Trading Co., York, 2013–; non-exec. Dir, HC-One Ltd, 2014–. Trustee, Dunhill Medical Trust, 2013–. Hon. Sec., Assoc. of Dirs of Social Services, 1993–96. *Recreations:* theatre, foreign travel, current affairs. *E:* jaransford@gmail.com.

RANTZEN, Dame Esther (Louise), (Dame Esther Wilcox), DBE 2015 (CBE 2006; OBE 1991); television producer/presenter, since 1968; *b* 22 June 1940; *d* of late Harry Rantzen and Katherine Rantzen; *m* 1977, Desmond John Wilcox (*d* 2000); one *s* two *d.* *Educ:* North London Collegiate Sch.; Somerville Coll., Oxford (MA; Hon. Fellow 2011). Studio manager making dramatic sound effects, BBC Radio, 1963; BBC TV: Researcher, 1965; Dir, 1967; Reporter, Braden's Week, 1968–72; Producer/Presenter, That's Life, 1973–94, scriptwriter, 1976–94; Producer, documentary series, The Big Time, 1976; Presenter: Esther Interviews …, 1988; Hearts of Gold, 1988; Esther, 1994–2002; That's Esther, 1999–; Producer/Presenter, Drugwatch, Childwatch, The Lost Babies, How to Have a Good Death and other progs on social issues; reporter/producer, various documentaries, religious and current affairs TV progs. Member: Nat. Consumer Council, 1981–90; Health Educn Authority, 1989–95; Task Force to review services for drug misusers, DoH, 1994. President: ChildLine, 2006– (Chair, 1986–2006); Assoc. of Young People with ME, 1996–; Founder, 2012, Pres., 2014–, Silver Line (Chm., 2012–14); a Vice-President: Nat. Deaf Children's Soc.;

Rennie Grove Hospice Care (formerly Iain Rennie Hospice at Home); Action on Hearing Loss; Vice-Patron, Rose Road Appeal (people with disabilities in S Hants); Patron: DEMAND (furniture for the disabled); SIMR (Seriously Ill for Medical Research); Livability (formerly John Grooms Assoc.); Hillingdon Manor Sch. for Autistic Children, 1999–; The New Sch. at West Heath (The Princess Diana Sch.), 2000–; Campaign for Courtesy; North London Hospice; Nat. Assoc. for People Abused in Childhood; Families in Care; Bristol Grandparents' Support Gp; Siblings Together; Red Balloon; Erosh; Compassion in Dying; Ambassador, BHF. Champion, Community Legal Service, 2000. Chair, 4Children Commn into the Family, 2009–. Trustee, NSPCC, 2006– (Hon. Mem., 1989). Contested (Ind Rantzen) Luton South, 2010. FRTS 1995. Hon. DLitt: Southampton Inst. for FE, 1994; South Bank, 2000; Portsmouth, 2003; Wolverhampton, 2009; Staffordshire, 2009; Hon. Fellow, Liverpool John Moore's Univ., 2008. Personality of 1974, RTS award; BBC TV Personality of 1975, Variety Club of GB; European Soc. for Organ Transplant Award, 1985; Special Judges' Award for Journalism, RTS, 1986; Richard Dimbleby Award, BAFTA, 1988; Snowdon Award for Services to Disabled People, 1996; RTS Hall of Fame Award, 1998; Lifetime Achievement Award, Women in Film and TV, 2005. SSStJ 1992. *Publications:* (with Desmond Wilcox): Kill the Chocolate Biscuit, 1981; Baby Love, 1985; (with Shaun Woodward) Ben: the story of Ben Hardwick, 1985; Esther (autobiog.), 2001; A Secret Life (novel), 2003; If Not Now, When?: living the baby boomer adventure, 2008; Running Out of Tears, 2011. *Recreations:* family life, the countryside, appearing in pantomime. *Address:* c/o Billy Marsh Associates, 4a Exmoor Street, W10 6BD.

RAO, Prof. Calyampudi Radhakrishna, Padma Vibhushan, 2001; FRS 1967; Eberly Professor of Statistics, Pennsylvania State University, 1988–2001, now Emeritus; Adjunct Professor, University of Pittsburgh, since 1988 (University Professor, 1979–88); Research Professor, University at Buffalo, since 2010; *b* 10 Sept. 1920; *s* of C. D. Naidu and A. Laksmikantamma; *m* 1948, C. Bhargavi Rao; one *s* one *d.* *Educ:* Andhra Univ. (MA, 1st Class Maths); Calcutta Univ. (MA, 1st Class Statistics; Gold Medal); PhD, ScD, Cambridge (Hon. Fellow, King's Coll., Cambridge, 1975). Indian Statistical Institute: Superintending Statistician, 1943–49; Professor and Head of Division of Theoretical Research and Training, 1949–64; Dir, Res. and Training Sch., 1964–76 (Sec., 1972–76); Jawaharlal Nehru Professor, 1976–84. Nat. Prof., India, 1987–92. Co-editor, Sankhya, Indian Jl of Statistics, 1964–72, Editor, 1972–96. Member, Internat. Statistical Inst., 1951 (Mem. Statistical Educn Cttee, 1958–; Treasurer, 1962–65; Pres.-elect, 1975–77, Pres., 1977–79, Hon. Mem. 1982); Chm., Indian Nat. Cttee for Statistics, 1962–70; President: Biometric Soc., 1973–75 (Hon. Life Mem., 1986); Indian Econometric Soc., 1971–76; Forum for Interdisciplinary Mathematics, 1982–84. Fellow: Indian Nat. Sci. Acad., 1953 (Vice-Pres., 1973, 1974); Inst. of Math. Statistics, USA, 1958 (Pres., 1976–77); Amer. Statistical Assoc., 1972; Econometric Soc., 1972; Indian Acad. of Scis, 1974; Founder Fellow: Third World Sci. Acad., 1983; Nat. Acad. of Scis, India, 1988; Nat. Acad. of Scis, USA, 1995; Foreign Mem., Lithuanian Acad. of Scis, 1997. Hon. Fellow: Royal Stat. Soc., 1969; Amer. Acad. of Arts and Scis, 1975; Calcutta Stat. Assoc., 1985; Biometric Soc., 1986; Finnish Statistical Soc., 1990; Inst. of Combinatorics and its Applications, 1995; Portuguese Statistical Soc., 2002; Eur. Acad. of Scis. Shanti Swarup Bhatnagar Memorial Award, 1963; Guy Medal in Silver, 1965, Guy Medal in Gold, 2011, Royal Stat. Soc.; Padma Bhushan, 1968; Meghnad Saha Medal, 1969; J. C. Bose Gold Medal, 1979; S. S. Wilke's Meml Medal, 1989; Mahalanobis Birth Centenary Gold Medal, 1996; Dist. Achievement Medal, Sect. on Stats and Envmt, Amer. Stat. Assoc., 1997; Carol and Emanuel Parzen Prize for statistical innovation, Texas A&M Univ., 2000; US Nat. Medal of Sci., 2001; Army Wilkes Medal, 2002; Srinivasa Ramanujan Medal, 2003; Mahalanobis Award, ISI, 2003. Hon. DSc: Andhra; Leningrad; Athens; Osmania; Ohio State; Philippines; Tampere; Neuchatel; Poznan; Indian Statistical Inst.; Colorado State; Hyderabad; Barcelona; Slovak Acad. of Scis; Guelph; Munich; Venkateswara; Waterloo; Brasilia; Athens; Kent; Cyprus; Wollongong; Oakland; Calcutta; Pretoria; Nova de Lisboa; Madras; Visva-Bharati; Univ. of San Marcos; Lima; Univ. of Rhode Island; Jawaharlal Tech. Univ.; Univ. of Colombo; Karnataka; Univ. at Buffalo; Rashtria Vidyapeth; Tirupati; Indian Inst. of Technol., Kharagpur; Hon. DLit Delhi. Hon. Prof., Univ. of San Marcos, Lima. *Publications:* (with Mahalanobis and Majumdar) Anthropometric Survey of the United Provinces, 1941, a statistical study, 1949; Advanced Statistical Methods in Biometric Research, 1952; (with Mukherjee and Trevor) The Ancient Inhabitants of Jebal Moya, 1955; (with Majumdar) Bengal Anthropometric Survey, 1945, a statistical study, 1959; Linear Statistical Inference and its Applications, 1965; (with A. Matthai and S. K. Mitra) Formulae and Tables for Statistical Work, 1966; Computers and the Future of Human Society, 1968; (with S. K. Mitra) The Generalised Inverse of Matrices and its Applications, 1971; (with A. M. Kagan and Yu. V. Linnik) Characterization Problems of Mathematical Statistics, 1973; (with J. Kleffe) Estimation of Variance Components and its Applications, 1988; Statistics and Truth, 1989; (with H. Toutenburg) Linear Models, 1995; (with D. N. Shanbhag) Choquet-Deny Type Functional Equations with Applications to Stochastic Models, 1994; (with M. B. Rao) Matrix Algebra and its Applications to Statistics and Econometrics, 1998. *Address:* CR Rao Advanced Institute of Mathematics, Statistics and Computer Science, University of Hyderabad Campus, Prof. C. R. Rao Road, Hyderabad 500046, India.

RAO, Prof. Chintamani Nagesa Ramachandra, Padma Shri, 1974; Padma Vibhushan, 1985; Bharat Ratna, 2014; FRS 1982; CChem, FRSC; Hon. President and Linus Pauling Research Professor, since 2000, and National Research Professor, since 2006, Jawaharlal Nehru Centre for Advanced Scientific Research, Bangalore, India (President, 1989–99); *b* 30 June 1934; *s* of H. Nagesa Rao; *m* 1960, Indumati; one *s* one *d.* *Educ:* Univ. of Mysore (DSc); Univ. of Purdue, USA (PhD). Research Chemist, Univ. of California, Berkeley, 1958–59; Lectr, Indian Inst. of Science, 1959–63; Prof., Indian Inst. of Technology, Kanpur, 1963–76, Head of Chemistry Dept, 1964–68, Dean of Research, 1969–72; Jawaharlal Nehru Fellow, 1973–75; Indian Institute of Science, Bangalore: Chm., Solid State and Structural Chemistry Unit and Materials Res. Laboratory, 1977–84; Dir, 1984–94. Commonwealth Vis. Prof., Univ. of Oxford, and Fellow, St Catherine's Coll., 1974–75; Jawaharlal Nehru Vis. Prof., Univ. of Cambridge, and Professorial Fellow, King's Coll., Cambridge, 1983–84; Linnett Vis. Prof., Univ. of Cambridge, 1998; Gauss Prof., Acad. of Scis, Göttingen, 2003; Albert Einstein Prof., Chinese Acad. of Scis, 2012. Blackett Lectr, Royal Soc., 1991. US Nat. Acad. of Sci. Lect., 1993. President: INSA, 1985–86; IUPAC, 1985–87; Indian Sci. Congress, 1987–88; Indian Acad. of Scis, 1989–91; Materials Res. Soc. of India, 1989–91. Member: First Nat. Cttee of Science and Technology, Govt of India, 1971–74; Science Adv. Cttee to Union Cabinet of India, 1981–86 (Chm., 1997–98); Atomic Energy Commn of India, 1986–2014; Chm., Science Adv. Council to Prime Minister, 1985–89, 2004–14. Member: Gen. Council, ICSU; Internat. Sci. Adv. Bd, UNESCO, 1996–99. Foreign Member: Slovenian Acad. of Scis, 1983; Serbian Acad. of Scis, 1986; Amer. Acad. of Arts and Scis, 1986; USSR Acad. of Scis, 1988; Czechoslovak Acad. of Scis, 1988; Polish Acad. of Scis, 1988; US Nat. Acad. of Scis, 1990; Pontifical Acad. of Scis, 1990; Academia Europaea, 1997; Brazilian Acad. of Scis, 1997; European Acad. of Arts, Scis and Humanities, 1997; Japan Acad., 1998; Royal Spanish Acad. of Scis, 1999; French Acad. of Scis, 2000; Centennial Foreign Fellowship, Amer. Chemical Soc., 1976; Founder Mem., Third World Acad. of Scis, 1983– (Pres., 2000–); Internat. Mem. (formerly Foreign Mem.), Amer. Philosophical Soc., 1995. Hon. Fellow: UWCC, 1997; St Catherine's Coll., Oxford, 2007; Hon. FRSC 1989; Hon. FInstP 2006. Hon. DSc: Purdue, 1982; Bordeaux, 1983; Sri Venkateswara, 1984; Roorkee, 1985; Banaras, Osmania, Mangalore and Manipur, 1987; Anna, Mysore, Burdwan, 1988; Wroclaw, 1989; Andhra, Karnatak, 1990; Bangalore, Hyderabad, Indian Inst. of Technology, Kharagpur, 1991; Oxford, 2007. Many awards and medals, incl.: Marlow Medal of Faraday Soc. (London), 1967; Bhatnagar Prize, 1968; Royal Soc. of Chemistry (London) Medal, 1981; Centennial For. Fellowship of Amer. Chemical Soc., 1976; Hevrovsky Gold Medal, Czech. Acad. of Scis, 1989; Golden Jubilee Prize, CSIR, 1991; P. C. Ray Meml Award, 1994; Sahabdeen Award for Sci., Sri Lanka, 1994; Medal for Chemistry, Third World Acad. of Scis, 1995; Albert Einstein Gold Medal, UNESCO, 1996; Shatabdi Puraskar prize, Indian Sci. Congress Assoc., 1999; Centenary Medal, RSC, 2000; Hughes Medal, Royal Soc., 2000; Millennium Plaque of Honour, Indian Sci. Cong., 2001; Somiya Award, Internat. Union of Materials Res., 2004; India Sci. Prize, 2005; (jtly) Dan David Internat. Prize for Materials Sci., 2005; Chemical Pioneer, Amer. Inst. of Chemists, 2005; Nikkei Asia Prize for Sci. and Technol. and Innovation, 2008; Royal Medal, Royal Soc., 2009; August-Wilhelm-von-Hoffmann Medal, German Chem. Soc., 2010; Ernesto Illy Trieste Sci. Prize, 2011. Comdr, Order of Rio Branco (Brazil), 2002; Chevalier, Légion d'Honneur (France), 2005; Order of Rising Sun, Gold and Silver Star (Japan), 2015. *Publications:* 48 books including: Ultraviolet and Visible Spectroscopy, 1960, 3rd edn 1975; Chemical Applications of Infrared Spectroscopy, 1963; Spectroscopy in Inorganic Chemistry, 1970; Modern Aspects of Solid State Chemistry, 1970; University General Chemistry, 1973; Solid State Chemistry, 1974; Phase Transitions in Solids, 1978; Preparation and Characterization of Materials, 1981; The Metallic and the Non-metallic States of Matter, 1985; New Directions in Solid State Chemistry, 1986; Chemistry of Oxide Superconductors, 1988; Chemical and Structural Aspects of High Temperature Oxide Superconductors, 1988; Bismuth and Thallium Superconductors, 1989; Advances in Catalyst Design, 1991; Chemistry of High Temperature Superconductors, 1991; Chemistry of Advanced Materials, 1992; Chemical Approaches to the Synthesis of Inorganic Materials, 1994; Transition Metal Oxides, 1995; Metal-Insulator Transition Revisited, 1995; Understanding Chemistry, 1999; Superconductivity Today, 1999; 1600 research papers. *Recreations:* gourmet cooking, gardening. *Address:* Jawaharlal Nehru Centre for Advanced Scientific Research, Jakkur Post, Bangalore 560064, India. *T:* (office) (80) 23653075, *T:* (home) (80) 23601410.

RAPER, Maj.-Gen. Anthony John, CB 2006; CBE 1996 (MBE 1987); Quartermaster General, Ministry of Defence, 2002–06; *b* 14 April 1950. *Educ:* RMA Sandhurst; Selwyn Coll., Cambridge (BA 1974, MA 1976). Commnd Royal Signals, 1970; posts in UK, Germany, Cyprus, Bosnia and NATO; Commander: 4th Armoured Div. and Signal Regt, 1988–91; 1st Signal Bde, Allied Comd Europe, 1994–95; Defence Intelligence Staff; Directorate of Land Warfare; directing staff, RMA Sandhurst and Staff Coll.; Dir, Operational Requirements for Inf. and Communication Services; Chief Exec., Defence Communications Services Agency, 1998–2002; Dir Gen. Strategy and Logistics Develt, 2002–04; Defence Logistics Transformation Prog. Team Leader, 2004–06. Sen. Defence and Security Advr, PwC, 2011–.

RAPHAEL, Adam Eliot Geoffrey; Editor, The Good Hotel Guide, since 2004; Associate Editor, Transport Times, since 2005; *b* 22 April 1938; *s* of Geoffrey George Raphael and Nancy Raphael (*née* Rose); *m* 1970, Caroline Rayner Ellis; one *s* one *d.* *Educ:* Arnold House; Charterhouse; Oriel Coll., Oxford (BA Hons History). 2nd Lieut Royal Artillery, 1956–58. Copy Boy, Washington Post, USA, 1961; Swindon Evening Advertiser, 1962–63; Film Critic, Bath Evening Chronicle, 1963–64; The Guardian: Reporter, 1965; Motoring Correspondent, 1967–68; Foreign Correspondent, Washington and S Africa, 1969–73; Consumer Affairs Columnist, 1974–76; Political Correspondent, The Observer, 1976–81, Political Editor, 1981–86; Presenter, Newsnight, BBC TV, 1987–88; an Asst Editor, 1988, Exec. Editor, 1988–93, The Observer; writer on Home Affairs, 1994, political correspondent, 1994–2004, The Economist. Awards include: Granada Investigative Journalist of the Year, 1973; British Press Awards, Journalist of the Year, 1973. *Publications:* My Learned Friends, 1989; Ultimate Risk: the inside story of the Lloyd's catastrophe, 1994. *Recreations:* tennis, golf, ski-ing. *Address:* 50 Addison Avenue, W11 4QP. *T:* (020) 7603 9133. *Clubs:* Garrick, Hurlingham, Royal Automobile.

RAPHAEL, Caroline Sarah; Director, Dora Productions, since 2015; *b* 15 Jan. 1958; *d* of Arnold Raphael and Lily Suzanne (*née* Shaffer); *m* 1st, 1982, Michael Eaves (marr. diss. 2001); one *s*; 2nd, 2011, Paul Keers. *Educ:* Putney High Sch.; Manchester Univ. (BA Hons Drama). Theatre director: Nuffield Theatre, 1980–81; Bristol Old Vic, 1981–83; Gate Theatre, London, 1983; Literary Agent and Publisher, Chappel's Music, 1983; joined BBC Radio, 1984: Script Reader, Producer, Editor Drama, 1984–90; Editor Drama, Features, Youth Programmes, Radio 5, 1990–94; Hd of Drama, BBC Radio, 1994–97; Commng Editor, Comedy, Drama, Fiction, Arts Features, BBC Radio 4, 1997–2015; Editl Strategy for BBC Radio 4 Extra, 2012–15. Mem. Bd, Paines Plough Theatre Co., 1996–2000; Council Mem., NYT, 2005–07. FRSA. *Recreations:* listening to radio, reading, food, comedy, cinema. *E:* mail@doraproductions.co.uk.

RAPHAEL, Prof. David Daiches, DPhil, MA; Emeritus Professor of Philosophy, University of London, since 1983; *b* 25 Jan. 1916; 2nd *s* of late Jacob Raphael and Sarah Warshawsky, Liverpool; *m* 1942, Sylvia (*d* 1996), *er d* of late Rabbi Dr Salis Daiches and Flora Levin, Edinburgh; two *d.* *Educ:* Liverpool Collegiate School; University College, Oxford (scholar). 1st Class, Classical Moderations, 1936; Hall-Houghton Junior Septuagint Prizeman, 1937; 1st Class, Literae Humaniores, 1938; Robinson Senior Scholar of Oriel College, Oxford, 1938–40; Passmore Edwards Scholar, 1939. Served in Army, 1940–41. Temporary Assistant Principal, Ministry of Labour and National Service, 1941–44; temp. Principal, 1944–46. Professor of Philosophy, University of Otago, Dunedin, NZ, 1946–49; Lecturer in Moral Philosophy, Univ. of Glasgow, 1949–51; Senior Lecturer, 1951–60; Edward Caird Prof. of Political and Social Philosophy, Univ. of Glasgow, 1960–70; Prof. of Philosophy, Univ. of Reading, 1970–73; Prof. of Philosophy, Imperial Coll., Univ. of London, 1973–83 (Acad. Dir of Associated Studies, 1973–80; Head of Dept of Humanities, 1980–83; Hon. Fellow 1987). Visiting Professor of Philosophy, Hamilton Coll., Clinton, NY (under Chauncey S. Truax Foundation), and Univ. of Southern California, 1959; Mahlon Powell Lectr, Indiana Univ., 1959; Vis. Fellow, All Souls Coll., Oxford, 1967–68; John Hinkley Vis. Prof. of Political Sci., Johns Hopkins Univ., 1984. Independent Member: Cttee on Teaching Profession in Scotland (Wheatley Cttee), 1961–63; Scottish Agricultural Wages Board, 1962–84; Agricultural Wages Bd for England and Wales, 1972–78. Mem. Academic Adv. Cttee, Heriot-Watt Univ., Edinburgh, 1964–71; Mem. Cttee on Distribution of Teachers in Scotland (Roberts Cttee), 1965–66; Independent Member Police Advisory Board for Scotland, 1965–70; Member Social Sciences Adv. Cttee, UK Nat. Commission, UNESCO, 1966–74; Vice-Pres., Internat. Assoc. Philosophy of Law and Social Philosophy, 1971–87; Pres., Aristotelian Soc., 1974–75. Academic Mem., Bd of Govs, Hebrew Univ. of Jerusalem, 1969–81, Hon. Gov., 1981–. Chm., Westminster Synagogue, 1987–89. *Publications:* The Moral Sense, 1947; Edition of Richard Price's Review of Morals, 1948; Moral Judgement, 1955; The Paradox of Tragedy, 1960; Political Theory and the Rights of Man, 1967; British Moralists 1650–1800, 1969; Problems of Political Philosophy, 1970, 2nd edn 1990; (ed jtly) Adam Smith's Theory of Moral Sentiments, 1976; Hobbes: Morals and Politics, 1977; (ed jtly) Adam Smith's Lectures on Jurisprudence, 1978; (ed jtly) Adam Smith's Essays on Philosophical Subjects, 1980; Justice and Liberty, 1980; Moral Philosophy, 1981, 2nd edn 1994; (trans. jtly with Sylvia Raphael) Richard Price as Moral Philosopher and Political Theorist, by Henri Laboucheix, 1982; Adam Smith, 1985; Concepts of Justice, 2001; The Impartial Spectator, 2007; articles in jls of philosophy and of political studies. *Address:* 54 Sandy Lane, Petersham, Richmond, Surrey TW10 7EL.

RAPHAEL, Frederic Michael; author; *b* 14 Aug. 1931; *s* of late Cedric Michael Raphael and of Irene Rose (*née* Mauser); *m* 1955, Sylvia Betty Glatt; two *s* (one *d* decd). *Educ:* Charterhouse; St John's Coll., Cambridge (Maj. Schol. in Classics; MA (Hons)). FRSL 1964.

Jackson Knight Meml Lectr, Exeter Univ., 2011. *Publications: novels:* Obbligato, 1956; The Earlsdon Way, 1958; The Limits of Love, 1960; A Wild Surmise, 1961; The Graduate Wife, 1962; The Trouble with England, 1962; Lindmann, 1963; Darling, 1965; Orchestra and Beginners, 1967; Like Men Betrayed, 1970; Who Were You With Last Night?, 1971; April, June and November, 1972; Richard's Things, 1973; California Time, 1975; The Glittering Prizes, 1976; Heaven and Earth, 1985; After the War, 1988 (adapted for television, 1989); The Hidden I, 1990; A Double Life, 1993; Old Scores, 1995; Coast to Coast, 1998; Fame and Fortune, 2007; Final Demands, 2010; Private Views, 2015; *short stories:* Sleeps Six, 1979; Oxbridge Blues, 1980 (also pubd as scripts of TV plays, 1984); Think of England, 1986; The Latin Lover, 1994; All His Sons, 1999; *biography:* Somerset Maugham and his World, 1977; Byron, 1982; *memoir:* Eyes Wide Open: a memoir of Stanley Kubrick and Eyes Wide Shut, 1999; A Spoilt Boy (autobiog.), 2003; Going Up (autobiog.), 2015; Personal Terms series: Personal Terms (notebooks 1951–1969), 2001; Rough Copy (notebooks 1970–1973), 2004; Cuts and Bruises (notebooks 1974–1978), 2006; Ticks and Crosses (notebooks 1978–1981), 2008; Ifs and Buts (notebooks 1978–79), 2011; There and Then (notebooks 1980–83), 2013; Shreds and Patches (notebooks 1983–88), 2016; *essays*: Bookmarks (ed), 1975; Cracks in the Ice, 1979; Of Gods and Men, 1992; France, the Four Seasons, 1994; The Necessity of Anti-Semitism, 1997; Karl Popper, 1998; (ed jtly and contrib.) The Great Philosophers from Socrates to Turing, 2000; The Benefits of Doubts, 2003; Some Talk of Alexander, 2006; A Jew Among the Romans: Flavius Josephus and his legacy, 2013; J. Robert Oppenheimer, For Example, 2013; For Gold, for Praise, for Glory: ambition in the ancient world, 2016; *screenplays:* Nothing but the Best, 1964; Darling, 1965 (Academy Award); Two For The Road, 1967; Far From the Madding Crowd, 1967; A Severed Head, 1972; Daisy Miller, 1974; The Glittering Prizes, 1976 (sequence of TV plays) (Writer of the Year 1976, Royal TV Soc.); Rogue Male, 1976; (and directed) Something's Wrong (TV), 1978; School Play (TV), 1979; The Best of Friends (TV), 1979; Richard's Things, 1981; After the War (TV series), 1989; (and directed) The Man In The Brooks Brothers Shirt, 1991 (ACE Award); Eyes Wide Shut, 1999; For God's Sake (TV documentary series), 1998; Coast to Coast, 2004; *plays:* From The Greek, Arts, Cambridge, 1979; The Daedalus Dimension (radio), 1982; The Thought of Lydia (radio), 1988; The Empty Jew (radio), 1993; A Thousand Kisses (radio), 2011; Jake Liebowitz (radio), 2013; *translations:* Petronius: Satyrica, 2003; (with Kenneth McLeish): Poems of Catullus, 1976; The Oresteia, 1978 (televised as The Serpent Son, BBC, 1979); The Complete Plays of Aeschylus, 1991; Medea, 1994; Hippolytus, 1997; Aias, 1998; Bacchae, 1999; *correspondence:* (with Joseph Epstein) Distant Intimacy, 2013; (with Joseph Epstein) Where Were We?: a deepening friendship, 2015. *Recreations:* tennis, bridge, having gardened. *Address:* c/o Ed Victor Ltd, 6 Bayley Street, WC1B 3HE.

RAPHAEL, Philip Montague, (Monty); Special Counsel, Peters & Peters Solicitors LLP, since 2005; *b* 8 Feb. 1937; *s* of Solomon and Sarah Raphael; *m* 1963, Leona Hartley; one *s* three *d* (and one *s* decd). *Educ:* Davenant Sch.; University Coll. London (LLB Hons). Admitted solicitor, 1962; Partner, Peters & Peters, 1965–2005. Vis. Prof., Kingston Univ., 2004–. Mem. Bd, Fraud Adv. Panel; Dir, Transparency Internat. (UK), 2006–. Trustee and Hon. Solicitor, Howard League for Penal Reform. Hon. QC 2011. *Publications:* The Proceeds of Crime Act: how it will work in practice, 2003; Blackstone's Guide to the Bribery Act, 2010. *Recreations:* obsessing about London, arts, travel, thinking very vigorously about exercise. *Address:* Peters & Peters Solicitors LLP, 15 Fetter Lane, EC4A 1BW. *T:* (020) 7822 7777, *Fax:* (020) 7822 7788. *E:* montyr@petersandpeters.com.

RAPHAEL, Ven. Timothy John; Archdeacon of Middlesex, 1983–96; *b* 26 Sept. 1929; *s* of Hector and Alix Raphael; *m* 1957, Anne Elizabeth Shepherd; one *s* two *d*. *Educ:* Christ's College, Christchurch, NZ; Leeds Univ. (BA). Asst Curate, St Stephen, Westminster, 1955–60; Vicar of St Mary, Welling, Kent, 1960–63; Vicar of St Michael, Christchurch, NZ, 1963–65; Dean of Dunedin, 1965–73; Vicar, St John's Wood, London, 1973–83. *Recreations:* contemporary poetry, theatre, beach-combing. *Address:* 121 Hales Road, Cheltenham, Glos GL52 6ST. *T:* (01242) 256075.

RAPHOE, Bishop of, (RC), since 1995; **Most Rev. Philip Boyce,** DD; *b* 25 Jan. 1940; *s* of Joseph Boyce and Brigid Gallagher. *Educ:* Downings, Co. Donegal; Castlemartyr Coll., Co. Cork; Carmelite House of Studies, Dublin; Pontifical Theol Faculty (Teresianum), Rome (DD). Entered Discalced Carmelites, 1958; studied philosophy in Dublin and theology in Rome; ordained priest, 1966; on teaching staff of Pontifical Theol Faculty (Teresianum), Rome, 1972–95. Mem., Congregation for Divine Worship and Discipline of Sacraments, 1999–2010. *Publications:* The Challenge of Sanctity: a study of Christian perfection in the writings of John Henry Newman, 1974; Spiritual Exodus of John Henry Newman and Thérèse of Lisieux, 1979; (ed) Mary: the Virgin Mary in the life and writings of John Henry Newman, 2001; articles on themes of spiritual theology. *Address:* Ard Adhamhnáin, Letterkenny, Co. Donegal, Ireland. *T:* (74) 9121208.

RAPIER, Gillian Barbara; *see* Westerman, G. B.

RAPINET, Michael William; a Vice-President, 1997–2002, and Acting Vice-President, 2003–05, Immigration Appeal Tribunal; *b* 13 April 1935; *s* of Charles Herbert Rapinet and Eleanor Adelaide Rapinet (*née* Hunt); *m* 1962, Christina Mary, *d* of Captain William Eric Brockman, CBE, RN; one *s* one *d*. *Educ:* St Edward's Coll., Malta; St Joseph's Coll., London. Admitted Solicitor, 1957; Sen. Partner, Kidd Rapinet, 1958–85. Pt-time Chm., Industrial Tribunals, 1987–91; pt-time Chm., 1989–92, Chm., 1992–97, Immigration Tribunal. Pres., Council of Immigration Judges, 2000–01. Member (C): Wandsworth LBC, 1958–62; Berks CC, 1968–75 (Chm., Schs Cttee; Member: Finance Cttee; Personnel and Mgt Cttee). Liveryman, Tallow Chandlers' Co. Founder: Order of Malta Homes Trust, 1975; Orders of St John Care Trust (formerly Orders of St John Trust), 1975. CStJ 1988; Kt of Magistral Grace, 1973, Kt Grand Cross, 1996, SMO (Malta). *Publications:* Our Lords the Sick: a history of the Orders of St John Care Trust, 2012. *Recreations:* fishing, gardening, walking, reading, theatre, music. *Address:* Greenlands, Townsend Road, Streatley-on-Thames, Berks RG8 9LH. *T:* (01491) 871740. *Club:* Carlton.

RAPLEY, Prof. Christopher Graham, CBE 2003; PhD; Professor of Climate Science, University College London, since 2009; *b* 8 April 1947; *s* of Ronald Rapley and Barbara Helen Rapley (*née* Stubbs); *m* 1970, Norma Khan; twin *d*. *Educ:* Jesus Coll., Oxford (BA Hons Physics 1969; MA 1974; four shooting half blues); Manchester Univ. (MSc Radio Astronomy 1970); UCL (PhD X-ray Astronomy 1976). Prof. of Remote Sensing Sci., UCL, 1991–97; Director: British Antarctic Survey, 1998–2007; Science Museum, 2007–10. Fellow: St Edmund's Coll., Cambridge, 1999–; UCL, 2008–. Exec. Dir, Internat. Geosphere-Biosphere Prog., Royal Swedish Acad. of Scis, 1994–97; Chm., ICSU Planning Gp, 2003–04, Mem., Jt Cttee, 2005–, for Internat. Polar Year 2007–08; Sen. Vis. Scientist, NASA Jet Propulsion Lab., 2006–; Chairman: UCL Communicating Climate Sci. Policy Commn, 2012–14; London Climate Change Partnership, 2013–. Pres., Internat. Scientific Cttee on Antarctic Res., 2006–08 (Vice Pres., 2000–04); Member: Earth Sci. Adv. Council, ESA, 2000–01; UK Deleg., Governing Council, ESF, 2000–03; Global Envmtl Res. Cttee, Royal Soc., 2007–; ESA Dir Gen's High Level Sci. Policy Adv. Cttee, 2013– (Chm., 2014–). Vis. Prof., Imperial Coll. London, 2009–. Hon. Professor: UCL, 1998; UEA, 1999–. Mem., Adv. Council, Winston Churchill Meml Trust, 2008–10, 2013–. MAE 2010. Hon. DSc: Bristol, 2008; UEA, 2010–. Edinburgh Science Medal, Edinburgh Internat. Sci. Fest., 2008. *Publications:* more than 150 res. papers on space astronomy, remote sensing, global change, earth system sci., sci. communication. *Recreation:* digital photography. *Address:* 22 Artington Walk, Guildford, Surrey GU2 4EA. *T:* (01483) 851538. *E:* christopher.rapley@ucl.ac.uk; Department of Earth Sciences, University College London, Room 224, Pearson Building, Gower Street, WC1E 6BT.

RAPSON, Sarah Oonagh; Director General, UK Visa and Immigration, Home Office, since 2014 (interim Director General, 2013–14); *b* London, 20 June 1967; *d* of Neil Rapson and Anne Rapson; *m* 2005, Rob McIvor; one *s*. *Educ:* Lancaster Univ. (BSc Maths 1988); London Business Sch. (MBA 2003). ACIB 1996. Manager, Branch Develt, Woolwich, later Barclays, 1991–2001; Strategy and Implementation Manager, American Express, 2003–05; Identity and Passport Service: Ops Dir, 2005–07; Exec. Dir, Service Planning and Delivery, 2007–10; Chief Exec., Identity and Passport Service, 2010–13; Registrar Gen. for England and Wales, 2010–14. *Recreations:* looking after pre-schooler, reading, cycling, walking. *Address:* Home Office, 2 Marsham Street, SW1P 4DF.

RAPSON, Sydney Norman John, BEM 1984; *b* 17 April 1942; *s* of late Sidney Rapson and of Doris Rapson (*née* Fisher); *m* 1967, Phyllis Edna, *d* of Frank and Beatrice Williams; one *s* one *d*. *Educ:* Southsea and Paulsgrove Secondary Modern Sch.; Portsmouth Dockyard Coll. Apprentice aircraft fitter, 1958–63, Aircraft Engr, 1963–97, MoD. Member (Lab): Portsmouth CC, 1971–97 (Lord Mayor, 1990–91; Hon. Alderman, 1999); Hants CC, 1973–76. Non-exec. Dir, Portsmouth Healthcare NHS Trust, 1993–97 (Gov., Portsmouth Hosp. Trust, 2007–). MP (Lab) Portsmouth N, 1997–2005; Team PPS, MoD, 2003–05. Dir, Paulsgrove Learning and Leisure Community, 2006–09. Freeman, City of London, 1990. Imperial Service Medal, 1998. *Address:* 79 Washbrook Road, Paulsgrove, Portsmouth, Hants PO6 3SB.

RASCH, Sir Simon (Anthony Carne), 4th Bt *cr* 1903, of Woodhill, Danbury, Essex; *b* 26 Feb. 1948; *s* of Sir Richard Guy Carne Rasch, 3rd Bt and Anne Mary (*d* 1989), *e d* of Maj. John Henry Dent-Brocklehurst, OBE; *S* father, 1996; *m* 1987, Julia, *er d* of Maj. Michael Godwin Plantagenet Stourton; one *s* one *d*. *Educ:* Eton; RAC Cirencester. MRICS (ARICS 1973). A Page of Honour to HM The Queen, 1962–64. *Heir: s* Toby Richard Carne Rasch, *b* 28 Sept. 1994. *Address:* Priors Farm, Semley, Shaftesbury, Dorset SP7 9BP.

RASHLEIGH, Sir Richard (Harry), 6th Bt *cr* 1831; management accountant; self-employed, since 1990; *b* 8 July 1958; *s* of Sir Harry Evelyn Battie Rashleigh, 5th Bt and Honora Elizabeth (*d* 1987), *d* of George Stuart Sneyd; *S* father, 1984; *m* 1996, Emma (*d* 2013), *o d* of John McGougan and Jennifer (*née* Dyke; she *m* 1987, Sir Antony Acland, *qv*); one *s* one *d*. *Educ:* Allhallows School, Dorset. Management Accountant with Arthur Guinness Son & Co., 1980–82; Dexion-Comino International Ltd, 1982–84; United Biscuits, 1985–88; Wessex Housing, 1988–90. *Recreations:* sailing, tennis, shooting. *Heir: s* David William Augustine Rashleigh, *b* 1 April 1997. *Address:* Menabilly, Par, Cornwall PL24 2TN. *T:* (01726) 815432. *Club:* Royal Fowey Yacht.

RASMUSSEN, Anders Fogh; Secretary-General, NATO, 2009–14; Founder and Chairman, Rasmussen Global, since 2014; *b* 26 Jan. 1953; *s* of Knud Rasmussen and Martha (*née* Fogh Andersen); *m* 1978, Anne-Mette; one *s* two *d*. *Educ:* Univ. of Aarhus (MSc Econs 1978). Consultant, Danish Fedn of Crafts and Small Industries, 1978–87. MP (L) Greve, Denmark, 1978–2009; Minister: for Taxation, 1987–92; for Econ. Affairs, 1990–92; spokesman for Liberal Party, 1992–98; Prime Minister of Denmark, 2001–09; Vice-Chairman: Housing Cttee, 1981–86; Econ. and Pol Affairs Cttee, 1993–98; Foreign Policy Bd, 1998–2001. Liberal Party: Mem., Mgt Cttee, 1984–87 and 1992–2009, Chm., 1998–2001, Parly Party; Vice-Chm., 1985–98, Chm., 1998–2009, nat. orgn. Nat. Chm., Liberal Youth of Denmark, 1974–76. Dr *hc*: George Washington, 2002; Corvinus, Budapest, 2008; Bucharest, 2013; Kaunas, 2014; Hon. LLD Hampden-Sydney Coll., Va, 2003; Hon. DPhil Haifa, 2008. Awards: Adam Smith Award, 1993; Politician of the Year, Danish Mktg Assoc., 1998; Liberal of the Year, Jongeren Organisatie Vrijheid en Democratie, Holland, 2002; European Leader, Polish Leaders Forum, 2003; European of the Year, Danish Eur. Movt, 2003; Robert Schuman Medal, EP, 2003; Best Leader in Denmark, 2005; Årets Erhvervspolitiker, Dansk Erhvervssammenslutning, 2005; Dist. Leadership Award, US Atlantic Council, 2013; Hillary Rodham Clinton Award, Georgetown Univ., 2014; Global Leadership Award, Chicago Council on Global Affairs, 2014. Medal of Merit in Gold (Denmark), 2002; Commander 1st Cl., Order of the Dannebrog (Denmark), 2002. Foreign decorations include: Grand Cross: Order of Merit (Portugal), 1992; Order of Merit (Germany), 2002; Order of Merit (Poland), 2003; Order of the Oak Crown (Luxembourg), 2003; Order of Nicaragua, 2003; Order of Star (Romania), 2004; Order of Polar Star (Sweden); Great Cross, Order Pedro Joaquín Chamorro (Nicaragua), 2003; Grand Duke Gediminas (Lithuania), 2004; Three Star Order (Latvia), 2005; Order of Stara Planina First Class (Bulgaria), 2006. *Publications:* Opgør med skattesystemet, 1979; Kampen om boligen, 1982; Fra socialstat til minimalstat, 1993.

RASMUSSEN, Lars Løkke; MP (L) Frederiksborg, Denmark, since 1994; Prime Minister of Denmark, 2009–11 and since 2015; *b* Vejle, Denmark, 15 May 1964; *m* 1998, Sólrun Jákupsdóttir; two *s* one *d*. *Educ:* Univ. of Copenhagen (LLM 1992). Mem., Græsted-Gilleleje Municipal Council, 1986–97; County Mayor, Frederiksborg County, 1998–2001. Minister for the Interior and Health, 2001–07, for Finance, 2007–09. Vice Chm., 1998–2009, Chm., 2009–, Liberal Party. Nat. Chm., Young Liberals, 1986–89. Comdr 1st Cl., Order of the Dannebrog (Denmark), 2009; Grand Cross, Order of the Phoenix (Greece), 2009. *Publications:* Foreningshåndbogen, 1994; Hvis jeg bli'r gammel (If I Get Old), 1997; Løkkeland: Lars Løkke Rasmussens Danmark, 2006. *Address:* Folketinget, Christiansborg, 1240 Copenhagen K, Denmark.

RASMUSSEN, Poul Nyrup; Member (Social Democrats) for Denmark, European Parliament, 2004–09; *b* 15 June 1943; *s* of Oluf Nyrup Rasmussen and Vera Nyrup Rasmussen; *m* 1st (marr. diss.); (one *c* decd); 2nd (marr. diss.); 3rd, 1994, Lone Dybkjær, MEP. *Educ:* Esbjerg Statsskole; Univ. of Copenhagen (MA Econs). With Danish Trade Union Council, 1980–86: in Brussels, 1980–81; Chief Economist, 1981–86; Man. Dir, Employees' Capital Pension Fund, 1986–88. Chm., SDP, 1992–2002 (Dep. Chm., 1987–92); MP (SDP) Herning-Kredsen, Denmark, 1988–2004; Prime Minister of Denmark, 1993–2001. Pres., PES, 2004–11. Former Chm. Bd, Lindoe Offshore Renewables Center.

RASSOOL, Bertrand Louis Maurice; Executive Director, Eden Offshore Ltd, Seychelles, since 2012; *b* 10 April 1957; *m* 1978, Estelle Gontier; one *s* two *d*. *Educ:* London Sch. of Econs (BSc Econs (Mathematical Econs and Econometrics)). Central Bank of Seychelles: economist, 1980; Asst Dir of Res., 1981–86; Dir of Res., 1986–88; Dir Gen., Planning and Econ. Co-operation Div., Min. of Planning and Ext. Relns, 1988–93; Principal Secretary: Min. of Foreign Affairs, Planning and Envmt, 1993–94; Min. of Industry, 1994–98; Min. of Tourism and Civil Aviation, 1998–99; High Comr of Seychelles to UK, 1999–2003. Gp Dep. CEO, British American Investment Gp (Mauritius), 2006–11 (Dir, 2005–11; Executive Chairman: Tourism and Leisure Div., 2008–09; Energy and Envmt Div., 2009–11). Non-executive Director: Trading Emissions plc (UK), 2007– (Advr, 2005–); Central Bank of Seychelles, 2012–. *Recreations:* fishing, chess, horse-racing. *Address:* Eden Offshore Ltd, PO Box 116, Victoria, Mahé, Seychelles.

RATCLIFF, Antony Robin Napier; Deputy Chairman and Chief Executive, Eagle Star Insurance, 1985–87; Visiting Professor, Sir John Cass Business School, City of London (formerly City University Business School), 1987–2005; *b* 26 Sept. 1925; *m* 1956, Helga Belohlawek, Vienna; one *s*. FIA 1953; Aktuar, DAV, 1994; ASA. Nat. Correspondent for England, Internat. Actuarial Assoc., 1965–70; Mem. Council, Assoc. of British Insurers (formerly British Insurance Assoc.), 1969–87. Pres., Inst. of Actuaries, 1980–82; Vice-

President: London Insce Inst., 1964–; Chartered Insce Inst., 1983–84. Hon. Mem., Assoc. internat. pour l'Etude de l'Economie de l'Assurance, 1991–2009 (Vice-Pres., 1986–90). Trustee, Soc. for the Protection of Life from Fire, 1989–2012 (Chm., 1998–2000). Mem., Evangelische Forschungs-akad., Berlin. Corresponding Member: Deutsche Gesellschaft für Versicherungsmathematik; Verein zur Förderung der Versicherungswirtschaft. Trustee, St Paul's German Evangelical Reformed Ch Trust; Extraordinary Mem. of Synod, German-speaking Protestant Congregations in GB, 2003–12. Messenger and Brown Prize-Winner, Inst. of Actuaries, 1963. Hon. DLitt City, 1986. Officer's Cross, Order of Merit (Germany), 2007. *Publications:* (jtly) Lessons from Central Forecasting, 1965; (jtly) Strategic Planning for Financial Institutions, 1974; (jtly) A House in Town, 1984; contribs to Jl of Inst. of Actuaries, Trans of Internat. Congress of Actuaries, Jl London Insce Inst., Jl Chartered Insce Inst., Blätter der Deutschen Gesellschaft für Versicherungsmathematik. *Address:* 8 Evelyn Terrace, Richmond, Surrey TW9 2TQ. *Clubs:* Actuaries, Anglo-Austrian Society.

RATCLIFFE, Frederick William, CBE 1994; MA, PhD; JP; University Librarian, University of Cambridge, 1980–94, now Emeritus; Life Fellow, since 1994 (Fellow, 1980–94), and Parker Librarian, 1995–2000, Corpus Christi College, Cambridge; *b* 28 May 1927; *y s* of late Sydney and Dora Ratcliffe, Leek, Staffs; *m* 1952, Joyce Brierley; two *s* one *d*. *Educ:* Leek High Sch., Staffs; Manchester Univ. (MA, PhD); MA Cantab. Served in N Staffs Regt, 1945–48. Manchester University: Graduate Res. Scholarship, 1951; Res. Studentship in Arts, 1952; Asst Cataloguer and Cataloguer, 1954–62; Sub-Librarian, Glasgow Univ., 1962–63; Dep. Librarian, Univ. of Newcastle upon Tyne, 1963–65; University Librarian, 1965–80, Dir, John Rylands University Library, 1972–80, Manchester University. Trustee, St Deiniol's Library, Hawarden, 1975–98 (Hon. Fellow, 2000). Hon. Lectr in Historical Bibliography, Manchester Univ., 1970–80; External Prof., Dept of Library and Inf. Studies, Loughborough Univ., 1981–86; Hon. Res. Fellow, Dept of Library, Archive and Inf. Studies, UCL, 1987; Sandars Reader in Bibliography, Cambridge Univ., 1988–89. Founder, later Pres., Consortium of Univ. Res. Libraries, 1984–94; Chm., Library Panel, The Wellcome Trust, 1988–94. Fellow, Chapter of Woodard Schools (Eastern Div.), 1981–97, now Emeritus (Vice-Provost, 1994–97). Chm., Adv. Cttee, Nat. Preservation Office, 1984–94. Trustee: Cambridge Foundn, 1989–94; Malaysian Commonwealth Studies Centre, 1994–98. Hon. FCLIP (Hon. FLA 1986). JP Stockport, 1972–80, Cambridge, 1981–97. Encomienda de la Orden del Merito Civil (Spain), 1988. *Publications:* Die Psalmenübersetzung Heinrichs von Mügeln, 1965; Preservation Policies and Conservation in British Libraries, 1984; many articles in learned journals. *Recreations:* book collecting, hand printing, cricket. *Address:* Ridge House, The Street, Rickinghall Superior, Diss, Norfolk IP22 1DY. *T:* (01379) 898232, (01379) 897199. *E:* frederick@ratcliffe7375.freeserve.co.uk.

RATCLIFFE, James A.; Chairman, and Founder, Ineos plc, since 1998; *b* 18 Oct. 1952; *s* of Alan and Marie Ratcliffe; two *s* one *d*. *Educ:* Univ. of Birmingham (BSc); London Business Sch. (MBA). ACMA. CEO, Inspec, 1992–98 (Founder, 1992). *Recreations:* ski-ing, running, mountains, wine.

RATCLIFFE, (John) Michael; writer and editor; *b* 15 June 1935; *s* of Donald Ratcliffe and Joyce Lilian Dilks; civil partnership 2006, *m* 2015, Howard Lichterman. *Educ:* Cheadle Hulme Sch.; Christ's Coll., Cambridge (MA). Trainee journalist, Sheffield Telegraph, 1959–61; Asst Literary and Arts Editor, Sunday Times, 1962–67; Literary Editor, 1967–72, chief book reviewer, 1972–82, The Times; freelance writer, 1982–83; theatre critic, 1984–89, Literary Ed., 1990–95, Contributing Ed., 1995–96, Observer; freelance writer, 1996–. Commended Critic of the Year, British Press Awards, 1989. Officer, Order of Merit (FRG), 2003. *Publications:* The Novel Today, 1968; The Bodley Head 1887–1987 (completed for J. W. Lambert), 1987. *Recreations:* music, travel, art, architecture, walking, gardening, cycling, reading, film, cooking. *Address:* Flat 6, The Design Works, 93–99 Goswell Road, EC1V 7EY. *T:* (020) 7490 8372. *E:* elia@dircon.co.uk.

RATCLIFFE, Sir Peter (John), Kt 2014; MD; FRCP, FMedSci; FRS 2002; Nuffield Professor of Clinical Medicine, since 2004, and Member, Ludwig Institute for Cancer Research, since 2013, University of Oxford; Fellow, Magdalen College, Oxford, since 2004; Honorary Consultant in Acute General Medicine, John Radcliffe Hospital, Oxford University Hospitals NHS Trust; *b* 14 May 1954; *s* of William and Alice Margaret Ratcliffe; *m* 1983, Fiona Mary MacDougall; two *s* two *d*. *Educ:* Lancaster Royal Grammar Sch.; Gonville and Caius Coll., Cambridge (MD 1987; Hon. Fellow); St Bartholomew's Hosp., London (MB ChB). FRCP 1995. University of Oxford: Wellcome Sen. Fellow, 1990–92; Fellow, Jesus Coll., 1992–2004; Prof. of Renal Medicine, 1996–2004. Hon. Consultant Physician, Radcliffe Trust, Oxford, 1990–. FMedSci 2002; Member: EMBO, 2006; Amer. Acad. of Arts and Scis, 2007. Louis-Jeantet Prize for Medicine, Fondation Louis-Jeantet, 2009; Canada Gairdner Award, Gairdner Foundn, 2010; Robert J. and Claire Pasarow Foundn Award, 2011; Baly Medal, RCP, 2011; Scientific Grand Prix of Instn Lefoulon-Delalande, Inst. of France, 2012; Jakob-Herz-Preis, Friedrich-Alexander-Universität, Erlangen-Nürnberg, 2012; Wiley Prize for Biomedical Res., 2014. *Publications:* contribs on aspects of renal and cell biology, particularly processes involved in cellular oxygen sensing. *Recreations:* fell-walking, gardening (when pressed). *Address:* Manor Farmhouse, 17 Church Street, Kidlington, Oxon OX5 2BA.

RATFORD, Sir David (John Edward), KCMG 1994 (CMG 1984); CVO 1979; HM Diplomatic Service, retired; translator and language consultant, University of Lund, Sweden, since 1997; *b* 22 April 1934; *s* of George Ratford and Lilian (*née* Jones); *m* 1960, Ulla Monica (*d* 2013), *d* of Oskar and Gurli Jerneck, Stockholm; two *d*. *Educ:* Whitgift Middle Sch.; Selwyn Coll., Cambridge (1st Cl. Hons Mod. and Med. Langs). National Service (Intell. Corps), 1953–55. Exchequer and Audit Dept, 1952; FO, 1955; 3rd Sec., Prague, 1959–61; 2nd Sec., Mogadishu, 1961–63; 2nd, later 1st Sec., FO, 1963–68; 1st Sec. (Commercial), Moscow, 1968–71; FCO, 1971–74; Counsellor (Agric. and Econ.), Paris, 1974–78; Counsellor, Copenhagen, 1978–82; Minister, Moscow, 1983–85; Asst Under-Sec., of State (Europe), 1986–90, and Dep. Political Dir, 1987–90, FCO; UK Rep., Permanent Council of WEU, 1986–90; Ambassador to Norway, 1990–94. Chm., Tushinskaya Trust, 1996–2011. Comdr, Order of the Dannebrog, Denmark, 1979. *Publications:* translations from Swedish: Zetterquist, A Europe of the Member States or of the Citizens?, 2002; Pihl Atmer, Stockholm Town Hall and its Architect, Ragnar Östberg, 2011; Jönsson, Jerneck and Arvidson, Politics and Development in a Globalised World, 2012; Gedin, Manilla, 2012. *Recreations:* music, walking. *Address:* Apt 4, 20 Cabanel Place, Kennington, SE11 6BD; Käringön, Bohuslän, Sweden. *Club:* Travellers.

RATHBAND, Very Rev. Kenneth William; Rector, St Ninian's, Alyth, with St Catherine's, Blairgowrie, and St Anne's, Coupar Angus, since 1991; Dean of St Andrews, Dunkeld and Dunblane, since 2007; *b* 1960. *Educ:* Edinburgh Theol Coll.; Edinburgh Univ. (BD 1986). Ordained deacon, 1986, priest, 1987; Asst Curate, St Paul's Cathedral, Dundee, 1986–88; Team Vicar, St Martin's, Dundee, 1988–89; Asst Curate, St Philips and St James', Edinburgh, 1990–91. *Address:* 10 Rosemount Park, Blairgowrie PH10 6TZ. *T:* (01250) 872431. *E:* krathband@btinternet.com.

RATHBONE, Prof. Dominic William, PhD; Professor of Ancient History, King's College London, since 2003; *b* 8 Feb. 1957; *s* of late Norman and Christine Rathbone; *m* 1993, Yvette Erete. *Educ:* Christ's Hosp., Horsham; Jesus Coll., Cambridge (BA Classics; PhD 1986). Lectr in Classics, Univ. of Aberdeen, 1981–84; Lectr, 1985–93, Reader, 1993–2003, in Ancient Hist., KCL. *Publications:* Economic Rationalism and Rural Society in Third-Century AD Egypt, 1991; (ed jtly) Cambridge Ancient History, vol. xi, 2001; (ed jtly) Egypt from Alexander to the Copts: an archaeological and historical guide, 2004. *Recreations:* travel, DIY. *Address:* Department of Classics, King's College London, Strand, WC2R 2LS. *T:* (020) 7848 2343. *E:* dominic.rathbone@kcl.ac.uk.

RATHBONE, Jenny; Member (Lab) Cardiff Central, National Assembly for Wales, since 2011; *b* Liverpool, 12 Feb. 1950; *d* of late Bertram Lyle Rathbone and Elizabeth Eleanor Rathbone; partner, John Uden; one *s* one *d*. *Educ:* Univ. of Essex (BA Govt (Latin America) 1972); London Metropolitan Univ. (Nat. Professional Qual. in Integrated Centre Leadership 2006). Researcher and reporter, World in Action, Granada TV, 1979–87; Producer, The Money Programme, BBC, 1989–96. Mem. (Lab) Islington LBC, 1998–2002. Contested (Lab) Cardiff Central, 2010. Chm., Ind. Rev. Panels, NHS London, 1995–2003; Prog. Manager, Sure Start Hillmarton, Islington, 2002–07. Chm., All Wales Prog. Monitoring Cttee, 2013–. Trustee: Eleanor Rathbone Charitable Trust, 1984–; Hybu, 2014–. *Recreations:* outdoor swimming, bicycling, films, family. *Address:* National Assembly for Wales, Cardiff Bay, Cardiff CF99 1NA. *T:* 0300 200 7135. *E:* Jenny.Rathbone@assembly.wales.

RATHBONE, William, OBE 2012; Director and Chief Executive, Royal United Kingdom Beneficent Association and Universal Beneficent Association, 1988–2001; *b* 5 June 1936; *s* of William Rathbone and Margaret Hester (*née* Lubbock); *m* 1st, 1960, Sarah Kynaston Mainwaring (*d* 2006); one *s* one *d*; 2nd, 2010, Carolyn Wendy Dorothy, *widow* of David O. Lloyd-Jacob, CBE. *Educ:* Radley Coll.; Christ Church, Oxford (MA 2nd Cl. Hons PPE 1959); IMEDE, Lausanne (Dip. Business Studies 1972). Nat. Service, RA, 1954–56. Ocean Group PLC, 1959–88: Elder Dempster Lines, 1959–69; tanker and bulk carrier div., 1969–71; Dir, Wm Cory & Sons Ltd, 1973–74; Gen. Manager, Ocean Inchcape Ltd, 1974–79; Exec. Dir, Gastransco Ltd, 1979–88. Dir, Rathbone Bros plc, 1994–2003. Trustee, Queen's Nursing Inst., 1974– (Vice-Chm., 1974–99); Pres., Community and Dist Nursing Assoc., 1984–99; Vice Pres., Christ Church (Oxford) United Clubs, 1991–. Trustee: Eleanor Rathbone Charitable Trust, 1958–; New England Co., 1974–; St Peter's Convent, Woking, 1992–2007; Hadfield Trust, 1997–; Southwark Cathedral Millennium Trust, 1998–2012; British Mus. Friends, 2003–12 (Vice-Chm., 2005–11). Mem., Develt Bd, Christ Church, 2002–. Gov., Centre for Policy on Ageing, 2000–02. Liveryman, Skinners' Co., 1969–. Trustee, Skinners' Almshouse Charity, 2009–12. *Recreations:* fishing, the arts, friends. *Address:* 7 Brynmaer Road, SW11 4EN. *T:* (020) 7978 1935. *Clubs:* Brooks's; Leander (Henley-on-Thames).

RATHCAVAN, 3rd Baron *cr* 1953, of The Braid, Co. Antrim; **Hugh Detmar Torrens O'Neill;** Bt 1929; *b* 14 June 1939; *o s* of 2nd Baron Rathcavan, PC (NI) and his 1st wife, Clare Désirée (*d* 1956), *d* of late Detmar Blow; *S* father, 1994; *m* 1983, Sylvie Marie-Thérèse Wichard du Perron; one *s*. *Educ:* Eton. Captain, Irish Guards. Financial journalism, Observer, Irish Times, FT; Dep. Chm., IPEC Europe, 1978–82; Chairman: Northern Ireland Airports, 1986–92; NI Tourist Board, 1988–96; Cleggan Estate Co. Ltd, 1996–; Brasserie St Quentin 2002 Ltd, 2002–08; non-executive Director: St Quentin, 1980–94; The Spectator, 1982–84; Old Bushmills Distillery Co., 1989–99; Savoy Management, 1989–94; Northern Bank Ltd, 1990–97; Berkeley Hotel Co. Ltd, 1995–97; Brompton Bar and Grill Ltd, 2008–14. Mem., BTA, 1988–96. Member: H of L European Select Cttee D, 1995–99; British-Irish Interparly Body, 1995–99. Trustee, Newman Foundn, 1998–. *Recreations:* food, travel. *Heir:* *s* Hon. François Hugh Nial O'Neill, *b* 26 June 1984. *Address:* Cleggan Lodge, Ballymena, Co. Antrim BT43 7JW. *T:* (028) 2568 4209, *Fax:* (028) 2568 4552; 14 Thurloe Place, SW7 2RZ. *T:* (020) 7584 5293, *Fax:* (020) 7823 8846. *E:* lordrathcavan@btopenworld.com. *Club:* Beefsteak.

RATHCREEDAN, 3rd Baron *cr* 1916; **Christopher John Norton;** Director, Norton & Brooksbank Ltd, Pedigree Livestock Auctioneers, since 2003; *b* 3 June 1949; *er s* of 2nd Baron Rathcreedan, TD and Ann Pauline (*d* 2007), *d* of late Surg.-Capt. William Bastian, RN; *S* father, 1990; *m* 1978, Lavinia Anne Ross, *d* of late A. G. R. Ormiston; two *d*. *Educ:* Wellington Coll.; RAC Cirencester. Partner, Hobsons, Pedigree Livestock Auctioneers; founded Norton & Brooksbank, 1983, Partner, 1983–2003. *Recreations:* horse racing, gardening. *Heir:* *b* Hon. Adam Gregory Norton [*b* 2 April 1952; *m* 1980, Hilary Shelton, *d* of Edmond Ryan; two *d*]. *Address:* Stoke Common House, Purton Stoke, Swindon, Wilts SN5 4LL. *T:* (01793) 772492. *Club:* Turf.

RATHDONNELL, 5th Baron *cr* 1868; **Thomas Benjamin McClintock Bunbury;** *b* 17 Sept. 1938; *o s* of William, 4th Baron Rathdonnell and Pamela (*d* 1989), *e d* of late John Malcolm Drew; *S* father, 1959; *m* 1965, Jessica Harriet, *d* of George Gilbert Butler, Scatorish, Bennettsbridge, Co. Kilkenny; three *s* one *d*. *Educ:* Charterhouse; Royal Naval College, Dartmouth. Lieutenant RN. *Heir:* *s* Hon. William Leopold McClintock Bunbury [*b* 6 July 1966; *m* 2002, Emily Henrietta Dacres Dixon]. *Address:* Lisnavagh, Rathvilly, County Carlow, Ireland. *T:* (59) 9161104.

RATLEDGE, Prof. Colin, PhD; CChem, FRSC; CBiol, FRSB; Professor of Microbial Biochemistry, University of Hull, 1983–2004, now Emeritus; *b* 9 Oct. 1936; *s* of Fred Ratledge and Freda Smith Ratledge (*née* Proudlock); *m* 1961, Janet Vivien Bottomley; one *s* two *d*. *Educ:* Bury High Sch.; Manchester Univ. (BSc Tech, PhD). AMCST; CChem, FRSC 1970; CBiol, FRSB (FIBiol 1982). Res. Fellowship, MRC Ireland, 1960–64; Res. Scientist, Unilever plc, 1964–67; Hull University, 1967–: Lectr, 1967–73; Sen. Lectr, 1973–77; Reader, 1977–83; Head of Dept of Biochemistry, 1986–88. Visiting Lecturer: Australian Soc. of Microbiol., 1986; NZ Soc. of Microbiol., 1986; Kathleen Barton Wright Meml Lectr (Inst. of Biol./Soc. Gen. Microbiol.), 1995; Visiting Professor: Univ. of Malaya, 1993; Hong Kong Poly., 1994, 2001–02; Univ. of OFS, Bloemfontein, 1994; Ben-Gurion Univ. of the Negev, Israel, 2008; Univ. of Malaysia, 2008; Jiangnan Univ., China, 2010–13. Mem., AFRC Food Res. Cttee, 1989–92; Chairman: AFRC Food Res. Grants Bd, 1989–92; AFRC Food-borne Pathogens Co-ord. Prog., 1992–95; Brit. Co-ordinating Cttee for Biotechnology, 1989–91; Inst. of Biol. Industrial Biol. Cttee, 1992–2001; Vice-Pres., SCI, 1993–96 (Chm. Biotechnol. Gp, 1990–91; Mem. Council, 1991–93); Sec., Internat. Cttee of Envmtl and Applied Microbiology, 1991–94; Mem., Biotechnology Cttee, Internat. Union of Biochemistry, 1984–97. Fellow, Internat. Inst. of Biotechnology, 1993. Editor: World Jl of Microbiol. and Biotechnol., 1987–2004; Biotechnology Techniques, 1988–99; Biotechnology Letters, 1996–. Stephen S. Chang Award, Amer. Oil Chemists' Soc., 2011. *Publications:* The Mycobacteria, 1977; Co-Editor: Microbial Technology: current state, future prospects, 1979; The Biology of the Mycobacteria, vol. 1 1982, vol. 2 1983, vol. 3 1989; Biotechnology for the Oils and Fats Industry, 1984; Microbial Technology in the Developing World, 1987; Microbial Lipids, vol. 1 1988, vol. 2 1989; Microbial Physiology and Manufacturing Industry, 1988; Biotechnology: Social and Economic Impact, 1992; Industrial Application of Single Cell Oils, 1992; Biochemistry of Microbial Degradation, 1993; Mycobacteria: molecular biology and virulence, 1999; Basic Biotechnology, 3rd edn 2006; Single Cell Oils, 2005, 2nd edn 2010; numerous scientific papers in biol science jls. *Recreations:* enjoying my grandchildren, hill walking, bonsai gardening, bridge. *Address:* Department of Biological Sciences, University of Hull, Hull HU6 7RX. *E:* c.ratledge@hull.ac.uk; (home) 49 Church Drive, Leven, Beverley, E Yorks HU17 5LH. *T:* (01964) 542690.

RATNER, Gerald Irving; Chief Executive, geraldonline, since 2003; after-dinner/conference speaker; *b* 1 Nov. 1949; *s* of Leslie and Rachelle Ratner; *m* 1st (marr. diss. 1989); two *d*; 2nd, 1989, Moira Day; one *s* one *d*. *Educ:* Hendon Co. Grammar Sch. Chm. and Chief Exec., Ratners Gp, 1986–92. Director: Norweb, 1989–91; Workshop Health & Fitness Club, Henley, 1997–2003. *Publications:* The Rise and Fall… and Rise Again (autobiog.), 2007. *Recreation:* road cycling.

RATTEE, Sir Donald (Keith), Kt 1989; a Judge of the High Court of Justice, Chancery Division, 1993–2000 (Family Division, 1989–93); *b* 9 March 1937; *s* of Charles Ronald and Dorothy Rattee; *m* 1964, Diana Mary, *d* of John Leslie and Florence Elizabeth Howl; four *d*. *Educ:* Clacton County High School; Trinity Hall, Cambridge (Schol.; 1st cl. Pts I and II Law Tripos; MA, LLB). Called to Bar, Lincoln's Inn, 1962, Bencher, 1985, Treas., 2006; Second Junior Counsel to the Inland Revenue (Chancery), 1972–77; QC 1977; Attorney Gen. of the Duchy of Lancaster, 1986–89; a Recorder, 1989. Liaison Judge, Family Div. (NE Circuit), 1990–93; Mem., Gen. Council of the Bar, 1970–74. Chm., Inns of Court and Bar Educnl Trust, 1997–2004. *Recreations:* reading, music, theatre. *Address:* 29 Shirley Avenue, Cheam, Surrey SM2 7QS. *Clubs:* Royal Automobile; Banstead Downs Golf (Banstead); Thurlestone Golf (Thurlestone, Devon).

RATTLE, Sir Simon, OM 2014; Kt 1994; CBE 1987; Chief Conductor and Artistic Director, Berlin Philharmonic Orchestra, since 2002; Principal Guest Conductor, Orchestra of the Age of Enlightenment, since 1992; *b* Liverpool, 19 Jan. 1955; *m* 1st, 1980, Elise Ross (marr. diss. 1995), American soprano; two *s*; 2nd, 1996, Candace Allen (marr. diss. 2008); 3rd, 2008, Magdalena Kozena; two *s* one *d*. Won Bournemouth John Player Internat. Conducting Comp., when aged 19. Has conducted: Bournemouth Sinfonietta; Philharmonia; Northern Sinfonia; London Philharmonic; London Sinfonietta; Berliner Philharmoniker; Boston Symphony; Chicago Symphony; Cleveland; Concertgebouw; Stockholm Philharmonic; Toronto Symphony, etc. Débuts: Festival Hall, 1976; Glyndebourne, 1977; ENO, 1985; Royal Opera, 1990; Vienna Philharmonic, 1993; Philadelphia, 1993; Royal Albert Hall (Proms etc), 1976–; Asst Conductor, BBC Scottish Symphony Orch., 1977–80; Principal Conductor and Artistic Advr, 1980–90, Music Dir, 1990–98, CBSO. Associate Conductor, Royal Liverpool Philharmonic Soc., 1977–80; Principal Conductor, London Choral Soc., 1979–84; Artistic Dir, South Bank Summer Music, 1981–83; Principal Guest Conductor: Rotterdam Philharmonic, 1981–84; Los Angeles Philharmonic, 1981–92. Exclusive contract with EMI Records. Hon. Fellow, St Anne's Coll., Oxford, 1991. Hon. DMus: Birmingham, 1985; Birmingham Poly., 1985; Oxford, 1999. Shakespeare Prize, Toepfer Foundn, Hamburg, 1996; Albert Medal, RSA, 1997; Comenius Award, 2004; Hon. Schiller Award, 2005; Urania Medal, 2006; Goldena Kamera Award, 2006. Chevalier des Arts et des Lettres (France), 1995. *Address:* c/o Askonas Holt Ltd, Lincoln House, 300 High Holborn, WC1V 7JH. *T:* (020) 7400 1700.

RATZINGER, Joseph Alois; *see* Benedict XVI, His Holiness.

RAU, Prof. Raghavendra, PhD; Sir Evelyn de Rothschild Professor of Finance, University of Cambridge, since 2011. *Educ:* Delhi Univ. (BSc Hons 1987); Indian Inst. of Mgt, Bangalore (MBA 1989); INSEAD (MSc 1993; PhD 1997). Associate Prof., Purdue Univ., 1997–2008; Principal, Barclays Global Investors, 2008–09. Vis. Associate Prof., UCLA, 2005–06; Vis. Prof., Univ. of Calif at Berkeley, 2009–11. *Publications:* articles in Jl of Finance, Jl of Financial Econs, Rev. of Financial Studies. *Recreations:* aikido, iaido. *Address:* Cambridge Judge Business School, University of Cambridge, Trumpington Street, Cambridge CB2 1AG.

RAUSING, Dr (Anna) Lisbet (Kristina), (Mrs Peter Baldwin), FLS; Founder, 2001, and Member, Donor Board, since 2006, Arcadia; Director, Ingleby Farms and Forests, since 2005; *b* Lund, Sweden, 9 June 1960; *d* of Hans A. Rausing, *qv*; *m* 1st, 1988, Prof. Joseph Leo Koerner (marr. diss. 2002); one *s* one *d*; 2nd, 2002, Prof. Peter Baldwin. *Educ:* Univ. of Calif, Berkeley (BA *summa cum laude* 1984); Harvard Univ. (MA Hist. 1987; PhD Hist. 1993). Lectr in Hist. of Sci., 1993–94, Asst Prof., 1994–96, Dept of Hist. of Sci., Harvard Univ.; Sen. Res. Investigator, 2000–02, Sen. Res. Fellow, 2002–11, Centre for Hist. of Sci., Technol. and Medicine, Imperial Coll. London. Dir, Tetra Laval Gp of Industries, 1984–95; Mem., Supervisory Bd, Ecolean, 2001–. Member: Bd of Overseers, Stockholm Sch. of Econs, 1993–2007; Founding Council, Inst. for Philanthropy, 2000–07; Bd, Courtauld Inst., 2004–08 (Mem., Investment Adv. Cttee, 2004–07); Bd of Overseers, Harvard Univ., 2005–11 (Mem., Cttee to Visit Harvard Liby, 1998–2011); Internat. Adv. Bd, Israel Nat. Liby, 2011–; Univ. Council Sub-Cttee, West Campus, Yale Univ., 2012–; Co-Chm., Planning Cttee, Harvard Campaign, Harvard Univ., 2012–. Vis. Scholar, Envmtl Studies, New York Univ., 2013–; Vis. Sen. Res. Fellow, Dept of Hist., KCL, 2013–14. Vice President: Fauna and Flora Internat., 2000– (Mem. Council, 2004–07); Kent Wildlife Trust, 2011–; Sussex Wildlife Trust, 2011–. Trustee, Yad Hanadiv, 2001–11; Member, Advisory Board: Sutton Trust, 2004–08; Smithsonian Nat. Mus. of Natural History, 2011–14; Cambridge Conservation Initiative, 2012–. FLS 2001. Fellow, Royal Swedish Acad. of Agric. and Forestry, 2015. Hon. FBA 2006; Hon. FRSB (Hon. FSB 2014). Hon. Dr: SOAS, 2004; Imperial Coll. London, 2007; Uppsala, 2007. *Publications:* Linnaeus: nature and nation, 1999; contrib. articles, newspaper commentary and book reviews. *Address:* Nyland, Sixth Floor, 5 Young Street, W8 5EH. *T:* (020) 7361 4911, *Fax:* (020) 7361 4949. *E:* celia.hamer@nyland.org.uk. *Clubs:* Athenæum, Reform, Farmers.

See also S. M. E. Rausing.

RAUSING, Dr Hans A., Hon. KBE 2006; *b* 25 March 1926; *s* of Ruben and Elisabeth Rausing; *m* 1958, Märit Norrby; one *s* two *d*. *Educ:* Univ. of Lund, Sweden. Tetra Pak: Man. Dir, 1954–83; Exec. Chm. and Chief Exec. Officer, 1983–91; Chm., Gp Bd, 1985–91; Chm. and Chief Exec. Officer, 1991–93, Hon. Chm., 1993–95, Tetra Laval Gp. Chm., Ecolean AB, Sweden, 2001–07 (Hon. Chm., 2008–); mem. of *c* 10 family-owned companies; Member, Board: Stockholms Enskilda Bank, Sweden, 1970–72; Skandinaviska Enskilda Banken, Sweden, 1973–82; South-Swedish Univs, Sweden, 1975–80; Business Internat., NY, 1975–79. Mem., Co-ordination Council for Foreign Investments, Russia, 1995. Hon. Prof., Univ. of Dubna, 1996; Vis. Prof., Mälardalens Högskola, Sweden, 2001. Mem., Russian Acad. of Inventors; Foreign Mem., Russian Acad. of Agriculture. Hon. Freeman and Liveryman, Stationers' and Newspaper Makers' Co., 2011. Hon. Member: Royal Swedish Acad. of Engrg Scis, 1994; Acad. of Natural Scis, Russia, 1994; Hon. Fellow, Isaac Newton Inst., Cambridge, 2001; Fellow, Ashmolean Mus., Oxford, 2006. Hon. doctorates: Econs: Lund, 1979; Stockholm Sch. of Econs, 1987; Amer. Univ. in London; DTech: Royal Inst. of Technol., Stockholm, 1985; Mälardalen Univ., 2004; MD Lund, 2001; ScD Imperial Coll. London, 2005. Swede of the Year in the World, Swedes in the World Assoc., 2007. *Address:* PO Box 216, Wadhurst, E Sussex TN5 6LW.

See also A. L. K. Rausing, S. M. E. Rausing.

RAUSING, Kirsten; Owner and General Manager, Lanwades Stud, since 1980; Director, British Bloodstock Agency Ltd, since 2010; *b* Lund, Sweden, 6 June 1952; *d* of Dr Gad Rausing and Dr Birgit Rausing (*née* Mayne). *Educ:* in Sweden, France and Ireland. Work at Airlie Stud, Ireland, 1977–80. Non-executive Director: Tetra Pak, 1983–; Tetra Laval Gp, 1983–. Director: British Bloodstock Agency plc, 2004–10; Jockey Club Estates Co. Ltd; National Stud. Chairman: Veterinary Commn (Paris), Eur. Fedn of Thoroughbred Breeders' Assocs, 1994–2004; Equine Industry Liaison Cttee, Animal Health Trust, 2002–; Fedn Européenne des Eleveurs de Pur Sang, Paris, 2002–05; Thoroughbred Breeders' Assoc., GB, 2008–. Mem., Cttee of Enquiry into Veterinary Res., RCVS. Member: Scientific Adv. Gp, Equine Fertility Unit, Univ. of Cambridge/Thoroughbred Breeders' Assoc.; Ext. Adv. Cttee, Liverpool Univ. Veterinary Coll.; Cataloguing Standards Cttee, Soc. of Internat. Thoroughbred Auctioneers. Founder and Chm., Alborada Trust, 2001–; Mem., Animal Health Trust. Patron, Asha Centre. Hon. Fellow, Wolfson Coll., Cambridge, 2009. Hon. Associate, RCVS, 2013. DUniv E Anglia, 2008. *Address:* c/o Tetra Laval International, SA, 70 Avenue Général-Guisan, PO Box 430, 1009 Pully, Switzerland. *Club:* Jockey.

RAUSING, Lisbet; *see* Rausing, A. L. K.

RAUSING, Sigrid Maria Elisabet; Publisher: Portobello Books, since 2005; Granta Publications, since 2005; Editor, Granta magazine, since 2014; *b* 29 Jan. 1962; *d* of Hans A. Rausing, *qv*; *m* 1st, 1996 (marr. diss. 2002); one *s*; 2nd, 2003, Eric Antony Abraham, *qv*. *Educ:* York Univ. (BA Hist.); University Coll. London (PhD Anthropol. 1997). Chm., Sigrid Rausing Trust, 1996–. Hon. Fellow, Dept of Anthropol., UCL, 1997–98. Emeritus Mem. Bd, Human Rights Watch Internat., 1997–; Mem., Adv. Bd, Coalition for Internat. Criminal Court, 2010–15; Emeritus Mem. Bd, Order of Teaspoon. Trustee, Charleston Trust, 2008–13. Judge: Amnesty Media Awards, 2009, 2010; Index on Censorship Media Awards, 2012; Per Anger Prize. Hon. Fellow: LSE, 2010; St Antony's Coll., Oxford, 2014; Morrell Fellow, Univ. of York, 2012. DUniv York, 2014. Human Rights Award, Internat. Service, 2004; Special Award for Philanthropy, Beacon Fellowship, 2005; Changing Face of Philanthropy Award, Women's Funding Network, 2006. *Publications:* History, Memory and Identity in Post-Soviet Estonia, 2004; Everything Is Wonderful, 2014. *Recreations:* walking, reading, conservation. *Address:* 12–14 Addison Avenue, W11 4QR.

See also A. L. K. Rausing.

RAVEN, Amanda; *see* Game, A.

RAVEN, Prof. James Russell, PhD, LittD; FSA, FRHistS; Professor of Modern History, University of Essex, since 2004; Senior Research Fellow, Magdalene College, Cambridge, since 2012; *b* Colchester, 13 April 1959; *s* of Leonard Raven and Eileen Raven; *m* 2000, Karen Jane Walden-Smith, *qv*; two *s*. *Educ:* Gilberd Sch., Colchester; Clare Coll., Cambridge (BA 1981; MA 1985; PhD 1985); MA Oxon 1997; LittD Cantab 2012. FRHistS 2000; FSA 2007. University of Cambridge: Drapers' Res. Fellow, 1985–89, Fellow, 1989–90, Pembroke Coll.; Munby Fellow, 1989–90; Dir, Studies in Hist., and Fellow and Lectr, Magdalene Coll., 1990–96; Newton Trust Lectr, Hist. Faculty, 1994–96; University of Oxford: Lectr, Mod. Hist. Faculty, 1996–2000; Reader in Social and Cultural Hist., 2000–04; Fellow, Mansfield Coll., 1996–2004. Dir, Cambridge Proj. for Book Trust, 1990–. Visiting Fellow: Newberry Liby, Chicago, 1986; Amer. Antiquarian Soc., 1986 and 1995 (Mem., 1997); Lewis Walpole Liby, Yale Univ., 1994–95; Magdalene Coll., Cambridge, 2003–04; Marsh's Liby, Dublin, 2015; McLean Fellow, Liby Co. of Philadelphia, 1996; Vis. Scholar, Pembroke Coll., Cambridge, 2005–07; British Acad. Res. Reader, 2005–07. Dep. Chm., ESU, 2014– (Gov., 2000–06 and 2012–); Chm., Lindemann Trust, 2015–. Gov., Wisbech Grammar Sch., 2014–. Member: Mid-Atlantic Gp, 1997–; Pilgrims Soc. of GB, 2006–. Vice-Pres., Bibliographical Soc., 2012–. Trustee, Marks Hall Estate, Essex, 2007–. Contested (Lib Dem): Colchester N, 1992; N Essex, 2005, 2010. Seeley Medal, 1986, Thirlwall Prize, 1986, Univ. of Cambridge. *Publications:* Judging New Wealth: popular publishing and responses to commerce in England, 1750–1800, 1992; (ed jtly) The Practice and Representation of Reading in England, 1996; (ed) Free Print and Non-Commercial Publishing since 1700, 2000; (jtly) The English Novel 1770–1829, 2 vols, 2000; London Booksellers and American Customers: Transatlantic literary community and the Charleston Library Society, 1748–1811, 2002; (ed) Lost Libraries: the destruction of book collections since antiquity, 2004; The Business of Books: booksellers and the English book trade 1450–1850, 2007 (DeLong Book Hist. Prize, Soc. for Hist. of Authorship, Reading and Publishing, 2008); (ed) Books Between Europe and the Americas, 2011; Bookscape: geographies of printing and publishing in London before 1800, 2014; Publishing Business in Eighteenth-Century England, 2014; Lost Mansions: essays on the destruction of the country house, 2015; over 80 articles in learned jls and chapters in books, 1985–. *Recreations:* family, painting, theatre, writing, tennis. *Address:* Magdalene College, Cambridge CB3 0AG. *T:* (01223) 332100. *E:* jr42@cam.ac.uk.

RAVEN, Prof. John Albert, FRS 1990; FRSE; CBiol, FRSB; Boyd Baxter Professor of Biology, University of Dundee, 1995–2008, now Emeritus; *b* 25 June 1941; *s* of John Harold Edward Raven and Evelyn Raven; *m* 1985, Linda Lea Handley. *Educ:* Wimbish County Primary Sch.; Friends' Sch., Saffron Walden; St John's College, Cambridge (MA, PhD). FRSE 1981; CBiol, FRSB (FIBiol 1998). University of Cambridge: Research Fellow, and Official Fellow, St John's Coll., 1966–71; Univ. Demonstrator in Botany, 1968–71; Lectr, and Reader, 1971–80, Prof. (personal chair), 1980–95, Dept of Biol Scis, Univ. of Dundee. Hon. PhD Umeå, Sweden, 1995. *Publications:* Energetics and Transport in Aquatic Plants, 1984; (with Paul Falkowski) Aquatic Photosynthesis, 1997, 2nd edn 2007; numerous papers in learned jls and chapters in multi-author vols. *Recreations:* aviation, walking, literature. *Address:* Spital Beag, Waterside, Invergowrie, Dundee DD2 5DQ.

RAVEN, Karen Jane; *see* Walden-Smith, K. J.

RAVEN, Martin Clark; HM Diplomatic Service, retired; Consul-General, São Paulo, and Director, Trade and Investment, Brazil, 2006–10; *b* 10 March 1954; *s* of Basil Raven and Betty Raven (*née* Gilbert); *m* 1978, Philippa Michale Morrice Ruddick; two *s*. *Educ:* Bury Grammar Sch., Lancs; Univ. of Sussex (BA Intellectual Hist.). Joined HM Diplomatic Service, 1976: Korea/Mongolia Desk, then Yugoslavia/Albania Desk, FCO, 1976–78; Third Sec., Lagos, 1978; Hindi lang. trng, SOAS, 1979; Third, later Second Sec., Delhi, 1979–83; First Secretary: N America, then Non-Proliferation Depts, FCO, 1983–88; Human Rights and Social Issues, UK Mission to UN, NY and Alternate Rep. to Commn on Human Rights, 1988–92; Dep. Hd, S Atlantic and Antarctic Dept, FCO and Dep. Comr, British Antarctic Territory, 1993–96; Hd, Drugs and Internat. Crime Dept, FCO, 1996–98; Counsellor, Dep. Hd of Mission and Consul Gen., Stockholm, 1998–2001; on secondment as Dir, Services, Aid and Export Finance, Business Gp, Trade Partners UK, later UK Trade & Investment, 2001–06. Dir, BESO, 2001–05. Non-exec. Chm., VG Partner, 2012–. Chairman: Anglo Latin American Foundn, 2010–; Nominations Cttee, EnglishUK, 2012–; Vice-Chm., Brazil Wkg Gp, TheCityUK, 2011–14. *Recreations:* cycling, cinema, food, theatre, reading novels, listening to music, watching football and cricket, eating olives. *E:* martin.raven@hotmail.com.

RAVENSCROFT, Ven. Raymond Lockwood; Archdeacon of Cornwall and Canon Librarian of Truro Cathedral, 1988–96; *b* 15 Sept. 1931; *s* of Cecil and Amy Ravenscroft; *m* 1957, Ann (*née* Stockwell) (*d* 2008); one *s* one *d*. *Educ:* Sea Point Boys' High School, Cape Town, SA; Leeds Univ. (BA Gen. 1953); College of the Resurrection, Mirfield. Assistant Curate: St Alban's, Goodwood, Cape, SA, 1955–58; St John's Pro-Cathedral, Bulawayo, S Rhodesia, 1958–59; Rector of Francistown, Bechuanaland, 1959–62; Asst Curate, St Ives, Cornwall, 1962–64; Vicar: All Saints, Falmouth, 1964–68; St Stephen by Launceston with St Thomas, 1968–74; Team Rector of Probus Team Ministry, 1974–88; RD of Powder, 1977–81; Hon. Canon of Truro Cathedral, 1982–88. *Recreations:* walking, reading, local history. *Address:* 19 Montpelier Court, St David's Hill, Exeter EX4 4DP. *T:* (01392) 430607.

RAVENSDALE, 3rd Baron *cr* 1911; **Nicholas Mosley,** MC 1944; Bt 1781; *b* 25 June 1923; *e s* of Sir Oswald Mosley, 6th Bt (*d* 1980) and Lady Cynthia (*d* 1933), *d* of 1st Marquess Curzon of Kedleston; *S* to barony of aunt, who was also Baroness Ravensdale of Kedleston (Life Peer), 1966, and to baronetcy of father, 1980; *m* 1st, 1947, Rosemary Laura Salmond (marr. diss. 1974; she *d* 1991); two *s* one *d* (and one *s* decd); 2nd, 1974, Mrs Verity Bailey; one *s*. *Educ:* Eton; Balliol College, Oxford. Served in the Rifle Brigade, Captain, 1942–46. *Publications:* (as Nicholas Mosley): Spaces of the Dark, 1951; The Rainbearers, 1955; Corruption, 1957; African Switchback, 1958; The Life of Raymond Raynes, 1961; Meeting Place, 1962; Accident, 1964; Experience and Religion, 1964; Assassins, 1966; Impossible Object, 1968; Natalie Natalia, 1971; The Assassination of Trotsky, 1972; Julian Grenfell: His Life and the Times of his Death, 1888–1915, 1976; The Rules of the Game: Sir Oswald and Lady Cynthia Mosley 1896–1933, 1982; Beyond the Pale: Sir Oswald Mosley 1933–1980, 1983; Efforts at Truth (autobiog.), 1995; Rules of the Game and Beyond the Pale, 1998; Time At War: a memoir, 2006; Paradoxes of Peace (autobiog.), 2010; *novels* (series): Catastrophe Practice, 1979; Imago Bird, 1980; Serpent, 1981; Judith, 1986; Hopeful Monsters (Whitbread Prize), 1990; Children of Darkness and Light, 1996; The Hesperides Tree, 2001; Inventing God, 2003; Look at the Dark, 2005; God's Hazard, 2009; A Garden of Trees, 2012. *Heir: g s* Daniel Nicholas Mosley, *b* 10 Oct. 1982. *Address:* 5 Hungerford Road, N7 9LA. *T:* (020) 7607 3579.

RAVENSWORTH, 9th Baron *cr* 1821; **Thomas Arthur Hamish Liddell;** Bt 1642; *b* 27 Oct. 1954; *s* of 8th Baron Ravensworth and Wendy, *d* of J. S. Bell; *S* father, 2004; *m* 1983, Linda, *d* of H. Thompson; one *s* one *d*. *Educ:* Gordonstoun; RAC Cirencester. *Heir: s* Hon. Henry Arthur Thomas Liddell, *b* 27 Nov. 1987.

RAVIV, Moshe; Ambassador of Israel to the Court of St James's, 1993–97; *b* Romania, 23 April 1935; *s* of David and Elka Raviv; *m* 1955, Hanna Kaspi; two *s* one *d*. *Educ:* Hebrew Univ., Jerusalem; Univ. of London (grad. Internat. Relations). Israel Ministry of Foreign Affairs: 2nd Sec., London, 1961–63; Office of Foreign Minister, Mrs Golda Meir, 1964–65; Political Sec. to Foreign Minister, Abba Eban, 1966–68; Counsellor, Washington, 1968–74; Dir, E European Div., 1974–76; Dir, N American Div., 1976–78; Ambassador to the Philippines, 1978–81; Dir, Economic Div., 1981–83; Minister, London, 1983–88; Dep. Dir Gen., i/c Information, 1988–93. *Publications:* Israel At Fifty: five decades of struggle for peace, 1998. *Recreations:* reading, chess, jogging.

RAWBONE, Rear-Adm. Alfred Raymond, CB 1976; AFC 1951; *b* 19 April 1923; *s* of A. Rawbone and Mrs E. D. Rawbone (*née* Wall); *m* 1943, Iris Alicia (*née* Willshaw); one *s* one *d*. *Educ:* Saltley Grammar Sch., Birmingham. Joined RN, 1942; 809 Sqdn War Service, 1943; CO 736 Sqdn, 1953; CO 897 Sqdn, 1955; CO Loch Killisport, 1959–60; Comdr (Air) Lossiemouth and HMS Ark Royal, 1961–63; Chief Staff Officer to Flag Officer Naval Air Comd, 1965–67; CO HMS Dido, 1968–69; CO RNAS Yeovilton, 1970–72; CO HMS Kent, 1972–73; Dep. ACOS (Operations), SHAPE, 1974–76. Comdr 1958; Captain 1964; Rear-Adm. 1974. Director: Vincents of Yeovil, 1983–86; Vindata, 1984–86; Vincents (Bridgewater) Ltd, 1984–86. *Address:* Wisteria House, 12 Wessex Court, Church Street, Henstridge, Templecombe, Som BA8 0AU.

RAWCLIFFE, Prof. Carole, PhD; FSA, FRHistS; Professor of Medieval History, University of East Anglia, since 2002; *b* 18 Sept. 1946; *d* of Lewis and Betty Rawcliffe. *Educ:* Univ. of Sheffield (BA; PhD 1975). FRHistS 1978; FSA 2004. Asst Keeper, Commn on Historical MSS, 1972–74; Co-ed., medieval vols of The History of Parliament, 1974–92; University of East Anglia: Sen. Res. Fellow, Sch. of Hist., 1992–95; Sen. Lectr, 1995–98; Dir, Centre of E Anglian Studies, 1997–98 and 2005–08; Reader in Medical Hist., 1998–2002. Vis. Fellow, Huntington Liby, Calif, 1984. Mem. Council, Norfolk Record Soc., 2008–. Trustee, Hungate Medieval Art Mus., Norwich, 2008–. Hon. Fellow, Norfolk Medico-Chirurgical Soc., 2003. *Publications:* The Staffords, Earls of Stafford and Dukes of Buckingham, 1978; (ed jtly) The History of Parliament: the House of Commons 1386–1421, 1993; Medicine and Society in Later Medieval England, 1995; Sources for the History of Medicine in Later Medieval England, 1995; The Hospitals of Medieval Norwich, 1995; Medicine for the Soul, 1999; (with R. G. Wilson) The History of Norwich, 2004; Leprosy in Medieval England, 2006; Urban Bodies: communal health in late medieval English towns and cities, 2013; contribs to numerous collections of essays and learned jls on medieval medical, social and religious history. *Recreations:* art, music, dog-walking. *Address:* School of History, University of East Anglia, Norwich NR4 7TJ. *T:* (01603) 592872, *Fax:* (01603) 593519. *E:* c.rawcliffe@uea.ac.uk.

RAWKINS, Jeremy John Bruce; His Honour Judge Jeremy Rawkins; a Circuit Judge, since 2008; Designated Family Judge for Lancashire, since 2011; *b* Preston; *s* of Robert Arthur Rawkins and Sally Joan Rawkins; *m* 1978, Jane Blake; one *s* two *d*. Admitted solicitor, 1974; Dep. District Judge, 1988–94; District judge, 1994–2008; Recorder, 2001–08. *Recreation:* spending frequent days in hot pursuit of sea and freshwater fish and endlessly analysing the reasons for absence of success. *Address:* c/o Designated Family Centre, Sessions House, Lancaster Road, Preston PR1 2PD.

RAWLINGS, Baroness *cr* 1994 (Life Peer), of Burnham Westgate in the County of Norfolk; **Patricia Elizabeth Rawlings;** a Baroness in Waiting (Government Whip), 2010–12; an Extra Baroness in Waiting, since 2012; *b* 27 Jan. 1939; *d* of Louis Rawlings and Mary (*née* Boas de Winter); *m* 1962, David Wolfson (*see* Baron Wolfson of Sunningdale) (marr. diss. 1967). *Educ:* Oak Hall, Haslemere, Surrey; Le Manoir, Lausanne; Florence Univ.; University Coll. London (BA Hons; Fellow 2005); London School of Economics (post grad. diploma course, Internat. Relns). Children's Care Cttee, LCC, 1959–61; WNHR Nursing, Westminster Hosp., until 1968. Contested (C): Sheffield Central, 1983; Doncaster Central, 1987. MEP (C) Essex SW, 1989–94; contested (C) Essex West and Hertfordshire East, Eur. parly elecns, 1994. European Parliament, 1989–94: EPP British Section Rep. on Conservative Nat. Union; Vice Pres., Albanian, Bulgarian and Romanian Delegn; EDG spokesman on Culture Cttee, substitute on Foreign Affairs Cttee; Dep. Whip, 1989–92. Opposition Whip, H of L, 1997–98; Shadow Minister for Internat. Develt and Foreign Affairs, H of L, 1998–2010; govt spokesman for DCMS and Scotland, 2010–12. British Red Cross Society: Mem., 1964–; Chm., Appeals, London Br., until 1988; Nat. Badge of Honour, 1981, Hon. Vice Pres., 1988; Patron, London Br., 1997–. Member Council: British Bd of Video Classification, 1986–89; Peace through NATO; British Assoc. for Central and Eastern Europe, 1994–2008; Mem. Adv. Council, PYBT, 1998–; Special Advr to Ministry on Inner Cities, DoE, 1987–88. President: NCVO, 2002–07; British Antique Dealers Assoc., 2005–12; Hon. Pres., Friends of BADA Trust, 2013–. Chm. Council, KCL, 1998–2007. Chm. of Govs, English Coll. Foundn, Prague, 2008–. Dir, English Chamber Orch. and Music Soc., 1980–2001. Trustee, Chevening Estate, 2002–. FKC 2003. Hon. LittD Buckingham, 1998. Hon. Plaquette, Nat. Assembly of Republic of Bulgaria, 2007. Order of the Rose, Silver Class (Bulgaria), 1991; Grand Official, Order of the Southern Cross (Brazil), 1997. *Recreations:* music, art, golf, ski-ing, travel. *Address:* House of Lords, SW1A 0PW. *Clubs:* Grillions, Pilgrims; Royal West Norfolk Golf.

RAWLINGS, Gillian Felicity; *see* Douglas, G. F.

RAWLINGS, Hugh Fenton, CB 2011; PhD; Director, Constitutional Affairs and Inter-Governmental Relations, Welsh Government (formerly Welsh Assembly Government), since 2011; *b* 24 Nov. 1950; *s* of William Rawlings and late Marion Rawlings (*née* Hughes), OBE; *m* 1981, (Felicity) Gillian Douglas, *qv*; one *s* one *d*. *Educ:* Worcester Coll., Oxford (BA Juris. 1973); London Sch. of Econs (PhD 1977). Lectr in Law, Univ. of Bristol, 1976–88; Welsh Office: Principal, Local Govt Finance Div., 1988–94; Hd, Culture and Recreation Div., 1994–97; Dep. Hd, Devolution Unit, 1997–99; National Assembly for Wales: Hd, European Affairs Div., 1999–2002; Sec., Commn on Local Govt Electoral Arrangements in Wales, 2002–03; Hd, Open Govt and Constitutional Affairs Div., 2003–04; Dir, Local Govt, Public Service and Culture, subseq. Local Govt and Culture, 2004–07; Dir, Strategic Policy, Legislation and Communications, later Constitutional Affairs, Equality and Communications, 2007–09, Dir, Dept of First Minister and Cabinet, 2009–11, Welsh Assembly Govt. Hon. Vis. Prof., Wales Governance Centre, Cardiff Univ., 2011–. *Publications:* Law and the Electoral Process, 1988; articles in acad. legal jls. *Recreations:* reading, music, theatre, worrying about Welsh Rugby. *Address:* 62 Adventurers Quay, Pierhead Road, Cardiff Bay, Cardiff CF10 4NQ; Welsh Government, Crown Buildings, Cathays Park, Cardiff CF10 3NQ. *T:* (029) 2082 6532. *E:* hugh.rawlings@wales.gsi.gov.uk.

RAWLINGS, Flt Lieut Jerry John; President, Republic of Ghana, 1992–2001; African Union High Representative for Somalia, 2010; *b* 22 June 1947; *s* of John Rawlings and Victoria Agbotui; *m* 1977, Nana Konadu Agyeman; one *s* three *d*. *Educ:* Achimota Sch., Accra; Ghana Military Acad. Enlisted in Ghana Air Force, 1967; commnd Pilot Officer, 1969; tried for mutiny, May 1979; forcibly released from cell, June 1979, by popular uprising; became Chm., Armed Forces Revolutionary Council; handed over to democratically elected Govt, Sept. 1979; overthrew Govt, Dec. 1981; Chm., Provisional Nat. Defence Council, 1982–92. *Recreations:* flying, swimming, riding, reading.

RAWLINGS, Ven. John Edmund Frank; Archdeacon of Totnes, 2005–14; *b* 15 April 1947; *s* of Edward and Ivy Rawlings; *m* 1969, Janette Mary Rawlings (*née* Alexander); one *s* one *d*. *Educ:* Godalming Grammar Sch.; King's Coll., London (AKC 1969); St Augustine's Coll., Canterbury. Ordained deacon, 1970, priest 1971; Curate: St Margaret's, Rainham, 1970–73; Tattenham Corner and Burgh Heath, 1973–76; Chaplain, RN, 1976–92; Vicar, Tavistock and Gulworthy, 1992–2005; RD Tavistock, 1997–2002; Preb., Exeter Cathedral, 1999–2005. *Recreations:* gardening, cooking, music (organ playing). *Address:* 9 Rosemount Lane, Honiton, Devon EX14 1RJ. *T:* (01404) 43404. *E:* rawlings1@btinternet.com.

RAWLINGS, Menna Frances, CMG 2014; HM Diplomatic Service; High Commissioner to Australia, since 2015; *b* Hillingdon, 16 Sept. 1967; *d* of Christopher and Ann Hornung; *m* 2001, Mark Rawlings; one *s* two *d*. *Educ:* Northwood Comprehensive Sch.; London Sch. of Econs and Pol Sci. (BSc (Econs) Internat. Relns 1989); Open Univ. (MBA 2011). FCIPD 2012. Entered FCO, 1989; Third, later Second Sec., UK Repn, Brussels, 1991–93; Second Sec. (Econ./Envmt), Nairobi, 1993–96; FCO, 1997; First Sec., Tel Aviv, 1998–2002; Private Sec. to Perm. Sec., FCO, 2002–04; Dep. Hd of Mission, Accra, 2005–08; Counsellor, Corporate Services and Consul-Gen., Washington, 2008–11; Dir, Human Resources, FCO, 2011–14. *Recreations:* family, sport (running, ski-ing, cycling), Chelsea FC, music. *Address:* c/o Foreign and Commonwealth Office, King Charles Street, SW1A 2AH.

RAWLINGS, Prof. Rees David, PhD, DSc; CEng; Professor of Materials Science, 1993–2007, now Emeritus, and Pro Rector (Educational Quality), 2000–08, Imperial College, London; *b* 30 Sept. 1942; *s* of Aubrey Rhys Islwyn Rawlings and Daphne Irene Rawlings (*née* Sangster); *m* 1964, Ann Margaret Halliday; two *d*. *Educ:* Sir Thomas Rich High Sch., Gloucester; Imperial Coll. (BSc Engrg 1st cl. Hons 1964; PhD Metallurgy 1967; Fellow 2009); ARSM 1964; DIC 1967; DSc London 1989. CEng 1980; FIMMM (FIM 1985); FHEA (ILTM 2000). Imperial College: Lectr, 1966–81; Reader, 1981–93; acting Hd, Earth Resources Engrg, 1996–98; Dean, Royal Sch. of Mines, 1995–98; Mem. Governing Body, 1995–98; Mem. Court, 1998–2008; Partner, Matcon (Materials Consultants), 1974–90. Vis. Prof., RCA, 2008–12. Subject Specialist Assessor: HEFCE, 1996–98; HEFCW, 1997–98. Mem., Dist. Adv. Bd, Jl Materials Science, 2015– (Dep. Ed., 1993–2002; Co-Ed.-in-Chief, 2002–08; Reviews Ed., 2008–15); Ed., Jl Materials Science Letters, 2002– (Dep. Ed., 1993–2002); Mem. Adv. Bd, Metal and Materials Internat., 2003–. Trustee, Montessori St Nicholas Charity, 2000–. Mem., Purbeck Arts Club. Hon. FRCA, 2001. FCGI 2002. L. B. Pfeil Medal and Prize, Inst. of Materials, 1990. *Publications:* (jtly) Materials Science, 1974, 5th edn 2003; (jtly) Composite Materials: engineering and science, 1994; articles in learned jls, conf. proceedings and books on materials science. *Recreations:* sport (Pres., Imperial Coll. Rugby Football Club, 2008–), gardening, art, theatre. *Address:* The Elms, 13 Wolverton Avenue, Kingston upon Thames, Surrey KT2 7QF. *Club:* Kingston Athletic and Polytechnic Harriers.

RAWLINS, Brig. Gordon John, OBE 1986; business development consultant, specialising in the Third Sector; *b* 22 April 1944; *s* of Arthur and Joyce Rawlins; *m* 1st, 1965, Ann Beard (*d* 1986); one *s*; 2nd, 1986, Margaret Anne Ravenscroft; one step *s* one step *d*. *Educ:* Peter Symond's, Winchester; Welbeck College; RMA Sandhurst; RMCS Shrivenham (BSc Eng). CEng, FIET, psc. Commissioned REME, 1964; served Aden, Oman, Jordan, Hong Kong, BAOR, UK, 1964–77; Staff Coll., 1978; MoD 1978–80; 2 i/c 5 Armd Wksp, REME, BAOR, 1981–82; CO 7 Armd Wksp, REME, BAOR, 1982–84; MoD, 1984–87 (Sec. to COS Cttee, 1987); Comd Maint., 1 (BR) Corps, BAOR, 1988. Sec., Instn of Production, subseq. Manufacturing, Engrs, 1988–91; Dep. Sec., 1991–2000, Dir, Members Services, 2000–02, IEE. Liveryman, Turners' Co., 1991. *Recreations:* travel, walking the dogs, watching Rugby and cricket. *Address:* Hall Barn Farm, Ingleby Arncliffe, Northallerton DL6 3PE. *Club:* Army and Navy.

RAWLINS, Hon. Sir Hugh (Anthony), Kt 2012; Chief Justice, Eastern Caribbean Supreme Court, 2008–12; Judge, International Administrative Tribunal, International Labour Organization, Geneva, since 2012; Course Director, LLM Legislative Drafting, Faculty of Law, University of the West Indies, 2012–14; *b* Gingerland, St Kitts and Nevis; *s* of William Joseph Rawlins and Veronica Rawlins; *m* Claudette Norville; two *d*. *Educ:* Univ. of West Indies (BA Hons 1974; LLB Hons 1983; LLM 1993); Norman Manley Law Sch., Jamaica (Legal Educn Cert. 1985); Inst. Advanced Legal Studies, Univ. of London. Undergrad. teacher, 1969–71, grad. teacher, 1974–76, high schs; Government of St Kitts and Nevis: Hd, Dept of Labour (Ag.), 1977–79; Asst Sec., Min. of Agric., Lands, Housing and Labour, 1976–85; Crown Counsel, 1985–88, Registrar of the High Court and Addnl Magistrate, 1988–89, Solicitor Gen. and Perm. Sec., Legal Dept, 1989–95, St Kitts and Nevis; Temp. Lectr in Law, 1994, Lectr in Law, 1995–2000, UWI; Master, Eastern Caribbean Supreme Court, 2000–02; High Court Judge, Antigua and Barbuda, Dominica and BVI, 2002–05; Mem., Judicial and Legal Services Commn, BVI, 2004–05; Justice of Appeal, Eastern Caribbean Supreme Court, 2005–08. Eastern Caribbean Supreme Court: Chm., Judicial Ethics Cttee, 2004–06; Chm., Judicial Educn Inst., 2004–07. Mem. Adv. Cttee, Commonwealth Judicial Educn Inst., Dalhousie Univ. Sch. of Law, Halifax, NS, 2006– (Fellow, 2004). UNITAR Fellow, Acad. Internat. Law, The Hague, 1986. Associate Fellow, Soc. of Advanced Legal Studies, Univ. of London, 1995–. *Publications:* contrib. articles on law subjects to Caribbean Law Rev., Caribbean Law Bulletin, Jl Transnat. Law and Policy. *Recreations:* athletics, soccer, cricket, tennis, swimming. *Address:* PO Box 720, Bridgetown, Barbados BB11000, West Indies. *T:* 2554798.

RAWLINS, Prof. (John) Nicholas (Pepys), DPhil; FMedSci; FBPsS; Watts Professor of Psychology, 2005–10, Associate Head, Medical Sciences Division, 2008–10, and Pro-Vice-Chancellor, Development and External Affairs, since 2010, University of Oxford; Professorial Fellow, Wolfson College, Oxford, since 2008; *b* 31 May 1949; *s* of Surg. Vice-Adm. Sir John Stuart Pepys Rawlins, KBE; *m* 1986, Prof. Susan Lynn Hurley (*d* 2007); two *s*. *Educ:* Winchester Coll.; University Coll., Oxford (BA 1971, MA 1976; DPhil 1977). Department of Experimental Psychology, University of Oxford: MRC Res. Asst, 1975–81; Royal Soc. Henry Head Fellow in Neurol., 1981–83; Univ. Lectr in Psychol., 1983–98; Prof. of Behavioural Neurosci., 1998–2005; University College, Oxford: Weir Jun. Res. Fellow, 1978–81; Sen. Res. Fellow, 1981–87; Sir Jules Thorne Fellow and Praelector in Psychol., 1987–2005; Professorial Fellow, 2005–07; Emeritus Fellow, 2008–. Special Vis. Prof., Univ. of Nottingham, 2009–; Fogarty Foundn Res. Fellow, Johns Hopkins Univ., 1979–80. Neurosci. Grants Cttee, MRC, 1986–90; Wellcome Trust: Neurosci. Grants Cttee, 1995–2000; Mem., 2000–02, Chm., 2002–04, Basic Sci. Interest Gp; Co-Chm., Neurosci. Panel, 2004–07; Chm., Neurosci. Panel Cognitive and Higher Systems, 2004–07; Mem., Neurosci. Strategy Cttee, 2004–07. Nuffield Council Panel on Bioethics, 2001–03. Trustee, Schizophrenia Res. Trust, 1995–. FMedSci 2006; FBPsS 2011. *Publications:* (jtly) Brain Power: working out the human mind, 1999; over 200 articles in learned jls. *Recreations:* wine, cooking, gardens, walking, landscape, architecture, ski-ing, snorkelling. *Address:* Wolfson College, Oxford OX2 6UD. *E:* nick.rawlins@psy.ox.ac.uk.

RAWLINS, Sir Michael (David), Kt 1999; MD; FRCP, FRCPE, FFPM, FMedSci; Ruth and Lionel Jacobson Professor of Clinical Pharmacology, University of Newcastle upon Tyne, 1973–2006, now Emeritus; Chairman, National Institute for Health and Clinical Excellence (formerly for Clinical Excellence), 1999–2013; President, Royal Society of Medicine, 2012–14; Chairman, Medicines and Healthcare Products Regulatory Agency, since 2014; *b* 28 March 1941; *s* of Rev. Jack and Evelyn Daphne Rawlins; *m* 1963, Elizabeth Cadbury Hambly (marr. diss. 2005); three *d*. *Educ:* St Thomas's Hosp. Med. Sch., London (BSc 1962; MB BS 1965); MD London 1973. FRCP 1977; FRCPE 1987; FFPM 1989. Lectr in Medicine, St Thomas's Hosp., London, 1967–71; Sen. Registrar, Hammersmith Hosp., London, 1971–72; Consultant Clinical Pharmacologist, Newcastle upon Tyne NHS Trust, 1973–2006. Chm., Eastern Academic Health Sci. Network, 2013–. Vis. Res. Fellow, Karolinska Inst., Stockholm, Sweden, 1972–73; Public Orator, Univ. of Newcastle upon Tyne, 1990–93; Ruiting van Swieten Vis. Prof., Academic Med. Centre, Amsterdam, 1998; Hon. Prof., LSHTM, 2000–; Guest Prof., Univ. of Remnin, Beijing, 2012–. Pres., NE Council on Addictions, 1991–2000; Chairman: Adv. Council on Misuse of Drugs, 1998–2008; UK Biobank, 2012–; Vice-Chm., Northern RHA, 1990–94; Member: Nat. Cttee on Pharmacology, 1977–83; Cttee on the Safety of Medicines, 1980–98 (Chm., 1993–98); Cttee on Toxicity, 1989–92; Standing Gp on Health Technology Assessment, 1993–95. Chm., Newcastle SDP, 1981–84. Bradshaw Lectr, RCP, 1986; Welcome Lectr, Soc. of Apothecaries, 1996; Samuel Gee Lectr, 2005, Harveian Orator, 2008, RCP; Stevens Lectr, RSocMed, 2010; Crookshank Lectr, RCR, 2010; Stanley Davidson Lectr, RCPE, 2010; Fear Meml Lectr, Univ. of Dalhousie, 2011; Jephcott Lectr, RSocMed, 2015. DL Tyne and Wear, 1999–2008. FRSocMed 1972; Founder FMedSci 1998. Hon. FRCA 2000; Hon. FBPhS (Hon. FBPharmacolS 2005); Hon. Fellow, Royal Statistical Soc. 2009; Hon. FRCS 2012; Hon. FRCGP 2013; Hon. FRCR 2013; FKC 2013. DUniv York, 2007; Hon. DCL Newcastle, 2008; Hon. DSc: Univ. of Scis, Philadelphia, 2010; Cambridge, 2015; Hon. MD Sheffield, 2011. Univ. Medal, Helsinki, 1978; William Withering Medal, RCP, 1994; Dixon Medal, Ulster Med. Soc., 1995; Lilly Medal, British Pharmacol Soc., 1997; Paracelsus Medal, Univ. of Amsterdam, 1998; Bradlaw Oration and Medal, FDS RCS, 2002; Hutchinson Medal, RSocMed, 2003; Galen Medal, Soc. of Apothecaries, 2011; Donebedian Lifetime Achievement Award, Internat. Soc. of Pharmacoeconomics and Outcomes Res., 2011; Prince Mahidol Award for Medicine, 2012; Lifetime Achievement Award, European Assoc. of Clinical Therapeutics, 2013. *Publications:* Variability in Human Drug Response, 1973; (ed) Textbook of Pharmaceutical Medicine, 1994; (ed) Patients, the Public and Priorities in Healthcare, 2009; Evidence for Decision-Making in Therapeutics, 2011; articles on clinical pharmacology in med. and scientific jls. *Recreation:* music. *Address:* 16 Friend Street, EC1V 7NS.

RAWLINS, Nicholas; *see* Rawlins, J. N. P.

RAWLINS, Brig. Peregrine Peter, MBE 1983; Clerk to the Grocers' Company, 1998–2006; *b* 3 March 1946; *s* of Lt-Col John Walter Rawlins, Northamptonshire Regt, and Elizabeth Joan Rawlins (*née* Delmé-Radcliffe); *m* 1976, Marlis Müller; one *s* one *d*. *Educ:* Malvern Coll.; RMA, Sandhurst; Lincoln Coll., Oxford (BA Hons Geography 1970). Royal Anglian Regiment: commnd 2nd Bn, 1966; Comd, 2nd Bn, 1985–87; Dep. Col, 1996–98. Staff Coll., 1978; Directing Staff, RMCS, 1988–90; COS, Directorate of Infantry, 1990–92; NATO Defence Coll., Rome, 1992; Defence Attaché, Bonn, 1992–96; Dep. Comdt, RMCS, 1996–98, retd. Gov., Dauntsey's Sch., 2007–. *Recreations:* bird watching, fishing, gardening, walking, golf. *Address:* The Grey House, Low Road, Little Cheverell, Devizes, Wilts SN10 4JS.

RAWLINS, Peter Jonathan, FCA; business strategy consultant and executive coach, Rawlins Strategy Consulting, since 1994; *b* 30 April 1951; *e s* of late Kenneth Raymond Ivan Rawlins and Constance Amande Rawlins (*née* Malzy); *m* 1st, 1973, Louise Langton (marr. diss. 1999); one *s* one *d*; 2nd, 2000, Christina Conway; three *s* one *d*. *Educ:* Arnold House Sch.; St Edward's Sch., Oxford; Keble Coll., Oxford (Hons English Lang. and Lit.; MA). Arthur Andersen & Co., 1972–85: Manager, 1977; Partner, 1983; UK Practice Develt Partner, 1984; full-time secondment to Lloyd's of London as PA to Chief Exec. and Dep. Chm., 1983–84; Dir, Sturge Holdings, and Man. Dir, R. W. Sturge & Co., 1985–89; Chief Exec., Internat., subseq. London, Stock Exchange, 1989–93; Director: Sturge Lloyd's Agencies, 1986–89; Wise Speke Holdings, 1987–89; non-exec. Dir, Lloyd-Roberts & Gilkes, 1989–94; Man. Dir (Europe, ME and Africa), Siegel & Gale Ltd, 1996–97; Director: Scala Business Solutions, NV, 1998–2000; Logistics Resources Ltd, 1999–2002; Oyster Partners Ltd, 2001–02; Cognito Ltd, 2007–09; Chm., Higham Gp plc, 2004–05. Mem., Cttee, Lloyd's Underwriting Agents Assoc., 1986–89 (Treasurer, 1986–87; Dep. Chm., 1988); Mem., standing cttees, Council of Lloyd's, 1985–89. Non-exec. Dir, Royal Bournemouth and Christchurch Hosps NHS Foundn Trust, 2005–07. Director: London Sinfonietta Trust, 1985–88; Half Moon Theatre, 1986–88; Mem. Council and Dir, ABSA, 1982–96; Dir and Trustee, London City Ballet Trust, 1986–93; Mem., Develt Council, RNT, 1991–95; Vice-Chm., 2000, Chm., 2000–02, Spitalfields Fest. Chairman: London First Neighbourhood Approach, 1993–95; Assoc. for Res. into Stammering in Children, 1993–. FRSA 1990. *Recreations:* performing arts, tennis, Rugby, travelling. *Address:* The White House, Hadlow Road, Tonbridge, Kent TN11 0AE. *T:* (01732) 852248. *E:* peter@pjrawlins.co.uk. *Clubs:* City of London, MCC.

RAWLINSON, Sir Anthony Henry John, 5th Bt *cr* 1891; photographer and inventor; *b* 1 May 1936; *s* of Sir Alfred Frederick Rawlinson, 4th Bt and Bessie Ford Taylor (*d* 1996), *d* of Frank Raymond Emmatt, Harrogate; *S* father, 1969; *m* 1st, 1960, Penelope Byng Noel (marr. diss. 1967), 2nd *d* of Rear-Adm. G. J. B. Noel, RN; one *s* one *d*; 2nd, 1967, Pauline Strickland (marr. diss. 1976), *d* of J. H. Hardy, Sydney; one *s*; 3rd, 1977, Helen Leone (marr. diss. 1997), *d* of T. M. Kennedy, Scotland; one *s*; 4th, 2013, Rosalind Snaith, *d* of Robert Everett. *Educ:* Millfield School. Coldstream Guards, 1954–56. *Recreations:* tennis, sailing. *Heir: s* Alexander Noel Rawlinson, *b* 15 July 1964.

RAWLINSON, Charles Frederick Melville, MBE 2012; Deputy Chairman, Britten Sinfonia, 1997–2013 (Director, 1988–2013; Member, Advisory Council, since 2013); *b* 18 March 1934; *s* of Rowland Henry Rawlinson and Olivia Melville Rawlinson; *m* 1962, Jill Rosalind Wesley; three *d*. *Educ:* Canford Sch.; Jesus Coll., Cambridge (MA). FCA, FCT. With A. E. Limehouse & Co., Chartered Accts, 1955–58; Peat Marwick Mitchell & Co., 1958–62; Morgan Grenfell & Co. Ltd, Bankers, 1962–94: Dir, 1970–87; Jt Chm., 1985–87; Morgan Grenfell Group PLC: Dir, 1985–88; Vice-Chm., 1987–88; Sen. Advr, 1988–94; Chm., Morgan Grenfell (Asia), Singapore, 1976–88, Hon. Pres., 1988–93; seconded as Man. Dir, Investment Bank of Ireland Ltd, Dublin, 1966–68; Director: Jefferson Smurfit Gp, 1969–83; Associated Paper Industries plc, 1972–91 (Chm., 1979–91); Yule Catto plc, 1975–85; Willis Faber plc, 1981–89; Hedley Wright & Co. Ltd, 1994–99; Chm., Boxford Suffolk Gp, 1992–2000. Sen. Advr, West Merchant Bank, 1994–97. Chairman: The Hundred Gp of Finance Dirs, 1984–86; Industrial Mems Adv. Cttee on Ethics, ICAEW, 1991–99; Member: Chartered Accountants' Jt Ethics Cttee, 1994–2001; Council, ICAEW, 1995–97; Exec. Cttee, Jt Disciplinary Scheme, 1995–2010. Mem., Council, Order of St Etheldreda, Ely Cathedral, 1999–; Trustee, Ely Cathedral Trust, 2007–. Chm., Peache Trustees, 1980–2002; Hon. Vice Pres., Ambition (formerly NABC—Clubs for Young People), 1995– (Jt Hon. Treas., 1983–91; Dep. Chm., 1989–92; Chm., 1992–94). Member: Soc. of St Radegund, Jesus Coll., Cambridge, 1994–; Vice Chancellor's Circle, Univ. of Cambridge, 2011–. FRSA. *Recreations:* music, sailing, travel. *Address:* The Old Forge, Arkesden, Saffron Walden, Essex CB11 4EX. *Club:* Brooks's.

See also under Royal Family.

RAWLINSON, David Ian, (Iain); Executive Chairman (formerly Chairman), Monarch Group, 2009–14; *b* Liverpool, 18 Sept. 1958; *s* of (James) Keith McClure Rawlinson and Griselda Maxwell Rawlinson (*née* Carlisle); *m* 1st, 1991 (marr. diss. 1995); 2nd, 1997 (marr. diss. 2013); one *s* one *d*. *Educ:* Birkenhead Sch.; Jesus Coll., Cambridge (BA 1980). Called to the Bar, Lincoln's Inn, 1981; corporate finance roles, Lazard Brothers & Co. Ltd, 1986–94; Robert Fleming London, 1994–95; Robert Fleming Johannesburg, 1995–2000; Hd, Corporate Finance, Robert Fleming South Africa, subseq. Fleming Martin, 1997–2000; Dir, SA Hldg Bd, RF Hldgs SA Ltd, 2000; Chief Operating Officer, Fleming Family & Partners Ltd, 2000–02; Chief Exec., FF&P Advisory Ltd, 2000–04; Sen. Advr, Fleming Family & Partners Ltd, 2004–05; Chief Exec., Highland Star Gp, 2004–05; Dir, Strategy, Good Governance Gp, 2004–08; Chm., Monarch Airlines Ltd, 2009–11. Non-executive Director: Dana Petroleum plc, 2004–10; Sindicatum Carbon Capital Ltd, 2007–10; Edgo Energy Ltd, 2007–09; Lithic Metals and Energy Ltd, 2007–09; Parkmead Gp plc, 2010–. Chairman: Tusk Trust, 2005–13; StudyVox Ltd, 2009–; StudyVox Foundn, 2009–; Rainmaker Foundn, 2013–; Dep. Chm., Global Philanthropic Ltd, 2007–13. *Recreations:* sailing, mountaineering, writing, military history, flying, music, Africa, Scotland. *T:* 07799 882382. *E:* iain@rawlinsonpartners.com. *Clubs:* Beaulieu River Sailing, Royal Southampton Yacht.

RAWLINSON, Iain; *see* Rawlinson, D. I.

RAWLINSON, Ivor Jon, OBE 1988; HM Diplomatic Service, retired; *b* 24 Jan. 1942; *s* of Vivian Hugh Rawlinson and Hermione (*née* Curry); *m* 1976, Catherine Paule Caudal; one *s* two *d*. *Educ:* Christ Church, Oxford (MA). Joined FO, 1964; Polish lang. student, 1965–66; Warsaw, 1966–69; Bridgetown, 1969–71 (course at Univ. of W Indies); Second Sec., News Dept, FCO, 1971–73; Asst Private Sec. to Minister of State, FCO, 1973–74; Second Sec. (Econ.), Paris, 1974–78; First Secretary: FCO, 1978–80; (Commercial), Mexico City, 1980–84; Consul, Florence and Consul-Gen., San Marino, 1984–88; First Sec., later Counsellor (Inspectorate), FCO, 1988–93; RCDS, 1993; Consul-Gen., Montreal, 1993–98; Ambassador to Tunisia, 1999–2002; Hd, FCO Outplacement, 2002–07. Dir, Northcote Books Ltd, 2013–. Gov., Ryde Sch., IoW, 2005–12 (Vice-Chm., 2006–11). Chm., Pimpernel Trust, 2013– (Trustee, 2006–13). *Publications:* Tunisian Dreams: a novel, 2012. *Recreations:* painting, writing, lecturing, collecting books, restoring farmhouse in France. *Address:* 29 Broxash Road, SW11 6AD. *T:* (020) 7228 5261.

RAWLINSON, Mark Stobart; Mergers and Acquisitions Partner, Freshfields Bruckhaus Deringer LLP (formerly Freshfields), since 1990 (Managing Partner, London office, 2011–14); *b* Eccles, Manchester, 3 May 1957; *s* of Thomas Stobart Rawlinson and Barbara Rawlinson; *m* 1984, Julia Shepherd; three *s*. *Educ:* Haberdashers' Aske's Sch., Elstree; Sidney Sussex Coll., Cambridge (BA Hons 1979; MA Hons Law 1980); Guildford Law Sch. (Professional Exams Pt II). Freshfields Bruckhaus Deringer LLP (formerly Freshfields): articled clerk, 1982–84; Associate, 1984–90; Hd, Trainee Recruitment, 2008–09; Hd, Corporate Dept, 2008–11. *Recreations:* sport (4 Peaks Challenge, 1997, Engadin cross country ski marathon, 2005), Rugby, cricket, golf. *Address:* Freshfields Bruckhaus Deringer LLP, 65 Fleet Street, EC4Y 1HS. *T:* (020) 7832 7105, *Fax:* (020) 7108 7105. *Club:* Hawks (Cambridge).

RAWLINSON, Richard Anthony; Managing Director, Axion Leadership Ltd, since 2015; *b* 11 Feb. 1957; *s* of Sir Anthony Rawlinson, KCB and Lady (Mary) Rawlinson; *m* 1991, Sharon Sofer; two *s*. *Educ:* Eton Coll. (King's Schol.); Christ Church, Oxford (BA Politics and Econs 1978; MA); Harvard Business Sch. (Baker Schol.; MBA 1983). J. Henry Schroder Wagg & Co. Ltd, 1978–81; Associates Fellow, Harvard Business Sch., 1983–84; Monitor Company: Cambridge, Mass, 1984–85; London, 1985–89; Tokyo, 1989–93; Hong Kong, 1994–96; London, 1996–2001; Partner (formerly Dir), Monitor Co. Gp LP, 1993–2001. Chm. and Man. Dir, W. P. Stewart & Co. (Europe) Ltd, 2001–02; Dep. Man. Dir, W. P. Stewart & Co. Ltd, Bermuda, 2001–02; Vice Pres., Booz Allen Hamilton Inc., later Booz & Co., then Strategy&, 2004–15 (Dir, 2010–13). Mem., Competition (formerly Monopolies and Mergers) Commn, 1998–2005. FRGS 2002. *Publications:* (contrib.) Competition in Global Industries, 1986; articles in Harvard Business Review, Strategy & Business. *Recreation:* mountain walking. *Address:* 3 Britannia Studios, 49A Britannia Road, SW6 2HJ. *Clubs:* Oxford and Cambridge, Hurlingham.

RAWNSLEY, Andrew Nicholas James; author, broadcaster and journalist; Chief Political Commentator and Associate Editor, The Observer, since 1993; *b* 5 Jan. 1962; *s* of Eric Rawnsley and Barbara Rawnsley (*née* Butler); *m* 1990, Jane Leslie Hall; three *d*. *Educ:* Lawrence Sheriff Grammar Sch., Rugby; Rugby Sch.; Sidney Sussex Coll., Cambridge (schol.; 1st Cl. Hons Hist.; MA). BBC, 1983–85; The Guardian: reporter, 1985–87; sketchwriter, 1987–93. Ed.-in-Chief, PoliticsHome.com, 2008–09. TV presenter: A Week in Politics, 1989–97; series: The Agenda, 1996; Bye Bye Blues, 1997; Blair's Year, 1998; What the Papers Say, incl. Rev. of the Year, 2002–07; The Sunday Edition, 2006–08; The Rise and Fall of Tony Blair, 2007; Gordon Brown: where did it all go wrong?, 2008; Crash Gordon: the inside story of the financial crisis, 2009; Cameron Uncovered, 2010; Roses and Thorns: the inside story of the coalition, 2011. Radio presenter: The Westminster Hour, 1998–2006; The Unauthorised Biography of the United Kingdom, 1999; Leader Conference, 2011–; Beyond Westminster, 2008–11. FRSA 2001. Student Journalist of Year, Guardian/NUS Student Media Awards, 1982; Young Journalist of Year, British Press Awards, 1987; Columnist of Year, What the Papers Say Awards, 2000; Journalist of the Year, Channel Four Pol Awards, 2003; Political Journalist of the Year, Public Affairs Awards, 2006; Commentator of Year, House Mag. Awards, 2008. *Publications:* Servants of the People: the inside story of New Labour, 2000, revd edn 2001 (Channel 4/Politico Book of the Year, 2001); Crash Gordon: the inside story of the financial crisis, 2009; The End of the Party: the rise and fall of New Labour, 2010. *Recreations:* books, movies, mah-jong, sailing, ski-ing. *Address:* The Observer, Kings Place, 90 York Way, N1 9GU. *T:* (020) 3353 4255. *E:* Andrew.Rawnsley@Observer.co.uk; Press Gallery, House of Commons, SW1A 1AA.

RAWORTH, Sophie; Presenter, BBC News; *b* Redhill, Surrey, 15 May 1968; *d* of Richard and Jenny Raworth; *m* 2003, Richard Winter; one *s* two *d*. *Educ:* Bute House Prep. Sch., Hammersmith; Putney High Sch.; St Paul's Girls' Sch.; Univ. of Manchester (BA Jt Hons French and German 1991); City Univ., London (Postgrad. Dip. Broadcast Journalism 1992). Joined BBC as trainee, 1992; reporter, BBC GMR Manchester, 1992–93; producer, Brussels office, 1993–95; Presenter: (and reporter) BBC Look North Leeds, 1995–97; BBC Breakfast, 1997–2002; (and reporter) Tomorrow's World, 1999–2002; BBC Six O'Clock News, 2003–06; BBC One O'Clock News, 2006–. TV presenter: Dream Lives, 2001; Judgemental, 2002; The Trouble with Working Women, 2009; Crimewatch Roadshow, 2009; Panorama: Swine Flu, 2009, Too Much Too Young?, 2011; The Big Personality Test, 2010; Moneywatch, 2010; Parents Under Pressure, 2010; Britain's Royal Weddings, 2011; The Royal Wedding, 2011; Watchdog Daily, 2013; The Watchdog Test House, 2014; Chelsea Flower Show, 2014–; The Queen's Longest Reign, 2015. Judge, Baileys Women's Prize for Fiction, 2014. Hon. DArts City, 2013. *Recreations:* running, cycling, books, theatre. *Address:* BBC News Centre, Broadcasting House, Portland Place, W1A 1AA.

RAWSON, Prof. Dame Jessica (Mary), DBE 2002 (CBE 1994); LittD; FBA 1990; Warden, Merton College, Oxford, 1994–2010, now Honorary Fellow; Professor of Chinese Art and Archaeology, University of Oxford, since 2000; Slade Professor of Fine Art, University of Cambridge, 2013–14; Fellow, St John's College, Cambridge, 2013–14; *b* 20 Jan. 1943; *d* of Roger Nathaniel Quirk and Paula Quirk; *m* 1968, John Rawson; one *d*. *Educ:* New Hall, Cambridge (BA Hons History; LittD 1991; Hon. Fellow, 1997); London Univ. (BA Hons Chinese Lang. and Lit.). Asst Principal, Min. of Health, 1965–67; Department of Oriental

Antiquities, British Museum: Asst Keeper II, 1967–71; Asst Keeper I, 1971–76; Dep. Keeper, 1976–87; Keeper, 1987–94; Pro-Vice-Chancellor, Univ. of Oxford, 2005–10. Visiting Professor: Kunsthistorisches Inst., Heidelberg, 1989, 2011; Dept of Art, Univ. of Chicago, 1994; Hon. Professor: Xi'an Jiaotong Univ., 2007–; Univ. of Sci. and Technol., Beijing, 2008–. Lectures: Barlow, Sussex Univ., 1979; Leventritt Meml, Harvard, 1989; A. J. Pope, Smithsonian Instn, 1991; Harvey Buchanan, Cleveland Mus. of Art, 1993; Pratt Inst., 1998; Beatrice Blackwood, Oxford, 1999; Millennium, Oxford, 2000; Creighton, Univ. of London, 2000; K. S. Lo, Hong Kong, 2009; Heinz-Goetze, Heidelberg, 2011; Frederick Mote, Princeton, 2011; Mok, Chinese Univ. of Hong Kong, 2011; Leon Levy, New York Univ., 2015. Member: Nuffield Langs Inquiry, 1998–99; British Library Bd, 1999–2003; Scholars' Council, Library of Congress, Washington, 2005–11. Academic Advr to Centre for Ancient Civilization, Inst. of Archaeol., Chinese Acad. of Social Scis, 2000–; Consultant to Res. Dept, Palace Mus., Beijing, 2014–; Ambassador, Inst. of Archaeol., Shaanxi Province, 2014–. Chm., Oriental Ceramic Soc., 1993–96; Vice-Chm., Exec. Cttee, GB-China Centre, 1985–87. Governor: SOAS, Univ. of London, 1998–2003; Latymer and Godolphin Sch., 2004–08; St Paul's Girls' Sch., 2009–14. Hon. DSc St Andrews, 1997; Hon. DLitt: London, 1998; Sussex, 1998; Newcastle, 1999; Hon. Dr: Xi'an Jiaotong, 2007; Univ. of Sci. and Technol., Beijing, 2008. *Publications:* Chinese Jade Throughout the Ages (with John Ayers), 1975; Animals in Art, 1977; Ancient China, Art and Archaeology, 1980; Chinese Ornament: the lotus and the dragon, 1984; Chinese Bronzes: art and ritual, 1987; The Bella and P. P. Chiu Collection of Ancient Chinese Bronzes, 1988; Western Zhou Ritual Bronzes from the Arthur M. Sackler Collections, 1990; (with Emma Bunker) Ancient Chinese and Ordos Bronzes, 1990; (ed) The British Museum Book of Chinese Art, 1992; Chinese Jade from the Neolithic to the Qing, 1995; Mysteries of Ancient China, 1996; (with Evelyn Rawski) China, The Three Emperors 1662–1795, 2005; Treasures from Shanghai, Ancient Chinese Bronzes and Jades, 2009; (ed with Kristian Göransson) China's Terracotta Army, 2010; Ancestors and Eternity: essays on Chinese archaeology and art, 2011; contrib. Proc. of British Acad. and learned jls. *Address:* Institute of Archaeology, University of Oxford, 34–36 Beaumont Street, Oxford OX1 2PG. *T:* (01865) 278240, *Fax:* (01865) 278254.

RAWSON, Prof. Kenneth John, MSc; FREng; RCNC; consultant; Professor and Head of Department of Design and Technology, 1983–89, Dean of Education and Design, 1983–89, Brunel University; *b* 27 Oct. 1926; *s* of late Arthur William Rawson and Beatrice Anne Rawson; *m* 1950, Rhona Florence Gill; two *s* one *d*. *Educ:* Northern Grammar Sch., Portsmouth; HM Dockyard Technical Coll., Portsmouth; RN Colls, Keyham and Greenwich. RCNC; FREng (FEng 1984); FRINA. WhSch. At sea, 1950–51; Naval Construction Res. Estabt, Dunfermline, 1951–53; Ship Design, Admiralty, 1953–57; Lloyd's Register of Shipping, 1957–59; Ship and Weapons Design, MoD, Bath, 1959–69; Naval Staff, London, 1969–72; Prof. of Naval Architecture, University Coll., Univ. of London, 1972–77; Ministry of Defence, Bath: Head of Forward Design, Ship Dept, 1977–79; Dep. Dir, Ship Design and Chief Naval Architect (Under Sec.), 1979–83. Hon. DEng Portsmouth, 1995. *Publications:* Photoelasticity and the Engineer, 1953; (with E. C. Tupper) Basic Ship Theory, 1968, 5th edn 2001; Ever the Apprentice, 2006; contrib. numerous technical publications. *Recreations:* cabinet making, gardening, walking. *Address:* Moorlands, The Street, Chilcompton, Radstock BA3 4HB. *T:* (01761) 232793.

RAWSON, Air Vice-Marshal Paul David, CB 2007; Regional Director (Riyadh), Rolls-Royce International, since 2007; Chief Executive Officer, Rolls-Royce Saudi Arabia Ltd, since 2009; *b* 13 March 1953; *s* of Geoffrey and Joyce Rawson; *m* 1975, Janet Elizabeth Fewster; one *s*. *Educ:* RAF Cranwell (HND Mech. Engrg); Open Univ. (BA). Joined RAF, 1972; completed Engr Officer trng, 1975; appts at Brize Norton, Waddington, Farnborough and Binbrook, 1975–83; Tech. Staff Officer, Ordnance Bd, then RAF Marham, subseq. Sen. Engr Officer, RAF Unit, Goose Bay, Canada, 1983–90; RAF St Athan, 1991–93; leader, VC10 Support Authy, Wyton, 1993–95; Sen. Engr Officer, St Athan, 1996–98; Logistics Support Services Agency, Wyton, 1998–2000; RCDS, 2000; ACOS Logistics, HQ Strike Comd, 2002–04; Team Comdr, MoD Saudi Arabian Armed Forces Project, 2004–06; Chief of Staff Support, HQ Strike Comd, 2006–07. *Recreations:* DIY, travel, golf, hill walking, ski-ing. *Address:* PO Box 88215, Riyadh 1162, Kingdom of Saudi Arabia. *T:* 07772 224820. *E:* rawsonpd@hotmail.com.

RAWSTHORN, Alice, OBE 2014; Design Critic, International New York Times (formerly International Herald Tribune), since 2006; *b* 15 Nov. 1958; *née* Judith Alison Rawsthorn; *d* of Peter Rawsthorn and Joan Rawsthorn (*née* Schofield). *Educ:* Clare Coll., Cambridge (MA). Grad. trainee journalist, Thomson Org., 1980–83; Journalist: Campaign Mag., 1983–85; Financial Times, 1985–2001; Dir, Design Mus., 2001–06; Columnist, NY Times, 2006–. Chm., Design Adv. Gp, British Council, 2003–07; Mem., Arts Council England, 2007–13 (Lead Advr on Visual Arts, 2004–07; Chm., Turning Point Review of Contemporary Visual Arts, 2003–06; Member: Visual Arts Bd, 2008–09; Arts Policy Cttee, 2010–13). Chm., Trustees, Chisenhale Gall., 2013–; Trustee: Whitechapel Gall., 1998–; Michael Clark Co., 2013–. Member: Global Agenda Council on Design, WEF, 2008–15; Writers at Liberty, 2014–. Hon. Sen. FRCA. Hon. Dr UAL, 2014. *Publications:* Yves Saint Laurent: a biography, 1996; Marc Newson, 2000; Hello World: where design meets life, 2013; *contributor:* Frieze Projects 2003–2005, 2006; Fashion Theory: a reader, 2007; Marti Guixe: don't buy it if you don't need it, 2007; Women of Design, 2008; Rises in the East: a gallery in Whitechapel, 2009; AC|DC: contemporary art, contemporary design, 2009; Articulado, 2010; 220° Virus Monobloc, 2010; Hella Jongerius: misfit, 2011; Ronan and Erwan Bouroullec: bivouac, 2012; Formafantasma, 2014; Martino Gamper: design is a state of mind, 2014; Richard Hamilton, 2014; How Social Design Changes Our World, 2014; Design and Violence, 2015; Designing Everyday Life, 2015. *Recreations:* art, architecture, film, literature, fashion, cycling, hiking, Manchester United. *Address:* International New York Times, 1 New Oxford Street, WC1A 1NU. *W:* www.alicerawsthorn.com.

RAWSTHORNE, Anthony Robert; a Senior Clerk, House of Lords, 2001–05; *b* 25 Jan. 1943; *s* of Frederic Leslie and Nora Rawsthorne; *m* 1967, Beverley Jean Osborne; one *s* two *d*. *Educ:* Ampleforth College; Wadham College, Oxford. Home Office, 1966–97: Asst Sec., 1977; Crime Policy Planning Unit, 1977–79; Establishment Dept, 1979–82; Sec., Falkland Islands Review Cttee, 1982; Principal Private Sec., 1983; Immigration and Nationality Dept, 1983–86; Assistant Under-Secretary: Establishment Dept, 1986–91; Equal Opportunities and Gen. Dept, 1991; Asst Under-Sec., then Dep. Dir-Gen., Policy, Immigration and Nationality Directorate, 1991–97; Dir, Customs Policy, and a Comr, HM Customs and Excise, 1997–2000. Mem., Fitness to Practise Panel (formerly Professional Conduct Cttee), GMC, 2001–12. *Recreations:* bridge, squash, holidays in France and Italy.

RAWSTHORNE, Rt Rev. John; Bishop of Hallam, (RC), 1997–2014, now Bishop Emeritus; *b* Crosby, Merseyside, 12 Nov. 1936. Priest, 1962; Titular Bishop of Rotdon and an Auxiliary Bishop of Liverpool, 1981–97. Pres., St Joseph's Coll., 1982–90.

RAY, Christopher, PhD; Reporting Inspector, Independent Schools Inspectorate, since 2014; *b* 10 Dec. 1951; *m* 1976, Carol Elizabeth Morrison. *Educ:* Rochdale Grammar Sch.; UCL (BA; Pres. Students' Union, 1974–75); Churchill Coll., Cambridge (PhD 1982); Balliol Coll., Oxford. MInstP 1996; CPhys 1996. Admin and Overseas Depts, Bank of England, 1976–78; Asst Master Physics, Marlborough Coll., 1982–83; Sci. Educn Ed., OUP, 1984–88; Fellow, Nat. Univ. of Singapore, 1988–89; Asst Prof., Portland State Univ., Oregon, 1989–91; Teacher and Director of Studies: Framlingham Coll., 1991–96; King's Coll. Sch., Wimbledon, 1996–2001; Headmaster, John Lyon Sch., Harrow, 2001–04; High Master, Manchester Grammar Sch., 2004–13; Head Master, British Sch. Al Khubairat, Abu Dhabi, 2013–14. Vis. Lectr in Philos. of Space and Time, Univ. of Oxford, 1987–88. Principal Sci. Scrutineer, QCA, 2000–02. Chm., HMC, 2012–13; Mem., UK Internat. Educn Council, BIS, 2013–. Gov., King's Sch., Chester, 2011–13. FRSA 2004. *Publications:* The Evolution of Relativity, 1987; Time, Space and Philosophy, 1991; (contrib.) A Companion to the Philosophy of Science, 2000; (contrib.) The Head Speaks Out, 2008. *Recreations:* fell-walking, opera and ballet, crime fiction. *Club:* East India.

RAY, Edward Ernest, CBE 1988; Director, 1986–2013, and Chairman, 1995–2013, C. T. Baker Ltd; Senior Partner, Spicer and Pegler, Chartered Accountants, 1984–88 (Partner, 1957); *b* 6 Nov. 1924; *s* of Walter James Ray and Cecilia May Ray; *m* 1949, Margaret Elizabeth, *d* of George Bull; two *s*. *Educ:* Holloway Co. Sch.; London Univ. (External) (BCom). Served RN, 1943–46. Inst. of Chartered Accountants: Mem., 1950; FCA 1955; Council Mem., 1973; Vice Pres., 1980; Dep. Pres., 1981; Pres., 1982, 1983. Chm., London Chartered Accountants, 1972–73. Dir, SIB, 1985–90; Chm., Investors' Compensation Scheme Ltd, 1988–91; Member: City Capital Markets Cttee, 1984–88; Marketing of Investments Bd Organising Cttee, 1984–88. *Publications:* Partnership Taxation, 1972, 3rd edn 1987; (jtly) VAT for Accountants and Businessmen, 1972; contrib. accountancy magazines. *Recreations:* walking, birdwatching, golf.

RAY, Jane Rosemary; illustrator of children's books; *b* 11 June 1960; *d* of Donald Edwin Ray and Barbara May Ray (*née* Rowley); *m* 1988, David Temple; one *s* two *d*. *Educ:* Middlesex Univ. (BA Hons 3-D Design (Ceramics)). *Publications:* author and illustrator: Noah's Ark, 1991; The Story of Creation, 1992; The Story of Christmas, 1992; Twelve Dancing Princesses, 1996; Hansel and Gretel, 1997; Can you catch a Mermaid, 2002; Adam and Eve and the Garden of Eden, 2004; The Apple Pip Princess, 2007; The Dolls House Fairy, 2009; Snow White, 2009; Ahmed and the Feathergirl, 2010; The Twelve Days of Christmas, 2011; Cinderella, 2012; The Emperor's Nightingale and other Feathery Tales, 2013; illustrator: A Balloon for Grandad, by Nigel Gray, 1989; The Happy Prince, by Oscar Wilde, 1994; Song of the Earth, by Mary Hoffman, 1995; Sun, Moon and Stars, by Mary Hoffman, 1998; Fairy Tales, by Berlie Doherty, 2000; Orchard Book of Love and Friendship, by Geraldine McCaughrean, 2000; The Bold Boy, by Malachy Doyle, 2001; The King of Capri, by Jeanette Winterson, 2003; Romeo and Juliet, re-written by Michael Rosen, 2004; Jinnie Ghost, by Berlie Doherty, 2005; Moonbird, by Joyce Dunbar, 2006; The Lost Happy Endings, by Carol Ann Duffy, 2006; Stories of Sun, Stone and Sea, by Sally Pomme Clayton, 2012; Zeraffa Giraffa, by Di Hofmeyr, 2014; various books illus. for Folio Soc., including: Myths and Legends of the Near and Middle East, 2003; Celtic Myths and Legends, 2006. *Recreations:* reading, gardening, listening to music, singing, general domesticity. *Address:* c/o Hilary Delamere, The Agency, 24 Pottery Lane, Holland Park, W11 4LZ. *T:* (home) (020) 8442 1748. *E:* janeray41@gmail.com. *W:* www.janeray.com.

RAY, Prof. John David, FBA 2004; FSA; Herbert Thompson Professor of Egyptology, University of Cambridge, 2005–13, now Emeritus (Reader, 1977–2005); Fellow, Selwyn College, Cambridge, since 1979; *b* 22 Dec. 1945; *s* of late Albert Ray and Edith Ray (*née* Millward); *m* 1997, Sonia Ofelia Falaschi. *Educ:* Latymer Upper Sch.; Trinity Hall, Cambridge (BA 1968, MA 1971; Thomas Young Medal). Res. Asst, Dept of Egyptian Antiquities, BM, 1970; Lectr in Egyptology, Univ. of Birmingham, 1970–77. Visiting Professor: Univ. of Chicago, 1984; Yale Univ., 1988. Reviewer: TLS, 1981–; The Times, 2001–. FSA 2000. *Publications:* The Archive of Hor, 1976; Reflections of Osiris: lives from Ancient Egypt, 2001; Demotic Papyri and Ostraca from Qasr Ibrim, 2005; The Rosetta Stone, 2007; Demotic, Hieroglyphic and Greek Inscriptions from the Sacred Animal Necropolis, North Saqqâra, 2011; Demotic Ostraca from the Sacred Animal Necropolis, North Saqqâra, 2013; articles in Jl of Egyptian Archaeology, Lingua Aegyptia, Kadmos, etc. *Recreations:* listening to Beethoven, reading Patrick O'Brian, being walked by a golden retriever. *Address:* Selwyn College, Cambridge CB3 9DQ. *E:* jdr1000@cam.ac.uk.

RAY, Kenneth Richard, OBE 1996; FDSRCS, FRCS; Dean, Faculty of Dental Surgery, Royal College of Surgeons of England, 1992–95; Chairman, Joint Committee for Specialist Training in Dentistry, 1996–98; *b* 25 Jan. 1930; *s* of late John Thomas Ray and Edith Rose (*née* Hobbs); *m* 1958, Pamela Ann Thomas; one *s* two *d*. *Educ:* City of Oxford High Sch.; Univ. of Birmingham (LDS, BDS). FDSRCS 1959; FRCS 1995; FRACDS 1995. Hse Surgeon, Gen. Hosp., Birmingham, 1955; Sen. Hse Officer, Midlands Regl Plastic and Jaw Surgery Centre, 1956; Registrar, then Sen. Registrar, Royal Dental Hosp. of London and St George's Hosp., 1957–60; Sen. Lectr and Hon. Cons. in Oral Surgery, Univ. of London at Royal Dental Hosp. Sch. of Dental Surgery, 1960–73; Cons. in Oral Surgery, Royal Berks Hosp., Reading and Oxford RHA, 1963–92. Mem., GDC, 1993–95. Chm., Central Cttee for Hosp. Dental Services, 1979–86; Mem., Jt Consultants Cttee, 1979–86 and 1992–95. Royal College of Surgeons: Mem. Bd, Fac. of Dental Surgery, 1981–95; Vice-Dean, 1989; Colyer Gold Medal, 1999; British Dental Association: Mem. Council, 1979–87; Pres., Berks, Bucks and Oxon Br., 1978; Pres., Hosp. Gp, 1979; Pres., BAOMS, 1985. UK Rep., EC Dental Liaison Cttee, 1981–89; UK Rep., EC Adv. Cttee on Trng of Dental Practitioners, 1981–92. Hon. Fellow, BDA, 1990; Hon. FDSRCSE 1997; Hon. FDSRCPSGlas 1998. *Publications:* articles in learned jls and contrib. to textbooks on oral and maxillofacial surgery, local analgesia and health service planning. *Recreations:* fell-walking, natural history, English inns. *Address:* Jacobs Spinney, Rag Hill, Aldermaston, Berks RG7 4NS. *T:* (0118) 971 2550. *Club:* Royal Society of Medicine.

RAY, Hon. Robert (Francis); Chairman, Australian Political Exchange Council, 2009–13; Senator for Victoria, 1981–2008; *b* Melbourne, 8 April 1947; *m* (Victoria) Jane Petheram. *Educ:* Monash Univ.; Rusden State Coll. Former technical sch. teacher. Australian Labor Party: Mem., 1966–; Deleg., Vic. State Conf., 1970–96; Mem., Nat. Exec., 1983–98; Minister for Home Affairs and Dep. Manager of Govt Business in the Senate, 1987; Minister assisting the Minister for Transport and Communications, 1988; Minister for Immigration, Local Govt and Ethnic Affairs, 1988–90; Manager of Govt Business in the Senate, 1988–91; Minister for Defence, 1990–96; Dep. Leader of Govt in Senate, 1993–96. Chm., Victorian Managed Insurance Authy, 2010–11. Mem. Council, Australian Strategic Policy Inst., 2010.

RAY, Vincent Edward; journalist, since 1987; writer, trainer; editorial adviser to BBC Trust; *b* London, 2 June 1957; *s* of Victor and Peggy Ray; partner, Sara Lee; two *s* one *d*. *Educ:* Wallington Co. Grammar Sch.; Bristol Coll. of Art (BA Hons Ceramics 1978); City of London Poly. (MA Politics 1987). Dir, Lincoln Hannah Ltd, 1981–87; BBC: Ceefax, 1987–88; producer, Nine O'Clock News, 1988–90; Foreign Field producer, 1990–93; Foreign Ed., 1993–96; World News Ed., 1996–99; Exec. Ed., News, 1999–2002; Dep. Hd, Newsgathering, 2002–05; Dir, BBC Coll. of Journalism, 2005–10. Visiting Professor: New York Univ., 2003–06; Bournemouth Univ., 2010–. Trustee, Rory Peck Trust, 1997–2004. Mem., Flying Gazebo Walking Soc. Distinguished Media Leadership Award, Dart Centre, 2004. *Publications:* The Reporter's Friend, 2002; The Television News Handbook, 2003. *Recreations:* walking in Greenwich Park, reading, art, storytelling, gadgets. *E:* vinray@me.com. *Club:* Frontline.

RAY, Rt Rev. William James; *see* Queensland, North, Bishop of.

RAYFIELD, Rt Rev. Lee Stephen; *see* Swindon, Bishop Suffragan of.

RAYLEIGH, 6th Baron *cr* 1821; **John Gerald Strutt;** Company Chairman, since 1988; *b* 4 June 1960; *s* of Hon. Charles Richard Strutt (*d* 1981) (2nd *s* of 4th Baron) and of Hon. Jean Elizabeth, *d* of 1st Viscount Davidson, GCVO, CH, CB, PC; *S* uncle, 1988; *m* 1991, Annabel Kate, *d* of late W. G. Patterson; four *s*. *Educ:* Eton College; Royal Agricultural College,

Cirencester. Welsh Guards, 1980–84. Chairman: Lord Rayleigh's Farms Ltd, 1988–; Eastern Data Gp Ltd, 2005–. MRI. *Recreations:* cricket, gardening, shooting, silviculture. *Heir:* s Hon. John Frederick Strutt, *b* 29 March 1993. *Clubs:* Brooks's, White's, MCC.

See also Baroness Jenkin of Kennington, Hon. B. C. Jenkin.

RAYMOND, Robert Jacques; director of banks and funds, retired 2014; *b* 30 June 1933; *s* of Henri Raymond and Andrée (*née* Aubrière); *m* 1970, Monique Brémond, MD. *Educ:* Sorbonne (Masters Econs 1955). With Bank of France, 1951–94: Audit Dept, 1958–66; Rep. in NY, 1966–67; Hd, Balance of Payments Div., 1969–73; Director: Internat. Affairs, 1973–75; Monetary Stats and Analysis, 1975–76; Dep. Sec. Gen., Conseil Nat. du Crédit, 1975–81; Dep. Hd, 1976–82, Dir Gen., 1982–90, Res. Dept; Dir Gen., Credit Dept, 1990–94; Dir Gen., European Monetary Inst., 1994–98; Perm. Rep. of European Central Bank to IMF, Washington, 1999; Chm. and CEO, Banque CPR-Paris, 1999–2001. Mem. Bd, various public financial instns in Paris, 1981–94. Chm., monetary experts, Cttee of Govs of EEC, 1981–91. Officier de la Légion d'Honneur (France), 1996 (Chevalier, 1984); Officier, Ordre national du Mérite (France), 1988. *Publications:* La Monnaie, 1976; (jtly) Les relations économiques et monétaires internationales, 1982, 3rd edn 1986; Les institutions monétaires en France, 1991, 2nd edn 1996; L'unification monétaire en Europe, 1993, 2nd edn 1996; L'Euro et l'unité de l'Europe, 2001. *Address:* 5 rue de Beaujolais, 75001 Paris, France.

RAYNE, Hon. Robert (Anthony); Chairman, Derwent London plc, since 2007; *b* 30 Jan. 1949; *s* of Baron Rayne and late Margaret Marco; *m* 1974, Jane Blackburn (separated); one *s* one *d*. *Educ:* Malvern Coll.; New York Inst. of Finance. Dir, 1983–2001, CEO, 2001–07, London Merchant Securities plc; CEO, 2007–10, Chm., 2010–11, LMS (formerly Leo) Capital plc (Dir, 2006–); Director: First Leisure Corp. plc, 1983–2000; Westpool Investment Trust plc, 1984–; Weatherford Internat. Inc. (US), 1987–; First Call Gp plc, 1996–98; Crown Sports plc, 2001–03; Chairman: Golden Rose Communications plc, 1991–99; London Jazz Radio, 1991–99. Trustee: Rayne Foundn, 1977– (Chm., 2004–); The Place To Be, 1993–; Royal Nat. Theatre Foundn, 2005–; Imperial Coll. Fund, 2007–. MInstD. *Recreations:* art, theatre, music. *Address:* LMS Capital plc, 100 George Street, W1U 8NU. *E:* rrayne@lmscapital.com.

RAYNER, Angela; MP (Lab) Ashton-under-Lyne, since 2015; *b* Stockport, 28 March 1980; *d* of Martyn and Lynne Bowen; one *s*; *m* 2010, Mark Rayner; two *s*. *Educ:* Bridgehall Primary Sch.; Avondale High Sch.; Stockport Coll. (British Sign Lang., Care, Counselling). Home help, private sector and local govt, 1998–2005. Trade union lay activist, 2002–15. Samaritan, 1997–2000. *Address:* House of Commons, SW1A 0AA. *T:* (020) 7219 8782. *E:* angela.rayner.mp@parliament.uk.

RAYNER, David Edward, CBE 1992; FCILT; Director, South East Trains Ltd, 2003–06; *b* 26 Jan. 1940; *s* of Marjory and Gilbert Rayner; *m* 1966, Enid Cutty; two *d*. *Educ:* St Peter's School, York; Durham University (BSc Hons). Joined British Railways, 1963; Passenger Marketing Manager, BR Board, 1982; Dep. Gen. Manager, BR, London Midland Region, 1984–86; Gen. Manager, BR, Eastern Region, 1986–87; British Railways Board: Mem., 1987–94; Jt Man. Dir, 1987–89; Man. Dir, Engrg and Operations, 1989–92; Man. Dir, Safety and Operations, 1992–94; Bd Mem., Railtrack Gp, 1994–97; Dir Safety and Standards, Railtrack, 1994–97. Non-executive Chairman: Rail Investments Ltd, 1998–99; Oakburn Properties plc, 1998–2004; non-executive Director: Coll. of Railway Technol., subseq. Catalis Rail Trng, Ltd, 1998–2003 (Chm., 1998–2002); Connex Transport UK (formerly Connex Rail) Ltd, 1998–2003. Chm., Rail Industry Training Council, 1992–95. Vis. Prof., UCL, 1998–2008. Trustee: Science Mus., 1997–2006; York and N Yorks Community Foundn, 2000–07; York Museums (formerly York Museums and Gall.) Trust, 2002–07; York Glaziers Trust, 2004–; St Peter's Foundn, 2005–10. Gov., York Co. of Merchant Adventurers, 2012–13. Hon. Col, Railway Sqn, RLC (TA), 1992–99. *Recreation:* collector.

RAYNER, Jay; freelance writer, journalist and broadcaster; *b* 14 Sept. 1966; *s* of late Desmond Rayner and Claire Berenice Rayner, OBE; *m* 1992, Pat Gordon Smith; two *s*. *Educ:* Leeds Univ. (BA Hons Pol Studies 1987). Editor, Leeds Student newspaper, 1987–88; freelance journalist, The Observer, The Guardian, Independent on Sunday, Cosmopolitan and others, 1988–92; Feature Writer: The Guardian, 1992–93; Mail on Sunday, 1993–96; The Observer, 1996–, Restaurant Critic, 1999–. Presenter, BBC Radio: Stop Press, 1995–97; Papertalk, 1997–99 (Magazine Prog. of the Year, Sony Radio Awards, 1999); The Food Quiz, 2003–06; The Kitchen Cabinet, 2012–; contributor: Masterchef, 2006–, The One Show, 2009–, BBC TV; Top Chef Masters, US TV, 2009–. Young Journalist of the Year, 1991, Critic of the Year, 2006, British Press Awards; Restaurant Critic of the Year, Glenfiddich Food and Drink Awards, 2001; Derek Cooper Award for Campaigning and Investigative Food Writing, Guild of Food Writers, 2013. *Publications:* Star Dust Falling, 2002; The Man Who Ate the World, 2008; A Greedy Man in a Hungry World, 2013; My Dining Hell: twenty ways to have a lousy night out, 2015; *novels:* The Marble Kiss, 1994; Day of Atonement, 1998; The Apologist, 2004; The Oyster House Siege, 2007; contrib. to Arena, Esquire, Gourmet, Food and Wine. *Recreations:* lousy jazz pianist, cooking, my kids. *Address:* c/o Curtis Brown Group Ltd, Haymarket House, 28–29 Haymarket, SW1Y 4SP. *T:* (020) 7393 4400, *Fax:* (020) 7393 4401. *E:* jay.rayner@observer.co.uk.

RAYNER, Rt Rev. Keith, AO 1987; Archbishop of Melbourne and Metropolitan of the Province of Victoria, 1990–99; Primate of Australia, 1991–99 (Acting Primate, 1989–91); *b* 22 Nov. 1929; *s* of Sidney and Gladys Rayner, Brisbane; *m* 1963, Audrey Fletcher (*d* 2011); one *s* two *d*. *Educ:* C of E Grammar Sch., Brisbane; Univ. of Queensland (BA 1951; PhD 1964). Deacon, 1953; Priest, 1953. Chaplain, St Francis' Theol Coll., Brisbane, 1954; Mem., Brotherhood of St John, Dalby, 1955–58; Vice-Warden, St John's Coll., Brisbane, 1958; Rotary Foundn Fellow, Harvard Univ., 1958–59; Vicar, St Barnabas', Sunnybank, 1959–63; Rector, St Peter's, Wynnum, 1963–69; Bishop of Wangaratta, 1969–75; Archbishop of Adelaide and Metropolitan of South Australia, 1975–90. Pres., Christian Conference of Asia, 1977–81; Chm., International Anglican Theological and Doctrinal Commission, 1980–88. Hon. ThD Aust. Coll. of Theology, 1987; DUniv Griffith, 2001. *Address:* 36 Highfield Avenue, St Georges, SA 5064, Australia.

RAYNER, Miranda; *see* Hughes, Miranda.

RAYNER, Prof. Peter John Wynn, PhD; Professor of Signal Processing, University of Cambridge, 1998–2002, now Emeritus; Fellow, Christ's College, Cambridge, 1969–2002, now Emeritus; *b* 22 July 1941; *s* of John Austin Rayner and Amelia Victoria Rayner; *m* 1960, Patricia Ann Gray; two *d*. *Educ:* Univ. of Aston (PhD 1968); MA Cantab 1969. Student apprentice, Pye TVT Ltd, 1957–62; Sen. Engr, Cambridge Consultants, 1962–65; Res. Student, Univ. of Aston, 1965–68; Cambridge University: Lectr, Dept of Engrg, 1968–90; Dir, Studies in Engrg, Christ's Coll., 1971–99; Reader in Inf. Engrg, 1990–98. Dir, Cedar Audio Ltd, 1989–; Advr to Bd, Autonomy Corp., 2000–. *Publications:* (with S. J. Godsill) Digital Audio Restoration, 1998; book chapters; numerous contribs to learned jls. *Recreations:* scuba-diving, flamenco and blues guitar, gardening, cycling. *Address:* 69 High Street, Oakington, Cambs CB24 3AG. *T:* (01223) 234203.

RAYNER, Samuel Alan Miles; Managing Director, Lakeland Ltd (formerly Lakeland Plastics Ltd), since 1974; *b* 31 May 1953; *s* of Alan and Dorothy Rayner; *m* 1978, Judy McIlvenny; two *s* one *d*. High Sheriff, Cumbria, 2015–16. *Address:* Lakeland Ltd, Alexandra Buildings, Windermere LA23 1BQ.

RAYNER, Prof. Steve, PhD; James Martin Professor of Science and Civilization and Director, Institute for Science, Innovation and Society (formerly James Martin Institute for Science and Civilization), University of Oxford, since 2003; Fellow, Keble College, Oxford, since 2003; *b* 22 May 1953; *s* of Harry Rayner and Esmé Rayner; *m* 1994, Heather Katz; one *d*. *Educ:* Univ. of Kent (BA Philos. and Theol. 1974); University Coll. London (PhD Anthropol. 1979). Res. Associate, Russell Sage Foundn, 1980–81; Vis. Schol., Boston Univ. Sch. of Public Health, 1982; Sen. Res. Staff, Oak Ridge Nat. Lab., 1983–91; Chief Scientist, Pacific Northwest Nat. Lab., 1991–99; Prof. of Envmt and Public Affairs, Columbia Univ., 1999–2003. Adjunct Asst Prof., Univ. of Tennessee, 1986; Vis. Associate Prof., Cornell Univ., 1990; Adjunct Associate Prof., Virginia Polytech., 1997–98; Hon. Prof. of Climate Change and Society, Univ. of Copenhagen, 2008–13; ANZSOG Goyder Vis. Prof. in Public Sector Policy and Mgt, Flinders Univ., 2013–14. Dir, ESRC Sci. in Society Prog., 2002–08. Member: Intergovtl Panel on Climate Change, 1999–2007; Royal Commn on Envmtl Pollution, 2003–09; Adv. Bd, UK Climate Impacts Prog., 2004–11; Wkg Gp on Geoengrg the Climate, Royal Soc., 2009. Mem., Lead Expert Gp, UK Foresight Prog. on Future of Cities, 2013–. Mem., Bd of Dirs, Foundn for Law, Justice and Soc., 2006–12. Sen. Fellow, Breakthrough Inst., 2010–. *Publications:* (with Jonathan Gross) Measuring Culture, 1985; (with James Flanagan) Rules, Decisions and Inequality, 1988; (with Robin Cantor and Stuart Henry) Making Markets, 1992; (with Elizabeth Malone) Human Choice and Climate Change, 4 vols, 1998; (with Peter Healey) Unnatural Selection, 2009; (with Mark Caine) The Hartwell Approach to Climate Policy, 2015; articles in Climatic Change, Global Envmtl Change, Ecol Econs, Energy Policy, Sci. and Public Policy, Science, Nature, Govt and Opposition, Social Studies of Sci., Risk Analysis, Evaluation Review, Econ. and Political Wkly, Industry and Higher Educn. *Recreations:* gardening, narrowboating. *Address:* Institute for Science, Innovation and Society, University of Oxford, 64 Banbury Road, Oxford OX1 6PN. *T:* (01865) 288938. *E:* steve.rayner@insis.ox.ac.uk.

RAYNER JAMES, Jonathan Elwyn; *see* James, Jonathan E. R.

RAYNES, Prof. (Edward) Peter, FRS 1987; Professor of Optoelectronic Engineering, University of Oxford, 1998–2010, now Emeritus; Fellow of St Cross College, Oxford, 1998–2010, now Emeritus; Honorary Visiting Professor, Department of Chemistry, University of York, since 2011 (Leverhulme Emeritus Fellow, 2010–12); *b* 4 July 1945; *s* of Edward Gordon and Ethel Mary Raynes; *m* 1970, Madeline Ord; two *s*. *Educ:* St Peter's School, York; Gonville and Caius College, Cambridge (MA, PhD). CPhys, FInstP. Royal Signals and Radar Establishment, 1971–92: SPSO, 1981; DCSO, 1988–92; Chief Scientist, 1992–95, Dir of Res., 1995–98, Sharp Labs of Europe Ltd, Oxford. Hon. DSc Hull, 2012. Rank Prize for Opto-electronics, 1980; Paterson Medal, Inst. of Physics, 1986; Special Recognition Award, 1987, Jan Rajchman Prize, 2009, Soc. for Information Display. *Publications:* (ed jtly) Liquid Crystals: their physics, chemistry and applications, 1983; (ed jtly) Handbook of Visual Display Technology, 2012; (ed jtly) Handbook of Liquid Crystals, 2014; numerous scientific papers and patents. *Recreations:* choral singing, hill walking. *Address:* Department of Chemistry, University of York, York YO24 5DD. *T:* (01904) 322527.

RAYNHAM, Viscount; Thomas Charles Townshend; *b* 2 Nov. 1977; *s* and *heir* of Marquess Townshend, *qv*; *m* 2011, Octavia Legge; one *s*. *Educ:* Oundle; RAC Cirencester (BSc Estate Mgt 2000). Chartered Surveyor. Land Agent, Bidwells, Cambridge, 2002–06; Hd of Agricultural Investment, Knight Frank, 2006–.

RAYNOR, Andrew Paul; entrepreneur; Chief Executive, Shakespeares Legal LLP, since 2015; *b* 24 May 1957; *s* of Laurence Edwin Raynor and Pamela Sylvia Raynor (*née* Skelton); *m* 1980, Karen Jane Robertson; three *d*. *Educ:* Leicester Polytech. (BA Hons Business Studies). FCA 1981. Partner, Stoy Hayward East Midlands, 1986; BDO Stoy Hayward East Midlands: Hd, Corporate Finance, 1994–97; Hd, Business Develt, 1997–2000; Managing Partner, 2000–01; Finance Dir, Tenon Group plc, 2002–03; Chief Exec., Tenon Gp, later RSM Tenon Gp plc, 2003–12; Chief Client Officer, Shakespeares Legal LLP, 2013–15. *Publications:* various articles in financial related jls. *Recreations:* running, travel, old and new motorcycles. *E:* andypraynor@gmail.com.

RAYNOR, Keith Hugh; His Honour Judge Keith Raynor; a Circuit Judge, since 2015; Diversity and Community Relations Judge, since 2015; *b* Nairobi, Kenya, 3 May 1964; *s* of Regtl Sgt Major Granville Vincent Raynor, Royal Norfolk Regt and Audrey Kathleen Raynor (*née* Ward); *m* 1994, Joanna Carolyn Truman; two *s*. *Educ:* Duke of York's Royal Mil. Sch.; Trent Poly. (LLB Hons). Admitted Solicitor, 1990; Asst Solicitor, Lovell White Durrant, 1990–91; Army Officer, Army Legal Services, 1991–94; called to the Bar, Lincoln's Inn, 1995; Sen. Associate, Clayton Utz, Perth, WA, 1995–96; in practice as solicitor advocate, 1996–2004, as barrister, 2004–15; a Recorder, 2005–15; UN Prosecutor: Extraordinary Chambers in Courts of Cambodia (Khmer Rouge Tribunal), 2012–14; Iraq Historic Allegations Prosecutions Team, 2014–15; Deployable Civilian Expert, Stabilisation Unit, 2012–. *Recreations:* adventurous travelling with my family, veterans' Rugby, open water swimming, Hindustan Ambassador cars. *Address:* Woolwich Crown Court, 2 Belmarsh Road, Thamesmead, SE28 0EY. *Clubs:* Victory Services; Derby Rugby Football.

RAYNOR, Philip Ronald; QC 1994; **His Honour Judge Raynor;** a Circuit Judge, since 2001; Specialist Circuit Judge, Technology and Construction Court, Manchester, since 2006; *b* 20 Jan. 1950; *s* of Wilfred and Sheila Raynor; *m* 1974, Judith Braunsberg; one *s* one *d*. *Educ:* Roundhay Sch., Leeds; Christ's Coll., Cambridge (Schol., MA). Lectr in Law, Univ. of Manchester, 1971–74; called to the Bar, Inner Temple, 1973; in practice, 1973–2001; a Recorder, 1993–2001; Head of Chambers, 40 King Street, Manchester, 1996–2001. *Recreations:* travel, opera, dining out. *Address:* Manchester Civil Justice Centre, 1 Bridge Street West, Manchester M60 9DJ.

RAYNSFORD, Rt Hon. Wyvill Richard Nicolls, (Rt Hon. Nick); PC 2001; *b* 28 Jan. 1945; *s* of Wyvill Raynsford and Patricia Raynsford (*née* Dunn); *m* 1st, 1968, Anne Raynsford (*née* Jelley) (marr. diss. 2011); three *d*; 2nd, 2012, Alison Jane Seabeck, *qv*. *Educ:* Repton Sch.; Sidney Sussex Coll., Cambridge (MA); Chelsea Sch. of Art (DipAD). Market research, A. C. Nielsen Co. Ltd, 1966–68; Gen. Sec., Soc. for Co-operative Dwellings, 1972–73; SHAC: Emergency Officer, 1973–74; Research Officer, 1974–76; Dir, 1976–86; Partner, 1987–90, Dir, 1990–92, Raynsford and Morris, housing consultants; Dir, Raynsford Dallison Associates, housing consultants, 1992–93; Consultant, HACAS, 1993–97. Councillor (Lab) London Borough of Hammersmith & Fulham, 1971–75 (Chm., Leisure and Recreation Cttee, 1972–74). MP (Lab) Fulham, April 1986–1987; contested (Lab) same seat, 1987; MP (Lab) Greenwich, 1992–97, Greenwich and Woolwich, 1997–2015. Opposition front bench spokesman on London, 1993–97, on housing, 1994–97; Parly Under-Sec. of State, DoE and Dept of Transport, subseq. DETR, 1997–99; Minister of State: DETR, 1999–2001; DTLR, 2001–02; ODPM, 2002–05. Mem., Envmt Select Cttee, 1992–93. Chairman: NHBC Foundn, 2006–; Triathlon Homes, 2010–; Hon. Vice Chm., Construction Industry Council, 2010– (Chm., 2006–08). President: Nat. Home Improvement Council, 2008–; Constructionarium, 2008–. Hon. FICE 2005; Hon. FRTPI 2006; Hon. FRIBA 2007; Hon. MRICS 2008; Hon. MCIH 2009. *Publications:* A Guide to Housing Benefit, 1982, 7th edn 1986. *Recreation:* photography.

RAZ, Prof. Joseph, FBA 1987; Professor of the Philosophy of Law, 1985–2006, Research Professor in the Philosophy of Law, 2006–09, University of Oxford; Fellow of Balliol College, Oxford, 1985–2006, now Emeritus; Professor, Columbia Law School, New York, since 2002; Research Professor (part-time), King's College London, since 2011; *b* 21 March 1939. *Educ:* Hebrew University, Jerusalem (MJur 1963); University Coll., Oxford (DPhil 1967). Lectr,

Hebrew Univ., Jerusalem, 1967–70; Research Fellow, Nuffield Coll., Oxford, 1970–72; Tutorial Fellow, Balliol Coll., Oxford, 1972–85. Vis. Prof., Columbia Law Sch., NY, 1995–2002. For. Hon. Mem., Amer. Acad. of Arts and Scis, 1992. Hon. Dr: Catholic Univ., Brussels, 1993; Hebrew Univ., Jerusalem, 2014; Hon. PhD, KCL, 2008. *Publications:* The Concept of a Legal System, 1970, 2nd edn 1980; Practical Reason and Norms, 1975, 2nd edn 1990; The Authority of Law, 1979; The Morality of Freedom, 1986; Ethics in the Public Domain, 1994, rev. edn 1995; Engaging Reason, 2000; Value, Respect and Attachment, 2001; The Practice of Value, 2003; Between Authority and Interpretation, 2009; From Normativity to Responsibility, 2011. *Address:* Columbia Law School, 435 W 110 Street, New York, NY 10027, USA.

RAZZALL, family name of **Baron Razzall**.

RAZZALL, Baron *cr* 1997 (Life Peer), of Mortlake in the London Borough of Richmond; **Edward Timothy Razzall,** CBE 1993; Partner, Argonaut Associates, since 1996; *b* 12 June 1943; *s* of late Leonard Humphrey and Muriel Razzall; *m* 1st, 1965, Elizabeth Christina Wilkinson (marr. diss. 1974); one *s* one *d*; 2nd, 1982, Deirdre Bourke Martineau (*née* Taylor Smith) (marr. diss. 2003). *Educ:* St Paul's Sch.; Worcester Coll., Oxford (Open Schol.; BA). Teaching Associate, Northwestern Univ., Chicago, 1965–66; with Frere Cholmeley Bischoff, solicitors, 1966–96 (Partner, 1973–96). Councillor (L), Mortlake Ward, London Borough of Richmond, 1974–98; Dep. Leader, Richmond Council, 1983–97. Treasurer: Liberal Party, 1986–87; Liberal Democrats, 1987–2000; Chm., Lib Dem Campaign Cttee, 2000–06; Lib Dem spokesman on trade and industry, H of L, 1998–2014; Lib Dem Treasury spokesman, H of L, 2014–. Pres., Assoc. of Lib Dem Councillors, 1990–95. European Lawyer of Year, Inst. of Lawyers in Europe, 1992. *Publications:* Chance Encounters: tales from a varied life, 2014. *Recreation:* all sports. *Address:* Spring Cottage, Swallowcliffe, Salisbury, Wilts SP3 5PA. *Clubs:* National Liberal, Soho House, MCC.

REA, family name of **Baron Rea**.

REA, 3rd Baron *cr* 1937, of Eskdale; **John Nicolas Rea,** MD; Bt 1935; General Medical Practitioner, Kentish Town, NW5, 1957–62 and 1968–93; *b* 6 June 1928; *s* of Hon. James Russell Rea (*d* 1954) (2nd *s* of 1st Baron) and Betty Marion (*d* 1965), *d* of Arthur Bevan, MD; *S* uncle, 1981; *m* 1st, 1951, Elizabeth Anne (marr. diss. 1991), *d* of late William Hensman Robinson; four *s* two *d*; 2nd, 1991, Judith Mary, *d* of late Norman Powell. *Educ:* Dartington Hall School; Belmont Hill School, Mass, USA; Dauntsey's School; Christ's Coll., Cambridge Univ.; UCH Medical School. MA, MD (Cantab); FRCGP; DPH, DCH, DObstRCOG. Research Fellow in Paediatrics, Lagos, Nigeria, 1962–65; Lecturer in Social Medicine, St Thomas's Hosp. Medical School, 1966–68. Trustee, 1985–2015, Pres., 2015–, UK Health Forum (formerly Nat. Forum for Prevention of Coronary Heart Disease, then Nat. Heart Forum); Chm., Parly Food & Health Forum, 1997–2014. Opposition spokesman on health, develt and co-operation, H of L, 1992–97; elected Mem., H of L, 1999. FRSocMed (Pres., Section of Gen. Practice, 1985–86). *Publications:* Interactions of Infection and Nutrition (MD Thesis, Cambridge Univ.), 1969; (jtly) Learning Teaching—an evaluation of a course for GP Teachers, 1980; articles on epidemiology and medical education in various journals. *Recreations:* music (bassoon), gardening. *Heir:* *s* Hon. Matthew James Rea, *b* 28 March 1956. *Address:* 1–2 Littledene Cottages, Glynde, E Sussex BN8 6LA. *T:* (weekdays) (020) 7607 0546.

REA, Christopher William Wallace; Broadcast Consultant, International Rugby Board, since 2014 (Controller, Broadcast Productions (formerly Head of Communications), 2000–14); *b* 22 Oct. 1943; *s* of Col William Wallace Rea and Helen Rea; *m* 1974, Daphne Theresa Manning; one *d*. *Educ:* High Sch. of Dundee; Univ. of St Andrews (MA). With BBC Radio Sports Dept, 1972–81; Rugby and Golf Corresp., Scotsman, 1981–84; Publisher and Ed., Rugby News Mag., 1984–88; Presenter, BBV TV Rugby Special, 1988–94; Asst Sec., then Head, Marketing and Public Affairs, MCC, 1995–2000. Rugby Corresp., Independent on Sunday, 1990–2000. Played Rugby Union for Scotland, 1968–71 (13 Caps); Mem., British Lions tour to NZ, 1971; played for Barbarians, 1971. *Publications:* Illustrated History of Rugby Union, 1977; Injured Pride, 1980; Scotland's Grand Slam, 1984. *Recreations:* golf, hill walking. *Address:* Artifex Media, Unit B2, Coxbridge Business Park, Farnham, Surrey GU10 5EH. *Clubs:* Royal and Ancient (St Andrews), Huntercombe Golf.

REA, Prof. Sir Desmond, Kt 2005; OBE 1996; PhD; non-executive Chairman, NIJobs.com, 2010–14; non-executive Director, Security Industry Authority, since 2013; *b* 4 March 1937; *s* of Samuel and Annie Rea; *m* 1969, Dr Irene Maeve Williamson; four *d*. *Educ:* Queen's Univ., Belfast (BSc Econs, MSc Econs; PhD); Univ. of Calif, Berkeley (MBA). Queen's University, Belfast: Lectr, then Sen. Lectr, in Business Admin, 1969–75; Asst Dean, Faculty of Econs and Social Scis, 1973–75; Hd of Dept and Prof. of Human Resource Mgt, Ulster Polytech., subseq. Univ. of Ulster, 1975–95, now Prof. Emeritus. Chairman (part-time): NI Schs Exams Council, 1987–90; NI Schs Exams and Assessment Council, 1990–94; NI Council for Curriculum, Exams and Assessment, 1994–98; NI Local Govt Staff Commn, 1989–96; NI Lab. Relns Agency, 1996–2002; Chm., 2001–09, Ind. Mem., 2001–11, NI Policing Bd. Sec., Jt Ind. Gp for Study and Action, 1980–2004. Mem. Bd, Anglo-Irish Encounter, 1983–2004. Chm., Ulster Orchestra Soc. Ltd, 2008–12. Chm., Bd of Govs, Methodist Coll., Belfast, 2000–04; non-exec. Chm., Stranmillis Univ. Coll., QUB, 2013–. Ed., Quarterly Economic Outlook and Business Review, First Trust Bank, 1984–2010. Hon. LLD Ulster, 2010. *Publications:* (ed) Political Co-operation in Divided Societies: a series of papers relevant to the conflict in Northern Ireland, 1981; (with Robin Mansfield) Policing in Northern Ireland: delivering the new beginning, 2014. *Recreations:* reading, classical music, Rugby. *Address:* c/o Stranmillis University College, Queen's University Belfast, Stranmillis Road, Belfast BT9 5DY.

REA, Rev. Ernest; freelance broadcaster and writer; Head of Religious Broadcasting, BBC, 1989–2001; *b* 6 Sept. 1945; *s* of Ernest Rea and Mary Wylie (*née* Blue); *m* 1st, 1973, Kay (*née* Kilpatrick) (marr. diss 1994); two *s*; 2nd, 1995, Gaynor (*née* Vaughan Jones). *Educ:* Methodist Coll., Belfast; Queen's Univ., Belfast; Union Theological Coll., Belfast. Asst Minister, Woodvale Park Presb. Ch, Belfast, 1971–74; Minister, Bannside Presb. Ch, Banbridge, Co. Down, 1974–79; Religious Broadcasting Producer, BBC Belfast, 1979–84; Sen. Religious Broadcasting Producer, BBC S and W, 1984–88; Editor, Network Radio, BBC S and W, 1988–89; Hd of Religious Progs, BBC Radio, 1989–93. Presenter, Beyond Belief, BBC Radio 4, 2001–. *Recreations:* reading, watching cricket, playing golf, theatre, music. *Address:* The Coach House, Beechfield Road, Alderley Edge, Cheshire SK9 7AU.

REA, Dr John Rowland, FBA 1981; Lecturer in Documentary Papyrology, University of Oxford, 1965–96; Senior Research Fellow, Balliol College, Oxford, 1969–96, now Emeritus Fellow; *b* 28 Oct. 1933; *s* of Thomas Arthur Rea and Elsie Rea (*née* Ward); *m* 1959, Mary Ogden. *Educ:* Methodist Coll., Belfast; Queen's Univ., Belfast (BA); University Coll. London (PhD). Asst Keeper, Public Record Office, 1957–61; Res. Lectr, Christ Church, Oxford, 1961–65. *Publications:* The Oxyrhynchus Papyri, Vol. XL, 1972, Vol. XLVI, 1978, Vol. LI, 1984, Vol LV, 1988, Vol. LVIII, 1991, LXIII, 1996, also contribs to Vols XXVII, XXXI, XXXIII, XXXIV, XXXVI, XLI, XLIII, XLIX, L, LXII, LXIV; (with P. J. Sijpesteijn) Corpus Papyrorum Raineri V, 1976; articles in classical jls. *Address:* Aurolaine, 1 Shirley Drive, St Leonards-on-Sea, East Sussex TN37 7JW.

REA, Rupert Lascelles P.; *see* Pennant-Rea.

REA, Stephen James; actor and director; *b* Belfast, 31 Oct. 1949; *s* of James Rea and Jane Rea (*née* Logue); *m* 1983, Dolours Price (marr. diss.; she *d* 2013); two *s*. *Educ:* Queen's Univ., Belfast. Trained at Abbey Theatre Sch., Dublin. Jt Founder, Field Day Theatre Co., 1980. *Theatre includes:* The Shadow of a Gunman; The Cherry Orchard; Miss Julie; High Society; Endgame; The Freedom of the City; Translations; The Communication Cord; Saint Oscar; Boesman and Lena; Hightime and Riot Act; Double Cross; Pentecost; Making History; Someone Who'll Watch Over Me; Uncle Vanya; Ashes to Ashes; Playboy of the Western World; Comedians; The Shaughraun; Cyrano de Bergerac, 2004; Kicking a Dead Horse, 2008; Ballyturk, 2014; *director:* Three Sisters; The Cure at Troy; Northern Star. *Films include:* Angel, Loose Connections, 1983; Company of Wolves, 1984; The Doctor and the Devils, 1986; Life is Sweet, 1991; The Crying Game, 1992; Bad Behaviour, 1993; Princess Caraboo, Angie, Interview with the Vampire, 1994; Prêt-à-Porter, Between the Devil and the Deep Blue Sea, 1995; All Men are Mortal, Michael Collins, 1996; Trojan Eddie, A Further Gesture, 1997; The Butcher Boy, Still Crazy, 1998; In Dreams, The Life Before This, Guinevere, 1999; The End of the Affair, I Could Read the Sky, 2000; Evelyn, 2003; Bloom, Breakfast at Pluto, V for Vendetta, 2006; River Queen, 2008; Stuck, Nothing Personal, 2009; Ondine, The Heavy, 2010; Blackthorn, Stella Days, Underworld: Awakening, 2012. *Television includes:* Four Days in July, 1984; The Kidnapper in Shergar, 1986; Hedda Gabler, 1993; The Shadow of a Gunman, 1995; Citizen X, 1995; Crime of the Century, 1996; Father & Son, 2010; The Shadow Line, 2011; Utopia, 2013; The Honourable Woman, 2014 (BAFTA Award for Best Supporting Actor, 2015). *Address:* c/o Independent Talent Group Ltd, 40 Whitfield Street, W1T 2RH.

REA PRICE, (William) John, OBE 1991; Director, National Children's Bureau, 1991–98; *b* 15 March 1937; *s* of late John Caxton Rea Price and of Mary Hilda Rea Price. *Educ:* University College Sch.; Corpus Christi Coll., Cambridge (MA); LSE (DSA; Cert. Applied Social Studies). London Probation Service, 1962–65; London Borough of Islington Children's Dept, 1965–68; Nat. Inst. for Social Work, 1968–69; Home Office, Community Develt Project, 1969–72; Dir of Social Services, London Borough of Islington, 1972–90. Lead Inspector, Children and Young People, HM Inspectorate of Prisons, 1999–2005. Pres., Assoc. of Dirs of Social Services, 1989–90. *Recreations:* cycling, archaeology, history of landscape. *E:* John.Reaprice@btinternet.com.

READ, Catherine Emma; *see* Ostler, C. E.

READ, Sir David (John), Kt 2007; PhD; FRS 1990; Professor of Plant Sciences, Sheffield University, 1990–2004, now Emeritus; *b* 20 Jan. 1939; *s* of O. Read; *m* (marr. diss.); one *s*. *Educ:* Sexey's Sch., Bruton, Som; Hull Univ. (BSc 1960; PhD 1963). Sheffield University: Jun. Res. Fellow, 1963–66; Asst Lectr, 1966–69; Lectr, 1969–79; Sen. Lectr, 1979–81; Reader in Plant Sci., 1981–90. Chairman: Bd of Dirs, Rothamsted Research, 2003–09; Res. Adv. Bd, Forestry Commn, 2004. Vice-Pres. and Biol Sec., Royal Soc., 2003–08. Mem. Bd Govs, Macaulay Land Res. Inst., 2003. *Publications:* editor of numerous books and author of papers in learned jls mostly on subject of symbiosis, specifically the mycorrhizal symbiosis between plant roots and fungi. *Recreations:* walking, botany. *Address:* Minestone Cottage, Youlgrave, Bakewell, Derbys DE45 1WD. *T:* (01629) 636360.

READ, Emma Rosemary; Founder and Managing Director, Emporium Productions, since 2015; *b* London, 1962; *d* of Anthony Read and Rosemary Elizabeth Read; *m* 2001, Robert Blagden; two *s*. *Educ:* Girton Coll., Cambridge (BA Natural Scis 1983). TV producer, BBC TV and freelance, 1983–98, series incl. Video Diaries; Hd, UK Documentaries, Mosaic Films, 1998–2000; Commissioning Editor: UK and EMEA, Discovery Communications, 2000–05; Factual and Features, BSkyB, 2005–10; Creative Dir, 2010, Hd, 2010–15, Factual and Features, ITN Prodns. Dir, Bd, Internat. Documentary Fest., Sheffield, 2004–13; Mem., Adv. Cttee, Guardian Edinburgh Internat. Television Fest., 2015. Member: Faraday and Kohn Awards Cttee, Royal Soc., 2008–14; Winton Book Prize Jury, Royal Soc., 2015. Mem., BAFTA. *Recreations:* cinema, theatre, reading, writing, walking, restoring derelict French houses. *Address:* Emporium Productions, 33 Oval Road, NW1 7EA. *T:* (020) 7184 7777. *E:* emmar@emporiumproductions.co.uk.

READ, Prof. Frank Henry, FRS 1984; consultant engineer in charged particle optics, since 2002; Founder Director, CPO Ltd, since 2000; Professor Emeritus, University of Manchester (formerly Victoria University of Manchester), since 2002; *b* 6 Oct. 1934; *s* of late Frank Charles Read and Florence Louise (*née* Wright); *m* 1961, Anne Stuart (*née* Wallace); two *s* two *d*. *Educ:* Haberdashers' Aske's Hampstead Sch. (Foundn Scholar, 1946); Royal Coll. of Science, Univ. of London (Royal Scholar, 1952; ARCS 1955; BSc 1955). PhD 1959, DSc 1975, Victoria Univ. of Manchester. FInstP 1968; FIET (FIEE 1998); CEng; CPhys. University of Manchester: Lectr, 1959; Sen. Lectr, 1969; Reader, 1974; Prof. of Physics, 1975–98; Langworthy Prof. of Physics, 1998–2001; Res. Dean, Faculty of Sci., 1993–95; Res. Prof., 2001–02. Vis. Scientist: Univ. of Paris, 1974; Univ. of Colorado, 1974–75; Inst. for Atomic and Molecular Physics, Amsterdam, 1979–80. Consultant to industry, 1976–. Vice Pres., Inst. of Physics, 1985–89 (Chm., IOP Publishing Ltd, 1985–89); Member: Science Bd, SERC, 1987–90; Council, Royal Soc., 1987–89. Holweck Medal and Prize, Inst. of Physics and Soc. Française de Physique, 2000. Hon. Editor, Jl of Physics B, Atomic and Molecular Physics, 1980–84. *Publications:* (with E. Harting) Electrostatic Lenses, 1976; Electromagnetic Radiation, 1980; over 200 papers in physics and instrumentation jls. *Recreations:* stonemasonry, landscaping, riding. *Address:* Deakins Cottage, Orleton, Ludlow SY8 4HN.

READ, Graham Stephen; QC 2003; *b* 17 Sept. 1957; *s* of Peter Denis Read and Dorothy Ruby Read; *m* 1983, Frances Margaret Catherine Daley; two *d*. *Educ:* Queen Mary's, Basingstoke; Trinity Hall, Cambridge (MA). Called to the Bar, Gray's Inn, 1981 (Arden Schol. 1980; Holker Schol. 1981). *Publications:* contrib. to various legal pubns. *Recreations:* walking, Roman and 20th century European history, concerts. *Address:* Devereux Chambers, Queen Elizabeth Building, Temple, EC4Y 9BS. *T:* (020) 7353 7534, *Fax:* (020) 7353 1724.
See also M. P. Read.

READ, Harry; British Commissioner, Salvation Army, 1987–90; Editor, Words of Life, 1990–2000; *b* 17 May 1924; *s* of Robert and Florence Read; *m* 1950, Winifred Humphries (*d* 2007); one *s* one *d*. *Educ:* Sir William Worsley Sch., Grange Town, Middlesbrough. Served RCS, 1942–47 (6th Airborne Div., 1943–45). Commnd Salvation Army Officer, 1948; pastoral work, 1948–54; Lectr, Internat. Training Coll., 1954–62; pastoral work, 1962–64; Divl Youth Sec., 1964–66; Lectr, Internat. Training Coll., 1966–72; Dir, Information Services, 1972–75; Divl Comdr, 1975–78; Principal, Internat. Training Coll., 1978–81; Chief Sec., Canada Territory, 1981–84; Territorial Comdr, Australia Eastern Territory, 1984–87. *Publications:* No Heart More Tender, 2010; Heart-Talk, 2013. *Recreations:* writing, hymns, poetry. *Address:* Flat 1 Dean Park Grange, 15A Cavendish Road, Bournemouth, Dorset BH1 1QX. *T:* (01202) 381758.

READ, Imelda Mary, (Mel); Member (Lab) East Midlands Region, European Parliament, 1999–2004 (Leicester, 1989–94; Nottingham and Leicestershire North West, 1994–99); *b* Hillingdon, 8 Jan. 1939; *d* of Robert Alan Hocking and Teresa Mary Hocking; *m*; one *s* one *d*, and one step *s*. *Educ:* Bishopshalt Sch., Hillingdon, Middx; Nottingham Univ. (BA Hons 1977). Laboratory technician, Plessey, 1963–74; researcher, Trent Polytechnic, 1977–80; Lectr, Trent Polytechnic and other instns, 1980–84; Employment Officer, Nottingham Community Relations Council, 1984–89. European Parliament: Chair, British Labour Gp, 1990–92; Quaestor, 1992–94. Contested (Lab): Melton, 1979; Leicestershire NW, 1983.

Member: Nat Exec. Council, ASTMS, 1975; NEC, MSF; TUC Women's Adv. Cttee; Chair, Regl TUC Women's Cttee. Hon. Pres., European Cervical Cancer Assoc., 2003–09. *Publications:* (jtly) Against a Rising Tide, 1992. *Recreations:* beekeeping, gardening.

READ, Joanna; Principal, London Academy of Music and Dramatic Art, since 2010; *b* Stroud, 8 March 1968; *d* of Michael Read and April Read; *m* 1997, Nicolas Pitt; two *d*. *Educ:* Bristol Univ. (BA Hons Drama). Asst Dir, Young Vic, 1991–92; Educn Dir, Birmingham Repertory Th., 1993–97; Associate Dir, Bolton Octagon Th., 1997–99; Artistic Dir and Jt Chief Exec., Salisbury Playhouse, 1999–2007; freelance dir and writer, 2007–10. Chm., Guildford Shakespeare Co., 2011–14. Trustee, Regl Th. Young Dirs Scheme, 2013–. *Recreations:* writing pantomimes, running. *Address:* London Academy of Music and Dramatic Art, 155 Talgarth Road, W14 9DA. *T:* (020) 8834 0502. *E:* joanna.read@lamda.org.uk.

READ, Keith Frank, CBE 1997; CEng; FIET; FCGI; consultant; Chief Executive (formerly Director General), Institute of Marine Engineering, Science and Technology (formerly Institute of Marine Engineers), 1999–2009; *b* 25 April 1944; *s* of Alan George Read, OBE and Dorothy Maud Read (*née* Richardson); *m* 1966, Sheila Roberts; one *s* two *d*. *Educ:* King's Sch., Bruton; Britannia Royal Naval Coll., Dartmouth; Royal Naval Engrg Coll., Manadon. CEng 1972; FIET (FIEE 1988); FIMarEST (FIMarE 1998), Hon. FIMarEST 2009. Joined Royal Navy, 1962: trng appts, 1963–67; HM Submarine Ocelot, 1968–69; Nuclear Reactor Course, RNC, Greenwich, 1969; HM Submarine Sovereign, 1970–73; Sen. Engr, HM Submarine Repulse, 1974–76; Staff of Capt. Submarine Sea Trng, 1976–79; Comdr 1980; Sch. Comdr, HMS Collingwood, 1980; Ops (E), MoD, 1981–84; jsdc 1984; Exec. Officer, Clyde Submarine Base, 1984–88; Capt. 1988; Dep. Dir, Naval Logistic Plans, 1989; rcds 1990; Capt. Surface Ship Acceptance, 1991–92; Naval Attaché, Rome and Albania, 1992–96; retd RN, 1996; Manager, Southern Europe, Ganley Gp, 1997–98. Dir, Engrg and Technol. Bd, 2001–02, 2008–09; Mem. Bd, Science Council, 2003–12 (Vice Chair, 2009–12). Dir, Marine South East, 2008–12. Chm., Cttee of Chief Execs of Engrg Instns, 2004–09. Member: Adv. Bd, Greenwich Maritime Inst., 1999–2010; Tech. Cttee, 2002–14, Council, 2010–14, RNLI (Vice Pres., 2014–). Trustee: RSA, 2012–; IMarEST Pension Fund, 2013–. FRSA 2000; FCGI 2009. *Recreations:* family, Italy, music, theatre, sailing.

READ, Leonard Ernest, (Nipper), QPM 1976; National Security Adviser to the Museums and Galleries Commission, 1978–86; *b* 31 March 1925; *m* 1st, 1951, Marion Alexandra Millar (marr. diss. 1979); one *d*; 2nd, 1980, Patricia Margaret Allen. *Educ:* elementary schools. Worked at Players Tobacco factory, Nottingham, 1939–43; Petty Officer, RN, 1943–46; joined Metropolitan Police, 1947; served in all ranks of CID; Det. Chief Supt on Murder Squad, 1967; Asst Chief Constable, Notts Combined Constabulary, 1970; National Co-ordinator of Regional Crime Squads for England and Wales, 1972–76. British Boxing Board of Control: Mem. Council, 1976–82; Admin. Steward, 1982–88; Vice Chm., 1988–96, Chm., 1996–2000; Vice Pres., 1991–97, Pres., 1997–2005; Vice Pres., 1989–, Sen. Vice Pres., 1997–2001, World Boxing Council; Vice-Pres., World Boxing Assoc., 1989–2001. Freeman, City of London, 1983. *Publications:* with James Morton: Nipper (autobiog.), 1991; Nipper Read: the man who nicked the Krays (autobiog.), 2001. *Recreations:* home computing, playing the keyboard. *Address:* 23 North Barn, Broxbourne, Herts EN10 6RR.

READ, Lionel Frank; QC 1973; a Recorder of the Crown Court, 1974–98; a Deputy High Court Judge, 1989–98; *b* 7 Sept. 1929; *s* of late F. W. C. Read and Lilian (*née* Chatwin); *m* 1956, Shirley Greenhalgh; two *s* one *d*. *Educ:* Oundle Sch.; St John's Coll., Cambridge (MA). Mons OCS Stick of Honour; commnd 4 RHA, 1949. Called to Bar, Gray's Inn, 1954, Bencher, 1981 (Treas., 2001); Mem., Senate of the Inns of Court and the Bar, 1974–77. A Gen. Comr of Income Tax, Gray's Inn Div., 1986–90. Chm., Local Government and Planning Bar Assoc., 1990–94 (Vice-Chm., 1986–90); Member: Bar Council, 1990–94; Council on Tribunals, 1990–96. *Recreations:* reading, travel. *Address:* Cedarwood, Church Road, Ham Common, Surrey TW10 5HG. *T:* (020) 8940 5247. *Clubs:* Garrick; Hawks (Cambridge).

READ, Malcolm James; District Judge (Magistrates' Courts) (formerly Metropolitan Stipendiary Magistrate), 1993–2013; *b* 4 May 1948; *s* of Frank James Cruickshank Read and Anne Elizabeth (*née* Oldershaw); *m*; one *s* by previous marriage. *Educ:* Wallington Independent Grammar Sch.; Council of Legal Educn. Called to the Bar, Gray's Inn, 1979; Clerk to Justices, Lewes Magistrates' Court, 1980–81; Clerk to: Hastings, Bexhill, Battle and Rye Justices, 1981–91; E Sussex Magistrates' Courts Cttee, 1981–91; in private practice, Brighton, 1991–93. *Recreations:* motor-cycling, golf (occasionally).

READ, Mark; Chief Executive Officer, WPP Digital, since 2006; Executive Director, WPP plc; *b* London, 19 Nov. 1966; *s* of Ian and Linda Read. *Educ:* Trinity Coll., Cambridge (MA Econs 1988); Harvard Univ. (Henry Fellow 1999); INSEAD (MBA 2003). Corporate Develt, WPP, 1989–95; Principal, Booz Allen & Hamilton, 1995–99; CEO, Webrewards, 1999–2001; Dir of Strategy, WPP plc, 2002. *Recreations:* ski-ing, sailing, wine, food. *Address:* WPP, 27 Farm Street, W1J 5RJ. *T:* (020) 7408 2204. *E:* mread@wpp.com.

READ, Dr Martin Peter, CBE 2011; Chairman: Laird plc, since 2014; Low Carbon Contracts Company, since 2014; Electricity Settlements Company, since 2014; Remuneration Consultants Group, since 2010; Senior Salaries Review Body, since 2015; non-executive Director, Lloyd's, since 2009; *b* 16 Feb. 1950; *s* of late Peter Denis Read and Dorothy Ruby Read; *m* 1974, Marian Eleanor Gilbart; one *s* one *d*. *Educ:* Queen Mary's Grammar Sch., Basingstoke; Peterhouse, Cambridge (BA Nat. Scis 1971); Merton Coll., Oxford (DPhil Physics 1974; Hon. Fellow, 2006). CDipAF 1976; FIET (FIEE 2005). Posts in sales and marketing, finance, ops, and systems develt, UK and overseas, Overseas Containers Ltd, 1974–81; Corp. Commercial Dir, Marine Coatings, 1981–84, Gen. Manager, Europe, 1984–85, International Paint, part of Courtaulds; joined GEC Marconi, 1985; Gen. Manager, Marconi Secure Radio, 1986–87; Dir, Marconi Defence Systems Ltd, 1987–89; Man. Dir, Marconi Command and Control Systems Ltd, 1989–91; Gp Man. Dir, Marconi Radar and Control Systems Gp, 1991–93; Gp Chief Exec., Logica, later LogicaCMG plc, 1993–2007. Non-executive Director: ASDA Gp plc, 1996–99; Southampton Innovations Ltd, 1999–2003; Boots Gp plc, 1999–2006; British Airways plc, 2000–09; Siemens Hldgs plc, 2008–09; Aegis Gp plc, 2009–13; Invensys plc, 2009–14. Senior Adviser: Candover Partners, 2008–09; HCL, 2008–12; Actis, 2011–13; Zensar Technologies, 2013–. Mem., President's Cttee, 2004–07, Internat. Adv. Bd, 2007–10, CBI; Dir, Strategy Bd, DTI, 2005–06; led govt review on improving efficiency of back office systems and IT across the public sector, 2008–09; led govt review on mgt information, 2012; non-exec. Dir, UK Govt Efficiency and Reform Bd, 2010–15. Director: Portsmouth Housing Assoc., 1993–2007; Shelter, 2004–10 (Mem. Finance Cttee, 2000–04); Trustee: Hampshire Technology Centre, 1990–; Southern Focus (formerly Portsmouth Housing) Trust, 1992–2000. Mem., Nat. Centre for Univs and Business (formerly Council for Industry and Higher Educn), 2000–07 (Trustee, 2007–14). Gov., Highbury Coll., Portsmouth, 1989–99; Member: Council, Southampton Univ., 1999–2015 (Vice Chm., 2008–15); Cambridge Univ. Library Adv. (formerly Vis.) Cttee, 2007– (Chm., 2015–); Council, Shakespeare's Globe, 2010–. Hon. DTech Loughborough, 2000. Gold Medal, Chartered Mgt Inst., 2007. *Publications:* article in Jl of Applied Physics. *Recreations:* French and German novels, drama, military history, travel, gardening. *Address:* c/o Company Secretary, Laird plc, 100 Pall Mall, SW1Y 5NQ.

See also G. S. Read.

READ, Mel; *see* Read, I. M.

READ, Paul John Z.; *see* Zollinger-Read.

READ, Piers Paul, FRSL; author; *b* 7 March 1941; 3rd *s* of Sir Herbert Read, DSO, MC and late Margaret Read, Stonegrave, York; *m* 1967, Emily Albertine, *o d* of Evelyn Basil Boothby, CMG and of Susan Asquith; two *s* two *d*. *Educ:* Ampleforth Coll.; St John's Coll., Cambridge (MA). Artist-in-residence, Ford Foundn, Berlin, 1963–64; Sub-Editor, Times Literary Supplement, 1965; Harkness Fellow, Commonwealth Fund, NY, 1967–68. Member: Council, Inst. of Contemporary Arts, 1971–75; Cttee of Management, Soc. of Authors, 1973–76; Literature Panel, Arts Council, 1975–77; Council, RSL, 2001–07. Adjunct Prof. of Writing, Columbia Univ., NY, 1980. Bd Mem., Aid to the Church in Need, 1988–2012. Trustee, Catholic Nat. Liby, 1998–2010. Governor: Cardinal Manning Boys' Sch., 1985–91; More House Sch., 1996–2000. Chm., Catholic Writers' Guild (the Keys), 1992–97 (Vice-Pres., 1997–). Screenplay: Verbrechen mit Vorbedacht, 1967; TV plays: Coincidence, 1968; The House on Highbury Hill, 1972; The Childhood Friend, 1974; Margaret Clitheroe, 1977; radio play: The Family Firm, 1970. *Publications: novels:* Game in Heaven with Tussy Marx, 1966; The Junkers, 1968 (Sir Geoffrey Faber Meml Prize); Monk Dawson, 1969 (Hawthornden Prize and Somerset Maugham Award; filmed 1997); The Professor's Daughter, 1971; The Upstart, 1973; Polonaise, 1976; A Married Man, 1979 (televised 1983); The Villa Golitsyn, 1981; The Free Frenchman, 1986 (televised 1989); A Season in the West, 1988 (James Tait Black Meml Prize); On the Third Day, 1990; A Patriot in Berlin, 1995; Knights of the Cross, 1997; Alice in Exile, 2001; The Death of a Pope, 2009; The Misogynist, 2010; Scarpia, 2015; *non-fiction:* Alive, 1974 (filmed 1992); The Train Robbers, 1978; Quo Vadis? the subversion of the Catholic Church, 1991; Ablaze: the story of Chernobyl, 1993; The Templars, 1999; Alec Guinness, The Authorised Biography, 2003; Hell and Other Destinations, 2006; The Dreyfus Affair: the story of the most infamous miscarriage of justice in French history, 2012. *Address:* 23 Ashchurch Park Villas, W12 9SP.

See also C. E. Ostler.

READ, Prof. Randy John, PhD; FRS 2014; Professor of Protein Crystallography, University of Cambridge, since 1998; *b* 9 June 1957; *s* of John and Anne Read; *m* 1995, Penelope Effie Stein; one *s* one *d*. *Educ:* Univ. of Alberta, Edmonton (BSc 1979; PhD 1986). Asst Prof., 1988–93, Associate Prof., 1993–98, Univ. of Alberta. Max Perutz Prize, Eur. Crystallographic Assoc., 2013; Rosario Prize, Instituto de Física de São Carlos, 2014. *Publications:* contrib. papers on methods in protein crystallography and applications to medically relevant proteins. *Address:* Cambridge Institute for Medical Research, Wellcome Trust/MRC Building, Hills Road, Cambridge CB2 0XY. *T:* (01223) 336500, *Fax:* (01223) 336827. *E:* rjr27@cam.ac.uk.

READE, Brian Anthony; HM Diplomatic Service, retired; *b* 5 Feb. 1940; *s* of Stanley Robert Reade and Emily Doris (*née* Lee); *m* 1964, Averille van Eugen; one *s* one *d*. *Educ:* King Henry VIII Sch., Coventry; Univ. of Leeds (BA Hons 1963). Interlang Ltd, 1963–64; Lectr, City of Westminster Coll., 1964–65; 2nd Sec., FCO, 1965–69; 2nd Sec., Bangkok, 1970–71, 1st Sec., 1971–74; FCO, 1974–77; Consul (Econ.), Consulate-General, Düsseldorf, 1977–81; FCO, 1981–82; 1st Sec., Bangkok, 1982–84; Counsellor (ESCAP), Bangkok, 1984–86; Counsellor, FCO, 1986–93. *Recreations:* watching sport, conversation, reading. *Clubs:* Coventry Rugby Football; Royal Bangkok Sports (Thailand).

READE, David Jarrett; QC 2006; *b* 20 April 1961; *s* of John and Margaret Reade; *m* 1989, Linda Jane Whitfield; two *d*. *Educ:* Prince Henry's High Sch., Evesham; Univ. of Birmingham (LLB 1982). Called to the Bar, Middle Temple, 1983, Bencher, 2009. Mem., Tufty Club, RoSPA, 1967–. Trustee, London Library, 2012. *Publications:* (jtly) the Law of Industrial Action and Trade Union Recognition, 2004; (contrib.) Transfer of Undertakings, 2007; (jtly) A guide to the Equality Act, 2010; (jtly) Blackstone's Employment Law Manual, 2013. *Recreations:* tennis, football (W Bromwich Albion), Rugby, music. *Address:* Littleton Chambers, 3 King's Bench Walk North, Temple, EC4Y 7HR. *T:* (020) 7797 8600. *E:* dr@djreade.com.

READE, Sir Kenneth Roy, 13th Bt *cr* 1661, of Barton, Berkshire; *b* 23 March 1926; *s* of Leverne Elton Reade (*d* 1943; 5th *s* of Sir George Compton Reade, 9th Bt), and Norma B. Ward; *S* cousin, 1982; *m* 1944, Doreen D. Vinsant; three *d*. *Heir:* none.

READE, Rt Rev. Nicholas Stewart; Bishop of Blackburn, 2004–12; an Honorary Assistant Bishop: Diocese of Europe, since 2013; Diocese of Chichester, since 2014; *b* 9 Dec. 1946; *s* of late Sqdn Ldr Charles Sturrock Reade and Eileen Vandermere (*née* Fleming); *m* 1971, Christine Jasper, *d* of late Very Rev. R. C. D. Jasper, CBE, DD and Ethel Jasper; one *d*. *Educ:* Elizabeth Coll., Guernsey; Univ. of Leeds (BA, DipTh); Coll. of the Resurrection, Mirfield. Ordained deacon, 1973, priest, 1974; Assistant Curate: St Chad's, Coseley, 1973–75; St Nicholas, Codsall, and Priest-in-charge of Holy Cross, Bilbrook, 1975–78; Vicar, St Peter's, Upper Gornal and Chaplain, Burton Road Hosp., Dudley, 1978–82; Vicar: St Dunstan's, Mayfield, 1982–88; St Mary's, Eastbourne, 1988–97; Archdeacon of Lewes and Hastings, 1997–2004. Rural Dean: Dallington, 1982–88; Eastbourne, 1988–97; Canon of Chichester Cathedral, 1990–2004 (Prebendary, 1990–97). Hon. Asst Priest, All Saints, Sidley, 2013–; Actg Priest in Charge, St Barnabas', Bexhill, 2014–. Member: Gen. Synod of C of E, 1995–2000, 2002–; Dioceses Commn, 2001–05; Sen. Appts Gp (Episcopal), 2007–12; Urban Bishops' Panel, 2010–12; Chairman: Chichester Dio. Liturgical Cttee, 1989–97; Ministry Div., Cttee for Ministry of and among Deaf and Disabled People, 2008–12. Entered H of L, 2009. President: Eastbourne and Dist Police Court Mission, 1994–; Crowhurst Christian Healing Centre, 2001–13; Vice Pres., Blackburn Diocesan Prayer Book Soc., 2010–12. Trustee: St Wilfrid's Hospice, Eastbourne, 1995–98; UC, Chichester, 2000–03; House of Bishops Healing Group, 2005–11. Patron: Rosemere Cancer Foundn, 2005–12; Derian House Children's Hospice, Chorley, 2006–12; Skipton-East Lancs Rail Action Partnership, 2006–; Stonyhurst Christian Heritage Centre, 2011–. Warden, Guild of St Raphael, 2009–13. FRSA 2010. Companion, Order of Star of Ethiopia, 2012. *Recreations:* cycling, steam trains, modern ecclesiastical and political biographies. *Address:* 5 Warnham Gardens, Cooden, Bexhill-on-Sea, E Sussex TN39 3SP. *T:* (01424) 842673. *E:* nicholas.reade@btinternet.com.

READER, David George; HM Diplomatic Service, retired; Special Representative for Secretary of State for Foreign and Commonwealth Affairs, since 2009; *b* 1 Oct. 1947; *s* of late Stanley Reader and of Annie Reader; *m* 1969, Elaine McKnight; one *s* one *d*. *Educ:* Barrow Grammar Sch. Entered FO, later FCO, 1964; Warsaw, 1969–72; Paris, 1972–74; Bucharest, 1974–76; FCO, 1976–79; Kinshasa, 1979–82; Kathmandu, 1982–84; FCO, 1984–87; Consul, Brisbane, 1987–92; First Sec. (Mgt) and Consul, Belgrade, 1992–96; FCO, 1996–98; Dir, Trade & Investment, Cairo, 1998–2001; High Comr, Kingdom of Swaziland, 2001–05; Ambassador to Cambodia, 2005–08. *Address:* c/o Foreign and Commonwealth Office, King Charles Street, SW1A 2AH. *Club:* Royal Over-Seas League.

READER, Martin Sheldon; Headmaster, Cranleigh School, since 2014; *b* 28 May 1967; *s* of Phillip John Reader and Juliet Elaine Reader; *m* 1994, Amanda Elizabeth Dyton; one *s* one *d*. *Educ:* St Olave's Grammar Sch.; University Coll., Oxford (Exhibitioner; BA Hons Eng. Lang. and Lit. 1989; MPhil Eng. Studies 1991; MA 1993); Homerton Coll., Cambridge (QTS 2002); Univ. of Hull (MBA 2004). Assistant Master: St Edward's Sch., Oxford, 1991–97; Oundle Sch., 1997–2002; Dep. Head, Laxton Sch. (subseq. merged with Oundle), 2000–02; Dep. Head, 2002–04, Sen. Dep. Head, 2004–06, Reigate Grammar Sch.; Headmaster, Wellington Sch., Somerset, 2006–14. *Recreations:* birdwatching, ski-ing, gym, reading, spending time with family, local church involvement. *Address:* Cranleigh School, Horseshoe Lane, Cranleigh, Surrey GU6 8QQ. *T:* (01483) 273677, *Fax:* (01483) 273696. *E:* mrp@cranleigh.org.

READER, Ven. Trevor Alan John, PhD; Archdeacon of Portsdown, 2006–13; *b* 3 Aug. 1946; *s* of Clement and Lucy Reader; *m* 1st, 1968, Lesley Suzanne Taubman (*d* 2005); six *d*; 2nd, 2008, Linda Margaret Parks. *Educ:* Portsmouth Poly. (BSc 1968, MSc 1970, Zoology (London Univ. external); PhD 1972); Southern Dios, MTS, Salisbury and Wells Theol Coll. Research Asst, 1968–72, Lectr/Sen. Lectr, 1972–86, Portsmouth Poly. Ordained deacon, 1986, priest, 1987; Asst Curate, St Mary, Alverstoke, 1986–89; Priest i/c, St Mary, Hook-with-Warsash, 1989–98; Priest i/c, Holy Trinity, Blendworth, with St Michael and all Angels, Chalton, with St Hubert, Idsworth, and Diocesan Dir of Non-Stipendiary Ministry, dio. Portsmouth, 1998–2003; Archdeacon of IoW, 2003–06. Bp of Portsmouth's Liaison Officer for Prisons, 2003–06; Bp of Portsmouth's Advr to Hospital Chaplaincy, 2006–13. Dir, Portsmouth Educn Business Partnership, 2004–10. *Publications:* (jtly) Teaching Christianity at Key Stage 2, 2001; (jtly) Reflective Learning, 2009; 16 articles relating to work in parasitology in scientific jls. *Recreations:* walking, surfing, reading, vegetable gardening, relaxing with family. *Address:* 54 David Newberry Drive, Lee on the Solent, Hants PO13 8FE.

READHEAD, Simon John Howard; QC 2006; a Recorder of the Crown and County Court, since 2000; *b* 3 Feb. 1956; *s* of Frederick John Readhead and Kathleen Mary Readhead; *m* 1987, Siobhan Elizabeth Mary O'Mahony; two *s*. *Educ:* Tonbridge Sch.; Lincoln Coll., Oxford (MA, BCL). Called to the Bar, Middle Temple, 1979, Bencher, 2012; Jun., Midland and Oxford Circuit, 1989–90. Asst Recorder, 1995–2000. Lectr in Law, Hammersmith and W London Coll., 1979–81. Mem., Costs Panel, Gen. Council of the Bar, 1995–2009. Member, Management Committee: Permanent Exhibn of Judicial and Legal Costume, Royal Courts of Justice, 1979– (Trustee, 2009–); Rolls Building Art and Educnl Trust, 2011– (Trustee, 2011–). Chm. Govs, King's House Sch., Richmond, 2007–13. *Address:* 1 Chancery Lane, WC2A 1LF. *T:* 0845 634 6666, *Fax:* 0845 634 6667. *E:* sreadhead@1chancerylane.com.

READING, 4th Marquess of, *cr* 1926; **Simon Charles Henry Rufus Isaacs;** Baron 1914; Viscount 1916; Earl 1917; Viscount Erleigh 1917; Sino-British business consultant; *b* 18 May 1942; *e s* of 3rd Marquess of Reading, MBE, MC, and Margot Irene, *yr d* of late Percy Duke, OBE; *S* father, 1980; *m* 1979, Melinda Victoria, *yr d* of late Richard Dewar, Cecily Hill, Cirencester, Glos; one *s* two *d*. *Educ:* Eton. Served 1st Queen's Dragoon Guards, 1961–64. Member of Stock Exchange, 1970–74. Director: Cure Internat., 2004–; Mertens House (St Petersburg), 2008–; Consegna, 2012–. Trustee, Garden Tomb, Jerusalem, 2002–08. Patron: Nelson Trust, 1985–; Barnabas Fund, 1998–. *Heir: s* Viscount Erleigh, *qv*. *Address:* 7 Cecily Hill, Cirencester, Glos GL7 2EF. *Clubs:* Cavalry and Guards, White's, MCC, All England Lawn Tennis and Croquet; Stoke Park (Pres., 2005–07).

READING, Area Bishop of, since 2011; **Rt Rev. Andrew John Proud;** *b* 27 March 1954; *s* of late John Gascoigne Proud and of Joan Denise Proud; *m* 1977, Hon. (Fiona) Janice, PhD, *d* of 2nd Baron Brain; one *s* one *d*. *Educ:* King's Coll., London (BD 1979, AKC); Sch. of Oriental and African Studies, Univ. of London (MA 2001). Ordained deacon, 1980, priest, 1981; Asst Curate, Stansted Mountfitchet, 1980; Team Vicar, Borehamwood, 1983; Asst Priest, Bishop's Hatfield, 1990; Rector, E Barnet, 1992; Chaplain, St Matthew's, Addis Ababa, 2002; Bishop's Asst for the Horn of Africa, 2004; Canon of Cairo, 2005; Area Bishop of Ethiopia and the Horn of Africa, 2007–11. *Recreations:* cooking, music, bird watching, reading. *Address:* Bishop's House, Tidmarsh Lane, Tidmarsh, Reading RG8 8HA.

READING, David Michael Ronald, OBE 2005; Director, Food Allergy Support, since 2009; *b* 17 Aug. 1947; *s* of Ronald George Frederick and Winifred Mabel Reading; *m* 1987, Sylvia Anne Cruickshank; two *d* (and one *d* decd). *Educ:* Godalming County Grammar Sch. Reporter, Surrey Advertiser, 1965–69; Sub-editor: Aldershot News, 1970–72, 1975–80, 1982–88, 1993–98; Reading Evening Post, 1972–73; Bedfordshire Times, 1973–74; Oxford Mail, 1974–75; Licensee Mag., 1980–82; Dep. Ed., Wokingham Times, 1988–93. Dir, Anaphylaxis Campaign, 1996–2009. *Recreations:* writing novels, guitar playing, films, ornithology, tai chi, photography. *Address:* 8 Wey Close, Ash, Aldershot, Hants GU12 6LY.

READING, (Ian) Malcolm, RIBA; Founder, 1996, Malcolm Reading & Associates (now Malcolm Reading Consultants); specialist adviser on architecture and the built environment; *b* 11 June 1957; *s* of Harold William Reading and Margaret (*née* Fletcher); *m* 1988, Catherine Jane Ormell; one *s*. *Educ:* George Heriot's Sch., Edinburgh; Univ. of Bristol (BA Arch. 1979; DipArch 1983). RIBA 1986. Bernard Hartley, architects, 1983–86; Andrews Downie and Partners, architects, 1986–89; Moxley Frankl Architects, 1989–90; Dir, Architecture and Design, British Council, 1990–96. Chm., Consultative Cttee, Tower of London World Heritage Site, UNESCO, 2008–. Mem., Public Art Panel for Supreme Court of UK, 2007–09. Trustee: Historic Royal Palaces, London, 2005–14; Edinburgh World Heritage, 2012–. FRSA 1993. Hon. FRGS 2005. *Publications:* Lubetkin and Tecton: architecture and social commitment, 1981; Lubetkin and Tecton, 1992. *Recreations:* cycling, walking, photography. *Address:* (office) 10 Ely Place, EC1N 6RY. *E:* malcolm@malcolmreading.co.uk.

READING, Dr Peter Richard; Managing Director, Peter Reading Strategic Consulting Ltd, since 2007; Associate Director, PwC, since 2014; *b* 1 May 1956; *s* of Dr Harold Garnar Reading and late Barbara Mary Reading (*née* Hancock); *m* 2001, Dr Catherine Austin (*née* Fountain); one *s* two *d*, and two step *d*. *Educ:* St Edward's Sch., Oxford; Gonville and Caius Coll., Cambridge (MA; Exhibnr, Sen. Exhibnr); Birmingham Univ. (PhD); Moscow State Univ. (British Council Res. Schol.); London Sch. of Econs and Pol Sci. (Public Sector Mgt Prog.). Health service mgt posts in London, 1984–94; Chief Executive: Lewisham and Guy's Mental Health NHS Trust, 1994–98; UCL Hosps NHS Trust, 1998–2000; Univ. Hosps of Leicester NHS Trust, 2000–07; Interim Chief Executive: Doncaster and Bassetlaw NHS Foundn Trust, 2010–11; Peterborough and Stamford Hosps NHS Foundn Trust, 2012–14. CCMI 2006. *Recreations:* history, Oxford United, animals, 1960s pop and rock music. *T:* 07813 438932. *E:* info@peterreading.co.uk.

REAMSBOTTOM, Barry Arthur; a Senior Secretary to the Speaker of the House of Commons, 2002–09; *b* 4 April 1949; *s* of Agnes Reamsbottom. *Educ:* St Peter's RC Secondary Sch., Aberdeen; Aberdeen Academy. Scientific Asst, Isaac Spencer & Co., Aberdeen, 1966–69; Social Security Officer, DHSS, Aberdeen, 1969–76; Area Officer, NUPE, Edinburgh, 1976–79; Civil and Public Services Association: Head of Educn Dept, 1979–87; Editor, Press Officer, 1987–92; Gen. Sec., 1992–98; Gen. Sec., PCS, 1998–2002. Mem., NUJ, 1987–. Bereavement counsellor, Trinity Hospice, London, 2007–. *Recreations:* reading, golf, art appreciation, politics, music, taking photographs, laughter and the love of friends. *Address:* 156 Bedford Hill, SW12 9HW.

REANEY, Trevor Eccles; Clerk and Chief Executive (formerly Clerk and Director General), Northern Ireland Assembly, since 2008; *b* Lisburn, Co. Antrim, 3 July 1959; *s* of John James and Norah Violet Reaney; *m* 1978, Elizabeth Ann Dunlop; three *s* one *d*. *Educ:* Ballymena Acad.; Open Univ. (MBA 1995). Gen. Manager, Stormont Estate Refreshment Club, 1983–87; Sen. Operations Manager, Compass Services (UK), 1987–90; Dir, Commercial Services, Southern Educn and Liby Bd, 1990–96; Chief Executive: Cragavon BC, 1996–2003; NI Policing Bd, 2004–08. *Recreations:* walking, sport, local church. *Address:* Northern Ireland Assembly, Parliament Buildings, Ballymiscaw, Stormont, Belfast BT4 3XX. *T:* (028) 9052 1199. *E:* trevor.reaney@niassembly.gov.uk.

REARDON, Rev. John Patrick, OBE 1999; General Secretary, Council of Churches for Britain and Ireland, 1990–99; Moderator, General Assembly of the United Reformed Church, 1995–96; *b* 15 June 1933; *s* of John Samuel Reardon and Ivy Hilda Reardon; *m* 1957, Molly Pamela Young; four *s* one *d*. *Educ:* Gravesend Grammar Sch. for Boys; University College London (BA Hons English); King's College London (postgraduate Cert. in Educn). Teacher, London and Gravesend, 1958–61; Minister, Horsham Congregational Church, 1961–68 (Chm., Sussex Congregational Union, 1967); Minister, Trinity Congregational Church, St Albans, 1968–72 (Chm., Herts Congregational Union, 1971–72); Sec., Church and Society Dept, 1972–90, and Dep. Gen. Sec., 1983–90, URC. *Publications:* More Everyday Prayers (contrib.), 1982; (ed) Leaves from the Tree of Peace, 1986; (ed) Threads of Creation, 1989; Together Met, Together Bound, 2007. *Recreations:* modern literature, photography, philately, travel. *Address:* 1 Newbolt Close, Newport Pagnell, Bucks MK16 8ND. *T:* (01908) 217559.

REARDON, Katherine Genevieve, (Mrs Charles Gordon-Watson); Editor, Tatler, since 2011; *b* New York, 20 Nov. 1968; *d* of Patrick Reardon and Polly Reardon (*née* Peverley, later Wood); *m* 2013, Charles Gordon-Watson; one *s* one *d* (twins). *Educ:* Cheltenham Ladies' Coll.; Stowe Sch. Fashion Asst, US Vogue, 1988–90; Fashion Dir, Tatler, 1990–97; Contrib. Editor, Vanity Fair, 1999–2011; Founder, Toptips.com, 2007–11. Columnist, fashion, 1999–2001, jewellery, 2003–06, The Times. Mem., CRUK, 2007–. *Publications:* Top Tips for Girls, 2008; Top Tips for Life, 2010. *Recreations:* riding, tidying. *Address:* Tatler, Vogue House, Hanover Square, W1S 1JU.

REARDON SMITH, Sir (William) Antony (John), 4th Bt *cr* 1920, of Appledore, Devon; Chairman, GEM Containers Ltd; *b* 20 June 1937; *e s* of Sir William Reardon Reardon-Smith, 3rd Bt and his 1st wife, Nesta Florence Phillips (*d* 1959); *S* father, 1995; *m* 1962, Susan Wight, *d* of Henry Wight Gibson; three *s* one *d*. *Educ:* Wycliffe Coll. Nat. Service, RN, Suez, 1956. Sir William Reardon Smith & Sons Ltd and Reardon Smith Line plc, 1957–85 (Dir, 1959–85); Director: London World Trade Centre, 1986–87; Milford Haven Port Authority, 1988–99; Marine and Port Services Ltd, Milford Docks, 1990–99. Chm., N Eastern Rubber Co. Ltd, 1980–2004. Member: Baltic Exchange, 1959–87 (Dir, 1982–87; Assoc. Mem., 1990–92); Chamber of Shipping Documentary Cttee, 1963–72 (Chm., 1968–72); Documentary Council, Baltic and Internat. Conf., 1964–82. Dir, UK Protection and Indemnity Club and Freight, Demurrage and Defence Assoc., 1968–80. Trustee: Royal Merchant Navy Sch. Foundn, 1966–2003 (Vice-Pres., 1992–); Bearwood Coll., 1966–2003; Trustee and Chm., Joseph Strong Frazer Trust, 1980–; Member: Council, King George's Fund for Sailors, 1981–95; City of London Cttee, RNLI, 1976–2006. Clerk, Fuellers' Co., 2002–14 (Hon. Liveryman, 2014); Liveryman: World Traders' Co., 1986–; Poulters' Co., 1991–; Shipwrights' Co., 1994–. GCLJ 2002 (KLJ 1997; Bailiff, 2002–08, now Bailiff Emeritus). *Recreations:* golf, shooting. *Heir: s* William Nicolas Henry Reardon Smith [*b* 10 June 1963; *m* 2001, Julia, *er d* of D. Martin Slade]. *Address:* 26 Merrick Square, SE1 4JB. *T:* (020) 7403 5723.

REASON, Prof. James Tootle, CBE 2003; FBA 1999; FRAeS; FBPsS; Professor of Psychology, University of Manchester, 1977–2001, now Emeritus; *b* 1 May 1938; *s* of late George Stanley Tootle and Hilda Alice Reason; *m* 1964, Rea Jaari; two *d*. *Educ:* Royal Masonic Sch.; Univ. of Manchester (BSc 1962); Univ. of Leicester (PhD 1967). FBPsS 1988; FRAeS 1998. RAF Inst. of Aviation Medicine, 1962–64; Lectr and Reader, Dept of Psychology, Univ. of Leicester, 1964–76. Hon. DSc Aberdeen, 2002. Dist. Foreign Colleague Award, US Human Factors and Ergonomics Soc., 1995. Hon. FRCGP 2006; Hon. Fellow, Safety and Reliability Soc., 2011. Dist. Service Award, RoSPA, 2006. *Publications:* Man in Motion, 1974; Motion Sickness, 1975; Human Error, 1990; Beyond Aviation Human Factors, 1995; Managing the Risks of Organizational Accidents, 1997; Managing Maintenance Error, 2003; The Human Contribution: unsafe acts, accidents and heroic recoveries, 2008; A Life in Error, 2013. *Recreations:* reading, writing, viewing. *Address:* 96 Cliveden Gages, Taplow, Bucks SL6 0GB, *T:* (01268) 666485. *E:* jim@jamesreason.com.

REAY, 15th Lord *cr* 1628, of Reay, Caithness; **Aeneas Simon Mackay;** Bt (NS) 1627; Baron Mackay van Ophemert and Zennewijnen, Netherlands, 1822; Chief of Clan Mackay; Director, Montrose Advisers LLP, since 2011; Principal and Co-founder, Montrose Partners LLP, 2003–11; *b* 20 March 1965; *s* of 14th Lord Reay and of Hon. Annabel Thérèse Fraser (*see* A. T. Keswick); *S* father, 2013; *m* 2010, Mia, *er d* of Markus Ruulio, Helsinki; two *s* one *d*. *Educ:* Westminster School; Brown Univ., USA. Associate, Salomon Brothers, 1987–91; Robert Fleming, later JP Morgan, 1992–2003. *Recreations:* most sports, especially football, cricket and shooting. *Heir: s* Master of Reay, *qv*.

REAY, Master of; Hon. Alexander Shimi Markus Mackay; *b* 21 April 2010; *s* and *heir* of Lord Reay, *qv*.

REAY, David William; Chairman, Northumberland Mental Health NHS Trust, 1992–2001; *b* 28 May 1940; *s* of late Stanley Reay and Madge Reay (*née* Hall); *m* 1964, Constance Susan Gibney; two *d*. *Educ:* Monkwearmouth Grammar School, Sunderland; Newcastle upon Tyne Polytechnic. Independent Television Authority, 1960–62; Alpha Television (ATV and ABC) Services Ltd, 1962–64; Tyne Tees Television Ltd, 1964–72; HTV Ltd: Engineering Manager, 1972–75; Chief Engineer, 1975–79; Dir of Engineering, 1979–84; Man. Dir, 1984–91, Chief Exec., 1991, Tyne Tees Television Hldgs. Chairman: Hadrian Television Ltd, 1988–91; Legend Television Ltd, 1989–91; Man. Dir, Tyne Tees Television Ltd, 1984–91; Director: Tyne Tees Music, 1984–91; Tyne Tees Enterprises, 1984–91; ITCA, now ITVA, 1984–91; Independent Television Publications, 1984–89; Tube Productions, 1986–91; ITN, 1990–91; Tyne and Wear Develt Corp., 1986–88; The Wearside Opportunity Ltd, 1988–91. Mem. Council, Univ. of Newcastle upon Tyne, 1989–94. CCMI (CBIM 1987); FRTS 1984; FRSA 1992. *Recreations:* walking, reading, music, watching soccer (particularly Sunderland AFC). *Address:* 11 The Links, Ascot, Berks SL5 7TN.

REAY, Prof. Diane, PhD; Professor of Education, University of Cambridge, since 2005; *b* 21 July 1949; *d* of Arthur James Sutton and Lilian Mary Sutton (*née* Smart); *m* 1971, Keith Reay (marr. diss. 1995); one *s* one *d*. *Educ:* Ashby Girls' Grammar Sch., Ashby-de-la-Zouch; Univ. of Newcastle upon Tyne (BA Hons Pols and Econs 1970; PGCE 1971); Inst. of Educn, London (MA 1987); South Bank Univ. (PhD 1995). Teacher, ILEA, 1971–90; Advr, Islington LEA, 1990–92; Res. Scholar, South Bank Univ., 1992–95; Res. Fellow, 1995–2001, Sen. Lectr, 2001–03, KCL; Prof., London Metropolitan Univ., 2003–05. Member: 2008 RAE Educn Panel; 2014 REF Educn Panel; ESRC Res. Grants Bd, 2006–. FAcSS (AcSS 2007). *Publications:* Class Work: mothers' involvement in their children's schooling, 1998; (ed jtly) Activating Participation: parents and teachers working towards partnership, 2004; (jtly) Degrees of Choice: social class, race and gender in higher education, 2005; (jtly) White Middle Class Identities and Urban Schooling, 2011. *Address:* Faculty of Education, University of Cambridge, Hills Road, Cambridge CB2 8PQ. *T:* (01223) 767600, *Fax:* (01223) 767602.

REAY, Dr John Sinclair Shewan; Director, Warren Spring Laboratory, Department of Trade and Industry, 1985–92; *b* Aberdeen, 8 June 1932; *s* of late George Reay, CBE and Tina (*née* Shewan); *m* 1958, Rhoda Donald Robertson; two *s* one *d*. *Educ:* Robert Gordon's College, Aberdeen; Univ. of Aberdeen; Imperial College, London (Beit Fellow). BSc, PhD, DIC. CChem, FRSC. Joined Scottish Agricultural Industries, 1958; Warren Spring Lab., Min of Technology, 1968; Head of Air Pollution Div., DoI, 1972–77; Head, Policy and Perspectives Unit, DTI, 1977–79; Head of Branch, Research Technology Div., DoI, 1979–81; Dep. Dir, Warren Spring Lab., 1981–85. *Publications:* papers on surface chemistry and air pollution. *Recreations:* using computer, listening to music. *Address:* 13 Grange Hill, Welwyn, Herts AL6 9RH. *T:* (01438) 715587.

REAY-SMITH, Richard Philip Morley; DL; Chairman, Surrey Compact, since 2008; Vice-Chairman, Painshill Park Trust, since 1985 (first Chairman, 1980–85); *b* 24 Nov. 1941; *m* 1972, Susan Margaret Hill; two *s*. *Educ:* Stowe Sch.; Durham Univ. (LLB); Harvard Business Sch. (AMP). Barclays Bank, 1963–98: Local Dir, Shrewsbury, 1984–87; Dep. Chief Exec., Central Retail Services Div., 1987–91; Chief Exec., Barclaycard, 1991–94; Man. Dir, Personal Banking, 1995–98; Chm., Barclays Life Assurance Co. Ltd, 1996–98; Chief Exec., UK Retail Banking, 1998. Director: Visa Internat. Services Assoc., 1991–98; Legal & General Bank Ltd, 2001–03. DL Surrey, 2004. FRSA. *Recreations:* sailing, music, travel, classic and vintage motorsport.

REBUCK, Baroness *cr* 2014 (Life Peer), of Bloomsbury in the London Borough of Camden; **Gail Ruth Rebuck,** DBE 2009 (CBE 2000); Chairman, Penguin Random House UK, and Director, Penguin Random House, since 2013; *b* 10 Feb. 1952; *d* of Gordon and Mavis Rebuck; *m* 1985, Philip Gould (later Baron Gould of Brookwood; *d* 2011); two *d*. *Educ:* Lycée Français de Londres; Univ. of Sussex (BA). Production Asst, Grisewood & Dempsey, 1975–76; Editor, then Publisher, Robert Nicholson Publications, 1976–78; Publisher, Hamlyn Paperbacks, 1978–82; Publishing Dir, Century Publishing, 1982–85; Publisher, Century Hutchinson, 1985–89; Chm., Random House Div., Random Century, 1989–91; Chm. and Chief Exec., Random House UK, then Random House Gp Ltd, 1991–2013. Non-exec. Dir, BSkyB, 2002–12. Mem., Creative Industries Taskforce, 1997–2000. Non-exec. Dir, Work Foundn, 2001–08. Trustee: IPPR, 1993–2003; Nat. Literacy Trust, 2007–; Cheltenham Festivals, 2013– (Chm. Literature Fest., 2013–). Member: Court, Univ. of Sussex, 1997–; Council, RCA, 1999–. FRSA 1989. *Recreations:* reading, travel. *Address:* Penguin Random House UK, 20 Vauxhall Bridge Road, SW1V 2SA. *T:* (020) 7840 8886.

RECKLESS, Mark John; *b* 6 Dec. 1970; *m* 2011, Catriona; two *s*. *Educ:* Marlborough Coll.; Christ Church, Oxford (BA PPE); Columbia Business Sch., NY (MBA); Coll. of Law (LLB). UK Economist, Warburgs, 1993–97; Booz Allen Hamilton, 1999–2001; Cons. Party Policy Unit, 2002–04. Called to the Bar, Lincoln's Inn, 2007; Herbert Smith LLP, 2007–10. Mem. (C) Medway Council, 2007–11. Mem., Kent Police Authy, 2007–11. Contested (C) Medway, 2001, 2005. MP (C) Rochester and Strood, 2010–Sept. 2014, (UK Ind) Rochester and Strood, Nov. 2014–2015; contested (UK Ind) same seat, 2015. Mem., Home Affairs Select Cttee, 2010–14. *Publications:* Euromoney Guide to the London Financial Markets, 1996; The Euro: bad for business, 1998; Conveyor Belt to Crime, 2003; (jtly) The Drivers of Regulations, 2004; (jtly) Direct Democracy, 2005.

REDDAWAY, Sir David (Norman), KCMG 2013 (CMG 1993); MBE 1980; HM Diplomatic Service, retired; Ambassador to Turkey, 2009–14; *b* 26 April 1953; *s* of late George Frank Norman Reddaway, CBE and of Jean Reddaway, OBE (*née* Brett); *m* 1981, Roshan Taliyeh Firouz (separated); two *s* one *d*. *Educ:* Oundle Sch. (Schol.); Fitzwilliam Coll., Cambridge (Exhibnr; MA Hist.). Volunteer teacher, Ethiopia, 1972. Joined FCO, 1975; language student, SOAS, 1976 and Iran, 1977; Tehran: Third Sec. later Second Sec. (Commercial), 1977–78; Second Sec. later First Sec. (Chancery), 1978–80; First Secretary: (Chancery), Madrid, 1980–84; FCO, 1985–86; Private Sec. to Minister of State, 1986–88; (Chancery), New Delhi, 1988–90; Chargé d'Affaires, Tehran, 1990–93 (Counsellor, 1991); Minister, Buenos Aires, 1993–97; Hd, Southern European Dept, FCO, 1997–99; Dir, Public Services, FCO, 1999–2001; UK Special Rep. for Afghanistan, 2002; Vis. Fellow, Harvard Univ., 2002–03; High Comr, Canada, 2003–06; Ambassador to Ireland, 2006–09. Advr to Bd, 2014–15, non-exec. Dir, 2015–, Beko plc. Member: Adv. Bd, Sch. of Mgt, Univ. of Bath, 2014–; Governing Body, SOAS, Univ. of London, 2015–. Mem., Council of Experts, Democratic Progress Inst., 2015–. *Recreations:* ski-ing, tennis, kayaking, Persian carpets and art. *Clubs:* Royal Over-Seas League; Hawks (Cambridge); Leander (Henley-on-Thames).

REDDICLIFFE, Paul, OBE 1998; HM Diplomatic Service, retired; Research Analyst for Cambodia, Laos, Thailand, and Vietnam, Foreign and Commonwealth Office, 1997–2008; *b* March 1945; *m* 1974, Wee Siok Boi; two *s*. *Educ:* Bedford Mod. Sch.; Jesus Coll., Oxford (MA Lit. Hum. 1967); Sch. of Oriental and African Studies, Univ. of London (MA SE Asian Studies 1973); Univ. of Kent. VSO, Vientiane, Laos, 1968–70 and 1971–72; joined HM Diplomatic Service, 1977; Indochina Analyst, Res. Dept, FCO, 1977–85; First Sec., Canberra, 1985–89; Indochina Analyst, 1989–92, Hd, S and SE Asia Section, 1992–94, Res. later Res. and Analysis, Dept, FCO; Ambassador to Kingdom of Cambodia, 1994–97. *Recreations:* bird-watching, books, P. G. Wodehouse, history. *Address:* c/o Foreign and Commonwealth Office, King Charles Street, SW1A 2AH.

REDDIHOUGH, John Hargreaves; His Honour Judge Reddihough; a Circuit Judge, since 2000; *b* 6 Dec. 1947; *s* of Frank Hargreaves Reddihough and Mabel Grace Reddihough (*née* Warner); *m* 1981, Sally Margaret Fryer; one *s* one *d*. *Educ:* Manchester Grammar Sch.; Univ. of Birmingham (LLB Hons). Called to the Bar, Gray's Inn, 1969; barrister, 1971–2000; Asst Recorder, 1991–94; Recorder, 1994–2000; Resident Judge, Grimsby Combined Court, 2001–09. *Recreations:* ski-ing, gardening, music, travel, reading, sport. *Address:* Reading Crown Court, Old Shire Hall, The Forbury, Reading RG1 3EH. *T:* (0118) 9674400.

REDDINGTON, (Clifford) Michael; Chief Executive, Liverpool City Council, 1986–88; *b* 14 Sept. 1932; *s* of Thomas Reddington and Gertrude (*née* Kenny); *m* 1968 Ursula Moor. *Educ:* St Michael's Coll., Leeds; St Edward's Coll., Liverpool; Liverpool Univ. (BCom 1953); Open Univ. (Dip. Maths 2013). CPFA (IPFA 1958). Served RAF, 1958–60. City Treasury, Liverpool, 1953–58 and 1960–86; Dep. City Treasurer, 1974, City Treasurer, 1982–86. Mem., Ind. Inquiry into Capital Market Activities of London Borough of Hammersmith and Fulham, 1990. Investigating Accountant, Disciplinary Scheme, CIPFA, 1999–2008. Member: Disciplinary Cttee, CIPFA, 2011–; Appeals Cttee, Inst. of Financial Accountants, 2013–. Chairman: Liverpool Welsh Choral Union, 1990–93; Convocation, Univ. of Liverpool, 1993–96; Trust Fund Manager, Hillsborough Disaster Appeal Fund, 1989–98; Chm., James Bulger Meml Trust, 1993–98. Mem. Governing Body, and Chm. Finance Cttee, Nugent Care Soc., 1992–2005. Member: World Bank mission to govts of Macedonia, Latvia, Armenia and Yugoslavia, 1999–2010; IMF missions to govt of Bosnia-Herzegovina, 2003. *Recreations:* cycling, fell walking. *Address:* Entwood, 18 Westwood Road, Noctorum, Prenton CH43 9RQ. *T:* (0151) 652 6081. *Club:* Athenæum (Liverpool).

REDDROP, Gemma; *see* Bodinetz, G.

REDESDALE, 6th Baron *cr* 1902; **Rupert Bertram Mitford;** Baron Mitford (Life Peer), 2000; *b* 18 July 1967; *s* of 5th Baron and of Sarah Georgina Cranstoun, *d* of Brig. Alston Cranstoun Todd, OBE; *S* father, 1991; *m* 1998, Helen, *e d* of David Shipsey; two *s* two *d*. *Educ:* Highgate Sch.; Newcastle Univ. (BA Hons Archaeology). Outdoor instructor, Fernwood Adventure Centre, South Africa, 1990–91. Lib Dem spokesman on overseas development, H of L, 1993–99, on defence, 2000–05, on energy, 2005–09, on agriculture, 2006–09; Member: H of L Select Cttee on Sci. and Technology, 1994–97; EU (D) Agric. Select Cttee, 1998–2000. Mem. Council, IAM, 1995–; Pres., Natural Gas Vehicle Assoc., 1997–2004; Chairman: Anaerobic and Biogas Assoc., 2009–12; Low Energy Co. (UK), 2013–; Chief Executive Officer: Carbon Management Assoc., 2013–; Energy Managers Assoc., 2013–. Chair, Red Squirrel Protection Partnership, 2006–. Hon. Vice Pres., Raleigh Internat., 2000–. *Recreations:* caving, climbing, ski-ing. *Heir:* *s* Hon. Bertram David Mitford, *b* 29 May 2000. *Address:* House of Lords, SW1A 0PW. *Club:* Newcastle University Caving.

REDFERN, Baroness *cr* 2015 (Life Peer), of the Isle of Axholme in the County of Lincolnshire; **Elizabeth Marie Redfern;** Member (C), North Lincolnshire Council (Leader, 2004–07 and since 2011). Mem. (C), Belton Parish Council, 1987–. *Address:* House of Lords, SW1A 0PW.

REDFERN, Rt Rev. Alastair Llewellyn John; *see* Derby, Bishop of.

REDFERN, Michael Howard; QC 1993; a Recorder, since 1999; *b* 30 Nov. 1943; *s* of Lionel William Redfern and Kathleen Roylance Redfern (*née* Brownston); *m* 1st, 1966, Sylvia Newlands (marr. diss. 1989); one *d*; 2nd, 1991, Diana Barbara Eaglestone, *qv*; one *d*, and two step *d*. *Educ:* Stretford Grammar Sch. for Boys; Leeds Univ. (LLB Hons). Teacher, 1967–68; Lectr in Law, 1968–69; called to the Bar, Inner Temple, 1970, Bencher, 2002. *Recreations:* music, sport (preferably participating), travel, history. *Address:* 24a–28 St John Street, Manchester M3 4DJ.

REDFORD, (Charles) Robert; American actor and director; Founder, 1981, and President, Sundance Institute; *b* 18 Aug. 1937; *s* of Charles Redford and Martha (*née* Hart); *m* 1958, Lola Jean Van Wagenen (marr. diss. 1985); one *s* two *d*; *m* 2009, Sibylle Szaggars. *Educ:* Van Nuys High Sch.; Univ. of Colorado; Pratt Inst., Brooklyn; Amer. Acad. of Dramatic Arts. *Theatre:* appearances include: Tall Story, Broadway, 1959; Sunday in New York, Broadway, 1961–62; Barefoot in the Park, Biltmore, NY, 1963–64; *television:* appearances include, The Iceman Cometh, 1960; *films* include: as actor: War Hunt, 1962; Inside Daisy Clover, 1965; Barefoot in the Park, 1967; Butch Cassidy and the Sundance Kid, 1969; The Candidate, 1972; The Way We Were, 1973; The Sting, 1973; The Great Gatsby, 1974; All the President's Men, 1976; The Electric Horseman, 1979; The Natural, 1984; Out of Africa, 1985; Legal Eagles, 1986; Havana, 1990; Sneakers, 1992; Up Close and Personal, 1996; Spy Game, 2001; The Last Castle, 2002; The Clearing, 2004; An Unfinished Life, 2006; All is Lost, 2013; Captain America: The Winter Soldier, 2014; Truth, A Walk in the Woods, 2015; as director: Ordinary People, 1980 (Acad. Award for Best Dir, 1981); Milagro Beanfield War (also prod.), 1988; A River Runs Through It, 1992; Indecent Proposal (also actor), 1993; The River Wild, 1995; The Horse Whisperer (also actor), 1998; The Legend of Bagger Vance, 2001; Lions for Lambs (also actor), 2007; The Conspirator, 2011; The Company You Keep (also actor), 2012. Hon. Academy Award, 2002; Chaplin Award, Film Soc. of Lincoln Center, 2015. *Publications:* The Outlaw Trail, 1978. *Address:* c/o Sundance Institute, PO Box 684429, Park City, UT 84068, USA.

REDGRAVE, Adrian Robert Frank; QC 1992; a Recorder of the Crown Court, since 1985; *b* 1 Sept. 1944; *s* of Cecil Frank Redgrave and Doris Edith Redgrave; *m* 1967, Ann Cooper; two *s* one *d*. *Educ:* Abingdon Sch.; Univ. of Exeter (LLB 1966). Called to the Bar, Inner Temple, 1968. *Recreations:* tennis, wine, garden, France, Bangalore Phall. *Address:* 13 King's Bench Walk, EC4Y 7EN. *T:* (020) 7353 7204.

REDGRAVE, Diane Catherine; Her Honour Judge Redgrave; a Circuit Judge, since 2008; *b* 28 May 1953; *d* of Norman Redgrave and Kathleen Redgrave; *m* 1981, Nicholas Harvey; one *s* one *d*. *Educ:* Notre Dame Collegiate Sch. for Girls, Leeds; Bristol Polytech. (BA Hons (Law) 1974). Lectr in Law, Leeds Polytech., 1974–78; Vis. Lectr in Law, Dept of Econs, Bradford Univ., 1976–77. Called to the Bar, Middle Temple, 1977, Bencher, 2012; District Judge, Principal Registry, Family Div., 1998–2008; Recorder, 2002–08. *Recreations:* my family, walking, ski-ing, reading, gardening. *Address:* Bromley County Court, Court House, College Road, Bromley BR1 3PX.

REDGRAVE, Sir Steven (Geoffrey), Kt 2001; CBE 1997 (MBE 1987); DL; oarsman; sports consultant; *b* 23 March 1962; *m* 1988, Elizabeth Ann Callaway; one *s* two *d*. *Educ:* Great Marlow Sch. Represented: Marlow Rowing Club, 1976–2000; Leander, 1987–2000. Rowed coxless pairs with Andrew Holmes, until 1989, then with Matthew Pinsent; subseq. rowed coxless fours with Matthew Pinsent, James Cracknell and Tim Foster; winner: Commonwealth Games, 1986 (single sculls, coxed fours, coxless pairs); World Championships, coxed pairs, 1986, coxless pairs, 1987, 1991, 1993, 1994 and 1995; Gold Medal, Olympic Games, 1984 (coxed fours), 1988, 1992 and 1996 (coxless pairs), 2000 (coxless fours); Gold Medal, World Championships, coxless fours, 1997, 1998 and 1999. Founded Sir Steve Redgrave Charitable Trust, 2001; Pres., British Assoc. of Snowsport Instructors, 2012–; Chm., Henley Royal Regatta, 2014–; Vice President: Diabetes UK; British Olympic Assoc. Hon. DCL. DL Bucks, 2001. *Publications:* Steven Redgrave's Complete Book of Rowing, 1992; (with Nick Townsend): A Golden Age (autobiog.), 2000; You Can Win at Life!, 2005; Inspired, 2009; Enduring Success, 2010; Great Olympic Moments, 2011. *Address:* PO Box 3400, Marlow, Bucks SL7 3QE. *T:* (01628) 483021. *Club:* Leander (Henley-on-Thames).

REDGRAVE, Vanessa, CBE 1967; actress, since 1957; *b* 30 Jan. 1937; *d* of late Sir Michael Redgrave, CBE, and Rachel Kempson; *m* 1962, Tony Richardson (marr. diss. 1967; he *d* 1991); one *d* (and one *d* decd); one *s* by Franco Nero. *Educ:* Queensgate School; Central School of Speech and Drama. Frinton Summer Repertory, 1957; Touch of the Sun, Saville, 1958; Midsummer Night's Dream, Stratford, 1959; Look on Tempests, 1960; The Tiger and the Horse, 1960; Lady from the Sea, 1960; Royal Shakespeare Theatre Company: As You Like It, 1961, Taming of the Shrew, 1961, Cymbeline, 1962; The Seagull, 1964; The Prime of Miss Jean Brodie, Wyndham's, 1966; Daniel Deronda, 1969; Cato Street, 1971; The Threepenny Opera, Prince of Wales, 1972; Twelfth Night, Shaw Theatre, 1972; Antony and Cleopatra, Bankside Globe, 1973; Design for Living, Phoenix, 1973; Macbeth, LA, 1974; Lady from the Sea, NY, 1976, Roundhouse, 1979; The Aspern Papers, Haymarket, 1984; The Seagull, Queen's, 1985; Chekhov's Women, Lyric, 1985; The Taming of the Shrew and Antony and Cleopatra, Haymarket, 1986; Ghosts, Young Vic, transf. Wyndham's, 1986; Touch of the Poet, Young Vic, transf. Comedy, 1988; Orpheus Descending, Haymarket, 1988, NY, 1989; A Madhouse in Goa, Lyric, Hammersmith, 1989; Three Sisters, Queen's, 1990; When She Danced, Globe, 1991; Heartbreak House, Haymarket, 1992; The Liberation of Skopje, Antony and Cleopatra, Riverside, 1995; John Gabriel Borkman, NT, 1996; The Tempest, Globe, 2000; The Cherry Orchard, RNT, 2000; Lady Windermere's Fan, Haymarket, 2002; Long Day's Journey into Night, NY (Best Actress, Tony Award), 2003; Hecuba, Albery, 2005; The Year of Magical Thinking, NT, 2008; Driving Miss Daisy, Wyndham's, 2011; The Revisionist, Cherry Lane Th., NY, 2013; Much Ado About Nothing, Old Vic, 2013. *Films:* Morgan—A Suitable Case for Treatment, 1966 (Cannes Fest. Award, Best Actress 1966); The Sailor from Gibraltar, 1967; Blow-Up, 1967; Camelot, 1967; Red White and Zero, 1967; Charge of the Light Brigade, 1968; Isadora, 1968; A Quiet Place in the Country, 1968; The Seagull, 1969; Drop-Out, 1970; La Vacanza, 1970; The Trojan Women, 1971; The Devils, 1971; Mary, Queen of Scots, 1972; Murder on the Orient Express, 1974; Out of Season, 1975; Seven Per Cent Solution, 1975; Julia, 1976 (Academy Award, 1977; Golden Globe Award); Agatha, 1978; Yanks, 1978; Bear Island, 1978; Playing for Time, 1980; My Body, My Child, 1981; Wagner, 1983; The Bostonians, 1984; Wetherby, 1985; Steaming, 1985; Comrades, 1987; Prick Up Your Ears, 1987; Consuming Passions, 1988; A Man For All Seasons, 1988; Orpheus Descending, 1990; Young Catherine, 1990; Whatever Happened to Baby Jane, 1990; The Ballad of the Sad Café, 1991; Howards End, 1992; The House of the Spirits, 1994; Mother's Boys, 1994; Little Odessa, 1995; A Month by the Lake, 1996; Mission: Impossible, 1996; Looking for Richard, 1997; Wilde, 1997; Smilla's Feeling for Snow, 1997; Mrs Dalloway, 1998; Deep Impact, 1998; Cradle Will Rock, 2000; Venus, 2007; Evening, 2007; Letters to Juliet, 2010; Anonymous, 2011; Song for Marion, 2013; The Butler, 2013. Television incl. The Gathering Storm, 2002 (Best Actress, BPG awards, 2003); The Day of the Triffids, 2009; The Thirteenth Tale, 2013. Fellow, BAFTA, 2010. *Publications:* Pussies and Tigers (anthology of writings of school children), 1963; Vanessa Redgrave: an autobiography, 1991. *Address:* c/o Gavin Barker Associates, 2d Wimpole Street, W1G 0EB.

See also Joely Richardson.

REDHEAD, Prof. Michael Logan Gonne, FBA 1991; Professor of History and Philosophy of Science, Cambridge University, 1987–97; Fellow, Wolfson College, Cambridge, 1988–97, now Emeritus Fellow (Vice-President, 1992–96); *b* 30 Dec. 1929; *s* of Robert Arthur Redhead and Christabel Lucy Gonne Browning; *m* 1964, Jennifer Anne Hill (*d* 2010); three *s*. *Educ:* Westminster Sch.; University College London (BSc 1st Cl. Hons Physics 1950; PhD Mathematical Phys. 1970). FInstP 1982. Dir, Redhead Properties Ltd, 1962; Partner, Galveston Estates, 1970; Lectr, Sen. Lectr in Philosophy of Science, 1981–84, Prof., Philosophy of Physics, 1984–85, Chelsea Coll., Univ. of London; Prof. of Philosophy of Physics, King's College London, 1985–87; Hd, 1987–93, Chm., 1993–95, Dept of Hist. and Philosophy of Sci., Cambridge Univ.; Dir of Studies, Christ's Coll., Trinity Hall and St Catharine's Coll., Cambridge, 1989–97; London School of Economics: Actg Dir, 1998–2001, Co-Dir, 2001–, Centre for Philosophy of Natural and Social Sci.; Centennial Prof. of Philosophy, 1999–2002. Tarner Lectr, Trinity Coll., Cambridge, 1991–94; Visiting Fellow: Pittsburgh Univ., 1985; Princeton Univ., 1991; LSE, 1994; All Souls Coll., Oxford, 1995; Vis. Prof., Essex Univ., 2004–07. Leverhulme Emeritus Fellow, 2008. Pres., British Soc. for Philos. of Sci., 1989–91; Trustee, Archive Trust for Res. in Math. Scis and Philosophy, 2008–12. Mem., Acad. Internat. de Philosophie des Sciences, 1995. FKC 2000. Lakatos Award in Philosophy of Science, 1988. Editor, Studies in History and Philosophy of Modern Physics, 1993–2001. *Publications:* Incompleteness, Nonlocality and Realism, 1987; From Physics to Metaphysics, 1995; (with T. Debs) Objectivity, Invariance and Convention, 2007; (with S. Groom) God, Belief and Explanation, 2011; papers in learned jls. *Recreations:* tennis, poetry, books, music. *Address:* 119 Rivermead Court, Hurlingham, SW6 3SD. *T:* (020) 7736 6767. *Clubs:* Athenæum, Hurlingham.

REDHOUSE, Naomi; a District Judge (Magistrates' Courts), since 2010; *b* London, 1 Dec. 1955; *d* of late Alexander Redhouse and Diana Redhouse (*née* Behr); one *s* one *d*. *Educ:* Hendon Co. Grammar Sch.; King's Coll., Cambridge (BA 1977); Coll. of Law. Admitted solicitor, 1984; a Dep. District Judge (Magistrates' Courts), 2003–10. *Publications:* with Mark Ashford: Defending Young People in the Criminal Justice System, 3rd edn 2006; Blackstone's Youth Court Handbook 2014–15, 2013. *Recreations:* walking, eating, cooking, friends.

REDING, Dr Viviane; Member (Christian Democrats), European Parliament, since 2014; *b* 27 April 1951; *m*; three *s*. *Educ:* Sorbonne, Paris (PhD). Journalist, Luxemburger Wort, 1978–99; Pres., Luxembourg Union of Journalists, 1986–98. MP (PCS) Luxembourg, 1979–89; MEP (EPP) Luxembourg, 1989–99; Mem., 1999–2014, a Vice-Pres., 2010–14, EC. Nat. Pres., Christian-Social Women, 1988–93; Vice Pres., Parti Chrétien-Social, Luxembourg, 1995–99. *Address:* European Parliament, 60 rue Wiertz, 1047 Brussels, Belgium.

REDMAN, Rev. Anthony James, FRICS; Partner, Whitworth Co. Partnership LLP, Architects and Surveyors, since 1985 (Managing Partner, 1985–2002); *b* 1 May 1951; *s* of Alan Redman and Diana Redman (*née* Cooke); *m* 1974, Caroline Blackwood Ford; two *d*. *Educ:* Walton-on-Thames Secondary Modern Sch.; Surbiton Grammar Sch.; Univ. of Reading (BSc Hons Estate Mgt); East Anglian MTS; Anglia Ruskin Univ. (MA Pastoral Theol. 2005). FRICS 1998; IHBC 1998. Surveyor: Lister Drew and Associates, 1972–74; Suffolk CC, 1974–79; Asst Surveyor, Whitworth & Hall, 1979–85. Surveyor of Fabric, St Edmundsbury Cathedral, 1992–. Chm., RICS Bldg Conservation Gp, 1997–2000; Mem., RICS Conservation Bd, 2000–03. Ordained deacon, 2003, priest, 2004; NSM, N Bury Team, 2003–05; Asst priest NSM, Blackbourne Team, 2006–. Member: Gen. Synod of C of E, 1989–2003 and 2010– (Mem., Church Buildings Council, 2010–); Council for Care of Churches, 1990–2001 (Jt Vice Chm., 1996–2001); Westminster Abbey Fabric Adv. Commn, 1998–; St Albans DAC, 1998–2004; Cathedrals Fabric Commn for England, 1999–2003; Cathedrals Measure Revision Cttee, 2001–02; Peterborough DAC, 2010–. Mem., Baptist Union Listed Bldg Adv. Panel, 1997–2010. Mem., Romanian Hospice of Hope Appeal Cttee, 2003–09. Liveryman, Masons' Co., 2009–. Freeman, City of London, 2009. *Publications:* (ed jtly) A Guide to Church Inspection and Repair, 1996; (ed with M. Carnell) A Taste of Transylvania, 2006. *Recreations:* gardening, painting, Romania, architectural history, avoiding household maintenance. *Address:* (office) 18 Hatter Street, Bury St Edmunds, Suffolk IP33 1NE. *T:* (01284) 760421. *E:* TRedman@whitcp.co.uk.

REDMAN, Prof. Christopher Willard George, FRCP, FRCOG; Consultant and Clinical Professor of Obstetric Medicine, Nuffield Department of Obstetrics and Gynaecology, Oxford University, 1992–2009, now Emeritus; Fellow of Lady Margaret Hall, Oxford, 1988–2009, now Honorary Research Fellow; *b* 30 Nov. 1941; *s* of late Roderick Oliver Redman and Annie Kathleen Redman (*née* Bancroft); *m* 1964, Corinna Susan Page; four *s* one *d*. *Educ:* St John's Coll., Cambridge (MA; MB, BChir). FRCP 1981; FRCOG (*ad eund*) 1993. Oxford University: Clinical Lectr, Dept of Regius Prof. of Medicine, 1970–76; Univ. Lectr and Consultant, Nuffield Dept of Obstetrics and Gynaecol., 1976–89; Clinical Reader and Cons., 1989–92. Pres., Internat. Soc. for Study of Hypertension in Pregnancy, 2006–08. *Publications:* scientific articles about pre-eclampsia in med. jls. *Recreation:* hill-walking. *Address:* Nuffield Department of Obstetrics and Gynaecology, John Radcliffe Maternity Hospital, Headington, Oxford OX3 9DU. *T:* (01865) 221009.

REDMAYNE, Charles George Mariner; Chief Executive Officer, HarperCollins UK, since 2013; *b* London, 30 Aug. 1966; *s* of Richard Redmayne and late Maxine Redmayne (*née* Brodrick, later Gray); *m* 1993, Annabel Jane Grayburn; one *s* one *d*. *Educ:* Eton Coll.; RMA, Sandhurst. Work in advertising and mktg; Founder: RCL Communications, 1993; Blink TV, 1996; Mykindaplace Ltd, 2000–06; Hd, Commercial Partnerships, Sky Online Business Unit, BSkyB, 2006–08; HarperCollins: GP Digital Dir, HarperCollins UK, 2008–09; Exec. Vice Pres. and Chief Digital Officer, NY, 2009–11; CEO, Pottermore, 2011–13. *Recreations:* cricket, tennis, ski-ing, golf, shooting, wine, reading, Scrabble, friends. *Address:* HarperCollins UK, 77–85 Fulham Palace Road, W6 8JB. *T:* (020) 8307 4399. *E:* Charlie.Redmayne@HarperCollins.co.uk. *Club:* Hurlingham.

REDMAYNE, Clive; retired aeronautical engineer; *b* 27 July 1927; *s* of late Procter Hubert Redmayne and Emma (*née* Torkington); *m* 1952, Vera Muriel, *d* of late Wilfred Toplis and Elsie Maud Toplis; one *s* one *d*. *Educ:* Stockport Sch. BSc (Hons Maths) London External. CEng, MIMechE. Fairey Aviation Co.: apprentice, 1944–48; Stress Office, 1948–50; English Electric Co., Warton: Stress Office, 1950–51; A. V. Roe & Co., Chadderton: Stress Office, 1951–55; A. V. Roe & Co., Weapons Research Div., Woodford: Head of Structural Analysis, 1955–62; Structures Dept, RAE, 1962–67; Asst Director, Project Time and Cost Analysis, Min. of Technology, 1967–70; Sen. Officers' War Course, RNC, Greenwich, 1970; Asst Dir, MRCA, MoD(PE), 1970–74; Division Leader, Systems Engrg, NATO MRCA Management Agency (NAMMA), Munich, 1974–76; Chief Supt, A&AEE, Boscombe Down, 1976–78; Dir, Harrier Projects, MoD(PE), 1978–80; Director General, Future Projects, MoD(PE), 1980–81; Dir Gen. Aircraft 3, Procurement Exec., MoD, 1981–84. *Recreations:* reading, chess, bridge. *Address:* 6 Hanna Court, 195–199 Wilmslow Road, Handforth, Cheshire SK9 3JX. *T:* (01625) 526315.

REDMAYNE, Sir Giles (Martin), 3rd Bt *cr* 1964, of Rushcliffe, co. Nottingham; Managing Director, Purpose Design, since 2004; *b* Chelmsford, 1 Dec. 1968; *s* of Hon. Sir Nicholas John Redmayne, 2nd Bt, and Ann Redmayne (*née* Saunders) (*d* 1985); *S* father, 2008; *m* 1994, Claire Ann O'Halloran; three *s*. *Educ:* Radley Coll. Man. Dir, Reef Design, 1996–2010. *Recreations:* shooting, ski-ing. *Heir: s* George Martin John Redmayne, *b* 13 April 2001. *Address:* Walcote Lodge, Walcote, Lutterworth, Leics LE17 4JR. *E:* redmayne@atlas.co.uk.

REDMOND, Sir Anthony (Gerard), Kt 2011; CPFA; Chairman and Chief Executive, Commission for Local Administration, and Local Government Ombudsman, 2001–10; *b* 18 May 1945; *s* of Alfonso and Florence Redmond; *m* 1973, Christine Mary Pinnington; two *s* two *d*. *Educ:* St Mary's Coll., Crosby. CPFA 1968. IRRV 2011. Liverpool City Council: various accountancy and audit posts, 1962–75; Chief Accountant, 1975–78; Dep. Treas., Wigan MBC, 1978–82; Treasurer: and Dep. Chief Exec., Knowsley MBC, 1982–87; Merseyside Police Authy, 1985–87; W London Waste Authy, 1987–2001; Chief Exec., London Borough of Harrow, 1987–2001. Mem., Local Govt Boundary Commn for England, 2011–; Chm., Consumer Council for Water (London and SE), 2013–. Treas., UNICEF UK, 2011–. FRSA 1994; Fellow, CPA Australia, 2012. Friend: Royal Opera Hse; Royal Acad. *Recreations:* sport, theatre, ballet, good food and fine wines. *Clubs:* MCC; Wasps Rugby, Waterloo Rugby (Blundellsands), Lancashire Rugby.

REDMOND, Ian Michael, OBE 2006; CBiol, FZS, FLS; independent wildlife biologist, since 1979; Consultant to UN Food and Agriculture Organisation, since 2009; Ambassador, UNEP Convention on Migratory Species, since 2010; Ambassador and Consultant, Virtual Ecotourism, since 2012; *b* 11 April 1954; *s* of Maj. Peter Redmond, RAMC (retd) and Margaret Redmond; *m* 1982, Caroline Ireland; two *s*. *Educ:* Beverley Grammar Sch., E Yorks; Kelvin Hall High Sch.; Univ. of Keele (BSc Hons Biol. with Geol. 1976). FZS 1979; MRSB (MIBiol 1985), CBiol 1986. Res. Asst to Dr Dian Fossey, Karisoke Res. Centre, Rwanda, 1976–78; zoologist, Operation Drake, PNG, 1979; field conservationist, Fauna Preservation Soc., Mt Gorilla Project, Rwanda, 1980; zoologist/botanist, Operation Drake, Kenya, 1980; estabd Mt Elgon Elephant Caves Res. Project, Kenya, 1981–. Hon. Res. Associate, Dept of Psychol., Univ. of Hull, 1981–. Mem., Primate Specialist Gp, IUCN Species Survival Commn, 2000–. Scientific Advr for, and sometimes featured in, numerous natural history documentaries, e.g. by BBC, Nat. Geographic, US and French TV, 1977–; documentaries include: Pembe ya Ndovu (we want ivory and we want more now) (Exec. Producer), 2014; When Giants Fall (Prod./biol consultant), 2014; freelance lecturer: UK and Africa, 1978–; N America, 1986–; public speaker: Foyles Lecture Agency, 1980–2000; Gordon Poole Agency, 2006–; Vis. Lectr, Oxford Brookes Univ., 2011–. Freelance natural history photo-journalist, 1982–; reporter, BBC Wildlife Mag., 1983–84; Leader, Wildlife Special Interest Tours, 1983–. Consultant, 1986–, various conservation and animal welfare orgns, including: Dian Fossey Gorilla Fund (formerly Digit Fund); Born Free Foundn; Internat. Fund for Animal Welfare; Internat. Primate Protection League; WSPA, etc. Accredited observer: Convention on Internat. Trade in Endangered Species of Wild Fauna and Flora, Lausanne, 1989, Kyoto, 1992, Fort Lauderdale, 1994, Harare, 1997, Nairobi, 2000, Santiago, Chile, 2002, Bangkok, 2004 and 2013, The Hague, 2007, Doha, 2010, Bangkok, 2013; Convention on Biological Diversity, Kuala Lumpur, 2004, Curitiba, 2006, Bonn, 2008, Nagoya, 2010; UN Framework Convention on Climate Change, Bali, 2007, Poznan, 2008, Copenhagen, 2009; UNEP Convention on Migratory Species, Rome, 2008, Bergen, 2011. Founder: and Co-ordinator, African Ele-Fund, 1987– (Co-founder, Elefriends, subseq. part of Born Free Foundn, 1989); and Chm., UK Rhino Gp, 1993–2003; and Chm., Ape Alliance, 1996–; Hd, Tech. Support Team, 2001–05, Chief Consultant, 2005–09, Envoy, 2009–12, Consultant, 2012–, UNEP/UNESCO Great Ape Survival Partnership (formerly Project, and under contract to Born Free Foundn and UNEP, 2001–11); Consultant, The Last of the Great Apes (3D film), 2012. Mem., British Herpetological Soc., 1981–. Member: Yorks Wildlife Trust, 1970–; Jersey Wildlife Preservation Trust, 1973–; Fauna and Flora Internat., 1978–; E African Wildlife Soc., 1980–; Elephant Res. Foundn (formerly Elephant Interest Gp), 1982–; Primate Soc. of GB, 1982– (Mem. Conservation Wkg Party, 1988–; Mem. Council, 1996–99, 2012–); Wildlife Conservation Soc. of Tanzania, 1992–; Elephant, Primates and Rhino/Tiger Wkg Gps, Species Survival Network, 1995–. Trustee: Orangutan Foundn-UK, 1993–; The Gorilla Organization (formerly Dian Fossey Gorilla Fund Europe), 2004– (Chm., Bd of Trustees, 2012–); Great Ape Film Initiative, 2006–; Thin Green Line Foundn (UK), 2014–. Ambassador, UN Year of the Gorilla, 2009. FLS 2008. DUniv Oxford Brookes, 2011; Hon. DSc Roehampton, 2014. Conservation Award, Internat. Fund for Animal Welfare, 2013. *Publications:* The Elephant in the Bush, 1990; (with V. Harrison) The World of Elephants, 1990; Monkeys and Apes, 1990; Wildlife at Risk: Gorillas, 1990; Wildlife at Risk: Elephants, 1990; The Elephant Book, 1990, 2nd edn 2001 (Friends of the Earth Earthworm Award, 1991); (jtly) Elephants - the Deciding Decade (Canada), 1991, 2nd edn 1997, UK edn as Elephants, Saving the Gentle Giants, 1993; Eyewitness Elephant, 1993; Eyewitness Gorilla and other primates, 1995; The Primate Family Tree: primates of the world, 2008; (jtly) Last Stand of the Gorilla: environmental crime and conflict in the Congo Basin, 2010; (jtly) Stolen Apes, 2013; contrib. numerous scientific reports and papers, news reports and feature articles to wildlife mags worldwide, and newspapers incl. Guardian, Sunday Times, Kuwait Times, Arab Post, Hong Kong Standard, Jakarta Post. *Recreations:* natural history, travel, outdoor activities, collecting antiquarian books and 78rpm records, minimum-intervention gardening and home maintenance. *Address:* Ape Alliance, c/o RSPCA Building, Lansdown, Stroud, Glos GL5 1BG. *T:* and *Fax:* (01453) 765228. *E:* ele@globalnet.co.uk. *W:* www.twitter.com/4apes.

REDMOND, Imelda, CBE 2010; Chief Executive, 4Children, since 2015; *b* 7 June 1959; *d* of Andy and Alice Redmond; *m* Jo Clare; one step *s*. *Educ:* Froebel Inst. (BA Hons (Social Admin) Univ. of London). Dir, Markfield Project, 1989–98; Dep. CEO, 1998–2003, Chief Exec., 2003–11, Carers UK; Dir, Policy and Public Affairs, Marie Curie Cancer Care, 2011–14. *Address:* 4Children, 5 Greenwich View Place, E14 9NN.

REDMOND, Phil, CBE 2004; writer and television producer; Founder, The Mersey Television Co. Ltd (Chairman, 1981–2005); Chairman, Merseyfilm, since 2003; *m* Alexis Jane Redmond. *Educ:* Univ. of Liverpool (BA Hons). Writer, Grange Hill, 1978–81; Executive Producer: Brookside, 1982–2003; Hollyoaks, 1996–2005; Grange Hill, 2002–08. Creative Chair, 2008 Eur. Capital of Culture, Liverpool, 2007–09. Chm. of Trustees, National Museums and Galleries of Liverpool, 2008–. Hon. Prof. of Media, 1989, Fellow, 1989, Ambassador Fellow, 2010, Liverpool John Moores Univ. FRSA 1996. Hon. DLitt: Chester, 2010; Liverpool, 2010. *Recreations:* photography, boating, digital media. *Address:* (office) Merseyfilm, Tirley Garth, Willington, Tarporley, Cheshire CW6 0RQ.

REDSHAW, Peter Robert Gransden; HM Diplomatic Service, retired; Group Security Adviser, Gallaher Ltd, 1996–2004; *b* 16 April 1942; *s* of late Robert Henry Gransden Redshaw and Audrey Nita Redshaw (*née* Ward); *m* 1970, Margaret Shaun (*née* Mizon) (*d* 2013); one *s* two *d*. *Educ:* Boxgrove School; Charterhouse; Trinity College, Cambridge (MA). ACA. Price Waterhouse, 1964–67; FCO, 1968; Kampala, 1970–73; 1st Sec., 1971; FCO, 1973; Lagos, 1982–85; Counsellor, 1985; FCO, 1985–88; Kuala Lumpur, 1988–91; FCO, 1992–96. *Recreations:* books, history, sailing, travel. *Clubs:* Kampala; Woking Tennis & Croquet.

REDSHAW, Tina Susan; HM Diplomatic Service; Consul-General, Chongqing, China, since 2013; *b* 25 Jan. 1961; *d* of Trevor Redshaw and Doreen Cooper; *m* 2001, Phong Phun Khogapun; one *d*. *Educ:* York Univ. (BA Hons Lang./Linguistics); Open Univ. (MSc Develt Mgt). Voluntary Service Overseas: Prog. Dir, China, 1990–94; Regl Prog. Manager, SE Asia, 1994–99; entered FCO, 1999; China Hong Kong Dept, 1999–2000; First Sec., Beijing, 2000–03; Ambassador, E Timor, 2003–06; Hd of Environment, Energy and Infrastructure, UK Trade and Investment, Beijing, 2007–11; Dep. Hd, Climate Change, FCO, 2011–13. *Recreations:* photography, theatre, dance, jazz music, swimming, creative writing. *E:* tina.redshaw@fco.gov.uk.

REDWOOD, Rt Hon. John (Alan); PC 1993; DPhil; MP (C) Wokingham, since 1987; *b* 15 June 1951; *s* of William Charles Redwood and Amy Emma Redwood (*née* Champion); *m* 1974, Gail Felicity Chippington (marr. diss. 2004); one *s* one *d*. *Educ:* Kent Coll., Canterbury;

Magdalen and St Antony's Colls, Oxford; MA, DPhil Oxon. MCSI. Fellow, All Souls Coll., Oxford, 1972–87, 2003–05, 2007–. Investment Adviser, Robert Fleming & Co., 1973–77; Investment Manager and Dir, N. M. Rothschild & Sons, 1977–87; Norcros plc: Dir, 1985–89; Jt Dep. Chm., 1986–87; non-exec. Chm., 1987–89. Non-executive Chairman: Hare Hatch Hldgs Ltd (formerly Mabey Securities), 1999–2008; Concentric plc, 2003–08; Pan Asset Capital Mgt, 2007–09; non-exec. Dir, BNB, 2001–07. Investment Advr, CS (formerly Evercore) Pan Asset, 2007–. Adviser, Treasury and Civil Service Select Cttee, 1981; Head of PM's Policy Unit, 1983–85. Councillor, Oxfordshire CC, 1973–77. Parly Under Sec. of State, DTI, 1989–90; Minister of State: DTI, 1990–92; DoE, 1992–93; Sec. of State for Wales, 1993–95; Opposition front bench spokesman on trade and industry, 1997–99, on the envmt, 1999–2000; Shadow Sec. of State for De-regulation, 2004–05. Head, Cons. Parly Campaigns Unit, 2000–01; Chairman: Cons. Party Policy Review on Econ. Competitiveness, 2005–10; Cons. Economic Affairs Cttee, 2010–. Vis. Prof., Middx Business Sch., 2000–. Governor of various schools, 1974–83. Qualified Ind. Financial Advr, CISI, 2012. *Publications:* Reason, Ridicule and Religion, 1976; Public Enterprise in Crisis, 1980; (with John Hatch) Value for Money Audits, 1981; (with John Hatch) Controlling Public Industries, 1982; Going for Broke, 1984; Equity for Everyman, 1986; Popular Capitalism, 1988; The Global Marketplace, 1994; The Single Currency, 1995; Action Not Words, 1996; Our Currency, Our Country, 1997; The Death of Britain?, 1999; Stars and Strife, 2001; Just Say No, 2001; Singing the Blues, 2004; Superpower Struggles, 2005; I Want to Make a Difference, 2006; After the Credit Crunch, 2009; The Future of the Euro, 2012; pamphlets on Cons. matters. *Recreations:* water sports, village cricket, daily blog (www.johnredwood.com). *W:* www.johnredwoodsdiary.com. *Address:* House of Commons, SW1A 0AA. *T:* (office) (020) 7219 4205, (home) (020) 7976 6603.

REDWOOD, Sir Peter (Boverton), 3rd Bt *cr* 1911; Colonel, late King's Own Scottish Borderers, retired 1987; *b* 1 Dec. 1937; *o s* of Sir Thomas Boverton Redwood, 2nd Bt, TD, and Ruth Mary Redwood (*née* Creighton, then Blair); *S* father, 1974; *m* 1964, Gilian, *o d* of John Lee Waddington Wood, Limuru, Kenya; three *d. Educ:* Gordonstoun. National Service, 1956–58, 2nd Lieut, Seaforth Highlanders; regular commn, KOSB, 1959; served in UK (despatches 1972), BAOR, Netherlands, ME, Africa and Far East; Staff Coll., Camberley, 1970; Nat. Defence Coll., Latimer, 1978–79. Dir, SERCO-IAL Ltd, 1992–95. Vice-Pres., Royal Bath and West of England Soc. Mem., Queen's Body Guard for Scotland (Royal Co. of Archers). Liveryman, Goldsmiths' Co. *Recreations:* shooting, silver and silversmithing. *Heir: half-b* Robert Boverton Redwood [*b* 24 June 1953; *m* 1978, Mary Elizabeth Wright; one *s* one *d*]. *Address:* c/o Drummonds, Royal Bank of Scotland, 49 Charing Cross, SW1A 2DX.

REECE, Damian John; Managing Partner, Instinctif Partners (formerly Managing Partner and Deputy Chief Executive, College Hill Capital Markets), since 2013; *b* Yalding, Kent, 15 Oct. 1966; *s* of Malcolm Reece and Sheila Reece; *m* 1995, Page Shepherd; one *s* one *d. Educ:* St Joseph's RC Sch., Horwich; Thornleigh Salesian Coll., Bolton; Univ. of Manchester (BA Econs). Staff writer, Investors Chronicle, 1993–94; Dep. Personal Finance Ed., The Sunday Telegraph, 1994–98; Consumer Industries Corresp., Sunday Business, 1998–99; Asst City Ed., The Sunday Telegraph, 1999–2003; City Ed., The Independent, 2003–05; Dep. City Ed., 2005–06, City Ed., 2006–07, The Daily Telegraph; Hd of Business, Telegraph Media Gp, 2007–13. Personal Finance Journalist of Year, 1996; Consumer Industries Journalist of Year, 2000. *Publications:* The Sunday Telegraph A–Z Guide to Family Finance, 1996. *Recreations:* family, the great outdoors, music and the arts, sport, clocks. *Address:* 116 Wilberforce Road, N4 2SU. *T:* 07931 598593, (020) 7457 2020. *E:* damian.reece@instinctif.com.

REECE, His Honour (Edward Vans) Paynter; a Circuit Judge, 1982–2003; *b* 17 May 1936; *s* of Clifford Mansel Reece and Catherine Barbara Reece (*née* Hathorn); *m* 1967, Rosamund Mary Reece (*née* Roberts); three *s* one *d. Educ:* Blundell's Sch.; Magdalene Coll., Cambridge (MA). Called to the Bar, Inner Temple, 1960; a Recorder of the Crown Court, 1980–82. *Recreations:* fishing, golf. *Clubs:* Garrick; New Zealand Golf.

REECE, Dr Henry Michael; Secretary to Delegates, and Chief Executive, Oxford University Press, 1998–2009; Fellow of Jesus College, Oxford, 1998–2009, now Emeritus; *b* 10 Aug. 1953; *s* of David Reece and Persis Rebecca Reece; *m* 1993, Allison Jane King (marr. diss. 2005); *m* 2009, Susan Norine Froud. *Educ:* Univ. of Bristol (BA 1st Cl. Hons); St John's Coll., Oxford (DPhil Modern Hist. 1981; Hon. Fellow 2010). Tutor in Hist., Univ. of Exeter, 1977–78; Prentice Hall International: Field Sales Editor, 1979–82; Academic Sales Manager, 1982–84; UK Sales Manager, 1984–85; Asst Vice-Pres., Simon & Schuster Internat., 1985–88; Exec. Ed., Allyn & Bacon (US), 1988–91; Man. Dir, Pitman Publishing, 1991–94; Executive Director: Longman Gp Ltd, 1994–95; Pearson Professional, 1995–97. Mem. Council, Publishers Assoc., 1999–2006 (Pres., 2004–05). Hon. DLitt Oxford, 2010. *Publications:* The Army in Cromwellian England, 1649–1660, 2013. *Recreations:* reading crime novels, watching Wales win at Rugby, cycling, kayaking, walking the dog. *Address:* Jesus College, Turl Street, Oxford OX1 3DW.

REECE, Paynter; *see* Reece, His Honour E. V. P.

REECE, Richard Marsden, DPhil; FSA; Reader in Late Roman Archaeology and Numismatics, Institute of Archaeology, University College London, 1994–99; *b* 25 March 1939; *o s* of Richard Marsden Reece and Alice Reece (*née* Wedel). *Educ:* Cirencester Grammar Sch.; UCL (BSc Biochem. 1961); Wadham Coll., Oxford (DipEd 1962; DPhil 1972). FSA 1968. Asst Master, St John's Sch., Leatherhead, 1962–65; Head of Chem. Dept, St George's Sch., Harpenden, 1966–68; London Institute of Archaeology, subseq. Institute of Archaeology, University College London: Lectr, 1970–81; Sen. Lectr, 1981–93; Tutor to Arts students, 1988–91. Linecar Lectr, British Numismatic Soc., 2011. Membre d'Honneur, Romanian Numismatic Soc.; Hon. FRNS 2003 (RNS Medal 2009). Derek Allen Award, British Acad., 2014. *Publications:* Roman Coins, 1970; Excavations on Iona 1964–74, 1981; Coinage in Roman Britain, 1987, revd edn as Coinage of Roman Britain, 2002; My Roman Britain, 1988; Later Roman Empire, 1999; Roman Coins and Archaeology: collected papers, 2003; articles in learned jls. *Recreations:* reading novels, music. *Address:* The Apple Loft, The Waterloo, Cirencester, Glos GL7 2PU.

REED, Rt Hon. Lord; Robert John Reed; PC 2008; a Justice of the Supreme Court of the United Kingdom, since 2012; *b* 7 Sept. 1956; *s* of George and Elizabeth Reed; *m* 1988, Jane Mylne; two *d. Educ:* George Watson's Coll.; Univ. of Edinburgh (LLB 1st Cl. Hons; Vans Dunlop Schol.); Balliol Coll., Oxford (DPhil). Admitted to Faculty of Advocates, 1983; called to the Bar, Inner Temple, 1991, Bencher, 2012; Standing Junior Counsel: Scottish Educn Dept, 1988–89; Scottish Office Home and Health Dept, 1989–95; QC (Scot.) 1995; Advocate Depute, 1996–98; a Senator of the Coll. of Justice in Scotland, 1998–2012; a Judge of the Outer House of the Court of Session, 1998–2008; Principal Commercial Judge, 2006–08; Mem., Inner House, 2008–12; *ad hoc* Judge, European Court of Human Rights, 1999. Expert advr, EU/Council of Europe Jt Initiative with Turkey, 2002–04. Chm., Franco-British Judicial Co-operation Cttee, 2005–12; Pres., EU Forum of Judges for the Envmt, 2006–08; Member: Adv. Bd, British Inst. Internat. and Comparative Law, 2001–06; UN Task Force on Access to Justice, 2006–09. Convener, Children in Scotland, 2006–12. Chm., Centre for Commercial Law, Univ. of Edinburgh, 2008–12; Visitor, Balliol Coll., Oxford, 2011–. Hon. Prof., Univ. of Glasgow, 2006–. Scottish Ed., European Law Reports, 1997–2011. FRSE 2015. Hon. LLD Glasgow, 2013. *Publications:* (with J. M. Murdoch) Human Rights Law in Scotland, 2001, 3rd edn 2011; contribs to various books and jls on public law. *Recreation:* music. *Address:* Supreme Court of the United Kingdom, Parliament Square, SW1P 3BD.

REED, Sir Alec (Edward), Kt 2011; CBE 1994; Founder, Reed Executive PLC, 1960; *b* 16 Feb. 1934; *s* of Leonard Reed and Annie Underwood; *m* 1961, Adrianne Mary Eyre; two *s* one *d. Educ:* Grammar School. FCMA. Founded: Medicare PLC; ICC PLC; Reed Business Sch.; Womankind Worldwide; Ethiopiaid UK, Australia, Ireland, Canada; Women @ Risk; Acad. of Enterprise; Alec Reed Acad.; The Big Give. President: Inst. of Employment Consultants, 1974–78; Internat. Confedn of Private Employment Agency Assocs, 1978–81. Hon. Prof., Enterprise and Innovation, Royal Holloway, Univ. of London, 1993–2003 (Hon. Fellow; Fellow, RHBNC, 1988); Vis. Prof., London Metropolitan (formerly London Guildhall) Univ., 1999–2004; Hon. Prof., Warwick Univ., 2001–14. Mem. Council, RHC, 1979–85. Fellow, Beacon Fellowship Charitable Trust, 2010 (Beacon Prize, 2010). Hon. PhD London Guildhall, 1999; DUniv Open, 2012. *Publications:* Innovation in Human Resource Management, 2002; Capitalism is Dead, Peoplism Rules, 2003; I Love Mondays (autobiog.), 2012. *Recreations:* family, ballet, cinema, tennis, riding, portrait painting, bridge. *Address:* Reed Foundation, The Peak, 5 Wilton Road, SW1V 1AN.

See also J. A. Reed.

REED, Andrew John, OBE 2012; Director, Saje Impact, since 2010; Senior Partner, Green & Gold Partnership, since 2013; *b* 17 Sept. 1964; *s* of James Donald Reed and Margaret Anne Reed; *m* 1992, Sarah Elizabeth Chester. *Educ:* Riverside Jun. Sch.; Stonehill High Sch.; Longslade Community Coll.; Leicester Poly. (BA Hons Public Admin 1987). Parly Asst to Keith Vaz, MP, 1987–88; Urban Regeneration Officer, Leicester CC, 1988–90; Sen. Economic Develt Officer, 1990–94, European Officer, 1994–97, Leics CC. MP (Lab and Co-op) Loughborough, 1997–2010; contested (Lab and Co-op) same seat, 2010. Parliamentary Private Secretary: to Minister for Sport, 2000–01; to Sec. of State for Envmt, Food and Rural Affairs, 2001–03; to Paymaster General, 2005–07. Director: Special Olympics Bd, 2010–; Amateur Swimming Assoc., 2010–13; Sports Think Tank, 2011–; Chair: Sport and Recreation Alliance, 2011–; Volleyball England Foundn, 2011–13; Mem. Bd, British Basketball League Foundn, 2011–. Mem., Evangelical Alliance Council, 2009–14. Trustee: Richard Engelhardt Trust, 2010–; Sports Chaplaincy UK, 2013–; Dir, World Vision UK, 2013–. Vis. Prof. of Sports Policy and Develt, Liverpool John Moores Univ., 2014–. *Recreations:* Rugby, volleyball, tennis, running. *Address:* 17 Nursery Lane, Quorn, Loughborough, Leics LE12 8BH. *Clubs:* Birstall Rugby Football, Leicester Rugby Football.

REED, Air Cdre April Anne, RRC 1981; Director of RAF Nursing Services, 1984–85, retired; *b* 25 Jan. 1930; *d* of Captain Basil Duck Reed, RN, and Nancy Mignon Ethel Reed. *Educ:* Channing Sch., Highgate. SRN, SCM. SRN training, Middlesex Hosp., 1948–52; midwifery training, Royal Maternity Hosp., Belfast, 1953; joined Royal Air Force, 1954; Dep. Matron, 1970; Sen. Matron, 1976; Principal Matron, 1981; Matron in Chief (Director), 1984. *Recreations:* sailing, ornithology, antiques, gardening, interest in oriental carpets. *Address:* 1 Garners Row, Walsingham Road, Burnham Thorpe, King's Lynn, Norfolk PE31 8HN. *Club:* Royal Air Force.

REED, Barry St George Austin, CBE 1988; MC 1951; Chairman, Austin Reed Group PLC, 1973–96; *b* 5 May 1931; *s* of late Douglas Austin Reed and Mary Ellen (*née* Philpott); *m* 1st 1956, Patricia (*née* Bristow) (*d* 2002); one *s* one *d*; 2nd, 2005, Mary Rose (*née* Lee Warner), *widow* of N. S. Farquharson. *Educ:* Rugby Sch. Commnd Middlesex Regt (DCO), 1950; served Korea, 1950–51; TA, 1951–60. Joined Austin Reed Group, 1953; Dir, 1958–99; Man. Dir, 1966–85. National Westminster Bank: Dir, City and West End Regions, 1980–87; Dir, 1987–90; Chm., Eastern Regl Adv. Bd, 1987–92; Dir, UK Adv. Bd, 1990–92. Pres., Menswear Assoc. of Britain, 1966–67; Chairman: Retail Alliance, 1967–70; British Knitting and Clothing Export Council, 1985–89; Dir, British Apparel and Textile Confedn, 1992–99; Member: Bd, Retail Trading-Standards Assoc., 1964–78; Consumer Protection Adv. Cttee, 1973–79; European Trade Cttee, 1975–84; Cttee, Fleming American Exempt Fund, 1979–94; Council, Royal Warrant Holders Assoc., 1980–2012 (Pres., 1990). Dir, Independent Broadcasting Telethon Trust Ltd, 1991–94. Pres., Vale of York Cons. Assoc., 1995–2000. Dir, Hambleton and Richmondshire Partnership Against Crime, 1997–99. Chm., Queen Elizabeth Scholarship Trust, 1990–95; Trustee, Third Age Challenge Trust, 1994–96. Member: Ripon and Leeds Dio. Synod, 1997–2006; Ripon and Leeds Dio. Bd of Finance, 1997–2009; Vice-Chm., 1997–2000, Chm., 2000–03, Ripon and Leeds Dio. Parsonages Bd; Chm., Ripon and Leeds Dio. Property and Estates Cttee, 2003–09. Freeman, City of London, 1963; Liveryman, Glovers' Co., 1963– (Master, 1980–81). DL Greater London, 1977–99; Rep. DL, London Borough of Hackney, 1980–86. FRSA. *Publications:* papers in clothing, textile and banking jls. *Recreations:* travel, gardens, reading. *Address:* The Old School, East Witton, Leyburn, N Yorks DL8 4SN. *T:* (01969) 625817. *Clubs:* Army and Navy, Pilgrims, MCC.

See also L. D. Reed.

REED, David; Director of Corporate Communications, Whitbread plc, 1990–2005; *b* 24 April 1945; *s* of Wilfred Reed and Elsie Swindon; *m* 1973, Susan Garrett, MA Oxon, MScEcon. *Educ:* West Hartlepool Grammar Sch. Former journalist and public relations adviser to Investors in Industry, Rank Xerox, Ernst & Young (formerly Ernst & Whinney), Hewlett-Packard. Dir and Hd of Corporate and Financial PR, Ogilvy and Mather. MP (Lab) Sedgefield, Co. Durham, 1970–Feb. 1974. Trustee: Leonard Cheshire Foundn, 2005–12; TB Alert, 2006–. *Publications:* many articles in national newspapers and other jls. *Recreations:* theatre, music, walking the dog. *Address:* St Luke's Cottage, Stonor, Oxon RG9 6HE.

REED, David; Regional Employment Judge (formerly Regional Chairman of Employment Tribunals), Newcastle upon Tyne, since 1998; *b* 11 Oct. 1946; *s* of Thomas and Olive Reed; *m* 1976, Sylvia Mary Thompson. *Educ:* London Univ. (LLB ext.). Admitted Solicitor (William Hutton Prize), 1972, in practice, 1972–91; full-time Chm., Industrial Tribunals, 1991–. *Address:* Quayside House, 110 Quayside, Newcastle upon Tyne NE1 3DX. *T:* (0191) 260 6900.

REED, Gavin Barras; *b* 13 Nov. 1934; *s* of late Lt-Col Edward Reed and Greta Milburn (*née* Pybus); *m* 1957, Muriel Joyce, *d* of late Humphrey Vaughan Rowlands; one *s* three *d. Educ:* Eton; Trinity Coll., Cambridge (BA). National Service, Fleet Air Arm Pilot, 1953–55. Joined Newcastle Breweries Ltd, 1958; Dir, Scottish & Newcastle Breweries Ltd, 1970–94; Gp Man. Dir, 1988–91, Gp Vice-Chm., 1991–94, Scottish & Newcastle plc; Chairman: Wainhomes plc, 1994–98; Harmeny Educn Trust Ltd, 1995–2005; John Menzies plc, 1997–2002 (Dir, 1992–2002); Hamilton & Inches Ltd, 1998–2011; Maclay Gp plc, 2001–12; Dir, Burtonwood Brewery plc, 1996–2005. Chm., N Region, CBI, 1987–88. Liveryman, Brewers' Co., 1992–. *Recreation:* shooting. *Address:* West Farnley Grange, Corbridge, Northumberland NE45 5RP. *Club:* New (Edinburgh).

REED, James Andrew; Chairman: Reed Executive Ltd, since 2004; Reed Global Ltd, since 2008; *b* Woking, 12 April 1963; *s* of Sir Alec Edward Reed, *qv*; *m* 1991, Nicola Arkell; three *s* three *d. Educ:* St Paul's Sch., London; Christ Church, Oxford (MA Hons PPE); Harvard Business Sch. (MBA). Exec. Asst, Body Shop plc, 1984–85; Media Planner and Buyer, Saatchi & Saatchi plc, 1986; Project Adminr, Afghanaid, 1987–88; Producer, BBC Television, 1990–94; Reed Executive plc: non-exec. Dir, 1991–94; Ops Dir, 1994–96; Chief Operating Officer, 1996–97; Chief Exec., 1997–2004; Chairman: Reed Learning Ltd, 2004–; Reed in Partnership, 2004–; Reed Online Ltd, 2004–. Founder, Keep Britain Working Campaign, 2009. FCIPD 2003. *Publications:* (jtly) Put Your Mindset to Work, 2011; Why You?: 101

interview questions you'll never fear again, 2014. *Recreations:* cinema, horse riding, mountaineering, running, scuba diving, tennis. *Address:* Reed Executive Ltd, The Peak, 5 Wilton Road, SW1V 1AN. *T:* (020) 7616 2301. *E:* james.reed@reedglobal.com. *Club:* Brooks's.

REED, Jamieson Ronald, (Jamie); MP (Lab) Copeland, since 2005; *b* 4 Aug. 1973; *s* of Ronald and Gloria Reed; *m*; three *s* one *d*. *Educ:* Whitehaven Sch.; Manchester Univ. (BA English 1994); Univ. of Leicester (MA Mass Communications 2000). Researcher: EP, 1995–97; and Advr, Labour Gp, Cumbria CC, 1997–2000; Manager, TU and Community Sellafield Campaign, 2000–01; Public Affairs, BNFL, 2001–05. *Recreations:* spending time with my family, American literature, modern history, music, football, fell walking, Rugby League. *Address:* House of Commons, SW1A 0AA. *T:* (office) (01946) 816723. *E:* andersenj@parliament.uk.

REED, Jane Barbara, CBE 2000; Director, Times Newspaper Holdings Ltd, since 2002; Director of Corporate Affairs, News International plc, 1989–2000; 2nd *d* of late William and Gwendoline Reed, Letchworth, Herts. *Educ:* Royal Masonic Sch.; sundry further educational establishments. Journalist on numerous magazines; returned to Woman's Own, 1965; Editor, 1970–79; Publisher, IPC Women's Monthly Group, 1979–81; Editor-in-Chief, Woman magazine, 1981–82; IPC Magazines: Asst Man. Dir, Specialist Educn and Leisure Gp, 1983; Man. Dir, Holborn Publishing Gp, 1983–85; Man. Editor (Features), Today, News (UK) Ltd, 1985–86; Man. Editor, Today, 1986–89. Mem., Editl Bd, British Journalism Rev., 2004–12. Pres., Media Soc., 1995. Trustee: Nat. Literacy Trust, 1992–; Media Trust, 1994–2014. Member: Royal Soc. COPUS, 1986–96; Council, Nat. Acad. of Writing, 2001–09. Trustee, St Katharine and Shadwell Trust, 1992–2009. Gov., Lady Margaret Sch., Fulham, 2011–. *Publications:* Girl About Town, 1964; (jtly) Kitchen Sink—or Swim?, 1982. *Address:* Fulham.

REED, Ven. John Peter Cyril; Archdeacon of Taunton, since 1999; *b* 21 May 1951; *s* of C. Gordon Reed and M. Joan Reed (*née* Stenning); *m* 1979, Gillian Mary Coles; one *s* one *d*. *Educ:* Monkton Combe Sch., Bath; King's Coll. London (BD, AKC 1978); Ripon Coll., Cuddesdon. With Imperial Group, 1969–73; Research and Marketing, Wales & the West Ltd, Cardiff, 1973–75. Deacon 1979, priest 1980; Curate, Croydon Parish Church, 1979–82; Precentor, St Albans Abbey, 1982–86; Rector, Timsbury and Priston and Chaplain for Rural Affairs, Archdeaconry of Bath, 1986–93; Team Rector, Ilminster and Dist Team Ministry, 1993–99. *Recreations:* family, cricket, tennis, fishing, countryside. *Address:* 2 Monkton Heights, West Monkton, Taunton TA2 8LU. *T:* (01823) 413315. *E:* adtaunton@bathwells.anglican.org.

REED, (John William) Rupert; QC 2014; *b* Dunfermline, 27 Nov. 1969; *s* of Comdr Robert Reed, RN and Joan Reed; *m* 2004, Anna Jane Boase; one *s* two *d*. *Educ:* Sandroyd Sch.; Sherborne Sch.; Lincoln Coll., Oxford (BA Mod. Hist. and French 1992); Downing Coll., Cambridge (BA Law 1994); Harvard Law Sch. (LLM Law 1995). Called to the Bar, Lincoln's Inn, 1996, Cayman Is (ad hoc), 1999; in practice as a barrister, Wilberforce Chambers, 1997–; Attorney Gen.'s C Panel of Treasury Counsel, 2000–05; Registered Advocate, DIFC Courts, 2009–. *Publications:* articles in Company, Banking and Commercial Law. *Recreations:* family, working from home, lunching with newspaper, cycling, classical and world music, French cinema, Arab news media. *Address:* Wilberforce Chambers, 8 New Square, Lincoln's Inn, WC2A 3QP. *T:* (020) 7306 0102. *E:* rreed@wilberforce.co.uk.

REED, Dame Julie Thérèse; *see* Mellor, Dame J. T.

REED, Laurance Douglas; *b* 4 Dec. 1937; *s* of late Douglas Austin Reed and Mary Ellen Reed (*née* Philpott). *Educ:* Gresham's Sch., Holt; University Coll., Oxford (MA). Nat. Service, RN, 1956–58; worked and studied on Continent (Brussels, Bruges, Leyden, Luxembourg, Strasbourg, Paris, Rome, Bologna, Geneva), 1963–66; Public Sector Research Unit, 1967–69. MP (C) Bolton East, 1970–Feb. 1974; PPS to Chancellor of Duchy of Lancaster, 1973–74. Jt Sec., Parly and Scientific Cttee, 1971–74; Mem., Select Cttee on Science and Technology, 1971–74. *Publications:* Europe in a Shrinking World, 1967; An Ocean of Waste, 1972; Political Consequences of North Sea Oil, 1973; The Soay of Our Forefathers, 1986; Philpott of Fordingbridge, 1994; A Marginal Seat, 2012; Mary's Letters, 2013; A Midshipman on the Warrior, 2014. *Recreations:* gardening, historical research. *Address:* 1 Disraeli Park, Beaconsfield, Bucks HP9 2QE. *T:* (01494) 673153. *Clubs:* Carlton; Coningsby.

See also B. St G. A. Reed.

REED, Leslie Edwin, PhD; Chief Industrial Air Pollution Inspector, Health and Safety Executive, 1981–85; *b* 6 Feb. 1925; *s* of Edwin George and Maud Gladys Reed; *m* 1947, Ruby; two *s*. *Educ:* Sir George Monoux Grammar Sch., Walthamstow; University Coll. London (BScEng, MScEng, PhD). Engineering Officer, RNVR, 1945–47; Fuel Research Station, 1950–58; Warren Spring Laboratory, 1958–70; Central Unit on Environmental Pollution, DoE, 1970–79; Head, Air and Noise Div., DoE, 1979–81. *Address:* 5 Devey Close, Knebworth, Herts SG3 6EN. *T:* (01438) 813272.

REED, Dr Malcolm Christopher, CBE 2004; FCILT, FCIHT, FIES; Chief Executive, Transport Scotland, 2005–09; Adviser, Virgin Trains, 2009–14; *b* 24 Nov. 1944; *s* of James and Lilian Reed; marr. diss.; two *d*. *Educ:* Blue Coat Sch., Durham; Royal Grammar Sch., Newcastle upon Tyne; St Catherine's Coll., Oxford (MA); Nuffield Coll., Oxford; DPhil Oxon 1971. Asst Grade 1, Bodleian Liby, Oxford, 1968–69; Lectr, Dept of Econ. Hist., Univ. of Glasgow, 1969–74; Researcher, then Associate Dir, Planning Exchange, Glasgow, 1974–75; Planner, then Chief Public Transport Co-ordinator, Gtr Glasgow PTE, 1975–79; Strathclyde Regional Council: Chief Policy Planner, 1979–80; Sen. Exec. Officer, 1980–90; Asst Chief Exec., 1990–96; Dir Gen., Strathclyde PTE, 1997–2005. Interim Clerk, E Ayrshire Council, 1995. Chair, Contract Assurance Cttee, Nexus (Tyne and Wear Passenger Transport Exec.), 2009. Railway Heritage Committee: Mem., 1994–99; Dep. Chm., 1996–99; Member: Adv. Cttee, Rail Safety & Standards Bd, 2003–05; Adv. Panel, Railway Heritage Trust, 2007–; Council, Instn of Engrs and Shipbuilders in Scotland, 2008–11. Trustee, City of Durham Trust, 2011–. FCILT (FCIT 1993); FCIHT (FIHT 2006); CIES 2007, FIES 2014. Hon. Fellow, Instn of Railway Operators, 2014. FRSA. *Publications:* (ed) Railways in the Victorian Economy, 1969; Investment in Railways in Britain, 1975; A History of James Capel & Co., 1975; The London & North Western Railway: a history, 1996; contribs to Econ. Hist. Rev., Transport Hist., Scottish Jl Political Econ. *Recreations:* hill-walking, gardening, listening to music. *E:* malcolm.reed@clara.co.uk. *Club:* Western (Glasgow).

REED, Matthew Graham; Chief Executive, Children's Society, since 2012 (Trustee, 2010–12); *b* Reading, 29 Aug. 1968; *s* of Graham and Patricia Reed; *m* 1995, Jennifer Candy; one *s* one *d*. *Educ:* Ranelagh Sch.; Univ. of Nottingham (BEng 1989); Ripon Coll. Cuddesdon (BA Oxon 1992); Univ. of Surrey (MSc 2003). Ordained deacon, 1993, priest, 1994; Parish priest: Oxton, Merseyside, 1993–97; Marlow, Bucks, 1997–2002; Christian Aid: Mktg Manager, 2002–04; Community Dir, 2004–08; Mktg Dir, 2008–10; Chief Exec., Cystic Fibrosis Trust, 2010–12. Trustee, Children England, 2013–. FRSA 2013. *Address:* Children's Society, Edward Rudolf House, Margery Street, WC1X 0JL. *T:* (020) 7841 4446. *E:* matthew.reed@childrenssociety.org.uk.

REED, Paul Stuart Malcolm; QC 2010; *b* London, 16 June 1959; *s* of Alfred Reed and Betty Patricia Reed (*née* Bryant); *m* 1990, Helen Garthwaite; one *s* one *d*. *Educ:* Skinners' Sch., Tunbridge Wells; King's Coll. London (LLB 1987; MSc 1990). Called to the Bar, Inner Temple, 1988; in practice as a barrister, specialising in commercial, insurance and construction; Head of Chambers, 2011–. *Publications:* Accessory Liability and Remedies, 2010; Cases That Changed The World, 2011; Construction All Risks Insurance, 2014. *Recreation:* sailing. *Address:* Hardwicke Building, New Square, Lincoln's Inn, WC2A 3SB. *T:* (020) 7242 2523. *E:* paul.reed@hardwicke.co.uk. *Club:* Bar Yacht.

REED, Penelope Jane; QC 2009; a Recorder, since 2010; a Deputy High Court Judge, since 2013; mediator, since 2009; *b* Epping, Essex, 13 June 1961; *d* of Robert Arthur Reed and Jean Audrey Reed; *m* 1986, Mark Simon Wilce; one *s* one *d*. *Educ:* Loughton Co. High Sch.; King's Coll., London (LLB); Inns of Court Sch. of Law. Called to the Bar, Inner Temple, 1983; in practice as barrister specialising in Chancery law. Chair, Chancery Bar Assoc., 2014–15 (Vice Chair, 2013–14). *Publications:* A Practical Guide to the Trustee Act 2000, 2001; With the Best Will in the World, 2002; Trusts and Estates Law Handbook, 2002, 3rd edn 2008; Inheritance Act Claims, 2007; Risk and Negligence in Wills, Trusts and Estates, 2009, 2nd edn 2014. *Recreations:* walking, reading, theatre. *Address:* 5 Stone Buildings, Lincoln's Inn, WC2A 3XT. *T:* (020) 7242 6201, *Fax:* (020) 7831 8102. *E:* preed@5sblaw.com.

REED, Philip Howard, OBE 2008; Director, Churchill War Rooms (formerly Cabinet War Rooms, then Churchill Museum and Cabinet War Rooms), since 1993, and HMS Belfast, since 2010, and Executive Director, American Air Museum in Britain, since 2014, Imperial War Museum; *b* 2 Nov. 1950; *s* of late William Reed and Mary Reed (*née* Fearon); *m* 1982, Sally Blaxland. *Educ:* Univ. of Leicester (BA Hons German 1973); Univ. of Bristol (MA 1974). Lexicographer, Harrap's Ltd, 1973–74; Dep. Keeper, Dept of Documents, Imperial War Mus., 1974–93. Exec. Vice Pres. (Exec. Dir), Churchill Centre, 2008–10. *Publications:* various academic articles, papers and forewords. *Recreations:* opera, fine wines and haute cuisine. *Address:* c/o Churchill War Rooms, Clive Steps, King Charles Street, SW1A 2AQ. *T:* (020) 7766 0120. *E:* preed@iwm.org.uk.

REED, Robert John; *see* Reed, Rt Hon. Lord.

REED, Roger William Hampson; FCIS; Chairman, South East Arts Board, 1995–2001; Member, Arts Council of England, 1996–98; Chairman, Pallant House Gallery Trust, 2002–07; *b* 23 Oct. 1938; *s* of late Thomas Henry Walter Reed and Lily Reed (*née* Hampson); *m* 1961, Jane Noelle Madeline Bowring Gabriel; one *s* one *d*. *Educ:* Trinity Sch. of John Whitgift; City of London Coll. FCIS 1968; FIET (FIEE 1990). Mgt trainee, Albright and Wilson Gp, 1957–61; Asst Co. Sec., Powell Duffryn Gp, 1961–62; Jt Chief Accountant, John Mowlem Gp, 1962–68; Ewbank Preece Group: Dir and Co. Sec., 1968–91; Chm., 1991–93; Chm., Old Ship Hotel (Brighton) Ltd, 1979–93; Dir, Regency Bldg Soc., 1984–88. Partner, Gratwicke Farm, 1982–. Founder Dir, Sussex Enterprise (formerly Sussex TEC), 1991–95. Chm., Sussex Br., Inst. Dirs, 1986–89. Trustee, Brighton Fest. Trust and Dir, Brighton Fest. Soc., 1980–95. Chm., Royal Alexandra Hosp. for Sick Children Centenary Fund and Rockinghorse Appeal, 1991–2004. Gov., Hurstpierpoint Coll., 1989–2001. Fellow, Woodard Foundn, 1993–2001. High Sheriff, 2004–05, DL 2005, W Sussex. FCIM 1982. *Recreations:* the arts, cooking and entertaining, sport. *Address:* 37 St Luke's Street, Chelsea, SW3 3RP. *Clubs:* Savile, MCC; Sussex; W Sussex Golf (Pulborough).

REED, Rupert; *see* Reed, J. W. R.

REED, Ruth Madeline, RIBA; Director, Green Planning Studio Ltd (formerly Green Planning Solutions LLP), since 2013 (Partner (part-time), 2007–13); President, Royal Institute of British Architects, 2009–11; *b* Winchester, 28 Sept. 1956; *d* of Roger and Pamela Green; *m* Donald Reed (marr. diss. 2010); two *d*. *Educ:* Harlescott Grange Prim. Sch., Shrewsbury; Wakeman Sch., Shrewsbury; Sheffield Univ. (BA 1978; DipArch 1981; MA 1982). RIBA 1983. Architectural Asst, Welmar (Yorkshire) Ltd, 1981–83; Architect, Hadfield Cawkwell Davidson and Partners, 1983–87; Sen. Architect, S Yorks Housing Assoc., 1988–90; Sole Practitioner, 1992–2002, Partner, 2002–06, Reed Architects. Course Dir, 2005–12, Prof. of Archtl Practice and Dir of Archtl Studies, 2012–13, Birmingham Sch. of Architecture, UCE, later Birmingham City Univ. Pres., Royal Soc. of Architects in Wales, 2003–05; Vice Pres. Membership, RIBA, 2005–07. *Recreations:* gardening and collecting plants, walking, photography, reading maps. *Address:* Green Planning Studio Ltd, Unit D - Lunesdale, Upton Magna Business Park, Upton Magna, Shrewsbury SY4 4TT. *E:* ruth.reed@gpsltd.co.uk.

REED, Steven Mark Ward, OBE 2013; MP (Lab) Croydon North, since Nov. 2012; *b* St Albans, 12 Nov. 1963; *s* of Royston and Thelma Reed. *Educ:* Sheffield Univ. (BA English). Thomson, 1990–97; Law Soc., 1997–2001; Home Office, 1997–98; Pannell Kerr Forster, Accountants, 1998–99; Thomson, 2001–02; Wolters Kluwer, 2002–08. Mem. (Lab) Lambeth LBC, 1998–12 (Leader, 2006–12). Member: Exec. Bd, for Housing, 2009–10, for Children and Young People's Services, 2010–12, London Councils; Bd, London Enterprise Partnership, 2010–12; Chm., London Young People's Educn and Skills Bd, 2010–12; Co-Chair, Nine Elms Strategy Bd, 2010–12; Dep. Chm., LGA, 2010–12; Chm., Central London Forward; Chair, Cooperative Councils Innovation Network, 2010–12 (Patron, 2012–). *Address:* House of Commons, SW1A 0AA; (office) 908 London Road, Thornton Heath CR7 7PE.

REED, Prof. Terence James, (Jim), FBA 1987; Taylor Professor of the German Language and Literature, University of Oxford, 1989–2004, now Emeritus; Fellow, Queen's College, Oxford, 1989–2004, Hon. Fellow, 2007; *b* 16 April 1937; *s* of William Reed and Ellen (*née* Silcox); *m* 1960, Ann Macpherson; one *s* one *d*. *Educ:* Shooters Hill Grammar Sch., Woolwich; Brasenose Coll., Oxford (MA). Sen. Scholar, Christ Church, Oxford, 1960–61; Jun. Res. Fellow, Brasenose Coll., Oxford, 1961–63; Fellow and Tutor in Mod. Langs, St John's Coll., Oxford, 1963–88 (Hon. Fellow, 1997). Schiller Prof., Univ. of Jena, 1999. Vis. Res. Scholar, Univ. of Göttingen, 2004–05. Pres., English Goethe Soc., 1995–; Mem., Council, Goethe Soc., Weimar, 2003–11. Corresponding Member: Collegium Europaeum, Jena, 1991; Göttingen Acad. of Scis, 1997. Hon. DPhil Freiburg, 2010. Gold Medal, Goethe Soc., Weimar, 1999; Res. Prize, Humboldt Foundn, 2002. Co-founder and Editor, Oxford German Studies, 1965–; Editor, Oxford Magazine, 1985–2004. *Publications:* (ed) Death in Venice, 1972 (German edn 1983); Thomas Mann, The Uses of Tradition, 1974, 2nd edn 1997; The Classical Centre: Goethe and Weimar 1775–1832, 1980 (German edn 1982); Goethe, 1984 (German edn 1999; also Hebrew, Japanese, Korean, Persian and Spanish edns); (trans.) Heinrich Heine: Deutschland, a not so sentimental journey, 1986; Schiller, 1991; Death in Venice: making and unmaking a master, 1994; (trans. with D. Cram) Heinrich Heine, Poems, 1997; (trans.) Goethe: The Flight to Italy: diaries and letters 1786, 1999; (ed) Goethe: poems, 1999; (ed and trans. jtly) Goethe: poems, 2000; Humanpraxis Literatur (essays), 2001; (ed jtly) Thomas Mann: Erzählungen 1893–1912, 2 vols (text and commentary), 2004; Mehr Licht in Deutschland: kleine Geschichte der Aufklärung, 2009; Light in Germany: scenes from an unknown Enlightenment, 2015. *Recreations:* hill walking, talking to people. *Address:* 91 Eynsham Road, Oxford OX2 9BY. *T:* (01865) 862946.

REED-PURVIS, Air Vice-Marshal Henry, CB 1982; OBE 1972; Sales Director, British Aerospace Dynamics Group, 1983–89; *b* 1 July 1928; *s* of late Henry Reed and of Nancy Reed-Purvis; *m* 1951, Isabel Price; three *d*. *Educ:* King James I School, Durham; Durham Univ. BSc Hons 1950. Entered RAF, 1950; various Op. Sqdns, 1951–58; Instr, Jt Nuclear Biological and Chemical Sch., 1958–60; RMCS Shrivenham (Nuclear Sci. and Tech.), 1961; MoD Staff, 1962–64; OC No 63 Sqdn, RAF Regt, Malaya, 1964–66; Exchange Duties, USAF, 1966–69; USAF War Coll., 1969–70; OC No 5 Wing RAF Regt, 1970–72; Gp Capt. Regt, HQ Strike Comd, 1972–74, HQ RAF Germany, 1974–76; ADC to the Queen, 1974–76; Dir, RAF Regt, 1976–79; Comdt Gen. RAF Regt and Dir Gen. of Security (RAF) 1979–83. Dir, Forces Help Soc. and Lord Roberts Workshops, 1986–97; Council Mem.,

Trustee and Dir, SSAFA/Forces Help, 1997–99. Vice Pres., Council for Cadet Rifle Shooting, 1985–. Pres., 2120 Sqdn ATC Welfare Cttee, 1995–2000. *Recreations:* golf, bridge and music. *Address:* 9 Turville Barns, Eastleach, near Cirencester, Glos GL7 3QB.

REEDER, John; QC 1989; *b* 18 Jan. 1949; *s* of Frederick and Barbara Reeder; *m* 1st, 1971, Barbara Kotlarz (marr. diss. 1994); 2nd, 1995, Pauline Madden. *Educ:* Catholic Coll., Preston; University Coll. London (LLM); PhD Birmingham 1976. Called to the Bar, Gray's Inn, 1971, NSW 1986. Lectr in Law, Univ. of Birmingham, 1971–76; commenced practice, 1976; Junior Counsel to the Treasury (Admiralty), 1981–89; a Recorder, 1991–97; Lloyd's salvage arbitrator, 1991–; CEDR Mediator, 2003–. Lawyer, PNG, 1984. Mem., Ferrari Owners' Club, 2003–. *Recreations:* motorsport, travel. *Address:* Stone Chambers, 4 Field Court, Gray's Inn, WC1R 5EA. *T:* (020) 7440 6900; 72 Bracondale Road, Norwich NR1 2BE.

REEDIE, Sir Craig (Collins), Kt 2006; CBE 1999; President, World Anti-Doping Agency, since 2014 (Board Member, since 2000); Vice-President, International Olympic Committee, since 2012 (Member, since 1994; Member, Executive Board, since 2009); *b* 6 May 1941; *s* of late Robert Lindsay Reedie and Anne Reedie; *m* 1967, Rosemary Jane Biggart; one *s* one *d*. *Educ:* High Sch., Stirling; Univ. of Glasgow (MA, LLB). Sec. and Pres., Scottish Badminton Union, 1966–81; Council Mem., Chm. and Pres., Internat. Badminton Fedn, 1970–84; Mem. Council and Treas., Gen. Assoc. of Internat. Sports Fedns, 1984–92; Chm., British Olympic Assoc., 1992–2005. Board Member: Manchester 2002 Ltd, 2000–02; London 2012, 2003–05; London Organising Cttee for the Olympic Games, 2005–13; Olympic Lottery Distributor, 2005–13. Mem., NHS Resource Allocation Steering Gp, 1998–99. FRSA 1995. DUniv: Glasgow, 2001; Stirling, 2014; Hon. LLD St Andrews, 2005; Hon. LLD: Brunel, 2007; W of Scotland, 2011; Hon. DBA Lincoln, 2009; Hon. DSc Glasgow Caledonian, 2013. *Recreations:* reading, golf, sport, sport and more sport. *Address:* Senara, Hazelwood Road, Bridge of Weir PA11 3DB. *T:* (01505) 613434. *Clubs:* East India; Royal & Ancient Golf (St Andrews), Western Gailes Golf, Ranfurly Castle Golf.

REEDIJK, Alexander; General Director, Scottish Opera, since 2006; *b* Lower Hutt, Wellington, NZ, 31 Dec. 1960; *s* of Leendert and Jacoba Reedijk; *m* 2002, Anne Goldrick; one *s* one *d*. *Educ:* Wainuiomata Coll., NZ; Victoria Univ., Wellington, NZ. Freelance roles incl. stage manager, dresser, lighting designer for shows and events in NZ, Ireland, England and Scotland, 1982–88; Production Manager: Opera Ireland, 1985–89; Assembly Th., Edinburgh Fest., 1988–94; Wexford Opera Fest., 1989–91; Tech. Dir, May Fest., Glasgow, 1989–91; New Zealand Festival: Tech. Dir, 1991–2008; Dep. Exec. Dir, 1998–2000 (incl. Producer, Edinburgh Mil. Tattoo in NZ); Exec. Dir, 2000–02; Studio Manager, Riverside Studios, 1994–96; Gen. Dir, Nat. Business Rev., NZ Opera, 2002–06. Convener, NZ Entry to Prague Quadrennial, 1999; Assessor, Creative NZ, 2002–04. Trustee: Downstage Th., Wellington, 1999–2002; Christchurch Arts Fest., 2001–05; NZ Opera Trng Sch., 2002–; Auckland Fest., 2003–06; Nat. Opera Studio, London, 2006–. Fellow, Royal Conservatoire of Scotland, 2011. *Recreations:* opera, sailing, family, theatre. *Address:* Scottish Opera, 39 Elmbank Crescent, Glasgow G2 4PT. *T:* (0141) 248 4567. *E:* alex.reedijk@scottishopera.org.uk. *Clubs:* Glasgow Art; Royal Scots (Edinburgh).

REEDS, Graham Joseph; QC 2009; a Principal Advocate for the Crown Prosecution Service, since 2008 (Principal Counsel, since 2010); a Recorder, since 2002; *b* Glossop, Derbys; *s* of Ernest Reeds and Glenys Reeds; *m* 1988, Madeleine Carne; one *s* one *d*. *Educ:* Hulme Grammar Sch., Oldham; Univ. of Sheffield (LLB Hons). Called to the Bar, Middle Temple, 1984; barrister, 11 King's Bench Walk, 1986–2006; Sen. Counsel, Serious Organised Crime Agency, 2006–09. CD-ROMs: (jtly) Family Finance Toolkit, 1996–2003; (jtly) Personal Injury Toolkit, 1997, 7th edn 2011. *Recreations:* football, high altitude mountaineering (climbed to 7,000m on Everest, 2002). *Address:* Crown Prosecution Service, United House, Piccadilly, York YO1 9PQ. *T:* (01904) 545652. *E:* graham.reeds@cps.gsi.gov.uk.

REEDY, Norris John, (Jack); media consultant and lecturer, since 1994; *b* 1934; *s* of John Reedy; *m* 1964, Sheila Campbell McGregor; one *d*. *Educ:* Chorlton High Sch., Manchester; Univ. of Sheffield. Newspaper journalist, 1956–82, incl. Sunday Times and Guardian; Birmingham Post, 1964–82 (Editor, 1974–82); Regl Officer, Midlands, IBA, 1983–88; Sen. Nat. and Regl Officer, ITC, 1988–94; PRO, Inst. of Dirs (Midland Br.), 1994–99. Tutor in media skills and public speaking, RCN, 1995–2008. Mem., Coventry and Warwickshire Selection Panel, The Prince's Trust, 1998–; Chm., Warwickshire Badger Gp, 2005–; Vice Chm., Badger Trust, 2006–10. Former Chm. W Midlands Region, and Nat. Vice-Pres., Guild of British Newspaper Editors; Sec., Midlands Centre, Royal Television Soc. Chm., House Cttee, Birmingham Press Club. Churchwarden, St Laurence, Rowington, 2005–. *Recreations:* astronomy, riding, natural history, painting, photography. *Address:* The Old Manor, Rowington, near Warwick CV35 7DJ. *T:* (01564) 783129.

REEKIE, Jonathan Alistair James, CBE 2013; Director, Somerset House Trust, since 2014; *b* 2 Sept. 1964; *s* of Dr Andrew Reekie and Virginia Reekie; two *d*. *Educ:* Bristol Poly. (BA Business Studies). Co. Co-ordinator, Glyndebourne Fest., 1987–91; Gen. Manager, Almeida Th., 1991–97; Dir, Almeida Opera, 1991–2003; Chief Exec., Aldeburgh Music, 1997–2014 (Trustee, 2009–12). Mem., Bd of Dirs, Musica Nel Chiostro, Batignano, Italy, 1989–2005. Advr, Arts Prog. Cttee, Paul Hamlyn Foundn, 2007–. Trustee, Arts Foundn, 2000–. Hon. FRAM 2010; Hon. DMus UEA, 2010. *Address:* Somerset House Trust, Somerset House, Strand, WC2R 1LA.

REEKS, David Robin, MBE 2015; TD 1974; Vice Lord-Lieutenant of Lanarkshire, 2002–10; *b* 15 June 1935; *s* of Harry and Dorothy Reeks; *m* 1958, Kathleen Stephens; one *s* one *d*. *Educ:* Canford Sch.; London Univ. (BSc Eng ext.). Rig Design Engr, UKAEA, Dounreay, 1962–67; Reactor Thermal Engr, SSEB, 1967–89; Reactor Performance and Safety Engr, Scottish Nuclear, 1989–94. Mem. Cttee, and Volunteer Convoy Leader, Edinburgh Direct Aid to Bosnia and Kosovo, 1994–. TA, RE and RCT, 1962–90. DL Lanarks, 1989. *Recreations:* hill-walking, Scottish country dancing, part-time tour manager Great Rail Journeys. *Address:* 3 Cedar Place, Strathaven, Lanarks ML10 6DW. *T:* and *Fax:* (01357) 521695. *E:* d.reeks@talktalk.net.

REEMAN, Douglas Edward; writer (also as Alexander Kent); *b* 1924; *m* 1985, Kimberley Jordan. Served RN. *Publications: as Douglas Reeman:* A Prayer for the Ship, 1958; High Water, 1959; Send a Gunboat, 1960; Dive in the Sea, 1961; The Hostile Shore, 1962; The Last Raider, 1963; With Blood and Iron, 1964; HMS Saracen, 1965; Path of the Storm, 1966; The Deep Silence, 1967; The Pride and the Anguish, 1968; To Risks Unknown, 1969; The Greatest Enemy, 1970; Rendezvous - South Atlantic, 1972; Go in and Sink!, 1973; The Destroyers, 1974; Winged Escort, 1975; Surface with Daring, 1976; Strike from the Sea, 1978; A Ship Must Die, 1979; Torpedo Run, 1981; Badge of Glory, 1982; The First to Land, 1984; D-Day: a personal reminiscence (non-fiction), 1984; The Volunteers, 1985; The Iron Pirate, 1986; In Danger's Hour, 1988; The White Guns, 1989; Killing Ground, 1992; The Horizon, 1993; Sunset, 1994; A Dawn Like Thunder, 1996; Battlecruiser, 1997; Dust on the Sea, 1999; For Valour, 2000; Twelve Seconds to Live, 2002; Knife Edge, 2004; The Glory Boys, 2008; *as Alexander Kent:* To Glory We Steer, 1968; Form Line of Battle, 1969; Enemy in Sight!, 1970; The Flag Captain, 1971; Sloop of War, 1972; Command a King's Ship, 1973; Signal - Close Action!, 1974; Richard Bolitho, Midshipman, 1975; Passage to Mutiny, 1976; In Gallant Company, 1977; The Inshore Squadron, 1977; Midshipman Bolitho and the Avenger, 1978; Stand into Danger, 1980; A Tradition of Victory, 1981; Success to the Brave, 1983; Colours Aloft!, 1986; Honour this Day, 1987; With All Despatch, 1988; The Only Victor, 1990; Beyond the Reef, 1992; The Darkening Sea, 1993; For My Country's Freedom, 1995; Cross of St George, 1996; Sword of Honour, 1998; Second to None, 1999; Relentless Pursuit, 2001; Man of War, 2003; Band of Brothers, 2005; Heart of Oak, 2007; In the King's Name, 2011. *Address:* c/o United Agents, 12–26 Lexington Street, W1F 0LE.

REES OF LUDLOW, Baron *cr* 2005 (Life Peer), of Ludlow in the county of Shropshire; **Martin John Rees,** OM 2007; Kt 1992; FRS 1979; Fellow, Trinity College, Cambridge, since 2012 (Master, 2004–12); Astronomer Royal, since 1995; *b* 23 June 1942; *s* of late Reginald J. and Joan Rees; *m* 1986, Caroline Humphrey (*see* Dame C. Humphrey). *Educ:* Shrewsbury Sch.; Trinity Coll., Cambridge; MA, PhD (Cantab). Fellow, Jesus Coll., Cambridge, 1967–69 (Hon. Fellow, 1996); Research Associate, California Inst. of Technology, 1967–68 and 1971; Mem., Inst. for Advanced Study, Princeton, 1969–70; Prof., Univ. of Sussex, 1972–73; Cambridge University: Plumian Prof. of Astronomy and Experimental Philosophy, 1973–91; Dir, Inst. of Astronomy, 1977–82 and 1987–91; Royal Soc. Res. Prof., 1992–2003; Prof. of Cosmology and Astrophysics, 2002–09; Fellow of King's Coll., Cambridge, 1969–72 and 1973–2003. Visiting Professor: Harvard Univ., 1972, 1986–88; Inst. for Advanced Studies, Princeton, 1982, 1995; Imperial Coll., London, 2001–; Hitchcock Vis. Prof., UC Berkeley, 1994; Regents Fellow of Smithsonian Instn, Washington, 1984–88; Oort Prof., Leiden, 1999. Lectures: H. P. Robertson Meml, US Nat. Acad. Sci., 1975; Bakerian, Royal Soc., 1982; Danz, Univ. of Washington, 1984; Pauli, Zurich, 1999; Leverhulme, 1999; Scribner, Princeton, 2000; Russell, Amer. Astron. Soc., 2004; Messenger, Cornell Univ., 2005; Gifford, Scottish Univs, 2007; Reith, BBC, 2010; Romanes, Oxford, 2011. Trustee: BM, 1996–2002; NESTA, 1998–2001; Inst. for Adv. Study, Princeton, 1998–; Kennedy Meml Trust, 1999–2004; IPPR, 2001–09; Nat. Mus. of Sci. and Industry, 2003–11; Gates Cambridge Trust, 2007–14. President: RAS, 1992–94; BAAS, 1994–95; Royal Soc., 2005–10; Chm., Science Adv. Cttee, ESA, 1976–78; Member: Council, Royal Soc., 1983–85 and 1993–95; PPARC, 1994–97. Member: Academia Europaea, 1989; Pontifical Acad. of Sci., 1990; For. Hon. Mem., Amer. Acad. of Arts and Sciences, 1975; Foreign Associate, Nat. Acad. of Sciences, USA, 1982; Foreign Member: Amer. Phil. Soc., 1993; Royal Swedish Acad. Sci., 1993; Russian Acad. of Sci., 1994; Norwegian Acad. of Arts and Letters, 1996; Accademia Lincei, Rome, 1996; Royal Netherlands Acad. of Arts and Sciences, 1998; Finnish Acad. of Sci. and Letters, 2004; Japan Acad., 2015; Associate Mem., TWAS: the Acad. of Scis for the Developing World, 2008. Hon. FInstP 2001; Hon. FREng 2007; Hon. FMedSci 2011; Hon. FBA 2012. Hon. Fellow: Cardiff Univ., 1998; Darwin Coll., Cambridge, 2004; John Moores Univ., 2008; King's Coll., Cambridge, 2007. Hon. DSc: Sussex, 1990; Leicester, 1993; Copenhagen, 1994; Keele, Newcastle and Uppsala, 1995; Toronto, 1997; Durham, 1999; Oxford, 2000; Ohio and Exeter, 2006; Hull, 2007; Liverpool, 2008; Yale, 2008; McMaster, 2009; E Anglia, 2009; Melbourne, 2010; Portsmouth, 2011; Sydney, 2012; ETH Zurich, 2012; Cambridge, 2014; Greenwich, 2014; DUniv Open, 2008; Hon. DLitt London, 2011; Bath, 2015. Heinemann Prize, Amer. Inst. Physics, 1984; Gold Medal, RAS, 1987; Guthrie Medal and Prize, Inst. of Physics, 1989; Balzan Prize, Balzan Foundn, 1989; Schwarzschild Medal, Astron. ges., 1989; Bruce Gold Medal, Astron. Soc. of Pacific, 1993; Bower Award for Science, Franklin Inst., 1998; Rossi Prize, American Astron. Soc., 2000; Cosmology Prize, Gruber Foundn, 2001; Einstein Award, World Cultural Council, 2003; Michael Faraday Award, Royal Soc., 2004; (jtly) Crafoord Prize, Royal Swedish Acad., 2005; Niels Bohr Medal, UNESCO, 2005; Templeton Prize, John Templeton Foundn, 2011; Newton Prize, Inst. of Physics, 2012; Chancellor's Medal, Univ. of Calif, Santa Cruz, 2012; Dirac Prize, ICTP Trieste, 2013; Nierenberg Prize, Scripps Inst., 2015. Officier, Ordre des Arts et des Lettres (France), 1991. *Publications:* Perspectives in Astrophysical Cosmology, 1995; (with M. Begelman) Gravity's Fatal Attraction: black holes in the universe, 1996, 2nd edn 2010; Before the Beginning, 1997; Just Six Numbers, 1999; Our Cosmic Habitat, 2001; Our Final Century?, 2003; From Here to Infinity: scientific horizons, 2011; (ed) Universe, 2012; What We Still Don't Know, 2016; mainly scientific papers; numerous general articles. *Address:* c/o Trinity College, Cambridge CB2 1TQ. *T:* (01223) 338412, (office) (01223) 337548.

REES, Allen Brynmor; Regional Chairman, Employment (formerly Industrial) Tribunals, Birmingham, 1995–2004; *b* 11 May 1936; *s* of late Allen Brynmor Rees and Elsie Louise Rees (*née* Hitchcock); *m* 1961, Nerys Eleanor Evans; two *d*. *Educ:* Monmouth Sch.; UCW, Aberystwyth (LLB Hons 1958). Admitted Solicitor (with Hons), 1961. Partner, Francis Ryan and Co., 1961–62; Solicitor, SW Div., NCB, 1962; Rexall Drug and Chemical Co., 1962–65; Rees Page (incorp. Page Son and Elias, Skidmore Hares and Co., and Darbey-Scott-Rees), 1965–93, Sen. Partner, 1974–93; Chm., Employment (formerly Industrial) Tribunals, 1993–2004. Prin. Solicitor, Birmingham Midshires Building Soc., 1976–93. Chairman: W Midlands Rent Assessment Panel, 1968–93; Social Security Tribunals, 1980–93; Employment (formerly Industrial) Tribunals, Birmingham, 1993–95; Reserve Forces Appeal Tribunal, 2003–; Mem. Cttee, Legal Aid Bd, 1975–93. Columnist (Solicitors' Notebook), Solicitors' Jl, 1968–92; Ed., Employment Tribunals Chairman's Handbook, 1999–2006. *Recreations:* canoeing, ski-ing, gardening, walking, watching Rugby. *Address:* Rossleigh, Shaw Lane, Albrighton, Wolverhampton WV7 3DS; Yr Hen Ystabl, Meifod, Powys SY22 6BP. *Club:* Old Monmothians (Monmouth).

REES, Prof. Andrew Jackson; Professorial Fellow, Medical University of Vienna, since 2010 (Marie Curie Professor, 2007–10); *b* 11 June 1946; *s* of late Gordon Jackson Rees and of Elisabeth Rees; *m* 1st, 1972, Ann Duncan (marr. diss. 1974); 2nd, 1979, Daphne Elizabeth Wood (marr. diss. 1985); two *d*; 3rd, 1999, Renate Kain; two *c*. *Educ:* King William's Coll., Isle of Man; Liverpool Univ. (MB ChB 1969); London Univ. (MSc). Trained in gen. medicine and nephrology, at Liverpool, Guy's, and Hammersmith Hosps, 1969–79; Consultant Physician, Hammersmith Hosp., 1979–90; Prof. of Nephrology, RPMS, 1990–94; Regius Prof. of Medicine, Univ. of Aberdeen, 1994–2007. Vis. Prof., Nat. Jewish Hosp., Denver, 1983–84; Goulstonian Lectr, RCP, 1984. Chair: UK Renal Genetics Gp, 2005–07; European Kidney Health Alliance, 2007–11. Pres., Nephrology Section, RSocMed, 1994–95. Vice-Pres., Kidney Res. UK (formerly Nat. Kidney Res. Fund), 2000– (Chm., 1995–2000); Pres., Renal Assoc. of GB and Ireland, 2001–04; Mem. Council, Internat. Soc. of Nephrology, 1998–2003. FMedSci 2000; FRSB (FSB 2009). *Publications:* (ed with C. D. Pusey) Rapidly Progressive Glomerulonephritis, 1998; papers on pathogenesis and treatment of glomerulonephritis. *Recreations:* contemporary theatre and music, ski-ing. *Address:* Mauerbachstrasse 10, 1140 Vienna, Austria.

REES, (Anthony) John (David); educational consultant, since 2003; *b* 20 July 1943; *s* of Richard Frederick and Betty Rees; one *s* one *d* (and one *d* decd). *Educ:* Newcastle Royal Grammar Sch.; Clare Coll., Cambridge (Exhibnr; BA 2nd Cl. Hons Geog.); PGCE 1966. Head of Economics, Harrow Sch., 1966–80; Head Master, Blundell's Sch., Tiverton, Devon, 1980–92; Rector, Edinburgh Acad., 1992–95; Director: Harrow Sch. Devlt Trust, 1995–97; The Bradfield Foundn, 1998–2000; school master, Cheltenham Coll., 2000–03. Established Notting Dale Urban Study Centre, 1972; Vis. Tutor, London Inst. of Education, 1973–2007. Member Executive Committee: Queen's Silver Jubilee Appeal, 1976–82; and Admin. Council, Royal Jubilee Trusts, 1978–82; Chairman: Prince's Trust for Devon, 1981–83; Youth Clubs UK, 1987–89; Founder Dir, Mid Devon Enterprise Agency, 1984–91; Chm., Crested, 1996–97. Member: CoSIRA Cttee for Devon, 1981–83; Council, Drake Fellowship, 1981–; Admiralty Interview Bd, 1981–2005; Cttee, HMC, 1986–91; Prince of Wales Community Venture, 1985–; Council, Prince's Trust for Wales, 2009–; Board: Devon and Cornwall Prince's Youth Business Trust, 1987–92; Fairbridge in Scotland, 1992–95; Trustee: SFIA Educnl Trust, 1996–2014; Talley Community Woodland, 2007– (Chm., 2009–). *Publications:* articles on economics and community service in many jls incl. Economics, Youth in Society, etc. *Recreations:* hill walking, family and friends.

REES, Barbara; *see* Wilding, B.

REES, Brian, MA Cantab; Headmaster, Rugby School, 1981–84; *b* 20 Aug. 1929; *s* of late Frederick T. Rees; *m* 1st, 1959, Julia (*d* 1978), *d* of Sir Robert Birley, KCMG; two *s* three *d*; 2nd, 1987, Juliet Akehurst (*née* Gowan). *Educ:* Bede Grammar Sch., Sunderland; Trinity Coll., Cambridge (Scholar). 1st cl. Historical Tripos, Part I, 1951; Part II, 1952. Eton College: Asst Master, 1952–65; Housemaster, 1963–65; Headmaster: Merchant Taylors' Sch., 1965–73; Charterhouse, 1973–81. Pres., Conference for Independent Further Education, 1973–82; Chm., ISIS, 1982–84. Res. Fellow, City Univ., 1989–90. Patron, UC of Buckingham, 1973–91. Liveryman, Merchant Taylors' Co., 1981. *Publications:* A Musical Peacemaker: biography of Sir Edward German, 1987; (ed) History and Idealism: essays, addresses and letters of Sir Robert Birley, 1990; Camille Saint-Saëns: a life, 1999; Stowe: the history of a public school 1923–1989, 2008; contrib. Oxford DNB. *Recreation:* music. *Address:* Windermere, 147 Woodnesborough Road, Sandwich, Kent CT13 0BA. *T:* (01304) 614311.

REES, Caroline, (Lady Rees of Ludlow); *see* Humphrey, Dame Caroline.

REES, Celia, FEA; writer; *b* Solihull, 17 June 1949; *d* of Wilfred Taylor and Lilla Taylor (*née* Goodway); *m* 1972, Terence Rees; one *d*. *Educ:* Tudor Grange Grammar Sch. for Girls, Solihull; Univ. of Warwick (BA Hons Hist. and Politics); Birmingham Univ. (PGCE, MEd). Teacher of English: Binley Park Comp. Sch., Coventry, 1972–81; Stoke Park Sch. and Community Coll., Coventry, 1981–82; Whitley Abbey Sch., Coventry, 1983–89; further educn lectr (pt-time), Henley Coll. of Further Educn, Coventry, 1990–97; Tutor in Open Studies (pt-time), Univ. of Warwick, 1997–2001. Chair, Children's Writers and Illustrators Gp, Soc. of Authors', 2007–09. FEA 2011. *Publications:* Every Step You Take, 1993; The Bailey Game, 1994; Colour her Dead, 1994; Blood Sinister, 1996; Midnight Hour, 1997; Ghost Chamber, 1997; The Vanished, 1997; Soul Taker, 1998; Truth or Dare, 2000 (Stockport Book Award, 2001); The Cunning Man, 2000; Witch Child, 2000 (Cassa di Risparmio di Cento di Letteratura per Ragazzi, 2001; Prix Sorcières, 2003); Trap in Time, 2001; City of Shadows, 2002; The Host Rides Out, 2002; Sorceress, 2002; Pirates!, 2003 (Thumbs Up!, Michigan Libraries Award, 2004); The Wish House, 2005; The Stone Testament, 2007; Sovay, 2008; The Fool's Girl, 2010; This Is Not Forgiveness, 2012. *Recreations:* reading, film, walking, swimming, yoga and pilates, travel, seeing friends. *Address:* 195 Rugby Road, Milverton, Leamington Spa, Warwickshire CV32 6DX.

REES, Christina Elizabeth; MP (Lab) Neath, since 2015; *b* 21 Feb. 1954; *m* 1981, Rt Hon. Ronald Davies, *qv* (marr. diss. 2000); one *d*. *Educ:* Cynffig Comprehensive Sch.; Ystrad Mynach Coll.; Univ. of Wales Coll. of Cardiff (LLB Hons 1995). Auditor, S Glamorgan CC, 1979–84; Constituency Sec., H of C, 1984–96; called to the Bar, 1996; in practice as barrister, Cardiff, 1997–98; Develt Officer and Nat. Coach, Wales Squash and Racketball, 2003–15; Squash Professional, Vale Hotel, 2004–14. Mem. (Lab): Mid-Glamorgan CC, 1988–95; Porthcawl Town Council, 2012–15; Bridgend CBC, 2012–15. Member: Welsh Affairs Select Cttee, 2015–; Justice Select Cttee, 2015–. Contested (Lab): Arfon, Nat. Assembly for Wales, 2011; Wales, EP, 2014. JP 1990. Female Coach of Year, Sport Wales, 2008. *Address:* House of Commons, SW1A 0AA.

REES, Christina Henking Muller, CBE 2015; communications, media and public relations consultant, since 1985; writer, since 1986; broadcaster, since 1990; campaigner, since 1990; executive coach, since 2003; *b* 6 July 1953; *d* of John Muller, Jr and Carol Benton Muller; *m* 1978, Christopher Rees, *s* of late Richard Rees and Margaret (*née* Head); two *d*. *Educ:* Pomona Coll., Calif (BA English 1975); King's Coll., London (MA Theology 1998). Asst PR Officer, Children's Soc., 1985–87. Sen. Partner, Media Maxima, 1990–. Member: Gen. Synod of C of E, 1990–2015; Archbishops' Council, 1999–2000, 2006–15; Chair: Women and the Church, 1996–2010; Women on the Move, 1999–; spokesperson, Movt for Ordination of Women, 1992–94. Mem., Central Religious Adv. Cttee, 2003–08. Trustee: Li Tim-Oi Foundn, 1997– (Vice Chm.); Christian Assoc. of Business Executives, 2007–; Bible Soc., 2013–; Dir, The Churchfield Trust, 2000–12. Consultant: IBA, 1979; BBC Children in Need Appeal, 1997–2000; Ernst & Young, 2011–13. Gov., Ripon Coll. Cuddesdon, 2000–15 (Hon. Fellow, 2014). Contribs to radio and TV progs, 1990–, incl. Thought for the Day, Radio 4, 1991–2006, Pause for Thought, Radio 2, 2008–10. FRSA 2005. *Publications:* Sea Urchin, 1990; The Divine Embrace, 2000; (ed) Voices of This Calling, 2002; Feast + Fast: food for Lent and Easter, 2011; Feast + Fast: food for Advent and Christmas, 2012; contrib. to The Times, Guardian, Independent, Christian publications, etc. *Recreations:* beachcombing, improving Anglo-American relations, cross country walking. *Address:* PO Box 43, Royston, Herts SG8 8LG. *E:* christina@mediamaxima.com.

See also Rev. Canon R. M. Rees.

REES, Sir Dai; *see* Rees, Sir David A.

REES, Sir David Allan, (Sir Dai Rees), Kt 1993; BSc, PhD, DSc; FRCPE, FMedSci; FRS 1981; FRSC, FRSB, FLSW; Medical Research Council scientist, 1996–2001; *b* 28 April 1936; *s* of James Allan Rees and Elsie Bolam; *m* 1959, Myfanwy Margaret Parry Owen; two *s* one *d*. *Educ:* Hawarden Grammar Sch., Clwyd; University Coll. of N Wales, Bangor, Gwynedd (BSc 1956; PhD 1959; Hon. Fellow, 1988); DSc Edinburgh, 1970. FRCPE 1999. DSIR Res. Fellow, University Coll., Bangor, 1959, and Univ. of Edinburgh, 1960; Asst Lectr in Chem., 1961, Lectr, 1962–70, Univ. of Edinburgh; Section Manager, 1970–72, Principal Scientist, 1972–82, and Sci. Policy Exec., 1978–82, Unilever Res., Colworth Lab.; Chm., Science Policy Gp for Unilever Res., 1979–82. Associate Dir (pt-time), MRC Unit for Cell Biophysics, KCL, 1980–82; Dir, Nat. Inst. for Med. Res., Mill Hill, 1982–87; Sec., subseq. Chief Exec., MRC, 1987–96. Vis. Professorial Fellow, University Coll., Cardiff, 1972–77. Philips Lecture, Royal Soc., 1984. Member: MRC, 1984–96; Council, Royal Soc., 1985–87. Pres., ESF, 1994–99. FKC 1989. Founder FMedSci 1998; FLSW 2010. Hon. FRCP 1986. Hon. DSc: Edinburgh, 1989; Wales, 1991; Stirling, 1995; Leicester, 1997; DUniv York, 2007. Colworth Medal, Biochemical Soc., 1970; Carbohydrate Award, Chemical Soc., 1970. *Publications:* various, on carbohydrate chem. and biochem. and cell biology. *Recreations:* river boats, reading, listening to music. *Address:* Ford Cottage, 1 High Street, Denford, Kettering, Northants NN14 4EQ. *T:* (01832) 733502. *E:* drees@nimr.mrc.ac.uk.

REES, His Honour (David) Wyn; a Circuit Judge, 2005–13; Deputy Designated Family Judge for South Wales, 2006–13; authorised to sit as a Judge of the High Court, Family Division, 2011–13; a Deputy Circuit Judge, since 2013; *b* 6 Jan. 1948; *s* of late David Daniel Rees and Mariann Rees; *m* 1972, Gillian Anne Davies; two *d*. *Educ:* Ysgol Gynradd Gymraeg Aberdâr; Mountain Ash Grammar Sch.; University Coll. of Wales, Aberystwyth (BSc Hons 1969). Admitted solicitor, 1973; Partner, Spicketts, Solicitors, Pontypridd, 1974–88; Dep. Dist Judge, 1984–88; Dist Judge, 1988–2005; Asst Recorder, 1994–98; Recorder, 1998–2005; Diversity and Community Relations Judge (formerly Ethnic Minority Liaison Judge) for SE Wales (formerly S Wales), 2005–11. Judicial Studies Board: Dir, Seminars for Dist Judges, 1996–2001; Mem., Civil and Family Cttees, 1996–2001; Mem., Main Bd, 1999–2001; Mem., Equal Treatment Adv. Cttee, 2007–11. Member: Lord Chancellor's Standing Cttee for Welsh Lang., 1999–2005; Law and Admin of Justice Terminology Subject Gp, Welsh Language Bd, 2007–12; Chm., Mgt Cttee, Pontypridd Children's Contact Centre, 2006–12; Mem., Expert Wkg Gp on Future Direction for Child Contact Centres, 2011–13. Chm., Legislative Sub-Cttee, 2012–13, Mem., 2013–, Assoc. of Judges of Wales. Pres., Pontypridd and Rhondda Law Soc., 1985–86. Hon. Mem., Gorsedd of Bards, 2003–. *Recreations:* walking Wales, foreign travel, golf, the company of family and friends.

REES, Edward Parry; QC 1998; *b* 18 June 1949; *s* of Edward Howell Rees and Margaret Rees Parry; *m* 1983, Kathleen Wiltshire; one *s* one *d*. *Educ:* University Coll. of Wales, Aberystwyth (LLB Hons). Called to the Bar, Gray's Inn, 1973. Hon. Fellow in Criminal Process, Univ. of Kent, 1992. *Publications:* Blackstone's Guide to the Proceeds of Crime Act 2002, 2003, 5th edn 2013; The Law of Public Order and Protest, 2010. *Recreations:* family, garden. *Address:* 53–54 Doughty Street, WC1N 2LS. *T:* (020) 7404 1313.

REES, Eleri Mair; Her Honour Judge Rees; a Circuit Judge, and Liaison Judge for the Welsh Language, since 2002; a Senior Circuit Judge, Resident Judge, Cardiff Crown Court, and Recorder of Cardiff, since 2012; *b* 7 July 1953; *d* of late Ieuan Morgan and Sarah Alice Morgan (*née* James); *m* 1975, Alan Rees. *Educ:* Ardwyn Grammar Sch., Aberystwyth; Univ. of Liverpool (LLB Hons). Called to the Bar, Gray's Inn, 1975, Bencher, 2013. Clerk to Justices, Bexley Magistrates' Court, 1983–94; Metropolitan Stipendiary Magistrate, subseq. Dist Judge (Magistrates' Courts), 1994–2002; a Recorder, 1997–2002. Editor, Family Court Reporter, 1992–94. Mem., Magisterial Cttee, Judicial Studies Bd, 1989–94. *Publications:* contrib. various jls on subject of family law. *Recreations:* travel, cookery, ski-ing. *Address:* c/o Cardiff Crown Court, The Law Courts, Cathays Park, Cardiff CF10 3PG.

REES, Gareth David; QC 2003; General Counsel, Financial Reporting Council (formerly Executive Counsel, Accountancy and Actuarial Discipline Board), since 2012; *b* 2 July 1956; *s* of Baron Merlyn-Rees, PC and Colleen (*née* Cleveley); *m* 2000, Lucia Boddington; two *d*, and one *s* two *d* from former marriage. *Educ:* Harrow Co. Sch. for Boys; Reading Univ. (BA Hons). Called to the Bar, Gray's Inn, 1981; in practice as barrister, 1981–2012. *Recreations:* sport, music, family, cinema. *Address:* Financial Reporting Council, 5th Floor, Aldwych House, 71–91 Aldwych, WC2B 4HN. *E:* gr@garethreesqc.com. *Club:* MCC.

REES, Prof. Geraint Ellis, PhD; FMedSci; Wellcome Senior Clinical Fellow, Wellcome Trust Centre for Neuroimaging, Institute of Neurology, since 2003, Professor of Cognitive Neurology, since 2006, and Dean, Faculty of Life Sciences, since 2014, University College London; *b* 27 Nov. 1967; *s* of Olav Anelyf Rees and Rosemary Ann Rees (*née* Dawson); *m* 2000, Rebecca Ruth Roylance; one *s* one *d*. *Educ:* Gonville and Caius Coll., Cambridge (BA Med. Sci. Tripos 1988); New Coll., Oxford (BM BCh 1991); University Coll. London (PhD 1999). MRCP 1994; FRCP 2008. Pre-registration surgery, Glasgow Royal Infirmary, and medicine, John Radcliffe Hosp., Oxford, 1991–92; post-registration SHO posts at Hammersmith Hosp., Royal Brompton Hosp., St Thomas' Hosp. and National Hosp., 1991–94; Registrar, Queen Mary's Hosp., Roehampton, 1994–95; University College London: Clin. Res. Fellow, Inst. of Neurol., 1995–99; Dir, Inst. of Cognitive Neurosci., 2009–14; Dep. Hd, Faculty of Brain Scis, 2011–14; Wellcome Advanced Fellow: CIT, 1999–2001; Inst. of Cognitive Neurosci., UCL, 2001–02. Hon. Consultant, National Hosp. for Neurol. and Neurosurgery, 2004–. FMedSci 2010. *Publications:* (ed jtly) Neurobiology of Attention, 2005; contrib. numerous articles to acad. jls and acad. monographs. *Recreation:* attempting to achieve a better work/life balance. *Address:* Wellcome Trust Centre for Neuroimaging, 12 Queen Square, WC1N 3BG. *T:* (020) 7679 5496, *Fax:* (020) 7813 1420. *E:* g.rees@ucl.ac.uk.

REES, Hefin Ednyfed; QC 2013; a Recorder, since 2008; *b* Liverpool, 1969; *s* of Rev. Dr D. Ben Rees and Meinwen Rees; *m* 1995, Dr Bethan; two *s*. *Educ:* King David High Sch., Liverpool; Durham Univ. (BA (Hons) Law); Inns of Court Sch. of Law. Called to the Bar: Inner Temple, 1992; St Vincent and the Grenadines, E Caribbean Circuit, 2010; Ireland, 2012. FCIArb 2011. *Publications:* (contrib.) Construction Contracts, 2013; contrib. Suffolk Transnational Law Rev., 2000. *Recreations:* charity work in Africa, travelling. *Address:* Thirty Nine Essex Street Chambers, 39 Essex Street, WC2R 3AT. *T:* (020) 7832 1111, *Fax:* (020) 7353 3978. *E:* hefin.reesqc@39essex.com. *Club:* Travellers.

REES, Helen; *see* Young, H.

REES, Hugh Francis E.; *see* Ellis-Rees.

REES, John; *see* Rees, A. J. D., and Rees, P. J.

REES, Rev. Canon John; *see* Rees, Rev. Canon V. J. H.

REES, John Charles; QC 1991; *b* 22 May 1949; *s* of Ronald Leslie Rees and Martha Therese Rees; *m* 1970, Dianne Elizabeth Kirby; three *s* one *d*. *Educ:* St Illtyd's College, Cardiff; Jesus College, Cambridge (double first class Hons; BA (Law), LLB (Internat. Law), MA, LLM; repr. Univ. in boxing and Association Football; boxing Blue). Called to the Bar, Lincoln's Inn, 1972. Trustee and Governor, St John's College, Cardiff, 1987–2010. Chm., British Boxing Board of Control, 2014–. *Recreations:* all sport, esp. boxing and Association Football; theatre. *Address:* Marleigh Lodge, Druidstone Road, Old St Mellons, Cardiff CF3 6XD. *T:* (029) 2079 4918; 28 Cathedral Road, Cardiff CF11 9LJ. *Club:* Hawks (Cambridge).

REES, John Samuel; Editor, Western Mail, 1981–87; *b* 23 Oct. 1931; *s* of John Richard Rees and Mary Jane Rees; *m* 1957, Ruth Jewell; one *s* one *d*. *Educ:* Cyfarthfa Castle Grammar Sch., Merthyr Tydfil. Nat. Service, Welch Regt and RAEC, 1950–52. Reporter, 1948–50, Sports Editor, 1952–54, Merthyr Express; The Star, Sheffield: Reporter, 1954–56; Sub Editor, 1956–58; Dep. Chief Sub Editor, 1958–59; Dep. Sports Editor, 1959–61; Asst Editor, 1961–66; Dep. Editor, Evening Echo, Hemel Hempstead, 1966–69; Editor: Evening Mail, Slough and Hounslow, 1969–72; The Journal, Newcastle upon Tyne, 1972–76; Evening Post-Echo, Hemel Hempstead, 1976–79, Asst Man. Dir, Evening Post-Echo Ltd, 1979–81. Lectr, Centre for Journalism Studies, Univ. of Wales Coll. of Cardiff, 1988–92. *Recreations:* marquetry, watching cricket and rugby, walking, gardening.

REES, Jonathan David; QC 2010; Senior Treasury Counsel, since 2008; *b* Cardiff, 18 Oct. 1961; *s* of John Geraint Rees and Caroline Fay Rees; *m* 1988, Clare Marian Gray; one *s* one *d*. *Educ:* Stowe Sch.; Jesus Coll., Oxford (BA Hons 1984). Called to the Bar, Gray's Inn, 1987; Jun. Treasury Counsel, 2002–08. *Recreations:* Welsh Rugby, Spurs, everything London has to offer. *Address:* 2 Hare Court, Temple, EC4Y 7BH. *T:* (020) 7353 5324. *E:* Jonathan.Rees@cps.gsi.gov.uk. *Club:* Cardiff and County.

REES, Prof. Jonathan Laurence, FRCP, FRCPE, FMedSci; Grant Professor of Dermatology, University of Edinburgh, since 2000; *b* 10 Oct. 1957; *s* of William Rees and Maura (*née* West); *m* 1983, Anne Bradbury (marr. diss. 2006); two *d*; *m* 2007, Lisa Naysmith. *Educ:* Newcastle Univ. (BMedSci 1st Cl. Hons 1981; MB BS Hons 1982). MRCP 1985, FRCP 1993; FRCPE 2001. Vis. Fellow, 1st Hautklinik, Allgemeines Krankenhaus der Stadt Wien, Vienna, 1986; MRC Trng Fellow, Univ. of Newcastle upon Tyne, 1987–89; MRC Clinician Scientist, CNRS/INSERM Lab. de Génétique Moléculaire des Eucaryotes, Strasbourg, 1989–91; Prof. of Dermatology, Univ. of Newcastle upon Tyne, 1992–99. FMedSci 1998. *Publications:* papers on genetics of skin disease, particularly pigment genetics ("red hair gene") and skin cancer; more recently, papers on semi-automated skin cancer diagnostic systems and learning in dermatology. *Recreations:* Rugby, avoiding formal occasions and wondering when the machines will take over. *Address:* Department of Dermatology, University of Edinburgh, Level 1, The Lauriston Building, Lauriston Place, Edinburgh EH3 9HA. *T:* (0131) 536 2041, *Fax:* (0131) 229 8769. *E:* reestheskin@me.com.

REES, Jonathan Nigel; Director General and Accounting Officer, Government Equalities Office, 2008–13; *b* 29 Sept. 1955; *s* of late Arthur Ernest Rees and of Thelma Maureen Rees; *m* 1996, Kathryn Jayne Taylor; one *s* one *d*. *Educ:* Jesus Coll., Oxford (MA Hons Modern History). Joined DTI, 1977; Private Sec. to Minister for Trade, 1981–84; EC, 1984–86 (on secondment); DTI, 1986–89; Industry Counsellor, UK Rep. to EU, 1989–94; Prime

Minister's Policy Unit, 1994–97; Dir, Citizen's Charter Unit, then Modernising Public Services Gp, Cabinet Office, 1997–2000; Dir, Consumer and Competition Policy, DTI, 2000–04; Dep. Dir Gen., later Dep. Chief Exec. (Policy), HSE, 2004–08. Ind. Dir, Lending Standards Bd, 2014–. Non-exec. Dir, Ombudsman Services, 2013–. Trustee: Citizens Advice, 2011–; NACAB Pension Fund, 2012–; Employers Network on Equality and Inclusion, 2013–. Ind. Dir, Personal Finance Soc., 2015–. *Recreations:* sport, travel, theatre. *Club:* MCC.

REES, Dame Judith (Anne), DBE 2013 (CBE 2005); PhD; Professor of Environmental and Resources Management, since 1995, and Vice-Chair, Grantham Research Institute on Climate Change and the Environment, since 2014 (Director, 2008–12; Co-Director, 2012–14), London School of Economics and Political Science; *b* 26 Aug. 1944; *d* of late Douglas S. Hart and Eva M. Hart (*née* Haynes); *m* 1st, 1968, Prof. Raymond Rees, *qv* (marr. diss. 1972); 2nd, 1981, Prof. David Keith Crozier Jones. *Educ:* Bilborough Grammar Sch., Nottingham; London Sch. of Economics (BSc Econ 1965; MPhil 1967; PhD 1978). Lectr, Agricl Econs, Wye Coll., London Univ., 1967–69; Lectr, 1969–85, Sen. Lectr, 1985–89, in Geography, LSE; University of Hull: Prof. of Geography, 1989–95; Dean of Sch. of Geography and Earth Resources, 1991–93; Pro-Vice Chancellor, 1993–95; London School of Economics and Political Science: Pro-Dir, then Dep. Dir, 1998–2004; Dir, 2011–12; Dir, ESRC Centre for Climate Change Econs and Policy, 2008–13. Nat. Water and Sewerage Policy Advr, Australian Dept of Urban and Regl Develt, 1974–75. Economic and Social Research Council: Member: Trng Bd, 1994–98; Global Envmtl Change Cttee, 1995–98; Council, 2004–10; Dutch Nat. Climate Res. Progs, Internat. Scientific Adv. Council, 2011–14; Chm., Trng and Develt Bd, 2004–; Member: Exec. Panel on Pollution Res., SSRC, 1977–80; Adv. Cttee, Centre for Regulated Industries, 1990–; Technical Adv. Cttee, Global Water Partnership, 1996–2010; Competition (formerly Monopolies and Mergers) Commn, 1996–2002; Link/Teaching Co. Scheme Bd, OST, 1997–2002; UN Sec. Gen's Adv. Bd on Water and Sanitation, 2004–; UN Water Task Force on Water and Climate Change, 2010–14; Scientific Adv. Cttee, Energy Climate House, Centre for Eur. Policy Studies; Chm., Ofwat Southern Customer Service Cttee, 1990–96. Royal Geographical Society: Mem. Council, 1979–82; Vice Pres., 1995–97; Pres., 2012–15; Mem. Council, Inst. of British Geographers, 1981–83. Hon. Dr Hull, 2012. *Publications:* Industrial Demands for Water, 1969; Natural Resources Allocation, Economics and Policy, 1985, 2nd edn 1990; (jtly) The International Oil Industry: an interdisciplinary perspective, 1987; (jtly) Troubled Water, 1987; Water for Life, 1993; articles on water resources and envmtl mgt in books and learned jls. *Address:* Grantham Research Institute, Tower 3, London School of Economics and Political Science, Houghton Street, WC2A 2AE. *T:* (020) 7955 6228.

REES, Laurence Mark; Chairman, LR History TV Ltd (formerly History Media LLP, then LR History LLP), since 2009; *b* 19 Jan. 1957; *s* of late Alan Rees and Margaret Julia Rees (*née* Mark); *m* 1987, Helena Brewer; two *s* one *d. Educ:* Solihull Sch.; Worcester Coll., Oxford (BA). Joined BBC TV, 1978: prodn trainee, 1978–79; writer/producer/dir, 1982–; Ed., Timewatch, BBC2, 1992–2002; Hd, History Progs Unit, BBC TV, 1999–2000; Creative Dir, BBC TV History Progs, 2000–08. Founder, writer and producer, WW2History.com, 2009– (Best in Class in Educn and Ref., Interactive Media Awards, 2011). Sen. Vis. Fellow, Internat. Hist. Dept, LSE, 2009–. *Productions* include: Crisis (drama documentary), 1987; A British Betrayal, 1991; We Have Ways of Making You Think (History of Propaganda series), 1992; Nazis: a warning from history (series; awards include: BAFTA, IDA, Peabody, BPG), 1997; War of the Century (series), 1999; Horror in the East (series), 2000; Auschwitz: the Nazis and the 'Final Solution' (series; Grierson Award, History Today Prize), 2005; World War Two: behind closed doors, 2008; The Dark Charisma of Adolf Hitler (series), 2012; Touched by Auschwitz, 2015; as Executive Producer, awards include: Emmy Awards, 1994 (2) and 1996; Amnesty Press Award, 1994; Internat. Documentary Assoc. Award, 1997; Western Heritage Award, 2000. Hon. DLitt Sheffield, 2005; DUniv Open, 2011. Lifetime Achievement Award, History Makers, 2009. *Publications:* Electric Beach (novel), 1990; Selling Politics, 1992; Nazis: a warning from history, 1997; War of the Century, 1999; Horror in the East, 2001; Auschwitz: the Nazis and the 'Final Solution', 2005 (History Book of the Year, British Book Awards, 2006); Their Darkest Hour: people tested to the extreme in World War Two, 2007; World War Two: behind closed doors, 2008; The Dark Charisma of Adolf Hitler: leading millions into the abyss, 2012. *Recreation:* my three children. *Address:* c/o Andrew Nurnberg Associates, 20–23 Greville Street, EC1N 8SS. *T:* (020) 7327 0400.

REES, Prof. Dame Lesley Howard, DBE 2001; MD, DSc; FRCP; FRCPath; FMedSci; Professor of Chemical Endocrinology, Bart's and The London School of Medicine and Dentistry, Queen Mary (formerly St Bartholomew's Hospital Medical College), University of London, 1978–2006, now Emeritus; *b* 17 Nov. 1942; *d* of Howard Leslie Davis and Charlotte Patricia Siegrid Young; *m* 1969, Gareth Mervyn Rees. *Educ:* Pate's Grammar Sch. for Girls, Cheltenham; Malvern Girls' Coll.; London Univ. (MB BS 1965; MD 1972; MSc 1974; DSc 1989). MRCP 1967, FRCP 1979; MRCPath 1976, FRCPath 1988. Editor, Clinical Endocrinology, 1979–84; Sub-dean, 1983–88, Dean, 1989–95, St Bartholomew's Hosp. Med. Coll.; Public Orator, London Univ., 1984–86. Chm., Soc. for Endocrinology, 1984–87; Sec.-Gen., Internat. Soc. of Endocrinology, 1984–2005. Mem., Press Complaints Commn, 1991–94. Royal College of Physicians: Dir, Internat. Office, 1997–99; Dir, Educn Dept, 1997–2001. Founder FMedSci 1998. Hon. Fellow, QMUL, 2006. *Recreations:* music, poetry, reading, administrative gardening. *Address:* 23 Church Row, Hampstead, NW3 6UP. *T:* and *Fax:* (020) 7794 4936; 2 Impasse du Petit St Martin, La Flotte en Ré, 17630 Ile de Ré, France. *Club:* Royal Air Force.

REES, Mary; *see* Rees, S. M.

REES, Sir Meuric; *see* Rees, Sir R. E. M.

REES, Rev. Canon Michael; *see* Rees, Rev. Canon R. M.

REES, Prof. Michael Ralph, FRCP, FRCR; Professor of Cardiovascular Studies, since 2005 and University Director of Medical Development, since 2012, Bangor University (formerly University of Wales, Bangor); *b* Hammersmith, 19 April 1950; *s* of William Morris Rees and Herta Klara Rees (*née* Teichmann); *m* 1992, Ann Patricia Clements; two *d. Educ:* Shene Grammar Sch., East Sheen; Univ. of East Anglia (BSc 1971); Univ. of Sheffield (MB ChB 1976). DMRD 1982; Eur. Bd of Cardiac Radiol. 2011; Cert Ed 2011. FRCR 1983; FRCP 1999. Consultant Cardioradiologist, Leeds, 1984–93; Consulting Prof., Stanford Univ., Calif, 1992–93; Prof. of Radiol Scis, Keele Univ., 1993–95; Prof. of Clinical Radiol., Univ. of Bristol, 1995–2005. Hon. Clinical Sen. Lectr, Univ. of Leeds, 1998–2002. Mem. Council, BMA, 2008– (Chm., 2003–07, Co-Chm., 2007–, Academic Staff Cttee). Pres., Eur. Soc. of Cardiac Radiol., 2008–11. FHEA 2005. Member: UK Healthcare Educn Adv. Cttee, 2009–12; Health Educn Nat. Strategic Exchange, 2009–. Hon. PhD Ionnina, 2006. Medal, BMA, 2008. *Publications:* book chapters and over 100 papers in scientific jls. *Recreation:* medical politics. *Address:* 3 Kings Oak, Colwyn Bay, Conwy LL29 0AJ. *T:* (01492) 531242. *E:* michael.rees@bangor.ac.uk.

REES, Owen, CB 1991; Deputy Chairman, Qualifications, Curriculum and Assessment Authority for Wales, 1997–2006; *b* 26 Dec. 1934; *s* of late John Trevor and Esther Rees, Trimsaran, Dyfed; *m* 1958, Elizabeth Gosby (*d* 1991); one *s* two *d. Educ:* Llanelli Grammar Sch.; Univ. of Manchester. BA(Econ). Bank of London and South America, 1957; regional development work in Cardiff, Birmingham and London, BoT, 1959–69; Cabinet Office, 1969–71; Welsh Office, 1971–94: Asst Sec. (European Div.), 1972; Under Sec., 1977–94; Sec. for Welsh Educn, 1977–78; Head, Educn Dept, 1978–80; Dir, Industry Dept, 1980–85; Head, Economic and Regl Policy Gp, 1985–90; Head, Agriculture Dept, 1990–94. *Address:* 4 Llandennis Green, Cyncoed, Cardiff CF23 6JX. *T:* (029) 2075 9712.

REES, Prof. (Peter) John, FRCP, FRCPE; Professor of Medical Education, King's College London School of Medicine, 2006, now Emeritus; *b* 2 March 1949; *s* of Joseph Thomas Rees and Doris Mary Williams; *m* 1973, Helen Mary Heath; one *s* one *d. Educ:* Whitchurch Grammar Sch., Cardiff; Christ's Coll., Cambridge (MB BChir; MA; MD); Guy's Hosp., London. FRCP 1988; FRCPE 2002. Guy's Hospital, later UMDS of Guy's and St Thomas' Hospitals, then Guy's, King's and St Thomas' Hospitals Medical and Dental School of King's College London, subseq. King's College London School of Medicine: Lectr, 1979–83; Sen. Lectr in Medicine, 1983–2006; Consultant Physician, 1983–2010; Asst Clin. Dean, 1993–2000; Gp Clin. Dir for Acute Med. Services, 1995–2000; Dep. Chm., Academic Bd, 1996–98; Site Dean, Guy's Hosp., 2000–05; Dean, Undergrad. Educn, 2005–10; Mem. Bd, Global Health Centre, 2010–. Non-exec. Mem., Lewisham and N Southwark HA, 1990–92; non-executive Director: Mildmay Mission Hosp., 1992–2005; Lewisham Hosp. Trust Bd, 1995–2006; Mem. Exec. Cttee, British Lung Foundn, 1988–95. FKC 2010. *Publications:* (jtly) ABC of Asthma, 1984, 6th edn 2009; (jtly) Practical Management of Asthma, 1985, 2nd edn 1996; A Medical Catechism, 1986; (jtly) A New Short Textbook of Medicine, 1988; Diagnostic Tests in Respiratory Medicine, 1988; Asthma: family doctor guide, 1988; (jtly) A Colour Atlas of Asthma, 1989; (jtly) Aids to Clinical Pharmacology and Therapeutics, 1993; (jtly) Principles of Clinical Medicine, 1995; (jtly) Asthma: current perspectives, 1996; (jtly) 100 Cases in Clinical Medicine, 2000, 3rd edn 2014; (jtly) Essential Clinical Medicine, 2009. *Recreations:* theatre, opera, cricket, squash, running. *Address:* Guy's Hospital, London Bridge, SE1 9RT. *T:* (020) 8693 2763.

REES, Peter John; QC 2009; FCIArb; Counsel and Arbitrator, Thirty Nine Essex Chambers, since 2014; *b* Wendover, 21 April 1957; *s* of Leslie Marchant Rees and Betty Rees; *m* 1st; one *d*; 2nd, 1999, Nicola Jane Mumford. *Educ:* Downing Coll., Cambridge (BA 1978); Nottingham Trent Univ. (MBA 1999). FCIArb 1997. Admitted solicitor, 1981; Partner, Norton Rose, 1987–2006; Partner, Debevoise & Plimpton LLP, 2006–10; Legal Dir and Exec. Cttee Mem., Royal Dutch Shell plc, 2011–14. Co-Chm., Internat. Construction Projs Cttee, IBA, 1999–2001; Chairman: Technol. and Construction Solicitors Assoc., 2000–04; Bd of Mgt, CIArb, 2008–09. Member: Council, ICC UK, 2006–; Court, London Court of Internat. Arbitration, 2012–; Bd, Internat. Inst. for Conflict Prevention and Resolution, 2012–; Governing Body, Internat. Court of Arbitration, ICC, 2012–14. *Publications:* (with A. Briggs) Civil Jurisdiction and Judgments, 1993, 5th edn 2009. *Recreations:* Association Football, golf, scuba diving, gardening. *Address:* 39 Essex Street, WC2R 3AT. *E:* peter.rees@39essex.com. *Clubs:* Hawks; Richmond Golf.

REES, Prof. Peter Wynne, CBE 2015; FRTPI; Professor of Places and City Planning, The Bartlett, UCL Faculty of the Built Environment, since 2014; *b* 26 Sept. 1948; *s* of Gwynne Rees, MM, CEng, MIMechE, FMES, and late Elizabeth Rodda Rees (*née* Hynam). *Educ:* Pontardawe Grammar Sch.; Whitchurch Grammar Sch., Cardiff; Bartlett Sch. of Architecture, UCL (BSc Hons); Welsh Sch. of Architecture, Univ. of Wales (BArch); Polytechnic of the South Bank (BTP). Architectural Asst, Historic Bldgs Div., GLC, 1971–72; Asst to Gordon Cullen, CBE, RDI, FSIA, 1973–75; Architect, Historic Areas Conservation, DoE, 1975–79; UK Rep., Council of Europe Wkg Parties studying New Uses for Historic Buildings and The Economics of Building Conservation, 1977–78; Asst Chief Planning Officer, London Bor. of Lambeth, 1979–85; Controller of Planning, 1985–87, The City Planning Officer, 1987–2014, Corp. of London, later City of London Corp. Trustee, Building Conservation Trust, 1985–91. Founder Mem. and Dir, British Council for Offices, 1989–. London Rep., EC (formerly European) Working Party on Technological Impact on Future Urban Change, 1989–92; Member: Steering Gp, London World City Study, 1990–91; Officers' Gp, London Pride Partnership, 1994–98; London Office Review Panel, 1996–. Hon. Mem., AA, 2014. FRSA 1988. Hon. FRIBA 2011. Hon. DSc London South Bank, 2014. President's Award, British Council for Offices, 2003; Barbara Miller Award, Faculty of Building, 2004; Outstanding Contribution, Offices Awards, 2010; Award for Outstanding Contribn to Property, Estates Gazette, 2013; Property Award, Coll. of Estate Mgt, 2014. *Publications:* City of London Local Plan, 1989; City of London Unitary Development Plans, 1994 and 2002; contribs to professional studies and jls. *Recreations:* swimming, playing the viola, tidying. *Address:* The Bartlett, UCL Faculty of the Built Environment, Central House, 14 Upper Woburn Place, WC1H 0NN. *E:* peter.rees@ucl.ac.uk.

REES, Philip; a Recorder of the Crown Court, 1983–2008; *b* 1 Dec. 1941; *s* of John Trevor Rees and Olwen Muriel Rees; *m* 1969, Catherine Good; one *s* one *d. Educ:* Monmouth Sch.; Bristol Univ. (LLB Hons). Called to the Bar, Middle Temple, 1965. Asst Boundary Comr, 1996–2008. *Recreations:* music, sport. *Address:* 35 South Rise, Llanishen, Cardiff CF14 0RF. *T:* (029) 2075 4364. *Club:* Cardiff and County (Cardiff).

REES, Prof. Philip Howell, CBE 2004; PhD; FBA 1998; FAcSS; Professor of Population Geography, University of Leeds, 1990–2009, now Emeritus; *b* 17 Sept. 1944; *s* of Foster and Mona Rees; *m* 1968, Laura Campbell; one *s* one *d. Educ:* King Edward's Sch., Birmingham; St Catharine's Coll., Cambridge (BA Geog. 1966; MA 1970); Univ. of Chicago (MA Geog. 1968; PhD 1973). University of Leeds: Lectr, 1970–80; Reader, 1980–90. Hofstee Vis. Fellow, Netherlands Interdisciplinary Demographic Inst., The Hague, 1995; Dist. Vis. Fellow, Univ. of Adelaide, 1996. FAcSS (AcSS 2013). Gill Meml Award, 1996, Victoria Medal, 2009, RGS. *Publications:* Spatial Population Analysis, 1977; Residential Patterns in American Cities, 1979; (ed jtly) Population Structures and Models, 1985; (ed jtly) Migration Processes and Patterns, Vol. 2, 1992; (ed jtly) Population Migration in the European Union, 1996; (jtly) The Determinants of Migration Flows in England, 1998; (ed jtly) The Census Data System, 2002; (jtly) The Development of a Migration Model, 2002; e-Learning for Geographers, 2009. *Recreation:* walking. *Address:* School of Geography, University of Leeds, Leeds LS2 9JT. *T:* (0113) 233 3341; (home) 3 Mavis Lane, Cookridge, Leeds LS16 7LL. *T:* (0113) 267 6968.

REES, Prof. Ray; Professor of Economics, University of Munich, 1993–2008, now Emeritus (Dean of Economics Faculty, 1999–2000); *b* 19 Sept. 1943; *s* of Gwyn Rees and Violet May (*née* Powell); *m* 1976, Denise Sylvia (*née* Stinson); two *s. Educ:* Dyffryn Grammar Sch., Port Talbot; London School of Economics and Political Science (MScEcon). Lectr 1966–76, Reader 1976–78, Queen Mary Coll., Univ. of London; Economic Advr, HM Treasury (on secondment), 1968–72; Prof. of Econs, UC, Cardiff, 1978–87; Prof. of Econs, Univ. of Guelph, Ont, 1987–93. Member (part-time), Monopolies and Mergers Commn, 1985–87. *Publications:* A Dictionary of Economics, 1968, 3rd edn 1984; Public Enterprise Economics, 1975, 3rd edn 1992; Microeconomics, 1981, 3rd edn 2004; Economics: a mathematical introduction, 1991; Introduction to Game Theory, 1992; The Theory of Principal and Agent, 1992; Mathematics for Economics, 1996, 3rd edn 2011; The Economics of Public Utilities, 2006; The Microeconomics of Insurance, 2008; Public Economics and the Household, 2009; articles in Economic Jl, Amer. Econ. Rev., Jl of Political Econ., Jl of Public Econs, Economica, and others. *Recreations:* playing the guitar, walking in the Alps and the Snowdonia National Park. *Address:* Bwlchcoediog Uchaf, Cwm Cewydd, Machynlleth, Powys SY20 9EE. *T:* (01650) 531652.

REES, Sir (Richard Ellis) Meuric, Kt 2007; CBE 1982; JP; FRAgS; Lord-Lieutenant for Gwynedd, 1990–99; Vice Chairman, Hill Farming Advisory Committee (Chairman, Committee for Wales); *b* Pantydwr, Radnorshire, 1924; *m*; three *d.* President: YFC in Wales, 1961; Merioneth Agricl Soc., 1972; Royal Welsh Agricl Show, 1978; former Chm., Welsh

Council of NFU; Mem., CLA. Member: Agricl Trng Bd, 1974 (Chm., Cttee for Wales); Countryside Commn, 1981 (Chm., Cttee for Wales). Governor: Welsh Agricl Coll., Aberystwyth; Coleg Meirionnydd, Dolgellau; Inst. of Grassland and Animal Production, 1987; Inst. of Grassland and Environmental Res., 1990. Mem., Tywyn UDC, 1967–73. Chm., N Wales Police Authority, 1982–84. JP Tywyn, 1957 (Chm. of Bench, 1974–94); High Sheriff of Gwynedd, 1982–83; DL Gwynedd, 1988. FRAgS 1973. Hon. MSc Wales, 1999. KStJ 1997. *Address:* Escuan Hall, Tywyn, Gwynedd LL36 9HR.

REES, Rev. Canon (Richard) Michael; Canon Emeritus, Chester Cathedral, since 2000; *b* 31 July 1935; *s* of late Richard and Margaret (*née* Head); *m* 1958, Yoma Patricia; one *s* one *d*. *Educ:* Brighton College; St Peter's College, Oxford (MA Theol); Tyndale Hall, Bristol. Curate: Crowborough, 1959–62; Christ Church, Clifton, Bristol, 1962–64; Vicar: Christ Church, Clevedon, 1964–72; Holy Trinity, Cambridge, 1972–84; Chaplain, Darwin Coll., Cambridge, 1972–84; Proctor, General Synod for Ely Diocese, 1975–85; Chief Sec., Church Army, 1984–90; Residentiary Canon, Chester Cathedral and Canon Missioner, Dio. of Chester, 1990–2000; Vice-Dean, Chester Cathedral, 1993–2000; Cheshire County Ecumenical Officer, 1991–99. C of E Rep., BCC, 1983–90 (Moderator, Evangelism Cttee, 1986–90). Editor, Missionary Mandate, 1955–68. *Publications:* Celebrating the Millennium in the Local Church, 1997; (jtly) Silhouettes and Skeletons: Charles Simeon of Cambridge, 2013; (contrib.) Proclaiming Marriage: 27 timeless talks and sermons, 2014. *Recreations:* photography, filling waste paper baskets. *Address:* 15 Norfolk House, County Court Road, King's Lynn, Norfolk PE30 5RP. *T:* (01553) 691982.

REES, Prof. (Susan) Mary, PhD; FRS 2002; Professor of Mathematics, University of Liverpool, since 2002; *b* 31 July 1953; *d* of Prof. David Rees, FRS and Joan Rees. *Educ:* St Hugh's Coll., Oxford (BA 1974, MSc 1975); Univ. of Warwick (PhD Maths 1978). Asst, then Associate Prof. of Maths, Univ. of Minnesota, 1982–84; Lectr, 1984–90, Sen. Lectr, 1990–2002, Univ. of Liverpool. *Publications:* contribs to Acta Mathematicae, Annales de l'Ecole Normale Supérieure, Jls of London Mathematical Soc., Inventiones Mathematicae, Ergodic Theory and Dynamical Systems, Asterisque, etc. *Recreations:* walking, running, choir-singing, listening to music, reading, gardening. *Address:* Department of Mathematical Sciences, Mathematics and Oceanography Building, University of Liverpool, Peach Street, Liverpool L69 7ZL. *T:* (0151) 794 4063, *Fax:* (0151) 794 4061. *E:* maryrees@liverpool.ac.uk.

REES, Prof. Dame Teresa Lesley, DBE 2015 (CBE 2003); PhD; FAcSS; FLSW; Professor of Social Sciences, Cardiff University, 2000–15, now Emerita (Pro Vice Chancellor, 2004–10); Director for Wales (formerly Associate Director), Leadership Foundation for Higher Education, 2010–13; *b* 11 June 1949; *d* of Gordon Leslie Baggs and Vera Geddes-Ruffle; *m* 1974, Gareth Meredydd Rees (marr. diss. 2004); two *s*. *Educ:* Univ. of Exeter (BA Hons Sociology and Politics); PhD Wales 1993. Res. Officer, Univ. of Exeter, 1970–73; Res. Fellow, UWIST, 1973–76; Sen. Res. Asst, Mid Glamorgan CC, 1977–78; University College, Cardiff: Res. Fellow, 1976–77, 1978–88; Dir, Social Res. Unit, and Lectr in Sociology, 1988–92; Bristol University: Sen. Res. Fellow, 1993–94; Reader, 1994–95; Prof. of Labour Mkt Studies, 1995–2000. Fellow, Sunningdale Inst., Nat. Sch. of Govt, 2007–12. Member: EOC, 1996–2002; BBC Audience Council Wales, 2007–12. Hon. Pres., S Wales Br., WEA, 1996–2014. FAcSS (AcSS 2001); FLSW 2012. FRSA. Hon. Fellow, Univ. of Lampeter, 2006. Hon. DSocSci QUB, 2012; Hon. LLD: Bath, 2012; Exeter, 2014. *Publications:* (ed jtly) Youth Unemployment and State Intervention, 1982; (ed jtly) Our Sisters' Land: the changing identities of women in Wales, 1994; Women and the Labour Market, 1992; Mainstreaming Equality in the European Union, 1998; Women and Work, 1999; (jtly) Adult Guidance and the Learning Society, 2000. *Recreation:* campaigning for gender equality. *Address:* School of Social Sciences, Cardiff University, Glamorgan Building, King Edward VII Avenue, Cardiff CF10 3WT.

REES, Victoria Kirstyn; *see* Williams, V. K.

REES, Rev. Canon (Vivian) John (Howard); Principal Registrar, Province of Canterbury, since 2000; Chaplain to the Queen, since 2014; *b* 21 April 1951; *s* of Herbert John Rees and Beryl Rees; *m* 1980, Dianne Elizabeth Hamilton; two *d*. *Educ:* Skinners' Sch., Tunbridge Wells; Southampton Univ. (LLB 1972); Wycliffe Hall, Oxford (MA); MPhil Leeds 1984. Admitted Solicitor, 1975; Ecclesiastical Notary; Asst Solicitor, Cooke Matheson & Co., 1975–76; Hosp. Administrator, Multan, Pakistan, 1976; ordained deacon 1979, priest 1980; Asst Curate, Moor Allerton Team Ministry, Leeds, 1979–82; Chaplain and Tutor, Sierra Leone Theol Hall, Freetown, 1982–85; with Winckworth Sherwood, 1986– (Partner, 1988–; Sen. Partner, 2013–). Proctor in Convocation for Oxford, 1995–2000; Legal Advr, ACC, 1996–; Diocesan Registrar, Dio. Oxford, 1998–; Registrar: Court of Arches and Court of Ecclesiastical Causes Reserved, 2000–; Clergy Discipline Tribunals, 2006–. Provincial Canon, Canterbury Cathedral, 2001–. Mem., Legal Adv. Commn, General Synod, 2000– (Vice-Chm., 2001–). Treas., 1995–2015, Chm., 2015–, Ecclesiastical Law Soc. *Recreations:* photography, walking, cycling, second-hand bookshops. *Address:* (office) 16 Beaumont Street, Oxford OX1 2LZ. *T:* (01865) 297200, *Fax:* (01865) 726274. *E:* jrees@wslaw.co.uk; (home) 36 Cumnor Hill, Oxford OX2 9HB. *T:* and *Fax:* (01865) 865875. *E:* vjhrees@btinternet.com. *Clubs:* Athenæum, Nobody's Friends.

REES, William Howard Guest, CB 1988; Chief Veterinary Officer, State Veterinary Service, 1980–88; *b* 21 May 1928; *s* of Walter Guest Rees and Margaret Elizabeth Rees; *m* 1952, Charlotte Mollie (*née* Collins); three *s* one *d*. *Educ:* Llanelli Grammar Sch.; Royal Veterinary Coll., London (BSc). MRCVS; DVSM. Private practice, Deal, Kent, 1952–53; joined MAFF as Veterinary Officer, 1953; stationed Stafford, 1953–66; Divl Vet. Officer, Vet. Service HQ, Tolworth, 1966–69; Divl Vet. Officer, Berks, 1969–71; Dep. Regional Vet. Officer, SE Reg., 1971–73; Regional Vet. Officer, Tolworth, 1973–76, Asst Chief Vet. Officer, 1976–80. Mem., AFRC, 1980–88. FRASE 1988. Hon. FRCVS 2000. Bledisloe Award, RASE, 1988; Gold Medal, Office Internat. des Epizooties, 1994. *Recreations:* Rugby and cricket follower, golf.

REES, His Honour Wyn; *see* Rees, His Honour D. W.

REES LEAHY, Prof. Helen Blodwen, PhD; Director, Centre for Museology, since 2002, and Professor of Museology, since 2013, School of Arts, Languages and Cultures (formerly School of Art History and Archaeology, then School of Arts, Histories and Cultures), University of Manchester; *b* 23 Aug. 1960; *d* of late Edward Elgar Rees and of Dorothy Rees (*née* Banham); *m* 1997, Dr Michael Gordon Leahy. *Educ:* Gaisford High Sch. for Girls, Worthing; New Hall, Cambridge (MA); City Univ.; Univ. of Manchester (PhD 1999). Information Officer, Conran Foundn, 1984–86; Curator, 1986–89, Dir, 1989–92, Design Mus.; Communications Dir, Eureka!, The Mus. for Children, 1992; Asst Dir and Head of Public Affairs, NACF, 1992–95; University of Manchester: Lectr in Art Gall. and Mus. Studies, 2000–07, Sen. Lectr, 2007–13, Sch. of Arts, Histories and Cultures (formerly Sch. of Art History and Archaeol); Dir, External Relns, 2010–13. Curatorial Consultant, Elizabeth Gaskell's House, Manchester, 2013–. Member: Adv. Panel, Arts Council of England, 1992–95; Design Adv. Cttee, RSA, 1990–94; Visual Arts Advr, NW Arts Bd, 1996–. Gov., Dean Clough Foundn (formerly Design Dimension Educnl Trust), 1990–. Trustee: Cardiff Old Library Trust, 1995–2000; Cornerhouse, Manchester, 1996–2003; Yorkshire Sculpture Park, 2002–. Editor (and contrib.) Design Museum Publications, 1989–92. *Publications:* 14:24 British Youth Culture, 1986; (contrib.) The Authority of the Consumer, ed Nigel Whiteley, 1993; (contrib.) The Culture of Craft, ed Peter Dormer, 1997; (contrib.) Art History and its Institutions, ed Elizabeth Mansfield, 2002; (contrib.) Museum Materialities, 2009; (ed) Art City Spectacle: the 1857 Manchester Art Treasures Exhibition revisited, 2009; (contrib.) Performance, Learning, Heritage, 2010; (contrib.) The Thing About Museums, 2011; (contrib.) Sculpture and Archaeology, 2011; Museum Bodies: the politics and practices of visiting and viewing, 2012; (contrib.) Museums and Biographies, 2012; articles in jls. *Recreations:* Bach, listening and playing. *Address:* 17 River Street, Manchester M1 5BG. *T:* (0161) 236 2717; Centre for Museology, School of Arts, Languages and Cultures, University of Manchester, Oxford Road, Manchester M13 9PL. *E:* helen.rees@manchester.ac.uk.

REES-MOGG, Jacob William; MP (C) North East Somerset, since 2010; *b* 24 May 1969; *s* of Baron Rees-Mogg and of Gillian Shakespeare Rees-Mogg (*née* Morris); *m* 2007, Helena de Chair; three *s* one *d*. *Educ:* Eton Coll.; Trinity Coll., Oxford (BA Hist. 1991). Investment Analyst, J. Rothschild Investment Mgt, 1991–93; Dir, Lloyd George Mgt, Hong Kong, 1992–96, London, 1996–2007; Sen. Partner and Founder, Somerset Capital Mgt, 2007–. Contested (C): Central Fife, 1997; The Wrekin, 2001. Member, Select Committee: on Procedure, 2010–15; on Eur. Scrutiny, 2010–; Treasury, 2015–. *Address:* House of Commons, SW1A 0AA; Gournay Court, West Harptree, Somerset BS40 6EB. *T:* (01761) 221027.

REES-WILLIAMS, family name of **Baron Ogmore**.

REES-WILLIAMS, Jonathan, FRCO; Organist and Master of the Choristers, St George's Chapel, Windsor Castle, 1991–2002; *b* 10 Feb. 1949; *s* of Ivor and Barbara Rees-Williams; *m* 1985, Helen Patricia Harling; one *s* two *d*. *Educ:* Kilburn Grammar Sch.; Royal Academy of Music; New Coll., Oxford (Organ Scholar; MA 1972). LRAM, DipRAM 1969; ARAM 1984; FRCO 1968. Organist: St Edmund, Yeading, 1967; Church of the Ascension, Wembley, 1968; Actg Organist, New Coll., Oxford, 1972; Assistant Organist: Hampstead Parish Church and St Clement Danes, 1972–74; Salisbury Cathedral, 1974–78; Dir of Music, Salisbury Cathedral Sch., 1974–78; Organist and Master of Choristers, Lichfield Cathedral, 1978–91; Conductor, Lichfield Cathedral Special Choir, 1978–91. Chorusmaster, Portsmouth Festival Choir, 1974–78; Accompanist and Asst Dir, Salisbury Musical Soc., 1974–78. *Recreations:* cycling, wine, railways, vintage model railways.

REESE, Prof. Colin Bernard, PhD, ScD; FRS 1981; FRSC; Daniell Professor of Chemistry, King's College, University of London, 1973–98, now Emeritus; *b* 29 July 1930; *s* of Joseph and Emily Reese; *m* 1968, Susanne Bird; one *s* one *d*. *Educ:* Dartington Hall Sch.; Clare Coll., Cambridge (BA 1953, PhD 1956, MA 1957, ScD 1972). 1851 Sen. Student, 1956–58; Research Fellow: Clare Coll., Cambridge, 1956–59; Harvard Univ., 1957–58; Official Fellow and Dir of Studies in Chem., Clare Coll., 1959–73; Cambridge University: Univ. Demonstrator in Chem., 1959–63; Asst Dir of Res., 1963–64; Univ. Lectr in Chem., 1964–73. FKC 1989. *Publications:* scientific papers, mainly in chemical jls. *Address:* 21 Rozel Road, SW4 0EY. *T:* (020) 7498 0230.

REESE, Colin Edward; QC 1987; a Recorder, 1994–2015; Deputy Judge, Technology and Construction Court (formerly Deputy Official Referee), High Court, 1994–2015; *b* 28 March 1950; *s* of late Robert Edward Reese and Katharine Reese (*née* Moore); *m* 1978, Diana Janet Anderson; two *s* one *d*. *Educ:* Hawarden Grammar School; King Edward VI School, Southampton; Fitzwilliam College, Cambridge (BA 1972; MA 1976). Called to the Bar, Gray's Inn, 1973 (Mould Schol., 1974; Bencher, 1998); admitted, *ad eund*, Lincoln's Inn, 1976; in practice, 1975–2014. An Asst Parly Boundary Comr, 1992–2006. Legal Mem., Restricted Patients' Panel, First-tier Tribunal (Mental Health) (formerly Mental Health Review Tribunals), 2000–15. Vice-Chm., Qualifications Cttee, 2006–11, Mem., Complaints Cttee, 2004–09, Bar Standards Bd. Vice Chm., 1997–2000, Chm., 2000–03, Technol. and Construction (formerly Official Referees) Bar Assoc. Dir, Bar Mutual Indemnity Fund Ltd, 2001–13. Pres., Cambridge Univ. Law Soc., 1971–72. Liveryman, Bakers' Co., 1991– (Mem., Ct of Assts, 2010; Master, 2015–16). *Address:* c/o 1 Atkin Building, Gray's Inn, WC1R 5AT. *T:* (020) 7404 0102.

REESE, Prof. Jason Meredith; Regius Professor of Engineering, University of Edinburgh, since 2013; *b* Wimbledon, 24 June 1967; *s* of late Dr Trevor R. Reese and of Hilary E. Reese (*née* Charker); *m* 2001, Dr Alexandra J. Shepard; one *d*. *Educ:* St Paul's Sch., London; Imperial Coll. London (BSc Hons Physics 1988; ARCS); St Edmund Hall, Oxford (MSc 1989; DPhil Applied Maths 1993). FInstP 2005; CEng 2006; FIMechE 2006; FREng 2011. Res. Fellow, Technische Universität Berlin, 1994–95; Res. Associate, Engrg Dept, Univ. of Cambridge, 1995–96; Lectr, Engrg Dept, Aberdeen Univ., 1996–2000; Lectr and Exxon Mobil Fellow, Mechanical Engrg Dept, KCL, 2001–03; Weir Prof. of Thermodynamics and Fluid Mechanics, 2003–13, Hd, Mechanical and Aerospace Engrg Dept, 2011–13, Univ. of Strathclyde. Mem., Scottish Sci. Adv. Council, 2012–. FRSE 2006. Lord Kelvin Medal, RSE, 2015. *Publications:* numerous res. papers in internat. res. jls incl. Jl of Fluid Mechanics, Physics of Fluids, Physical Rev. E. *Recreations:* conversation, music, Byzantine history. *Address:* School of Engineering, University of Edinburgh, Edinburgh EH9 3JL. *E:* jason.reese@ed.ac.uk. *Clubs:* Oxford Union; Western (Glasgow).

REEVE, Anne Elizabeth; *see* Longfield, A. E.

REEVE, Derek Charles; financial consultant; Director of Finance and Information Systems, Deputy Town Clerk and Deputy Chief Executive, Royal Borough of Kensington and Chelsea, 1991–2002; *b* 7 Dec. 1946; *s* of Charles Reeve and Sylvia Reeve (*née* Prynne); *m* 1968, Janice Rosina Williamson; one *s* one *d*. *Educ:* Dame Alice Owen's Grammar Sch. for Boys, Islington; Tottenham and E Ham Tech. Colls. Various posts, Islington LBC, 1965–74; Asst Borough Treas., Greenwich LBC, 1974–79; Dep. Dir of Finance, RBK&C, 1979–91. Actg Clerk, Western Riverside Waste Authy, 2005–06. Pres., Soc. of London Treasurers, 2000–01. Vice-Chairman of Governors: Sweyne Co. Primary Sch., Swanscombe, Kent, 2002– (Chm., Finance Cttee, 2002–); Manor Sch., Swanscombe, Dartford, 2009– (Chm., Interim Governing Body, 2008–09). *Recreations:* golf, painting (watercolours), reading, gardening, music, following Arsenal FC, genealogy, fly-fishing, running art clubs for primary schoolchildren. *Address:* 5 Red Lodge Crescent, Bexley, Kent DA5 2JR. *Clubs:* The Warren; Birchwood Park Golf (Wilmington).

REEVE, John; non-executive Chairman, Temple Bar Investment Trust PLC, since 2003 (Director, since 1992); Director, Premium Credit Ltd, since 2012; *b* 13 July 1944; *s* of Clifford Alfred Reeve and Irene Mary Turnidge Reeve; *m* 1974, Sally Diane Welton; one *d*. *Educ:* Westcliff High School (Grammar). FCA. Selbey Smith & Earle, 1962–67; Peat Marwick McLintock, 1967–68; Vickers, Roneo Vickers Group, 1968–76; Wilkinson Match, 1976–77; Amalgamated Metal Corp., 1977–80; Group Finance Director: British Aluminium Co., 1980–83; Mercantile House Holdings, 1983–87; Dep. Man. Dir, 1988, Man. Dir, 1989, Sun Life Assurance Society plc; Gp Man. Dir, 1990–95, non-exec. Dir, 1995–96, Sun Life Corp. plc; Exec. Chm., Willis Corroon, subseq. Willis, Gp Ltd, 1995–2000. Non-executive Chairman: Alea Gp Hldgs (Bermuda) Ltd, 2003–07; Coverzones Ltd, 2007–10. Director: The English Concert, 1987– (Chm., 1993–2006); HMC Group plc, 1988–94; London First, 1998–2002. Pres., Inst. of Business Ethics, 1997–2000 (Mem. Adv. Council, 1986–91; Dep. Pres., 1991–96). Chm., E London Business Alliance, 2000–02; Member: E London Partnership Bd, 1991–2000 (Chm., 1996–2000); Council, BITC, 1995–2000; Life Insce Council, 1991–94, Bd, 1993–95, ABI; Bd, 1993–2001, Exec. Cttee, 1996–2001, Internat. Insurance Soc. Inc. Governor: Res. into Ageing, 1991–96; NIESR, 1995–2000. CCMI. FRSA 1999. *Recreations:* yachting, music, theatre. *Address:* Cliff Dene, 24 Cliff Parade, Leigh-on-Sea, Essex SS9 1BB. *T:* (01702) 477563, *Fax:* (01702) 479092. *E:* reevej@compuserve.com. *Clubs:* Athenæum, Royal Ocean Racing; Essex Yacht.

REEVE, Rear Adm. Jonathon, CB 2003; CEng; Deputy Chief Executive, Warship Support Agency, and Navy Board Member for Logistics, 2001–04; *b* 1 Oct. 1949; *e s* of late Lawrence Alick Reeve and of Joan Reeve; *m* 1980, Jennifer Anne, *d* of late Guy and of Betty Wickman; one *s* one *d*. *Educ:* Marlborough Coll.; St Catharine's Coll., Cambridge (MA 1972). CEng, MIEE 1978, FIET (FIEE 2000). Joined Royal Navy, 1967: qualified submarines, 1974; HMS Renown, 1974–76; HMS Dreadnought, 1979–82; RNSC, 1982; Naval Sec.'s Dept, MoD, 1982–84; Strategic Systems Exec., 1985–88; Naval Manpower Trng, 1989–91; Capt. 1991; Asst Dir, MoD Defence Systems, 1991–93; Head of Integrated Logistics Support (Navy), Ship Support Agency, MoD, 1994–96; rcds 1997; Cdre 1998; Naval Base Comdr, Devonport, 1998–2000; COS (Corporate Develt) to C-in-C Fleet, 2000. Dir, OMG, 2006–. *Recreations:* golf, tennis, gardening, dancing. *Address:* c/o Naval Secretary, Fleet Headquarters, Whale Island, Portsmouth, Hants PO1 3LS.

REEVE, Prof. Michael David, FBA 1984; Fellow, Pembroke College, Cambridge, since 1984; *b* 11 Jan. 1943; *s* of Arthur Reeve and Edith Mary Barrett; *m* 1970, Elizabeth Klingaman (marr. diss. 1999); two *s* one *d*. *Educ:* King Edward's Sch., Birmingham; Balliol Coll., Oxford (MA). Harmsworth Senior Scholar, Merton Coll., Oxford, 1964–65; Woodhouse Research Fellow, St John's Coll., Oxford, 1965–66; Tutorial Fellow, Exeter Coll., Oxford, 1966–84, now Emeritus Fellow; Kennedy Prof. of Latin, 1984–2006, Dir of Res., Faculty of Classics, 2006–07, Sandars Reader in Bibliography, 2012, Cambridge Univ. Visiting Professor: Univ. of Hamburg, 1976; McMaster Univ., 1979; Univ. of Toronto, 1982–83. Chm., Adv. Council, Warburg Inst., 2008–13. Fellow, Società Internazionale per lo Studio del Medioevo Latino, 1996; Corresp. Mem., Akademie der Wissenschaften, Göttingen, 1990; For. Mem., Istituto Lombardo, Milan, 1993; Accademico della Classe di Studi Greci e Latini, Biblioteca Ambrosiana, Milan, 2014. Editor, Classical Quarterly, 1981–86. *Publications:* Longus, Daphnis and Chloe, 1982; contribs to Texts and Transmission, ed L. D. Reynolds, 1983; Cicero, Pro Quinctio, 1992; Vegetius, Epitoma rei militaris, 2004; Geoffrey of Monmouth, De gestis Britonum, 2007; Manuscripts and Methods, 2011; articles in European and transatlantic jls. *Recreations:* chess, music, gardening, mountain walking. *Address:* Pembroke College, Cambridge CB2 1RF.

REEVE, Philip John; author and illustrator; *b* Brighton, 28 Feb. 1966; *s* of Michael and Jean Reeve; *m* 1998, Sarah Hedley; one *s*. *Educ:* Stanley Deason High Sch., Brighton; Cambs Coll. of Arts and Technol. (HND BTEC (Illustration)). Freelance illustrator, 1990–; author, 2001–. *Publications:* Mortal Engines, 2001 (Guardian Children's Fiction Prize, Nestlé Book Prize, Blue Peter Book of Year); Predator's Gold, 2003; Infernal Devices, 2005; A Darkling Plain, 2006; Larklight, 2006; Here Lies Arthur, 2007 (Carnegie Medal, CLIP, 2008); Starcross, 2007; Mothstorm, 2008; Fever Crumb, 2009; No Such Thing as Dragons, 2009; A Web of Air, 2010; Scrivener's Moon, 2011; Goblins, 2012; Goblin Quest, 2014; with Sarah McIntyre: Oliver and the Seawigs, 2013; Cakes in Space, 2014; Railhead, 2015. *Recreation:* exploring Dartmoor on foot, horseback and bicycle. *Address:* c/o Lucas Alexander Whitley, 14 Vernon Street, W14 0RJ. *T:* (020) 7471 7900.

REEVE, Robin Martin, MA; Head Master, King's College School, Wimbledon, 1980–97; *b* 22 Nov. 1934; *s* of Percy Martin Reeve and Cicely Nora Parker; *m* 1959, Brianne Ruth Hall; one *s* two *d*. *Educ:* Hampton Sch.; Gonville and Caius Coll., Cambridge (Foundation Schol.; BA 1957; MA). Asst Master, King's Coll. Sch., Wimbledon, 1958–62; Head of History Dept, 1962–80, and Dir of Studies, 1975–80, Lancing Coll. Member: CATE, 1993–94; ISC (formerly ISJC), 1991–99; Council, Brighton Coll., 1997–99; Council, Lancing Coll., 1997–2009 (Chm., 1999–2008). *Publications:* The Industrial Revolution 1750–1850, 1971. *Recreations:* English history and architecture, gardening. *Address:* The Old Rectory, Coombes, Lancing, W Sussex BN15 0RS. *Club:* Athenæum.

REEVE, Roy Stephen, CMG 1998; HM Diplomatic Service, retired; Consultant, Conciliation Resources, since 2010; *b* 20 Aug. 1941; *s* of Ernest Arthur Reeve and Joan Elizabeth (*née* Thomas); *m* 1964, Gill Lee; two *d*. *Educ:* Dulwich Coll.; LSE (BSc Econs 1965; MSc 1966). Joined FCO, 1966; Moscow, 1968–71; First Secretary: FCO, 1973–78; (Commercial) Moscow, 1978–80; Counsellor on loan to Home Civil Service, 1983–85; Dep. Consul-General, Johannesburg, 1985–88; Hd, Commercial Management and Export Dept, FCO, 1988–91; Consul-Gen., Sydney, 1991–95; Ambassador to Ukraine, 1995–99; OSCE Ambassador: to Armenia, 1999–2003; to Georgia, 2003–07; Hd, EU Planning Team, and Dep. Hd, EU Rule of Law Mission, Kosovo, 2008–10. Hon. Sen. Res. Fellow, Centre for Russian and E European Studies, Univ. of Birmingham, 1999–. Chair, British Georgian Soc., 2014–. *Recreations:* Rugby Union, scuba diving.

REEVELL, Simon Justin; *b* Doncaster, 2 March 1966; *s* of Stephen and Jean Reevell; *m* 2001, Louise Cooke. *Educ:* Boston Spa Comprehensive Sch. (MoD (Army) VI Form Scholarship); Manchester Poly. (BA Hons Econs; MoD (Army) Univ. Cadetship); Poly. of Central London (DipLaw); Inns of Court Sch. of Law (Denning Scholar, Hardwicke Scholar, Thomas More Bursar). PWO Regt of Yorks, 1985–89. Called to the Bar, Lincoln's Inn, 1990; in practice as a barrister, specialising in military and criminal law, Leeds and London, 1990–. MP (C) Dewsbury, 2010–15; contested (C) same seat, 2015. Court Martial Ed., Westlaw UK Insight, 2013–. *Club:* Farmers.

REEVES, Antony Robert; Partner, Audit, Deloitte, since 2015; *b* 10 Feb. 1965; *s* of Bob and Jackie Reeves; *m* 2002, Kathryn; one *s*. *Educ:* Bristol Poly. (BA Hons); Huddersfield Univ. (MBA 1996). Housing Officer, 1989, Sen. Housing Officer, 1989–90, Stockport MBC; Estate Action Team Leader, 1990, District Housing Manager, 1990–92, Calderdale MBC; Barnsley Metropolitan Borough Council: Prin. Housing Officer, 1992–93; Hd of Housing Ops, 1993–95; Hd of Housing, 1995–99; Actg Prog. Dir of Health, Home Care Services, 1999–2000; Exec. Dir of Housing and Property Services, 2000–03; Dep. Chief Exec., Wakefield MDC, 2003–06; Chief Exec., City of Bradford MDC, 2006–14. *Recreations:* scuba diving, walking, golf, Rugby, reading, travel. *Address:* Deloitte, 1 City Square, Leeds LS1 2AL. *E:* toreeves@deloitte.co.uk.

REEVES, Dr Colin Leslie, CBE 1999; self-employed healthcare consultant, since 2003; *b* 4 April 1949; *s* of Leslie and Isabelle Reeves; *m* 1978, Christine Lloyd; two *d*. *Educ:* Birkenhead Sch.; Clare Coll., Cambridge (BA 1970; MA); UCNW, Bangor (MSc 1971; PhD 1973); DBA Cornell Univ. 1990. CPFA (IPFA 1976). Lectr, UCNW, Bangor, 1971–73; Accountancy and Audit Assistant, Warrington County Borough, 1973–75; Asst Treas., Ellesmere Port and Neston BC, 1975–80; Deputy Director of Finance: Stratford-on-Avon DC, 1980–84; NW Thames RHA, 1984–85; Director of Finance: Paddington and N Kensington DHA, 1985–86; NW Thames RHA, 1986–94; Dir of Finance and Performance, NHS Exec., 1994–2001; Dir, Accountancy Foundn Rev. Bd, 2001–03. Vice Chm. and Chm., Audit Cttee, Oxford Radcliffe Hosps NHS Trust, 2005–09. Member: Adv. Cttee on Mentally Disordered Offenders, 1993–94; Culyer Cttee on R&D, 1993–94; NHS Steering Gps on Capitation and on Capital, 1993–94; Chancellor of Exchequer's Pvte Finance Panel, 1994–95; Butler Cttee on review of Audit Commn, 1995; CMO's Nat. Screening Cttee, 1996–2001; Review of ONS, reporting to HM Treasury, 1999; Bd, Accountancy NTO, 1999–2001; Co-ordinating Gp on Audit and Accounting Issues, DTI/HM Treasury, 2002; Consultative Cttee on Review of the Listing Regime, FSA, 2002. Mem., Finance and Audit Cttee, Oxfam Internat., 2009–10. Hon. Treasurer: Headway (brain injury charity), 2002–; Florence Nightingale Foundn, 2011–; Goring and Streatley Fest., 2014–. Member: NT; RSPB; Woodland Trust. *Publications:* The Applicability of the Monetary Base Hypothesis to the UK, the USA, France and West Germany, 1974; contrib. professional jls. *Recreations:* sport, especially cricket and golf, history of Test Match cricket, hockey (former regl internat. and county player). *Address:* Battle Hill, Elvendon Road, Goring-on-Thames, Oxon RG8 0DT. *T:* (01491) 872166; La Loma, Las Lomas, 29500 Alora, Malaga, Spain. *Clubs:* Royal Automobile, MCC; Goring and Streatley Golf; Flying Ferrets Golf Soc.; Henley Hawks Rugby Football.

REEVES, Dr David Alan; Managing Director, DRC Consulting Ltd, since 2009; Consultant: Quantic Group, since 2012; Chairman, Near East Digital Ventures, Dubai, since 2012; *b* London, UK, 8 March 1947; *s* of Edward Arthur and Madge Dora Reeves; *m* 1st, 1968, Margaret Micklethwaite (marr. diss.); two *d*; 2nd, 1998, Eiko Yamanouchi; one *d*. *Educ:* Univ. of East Anglia (BSc); Univ. of Cambridge and Univ. of East Anglia (PhD 1971). Regl Manager, S Africa, RJR Nabisco, 1984–87; Mktg Dir, RJR Switzerland and Austria, 1987–89; Global Brand Manager, RJR Camel, 1989–91; Vice Pres., Mktg, RJR Mitsubishi TV, Tokyo, 1991–95; Sony Computer Entertainment (Europe): Man. Dir, Germany, Austria and Switzerland, 1995–99; Vice Pres., Mktg and Sales, London, 1999–2003; Pres. and Chief Operating Officer, 2003–09; CEO, 2005–09; Chief Operating Officer, Capcom EMEA, 2010–13. Dir, RED Entertainment Dubai, 2011–; Sen. Ind. Dir, Keywords Internat. plc, Dublin, 2012–. Trustee: Rabin Ezra Scholarship Trust, 2007–; Sense, 2009–; Autistica, UK, 2013–. *Recreations:* National Ski Patrol (Instructor), tennis, PADI scuba. *Address:* 2 Midgarth Close, Oxshott, Surrey KT22 0JY. *T:* (01372) 841527. *E:* David.Reeves26@yahoo.co.uk.

REEVES, Rev. Donald St John, MBE 2008; Rector, St James's Church, Piccadilly, 1980–98; *b* 18 May 1934; *s* of Henry and Barbara Reeves. *Educ:* Sherborne; Queens' Coll., Cambridge (BA Hons 1957); Cuddesdon Theol Coll. 2nd Lieut, Royal Sussex Regt, 1952–54. Lectr, British Council, Beirut, 1957–60; Tutor, Brasted Theol Coll., 1960–61; Cuddesdon Theol Coll., 1961–63; deacon, 1963, priest, 1964; Curate, All Saints, Maidstone, 1963–65; Chaplain to Bishop of Southwark, 1965–68; Vicar of St Peter's, Morden, 1969–80. Mem., Gen. Synod of C of E, 1990–94. Dir, The Soul of Europe, 1999–. MLitt Lambeth, 2003. *Publications:* (ed) Church and State, 1984; For God's Sake, 1988; Making Sense of Religion, 1989; Down to Earth: a new vision, 1995; The Memoirs of "A Very Dangerous Man", 2009. *Recreations:* playing the organ, watching TV soaps. *Address:* The Coach House, Church Street, Crediton EX17 2AQ. *T:* (01363) 775100, *Fax:* (01363) 773911. *Club:* Athenæum.

REEVES, Gordon; *see* Reeves, W. G.

REEVES, Dame Helen May, DBE 1999 (OBE 1986); Chief Executive (formerly Director), Victim Support (formerly National Association of Victim Support Schemes), 1980–2005; *b* 22 Aug. 1945; *d* of Leslie Percival William Reeves and Helen Edith Reeves (*née* Brown). *Educ:* Dartford Grammar School for Girls; Nottingham University (BA Hons Social Admin. 1966). Probation Officer, Inner London Probation Service, 1967–79 (Senior Probation Officer, 1975–79). Member: Nat. Bd for Crime Prevention, 1993–95; Govt Working Gp on Vulnerable and Intimidated Witnesses, 1998–99; Home Office Steering Gp on Review of Sexual Offences, 1999; EU Cttee of Experts on Victims of Crime, 1998–99; Ind. Review of Criminal Stats, 2006; Chm., Council of Europe Expert Cttee on Victims of Crime and Terrorism, 2005–06. Vice Pres., World Soc. of Victimology, 1994–2006; Chm., Eur. Forum for Victim Services, 2001–05. Member: Howard League Commn on Future of English Prisons, 2005–09; RSA Risk Commn, 2006–09; Adv. Bd, Tim Parry Johnathan Ball Foundn for Peace, 2005–11 (Trustee, 2011–). Chair: Blackheath Decorative and Fine Arts Soc., 2011–14; Blackheath Soc., 2014–. Hon. MA Nottingham, 1998; Hon. LLD: Warwick, 2001; Southampton Solent, 2004; Nottingham, 2014. *Recreations:* social and local history and architecture, food, gardens, fine and decorative arts.

REEVES, Marc Barnaby; Publishing Director, Trinity Mirror Midlands, since 2013; Editor, Birmingham Mail, since 2014; *b* 25 Nov. 1965; *s* of late Frederick Reeves and Mai Reeves (then Barnes); *m* 1st, 1988 (marr. diss.); two *d*; 2nd, 2014, Claire Procter. *Educ:* St Teresa's Primary Sch., Birmingham; Handsworth Grammar Sch., Birmingham; Birmingham Poly.; Oxford Brookes Univ. (CMS 2002; DMS 2003). Dep. Ed., Walsall Advertiser, 1988–89; Sub-ed., Focus Newspapers. Birmingham, 1989–91; Revise Ed., Computer Newspaper Services, Howden, 1991–92; Prodn Ed., Northampton Chronicle & Echo, 1992–94; Dep. Ed., Cumberland News, 1994–97; Ed., Reading Chronicle, 1997–2000; Editl Dir, Trinity Mirror Southern, 2000–06; Editor: Birmingham Post, 2006–09; TheBusinessDesk.com W Midlands, 2010–12; Partner, RJF Public Affairs Ltd, 2011–13. Mem., Lunar Soc. *Recreations:* collecting music and music trivia, military and political history, lazing in the garden.

REEVES, Martin Robert, PhD; Chief Executive, Coventry City Council, since 2009; *b* Chatham, Kent, 30 May 1970; *s* of David Reeves and Margaret Reeves; *m* 2006, Lucy Ann Parker; two *d*. *Educ:* Sheffield City Poly. (BA Hons Mgt 1991); Loughborough Univ. (MSc (dist.) Rec. Mgt 1993); Cheltenham and Gloucester Coll. of HE (PGCFHE 1998); Loughborough Univ. (PhD 2000). Nat. Press and PR Officer, Disability Sport England, 1991–92; Lectr and Researcher, Cheltenham and Gloucester Coll. of HE, 1997–2000; Policy and Res. Manager, Reigate and Banstead BC, 2000–01; Hd of Policy, Performance and Business Support, Waltham Forest LBC, 2001–03; Hd, Performance Improvement, Westminster CC, 2003–06; Asst Chief Exec., 2006–08, Chief Exec., 2008–09, Beds CC. *Recreations:* all sport, travel, photography. *Address:* Coventry City Council, Council House, Earl Street, Coventry CV1 5RR. *T:* (024) 7683 1100, *Fax:* (024) 7683 3680. *E:* martin.reeves@coventry.gov.uk.

REEVES, Prof. Nigel Barrie Reginald, OBE 1987; DPhil; Pro-Vice-Chancellor for External Relations, Aston University, 1996–2007, now Professor Emeritus; *b* 9 Nov. 1939; *s* of Reginald Arthur Reeves and Marjorie Joyce Reeves; *m* 1982, Minou (*née* Samimi); one *s* one *d*. *Educ:* Merchant Taylors' Sch.; Worcester Coll., Oxford (MA); St John's Coll., Oxford (DPhil 1970). FIL 1981. Lectr in English, Univ. of Lund, Sweden, 1964–66; Lectr in German, Univ. of Reading, 1968–74; Alexander von Humboldt Fellow, Univ. of Tübingen, 1974–75; University of Surrey: Prof. of German, 1975–90; Hd of Dept of Linguistic and Internat. Studies, 1979–90; Dean, Faculty of Human Studies, 1986–90; Prof. of German and Head of Dept of Modern Langs, Aston Univ., 1990–96. Guest Prof. of German, Royal Holloway Coll., London Univ., 1976; Vis. Prof., European Business Sch., 1981–88; Sen. Alexander von Humboldt Fellow, Univ. of Hamburg, 1986; UK Short-term Visitor to Japan, Japan Foundn, 1997. Chm., Nat. Congress on Langs in Educn, 1986–90; President: Nat. Assoc. of Language Advisers, 1986–91; Assoc. of Teachers of German, 1988–89; Vice-President: Conf. of University Teachers of German, 1995–97 (Vice-Chm., 1988–91); Inst. of Linguists, 1990–2008 (Chm. Council, 1985–88); Convenor, British Inst. of Traffic Educn Res., 2001–02; Member: Academic Adv. Council, Linguaphone Inst., 1991–2005; Modern Langs Steering Cttee, Open Univ., 1991–96; Academic Adv. Council, Univ. of Buckingham, 1994–2002; Bd, British Trng Internat., 1998–2001; SCOTLANG (SHEFC), 2000–02; Exec. Cttee, Univ. Council for Modern Langs, 2003–07; Steering Gp for Benchmarking, QAA, 2003–07; Assessor, Irish Res. Council for Humanities and Social Scis, 2001–02. Consultant, QCA, 2001–03; Mem., Langs Ladder Wkg Gp, DfES, 2004–06. Governor: Germanic Inst., Univ. of London, 1989–94; Matthew Boulton Further and Higher Educn Corp., Birmingham, 2002–07 (Chm., 1999–2002). Mem., Adv. Council, Worcester Coll. Soc., Oxford, 2000–08. Trustee, London Chamber of Commerce and Industry Commercial Educn Trust, 2001–08. FRSA 1986; CIEx 1987. Hon. Fellow, Hong Kong Translation Soc., 2006. Goethe Medal, Goethe Inst., Munich, 1989; Medal, European Foundn for Quality Management, 1996. Officer's Cross, Order of Merit (Germany), 1999. *Publications:* Merkantil-Tekniska Stilar, 2 Vols, 1965–66; Heinrich Heine: poetry and politics, 1974; (with K. Dewhurst) Friedrich Schiller: medicine, psychology and literature, 1978; (with D. Luke) Heinrich von Kleist, The Marquise von O. and other stories, 1978; (with D. Liston) Business

Studies, Languages and Overseas Trade, 1985; (jtly) Making Your Mark: effective business communication in Germany, 1988; (with D. Liston) The Invisible Economy: a profile of Britain's invisible exports, 1988; (jtly) Franc Exchange, effective business communication in France, 1991; (jtly) Spanish Venture, basic business communication in Spain, 1992; (with C. Wright) Linguistic Auditing, 1996; (ed with H. Kelly-Holmes) The European Business Environment: Germany, 1997; (with R. West and A. Simpson) Pathways to Proficiency: the alignment of language proficiency scales for assessing competence in English Language, 2003; over 100 articles in learned jls on language, language educn, literature and overseas trade. *Recreations:* gardening, walking. *Address:* c/o Pro-Vice-Chancellor's Office, Aston University, Aston Triangle, Birmingham B4 7ET.

REEVES, Philip Thomas Langford, RE 1964; RSA 1976 (ARSA 1971); PPRSW; artist in etching and other mediums; Senior Lecturer, Glasgow School of Art, 1973–91; President, Royal Scottish Society of Painters in Water Colours, 1998–2005; *b* 7 July 1931; *s* of Herbert Reeves and Lilian; *m* 1964, Christine MacLaren (*d* 1994); one *d. Educ:* Naunton Park Sch., Cheltenham. Student, Cheltenham Sch. of Art, 1947–49. Army service, 4th/7th Royal Dragoon Guards, Middle East, 1949–51. RCA, 1951–54 (ARCA 1st Cl.); Lectr, Glasgow Sch. of Art, 1954–73. Founder Member: Edinburgh Printmakers Workshop, 1967; Glasgow Print Studio, 1972. Associate, Royal Soc. of Painter Etchers, 1954; RSW 1962; RGI 1981. Works in permanent collections: Arts Council; V&A; Gall. of Modern Art, Edinburgh; Glasgow Art Gall.; Glasgow Univ. Print Collection; Hunterian Art Gall., Glasgow; Manchester City Art Gall.; Royal Scottish Acad.; Aberdeen Art Gall.; Paisley Art Gall.; Inverness Art Gall.; Milngavie Art Gall.; Dept of the Environment; Dundee Art Gall.; Scottish Develt Agency; Stirling and Strathclyde Univs; British Govt Art Collection; Contemporary Art Soc. *Recreation:* walking. *Address:* 13 Hamilton Drive, Glasgow G12 8DN.

REEVES, Rachel Jane; MP (Lab) Leeds West, since 2010; *b* 13 Feb. 1979; *d* of Graham Reeves and Sally Reeves. *Educ:* New Coll., Oxford (BA Hons PPE); London Sch. of Econs and Pol Sci. (MSc Econs). Economist: Bank of England, 2000–02, 2003–09; British Embassy, Washington, 2002–03; Business Planner, Halifax Bank of Scotland, 2006–09. Shadow Chief Sec. to the Treasury, 2011–13; Shadow Sec. of State for Work and Pensions, 2013–15. Contested (Lab) Bromley and Chislehurst, 2005, June 2006. *Publications:* Why Vote Labour?, 2010; contrib. Jl of Pol Econ. *Recreations:* swimming, walking, tennis, theatre. *Address:* House of Commons, SW1A 0AA; (office) Unit 8A, Bramley Shopping Centre, Bramley, Leeds LS13 2ET. *T:* (0113) 255 2311. *E:* rreevesmp@gmail.com.

REEVES, William Desmond, CB 1993; Secretary, UK Management Board, PricewaterhouseCoopers, 1998–2004; *b* 26 May 1937; *s* of late Thomas Norman and Anne Reeves; *m* 1967, Aase Birte Christensen; two *d. Educ:* Darwen Grammar Sch.; King's Coll., Cambridge (BA Hist.). National service, RAEC, 1959–61. Joined Admiralty as Asst Principal, 1961; MoD, 1964; Asst Sec., 1973; seconded to Pay Board, 1973–74; Asst Under Sec. of State, Air, MoD (PE), 1982–84, Resources and Progs, MoD, 1984, Systems, Office of Management and Budget, MoD, 1985–88; Under Sec., Cabinet Office, 1989–92; Asst Under Sec. of State (Commitments), MoD, 1992–94. Partnership Sec., Coopers & Lybrand, 1994–98. *Recreation:* supporting Blackburn Rovers. *Address:* 2 Downs Bridge Road, Beckenham, Kent BR3 5HX.

REEVES, Prof. (William) Gordon, FRCP, FRCPath; Professor and Head of Department of Microbiology and Immunology, College of Medicine, Sultan Qaboos University, Muscat, Oman, 1993–98; *b* 9 July 1938; *s* of Rev. W. H. and Mrs E. L. Reeves; *m* 1970, Elizabeth Susan, *d* of Surg.-Comdr L. A. and Mrs P. Moules; one *s* one *d. Educ:* Perse Sch., Cambridge; Guy's Hosp. Med. Sch. (BSc, MB BS). MRCS, LRCP 1964; MRCP 1966; FRCP 1978; FRCPath 1985. HO and Med. Registrar appts at Guy's, Central Middx, Brompton, National, Middx, and University Coll. Hosps, 1964–68; Lecturer: Clinical Pharmacology, Guy's Hosp. Med. Sch., 1968–71; Immunology and Medicine, Royal Postgrad. Med. Sch., 1971–73; Consultant Immunologist, Nottingham HA, 1973–88; Nottingham University: Sen. Lectr, 1975–85; Prof. of Immunology, 1985–88; Editor, The Lancet, 1989–90; Med. Editor and Consultant, Communicable Disease Surveillance Centre, PHLS, 1991–93. Vis. Prof. in Immunology of Infectious Disease, St Mary's Hosp. Med. Sch., 1992–97. Member: Soc. of Authors; Friends of Cathedral Music; Friends of King's Coll., Cambridge; Bury Soc.; Devonshire Assoc.; Norfolk Heraldry Soc.; Suffolk Preservation Soc.; Suffolk Records Soc.; Soc. des Etudes du Lot. *Publications:* contribs to books and jls on medicine, immunology and medieval history. *Recreations:* unspoiled countryside, cottage gardens, vineyards of the Côte d'Or.

REFFELL, Adm. Sir Derek (Roy), KCB 1984; Governor and Commander-in-Chief, Gibraltar, 1989–93; *b* 6 Oct. 1928; *s* of late Edward (Roy) and Murielle Reffell; *m* 1956, Janne Gronow Davis (*d* 2013); one *s* one *d. Educ:* Culford Sch., Suffolk; Royal Naval Coll., Dartmouth. Various ships at Home, Mediterranean, West Indies and Far East, 1946–63; qualified Navigating Officer, 1954; Comdr 1963; Comd HMS Sirius, 1966–67; Comdr BRNC Dartmouth, 1968–69; Captain 1970; Naval Staff, 1971–74; Comd HMS Hermes, 1974–76; Director Naval Warfare, 1976–78; Commodore Amphibious Warfare, 1978–79; Asst Chief of Naval Staff (Policy), 1979–82; Flag Officer Third Flotilla and Comdr Anti-Submarine Group Two, 1982–83; Flag Officer, Naval Air Comd, 1983–84; Controller of the Navy, 1984–89, retd. Governor, Royal Sch., Hindhead, 1995–98. Trustee, Special Olympics UK, 1998–2002. Chm., Friends of Gibraltar Heritage Soc., 1994–2004. Master, Coachmakers' Company, 1998–99. KStJ 1989. *Recreations:* golf, watching birds.

REFFO, Geraldine Mary Nicole, CMG 2009; Founder and Managing Director, Gerry Reffo Coaching and Consulting Ltd, since 2009; *b* London, 17 Jan. 1959; *d* of Gerald Francis Reffo and Josephine Mary Reffo. *Educ:* Open Univ. (MBA 1995). Clerical Officer, 1975–82, Auditor, 1982–89, Dept of Employment; Foreign and Commonwealth Office: Sen. Auditor, 1989–93; Dep. Hd, Internal Audit, 1993–96; Hd, Personnel Mgt Unit, 1998–2001; Asst Dir, Human Resources, 2001–03; Hd, Learning and Develt, 2003–09. Mem., Inst. of Internal Auditors, 1985; MInstD 2010. *Publications:* (with V. Wark) Leadership PQ, 2014. *Recreations:* walking (dog), reading, horse racing, house in France. *E:* greffo2000@yahoo.co.uk. *T:* 07788 428340.

REFSON, Benita Margaret, OBE 2007; President, Place2Be, since 2014; *b* London, 9 Sept. 1947; *d* of late Gerald and Anne Ronson; one *s* two *d. Educ:* Sarum Hall; Roedean Sch.; Paris; Regent's Coll. and Westminster Pastoral Foundn (Qualified Counsellor). Trainee psychiatric social worker; fashion ed., Vogue; Founding Trustee and Dir, 1994–2002, CEO, 2002–13, Place2Be. Advr, Educn and Learning Cttee, Paul Hamlyn Foundn. Trustee: Children and Success Schs Trust, 2013–; RAPt, 2013–. Hon. LLD E London, 2009; Hon. DLit (Educn) Inst. of Educn, 2014. *Recreations:* walking, piano lessons, dog walking, fashion, spending time with children and grandchildren, film and theatre. *Address:* Place2B, 13/14 Angel Gate, 326 City Road, EC1V 2PT. *T:* (020) 7923 5500. *Club:* Reform.

REGAN, Rt Rev. Edwin; Bishop of Wrexham, (RC), 1994–2012, now Bishop Emeritus; *b* 31 Dec. 1935; *s* of James Regan and Elizabeth Ellen Regan (*née* Hoskins). *Educ:* St Joseph's RC Primary Sch., Aberavon; Port Talbot County Grammar Sch.; St John's Coll., Waterford, Eire; Corpus Christi Coll., London. Priest, 1959; Curate, Neath, 1959–66; Adviser in RE, Archdio. Cardiff, 1967–87; Chaplain, St Clare's Convent, Porthcawl, 1967–71; Administrator, St David's Cathedral, Cardiff, 1971–84; Parish Priest: St Helen's, Barry, 1984–89; St Mary's, Bridgend, 1989–94; Blaenau Ffestiniog, 2012–. Apostolic Administrator, Archdio. of Cardiff, 2000–01. *Recreation:* gentle hill-walking. *Address:* Bethania, 6 Geufron Terrace, Blaenau Ffestiniog, Gwynedd LL41 3BW.

REGAN, Prof. Lesley, (Mrs John Summerfield), MD; FRCOG; Professor and Head of Department of Obstetrics and Gynaecology, Imperial College at St Mary's Hospital, London, since 1996; Deputy Head, Division of Surgery, Oncology, Reproductive Biology and Anaesthetics, Imperial College London, since 2005; *b* 8 March 1956; *d* of Jack Regan and Dorothy Hull (*née* Thorne); *m* 1990, Prof. John Summerfield; twin *d*, and two step *s* two step *d. Educ:* Royal Free Hosp. Sch. of Medicine (MB BS 1980; MD 1989). MRCOG 1985, FRCOG 1998. Sen. Registrar in Obstetrics and Gynaecology, Addenbrooke's Hosp., Cambridge, 1986–90; Teaching Fellow (Medicine), 1986–90, Dir of Medical Studies, 1987–90, Girton Coll., Cambridge; Sen. Res. Associate, MRC Embryo and Gamete Res. Gp, Univ. of Cambridge, 1987–89; Sen. Lectr, ICSM, and Hon. Consultant in Obstetrics and Gynaecology, St Mary's Hosp., London, 1990–96; Director: Miscarriage Service, St Mary's Hosp., 1990–; Subspecialty Trng Prog. in Reproductive Medicine for ICSM at St Mary's and Hammersmith Hosps, 1995–; Clinical Dir, Maternity, 2000–03, Gynaecology, 2002–05, St Mary's Hosp. Rosenfelder Vis. Fellow, Boston, USA, 1999; Vis. Prof., Harvard Centre of Excellence for Women's Health, 2000–02; RCOG Vis. Lectr to S Africa, 2004; Lectures: Alexander Gordon, Aberdeen Univ., 2003; Lettsomian, Med. Soc. of London, 2004; Green-Armytage, RCOG, 2006. Non-exec. Dir, W Middx Univ. Hosp. NHS Trust, 2006–08. Mem., HFEA, 2008–. Professional Advisor: Miscarriage Assoc., 1992–; CHANA, 1994–; Industrial Relns Soc., 1994–; Twins and Multiple Births Assoc., 1996–. Mem., Expert Adv. Panels in Reproductive Medicine and Contraception, 1997, Women's Sexual and Reproduction Rights Cttee, 2008–, FIGO; Member: Wellcome Trust Adv. Bd (Clinical Interest Gp), 2002–04; Gynaecol Vis. Soc.; Soc. for Gynaecol Investigation, USA; Council, 2006–, Academic Cttee, 2006–, Finance and Exec., 2008–, RCOG. Sec., Assoc. of Professors and Gynaecologists, 2001–07; Pres., Assoc. of Early Pregnancy Units in the UK, 2005–. Trustee: Inst. of Obstetrics and Gynaecology, 1996–; Save the Baby, 1998–; Wellbeing of Women, 2009–. Woman of Achievement Award, 2005, for services to reproductive medicine. *Publications:* Miscarriage: what every woman needs to know, 1997, 2nd edn 2001; Your Pregnancy Week by Week, 2005; numerous chapters in reproductive medicine textbooks; scientific articles on sporadic and recurrent pregnancy loss and uterine fibroids in BMJ, Lancet, Human Reproduction, British Jl of Obstetrics and Gynaecol., Amer. Jls of Obstetrics and Gynaecol. *Recreations:* mother to my twin girls, opera, creating a garden in the South of France. *Address:* Department of Obstetrics and Gynaecology, Imperial College at St Mary's Hospital London, South Wharf Road, Paddington, W2 1NY. *T:* (020) 7886 1798. *E:* l.regan@imperial.ac.uk.

REGAN, Maj.-Gen. Michael Dalrymple, CB 1996; OBE 1985; Controller, The Army Benevolent Fund, 1997–2003; *b* 6 Jan. 1942; *s* of late M. L. R. Regan and G. I. Regan (*née* Dalrymple); *m* 1974, Victoria, *o d* of late Comdr V. C. Grenfell, DSO; two *d. Educ:* St Boniface's Coll.; RMA, Sandhurst. Commnd 1st KSLI, 1962; served Germany, Malaysia, Cyprus and NI; Instructor, Sch. of Infantry, 1968–70; Adjutant, 3rd LI, 1971–73; Staff Coll., Camberley, 1973–74; BM, 12th Mech. Bde, 1975–76; Company Comdr, 1st LI, 1977–78; MA to C-in-C, UKLF, 1979–82; CO, 3rd LI, 1982–84 (mentioned in Despatches); Col MS 2, MoD, 1985; Comdr, 20th Armd Bde, 1986–87; RCDS, 1988; DCOS, HQ UKLF, 1989–91; GOC Wales and Western Dist, 1991–94; Dir Gen., AGC, 1994–95; COS, HQ Adjt Gen., 1995–96. Col, LI, 1992–96; Asst Col Comdt, AGC, 1995–96. Chm. Trustees, Shropshire Regimental Mus., 1998–2003; Trustee: Army Dependants Assurance Trust, 2003–12; Royal Commonwealth Ex-Services League, 2006–12 (Council Mem., 2003–12). *Recreations:* golf, ski-ing, sailing. *Clubs:* MCC, Army and Navy; Royal Yacht Squadron (Cowes).

REGAN, Michael John; HM Diplomatic Service, retired; Managing Partner (formerly Executive Director), G3 Good Governance Group Ltd, since 2010; *b* 17 Aug. 1955; *s* of late Brig. John Joseph Regan, OBE and Edith Nancy Cunliffe; *m* 1986, Carolyn Gaye Black; two *s. Educ:* St George's Coll., Weybridge; Nottingham Univ. (BA Jt Hons Econs and Agricl Econs). SSC, 3rd RTR, 1977–82. Insurance Broker, Fenchurch Gp, 1982–83; joined Diplomatic Service, 1983; FCO, 1983–86; Kabul, 1986–88; FCO, 1988–89; First Sec. (Chancery/Economic), Dubai, 1989–91, FCO, 1991–95; Counsellor (ESCAP), Bangkok, 1995–98; FCO, 1998–2004; Counsellor, Harare, 2004–07; Baghdad, 2007–08; Counsellor, FCO, 2008–10. *Recreations:* hockey, tennis, golf, sailing, walking. *Clubs:* Frontline; Hankley Common Golf; Frensham Fly Fishers.

REGO, Dame (Maria) Paula (Figueiroa), DBE 2010; artist; *b* 26 Jan. 1935; *d* of José Fernandes Figueiroa Rego and Maria de S José Paiva Figueiroa Rego; *m* 1959, Victor Willing (*d* 1988); one *s* two *d. Educ:* St Julian's Sch., Carcavelos, Portugal; Slade School of Fine Art, UCL. First Associate Artist, Nat. Gall., Jan.–Dec. 1990. Selected solo exhibitions: (1st at) Soc. Nat. de Belas Artes, Lisbon, 1965; Gal. S Mamede, Lisbon, 1971; Gal. Modulo, Porto, 1977; Gal. III, Lisbon, 1978; Air Gall., London, 1981; Edward Totah Gall., 1982, 1985, 1987; Arnolfini, 1983; Art Palace, NY, 1985; Gulbenkian Foundn, 1988, 1999, 2012; Serpentine Gall. (retrospective), 1988; Marlborough Graphics (nursery rhymes), 1989; Nat. Gall., 1991–92; Marlborough Gall., 1992, 1994; Tate Gall., Liverpool (retrospective), 1997; Dulwich Picture Gall., 1998; Gulbenkian Foundn, Lisbon, 1999; Abbot Hall, Kendal, 2001; Yale Centre for British Art, 2002; Marlborough Fine Art, 2003, 2006, 2008, 2010; Tate Britain, 2004; Serralves Museum, Oporto, 2004–05; prints (retrospective), Talbot Rice Gall., Edinburgh, then Brighton Mus. and tour, 2005–07; Mus. Nacional Centro de Arte Reina Sofia, Madrid (retrospective), 2007, then Nat. Mus. of Women in the Arts, Washington, DC; Marlborough, NY, 2008; print retrospective, École des Beaux Arts, Nîmes, 2008; Marco Monterrey, 2010, then Pinacoteca do Estado, São Paulo, 2011; Marlborough Fine Art, 2013, 2014. Many collective shows include: ICA, 1965; S Paulo Biennale, 1969, 1985; British Art Show, 1985, 2000; Hayward Gall., 1994 and 1996; Saatchi Gall., 1994–95; Encounters, Nat. Gall., 2000; also in Japan, Australia, all over Europe. Large painting, Crivelli's Garden, in restaurant of Sainsbury Wing, Nat. Gall., 1992. Sen. Fellow, RCA, 1989. Hon. Fellow, Murray Edwards Coll., Cambridge, 2013. Hon. DLitt: St Andrews, 1999; E Anglia, 1999; Oxford, 2005; Hon. DFA Rhode Island Sch. of Design, 2000; Hon. Dr: London Inst., 2002; UCL, 2004; DUniv Roehampton, 2005; Hon. LittD Cambridge, 2015. Premio Penagos, Fundación MAPFRE, 2010. *Relevant Publications:* Paula Rego, by John McEwen, 1992, 3rd edn 2006; Paula Rego, by Fiona Bradley, 2002; Paula Rego: the complete graphic work, by T. G. Rosenthal, 2003, 2nd edn 2012; Paula Rego's Map of Memory, by Dr Maria Lisboa, 2003; Behind the Scenes, by John McEwen, 2008. *Recreations:* going to the movies, plays. *Address:* c/o Marlborough Fine Art, 6 Albemarle Street, W1S 4BY. *T:* (020) 7629 5161.

REHN, Olli Ilmari, DPhil; Member (Alliance of Liberals and Democrats for Europe) for Finland, European Parliament, since 2014; *b* Mikkeli, Finland, 31 March 1962; *s* of Tauno and Vuokko Rehn; *m* 1995, Merja Maria Hakkarainen; one *d. Educ:* Macalester Coll., St Paul, Minn; Univ. of Helsinki (Master Soc. Sci. Political Sci. 1989); St Antony's Coll., Oxford (DPhil Internat. Political Econ. 1996). Mem., City Council, Helsinki, 1988–94; MP (Centre Party), 1991–95; Special Advr to Prime Minister, 1992–93; MEP, 1995–96; Hd of Cabinet, EC, 1998–2002; Prof. and Dir of Res., Dept of Political Sci. and Centre for European Studies, Univ. of Helsinki, 2002–03; Econ. Policy Advr to Prime Minister, 2003–04; Mem., EC, 2004–14. Chm., Centre Youth, Finland, 1987–89; Dep. Chm., Centre Party, 1988–94. Chm., Finnish Delegn to Council of Europe, 1991–95; Vice-Pres., European Movement of Finland, 1996–98. Chm., Football League of Finland, 1996–97. Player, association football, 1968–: FC Mikkelin Palloilijat (youth teams, 1968–78; 1st team, 1979–82); FC Finnish Parliament, 1991–; CS Eurocommission II, 1998–2002. Columnist in several newspapers and mags, 1985–. *Publications:* Pieni valtio Euroopan Unionissa (A Small State in the European Union), 1996; European Challenges of the Finnish EU Presidency, 2nd edn 1998; (contrib.)

Liberalism in the European Union: the way forward, 2004; Europe's Next Frontiers, 2006; Suomen eurooppalainen valinta ei ole suhdannepolitikkaa, 2006; Myrskyn silmässä, 2012. *Recreations:* political economy, rock and jazz, reading. *Address:* European Parliament, Rue Wiertz, 1047 Brussels, Belgium.

REICH, Sir Erich (Arieh), Kt 2010; Founder and Managing Director, Classic Tours, since 1989; *b* Vienna, 1935; *s* of late Sigmund Reich and Mina Reich; *m* 2003, Linda Esther Haase; three *s* two *d.* Manager, Client Services, 1970–76, Ops Dir, 1976–80, Thomson Holidays; Gen. Manager, 1980–84, Man. Dir of Tour Ops, 1984–89, Thomas Cook. Chm., Kindertransport Gp, Assoc. of Jewish Refugees, 2007–. *Recreations:* classical music, swimming. *Address:* 95H Hornsey Lane, Highgate, N6 5LW. *T:* (020) 8340 0751. *E:* reich@blueyonder.co.uk.

REICH, Peter Gordon; Assistant Chief Scientist (G), Royal Air Force, 1984–86; *b* 16 Sept. 1926; *s* of Douglas Gordon Reich and Josephine Grace Reich; *m* 1948, Kathleen, *d* of Alan and Florence Lessiter, Banstead; three *d. Educ:* Sutton Grammar Sch.; London Univ. (BSc). FRIN 1967 (Bronze Medal, 1967). Served RN, 1944–47. Entered Civil Service as Scientific Officer, 1952; Armament Res. Estab., 1952–54; Opl Res. Br., Min. of Transport and Civil Aviation, 1955–60; RAE, 1960–68; Asst Dir of Electronics Res. and Develt (2), Min. of Technol., 1968–70; Asst Dir of Res. (Avionics, Space and Air Traffic), Min. of Aviation Supply, 1971–73; Supt, Def. Opl Analysis Estab., MoD, 1973–76; Mem., Reliability and Costing Study Gp, MoD, 1976–79; Counsellor (Defence Res.), Canberra, and Head of British Defence Res. and Supply Staffs, Australia, 1979–83. *Publications:* papers in Jl of Inst. of Nav., and Jl of Opl Res. Soc. *Recreations:* racquet games, walking, aural pleasures.

REICH, Steve; composer; *b* 3 Oct. 1936; *s* of Leonard Reich and June Carroll (*née* Sillman); *m* 1976, Beryl Korot; one *s*, and one *s* from previous *m. Educ:* Cornell Univ. (BA Hons Philos. 1957); Juilliard Sch. of Music; Mills Coll. (MA Music 1963); Inst. for African Studies, Univ. of Ghana. Guggenheim Fellow, 1978; Montgomery Fellow, Dartmouth Coll., 2000. Mem., AAAL, 1994. Founded ensemble, Steve Reich and Musicians, 1966, toured the world, 1971–. Music performed by major orchestras, including: NY Philharmonic; San Francisco Symphony; St Louis Symphony; Brooklyn Philharmonic; LA Philharmonic; BBC Symphony; London Symphony Orch.; commissions received include: Fest. d'Automne, Paris for 200th Anniv. of French Revolution, 1989; BBC Proms in honour of centennial, 1995. Member: Amer. Acad. of Arts and Letters, 1994; Bavarian Acad. of Fine Arts, 1995. Hon. DMus: Calif Inst. of the Arts, 2002; SUNY, Buffalo, 2008; New England Conservatory of Music, 2009; Juilliard Sch. of Music, 2010. Schuman Prize, Columbia Univ., 2000; Premium Imperial in Music, 2006; Polar Prize, 2007; Pulitzer Prize in Music, 2009. Commandeur, Ordre des Arts et des Lettres (France), 1999. *Compositions include:* Drumming, 1971; Music for 18 Musicians, 1976 (Grammy Award for Best Small Ensemble recording, 1996); Eight Lines, 1979–83; Tehillim, 1981; The Desert Music, 1984; Sextet, 1985; Different Trains, 1988 (Grammy Award for Best Contemporary Composition, 1990); The Cave, 1993; Nagoyd Marimba, 1994; City Life, 1995; Proverb, 1995; Triple Quartet, 1999; Three Tales, 2002; Cello Counterpoint, 2003; You Are (variations), 2004; Daniel Variations, 2006; 2x5, 2007; Double Sextet, 2008 (Pulitzer Prize, 2009); Mallet Quartet, 2009; WTC 9/11, 2010; Radio Rewrite, 2013; Quartet, 2014; music for winds, strings, piano and electric bass, 2016; Runner, 2016. *Publications:* Writings About Music, 1974; Writings on Music 1965–2000, 2002. *Address:* c/o Andrew Rosner, Rayfield Allied, Southbank House, Black Prince Road, SE1 7SJ.

REID, family name of **Baron Reid of Cardowan**.

REID OF CARDOWAN, Baron *cr* 2010 (Life Peer), of Stepps in Lanarkshire; **John Reid;** PC 1998; PhD; Chairman, Celtic plc, 2007–11; a Senior Advisor, Chertoff Group, since 2010; *b* 8 May 1947; *s* of late Thomas Reid and Mary Reid; *m* 1st, 1969, Catherine (*née* McGowan) (*d* 1998); two *s*; 2nd, 2002, Carine Adler. *Educ:* St Patrick's Senior Secondary Sch., Coatbridge; Stirling Univ. (BA History, PhD Economic History). Scottish Research Officer, Labour Party, 1979–83; Political Adviser to Rt Hon. Neil Kinnock, 1983–86; Scottish Organiser, Trades Unionists for Labour, 1986–87. MP (Lab) Motherwell N, 1987–97, Hamilton N and Bellshill, 1997–2005, Airdrie and Shotts, 2005–10. Opposition spokesman on children, 1989–90, on defence, 1990–97; Minister of State, MoD, 1997–98; Minister of Transport, 1998–99; Secretary of State: for Scotland, 1999–2001; for Northern Ireland, 2001–02; Minister without Portfolio and Chair, Labour Party, 2002–03; Leader of the H of C and Pres. of the Council, 2003; Secretary of State: for Health, 2003–05; for Defence, 2005–06; for the Home Dept, 2006–07. Member: Public Accounts Cttee, 1988–89; Armed Forces Cttee and Reserved Forces Cttee, 1996–97. Hon. Prof. and Chair, Inst. for Security and Resilience Studies, UCL, 2008–. Fellow, Armed Forces Parly Scheme, 1990–. *Publications:* (jtly) Cyber Doctrine: toward a framework for learning resilience, 2011. *Recreations:* football, reading history, crossword puzzles. *Address:* House of Lords, SW1A 0PW.

REID, Sir Alan; *see* Reid, Sir P. A.

REID, Alan; *b* 7 Aug. 1954; *s* of James Smith Reid and Catherine Graham Reid (*née* Steele). *Educ:* Prestwick Acad.; Ayr Acad.; Strathclyde Univ. (BSc Hons Pure & Applied Maths). Strathclyde Regional Council: Maths Teacher, 1976–77; Computer Programmer, 1977–85; Computer Project Manager, Glasgow Univ., 1985–2001. MP (Lib Dem) Argyll and Bute, 2001–15; contested (Lib Dem) same seat, 2015. *Recreations:* playing chess, walking, reading, watching TV.

REID, Dr Alexander Arthur Luttrell; Director-General, Royal Institute of British Architects, 1994–2000; *b* 11 Jan. 1941; *s* of late Capt. Philip Reid, RN and of Louisa (*née* Luttrell); *m* 1st, 1964, Sara Louise Coleridge (marr. diss. 1987); two *d*; 2nd, 1988, Sian Tudor Roberts; one *s* one *d. Educ:* Winchester Coll. (Schol.); Trinity Coll., Cambridge (MA); University Coll., London (MSc; PhD 1974). Served RN, Lieut (helicopter pilot), 1962–67. Post Office Telecommunications: Hd, Long Range Studies, 1972–77; Director: Prestel, 1977–80; Business Systems, 1980–83; Acorn Computer Gp PLC, 1984–85; Octagon Investment Mgt Ltd, 1984–2010; MJP Architects Ltd, 2007–; Chief Exec., DEGW Ltd, 1991–94. Mem. (Lib Dem), Cambs CC, 2003–09. Royal College of Art: Council Mem., 1988–90; Chm., 1990–93. *Recreations:* carpentry, sailing. *Address:* 27 Millington Road, Cambridge CB3 9HW. *T:* (01223) 356100.

REID, Sir Alexander (James), 3rd Bt *cr* 1897; JP; DL; *b* 6 Dec. 1932; *s* of Sir Edward James Reid, 2nd Bt, KBE, and Tatiana (*d* 1992), *d* of Col Alexander Fenoult, formerly of Russian Imperial Guard; *S* father, 1972; *m* 1955, Michaela Ann, *d* of late Olaf Kier, CBE; one *s* three *d. Educ:* Eton; Magdalene Coll., Cambridge. Nat. Certificate Agriculture (NCA). 2nd Lieut, 1st Bn Gordon Highlanders, 1951; served Malaya; Captain, 3rd Bn Gordon Highlanders (TA), retired 1964. Director: Ellon Castle Estates Co. Ltd, 1965–96; Cristina Securities Ltd, 1970–. Chm., 1994–2003, Hon. Pres., 2004–, Clan Donnachaidh Soc. Gov., Heath Mount Prep. Sch., Hertford, 1970–92 (Chm., Govs, 1976–92). JP Cambridgeshire and Isle of Ely, 1971, DL 1973; High Sheriff, Cambridgeshire, 1987–88. *Heir: s* Charles Edward James Reid, *b* 24 June 1956. *Address:* Lanton Tower, Jedburgh, Roxburghshire TD8 6SU. *T:* (01835) 863443. *Club:* Caledonian.

REID, Andrew Milton; Deputy Chairman, Imperial Group, 1986–89; *b* 21 July 1929; *s* of late Rev. A. R. R. Reid, DD and of Lilias Symington Tindal; *m* 1st, 1953, Norma Mackenzie Davidson (*d* 1993); two *s*; 2nd, 1995, Audrey Janet Wilson Bruell. *Educ:* Glasgow Academy; Jesus Coll., Oxford. Imperial Tobacco Management Pupil, 1952; Asst Managing Director, John Player & Sons, 1975; Dir, Imperial Group Ltd, 1978; Chm., Imperial Tobacco Ltd, 1979–86. Dep. Chm., Trade Indemnity plc, 1994–96 (Dir, 1982–96); Dir, Renold PLC, 1983–96. Member, Tobacco Adv. Council, 1977–86. Member: Council, RSCM, 1987–89; Court and Council, Bristol Univ., 1986–99; Board, Bristol Develt Corp., 1989–96 (Dep. Chm., 1993–). Chm. Governors, Colston's Collegiate Sch., 1986–94. Master, Soc. of Merchant Venturers of Bristol, 1991–92. High Sheriff of Avon, 1991. *Recreations:* sailing, golf, fishing. *Address:* Chew Magna, Somerset.

REID, Andrew Scott; HM Coroner, Inner North London District of Greater London, 2002–12; *b* 2 March 1965; *m* 2007, Suzanne Ellen Greenaway; twin *s* two *d* from a previous marriage. *Educ:* Univ. of Nottingham Med. Sch. (BMedSci 1986; BM BS 1988); Nottingham Trent Univ. Sch. of Law (Postgrad. Dip. Law 1992; Solicitors Final Exam 1993). Pre-registration, sen. house officer and registrar posts in gen. medicine, surgery and histopathol., 1988–92; temp. Lectr in Human Morphol., Univ. of Nottingham, 1989–90; admitted solicitor, specialising in med. law and clin. negligence, 1995; In-house Solicitor and/or Clinical Risk Manager: NHS Litigation Authy, 1998–99; NHS Exec. Regl Medicolegal Service, 1999–2001; NW London Hosps NHS Trust, 2001–02. Asst Dep. Coroner, Notts, 1995–98; Dep. Coroner, N London, 1998–2002. Hon. Sen. Lectr in Pathology, Inst. of Cell and Molecular Sci., Queen Mary's Sch. of Medicine and Dentistry, London Univ., 2005–08. Legal Mem., Mental Health Rev. Tribunal, 2002. Mem., Human Tissue Authy, 2005–12. Member: BMA, 1987–; Coroners' Soc. of England and Wales, 1995–. FRSocMed 1997; FFFLM 2006 (Vice Pres., 2010–12). *Publications:* (contrib.) The Pathology of Trauma, ed Prof. J. K. Mason, 2nd edn 1993; contrib. papers on epithelial cell kinetics, breast cancer and industrial disease to med. jls. *Recreation:* trying to enjoy life between moderation and excess as appropriate.

REID, Andrew Stephen; Senior Partner, RMPI (formerly Reid Minty) LLP, Solicitors, since 1980; Deputy High Court Costs Judge (formerly Deputy Supreme Court Taxing Master), since 1991; Deputy District Judge: Principal Registry of the Family Division, since 2001; South Eastern Circuit, since 2002; Deputy Adjudicator, HM Land Registry, since 2007; *b* 2 March 1954; *s* of Leon Ralph Reid and Fay Marion Reid; partner, Corrina Bithell; one *d. Educ:* University College Sch.; University Coll. London (LLB Hons). ACIArb 1979, MCIArb. Admitted solicitor, 1979; founded Reid Minty, Solicitors, 1980. Mem., Radio Authy, 1994–99. Farmer, 1981–, established Belmont Children's Farm, Mill Hill, 2009–. Racehorse trainer/breeder, London (trained and bred winner of All Weather Derby, 2005, plus 200 other winners). Non-exec. Dep. Treas., 2013–14, Nat. Treas., 2014–15, UKIP. Trustee, RAF Mus., 2011–. Liveryman, Coachmakers' Co., 2008. *Recreations:* polo, hunting, gardening, horse breeding, shooting, carriage driving, sailing, flying, classic car collector. *Address:* (office) Moss House, 16 Brooks Mews, W1K 4DS. *Clubs:* MCC, Alfred's; Belmont Polo; Guards' Polo; Oakley Hunt; Leander (Henley-on-Thames); Royal Dart Yacht; Stoke Gabriel Boating Assoc.

REID, Caroline Jean Vernon; Hon. Director General, European Investment Bank, since 2004; *b* 6 April 1948; *d* of late Colin Beever and of Dorothy Beever; *m* 1970, Michael Francis Reid; two *s. Educ:* Lycée Châteaubriand, Rome; Bedford High Sch. for Girls; Univ. of Bristol (BSc Hons Econs and Stats). Asst economist, British Gas Council, 1969–71; with NIESR, 1972–74; joined European Investment Bank, 1974: Energy Economist, 1974–85; loan officer, Energy/Envmt Div., Dept for Lending, Rome, 1985–88, Hd of Div., 1988–94; Dir, Italy Dept, 1994–99; Dir Gen., Projects Directorate, 1999–2001; Hd of Infrastructure and Project Finance, Banca OPI SpA, SanPaolo Imi Banking Gp, 2001–07. *Address:* Via Palestro 11, 00185 Rome, Italy. *E:* cjvreid@gmail.com.

REID, Caroline Oldcorn, PhD; a District Judge, Principal Registry, Family Division, 2006–15 (Deputy District Judge, 2003–06); *b* 6 April 1948; *d* of late John Patterson Reid and Olwen Reid; *m* 1983, Dr Frank Patrick Burton, *qv*; two *s* one *d. Educ:* Holt Grammar Sch., Wokingham; Univ. of Sheffield (BA Hons Hist. 1969; PhD 1976); City Univ. (Dip Law 1981). Tutor Organiser, WEA, Sheffield, 1974–80; called to the Bar, Middle Temple, 1982; in practice as a barrister, 1984–2006, 14 Gray's Inn Square, 1994–2006. *Publications:* (contrib.) Evidence in Family Proceedings, 1999; (contrib.) Child Abuse, 3rd edn 2003; (contrib.) The Family Court Practice, 2007–. *Recreations:* relaxing with my family, Suffolk, reading, cooking, old things, garden design.

REID, Sir David (Edward), Kt 2012; Chairman, Intertek Group plc, since 2012; *b* Ndola, Zambia, 5 Feb. 1947; *s* of late Robert Barron Reid and Mary Reid (*née* Johnston); *m* 1973, Prunella Alexandra Hiatt; two *d. Educ:* Fettes Coll., Edinburgh. CA 1970. Supervisor, then Sen. Auditor, Peat Marwick Mitchell, Paris, 1970–73; Chief Accountant, Philips Electronics (UK) Ltd, 1973–79; Finance Dir, Internat. Stores Ltd, British American Tobacco plc, 1979–85; Director: Tesco plc, 1985– (Chm., 2004–11); Westbury plc, 1989–96; De Vere Gp (formerly Greenalls Gp plc), 1994–2002; Legal and General Gp plc, 1995–97; non-exec. Dir, Reed Elsevier plc, 2003–13; Chm., Kwik-Fit Gp Ltd, 2006–11. Mem., Global Sen. Adv. Bd, Jefferies Internat., 2012–. Business Ambassador, UK Trade & Investment, 2010–. Chm., Whizz-Kidz Ltd, 2008–. Hon. DBA Robert Gordon, 2005; Hon. LLD Aberdeen, 2006. *Recreations:* Rugby (Chm., London Scottish Rugby Club), golf. *Address:* Intertek Group plc, 25 Savile Row, W1S 2ES. *T:* (020) 7396 3400, *Fax:* (020) 7396 3480. *E:* david.reid@intertek.com. *Club:* Caledonian.

REID, David James Glover; Member, Arts Council of England, 1995–98 (Acting Deputy Chairman, 1997–98; Chairman, Audit Committee, 1996–98); *b* 14 Aug. 1936; *s* of Alexander Robert Reid and Maisie Cullen Mowat; *m* 1963, Norma Scott Elder Chalmers; two *s. Educ:* Edinburgh Royal High Sch.; Univ. of Edinburgh (BSc Maths and Math. Physics). Joined IBM, 1962; USA, 1967–75; Manager, IBM Product 3250, 1977; Graphics Product Manager, 1979; lab. ops Manager, 1983; Resident Dir for Scotland, N England and NI, 1985, for England, Wales and NI, 1990; retired, 1993. Chairman: Scottish Cttee, ABSA, 1986; Scottish Enterprise Foundn, 1986; Southern Regl Arts Bd, 1991–98; Business in the Arts South, 1991–98; Member: Scottish Econ. Council, 1988; Exec., Scottish Business in the Community, 1988. Trustee, Arts Foundn, 1996–98. Gov., Univ. of Portsmouth, 1991–96. *Recreations:* bridge, computing, music, sailing, theatre, walking.

REID, Derek Donald; Chairman, Harris Tweed Textiles Ltd, since 2005; Board Member, Scottish Enterprise Tayside, 1996–2003; *b* 30 Nov. 1944; *s* of Robert Slorach Reid and Selina Mons Lewis Reid (*née* Donald); *m* 1977, Janice Anne Reid; one *s* one *d. Educ:* Inverurie Acad., Aberdeen; Aberdeen Univ. (MA); Robert Gordon Inst. of Technol. (Dip. Personnel Mgt). Cadbury Schweppes: mgt trainee, 1968; Divl Dir, 1982–86; Founder Mem., Premier Brands and Dir, Tea Business after mgt buy-out, 1986–89; Man. Dir, Tea Business, 1989–90; Chief Exec., Scottish Tourist Bd, 1994–96; Dep. Chm., Sea Fish Industry Authy, 1996–2000; Chm., Scotland's Hotels of Distinction, 1998–2001; dir, various small cos. Vis. Prof. of Tourism, Abertay Univ. (formerly Univ. of Abertay Dundee), 2000–. Hon. DBA Robert Gordon Univ., Aberdeen, 1995. *Recreations:* golf, cricket, fishing, art appreciation, classical music. *Address:* Broomhill, Kinclaven, Stanley, Perthshire PH14 4QL. *T:* (01250) 883209. *Clubs:* Royal Perth Golf, Blairgowrie Golf.

REID, Dominic; *see* Reid, J. D.

REID, Elizabeth Margaret; Chief Executive, Specialist Schools and Academies Trust (formerly Technology Colleges, then Specialist Schools, Trust), 2001–11; *b* 16 April 1947; *d* of late John A. McConachie, MB ChB, FRCPE and J. Margaret McConachie, MB ChB; *m* 1st, 1970, Robin Reid, MA (marr. diss. 1975); 2nd, 1982, Martin J. Monk, BA Hons Oxon (marr. diss. 2000). *Educ:* Aberdeen Univ. (MA Hons 1969); London Univ. (MA Educnl

Admin 1980); Courtauld Inst. of Art (Grad. Dip. 2014). Asst Principal, CS, 1969–70; Inner London Education Authority: schoolteacher, 1970–78; Advr for 16–19 educn, 1978–79; Professional Asst, London Borough of Ealing, 1979–80; Asst Educn Officer, London Borough of Haringey, 1980–83; Sen. Principal Officer (Educn), AMA, 1983–85; Inner London Education Authority: Admin. Head, Further and Higher Educn Br., 1985–88; Dep. Dir of Educn (Further and Higher Educn), 1988–89; Dep. Provost, London Guildhall Univ. (formerly City of London Poly.), 1989–93; Director of Education: Lothian Regional Council, 1993–96; City of Edinburgh Council, 1996–98; London Borough of Hackney, 1998–2000. Vice Chm., Scottish Qualifications Authy, 1996–98; Mem. Bd, QCDA (formerly QCA), 2009–11. Mem. Bd, Enterprise Educn Trust (formerly Understanding Industry), 2000–; Dir, Muban Educnl Trust, 2009–. Member: Ct of Govs, Univ. of the Arts, London (formerly London Inst.), 2001–13 (Chair, Finance Cttee, 2009–13); Fashion Retail Acad., 2006–15; Bd, City and Islington Coll., 2007–14. Trustee, Royal Female Sch. of Art Foundn, 2015–. Fellow, Inst. of Educn, 2008. FRSA 1989; FSQA 1998; Fellow and Icebreaker of the Year, 48 Gp Club, 2007. *Publications:* (contrib.) Central and Local Control of Education After the Education Reform Act 1988, ed R. Morris, 1990; (contrib.) The Future of Higher Education, ed T. Schuller, 1991; (with R. Morris and J. Fowler) Education Act 93: a critical guide, 1993. *Recreations:* theatre, opera, music, reading, gardening, China. *E:* elizabethreid@sky.com.

REID, Prof. Gavin Clydesdale, PhD, DLitt; Professor of Business Management and Strategy, and Head, Dundee Business School, Abertay University, since 2014; Member, Competition Appeal Tribunal, since 2011; Professor of Economics, University of St Andrews, 1991–2013, now Honorary Professor of Economics and Finance; *b* Glasgow, 25 Aug. 1946; *s* of late Lt Col Alexander Macfarlane Reid, BSc and Sheila Macgregor Reid (*née* Jackson); *m* 1st, 1967, Margaret Morrice McGregor, MA, JP, DL (marr. diss. 1983); one *s* and one step *s*; 2nd, 1986, Maureen Johnson Bagnall, MB, ChB, BSc (marr. diss. 2007); one *s* two *d* and one step *s*; 3rd, 2008, Julia Anne Smith, BCom, PhD, FCMA; two *d*. *Educ:* Lyndhurst Prep. Sch.; Frimley and Camberley Grammar Sch.; Univ. of Aberdeen (MA 1st Cl. Hons Econ. Sci. 1969; Stephen Schol.); Univ. of Southampton (MSc Econ. Theory and Econometrics 1971); Univ. of Edinburgh (PhD Industrial Orgn 1975); Univ. of Aberdeen (DLitt Small Business Enterprise 2012). Lectr, 1971–84, Sen. Lectr, 1984–90, Reader in Econs, 1990–91, Univ. of Edinburgh; Founder and Dir, Centre for Res. into Industry, Enterprise, Finance and the Firm, Univ. of St Andrews, 1991–2013; Prof. of Enterprise and Innovation, Business Sch., UWS, 2013–14. Visiting Professor: Queen's Univ., Ont, 1981–82; Univ. of Denver, 1984; Univ. of Nice, 1998; Vis. Schol., Darwin Coll., Cambridge, 1987–88; Vis. Prof. in Accounting and Finance, Univ. of Strathclyde, 2007–. Research Fellow: Leverhulme Trust, 1989–90; Nuffield Foundn, 1997–98. President: Scottish Econ. Soc., 1999–2002; Nat. Conf. of Univ. Profs, 2003–06; Inst. of Contemporary Scotland, 2005–06. Chairman: ESRC Network of Industrial Economists, 1997–2001; Scottish Inst. for Enterprise Res. Forum, 2002–03; ESRC Seminars in Accounting, Finance and Econs, 2006–08. FFCS 2000; FRSA 2000. Hon. DBA Abertay Dundee, 2010; DLitt Aberdeen, 2012. *Publications:* The Kinked Demand Curve Analysis of Oligopoly, 1981; Theories of Industrial Organization, 1987; (jtly) The Small Entrepreneurial Firm, 1988; Classical Economic Growth, 1989; Small Business Enterprise, 1993; (jtly) Profiles in Small Business, 1993; Venture Capital Investment, 1998; (jtly) Information System Development in the Small Firm, 2000; The Foundations of Small Business Enterprise, 2007; (jtly) Risk Appraisal and Venture Capital in High Technology New Ventures, 2008; contrib. papers to learned jls in economics, accounting and finance. *Recreations:* reading, poetry, music, running, badminton. *Address:* Dundee Business School, Abertay University, Bell Street, Dundee DD1 1HG. *E:* gavin.reid@abertay.ac.uk. *Clubs:* Reform, Royal Over-Seas League; St Andrews Golf.

REID, Rt Rev. Gavin Hunter, OBE 2000; Bishop Suffragan of Maidstone, 1992–2000; an Honorary Assistant Bishop, Diocese of St Edmundsbury and Ipswich, since 2008; *b* 24 May 1934; *s* of Arthur William Reid and Jean Smith Reid (*née* Guthrie); *m* 1959, Mary Eleanor Smith; two *s* one *d*. *Educ:* Roan Sch., Greenwich; Queen Mary Coll. and King's Coll., London Univ. (BA 1956); Oak Hill Theol Coll. Ordained, Chelmsford Cathedral: deacon, 1960; priest, 1961; Assistant Curate: St Paul's, East Ham, 1960–63; Rainham Parish Church, 1963–66; Publications Sec., CPAS, 1966–71; Editorial Sec., United Soc. for Christian Lit., 1971–74; Sec. for Evangelism, 1974–90, Consultant Missioner, 1990–92, CPAS; Advr, Gen. Synod Bd of Mission, 1990–92. Seconded: Nat. Dir, Mission England, 1982–85; Project Dir, Mission 89, 1988–89. Chairman: Archbishops' Adv. Gp for the Millennium, 1995–2000; CPAS Council of Reference, 2005–08. Pres., British Youth for Christ, 2001–04. *Publications:* The Gagging of God, 1969; The Elaborate Funeral, 1972; A New Happiness, 1974; To Be Confirmed, 1977; Good News to Share, 1979; Starting Out Together, 1981; To Reach a Nation, 1987; Beyond Aids, 1987; Lights that Shine, 1991; Brushing up on Believing, 1991; Our Place in his Story, 1994; To Canterbury with Love, 2002; various symposia. *Recreations:* golf, sailing, walking, birdwatching. *Address:* 17 Richard Crampton Road, Beccles, Suffolk NR34 9HN.

REID, Rt Hon. Sir George (Newlands), Kt 2012; PC 2004; Member, UK Electoral Commission, 2010–13; Chairman, Remuneration Board, National Assembly for Wales, 2010–13; Lord-Lieutenant of Clackmannanshire, 2011–14; Professorial Fellow, University of Stirling and London Academy of Diplomacy, since 2014; *b* 4 June 1939; *s* of late George Reid, company director, and of Margaret Forsyth; *m* 1968, Daphne Ann MacColl; one *d*, and one *d* from previous marriage. *Educ:* Tullibody Sch.; Dollar Academy; Univ. of St Andrews (MA Hons). Pres., Students' Representative Council. Features Writer, Scottish Daily Express, 1962; Reporter, Scottish Television, 1964; Producer, Granada Television, 1965; Head of News and Current Affairs (Scottish Television), 1968; presenter, BBC, 1979. Head of Inf., 1984–86, Dir of Public Affairs, 1986–90, Dir of Internat. Campaign for Victims of War, 1990–92, League of Red Cross and Red Crescent Socs, Geneva. MP (SNP) Stirlingshire E and Clackmannan, Feb. 1974–1979; Mem., British Parly Delegn to Council of Europe and WEU, 1977–79. Scottish Parliament: Mem. Mid Scotland & Fife, 1999–2003, Ochil, 2003–07 (SNP, 1999–2003, when elected Presiding Officer); Dep. Presiding Officer, 1999–2003; Presiding Officer, 2003–07; Convener: Scottish Parly Bureau, 2003–07; Scottish Parly Corporate Body, 2003–07. Chair, Strategic Rev. of Governance, NI Assembly, 2007–08. Dir, Strategic Rev., NT for Scotland, 2009–10. Vice-Convener, SNP, 1997–99. Contested (SNP) Ochil, 1997. Ind. Advr, Scottish Ministerial Code, 2008–11. Lord High Comr, Gen. Assembly, Ch of Scotland, 2008 and 2009. Dir, Scottish Council Res. Inst., 1974–77. Visiting Professor: Glasgow Univ., 2006–; Stirling Univ., 2008–. Vice Chm., Carnegie Commn on Civil Soc., 2006–09; Mem., Caucasus-Caspian Commn, 2007–08. Chair, Scottish Press Awards, 2008–11. Trustee: Glasgow Culture and Sport, 2007–13; Royal Edinburgh (formerly Edinburgh) Military Tattoo, 2007–13 (Vice-Patron, 2013–). Chief Red Cross deleg. to Armenia, Dec. 1988–Jan. 1989. FRSE 2015. Hon LLD: St Andrews, 2005; Glasgow, 2009; DUniv: Queen Margaret UC, 2006; Edinburgh, 2007; Stirling, 2008. *Address:* Coneyhill House, Bridge of Allan, Stirling FK9 4DU.

REID, Gordon; *see* Reid, J. G.

REID, Rev. Canon Gordon; *see* Reid, Rev. Canon W. G.

REID, Graham Livingstone, CB 1991; Director General of Strategy, International and Analytical Services, Department for Education and Employment, 1995–97; *b* 30 June 1937; *s* of late William L. Reid and of Louise M. Reid; *m* 1st, 1973, Eileen M. Loudfoot (marr. diss. 1983); 2nd, 1985, Sheila Rothwell (*d* 1997); 3rd, 2008, Mavis Waller. *Educ:* Univ. of St Andrews (MA); Queen's Univ., Kingston, Canada (MA). Dept of Social and Economic Res., Univ. of Glasgow: Asst Lectr in Applied Economics, 1960, Lectr 1963, Sen. Lectr 1968, Reader 1971; Sen. Econ. Adviser and Head of Econs and Statistics Unit, Scottish Office, 1973–75; Dir, Manpower Intelligence and Planning Div., MSC, 1975–84; Department of Employment: Chief Economic Adviser and Hd, Economic and Social Div., 1984–88 and Dir, Enterprise and Deregulation Unit, 1987; Dep. Sec., Manpower Policy, 1988–90, Resources and Strategy, 1991, Indust. Relns and Internat. Directorate, 1991–95. Vis. Associate Prof., Mich State Univ., 1967; Vis. Res. Fellow, Queen's Univ., Canada, 1969. FRSA 1996. *Publications:* Fringe Benefits, Labour Costs and Social Security (ed with D. J. Robertson), 1965; (with K. J. Allen) Nationalised Industries, 1970, 3rd edn 1975; (with L. C. Hunter and D. Boddy) Labour Problems of Technological Change, 1970; (with K. J. Allen and D. J. Harris) The Nationalised Fuel Industries, 1973; contrib. to Econ. Jl, Brit. Jl of Indust. Relations, Scot. Jl of Polit. Econ., Indust & Lab. Relns Rev. *Recreations:* golf, music. *Address:* 24 Barley Way, Marlow SL7 2UG. *T:* (01628) 483720. *Club:* Phyllis Court (Henley-on-Thames).

REID, Henry William, (Harry); writer; *b* 23 Sept. 1947; *s* of late William Reid and of Catherine Robertson Craighead Reid (*née* Maclean); *m* 1980, Julie Wilson Davidson; one *d*. *Educ:* Aberdeen Grammar Sch.; Fettes Coll.; Worcester Coll., Oxford (BA). The Scotsman: reporter, sports writer, leader writer, 1970–73; educn correspondent, 1973–77; Features Ed., 1977–81; Sport and Leisure Ed., Sunday Standard, 1981–82; Exec. Ed., 1982–83, Dep. Ed., 1983–97, Ed., 1997–2000, columnist, 2004–, The Herald, Glasgow. Vis. Fellow, Faculty of Divinity, Univ. of Edinburgh, 2001–02. Mem., Church and Soc. Council, Ch of Scotland, 2005–06. Gov., Fettes Coll., 2002–12. DUniv Glasgow, 2001; Dr *hc* Edinburgh, 2001. Oliver Brown Award, Scots Independent, 2008. *Publications:* Dear Country: a quest for England, 1992; Outside Verdict: an old kirk in a new Scotland, 2002; Deadline: the story of the Scottish press, 2006; Reformation: the dangerous birth of the modern world, 2009. *Recreations:* exploring Scotland and European cities, hill walking, supporting Aberdeen FC, reading novels, listening to Bob Dylan. *Address:* 12 Comely Bank, Edinburgh EH4 1AN. *T:* (0131) 332 6690.

REID, Iain; arts consultant; *b* 27 March 1942; *s* of Jean Reid (*née* Money) and George Aitken Reid; *m* 1st, 1968, Judith Coke; 2nd, 1982, Kay Barlow; one *s* one *d*. *Educ:* Uppingham; RADA; Lancaster Univ. (MA). Actor, 1963–73; theatre administrator, 1973–77; Drama Officer, Greater London Arts, 1977–82; Dir of Arts, Calouste Gulbenkian Foundn (UK), 1982–89; Dir, Arts Co-ordination, later Arts Develt, Arts Council of GB, 1989–94; Dir of Combined Arts, Arts Council of England, 1994–98; Dean, Arts Educnl Sch., London, 1998–2006. Examnr, Trinity Coll., London, 2008–. FRSA 1992. *E:* Kay.in@btinternet.com.

REID, (James) Gordon; QC (Scot.) 1993; a Temporary Judge of the Court of Session and High Court of Justiciary, since 2002; *b* 24 July 1952; *s* of James R. Reid and Constance M. Lawrie or Reid; *m* 1984, Hannah Hogg Hopkins; two *s* one *d* (and one *s* decd). *Educ:* Melville Coll., Edinburgh; Edinburgh Univ. (LLB Hons). Solicitor, 1976–80; Advocate, 1980–; called to the Bar, Inner Temple, 1991; Chm., Terra Firma Chambers, 2012–. Part-time Chm., VAT and Duties Tribunals, 1997–2009; Dep. Special Comr for Income Tax Purposes, 1997–2009; part-time First-tier Tribunal Judge (Tax Chamber), 2009–; Dep. Tribunal Judge, Upper Tribunal (Tax and Chancery Chamber, formerly Tax Chamber), 2009–. Arbitrator, Motor Insurers' Bureau Agreement, 2003–. FCIArb 1994. *Recreation:* classical guitar. *Address:* Blebo House, by St Andrews, Fife KY15 5TZ.

REID, His Honour James Robert; QC 1980; a Circuit Judge, 1999–2013; *b* 23 Jan. 1943; *s* of late Judge J. A. Reid, MC and Jean Ethel Reid; *m* 1st, 1974, Anne Prudence Wakefield, *qv* (marr. diss. 2002); two *s* one *d*; 2nd, 2012, Rosalba Effenberg (*née* de Lisi). *Educ:* Marlborough Coll.; New Coll., Oxford (MA). FCIArb 1992. Called to the Bar, Lincoln's Inn, 1965, Bencher, 1988 (Treas., 2011); Recorder, 1985–99; Dep. High Court Judge, 1985–2013; Additional Judge of Employment Appeal Tribunal, 2000–11; Designated Civil Judge, Surrey Courts, 2004–12; Legal Mem., Lands Tribunal, subseq. Judge of the Upper Chamber (Lands), 2006–11. Mem., Senate of Inns of Court and the Bar, 1977–80; Mem., Gen. Council of the Bar, 1990–96 (Chm., Professional Conduct Cttee, 1995–96). Chm., Barristers Benevolent Assoc., 1995–99 (Hon. Jt Treas., 1986–91; Dep. Chm., 1991–95). Dir, Bar Mutual Indemnity Fund Ltd, 1996–99. Mem., Court of Arbitration for Sport, 1999–; Chairman: Football League Appeal Cttee, 2000–; Professional Football Compensation Cttee, 2008–.

REID, Prof. Janice Clare, AC 2015 (AM 1998); FASSA; Vice-Chancellor and President, University of Western Sydney, 1998–2013; *b* 19 Sept. 1947; *d* of Keith M. Reid and Joan C. Reid; one *d*. *Educ:* Presbyterian Girls' Coll., Adelaide; Univ. of Adelaide (BSc); Univ. of Hawaii (MA); Stanford Univ., USA (MA, PhD). FASSA 1991. High sch. teacher, PNG, 1968–69; Res. Officer/Asst, Dept of Community Medicine, Univ. of NSW, 1974–75; Sen. Lectr, then Associate Prof., Sch. of Public Health and Tropical Medicine, 1979–90, and Dir, Centre for Crosscultural Studies in Health and Medicine, 1988–92, Univ. of Sydney; Foundn Hd, Sch. of Community Health, Cumberland Coll. of Health Scis, 1987–91; Prof. of Community Health, Univ. of Sydney, 1990–91; Pro Vice-Chancellor (Acad.), Qld Univ. of Technol., 1991–98. Chm. or mem., various Nat. Health and MRC standing cttees, 1992–96; Member: Higher Educn Council, 1996–98; Gtr Western Sydney Econ. Develt Bd, 1998–2000; Council, ACU, 1999; Integral Energy Bd, 2000–06; Fed. Council on Australian/Latin American Relns, 2001–06 (Chm., Educn Action Gp, 2003–06); Higher Educn Cttee, Ministerial Ref. Gp, Nat. Higher Educn Rev., 2002; Governing Bd, OECD Instnl Mgt in Higher Educn Prog., 2005– (Vice-Chm., 2007–08); Steering Cttee, Internat. Talloires Univ. Network, 2005– (Vice-Chm., 2011–); Bd, NSW Health Clinical Excellence Commn, 2007–14; Bd, Agency for Clinical Innovation, 2007–14; Expert Ref. Gp, Commonwealth Tertiary Educn Quality Standards, 2009–10; Innovation and Productivity Council, NSW, 2011–12; Convenor, NSW Vice-Chancellors' Cttee, 2012. Mem., Regl Adv. Bd, St Vincent's Hosp., NSW, 2014–. Mem. Bd, UniSuper Ltd, 2006–12. Mem., Australian Inst. Aboriginal and Torres Is Studies, 1981–; Dep. Chm., Qld Inst. Med. Res., 1994–97. Chm., Founder and Convener, Australian Soc. of Med. Anthropol., 1981–82. Member: Qld Mus. Bd, 1992–97; Nat. Cultural Heritage Cttee, 2011–13; Council, Nat. Liby of Australia, 2012–15; Council, Univ. of S Pacific, 2014–. Mem. Council, Blue Mts GS, 1998–2002; Gov., Westmead Millennium Inst., 2001–05. Mem. Adv. Bd, Western Sydney Salvation Army, 2001–10. Trustee, Kedumba Drawing Award, 2001–02, 2004–10; Mem. Trust, NSW Art Gall., 2004–12. Hon. DLitt Western Sydney, 2013. Wellcome Medal, RAI, 1984. Centenary Medal, Australia, 2003. *Publications:* (ed) Body Land and Spirit, 1982; Sorcerers and Healing Spirits, 1983; edited with P. Trompf: The Health of Immigrant Australia, 1990; The Health of Aboriginal Australia, 1991; contrib. numerous chapters, papers and reports to various jls, incl. Social Sci. and Medicine, particularly on Aborigines, migrants and refugees and health. *Address:* NSW, Australia. *E:* janice.reid@uws.edu.au.

REID, John Boyd, AO 1980; LLB; FAIM, FAICD; CPEng, FIEAust; Chairman Emeritus, Australian Graduate School of Management, since 2000 (Board Member, 1991–2002); Chairman, James Hardie Industries Ltd, 1973–96 (Director, 1964–96); *b* 27 Dec. 1929; *s* of Sir John Thyne Reid, CMG. *Educ:* Scotch College; Melbourne Univ. Chm., Comsteel Vickers Ltd, 1983–86; Vice-Chm., Qantas Airways, 1981–86 (Dir, 1977–86); Director: Broken Hill Pty Co., 1972–97; Barclays Internat. Australia, 1982–85; Bell Resources Ltd, 1987–88; Peregrine Capital Australia Ltd, 1991–95; Focus Publishing, 1991–2003. Chm., Australian Bicentennial Authy, 1979–85; Dir, World Expo 88, 1986–89; Member: Admin. Review Cttee, 1975–76; Ind. Inquiry into Commonwealth Serum Labs, 1978; Patron, Australia Indonesia Business Co-operation Cttee, 1979–88 (Pres., 1973–79); Dir, Thailand-Australia Foundn Ltd, 1993–96; Mem., Internat. Adv. Bd, Swiss Banking Corp., 1986–97;

Chm., Review of Commonwealth Admin, 1981–82. Trustee and Internat. Counsellor, Conference Bd USA; Internat. Council, Stanford Res. Inst., USA. Chairman: NSW Educn and Trng Foundn, 1989–93; Cttee, Aust. Scout Educn and Trng Foundn, 1991; Museum of Contemp. Art, 1994–98. Chm. Council, Pymble Ladies Coll., 1975–82 (Mem., 1965–75); Governor, Ian Clunies Ross Meml Foundn, 1975–2000; Chm., Sydney Adv. Cttee, 1995–97, and Red Shield Appeal, 1993–94, Salvation Army. Mem., Inst. of Company Dirs. Life Governor, AIM (Sydney Div.). Hon. Fellow, Univ. of Sydney, 2004. Hon. DBus Charles Sturt Univ., NSW; Hon. PhD Queensland; DUniv Qld Univ. of Technol., 2002. Melbourne Univ. Graduate Sch. of Business Admin Award, 1983; John Storey Medal, AIM, 1985. *Address:* PO Box 15557, 42 Albert Street, Brisbane, Qld 4002, Australia. *Club:* Queensland.

REID, (John) Dominic, OBE 2003; Pageantmaster, Lord Mayor's Show, since 1992; Principal, Reid and Reid, since 1992; Managing Director, Invictus Games Foundation, since 2014; *b* 24 Sept. 1961; *s* of late John Reid, OBE, DL and of Sylvia Reid; *m* 1991, Suzanne Jessup (*née* Schultz); one *d*. *Educ:* Oundle Sch. (Music Scholar); Downing Coll., Cambridge; University College London. RIBA 1991. 2nd Lt, 49 Field Regt, Royal Artillery, 1981. Architect: Doshi-Raje, Ahmedabad, India, 1984–85; Austin-Smith:Lord, 1986–89; Richard Horden Associates Ltd, 1989–90; John and Sylvia Reid, 1990–92; Dir, Designer's Collaborative, 1996–2000; Chief Exec., London Film Commission, 1999–2000; Exec. Dir, Oxford and Cambridge Boat Race, 2000–04; Pageantmaster, The Queen's Golden Jubilee, 2002; Dir, 2010 Anniversary Prog., Royal Soc., 2007–10; Dir of Events, Invictus Games, 2014. Director: Chatsworth Country Fair, 2013; Holkham Country Fair, 2013. Gov., Mus. of London, 2013–. Hon. Col, City of London and NE Sector ACF, 2015–. Sergeant-at-Mace, Royal Soc., 2010–. HM Lieut for City of London, 2009–. Liveryman, Grocers' Co., 1999–. OStJ 1999. *Recreations:* telemarking, sailing, cycling, shooting, sartorial correctness. *E:* dominic@reidandreid.com. *Clubs:* HAC; Leander.

REID, Prof. John Low, OBE 2001; DM; Regius Professor of Medicine and Therapeutics, University of Glasgow, 1989–2009, now Emeritus Professor and Hon. Senior Research Fellow; Medical Director, Scottish Advisory Committee on Distinction Awards, Scottish Government (formerly Executive) Health Department, 2005–09; *b* 1 Oct. 1943; *s* of Dr James Reid and Irene M. Dale; *m* 1964, Randa Pharaon; one *s* one *d*. *Educ:* Fettes Coll., Edinburgh; Magdalen Coll., Oxford. MA; DM. FRCP 1986; FRCPGlas 1979; FRCPI 1997; FRSE 1995; FBPhS (FBPharmacolS 2009). House Officer, Radcliffe Infirmary, Oxford, and Brompton Hosp., 1967–70; Res. Fellow, RPMS, 1970–73; Vis. Fellow, Nat. Inst. of Mental Health, USA, 1973–74; Royal Postgraduate Medical School: Sen. Lectr in Clin. Pharmacol., and Consultant Physician, 1975–77; Reader in Clin. Pharmacol., 1977–78; Regius Prof. of Materia Medica, Univ. of Glasgow, 1978–89; Clinical Dir, Acute Medicine, 1993–2000, Chm., Div. of Medicine, 2000–06, N Glasgow Univ. Hosps NHS Trust. Founder FMedSci 1998. *Publications:* Central Action of Drugs in Regulation of Blood Pressure, 1975; Lecture Notes in Clinical Pharmacology, 1982; Handbook of Hypertension, 1983; papers on cardiovascular and neurological diseases in clinical and pharmacological journals. *Recreations:* books, gardening, the outdoors. *Address:* Maryland, Black Bull Lane, Fencott, Oxon OX5 2RD. *T:* (01865) 331023.

REID, Rt Rev. John Robert; United Mission to Nepal, 1995–97; Bishop of South Sydney, 1983–93 (Assistant Bishop, Diocese of Sydney, 1972–93); *b* 15 July 1928; *s* of John and Edna Reid; *m* 1955, Alison Gertrude Dunn; two *s* four *d*. *Educ:* Melbourne Univ. (BA); Moore Coll., Sydney (ThL). Deacon 1955, Priest 1955; Curate, Manly, 1955–56; Rector, Christ Church, Gladesville, NSW, 1956–69; Archdeacon of Cumberland, NSW, 1969–72. *Recreation:* walking. *Address:* Tarragal House, 107 Karalta Road, Erina, NSW 2050, Australia.

REID, Dr Julia; Member (UK Ind) South West Region and Gibraltar, European Parliament, since 2014; *b* Brockley, SE London, 16 July 1952; *d* of John and Joan Rudman; *m* 1st, 1970 (marr. diss. 1986); one *s*; 2nd, 1987, Kenneth Reid. *Educ:* Honor Oak Grammar Sch.; Sudbury Girls' High Sch.; John Bentley Sch., Calne; Univ. of Bath (BSc Hons Biochem. 1990; PhD Pharmacol. 1998). Hd of Academic Res. and Lab. Manager, Diabetes and Lipid Res. Lab., Royal United Hosp., Bath, 1999–2009. Parly Asst to Trevor Colman, MEP, 2011. Mem. (UK Ind) Calne Town Council, 2013–. Contested (UK Ind): SW Reg., EP, 2009; Chippenham, 2010, 2015. *Address:* European Parliament, 60 Rue Wiertz, 1047 Brussels, Belgium; (office) 40 Market Place, Chippenham, Wilts SN15 3HT.

REID, Prof. Kenneth Bannerman Milne, PhD; FRS 1997; Professor of Immunochemistry, University of Oxford, 1993–2008; Fellow, Green College, Oxford, 1986–2008, now Emeritus; Director, MRC Immunochemistry Unit, Oxford University, 1985–2008; *b* 22 Sept. 1943; *s* of John McBean Reid and Maria Anderson (*née* Smith); *m* 1969, Margery Robertson Gilmour; one *s* two *d*. *Educ:* Univ. of Aberdeen (BSc 1965; PhD 1968). SO, Fisheries Res. Unit, Aberdeen Univ., 1968–69; ICI Res. Fellowship, Dept Biochem., Univ. of Oxford, 1969–70; Mem., Scientific Staff, 1970–84, Dep. Dir, 1984–85, MRC Immunochemistry Unit, Dept of Biochemistry, Univ. of Oxford. Fellow, EMBO, 1991; Founder FMedSci 1998. Second Wellcome Trust Lecture Award, 1981. *Publications:* Complement, 1988, 2nd edn 1995; author or co-author of numerous papers in jls such as Nature, Biochem. Jl, Jl Immunology. *Recreations:* hill-walking, racket sports (squash, tennis). *Address:* 4 Peacock Road, Headington, Oxford OX3 0DQ; Green Templeton College, at the Radcliffe Observatory, Woodstock Road, Oxford OX2 6HG.

REID, Prof. Kenneth Gilbert Cameron, CBE 2005; WS; FRSE; FBA 2008; Professor of Scots Law, University of Edinburgh, since 2008; *b* 25 March 1954; *s* of Gilbert Beith Reid and Mary Henry Reid (*née* Sinclair); *m* 1981, Elspeth Christie; two *s* one *d*. *Educ:* Loretto; St John's Coll., Cambridge (MA); Univ. of Edinburgh (LLB). Admitted solicitor, 1980; WS 1999. University of Edinburgh: Lectr in Law, 1980–91; Sen. Lectr, 1991–94; Prof. of Property Law, 1994–2008; Mem., Scottish Law Commn, 1995–2005. Visiting Professor: Tulane Law Sch., New Orleans, 2003; Loyola Univ., New Orleans, 2013. Fellow: Business and Law Res. Centre, Radboud Univ., Nijmegen, 2005–09; Stellenbosch Inst. for Advanced Study, 2015. Ed., Edinburgh Law Review, 2006–10. FRSE 2000. *Publications:* (jtly) The Laws of Scotland: Stair Memorial Encyclopaedia, Vol. 18, 1993, rev. edn as The Law of Property in Scotland, 1996; (with G. L. Gretton) Conveyancing, 1993, 4th edn 2011; (ed jtly) A History of Private Law in Scotland, 2000; Abolition of Feudal Tenure in Scotland, 2003; (ed jtly) Mixed Legal Systems in Comparative Perspective: property and obligations in Scotland and South Africa, 2004; (ed jtly) Exploring the Law of Succession: studies national, historical and comparative, 2007; (ed jtly) Towards an EU Directive on Protected Funds, 2009; (ed jtly) Testamentary Formalities, 2011; (ed jtly) Intestate Succession, 2015; numerous papers in learned jls. *Recreations:* classical music, both listening and doing. *Address:* School of Law, University of Edinburgh, Old College, South Bridge, Edinburgh EH8 9YL. *T:* (0131) 650 2015.

REID, Lesley Munro; *see* Shand, L. M.

REID, Leslie, CBE 1978; HM Diplomatic Service, retired; Director General, The Association of British Mining Equipment Companies, 1980–83; *b* 24 May 1919; *s* of late Frederick Sharples and Mary Reid; *m* 1942, Norah Moorcroft; three *d*. *Educ:* King George V Sch., Southport, Lancs. Served War of 1939–45, W Europe and SEAC, Major, XX The Lancashire Fusiliers. Board of Trade, 1947–49; Asst Trade Commissioner: Salisbury, Rhodesia, 1949–55; Edmonton, Alberta, 1955–56; Trade Comr, Vancouver, 1956–60; Principal, BoT, 1960–62; Trade Comr and Economic Advisor, British High Commn, Cyprus, 1962–64; BoT, 1964–66; 1st Sec., FCO, 1966–68; Sen. Commercial Sec., British High Commn, Jamaica, and 1st Sec., British Embassy, Port-au-Prince, Haiti, 1968–70; Commercial and Economic Counsellor, Ghana, 1970–73; Consul Gen., Cleveland, Ohio, 1973–79. *Recreations:* golf, reading. *Address:* Kingsdowne, Albert Terrace, Norwich NR2 2JD.

REID, Lynne Elizabeth; *see* Frostick, L. E.

REID, Malcolm Herbert Marcus; Chief Executive, Life Assurance and Unit Trust Regulatory Organisation, 1986–89; *b* 2 March 1927; *s* of late Marcus Reid and Winifred Stephens; *m* 1st, 1956, Eleanor (*d* 1974), *d* of late H. G. Evans, MC; four *s*; 2nd, 1975, Daphne (*d* 2000), *e d* of Sir John Griffin, QC; 3rd, 2004, Carol Stephens, *d* of late E. Deason. *Educ:* Merchant Taylors' Sch.; St John's Coll., Oxford. Served in Navy, 1945–48 and in RNVR, 1949–53. Entered Board of Trade, 1951; Private Secretary to Permanent Secretary, 1954–57; Trade Comr in Ottawa, 1957–60; Board of Trade, 1960–63; Private Secretary to successive Prime Ministers, 1963–66; Commercial Counsellor, Madrid, 1967–71; Asst Sec., DTI, 1972–74; Under Sec., Dept of Industry, 1974–78, of Trade, 1978–83, DTI, 1983–84; Registrar, Registry of Life Assurance Commn, 1984–86. Dir, Mercury Life Assurance Co. Ltd, 1989–97. Mem., Appeal Cttee, ICA, 1990–96. *Recreations:* National Hunt racing, inland waterways. *Address:* 3 Church Street, St Ives, Cambs PE27 6DG. *T:* (01480) 468367. *Club:* Oxford and Cambridge.

REID, Melanie Frances; columnist, since 2007, and writer, Spinal Column, since 2010, The Times; *b* Barnet, Herts, 13 April 1957; *d* of Ronald Ogilvy Reid and Edith Elizabeth Reid (*née* Oakman); *m* 1st, 1982, Clifford Martin (marr. diss. 1992); one *s*; 2nd, 1996, David McNeil. *Educ:* Ormskirk Grammar Sch.; Univ. of Edinburgh (MA Hons 1980). Graduate trainee, 1980–82, Woman's Editor, 1983–87, The Scotsman; Associate Ed., Sunday Mail, 1987–2000; Sen. Writer, The Express, 2000–01; Sen. Asst Ed., The Herald, 2001–07. Mem., Carnegie Commn for Rural Community Develt, 2004–07. Journalist of the Year, Scottish Press Awards, 2010; Columnist of the Year - Broadsheet, Press Awards, 2011. DUniv Stirling, 2014. *Recreations:* amateur bird-watching, painful physiotherapy. *Address:* The Times, 1 London Bridge Street, SE1 9GF. *E:* melanie.reid@thetimes.co.uk.

REID, Prof. Miles Anthony, PhD; FRS 2002; Professor, Mathematics Institute, University of Warwick, since 1992; *b* 30 Jan. 1948; *s* of John Rollo Reid and Edna Mary Reid (*née* Frost); *m* 1978, Nayo Hagino; three *d*. *Educ:* Petit Lycée Condorcet, Paris; Bournemouth Sch. for Boys; Trinity Coll., Cambridge (BA 1969, PhD 1972, MA 1973). Res. Fellow, Christ's Coll., Cambridge, 1973–78; Lectr, 1978–89, Reader, 1989–92, Maths Inst., Univ. of Warwick. Visiting Professor: Univ. of Tokyo, 1990; Nagoya Univ., 1996–97; British Hispanic Foundn Queen Victoria Eugenia Prof. of Doctoral Studies, Complutense Univ., Madrid, 2002–03. *Address:* Mathematics Institute, University of Warwick, Coventry CV4 7AL. *T:* (024) 7652 3523, *Fax:* (024) 7652 4182. *E:* miles@maths.warwick.ac.uk.

REID, Paul Campbell; QC 2001; a Recorder of the Crown Court, since 1993; *b* 27 March 1949; *s* of Stuart Wemyss Reid and Elsie Reid; *m* 1978, Pauline Brown; two *s*. *Educ:* Merchant Taylors' Sch., Crosby; Christ's Coll., Cambridge (MA). Called to the Bar, Gray's Inn, 1973; an Assistant Recorder, 1989–93. *Recreations:* tennis, amateur dramatics, acoustic guitar. *Address:* Lincoln House Chambers, Tower 12, The Avenue North, Spinningfields, 18–22 Bridge Street, Manchester M3 3BZ. *T:* (0161) 832 5701.

REID, Maj.-Gen. Peter Daer, CB 1981; *b* 5 Aug. 1925; *s* of Col S. D. Reid and Dorothy Hungerford (*née* Jackson); *m* 1958, Catherine Fleetwood (*née* Boodle); two *s* two *d*. *Educ:* Cheltenham College; Wadham Coll., Oxford. Commissioned into Coldstream Guards, 1945; transferred Royal Dragoons, 1947; served: Germany, Egypt, Malaya, Gibraltar, Morocco; Staff Coll., 1959; Comdg Officer, The Royal Dragoons, 1965–68; student, Royal College of Defence Studies, 1973; Commander RAC, 3rd Div., 1974–76; Dir, RAC, 1976–78; Chief Exec., Main Battle Tank 80 Proj., 1979–80; Dir, Armoured Warfare Studies, 1981; Defence Advr, GKN, 1983–88; Mil. Advr, Howden Airdynamics, 1982–88; Associate Mem., Burdeshaw Associates Ltd (USA), 1982–94; Defence Consultant, Vickers Defence Systems Ltd, 1989–94. *Publications:* A Brief History of Medieval Warfare, 2008. *Recreations:* sailing, ski-ing, fishing, bird watching. *Clubs:* Army and Navy; Royal Western Yacht; Kandahar Ski.

REID, Philip; *see* under Ingrams, R. R.

REID, Sir (Philip) Alan, GCVO 2012 (KCVO 2007); Keeper of the Privy Purse, Treasurer to the Queen, and Receiver-General of the Duchy of Lancaster, since 2002; *b* 18 Jan. 1947; *s* of Philip Reid and Margaret Reid (*née* McKerracher); *m* 1971, Maureen Petrie; one *s* one *d*. *Educ:* Fettes Coll.; St Andrews Univ. (LLB Hons). Internat. Chm., KMG Tax Advisors, 1982–87; Nat. Dir of Taxation, KMG Thomson McLintock, 1983–87; KPMG Management Consultancy: Eur. Exec. Chm., 1994–98; UK Head, 1994–98; Global Chm., 1996–98; KPMG: UK Chief Financial Officer, 1998–2001; Eur. Chief Financial Officer, 1999–2001; Global Chief Financial Officer, 1999–2001; UK Chief Operating Officer, 2001–02. Pres., Mgt Consultancies' Assoc., 1997. Mem. Council, King's Fund, 2002–12. Trustee: Royal Collection Trust, 2002–; Historic Royal Palaces, 2002–15 (Dep. Chm., 2007–15); Chm., Queen's Trust (formerly Queen's Silver Jubilee Trust), 2007–. Pres., King George Fund for Actors and Actresses, 2011–. Vice Pres., RNLI, 2014– (Trustee, 2009–14; Treas., 2011–14). Gov., King Edward VII's Hosp. Sister Agnes, 2004–13. Mem., ICAS, 1973; Fellow, Inst. Taxation, 1979. *Recreations:* family, Arsenal, cinema, theatre, golf, ski-ing. *Address:* Buckingham Palace, SW1A 1AA. *Club:* MCC.

REID, Sir Robert Paul, (Sir Bob), Kt 1990; Chairman, ICE Futures Europe (formerly International Petroleum Exchange), since 1999; Deputy Governor, Bank of Scotland, 1997–2004 (Director, 1987–2004); non-executive Director, HBOS, 2001–04; *b* 1 May 1934; *m* 1958, Joan Mary; three *s*. *Educ:* St Andrews Univ. (MA Pol Econ. and Mod. Hist.). Joined Shell, 1956; Sarawak Oilfields and Brunei, 1956–59; Nigeria 1959–67 (Head of Personnel); Africa and S Asia Regional Orgn, 1967–68; PA and Planning Adviser to Chairman, Shell & BP Services, Kenya, 1968–70; Man. Dir, Nigeria, 1970–74; Man. Dir, Thailand, 1974–78; Vice-Pres., Internat. Aviation and Products Trading, 1978–80; Exec. Dir, Downstream Oil, Shell Co. of Australia, 1980–83; Co-Ordinator for Supply and Marketing, London, 1983; Dir, Shell International Petroleum Co., 1984–90; Chm. and Chief Exec., Shell UK, 1985–90; Chairman: BRB, 1990–95; London Electricity plc, 1994–97; Sears plc, 1995–99; British-Borneo Oil & Gas plc, 1995–2000; Sondex Ltd, 1999–2002. Director: British Borneo Petroleum, 1993–2000; AVIS Europe, 1997–2004 (Chm., 2002–04); Sun Life Assurance Co. of Canada, subseq. Sun Life Financial, 1997–2004; Siemens plc, 1998–2006; Diligenta Ltd, 2005–; Jubilant Energy NV, 2007–; EEA Helicopter Operations, 2008–. Chairman: Foundn for Management Educn, 1986–2003; BIM, 1988–90; Council, Industrial Soc., 1993–98; Foundn for Young Musicians, 1994–; Learning Through Landscapes, 2000–; Conservatoire for Dance and Drama, 2001–11. Dir, Merchants Trust, 1995–2008. Chancellor, Robert Gordon Univ., 1993–2004. CCMI. Hon. LLD: St Andrews, 1987; Aberdeen, 1988; Sheffield Hallam, 1995; South Bank, 1995; Hon. DSc Salford, 1990. *Recreations:* golf, opera. *Address:* ICE Futures, 5th Floor, Milton Gate, 60 Chiswell Street, EC1Y 4SA. *T:* (020) 7065 7708. *E:* Kathleen.Murray@theice.com. *Clubs:* MCC; Royal and Ancient Golf; Royal Melbourne (Melbourne); Royal Mid-Surrey Golf, Frilford Heath Golf.

REID, Dame Seona (Elizabeth), DBE 2014 (CBE 2008); FRSE; Director, Glasgow School of Art, 1999–2013; *b* 21 Jan. 1950; *d* of George Robert Hall and Isobel Margaret Reid. *Educ:* Park Sch., Glasgow; Strathclyde Univ. (BA Hons Sociology); Liverpool Univ. (DBA). Business Manager, Lincoln Theatre Royal, 1972–73; Press and Publicity Officer, Northern Dance Theatre, 1973–76; Press and PRO, Ballet Rambert, 1976–79; freelance Arts consultant, 1979–80; Dir, Shape, 1980–87; Asst Dir, Strategy and Regl Develt, Greater London Arts, 1987–90; Dir, Scottish Arts Council, 1990–99. Bd Mem., Cove Park, 2004– (Chm., 2013–). Hon. Prof., Univ. of Glasgow, 1999. Dep. Chm., NHMF and Chm., Scottish Cttee, Heritage Lottery Fund (formerly Trustee for Scotland, NHMF), 2011–14; Scottish Comr to Fulbright Commn, 2011–. Chm., Nat. Theatre of Scotland, 2013–. Trustee, Tate Gall., 2013–. FRSA 1991; FRSE 2015. Hon. DArts Robert Gordon Univ., Aberdeen, 1995; Hon. DLitt: Glasgow, 2001; Strathclyde, 2009; Hon. DLit Glasgow Caledonian, 2004. *Recreations:* walking, birdwatching, travel, arts.

REID, Simon H. C.; Principal, Gordonstoun School, since 2011; *b* Johannesburg, 19 Oct. 1961; *s* of Derric Reid and Pamela Reid (*née* Gray); *m* 1985, Michèle C. La Hausse de Lalouvière; one *s* one *d*. *Educ:* Hilton Coll., Natal; Univ. of the Witwatersrand (BA; Higher Dip. Educn). Teacher of English: Brentwood School, 1986–88; Stowe Sch., 1988–93; Dep. Hd of English, 1993–98, Housemaster, 1998–2004, Christ's Hospital Sch.; Dep. Hd, Worksop Coll., Notts, 2004–11. Gov., St Mary's Prep. Sch., Lincoln, 2009–11. *Recreations:* reading, photography, ski-ing. *Address:* Gordonstoun School, Elgin, Moray IV30 5RF.

REID, Stephen Ashton; Deputy Vice Chancellor (formerly Deputy Rector), Strategic Development, University of the Arts, London, since 2011; *b* 13 May 1949; *s* of Tom and Enid Reid. *Educ:* Brighton, Hove & Sussex Grammar Sch.; City of Westminster Coll.; UMIST; Pembroke Coll., Oxford; Harvard Business Sch. Personnel Mgt, BBC, 1975–79; Industrial Relns and Design Mgt, Granada TV, 1980–87; General Manager: Granada TV News Ops, 1987–90; BBC Wales, 1991–93; Controller: Resources Regs BBC, 1993–95; Services, BBC, 1995–97; Projects Dir, BBC Resources, 1998–99; Chief Exec., energywatch, 2000–03; Dir of Ops, Tanaka Business Sch., 2004–08, Project Prog. Dir, 2009–10, Imperial Coll. London. *Recreations:* piano playing, sport, modern fiction. *Address:* 272 High Holborn, WC1V 7EY.

REID, Rev. Canon William Gordon; Rector of St Clement's, Philadelphia, USA, 2004–15, now Rector Emeritus; *b* 28 Jan. 1943; *s* of William Albert Reid and Elizabeth Jean Inglis. *Educ:* Galashiels Academy; Edinburgh Univ. (MA); Keble Coll., Oxford (MA); Cuddesdon College. Deacon 1967, priest 1968; Curate, St Salvador's, Edinburgh, 1967–69; Chaplain and Tutor, Salisbury Theological Coll., 1969–72; Rector, St Michael and All Saints, Edinburgh, 1972–84; Provost of St Andrew's Cathedral, Inverness, 1984–88; Chaplain of St Nicolas, Ankara, 1988–89, of St Peter and St Sigfrid's Church, Stockholm, 1989–92; Canon, Gibraltar Cathedral, 1992–98; Vicar-Gen., Dio. of Gibraltar in Europe, 1992–2003; Archdeacon in Europe, 1996–98; Priest-in-Charge, St Michael, Cornhill with St Peter le Poer, 1997–98; Dean of Gibraltar, 1998–2000; Archdeacon of Italy and Malta, and Chaplain of All Saints, Milan, 2000–03. Canon Emeritus, Gibraltar Cathedral, 2004. Councillor, Lothian Regional Council, 1974–84; Chm., Lothian and Borders Police Bd, 1982–84. *Publications:* (ed) The Wind from the Stars, 1992; Every Comfort at Golgotha, 1999. *Recreations:* travel and languages, Church and politics. *Address:* 1027 Arch Street, Apt 406, Philadelphia, PA 19107, USA. *Clubs:* New (Edinburgh); Union League (Philadelphia).

REID, Sir William (Kennedy), KCB 1996 (CB 1981); Chairman: Advisory Committee on Distinction Awards, 1997–2000; Mental Welfare Commission for Scotland, 1997–2000; Parliamentary Commissioner for Administration, and Health Service Commissioner for England, Scotland and Wales, 1990–96; *b* 15 Feb. 1931; 3rd *s* of late James and Elspet Reid; *m* 1959, Ann, *d* of Rev. Donald Campbell; two *s* one *d*. *Educ:* Robert Gordon's Coll.; George Watson's Coll.; Univ. of Edinburgh; Trinity Coll., Cambridge. MA 1st cl. Classics Edinburgh and Cantab. Ferguson scholar 1952; Craven scholar 1956. Nat. service, 1952–54. Min. of Educn, 1956; Cabinet Office, 1964; Private Sec. to Sec. of Cabinet, 1965–67; Sec., Council for Scientific Policy, 1967–72; Under Sec., 1974–78, Accountant-General, 1976–78, DES; Dep. Sec. (Central Services), Scottish Office, 1978–84; Sec., SHHD, 1984–90. Chm. of Govs, Scottish Police Coll., 1984–90. Member: Council on Tribunals, 1990–96; Commns for Local Administration in England and in Wales, 1990–96. A Dir, Internat. Ombudsman Inst., 1992–96. Chm. Council, St George's Sch. for Girls, 1997–2003. Lectures: Crookshank, RCR, 1994; Sydenham, Soc. of Apothecaries, 1994; Hunt, RCGP, 1996. Chm., Edinburgh Fest. of Music, Speech and Drama, 2006–10. Chm., Scottish Churches Architectural Heritage Trust, 2011–12. Queen Mother Fellow, Nuffield Trust, 1998. FRCPE 1997; FRSE 1999; Hon. FRCSE 2002. Hon. LLD: Aberdeen, 1996; Reading, 1998; Hon. DLitt Napier, 1998. *Recreation:* versification. *Address:* Darroch House, 9/1 East Suffolk Park, Edinburgh EH16 5PL. *Club:* New (Edinburgh).

REID, William Macpherson; Sheriff of Tayside, Central and Fife, 1983–2004; *b* 6 April 1938; *s* of William Andrew Reid and Mabel McLeod; *m* 1971, Vivien Anne Eddy; three *d*. *Educ:* Elgin Academy; Aberdeen Univ.; Edinburgh Univ. MA; LLB. Admitted Advocate, 1963; Sheriff of: Lothian and Borders, 1978; Glasgow and Strathkelvin, 1978–83. *Address:* 28 Impasse des Darbounelles, 30400 St Siffret, Gard, France.

REID BANKS, Lynne; *see* Banks.

REIDHAVEN, Viscount, (Master of Seafield); James Andrew Ogilvie-Grant; *b* 30 Nov. 1963; *s* and *heir* of Earl of Seafield, *qv*. *Educ:* Harrow.

REIDY, Andrea Jane, OBE 2005; HM Diplomatic Service, retired; international political risk and governance consultant, since 2010; *b* 24 Nov. 1958; one *d*. *Educ:* South Bank Univ. (BA Hons Modern Langs and Internat. Business). Teaching, Caracas, Venezuela and British Embassy, Caracas, 1977–89; Internat. Policy, DoE, 1994–95; entered FCO, 1995; Desk Officer, Venezuela, Ecuador and Peru, Latin America Dept, FCO, 1995–97; Second Sec., Bratislava, 1997–2000; Dep. High Comr, Freetown, 2000–02; Hd, Global Opportunity Fund, FCO, 2003; Hd, UK Office, Coalition Provisional Authy, 2003–04, First Sec. (Political), 2004–05, Baghdad; Communications Team Leader, Prism Prog., FCO, 2005–06; Consul Gen. for Northern Iraq, Ebril, 2006–07; Ambassador to Eritrea, 2008–10. *Recreations:* running, swimming, reading, travelling.

REIF, Prof. Stefan Clive, PhD, LittD; Professor of Medieval Hebrew Studies, Faculty of Oriental Studies, University of Cambridge, 1998–2006, now Emeritus; Fellow of St John's College, Cambridge, since 1998; Founder Director, Genizah Research Unit, 1973–2006, and Head, Oriental Division, 1983–2006, Cambridge University Library; *b* 21 Jan. 1944; *s* of late Peter and Annie Reif (*née* Rapstoff); *m* 1967, Shulamit (*d* 2010), *d* of late Edmund and Ella Stekel; one *s* one *d*. *Educ:* Jews' Coll., Univ. of London (BA 1964); PhD London 1969; MA Cantab 1976; LittD Cantab 2002. Lectr in Hebrew and Semitic Langs, Univ. of Glasgow, 1968–72; Asst Prof. of Hebrew Lang. and Lit., Dropsie Coll., Philadelphia, 1972–73. Visiting Professor: Hebrew Univ. of Jerusalem, 1989, 1996–97; Univ. of Pennsylvania, 2001. President: Jewish Historical Soc. of England, 1991–92; British Assoc. for Jewish Studies, 1992; Cambridge Theological Soc., 2002–04. Hon. PhD Haifa, 2014. *Publications:* Shabbethai Sofer and his Prayer-Book, 1979; (ed) Interpreting the Hebrew Bible, 1982; Published Material from the Cambridge Genizah Collections, 1988; (ed) Genizah Research After Ninety Years, 1992; Judaism and Hebrew Prayer, 1993; Hebrew Manuscripts at Cambridge University Library, 1997; A Jewish Archive from Old Cairo, 2000; Why Medieval Hebrew Studies?, 2001; (ed) The Cambridge Genizah Collections: their contents and significance, 2002; Problems with Prayers, 2006; Charles Taylor and the Genizah Collection, 2009; Ha-Tefillah Ha-Yehudit, 2010; (ed) Death in Jewish Life: burial and mourning customs among the Jews of Europe and nearby communities, 2014; (ed) Religious Identity Markers, 2015; about 400 articles. *Recreations:* football, cooking matza-brei for his grandchildren, opera. *Address:* St John's College, Cambridge CB2 1TP. *T:* (01223) 766370.

REIGATE, Archdeacon of; *see* Kajumba, Ven. D. S. K.

REIHER, Sir Frederick (Bernard Carl), KCMG 2010 (CMG 1982); KBE 1992; Investment and finance consultant, 1992; Chairman, Air Niugini, since 2014 (Director, since 2005; Deputy Chairman, 2013–14); *b* 7 Feb. 1945; *s* of William and Ruth Reiher; *m* 1974, Helen Perpetua; two *s* two *d*. *Educ:* Chanel Coll., Rabaul; Holy Spirit National Seminary, Port Moresby; Univ. of Papua New Guinea (BD). Private Sec. to Minister for Finance, PNG, 1973–76. Joined Diplomatic Service, 1976; established Diplomatic Mission for PNG in London, 1977; High Comr for PNG in London, 1978–80, concurrently accredited Ambassador to FRG, Belgium, EEC and Israel; Sec. of Dept of Prime Minister, PNG, 1980–82; formerly High Comr for PNG in Canberra; COS to Prime Minister of PNG, 2001. Chairman: Harcos Trading (PNG) Ltd, 1982–91; PNG Agriculture Bank, 1986–91; PNG Nat. Airline Commn, 1992; Dir, Harrisons & Crosfield (PNG) Ltd, 1982–91. Chm., Nat. Honours and Awards Council, 2005–11. *Address:* PO Box 7500, Boroko, Papua New Guinea. *Clubs:* Aviat Social & Sporting, South Pacific Motor Sports, Royal Yacht, PNG Pistol.

REIK, Prof. Wolf, MD; FRS 2010; FMedSci; Principal Investigator, since 1989, and Head, Laboratory of Developmental Genetics and Imprinting, since 1992, Babraham Institute, Cambridge; *b* Aachen, Germany, 22 Aug. 1957; *s* of Prof. Dr Helmut Reik and Rosemarie Reik; *m* 1989, Dr Cristina Rada; one *s* one *d*. *Educ:* Univ. of Hamburg (MD 1985). EMBO Postdoctoral Fellow, Univ. of Cambridge, 1985–87; Fellow, Lister Inst. of Preventive Medicine, Cambridge, 1987–93; Babraham Institute, Cambridge: Hd, Prog. of Develtl Genetics, 1997–2004; Associate Dir of Res., 2004–; Hd, Epigenetics (formerly Epigenetics and Chromatin) Prog., 2008–. Mem., EMBO 2003; MAE 2011. Hon. Prof. of Epigenetics, Dept of Physiol., Develt and Neurosci., Univ. of Cambridge, 2008–. FMedSci 2003. Wellcome Prize in Physiol., 1994. *Publications:* contrib. articles on epigenetics to res. jls. *Recreations:* music, reading, cooking, ski-ing, bicycling. *Address:* Babraham Institute, Cambridge CB22 3AT. *T:* (01223) 496336. *E:* wolf.reik@babraham.ac.uk.

REILLY, David, FRCP; Lead Consultant Physician, Centre for Integrative Care, Glasgow Homoeopathic Hospital, since 1990 (Director, Adhom Academic Departments, since 1985); National Lead Clinician for Integrative Care, Scottish Government Health Department, 2008–11 (part-time secondment); Founding Director, WEL: Wellness Enhancement Learning Programme, since 2005; Hon. Senior Lecturer in Medicine, Glasgow University, since 1991; *b* 4 May 1955. *Educ:* Glasgow Univ. (MB ChB with commendation). MRCP 1981, FRCP 1993; MRCGP 1982; MFHom 1983, FFHom 1989. Various trng posts in conventional medicine and complementary medicine, mind body medicine and holism; Hon. Sen. Registrar in Gen. Medicine and RCCM/MRC Res. Fellow, Univ. Dept of Medicine, Glasgow Royal Infirmary, 1987–90. Vis. Faculty Mem., Harvard Med. Sch., 1994–; Vis. Prof., Univ. of Maryland Sch. of Med., 1999–. Co-founding Ed., Interprofessional Care, 1992–96; Internat. Ed., Alternative Therapies in Health and Medicine, 1995–96. Co-Founder and Dir, AdHominem charity, 1998–. RAMC Meml Prize, 1978; Merit Award, Gtr Glasgow Health Council, 1998; NHS Merit Award, 2001; Person of the Year, Dynamic Place Awards, 2004. *Publications:* contrib. to numerous scientific pubns and book chapters exploring human healing and integrative processes. *Recreations:* living, loving, lounging and laughing. *Address:* NHS Centre for Integrative Care, 1053 Great Western Road, Glasgow G12 0XQ. *T:* (0141) 211 1621. *W:* www.davidreilly.net.

REILLY, David Nicholas, (Nick), CBE 2000; Chairman, Asia-Pacific, MSX International Inc., since 2012; *b* 17 Dec. 1949; *s* of late John Reilly and of Mona Reilly; *m* 1976, Susan Haig; one *s* two *d*. *Educ:* Harrow Sch.; St Catharine's Coll., Cambridge (MA). Investment Analyst, 1971–74; joined Gen. Motors, 1974; Finance Dir, Moto Diesel Mexicana, 1980–83; Supply Dir, Vauxhall Motors, 1984–87; Vice Pres., IBC, 1987–90; Manufg Dir, Vauxhall Ellesmere Port, 1990–94; Vice Pres., Quality, Gen. Motors Europe, 1994–96; Man. Dir, 1996–2001, Chm., 1996–2001, Vauxhall Motors Ltd; Chm., IBC Vehicles, 1996–2001; Vice Pres., 1997–2006, Gp Vice-Pres., 2006–09, Gen. Motors Corp.; Vice-Pres. of Sales, Mktg and Aftersales, Gen. Motors Europe, 2001–02; Pres. and CEO, 2002–06, Chm., 2006–09, GM Daewoo Auto and Technol.; Pres., Gen. Motors Asia Pacific Ops, 2006–09; Pres., Gen. Motors Internat. Ops, 2009; Exec. Vice-Pres., Gen. Motors Corp., 2009–12; Pres., Gen. Motors Europe, 2009–11; Chief Exec., 2009–11, Chm., 2011–12, Supervisory Bd, Opel/Vauxhall. Mem. Bd, Saab GB, 1996–. Chairman: Chester, Ellesmere, Wirral TEC, 1990–94; Trng Standards Council, 1997–2001; Adult Learning Inspectorate, 2001. Mem., Commn for Integrated Transport, 1999–2001. Pres., SMMT, 2001–02 (Vice Pres., 1996–2001). Chm., Econ. Affairs Cttee, CBI, 1999–2001. Chm., Oundle Sch. Foundn, 1997–2001. FIMI 1990 (Vice Pres., 1995).

REILLY, Lt-Gen. Sir Jeremy (Calcott), KCB 1987; DSO 1973; Commander Training and Arms Directors, 1986–89, retired; *b* 7 April 1934; *s* of late Lt-Col J. F. C. Reilly and E. N. Reilly (*née* Moreton); *m* 1960, Julia Elizabeth (*née* Forrester); two *d* (and one *d* decd). *Educ:* Uppingham; RMA Sandhurst. Commissioned Royal Warwickshire Regt, 1954; served Egypt, Cyprus (Despatches), Ireland, Hong Kong, Germany, Borneo, BJSM Washington DC; psc 1965; Brigade Major, BAOR, 1967–69; Chief Instructor, RMA, 1969–71; CO 2nd Bn Royal Regt of Fusiliers, 1971–73 (DSO); Instructor, Staff Coll., 1974–75; Col GS (Army Deployment), MoD, 1975–77; PSO to Field Marshal Lord Carver and attached FCO (Rhodesia), 1977–79; Comdr 6 Field Force and UK Mobile Force, 1979–81; Comdr 4th Armoured Div., BAOR, 1981–83; Dir Battle Develt, MoD, 1983–84; ACDS (Concepts), MoD, 1985–86. Dep. Col, RRF (Warwickshire), 1981–86; Col, RRF, 1986–96; Col Comdt, The Queen's Div., 1988–90. *Address:* RHQ RRF, HM Tower of London, EC3N 4AB.

REILLY, Mary Margaret; CA; Partner, Deloitte (formerly Deloitte & Touche) LLP, 1987–2013; *b* 22 May 1953; *d* of John Reilly and Helena Reilly; *m* 1979, Mark Corby; one *s* one *d*. *Educ:* Notre Dame Collegiate Sch., Leeds; University Coll. London (BA Hist.); London Business Sch. ACA 1978, FCA 1988. Chm., London Develt Agency, 2004–08. Chm. London Reg., Council, CBI, 2004–06. Non-executive Director: Crown Agents for Overseas Govts and Admin Ltd, 2013–; DfT, 2013–; Travelzoo Inc., 2013–; Woodford Investment Mgt LLP, 2014–. Fellow, UCL, 2010. *Recreations:* travel, theatre, music, cooking. *Club:* Reform.

REILLY, Michael David, PhD; HM Diplomatic Service, retired; Chief Representative, China, BAE Systems, 2011–14; *b* 1 March 1955; *s* of late Hugh Aidan Reilly and Mary Sheila Reilly; *m* 1981, Won-Kyong Kang; one *s* one *d*. *Educ:* Ulverston Grammar Sch.; Barnard Castle Sch.; Univ. of Liverpool (BA 1975; PhD 1986); Yonsei Univ., Seoul. Joined HM Diplomatic Service, 1978: Seoul, 1979–84; First Secretary: FCO, 1984–88; UK Delegn to OECD, Paris, 1988–91; Seoul, 1991–93; FCO, 1994–96; Dep. Hd of Mission, Manila, 1997–2000; Head: Cultural Relns, subseq. Culture, Scholarships and Sport, Dept, FCO, 2000–02; SE Asia Dept, FCO, 2003–05; Dir, British Trade and Cultural Office, Taipei, 2005–09; on secondment to BAE Systems, 2009–10. Dir, Visiting Arts, 2000–03. Chairman: Coral Cay Conservation Trust, 2013–; Coral Restoration Foundn Europe, 2014–. Taiwan Friendship Medal. *Publications:* articles in academic jls and railway press. *Recreations:* hiking, cycling, ski-ing, steam engines. *Address:* c/o BAE Systems, PO Box 87, Warwick House, Farnborough GU14 6YU. *T:* (01252) 373232.

REILLY, Nick; *see* Reilly, D. N.

REIMAN, Dr Donald Henry; Editor, Shelley and his Circle, Carl H. Pforzheimer Collection, New York Public Library, since 1986; Adjunct Professor of English, University of Delaware, 1992; *b* 17 May 1934; *s* of Mildred A. (Pearce) Reiman and Henry Ward

Reiman; *m* 1st, 1958, Mary A. Warner (marr. diss. 1974); one *d*; 2nd, 1975, Hélène Dworzan. *Educ:* Coll. of Wooster, Ohio (BA 1956; Hon. LittD 1981); Univ. of Illinois (MA 1957; PhD 1960). Instructor, 1960–62, Asst Prof. 1962–64, Duke Univ.; Associate Prof., Univ. of Wisconsin, Milwaukee, 1964–65; Editor, Shelley and his Circle, Carl H. Pforzheimer Liby, 1965–86. James P. R. Lyell Reader in Bibliography, Oxford Univ., 1988–89. Gen. Editor, Manuscripts of the Younger Romantics, 1984–98 (29 vols); Editor-in-Chief, Bodleian Shelley MSS, 1984–2000 (23 vols). *Publications:* Shelley's The Triumph of Life, 1965; Percy Bysshe Shelley, 1969, 2nd edn 1990; (ed) The Romantics Reviewed, 9 Vols, 1972; (ed) Shelley and his Circle, vols V–VI, 1973, Vols VII–VIII, 1986, (ed with D. D. Fischer) Vols IX–X, 2002; (ed with D. D. Fischer) Byron on the Continent, 1974; (ed with S. B. Powers) Shelley's Poetry and Prose, 1977, 2nd edn (with N. Fraistat), 2001; (ed) The Romantic Context: Poetry, 128 vols, 1976–79; (ed jtly) The Evidence of the Imagination, 1978; English Romantic Poetry 1800–1835, 1979; Romantic Texts and Contexts, 1987; Intervals of Inspiration, 1988; The Study of Modern Manuscripts, 1993; (ed with N. Fraistat) The Complete Poetry of Percy Bysshe Shelley, vol. I, 2000, vol. II, 2004; contribs to scholarly books, reviews and learned jls. *Address:* 907 Aster Avenue, Newark, DE 19711–2631, USA. *E:* dhreiman@udel.edu.

REINFELDT, Fredrik; Prime Minister of Sweden, 2006–14; Chairman, Moderate Party of Sweden, 2003–15; *b* 4 Aug. 1965; *s* of Bruno and Birgitta Reinfeldt; *m* 1992, Filippa; two *s* one *d*. *Educ:* Stockholm Univ. (BSc Business Admin and Econs 1990). Dep. Chm., Swedish Conscripts Council, Swedish Defence Staff, 1986; Skandinaviska Enskilda Banken, Täby, 1986, 1987. Young Moderates: Dep. Chm., 1988–90, Chm., 1990–92, Regl Section, Stockholm; Mem., 1990–92, Chm., 1992–95, Exec. Cttee. Dep. Sec., 1990–91, Sec., 1991, to Stockholm City Comr. Mem., Riksdag, 1991–2014; Alternate, Riksdag Cttee, on Taxation, 1991–94, on EU Affairs, 2001–02; Mem., 1994–2001, Dep. Chm., 2002–03, Riksdag Cttee on Finance, 1994–2001; Chm., Riksdag Cttee on Justice, 2001–02; Alternate, 2002–03, Mem., 2003–06, Riksdag Adv. Council on For. Affairs. Moderate Party: Mem. Regl Section, Stockholm, 1992–2003; Mem., 1999–2003, Leader and First Dep. Chm., 2002–03, Chm., 2003–15, Exec. Cttee, Moderate Party Gp, Riksdag. *Publications:* Det sovande folket, 1993; Projekt Europa: sex unga européer om Europasamarbetet, 1993; Nostalgitrippen, 1995; Stenen i handen på den starke, 1995; Väljarkryss: personvalshandbok, 2001.

REINHARDT, Prof. Tobias, DPhil; Corpus Christi Professor of the Latin Language and Literature, University of Oxford, since 2008; Fellow, Corpus Christi College, Oxford, since 2008; *b* Gross-Gerau, Germany, 31 Aug. 1971; *s* of Mathias and Sabine Reinhardt; *m* 1997, Eva Maria Martin; one *s* one *d*. *Educ:* Kronberg-Gymnasium, Aschaffenburg, Germany; Univ. of Frankfurt (Staatsexamen); Corpus Christi Coll., Oxford (DPhil 2000). Jun. Res. Fellow in Ancient Philosophy, Merton Coll., Oxford, 2001–02; Lectr in Classical Langs and Lit., Univ. of Oxford, 2002–08; Fellow and Tutor in Latin and Greek, Somerville Coll., Oxford, 2002–08. *Publications:* Das Buch E der Aristotelischen Topik, 2000; Cicero's Topica, 2003; (with M. Winterbottom) Quintilian Book 2, 2006; contrib. learned jls. *Address:* Corpus Christi College, Oxford OX1 4JF.

REINTON, Sigurd Evang, Hon. CBE 2007; Director: NATS Holdings Ltd, 2007–13; Monitor, since 2012; *b* 9 Nov. 1941; *s* of Dr Lars Reinton and Ingrid Evang Reinton (*née* Evang); *m* 1966, Arlette Jeanne Gisele Dufresne; two *d*. *Educ:* Lund Univ. (MBA 1964). Sales Dir, Audio-Nike AB, 1964–66; Account Supervisor, Young & Rubicam, 1966–68; Associate, 1968–76, Principal, 1976–81, Dir, 1981–88, McKinsey & Co., Inc.; Chm., Express Aviation Services, 1988–91; Dir, Aubin Hldgs Ltd, 1988–98; Chairman: Mayday Healthcare NHS Trust, 1997–99; London Ambulance Service NHS Trust, 1999–2009. Dir, Freewheel Film Finance Ltd, 2000–03. Mem., Nat. Council, NHS Confedn, 1998–2007; Dir, Ambulance Services Network (formerly Ambulance Services Assoc.), 2005–09 (Mem. Nat. Council, 2001–05); Mem., Adv. Bd, The Foundation, 2005–10. *Publications:* contrib. McKinsey Qly and Financial Times on corporate leadership. *Recreations:* flying (private pilot's licence/instrument rating), sailing, theatre. *Address:* 8 Wickham Way, Beckenham, Kent BR3 3AA. *Club:* Royal Automobile.

REIS e SOUSA, Caetano, DPhil; FMedSci; Group Leader, Francis Crick Institute, since 2015 (Head, Immunobiology Laboratory, Cancer Research UK, London Research Institute (formerly Imperial Cancer Research Fund), 1998–2015); *b* 24 Feb. 1968; *s* of Artur and Margarida Reis e Sousa. *Educ:* United World Coll. of the Atlantic; Imperial Coll. of Sci., Technol. and Medicine, London (BSc Hons Biol. 1989); Hertford Coll., Oxford (DPhil Immunology 1992). Vis. Fellow, 1993–97, Vis. Associate, 1998, Nat. Inst. of Allergy and Infectious Diseases, NIH, Bethesda; Res. Scientist, 1998–2003, Sen. Scientist, 2003–05, Sen. Gp Leader, 2003–15, CRUK, London Res. Inst. (formerly ICRF); Prof. of Immunol., Dept of Medicine, Imperial Coll. London, 2013–15. Hon. Sen. Res. Fellow, 1998–2003, Hon. Reader, 2003–05, Hon. Prof., 2005–, Dept of Immunology and Molecular Pathology, UCL; Hon. Reader, 2004–05, Hon. Prof., 2005–09, Centre for Molecular Oncology, Inst. of Cancer, QMUL; Hon. Prof., KCL, 2014–. FMedSci 2006. Mem., EMBO, 2006. BD Bioscis Award, Eur. Macrophage and Dendritic Cell Soc., 2003; Liliane Bettencourt Award for Life Scis, Fondation Bettencourt-Schueller, 2008; Eur. Soc. for Clinical Investigation Award for Excellence in Basic/Translational Res., 2011. Officer, Order of Sant'iago da Espada (Portugal), 2009. *Publications:* numerous articles in scientific jls. *Recreations:* reading, music, diving. *Address:* Francis Crick Institute, Lincoln's Inn Fields Laboratories, 44 Lincoln's Inn Fields, WC2A 3LY. *T:* (020) 7269 2832, (Assistant) (020) 7269 3598, (Lab) (020) 7269 2859, *Fax:* (020) 7269 2833. *E:* caetano@crick.ac.uk.

REISS, Charles Alexander; Political Editor, Evening Standard, 1985–2004; *b* 23 March 1942; *s* of Dr Joseph Charles Reiss and Jenny Francisca Reiss; *m* 1978, Sue Rosemary Newson-Smith; three *d*. *Educ:* Bryanston Sch., Dorset. Reporter: Hampstead & Highgate Express, 1964–66; London office, Glasgow Citizen, and Scottish Daily Express, 1966–68; Press Officer, Labour Party, 1968–71; Lobby Correspondent: E Anglia Daily Times, etc, 1971–73; Birmingham Post, 1973–75; Political Correspondent: and leader writer, Evening News, 1975–80; and chief leader writer, Evening Standard, 1980–85. Chm., Parly Lobby Journalists, 1995–96. Mem., Govt Communications Review Gp, 2003. Trustee, Kennet and Avon Canal Trust, 2009. *Recreations:* opera, walking, reading, teaching, travel. *Club:* Royal Automobile.

REISS, David Anthony; Managing Director and Chairman, Reiss (Holdings) Ltd, since 1992; *b* London, 15 May 1943; *s* of late Joshua Reiss and Rita Reiss; *m* 1966, Rosemary June; one *s* two *d*. *Educ:* Carmel Coll.; Kingsway Day Coll., Oxon. Manufacturers' agent, 1964–66; co-founder, Oliver Shirts, shirt manufg co., 1966–71; opened Reiss store, Bishopsgate, London, 1971; opened flagship store, King's Road, Chelsea, 1980; own label brand, 1992; launched Women's Wear Div., 2000; opened flagship store, NY, 2003. *Recreations:* sport, soccer (Mem., Diamond Club), Arsenal, plays tennis and golf, running. *Address:* Reiss Building, 12 Picton Place, W1U 1BW. *T:* (020) 3075 2000, *Fax:* (020) 3075 2001. *E:* david.reiss@reiss.com.

REISS, Rev. Prof. Michael Jonathan, PhD; FRSB, FAcSS; Professor of Science Education, UCL Institute of Education, University College London (formerly Institute of Education, University of London), since 2001 (Head, School of Science, Mathematics and Technology, 2001–07; Associate Director, then Pro-Director, Research and Development, 2009–14); *b* 11 Jan. 1958; *s* of Herbert and Ann Reiss (*née* Scott); *m* 1982, Jenny L. Chapman. *Educ:* Westminster Sch., London; Trinity Coll., Cambridge (BA 1st Cl. Hons Natural Scis 1978; MA 1982; PhD 1982; PGCE 1983); E Anglian Ministerial Trng Course; Cambs Consultancy in Counselling (Grad. Counsellor 1993); Open Univ. (MBA 2002). FRSB (FIBiol 1990); FAcSS (AcSS 2010). Teacher, Hills Rd VIth Form Coll., Cambridge, 1983–88 (Hd, Social Biol., 1987); University of Cambridge: Lectr and Tutor, Dept of Educn, 1988–94; Sen. Lectr, 1994–98; Reader in Educn and Bioethics, 1998–2000; Tutor, Homerton Coll., 1994–2000. Inaugural Ed., Sex Education, 1999–2011. Dir of Educn, Royal Soc., 2006–08. Chief Exec., Sci. Learning Centre, London, 2003–. Ordained deacon, 1990, priest, 1991; Priest-in-charge, Boxworth, Elsworth and Knapwell, 1996–99, Toft, 2003–05, Dio. Ely. Specialist Adviser: to H of L Select Cttee on Animals in Scientific Procedures, 2001–02; to H of C Educn Cttee on Personal, Social, Health and Econ, Educn, 2014–15. Chm., Biosci. for Society Strategy Panel, BBSRC, 2004–07. Member: Adv. Cttee on Novel Foods and Processes, 1998–2001; Farm Animal Welfare Council, 2004–. Vice-President: Inst. Biol., 1994–97; British Sci. Assoc., 2009–. Hon. Visiting Professor: Univ. of York, 2000–; Univ. of Birmingham, 2009–12; RVC, 2012–; Univ. of Leeds, 2013–; Vis. Prof., Kristianstad Univ., Sweden, 2002; Docent, Univ. of Helsinki, 2004–; Hon. Prof., RVC, 2012. Hon. FCT, 2010; Hon. Fellow, British Sci. Assoc., 2010. FRSA 2006. Freeman, Salters' Co., 2004 (Liveryman, 2010; Mem. Court, 2014). *Publications:* The Allometry of Growth and Reproduction, 1989; Science Education for a Pluralist Society, 1993; (with R. Straughan) Improving Nature?: the science and ethics of genetic engineering, 1996 (trans. Chinese, Croatian, Japanese, Polish and Portuguese); (with J. L. Chapman) Ecology: principles and applications, 1992, 2nd edn 1999 (trans. Italian); Understanding Science Lessons: five years of science teaching, 2000; (with J. M. Halstead) Values in Sex Education: from principles to practice, 2003; (with J. White) An Aims-Based Curriculum, 2013; contrib. numerous acad. papers, chapters, curriculum materials, reports and other books. *Recreations:* visiting art galleries and museums, trying to keep fit. *Address:* UCL Institute of Education, University College London, WC1H 0AL. *T:* (020) 7612 6092, *Fax:* (020) 7612 6089. *E:* m.reiss@ioe.ac.uk. *Club:* Athenæum.

REISS, Rev. Canon Robert Paul; Canon Treasurer, 2005–13, and Sub-Dean, 2011–13, Westminster Abbey, now Canon Emeritus; *b* 20 Jan. 1943; *s* of Paul Michael Reiss and Beryl Aileen Reiss (*née* Bryant); *m* 1985, Dixie Nichols; one *d*. *Educ:* Haberdashers' Aske's Sch., Hampstead; Trinity Coll., Cambridge (MA); Westcott House, Cambridge; Theol Inst., Bucharest, Rumania; PhD Lambeth 2012. Ordained deacon, 1969, priest, 1970; Asst Curate, St John's Wood Parish Church, London, 1969–73; Asst Missioner, Rajshahi, dio. of Dacca, Bangladesh, 1973; Chaplain, Trinity Coll., Cambridge, 1973–78; Selection Sec., ACCM, 1978–85 (Sen. Selection Sec., 1983–85); Team Rector of Grantham, dio. of Lincoln, 1986–96; Archdeacon of Surrey, 1996–2005. Mem., General Synod of C of E, 1990–2005. Trustee, Churches Conservation Trust, 2002–08. *Publications:* (contrib.) Say One for Me, 1992; The Testing of Vocation: 100 years of ministry selection in the Church of England, 2013. *Recreations:* cricket, golf. *Address:* 35 Addington Square, SE5 7LB. *Clubs:* Garrick, MCC; Worplesdon Golf.

REITH; Barony of (*cr* 1940); title disclaimed by 2nd Baron.
See under Reith, Christopher John.

REITH, Christopher John; retired farmer; *b* 27 May 1928; *s* of 1st Baron Reith, KT, PC, GCVO, GBE, CB, TD, of Stonehaven, and Muriel Katharine, *y d* of late John Lynch Odhams; *S* father, 1971, as 2nd Baron Reith, but disclaimed his peerage for life, 1972; *m* 1969, Penelope Margaret Ann, *er d* of late H. R. Morris; one *s* one *d*. *Educ:* Eton; Worcester College, Oxford (MA Agriculture). Served in Royal Navy, 1946–48. *Recreations:* fishing, gardening, forestry. *Heir: (to disclaimed peerage): s* Hon. James Harry John Reith, *b* 2 June 1971. *Address:* Glendene, 13 Polinard, Comrie, Perthshire PH6 2HJ.

REITH, Fiona Lennox; QC (Scot.) 1996; Sheriff of Lothian and Borders at Edinburgh, since 2007; *b* 17 July 1955; *d* of late Patrick Donald Metcalfe Munro and Francesca Diana Munro (*née* Fendall, later Sutherland); *m* 1979, David Stewart Reith, WS (marr. diss. 1990). *Educ:* Perth Acad.; Aberdeen Univ. (LLB). Solicitor, Edinburgh, 1979–82; admitted WS 1981; admitted to Faculty of Advocates, 1983; Standing Jun. Counsel in Scotland to Home Office, 1989–92; Advocate-Depute, 1992–95; Standing Jun. Counsel to Scottish Office Envmt Dept, 1995–96; Sheriff: of Tayside Central and Fife at Perth, 1999–2000; of Glasgow and Strathkelvin, 2000–07. Member: Sheriff Courts Rules Council, 1989–93; Council, Sheriffs' Assoc., 2003–06, 2009–12; Criminal Courts Rules Council, 2004–11; Parole Bd for Scotland, 2004–07 (Vice-Chm., 2008–09); Civil Justice Adv. Gp, 2004–05; Information and Communications Technol. Cttee, Judicial Council for Scotland, 2011–12. External Examr in Professional Conduct, Faculty of Advocates, 2000–06. FSAScot. Mem., Scotch Malt Whisky Soc., Edinburgh. *Recreations:* walking, theatre, good food and wine, travel, pilates, enthusiastic supporter of Edinburgh International Book Festival and Edinburgh International Festival. *Address:* Sheriffs' Chambers, Sheriff Court House, 27 Chambers Street, Edinburgh EH1 1LB. *T:* (0131) 225 2525. *Club:* New (Edinburgh).

REITH, Gen. Sir John (George), KCB 2003 (CB 2000); CBE 1991 (OBE 1989); Lead Senior Mentor, NATO, 2008–14; Deputy Supreme Allied Commander Europe, 2004–07; *b* 17 Nov. 1948; *s* of John and Jean Reith; *m* 1st, 1971, Cherry Parker; one *s* one *d*; 2nd, 1987, June Nightingale; two *s*. *Educ:* Elliots Green; RMA Sandhurst. Commnd, 1969; CO 1st Bn Parachute Regt, 1986–88 (despatches 1986); COS 1 Armd Div., 1988–91; Comd, 4 Armd Bde, 1992–94; Comd, UN Sector SW Bosnia, 1994; Dir, Internat. Orgns, 1994, Dir, Mil. Ops, 1995–97, MoD; Comdr, ACE Mobile Force (Land), 1997–99; Comdr, Albania Force, 1999; ACDS (Policy), MoD, 2000–01; Chief of Jt Ops, Permt Jt HQ, 2001–04. Chm. of Govs, Millfield Sch., 2010–. Freeman, City of London, 2000. QCVS 1994. *Recreations:* hill walking, gardening, good food. *Club:* Army and Navy.

REITH, Lesley-Anne; *see* Alexander, L.-A.

REITH, Martin; HM Diplomatic Service, retired; *b* 6 Dec. 1935; *s* of late James Reith and Christian (*née* Innes); *m* 1964, Ann Purves; four *s*. *Educ:* Royal High Sch. of Edinburgh. Served: India (Calcutta), 1957–59; Uganda, 1962–66; Scottish Office, Edinburgh, 1966–68; Australia (Canberra), 1969–72; Asst Head of Central and Southern Africa Dept, FCO, 1974–77; Commercial Sec., Beirut, 1977–78; Dep. Hd, UN Dept, FCO, 1979; Counsellor, NATO Def. Coll., Rome, 1980; Dep. High Comr, Malta, 1980–83; High Comr, Swaziland, 1983–87; Ambassador, Republic of Cameroon, 1987–91. *Recreations:* bridge, bowling, family history, bird-watching, travel. *Address:* Ardnagaul House, Strathtay, by Pitlochry, Perthshire PH9 0PG.

REITH, Hon. Peter Keaston; writer and political commentator; *b* 15 July 1950; *s* of Dr A. C. Reith and E. V. Sambell; *m* (marr. diss.); four *s*. *Educ:* Brighton Grammar Sch., Vic; Monash Univ. (BEc, LLB). Solicitor, 1974–82. MP (L) Flinders, Victoria, 1984–2001; Shadow Attorney-Gen., 1987–88; Shadow Industrial Relns, 1988–89; Shadow Minister of Educn, 1989–90; Shadow Treas., 1990–93; Dep. Leader of Opposition, 1990–93; Shadow Special Minister of State, 1993; Shadow Minister for Defence, 1994; responsibility for Native Title legislation, 1994; Shadow Minister: for Foreign Affairs, 1994–95; of Industrial Relns and Manager, Opposition Business in the House, 1995–96; Leader, House of Representatives, 1996–2001; Minister assisting Prime Minister for Public Service, 1996–97; Minister: for Industrial Relns, 1996–97; for Employment, Workplace Relns and Small Business, 1998–2000; for Defence, 2000–01. Dir, EBRD, 2003–09. Chm., Gas Market Rev. for Govt of Victoria, 2013. Pres., Shire, Phillip Is. Council, 1980–81. Sec., Newhaven Coll., Phillip Is., 1977–82. *Recreations:* farming, reading. *E:* peter@reith.com.au.

RELLIE, Alastair James Carl Euan, CMG 1987; HM Diplomatic Service, retired; adviser, Kroll, 2003–12; *b* 5 April 1935; *s* of William and Lucy Rellie; *m* 1961, Annalisa (*née* Modin) (*d* 2014); one *s* two *d*. *Educ:* Michaelhouse, SA; Harvard Univ., USA (BA). Rifle Bde, 1958–60. Second Sec., FCO, 1963–64; Vice-Consul, Geneva, 1964–67; First Secretary: FCO, 1967–68; (Commercial), Cairo, 1968–70; Kinshasa, 1970–72; FCO, 1972–74; (and later Counsellor), UK Mission to UN, New York, 1974–79; FCO, 1979–92. Dir, Market Relations, BAE Systems (formerly British Aerospace), 1993–2000. Mem. Bd, Eur. Defence Industries Gp, 1994–2000, and NATO Industrial Adv. Gp, 1994–2000 (Head, UK delegn to both Gps, 1998–2000). Mem. Council, UK Defence Manufrs Assoc., 1994–2000. *Address:* 50 Smith Street, SW3 4EP. *T:* (020) 7352 5734. *Club:* Brooks's.

RELPH, Simon George Michael, CBE 2004; independent film producer; Director: Skreba Films, since 1980; Greenpoint Films, since 1980; *b* 13 April 1940; *s* of Michael Leighton George Relph; *m* 1963, Amanda, *d* of Anthony Grinling, MC; one *s* one *d*. *Educ:* Bryanston School; King's College, Cambridge (MA Mech. Scis). Asst Dir, Feature Films, 1961–73; Production Administrator, Nat. Theatre, 1974–78; Chief Exec., British Screen Finance Ltd, 1985–90. Chairman: Children's Film and TV Foundn, 1999–2005; BAFTA, 2000–02 (Vice Chm., 1994–98; Dep. Chm., 1999–2000; Trustee, 2004–08); David Lean BAFTA Foundn, 2009–11; Director: Bristol Old Vic, 2000–06; South West Screen, 2001–09; Mem. Council, RCA, 1989–99 (Hon. Fellow, 1999). Non-executive Director: Arts Alliance Media, 2006–; Ritzy Cinema and Picturehouse, Exeter, 2006–12. Chm., Screenwriters Fest., 2006–09. Governor: BFI, 1991–97; Nat. Film and Television Sch., 2002–14. *Films* include: Production Supervisor, Yanks, 1978; Executive Producer: Reds, 1980; Laughterhouse, 1984; Enchanted April, 1991; Hideous Kinky, 1998; Bugs, 2002; Producer/Co-Producer: The Return of the Soldier, 1981; Privates on Parade, 1982; Ploughman's Lunch, 1983; Secret Places, 1984; Wetherby, 1985; Comrades, 1986; Damage, 1992; The Secret Rapture, 1992; Camilla, 1993; Look Me in the Eye, 1994; Blue Juice, 1995; The Slab Boys, 1996; Land Girls, 1997. Trustee, Bradford on Avon Preservation Trust, 2012–. Hon. DLit Bath Spa, 2010. Chevalier, Ordre des Arts et des Lettres (France), 1992. *Publications:* Relph Report, 2002. *Recreations:* gardening, photography, golf. *Address:* Barton Farm, Pound Lane, Bradford-on-Avon, Wilts BA15 1LF.

REMEDIOS, Alberto Telisforo, CBE 1981; opera and concert singer; *b* 27 Feb. 1935; *s* of Albert and Ida Remedios; *m* 1st, 1958, Shirley Swindells (marr. diss.); one *s*; 2nd, 1965, Judith Annette Hosken; one *s* one *d*. *Educ:* studied with Edwin Francis, Liverpool, and with Joseph Hislop. Début: Sadler's Wells Opera, 1956; Proms, 1960; Royal Opera, Covent Gdn, 1965; San Francisco, 1973; Los Angeles, 1974; WNO, 1975; NY Met., 1976; San Diego, 1978; Scottish Opera, 1977. Principal tenor, Frankfurt Opera, 1968–70; Member: Royal Opera Co., 1982–84; Australian Opera Co., 1984–86. Repertoire of over 80 principal roles; notable for Wagner interpretations, esp. Walther von Stolzing, Siegmund, Siegfried and Tristan, Sadler's Wells/ENO, under direction of Sir Reginald Goodall, 1968–81; first British tenor since 1935 to sing Siegfried at Covent Gdn, 1980–81 and 1981–82 seasons. Conductors worked with include: Richard Bonynge, Sir Colin Davis, Sir Edward Downes and Sir Charles Mackerras. Gives lectures, workshops, masterclasses. Recordings include Wagner's Ring; Tippett's A Midsummer Marriage; Stravinsky's Oedipus Rex. Mem., Wagner Soc. Queen's Prize, RCM, 1957; 1st prize for Tenor (Bulgarian Song), Union of Bulgarian Composers, and 1st prize, Bulgarian Internat. Opera Contest, 1963; Sir Reginald Goodall Award, Wagner Soc., 1995. *Recreations:* soccer (Hon. Mem., Liverpool FC), motoring, record collecting, old radios and record players.

REMEDIOS, Prof. John Joseph, DPhil; Professor of Earth Observation Science, since 2010, and Director, National Centre for Earth Observation, since 2014, University of Leicester; *b* Addis Ababa, 20 July 1964; *s* of Lucas and Anne Remedios; *m* 2001, Gabrielle Loftus; one *s* one *d*. *Educ:* Salesian Coll., Battersea; University Coll., Oxford (BA; MA; DPhil 1991). Res. Associate in Atmospheric Oceanic and Planetary Physics, Univ. of Oxford, 1988–2000; Res. Fellow, St Peter's Coll., Oxford, 1991–2001; Leicester University: Lectr, 2000–06; Sen. Lectr, 2006–10; Hd, Earth Observation Sci., 2002–14. *Publications:* contrib. articles to Jl Geophysical Res., Atmospheric Chemistry and Physics, Remote Sensing of Envmt. *Recreations:* sport, parish and lay community life, music. *Address:* National Centre for Earth Observation, Michael Atiyah Building, University of Leicester, University Road, Leicester LE1 7RH.

REMFRY, David, MBE 2001; RA 2006; RWS 1987; artist; *b* Worthing, 1942. *Educ:* Hull Coll. of Art. *Solo exhibitions* include: Ferens Art Gall., Hull, 1975, 2005; Middlesbrough Art Gall., 1981; NPG, 1992; MoMA PSI Contemp. Art Center, NY, 2001; V&A Mus., 2003; has exhibited in USA, Holland and Germany in solo and gp exhibns. Hon. DA Lincoln, 2007. Hugh Casson Drawing Prize, Royal Acad. Arts, 2010. *Publications:* David Remfry Dancers, 2001; We Think the World of You, 2015. *Address:* c/o Royal Academy of Arts, Piccadilly, W1J 0BD. *E:* studio@davidremfry.com. *Clubs:* Groucho, Soho House, Chelsea Arts, Arts.

REMNANT, family name of **Baron Remnant**.

REMNANT, 3rd Baron *cr* 1928, of Wenhaston; **James Wogan Remnant,** CVO 1979; FCA; Bt 1917; Director, Bank of Scotland, 1989–96 (Director 1973–96, and Chairman, 1979–92, London Board); Chairman, National Provident Institution, 1990–95 (Director, 1963–95); *b* 23 Oct. 1930; *s* of 2nd Baron Remnant, MBE and Dowager Lady Remnant (*d* 1990); *S* father, 1967; *m* 1953, Serena Jane Loehnis, *o d* of Sir Clive Loehnis, KCMG; three *s* one *d*. *Educ:* Eton. FCA 1955. Nat. Service, Coldstream Guards, 1948–50 (Lt). Partner, Touche Ross & Co., 1958–70; Man. Dir, 1970–80, Chm., 1981–89, Touche, Remnant & Co.; Chairman: TR City of London Trust, 1978–90 (Dir, 1973–90); TR Pacific Investment Trust, 1987–94. Dep. Chm., Ultramar, 1981–91 (Dir, 1970–91); Director: Australia and New Zealand Banking Group, 1968–81 (Mem., Internat. Bd of Advice, 1987–91); Union Discount Co. of London, 1968–92 (Dep. Chm., 1970–86); London Merchant Securities, 1994–2002; London Authorities Mutual, 2007–09, and other cos. Chm., Assoc. of Investment Trust Cos, 1977–79. A Church Comr, 1976–84. Chm., Institutional Shareholders Cttee 1977–78. Trustee, Royal Jubilee Trusts, 1990–2000 (Hon. Treasurer, 1972–80; Chm., 1980–89); President: Wokingham Constituency Cons. Assoc., 1981–96; Nat. Council of YMCAs, 1983–96; Florence Nightingale Foundn, 1987–2004; Chairman: Learning Through Landscapes Trust, 1989–2000; Friends of Anglican Communion Fund, 2009–14; Patron, Orders of St John Care Trust, 2002–14. Master, Salters' Co., 1995–96. GCStJ (Bailiff of Egle, 1993–99). *Heir:* *s* Hon. Philip John Remnant, *qv*. *Address:* 53a Northfield End, Henley-on-Thames RG9 2JJ.

REMNANT, Hon. Philip John, CBE 2011; Senior Adviser, Credit Suisse, 2006–13; Chairman, Shareholder Executive, 2007–12; *b* 20 Dec. 1954; *s* and *heir* of Baron Remnant, *qv*; *m* 1977, Caroline Elizabeth Clare Cavendish; one *s* two *d*. *Educ:* Eton Coll.; New Coll., Oxford (MA Law). ACA 1979. Peat, Marwick, Mitchell & Co., 1976–82; Kleinwort Benson Ltd, 1982–90 (Dir, 1988–90); Barclays de Zoete Wedd, 1990–97: Man. Dir, 1992–97; Hd, UK Corporate Finance, 1993–94; Dep. Hd, Global Corporate Finance, 1995–96; Co-Hd, Global M&A, 1997; Man. Dir and Dep. Hd, UK Investment Banking, Credit Suisse First Boston, 1997–2001; Dir Gen., 2001–03 (on secondment) and 2010, Dep. Chm., 2012–, Takeover Panel; Hd, UK Investment Banking, Credit Suisse First Boston, 2003–04; Vice-Chm., Credit Suisse First Boston Europe, 2003–06. Member Board: Northern Rock plc, 2008–09; UK Financial Investments Ltd, 2009– (Sen. Ind. Dir); Northern Rock (Asset Mgt) plc, 2009–10; Chm., City of London Investment Trust plc, 2011–; Sen. Ind. Dir, Prudential plc, 2013–; non-exec. Dir, Severn Trent plc, 2014–. Bencher, Inner Temple, 2015. *Address:* Ham Farm House, Baughurst, Basingstoke, Hants RG26 5SD.

REMNICK, David Jay; Editor, The New Yorker, since 1998; *b* 29 Oct. 1958; *m* 1987, Esther B. Fein; two *s* one *d*. *Educ:* Princeton Univ. (BA). Washington Post: staff writer, 1982–88; Moscow corresp., 1988–92; staff writer, The New Yorker, 1992–98. Vis. Fellow, Council on Foreign Relns. *Publications:* Lenin's Tomb, 1993 (Pulitzer Prize, George Polk Award, 1994); Resurrection, 1997; The Devil Problem (and Other True Stories), 1997; King of the World, 1998; Reporting: writings from The New Yorker, 2007; The Bridge: the life and rise of Barack Obama, 2010. *Address:* The New Yorker, 4 Times Square, New York, NY 10036, USA.

RENALS, Sir Stanley, 4th Bt *cr* 1895; formerly in the Merchant Navy; *b* 20 May 1923; 2nd *s* of Sir James Herbert Renals, 2nd Bt; *S* brother, Sir Herbert Renals, 3rd Bt, 1961; *m* 1957, Maria Dolores Rodriguez Pinto, *d* of late José Rodriguez Ruiz; one *s*. *Educ:* City of London Freemen's School. *Heir:* *s* Stanley Michael Renals, BSc, CEng, MIMechE, MIProdE [*b* 14 Jan. 1958; *m* 1982, Jacqueline Riley; one *s* one *d*]. *Address:* 52 North Lane, Portslade, East Sussex BN41 2HG.

RENDEL, David Digby; Member (Lib Dem), West Berkshire Council, 2007–15; *b* 15 April 1949; *s* of late Alexander Rendel and Elizabeth (*née* Williams); *m* 1974, Dr Susan Taylor; three *s*. *Educ:* Eton (schol.); Magdalen Coll., Oxford (BA); St Cross Coll., Oxford. Shell Internat., 1974–77; British Gas, 1977–78; Esso Petroleum, 1978–90. Mem., Newbury DC, 1987–95. MP (Lib Dem) Newbury, May 1993–2005; contested (Lib Dem) same seat, 2005, 2010; contested (Lib Dem) Somerton and Frome, 2015. Lib Dem spokesman: on Local Govt, 1993–97; on Higher Educn, 2001–05. Member: Public Accounts Cttee, 1999–2003; Procedures Cttee, 2001–02. Ldr, Lib Dem Parly Welfare Team, 1997–99. *Address:* Hilltop Cottage, Hopgoods Green, Upper Bucklebury, Berks RG7 6TA. *T:* (01635) 862534.

RENDLESHAM, 9th Baron *cr* 1806 (Ire.); **Charles William Brooke Thellusson;** *b* 10 Jan. 1954; *o s* of 8th Baron Rendlesham and his 2nd wife, Clare, *d* of Lt-Col D. H. G. McCririck; *S* father, 1999; *m* 1988, Lucille Clare, *d* of Rev. Henry Ian Gordon Cumming; one *d*. *Educ:* Eton. *Heir:* *cousin* James Hugh Thellusson [*b* 7 Jan. 1961; *m* 1995, Jennifer Louise Owers; one *s* one *d*].

RENÉ, (France) Albert; barrister-at-law; President of the Republic of Seychelles, 1977–2004 (re-elected, 1979, 1984, 1989, 1993, 1998, 2001); *b* Mahé, Seychelles, 16 Nov. 1935; *s* of Price René and Louisa Morgan; *m* 1st, 1956, Karen Handlay; one *d*; 2nd, 1975, Geva Adam; one *s*; 3rd, 1993, Sarah Zarqani; three *d*. *Educ:* St Louis Coll., Seychelles; Collège du Sacré Cœur, St Maurice, Valais, Switzerland; St Mary's Coll., Southampton, England; King's Coll., Univ. of London; Council of Legal Educn, 1956; LSE, 1961. Called to Bar, 1957. Leader, Founder, Pres., 1964–78, Seychelles People's United Party (first effective political party and liberation movement in Seychelles); MP, 1965; Mem. in Governing Council, 1967; Mem., Legal Assembly, 1970 and 1974; Minister of Works and Land Development, 1975; Prime Minister, 1976–77; Minister: of Transport, 1984–86; of Admin, Finance and Industries, Planning and External Relns, 1984–89; of Defence, 1986–92. Founder, Leader and Sec.-Gen., Seychelles People's Progressive Front, 1978. Order of the Golden Ark (1st cl.), 1982. *Address:* c/o President's Office, State House, Republic of Seychelles.

RENFREW, family name of **Baron Renfrew of Kaimsthorn**.

RENFREW OF KAIMSTHORN, Baron *cr* 1991 (Life Peer), of Hurlet in the District of Renfrew; **Andrew Colin Renfrew,** FBA 1980; Disney Professor of Archaeology, University of Cambridge, 1981–2004; Director, 1991–2004, Senior Fellow, since 2004, McDonald Institute for Archaeological Research, Cambridge; *b* 25 July 1937; *s* of late Archibald Renfrew and Helena Douglas Renfrew (*née* Savage); *m* 1965, Jane Margaret, *d* of Ven. Walter Frederick Ewbank; two *s* one *d*. *Educ:* St Albans Sch.; St John's Coll., Cambridge (Exhibnr; Hon. Fellow, 2004); British Sch. of Archaeology, Athens. Pt I Nat. Scis Tripos 1960; BA 1st cl. hons Archaeol. and Anthrop. Tripos 1962; MA 1964; PhD 1965; ScD 1976. Pres., Cambridge Union Soc., 1961; Sir Joseph Larmor Award 1961. Nat. Service, Flying Officer (Signals), RAF, 1956–58. Res. Fellow, St John's Coll., Cambridge, 1968; Bulgarian Govt Schol., 1966; University of Sheffield: Lectr in Prehistory and Archaeol., 1965–70; Sen. Lectr, 1970–72; Reader, 1972; Prof. of Archaeology, Southampton Univ., 1972–81; Professorial Fellow, St John's Coll., Cambridge, 1981–86; Jesus College, Cambridge: Master, 1986–97; Professorial Fellow, 1997–2004; Emeritus Fellow and Hon. Fellow, 2004–. Vis. Lectr, Univ. of Calif at Los Angeles, 1967 and 2005. Contested (C) Sheffield Brightside, 1968; Chm., Sheffield Brightside Conserv. Assoc., 1968–72. Member: Ancient Monuments Bd for England, 1974–84; Royal Commn on Historical Monuments (England), 1977–87; Historic Buildings and Monuments Commn for England, 1984–86; Ancient Monuments Adv. Cttee, 1984–2001; UK Nat. Commn for UNESCO, 1984–86 (Mem. Culture Adv. Cttee, 1984–86); Exec. Cttee, NACF, 2001–10; Trustee: Antiquity Trust, 1974–2014; British Mus., 1991–2001; Chm., Hants Archaeol Cttee, 1974–81; a Vice-Pres., RAI, 1982–85. Chm., Governors, The Leys, 1984–92; Chm. Council, British Sch. at Athens, 2004–10. Chairman: All Party Parly Archaeol Cttee, 2002–; Treasure Valuation Cttee, 2011–. Lectures: Dalrymple in Archaeol., Univ. of Glasgow, 1975 and 2000; George Grant MacCurdy, Harvard, 1977; Patten, Indiana Univ., 1982; Harvey, New Mexico Univ., 1982; Hill, Univ. of Minnesota, 1987; Tanner, Stanford Univ., 1993; Neubergh, Univ. of Göteborg, 1997; Hitchcock, Univ. of Calif, Berkeley, 1997; Kroon, Amsterdam, 1999; McDonald, Cambridge Univ., 1999; Rhind, Edinburgh, 2001; Sackler, Nat. Acad. of Scis, Washington, DC, 2005. Excavations: Saliagos near Antiparos, 1964–65; Sitagroi, Macedonia, 1968–70; Phylakopi in Melos, 1974–76; Quanterness, Orkney, 1972–74; Maes Howe, 1973–74; Ring of Brodgar, 1974; Liddle Farm, 1973–74; Markiani, Amorgos, 1987; Keros, 2006–08. FSA 1968 (Vice-Pres., 1987–92); FSAScot 1970 (Hon. FSAScot 2001); Hon. FRSE 2001; Hon. Fellow, Archaeol. Soc. of Athens, 1990. For. Associate, Nat. Acad. of Scis, USA, 1997; Corresponding Member: Österreichische Akad. der Wissenschaften, 2000; Deutsches Archaeologisches Institut, 2004; Russian Acad. of Scis, 2006; Amer. Philosophical Soc., 2006. Freeman, City of London, 1987. Hon. LittD: Sheffield, 1987; Southampton, 1995; Liverpool, 2005; Dr *hc*: Athens, 1991; Pontificia Univ. Católica del Peru, 2009; Hon. DLitt: Edinburgh, 2005; St Andrews, 2006; Kent, 2007; London, 2008. Rivers Meml Medal, 1979, Huxley Meml Medal, 1991, RAI; Fyssen Prize, Fyssen Foundn, Paris, 1996; Lucy Wharton Drexel Medal, Univ. of Pennsylvania Mus., 2003; Latsis Prize, Eur. Sci. Foundn, 2003; Balzan Foundn Prize, 2004. *Publications:* (with J. D. Evans) Excavations at Saliagos near Antiparos, 1968; The Emergence of Civilisation, 1972; (ed) The Explanation of Culture Change, 1973; Before Civilisation, 1973; (ed) British Prehistory, a New Outline, 1974; Investigations in Orkney, 1979; (ed) Transformations: Mathematical Approaches to Culture Change, 1979; Problems in European Prehistory, 1979; (with J. M. Wagstaff) An Island Polity, 1982; (ed) Theory and Explanation in Archaeology, 1982; Approaches to Social Archaeology, 1984; The Prehistory of Orkney, 1985; The Archaeology of Cult, 1985; Archaeology and Language, 1987; (with G. Daniel) The Idea of Prehistory, 1988; The Cycladic Spirit, 1991; (with P. Bahn) Archaeology, 1991; (ed) America Past, America Present, 2000; Loot, Legitimacy and Ownership, 2000; (ed) Archaeogenetics, 2000; Figuring It Out, 2003; (with P. Bahn) Archaeology, the Key Concepts, 2005; (ed with P. Forster) Phylogenetic Methods and the Prehistory of Languages, 2006; (ed jtly) Markiani, Amorgos: an early bronze age fortified settlement, 2006; Prehistory, the Making of the Human Mind, 2007; (ed) Excavations at Phylakopi in Melos 1974–77, 2007; (with I. Morley) The Archaeology of Measurement, 2010; (ed jtly) The Settlement at Dhaskalio, 2013; articles in archaeol jls. *Recreations:* modern art, travel. *Address:* McDonald Institute for Archaeological Research, Downing Street, Cambridge CB2 3ER. *T:* (01223) 333521. *Clubs:* Athenæum, Oxford and Cambridge.

See also Hon. M. A. Renfrew.

RENFREW, Hon. Magnus Archibald; Deputy Chairman, Asia, and Director of Fine Arts, Asia, Bonhams, since 2014; *b* Winchester, 5 Nov. 1975; *s* of Baron Renfrew of Kaimsthorn, *qv*; *m* 2004, Emma Louise Williamson; two *s*. *Educ:* St Faith's, Cambridge; Leys Sch., Cambridge; Univ. of St Andrews (MA 1st Cl. Hons Art Hist. 1999; OE Saunders Prize for Art Hist. 1999). Specialist in Scottish Art, Bonhams, Edinburgh, 1999–2002; Bonhams, London: Specialist: in 20th Century British Art, 2002–04; in Modern and Contemporary Art, 2004–06; in Contemporary Asian Art, 2004–06; Manager and Hd of Exhibns, Contrasts Gall., Shanghai, 2006–07; Fair Dir, ART HK, Hong Kong Internat. Art Fair, Hong Kong, 2007–12; Dir, Asia, and Mem., Exec. Cttee, Art Basel, 2012–14. Mem., Hong Kong Arts Develt Council, 2014–; Chm., Adv. Council, Para Site, Hong Kong, 2015–. FSAScot 2001. Young Global Leader, WEF, 2013. *Recreations:* family, art. *Address:* 1D Tower 1, Hillsborough Court, 18 Old Peak Road, Hong Kong. *E:* info@magnusrenfrew.com. *Club:* Brooks's.

RENNARD, Baron *cr* 1999 (Life Peer), of Wavertree in the county of Merseyside; **Christopher John Rennard,** MBE 1989; Chief Executive, Liberal Democrats, 2003–09 (Director of Campaigns and Elections, 1989–2003); *b* 8 July 1960; *s* of late Cecil Langton Rennard and Jean Winifred Rennard (*née* Watson); *m* 1989, Ann McTegart. *Educ:* Mosspits Lane County Primary Sch.; Liverpool Blue Coat Sch.; Univ. of Liverpool (BA Hons Politics and Economics). Liberal Party: Agent, Liverpool Mossley Hill constituency, 1982–84; Area Agent, East Midlands region, 1984–88; Election Co-ordinator, Social & Liberal Democrats, 1988–89. *Recreations:* cooking, wine, France. *Address:* 19 Stockwell Park Road, SW9 0AP.

RENNELL, 4th Baron *cr* 1933, of Rodd, co. Hereford; **James Roderick David Tremayne Rodd;** Event Marketing Manager, Vision Nine (formerly Sports Vision); *b* 9 March 1978; *o s* of 3rd Baron Rennell and Phyllis (*née* Neill); *S* father, 2006. *Educ:* Wellesley House; Bryanston; Latymer; De Montfort Univ. *Recreations:* wide range of sports, esp. surfing, golf, cricket. *Heir:* none. *E:* jamesrodd9@me.com.

RENNET, Roderick James, CBE 2000; CEng; FICE; Chief Executive, East of Scotland Water, 1996–2000; *b* 25 March 1942; *s* of James Mowat Rennet and Rachel Rennet; *m* 1965, Lesley Margaret Irving Love; one *s* one *d*. *Educ:* Dundee Inst. of Technol. (BSc Hons). CEng 1969; FICE 1986; FCIWEM (FIWEM 1987); FIWO 1992. Civil engrg apprentice, Dundee Harbour Trust, 1960–62; asst engr, Chester CBC, 1966–68; asst engr, then sen. engr, Durham CC, 1969–70; sen. engr, then principal engr, Dundee Corp., 1970–75; Tayside Regional Council: Depute Dir of Water Services, 1975–87; Dir of Water Services, 1988–95. *Recreations:* hill-walking, photography, cycling. *Address:* 1A Polwarth Terrace, Edinburgh EH11 1NF.

RENNIE, Archibald Louden, CB 1980; Secretary, Scottish Home and Health Department, 1977–84, retired; *b* 4 June 1924; *s* of John and Isabella Rennie; *m* 1950, Kathleen Harkess; four *s*. *Educ:* Madras Coll.; St Andrews University (BSc). Minesweeping Res. Div., Admty, 1944–47; Dept of Health for Scotland, 1947–62; Private Sec. to Sec. of State for Scotland, 1962–63; Asst Sec., SHHD, 1963–69; Registrar Gen. for Scotland, 1969–73; Under-Sec., Scottish Office, 1973–77. Member: Scottish Records Adv. Council, 1985–94; Council on Tribunals, 1987–88. Gen. Council Assessor, St Andrews Univ. Court, 1984–85; Chancellor's Assessor and Finance Convener, 1985–89; Vice-Chm., Adv. Cttee on Distinction Awards for Consultants, 1985–94; Chm., Disciplined Services Pay Review Cttee, Hong Kong, 1988. Trustee, Lockerbie Air Disaster Trust, 1988–91; Dir, Elie Harbour Trust, 1989–2008 (Chm., 1994–98). Mem. Bd, Madras Coll., 1994–99. Chm., Elie and Royal Burgh of Earlsferry Community Council, 2001–03. Cdre, Elie and Earlsferry Sailing Club, 1991–93. Hon. FDSRCS 1995. Hon. LLD St Andrews, 1990. *Publications:* Fringe of Gold: the East Neuk through nine millennia, 2000; The Harbours of Elie Bay: a history, 2008; odd verses. *Recreations:* reading, pottering, firth-watching. *Address:* The Laigh House, 6A South Street, Elie, Fife KY9 1DN. *T:* (01333) 330741.

RENNIE, David James; His Honour Judge Rennie; a Circuit Judge, since 2001; *b* 8 March 1953; *s* of Michael Rennie and Margaret Rennie (*nee* McGrath); partner, Catherine O'Shea; two *s*. *Educ:* Cranleigh Sch.; Kingston Poly. (BA Hons Law). Called to the Bar, Inner Temple, 1976; in practice, specialising in criminal law; a Recorder, 1998–2001. *Recreations:* spending time in France, cooking, cinema, painting. *Address:* Lewes Crown Court, High Street, Lewes, E Sussex BN7 1YB.

RENNIE, William Cowan; Member (Lib Dem) Scotland Mid and Fife, Scottish Parliament, since 2011; Leader, Scottish Lib Dems, since 2011; *b* 27 Sept. 1967; *s* of Alexander and Peta Rennie; *m* 1992, Janet Macfarlane; two *s*. *Educ:* Paisley Coll. of Technol. (BSc 1989). Agent for Paul Tyler, MP, 1990–94; Campaign Officer, Liberal Democrats, 1994–97; Chief Exec., Scottish Liberal Democrats, 1997–2001; self-employed consultant, 2001–03; Account Dir, McEwan Purvis, 2003–06; self-employed communications consultant, 2010–11. MP (Lib Dem) Dunfermline and W Fife, Feb. 2006–2010; contested (Lib Dem) same seat, 2010. *Recreation:* running. *Address:* Scottish Parliament, Edinburgh EH99 1SP. *Club:* Carnegie Harriers.

RENNISON, Air Vice-Marshal David Ralph Grey, CB 2005; Vice President, Saudi Arabia Typhoon Aircraft Programme, BAE Systems Saudi Arabia, 2009–14; consultant in defence sector, since 2014; *b* 28 June 1951; *s* of Brian and Elizabeth Rennison; *m* 1975, Anne Scarth; one *s* one *d*. *Educ:* Royal Sch., Armagh; UMIST (BSc Electrical Engrg and Electronics); Univ. of Cranfield (MSc Corporate Mgt); RAF Coll., Cranwell. Joined RAF, 1970; various jun. officer appts, 1975–82; 3 Sqn Ldr appts, 1982–89; student, RAF Staff Coll., 1989; OC Engrg Wing, RAF Wildenrath, 1990–92; Wing Comdr Appointer, RAF Personnel Agency, 1992–94; Gp Capt., RAF Signals Engrg Estabt, 1994–97; Station Comdr, RAF Sealand, 1997–98; ACOS Communications and Inf. Systems, HQ Strike Comd, 1999–2002; Dir, Defence Inf. Infrastructure Prog., MoD, 2002–03; COS (Support), HQ Strike Comd, 2003–05; Air Mem. for Logistics, and Dir Gen. Logistics (Strike Envmt), Defence Logistics Orgn, MoD, 2006–07; Dir, Internat. Maintenance and Logistics Ops, later Future Capability and Internat. Support, Military Air Solutions, BAE Systems, 2007–09. *Recreations:* social golf, walking, jogging. *Address:* Pear Tree Cottage, Mill Lane, Calcot, Reading, Berks RG31 7RF. *Club:* Royal Air Force.

RENO, Janet; Attorney General of the United States of America, 1993–2001; *b* 21 July 1938. *Educ:* Cornell Univ. (AB Chem. 1960); Harvard Law Sch. (LLB 1963). Started legal career in private practice; Staff Dir, Judiciary Cttee, Florida House of Reps, 1971–72; Asst State Attorney, Florida, 1973–76; Partner, Steel, Hector & Davis, Miami, 1976–78; State Attorney, Miami, 1978–93. Pres., Fla Prosecuting Attorneys Assoc., 1984–85; American Bar Association: Member: Special Cttee on Criminal Justice in a Free Soc., 1986–88; Task Force on Minorities and the Justice System, 1992. Herbert Harley Award, Amer. Judicature Soc., 1981; Medal of Honor, Fla Bar Assoc., 1990. *Address:* c/o Department of Justice, 10th & Constitution Avenue NW, Washington, DC 20530, USA.

RENSHAW, Sir (John) David, 4th Bt *cr* 1903, of Coldharbour, Wivelsfield, Sussex; *b* 9 Oct. 1945; *s* of Sir Maurice Renshaw, 3rd Bt and his 1st wife, Isabel Bassett (*née* Popkin); *S* father, 2002; *m* 1970, Jennifer Murray (marr. diss. 1988); one *s* two *d*. *Educ:* Ashmole Sch., Southgate. Army, 1960–69; NAAFI, 1970–74; Meat and Livestock Commn, 1974–88; self-employed furniture maker, 1990–2002. *Recreations:* ski-ing, narrowboating, travel. *Heir:* *s* Thomas Charles Bine Renshaw, *b* 3 March 1976. *Address:* 3 Hunts Field Drive, Gretton, Northants NN17 3GD.

RENTON, family name of **Baron Renton of Mount Harry**.

RENTON OF MOUNT HARRY, Baron *cr* 1997 (Life Peer), of Offham in the co. of Sussex; **Ronald Timothy Renton;** PC 1989; DL; *b* 28 May 1932; *yr s* of R. K. D. Renton, CBE, and Mrs Renton, MBE; *m* 1960, Alice Fergusson of Kilkerran, Ayrshire; two *s* two *d* (and one *d* decd). *Educ:* Eton Coll. (King's Schol.); Magdalen Coll., Oxford (Roberts Gawen Schol.). First cl. degree in History, MA Oxon. Joined C. Tennant Sons & Co. Ltd, London, 1954; with Tennants' subsidiaries in Canada, 1957–62; Dir, C. Tennant Sons & Co. Ltd and Managing Dir of Tennant Trading Ltd, 1964–73; Director: Silvermines Ltd, 1967–84; Australia & New Zealand Banking Group, 1967–76; Fleming Continental European Investment Trust, 1992–2003 (Chm., 1999–2003), and other cos. Mem., BBC Gen. Adv. Council, 1982–84; Vice Chm., British Council, 1992–97; Mem., British Council Bd, 1997–99. Contested (C) Sheffield Park Div., 1970. MP (C) Mid-Sussex, Feb. 1974–1997. PPS to Rt Hon. John Biffen, MP, 1979–81, to Rt Hon. Geoffrey Howe, MP, 1983–84; Parly Under Sec. of State, FCO, 1984–85; Minister of State: FCO, 1985–87; Home Office, 1987–89; Parly Sec. to HM Treasury and Govt Chief Whip, 1989–90; Minister of State, Privy Council Office (Minister for the Arts), 1990–92. Member: Select Cttee on Nationalised Industries, 1974–79; Select Cttee on Nat. Heritage, 1995–97; Vice-Chm., Cons. Parly Trade Cttee, 1974–79; Chairman: Parly British-Hong Kong All-Party Gp, 1992–97; Cons. Foreign and Commonwealth Council, 1982–84; Member: Sub-Cttee A, 1997–2001, Sub-Cttee D, 2002– (Chm., 2003–06), EC Cttee, H of L; Chm., Information Cttee, H of L, 2006–; Vice-Pres., 1978–80, Pres., 1980–84, Cons. Trade Unionists; Fellow, Industry and Parlt Trust, 1977–79. Member: Adv. Bd, Know-How Fund for Central and Eastern Europe, 1992–2000; Develt Council, Parham Trust, 1992–2000; Criterion Theatre Trust, 1992–97; APEX. DL East Sussex, 2004. Pres. Council, Roedean Sch., 1998–2005 (Mem., 1982–97). Trustee: Mental Health Foundn, 1985–89; Brighton West Pier Trust, 1997–2005. Founding Pres. (with Mick Jagger), Nat. Music Day, 1992–97; Chairman: Outsider Art Archive, 1995–2001; Sussex Downs Conservation Bd, 1997–2005; South Downs Jt Cttee, 2005–09; Pres., Fedn of Sussex Amenity Socs, 2009–14. Mem. Council, Univ. of Sussex, 2000–07; Pres. Council, Brighton Coll., 2007–11. *Publications:* The Dangerous Edge (novel), 1994; Hostage to Fortune (novel), 1997; Chief Whip: the role, history and black arts of parliamentary whipping, 2004. *Recreations:* writing, messing about in boats, listening to opera, cultivating a Sussex vineyard. *Address:* House of Lords, SW1A 0PW.

RENTON, Air Cdre Helen Ferguson, CB 1982; Director, Women's Royal Air Force, 1980–86; *b* 13 March 1931; *d* of late John Paul Renton and Sarah Graham Renton (*née* Cook). *Educ:* Stirling High Sch.; Glasgow Univ. (MA). Joined WRAF, 1954; commnd, 1955; served in UK, 1955–60; Cyprus, 1960–62; UK, 1963–66; RAF HQ Staff, Germany, 1967; MoD Staff, 1968–71; NEAF, 1971–73; Training Comd, 1973–76; MoD Staff, 1976–78. Hon. ADC to the Queen, 1980–86. Hon. LLD Glasgow, 1981. *Publications:* (jtly) Service Women, 1977. *Recreations:* needlework, reading.

RENTON, Ian; *see* Renton, R. I.

RENTON, Nicholas William; Resident Judge (formerly Regional Adjudicator), since 2004, and Upper Tribunal Judge, since 2008, Birmingham; *b* Crewe, 25 July 1948; *s* of William John Renton and Mary Renton (*née* Holland); *m* 1975, Mary Joyce Garrett; one *s* one *d*. *Educ:* Warwick Sch.; Univ. of Kent, Canterbury (BA Hons 1970). Admitted solicitor, 1974; in private practice, Coventry, 1974–92. Part-time Chairman: Social Security Appeal Tribunal, 1985–2000; Disability Appeal Tribunal, 1985–2000; Child Support Appeal Tribunal, 1985–2000; pt-time Immigration Adjudicator, 1990–2000; salaried Immigration Adjudicator, 2000–04. *Recreations:* Coventry City FC, reading, history. *Address:* Tribunal Service, Sheldon Court, 1 Wagon Lane, Sheldon, Birmingham B26 3DU. *T:* (0121) 722 7929, *Fax:* (0121) 722 7948. *E:* nicholas.renton@judiciary.gsi.gov.uk.

RENTON, (Robert) Ian; Regional Director, South West, Jockey Club, since 2012; *b* London, 1 Nov. 1958; *s* of Alec Renton and Susan Renton; *m* 2007, Jean Keane; one *s* one *d*. *Educ:* Shrewsbury Sch.; Magdalene Coll., Cambridge (BA 1981). Manager, Davy's of London, 1982–84; Asst Manager, Cheltenham Racecourse, 1985–87; Manager, Salisbury and Wincanton Racecourse, 1988–2001; Clerk of the Course, Aintree Racecourse, 1993–2001; Man. Dir, Arena Leisure, 2001–12. Director: Racecourse Assoc., 2000–07; British Horseracing Authy, 2007–09. *Recreations:* tennis, ski-ing, wine. *Address:* Cheltenham Racecourse, Cheltenham, Glos GL50 4SH. *T:* (01242) 513014. *E:* ian.renton@thejockeyclub.co.uk.

RENTOUL, John Tindal; journalist; Chief Political Commentator, Independent on Sunday, since 2004; *b* Kalimpong, India, 25 Sept. 1958; *s* of Robert Wylie Rentoul and Mary Claire Rentoul (*née* Tindal); *m* 2003; one *s* two *d*. *Educ:* Bristol Grammar Sch.; Wolverhampton Grammar Sch.; King's Coll., Cambridge (BA Eng. Lit. 1980). Reporter, Accountancy Age, 1981–83; reporter, 1983–87, Dep. Editor, 1987–88, New Statesman; reporter, On The Record, BBC1, 1988–95; Political Corresp., 1995–97, Chief Leader Writer, 1997–2004, The Independent. Vis. Fellow, 2008–12, Vis. Prof., 2012–, contemp. hist., QMUL; Vis. Prof., KCL, 2014–. *Publications:* The Rich Get Richer: the growth of inequality in Britain in the 1980s, 1987; Me and Mine: the triumph of the new individualism?, 1989; Tony Blair, 1995, 2nd edn 1996; Tony Blair: Prime Minister, 2001, 3rd edn 2013; The Banned List: a manifesto against jargon and cliché, 2011; Questions to Which the Answer is No, 2012; Listellany: a miscellany of very British top tens from politics to pop, 2014. *Recreation:* watching American football. *Address:* Independent on Sunday, Northcliffe House, 2 Derry Street, W8 5HF. *E:* j.rentoul@independent.co.uk.

RENTZENBRINK, Catherine Marion; Project Director, Quick Reads, since 2012; Associate Editor, The Bookseller, since 2013; *b* Truro, Cornwall, 8 Jan. 1973; *d* of (Matthew) Kevin Mintern and Margaret Mintern; *m* 2009, Erwyn Rentzenbrink; one *s*. *Educ:* Univ. of Leeds (BA Hons 1996). Bell and Crown pub and travel, 1996–2002; Waterstone's: bookseller, Harrods, 2002–04; Events Manager, Oxford St, 2004–06; Asst Manager, Hatchards, 2006–08; Manager, Teddington, 2008–09, Richmond, 2009–10; Publisher Relationship Manager, 2010–11; Publisher Liaison Manager, 2011–12; New Fiction Reviewer, The Bookseller, 2012–13. *Publications:* The Last Act of Love (memoir), 2015. *Recreations:* reading excessively, day dreaming. *Address:* The Bookseller, Crowne House, 56–58 Southwark Street, SE1 1UN. *T:* (020) 3358 0372. *E:* cathyrentzenbrink@hotmail.com.

RENWICK, family name of **Barons Renwick** and **Renwick of Clifton**.

RENWICK, 2nd Baron *cr* 1964, of Coombe; **Harry Andrew Renwick;** Bt 1927; *b* 10 Oct. 1935; *s* of 1st Baron Renwick, KBE, and Mrs John Ormiston, Miserden House, Stroud, *er d* of late Major Harold Parkes, Alveston, Stratford-on-Avon; *S* father, 1973; *m* 1st, 1965, Susan Jane (marr. diss. 1989), *d* of late Captain Kenneth S. B. Lucking and Mrs Moir P. Stormonth-Darling, Lednathie, Glen Prosen, Angus; two *s*; 2nd, 1989, Mrs Homayoun Mazandi, *d* of late Col Mahmoud Yazdanparst Pakzad. *Educ:* Eton. Grenadier Guards (National Service), 1955–56. Partner, W. Greenwell & Co., 1964–80; Dir, General Technology Systems Ltd, 1975–93; Chm., European Information Society Group, 1994–2000 (Pres., 2000–). Mem., H of L Select Cttee on the European Communities, 1988–92, on Science and Technology, 1992–95; Hon. Sec., Parly Information Technology Cttee, 1991–2000 (Vice-Pres., 2006–). Vice-Pres., British Dyslexia Assoc., 1982– (Chm., 1977–82); Chm., Dyslexia Educnl Trust, 1986–2002. *Heir:* *s* Hon. Robert James Renwick, *b* 19 Aug. 1966. *Address:* 38 Cadogan Square, SW1X 0JL. *Club:* Turf.

RENWICK OF CLIFTON, Baron *cr* 1997 (Life Peer), of Chelsea in the Royal Borough of Kensington and Chelsea; **Robin William Renwick,** KCMG 1989 (CMG 1980); Member, International Advisory Council, JP Morgan Europe, since 2014 (Vice-Chairman, Investment Banking, 2001–14); Vice-Chairman, JP Morgan Cazenove, 2005–14; Director, Stonehage Fleming Family and Partners, since 2014 (Deputy Chairman, Fleming Family and Partners, 2000–14); *b* 13 Dec. 1937; *s* of late Richard Renwick, Edinburgh, and Clarice (*née* Henderson); *m* Annie; one *s* one *d*. *Educ:* St Paul's Sch.; Jesus Coll., Cambridge (Hon. Fellow, 1992); Univ. of Paris (Sorbonne). Army, 1956–58. Entered Foreign Service, 1963; Dakar, 1963–64; FO, 1964–66; New Delhi, 1966–69; Private Sec. to Minister of State, FCO, 1970–72; First Sec., Paris, 1972–76; Counsellor, Cabinet Office, 1976–78; Rhodesia Dept, FCO, 1978–80; Political Adviser to Governor of Rhodesia, 1980; Vis. Fellow, Center for Internat. Affairs, Harvard, 1980–81; Head of Chancery, Washington, 1981–84; Asst Under Sec. of State, FCO, 1984–87; Ambassador to S Africa, 1987–91; Ambassador to Washington, 1991–95. Dir, 1996–2000, Dep. Chm., 1999–2000, Robert Fleming Hldgs Ltd. Chairman: Save & Prosper Gp, 1996–98; Fluor Ltd, 1996–2011; Director: Compagnie Financière Richemont AG, 1995–; British Airways plc, 1996–2005; Liberty Internat., 1996–2000; Canal Plus, 1997–2000; BHP Billiton plc, 1997–2005; Fluor Corp., 1997–2008; SABMiller plc (formerly South African Breweries), 1999–2008; Harmony Gold, 1999–2004; KAZ Minerals (formerly Kazakhmys) plc, 2005–15; Gem Diamonds Ltd, 2007–08; Excelsior Mining Co., 2014–. Trustee, The Economist, 1996–2009. Dir, Open Europe, 2012–. FRSA. Hon. LLD: Wits Univ., 1990; Amer. Univ. in London, 1993; Hon. DLitt: Coll. of William and Mary, 1993; Oglethorpe Univ., 1995. *Publications:* Economic Sanctions, 1981; Fighting with Allies, 1996; Unconventional Diplomacy, 1997; A Journey with Margaret Thatcher: foreign policy under the Iron Lady, 2013; Helen Suzman, 2014; Ready for Hillary?, 2014; The End of Apartheid: a diary of a revolution, 2015. *Recreations:* tennis, fly fishing. *Address:* 9 South Street, W1K 2XA. *T:* (020) 7907 2618. *Clubs:* Brooks's, Hurlingham, Queen's.

RENWICK, David Peter; scriptwriter and author, since 1974; *b* 4 Sept. 1951; *s* of James George Renwick and Winifred May Renwick (*née* Smith); *m* 1994, Eleanor Florence (*née* Hogarth). *Educ:* Luton Grammar Sch.; Luton Sixth Form Coll.; Harlow Tech. Coll. (Nat. Proficiency Cert. in Journalism). Reporter/Sub-Editor, Luton News, 1970–74. (With Andrew Marshall) creator and writer: The Burkiss Way, BBC Radio 4; television: End of Part One, 1979–80; Whoops Apocalypse, 1982; The Steam Video Company, 1984; Hot Metal, 1986–88; Alexei Sayle's Stuff, 1989–91; If You See God, Tell Him, 1993; solo creator and writer: One Foot in the Grave, 1989–2000; Jonathan Creek, 1997–2014 (also dir, 2009–13); Love Soup, 2005–08; stage play, Angry Old Men, 1994. *Publications:* One Foot in the Grave, 1993. *Address:* c/o Roger Hancock Ltd, 7 Broadbent Close, Highgate Village, N6 5JW. *T:* (020) 8341 7243.

RENWICK, Sir Richard Eustace, 4th Bt *cr* 1921; *b* 13 Jan. 1938; *er s* of Sir Eustace Deuchar Renwick, 3rd Bt, and Diana Mary, *e d* of Colonel Bernard Cruddas, DSO; *S* father, 1973; *m* 1966, Caroline Anne, *er d* of Major Rupert Milburn; three *s*. *Educ:* Eton. *Heir:* *s* Charles Richard Renwick [*b* 10 April 1967; *m* 1993, Jane Ann Lyles (*née* Bush) (marr. diss. 2003); two *s*]. *Address:* Whalton House, Whalton, Morpeth, Northumberland NE61 3UZ. *T:* (01670) 775383. *Club:* Northern Counties (Newcastle).

REPP, Richard Cooper, DPhil; Master, St Cross College, Oxford, 1987–2003; *b* 1 April 1936; *s* of Robert Mathias Repp, Jun., and Martha Repp (*née* Cooper); *m* 1972, Catherine Ross MacLennan; one *s* one *d*. *Educ:* Shady Side Acad., Pittsburgh; Williams Coll., Mass (BA); Worcester Coll., Oxford (1st Cl. Hons Oriental Studies, MA, DPhil; Hon. Fellow 1989). Instr in Humanities, Robert Coll., Istanbul, 1959–62; Oxford University: Univ. Lectr in Turkish History, 1963–2003; Sen. Proctor, 1979–80; Vice-Chm., Staff Cttee, 1982–84; Member: Gen. Bd of the Faculties, 1982–84, 1985–89; Hebdomadal Council, 1991–2000; Pro-Vice-Chancellor, 1994–2003; Linacre College: Fellow, 1964–87, Hon. Fellow, 1987; Sen. Tutor, 1985–87. Boskey Distinguished Vis. Prof. of History, Williams Coll., Mass., 2008. Chm., Visitors of the Ashmolean Mus., 1995–2002. Hon. Fellow, St Cross Coll., Oxford, 2003. Bicentennial Medal, Williams Coll., Mass, 2004. *Publications:* The Müfti of Istanbul, 1986; various articles on Ottoman history. *Recreations:* gardening, music. *Address:* St Cross College, Oxford OX1 3LZ. *T:* (01865) 278490.

REPTON, Bishop Suffragan of; *no new appointment at time of going to press.*

RESTIEAUX, Mary Catherine, RDI 2011; freelance weaver and textile designer, since 1974; *b* Norwich, 31 Aug. 1945; *d* of late Stephen Restieaux and Catherine Restieaux (*née* Freeman); *m* 2003, Robin White; one *d*. *Educ:* Cambridge Coll. of Art and Technol. (BA 1967); Hammersmith Coll. of Art, London (Cert. Textiles 1972); Royal Coll. of Art (MA Textiles 1974). Established studio, 1974; Textile Res. Fellow, RCA, 1974–80; Index of Selected Makers, Crafts Council, 1979; Mem., First Eleven Studio, textile design, 1991–. Vis. Lectr, Chelsea Coll. of Art and Design, Goldsmiths' Coll., Central St Martins Coll. of Art and Design, Surrey (formerly West Surrey) Coll. of Art and Design, Camberwell Coll. of Art, 1976–98; study days in own studio for students from RCA, Chelsea Coll. of Art and Design, Central St Martins Coll. of Art and Design, and Middlesex Univ. (formerly Middlesex Poly.), 1988–. Work in public collections including: V&A; British Acad.; Govt Art Collection; Craft Study Centre, Farnham; Crafts Council; Nat. Mus. of Mod. Art, Kyoto. Hon. FRCA 2005. Gold Medal, Gestaltendes Handwerk, Munich, 1993; Traditional Technique Prize, 4th Internat. Textile Competition, Kyoto, 1994; Silver Medal, Weavers' Co., 2009. *Address:* 19 Rollscourt Avenue, SE24 0EA. *T:* (020) 7733 3637.

RESTREPO-LONDOÑO, Andrés; Order of Boyacá, Colombia; private financial consultant, since 1993; President, Empresa Colombiana de Petróleos-ECOPETROL, 1988–92; *b* 20 Jan. 1942; *m* 1968, Ghislaine Ibiza; one *s* three *d*. *Educ:* Universidad de Antioquia; Université de Paris (postgraduate courses, 1966). Professor and Head of Economic Dept, Univ. de Antioquia, 1967–68; Gen. Man., La Primavera chain of stores, 1969–76; Finance Man., Empresas Públicas de Medellín, 1976–79; Gen. Man., Carbones de Colombia (Colombian Coal Bd), 1979–80; Minister for Economic Develt, 1980–81; Ambassador to UK, 1981–82. Chm., Proban SA (Banana Exporting Co.), 1983–84; Pres., Industrias e Inversiones Samper SA (Cement Co.), 1985–88. Order Sol of Perú; Order Cruzeiro do Sul, Brazil. *Publications:* Carbones Térmicos en Colombia, Bases para una Política Contractual, 1981; several articles in El Colombiano, daily newspaper of Medellín, Colombia. *Recreations:* fishing, tennis. *Address:* Calle 136A No. 73–17, Bogotá, Colombia; (office) Calle 93B No. 12–30 Of. 305, Bogotá, Colombia. *T:* (1) 6217905, 6217954. *Club:* Lagartos (Bogotá).

REUBEN, David; Joint Chief Executive Officer, Reuben Brothers SA, since 1988; Trustee, Reuben Brothers Foundation, since 2002; *b* 14 Sept. 1938; *s* of David Sassoon Reuben and Nancy Reuben; *m* 1976, Debra; two *s* one *d*. *Educ:* Sir Jacob Sassoon High Sch.; Sir John Cass Coll., London (non-degree course Metallurgy). Mountstar Metals, 1958–74, Dir, until 1972; Dir, Metal Traders Gp, 1974–77; Chm., Trans World Metals Gp, 1977–2000. *Recreations:* painting, writing, golf, other sports. *Clubs:* Hurlingham; Wentworth, Coombe Hill Golf.

REUBEN, Simon David; Director, Reuben Brothers Ltd, since 1988; Trustee, Reuben Foundation, since 2002; *s* of David Sassoon Reuben and Nancy Reuben; *m* 1973, Joyce Nounou; one *d*. *Educ:* Sir Jacob Sassoon High Sch.; Sir John Cass Coll., London (degree not completed). Principal and Managing Director: J. Holdsworth & Co. Ltd, 1966–77; Devereux Gp of Cos, 1970–77; Dir and Jt Principal, Trans World Metals Gp, 1977–2000. *Recreations:* film, history, politics, avoiding cocktail parties. *E:* sreuben@libello.com. *Clubs:* Hurlingham; Yacht Club de Monaco; Monte-Carlo Tennis; Automobile Club de Monaco.

REUPKE, Michael; journalist, 1962–89; *b* Potsdam, Germany, 20 Nov. 1936; *s* of Dr Willm Reupke and Dr Frances G. Reupke (*née* Kinnear); *m* 1963, (Helen) Elizabeth Restrick; one *s* two *d*. *Educ:* Latymer Upper Sch., London; Jesus Coll., Cambridge (MA Mod. Langs); Collège d'Europe, Bruges. Pilot Officer, RAF, 1957–58. Joined Reuters, 1962; reporter, France, Switzerland, Guinea and West Germany, 1962–69; Asst European Manager, Gen. News Div., 1970–72; Chief Rep., West Germany, 1973–74; Manager, Latin America and the Caribbean, 1975–77; Editor-in-Chief, 1978–89; Gen. Manager, 1989. Director: Visnews, 1985–89; Compex (formerly Company Information Exchange), 1992–2009. Mem. Bd, Radio Authy, 1994–99. Member: IPI, 1978–97; Internat. Inst. of Communications, 1987–2003. Trustee, Reuter Foundn, 1982–89. Founder Chm., Michael Reupke Foundn, 2015–. Volunteer in post-stroke rehabilitation res., Oxford Univ., 2009–; Founder Mem., Stroke Survivors' Club, Chinnor, 2009–. *Recreations:* travel, cooking, wine (dégustateur officiel, concours des grands vins de France, 1997–2013). *Address:* 27A Upper High Street, Thame, Oxon OX9 3EX; 60 rue St Georges, 75009 Paris, France. *Clubs:* Royal Automobile; Leander (Henley-on-Thames).

REUTER, Edzard; Chairman, Board of Management, Daimler-Benz, 1987–95. *Educ:* Univs of Berlin and Göttingen (maths and physics); Free Univ. of Berlin (law). Research Asst, Free Univ. of Berlin Law Faculty, 1954–56; Universum Film, 1957–62; Manager, TV prod. section, Bertelsmann Group, Munich, 1962–64; Daimler-Benz: exec., finance dept, 1964; responsible for management planning and organization, 1971; Dep. Mem., Bd, 1973; Full Mem., Exec. Bd, 1976. Mem., Bd of Trustees, Ernst Reuter Foundn, Berlin, 1988–; Chm., Bd of Trustees, Helga and Edzard Foundn, Stuttgart, 1998–. Hon. Citizen, Berlin, 1998. *Publications:* Vom Geist der Wirtschaft, 1986; Horizonte der Wirtschaft, 1993; Schein und Wirklichkeit, 1998; Der schmale Grat des Lebens, 2007; Die Stunde der Heuchler, 2010. *Address:* Taldorfer Strasse 14A, 70599 Stuttgart, Germany.

REVELL, Surg. Vice-Adm. Anthony Leslie, CB 1997; FRCA; Surgeon General, Ministry of Defence, 1994–97; *b* 26 April 1935; *s* of Leslie Frederick Revell and Florence Mabel (*née* Styles). *Educ:* King's Coll. Sch., Wimbledon; Ashford and Eastbourne Grammar Schs; Univ. of Birmingham Med. Sch. (MB, ChB); DA 1968. FRCA (FFARCS 1969). Joined RN, 1960; HMS Troubridge, 1960–62; HMS Dampier, 1962; HMS Loch Fada and 5th Frigate Sqdn, 1963; Anæsthetist, RN Hosp., Plymouth, 1964–65; HMS Eagle, 1965–67; Clin. Assistant, Radcliffe Infirmary, Oxford, Alder Hey Children's Hosp., Liverpool, and various courses, 1967–69; Anæsthetist, RN Hosp., Plymouth, 1969–70; RAF Hosps Nocton Hall and Akrotiri, Cyprus, 1970–72; ANZUK Mil. Hosp., Singapore, 1972–74; Cons. Anæsthetist, RN Hosp., Haslar, 1974–79; *ndc*, Latimer, 1979–80; Recruiter, MoD, 1980; Dir of Studies, Inst. of Naval Medicine, 1980–82; on staff, Surg. Rear-Adm. (Naval Hosps), 1982–84; Dir, Med. Personnel, 1984–86; RCDS, 1986; MO i/c, RN Hosp., Plymouth, 1987–88; on staff, C-in-C Fleet, 1988–90; Dir, Clinical Services, Defence Med. Directorate, 1990–91; Surg. Rear-Adm., Operational Med. Services, 1991–92; CSO (Med. and Dental) to C-in-C Fleet, 1992–93; Med. Dir Gen. (Navy), 1993–94; QHS, 1989–97. Member Council: Epsom Coll., 1997–2010; Royal Med. Foundn, 1997– (Vice Chm., 1999–2006; Chm., 2006–09); Pilgrims Sch., Winchester, 1997–2010; Winchester Cathedral, 2010–. Trustee, John Ellerman Foundn, 1997–2009. Chairman: Winchester Fest., 2007–; Hampshire Singing Competition, 2000–13. FRSocMed 1970. Hon. MD Birmingham, 1996. CStJ 1993. *Publications:* Haslar: the Royal Hospital, 1979; (ed jtly) Proc. World Assoc. Anæsthetists, 1970. *Recreation:* choral music. *Address:* Willow Cottage, Domum Road, Winchester, Hants SO23 9NN.

REVELSTOKE, 7th Baron *cr* 1885, of Membland, Devon; **Alexander Rupert Baring;** *b* 9 April 1970; *er s* of 6th Baron Revelstoke and Aneta (*née* Fisher); *S* father, 2012. *Heir:* *b* Hon. Thomas James Baring, *b* 4 Dec. 1971. *Address:* Lambay, Rush, Co. Dublin, Eire.

REW, Paul Francis, FCA; Partner, PricewaterhouseCoopers (formerly Price Waterhouse), 1987–2010; non-executive Director, Northumbrian Water Group plc, since 2010; *b* 1953; *s* of late Lt Col Peter Rew and of Diana Edith Rew; *m* 1982, Mary Ellen Pleasant; two *d*. *Educ:* Churcher's Coll., Petersfield; Exeter Univ. (BSc Engrg Sci.). ACA 1977; FCA 1983. Price Waterhouse: articled, London, 1974; Johannesburg office, 1982–84; Partner, 1987; UK Energy and Utilities leader, 2001–07; on secondment to DTI as Under Sec. and Dir, Industrial Develt Unit, 1992–94. Non-executive Director: Met Office, 2010–; Sustainable Develt Commn, 2010–11; DEFRA, 2011–; Care Quality Commn, 2014–. Mem., Steering Bd, Insolvency Service, 1992–94. Member: Bd of Mgt, St Bartholomew's and Queen Alexandra's Coll. of Nursing and Midwifery, 1990–95; Adv. Bd, Univ. of Exeter Business Sch., 2010–.

REY, Prof. Hélène, PhD; FBA 2011; Professor of Economics, London Business School, since 2007; *b* Brioude, France, 13 March 1970; *d* of Denis and Andrée Rey; *m* 2006, Prof. Richard David Portes, *qv*; one *d*. *Educ:* Ecole Nationale de la Statistique et de l'Administration Economique; Stanford Univ. (MSc 1994); Ecole des Hautes Etudes en Sciences Sociales (PhD 1998); London Sch. of Econs and Pol Sci. (PhD 1998). London School of Economics and Political Science: Lectr, 1997–2000; Asst Prof., 2000–06; Prof. of Econs and Internat. Affairs, Econs Dept, Woodrow Wilson Sch., Princeton Univ., 2006–07. Alfred P. Sloan Fellow, 2005–07. Member: Bd, Autorité de Contrôle Prudentiel, France, 2010– (Founding Chair, Scientific Cttee); Conseil d'Analyse Economique, France, 2010–. Bernácer Prize, 2006. *Publications:* Reforming the International Monetary System, 2011; contribs to Political Econ., Amer. Econ. Rev., Qly Jl Econs, Rev. of Econ. Studies. *Address:* London Business School, Regent's Park, NW1 4SA. *T:* 07966 908412, *Fax:* (020) 7000 7001. *E:* hrey@london.edu.

REYNOLD, Frederic; QC 1982; *b* 7 Jan. 1936; *s* of late Henry and Regina Reynold. *Educ:* Battersea Grammar School; Magdalen College, Oxford. BA Hons Jurisprudence. Called to the Bar, Gray's Inn, 1960, Bencher, 1991; commenced practice, 1963. *Publications:* The Judge as Lawmaker, 1967; Disagreement and Dissent in Judicial Decision-Making, 2013. *Recreations:* too numerous to specify. *Address:* 5 Hillcrest, 51 Ladbroke Grove, W11 3AX. *T:* (020) 7229 3848.

REYNOLDS, Christopher Douglas; Chief Executive Officer, Games Marketing Ltd, since 2004; *b* 24 March 1957; *s* of Geoffrey Butler and Margaret Williams (*née* Reynolds); *m* 1993, Deborah Pegden; one *s* one *d*. *Educ:* Ellesmere Coll.; St John's Coll., Durham Univ. (BA 1978). Mktg trainee, Grants of St James's, 1978–80; Product Manager, Eden Vale, 1980–82; various mktg roles, incl. Mktg and Sales Dir, Europe, Dunlop Slazenger Internat. Ltd, 1982–90; Vice-Pres., Apparel, Internat. Div., Reebok Internat. Ltd, 1990–93; Brand Dir, Pringle of Scotland, 1994–95; Vice-Pres., Mktg, Sara Lee Champion Europe, Florence, 1995–97; Founder Partner, Pegden Reynolds Consultancy, 1997–2000; Man. Dir, British Horseracing Bd, 2000–02. Non-executive Chairman: iKnowledge Ltd, 2002–06; Sound Decisions Ltd, 2007–12 (non-exec. Dir, 2002–07). MInstD 2000. *Recreations:* golf, tennis, squash, lapsed Rugby/cricket - too slow/old, family, wines - passionate collector/imbiber. *T:* (01483) 417679. *Clubs:* MCC; Hankley Common Golf (Tilford, Surrey); Guildford and Godalming Rugby.

REYNOLDS, Prof. David, CBE 2002; Professor of Educational Effectiveness, University of Southampton, since 2011; *b* 3 May 1949; *s* of Colin Reynolds and Joyce Reynolds (*née* Jones); *m* 1994, Meriel Jones; two step *s*. *Educ:* Norwich Sch.; Univ. of Essex. Mem., Scientific Staff, MRC, 1971–75; Lectr in Social Admin, UC Cardiff, 1976–82; Lectr, then Sen. Lectr in Educn, UC Cardiff, subseq. UWCC, 1983–93; Professor: of Educn, Univ. of Newcastle upon Tyne, 1993–99; of Sch. Effectiveness and Sch. Improvement, Loughborough Univ., 1999–2000; of Leadership and Sch. Effectiveness, Univ. of Exeter, 2000–05; of Educn, Univ. of Plymouth, 2005–11. Guest Prof., Univ. of Shenyang, China, 2005–; Visiting Professor: Univ. of Southampton, 2007–10; Univ. of Balearic Isles, 2008–. Mem., Literacy Task Force,

1996–97; Chm., Numeracy Task Force, 1997–98; Department for Education and Employment, subseq. Department for Education and Skills: Member: Literacy and Numeracy Strategy Gp, 1998–2001; Value Added Adv. Gp, 2003–05; Adviser: Teachers' Gp, 1999–2000; Standards and Effectiveness Unit, 2001–01; City Acad. Support Service, 2002–03; Innovation Unit, 2003–06; Sen. Educnl Policy Advr, Dept for Educn and Skills, Welsh Govt, 2011–13. Member Board: British Educnl Communications and Technol. Agency, 1999–2003; TDA (formerly TTA), 2000–06; Educnl Broadcasting Council for Wales, 2005–07. Consultant, Tribal Educn, 2003–10. Non-exec. Dir, Goal plc, 2000–02. Trustee/Dir, E-ACT Academies, 2009–13. Gov., Clifton Coll., 2003–; Chm., The Innovation Trust (Monkseaton Community High Sch.), 2007–13. FRSA 1996. Co-Ed., School Effectiveness and Improvement: an internat. jl of res., policy and practice, 1991–2005. *Publications:* jointly: (ed) Studying School Effectiveness, 1985; The Comprehensive Experiment, 1987; Education Policies: controversies and critiques, 1989; (ed) School Effectiveness and School Improvement, 1989; International School Effects Research, 1992; (ed) School Effectiveness, 1992; Advances in School Effectiveness Research, 1994; (ed) Merging Traditions, 1996; Making Good Schools, 1996; (ed) Dilemmas of Decentralisation, 1996; Worlds Apart?, 1996; Improving Schools: performance and potential, 1999; The International Handbook of School Effectiveness Research, 2000; World Class Schools, 2002; Effective Teaching, 2001, 3rd edn as Effective Teaching: evidence practice, 2010; Failure Free Education? The Past, Present and Future of School Effectiveness and Improvement, 2010; School Effectiveness and Improvement: research, policy and practice, 2012; contrib. articles to acad. jls, professional jls and popular media. *Recreations:* walking, wine, travelling, opera. *Address:* Tondrugwaer Farm, Cross Inn, Llantrisant CF72 8NZ. *T:* (01443) 223417. *E:* d.reynolds@southampton.ac.uk, david@davidreynoldsconsulting.com.

REYNOLDS, Prof. David James, PhD; FBA 2005; Professor of International History, University of Cambridge, since 2002; Fellow of Christ's College, Cambridge, since 1983; *b* 17 Feb. 1952; *s* of late Leslie Reynolds and Marian Reynolds (*née* Kay); *m* 1977, Margaret Philpott Ray; one *s*. *Educ:* Dulwich Coll.; Gonville and Caius Coll., Cambridge (BA, MA, PhD 1980). Choate Fellow, 1973–74, Warren Fellow, 1980–81, Harvard Univ.; Res. Fellow, Gonville and Caius Coll., Cambridge, 1978–80, 1981–83; University of Cambridge: Asst Lectr in History, 1984–88; Lectr, 1988–97; Reader in Internat. History, 1997–2002; Chm., History Faculty, 2013–15. Writer and presenter, BBC TV: Churchill's Forgotten Years, 2005; The Improbable Mr Attlee, 2005; Summits (3-part series), 2008; Armistice, 2008; Nixon in the Den, 2010; World War Two: 1941 and the Man of Steel, 2011; World War Two: 1942 and Hitler's soft underbelly, 2012; Long Shadow (3-part series), 2014; World War Two: 1945 and the Wheelchair President, 2015; America, Empire of Liberty (90-part series), BBC Radio 4, 2008–09 (Voice of the Listener and Viewer Award for Best New Radio Prog., 2008). *Publications:* The Creation of the Anglo-American Alliance, 1937–41, 1981 (Bernath Prize, Soc. for Historians of Amer. For. Relns, 1982); (jtly) An Ocean Apart: the relationship between Britain and America in the 20th century, 1988; Britannia Overruled: British policy and world power in the 20th century, 1991; (ed jtly) Allies at War: the Soviet, American, and British experience 1939–45, 1994; (ed) The Origins of the Cold War in Europe, 1994; Rich Relations: the American occupation of Britain 1942–45, 1995 (Soc. for Mil. Hist. Distinguished Book Award, 1996); One World Divisible: a global history since 1945, 2000; From Munich to Pearl Harbor: Roosevelt's America and the origins of the Second World War, 2001; In Command of History: Churchill fighting and writing the Second World War, 2004 (Wolfson Hist. Prize, 2005); From World War to Cold War: Churchill, Roosevelt and the international history of the 1940s, 2006; Summits: six meetings that shaped the twentieth century, 2007; (ed jtly) FDR's World: war, peace and legacies, 2008; America, Empire of Liberty: a new history, 2009; The Long Shadow: the Great War and the twentieth century, 2013 (Hessell-Tiltman Prize, English PEN, 2014). *Address:* Christ's College, Cambridge CB2 3BU. *T:* (01223) 334900.

REYNOLDS, Deborah, CB 2008; PhD; Chief Veterinary Officer and Director General, Animal Health and Welfare, Department for Environment, Food and Rural Affairs, 2004–07; Visiting Professor, Royal Veterinary College, since 2008; *b* 29 May 1952; *m*; one *s*. *Educ:* Univ. of Bristol (BVSc 1975); Univ. of Reading (PhD 1983). MRCVS. Vet. Res. Officer, Inst. of Animal Health; Vet. Investigation Service, State Vet. Service, MAFF, 1984–91; MAFF, 1991–94; Hd, Bacteriol. Dept, Vet. Labs Agency, 1994–97; Hd of Endemic Animal Diseases and Zoonoses, MAFF, 1997–2001; Veterinary Dir, Food Standards Agency, 2001–04. Member, Board: HPA, 2008–13; Berkshire West NHS PCT, 2008–11; Partner Gov., Royal Berks Hosp. Foundn Trust, 2009–11. Chm., Natural Envmt (formerly Nature Conservation) Panel, NT, 2009–. Affiliate Prof., Colorado State Univ., 2008–. *Address:* Brimstone Cottage, Upper Bucklebury, near Reading, Berks RG7 6QX. *T:* (01635) 860254, 07976 297190.

REYNOLDS, Prof. (Edward) Osmund (Royle), CBE 1995; MD; FRCP, FRCOG, FMedSci; FRS 1993; Professor of Neonatal Paediatrics, University College London (formerly University College Hospital) Medical School, 1976–96, now Emeritus Professor, University of London; *b* 3 Feb. 1933; *s* of Edward Royle Reynolds and Edna Reynolds; *m* 1956, Margaret Lindsay Ballard; two *s*. *Educ:* St Paul's Sch.; St Thomas' Hosp. Med. Sch. (Henry Myers Exhibn, 1958). BSc, MD London; DCH; FRCP 1975; FRCOG (*ad eundem*) 1983. Posts at St Thomas' Hosp., 1959–63; Research Fellow in Pediatrics: Harvard Med. Sch., 1963–64; Yale Med. Sch., 1964; Res. Asst, then Lectr and Sen. Lectr, UCH Med. Sch., 1964–76; Hd, Dept of Paediatrics, UCMSM, 1987–93. Consultant Paediatrician, UCH, 1969–94. Hon. Prof. of Paediatrics, Inst. of Child Health, 1994; William Julius Mickle fellow, Univ. of London, 1976–77. Numerous visiting professorships, incl. RSocMed Foundn Vis. Prof. to Amer. Acad. of Pediatrics, 1989. Specialist Advr (perinatal medicine), H of C Social Services and Health Select Cttees, 1978–92; Member: Scientific Adv. Panel, Foundn for Study of Infant Deaths, 1994–98; Bd of Management, Inst. of Child Health, 1990–96 (Hon. Fellow, 1996). President: BLISS (Baby Life Support Systems), 1982–97; Neonatal Soc., 1991–94. Trustee, Action Medical Research (formerly Action Research), 2002–04 (Mem., Scientific Adv. Cttee, 1981–87). Founding Scientific Patron, Liggins Inst., Univ. of Auckland, 2001. Foundn Fellow, UCL Hosps, 1999. Founder FMedSci 1998. Hon. FRCPCH 1997; Hon. FRSocMed 2000. Hon. Member: Argentine Paediatric Assoc.; Italian Soc. for Perinatal Medicine; British Assoc. of Perinatal Medicine, 1992 (Founder's Lectr, 1992). Lectures: Charles West, RCP, 1989; George Frederic Still Meml, BPA, 1995; Perinatal, Belfast, 1997. Dawson Williams Meml Prize, BMA, 1992; James Spence Medal, BPA, 1994; Maternité Prize, Eur. Assoc. of Perinatal Medicine, 1994; Harding Award, Action Research, 1995; Perinatal Pioneer Award, Amer. Acad. Pediatrics, 2008. *Publications:* chapters and papers on neonatal physiology and medicine. *Recreations:* travel, music, photography, sport (particularly fencing; mem., British foil team, 3rd in World Championship, Rome, 1955). *Address:* 72 Barrowgate Road, Chiswick, W4 4QU. *T:* (020) 8994 3326.

REYNOLDS, Emma; MP (Lab) Wolverhampton North East, since 2010; *b* Wolverhampton, 2 Nov. 1977. *Educ:* Wadham Coll., Oxford (BA PPE). Policy Researcher, Small Business Europe, Brussels, 2001–03; Pol Advr to Pres., Party of Eur. Socialists, 2004–06; Special Advr to Minister of State for Europe, FCO, 2006–07, to Parly Sec. to HM Treasury (Govt Chief Whip), 2007–08; Sen. Consultant, Cogitamus Ltd, 2009–10. Shadow Minister for Housing, 2013–15; Shadow Sec. of State for Communities and Local Govt, 2015. *Recreations:* running, swimming, cinema. *Address:* (office) 492A Stafford Street, Wolverhampton WV10 6AN. *E:* emma.reynolds.mp@parliament.uk.

REYNOLDS, Dame Fiona Claire, (Mrs R. W. T. Merrill), DBE 2008 (CBE 1998); Master, Emmanuel College, Cambridge, since 2013; *b* 29 March 1958; *d* of Jeffrey Alan Reynolds and Margaret Mary (*née* Watson); *m* 1981, Robert William Tinsley Merrill; three *d*. *Educ:* Rugby High Sch. for Girls; Newnham Coll., Cambridge (MA, MPhil 1980). Sec., Council for Nat. Parks, 1980–87; Asst Dir, 1987–91, Dir, 1992–98, CPRE; Dir, Women's Unit, Cabinet Office, 1998–2000; Dir-Gen., Nat. Trust, 2001–12. Non-exec. Dir, Wessex Water Services, 2012–; Sen. non-exec. Dir, BBC, 2012–. Hon. FBA 2012. Global 500 Award, UN Envmt Programme, 1990. *Recreations:* hillwalking, classical music and opera, reading. *Address:* Master's Lodge, Emmanuel College, Cambridge CB2 3AP.

REYNOLDS, Prof. Francis Martin Baillie, DCL; FBA 1988; Professor of Law, University of Oxford, 1992–2000, now Emeritus; Fellow of Worcester College, Oxford, 1960–2000, now Emeritus; *b* 11 Nov. 1932; *s* of Eustace Baillie Reynolds and Emma Margaret Hanby Reynolds (*née* Holmes); *m* 1965, Susan Claire Shillito; two *s* one *d*. *Educ:* Winchester Coll.; Worcester Coll., Oxford (BA 1956; BCL 1957; MA 1960; DCL 1986). Bigelow Teaching Fellow, Univ. of Chicago, 1957–58. Called to the Bar, Inner Temple, 1961, Hon. Bencher 1979. Reader in Law, Oxford Univ., 1977–92. Visiting Professor, Nat. Univ. of Singapore, UCL, Univ. of Melbourne, Monash Univ., Otago Univ., Univ. of Sydney, Univ. of Auckland, Univ. of Hong Kong, Singapore Mgt Univ.; Hon. Prof. of Internat. Maritime Law, Internat. Maritime Law Inst., Malta. Hon. QC 1993. Gen. Editor, Lloyd's Maritime and Commercial Law Qly, 1983–87; Editor, Law Qly Review, 1987–2014. *Publications:* (ed jtly) Chitty on Contracts, 24th edn 1977 to 31st edn 2012; (ed jtly) Benjamin's Sale of Goods, 1st edn 1974, to 9th edn 2014; Bowstead on Agency, (ed jtly) 13th edn 1968 to 18th edn as Bowstead and Reynolds on Agency 2006, (contrib.) 19th edn 2010 to 20th edn 2014; (ed jtly) English Private Law, 2000, 2nd edn 2008; (with Sir Guenter Treitel) Carver on Bills of Lading, 2001, 3rd edn 2011; published lectures and contribs to legal jls. *Recreations:* music, walking. *Address:* 61 Charlbury Road, Oxford OX2 6UX. *T:* (01865) 559323.

REYNOLDS, Gillian, MBE 1999; Radio Critic, The Daily Telegraph, since 1975; *b* 15 Nov. 1935; *d* of Charles Morton and Ada (*née* Kelly); *m* 1958, Stanley Reynolds (marr. diss. 1982); three *s*. *Educ:* St Anne's Coll., Oxford (MA; Hon. Fellow, 1996); Mount Holyoke Coll., South Hadley, Mass, USA. TV journalist, 1964–; Radio Critic, The Guardian, 1967–74; Programme Controller, Radio City, Liverpool, 1974–75. Vis. Fellow, Bournemouth Univ. Media Sch., 2002. Trustee: Nat. Museums Liverpool (formerly Nat. Museums and Galls on Merseyside), 2001–08; Nat. Media Mus., 2009–. Chm., Charles Parker Archive Trust, 1986–2009. Fellow (first to be apptd), Radio Acad., 1990; FRTS 1996. Hon. Fellow, Liverpool John Moores Univ., 2004. Hon. DLit Lancaster, 2012. Media Soc. Award for distinguished contrib. to journalism, 1999. *Recreation:* listening to the radio. *Address:* Flat 3, 1 Linden Gardens, W2 4HA. *T:* (020) 7229 1893.

REYNOLDS, Guy Edwin K.; *see* King-Reynolds.

REYNOLDS, James Edward; BBC News Correspondent, since 1998; *b* 20 May 1974; *s* of Paul and Louise Reynolds. *Educ:* Westminster Sch.; Christ's Coll., Cambridge (BA Hons Modern Langs 1996). Joined BBC, 1997; S America corresp., 1998–2001; Middle East corresp., 2001–06; China corresp., 2006–09; Iranian affairs corresp., 2010–12; Istanbul corresp., 2012–14; Rome corresp., 2014–. Nieman Fellow, Harvard Univ., 2009–10. *Recreations:* studying the effects of galactic trash, floating in the Dead Sea. *Address:* c/o BBC Broadcasting House, Portland Place, W1A 1AA. *T:* (020) 7743 8000. *E:* james.reynolds@bbc.co.uk. *Club:* Frontline.

REYNOLDS, Sir James Francis, 4th Bt *cr* 1923, of Woolton, co. Lancaster; music producer and mix engineer; *b* 10 July 1971; *s* of Sir David James Reynolds, 3rd Bt and of Charlotte Reynolds (*née* Baumgartner); *S* father, 2015, but his name does not appear on the Official Roll of the Baronetage; *m* 2004, Camilla Anne Stewart; one *s* one *d*. *Educ:* Worth Abbey. *Recreation:* sport. *Heir:* *s* Frederik James Reynolds, *b* 9 Sept. 2005.

REYNOLDS, (James) Kirk; QC 1993; *b* 24 March 1951; *s* of late James Reynolds, sometime Judge of the High Ct, Eastern Reg. of Nigeria, and of Alexandra Mary (*née* Strain); civil partnership 2007, Holger Andreas Baehr. *Educ:* Campbell Coll., Belfast; Peterhouse, Cambridge (MA). Called to the Bar, Middle Temple, 1974; Bencher, 2000. FCIArb 2014. Hon. Mem., RICS, 1997. Hon. LLD Bedfordshire, 2009. *Publications:* The Handbook of Rent Review, 1981 (Australian edn 2009); The Renewal of Business Tenancies, 1985, 4th edn 2012; Dilapidations: the modern law and practice, 1995, 5th edn 2013; Essentials of Rent Review, 1995. *Address:* Falcon Chambers, Falcon Court, EC4Y 1AA. *T:* (020) 7353 2484.

REYNOLDS, John; Director and Fellow, SAMI Consulting, St Andrews Management Institute, since 2006; *b* 14 Nov. 1950; *s* of Albert Victor Reynolds and Nina Eileen Reynolds (*née* Wolfenden); *m* 1973, Brenda O'Doherty; one *s* one *d*. *Educ:* HMS Worcester; UWIST (BSc Maritime Studies 1975). Navigating Officer, P&OSNCo., 1966–75; Res Scientist, Nat. Maritime Inst., 1975–84; Department of Trade and Industry, 1984–89: Shipbuilding Policy Div., 1984–87; Eur. Mgt of Technol. Prog., 1985–86; Tech. Asst to Chief Engr and Scientist, 1987–89; Head of Mobile Radio Licensing, Radiocommunications Agency, 1989–90; Dir of Resources, Lab. of Govt Chemist, 1991–96; Director: Radiocommunications Agency, 1996–98; Future and Innovation Unit, DTI, 1998–2001; Gp Dir, Strategy and Communications Gp, British Trade Internat., subseq. UK Trade and Investment, 2001–04; Dir, Capabilities Programme, DTI, 2005–06. *Recreations:* tennis, cycling, gardening. *Address:* SAMI Consulting, The Rectory, 1 Toomers' Wharf, Canal Walk, Newbury RG14 1DY.

REYNOLDS, John; Depute Provost, City of Aberdeen, since 2012 (Lord Provost and Lord-Lieutenant, 2003–07); *b* 5 April 1949; *s* of William and Anne Reynolds; *m* 1970, Helen Will; one *s* two *d*. *Educ:* Blackpool Grammar Sch. Posts in: entertainment ind. throughout UK, 1966–70; electrical retail trade, with Electric Rentals Gp/Granada, and John Reynolds news agency, 1970–96; self employed in travel business, Scottish Choice Itineraries, and news agency, 1996–. Member (Lib Dem): Aberdeen DC, 1986–96; Grampian Regl Council, 1994–96; Mem., Aberdeen CC, 1995– (Lib Dem, 1995–2012, Ind, 2012–) (Mem., Licensing Cttee, 1996–). Member: Grampian Jt Fire Bd; Aberdeen Licensing Bd. Comr, Northern Lighthouse Bd, 2003–07. Director: Aberdeen YMCA, 2007–; Aberdeen Seafarers Centre, 2011–; Aberdeen Exhibn and Conf. Centre, 2012–. President: Voluntary Service Aberdeen, 2003–07; Aberdeen Br., RNLI, 2003–07; Vice-Pres., Shipwrecked Fishermen and Mariners' Royal Benevolent Soc., 2003–07; Mem., Local Adv. Cttee, Royal Nat. Mission to Deep Sea Fishermen. Trustee, Nat. Liby of Scotland, 2003–07. Patron: Mental Health Aberdeen, 2003–07; Aberdeen Internat. Youth Fest., 2003–. Hon. Pres., Aberdeen Scout Council. JP Aberdeen, 2003–07 (Chm., JPs Adv. Cttee). OStJ 2005. *Recreations:* music, theatre, DIY, socialising. *Address:* Aberdeen City Council, Town House, Aberdeen AB10 1LP. *T:* (01224) 522637, *Fax:* (01224) 523747. *E:* jreynolds@aberdeencity.gov.uk.

REYNOLDS, Jonathan Neil; MP (Lab Co-op) Stalybridge and Hyde, since 2010; *b* 28 Aug. 1980; *s* of Keith and Judith Reynolds; *m* 2008, Claire Johnston; one *s* one *d*. *Educ:* Houghton Kepier Comprehensive Sch.; Sunderland City Coll.; Manchester Univ. (BA Politics and Modern Hist.); BPP Law Sch., Manchester. Political asst to James Purnell, MP; trainee solicitor, Addleshaw Goddard LLP, Manchester until 2010. Mem. (Lab Co-op) Tameside MBC, 2007–11. Mem., Select Cttee on Sci. and Technol., 2010–12; Sec., All Party Parly Gp on the Armed Forces, 2010–. *Address:* House of Commons, SW1A 0AA.

REYNOLDS, Joyce Maire, FBA 1982; Fellow of Newnham College, 1951–84, now Hon. Fellow, and Reader in Roman Historical Epigraphy, 1983–84, University of Cambridge; *b* 18 Dec. 1918; *d* of late William Howe Reynolds and Nellie Farmer Reynolds. *Educ:* Walthamstow County High Sch. for Girls; St Paul's Girls' Sch., Hammersmith; Somerville Coll., Oxford (Hon. Fellow, 1988). Temp. Civil Servant, BoT, 1941–46; Rome Scholar, British Sch. at Rome, 1946–48; Lectr in Ancient History, King's Coll., Newcastle upon Tyne, 1948–51; Cambridge University: Asst Lectr in Classics, 1952–57; Univ. Lectr 1957–83; Dir of Studies in Classics, 1951–79 and Lectr in Classics, 1951–84, Newnham Coll. Woolley Travelling Fellow, Somerville Coll., Oxford, 1961; Mem., Inst. for Advanced Study, Princeton, USA, 1984–85; Vis. Prof., Univ. of Calif at Berkeley, 1987. President: Soc. for Libyan Studies, 1981–86; Soc. for the Promotion of Roman Studies, 1986–89. Corresponding Member: German Archaeol Inst., 1971–; Austrian Archaeol Inst., 1991–. Hon. DLitt Newcastle upon Tyne, 1984. Gold Medal, Soc. of Antiquaries of London, 2004. *Publications:* (with J. B. Ward Perkins) The Inscriptions of Roman Tripolitania, 1952; Aphrodisias and Rome, 1982; (with R. Tannenbaum) Jews and Godfearers at Aphrodisias, 1987; (ed) Christian Monuments of Cyrenaica, 2003; articles on Roman history and epigraphy in jls, 1951–. *Recreation:* walking. *Address:* Newnham College, Cambridge CB3 9DF.

REYNOLDS, Kirk; *see* Reynolds, J. K.

REYNOLDS, His Honour Martin Paul; a Circuit Judge, 1995–2006; a Deputy Circuit Judge, 2006–11; *b* 25 Dec. 1936; *s* of Cedric Hinton Fleetwood Reynolds and Doris Margaret (*née* Bryan); *m* 1961, Gaynor Margaret Phillips; three *s*. *Educ:* University College Sch., Hampstead; St Edmund Hall, Oxford (MA). ACIArb 1982. Called to the Bar, Inner Temple, 1962. Mem., Parole Bd, 2006–Aug. 2016; Pres., later Tribunal Judge, Mental Health Rev. Tribunal (Restricted Cases), 1997–2011. Councillor, London Borough of Islington, 1968–71 and 1972–82. Contested (Lab) Harrow West, Oct. 1994. *Recreations:* navigating waterways in a Dutch barge, foreign travel, gastronomy, music, grandchildren. *Clubs:* Savage; Bar Yacht.

REYNOLDS, Dr Martin Richard Finch; Associate Director of Health Policy and Public Health, East Riding Health Authority, 1993–99; *b* 26 July 1943; 2nd *s* of Gerald Finch Reynolds and Frances Bertha (*née* Locke); *m* 1965, Shelagh (*née* Gray) (*d* 2010); two *d*. *Educ:* Newton Abbot Grammar Sch.; Univ. of Bristol. MB ChB, DPH; FFPHM; FRCP. House posts in medicine, surgery, infectious diseases and paediatrics, 1966–67; Dep. Med. Officer, Glos CC, 1967–70; Sen. Dep. Med. Officer, Bristol City and Asst Sen. Med. Officer, SW Regional Hosp. Bd, 1970–74; Dist Community Physician, Southmead Dist of Avon AHA (Teaching) and Med. Officer for Environmental Health, Northavon Dist Council, 1974–79; Area Med. Officer, Wilts AHA, 1979–80; Regional MO/Chief Med. Advr, South Western RHA, 1980–86; Specialist in Community Medicine, 1986–89, Consultant in Public Health Medicine, 1989–93, Hull HA. Registrar, FPHM, 1995–97. Voluntary work with Mission Assist (formerly Wycliffe Associates) for Bible trans., 1999–. *Publications:* contrib. various articles in professional jls on subjects in community medicine.

REYNOLDS, Maj.-Gen. Michael Frank, CB 1983; author (military history); *b* 3 June 1930; *s* of Frank Reynolds and Gwendolen Reynolds (*née* Griffiths); *m* 1955, Anne Bernice (*née* Truman); three *d*. *Educ:* Cranleigh; RMA Sandhurst (Infantry Prize). Commnd Queen's Royal Regt, 1950 (last Adjt, 1959); served Germany, Korea (severely wounded), Cyprus (EOKA emergency), Canada (exchange officer), Persian Gulf, Netherlands, Belgium; psc 1960; GSO 1 Ops, HQ AFCENT, 1970–71; CO 2 Queen's, BAOR and Ulster, 1971–73; GSO 1 Ops, N Ireland, 1973–74; Comdr 12 Mech. Bde, BAOR, 1974–76; RCDS, 1977; Dep. Adjt Gen., BAOR, 1978–80; Comdr, Allied Command Europe Mobile Force (Land), 1980–83; Asst Dir, IMS (Plans and Policy), HQ NATO, 1983–86. Col Comdt, The Queen's Division, 1984–86; (Last) Col, The Queen's Regt, 1989–92. Pres., E Anglian Aviation Soc., 1996–98. Comdr First Cl., Order of the Dannebrog (Denmark), 1990; Grand Cross, Order of Orange-Nassau (Netherlands), 1992. *Publications:* The Devil's Adjutant, 1995; Steel Inferno, 1997; Men of Steel, 1999; Sons of the Reich, 2002; Eagles and Bulldogs in Normandy 1944, 2003; Monty and Patton - Two Paths to Victory, 2005; Soldier at Heart - Private to General, 2012; Soldier at Heart: from Private to General, 2013. *Recreations:* military history (especially Normandy and Battle of the Ardennes, 1944), writing.

REYNOLDS, Osmund; *see* Reynolds, E. O. R.

REYNOLDS, Sir Peter (William John), Kt 1985; CBE 1975; Director, Cilva Holdings plc, 1989–96; *b* 10 Sept. 1929; *s* of Harry and Gladys Victoria Reynolds; *m* 1955, Barbara Anne, *d* of Vincent Kenneth Johnson, OBE; two *s* decd. *Educ:* Haileybury Coll., Herts. National Service, 2nd Lieut, RA, 1948–50. Unilever Ltd, 1950–70: Trainee Dir, Managing Dir, then Chm., Walls (Meat & Handy Foods) Ltd. Ranks Hovis McDougall: Asst Gp Managing Dir, 1971; Gp Man. Dir, 1972–81; Chm., 1981–89; Dep. Chm., 1989–93. Director: Guardian Royal Exchange Assurance plc, 1986–99; Boots Co. plc, 1986–2000; Avis Europe Ltd, 1988–2001; Pioneer International, until 1999; Nationwide Anglia Building Soc., 1990–92; Chm., Pioneer Concrete (Hldgs), 1990–99. Chairman: EDC Employment and Trng Cttee, 1982–87; Resources Cttee, Food and Drink Fedn (formerly Food and Drink Industries Council), 1983–86; Member: EDC for Food and Drink Manufg Industry, 1976–87; Consultative Bd for Resources Develt in Agriculture, 1982–84; Covent Garden Market Authority, 1989–97; Dir, Industrial Develt Bd for NI, 1982–89; Mem., Peacock Cttee on Financing the BBC, 1985–86. Dir, Freemantle Trust (formerly Bucks Comm. Housing Trust), 1992–2001. Gov., Berkhamsted Sch., 1985–2001; Life Gov., Haileybury, 1985. High Sheriff, Bucks, 1990–91. *Address:* Rignall Farm, Rignall Road, Great Missenden, Bucks HP16 9PE. *T:* (01240) 64714.

REYNOLDS, Dr Roy Gregory, CMG 2000; Chief Executive, Commonwealth Development Corporation, 1994–99; *b* 4 May 1939; *s* of Henry Herbert Reynolds and Alice Emily Reynolds; *m* 1963, Monica Cecelia; one *s* one *d*. *Educ:* George Dixon Grammar Sch., Birmingham; Birmingham Univ. (BSc Chem. Eng 1960); Imperial Coll., London (PhD 1964). Shell Internat. Petroleum Co., 1964–92. Dir, 1999–2009, Chm., 2003–09, J P Morgan Emerging Markets Investment Trust (formerly Fleming Emerging Markets Trust). Non-exec. Dir, LASMO plc, 1997–2001. *Recreations:* keeping fit, golf. *Club:* Royal Automobile.

REYNOLDS, Susan Mary Grace, FRHistS; FBA 1993; Senior Research Fellow, Institute of Historical Research, since 1993; Hon. Research Fellow, History Department of University College London, since 1987, and of Birkbeck College, since 1995; *b* 27 Jan. 1929; *d* of Hugh Reynolds and Maisie Reynolds (*née* Morten). *Educ:* The Study, Montreal; Howell's Sch., Denbigh; Lady Margaret Hall, Oxford (History Cl. II, MA); Dip. Archive Admin, UCL. FRHistS 1968. Archive Asst, 1951–52; Victoria County Histories, 1952–59; school teacher, 1959–64; Fellow and Tutor in Modern History, LMH, Oxford, 1964–86, Emeritus Fellow, 1986; Lectr in Modern History, Oxford Univ., 1965–86. Visiting Professor: Dartmouth Coll., USA, 1986–87; Central European Univ., Budapest, 1994. *Publications:* (ed) Register of Roger Martival, Bishop of Salisbury, vol. 3, 1965; Introduction to the History of English Medieval Towns, 1977; Kingdoms and Communities in Western Europe 900–1300, 1984, 2nd edn 1997; Fiefs and Vassals, 1994; Ideas and Solidarities of the Medieval Laity, 1995; Before Eminent Domain: toward a history of expropriation for the common good, 2010; The Middle Ages without Feudalism, 2012; articles in historical jls. *Address:* 19 Ridgmount Gardens, WC1E 7AR. *T:* (020) 7636 9043.

REYNOLDS, Prof. Vernon, PhD; Professor of Biological Anthropology, University of Oxford, 1996–2001, now Professor Emeritus; Fellow, Magdalen College, Oxford, 1987–2001, now Fellow Emeritus; Emeritus Fellow, School of Anthropology, University of Oxford, since 2008; *b* 14 Dec. 1935; *s* of Heinz Emil Max Rheinhold and Eva Marianne Rheinhold (*née* Rudenberg); name changed to Reynolds, 1949; *m* 1960, Frances Glover; one *s* one *d*. *Educ:* Collyer's Sch.; University Coll. London (BA Hons; PhD 1962). Univ. of London Travelling Schol. to study wild chimpanzees in Uganda, 1962; Lecturer: in Anthropol., Bristol Univ., 1966–72; in Biol Anthropol., Oxford Univ., 1972–96. Hon. Sen. Res. Fellow, Univ. of Sussex, 2002–. Founder and Hd, Budongo Forest Project, Uganda, 1990–. President's Award, Amer. Soc. Primatologists, 2000; Chm.'s Award, Cttee for Res. and Exploration, Nat. Geographic Soc., 2000. *Publications:* Budongo: a forest and its chimpanzees, 1965; The Apes, 1967; The Biology of Human Action, 1976, 2nd edn 1980; (jtly) Primate Social Behaviour, 1993; (jtly) The Biology of Religion, 1983, 2nd edn 1994; The Chimpanzees of the Budongo Forest, 2005; edited jointly: Human Behaviour and Adaptation, 1978; The Meaning of Primate Signals, 1984; The Sociobiology of Ethnocentrism, 1987; Fertility and Resources, 1990; Mating and Marriage, 1991; The Aquatic Ape: fact or fiction?, 1991; Human Populations: diversity and adaptation, 1995; Survival and Religion, 1995; contributed chapters; contrib. scientific jls. *Recreations:* dinghy sailing, bee-keeping. *Address:* Orchard House, West Street, Alfriston, E Sussex BN26 5UX. *T:* (01323) 871136. *E:* vreynolds@btopenworld.com.

REYNTIENS, Nicholas Patrick, OBE 1976; Head of Fine Art, Central School of Art and Design, London, 1976–86; *b* 11 Dec. 1925; *s* of Nicholas Serge Reyntiens, OBE, and Janet MacRae; *m* 1953, Anne Bruce (*d* 2006); two *s* two *d*. *Educ:* Ampleforth; Edinburgh Coll. of Art (DA). Served Scots Guards, 1943–47. St Marylebone Sch. of Art, 1947–50; Edinburgh Coll. of Art, 1950–51. Founder (with wife, Anne Bruce, the painter), Reyntiens Trust, which ran art sch., Burleighfield, where pupils from UK, Ireland, France, Germany, Japan, Canada, Australia, New Zealand, US and Iceland learned art of stained glass, and which had facilities for tapestry design and teaching, a printing house for editioning in lithography, etching and silkscreen, as well as workshops for stained glass, ceramics, drawing and painting. Has lectured in USA, Spain, Mexico, France and Switzerland; British Council lectr, India, 1995–96; occasional Vis. Prof., Pilchuck Sch. of Glass, Washington State, USA. Many commissions, including glass for Liverpool RC Metropolitan Cathedral; for 35 years interpreted painters' designs into stained glass, as well as own commissions for stained glass, 1953–, including baptistery window, Coventry Cathedral, Eton Coll. Chapel, Churchill Coll., Cambridge, Robinson Coll., Cambridge, St Margaret's Westminster (all with John Piper), Derby Cathedral and Liverpool Metropolitan Cathedral Blessed Sacrament Chapel (with Ceri Richards), All Saints Basingstoke (with Cecil Collins); completed glazing of Christ Church Hall, Oxford, 1980–84; designed and painted Great West Window, Southwell Minster, Notts, 1995; commnd with son, John, to design and paint Lady Chapel, and entire south transept, Ampleforth Abbey, 2002; collaboration with G. Jones, designed and painted eight windows, Church of St Martin, Cochem, Germany, 2009. Retrospective exhibn of autonomous panels, Ontario, 1990. Member: Court, RCA; Adv. Cttee in Decoration, Brompton Oratory; Adv. Cttee in Decoration, Westminster Cathedral; Adv. Cttee, Westminster Abbey, 1981–95. Art Critic, Catholic Herald; art correspondent, The Oldie. *Publications:* Technique of Stained Glass, 1967, 2nd edn 1977; The Beauty of Stained Glass, 1990; has written for architectural, art, literary and political magazines and on cooking for Harpers & Queen. *Address:* Winterbourne Lodge, Ilford Bridges Farm, close Stocklinch, Ilminster, Som TA19 9HZ. *T:* (01460) 52241.

RHIND, Prof. David William, CBE 2001; FRS 2002; Vice-Chancellor and Principal, City University, 1998–2007; Member of Court, Bank of England, 2006–09; *b* 29 Nov. 1943; *s* of late William Rhind and Christina Rhind; *m* 1966, Christine Young; one *s* two *d*. *Educ:* Berwick Grammar School; Bristol Univ. (BSc); Edinburgh Univ. (PhD); London Univ. (DSc). FRGS; FRICS 1991; FSS 2004. Research Fellow, Royal College of Art, 1969–73; Lectr then Reader, Univ. of Durham, 1973–81; Birkbeck College, London University: Prof. of Geography, 1982–91; Dean, Faculty of Economics, 1984–86; Governor, 1986–90; Hon. Fellow, 2000; Dir Gen. and Chief Exec., Ordnance Survey, 1992–98. Visiting Fellow: Internat. Trng Centre, Netherlands, 1975; ANU, 1979. Vice-Pres., Internat. Cartographic Assoc., 1984–91; Mem., Govt Cttee on Enquiry into handling of geographic inf., 1985–87; Advisor, H of L Select Cttee on Sci. and Tech., 1983–84; Mem., ESRC, 1996–2000. Chm., Portsmouth Hosps NHS Trust, 2009–12. Chairman: Bloomsbury Computing Consortium Mgt Cttee, 1988–91; Royal Soc. Ordnance Survey Scientific Cttee, 1989–91; Commn on Social Scis, Acad. of Learned Socs for Social Scis, 2000–03; Statistics Commn, 2003–08 (Mem., 2000–03); Higher Educn Staff Develt Agency, 2001–04; Islington Improvement Bd, 2003–04; Socio-Econ. Cttee, Nuclear Decommng Authy, 2006–08; Adv. Panel on Public Sector Inf., 2008–15; Governing Bd, Cohort and Longitudinal Studies Enhancement Resources, ESRC, 2013–; Member: UK Statistics Authy, 2008– (Dep. Chm., 2012–15); Royal Soc. Section 10 Cttee, 2010–12; Public Sector Transparency Bd, 2013–. President: Remote Sensing and Photogrammetric Soc., 2003–09; British Exploring (formerly British Schs Exploring) Soc., 2010– (Vice-Pres., 2007–10). Trustee, Nuffield Foundn, 2008– (Chm., 2010–); Chm., Bank of England Pension Trustees, 2009–12. Governor: City of London Girls' Sch., 1999–2001; Ashridge Mgt Coll., 2000–04; NIESR, 2004–. Mem. Council, 2003–04, Mem. F and GP Cttee, 2003–08, Royal Soc.; Hon. Sec., RGS, 1988–91. CCMI (CIMgt 1998). Hon. FBA 2002; Hon. FCII 2004. Hon. Fellow, QMUL, 2007. Hon. DSc: Bristol, 1993; Loughborough, 1996; Southampton, 1998; Kingston, 1999; Durham, 2001; London Metropolitan, 2003; Royal Holloway, London, 2004; St Petersburg State Poly., 2007; Edinburgh, 2009; City Univ. London, 2011; Aberdeen, 2015. Centenary Medal, RSGS, 1992; Patron's Medal, RGS, 1997; Decade Award for Achievement, Assoc. for Geographic Inf., 1997. *Publications:* (jtly) Land Use, 1980; The Census User's Handbook, 1983; (jtly) Atlas of EEC Affairs, 1984; (jtly) Geographical Information Systems, 1991, revised 1999; (jtly) Postcodes: the new geography, 1992; Framework for the World, 1997; (jtly) Geographical Information Systems and Science, 2001, 4th edn 2015; numerous papers on map-making, geographical information systems and information policy. *Recreations:* travelling, mowing the lawn, coping with grandchildren. *Address:* 1 Cold Harbour Close, Wickham, Hants PO17 5PT.

RHODES, Prof. Daniela, PhD; FRS 2007; Professor, School of Biological Sciences, Nanyang Technological University, Singapore, since 2011. *Educ:* Tekniska Hogskolan, Orebro (Dip. Chem. Engrg 1969); Univ. of Cambridge (PhD 1982). MRC Laboratory of Molecular Biology: Gp Leader, 1983–94; Sen. Scientist, 1994–2011; Dir of Studies, 2003–06; Fellow, Clare Hall, Cambridge, 1992. Former Visiting Professor: La Sapienza, Rome; Rockefeller Univ., NY. Mem., EMBO, 1996 (Mem., 2007–12, Chm., 2009–12, Council). MAE 2011. *Publications:* contribs to jls incl. Molecular Cell, Molecular Biol., Proc. NAS. *Address:* School of Biological Sciences, Nanyang Technological University, 50 Nanyang Avenue, Singapore 639798.

RHODES, Gary, OBE 2006; chef and restaurateur; *b* 22 April 1960; *s* of Jean Rhodes (*née* Ferris) and step *s* of John Smellie; *m* 1989, (Yolanda) Jennifer Adkins; two *s*. *Educ:* Thanet Technical Coll., Broadstairs (C&G qualifs; Student of the Year, Chef of the Year, 1979). Commis, then Chef de Partie, Amsterdam Hilton, 1979–81; Sous Chef: Reform Club, 1982–83; Capital Hotel, Knightsbridge, 1983–85; Head Chef: Whitehall, Broxted, 1985–86; Castle Hotel, Taunton, 1986–90 (Michelin Star, annually, 1986–90); The Greenhouse, London, 1990–96 (Michelin Star, 1996); Chef and Co-Proprietor: city rhodes, 1997–2003 (Michelin Star, annually 1997–2003); Rhodes in the Square, 1998–2003 (Michelin Star, 1998–2003); Rhodes & Co., Manchester, and Edinburgh, 1999–2002 (Bib Gourmand Award, 2001); Rhodes at the Calabash Hotel, Grenada, 2003–; Rhodes Twenty Four, 2003– (Michelin Star, 2004–); Arcadian Rhodes, P&O liner, 2005–11; Oriana Rhodes, P&O liner,

2006–11; Rhodes D7, Dublin, 2006–09; Rhodes W1 Restaurant, London, 2007– (Michelin Star, 2008–); Rhodes Mezzanine, Dubai, 2007–; Kings Rhodes, 2008–09; Rhodes South, 2008–10. Jt owner, Rhokett Patisserie, 2002–. Hon. Prof., Thames Valley Univ., 2003. FCGI 2005. *Television series:* Hot Chefs, 1988; Rhodes Around Britain, 1994; More Rhodes Around Britain, 1995; Open Rhodes Around Britain, 1996; Gary Rhodes, 1997; Gary's Perfect Christmas, 1998; Gary Rhodes' New British Classics, 1999; Masterchef, 2001; At the Table, 2001; Spring into Summer, 2002; Autumn into Winter, 2002; Hell's Kitchen, 2005; Rhodes Across India, 2007; Rhodes Across China, 2008; Rhodes Across the Caribbean, 2009; Rhodes Across Italy, 2010; columnist, BBC Good Food magazine, 1996–. *Publications:* Rhodes Around Britain, 1994; More Rhodes Around Britain, 1995; Open Rhodes Around Britain, 1996; Short-cut Rhodes, 1997; Fabulous Food, 1997; Sweet Dreams, 1998; New British Classics, 1999; At the Table, 2000; Spring into Summer, 2002; Autumn into Winter, 2002; The Complete Cookery Year, 2003; Keeping it Simple, 2005; Time to Eat, 2007; Rhodes 365, 2008. *Recreations:* driving, art, fashion. *Address:* Restaurant Associates, 4th Floor, 24 Martin Lane, EC4R 0DR. *Clubs:* Les Ambassadeurs, St James's.

RHODES, George Harold Lancashire, TD 1946; Regional Chairman of Industrial Tribunals, Manchester, 1985–88; *b* 29 Feb. 1916; *er s* of Judge Harold and Ena Rhodes of Bowdon, Cheshire. *Educ:* Abberley Hall; Shrewsbury School; The Queen's College, Oxford (MA 1941). Commissioned 52nd Field Regt RA TA, 1938; war service, BEF, 1940, Middle East, 1942, Italy, 1943–46 (Major). Called to the Bar, Gray's Inn, 1947; practised on N Circuit; the Junior, 1948; Office of Judge Advocate General (Army and RAF), 1953; Asst Judge Advocate General, 1967; Chm., Industrial Tribunals (Manchester), 1974, Dep. Regional Chm., 1975. *Address:* 42 Custerson Court, Saffron Walden, Essex CB11 3HF.

RHODES, John Andrew; independent public transport consultant, 1999–2014; *b* 22 May 1949; *s* of George and Elsie Rhodes; *m* 1985, Marie Catherine Carleton. *Educ:* Queen Elizabeth Sch., Barnet; Wadham Coll., Oxford (MA Mod. History). Civil Service: various posts in DoE, Cabinet Office, Dept of Transport, 1971–87; Dir Gen., W Yorks PTE, 1988–92; Strategy and Planning Advr, BRB, 1992–93; Dir, Passenger Services Gp, Office of Rail Regulator, 1993–99. Chm., railway industry Delay Attribution Bd, 2004–14. Non-exec. Dir, E and N Herts NHS Trust, 2000–02. Chm., Bishop's Stortford Civic Soc., 2000–07; Pres., Bishop's Stortford Civic Fedn, 2014– (Vice-Chm., 2007–12). Hon. Sen. Res. Fellow, Constitution Unit, UCL, 2001–12. *Recreations:* music, history, gardening. *Address:* 26 Warwick Road, Bishop's Stortford, Herts CM23 5NW. *T:* (01279) 656482.

See also P. J. Rhodes.

RHODES, Sir John (Christopher Douglas), 4th Bt *cr* 1919; *b* 24 May 1946; *s* of Sir Christopher Rhodes, 3rd Bt, and Mary Florence, *d* of late Dr Douglas Wardleworth; *S* father, 1964. *Heir: b* Michael Philip James Rhodes [*b* 3 April 1948; *m* 1973, Susan, *d* of Patrick Roney-Dougal; one *d*].

RHODES, Prof. John David, CBE 2000 (OBE 1992); PhD, DSc; FRS 1993; FREng; Chairman, 1994, Group Chief Executive, 2006, Filtronic plc (formerly Filtronic Comtek plc); Industrial Professor, Leeds University, since 1981, now Emeritus; *b* 9 Oct. 1943; *s* of Jack and Florence Rhodes; *m* 1965, Barbara Margaret Pearce; one *s* one *d*. *Educ:* Univ. of Leeds (BSc, PhD, DSc). FIEEE 1980; FIET (FIEE 1984); FREng (FEng 1987). Leeds University: Res. Asst, 1964–66; Res. Fellow, 1966–67; Sen. Res. Engr, Microwave Develt Labs, USA, 1967–69; Leeds University: Lectr, 1969–72; Reader, 1972–75; Prof., 1975–81. Chm., and CEO Filtronic Ltd, 1977–2004. Hon. DEng: Bradford, 1988; Leeds, 2004; Hon. DSc Napier, 1995. Prince Philip Medal, Royal Acad. of Engrg, 2003. *Publications:* Theory of Electrical Filters, 1976. *Recreation:* golf. *Address:* Dabarda, West Winds, Moor Lane, Menston, Ilkley LS29 6QD.

RHODES, John David McKinnon; Development Volunteer, Southwark Legal Advice Network Development, since 2011; Advice Volunteer, Southwark Citizens Advice Bureau, since 2012; *b* 20 Aug. 1950; *s* of late John Ivor McKinnon Rhodes, CMG and Eden Annetta Rhodes; *m* 1984, Sarah Elizabeth Rickard; two *s* one *d*. *Educ:* Dulwich Coll.; Sussex Univ. (BA Hons); London Business Sch. (Sloan Fellow 1983). With Lithotype Inc., 1971–72; joined Department of Trade and Industry, 1972: Principal Private Sec. to Sec. of State for Trade, 1981–83; Asst Sec., Internat. Projects, 1984–86; Director: British Trade and Investment Office (USA), NY, 1987–90; EC Single Market Policy, 1991–94; Electricity and Nuclear Fuels, 1994–96; Nuclear Sponsorship, 1996–97; Sec., Low Pay Commn, 1997–98; Director: Infrastructure and Energy Projects, 1998–2000; BNFL Partnership Team, 2000–02; Dir, Innovation Gp, 2002–04; voluntary and public sector consultancy, 2005; Hd of Financial Capability, Citizens Advice, 2006–11. Trustee, St Andrew's Youth Club, 2015–. *Recreations:* family, cooking, house restoration. *Address:* 31 Holly Grove, SE15 5DF. *E:* jdmrhodes@btinternet.com.

RHODES, Prof. Jonathan Michael, MD; FRCP, FMedSci; Professor of Medicine, University of Liverpool, 1995–2014, now Emeritus; Consultant Gastroenterologist, Royal Liverpool University Hospital, since 1991; *b* 21 April 1949; *s* of late Wilfred Harry Rhodes and Ellen Linda Rhodes (*née* Wreford); *m* 1st, 1978, Elizabeth Geraldine Helen Morris (*d* 2007); three *d*; 2nd, 2009, Collette Marie Clifford. *Educ:* Kingston Grammar Sch.; St John's Coll., Cambridge (MA); St Thomas's Hosp. Med. Sch. (MD 1982). FRCP 1989. House surgeon, St Thomas' Hosp., 1973; house physician and SHO, Kingston Hosp., 1974–75; SHO, Hammersmith Hosp., 1976; Registrar and Res. Fellow, Royal Free Hosp., 1976–81; Sen. Registrar, Queen Elizabeth and Selly Oak Hosps, Birmingham, 1981–85; Sen. Lectr, 1985–91, Reader, 1991–95, Univ. of Liverpool. Pres.-elect, 2002–03, Pres., 2003–04, Liverpool Medical Inst. Pres., British Soc. Gastroenterology, 2010–12; Chm., Gastroenterology Speciality Cttee, RCP, 1997–2001; Member: Exec. Cttee, Assoc. Physicians, 1999–2001; Council, RCP, 2003–06. FMedSci 1999. Avery Jones Res. Medal, British Soc. Gastroenterology, 1989; Bengt Ihre Medal, Swedish Med. Assoc., 2005. *Publications:* (ed jtly) Inflammatory Bowel Disease, 3rd edn 1997; contrib. papers on inflammatory bowel disease, colon cancer, lectins and glycobiology. *Recreations:* fell-walking, classical guitar, rowing coaching. *Address:* Department of Gastroenterology, Institute of Translational Medicine, University of Liverpool, Henry Wellcome Laboratory, Nuffield Building, Crown Street, Liverpool L69 3GE. *T:* (0151) 794 6822. *Clubs:* Hawks (Cambridge); Leander (Henley); Bristol Owners.

RHODES, Nicholas Piers; QC 2008; a Recorder, since 2002; *b* 26 April 1958; *s* of Colin and Charlotte Rhodes; *m* 1999, Sally Ann Matthews; two *s*. *Educ:* Dover Coll. Jun. Sch.; Dover Coll.; Univ. of E Anglia (LLB Hons); Inns of Court Sch. of Law. Called to the Bar, Lincoln's Inn, 1981. *Recreation:* military history. *Address:* Charter Chambers, 33 John Street, WC1N 2AT. *T:* (020) 7618 4400, *Fax:* (020) 7618 4401. *E:* Nick.Rhodes@charterchambers.com.

RHODES, Prof. Peter John, FBA 1987; Professor of Ancient History, University of Durham, 1983–2005, Hon. Professor, since 2005; *b* 10 Aug. 1940; *s* of George Thomas Rhodes and Elsie Leonora Rhodes (*née* Pugh); *m* 1971, Jan Teresa Adamson (marr. diss. 2001). *Educ:* Queen Elizabeth's Boys' Grammar Sch., Barnet; Wadham Coll., Oxford (minor schol.; BA (1st cl. Mods, 1st cl. Greats); MA; DPhil). Harmsworth Schol., Merton Coll., Oxford, 1963–65; Craven Fellow, Oxford Univ., 1963–65; Lectr in Classics and Ancient History, 1965, Sen. Lectr, 1977, Durham Univ. Jun. Fellow, Center for Hellenic Studies, Washington, DC, 1978–79; Visiting Fellow: Wolfson Coll., Oxford, 1984; Univ. of New England, Aust., 1988; Corpus Christi Coll., Oxford, 1993; All Souls Coll., Oxford, 1998; Leverhulme Res. Fellow, 1994–95; Langford Family Eminent Scholar, Florida State Univ., 2002; Mem., Inst. for Advanced Study, Princeton, USA, 1988–89; Invitation Fellow, Japan Soc. for the Promotion of Sci., 2005; Fellow, Fondazione Lorenzo Valla, 2010. Sackler Lectr, Tel Aviv Univ., 2013. Pres., Classical Assoc., 2014–15. Foreign Mem., Royal Danish Acad., 2005. Chancellor's Medal, Durham Univ., 2015. *Publications:* The Athenian Boule, 1972; Greek Historical Inscriptions 359–323 BC, 1972; Commentary on the Aristotelian Athenaion Politeia, 1981; (trans.) Aristotle: the Athenian Constitution, 1984; The Athenian Empire, 1985; The Greek City States: a source book, 1986, 2nd edn 2007; (ed) Thucydides Book II, 1988; (ed) Thucydides Book III, 1994; (with D. M. Lewis) The Decrees of the Greek States, 1997; (ed with L. G. Mitchell) The Development of the Polis in Archaic Greece, 1997; (ed) Thucydides Book IV.1–Book V.24, 1999; Ancient Democracy and Modern Ideology, 2003; (with R. Osborne) Greek Historical Inscriptions 404–323 BC, 2003; (ed) Athenian Democracy, 2004; A History of the Classical Greek World 478–323 BC, 2005, 2nd edn 2010; (ed with E. E. Bridges and E. M. Hall) Cultural Responses to the Persian Wars, 2007; (ed with J. L. Marr) The 'Old Oligarch', 2008; (trans. and commentary with M. Hammond) Thucydides: the Peloponnesian War, 2009; Alcibiades, 2011; A Short History of Ancient Greece, 2014; (ed) Thucydides Book I, 2014; Atthis, 2014; articles and reviews in jls. *Recreations:* music, typography, travel. *Address:* Department of Classics, University of Durham, 38 North Bailey, Durham DH1 3EU. *T:* (0191) 334 1670.

See also J. A. Rhodes.

RHODES, Richard David Walton; JP; Police and Crime Commissioner (C) for Cumbria, since 2012; *b* 20 April 1942; *er s* of Harry Walton Rhodes and Dorothy Rhodes (*née* Fairhurst); *m* 1966, Stephanie Heyes, 2nd *d* of Frederic William Heyes and Catherine Heyes; two *d*. *Educ:* Rossall Sch.; St John's Coll., Durham (BA 1963). Asst Master, St John's Sch., Leatherhead, 1964–75 (Founder Housemaster, Montgomery House, 1973–75); Deputy Headmaster, Arnold Sch., Blackpool, 1975–79, Headmaster, 1979–87; Headmaster, then Principal, Rossall Sch., 1987–2001. Member: Lancs CC Social Services Adv. Cttee, 1992–2001; Lancs Magistrates' Courts Cttee, 1993–96. Chairman: NW Div., HMC, 1987; Northern ISIS, 1993–95. Lay Member: Family Health Services Appeal Authy, 2002–10; First-tier Tribunal Service, 2010–12. Member: Independent Remuneration Panel, South Lakeland DC, 2003–08; Cumbria Probation Bd, 2004–08; Chair: Cumbria Bd, Nat. Probation Service, 2008–10; Cumbria Probation Trust, 2011–12; non-exec. Dir, Probation Assoc., 2011–12. JP Member: Cumbria Courts Bd, 2004–07; Cumbrian Lancs Courts Bd, 2007–11. Member Council: Univ. of Salford, 1987–93; Lawrence House Sch., Lytham St Annes, 1988–93; Trustee, Lawrence House Trust, 1994–97 (Chm., 2000–08); Gov., Terra Nova Sch., Jodrell Bank, 1989–2005 (Chm. Govs, 2000–05). JP Fylde, 1978, Wyre, 1999, Furness, 2002. *Recreations:* photography, sports, motoring, gardening in the Lake District. *Address:* Fairview, Staveley in Cartmel, Newby Bridge, Ulverston, Cumbria LA12 8NS. *T:* (01539) 531634; Office of the Police and Crime Commissioner for Cumbria, Carleton Hall, Penrith CA10 2AU. *T:* (01768) 217734. *E:* commissioner@cumbria.police.uk. *Club:* East India, Devonshire, Sports and Public Schools.

RHODES, Robert Elliott; QC 1989; a Recorder, since 1987; *b* 2 Aug. 1945; *s* of late Gilbert G. Rhodes, FCA and of Elly, who *m* 2nd, Leopold Brook (he *d* 2007); *m* 1971, Georgina Caroline (marr. diss. 1996), *d* of late Jack Gerald Clarfelt; two *s* one *d*. *Educ:* St Paul's School; Pembroke Coll., Oxford (MA). Called to the Bar, Inner Temple, 1968, Bencher, 2007. Accredited Mediator, 2007; qualified Arbitrator, 2013. Second Prosecuting Counsel to Inland Revenue at Central Criminal Court and Inner London Crown Courts, 1979, First Prosecuting Counsel, 1981–89. Hd of Chambers, 1998–2003. Deputy Chairman: IMRO Membership Tribunal Panel, 1992–2001; ICAEW Appeal Cttee, 1998–2004; a Financial Reporting Council (formerly AIDB, then AADB) Chm. of Disciplinary Tribunals, 2004–14. Advr, Arbitration and ADR Center, Central Univ. of Finance and Econs, Beijing, 2012–; Member: Panel of Mediators, China Council for Promotion of Internat. Trade, 2013–; Panel of Mediators and Arbitrators, Lang Fang Arbitration Commn, People's Republic of China, 2013; Panel of Arbitrators: Thai Arbitration Inst., 2013–; Chinese Arbitration Inst., 2013–; arbitrator, Global Panel of Dist. Neutrals, Internat. Inst. for Conflict Prevention and Resolution, 2014–. *Recreations:* opera, ballet, theatre, reading, art, cricket, real tennis, former international fencer. *Address:* Outer Temple, 222–225 Strand, WC2R 1BA. *T:* (020) 7353 6381. *Clubs:* Garrick, Annabel's, MCC; Epee.

RHODES, Dame Zandra (Lindsey), DBE 2014 (CBE 1997); RDI 1976; DesRCA, FCSD; Managing Director, Zandra Rhodes Enterprises; Chancellor, University for the Creative Arts, since 2010; *b* 19 Sept. 1940; *d* of Albert James Rhodes and Beatrice Ellen (*née* Twigg). *Educ:* Medway Technical Sch. for Girls, Chatham; Medway Coll. of Art; Royal Coll. of Art (DesRCA 1964). FSIAD 1982. With Alexander MacIntyre, set up print factory and studio, 1965; sold designs (and converted them on to cloth) to Foale and Tuffin and Roger Nelson; formed partnership with Sylvia Ayton and began producing dresses using her own prints, 1966; opened Fulham Road Clothes Shop, designing dresses as well as prints, first in partnership, 1967–68, then (Fulham Road shop closed) alone, producing first clothes range in which she revolutionised use of prints in clothes by cutting round patterns to make shapes never before used; took collection to USA, 1969; sold to Fortnum and Mason, London, 1969, Piero de Monzi, 1971; began building up name and business in USA (known for her annual spectacular Fantasy Shows); also started designing in jersey and revolutionised its treatment with lettuce edges and seams on the outside; with Knight and Stirling founded Zandra Rhodes (UK) Ltd and Zandra Rhodes (Shops) Ltd, 1975–86; opened first shop in London, 1975; others opened in Bloomingdale's NY, Marshall Field, Chicago, Seibu, Tokyo and Harrods, London, 1976; new factory premises opened in Hammersmith, London, 1984; closed Mayfair shop, 1991, to show on a more personal and individual scale in her Hammersmith showroom. Since 1976 Zandra Rhodes has tried to reach a wider public through licensing her name in UK, USA, Australia and Japan, making full use of the Zandra Rhodes textile design talent for: wallpapers and furnishing fabrics, bathmats, men's ties, sheets and bed linen, printed shawls and scarves, hosiery, teatowels, kitchen accessories and jewellery. Notable licences include: Eve Stillman Lingerie (USA), 1977, Wamsutta sheets and pillowcases (USA), 1976, CVP Designs interior fabrics and settings (UK), 1977, Philip Hockley Decorative Furs (UK), 1986 and Zandra Rhodes Saris (India), 1987 (which she launched with 'West meets East' shows of Saris and Shalwar Chamises in Bombay and Delhi—the first Western designer to do so), Littlewoods Catalogues (UK), 1988 for printed T-shirts and Intasia sweaters; Hilmet silk scarves and men's ties (UK), 1989; Bonnay perfume, Coats Patons needlepoint (UK), 1993; Pologeorgis Furs (USA), Zandra Rhodes II handpainted ready-to-wear collection (HK, China), 1995; Grattons Catalogue sheets and duvets (UK), 1996; range of printed tops for Topshop (UK), 2002; Jewellery Licence, 2002; China licence for Royal Doulton, 2004. Designed stand with furniture and carpet for Hanover Expo, 2000. Designed: costumes for Magic Flute, San Diego Opera, 2001; costumes and sets for: Pearl Fishers, San Diego and Michigan, 2004, San Francisco and NY, 2005; Aida, ENO, 2007. Solo exhibitions: Oriel, Cardiff (Welsh Arts Council), 1978; Texas Gall., Houston, 1981; Otis Parsons, Los Angeles, 1981; La Jolla Museum of Contemporary Art, San Diego, 1982; ADITI Creative Power, Barbican Centre, 1982; Sch. of Art Inst., Chicago, 1982; Parsons Sch. of Design, NY, 1982; Art Museum of Santa Cruz Co., Calif, 1983; retrospective exhibition of 'Works of Art' with textiles, Museum of Art, El Paso, Texas, 1984; retrospective of Garments & Textiles (also Lead Speaker for Art to Wear exhibn), Columbus, Ohio, 1987; retrospectives for Seibu Seed Hall, Seibu, Tokyo, 1987 and 1991; Mint Mus., N Carolina, 1992; Athenæum Liby, La Jolla, 1996; water colour exhibition: Dyansen Galls, NY, LA and New Orleans, 1989; major group exhibitions: Nat. Gall. of Australia, 1993; V&A, 1994; RCA 1996. Work represented in major costume collections: UK: V&A; City Mus. and Art Gall., Stoke-on-Trent; Bath Mus.; Royal

Pavilion Brighton Mus.; Platt Fields Costume Mus., Manchester; City Art Gall., Leeds; overseas: Metropolitan Mus., NY; Chicago Historical Soc.; Smithsonian Instn; Royal Ontario Mus.; Mus. of Applied Arts and Scis, Sydney; Nat. Mus. of Victoria, Melbourne; La Jolla Mus. of Contemp. Art; LA County Mus. of Art. Opening speaker, Famous Women of Fashion, Smithsonian Instn, Washington, 1978. Founded Fashion & Textile Mus., Bermondsey, 1996, opened to public, 2003. Hon. DFA Internat. Fine Arts Coll., Miami, Florida, 1986; Hon. Dr RCA, 1986; Hon. DD CNAA, 1987; Hon. DLitt Westminster, 2000; Hon. Dr London Inst., 2000; Hon. DHL Acad. of Art Coll., San Francisco, 2001. Designer of the Year, English Fashion Trade UK, 1972; Emmy Award for Best Costume Designs in Romeo and Juliet on Ice, CBS TV, 1984; Woman of Distinction award, Northwood Inst., Dallas, 1986; Top UK Textile Designer, Observer, 1990; Hall of Fame Award, British Fashion Council, 1995; citations and commendations from USA estabs. *Publications:* The Art of Zandra Rhodes, 1984, US edn 1985; The Zandra Rhodes Collection by Brother, 1988. *Recreations:* travelling, drawing, gardening, cooking. *Address:* (office) 79–85 Bermondsey Street, SE1 3XF. *T:* (020) 7403 5333, *Fax:* (020) 7403 0555. *E:* zrhodesent@aol.com, zrhodesent@newham.ac.uk.

RHYMES, Rupert John, OBE 2002; Trustee and Chairman, The Theatres Trust, 2002–09; Director, 2002–07, and Chairman, 2003–07, Bristol Old Vic; Chairman, Frank Matcham Society, since 2011; *b* 24 June 1940; *s* of Elson John Rhymes and Phyllis Rhymes (*née* Rawlings); *m* 1970, Susan Mary Chennells; one *s* one *d*. *Educ:* King Edward's Sch., Bath; Magdalen Coll., Oxford (BA Mod. Hist. 1962; MA). Box Office Clerk, RSC, Aldwych Theatre, 1962; Asst Manager, Sadler's Wells Theatre, 1963; Theatre Manager, Nat. Theatre, Old Vic, 1963–69; Sadler's Wells Opera, then English National Opera, 1969–87: Asst to Admin. Dir, then Head of Press and Publicity, then Gen. Manager, 1969–72, Co. Sec., and Admin. Dir, 1972–87; Chief Executive: SOLT, 1987–2001; Theatrical Mgt Assoc., 1987–2001. Chm., Oxford Stage Co., 1987–97. Director: West End Theatre Managers, 1978–87 (Pres., 1979–82; Vice Pres., 1982–83); Theatre Investment Fund, 1982–2010; Nat. Campaign for the Arts, 1988–2001 (Vice Chm., 1999–2001); Nat. Council for Drama Trng, 1997–2001. Director: JFMG Ltd, 1997–2009; Wheelshare, 2007–12; Peter Saunders Gp Ltd, 2007–. Founding Mem., later Mem. Exec. Council, Performing Arts Employers Assocs League, Europe, 1991–2001 (Chm., 2000–01). Trustee: Raymond Mander and Joe Mitchenson Theatre Collection, 1977–2001 (Chm., 1986–2001); Motley Design Course, 1985–; Chichester Fest. Theatre, 1998–2000; Stephen Arlen Meml Fund, 1993–; Olivier Foundn, 2007–09; Peggy Ramsay Foundn, 2009–. Gov., Central Sch. of Speech and Drama, 1990–2002 (Vice Chm., 1991–92). *Recreations:* finding time for theatre, protesting against further destruction in the city of Bath. *Address:* Honeysuckle Farm, Perrymead, Bath BA2 5AU. *T:* (01225) 834188.

RHYS, family name of **Baron Dynevor**.

RHYS, Prof. (David) Garel, CBE 2007 (OBE 1989); FIMI; SMMT Professor Emeritus of Motor Industry Economics, and former Director, Centre for Automotive Industry Research, Cardiff Business School, Cardiff University; *b* 28 Feb. 1940; *s* of Emyr Lewys Rhys and Edith Phyllis Rhys (*née* Williams); *m* 1965, Charlotte Mavis Walters; one *s* two *d*. *Educ:* Ystalyfera Grammar Sch.; University Coll., Swansea (BA); Univ. of Birmingham (MCom). IOTA 1972. Asst Lectr, then Lectr in Econs, Univ. of Hull, 1965–70; University College, Cardiff, subseq. University of Wales College of Cardiff, now Cardiff University: Lectr in Econs, 1971–77; Sen. Lectr, 1977–84; Prof. of Motor Industry Econs, 1984–2005; seconded to Cardiff Business Sch., UWIST, 1987–88, until merger with UC Cardiff to form UWCC; Head of Economics, 1987–99; Dir, Centre for Automotive Industry Res., 1991–2005. Member: RPI Adv. Cttee, 1992–96; Bd, WDA, 1994–99 (Special Advr, 1999–2006); UK Round Table on Sustainable Develt, 1996–2000; Motor Racing Industry Competitiveness Panel, DTI, 2003–09; HEFCW, 2003–09; National Assembly for Wales: Member: Enterprise, Innovation and Ministerial Adv. Gp, 2006–12; Bd, Sector Develt, Industry Wales (formerly Wales Partnership), 2013–; Chairman: Economic Res. Adv. Panel, 2002–12; Low Carbon Vehicle Steering Gp, 2013–. Chm., Welsh Automotive Forum, 2000–. Co-Chair, Wales Adv. Panel, Green Growth, 2013–. Consultant, EC, 2005–06. Mem. and Dir, Capital Region Tourism, 2011–14; Chm., St Athan Enterprise Zone, 2012–. Advr to H of C and H of L select cttees, 1975–96. Pres., Inst. of the Motor Industry, 2004–09 (Vice-Pres., 1990–2004, 2009–). Chm. of Trustees, Wales Video Gall., 2001–14. FLSW 2013. FRSA 1991. Freeman, City of London, 2000; Liveryman, Carmen's Co., 2000–. *Publications:* The Motor Industry: an economic survey, 1972; The Motor Industry in the European Community, 1989; (contrib.) Industries in Europe: competition, trends and policy issues, 2003; (contrib.) Deep Integration: how transatlantic markets are leading globalisation, 2005; (contrib.) Outsourcing and Human Resource Management: an international survey, 2008; contrib. Jl Industrial Econs, Jl Transport Hist., Jl Transport Econs and Policy, Bulletin of Econ. Res., Scottish Jl of Political Economy, Industrial Relns Jl, Accounting and Business Res., Jl Econ. Studies, World Econs, Long Range Planning. *Recreations:* walking, gardening, theatre and opera, sports' spectator, still amusing my grandchildren. *Address:* 14 Maes Yr Awel, Radyr, Cardiff CF15 8AN. *T:* (029) 2084 2714. *Club:* Royal Automobile.

RHYS-JAMES, Shani, MBE 2006; artist; *b* 2 May 1953; *d* of Harold Marcus Rhys-James and Jean (*née* Barker); *m* 1977, Stephen Alexander West; two *s*. *Educ:* Parliament Hill Girls' Sch.; Loughborough Coll. of Art; St Martin's Sch. of Art (BA Hons). Major touring exhibitions: Blood Ties, Wrexham Arts Centre, 1993; Facing the Self, Oriel Mostyn, Llandudno, 1997; The Black Cot, Aberystwyth Arts Centre, 2003; one person shows: Beaux Arts Gall., Bath, 1992; Martin Tinney Gall., Cardiff, 1993, 1995, 1998, 2003, 2005, 2008, 2010; The Inner Room, Stephen Lacey Gall., London, 2000; Connaught Brown Gall., London, 2009, 2012, 2015; Hillsboro Fine Art, Dublin, 2010; Aberystwyth Arts Centre, and tour, 2013; The Rivalry of Flowers, Kings Place Gall., London, and tour, 2013; Oriel Tegfryn, 2014; Distillation, Nat. Liby of Wales, 2015; Ceredigion Mus., 2015. Artist Advr, Purchasing Panel, Derek Williams Trust, Nat. Mus. Wales, 2006–11. Residency, Columbia Univ., NY, 2015. Hon. Fellow: UWIC, 2007; Hereford Coll. of Art, 2008. Mem., RCA, 1994. Gold Medal, Nat. Eisteddfod, 1992; Hunting/Observer Prize 1993; Welsh BBC Artist of the Year Award, 1994; Jerwood Painting Prize, 2003; Creative Wales Award, Welsh Arts Council, 2006. *Publications:* Facing the Self, 1997; The Inner Room, 2000; (with Eve Ropek) The Black Cot, 2003; Imaging the Imagination, 2005; 'Cassandra's Rant' artists book, 2006; The Rivalry of Flowers, 2013; The Spider, the Plants and the Black Black Cot, 2015; exhibition catalogues. *Recreations:* writing, vegetable gardening, restoring, music. *Address:* Dolpebyll, Llangadfan, Powys SY21 0PU. *T:* (01938) 820469. *E:* shanirhysjames@btinternet.com.

RHYS JONES, Griffith; actor, writer, director and producer; *b* 16 Nov. 1953; *s* of Elwyn Rhys Jones and Gwynneth Margaret Jones; *m* 1981, Joanna Frances Harris; one *s* one *d*. *Educ:* Brentwood Sch.; Emmanuel Coll., Cambridge (Hon. Fellow 2007). BBC Radio Producer, 1976–79; *television:* Not the Nine O'Clock News (also co-writer), 1979–81; Alas Smith and Jones (also co-writer), 1982–87; Porterhouse Blue (serial), 1987; The World according to Smith and Jones, 1987; Small Doses (series of short plays) (writer, Boat People), 1989; A View of Harry Clark, 1989; Smith and Jones (also co-writer), 1992, 1995, 1997, 1998; Demob (drama series), 1993; Bookworm (presenter), 1994–2000; Restoration (presenter), 2003, 2004; Mine All Mine (drama serial), 2004; The Secret Life of Arthur Ransome, 2005; Betjeman and Me, 2006; Kipling: a remembrance tale, 2006; Restoration Village (presenter), 2006; Building Britain, 2007; A Pembrokeshire Farm, 2006, 2009; Three Men in a Boat, 2006, 2008–11; Mountain (writer and presenter), 2007; Charles Dickens and the Invention of Christmas, 2007; Greatest Cities of the World with Griff Rhys Jones, 2008, 2010; The Heart of Thomas Hardy, 2008; It'll be Alright on the Night, 2008; Losing It, 2008; Why Poetry Matters, 2009; Rivers with Griff Rhys Jones, 2009; The Prince's Welsh Village, 2010; Hidden Treasures of… (presenter), 2011; Three Men Go to Venice, 2011; A Short History of Everything Else, 2012; Britain's Lost Routes with Griff Rhys Jones, 2012; The Wind in the Willows, 2012; A Great Welsh Adventure with Griff Rhys Jones, 2014; A Poet in New York (exec. prod.), 2014; National Treasures of Wales, 2014; The Quizeum, 2015; Slow Train Through Africa, 2015; *theatre:* Charley's Aunt, 1983; Trumpets and Raspberries, 1985; The Alchemist, 1985; Arturo Ui, 1987; Smith & Jones (also co-writer), 1989–; Thark, 1989; The Wind in the Willows, RNT, 1990; dir, Twelfth Night, RSC, 1991; The Revengers' Comedies, Strand, 1991; An Absolute Turkey, Globe, 1994; Plunder, Savoy, 1996; The Front Page, Donmar, 1997; Horse and Carriage, W Yorks Playhouse, 2001; Oliver, Drury Lane, 2009–10; *films:* Morons from Outer Space, 1985; Wilt, 1989; As You Like It, 1992; Staggered, 1994; Up and Under, 1998; Taliesin Jones, 2000; Puckoon, 2003; *opera:* Die Fledermaus, Royal Opera Covent Garden, 1989; *radio* series: (also writer) Do Go On, 1997–; (also writer) Griff Rhys Jones show, 2000–03. President: Civic Trust, 2008–09; Civic Voice, 2009–; Vice Pres., Victorian Soc. Director: TalkBack, Advertising and Production; Playback, 1987–; Smith Jones Campbell (formerly Smith Jones Brown & Cassie), 1988–99; Modern Television, 2005–. Chm., Hackney Empire Appeal Cttee, 1998–2004. FRWCMD (FWCMD 1997); FRSA 2002. *Publications:* (jtly) The Smith and Jones World Atlas, 1983; The Lavishly Tooled Smith and Jones, 1986; (jtly) Janet lives with Mel and Griff, 1988; (jtly) Smith & Jones Head to Head, 1992; To the Baltic with Bob, 2003; Semi-Detached, 2006; Mountain: exploring Britain's high places, 2007; Rivers: a voyage into the heart of Britain, 2009; Insufficiently Welsh, 2014. *Address:* c/o Troika, 10a Christina Street, EC2A 4PA.

RHYS JONES, Sandra Yvonne, (Sandi), OBE 1998; FCIOB; advocate and change agent for construction and engineering, especially the role of women; Founding Partner, RhysJones Consultants, since 1976; *b* 26 May 1946; *d* of Ralph and Stella Wyndham; *m* 1968, Roderick Rhys Jones; three *s*. *Educ:* King's Coll., London (MSc Construction Law and Arbitration 1994). Accredited Mediator, Centre for Dispute Resolution, 1995. FCIOB 2003. Media librarian, J Walter Thompson, 1964–65; journalist, Construction News, 1965–67; Dep. Fashion Ed., Drapers Record, 1968–70; Exec., Public Relns Partners, 1970–72; tech. journalist and ed., 1972–76. Non-executive Director: DLR, 1998–2000; Simons Gp Ltd, 2002–09; Engrg UK, 2008–. Chair: Wkg Gp 8, Construction Industry Bd, 1994–97; Assessment Panel for Construction Res., DoE, 1996–97; Construction Industry Wkg Gp, Centre for Dispute Resolution, 1996–2000. Chair of Trustees, Women's Educn in Building, 1997–2002; Mem., Nat. Strategy Panel, Rethinking Construction, 2002–04. Deputy Chair of Trustees: UK Resource Centre for Women in Sci., Engrg and Technol., 2008–10; Royal Marines Mus., 2002–12. ACIArb 1993; MCIM 1998; CCMI 2012. Hon. Dr Sheffield Hallam, 2005. *Publications:* Tomorrow's Team: women and men in construction, 1996; (contrib.) Managing Diversity and Equality in Construction, 2006; Never Waste a Good Crisis, 2009. *Recreations:* building projects, slow food, fast conversation with family and friends, music, trying to write better haiku in less time. *E:* sandi@rhysjones.com.

RHYS WILLIAMS, Sir (Arthur) Gareth (Ludovic Emrys), 3rd Bt *cr* 1918, of Miskin, Parish of Llantrisant, Co. Glamorgan; CEng, FIET, FIMechE; Chief Executive Officer, PHS Group plc, since 2012; *b* 9 Nov. 1961; *s* of Sir Brandon Rhys Williams, 2nd Bt, MP and Caroline Susan, *e d* of L. A. Foster; *S* father, 1988; *m* 1996, Harriet, *d* of Maj. Tom Codner; two *s* one *d*. *Educ:* Eton; Durham Univ. (BSc Hons Eng); Insead (MBA). CCMI. Materials Manager, Lucas CAV, 1987–88; Managing Director: NFI Electronics, 1990–93; Rexam Custom Europe, 1992–96; Reg. Man. Dir, Central Europe, BPB plc, 1996–2000; Chief Executive Officer: Vitec Gp plc, 2001–08; Capital Safety Ltd, 2008–10; Charter Internat. plc, 2011–12. Mem. Council, FFI, 2012–. *Recreations:* sailing, conjuring, shooting, travel. *Heir: s* Ludo Dhaulagiri Rhys Williams, *b* 12 Oct. 2001. *Address:* 9 Matheson Road, W14 8SN. *Club:* Garrick.

RIBBANS, Prof. Geoffrey Wilfrid, MA; Kenan University Professor of Hispanic Studies, Brown University, USA, 1978–99, now Emeritus; *b* 15 April 1927; *o s* of late Wilfrid Henry Ribbans and Rose Matilda Burton; *m* 1956, Magdalena Cumming (*née* Willmann) (*d* 2004), Cologne; one *s* two *d*. *Educ:* Sir George Monoux Grammar Sch., Walthamstow; King's Coll., Univ. of London. BA Hons Spanish 1st cl., 1948; MA 1953. Asst Lectr, Queen's Univ., Belfast, 1951–52; Asst, St Salvator's Coll., Univ. of St Andrews, 1952–53; Univ. of Sheffield: Asst Lectr, 1953–55; Lectr, 1955–61; Sen. Lectr, 1961–63; Gilmour Prof. of Spanish, Univ. of Liverpool, 1963–78; First Director, Centre for Latin-American Studies, 1966–70; Dean, Faculty of Arts, 1977–78; Chm., Dept of Hispanic and Italian Studies, Brown Univ., USA, 1981–84. Andrew Mellon Vis. Prof., Univ. of Pittsburgh, 1970–71; Leverhulme Res. Fellow, 1975; NEH Univ. Fellowship, 1991; Hon. Prof., Univ. of Sheffield, 1994–; Vis. Prof., Univ. of Salamanca, 1995. Lectures: Fundación Juan March, Madrid, 1984; E. Allison Peers, Univ. of Liverpool, 1985, 1994; Norman Maccoll, Univ. of Cambridge, 1985; Fordham Cervantes, NY, 1988; Raimundo Lida Meml, Harvard, 1998; Joan Gili Meml, Anglo-Catalan Soc., Edinburgh, 2009. Vice-Pres., Internat. Assoc. of Hispanists, 1974–80 (Pres., Local Organising Cttee, 8th Congress, Brown Univ., 1983); Pres., Anglo-Catalan Soc., 1976–78. Dir, Liverpool Playhouse, 1974–78. Editor, Bulletin of Hispanic Studies, 1964–78. Hon. Fellow, Inst. of Linguists, 1972. Corresp. Member: Real Academia de Buenas Letras, Barcelona, 1978; Hispanic Soc. of Amer., 1981. Hon. Mem., N American Catalan Soc., 2001. MA *ad eund* Brown Univ., 1979. Special Prize for excellence in Galdós Studies, Las Palmas, 1997. Encomienda de la Orden de Isabel la Católica (Spain), 1997; J. M. Batista i Roca Prize for contributions to Catalan studies, Barcelona, 2000. *Publications:* Catalunya i València vistes pels viatgers anglesos del segle XVIIIè, 1955, 2nd edn 1993; Niebla y Soledad: aspectos de Unamuno y Machado, 1971; ed, Soledades, Galerías, otros poemas, by Antonio Machado, 1975, 17th rev. edn 2008; Antonio Machado (1875–1939): poetry and integrity, 1975; B. Pérez Galdós: Fortunata y Jacinta, a critical guide, 1977 (trans. Spanish 1989); (ed) Campos de Castilla, by Antonio Machado, 1989, 14th rev. edn 2003; History and Fiction in Galdós's Narratives, 1993; Conflicts and Conciliations: the evolution of Galdós's Fortunata y Jacinta, 1997; numerous articles on Spanish and Catalan literature in specialised publications; *festschrift:* Hispanic Studies in Honour of Geoffrey Ribbans, 1992. *Recreations:* travel, fine art. *Address:* c/o Department of Hispanic Studies, Box 1961, Brown University, Providence, Rhode Island 02912, USA.

RIBBINS, Maureen Margaret; Headmistress, Woldingham School, 1997–2000; *b* 16 Aug. 1947; *d* of Guy and Eileen Shoebridge; *m* 1969, Peter Michael St John Ribbins, Prof. of Educn Mgt, Birmingham Univ. *Educ:* St Joseph's Convent GS, Abbey Wood; Lady Margaret Hall, Oxford (MA Hons Physics 1968; PGCE 1969); Thames Poly. (MSc Hons Solid State Physics, London, 1972); Birkbeck Coll., London Univ. (BSc Botany 1977); Birmingham Univ. (Cert. in Higher Educn in Botanical Illustration, 2003). Teacher of Mathematics and Physics, Farringtons Sch., Chislehurst, 1969–73; Head of Science, Dartford Girls' GS, 1973–80; Headmistress: Walton Girls' High Sch., 1980–83; Wolverhampton Girls' High Sch., 1983–97. Assessor, Nat. Educn Assessment Centre, 1991–2001; accredited OFSTED Inspector, 1995–2001. Mem., Birmingham Soc. of Botanical Painters. *Publications:* reviews and articles in Jl of Educnl Admin, and Pastoral Care in Educn. *Recreations:* reading modern literature, Chinese brush painting, botanical illustration, walking dog, music.

RIBEIRO, family name of **Baron Ribeiro**.

RIBEIRO, Baron *cr* 2010 (Life Peer), of Achimota in the Republic of Ghana and of Ovington in the County of Hampshire; **Bernard Francisco Ribeiro,** Kt 2009; CBE 2004; FRCS; FRCP; Consultant General Surgeon, Basildon University Hospital, 1979–2008; President, Royal College of Surgeons of England, 2005–08; *b* 20 Jan. 1944; *s* of Miguel Augustus

Ribeiro and Matilda Ribeiro; *m* 1968, Elisabeth Jean Orr; one *s* three *d* (incl. twin *d*). *Educ:* Dean Close Sch., Cheltenham; Middlesex Hosp. Med. Sch., London (MB BS 1967). LRCP 1967; MRCS 1967, FRCS 1972; FRCSEd (*ad hominem*) 2000; FRCP 2006; FRCA 2008; FRCPSGlas (*qua surgeon ad eundem*) 2008. Registrar, then Sen. Registrar, Middlesex Hosp., 1972–78; Lectr in Urology, Ghana Med. Sch., Accra, 1974. Mem. Bd of Visitors, HM Prison Chelmsford, 1982–92; Surgical Advr to Expert Adv. Gp on Aids (EAGA) and UK Adv. Panel for health care workers infected with blood-borne viruses (UKAP), DoH, 1994–2003; Vis. Prof., Dept of Surgery, Univ. of N Carolina, 2006–07. Hon. Sec., 1991–96, Pres., 1999–2000, Assoc. of Surgeons of GB and Ire; Mem. Council, RCS, 1998–2008 (Mem., Ct of Examrs, 1998–2004; Chm., Quality Assurance and Inspection, 2002–05; Sen. Vice-Pres., 2004–05); Med. Vice Chm. E England, Adv. Cttee on Clinical Excellence Awards, 2002–05; Consultant, Adv. Bd, Amer. Coll. of Surgeons/Health Policy Res. Inst., 2009–14; Chairman: Res. Panel, Pelican Cancer Foundn, 2009–; Ind. Reconfiguration Panel, 2012–; Confidential Reporting System in Surgery, 2012–. Charles Saint Lect., S Africa, 2007; Arthur Li Oration, Hong Kong, 2007; Vicary Lect., RCS, 2008; Joseph H. Ogura Lect., Triological Soc., Chicago, 2011. Patron: Achimota Trust, 2011–; Operation Hernia, 2011–12; RCS, 2011; Lifebox, 2012–; Phi, 2013–. Mem., Exec. Cttee, Assoc. of Cons. Peers, 2012–15. Mem., Test and Itchen Assoc., 1989–. Liveryman, Co. of Barbers, 1997– (Mem., Ct of Assts, 2006–; Master, 2013–14). Mem., Editl Internat. Adv. Bd, Archives of Surgery, 2000–09. Mem. Council, Dean Close Sch., Cheltenham, 2006– (Trustee, 2010–12); Pres., Old Decanians Soc., 2014–. Fellow, Acad. of Medicine, Malaysia, 2006; Hon. Fellow: Ghana Coll. of Physicians and Surgeons, 2006; Caribbean Coll. of Surgeons, 2007; Hon. FDSRCS 2006; Hon. FRCSI 2008; Hon. FACS 2008; Hon. FFGDP(UK) 2009; Hon. Mem., Acad. Nationale de Chirurgie, 2008. Hon. DSc Anglia Ruskin, 2008; Hon. DEng Bath, 2012. Hon. Liveryman, Cutlers' Co., 2008. Officer, Order of the Volta (Ghana), 2008. *Publications:* (contrib.) Concise Surgery, 1998; (contrib.) Emergency Surgery: principles and practice, 2006; contrib. Archives of Surgery, Bull. of RCS. *Recreations:* fishing, riparian activities, shooting, interest in the history of war. *Address:* House of Lords, SW1A 0PW. *T:* (020) 7219 5353. *E:* ribeirob@parliament.uk. *Clubs:* Flyfishers'; Surgical Sixty Travelling.

RIBEIRO, Roberto Alexandre Vieira; Hon. Mr Justice Ribeiro; Permanent Judge, Hong Kong Court of Final Appeal, since 2000; *b* 20 March 1949; *s* of late Gilberto and Eleanora Vieira Ribeiro; *m* 1974, Susan Elizabeth Swan. *Educ:* La Salle Coll., Hong Kong; London Sch. of Econs (LLB 1971, LLM 1972; Hon. Fellow, 2007). Called to the Bar, Inner Temple (Hon. Bencher, 2003) and Hong Kong, 1978; Lectr, Faculty of Law, Univ. of Hong Kong, 1972–79; in practice at Hong Kong Bar, 1979–99; QC (Hong Kong) 1990; Judge, Court of First Instance, 1999, Justice of Appeal, 2000, Hong Kong. Mem., Judicial Officers Recommendation Commn, 2008–. Pres., Alliance Française, Hong Kong, 2000–. Board Member: Hong Kong Internat. Film Fest., 2004–; Hong Kong Arts Fest. Soc., 2008–. Chevalier, l'Ordre des Arts et des Lettres (France), 2002; Comdr, Ordre des Palmes Académiques (France), 2007; Officier de la Légion d'Honneur (France), 2015 (Chevalier, 2002). *Recreations:* dogs, wine, books, music. *Address:* Court of Final Appeal, 8 Jackson Road, Central, Hong Kong. *T:* 21230012, *Fax:* 21210303. *E:* rribeiro@netvigator.com. *Clubs:* Hong Kong, Lusitano (Hong Kong).

RICARD, Alexandre; Chairman and Chief Executive Officer, Pernod Ricard, since 2015. *Educ:* Ecole Supérieure de Commerce, Paris; Univ. of Pennsylvania (MA Internat. Global Studies 2001); Wharton Sch., Univ. of Pennsylvania (MBA 2001). Strategy consultant, Accenture; Mergers and Acquisitions Consultant, Morgan Stanley; joined Audit and Develt Dept, Pernod Ricard, 2003; Chief Financial Officer, Irish Distillers Pernod Ricard, Dublin, 2004–06; Chm. and CEO, Pernod Ricard Asia Duty Free, Hong Kong, 2006–08; CEO, Irish Distillers Pernod Ricard, 2008–11; Pernod Ricard: Man. Dir, Distribn Network, Paris, 2011–12; Mem., Exec. Bd, 2011–; Dep. CEO and Chief Operating Officer, 2012–15. *Address:* Pernod Ricard, 12 place des Etats-Unis, 75783 Paris Cedex 16, France.

RICE; *see* Spring Rice, family name of Baron Monteagle of Brandon.

RICE; *see* Talbot Rice.

RICE, Sir (Charles) Duncan, Kt 2009; FRSE; Principal and Vice-Chancellor, University of Aberdeen, 1996–2010; *b* 20 Oct. 1942; *s* of James Inglis Rice and Jane Meauras Findlay (*née* Scroggie); *m* 1967, Susan Ilene Wunsch (*see* S. I. Rice); two *s* one *d*. *Educ:* Univ. of Aberdeen (MA 1st Cl. Hons Hist. 1964); Univ. of Edinburgh (PhD 1969). FRHistS 1996; FRSE 1998. Lectr, Univ. of Aberdeen, 1966–69; Yale University: Asst Prof. of Hist., 1970–75; Associate Prof., 1975–79; Prof. of History, Hamilton Coll., Clinton, NY, 1979–85; New York University: Prof. of History, 1985–96; Dean, Faculty of Arts and Sci., 1985–94; Vice-Chancellor, 1994–96. Dir, BT Scotland, 1998–2002; Vice Chm., Grampian Enterprise Ltd, 1999–2006. Board Member: Univs and Colls Employers' Assoc., 1997–2007; Rowett Res. Inst., 1998–; Scottish Opera, 1998–2004; Scottish Ballet, 1998–2003; Glasgow Life, 2011–; Member: Council, Nat. Trust for Scotland, 1998–2004; Heritage Lottery Fund Cttee for Scotland, 2005–10. Chm., Global Philanthropic, Europe, 2011–. Trustee, CASE Europe, 2005–10 (Chm. Bd, 2007–10). Chm., UK Socrates-Erasmus Council, 1999–2008. FRSA 1996. Hon. DHL New York, 2004; Hon. DEd Robert Gordon, 2005; Hon. DHC Edinburgh, 2010; Hon. LLD Aberdeen, 2011. *Publications:* The Rise and Fall of Black Slavery, 1975; The Scots Abolitionists 1831–1961, 1982. *Recreations:* contemporary Scottish literature, opera, studio ceramics, salmon fishing.

RICE, Condoleezza, PhD; Professor of Political Science, and Senior Fellow, Hoover Institution, since 2009, and Professor of Political Economy, Graduate School of Business, Stanford University; *b* Birmingham, Ala, 14 Nov. 1954. *Educ:* Univ. of Denver (BA Internat. Relns 1974; PhD 1981); Univ. of Notre Dame, Indiana. Prof., Stanford Univ., Calif, 1981–88; Dir, Soviet and E Eur. Affairs, Nat. Security Council, Special Asst to Pres. for nat. security affairs and Sen. Dir for Soviet Affairs, 1988–91; Stanford University, California: Prof., 1991–93; Provost, 1993–99; on leave of absence as foreign policy advr to George W. Bush, 2000–01; Nat. Security Advr, and Asst to the Pres. for Nat. Security Affairs, 2001–05; Secretary of State, USA, 2005–09. Dir, KiOR, 2011–. Hon. Dr Notre Dame, 1995. *Publications:* Uncertain Allegiance: the Soviet Union and the Czechoslovak Army, 1984; (with A. Dallin) The Gorbachev Era, 1986; (with P. Zelikow) Germany Unified and Europe Transformed, 1995; Extraordinary, Ordinary People: a memoir of family, 2010; No Higher Honour: a memoir of my years in Washington, 2011; contrib. numerous articles on Soviet and E European foreign and defense policy. *Address:* Hoover Institution, Stanford University, Stanford, CA 94305–6010, USA.

RICE, Dennis George, PhD; Social Security (formerly National Insurance) Commissioner, 1979–98; a Child Support Commissioner, 1993–98; a Recorder, 1991–97; *b* 27 Nov. 1927; *s* of George Henry Rice and Ethel Emily Rice; *m* 1959, Jean Beryl Wakefield; one *s*. *Educ:* City of London Sch.; King's Coll., Cambridge (Scholar and Prizeman; BA 1950, LLB 1951, MA 1955); London Sch. of Econs (PhD 1956). Called to the Bar, Lincoln's Inn, 1952. Served RAF, 1946–48. Entered J. Thorn and Sons Ltd, 1952; Dir, 1955; Man. Dir, 1956; Chm. and Man. Dir, 1958–69; in practice at Chancery Bar, 1970–79. Member: Cttee of Timber Bldg Manufrs Assoc., 1967–69; Cttee of Joinery and Woodwork Employers Fedn, 1968–69. *Publications:* Rockingham Ornamental Porcelain, 1965; Illustrated Guide to Rockingham Pottery and Porcelain, 1971; Derby Porcelain: the golden years, 1750–1770, 1983; English Porcelain Animals of the Nineteenth Century, 1989; Cats in English Porcelain of the Nineteenth Century, 2002; Dogs in English Porcelain of the Nineteenth Century, 2002; articles on company law in legal jls and on Rockingham porcelain in art magazines. *Recreations:* history of English porcelain, gardening. *Address:* Mouse Cottage, 28 Springett Avenue, Ringmer, E Sussex BN8 5HE. *Club:* Reform.

RICE, Maj.-Gen. Sir Desmond (Hind Garrett), KCVO 1989 (CVO 1985); CBE 1976 (OBE 1970); Vice Adjutant General, 1978–79; *b* 1 Dec. 1924; *s* of Arthur Garrett Rice and Alice Constance (*née* Henman); *m* 1954, Denise Ann (*née* Ravenscroft); one *d*. *Educ:* Marlborough College. Commissioned into The Queen's Bays, 1944; psc 1954; 1st The Queen's Dragoon Guards, 1958; jssc 1963; First Comdg Officer, The Royal Yeomanry, 1967–69; Col GS 4 Div., 1970–73; BGS (MO) MoD, 1973–75; rcds 1976; Director of Manning (Army), 1977–78. Col, 1st The Queen's Dragoon Guards, 1980–86. Sec., Central Chancery of Orders of Knighthood, 1980–89. An Extra Gentleman Usher to HM Queen, 1989–. *Recreations:* field sports, gardening. *Address:* Fairway, Malacca Farm, West Clandon, Surrey GU4 7UQ. *T:* (01483) 222677. *Club:* Cavalry and Guards.

RICE, Sir Duncan; *see* Rice, Sir C. D.

RICE, Maureen; *see* Rice-Knight, M.

RICE, Maurice; *see* Rice, T. M.

RICE, Noel Stephen Cracroft, MD; FRCS, FRCOphth; Consulting Surgeon, Moorfields Eye Hospital, since 1996 (Consultant Surgeon, 1967–96); Hospitaller, St John of Jerusalem, 1996–2002; *b* 26 Dec. 1931; *s* of late Raymond Arthur Cracroft Rice and Doris Ivy Rice (*née* Slater); *m* 1st, 1957, Karin Elsa Brita Linell (*d* 1992); two *s* one *d*; 2nd, 1997, Countess Ulla Mörner. *Educ:* Haileybury and ISC; Clare Coll., Cambridge (MA, BChir, MD); St Bartholomew's Hosp. House appts, St Bartholomew's Hosp., 1956–57; Jun. Specialist, RAF, 1957–60 (Flt Lt); Registrar, Sen. Registrar, Moorfields Eye Hosp., 1962–65; Sen. Lectr, 1965–70, Clin. Teacher, 1970–91, Dean, 1991–96, Inst. of Ophthalmology. Vice-Pres., Ophthalmol Soc.; Member: Council, Coll. of Ophthalmologists; Internat. Council of Ophthalmol.; Acad. Ophth. Internat. Vis. Prof., Nat. Univ. of Singapore. St Eric's Medal, Karolinska Inst., Stockholm. KStJ 1996. Order of the Falcon (Iceland). *Publications:* contribs to sci. jls on subjects related to ophthalmology. *Recreation:* fly fishing.

RICE, Dr Patricia; Senior Research Fellow and Strategy Officer, Department of Economics, University of Oxford, since 2007; *b* Plymouth, 17 Nov. 1951; *d* of George Alfred Rice and Marion Annette Rice (*née* Gale); *m* 1983, Prof. Anthony James Venables, *qv*; one *s* one *d*. *Educ:* Plymouth High Sch. for Girls; Univ. of Warwick (BSc 1st Cl. Hons 1973; MA 1974); Harvard Univ. (Frank Knox Schol.); Nuffield Coll., Oxford (DPhil 1981). Lectr in Econs, Univ. of Sussex, 1977–89; University of Southampton: Lectr in Econs, 1989–99; Sen. Lectr, 1999–2007; Hd of Econs, 2003–06. Vis. Prof. of Econs, Univ. of BC, 1982–83. Res. Consultant, World Bank, 1999. Academic Assessor for Fast Stream Economist Recruitment Service, HM Govt, 1994–97; Member: Adv. Panel, DCLG, 2007–10; Sch. Teacher Rev. Bd, 2011– (Chair, 2014–). Mem. Council, REconS, 2006–11. *Publications:* contribs to acad. jls on labour econs and regl econs. *Address:* Department of Economics, University of Oxford, Manor Road Building, Manor Road, Oxford OX1 3UQ.

RICE, Peter Anthony Morrish; stage designer; *b* 13 Sept. 1928; *s* of Cecil Morrish Rice and Ethel (*née* Blacklaw); *m* 1954, Patricia Albeck; one *s*. *Educ:* St Dunstan's Coll., Surrey; Royal Coll. of Art (ARCA 1951). Designed first professional prodn, Sex and the Seraphim, Watergate Theatre, London, 1951, followed by The Seraglio, Sadler's Wells Opera, 1952, and Arlecchino, Glyndebourne, 1954; subsequently has designed over 100 plays, operas and ballets, including: *plays:* Time Remembered, 1954; The Winter's Tale, and Much Ado About Nothing, Old Vic, 1956; Living for Pleasure, 1956; A Day in the Life of…, 1958; The Lord Chamberlain Regrets, and Toad of Toad Hall, 1961; The Farmer's Wife, The Italian Straw Hat, and Heartbreak House, Chichester, 1966; Flint, and Arms and the Man, 1970; Happy Birthday, 1977; Private Lives, Greenwich and West End, 1980; Present Laughter, Greenwich and West End, 1981; Cavell, and Goodbye Mr Chips, Chichester, 1982; The Sleeping Prince, Chichester and West End, 1983; Forty Years On, Chichester and West End, 1984; Thursday's Ladies, Apollo, 1987; Hay Fever, Chichester, and Re: Joyce!, Fortune, 1988; Don't Dress for Dinner, Apollo, 1990; Night Must Fall, Haymarket, 1996; The Importance of Being Earnest, Chichester, transf. Haymarket, 1999; *operas:* Count Ory, Sadler's Wells, 1962; Arabella, Royal Opera, 1964, Paris Opera, 1981, Chicago, 1984, and Covent Garden, 1986; The Thieving Magpie, and The Violins of St Jacques, Sadler's Wells, 1967; La Bohème, Scottish Opera, 1970; The Magic Flute, Ottawa, 1974; Tosca, Scottish Opera, 1980; The Secret Marriage, Buxton Fest., 1981; The Count of Luxembourg, Sadler's Wells, 1982, 1987; Death in Venice, Antwerp, and Die Fledermaus, St Louis, USA, 1983; Manon, Covent Garden, 1987; Cosi Fan Tutte, Ottawa, 1990, Hong Kong, 1991; Carmen, Hong Kong, 1992; Ottone, Tokyo, 1992, QEH, 1993; Madama Butterfly, Holland, 1993; L'Infedelta Delusa, Garsington, 1993; L'Etoile, La Bohème, Carmen, 1995–97, Martha, 2000, Castleward Opera, NI; Un Ballo in Maschera, Iris, Eugene Onegin, 1996–97, Cosi fan tutte, The Yeomen of the Guard, 2000, The Merry Widow, 2006, Lakmé, 2007, Orpheus in the Underworld, 2009, Opera Holland Park; Tosca (revival), Opera di Orviedo, 2009; *ballets:* Romeo and Juliet, Royal Danish Ballet, 1955, new prodn 1995, and London Festival Ballet, 1985; Sinfonietta, Royal Ballet, 1966; The Four Seasons, Royal Ballet, 1974. Theatre interiors: Vaudeville Theatre, London; Grand Theatre, Blackpool; His Majesty's Theatre, Aberdeen; Minerva Studio Theatre, Chichester. *Publications:* The Clothes Children Wore, 1973; Farming, 1974; Narrow Boats, 1976. *Recreation:* ancient films. *Club:* Garrick.

RICE, Rowena C.; *see* Collins Rice.

RICE, Susan Ilene, (Lady Rice), CBE 2005; FCIBS; FRSE; Chairman: Scottish Water, since 2015; Scottish Fiscal Commission, since 2014; *b* 7 March 1946; *m* 1967, C(harles) Duncan Rice (*see* Sir C. D. Rice); two *s* one *d*. *Educ:* Wellesley Coll., Mass (BA); Univ. of Aberdeen (MLitt). Chartered Banker; FCIBS 2000; FRSE 2001. Dean, Saybrook Coll., Yale Univ., 1973–79; Staff Aide to Pres., Hamilton Coll., 1980–81; Dean of Students, Colgate Univ., 1981–86; Sen. Vice Pres. and Div. Hd, Nat West Bancorp, 1986–96; Dir, Business Projects, Hd, Branch Banking, then Man. Dir, Personal Banking, Bank of Scotland, 1997–2000; Chm. and Chief Exec., Lloyds TSB Scotland, 2000–09; Man. Dir, Lloyds Banking Gp Scotland, 2009–14. Non-executive Director: SSE plc (formerly Scottish & Southern Energy plc), 2003–14; Bank of England, 2007–14; Big Society Capital, 2011–; J Sainsbury plc, 2013–; Nat. Centre for Univs and Business, 2013–14; Banking Standards Bd, 2015–; North American Income Trust, 2015–. Pres., Scottish Council of Develt and Industry, 2012–. Regent, RCSE, 2011. CCMI 2003; FRSA 2004. Hon. DBA: Robert Gordon Univ., 2001; Queen Margaret, 2008; Dr *hc* Edinburgh, 2003; Hon. DLitt Heriot-Watt, 2004; DUniv: Paisley, 2005; Glasgow, 2007; Hon. LLD Aberdeen, 2008. *Recreations:* modern art, fly fishing, opera, walking. *Address:* Scottish Water, Castle House, 6 Castle Drive, Carnegie Campus, Dunfermline KY11 8GG.

RICE, Prof. (Thomas) Maurice, PhD; FRS 2002; Professor of Physics, Eidgenössische Technische Hochschule Hönggerberg, Zürich, 1981–2004, now Emeritus; *b* 26 Jan. 1939; *s* of James P. Rice and Maureen K. Rice (*née* Quinn); *m* 1966, Helen D. Spreiter; one *s* two *d*. *Educ:* University Coll., Dublin (BSc 1959, MSc 1960); Churchill Coll., Cambridge (PhD 1964). Asst Lectr, Birmingham Univ., 1963–64; Res. Associate, Univ. of Calif., San Diego, 1964–66; Mem., tech. staff, Bell Labs, Murray Hill, NJ, 1966–81. *Address:* Theoretische Physik, ETH Hönggerberg, 8093 Zürich, Switzerland. *T:* (1) 6332581, *Fax:* (1) 6331115. *E:* rice@itp.phys.ethz.ch.

RICE, Sir Timothy (Miles Bindon), Kt 1994; writer and broadcaster; *b* 10 Nov. 1944; *s* of late Hugh Gordon Rice and Joan Odette Rice; *m* 1974, Jane Artereta McIntosh; one *s* one *d*; partner, Nell Sully; one *d*. *Educ:* Lancing Coll. EMI Records, 1966–68; Norrie Paramor Org., 1968–69. Lyrics for stage musicals (with music by Andrew Lloyd Webber): The Likes of Us, 1965; Joseph and the Amazing Technicolor Dreamcoat, 1968; Jesus Christ Superstar, 1970; Evita, 1976; Cricket, 1986; The Wizard of Oz, 2011 (some songs only); (with music by Stephen Oliver) Blondel, 1983; (with music by Benny Andersson and Björn Ulvaeus) Chess, 1984; (with music by Michel Berger and book by Luc Plamondon) Tycoon, 1992; (with music by Alan Menken) Beauty and the Beast, 1994 (some songs only); (with music by John Farrar) Heathcliff, 1996; (with music by Alan Menken) King David, 1997; (with music by Elton John) Aida, 1998; (with music by Stuart Brayson) From Here to Eternity, 2013; lyrics for film musicals: (with music by Alan Menken) Aladdin, 1992, expanded for theatre, 2014; (with music by Elton John) The Lion King, 1994, expanded for theatre, 1997; (with music by Elton John) The Road to El Dorado, 2000; (with music by Tchaikovsky) Nutcracker - The True Story, 2009; (with various composers) Jock of the Bushfeld, 2010. Producer, Anything Goes, Prince Edward Theatre, 1989. Lyrics for songs, 1975–, with other composers, incl. Marvin Hamlisch, Rick Wakeman, Vangelis, Paul McCartney, Mike Batt, Francis Lai, John Barry, Freddie Mercury, Richard Kerr, Burt Bacharach, Graham Gouldman, Michael Kamen, Malcolm Arnold and Lalo Schifrin. Awards include: Oscar and Golden Globe for Best Original Film Song, A Whole New World (music by Alan Menken), 1992, for Can You Feel the Love Tonight (music by Elton John), 1994 and for You Must Love Me (music by Andrew Lloyd Webber), 1996; gold and platinum records in over 20 countries, 13 Ivor Novello Awards, 3 Tony Awards and 6 Grammy Awards (incl. Song of the Year for A Whole New World, 1993); Star, Hollywood Walk of Fame, 2008; Olivier Special Award, 2012. Researcher, writer and presenter, Tim Rice's American Pie (52-part series), BBC Radio 2, 2010–11. Film début as actor in insultingly small rôle, The Survivor, 1980; even smaller rôle in About A Boy, 2002. Cameron Mackintosh Vis. Prof. of Contemporary Theatre, Univ. of Oxford, 2003. Chairman: Foundn for Sport and the Arts, 1991–; Lancing Coll. Develt, 2006–; Trustee, Chance to Shine, 2005–. Former Pres., Lord's Taverners. Fellow, BASCA, 2010. *Publications:* Heartaches Cricketers' Almanack, yearly, 1975–; (ed) Lord's Taverners Sticky Wicket Book, 1979; Treasures of Lord's, 1989; Oh, What a Circus (autobiog.), 1999; (with Andrew Lloyd Webber): Evita, 1978; Joseph and the Amazing Technicolor Dreamcoat, 1982; (jtly) Guinness Books of British Hit Singles and Albums and associated pubns, 1977–96, 31 books in all; (jtly) The Complete Eurovision Song Contest Companion, 1998. *Recreations:* cricket, history of popular music, chickens. *Clubs:* Garrick, MCC (Pres., 2002–03; Trustee, 2006–11), Groucho, Dramatists', Saints and Sinners (Chm., 1990), Soho House; Cricket Writers.

RICE, Victor Albert; Chief Executive, LucasVarity plc, 1996–99; President, Ravelin LLC, 1999; *b* 7 March 1941; *o s* of late Albert Edward Rice and of Rosina Emmeline (*née* Pallant); *m* 1984, Corinne Sutcliffe. Left sch. at 16 to join Finance Dept, Ford UK, 1957; various finance posts with Ford, Cummins and Chrysler, 1957–70; Comptroller, Northern European Ops, Perkins Engines Gp, 1970–75; Corporate Comptroller, Massey Ferguson (Perkins' parent co.), 1975–78; Varity Corporation: Pres. and Chief Operating Officer, 1978–80; Chm. and CEO, 1980–96. Liveryman, Glaziers' Co., 1978–. Mem. Council, Univ. of Buffalo, 1999. *Recreations:* golf, gardening, opera, ballet, theatre.

RICE-KNIGHT, Maureen, (Maureen Rice); Editor-in-Chief (formerly Editorial Director), Cedar Publishing, since 2010; *b* 13 Dec. 1958; *d* of Patrick Rice and Anastasia Rice (*née* McGuire); *m* 1986, David Peter Knight; one *s* one *d*. *Educ:* Gumley House Convent Grammar Sch., Isleworth; Polytechnic of Central London (BA Hons Media Studies; BA Hons Journalism). Magazines: Features Editor, Mizz, 1985; Dep. Editor, No 1, 1985; Editor, Mizz, 1986; Editor, 19, 1988; Editor, Options, 1991–98; Editor, Psychologies, 2005–09. Mem. Cttee, Women in Journalism (Co-Chm., 2010–11). FRSA. Editor of Year Awards: (Consumer Mags), PPA, 2008; (Lifestyle Mags), BSME, 2008. *Recreations:* reading, cinema, food, walking, arts.

RICH, Harry Paul; Chief Executive, Royal Institute of British Architects, since 2009; *b* Birmingham, 15 Jan. 1958; *s* of late Walter Rich and of Doreen Rich (*née* Seager, now Coleman); civil partnership 2006, Richard Scandrett. *Educ:* King Edward VI Camp Hill Sch., Birmingham; Birmingham Univ. (LLB Hons); Coll. of Law, London. Admitted as solicitor, 1983; Solicitor, Warner Cranston, 1981–83; Managing Director: Rich & Pattison Ltd, 1984–94; Tandem (UK) Ltd, 1995–98; Dir, 1999–2003, Dep. Chief Exec., 2003–07, Design Council; Chief Exec., Enterprise Insight, 2007–09. Chm., New Moon Pubns plc, 1990–93. Member: Council, ASA, 1997–2003; Charter Compliance Panel, Press Complaints Commn, 2007–09; Bd, Press Recognition Panel, 2014–. Chm., Student and Academic Campaign for Soviet Jews, 1983–88; Mem., Exec. Cttee, Bd of Deputies of British Jews, 1985–94. Mem., Internat. Adv. Council, Design Mgt Inst., USA, 2004–11; Gov., Univ. for Creative Arts, 2009–. Chm., JAT (Jewish sexual health charity), 1998–2007. Mem., Law Soc., 1983–; Affiliate Mem., RIBA, 2010. MInstD 2000; CCMI 2012. FRSA. JP London 1998–2001. *Recreations:* theatre and music, enquiring and understanding. *Address:* Royal Institute of British Architects, 66 Portland Place, W1B 1AD. *T:* (020) 7307 3664. *E:* harry.rich@riba.org. *Club:* Groucho.

RICH, Marcus; Chief Executive, Time Inc. (UK) Ltd (formerly IPC Media Ltd), since 2014; *b* Wisbech, 21 June 1959; *s* of Eric Rich and Pamela Rich (*née* White); *m* 2004, Liza Hill; three *s* one *d*. *Educ:* King's Lynn Grammar Sch. Norfolk Coll. of Arts and Technol. (HND 1980); Coll. for Distributive Trades (CAM Dip. 1982). Mgt Trainee, Foster Refrigeration UK, 1978–82; Res. Manager, Emap Nationals, 1982–83; Mktg Manager, Emap Business, 1983–85; Gp Account Dir, McCann Erickson, 1985–92; Mktg Dir, Emap Images, 1992–94; Publishing Dir, Emap Metro, 1994–97; Man. Dir, Emap Australia, 1997–99; Pres., Emap Metro LLC USA, 1999–2002; Managing Director: FHM Worldwide, 2002–04; Emap Performance, 2004–05; Emap Advertising, 2005–06; Gp Man. Dir, Bauer Advertising and Bauer Consumer Media Lifestyle Mags, 2006–14. *Recreations:* horse riding, ski-ing, music. *Address:* Time Inc. (UK) Ltd, Blue Fin Building, 110 Southwark Street, SE1 0SU. *T:* (020) 3148 5102. *E:* marcus.rich@timeinc.com. *Clubs:* Soho House, Solus.

RICH, Michael Anthony; Regional Chairman, Industrial Tribunals, Southampton, 1987–96; *b* 16 March 1931; *s* of Joseph and Kate Alexandra Rich; *m* 1959, Helen Kit Marston, MB, BS; one *s* one *d*. *Educ:* Kimbolton Sch., Hunts; Leicester Univ. (LLM). Admitted Solicitor, 1954. Army Legal Aid, 1954–56; Partner, Rich and Carr, Leicester, 1960–76; Part-time Chm., 1972 and 1996–99, Permanent Chm., 1976, Industrial Tribunals. President: Leicester Law Soc., 1976–77; Council of Industrial Tribunal Chairmen, 1993–94. Trustee: Ulverscroft Foundn, 1972–97; Millennium Meml Hall Trust, 2005–10. *Publications:* (with I. A. Edwards) Mead's Unfair Dismissal, 5th edn, 1994; Industrial Tribunal Chairmen's Handbook, 1997. *Recreations:* railway modelling, France. *Address:* 4 Hickory Drive, Harestock, Winchester, Hants SO22 6NJ.

RICH, His Honour Michael Samuel; QC 1980; a Circuit Judge, 1991–2005; *b* 18 Aug. 1933; *s* of late Sidney Frank Rich, OBE and of Erna Babette; *m* 1963, Janice Sarita Benedictus (*d* 2011); three *s* one *d*. *Educ:* Dulwich Coll.; Wadham Coll., Oxford (MA, 1st Class Hons PPE). Called to the Bar, Middle Temple, 1958 (Bencher, 1985; Reader, 2006); a Recorder, 1986–91; Deputy High Court Judge: Chancery Div., 1992–2005; QBD, 1993–2005. Mem., Lands Tribunal, 1993–2006. Hon. Pres., Dulwich Soc., 2001–11. Medal of Merit, Boy Scouts Assoc., 1970. *Publications:* (jtly) Hill's Law of Town and Country Planning, 5th edn, 1968. *Address:* 5 John Adam House, 17–19 John Adam Street, WC2N 6JG. *Clubs:* Garrick, Dulwich; Maccabæans.

RICH, Nigel Mervyn Sutherland, CBE 1995; Chairman, SEGRO (formerly Slough Estates) plc, since 2006; *b* 30 Oct. 1945; *s* of Charles Albert Rich and Mina Mackintosh Rich; *m* 1970, Cynthia Elizabeth (*née* Davies); two *s* two *d*. *Educ:* Sedbergh Sch.; New Coll., Oxford (MA). FCA. Deloittes, London and New York, 1967–73; Jardine Matheson, Hong Kong, Johannesburg, Manila, 1974–94; Man. Dir, Jardine Matheson Holdings, 1989–94; Chief Exec., Trafalgar House, 1994–96. Chairman: Hamptons Gp, 1997–2005; Exel plc, 2002–05; CP Ships, 2005; Xchanging plc, 2008–11 (Dep. Chm., 2006–08); Director: Matheson & Co., 1994–; Pacific Assets, 1997–; British Empire Securities, 2012–. Co-Chm., Philippine British Business Council, 2001–. Hon. Steward, HK Jockey Club, 1994–. Freeman, City of London, 1970; Master, Tobacco Pipemakers' and Tobacco Blenders' Co., 2008–09. *Recreations:* golf, horseracing. *Address:* SEGRO plc, Cunard House, 15 Regent Street, SW1Y 4LR. *Clubs:* Boodle's, Hurlingham, Turf, MCC; Denham Golf; Royal and Ancient Golf (Mem., Gen. Cttee, 2012–; Chm., Business Affairs Cttee, 2013–); Royal St George's Golf; Royal County Down Golf; New Zealand Golf; Leopard Creek Golf (S Africa).

RICHARD, family name of **Baron Richard**.

RICHARD, Baron *cr* 1990 (Life Peer), of Ammanford in the County of Dyfed; **Ivor Seward Richard;** PC 1993; QC 1971; *b* 30 May 1932; *s* of Seward Thomas Richard, mining and electrical engineer, and Isabella Irene Richard; *m* 1st, 1956, Geraldine Moore (marr. diss. 1962); one *s*; 2nd, 1962, Alison Imrie (marr. diss. 1983); one *s* one *d*; 3rd, 1989, Janet Jones; one *s*. *Educ:* St Michael's Sch., Bryn, Llanelly; Cheltenham Coll.; Pembroke Coll., Oxford (Wightwick Scholar; BA (Jurisprudence) 1953, MA 1970; Hon Fellow, 1981). Called to Bar, Inner Temple, 1955, Bencher, 1985. Practised in chambers, London, 1955–74. UK Perm. Representative to UN, 1974–79; Mem., Commn of EEC, 1981–84; Chm., Rhodesia Conf., Geneva, 1976. Chm., Commn on Powers and Electoral Arrangements of Nat. Assembly for Wales, 2002–04. Parly Candidate, S Kensington, 1959; MP (Lab) Barons Court, 1964–Feb. 1974. Delegate: Assembly, Council of Europe, 1965–68; Western European Union, 1965–68; Vice-Chm., Legal Cttee, Council of Europe, 1966–67; PPS, Sec. of State for Defence, 1966–69; Parly Under-Sec. (Army), Min. of Defence, 1969–70; Opposition Spokesman, Broadcasting, Posts and Telecommunications, 1970–71; Dep. Spokesman, Foreign Affairs, 1971–74; Leader of the Opposition, H of L, 1992–97; Lord Privy Seal and Leader, H of L, 1997–98; Chairman: H of L Select Cttee on Constitutional Reform Bill, 2004; Jt Cttee on H of L Reform Bill, 2011–12. Chm., World Trade Centre Wales Ltd (Cardiff), 1985–97; Dir, World Trade Centre (Hldgs) Ltd, 2002–. Pres., UK-Korea Forum for the Future, 2000–07. Member: Fabian Society; Society of Labour Lawyers. *Publications:* (jtly) Europe or the Open Sea, 1971; We, the British, 1983 (USA); (jtly) Unfinished Business, 1999; articles in various political jls. *Recreations:* playing piano, watching football matches, talking. *Address:* House of Lords, SW1A 0PW.

RICHARD, Dame Alison (Fettes), DBE 2010; PhD; Vice-Chancellor, Cambridge University, 2003–10; Fellow of Newnham College, Cambridge, 2003–10, now Hon. Fellow; *b* 1 March 1948; *d* of Gavin and Joyce Richard; *m* 1976, Robert E. Dewar (*d* 2013); two *d* (one *s* decd). *Educ:* Queenswood; Newnham Coll., Cambridge (BA 1969, MA); Queen Elizabeth Coll., London (PhD 1973). Yale University: Asst Prof., 1972–80; Associate Prof., 1980–86; Prof. of Anthropol., 1986–2003; Provost, 1994–2002; Franklin Muzzy Crosby Prof. of the Human Envmt, 1998–2003, Emerita, 2003–; Sen. Res. Scientist, 2011–; Dir, Yale Peabody Mus. of Natural Hist., 1991–94; Co-dir, Prog. of Conservation and Develt in Southern Madagascar, 1977–. Consultant, Species Survival Commn, IUCN, 1982–90. Chair, Advisory Board: Cambridge Conservation Initiative, 2011–; Perrett Laver, 2012–; Member, Editorial Board: Folia Primatologica, 1982–95; Amer. Jl of Primatology, 1988–97. Member: Sci. Adv. Council, L. S. B. Leakey Foundn, 1986–96; Physical Anthropol. Rev. Panel, NSF, 1988–91; Sci. Adv. Council, Wenner-Gren Foundn for Anthropol Res., 1991–94; Nat. Council, 1992–95, Bd, 1995–2004, WWF-US; Bd, Liz Claiborne/Art Ortenberg Foundn, 1998–2014. Trustee: WWF Internat., 2007–; Howard Hughes Med. Inst., 2008–; Liz Claiborne/Art Ortenberg Foundn, 2014–. DL Cambs, 2004–10. Hon. Dr: Peking, 2004; Antananarivo, Madagascar, 2005; York, Canada, 2006; Edinburgh, 2006; QUB, 2008; Anglia Ruskin, 2008; Yale, 2009; Chinese Univ. of HK, 2009; EWHA Women's Univ., Korea, 2009; Exeter, 2010; Cambridge, 2011. Officier, Ordre National (Madagascar), 2005. *Publications:* Behavioral Variation: case study of a Malagasy lemur, 1978; Primates in Nature, 1985; contrib. numerous scientific articles on primate evolution, ecology and social behaviour to acad. jls. *Recreations:* opera, gardening, cooking. *Club:* Athenæum.

RICHARD, Sir Cliff, Kt 1995; OBE 1980; singer, actor; *b* 14 Oct. 1940; *s* of late Rodger Webb and Dorothy Webb; *né* Harry Rodger Webb; changed name to Cliff Richard, 1958. *Educ:* Riversmead Sch., Cheshunt. Awarded 14 Gold Discs for records: Living Doll, 1959; The Young Ones, 1962; Bachelor Boy, 1962; Lucky Lips, 1963; Congratulations, 1968; Power to all Our Friends, 1973; Devil Woman, 1976; We Don't Talk Anymore, 1979; Wired for Sound, 1981; Daddy's Home, 1981; Living Doll (with The Young Ones), 1986; All I Ask of You (with Sarah Brightman), 1986; Mistletoe and Wine, 1988; The Millennium Prayer, 1999; also 37 Silver Discs and 3 Platinum Discs (Daddy's Home, 1981; All I Ask of You, 1986; The Millennium Prayer, 1999). Films: Serious Charge, 1959; Expresso Bongo, 1960; The Young Ones, 1962; Summer Holiday, 1963; Wonderful Life, 1964; Finders Keepers, 1966; Two a Penny, 1968; His Land, 1970; Take Me High, 1973. Own TV series, ATV and BBC. Stage: rep. and variety seasons; Time, Dominion, 1986–87; Heathcliff, Apollo, 1997. Top Box Office Star of GB, 1962–63 and 1963–64; UK's best-selling singles artist of all time, 2004. 50th anniversary in music business, 2008–09; 50th anniversary internat. reunion tour with The Shadows, 2009–10; Bold as Brass tour, 2010; Soulicious UK tour, 2011; Still Reelin' and A Rockin' tour, 2013; 75th Birthday tour, 2015. *Publications:* Questions, 1970; The Way I See It, 1972; The Way I See It Now, 1975; Which One's Cliff, 1977; Happy Christmas from Cliff, 1980; You, Me and Jesus, 1983; Mine to Share, 1984; Jesus, Me and You, 1985; Single-minded, 1988; Mine Forever, 1989; Jesus Here and Now, 1996; My Story: a celebration of 40 years in show business, 1998; (with Penny Junor) My Life, My Way, 2008. *Recreation:* tennis. *Address:* c/o PO Box 46C, Esher, Surrey KT10 0RB. *T:* (01372) 467752. *Club:* All England Lawn Tennis and Croquet.

RICHARDS, family name of **Barons Milverton** and **Richards of Herstmonceux**.

RICHARDS OF HERSTMONCEUX, Baron *cr* 2014 (Life Peer), of Emsworth in the County of Hampshire; **Gen. David Julian Richards,** GCB 2011 (KCB 2007); CBE 2000; DSO 2001; DL; Chairman: Palliser Associates Ltd, since 2013; Equilibrium Global Ltd, since 2013; non-executive Chairman, Arturius International, since 2013; Chief of the Defence Staff, 2010–13; Aide-de-Camp General to the Queen, 2008–13; *b* 4 March 1952; *s* of John Downie Richards and Pamela Mary Richards (*née* Reeves); *m* 1978, Caroline Reyne (*née* Bond); two *d*. *Educ:* Eastbourne Coll. (Hd Boy, Capt. of Rugger); UWCC (BA Politics and Econs 1974). CO 3rd Regt RHA, 1991–94; Col Army Plans, 1994–96; Comdr 4th Armoured Bde, 1996–98; Comdr Jt Force HQ, 1998–2001; Commander British Joint Task Force: East Timor, 1999; Sierra Leone, 2000; COS ACE RRC, 2001–02; ACGS, 2002–04; Commander: ARRC, 2005–07; NATO Internat. Security and Assistance Force, Afghanistan, 2006–07; C-in-C, Land Forces, 2008–09; Chief of Gen. Staff, 2009–10. Mem., RUSI, 1992– (Mem. Council, 1995–96). Colonel Commandant: RA, 2005–12; Bde of Gurkhas, 2007–12; Media Ops Gp TA, 2008–12. Sen. Advr, IISS, 2013–. Dep. Grand Pres., Royal

Commonwealth Ex-Services League, 2013–. President: Combined Services Polo Assoc., 2010–; Combined Ops Pilotage Parties, 2011–; Mil. Historical Soc., 2012–; Vice Pres., Forces Pension Soc., 2014–. Patron: Afghan Appeal Fund, 2007–; Armed Forces Moslem Assoc., 2008–; Wilts Search and Rescue, 2009–11; Dougie Dalzell MC Trust, 2010–; Row to Recovery, 2010–; The Garrison, 2013–; UK Assoc. for the Blind Schs of Sierra Leone, 2014–; Vice Patron, Blind Veterans UK, 2012–; Contributor, Speakers for Schs, 2011–. Admiral, Army Sailing Assoc., 2008–10. DL Hants, 2014. *Publications:* (ed jtly) Victory Among People—Lessons from Countering Insurgency and Stabilising Fragile States, 2011; (contrib.) Oxford Handbook of War, 2012; (contrib.) Blair's Generals, 2013; (autobiog.) Taking Command, 2014; articles in RUSI Jl, SA Inst. of Internat. Affairs Jl, British Army Rev., RA Jl and other mil. pubns. *Recreations:* offshore sailing, military history, riding, gardening, opera. *Address:* c/o Regimental Headquarters Royal Artillery, Royal Artillery Barracks, Larkhill, Salisbury, Wilts SP4 8QT. *T:* (01980) 845788. *Clubs:* Army and Navy, Cavalry and Guards, Pitt; Royal Artillery Yacht (Adm., 2012–), Royal Cruising, British Kiel Yacht (Cdre, 2001–02; Adm., 2005–).

RICHARDS, Prof. (Adrian) John, PhD; Professor of Botany, University of Newcastle upon Tyne, 2002–04, now Professor Emeritus; *b* 26 Jan. 1943; *s* of Dr Taliesin Richards and Roonie Eileen Richards; *m* 1966, Sheila Mackie; one *s* two *d. Educ:* Leighton Park Sch., Reading; University Coll., Durham (BSc 1964; PhD 1968). Demonstrator, Botany Sch., Univ. of Oxford, 1967–70; University of Newcastle upon Tyne: Lectr, 1970–85; Sen. Lectr, 1985–96; Reader in Botany, 1996–2002. Mem., Jt Rock Gdn Cttee, RHS, 1995–. Vice-Pres., Botanical Soc. of British Isles, 2002–; Pres., Alpine Gdn Soc., 2003–06. *Publications:* Plant Breeding Systems, 1986, 2nd edn 1997; Primula, 1993, 2nd edn 2003; (with A. A. Dudman) Dandelions of the British Isles, 1997; Mountain Flower Walks: the Greek mainland, 2008; numerous botanical papers, esp. in New Phytologist and Heredity. *Recreations:* Alpine gardening, plant exploration, mountain walking (especially in Greece), birding, photographing butterflies. *Address:* School of Biology, Ridley Building, University of Newcastle upon Tyne NE1 7RU. *T:* (0191) 222 8839, *Fax:* (0191) 222 5229.

RICHARDS, Alun; *see* Richards, R. A.

RICHARDS, Anne Helen, CVO 2014; CBE 2015; Chief Investment Officer, since 2003, Executive Director, since 2011, Aberdeen Asset Management plc; *b* 7 Aug. 1964; *d* of Michael and Helen Finnigan; *m* 1991, Matthew John Richards; two *s. Educ:* Univ. of Edinburgh (BSc Hons Electronics and Elec. Engrg 1985); INSEAD (MBA 1992); CDipAF 1991. CEng 1992; MIET 1992; Chartered FCSI 2010 (FSI 2007). Res. Fellow, European Lab. for Particle Physics, CERN, 1985–88; Consultant, Cambridge Consultants Ltd, 1989–91; Analyst, Alliance Capital Ltd, 1992–94; Portfolio Manager, J P Morgan Investment Mgt, 1994–98; Man. Dir, Merrill Lynch Investment Managers, 1999–2002; Jt Man. Dir, Edinburgh Fund Managers plc, 2002–03. Non-exec. Dir, esure Gp plc, 2012–. Mem. Council, Duchy of Lancaster, 2005–14; Director: Scottish Financial Enterprise, 2006–12; Nuclear Liabilities Fund, 2008–11. Chm., CERN & Soc. Foundn Bd, 2014–; Dir and Trustee, EveryChild, 2005–13; Dir, Scottish Chamber Orch., 2008–14. Gov., Caledonian Res. Foundn, 2007–09. Mem., 2007–14, Vice Convener, 2014–, Ct, Univ. of Edinburgh. Hon. DLitt Heriot-Watt, 2013. *Recreations:* music, mountains, family, gardening. *Address:* Aberdeen Asset Management, 40 Princes Street, Edinburgh EH2 2BY.

RICHARDS, (Anthony) Charles, CVO 2012 (LVO 2006; MVO 1997); Deputy Master of HM Household and Equerry to the Queen, since 1999; *b* 20 Feb. 1953; *s* of Dudley Raymond Richards and Eleonora Caroline Richards (*née* Otter); *m* 1978, Serena Anne Spencer; three *s. Educ:* Marlborough Coll.; RMA Sandhurst. Commissioned Welsh Guards, 1973; served with 1st Bn Welsh Guards, UK and BAOR, 1973–82; seconded 1st Bn 2nd Gurkha Rifles, Hong Kong, 1982–84; Staff Coll., 1985; BAOR, 1986–90; 2 i/c 1st Bn Welsh Guards, UK, 1990–92; Staff Officer, HQ London Dist, 1992–94; Equerry to the Duke of Edinburgh, 1994–97; Div. Lt Col, Foot Guards, 1997–99, retired 1999. *Recreations:* shooting, fishing, travel. *Address:* Rotherby Grange, Melton Mowbray, Leics LE14 2LP. *T:* (01664) 434206.

RICHARDS, Brian Henry, CEng, FIET; *b* 19 July 1938; *s* of Alfred Edward Richards and Lilian Maud Richards (*née* Bennett); *m* 1961, Jane Wilkins; one *s* one *d. Educ:* Buckhurst Hill County Grammar Sch.; St John's College, Cambridge (Mech. Sci. Tripos, 1st Class Hons 1959, BA 1960; MA 1965). GEC Electronics, later Marconi Defence Systems, 1960–87: Guided Weapons Division: various develt, systems, project and gen. management appts, 1960–84; Dir, Guided Weapons, 1985; RCDS, 1986; Asst Man. Dir, 1987; Technical Dir, Hunting Engineering, 1988–90; Chief Exec., Atomic Weapons Estabt, 1990–94; Weapon Systems Dir, 1995–2001, Special Projects Dir, 2001–02, Dynamics Div., GEC-Marconi Dynamics, later Missile Systems Div., Alenia-Marconi Systems; Projects Advr, MBDA UK, 2002–03. Consultant, Defence Res. Progs, Soc. of British Aerospace Cos, subseq. ADS, 2002–10. *Recreations:* golf, listening to music, reading, travel, gardening, dabbling in the stock market, being a grandparent to four grandsons and one granddaughter!

RICHARDS, Sir Brian (Mansel), Kt 1997; CBE 1990; PhD; Chairman: Alizyme plc, 1996–2009; Xenetic plc (formerly Lipoxen plc), 2005–14; *b* 19 Sept. 1932; *s* of Cyril Mansel Richards and Gwendolyn Hyde Richards; *m* 1st, 1952, Joan Lambert Breese (marr. diss. 2003); one *s* one *d*; 2nd, 2003, June Clark-Richards. *Educ:* Lewis Sch., Pengam, Glam; University Coll. of Wales, Aberystwyth (BSc); King's College London (PhD). British Empire Cancer Fellowship, 1955–57; Nuffield Fellowship, 1957; MRC Biophysics Research Unit, 1957–64; Reader in Biology, Univ. of London, 1964–66; Research Div., G. D. Searle & Co., 1966–86; Vice-Pres., UK Preclinical R&D, 1980–86; Chairman: British Bio-technology Ltd, 1986–89; British Bio-technology Gp, 1989–94; Oxford BioMedica plc, 1996–98; CeNes Ltd, 1996–98; LGC (Holdings) Ltd, 1996–2001; Peptide Therapeutics Group plc, 1997 (Exec. Chm., 1995–97; Dir, 1998–2003); Cozart Biosciences Ltd, 2001–07; MAN Alternative Investments Ltd, 2001–07. Director: Prelude Trust plc, 1997–2003; Innogenetics SA, 1997–2005; Drug Royalty Corp., 1998–2002; Summit (formerly Vastox) plc, 2005–08; Aitua Ltd, 2006–. Hon. Prof. in Life Scis, UCW, Aberystwyth, 1991–. Chm., Biotechnology Working Party, CBI, 1988; Mem., Res. and Manufg Cttee, CBI, 1988; Mem., Sci. Bd, SERC, 1987; Chairman: Biotechnology Jt Adv. Bd, SERC/DTI, 1989; Science-based Cos Cttee, London Stock Exchange, 1994; Member: Adv. Cttee for Genetic Modification (previously Manipulation), HSE, 1984–96; Gene Therapy Adv. Cttee, DoH, 1994–98; BBSRC, 1994–97; Consultant on Biotechnology, OECD, 1987; Specialist Advr, H of L Select Cttee II on Biotechnol. Regulation, 1993. Chm., Roslin Inst., 1995–99. Hon. DSc Abertay Dundee, 1997. *Publications:* papers in sci. jls. *Recreation:* gastronomic travel.

RICHARDS, Carol Anne Seymour-; *see* Seymour, C. A.

RICHARDS, Charles; *see* Richards, Anthony C.

RICHARDS, Clare Mary Joan; *see* Spottiswoode, C. M. J.

RICHARDS, Rt Hon. Sir David (Anthony Stewart), Kt 2003; PC 2015; **Rt Hon. Lord Justice David Richards;** a Lord Justice of Appeal, since 2015; Vice Chancellor, County Palatine of Lancaster, 2008–11; *b* 9 June 1951; *s* of late Kenneth Richards, MBE and Winifred Richards; *m* 1979, Gillian, *er d* of Lt-Col W. A. Taylor; one *s* twin *d. Educ:* Oundle; Trinity Coll., Cambridge (BA 1973; MA 1980). Called to the Bar, Inner Temple, 1974; Bencher, Lincoln's Inn, 2000; a Judge of the High Court, Chancery Div., 2003–15. Junior Counsel (Chancery), DTI, 1989–92; QC 1992. Contrib., 2000–, Jt Gen. Ed., 2009–, Buckley on the Companies Acts. *Address:* Royal Courts of Justice, Strand, WC2A 2LL. *Club:* Garrick.

RICHARDS, Sir David (Gerald), Kt 2006; Chairman, Leicester City Football Club, since 2013; *b* 3 Oct. 1943; *m* Janet; one *s* one *d. Educ:* Comprehensive sch. Mech. engr with own business, 1970–2000; Chairman: Sheffield Wednesday FC, 1990–2000; Premier League (formerly FA Premier League), 1999–2013; Football Foundn, 2003–08. *Address:* c/o Leicester City Football Club, King Power Stadium, Filbert Way, Leicester LE2 7FL.

RICHARDS, David Pender, CBE 2005; Chairman: Prodrive, since 1984; Aston Martin Lagonda Ltd, 2007–14; *b* 3 June 1952; *s* of Geoffrey and Eileen Richards; *m* 1976, Karen Danahur; two *s* one *d. Educ:* Brynhyfryd Sch., Ruthin. Chartered accountancy articles, Cooke & Co., Liverpool, 1970–75; professional rally driver, 1976–81; World Rally Champion, 1981; Team Principal, BAR F1, 2002–04. *Recreations:* flying helicopters, tennis, classic sports cars, sailing, time with the family. *Address:* Prodrive, Banbury, Oxon OX16 3ER. *Clubs:* Royal Automobile; British Racing Drivers' (Silverstone).

RICHARDS, David Thomas; Director of Governance, Welsh Government (formerly Welsh Assembly Government), since 2010; *b* 30 Nov. 1954; *s* of Ralph Henry Richards and Brenda Mary Elizabeth Richards; *m* 1979, Veryan Cumming Black; one *s* two *d. Educ:* Whitchurch High Sch., Cardiff; New Univ. of Ulster, Coleraine (BA Philosophy). Exec. Officer, DTI, 1978–79; Welsh Office: fast stream trainee, 1979–83; Principal: Housing Div., 1983–86; Local Govt Finance Div., 1986–90; Assistant Secretary: Econ. Policy Div., 1990–92; Industrial Policy Div., 1992–94; Finance Programmes Div., 1994–97; Principal Finance Officer, 1997–99; Welsh Assembly Government: Finance Dir, 1999–2006; Dir, Governance in Health Project, later Governance in Wales Prog., 2006–08; Dir of Public Private Partnerships, 2008–10; Dir of Strategic Investment, 2010. Chm., Steering Bd, UK Intellectual Property Office (formerly Patent Office), 2001–. *Recreations:* books, playing the harp, cooking, tennis. *Address:* Welsh Government, Cathays Park, Cardiff CF10 3NQ. *T:* (029) 2082 5931.

RICHARDS, His Honour (David) Wyn; a Circuit Judge, 1998–2008; *b* 22 Sept. 1943; *s* of late Evan Gwylfa Richards and Florence Margretta Richards (*née* Evans); *m* 1972, Thelma Frances Hall; five *s. Educ:* Gwendraeth GS; Llanelli GS; Trinity Hall, Cambridge. Called to the Bar, 1968; a Recorder, 1985–98. Asst Comr, Boundary Commn for Wales, 1982–86, 1992–96. *Address:* c/o Swansea Civil Justice Centre, Caravella House, Quay West, Quay Parade, Swansea SA1 1SP.

RICHARDS, Edward Charles, CBE 2015; Chief Executive, Ofcom, 2006–14; *b* 29 Aug. 1965; *s* of Donald and Pat Richards; partner, Delyth Evans, *qv*; one *s* one *d. Educ:* London Sch. of Econs (BSc 1987; MSc 1989); London Business Sch. (Corp. Finance 1996); Harvard Business Sch. (AMP 2005). Researcher, Diverse Prodns, 1988–89; Policy Advr, Nat. Communications Union, 1989–90; Advr to Gordon Brown, MP, 1990–92; Sen. Consultant, London Econs, 1992–95; Controller, Corporate Strategy, BBC, 1995–99; Sen. Advr, Prime Minister's Office, 1999–2003; Sen. Partner, 2003–05, Chief Operating Officer, 2005–06, Ofcom. *Recreations:* music, fiction, film/theatre, sport.

RICHARDS, Sir Francis Neville, KCMG 2002 (CMG 1994); CVO 1991; DL; Chairman, National Security Inspectorate, 2007–13; Governor and Commander-in-Chief, Gibraltar, 2003–06; *b* 18 Nov. 1945; *s* of Sir (Francis) Brooks Richards, KCMG, DSC and Hazel Myfanwy, *d* of Lt-Col Stanley Price Williams, CIE; *m* 1971, Gillian Bruce Nevill, *d* of late I. S. Nevill, MC and of Dr L. M. B. Dawson; one *s* one *d. Educ:* Eton; King's Coll., Cambridge (MA). Royal Green Jackets, 1967 (invalided, 1969). FCO, 1969; Moscow, 1971; UK Delegn to MBFR negotiations, Vienna, 1973; FCO, 1976–85 (Asst Private Sec. to Sec. of State, 1981–82); Economic and Commercial Counsellor, New Delhi, 1985–88; FCO, 1988–90 (Head, S Asian Dept); High Comr, Windhoek, 1990–92; Minister, Moscow, 1992–95; Dir (Europe), FCO, 1995–97; Dep. Under-Sec. of State, FCO, 1997–98; Dir, GCHQ, 1998–2003. Dir, Centre for Studies in Security and Diplomacy, 2007–10, Hon. Sen. Fellow, 2010–, Univ. of Birmingham. Chm., Internat. Adv. Bd, Altimo, 2008–13. Co. Pres., SSAFA Glos, 2007–. Chm., Bletchley Park Trust, 2007–12; Trustee, Imperial War Mus., 2007– (Dep. Chm., 2009–11; Chm., 2011–). Hon. Col Catering Support Regt, RLC (Vol), 2012–. DL Glos, 2007. DUniv Birmingham, 2012. KStJ 2003. *Recreations:* walking, travelling, riding. *Clubs:* Special Forces, Brooks's.

RICHARDS, Prof. George Maxwell, (Max), TC 2003; PhD; President, Trinidad and Tobago, 2003–13; *b* 1 Dec. 1931; *m* Jean Ramjohn; one *s* one *d. Educ:* Queen's Royal Coll., Port of Spain; Univ. of Manchester (BSc Tech 1955, MSc Tech 1957; Outstanding Alumnus Award, UMIST, 2003); Pembroke Coll., Cambridge (PhD 1963; Hon. Fellow, 2004). Trainee, United British Oilfields of Trinidad Ltd, 1950–51; Shell Trinidad Ltd: Asst Chemist, 1957–58, Chief Chemist, 1958–59; Auxiliary Plants Supervisor, 1959–60; Section Head: Distillation Processes, 1963–64; Catalytic Conversion Processes, 1964–65; Hd, Refinery Ops, 1965; University of the West Indies: Sen Lectr, 1965–70; Hd, Dept of Chem. Engrg, 1969–74; Prof. of Chem. Engrg, 1970–85, now Emeritus; Asst Dean, 1970–74, Dean, 1974–79, Faculty of Engrg; Dep. Principal, St Augustine Campus, and Pro-Vice-Chancellor, 1980–85; Principal, St Augustine, and Pro-Vice-Chancellor, 1985–96; Chancellor, Univ. of Trinidad and Tobago, 2006–11. Chm., Salaries Review Commn, 1977–2003. Hon. FIChemE, 2003. Hon. DLitt Sheffield, 2005; Hon. LLD West Indies, 2006; DUniv Heriot-Watt, 2007. CMT (1st Class), 1977.

RICHARDS, Graham; *see* Richards, William G.

RICHARDS, Sir (Isaac) Vivian (Alexander), KGN 1999; OBE 1994; cricketer; Chairman, West Indies Selection Committee, 2002–04; *b* St Johns, Antigua, 7 March 1952; *s* of Malcolm Richards; *m* Miriam Lewis; one *s* one *d. Educ:* Antigua Grammar School. First class débuts, Leeward Islands, 1971, India (for WI), 1974; played for: Somerset, 1974–86; Queensland, 1976–77; Rishton, Lancs League, 1987; Glamorgan, 1990–93; Capt., WI Cricket Team, 1985–91; played in 100th Test Match, 1988; scored 100th first class century, 1988; 100th Test Match catch, 1988; highest Test score, 291, *v* England, Oval, 1976; highest first class score, 322, *v* Warwicks, Taunton, 1985; fastest Test century *v* England, Antigua, 1986; highest number of Test runs by a West Indian batsman, 1991. WI team coach, tour of NZ, 1999. An ICC Ambassador. Hon. DLitt Exeter, 1986. *Publications:* (with David Foot) Viv Richards (autobiog.), 1982; (with Patrick Murphy) Cricket Masterclass, 1988; (with Michael Middles) Hitting across the Line (autobiog.), 1991; (with Bob Harris) Sir Vivian (autobiog.), 2000. *Recreations:* golf, tennis, music, football. *Address:* 36 Novello Street, SW6 4JB. *T:* (020) 7736 7420.

RICHARDS, Jeremy Simon; His Honour Judge Jeremy Richards; a Circuit Judge, since 2004; Designated Family Judge for Norfolk, since 2007; *b* 18 Sept. 1959; *s* of Richard Elwyn Richards and Rosemary Isobel Richards; *m* 1990, Lesley Isobel Seaton (*née* Buist); one *s* one *d. Educ:* Tywyn Sch.; UCW, Aberystwyth (LLB Hons). Called to the Bar, Gray's Inn, 1981; in practice as barrister, 1981–2004, specialising in children and family work for Official Solicitor, guardians and local authorities. Chm. (pt-time), Employment Tribunals, 1996–2004; Asst Recorder, 1998–2000, Recorder, 2000–04. *Recreations:* sailing, cooking. *Address:* Norwich County Court, The Law Courts, Bishopgate, Norwich NR3 1UR. *T:* (01603) 728200. *Clubs:* Norfolk (Norwich); Norfolk Punt.

RICHARDS, John; *see* Richards, Adrian J. and Richards, Robert J. G.

RICHARDS, Dr John Arthur, OBE 1997; Leader, Climate Change Programme, British Council, 2007–08; Secretary, Putney Bridge Canoe Club, since 2009; *b* 28 Nov. 1946; *s* of Clifford Alban Richards and Helen Mary Richards (*née* Shaw); *m* 1980, Asha Kasbekar; two *s. Educ:* Faringdon Sch.; The Coll., Swindon; Univ. of Surrey (BSc Hons (Chem.) 1969);

Univ. of Nottingham (PhD (Organometallic Chem.) 1975). Plessey Co. Ltd: res., Allen Clarke Res. Centre, 1967–68; Manager, Components Gp, 1969–72; res., Centre de la recherche scientifique, Bordeaux, 1975–76; British Council: London, 1976–77; Bombay, 1977–80; Sci. Officer and Dep. Dir, Japan, 1981–87; on secondment to Cabinet Office, 1987–89; Dir, Sci. and Technol. Dept, London, 1989–92; Hd, Educn and Sci. Dept, 1992–94; Director: Thailand, 1995–2000; Hungary, 2000–03; Nigeria, 2003–06. *Recreations:* reading, canoeing and other water sports, travelling. *Address:* c/o Putney Bridge Canoe Club, 28 Cristowe Road, SW6 3QE. *Club:* Canoe England.

RICHARDS, Julian Charles, FSA; independent archaeologist, broadcaster, writer and educator, since 2004; *b* Nottingham, 22 Nov. 1951; *s* of Albert Charles Richards and Helen Mary Richards; *m* 1987, Susan Jean Lobb; one *s*. *Educ:* Nottingham Boys High Sch.; Reading Univ. (BA Hons Archaeol.). FSA 1992. Field archaeologist and project manager, Berks Archaeol Unit and Wessex Archaeol., 1975–91; Partner, AC Archaeol., 1991–94; fieldworker, English Heritage, 1994–97; presenter and writer: Meet the Ancestors, 1998–2004, Blood of the Vikings, 2002, BBC TV; Mapping the Town, BBC Radio 4, 1999–2005. *Publications:* Stonehenge, 1991; Meet the Ancestors, 1999; Blood of the Vikings, 2001, rev. edn 2002; Stonehenge: a history in photographs, 2004; Stonehenge: the story so far, 2007. *Recreations:* classic cars and historic motorsport, Stonehenge trivia, lecturing. *Address:* Foyle Hill House, Foyle Hill, Shaftesbury, Dorset SP7 0PT. *T:* (01747) 851531. *E:* julian@archaemedia.co.uk.

RICHARDS, Prof. Keith Sheldon, PhD; Professor of Geography, University of Cambridge, 1995–2014, now Emeritus; Fellow of Emmanuel College, Cambridge, since 1984 (Professorial Fellow, since 1995); *b* 25 May 1949; *s* of Maurice and Jean Richards; *m* 1973, Susan Mary Brooks. *Educ:* Falmouth Grammar Sch.; Jesus Coll., Cambridge (MA 1974; PhD 1975). Lectr, then Sen. Lectr, Lanchester Poly., 1973–78; Lectr, then Sen. Lectr, Univ. of Hull, 1978–84; University of Cambridge: Lectr, 1984–95; Reader in Physical Geog., 1995; Head of Geography Dept, 1994–99; Dir, Scott Polar Res. Inst., 1997–2002. Chm., Brit. Geomorph. Res. Gp, 1994–95; Member: various NERC Cttees, 1990–93, 1995–97, Peer Review Coll., 2004–07; ESRC Peer Rev. Coll., 2010–12. Vice-Pres. (Research), RGS, 2004–07; Pres., BAAS Geography Section, 2005–06. Mem./Chm., 2001 and 2008 RAE Panels, and 2013 REF Panels. FRSA 2005; Fellow, British Soc. for Geomorph., 2014. Cuthbert Peek Award, 1983, Founders Medal, 2013, RGS; Linton Award, British Soc. for Geomorph., 2015. *Publications:* Stochastic Processes in One-dimensional Series: an introduction, 1979; (ed jtly) Geomorphological Techniques, 1982; Rivers: form and process in alluvial channels, 1982; (ed jtly) Geomorphology and Soils, 1985; (ed) River Channels: environment and process, 1987; (ed jtly) Slope Stability: geotechnical engineering and geomorphology, 1987; (ed jtly) Landform Monitoring, Modelling and Analysis, 1998; (ed jtly) Glacier Hydrology and Hydrochemistry, 1998; (jtly) Arsenic Pollution: a global synthesis, 2009; numerous papers on geomorphol., hydrology, river and slope processes in various jls. *Recreations:* reading, travel, opera. *Address:* Department of Geography, University of Cambridge, Cambridge CB2 3EN. *T:* (01223) 333393.

RICHARDS, Louise; Director of Policy and Campaigns, Institute of Fundraising, 2009–12; *b* 11 July 1951; *d* of William and Evelyn Greene; *m* 1977, Anthony Richards. *Educ:* Univ. of Leicester (BA Hons). Head of International Department: NALGO, 1983–93; UNISON, 1993–2003; Chief Executive: War on Want, 2003–07; Computer Aid Internat., 2007–09. Bd Mem., Community HEART, 2003–. *Recreations:* music, theatre, film.

RICHARDS, Prof. Martin Paul Meredith; Professor of Family Research, 1997–2005, now Emeritus, and Director of the Centre for Family Research, 1969–2005, Cambridge University; *b* 26 Jan. 1940; *s* of Paul Westmacott Richards and Sarah Anne Richards (*née* Hotham); *m* 1st, 1961, Evelyn Cowdy (marr. diss. 1966); 2nd, 1999, Sarah Smalley. *Educ:* Westminster Sch.; Trinity Coll., Cambridge (BA 1962; MA 1965; PhD 1965; ScD 1999). SRC Post-Doctoral Fellow, 1965–67; University of Cambridge: Res. Fellow, Trinity Coll., 1965–69; Mental Health Res. Fund Fellowship, 1970; Lectr in Social Psychology, 1970–89; Reader in Human Develt, 1989–97; Chm., Faculty of Soc. and Pol Scis, 1997, Head of Dept, 1996–99. Member: Biomedical Ethics (formerly Medicine and Society) Panel, Wellcome Trust, 1998–2006; Human Genetics Commn, 2000–05; Ethics and Governance Council, UK Biobank, 2006–14 (Vice Chm., 2008–14); Nuffield Council on Bioethics, 2012–15. Vis. Fellow, Princeton Univ., 1966–67; Visitor, Centre for Cognitive Studies, Harvard Univ., 1967 and 1968; Winegard Vis. Prof., Univ. of Guelph, 1987; Hon. Vis. Prof., City Univ., 1992–94; de Lissa Fellow, Univ. of SA, 1993; William Evans Vis. Fellow, Univ. of Otago, 1997. Chm., Bardsey Is Trust, 1993–2000. *Publications:* (ed jtly) Race, Culture and Intelligence, 1972; (ed) The Integration of a Child into a Social World, 1974; (ed jtly) Benefits and Hazards of the New Obstetrics, 1977; (ed jtly) Separation and Special Care Baby Units, 1978; Infancy: the world of the newborn, 1980; (ed jtly) Parent-Baby Attachment in Premature Infants, 1983; Children in Social Worlds, 1986; (with J. Burgoyne and R. Ormrod) Divorce Matters, 1987; (ed jtly) The Politics of Maternity Care, 1990; (ed jtly) Obstetrics in the 1990s, 1992; (with J. Reibstein) Sexual Arrangements, 1992; (ed jtly) The Troubled Helix, 1996; (ed jtly) What is a Parent?, 1999; (ed jtly) Body Lore and Laws, 2002; (ed jtly) The Blackwell Companion to the Sociology of Families, 2003; (ed jtly) Children and their Families: contact, rights and welfare, 2003; (jtly) Supporting Children Through Family Change, 2003; (ed jtly) Kinship Matters, 2006; (ed jtly) Death Rites and Rights, 2007; (ed jtly) The Limits of Consent, 2009; (ed jtly) Regulating Autonomy, 2009; (ed jtly) Birth Rites and Rights, 2011; (ed jtly) Reproductive Donation, 2012; (ed jtly) Relatedness in Assisted Reproduction, 2014; (ed jtly) The Wiley Blackwell Companion to the Sociology of Families, 2014; (ed jtly) Regulating Reproductive Donation, 2015. *Recreations:* bird-watching, listening to blue grass music, alpine gardening, grandchildren. *Address:* c/o Centre for Family Research, University of Cambridge, Free School Lane, Cambridge CB2 3RQ.

RICHARDS, Max; *see* Richards, George M.

RICHARDS, Menna, OBE 2010; Director (formerly Controller), BBC Wales, 2000–11; *b* 27 Feb. 1953; *d* of late Penri T. Richards and of Dilys M. Richards; *m* 1985, Patrick Hannan (MBE 1994), journalist and broadcaster (*d* 2009). *Educ:* Maesteg Grammar Sch.; UCW, Aberystwyth (BA). Journalist, BBC Wales, 1975–83; HTV Wales: journalist, 1983–91; Controller, Factual and Gen. Programmes, 1991–93; Dir of Programmes, 1993–97; Man. Dir, 1997–99. Non-executive Director: Welsh Water, 2010–; Principality Building Soc., 2012–. Non-exec. Dir, WNO, 2010–; Vice-Pres., RWCMD, 2007–. Trustee, Aloud Charity, 2012–. Hon. Fellow: Univ. of Wales, Aberystwyth, 1999; NE Wales Inst., 2004; Cardiff Univ., 2007; Univ. of Wales, Lampeter, 2008; Cardiff Metropolitan Univ., 2012. FRTS 2001. DUniv Glamorgan, 2008; Hon. Dr Swansea, 2013. *Recreations:* music, family, friends. *Clubs:* Royal Over-Seas League; Newport Boat.

RICHARDS, Prof. Sir Michael (Adrian), Kt 2010; CBE 2001; MD; FRCP; Sainsbury Professor of Palliative Medicine, King's College London School of Medicine (formerly Guy's, King's and St Thomas' School of Medicine, King's College London), 1995–99; Chairman, National Cancer Research Institute, 2006–08; Chief Inspector of Hospitals, Care Quality Commission, since 2013; *b* 14 July 1951; *s* of Donald Hibbert Richards and Peronelle Imogen (*née* Armitage-Smith). *Educ:* Dragon Sch., Oxford; Radley Coll.; Trinity Coll., Cambridge (MA); St Bartholomew's Hosp., London (MB BChir, MD 1988). FRCP 1993. ICRF Res. Fellow, St Bartholomew's Hosp., 1982–86; ICRF Sen. Lectr, 1986–91, Reader in Med. Oncology, 1991–95, Guy's Hosp., London; Clinical Dir of Cancer Services, Guy's and St Thomas' Hosps, 1993–99; Nat. Cancer Dir, DoH, 1999–2013; Dir for Reducing Premature Mortality (Domain 1), NHS England, 2012–13. *Publications:* papers on breast cancer, cancer service delivery, palliative care, quality of life. *Recreations:* hill-walking, classical music. *Address:* Care Quality Commission, Finsbury Tower, 103–105 Bunhill Row, EC1Y 8TG; 42 Liberia Road, N5 1JR.

RICHARDS, Maj.-Gen. Nigel William Fairbairn, CB 1998; OBE 1987; Chairman, Confederation of British Service and Ex-Service Organisations, 1999–2002; *b* 15 Aug. 1945; *s* of late Lt-Col William Fairbairn Richards RA and of Marjorie May Richards; *m* 1968, Christine Anne Helen Woods; two *s* one *d*. *Educ:* Eastbourne Coll.; RMA Sandhurst; Peterhouse, Cambridge (MA). Commissioned, RA, 1965; regtl duty, 1966–76, UK, Germany, NI, Cyprus, Malaya; RN Staff Coll., 1976–77; MoD, 1978–80; Comd J Anti-Tank Battery, RHA, 1980–81; Directing Staff, RMCS, 1982–83; CO 7 Para Regt, RHA, 1983–86; MoD, 1986–88; Higher Comd and Staff Course, 1988; Comdr 5 Airborne Brigade, 1989–90; RCDS 1991; Dir Army Staff Duties, MoD, 1991–93; Chief of Combat Support, HQ Allied Command Europe Rapid Reaction Corps, 1994–96; GOC 4th Div., 1996–98. President: British Scouts Western Europe, 1994–96; Army Boxing and Hockey, 1996–98. Hon. Col, 7 Para Regt RHA, 1999–2005; Col Comdt, RA, 2001–06. Chm., Peterhouse Soc., 2001–04. *Recreations:* cricket, fishing, ski-ing, golf. *Address:* 6 Park Road, Winchester, Hants SO22 6AA. *Club:* Army and Navy.

RICHARDS, Peter Graham Gordon; a District Judge (Magistrates' Courts) (formerly Stipendiary Magistrate), Staffordshire, 1991–2008; *b* 16 July 1939; *s* of David Gordon and Irene Florence Richards; *m* 1965, Jeanette Uncles (*d* 1997); two *d*. *Educ:* Univ. of London (LLM 1966). Schoolmaster, 1962–65; Lectr, 1965–68; called to the Bar, Middle Temple, 1968; Midland and Oxford Circuit, 1968–91. *Recreations:* sports broadcasting, travel, theatre, astronomy. *Address:* c/o Law Courts, Baker Street, Fenton, Stoke on Trent ST4 3BX.

RICHARDS, Philip Brian; His Honour Judge Philip Richards; a Circuit Judge, since 2001; *b* 3 Aug. 1946; *s* of late Glyn Bevan Richards and Nancy Gwenhwyfar Richards (*née* Evans); *m* 1st, 1971, Dorothy Louise George (marr. diss.); two *d*; 2nd, 1994, Julia Jones; one *d*, and one step *s*. *Educ:* Univ. of Bristol (LLB Hons). Called to the Bar, Inner Temple, 1969; Asst Recorder, 1995–2000; Recorder, 2000–01. *Publications:* (jtly) Government of Wales Bill, 1996; Report on Judicial training in the Welsh language, 2003. *Recreations:* music, sport, theatre, literature, the history, culture, languages and constitution of Wales. *Address:* Cardiff Crown Court, Cathays Park, Cardiff CF10 3PG. *T:* (029) 2041 4400. *Clubs:* Cardiff and County; Mountain Ash Rugby Football.

RICHARDS, Sir Rex (Edward), Kt 1977; DSc Oxon 1970; FRS 1959; FRSC; Chancellor, Exeter University, 1982–98; *b* 28 Oct. 1922; *s* of H. W. and E. N. Richards; *m* 1948, Eva Edith Vago; two *d*. *Educ:* Colyton Grammar School, Devon; St John's College, Oxford. Senior Demy, Magdalen College, Oxford, 1946; MA; DPhil; Fellow, Lincoln College, Oxford, 1947–64, Hon. Fellow, 1968; Research Fellow, Harvard University, 1955; Dr Lee's Prof. of Chemistry, Oxford, 1964–70; Fellow, Exeter College, 1964–69; Warden, Merton Coll., Oxford, 1969–84, Hon. Fellow, 1984; Vice-Chancellor, Oxford Univ., 1977–81; Hon. Fellow, St John's Coll., Oxford, 1968; Associate Fellow, Morse Coll., Yale, 1974–79. Director: IBM-UK Ltd, 1978–83; Oxford Instruments Group, 1982–91. Chm., BPMF, 1986–93; Dir, Leverhulme Trust, 1984–93; Chm., Task Force on Clinical Academic Careers, 1996–97. Member: Chemical Society Council, 1957, 1987–93; Faraday Society Council, 1963; Royal Soc. Council, 1973–75; Scientific Adv. Cttee, Nat. Gall., 1978–2007; ABRC, 1980–83; ACARD, 1984–87; Comr, Royal Commn for the Exhibition of 1851, 1984–97; Pres., Royal Soc. of Chemistry, 1990–92; Trustee: CIBA Foundn, 1978–97; Nat. Heritage Memorial Fund, 1980–84; Tate Gall., 1982–88, 1991–93; Nat. Gall., 1982–88, 1989–93; Henry Moore Foundn, 1989–2003 (Vice-Chm., 1993–94; Chm., 1994–2001); Chm., Nat. Gall. Trust, 1995–99 (Trustee, 1995–2007). Tilden Lectr, 1962. FRIC 1970. Hon. FRCP 1987; Hon. FBA 1990; Hon. FRAM 1991. Hon. DSc: East Anglia, 1971; Exeter, 1975; Leicester, 1978; Salford, 1979; Edinburgh, 1981; Leeds, 1984; Kent, 1987; Birmingham, 1993; London, 1994; Oxford Brookes, 1998; Warwick, 1999; Hon. LLD Dundee, 1977; Hon. ScD Cambridge, 1987. Centenary Fellow, Thames Polytechnic (subseq. Univ. of Greenwich), 1990. For. Associate, Académie des Sciences, France, 1995. Corday-Morgan Medal of Chemical Soc., 1954; Davy Medal, Royal Soc., 1976; Award in Theoretical Chemistry and Spectroscopy, Chem. Soc., 1977; Educn in Partnership with Industry or Commerce Award, DTI, 1982; Medal of Honour, Rheinische Friedrich-Wilhelms Univ., Bonn, 1983; Royal Medal, Royal Soc., 1986; President's Medal, Soc. of Chemical Ind., 1991. *Publications:* various contributions to scientific journals. *Recreations:* enjoying painting and sculpture, keeping fit in old age. *Address:* Unit 4, West Heanton, Buckland Filleigh, Beaworthy, Devon EX21 5PJ. *T:* (01409) 281985.

RICHARDS, (Richard) Alun; Welsh Secretary in charge of Welsh Office Agriculture Department, 1978–81, retired; *b* 2 Jan. 1920; *s* of Sylvanus and Gwladys Richards, Llanbrynmair, Powys; *m* 1944, Ann Elonwy Mary, (Nansi), Price (decd), Morriston, Swansea; two *s*. *Educ:* Machynlleth County Sch.; Liverpool Univ. (BVSc, MRCVS, 1942). Veterinary Officer with State Vet. Service, Caernarfon and Glamorgan, 1943–57; Divl Vet. Officer, HQ Tolworth and in Warwick, 1957–65; Dep. Reg. Vet. Officer (Wales), 1965–67; seconded to NZ Govt to advise on control of Foot and Mouth disease, 1967–68; Reg. Vet. Officer, HQ Tolworth, 1968–71; Asst Chief Vet. Officer, 1971–77; Asst Sec., Welsh Dept, MAFF, 1977–78; Under-Sec., 1978. *Publications:* contrib. to vet. jls. *Recreations:* fishing, playing bridge. *Address:* Penrhiw, Cefnllan, Waunfawr, Aberystwyth SY23 3QB. *T:* (01970) 617107.

See also Rt Hon. Sir S. P. Richards.

RICHARDS, (Robert) John (Godwin); Senior Advisor, Värde Partners Europe Ltd, since 2011; *b* 11 Jan. 1956; *m* 1987, Amanda Joseph; two *s*. *Educ:* Poly. of Wales (BSc). FRICS. Joined Hammerson plc, 1981; Dir, 1990–2009; UK Develt Dir, 1990–93; UK Man. Dir, 1993–97; Internat. Man. Dir, 1997–99; Chief Exec., 1999–2009. President: British Council of Shopping Centres, 2003–04; British Property Fedn, 2010–11.

RICHARDS, Roderick; Member (C) Wales North, National Assembly for Wales, 1999–2002; *b* 12 March 1947; *s* of Ivor George Richards and Lizzie Jane Richards (*née* Evans); *m* 1975, Elizabeth Knight; two *s* one *d*. *Educ:* Llandovery College; Univ. of Wales (BSc Econ). Short service commn, RM, 1969–71. Ministry of Defence, 1977–83; broadcaster and journalist, 1983–89; Special Adviser to Sec. of State for Wales, 1990. Contested (C): Carmarthen, 1987; Vale of Glamorgan, May 1989. MP (C) Clwyd North West, 1992–97; contested (C) Clwyd West, 1997. PPS to Minister of State, FCO, 1993–94; Parly Under-Sec. of State, Welsh Office, 1994–96. Mem. Welsh Affairs Select Cttee, 1992–93. Welsh Cons. Leader, 1998–99. *Recreations:* Rugby, cricket, walking, games. *Clubs:* Special Forces; Llanelli Rugby; Colwyn Bay Cricket.

RICHARDS, Sandra Anne; *see* Phinbow, S. A.

RICHARDS, Stephen; Chief Political Commentator, Independent, since 2000; *b* London, 6 June 1960; *s* of Keith and Val Richards; *m* 2010, Barbara Schofield; one *s* one *d*. *Educ:* Christ's Coll., Finchley; Univ. of York (BA Hons Hist.). BBC: Community Affairs Corresp., 1987–90; Political Corresp., 1990–96; Political Ed., New Statesman, 1996–2000. *Publications:* Preparing for Power, 1997; Whatever it Takes: a history of New Labour, 2010. *Recreations:* running, watching football, performing one-man show. *Address:* Independent, 2 Derry Street, W8 5HF. *T:* (020) 7005 2000. *E:* S.Richards@independent.co.uk.

RICHARDS, Rt Hon. Sir Stephen (Price), Kt 1997; PC 2005; **Rt Hon. Lord Justice Richards;** a Lord Justice of Appeal, since 2005; *b* 8 Dec. 1950; *s* of Richard Alun Richards, *qv*; *m* 1976, Lucy Elizabeth Stubbings, MA; two *s* one *d*. *Educ:* King's Coll. Sch., Wimbledon; St John's Coll., Oxford (open schol.; BA Lit.Hum. 1972; BA Jurisprudence 1974; MA 1977; Hon. Fellow, 2008). Called to the Bar, Gray's Inn, 1975 (Arden Schol. and Bacon Schol.; Bencher, 1992); Second Jun. Counsel, 1987–89, Standing Counsel, 1989–91, to Dir Gen. of Fair Trading; a Jun. Counsel to the Crown, 1990–91, First Jun. Treasury Counsel, Common Law, 1992–97; an Asst Recorder, 1992–96; a Recorder, 1996–97; a Judge of High Court of Justice, QBD, 1997–2005; a Presiding Judge, Wales and Chester Circuit, 2000–03; Dep. Hd of Civil Justice, 2013–Jan. 2016. Dep. Chm., Boundary Commn for Wales, 2001–05. Governor, King's Coll. Sch., Wimbledon, 1998–2007 (Chm., 2004–07). Hon. LLD Glamorgan, 2004. *Publications:* (ed jtly) Chitty on Contracts, 25th edn 1983, 26th edn 1989. *Recreations:* walking, relaxing in the Welsh hills. *Address:* Royal Courts of Justice, Strand, WC2A 2LL.

RICHARDS, Sir Vivian; *see* Richards, Sir I. V. A.

RICHARDS, Prof. (William) Graham, CBE 2001; DPhil, DSc; Professor of Chemistry, 1996–2007, now Emeritus, and Chairman of Chemistry, 1997–2006, Oxford University; Fellow of Brasenose College, Oxford, since 1966; *b* 1 Oct. 1939; *o s* of Percy Richards and Julia Richards (*née* Evans); *m* 1st, 1970, Jessamy Kershaw (*d* 1988); two *s*; 2nd, 1996, Mary Elizabeth Phillips. *Educ:* Birkenhead Sch.; Brasenose Coll., Oxford (MA; DPhil 1964; DSc 1985). ICI Res. Fellow, Balliol Coll., Oxford, 1964 (Hon. Fellow, 2006); Res. Fellow, CNRS, Paris, 1965; Lectr, 1966–94, Reader in Computational Chemistry, 1994–96, Dept of Physical Chemistry, Oxford Univ. Director: Oxford Molecular Gp plc, 1989–99 (Founding Scientist, 1989, Chm., 1990–93); Isis Innovation Ltd, 1994–2007; Catalyst Biomedica Ltd, 1998–2003; IP Gp Plc (formerly IP2IPO Gp), 2000–13 (Chm., 2004–06; Venture Partner, 2013–); Oxeco Plc, 2006–10; TdeltaS, 2007–12; Crysalin Ltd, 2008–10; Chm. and Founding Scientist, Inhibox Ltd, 2002–. Res. Schol., Stanford Univ., 1975–76; Visiting Professor: Univ. of Calif at Berkeley, 1975–76; Stanford Univ., 1978–82. Mem., Bd of Dirs, Assoc. for Internat. Cancer Res., 1995–99. Member: Council, RSC, 2005–12; African Inst. of Mathematical Scis, 2005–; Council, Royal Inst., 2006–08. Editor, Jl of Molecular Graphics, 1984–96. Marlow Medal, 1972, Award for Theoretical Chem., 1989, RSC; Lloyd of Kilgerran Prize, Foundn for Sci. and Technol., 1996; Mullard Award, Royal Soc., 1998; Italgas Prize, 2001; Award for Computers in Chemical and Pharmaceutical Res., American Chemical Soc., 2004. *Publications:* Ab Initio Molecular Orbital Calculations for Chemists, 1970, 2nd edn 1983; Bibliography of Ab Initio Wave Functions, 1971, supplements, 1974, 1978, 1981; Entropy and Energy Levels, 1974; Structure and Spectra of Atoms, 1976; Quantum Pharmacology, 1977, 2nd edn 1983; Spin-Orbit Coupling in Molecules, 1981; Structure and Spectra of Molecules, 1985; The Problems of Chemistry, 1986; Computer-Aided Molecular Design, 1989; Energy Levels of Atoms and Molecules, 1994; Computational Chemistry, 1995; An Introduction to Statistical Thermodynamics, 1995; Spin-outs: creating business from university intellectual property, 2009; 50 Years at Oxford, 2011; University Intellectual Property: a source of finance and impact, 2012. *Recreations:* sport, running, swimming. *Address:* Brasenose College, Oxford OX1 4AJ. *T:* (01865) 277830. *Club:* Vincent's (Oxford).

RICHARDS, Wyn; *see* Richards, His Honour D. W.

RICHARDSON, family name of **Baroness Richardson of Calow**.

RICHARDSON OF CALOW, Baroness *cr* 1998 (Life Peer), of Calow in the co. of Derbyshire; **Rev. Kathleen Margaret Richardson,** OBE 1996; Moderator, Churches' Commission for Inter-Faith Relations, 1999–2006; *b* 24 Feb. 1938; *d* of Francis and Margaret Fountain; *m* 1964, Ian David Godfrey Richardson; three *d*. *Educ:* St Helena Sch., Chesterfield; Stockwell Coll. (Cert Ed); Deaconess Coll., Ilkley; Wesley House, Cambridge. School teacher, 1958–61. Wesley Deaconess, Champness Hall, Rochdale, 1961–64; Lay Worker, Team Ministry, Stevenage, 1973–77; Minister, Denby Dale and Clayton West Circuit, 1979–87; ordained presbyter, 1980; Chm., West Yorks Dist, 1987–95. Pres., Methodist Conf., 1992–93; Moderator, Free Church Federal Council, subseq. Free Churches' Council, 1995–99; a President, Churches Together in England, 1995–99; Chm., Commn on Urban Life and Faith, 2004–06. Hon. DLitt Bradford, 1994; Hon. LLD Liverpool, 1999; Hon. DD Birmingham, 2000. *Recreations:* reading, needlework.

RICHARDSON, Sir Anthony (Lewis), 3rd Bt *cr* 1924; *b* 5 Aug. 1950; *s* of Sir Leslie Lewis Richardson, 2nd Bt, and of Joy Patricia, Lady Richardson, *d* of P. J. Rillstone, Johannesburg; *S* father, 1985; *m* 1985, Honor Gillian Dauney; one *s* one *d*. *Educ:* Diocesan College, Cape Town, S Africa. Stockbroker with L. Messel & Co., London, 1973–75; Insurance Broker with C. T. Bowring, London and Johannesburg, 1975–76; Stockbroker with Fergusson Bros, Hall, Stewart & Co., Johannesburg and Cape Town, 1976–78; Stockbroker with W. Greenwell & Co., London, 1979–81; with Rowe & Pitman, subseq. S. G. Warburg Securities, then SBC Warburg, London, 1981–99 (Dir, 1986–99), seconded to Potter Partners, Melbourne and Sydney, 1986–89, seconded to SBC Warburg, Johannesburg, 1996–99; Dir, Barclays Private Bank, London, 1999–. *Recreations:* various sports, photography. *Heir:* *s* William Lewis Richardson, *b* 15 Oct. 1992. *Clubs:* Boodle's, Hurlingham.

RICHARDSON, Prof. Brian Frederick, FBA 2003; Professor of Italian Language, University of Leeds, 1996–2012, now Emeritus; *b* 6 Dec. 1946; *s* of late Ronald Frederick Richardson, CBE and Anne Elizabeth Richardson (*née* McArdle); *m* 1973, Catherine Normand; three *d*. *Educ:* Lincoln Coll., Oxford (MA); Bedford Coll., London (MPhil). Lecturer in Italian: Univ. of Strathclyde, 1970–72; Univ. of Aberdeen, 1972–76; Lectr, 1977–89, Sen. Lectr, 1989–96, Univ. of Leeds. Gen. Editor, Modern Language Review, 2004–13. *Publications:* (ed) N. Machiavelli, Il principe, 1979; (ed) Trattati sull'ortografia del volgare, 1984; Print Culture in Renaissance Italy, 1994; Printing, Writers and Readers in Renaissance Italy, 1999; (ed) G. F. Fortunio, Regole grammaticali della volgar lingua, 2001; Manuscript Culture in Renaissance Italy, 2009. *Recreations:* music, walking, gardening. *Address:* School of Languages, Cultures and Societies, University of Leeds, Leeds LS2 9JT.

RICHARDSON, David; Director, London Office, International Labour Organisation, 1982–91; *b* 24 April 1928; *s* of Harold George Richardson and Madeleine Raphaële Richardson (*née* Lebret); *m* 1951, Frances Joan Pring; three *s* one *d*. *Educ:* Wimbledon Coll.; King's Coll., London (BA Hons). FIPM 1986. RAF, 1949. Unilever, 1951. Inland Revenue, 1953; Min. of Labour, 1956; Sec., Construction Industry Training Bd, 1964; Chm., Central Youth Employment Exec., 1969; Royal Coll. of Defence Studies, 1971; Under Sec., Dept of Employment, 1972; Dir, Safety and Gen. Gp, Health and Safety Exec., 1975; Dir and Sec., ACAS, 1977. Director: The Tablet, 1985–98; Industrial Training Service Ltd, 1987–93. *Recreations:* music, walking, landscape gardening, ceramics. *Address:* 2 Bellingham Drive, Reigate, Surrey RH2 9BB. *T:* (01737) 225335. *E:* richardson.183@blueyonder.co.uk.
See also S. M. Richardson.

RICHARDSON, Rev. David John; His Honour Judge Richardson; a Circuit Judge, since 2000; an Additional Judge of the Employment Appeal Tribunal, since 2003; *b* 23 June 1950; *s* of Abraham Eric Richardson and Gwendoline Richardson (*née* Ballard); *m* 1980, Jennifer Margaret Richardson (*née* Cooke); one *s* one *d*. *Educ:* John Ruskin Grammar Sch., Croydon; Trinity Hall, Cambridge (BA 1971, MA; LLB 1972); Southwark Ordination Trng Course. Called to the Bar, Middle Temple, 1973; in practice, 1973–2000; an Asst Recorder, 1992–97; a Recorder, 1997–2000. Ordained deacon, 1985, priest, 1986; Hon. Curate, Emmanuel Church, S Croydon, 1985–2006. *Recreations:* walking, reading, supporter of Crystal Palace FC.

RICHARDSON, David John; Chief Executive, International Cricket Council, since 2012; *b* Johannesburg, 16 Sept. 1959; *s* of John Henry Richardson and Margaret Ann Richardson; *m* 1985, Jennifer Elizabeth Grüttner; three *s*. *Educ:* Marist Brothers Coll., Port Elizabeth; Univ. of Port Elizabeth (BComm; LLB 1982); London Business Sch. (Sen. Exec. Prog. 2008). Played 1st class cricket for Eastern Province and South Africa, 1978–98 (Captain, Eastern Province, 1987–88); represented South Africa (wicket keeper/batsman) in 42 Tests and 122 One Day Internats. Dir, Pagdens Inc., attorneys, 1985–98; Business Dir, ESPM Legends (Pty) Ltd, subseq. Octagon SA (Pty) Ltd, sports mktg and events, 1998–2002; Gen. Manager, Cricket, ICC, 2002–12. Cricket Commentator, M-Net Supersport, 2000–02. Member: World Cricket Cttee, MCC, 2009–; Internat. Adv. Bd, World Acad. of Sport, 2013. Alumni Achievers Award, Nelson Mandela Metropolitan Univ., 2010. *Recreations:* golf, reading, family. *Address:* International Cricket Council, Dubai Sport City, PO Box 500070, Dubai, United Arab Emirates. *T:* (4) 3828800, *Fax:* (4) 3828600. *Club:* MCC (Hon. Life Mem., 2002).

RICHARDSON, Very Rev. Canon David John Leyburn, OBE 2013; Archbishop of Canterbury's Representative to the Holy See, and Director, Anglican Centre in Rome, 2008–13; *b* Townsville, Qld, 14 March 1946; *s* of David James Leyburn Richardson and Alice May Richardson (*née* Tansey); *m* 1972, Margaret Rosalind Lewis; one *s* one *d*. *Educ:* Univ. of Queensland (BA 1969); St Barnabas' Coll., Adelaide (ThL 1970); Melbourne Coll. of Divinity (BD 1975); Univ. of Birmingham (Dip. in Pastoral Theol. 1976). Ordained deacon, 1970, priest, 1971; Assistant: St Paul's, Maryborough, 1972–73; Ipswich, 1974–75; St Francis, Birmingham, 1975–76; Chaplain, Girton Coll., Cambridge and Asst Curate, Great St Mary's Univ. Church, 1976–79; Sub-Warden, St Barnabas' Coll., Adelaide, 1979–82; Rector, Christ Church, St Lucia, Brisbane, 1982–88; Rector, 1988–89, Dean, 1989–99, St Peter's Cathedral, Adelaide; Dean, St Paul's Cathedral, Melbourne, 1999–2008, now Emeritus. Member: Gen. Synod, and Standing Cttee of Gen. Synod, Anglican Ch of Australia, 1988–2007; Bd of Election of Primate of Anglican Ch of Australia, 2007–08. Hon. Canon, Canterbury Cathedral, 2010–. Exec. Sec., Nat. Liturgical Commn, 1985–99; Nat. Rep., Anglican Consultative Council, 1992–2002. Mem., Ethics Cttee, Wakefield St Hosp., Adelaide, 1991–99. Gov., St Peter's Collegiate Girls Sch., Adelaide, 1989–98; Dep. Chm., Council, St Peter's Coll., Adelaide, 1998–99; Mem. Council, Melbourne Girls Grammar, 1999–2008. ChStJ 1996. *Recreations:* music, literature. *Clubs:* Adelaide, Melbourne.

RICHARDSON, Prof. Genevra Mercy, CBE 2007; FBA 2007; Professor of Law, King's College London, since 2005; *b* 1 Sept. 1948; *d* of John Lawrence Richardson and Josephine Juliet Richardson; *m* 1977, Oliver Thorold (*see* Sir A. O. Thorold); one *s* one *d*. *Educ:* King's Coll., London (LLB, LLM). Res. Officer, Centre for Socio-Legal Studies, Oxford, 1974–78; Lectr, UEA, 1979–87; Lectr, 1987–89, Reader, 1989–94, Prof. of Public Law, 1994–2005, Dean, Faculty of Law, 1996–99, QMW, subseq. Queen Mary, Univ. of London. Chm., Expert Cttee Advising Ministers on Reform of Mental Health Legislation, 1998–99. Mem., Administrative Justice & Tribunals Council (formerly Council on Tribunals), 2001–10. Member: Mental Health Act Commn, 1987–92; Animal Procedures Cttee, 1998–2006; Chairman: Prisoner's Advice Service, 1994–2002; Appointing Authy for Phase 1 Ethics Cttees, 2009–12. Mem. Council, MRC, 2001–08. Trustee: Nuffield Foundn, 2002–14; Med. Res. Foundn, 2006–14. Hon. FRCPsych 2004. *Recreations:* walking, travel. *Address:* School of Law, King's College, Strand, WC2R 2LS. *E:* genevra.richardson@kcl.ac.uk.

RICHARDSON, George Barclay, CBE 1978; Warden, Keble College, Oxford, 1989–94 (Hon. Fellow, 1994); Pro-Vice-Chancellor, Oxford University, 1988–94; *b* 19 Sept. 1924; *s* of George and Christina Richardson; *m* 1957, Isabel Alison Chalk (marr. diss. 1998); two *s*. *Educ:* Aberdeen Central Secondary Sch. and other schs in Scotland; Aberdeen Univ. (BSc Physics and Maths, 1944); Corpus Christi Coll., Oxford (MA PPE 1949; Hon. Fellow, 1987). Admty Scientific Res. Dept, 1944; Lieut, RNVR, 1945. Intell. Officer, HQ Intell. Div. BAOR, 1946–47; Third Sec., HM Foreign Service, 1949; Student, Nuffield Coll., Oxford, 1950; Fellow, St John's Coll., Oxford, 1951–89, Hon. Fellow, 1989; University Reader in Economics, Oxford, 1969–73; Sec. to Delegates and Chief Exec., OUP, 1974–88 (Deleg., 1971–74). Economic Advr, UKAEA, 1968–74. Member: Economic Develt Cttee for Electrical Engineering Industry, 1964–73; Monopolies Commn, 1969–74; Royal Commn on Environmental Pollution, 1973–74; Council, Publishers Assoc., 1981–87. Mem., UK Delegation, CSCE Cultural Forum, 1985. Visitor, Ashmolean Mus., 1992–96. Hon. DCL Oxon, 1988; Hon. LLD Aberdeen, 1996. *Publications:* Information and Investment, 1960, 2nd edn 1991; Economic Theory, 1964; The Economics of Imperfect Knowledge, 1998; articles in academic jls. *Address:* 33 Belsyre Court, Woodstock Road, Oxford OX2 6HU.

RICHARDSON, Prof. Guy Peel, PhD; FRS 2009; Professorial Fellow, Hearing Research Centre, School of Life Sciences, University of Sussex, since 2004. *Educ:* Univ. of Sussex (BSc Neurosci. 1975; PhD 1980). Univ. of Sussex, 1984–. Member, Research Advisory Panel: Deafness Research UK; RNID. FMedSci 2013. *Publications:* articles in jls. *Address:* School of Life Sciences, University of Sussex, Falmer, Brighton BN1 9QG.

RICHARDSON, Hugh; Head, Delegation of European Commission to Tokyo, 2006–09; Ambassador of European Union to Japan, 2009–10; *b* 12 May 1947; *s* of Robert Richardson and Pauline (*née* Broadhurst); *m* (marr. diss.); two *s* three *d*; *m* 2000, Lisbeth Van Impe. *Educ:* Pembroke Coll., Oxford (BA 1969; BCL 1970; MA 2002). Commission of the European Communities: with Secretariat Gen., 1974–79; Directorate-Gen. for External Relns, 1979–84; Counsellor and Dep. Head, Tokyo Delegn, 1984–88; Asst to DG for External Relns, 1988–91; Dir, Rights and Obligations, Directorate-Gen. for Personnel and Admin, 1991–96; Deputy Director General: Jt Res. Centre, 1996–2002; DG Res., 2002–04; DG EuropeAid Co-operation Office, 2004–06. *Publications:* EC-Japan Relations: after adolescence, 1989. *Recreations:* sailing, ski-ing, running.

RICHARDSON, James Colin, PhD; Director, Fiscal, and Deputy Chief Economic Adviser, HM Treasury, since 2012; *b* Windsor, 5 Oct. 1965; *s* of Colin Richardson and Anne Richardson; *m* 2001, Rebecca Stanley; one *d*. *Educ:* Balliol Coll., Oxford (BA Hons PPE 1988); London Sch. of Econs and Pol Sci. (PhD Econs 1999). Chief Microeconomist, 2007–12, Dir, Public Spending, 2008–12, HM Treasury. Dir, HM Treasury UK Sovereign Sukuk, 2014–. Mem., ESRC, 2013–. *Recreations:* photography, walking, family, reading. *E:* James.Richardson@hmtreasury.gsi.gov.uk.

RICHARDSON, Rev. Canon James John, OBE 2007; Hon. Canon Pastor, 2009–14, Hon. Assistant Priest, since 2014, Sherborne Abbey; *b* 28 March 1941; *s* of late James John Richardson and of Gladys May (*née* Evans); *m* 1966, Janet Rosemary Welstand; two *s* one *d*. *Educ:* Catford Central Sch.; Hull Univ. (BA); Sheffield Univ. (DipEd); Cuddesdon Coll., Oxford. Assistant Master, Westfield Comp. Sch., Sheffield, 1964–66; Curate, St Peter's Collegiate Church, Wolverhampton, 1969–72; Priest i/c, All Saints, Hanley, Stoke-on-Trent, 1972–75; Rector of Nantwich, 1975–82; Vicar of Leeds, 1982–88; Exec. Dir, CCJ, 1988–92; Priest-in-Charge: Gt Brington, Whilton and Norton (Northampton), dio. of Peterborough, 1993–96; E Haddon and Holdenby, Church and Chapel Brampton and Harlestone, 1994–96; St Augustine, Bournemouth, 2001–08; Team Rector, Bournemouth Town Centre Parish, 1996–2008. Hon. Canon, 1982–88, Canon Emeritus, 1988–, Ripon Cathedral. Chaplain: to Earl Spencer, 1993–96; to High Sheriff of Northants, 1995–96; to Mayor of Bournemouth, 2002–03 and 2006–07; to High Sheriff of Dorset, 2007–08. Chm., Racial Harassment

Commn, Leeds, 1986–87; N of England Vice-Pres., UN Year of Peace, 1986–87. Chairman: Bournemouth Town Centre Detached Youth Project, 1997–2008; Churches Together in Bournemouth, 1998–2002; Director: Bournemouth Millennium Co., 1998–99; Hope FM Radio, 1998–2001. Member: Council, Centre for the Study of Judaism and Jewish/Christian Relations, Selly Oak Coll., 1989–94; Internat. Council of Christians and Jews Adv. Cttee, 1992–96; Council, Order of St John, Dorset, 2010–13. Member: Partnership Steering Cttee, Bournemouth BC, 2001–03; Bournemouth BC Standards Bd, 2003– (Vice-Chm., 2003–07; Chm., 2007–08); Bournemouth BC Schs Orgn Cttee, 2003–06; Bournemouth Town Centre Mgt Bd, 2003–08. Mem. Court, Leeds Univ., 1986–88; Chairman of Governors: Abbey Grange High Sch., Leeds, 1982–86; Leeds Grammar Sch., 1983–88; Governor: Leeds Girls' High Sch., 1982–88; Leeds Music Fest., 1982–88; Chm. Steering Gp, New Church Secondary Sch. for Bournemouth, 2001–03. FRSA 1991. Hon. Freeman, Bor. of Bournemouth, 2008. *Publications:* (contrib.) Four Score Years, 1989; contrib. Yorkshire Post, 1982–90. *Recreations:* leading pilgrimages to Israel, biography—especially life and times of Rupert Brooke, deciphering Tudor churchwardens' accounts. *Address:* 6 St Johns' Almshouse, Half Moon Street, Sherborne, Dorset DT9 3LJ. *T:* (01935) 814984. *E:* Canonrichardson@btinternet.com.

RICHARDSON, Jenny; *see* Brown, J.

RICHARDSON, Prof. Jeremy John, PhD; Fellow, 1998–2003, and Senior Tutor, 2001–03, Nuffield College, Oxford, now Emeritus Fellow; Professor, National Centre for Research on Europe, University of Canterbury, New Zealand, since 2008; *b* 15 June 1942; *s* of Samuel Radcliffe Richardson and Sarah Doris Richardson; *m* 1966, Anne Philippsen (marr. diss. 1993); one *s* one *d*; *m* 1994, Sonia Pauline Mazey; two *d*. *Educ:* Univ. of Keele (BA Hons Politics and Econs); Univ. of Manchester (MA Econ; PhD 1970). Asst Lectr, Lectr, then Reader, Univ. of Keele, 1966–82; Professor: Dept of Politics, Univ. of Strathclyde, 1982–92; Univ. of Warwick, 1992–95; Univ. of Essex, 1995–98; Nuffield Prof. of Comparative European Politics and Dir, Centre for European Politics, Economics and Society, Oxford Univ., 1998–2001. Ed., Jl of European Public Policy, 1993–. Hon. Dr Pol Sci., Umeå, 1995. *Publications:* The Policy-Making Process, 1969; (ed with R. Kimber) Campaigning for the Environment, 1974; (ed with R. Kimber) Pressure Groups in Britain: a reader, 1974; (with A. Grant Jordan) Governing Under Pressure: the policy process in a post-parliamentary democracy, 1979; (ed with R. Henning) Policy Responses to Unemployment in Western Democracies, 1984; (with J. Moon) Unemployment in the UK: politics and policies, 1985; (with A Grant Jordan) Government & Pressure Groups in Britain, 1987; (ed jtly) The Politics of Economic Crisis: lessons from Western Europe, 1989; (jtly) Local Partnership and the Unemployment Crisis in Britain, 1989; (with G. Dudley) Politics and Steel in Britain 1967–1988, 1990; (ed) Privatisation and Deregulation in Canada and Britain, 1990; (with S. Mazey) Lobbying in the European Community, 1993; (ed) Pressure Groups, 1993; (jtly) True Blues: the politics of Conservative Party membership, 1994; (jtly) Networks for Water Policy: a comparative perspective, 1994; (with W. Maloney) Managing Policy Change in Britain: the politics of water policy, 1995; (ed) European Union: power and policy-making, 1996, 4th edn (ed with S. Mazey) 2015; (with G. Dudley) Why Does Policy Change?: lessons from British transport policy 1945–1999, 2000; (with D. Coen) Lobbying in the European Union: institutions, actors and issues, 2009; Constructing a Policy-Making State?: policy dynamics in the European Union, 2012. *Recreations:* gardening, DIY, walking, acting as a taxi driver for the children. *Address:* 30 Queen's Avenue, Fendalton, Christchurch 8014, New Zealand. *T:* (3) 3559161.

RICHARDSON, Jeremy William; QC 2000; **His Honour Judge Jeremy Richardson;** a Circuit Judge, since 2009; Designated Civil Judge for Humberside, since 2009; Resident Judge, Hull, since 2014; *b* 3 April 1958; *s* of late Thomas William Sydney Raymond Richardson and of Jean Mary Richardson (*née* Revill); civil partnership 2006, David Carruthers. *Educ:* Forest Sch.; Queen Mary Coll., Univ. of London (LLB Hons 1979). Called to the Bar, Inner Temple, 1980, Bencher, 2007; in practice at the Bar, NE Circuit, 1982–2009; Asst Recorder, 1998–2000; Recorder, 2000–09; Dep. High Court Judge, Family Div., 2004–09. Mem., Gen. Council of the Bar, 1992–94. Sec., NE Circuit, 1991–96. *Address:* Kingston upon Hull Combined Court Centre, Lowgate, Hull HU1 2EZ. *T:* (01482) 586161.

RICHARDSON, Joely; actress; *b* 9 Jan. 1965; *d* of late Tony Richardson and of Vanessa Redgrave, *qv*; *m* 1992, Tim Bevan, *qv* (marr. diss. 2001); one *d*. *Educ:* Lycée Français de Londres; St Paul's Girls' Sch.; Pinellas Park High Sch., Florida; Thacher Sch., Calif; RADA. West End début, Steel Magnolias, Lyric, 1989; Lady Windermere's Fan, Haymarket, 2002; The Lady from the Sea, Rose Th., 2012; Ivanov, Classic Stage Co., NY, 2012. *Films include:* Wetherby, 1985; Drowning by Numbers, 1988; Shining Through, Rebecca's Daughters, 1992; Sister, My Sister, 1995; Loch Ness, Believe Me, 101 Dalmatians, Hollow Reed, 1996; Event Horizon, 1997; Wrestling with Alligators, Under Heaven, 1998; Maybe Baby, Return to Me, The Patriot, 2000; The Affair of the Necklace, 2002; Anonymous, 2011; *television includes:* Body Contact, 1987; Behaving Badly, 1989; Heading Home, 1991; The Storyteller, Lady Chatterley's Lover, 1993; The Tribe, Echo, 1998; Nip/Tuck, 2004–10; Wallis and Edward, 2005; Fatal Contact, 2007; Day of the Triffids, 2009. *Address:* c/o Finch and Partners, Top Floor, 29–37 Heddon Street, W1B 4BR.

RICHARDSON, John Burke; Senior Resident Fellow, German Marshall Fund, since 2010 (Director, Brussels Forum, 2008–10); *b* 22 Dec. 1944; *s* of Alan and Mary Richardson; *m* 1969, Irmtraud Hübner; three *d*. *Educ:* Downing Coll., Cambridge (BA Chemistry; MA 1970); University Coll. London (MSc Econs 1969). Economist, Unilever, 1969–73; joined European Commn, 1973: Negotiator for Internat. Trade in Services, 1982–88; Head of Unit: for USA, 1988–92; for Japan, 1992–96; Dep. Hd of Delegn to USA, 1996–2001; Ambassador and Hd, EC Delegn to UN, NY, 2001–05; Head, Maritime Policy Task Force, EU, 2005–08. Trustee, Sail Trng Internat., 2009–. *Publications:* contrib. on trade in services and internat. relations to learned jls. *Recreations:* gardening, bird watching, Mediterranean life. *Address:* German Marshall Fund, 155 rue de la Loi, 1040 Brussels, Belgium. *Club:* International Château St Anne (Brussels).

RICHARDSON, John Charles; Managing Director, Historical Publications Ltd, since 1971; *b* 7 June 1935; *s* of Joseph and Vera Richardson; *m* 1st, 1957, Laura Caroline Bourne Webb (marr. diss. 1962); two *s*; 2nd, 1966, Elizabeth Noel Ballard (marr. diss. 1981); two *s*; 3rd, 1981, Helen Warnock English. *Educ:* Barking Abbey GS. J. Walter Thompson, 1965–72; KMP, 1974–84. Member: St Pancras BC, 1959–66; Camden BC, 1966–71. Joint Founder: GLAA, 1966; Camden Arts Centre, 1966; Chm., Bubble Theatre Co., 1968–74. Chm., Camden Hist. Soc., 1970–. *Publications:* The Local Historian's Encyclopedia, 1974; Covent Garden, 1979; Highgate: its history since the fifteenth century, 1983; Hampstead One Thousand, 1985; Islington Past, 1986; Highgate Past, 1989; Camden Town and Primrose Hill Past, 1991; London and its People, 1995; Covent Garden Past, 1995; Kentish Town Past, 1997; A History of Camden, 1999; The Annals of London, 2000; The Camden Town Book, 2007. *Recreations:* visiting the London Library, architecture. *Address:* 14 Saddleton Road, Whitstable, Kent CT5 4JD. *T:* (01227) 272605.

RICHARDSON, Rt Rev. John Henry; Suffragan Bishop of Bedford, 1994–2002; an Hon. Assistant Bishop, Dioceses of Carlisle and Newcastle, since 2003; *b* 11 July 1937; *s* of John Farquhar Richardson and Elizabeth Mary Richardson; *m* 1963, Felicity-Anne Lowes; three *d*. *Educ:* Winchester; Trinity Hall, Cambridge (BA 1961; MA 1965); Cuddesdon Coll., Oxford. Nat. Service, 1956–58 (despatches, Malaya, 1958). Ordained deacon, 1963, priest, 1964; Asst Curate, St George's, Stevenage, 1963–66; Curate, St Mary's, Eastbourne, 1966–68; Vicar: St Paul's, Chipperfield, 1968–75; St Mary's, Rickmansworth, 1975–86; RD, Rickmansworth, 1977–86; Vicar, St Michael's, Bishop's Stortford, 1986–93; Hon. Canon, St Albans Cathedral, 1986–2002. Hon. Fellow, Luton Univ., 2003. *Recreations:* walking, bird-watching, fishing, energetic gardening. *Address:* The Old Rectory, Bewcastle, Carlisle, Cumbria CA6 6PS. *T:* (016977) 48389. *Clubs:* Royal Automobile; Leander.

RICHARDSON, Sir John Patrick, KBE 2012; writer; *b* 6 Feb. 1924; *s* of Sir Wodehouse Richardson, KCB, DSO and Clara Pattie (*née* Crocker). *Educ:* Stowe; Slade Sch. of Art. US Rep., Christie's, 1964–72; Vice-Pres., M. Knoedler & Co., NYC, 1972–76; Man. Dir, Artemis Gp, London and New York, 1976–78; Editor-at-large, House and Garden (US), 1981–91; Contributing Ed., Vanity Fair, 1990–2006. Slade Prof. of Art History, Oxford, 1995–96. Corresp. FBA 1993. Whitbread Book of Year Award, 1991; La Vanguardia Book of Year Award, Barcelona, 1997. *Publications:* Picasso: watercolors and gouaches, 1956; Manet, 1958; Braque, 1959; A Life of Picasso, Vol. I, 1991, Vol. II, 1996, Vol. III, 2007; The Sorcerer's Apprentice: Picasso, Provence, and Douglas Cooper, 1999; Sacred Monsters, Sacred Masters: Beaton, Capote, Dali, Picasso, Freud, Warhol, and more, 2001; contrib. to TLS, Burlington Mag., New York Rev. of Books, New Yorker, etc. *Address:* 73 Fifth Avenue, New York City, NY 10003, USA; 263 West Meeting House Road, New Milford, CT 06776, USA.

RICHARDSON, Very Rev. John Stephen; Priest-in-charge, Holy Trinity, Margate, since 2009; Chairman, AQUILA, Diocese of Canterbury Academies Trust, since 2014; *b* 2 April 1950; *s* of James Geoffrey and Myra Richardson; *m* 1972, Elizabeth Susan Wiltshire; one *s* two *d* (and one *s* decd). *Educ:* Haslingden Grammar Sch.; Univ. of Southampton (BA Hons Theology); St John's Theological Coll., Nottingham. Deacon 1974, priest 1975; Asst Curate, St Michael's, Bramcote, 1974–77; Priest-in-Charge, Emmanuel Church, Radipole and Melcombe Regis, 1977–80; Asst Diocesan Missioner and Lay Trainer Adviser, dio. of Salisbury and Priest-in-Charge of Stinsford, Winterborne Monkton and Winterborne Came with Witcombe, 1980–83; Vicar of Christ Church, Nailsea, 1983–90; Adviser in Evangelism, dio. of Bath and Wells, 1985–90; Provost, subseq. Dean, of Bradford, 1990–2001; Vicar of Wye and Brook with Hastingleigh, and Chaplain, Imperial Coll. London (Wye Agricultural Coll., later Wye Coll.), 2001–09; Area Dean of West Bridge, 2003–09; Priest-in-charge, Boughton Aluph and Eastwell, 2004–09, and of Hinxhill, 2007–09; Asst Area Dean of Thanet, 2009–; Advr to Bishop of Dover on Deliverance Ministry, 2010–. Dir, Spring Harvest, 1998–2003 and 2007–11; Chm., Spring Harvest Charitable Trust, 1998–2012. Chaplain, W Yorks Police, 1995–2001. Bishop's Selector, ABM, 1993–97. Mem., General Synod, 1993–2001. Member: Exec. Bd, Common Purpose, 1992–2000; BBC North Adv. Panel, 1990–94; Bradford Breakthrough, 1992–2001; Council, Evangelical Alliance Management Gp, 1994–2000; Council, Scripture Union, 2000–07; Archbishop's Council, Dio. of Canterbury, 2013–; Canterbury Diocesan Bd of Educn, 2013–. Mem. Council, Bradford Chamber of Commerce, 1992–2001. Director: Mildmay Hosp., 2004– (Chm., 2007–); Kent Community Housing Trust, 2005–08. Trustee: Acorn Healing Trust, 1990–2007; Spennithorne Hall, 1990–98; Northumbria Community, 2006–09. Council Mem., St John's Theological Coll., Nottingham, 1988–94; Governor: Bradford Grammar Sch., 1990–2001; Giggleswick Sch., 1993–2001; Bradford Cathedral Community Coll. (formerly Fairfax Sch., then Bowling Community Coll.), 1994–2001. Chaplain to: High Sheriff, W Yorks, 1994–95, 2000–01; High Sheriff, Kent, 2004–05. Dir, Monnaie Chapel, Guernsey, 2013–. MInstD 1994. *Publications:* Ten Rural Churches, 1988. *Recreations:* football, cricket, North Western Municipal Bus Operators, walking, writing, broadcasting. *Address:* 5 Devonshire Gardens, Cliftonville, Margate, Kent CT9 3AF. *T:* (01843) 294129, (01843) 221864. *E:* vicarjohnsrichardson@googlemail.com.

RICHARDSON, John Stephen; Headmaster, Cheltenham College, 2004–10; education consultant, since 2010; *b* 2 Dec. 1953; *s* of Rev. James H. Richardson and Rachel Richardson (*née* Varley); *m* 1989, Ruth W. Vardy; two *s* one *d*. *Educ:* Rossall Sch.; Selwyn Coll., Cambridge (BA 1976; PGCE 1977; MA 1978). Dean Close School, Cheltenham, 1977–84: Teacher of Maths, Housemaster and Curriculum Dir; OC CCF/RAF Section; Eton College, 1984–92: Teacher of Maths, House List, Chapel Steward; Master i/c U16 Rowing; OC CCF/RAF Section; Treas., Eton Action; Headmaster, Culford Sch., Bury St Edmunds, 1992–2004. ISI Inspector, 1993–2004; Chm., East Div., HMC, 2000–02; Mem., NAHT, 1992–2010. Vice Chm., Curriculum Evaluation and Mgt Centre, Durham Univ., 2000–04. Mem. Council of Reference, Cheltenham Youth for Christ, 2007–08. Trustee, Ind. Schs Christian Alliance, 1994–2002. Chm. Govs, Kingham Hill Sch., 2012–; Trustee, Kingham Hill Trust, 2012; Vice Chm. Govs, Elstree Sch., 2012–15; Gov., Wrekin Old Hall Schs, 2015–. FRSA 2007. Foundn Fellow, Univ. of Gloucester, 2006–10. *Recreations:* reading, sailing, mountaineering. *Address:* White Gables, Moorend Road, Charlton Kings, Cheltenham, Glos GL53 9BN. *T:* (01242) 250754. *E:* jsr1253@gmail.com.

RICHARDSON, Kenneth Augustus, CVO 1994; CBE 1989; JP; Secretary to the Cabinet, Bermuda, 1984–93; *b* 13 Feb. 1939; *s* of Augustus J. Richardson; *m* 1966, Brenda Joyce (*née* Smith); one *s* one *d*. *Educ:* Howard Univ., Washington (BSc); Manchester Polytechnic (Dip. Personnel Admin and Labour Relations). Teacher, Sandys Secondary School, Bermuda, 1964; Admin. Cadet, Colonial Sec.'s Office, 1967; Training and Recruitment Officer, Bermuda Govt, 1969; Perm. Sec., Labour and Home Affairs, 1974. Chm., Employment Tribunal, 1990–. Hon. Life Vice Pres., Bermuda Football Assoc., 1994. MIPM 1973; MInstD 1988. JP 1984. *Recreation:* sport (soccer, tennis). *Address:* Mahogany, 19 Trimingham Hill, Paget PG 05, Bermuda; PO Box HM 1703, Hamilton HM GX, Bermuda. *T:* 236 1788.

RICHARDSON, Prof. Louise Mary, PhD; FRSE; Vice-Chancellor, University of Oxford, from Jan. 2016; *b* Dublin, 8 June; *d* of Arthur and Julie Richardson; *m* 1988, Thomas Jevon; one *s* two *d*. *Educ:* Trinity Coll., Dublin (BA Hist., 1980; MA Hist. 1982); Univ. of California, Los Angeles (MA Pol Sci. 1981); Harvard Univ., (MA Govt 1984; PhD Govt 1989). FRSE 2010. Asst Prof. of Govt, 1989–94, Associate Prof., 1994–2001, Harvard Univ.; Lectr on Law, Harvard Law Sch., 2001–08; Exec. Dean, Radcliffe Inst. for Advanced Study, 2001–08; Principal and Vice-Chancellor, 2009–15, Prof. of Internat. Relns, 2010–15, Univ. of St Andrews. Mem., Council of Econ. Advrs, Scottish Govt, 2011–15. Hon. DSSc QUB, 2015; Hon. LLD Aberdeen, 2015. *Publications:* When Allies Differ, 1996; What Terrorists Want, 2006; (ed) The Roots of Terrorism, 2006; (ed jtly) Democracy and Counterterrorism: lessons from the past, 2007. *Address:* University of Oxford, Wellington Square, Oxford OX1 2JD.

RICHARDSON, Margaret Ann, OBE 2005; FSA; Curator, Sir John Soane's Museum, 1995–2005 (Assistant Curator, 1985–95); *b* 11 Sept. 1937; *d* of late James Ballard and Edna (*née* Johnstone); *m* 1963, Anthony George Richardson; two *d*. *Educ:* Harrogate Coll.; University Coll. London (BA Hons; Fellow, 2001); Courtauld Inst. of Art (Acad. Dip.). FSA 1996. Asst Curator, 1963–68, Jt Dep. Curator, 1972–85, Drawings Collection, British Architectural Liby. Pres., Twentieth Century Soc., 1995–2003 (Mem. Cttee, 1984–2003); Trustee: Save Britain's Heritage, 1975–; Lutyens Trust, 1984– (Chm., 1994–2001); Greenwich Foundn for RNC, 1997–2004; Member, Council: Nat. Trust, 2002–11; Soc. of Antiquaries, 2010–14. Hon. Curator of Architecture, RA, 2005–. Hon. FRIBA 1994. *Publications:* (ed) RIBA Catalogue series, vols A, B, C–F, and S, 1969–76; Edwin Lutyens, 1973; Lutyens and the Sea Captain, 1981; (jtly) Great Drawings from the RIBA, 1983; Architects of the Arts and Crafts Movement, 1983; 66 Portland Place: the London headquarters of the RIBA, 1984; (jtly) The Art of the Architect, 1984; Sketches by Lutyens, 1994; (ed jtly) John Soane Architect: master of space and light, 1999. *Address:* 64 Albert Street, NW1 7NR. *T:* (020) 7387 7940.

See also V. Richardson.

RICHARDSON, Dame Mary, DBE 2001; Chief Executive, HSBC Global Education Trust, 1999–2008; *b* 26 Feb. 1936; *d* of Lt George Arthur Habgood, RN, and Anna Jane Habgood; *m* 1960, Dr Donald Arthur Richardson; one *s* one *d*. *Educ:* Notre Dame High Sch., Wigan; Liverpool Univ. (BA 1957; DipEd 1958). Officer, WRAC, 1954–60. Pt-time teacher, St Adrian's Jun. Sch., 1963–72; Hd of Sixth Form, then Hd of English, Marlborough Sch., St Albans, 1977–85; Dep. Hd, Convent of Jesus and Mary, Willesden, 1985–86; Principal, Convent of Jesus and Mary Lang. Coll., Harlesden, 1986–99. Chm., Steering Gp, London Challenge Cadet Partnership Pilot Project, DFE/MoD, 2007–11. Chm., Adv. Cttee on educn to HRH Prince Seeiso. Member: Adv. Cttee on Ind./State Schs Partnerships, 1999–2002; Bd of Visitors, HM Prison Wormwood Scrubs, 1995–2002. Director: Technol. Colls, subseq. Specialist Schs and Academies, Trust, 2000– (Fellow 2005); Nat. Coll. Sch. Leadership, 2008–; Founding Ambassador, Teach First, 2008–; Member, Board: Teach for All, 2008–; Grant Making Trusts and Foundns; Trustee, CfBT, 2001–06. President: London Youth Trust, 2003–05; SOS Children's Villages, UK, 2008–; Vice Pres., Internat. Friendship League, 2012–. Governor: Thornton Coll., Bucks, 1994–; City of London Schs (Boys), 2000–; ESU, 2005–14 (Dep. Chm., 2008–11; Chm., 2011–14); Mem. Council, Royal Alexandra and Albert Sch., Reigate, 2007–09 (Gov., 2009–); Mem., Develt Cttee, Ripon Theol Coll., Cuddesdon, 2008–; Hon. Vice-Pres., Commonwealth Youth Orch. and Choir, 2012–. Trustee: Waterford Coll., Swaziland, 2002–04 and 2008–; Dulverton Trust, 2003–; Marine Soc. and Sea Cadets, 2007–; Future Hope, Calcutta, 2008–; Vitol Foundn, 2008–; Shakespeare's Globe, 2008–; Internat. Centre for Circulatory Health, Imperial Coll. London, 2011–; Patron, Four Pillars (of Good Governance), 2009–. FRSA 1996. CCMI 2011. Member: Newman Assoc., 1964; Baconian Soc., 2002 (Chm., 2008–09); NADFAS, 2000. Freeman, City of London, 2000; Guild of Educators; Basketmakers' Co. Hon. Dr Brunel, 2005; Hon. DHumLit Richmond, 2007; Hon. DSc City, 2008. *Publications:* Free to Play, Free to Pretend, Free to Imagine, drama textbooks for use in primary schs, 1972; contrib. professional periodicals. *Address:* 1A Abbey Avenue, St Albans, Herts AL3 4BJ. *T:* (01727) 859039. *E:* MRicha3539@aol.com. *Clubs:* Army and Navy, Victory Services.

RICHARDSON, Michael Elliot; Director of Continuing Education and Lifelong Learning and Director, Institute of Continuing Education (formerly Director of Continuing Education and Secretary, Board of Continuing Education), University of Cambridge, 1990–2003; Fellow of Wolfson College, Cambridge, 1990–2003, now Emeritus; *b* 29 Sept. 1938; *s* of late Rev. Emery Lonsdale Richardson and Margaret Ann Richardson (*née* Elliot); *m* 1968, Gillian Miles Jones; two *d*. *Educ:* Pocklington Sch., York; St John's Coll., Cambridge (MA 1967); Lincoln Theol Coll.; Univ. of Nottingham (DipAE 1970). FCIPD. Schoolmaster, Middlesbrough Boys' High Sch., 1964–65; Adult Educn Tutor, Ibstock Community Coll., 1965–67; Principal, Alfreton Hall Adult Educn Centre, 1967–69; Open University, 1969–90: Dep. Regl Dir, Northern, 1969–76; Regl Dir, NW, 1976–79; Dir, Educnl Services for Contg Educn, 1979–81; Pro-Dir, 1981–84, Dir, 1984–86, Centre for Contg Educn; Pro-Vice Chancellor, Contg Educn, 1985–90. Chm., Council for Educn and Training of Youth and Community Workers, 1985–90; Sec., UACE, 1998–2002 (Mem. Council, 1990–2003, now Life Mem.); Mem. Council, CRAC, 1990–98; Mem., numerous cttees and boards, 1980–. Trustee, Nat. Extension Coll., 1988–2003. Pres., Rotary Club of Tynedale, 2009–10. DUniv Open 1994. FRSA. *Publications:* Preparing to Study, 1979; Continuing Education for the Post Industrial Society, 1982; contribs to educn jls. *Recreations:* gardening, angling, walking. *Address:* Holmlea, Station Road, Corbridge, Northumberland NE45 5AY.

RICHARDSON, Michael John, CB 2005; Chairman, Teachers Pension Scheme Pensions Board, since 2014; *b* 17 March 1946; *s* of Philip George Richardson, MBE and Susan Rowena (*née* Pearce); *m* 1967, Celia, *d* of Rev. Canon Peter and Daphne Bradshaw; one *s* one *d*. *Educ:* Eton Coll.; St Edmund Hall, Oxford (BA Lit.Hum. 1968). Joined HM Diplomatic Service, 1968; Hong Kong, 1969–71; 3rd, later 2nd Sec., Peking, 1972–74; 1st Secretary: FCO, 1974–75; EEC, 1976; Western European Dept, FCO, 1977–78; Private Secretary to: Minister of State, 1978–79; Lord Privy Seal, 1979–80; 1st Sec., Rome, 1980–85; Asst Head, EC Dept, 1985; Head, EC Presidency Unit, FCO, 1986–87; Department for Education, later DFEE, 1987–2001: Under Sec., 1992; Dir for Qualifications, 1995–98; Dir for Employment Policy, 1998–2001; Department for Work and Pensions: Director: for Work, Welfare and Fraud, 2001–02; for Work and Welfare Strategy, 2002–03; for Work, Welfare and Poverty, 2003–06. Dep. Chm., London & Quadrant Housing Assoc., 1998–2010. Chairman: Lewisham PCT, subseq. NHS Lewisham, 2007–11; Jt Cttee of SE London NHS PCTs, 2009–11. Trustee, Transformation Trust, 2013–. *Recreations:* family, reading, gardening, theatre-going, adventurous travel, visiting parish churches. *Address:* 12 Northumberland Place, W2 5BS.

RICHARDSON, Miranda; actress; *b* 3 March 1958; *d* of William Alan Richardson and Marian Georgina Townsend. *Educ:* St Wyburn, Southport, Merseyside; Southport High Sch. for Girls; Bristol Old Vic Theatre Sch. Repertory: Manchester Library Theatre, 1979–80; Derby Playhouse, Duke's Playhouse, Lancaster, Bristol Old Vic and Leicester Haymarket, 1982–83; West End début, Moving, Queen's, 1980–81; Royal Court: Edmund, 1985; A Lie of the Mind, 1987; Etta Jenks, 1990; Grasses of a Thousand Colours, 2009; National Theatre: The Changeling, and Mountain Language, 1988; The Designated Mourner, 1996; Orlando, Edinburgh Fest., 1996; Aunt Dan and Lemon, Almeida, 1999. *Television:* series include: Agony; Sorrell and Son; Blackadder II and III; Die Kinder, 1990; The True Adventures of Christopher Columbus, 1992; A Dance to the Music of Time, 1998; The Life and Times of Vivienne Vyle, 2007; Parade's End, 2012; World Without End, 2013; plays include: The Master Builder; The Demon Lover; After Pilkington; Sweet as You Are (RTS Award, 1987–88); Ball-trap on the Côte Sauvage, 1989; Old Times, 1991; Merlin, 1998; Alice in Wonderland, 2000; The Lost Prince, 2003; Gideon's Daughter, 2006; Mapp and Lucia, 2014; An Inspector Calls, 2015; *films:* Dance with a Stranger (role, Ruth Ellis) (City Limits Best Film Actress, 1985; Evening Standard Best Actress, 1985; Variety Club Most Promising Artiste, 1985); Underworld; Death of the Heart; Empire of the Sun; The Mad Monkey; Eat the Rich; Redemption, 1991; Enchanted April, 1992 (Golden Globe Award, Best Comedy Actress, 1993); Mr Wakefield's Crusade, The Bachelor, 1992; Damage (BAFTA Award, Best Supporting Actress, 1993; NY Critics Circle Award; Film Critics Circle, Best Actress 1994; Royal Variety Club of GB, Best Film Actress of 1994); The Crying Game, 1992; Century, 1993; Tom and Viv (Best Actress, Nat. Bd of Review of Motion Pictures), La Nuit et Le Moment, 1994; Kansas City, Evening Star, 1996; Swann, 1997; Designated Mourner, Apostle, All For Love, Jacob Two Two and the Hooded Fang, The Big Brass Ring, 1998; Sleepy Hollow, Chicken Run (voice), Snow White, 2000; The Hours, Spider, 2001; The Actors, 2002; Rage on Placid Lake, Falling Angels, The Prince and Me, Phantom of the Opera, 2003; Harry Potter and the Goblet of Fire, 2005; Wah Wah, Spinning into Butter, Puffball, Southland Tales, 2006; Fred Claus, Provoked: a True Story, 2007; The Young Victoria, 2009; Harry Potter and the Deathly Hallows, Pt 1, Made in Dagenham, 2010; Belle, 2014; Testament of Youth, 2015. Chm. Judges, Women's Prize for Fiction, 2013. *Recreations:* reading, walking, softball, gardening, music, junkshops, occasional art, animals. *Address:* c/o Independent Talent Group Ltd, 40 Whitfield Street, W1T 2RH.

RICHARDSON, Rev. Neil Graham, PhD; President, Methodist Conference, 2003–04; *b* 2 Dec. 1943; *s* of John and Ethel Richardson; *m* 1972, Rhiannon Bradshaw; three *s*. *Educ:* Queen's Coll., Oxford (BA Classics, Modern Hist.; MA 1970); Wesley House, Cambridge (BA Theol. 1971); Bristol Univ. (MLitt 1977, PhD 1992). Asst Tutor, Wesley Coll., Bristol, 1971–73; Minister, Oxford Circuit, 1973–77; Ecumenical Lectr, Bishop's Hostel, Lincoln, 1977–81; Minister, Manchester Mission Circuit, and Chaplain to Manchester Univ., 1981–84; Wesley College, Bristol: Tutor in New Testament Studies, 1984–95; Principal, 1995–2001; Superintendent Minister, Leeds NE Circuit, 2001–07. Res. Fellow, Queen's Coll., Birmingham, 2007–08. *Publications:* Was Jesus Divine?, 1979; The Panorama of Luke, 1982; Preaching from Scripture, 1983; Paul's Language About God, 1994; God in the New Testament, 1999; Paul for Today: new perspectives on a controversial apostle, 2009; John for Today, 2010; (with G. Lovell) Sustaining Preachers and Preaching, 2011; Who on Earth is God?, 2014. *Recreation:* marathon running (London Marathon, 1995, 1999, 2000, 2004–07, 2010; first UK national Church leader to run the London Marathon whilst in office). *Address:* 14 Mortimer Drive, Orleton SY8 4JW.

RICHARDSON, Dr Nigel Peter Vincent; education consultant, appraiser and author; Headmaster, The Perse School, Cambridge, 1994–2008; *b* 29 June 1948; *s* of Vincent Boys Richardson and Jean Frances (*née* Wrangles); *m* 1979, (Averon) Joy James; two *s*. *Educ:* Highgate Sch.; Trinity Hall, Cambridge (MA Hist.); Bristol Univ. (PGCE); University Coll. London (PhD 2007). Uppingham School: Hist. Dept, 1971–89; Sixth Form Tutor, 1977–83; Second Master, 1983–89; Headmaster, Dragon Sch., Oxford, 1989–92; Dep. Headmaster and Dir of Studies, King's Sch., Macclesfield, 1992–94. Course Dir, Bell Sch., Cambridge, 1976–82. Chm., HMC, 2007 (Vice-Chm., 2007–08). Syndic, Cambridge Univ. Press, 2009–14. Question compiler, Top of the Form, BBC Radio 4, 1982–87. Governor: Greycotes Sch., Oxford, 1989–92; King's Coll. Sch., Cambridge, 1998–2004; King's Sch., Ely, 2008–13 (Chm., Educn Cttee, 2010–13); Norwich Sch., 2008–13; Magdalen Coll. Sch., Oxford, 2008–; Mem., Educn Cttee, 2008– (Chm., 2014–), Mem., Council, 2013–, Haileybury Coll.; Mem. Bd, Assoc. of Governing Bodies of Ind. Schs, 2014–. Walter Hines Page Scholar, ESU, 2003. Ed., Conference and Common Room, 1999–2002; Series Ed. and Contrib., Leading Schools book series, HMC, 2006–12. *Publications:* The Effective Use of Time, 1984, 2nd edn 1989; First Steps in Leadership, 1987; Typhoid in Uppingham: analysis of a Victorian town and school in crisis 1875–77, 2008 (British Assoc. for Local Hist. Award, 2008); Thring of Uppingham: Victorian educator, 2014; various histories and biographies for school use; contrib. TES, The Times, Daily Telegraph, Daily Mail, etc. *Recreations:* history, music, writing, sport, gardening, travel. *Address:* 6 High Meadow, Harston, Cambridge CB22 7TR. *T:* (01223) 872469. *E:* NPVRichardson@btinternet.com.

RICHARDSON, Rev. Paul; Assistant Bishop of Newcastle, 1998–2009; *b* 16 Jan. 1947; *s* of late William and Ilene Richardson. *Educ:* Keswick Sch.; The Queen's Coll., Oxford (BA (Mod. History) 1968, (Theol.) 1970; MA 1975); Harvard Divinity Sch.; Cuddesdon Theol Coll. Ordained deacon, 1972, priest, 1973; Asst Curate, St John's, Earlsfield, 1972–75; Asst Chaplain, Oslo, Norway, 1975–77; Mission Priest, Nambaiyufa, PNG, 1977–79; Lectr, 1979–81, Principal, 1981–85, Newton Theol Coll.; Dean, St John's Cathedral, Port Moresby, 1985–86; Bishop of Aipo Rongo, PNG, 1987–95; Bishop of Wangaratta, 1995–97. Re-ordained in RC Church, 2011. *Recreations:* reading, walking, travel. *Address:* 86 Fitzalan Street, Lambeth, SE11 6QU. *T:* (020) 7091 4299. *Club:* Oxford and Cambridge.

RICHARDSON, Paul Brayshaw; a District Judge (Magistrates' Courts), 2002–14; *b* 21 June 1948; *s* of Ronald and Enid Richardson; *m* 1973, Valerie Madeleine Hine; one *s* one *d*. *Educ:* Berkhamsted Sch.; Trinity Coll., Oxford (MA). Called to the Bar, Middle Temple, 1972; in practice as barrister, Northern Circuit, with chambers in Manchester, 1973–2002; Actg Stipendiary Magistrate, 1995–2002. *Recreations:* fly fishing, cricket, jugband music.

RICHARDSON, Prof. Peter Damian, FRS 1986; Professor of Engineering and Physiology, Brown University, USA, since 1984; *b* West Wickham, Kent, 22 Aug. 1935; *s* of late Reginald William Merrells Richardson and Marie Stuart Naomi (*née* Ouseley). *Educ:* Imperial College, Univ. of London (BSc (Eng) 1955; PhD 1958; DSc (Eng) 1974; ACGI 1955; DIC 1958; DSc 1983); MA Brown Univ. 1965. Demonstrator, Imperial Coll., 1955–58; Brown University: Vis. Lectr, 1958–59; Research Associate, 1959–60; Asst Prof. of Engrg, 1960–65; Associate Prof. of Engrg, 1965–68; Prof. of Engrg, 1968–84; Chair, University Faculty, 1987– (Vice-Chair, 1986–87; Parliamentarian, 1989–). Sen. Vis. Fellow, Univ. of London, 1967; Prof. d'échange, Univ. of Paris, 1968; leave at: Orta Doğu Teknik Univ., Ankara, 1969; Abteilung Physiologie, Medizinische Fakultat, RWTH Aachen, 1976; Univ. of Pisa, 1983; Lab. de Recherche sur les macromolecules, Univ. de Paris XIII, 1991. FASME 1983; Founding Fellow, AIMBE, 1991; FCGI 2003; Inaugural Fellow, Biomedical Engrg Soc., 2005. Hon. FRCP 2010. Humboldt-Preis, A. von Humboldt Sen. Scientist Award, 1976; Laureate in Medicine, Ernst Jung Foundn, 1987; President's Award for Excellence in Faculty Governance, Brown Univ., 2010. *Publications:* (with M. Steiner) Principles of Cell Adhesion, 1995; numerous articles in learned jls. *Recreations:* photography, travel, country life. *Address:* Box D, Brown University, 184 Hope Street, Providence, Rhode Island 02912–9104, USA. *T:* (401) 8632687.

RICHARDSON, Hon. Ruth Margaret; consultant and company director; Ruth Richardson (NZ) Ltd, strategic and economic policy advice, since 1994; *b* 13 Dec. 1950; *d* of Ross Pearce Richardson and Rita Joan Richardson; *m* 1975, Andrew Evan Wright; one *s* one *d*. *Educ:* Canterbury Univ., NZ (LLB Hons 1971). Admitted to the Bar, 1973; Legal Adviser: Law Reform Div., Dept of Justice, 1972–75; Federated Farmers of NZ, 1975–80. MP (Nat. Party) Selwyn, NZ, 1981–94; Opposition spokesman: on Education and on Youth Issues, 1984–87; on Finance, 1987–90; Minister of Finance, 1990–93. Dir, Reserve Bank of NZ, 1999–2004. Chairman: Jade Software Corp. Ltd; NZ Merino Co. Ltd; Adv. Cttee, Kula Fund II; Syft Technologies Ltd; Kiwi Innovation Network; Director: Synlait Milk Ltd; Bank of China (NZ). *Recreations:* running, swimming, gardening. *Address:* 713 Newtons Road, RD5, Christchurch 7675, New Zealand. *T:* (3) 3479146.

RICHARDSON, Sarah Jane; Her Honour Judge Sarah Richardson; a Circuit Judge, since 2015. *Educ:* Nottingham Univ. (BA 1st Cl. Hons Law 1992). Called to the Bar, Inner Temple, 1993; a Dep. Dist Judge, 2005–08; a Dist Judge, 2008–15. *Address:* Leeds Combined Court Centre, The Courthouse, 1 Oxford Row, Leeds LS1 3BG.

RICHARDSON, Sir Simon Alaisdair S.; *see* Stewart-Richardson.

RICHARDSON, Prof. Stephen Michael, CBE 2015; PhD; FREng; FIChemE; Professor of Chemical Engineering, since 1994, and Associate Provost, since 2013, Imperial College London; *b* London, 8 Dec. 1951; *s* of David Richardson, *qv*; *m* 1976, Hilary Joy Burgess; one *s* two *d*. *Educ:* Imperial Coll., London (BSc (Eng) 1972; PhD 1976). FIChemE 1990; FREng 1996. Rolls-Royce Res. Asst, 1975, 1851 Res. Fellow, 1976–78, Univ. of Cambridge; Imperial College, London: Lectr, Dept of Chem. Engrg, 1978–87; Sen. Lectr, 1987–92; Reader, 1992–94; Hd of Dept, 2001–08; Principal, Faculty of Engrg, 2008–10; Dep. Rector, 2009–13. FCGI 1999; FHEA 2007. *Publications:* Fluid Mechanics, 1989. *Recreations:* gardening, walking, classical music. *Address:* Faculty Building, Imperial College London, S Kensington, SW7 2AZ. *T:* (020) 7594 5039. *E:* s.m.richardson@imperial.ac.uk.

RICHARDSON, Sir Thomas (Legh), KCMG 2000 (CMG 1991); HM Diplomatic Service; Ambassador to Italy, 1996–2000; *b* 6 Feb. 1941; *s* of Arthur Legh Turnour Richardson and Penelope Margaret Richardson; *m* 1979, Alexandra Frazier Wasiqullah (*née* Ratcliff). *Educ:* Westminster Sch.; Christ Church, Oxford. MA (Hist.). Joined Foreign Office, 1962; seconded to Univ. of Ghana, 1962–63; FO, 1963–65; Third Sec., Dar-es-Salaam, 1965–66; Vice-Consul (Commercial), Milan, 1967–70; seconded to N. M. Rothschild & Sons, 1970; FCO, 1971–74; First Sec., UK Mission to UN, 1974–78; FCO, 1978–80; seconded to

Central Policy Review Staff, Cabinet Office, 1980–81; Head of Chancery, Rome, 1982–86; Head of Economic Relns Dept, FCO, 1986–89; UK Dep. Perm. Rep. to UN, with personal rank of Ambassador, 1989–94; Dep. Pol Dir and Asst Under-Sec. of State (Western Europe), FCO, 1994–96. Governor: British Inst. of Florence, 2001–08 (Chm., 2003–08); Monte San Martino Trust, 2003–; Mem. Council, British Sch. at Rome, 2002–06. Hon. Pres., British-Italian Soc., 2007–. *Recreations:* reading, walking, travel, music.

RICHARDSON, Victoria; Director, Architecture, Design and Fashion, British Council, since 2010; *b* London, 16 Oct. 1968; *d* of Anthony Richardson and Margaret Ann Richardson, *qv*; *m* 1999, Adrian Friend; three *d*. *Educ:* Central St Martins (Foundn in Art 1988); Univ. of Westminster (BA Hons Arch. 1992); Napier Univ. (NCTJ Newspaper Writing 1995). Asst Ed., Public Sector Bldg, 1995–96; Ed., Public Service & Local Govt, 1996–97; Sen. Reporter, 1997–2000, Dep. Ed., 2000–02, RIBA Jl; Ed., Blueprint, 2004–10. Co-Dir, London Fest. of Architecture, 2010–14. Chair, Architecture Centre Network, 2007–09; Member: London Cultural Strategy Gp, 2008–; Adv. Cttee, V&A Dundee, 2014–. Mem. Council, AA, 2015–. Trustee, Campaign for Drawing, 2004–11. Hon. FRIBA 2015. *Publications:* In Defence of the Dome, 1999; New Vernacular Architecture, 2001; The Dungeness Box, 2003. *Address:* British Council, 10 Spring Gardens, SW1A 2BN. *T:* (020) 7389 3155. *E:* Vicky.Richardson@britishcouncil.org.

RICHARDSON, Prof. William Boys, DPhil; General Secretary, Headmasters' and Headmistresses' Conference, since 2011; *b* Barnet, 13 July 1956; *s* of late Vincent Richardson and of Jean Richardson (*née* Wrangles); partner, Susan Shallcross; one *s*; *m* 1991, Ellen Renner; one *s*. *Educ:* Highgate Sch.; Univ. of Bristol (BA); New Coll., Oxford (DPhil 1993). Gen. mgt trainee, industrial relns manager, Unilever plc, 1982–85; British Petroleum Fellow, Univ. of Warwick, 1986–95; Lectr, then Sen. Lectr, Univ. of Sheffield, 1995–2000; Prof. of Educn, and Dir, Res. Centre for the Learning Society, 2000–11, Public Orator, 2003–05, Univ. of Exeter. Hon. Prof., Univ. of Exeter, 2011–. Mem. Editl Bd, 1998–, Reviews Ed., 1998–2010, Hist. of Educn. Dir, Educn Policy MA prog., DfEE, 2003–07. Chief Examr, Inst. of Educn, Univ. of London, 2002–05. Dir, ISC, 2011–. Mem., Governing Council, Univ. of Exeter, 2004–07. Trustee: Coombeshead Coll. Trust, 2007–11 (Chm., 2010–11); Creative Educn Trust, 2010– (Vice Chm., 2013–). *Publications:* (jtly) Teachers into Business and Industry, 1989; (jtly) The Reform of Post-16 Education and Training in England and Wales, 1993; (jtly) Something Borrowed, Something Learned?: the transatlantic market in education and training reform, 1993; (with G. Stanton) Qualifications for the Future: a study of tripartite and other divisions in post-16 education and training, 1997; (with G. McCulloch) Educational Research in Historical Settings, 2000; (jtly) Social Change in the History of British Education, 2008; (contrib.) Oxford Dictionary of National Biography (1532–1677), 2004; res. reports, evaluation studies and teaching pubns. *Recreations:* histories, landscapes, lost causes. *Address:* Headmasters' and Headmistresses' Conference, 12 The Point, Rockingham Road, Market Harborough, Leics LE16 7QU. *E:* gensec@hmc.org.uk. *Club:* Athenæum.

RICHARDSON, Prof. William David, PhD; FRS 2013; FMedSci; Professor of Biology, since 1993, and Director, since 2012, Wolfson Institute for Biomedical Research, University College London; *b* Belfast, 18 Aug. 1951; *s* of Walter Richardson and Olive Richardson (*née* Woods); *m* 1977, Susan Anne Powell (*née* Wray); one *s* one *d*. *Educ:* Royal Belfast Academical Instn; Univ. of Manchester (BSc 1st Cl. Phys 1973); King's Coll. London (PhD Biophys 1978). Internat. Fellow, NIH, Bethesda, Md, 1978–82; Staff Scientist, NIMR, Mill Hill, London, 1982–85; University College London: Lectr in Molecular Genetics, 1985–90; Reader in Biology, 1990–93; Hd of Dept, 2000–06; Wolfson Inst. for Biological Res., 1999–. FLS 2008; FMedSci 2010. *Publications:* over 100 articles in scientific jls and books, mainly on develtl neurosci. (specialty oligodendrocytes, the myelin-forming cells of central nervous system). *Recreations:* fencing in earlier years, more recently squash, lifelong motorcyclist. *Address:* Wolfson Institute for Biomedical Research, University College London, Gower Street, WC1E 6BT. *T:* (020) 7679 6729. *E:* w.richardson@ucl.ac.uk.

RICHARDSON-BUNBURY, Sir (Richard David) Michael; *see* Bunbury.

RICHBOROUGH, Bishop Suffragan of, since 2011; **Rt Rev. Norman Banks;** Provincial Episcopal Visitor, Province of Canterbury, since 2011; an Honorary Assistant Bishop: Diocese of St Edmundsbury and Ipswich, since 2011; Diocese of Norwich, since 2012; Diocese of Ely, since 2012; Diocese of Guildford, since 2012; Diocese of Chelmsford, since 2012; Diocese of St Albans, since 2013; Diocese of Lincoln, since 2015; Diocese of Gibraltar in Europe, since 2015; *b* Wallsend, Tyne and Wear, 4 April 1954; *s* of Francis John Banks and Elizabeth Jane Banks. *Educ:* Oriel Coll., Oxford (MA 1980); St Stephen's House, Oxford (CTh 1982). Ordained deacon, 1982, priest, 1983; Curate, 1982–87, Priest-in-charge, 1987–90, Christchurch with St Ann, Newcastle; Vicar, St Paul's, Whitley Bay, 1990–2000; Vicar, Walsingham, Houghton and the Barshams, Norfolk, 2000–11; Rural Dean, Burnham and Walsingham, 2008–11; Chaplain to the Queen, 2008–11; Chaplain to the High Sheriff of Norfolk, 2011. *Address:* Parkside House, Abbey Mill Lane, St Albans, Herts AL3 4HE. *T:* (01727) 836358. *E:* bishop@richborough.org.uk, secretary@richborough.org.uk.

RICHENS, Prof. Paul Nicholas, RIBA; Professor of Architectural Computing, University of Bath, 2005; *b* Cambridge, 24 July 1946; *s* of Richard Hook Richens and Ruth Hamilton Richens (*née* Scott); partner, Clare Gilmour; two *s* two *d*; *m* 2004, Megan Yakeley (marr. diss. 2013); one *d*; *m* 2014, Prof. Heather van der Lely (*d* 2014); partner, Prof. Mary Target. *Educ:* Cambridgeshire High Sch. for Boys; King's Coll., Cambridge (BA 1968; DipArch). RIBA 1989. Software developer, 1969–84, Dir, 1984–86, Applied Research of Cambridge; Technical Dir, McDonnell Douglas AEC Systems Co., 1986–89; University of Cambridge: Asst Dir of Res., 1989–2000; Dir, Martin Centre for Architectural and Urban Studies, 1992–2002; Reader in Architectural Computing, 2000–05; Vice Master, Churchill Coll., Cambridge, 2000–05; Dir, Centre for Advanced Studies in Arch., Univ. of Bath, 2007–09. *Recreations:* feeding friends, trespassing. *Address:* 33 Belvedere, Bath BA1 5HR.

RICHER, family name of **Baroness Altmann**.

RICHER, Julian, LVO 2007; Founder and Managing Director, Richer Sounds plc, since 1978; *b* 9 March 1959; *s* of Percy Isaac Richer and Ursula Marion (*née* Haller); *m* 1982, Rosemary Louise Hamlet. *Educ:* Clifton Coll., Bristol. Salesman, Hi-Fi Markets Ltd, 1977; Founder and Chairman: JR Properties, 1989–; Audio Partnership plc, 1994–2010; Richer Consulting Ltd, 1996–2002; The Richer Partnership, 1997–2009; JR Publishing, 1998–; Lomo Ltd, 1998–2007; Definitely Mktg Ltd, 2000–05; Chairman: Home Ltd, 1999–2003; Grey Frog plc, 2000–04. Non-executive Director: Duchy Originals Ltd, 1998–2006; Urban Spaces Ltd, 1999–2003; Knutsford plc, 1999–2002; Poptones plc, 2000–05; WILink.com plc, 2000–03. Chm., Business Develt Gp, Henry Doubleday Res. Assoc., 1998–2002. Founder and Trustee: Persula Foundn, 1994–; Acts 435, 2009–; ASB Help, 2013–; Mem., Leadership Gp, Amnesty Internat., 2004–07; Ambassador for Youth, 1998–; Patron: Gold Service Panel, Irwell Valley Housing Assoc., 1998– (Chm., Gold Service Evaluation Panel, 1998–2005); Big Issue, 1999; Youth Clubs UK 90th Anniv., 2000; Ambassador, Centrepoint, 2000–01; Vice-Pres., RSPCA, 2002–; Dep. Chm. and Mem., New Horizons Develt Bd, 1997–2002, Mem., Adv. Bd, 2002–04, RNIB. Dir, Whizz-Kids 10th Birthday Bd, 1999–2007. Hon. DBA: Kingston, 2001; Bournemouth, 2002. Richer Sounds plc awarded Royal Warrant, 2011. *Publications:* The Richer Way, 1995, 5th edn 2009; Richer on Leadership, 1999; A Richer Life (private pubn), 2010. *Recreations:* managing and drumming in a band, hosting weekly bible study meetings, travelling. *Address:* c/o Richer Sounds plc, Richer House, Hankey Place, SE1 4BB. *T:* (020) 7403 1310.

RICHES, Anne Clare, (Mrs T. C. Coltman), OBE 1999; DL; FSA; free-lance architectural historian, since 1989; *b* 12 April 1943; *d* of late Rt Rev. Kenneth Riches and of Kathleen Mary Riches (*née* Dixon); *m* 1989, Timothy Charles Coltman. *Educ:* Headington Sch., Oxford; Edinburgh Univ. (MA 1965; Dip. Hist. of Art 1966). FSA 1985. Historian, Historic Bldgs Div., GLC, 1966–78; Inspector, then Principal Inspector, Historic Bldgs and Monuments Directorate, Scottish Develt Dept, 1978–89. Society of Architectural Historians of Great Britain: Sec., 1978–83; Conf. Sec., 1978–85; Chm., 1985–88. Member: Adv. Panel, Railway Heritage Trust, 1985–2006; Nat. Cttee, Assoc. of Preservation Trusts, 1989–95; RCHME, 1991–99; Royal Commn on Ancient and Historical Monuments of Scotland, 1995–2004; Church Bldgs Council (formerly Council for Care of Churches), 2001–13. Trustee: Scottish Historic Bldgs Trust, 1989–2009; Theatres Trust, 1996–2005; Heritage Trust for Lincolnshire: Dir, 1990–; Chm., 2002–12; Chm., Archaeol. Adv. Cttee, 1991–94; Chm., Bldgs Adv. Cttee, 1992–. Mem., Lincoln Cathedral Fabric Council, 1998–. DL Lincs, 2006. Chancellor's Medal, Univ. of Lincoln, 2013. *Publications:* (with R. Barber) A Dictionary of Fabulous Beasts, 1972; Victorian Church Building and Restoration in Suffolk, 1982; (jtly) Building of Scotland: Glasgow, 1990; (with R. Close) Buildings of Scotland: Ayrshire and Arran, 2012; contrib. Architectl Hist. *Recreations:* gardening, hill-farming, visiting buildings. *Address:* Skellingthorpe Hall, Lincoln LN6 5UU. *T:* (01522) 694609.

RICHES, Lucinda Jane; non-executive Director: UK Financial Investments Ltd, since 2009; Diverse Income Trust plc, since 2011; Graphite Enterprise Trust plc, since 2011; British Standards Institution, since 2012 (Adviser, 2011–12); CRH plc, since 2015; *b* Dorking, Surrey, 26 July 1961; *d* of late Kenneth Riches and Margaret Riches; three *d*. *Educ:* St Teresa's Convent, Effingham; Rosebery Grammar Sch., Epsom; Brasenose Coll., Oxford (BA PPE 1983; Exhibnr); Univ. of Pennsylvania (MA Pol Sci. 1984, Thouron Scholar). Grad. trng course, Chase Manhattan Bank, 1984–85; S. G. Warburg, and subseq. firms, then UBS, 1986–2007: Hd, US Equity Capital Mkts, NY, 1992–94; Hd, Eur. Equity Capital Mkts, 1995–99; Global Hd, Equity Capital Mkts, 1999–2007; Mem. Bd, UBS Investment Bank, 2001–07; non-exec. Mem., Partnership Bd, King & Wood Mallesons LLP (formerly S J Berwin LLP), 2012–. Pres., Brasenose Soc., 2011–12. Trustee, Sue Ryder (formerly Sue Ryder Care), 2008–. *Recreations:* family, walking, theatre, music. *E:* lucinda.riches@hotmail.co.uk.

RICHMOND, 10th Duke of, *cr* 1675, **LENNOX,** 10th Duke of, *cr* 1675 (Scot.), **AND GORDON,** 5th Duke of, *cr* 1876; **Charles Henry Gordon Lennox;** Baron Settrington, Earl of March, 1675; Lord of Torboulton, Earl of Darnley (Scot.), 1675; Earl of Kinrara, 1876; Duc d'Aubigny (France), 1684; Hereditary Constable of Inverness Castle; Lord-Lieutenant of West Sussex, 1990–94; *b* 19 Sept. 1929; *s* of 9th Duke of Richmond and Gordon, and Elizabeth Grace (*d* 1992), *y d* of late Rev. T. W. Hudson; *S* father, 1989; *m* 1951, Susan Monica, *o d* of late Colonel C. E. Grenville-Grey, CBE, Hall Barn, Blewbury, Berks; one *s* four *d*. *Educ:* Eton; William Temple Coll. 2nd Lieut, 60th Rifles, 1949–50. Chartered Accountant, 1956. Financial Controllers Dept, Courtaulds Ltd, Coventry, 1960–64; Dir of Industrial Studies, William Temple Coll., 1964–68; Chancellor, Univ. of Sussex, 1985–98 (Treasurer, 1979–82). Church Commissioner, 1963–76; Mem. Gen. Synod of Church of England, formerly Church Assembly, 1960–80 (Chm., Bd for Mission and Unity, 1967–77); Mem., Central and Exec. Cttees, World Council of Churches, 1968–75; Chairman: Christian Orgn Res. and Adv. Trust, 1965–87; House of Laity, Chichester Diocesan Synod, 1976–79; Vice-Chm., Archbishop's Commn on Church and State, 1966–70; Member: W Midlands Regional Economic Planning Council, 1965–68; Steering Gp, W Sussex Economic Forum, 1997–2003; Bognor Regis Jt Regeneration Steering Gp, 2001–07; Chm., W Sussex Coastal Strip Enterprise Gateway Hub, 2000–06. Chairman: Goodwood Group of Cos, 1969–2009; Dexam International Holdings Ltd, 1969–2011; Ajax Insurance (Holdings) Ltd, 1987–89; John Wiley and Sons Ltd, 1992–99 (Dir, 1984–92); Dir, Radio Victory Ltd, 1982–87. Historic Houses Association: Hon. Treas., 1975–82; Chm., SE Region, 1975–78; Dep. Pres., 1982–86; President: Action in Rural Sussex (formerly Sussex Rural Community Council), 1973–2006 (Chm., Rural Housing Adv. Cttee, 1996–2006); British Horse Soc., 1976–78; South of England Agricultural Soc., 1981–82; SE England Tourist Bd, 1990–2003 (Vice-Pres., 1974–90); Chm., Assoc. of Internat. Dressage Event Organisers, 1987–94; Chairman: Rugby Council of Social Service, 1961–68; Dunford Coll., (YMCA), 1969–82; Dir, Country Gentlemen's Assoc. Ltd, 1975–89. Pres. (UK), African Med. and Res. Foundn, 1996–. Chairman: of Trustees, Sussex Heritage Trust, 1978–2001; Planning for Economic Prosperity in Chichester and Arun, 1984–89 (Pres., 1989–2010); Chichester Cathedral Develt Trust, 1985–91 (Pres., 1991–); Sussex Community Foundn, 2005–10. President: Chichester Festivities, 1975–2012; Sussex CCC, 1991–2001 (Patron, 2001–). DL W Sussex, 1975–90. CCMI (CBIM 1982). Freeman, City of Chichester, 2008. Hon LLD Sussex, 1986. Medal of Honour, British Equestrian Fedn, 1983. *Heir: s* Earl of March and Kinrara, *qv*. *Address:* Carne's Seat, Goodwood, Chichester, W Sussex PO18 0PX. *T:* (office) (01243) 755000, (home) (01243) 527861, *Fax:* (office) (01243) 755005. *E:* richmond@goodwood.com.

RICHMOND, Bishop Suffragan of, since 2015; **Rt Rev. Paul John Slater;** *b* 22 March 1958; *s* of Norman and Jean Slater; *m* 1981, Beverley Louise (*née* Knight); two *s* (and one *s* decd). *Educ:* Corpus Christi Coll., Oxford (MA (Natural Sci.) 1983); St John's Coll., Durham (BA (Theol.) 1983). Ordained deacon, 1984, priest, 1985; Asst Curate, St Andrew's, Keighley, 1984–88; Priest-in-charge, St John's, Cullingworth, 1988–93; Dir, Lay Trng Foundn Course, 1988–93; PA to Bishop of Bradford, 1993–95; Rector, St Michael's, Haworth, 1995–2001; Bishop's Officer for Ministry and Mission, Dio. of Bradford, 2001–14; Archdeacon of Craven, 2005–14; Archdeacon of Richmond and Craven, 2014–15. Mem., Gen. Synod, C of E, 2013–. Mem., Brontë Soc., 1996–2005. Trustee, Craven Trust, 2005–. *Recreations:* playing and watching cricket, playing tennis, reading novels, learning Spanish. *Address:* 4 Borrowdale Court, 5 Clifton Drive, Menston, Ilkley LS29 6FZ. *E:* paul.slater@westyorkshiredales.anglican.org.

RICHMOND, Bernard Grant; QC 2006; a Recorder, since 2002; an Assistant Coroner (formerly Assistant Deputy Coroner), since 2012; *b* 25 May 1965; *s* of James Richmond and Carol Richmond (*née* Linstead); *m* 1995, Christa Elfriede, *d* of Rudolf and Ruth Veile. *Educ:* Stratford Comp. Sch.; City of London Poly. (LLB Hons 1986). Called to the Bar, Middle Temple, 1988, Bencher, 2005; in practice as a barrister, 1988–; apptd to Faculty, Middle Temple Advocacy, 1995, Dir of Studies, 2006–09 and 2011–. Chair, Mgt Cttee, 2007–, Dep. Vice Pres., 2012–, British Judo Council. *Recreations:* judo, Real tennis, battling with German grammar, conversing with my cats, alto saxophone. *Address:* Lamb Building, Temple, EC4Y 7AS. *T:* (020) 7797 7788. *E:* bernardrichmond@lambbuilding.co.uk. *Clubs:* Dantai Seishin Judokwai; Hyde Real Tennis.

RICHMOND, Sir David (Frank), KBE 2008; CMG 2004; HM Diplomatic Service, retired; Director General, Defence and Intelligence, Foreign and Commonwealth Office, 2004–07; Adviser, Bell Pottinger, since 2007; *b* 9 July 1954; *s* of Frank George Richmond and Constance Lillian Richmond (*née* Hilling); *m* 1990, Caroline Matagne; one *s* one *d*. *Educ:* Merchant Taylors' Sch.; Trinity Hall, Cambridge (BA). FCO, 1976; MECAS, 1977–78; Baghdad, 1979–82; Second, later First Sec., FCO, 1982–87; UK Rep., Brussels, 1987–91; Dep. Head, Near East and N Africa Dept, FCO, 1991–94; Head, Economic Relations Dept, FCO, 1994–96; Head of Chancery, UK Mission to UN, NY, 1996–2000; UK Rep. to Pol and Security Cttee, EU and UK Perm. Rep. to WEU, Brussels, with rank of Ambassador, 2000–03; UK Special Rep. for Iraq, 2004. Gov., Ditchley Foundn, 2004–12. Chm., British Lebanese Assoc., 2012–. *Address:* 12 Carlisle Mansions, Carlisle Place, SW1P 1HX.

RICHMOND, Rt Rev. (Francis) Henry (Arthur); Hon. Assistant Bishop, Diocese of Oxford, since 1999; *b* 6 Jan. 1936; *s* of Frank and Lena Richmond; *m* 1966, Caroline Mary Berent; two *s* one *d*. *Educ:* Portora Royal School, Enniskillen; Trinity Coll., Dublin (MA); Univ. of Strasbourg (BTh); Linacre Coll., Oxford (MLitt); Wycliffe Hall, Oxford. Deacon, 1963, priest, 1964; Asst Curate, Woodlands, Doncaster, 1963–66; Sir Henry Stephenson Research Fellow, Sheffield Univ. and Chaplain, Sheffield Cathedral, 1966–69; Vicar, St George's, Sheffield, 1969–77; Anglican Chaplain to Sheffield Univ. and Mem. Sheffield Chaplaincy for Higher Education, 1974–77; Warden, Lincoln Theol Coll., and Canon and Prebendary of Lincoln Cathedral, 1977–85; Bishop Suffragan of Repton, 1986–98. Examng Chaplain to Bishop of Lincoln; Proctor in Convocation for Lincoln, 1980. Archbishop's ecumenical bishop for Old Catholic Churches, 1991–98. Hon. Asst Chaplain, Christ Church Cathedral, Oxford, 2006–12. *Recreations:* listening to classical music, reading, theatre, walking, gardening, learning Irish (Gaelic). *Address:* 39 Hodges Court, Oxford OX1 4NZ. *T:* (01865) 790466.

RICHMOND, Sir Mark (Henry), Kt 1986; PhD, ScD; FRS 1980; Member, School of Public Policy, University College London, 1996–2005; *b* 1 Feb. 1931; *s* of Harold Sylvester Richmond and Dorothy Plaistowe Richmond; *m* 1st, 1958, Shirley Jean Townrow (marr. diss. 1999); one *s* one *d* (and one *d* decd); 2nd, 2000, Sheila Travers. *Educ:* Epsom College; Clare Coll., Cambridge (BA, PhD, ScD). Scientific Staff, MRC, 1958–65; Reader in Molecular Biology, Univ. of Edinburgh, 1965–68; Prof. of Bacteriology, Univ. of Bristol, 1968–81; Vice-Chancellor, and Prof. of Molecular Microbiol., Victoria Univ. of Manchester, 1981–90; Chm., SERC, 1990–94 (Mem., 1981–85); Gp Hd of Res., Glaxo Hldgs, 1993–95. Director: Whittington Hosp. NHS Trust, 1996–98; Core Gp plc, 1997–99; Ark Therapeutics plc, 1997–2010; Genentech Inc., 1999–2005; OSI Pharmaceuticals Inc., 1999–2006; Cytos AG, 1999–2011. Member: Bd, PHLS, 1976–85; Fulbright Cttee, 1980–84; Chairman: British Nat. Cttee for Microbiol., 1980–85; CVCP, 1987–89; Cttee on Microbiological Food Safety, 1989–91; Member: Genetic Manipulation Adv. Gp, 1976–84; Adv. Cttee on Genetic Manipulation, 1984–85; Internat. Scientific Adv. Bd, UNESCO, 1996–2001; Council, Cancer Res. UK (formerly CRC), 1997–2002 (Chm., CRC Technology, 1997–2002; Chm., Cancer Res. Ventures, 1999–2002). Pres., Epsom Coll., 1992–2001. Member: IBM Academic Adv. Bd, 1984–90; Knox Fellowship Cttee, 1984–87; CIBA-Geigy Fellowship Trust, 1984–91; Jarrett Cttee for University Efficiency, 1985; Governing Body, Lister Inst., 1987–90; Council, ACU, 1988–90; Council, Royal Northern Coll. of Music, 1990–92; Educn Cttee, Royal Anniversary Trust, 1994–97; Trustee: Nat. Gall., 1994–2000; Tate Gall., 1995–99; Dyson Perrins Mus., Worcester, 1993–2001. Hon. Fellow, Pembroke Coll., Cambridge, 2011. *Publications:* several in microbiology and biochemistry jls. *Recreation:* hill-walking. *Address:* School of Public Policy, University College London, 29 Tavistock Square, WC1H 9QU. *Club:* Athenæum.

RICHMOND, Prof. Peter, PhD, DSc; FInstP; Chairman, Physics of Competition and Conflict, European Co-operation in Scientific and Technical Research, 2008–12; *b* 4 March 1943; *s* of John Eric Richmond and Nellie (*née* Scholey); *m* 1st, 1967, Christine M. Jackson (*d* 1995); one *s* one *d*; 2nd, 2005, Mairin Breathnach. *Educ:* Whitcliffe Mount Grammar Sch., Cleckheaton; Queen Mary Coll., London (BSc, PhD); London Univ. (DSc). ICI Res. Fellow, Univ. of Kent, 1967–69; Univ. of NSW, 1969–71; Queen Elizabeth II Res. Fellow, Inst. of Advanced Studies, ANU, 1971–73; Unilever Res., 1973–82; Hd, Process Physics, AFRC Food Res. Inst., Norwich, 1982–86; Prof., Univ. of Loughborough, 1985–88; Dir, AFRC Inst. of Food Res., Norwich Lab., 1986–92; Gen. Manager, CWS, 1992–96; Dir, EPM Associates Ltd, 1998–2008. Hon. Prof., UEA, 1986–; EU Marie Curie Fellow, 1998, Vis. Prof., Dept of Physics, 1998–2008, TCD; Sen. Vis. Fellow, Univ. Coll. Dublin, 2008–; Vis. Prof., Open Univ., 2010–13. Mem., MAFF/DoH Adv. Cttee on novel foods and processes, 1988–94; Chm., Eur. Co-operation in Scientific and Tech. Res. P10, Physics of Risk, 2004–07. Mem., Exam. Cttee, Radio Communications Foundn. *Publications:* (with R. D. Bee and J. Mingins) Food Colloids, 1989; (with P. J. Frazier and A. Donald) Starch Structure and Functionality, 1997; (with J. Mimkes and S. Hutzler) Econophysics and Physical Economics: an introduction, 2013; contribs to learned jls on econophysics, complex systems, statistical physics, colloid and polymer physics and food physics. *Recreations:* music, walking, talking and eating with friends. *Club:* Athenæum.

RICHMOND, Timothy Stewart, MBE 1985; TD 1982; FCA; Vice Lord-Lieutenant of Nottinghamshire, since 2008; chartered accountant, consultant and adviser in business direction; *b* Edingley, 17 Nov. 1947; *s* of Stewart McKenzie Sylvester Richmond and Nancie Richmond (*née* Barber); *m* 1974, Susan Carol Spencer; two *s* two *d*. *Educ:* Birkdale Sch., Sheffield; Nottingham High Sch. ACA 1970; FCA 1979. Pannell Kerr Forster (PKF), Chartered Accountants: articles, 1966–70; qualified Asst, Manager, 1970–74; Partner, 1974–98; Man. Partner, Nottingham firm, 1980–85; Nat. Man. Partner, UK firm, 1985–94; Chm., internat. firm, 1994–98; Partner: Richmond Waine, later GTN, 1998–2008; Mazars, 2002–03; Arc Mediators LLP, 2009–11; Arc Partnership Consultants LLP, 2011–13. Chairman: Huthwaite Internat. Ltd, 1998–; Clegg Gp Ltd, 2008–10 (non-exec. Dir, 2000–); Dir, Legal Practice Consortium Ltd, 2006–11. Mem., Monopolies and Mergers Commn, subseq. Competition Commn, 1997–2003. Dir, Nottingham HA, 1989–91. Chm., Nottingham and Notts Futures (formerly Connexions Notts) Ltd, 2001–. Dir, Notts Community Foundn, 2003–05. Chm., English Churches Housing Gp, 1994–98. Pres., Nottingham, Derby and Lincoln Dist Soc. of Chartered Accountants, 2006–07 (Vice and Dep. Pres., 2004–06); Mem., Members Services Bd, ICAEW, 2007–12. Mem. Council, Chartered Mgt Inst., 1998–2002 (CCMI). Dep. Chm., Nottingham Trent Univ. (formerly Nottingham Poly.), 1989–97 (Gov., 1984–98); Gov., New Coll., Nottingham, 2008–10; Chm., Portland Coll., 2014– (Gov., 2013). Member: Southwell Cath. Council, 2000–07, 2012–; Council of Friends of Southwell Cath., 2006–. Trustee, Notts Community Safety Trust, 2002–09; Patron, Notts Hospice, 2011–. Chm. Bd, Nat. Council, Reserve Forces and Cadets Assoc., 2011–14 (Vice Chm. (Army), 2003–11; Chm., E Midlands Assoc., 2003–12); Mem., Ext. Scrutiny Gp into Future Reserves 2020. Commnd Royal Regt of Artillery TA, 1971 (2nd Lieut); OC (Maj.) 307 (S Notts Hussars Yeo. RHA) Observation Post Battery (V), 1982–85 (Sen. Officer, 1995–2008; Hon. Col, 2002–14); CO (Lt Col), E Midlands Univs OTC, 1988–91 (Hon. Col, 2005–13); Dep. Bde Comdr (Col), 49 and 54 Bdes and TA Col for E Midlands, 1991–95; ADC (TA) to the Queen, 1992–95; Comdt, Notts ACF, 1997–2001. Hon. Col, S Notts Hussars. DL 1990, High Sheriff, 2002–03, Notts. Hon. DBA Nottingham Trent, 1998. *Recreations:* sailing, gardening. *Address:* Newark, Notts. *Clubs:* Army and Navy; Nottingham.

RICHMOND-WATSON, Julian Howard; Chairman, Newmarket Racecourse, since 2010; *b* 6 Dec. 1947; *s* of late Sonny and Jean Richmond-Watson; *m* 1972, Sarah Gee; four *s*. *Educ:* Hawtreys Sch.; Radley Coll. Man. Dir and Chm. of private cos in the property, quarrying and packing fields. Mem., various racecourse boards. Senior Steward, Jockey Club, 2003–09. *Recreations:* horse-racing, shooting. *Address:* Wakefield Lodge, Potterspury, Northants NN12 7QX. *E:* Julianrw@wakefieldestate.co.uk. *Clubs:* Boodle's, Jockey.

RICHMOND AND CRAVEN, Archdeacon of; *no new appointment at time of going to press.*

RICHTER, Prof. Burton; Paul Pigott Professor in the Physical Sciences, Stanford University, USA, 1980–2006 (Professor of Physics, 1967–2005, now Emeritus); Director, Stanford Linear Accelerator Center, 1984–99, now Emeritus (Technical Director, 1982–84); *b* 22 March 1931; *s* of Abraham Richter and Fannie Pollack; *m* 1960, Laurose Becker; one *s* one *d*. *Educ:* Massachusetts Inst. of Technology. BS 1952, PhD (Physics) 1956. Stanford University: Research Associate, Physics, High Energy Physics Lab., 1956–60; Asst Prof., 1960–63; Associate Prof., 1963–67; full Prof., 1967; Sen. Fellow, Freeman Spogli Inst. for Internat. Studies, 2006–. Loeb Lectr, Harvard, 1974; De Shalit Lectr, Weizmann Inst., 1975; Astor Vis. Lectr, Oxford Univ., 2000. Member, Board of Directors: Varian Corp., then Varian Associates, 1989–99; Litel Instruments, 1990–; Varian Med. Systems, 1999–2002; AREVA Enterprises, 2003–. Chm., Bd on Physics and Astronomy, Nat. Res. Council/Nat. Acads of Sci., USA, 2003–06. Pres., IUPAP, 1999–2002 (Pres. Designate, 1997–99). FAPS 1984 (Pres., 1994); Fellow, Amer. Acad. of Arts and Scis, 1990 (Mem., 1989); Mem., Nat. Acad. of Scis, 1977. Laurea *hc* in Physics, Univ. of Pisa, 2001. E. O. Lawrence Award, 1975; Nobel Prize for Physics (jointly), 1976; Enrico Fermi Award, US Dept of Energy, 2010; Nat. Medal of Sci. (US), 2014. *Publications:* Beyond Smoke and Mirrors: climate change and energy in the 21st century, 2010, 2nd edn 2014; over 300 articles in various scientific journals. *Address:* Stanford Linear Accelerator Center MS–80, 2575 Sand Hill Road, Menlo Park, CA 94025, USA.

RICHTER, Max; composer; *b* Hamelin, Germany, 22 March 1966; *s* of Lutz Richter and Ursula Meyer; *m* 1991, Yulia Mahr; one *s* two *d*. *Educ:* Bedford Modern Sch.; Univ. of Edinburgh; Royal Acad. of Music (BMus Hons; ARAM 2013). Co-founder, Piano Circus, classical ensemble, 1989–99. Solo albums: Memoryhouse, 2002; The Blue Notebooks, 2004; Songs From Before, 2006; 24 Postcards in Full Colour, 2008; Infra, 2010; Recomposed: Vivaldi's Four Seasons, 2012 (ECHO Klassik Award, 2013); SLEEP, 2015; film, ballet and theatre collaborations, 2004–; film soundtracks include: Waltz with Bashir, 2008 (Best Composer, Eur. Film Prize); Shutter Island, 2010; Sarah's Key, 2010; Perfect Sense, 2011; Lore, 2012 (Best Film Music, Bavarian Film Awards, 2013); Disconnect, 2012; Testament of Youth, 2014; television soundtracks incl. The Leftovers, 2014; theatre includes: Black Watch, NT of Scotland, 2011; Macbeth, NY, 2012; chamber opera, Sum, 2012; work with Royal Ballet in collaboration with choreographer, Wayne McGregor incl. Infra, 2008, Woolf Works, 2015; Kairos for Ballet Zurich, 2015; works used by Joffrey Ballet, Nederlands Dans Teatre, NYC Ballet, Amer. Ballet Th., Dutch Nat. Ballet, Dresden Semper Oper, Ballet du Rhin, Northern Ballet; art collaborations: at White Cube; Future Self, Lunds Konsthall, Sweden, 2011; Rain Room, Barbican and MOMA, 2012. *Publications:* Memoryhouse, 2002; The Blue Notebooks, 2004; Songs From Before, 2006; 24 Postcards in Full Colour, 2008; Infra, 2010; SUM, 2012; The Four Seasons Recomposed, 2013; Woolf Works, 2015; SLEEP, 2015. *Recreations:* butterflies, astronomy, analogue synthesis, poetry. *E:* directors@studiorichtermahr.com.

RICKARD, Rear Adm. Hugh Wilson, CBE 1996; business consultant, since 2013; Director, Hugh Rickard Associates Ltd, since 2013; South Division Strategic Business Partner, BrightHouse, 2012–13; *b* 1 Sept. 1948; *s* of Charles Thomas Rickard and Isobel Rickard; *m* 1982, Patricia Ann Seager; two *s* one *d*. *Educ:* Surbiton Co. Grammar Sch.; Northern Poly. (BSc London Hons). MCIL (MIL 1994). Joined RN, 1972; qualified as Meteorological and Oceanographic Officer, 1974; Naval Staff Course, 1982; UK Defence and Naval Attaché, The Hague, 1992–95; CO, HMS Raleigh, 1995–98; Sen. Naval DS, RCDS, 1998–2000. Chief Exec., Lib Dems, 2000–03. Chief Exec., Royal Anniversary Trust, 2004–06; Bursar, Claremont Fan Court Sch., 2006–09; BrightHouse: Learning and Develt Manager, 2009–10; Nat. Customer Service Manager, 2010–11; Regl Manager, 2011–12. *Recreations:* sailing, hill-walking. *Address:* High Burrows, The Drive, Sutton, Surrey SM2 7DP. *T:* (020) 8661 6258.

RICKARD, Dr John Hellyar; independent consultant economist; *b* 27 Jan. 1940; *s* of Peter John Rickard and Irene Eleanor (*née* Hales); *m* 1963, Christine Dorothy Hudson; one *s* two *d*. *Educ:* Ilford County High Sch.; St John's Coll., Oxford (MA 1966; DPhil 1976); Univ. of Aston in Birmingham (MSc 1969). Lectr, Univ. of Aston, 1967–70; Economist, Programmes Analysis Unit, AEA, Harwell, 1970–72; Res. Associate, and Dep. Head, Health Services Evaluation Gp, Dept of Regius Prof. of Medicine, Univ. of Oxford, 1972–74; Econ. Adviser, Dept of Health, 1974–76; Sen. Econ. Adviser: Dept of Prices and Consumer Protection, 1976–78; Central Policy Review Staff, Cabinet Office, 1978–82; HM Treasury, 1982–84; Econ. Adviser, State of Bahrain, 1984–87; Chief Economic Advr, Dept of Transport, 1987–91; Under Sec. (Econs), HM Treasury, 1991–94; Chief Econ. Advr, Dept of Transport, 1994–95; IMF Fiscal Advr, Min. of Finance, Republic of Moldova, 1995. Trustee, Earl Mountbatten Hospice, IoW, 2003– (Chm., 2010–13). *Publications:* (with D. Aston) Macro-Economics: a critical introduction, 1970; Longer Term Issues in Transport, 1991; articles in books and learned jls. *Recreations:* sailing, music. *Address:* Bay House, Lanes End, Totland Bay, Isle of Wight PO39 0BE. *T:* (01983) 754669. *Club:* Island Sailing.

RICKARD, Josanne Penelope Jeanne; Partner, Shearman & Sterling (London) LLP, since 2006; *b* Redruth, 1 Oct. 1949; *d* of John and Jeanne Rickard; *m* 1981, John Sawrey King; two *d*. *Educ:* Malvern Girls' Coll.; King's Coll. London (LLB). Articled Clerk, Kenneth Brown Baker Baker, 1971–73; admitted as solicitor, 1973; Associate, Cameron Kemm, 1973–75; Freshfields Bruckhaus Deringer: Associate, 1975–81; Partner, 1981–2006; on secondment to Lloyd's of London as Dir, Legal Services, 1994–96; Hd, London Dispute Resolution, 1996–2000; Jt Hd, Global Dispute Resolution, 2000–05. Chm., Mkt Supervision and Rev. Cttee, Lloyd's of London, 2013–. Dep. Chm., St Paul's Sch., 2010–14. *Recreations:* family, golf, tennis, travel. *Address:* Shearman & Sterling (London) LLP, 9 Appold Street, EC2A 2AP. *T:* (020) 7655 5781. *E:* josanne.rickard@shearman.com. *Club:* Roehampton.

RICKARDS, Joanne Elisabeth; Partner, Kingsley Napley LLP, since 2014; *b* Harbury, Warwickshire, 7 Oct. 1963; *d* of Stan Rickards and Maureen Rickards; *m* (marr. diss.); one *s* one *d*. *Educ:* Leamington Coll. for Girls; University Coll. London (LLB Hons). Admitted as solicitor, 1989; articled, 1986, Partner, 1992–2009, Peters & Peters; Partner, DLA Piper (UK) LLP, 2010–14. *Recreations:* dancing, reading, collecting twentieth century ceramics, gardening, theatre and ballet, flea markets. *Address:* Kingsley Napley LLP, Knights Quarter, 14 St John's Lane, EC1M 4AJ. *T:* (020) 7369 3848. *E:* jrickards@kingsleynapley.co.uk.

RICKERD, Martin John Kilburn, OBE 2004; MVO 1985; HM Diplomatic Service, retired; freelance copy-editor, writer and proofreader; *b* 17 Aug. 1954; *s* of John Rickerd and Anne Rickerd (*née* Kilburn, later Greener); *m* 1976, Charmain Gwendoline Napier; two *s*. *Educ:* Lord Weymouth Sch. HM Diplomatic Service, 1972–2010: FCO, 1972–75; UK Delegn to NATO, Brussels, 1975–77; Wellington, 1977–80; Asst Private Sec. to Parly Under Sec. of State, FCO, 1980–82; Third Sec., Bridgetown, 1982–86; Consul, Milan, 1986–91; First Sec., FCO, 1991–95; Hd of Chancery, Singapore, 1995–98; on secondment to Standard Chartered Bank, London, 1998–2000; Dep. Hd of Mission, Abidjan, 2000–03; Hd, N America Team, FCO, 2003–05; Consul Gen., Atlanta, USA, 2005–09. Mem., Soc. for Editors and Proofreaders, 2013– (Associate, 2011–13; E of England Coordinator, 2015–). Vice-Chm., Friends of Tiddenfoot Waterside Park, 2011–14. *Publications:* The Patriotic Art: random recollections from a (mostly) diplomatic career, 2012. *E:* m.rickerd@lycos.com.

RICKETS, Brig. Reginald Anthony Scott, (Tony); Chairman, Relate Glasgow, 2008–11; *b* 13 Dec. 1929; *s* of Captain R. H. Rickets and Mrs V. C. Rickets (*née* Morgan); *m* 1952, Elizabeth Ann Serjeant; one *s* one *d*. *Educ:* St George's Coll., Weybridge; RMA Sandhurst. 2nd Lieut, RE, 1949; served with airborne, armoured and field engrs in UK, Cyrenaica, Egypt, Malaya, Borneo, Hong Kong and BAOR; special employment military forces Malaya, 1955–59; Staff Coll., Camberley, 1962; BM Engr Gp, BAOR, 1963–66; OC 67 Gurkha Ind. Field Sqn, 1966–68; DS Staff Coll., 1968–70; Comdt Gurkha Engrs/CRE Hong Kong, 1970–73; COS British Sector, Berlin, 1973–77; Col GS RSME, 1977–78; Chief Engr UKLF, 1978–81. Man. Dir, Irvine Develt Corp., 1981–95. Director: Enterprise Ayrshire, 1990–97; Kelvin Travel, 1995–98; Nobel Exhibn Trust, (The Big Idea), 1997–2002; Chm., Irvine Housing Assoc., 2002–07. President: Ayrshire Chamber of Industries, 1983–86; Ayrshire Chamber of Commerce and Industry, 1989–91; German-British Chamber of Industry and

Commerce in Scotland, 1998–; Mem. Exec. Bd, Scottish Council (Develt and Industry), 1990–92. Chm., ASSET Enterprise Trust, 1996–97. Mem. Exec. Bd, Scottish Maritime Mus., 1986–. *Recreation:* sailing. *Address:* Burnbrae Cottage, Montgreenan, Ayrshire KA13 7QZ. *Club:* Royal Engineer Yacht (Commodore, 1979–81).

RICKETT, William Francis Sebastian, CB 2010; Director General, Energy Markets and Infrastructure (formerly Energy), Department of Energy and Climate Change (formerly Department of Trade and Industry, then Department for Business, Enterprise and Regulatory Reform), 2006–09; *b* 23 Feb. 1953; *s* of Sir Denis Rickett, KCMG, CB; *m* 1979, Lucy Caroline Clark; one *s* one *d. Educ:* Trinity Coll., Cambridge (BA 1974). Joined Department of Energy, 1975; Private Sec. to Perm. Under Sec. of State, 1977; Principal, 1978; Private Sec. to Prime Minister, 1981–83; seconded to Kleinwort Benson Ltd, 1983–85; Asst Sec., Oil Div., Dept of Energy, 1985; Asst Sec., Electricity Privatisation, 1987; Grade 4, Electricity Div., 1989; Under Sec., 1990; Dir Gen., Energy Efficiency Office, Dept of Energy, 1990–92, DoE, 1992–93; Dir of Finance (Central) and Principal Finance Officer, DoE, 1993–97; Dir of Town and Country Planning, DoE, then DETR, 1997–98; Dep. Sec. and Hd, Economic and Domestic Secretariat, Cabinet Office, 1998–2000; Hd, Integrated Transport Taskforce, subseq. Dir-Gen., Transport Strategy and Planning, DETR, 2000–01; Dir-Gen., Transport Strategy, Roads, Local and Maritime Transport, then Transport Strategy, Roads and Local Transport, then Strategy, Finance and Delivery, DTLR, subseq. DfT, 2001–04; on secondment to Ernst & Young from DfT, 2004–06. Chm., Governing Bd, Internat. Energy Agency, 2007–09. Director: Cambridge Econ. Policy Associates Ltd, 2009– (Chm., 2013–); Nat. Renewable Energy Centre Ltd, 2010–13; Eggborough Power Ltd, 2010–15; Impax Envmtl Markets plc, 2011–; Helius Energy plc, 2011–15; Greencoat UK Wind plc, 2013–; Smart DCC Ltd, 2013–. Ind. energy expert, Which?, 2011–12; Sen. Advr, Cleveland Associates Ltd, 2011–. Mem. Adv. Bd, Electricity Policy Res. Gp, Cambridge Univ., 2009–. Hon. FEI 2010. *Recreations:* children, painting, sports.

RICKETTS, Prof. Martin John, DPhil; Professor of Economic Organisation, University of Buckingham, since 1987; *b* 10 May 1948; *s* of Leonard Alfred Ricketts and Gertrude Dorothy (*née* Elgar); *m* 1975, Diana Barbara Greenwood; one *s* one *d. Educ:* City of Bath Boys' Sch.; Univ. of Newcastle upon Tyne (BA Hons Econ.); Univ. of York (DPhil). Econ. Asst, Industrial Policy Gp, 1970–72; Res. Fellow, Inst. Econ. and Social Res., Univ. of York, 1975–77; University College at Buckingham, later University of Buckingham: Lectr in Econs, 1977–82; Sen. Lectr, 1982–85; Reader, 1985–87; Dean, Sch. of Business (formerly Sch. of Accountancy, Business and Econs), 1993–97; Pro-Vice-Chancellor, 1993; Dean of Humanities, 2002–15. Economic Dir, NEDO, 1991–92. Vis. Prof., Virginia Poly. Inst. and State Univ., 1984. Hon. Prof., Heriot-Watt Univ., 1996. Trustee, Inst. of Econ. Affairs, 1992–. Chm., Buckingham Summer Fest., 2004–. *Publications:* (with M. G. Webb) The Economics of Energy, 1980; The Economics of Business Enterprise: new approaches to the firm, 1987, 3rd edn 2002; The Many Ways of Governance: perspectives on the control of the firm, 1999; papers on public finance, public choice, housing econs and econ. orgn. *Recreations:* music, student of piano and oboe. *Address:* 22 Bradfield Avenue, Buckingham MK18 1PR; Department of Economics and International Studies, University of Buckingham, Hunter Street, Buckingham MK18 1EG.

RICKETTS, Sir Peter (Forbes), GCMG 2011 (KCMG 2003; CMG 1999); GCVO 2014; HM Diplomatic Service; Ambassador to France, since 2012; *b* 30 Sept. 1952; *s* of Maurice and Dilys Ricketts; *m* 1980, Suzanne Julia Horlington; one *s* one *d. Educ:* Bishop Vesey's Grammar Sch.; Pembroke Coll., Oxford (MA; Hon. Fellow, 2007). Joined FCO, 1974; Singapore, 1975–78; UK Delegn to NATO, 1978–81; FCO, 1981–86, Private Sec. to Sec. of State for Foreign and Commonwealth Affairs, 1983–86; Washington, 1986–89; FCO, 1989–94, Head, Hong Kong Dept, 1991–94; Economic and Financial Counsellor, Paris, 1994–97; Dep. Pol Dir, FCO, 1997–99; Dir, Internat. Security, FCO, 1999–2000; Chm., Jt Intelligence Cttee, Cabinet Office (on secondment), 2000–01; Pol Dir, FCO, 2001–03; UK Perm. Rep., UK Delegn to NATO, 2003–06; Permanent Under-Sec. of State, and Hd of Diplomatic Service, 2006–10; Nat. Security Advr, 2010–11. *Recreation:* Victorian art and literature. *Address:* c/o Foreign and Commonwealth Office, King Charles Street, SW1A 2AH.

RICKETTS, Simon Anthony; Chief Information Officer, Rolls Royce plc, since 2009; *b* Shoreham by Sea, Sussex, 17 Dec. 1954; *s* of late Herbert Arthur Ricketts and Pamela Anne Ricketts (*née* Forteware); *m* 1st, 1978, Monica Anne Ball (marr. diss. 2004); one *d*; 2nd, 2004, Jo Mary Fearn. *Educ:* Hastings Secondary Sch. for Boys; Univ. of East Anglia (BSc Hons Maths 1976); Univ. of Sussex (MSc Statistics 1980). British Steel Corporation: Operational Res. Gp, 1980–84; BSC Cumbria, 1984–86; Central Mgt Services, 1986–90; Cadbury Schweppes plc: Man. Dir, ITNet Ltd, 1990–94 (non-exec. Dir, ITNet Ltd, subseq. ITNet plc, 1994–2004); Ops Dir, Trebor Bassett Ltd, 1994–98; Gp IT Dir, 1998–2000; Chief Information Officer, 2000–03; Gp Information Systems Dir, Scottish & Newcastle plc, 2003–07; Global Transformation Dir, Logica plc, 2008–09. Director: Bar Box Ltd, 2004–08; UKCeB, 2010–. Non-executive Director: Strategic Thought plc, 2005–09 (Mem., Audit Cttee, 2005–09; Chm., Remuneration Cttee, 2005–09); National Savings and Investments, 2007–14 (Mem., Audit Cttee, 2007–14); HMRC, 2014–. Associate Fellow, Warwick Univ. Business Sch., 2014–. *Recreations:* historic motor vehicles, running, cycling, political and economic history, music, house restoration. *Address:* c/o Rolls Royce plc, 65 Buckingham Gate, SW1E 6AT. *T:* 07733 308766. *E:* simonrickett_s@yahoo.co.uk. *Clubs:* Royal Automobile; Warwickshire Golf and Country.

RICKETTS, Simon Henry Martin, CB 2000; Ministry of Defence, 1975–2011; *b* 23 July 1941; *s* of late Ralph Robert Ricketts and Margaret Adeliza Mary (*née* Royds); *m* 1973, Annabel Ophelia Clare Lea (*d* 2003); one *s* one *d. Educ:* Ampleforth; Magdalen Coll., Oxford (BA Hons History). Senior Systems Analyst, George Wimpey & Co., 1963–71; Lectr in Liberal Studies, Hammersmith Coll. of Art and Building, 1967–68; Kulu Trekking Agency, 1971; Teacher, British Inst. of Florence, 1971–73; Royalties Clerk, Cape & Chatto Services, 1973–75. Mem., Friends of Georgian Soc. of Jamaica, 2001– (Trustee, 2004–07). *Publications:* (ed) The English Country House Chapel: building a Protestant tradition, by Annabel Ricketts, 2007. *Address:* c/o Lloyds, 8 Fore Street, Budleigh Salterton, Devon EX9 6NQ. *Club:* Athenæum.

RICKETTS, Sir Stephen Tristram, 9th Bt *cr* 1828, of The Elms, Gloucestershire, and Beaumont Leys, Leicestershire; *b* 24 Dec. 1974; *s* of Sir (Robert) Tristram Ricketts, 8th Bt and of Ann Ricketts (*née* Lewis); *S* father, 2007; *m* 2009, Amy, *d* of Richard Robinson-Horley; two *s. Educ:* Winchester; Exeter Univ. *Heir: s* Freddy Tristram Ricketts, *b* 2 Aug. 2010.

RICKFORD, Jonathan Braithwaite Keevil, CBE 2001; solicitor, 1985–2010; regulatory consultant, 1996–2010; Professorial Fellow, British Institute of International and Comparative Law, 2006–08 (Director, Company Law Centre, 2003–06); *b* 7 Dec. 1944; *s* of R. B. K. Rickford, MD, FRCS, FRCOG and of Dorothy Rickford (*née* Lathan); *m* 1968, Dora R. Sargant; one *s* two *d. Educ:* Sherborne School; Magdalen College, Oxford (MA (Jurisp.); BCL). Barrister, 1970–85. Teaching Associate, Univ. of California Sch. of Law, 1968–69; Lectr in Law, LSE, 1969–72; Legal Asst, Dept of Trade, 1972–73; Senior Legal Assistant: Dept of Prices and Consumer Protection, 1974–76; Law Officers' Dept, Attorney General's Chambers, 1976–79; Dept of Trade and Industry (formerly Dept of Trade): Asst Solicitor (Company Law), 1979–82; Under Sec. (Legal), 1982–85; Solicitor, 1985–87; British Telecom: Solicitor and Chief Legal Advr, 1987–89; Dir of Govt Relns, 1989–93; Dir of Corporate Strategy, 1993–96; Project Dir, DTI's Review of Company Law, 1998–2001; Unilever Prof. in Eur. Corporate Law, Univ. of Leiden, Netherlands, 2002. Vis. Prof. of Law, LSE, 2003–09. Mem., Competition (formerly Monopolies and Mergers) Commn, 1997–2004. Member: Europe Cttee, CBI, 1993–98; Council, European Policy Forum, 1993–2014. FRSA 1992. *Publications:* (ed) The European Company, 2002; articles in learned jls. *Recreation:* sailing.

RICKINSON, Prof. Alan Bernard, PhD; FRS 1997; Professor of Cancer Studies, University of Birmingham, since 1983; *b* 12 Nov. 1943; *s* of Lawrence and Annie Rickinson; *m* 1968, Barbara; one *s* two *d. Educ:* Corpus Christi Coll., Cambridge (MA, PhD 1969). Hon. FRCP 1996. *Recreations:* walking, poetry. *Address:* School of Cancer Sciences, University of Birmingham, Edgbaston, Birmingham B15 2TT. *T:* (0121) 414 4492.

RICKLETON, James David John; Finance Director, Market Operator Services Ltd, since 2015; *b* 26 Aug. 1959; *s* of Jack and Jenifer Mary Rickleton; *m* 1998, Carol Anne Lyons; one *s* one *d. Educ:* Newcastle upon Tyne Poly. (BA Hons (Econs) 1980); City of London Poly. IPFA 1985. National Audit Office, 1981–2014: Audit trainee, 1981–86; Sen. Auditor, Financial Audit Tech. Support Team, 1986–88; Audit Manager, DES, 1988–92; Private Sec. to Comptroller and Auditor Gen., 1992–95; Dir of Audit, 1995–2003; Asst Auditor Gen., 2003–09; Dir Gen., Finance and Commerce, 2009–14. *Recreations:* golf, reading, Newcastle United FC.

RICKMAN, Alan; actor. *Educ:* Latymer Upper Sch.; Chelsea Sch. of Art (DipAD); Royal Coll. of Art; RADA. *Theatre* includes: The Devil is an Ass, Measure for Measure, Birmingham, Edinburgh Fest., Nat. Theatre, European tour, 1976–77; The Tempest, Captain Swing, Love's Labour's Lost, Antony and Cleopatra, RSC, 1978–79; The Summer Party, Crucible, 1980; Commitments, Bush, 1980; The Devil Himself, Lyric Studio, 1980; Philadelphia Story, Oxford Playhouse, 1981; The Seagull, Royal Court, 1981; Brothers Karamazov, Edinburgh Fest. and USSR, 1981; The Last Elephant, Bush, 1981; Bad Language, Hampstead, 1983; The Grass Widow, 1983, The Lucky Chance, 1984, Royal Court; As You Like It, Troilus and Cressida, Les Liaisons Dangereuses, Mephisto, RSC, 1985–86; Les Liaisons Dangereuses, West End and Broadway, 1986–87; Tango at the End of Winter, Edinburgh and West End, 1991; Hamlet, Riverside Studios and Brit. Tour, 1992; Antony and Cleopatra, RNT, 1998; Private Lives, Albery, 2001, NY, 2002; John Gabriel Borkman, Abbey Th., Dublin, 2010, NY, 2011; *director:* Desperately Yours, NY, 1980; (asst dir) Other Worlds, Royal Ct, 1983; Live Wax, Edin. Fest., 1986; Wax Acts, West End and tour, 1992; The Winter Guest, Almeida, 1995; My Name is Rachel Corrie, Royal Court, 2005, West End, Edin. Fest. and NY, 2006; Creditors, Donmar Warehouse, 2008, NY, 2010; *films:* Die Hard, 1988; The January Man, 1989; Quigley Down Under, 1990; Truly, Madly, Deeply, Closetland, Close My Eyes, Robin Hood, Prince of Thieves, 1991; Bob Roberts, 1992; Fallen Angels (TV, USA), Mesmer, 1993; An Awfully Big Adventure, 1995; Sense and Sensibility, Michael Collins, Rasputin, 1996; (dir) The Winter Guest (Best Film, Chicago Film Fest.; Premio Cinema Avvenire, OCIC Award, Venice Film Fest.), 1997; Dark Harbor, Judas Kiss, Dogma, 1999; Galaxy Quest, The Search for John Gissing, 2000; Blow Dry, Play, Harry Potter and the Philosopher's Stone, 2001; Harry Potter and the Chamber of Secrets, 2002; Love, Actually, 2003; Harry Potter and the Prisoner of Azkaban, Something the Lord Made, 2004; The Hitchhiker's Guide to the Galaxy, Harry Potter and the Goblet of Fire, 2005; Snow Cake, Perfume, Nobel Son, 2006; Harry Potter and the Order of the Phoenix, 2007; Sweeney Todd: The Demon Barber of Fleet Street, Bottle Shock, 2008; Harry Potter and the Half-Blood Prince, 2009; Alice in Wonderland, Harry Potter and the Deathly Hallows, Pt 1, 2010, Pt 2, 2011; Gambit, 2012; The Butler, 2013; A Promise, 2014; A Little Chaos (also dir), 2015; *television* includes: Thérèse Raquin, 1979; Barchester Chronicles, 1982; Pity in History, 1984; Revolutionary Witness, Spirit of Man, 1989; also radio performances. Bancroft Gold Medal, RADA, 1974; Seattle Film Fest. Best Actor, 1991, 2008; Time Out Award for Tango at the End of Winter, 1992; BAFTA Film Award for Best Supporting Actor, 1992; Evening Standard Film Award for Best Actor, 1992; Best Actor, Montreal Film Fest., 1994; Emmy Award for Best Actor, 1996; Golden Globe Award for Best Actor, 1997; Screen Actors Guild Award for Best Actor, 1997; Variety Club Award for Best Actor, 2002. *Publications:* (contrib.) Players of Shakespeare, Vol. 2, 1989. *Address:* c/o Independent Talent Group Ltd, 40 Whitfield Street, W1T 2RH.

RICKS, Dr Catherine Louise; Head, Sevenoaks School, since 2002; *b* 16 March 1961; *d* of Paul George Koralek, *qv*; *m* 1983, David Bruce Ricks. *Educ:* Camden Sch. for Girls, London; Balliol Coll., Oxford (MA Eng. Lit. 1982; DPhil Eng. Lit. 2014). Assistant Teacher: St Paul's Girls' Sch., 1985–87; King Edward's Sch., Birmingham, 1987–90; Latymer Upper Sch., 1990–92; Hd of Eng., St Edward's Sch., Oxford, 1992–97; Dep. Hd (Academic), Highgate Sch., 1997–2002. *Address:* Sevenoaks School, Sevenoaks, Kent TN13 1HU. *T:* (01732) 455133, *Fax:* (01732) 456143.

RICKS, Sir Christopher Bruce, Kt 2009; FBA 1975; Warren Professor of the Humanities, since 1998, and Co-Director, Editorial Institute, since 1999, Boston University (Professor of English, 1986–97); Professor of Poetry, University of Oxford, 2004–09; *b* 18 Sept. 1933; *s* of James Bruce Ricks and Gabrielle Roszak; *m* 1st, 1956, Kirsten Jensen (marr. diss.); two *s* two *d*; 2nd, 1977, Judith Aronson; one *s* two *d. Educ:* King Alfred's Sch., Wantage; Balliol Coll., Oxford (BA 1956; BLitt 1958; MA 1960; Hon. Fellow, 1989). 2nd Lieut, Green Howards, 1952. Andrew Bradley Jun. Res. Fellow, Balliol Coll., Oxford, 1957; Fellow of Worcester Coll., Oxford, 1958–68 (Hon. Fellow, 1990); Prof. of English, Bristol Univ., 1968–75; University of Cambridge: Prof. of English, 1975–82; King Edward VII Prof. of English Lit., 1982–86; Fellow, Christ's Coll., 1975–86 (Hon. Fellow, 1993). Visiting Professor: Berkeley and Stanford, 1965; Smith Coll., 1967; Harvard, 1971; Wesleyan, 1974; Brandeis, 1977, 1981, 1984. Lectures: Lord Northcliffe, UCL, 1972; Alexander, Univ. of Toronto, 1987; T. S. Eliot, Univ. of Kent, 1988; Clarendon, Univ. of Oxford, 1990; Clark, Trinity Coll., Cambridge, 1991. Pres., Assoc. of Literary Scholars and Critics, 2007–08. A Vice-Pres., Tennyson Soc.; Pres., Housman Soc. Chm. Judges, Man Booker Internat. Prize, 2013. Co-editor, Essays in Criticism. Fellow, American Acad. of Arts and Scis, 1991. Hon. DLitt: Oxon, 1998; Bristol, 2003. George Orwell Meml Prize, 1979; Beefeater Club Prize for Literature, 1980; Andrew W. Mellon Dist. Achievement Award, 2004. *Publications:* Milton's Grand Style, 1963; (ed) The Poems of Tennyson, 1969, rev. edn 1987; Tennyson, 1972, rev. edn 1989; Keats and Embarrassment, 1974; (ed with Leonard Michaels) The State of the Language, 1980, new edn 1990; The Force of Poetry, 1984; (ed) The New Oxford Book of Victorian Verse, 1987; (ed) A. E. Housman: Collected Poems and Selected Prose, 1988; T. S. Eliot and Prejudice, 1988; (ed with William Vance) The Faber Book of America, 1992; Beckett's Dying Words, 1993; Essays in Appreciation, 1996; (ed) Inventions of the March Hare: poems 1909–1917 by T. S. Eliot, 1996; (ed) The Oxford Book of English Verse, 1999; (ed) Selected Poems of James Henry, 2002; Reviewery, 2002; Allusion to the Poets, 2002; Dylan's Visions of Sin, 2003; Decisions and Revisions in T. S. Eliot, 2003; (ed) New and Selected Poems of Samuel Menashe, 2005; Tennyson: selected poems, 2007; True Friendship: Geoffrey Hill, Anthony Hecht, and Robert Lowell under the sign of Eliot and Pound, 2010; (ed) What Maisie Knew, 2010; (ed) Joining Music with Reason: 34 poets, British and American, Oxford 2004–2009, 2010; (ed) Samuel Rogers: table-talk and recollections, 2011; (ed with Lisa Nemrow and Julie Nemrow) The Lyrics: since 1962, by Bob Dylan, 2014. *Address:* 39 Martin Street, Cambridge, MA 02138, USA. *T:* (617) 3547887; Lasborough Cottage, Lasborough Park, near Tetbury, Glos GL8 8UF. *T:* (01666) 890252.

RICKS, David Trulock, CMG 1997; OBE 1981; British Council Director, France, and Cultural Counsellor, British Embassy, Paris, 1990–96; *b* 28 June 1936; *s* of Percival Trulock Ricks and Annetta Helen (*née* Hood); *m* 1960, Nicole Estelle Aimée Chupeau (*d* 2013); two *s. Educ:* Kilburn Grammar Sch.; Royal Acad. of Music; Merton Coll., Oxford (MA); Univ. of London Inst. of Educn; Univ. of Lille (LèsL). Teaching in Britain, 1960–67; joined British Council, 1967: Rabat, 1967–70; Univ. of Essex, 1970–71; Jaipur, 1971–74, New Delhi, 1974; Dar Es Salaam, 1974–76; Tehran, 1976–80; London, 1980–85; Rep., Italy, and Cultural Counsellor, British Embassy, Rome, 1985–90. Mem., Rome Cttee, Keats-Shelley Meml House, Rome, 1985–90; Founder Mem., Assoc. Bourses Entente Cordiale, 1996. Gov., British Inst., Florence, 1985–90. Mem., Municipal Council, Forcalquier, France, 2001–08. *Publications:* (jtly) Penguin French Reader, 1967; (jtly) New Penguin French Reader, 1992. *Recreations:* music, playing the piano. *Address:* Saint Jean, Boulevard Raoul Dufy, 04300 Forcalquier, France. *T:* 492752063. *Club:* Oxford and Cambridge.

RICKS, Robert Neville; Deputy Legal Adviser, Treasury Advisory Division, Treasury Solicitor's Department, 1998–2002; *b* 29 June 1942; *s* of Sir John Plowman Ricks. *Educ:* Highgate Sch.; Worcester Coll., Oxford (MA). Admitted Solicitor, 1967. Entered Treasury Solicitor's Dept as Legal Asst, 1969; Sen. Legal Asst, 1973; Asst Solicitor, 1981; Prin. Asst Solicitor, 1986; Legal Advr, DES, then DfEE, 1990–97; Special Projects Dir, Treasury Solicitor's Dept, 1997–98. *Recreations:* collecting original cartoons, wine. *Address:* 2 Eaton Terrace, Aberavon Road, E3 5AJ. *T:* (020) 8981 3722.

RICKSON, Ian; freelance director; *b* 8 Nov. 1963; *s* of Richard and Eileen Rickson; one *s* by Kate Gould; *m* 2006, Polly Teale; one *d. Educ:* Essex Univ. (BA Eng and Eur. Lit. Hons); Goldsmiths' Coll., London Univ. (PGTC; Hon. Fellow, 2005). Freelance Dir, King's Head, The Gate, Chichester Fest. Theatre; Special Projects Dir, Young People's Th., 1991–92, Associate Dir, 1993–98, Royal Court Theatre; Artistic Dir, Royal Court Th., 1998–2006. Plays directed include: Me and My Friend, Chichester, 1992; The House of Yes, Gate Th., 1993; La Serva Padrona (opera), Broomhill, 1993; The Day I Stood Still, RNT, 1997; The Hothouse, NT, 2007; Parlour Song, Almeida, 2009; Hedda Gabler, NY, 2009; The Children's Hour, Betrayal, Comedy, 2011; Hamlet, Young Vic, 2011; Old Times, Harold Pinter Th., 2013; Electra, Old Vic, 2014; The Red Lion, RNT, 2015; *Royal Court Theatre:* Wildfire, Sab, Killers, 1992; Some Voices, Ashes and Sand, 1994; Mojo, transf. Chicago, Pale Horse, 1995, Harold Pinter Th., 2013; Chicago, The Lights, 1996; The Weir, 1997, transf. Duke of York's, then NY, 1998; Dublin Carol, 2000; Mouth to Mouth, transf. Albery, 2001; The Night Heron, 2002; Fallout, 2003; The Sweetest Swing in Baseball, 2004; Alice Trilogy, 2005; The Winterling, Krapp's Last Tape, 2006; The Seagull, 2007, transf. NY, 2008; Jerusalem, 2009, transf. Apollo, 2010, NY 2011; The River, 2012. Films directed: Krapp's Last Tape (BBC), 2007; Fallout (C4), 2008; The Clear Road Ahead, 2010.

RIDDELL, Alan Gordon; Associate Director, IRIS Consulting, since 2007; *b* 8 Sept. 1948; *s* of George Riddell and Elizabeth (*née* Mellin); *m* 1976, Barbara Kelly; two *d. Educ:* Greenock Acad.; Glasgow Univ. (MA Hons Mod. Hist. and Pol Econ.). History teacher, Greenock Acad., 1971–74; Hd of History, Eyemouth High Sch., 1974–75; Department of the Environment, 1975–97: Asst Private Sec. to Minister of Housing, 1981–83; Inner Cities Div., 1983–86; Private Rented Sector Div., 1986–87; Private Sec. to Minister for Local Govt, 1987–90; Hd, Private Rented Sector Div., 1990–92; Principal Private Sec. to Sec. of State, 1992–94; Sec., Cttee on Standards in Public Life (Nolan Cttee), 1994–97; Hd, Regeneration Policy Div., DETR, 1997–98; Regl Dir, Govt Office for E of England, 1998–2002; Dir of Ops, Neighbourhood Renewal Unit, subseq. Dir of Local Develt and Renewal, ODPM, then DCLG, 2002–07. Chm., Standards Cttee, Sevenoaks DC, 2001. *Recreations:* walking, boats.

RIDDELL, Alexander Hill, (Sandy); Director, Health and Social Care Partnership, Fife, since 2014; *b* Inverness, 30 July 1956; *s* of Malcolm and Esther Riddell; *m* 1978, Sheila Fraser; two *d. Educ:* Moray Hse Coll., Edinburgh (DipSW 1978); Open Univ. (BA Hons Social Sci. 1994); Univ. of Stirling (MSc Social Work Mgt 1997). Highland Regional Council: Social Worker, 1978–85; Area Team Leader, 1985–89; Principal Officer, Community Care, 1989–94; Asst Dir, Elderly Services, 1994–96; Hd, Client Services, 1996–2002, Hd of Ops, 2002–05, Highland Council; Dir, Community Services, 2005–11, Corporate Dir, Educn and Social Care, 2011–14, Moray Council. *Recreations:* family, travel, music, gardening. *Address:* Health and Social Care Partnership, Rothesay House, Rothesay Place, Glenrothes, Fife KY7 5PQ. *T:* 0345 155 5555, ext. 444112. *E:* Sandy.riddell@fife.gov.uk.

RIDDELL, Christopher Barry; political cartoonist and illustrator; Political Cartoonist, The Observer, since 1995; Children's Laureate, since 2015; *b* 13 April 1962; *s* of Morris and Pamela Riddell; *m* 1987, Joanna Burroughes; two *s* one *d. Educ:* Archbishop Tenison's Grammar Sch., London; Epsom Sch. of Art and Design (Foundn); Brighton Polytech. Art Sch. (BA 1st cl. Hons (Illustration)). Cartoonist: The Economist, 1988–96; The New Statesman, 1998–2006; Political Cartoonist, Independent and Independent on Sunday, 1990–95; Cover Artist, Literary Review, 1996–. *Publications:* Ben and the Bear, 1986; Humphrey Goes to the Ball, 1986; Humphrey of the Rovers, 1986; Humphrey the Hippo, 1986; Humphrey's New Trousers, 1986; Mr Underbed, 1986, 2nd edn 1997; Bird's New Shoes, 1987; The Fibbs, 1987; The Trouble with Elephants, 1988; When the Walrus Comes, 1989; The Wish Factory, 1990; The Bear Dance, 1990; The Emperor of Absurdia, 2006; The Da Vinci Cod: and other illustrations to unwritten books, 2006; Ottoline and the Yellow Cat, 2007; Ottoline Goes to School, 2007; Ottoline at Sea, 2007; Alienography, 2010; Goth Girl and the Ghost of a Mouse (Costa Children's Book Award), 2013; with Richard Platt: The Castle Diary: the journal of Tobias Burgess, 1999; The Pirate Diary: the journal of Jake Carpenter, 2001 (Kate Greenaway Medal, 2002); Platypus, 2001; Platypus and the Lucky Day, 2002; with Martin Jenkins: Jonathan Swift's Gulliver (Kate Greenaway Medal), 2004; Don Quixote, 2009; with Paul Stewart: The Edge Chronicles series, 1998–; The Rabbit and Hedgehog series, 1998–2001; The Blobheads series, 2000; The Muddle Earth series, 2003; Fergus Crane (Smarties Book Prize), 2004; Corby Flood (Nestlé Book Prize), 2005; Hugo Pepper (Nestlé Book Prize), 2006; Barnaby Grimes: curse of the nightwolf, 2007; Wyrmeweald, 2010; with Neil Gaiman: The Graveyard Book, 2008 (Carnegie Prize, 2010); Coraline, 2012; Fortunately, the Milk, 2013; illus. for many other authors. *Recreations:* writing, drawing, talking. *Address:* The Observer, Kings Place, 90 York Way, N1 9GU. *Club:* Academy.

RIDDELL, His Honour Nicholas Peter; a Circuit Judge, 1995–2008; *b* 24 April 1941; *s* of late Peter John Archibald Riddell and Cynthia Mary Riddell (later Douglas); *m* 1976, Barbara Helen Glucksmann; three *d. Educ:* Harrow; Magdalene Coll., Cambridge (BA Cantab). Called to the Bar, Inner Temple, 1964; practised at the Bar, 1964–95. Mem. Bd, Circle 33 Housing Trust Ltd, 1998. *Address:* 18 Myddelton Square, EC1R 1YE. *T:* (020) 7837 4034.

RIDDELL, Norman Malcolm Marshall; Vice Chairman, OneFamily (formerly Family Investments), 2006–14 and since 2015 (Chairman, 2014–15); *b* 30 June 1947; *s* of Malcolm Riddell and Euphemia Richardson Riddell (*née* Wight); *m* 1969, Leila Jean White; three *s. Educ:* George Heriot's Sch., Edinburgh. MCIBS; AIIMR. National Commercial Bank and Royal Bank of Scotland, 1965–78; Man. Dir, Britannia Investment Services, 1978–86; Chief Executive: Capital House Investment Management, 1986–93; INVESCO plc, 1993–96; Chairman: United Overseas Gp plc, 1997–99; Savoy Asset Mgt plc, 1997–2000; Norman Riddell and Associates Ltd, subseq. Novitas Partners LLP, 1997–2009. Director: Charterhouse Gp, 1986–89; Life Assce Hldg Corp., 1995–2004; Asset Management Investment Co., 1997–2002; Clubhaus, 1999–2004; Improvement Pathway, 1999–2002; Pathway One VCT plc, 2001–07; Invesco UK Ltd, 2011–. *Recreations:* gardening, most sports, travel, music, fine wine. *Address:* OneFamily, 17 West Street, Brighton, E Sussex BN1 2RL.

RIDDELL, Rt Hon. Peter (John Robert), CBE 2012; PC 2010; Director, Institute for Government, since 2012 (Senior Fellow, 2008–11); *b* 14 Oct. 1948; *s* of late Kenneth Robert Riddell and Freda Riddell (*née* Young); *m* 1994, Avril Walker; one *d. Educ:* Dulwich Coll.; Sidney Sussex Coll., Cambridge (BA Hist. and Econs 1970, MA; Hon. Fellow, 2005). Joined Financial Times, 1970: Property Corresp., 1972–74; Lex Column, 1975–76; Economics Corresp., 1976–81; Political Editor, 1981–88; US Editor and Washington Bureau Chief, 1989–91; joined The Times, 1991; Political Columnist, 1991–2010; Political Editor, 1992–93; Asst Editor (Politics), subseq. Chief Political Commentator, 1993–2010. Mem., Privy Council Review of Treatment of UK Detainees, 2010–11. Regular broadcaster, Week in Westminster, Talking Politics, Radio 4, and on TV. Vis. Prof. of Political History, QMW, 2000–03. Chairman: Parly Press Gall., 1997; Council, Hansard Soc., 2007– (Mem., 1995–). Mem. Cttee, Centre for (formerly Inst. of) Contemp. British Hist., 1996–. Gov., Dulwich Coll., 2009–. FRHistS 1998; FAcSS (AcSS 2012). Hon. Fellow, Pol Studies Assoc., 2007. Freeman, City of London, 2012. Hon. DLitt: Greenwich, 2001; Edinburgh, 2007. Wincott Award for Economic and Financial Journalism, 1981; House Magazine Political Journalist of the Year, 1986; Political Columnist of the Year, Political Studies Assoc., 2004; Pres.'s Medal, British Acad., 2010. *Publications:* The Thatcher Government, 1983, rev. edn 1985; The Thatcher Decade, 1989, rev. edn as The Thatcher Era, 1991; Honest Opportunism, the rise of the career politician, 1993, rev. edn 1996; Parliament under Pressure, 1998, rev. edn as Parliament under Blair, 2000; Hug Them Close, 2003 (Pol Book of Year, Channel 4 Pol Awards, 2004); The Unfulfilled Prime Minister, 2005; In Defence of Politicians - In Spite of Themselves, 2011; contrib. chaps in books, including: A Conservative Revolution?, 1994; The Major Effect, 1994; The Blair Effect, 2001; British Politics since 1945, 2001; Reinventing Britain: Constitutional change under New Labour, 2007; So You Want to be a Political Journalist, 2011; contrib. to Spectator, New Statesman, Political Qly, British Journalism Rev., TLS, Jl of Legislative Studies. *Recreations:* watching cricket, opera, theatre. *Address:* Institute for Government, 2 Carlton Gardens, SW1Y 5AA. *Clubs:* Garrick, MCC.

RIDDELL, Richard Rodford, PhD; education academic, freelance writer and researcher; Senior Lecturer, Bath Spa University, since 2009; *b* 28 Jan. 1953; *m* 1975, Millie Mitchell; one *s* one *d. Educ:* Manchester Grammar Sch.; Magdalen Coll., Oxford (MA); Madeley Coll. of Educn (PGCE); Bulmershe Coll. of Higher Educn (MPhil); Bath Spa Univ. (PhD 2012). Teacher: John Mason Sch., Abingdon, 1975–77; Waingel's Copse Sch., Reading, 1977–81; Asst Educn Officer, Wilts CC, 1981–86; Educn Officer, Notts CC, 1986–90; Asst Dir of Educn, Avon CC, 1990–95; Dir of Educn, Bristol CC, 1995–2002; Jt Hd of Educn, Amnesty Internat. UK, 2005–08. Vis. Fellow, UWE, 2002–. FRSA 1999. *Publications:* Schools For Our Cities, 2003; Aspiration, Identity and Self-Belief, 2010. *E:* richardxvriddell@gmail.com.

RIDDELL, Sandy; *see* Riddell, A. H.

RIDDELL, Sir Walter (John Buchanan), 14th Bt *cr* 1628 (NS), of Riddell, Roxburghshire; *b* 10 June 1974; *e s* of Sir John Riddell, 13th Bt, KCVO and of Hon. Sarah, LVO, *o d* of Baron Richardson of Duntisbourne, KG, MBE, TD, PC; *S* father, 2010; *m* 2003, Lucy, *d* of Selwyn J. Awdry; one *s* three *d* (of whom one *s* one *d* are twins). *Heir: s* Finlay John Buchanan Riddell, *b* 2 June 2004.

RIDDICK, Graham Edward Galloway; Director: Norman Broadbent, 2007–09; Ashurst Executives, since 2010; *b* 26 Aug. 1955; *s* of late John Julian Riddick and Cecilia Margaret Riddick (*née* Ruggles-Brise); *m* 1988, Sarah Northcroft; one *s* two *d. Educ:* Stowe Sch., Buckingham; Univ. of Warwick (Chm., Warwick Univ. Cons. Assoc.). Sales management with Procter & Gamble, 1977–82; Coca-Cola, 1982–87. Gp Mktg Dir, subseq. Gp Mktg and Communications Dir, Onyx Environmental Gp plc, 1997–2000; Business Develt Dir, DeHavilland Information Services plc, 2000–05; Commercial Dir, Adfero Ltd, 2005–07. MP (C) Colne Valley, 1987–97 (first Cons. MP in Colne Valley for 102 years); contested (C) same seat, 1997. PPS to Financial Sec. to HM Treasury, 1990–92, to Sec. of State for Transport, 1992–94. Mem., Educn Select Cttee, 1994–96; Vice Chm., Cons. Trade and Industry Cttee, 1990; Secretary: Cons. Employment Cttee, 1988–90; All Party Textiles Gp, 1988–97. Pres., Yorks CPC, 1993–97. *Recreations:* fishing, shooting, sports, photography, bridge.

RIDDING, John Joseph; Chief Executive, Financial Times Group, since 2006; President, Pearson Professional, since 2013; *b* Birmingham, 25 June 1965; *s* of Mike and Moira Ridding; *m* 2003, Lizzie; one *s* two *d. Educ:* Bedales Sch.; Oxford Univ. (BA 1st Cl. PPE). Hd, Econs and Asia Pacific desks, Oxford Analytica, 1987; joined Financial Times, 1988: Korea corresp.; Paris corresp.; Companies Reporter; Man. Ed.; Dep. Ed.; Ed. and Publisher, FT Asia; Chm., Pearson Asia. *Recreations:* music, running, surfing, scuba diving. *Address:* Financial Times, 1 Southwark Bridge, SE1 9HL. *E:* john.ridding@ft.com.

RIDDLE, Howard Charles Fraser; Senior District Judge (Chief Magistrate), since 2010; a District Judge (Magistrates' Courts) (formerly Metropolitan Stipendiary Magistrate), since 1995; *b* 13 Aug. 1947; *s* of Cecil Riddle and Eithne Riddle (*née* McKenna); *m* 1974, Susan Hilary Hurst; two *d. Educ:* Judd Sch., Tonbridge; London School of Economics (LLB); Coll. of Law. Admitted Solicitor, 1978. Sub-Editor, Penguin Books, 1969–70; Editor, McGill-Queens University Press, 1970–71; Publications Officer, Humanities and Social Science Res. Council, Canada, 1971–76; Solicitor, Edward Fail, Bradshaw and Waterson, 1976–95 (Sen. Partner, 1985–95). Vice-Chm., London Area Cttee, Legal Aid Bd, 1993–95; Mem., Sentencing Adv. Panel, 2004–10 (Vice-Chm., 2007–10); Chm., Legal Cttee, Council of Dist Judges (Magistrates' Courts), 2008–11; Mem., Criminal Law Cttee, Law Commn, 2009–. Hon. Bencher, Gray's Inn, 2012. Member, Editorial Board: Blackstone's Criminal Practice, 2012–; Criminal Law Review, 2012–. *Publications:* (Contrib. Ed.) Wilkinson's Road Traffic Offences, 2008–12; (contrib.) Blackstone's Criminal Practice, 2011–12. *Recreations:* village activities, Rugby football, tennis, visiting France. *Address:* c/o Westminster Magistrates' Court, 181 Marylebone Road, NW1 5BR. *Clubs:* Druidstone (Pembrokeshire); Tonbridge Juddians Rugby Football.

RIDDLE, Kathryn Elizabeth, OBE 2013; JP; DL; Chairman, Health Education Yorkshire and the Humber, since 2013; *b* Halifax, 4 Aug. 1945; *d* of Maj. George Foster, MBE and Doris Foster; *m* 1967, Anthony Riddle; three *s. Educ:* High Sch., Retford, Notts; Univ. of Sheffield (BA Hons Econs 1967; LLB 1986). Tutor in Law, Univ. of Sheffield, 1986–98. Chairman: Sheffield FHSA, 1994–96; Sheffield HA, 1996–2001; S Yorks HA, 2001–06; Yorks and the Humber Strategic HA, later NHS N of England, 2006–13. Pro Chancellor and Chm. Council, Univ. of Sheffield, 2003–13. Hon. Col, Univ. of Sheffield OTC, 2009–14. JP Sheffield, 1975; High Sheriff, 1998–99, DL, 1999, S Yorks. *Recreations:* family, friends, cooking, Rugby Union, travelling in Spain.

RIDDLE, Philip Keitch, OBE 2008; Chief Executive, VisitScotland, 2001–10; Hon. Professor, Queen Margaret University, Edinburgh, since 2011; *b* 6 May 1952; *s* of Clifford Stanley Frederick Riddle and Anne Munro Riddle (*née* Black); *m* 1977, Catherine Mary Riddle (*née* Adams); three *s. Educ:* Dunfermline High Sch.; Trinity Hall, Cambridge (BA 1973, MA 1977); Univ. of Edinburgh (MBA 1977). Shell Group: various posts, marketing and trading, 1977–82; Hd, Oil and Gas Trading, Brunei Shell, 1982–85; Business Develt Manager, Shell Internat. Gas, 1985–88; Area Co-ordination, S America, Shell Internat., 1988–91; Man. Dir, Shell Namibia, 1991–94; Regl Develt Dir, Shell S Africa, 1994–95; Vice-Pres., Shell LPG Europe, 1995–99; Chm., Maximedia, 2000–01. Hon. Consul (Namibia), Govt of the Netherlands, 1991–94. Counsellor, Prince's Scotland Youth Business Trust, 2000–10. Tourism Develt Advr, Tajikistan, 2013. Researching competitive advantage, Univ. of Edinburgh Business Sch., 2015. *Recreations:* ski-ing, walking, reading, travel, making sense of Scotland. *E:* philriddle@blueyonder.co.uk.

RIDEOUT, Prof. Roger William; Professor of Labour Law, University College, London, 1973–2000; *b* 9 Jan. 1935; *s* of Sidney and Hilda Rideout; *m* 1st, 1959, Marjorie Roberts (marr. diss. 1976); one *d*; 2nd, 1977, Gillian Margaret Lynch (*d* 2005). *Educ:* Bedford School; University Coll., London (LLB, PhD). Called to the Bar, Gray's Inn, 1964. National Service, 1958–60; 2nd Lt RAEC, Educn Officer, 1st Bn Coldstream Guards. Lecturer: Univ. of Sheffield, 1960–63; Univ. of Bristol, 1963–64. University Coll., London: Sen. Lectr, 1964–65; Reader, 1965–73; Dean of Faculty of Laws, 1975–77; Fellow, 1997. ILO missions to The Gambia, 1982–83, Somalia, 1989–90, Egypt, 1992–94. Part-time Chm., Industrial Tribunal, subseq. Employment Tribunals, 1984–2007, salaried 2003–07. ACAS panel arbitrator, 1981–; Vice-Pres., Industrial Law Society. FZS 1974. Jt Editor, Current Legal Problems, 1975–92; Gen. Editor, Federation News, 1989–2001. *Publications:* The Right to Membership of a Trade Union, 1962; The Practice and Procedure of the NIRC, 1973; Trade Unions and the Law, 1973; Principles of Labour Law, 1972, 5th edn 1989; Bromham in Bedfordshire – a history, 2003. *Address:* 255 Chipstead Way, Woodmansterne, Surrey SM7 3JW. *T:* (01737) 213489.

RIDER, Prof. Barry Alexander Kenneth, OBE 2014; PhD; Director, Institute of Advanced Legal Studies, University of London, 1995–2004, Hon. Senior Research Fellow, since 2004; Fellow Commoner, Jesus College, Cambridge, since 2001; Professorial Fellow, Centre of Development Studies (formerly Development Studies Committee), University of Cambridge, since 2008; Professor of Comparative Law, Renmin University, China, since 2011; *b* 30 May 1952; *s* of Kenneth Leopold Rider and Alexina Elsie Rider (*née* Bremner); *m* 1976, Normalita Antonina Furto Rosales; one *d*. *Educ:* Bexleyheath Boys' Secondary Modern Sch.; Poly. of N London (Intermediate Ext. LLB 1970); Queen Mary Coll., London (LLB Hons 1973; PhD 1976); Jesus Coll., Cambridge (MA 1976; PhD 1978). Called to the Bar, Inner Temple, 1977, Bencher, 2010. Univ. teaching officer, Univ. of Cambridge, 1980–95; Fellow, 1976–2001, Dean, 1989–96, Jesus Coll., Cambridge. Master of Witan Hall, incorp. Gyosei Internat. Coll., 2002–03. Vis. Sen. Fellow, Centre for Commercial Law Studies, QMC, 1979–90; University of London: Chm., Acad. Policy and Standards Cttee, Sch. of Advanced Study, 1997–2004; Mem., Bd of Mgt, Inst. of US Studies, 1997–2004. Prof. of Law, and Dir, LLM Progs, Law Sch., BPP Univ. (formerly BPP University Coll.), 2008–. Various visiting academic appts, inc. Florida Univ., 1990–; Paul Hastings Prof. of Commercial Law, Univ. of Hong Kong, 2003. Honorary Professor: Dept of Mercantile Law, Univ. of the Free State (formerly Univ. of OFS), RSA, 1998–; Beijing Normal Univ., 2006–; Supreme People's Procuratorate Univ., PRC, 2006–; Renmin Univ., 2006– (Special Counsellor, Develt, Renmin Law Sch., 2015–). General Editor: Company Lawyer, 1980–; European Business Law Rev., 1996–2005; Jl Financial Crime, 1994–; Jl Money Laundering Control, 1996–; Amicus Curiae, 1997–; Internat. and Comparative Corporate Law Jl, 1998–; Internat. Jl of Disclosure and Governance, 2003–; Editor: CUP series on Corporate Law, 1996–; Kluwer series on Company and Financial Law, 1997–2006; Butterworth's series on Compliance, 2002–06. Hd, Commonwealth Commercial Crime Unit, 1981–89; Exec. Dir, Centre for Internat. Documentation on Organised and Econ. Crime, 1989–. Special Advr to H of C Select Cttee on Trade and Industry, 1989–93. Internat. Gen. Counsel, Internat. Compliance Assoc., 2007–09. Chairman: Exec. Cttee, Soc. for Advanced Legal Studies, 1997–2004 (Mem., 2006–); Hamlyn Trust for Legal Educn, 2001–05. Former Consultant to various govtl agencies and to internat. bodies, incl. UNDP, IMF, Commonwealth Fund for Tech. Co-operation, Asian Develt Bank, and Commonwealth Secretariat. Consultant: Beachcroft LLP (formerly Beachcroft Wansbroughs), 2004–06; Islamic Financial Services Bd, 2005–; of Counsel, Bryan Cave LLP, 2008–12. Member: Bd of Advrs, Internat. Council for Capital Formation, 2003–07; Adv. Bd, Centre for Financial Crime and Security Studies, RUSI, 2015–; Adv. Cttee, China Overseas-educated Scholars Foundn, YICAI Foundn, 2015–. International Advisor: New England Sch. of Law, 2002–; Faculty of Law, Univ. of Cyprus, 2003–; Centre for Criminology, Univ. of Hong Kong, 2004–; Inst. of Criminal Justice, Beijing, 2006–. Mem. Court, City Univ., 2001–. Freeman, City of London, 1984; Mem., Court of Assts, 1998–, Master, 2007–08, Co. of Pattenmakers; Freeman, Guild of Educators, 2008–. Fellow, Inst. of Professional Investigators, 1980; FRSA 1997. Hon. Fellow, Soc. for Advanced Legal Studies, 2004. Hon. LLD: Dickinson Law Sch., USA, 1996; Free State, RSA, 2001. *Publications:* (jtly) The Regulation of Insider Trading, 1979; Insider Trading, 1983; (jtly) Guide to the Financial Services Act, 1987, 2nd edn 1989; (jtly) Insider Crime, 1993; (jtly) Guide to Financial Services Regulation, 1997; (jtly) Anti-Money Laundering Guide, 1999; (jtly) Market Abuse and Insider Dealing, 2002, 2nd edn 2009; *edited:* The Regulation of the British Securities Industry, 1979, CCH Financial Services Reporter, 3 vols, 1987; The Fiduciary, the Insider and the Conflict, 1995; Money Laundering Control, 1996; Corruption: the enemy within, 1997; Developments in European Company Law, vol. I 1997, vol. II 1998; International Tracing of Assets, 2 vols, 1997; Commercial Law in a Global Context, 1998; The Corporate Dimension, 1998; The Realm of Company Law, 1998; (jtly) The Prevention and Control of International Financial Crime, 2010; (jtly) Strategies for the Development of Islamic Capital Markets, 2011; International Financial Crime, 2015; contrib. to numerous books and legal periodicals on company law, financial law and control of economic crime. *Recreations:* riding, historic houses. *Address:* Institute of Advanced Legal Studies, Charles Clore House, 17 Russell Square, WC1B 5DR. *T:* (020) 7862 5800; Jesus College, Cambridge CB5 8BL. *T:* (01223) 339339. *E:* b.rider@jesus.cam.ac.uk. *Clubs:* Athenæum, Oxford and Cambridge, Civil Service.

RIDER, Gill, CB 2011; non-executive Director: De La Rue plc, since 2006; Charles Taylor plc, since 2012; Pennon plc, since 2012; President, Chartered Institute of Personnel and Development, since 2010; *b* London, 24 Oct. 1954; *d* of William and Ethel Rider; *m* 1986, David Paul Burke. *Educ:* Univ. of Southampton (BSc Hons Biol.; PhD Botany). FCIPD 2008. Accenture, 1979–2006: Man. Partner, Utilities Practice, Europe and S Africa, 1998–99; Mem., Global Exec. Cttee, 1999–2006; Man. Partner, Resources Operating Unit, EMEA, India and S America, 1999–2002; Chief Leadership Officer, 2002–06; Dir-Gen., CS Capability Gp, Cabinet Office, 2006–11. Chm. Council, Univ. of Southampton, 2012–. *Recreations:* entertaining, gardening, motor-racing, travel. *E:* gill.rider@mac.com.

RIDER, Stephen Henry; Presenter: Legends series, Sky Sports F1, since 2012; British Touring Car Championship, ITV; *b* 28 April 1950; *s* of Alfred Charles Rider and Shirley Jeanette (*née* Walls); *m* 1985, Jane Eydmann; one *s* one *d*. *Educ:* Roan Grammar Sch., Blackheath. Local sports journalist, S London and sports presenter for London Broadcasting, 1969–76; Sports Presenter: Anglia TV, 1976–80; ITV Network, incl., World of Sport, 1980 Olympics, Midweek Sports Special, Network Golf, 1980–85; Network Presenter for BBC Sport: Main Presenter, Sportsnight, 1985–92; network golf coverage; Olympic Games, Seoul, 1988, Barcelona, 1992, Atlanta, 1996, Sydney, 2000, Athens, 2004; Commonwealth Games, 1986, 1990, 1994, 1998 and 2002; main network golf presenter, 1991–2005; motor sport specialist; Presenter: Grandstand, 1985–2005 (Main Presenter, 1992–2005); BBC Sports Personality of the Year, 1986–2005; F1 Grand Prix, ITV, 2006–08; ITV Football (incl. Champions League and World Cup, 2006), 2006–10; Rugby World Cup, ITV, 2011. Sports Presenter of Year, TRIC, 1994, RTS, 1995. *Publications:* 50 Years of Sports Personality of the Year, 2003; Europe at the Masters, 2006; My Chequered Career: thirty-five years of televising motorsport, 2012. *Recreations:* golf, family. *Address:* c/o Blackburn Sachs Associates, Argyll House, All Saints Passage, SW18 1EP.

RIDGE, Keith William, CBE 2014; PhD; Chief Pharmaceutical Officer, NHS England, Department of Health and Health Education England (formerly Chief Pharmaceutical Officer, Department of Health), since 2006; *b* Romford, Essex, 15 Feb. 1962; *s* of Cyril Ridge and Gwen Ridge; *m* 1989, Susan Caroline Sands; one *s* one *d*. *Educ:* University College London (BPharm 1st Cl. Hons 1987; MSc (Dist.) 1991); Univ. of Manchester (PhD 1998). Registered Pharmacist 1988. Res. Pharmacist, Roche Pharmaceuticals, 1988–90; various hosp. pharmacist posts, Whittington Hosp. NHS Trust, 1990–96; Principal Pharmacist, DoH, 1996–2000; Chief Pharmacist: North Glasgow Univ. NHS Trust, 2000–05; Univ. Hosps Birmingham, 2005–06. Vis. Prof., Dept of Medicine, Imperial Coll. London, 2013–. *Publications:* articles in learned jls. *Recreations:* family, angling, theatre, cooking. *Address:* NHS England, Skipton House, 80 London Road, SE1 6LH. *T:* (020) 7972 2833, *Fax:* (020) 7972 1186. *E:* Keith.Ridge@dh.gsi.gov.uk, Keith.Ridge@nhs.net.

RIDGE, Rupert Leander Pattle; Adviser, Motivation Charitable Trust, since 2004; *b* 18 May 1947; *y s* of late Major Robert Vaughan Ridge and Marian Ivy Edith Ridge (*née* Pattle); *m* 1971, Mary Blanche Gibbs; two *s* two *d*. *Educ:* King's Coll., Taunton. Officer, LI, 1969–73. BAC, then British Aerospace Defence Ltd, 1973–94; Internat. Dir, Leonard Cheshire Foundn, then Dir, Leonard Cheshire Internat., 1994–2004. Trustee: Action around Bethlehem Children with Disability, 1994–2005 (Chm., 1998–2005; Patron, 2008–); Wellspring Counselling, 2004–11 (Chm., 2006–09). *Recreations:* gardening, being in the country. *Address:* (office) Motivation Charitable Trust, Brockley Academy, Brockley Lane, Backwell, Bristol BS48 4AQ.

RIDGWAY, Lt-Gen. Sir Andrew Peter, KBE 2011 (CBE 1995); CB 2001; Lieutenant-Governor and Commander-in-Chief, Jersey, 2006–11; Executive Chairman, Confederation of Service Charities, since 2014; *b* 20 March 1950; *s* of late Robert Hamilton Ridgway and Betty Patricia Ridgway (*née* Crane); *m* 1974, Valerie Elizabeth Shawe; three *s* one *d*. *Educ:* Hele's Sch., Exeter; RMA, Sandhurst; St John's Coll., Cambridge (MPhil). Commnd RTR, 1970: served Germany, NI, Belize, Bosnia, Kuwait, Macedonia, Kosovo and UK; CO, 3 RTR, 1991–92; Col, Army Prog., MoD, 1992–93; Comdr, 7 Armd Bde, 1993–95 (Comdr, UN Sector SW Bosnia Herzegovina, Feb.–Nov. 1994); Dir, Operational Capability, MoD, 1995–97; Chief, Jt Rapid Deployment Force, 1997–98; COS, ACE RRC, 1998–2001 (COS, Kosovo Force, 1999); Hd, Defence Trng Review Implementation Team, 2001–02; Dir Gen. Trng and Educn, MoD, 2002; Chief of Defence Intelligence, MoD, 2003–06. Col Comdt, RTR, 1999–2006; Hon. Colonel: Cambridge Univ. OTC, 2003–13; Westminster Dragoons, 2008–14; Jersey Field Sqdn RE, 2010–14. Dir, Army Ice Sports, 1999–2006; Chm., British Bobsleigh, 2010–14. Mem., Judicial Appts Commn, 2012–; Chm., Adv. Cttee, War Pension Tribunals, 2014–. Mem., Adv. Bd, King's Centre for Mil. Health Res., KCL. KStJ 2009 (CStJ 2007). *Recreations:* golf, fishing, walking, bobsleigh, beekeeping. *Club:* Army and Navy.

RIDGWAY, David Frederick Charles, CMG 2000; OBE 1988; HM Diplomatic Service, retired; Assessor, Foreign and Commonwealth Office, 2001–07; Partner, CONSULAT Business Consultancy, 2002–14; *b* 9 June 1941; *m* 1966, Dora Beatriz Siles; one *s* one *d*. Entered FO, 1960; served La Paz, Colombo and Durban, 1963–77; First Sec. (Commercial), Buenos Aires, 1980–82; FCO, 1982–84; Chargé d'Affaires *ai*, San Salvador, 1984–87; FCO, 1988–91; Dir of Trade Promotion, Madrid, 1991–95; Ambassador to: Bolivia, 1995–98; Cuba, 1998–2001. Chairman: Anglo-Central American Soc., 2005–07; Cuba Studies Trust, 2007–13. *Address:* 4 Heath Rise, Kersfield Road, SW15 3HF.

RIDGWELL, Angela; Director General, Corporate Services, Department of Energy and Climate Change, since 2013; *b* Cambridge, 24 July 1964; *d* of Ronald Stenning and Jean Stenning; *m* 1985, Howard Ridgwell; one *d*. CIPFA 1991. Dir, Resources, Bridgnorth DC, 2000–02; Dir, Finance and ICT, Coventry CC, 2002–06; Chief Exec., Thurrock BC, 2007–08; Man. Dir, Angie Ridgwell Associates Ltd, 2009–; Strategic Dir, Business Change, Bristol CC, 2013. *Recreations:* triathlon, walking, family, theatre, ballet. *Address:* Department of Energy and Climate Change, 3 Whitehall Place, SW1A 2AW. *T:* 0300 068 5115. *E:* angie.ridgwell@decc.gsi.gov.uk.

RIDLEY, family name of **Viscount Ridley**.

RIDLEY, 5th Viscount *cr* 1900; **Matthew White Ridley,** DL; DPhil; FRSL; FMedSci; Baron Wensleydale 1900; Bt 1756; *b* 7 Feb. 1958; *o s* of 4th Viscount Ridley, KG, GCVO, TD and Lady Anne Lumley (*d* 2006), 3rd *d* of 11th Earl of Scarborough, KG, GCSI, GCIE, GCVO, PC; *S* father, 2012; *m* 1989, Prof. Anya Hurlbert, *d* of Dr Robert Hurlbert, Houston, Texas; one *s* one *d*. *Educ:* Eton Coll.; Magdalen Coll., Oxford (BA Zoology 1979; DPhil Zoology 1983). Science Editor, 1983–87, Washington corresp., 1987–90, American Editor, 1990–92, The Economist; columnist, Sunday and Daily Telegraph, 1993–2000. Chairman: Northern 2 VCT, 1999–2008; Northern Rock plc, 2004–07 (Dir, 1994–2007); Director: Northern Investors, 1994–2007; PA Holdings Ltd, 1999–2008. Chm., Internat. Centre for Life, 1996–2003. Elected Mem., H of L, 2013. DL Northumberland, 2007. FRSL 1999; FMedSci 2004. *Publications:* Warts and All, 1989; The Red Queen, 1993; The Origins of Virtue, 1996; Genome, 1999; Nature Via Nurture, 2003; Francis Crick, 2006; The Rational Optimist: how prosperity evolves, 2010. *Recreations:* fly fishing, natural history. *Heir: s* Hon. Matthew White Ridley, *b* 27 Sept. 1993. *Address:* Blagdon Hall, Seaton Burn, Newcastle upon Tyne NE13 6DD.

RIDLEY, Sir Adam (Nicholas), Kt 1985; Director General, London Investment Banking Association, 2000–05, Senior Adviser, 2005–06; Chairman of Trustees, Equitas Group of Companies, since 1996; *b* 14 May 1942; *s* of late Jasper Maurice Alexander Ridley and Helen Cressida Ridley (*née* Bonham Carter); *m* 1981, Margaret Anne Passmore; three *s* (inc. twin *s*). *Educ:* Eton Coll.; Balliol Coll., Oxford (1st cl. hons PPE 1965); Univ. of California, Berkeley. Foreign Office, 1965, seconded to DEA, 1965–68; Harkness Fellow, Univ. of California, Berkeley, 1968–69; HM Treasury, 1970–71, seconded to CPRS, 1971–74; Economic Advr to shadow cabinet and Asst Dir, 1974–79, Dir, 1979, Cons. Res. Dept; Special Advr to Chancellor of the Exchequer, 1979–84, to Chancellor of the Duchy of Lancaster, 1985. Director: Hambros Bank, 1985–97; Hambros PLC, 1985–97; Sunday Newspaper Publishing PLC, 1988–90 (Chm., 1990); non-executive Director: Leopold Joseph Holdings, 1997–2004; Morgan Stanley Bank Internat., 2006–13; Hampden Agencies Ltd, 2007–12; Equitas Ltd, 2009–; Equitas Reinsce Ltd, 2009–; Equitas Hldgs Ltd, 2009–; Equitas Insce Ltd, 2009–. Chm., Names Adv. Cttee, 1995–96, Mem. Council, 1997–99, Mem., Regulatory Bd, 1997–99, Lloyds of London. Mem., National Lottery Charities Bd, 1994–2000 (Dep. Chm., 1995–2000). Mem. Council, British Sch. at Athens, 2003– (Vice Chm., 2010–). *Publications:* articles on regional policy, public spending, international and Eastern European economics, charities, and financial regulation. *Recreations:* music, pictures, travel. *Clubs:* Garrick, Political Economy.

RIDLEY, Prof. Anne Jacqueline, PhD; FMedSci; Professor of Cell Biology, King's College London, since 2007; *b* Oxford, 3 April 1963; *d* of Kenneth Ridley and Jane Ridley; *m* 1990, Edward Kay; two *d*. *Educ:* Clare Coll., Cambridge (BA Hons Natural Scis 1985); Imperial Cancer Res. Fund, Univ. of London (PhD 1989). Post-doctoral Fellow: MIT, Cambridge, 1989–90; Inst. of Cancer Res., London, 1990–93; University College London: Mem., Ludwig Inst. for Cancer Res., 1993–2007; Lectr, 1995–2001; Reader, 2001–03; Prof., 2003–07. Mem. Council, Amer. Soc. for Cell Biol., 2006–08. Mem., EMBO, 2003. FMedSci 2012. *Publications:* over 150 articles in biochem., cell biol. and med. jls. *Recreation:* music (play viola and piano). *Address:* Randall Division of Cell and Molecular Biophysics, King's College London, New Hunt's House, Guy's Campus, SE1 1UL. *E:* anne.ridley@kcl.ac.uk.

RIDLEY, Prof. Brian Kidd, FRS 1994; Research Professor of Physics, University of Essex, 1991–2008, now Professor Emeritus; *b* 2 March 1931; *s* of Oliver Archbold Ridley and Lillian Beatrice Ridley; *m* 1959, Sylvia Jean Nicholls; one *s* one *d*. *Educ:* Univ. of Durham (BSc 1st Cl. Hons Physics, PhD). CPhys, FInstP. Research Physicist, Mullard Research Lab., Redhill,

1956–64; Essex University: Lectr in Physics, 1964–67; Sen. Lectr, 1967–71; Reader, 1971–84; Prof., 1984–91. Dist. Vis. Prof., Cornell Univ., 1967; Vis. Prof. at univs in USA, Denmark, Sweden and Holland. Paul Dirac Medal and Prize, Inst. of Physics, 2001. *Publications:* Time, Space and Things, 1976, 3rd edn 1995; The Physical Environment, 1979; Quantum Processors in Semiconductors, 1982, 5th edn 2013; Electrons and Phonons in Semiconductor Multilayers, 1997, 2nd edn 2009; On Science, 2001; Reforming Science: beyond belief, 2010. *Recreations:* tennis, piano.

RIDLEY, Prof. Frederick Fernand, OBE 1978; PhD; Professor of Political Theory and Institutions, University of Liverpool, 1965–95, now Emeritus, and Senior Fellow, School of Management (formerly Institute of Public Administration and Management), 1995–2005; *b* 11 Aug. 1928; *s* of late J. and G. A. Ridley; *m* 1967, Paula Frances Cooper Ridley, *qv*; two *s* one *d*. *Educ:* The Hall, Hampstead; Highgate Sch.; LSE (BScEcon, PhD); Univs of Paris and Berlin. Lectr, Univ. of Liverpool, 1958–65. Vis. Professor: Graduate Sch. of Public Affairs, Univ. of Pittsburgh, 1968; Coll. of Europe, Bruges, 1975–83. Manpower Services Commission, Merseyside: Chm., Job Creation Prog., 1975–77; Vice-Chm., 1978–87, Chm., 1987–88, Area Manpower Bd. Member: Jt Univ. Council for Social and Public Admin, 1964–95 (Chm., 1972–74); Exec., Pol Studies Assoc., 1967–75 (Hon. Vice-Pres., 1995–); Council, Hansard Soc., 1970–94; Pol Science Cttee, SSRC, 1972–76; Cttee, European Gp on Public Admin, 1973–92; Public and Social Admin Bd, CNAA, 1975–82; Social Studies Res. Cttee, CNAA, 1980–83 (Chm.); Academic Cttee, Assoc. Internat. de la Fonction Publique, 1988–93; Vice-Pres., Rencontres Européennes des Fonctions Publiques/Entretiens Universitaires pour l'Admin en Europe, 1990–2001. Member: Exec., Merseyside Arts (RAA), 1979–84; Adv. Council, Granada Foundn, 1984–98; Council, Hochschule für Verwaltungswissenschaft, Speyer, 1993–2005; Trustee, Friends of Merseyside Museums and Galleries, 1977–85. Pres., Politics Assoc., 1976–81 (Hon. Fellow, 1995). Editor: Political Studies, 1969–75; Parliamentary Affairs, 1975–2004. *Publications:* Public Administration in France, 1964; Revolutionary Syndicalism in France, 1970; The Study of Government, 1975; numerous articles and edited vols on political sci. and public admin. *Address:* Riversdale House, Grassendale Park, Liverpool L19 0LR. *T:* (0151) 427 1630.

RIDLEY, Michael; *see* Ridley, R. M.

RIDLEY, Sir Michael (Kershaw), KCVO 2000 (CVO 1992); Clerk of the Council, Duchy of Lancaster, 1981–2000; *b* 7 Dec. 1937; *s* of late George K. and Mary Ridley; *m* 1968, Diana Loraine McLernon; two *s*. *Educ:* Stowe; Magdalene College, Cambridge. MA. FRICS. Grosvenor Estate, Canada and USA, 1965–69, London, 1969–72; Property Manager, British & Commonwealth Shipping Co., 1972–81. A Gen. Comr of Income Tax, 1984–98. Chm., Standards Cttee, RBK&C, 2001–06. Mem., Adv. Panel, Greenwich Hosp., 1978–2002. Mem. Court, Lancaster Univ., 1981–2000. Trustee: St Martin-in-the-Fields Almshouse Assoc., 1991–2005; Anne Duchess of Westminster Charity, 2004–. Pres., Assoc. of Lancastrians in London, 2000. *Recreation:* golf. *Address:* 27 Musgrave Crescent, SW6 4QE. *Clubs:* Garrick; Royal Mid-Surrey Golf.

RIDLEY, Paula Frances Cooper, CBE 2008 (OBE 1996); JP; DL; MA; Chairman, Board of Trustees, Victoria and Albert Museum, 1998–2007; Director: Gulbenkian Foundation (UK), 1999–2007; English National Ballet, 2011–13; *b* 27 Sept. 1944; *d* of Ondrej Clyne and Ellen (*née* Cooper); *m* 1967, Frederick Fernand Ridley, *qv*; two *s* one *d*. *Educ:* Kendal High Sch., Westmorland; Univ. of Liverpool (BA, MA). Lectr in Politics and Public Admin, Liverpool Polytechnic, 1966–71; Proj. Co-ordinator, Regeneration Projects Ltd, 1981–84; Dir, Community Initiatives Res. Trust, 1983–90; Consultant, BAT Industries Small Businesses Ltd, 1983–95; Bd Mem., Brunswick Small Business Centre Ltd, 1984–95; Associate, CEI Consultants, 1984–88. Chairman: Liverpool Housing Action Trust, 1992–2005; Public Interest Gen. Council, Office for Public Mgt, 2003–07; Dir, Merseyside Develt Corp., 1991–98. Mem., Royal Commn on Long Term Care for the Elderly, 1997–99. Presenter and Assoc. Editor, Granada Action, 1989–92; Mem., IBA, 1982–88. Chm., Stocktonwood County Primary Sch., 1976–79; Member: Liverpool Heritage Bureau, 1971–88; Management Cttee, Liverpool Victoria Settlement, 1971–86 (Vice-Chm., 1977–86); Granada Telethon Trust, 1988–94. Trustee: Tate Gall., 1988–98; Nat. Gall., 1995–98; Chm., Tate Gall., Liverpool, 1988–98. Liverpool University: Lady Pres., Guild of Undergraduates, Clerk of Convocation, 1972–74; Member: Court, 1972–; Council, 1998–2007; Life Governor, Liverpool and Huyton Colls, 1979–94. Merseyside Civic Society: Hon. Sec., 1971–82; Vice-Chm., 1982–86; Chm., 1986–91. Chm., Liverpool Biennial of Contemporary Art, 2008–; Chair: Nat. Student Drama Fest., 2009–12; Civic Voice, 2010–13. JP Liverpool, 1977. DL Merseyside, 1989. Hon. FRIBA 2005. Hon. Fellow, Liverpool John Moores Univ., 2002. Hon. LLD Liverpool, 2003. *Address:* Riversdale House, Grassendale Park, Liverpool L19 0LR. *T:* (0151) 427 1630; 69 Thomas More House, Barbican, EC2Y 8BT. *T:* (020) 7628 8573.

RIDLEY, (Robert) Michael; Principal, Royal Belfast Academical Institution, 1990–2006; *b* 8 Jan. 1947; *s* of Maurice Roy Ridley and Jean Evelyn Lawther (*née* Carlisle); *m* 1985, Jennifer Mary Pearson; two *d*. *Educ:* Clifton Coll.; St Edmund Hall, Oxford (MA, Cert Ed). Wellington Coll., Berks, 1970–82 (Housemaster, 1975–82); Hd of English, Merchiston Castle Sch., Edinburgh, 1982–86; Headmaster, Denstone Coll., 1986–90. Mem., Rotary Club, Belfast, 1990–. *Recreations:* cricket (Oxford Blue, 1968–70; Ireland 1968), golf, reading, travel. *Clubs:* Ulster Reform (Belfast); Vincent's (Oxford); Royal County Down Golf (Newcastle, Co. Down); Boat of Garten Golf (Inverness-shire).

RIDLEY, Prof. Tony Melville, CBE 1986; FREng, FICE, FCILT; Professor of Transport Engineering (formerly Rees Jeffreys Professor), 1991–99, and Head of Department of Civil and Environmental Engineering (formerly Department of Civil Engineering), 1997–99, Imperial College of Science, Technology and Medicine, University of London, now Professor Emeritus, Imperial College London; *b* 10 Nov. 1933; *s* of late John Edward and Olive Ridley; *m* 1959, Jane (*née* Dickinson); two *s* one *d*. *Educ:* Durham Sch.; King's Coll. Newcastle, Univ. of Durham (BSc); Northwestern Univ., Ill (MS); Univ. of California, Berkeley (PhD); Stanford Univ., Calif (Sen. Exec. Prog.). Nuclear Power Group, 1957–62; Univ. of California, 1962–65; Chief Research Officer, Highways and Transportation, GLC, 1965–69; Director General, Tyne and Wear Passenger Transport Exec., 1969–75; Man. Dir, Hong Kong Mass Transit Rly Corp., 1975–80; Bd Mem., 1980–88, Man. Dir (Rlys), 1980–85, LTE, then LRT; Chm., 1985–88, Man. Dir, 1985–88, Chief Exec., 1988, London Underground Ltd; Man. Dir-Project, Eurotunnel, 1989–90 (Dir, 1987–90). Chm., Docklands Light Railway Ltd, 1987–88; Dir, London Transport Internat., 1982–88. Sen. Transport Advr, London 2012 Olympic Bid, 2004–05; Mem., Ind. Dispute Avoidance Panel for London 2012, 2008–. Chm., Building Schs for the Future Investments LLP, 2007–10. Dir, Major Projects Assoc., 1995–2009. President: Light Rail Transit Assoc., 1974–92; Assoc. for Project Mgt, 1999–2003; Commonwealth Engineers Council, 2000–09; Internat. Pres., CILT (formerly CIT), 1999–2001 (Vice-Pres., 1987–90); Member: Council, ICE, 1990–97 (Chm., Transport Bd, 1990–93; Vice Pres., 1992–95; Pres., 1995–96); Senate, Engrg Council, 1997–2000 (Chm., Bd for the Engrg Profession, 1997–99); Exec. Council, WFEO, 2000–09; Task Force 10 (Sci., Technol. and Innovation), UN Millennium Project, 2002–05; Minister of Transport's Internat. Adv. Panel, Singapore, 2007–10; Chm., Steering Gp, Global Transport Knowledge Partnership, 2008–10. Trustee, RAC Foundn for Motoring, 1999–2009 (Mem., Public Policy Cttee, 1997–2010). Freeman, City of London, 1982; Hon. Fellow, Paviors' Co., 2006. FREng (FEng 1992); FHKIE, FITE, FCIHT (FIHT 1992) (Highways Award, 1988). FCGI 1996. Hon. FAPM 1996; Hon. FIA 1999. Hon. DTech Napier, 1996; Hon. DEng Newcastle upon Tyne, 1997. Herbert Crow Award (1st recipient), Carmen's Co., 2001; President's Award, Engrg Council, 2002. *Publications:* articles in transport, engrg and other jls. *Recreations:* walking, theatre, music, international affairs. *Address:* Orchard Lodge, Stichens Green, Streatley, Berks RG8 9SU. *T:* (01491) 871075. *Clubs:* Royal Automobile; Hong Kong, Jockey (Hong Kong).

RIDLEY-THOMAS, Roger; Managing Director, Thomson Regional Newspapers Ltd, 1989–94; *b* 14 July 1939; *s* of late John Montague Ridley-Thomas, MB, ChB, FRCSE, Norwich, and Christina Anne (*née* Seex); *m* 1962, Sandra Grace McBeth Young; two *s* two *d*. *Educ:* Gresham's Sch. Served Royal Norfolk Regt, 1958–60. Newspaper Publisher: Eastern Counties Newspapers, 1960–65; Thomson Regional Newspapers, 1965–94 (Dir, 1985–94); Managing Director: Aberdeen Journals, 1980–84; Scotsman Publications, 1984–89; Director: Caledonian Offset, 1979–94; Radio Forth, 1978–81; TRN Viewdata, 1978–89; Thomson Scottish Organisation, 1984–89; Northfield Newspapers, 1984–89; The Scotsman Communications, 1984–94; The Scotsman Publications, 1984–94; Central Publications, 1984–94; Aberdeen Journals, 1980–84, 1990–94; Belfast Telegraph Newspapers, 1990–94; Chester Chronicle, 1990–94; Newcastle Chronicle & Journal, 1990–94; Western Mail & Echo, 1990–94; Cardrona Ltd, 1995–; Milex Ltd, 1996–2005; Adscene Gp plc, 1996–99; Roys (Wroxham) Ltd, 1997– (Chm., 2004–14); Norfolk Christmas Trees Ltd, 2000–08; Chairman: Anglia FM, 1996–98; NorCor Hldgs plc, 1996–2000. Director: Aberdeen Chamber of Commerce, 1981–84; Scottish Business in the Community, 1984–89; Scottish Business Achievement Award Trust, 1985–2003; Edinburgh Ch. of Commerce and Manufrs, 1985–88. Pres., Scottish Daily Newspaper Soc., 1983–85; Mem. Council, CBI, 1983–86; Mem., Scottish Wildlife Appeal Cttee, 1985–88. *Recreations:* shooting, golf, tennis, travel.

RIDPATH, Ian William; author, broadcaster and lecturer on astronomy and space; *b* 1 May 1947; *s* of late Alfred William Joseph Ridpath and Irene Florence Ridpath (*née* Walton). *Educ:* Beal Grammar Sch., Woodford. FRAS 1988 (Council Mem., 2004–07); Mem., Soc. of Authors; Assoc. of British Sci. Writers. Editor: Popular Astronomy (qly mag.), 1986–89; The Antiquarian Astronomer, 2015–. Klumpke-Roberts Award, Astronomical Soc. of the Pacific, 2012. *Publications:* Worlds Beyond, 1975; (ed) Encyclopedia of Astronomy and Space, 1976; Messages from the Stars, 1978; The Young Astronomer's Handbook, 1981; Hamlyn Encyclopedia of Space, 1981; Life off Earth, 1983; Collins Pocket Guide to Stars and Planets, 1984, 4th edn as Collins Stars and Planets Guide, 2007; The Night Sky, 1985; (jtly) A Comet Called Halley, 1985; Concise Handbook of Astronomy, 1986; Dictionary of Astronomy and Astronautics, 1987; The Monthly Sky Guide, 1987, 9th edn 2012; Go Skywatching, 1987; Star Tales, 1988; (ed) Norton's Star Atlas, 18th edn 1989, 20th edn 2003; Giant Book of Space, 1989; Pocket Guide to Astronomy, 1990; Space, 1991; Book of the Universe, 1991; Philip's Atlas of Stars and Planets, 1992, 4th edn 2004; (ed) Oxford Dictionary of Astronomy, 1997, 2nd edn 2007; Handbook of Stars and Planets, 1998, 3rd edn 2010; Gem Stars, 1999; (ed) Collins Encyclopedia of the Universe, 2001; The Times Space, 2002; The Times Universe, 2004; Eyewitness Companion to Astronomy, 2006; Philip's Astronomy Starter Pack, 2011; Exploring Stars and Planets, 2011; *for children:* Discovering Space, 1972; (ed) Man and Materials (series): Oil, Coal, Gas, Stone, Plastics, Minerals, 1975; Signs of Life, 1977; Space, 1979; Secrets of Space, 1980; Spacecraft, 1981; Stars and Planets, 1981; Secrets of the Sky, 1985; The Sun, 1987; The Stars, 1987; Outer Space, 1987; *contributions to:* Reader's Digest Library of Modern Knowledge, 1978; Hutchinson 20th Century Encyclopedia, 1987; Microsoft Encarta Encyclopedia, 1997–2008; Universe, 2005–. *Recreations:* collecting antique star atlases and astronomically related stamps, distance running (Race Dir, Polytechnic Marathon, 1993–95), horse racing and riding. *Address:* 48 Otho Court, Brentford, Middlesex TW8 8PY. *T:* (020) 8568 6100. *E:* ian@ianridpath.com. *W:* www.ianridpath.com.

RIESEBERG, Prof. Loren Henry, PhD; FRS 2010; FRSC; FRSB; Professor of Botany, University of British Columbia, since 2006. *Educ:* Southern Coll., Chattanooga (BA Biol. 1981); Univ. of Tennessee (MS Botany 1984); Washington State Univ. (PhD Botany 1987). Asst Prof. of Botany, Claremont Graduate Sch., 1987–93; Department of Biology, Indiana University: Associate Prof., 1993–97; Prof., 1997–2004; Distinguished Prof., 2004–; Dir, Plant Scis Prog., 1996–2000; Associate Chair for Res. and Facilities, 2000–04. Pres., Amer. Genetics Assoc., 2006. FAAAS 2003; Fellow, Amer. Acad. of Arts and Scis, 2004; FRSB (FSB 2010); FRSC 2010. *Address:* Rieseberg Laboratory, Department of Botany, University of British Columbia, 6270 University Boulevard, Vancouver, BC V6T 1Z4, Canada.

RIESS, Prof. Adam Guy, PhD; Distinguished Astronomer, Space Telescope Science Institute, since 1999; Thomas J. Barber Professor of Physics and Astronomy, Johns Hopkins University, since 2006; *b* Washington, DC, 16 Dec. 1969; *s* of late Michael and Doris Riess; *m* 1998, Nancy Joy Schondorf. *Educ:* Massachusetts Inst. of Technol. (AB Physics 1992); Harvard Univ. (AM Astrophysics 1994; PhD Astrophysics 1996). Miller Fellow, Univ. of Calif, Berkeley, 1996–99. Kavli Frontier of Sci. Fellow, 2007; MacArthur Fellow, 2008. Fellow, Amer. Physical Soc., 2011. Mem., NAS, 2009. Hon. Mem., Amer. Acad. Arts and Scis, 2008. Trumpler Award, Astronomical Soc. of Pacific, 1999; Sci. Award, Assoc. of Univs for Res. in Astronomy, 2000; Bok Prize, Harvard Univ., 2001; Helen B. Warner Prize, Amer. Astronomical Soc., 2003; Raymond and Beverley Sackler Prize, Tel-Aviv Univ., 2004; Shaw Prize, Shaw Foundn, 2006; Gruber Prize in Cosmol., Gruber Foundn, 2007; Einstein Medal, Albert Einstein Soc., 2011; Exceptional Scientific Achievement Award, NASA, 2011; (jtly) Nobel Prize in Physics, 2011. *Publications:* contribs to jls incl. Astrophysical Jl, Astronomical Jl. *Address:* Department of Physics and Astronomy, Bloomberg 207, Johns Hopkins University, 3400 N Charles Street, Baltimore, MD 21218–2686, USA.

RIFKIN, Joshua; Founder, and Director, The Bach Ensemble, since 1978; *b* 22 April 1944; *s* of Harry H. Rifkin and Dorothy (*née* Helsh); *m* 1st, 1970, Louise Litterick (marr. diss. 1984); 2nd, 1995, Helen Palmer; one *d*. *Educ:* Juilliard Sch. of Music (BS 1964); Princeton Univ. (MFA 1969). Musical Consultant, later Musical Dir, Nonesuch Records, NY, 1963–75; Brandeis University: Instructor, 1970–71; Asst Prof., 1971–77; Associate Prof., 1977–82. Visiting Professor, 1973–2002: NY Univ.; Harvard Univ.; Yale Univ.; Rutgers Univ.; Bard Coll.; Princeton Univ.; Stanford Univ.; King's Coll. London; Basel Univ.; Ohio State Univ.; Dortmund Univ. (Gambrinus Prof.); Munich Univ.; Univ. of N Carolina at Chapel Hill. Numerous concerts with Bach Ensemble in UK, Europe, US and Canada; Guest Conductor: English Chamber Orch., 1983, 1984; Scottish Chamber Orch., 1984, 1994; St Louis SO, 1985; Schola Cantorum Basiliensis, 1986, 1990, 1993, 1997, 2000; Victoria State SO, 1989; San Francisco SO, 1989; St Paul Chamber Orch., 1989; LA Chamber Orch., 1990; City of Glasgow SO, 1992; Cappella Coloniensis, Germany, 1993, 1994; Orch. Haydn/Bolzano, 1995; Solistas de México, BBC Concert Orch., and City of London Sinfonia, 1996; Jerusalem SO, Prague Chamber Orch., 1997; Nat. Arts Centre Orch., Houston SO, Camerata de las Américas, 1999; Bayerische Staatsoper, Munich, 2001; Israel Camerata, Jerusalem, 2002. Numerous recordings. Fellow, Wissenschaftskolleg, Berlin, 1984–86. Hon. PhD Dortmund, 1999. *Publications:* contrib. New Grove Dictionary of Music and Musicians, 1980; numerous articles in scholarly jls. *Recreations:* food, wine, cinema, theatre, computers, fiction. *E:* jrifkin@compuserve.com.

RIFKIND, (Gabriel) Charles; Director, Rifkind Levy Partnership, property development, since 1981; *b* Wolverhampton, 24 Jan. 1958; *s* of late Dr Joseph Rifkind and Renee Rifkind; *m* 1986, Simone Frances Sandelson; two *s*, and two step *s*. *Educ:* Clifton Coll. BA Law. Called to the Bar, Gray's Inn, 1981. Partner, MCC, Vision for Lord's, 2003–13. Facilitated Global Cities Exhibn, 2007, Mem., Corp. Adv. Gp, 2011–, Tate Mus.; Mem., Develt Cttee, 2011–, Trustee, 2012–, Design Mus. Fellow, Duke of Edinburgh's Internat. Awards, 2008, Chm., Business Adv. Gp, Duke of Edinburgh's Internat. Award Foundn, 2010–11. Chm., Develt Gp, Juvenile Diabetes Res. Foundn, 2010–; Member, Board: Wellington Hosp. Appeal,

2010–; Internat. Med. and Scis Fundraising Cttee, British Red Cross, 2011–. Gov., Arnold House Sch., 2002–. *Recreations:* golf, playing and watching tennis, cycling. *Address:* Rifkind Levy Partnership, 15 Hall Road, St John's Wood, NW8 9RD. *T:* (020) 7289 4444, *Fax:* (020) 7289 2028. *E:* charles@rifkind.co.uk. *Club:* Queen's.

RIFKIND, Rt Hon. Sir Malcolm (Leslie), KCMG 1997; PC 1986; QC (Scot.) 1985; *b* 21 June 1946; *yr s* of late E. Rifkind, Edinburgh; *m* 1970, Edith Amalia Rifkind (*née* Steinberg); one *s* one *d*. *Educ:* George Watson's Coll.; Edinburgh Univ. LLB, MSc. Lectured at Univ. of Rhodesia, 1967–68. Vis. Prof., Inst. for Advanced Studies in the Humanities, Edinburgh Univ., 1998. Called to Scottish Bar, 1970. Contested (C) Edinburgh, Central, 1970; MP (C) Edinburgh, Pentlands, Feb. 1974–1997; contested (C) same seat, 1997, 2001; MP (C) Kensington and Chelsea, 2005–10, Kensington, 2010–15. Opposition front bench spokesman on Scottish Affairs, 1975–76; Parly Under Sec. of State, Scottish Office, 1979–82, FCO, 1982–83; Minister of State, FCO, 1983–86; Secretary of State: for Scotland, 1986–90; for Transport, 1990–92; for Defence, 1992–95; for Foreign and Commonwealth Affairs, 1995–97; Opposition front bench spokesman on work and pensions, 2005. Jt Sec., Cons. Foreign and Commonwealth Affairs Cttee, 1978; Member: Select Cttee on Eur. Secondary Legislation, 1975–76; Select Cttee on Overseas Develt, 1978–79; Chm., Intelligence and Security Cttee, 2010–15. Non-exec. Dir, Unilever plc, 2010–15. Member: Bd, Nuclear Threat Initiative, 2014–; Panel of Eminent Persons on Eur. Security, OSCE, 2015–. Hon. Pres., Scottish Young Conservatives, 1975–76; Pres., Scottish Cons.-Unionist Party, 1998–2002. Mem., Royal Co. of Archers, Queen's Body Guard for Scotland, 1992; Hon. Col, 162 Movt Control Regt (V), RLC, 1997–2005; Hon. Col, City of Edinburgh Univs OTC, 2004–14 (Hon. Dep. Col, 1999–2004). Pres., Edinburgh Univ. Develt Trust, until 2014. Hon. LLD Napier, 1998; Dr *hc* Edinburgh, 2003. Commander: Order of Merit (Poland), 1998; Order of Grand Duke Gediminas (Lithuania), 2002. *Recreations:* walking, reading, field sports. *E:* m.rifkind@btinternet.com. *Clubs:* Pratt's, White's; New (Edinburgh).

RIGBY, Sir Anthony (John), 3rd Bt *cr* 1929, of Long Durford, Rogate. co. Sussex; *b* 3 Oct. 1946; *e s* of Lt-Col Sir (Hugh) John (Macbeth) Rigby, 2nd Bt and Mary Patricia Erskine Rigby (*née* Leacock); *S* father, 1999; *m* 1978, Mary Oliver; three *s* one *d*. *Educ:* Rugby. *Heir: e s* Oliver Hugh Rigby, *b* 20 Aug. 1979.

RIGBY, Brian, CBE 2003; Chairman, Walnut Tree Enterprises Ltd, since 2003; *b* 30 Aug. 1944; *s* of Donald Rigby and Margaret Rigby (*née* Dorrity); *m* 1986, Ann Passmore; one *s*. *Educ:* Birkenhead Sch.; Hertford Coll., Oxford (MA 1970); LSE (MSc 1972). Principal, DoE, 1971–77; British Telecommunications: joined, 1977; Dir, London, 1984–88; Dep. Man. Dir, Enterprises, 1988–92; Dir, Supply Mgt, 1992–97; Dir, Procurement Gp, HM Treasury, 1997–2000; Dep. Chief Exec., Office of Govt Commerce, 2000–03. Vis. Fellow, Warwick Business Sch., 2003–. Director: Oxford Radcliffe Hosp. NHS Trust, 2004–10; Partnership for Schools, 2005–12; Educn Funding Agency, 2012–. *Recreations:* people, places.

RIGBY, Bryan; Chairman, Anglo German Foundation, 1998–2009 (Trustee, since 1992); *b* 9 Jan. 1933; *s* of William George Rigby and Lily Rigby; *m* 1978, Marian Rosamund; one *s* one *d* of a former marriage, and one step *s* one step *d*. *Educ:* Wigan Grammar Sch.; King's Coll., London (BSc Special Chemistry, Dip. Chem. Engrg). UKAEA Industrial Gp, Capenhurst, 1955–60; Beecham Gp, London and Amsterdam, 1960–64; Laporte Industries (Holdings) Ltd, 1964–78; Dep. Dir-Gen., CBI, 1978–83; Man. Dir, UK Ops, 1984–87, UK, Ireland and Scandinavia, 1987–93, BASF Group; Chairman: Streamline Hldgs, 1994–98; Elliott Ross Associates, 1998–2003. Dir, MEDEVA plc, 1993–99. Mem., Social Security Adv. Cttee, 1994–99; Chm., Nurses' Pay Review Body, 1995–98. Vice-Pres., BAAS, 1992–96; Gov., Henley Management Coll., 1993–2002. Chm., Scannappeal, 1999–2011. *Recreations:* music, golf, gardening. *Address:* Cluny, 61 Penn Road, Beaconsfield, Bucks HP9 2LW. *T:* (01494) 673206. *Club:* Reform.

RIGBY, Jean Prescott, (Mrs Jamie Hayes); mezzo-soprano; Principal, English National Opera, 1982–90; *d* of late Thomas Boulton Rigby and of Margaret Annie Rigby; *m* 1987, Jamie Hayes; three *s*. *Educ:* Birmingham Sch. of Music (ABSM 1976); Royal Acad. of Music (Dip. RAM; Hon. ARAM 1984; Hon. FRAM 1989). ARCM 1979; ABC 1996. Début: Royal Opera House, Covent Garden, 1983; Glyndebourne Festival Opera, 1984; rôles, 1990–, include: Nicklaus, in The Tales of Hoffmann, Olga in Eugene Onegin, Royal Opera; Isabella, in The Italian Girl in Algiers, Buxton; title rôle, La Cenerentola, and Idamante in Idomeneo, Garsington; Charlotte, in Werther, San Diego and Seattle; Irene, in Theodora, Geneviève, in Pelléas and Mélisande, Eduige, in Rodelinda, Hippolyta, in A Midsummer Night's Dream, and Emilia, in Otello, Glyndebourne; *English National Opera:* Penelope, in The Return of Ulysses; title rôle, in The Rape of Lucretia; Amastris, in Xerxes; Rosina, in The Barber of Seville; Helen, in King Priam; Maddalena, in Rigoletto; Ruth, in The Pirates of Penzance; Suzuki, in Madam Butterfly; Mrs Ford, in Sir John in Love. Several TV performances, videos and over fifty recordings. Hon. Fellow, Birmingham Conservatoire, 2007. *Recreations:* British heritage, sport, cooking.

RIGBY, Sir Peter, Kt 2002; Founder, Chairman and Chief Executive, Rigby Group Plc (formerly Specialist Computer Holdings Plc), since 1975; *b* 29 Sept. 1943; *s* of late John and Phyllis Rigby; two *s*. Chm. and CEO, SCC Plc and subsidiaries, 1982–; President: SCC SA France, and subsidiaries, 2001–; SCC Holland BV, 2001–; SCC Spain SL, 2001–; SCC Romania, 2007–; SCD Middle East, Dubai, 2010–; SCD N Africa and Morocco, Casablanca, 2010–; Chairman: Eden Hotel Collection (formerly Mallory Court Hotel), 1995–; Patriot Aerospace Gp, 2002–, incorporating British Internat. Helicopters Ltd, Veritair Aviation Ltd, Patriot Aviation Ltd, London Helicopter Centres Ltd; Coventry and Warwicks Develt Partnership LLP, 2011–; Regl and City Airports Mgt, 2013–. Chm., Millennium Point Trust, 1996–2003; Founder and Trustee, Rigby Foundn, 1995–. Patron, Acorns Children's Hospice, 1993–. Chm., Coventry and Warwicks Local Enterprise Partnership, 2012–14 (Mem. Bd, 2011–). DL W Midlands, 2000. Liveryman, Hon. Co. of Air Pilots (formerly GAPAN), 2009–. FRAeS 2014. DUniv UCE, 1998; Hon. DSc Aston, 2003. *Recreations:* flying, classical music. *Address:* Rigby Group Plc, James House, Warwick Road, Birmingham B11 2LE. *T:* (0121) 766 7000, *Fax:* (0121) 766 2601. *E:* peter.rigby@scc.com.

RIGBY, Prof. Peter William Jack, PhD; FRS 2010; FMedSci; Professor of Developmental Biology, Institute of Cancer Research, University of London, 2001–12, now Emeritus; Member, Board of Governors, Wellcome Trust, 2008–June 2016 (Deputy Chairman, 2010–13); *b* 7 July 1947; *s* of late Jack Rigby and Lorna Rigby; *m* 1st, 1971, Paula Webb (marr. diss. 1983); 2nd, 1985, Julia Maidment; one *s*. *Educ:* Lower Sch. of John Lyon, Harrow; Jesus Coll., Cambridge (BA, PhD). MRC Lab. of Molecular Biol., Cambridge, 1971–73; Helen Hay Whitney Foundn Fellow, Stanford Univ. Med. Sch., 1973–76; Imperial College London: Lectr, then Sen. Lectr in Biochem., 1976–83; Reader in Tumour Virology, 1983–86; Vis. Prof., 1986–94 and 2000–08; Head, Div. of Eukaryotic Molecular Genetics, NIMR, MRC, 1986–2000 (Head, Genes and Cellular Controls Gp, 1986–96); Chief Exec., Inst. of Cancer Res., 1999–2011. Chm., MRC Gene Therapy Co-ordinating Cttee, 1992–96; Member: MRC Cell Bd, 1988–92; EMBO, 1979; Science Council, Celltech, 1982–2003; Scientific Cttee, Cancer Res. Campaign, 1983–88, 1996–99; Strategy Bd, BBSRC, 2004–06; Bd, Genome Res. Ltd, The Wellcome Trust Sanger Inst., 2006–14; Mem. Council, Marie Curie Cancer Care, 2008– (Chm., Cancer Res. Cttee, 2008–10). Chairman, Scientific Advisory Board: Topotarget (formerly Prolifix Ltd), 1996–2008; Hexagen Technology Ltd, 1996–98; Oxford Gene Technology, 2012–; Member, Scientific Advisory Board: Somatix Therapy Corp., 1989–97; deVGen NV, 1998–2000; KuDOS Pharmaceuticals, 1999–2006; Australian Regenerative Medicine Inst., 2011–. Non-executive Director: Royal Marsden NHS Foundn Trust, 2001–11; Proacta Therapeutics, 2001–03. Member: Council, Acad. of Med. Scis, 2002–04; Bd of Govs, Beatson Inst. for Cancer Res., Glasgow, 2003–06 (Dep. Chm., 2006–07); Council, St George's, Univ. of London (formerly St George's Hosp. Med. Sch.), 2003–10; Bd of Trustees, Univ. of London, 2008–11; Bd of Govs, Royal Brompton and Harefield NHS Foundn Trust, 2009–13; Chair, Bd of Trustee Dirs, Babraham Inst., 2014–. Chm. Medical Res. Cttee, and Mem. Nat. Council, Muscular Dystrophy Campaign, 2003–07; Chm., Wellcome Trust Principal Res. Fellowship Interview Cttee, 2004–07. FMedSci 1999. European Editor, Cell, 1984–97. *Publications:* papers on molecular biology in sci. jls. *Recreations:* narrow boats, listening to music, sport. *Address:* Chester Beatty Laboratories: Institute of Cancer Research, 237 Fulham Road, SW3 6JB. *T:* (020) 7153 5125. *Club:* Athenæum.

RIGG, Dame Diana, DBE 1994 (CBE 1988); actress; *b* Doncaster, Yorks, 20 July 1938; *d* of Louis Rigg and Beryl Helliwell; *m* 1982, Archibald Stirling; one *d*. *Educ:* Fulneck Girls' Sch., Pudsey. Trained for the stage at Royal Academy of Dramatic Art. First appearance on stage in RADA prod. in York Festival, at Theatre Royal, York, summer, 1957 (Natella Abashwili in The Caucasian Chalk Circle); after appearing in repertory in Chesterfield and in York she joined the Royal Shakespeare Company, Stratford-upon-Avon, 1959; first appearance in London, Aldwych Theatre, 1961 (2nd Ondine, Violanta and Princess Berthe in Ondine); at same theatre, in repertory (The Devils, Becket, The Taming of the Shrew), 1961; (Madame de Tourvel, The Art of Seduction), 1962; Royal Shakespeare, Stratford-upon-Avon, April 1962 (Helena in A Midsummer Night's Dream, Bianca in The Taming of the Shrew, Lady Macduff in Macbeth, Adriana in The Comedy of Errors, Cordelia in King Lear); subseq. appeared in the last production at the Aldwych, Dec. 1962, followed by Adriana in The Comedy of Errors and Monica Stettler in The Physicists, 1963. Toured the provinces, spring, 1963, in A Midsummer Night's Dream; subseq. appeared at the Royal Shakespeare, Stratford, and at the Aldwych, in Comedy of Errors, Dec. 1963; again played Cordelia in King Lear, 1964, prior to touring with both plays for the British Council, in Europe, the USSR, and the US; during this tour she first appeared in New York (State Theatre), 1964, in same plays; Viola in Twelfth Night, Stratford, June 1966; Heloise in Abelard and Heloise, Wyndham's, 1970, also at the Atkinson, New York, 1971; joined The National Theatre, 1972: in Jumpers, 'Tis Pity She's a Whore and Lady Macbeth in Macbeth, 1972; The Misanthrope, 1973, Washington and NY, 1975; Phaedra Britannica, 1975 (Plays and Players Award for Best Actress); The Guardsman, 1978; Pygmalion, Albery, 1974; Night and Day, Phoenix, 1978 (Plays and Players award, 1979); Colette, USA, 1982; Heartbreak House, Haymarket, 1983; Little Eyolf, Lyric, Hammersmith, 1985; Antony and Cleopatra, Chichester, 1985; Wildfire, Phoenix, 1986; Follies, Shaftesbury, 1987; Love Letters, San Francisco, 1990; All for Love, Almeida, 1991; Berlin Bertie, Royal Court, 1992; Medea, Almeida, 1992, transf. Wyndhams, 1993–94 (Evening Standard Drama Award), then NY, 1994 (Tony Award); Mother Courage, RNT, 1995; Who's Afraid of Virginia Woolf?, Almeida, 1996; Phèdre, and Britannicus, Albery, 1998; Humble Boy, RNT, 2001; Suddenly Last Summer, Albery, 2004; Honour, Wyndham's, 2006; All About my Mother, Old Vic, 2007; The Cherry Orchard, Chichester, 2008; Hay Fever, Chichester, 2009; *films include:* A Midsummer Night's Dream, Assassination Bureau, On Her Majesty's Secret Service, Julius Caesar, The Hospital, Theatre of Blood, A Little Night Music, The Great Muppet Caper, Evil Under the Sun (Film Actress of the Year Award, Variety Club, 1983), A Good Man in Africa, Heidi, The Painted Veil; *television appearances include:* Sentimental Agent, The Comedy of Errors, The Avengers (Special Award, BAFTA, 2000), Married Alive, Diana (US series), In This House of Brede (US), Three Piece Suite, The Serpent Son, Hedda Gabler, The Marquise, Little Eyolf, King Lear, Witness of the Prosecution, Bleak House, Mother Love (BAFTA award), Unexplained Laughter, Moll Flanders (serial), Rebecca (Emmy Award for Best Supporting Actress, 1997), The Mrs Bradley Mysteries, Victoria and Albert, Charles II: The Power and the Passion, Game of Thrones, and others. Chair, MacRoberts Arts Centre; Mem., BM Develt Fund. A Vice-Pres., Baby Life Support Systems (BLISS), 1984–. Cameron Mackintosh Vis. Prof. of Contemporary Theatre, Oxford Univ., 1999; Emeritus Fellow, St Catherine's Coll., Oxford. Chancellor, Stirling Univ., 1997–2008. Foreign Hon. Mem., American Acad. of Arts and Scis. *Publications:* No Turn Unstoned, 1982; So to the Land, 1994. *Recreations:* reading, trying to get organized. *Address:* c/o Dalzell and Beresford, Paddock Suite, The Courtyard, 55 Charterhouse Street, EC1M 6HA.

RIGG, (Ian) Malcolm; Director, Policy Studies Institute, 2004–13, now Visiting Research Fellow; *b* 31 Jan. 1947; *s* of Donald Appleby Rigg and Marjorie Isobel Connell Rigg (*née* Smiley); *m* 1982, Lesley Saunders, DPhil; one *s*, and one step *s* one step *d*. *Educ:* Magdalen College Sch., Oxford; Enfield Coll. of Technol. (BA Business Studies). Director: IFF Res., 1978–82; Sample Surveys, 1982–83; Sen. Res. Fellow, PSI, 1984–90; Head of Inf., Consumers' Assoc., 1990–94; Dir of Res., COI Communications, 1994–97; Managing Director: BMRB Social Res., 1997–2000; BMRB Internat., 2001–04. Mem., Ofgem Panel for Electricity Stakeholder Engagement Scheme, 2012–. Market Research Society: Mem. Council, 1995–97; Vice-Chm., 1996–97; Chairman: Professional Standards Cttee, 1995–97; Professional Develt Adv. Bd, 1997–2004. Mem. Cttee, Assoc. of Res. Centres in Soc. Scis, 2005–. Mem., Bd of Trustees, Involve, 2010–. Chm., Slough CAB, 2013–; Exec. Dir, Slough Healthwatch, 2013–. FAcSS. Mem., PSI Team, HEFCE Strategic Rev. of Sustainable Develt in Higher Educn in England, 2008. *Publications:* Training in Britain: individuals' perspectives, 1989; Continuing Training in Firms and Trainer Development in Britain, 1991; (jtly) Electronic Government: the view from the queue, 1999; (jtly) Food Labels and Food Choice: what do people actually understand and use?, 2012. *Recreations:* tandem triathlon, cycling up hills, social justice, music festivals, avant-garde jazz, poetry, Tottenham Hotspur season ticket holder (an annual entitlement to hope with minimal chance of fulfilment). *Address:* 15 Herschel Street, Slough SL1 1PB. *T:* (01753) 576432. *E:* malcolm.rigg@btinternet.com.

RIGGE, Marianne, (Mrs Trevor Goodchild), OBE 2000; Director, College of Health, 1983–2003; *b* 10 May 1948; *d* of late Dr Patrick Noel O'Mahony and Elizabeth Nora O'Mahony (*née* Daly); *m* 1st, 1968, John Simon Rigge; two *d* (one *s* decd); 2nd, 1990, Trevor Goodchild. *Educ:* St Angela's Ursuline Convent, London; University College London (BA Hons French). PA, Consumers' Assoc., 1971–76; Res. Asst to Chm., Nat. Consumer Council, 1976–77; founder Dir, Mutual Aid Centre, 1977–83. Member: Clinical Outcomes Gp, 1993–97; Clinical Systems Gp, 1997–2000; NICE Partners Council, 1999–2002; Nat. Access Taskforce, 2000–02. Non-exec. Dir, Whipps Cross Univ. Hosp. NHS Trust, 2001–08. Editor, Self Health, 1985–87; columnist, Health Service Jl, 1999–2003. *Publications:* (with Michael Young) Mutual Aid in a Selfish Society, 1979; Building Societies and the Consumer, 1981; Hello, Can I Help You, 1981; Prospects for Worker Co-operatives in Europe, 1981; (with Michael Young) Revolution from Within, 1983; Annual Guide to Hospital Waiting Lists, 1984–92. *Recreations:* gardening, cooking, music. *Address:* 157 Whipps Cross Road, E11 1NP. *T:* (020) 8530 4420.

RIGGS, David George; Corporate Finance Executive, Australian Government Solicitor, since 2014 (Chief Financial Officer, 1998–2014); *b* 6 May 1942. *Educ:* Bury GS; Manchester Univ. (BA Econ.). CPFA (IPFA 1963). With Bury CBC, 1958–68; Greater London Council, 1968–82: Finance Officer, 1968–74; Hd of Public Services Finance, 1974–76; Asst Comptroller of Finance, 1976–82; Dir of Finance, ILEA, 1982–90; Dir of Finance, Benefits Agency, 1991–98. *Address:* 48 Jacka Crescent, Campbell, ACT 2612, Australia.

RIGNEY, Andrew James; QC 2010; *b* Oldham, 26 Aug. 1967; *s* of Arthur George Rigney and Mary Rigney; *m* 1998, Jane Allison; one *s* two *d*. *Educ:* Hulme Grammar Sch., Oldham; Christ's Coll., Cambridge (BA 1989; MA 1993); City Univ. (DipLaw 1998). Called to the

Bar, Gray's Inn, 1992; in practice as barrister, specialising in construction, insurance and professional indemnity. *Recreations:* family, reading, music, travel. *Address:* Crown Office Chambers, 2 Crown Office Row, Temple, EC4Y 7HJ. *T:* (020) 7797 8100, *Fax:* (020) 7797 8101.

RIIS-JØRGENSEN, Birger; Ambassador of Denmark to Italy and also accredited to Malta and San Marino, since 2011; *b* 13 Jan. 1949; *s* of Jens and Thyra Jørgensen; *m* 1978, Karin Rasmussen; two *s*. *Educ:* Univ. of Copenhagen (MA Hist. 1974); studies in Sweden and USA. Res. Librarian, Royal Liby, Copenhagen, 1975; joined Danish Foreign Service, 1976; First Sec., Danish Delegn to NATO, Brussels, 1979–83; Hd of Section, Min. of For. Affairs, and Sec. to For. Affairs Cttee of Parlt, 1983–86; Counsellor, Secretariat for Eur. Political Co-operation, Brussels, 1987–88; Hd of Section and Dep. Hd of Dept, Danish Internat. Develt Agency, 1989–91; Ministry of Foreign Affairs: Hd, Africa Dept, 1991–94; Hd, Middle East and Latin America Dept, 1994–96; Under-Sec. for Bilateral Affairs, 1996–2000; State Sec. and Hd of Trade Council of Denmark, 2000–06; Ambassador to the Court of St James's, 2006–11. Member Board of Directors: Industrialisation Fund for Developing Countries, 1996–2000; Fund for Industrialisation of Eastern Europe, 1996–2000; Danish Co-Chm., US/Denmark/ Greenland Cttee for Econ., Technical, Scientific and Cultural Co-operation, 2004–06. Comdr of First Class, Order of the Dannebrog (Denmark), 2009. *Recreations:* tennis, bicycling, sea-kayaking, swimming, modern history, classical music. *Address:* Ambasciata di Danimarca, Via dei Monti Parioli 50, 00197 Rome, Italy. *T:* (06) 9774831, *Fax:* (06) 97748399. *E:* birrii@um.dk. *Club:* Athenæum.

RILEY, Bridget Louise, CH 1999; CBE 1972; artist; *b* 24 April 1931; *d* of late John Riley and Louise (*née* Gladstone). *Educ:* Cheltenham Ladies' College; Goldsmiths' School of Art; Royal College of Art. ARCA 1955. Mem., RSA. Exhibitions: Gall. One, London, 1962–63; Drawings, Mus. of Modern Art, NY, 1966–67; (with Philip King) XXXIV Biennale Venice, 1968; (retrospective) British Council touring exhibn, Hanover, Berne, Dusseldorf, Turin, Prague, 1970–72; (retrospective) touring exhibn, US, Aust., Japan, 1978–80; Working with Colour, Arts Council of GB touring exhibn, 1984–85; According to Sensation: Paintings 82–92, Arts Council of GB touring exhibn, Germany and Hayward Gall., London, 1992; Paintings from the 60s and 70s, Serpentine Gall., London, 1999; Paintings 1982–2000 and Early Works on Paper, PaceWildenstein, NY, 2000; Reconnaissance, DIA Center for Arts, NY, 2001; (retrospective) Tate Britain, 2003; New Work, Krefeld, Germany, 2004; Mus. of Contemp. Art, Sydney, Aust., 2004–05; (retrospective) Colour, Stripes, Planes and Curves, Kettle's Yard, Cambridge, 2011; (retrospective) Works 1960–66, Karsten Schubert, London and Hazlitt Holland-Hibbert, London, 2012; (retrospective) The Stripe Paintings, David Zwirner Gall., 2014; The Curve Paintings 1961–2014, De La Warr Pavilion, 2015; (retrospective) Learning from Seurat, Courtauld Gall., 2015–16. Public collections include: Tate Gallery; Victoria and Albert Museum; Arts Council; British Council; Museum of Modern Art, New York; Australian Nat. Gallery, Canberra; Museum of Modern Art, Pasadena; Ferens Art Gallery, Hull; Allbright Knox, Buffalo, USA; Museum of Contemporary Art, Chicago; Ulster Museum, Ireland; Stedelijk Museum, Amsterdam; Berne Kunsthalle; Mus. of Modern Art, Tokyo. Designed Colour Moves, for Ballet Rambert, 1983. Trustee, Nat. Gallery, 1981–88. Hon. DLitt: Manchester, 1976; Ulster, 1986; Oxford, 1993; Cambridge, 1995; De Montfort, 1996; Exeter, 1997; London, 2005. AICA critics Prize, 1963; Stuyvesant Bursary, 1964; Ohara Mus. Prize, Tokyo, 1972; Gold Medal, Grafik Biennale, Norway, 1980; Praemium Imperiale for Painting, 2003. *Address:* c/o Karsten Schubert, 46 Lexington Street, W1F 0LP.

RILEY, Christopher John; Associate, Oxera Consulting Ltd, since 2005; *b* 20 Jan. 1947; *s* of Bernard Francis Riley and Phyllis (*née* Wigley); *m* 1982, Helen Marion Mynett; two *s*. *Educ:* Ratcliffe Coll., Leicester; Wadham Coll., Oxford (MA Maths); Univ. of East Anglia (MA Econs). Economist, HM Treasury, 1969–77; Res. Fellow, Nuffield Coll., Oxford, 1977–78; Sen. Economic Advr, 1978–88, Under Sec., 1988–95, HM Treasury; Chief Economist, DoE, subseq. DETR, then DTLR, later DfT, 1995–2005. *Publications:* various articles in books and learned jls. *Recreation:* music - especially choral singing. *Address:* 10 Briarwood Road, SW4 9PX. *T:* (020) 7720 6263. *E:* chris@h-riley.gotadsl.co.uk.

RILEY, Prof. Eleanor Mary, PhD; FMedSci; FRSB; Professor of Infectious Disease Immunology, London School of Hygiene and Tropical Medicine, University of London, since 1998; *b* Wrexham, N Wales, 30 June 1956; *d* of Robert Malcolm Riley and Yvonne Mary Riley (*née* Hall). *Educ:* Banbury Grammar Sch.; Univ. of Bristol (BSc Cellular Pathol. 1978; BVSc 1980); Univ. of Liverpool (PhD 1985). Intern in Veterinary Pathol., Cornell Univ., 1980–81; Sen. Scientist, MRC Labs, The Gambia, 1985–90; Wellcome Trust Sen. Res. Fellow, Univ. of Edinburgh, 1990–98. Consultant, USAID Malaria Vaccine Develt Prog., 2013–. Chair, Biosci. for Health Strategy Adv. Panel, BBSRC, 2014–; Dep. Chair, Infections and Immunity Bd, MRC, 2015–. FMedSci 2014; FRSB (FSB 2015). Ed., Parasite Immunol., 2002–. *Recreations:* walking, local politics, yoga, theatre, tidying the garden, coffee. *Address:* London School of Hygiene and Tropical Medicine, Keppel Street, WC1E 7HT. *T:* (020) 7927 2706. *E:* eleanor.riley@lshtm.ac.uk.

RILEY, Lt-Gen. Jonathon Peter, CB 2008; DSO 1996; Director-General and Master of the Royal Armouries, 2009–12; *b* 16 Jan. 1955; *s* of John Sisson Riley and Joyce Riley (*née* Outen); *m* 1st, 1980, Kathryn Mary Beard (marr. diss. 2000); one *s* one *d*; 2nd, 2009, Sara Elinor Edwards, *qv*; one *d*. *Educ:* St Mary's, Beverley; Kingston Sch.; UCL (BA Geog. 1979); Leeds Univ. (MA Hist. 1989); Cranfield Univ. (PhD 2006). Commnd Queen's Royal Regt, 1974; Staff Coll., 1987; Bde Major, 6th Armd Bde, 1989; transferred to RWF, 1990; mil. observer, Balkan war, 1992–93; DS, Staff Coll., 1993–94; CO, 1 RWF, 1994–96; COS, 1st Armd Div., 1996–98; Dep. Comdt, Multinat. Div. (SW), Bosnia, 1998–99; Commander: 1 Mechanized Bde, Sierra Leone, 1999–2001; Jt Task Force Comd, and Mil. Advr to Govt of Sierra Leone, 2000–01; Dep. Comdt, Staff Coll., 2001–03; Dep. Comdg Gen., New Iraqi Army, 2003; rcds 2004; GOC British Troops, Iraq, and Comdg Gen., Multinat. Div. (SE), Iraq, 2004–05; Sen. British Mil. Advr, US Central Comd, 2005–07; Dep. Comdr, NATO Internat. Security Assistance Force, Afghanistan, 2007–08. Col, Royal Welch Fusiliers, 2005–06. Vis. Prof. in War Studies, KCL, 2010, 2012–; Fellow in Internat. Politics, Univ. of Aberystwyth, 2011–12; ext. examiner in defence mgt and technol., Cranfield Univ., 2009–14. Mem., Welsh Govt World War I Commemoration Prog. Bd, 2013–. Expert Witness, Internat. Criminal Court, 2012–. Trustee, CDISS, 2006–08; Mem., Catholic Records Soc., 2005–. Liveryman, Armourers' and Brasiers' Co., 2011. Officer, Legion of Merit (US), 2005; NATO MSM, 2009. *Publications:* History of the Queen's, 1988; From Pole to Pole, 1989, 2nd edn 2001; Soldiers of the Queen, 1992; White Dragon, 1995; Napoleon and the World War 1813, 2000; The Royal Welch Fusiliers 1945–2000, 2001; The Life and Campaigns of General Hughie Stockwell, 2006; Napoleon as a General, 2007; (ed) That Astonishing Infantry, 2007; Decisive Battles, 2010; (ed) Up to Mametz and Beyond, 2010; A Matter of Honour, 2011; 1813: empire at bay, 2013; The Last Ironsides, 2014; The First Colonial Soldiers, vol. 1, 2014, vol. 2, 2015; Oft in Danger: the life and campaigns of General Sir Anthony Farrar-Hockley, 2015. *Recreations:* field sports, white water rafting, rowing, historical research, poetry and English literature. *Club:* Naval and Military.

RILEY, Very Rev. Kenneth Joseph, OBE 2003; Dean of Manchester, 1993–2005, now Emeritus; *b* 25 June 1940; *s* of Arthur and Mary Josephine Riley; *m* 1968, Margaret; two *d*. *Educ:* Holywell GS; UCW, Aberystwyth (BA 1961); Linacre Coll., Oxford (BA 1964; MA); Wycliffe Hall, Oxford. Ordained deacon, 1964, priest, 1965; Asst Curate, Emmanuel Ch, Fazakerley, Liverpool, 1964–66; Chaplain: Brasted Place Coll., 1966–69; Oundle Sch., 1969–74; Liverpool Univ., 1974–83; Vicar, Mossley Hill, Liverpool, 1975–83; RD, Childwall, 1982–83; Canon Treas., 1983–87, Canon Precentor, 1987–93, Liverpool Cathedral. *Publications:* Liverpool Cathedral, 1987. *Recreations:* music, drama, films. *Address:* 145 Turning Lane, Southport PR8 5HZ. *T:* (01704) 542155.

RILEY, Philip Stephen; Chairman, Orion Media Ltd, since 2015 (Chief Executive, 2009–15); *b* 4 June 1959; *s* of James and Marie Riley; *m* 1992, Jean Fiveash; one *s* two *d*. *Educ:* Loughborough Univ. (BSc Hons 1980); Columbia Business Sch. (MBA Beta Gamma Sigma 1988). Prog. Dir, BRMB Radio, 1989–90; Managing Director: Radio Aire, 1990–94; 100.7 Heart FM, 1994–96; Man. Dir, 1996–99, Chief Exec., 1999–2007, Chrysalis Radio. Member, Board: Commercial Radio Companies' Assoc., 1994–2007; Radio Advertising Bureau, 1996–2007; RAJAR, 2004–07. Trustee, Acorns Children's Hospice Trust, 2014–.

RILEY, Sara Elinor; *see* Edwards, S. E.

RILEY, Stephen Michael, FSA; Director, Maritime Heritage, National Maritime Museum, Greenwich, 2002–07; *b* 4 April 1950; *s* of Jack and Constance Riley; partner, Jane Avard Weeks; one *s* one *d*. *Educ:* Liverpool Univ. (BA Hons 1972); Univ. of Leicester (Post-grad. Cert. in Mus. Studies 1974). FSA 2007. Curatorial trainee, Maritime Hist., Merseyside Co. Mus, Liverpool, 1972–76; National Maritime Museum, Greenwich: Dep. Hd, Dept of Ships and Antiquities, 1986–92; Director: Property and Tech. Services, 1993–95; Display Div., 1995–98; Neptune Court Re-develt Project, 1998–99; Nat. Maritime Mus. Galls, 1999–2001. *Recreations:* classic boats and classic cars, photography, travel, reading, music, gardening.

RILEY-SMITH, Prof. Jonathan Simon Christopher, FRHistS; Dixie Professor of Ecclesiastical History, Cambridge University, 1994–2005, now Emeritus; Fellow, Emmanuel College, Cambridge, 1994–2005; Librarian, Order of St John, since 2005; *b* 27 June 1938; *s* of late William Henry Douglas Riley-Smith and Elspeth Agnes Mary Riley-Smith (*née* Craik Henderson); *m* 1968, Marie-Louise Jeannetta, *d* of Wilfred John Sutcliffe Field; one *s* two *d*. *Educ:* Eton College; Trinity College, Cambridge (MA, PhD, LittD). Dept of Mediaeval History, University of St Andrews: Asst Lectr, 1964–65; Lectr, 1966–72; Faculty of History, Cambridge: Asst Lectr, 1972–75; Lectr, 1975–78; Chm., Bd, 1997–99; Queens' College, Cambridge: Fellow and Dir of Studies in History, 1972–78; Praelector, 1973–75; Librarian, 1973, 1977–78; Prof. of History, Univ. of London, 1978–94 (at RHC, 1978–85, at RHBNC, 1985–94); Head of Dept of History, RHC, then RHBNC, 1984–90. Stewart Short-Term Vis. Fellow, Princeton Univ., 2001. Lectures: Bampton, Columbia Univ., 2007; Robert M. Conway, Univ. of Notre Dame, 2008. Chairman: Bd of Management, Inst. of Historical Res., 1988–94 (Hon. Fellow, 1997); Victoria County Hist. Cttee, 1989–97; Pres., Soc. for the Study of the Crusades and the Latin East, 1990–95. Corresp. Fellow, Medieval Acad. of America, 2006. BGCStJ 2013 (Librarian: Priory of Scotland, 1966–78; Grand Priory, subseq. Priory of England and the Islands, 1982–2007); KM 1971 (Officer of Merit, 1985); Knight Grand Cross of Grace and Devotion, Order of Malta, 2007. Prix Schlumberger, Acad. des Inscriptions et Belles-Lettres, Paris, 1988. Gold Medal of Merit, Johanniter Orde (Netherlands), 2013. *Publications:* The Knights of St John in Jerusalem and Cyprus, 1967; (with U. and M. C. Lyons) Ayyubids, Mamlukes and Crusaders, 1971; The Feudal Nobility and the Kingdom of Jerusalem, 1973; What were the Crusades?, 1977, 4th edn 2009 (trans. German 2003, Croatian 2007); (with L. Riley-Smith) The Crusades: idea and reality, 1981; The First Crusade and the Idea of Crusading, 1986; The Crusades: a short history, 1987, 3rd edn 2014 (trans. French 1990, Italian 1994); (ed) The Atlas of the Crusades, 1991 (trans. German 1992, French 1996); The Oxford Illustrated History of the Crusades, 1995; (with N. Coureas) Cyprus and the Crusades, 1995; (jtly) Montjoie, 1997; The First Crusaders, 1997; Hospitallers: the history of the Order of St John, 1999; Al seguito delle Crociate, 2000; (jtly) Dei gesta per Francos, 2001; (jtly) In Laudem Hierosolymitani, 2007; The Crusades, Christianity and Islam, 2008; Crusaders and Settlers in the Latin East, 2009; Templars and Hospitallers as Professed Religious in the Holy Land, 2010; The Knights Hospitaller in the Levant, *c* 1070–1309, 2012; articles in learned jls. *Recreation:* the past and present of own family. *Address:* Emmanuel College, Cambridge CB2 3AP. *T:* (01223) 334200.

RIMER, Rt Hon. Sir Colin (Percy Farquharson), Kt 1994; PC 2007; a Lord Justice of Appeal, 2007–14; *b* 30 Jan. 1944; *s* of late Kenneth Rowland Rimer and Maria Eugenia Rimer (*née* Farquharson); *m* 1970, Penelope Ann Gibbs; two *s* one *d*. *Educ:* Dulwich Coll.; Trinity Hall, Cambridge (MA, LLB; Hon. Fellow, 2009). Legal Assistant, Inst. of Comparative Law, Paris, 1967–68; called to the Bar, Lincoln's Inn, 1968, Bencher, 1994; QC 1988; in practice, 1969–94; a Judge of the High Court of Justice, Chancery Div., 1994–2007. *Recreations:* music, novels, walking.

RIMER, Jennifer; Head Teacher, St Mary's Music School, Edinburgh, 1996–2013; *b* Kirkcaldy; *d* of James and Margaret Whitelaw; *m* 1971, David Rimer; three *d*. *Educ:* Buckhaven High Sch., Fife; Univ. of Edinburgh (BMus Hons 1969; DipEd 1970). LRAM 1968; Hon. ARAM 2009. Teacher, Church High Sch., Newcastle, 1970–72; Principal Teacher, Music, St David's High Sch., Dalkeith, 1972–77; Music and Piano Teacher, 1982–93, Hd, Acad. Music, Careers and Guidance, 1993–96, St Mary's Music Sch., Edinburgh. Music and Piano Teacher, George Heriot's Sch., Edinburgh, 2013–15. Examiner, setter and marker, SQA, 1978–2015. Founder Fellow, Inst. of Contemp. Scotland, 2000; Member: Eur. Piano Teachers' Assoc., 1975–; Sch. Leaders Scotland (formerly Headteachers' Assoc. of Scotland), 2001–. Gov., George Heriot's Sch., 1990–2000; Director: Edinburgh Youth Orch., 1990–93; Nat. Youth Orch. of Scotland, 2009–. *Publications:* contrib. Jl of Scottish Educn. *Recreations:* family, theatre, opera, concerts, art galleries, piano, viola, books, youth orchestras, walking, yoga. *E:* jennifer_rimer@hotmail.com.

RIMINGTON, John David, CB 1987; Director-General, Health and Safety Executive, 1984–95; *b* 27 June 1935; *s* of late John William Rimington, MBE, and of Mabel Dorrington; *m* 1963, Dame Stella Rimington, *qv*; two *d*. *Educ:* Nottingham High Sch.; Jesus Coll., Cambridge (Cl. I Hons History, MA). Nat. Service Commn, RA, 1954–56. Joined BoT, 1959; seconded HM Treasury (work on decimal currency), 1961; Principal, Tariff Div., BoT, 1963; 1st Sec. (Economic), New Delhi, 1965; Mergers Div., DTI, 1969; Dept of Employment, 1970; Asst Sec. 1972 (Employment Policy and Manpower); Counsellor, Social and Regional Policy, UK perm. representation to EEC, Brussels, 1974; MSC, 1977–81; Under Sec. 1978; Dir, Safety Policy Div., HSE, 1981–83; Dep. Sec., 1984; Permanent Sec., 1992. Non-executive Director: Magnox Electric, 1996–98; BNFL, 1998–2000; Angel Trains Gp (formerly Angel Train Contracts) Ltd, 1999–2006. Mem. Nat. Council, 1995–2008, Vice Chm., 2001–07, Hon. Vice-Pres., 2008–, Consumers' Assoc. Visiting Professor: Univ. of Strathclyde, 1997–99; Salford Univ., 1999–. CCMI (CIMgt 1993). Hon. DSc Sheffield, 1995. *Publications:* articles on risk; contrib. to RIPA Jl, New Asia Review, Trans IChemE, Pol Quarterly, etc. *Recreations:* playing the piano, gardening, watching cricket. *Address:* 9 Highbury Hill, N5 1SU. *Club:* Athenæum.

RIMINGTON, Dame Stella, DCB 1996; Director General, Security Service, 1992–96; *b* 1935; *m* 1963, John David Rimington, *qv*; two *d*. *Educ:* Nottingham High Sch. for Girls; Edinburgh Univ. (MA). Security Service, 1969. Non-executive Director: Marks & Spencer plc, 1997–2004; Whitehead Mann GKR (formerly GKR), 1997–2001; BG plc, 1997–2000; BG Gp, 2000–05; Royal Marsden NHS Trust, 1998–2001. Chm., Inst. of Cancer Res., 1997–2001. Chm. of Judges, Man Booker Prize, 2011. Trustee: RAF Mus., 1998–2001; Refuge, 2007–. Hon. Air Cdre, No 7006 (VR) Intelligence Sqn, RAuxAF, 1997–2001. Hon. LLD: Nottingham, 1995; Exeter, 1996; London Metropolitan, 2004; Liverpool, 2005; Hon. DSocSc Nottingham Trent, 2009. *Publications:* Open Secret (autobiog.), 2001; novels: At

Risk, 2004; Secret Asset, 2006; Illegal Action, 2007; Dead Line, 2008; Present Danger, 2009; Rip Tide, 2011; The Geneva Trap, 2012; Close Call, 2014. *Address:* PO Box 1604, SW1P 1XB.

RIMMER, Henry, (Harry), CBE 1994; DL; Member (Lab) Liverpool City Council, 1952–53 and 1987–96; Leader, Liverpool City Council, 1990–96; *b* 19 May 1928; *s* of Thomas and Sarah Ellen Rimmer; *m* 1st, 1951, Doreen Taylor (marr. diss. 1978); three *s* one *d*; 2nd, 1978, Joan Conder. *Educ:* Oulton High Sch.; Liverpool Collegiate Sch. Mem., Merseyside CC, 1981–86 (Dep. Leader, 1982–86). Member: Merseyside Police Authy, 1987–96 (Vice-Chm., 1990–92); Bd, Merseyside Develt Corp., 1991–98. Director: Wavertree Technology Park Co., 1987–96; Liverpool Airport PLC, 1989–96. DL Merseyside, 1997. *Recreations:* country walking, supporting Liverpool Football Club. *Address:* Flat 103 Ash Grange, Brookside Avenue, Knotty Ash, Liverpool L14 7NQ. *T:* (0151) 220 6022.

RIMMER, Marie Elizabeth, CBE 2005; MP (Lab) St Helens South and Whiston, since 2015; *b* St Helens, 27 April 1947. With Pilkington Glass, 1962–99, incl. Stats and Accounts Dept, buyer of engrg equipt for glass prodn lines, and Health and Safety Advr, Float Glass Manufg. Mem. (Lab), St Helens MBC, 1978– (Leader, 1985–93, 1999–2013). Trustee, St Helens Hope Centre. *Address:* House of Commons, SW1A 0AA.

RIMMER, Paul Derek James; Director, Ministry of Defence, since 2014; *b* Birmingham, 17 April 1960; *s* of James Derek Rimmer and Sylvia Rimmer (*née* Baker-Sherman); *m* 1990, Jill Mary Venables Turner; two *s*. *Educ:* Bishop Vesey's Grammar Sch., Sutton Coldfield; Univ. of Keele (BA (Hons) Internat. Relns). Ministry of Defence: Defence Intelligence Staff, 1983; jsdc, 1993–94; Procurement Exec., 1994; Overseas Secretariat, 2000; Principal Private Sec. to Sec. of State for Defence, 2008–09; Chief of the Assessments Staff, Cabinet Office, 2009 (on secondment); COS (Policy and Finance), Perm. Jt HQ, 2012–14. Hon. Col, 3MI Bn Intelligence Corps, 2011–. *Recreations:* my family, hill walking, military history. *Address:* c/o Ministry of Defence, Main Building, Whitehall, SW1A 2HB.

RIMMER, Air Vice-Marshal Thomas William, CB 2001; OBE 1987; FRAeS, FRGS; Commander, British Forces Cyprus, 2000–03; *b* 16 Dec. 1948; *s* of William Thompson Rimmer and Elizabeth Comrie Rimmer (*née* Baird); *m* 1976, Sarah Caroline Hale; one *s* one *d*. *Educ:* Morrison's Academy, Crieff; Montpelier Univ., France; Edinburgh Univ. (MA Hons 1970). FRAeS 1997. Graduated RAF Cranwell, 1972; served Central Flying Sch., RAF Linton-on-Ouse, RAF Bruggen, RAF Coltishall, to 1983; French Air Force Staff Coll., 1983–84; Chief Instructor, RAF Cottesmore, 1984–87; HQ RAF Germany, 1987–89; Head, RAF Presentation Team, 1989–90; Station Comdr, RAF Cottesmore, 1990–92; Senior UK Mil. Officer, WEU, 1992–94; rcds 1995; MoD, 1996–98; AOC and Comdt, RAF Coll., Cranwell, 1999–2000. FRGS 2010. Liveryman, Tallow Chandlers' Co., 1992– (Warden, 2011–14). QCVSA 1983. *Recreations:* offshore sailing, golf, gardening (mechanical), vintage tractors. *Clubs:* Royal Air Force; RAF Yacht, RAF Sailing Assoc.

RIMMINGTON, Rosemary Jean Neil; *see* Conley, R. J. N.

RINGEN, Mary Christina; *see* Chamberlain, M. C.

RINGEN, Prof. Stein; Professor of Sociology and Social Policy, University of Oxford, 1990–2012, now Emeritus; Fellow of Green Templeton College (formerly Green College), Oxford, 1990–2012, now Emeritus; *b* 5 July 1945; *s* of John Ringen and Anna Ringen (*née* Simengard); *m* 2002, Prof. Mary Christina Chamberlain, *qv*. *Educ:* Univ. of Oslo (MA, dr. philos.). Broadcasting reporter, Norwegian Broadcasting Corp., 1970–71; Fellow, Internat. Peace Res. Inst., Oslo, 1971–72; Head of Secretariat, Norwegian Level of Living Study, 1972–76; Fellow, Inst. for Social Res., Oslo, 1976–78; Head of Res., Min. of Consumer Affairs and Govt Admin, Oslo, 1978–83; Prof. of Welfare Studies, Univ. of Stockholm, 1983–86; Sen. Res. Scientist, Central Bureau of Statistics, Oslo, 1986–88; Asst Dir Gen., Min. of Justice, Oslo, 1988–90. Mem., Royal Commn on Human Values, Norway, 1998–2001. Adjunct Prof., Lillehammer University Coll., 2009–15; Hon. Professor: Central China Normal Univ., 2012–; Sun Yat-sen Univ., 2014–; Vis. Prof., Richmond, the American Internat. Univ., London, 2012–. Fellow, European Acad. of Sociol., 2009. FRSA. Hon. Dr Masaryk Univ., Czech Republic, 2008. *Publications:* The Possibility of Politics, 1987, 3rd edn 2006; Citizens, Families and Reform, 1997, 2nd edn 2005; Reformdemokratiet, 1997; The Family in Question, 1998; Veien til det gode liv, 2000; What Democracy Is For, 2007; The Liberal Vision and Other Essays on Democracy and Progress, 2007; The Economic Consequences of Mr Brown: how a strong government was defeated by a weak system of governance, 2009; The Korean State and Social Policy: how South Korea lifted itself from poverty and dictatorship to affluence and democracy, 2011; Nation of Devils: democracy and the problem of obedience, 2013. *Address:* St Antony's College, Asian Studies Centre, Oxford OX2 6JF. *T:* (01865) 274559. *E:* stein.ringen@gtc.ox.ac.uk.

RINGROSE, Adrian Michael; Chief Executive, Interserve plc, since 2003; *b* 9 April 1967; *s* of Prof. John Robert Ringrose, *qv*; *m* 1995, Frances Jacombs; one *s* two *d*. *Educ:* Univ. of Liverpool (BA Hons Pol Theory and Instns 1988). MCIM 1991. London Electricity plc: Business Analyst, 1990–92; Commercial Manager, 1992–97; Hd, Business Develt, Building & Property Gp, 1997–2001; Man. Dir, Interserve FM Ltd, 2001–03. Chm., Public Services Strategy Bd, CBI, 2009–13. Pres., Business Services Assoc., 2007–10. *Recreations:* family, sport, music, film, travel. *Address:* Interserve plc, Ruscombe Park, Twyford, Berks RG10 9JU.

RINGROSE, Ven. Hedley Sidney; Archdeacon of Cheltenham, 1998–2009, now Emeritus; *b* 29 June 1942; *s* of Sidney and Clara Ringrose; *m* 1969, Rosemary Anne Palmer; one *s* two *d*. *Educ:* West Oxfordshire Coll.; Salisbury Theol Coll.; BA Open Univ. 1979. Deacon 1968, priest 1969; Curate: Bishopston, Bristol, 1968–71; Easthampstead, Berks, 1971–75; Vicar, St George, Gloucester with Whaddon, 1975–88; RD Gloucester City, 1983–88; Vicar of Cirencester, 1988–98; RD Cirencester, 1989–97; Hon. Canon, 1986–98, Reserved Canonry, 1998–2009, Gloucester Cathedral; Actg Archdeacon of Malmesbury, dio. Bristol, 2010–11; Interim Archdeacon of Oxford, 2011–13. Chairman: Dio. Bd of Patronage, 1990–98; Dio. House of Clergy, 1994–98; Dio. Bd of Education, 1998–2009. Mem., Gen. Synod of C of E, 1990–2005. Governor: Rendcomb Coll., 2000–; St Mary's and St Margaret's Schs, Calne, 2011–; Dir, Oxford Diocesan Schs Trust, 2012–14. Trustee: Glenfall House, 1998–2009; Foundn of St Matthias, 1998–2009 (Chm., 2005–10); Sylvanus Lysons Trust, 2000–09. Mem., Conservation Bd, Cotswold AONB, 2015. *Recreations:* travel, family and friends, grandchildren, cycling, driving, DIY, gardening. *Address:* 131 North Street, Calne, Wilts SN11 0HL. *T:* (01249) 821215. *E:* hedleyringrose@gmail.com.

RINGROSE, Prof. John Robert, FRS 1977; FRSE; Professor of Pure Mathematics, 1964–93, now Emeritus, and a Pro-Vice-Chancellor, 1983–88, University of Newcastle upon Tyne; *b* 21 Dec. 1932; *s* of Albert Frederick Ringrose and Elsie Lilian Ringrose (*née* Roberts); *m* 1956, Jean Margaret Bates; three *s*. *Educ:* Buckhurst Hill County High School, Chigwell, Essex; St John's Coll., Cambridge (MA, PhD). Lecturer in Mathematics: King's Coll., Newcastle upon Tyne, 1957–61; Univ. of Cambridge (also Fellow of St John's Coll.), 1961–63; Sen. Lectr in Mathematics, Univ. of Newcastle upon Tyne, 1963–64. Pres., London Mathematical Soc., 1992–94. *Publications:* Compact Non-self-adjoint Operators, 1971; (with R. V. Kadison) Fundamentals of the Theory of Operator Algebras, 1983; mathematical papers in various research jls. *Address:* 15 Longmeadows, Ponteland, Newcastle upon Tyne NE20 9DX.

See also A. M. Ringrose.

RINGROSE, Peter Stuart, PhD; Chairman, Biotechnology and Biological Sciences Research Council, 2003–09; *b* 9 Oct. 1945; *s* of Arthur Ringrose and Roma Margaret Ringrose (*née* Roberts); *m* 1966, Nancy Elaine Palmer; two *s* one *d*. *Educ:* Alderman Newton's Grammar Sch., Leicester; Corpus Christi Coll., Cambridge (BA 1967; PhD 1971). Hd Biochemistry, Hoffmann La Roche, UK, 1970–79; Div. Dir, Sandoz Forschungs-Institut, Vienna, 1979–82; Sen. Vice Pres., Global Drug Discovery, Pfizer Inc., UK, 1982–96; CSO, Bristol-Myers Squibb Co., NY, and Pres., Pharmaceutical Res. Inst., Princeton, 1997–2002. Chm. Pharmaceutical R&D Heads, Hever Gp, 1999–2002; non-exec. Director: Cambridge Antibody Technology, 2003–06 (Chm., Scientific Adv. Bd, 2003–06); Astex Therapeutics, 2005–11; Rigel Pharmaceuticals, 2005–; Biotica Technology Ltd, 2007–12; Technol. Strategy Bd, 2007–09; Theravance Inc., 2010–14; Theravance Biopharma, 2014– (Chm., Sci. and Technol. Adv. Cttee); Member Scientific Advisory Board: Accenture Life Sciences, 2003–07; Merlin Biosciences, 2003–05; Cempra Pharmaceuticals, 2006–12; Schering-Plough Inc., 2007–09. Council Mem., Foundn for Sci. and Technol., UK, 2003–. Member: Policy Adv. Bd, Centre for Medicines Res. Internat., 1994–2001; Sci. and Regulatory Exec., Pharmaceutical Res. and Manufacturers of America, 1997–2002; US Council on Competitiveness, 1998–2002. Member: Chancellor's Ct of Benefactors, Oxford Univ., 1998–2003; Chemistry Adv. Bd, Cambridge Univ., 2001–13; Bd of Governors, NY Acad. of Sciences, 2001–05. William Pitt Fellow, Pembroke Coll., Cambridge, 1998–2006 (Life Hon. Fellow, 2006). Mem., Speldhurst Parish Council, 2011–12. *Recreations:* grandchildren, sketching, historical fiction, swimming, travelling, archaeology. *Club:* Athenæum.

RINK, John Stuart; Managing Partner, Allen & Overy, 1994–2003; *b* 25 Oct. 1946; *s* of Paul Lothar Max Rink and Mary Ida McCall Rink (*née* Moore); *m* 1971, Elizabeth Mary Pitkethly; one *s* one *d*. *Educ:* Sedbergh Sch.; London Univ. (LLB ext.). Allen & Overy: Trainee Solicitor, 1970–72; Asst Solicitor, 1972–77; Partner, 1977–2003; Man. Partner, Litigation Dept, 1989–94; Legal Dir, British Aerospace, 1994–95 (on secondment). Director: Brixton plc, 2003–06; Eversheds, 2004–09; RSM Robson Rhodes, 2004–06. Dep. Chm., Teach First, 2008– (Trustee, 2006–). Gov., Sedbergh Sch., 2008–. *Recreations:* golf, Rugby, walking, opera. *Address:* 2 Camp View, Wimbledon, SW19 4UL. *T:* (020) 8947 4800. *Clubs:* MCC, City Law; Royal Wimbledon Golf; Royal West Norfolk Golf; Windermere Golf; Silloth Golf; Windermere Motor Boat Racing.

RINTOUL, Dr Gordon Charles, CBE 2012; Director, National Museums Scotland, since 2002; *b* 29 May 1955; *s* of Henry Rintoul and Janet Rintoul (*née* Brown); *m* 1997, Stephanie Jane Budden; one *s*. *Educ:* Allan Glen's Sch., Glasgow; Univ. of Edinburgh (BSc Hons Physics); Univ. of Manchester (MSc Sci., Technol. and Society; PhD Hist. of Sci. and Technol. 1982). Dip. Museums Assoc. Res. Supervisor, Chem. Mus. Develt Project, 1982–84; Consultant and Tutor, Open Univ., Milton Keynes, 1984; Curator, Colour Mus., Bradford, 1984–87; Dir, Catalyst: Mus. of the Chem. Industry, 1987–98; Chief Exec., Sheffield Galls and Museums Trust, 1998–2002. Member: Registration Cttee, Resource: Council for Museums, Archives and Libraries, 1995–2002; Bd, Scottish Cultural Resources Access Network (SCRAN), 2002–06; Leadership Gp, Scottish Tourism Forum, 2010–12; Bd, Destination Edinburgh Ltd, 2010–11; Bd of Dirs, Marketing Edinburgh Ltd, 2011–. Member Council: Assoc. of Ind. Museums, 1989–2002 (Treas., 1991–97); Museums Assoc., 1998–2004 (Mem., Collections Strategy Gp, 2009–12). Hon. Prof., Univ. of Edinburgh, 2007–. Dr *hc* Edinburgh, 2013; DUniv Edinburgh Napier, 2013. *Recreations:* travel, reading, cooking. *Address:* National Museums Scotland, Chambers Street, Edinburgh EH1 1JF. *T:* (0131) 247 4260, *Fax:* (0131) 247 4308. *E:* g.rintoul@nms.ac.uk.

RIORDAN, Prof. Colin Bryan, PhD; President and Vice-Chancellor, Cardiff University, since 2012; *b* Paderborn, 27 July 1959; *s* of late Bryan Victor Riordan and Elisabeth Riordan; *m* 1991, Karin Alderson (marr. diss. 2013); two *d*. *Educ:* Liverpool Collegiate Sch.; Univ. of Manchester (BA 1st Cl. Hons German 1981; PhD 1986). Lektor, Julius-Maximilians Univ., Würzburg, 1982–84; University of Wales, Swansea: Lectr in German, 1986–94; Sen. Lectr in German, 1994–98; Hd, Dept of German, 1992–93; University of Newcastle upon Tyne: Prof. of German, 1998–2007; Hd, Sch. of Modern Langs, 2001–04; Dean, Postgrad. Studies, Faculty of Humanities and Social Scis, 2004–05; Provost and Pro-Vice-Chancellor, 2005–07; Vice-Chancellor, Univ. of Essex, 2007–12. *Publications:* The Ethics of Narration, 1989; (with G. Butzphal) Studium Wirtschaftsdeutsch, 1990; (ed) Peter Schneider, 1993; (ed) Peter Schneider, 1995; (ed jtly) German Writers and the Cold War, 1945–61, 1992; (ed) Green Thought in German Culture, 1997; (ed) Jurek Becker, 1998; (ed jtly) Aesthetics and Politics in Modern German Culture: festschrift in honour of Rhys W. Williams, 2010; contribs to jls incl. Jl Eur. Studies, Modern Lang. Rev., Johnson-Jahrbuch. *Address:* Vice-Chancellor's Office, Cardiff University, Main Building, Park Place, Cardiff CF10 3AT.

RIORDAN, Linda; *b* 31 May 1953; *d* of John Foulds Haigh and Mary Alice Haigh (*née* Helliwell); *m* 1979, Alan Riordan (*d* 2007). *Educ:* Univ. of Bradford (BSc Hons). Formerly in banking. Pvte Sec. to Alice Mahon, MP, 2001–05. Mem. (Lab), Calderdale MBC, 1995–2006. MP (Lab and Co-op) Halifax, 2005–15.

RIORDAN, Stephen Vaughan; QC 1992; a Recorder, since 1990; *b* 18 Feb. 1950; *s* of Charles Maurice Riordan and Betty Morfydd Riordan; *m* 1983, Jane Elizabeth Thomas; two *d*. *Educ:* Wimbledon Coll.; Univ. of Liverpool (LLB Hons). Called to the Bar, Inner Temple, 1972; Asst Recorder, 1986–90. *Recreation:* singing. *Address:* KCH Garden Square, 1 Oxford Street, Nottingham NG1 5BH.

RIORDAN, Thomas Messenger; Chief Executive, Leeds City Council, since 2010; *b* 9 April 1968; *s* of late Michael Riordan and of Juliet Riordan; *m* Louise; one *s* one *d*. *Educ:* Trinity Coll., Oxford (BA Hons Mod. Hist. 1989); Imperial Coll., London (MBA 1st Cl. 1997). Joined Civil Service, 1990, fast stream incl. rep. UK on internat. envmtl policy negotiations (climate change and biodiversity), 1990–96; Operational Hd, RDA Proj. Team, Govt Office for Yorkshire and Humber, 1997–99; Yorkshire Forward: Hd, Strategy, 1999–2000; Exec. Dir, Strategy and Policy, 2000–05; Dep. Chief Exec., 2005–06; Chief Exec., 2006–10. Trustee, Centre for Cities. Patron, St Gemma's Hospice, Leeds. Hon. DLitt Bradford, 2008. *Publications:* articles on regl develt for Smith Inst. and New Local Govt Network. *Recreations:* football, Middlesbrough Football Club, horse racing, competitive dominoes, music. *Address:* Leeds City Council, Civic Hall, Calverley Street, Leeds LS1 1UR. *T:* (0113) 247 4554, *Fax:* (0113) 247 4870. *E:* tom.riordan@leeds.gov.uk. *W:* www.twitter.com/tomriordan. *Club:* Northallerton Working Men's.

RIPA di MEANA, Carlo; Member for Italy, European Parliament, 1979–84 and 1994–99; *b* 15 Aug. 1929; *m* 1982, Marina Punturieri. Editor, Il Lavoro (Ital. Gen. Conf. of Labour weekly newspaper), and Editor, foreign dept, Unita (Ital. Communist Party daily paper), 1950–53; rep. of Italy on UIE, Prague, 1953–56; founded jointly Nuova Generazione, 1956; left Ital. Communist Party, 1957; founded jointly Passato e Presente, 1957 (chief editor); joined Italian Socialist Party (PSI), 1958; worked in publishing, Feltrinelli, Rizzoli, until 1966; Councillor for Lombardy (PSI), 1970–74 (Chm., Constitutional Cttee); leader, PSI Group, regional council; head, international relations PSI, 1979–80; left PSI 1993; Leader, Green Party, Italy, 1993–95. Comr, EEC Exec. Cttee, 1985–92; Minister for Environment, Italy, 1992–93. Councillor for Umbria, 2000–05. Pres., Inst. for Internat. Economic Cooperation and Develt Problems, 1983. Nat. Pres., Italia Nostra, 2005–07, Pres., Italia Nostra Roma, 2007. Sec.-Gen., Club Turati, Milan, 1967–76; Mem. Board, Scala Theatre, Milan, 1970–74; Mem. Council, Venice Biennale, 1974–82 (Pres., 1974–79); founder Mem., Crocodile Club; Pres., Fernando Santi Inst.; Pres., Unitary Fedn, Italian Press abroad; Vice-Chm., Internat. Cttee for Solidarity with Afghan People, 1980–85. *Publications:* Un viaggio in Viet-Nam (A

Voyage to Vietnam), 1956; A tribute to Raymond Roussel and his Impressions of Africa, 1965; Il governo audiovisivo (Audiovisual Government), 1973; Adieu La Terre, 1993; Salvare Il Pianeta, 1995; Sorci Verdi, 1997; Cane Sciolto, 2000; L'Ordine di Mosca: fernate la biennale del dissenso, 2007. *Recreations:* horse riding, sailing. *Address:* Via Ovidio 26, Int.2–00193 Rome, Italy.

RIPLEY, Prof. Brian David, PhD; FRSE; Professor of Applied Statistics, and Fellow of St Peter's College, University of Oxford, 1990–2014; *b* 29 April 1952; *s* of Eric Lewis Ripley and Sylvia May Ripley (*née* Gould); *m* 1973, Ruth Mary Appleton. *Educ:* Farnborough Grammar Sch.; Churchill Coll., Cambridge (MA, PhD). FIMS 1987; FRSE 1990. Lectr in Statistics, Imperial Coll., London, 1976–80; Reader, Univ. of London, 1980–83; Prof. of Statistics, Univ. of Strathclyde, 1983–90. Mem., Internat. Statistical Inst., 1982. Adams Prize, Univ. of Cambridge, 1987. *Publications:* Spatial Statistics, 1981; Stochastic Simulation, 1987; Statistical Inference for Spatial Processes, 1988; Modern Applied Statistics with S-Plus, 1994, 3rd edn 1999; Pattern Recognition and Neural Networks, 1996; S Programming, 2000; numerous papers on statistics and applications in astronomy, biology, chemistry and earth sciences. *Recreation:* natural history. *Address:* Department of Statistics, University of Oxford, 1 South Parks Road, Oxford OX1 3TG. *T:* (01865) 272861.

RIPLEY, John Kenneth, ACMA, CGMA; Chair: CABI (formerly CAB International), since 2011 (Director, since 2009); Church Mission Society, since 2010; *b* Farnborough, 29 April 1952; *s* of Eric Ripley and Sylvia May Ripley (*née* Gould); *m* 1978, Anne Waring; two *d* (and one *d* decd). *Educ:* Farnborough Grammar Sch.; Trinity Coll., Cambridge (BA 1973). ACMA, CGMA 1980. Unilever: specialist, 1973–76; Mgt Accountant, van den Berghs, 1976–80, Internat. Specialities Div., Netherlands, 1980–82, Lever Bros, 1982–85; Commercial Dir, Loders Croklaan, Netherlands, 1985–89, Agribusiness, 1989–92; Finance Dir, Central Asia and Latin America, 1992–96; Hd, Strategy, 1996–2000; Chief Financial Officer, HPC Div., 2001–05; Dep. Chief Financial Officer, 2005–08; Hd, Corporate Develt, 2008. Gov., Kingston Univ., 2010–. Non-exec. Dir, Great Ormond Street Hosp., 2012–. *Recreations:* travel, photography. *T:* (01372) 458054.
See also B. D. Ripley.

RIPLEY, Sir William (Huw), 5th Bt *cr* 1880, of Rawdon, Yorkshire and Bedstone, Salop; *b* 13 April 1950; *s* of Major Sir Hugh Ripley, 4th Bt, American Silver Star, and Dorothy Mary Dunlop Ripley (*née* Bruce-Jones); *S* father, 2003. *Educ:* Eton; McGill Univ., Montreal (BA Pol Sci. and Eng. Lit.). Published poet; local journalist; bookseller; printer; smallholder; factory worker (nightshift). Patron, St Edward's Church, Hopton Castle. Mem., Leintwardine History Soc. Friend, Gwasg Gregynog. *Publications:* (jtly) Bedstone Court: the story of a calendar house, 2007. *Recreations:* white wine, the occasional whiskey, rare books, writing, the Welsh borderland, border people, the Clun Valley, gardening, peace and quiet, a private life, a little alchemy from time to time. *Heir:* none. *Address:* The Old Post Office and Forge, Bedstone, Bucknell, Salop SY7 0BE; The Carpenter's Cottage, Bedstone, Bucknell, Salop.

RIPLEY-DUGGAN, Gregory Alan; Executive Producer, Hampstead Theatre, London, since 2010; *b* Leatherhead, 20 July 1958; *s* of Eric Ripley-Duggan and Olive Adelaide Ripley-Duggan; partner, Pascale Giudicelli; one *d*. *Educ:* St Peter's and Merrow Grange Comp. Sch.; Downing Coll., Cambridge (BA Eng. Lit. 1980). Independent West End producer, 1990–; Exec. Producer, Shakespeare's Globe, 1996–2006; Interim Exec. Producer, Headlong, 2008–09; Associate Producer, Kingston Rose, 2010–. Chm., League of Independent Producers, 2011–; Mem., SOLT, 2001–. *Recreations:* classical music, literature, following cricket, carpentry. *Address:* Hampstead Theatre, Eton Avenue, NW3 3EU. *T:* (020) 7449 4200. *E:* grd@ripleyduggan.com. *Club:* Groucho.

RIPON, Area Bishop of, since 2014; **Rt Rev. James Harold Bell;** *b* 20 Nov. 1950; *s* of James and Melita Jane Bell. *Educ:* St John's Coll., Durham Univ. (BA (Mod. Hist.) 1972); Wycliffe Hall, Oxford (BA (Theol.) 1974, MA 1978). Ordained deacon, 1975, priest, 1976; Chaplain and Lectr, 1976–82, Official Fellow, 1979–82, Brasenose Coll., Oxford; Pro-proctor, Oxford Univ., 1982; Rector, St Mary, Northolt, 1982–93; Area Dean, Ealing, 1991–93; Willesden Area Advr for Ministry, and Dir, Willesden Ministry Trng Prog., 1993–97; Dir of Ministry and Trng, Dio. Ripon, and Res. Canon, Ripon Cathedral, 1997–99; Dir of Mission, Dio. Ripon and Leeds, 1999–2004; Bishop Suffragan of Knaresborough, 2004–14. Mem., Gen. Synod, 2010 (Chm., Rural Affairs Gp, 2009–). Hon. Canon, Ripon Cathedral, 1999–2004. Dir, Methodist Chapel Aid, 2007–12. Mem. Council, Yorks Ministry Course, 2011– (Chm., 2012–). Gov., York St John Univ., 2009–; Mem., Consultative Gp, Harrogate Coll., 2008–. Trustee, St Michael's Hospice, Harrogate, 2014–. *Publications:* (ed jtly) Re-shaping Rural Ministry, 2009. *Recreations:* entertaining (and being entertained), collecting, gardening (as required). *Address:* Thistledown, Main Street, Exelby, Bedale, N Yorks DL8 2HD. *T:* (01677) 423525, *Fax:* (01677) 423525. *E:* bishop.james@westyorkshiredales.anglican.org.

RIPON, Dean of; *see* Dobson, Very Rev. J. R.

RIPPENGAL, Derek, CB 1982; QC 1980; Counsel to Chairman of Committees, House of Lords, 1977–99; *b* 8 Sept. 1928; *s* of William Thomas Rippengal and Margaret Mary Rippengal (*née* Parry); *m* 1963, Elizabeth Melrose (*d* 1973); one *d* (one *s* decd). *Educ:* Hampton Grammar Sch.; St Catharine's Coll., Cambridge (Scholar; MA). Called to Bar, Middle Temple, 1953 (Harmsworth schol.). Entered Treasury Solicitor's Office, 1958, after Chancery Bar and univ. posts; Sen. Legal Asst, 1961; Asst Treasury Solicitor, 1967; Principal Asst Treasury Solicitor, 1971; Solicitor to DTI, 1972–73; Dep. Parly Counsel, 1973–74, Parly Counsel, 1974–76, Law Commn. *Publications:* (contrib.) Halsbury's Laws of England, vol. 34 (Parliament), 4th edn, 1997. *Recreations:* music, fishing. *Address:* 62 Gwydir Street, Cambridge CB1 2LL. *Club:* Athenæum.

RIPPON, Angela, OBE 2004; broadcaster; presenter, Rip Off Britain, BBC TV, since 2010; *b* 12 Oct. 1944; *d* of late John Rippon and Edna Rippon; *m* 1967, Christopher Dare (marr. diss.). *Educ:* Plymouth Public Grammar Sch. Journalist, The Independent, Plymouth; presenter and reporter, BBC TV, Plymouth, 1966–69; editor, producer and presenter, Westward TV, 1967–73; reporter, nat. news, 1973–75, newsreader, 1975–81, BBC TV; co-founder, and presenter, TV-am, 1983; arts and entertainment correspondent, WNEV-TV, Boston, USA, 1984–85; presenter, LBC, 1990–94. *Television series include:* presenter: Angela Rippon Reporting, 1980–81; Antiques Roadshow, 1980–83; In the Country, 1980–83; Top Gear, 1980–83; Masterteam, 1985–87; Come Dancing, 1988–91; What's My Line, 1988–90; Live with Angela Rippon, 2002–04; Sun, Sea and Bargain Spotting, 2004–09; Cash in the Attic, 2006–; Holiday Hit Squad, 2012–; Amazing Greys, 2014; compère, Eurovision Song Contest, 1976; also presenter, radio progs. Vis. Prof., Consumer Journalism, Lincoln Univ., 2010–. Chm., English Nat. Ballet, 2000–04. Vice-Pres., British Red Cross, 1999–; Ambassador, Alzheimer's Soc., 2009–; Patron, Kidney Res. UK, 2009–11; Co-Chm., Prime Minister's Dementia Friendly Communities Cttee, 2011–. Pres., Lady Taverners, 2011–. TRIC Newsreader of the Year, 1975, 1976, 1977. Hon. DHum Amer. Coll. in London, 1994; Hon. DArts Plymouth, 2012; Hon. DCL Newcastle, 2014. European Woman of Achievement, Women's EU, 2002; Lifetime Achievement Award, Women in Film and TV Awards, 2013. *Publications:* Riding, 1980; In the Country, 1980; Victoria Plum (children's stories), 1981; Mark Phillips: the man and his horses, 1982; Angela Rippon's West Country, 1983; Badminton: a celebration, 1987; Fabulous at 50 and Beyond, 2003. *Address:* c/o Knight Ayton Management, 35 Great James Street, WC1N 3HB.

RISBY, Baron *cr* 2010 (Life Peer), of Haverhill in the County of Suffolk; **Richard John Grenville Spring;** *b* 24 Sept. 1946; *s* of late H. J. A. Spring and Marjorie (*née* Watson-Morris); *m* 1979, Hon. Jane (marr. diss. 1993), *o d* of 8th Baron Henniker, KCMG, CVO, MC; one *s* one *d*. *Educ:* Rondebosch, Cape; Univ. of Cape Town; Magdalene Coll., Cambridge (MA Econs). Vice-Pres., Merrill Lynch Ltd, 1976–86; Dep. Man. Dir, E. F. Hutton Internat. Associates, 1986–88; Exec. Dir, Shearson Lehman Hutton, 1988–89; Man. Director, Xerox Furman Selz, 1989–92. Contested (C) Ashton-under-Lyne, 1983. MP (C) Bury St Edmunds, 1992–97, W Suffolk, 1997–2010. PPS to Min. of State, DTI, 1996, to Ministers for the armed forces and for defence procurement, 1996–97; Opposition front bench spokesman on culture, media and sport, 1997–2000, on foreign and Commonwealth affairs, 2000–04; Shadow Financial Services Minister, 2004–05; Shadow Paymaster Gen., 2005; Prime Ministerial Trade Envoy to Algeria, 2012–. Member: Employment Select Cttee, 1992–94; NI Select Cttee, 1994–97; Health Select Cttee, 1995–97; Vice Chairman: All Party Racing and Bloodstock Cttee, 1997–98; All Party Mobile Telephone Gp, 2004; Chm., All Party Mauritius Gp, 2008–10. A Vice Chm., Cons. Party, and Co-Chm., Cons. City Circle, 2006–10. Pres., Arts and Heritage Cttee, Bow Gp, 1992–97. European Elections Campaign Co-ordinator, 1989; Chm., Westminster CPC, 1990; Dep.-Chm., Small Business Bureau, 1997– (Chm., Parly Adv. Gp, 1992–2010). Chm., British-Ukranian Soc., 2007–. Gov., Westminster Foundn for Democracy, 2001–10. Pres., Assoc. for Decentralised Energy, 2013–. Mem., Adv. Bd, Newsmax, 2013–. Patron: Cons. City Future, 2010–; London Mag., 2013–; Open Reach, 2013–. *Recreations:* country pursuits, English watercolours. *Address:* House of Lords, SW1A 0PW. *Club:* Boodle's.

RISELEY-PRICHARD, Air Vice-Marshal Richard Augustin; Principal Medical Officer, Royal Air Force Support Command, 1980–85; *b* 19 Feb. 1925; *s* of late Dr J. A. Prichard and Elizabeth (*née* Riseley); *m* 1953, Alannah, *d* of late Air Cdre C. W. Busk, CB, MC, AFC; four *d*. *Educ:* Beaudesert Park; Radley Coll.; Trinity Coll., Oxford (MA, BM, BCh); St Bartholomew's Hosp., London. FFCM. Commnd RAF Med. Br., 1951; pilot trng, 1951–52; served at RAF Coll., Cranwell, 1953–56; Dep. Principal Med. Officer (Flying), HQ Transport Comd and HQ RAF Germany, 1956–63; RAF Staff Coll., 1964; SMO, British Forces, Aden, 1967; Dep. Principal Med. Officer, HQ Strike Comd, 1970–73; Commanding Officer: RAF Hosp. Wegberg, Germany, 1973–76; Princess Alexandra Hosp., Wroughton, 1977–80. QHS 1980–85. Hon. Air Cdre, No 4626, RAuxAF Sqn, 1986–2002. Gen. Comr of Income Tax, 1987–95. Mem., 1988–90, Associate Mem., 1990–93, Swindon DHA. Dir (non-exec.) and Vice Chm., Wiltshire Ambulance Service NHS Trust, 1993–2000. Mem., Armed Forces Cttee, BMA, 1989–99. Chm. of Trustees, Dauntsey's Sch., 1999–2005 (Gov., 1982–99; Vice-Chm., 1985–86; Chm., 1986–99); Gov., BUPA Medical Foundn, 1990–96. CStJ. *Recreations:* tennis, squash, bridge, gardening. *Address:* The Little House, Allington, Devizes, Wilts SN10 3NN. *T:* (01380) 860662. *Clubs:* Royal Air Force; All England Lawn Tennis.

RISIUS, His Honour Maj. Gen. Gordon, CB 2000; a Circuit Judge, 2003–14; *b* 10 July 1945; *s* of late Rudolf Risius and Irene Risius (*née* Spier); *m* 1980, Lucinda Mary, *d* of Marshal of the Royal Air Force Sir Michael Beetham, *qv*; one *s* two *d*. *Educ:* University College Sch.; Coll. of Law. Admitted Solicitor, 1972; commnd as Capt., Army Legal Services, 1973; served HQ Land Forces Hong Kong, HQ BAOR, HQ NI, MoD, HQ 4th Armd Div., HQ Land Forces Cyprus; Col, Army Legal Services 2, MoD, 1992–94; Brig. Legal, HQ BAOR/UKSC (Germany), 1994–95; Brig. Legal, HQ Land Command, 1995–96; Brig. Prosecutions, 1997; Dir, Army Legal Services and Army Prosecuting Authy, 1997–2003. Asst Recorder, 1991–95; a Recorder, 1995–2003; a Vice-Pres., Immigration Appeal Tribunal, 2003–05; a Sen. Judge, Sovereign Base Areas Court, Cyprus, 2007–14; Resident Judge, Oxford Crown Court, 2010–14. Dep. Col Comdt, AGC, 2004–09. Vice-Pres., 1997–2003, Hon. Pres., 2003–, Internat. Soc. for Military Law and the Law of War; Mem., Internat. Inst. of Humanitarian Law, 1994–2003. Hon. Recorder of Oxford, 2011–14. *Publications:* articles on the law of war. *Recreations:* music, reading, computers, travel.

RISK, Douglas James; QC (Scot.) 1992; Sheriff Principal of Grampian, Highland and Islands, 1993–2001; *b* 23 Jan. 1941; *s* of James Risk and Isobel Katherine Taylor Risk (*née* Dow); *m* 1967, Jennifer Hood Davidson; three *s* one *d*. *Educ:* Glasgow Academy; Gonville and Caius Coll., Cambridge (BA 1963, MA 1967); Glasgow Univ. (LLB 1965). Admitted to Faculty of Advocates, 1966; Standing Junior Counsel, Scottish Education Dept, 1975; Sheriff of Lothian and Borders at Edinburgh, 1977–79; Sheriff of Grampian, Highland and Islands at Aberdeen and Stonehaven, 1979–93. Hon. Prof., Faculty of Law, Univ. of Aberdeen, 1994–2007 (Hon. Lectr, 1981–94). Burgess of Guild, City of Aberdeen, 2008–. *Club:* Royal Northern and University (Aberdeen).

RIST, Prof. John Michael, FRSC; Professore Incaricato, Istituto Patristico Augustinianum, Rome, since 1998; *b* 6 July 1936; *s* of Robert Ward Rist and Phoebe May (*née* Mansfield); *m* 1960, Anna Thérèse (*née* Vogler); two *s* two *d*. *Educ:* Trinity Coll., Cambridge (BA 1959, MA 1963). FRSC 1976. Univ. of Toronto: firstly Lectr, finally Prof. of Classics, 1959–80; Chm., Grad. Dept of Classics, 1971–75; Regius Prof. of Classics, Aberdeen Univ., 1980–83; Prof. of Classics and Philosophy, Univ. of Toronto, 1983–96, Emeritus Prof., 1997. Kurt Pritzl O. P. Prof. of Philosophy, Catholic Univ. of America, 2012–14. Hon. PhilDr Santa Croce, Rome, 2002. Aquinas Medal, Amer. Catholic Philosophical Assoc., 2014. *Publications:* Eros and Psyche, Canada 1964; Plotinus: the road to reality, 1967; Stoic Philosophy, 1969; Epicurus: an introduction, 1972; (ed) The Stoics, USA 1978; On the Independence of Matthew and Mark, 1978; Human Value, 1982; Platonism and its Christian Heritage, 1985; The Mind of Aristotle, 1989; Augustine, 1994; Man, Soul and Body, 1996; On Inoculating Moral Philosophy Against God, 2000; Real Ethics, 2001; What is Truth?, 2008; Plato: the discovery of the foundations of ethics, 2012; Augustine Deformed, 2014; contrib. classical and phil jls. *Recreations:* travel, swimming, hill-walking. *Address:* 14 St Luke's Street, Cambridge CB4 3DA.

RITBLAT, Jamie William Jeremy; Chief Executive, since 1995 and Chairman, since 2001, Delancey; *b* London, 18 Feb. 1967; *s* of Sir John Henry Ritblat, *qv*; *m* 1995, Joanna Henrietta Jackson; one *s* three *d*. *Educ:* Hall Sch.; Eton Coll.; Univ. of Bristol. Morgan Grenfell, 1986–90, Associate Dir, 1989–90; British Land Company plc, 1990–95, Dir, 1992–95 (Consultant, 1995–97); Founder, Freehold Portfolios Estates, 1995. Trustee: Gordon Russell Trust, 2002–12 (Patron, 2012–); Bathurst Estate, 2012–; Dir, Main Bd, 2005–14, Nat. Campaign Bd, 2007–11, Maggie's Cancer Caring Centres. Mem. Council, KCL, 2006– (Vice Chm., 2014; Chm., Estates Bd, 2007–; Mem., Chm.'s Cttee, 2008–); FKC 2012. Dep. Chm., Real Estates Adv. Bd, Tate Britain, 2008–; Gov., 2009–, Chm. Estates Cttee, 2010–, Southbank Centre. Freeman, City of London, 1996. FRSA. *Recreations:* ski-ing, Real tennis, farming, shooting, bees, art. *Address:* Delancey, Lansdowne House, Berkeley Square, W1J 6ER. *E:* jamie.ritblat@delancey.com. *Clubs:* MCC (Mem., Estates Cttee, 2011); Boodle's, Queen's, Royal Automobile.

RITBLAT, Jillian Rosemary, (Lady Ritblat); Vice-Chairman, New Contemporaries, since 1992 (Board Member, since 1991); Member of Council, Royal College of Art, since 2010 (Chair, Fashion Gala, 2012–14); Trustee, Design Museum, since 2010; *b* Newcastle upon Tyne, 14 Dec. 1942; *d* of Max Leonard Slotover and Peggy Cherna (*née* Cohen); *m* 1st, 1966, Elie Zilkha (marr. diss. 1981); one *s* one *d*; 2nd, 1986, Sir John Henry Ritblat, *qv*. *Educ:* Newcastle-upon-Tyne Ch High Sch.; Roedean; Westfield Coll., Univ. of London (BA Hons Hist. of Art). Called to the Bar, Gray's Inn, 1964; pupillage to Robin Simpson, QC, 1964–65; Alt. Deleg. for Internat. Council of Jewish Women, UN, Geneva, 1977–79; Patrons of New Art Tate Gallery: events organiser, 1984–87; Chm., 1987–90; Mem., Acquisitions Sub-Cttee,

1992–93 and 2000–01; Mem., Internat. Council, Tate Gall., 1995– (Vice-Chm., 1996–2001). Member: Cttee, British Friends of Art Museums of Israel, 1980–; Modern Art Oxford (formerly MOMA, Oxford), 1986– (Mem. Council, 1993–2010); Internat. Council, Jerusalem Mus., 1987–; Adv. Council, Friends of Tate Gall., 1990–; Special Events Cttee, NACF, 1991–92; William Townsend Mems Lecture Cttee, 1991–; Bd, Jerusalem Music Centre, 1991–; Arts Council Appraisal for W Midlands Arts, 1994; Develt Cttee, RAM, 2002–10 (Cttee of Honour, 2010–); Bd, British Archtl Trust Bd (formerly RIBA Trust), 2006–12; Internat. Council, Wallace Collection, 2008–. Design Trustee, Public Art Comrs Agency, 1996–99; Trustee: Tate Foundn, 2006–; Garden Mus., 2010–; Patron, Nat. Alliance for Art, Architecture and Design, 1994–97; Founding Patron, South Downs Soc., 2014–. Co-Curator: The Curator's Egg, Anthony Reynolds Gall., 1994; One Woman's Wardrobe, V&A, 1998–99 (Catalogue Design and Art Direction Silver Award for Graphic Design, D&AD, 1999); Exec. Producer, Normal Conservative Rebels: Gilbert & George in China, Edinburgh Film Fest., 1996 (Gold Medal, Chicago Film Fest.). Jury Member: Painting in the Eighties, 1987; Turner Prize, 1988; BA New Artist Award, 1990; Swiss Bank Corp. Euro Art Competition, 1994 and 1995; NatWest 90s Prize for Art, 1994 and 1995; FT Arts and Business Awards, 2000 and 2001; RIBA Regl Award, Building Commn, 2001; Royal Instn Nature Niche Prize, 2007; Manser Prize, RIBA, 2012. Hon. FRAM 2011; Hon. FRIBA 2013. *Recreations:* art, opera, travel, food, people. *Address:* Lansdowne House, Berkeley Square, W1J 6ER.

RITBLAT, Sir John (Henry), Kt 2006; FRICS; Chairman, The British Land Company PLC, 1970–2006 (Managing Director, 1970–2004; Hon. President, 2007); *b* 3 Oct. 1935; *m* 1st, 1960, Isabel Paja (*d* 1979); two *s* one *d*; 2nd, 1986, Jillian Rosemary Zilkha (*see* J. R. Ritblat). *Educ:* Dulwich Coll.; London Univ. College of Estate Management. FRICS 2000. Articles with West End firm of Surveyors and Valuers, 1952–58. Founder Partner, Conrad Ritblat & Co., Consultant Surveyors and Valuers, 1958; Chairman: Conrad Ritblat Gp plc, 1993–97; Colliers Conrad Ritblat Erdman, 2000–; Colliers Internat. (UK) Ltd, 2010–12. Comr, Crown Estate Paving Commn, 1969–2012, now Comr Emeritus. Hon. Surveyor, Seafarers UK (formerly King George's Fund for Sailors), 1979– (Vice Pres., 2010). Member: Council, Business in the Community, 1987–; Prince of Wales' Royal Parks Tree Appeal Cttee, 1987–; British Olympic Assoc., 1979; Olympic Appeal Cttee, 1984, 1988, 1996 and 2000. Chairman: Trustees, Wallace Collection, 2005–14; Hertford House Trust, 2014–; Trustee, Tate Gall., 2006–; Member: Patrons of British Art, Tate Gall.; English Heritage; Royal Horticultural Soc.; Architecture Club; SPAB; NACF; British Library Bd, 1995–2003 and 2015–; Council, Royal Instn, 2002 (Life Fellow, 2001; Vice-Pres., 2008); Life Member: Nat. Trust; Zool Soc. of London; Georgian Gp; RGS; Trollope Soc. Patron, Investment Property Forum, 1999–. Pres., London Festival of Architecture, 2010. Trustee, Zool Soc. of London Develt Trust, 1986–89. Trustee, Internat. Students' Trust; Mem., Council of Govs, Internat. Students' House (Vice-Chm., 2007–14; Vice-Pres., 2014–). Patron, London Fedn of Boys' Clubs Centenary Appeal; Founder Sponsor, Young Explorers Trust; Sponsor: RGS, 1982–85; (sole), British Nat. Ski Championships, 1978–; Pres., British Ski and Snowboard (formerly British Ski Fedn, then British Ski and Snowboard Fedn), 1994– (Vice-Pres., 1984–89). Member, Board of Governors: London Business Sch., 1990–2014 (Hon. Fellow, 2000; Chm. Govs, 2006–14; Chm., 2013–14, Mem., 2014–, Estates Cttee); The Weizmann Inst., 1991–; Dir and Gov., RAM, 1998–2012 (Dep. Chm., 1999–2012; Hon. Fellow, 2000; Hon. Trustee, 2014–); Gov., 2003–12, Consultant, 2012–, Dulwich Coll. FRGS 1982; CCMI; Life FRSA; Hon. FRIBA 2006. Hon. DLitt: London Metropolitan, 2005; Buckingham, 2013; Hon. DSc London Business Sch., 2014. *Recreations:* antiquarian books and libraries, bees, Real tennis, golf, ski-ing, opera, ballet. *Address:* Lansdowne House, 57 Berkeley Square, W1J 6ER. *Clubs:* Carlton, Royal Automobile, MCC, The Pilgrims, Queen's; Cresta (St Moritz).

See also J. W. J. Ritblat.

RITCHIE, family name of **Baron Ritchie of Dundee**.

RITCHIE OF DUNDEE, 6th Baron *cr* 1905; **Charles Rupert Rendall Ritchie;** *b* 15 March 1958; *s* of 5th Baron Ritchie of Dundee and Anne (*née* Johnstone); *S* father, 2008; *m* 1st, 1984, Tara Van Tuyl Koch (marr. diss. 1992); 2nd, 2003, Celina Lucie Traill (marr. diss. 2005); one *s* one *d* (twins); one *s*, *b* 1994; 3rd, 2010, Mrs Harriet J. Draper (*née* Hague). *Educ:* Brickwall Sch., Northiam. *Heir: s* Hon. Sebastian Ritchie, *b* 31 July 2004.

RITCHIE, Andrew George; QC 2009; *b* 4 April 1960; *s* of H. D. Ritchie and J. P. Ritchie; *m* 1988, Victoria Wilberforce (marr. diss. 2011); one *s* one *d*. *Educ:* Magdalene Coll., Cambridge (BA 1981). Admitted solicitor, 1984; called to the Bar, Inner Temple, 1985. Mem., Funding Appeal Cttee, LSC, 1998–2001. Member, Executive Committee: Assoc. of Personal Injury Lawyers, 1996–99; Personal Injury Bar Assoc., 2003–10. Gen. Ed., Kemp & Kemp: Law Practice and Procedure, 2005–; Mem., Editl Bd, Kemp & Kemp on Quantum, 2004–09. *Publications:* Medical Evidence in Whiplash Cases, 1998; MIB Claims, 2001, 3rd edn 2008; Asbestos Claims, 2007; Manual Handling Claims, 2008; (ed) Guide to RTA Liability, 2009, 2nd edn 2012. *Recreations:* ski-ing, sailing. *Address:* 9 Gough Square, EC4A 3DG. *T:* (020) 7832 0500, *Fax:* (020) 7353 1344.

RITCHIE, Maj.-Gen. Andrew Stephenson, CBE 1999; Director, Goodenough College, since 2006; *b* 30 July 1953; *er s* of Rev. Canon David Caldwell Ritchie and Dilys (*née* Stephenson); *m* 1981, Camilla Trollope; one *s* two *d*. *Educ:* Harrow County Boys' Sch.; RMA Sandhurst; Durham Univ. (BA Hons). Commnd RA 1973; regtl service, UK, Belize, Rhodesia, Germany, 1974–84; sc 1985; SO 2 Dir of Mil. Ops, MoD, 1986–87; 3 RHA, Germany, Cyprus, UK, 1988–90; SO 1 Dir of Army Plans, MoD, 1990–92; CO 1 RHA, UK, 1992–95; COS 3 (UK) Div./Multinational Div. SW, Bosnia, 1995–96; hcsc, 1997; Comdr RA 3 (UK) Div., 1997–98; Dir Personal Services (Army), 1998–2000; rcds, 2001; Dir Corporate Communications (Army), MoD, 2001–02; GOC 4th Div., 2002–03; Comdt, RMA Sandhurst, 2003–06. Trustee, Larkhill Racecourse, 2008–. Director: Goodenough Club Ltd, 2006–; Regular Forces Employment Assoc., 2010–; Goodenough Ventures Ltd, 2014–. Mem. Council, Marlborough Coll., 2006–. *Recreations:* hunting, opera, tennis, golf. *Address:* Goodenough College, Mecklenburgh Square, WC1N 2AB. *E:* andrew.ritchie@goodenough.ac.uk. *Club:* Boodle's.

RITCHIE, Anna, OBE 1997; PhD; FSA; consultant archaeologist; *b* 28 Sept. 1943; *d* of George and Margaret Bachelier; *m* 1968, Graham Ritchie; one *s* one *d*. *Educ:* UC, Cardiff (BA Hons); Univ. of Edinburgh (PhD 1970; Hon. Fellow, 2000). FSA 1977. Member, Ancient Monuments Bd for Scotland, 1990–99. Trustee: Nat. Museums of Scotland, 1993–2003; BM, 1999–2004. Vice-Pres., Soc. of Antiquaries of London, 1988–92; Pres., Soc. of Antiquaries of Scotland, 1990–93. Hon. FSAScot 2007. *Publications:* Orkney and Shetland, 1985; Picts, 1989; Viking Scotland, 1993; Perceptions of the Picts from Eumenius to John Buchan, 1994; Prehistoric Orkney, 1995; Orkney, 1996; Shetland, 1997; Iona, 1997; Govan and its Carved Stones, 1999; Hogbacks at Govan and Beyond, 2004; Kilellan Farm, Ardnave, Islay, 2005; On the Fringe of Neolithic Europe: excavation of a chambered cairn, Holm of Papa Westray, Orkney, 2009; A Shetland Antiquarian: James Thomas Irvine of Yell, 2011; with G. Ritchie: Scotland: archaeology and early history, 1981; Scotland: an Oxford archaeological guide, 1998; with I. Scott: People of Early Scotland from Contemporary Images, 2006; Pictish and Viking-Age Carvings from Shetland, 2009. *Address:* 11 Powderhall Rigg, Edinburgh EH7 4GG. *T:* (0131) 556 1128.

RITCHIE, Cameron; President, Law Society of Scotland, 2011–12 (Vice President, 2010–11); *b* Paisley, 25 Sept. 1952; *s* of Alexander McPherson Ritchie and Jane Cameron Ritchie (*née* Brown); *m* 1981, Hazel Fraser; two *s*. *Educ:* John Neilson Instn, Paisley; Univ. of Glasgow (LLB). Admitted as solicitor Advocate in criminal law, 1995; Procurator Fiscal, Stirling and Alloa, 1996–2002; Area Procurator Fiscal, Fife, 2002–10. *Recreations:* golf, walking. *Address:* 9 Coxburn Brae, Bridge of Allan FK9 4PS. *T:* (01786) 834200. *E:* cameron3@btinternet.com.

RITCHIE, Prof. David Alastair, DPhil; FInstP; Professor of Experimental Physics, Cavendish Laboratory, University of Cambridge, since 2002; Fellow, Robinson College, Cambridge, since 1991; *b* Watford, 11 March 1959; *s* of Charles and Patricia, (Betty), Ritchie; *m* 1989, Linda Elizabeth Miller (marr. diss. 2013); two *d*. *Educ:* Watford Grammar Sch. for Boys; Hertford Coll., Oxford (BA Physics 1980); Univ. of Sussex (DPhil Physics 1986). FInstP 2005. Res. Asst, Univ. of Sussex, 1984–85; University of Cambridge: Res. Associate, 1985–91; Asst Dir of Res., 1991–99; Reader of Exptl Physics, 1999–2002; Dep. Hd, Cavendish Lab., 2009–13. Gov., Watford GS for Boys, 2005–. Tabor Medal and Prize, Inst. of Physics, 2008. *Publications:* contrib. jl papers on physics and technol. of III–V semiconductors. *Recreations:* reading, running, cycling, exploring the Gower peninsula. *Address:* Cavendish Laboratory, J. J. Thomson Avenue, Cambridge CB3 0HE. *T:* (01223) 337331, *Fax:* (01223) 337271. *E:* dar11@cam.ac.uk.

RITCHIE, David Robert, CB 2001; Regional Director, Government Office for West Midlands, 1994–2001; *b* 10 March 1948; *s* of late James Ritchie and Edith Ritchie (*née* Watts); *m* 1989, Joan Gibbons. *Educ:* Manchester Grammar School; St John's College, Cambridge (BA, MA). Min. of Transport, 1970; DoE, 1970; Regl Dir, W Midlands Regl Office, Depts of the Envmt and Transport, 1989–94. Mem., First-tier Tribunal, Gen. Regulatory Chamber (formerly Adjudication Panel for England), 2002–; Chm., Nat. Urban Forestry Unit, 2003–06. Mem., Bishop's Council, Dio. Birmingham, 1992–2004. Dir, Univ. Hosp. Birmingham NHS Foundn Trust, 2006–13. Gov., The Queen's Foundn, 2013– (Vice-Pres., 2002–07; Pres., 2007–13). *Recreations:* fell-walking, cooking. *Address:* 14 Ashfield Road, Birmingham B14 7AS.

RITCHIE, Prof. Donald Andrew, CBE 2005; DL; FRSE; Professor of Genetics, University of Liverpool, 1978–2003, now Emeritus; Deputy Chairman, Environment Agency, 2000–05; *b* 9 July 1938; *s* of Andrew Ritchie and Winifred Laura (*née* Parkinson); *m* 1962, Margaret Jeanne (*née* Collister); one *s* one *d*. *Educ:* Latymer Sch., London; Univ. of Leicester (BSc 1959); RPMS, London (PhD 1964). FRSB (FIBiol 1978), CBiol 1985; FRSE 1979. MRC Microbial Genetics Res. Unit, London, 1959–64; Res. Associate, Biophysics Dept, Johns Hopkins Univ., 1964–66; Lectr, 1966–72, Sen. Lectr, 1972–78, Virology Dept, Univ. of Glasgow; Pro-Vice-Chancellor, Liverpool Univ., 1992–95. Royal Soc. Leverhulme Trust Sen. Res. Fellow, 1991–92; Royal Acad. of Engrg Vis. Prof., Univ. of Liverpool, 2004–06. Member: Science Bd, SERC, 1989–92; Biotechnol. Jt Adv. Bd, DTI, 1990–95; NERC, 1990–95; Bd, Envmt Agency, 1998–2005 (Dep. Chm., 2001–05). Mem. Council, Marine Biol Assoc., 1991–94; Professional Affairs Officer, Soc. for Gen. Microbiol., 1998–2001; Mem., Environment Cttee, 1996–99 and Finance Cttee, 1996–2002, Inst. of Biol. Chairman: Mil. Educn Cttee, Liverpool Univ., 1995–2006; Council of Mil. Educn Cttees of UK Univs, 2004–12; Mem., Mil. Educn Cttee, City of Edinburgh Univs, 2012–. Member: Council, Liverpool Sch. of Tropical Medicine, 1993–99; RFCA (formerly TAVRA), NW England & IOM, 1995–2011; Bd of Mgt, Shrewsbury House Youth Club, Everton, 2007–. Chairman: Merseyside Reg., NACF, 1996–2000; Liverpool Scottish Mus. Trust, 1999–; King's Regt Mus. Trust, 2006–. Trustee, RSE Scotland Foundn, 2009– (Chm., 2013–). Governor: IOM Internat. Business Sch., 2000–11; Shrewsbury Sch., 2003–12 (Dep. Chm., 2007–12). One-man show of paintings, Shrewsbury Sch., 2012. Mem., SE Scotland Cttee, St John Priory of Scotland, 2012–. Hon. Col Liverpool Univ. OTC, 2001–07. DL Merseyside, 2002. *Publications:* (with T. H. Pennington) Molecular Virology, 1971; (with K. M. Smith) Introduction to Virology, 1980; pubns on microbial molecular genetics and environmental microbiology in learned jls. *Recreations:* painting, gardening, walking, photography. *Address:* Allanbank, Gavinton, Duns, Berwickshire TD11 3QT. *T:* (01361) 882547. *E:* donald.ritchie167@btinternet.com. *Clubs:* Army and Navy; Athenæum (Liverpool).

RITCHIE, Sister Frances Dorothy Lyon, (Sister Frances Dominica), OBE 2006; DL; FRCN; Sister of All Saints Community, since 1966; Founder: Helen House Children's Hospice, 1982; Douglas House, Respice for Young People, 2003; *b* 21 Dec. 1942; *d* of Thomas Norman Ritchie and Margaret Armstrong Ritchie (*née* Paterson). *Educ:* Cheltenham Ladies' Coll.; Hosp. for Sick Children, Gt Ormond St (RSCN); Middlesex Hosp. (RGN). FRCN 1983. Entered Soc. of All Saints, Sisters of the Poor, 1966; professed, 1969; Mother Superior, 1977–89. Trustee, Helen & Douglas House, 2002–. Hon. FRCPCH 1998. MUniv Open, 2003; Hon. Dr: Oxford Brookes, 2003; London Metropolitan, 2004; Northampton, 2012. DL Oxon, 2001. *Publications:* Just My Reflection: helping families to do things their way when their child dies, 1997, 2nd edn 2007. *Recreations:* dog walking at dawn, being alone in a country cottage with no television, telephone or alarm clock for a week at a time, friends. *Address:* All Saints, 15A Magdalen Road, Oxford OX4 1RW. *T:* 07762 019357.

RITCHIE, Hamish Martin Johnston; Chairman, Marsh & McLennan Companies UK Ltd, 2000–04; *b* 22 Feb. 1942; *s* of late James Martin Ritchie and Noreen Mary Louise Ritchie; *m* 1967, Judith Carol Young; one *s* one *d*. *Educ:* Loretto Sch.; Christ Church, Oxford (MA). Man. Dir, Hogg Robinson UK Ltd, 1980–81 (Dir, 1974–80); Chairman: Bowring London Ltd, 1981–93; Marsh Mercer Holdings Ltd (formerly Bowring Gp), 1983–; and Chief Exec., Bowring Marsh & McLennan Ltd, 1985–96; Marsh Europe SA, 1992–2001; Dir, Marsh Ltd, 1997–2005. Director: RAC, 1990–99; Halma plc, 1997–2002. Chm., BIBA, 2002–04 (Dep. Chm., 1987–91); Pres., Insurance Inst. of London, 1995–96. CCMI (CIMgt 1985). Trustee: Princess Royal Trust for Carers, 2000–05; Tower Hill Improvement Trust, 2005–11; Chm., Oldhurst Trust, 2003–. Member: Barbican Centre Cttee, 2005–06; Develt Council, Historic Royal Palaces, 2005–06. Gov., English Nat. Ballet, 2001–05. *Recreations:* music, golf. *Address:* Oldhurst, 35 Bulstrode Way, Gerrards Cross, Bucks SL9 7QT. *T:* (01753) 883262. *Clubs:* MCC, Royal Automobile; Royal & Ancient Golf (St Andrews) (Capt. 2008–09), Denham Golf, Rye Golf.

See also S. M. Ritchie.

RITCHIE, Ian Carl, CBE 2000; RA 1998; RIBA; RIAI; Principal, Ian Ritchie Architects, since 1981; *b* 24 June 1947; *s* of Christopher Charles Ritchie and Mabel Berenice (*née* Long); *m* 1972, Jocelyne van den Bossche; one *s*. *Educ:* Varndean, Brighton; Liverpool Sch. of Architecture; Polytechnic of Central London Sch. of Architecture (Dip. Arch. distinction). With Foster Associates, 1972–76; in private practice in France, 1976–78; Partner, Chrysalis Architects, 1979–81; Co-founder and Dir, RFR (Rice Francis Ritchie), 1981–87. Major works include: Ecology Gall., Nat. Hist. Mus.; B8, Stockley Park, London; Roy Square housing, Limehouse, London; Eagle Rock House, E Sussex; Culture Centre, Albert, France; roofs, Louvre Sculpture Courts, Paris; roof and glass facades, Mus. Nat. de Science, Techniques et de l'Industrie, La Villette, Paris; pharmacy, Boves, France; Fluy House, Picardy, France; Terrasson Cultural Greenhouse, France; HV Pylons for EDF, France (Millennium Product award, Design Council, 1999); glass towers, Centro de Arte Reina Sofia, Madrid; Leipzig Glashalle; Bermondsey Underground Stn, Crystal Palace Concert Platform (Millennium Product award, Design Council, 1999), and Wood Lane Underground Stn, London (Stn Excellence, HSBC Rail Bus. Awards, Rail Stn of Year Award, Nat. Transport Awards, 2009); Scotland's Home of the Future, Glasgow (Regeneration of Scotland Supreme Award); White City, London; Spire Monument, Dublin; Internat. Rowing Centre, Royal Albert Dock, London; Light Monument, Milan; Plymouth Th. Royal Production Centre; RSC Courtyard Th.; King Solomon Acad., Westminster; Sainsbury Wellcome Centre, UCL; works in public collections: RA; Centro de Arte Reina Sofia, Madrid; Lodz Gall., Poland;

Hugh Lane Gall., Dublin. Mem., Royal Fine Art Commn, now CABE, 1995–2001, now Emeritus Comr; Mem., Design and Built Envmt Cttees, Royal Commn for the Exhibn of 1851, 1999–2011. Architectural Adviser: Natural Hist. Mus., 1991–95; to the Lord Chancellor, 1999–2004; BM, 2004–06; Adviser: Ove Arup Foundn, 2002–; to Pres., Columbia Univ., NY, 2008–; to Centre for Urban Sci. and Progress, New York Univ., 2013–. External examiner, RIBA, 1986–. Vis. Prof., Vienna Technical Univ., 1994–95; Special Prof., Sch. of Civil Engrg, Leeds Univ., 2001–04; Prof. of Architecture, RA, 2005–12; Hon. Vis. Prof., Liverpool Univ., 2009–. Mem., Technology Foresight Construction Panel, 1996–98. Chm., Europan UK, 1997–2003. Mem. Council, 1999, 2005–07, 2014–16, Chm., Collections and Library Cttee, 2000–09, RA. Council Mem., Steel Construction Inst., 1994–97; Architects' Council of Europe rep. on European Construction Technology Platform, 2005–07. Gov., RSC, 2000– (Mem., Internat. Council, 2005–11). Chairman: RIBA Stirling Awards, 2006; RIAS Andrew Doolan Award, 2009. FRSA; Fellow, Soc. of Facade Engrg, 2012; Mem., Akademie der Künste, Berlin, 2013. Hon. FRIAS 2009; Hon. FAIA 2010. Hon. DLitt Westminster, 2000. Tableau de l'Ordre des Architectes Français, 1982; Architectural Design Silver Medal, 1982; IRITECNA (Italian state construction industry) European Prize, 1992; Eric Lyons Meml Award, for European housing, 1992; Robert Matthew Award, Commonwealth Assoc. of Architects, 1994; AIA Awards, 1997, 2003, 2008; Civic Trust Awards, 1993, 1998, 2003 (two); Arts Bldg of the Year Award, Royal Fine Art Commn, 1998; Stephen Lawrence Prize, 1998; RIBA Awards, 1998 (two), 2000, 2003, 2004, 2007; Acad. d'Architecture Grand Médaille d'Argent, 2000; Sports Bldg of the Year Award, Royal Fine Art Commn, 2000; Internat. Outstanding Structure Award, IABSE, 2000; Bldg of the Year Award, Royal Fine Art Commn, 2003; Innovation in Copper Award, Copper Develt Assoc. (UK), 2000, 2003. *Publications:* (Well) Connected Architecture, 1994; The Biggest Glass Palace in the World, 1997; Ian Ritchie Technoecology, 1999; Plymouth Theatre Royal TR2, 2003; The Spire, 2004; The RSC Courtyard Theatre, 2006; The Leipzig Glass Hall, 2007; Lines: poems and etchings, 2010; (with Roger Connah) Being: an architect, 2014. *Recreations:* art, swimming, reading, writing, theatre, supporting the Reds. *Address:* (office) 110 Three Colt Street, E14 8AZ. *T:* (020) 7338 1100. *E:* iritchie@ianritchiearchitects.co.uk.

RITCHIE, Ian Charles Stewart; festival director, artistic curator and music specialist; Director, City of London Festival, 2005–13; *b* 19 June 1953; *s* of Kenneth John Stewart Ritchie and Wanda Margaret Angela Ritchie; *m* 1st, 1977, Angela Mary (marr. diss. 1993); two *d*; 2nd, 1997, Kathryn Alexandra McDowell, *qv*. *Educ:* Stowe Sch.; Royal Coll. of Music; Trinity Coll., Cambridge (MA); Guildhall Sch. of Music and Drama. General Manager, City of London Sinfonia, 1979–84; Artistic Dir, City of London Fest., 1983–84; Man. Dir, Scottish Chamber Orchestra, 1984–93; Gen. Dir, Opera North, 1993–94; arts mgt consultant, 1994–2005. Artistic Co-Dir, 1988–93, Dir, 2004–05, St Magnus Fest., Orkney; Artistic Director: Setúbal Music Fest., 2010–; The Musical Brain, 2010–. Director/Trustee: Choirbook Trust; Musicians Without Borders; Tenebrae Choir. Vis. Prof., London Metropolitan Univ., 2012–; Associate Fellow, Inst. of Musical Res., Univ. of London, 2013–. *Recreations:* wine, walking, song. *Address:* 167 Liverpool Road, N1 0RF. *T:* (020) 7837 6665. *E:* ian@ianritchie.org. *Clubs:* MCC; New (Edinburgh).

RITCHIE, Ian Cleland, CBE 2003; FRSE; CEng, FREng, FBCS; Chairman: Computer Application Services Ltd, since 2005; Interactive Design Institute Ltd, since 2007; Iomart plc, since 2008; Red Fox Media Ltd, since 2012; Cogbooks Ltd, since 2013; *b* 29 June 1950; *s* of late Alexander Ritchie and Jean Russell Ritchie (*née* Fowler); *m* 1974, Barbara Allan Cowie (*d* 2001); one *s* one *d*. *Educ:* Heriot-Watt Univ. (BSc Hons Computer Sci. 1973). CEng 1991; FBCS 1992. Develt Engr/Manager, ICL, 1974–83; CEO and Man. Dir, Office Workstations Ltd (OWL), Edinburgh and Seattle, 1984–92 (OWL pioneered develt of hypertext (web-browsing) technol.; sold to Panasonic, 1989); special project, Heriot-Watt Univ., 1992–94. Chairman: Voxar Ltd, 1994–2002 (non-exec. Dir, 1994–2004); Orbital Software Gp Ltd, 1995–2001; Active Navigation (formerly Multicosm) Ltd, 1997–2004; Digital Bridges Ltd, 2000–03 (Dir, 2003–05); Sonaptic Ltd, 2003–06; Interactive University Ltd, 2003–08; Scapa Ltd, 2006–10; Caspian Learning Ltd, 2007–11; Blipfoto Ltd, 2012–15; Dep. Chm., Vis Entertainment (formerly Vis Interactive) plc, 1995–2004. Director: Northern Venture Trust PLC, 1996–2001; Scran, 1996–2004; Indigo Active Vision Systems Ltd, 1997–2000; Epic Gp PLC, 1998–2004; Scottish Enterprise, 1999–2005; Channel 4 TV, 2000–06; Bletchley Park Trust, 2000–09; Scottish Science Trust, 2001–03; Mindwarp Pavilion Ltd, 2001–02; Dynamic Earth, 2004– (Chm., 2010–); GO Gp, 2008–12. Chairman: Generation Science, 2005–09; Connect Scotland, 2006–08. Director: Edinburgh Internat. Film Fest., 2002–10; Nat. Museums Scotland (formerly Nat. Museums of Scotland), 2003–10; Edinburgh Internat. Sci. Fest., 2005–. Member: PPARC, 1999–2002; SHEFC, 2002–05; SFC, 2005–07. Dir, Scottish Inst. for Enterprise, 2001–06. Trustee: Nominet Trust, 2008–14; Saltire Foundn, 2009–; Dave Hume Trust, 2008–. Pres., BCS, 1998–99; Vice Pres., Business, RSE, 2012–; Hon. Treas., RAEng, 2012–. Hon. Prof., Heriot-Watt Univ., 1993–. FREng 2001; FRSE 2002. DUniv Heriot-Watt, 2000; Hon. DSc Robert Gordon, 2001; Hon. DBA Abertay Dundee, 2002; Dr *hc* Edinburgh, 2003. *Publications:* New Media Publishing: opportunities from the digital revolution, 1996; contrib. various technol. papers and articles. *Recreations:* travel, theatre and arts, web-browsing. *Address:* Coppertop, Green Lane, Lasswade EH18 1HE. *T:* (0131) 663 9486.

RITCHIE, Ian Kristensen, FRCSE, FRCSE(Orth); Consultant Orthopaedic Surgeon, Forth Valley, 1992–2012; President, Royal College of Surgeons of Edinburgh, 2012–15 (Vice-President, 2009–12); *b* Syria, 2 Jan. 1953; *s* of James Ritchie and Mette Ritchie (*née* Kristensen); *m* 1986, Alyson M. Dow; three *d*. *Educ:* Lochaber High Sch.; Gordon Schs, Huntly; Univ. of Aberdeen (MB ChB 1977). FRCSE 1984; FRCSE(Orth) 1990. Surgeon Lieut, RN, 1978–83; Surgical Trng, Aberdeen, 1983–92. Convener, Trainer Trng, 1996–2009, Dir, Surgical Trng, 2005–09, RCSE. *Recreations:* music, family, walking. *Address:* 13 Abercromby Place, Stirling FK8 2QP.

RITCHIE, Ian Russell; Chief Executive, Rugby Football Union, since 2012; *b* 27 Nov. 1953; *s* of Hugh Russell Ritchie and Sheelah Ritchie; *m* 1982, Jill Evelyn Middleton-Walker; two *s*. *Educ:* Leeds Grammar Sch.; Trinity Coll., Oxford (MA Jurisprudence). Called to the Bar, Middle Temple, 1976. Practised at the Bar, 1976–78; Industrial Relations Advr, EEF, 1978–80; Granada TV, 1980–88 (Head of Prodn Services, 1987–88); Dir of Resources, 1988–91, Man. Dir, 1991–93, Tyne Tees TV; Gp Dep. Chief Exec., Yorkshire Tyne Tees TV, 1992–93; Managing Director: Nottingham Studios, Central Television, 1993–94; London News Network, 1994–96; Chief Exec., 1996, Chief Operating Officer, 1996–97, Channel 5 Broadcasting; Partner and Man. Dir, Russell Reynolds Associates, 1997–98; CEO, Middle East Broadcasting, 1998–2000; CEO, Associated Press Television News, 2000–03; Vice-Pres., Global Business, and Man. Dir, Associated Press Internat., 2003–05; Chief Exec., AELTC, 2005–12. Director: West Ham United plc, 1999–2002; Wembley Nat. Stadium Ltd, 2008–11; Ind. Dir, Football League Ltd, 2004–12. Member Council: LTA, 2006–09; FA, 2008–12. FRSA. *Recreations:* golf, tennis, theatre, music. *Address:* Virginia Water, Surrey. *Club:* Vincent's (Oxford).

RITCHIE, Jean Harris, (Mrs G. T. K. Boney); QC 1992; *b* 6 April 1947; *d* of late Walter Weir Ritchie and Lily (*née* Goodwin); *m* 1976, Guy Thomas Knowles Boney, *qv*; two *s*. *Educ:* King's Coll., London (LLB); McGill Univ., Montreal (LLM); Open Univ. (BA). Called to the Bar, Gray's Inn, 1970 (Churchill Schol., 1968; Bencher, 2000); on Western Circuit; a Recorder, 1993–2009; Head of Chambers, 2000–04. Chairman: Clunis Inquiry (care in the community for patients suffering from schizophrenia), 1993–94; Inquiry into Clinical Governance (arising from actions of Rodney Ledward), 1999–2000. Member: Supreme Ct Rule Cttee, 1993–97; Judicial Studies Bd, 1998–2001 (Mem., Civil Cttee, 1997–2001); QC Selection Panel, 2006–12. Chm. Council, Winchester Cathedral, 2011–. Member: Med. Ethics Cttee, King Edward VII Hosp., 2003–; City Panel, Treloar Trust, 2005–08. Trustee, Bromley Trust, 2007–. Fellow, Winchester Coll., 2008–. Chm. Govs, Norman Court Prep. Sch., W Tytherley, 1996–2000. *Publications:* (contrib.) Safe Practice in Obstetrics and Gynaecology, ed R. V. Clements, 1994. *Recreations:* family, grandchildren, dog walking. *Address:* King's Head House, Stockbridge, Hants SO20 6EU.

RITCHIE, Dr John Hindle, MBE 1985; architect; development management consultant; *b* 4 June 1937; *s* of Charles A. Ritchie; *m* 1963, Anne B. M. Leyland; two *d*. *Educ:* Royal Grammar School, Newcastle upon Tyne; Univ. of Liverpool (BArch Hons); Univ. of Sheffield (PhD Building Science). RIBA 1965. Served RN, 1956–58. Science Research Council, 1963–66; Town Planner, Liverpool City Council, 1966–69; Rowntree Housing Trust, Univ. of Liverpool, 1969–72; R&D Architect, Cheshire County Council, 1972–74; Asst County Planner (Envmt), Merseyside CC, 1974–80; Merseyside Development Corporation: Dir of Develt, 1980–85; Chief Exec. and Mem., 1985–91. Chm., Merseyside Educn Training Enterprise Ltd, 1986–91; Member: Merseyside Tourism Bd, 1986–88; Internat. Organising Cttee, Grand Regatta Columbus '92, 1986–92; Board: Gardners Row Business Centre, 1987–90; Merseyside Enterprise Trust, 1988–91; Instant Muscle Ltd, 1993–95; Merseyside Sculptors Guild, 1993–97; Wirral Community Healthcare Trust, 1993–95; Landscape Trust, 1996–2001. Mem., Lord Chancellor's Panel of Ind. Inspectors, 1994–2003; consultant inspector, Planning Inspectorate, 2003–05. Gov., Liverpool Community Coll., 1995–2011. Major projects include: natural resource management, pollution control, land reclamation and urban conservation progs and projects, Merseyside Strategic Plan; Liverpool South Docks and Riverside reclamation and develt, Liverpool Internat. Garden Fest., 1984 (Civic Trust Award; Landscape Inst. 75th Anniv. Award, 2004); Albert Dock Conservation (European Gold Medal, 1986; Civic Trust Jubilee Award, 1987). CCMI; CBIM; FRSA. *Publications:* scientific and planning papers on urban environment obsolescence and regeneration. *Address:* Cartref, 46 The Mount, Heswall, Wirral CH60 4RD. *E:* johnritchie37@talktalk.net.

RITCHIE, Kathryn Alexandra; *see* McDowell, K. A.

RITCHIE, Dr Kenneth George Hutchison; Chief Executive, Electoral Reform Society, 1997–2010 (Member, Board, since 2012); *b* 8 Dec. 1946; *s* of late William Ritchie and Margaret Morton Ritchie (*née* Hutchison); *m* 1985, Elizabeth Anne Black; one *s* one *d*. *Educ:* George Heriot's Sch., Edinburgh; Edinburgh Univ. (BSc); Aston Univ. (PhD 1981). Maths teacher, VSO, Tanzania, 1968–69; systems analyst, ICI, 1970–73; Hd, Internat. Service, UNA, 1976–83; Exec. Dir, Appropriate Health Resources and Technologies Action Gp, 1983–88; Dep. Dir, British Refugee Council, 1988–94; UK Dir, Intermediate Technol., 1994–96. Co-ordinator, All-Party Parly Human Rights Gp, 2011. Hon. Treas., War on Want, 1980–85; Treas., Western Sahara Campaign, 1984–. Mem., Council for Advancement of Arab-British Understanding, 1989–94. Dir, Make Votes Count, 1998–2010; Bd Mem., FairVote/Center for Voting and Democracy, Washington, 2004–10. Member: Exec. Cttee, Labour Campaign for Electoral Reform, 2010–; Republic, 2011–; Reform Foundn, 2011– (Chm., 2011–). Contested (Lab): Beckenham, 1987 and 1992; Daventry, 1997. *Publications:* (with L. Baston) Don't Take No for an Answer: the 2011 referendum and the future of electoral reform, 2011; (contrib.) Electoral Systems, 2012; Fixing our Broken Democracy: the case for total representation, 2012; The Saharawi Struggle for Self-Determination: a history of the campaign in Britain, 2014; Total Representation: an electoral system to resolve Italy's democratic crisis, 2014; The Elephant in the House, 2015. *Recreations:* golf, music, walking the dog. *Address:* 37 Ware Road, Barby, Rugby CV23 8UE. *T:* (01788) 890942.

RITCHIE, Prof. Sir Lewis (Duthie), Kt 2011; OBE 2001; James Mackenzie Professor of General Practice, University of Aberdeen, since 1992; assistant general practitioner, since 2012; *b* Fraserburgh, 26 June 1952; *s* of Lewis Duthie Ritchie and Sheila Gladys Ritchie; *m* 1978, Heather Skelton. *Educ:* Fraserburgh Acad.; Univ. of Aberdeen (BSc Chem. 1978; MB ChB (Commendation) 1978; MD 1993); Univ. of Edinburgh (MSc Community Medicine 1982). DRCOG 1980; FFPH (FFPHM 1993); FRCGP 1994; FRCPEd 1995; FBCS 2004; CEng 1993; CITP 2004. Principal GP, Peterhead Health Centre and Community Hosp., 1984–2012; Lectr in Gen. Practice, 1984–92, Hd, Dept of Gen. Practice and Primary Care, 1992–2007, Univ. of Aberdeen; Consultant in Public Health Medicine, Grampian Health Bd, 1987–92; Hon. Consultant in Public Health Medicine, 1993–2012 and 2014–, Dir of Public Health, 2012–14, NHS Grampian. Hon. Prof. of Primary Care and Public Health, Univ. of Highlands and Is, 2014–. Lectures: Richard Scott, Univ. of Edinburgh, 2007; James Mackenzie, RCGP, 2010; Stock Meml, Assoc. of Port Health Authorities, 2012; Fulton, RCGP W Scotland, 2012; DARE, FPH, 2014. Hon. FRCPGlas 2015. John Perry Prize, BCS, 1991; Stokoe Award, RCGP, 1992; Blackwell Prize, Univ. of Aberdeen, 1995; Eric Elder Medal, Royal NZ Coll. of GPs, 2007; Provost Medal, RCGP NE Scotland, 2010. *Publications:* Computers in Primary Care, 1984, 2nd edn 1986 (trans. Spanish 1991); contrib. chapters, reports and papers on computers, telemedicine, cardiovascular prevention and mgt, cancer, community hosps and intermediate care, immunisation, community pharmacy, professionalism and excellence in medicine. *Recreations:* Church, classical music, art appreciation, reading (particularly military and naval history), dog walking, civilian gallantry, RNLI. *Address:* Cramond, 79 Strichen Road, Fraserburgh, Aberdeenshire AB34 9QJ. *T:* (01346) 510191, *Fax:* (01346) 515598. *E:* l.d.ritchie@abdn.ac.uk.

RITCHIE, Margaret; MP (SDLP) South Down, since 2010; *b* 25 March 1958; *d* of late John Ritchie and Rose Ritchie (*née* Drumm). *Educ:* Queen's Univ., Belfast (BA). Mem. (SDLP) Down DC, 1985–2009. Mem., NI Forum, 1996. Parly Asst to Edward McGrady, MP, 1987–2003. Mem. (SDLP) S Down, NI Assembly, 2003–12; Minister for Social Develt, NI, 2007–10. Mem., Envmt, Food and Rural Affairs Select Cttee, 2012–. Leader, SDLP, 2010–11. *Address:* (office) 32 Saul Street, Downpatrick, Co. Down BT30 6NQ.

RITCHIE, Margaret Claire; Headmistress of Queen Mary School, Lytham, 1981–98; *b* 18 Sept. 1937; *d* of Roderick M. Ritchie, Edinburgh. *Educ:* Leeds Girls' High Sch.; Univ. of Leeds (BSc); London Univ. (PGCE). Asst Mistress, St Leonards Sch., St Andrews, 1960–64; Head of Science Dept, Wycombe Abbey Sch., High Wycombe, 1964–71; Headmistress, Queenswood Sch., 1972–81. JP Fylde, 1991–99, Preston PSD, 1999–2007. *Address:* 29 Walmer Road, Lytham St Annes, Lancs FY8 3HL.

RITCHIE, Peter, FCCA; Head of Finance, Fife Council, 1995–2001; *b* 16 March 1951. *Educ:* Kirkland High Sch.; Buckhaven High Sch.; Dundee Coll. of Commerce. FCCA 1975. Fife CC, 1969–75; Fife Regional Council, 1975–2001: Chief Accountant, 1980–84; Sen. Asst Dir of Finance, 1984–88; Dep. Dir of Finance, 1988–95. *Recreations:* travelling, hill-walking, gardening, theatre, cinema, photography.

RITCHIE, Shirley Anne; *see* Anwyl, Her Honour S. A.

RITCHIE, Stuart Martin; QC 2012; *b* Beaconsfield, 27 July 1970; *s* of Hamish Martin Johnston Ritchie, *qv*; *m* 2001, Victoria Maclean; one *s* one *d*. *Educ:* Radley Coll., Abingdon; Christ Church, Oxford (BA Mod Langs 1993); Coll. of Law (CPE 1994). Called to the Bar, Middle Temple, 1995; in practice as a barrister, Littleton Chambers, 1996–. Mediator. *Publications:* Fiduciary Duties: directors and employees, 2008, 2nd edn 2015. *Recreations:* classical music, piano and organ, golf, school governor, trustee of Gerald Finzi charitable trust, Ripon Cathedral Music Trust. *Address:* Littleton Chambers, 3 King's Bench Walk,

North Temple, EC4Y 7HR. *T:* (020) 7797 8600, *Fax:* (020) 7797 8699. *E:* sr@littletonchambers.co.uk. *Clubs:* Hurlingham; Denham Golf, Rye Golf, Royal and Ancient Golf.

RITCHIE, Susan Rosemary; *see* Foister, S. R.

RITCHIE, Prof. William, OBE 1994; PhD; FRSGS; FRICS; FRSE; Director, Aberdeen Institute of Coastal Science and Management, King's College, University of Aberdeen, 2002–11; *b* 22 March 1940; *s* of Alexander Ritchie and Rebecca Smith Ritchie; *m* 1965, Elizabeth A. Bell; two *s* one *d*. *Educ:* Glasgow Univ. (BSc, PhD 1966). FRSGS 1980; FRSE 1982; FRICS 1989. Research Asst, Glasgow Univ., 1963; Aberdeen University: Lectr, 1964–72; Sen. Lectr, 1972–79; Prof., 1979–95; Dean, 1988–89; Vice Principal, 1989–95; Vice-Chancellor, Lancaster Univ., 1995–2002; Interim Dir, Macaulay Inst., Aberdeen, 2006. Post-doctoral Vis. Prof. and Hon. Prof. appts in geog. and coastal geog., Louisiana State Univ., USA, at various times, 1971–95; Adjunct Prof., World Maritime Univ., Malmo, 2003–. Chm., Scottish Aquaculture Res. Forum, 2003–. DUniv Stirling, 2003; Hon. DSc Lancaster, 2003. *Publications:* Mapping for Field Scientists, 1977; Surveying and Mapping for Field Scientists, 1988, 4th edn 1996; The Environmental Impact of the Wreck of the Braer, 1994; numerous papers mainly in jls of physical and coastal geog. and envmtl mgt. *Address:* Aberdeen Institute of Coastal Science and Management, School of Geosciences, King's College, University of Aberdeen, Aberdeen AB24 3UE.

RITTER, Prof. Mary Alice, OBE 2014; DPhil; FRCPath, FRSB, FCGI; Professor of Immunology, Imperial College London, 1991–2011, now Emeritus; Chief Executive Officer, Climate-KIC, since 2010; *b* 19 Dec. 1943; *d* of Douglas and Iris Buchanan Smith; *m* 1st, 1967, James Ritter (marr. diss. 1973); 2nd, 1976, Roger Morris; three *s*. *Educ:* Berkhamsted Sch. for Girls; St Hilda's Coll., Oxford (BA Hons Zool. 1966; Dip. Physical Anthropol. 1967; MA 1971); Wolfson Coll., Oxford (DPhil 1971). FRCPath 2006. FCGI 2006. Res. Associate, Univ. of Conn, 1976–78; Res. Fellow, ICRF, 1978–84; Royal Postgraduate Medical School, London, later Imperial College, London: Lectr in Immunol., 1982–86; Sen. Lectr, 1986–88; Reader, 1988–91; Vice Dean (Educn), 1992–97; Asst Vice Principal (Postgrad. Medicine), 1998–2000; Dir, Grad. Sch. of Life Scis and Medicine, 1999–2006; Hd, Dept of Immunol., 2004–06; Pro-Rector: for Postgrad. Affairs, 2004–07; for Internat. Affairs, 2005–11. Mem. Council, and Chm. Scientific Adv. Panel, Action Res., 1997–2000; Member: Non-Clin. Trng and Career Develt Panel, MRC, 2005–09; Non-Clin. Careers Cttee, Acad. of Med. Scis, 2006–11; Prime Minister's Initiative for Higher Educn, 2006–11. Chm., Evaluation Panel, UK-India Educn and Res. Initiative, 2006–08; Vice Chm., Council for Doctoral Educn, European Univs Assoc., 2007–12; Chm., External Adv. Bd, Res. Councils UK Vitae Prog., 2008– (Chm., Annual Conf., UKGRAD Prog., subseq. Vitae Prog., 2005–10). Member: AgroParisTech Council, 2007–; Internat. Adv. Panel, A*Star Grad. Acad., Singapore, 2007–12; Internat. Panel of Advrs, Inst. of Advanced Studies, Singapore, 2008–; Mgt Bd, GlobalTech, 2008–11; Pro Tem Gov. Bd, Lee Kong Chian Sch. of Medicine, 2010–12; Rectors' Bd, League of Eur. Res. Univs, 2010–11; Strategic Cttee, Univ. Pierre et Marie Curie, Paris VI, 2011–. FRSA 2004. *Publications:* (with I. N. Crispe) The Thymus, 1992 (trans. Japanese 1993); contrib. numerous articles to peer-reviewed scientific learned jls. *Recreations:* travelling, gardening, cycling, biography, baroque music, ballet, opera. *Address:* Climate-KIC, Central Office, 31–35 Kirby Street, EC1N 8TE. *T:* (020) 7492 1921. *E:* m.ritter@imperial.ac.uk.

RITTERMAN, Dame Janet (Elizabeth), DBE 2002; PhD; Vice-President, Royal College of Music, since 2005 (Director, 1993–2005); *b* 1 Dec. 1941; *d* of Charles Eric Palmer and Laurie Helen Palmer; *m* 1970, Gerrard Peter Ritterman. *Educ:* North Sydney Girls' High Sch.; NSW State Conservatorium of Music; Univ. of Durham (BMus 1971); King's Coll. London (MMus 1977; PhD 1985). Pianist, accompanist, chamber music player; Senior Lecturer in Music: Middlesex Poly., 1975–79; Goldsmiths' Coll., Univ. of London, 1980–87; Dartington College of Arts: Head of Music, 1987–90; Dean, Academic Affairs, 1988–90; Acting Principal, 1990–91; Principal, 1991–93; Hon. Vis. Prof. of Music Educn, Univ. of Plymouth, 1993–2005. Chm., Assoc. Bd of Royal Schs of Music (Publishing) Ltd, 1993–2005. Former Mem., music educn and arts orgns; Member: Arts Council, 2000–02 (Mem., Music Panel, 1992–98); DfES Adv. Cttee, Music and Dance Scheme, 2001–05; Chm., Postgrad. Cttee, AHRB, 2002–04 (Mem. Postgrad. Panel, 1999–2002); Mem., Nominating Cttee, AHRC, 2005–08. Member: Council, Royal Musical Assoc., 1994–2004 (Vice-Pres., 1998–2004); Bd, ENO, 1996–2004; Bd, NYO, 1999–2008; Bd of Dirs, The Voices Foundn, 2005–12; Adv. Council, Inst. of Germanic and Romance Studies, 2005–11, Inst. of Musical Res., 2006–14, Univ. of London; Adv. Bd, Inst. for Advanced Studies in the Humanities, Univ. of Edinburgh, 2005–13; Bd, Sch. of Advanced Study, Univ. of London, 2008–14; Vice-Pres., Nat. Assoc. of Youth Orchestras, 1993–2005. Chairman: Adv. Council, Arts Res. Ltd, 1997–2005; Fedn of British Conservatoires, 1998–2003; Arts Res. Bd, Fonds zur Förderung der wissenschaftlichen Forschung, Austria, 2009–; Member: Wissenschaftsrat, Bundesministerium für Wissenschaft und Forschung, Austria, 2003–12; Bd of Dirs, Anglo-Austrian Soc., 2005–11; Conseil de fondation, Haute École de Musique Genève, Switzerland, 2009–. Strategic Develt Advr, Orpheus Inst., Ghent, Belgium, 2009–. Chancellor, Middlesex Univ., 2013– (Mem., Governing Body, 2006–13); Member: Governing Body: Heythrop Coll., 1996–2006; Dartington Coll. of Arts, 2005–08; Falmouth Univ. (formerly UC Falmouth), 2008– (Dep. Chm., 2013–); RWCMD, 2010–; Council, Goldsmiths Coll., later Goldsmiths, Univ. of London, 2002–07; Governor: Assoc. Bd, Royal Schs of Music, 1993–2005; Purcell Sch., 1996–2000. Mem., Nuffield Foundn Educn Adv. Cttee, 2007–10. Trustee: Countess of Munster Musical Trust, 1993–; Plymouth Chamber Music Trust, 2006–10; EU Chamber Orch., 2012–; Belcea Quartet Trust, 2012–. Mem. Ct, Musicians' Co., 2005–11. FRNCM 1996; Fellow: Nene Coll., 1997; Dartington Coll. of Arts, 1997; High Educn Acad., 2007; Heythrop Coll., Univ. of London, 2008; Goldsmiths, Univ. of London, 2009. Hon. RAM 1995; Hon. GSMD 2000; Hon. Sen. Fellow, RCA 2004. DUniv: Central England, 1996; Middx, 2005; Hon. DLitt Ulster, 2004; Hon. DMus Sydney, 2010. *Publications:* articles in learned jls, France and UK. *Recreations:* reading, theatre-going, country walking. *E:* jritterman@blueyonder.co.uk. *Club:* Athenæum.

RITTNER, Luke Philip Hardwick; Chief Executive, Royal Academy of Dance (formerly of Dancing), since 1999; *b* 24 May 1947; *s* of late George Stephen Hardwick Rittner and Joane (*née* Thunder); *m* 1974, Corinna Frances Edholm; one *d*. *Educ:* Blackfriars School, Laxton; City of Bath Technical Coll.; Dartington Coll. of Arts; London Acad. of Music and Dramatic Art. Asst Administrator, Bath Festival, 1968–71, Jt Administrator, 1971–74, Administrative Director, 1974–76; Founder, and Dir, Assoc. for Business Sponsorship of the Arts, 1976–83; Sec. Gen., Arts Council of GB, 1983–90; Dir, Marketing and Communications, then Corporate Affairs, Sotheby's Europe, 1992–99. Chm., English Shakespeare Co., 1990–94. UK Cultural Dir, Expo '92, Seville; Corporate Advr on cultural sponsorship to: Eurotunnel; J. Sainsbury plc. Non-exec. Bd Mem., Carlton Television, 1991–93. Member: Adv. Council, V&A Museum, 1980–83; Music Panel, British Council, 1979–83; Drama Panel, 1992–94, 2007–09, 2012–13, Dance Panel, 2003–04, Olivier Awards; Council, and Chm., Exec. Bd, LAMDA, 1994–; Jury, Walpole Awards for Cultural Excellence, 2006–; Arts and Media Honours Adv. Cttee, 2012–; Judging Panel, Legacy 10 Awards, 2013–; Founder Mem., Adv. Develt Bd, Cambridge Summer Music Fest., 2010–. Chm., London Choral Soc., subseq. London Chorus, 1994–2005. Trustee: Bath Preservation Trust, 1968–73; Theatre Royal, Bath, 1979–82; City Ballet of London, 1997–2000; Foundn Trustee, Holburne Museum, Bath, 1981–83; Gov., Conservatoire for Dance and Drama, 2004–13. Patron, Dartington Coll. of Arts, 2002–. Hon. DA Bath, 2004; Hon. DCL Durham, 2005. *Recreations:* the arts, people, travel. *Address:* Royal Academy of Dance, 36 Battersea Square, SW11 3RA. *Club:* Garrick.

RIVA, Hilary, OBE 2009; Chairman, Development Committee, British Fashion Council, 2009–10 (Chief Executive, 2005–09); *b* Mansfield, 3 April 1957; three *s*. *Educ:* Poly. of Central London (BA Hons Soc. Sci. 1984). Arcadia Group: Buying and Merchandising Controller, Topshop, 1980–90; Buying and Merchandising Dir, Burton Gp, 1990–96; Man. Dir, Evans, 1996–98; Man. Dir, Dorothy Perkins, Topshop, Evans, Principles, 1998–2000; Man. Dir, Evans, Wallis, Warehouse, Principles, 2000–01; Man. Dir, Rubicon Retail Ltd, 2001–05. Non-executive Director: Shaftesbury plc, 2010–; London & Partners Ltd, 2011–; Asos plc, 2014–. *Address:* Abbey House, Abbey Road, Faversham ME13 7BE. *T:* (01795) 834744.

RIVERDALE, 3rd Baron *cr* 1935, of Sheffield, co. York; **Anthony Robert Balfour;** Bt 1929; *b* 23 Feb. 1960; *s* of Hon. Mark Robin Balfour (*d* 1995) and Susan Ann Phillips (*d* 1996); *S* grandfather, 1998. *Educ:* Wellington. *Heir: cousin* Arthur Michael Balfour [*b* 24 Nov. 1938; *m* 1962, Rita Ann Fance; two *s* one *d*].

RIVERINA, Bishop of, since 2014; **Rt Rev. (Alan) Robert Gillion;** *b* Docking, Norfolk, 7 Sept. 1951; *s* of Arthur and Barbara Gillion; *m* 1974, Janine Ellis; two *s*. *Educ:* Norwich Sch.; New Coll. of Speech and Drama; London Univ. (Dip. in Dramatic Art; DipEd); Salisbury and Wells Theol Coll. (DipTh). LRAM 1973. Actor and theatre dir, 1970–81; ordained deacon, 1983, priest, 1984; Curate, East Dereham, 1983–86; Team Vicar, Richmond, Surrey, 1986–90; Priest-in-charge, Discovery Bay Church, Hong Kong, 1990–98; Bishop of Kensington's Officer for Evangelism, 1998–2001; Vicar, St Simon Zelotes and St Saviour, London, 2001–08; Area Dean of Chelsea, 2004–11; Rector, Holy Trinity and St Saviour, Upper Chelsea, 2008–14. Chaplain: St John's Cathedral, Hong Kong, 1990–98; Shek Pik Prison, Hong Kong, 1990–98; Exec. Sec. for Religious Broadcasting, Hong Kong Christian Council, 1990–98. Chaplain to Harrods, 2004–14; Sen. Chaplain, Actors Church Union, 2006–13. Trustee, Bible Reading Fellowship, 2008–14. Freelance broadcaster, BBC, 1998–2014; contrib. to New Daylights, 1998–2005. *Recreations:* family, theatre, sport, golf, tennis. *Address:* The Registry, PO Box 10, 58 Arthur Street, Narrandera, NSW 2700, Australia. *T:* (2) 69591648, *Fax:* (2) 69592903. *E:* robgillion@hotmail.com, rivdio@bigpond.com. *Club:* Sloane.

RIVERS, Deborah Ann; *see* Cadman, D. A.

RIVERS, Valerie Lane-Fox P.; *see* Pitt-Rivers.

RIVETT, Dr Geoffrey Christopher; Senior Principal Medical Officer, Department of Health (formerly of Health and Social Security), 1985–92; *b* 11 Aug. 1932; *s* of Frank Andrew James Rivett and Catherine Mary Rivett; *m* 1976, Elizabeth Barbara Hartman; two *s* by previous marriage. *Educ:* Manchester Grammar Sch.; Brasenose Coll., Oxford (MA 1st Cl. Hons Animal Physiol.); University Coll. Hosp. (BM, BCh); FRCGP, DObst RCOG. House Officer, Radcliffe Inf., Oxford, 1957; House Phys., London Chest Hosp., 1958; RAMC, 1958–60; GP, Milton Keynes, 1960–72; DHSS, subseq. DoH, 1972–92. Vice Chm., Council of Govs, Homerton NHS Foundn Trust, 2007–13. Liveryman: Soc. of Apothecaries, 1981–; Co. of Barbers, 1993–. ARPS 1971. *Publications:* The Development of the London Hospital System 1823–1982, 1986, 2nd edn as The Development of the London Hospital System 1823–2015, 2015; From Cradle to Grave: fifty years of the NHS, 1998. *Recreations:* photography, contemporary history, web authoring. *Address:* 173 Shakespeare Tower, Barbican, EC2Y 8DR. *T:* (020) 7786 9617. *E:* geoffrey@rivett.net. *W:* www.nhshistory.net. *Club:* Royal Society of Medicine.

RIVETT-CARNAC, Sir Jonathan James, 10th Bt *cr* 1836, of Derby; Chairman, Finch & Partners, since 2012; *b* 14 June 1962; *er s* of Sir Miles James Rivett-Carnac, 9th Bt and of April Sally (*née* Villar); *S* father, 2009; *m* 2013, Reiko, *d* of Setsuko Kiuchi, Tokyo, Japan; one *d*. *Educ:* Harrow. Dir, Lulu Guinness Ltd, 2011–. *Heir: b* Simon Miles Rivett-Carnac [*b* 10 Feb. 1966; *m* 1994, Sarah Jane Petrie; two *s*]. *Clubs:* White's, Brooks's.

RIVIERE, Rev. Canon Jonathan Byam Valentine, LVO 2015; Rector, Sandringham Group of Parishes, and Domestic Chaplain to the Queen, since 2003; Chaplain to the Queen, since 2007; Rural Dean of Heacham and Rising, since 2013; *b* 4 Feb. 1954; *s* of late Anthony and of Ann Riviere; *m* 1987, Clare Hudson; two *s* one *d*. *Educ:* Westminster; RAC Cirencester; Cuddesdon Coll. Ordained deacon, 1983, priest, 1984; Curate, Wymondham, 1983–88; Team Vicar, Quidenham, 1988–94; Priest i/c, 1994, Rector, 1995–2003, Somerleyton Gp of Parishes. Hon. Canon, Norwich Cathedral, 2014–. *Recreation:* sailing. *Address:* The Rectory, Sandringham, Norfolk PE35 6EH. *T:* (01485) 540587.

RIVLIN, His Honour Geoffrey; QC 1979; Adviser to Director, Serious Fraud Office, since 2012; *b* 28 Nov. 1940; *s* of late M. Allenby Rivlin and late May Rivlin; *m* 1974, Maureen Smith, Hon. ARAM, Prof. of Violin, RAM; two *d*. *Educ:* Bootham Sch.; Leeds Univ. (LLB). Called to the Bar, Middle Temple, 1963 (Colombos Prize, Internat. Law); Bencher, 1987; Reader, 2007. NE Circuit Junior 1967; a Recorder, 1978–89; a Circuit Judge, 1989–2004; a Sen. Circuit Judge, 2004–11. Mem., Senate of Inns of Court and the Bar, 1976–79. Chm. Adv. Bd, Computer Crime Centre, QMW, 1996–2002. Mem., Investigatory Powers Tribunal, 2012–. Mem. (Ind), Westminster CC, 2012–. Hon. Recorder, City of Westminster, 2008–11. Chm., Bar Council review into future of criminal bar, 2014–. Trustee, Fine Cell Work charity, 2012– (Chm., 2012–14). Governor: St Christopher's Sch., Hampstead, 1990–99; NLCS, Edgware, 1993–2003. *Publications:* First Steps in the Law, 1999, 7th edn 2015; Judges and Schools, 2002. *Address:* Serious Fraud Office, 2–4 Cockspur Street, SW1Y 5BS.

RIX, family name of **Baron Rix**.

RIX, Baron *cr* 1992 (Life Peer), of Whitehall in the City of Westminster and of Hornsea in Yorkshire; **Brian Norman Roger Rix,** Kt 1986; CBE 1977; DL; actor-manager, 1948–77; President, Mencap (The Royal Mencap Society, formerly Royal Society for Mentally Handicapped Children and Adults), since 1998 (Secretary-General, 1980–87; Chairman, 1988–98); Chairman, The Rix-Thompson-Rothenberg Foundation (formerly Mencap City Foundation), since 1988 (Founder and Governor, since 1984); *b* 27 Jan. 1924; *s* of late Herbert and Fanny Rix; *m* 1949, Elspet Jeans Macgregor-Gray (*d* 2013); two *s* one *d* (and one *d* decd). *Educ:* Bootham Sch., York. Stage career: joined Donald Wolfit, 1942; first West End appearance, Sebastian in Twelfth Night, St James's, 1943; White Rose Players, Harrogate, 1943–44. Served War of 1939–45, RAF and Bevin Boy. Became actor-manager, 1948; ran repertory cos at Ilkley, Bridlington and Margate, 1950; toured Reluctant Heroes and brought to Whitehall Theatre, 1950–54; Dry Rot, 1954–58; Simple Spymen, 1958–61; One For the Pot, 1961–64; Chase Me Comrade, 1964–66; went to Garrick Theatre, 1967, with repertoire of farce: Stand By Your Bedouin; Uproar in the House; Let Sleeping Wives Lie; after 6 months went over to latter, only, which ran till 1969; then followed: She's Done It Again, 1969–70; Don't Just Lie There, Say Something!, 1971–73 (filmed 1973); New Theatre, Cardiff, Robinson Crusoe, 1973; Cambridge Theatre, A Bit Between The Teeth, 1974; Fringe Benefits, Whitehall Theatre, 1976; returned to a theatre season with Dry Rot, Lyric Theatre, 1989; dir., You'll Do For Me!, tour, 1989. Entered films, 1951: subsequently made eleven, including Reluctant Heroes, 1951, Dry Rot, 1956. BBC TV contract to present farces on TV, 1956–72; first ITV series Men of Affairs, 1973; A Roof Over My Head, BBC TV series, 1977. Presenter, Let's Go …, BBC TV series (first ever for people with a learning disability), 1978–83; BBC Radio 2 series, 1978–80; occasional appearances in A Peer Round Whitehall, 2008–12. Dir and Theatre Controller, Cooney-Marsh Group, 1977–80; Trustee, Theatre of Comedy, 1983–93; Arts Council: Mem., 1986–93; Chairman: Drama Panel, 1986–93; Monitoring Cttee, Arts and Disabled People, 1988–93; Ind. Develt Council for People with Mental Handicap, 1981–86; Normansfield and Richmond Foundn (formerly Friends of Normansfield), 1975–2003 (Pres., 2003–); Libertas, 1987–2006. Chancellor, Univ. of E London, 1997–2011, now Chancellor Emeritus. DL Greater London, 1987; Vice Lord-Lieut of Greater London, 1988–97. Hon. Fellow: Humberside Coll. of Higher Educn, 1984; Myerscough Coll., 2002; Hon. FRSocMed 1998; Hon. FRCPsych 1999. Hon. MA: Hull, 1981; Open, 1983; DUniv: Essex, 1984; Bradford, 2000; East London, 2013; Hon. LLD: Manchester, 1986; Dundee, 1994; Exeter, 1997; Hon. DSc Nottingham, 1987; Hon. DLitt Kingston, 2012. Evian Health Award, 1988; Communicator of the Year, RNID, 1990; Campaigner of the Year, Spectator, 1999; Yorks Lifetime Achievement Award, Yorkshire Awards, 1999; Lifetime Achievement Award, UK Charity Awards, 2001; Public Service Award, British Neurosci. Assoc., 2001; Lifetime Achievement Award, ePolitix Charity Champions Awards, 2004; Bevin Boy Veteran Badge, 2008. *Publications:* My Farce from My Elbow: an autobiography, 1975; Farce about Face (autobiog.), 1989; Tour de Farce, 1992; Life in the Farce Lane, 1995; (ed and contrib.) Gullible's Travails, 1996; All About Us!: the story of people with a learning disability and Mencap, 2006. *Recreations:* cricket, amateur radio (G2DQU; Hon. Vice-Pres., Radio Soc. of GB, 1979), gardening. *Address:* House of Lords, SW1A 0PW. *Clubs:* Garrick, MCC, Lord's Taverners (Pres., 1970).

RIX, Rear Adm. Anthony John, CB 2009; defence and security consultant, since 2010; Director, Maritime Security, Salamanca Group, since 2011; *b* 12 Aug. 1956; *s* of Sir John Rix, MBE, and of Sylvia Gene Rix (*née* Howe). *Educ:* Sherborne Sch.; Britannia RNC. Joined RN, 1975; Commanding Officer: HMS Glasgow, 1995–96; HMS Marlborough, 1999–2000; Flag Officer Sea Trng, 2006–07; COS to Comdr Allied Naval Forces Southern Europe, 2007–09. QCVS 2006. *Recreations:* tennis, shooting, fishing, sailing. *Address:* c/o Salamanca Group, 50 Berkeley Street, W1J 8HA. *E:* Anthony.Rix@btinternet.com. *Clubs:* Royal Yacht Squadron; Trinity House.

RIX, Rt Hon. Sir Bernard (Anthony), Kt 1993; PC 2000; a Lord Justice of Appeal, 2000–13; Professor of International Commercial Law, Queen Mary University of London, since 2013; international arbitrator and mediator; *b* 8 Dec. 1944; *s* of late Otto Rix and Sadie Silverberg; *m* 1983, Hon. Karen Debra, *er d* of Baron Young of Graffham, *qv*; three *s* two *d* (incl. twin *s*). *Educ:* St Paul's School, London; New College, Oxford (BA: Lit.Hum. 1966, Jur. 1968; MA; Hon. Fellow 2007); Harvard Law School (Kennedy Scholar 1968; LLM 1969). FCIArb 1999. Called to Bar, Inner Temple, 1970 (Bencher, 1990; Reader, 2004, Treasurer, 2005); QC 1981; a Recorder, 1990–93; a Judge of the High Court, QBD, 1993–2000; Judge in charge of Commercial List, 1998–99; a Judge of the Court of Appeal, Cayman Islands, 2013–. Member: Senate, Inns of Court and Bar, 1981–83; Bar Council, 1981–83. Chm., Commercial Bar Assoc., 1992–93. Pres., Harvard Law Sch. Assoc. of UK, 2002–; Vice-Pres., British Insurance Law Assoc., 2006–. Dir, London Philharmonic Orchestra, 1986–. Vice-Chm., Central Council for Jewish Community Services, 1994–96 (author, report on youth services and orgns, 1994). Dir, Spiro Inst., 1995–99. Chm., British Friends of Bar-Ilan Univ., 1987–99 (Hon. Vice-Pres., 1999–); Mem. Bd of Trustees, Bar-Ilan Univ., 1988–99; Chm., Adv. Council, Centre of Commercial Law Studies, QMUL, 2003–; Trustee and Dir, British Inst. of Internat. and Comparative Law, 2003–12. Patron, Wiener Library, 2006–. Hon. Fellow, QMUL, 2008. *Recreations:* music, opera, Italy, formerly fencing. *Address:* 20 Essex Street, WC2R 3AL. *T:* (020) 7842 1200.

RIX, Dr (Edward) Martyn; freelance writer and botanist, since 1978; Editor, Curtis's Botanical Magazine, since 2003; *b* 15 Aug. 1943; *s* of Edward Lionel Reussner Rix and Elizabeth Joyce Rix; *m* 1983, Alison Jane Goatcher; two *d*. *Educ:* Sherborne Sch., Dorset; Trinity Coll., Dublin (MA); Corpus Christi Coll., Cambridge (PhD). Res. Fellow, Univ. of Zürich, 1971–73; botanist, RHS, Wisley, 1974–78. FLS 2006. Gold Veitch Meml Medal, RHS, 1999; Tercentenary Bronze Medal, Linnean Soc. of London, 2008. *Publications:* The Art of the Botanist, 1981; Growing Bulbs, 1983; The Redouté Album, 1990; Subtropical and Dry Climate Plants, 2006; with R. Phillips: Bulbs, 1981; Freshwater Fish, 1985; Roses, 1988; Shrubs, 1989; Perennials, 2 vols, 1991; Vegetables, 1993; The Quest for the Rose, 1993; Conservatory and Indoor Plants, 1997; Annuals, 1999; The Botanical Garden, 2002; (with S. Sherwood) Treasures of Botanical Art, 2008. *Recreations:* fishing, sailing, travel. *Address:* c/o Macmillan Publishers Ltd, 20 New Wharf Road, N1 9RR.

RIX, Michael David; National Executive Officer, GMB, since 2005; *b* 11 April 1963; *s* of Roy Rix; *m* 1984; one *s* one *d*. *Educ:* Primrose Hill High Sch., Leeds; Bradford and Ilkley TUC Coll.; various TUC/ASLEF educn projects. Left sch. at 16 with no formal qualifications; work experience, Yorks copper works, 1979; trainee driver, BR, Leeds, 1979–86; qualified BR driver, 1986. Leeds ASLEF: Mem., Br. Cttee, 1980–84; Asst Br. Sec., 1984–98; Br. Sec., 1988–98; Negotiating Chair, 1992; Dist Council Chm., 1995; Dist Sec., No 3 Reg., 1998; Gen. Sec., ASLEF, 1998–2003. Mem., TUC General Council, 2001–03. Mem., Labour Party, 1980–97, 2000–. Mem., Co-op Soc., Wortley Hall, PPPS. *Recreations:* football, especially Leeds United, watching Rugby league, watching Yorkshire CCC, swimming, reading, very little time though to pursue. *Address:* c/o GMB National Office, 22 Stephenson Way, Euston, NW1 2HD.

RIZA, Alper Ali; QC 1991; a Recorder of the Crown Court, since 2000; *b* 16 March 1948; *s* of Ali Riza and Elli Liasides; *m* 1981, Vanessa Frances Hall-Smith, *qv* (marr. diss. 2009); two *d*. *Educ:* American Academy, Larnaca, Cyprus; English Sch., Nicosia. Called to the Bar, Gray's Inn, 1973. Pupillage, 1974–75; Turnpike Lane Law and Advice, 1975–77; Appeals Lawyer, Jt Council for Welfare of Immigrants, 1977–82; private practice, 1982–. Founder Mem., Assoc. of Greek, Turkish and Cypriot Affairs, 1990–. Fellow, Inst. of Advanced Legal Studies; Mem., RIIA. *Recreations:* music, philosophy, drinking and smoking, sport, walking around London W2 and W11 esp. Hyde Park, Kensington Gardens and Holland Park. *Address:* Goldsmith Chambers, Goldsmith Building, Temple, EC4Y 7BL.

RIZZARDO, Dr Ezio, FRS 2010; CSIRO Fellow, since 2000, Project Leader, Engineered Polymers, since 1978, and Leader, Polymer Production Program, Cooperative Research Centre, since 1994, CSIRO; *b* Onigo, Italy, 26 Dec. 1943; *s* of Gino Rizzardo and Ottorina Bresolin; *m* 1968, Jeannette Angela Dodds; one *s* one *d*. *Educ:* Univ. of NSW (BSc 1st Cl. Hons 1966); Univ. of Sydney (PhD 1969). Postdoctoral Fellow: Rice Univ., Houston, 1969–71; Research Inst. for Medicine and Chem., Cambridge, Mass, 1971–73; Res. Fellow, ANU, 1973–76; CSIRO: Sen. Res. Scientist, 1976–2000; Manager, Polymers Prog., 1980–98; Proj. Leader, Polymeric Biomaterials, 1988–92; Chief Res. Scientist, 1992–2000. FRACI 1981; FTSE 1994; FAA 2002. Aust. Polymer Medal, 1992, Applied Res. Medal, 1996, H. G. Smith Meml Medal, 2003, RACI; Most Prolific Inventor Award, 2001, Chairman's Gold Medal, CSIRO; Centenary Medal, Australia, 2003; Prime Minister's Prize for Sci., Australia, 2011. *Publications:* articles and book chapters on organic chemistry and polymer sci. *Address:* CSIRO, Locked Bag 10, Clayton South, Vic 3169, Australia.

RIZZI, Carlo; conductor; Musical Director, Welsh National Opera, 1992–2001 and 2004–08; *b* 19 July 1960. *Educ:* Milan Conservatoire; Accademia Musicale Chigiana, Siena. Débuts: Australian Opera Co., 1989; Netherlands Opera, 1989; Royal Opera, 1990; WNO, 1991; Deutsche Oper, Berlin, 1992; Cologne Opera, 1992; La Scala, 1992; Israel Philharmonic, 1993; Metropolitan Opera, NY, 1993; Pesaro, 1994; Edinburgh Fest., 1996; Chicago Lyric Opera, 1996; has made numerous recordings.

ROADS, Dr Christopher Herbert; Acting Chairman and (Founding) Managing Director, Historic Arms Exhibitions and Forts LLC, Oman, since 2001; consultant in museums and audio visual archives; *b* 3 Jan. 1934; *s* of late Herbert Clifford Roads and Vera Iris Roads; *m* 1976, Charlotte Alicia Dorothy Mary Lothian (marr. diss.); one *d*. *Educ:* Cambridge and County Sch.; Trinity Hall, Cambridge (Double 1st Cl. Hist.; PhD 1961). Nat. Service, 2nd Lieut, RA, Egypt, 1952–54. Adviser to WO on Disposal of Amnesty Arms, 1961–62; Imperial War Museum: Keeper of Dept of Records, 1962–70; Dep. Dir-Gen. at Main Building, Southwark, 1964–79, at Duxford, Cambridge, 1976–79, HMS Belfast, Pool of London, 1978–79; Dir, Museums & Archives Develt Associates Ltd, 1977–85; Dir, Nat. Sound Archive, 1983–92; Associate Dir (Consultancy), R&D Dept, BL, 1992–94. UNESCO consultant designing major audio visual archives or museums in Philippines, Panama, Bolivia, Kuwait, Jordan, Saudi Arabia, etc, 1976–. Founder and Dir, Cambridge Coral/Starfish Res. Gp, 1968–; Founding Chairman: Sudanese British Develt Co., 1972–79; Photoair Services Ltd, 1972–80; Director: Nat. Discography Ltd, 1986–92; Historic Cable Ship John W. Mackay, 1986–; AVT Communications Ltd, 1988–92; Cedar Audio Ltd, 1989–92; Green Metals Ltd, 2011; Founding Consultant: Oman Titanium LLC, 2013–; Nizbridge LLC, 2013–. Founder, Dept of Materials Sci. and Metallurgy, Univ. of Nizwa in association with Dept of Materials Sci. and Metallurgy, Univ. of Cambridge, 2013, Consultant to Univ. of Nizwa, 2013–. Chm., Coral Conservation Trust, 1972–; President: Historical Breechloading Small Arms Assoc., 1973–, Pres. for Life, 2003; Internat. Film and TV Council (UNESCO Category A), 1990–92 (Pres., Archives Commn, 1970–); Hon. Pres., World Expeditionary Assoc. (Vice Pres., 1971); Vice President: Duxford Aviation Soc., 1974–; English Eight Club, 1980–; Cambridge Univ. Rifle Assoc., 1987– (Mem. Council, 1955–87; Double Half Blue in Rifle Shooting); Mem. Council, Scientific Exploration Soc., 1971–82; Sec., Nat. Archives Cttee, Internat. Assoc. of Sound Archives, 1988–92; Hon. Sec., Cambridge Univ. Long Range Rifle Club, 1979–2008 (Pres., 2008–); Mem., Home Office Reference Panel for Historic Firearms, 1997–2003; Chm., Heritage Arms Rescue, 1996–. Trustee: HMS Belfast Trust, 1970–78; Nat. Life Stories Collection, 1986–92; NSA Wild Life Sound Trust, 1986–92. Adjt, English VIII, 1964–88. Churchill Fellowship, 1970; Vis. Fellow, Centre of Internat. Studies, Univ. of Cambridge, 1983–84. FRGS. Liveryman, Gunmakers' Co., 1996; Freeman, City of London, 1996. Silver Jubilee Medal, 1977. Order of Independence, 2nd cl. (Jordan), 1977. *Publications:* The British Soldier's Firearm, 1850–1864, 1964; (jtly) New Studies on the Crown of Thorns Starfish, 1970; The Story of the Gun, 1978. *Recreations:* rifle shooting, marine and submarine exploration, wind surfing, motorcycling, videography. *Address:* The White House, 90 High Street, Melbourn, near Royston, Herts SG8 6AL. *T:* (01763) 260866, *Fax:* (01763) 262521; DX 12 Urbanización Bahia Dorada, 29693 Estepona, Málaga, Spain. *T:* and *Fax:* (95) 2796407; Historic Arms Exhibitions and Forts LLC, PO Box 3726, P. Code 112, Ruwi, Muscat, Sultanate of Oman. *T:* (residence) 99797326, *T:* and *Fax:* (office) 24501218. *Clubs:* Oxford and Cambridge; Hawks (Cambridge).

ROADS, Elizabeth Ann, LVO 2012 (MVO 1990); Lyon Clerk and Keeper of the Records, since 1986, Snawdoun Herald of Arms, since 2010 and Secretary, Order of the Thistle, since 2014; *b* Iserlohn, Germany, 5 July 1951; *d* of Lt Col James Bruce, MC and Mary Hope Bruce (*née* Sinclair); *m* 1983, Maj. Christopher George William Roads, TD; two *s* one *d*. *Educ:* Lansdowne House Sch., Edinburgh; Edinburgh Napier Univ. (LLB 2012). Christie, Manson & Woods, London, 1970–74; Court of the Lord Lyon, 1975–: Linlithgow Pursuivant Extraordinary, 1987; Carrick Pursuivant of Arms, 1992–2010; Asst Sec., Order of the Thistle, 2008–14. Hon. Treas., Scottish Record Soc., 1997–2011; Chm., Scottish Records Assoc., 2010–15; Trustee, Scottish Council on Archives, 2015–. Pres., Old Edinburgh Club, 2013– (Hon. Sec., 2012–13). FSAScot 1986; FSA 2013; Fellow: Heraldry Soc. of Scotland, 1996; Royal Heraldry Soc. of Canada, 2004; Academician, Academie Internationale d'Heraldique, 2008. Silver Jubilee Medal, 1977; Golden Jubilee Medal, 2002; Diamond Jubilee Medal, 2012. OStJ 1999. *Publications:* The Chapel of the Order of the Thistle, 2009; articles in heraldic and genealogical jls. *Recreations:* history, reading, genealogical research, the countryside. *Address:* Court of the Lord Lyon, HM New Register House, Edinburgh EH1 3YT. *T:* (0131) 556 7255.

ROBARDS, Prof. Anthony William, OBE 2002; PhD, DSc; FRSB; HSBC Professor of Innovation, University of York, 2001–09, now Emeritus Professor; Consultant, AWR1 Associates, since 2009; *b* 9 April 1940; *s* of Albert Charles Robards, Lamberhurst, Kent, and Kathleen Emily Robards; *m* 1st, 1962, Ruth Bulpett (marr. diss. 1985); one *s* one *d*; 2nd, 1987, Eva Christina, *d* of Bo Knutson-Ek, Lidingo, Sweden. *Educ:* Skinners' Sch.; UCL (BSc 1962; PhD 1966; DSc 1977); Inst. of Educn, Univ. of London (PGCE 1963); Dip RMS 1976. FRSB (FIBiol 1978). Department of Biology, University of York: Lectr, 1966–70; Sen. Lectr, 1970–79; Reader, 1979–88; Prof. of Biol., 1988–2003; Pro-Vice-Chancellor for Ext. Relns, 1996–2004; Director: Inst. for Applied Biol., 1986–95; Industrial Develt, 1988–96. Visiting Research Fellow: ANU, 1975; Univ. of Stockholm, 1986. Dir, York Science Park (Innovation Centre) Ltd, 1994– (Chm., 1995–2006); Chm., York Science Park Ltd, 1999–2008; Exec. Chm., York Sci. and Innovation Grand Tour Ltd, 2011–; non-exec. Chm., YorkTest Gp Ltd, 1999–2009. Trustee, Yorks Cancer Res., 2006– (Dep. Chm., 2009–10; Chm., 2010–). Mem., Co. of Merchant Adventurers, City of York, 1991– (Gov., 2008–09). *Publications:* (with U. B. Sleytr) Low Temperature Methods in Biological Electron Microscopy, 1985; 130 scientific articles. *Recreations:* horology, sailing, opera, photography. *Address:* Shrubbery Cottage, Nun Monkton, Yorks YO26 8EW. *T:* (01423) 331023; The Innovation Centre, York Science Park, York YO10 5DG. *T:* (01904) 435105. *E:* Anthony.Robards@york.ac.uk, AnthonyRobards@aol.com.

ROBARTS, (Anthony) Julian; Director and Chief Executive, Iveagh Trustees Ltd, 1993–98; Managing Director, Coutts & Co., 1986–91; *b* 6 May 1937; *s* of late Lt-Col Anthony V. C. Robarts, DL and Grizel Mary Robarts (Grant); *m* 1961, Edwina Beryl Hobson; two *s* one *d*. *Educ:* Eton College. National Service, 11th Hussars (PAO), 1955–57; joined Coutts & Co., 1958, Dir, 1963, Dep. Man. Dir, 1976–86; Director: Coutts Finance Co., 1967–91; F. Bolton Group, 1970–2008; International Fund for Institutions Inc., USA, 1983–93; Chm., Hill Martin, 1993–2004; Regional Dir, Nat. Westminster Bank, 1971–92. Hon. Treasurer, 1969–2001, Vice-Pres., 2001–09, Union Jack Club. Trustee: Beit Med. Meml Fellowships, 1993–2001; Sargent Cancer Care for Children, 1997–2000. *Recreations:* shooting, gardening, opera. *Address:* Bromley Hall, Standon, Ware, Herts SG11 1NY. *Clubs:* Brooks's, Pratt's, MCC.

ROBATHAN, Rt Hon. Andrew (Robert George); PC 2010; *b* 17 July 1951; *s* of late Robert Douglas Brice Robathan and Sheena Mary Martin (*née* Gimson); *m* 1991, Rachael Maunder; one *s* one *d*. *Educ:* Merchant Taylors' Sch., Northwood; Oriel Coll., Oxford (MA). Served Coldstream Guards, 1974–89 (Officer, SAS, 1981–83, HQ, 1984–87), resigned as Major; rejoined Army for Gulf War, Jan.–April 1991 (COS, POW Guard Force). Councillor, London Borough of Hammersmith and Fulham, 1990–92. MP (C) Blaby, 1992–2010, S Leicestershire, 2010–15. PPS to Minister of State for Nat. Heritage, 1995–97; opposition spokesman on: trade and industry, 2002–03; internat. develt, 2003; defence, 2004–05; Dep. Opposition Chief Whip, 2005–10; Parly Under-Sec. of State, 2010–12, Minister of State, 2012–13, MoD; Minister of State, NI Office, 2013–14. Mem., Internat. Develt Select Cttee, 1997–2002, 2003–04; Chm., 1994–97, Vice-Chm., 1997–2010, All-Party Cycling Gp; Vice Chairman: Parly Renewable and Sustainable Energy Gp, 1992–94, 1997–2010; Cons. back bench Defence Cttee, 1993–94, 1997–2001 (Chm., 1994–95); Cons. NI Cttee, 1994–95, 1997–2001; Cons. Defence and Internat. Affairs Policy Gp, 2001–02. Captain, Tug of War Team, 1995–2000, Clay Pigeon Team, 1997–2007, H of C. Mem. Bd, Indict, 1998–2001;

Trustee, Halo Trust, 2000–06 (Chm., 2003–06). *Recreations:* hill-walking, ski-ing, shooting, architecture, history, conservation.

[Created a Baron (Life Peer) 2015 but title not yet gazetted at time of going to press.]

ROBB, Andrew Mackenzie, FCMA, FCT; Chairman, Tata Steel Europe Ltd, since 2009 (Independent Director, since 2003); Independent Director: Tata Steel Ltd (India), since 2007; Jaguar Land Rover plc, since 2009; *b* Birmingham, Sept. 1942; *s* of William and Kathleen Robb; *m*; two *d. Educ:* Rugby Sch. FCMA 1968; JDipMA 1973; FCT 1980. Accountant: T. Wall & Sons Ltd, 1964–69; Hoskyns Gp Ltd, 1969–71; Financial Controller, 1971–83, Gp Finance Dir, 1983–89, P & O Steam Navigation Co.; Exec. Dir, Pilkington plc, 1989–2003 (Gp Finance Dir, 1989–2001). Independent Director: Kesa Electricals plc, 2003–12; Paypoint plc, 2004–14; Laird plc, 2004–12. Mem., Urgent Issues Taskforce, Accounting Standards Bd, 1992–97. Chm. Trustees, Pilkington Superannuation Scheme, 2000–14. Freeman, City of London, 1998. *Address:* Tata Steel Europe Ltd, 30 Millbank, SW1P 4WY. *T:* (020) 7717 4553. *E:* andrewmrobb1@gmail.com.

ROBB, (David) Campbell; Chief Executive, Shelter, since 2010; *b* Glasgow, 14 May 1969; *m* 2007, Donna Murray; two *d. Educ:* Univ. of Edinburgh (MA Hons Pols and Mod. Hist.). Researcher for David Blunkett, MP, 1993–94; Press Officer for Chris Smith, MP, 1996–97; Hd of Campaigns, 1998–2001, Dir, Public Policy, 2001–05, NCVO; Advr to HM Treasury, 2005; Dir Gen., Office of the Third Sector, 2006–09 and Social Exclusion Task Force, 2009, Cabinet Office. *Recreations:* music, cooking, escaping to our allotment, reading. *Address:* Shelter, 88 Old Street, EC1V 9HU. *T:* 0844 515 2124.

ROBB, Dr Graham Macdonald, FRSL; writer; *b* Manchester, 2 June 1958; *s* of Gordon James Robb and Joyce Robb (*née* Gall); *m* 1986, Margaret Gay Hambrick. *Educ:* Worcester Royal Grammar Sch.; Exeter Coll., Oxford (BA, MA); Goldsmiths' Coll., London (PGCE); Vanderbilt Univ. (MA; PhD 1986). British Acad. Post-doctoral Fellow, Exeter Coll., Oxford, 1987–90. FRSL 1999. Grande Médaille de la Ville de Paris, 2012. Chevalier, Ordre des Arts et des Lettres (France), 2009. *Publications:* Le Corsaire-Satan en Silhouette, 1985; Baudelaire lecteur de Balzac, 1988; (ed) Scènes de la vie de bohème, 1988; (adapted trans.) Baudelaire, 1989; La Poésie de Baudelaire et la poésie française, 1993; Balzac, 1994; Unlocking Mallarmé, 1996 (MLA Prize for Ind. Scholars, 1997); Victor Hugo, 1997 (Whitbread Biog. Prize; Heinemann Award, RSL); Rimbaud, 2000; Strangers: homosexual love in the nineteenth century, 2003; The Discovery of France, 2007 (Duff Cooper Prize, 2008; Ondaatje Prize, RSL, 2008); Parisians: an adventure history of Paris, 2010; The Ancient Paths: discovering the lost map of Celtic Europe, 2013; contribs to TLS, London Rev. of Books, NY Rev. of Books. *Recreations:* road cycling, sylviculture. *Address:* c/o Rogers, Coleridge & White Ltd, 20 Powis Mews, W11 1JN. *E:* info@rcwlitagency.com.

ROBB, Sir John (Weddell), Kt 1999; Chairman, British Energy, 1995–2001; *b* 27 April 1936; *s* of John and Isabella Robb; *m* 1965, Janet Teanby; two *s* one *d. Educ:* Daniel Stewart's College, Edinburgh. Beecham Group: Marketing Exec., Toiletry Div., Beecham Products, 1966; Man. Dir, Beecham (Far East), Kuala Lumpur, 1971; Vice-Pres., W. Hemisphere Div., Beecham Products, USA, 1974; Man. Dir, Food and Drink Div., Beecham Products, 1976; Group Board, 1980; Chm., Food and Drink Div., 1980; Chm., Beecham Products, 1984–85; Gp Man. Dir, 1985–88; Wellcome Plc: Dep. Chief Exec., 1989–90; Chief Exec., 1990–95; Chm., 1994–95. Non-exec. Dir, Uniq plc (formerly Unigate), 1996–2002. Dep. Chm., Horserace Betting Levy Bd, 1993–2006; Trustee, Royal Botanic Gdn, Edinburgh, 1997–2002. *Recreations:* golf, gardening, racing. *Clubs:* Turf; Sunningdale.

ROBB, Kenneth Richard; Sheriff of South Strathclyde, Dumfries and Galloway at Stranraer, since 2008 and at Dumfries, since 2013 (at Kirkcudbright, 2008–13); *b* Larbert, 3 Sept. 1954; *s* of Richard Robb and Mary Robb; *m* 1977, Susan Ringrose; one *d. Educ:* Falkirk High Sch.; Edinburgh Univ. (LLB Hons). Admitted solicitor, 1978; private legal practice, 1976–2000; pt-time Immigration Judge, 2002–08; pt-time Employment Judge, 2005–08; pt-time Sheriff, 2006–08. Mem., Scottish Solicitors' Discipline Tribunal, 1998–2008. Mem. Council, Law Soc. of Scotland, 1987–97. Member, disciplinary panels: GMC, 2000–05; ACCA, 2002–08; Soc. of Actuaries, 2003–07. Mem. Council, Sheriffs' Assoc., 2012–15. *Publications:* (contrib. ed) Scottish Family Law Service, 1995. *Recreations:* hill-walking, history, holidays. *Address:* Sheriff Courthouse, Lewis Street, Stranraer DG9 7AA.

ROBB, Prof. Michael Alfred, PhD, DSc; FRS 2000; Professor of Chemistry, Imperial College, London, since 2004; *b* 19 Feb. 1944; *s* of Robert Fredrick Robb and Dorothy Estelle Robb; *m* 1st, 1967, Brenda Elizabeth Donald (*d* 2000); one *s*; 2nd, 2001, Elaine Murphy (*see* Baroness Murphy). *Educ:* Toronto Univ. (PhD 1970); DSc London 1987. King's College, London: Lectr, 1971–88; Reader, 1988–92; Prof. of Chemistry, 1992–2003; Hd, Dept of Chemistry, 2000–03. *Publications:* contrib. to chemistry jls. *Address:* Department of Chemistry, Imperial College London, SW7 2AZ. *T:* (020) 7594 5757.

ROBBIE, David Andrew; Finance Director, Rexam plc, since 2005; *b* Greenmount, Lancs; *s* of Frank Robbie and Dorothy Robbie (*née* Holt). *Educ:* St Andrews Univ. (MA). ACA 1990. Finance Director: CMG plc, 2000–03; Royal P&O Nedlloyd NV, 2004–05. Non-executive Director: BBC, 2007–10; Almeida Theatre, 2007–10. Trustee, Aldeburgh Music, 2010–. *Recreations:* theatre, opera, travelling. *Address:* Rexam plc, 4 Millbank, SW1P 3XR. *T:* (020) 7227 4155. *E:* david.robbie@rexam.com.

ROBBINS, Christopher William; academic; HM Diplomatic Service, retired; *b* 16 June 1946. *Educ:* Skinners' Sch., Tunbridge Wells; Univ. of Sussex (BA); Warburg Inst., Univ. of London (MPhil). Lectr in Philosophy, Univ. of York, 1969–75; Principal, Welsh Office, 1975–77; Adminr, Directorate of Economic and Social Affairs, Council of Europe, 1977–84; joined HM Diplomatic Service, 1984; EC Dept, FCO, 1984–87; First Sec., New Delhi, 1987–90; Asst Head, Central and Southern Africa Dept, 1990–91; Head, Projects and Export Policy Branch I, DTI (on secondment), 1991–94; Commercial Counsellor, The Hague, 1994–98, and Consul-Gen., Amsterdam, 1996–98; Ambassador to Lithuania, 1998–2001; Minister-Counsellor (formerly Consul Gen.) and Dep. Hd of Mission, Seoul, 2001–05. Leader of Philosophy Gp, Mallorca, 2006–12. Tutor in Philosophy, Univ. of York, 2013–. *Publications:* (contrib.) La Santé Rationnée?, 1981; (contrib.) The End of an Illusion, 1984; articles in philosophical and social policy jls. *Recreation:* the enjoyment of beauty.

ROBBINS, James; Diplomatic Correspondent, BBC, since 1998; *b* 19 Jan. 1954; *s* of late (Richard) Michael Robbins, CBE and (Rose Margaret) Elspeth Robbins (*née* Bannatyne); *m* 1981, Gillian Gee; one *d. Educ:* Westminster Sch.; Christ Church, Oxford (BA Hons PPE). BBC: News Trainee, 1977; Reporter: Belfast, 1979–83; BBC News, 1983–87; Southern Africa Corresp., 1987–92; Europe Corresp., 1993–97. *Recreations:* opera, music, tennis, cooking, walking, looking out of train windows. *Address:* BBC News Centre, Broadcasting House, Portland Place, W1A 1AA. *E:* james.robbins@bbc.co.uk.

ROBBINS, Prof. Keith Gilbert; Vice-Chancellor (formerly Principal), University of Wales (formerly St David's University College), Lampeter, 1992–2003; Senior Vice-Chancellor, University of Wales, 1995–2001; *b* 9 April 1940; *s* of Gilbert Henry John and Edith Mary Robbins; *m* 1963, Janet Carey Thomson; three *s* one *d. Educ:* Bristol Grammar Sch.; Magdalen and St Antony's Colls, Oxford (MA, DPhil); DLitt Glasgow. FRSE 1991. University of York: Asst Lectr in History, 1963; Lectr in Hist., 1964; Prof. of History, 1971–79, Dean of Faculty of Arts, 1977–79, UCNW, Bangor; Prof. of Modern Hist., Glasgow Univ., 1980–91. Visiting Professor: British Columbia Univ., 1983; Univ. of Western Australia, 1995. Lectures: Enid Muir, Newcastle Univ., 1981; A. H. Dodd, UCNW, Bangor, 1984; Raleigh, British Acad., 1984; Ford, Oxford Univ., 1986–87. Winston Churchill Travelling Fellow, 1990. Pres., Historical Assoc., 1988–91; Chm. Cttee, Hds of Higher Educn, Wales, 1996–98. Mem., and Chm. Res. Cttee, Humanities Res. Bd, British Acad., 1994–97; Mem., Arts and Humanities Res. Bd, 1998–2003. Pres., Old Bristolians' Soc., 1995–96. Founding FLSW 2010. Honorary Fellow: Univ. of Wales, Lampeter, 2006; Bangor Univ., 2010. Editor, History, 1977–86; Member: Editorial Bd, Jl of Ecclesiastical History, 1978–93. Hon. DLitt: UWE, 1999; Wales, 2005. *Publications:* Munich 1938, 1968; Sir Edward Grey, 1971; The Abolition of War: The British Peace Movement 1914–1919, 1976; John Bright, 1979; The Eclipse of a Great Power: Modern Britain 1870–1975, 1983; The First World War, 1984; Nineteenth-Century Britain: integration and diversity, 1988; Appeasement, 1988; (ed) Blackwell Biographical Dictionary of British Political Life in the Twentieth Century, 1990; (ed) Protestant Evangelicalism, 1991; Churchill, 1992; History, Religion and Identity in Modern British History, 1993; Politicians, Diplomacy and War in Modern British History, 1994; A Bibliography of British History 1914–1989, 1996; Great Britain: identities, institutions and the idea of Britishness, 1997; The World since 1945: a concise history, 1998; The British Isles 1901–1951, 2002; Britain and Europe 1789–2005, 2005; England, Ireland, Scotland, Wales: the Christian Church 1900–2000, 2008; Pride of Place: a modern history of Bristol Grammar School, 2010; (ed) Religion and British Foreign Policy, 1815–1941, 2010; (ed) The Dynamics of Religious Reform in Northern Europe, 1780–1920, 2010; Transforming the World: global political history since World War II, 2013; articles in Historical Jl, Internat. Affairs, Jl of Contemporary Hist., Jl of Ecclesiastical Hist., Jl of Commonwealth and Imperial Hist., etc. *Recreations:* music, gardening, walking. *Address:* Gothic House, 48 Bridge Street, Pershore, Worcs WR10 1AT. *T:* (01386) 555709. *E:* profkgr@clara.co.uk.

ROBBINS, Lydia Akrigg; *see* Brown, L. A.

ROBBINS, Oliver, CB 2015; Second Permanent Secretary, Home Office, since 2015; *b* 20 April 1975; *s* of Derek and Diana Robbins; *m* 2005, Sherry Birkbeck; three *s. Educ:* Hertford Coll., Oxford (BA Hons PPE 1996). HM Treasury, 1996–2006: Hd, Corporate and Private Finance, 2003–06; Hd, Defence, Diplomacy and Intelligence, 2006; Principal Private Sec. to the Prime Minister, 2006–07; Dir, Prime Minister's Private Office, 2007; Cabinet Office: Dir, Intelligence and Security, 2007–10; Dep. Nat. Security Advr and Dir Gen., 2010–12; Dir Gen., Civil Service, Cabinet Office, 2014–15. *Recreations:* walking, cooking. *Club:* National Liberal.

ROBBINS, Ven. Stephen, CB 2011; Archdeacon for the Army, 2004–11; Chaplain General, Ministry of Defence Chaplains (Army), 2008–11; Honorary Canon, Salisbury Cathedral, 2007–11, now Canon Emeritus; *b* 11 Aug. 1953; *s* of Joseph and Jane Robbins; *m* 1976, Susan Florence McCann (*d* 2009); one *s* one *d*; *m* 2011, Dr Lydia Akrigg Brown, *qv. Educ:* Jarrow Grammar Sch.; King's Coll., London (BD, AKC 1974). Ordained deacon, 1976, priest, 1977; Curate, Tudhoe Grange, Spennymoor, 1976–80; Priest-in-charge, then Vicar, Harlow Green, Gateshead, 1980–87; joined RAChD, 1987; Regtl Chaplain in Germany, 1987–94; Chaplain, Army Trng Regt, Bassingbourn, 1994–97; Sen. Chaplain, 8 Infantry Bde, Londonderry, 1997–99; Armed Forces Chaplaincy Centre, 1999–2001; Chaplain, RMA Sandhurst, 2001–02; Assistant Chaplain General: Germany, 2002–03; HQ Land Comd, 2003–06; Dir of Training, 2006–07, Dep. Chaplain Gen., 2007–08, MoD Chaplains (Army). QHC 2005–11. Permission to Officiate, Salisbury, Newcastle and Europe, 2011; Chaplain to Bishop of Salisbury, 2012–15. Pres., SSAFA Wilts, 2012–. *Recreations:* exploring Neolithic and Bronze Age earthworks, Newcastle United, trying to find a beer I don't like. *Address:* Mill Leat, West Gomeldon, Salisbury, Wilts SP4 6JY. *E:* venstephen@gmail.com.

ROBBINS, Stephen Dennis; His Honour Judge Robbins; a Circuit Judge, since 1994; *b* 11 Jan. 1948; *s* of late Lt-Col Dennis Robbins, OBE, TD and Joan Robbins (*née* Mason); *m* 1974, Amanda Smith, JP; three *d. Educ:* Orwell Park; Marlborough; Coll. d'Europe, Bruges (Churchill Award). Infantry, HAC, 1966–69. Called to the Bar, Gray's Inn, 1969; practised SE Circuit, 1972–94; Asst Recorder, 1983–87; Recorder, 1987–94. Former Mem., Overseas Cttee, Bar Council; Hon. Sec., London Common Law Bar Cttee; Hon. Legal Advr, Katharine Lowe Centre, Battersea, 1974–79. Pres., Mental Health Rev. Tribunals, 1994–. Mem., Parole Bd, 2001–07. *Recreations:* collecting ephemera, shooting, swimming, walking, music. *Address:* Hillcrest Farm, Sevington, near Ashford, Kent TN24 0LJ. *T:* (01233) 502732; 1/2 The Studios, 17/19 Edge Street, Kensington Church Street, W8 7PN. *T:* (020) 7727 7216.

ROBBINS, Prof. Trevor William, CBE 2012; PhD; FBPsS, FMedSci; FRS 2005; Professor of Experimental Psychology and Head of Department of Psychology (formerly Department of Experimental Psychology), since 2002, and Director, MRC Centre for Behavioural and Clinical Neuroscience Institute, since 2005, University of Cambridge (Professor of Cognitive Neuroscience, 1997–2002); Fellow, since 1990, and Angharad Dodds John Fellow in Mental Health and Neuropsychiatry, since 2012, Downing College, Cambridge; *b* 26 Nov. 1949; *s* of William Walter Robbins and Eileen Hilda Robbins; *m* 1979, Barbara Jacquelyn Sahakian; two *d. Educ:* Battersea GS; Jesus Coll., Cambridge (Schol.; BA 1st cl. Hons; MA; PhD). FBPsS 1990. Univ. Demonstrator, 1973–78, Univ. Lectr, 1978–92, Reader in Cognitive Neuroscience, 1992–97, Dept of Exptl Psychology, Univ. of Cambridge. Chm. and Council Mem., Neuroscience Bd, MRC, 1995–99 (Mem., 1989–93); Council Mem., European Neuroscience Assoc., 1996–98; President: European Behavioural Pharmacology Soc., 1992–94; British Assoc. for Psychopharmacology, 1996–98; British Neurosci. Assoc., 2009–11. Ed., Psychopharmacology, 1980–. Fred Kavli Dist. Internat. Scientist Lectr, Soc. for Neurosci., 2005. Foreign Mem., Amer. Coll. of Neuropsychopharmacology, 1994–. FMedSci 1999; Fellow, Amer. Acad. of Psychol Sci., 2010. Spearman Medal, BPsS, 1982; D. G. Marquis Award, Amer. Psychol Assoc., 1997; Dist. Scientist Award, European Behavioural Pharmacol. Soc., 2001; Medal, Coll. de France, 2004; Prize for Neuronal Plasticity, Fondn Ipsen, 2005; (jtly) Distinguished Scientific Contribn Award, American Psychol Assoc., 2011; (jtly) Brain Prize, Grete Lundbeck Foundn, 2014. *Publications:* (ed jtly) Psychology for Medicine, 1988; (ed jtly) The Prefrontal Cortex, 1998; Disorders of Brain and Mind 2, 2003; (ed jtly) Drugs and the Future, 2007; (ed jtly) Neurobiology of Addiction: new vistas, 2010; (ed jtly) Decision-making, Affect and Learning, 2011; (ed jtly) Cognitive Search: evolution, algorithms and the brain, 2012; more than 700 articles in learned books and jls. *Recreations:* chess, cricket, cinema, theatre, modern literature, visual arts. *Address:* Department of Psychology, University of Cambridge, Downing Street, Cambridge CB2 3EB. *T:* (01223) 333551, *Fax:* (01223) 333564. *E:* twr2@cam.ac.uk.

ROBBS, John Edward; Director, Marine and Fisheries, Department for Environment, Food and Rural Affairs, 2011–15; *b* 26 June 1955; *s* of Eric and Christine Robbs; *m* 1989, Jacqueline Tozer; two *s. Educ:* King Edward VII Sch., King's Lynn; Queens' Coll., Cambridge (MA); London Sch. of Econs (MSc Econ). Joined Ministry of Agriculture, Fisheries and Food, 1977: Private Sec. to Perm. Sec., 1981–82; Private Sec. to Minister, 1982–83; on secondment to UK Perm. Repn to EU, Brussels, 1985–89; Head: of Envmt Task Force Div., 1991–94; of Conservation Policy Div., 1994–95; of Fisheries (Common Fisheries Policy) Div., 1995–99; of EU Internat. Div., 1999–2000; of Food Industry, Competitiveness and Flood Defence Gp, 2000–01; Dir, Food Industry and Crops, 2001–06, Wildlife and Countryside, 2006–11, DEFRA. *Recreations:* family, friends, gardening.

ROBERG, Rabbi Meir; Inspector of schools, UK, since 1997; Senior Advisor, Lauder Yeshurun Foundation, Berlin, since 2007; Rabbi, Kehal Adass Yisroel congregation, Berlin, since 2012; *b* 25 June 1937; *s* of late Julius and Hannchen Roberg; *m* 1961, Mirjam Nager; three *s* two *d. Educ:* Manchester Grammar Sch. (Gratrix Scholar); Talmudical Coll., Israel

(Rabbinical Diploma); Univ. of London (BA 1st Cl. Hons 1960; DipEd 1970; MPhil 1972). Asst Teacher, 1960–62, Dep. Head, 1962–65, Yavneh Grammar Sch., London; Hasmonean High School: Asst Teacher and Head of Classics, 1965–71; Dep. Head, 1971–80; Headmaster, 1980–93; Principal of Jewish Day Schs and Dean of Talmudical Coll., Kiev, 1993–95; Hon. Consultant for Jewish schs and colls estabd in Ukraine following independence, 1995–2005. Lectr, Colls of Further Educn, 1962–93; Headmaster, Middx Regl Centre, 1965–73. Delegate, Internat. Religious Conf., Jerusalem, 1963 and 1980. Member: Keren Hatorah; Hendon Adass; Massoret Inst. (Chm., 1980–95); Assoc. of Headteachers of Jewish Day Schs (Pres., 1991–93; Life Pres., 1993–). *Publications:* (contrib.) Responsa Literature, 1996, 1998, 2000; reviews for Comparative Education, Jewish Tribune, and Parent-Teacher Monthly (NY). *Recreations:* Talmudic research, hiking. *Address:* 19 Sorotzkin Street, Jerusalem, Israel.

ROBERTS, family name of **Barons Clwyd** and **Roberts of Llandudno**.

ROBERTS OF LLANDUDNO, Baron *cr* 2004 (Life Peer), of Llandudno in the County of Gwynedd; **Rev. John Roger Roberts;** Superintendent Methodist Minister: Llangollen, 1965–70, Llandudno, 1983–2002; *b* 23 Oct. 1935; *s* of Thomas Charles and Alice Ellen Roberts; *m* 1962, Eirlys Ann (*d* 1995); one *s* two *d*. *Educ:* John Bright Grammar Sch., Llandudno; Univ. of Wales, Bangor (BA Hons); Handsworth Methodist Coll., Birmingham. Methodist Minister, 1958–. President: Welsh Liberal Party, 1981–84; Welsh Lib Dems, 1990–96. Contested Conwy: (L) 1979; (L/Alliance) 1983, 1987; (Lib Dem) 1992, 1997. *Recreations:* travel, walking, music. *Address:* 22 Garth Court, Abbey Road, Llandudno, Conwy LL30 2HF. *T:* (01492) 876690; House of Lords, SW1A 0PW. *E:* jrogerroberts@aol.com.

ROBERTS, Sir Adam; *see* Roberts, Sir E. A.

ROBERTS, Prof. Alan Clive, OBE 2001 (MBE 1982); TD 1969; JP; DL; PhD; Professor of Biomaterials in Surgery, University of Hull, since 1994; Consultant: Nuffield Hospital, Leeds, 2002–10; Bradford Institute for Health Research, since 2012; *b* 28 April 1934; *s* of Major William Roberts, MBE and Kathleen Roberts; *m* 1956, Margaret Mary Shaw; two *s*. *Educ:* Gregg Sch., Newcastle upon Tyne; MPhil CNAA 1975; PhD Bradford Univ. 1988. CBiol 1971; FRSB (FIBiol 1987); CIMechE 1995. Nat. Service, 1950–54. Scientific Officer, Royal Victoria Infirmary, Newcastle, 1954–56; Sen. Scientific Officer, Leeds Hosps, 1956–60; Prin. Clin. Scientist, Dept of Plastic Surgery, 1960–67, Consultant Clin. Scientist, 1990–, St Luke's Hosp., Bradford; Vis. Sen. Res. Fellow, Biomedical Scis, 1961–, Dir, Biomaterials Res. Unit, 1990–, Jt Dir, Inst. of Health Res., 1993–2003, Hon. Prof., 2000, Univ. of Bradford; Dir of R&D, Bradford Hosps NHS Trust, 1992–2003. Council of Europe Res. Fellow, Sweden, 1968. ADC to the Queen, 1980–83. Royal Society of Medicine: Mem. Council, 2000–09; Hon. Sub Dean, N Yorks, 2001–04; Treas., 2004–07; Vice Pres., 2007–09; Stuart Lectr, Edinburgh, 2009; Pres., Technol. in Medicine Sect., 2010–; Chm., Academic Bd, 2015–; Stevens Lect., 2015. President: British Inst. of Surgical Tech., 1998– (Vice-Pres., 1996–98); Bradford Medico-Chirurgical Soc., 1995; Chm., Bradford Res. Ethics Cttee, 2003–12; Partner, Health Professions Council, 2004–06; Clin. Dir, Prosthetic Solutions, Univ. of Bradford, 2005. Mem., NY Acad. of Scis, 1987. Chm., COMEC, 1990–96; University of Leeds: Crown Rep., 1985–86; Chm., Court and Council, 1986–; Pro-Chancellor, 1986–2000; Dir, Westwood Hall, 1987–; Chm., Mil. Educn Cttee, 1996–; Dir, Univ. of Leeds Foundn, 1986–2000; Examiner: Sch. of Clin. Dentistry, Univ. of Sheffield, 1995–; Dental Sch., Univ. of Malta, 2004–; Chm., Adv. Bd, Inst. of Cancer Therapeutics, Univ. of Bradford, 2009–. Vis. Prof., Inst. of Bioengrg, Brunel Univ., 2009–. Trustee: Edward Boyle Trust, 1986–97; Yorks Sculpture Park, 1995–; Isherwood Trust, 2004–. Mem. Council, BRCS, 1995 (Pres., W Yorks, 1983–2004; Badge of Honour, 1992); Vice Chm., Mil., Yorks and Humber, RFCA, 1997–2001. President: Leeds RBL; W Yorks SSAFA, 2000– (Chm., 1985–99); Leeds NSPCC, 2002–; Chm., W Riding Artillery Trust, 1983–; Trustee: ARNI Trust, 2007–; Maritime Heritage Foundn (formerly British Maritime Heritage Foundn), 2011–. Lt-Col Comdg, 1972–79, Hon. Col, 1980–90, Regtl Col, 2000–, Leeds Univ. OTC; Col and Dep. Comdr, NE Dist TA, 1980–83; Hon. Col, 269 Batt., RA, 1990–; Col Comdt, RA, 1996–; Mem., HAC, 2000–. Patron, Age Concern, 1994–. Governor: Pocklington Sch., 1990–2001; Gateways Sch., Leeds, 2000–06. Hon. Freeman and Liveryman, Clothworkers' Co., 2000–. JP Leeds, 1977; DL W Yorks, 1982. CGIA, 1969, 1976, FCGI 1990 (Pres., City and Guilds Assoc., 1998–2003); FRSocMed 1993, Hon. FRSocMed, 2010; FLS 1998; Fellow, Med. Soc. of London, 2009–. Hon. LLD Leeds, 2000; Hon. DSc: London, 2005; Bradford, 2007; Hon. DTech Brunel, 2007. Prince Philip Medal for Science, C&G, 1970; Convocation Medal, Univ. of Leeds, 2008. Lead researcher and inventor of: Indermil Tissue Adhesive, 1993; Zeflosil Prosthetic Adhesive, 2007. KStJ 2010 (CStJ 2002; Chm. Council, S & W Yorks, 2004–); Kt Comdr of Merit, Mil. Constantinian Order of St George, 2011. Companion, Order of the League of Mercy, 2002. Gentleman Usher, Imperial Soc. of Kts Bachelor, 2009–. Kt Grand Officer, Royal Order of Eagle of Georgia, 2015. *Publications:* Obturators and Prosthesis for Cleft Palate, 1968; Facial Restoration by Prosthetic Means, 1975; Maxillo-Facial Prosthetics: a multi-disciplinary practice, 1975; numerous articles in med. and dental jls. *Recreations:* sculpture, silversmithing, avoiding holidays. *Address:* The Grange, Rein Road, Morley, Leeds, W Yorks LS27 0HZ. *T:* (0113) 253 4632. *E:* roberts@132acr.com. *Club:* Army and Navy.

ROBERTS, Prof. Alan Madoc, PhD; FRS 2015; Professor of Zoology, University of Bristol, 1991–2013, now Emeritus; *b* Rugby, Warwickshire, 24 Aug. 1941; *s* of Vernon and Mary Roberts; *m* 1st, 1963, Naomi Collet (marr. diss. 1973); one *s* one *d*; 2nd, 1973, Pamela Reynolds (marr. diss. 1985); one *d*; 3rd, 1991, Joanna Wright. *Educ:* Rugby Sch.; Trinity Coll., Cambridge (BA Natural Scis 1963); Univ. of Calif, Los Angeles (PhD Zool. 1967). University of Bristol: SRC Fellow, 1967–70; Lectr in Zool., 1970–82; Reader in Zool., 1982–91. *Publications:* contrib. papers to scientific jls. *Recreations:* gardening, making things, early music, collecting porcelain. *Address:* School of Biological Sciences, University of Bristol, Life Science Building, 24 Tyndall Avenue, Bristol BS8 1TQ. *T:* (0117) 394 1328. *E:* a.roberts@bristol.ac.uk.

ROBERTS, Alfred, PhD; Chief Executive, Institution of Engineering and Technology (formerly Institution of Electrical Engineers), 1999–2007; *b* 24 June 1945; *s* of Oswald and Ellen Roberts; *m* 1978, Elizabeth Ann King; one *s* one *d*. *Educ:* University Coll. London (BSc 1st cl. Hons 1967); Univ. of Manchester (PhD 1970). Central Electricity Generating Board: Res. Officer, 1971–73; Section Manager, Applied Physics, 1973–75; Div. Head, Engrg Sci., 1975–81; Regl Financial Controller, 1981–85; Gp Financial Controller, 1985–88; Dir, Engrg Services, 1988–89; Commercial Dir, PowerGen plc, 1989–98. *Publications:* articles in Nuclear Physics; conf. proceedings on nucleon transfer reactions; conf. papers on privatisation and deregulation of the electricity industry. *Recreations:* science, technology, history, music, literature, football.

ROBERTS, Allan Deverell, CB 2013; Counsel to the Chairman of Committees, House of Lords, 2002–13; *b* 14 July 1950; *s* of Irfon Roberts and Patricia Mary (*née* Allan); *m* 1991, Irene Anne Graham Reilly; two *s* (and one *s* decd). *Educ:* Eton Coll. (King's Schol.); Magdalen Coll., Oxford (MA). Solicitor in private practice, 1974–76; Solicitor's Office, DHSS, 1976–96, Under-Sec. (Legal), 1989–96; Dir, Legal (Envmt, Planning and Countryside), DoE, 1996–97; Dir, Legal (Envmt, Housing and Local Govt), DETR, 1997–99; Dir, Legal (Legislation Unit), DETR, subseq. DTLR, 1999–2002. *Recreations:* tegestology, football, gardening, decorative arts.

ROBERTS, Alwyn; Pro Vice Chancellor, University of Wales, Bangor, 1994–97; *b* 26 Aug. 1933; *s* of late Rev. Howell Roberts and Buddug Roberts; *m* 1960, Mair Rowlands Williams; one *s*. *Educ:* Penygroes Grammar Sch.; Univ. of Wales, Aberystwyth and Bangor (BA, LLB); Univ. of Cambridge (MA). Tutor, Westminster Coll., Cambridge, 1959; Principal, Pachhunga Meml Govt Coll., Aijal, Assam, India, 1960–67; Lectr in Social Admin, University Coll., Swansea, 1967–70; University College of North Wales, later University of Wales, Bangor: Lectr, subseq. Sen. Lectr, Dept of Social Theory and Instns, 1970–79; Dir of Extra Mural Studies, 1979–95; Vice Principal, 1985–94. BBC National Governor for Wales, 1979–86; Chm., Broadcasting Council for Wales, 1979–86 (Mem., 1974–78); Member: Welsh Fourth TV Channel Authy, 1981–86; Gwynedd CC, 1973–81 (Chm., Social Services Cttee, 1977–81); Gwynedd AHA, 1973–80; Royal Commn on Legal Services, 1976–79; Parole Bd, 1987–90. Pres., Royal National Eisteddfod of Wales, 1994–96 (Vice-Chm., 1987–89; Chm., 1989–92; Mem. Council, 1979–); Chm., Acen (Cyf.), 1989–2010; Vice Chm., Arts Council of Wales, 1994–2000; Mem. Bd, Cwmni Theatr Cymru, 1982–86. Pro Chancellor, Bangor Univ., 2013– (Mem., Council, 2005–12). Fellow, Nat. Eisteddfod of Wales, 2005. Hon. Fellow, Univ. of Wales, Aberystwyth, 1999. Hon. LLD Wales, 2000. *Address:* Brithdir, 43 Talycae, Tregarth, Bangor, Gwynedd LL57 4AE. *T:* (01248) 600007.

ROBERTS, Andrew, PhD; FRSL; writer; *b* 13 Jan. 1963; *s* of Simon and Katie Roberts; *m* 1st, 1995, Camilla Henderson (marr. diss. 2001); one *s* one *d*; 2nd, 2007, Susan Gilchrist, *qv*. *Educ:* Cranleigh Sch.; Gonville and Caius Coll., Cambridge (exhibnr, Hon. Sen. Schol.; BA 1st Cl. Hons Hist.; MA; Chm., CU Cons. Assoc., 1984; Mem., Ct of Benefactors, 2002–06); PhD Cantab 2011. Corporate broker, Robert Fleming Securities Ltd, 1985–88; freelance journalist, broadcaster and book reviewer, 1988–; USA corresp., Standpoint mag., 2011–. Guest Curator, Morgan Liby, NYC, 2001–12, incl. 'Churchill and the Power of Words', 2011–12. Merrill Family Vis. Prof., Cornell Univ., 2013. Trustee: Roberts Foundn, 1989–; Margaret Thatcher Archive Trust, 2005–; NPG, 2013–; Dir, Frank Harry Guggenheim Foundn, 2009; Member: Exec. Cttee, Friends of Lambeth Palace Library, 2003–11; Bd, Internat. Friends of London Liby, 2011–; Acad. Adv. Cttee, Nat. Churchill Liby and Center, George Washington Univ., 2013–. Member, Council: Bruges Gp, 2003–; Freedom Assoc., 2003–; British Weights and Measures Assoc., 2003–; Centre for Policy Studies, 2003–; Centre for Social Cohesion, 2007–; Global Vision, 2008–; European Foundn, 2008–; Hougoumont Project, 2008–; Mem., Adv. Council, UK Nat. Defence Assoc., 2009–; Mem., Internat. Bd, Canadian Inst. for Jewish Res., 2010–; Contributing Mem. Bd, Wkg Gp on Mil. Hist. and Contemporary Conflict, Hoover Instn, 2013–; Mem., Academic Bd, Historians for Britain, 2014–. Founder Mem., Friends of Israel Initiative, 2010–. Chm., Cons. Party Adv. Panel on Sch. History Teaching, 2005. Mem. Academic Council, Henry Jackson Soc., 2011. Judge, Elizabeth Longford Historical Biography Prize, 2003, 2005–; Chairman: Judges Panel, Hessell-Tiltman History Prize, 2009; Judges, Guggenheim-Lehrman Prize for Mil. Hist., 2012–; Mem., Rev. Cttee, Dan David Prize, 2012. Hon. Co-Chair, Chms' Council, 2011–, Lewis Lehrman Dist. Fellow, 2014–, NY Histl Soc.; Hon. Member: Guild of Battlefield Guides, 2006; Internat. Churchill Soc. (UK), 2007; Vice-Pres., Internat. Guild of Battlefield Guides, 2010–. FRSL 2001. Hon. DHL Westminster Coll., Fulton, Mo, 2000. Lion of Judah Award, Canadian Inst. for Jewish Res., 2010; William Penn Award, Penn Club, 2012; Pride of Century Award, British Schs and Univs Club, USA, 2012. *Publications:* The Holy Fox: a life of Lord Halifax, 1991; Eminent Churchillians, 1994; The Aachen Memorandum, 1995; Salisbury: Victorian Titan, 1999 (James Stern Silver Pen Award, Wolfson Award for Hist., 2000); The House of Windsor, 2000; Napoleon and Wellington, 2001; Hitler and Churchill: secrets of leadership, 2003; (ed) What Might Have Been, 2004; Waterloo: Napoleon's Last Gamble, 2005; (ed) The Correspondence Between Mr Disraeli and Mrs Brydges Willyams, 2006; A History of the English-Speaking Peoples since 1900, 2006 (Intercollegiate Studies Inst. Book Award, 2007); (ed) The Art of War, vol. 1 2008, vol. 2 2009; Masters and Commanders, 2008 (Emery Reves Prize, Churchill Centre, 2009); The Storm of War: a new history of the Second World War, 2009 (British Army Mil. Book of Year, 2010); (ed) Letters to Vicky: the correspondence between Queen Victoria and her daughter Vicky, Empress of Germany, 1858–1901, 2011; (ed) Love, Tommy, 2012; Napoleon the Great, 2014; Elegy: the first day on the Somme, 2015. *Recreation:* Corinthian Bagatelle. *Address:* 22 South Eaton Place, SW1W 9JA. *T:* (020) 7730 3091. *E:* andrew@roberts-london.fsnet.co.uk. *Clubs:* Pratt's, Brooks's, Garrick, Beefsteak, Saintsbury, Miller's Academy (Hon. Mem.), Fox, 5 Hertford Street (Hon. Mem.); Brook (New York); Spectacle (Milwaukee) (Hon. Mem.).

ROBERTS, Air Vice-Marshal Andrew Lyle, CB 1992; CBE 1983; AFC 1969; FRAeS; General Manager for Jennifer Bate, international concert organist, since 2001; *b* 19 May 1938; *s* of Ronald and Norah Roberts; *m* 1962; three *d*. *Educ:* Cranbrook Sch.; RAF Coll., Cranwell. Commnd RAF, 1958; ADC to AOC No 18 Gp, 1965–66; Flight Comdr, 201 Sqdn, 1967–68 (AFC); RNSC, 1969; Personal Air Sec. to Parly Under-Sec. of State (RAF), MoD, 1970–71; i/c 236 Operational Conversion Unit, 1972–74; US Armed Forces Staff Coll., 1974; staff, SACLANT, 1975–77; i/c RAF Kinloss, 1977–79; Gp Capt. Ops, HQ Strike Command, 1980–82 (CBE); RCDS, 1983; Dir, Air Plans, MoD, 1984–86; C of S, HQ No 18 Gp, 1987–89; ACDS (Concepts), 1987–92; Hd of RAF Manpower Structure Study Team, 1992–94. Chm. of Public Inquiries, Lord Chancellor's Panel of Ind. Inspectors, 1994–2010. Vice-Pres., Coastal Comd and Maritime Air Assoc., 2002– (founding Chm., 1995–2002); Pres., Brockenhurst Br., RBL, 2006–. Trustee, Gwennili Trust (sailing for the disabled), 1995–2011. Organist, St Paul's Cathedral, Valletta, 1961. *Recreations:* cross-country and hill walking, natural history, classical music, church organ, choral singing, off-shore sailing. *Address:* 28 Oakenbrow, Sway, Lymington, Hants SO41 6DY. *Club:* Royal Air Force.

ROBERTS, Ann; *see* Clwyd, Rt Hon. Ann.

ROBERTS, (Anthony) John, CBE 1991; Board Member, 1985–2002, and Chief Executive, 1995–2002, Royal Mail Group (formerly The Post Office, then Consignia plc); Chairman, Post Office Ltd (formerly Post Office Counters Ltd), 1993–2002; *b* 26 Aug. 1944; *s* of Douglas and Margaret Roberts; *m* 1970, Diana June (*née* Lamdin); two *s*. *Educ:* Hampton Sch.; Exeter Univ. (BA Hons). Open Entrant, Administrative Class Civil Service, The Post Office, 1967; PA to Dep. Chairman and Chief Executive, 1969–71; Principal, Long Range Planning, 1971–74; Controller Personnel and Finance, North Western Postal Board, 1974–76; Principal Private Sec. to Chairman, 1976–77; Director, Chairman's Office, 1977–80; Secretary Designate, 1980–81, Sec., 1981–82; Dir, 1981–85, Man. Dir, 1985–93, Counter Services, subseq. Post Office Counters Ltd; Man. Dir, Gp Services, 1993–95; Chm., Subscription Services, 1993–95. Advr, Deloitte Consulting, 2003–05. Chm., South Thames TEC, 1989–92; Dir, Internat. Posts Corp., 1996–2003; Bd Mem., 2004–11, Dep. Chm., 2005–11, British Educnl Communications and Technol. Agency; Member: Govt New Deal Task Force, 1997–2003; CBI Educn and Trng Affairs Cttee, 1998–2003; Home Office Strategic Delivery Bd, 2003–05; Royal Mail Stamp Adv. Cttee, 2003–; Bd, Ofsted, 2007–. Mem. Council, Inst. of Employment Studies, 1995–2003 (Pres., 1998–2003); Governor: Henley Mgt Coll., 1996–2006 (Hon. Fellow, 2008); Eur. Foundn for Quality Management, 1996–2001 (Pres., 1998–2001); Chm., Bd of Pension Trustees, Inst. of Cancer Res. Pension Fund, 2013– (Mem., 2012–13; Mem. Inst. of Cancer Res., 2012). FRSA 1992. Freeman, City of London, 1983. *Recreations:* golf, gardening, music. *Clubs:* MCC; Betchworth Park Golf; Harlequins Rugby Football.

ROBERTS, Barbara Haig; *see* MacGibbon, B. H.

ROBERTS, Benjamin Andrew; Director, Lottery Film Fund, British Film Institute, since 2012; *b* Coventry, 1 April 1975; *s* of James and Jennifer Roberts; civil partnership 2012, Chris Morriss. *Educ:* Bablake Sch., Coventry; Coventry Univ. (Dip. Fine Art 1994); Leeds Univ. (BA Hons English 1997). Hd of Distribn, Metrodome, 1998–2003; Vice Pres., Worldwide

Acquisitions, Universal Pictures, 2003–07; CEO, Protagonist Pictures, 2007–12. Member: BAFTA; Eur. Film Acad. *Address:* British Film Institute, 21 Stephen Street, W1T 1LN. *T:* (020) 7173 3222. *E:* ben.roberts@bfi.org.uk. *Club:* Soho House.

ROBERTS, Brian Stanley; HM Diplomatic Service, retired; *b* 1 Feb. 1936; *s* of Stanley Victor Roberts and Flora May (*née* McInnes); *m* 1st, 1961, Phyllis Hazel Barber (marr. diss. 1976); two *s*; 2nd, 1985, Jane Catharine Chisholm; one *d*. *Educ:* Christ's Coll., Cambridge (MA); Courtauld Institute, London (MA). Served Royal Navy, 1955–57. Staff, Edinburgh Univ., 1960–62; Lecturer in Art History, Goldsmiths' Coll., London, 1962–69; entered FCO, 1970: First Secretary, Cape Town/Pretoria, 1972; FCO, 1974; attached to Hong Kong Govt, 1977; FCO, 1980; Counsellor, Stockholm, 1983–87; Cabinet Office, 1987. Teacher, Art Hist., Cheltenham Ladies' Coll., 1988–89; Head of Art Hist., Putney High Sch., 1989–97. *Recreations:* walking, looking at pictures. *Club:* Lansdowne.

ROBERTS, Dr Brynley Francis, CBE 1993; Librarian, National Library of Wales, 1985–94; Moderator, General Assembly of the Presbyterian Church of Wales, 2001–02; *b* 3 Feb. 1931; *s* of Robert F. Roberts and Laura Jane Roberts (*née* Williams); *m* 1957, Rhiannon Campbell; twin *s*. *Educ:* Grammar School, Aberdare; University College of Wales, Aberystwyth (BA Hons Welsh, MA, PhD). Fellow, Univ. of Wales, 1956–57; Lectr, Sen. Lectr, Reader, Dept of Welsh, University Coll. of Wales, Aberystwyth, 1957–78; Prof. of Welsh Language and Literature, University Coll. Swansea, 1978–85. Sir John Rhys Fellow, Jesus Coll., Oxford, 1973–74; Leverhulme Emeritus Fellow, 1997; Res. Associate, Dublin Inst. for Advanced Studies, 2000–11. Chairman: United Theological Coll., Aberystwyth, 1977–98; Gwasg Pantycelyn, Caernarfon, 1977–98. Pres., Welsh Library Assoc., 1985–94; Chm., Welsh Books Council, 1989–94 (Vice-Chm., 1986–89; Mem., 1994–2012); Mem., HEFCW, 1993–2000. Editor: Dictionary of Welsh Biography, 1987–2014; Y Traethodydd, 1999–2015. Hon. Fellow, Univ. of Wales, Swansea, 1996, Aberystwyth, 2000; Hon. Prof., Cardiff, 2001; Hon. Sen. Res. Fellow, Centre for Advanced Welsh and Celtic Studies, Univ. of Wales, 2009. FLSW 2011. Hon. FCLIP (Hon. FLA 1994). Hon. DLitt Wales, 1996. Sir Ellis Griffith Prize, 1962, Vernam Hull Prize, 2005, Univ. of Wales; Medal, Hon. Soc. of Cymmrodorion, 2007. *Publications:* Gwassanaeth Meir, 1961; Brut y Brenhinedd, 1971, 2nd edn 1984; Cyfranc Lludd a Llefelys, 1975; Brut Tysilio, 1980; Edward Lhuyd: the making of a scientist, 1980; Gerald of Wales, 1982; Itinerary through Wales, 1989; Studies on Middle Welsh Literature, 1992; (ed) Y Bywgraffiadur Cymreig 1951–1970, 1997; (ed) Dictionary of Welsh Biography 1941–1970, 2001; Breudwyt Maxen Wledic, 2005; (with Dewi W. Evans) Edward Lhwyd, Archaeologia Britannica: texts and translations, 2009; Anwir Anwedhys Y Mae Yn I Ysgrivenny Ymma: rhai o ymylnodau Edward Lhwyd, 2009; Ar drywydd Edward Lhwyd, 2013; articles in learned jls. *Recreations:* reminiscing, gardening, music. *Address:* Hengwrt, Llanbadarn Road, Aberystwyth SY23 1HB. *T:* (01970) 623577.

ROBERTS, Prof. Callum Michael, PhD; Professor of Marine Conservation, University of York, since 2002; *b* Pitlochry, 14 April 1962; *s* of Peter Alva Roberts and Margaret Jean Roberts; *m* 1987, Julie Patricia Hawkins; two *d*. *Educ:* York Univ. (BSc Hons Biol. 1983; PhD Biol. 1986). Research Associate: Univ. of York, 1987; Univ. of Liverpool and Suez Canal Univ., 1987–90; Sen. Res. Associate, Univ. of Newcastle upon Tyne, 1990–92; Res. Asst Prof., Univ. of Virgin Is, 1992–95. Hrdy Vis. Prof., Harvard Univ., 2001. *Publications:* Marine Ecology of the Arabian Region, 1992; Reef Fisheries, 1996; Fully Protected Marine Reserves: a guide, 1999; The Unnatural History of the Sea, 2007; Ocean of Life: how our seas are changing, 2012. *Recreations:* scuba-diving, hiking, collecting and reading old books, writing, fish watching. *Address:* Environment Department, University of York, York YO10 5DD. *T:* (01904) 324066, *Fax:* (01904) 324998. *E:* callum.roberts@york.ac.uk.

ROBERTS, Carl Bertrand Westerby, CMG 2012; High Commissioner of Antigua and Barbuda to the Court of St James's, and concurrently Ambassador to France, Germany, Spain and Italy, 2004–14; *b* St John's, Antigua and Barbuda, 13 Oct. 1948; *s* of late Arthur E. S. Roberts and of Audrey E. Roberts; *m* 1974, Pauline Margaret A.; two *s* one *d*. *Educ:* Antigua Grammar Sch.; Northeastern Univ., Boston (BSEE Hons *magna cum laude* 1982); Univ. of WI, Barbados (MBA 1995); Univ. of Bradford (DBA 2004). Joined Cable & Wireless (WI) Ltd, 1967; Gen. Manager, Montserrat, 1995–97; Chief Executive: Cable & Wireless Dominica, 1997–2002; Cable & Wireless St Kitts & Nevis, 2002–04. Perm. Rep., UNESCO, Paris, 2004–; Dep. Perm. Rep., WTO, Geneva, 2004–. *Recreations:* cricket, tennis, golf, reading, singing. *Address:* c/o High Commission for Antigua and Barbuda, 2nd Floor, 45 Crawford Place, W1H 4LP. *Club:* Rotary (London).

ROBERTS, Cedric P.; *see* Prys-Roberts.

ROBERTS, Prof. Charlotte Ann, (Mrs S. J. Gardner), PhD; FBA 2014; Professor of Archaeology, Durham University, since 2004; *b* Harrogate, 25 May 1957; *d* of Neville Harpin Roberts and Elizabeth Ann Roberts; *m* 2003, Stewart James Gardner. *Educ:* St James' Hosp., Leeds (SRN 1978); Leicester Univ. (BA Hons Archaeol Studies 1982); Sheffield Univ. (MA Envmtl Archaeol. 1983); Bradford Univ. (PhD Human Bioarchaeol. 1988). Staff Nurse, Burns Unit, St Lawrence Hosp., Chepstow, 1979; University of Bradford: Res. Asst, 1983–88; Lectr in Palaeopathol., 1989–94; Sen. Lectr in Biol Anthropol., 1994–99; Reader in Archaeol., Durham Univ., 2000–04. Leverhulme Trust Sen. Res. Fellow, 2006–08; Nuffield Foundn Res. Fellow, 2006–07. Mem., REF 2014 Panel (Archaeol.). Pres., Paleopathol. Assoc., 2011–13. Excellence in Teaching Award, Univ. of Bradford, 1999; Excellence in Doctoral Supervision Award, Durham Univ., 2009. *Publications:* (ed jtly) Burial Archaeology: current research, methods and developments, 1989; (ed jtly) Studies in Crime: an introduction to forensic archaeology, 1995; (with K. Manchester) The Archaeology of Disease, 1995, 3rd edn 2005; (ed jtly) Proceedings of the International Congress on the Evolution and Palaeoepidemiology of the Infectious Diseases, 2002; (with M. Cox) Health and Disease in Britain: from prehistory to the present day, 2003; (with J. E. Buikstra) The Bioarchaeology of Tuberculosis: a global perspective on a re-emerging disease, 2003; Human Remains in Archaeology: a handbook, 2009; (ed jtly) The Global History of Paleopathology: pioneers and prospects, 2012; contrib. papers to jls, incl. Amer. Jl Physical Anthropol. and chapters in books. *Recreations:* fell running, cycling, hiking, gardening, border collies, flower arranging, bell ringing, WI, flute playing, Scotland exploring, travel to developing countries, folk music, cross country ski-ing. *Address:* Department of Archaeology, Durham University, South Road, Durham DH1 3LE. *T:* (0191) 334 1154, *Fax:* (0191) 334 1101.

ROBERTS, Christine Elizabeth; a Judge of the Upper Tribunal (Immigration and Asylum Chamber), since 2010; *b* Newcastle upon Tyne, 31 May 1950; *d* of William Crawford and Edna Crawford (*née* Osborne); *m* 1972, Adrian Roberts; one *s*. *Educ:* Whitley Bay Grammar Sch.; Univ. of Manchester (LLB Hons). Admitted solicitor, 1975; in practice as a solicitor, 1975–95; Immigration Adjudicator (full-time), 1995–2002; Regl Adjudicator, Bradford, 2002–05; Resident Judge, Bradford, 2005–. *Recreations:* reading, world cinema, theatre, cricket, walking. *Address:* Tribunals Service (Immigration and Asylum Chamber), Phoenix House, Rushton Avenue, Bradford BD3 7BH.

ROBERTS, Christopher William, CB 1986; Deputy Secretary, 1983–97, and Director-General of Trade Policy, 1987–97, Department of Trade and Industry; Senior Trade Adviser, Covington and Burling, 1998–2011; *b* 4 Nov. 1937; *s* of Frank Roberts and Evelyn Dorothy Roberts. *Educ:* Rugby Sch.; Magdalen Coll., Oxford (MA). Lectr in Classics, Pembroke Coll., Oxford, 1959–60; Asst Principal, BoT, 1960; Second Sec. (Commercial), British High Commn, New Delhi, 1962–64; Asst Private Sec. to Pres. of BoT, 1964–65; Principal, 1965; Cabinet Office, 1966–68; Private Sec. to Prime Minister, 1970–73; Asst Sec., 1972; Dept of Trade, 1973–77; Under Secretary: Dept of Prices and Consumer Protection, 1977–79; Dept of Trade, 1979–82; Chief Exec., BOTB, 1983–87. Non-exec. Dir, NHBC, 1998–2004. Chairman: Wine Standards Bd, 1999–2006; Liberalisation of Trade in Services Cttee, Internat. Financial Services London, 2000–05; Policy Cttee, European Services Forum, 2002–08. Master, Turners Co., 2009–10. *Recreations:* travel, cricket, opera. *Address:* Tall Timbers, High Drive, Woldingham, Surrey CR3 7ED. *Clubs:* Oxford and Cambridge, MCC.

ROBERTS, Colin, MD; FRCP, FMedSci; Consultant Medical Microbiologist, and Medical and Scientific Postgraduate Dean, Public Health Laboratory Service, 1993–99; Hon. Clinical Scientist (non-medical), Oxford University Hospitals NHS Trust (formerly Oxford Radcliffe Hospitals NHS Trust), 2011–13 (locum consultant microbiologist, 2000–07, Hon. Consultant Microbiologist, 2007–10); *b* 25 Jan. 1937; *s* of Theophilus and Daisy Roberts; *m* 1961, Marjorie Frances Conway; two *s*. *Educ:* Univ. of Liverpool (BSc 1960; MB ChB 1963; MD 1968); Univ. of Manchester (Dip. Bact. (Dist.) 1972). FRCPath 1986; FRCP 1999; FRIPH 1992. House physician/surgeon, 1963–64, Registrar in Pathology, 1964–66, Sefton Gen. Hosp., Liverpool; Hon. Sen. Registrar, United Liverpool Hosps, 1966–70, and Lectr in Pathology, 1966–69, in Med. Microbiol., 1969–70, Univ. of Liverpool; Asst Microbiologist (Sen. Registrar), Regl Public Health Lab., Fazakerley Hosp., Liverpool, 1970–73; Liverpool Public Health Laboratory: Sen. Microbiologist, 1973–75; Consultant Med. Microbiologist, 1975–87; Dep. Dir, 1977–87; Dep. Dir, PHLS, London, 1987–93. Study Unit Tutor in Hosp. Infection, Distance Learning, 2004–08, Chm., Dip. HIC Examiners' Cttee, 2007–08, LSHTM. Sec., Assoc. of Acad. Clin. Bacteriologists and Virologists, 2000–07; Hon. Treas., 2003–06, Pres., Pathology Sect., 2009–10, RSocMed. Chm., Central Sterilising Club, 1992–96. Mem. Editl Bd, Jl Clin. Pathol., 1992–97; Asst Ed., Jl of Hosp. Infection, 2004–. Founder FMedSci 1998; Fellow, Acad. of Med. Educators, 2010 (Founder Mem., 2007). Hon. FRCPCH 1996; Hon. FFPH (FFPHM 1997); Hon. FFPath, RCPI, 2000; Hon. Fellow, Liverpool John Moores Univ., 2001; Hon. FRCS 2013. Hon. Dip. HIC 1999. Harold Ellis Award, RCS, 2012. *Publications:* contrib. chapters, papers and proceedings, including: (contrib.) Infectious and Communicable Diseases in England and Wales, 1990; (ed jtly) Quality Control: principles and practice in the microbiology laboratory, 1991, 2nd edn 1999; (jtly) A Supervisor's Handbook of Food Hygiene and Safety, 1995; contribs to academic jls. *Recreations:* theatre, music, art, literature, sport (represented Wales at schoolboy level in soccer). *Address:* Microbiology Department, Level 6, John Radcliffe Hospital, Headington, Oxford OX3 9DU. *T:* (01865) 220886. *Club:* Royal Society of Medicine.

ROBERTS, Colin, CVO 2006; HM Diplomatic Service; Governor of the Falkland Islands and Commissioner of South Georgia and the South Sandwich Islands, since 2014; *b* 31 July 1959; *s* of John Jeffrey Roberts and Avril Joyce Roberts (*née* Dowding); *m* 2000, Camilla Frances Mary Blair; two *s*. *Educ:* Winchester Coll.; King's Coll., Cambridge (BA Eng. Lit., MA); Courtauld Inst. of Art (MPhil 1982). Lectr, Ritsumeikan Univ., Kyoto, 1983–84; called to the Bar, Inner Temple, 1986; in private legal practice, 1986–89; entered HM Diplomatic Service, 1989; Second Sec. (Econ.), later First Sec. (Pol), Tokyo, 1990–94; First Secretary: EU Dept (Internal), FCO, 1995–96; (Pol/Mil.), Paris, 1997–98; Hd, Common Foreign and Security Policy Dept, FCO, 1998–2000; Pol Counsellor, Tokyo, 2001–04; Ambassador to Lithuania, 2004–08; Dir, Overseas Territories, FCO, 2008–12; Comr, British Indian Ocean Territory and British Antarctic Territory, 2008–12; Dir, Eastern Europe and Central Asia, FCO, 2012–13. *Recreations:* mountain sports, natural history, tennis, reading. *Address:* c/o Foreign and Commonwealth Office, King Charles Street, SW1A 2AH. *Club:* Travellers.

ROBERTS, David Francis, CMG 2003; consultant on agricultural trade issues; Deputy Director General responsible for agricultural trade issues, European Commission, 1996–2002; *m* 1974, Astrid Suhr Henriksen; two *s* one *d*. *Educ:* Priory Grammar School, Shrewsbury; Worcester College, Oxford (MA). Joined MAFF, 1964; seconded to FCO as First Sec. (Agric.), Copenhagen, 1971–74; Principal Private Sec. to Minister of Agriculture, 1975–76; seconded to HM Treasury as Head of Agric. Div., 1979–80; Under Sec., 1985, seconded to FCO as Minister (Agric.), UK Repn to the European Communities, Brussels, 1985–90; Dep. Dir Gen., resp. for agricl support, DG VI, EC, 1990–96. *Recreations:* sailing, squash, rowing, racketball.

ROBERTS, David George; HM Diplomatic Service, retired; Founder and Director, Dagero Ltd, international business advice, since 2010; *b* 11 April 1955; *s* of David Ceredig Roberts, Dolgellau, and Margaret Roberts (*née* Burns); *m* 1985, Rosmarie Rita Kunz, Winterthur, Switzerland; one *s* one *d*. *Educ:* Bishop Vesey's Grammar Sch., Sutton Coldfield; Pembroke Coll., Oxford (BA Hons Mod. Hist. 1976; MA 1983). Joined FCO, 1976: Desk Officer, E Germany and WEU, 1976–77; Third, later Second, Sec. (Chancery), Jakarta, 1977–81; Second Sec. (Chancery), Havana, 1981–83; Desk Officer for nuclear deterrence, strategic defence and test ban matters, Defence and Arms Control and Disarmament Depts, FCO, 1983–86; Section Head for N Africa, Near East and N Africa Dept, FCO, 1986–88; First Secretary: (Eur. and Econ. Affairs), Madrid, 1988–90; (EU and Financial Affairs), Paris, 1990–94; Deputy Head: Hong Kong Dept, FCO, 1994–96; of Mission, and Consul Gen., Santiago, 1996–2000; of Mission, Dir of Trade and Investment and Consul Gen., Switzerland and Liechtenstein, 2000–05; Hd, Global Business, subseq. Sustainable Devlt and Business, Gp, FCO, 2005–08. Internat. Advr, 3i Gp plc, 2008–09; Sen. Advr to Gov., Turks and Caicos Is, 2009. *Recreations:* enjoying languages (Spanish, French, German, Indonesian), attempting to keep fit, reading, gardening, listening to classical music, eating and drinking, rowing.

ROBERTS, (David) Gwilym (Morris), CBE 1987; FREng; Chairman, Acer Group Ltd, 1987–92; *b* 24 July 1925; *er s* of late Edward and Edith Roberts of Crosby; *m* 1st, 1960, Rosemary Elizabeth Emily (*d* 1973), *d* of late J. E. Giles of Tavistock; one *s* one *d*; 2nd, 1978, Wendy Ann, *d* of late Dr J. K. Moore of Beckenham and Alfriston. *Educ:* Merchant Taylors' School, Crosby; Sidney Sussex College, Cambridge (Minor Scholar, MA; Hon. Fellow, 1993). FICE, FIMechE; FREng (FEng 1986). Engineering Officer, RNVR, 1945–47; Lieut Comdr RNR, retired 1961. Asst Engineer, 1947–55, Partner, 1956–90 (Sen. Partner, 1981–90), John Taylor & Sons; principally development of water and wastewater projects, UK towns and regions, and Abu Dhabi, Bahrain, Egypt, Iraq, Kuwait, Mauritius, Qatar, Saudi Arabia and Thailand. Director: Acer Gp Ltd, 1987–92; various transportation projects in UK and abroad. Vis. Prof., Loughborough Univ., 1991–95. Chairman: BGS Programme Bd, 1989–93; Football Stadia Adv. Design Council, 1990–93; 2nd Severn Crossing Technical Adjudication Panel, 1991–97; Member: UK Cttee, IAWPRC, 1967–83; Bd of Control, AMBRIC (American British Consultants), 1978–92; (Construction Industry) Group of Eight, 1983–85, 1987–88; President: IPHE, 1968–69 (IPHE Silver Medal 1974; Gold Medal 1987); ICE, 1986–87 (Vice-Pres., 1983–86; Overseas Premium, 1978; Halcrow Premium, 1985; George Stephenson Medal, 1986); Smeatonian Soc. of Civil Engrs, 2009. Council Member: Brighton Polytechnic, 1983–86; NERC, 1987–93; CIRIA, 1988–92. Member: Exec. Cttee, British Egyptian Soc., 1991–93; Nat. Cttee, British-Arab Univ. Assoc., 1991–93; Council, Newcomen Soc., 2010–12. Governor: Chailey Sch., 1988–92; Roedean Sch., 1989–93. Freeman, City of London, 1977; Liveryman: Engineers' Co., 1985; Constructors' Co., 1990; Water Conservators' Co., 2000. Hon. FCIWEM. *Publications:* (co-author) Civil Engineering Procedure, 3rd edn 1979; Built By Oil, 1995; From Kendal's Coffee House to Great George Street, 1995; Chelsea to Cairo, 2006; papers to Royal Soc., Arab League, ICE, IPHE, Newcomen Soc. *Recreations:* golf, engineering history, family history. *Address:* 33 High Hurst Close, Newick, E Sussex BN8 4NJ. *T:* (01825) 722603. *Clubs:* Oxford and Cambridge; Piltdown Golf.

ROBERTS, David Ian; Co-Founder and Chief Executive, Edinburgh House Holdings Ltd, since 2001; Co-Founder, Estama EMBH, since 2007; *b* Greenock, 29 Sept. 1956; *s* of Romley Lewis Roberts and Anne Roberts; *m* 1993, Philippa Thornton (marr. diss. 2011); three *s* three *d. Educ:* Paisley Univ. (BA Land Econs). Chief Executive: Bourne End Properties plc, 1997–2001; Edinburgh House Estates (Hldgs) Ltd, 2001–10. Founder, David Roberts Art Foundn, 2007. *Recreations:* art collecting, ski-ing, fishing, golf. *Address:* Edinburgh House Holdings Ltd, 4th Floor, Adam House, 1 Fitzroy Square, W1T 5HE. *T:* (020) 7383 8300. *E:* dir@ehel.co.uk. *Clubs:* Annabel's, Harry's Bar, Morton's, Arts.

ROBERTS, (David) Paul, OBE 2008; Managing Director, Improvement and Development Agency, 2009–10; Chairman: of Trustees, Creativity, Culture and Education, since 2008; Board of Directors, Innovation Unit, since 2014 (Director, since 2011); *b* 6 Sept. 1947; *s* of Percival and Nancy Roberts; *m* 1969, Helen Margaret Shone; two *d. Educ:* Univ. of Bristol (BSc Hons 1969; CertEd 1970); Cambridge Inst. Educn (AdvDip 1982). Maths Teacher, then Dir of Studies, Ipswich Sch., 1970–74; Dep. Hd Teacher, Harlington Upper Sch., Beds, 1974–83; Chief Inspector, then Dep. Dir of Educn, Notts CC, 1983–97; Dir of Educn, Nottingham CC, 1997–2001. Dir, Guideline Careers Co. Ltd, 1997–2001; Dir, Capita Strategic Educn Services, and Dir of Educn, Haringey Council, 2001–04; Improvement and Development Agency: Strategic Advr, Educn and Children's Services, 2004–05; Dir, Strategy and Develt, 2005–09. Advr to DCMS and DFE (formerly DfES, then DCSF) Ministers on Creativity in Schs, 2005–10; Chm., Creative and Cultural Educn Bd, DCSF and DCMS, 2007–08; Mem., Cultural Educn Bd, DfE and DCMS, 2013–. National Endowment for Science, Technology and the Arts: Member: Fellowship Prog. Cttee, 2004–06; Innovation Cttee, 2006–10; Public Services Innovation Lab. Bd, 2009–12; Creative Councils Steering Gp, 2012–13. Mem., Warwick Commn on Future of Cultural Value, 2014–15. Chm., Nottingham Music Educn Hub; Member, Board of Directors: Mountview Acad. of Theatre Arts, 2010– (Dep. Chm., 2013–); Nottingham Contemp., 2010– (Dep. Chm., 2012–); Greenwood Acads Trust, 2010–14. FRSA 1999. *Publications:* Nurturing Creativity in Young People, 2006; (jtly) Organisational Innovation in Public Services, 2013; (jtly) The Virtuous Circle: why creativity and cultural education matter, 2014; articles in educnl and maths jls. *Recreations:* arts, hill-walking. *Address:* 55 Dunster Road, West Bridgford, Nottingham NG2 6JE. *T:* 07799 408229. *E:* paul.roberts@cceengland.org.

ROBERTS, Dennis Laurie Harold; Director of Methodology, Office for National Statistics, 2011–12; *b* 24 Jan. 1949; *s* of William Roberts and Vera Roberts; *m* 1980, Anne Mary Hillhouse; one *s. Educ:* Sheffield Univ. (BA, MSc). CSO, 1971–76; DoE, 1976–83; MoD, 1983–85; Department of the Environment: Head: Local Govt Finance Div., 1985–89; Water Envmt Div., 1989–92; Finance Div., 1992–94; OPCS, 1994–96; Dir, Socio-Economic Stats and Analysis Gp, 1996–98, Dir, Corp. Services Gp, 1998–99, ONS; Dir, Roads and Traffic Directorate, DETR, 2000–01; Dir, Road Transport Directorate, DTLR, then DfT, 2001–03; Dir, Registration Services and Dep. Registrar General for England and Wales, 2004–08, Dir, Surveys and Admin. Sources, 2008–11, ONS. *Recreations:* walking, reading, watching football.

ROBERTS, Derek Franklyn, FCII, FCIB; Chairman, Yorkshire Building Society, 1997–2001; *b* 16 Oct. 1942; *s* of Frank Roberts, MBE, and May Evelyn Roberts; *m* 1969, Jacqueline (*née* Velho); two *s* one *d. Educ:* Park High Grammar Sch., Birkenhead; Liverpool Coll. of Commerce; Harvard Business Sch. (AMP (Grad.)). Royal Insurance Co. Ltd, 1961–72; Huddersfield Building Society: Insce Services Man., 1972; apptd to Executive, as Business Develt Man., 1975; Develt Man., 1979; on formation of Yorkshire Building Soc., 1982, apptd Asst Gen. Man. (Marketing); Dir and Chief Exec., 1987–96. Director: BWD Securities plc, 1988–92; Yorkshire Water Services (formerly Yorkshire Water), 1996–2005; Kelda Gp plc, 1999–2005. Dir, Bradford City Challenge Ltd, 1993–97; Mem., W Yorks Rural Develt Cttee, 1992–96. CCMI. *Recreations:* golf, gardening, ski-ing, keeping friendships in constant repair. *Address:* The Ark, 20 Arkenley Lane, Almondbury, Huddersfield HD4 6SQ. *T:* (01484) 426414. *Clubs:* Huddersfield Golf, Royal Liverpool Golf, Woodsome Hall Golf; Huddersfield Rugby Union FC.

ROBERTS, Sir Derek (Harry), Kt 1995; CBE 1983; FRS 1980; FREng, FInstP; Provost of University College London, 1989–99 and 2002–03; *b* 28 March 1932; *s* of Harry and Alice Roberts; *m* 1958, Winifred (*née* Short); one *s* one *d. Educ:* Manchester Central High Sch.; Manchester Univ. (BSc). Joined Plessey Co.'s Caswell Res. Lab., 1953; Gen. Man., Plessey Semiconductors, 1967; Dir, Allen Clark Res. Centre, 1969; Man. Dir, Plessey Microelectronics Div., 1973; Technical Dir, 1983–85, Jt Dep. Man. Dir (Technical), 1985–88, GEC. Pres., BAAS, 1996–97. Hon. DSc: Bath, 1982; Loughborough, 1984; City, 1985; Lancaster, 1986; Manchester, 1987; Salford, Essex, London, 1988; DUniv Open, 1984. *Publications:* about 20 pubns in scientific and technical jls. *Recreations:* reading, gardening. *Address:* University College London, Gower Street, WC1E 6BT. *T:* (020) 7679 7234.

ROBERTS, Sir (Edward) Adam, KCMG 2002; FBA 1990; Montague Burton Professor of International Relations, 1986–2007, Senior Research Fellow, Department of Politics and International Relations, since 2008, Oxford University; Fellow of Balliol College, Oxford, 1986–2007, now Emeritus; President, British Academy, 2009–13; *b* 29 Aug. 1940; *s* of late Michael Roberts, poet and Janet Roberts, OBE, writer (as Janet Adam Smith); *m* 1966, Frances P. Dunn; one *s* one *d. Educ:* Westminster School; Magdalen College, Oxford (Open Schol.; Stanhope Hist. Essay Prize, 1961; BA 1962, MA 1981). Asst Editor, Peace News Ltd, 1962–65; Noel Buxton Student in Internat. Relations, LSE, 1965–68; Lectr in Internat. Relations, LSE, 1968–81; Alastair Buchan Reader in Internat. Relations, Oxford Univ., and Professorial Fellow, St Antony's Coll., Oxford, 1981–86; Leverhulme Res. Fellow, 2000–03. Mem., Council for Sci. and Technol., 2010–13. Member, Council: RIIA, 1985–91; IISS, 2002–08; Mem. Adv. Bd, UK Defence Acad., 2003–15. Gov., Ditchley Foundn, 2001–11. Hon. Fellow: LSE, 1997; St Antony's Coll., Oxford, 2006; Cumbria Univ., 2014. For. Mem., Amer. Acad. of Arts and Scis, 2011; Mem., Amer. Philosophical Soc., 2013; MAE 2013. Hon. DSocSc KCL, 2010; Hon. LLD Aberdeen, 2012; Hon. Dr Internat. Politics Aoyama Gakuin, Tokyo, 2012; Hon. DLitt Bath, 2014. *Publications:* (ed) The Strategy of Civilian Defence, 1967; (jtly) Czechoslovakia 1968, 1969; Nations in Arms, 1976, 2nd edn, 1986; (ed jtly) Documents on the Laws of War, 1982, 3rd edn 2000; (ed jtly) United Nations, Divided World, 1988, 2nd edn 1993; (ed jtly) Hugo Grotius and International Relations, 1990; Humanitarian Action in War, 1996; (ed jtly) The United Nations Security Council and War, 2008; (ed jtly) Civil Resistance and Power Politics, 2009; (ed) Democracy, Sovereignty and Terror, 2012. *Recreations:* mountaineering, cycling. *Address:* Balliol College, Oxford OX1 3BJ. *Club:* Alpine (Trustee, 2013–).

ROBERTS, Eifion; *see* Roberts, His Honour H. E. P.

ROBERTS, Elizabeth S.; *see* Saville Roberts, E.

ROBERTS, Emyr Gordon, PhD; Chief Executive, Natural Resources Wales, since 2012; *b* 6 Sept. 1958; *s* of Gordon and Awena Wyn Roberts; *m* 1999, Karen Turner; one *s* one *d. Educ:* Univ. of Reading (BA Hons 1979); Univ. of Wales, Aberystwyth (PhD 1982). NFU, 1982–91; Welsh Office: Principal, 1991–97; Hd, Financial Planning Div., 1997–2000; Hd, Econ. Planning Div., Nat. Assembly for Wales, 2001–03; Chief Exec., Welsh European Funding Office, 2003–05; Welsh Assembly Government, subseq. Welsh Government: Dir, Dept for Social Justice and Regeneration, later Social Justice and Local Govt, 2005–09; Dir Gen., Public Services and Local Govt Delivery, 2009–10; Dir Gen., Children, Educn, Lifelong Learning and Skills, subseq. Dept for Educn and Skills, 2010–12. Trustee, Alzheimer's Soc., 2014–. Fellow, Aberystwyth Univ., 2013. *Address:* Natural Resources Wales, Tŷ Cambria, 29 Newport Road, Cardiff CF24 0TP. *T:* 0300 065 4444. *E:* emyr.roberts@cyfoethnaturiolcymru.gov.uk.

ROBERTS, Prof. Gareth Owen, PhD; FRS 2013; Professor of Statistics and Director, Centre for Research in Statistical Methodology, University of Warwick, since 2007; *b* Liverpool, 1964; *s* of Alun Roberts and Ceri Roberts; *m* 1998, Deborah Tait; one *s* one *d. Educ:* Blue Coat Sch., Liverpool; Jesus Coll., Oxford (BA 1st Cl. Hons Maths 1985); Univ. of Warwick (PhD Statistics 1988). Lecturer in Statistics: Dept of Maths, Univ. of Nottingham, 1988–91; Dept of Pure Maths and Mathematical Statistics, Univ. of Cambridge, 1992–98; Prof. of Statistics, Dept of Maths and Statistics, Lancaster Univ., 1998–2007. FSS 1998. Medallion Lect., 2009, Blackwell Lect., 2014, Inst. for Mathematical Statistics. Guy Medal, Bronze, 1997, Silver, 2008, Royal Statistical Soc.; Rollo Davidson Prize, 1999. *Publications:* over 140 articles in acad. jls. *Recreations:* bridge, music, cycling, walking. *Address:* Department of Statistics, University of Warwick, Coventry CV4 7AL. *T:* (024) 7657 4812, *Fax:* (024) 7652 4532. *E:* gareth.o.roberts@warwick.ac.uk.

ROBERTS, George Arnott; Head of Administration Department, House of Commons, 1988–91; *b* 16 April 1930; *s* of David Roberts and Doris (*née* Sykes); *m* 1956, Georgina (*née* Gower); two *s* one *d. Educ:* Rastrick Grammar Sch.; London Univ. (extra-mural). Min. of Labour, then Dept of Employment, 1947–74; Advisory, Conciliation and Arbitration Service, 1974–85: Sec., Central Arbitration Cttee, 1978–80; Dir of Administration, 1980–83; Dir, London Region, 1983–85; House of Commons, 1985–91: Hd of Establishment Office, 1985–88. *Recreations:* golf, gardening.

ROBERTS, Sir Gilbert (Howland Rookehurst), 7th Bt *cr* 1809; *b* 31 May 1934; *s* of Sir Thomas Langdon Howland Roberts, 6th Bt, CBE, and of Evelyn Margaret, *o d* of late H. Fielding-Hall; *S* father, 1979; *m* 1958, Ines, *o d* of late A. Labunski; one *s* one *d. Educ:* Rugby; Gonville and Caius Coll., Cambridge (BA 1957). CEng, MIMechE. *Heir: s* Howland Langdon Roberts, *b* 19 Aug. 1961. *Address:* 3340 Cliff Drive, Santa Barbara, CA 93109–1079, USA.

ROBERTS, Prof. Gordon Carl Kenmure, PhD; Professor of Biochemistry, University of Leicester, 1986–2008, Emeritus Professor, 2011 (Honorary Professor, 2008–11); *b* 28 May 1943; *s* of Rev. Douglas M. A. K. Roberts and Hilda (*née* Engelmann); *m* 1963, Hilary Margaret Lepper; two *s* one *d. Educ:* University Coll., London (BSc Hons Biochem. 1964); PhD Biochem. London 1967. Res. Chemist, Merck Sharp & Dohme Res. Labs, Rahway, NJ, 1967–69; Member scientific staff: MRC Molecular Pharmacol. Res. Unit, Dept of Pharmacol., Univ. of Cambridge, 1969–72; NIMR, 1972–86; University of Leicester: Director: Henry Wellcome Labs for Structural Biol. (formerly Leicester Biol NMR Centre), 1986–2008; Centre for Mechanisms of Human Toxicity, 1991–2000; Head: Dept of Biochemistry, 2000–04; Sch. of Biol Scis, 2004–08. Pres., IUPAB, 2011–14. Ed.-in-Chief, Encyclopaedia of Biophysics, 5 vols, 2012. *Publications:* NMR in Molecular Biology (with O. Jardetzky), 1981; (ed) NMR of Biological Macromolecules, 1993; (ed with L.-Y. Lian) Protein NMR: practical techniques and applications, 2011; numerous papers in scientific jls. *Recreation:* gardening. *Address:* Henry Wellcome Laboratories for Structural Biology, Henry Wellcome Building, University of Leicester, PO Box 138, Lancaster Road, Leicester LE1 9HN. *T:* (0116) 229 7106.

ROBERTS, Gwilym; *see* Roberts, D. G. M.

ROBERTS, Gwilym Edffrwd, PhD; Member (Lab), Staffordshire County Council, 2005–09; *b* 7 Aug. 1928; *s* of William and Jane Ann Roberts; *m* 1954, Mair Griffiths; no *c. Educ:* Brynrefail Gram. Sch.; UCW (Bangor); City Univ. BSc. Industrial Management, 1952–57; Lecturer (Polytechnic and University), 1957–66, 1970–74. Mem., Cannock Chase DC, 1983–2002 (Leader, 1992–99). MP (Lab): South Bedfordshire, 1966–70; Cannock, Feb. 1974–1983; PPS, DoI, 1976–79. Contested (Lab): Ormskirk, 1959; Conway, 1964; S Beds, 1970; Cannock and Burntwood, 1983, 1987. Chm., First Community NHS Trust, 1998–2001. Business Analyst, Economic Forecasting, Market and Operational Research, 1957. Institute of Statisticians: Vice-Pres., 1978; Hon. Officer, 1983–84; Editor, Newsletter, 1967–78. FCMI. Hon. FSS 1993. *Publications:* many articles on technical, political, parliamentary and European matters. *Recreations:* cricket, table tennis. *Address:* 18 Church Street, Rugeley, Staffs WS15 2AB. *T:* (01889) 583601.

ROBERTS, Howard Edward; QC (Guernsey) 2000; HM Procureur (Attorney-General) and Receiver General, Guernsey, since 2009; *b* Suffolkbrowse, 19 April 1956; *s* of Basil Roberts and Lorna Roberts (*née* Heyworth); *m* 1977, Janice Dronsfield; two *s. Educ:* Cheadle Mosely Grammar Sch., Cheshire; Gonville and Caius Coll., Cambridge (MA); Univ. of Caen, France. Called to the Bar, Middle Temple, 1978, Guernsey, 1988; Legal Asst, MAFF, 1980–83; Legislative Draftsman, Guernsey, 1983–90; Crown Advocate, Guernsey, 1990–99; HM Comptroller (Solicitor-Gen.), Guernsey, 1999–2009. Mem., Guernsey Choral and Orchestral Soc. *Recreations:* choral music, gardening. *Address:* St James Chambers, St Peter Port, Guernsey GY1 2PA. *T:* (01481) 723355, *Fax:* (01481) 725439. *E:* howard.roberts@gov.gg.

ROBERTS, Sir Hugh (Ashley), GCVO 2010 (KCVO 2001; CVO 1998; LVO 1995); FSA; Director of the Royal Collection and Surveyor of the Queen's Works of Art, 1996–2010, now Surveyor Emeritus; *b* 20 April 1948; *s* of late Rt Rev. Edward James Keymer Roberts, sometime Bishop of Ely, and Dorothy Frances, *d* of Rev. Canon Edwin David Bowser; *m* 1975, Hon. Priscilla Jane Stephanie Low (*see* Hon. Dame P. J. S. Roberts); two *d. Educ:* Winchester Coll.; Corpus Christi Coll., Cambridge (MA; Hon. Fellow 2011). FSA 1994. With Christie Manson and Woods, 1970–87 (Dir, 1978–87); Dep. Surveyor of the Queen's Works of Art, 1988–96. Mem., Sec. of State's Adv. Gp, Historic Royal Palaces Agency, 1990–98. Mem., Fabric Adv. Cttee, St George's Chapel, Windsor, 1998–. Member: Exec. Cttee, NACF, 1988–2000; Arts Panel, NT, 1988–2014 (Chm., 1997–2010); Council, Attingham Trust, 1988–2010 (Patron, 2010–); Conservation Cttee, Devonshire Collection, 2008–. Trustee: Harewood House Trust, 1986–; Cobbe Collection Trust, 1997–; Historic Royal Palaces Trust, 1998–2010; Great Steward of Scotland's Dumfries House Trust, 2007–14; Wallace Collection, 2013–; Trustee and Gov., Royal Pavilion and Museums Foundn (formerly Friends of Royal Pavilion Art Gall. and Brighton Mus.), 2008–. Mem., Internat. Council, Preservation Soc. of Newport Co., RI, 2011–. Mem., Soc. of Dilettanti, 1991–. *Publications:* For the King's Pleasure: the furnishing and decoration of George IV's apartments at Windsor Castle, 2001; The Queen's Diamonds, 2012; contrib. to Furniture History, Burlington Mag., Apollo, etc. *Recreation:* gardening. *Address:* 33 East Lockinge, near Wantage, Oxon OX12 8QG. *T:* (01235) 835708. *Clubs:* Brooks's, Grillions; Nobody's Friends.

ROBERTS, His Honour (Hugh) Eifion (Pritchard); QC 1971; DL; a Circuit Judge, 1977–98; *b* 22 Nov. 1927; *er s* of late Rev. and Mrs E. P. Roberts, Anglesey; *m* 1958, Buddug Williams; one *s* two *d. Educ:* Beaumaris Grammar Sch.; University Coll. of Wales, Aberystwyth (LLB); Exeter Coll., Oxford (BCL). Called to Bar, Gray's Inn, 1953; practised on Wales and Chester Circuit, Sept. 1953–July 1977. Dep. Chairman: Anglesey QS, 1966–71; Denbighshire QS, 1970–71; a Recorder of the Crown Court, 1972–77. Formerly Asst Parly Boundary Comr for Wales; Mem. for Wales of the Crawford Cttee on Broadcasting Coverage. Hon. Fellow, Bangor Univ., 2009. Hon. LLD Wales, 2014. *Recreation:* gardening. *Address:* Maes-y-Rhedyn, Gresford Road, Llay, Wrexham LL12 0NN. *T:* (01978) 852292.

ROBERTS, Hugh Martin P.; *see* Plowden Roberts.

ROBERTS, Prof. Ian Gareth, PhD, LittD; FBA 2007; Professor of Linguistics, since 2000 and Chair, Faculty of Modern and Medieval Languages, since 2011, University of Cambridge (Head of Department of Linguistics, 2001–05); Fellow, Downing College, Cambridge, since 2000; *b* 23 Oct. 1957; *s* of Idris Michael Roberts and Dorothy Sybil Roberts (*née* Moody); *m* 1993, Lucia Cavalli; one *s* one *d*. *Educ:* Stamford Sch.; Eirias High Sch., Colwyn Bay; UCNW (Bangor) (BA Hons Linguistics 1979); Univ. of Southern Calif (PhD 1985); LittD Cantab 2006. Translator, Motor Ind. Res. Assoc., Nuneaton, 1980–81; University of Geneva: Asst de linguistique anglaise, 1985–86; Maître-asst de linguistique générale, 1986–91; Professor: of Linguistics, UCNW (Bangor), then Univ. of Wales, Bangor, 1991–96; of English Linguistics, Univ. of Stuttgart, 1996–2000. Ed., Jl Linguistics, 1994–2000. MAE 2008. Pres., Soc. Linguistica Europaea, 2012–13. Hon. Dr Bucharest, 2013. *Publications:* The Representation of Implicit and Dethematised Subjects, 1987; Verbs and Diachronic Syntax, 1993; Comparative Syntax, 1996; Syntactic Change, 2003; Principles and Parameters in a VSO Language, 2005; Diachronic Syntax, 2007; Agreement and Head Movement, 2010; contrib. numerous articles to learned jls. *Recreations:* reading, walking, music. *Address:* Downing College, Cambridge CB2 1DQ. *T:* (01223) 334834.

ROBERTS, Ian White; HM Diplomatic Service, retired; Hon. Visiting Fellow, 1985–99, Official Historian, since 1999, School of Slavonic and East European Studies, University College London; *b* 29 March 1927; *s* of George Dodd Roberts and Jessie Dickson Roberts (*née* White); *m* 1956, Pamela Johnston; one *d*. *Educ:* Royal Masonic Sch., Bushey, Herts; Gonville and Caius Coll., Cambridge (MA 1st Cl. Hons Mod. Langs). Served Royal Air Force (Pilot Officer), 1948–50; postgrad. student, Cambridge (Scarbrough Award), 1950. Joined Foreign Office, 1951; Klagenfurt, 1952; Munich, 1954; Berlin, 1955; FCO, 1957–61; Second (later First) Secretary, Budapest, 1961–63; FCO, 1963; Bujumbura, 1965; FCO, 1965–66; Buenos Aires, 1966; FCO, 1969–74; Oslo, 1974–76; FCO, 1976–84; Counsellor, 1976. Special Advr, Finnish Inst., London, 2009. *Publications:* Nicholas I and the Russian Intervention in Hungary, 1991; History of School of Slavonic and East European Studies, University College London, 1991, 2nd edn 2009; articles in philatelic and other jls incl. East-West Rev. and publications of FCO Historical Dept. *Recreations:* music, reading, philately. *Address:* c/o Lloyds, 1 Butler Place, SW1H 0PR. *Club:* Travellers.

ROBERTS, Sir Ivor (Anthony), KCMG 2000 (CMG 1995); President, Trinity College, Oxford, since 2006; HM Diplomatic Service, retired; *b* 24 Sept. 1946; *s* of late Leonard Moore Roberts and Rosa Maria Roberts (*née* Fusco); *m* 1974, Elizabeth Bray Bernard Smith; two *s* one *d*. *Educ:* St Mary's Coll., Crosby; Keble Coll., Oxford (Gomm schol.; MA; Hon. Fellow 2001); FCIL (FIL 1991). Entered HM Diplomatic Service, 1968; MECAS, 1969; Third, later Second Sec., Paris, 1970–73; Second, later First Sec., FCO, 1973–78; First Sec., Canberra, 1978–82; First Sec., later Counsellor, FCO, 1982–88; Minister and Dep. Head of Mission, Madrid, 1989–93; Chargé d'Affaires, Belgrade, 1994–96; Ambassador to Yugoslavia, 1996–97; Sen. Associate Mem., St Antony's Coll., Oxford, 1997–98; Ambassador: to Ireland, 1999–2003; to Italy and to San Marino, 2003–06. Chm. Council, British Sch. of Archaeol. and Fine Arts, Rome, 2008–12. Patron, Venice in Peril Fund, 2006–. Freeman, City of London, 2009. *Publications:* (ed) Satow's Diplomatic Practice, 6th edn 2009; Razgovori s Miloševićem, 2012; (contrib.) The Past is Never Dead: Balkan legacies of the Great War, 2015; Conversations with Milošević, 2015. *Recreations:* opera, ski-ing, golf, photography. *Address:* President's Lodgings, Trinity College, Oxford OX1 3BH. *Clubs:* Oxford and Cambridge, Beefsteak; Downhill Only (Wengen).

ROBERTS, Sir James Elton Denby Buchanan, 4th Bt *cr* 1909, of Milner Field, Bingley, W Riding of Yorks; *b* 12 July 1966; *o s* of David Gordon Denby Roberts (*d* 1971), 3rd *s* of 2nd Bt, and of Diana Frances Roberts (*née* Wilson-Jones, now Buchanan); adopted by his step-father and assumed surname of Roberts-Buchanan, later reverted to Roberts and assumed Buchanan as a forename; *S* uncle, 2012, but his name does not appear on the Official Roll of the Baronetage; *m* 1994, Lisa Jane, *d* of Ian Ross Stirling; one *s* three *d*. *Educ:* George Watson's Coll., Edinburgh; Harper Adams Agric. Coll. *Heir:* *s* John David Denby Roberts, *b* 29 Dec. 1999. *Address:* Lawhill House, Trinity Gask, by Auchterarder, Perthshire PH3 1LJ.

ROBERTS, Hon. Jane; *see* Roberts, Hon. P. J. S.

ROBERTS, Dame Jane (Elisabeth), DBE 2004; FRCPsych; Consultant Child and Adolescent Psychiatrist, Whittington Health (formerly Islington Primary Care Trust), since 1993 (Medical Director, 2002–06; Director, Quality and Performance, 2006–10); *b* 23 Aug. 1955; *d* of Rev. Dr Fred Roberts and Nia Lora Roberts; *m* 2005, Prof. David Brian Dunger, *qv*; one *s* and one step *d*. *Educ:* Bristol Univ. (MB ChB 1980); Brunel Univ. (MSc 1991). MRCP 1983; MRCPsych 1986, FRCPsych 2004. Jun. posts in paediatrics, 1980–84; Registrar, Psychiatry, Maudsley Hosp., 1984–87; Sen. Registrar, Child and Adolescent Psychiatry, Tavistock Clinic, 1987–92; Locum Consultant, Child and Adolescent Psychiatry, Camden and Islington Community Health Services, NHS Trust, 1992–93. London Borough of Camden Council: Mem., 1990–2006; Dep. Leader, 1994–98, Leader, 2000–05; Chair, Educn Cttee, 1998–2000. Chair, Councillors' Commn, 2007–09. Interim Clin. Dir, Commissioning Support for London, 2010. Mem. Bd, OFSTED, 2007–11. Trustee: IPPR, 2005–; Parenting UK, 2006–12 (Chair, 2006–12); Dir, New Local Govt Network, 2006– (Chair, 2012–); Member: Central Council, Socialist Health Assoc., 2006–; Dr Foster Ethics Cttee, 2008–; Ethics Cttee, Assoc. of Child Psychotherapists, 2012–; Chm., Adv. Council, Compass Educn Inquiry, 2013–14. Lay Rep., Ethics Cttee, Zool Soc. of London, 2007–. Trustee, Freedom from Torture (formerly Med. Foundn for the Care of Victims of Torture), 2010–14. Sen. Associate Fellow, Warwick Business Sch., 2006–15; Vis. Fellow, Open Univ., 2015–. Governor: Eleanor Palmer Primary Sch., Camden, 2010–14; Regent High Sch., Camden, 2012–; Mem., Camden Partnership for Educnl Excellence, 2012–. Hon. Fellow, UCL, 2005. Hon. DLaws Bristol, 2007. *Publications:* (ed with Dr S. Kraemer) The Politics of Attachment, 1996; Losing Political Office, 2015; academic articles in paediatrics and psychiatry. *Address:* 1 Countess Road, NW5 2NS.

ROBERTS, Hon. Dame Jennifer (Mary), DBE 2014; **Hon. Mrs Justice Roberts;** a Judge of the High Court, Family Division, since 2014. *Educ:* LLB 1st Cl. Hons. Called to the Bar, Inner Temple, 1988; Recorder, 2000–14; QC 2009; Dep. High Ct Judge, 2011–14. MCIArb 2013. Fellow, Internat. Acad. of Matrimonial Lawyers, 2011. *Address:* Royal Courts of Justice, Rolls Building, Fetter Lane, EC4A 1NL.

ROBERTS, His Honour Jeremy Michael Graham; QC 1982; Member, Parole Board, since 2010; *b* 26 April 1941; *s* of late Lt-Col J. M. H. Roberts and E. D. Roberts; *m* 1964, Sally Priscilla Johnson, *d* of late Col F. P. Johnson, OBE. *Educ:* Winchester; Brasenose Coll., Oxford (BA). Called to the Bar, Inner Temple, 1965, Bencher, 1992. Recorder, 1981–2000; Perm. Judge, Central Criminal Court, 2000–11. Head of Chambers, 1997–2000. Mem., Press Complaints Commn, 2011–14. *Recreations:* racing, reading, theatre, opera, canals. *Address:* 21 The Butts, Brentford, Middx TW8 8BJ.

ROBERTS, John; *see* Roberts, A. J.

ROBERTS, John Anthony, CBE 2011; QC 1988; FCIArb; a Recorder of the Crown Court, 1987–98; *b* Sierra Leone, 17 May 1928; *s* of late John Anthony Roberts of Brazil and Regina Roberts of Sierra Leone; *m* 1961, Eulette Valerie; one *s*. *Educ:* St Edward's RC Secondary Sch., Sierra Leone; Inns of Court Sch. of Law. Costs Clerk, Taylor Woodrow W Africa Ltd; Civil Servant, Sierra Leone; RAF 1952–62 (GSM Malaya), served UK, Europe, Near East, Far East, S Pacific; qualified Air Traffic Control Officer, 1962–64; qualified pilot; Civil Service, UK, 1964–69, incl. Inland Revenue; part time law student; called to the Bar, Gray's Inn, 1969, Bencher, 1996; Mem., Lincoln's Inn, 1972; Head of Chambers, 1975; Asst Recorder, 1983–87. First person of African ancestry to be appointed QC at the English Bar; called to the Bar in: Jamaica, 1973; Sierra Leone, 1975; Trinidad and Tobago, 1978; Bahamas, 1984; St Kitts and Nevis, 1988; Antigua, 2002; Barbados, 2002; Bermuda, 2003; Anguilla, 2006; Grenada, 2007. Judge, Supreme Cts of BVI and Anguilla, BWI, 1992–93. Bencher, Council of Legal Educn, Sierra Leone, 1990. Tutor, Inns of Ct Sch. of Law, London, 1990–92. Pres., UK Br., W Indian Ex-Servicemen's and Ex-Servicewomen's Assoc., 2000–03; Jt Pres., British Caribbean Assoc., UK, 2002–06. Hon. Citizen, Atlanta, Ga, USA, 1991. Freeman, City of London, 1996; Mem. Guild of Freemen, 1997. Hon. Citizen, BVI, 2000. Hon. DCL City, 1996. *Recreations:* music, singing in a choir (Latin Mass and Gregorian Chant), flying light aircraft, playing piano, organ and guitar, reading, dancing, athletics, boxing (former sprinter and boxer, RAF).

ROBERTS, John Charles Quentin; Hon. Chairman, International Advisory Board of All-Russia State Library for Foreign Literature, Moscow, since 2004 (Member, 1991–93; Co-Chairman, 1994–2004); Director, Britain-Russia Centre (formerly Great Britain-USSR Association), 1974–93; *b* 4 April 1933; *s* of Hubert and Emilie Roberts; *m* 1959, Dinah Webster-Williams (marr. diss.); one *s* one *d*. *Educ:* Quainton Hall; King's Coll., Taunton (open scholar); Merton Coll., Oxford (MA). Royal Air Force CSC Interpreter, 1953; Russian Language Tutor, SSEES, Univ. of London, 1953; Shell International Petroleum Co. Ltd, 1956; Shell Co. of E Africa Ltd: Representative, Zanzibar and S Tanganyika, 1957, Kenya Highlands, 1958; PA to Man. Dir, Shell Austria AG Vienna, 1960; Pressed Steel Co. Ltd, Oxford, 1961; Asst Master, Marlborough Coll., 1963–74. Chairman: Organising Cttee for British Week in Siberia, 1978; Steering Cttee, British Month in USSR (Kiev), 1990. Mem. Council, Amer. Friends of the Russian Country Estate Inc., Washington, 1998–2003. Member Council: SSEES, Univ. of London, 1981–93; Academia Rossica, 2000–06; Vice Pres., Assoc. of Teachers of Russian, 1984–89. Governor, Cobham Hall, 1984–88. Trustee: Serge Rachmaninoff Foundn, 2002–06; Keston Inst., Oxford, 2003–07; Friends of Chelsea & Westminster Hosp., 2005–11. Hon. Life Mem., GB-Russia Soc., 2002. Mem., Editl Adv. Bd, Herald of Europe, Moscow, 2001–. Tyutchev Gold Medal, Internat. Pushkin Foundn, 2004; Internat. Nikolai Karamzin Medal, Herald of Europe and Egor Gaidar Foundn, 2012. *Publications:* Speak Clearly into the Chandelier: cultural politics between Britain and Russia 1973–2000, 2000 (Russian lang. edn 2001, Znamya Award); The Colour of Poppies (trans. from French), 2005; If Only I Could Fly: children's poems from Russia, 2012; contribs to specialist jls. *Recreations:* family, friends old and new, the arts. *Address:* 147 Beaufort Street, SW3 6BS. *T:* (020) 7376 3452. *Club:* Athenæum.

ROBERTS, John Edward, CBE 2004; FREng, FIET, FCCA; Chairman: RBC Europe Ltd, since 2009; Halite Energy Group, since 2010; First Utility, since 2013; Electricity North West, since 2014; *b* 2 March 1946; *s* of Arthur and Dora Roberts; *m* 1970, Pamela Baxter; one *s* one *d*. *Educ:* Liverpool Univ. (BEng). FCCA 1983; CEng, FIET (FIEE 1988); FREng 2002; DMS. Merseyside and North Wales Electricity Board, subseq. Manweb: Chief Accountant, 1984–90; Finance Dir, 1990–91; Man. Dir, 1991–92; Chief Exec., 1992–95; Chief Executive: S Wales Electricity, then Hyder Utilities, 1996–99; United Utilities, 1999–2006. Dir, Hyder Gp, 1996–99. Chm., Black Rock New Energy Investment Trust, 2011–14. Mem., Royal Commn on Envmtl Pollution, 1998–2002. CCMI. Hon. Fellow, Liverpool John Moores Univ., 2004. DL Merseyside, 2006. Hon. DEng Liverpool, 2004. *Recreations:* scuba diving, walking, gardening.

ROBERTS, Dr John Esmond; Deputy Director (part time), Common Agricultural Policy Direct Payments, Department for Environment, Food and Rural Affairs, 2011–15; Secretary, Royal Commission on Environmental Pollution, 2009–11; *b* Bristol, 29 June 1951; *s* of Bill and Marian Roberts; *m* 1989, Lucy-Anne Collier; one *s* one *d*. *Educ:* Bishop Wordsworth Sch., Salisbury; Keble Coll., Oxford (MA, DPhil Chem. 1975). DoE, later DEFRA, 1975–2015; on secondment to Cabinet Secretariat, 1985–87; Divisional Manager: Local Govt Finance – Grants, 1987–91; Housing Gp Secretariat, 1991–92; Housing, Private Rented Sector, 1992–96; on secondment to LGA, 1996–97; Divisional Manager: Urban Policy, 1997–2001; Marine Envmt, 2001–06; Hd, Chemicals and Nanotechnologies, 2006–09, Hd, Noise and Local Envmtl Quality, 2008–09. Mem., Mgt Bd, Eur. Chemicals Agency, 2007–09. Vice Pres., Stockholm Convention on Persistent Organic Pollutants, 2007–09. *Recreations:* St Luke's Church, Wimbledon Park, Fulham Football Club.

ROBERTS, John Herbert; former tax administrator; *b* 18 Aug. 1933; *s* of late John Emanuel Roberts and Hilda Mary Roberts; *m* 1965, Patricia Iris; one *s* three *d*. *Educ:* Canton High Sch.; London School of Economics (BScEcon Hons). Entered Civil Service by Open Competition as Inspector of Taxes, 1954; National Service, commnd RASC, 1955–57; returned to Inland Revenue, 1957; Principal Inspector, 1974; Sen. Principal Inspector, 1979; Under Secretary, 1981; Director of Operations, 1981–85; Dir, Technical Div. 2, 1985–88; Dir, Compliance and Collection Div., 1988–92; Dir of Ops (DO2), 1992–93; consultant, overseas tax admin, 1994–99. *Recreations:* music, walking.

ROBERTS, His Honour John Houghton; a Circuit Judge, 1993–2012; *b* 14 Dec. 1947; *s* of John Noel Roberts and Ida Roberts, Irby, Wirral; *m* 1st, 1972, Anna Elizabeth (marr. diss. 1990), *e d* of Peter and Elizabeth Sheppard; three *s*; 2nd, 1991, Mary, *er d* of Frederic and Patricia Wilkinson, Blundellsands. *Educ:* Calday Grange Grammar Sch., West Kirby; Trinity Hall, Cambridge (Schol.; BA 1st Cl. Hons Law Tripos; MA). Lectr in Law, Liverpool Univ., 1969–71; called to the Bar, Middle Temple, 1970 (Harmsworth Major Entrance Exhibn 1968; Astbury Law Schol. 1970). Practised Northern Circuit, 1970–93. Asst Recorder, 1983; Recorder, 1988–93; Resident Judge, Bolton Crown Court, 1997–2001. President: Wirral Hospice St John's, 2014–; Cheshire Union of Golf Clubs, 2015. Mem., Bd of Regents, Liverpool Hope Univ. Church Warden, 2013–15. *Recreations:* Rugby football, golf, cricket, music. *Clubs:* Athenæum, Artists (Liverpool); Heswall Golf; Oxton Cricket.

ROBERTS, Dr John Laing; independent consultant in health and economic and sustainable development policy, since 1997; Adviser: to the Indian Ocean Commission, since 2004; to the Commonwealth Secretariat, since 2004; *b* 26 Dec. 1939; *s* of Charles F. Roberts and May Roberts; *m* 1st, 1963, Meriel F. Dawes (marr. diss. 1980); three *d*; 2nd, 1981, Judith Mary Hare (marr. diss. 2002); 3rd, 2002, Bibi Bilkis Sheik Janny. *Educ:* Latymer Upper School; Univ. of Birmingham. PhD, MSc, BSocSc. FHA. NHS Nat. Administrative Trainee, 1962–63; Senior Administrative Asst, United Birmingham Hosps, 1964–66; Sen. Res. Associate, Dept of Social Medicine, Univ. of Birmingham, 1966–69; Dep. Dir, Res. Div., Health Education Council, 1969–74; Operational Services Gen. Administrator, S Glamorgan AHA (T), 1974–77; Regional Gen. Administrator, W Midlands RHA, 1977–82; Regional Administrator, 1983–85, Regl Prevention Manager, 1985–89, N Western RHA; Regl Advr in Health Services, WHO Office for Europe, Copenhagen, 1990–92; Consultant, WHO Office for Europe, 1992–94; Health Economist/Planner, Min. of Econ. Planning and Develt, Mauritius, 1994–98. Adviser to Government: of Malaŵi, 1999–2001; of Mauritius, 2000–04; consultant to UNEP on Africa envmt outlook, 2001–02; advr to UNEP, 2002–; consulting Ed. to Bank of Mauritius, 2013–. Associate Prof., Dept of Econs and Statistics, Univ. of Mauritius, 2006–08. Dir, Adhealth, 1989–96. Hon. Sen. Res. Fellow, Manchester Univ., 1990–2000. Vice Pres., Mauritian Writers' Assoc., 2014–. Mem. Editl Bd, Internat. Jl of Health Promotion, 1996–. *Publications:* If Only: death and injury from accidents, 1977; The Big Kill: death, disease and cost of smoking in England and Wales, 1985; (ed jtly) Saving Small and Island States, 2010; (ed jtly) Tools for Mainstreaming Sustainable Development in Small States, 2011; The Big Divide: progress with MDGs in small states, 2012; papers on health education, health service administration, health and economics, the environment and sustainable development; PhD thesis, Studies of Information Systems for Health Service Resource Planning and Control. *Recreations:* swimming, beach walking, tennis, travel writing, poetry. *Address:* 5 Ranmore Court, 101 Worple Road, SW19 8HB; Habasha, Morcellement Mont Choisy, Mont Choisy, Mauritius. *T:* 2655187. *E:* john.laing@hotmail.com.

ROBERTS, His Honour John Mervyn; a Circuit Judge, 1999–2011; *b* 19 Feb. 1941; *s* of late Mervyn and Catherine Roberts; *m* 1972, Phillippa Ann Critien; one *d. Educ:* Hereford Cathedral Sch.; King's Coll., London (LLB Hons 1962). Called to the Bar, Inner Temple, 1963, Bencher, 2007; in practice at the Bar, 1963–99; a Recorder, 1994–99. Member: Criminal Injuries Compensation Bd, 1998–99; Parole Bd, 2002–14. *Recreations:* music, golf, travel. *Address:* c/o 5 Essex Court, Temple, EC4Y 9AH.

ROBERTS, Rear-Adm. John Oliver, CB 1976; MNI; Managing Director, Demak Ltd, International Consultants, 1983–98; *b* 4 April 1924; *er s* of J. V. and M. C. Roberts; *m* 1st, 1950, Lady Hermione Mary Morton Stuart (marr. diss. 1960; she *d* 1969); one *d*; 2nd, 1963, Honor Marigold Gordon Gray (marr. diss. 1987); one *s* one *d*; 3rd, 1987, Sheila Violet Mary Traub (*née* Barker) (*d* 2012); 4th, 2014, Gillian Ffrench Reckitt (*née* Nobbs). *Educ:* RN Coll., Dartmouth. Served War: Midshipman, HM Ships Renown and Tartar, 1941–43; Sub-Lt, HMS Serapis, 1943–44; Lieut, 1945; Pilot Trng, 1944–46. HMS Triumph, 1947–49; RNAS, Lossiemouth, 1949–51; Flag-Lt to FOGT, 1952; Lt-Comdr, 1953; HMAS Vengeance and Sydney, 1953–54; RNVR, Southern Air Div., 1954–56; CO, No 803 Sqdn, HMS Eagle, 1957–58; Comdr, 1958; RNAS, Brawdy, 1958–60; CO, HMS St Bride's Bay, 1960–61; Naval Staff, 1962–64; Captain, 1964; CSO, Flag Officer Aircraft Carriers, 1964–66; CO, HMS Galatea, 1966–68; Naval Staff, 1968–70; CO, HMS Ark Royal, 1971–72; Rear-Adm., 1972; Flag Officer Sea Training, 1972–74; COS to C-in-C Fleet, 1974–76; Flag Officer, Naval Air Command, 1976–78. Non-exec. Dir, Aeronautical & General Instruments Ltd, 1981–82 (Head of Marketing and Sales, Defence Systems Div., 1980–81); Dir Gen., British Printing Industries Fedn, 1981–82. FRSA. *Recreations:* Rugby football, cricket, athletics, sailing, ski-ing. *Address:* 22 St Anne's Road, Whitstable, Kent CT5 2DW. *Club:* East India, Devonshire, Sports and Public Schools.

ROBERTS, Julia Fiona; actress; *b* Smyrna, Georgia, 28 Oct. 1967; *d* of late Walter Roberts and of Betty Roberts; *m* 1st, 1993, Lyle Lovett (marr. diss. 1995); 2nd, 2002, Danny Moder; two *s* one *d* (of whom one *s* one *d* are twins). *Educ:* Campbell High Sch., Georgia. *Stage:* Three Days of Rain, NY, 2006; *films include:* Satisfaction, Mystic Pizza, 1988; Steel Magnolias, 1989 (Best Supporting Actress, Golden Globe Awards, 1990); Blood Red, Pretty Woman (Best Actress, Golden Globe Awards, 1991), Flatliners, 1990; Sleeping with the Enemy, Hook, Dying Young, 1991; The Pelican Brief, I Love Trouble, Prêt-à-Porter, 1994; Something to Talk About, 1995; Mary Reilly, Everybody Says I Love You, Michael Collins, 1996; My Best Friend's Wedding, Conspiracy Theory, 1997; Stepmom, 1998; Notting Hill, Runaway Bride, 1999; Erin Brockovich, 2000 (Academy Award for Best Actress, 2000; Best Actress, BAFTA Awards, Golden Globe Awards, Screen Actors' Guild Awards, 2001); The Mexican, America's Sweethearts, 2001; Ocean's Eleven, 2002; Confessions of a Dangerous Mind, Full Frontal, 2003; Mona Lisa Smile, 2004; Closer, Ocean's Twelve, 2005; Ocean's Thirteen, Charlie Wilson's War, 2007; Duplicity, Fireflies in the Garden, 2009; Valentine's Day, Eat Pray Love, 2010; Larry Crowne, 2011; Mirror, Mirror, 2012; August: Osage County, 2014 (also prod.); *television includes:* Crime Story, 1988; Baja Oklahoma, 1988; In the Wild, 1988.

ROBERTS, Ven. Kevin Thomas; Archdeacon of Carlisle, and Canon Residentiary, Carlisle Cathedral, since 2009; *b* Saltburn by the Sea, 11 Oct. 1955; *s* of Abel and Margaret Roberts; *m* 1982, Anne Waine; two *s* one *d. Educ:* Queens' Coll., Cambridge (BA Hons 1978; MA 1982); Nottingham Univ. (BA Hons 1982). Ordained deacon, 1983, priest, 1984; Assistant Curate: Beverley Minster, 1983–86; St John the Evangelist, Woodley, Oxfordshire, 1986–91; Vicar, Holy Trinity, Meole Brace, 1991–2009; Rural Dean, Shrewsbury, 1998–2008. Preb., Lichfield Cathedral, 2002–08. Chm., Carlisle Diocesan Bd of Educn, 2009–. *Recreations:* reading, photography, Middlesbrough FC. *Address:* 2 The Abbey, Carlisle CA3 8TZ. *T:* (01228) 523026. *E:* archdeacon.north@carlislediocese.org.uk.

ROBERTS, Prof. Kevin William Stuart, DPhil; FBA 2007; Sir John Hicks Professor of Economics, University of Oxford, since 1999; Fellow, Nuffield College, Oxford, since 1999; *b* 29 Feb. 1952; *s* of Basil Roberts and Dorothy Roberts (*née* Heaven); *m* 1981, Julia Clarke (marr. diss. 1996); two *d*; *m* 2014, Sophie Petersen. *Educ:* Cheltenham Grammar Sch.; Univ. of Essex (BA Math. Econ. 1973); Nuffield Coll., Oxford (BPhil Econ. 1975; DPhil Econ. 1977). Jun. Res. Fellow, St John's Coll., Oxford, 1975–77; Asst Prof., MIT, 1977–78; Univ. Lectr and Official Fellow, St Catherine's Coll., Oxford, 1978–82; Professor: of Econ. Theory, Univ. of Warwick, 1982–87; of Economics, LSE, 1987–99. Fellow, Econometric Soc., 1984. *Publications:* articles in internat. learned jls incl. Econometrica and Rev. Econ. Studies. *Address:* Nuffield College, Oxford OX1 1NF. *T:* (01865) 278601.

ROBERTS, Lisa; QC 2015; *b* Manchester, 2 Feb. 1969; *d* of Dr Geraint Roberts and Shirley Roberts; *m* 1994, Jonathan Bourne; one *s* one *d. Educ:* Salendine Nook Comprehensive Sch., Huddersfield; Huddersfield New Coll.; St Catherine's Coll., Oxford (BA Hons); Huddersfield Univ. (CPE); Inns of Court Sch. of Law (BVC). Called to the Bar, Lincoln's Inn, 1993; in practice as barrister, specialising in criminal and regulatory law, 1993–. Member: Criminal Bar Assoc.; Health and Safety Lawyers Assoc. *Recreations:* tennis, eating out, concerts, theatre, holidaying with family. *Address:* Lincoln House Chambers, Tower 12, Bridge Street, Manchester M3 3BZ. *T:* (0161) 832 5701, (0870) 458 0592. *E:* lisa.roberts@lincolnhousechambers.com.

ROBERTS, Lynn Deborah; a Circuit Judge, since 2012; **Her Honour Judge Lynn Roberts;** *b* 25 Oct. 1956; *d* of Henry and Eva Roberts; *m* 1994, John Watson (*d* 2007); one *s* one *d*, and one step *s* one step *d. Educ:* South Hampstead High Sch.; Brasenose Coll., Oxford (BA Hons (Mod. Hist.) 1979); Coll. of Law. Solicitor, 1986–88, Partner, 1988–2001, Hodge Jones and Allen; Dep. District Judge, County Courts, 1999–2001; Dep. District Judge, 1999–2001, District Judge, 2001–12, Principal Registry, Family Div.; Designated Family Judge for Essex and Suffolk, 2014–. Chair of Trustees, Melos Sinfonia, 2014–. *Publications:* (contrib.) Raydon and Jackson, Divorce and Family Matters, 18th edn 2004. *Recreations:* music, crosswords, country walks. *Address:* Chelmsford County Court, Priory Place, New London Road, Chelmsford, Essex CM2 0PP.

ROBERTS, Martin Geoffrey; Member, St Helena Financial Services Regulatory Authority, since 2011; *b* 3 July 1946; *s* of Arthur and Mary Roberts; *m* 1969, Christine Muriel George (*d* 2008); two *s. Educ:* Priory Grammar Sch., Shrewsbury; Worcester Coll., Oxford (MA). Min. of Technology, 1970; Private Sec. to Minister without Portfolio, 1973–74; seconded: to FCO, 1979–82; to DoE as Controller, Yorks and Humberside Regl Office, 1984–85; Sec., BOTB, 1985–89; Hd of Investigations Div., 1992–96, Dir, Finance and Resource Mgt, 1996–98, DTI; Dir, Insurance, HM Treasury, 1998; Dir, Insce and Friendly Socs, 1999–2002, Sen. Insce Advr, 2002–03, FSA; Sen. Consultant, Beachcroft Regulatory (formerly Beachcroft Wansbroughs) Consulting, 2003–09; Dir, PensionsRisk LLP, 2007–09. Chm., Friendly Socs Commn, 1998–2002; Mem., Exports Guarantee Adv. Council, 2003–12. Non-executive Director: Ealing PCT, 2009–13; Hillingdon PCT, 2011–13 (Interim Chm., 2010–11); NHS Outer NW London, 2011–12; NHS NW London, 2012–13. Mem., Exec. Cttee, 1998–2003, Chm., Tech. Cttee, 2000–03, Internat. Assoc. of Insce Supervisors. *Recreation:* sailing.

ROBERTS, Michael; *see* Roberts, Thomas M.

ROBERTS, Michael Andrew; Chief Executive, Association of Train Operating Companies, since 2008; Director-General, Rail Delivery Group, since 2013; *b* Santiago de Chile, 14 May 1966; *s* of Michael Francis Roberts and Georgina Sara Olmos Adriazola; *m* 1st, 2004, Michelle Cora Farrell (*d* 2008); 2nd, 2012, Emma Kate Wild; one *d. Educ:* Prior Park Coll., Bath; St Benet's Hall, Oxford (BA Hons Mod. Hist. 1987). Account Manager, Decision Makers, 1989–91; CBI, 1991–2008, Dir, Business Envmt, 2000–08. Member: Standing Adv. Cttee on Trunk Road Assessment, 1996–99; Dep. Prime Minister's Panel on Transport White Paper, 1997–98; Commn for Integrated Transport, 2000–08. Non-exec. Dir, Carbon Trust, 2001–08. *Recreations:* football, running, ski-ing, rowing. *Address:* Association of Train Operating Companies and Rail Delivery Group, 2nd Floor, 200 Aldersgate Street, EC1A 4HD. *T:* (020) 7841 8001. *E:* michael.roberts@atoc.org. *Club:* Molesey Boat.

ROBERTS, Surgeon Rear Adm. Michael Atholl F.; *see* Farquharson-Roberts.

ROBERTS, Rev. Canon Michael Graham Vernon; Principal, Westcott House, Cambridge, 1993–2006; *b* 4 Aug. 1943; *s* of Walter Graham Southall Roberts and Pamela Middleton Roberts (*née* Abel, now Murray); *m* 1970, Susan Elizabeth (*née* Merry); one *s* two *d. Educ:* Eton Coll.; Keble Coll., Oxford (BA 1965; MA); Cuddesdon Coll.; Church Divinity Sch. of Pacific, Berkeley, Calif. (MDiv 1967). Curate, Exmouth, 1967–70; Chaplain, Clare Coll., Cambridge, 1970–74; Vicar, St Mark, Bromley, 1974–79; Tutor, Queen's Coll., Birmingham, 1979–85; Team Rector, High Wycombe, 1985–90; Vice-Principal, Westcott House, Cambridge, 1990–93. Hon. Canon, Ely Cathedral, 2004–. *Recreations:* gardening, walking, theological education, reading. *Address:* Flat 1, 5 Salterton Road, Exmouth, Devon EX8 2BW.

ROBERTS, Michael John Wyn, CVO 2008; HM Diplomatic Service, retired; Ambassador to Slovakia, 2007–10; consultant on governance and international affairs, since 2011; *b* 4 July 1960; *s* of late Denys Murray Wyn Roberts and of Diana Roberts (*née* Marshall); *m* 1985, Margaret Anne Ozanne; one *s* two *d. Educ:* Bryanston Sch.; Brasenose Coll., Oxford (MA). Joined HM Diplomatic Service, 1984; Second, then First Sec., Athens, 1987–91; FCO, 1991–95; First Sec., UK Perm. Repn to EU, Brussels, 1995–99; Hd of Div., European Secretariat, Cabinet Office, 1999–2003; Dep. Hd of Mission, Ankara, 2004–07. Chm., British Czech and Slovak Assoc. Trustee: EU Baroque Orch.; Depaul Slovensko. *Recreations:* music, Chelsea FC, walking.

ROBERTS, Prof. Michael Symmons, FRSL; poet; Professor of Poetry, Manchester Metropolitan University, since 2009; *b* Preston, Lancs, 13 Oct. 1963; *s* of David Symmons Roberts and Iris Roberts; *m* 1991, Ruth Humphreys; three *s. Educ:* St Bartholomew's Comprehensive Sch., Newbury; Regent's Park Coll., Oxford (BA Hons Philosophy and Theol. 1986). Radio producer, 1989–95, TV producer (documentaries), 1995–99, BBC; Hd of Develt, BBC Religion and Ethics, 1999–2001; freelance writer, 2001–05; Sen. Lectr in English, Manchester Metropolitan Univ., 2005–09. FEA 2012; FRSL 2014. *Publications: poetry*: Soft Keys, 1993; Raising Sparks, 1996; Burning Babylon, 2001; Corpus, 2004 (Whitbread Poetry Award, 2004); The Half Healed, 2008; Drysalter, 2013 (Costa Poetry Award, 2013; Forward Poetry Prize, 2013); Selected Poems, 2016; *fiction:* Patrick's Alphabet, 2006; Breath, 2008; *non-fiction:* (with Paul Farley) Edgelands, 2011; *libretti*: (with composer James MacMillan): Raising Sparks, 1997; Quickening, 1998; Parthenogenesis, 2000; The Birds of Rhiannon, 2002; Chosen, 2003; Sun Dogs, 2006; The Sacrifice, 2007; Clemency, 2011; New-Made for a King, 2011; *translation*: Schubert's Winterreise, 2009. *Recreations:* music, film, theatre, sport, season ticket holder at Old Trafford. *Address:* c/o Anna Webber, United Agents, 12–26 Lexington Street, W1F 0LE. *T:* (020) 3214 0876. *E:* awebber@unitedagents.co.uk. *W:* www.symmonsroberts.com.

ROBERTS, Michèle Brigitte; novelist and poet; Professor of Creative Writing, University of East Anglia, 2002–07, now Emeritus; *b* 20 May 1949; *d* of Reginald George Roberts and Monique Pauline Joseph (*née* Caulle); *m* 1st, 1983, Howard Burns (marr. diss. 1987); 2nd, 1991, Laurence James Latter (marr. diss. 2005). *Educ:* Somerville Coll., Oxford (MA); University Coll. London. MCLIP (ALA 1972); FRSL 1999. British Council Librarian, Bangkok, 1973–74; writer, 1974–; Poetry Editor: Spare Rib, 1974; City Limits, 1981–83. Vis. Fellow in Creative Writing, UEA, 1992; Research Fellow in Writing, 1995–96, Vis. Prof., 1996–2001, Nottingham Trent Univ.; Writer-in-Residence, York Univ., 2008. Tutor, Autobiog. Unit, MA in Life-Writing, UEA, 2009–. Chm., Lit. Cttee, British Council, 1998–2001. Member: Soc. of Authors; PEN Translation Cttee. Chevalier, Ordre des Arts et des Lettres (France), 2001. *Publications: novels:* A Piece of the Night, 1978; The Visitation, 1983; The Wild Girl, 1984; The Book of Mrs Noah, 1987; In the Red Kitchen, 1990; Daughters of the House, 1992 (W. H. Smith Literary Award, 1993); Flesh and Blood, 1994; Impossible Saints, 1997; Fair Exchange, 1999; The Looking-Glass, 2000; The Mistressclass, 2003; Reader, I Married Him, 2005; Ignorance, 2012; *stories:* During Mother's Absence, 1993; Playing Sardines, 2001; Mud: stories of sex and love, 2010; *memoir:* Paper Houses, 2007; *poetry:* The Mirror of the Mother, 1986; Psyche and the Hurricane, 1991; All the Selves I Was, 1995; The Hunter's House, 2013; *plays:* The Journeywoman, 1988; Child-Lover, 1995; *film:* The Heavenly Twins, 1993; *essays:* Food, Sex and God: on inspiration and writing, 1998; *artist's books* (jointly): Poems, 2001; Fifteen Beads, 2003; Dark City Light City, 2007; The Secret Staircase, 2008; The Dark and Marvellous Room, 2013; *anthology:* (ed jtly) Mind Readings, 1996. *Recreations:* cooking, gardening. *Address:* c/o Ayesha Karim, Aitken Alexander Associates, 291 Gray's Inn Road, WC1X 8EB. *T:* (020) 7373 8672.

ROBERTS, Patrick John; Director, Cognis Public Relations, since 2006; *b* 21 Oct. 1942; *s* of Frank and Hilda Mary Roberts; *m* 1978, Alison Mary Taylor; one *s* one *d. Educ:* Rotherham Grammar Sch.; Lincoln Coll., Oxford (BA Hons Modern Langs). Foreign Office, 1965; Bangkok, 1966; FCO, 1970; First Sec., Lagos, 1971; FCO, 1974; UK Repn to EEC, Brussels, 1977; FCO, 1980; Counsellor (Inf.), Paris, 1984. Edelman Public Relations Worldwide: Dir of Eur. Affairs, 1989–90; Dir of Public, then Business and Corporate, Affairs, 1991–95; Dep. Man. Dir, 1995–99. Consultant, Abel Hadden and Co. Ltd, 1999–2002; Principal Consultant, Kaizo, 2002–06. *Recreations:* cooking, photography. *Address:* 81 Fawnbrake Avenue, SE24 0BG. *T:* (020) 7274 3530. *Club:* Oxford and Cambridge.

ROBERTS, Paul; *see* Roberts, D. P.

ROBERTS, Prof. Paul Harry, PhD, ScD; FRS 1979; FRAS; Professor of Mathematics, 1986–2010, now Emeritus, and Professor of Geophysical Sciences, Institute of Geophysics and Planetary Physics, now Distinguished Research Professor of Mathematics, University of California at Los Angeles; *b* 13 Sept. 1929; *s* of Percy Harry Roberts and Ethel Frances (*née* Mann); *m* 1989, Mary Frances (*née* Tabrett). *Educ:* Ardwyn Grammar Sch., Aberystwyth; University Coll. of Wales, Aberystwyth; Gonville and Caius Coll., Cambridge (George Green Student; BA, MA, PhD, ScD). FRAS 1955. Res. Associate, Univ. of Chicago, 1954–55; Scientific Officer, AWRE, 1955–56; ICI Fellow in Physics, 1956–59, Lectr in Phys, 1959–61, Univ. of Durham; Associate Prof. of Astronomy, Univ. of Chicago, 1961–63; Prof. of Applied Maths, Univ. of Newcastle upon Tyne, 1963–85. Fellow: Amer. Geophysical Union; Amer. Acad. of Arts and Scis. Editor, 1976–91, Mem. Editl Bd, 1991–, Geophysical and Astrophysical Fluid Dynamics. John Adam Fleming Medal, Amer. Geophysical Union, 1999. *Publications:* An Introduction to Magnetohydrodynamics, 1967; contrib. to Geophys. and Astrophys. Fluid Dyn., Jl Low Temp. Phys., Astrophys. Jl, Jl Fluid Mech., Jl Phys. Soc., Nature, Science, and Proc. and Trans Royal Soc. *Recreations:* playing bassoon, chess. *Address:* Department of Mathematics, University of California at Los Angeles, Los Angeles, CA 90095–1555, USA.

ROBERTS, Peter John Martin; Headmaster, King's School, Canterbury, since 2011; *b* 31 May 1963; *s* of Alfred John Victor and Pamela Roberts; *m* 1990, Marie Toudic; three *d*. *Educ:* Tiffin Boys' Sch., Kingston upon Thames; Merton Coll., Oxford (MA 1st cl. Hons (Mod. Hist.) 1985); Inst. of Educn, London (PGCE 1986). Winchester College: Asst Master, 1986–90; Hd of History, 1990–97; Master in Coll. (Housemaster to the Scholars), 1991–2003; Headmaster, Bradfield Coll., 2003–11. Hon. Canon, Canterbury Cathedral, 2012. *Recreations:* sailing, book binding, calligraphy. *Address:* King's School, Canterbury, Kent CT1 2ES.

ROBERTS, Philip Bedlington; a Recorder of the Crown Court, 1982–93; Consultant, Scholfield Roberts & Hill, 1990–97; *b* 15 Dec. 1921; *s* of late R. J. S. Roberts, solicitor and A. M. Roberts; *m* 1944, Olive Margaret, *d* of E. R. Payne, Mugswell, Chipstead, Surrey; one *s* one *d*. *Educ:* Dawson Court, Kensington; St Matthew's Sch., Bayswater. RAFVR, 1940–46. Admitted solicitor, 1949; in private practice with Scholfield Roberts & Hill, 1950–75; part-time Chm. of Industrial Tribunals, 1966–75, 1990–94, Chm., 1975–84, Regional Chm. (Bristol), 1984–90, retd. Chairman: Nat. Insce Tribunals, 1959–75; Compensation Appeals Tribunal, 1962. Solicitor, Somerset British Legion, 1960–75. *Publications:* contribs to professional jls. *Recreations:* illiterate computing, fair weather gardening. *Club:* Royal Air Force.

ROBERTS, Phyllida Katharine S.; *see* Stewart-Roberts.

ROBERTS, Hon. Dame (Priscilla) Jane (Stephanie), (Hon. Lady Roberts), DCVO 2013 (CVO 2004; LVO 1995; MVO 1985); Curator of the Print Room, 1975–2013 and Librarian, 2002–13, Royal Library, Windsor Castle; *b* 4 Sept. 1949; *d* of 1st Baron Aldington, KCMG, CBE, DSO, TD, PC; *m* 1975, Hugh Ashley Roberts (*see* Sir H. A. Roberts); two *d*. *Educ:* Cranborne Chase School; Westfield College, Univ. of London (BA Hons); Courtauld Inst., Univ. of London (MA). Gov., British Inst. of Florence, 2002–; Trustee, Royal Drawing Sch., 2014–. *Publications:* Holbein, 1979; Leonardo: Codex Hammer, 1981; Master Drawings in the Royal Collection, 1985; Royal Artists, 1987; A Dictionary of Michelangelo's Watermarks, 1988; (jtly) Leonardo da Vinci, 1989; A Souvenir Album of Sandby Views of Windsor, 1990; A King's Purchase: King George III and the Collection of Consul Smith, 1993; Holbein and the Court of Henry VIII, 1993; Views of Windsor: watercolours by Thomas and Paul Sandby, 1995; Royal Landscape: the gardens and parks of Windsor, 1997; Ten Religious Masterpieces: a Millennium Celebration, 2000; (ed and contrib.) Royal Treasures: a Golden Jubilee celebration, 2002; (ed and contrib.) George III and Queen Charlotte: patronage, collecting and Court taste, 2004; (jtly) Unfolding Pictures: fans in the Royal Collection, 2005; Queen Elizabeth II: a birthday souvenir album, 2006; Five Gold Rings: a royal wedding souvenir album, 2007; Charles, Prince of Wales: a birthday souvenir album, 2008; Queen Elizabeth II: a Diamond Jubilee souvenir album, 2011; articles in Burlington Magazine, Apollo, Report of Soc. of Friends of St George's. *Recreations:* singing, sewing. *Address:* 33 East Lockinge, Wantage, Oxon OX12 8QG. *Clubs:* Athenæum, Roxburghe, Grillions.

ROBERTS, Ven. Raymond Harcourt, CB 1984; Chairman, Customer Service Committee for Wales, Office of Water Services, 1990–2001; licensed to officiate, diocese of Llandaff, since 1995; *b* 14 April 1931; *s* of Thomas Roberts and Carrie Maud Roberts. *Educ:* Pontywaun Grammar Sch., Risca, Mon; St Edmund Hall, Oxford (MA English); St Michael's Theol Coll., Llandaff. Nat. Service, RN, 1949–51. Deacon 1956, priest 1957, dio. of Monmouth (Curate of Bassaleg); Chaplain RNVR, 1958, RN, 1959; Destroyers and Frigates, Far East, 1959; HMS Pembroke, 1962; Dartmouth Trng Sqdn, 1963; RM Commando Course, 1965; 45 Commando, S. Arabia, 1965; RN Engrg Coll., 1967; HMS Bulwark, 1968; BRNC Dartmouth, 1970; HMS Ark Royal, 1974; Commando Trng Centre, RM, 1975; HMS Drake and HM Naval Base, Plymouth, 1979; Chaplain of the Fleet and Archdeacon for RN, 1980–84, Archdeacon Emeritus, 1985–; QHC, 1980–84; Hon. Canon, Cathedral of Holy Trinity, Gibraltar, 1980–84; Gen. Sec., Jerusalem and ME Church Assoc., 1985–89; licensed, dio. of Guildford, 1986–91; Hon. Chaplain, Llandaff Cathedral, 1991–95. Mem., Nat. Customer Council, Ofwat, 1993–2001. Liveryman, Livery Co. of Wales (formerly Welsh Livery Guild), 1993– (Chaplain, 1993–2007); Chaplain: to the High Sheriff of S Glam, 1993–94; Drapers' Co., 1996–97; Submariners Assoc., 2000–06. Governor, Rougemont Sch., Gwent, 1993–2004. *Recreations:* cooking and listening to Mozart, not necessarily simultaneously. *Address:* 13 Cwm Lane, Rogerstone, Newport, S Wales NP10 9AF. *T:* (01633) 895721.

ROBERTS, Richard (David Hallam); occasional academic and writer (seldom published), yachtmaster (unqualified), bookbinder's mate, competent househusband, gardener, woodman, antiquarian cyclist; *b* 27 July 1931; *s* of Arthur Hallam Roberts, Barrister-at-law, sometime Attorney-General, Zanzibar, and Ruvé Constance Jessie Roberts; *m* 1960, Wendy Ewen Mount; three *s*. *Educ:* King's Sch., Canterbury; Jesus Coll., Cambridge. Commissioned into RA 6th Field Regt, 1952. Asst Master, King's Sch., Canterbury, 1956; Housemaster, 1957; Head of Modern Language Dept, 1961; Senior Housemaster, 1965; Headmaster: Wycliffe Coll., Stonehouse, 1967–80; King Edward's Sch., Witley, 1980–85. Chairman: Alde and Ore Assoc., 1991–94; Orford Town Trust, 1995–99. *Club:* Orford Sailing.

ROBERTS, Richard James Lloyd; a Master of the Senior (formerly Supreme) Court, Queen's Bench Division, since 2009; *b* Coalville, Leics, 19 Aug. 1961; *s* of Rev. Richard Lloyd Roberts and Mary Roberts; *m* 2000, Catriona Mackenzie Smith; one *s* two *d*. *Educ:* St Martin's Sch., Brentwood; Anglia Ruskin Univ. (BA Hons). Called to the Bar, Middle Temple, 1983; in practice as a barrister, Temple Garden Chambers, specialising in personal injury and clinical negligence, 1984–2009; an Immigration Judge, 2007–09; Mem., CICAP, 2008–09. Mem., Injury Cttee, Civil Justice Council, 2010. Sec., Assoc. of High Court Masters, 2010. *Publications:* (ed jtly) Civil Procedure (The White Book), 2010. *Recreations:* playing the piano, listening to classical and popular music, literature, travel. *Address:* Royal Courts of Justice, Strand, WC2A 2LL.

ROBERTS, Sir Richard (John), Kt 2008; PhD; FRS 1995; Chief Scientific Officer, New England Biolabs, since 2005 (Director of Research, 1992–2005); *b* Derby, 6 Sept. 1943; *s* of John Walter Roberts and Edna Wilhelmina Roberts; *m* 1st, 1965, Elizabeth Dyson; one *s* one *d*; 2nd, 1986, Jean (*née* Tagliabue); one *s* one *d*. *Educ:* City of Bath Boys' Sch.; Sheffield Univ. (BSc Chem. 1965; PhD 1968). Harvard University: Res. Fellow, 1969–70; Res. Associate in Biochem., 1971–72; Cold Spring Harbor Laboratory: Sen. Staff Investigator, 1972–86; Asst Dir for Research, 1986–92. Miller Prof., UC Berkeley, 1991. Dist. Scientist and Res. Schol., Boston Univ., 2003–. Chm., Scientific Adv. Bd, Celera, 1998–2002; Advr to Dir, NASA Astrobiol. Prog., 2000–. Dir, InVivo Therapeutics, 2009–. Exec. Editor, Nucleic Acids Res., 1987–2009 (Mem. Editl Bd, 1977–87); Panel Mem., NLM Study Section, Comp. Biol., 1993–95. Fellow, Science Mus., London, 2009. Hon. MD: Uppsala, 1992; Bath, 1994; Hon. DSc Sheffield, 1994. (Jtly) Nobel Prize in Physiology or Medicine, 1993. *Publications:* numerous papers on restriction endonucleases, DNA methylases, computational molecular biology. *Recreations:* collecting games, croquet. *Address:* New England Biolabs, 240 County Road, Ipswich, MA 01938–2723, USA. *T:* (978) 3807405.

ROBERTS, Prof. Richard Whitfield, PhD; Professor of Contemporary Financial History, Institute of Contemporary British History, King's College London, since 2010; *b* London; *s* of late Prof. Benjamin Charles Roberts and Veronica Lilian Roberts (*née* Vine-Lott); *m* 2001, Sarah Robson; two *d*. *Educ:* Haberdashers' Aske's Boys' Sch.; University Coll. London (BA 1st Cl. Hist.); Downing Coll., Cambridge (PhD 1982); Princeton Univ. (Procter Fellow). Analyst, British Petroleum Co.; Univ. of Sussex, 1985–2006; Prof., Sch. of Advanced Studies, Univ. of London, 2007–10. Houblon-Norman Fellow, Bank of England, 2002. Associate, Lombard St Res., 2008–. Member, Advisory Board: OMFIF, 2012–; Gulbenkian Foundn, Lisbon, 2013–. Co-organiser, Monetary Hist. Gp, 2008–. *Publications:* Schroders: merchants and bankers, 1992; (ed) International Financial Centres, 1994; (ed with D. Kynaston) Bank of England 1694–1994, 1995; Get Lucky, 1995; Inside International Finance, 1998; Take Your Partners, 2001; (with D. Kynaston) City State, 2002; Wall Street, 2003; The City, 2004, 2nd edn 2008; Did Anyone Learn Anything from the Equitable Life?: lessons and learning from financial crises, 2012; Saving the City: the great financial crisis of 1914, 2013; (with D. Kynaston) The Lion Wakes: a modern history of HSBC, 2015. *Recreations:* family, financial history, investment analysis, cinema and screenwriting, music, modern dance, le Gers. *Address:* King's College London, Strand, WC2R 2LS. *E:* Richard.Roberts@kcl.ac.uk. *Clubs:* Political Economy, Union.

ROBERTS, Prof. Ronald John, PhD; FRCPath, FRSB, FRCVS; FRSE; Professor of Aquatic Pathobiology and Director, Institute of Aquaculture, University of Stirling, 1971–96, now Professor Emeritus; *b* 28 March 1941; *s* of Ronald George Roberts and Marjorie Kneale; *m* 1964, Helen, *d* of Gordon Gregor Macgregor; two *s*. *Educ:* Campbeltown Grammar Sch., Argyll; Univ. of Glasgow Vet. Sch. (PhD, BVMS). FRSB (FIBiol 1984); FRCPath 1988; FRCVS 1992; FRSE 1978. Univ. of Glasgow: Asst in Microbiology, 1964–66; Lectr in Vet. Pathology, 1966–71. Hagerman Dist. Vis. Prof., Univ. of Idaho, 1997–; Vis. Prof., Univ. of Malaysia Terengganu, 2009–; Adjunct Prof., Washington State Univ., 2010–. Consultant in Fish Diseases: Dept Agric. and Fisheries for Scotland, 1968–71; ODA, subseq. DFID, 1974–2001; FAO, Rome, 1978–83; World Bank, 1989. Dir, Machrihanish Marine Envmtl Res. Lab., 1991–96. Member: Cabinet Office Science Panel, 1993–94; Res. Grants Panel, SFHEFC (formerly SHEFC), 2001–10; Vice-Chm., 2003–06, Mem., 2006–09, Animal Health and Welfare Panel, European Food Safety Authy. Editor: Jl Fish Diseases, 1978–; Aquaculture Research (formerly Aquaculture and Fisheries Management), 1988–2000. Chairman: Stirling Aquaculture, 1987–95; Heronpisces Ltd, 2003–; Bradan Ltd, 2003–; Director: Stirling Salmon, 1987–94; Tarbert Fyne Foods, 1987–90; Stirling Aquatic Technology, 1987–90; Campbeltown and Kintyre Enterprise, 1992–2005 (Chm., 1996–2005); Landcatch Ltd, 1996–2011. Scientific Advr, Lithgow Gp, 1996–2011. Chm., Argyll and Bute Countryside Trust, 1994–2004; Sec., Lady Linda McCartney Meml Trust, 2000–. Foundn Fellow, World Aquatic Veterinary Medical Assoc., 2013. Buckland Prof. and Medallist, 1985–86; C-Vet Award, BVA, 1989; Dalrymple-Champneys Cup and Medal, BVA, 1990. Commander, Most Noble Order of the Crown (Thailand), 1992. *Publications:* (with C. J. Shepherd) Handbook of Salmon and Trout Diseases, 1974, 3rd edn 1996; Fish Pathology, 1978, 4th edn 2012; various scientific publications on histopathology of fishes. *Recreations:* arboriculture, rhododendron culture, golf, squash, admiring and conserving the Scottish natural environment. *Address:* 9 Alexander Drive, Bridge of Allan, Stirling FK9 4QB. *T:* (01786) 833078; Carrick Point Farm, Ardnacross Shorelands, by Campbeltown, Argyll PA28 5QR. *T:* (01586) 554417. *Club:* Machrihanish Golf (Kintyre).

ROBERTS, Sir Samuel, 4th Bt *cr* 1919, of Ecclesall and Queen's Tower, City of Sheffield; barrister; *b* 16 April 1948; *s* of Sir Peter Geoffrey Roberts, 3rd Bt, and Judith Randell (*d* 1998), *d* of late Randell G. Hempson; *S* father, 1985; *m* 1977, Georgina Ann (DL Norfolk, 2013), *yr d* of David Cory; one *s* three *d*. *Educ:* Harrow School; Sheffield Univ. (LLB); Manchester Business School. Called to the Bar, Inner Temple, 1972. Chairman: Cleyfield Properties Ltd, 1984–; Wiltshire and Co. Ltd, 1988–2013; Angermann, Goddard and Loyd Ltd, 1994–2010. *Heir: s* Samuel Roberts, *b* 12 Aug. 1989.

ROBERTS, Maj. Gen. Sir Sebastian (John Lechmere), KCVO 2007; OBE 1993; Chairman, The Military Mutual, since 2014; General Officer Commanding London District and Officer Commanding Household Division, 2003–07; *b* 7 Jan. 1954; *s* of Brig. John Mark Herbert Roberts, OBE and Nicola Helen Lechmere Roberts (*née* Macaskie); *m* 1979, Elizabeth Anne Muir; two *s* two *d*. *Educ:* Ampleforth; Balliol Coll., Oxford (BA, MA); RMA, Sandhurst; Army Staff Coll., Camberley. Commnd Irish Guards, 1977; Captain, Rendezvous Point Comdr, Op AGILA, Southern Rhodesia, 1979–80; Major, COS, 4th Armd Bde, Münster, 1987–89; Co. Comdr, Irish Guards, Belize and Berlin, 1989–91; Lt Col, MA to CGS, MoD, 1991–93; CO, 1st Bn, Irish Guards, London and E Tyrone, 1993–96; Col, Land Warfare 2 (Doctrine), Upavon, 1996–99; Brig., Dir Public Relns (Army), MoD, 1999–2002; rcds 2003. COS, RCDS, 2007–09. Regtl Lt Col, 1999–2008, Col, 2008–11, Irish Guards; Col Comdt, Media Ops Gp (Volunteers), 2006–09. Hon. Col, 256 (City of London) Field Hosp. (Volunteers), 2007–13; Hon. Col, London Irish Rifles, 2012–. Chm., Soc. for Army Historical Res., 2009–13. Gov., St Mary's Sch., Shaftesbury, 2009– (Chm. Govs, 2010–). Queen's Rep., Trustees of Royal Armouries, 2011–. Liveryman, Girdlers' Co., 2005. *Publications:* The Bullingdon War Mag, 1976; Bertie Meets the Queen, 1978; Soldiering: the military covenant, 1998; RCDS Strategy Handbook, 2009. *Recreations:* painting and drawing, conversation, rebus letters, public speaking, prayer, eating, drinking, travelling, reading, writing, 9 brothers and sisters, shooting. *Clubs:* Beefsteak, Pitt, Aspinalls, Buck's, Cavalry and Guards.

ROBERTS, Stephen Cheveley; Principal, Stamford Endowed Schools, since 2008; *b* 23 Aug. 1956; *s* of David Roberts and Elizabeth Roberts (*née* Thornborough); *m* 1985, Joanna Meryl Cunnison; two *s*. *Educ:* Mill Hill Sch.; University Coll., Oxford (BA 1978; PGCE 1979; MA 1982). Credit Analyst, Orion Bank, 1979–80; Asst Master, Christ's Hosp., Horsham, 1980–86; Oundle School: Hd of Physics, 1986–90; Housemaster, 1990–93; Headmaster, Felsted Sch., 1993–2008. Gov., Royal Hosp. Sch., Holbeach, 2009–12. *Recreations:* golf, hockey, music, reading. *Address:* Stamford Endowed Schools, St Paul's Street, Stamford, Lincs PE9 2BS. *T:* (01780) 750310. *Clubs:* East India; Vincent's (Oxford).

ROBERTS, Rev. Canon Stephen John; Archdeacon of Wandsworth, 2005–15, now Archdeacon Emeritus; Deputy Diocesan Secretary, and Bishop's Officer for Non-stipendiary Clergy, Diocese of Southwark, since 2015; *b* 6 Dec. 1958; *s* of Percy Stanley Roberts and Brenda May Roberts. *Educ:* Newcastle-under-Lyme High Sch.; King's Coll. London (BD Hons 1981); Westcott House, Cambridge; Heythrop Coll. London (MTh 1999). Ordained deacon, 1983, priest, 1984; Asst Curate, St Mary, Riverhead, with St John, Dunton Green, 1983–86; Curate, St Martin-in-the-Fields, 1986–89; Vicar, St George, Camberwell, and Warden, Trinity Coll. Centre, Peckham, 1989–2000; Canon Treas., Southwark Cathedral, and Sen. Dir of Ordinands, Southwark Dio., 2000–05. Hon. Canon, Southwark Cathedral, 2015–. *Recreations:* cycling, walking, music, travel. *Address:* 2 Alma Road, Wandsworth, SW18 1AB. *T:* (020) 8874 8567.

ROBERTS, Stephen Pritchard; baritone; professional singer, since 1972; *b* 8 Feb. 1949; *s* of Edward Henry Roberts and Violet Pritchard. *Educ:* Royal College of Music (schol.). ARCM 1969; GRSM 1971. Professional Lay-Cleric, Westminster Cathedral Choir, 1972–76; now sings regularly in London, UK and Europe, with all major orchs and choral socs; has also sung in USA, Canada, Israel, Hong Kong, Singapore and S America. Mem., Vocal Faculty, RCM, 1993–. *Opera* rôles include: Count, in Marriage of Figaro; Falke, in Die Fledermaus; Ubalde, in Armide; Ramiro, in Ravel's L'Heure Espagnole; Aeneas, in Dido and Aeneas; Don Quixote, in Master Peter's Puppet Show; Mittenhofer, in Elegy for Young Lovers; *television* appearances include: Britten's War Requiem; Weill's Seven Deadly Sins; Delius' Sea Drift; Handel's Jeptha; Handel's Judas Maccabaeus; Penderecki's St Luke Passion, 1983 Proms; Walton's Belshazzar's Feast, 1984 Proms; *recordings* include: Tippett's King Priam; Birtwistle's Punch and Judy; Gluck's Armide; Orff's Carmina Burana; Vaughan Williams' Five Mystical Songs, Epithalamion, Sea Symphony, Fantasia on Christmas Carols, Hodie, and Serenade; Elgar's Apostles, and Caractacus; Penderecki's St Luke Passion; Fauré's Requiem; Dyson's

Canterbury Pilgrims; Stravinsky songs; English song recordings incl. Gurney, Finzi, Somervell, Bennett and Howells; works by J. S. Bach, C. P. E. Bach and Duruflé. *Address:* 144 Gleneagle Road, SW16 6BA. *T:* (020) 8516 8830.

ROBERTS, Stewart Brian, MA; Headmaster, Dauntsey's School, 1997–2012; *b* 21 March 1952; *s* of late Evan John and Joyce Roberts; *m* 1985, Anna Susan Norman (*d* 2011); one *s* one *d. Educ:* Birkenhead Sch.; St Peter's Coll., Oxford (BA 1974; PGCE 1975; MA 1978). Asst Master, Birkenhead Sch., 1975–78; Asst Master, 1978–93, (Housemaster, 1984–93), Shrewsbury Sch.; Headmaster-des., Chand Bagh Sch., Lahore, 1994; Second Master, Dauntsey's Sch., 1995–97. Mem., P&O Scholarship Bd, 2001–05. Governor: St Francis Sch., Pewsey, 1997–2002; Shiplake Coll., 2003–11; Thomas Telford Sch., 2012–; Moreton Hall, 2012–; Madeley Acad., 2014–; Walsall Acad., 2015–. Freeman, City of London, 2000. *Address:* Upper Stanway, Rushbury, Shropshire SY6 7EF.

ROBERTS, Susan; *see* Gilchrist, S.

ROBERTS, Susan Holt, CBE 2009; FRCP; National Clinical Director for Diabetes, Department of Health, 2003–08; *b* 28 Aug. 1945; *d* of David Holt Roberts and Joyce Eastoe Roberts (*née* How); *m* 1971, Christopher Kenneth Drinkwater; two *d. Educ:* Middlesex Hospital Medical Sch., London (BSc 1966; MB BS 1969); Univ. of Newcastle upon Tyne (MSc Clin. Biochem. 1975). FRCP 1986. Lectr in Medicine, Meml Univ. of Newfoundland, 1974–76; Consultant Physician, Northumbria Healthcare Trust, 1978–2008 (Chair, Year of Care Partnerships, 2010–). Hon. FRCGP 2012. *Publications:* articles and book chapters on med. topics incl. women in medicine, diabetes, healthcare delivery and patient educn. *Recreations:* walking, gardening, knitting, cats. *Address:* 30 Battle Hill, Hexham, Northumberland NE46 2EB. *T:* (01434) 600352. *E:* sue.roberts@gofo.co.uk.

ROBERTS, Dr (Thomas) Michael, CBE 2009; CBiol, FRSB; Chief Executive, Central Science Laboratory, Department for Environment, Food and Rural Affairs, 2001–08, now Consultant; *b* 12 May 1948; *e s* of late Robert Stanley Roberts and Mary Roberts (*née* Cliffe); *m* 1968, Ann Vaughan-Williams; one *s* two *d. Educ:* St Asaph Grammar Sch.; Univ. of Wales, Swansea (BSc 1969; PhD 1972). CBiol 1991; FRSB (FIBiol 1991); MCIEEM (MIEEM 1995). Asst Prof., Dept of Botany, Univ. of Toronto, 1972–74; Lectr, Dept of Botany, Univ. of Liverpool, 1974–78; Section Head, Terrestrial Ecology, Biology Section, CEGB, 1978–89; Dir, Inst. of Terrestrial Ecology, 1989–99, Dir, Centre for Ecology and Hydrology, 1999–2001, NERC. Ext. Examiner, York Univ., 1993–2008. Member: DoE Adv. Cttee on Hazardous Substances, 1992–2000; HSE Adv. Cttee on Genetic Modification, 1994–99; MAFF Adv. Cttee on Pesticides, 1996–2001; Adv. Bd, Jt Inst. for Food and Nutrition, Food and Drug Admin/Univ. of Maryland, USA, 2002–08; Veterinary Residues Cttee, DEFRA, 2005–; Royal Commn on Envmtl Pollution, 2009–11; non-exec. Bd Mem., Nat. Non-Food Crops Centre, 2008–13 (Chm., 2013–); Chm., UK Man and Biosphere Cttee, 1993–2001; Trustee, Nat. Biodiversity Network, 2000–01. Mem. Bd, Yorks and Humber Sci. and Innovation Council, 2006–08. Mem., Yorks Philosophical Soc., 2003–. Vice-Pres., Reigate Priory CC and Little Shelford CC, 2000–. Ed., Jl of Applied Ecology, 1981–86. *Publications:* Planning and Ecology, 1984; Ecological Aspects of Radionuclide Releases, 1985; numerous articles on applied ecology in learned jls. *Recreations:* club cricket, golf, gardening. *Club:* Easingwold Golf (Chm., 2011–).

ROBERTS, Timothy David; QC 2003; a Recorder, since 1993; *b* 4 Oct. 1955; *s* of Norman and Heather Roberts; *m* 1986, Angela Shakespeare; two *d. Educ:* Guisborough Grammar Sch.; Southampton Univ. (LLB Hons). Called to the Bar, Gray's Inn, 1978, Bencher, 2007; Public Solicitor, Solomon Islands, 1979–81; joined Fountain Chambers, 1982, Hd of Chambers, 2000–10; in practice, specialising in criminal law. *Recreations:* music, sailing. *Address:* Fountain Chambers, Cleveland Business Centre, 1 Watson Street, Middlesbrough, Cleveland TS1 2RQ. *T:* (01642) 804040, *Fax:* (01642) 804060. *Club:* Runswick Bay Sailing.

ROBERTS CAIRNS, Patricia Rose Marie, (Mrs D. A. O. Cairns), OBE 2000; freelance editorial consultant; Consultant, National Magazine Co., since 1999; *b* 27 Nov. 1947; *d* of late Maj. William Roberts, MBE, RA and Catherine (*née* Slawson); *m* 1993, Dr David A. O. Cairns (*d* 2014). *Educ:* St Barnabas Sch., Woodford Green; Open Univ. (BA 2007). Reporter, Independent Newspapers, Essex, 1965–68; features writer, IPC mags, 1968–72; Founder Editor, Girl About Town (London's first free mag.), 1972–80; feature writer, Femail, Daily Mail, 1980–82; Associate Editor, Family Circle, 1982–84; Editor, Over 21, 1984–89; Founder Editor, House Beautiful, 1989–95; Editor-in-Chief, Good Housekeeping, 1995–99. Member: Editl Cttee, Periodical Trng Council, 1992–; Women of Year Cttee, 1993–; BSME Cttee, 1993–99; Editl Public Affairs Cttee, PPA, 1993–99; Press Complaints Commn, 1998–99. FRSA. Launch Editor of Year, BSME, 1990; Editor of Year, PPA, 1992. *Publications:* Living Images: styling yourself to success, 1990; House Beautiful Home Handbook, 1992. *Address:* Cliff Cottage, 49 Meads Street, Eastbourne BN20 7RN.

ROBERTS-WEST, Lt-Col George Arthur Alston-; *see* West.

ROBERTSHAW, His Honour Patrick Edward; a Circuit Judge, 1994–2010; *b* 7 July 1945; *s* of late George Edward Robertshaw and May (*née* Tallis); *m* 1972, Sally Christine Greenburgh (*née* Searle); two *s* two *d. Educ:* Hipperholme Grammar Sch.; Southampton Univ. (LLB). Called to the Bar, Inner Temple, 1968; a Recorder, 1989–94. Mem., Parole Bd, 2010–. *Publications:* The Inglorious Twelfth: the study of a 1950s murder trial, 2005; No Smoking Gun: exposure of a 1950s miscarriage of justice, 2012; contrib. to legal periodicals. *Recreations:* reading, listening to music, travel, photography.

ROBERTSON, family name of **Barons Robertson of Oakridge, Robertson of Port Ellen** and **Wharton.**

ROBERTSON OF OAKRIDGE, 3rd Baron *cr* 1961; **William Brian Elworthy Robertson;** Bt 1919; Investment Agent, Strutt and Parker LLP, since 2006; *b* Roehampton, 15 Nov. 1975; *o s* of 2nd Baron Robertson of Oakridge and of Celia Jane, *d* of William R. Elworthy; *S* father, 2009. *Educ:* BA Hons English Lit. MRICS. Admitted Solicitor of the Supreme Court; Solicitor: Ashurst, 2001–05; Reed Smith, 2005; Schulte Roth & Zabel, 2006. Mem., Salters' Co. *Heir:* none. *T:* 07970 822274. *E:* willahr@hotmail.com.

ROBERTSON OF PORT ELLEN, Baron *cr* 1999 (Life Peer), of Islay in Argyll and Bute; **George Islay MacNeill Robertson,** KT 2004; GCMG 2004; PC 1997; Special Adviser to BP plc, since 2013; Chancellor of the Order of St Michael and St George, since 2011; *b* 12 April 1946; *s* of George Philip Robertson and Marion I. Robertson; *m* 1970, Sandra Wallace; two *s* one *d. Educ:* Dunoon Grammar Sch.; Univ. of Dundee (MA Hons 1968). Res. Asst, Tayside Study, 1968–69; Scottish Organiser, G&MWU, 1970–78. MP (Lab) Hamilton, 1978–97, Hamilton South, 1997–99. PPS to Sec. of State for Social Services, 1979; opposition spokesman on Scottish Affairs, 1979–80, on Defence, 1980–81, on Foreign and Commonwealth Affairs, 1981–93; principal spokesman on European Affairs, 1984–93; principal opposition front bench spokesman on Scotland, 1993–97; Sec. of State for Defence, 1997–99. Sec.-Gen., NATO, 1999–2003. Chm., Scottish Labour Party, 1977–78; Mem., Scottish Exec. of Lab. Party, 1973–79, 1993–97. Dep. Chm., 2004–06, Sen. Internat. Advr, 2007–10, Cable & Wireless plc; Chm., Cable & Wireless Internat., 2006–10; Sen. Internat. Advr, Cable and Wireless Communications plc, 2010–; Dep. Chm., TNK-BP, 2006–13; non-executive Director: Smiths Gp plc, 2004–06; Weir Gp plc, 2004–14; Edinburgh Military Tattoo, 2015–. Adviser: Cohen Gp, USA, 2004–; Engelfield Capital, 2004–11; Royal Bank of Canada, 2004–06. Vice Chm. Bd, British Council, 1985–94; Member: Council, RIIA, 1984–91 (Jt Pres., 2001–11); Adv. Council, European Council on Foreign Relations, 2008–; Council, IISS, 2013–; Adv. Bd, Centre for European Reform, 2014–. Chm., Commn on Global Road Safety (Make Roads Safe), 2004–. Chm., John Smith Meml Trust, 2004–08; Trustee: British Forces Foundn, 2006–; Queen Elizabeth Diamond Jubilee Trust, 2012–; FIA Foundn, 2015–; Patron: Scottish Burned Children Trust, 2001–; Islay Book Fest., 2009–; Dunblane Centre, 2009–; Disability Trust, 2010–; Paratroop Regt Afghanistan Trust, 2012–; Mus. of Islay Trust, 2013–. Chm., Council, Ditchley Foundn, 2009– (Gov., 1989–; Dep. Chm., 2008). Mem. Adv. Bd, Commemoration of World War One, 2012–. Hon. Regtl Col, London Scottish (Volunteers), 2000–. Mem. Court and Elder Brother, Trinity Hse, 2001–. Pres., Hamilton Burns Club, 2002. Hon. Guild Brother, Guildry of Stirling, 2004. FRSA 1999. Hon. FRSE 2003; Hon. Sen. Fellow, Foreign Policy Assoc., USA, 2000; Hon. Prof. of Politics, Stirling Univ., 2009–. Hon. LLD: Dundee, Bradford, 2000; Baku State Univ., Azerbaijan, 2001; Romanian Nat. Sch. of Pol and Admin. Studies, 2003; French Univ., Yerevan, Armenia, 2003; Azerbaijan Acad. of Scis, 2003; St Andrews, 2003; Glasgow Caledonian, 2004; Hon. DSc RMCS Cranfield, 2000; DUniv: Paisley, 2006; Stirling, 2008; Lincoln, 2008. Knight Grand Cross: Order of Merit (Italy), 2003; Order of Oranje-Nassau (Netherlands), 2003; Comdr Grand Cross, Order of Three Stars (Latvia), 2004; Grand Cross: Order of the Star (Romania), 2000; Order of Merit (Germany), 2003; Order of Merit (Poland), 2003; Order of Merit (Hungary), 2003; Order of Merit (Luxembourg), 2003; Order of Isabel the Catholic (Spain), 2003; Order of Jesus (Portugal), 2003; Order of Grand Duke Gedeminos (Lithuania), 2003; Order of Stara Planina (Bulgaria), 2003; Order of King Petar Kresimir IV (Croatia), 2003; Order of Yaroslav the Wise (Ukraine), 2005; Grand Cordon, Order of Leopold (Belgium), 2003; Presidential Medal of Freedom (USA), 2003; First Class: Order of the Tarra Mariana (Estonia), 2004; Order of the White Two-Arm Cross (Slovakia), 2004; Order for Exceptional Services (Slovenia), 2006. *Publications:* Islay and Jura: photographs, 2006; (jtly) Dunblane: its people in a century of change, 2012. *Recreations:* reading, family, photography, golf. *Address:* House of Lords, SW1A 0PW. *E:* robertsong@parliament.uk. *Clubs:* Army and Navy; Islay Golf; Dunblane New Golf.

ROBERTSON, Aidan Malcolm David; QC 2009; *b* Newcastle upon Tyne, 19 Dec. 1961; *s* of William David Duncan and Veronica Gloria Robertson; *m* 2005, Beverley Anne Blakeney; one *s* two *d* (of whom one *s* one *d* are twins). *Educ:* Jesus Coll., Cambridge (BA 1984; LLM 1985). Solicitor, 1988–95; called to the Bar, Middle Temple, 1995. Lectr in Law, Univ. of Oxford, 1990–96, Vis. Prof. in Law, 2015– (Vis. Lectr, 2002–15); Fellow and Tutor in Law, Wadham Coll., Oxford, 1990–99. *Publications:* (with N. Green) Commercial Agreements and Competition Law, 2nd edn 1997; (with D. Vaughan) Law of the European Union (looseleaf encyclopedia), 2003. *Recreations:* swimming, Newcastle United. *Address:* Brick Court Chambers, 7–8 Essex Street, WC2R 7LD. *T:* (020) 7379 3550, *Fax:* (020) 7379 7558. *E:* aidan.robertson@brickcourt.co.uk. *Club:* Royal Automobile.

ROBERTSON, Alastair, PhD; consultant on research strategy and agribusiness; Group Executive, Food, Health and Life Science Industries, CSIRO, 2009–13; *b* 18 July 1949; *s* of Robert Russell Robertson and Brenda Scott Robertson; *m* 1975, Wendy Kathleen Purchase; one *s* one *d. Educ:* Univ. of Bath (BSc Hons Applied Biology 1973; PhD Plant Biochemistry 1976). FRSC 1983; FIFST 1983. Postdoctoral Fellow, Univ. of Cambridge, 1976–79; Process Biochemist, Sigma Chemical Co., 1979–81; Head of Chemistry and Biochemistry, 1981–86, Dir of Food Science, 1986–92, Campden and Chorley Wood Food Res. Assoc.; Head of Res. and Devclt, 1992–95, Technical Dir, 1995–2000, Safeway Stores plc; Dir, Inst. of Food Res., BBSRC, 2000–03; Chief Exec., Food Sci. Australia, 2003–05; Gp Exec., CSIRO Agribusiness, 2005–07; Dep. Chief Exec., CSIRO Sci. Strategy and Investment, 2007–09. Hon. Prof., UEA, 2000–03; Res. Prof., Univ. of Tasmania, 2004–13. *Publications:* 50 articles in jls on biochemistry and food sci. areas. *Recreations:* gardening, music, angling, sports. *E:* aw1.robertson@gmail.com.

ROBERTSON, Andrew James; QC 1996; *b* 14 May 1953; *s* of Pearson Robertson and Zillah Robertson (*née* Robinson); *m* 1981, Gillian Amanda Frankel; two *s* one *d. Educ:* Bradford GS; Christ's Coll., Cambridge (MA). Called to the Bar, Middle Temple, 1975; North Eastern Circuit; a Recorder, 1994–2002; Hd of Chambers, King's Bench Walk, 2006–. *Recreations:* climbing, history. *Address:* KBW, The Engine House, 1 Foundry Square, Leeds LS11 5DL.

ROBERTSON, Andrew Ogilvie, OBE 1994; Senior Partner, T. C. Young, 1994–2006; *b* 30 June 1943; *s* of Alexander McArthur Ogilvie Robertson and Charlotte Rachel Robertson (*née* Cuthbert); *m* 1974, Sheila Sturton; two *s. Educ:* Sedbergh Sch.; Edinburgh Univ. (LLB 1964). Apprentice Solicitor, Maclay Murray & Spens, 1964–67; Asst Solicitor, 1967–68, Partner, 1968, T. C. Young. Secretary: Erskine Hosp., 1976–2002 (Vice-Chm., 2006; Chm., 2011–); Fedn of Community Clydeside-based Housing Assocs, 1978–93 (also Treas.); Briggait Co. Ltd, 1983–88; Princess Royal Trust for Carers, 1990–2006 (Legal Advr, 1990–2006; Trustee, 2006–12); Chairman: Post Office Users' Council for Scotland, 1988–99; Gtr Glasgow Community and Mental Health Services NHS Trust, 1994–97; Glasgow Royal Infirmary Univ. NHS Trust, 1997–99; Gtr Glasgow Primary Care NHS Trust, 1998–2004; Member: POUNC, 1988–99; Gtr Glasgow Health Bd, 1999– (Vice-Chm., 2004–07; Chm., 2007–). Chm., Lintel Trust (formerly Scottish Housing Assocs Charitable Trust), 1990–2007; Trustee: Housing Assocs Charitable Trust (UK), 1990–97; Music in Hosps, 2006–13; Vice Pres., Carers Trust, 2012–. Non-exec. Dir, Scottish Building Soc., 1994–2008 (Chm., 2003–06). Dir, Scotcash, 2007–11. Gov., Sedbergh Sch., 2000–08. *Recreations:* climbing, sailing, swimming, reading, fishing. *Address:* Burnside Cottage, Main Street, Drymen G63 0BQ. *Clubs:* East India; Western (Glasgow).

ROBERTSON, Rt Hon. Angus; PC 2015; MP (SNP) Moray, since 2001; *b* 28 Sept. 1969. *Educ:* Broughton High Sch., Edinburgh; Univ. of Aberdeen (MA 1991). News Editor, Austrian Broadcasting Corp., 1991; reporter, BBC, Austria, etc, 1991–99; communications consultant and journalist, 1999–. SNP spokesman on foreign affairs, 2001–15, on defence, 2003; SNP Leader, H of C, 2007–. SNP Campaign Director: Scottish Parlt elections 2007 and 2011, Scottish independence referendum, 2014. Mem., Intelligence and Security Cttee, 2015–. Contested (SNP) Midlothian, Scottish Parlt, 1999. *Address:* (constituency office) 9 Wards Road, Elgin, Moray IV30 1NL; c/o House of Commons, SW1A 0AA.

ROBERTSON, Hon. Sir Bruce; *see* Robertson, Hon. Sir J. B.

ROBERTSON, Rev. Charles, LVO 2005; Parish Minister, Canongate (The Kirk of Holyroodhouse), 1978–2005, now Minister Emeritus; Chaplain to the Queen in Scotland, 1991–2010, Extra Chaplain to the Queen in Scotland, since 2010; *b* 22 Oct. 1940; *s* of late Thomas Robertson and Elizabeth Halley; *m* 1965, Alison Margaret Malloch; one *s* two *d. Educ:* Camphill School, Paisley; Edinburgh Univ. (MA); New College, Edinburgh. Asst Minister, North Morningside, Edinburgh, 1964–65; Parish Minister, Kiltearn, Ross-shire, 1965–78. Chaplain to Lord High Comr, 1990, 1991, 1996 (the Princess Royal). Convener, Gen. Assembly's Panel on Worship, 1995–99 (Sec., 1982–95); C of S rep. on Joint Liturgical Group, 1984–99 (Chm., 1994–99). Mem., Broadcasting Standards Council, 1988–91, 1992–93. Chaplain: Clan Donnachaidh Soc., 1981–96; New Club, Edinburgh, 1986–2015; Moray House Coll. of Educn, then Edinburgh Univ. at Moray House, 1986–2002; No 2 (City of Edinburgh) Maritime HQ Unit, 1987–99, No 603 (City of Edinburgh) Sqn, 1999–2015, RAAF; to the High Constables and Guard of Honour of Holyroodhouse, 1993–2009 (Chaplain Emeritus, 2009); Incorp. of Goldsmiths of City of Edinburgh, 2000–; Edinburgh Merchants' Co., 2002–; Convenery of Trades of Edinburgh, 2005–; Incorporation of Bonnetmakers and Dyers of Edinburgh, 2008–. Lectr, St Colm's Coll., 1980–94. Mem., Historic Buildings Council for Scotland, 1990–99. Chairman: Bd of Queensberry House

Hosp., 1989–96 (Mem., 1978–96); Queensberry Trust, 1996–; Gov., St Columba's Hospice, 1986–2005; Trustee: Edinburgh Old Town Trust, 1987–94; Edinburgh Old Town Charitable Trust, 1994–; Edinburgh World Heritage Trust, 1999–2000; Church Hymnary Trust, 1987–; Carnegie Trust for the Univs of Scotland, 2005–15; Soc. for the Benefit of Sons and Daughters of the Clergy of the Church of Scotland, 2003– (Chm., 2009–); Pres., Church Service Soc., 1988–91. Hon. Life Mem. No 603 (City of Edinburgh) Squadron Assoc., 2013. JP Edinburgh, 1980–2006. Sec. of cttees which compiled Hymns for a Day, 1983, Songs of God's People, 1988, Worshipping Together, 1991, Clann ag Urnaigh, 1991, Common Order, 1994, Common Ground, 1998; Sec., Cttee to Revise Church Hymnary, 1995–2004. *Publications:* (ed) Singing the Faith, 1990; (ed) St Margaret Queen of Scotland and her Chapel, 1994; (jtly) By Lamplight, 2000. *Recreations:* Scottish and Edinburgh history and literature, hymnody, collecting Canongate miscellanea. *Address:* 3 Ross Gardens, Edinburgh EH9 3BS. *T:* (0131) 662 9025. *Clubs:* Puffin's, New (Hon. Mem.), Royal Scots (Hon. Mem.) (Edinburgh).

ROBERTSON, Christine Joyce; *see* Howe, C. J.

ROBERTSON, Daphne Jean Black, WS; Sheriff of Lothian and Borders at Edinburgh, 1996–2000; *b* 31 March 1937; *d* of Rev. Robert Black Kincaid and Ann Parker Collins; *m* 1965, Donald Buchanan Robertson, QC (*d* 2012). *Educ:* Hillhead High Sch.; Greenock Acad.; Edinburgh Univ. (MA); Glasgow Univ. (LLB). Admitted solicitor, 1961; WS 1977; Sheriff of Glasgow and Strathkelvin, 1979–96.

ROBERTSON, Douglas; *see* Robertson, J. D. M.

ROBERTSON, Fiona Mary Cecile; physiotherapist, since 1977; Vice Lord-Lieutenant of Fife, since 2015; *b* Greenock, 25 Aug. 1954; *d* of David and Pamela Collen; *m* 1993, William Brian Robertson; two *s*. *Educ:* St Leonard's Sch., St Andrews; Aberdeen Sch. of Physiotherapy (MCSP 1976); Univ. of Southampton (MSc Rehabilitation Studies 1993). Res. Physiotherapist, Univ. of Oxford, 1988–90; Physiotherapy Lectr, Queen Margaret Univ., Edinburgh, 1994–2004. Trustee, Carnegie Dunfermline and Hero Fund Trusts, 2005–. DL Fife, 2007. *Recreations:* family, keeping fit, family history research, arts. *E:* fionarobertson13@gmail.com.

ROBERTSON, Geoffrey Ronald; QC 1988; barrister; author; *b* 30 Sept. 1946; *s* of Francis Albert Robertson and Bernice Joy (*née* Beattie); *m* 1990, Kathryn Marie Lette, *qv*; one *s* one *d*. *Educ:* Epping Boys' High Sch.; Univ. of Sydney (BA 1966; LLB Hons 1970); University Coll., Oxford (BCL 1972; Rhodes Schol.). Called to the Bar, Middle Temple, 1973, Bencher, 1997; Supreme Court of NSW, 1977, of Antigua, 1990, of Trinidad, 1992, of Malaysia, 1998, of Hong Kong, 2001, of Fiji, 2002, of Anguilla, 2007. An Asst Recorder, 1993–99; a Recorder, 1999–2012. Founder and Head, Doughty Street Chambers, 1990–. Visiting Professor: Univ. of NSW, 1977; Birkbeck Coll., and Queen Mary, London Univ., 1997–; New Coll. of the Humanities, 2012–; Vis. Fellow, Warwick Univ., 1980–81. Consultant on Human Rights to Attorney Gen. of Australia, 1983; Consultant (Commonwealth Secretariat) to Constitutional Convention, Seychelles, 1993. Chm., Inquiry into Press Council, 1982–83; Counsel: Royal Commn on Arms Trafficking, Antigua, 1990–91; Commn on Admin of Justice, Trinidad, 2000. Appeal Judge, UN Special Ct for Sierra Leone, 2002–07 (and Pres., 2002–04). Chm., Commn on UN Internal Justice Reform, 2006–07; Mem., UN Internal Justice Council, 2008–12. Member: BFI Wkg Party on New Technologies, 1984; Exec. Council, ICA, 1987–97; Freedom of Inf. Campaign, 1987–; Charter 88, 1988–96; Justice, 1991–. Chm., BMA Cttee on Medical Inf. and Patient Privacy, 1994. Chm., Common Sense, 1998–. *Television:* Moderator, Hypotheticals, 1981–; writer and presenter, Tree of Liberty, 1982; Chm., The World This Week, 1987; writer and narrator, 44 Days (documentary), 1992. Editor, legal column, The Guardian, 1980–85. Hon. LLD: Sydney, 2008; Brunel, 2010; Romanian Nat. Sch. of Pol Scis, 2011. Freedom of Information Award, 1993; Award for dist. in internat. law, NY Bar Assoc., 2011. *Publications:* The Trials of Oz (play), 1973 (televised 1991); Whose Conspiracy?, 1974; Reluctant Judas, 1976; Obscenity, 1979; People Against the Press, 1983; (with A. Nicol) Media Law, 1984, 5th edn 2007; Hypotheticals, 1986; Does Dracula have Aids?, 1987; Freedom, the Individual and the Law, 6th edn 1989, 7th edn 1993; Geoffrey Robertson's Hypotheticals, 1991; The Justice Game, 1998; Crimes Against Humanity, 1999, 4th edn 2012; The Tyrannicide Brief, 2005; The Levellers: the Putney debates, 2007; Statute of Liberty, 2009; Was there an Armenian Genocide?, 2009; The Case of the Pope: Vatican accountability for human rights abuses, 2010; The 1988 Iranian Prison Massacres, 2010; Human Rights Fact-Finding: some legal and ethical dilemmas, 2010; Who Wants Diego Garcia? Decolonisation, Torture and Indigenous Rights, 2012; Mullahs Without Mercy: human rights and nuclear weapons, 2012; Dreaming Too Loud: reflections on a race apart, 2013; Stephen Ward Was Innocent, OK, 2013; An Inconvenient Genocide: who now remembers the Armenians?, 2014; contribs to anthologies and learned jls. *Recreations:* tennis, opera, fishing. *Address:* Doughty Street Chambers, 54 Doughty Street, WC1N 2LS. *T:* (020) 7404 1313, *Fax:* (020) 7404 2283. *E:* g.robertson@doughtystreet.co.uk.

ROBERTSON, Air Marshal Graeme Alan, CBE 1988 (OBE 1985); Managing Director, Blackbourne Wells Ltd, since 2003; *b* 22 Feb. 1945; *s* of Ronald James Harold Robertson, DFC and Constance Rosemary (*née* Freeman); *m* 1972, Barbara Ellen (*née* Mardon); one *d*. *Educ:* Bancroft's Sch.; RAF Coll., Cranwell; BA Open Univ. Pilot: 8 Sqn, 1968–69; 6 Sqn, 1970–72; 228 OCU, 1972–73; Flight Commander: 550 TFTS, USAF, 1973–76; 56 Sqn, 1976–77; RAF Staff Coll., 1977–78; OR/Air Plans Staff, MoD, 1978–82; Commanding Officer: 92 Sqn, 1982–84; 23 Sqn, 1984–85; RAF Wattisham, 1985–87; Hon. ADC to the Queen, 1985–87; Dir of Air Staff Briefing and Co-ordination, MoD, 1987–88; RCDS, 1989; Dir of Defence Programmes, MoD, 1990–91; Dep. C-in-C, RAF Germany, 1991–93; AOC No 2 Gp, 1993–94; ACDS (Programmes), MoD, 1994–96; C of S and Dep. C-in-C, Strike Comd, 1996–98; Hon. Col, 77 Engr Regt (Vols), 1996–99. Defence and Air Advr, BAe, subseq. Sen. Mil. Advr, BAE Systems, 1999–2003. Co-ordinator, British-American Community Relns, MoD, 2004–10. FRSA 1995; FRAeS 1997. Freeman, City of London, 1997; Clerk, Hon. Co. of Glos, 2013–. QCVSA 1973. *Recreations:* field sports, sailing, winter sports, the arts. *Address:* c/o National Westminster Bank, Sleaford, Lincs NG34 7BF. *Clubs:* Royal Air Force, MCC.

ROBERTSON, Rt Hon. Sir Hugh (Michael), KCMG 2014; PC 2012; DL; FRGS; Director, International Relations, Falcon and Associates, since 2015; *b* 9 Oct. 1962; *s* of George and June Robertson; *m* 2002, Anna Copson; one *s*. *Educ:* King's Sch., Canterbury; RMA Sandhurst; Reading Univ. (BSc Hons Land Mgt (Property Investment); Dist. Fellow, 2014). Served Life Guards, 1985–95 (Armourers' and Brasiers' Prize, 1986): active service: NI, 1988; UN Cyprus, 1988; Gulf War, 1991; Bosnia, 1994; i/c Household Cavalry on Queen's Birthday Parade and State Opening of Parlt as Field Officer of the Escort, 1993; Silver Stick Adjutant, 1994–95; retd in rank of Major; Schroder Investment Mgt, 1995–2001 (Asst Dir, 1999–2001). MP (C) Faversham and Mid Kent, 2001–15. An Opposition Whip, 2002–04; Shadow Sports Minister, 2004–05; Shadow Minister for Sport and the Olympics, 2005–10; Parly Under-Sec. of State (Minister for Sport and the Olympics), 2010–12, Minister of State (Minister for Sport and Tourism), 2012–13, DCMS; Minister of State, FCO, 2013–14. Sec., Parly Fruit Gp, 2001–10; Chm., All Party UN Gp, 2005–08. Gov., Westminster Foundn for Democracy, 2005–08. DL Kent, 2015. FRGS 1995. Sultan of Brunei's Personal Order of Merit, 1993; Internat. Paralympic Cttee Merit Award, 2012; Sport and Recreation Alliance Emeritus Award, 2014. *Recreations:* cricket, hockey. *Clubs:* Cavalry and Guards, Pratt's, MCC (Playing Mem.).

ROBERTSON, Iain Samuel, CBE 2002; CA; Chairman, Corporate Banking and Financial Markets, Royal Bank of Scotland, 2001–05 (Chief Executive, 2000–01); *b* 27 Dec. 1945; *s* of Alfred and Kathleen Robertson; *m* 1972, Morag; two *s* two *d*. *Educ:* Jordanhill College Sch.; Glasgow Univ. (LLB). Industry and professional practice, 1966–72; Civil Servant, 1972–83; Dir, Locate in Scotland, 1983–86; Chief Exec., SDA, 1987–90; Gp Finance Dir, County Natwest, 1990–92; Royal Bank of Scotland: Man. Dir, Corporate and Instnl Banking Div., 1992–98; Chief Exec., UK Bank, 1998–2000. Non-executive Director: Scottish Development Finance, 1983–90; Selective Assets Trust plc, 1989–96; British Empire Securities & Gen. Trust plc, 1995–2007; BT (Scotland), 2004–08; Cairn Capital Ltd, 2004–08; John Menzies plc, 2004–09. *Recreations:* golf, reading.

ROBERTSON, Ian, CA; President, Institute of Chartered Accountants of Scotland, 2004–05; *b* 10 Aug. 1947; *s* of James Love Robertson and Mary Hughes Robertson (*née* Reid); *m* 1st, 1968, Susan Moira Scott (marr. diss.); two *s* one *d*; 2nd, 2001, Fiona Ann Hervey. *Educ:* Queen's Park Sch., Glasgow. CA 1969. Chief Accountant, Whitbread Scotland Ltd, 1973–76; Dir, J. & A. Ferguson Ltd, 1976–82; Chief Accountant, United Biscuits, Glasgow, 1982–84; Financial Controller, Terry's of York, 1984–87; Finance Dir, Dairy Div., 1987–90, Gp Finance Controller, 1991–94, Northern Foods plc; Finance Dir, 1994–2003, Gp Chief Exec., 2003–07, Wilson Bowden plc. Non-executive Director: Homes & Communities Agency, 2008– (Chm., Audit Cttee, 2008–); Leeds Building Soc., 2008– (Chm., Audit Cttee, 2010–). Member: Financial Reporting Council, 2004–07; Audit Adv. Bd, Scottish Parlt Corporate Body, 2007–14 (Chm., 2009–14); Ind. Mem., Audit Cttee, DCLG, 2012–. Ext. Expert, Audit Cttee, UN Jt Staff Pension Fund, 2010–14 (Dep. Chm., 2012–14). Mem. (C), 1973–84, Chm., 1980–84, Eastwood DC. Institute of Chartered Accountants, Scotland: Mem. Council, 1996–2003; Sen. Vice-Pres., 2003–04; Convener, Investigations Cttee, 2010–. CCMI 2004 (FCMI 1976). *Recreations:* reading, music, travel, walking. *E:* ianrobertsonca@aol.com.

ROBERTSON, Prof. Ian Hamilton, PhD; Professor of Psychology, Trinity College Dublin, since 1999; *b* Lennoxtown, Scotland, 26 April 1951; *s* of John M. Robertson and Anne D. Robertson; *m* 1984, Dr Fiona O'Doherty; two *s* one *d*. *Educ:* Allan Glen's Sch., Glasgow; Univ. of Glasgow (BSc Psychol. 1973); Inst. of Psychiatry, Univ. of London (MPhil 1978); Univ. of London (PhD 1988). FBPsS 1987. Clin. Psychologist, Tayside Health Bd, 1978–82; Sen. Clin. Psychologist, Royal Edinburgh Hosp., 1982–84; Hd Neuropsychologist, Astley Ainslie Hosp., Edinburgh, 1984–91; Sen. Scientist, MRC Cognition and Brain Scis Unit, Cambridge, 1991–99. Fellow, Hughes Hall, Cambridge, 1994–99. MRC Travelling Fellow, Univ. La Sapienza, Rome, 1989; Visiting Professor: UCL, 1996–; Bangor Univ., 1996–; Staff Scientist, Rotman Res. Inst., Univ. of Toronto, 1995–. MRIA 2007; Fellow, Amer. Assoc. for Psychological Sci., 2013. FRSA 2011. *Publications:* Problem Drinking, 1981, 3rd edn 1997; Controlled Drinking, 1981; Unilateral Neglect, 1993; Spatial Neglect, 1999; Mind Sculpture, 1999; Cognitive Neurorehabilitation, 2002, 2nd edn 2008; The Mind's Eye, 2002; Handbook of Neuropsychology, vol. 9, 2003; Stay Sharp, 2006; The Winner Effect, 2012. *Recreations:* boating, fishing, choral singing, tennis. *Address:* Institute of Neuroscience, Trinity College Dublin, Lloyd Building, Dublin 2, Ireland. *T:* (87) 2850478, (1) 8962684. *E:* iroberts@tcd.ie.

ROBERTSON, Ian Stuart, CMG 2012; Member, Board of Management, BMW AG, and Head of Sales and Marketing, BMW, since 2008; *b* Shropshire, 5 June 1958. *Educ:* University Coll. Cardiff (BSc Maritime Studies 1979). Joined Rover Gp, 1979: Plant Director: Drews Lane, 1988–90; Powertrain, 1990–91; Purchasing Dir, 1991–94; Man. Dir, Land Rover Vehicles, 1994–99; Man. Dir, BMW SA, 1999–2005; Chm. and Chief Exec., Rolls-Royce Motor Cars Ltd, 2005–12. Non-exec. Dir, Dyson, 2013–. Hon. DSc Aston, 2011. *Address:* BMW AG, Petuelring 130, 80809 Munich, Germany. *T:* 893820.

ROBERTSON, James Andrew Stainton, PhD; Director, Health, Value for Money Studies, 1995–2005, Private Finance Value for Money Studies, 2005–10 and Chief Economist, 2006–10, National Audit Office; *b* 23 April 1949; *s* of James Robertson and Margaret Elodie Robertson (*née* Stainton); *m* 1979, Ann Leatherbarrow; one *s* one *d*. *Educ:* Highgate Sch.; Univ. of Essex (BA Econs); LSE (MSc Econs, PhD). Sen. Econ. Asst and Econ. Advr, Dept of Employment, 1975–82; Econ. Advr, Dept of Energy, 1982–86; Senior Economic Adviser: DTI, 1986–89; Dept of Transport, 1989–90; Hd of Industrial and Regl Econs, DTI, 1990–93; Chief Econ. Advr, Dept of Employment, subseq. DFEE, 1993–95. *Publications:* contrib. various learned jls. *Recreations:* family, do-it-yourself, gardening.

ROBERTSON, Hon. Sir (James) Bruce, KNZM 2010; Presiding Judge, Court of Appeal of Vanuatu, since 1996; President, Court of Appeal of Pitcairn, since 2011; Judge of the Qatar Financial Centre Civil and Commercial Court, since 2011; Judge of the High Court, Turks and Caicos Islands, since 2014; *b* Dunedin, NZ, 15 Feb. 1944; *s* of Finlay and Olive Mary Robertson; *m* 1969, Lyn Radford; two *s* one *d*. *Educ:* Otago Boys' High Sch.; Univ. of Otago (BA, LLB); Univ. of Virginia (LLM). Lectr (pt-time), Univ. of Otago, 1968–85; Partner, Ross Dowling Marquet & Griffin, Dunedin, 1969–87; Judge, High Court of NZ, 1987–2005; Judge of Ct of Appeal, NZ, 2005–10. Mem., PNG Leadership Tribunal, 2011; Chm., Financial Advrs Disciplinary Cttee, 2011–; Chair, NZ Sports Tribunal, 2012–; Commonwealth Secretariat Sen. Internat. Judicial Advr to Commn of Nat. Inquiry, Maldives, 2012; Comr for Security Warrants, 2013–. Pres., NZ Law Commn, 2001–05. Mem. Council, Univ. of Otago, 1969–88 (Pro-Chancellor, 1982–88). Pres., Legal Res. Foundn, 1990–99. Chairman: Rugby World Cup Authy, 2010–12; Online Media Standards Authy, 2012–. Chm., Bd, Presbyterian Support Central, 2010–13. Visitor, Univ. of S Pacific, 2012–. Hon. LLD Otago, 1990. Consulting Ed., Adams on Criminal Law, 1992–; Ed. in Chief, Introduction to Advocacy, 2000–. Gen. Service Medal (Vanuatu), 2012. *Publications:* (consulting ed.) Essays on Criminal Law, 2004; (contrib.) The Promise of Law Reform, 2005. *Recreations:* reading, walking, bridge. *Address:* 22A Orchard Street, Wadestown, Wellington 6012, New Zealand. *T:* 44721935, (mobile) 21657726. *E:* jbruce.robertson@gmail.com. *Clubs:* Dunedin, Wellington.

ROBERTSON, (James) Douglas (Moir), CBE 1992; DL; Chairman, Surrey Primary Care Trust, 2006–10; *b* Stalybridge, 15 Nov. 1938; *s* of late George Robertson and Jessie Barrie (*née* Brough); *m* 1963, Caroline Blanche; two *s* one *d*. *Educ:* Dunfermline High Sch.; Trinity Acad., Edinburgh; Heriot-Watt Coll. Chartered Quantity Surveyor; ARICS 1961, FRICS 1969. Founder and Principal, Surveyors Collaborative, 1969–95. Director: Building Cost Information Service Ltd, RICS, 1962–95; Bobbett and Robertson, 1994–96; Research Park Developments Ltd, 1995–; Surrey Social and Market Research Ltd, 1999–2011; Chairman: Airports Policy Consortium, 1984–93; Building Data Banks Ltd, 1985–95. Chm., 1987–90, Leader, 1990–93, Surrey CC. Chm., Envmt Cttee, Assoc. of CCs, 1990–92. Pro-Chancellor, Univ. of Surrey, 1998–2007, now Emeritus (Chm. Council, 1995–98); Chm. Council, Federal Univ. of Surrey, 2000–04. Chairman: Bournewood Community and Mental Health NHS Trust, 1997–2002; N Surrey PCT, 2002–06. Chm., Nat. Crimebeat, 1998–2005. Trustee, Surrey Hist. Trust, 1998–. FCMI 1971; FRSA 1989. DL 1988, High Sheriff 1997, Surrey. Hon. Dr Laws Roehampton, 2006; DUniv Surrey, 2007. *Publications:* Property Occupancy Analysis, 1970; Maintenance Price Book, 1980; Guide to House Rebuilding Costs, 1988; papers on economics of construction industry, cost indices and trends, and regl govts. *Recreations:* golf, music, travel. *Address:* 16 Homewaters Avenue, Sunbury-on-Thames, Middx TW16 6NS. *T:* (01932) 786624, *Fax:* (01932) 786190. *E:* jdmrobertson@aol.com.

ROBERTSON, Jane Elizabeth Louise; *see* Cooper, J. E. L.

ROBERTSON, John; *b* 17 April 1952; *s* of Charles Robertson and Agnes Millen Robertson (*née* Webster); *m* 1973, Eleanor Munro; three *d*. *Educ:* Shawlands Acad.; Langside Coll.; Stow Coll. (HNC Electrical Engrg). GPO, subseq. PO, then British Telecom, 1969–2000 (Customer Service Field Manager, BT, 1991–2000). MP (Lab) Glasgow Anniesland, Nov. 2000–2005, Glasgow NW, 2005–15; contested (Lab) same seat, 2015. Parliamentary Private Secretary: to Minister of State for ME, FCO, 2005–08; to Chief Sec. to the Treasury, 2008–09; to Sec. of State, DWP, 2009–10; to Shadow Sec. of State, Home Office, 2010–15. Mem., Select Cttee on Energy and Climate Change, 2009–15; Chairman, All Party Parliamentary Groups: on telecommunications, subseq. communications, 2002–15; on music, 2005–15 (Sec., 2003–05); on nuclear energy, 2005–15; on Nigeria, 2005; on Angola, 2007. *Recreations:* football, cricket, reading, music. *Clubs:* Garrowhill Cricket, Cambus Athletic Football, Old Kilpatrick Bowling (Glasgow).

ROBERTSON, Prof. John, PhD; FRS 2015; FIEEE; Professor of Electronics, since 2002 and Head, Electrical Engineering Division, Engineering Department, since 2014, University of Cambridge; *b* Manchester, 1950; *s* of John Alexander and Jeannette Robertson; *m* 1983, Christine Ann Girling; one *s* one *d*. *Educ:* Sandbach Sch.; Churchill Coll., Cambridge (BA Natural Scis 1971; PhD Physics 1975). FIEEE 2012. Research Officer: Central Electricity Res. Labs, Leatherhead, CEGB, 1975–90; Nat. Power, 1990–94; University of Cambridge: Res. Associate, 1994–96; Lectr, 1996–99, Reader, 1999–2002, Engrg Dept. Vis. Associate Prof., Univ. of Illinois, Urbana Champagne, 1981–82; Vis. Prof., Waseda Univ., Tokyo, 2007–09. Fellow: Materials Res. Soc., 2010; Amer. Physical Soc., 2011. *Publications:* contrib. papers to scientific jls. *Recreations:* squash, tennis, walking. *Address:* Department of Engineering, University of Cambridge, 9 J J Thomson Avenue, Cambridge CB3 0FA. *T:* (01223) 748331. *E:* jr214@cam.ac.uk.

ROBERTSON, Prof. John Charles, DPhil; Professor of the History of Political Thought, University of Cambridge, since 2010; Fellow, Clare College, Cambridge, since 2010; *b* Dundee, 28 Sept. 1951; *s* of Sir Lewis Findlay Robertson, CBE and Elspeth Robertson (*née* Badenoch); *m* 1977, Prof. Maxine Louise Berg, *qv*; three *d*. *Educ:* Trinity Coll., Glenalmond; Wadham Coll., Oxford (BA Mod. Hist. 1972; DPhil Mod. Hist. 1980). Res. Lectr, Christ Church, Oxford, 1975–80; Lectr in Mod. Hist., Univ. of Oxford, 1980–2010; Fellow and Tutor in Mod. Hist., St Hugh's Coll., Oxford, 1980–2010. Vis. appointments: Inst. for Advanced Studies in the Humanities, Univ. of Edinburgh, 1986; Folger Shakespeare Liby, Washington, DC, 1991; École des Hautes Études en Sciences Sociales, Paris, 2013. *Publications:* The Scottish Enlightenment and the Militia Issue, 1985; (ed) A Union for Empire: political thought and the British Union of 1707, 1995; The Case for the Enlightenment: Scotland and Naples 1680–1760, 2005; (ed with S. Mortimer) The Intellectual Consequences of Religious Heterodoxy 1600–1750, 2012; The Enlightenment: a very short introduction, 2015; articles in histl jls and collected vols on enlightenment, historiography and political thought 1600–1800. *Recreations:* cricket, walking, Italy (esp. Naples and the South). *Address:* Clare College, Cambridge CB2 1TL. *T:* (01223) 333277. *E:* jcr57@cam.ac.uk; 99 Glisson Road, Cambridge CB1 2HQ. *T:* (01223) 353228.

ROBERTSON, John David H.; *see* Home Robertson.

ROBERTSON, John Davie Manson, CBE 1993 (OBE 1978); DL; FRSE; Chairman, S. & J. D. Robertson Group, 1979–2010; *b* 6 Nov. 1929; *s* of late John Robertson and Margaret Gibson (*née* Wright); *m* 1959, Elizabeth Amelia Macpherson; two *s* two *d*. *Educ:* Kirkwall Grammar Sch.; Univ. of Edinburgh (BL). Anglo Iranian Oil Co., later BP, UK and ME, 1953–58; S. & J. D. Robertson Gp, 1958–. Dir, Stanley Services, Falkland Is, 1987–; Founder Chm., Orkney Today, 2003–10; Chm., Orkney Media Gp, 2007–10. Chairman: Kirkwall Ba' Cttee, 1977–2010; Orkney Health Bd, 1983–91 (Mem., 1974–79, Vice-Chm., 1979–83); Highland Health Bd, 1991–97; N of Scotland Water Authy, 1995–98. Member: Bd of Mgt, Orkney Hosps, 1970–74; Highlands and Is Consultative Council, 1988–91; Highlands and Is Enterprise, 1990–95; NHS Tribunal, 1990–2012; Chairman: Children's Panel, Orkney, 1971–76 (Chm., Adv. Cttee, 1977–82); Highlands and Is Savings Cttee, 1975–78; Scottish Health Mgt Efficiency Gp, 1985–95; Chm. and Vice-Chm., Scottish Health Bds Chairmen's Gp, 1995–97. Chm., Lloyds TSB Foundn for Scotland, 1997–99 (Trustee, 1989–99). Hon. Sheriff, Grampian Highland and Islands, 1977–. Hon. Vice Consul for Denmark, 1972–2004; Hon. Consul for Germany, 1976–2007. DL Sutherland, 1999. FRSE 2000; FRSA 1993. Hon. FCIWEM 1996. Knight, Order of Dannebrog (Denmark), 1982; Officer's Cross, Order of Merit (Germany), 1999 (Cavalier's Cross, 1986). *Publications:* Uppies and Doonies, 1967; (ed) An Orkney Anthology, vol. I, 1991, vol. II, 2012; Spinningdale and its Mill 1791–2000, 2000; The Kirkwall Ba', 2004; The Island of Fara 1739–2008, 2009; The Press Gang in Orkney and Shetland, 2011. *Recreations:* history, art. *Address:* S. & J. D. Robertson Gp, Dunkirk, Shore Street, Kirkwall, Orkney KW15 1LG; Spinningdale House, Spinningdale, Sutherland IV24 3AD. *T:* (01862) 881240. *Club:* New (Edinburgh).

ROBERTSON, Rear Adm. John Keith, CB 1983; FIET; *b* 16 July 1926; *s* of G. M. and J. L. Robertson; *m* 1951, Kathleen (*née* Bayntun); one *s* three *d*. *Educ:* RNC Dartmouth; Clare Coll., Cambridge (BA 1949). FIET (FIEE 1981). RNC Dartmouth, 1940–43; served, 1943–83 (Clare Coll., Cambridge, 1946–49): HM Ships Queen Elizabeth, Zest, Gabbard, Aisne and Decoy; Staff, RNC Dartmouth; Grad. Recruiting; Weapon Engr Officer, HMS Centaur; Comdr, RNEC Manadon; RCDS; Captain Technical Intell. (Navy), 1974–76; Captain Fleet Maintenance, Portsmouth, 1976–78; Dir, Naval Recruiting, 1978–79; Dir, Management and Support of Intelligence, MoD, 1980–82; ACDS (Intelligence), 1982–83. *Recreations:* hockey, tennis, golf, wood carving. *Address:* Alpina, Kingsdown, Corsham, Wilts SN13 8BJ. *Clubs:* Corkscrew (Bath); Kingsdown Golf.

ROBERTSON, John Shaw; educational consultant, since 2010; Rector, Dollar Academy, 1994–2010; *b* Glasgow, 7 April 1950; *s* of David and Margaret Robertson; *m* 1973, Mary Roy; one *s* one *d*. *Educ:* Univ. of Glasgow (MA English Lang. and Lit.; DipEd). English master, Housemaster, then Asst Headmaster, Daniel Stewart's & Melville Coll., 1973–87; Dep. Rector, Dollar Acad., 1987–93. Principal Examr, English (H), Scottish Exam. Bd, 1990–94. Headmasters' and Headmistresses' Conference: Member: Academic Policy Cttee, 1997–2003; Membership Cttee, 2003– (Chm., 2007–10); Chm., Scottish Div., 2000. Governor: Longridge Towers Sch., 2007–; St Mary's, Melrose, 2008–; High Sch. of Dundee, 2010–; various educnl consultancies. Hon. Life Mem., Dollar Burns Club. *Publications:* Stewart's Melville: the first ten years, 1984; contrib. articles on educn, curriculum, assessment and on Robertson Davies, Canadian novelist. *Recreations:* cricket (Scottish), music (English), literature (international). *Address:* Sheardale, 11 Riverside Drive, Kelso TD5 7RH. *E:* johnandmaryrobertson@gmail.com. *Clubs:* East India, Lansdowne; Scottish Cricket Union (Life Member).

ROBERTSON, John William; Director, John Robertson Architects, since 2005; *b* 27 Aug. 1956; *s* of Ian Middleton Strachan Robertson and Agnes Ramsey Seaton Robertson; *m* 1984, Judy Peacock; one *s* two *d*. *Educ:* Univ. of Dundee (BSc 1976); Univ. of Liverpool (BArch Hons 1979). RIBA 1981. Partner, Fitzroy Robinson Partnership, 1986–93; Dir, Hurley Robertson and Associates, 1993–2005. Projects include: One Great St Helens, London (British Council for Offices Award, 2000); restoration and refurbishment of Daily Express Bldg, Fleet Street (Royal Fine Art Commn Award, 2001; City Heritage Award, 2002); 10 Queen St Place, EC4 (British Council for Offices Award, 2007); Park House, Finsbury Circus, 2008; 107 Cheapside, EC2, 199 Bishopsgate, EC2, Bush House, Aldwych, 2013; refurbishment of Great Arthur House, EC1; Crossrail over-station developments at Moorgate and Farringdon stations. Mem., City Architectural Forum, 1994–. *Publications:* contrib. Architecture Today, RIBA Jl. *Recreations:* bagpiping, golf, ski-ing, Norfolk terriers, cycling, mountain walking. *Address:* John Robertson Architects, 111 Southwark Street, SE1 0JF. *T:* (020) 7633 5100, *Fax:* (020) 7620 0091. *E:* john.robertson@jra.co.uk. *Clubs:* Royal Automobile; Berkshire Golf.

ROBERTSON, Kathryn Marie; *see* Lette, K. M.

ROBERTSON, Rt Rev. Larry; *see* Yukon, Bishop of.

ROBERTSON, Laurence Anthony; MP (C) Tewkesbury, since 1997; *b* 29 March 1958; *s* of James Robertson and Jean (*née* Larkin); *m* 1989, Susan (*née* Lees) (marr. diss. 2014); two step *d*; *m* 2015, Anne Marie (*née* Adams). *Educ:* St James C of E Sch., Farnworth; Farnworth Grammar Sch.; Bolton Inst. Higher Educn. Work study engr, 1976–82; industrial consultant, 1982–92; charity fundraising, 1992–97 (raised about £2 million for various charities). Contested (C): Makerfield, 1987; Ashfield, 1992. An Opposition Whip, 2001–03; Opposition front bench spokesman on economic affairs, 2003–05; Shadow Minister for NI, 2005–10. Chm., NI Affairs Select Cttee, 2010–; Member: Envmt Audit Select Cttee, 1997–99; Social Security Select Cttee, 1999–2001; European Scrutiny Select Cttee, 1999–2002; Educn and Skills Select Cttee, 2001; Jt Cttee on Consolidation of Bills, 1997–2001; Chm., All Party Gp on Ethiopia and Djibouti, 2009–; Jt Chm., All Party Gp on Racing and Bloodstock, 2010–; Co-Chm., British Irish Parly Assembly, 2011–. Secretary: Cons. Back Bench Constitutional Cttee, 1997–2001; 92 Gp, 2001–02. *Recreations:* sport (ran 6 marathons), particularly horseracing and golf, reading, writing, history. *Address:* House of Commons, SW1A 0AA. *T:* (020) 7219 4196; 22 High Street, Tewkesbury GL20 6DL. *T:* (01684) 291640.

ROBERTSON, Nelson; *see* Robertson, W. N.

ROBERTSON, Nicholas John, OBE 2011; Chief Executive Officer, ASOS.com, 1999–2015 (non-executive Director, since 2015); *b* Woking, Nov. 1967; *s* of John Spencer Robertson and Cynthia Mary Robertson; *m* 2004, Janine Coulson; one *d*. *Educ:* Canford Sch., Wimborne. Young and Rubicam, 1987–92; Carat UK, 1992–96; Entertainment Marketing UK Ltd, 1996–99. *Recreations:* ski-ing, Chelsea FC, cycling. *Address:* ASOS.com, Greater London House, Hampstead Road, NW1 7FB. *T:* (020) 7756 1000, *Fax:* (020) 7756 1001.

ROBERTSON, Prof. Norman Robert Ean, CBE 1991; FDSRCPSGlas; Professor of Orthodontics, 1970–92, Dean of the Dental School, 1985–92, University of Wales College of Medicine; Hon. Consulting Orthodontist, South Glamorgan Health Authority, since 1992 (Hon. Consultant in Orthodontics, 1970–92); *b* 13 March 1931; *s* of late Robert Robertson and Jean Robertson (*née* Dunbar); *m* 1954, Morag Wyllie (*d* 2014), *d* of George McNicol, MA; three *s* two *d*. *Educ:* Hamilton Acad.; Glasgow Univ. (BDS); Manchester Univ. (MDS 1962; DDS 1969). FDSRCPSGlas 1967. Registrar, then Sen. Registrar in Orthodontics, Glasgow Dental Hosp., 1957–59; Lectr in Orthodontics, 1960–62, Sen. Lectr in Orthodontics, 1962–70, Manchester Univ. Member: GDC, 1985–94; Standing Dental Adv. Cttee, 1989–92; S Glamorgan HA, 1976–92. *Publications:* Oral Orthopaedics and Orthodontics for Cleft Lip and Palate, 1983; articles in dental and med. jls. *Recreation:* painting. *Address:* 26 Heol Tyn y Cae, Rhiwbina, Cardiff CF14 6DJ. *T:* (029) 2061 3439.

ROBERTSON, Patricia; QC 2006; *b* 1 Aug. 1964; *d* of George and Sheila Robertson; *m* 1991, Tom Henry; two *s* one *d*. *Educ:* St George's Sch., Edinburgh; Balliol Coll., Oxford (BA Mod. Hist.); City Univ. (Dip. Law). Called to the Bar, Inner Temple, 1988, Bencher, 2011; in practice as a barrister, 1989–, specialising in commercial law, banking and financial services, professional negligence and regulatory law. CEDR accredited mediator, 2004–. Mem., Bar Standards Bd, 2010– (Vice Chm., 2013–). Mem., Mediterranean Gardening Soc. *Publications:* (contrib.) Law of Bank Payment, ed by Brindle and Cox, 1996, 2004; (contrib.) Professional Negligence and Liability, ed by M. Simpson, 2006. *Recreations:* gardening on a grand scale, faking Renaissance masterpieces (for pleasure, not profit). *Address:* Fountain Court, Temple, EC4Y 9DH. *T:* (020) 7583 3335, *Fax:* (020) 7353 0329. *E:* pr@fountaincourt.co.uk.

ROBERTSON, Raymond Scott; Director of Public Affairs (formerly Development Director), Halogen Communications, since 2002; *b* 11 Dec. 1959; *s* of late James Robertson and Marion Robertson. *Educ:* Glasgow Univ. (MA Hist. and Politics); Jordanhill Coll. Teacher, Hist. and Mod. Studies, Smithycroft Secondary Sch., Glasgow, 1982–83, Dumbarton Acad., 1983–89; NE Political Dir, 1989–92, Vice-Chm., 1993–95, Chm., 1997–2001, Scottish Cons Party. MP (C) Aberdeen South, 1992–97; contested (C): same seat, 1997; Eastwood, 2001. PPS to Min. of State, NI Office, 1994–95; Parly Under-Sec. of State, Scottish Office, 1995–97.

ROBERTSON, Prof. Ritchie Neil Ninian, DPhil; FBA 2004; Taylor Professor of German Language and Literature, University of Oxford, since 2010; Fellow of Queen's College, Oxford, since 2010; *b* 25 Dec. 1952; *s* of Alexander Ritchie Robertson and Elizabeth Robertson (*née* Ninian); *m* 1999, Katharine Mary Nicholas; one step *s* one step *d*. *Educ:* Nairn Acad.; Univ. of Edinburgh (MA 1st class Honours: English 1974; German 1976); Lincoln Coll., Oxford (DPhil 1981). Montgomery Tutorial Fellow, Lincoln Coll., Oxford, 1979–84; Fellow and Dir of Studies in Modern Langs, Downing Coll., Cambridge, 1984–89; Lectr in German, 1989–99, Prof. of German, 1999–2010, Univ. of Oxford; Official Fellow, St John's Coll., Oxford, 1989–2010. Ed., Austrian Studies, 1990–99; Germanic Ed., MLR, 2000–10. *Publications:* Kafka: Judaism, politics and literature, 1985 (trans. German 1988); Heine, 1988 (trans. German 1997); The 'Jewish Question' in German Literature 1749–1939, 1999; (ed) The Cambridge Companion to Thomas Mann, 2002; Kafka: a very short introduction, 2004 (trans. Japanese 2007, Chinese 2008, German 2009); (ed with Katrin Kohl) A History of Austrian Literature 1918–2000, 2006; Mock-Epic Poetry from Pope to Heine, 2009; (ed) Lessing and the German Enlightenment, 2013. *Address:* 31 Frenchay Road, Oxford OX2 6TG; Faculty of Modern Languages, 47 Wellington Square, Oxford OX1 2JF. *E:* ritchie.robertson@mod-langs.ox.ac.uk.

ROBERTSON, Robert Henry; Australian diplomat, retired; *b* 23 Dec. 1929; *s* of James Rowland Robertson and Hester Mary (*née* Kay); *m* 2nd, 1958, Jill Bryant Uther (marr. diss. 1982); two *s* one *d*; 3rd, 1986, Isabelle Costa de Beauregard, *d* of Comte and Comtesse René Costa de Beauregard. *Educ:* Geelong Church of England Grammar Sch.; Trinity Coll., Univ. of Melbourne (LLB). Third Secretary, Australian High Commn, Karachi, 1954–56; Second Sec., Mission to UN, New York, 1958–61; First Sec., later Counsellor, Washington, 1964–67; Ambassador to Jugoslavia, Romania and Bulgaria, 1971–73; Asst Sec., Personnel Br., Dept of Foreign Affairs, Canberra, 1974–75; First Asst Sec., Western Div., 1975–76, Management and Foreign Service Div., 1976–77; Ambassador to Italy, 1977–81; Dep. High Comr in London, 1981–84; Perm. Rep. to UN in Geneva, 1984–88; Ambassador to Argentina, Uruguay and Paraguay, 1989–92. Chm., Exec. Cttee, UN High Comr for Refugees, 1987–88. *Address:* 53 Williams Road, Mount Eliza, Vic 3930, Australia. *T:* and *Fax:* (3) 97752078. *Club:* Melbourne.

ROBERTSON, Shirley Ann, (Mrs J. Boag), OBE 2005 (MBE 2001); DL; sailor and television presenter; *b* 15 July 1968; *d* of Iain Robertson and Elizabeth Ann Robertson (*née* Burnett); *m* 2001, Jamie Boag; one *s* one *d* (twins). *Educ:* Moray House, Edinburgh (BA Hons Recreation Mgt). Competitive Laser Cl. sailing, 1983–88, Europe Cl., 1988–2000; Extreme 40 Catamaran Sailing Series, 2007–. Member GB sailing team, Olympic Games: Barcelona, 1992; Atlanta, 1996; Gold Medal: Women's Singlehanded Europe Cl., Olympic Games, Sydney, 2000; three-person Women's Yngling Keelboat Cl., Olympic Games, Athens, 2004. World Sailor of the Year, ISAF, 2000. DL Isle of Wight, 2014. *Address:* c/o Into the Blue, One The Parade, Cowes PO31 7QJ. *Club:* Royal Corinthian Yacht.

ROBERTSON, Sir Simon (Manwaring), Kt 2010; Partner, Simon Robertson Associates LLP (formerly Managing Partner, Simon Robertson Associates, then Partner, Robertson Robey Associates, since 2005; *b* 4 March 1941; *s* of David Lars Manwaring Robertson, CVO; *m* 1965, Virginia Stewart Norman; one *s* two *d*. *Educ:* Eton. Joined Kleinwort Benson, 1963; Dir, 1977–97; Dep. Chm., 1992–96; Chm., 1996–97; Man. Dir, Goldman Sachs Internat. and Pres., Goldman Sachs Europe Ltd, 1997–2005. Chm., Rolls-Royce plc, 2005–13 (Dir, 2004–13); non-executive Director: Inchcape, 1996–2005; London Stock Exchange, 1998–2001; Berry Bros & Rudd, 1998–; Invensys, 1999–2005; Royal Opera House Covent Garden Ltd, 2002–12; Economist Newspaper Ltd, 2005–; HSBC Hldgs PLC, 2006– (Sen. Ind. Dir, 2007–15; Dep. Chm., 2010–); Troy Asset Mgt Ltd, 2012–. Trustee: Eden Project, 2000–15; St Paul's Foundn, 2000–05; Royal Acad. Trust, 2001–07; Royal Opera Hse Endowment Fund 2000, 2001–. Officier: Ordre des Arts et des Lettres (France), 2011; Legion d'Honneur (France), 2014. *Recreations:* ski-ing, walking in the Alps. *Clubs:* Boodle's, White's; Racquet (New York).

ROBERTSON, Stanley Stewart John, CBE 1998; safety engineering consultant; Managing Director, Robertson Safety Engineering Services Ltd, 1998–2010; Director, Metro Solutions Ltd, 2005–12; *b* 14 July 1938; *s* of Jock Stanley Robertson and Florence Kathleen Robertson (*née* Carpenter); *m* 1961, Valerie Housley; two *s* two *d*. *Educ:* Liverpool Poly. (Dip. EE 1961). CEng 1973; FIET (FIEE 1987); FCILT (FCIT 1998). Student engrg apprentice, UKAEA, 1956–62; Asst Electrical Engr, CEGB, 1961–67; Elec. Engrg Manager, Shell Chemicals UK, 1967–74; Health and Safety Executive: Sen. Electrical Inspector, 1974–77; Dep. Superintending Inspector, 1977–80; Superintending Inspector, 1980–91; Dep. Chief Inspector and Regl Dir, 1991–93; HM Chief Inspector of Railways, 1993–98. Chairman: HSE Tech. Cttee investigating radio frequency ignition hazards, St Fergus, Scotland, 1979; Rly Industry Adv. Cttee, HSC, 1993–98; HSE Cttee investigating safety of Forth Rail Bridge, 1995–96; Mem., HSE Tech. Cttee investigating collapse of railway tunnels at Heathrow Airport and New Austrian Tunnelling Method, 1994. Health and Safety Advr, Taiwan High Speed Rail Corp., 1999–2006; Railway Safety Advr, Roads & Transport Authy, Dubai, 2008–09. Chm., Nat. Inspection Council for Elec. Installation Contracting, 1993–95. Non-exec. Dir, NQA Ltd, 1993–95. *Publications:* several tech. papers on electrical and railway safety matters. *Recreations:* music, gardening. *E:* ssjrcbe@hotmail.com.

ROBERTSON, Stephen Peter; Chairman, Business West, since 2013; *b* Essex, 1954; *m* Susan; three *s* two *d*. *Educ:* Univ. of Nottingham (BSc Hons Chem.). Eur. Mktg Manager, Mars Inc., 1986–92; Marketing Director: Mattel Toys, 1992–93; B&Q plc, 1993–2000; Chm., Screwfix Direct, 2000–02; Dir, Gp Communications, Kingfisher plc, 2002–04 (incl. Man. Dir, Ellen MacArthur sponsorship); Marketing Director: (interim) WH Smith plc, 2004; Woolworths Gp plc, 2004–07; Dir Gen., British Retail Consortium, 2008–12. Non-executive Director: Fresca Gp Ltd, 2005–08; Nat. Portrait Gall. Co., 2008–11; Timpson Gp, 2010–; Hargreaves Lansdown plc, 2011–; Clipper Logistics plc, 2014–. Mem., Adv. Bd, PrismaStar Ltd, 2014–. Fellow and former Chm., Marketing Soc. CCMI 2013. FRSA 2013.

ROBERTSON, Stuart Douglas; Regional Employment Judge for the North West Region, Employment Tribunals (England and Wales), since 2015; *b* Bradford, 1 May 1957; *s* of Ian and Joan Robertson; one *s* one *d*. *Educ:* Bradford Grammar Sch.; Trinity Hall, Cambridge (BA Law 1979; MA 1983); Coll. of Law, Chester. Solicitor in private practice, 1982–2004; Fee-paid Employment Judge, 1994; Salaried Employment Judge, 2004; Registrar, Dio. Bradford, 2002–04. *Recreations:* long-distance walking, hill-walking, Rugby League. *Address:* Regional Office of the Employment Tribunals, Alexandra House, 14–22 The Parsonage, Manchester M3 2JA. *T:* (0161) 833 6161.

ROBERTSON, Tina; *see* Tietjen, T.

ROBERTSON, (William) Nelson, CBE 1996; FCII; Director, Alliance Trust, 1996–2002; *b* 14 Dec. 1933; *s* of James Bogue and Eleanor Robertson; *m* 1964, Sheila Catherine Spence (*d* 2013); two *d*. *Educ:* Berwick Grammar Sch.; Edinburgh Univ. (MA). FCII 1963. Served RA, 1955–57. General Accident Fire & Life Assurance Corporation Ltd, later General Accident plc, 1958–95: Asst Gen. Man. (Overseas), 1972; Gen. Man., 1980; Dir, 1984; Dep. Chief Gen. Man., 1989; Gp Chief Exec., 1990–95. Director: Morrison Construction Gp, 1995–2001; Second Alliance Trust, 1996–2002; Edinburgh New Tiger Trust, 1996–2001; Scottish Community (formerly Caledonian) Foundn, 1996–99; Supervisory Bd, Scottish Amicable, 1997–2004; Edinburgh Leveraged Income Trust plc, 2001–02; Edinburgh Zeros 2008 plc, 2001–02. Bd Mem., ABI, 1991–95. Mem. Court, Univ. of Abertay, Dundee, 1996–99. *Recreations:* hill-walking, gardening. *Club:* Caledonian.

ROBERTSON-MACLEOD, (Roderick) James (Andrew); Consultant, G4S (formerly Group 4 Securicor), 2006–15; *b* 5 March 1951; *s* of Col Roderick Robertson-Macleod and Daphne Robertson-Macleod; *m* 1992, Karen Barclay; one *s* two *d*. *Educ:* Milton Abbey. Commnd Royal Green Jackets, 1970–80; Private Sec. to HSH Princess Grace of Monaco, 1980–82; Dir, Markham Sports Sponsorship, 1982–91; Chief Exec., Raleigh International, 1991–2003; Dir, Project Support, AEGIS Defence Services, 2004–06. *Recreations:* tennis, Real tennis, ski-ing, walking. *Address:* Hill House, Coneyhurst, W Sussex RH14 9DL. *T:* (01403) 786877. *E:* jrobmac@btinternet.com.

ROBINS, David Anthony; Chairman: Asian Total Return Investment Company plc (formerly Henderson TR Pacific Investment Trust plc, then Henderson Asian Growth Trust), since 2004 (Director, since 2002); Fidelity Japanese Values plc, since 2012 (Director, since 2011); Hackney Empire Ltd, 2003–13 (Director, 2001–13); Oriel Securities Ltd, 2007–14; *b* 2 Sept. 1949; *s* of John Anthony Robins and Ruth Wenefrede Robins (*née* Thomas); *m* 1981, Joanna Christina Botting; two *s* one *d*. *Educ:* University Coll. London (BSc Econ). Economic Analyst, Investment and Res. Dept, Commonwealth Bank, Sydney, Australia, 1973–74; Economist, Overseas Dept, Bank of England, 1976–78; Exec., Japanese Dept, James Capel, 1978–80; Chief Internat. Economist, Phillips & Drew, 1980–86; Hd of Res., UBS Phillips & Drew Ltd, Tokyo, 1986–88; Hd, Internat. Securities Dept, UBS Securities Inc., NY, 1988–90; Functional Advr, Securities and Res., Union Bank of Switzerland, Zurich, 1990–93; Chief Exec. Officer, UBS UK Ltd, 1994–98; Exec. Vice Pres. and Hd, Region Europe, Union Bank of Switzerland, 1997–98; Chm. and Chief Exec. Officer, ING Barings, 1998–2000; Mem., Exec. Bd, ING Gp, 2000. Chm., New Philanthropy Capital, 2001–09; Non-executive Director: MPC Investors Ltd, 2001–07; Bending Light Ltd, 2001–; LCH Clearnet Ltd, 2001–07 (Chm., 2003–07); Meggitt plc, 2002–14; EMG Gp Ltd, 2004–10; Serrasolar Inc., 2011–; Pemberton Capital Advrs LLP, 2013–14; NHBS Ltd, 2014–; Sen. Ind. Dir, SVG Capital plc, 2013–. Dep. Chm., E London Business Alliance, 2000–06. Mem., Investment Adv. Cttee, Univs Superannuation Scheme, 2004–08. Mem., RIIA, 1982; MCSI 1997; FInstD 2011 (MInstD 2002); FRSA 2003. Gov., Eltham Coll., 2001–13 (Chm., 2004–13). *Recreations:* travel, walking, gardening, wine.

ROBINS, John Vernon Harry; Chairman, Xchanging plc, 2000–08; *b* 21 Feb. 1939; *s* of Col William Vernon Harry Robins, DSO and Charlotte Mary (*née* Grier); *m* 1962, Elizabeth Mary Banister; two *s* one *d*. *Educ:* Winchester Coll. Nat. Service, 2nd Lieut 2/10 Princess Mary's Own Gurkha Rifles, 1959–61. Man. Dir, SNS Communications Ltd, 1966–74; Chief Exec., Bally Gp (UK) Ltd, 1974–79; Group Financial Director: Fitch Lovell plc, 1979–84; Willis Faber, subseq. Willis Corroon Gp plc, 1984–94; Chief Exec., Guardian Royal Exchange plc, 1994–99; Chairman: Hyder plc, 1998–2000; Lane, Clark and Peacock (Actuaries), 2000–03; Austin Reed Gp plc, 2000–06. Director: Wellington Underwriting plc, 1999–2001; Axa Asia Pacific Hldgs Ltd, Melbourne, 1999–2002; Alexander Forbes Ltd (SA), 2002– (Dep. Chm., 2004–07); Xchanging Insure Hldgs Ltd, 2008–12. Chm., Policyholders Protection Bd, 1998–2000. Mem., Barbican Centre Bd, 2003–08. *Recreations:* clocks, Baroque music, grandchildren. *Club:* Brooks's.

ROBINS, Group Captain Leonard Edward, CBE (mil.) 1979; AE 1958 (and 2 clasps); Inspector, Royal Auxiliary Air Force, 1973–83; *b* 2 Nov. 1921; *yr s* of late Joseph Robins, Bandmaster RM, and late Louisa Josephine (*née* Kent); *m* 1949, Jean Ethelwynne (Headteacher) (*d* 1985), *d* of late Roy and Bessie Searle, Ryde, IoW. *Educ:* Singlegate, Mitcham, Surrey; City Day Continuation School, EC. Entered Civil Service, GPO, 1936; War service, Radar Br., RAF, UK, SEAC, Ceylon, India, 1941–46; resumed with GPO, 1946; Min. of Health, 1948; Min. of Housing and Local Govt, 1962; DoE, 1970–80, retired. Airman, No 3700 (Co. of London) Radar Reporting Unit RAuxAF, 1950; Commissioned 1953, radar branch; transf. to No 1 (Co. of Hertford) Maritime HQ Unit RAuxAF, intelligence duties, 1960; OC No 1 Maritime Headquarters Unit, RAuxAF, 1969–73; Gp Capt., Inspector RAuxAF, 1973–83. ADC to the Queen, 1974–83. Selected Air Force Mem., Greater London TAVRA, 1973–83 and City of London TAVRA, 1980–84; Mem., HAC, 1997–. Patron, World War II Air Forces Radar Reunion, 2001, presided at Reunions, annually, 2003–10. Lord Mayor of London's personal staff, as researcher and speech writer, 1977–78, 1980–81, 1982–83 and 1986–94. Pres., Wandsworth Victim Support Scheme, 1980–87. Trustee, Royal Foundn of Greycoat Hosp., 1983–88. Freeman, City of London, 1976. Coronation Medal, 1953; Silver Jubilee Medal, 1977. Officer of Merit with Swords, SMO Malta, 1986. DL Greater London, 1978–97, Rep. DL, Bor. of Wandsworth, 1979–97. FCMI. *Recreations:* naval, military and aviation history, book hunting, kipping, speech writing. *Address:* 5 Varley Terrace, Dean Street, Liskeard, Cornwall PL14 4AN. *T:* (01579) 348740. *Club:* Royal Air Force.

ROBINS, Sir Ralph (Harry), Kt 1988; DL; FREng; FRAeS; Chairman, Rolls-Royce plc, 1992–2003; *b* 16 June 1932; *s* of Leonard Haddon and Maud Lillian Robins; *m* 1962, Patricia Maureen Grimes; two *d*. *Educ:* Imperial Coll., Univ. of London (BSc; ACGI; FIC 1993). MIMechE; FREng (FEng 1988); FRAeS 1990. Development Engr, Rolls-Royce, Derby, 1955–66; Exec. Vice-Pres., Rolls-Royce Inc., 1971; Man. Dir, RR Industrial & Marine Div., 1973; Commercial Dir, RR Ltd, 1978; Chm., International Aero Engines AG, 1983–84; Rolls-Royce plc: Man. Dir, 1984–89; Dep. Chm., 1989–92; Chief Exec., 1990–92. Chairman: Adv. Bd, Hakluyt, 2005–13; Freastream Aircraft Ltd, 2005–; GAMA Aviation plc, 2015–. Non-executive Director: Standard Chartered plc, 1988–2004; Schroders plc, 1990–2002; Marks & Spencer plc, 1992–2001; Cable and Wireless plc, 1994–2003 (non-exec. Chm., 1998–2003); Marshall of Cambridge Hldgs (formerly Marshall Hldgs) Ltd, 2004–. Chm., Defence Industries Council, 1986–2003; Pres., SBAC, 1986–87. Mem., Council for Sci. and Technology, 1993–98. DL Derbys, 2000. FCGI 1990. Hon. FRAeS; Hon. FIMechE 1996. Hon. DSc: Cranfield, 1990; Nottingham, 2002; Cambridge, 2008; DUniv Derby, 1992; Hon. DBA Strathclyde, 1996; Hon. DEng Sheffield, 2001. Commander's Cross, Order of Merit (Germany), 1996. *Recreations:* golf, music, classic cars. *Clubs:* Athenæum, Royal Air Force.

ROBINS, Maj.-Gen. William John Pherrick, CB 1998; OBE 1984 (MBE 1979); CEng, FIET; FBCS; Director, Bill Robins Ltd, since 2003; *b* 28 July 1941; *s* of John Robins and Helen Hamilton (*née* Urry); *m* 1st, 1967, Anne Marie Cornu (marr. diss. 1985); one *s* one *d*; 2nd, 1993, Kathy Walsh. *Educ:* Henry Mellish Grammar Sch., Nottingham; Welbeck Coll.; RMA Sandhurst; RMCS Shrivenham (BSc (Eng) London, 1966); Staff Coll., Camberley; Cranfield Inst. of Technology (MPhil (Information Systems) 1993). CEng 1991, FIET (FIEE 1992); FBCS 1995. 16 Parachute Bde, 1966–70; Special Communications, 1970–72; Germany and UK, 1972–79; CO 14 Signal Regt (Electronic Warfare), 1979–82; Mil. Asst to MGO, 1982–84; Army ADP Co-ordinator, 1984–87; Project Dir, 1987–89; Dir, CIS (Army), 1989–92; ACDS (Command, Control, Communications and Information Systems), 1992–94; Dir Gen., Information and Communication Services, MoD, 1995–98. Director: Marconi Radar and Defence Systems, 1998–99; Alenia Marconi Systems, 1999–2000; BAE SYSTEMS: Future Systems Dir, 2000–01; Dir, C4ISTAR Develt Avionics Gp, 2001–02; Dir, Advanced Concepts C4ISR Gp, 2002–03. Vis. Prof., Cranfield Univ., 2003–. Freeman, Information Technologists' Co., 2004. Hon. Fellow, Sch. of Defence Management, Cranfield Univ., 1994; Associate FRUSI 2002. *Recreations:* cartoons, looking at pictures, making high quality compost, running, hill walking. *Address:* c/o RHQ Royal Signals, Blandford Camp, Dorset DT11 8RH. *Clubs:* Special Forces, Army and Navy.

ROBINSON, family name of **Baron Martonmere**.

ROBINSON, Alastair; *see* Robinson, F. A. L.

ROBINSON, Alice; Her Honour Judge Alice Robinson; a Circuit Judge, since 2007; a Deputy High Court Judge of the Administrative Court, since 2010; *b* Brentwood, Essex, 13 June 1959; *d* of Anthony Robinson and Anne Mary Robinson; *m* 1988, Antony John Cronk; one *s* one *d*. *Educ:* Haverstock Comp. Sch., London; University Coll., Cardiff (LLB 1st Cl. Hons 1982). Called to the Bar, Gray's Inn, 1983; in practice as barrister specialising in planning, property and public law; Supplementary Panel of Jun. Counsel to the Crown, Common Law, 1992–99; Recorder, 2003–07. Sen. Judge of Sovereign Base Areas of Akrotiri and Dhekelia, Cyprus, 2012–. Legal Mem., 2007–, Mem., Restricted Patients Panel, 2007–, Mental Health Rev. Tribunal; Mem., Lands Tribunal, 2009–. Asst Ed., Encyclopaedia of Planning Law and Practice, 2004–07. *Publications:* various articles in Jl of Planning Law and Judicial Rev. on Planning and Public Law. *Recreations:* hill walking, choral singing, films, cooking. *Address:* Woolwich Crown Court, 2 Belmarsh Road, SE28 0EY.

ROBINSON, Alwyn Arnold; Managing Director, Daily Mail, 1975–89; *b* 15 Nov. 1929. Mem., Press Council, 1977–87 (Jt Vice-Chm., 1982–83).

ROBINSON, Ann; *see* Robinson, M. A.

ROBINSON, Dr Ann; Director General, National Association of Pension Funds Ltd, 1995–2000; *b* 28 Jan. 1937; *d* of Edwin Samuel James and Dora (*née* Thorne); *m* 1961, Michael Finlay Robinson; two *s*. *Educ:* St Anne's Coll., Oxford (MA); McGill Univ. (MA, PhD). Financial journalist, Beaverbrook Newspapers, 1959–61; University Lecturer: Durham, 1962–65; Bristol, 1970–72; Bath, 1972–75; Cardiff, 1972–89 (Sen. Lectr, 1987–89); Head of Policy Unit, Inst. of Dirs, 1989–95. Director: Great Western Hldgs, 1996–98; Almeida Capital, 2001–09. ICSA Vis. Prof. of Corporate Governance, Bournemouth Univ., 2000–03. Member: Equal Opportunities Commn, 1980–85; Econ. and Social Cttee, EEC, 1986–93 (Chm., Industry Section, 1990–92); Welsh Arts Council, 1991–93; HEFCW, 1993–97; Competition (formerly Monopolies and Mergers) Commn, 1993–99; Bd, Harwich Haven Authy, 1999–2006; Pensions Protection and Investments Accreditation Bd, 2001–06; London Pensions Fund Authy, 2001–05. Dir, WNO, 1992–94. Member: Council, RIIA, 1991–97; Bd of Academic Govs, Richmond Coll., London, 1992–2014; Bd of Govs, Commonwealth Inst., 1992–97; Council, Clifton Coll. (Vice-Chm. Council, 1998–2003); Council, City Univ., 1998–2002. Trustee: Foundn for Business Responsibilities, 1997–2003; Dixons Retirement and Employee Security Scheme, 2000–06; Wye Valley Chamber Music Festival, 2009–. Contested (C) S E Wales, EP election, 1979. *Publications:* Parliament and Public Spending, 1978; (jtly) Tax Policy Making in the United Kingdom, 1984; articles in acad. jls and chapters on public expenditure control by Parliament. *Recreation:* gardening. *Address:* Northridge House, Usk Road, Shirenewton, Monmouthshire NP16 6RZ. *Club:* Reform.

ROBINSON, Anne Josephine; journalist; *b* 26 Sept. 1944; *d* of late Bernard James Robinson and Anne Josephine Robinson (*née* Wilson); *m* 1st, 1968, Charles Martin Wilson, *qv* (marr. diss. 1973); one *d*; 2nd, 1980, John Penrose (marr. diss. 2008). *Educ:* Farnborough Hill Convent; Les Ambassadrices, Paris. Reporter: Daily Mail, 1967–68; Sunday Times, 1968–77; Daily Mirror: Women's Editor, 1979–80; Asst Editor, 1980–93; columnist, 1983–93; columnist: Today, 1993–95; The Times, 1993–95; The Sun, 1995–97; The Express, 1997–98; The Times, 1998–2001; The Daily Telegraph, 2003–05. Presenter: Anne Robinson Show, Radio 2, 1988–93; Watchdog, 1993–2001 and 2009; Guess Who Is Coming to Dinner, 2003; for BBC Television: Points of View, 1987–98 (also writer); Weekend Watchdog, 1997–2001; Going for a Song, 2000; The Weakest Link, 2000–12 (also USA, 2001–02); Test the Nation, 2002–07; Outtake TV, 2003–09; Travels with an Unfit Mother, 2004; What's the Problem?, 2005; Watchdog with Anne Robinson, 2009–; My Life in Books, 2011–12; Britain's Spending Secrets, 2015. Hon. Fellow, Liverpool John Moores Univ., 1996. *Publications:* Memoirs of an Unfit Mother, 2001. *Recreations:* dogs, houses, gossip, decently cooked food, having opinions. *Address:* PO Box 50445, London, W8 9BE. *E:* office@victoriagrove.co.uk.

ROBINSON, Sir Anthony, (Sir Tony), Kt 2013; actor and writer; Vice-President, British Actors' Equity, 1996–2000; Member, Labour Party National Executive, 2001–04; Ambassador, Alzheimer's Society, since 2009; *b* 15 Aug. 1946; *s* of Leslie Kenneth Robinson and Phyllis Joan Robinson; one *s* one *d*; *m* 2011, Louise Hobbs. *Educ:* Wanstead Co. High Sch.; Central Sch. of Speech and Drama. Numerous appearances as child actor, incl. original stage version of Oliver!; theatre dir, 1968–78; work with Chichester Festival Th., RSC and NT; nationwide tour of 40 Years On, 1997; Tony Robinson's Cunning Night Out (on tour), 2005–07; The Wind in the Willows, Duchess Th., 2013; *television* includes: Joey (documentary); Baldrick in Blackadder (4 series), 1983–89; Sheriff of Nottingham in Maid Marian and Her Merry Men (4 series) (also writer); My Wonderful Life (3 series), 1997–99; presenter of TV programmes, incl. Blood and Honey (OT series) (also writer); Time Team (20 series); The Good Book Guide; The Worst Jobs in History (2 series); The Real Da Vinci Code, 2005; Me & My Mum, 2006; Tony Robinson's Crime and Punishment, 2008; Blitz Street, 2010; Birth of Britain, 2010; Tony Robinson's Gods and Monsters, 2011; Tony Robinson's Walking Through History, 2012; Tony Robinson's World War One, 2014; Time Crashers, 2015; documentaries in Africa for Comic Relief; writer for TV: Fat Tulip's Garden; Odysseus: the greatest hero of them all (13 episodes); *film:* The Never Ending Story III. Hon. MA: Bristol, 1999; East London, 2003; Hon. PhD: Open, 2005; Exeter, 2005; Oxford Brookes, 2006; Chester, 2011. RTS and BAFTA awards; Internat. Prix Jeunesse. *Publications:* for children: Boodicaa and the Romans, 1989; Robert the Incredible Chicken, 1989; Keeping Mum/Driving Ambition, 1992; Hit Plays, 1992; Blood and Honey: story of Saul and David, 1993; Tony Robinson's Kings and Queens, 2000; Maid Marian and Her Merry Men series: How the Band Got Together, 1989; Beast of Bolsover, 1990; Whitish Knight, 1990; Rabies in Love, 1991; Worksop Egg Fairy, 1991; It Came From Outer Space, 1992; with Richard Curtis: Odysseus Goes Through Hell, 1996; Odysseus, Superhero!, 1996; Theseus, Monster-killer!, 1996; The Worst Children's Jobs in History, 2005 (Blue Peter Factual Book of the Yr, 2005); Bad Kids, 2009; (series) Tony Robinson's Weird World of Wonders, 2012–14 (Blue Peter Factual Book of the Yr, 2013, for World War II); for adults: (with Mick Aston) Archaeology is Rubbish: a beginners guide to excavation, 2002; In Search of British Heroes, 2003; The Worst Jobs in History, 2004; Tony Robinson's History of Australia, 2011. *Recreations:* politics, Bristol City Football Club. *Address:* c/o Jeremy Hicks Associates, 3 Stedham Place, WC1A 1HU.

ROBINSON, Anthony John de G.; *see* de Garr Robinson.

ROBINSON, Rt Rev. Anthony William; *see* Wakefield, Area Bishop of.

ROBINSON, Ariadne Elizabeth S.; *see* Singares Robinson.

ROBINSON, Bill; *see* Robinson, Patrick W.

ROBINSON, Boz; *see* Robinson, Air Vice-Marshal B. L.

ROBINSON, Brian Gordon, CBE 1996; QFSM 1992; FIFireE; Commissioner for Fire and Emergency Planning (formerly Chief Officer, then Chief Fire Officer and Chief Executive), London Fire Brigade, 1991–2003; *b* 21 April 1947; *s* of Gordon and Theodora Robinson, Colchester, Essex; *m* 1996, Charmian Lesley Houslander-Green. FIFireE 1992. Joined London Fire Brigade, 1968; Accelerated Promotion Course, 1974, Sen. Course Dir, 1982, Fire Service Coll.; Divl Comdr, London, 1983; Asst Chief Officer, 1985; Dep. Chief Officer, 1990. Pres., Assoc. for Specialist Fire Protection. OStJ 1992. *Recreation:* golf. *Address:* c/o London Fire Brigade Headquarters, 8 Albert Embankment, SE1 7SD. *T:* (020) 7587 4000.

ROBINSON, Air Vice-Marshal Brian Lewis, (Boz); Managing Director, Boz! Ltd, 2002–07; Joint Managing Director, Boz Asia Co. Ltd, since 2007; *b* 2 July 1936; *s* of Frederick Lewis Robinson and Ida (*née* Croft); *m* 1962, Ann Faithfull; one *s* one *d*. *Educ:* Bradford Grammar Sch. (Queen's Scout). Served, 1956–76: 74 Sqn; Oxford Univ. Air Sqn; 73 Sqn; Canberra Trials and Tactical Evaluation Unit; Directorate of Flight Safety, MoD; 60 Course RAF Staff Coll., 1970; RAF Valley; 2 ATAF Germany; Canadian Forces Comd and Staff Coll., and 411 Air Reserve Sqn, Toronto; Chief Instr, 4 Flying Trng Sch., 1976–78, OC, RAF Valley, 1978–80; Internat. Mil. Staff HQ, NATO, Brussels, 1980–82; Defence and Air Attaché, Moscow, 1983–86; Dir of Orgn and Quartering, RAF, MoD, 1986–88; RAF Long-term Deployment Study, 1988; AOC Directly Administered Units, and AO Admin, HQ Strike Command, 1989–91. Sen. Partner, Belmont Consultants, then Sole Exec., Belmont Aviation, 1991–2001. Display pilot: (Gnat), Kennet Aviation, 1997–2001; (Hunter): Classic Jets, 2001–02; Thunder City, Cape Town, 2001–02; Hunter Flying Club, 2002; (Gnat and Hunter), Delta Jets, 2002; Flying Instr, Bristol Flying Centre, 1997–2001; Mem., British Precision Flying Team, Krakow, 1998. Editor, Flight Safety section, Air Clues, 1967–69. RAF Rally Champion, 1962; Mem., RAF and British Bobsleigh teams, 1967–74. President: 74 Tiger Sqdn Assoc., 1992–2008; British Aviation Archaeol. Council, 2000–. Gov., Edgehill Coll., Bideford, 1997–2001. Humanities Teacher, Utaloy Internat. Sch., Guangzhou, China, 2006–07. FRAeS 2000–08. King Hussein Meml Sword, Royal Internat. Air Tattoo Cottesmore, 2001. *Recreations:* writing, travel. *Address:* The Old White House, Dixton Road, Monmouth NP25 3PL. *E:* bozbozrob@gmail.com.
See also (Sir) N. J. Wakeley (Bt).

ROBINSON, Dame Carol Vivien, DBE 2013; PhD; FRS 2004; Royal Society Professor of Chemistry and Dr Lee's Professor of Chemistry, University of Oxford, since 2009; Fellow of Exeter College, Oxford, since 2009; *b* 10 April 1956; *m* 1982, Martin Robinson; two *s* one *d*. *Educ:* Canterbury Coll. of Technol. (ONC; HNC); Medway and Maidstone Coll.; RSC (grad.); Univ. of Swansea (MSc); Churchill Coll., Cambridge (PhD 1982). Res. Technician, Pfizer, 1972–79; MRC Trng Fellow, Univ. of Bristol, 1982–83; Post Doctoral Fellow, 1993–95, Royal Soc. Univ. Res. Fellow, 1995–2001, Univ. of Oxford; Prof. of Mass Spectrometry, 2001–06, Royal Soc. Res. Prof. of Biol Chemistry, 2006–09, Univ. of Cambridge. FMedSci 2009. Biemann Medal, Amer. Soc. for Mass Spectrometry, 2003; Rosalind Franklin Award, Royal Soc., 2004. *Publications:* 120 pubns inc. book chapters, etc. *Recreations:* gardening, sport. *Address:* Exeter College, Oxford OX1 3DP.

ROBINSON, Christopher John, CVO 1992 (LVO 1986); CBE 2004; Fellow, since 1991, and Organist and Director of Music, 1991–2003, St John's College, Cambridge; *b* 20 April 1936; *s* of late Prebendary John Robinson, Malvern, Worcs; *m* 1962, Shirley Ann, *d* of H. F. Churchman, Sawston, Cambs; one *s* one *d*. *Educ:* St Michael's Coll., Tenbury; Rugby; Christ Church, Oxford (BMus); MA (Oxon and Cantab). FRCO; Hon. RAM. Assistant Organist of Christ Church, Oxford, 1955–58; Assistant Organist of New College, Oxford, 1957–58; Music Master at Oundle School, 1959–62; Assistant Organist of Worcester Cathedral, 1962–63; Organist and Master of Choristers: Worcester Cathedral, 1963–74; St George's Chapel, Windsor Castle, 1975–91; Acting Dir of Music, Clare Coll., Cambridge, 2005–06. Conductor: City of Birmingham Choir, 1963–2002; Oxford Bach Choir, 1977–97; Leith Hill Musical Festival, 1977–80. President: RCO, 1982–84; Friends of Cathedral Music, 2004–June 2016; Vice-Pres., Herbert Howells Soc., 2012–. Chm., Ouseley Trust, 2002–07. Hon. Fellow, Birmingham City Univ. (formerly Birmingham Poly., later Univ. of Central England), 1990. Hon. FGCM 2002. Hon. MMus Birmingham, 1987; MusD Lambeth, 2002. *Recreations:* watching cricket, travel. *Address:* St John's College, Cambridge CB2 1TP.

ROBINSON, Sir Christopher Philipse, 8th Bt *cr* 1854, of Toronto; *b* 10 Nov. 1938; *s* of Christopher Robinson, QC (*d* 1974) (*g s* of 1st Bt) and Neville Taylor (*d* 1991), *d* of Rear-Adm. Walter Rockwell Gherardi, USN; *S* kinsman, Sir John Beverley Robinson, 7th Bt, 1988, but his name does not appear on the Official Roll of the Baronetage; *m* 1962, Barbara Judith, *d* of late Richard Duncan (marr. diss.); two *s* (and one *s* decd). *Heir:* *s* Peter Duncan Robinson [*b* 31 July 1967; *m* Jennifer Ann Martin; two *s* one *d*].

ROBINSON, Prof. Colin, FSS, FEI; Professor of Economics, University of Surrey, 1968–2000, now Emeritus; Editorial Director, Institute of Economic Affairs, 1992–2002; *b* 7 Sept. 1932; *s* of late James Robinson and Elsie (*née* Brownhill); *m* 1st, 1957, Olga West; two *s*; 2nd, 1983, Eileen Marshall; two *s* two *d*. *Educ:* Univ. of Manchester (BA Econ). FSS 1970; FEI (FInstPet 1985). Economist, Procter and Gamble, 1957–60; Economist, subseq. Head of Economics Dept, Esso Petroleum Co., 1960–66; Econ. Advr, Natural Gas, Esso Europe, 1966–68. Mem., Monopolies and Mergers Commn, 1992–98. Fellow, Soc. of Business Economists, 2000. Outstanding Contribution to the Profession Award, Internat. Assoc. for Energy Economics, 1998. *Publications:* Business Forecasting, 1970; (with Jon Morgan) North Sea Oil in the Future, 1978; (with Eileen Marshall) Can Coal Be Saved?, 1985; Energy Policy, 1993; Arthur Seldon: a life for liberty, 2009; papers on energy economics and regulation in learned jls. *Recreations:* walking, music, home improvements.

ROBINSON, Cynthia Ann; consultant in strategic development, since 2010; Chief Executive, Extend Exercise, since 2013; *b* 28 June 1951; *d* of Andrew Ian Robinson and Alys Congreve Sandys Robinson. *Educ:* Univ. of Nottingham (BSc Hons Biochem. 1972). Registered nutritionist, 1991; CDipAF 1993. Res. Biochemist, Roche Products, 1972–75; Res. Nutritionist, Slimming Magazine, 1975–80; Mkt Res. Exec., AGB Ltd, 1980–82; consultant nutritionist, 1982–; Hd of Communications, Cow & Gate, 1991–93; Dir of Communications, Marie Curie Cancer Care, 1993–98; Chief Exec., Fitness Industry Assoc., 1998–99; Chief Exec., Queen Elizabeth's Foundn for Disabled People, 2001–10; Personal Trainer, 2012, Exercise Referral, 2013, SkillsActive. Dir, RYA, 1999–2002, 2004–07. Mem. Council, Royal Inst. of Navigation, 2004–11 (Chm., Small Craft Gp, 2007–14). Freeman, Hon. Co. of Air Pilots (formerly GAPAN), 2005. Vice Cdre, City Livery Yacht Club, 2014 (Rear Cdre, 2013). FRIN 2004. J. E. D. Williams Medal for Outstanding Service, Royal Inst. of Navigation, 2014. *Publications:* (contrib.) Good Health Fact Book, 1995. *Recreations:* sailing (RYA Yachtmaster Offshore instructor, 1983–, examiner, 1994–), gliding (British Gliding Assoc. instructor, 1984–90), flying. *Address:* c/o Royal Institute of Navigation, 1 Kensington Gore, SW7 2AT.

ROBINSON, Prof. David Antony, PhD; Director, International Corporate Coaching Pty Ltd, 2003–11; Vice Chancellor and President, Monash University, 1997–2002; *b* 24 July 1941; *s* of Harry Robinson and Marjorie Newcombe Robinson (*née* Patchett); *m* 1st, 1965, Marjorie Rose Collins (marr. diss. 1970); 2nd, 1976, Yvonne Ann Salter (marr. diss. 2003); 3rd, 2006, Gael Edith Hayes. *Educ:* Royal Masonic Schs; University Coll., Swansea (BA, PhD 1967). University College, Swansea: Res. Asst, Dept of Sociol., 1964–67; Res. Fellow, DHSS Med. Sociol. Res. Centre, 1967–71; Lectr, then Sen. Lectr, DHSS-MRC Addiction Res. Unit, Inst. of Psychiatry, Univ. of London, 1974–80; University of Hull: Sen. Lectr and Actg Dir, 1980–82, Dir, 1982–91, Inst. for Health Studies; Prof. of Health Studies, 1984–91; Hd of Dept, Social Policy and Professional Studies, 1985–86; Dean, Sch. of Social and Pol Scis, 1986–89; Pro Vice-Chancellor, 1989–91; Co-Dir, ESRC Addiction Res. Centre, Univs of Hull and York, 1983–88; Dir, WHO Collaborating Centre for Res. and Trng in Psycho-social and Econ. Aspects of Health, 1986–91; Vice-Chancellor and Pres., Univ. of S Australia, 1992–96, Prof. Emeritus, 1999. Member: Editl Bd, Brit. Jl of Addiction, 1978–89; Editl Adv. Bd, Sociol. of Health and Illness, 1987–90. Member: Exec. Council of Soc. for Study of Addictions, 1979–82; Exec. Cttee, Nat. Council on Alcoholism, 1979–82; Exec. Cttee, Nat. Council on Gambling, 1980–87; Health Services Res. Cttee, MRC, 1981–84; Social Affairs Cttee, ESRC, 1982–85. Member: Australian Vice Chancellors Cttee, 1992–2002, Dir, 1995–96; Business/Higher Educn Round Table, 1992–97 (Dir, 1995–98); Australian Higher Educn Industrial Assoc., 1992–97 (Mem., Exec. Cttee, 1993–97; Vice Pres., 1995–97); Univ. Grants Cttee, HK, 2002; Aust. Govt Rep., Univ. Grants Cttee, Univ. of S Pacific, 2001–02. Chm., VERNet Pty Ltd, 2005–07. Director: Open Learning Agency of Australia Pty Ltd, 1994–2002; Foundn for Family and Private Business, 1997–2000; Monash Univ. Sunway Campus Malaysia Sdn Bhd, 1998–2002; Monash Univ. S Africa Ltd, 2000–02; Monash Southern Africa (Pty) Ltd, 2000–02; Vice-Chm., Olympic Games Knowledge Services Inc., 2002. Chm. Council, Victorian Inst. of Forensic Mental Health, 1998–2000. FAIM 1993; FAICD 2005. FRSA 1990. *Publications:* (jtly) Hospitals, Children and their Families, 1970; The Process of Becoming Ill, 1971; Patients, Practitioners and Medical Care: aspects of medical sociology, 1973, 2nd edn 1978; From Drinking to Alcoholism: a sociological commentary, 1976; (ed jtly) Studies in Everyday Medical Life, 1976; (with S. Henry) Self-help and Health: mutual aid for modern problems, 1977; Talking Out of Alcoholism: the self-help process of Alcoholics Anonymous, 1979; (with Y. Robinson) From Self-help to Health: a guide to self-help groups, 1979; (ed) Alcohol Problems: reviews, research and recommendations, 1979; (with P. Tether) Preventing Alcohol Problems: a guide to local action, 1986; (ed jtly) Local Action on Alcohol Problems, 1989; (ed jtly) Controlling Legal Addictions, 1989; (ed jtly) Manipulating Consumption: information, law and voluntary controls, 1990; (with A. Maynard et al) Social Care and HIV-AIDS, 1993; contrib. numerous pamphlets, book chapters and papers in learned and professional jls. *Recreations:* walking, bridge, painting, cinema. *Address:* 55/1 Sandilands Street, South Melbourne, Vic 3205, Australia. *E:* robinsond@ozemail.com.au. *Club:* Melbourne.

ROBINSON, (David) Duncan, CBE 2008; DL; Director and Marlay Curator, Fitzwilliam Museum, Cambridge, 1995–2007; Master, Magdalene College, Cambridge, 2002–12 (Hon. Fellow, 2012); Deputy Vice-Chancellor, University of Cambridge, 2005–12; *b* 27 June 1943; *s* of Tom and Ann Robinson; *m* 1967, Elizabeth Anne Sutton; one *s* two *d*. *Educ:* King Edward VI Sch., Macclesfield; Clare Coll., Cambridge (MA); Yale Univ. (Mellon Fellow, 1965–67; MA). Asst Keeper of Paintings and Drawings, 1970–76, Keeper, 1976–81, Fitzwilliam Museum, Cambridge; Fellow and Coll. Lectr, Clare Coll., Cambridge, 1975–81; Dir, Yale Center for British Art, New Haven, Conn, and Chief Exec., Paul Mellon Centre for Studies in British Art, London, 1981–95; Adjunct Prof. of History of Art, and Fellow of Berkeley Coll., Yale Univ., 1981–95; Professorial Fellow, Clare Coll., Cambridge, 1995–2002, Fellow Emeritus, 2002. Mem. Cttee of Management, Kettle's Yard, Cambridge Univ., 1970–81, 1995–2007 (Chm., Exhibns Cttee, 1970–81). Member: Art Panel, Eastern Arts Assoc., 1973–81 (Chm., 1979–81); Arts Council of GB, 1981 (Mem., 1978–81, Vice-Chm., 1981, Art Panel); Museums and Collections Cttee, English Heritage, 1996–2002; Assoc. of Art Mus. Dirs (USA), 1982–88; Bd of Managers, Lewis Walpole Library, Farmington Ct, USA,

1982–95; Council of Management, The William Blake Trust, 1983–2012; Vis. Cttee, Dept of Paintings Conservation, Metropolitan Museum of Art, NY, 1984–94; Walpole Soc., 1983–2005 (Mem. Council, 1985–87, 1995–2000); Connecticut Acad. of Arts and Scis, 1991–95; Univ. Museums Gp, 1995–2002 (Sec., 1997–99); Adv. Council, Paul Mellon Centre for Studies in British Art, 1997–2002; Arts and Humanities Res. Bd, 1998–2003; Chairman: Art and Artifacts Indemnity Adv. Panel (USA), 1992–94 (Mem., 1991); Jardine Foundn Scholarship Cttee, Hong Kong, 2006–12; City of Cambridge Public Art Panel, 2009–15. Member, Board of Directors: New Haven Colony Historical Soc., 1991–94; Amer. Friends of Georgian Gp, 1992–95; E of England Museums, Libraries and Archives Council (formerly Mus Service East of England), 2001–03; The Burlington Magazine Publications Ltd, 2003–11. Gov., Yale Univ. Press, 1987–95. Trustee: Yale Univ. Press, London, 1990–; Charleston Trust (USA), 1990–92; Fitzwilliam Mus. Trust, 1995–2007; Wingfield Arts Trust, 2001–03; Burlington Magazine Foundn, 2003–; Crafts Study Centre, Surrey Inst. of Art and Design, 2004–08; Henry Moore Foundn, 2006–14 (Chm., 2008–14); Royal Collection, 2006–12; The Chantrey Bequest, 2010–; Chairman of Trustees: Prince's Drawing Sch., 2007–13; Cambridge and County Folk Museum, 2011–13; Hon. Treas., NW Essex Collection Trust, 2003–07 (Chm., 2002–03). Governor: SE Museums Service, 1997–99; Gainsborough's House Soc., 1998–2002. Pres., Friends of Stanley Spencer Gall., Cookham, 1998–; Vice-Pres., NADFAS, 2000–06. FRSA 1990; FSA 2006. DL Cambs, 2004. Organised Arts Council exhibitions: Stanley Spencer, 1975; William Nicholson, 1980. *Publications:* Companion Volume to the Kelmscott Chaucer, 1975, re-issued as Morris, Burne-Jones and the Kelmscott Chaucer, 1982; Stanley Spencer, 1979, rev. edn 1990; (with Stephen Wildman) Morris & Company in Cambridge, 1980; Town, Country, Shore & Sea: English Watercolours from van Dyck to Paul Nash, 1982; Man and Measure: the paintings of Tom Wood, 1996; The Yale Center for British Art: a tribute to the genius of Louis I. Kahn, 1997; The Fitzwilliam Museum 1848–1998: one hundred and fifty years of collecting, 1998; catalogues; articles and reviews in Apollo, Burlington Magazine, etc. *Address:* c/o Magdalene College, Cambridge CB3 0AG. *Club:* Oxford and Cambridge.

ROBINSON, David Julien; film critic and historian and festival director; *b* 6 Aug. 1930; *s* of Edward Robinson and Dorothy Evelyn (*née* Overton). *Educ:* Lincoln Sch.; King's Coll., Cambridge (BA Hons). Associate Editor, Sight and Sound, and Editor, Monthly Film Bulletin, 1956–58; Programme Dir, NFT, 1959; Film Critic: Financial Times, 1959–74; The Times, 1973–92; Editor, Contrast, 1962–63. Director: Garrett Robinson Co., 1987–88; The Davids Film Co., 1988–2013. Dir, Edinburgh Film Fest., 1989–91; Director: Channel 4 Young Film Maker of the Year Comp., Edinburgh Film Fest., 1992–95; Pordenone Silent Film Fest., Italy, 1997–. Has curated exhibns, incl. Musique et Cinéma muet, Musée d'Orsay, Paris, 1995. Films produced and directed: Hetty King—Performer, 1969; (Co-dir) Keeping Love Alive, 1987; (Co-dir) Sophisticated Lady, 1989. *Publications:* Hollywood in the Twenties, 1969; Buster Keaton, 1969; The Great Funnies, 1972; World Cinema, 1973, 2nd edn 1980 (US edn The History of World Cinema, 1974, 1980); Chaplin: the mirror of opinion, 1983; Chaplin: his life and art, 1985, 2001; (ed and trans.) Luis Buñuel (J. F. Aranda); (ed and trans.) Cinema in Revolution (anthology); (ed jtly) The Illustrated History of the Cinema, 1986; Music of the Shadows, 1990; Masterpieces of Animation 1833–1908, 1991; Richard Attenborough, 1992; Georges Méliès, 1993; Lantern Images: iconography of the magic lantern 1440–1880, 1993; Sight and Sound Chronology of the Cinema, 1994–95; Musique et cinéma muet, 1995; Charlot—entre rires et larmes, 1995; Peepshow to Palace, 1995; (jtly) Light and Image: incunabula of the motion picture, 1996; Alexander Shiryaev, Master of Movement, 2009; The World of Limelight, 2014. *Recreations:* collecting optical toys, model theatres. *Address:* 1 Partis College, Bath BA1 3QD. *T:* (01225) 465838.

ROBINSON, Derek Anthony, DPhil; Keeper, Science Museum, London, 1978–99; *b* 21 April 1942; *e s* of late Charles Frederick Robinson and Mary Margaret Robinson; *m* 1965, Susan Gibson (*d* 1991); two *s*. *Educ:* Hymers Coll., Hull; The Queen's Coll., Oxford (Hastings Scholar; BA 1963; MA, DPhil 1967). MRSC 2001. Post-doctoral Res. Fellow, Dept of Chemistry, Univ. of Reading, 1967–69; Mem. scientific staff, Molecular Pharmacology Unit of MRC, Cambridge, 1969–72; Sen. Asst in Res., Dept of Haematol Medicine, Cambridge Univ. Med. Sch., 1972–74; Science Museum: Asst Keeper I, Dept of Chem., 1974–77; Dep. Keeper (formerly Asst Keeper I), Wellcome Mus. of History of Medicine, and Sec. of Adv. Council, 1977–78; Keeper, Dept of Museum Services, 1978–87; Keeper, Dept of Physical Scis, later Head of Sci. Gp, then Head of Phys. Scis and Engrg Gp, 1987–98; Asst Dir (actg) and Hd of Collections, 1998–99. Mem., British Nat. Cttee for History of Sci., Medicine and Technology, 1987–88; Mem., CGLI, 1984–; Dir, Bd, Mus. Documentation Assoc., 1989–92. Trustee, Nat. Gas Mus., 1999–. Hon. Sec., Artefacts annual internat. confs, 2000–09. *Publications: contributions to:* 2nd edn Acridines, ed R. M. Acheson, 1973; Vol. VI, The History of Technology, ed T. I. Williams, 1978; Cambridge General Encyclopaedia, ed D. Crystal, 1990; Making of the Modern World: milestones of science and technology, ed N. Cossons, 1992; Instruments of Science: an historical encyclopaedia, ed R. F. Bud and D. J. Warner, 1998; Musei, saperi e culture, Atti del Convegno, ed M. Gregorio, 2002; (ed jtly and contrib.) Chymica Acta: an autobiographical memoir, by Frank Greenaway, 2007; papers on heterocyclic chemistry, molecular pharmacol., and leukaemia chemotherapy, in Jl Chem. Soc., Brit. Jl Pharmacol., and Biochem. Soc. Trans. *Recreations:* living and gardening in France, travel. *Address:* 3 Broadwater Avenue, Letchworth Garden City, Herts SG6 3HE. *T:* (01462) 686961. *E:* derekanthonyrobinson@gmail.com. *Club:* Athenæum.

ROBINSON, Dickon Hugh Wheelwright, CBE 2003; RIBA; Member: Commission for Architecture and the Built Environment, 2000–07; Cathedrals Fabric Commission for England, since 2009; *b* 28 Dec. 1945; *s* of Hugh and Nancy Robinson (*née* Bartlett); *m* 1969, Charlotte Louise Clifton (*née* Gilmore); three *s* one *d*. *Educ:* St George's Sch., Hong Kong; King's Sch., Bruton; Portsmouth Coll. of Art (Dip Arch). RIBA 1971. Dept of Architecture, GLC, 1966–67; Scientific Control Systems (SCION), 1969–74; Sir John Burnet Tait Architects (hosp. design partnership), 1972–74; Westwood, Piet Poole and Smart, Architects, 1974–75; Housing Dept, Camden LBC, 1976–88; Dir, Develt and Tech. Services, Peabody Trust, 1988–2004; Man. Dir, Peabody Enterprises, 2004–05. Vis. Prof., Mackintosh Sch. of Architecture, 2004–09. Retained Advr, Grainger Trust plc, 2004–08; Mem., Urban Regeneration Panel, Bath & NE Som DC, 2004–. Chairman: Cabespace, 2003–07; Building Futures, 2005; Living Architecture, 2007–. Mem., Urban Panel, English Heritage, 2000. Founder Member: Save Piccadilly Campaign, 1972–74; and First Chm., Soho Housing Assoc., 1973–80. Mem., Policy Cttee, British Property Fedn, 2000–03. Member: Mgt Cttee, Vision for London, 1994–98; Mgt Cttee, Centrepoint, 1995–99; Council, Urban Villages Forum, 1996–99; Mgt Cttee, St Mungo's, 1999–2000. Mem., Foyer Fedn for Youth, 1992 (Chm., 1994–2001). FRSA 1995. *Recreations:* twentieth century fine and applied art, architecture and books, apples, cider-making, orchards and trees, challenging received wisdom. *Address:* 4 Morgan House, 127 Long Acre, Covent Garden, WC2E 9AA. *E:* dickon@ambooco.co.uk. *Club:* Architecture.

ROBINSON, Sir Dominick Christopher L.; *see* Lynch-Robinson.

ROBINSON, Rt Rev. Donald William Bradley, AO 1984; Archbishop of Sydney and Metropolitan of New South Wales, 1982–93; *b* 9 Nov. 1922; *s* of Rev. Richard Bradley Robinson and Gertrude Marston Robinson (*née* Ross); *m* 1949, Marie Elizabeth Taubman; three *s* one *d*. *Educ:* Sydney Church of England Grammar Sch.; Univ. of Sydney (BA); Queens' Coll., Cambridge (MA). Australian Army, 1941–45, Lieut Intell. Corps, 1944. Deacon 1950, Sydney; priest 1951; Curate, Manly, NSW, 1950–52; St Philip's, Sydney, 1952–53; Lecturer: Moore Coll., 1952–81 (Vice-Principal, 1959–72); Sydney Univ., 1964–81; Asst Bishop, Diocese of Sydney (Bishop in Parramatta), 1973–82. Hon. ThD Aust. Coll. of Theology, 1979. *Address:* 1 Jubilee Avenue, Pymble, NSW 2073, Australia. *T:* (2) 94493033.

ROBINSON, Duncan; *see* Robinson, David D.

ROBINSON, Emma-Jane, PhD; heritage consultant and researcher; University Librarian, University of London Library, 1994–2003; *b* 19 Aug. 1953; *d* of late Harold Frederick Wensley Cory and Yvonne Margaret Cory (*née* Hales); *m* 1974, Dr David John Robinson. *Educ:* Westonbirt Sch.; University Coll. of Wales, Aberystwyth (BSc); Inst. of Educn, London Univ. (PhD 2008). MCLIP (ALA 1981). Asst Librarian, then Sub-Librarian, Univ. of London Liby, 1989–94. Member: Consortium of Univ. Res. Libraries, 1994–2003; Consortium of European Res. Libraries, 1994–2003; Res. Libraries Gp, 1994–2003; BL Arts, Humanities and Social Scis Adv. Bd, 1997–2003. Chair and Co. Dir, Frome Heritage Mus., 2014–. FRSA 1995. *Publications:* articles on cultural landscapes in academic and professional jls. *Recreations:* walking, botanising, archaeologising. *Address:* 101 Colindeep Lane, Colindale, NW9 6DD.

ROBINSON, Eric; Chief Executive, Wirral Council, since 2015; *b* 28 May 1960; *s* of Eric Robinson and Margaret Robinson; partner, Jacqueline Pratt; one *s* two *d*. *Educ:* University Coll. Cardiff (BSc; DMS). Qualified as social worker, 1982; Assistant Director of Social Services: Knowsley MBC, 1995–97; Lincs CC, 1997–2001; Director of Social Services: Enfield LBC, 2001–03; Cambridgeshire CC, 2003–05; Corporate Dir, Social Care and Health, 2005–10, Dep. Chief Exec. and Dir for People, 2010–15, Staffordshire CC. *Recreations:* being a father, family life, Liverpool Football Club. *Address:* Wirral Council, Wallasey Town Hall, Brighton Street, Wallasey, Wirral CH44 8ED.

ROBINSON, (Francis) Alastair (Lavie); Group Vice-Chairman, Barclays Bank, 1992–96; *b* 19 Sept. 1937; *s* of late Stephen and Patricia Robinson; *m* 1961, Lavinia Elizabeth Napier; two *d*. *Educ:* Eton. Nat Service, 4th/7th Royal Dragoon Guards, 1956–58 (2nd Lieut). Mercantile Credit: management trainee, 1959; Gen. Manager, 1971; Mem. Board, 1978; Chief Exec. Officer and Pres., Barclays American, USA, 1981; Regional Gen. Manager, Asia-Barclays International, 1984; Barclays Bank: Dir Personnel, 1987; Exec. Dir, UK Ops, 1990–92; Exec. Dir, Banking Div., 1992–96. Non-executive Director: RMC Gp plc, 1996–2005; Marshall of Cambridge (Hldgs) Ltd, 1996–2006; Portman Bldg Soc., 1998–2004. Chm., St Nicholas Hospice, Bury St Edmunds, 2008–12. *Recreations:* music, country pursuits, gardening.

ROBINSON, Prof. Francis Christopher Rowland, CBE 2006; DL; PhD; Professor of History of South Asia, University of London, since 1990; *b* Southgate, 23 Nov. 1944; *s* of late Leonard Robinson and Joyce Robinson (*née* King); *m* 1971, Patricia Courtenay Hughes; one *s* one *d*. *Educ:* County Grammar Sch. for Boys, Bexhill-on-Sea; Trinity Coll., Cambridge (MA, PhD). Prize Fellow, Trinity Coll., Cambridge, 1969–73; Royal Holloway College, then Royal Holloway and Bedford New College, subseq. Royal Holloway, University of London: Lectr in History, 1973–85; Reader, 1985–90; Hd of Dept, 1990–96; Mem., Council, 1991–; Vice-Principal (Res. and Enterprise), 1997–2003; Sen. Vice-Principal, 2003–04; Mem., Academic Cttee, 1994–, Council, 1995–98, London Univ. Vis. Prof., S Asia Program, 1982 and 1986, Near East Program, 1985, Jackson Sch. of Internat. Studies, Univ. of Washington; Directeur d'Etudes Associé, Ecole des Hautes Etudes en Sciences Sociales, Paris, 1985, 2006–; Vis. Fellow, 2005–08, Sultan of Oman Fellow, 2008–11, Sen. Res. Associate, 2011–, Oxford Centre for Islamic Studies; Vis. Prof., Faculty of History, Oxford Univ., 2008–11; Sen. Golding Fellow, Brasenose Coll., Oxford, 2009–13; Mellon Vis. Prof. of Islamic Studies, Univ. of Chicago, 2015–June 2016. Member, Board of Management: Inst. of Histl Research, 1994–99; Inst. of Commonwealth Studies, 1994–99. Mem., SE England - India Adv. Bd, 2007–. Pres., RAS, 1997–2000, 2003–06 (Vice-Pres., 2000–03, 2014–); Mem. Council, Soc. for S Asian Studies, 1998–2002. Trustee: Charles Wallace (Pakistan) Trust, 1999–2006 (Chm. of Trustees, 2001–06); Surrey History Trust, 2001–; Sir Ernest Cassel Educnl Trust, 2005– (Chm., 2008–). Governor: King Edward's Sch., Witley, 2002–12; Jubilee High Sch., Addlestone, 2002–04 (Chm., Jubilee Internat. High Sch. Trust, 2012–13). Ed.-in-Chief, Past in the Present Books, 2006–11. FRSA 1997. DL Surrey, 2011. Iqbal Centenary Medal (Pakistan), 1978; Sheikh Zaki Yamani Medal, Iqbal Acad. UK, 2008. *Publications:* Separatism among Indian Muslims: the politics of the United Provinces' Muslims 1860–1923, 1974, 2nd edn 1993; (with F. Harcourt) Twentieth Century World History: a select bibliography, 1979; Atlas of the Islamic World since 1500, 1982; (with P. R. Brass) Indian National Congress and Indian Society 1885–1985, 1987; Varieties of South Asia Islam, 1988; (ed) Cambridge Encyclopedia of India, Pakistan, Bangladesh, Sri Lanka, 1989; (ed) Cambridge Illustrated History of the Islamic World, 1996; Islam and Muslim History in South Asia, 2000; The 'Ulama of Farangi Mahall and Islamic Culture in South Asia, 2001; Islam, South Asia and the West, 2007; The Mughal Emperors and the Islamic Dynasties of India, Iran and Central Asia 1206–1925, 2007; (ed) New Cambridge History of Islam, vol. 5: Islam in the Age of Western Dominance, 2010; contrib. Modern Asian Studies, Asian Affairs, S Asia, Jl of Islamic Studies, Encyclopedia of Islam, Indian Sociology, etc. *Recreations:* ball games, gardening, people, books, travel, food and wine. *Address:* Department of History, Royal Holloway, University of London, Egham, Surrey TW20 0EX. *T:* (01784) 443300. *Clubs:* Athenæum; Hawks.

ROBINSON, Gavin James; MP (DemU) Belfast East, since 2015; *b* Belfast, 22 Nov. 1984; *s* of John Calvert Robinson and Claire Allison Robinson (*née* Nesbitt); *m* 2011, Lindsay Witherow. *Educ:* Grosvenor Grammar Sch.; Univ. of Ulster (LLB Hons Law); Queen's Univ., Belfast (MA Irish Politics; CPLS). Called to the Bar, NI, 2008; Special Advr to First Minister of NI, 2011–12, 2013–15. Mem. (DemU), Belfast CC, 2010–15 (Alderman, 2012–15; Gp Leader, DUP); Lord Mayor of Belfast, 2012–13. *Recreations:* Rugby, reading, cooking, travel. *Address:* House of Commons, SW1A 0AA. *E:* g.j.robinson@hotmail.co.uk. *Club:* Ulster Reform.

ROBINSON, Geoffrey; MP (Lab) Coventry North West, since March 1976; *b* 25 May 1938; *s* of Robert Norman Robinson and Dorothy Jane Robinson (*née* Skelly); *m* 1967, Marie Elena Giorgio; one *s* one *d*. *Educ:* Emanuel School; Cambridge and Yale Univs. Labour Party Research Assistant, 1965–68; Senior Executive, Industrial Reorganisation Corporation, 1968–70; Financial Controller, British Leyland, 1971–72; Managing Director, Leyland Innocenti, Milan, 1972–73; Chief Exec., Jaguar Cars, Coventry, 1973–75; Chief Exec. (unpaid), Meriden Motor Cycle Workers' Co-op., 1978–80 (Dir, 1980–82). Chm., TransTec PLC, 1986–97. Dir, W Midlands Enterprise Bd, 1980–84. Opposition spokesman on science, 1982–83, on regional affairs and industry, 1983–86; HM Paymaster General, 1997–98. *Publications:* The Unconventional Minister: my life inside New Labour, 2000. *Recreations:* reading, architecture, gardens, football. *Address:* House of Commons, SW1A 0AA. *T:* (020) 7219 3000.

ROBINSON, Dr Geoffrey Walter, CBE 1998; FREng, FIET, FBCS; Director General and Chief Executive, Ordnance Survey, 1998–99; *b* 9 Nov. 1945; *s* of late George Robinson and Edith Margaret (*née* Wilson); *m* 1967, Edwina Jones; one *s* one *d*. *Educ:* Aireborough Grammar Sch.; Nottingham Univ. (BSc 1st Cl. Maths; PhD). IBM UK: Lab. posts, 1969–82; Manager of Scientific Centre, 1982–84; Technical Progs Advr, 1984–85; Technical Dir, 1986–88; Dir, Laboratories, 1988–92, 1994–96; Vice Pres., Networking Software Div., 1994–96; Dir of Technol., 1996–97; Chm., Transarc Corp., 1994–96; Dir, Pirelli UK, 2002–05. Chief Advr on Sci. and Technol., DTI, 1992–94. Dep. Chm., Foundn for Sci. and Technol., 1998–2000. Member: SERC, 1992–94; NERC, 1992–94; PPARC, 1994–98; CCLRC, 1995–98; Bd, QAA, 1997–2000; Bd, British Geol Survey, 2001– (Chm., 2002–04). Liveryman, Co. of Inf. Technologists, 1992. Gov., King Alfred's Coll., Winchester, 1993–99 (Hon. DTech 1992).

FBCS 1994 (Pres., 1995–96); FIET (FIEE 1994) (Vice Pres., IEE, 1998–2000); FREng (FEng 1994). DUniv Leeds Metropolitan, 1997. *Publications:* articles on science, technol. and society. *Recreation:* music. *Address:* Fardale, Hookwood Lane, Ampfield, Romsey, Hants SO51 9BZ. *T:* (023) 8026 1837. *E:* gwr@fardale.org.

ROBINSON, George, MBE 2015; Member (DemU) East Londonderry, Northern Ireland Assembly, since 2003; *b* Limavady, 30 May 1941; *m*; one *s* one *d*. *Educ:* Limavady Tech. Coll. Civil servant, retired. Mem. (DemU), Limavady BC, 1985– (Mayor, 2002). Mem., Regl Develt Cttee, NI Assembly. *Address:* (office) 6–8 Catherine Street, Limavady, Co. Londonderry BT49 9DB.

ROBINSON, Sir Gerrard Jude, (Sir Gerry), Kt 2004; Chairman, Nurse Plus Ltd, since 2015; Director, Fosterplus Ltd, since 2013; *b* 23 Oct. 1948; *s* of Anthony and Elizabeth Ann Robinson; *m* 1st, 1970, Maria Ann Borg (marr. diss. 1990); one *s* one *d*; 2nd, 1990, Heather Peta Leaman; one *s* one *d*. *Educ:* St Mary's Coll., Castlehead. FCMA 1991. Works Accountant, Lesney Products, 1970–74; Financial Controller, Lex Industrial Distribution and Hire, 1974–80; Coca Cola: Finance Dir, 1980–81; Sales and Mkting Dir, 1981–83; Man. Dir, 1983–84; Man. Dir, Grand Metropolitan Contract Services, 1984–87; Chief Exec., Compass Gp plc, 1987–91; Granada Group plc: Chief Exec., 1991–96; Chm., 1996–2000; Dir, 2001–03; Chairman: LWT, 1994–96; ITN, 1995–97; BSkyB, 1995–98; Granada Compass plc, 2000–01; Allied Domecq, 2002–05; Moto Hospitality Ltd, 2006–15. Presenter television documentaries: I'll Show Them Who's Boss, 2003; Can Gerry Robinson Fix the NHS? (series), 2007; Can Gerry Robinson Fix Dementia Care Homes?, 2009; Gerry's Big Decision, 2009; Can't Take It with You, 2011. Chm., Arts Council of England, later Arts Council England, 1998–2004. *Publications:* I'll Show Them Who's Boss: the six secrets of successful management, 2004. *Recreations:* golf, opera, chess, ski-ing, reading, music. *Club:* Wisley Golf.

ROBINSON, Helen Gillian, (Mrs Oliver Prenn), OBE 1992; Chief Executive, The New West End Co., 2000–05; *b* 4 Jan. 1940; *d* of Dr John Christopher Wharton and Gertrude Margaret (*née* Dingwall); *m* 1st, 1959, Philip Henry Robinson, *qv* (marr. diss. 1979); one *d* (one *s* decd); 2nd, 1980, Desmond Preston (*d* 1995); 3rd, 2009, Oliver Prenn. *Educ:* Roedean. Fashion Ed., UK and USA, Vogue Mag., 1960–70; Exec. Ed., Vogue Mag., 1970–75; Dir, Debenhams plc, 1975–86; Gp Mktg Dir, Condé Nast Pubns, 1986–88; Gp Man. Dir, Thomas Goode & Co. Ltd, 1988–93; general marketing and design mgt consultancies, 1993–96; Dir of Mktg, Asprey Gp, 1996–98; Mgt Consultant, MIA Pty Australia, 1999. Non-executive Director: BAA, 1978–95; LRT, 1984–95; London Electricity Plc, 1989–94; Churchill China Plc, 1996–98. Royal College of Art: Mem. Council, 1982–2000 (Vice Chm., 1992–2000); Chm., Staff Cttee, 1985–2000; Sen. Fellow, 2001. Gov. and Trustee (formerly Gov. and Mem., Exec. Cttee), Commonwealth Inst., 1994–2007; Trustee, Commonwealth Educn Trust, 2007–. Mem., Design Mgt Adv. Gp, London Business Sch., 1985–95. World Wide Fund for Nature: Trustee and Chm., WWF (UK) Ltd, 1989–95; Mem., Council of Ambassadors, 1999–2006 (Fellow, 2006–). Mem. Council, Cottage Homes (Retail Trade Charity), 1995–96. FRSA 1990; Hon. FCSD 1994. *Recreations:* performing and visual arts, cooking, nature, family. *Address:* 47 Hyde Park Gate, SW7 5DU. *T:* (020) 7584 8870, *Fax:* (020) 7584 8910.

ROBINSON, Sir Ian, Kt 2000; FREng, FIChemE; Chairman, Ladbrokes plc (formerly Hilton Group), 2001–09; *b* 3 May 1942; *s* of Thomas Mottram Robinson and Eva Iris Robinson (*née* Bird); *m* 1967, Kathleen Crawford Leay; one *s* one *d*. *Educ:* Leeds Univ. (BSc); Harvard Univ. FIChemE 1982; FREng (FEng 1994). With Kellogg International Co. Ltd, 1964–72; Managing Director: Ralph M. Parsons Co. Ltd, 1972–86; John Brown Engrs & Constructors, 1986–92; Dir and Chm., Engrg Div., Trafalgar House plc, 1992–95; Chief Exec., Scottish Power plc, 1995–2001; Chm., Amey plc, 2001–03. Non-executive Director: Siemens plc, 2002–13; Scottish & Newcastle plc, 2004–08; Compass Gp plc, 2006– (Sen. Ind. Dir). Member: Takeover Panel, 2003–; Adv. Bd, CVC Capital Partners, 2004–06. Chm., Scottish Enterprise, 2001–03. *Recreations:* golf, gardening. *Club:* Royal Automobile.

ROBINSON, Iris; *b* 6 Sept. 1949; *d* of Joseph and Mary Collins; *m* 1970, Peter David Robinson, *qv*; two *s* one *d*. *Educ:* Knockbreda Intermediate Sch.; Cregagh Tech. Coll. Mem. (DemU) Castlereagh BC, 1989–2010 (Mayor 1992, 1995, 2000). Mem. (DemU) Strangford, NI Assembly, 1999–2010. MP (DemU) Strangford, 2001–10. *Recreation:* interior design.

ROBINSON, Jancis Mary, (Mrs N. L. Lander), OBE 2003; MW; wine writer and online publisher; *b* 22 April 1950; *d* of late Thomas Edward Robinson and Ann Sheelagh Margaret Robinson (*née* Conacher); *m* 1981, Nicholas Laurence Lander, *qv*; one *s* two *d*. *Educ:* Carlisle and County High Sch. for Girls; St Anne's Coll., Oxford (MA). Editor, Wine & Spirit, 1976–80; Founder and Editor, Drinker's Digest (subseq. Which? Wine Monthly), 1977–82; Editor, Which? Wine Guide, 1980–82; Sunday Times Wine Corresp., 1980–86; Evening Standard Wine Corresp., 1987–88; Financial Times Wine Corresp., 1989–; freelance journalism, particularly on wine, food and people, 1980–; freelance television and radio broadcasting, on various subjects, 1983–; Writer/Presenter: The Wine Programme, 1983 (Glenfiddich Trophy), 1985, 1987; Jancis Robinson Meets…, 1987; Matters of Taste, 1989, 1991; Vintners' Tales, 1992, 1998; Jancis Robinson's Wine Course, 1995 (Glenfiddich Trophy); The Food Chain, 1996; Taste, 1999; wine judging and lecturing, 1983–; Wine Consultant, British Airways, 1995–2010. Director: Eden Productions Ltd, 1989–2003 and 2010–; JancisRobinson.com, 2003–. Proprietor and principal contrib., jancisrobinson.com, 2000–. Mem., Wine Cttee, Royal Household, 2005–. Hon. Pres., Wine and Spirit Educn Trust, 2012–. Freeman, City of London, 2013; Hon. Freeman, Vintners' Co., 2013. DUniv Open, 1997. Officier, Ordre du Mérite Agricole (France), 2010; Comendador da Ordem do Mérito Empresarial (Portugal). *Publications:* The Wine Book, 1979, rev. edn 1983; The Great Wine Book, 1982 (Glenfiddich Award); Masterglass, 1983, rev. edn 1987; How to Choose and Enjoy Wine, 1984; Vines, Grapes and Wines, 1986 (André Simon Meml Prize, Wine Guild Award, Clicquot Book of the Year); Jancis Robinson's Adventures with Food and Wine, 1987; Jancis Robinson on the Demon Drink, 1988; Vintage Timecharts, 1989; (ed) The Oxford Companion to Wine, 1994 (6 internat. awards), 4th edn 2015; Jancis Robinson's Wine Course, 1995, revd edn 2003; Jancis Robinson's Guide to Wine Grapes, 1996; Confessions of a Wine Lover (autobiog.), 1997; Jancis Robinson's Wine Tasting Workbook, 2000; Jancis Robinson's Concise Wine Companion, 2001; (with Hugh Johnson) The World Atlas of Wine, 5th edn 2001 to 7th edn 2013; How to Taste (Wine), 2008; (with Hugh Johnson) Concise World Atlas of Wine, 2009; (with J. Harding and J. Vouillamoz) Wine Grapes, 2012; (with Linda Murphy) American Wine, 2013. *Recreations:* wine, food and words. *E:* jancis@jancisrobinson.com. *W:* www.JancisRobinson.com.

ROBINSON, Jane; *see* Morrice, J.

ROBINSON, Joanna Lesley; *see* Simons, J. L.

ROBINSON, John Harris, CBE 2014; FREng, FIChemE; Chairman, Abbeyfield Society, since 2009; Operating Partner, Duke Street Capital, 2001–10; *b* 22 Dec. 1940; *s* of Thomas and Florence Robinson; *m* 1963, Doreen Alice Gardner; one *s* one *d*. *Educ:* Woodhouse Grove Sch.; Birmingham Univ. (BSc). CEng 1968, FREng (FEng 1998); FIChemE 1983. ICI plc, 1962–65; Fisons plc, 1965–70; PA Consulting Gp, 1970–75; Woodhouse and Rixson, 1975–79; Smith & Nephew plc: Man. Dir, Healthcare Div., 1979–82; Dir, 1982–89; Dep. Chief Exec., 1989–90; Chief Exec., 1990–97; Chm., 1997–2000; Chairman: Low & Bonar PLC, 1997–2001; UK Coal (formerly RJB Mining) plc, 1997–2003; George Wimpey plc, 1999–2007; Railtrack, 2001–02; Paragon Healthcare Gp, 2002–06; Bespak, later Consort Medical plc, 2004–09; Affinity Healthcare Ltd, 2005–10; Oasis Healthcare Ltd, 2007–10; non-executive Director: Delta plc, 1993–2001; Esporta Gp Ltd, 2006–07; Abbeyfield Soc., 2007–. Chm., Healthcare Sector Gp, DTI, 1996–2001; Mem., Industrial Develt Adv. Bd, DTI, 1998–2001. Mem., President's Cttee, CBI, 2001–07 (Chm., Technol. and Innovation Cttee, 1998–2001). Chm., MacRobert Award, RAEng, 2010–14. Governor: Hymers Coll., Hull, 1983–2012; Woodhouse Grove Sch., 2003–13; Chm. Council and Pro-Chancellor, Hull Univ., 1998–2006; Mem., Cttee of Univ. Chairmen, 1998–2006. Trustee: Methodist Ind. Schools Trust, 2012–; Livability, 2014–; RCS, 2014–; Chm., Engineers Trust, 2012–. President: IChemE, 1999; Inst. of Mgt, 2002. Liveryman, Engineers' Co. (Master, 2010–11). CCMI (CIMgt 1991); FRSA 1992. Hon. DEng Birmingham, 2000; DUniv Bradford, 2000; Hon. DBA Lincoln, 2002; Hon. DSc Hull, 2006. *Recreations:* golf, cricket, theatre, long distance walking. *Address:* 146 Artillery Mansions, Victoria Street, SW1H 0HX. *T:* (020) 7222 7303. *Clubs:* Athenæum; Brough Golf (E Yorks).

ROBINSON, Sir John (James Michael Laud), 11th Bt *cr* 1660; Vice Lord-Lieutenant of Northamptonshire, 2008–14; *b* 19 Jan. 1943; *s* of Michael Frederick Laud Robinson (*d* 1971) and Elizabeth (*née* Bridge); *S* grandfather, 1975; *m* 1968, Gayle Elizabeth (*née* Keyes) (High Sheriff, Northants, 2001–02); two *s* one *d*. *Educ:* Eton; Trinity Coll., Dublin (MA, Economics and Political Science). Chartered Financial Analyst. Chairman: St Andrews Hosp., Northampton, 1984–94; Northampton Gen. Hosp. NHS Trust, 1994–99. Pres., British Red Cross, Northants Br., 1982–90. DL Northants, 1984. *Heir:* *s* Mark Christopher Michael Villiers Robinson [*b* 23 April 1972; *m* 1st, 2002, Paula (marr. diss.), *d* of late Donald Hendrick; one *d*; 2nd, 2009, Emma, *d* of Douglas Ainscough; two *d*]. *Address:* Cranford Hall, Cranford, Kettering, Northants NN14 4AL.

ROBINSON, Very Rev. (John) Kenneth; Dean of Gibraltar, 2000–03, now Emeritus; *b* 17 Dec. 1936; *s* of John Robinson and Elizabeth Ellen Robinson (*née* Blackburn); *m* 1965, Merrylyn Kay (*née* Young); one *s* one *d*. *Educ:* Balshaw's Grammar Sch., Leyland, Lancs; KCL (BD 1961). Ordained deacon, 1962, priest 1963; Assistant Curate: St Chad, Poulton-le-Fylde, 1962–65; Lancaster Priory, 1965–66; Chaplain, St John's Army Children's Sch., Singapore, 1966–68; Vicar, Holy Trinity, Colne, Lancs, 1968–70; Dir of Educn, dio. Windward Is, WI, 1971–74; Vicar, St Luke, Skerton, Lancaster, 1974–81; Area Sec., USPG, 1981–91; Minor Canon, St Edmundsbury Cathedral, 1982–91; Chaplain, Greater Lisbon, Portugal, 1991–2000; Archdeacon of Gibraltar, 1994–2002. *Recreations:* swimming, crossword puzzles, cooking. *Address:* 9 Poplar Drive, Coppull, Chorley, Lancs PR7 4LS.

ROBINSON, John Martin Cotton, DPhil, DLitt; FSA; antiquary and writer; *b* 10 Sept. 1948; *s* of John Cotton Robinson and Ellen Anne Cecilia Robinson, *e d* of George Adams, Cape Town, S Africa. *Educ:* Fort Augustus Abbey; St Andrews Univ. (MA 1st Cl. Hons 1970; DLitt 2002); Oriel Coll., Oxford (DPhil 1974). FSA 1979. Historic Buildings Div., GLC, 1974–86; Inspector, English Heritage, 1986–88; Partner, Historic Buildings Consultants, 1989–2013. Librarian to Duke of Norfolk, 1978–. Fitzalan Pursuivant Extraordinary, 1982–88; Maltravers Herald Extraordinary, 1988–. Heraldic Advr, NT, 1996–. Vice-Chm., Georgian Gp, 1990–2014; Chm., Art and Architecture Cttee, Westminster Cathedral, 1996–; Member: Prince of Wales Restoration Cttee, Windsor Castle, 1993–94; NW Cttee, NT, 1994–2005; Trustee, Abbot Hall Art Gall., 1990–. KM 1980. Architectural Editor, Survey of London, 1978–80. *Publications:* The Wyatts, 1979; Georgian Model Farms, 1980; Dukes of Norfolk, 1982; Latest Country Houses, 1983; Cardinal Consalvi, 1987; (with Thomas Woodcock) Oxford Guide to Heraldry, 1988; Temples of Delight, 1990; Guide to Country Houses of the North West, 1991; Treasures of English Churches, 1995; (with David Neave) Francis Johnson, Architect, 2001; The Staffords, 2002; The Regency Country House, 2005; Grass Seed in June, 2006; Arundel Castle, 2011; Felling the Ancient Oaks, How England Lost its Great Estates, 2012; James Wyatt, Architect to George III, 2012; Requisitioned: the British country house in the Second World War, 2014. *Address:* Beckside House, Barbon, Carnforth, Lancs LA6 2LT. *T:* (office) (020) 7831 4398, 07810 188000. *E:* mentmore@historical-buildings.co.uk. *Clubs:* Travellers, Beefsteak, Pratt's, Pitt, XV, Roxburghe (Sec., 1990–).

ROBINSON, Dr Keith; Chief Executive, Wiltshire Council, 2009–10 (Chief Executive, Wiltshire County Council, 1996–2009); *b* 12 July 1951; *s* of Wes and Eileen Robinson; *m* 1976, Anne Elizabeth Wilkinson; one *s* one *d*. *Educ:* Sidney Sussex Coll., Cambridge (MA); Durham Univ. (MA); Manchester Univ. (PhD). Dept of Educn and Science, 1975–85; Leics CC, 1985–88; Bucks CC, 1988–93; Wilts CC, 1993–2009. *Recreations:* jazz, marathon running. *E:* robinson9thelays@btinternet.com.

ROBINSON, Very Rev. Kenneth; *see* Robinson, Very Rev. J. K.

ROBINSON, Sir Kenneth, Kt 2003; PhD; author, educator and educational consultant; *b* 4 March 1950; *s* of James Robinson and Ethel Robinson; *m* 1982, Marie Therese Watts; one *s* one *d*. *Educ:* Univ. of Leeds (BEd 1972); Inst. of Educn, Univ. of London (PhD 1982). Dir, Nat. Curriculum Council for Arts in Schs, 1985–89; Prof. of Educn, Univ. of Warwick, 1989–2001, now Emeritus; Sen. Advr, J. Paul Getty Trust, Los Angeles, 2001–06. Dir of Culture, Creativity and the Young, Council of Europe, 1996–98; Chm., Nat. Adv. Cttee on Creative and Cultural Educn, 1998–99. FRSA 1988. Athena Award, Rhode Island Sch. of Design, 2004; Peabody Medal, Peabody Inst., 2007; Benjamin Franklin Medal, RSA, 2008; LEGO Prize for Internat. Achievement in Educn, 2011; Sir Arthur C. Clarke Imagination Award, 2012. *Publications:* Learning Through Drama, 1977; Exploring Theatre and Education, 1980; (jtly) The Arts in Schools, 1982; The Arts and Higher Education, 1983; The Arts 5–16, 1990; Arts Education in Europe, 1997; All Our Futures: creativity, culture and education, 1999; Out of Our Minds: learning to be creative, 2001, rev. edn 2011; The Element: how finding your passion changes everything, 2009; (jtly) Creative Schools: revolutionizing education from the ground up, 2015. *Recreations:* theatre, music, cinema.

ROBINSON, Kenneth William; Member (UU) Antrim East, Northern Ireland Assembly, 1998–2011; *b* Belfast, 2 June 1942; *s* of Joseph Robinson and Anne Elizabeth (*née* Semple); *m* 1964, Louisa Morrison; three *s*. *Educ:* Whitehouse Primary Sch.; Ballyclare High Sch.; Stranmillis Coll. (Teacher's Cert. 1963); Queen's Univ., Belfast (BEd 1979). Principal Teacher: Lisfearty Primary Sch., 1975–77; Argyle Primary Sch., 1977–80; Cavehill Primary Sch., 1980–96. Mem., and Vice-Chm. Educn Cttee, N Eastern Educn and Liby Bd, 1985–93. Mem. (UU), Newtownabbey BC, 1985– (Mayor, 1991–92; Vice Chm., Econ. Develt Cttee, 1995–96, 2011–12); Mem., Newtownabbey Dist Partnership Bd, 1996–97. Chm., S Antrim Unionist Assoc., 1985–87. Governor: E Antrim Inst. Higher and Further Educn, 1985–93; Whiteabbey Primary Sch., 1985–; Hollybank Primary Sch., 1985–. Vice-Chm., Newtownabbey-Dorsten Twinning Assoc., 2001–03. *Recreations:* foreign travel, caravanning, historical research, Association Football, swimming. *Address:* 5 Sycamore Close, Jordanstown, Newtownabbey, Co. Antrim BT37 0PL. *T:* (028) 9086 6056.

ROBINSON, Lee Fisher, CEng; Chairman: HMC Technology plc, 1983–2011; Demetal Ltd, 2004–11; Metals Recovery Ltd, 2005–11; Director, HMC Technology (Asiatic) Ltd, 1997–2011; *b* 17 July 1923; *m* 1st, 1944; three *d*; 2nd, 1976, June Edna Hopkins. *Educ:* Howard Sch.; Cardiff Tech. College. CEng, MICE; MCIArb. Royal Engrs, Sappers and Miners, IE, 1942–45. Turriff Const. Corp. Ltd, HBM (BCC), 1963; Man. Dir, Power Gas Corp. Ltd, 1964; Chief Exec. and Dep. Chm., Turriff Construction Corp., 1970–73. Director: Davy-Ashmore Ltd, 1970; Combustion Systems (NRDC), 1972–96 (Chm., 1978); Redwood Internat. (UK) Ltd, 1972; Altech SA, 1976–96; Protech SA, 1976–96; BCS Ltd, 1976–96; Charterhouse Strategic Development Ltd, 1976–80 (Gp Indust. Adviser, Charterhouse Gp); Ingeco Laing SA, 1977–96; RTR (Oil Sands) Alberta, 1977–96; RTR Canada Ltd, 1977–96; RTR SA (also Chief Exec.), 1977–96; RTL SA (also Vice-Pres.), 1977–96; Thalassa (North Sea) Ltd, 1980–96; Marcent Natural Resources Ltd (Man. Dir),

1980–96; Roro Trading Ltd, 1982–2001; Hydromet Mineral Co., 1983–96; Solvex Corp., 1988–96; Chairman: Graesser (Contractors) Ltd, 1979–96; Biotechna Ltd, 1982–96; ABG Ltd, 1993–96; Bio-Electrical Ltd, 1993–96; Chm. and Chief Exec. Officer, Biotechna Environmental Ltd, 1994–96. Consultant, Internat. Management Consultants, 1972–96. Chm., Warren Spring Adv. Bd, 1969–72; Mem. Adv. Council for Technology, 1968–69. Mem., Academy of Experts, 1996. *Publications:* Cost and Financing of Fertiliser Projects in India, 1967; (poetry) Only Yesterday, Book 1, 2011, Book 2, 2014; various articles. *Address:* Suite F01, Sunrise of Chorleywood, High View, Rickmansworth, Herts WD3 5TQ.

ROBINSON, Louise Anne; Headmistress, Merchant Taylors' Girls' School, Crosby, since 2006; *b* Rochdale, 15 Dec. 1960; *m* 1986, Edward Philip Robinson; one *s*. *Educ:* Univ. of York (BA Hons Computer Sci. and Maths 1982); Univ. of Liverpool (PGCE 1983; MEd 2002). NPQH 1999. Teacher of Maths and Computer Sci., then Hd, Dept of Computing, later Sen. Teacher of Admin, Bolton Sch. Girls' Div., 1983–95; Dep. Hd, Manchester High Sch. for Girls, 1995–2001; Principal, Howell's Sch., Denbigh, 2001–06. Pres., GSA, 2012. *Recreations:* ski-ing, reading, sci-fi. *Address:* Merchant Taylors' Girls' School, Liverpool Road, Crosby L23 5SP. *T:* (0151) 924 3140. *E:* lar@merchanttaylors.com.

ROBINSON, Prof. Margaret Scott, PhD; FRS 2012; FMedSci; Professor of Molecular Cell Biology, University of Cambridge, since 2003; *b* Schenectady, NY, 29 Dec. 1951; *d* of Arthur W. Robinson, Jr and Cynthia Button Robinson; *m* 1985, John Vincent Kilmartin, *qv*; one *d*. *Educ:* Baldwin Sch., Bryn Mawr, USA; Smith Coll. (BA); Harvard Univ. (PhD 1982). Postdoctoral Fellow, MRC Lab. of Molecular Biology, 1982–89; University of Cambridge: Wellcome Sen. Res. Fellow, 1989–99; Wellcome Principal Fellow, 1999–. FMedSci 2001. Mem., EMBO, 2001. *Publications:* papers in sci. jls on cell biology. *Recreations:* reading, opera, theatre, swimming, knitting, cooking. *Address:* Cambridge Institute for Medical Research, Wellcome Trust/MRC Building, Hills Road, Cambridge CB2 0XY. *T:* (01223) 330163. *E:* msr12@cam.ac.uk.

ROBINSON, Mark; *see* Robinson, S. M. P.

ROBINSON, Mark Noel Foster; Executive Director, Commonwealth Press Union, 1997–2002; *b* 26 Dec. 1946; *s* of late John Foster Robinson, CBE, TD and Margaret Eve Hannah Paterson; *m* 1982, Vivien Radclyffe (*née* Pilkington) (*d* 2004); one *s* one *d*. *Educ:* Harrow School; Christ Church, Oxford. MA Hons Modern History. Called to the Bar, Middle Temple, 1975. Research Assistant to Patrick Cormack, MP, 1970–71; Special Asst to US Congressman Hon. F. Bradford Morse, 1971–72; Special Asst to Chief of UN Emergency Operation in Bangladesh, 1972–73; Second Officer, Exec. Office, UN Secretary-General, 1974–77; Asst Dir, Commonwealth Secretariat, 1977–83. Consultant, 1987, Dir, 1988–91, non-exec. Dir, 1991–94, Leopold Joseph & Sons Ltd; non-exec. Dir, Leopold Joseph Hldgs, 1994–95. MP (C): Newport West, 1983–87; Somerton and Frome, 1992–97; contested (C): Newport West, 1987; Somerton and Frome, 1997. PPS to Sec. of State for Wales, 1984–85; Parly Under Sec. of State, Welsh Office, 1985–87; PPS to Minister for Overseas Develt and to Parly Under-Sec. of State, FCO, 1992–94, to Sec. of State for Foreign and Commonwealth Affairs, 1994–95, to Chief Sec. to Treasury, 1995–97. Member: Foreign Affairs Select Cttee, 1983–84; Welsh Affairs Cttee, 1992–97. Chm., UN Parly Gp, 1992–98 (Hon. Sec., 1983–85; Vice Chm., 1996–97); Mem. Cttee, British American Parly Gp, 1996–97. Mem., Commonwealth Develt Corp., 1988–92; Chm., Council for Educn in the Commonwealth, 1999–2005; Dir, Friends of the Commonwealth Foundn, 2008–. Mem. Council, Winston Churchill Meml Trust, 1993–. Fellow, Industry and Parlt Trust, 1985. Member: RUSI, 1984; RIIA, 1984. FCMI (FBIM 1983); FRSA 1990. *Recreations:* include the countryside and fishing. *Clubs:* Brooks's, Pratt's, Travellers.

ROBINSON, Mary; President, and Chairman, Board of Trustees, Mary Robinson Foundation - Climate Justice, since 2010; *b* 21 May 1944; *d* of Aubrey and Tessa Bourke; *m* 1970, Nicholas Robinson; two *s* one *d*. *Educ:* Trinity Coll. Dublin (MA, LLB 1967; Hon. Fellow 1991); Harvard Law Sch. (LLM 1968). Called to the Bar, King's Inns, Dublin, 1967 (Hon. Bencher, 1991), Middle Temple, 1973 (Hon. Bencher, 1991); SC 1980. Reid Prof. of Constitutional and Criminal Law, 1969–75, Lectr in EC Law, 1975–90, TCD. Mem., Irish Senate, 1969–89; Pres. of Ireland, 1990–97; UN High Comr for Human Rights, 1997–2002; UN Special Envoy to Gt Lakes, 2013–14, for Climate Change, 2014–. Member: Adv. Bd, Common Market Law Review, 1976–90; Internat. Commn of Jurists, 1987–90 and 2004– (Pres., 2008–); Adv. Cttee, Inter-Rights, 1984–90; Vaccine Fund Bd, 2001–; Global Commn on Internat. Migration, 2003–. Pres., Realizing Rights, Ethical Globalization Initiative, 2002–10. Chair, Council of Women World Leaders, 2003–. Hon. Pres., Oxfam Ltd, 2002–. Chancellor, Dublin Univ., 1998–. Extraordinary Prof., Univ. of Pretoria, 2003–; Prof. of Practice, Columbia Univ., 2004–. Chair, Irish Chamber Orch., 2003–. Mem., Haut Conseil de la Francophonie, 2003–. Mem., Club of Madrid, 2002– (Vice Pres., 2004–). MRIA 1992; Mem., Amer. Phil Soc., 1998. Hon. Fellow: Hertford Coll., Oxford, 1999; LSE, 1999. Hon. FRCOG 1995; Hon. FRCPsych; Hon. FRCPI; Hon. FRCSI; Hon. FIEI. DCL Oxford (by diploma), 1993; hon. doctorates: Austin; Basle; Brown; Buenos Aires; Caledonian; Cambridge; Columbia; Costa Rica; Coventry; Dublin; Dublin City; Dublin Inst. of Technol.; Duke; Edinburgh; Emory; Essex; Florence; Fordham; Harvard; Leuven; Liverpool; London; McGill; Melbourne; Mongolia; Montpellier; Northeastern; Nottingham; Nova, Lisbon; NUI; Open; Poznan; QUB; Rennes; St Andrews; St Mary's, Halifax; Schweitzer Internat., Geneva; Seoul; S Africa; Toronto; Uppsala; Victoria; Wales; Wheaton; Winnipeg; Yale. Presidential Medal of Freedom (USA), 2009. Grand Cross: Order of Merit, Chile, 2002; Order of the Southern Cross (Brazil), 2002; Military Order of Christ (Portugal), 2003; Grand Officer, Légion d'Honneur (France), 2003; Condecoración, Aquila Azteca (Mexico), 2002. *Publications:* Everybody Matters (memoir), 2012. *Address:* Mary Robinson Foundation - Climate Justice, Trinity College, 6 Leinster Street South, Dublin 2, Ireland; Massbrook House, Ballina, Co. Mayo, Ireland.

ROBINSON, Mary Josephine; MP (C) Cheadle, since 2015; *b* 23 Aug. 1955; *m* Stephen Robinson; four *c*. Co-founder, Robinson Rose, Accountants, until 2008; proprietor, Mary Felicity Design, 2008. Mem. (C), S Ribble BC, 2007–13. Mem., Communities and Local Govt Select Cttee, 2015–. *Address:* House of Commons, SW1A 0AA.

ROBINSON, (Maurice) Richard; President, since 1974, Chief Executive Officer, since 1975 and Chairman, since 1982, Scholastic Corporation; *b* 15 May 1937; *s* of Maurice Richard Robinson and Florence Liddell; *m* 1986, Helen Benham (marr. diss.); two *s*. *Educ:* Harvard Univ. (BA magna cum laude); Teachers Coll., Columbia Univ.; St Catharine's Coll., Cambridge. Teacher, Evanston High Sch., Ill, 1960–62; Scholastic: Asst Editor, 1962–64; Editorial Dir, 1964–70; Publisher, 1971–74. Trustee, American Mus. of Natural History, NY. *Recreations:* tennis, swimming, jogging, books. *Address:* c/o Scholastic Corporation, 557 Broadway, New York, NY 10012, USA. *T:* (212) 3436700, *Fax:* (212) 3436701. *E:* drobinson@scholastic.com. *Clubs:* University, Century (New York).

ROBINSON, Michael John, CMG 1993; HM Diplomatic Service, retired; independent consultant to business and government, Albania and Montenegro, since 2007; *b* 19 Dec. 1946; *s* of George Robinson and Beryl Florence Naldrett Robinson; *m* 1971, Anne Jamieson Scott; two *s* two *d*. *Educ:* Cheadle Hulme Sch.; Worcester Coll., Oxford (BA Hons Mod. Langs). Third Sec., FCO, 1969; Russian lang. student, 1969; Third, subseq. Second, Sec., Moscow, 1970; Second, subseq. First, Sec., Madrid, 1972; FCO, 1977; UK Delegn to CSCE, Madrid, 1980; First Sec. and Head of Chancery, Madrid, 1981; Chef de Cabinet to Sec. Gen., OECD, Paris (on secondment), 1982; Dep. Head, UK Delegn to UNESCO, Paris, 1985; First Sec., subseq. Counsellor, FCO, 1986; Dep. Head of Mission and Consul-Gen., subseq. Chargé d'Affaires, Belgrade, 1990; Dep. Gov., Gibraltar, 1995–98; on secondment as: Pol Advr, OSCE Presence in Albania, Tirana, 1999–2001; Sen. Pol Advr, OSCE Mission to Belgrade, Yugoslavia, 2001–02; Head of OSCE Office, Podgorica, Montenegro, 2002–03; Anti-trafficking Adviser to Govt of Albania, Tirana, 2003–07 (on secondment to Internat. Criminal Investigative Trng Assistance Prog., US Dept of Justice). Vis. Fellow, RIIA, 1994. *Publications:* Managing Milosevic's Serbia, 1995. *Recreations:* reading, music, travel. *E:* mrobinson102@hotmail.com. *Club:* Royal Gibraltar Yacht.

ROBINSON, Air Vice-Marshal Michael Maurice Jeffries, CB 1982; *b* 11 Feb. 1927; *s* of Dr Maurice Robinson and Muriel (*née* Jeffries); *m* 1952, Drusilla Dallas Bush; one *s* two *d*. *Educ:* King's Sch., Bruton; Queen's Coll., Oxford; RAF Coll., Cranwell. psa 1961, jssc 1965. MA History, Univ. of West of England, 1994. Commnd, 1948; 45 Sqdn, Malaya, 1948–51; CFS, 1953–55; OC 100 Sqdn, 1962–64; Comd, RAF Lossiemouth, 1972–74; Asst Comdt, RAF Coll., Cranwell, 1974–77; SASO No 1 Gp, 1977–79; Dir Gen. of Organisation (RAF), 1979–82, retd. Wing Comdr 1961, Gp Captain 1970, Air Cdre 1976, Air Vice-Marshal 1980. *Recreations:* golf, gardening, going to the opera. *Address:* 70 Southover, Wells, Somerset BA5 1UH. *Club:* Royal Air Force.

ROBINSON, Michael R.; *see* Rowan-Robinson, G. M.

ROBINSON, Michael Stuart; Chief Executive, British Safety Council, since 2015; *b* 17 May 1964; *s* of Albert Edward Robinson and Mary Robinson; *m* 1994, Lucie Kate Bailey; one *s* one *d*. *Educ:* Portsmouth Poly. (BSc Hons Computer Sci.). ACA 1989. Audit Manager, Price Waterhouse, 1986–92; Chief Internal Auditor, Black Horse Financial Services, 1992–97; Chief Executive: Clerical Med. Internat., 1997–2005; HBOS Europe Financial Services, 2005–06; UK Hydrographic Office, 2006–11; Co-Founder and CEO, Global Navigation Solutions Ltd, 2012–14. *Recreations:* music, tennis, ski-ing, sailing.

ROBINSON, (Moureen) Ann; Partner, Rush Communication Strategic Consultancy, since 2003; Director of Consumer Policy, uSwitch, since 2005; Director of Public Awareness, Health Information Standard, 2008–14; *d* of William and Winifred Flatley; *m* Peter Crawford Robinson. DHSS, 1969–74; Central Policy Review Staff, 1974–77; nurses and midwives pay, educn and professional matters, 1981–85; liaison with Health Authorities, NHS planning and review, 1985–86; social security operations, 1986–93; Dir of Policy and Planning, Benefits Agency, DSS, 1990–93; Chief Exec., The Spastics Soc., then Scope, 1993–95; Head, Govt Consultancy Computer Sciences Corp., 1995–96; Dir-Gen., British Retail Consortium, 1997–99; Chairman: Gas Consumers Council, 2000; London Electricity Consumer Cttee, 2000; energywatch (formerly Gas and Electricity Consumers Council), 2000–03; Ascertiva Ltd, 2012–15. Member: GMC, 2003–12; Prison Service Pay Review Body, 2004–08. Chm., Victim Support London, 1999–2001; Trustee, Foundn for Credit Counselling, 2000–08. *Recreations:* walking, fine wine, bridge. *E:* annrob@ntlworld.com.

ROBINSON, Prof. Muriel Anita, OBE 2013; PhD; DL; Vice Chancellor, Bishop Grosseteste University (formerly Principal, Bishop Grosseteste College, then Bishop Grosseteste University College), Lincoln, 2003–13, now Emeritus Professor; *b* 21 Feb. 1954; *d* of Albert and Anita Robinson; *m* 1981, Richard Mosiewicz. *Educ:* Furzedown Coll., London (BEd English and Educn Studies 1976); Univ. of London Inst. of Educn (MA Lang. and Lit. 1985; PhD 1995). Teaching in primary schs, ILEA, 1976–85; Brighton Polytechnic, subseq. University of Brighton School of Education: Lectr, 1985, Sen. Lectr, 1987, English in Educn; Course Leader, 1990–97; Principal Lectr, 1993; Co-ordinator, Professional Develt Award Scheme, 1994–98; Dep. Hd of Sch., 1998–2000; Vice Principal, Newman Coll. of Higher Educn, Birmingham, 2000–03. Chair, Lincoln Diocesan Bd of Educn, 2012–; Mem. Bd, Open Coll. of Arts, 2013–. Trustee, Mukherjee Trust, 2012–. Fellow, Higher Educn Acad. DL Lincs, 2013. *Publications:* Children Reading Print and Television, 1997; extensive range of chapters in learned books and articles in jls, mainly in field of children and media educn. *Recreations:* music, reading, film, cycling, walking, travel. *Address:* Bishop Grosseteste University, Lincoln LN1 3DY. *E:* m.robinson@bishopg.ac.uk.

ROBINSON, Neil; Director, Global Marketing and Communications, ABP (China) Holdings, since 2013; *b* 25 April 1958; *s* of Arthur and Margery Robinson; *m* 1988, Susie Elizabeth Campbell; one *s*. *Educ:* Anfield Comprehensive Sch. Journalist: S Yorks Times, 1977–79; Evening Chronicle, Newcastle, 1979–86; freelance journalist various nat. newspapers, 1982; Border Television: News Ed., 1986–87; Producer (various programmes), 1987–88; Head of News and Current Affairs, 1988–90; Controller of Programmes, 1990–2000; Dir of Programmes, 2000–04; Interim Dir of Communications, Liverpool Culture Co., European Capital of Culture, 2005–06; Communications Consultant, London 2012 Olympic Games, 2006–09; Dir of Business Develt, Ten Alps Digital, 2007–09; Hd of Central Marketing, HM Treasury, 2009; Hd of Digital, British Army, MoD, 2010; Creative Dir, Global Cities Ltd, 2011–13. Dir, Cumbria Inward Investment Agency Ltd, 1997–. European Bd Mem., Co-op. Internat. de la Recherche et d'Actions en Matière de Communication, 1998–. Dir, NW Media Charitable Trust Ltd, 1998–99. Member: Northern Production Fund Panel, Northern Arts, 1993–2000; Cttee, BAFTA Scotland, 1998–2003. Mem., RTS, 1988; FRSA 1995. *Address:* Fayrefield, High Bank Hill, Kirkoswald, Cumbria CA10 1EZ. *Club:* Groucho.

ROBINSON, Nicholas Anthony; Presenter, Today Programme, BBC Radio Four, since 2015; *b* 5 Oct. 1963; *s* of E. D. (Robbie) Robinson and Evelyn Robinson; *m* 1991, Pippa Markus; two *s* one *d*. *Educ:* University Coll., Oxford (BA Hons PPE). BBC, 1986–2002: Producer, then Dep. Ed., On The Record, 1988–92; Ed., The Vote Race, 1992; Dep. Ed., Panorama, 1992–95; Political Corresp., BBC News, 1995–97; Presenter, Radio Five Live, 1997–98; Chief Political Corresp., News 24, 1999–2002; Presenter, Westminster Live, 2001–02; Political Editor: ITV News, 2003–05; BBC, 2005–15. Columnist, The Times, 2003–05. *Publications:* Live From Downing Street: the inside story of politics, power and the media, 2012; Election Notebook: the inside story of the battle over Britain's future and my personal battle to report it, 2015. *Recreations:* Alice, Will and Harry, sailing, theatre, Orford. *Address:* c/o BBC News Centre, New Broadcasting House, Portland Place, W1A 1AA. *E:* nick.robinson@bbc.co.uk.

ROBINSON, Dr Patrick William, (Bill); Chief Economist, KPMG, since 2015; *b* 6 Jan. 1943; *s* of Harold Desmond Robinson and Joyce Grover; *m* 1st, 1966, Heather Jackson (*d* 1995); two *s* one *d*; 2nd, 1997, Priscilla Stille; two step *s*. *Educ:* Bryanston Sch.; St Edmund Hall, Oxford; DPhil Sussex 1969; MSc LSE 1971. Economic Asst, 10 Downing Street, 1969–70; Cabinet Office, 1970–71; Economic Adviser, HM Treasury, 1971–74; Head of Div., European Commn, 1974–78; Sen. Res. Fellow, London Business Sch., 1979–86; Adviser, Treasury and Civil Service Cttee, 1981–86; Dir, Inst. for Fiscal Studies, 1986–91; econ. columnist, The Independent, 1989–91; Special Advr to Chancellor of Exchequer, 1991–93; Dir, London Economics, 1993–99; Hd UK Business Economist, Corporate Finance and Recovery (formerly Financial Adv. Services), PricewaterhouseCoopers, 1999–2007; Hd of Econs, 2007–12, Chm., Econs and Regulation, 2012–15, KPMG Forensic. Mem. Council, IFS, 2013–. Trustee, Tavistock Centre for Medical Psychology, 2006–11. Mem., Retail Prices Index Adv. Cttee, 1988–91. Editor: Exchange Rate Outlook, LBS, 1979–86; Economic Outlook, LBS, 1980–86; IFS Green Budget, 1987–91. *Publications:* Medium Term Exchange Rate Guidelines for Business Planning, 1983; Britain's Borrowing Problem, 1993; numerous articles. *Recreations:* bassoon playing, opera, bridge, ski-ing, windsurfing, writing musicals. *Address:* KPMG, 15 Canada Square, E14 5GL. *T:* (020) 7311 3515, 07715 704743. *Club:* Reform.

ROBINSON, Paul Anthony; Chief Executive and Chairman, Paul Robinson Associates, since 2014; *b* Birmingham, 9 Sept. 1953; *s* of Frank and Marie Robinson; *m* 1986, Alison Margaret Cheadle; one *s* one *d.* *Educ:* Leeds Univ. (BA Hons Hist. 1975); Christ's Coll., Liverpool (PGCE 1977). Auditor, Price Waterhouse, 1975–76; teacher, Doncaster GS, 1977–83; Professional Asst, Leics CC, 1983–85; Asst Educn Officer, Cambs CC, 1986–89; Asst Co. Educn Officer, Essex CC, 1989–92; Dep. Dir of Educn, 1992–94, Dir of Educn, 1994–2007, Dir of Children's Services, 2007–14, Wandsworth BC. Chm., London Aggregation Body, 2002–. Chm., Assoc. of London Chief Educn Officers, 1997–2004. Chm., London Grid for Learning Trust Co., 1995–. Mem., S London Local Educn and Trng Bd, 2012–. Gov., S Thames Further Educn Coll., 2001–. Chevalier, Ordre des Palmes Académiques (France), 2003. *Publications:* (contrib.) School Development Planning, 1989. *Recreations:* golf, gym, Rugby coaching, tennis, scuba-diving, theatre, cinema, eating and food, anything to do with castles. *Address:* Wandsworth Borough Council, Town Hall, Wandsworth High Street, SW18 2PU. *T:* (020) 8871 7890. *E:* paul.robinson93@ntlworld.com. *Clubs:* Richmond Golf; Sandown Sports.

ROBINSON, Air Vice-Marshal Paul Anthony, OBE 1994; FRAeS; defence and security consultant; *b* 8 Aug. 1949; *s* of Anthony and Eira Robinson; *m* 1971, Sarah Wood; one *s* one *d.* *Educ:* Peter Symonds' Sch., Winchester; RAF Coll., Cranwell; RAF Staff Coll., Bracknell. FRAeS 2001. Joined RAF, 1967; Harrier pilot, 1972–77, 1983–85 and 1989–91; qualified flying instructor, 1978; instructed on Gnat, Hawk, Harrier, Jetstream, Tutor and Vigilant aircraft; MoD (OR), 1987–89; OC 233 Operational Conversion Unit (Harrier), 1989–91; HQ 1 Gp, 1991–93; HQ 2 Gp, 1994–96; Stn Comdr, RAF Coll., Cranwell, 1996–98; COS, British Forces, Cyprus, 1998–2000; Comdt, CFS, 2000–01; Dep. Chief of Jt Ops, 2001–04. RAFR flying instructor, 2004–14. Mem., Mgt Bd, Lincs Bomber Command Meml Trust, 2013–. Mem. of Chapter and Lay Canon, Lincoln Cath., 2012–. Liveryman, Hon. Co. of Air Pilots (formerly GAPAN), 2007. *Recreations:* sailing, fishing, shooting, golf, charity and other voluntary work. *Club:* Royal Air Force.

ROBINSON, Paul Nicholas; Chief Executive Officer: Creative Media Partners, since 2013; Radio Academy, since 2013; President, International, A Squared Elxsi Entertainment LLC, since 2012; Executive Vice President, Your Family Entertainment, since 2014; Chairman, East London Radio, since 2015; *b* 31 Dec. 1957; *s* of Harold George Robert Robinson and Sonja Diana Robinson; *m* 1983, Gill; two *s.* *Educ:* Camberley Grammar Sch.; Manchester Univ. (BSc Hons Metallurgy 1978); Univ. of Bradford Sch. of Mgt (MBA Dist. 1996). Prog. Dir, Chiltern Radio Network, 1987–90; Head: of Programmes, BBC Radio 1, 1990–94; of Strategy and Develt, BBC, 1994–96; Man. Dir, Talk Radio UK, 1996–98; Vice-Pres., Walt Disney TV Internat., 1998–2000; Sen. Vice Pres., and Hd, Worldwide Prog. Strategy, Disney/ABC Cable Networks, 2000–03; Principal, PR Media Consulting, 2004–09; Man. Dir, KidsCo Ltd, 2007–11. Judge: BAFTA Awards; Sony Radio Awards. Member: Radio Acad., 1985; RTS 1998. *Recreations:* music, the gym, travel, freelance broadcasting.

ROBINSON, Rt Hon. Peter (David); PC 2007; Member (DemU) Belfast East, Northern Ireland Assembly, since 1998 (First Minister, 2008–15); *b* 29 Dec. 1948; *s* of David McCrea Robinson and Sheliah Robinson; *m* 1970, Iris Collins (*see* I. Robinson); two *s* one *d.* *Educ:* Annadale Grammar School; Castlereagh Further Education College. Gen. Secretary, Ulster Democratic Unionist Party, 1975–79, Dep. Leader, 1980–87, Leader, 2008–. MP (DemU) Belfast E, 1979–2010 (resigned seat Dec. 1985 in protest against Anglo-Irish Agreement; re-elected Jan. 1986); contested (DemU) same seat, 2010. Member: (DemU) Belfast E, NI Assembly, 1982–86; NI Forum, 1996–98. Minister for Regl Develt, 1999–2000 and 2001–02, of Finance and Personnel, 2007–08, NI. Member, Castlereagh Borough Council, 1977–2007; Deputy Mayor, 1978; Mayor of Castlereagh, 1986. Member: Select Cttee on NI, 1994–2005; All-Party Cttee on Shipbuilding, 1992. Mem., NI Sports Council, 1986. *Publications:* (jtly) Ulster—the facts, 1982; booklets include: The North Answers Back, 1970; Capital Punishment for Capital Crime, 1978; Ulster in Peril, 1981; Their Cry Was "No Surrender", 1989; The Union Under Fire, 1995. *Recreations:* golf, bowling. *Address:* 51 Gransha Road, Dundonald, Northern Ireland BT16 2HB; (office) Strandtown Hall, 96 Belmont Avenue, Belfast BT4 3DE. *E:* probin1690@aol.com.

ROBINSON, Sir Peter Frank, 4th Bt *cr* 1908 of Hawthornden, Cape Province and Dudley House, City of Westminster; *b* Cape Town, SA, 23 June 1949; *o s* of Sir Wilfred Henry Frederick Robinson, 3rd Bt and Margaret Alison Kathleen Mellish; *S* father, 2012; *m* 1988, Alison Jane Bradley; three *d.* *Educ:* Diocesan Coll. Sch., Rondebosch; Univ. of Cape Town (BA); St John's Coll., Cambridge (MA). Chm., Berwin Leighton Paisner, 1994–2012. *Heir:* none. *Address:* 14 Wellgarth Road, NW11 7HS. *Clubs:* Royal Wimbledon Golf, Hampstead Golf.

ROBINSON, Peter James, FCIS, FCIB; Chairman, Cobra Holdings plc, 2006–12; Group Chief Executive, Forester Holdings (Europe) Ltd (formerly Forester UK, then Foresters UK Group), 1998–2006 (non-executive Director, 2006–13); *b* 28 April 1941; *s* of Percival Albert Robinson and Lillian Caroline (*née* Pantling); *m* 1st, 1963 (marr. diss.); twin *s* one *d*; 2nd, 1984, Janice Helen Jones; two *d.* *Educ:* Erith Co. Grammar Sch.; City of London Poly. FCIS 1967; FCIB 1967. Woolwich Building Society: mgt trainee, 1963–68; PA to Jt CEOs, 1968–70; Ops and Mkting Manager, 1970–72; Co. Sec., 1972–75; Asst Gen. Manager (Develt), 1975–81; Gen. Manager (Ops), 1981–86; Dep. Chief Exec. and Dir, 1986–91; Man. Dir, 1991–95; Gp Chief Exec., Woolwich Building Soc., 1995; management consultant, 1997–98. Chm., Metropolitan Assoc. of Building Socs, 1992. Freeman, City of London, 1982. MInstD 1988; CCMI (CIMgt 1991). *Publications:* contrib. articles to Finance Gazette, Economist, Mgt Today, various newspapers. *Recreations:* cricket, golf, gardening, dogs. *Address:* Quakers, Brasted Chart, Kent TN16 1LY. *Clubs:* Royal Automobile, MCC.

ROBINSON, Ven. Peter John Alan; Archdeacon of Lindisfarne, since 2008; *b* Carshalton, Surrey, 8 Dec. 1961; *s* of Alan and Sylvia Robinson; *m* 1986, Sarah Frances Walker; two *s.* *Educ:* Tiffin Boys Grammar Sch., Kingston-upon-Thames; St John's Coll., Cambridge (BA Hons 1983); St John's Coll., Univ. of Durham (BA Hons 1992; PhD 1997). Exec., Burmah Castrol, 1983–90; ordained deacon, 1995, priest, 1996; Asst Curate, North Shields, 1995–99; Priest-in-charge: St Martin's, Byker, 1999–2008; St Michael's, Byker, 2001–08. Dir, Urban Ministry and Theology Project, Newcastle E Deanery, 1999–2008. Chair: Lindisfarne Regl Trng Partnership, 2009–; Newcastle Diocesan Educn Bd, 2014–. Chm., William Temple Foundn, 2009–. *Recreations:* fell-walking (especially in Northumberland), cricket, music (especially opera), reading (contemporary novels), travel (especially in Europe), family occasions, teaching theology. *Address:* 4 Acomb Close, Morpeth, Northumberland NE61 2YH. *T:* (01670) 503810, *Fax:* (01670) 503469. *E:* pjarobinson@btinternet.com.

ROBINSON, Prof. Peter Michael, FBA 2000; Tooke Professor of Economic Science and Statistics, London School of Economics and Political Science, since 1995 (Professor of Econometrics, 1984–95); Leverhulme Trust Personal Research Professor, 1998–2003; *b* 20 April 1947; *s* of Maurice Allan Robinson and Brenda Margaret (*née* Ponsford); *m* 1981, Wendy Rhea Brandmark; one *d.* *Educ:* Brockenhurst Grammar Sch.; University Coll. London (BSc); London School of Economics (MSc); Australian National Univ. (PhD). Lectr, LSE, 1969–70; Asst Prof. 1973–77, Associate Prof. 1977–79, Harvard Univ.; Associate Prof., Univ. of British Columbia, 1979–80; Prof., Univ. of Surrey, 1980–84. Fellow: Econometric Soc., 1989; Centre for Microdata Methods and Practice, 2003–; Spatial Econometrics Assoc., 2006–; Modelling and Simulation Soc. of Australia and NZ, 2007– (Biennial Medallist, 2007); Granger Centre for Time Series Econometrics, 2007–; FIMS 2000; FRSA 1999. Cátedra de Excelencia, Universidad Carlos III, Madrid, 2010, 2013. Mem., ISI, 2005–. Dr *hc* Universidad Carlos III, Madrid, 2000. Best Paper Award, Japan Statistical Soc., 2009. Co-Editor: Econometric Theory, 1989–91 (Mem., Adv. Bd, 2005–); Econometrica, 1991–96; Jl of Econometrics, 1997–2013 (Mem., Exec. Council, 2014–). *Publications:* (ed with M. Rosenblatt) Time Series Analysis, 1996; (ed) Time Series with Long Memory, 2003; articles in books, and in learned jls, incl. Econometrica, Annals of Statistics. *Recreation:* walking. *Address:* Department of Economics, London School of Economics and Political Science, Houghton Street, WC2A 2AE. *T:* (020) 7955 7516.

ROBINSON, Philip; Chief Executive, City of Bradford Metropolitan District Council, 2003–05; *b* 2 March 1949; *s* of late Clifford and Vera Robinson; *m* 1974, Irene Langdale. *Educ:* Grange Grammar Sch., Bradford. IPFA, IRRV. City of Bradford Metropolitan District Council: Principal Accountant, 1982–85; Asst Dir of Finance, 1985–87; Dir of Finance, 1987–95; Strategic Dir (Corporate Services), 1995–2000; Asst Chief Exec. (Policy and Corporate Support), 2000–03. *Recreations:* walking, music, theatre.

ROBINSON, Philip Edward Donald; Vice Chancellor, University of Chichester (formerly Principal, University College Chichester), 1996–2007; *b* 13 April 1943; *s* of late James Edward Robinson and Phyllis Robinson (*née* Colclough); *m* 1st, 1967, Pamela Joan Bolton (*d* 1972); one *d*; 2nd, 1975, Linda Jane Whitelaw (*d* 2009); one *s* two *d.* *Educ:* Haslingden Grammar Sch.; St Paul's Coll., Cheltenham (CertEd 1964); Goldsmiths' Coll., London (BScSoc 1969); Inst. of Educn, London (MSc Econ. 1971); Univ. of Oxford (Advanced Dip. in Local History, 2009; MSc English Local History, 2011). Lectr, then Sen. Lectr, Univ. of Keele, 1974–83; Hd of Educn, Westminster Coll., Oxford, 1983–87; Dean of Educn, then Sen. Pro Rector and Principal of Froebel Coll., Roehampton Inst., London, 1987–96. Inter-Univ. Council Vis. Fellow, Univ. Sains Malaysia, 1977–78. Chm., Council of Ch Univs and Colls, 2001–03; Vice Chm., GuildHE (formerly Standing Conf. of Principals), 2003–06; Bd Mem., QAA, 2000–04. Mem. Bd, Chichester Fest. Th., 2005–07. Vice Chm., Bd of Govs, Central Sch. of Speech and Drama, 2003–10; Gov., Chichester High Sch. for Girls, 1997–2003; Mem., Bd of Govs, South Downs Coll., 2005–09. *Publications:* Education and Poverty, 1976; Perspectives on the Sociology of Education, 1981 (trans. Korean 1991); (with F. J. Coffield and J. Sarsby) A Cycle of Deprivation?, 1981; articles relating to educnl policy. *Recreations:* theatre, 18th century maritime history, local history, Rugby Union football, long-distance walking, 18th and 19th century music. *Address:* The Drift, 11 Park Crescent, Emsworth, Hants PO10 7NT. *T:* (01243) 816050, *Fax:* (01243) 816063.

ROBINSON, Philip Henry; Member, Estates Committee, Canterbury Cathedral, 1993–99; *b* 4 Jan. 1926; *s* of Arthur Robinson and Frances M. Robinson; *m* 1st, 1959, Helen Gillian Wharton (*see* H. G. Robinson) (marr. diss. 1979); one *d* (one *s* decd); 2nd, 1985, Aneta Baring (*née* Fisher) (*d* 2010); two step *s.* *Educ:* Lincoln Sch.; Jesus Coll., Cambridge (Exhibnr, MA); Sch. of Oriental and African Studies, London Univ.; NY Univ. Graduate Sch. of Business Admin. Member, Gray's Inn. Royal Navy, 1944–47; N. M. Rothschild & Sons, 1950–54; Actg Sec., British Newfoundland Corp., Montreal, 1954–56; Asst Vice-Pres., J. Henry Schroder Banking Corp., New York, 1956–61; J. Henry Schroder Wagg & Co. Ltd, 1961; Director: J. Henry Schroder Wagg & Co. Ltd, 1966–85; Siemens Ltd, 1967–86; Schroders & Chartered Ltd Hong Kong, 1971–85; Schroder International Ltd, 1973–85 (Exec. Vice-Pres., 1977–85); Standard Chartered PLC, 1986–91 (Chm., Audit Cttee, 1989–91); Chairman: Schroder Leasing Ltd, 1979–85; Sunbury Investment Co. Ltd, 1985–94; Berkertex Hldgs Ltd, 1987–88; Man. Trustee, Municipal Mutual Insurance Ltd, 1977–92 (Dep. Chm., 1992). Dir and Chm., Audit Cttee, CLF Municipal Bank, 1993–96; Dir, Capital Re Corp., NY, 1993–99 (Chm., Audit Cttee, 1994–98). Mem., Nat. Coal Board, 1973–77. Hon. Treasurer, Nat. Council for One Parent Families, 1977–79. *Recreation:* music. *Address:* Stone Hall, Great Mongeham, Deal, Kent CT14 0HB. *Club:* Oxford and Cambridge.

See also Baron Revelstoke.

ROBINSON, Richard; *see* Robinson, Maurice R.

ROBINSON, Richard John; a District Judge, Principal Registry, Family Division, since 2002; *b* 4 Aug. 1952; *s* of Peter Norton and Patricia Helen Robinson; *m* 1987, Joanna Lesley Simons, *qv* (marr. diss. 2010). *Educ:* Trinity Hall, Cambridge (BA 1974); SOAS, London (LLM 1976). Called to the Bar, Middle Temple, 1977, also Gray's Inn *ad eundem*; in practice as barrister, 1977–2002. *Recreations:* nature conservation (London Wildlife Trust, Galapagos Conservation Trust), birdwatching (partic. in hot climates). *Address:* Principal Registry of the Family Division, First Avenue House, 42–49 High Holborn, WC1V 6NP. *T:* (020) 7947 6000. *Clubs:* Norwich City Football; Charlton Athletic Football.

ROBINSON, Sian Christina; *see* MacLeod, S. C.

ROBINSON, (Simon) Mark (Peter); Member (DemU) South Belfast, Northern Ireland Assembly, 1998–2007; *b* 12 May 1959; *s* of Desmond and Evelyne Robinson. *Educ:* Knockbreda High Sch.; Castlereagh Coll. of Further Educn (HNC); Belfast Coll. of Technol. Mechanical engr, 1977–89; Gen. Manager, 1989–95; Man. Dir, DCR Engrg, 1995–99. Mem. (DemU) Castlereagh BC, 1997–2005. Former Governor: Knockbreda High Sch.; Belvoir Park Primary Sch. *Recreations:* musical theatre, golf. *Address:* c/o Parliament Buildings, Stormont, Belfast BT4 3XX.

ROBINSON, Stella; *see* Robson, S.

ROBINSON, Stephen Joseph, OBE 1971; FRS 1976; FREng, FIET; FInstP; Managing Director, Cambridge Angle Management Co., since 1992; *b* 6 Aug. 1931; *s* of Joseph Allan Robinson and Ethel (*née* Bunting); *m* 1957, Monica Mabs Scott; one *s* one *d.* *Educ:* Sebright Sch., Wolverley; Jesus Coll., Cambridge (MA Natural Sciences). RAF, 1950–51. Mullard Res. Labs, 1954–72; MEL Div., Philips Industries (formerly MEL Equipment Co. Ltd), 1972–79; Product Dir, 1973–79; Man. Dir, Pye TVT Ltd, 1980–84; Dep. Dir, 1985–89, Dir, 1990–91, RSRE, MoD. Vis. Prof., Birmingham Univ., 1990–91. Mem. Council, Royal Soc., 1982–. Mem., Exec. Cttee, Campaign for Sci. and Engrg, 1995–2010. *Recreations:* sailing, skiing.

ROBINSON, Steve John; Chief Executive, Cheshire West and Chester Council, since 2009; *b* Evesham, Worcs, 2 March 1956; *s* of John and Lorna Robinson; *m* 1989, Nicola Dixon; one *s.* *Educ:* Abbey High Sch., Redditch; Univ. of Aston (BSc Envmtl Health 1979); Wolverhampton Poly. (Postgrad. Dip. Mgt Studies 1985). Trainee Envmtl Health Officer, Coventry CC, 1975–79; Envmtl Health Officer, 1979–81, Housing Agency Co-ordinator, 1981–86, Sandwell BC; Prin. Housing Officer, 1986–91, Chief Housing Renewal Officer, 1991–96, Wolverhampton BC; Hd, Urban Renewal Service, Liverpool CC, 1996–98; Chief Exec., S Liverpool Housing, 1998–99; Asst Dir, Regeneration, Liverpool CC, 1999–2001; Dir, Riverside Housing Assoc., Liverpool, 2001–02; Chief Exec., Walsall Housing Gp, 2002–03; Stoke-on-Trent City Council: Dir, Housing and Consumer Protection, 2003–05; Dir, Community and Adult Services, 2005–06; Chief Exec., 2006–08. Clerk to Lord Mayor of Chester, 2009–. *Recreations:* walking, gardening, cycling, golf. *Address:* Cheshire West and Chester Council, 58 Nicholas Street, Chester CH1 2NP. *T:* (01244) 977454. *E:* steve.robinson@cheshirewestandchester.gov.uk. *Club:* Chester Business.

ROBINSON, Timothy James; tenor; *b* 10 May 1964; *s* of John Robinson and Sheila Robinson; *m* 1990, Elizabeth Marcus; two *s.* *Educ:* Uppingham Sch.; New Coll., Oxford (BA 1985); Guildhall Sch. of Music and Drama. Operatic début, Kudrjas in Katya Kabanova, Glyndebourne Touring Opera, 1992; other Glyndebourne Fest. rôles incl. Jacquino in Fidelio, Grimoaldo in Rodelinda, Lysander in Midsummer Night's Dream; rôles with ENO incl. Fenton in Falstaff, Male Chorus in Rape of Lucretia, Captain Vere in Billy Budd, Peter

Quint in Turn of the Screw; Principal, Royal Opera House, Covent Garden, 1995–2001, rôles incl. Ferrando in Così fan tutte, Froh in Das Rheingold, Jupiter in Semele, Vasek in The Bartered Bride; has also sung with Aix Opera, Opéra National de Paris, Salzburg Opera, Hamburg Opera, Lyon Opera, Welsh Nat. Opera, Bavarian State Opera, Bilbao Opera. Has appeared in concert with leading orchestras incl. Royal Philharmonic, Berlin Philharmonic, Leipzig Gewandhaus and Vienna Philharmonic. Numerous recordings. *Recreations:* good food and wine, anything to do with sport, family holidays. *Address:* c/o Askonas Holt, Lincoln House, 300 High Holborn, WC1V 7JH.

ROBINSON, Timothy Michael; Chief Executive, LGC Group Ltd, since 2013; *b* Eaglescliffe, 9 Aug. 1963; *s* of Michael Robinson and Sheila Robinson; *m* 1992, Victoria Davies; one *s* one *d. Educ:* Pocklington Sch.; Univ. of Leeds (BSc Hons Physiology). Engr, mktg, Gen. Manager, IBM, 1984–94; Man. Dir, UK, Silicon Graphics, 1994–97; Chief Exec., DCS Gp plc, 1997–2001; Sen. Vice Pres., Thales, 2001–05; Chief Executive: Xafinity, 2005–10; Talaris, 2010–13. Non-exec. Dir, Camelot, 2002–10. Non-executive Member Board: UKTI, 2006–12; DFID, 2013–. Non-exec. Mem., Audit Cttee, Oxfam, 2006–12. FInstD 2009; FRSA. Freeman, Information Technologists' Co., 2000. *Recreations:* Real tennis, triathlon, vintage Alvis, trekking, making lists. *Address:* LGC Group Ltd, Queens Road, Teddington, Middx TW11 0LY. *T:* (020) 8943 7400. *E:* tim.robinson@lgcgroup.com. *Clubs:* Royal Automobile; Radley College Real Tennis.

ROBINSON, Maj. Gen. Timothy Patrick, CBE 2015 (OBE 2007); Chief of Staff, Field Army, since 2015; *b* Wegberg, W Germany, 25 Nov. 1967; *s* of Alan and Yvonne Robinson; *m* 1996, Kate Woodrow; two *d. Educ:* Rendcomb Coll.; Exeter Univ. (BA Law 1990); Cranfield Univ. (MBA 2000); King's Coll. London (MA Defence Studies 2001). Mil. Asst to CGS, 2000–02; SO1, Middle East Plans, PJHQ, 2005–07; CO, 9th/12th Royal Lancers, 2007–09; Asst Hd, Land Defence Concepts and Doctrine Centre, 1 Mechanised Bde, 2010–12; ACOS (Ops), 2012–14; Mem., RCDS, 2015. *Publications:* Operations, 2010. *Recreations:* theatre, art and music, German-style shooting, conservation. *Address:* c/o Army Headquarters, Blenheim Building, Marlborough Lines, Andover SP11 1HJ. *T:* (01264) 886006. *E:* armylf-comdgp-cos@mod.uk. *Clubs:* Cavalry and Guards, Royal Automobile.

ROBINSON, Sir Tony; *see* Robinson, Sir A.

ROBINSON, Vivian; QC 1986; a Recorder, since 1986; Partner, McGuireWoods London LLP, since 2011; *b* 29 July 1944; *s* of late William and Ann Robinson; *m* 1975, Louise Marriner; one *s* two *d. Educ:* Queen Elizabeth Grammar School, Wakefield; The Leys School, Cambridge; Sidney Sussex College, Cambridge (BA). Called to the Bar, Inner Temple, 1967 (Bencher, 1991; Treas., 2009). Gen. Counsel, SFO, 2009–11. Liveryman, Gardeners' Co., 1976– (Mem., Court of Assistants, 1989–; Master, 2000–01). *Address:* McGuireWoods, 11 Pilgrim Street, EC4V 6RN. *Clubs:* Garrick, MCC, Pilgrims.

ROBINSON, William Good; Deputy Secretary, Department of the Civil Service, Northern Ireland, 1978–80, retired; *b* 20 May 1919; *s* of William Robinson and Elizabeth Ann (*née* Good); *m* 1947, Wilhelmina Vaughan; two *d. Educ:* Clones High Sch.; Queen's Univ. of Belfast (BScEcon, BA). Served War, RAF, 1941–46 (Flt Lieut, Navigator). Entered NI Civil Service, 1938; Min. of Labour and National Insurance, NI, 1946–63; Principal, Min. of Home Affairs, NI, 1963; Asst Sec., 1967; Sen. Asst Sec., NI Office, 1973. *Recreations:* do-it-yourself, reading history. *Address:* Stormochree, 47 Castlehill Road, Belfast BT4 3GN. *T:* (028) 9020 7386.

ROBINSON, Yasmin; *see* Sewell, Y.

ROBISON, Maj. Gen. Garry Stuart, CB 2010; Chief of Staff (Capability) to Commander-in-Chief Fleet, 2008–11; Head of Global Security, Bechtel, since 2014 (Risk Manager, 2011–12; In Country Operations Manager (BP West Nile Delta, Egypt), 2012–14); *b* 10 June 1958; *s* of late George Desmond Robison and of Carole Margaret Robison (*née* Pugh); *m* 1982, Bridget Anne Clark; one *s* two *d. Educ:* Bemrose Grammar Sch., Derby; Christ's Coll., Cambridge (MPhil Internat. Relns 1999). Royal Marines: Officer trng, 1976–77; Company Comdr, 40 Commando, 1988–89; CO, 45 Commando, 1999–2000; Dep. Comdr, Iraq Survey Gp, 2003; Comdt, Commando Trng Centre, 2004–06; Comdr UK Amphibious Forces, 2006–08; Comdt Gen. RM, 2006–09, and Captain of Deal Castle, 2009; Dep. Comdr (Stability), HQ Internat. Security and Assistance Force, Afghanistan, 2007. Vice Pres., RN and RM Children's Fund, 2006–. Hon. Vice President: RN Cricket, 2011– (Pres., 2007–11); RN Football, 2011– (Vice Pres., 2009–11). Freeman, City of London, 2010; Liveryman, Plaisterers' Co., 2010. DUniv Derby, 2011. *Recreations:* cricket, football, music. *Club:* Free Foresters Cricket.

ROBISON, Shona; Member (SNP) Dundee City East, Scottish Parliament, since 2011 (North East Scotland, 1999–2003, Dundee East, 2003–11); Cabinet Secretary for Health, Wellbeing and Sport, since 2014; *b* 26 May 1966; *d* of Robin and Dorothy Robison; *m* 1997, Stewart Hosie, *qv*; one *d. Educ:* Alva Acad.; Glasgow Univ.; Jordanhill Coll. Sen. Community Worker, City of Glasgow Council, 1993–99. Scottish Parliament: Shadow Minister, Health (formerly Health and Community Care) Cttee, 2003–07; Minister for Public Health, 2007–11, for Sport, 2009–14, for Commonwealth Games, 2011–14. Contested (SNP) Dundee E, 1997. *Address:* Scottish Parliament, Edinburgh EH99 1SP.

ROBLES, Marisa, FRCM; harpist; Professor of Harp, Royal College of Music, 1971, now Visiting Professor; *b* 4 May 1937; *d* of Cristobal Robles and Maria Bonilla; *m* 1985, David Bean; two *s* one *d* by previous marriage. *Educ:* Madrid National Sch.; Royal Madrid Conservatoire. Prof. of Harp, Royal Madrid Conservatoire, 1958–60. Recitals and solo appearances with major orchestras in UK, Europe, Africa, Canada, USA, South America, Japan, China and Australia. Mem., UK Harp Assoc. Recordings include concerti by Handel, Dittersdorf, Boildieu, Debussy, Rodrigo, Moreno-Buendia, solo repertoire by Beethoven, Mozart, Fauré, Hasselmans, Tournier, Guridi and others, and chamber music by Alwyn, Roussel, Britten, Ravel, Debussy and others. Hon. Royal Madrid Conservatoire 1958; Hon. RCM 1973; FRCM 1983. *Recreations:* theatre, gardening, indoor plants, family life in general. *Address:* 38 Luttrell Avenue, Putney, SW15 6PE. *T:* (020) 8785 2204. *Club:* Royal Over-Seas League.

ROBOROUGH, 4th Baron *cr* 1938, of Maristow, co. Devon; **Massey John Henry Lopes;** Bt 1805; *b* 22 Dec. 1969; *s* of 3rd Baron Roborough and Robyn Zenda Carol Lopes (*née* Bromwich); *S* father, 2015; *m* 1996, Jean Campbell Sorell Underwood; two *s* one *d. Heir: s* Hon. Henry Massey Peter Lopes, *b* 30 July 1997.

ROBOTTOM, Dame Marlene (Anne), DBE 2000; education consultant; Headteacher, Mulberry School for Girls, Tower Hamlets, London, 1991–2006; *b* 10 July 1950; *d* of Alan Joseph Robottom and Patricia Annie Robottom (*née* Gilkes). *Educ:* Coll. of All Saints, London (CertEd 1971); NE London Poly. (BEd 1981); Poly. of E London (MSc 1989). Tower Hamlets, subseq. Mulberry School: Teacher, 1971–72; Dep. Head of Dept, 1972–77; Hd of Dept, 1977–78; Hd of House, 1979–80; Hd of House and Second Dep. Headteacher, 1980–87; First Dep. Headteacher (Curriculum), 1987–90. *Recreations:* theatre, music, the arts, antiques and restoration.

ROBSON, Agnes; Head of Corporate Services, Scottish Executive, 2000–04; *b* 6 Oct. 1946; *d* of John Wight and Agnes Margaret Wight (*née* Stark); *m* 1969, Godfrey Robson (marr. diss.); one *s. Educ:* Holy Cross Acad., Edinburgh; Edinburgh Univ. (MA Hons Politics and Mod. Hist.). Civil Servant, Dept of Employment, 1968–79; joined Scottish Office, 1985: Industry Department: Head: Energy Div., 1988–89; Nuclear Energy Div., 1989–90; Urban Policy Div., 1990–92; Dir, Primary Care, NHS Mgt Exec., Health Dept, 1992–2000. Mem., Scottish Health Council, 2005–11. Non-executive Director: Royal Scottish Nat. Orch., 2006–13; Citizens Advice Edinburgh, 2008–14; Citizens Advice Scotland, 2010–. Gov., Royal Conservatoire of Scotland, 2013–. *Recreations:* opera, contemporary Scottish painting.

ROBSON, Alan; General Secretary, Confederation of Shipbuilding and Engineering Unions, 1993–2005; *b* 24 Dec. 1941; *s* of John William Robson and Bridgit Robson; *m* 1964, Joyce Lydia. *Educ:* Ellison C of E Sch. Fitter-turner, 1958–90; Asst Gen. Sec., AEU, 1990–93. *Recreations:* reading, supporting the arts, football. *Address:* 20 York Avenue, Jarrow, Tyne and Wear NE32 5LT. *Clubs:* Labour, Elmfield, Ex-Service Men's (Jarrow).

ROBSON, Prof. Alan David, AO 2013 (AM 2003); PhD; FTSE, FAIAST; FACE; Hackett Professor of Agriculture, University of Western Australia, 1996–2012, now Emeritus Professor; *b* 1 Feb. 1945; *s* of Thomas Robson and Anne Robson (*née* Cummings); *m* 1966, Gwenda Clarice Ferris; one *s* two *d. Educ:* Univ. of Melbourne (BAgrSc); Univ. of Western Australia (PhD 1970). FACE 2004. Res. agronomist, 1972–73; University of Western Australia: Lectr, 1974–80; Sen. Lectr, 1980–82; Associate Prof., 1982–83; Prof., 1984–2012; Vice Chancellor, 2004–12; Dir, Centre for Legumes in Mediterranean Agric., 1992–93; Dep. Vice Chancellor, 1993–2004. Chairman: HE Standards Panel, Australian Govt, 2012–; WA Biosecurity Council, 2012–15. Chm. of Trustees, WA Mus., 2012–. FTSE 1989; FAIAST (FAIAS 1989). *Publications:* (ed) Copper in Soils and Plants, 1981; (ed) Soil Acidity and Plant Growth, 1989; (ed) Zinc in Soil and Plants, 1993; (ed) Management of Mycorrhizas in Agriculture, Horticulture and Forestry, 1994; numerous scientific contribs on mineral nutrition of plants. *Recreations:* sport, reading. *Address:* School of Earth and Environment, University of Western Australia, 35 Stirling Highway, Crawley, WA 6009, Australia. *E:* Alan.Robson@uwa.edu.au.

ROBSON, Bryan, OBE 1990; Manager, Sheffield United Football Club, 2007–08; Head Coach, Thailand National Football Team, 2009–11; *b* 11 Jan. 1957; *s* of Brian and Maureen Robson; *m* 1978, Denise Brindley; one *s* two *d. Educ:* Lord Lawson Comprehensive Sch., Birtley. Player: West Bromwich Albion FC, 1974–81; Manchester United FC, 1981–94 (captain, winning team: FA Cup, 1983, 1985, 1990; European Cup Winners' Cup, 1991; Premier League, 1993, 1994); Manager: Middlesbrough FC, 1994–2001 (player-manager, 1994–97); Bradford City FC, 2003–04; W Bromwich Albion FC, 2004–06. Player, England Football Team, 1980–91 (90 appearances, 65 as captain, 26 goals). Hon. BA: Manchester, 1992; Salford, 1992. *Publications:* United I Stand (autobiog.), 1983. *Recreations:* horse racing, golf. *Clubs:* West Bromwich Albion Football, Manchester United, Middlesbrough.

ROBSON, Carol; *see* Robson, E. C.

ROBSON, David Ernest Henry; QC 1980; a Recorder of the Crown Court (NE Circuit), 1979–2005; *b* 1 March 1940; *s* of late Joseph Robson and Caroline Robson; civil partnership 2006, Leslie Colwell. *Educ:* Robert Richardson Grammar Sch., Ryhope; Christ Church, Oxford (MA). Called to the Bar, Inner Temple, 1965 (Profumo Prize, 1963), Bencher, 1988. NE Circuit, 1965–. Artistic Dir, Royalty Studio Theatre, Sunderland, 1986–88. Pres., Herrington Burn YMCA, Sunderland 1987–2001. *Recreations:* acting, Italy. *Address:* 1 Tollgate Road, Hamsterley Mill, Rowlands Gill, Tyne and Wear NE39 1HF. *T:* (01207) 549989. *Club:* County (Durham).

ROBSON, Elizabeth; *see* Howlett, E.

ROBSON, Prof. Elizabeth Browel, (Mrs George MacBeth); Galton Professor of Human Genetics, University College London, 1978–93; *b* 10 Nov. 1928; *d* of Thomas Robson and Isabella (*née* Stoker); *m* 1955, George MacBeth, writer (marr. diss. 1975, he *d* 1992). *Educ:* Bishop Auckland Girls' Grammar Sch.; King's Coll., Newcastle upon Tyne; BSc Dunelm; PhD London, 1954; Dip. History of Art, Univ. of London, 2000. Rockefeller Fellowship, Columbia Univ., New York City, 1954–55; external scientific staff of MRC (London Hosp. Med. Coll. and King's Coll. London), 1955–62; Member and later Asst Director, MRC Human Biochemical Genetics Unit, University Coll. London, 1962–78; Hd, Dept of Genetics and Biometry, UCL, 1978–90. Jt Editor, Annals of Human Genetics, 1978–93. *Publications:* papers on biochemical human genetics and gene mapping in scientific jls.

ROBSON, (Elizabeth) Carol; HM Diplomatic Service, retired; Head, United Nations and Commonwealth Department, Department for International Development, 2004–05 (on secondment); *b* 14 Jan. 1955; *d* of James Henry Robson and Laura Robson (*née* Jacobson). *Educ:* Carlisle and County High Sch.; York Univ. (BA Physics 1977). Entered Diplomatic Service, 1977; Latin America floater, 1980–81; Russian lang. trng, 1981–82; Ulaanbaatar, 1983; Moscow, 1983–84; FCO, 1984; UKMIS, Geneva, 1987–92; Asst Head, SE Asia Dept, 1992–95; Head, Transcaucasus and Central Asia Unit, 1995–96; Counsellor, Consul-Gen. and Dep. Head of Mission, Stockholm, 1996–98; Dep. Dir, Ditchley Foundn, 1998–2001 (on special leave); Counsellor and Dep. Hd of Mission, Copenhagen, 2002–04. *Recreations:* diverse, including cooking, antiques, art, gardening, travel, visiting historic sites and houses, reading.

ROBSON, Eric; DL; freelance writer and broadcaster, since 1979; farmer, 1987–2009; *b* 31 Dec. 1946; *s* of James Walter Robson and Agnes Gourlay Robson; *m* 1st, 1976, Mary Armstrong (marr. diss. 1984); one *s* one *d*; 2nd, 1988, Annette Steinhilber; one *s* two *d. Educ:* Carlisle Grammar Sch. Border TV, 1966–; BBC TV and Radio, 1976–; BBC outside broadcast commentator, Trooping the Colour, the Cenotaph, handover of Hong Kong; Chm., Gardeners' Question Time, BBC Radio, 1995–; documentary producer and presenter. Partner, Osprey Communications, 2008–. Chairman: Striding Edge Ltd, 1994–; Cumbria Tourist Bd, 2002–; Wainwright Soc., 2002–. Trustee, Tullie House Mus. and Art Gall. Trust, 2012–. DL Cumbria, 2004. *Publications:* Great Railway Journeys of the World, 1981; Northumbria, 1998; Out of Town, 2002; After Wainwright, 2004; The Border Line, 2006; Outside Broadcaster, 2007; The Zoo, 2007; Wainwright's TV Walks, 2008; Abroad, 2014. *Recreations:* painting, fell walking, cooking, avoiding housework. *Address:* Crag House Farm, Wasdale, Cumbria CA19 1UT. *T:* (01946) 726301. *Club:* Farmers.

ROBSON, Euan Macfarlane; Associate, Caledonia Consulting, since 2008; *b* 17 Feb. 1954; *m* 1984, Valerie Young; two *d. Educ:* Univ. of Newcastle upon Tyne (BA Hons History 1976); Univ. of Strathclyde (MSc Political Sci. 1984). Teacher, King Edward VI Sch., Morpeth, 1977–79; Dep. Sec., Gas Consumers' Northern Council, Newcastle upon Tyne, 1981–86; Scottish Manager, Gas Consumers' Council, 1986–99. Mem. (L/All), Northumberland CC, 1981–89 (Chm., Highways Cttee, 1988–89; Hon. Alderman, 1989); L/All Gp Sec., 1981–87. Contested (L/All) Hexham, 1983, 1987. Scottish Parliament: Mem. (Lib Dem) Roxburgh and Berwickshire, 1999–2007; Lib Dem Rural Affairs spokesman, 1998–99, Justice and Home Affairs spokesman, 1999–2001, Health and Communities spokesman, 2005–07; Dep. Minister for Parlt, subseq. for Parly Business, 2001–03, for Educn and Young People, 2003–05; Convener, Lib Dem Parly party, 2005–07. Contested (Lib Dem): Roxburgh and Berwicks, 2007, Ettrick, Roxburgh and Berwicks, 2011, Scottish Parlt; Scotland, Eur. Parlt, 2009. River Tweed Comr, 1994–2001. Founding Mem., Consumer Safety Internat.; Life Mem., Nat. Trust for Scotland. Chair, Borders Consortium of CAB, 2013–. *Publications:* The Consumers' View of the 1990 EU Gas Appliances' Directive, 1991; George Houston: nature's limner, 1997; (contrib.) Kirkcudbright: 100 years of an artists' colony, 2000; Scotland, Poland and the European Union, 2002; Charles Oppenheimer: from craftsman to artist, 2012. *Recreation:* angling. *Address:* Elmbank, Tweedsyde Park, Kelso, Roxburghshire TD5 7RF. *T:* (01573) 225279.

ROBSON, Frank Elms, OBE 1991; Partner, Winckworth Sherwood (formerly Winckworth & Pemberton), Solicitors, Oxford and Westminster, 1962–98 (Senior Partner, 1990–94); *b* 14 Dec. 1931; *s* of Joseph A. Robson and Barbara Robson; *m* 1958, Helen (*née* Jackson) (*d* 2004); four *s* one *d*. *Educ:* King Edward VI Grammar Sch., Morpeth; Selwyn Coll., Cambridge (MA). Admitted solicitor, 1954. Registrar, Dio. Oxford, 1970–2000; Joint Registrar, Province of Canterbury, 1982–2000. Chm., Ecclesiastical Law Soc., 1996–2002; Vice-Chm., Legal Adv. Commn, Gen. Synod of C of E, 1990–2002. DCL Lambeth, 1991. *Recreation:* Northumberland. *Address:* 2 Simms Close, Middle Road, Stanton St John, Oxford OX33 1HB. *T:* (01865) 351393.

ROBSON, Godfrey, CB 2002; Chairman, Frontline Consultants, 2003–13 (Director, 2003–13); *b* 5 Nov. 1946; *s* of late William James Robson and Mary Finn; *m* (marr. diss.); one *s*. *Educ:* St Joseph's Coll., Dumfries; Edinburgh Univ. (MA). Joined Scottish Office, 1970; Pvte Sec. to Parly Under-Sec. of State, 1973–74, to Minister of State, 1974; Prin. Pvte Sec. to Sec. of State for Scotland, 1979–81; Assistant Secretary: Roads and Transport, 1981–86; Local Govt Finance, 1986–89; Under Sec., 1989; Scottish Fisheries Sec., 1989–93; Scottish Executive (formerly Scottish Office): Under Sec., Industrial Expansion, subseq. Economic and Industrial Affairs, 1993–2000; Dir of Health Policy, 2000–02. Sen. Policy Advr, ICAP, Washington DC, 2004–. Non-executive Director: Lloyds TSB Scotland, 2001–13; TSB Bank plc, 2013–. Founding Chm., Nat. Jubilee Hosp., Clydebank, 2002–03; Dir and Trustee, Caledonia Youth, 2003–12. *Recreations:* walking, travel by other means, reading history. *Address:* 50 East Trinity Road, Edinburgh EH5 3EN. *T:* (0131) 552 9519; Chemin Sous Baye, 84110 Vaison la Romaine, France. *T:* (4) 90371832.

ROBSON, Sir John (Adam), KCMG 1990 (CMG 1983); HM Diplomatic Service, retired; Ambassador to Norway, 1987–90; *b* 16 April 1930; *yr s* of Air Vice-Marshal Adam Henry Robson, CB, OBE, MC; *m* 1958, Maureen Molly, *er d* of E. H. S. Bullen; three *d*. *Educ:* Charterhouse; Gonville and Caius Coll., Cambridge (Major Scholar; BA 1952, MA 1955, PhD 1958). Fellow, Gonville and Caius Coll., 1954–58; Asst Lectr, University Coll. London, 1958–60. HM Foreign Service (later Diplomatic Service), 1961; Second Sec., British Embassy, Bonn, 1962–64; Second, later First, Secretary, Lima, 1964–66; First Sec., British High Commn, Madras, 1966–69; Asst Head, Latin American Dept, FCO, 1969–73; Head of Chancery, Lusaka, 1973–74; RCDS, 1975; Counsellor, Oslo, 1976–78; Head of E African Dept, FCO, and Comr for British Indian Ocean Territory, 1979–82; Ambassador to Colombia, 1982–87. Leader, UK Delegn, Conf. on Human Dimension, CSCE, 1990–91. Panel Mem., Home Office Assessment Consultancy Unit, 1992–2000. Chm. Mgt Cttee, Seven Springs Cheshire Home, 1992–96; Mem. Internat. Cttee, Cheshire Foundn, 1996–2000. Mem. Ct, Kent Univ., 1990–99. Chm., Anglo-Norse Soc., 1998–2003. Royal Order of Merit (Norway), 1988. *Publications:* Wyclif and the Oxford Schools, 1961; articles in historical jls. *Recreation:* gardening. *Address:* Biggenden Oast, Paddock Wood, Tonbridge, Kent TN12 6ND. *Club:* Oxford and Cambridge.

ROBSON, John Gair, PhD, ScD; FRS 2003; Senior Research Professor in Vision Science, University of Houston, since 1997; Fellow of Gonville and Caius College, Cambridge, since 1965 (Life Fellow, 1995); *b* 27 June 1936; *s* of Thomas Robson and Kathleen (*née* Elwell); *m* 1958, Jane Macdonald; two *s* two *d*. *Educ:* Shrewsbury Sch.; St John's Coll., Cambridge (BA; PhD 1962; ScD 2004). Vis. Scientist, Bell Labs, Murray Hill, 1964; Vis. Prof. Northwestern Univ., 1964; Demonstrator in Physiol., 1962–65, Lectr in Physiol., 1966–83, Reader in Neurophysiol., 1983–96, Univ. of Cambridge. Champness Lectr, Spectacle Makers' Co., 1990. (Jtly) Friedenwald Award, Assoc. for Res. in Vision and Ophthalmol., 1983; Edgar J. Tillyer Award, Optical Soc. of America, 1996. *Publications:* numerous contribs on vision and visual neurophysiology to learned jls. *Address:* Herring's House, Wilbraham Road, Fulbourn, Cambridge CB21 5EU. *T:* (01223) 880277.

ROBSON, Rev. John Phillips, LVO 1999; Chaplain to the Queen, 1993–2002; an Extra Chaplain to the Queen, since 2002; Chaplain of the Queen's Chapel of the Savoy and Chaplain of the Royal Victorian Order, 1989–2002; *b* 22 July 1932; *s* of Thomas Herbert and Nellie Julia Robson. *Educ:* Hele's School, Exeter; Brentwood School; St Edmund Hall, Oxford (Liddon Exhibnr 1954); King's College London (AKC 1958). Deacon 1959, priest 1960; Curate, Huddersfield Parish Church, 1959–62; Asst Chaplain 1962–65, Senior Chaplain 1965–80, Christ's Hospital, Horsham; Senior Chaplain of Wellington College, Berks, 1980–89. *Recreations:* cinema, theatre, technology. *Address:* Charterhouse, Charterhouse Square, EC1M 6AN. *T:* (020) 7253 1591. *Club:* Garrick.

ROBSON, Mark Hunter, FIMA, FCMA; CMath, CSci, CGMA; Agent for Central Southern England, Bank of England, since 2015; *b* Southend-on-Sea, 10 Aug. 1958; *s* of Peter William Robson and Shirley Marion Robson; *m* 1st, 1989, Amanda Louise Knox (marr. diss. 2000); two *d*; 2nd, 2006, Lara Jane Hays; two *s*. *Educ:* Westcliff High Sch. for Boys; St John's Coll., Oxford (BA Maths and Philosophy 1979; MA 1983; MPhil Econs 1985). FIMA 1990; CMath 1992; FCMA 2004; CSci 2005; CGMA 2012. HM Inspector of Taxes, 1980–83, Econ. Advr, 1985–90, Bd of Inland Revenue; Res. Fellow, Financial Mkts Gp, LSE, 1987–89; Sen. Manager, Tax Consultancy, KPMG Peat Marwick, 1990–93; Principal Administrator, Fiscal Affairs, OECD, 1993–95; Advr/Manager, Financial Stability, Bank of England, 1995–98; Tax Policy Advr, Thailand, IMF, 1998–99; Sen. Manager, Finance, Bank of England, 1999–2003; Treas. and Official Fellow, Lady Margaret Hall, Oxford, 2003–07, Hon. Res. Fellow, 2008–; Bank of England: Sen. Manager, Banking Services, 2008–09; Hd of Monetary and Financial Statistics, 2009–12; Hd of Statistics and Regulatory Data, 2012–15. Mem., Audit Cttee, London Bor. of Islington, 2008–12. Member: Grants Assessment Panel, 2010–14, Bd, 2015–, ESRC; Social Scis Main Panel, HEFCE REF 2014, 2011–14; Bd, HEFCE, 2012–; Commonwealth Scholarship Commn, 2014–. Mem. Council, IMA, 1997–2000; Mem. Council and Exec. Cttee, Inst. for Fiscal Studies, 1997–; Mem., Governing Council, Centre for the Study of Financial Innovation, 2004–. Treasurer: Royal Statistical Soc., 2003–07; REconS, 2008–; Science Council, 2013–15. Mem. Council, City Univ., 2002–11; Vice Chm., London Metropolitan Univ., 2010–14. Gov., City of London Acad., Islington, 2008–11. Liveryman, Internat. Bankers' Co., 2006–. *Recreations:* family, reading, music, theatre, Roman Catholicism, charity governance, collegiate rowing. *Address:* Bank of England, Threadneedle Street, EC2R 8AH. *T:* (020) 7601 4311, *Fax:* (020) 7601 3334. *E:* mark.robson@bankofengland.co.uk.

ROBSON, Mark William; Director, English and Examinations, British Council, since 2010; *b* Newcastle upon Tyne, 2 Nov. 1960; *s* of William and Doris Robson; *m* 1995, Patricia Voets; two *d*. *Educ:* Latymer Upper Sch.; Univ. of Southampton (BSc Econs and Stats 1982). Mkt Res. Exec., MORI, 1982–84; Mkt Res. Exec., 1984–86, Sen. Brand Manager, 1986–88, Mkt Res. Manager, 1988–91, Colgate-Palmolive; Market Research Manager: Jamont, 1991–93; Eridania Beghin-Say, 1993–95; Dir, Mktg and Export, Carapelli Firenze, 1995–98; Vice-Pres., Sales and Mktg, Georgia-Pacific EMEA, 1998–2007; Dir, Ops, British Council, 2007–10. *Recreations:* football, football coaching, running, music, family. *Address:* British Council, 10 Spring Gardens, SW1A 2BN.

ROBSON, Air Vice-Marshal Robert Michael, OBE 1971; freelance journalist; sheep farmer, 1987–96; *b* 22 April 1935; *s* of Dr John Alexander and Edith Robson; *m* 1959, Brenda Margaret (*née* Croysdill); one *s* two *d*. *Educ:* Sherborne; RMA Sandhurst. Commissioned 1955; RAF Regt, 1958; Navigator Training, 1959; Strike Squadrons, 1965; Sqdn Comdr, RAF Coll., 1968; Defence Adviser to British High Comr, Sri Lanka, 1972; Nat. Defence Coll., 1973; CO 27 Sqdn, 1974–75; MoD staff duties, 1978; CO RAF Gatow, 1978–80; ADC to the Queen, 1979–80; RCDS 1981; Dir of Initial Officer Training, RAF Coll., 1982–84; Dir of Public Relations, RAF, 1984–87; Hd, RAF Study of Officers' Terms of Service, 1987; retired. Chairman: Turbo (UK) Ltd, 1995–98; Fuel Mechanics Ltd, 1995–97; Dir, Advanced Technology Industries Ltd, 1993–97; Chm., Prince's Trust, Lincs, 1993–96; Dir and Chm., Witham Hall Trust, 1995–2003; Gov., Witham Hall Sch., 1988–2006 (Chm. Govs, 1995–2003; Vice-Pres., 2003–06). Pres., SSAFA Forces Help, Lincs, 2010 (Vice-Pres., 2001–10). FCMI (FBIM 1980). *Recreations:* fly fishing, gardening. *Club:* Royal Air Force.

ROBSON, Stella; Chair, Northern Sinfonia Board, 1998–2002; *b* 18 Feb. 1935; *d* of Charles Moreton Marchinton and Margaret Maude Backhouse; *m* 1998, Frank Robson (*d* 2011); one *s* one *d* by a previous marriage. *Educ:* Aireborough Grammar Sch.; Princess Mary High Sch., Halifax; Univ. of Leeds (BA Hons English 1956). Housing Officer: Joseph Rowntree Village Trust, York, 1956–57; Rotherham BC, 1957–59; Students Accommodation Officer, King's Coll., Newcastle, 1959–63; Chair, Northern Arts, 1990–98. Mem., Arts Council of England, 1993–98. Trustee, North Music Trust, 2000–07. Mem. Bd, Darlington Housing Assoc., 2001–05. Member (Lab): Darlington BC, 1972–79, 1995–2011 (Mayor of Darlington, 2005–06); Durham CC, 1981–97 (Hon. Alderman, 1997). *Recreations:* walking, the arts.

ROBSON, Rt Rev. Stephen; *see* Dunkeld, Bishop of, (RC).

ROBSON, Sir Stephen Arthur, (Sir Steve), Kt 2000; CB 1997; PhD; Second Permanent Secretary, Finance, Regulation and Industry, HM Treasury, 1997–2001; *b* 30 Sept. 1943; *s* of Arthur Cyril Robson and Lilian Marianne (*née* Peabody); *m* 1974, Meredith Hilary Lancashire; two *s*. *Educ:* Pocklington Sch.; St John's Coll., Cambridge (MA, PhD); Stanford Univ., USA (MA). Joined Civil Service (HM Treasury), 1969; Private Sec. to Chancellor of the Exchequer, 1974–76; seconded to Investors in Industry plc, 1976–78; Under Sec., Defence Policy and Material Gp, 1987–89, Public Enterprises and Privatisation Gp, 1990–93; Dep. Sec., Industry and Financial Instns, later Finance, Regulation and Industry, 1993–97. Non-executive Director: Royal Bank of Scotland, 2001–08; J P Morgan Cazenove (formerly Cazenove), 2001–10; Partnerships UK, 2001–08; Xstrata, 2002–13; Financial Reporting Council, 2007–13; KPMG, 2010–15; Kuwait Energy, 2014–. *Recreation:* sailing. *Club:* Bosham Sailing.

ROCARD, Michel Louis Léon; Prime Minister of France, 1988–91; French Ambassador for International Negotiations on the Arctic and Antarctic, since 2009; *b* 23 Aug. 1930; *s* of late Yves Rocard and of Renée (*née* Favre); *m* 1st; one *s* one *d*; 2nd, 1972, Michèle Legendre (marr. diss.); two *s*. *Educ:* Lycée Louis-le-Grand, Paris; Univ. of Paris (Nat. Sec., Association des étudiants socialistes, 1953–55); Ecole Nationale d'Administration, 1956–58. Inspecteur des Finances, 1958; Econ. and Financial Studies Service, 1962; Head of Econ. Budget Div., Forecasting Office, 1965; Sec.-Gen., Nat. Accounts Commn, 1965. Nat. Sec., Parti Socialiste Unifié, 1967–73; candidate for Presidency of France, 1969; Deputy for Yvelines, 1969–73, 1978–81, 1986–93; Minister of Planning and Regl Develt, 1981–83; Minister of Agriculture, 1983–85; Mem., Senate, 1995–97. MEP (Party of Eur. Socialists), 1994–2009; European Parliament: Chairman: Develt Cttee, 1997–99; Employment and Social Affairs Cttee, 1999–2001; Culture Cttee, 2002, 2004; Mem., Foreign Affairs Cttee, 2004. Joined Parti Socialiste, 1974: Mem., Exec. Bureau, 1975–81 and 1986–88; Nat. Sec. in charge of public sector, 1975–79; First Sec., 1993–94. Mayor, Conflans-Sainte-Honorine, 1977–94. *Publications:* Le PSU et l'avenir socialiste de la France, 1969; Des militants du PSU présentés par Michel Rocard, 1971; Questions à l'Etat socialiste, 1972; Un député, pour quoi faire?, 1973; (jtly) Le Marché commun contre l'Europe, 1973; (jtly) L'Inflation au cœur, 1975; Parler vrai, 1979; A l'épreuve des faits: textes politiques 1979–85, 1986; Le coeur à l'ouvrage, 1987; Un pays comme le nôtre, 1989; L'art de la Paix, 1997; Les moyens d'en sortir, 1997; Le français langue des Droits de l'Homme?, 1998; Mes idées pour demain, 2000; Entretiens, 2001; Si la gauche savait, 2005; (jtly) La gauche n'a plus droit à l'erreur, 2013.

ROCH, Rt Hon. Sir John (Ormond), Kt 1985; PC 1993; a Lord Justice of Appeal, 1993–2000; *b* 19 April 1934; *s* of Frederick Ormond Roch and Vera Elizabeth (*née* Chamberlain); *m* 1st, 1967, Anne Elizabeth Greany (*d* 1994); three *d*; 2nd, 1996, Mrs Susan Angela Parry. *Educ:* Wrekin Coll.; Clare Coll., Cambridge (BA, LLB). Called to Bar, Gray's Inn, 1961, Bencher, 1985; QC 1976; a Recorder, 1975–85; a Judge of the High Court of Justice, QBD, 1985–93; Presiding Judge, Wales and Chester Circuit, 1986–90. Vice-Pres., RNLI, 2006– (Gov. and Mem. Mgt Cttee, 1996–2006). President: Haverfordwest Civic Soc., 2006–; Old Wrekinian Assoc., 2007–13; Atlantic Challenge, Pembrokeshire Gig Assoc., 2010–14. *Recreations:* sailing, music. *Club:* Dale Yacht.

ROCHA, John, CBE 2002; fashion designer, since 1980; *b* Hong Kong, 23 Aug. 1953; *s* of Henry and Cecilia Rocha; *m* 1990, Odette Gleeson; one *s* two *d*. *Educ:* Croydon Coll. of Art and Design (Dip. Fashion). Estabd career, Dublin, late 1970s; worked in Milan, 1988–90, subseq. estabd John Rocha; launched: John Rocha at Waterford Crystal, 1997; John Rocha at Debenhams, 2000; John Rocha Jewellery, 2002; opened shop, 15A Dover St, London, 2007. Hon. DLitt Ulster, 1994; Hon. MA, Univ. of the Creative Arts, 2008. British Designer of the Year, British Fashion Awards, 1994. *Publications:* Texture, Form, Purity, Detail, 2002. *Recreation:* fly fishing. *Address:* 10 Ely Place, Dublin 2, Ireland. *T:* (1) 6629225, *Fax:* (1) 6629226. *E:* info@johnrocha.ie. *W:* www.johnrocha.ie. *Clubs:* Hospital, Groucho.

ROCHAT, Dr Philippe Henri Pierre; Secretary General, International Civil Aviation Organization, 1991–97; former Executive Director, Air Transport Action Group, Geneva; *b* 19 Oct. 1942; *m* 1967, Catherine Dupuy; two *s* one *d*. *Educ:* Gymnase de Lausanne; Lausanne Univ. (LLB 1966; LLD 1974). Journalist and reporter, Swiss Radio-TV, 1967–74; Asst to Dep. Dir, Federal Office for Civil Aviation, Bern, 1975–77; Admin. and Commercial Dir, Geneva Airport, 1977–85; International Civil Aviation Organisation Council: Alternate Rep. of Belgium, 1985–86; Rep. of Switzerland, 1986–89; Dir, Mkting and Envmt, Geneva Airport, 1989–91. Air Law Professor: Geneva Univ.; Lausanne Univ. *Publications:* articles, reports and lectures on civil aviation and envmt, airports' structure and mgt, challenges in civil aviation, etc. *Recreations:* ski-ing, tennis, hiking, various cultural activities.

ROCHDALE, 3rd Viscount *cr* 1960; **Jonathan Hugo Durival Kemp;** Managing Director, SmartWisdom, since 1999; Baron 1913; *b* Edinburgh, 10 June 1961; *s* of 2nd Viscount Rochdale and of Serena Jane Kemp (*née* Clark-Hall, now Hanson); *S* father 2015; *m* 1993, Ming Zhu; one *d*. *Educ:* Stowe Sch.; Westminster Univ. (Postgrad. Dip. Mgt); Cass Business Sch. (MSc Shipping, Trade and Finance). Metropolitan Police, 1982–93. MInstD. *Publications:* (jtly) two sci. papers on knowledge mgt. *Recreation:* photography. *Heir: nephew* George Thomas Kemp, *b* 2001. *T:* 07786 526529. *E:* jkemp@smartwisdom.com. *Club:* Royal Automobile.

ROCHDALE, Archdeacon of; *see* Vann, Ven. C. E.

ROCHE, family name of **Baron Fermoy**.

ROCHE, Most Rev. Arthur; Archbishop Secretary of the Congregation of Divine Worship and Discipline of the Sacraments, Vatican City, since 2012; *b* 6 March 1950; *s* of Arthur Francis Roche and Frances Roche (*née* Day). *Educ:* Christleton Hall, Chester; English Coll., Valladolid; Pontifical Gregorian Univ., Rome (STL). Ordained priest, 1975; Asst Priest, Holy Rood, Barnsley, 1975–77; Sec. to Rt Rev. Gordon Wheeler, Bishop of Leeds, 1977–82; Vice-Chancellor, 1979–89, Financial Administrator, 1986–90, Dio. of Leeds; Asst Priest, Leeds Cathedral, 1982–89; Parish Priest, St Wilfrids's, Leeds, 1989–91; Spiritual Dir,

Venerable English Coll., Rome, 1992–96; Gen. Sec. to Catholic Bps' Conf. of England and Wales, 1996–2001; Auxiliary Bishop of Westminster, 2001–02; Coadjutor Bishop of Leeds, 2002–04; Bishop of Leeds, (RC), 2004–12. Hon. Ecumenical Canon: Wakefield Cath., 2006–; Bradford Cath., 2008–. Titular Bishop of Rusticiana, 2001–02. Chm., Dept of Christian Life and Worship, Catholic Bps' Conf. of England and Wales, 2004–12. Chm., Internat. Commn for English in the Liturgy, 2002–12. Co-ordinator of the Papal Visit to York, 1982. Prelate of Honour to Pope John Paul II. *Recreations:* gardening, walking, travel. *Address:* Piazza Pio XII, 10, 00120 Città del Vaticano, Italy. *T:* (6) 69884005, *Fax:* (6) 69882866.

ROCHE, Barbara Maureen; Chairman: Migration Matters Trust, since 2012; Praxis, since 2013; *b* 13 April 1954; *d* of late Barnett Margolis and Hannah (*née* Lopes Dias); *m* 1977, Patrick Roche; one *d*. *Educ:* JFS Comprehensive Sch., Camden; Lady Margaret Hall, Oxford (BA). Called to the Bar, Middle Temple, 1977. MP (Lab) Hornsey and Wood Green, 1992–2005; contested (Lab) same seat, 2005. Parly Under-Sec. of State, DTI, 1997–98; Financial Sec., HM Treasury, 1999; Minister of State: Home Office, 1999–2001; Cabinet Office, 2001–02; ODPM, 2002–03. Chm., Metropolitan Housing Partnership, 2009–13 (Bd Mem., 2006–13; Dep. Chm., 2008–09). Chm., Metropolitan Support Trust, 2007–09; Trustee, Oxford Literary and Debating Union Trust, 2012–. Former Vis. Fellow, Univ. of Teesside; Vis. Prof., Univ. of Sunderland, 2008–11. Associate Fellow, IPPR, 2009–. Chm., Migration Mus. Project, 2006–. *Recreations:* theatre, detective fiction.

ROCHE, David Lawrence Redmond; owner, David Roche Enterprises Ltd, since 2011; Director, Entertainment Alliance, since 2015; *b* 8 May 1961; *s* of Lawrence and Jocelyn Roche; *m* 1987, Johanna Kari; three *s*. *Educ:* Worth Sch.; Durham Univ. (BA Hons Psychol. 1983). Prodn Planner, Burlington Klopman, 1984–86; Stock Control Manager, Hornes Ltd, 1986–89; Ops Manager, HMV UK Ltd, 1989–95; Product Director: HMV Europe Ltd, 1995–2002; Waterstone's Ltd, 2002–05; Chief Executive, Borders UK and Ireland Ltd, 2006–08; Gp Sales and Trade Mktg Dir, HarperCollins Publishing, 2008–11. Pres., Booksellers Assoc. UK & Ire. Chm., Adv. Bd, 2011–, non-exec. Chm., 2012–, London Book Fair. Trustee, Booktrust, 2008–. *Recreations:* travel, reading, arts, Rugby, golf, ski-ing, scuba diving, cooking. *Address:* 25 Kingston Hill Place, Kingston upon Thames, Surrey KT2 7QY. *T:* (020) 8546 1023. *Clubs:* Soho House, MCC; Royal Wimbledon Golf.

ROCHE, Sir David (O'Grady), 5th Bt *cr* 1838 of Carass, Limerick; FCA; *b* 21 Sept. 1947; *s* of Sir Standish O'Grady Roche, 4th Bt, DSO, and of Evelyn Laura, *d* of Major William Andon; *S* father, 1977; *m* 1971, Hon. (Helen) Alexandra Briscoe Frewen, *d* of 3rd Viscount Selby; one *s* one *d* (and one *s* decd). *Educ:* Wellington Coll., Berks; Trinity Coll., Dublin. Qualified as Chartered Accountant with Peat Marwick Mitchell, 1974; Sen. Manager, UK Banking, Samuel Montagu & Co. Ltd, 1976–78; Chm. and Finance Dir, Carlton Real Estate plc, 1978–82; Chairman: Echo Hotel plc, 1983–93; Plaza Hldgs Ltd, 2003–. Dir of private cos in sectors of energy, leisure, shipping and Eastern European property, 1994–2002. Dep. Chm., Standing Council of the Baronetage, 2012–. Clan Leader, rocheclan.org, 2012–. *Heir: s* David Alexander O'Grady Roche, *b* 28 Jan. 1976. *Address:* Bridge House, Starbotton, Skipton, N Yorks BD23 5HY. *T:* (01756) 760863; 20 Lancaster Mews, W2 3QE. *E:* davidroche20@yahoo.co.uk. *Club:* Royal Yacht Squadron.

ROCHE, Sir Henry John, (Sir Harry), Kt 1999; Chairman, Press Association, 1995–2008 (non-executive Director, 1988–2008); *b* 13 Jan. 1934; *s* of Henry Joseph Roche and Mary Ann Roche; *m* 1st, 1956, Shirley May Foreman (marr. diss. 1986); three *s*; 2nd, 1986, Heather Worthington. *Educ:* George Mitchell Sch., Leyton; Watford Coll. of Technol. (HND Printing Technol.). Apprentice engraver, until 1959; worked on shopfloor of Daily Mirror, 1959–69; Dep. Prodn Controller, Daily Mirror, 1969–70; Northern Prodn Controller, Mirror Gp Newspapers, Manchester, 1970–73; Prodn Dir, 1973–77, Man. Dir, 1977–85, Manchester Evening News; Man. Dir, The Guardian, 1985–88; Chm. and Chief Exec., Guardian Media Gp Plc, 1988–96; Chm., GMTV, 1989–92. Director: Johnston Press plc, 1993–2004 (Dep. Chm., 1995–2004); Jazz FM (formerly Golden Rose Communications) plc, 1995–2002 (Chm., 1999–2002). Chairman: Press Standards Bd of Finance Ltd, 1991–2003; Orgn for Promoting Understanding in Society, 1998–2002; Dep. Chm., Printers Charitable Corp., 1996–2000 (Dir, 1985–2000; Pres., 1993). Mem. Council, CPU, 1988–. FIP3 (FIOP 1993 (Pres., 1996–98)). Freeman, City of London, 1993. *Recreations:* golf, ski-ing, music (particularly jazz). *Clubs:* Royal Automobile; Dunham Forest Golf and Country (Cheshire).

ROCHE, Nicola, CBE 2013; Chief Executive, TdFHub2014 Ltd, 2013–14; *b* 27 Dec. 1956; *d* of Ronald and Shirley Roche. *Educ:* Harrogate Grammar Sch.; Univ. of York (BA Hons Hist. 1979); Birkbeck Coll., London (MA Hist. 1986). EDG, 1979–82; Prime Minister's Office, 1982–86; EDG, 1987–91; City and Inner London N TEC, 1991–93; Labour Attaché, Brussels, The Hague and Luxembourg, 1993–98; Private Office, DfEE, 1998–2001; Hd of Strategy, then Dir for Identity Cards, Children and Coroners, Home Office, 2001–04; Dir of Sport, 2004–07, Dir of Strategy, then of Staging, later of Ops, Govt Olympic Exec., 2007–13, DCMS. Non-exec. Dir, British Showjumping, 2013–. Mem. Bd, UK Sport, 2014–. Trustee, Care Leavers Foundn, 2013–. *Recreations:* athletics, walking, history, art, riding.

ROCHE, Patrick John; Member (NIU), Lagan Valley, Northern Ireland Assembly, 1999–2003 (UKU, 1998–99); *b* 4 March 1940; *m*. *Educ:* Trinity Coll., Dublin (BA Hons Econs and Politics); Durham Univ. (MA Politics). Posts in banking, 1957–66; Lecturer: in Economics, Ulster Univ., 1974–95; in Philosophy of Religion, Irish Baptist Coll., 1978–. *Publications:* (ed jtly) The Northern Ireland Question: myth and reality, 1991, perspectives and policies, 1994, Unionism, nationalism and partition, 1999; (jtly) An Economics Lesson for Irish Nationalists, 1996; The Appeasement of Terrorism and the Belfast Agreement, 2000; The Northern Ireland Question: the peace process and the Belfast Agreement, 2009; publications on political and econ. issues. *Recreation:* jogging.

ROCHESTER, 2nd Baron, of the 4th creation, *cr* 1931, of Rochester in the County of Kent; **Foster Charles Lowry Lamb;** DL; *b* 7 June 1916; *s* of 1st Baron Rochester, CMG, and Rosa Dorothea (*née* Hurst); *S* father, 1955; *m* 1942, Mary Carlisle (*d* 2000), *yr d* of T. B. Wheeler, CBE; two *s* one *d* (and one *d* decd). *Educ:* Mill Hill; Jesus College, Cambridge. MA. Served War of 1939–45: Captain 23rd Hussars; France, 1944. Joined ICI Ltd, 1946: Labour Manager, Alkali Div., 1955–63; Personnel Manager, Mond Div., 1964–72. Pro-Chancellor, Univ. of Keele, 1976–86. Chairman: Cheshire Scout Assoc., 1974–81; Governors of Chester Coll., 1974–83. DL Cheshire, 1979. DUniv Keele, 1986. *Heir: s* Hon. David Charles Lamb [*b* 8 Sept. 1944; *m* 1969, Jacqueline Stamp; two *s*. *Educ:* Shrewsbury Sch.; Univ. of Sussex]. *Address:* 337 Chester Road, Hartford, Northwich, Cheshire CW8 1QR. *T:* (01606) 74733. *Clubs:* Reform, National Liberal, MCC; Hawks (Cambridge).

See also Hon. T. M. Lamb.

ROCHESTER, Bishop of, since 2010; **Rt Rev. James Henry Langstaff;** Bishop to HM Prisons, since 2013; *b* 27 June 1956; *s* of Henry, (Harry), Langstaff and Jillian Langstaff (*née* Brooks, now Harper); *m* 1977, Bridget Streatfeild; one *s* one *d*. *Educ:* St Catherine's Coll., Oxford (BA (PPE) 1977, MA 1981); Univ. of Nottingham (BA (Theol.) 1980); St John's Coll., Nottingham (Dip. Pastoral Studies). Ordained deacon, 1981, priest, 1982; Asst Curate, St Peter, Farnborough, 1981–86; Vicar, St Matthew, Duddeston and St Clement, Nechells, 1986–96; RD, Birmingham City, 1995–96; Chaplain to Bp of Birmingham, 1996–2000; Rector, Holy Trinity, Sutton Coldfield, 2000–04; Area Dean, Sutton Coldfield, 2002–04; Bishop Suffragan of Lynn, 2004–10. Took seat in H of L, 2014. Tutor, Aston Trng Scheme, 1987–97. Mem., E of England Regl Assembly, 2006–10, Regl Strategy Bd, 2010. Non-exec. Dir, Good Hope Hosp. NHS Trust, 2003–04. Mem. Bd, FCH Housing and Care, 1988–2002; Chairman: Flagship Housing Gp, 2006–10; Housing Justice, 2008–. *Recreations:* ski-ing, walking, music, theatre, travel, current affairs. *Address:* Bishopscourt, 24 St Margaret's Street, Rochester, Kent ME1 1TS.

ROCHESTER, Dean of; *no new appointment at time of going to press.*

ROCHESTER, Archdeacon of; *see* Burton-Jones, Ven. S. D.

ROCHESTER, Terence Anthony, CB 1997; *b* 30 May 1937; *s* of Arthur Alfred Rochester and Winifred Mabel Rochester (*née* Smith); *m* 1966, Margaret Alexandra Fleming; one *s* one *d*. *Educ:* Southwest Essex Sch. British Rail, 1953–59, 1961–65; Nat. Service, 2nd Lieut, RE, 1959–61; joined Dept of Transport, 1965; various posts, 1965–87; Director: Transport Eastern Region, 1987–89; Transport W Midlands Region, 1989–90; Construction Programme, W Midlands, 1990–91; Chief Highway Engineer, 1991–97; Civil Engrg and Envmtl Policy Dir, 1994–96, Quality Services Dir, 1996–97, Highways Agency. Chairman: Tech. Cttee B/525 Bldg and Civil Engrg Structures, BSI, 1997–2000; Construction Clients' Forum, 1997–2000; Mem., Govt Cttee on Thaumasite, 1998–99. Res. Fellow, Transport Res. Foundn. Pres., CIRIA, 1998–2001; Hon. Mem., British World Road Assoc. *Recreations:* music, walking, DIY.

ROCK, David Annison, PPRIBA; FCSD; President, Royal Institute of British Architects, 1997–99; Partner, Camp 5, since 1992; *b* 27 May 1929; *s* of Thomas Henry Rock and Muriel Rock (*née* Barton); *m* 1st, 1954, Daphne Elizabeth Richards (marr. diss. 1986); three *s* two *d*; 2nd, 1989, Lesley Patricia Murray. *Educ:* Bede Grammar Sch., Sunderland; King's Coll., Durham (BArch 1952; CertTP 1953). ARIBA 1953, FRIBA 1967; MSIAD 1963, FCSD 1978. 2nd Lieut, RE, 1953–55. With Basil Spence and Partners, 1952–53 and 1955–59; David Rock Architect, 1958–59; Associate Partner, 1959–64, Equity Partner, 1964–71, Grenfell Baines & Hargreaves, later Building Design Partnership; Chm. and Man. Dir, Rock Townsend, 1971–92. Inventor, Workspace concept (sharing by several firms of central support services in a building), 1971; first RIBA/ARCUK approved Archt Developer, 1973. Major projects include: Bumpus Bookshop, W1, 1958; Univ. of Surrey Develt Plan, 1965; UN HQ and Austrian Nat. Conf. Centre, Vienna, 1970; Middlesex Poly., Bounds Green, 1975–88; (with Ralph Erskine) The London Ark, Hammersmith, 1993. Graham Willis Vis. Prof., Univ. of Sheffield, 1990–92. Founder Chairman and Director: 5 Dryden Street Collective, 1971–82; Barley Mow Workspace Ltd, 1973–92; Joint Founder: Construction Industry Council, 1986; Urban Design Alliance, 1997. Royal Institute of British Architects: Mem./Chm., Architecture Award Bds for 14 UK Regs, 1960–77; Mem., Vis. Bds, 20 univs and polys, 1973–81; Mem. Council, 1970–76, 1986–88, 1995–2001; Vice-Pres., 1987–88, 1995–97. Member: Architecture Bd, CNAA, 1975–81; Housing the Arts Cttee, Arts Council of GB, 1981–84; Lottery Awards Panel, Sports Council, 1995–97; Specialist Assessor, HEFCE, 1994–95; Hd, Lottery Architecture Unit, Arts Council of England, 1995–99. Finance Dir, HCL Ltd, 2003–05 and 2006–13. Chm., Soc. of Architect Artists, 1986–92; Pres., Architects Benevolent Soc., 2003–07 (Vice Pres., 2000–03, 2007–); Patron, Twentieth Century Soc., 2012–. Trustee: Montgomery Sculpture Trust, 2000–05; S Norfolk Buildings Preservation Trust, 2003–05. Hon. Treas., Harleston and Waveney Art Trail Collective, 2008–12. *Solo painting exhibitions:* Durham, and Covent Garden, 1977; Ditchling, 1994; Harleston, 2007; Spitalfields, London, 2010; Norwich, 2011. Hon. FAIA 2002 (Hon. AIA 1998). Glover Medal, Northern Architectl Assoc., 1949; Henry Bell Saint Bequest, Univ. of Durham, 1950; Crown Prize, Walpamur Co., 1951; Soane Medallion, 1954, Owen Jones Studentship prize, 1960, RIBA; President's Medal, AIA, 1998. *Publications:* Vivat Ware!: strategies to enhance a historic town, 1974; The Grassroot Developers: a handbook for town development trusts, 1979; *illustrated:* B. Allsopp, Decoration and Furniture, 1950; D. Senior, Your Architect, 1964; articles and reviews in prof. and technical pubns, 1961–. *Recreations:* work, painting, watching TV sport. *Address:* Camp 5, The Beeches, 13 London Road, Harleston, Norfolk IP20 9BH. *T:* and *Fax:* (01379) 854897. *E:* david.rock1@keme.co.uk.

ROCK, Kate Harriet Alexandra; Vice Chairman with special responsibility for business, Conservative Party, since 2015 (Head of Business Development, 2008–10; Director, Business Engagement, 2010–15); *b* London, 9 Oct. 1968; *d* of Thomas Pope and Anna Pope; *m* 1999, Caspar Rock; one *s* one *d*. *Educ:* Hanford Sch.; Sherborne Sch. of Girls; Oxford Poly. (BA Hons). Work in corporate communications and business relations; Partner, Retail and Luxury Brands team, College Hill PR, 1996–2008. Non-executive Director: Imagination Technologies, 2014–; First News, 2014–. Gov., Burlington Danes Acad., 2012–. *Recreations:* reading, running, ski-ing, tennis, Dorset countryside. *Clubs:* Queen's; Marden's (Klosters).

[Created a Baroness (Life Peer) 2015 but title not yet gazetted at time of going to press.]

ROCK, Prof. Paul Elliot, FBA 2000; Professor of Social Institutions, London School of Economics and Political Science, 1995–2008, now Emeritus; *b* 4 Aug. 1943; *s* of Ashley Rock and Charlotte (*née* Dickson); *m* 1965, Barbara Ravid (*d* 1998); two *s*. *Educ:* London School of Economics (BScSoc); Nuffield Coll., Oxford (DPhil). London School of Economics: Asst Lectr, 1967; Lectr, 1970; Sen. Lectr, 1976; Reader in Sociology, 1980; Reader in Social Institutions, 1981; Prof. of Sociology, 1986–95; Dir, Mannheim Centre for Study of Criminology and Criminal Justice, 1992–95. Vis. Prof., Princeton Univ., 1974–75; Vis. Schol., Ministry of Solicitor Gen. of Canada, 1981–82; Fellow, Center for Advanced Study of Behavioral Scis, Stanford, Calif, 1996; Resident, Rockefeller Foundn Study Center, Bellagio, 2003; Vis. Prof. of Criminology, Univ. of Pennsylvania, 2006–10. Apptd by Cabinet Office to work on official history of criminal justice, 2009–14. FRSA 1997. DUniv Middx, 2009. *Publications:* Making People Pay, 1973; Deviant Behaviour, 1973; The Making of Symbolic Interactionism, 1979; (with D. Downes) Understanding Deviance, 1982, 6th edn 2011; A View from the Shadows, 1986; Helping Victims of Crime, 1990; The Social World of an English Crown Court, 1993; Reconstructing a Women's Prison, 1996; After Homicide, 1998; Constructing Victims' Rights, 2004; Victims, Policy-Making and Criminology Theory: selected essays, 2010. *Address:* London School of Economics and Political Science, Houghton Street, Aldwych, WC2A 2AE. *T:* (020) 7955 7296.

ROCKEFELLER, David; banker; *b* New York City, 12 June 1915; *s* of John Davison Rockefeller, Jr and Abby Greene (Aldrich) Rockefeller; *m* 1940, Margaret (*d* 1996), *d* of Francis Sims McGrath, Mount Kisco, NY; one *s* four *d* (and one *s* decd). *Educ:* Lincoln School of Columbia University's Teachers College; Harvard Coll. (BS); London School of Economics; Univ. of Chicago (PhD). Sec. to Mayor Fiorello H. LaGuardia, 1940–41; Asst Regional Dir, US Office of Defense Health and Welfare Services, 1941. Served in US Army, N Africa and France, 1942–45 (Captain). Joined Chase National Bank, NYC, 1946; Asst Manager, Foreign Dept, 1946–47; Asst Cashier, 1947–48; Second Vice-Pres., 1948–49; Vice-Pres., 1949–51; Senior Vice-Pres., 1951–55; Chase Manhattan Bank (merger of Chase Nat. Bank and Bank of Manhattan Co.): Exec. Vice Pres., 1955–57; Dir, 1955–81; Vice-Chm., 1957–61; Pres. and Chm., Exec. Cttee, 1961–69; Chm. of Bd and Chief Exec. Officer, 1969–81; Chairman: Chase Internat. Investment Corp., 1961–75; Chase Internat. Adv. Cttee, 1980–2000; Rockefeller Brothers Fund Inc., 1981–87; The Rockefeller Group Inc., 1983–95; Rockefeller Center Properties Inc., 1985–92. Director: Internat. Exec. Service Corps (Chm., 1964–68); NY Clearing House, 1971–78; Center for Inter-American Relations (Chm. 1966–70); Overseas Develt Council; US-USSR Trade and Econ. Council, Inc.; Chairman: Rockefeller Univ., 1950–75; NYC Partnership, 1979–88; Hon. Chm., Americas Soc.; Hon. N America Chm., Trilateral Commn; Member: Council on Foreign Relations; Exec. Cttee, Museum of Modern Art (Chm., 1962–72, 1987–93); Harvard Coll. Bd of Overseers, 1954–60, 1962–68; Urban Develt Corp., NY State, Business Adv. Council, 1968–72; US Adv. Cttee on Reform of Internat. Monetary System, 1973–; Sen. Adv. Gp,

Bilderberg Meetings; US Exec. Cttee, Dartmouth Conf.; Bd, Inst. of Internat. Economics. Director: Downtown-Lower Manhattan Assoc., Inc. (Chm., 1958–65); Internat. House, NY, 1940–63; Morningside Heights Inc., 1947–70 (Pres., 1947–57, Chm., 1957–65); B. F. Goodrich Co., 1956–64; Equitable Life Assce Soc. of US, 1960–65. Trustee: Univ. of Chicago, 1947–62 (Life Trustee, 1966); Carnegie Endowment for Internat. Peace, 1947–60; Council of the Americas (Chm., 1965–70, 1983–92); Historic Hudson Valley (formerly Sleepy Hollow Restorations), 1981–. Member: American Friends of LSE; US Hon. Fellows, LSE; Founding Mem., Business Cttee for the Arts; Hon. Mem., Commn on White House Fellows, 1964–65; Hon. Chm., Japan Soc. World Brotherhood Award, Jewish Theol Seminary, 1953; Gold Medal, Nat. Inst. Social Sciences, 1967; Medal of Honor for city planning, Amer. Inst. Architects, 1968; C. Walter Nichols Award, NY Univ., 1970; Reg. Planning Assoc. Award, 1971. Hon. LLD: Columbia Univ., 1954; Bowdoin Coll., 1958; Jewish Theol Seminary, 1958; Williams Coll., 1966; Wagner Coll., 1967; Harvard, 1969; Pace Coll., 1970; St John's Univ., 1971; Middlebury, 1974; Univ. of Liberia, 1979; Rockefeller Univ., 1980; Hon. DEng: Colorado Sch. of Mines, 1974; Univ. of Notre Dame, 1987. Holds civic awards. Grand Croix, Legion of Honour, France, 2000 (Grand Officer, 1955); Order of Merit of the Republic, Italy; Order of the Southern Cross, Brazil; Order of the White Elephant and Order of the Crown, Thailand; Order of the Cedar, Lebanon; Order of the Sun, Peru; Order of Humane African Redemption, Liberia; Order of the Crown, Belgium; National Order of Ivory Coast; Grand Cordon, Order of Sacred Treasure, Japan, 1991. *Publications:* Unused Resources and Economic Waste, 1940; Creative Management in Banking, 1964; Memoirs, 2002. *Recreation:* sailing. *Address:* 30 Rockefeller Plaza, New York, NY 10112, USA. *Clubs:* Century, Harvard, River, Knickerbocker, Links, University, Recess (New York); New York Yacht.

ROCKEY, Patricia Mary, (Mrs D. C. Rockey); *see* Broadfoot, P. M.

ROCKHAMPTON, Bishop of, since 2003; **Rt Rev. Godfrey Charles Fryar;** *b* 5 Feb. 1950; *s* of Neville Gordon Fryar and Norma Emma Fryar (*née* Kloske); *m* 1977, Bronwyn Anne Horrocks; two *s* one *d*. *Educ:* All Souls' Sch., Charters Towers, Qld; St Francis Coll. (ThL 1972). Ordained deacon, 1973, priest, 1974; Bush Brother, Longreach, Cunnamulla and Quilpie, 1973–76; Parish Priest, Dawson Valley, N Rockhampton, N Mackay, Stafford, 1977–93; Dean, St Saviour's Cathedral, Goulburn, 1993–98; Asst Bishop, Wagga Wagga, and Vicar Gen., Dio. Canberra and Goulburn, 1998–2003. Protector Little Brother of St Francis, 2008–; Visitor, Soc. Sacred Advent Sisters, 2007–; Liaison Bp, Mission to Seafarers, 2004–09. Chm., Liturgy Commn, Anglican Ch Australia, 2008–. Chair: Refugee Settlement Cttee, dio. Brisbane, 1989–92 (active involvement in refugee settlement, 1989–); Anglicare dio. Canterbury and Goulburn, 2001–03; Anglicare Central Qld, 2004–05. Founding Mem. Bd, Riverina Anglican Coll., 1999–2003. *Recreation:* bush walking (walked Kokoda Track, 2006). *Address:* c/o Lis Escop, PO Box 710, Rockhampton, Qld 4700, Australia. *T:* (7) 49273188, *Fax:* (7) 49229325. *E:* bishop@anglicanrock.org.au.

ROCKLEY, 4th Baron *cr* 1934, of Lytchett Heath, Dorset; **Anthony Robert Cecil;** *b* 29 July 1961; *o s* of 3rd Baron Rockley and Lady Sarah Cadogan, *d* of 7th Earl Cadogan, MC; *S* father, 2011; *m* 1988, Katherine Jane, *d* of G. A. Whalley; one *s* two *d*. *Educ:* Eton; Gonville and Caius Coll., Cambridge (BA 1983; MA 1987). *Heir:* *s* Hon. William Evelyn Cecil, *b* 7 July 1996. *Address:* Lytchett Heath, Poole, Dorset BH16 6AE.

ROCKLIFFE, Victor Paul L.; *see* Lunn-Rockliffe.

ROCKLIN, David Samuel; Chairman, Norton Opax, 1973–89; *b* 15 Aug. 1931; *s* of Alfred Rocklin and Ada Rebecca Rocklin; *m* 1955, Dorothy Ann (*d* 2011); two *s* two *d*. *Educ:* Hele's School, Exeter. Managing Director, Norton Opax, 1969–73. *Recreations:* books, travel, music, painting, good food and conversation.

ROCKSAVAGE, Earl of; Alexander Hugh George Cholmondeley; *b* 12 Oct. 2009; *er* twin *s* and *heir* of Marquess of Cholmondeley, *qv*.

RODAN, Hon. Stephen Charles; MHK, Garff, since 1995; Speaker, House of Keys, Isle of Man, since 2006; *b* 19 April 1954; *s* of Robert W. Rodan and Betty Rodan (*née* Turner); *m* 1977, Ana Maria Valentina Ballesteros Torres, Mexico City; two *d*. *Educ:* High Sch., Glasgow; Univ. of Edinburgh; Heriot-Watt Univ. (BSc Hons Pharmacy 1977). MRPharmS 1978. Pharmacist, Elgin, Inverness, 1978–80; Pharmacy Manager, Bermuda, 1980–87; Pharmacy Proprietor, I of M, 1987–. Mem., Laxey Village Commn, 1991–95 (Chm., 1993–95). Isle of Man Government: Chm., Planning Cttee, 1997–99; Minister: for Educn, 1999–2004; for Health and Soc. Security, 2004–06. Chairman: Liberal Club, Univ. of Edinburgh, 1974–76; Scottish Young Liberals, 1974–76; Mem. Nat. Exec., Scottish Liberal Party, 1975–77. Contested (Scots L) Moray and Nairn, 1979. Pres., Caledonian Soc. of Bermuda, 1983–85. Pipe Major, Cair Vie Manx Pipe Band, 1992–95. Chm., Laxey and Lonan Heritage Trust, 1995–. Pres., Laxey and Lonan Br., 1998–, Isle of Man Co., 2012–, RBL. *Recreations:* playing the bagpipes, speaking at Burns' dinners, visiting art galleries, books, travel, Isle of Man heritage. *Address:* Orry's Mount, Ballaragh Road, Laxey, Isle of Man IM4 7PE. *T:* and *Fax:* (01624) 861514. *E:* steve.rodan@gov.im.

RODD, family name of **Baron Rennell**.

RODDA, James, (Jim), FCA; Financial Director, National Film and Television School, 1996–2005; *s* of George Rodda and Ruby (*née* Thompson); *m* 1967, Angela Hopkinson (*d* 2014); one *s* two *d*; *m* 2015, Elizabeth Hardy. *Educ:* Maldon Grammar Sch.; Reading Univ. (BA Hons); Leicester Univ. FCA 1971. Spicer and Pegler, 1967–71; Coopers and Lybrand, 1971–77; Thomas Cook Group, 1977–84; Lonconex Group, 1984–85; Mercantile Credit, 1985–86; London Commodity Exchange, 1986–91; Dir of Finance and Admin, House of Commons, 1991–96. Chm. then Treas., Berks, Bucks and Oxon Gp, 1994–, Nat. Treas., 2006–10, Nat. Council for Conservation of Plants and Gardens, later Plant Heritage. *Recreations:* railway rambling, Chiltern Soc. (No HS2 across the Chilterns Campaign).

RODDA, Dr John Carrol, FRMetS; FRGS; President, International Association of Hydrological Sciences, 1995–2001; *b* 15 Aug. 1934; *s* of late J. Allen Rodda and Eleanor M. Rodda; *m* 1961, Annabel Brailsford Edwards; two *s*. *Educ:* UCW, Aberystwyth (BSc 1956; DipEd 1957; PhD 1960; DSc 1979). FRMetS 1961; MCIWEM 1976. DSIR Res. Fellow, 1960–62, Hydrologist, 1962–65, Hydraulics Res. Station, Wallingford; Hd, Catchment Res., Inst. Hydrology, Wallingford, 1965–69 and 1970–72; Consultant, WMO, Geneva, 1969–70 (on secondment); Head: Envmtl Pollution and Resources Unit, Directorate Gen. of Res., DoE, 1972–74; Data Acquisition Br., Water Data Unit, Reading, DoE, 1974–82; Asst Dir, Inst. Hydrology, Wallingford, 1982–88; Dir, Hydrology and Water Resources Dept, WMO, Geneva, 1988–95. Visiting Professor: Dept of Geog., Univ. of Strathclyde, 1976–79; Internat. Inst. for Infrastructure, Hydraulics & Envmt, Delft, 1976–97; Univ. of Perugia, 1983; Hon. Prof., Inst. Geog. and Earth Scis, Univ. of Aberystwyth (formerly Univ. of Wales, Aberystwyth), 1995–. Ed., 1972–79, Sec.-Gen., 1979–87, Internat. Assoc. Hydrological Scis; Sec./Treas., ICSU/Union Internat. des Assocs et Organismes Techniques Cttee on Water Res., 1982–87; Mem., Scientific Cttee on Water Res., ICSU, 1991–95; Mem. Exec. Cttee, IUGG, 1995–2001. UN International Decade for Natural Disaster Reduction: Member: Prep. Cttee, 1988–90; Scientific and Tech. Cttee, 1990–95; Chm., UN Admin. Co-ordinating Cttee, Sub-cttee on Water Resources, 1990–92; Chairman: Prog. Rev. Gp IV, Centre for Ecol. and Hydrol., NERC, 1996–2000; Commn on Water, World Humanities Action Trust, 1998–2000; Member: Bd of Govs, World Water Council, 1999–2001; Regl Envmt Protection Adv. Cttee, Envmt Agency, 2007–11. Associate. Dir, Hydro-GIS Ltd, 2006–. Mem., Amer. Geophysical Union, 1960; Hon. Member: British Hydrological Soc., 1983; Amer. Water Resources Assoc., 1992; Hungarian Hydrological Soc., 1992. Chm., Oxon Agenda 21 Planning Gp, 1997–2001; Vice-Chm., Trust for Oxon's Envmt, 2001–03 (Mem. Bd, 1998–2000). Fellow: NERC Centre for Ecol. and Hydrol., 2004; IUGG, 2015. FRGS 2003. Hugh Robert Mill Prize, RMetS, 1980; Internat. Hydrology Prize, Internat. Assoc. of Hydrol Scis/UNESCO/WMO, 2004. *Publications:* (jtly) Systematic Hydrology, 1976; (ed) Facets of Hydrology, 1976, Facets of Hydrology II, 1985 (trans. Russian); (jtly) Global Water Resource Issues, 1994; (ed jtly) Land Surface Processes in Hydrology: trials and tribulations of modeling and measurement, 1997; (ed jtly) World Water Resources at the Beginning of the Twenty-First Century, 2003; (ed jtly) The Basis of Civilisation - Water Science?, 2004; (ed jtly) The Role of Hydrology in Water Resources Management, 2009; (ed jtly) Progress in Modern Hydrology: past, present and future, 2015. *Recreations:* music, painting, environment. *Address:* Ynyslas, Brightwell cum Sotwell, Wallingford, Oxon OX10 0RG. *E:* jandarodda@waitrose.com.

RODDAM; *see* Holderness-Roddam.

RODDICK, (George) Winston, CB 2004; QC 1986; Police and Crime Commissioner (Ind) for North Wales, since 2012; *b* Caernarfon, 2 Oct. 1940; *s* of William and Aelwen Roddick; *m* 1966, Cennin Parry; one *s* one *d*. *Educ:* Sir Huw Owen GS, Caernarfon; Tal Handak, Malta; University Coll. London (LLB, LLM). Called to the Bar, Gray's Inn, 1968, Bencher, 1997; a Recorder, 1987–2012; Counsel Gen. to Nat. Assembly for Wales, 1998–2003; Leader, Wales and Chester Circuit, 2007–10. Member: Gen. Council of the Bar, 1992–95 and 2007–12; Professional Conduct Cttee of the Bar, 1994–96; Employed Barristers Cttee, Bar Council, 2000–03; Chm., Bristol and Cardiff Chancery Bar Assoc., 1996–98. Hon. Recorder, Caernarfon, 2001–12. Member: ITC, 1998; S4C Authy, 2005–12. Member: Welsh Language Bd, 1988–93; Lord Chancellor's Adv. Cttee on Statute Law, 1999–2003; Standing Cttee on use of Welsh lang. in legal proceedings, 1999–2003. Vice Pres., Aberystwyth Univ. (formerly Univ. of Wales, Aberystwyth), 2000–11 (Hon. Fellow, 1999). Vice Pres., Caernarfon Male Voice Choir, 1994–. Patron, Caernarfon RFC, 1994–. Mem., Gorsedd of Bards, 2004–. *Recreation:* fishing. *T:* (office) (01492) 805486. *Clubs:* Caernarfon Sailing, Caernarfon Bowls.

RODECK, Prof. Charles Henry, DSc; FRCOG, FRCPath, FMedSci; Professor of Obstetrics and Gynaecology, University College London, 1990–2007, now Emeritus; *b* 23 Aug. 1944; *s* of Heinz and Charlotte Rodeck; *m* 1971, Elisabeth (*née* Rampton); one *s* one *d*. *Educ:* University College London (BSc Anatomy 1966; Fellow 2003); UCH Med. Sch. (MB BS 1969); DSc (Med) London 1991. MRCOG 1975; FRCOG 1987; FRCPath 1994. House appts to 1975; King's College Hospital Medical School: Registrar, 1975; Lectr, 1976; Sen. Lectr/Consultant, 1978; Dir, Harris Birthright Res. Centre for Fetal Medicine, 1983–86; Prof., Inst. of Obstetrics and Gynaecol., RPMS, Queen Charlotte's and Chelsea Hosp., 1986–90. Member, Council: Obst. and Gyn. Sect., RSocMed; British Assoc. of Perinatal Med.; RCOG, 1991–92, 1996–2001 (Chm., Subspeciality Bd, 1989–92); Mem., Working Party on Antenatal Diagnosis, RCP, 1986–89; Chm., Steering Gp for Fetal Tissue Bank, MRC, 1989–92; Mem., EEC Working Party on Chorion Villus Sampling, 1983–85; Mem., Antenatal Screening Subgroup, DoH, 2001–05. Examr, RCOG and Univs of Aberdeen, Brussels, Dublin, Leiden, London, Nottingham, Oxford, Reading, Singapore, Stockholm; Visiting Professor: USA Univs; Hong Kong Univ. Pres., Internat. Fetal Medicine and Surgery Soc., 1986; Chm., Assoc. of Profs of Obst. and Gyn., 1995–2000; Chm., Fedn of Assocs of Clinical Profs, 2000–07; Pres., Internat. Soc. for Prenatal Diagnosis, 2002–06. J. Y. Simpson Oration, 2000, William Meredith Fletcher Shaw Oration, 2002, Founder's Lect., 2010, RCOG. Founder FMedSci 1998. Hon. Member: Italian Soc. of Perinatol., 1982; Indian Soc. for Prenatal Diagnosis and Therapy, 1984; S African Soc. of Obstetrics and Gynaecol., 1985; British Assoc. of Perinatal Medicine, 1992; Soc. of Obstetrics and Gynaecol. of Nigeria, 1999; Soc. of Perinatol., Bogota, 2002. Hon. Fellow: Amer. Inst. of Ultrasound in Medicine, 1990; Soc. of Maternal Fetal Medicine of USA, 2008; Nat. Acad. of Medicine of Argentina, 2008. Mem., editl bds of professional jls, UK and overseas; Ed. for Europe, 1985–2005, Ed.-in-Chief, 2005–07, Prenatal Diagnosis. James Blundell Medal, British Blood Transfusion Soc., 2002; Eardley Holland Medal, RCOG, 2010; Ian Donald Gold Medal, Internat. Soc. of Ultrasound in Obst. and Gyn., 2014. *Publications:* (ed) Prenatal Diagnosis, 1984; (ed) Fetal Diagnosis of Genetic Defects, 1987; (ed) Fetal Medicine, 1989; (co-ed) Prenatal Diagnosis and Screening, 1992; (co-ed) Fetus and Neonate, 1993; (co-ed) Fetal Medicine: basic science and clinical practice, 1999, 2nd edn 2009; over 500 articles on prenatal diagnosis and fetal medicine. *Recreations:* stroking the cats, looking out of aeroplanes, the Wigmore Hall, Tottenham Hotspur. *Club:* Athenæum.

RODEN, 10th Earl of, *cr* 1771 (Ire.); **Robert John Jocelyn;** Baron Newport 1743; Viscount Jocelyn 1755; Bt 1665; *b* 25 Aug. 1938; *s* of 9th Earl of Roden and Clodagh Rose (*d* 1989), *d* of Edward Robert Kennedy; *S* father, 1993; *m* 1st, 1970, Sara Cecilia (marr. diss. 1982), *d* of Brig. Andrew Dunlop; one *d*; 2nd, 1986, Ann Margareta Maria, *d* of Dr Gunnar Henning; one *s*. *Educ:* Stowe. *Heir:* *s* Viscount Jocelyn, *qv*.

RODEN, Michael; Principal, University of Birmingham School, since 2014; *b* Rotherham, S Yorks, 15 Oct. 1959; *s* of Stanley and Kathleen Freda Roden; *m* 1982, Alison Mary Tonks; two *s* one *d*. *Educ:* Swinton Comprehensive Sch., Rotherham; Manchester Univ. (BSc Geog., PGCE). NPQH 2003. Asst Master, King Edward's Sch., Birmingham, 1982–89; Hd of Geog., Bristol GS, 1990–95; Dep. Headmaster, King Edward VI Camp Hill Sch. for Boys, 1995–2003; Asst Headmaster, King Edward's Sch., Birmingham, 2003–08; Headmaster, King Edward VI Camp Hill Sch. for Boys, Birmingham, 2008–14. Pres., Camp Hill Old Edwardian's Assoc., 2009–. *Recreations:* golf, reading crime novels, running, Rugby, travel, ski-ing. *Address:* University of Birmingham School, 12 Weoley Park Road, Birmingham B29 6QU. *Clubs:* Marston Lakes Golf (Sec., 2004–08, Captain, 2007); Camp Hill Rugby Football (Pres., 2008–14), Camp Hill Old Edwardian's Cricket (Pres., 2008–14).

RODENBURG, Patricia Anne, (Patsy), OBE 2005; Head of Voice, since 1981, and Professor, since 2014, Guildhall School of Speech and Drama; Head of Voice, Royal National Theatre, 1990–2006; *b* 2 Sept. 1953; *d* of late Marius Rodenburg and Margaret Edna Rodenburg (*née* Moody). *Educ:* St Christopher's Sch., Beckenham; Central Sch. of Speech and Drama. Voice Tutor, Royal Shakespeare Co., 1981–90; Head of Voice, Stratford Fest. Theatre, Canada, 1984–85; Associate: Michael Howard Studios, NY, 1994–; Royal Court Theatre, 1999–; Founding Dir, Voice and Speech Centre, London, 1989–; works regularly with Almeida Theatre, Shared Experience, Cheek-by-Jowl, Théâtre de Complicité, Donmar Warehouse; works extensively in theatre, TV and radio throughout Europe, N America, Australia, Africa and Asia with major theatre and opera cos. Presenter, writer and producer, DVD, Shakespeare in the Present, 2011. Distinguished Vis. Prof., Southern Methodist Univ., Dallas, 1987–. Mem. Bd, RSC, 2014–. *Publications:* The Right to Speak, 1992; The Need for Words, 1993; The Actor Speaks, 1997; Speaking Shakespeare, 2002; Presence, 2007; Power, Presentation, 2009; Shakespeare in the present, 2012. *Recreations:* travelling, reading. *Address:* c/o Guildhall School of Music and Drama, Silk Street, Barbican, EC2Y 8DT.

RODERICK, Edward Joseph; Co-Chairman, Envestors (MENA) Ltd, 2008–13; Group Chief Executive, Christian Salvesen PLC, 1997–2004; *b* 23 Oct. 1952; *s* of late Edward Deakin Roderick and Joan Roderick; *m* 1974, Denise Ann Rowan; two *s*. *Educ:* De La Salle Grammar Sch., Liverpool. National/International CPC. FCIL (FILog 1992). B&I Line, 1972–87 (Head, UK Freight Ops, 1984–87); Man. Dir, Alexandra Molyneux Transport, 1987–88; BET plc, 1988–90: Man. Dir, IFF, 1988–90; Gp Dir, UTCH Ltd, 1988–90; Director: UTL Ltd, 1988–90; Seawheel, 1988–90; Gen. Manager, UK and Iberia, Bell Lines,

1990–92; Divl Man. Dir, Hays Network Distribn and other directorships in Hays plc, 1992–95; Man. Dir, Industrial Div., 1996–97, Man. Dir, Logistics UK and Europe, 1997, Christian Salvesen PLC. Dir, Heywood Williams Gp plc, 2002–07. Non-exec. Dir, Cash For Mobiles Dubai, 2010–11. Chairman: Passim Internat. Ltd, 2005–07; Truck Project Ltd, 2005–08. Director: Road Haulage Assoc., 1998–2000; Freight Transport Assoc., 2000–07. Sen. Vice-Pres., Global Logistics Agility Inc., 2007–08. Dir, Northern Ballet Theatre, 1997–2000. MInstD 1987; CCMI (CIMgt 2000). Distinguished Fellow, Hult Internat. Business Sch., 2011. Hon. LLD De Montfort, 2001. *Recreations:* golf, opera, ballet, swimming, wife and family. *Address:* Campbell House, Northampton Road, Higham Ferrers, Rushden, Northants NN10 6AL. *T:* (01933) 419148, (Dubai) 506554527. *Clubs:* Royal Automobile; Wellingborough Golf; Jumeira Golf Estates (Dubai).

RODGER, Prof. Albert Alexander, DSc, PhD; FICE; FREng; Professor of Civil Engineering, University of Aberdeen, 1995–2014, now Emeritus; Visiting Professor of Civil and Environmental Engineering, University of Strathclyde, since 2015; *b* Greenock, Renfrewshire, 12 May 1951; *s* of Alexander Rodger and Grace Rodger; *m* 1973, Jane Helen Whyte; two *d. Educ:* Duncanrig Sch., East Kilbride; Univ. of Aberdeen (BSc 1st Cl. Engrg 1973; PhD 1976; DSc 2015). FGS 1975; CEng 1983; FICE 2001; FREng 2010. Res. Scientist, Cementation Research Ltd, 1977–79; University of Aberdeen: Lectr, 1979–89; Sen. Lectr, 1989–95; Dean, Sci. and Engrg, 2001–03; Vice Principal and Hd, Coll. of Physical Scis, 2003–11; Vice Principal, External Affairs, 2011–14. Mem. Bd, SFC, 2009–. CEO, Nat. Subsea Res. Inst., 2009–11. Hon. Citizen, Hadong County, Rep. of Korea, 2014. *Recreation:* photography. *Address:* 7 Mill Lade Wynd, Aberdeen AB22 8QN. *T:* (01224) 708905. *E:* a.a.rodger@abdn.ac.uk.

RODGER, Martin Owen; QC 2006; Deputy President, Upper Tribunal (Lands Chamber), since 2013; a Recorder, since 2003; *b* 11 Feb. 1962; *s* of William Rodger and Elizabeth Rodger (*née* Tunney); *m* 1991, Catherine Murphy; two *s* one *d. Educ:* St Aloysius Coll., Glasgow; University Coll., Oxford (BA 1983). Called to the Bar, Middle Temple, 1986. *Address:* Upper Tribunal (Lands Chamber), 5th floor, Rolls Building, 7 Rolls Buildings, Fetter Lane, EC4A 1NL. *T:* (020) 7612 9700. *E:* Martin.Rodger@judiciary.gsi.gov.uk.

RODGER, Mary Elizabeth; *see* Francis, M. E.

RODGER, Prof. Nicholas Andrew Martin, DPhil; FBA 2003; FSA, FRHistS; Senior Research Fellow, All Souls College, Oxford, since 2008; *b* 12 Nov. 1949; *s* of Lt Comdr Ian Rodger and Sara Rodger; *m* 1982, Susan Eleanor Farwell; three *s* one *d. Educ:* Ampleforth Coll., York; University Coll., Oxford (BA 1971, MA; DPhil 1974). FRHistS 1980; FSA 1985. Asst Keeper, PRO, 1974–91; Anderson Sen. Res. Fellow, Nat. Maritime Mus., 1992–99; Sen. Lectr in Hist., 1999–2000, Prof. of Naval Hist., 2000–08, Exeter Univ. *Publications:* The Admiralty, 1979; (ed with G. A. Osbon) The Black Battlefleet, by G. A. Ballard, 1980; Exchequer Ancient Deeds DD Series, 1101–1645 (E211), 1983; Naval Records for Genealogists, 1985, 3rd edn 1998; (ed) The Naval Miscellany, Vol. V, 1985; The Wooden World: an anatomy of the Georgian Navy, 1986, 2nd edn 1988; (ed with G. J. A. Raven) The Anglo-Dutch Relationship in War and Peace 1688–1988, 1990; The Insatiable Earl: a life of John Montagu, Fourth Earl of Sandwich, 1718–1792, 1993; (ed jtly) British Naval Documents 1204–1960, 1993; (ed) Naval Power in the Twentieth Century, 1996; The Safeguard of the Sea: a naval history of Britain, Vol. I, 660–1649, 1997; (ed) Memoirs of a Seafaring Life: the narrative of William Spavens, 2000; The Command of the Ocean: a naval history of Britain, Vol. II, 1649–1815, 2004; (ed with R. Cock) A Guide to the Naval Records in the National Archives, 2006; Essays in Naval History, from Medieval to Modern, 2009. *Address:* All Souls College, Oxford OX1 4AL. *T:* (01865) 279379, *Fax:* (01865) 279299. *E:* Nicholas.Rodger@all-souls.ox.ac.uk.

RODGERS, family name of **Baron Rodgers of Quarry Bank**.

RODGERS OF QUARRY BANK, Baron *cr* 1992 (Life Peer), of Kentish Town in the London Borough of Camden; **William Thomas Rodgers;** PC 1975; Chairman, Advertising Standards Authority, 1995–2001; Leader, Liberal Democrats, House of Lords, 1998–2001; *b* 28 Oct. 1928; *s* of William Arthur and Gertrude Helen Rodgers; *m* 1955, Silvia (*d* 2006), *d* of Hirsch Szulman; three *d. Educ:* Sudley Road Council Sch.; Quarry Bank High School, Liverpool; Magdalen College, Oxford (Open Exhibnr in Modern History). General Secretary, Fabian Society, 1953–60; publisher's editor, 1961–64, 1970–72; management recruiter, 1972–74. Contested: (Lab) Bristol West, March 1957; (SDP) Stockton N, 1983; (SDP/Alliance) Milton Keynes, 1987. MP (Lab 1962–81, SDP 1981–83) Stockton-on-Tees, 1962–74, Teesside, Stockton, 1974–83; Parly Under-Sec. of State: Dept of Econ. Affairs, 1964–67, Foreign Office, 1967–68; Leader, UK delegn to Council of Europe and Assembly of WEU, 1967–68; Minister of State: BoT, 1968–69; Treasury, 1969–70; MoD, 1974–76; Sec. of State for Transport, 1976–79. Chm., Expenditure Cttee on Trade and Industry, 1971–74. Vice-Pres., SDP, 1982–87. Dir-Gen., RIBA, 1987–94. Borough Councillor, St Marylebone, 1958–62. Hon. FRIBA 1994; Hon. FIStructE 1993. Hon. Fellow, Liverpool John Moores Univ., 2008. Hon. LLD Liverpool, 2008. *Publications:* Hugh Gaitskell, 1906–1963 (ed), 1964; (jt) The People into Parliament, 1966; The Politics of Change, 1982; (ed) Government and Industry, 1986; Fourth Among Equals, 2000; pamphlets, etc. *Address:* 43 North Road, N6 4BE.

RODGERS, Sir (Andrew) Piers (Wingate), 3rd Bt *cr* 1964, of Groombridge, Kent; Secretary, Royal Academy of Arts, London, 1982–96; *b* 24 Oct. 1944; second *s* of Sir John Rodgers, 1st Bt and Betsy (*d* 1998), *y d* of Francis W. Aikin-Sneath; *S* brother, 1997; *m* 1st, 1979, Marie Agathe Houette (marr. diss. 2000); two *s*; 2nd, 2004, Ilona Medvedeva; two *d. Educ:* Eton Coll.; Merton Coll., Oxford (BA 1st Cl. Honour Mods, Prox. acc. Hertford and De Paravicini Prizes). J. Henry Schroder Wagg & Co. Ltd, London, 1967–73: Personal Asst to Chairman, 1971–73; Director, International Council on Monuments and Sites (ICOMOS), Paris, 1973–79; Consultant, UNESCO, Paris, 1979–80; Member, Technical Review Team, Aga Khan Award for Architecture, 1980, 1983; Secretary, UK Committee of ICOMOS, 1981. Trustee, The Type Mus., London, 1991–2004 (Dir, 2001–04). Mem. Bd, Warburg Inst., Univ. of London, 1993–98. FRSA 1973. Mem., Court of Assts, Masons' Co., 1982–. Chevalier de l'Ordre des Arts et des Lettres (France), 1987; Chevalier de l'Ordre National du Mérite (France), 1991; Cavaliere dell'Ordine al Merito della Repubblica Italiana, 1992. *Publications:* articles on protection of cultural heritage. *Recreations:* books, music, Real tennis, Islamic art. *Heir: s* Thomas Rodgers, *b* 18 Dec. 1979. *Address:* Peverell, Bradford Peverell, Dorset DT2 9SE. *Club:* Brooks's.

RODGERS, Bríd; Director, Bord Bia, 2004–10; *b* 20 Feb. 1935; *d* of Tom Stratford and Josephine (*née* Coll); *m* 1960, Antoin Rodgers; three *s* three *d. Educ:* St Louis Convent, Monaghan; University Coll., Dublin (BA Hons Mod. Langs; Higher DipEd). Exec. Mem., NI Civil Rights Assoc., 1970–71. Mem., Irish Senate, 1983–87. Mem. (SDLP), Craigavon BC, 1985–93. Social Democratic and Labour Party: Vice Chair, 1976–78; Chair, 1978–80; Gen. Sec., 1981–83; Delegate to Brooke/Mayhew Talks, 1991–92; elected in Upper Bann to Negotiations, 1996, Chair, Negotiating Team, 1996–98; Dep. Leader, 2001–04. Mem. (SDLP) Upper Bann, NI Assembly, 1998–2003. Minister of Agriculture & Rural Develt, NI, 1999–2002. Contested (SDLP) Tyrone West, 2001. Hon. LLD NUI, 2003; Hon. DLitt Harper Adams, 2009. *Recreations:* reading, music, golf. *Address:* 34 Kilmore Road, Lurgan, Co. Armagh BT67 9BP.

RODGERS, Derek; *see* Rodgers, His Honour R. F.

RODGERS, Joan, CBE 2001; soprano; *b* 4 Nov. 1956; *d* of Thomas and Julia Rodgers; *m* 1988, Paul Daniel, *qv* (marr. diss. 2005); two *d. Educ:* Univ. of Liverpool (BA Hons Russian); RNCM. FRNCM. Kathleen Ferrier Meml Scholarship, 1981. Début, Aix-en-Provence, 1982; Covent Garden début, 1984; NY Met. début, 1995; has appeared with all major British opera cos; has worked with many conductors, incl. Barenboim, Solti, Abbado, Rattle, Gardiner, Colin Davis, Andrew Davis, Salonen, Mehta, Harnoncourt; Mozart rôles incl. Susanna, Zerlina, Ilia, Fiordiligi, Elvira, Sandrina, Countess; other rôles incl. Cleopatra in Giulio Cesare, Ginevra in Ariodante, Tatyana in Eugene Onegin, Mélisande, Theodora, Governess in The Turn of the Screw, Marschallin in Der Rosenkavalier, Blanche in The Carmelites; regular recitals and concert performances in London, Australia, Vienna, Madrid, Los Angeles, New York, Chicago, Paris and Brussels; many recordings. *Recreations:* walking, spending time with my family. *Address:* c/o Ingpen & Williams Ltd, 7 St George's Court, 131 Putney Bridge Road, SW15 2PA.

RODGERS, Dr Patricia Elaine Joan; Permanent Secretary, Ministry of Tourism, Commonwealth of the Bahamas, since 2013; *b* 13 July 1948; *d* of late Dr Kenneth V. A. Rodgers, OBE and Anatol C. Rodgers, MBE. *Educ:* Univ. of Aberdeen (MA Hons English, 1970); Inst. of Internat. Relations, St Augustine, Trinidad (Dip. in Internat. Relns (Hons) 1972); Inst. Univ. des Hautes Etudes Internationales, Geneva (PhD 1977). Joined Ministry of Foreign Affairs, Nassau, Bahamas, 1970; Minister-Counsellor, Washington, 1978–83; Actg High Comr to Canada, 1983–86, High Comr, 1986–88; High Comr to UK, 1988–92, also Ambassador (non-resident) to: FRG and Belgium, 1988–92, to EC and France, 1989–92; Perm. Rep. to IMO, 1991–92; Chief of Protocol, Min. of For. Affairs, 1993–94; Permanent Secretary: Min. of Tourism, 1995–2003; Min. of For. Affairs, 2003–07; Cabinet Office, 2007–08; Min. of For. Affairs, 2008–12. *Publications:* Mid-Ocean Archipelagos and International Law: a study of the progressive development of international law, 1981. *Recreations:* folk painting, gourmet cooking, theatre. *Address:* Ministry of Tourism, George Street, Bolam House, PO Box N3701, Nassau, Bahamas.

RODGERS, Paul David; Director, Commercial Operations, HS2, Department for Transport, since 2014; *b* Manchester, 21 June 1962; *s* of John Rodgers and Lillian Rodgers; *m* (marr. diss.); one *d. Educ:* Univ. of Southampton (BA Hons Archaeol.). MCIPS 2010. Shell UK, 1989–99; Regl Commercial Manager, Great Western, 1999–2003; Hd, Passenger Business, Network Rail, 2003–04; Department for Transport: Divl Manager, Midlands, 2004–08; Prog. Dir, 2008–11; Dir, Rail Commercial, 2011–14. *Recreations:* hillwalking, beekeeping. *Address:* Department for Transport, 33 Horseferry Road, SW1P 4DR. *T:* (020) 7944 4774, *Fax:* (020) 7944 2446. *E:* paul.rodgers@dft.gsi.gov.uk.

RODGERS, Sir Piers; *see* Rodgers, Sir A. P. W.

RODGERS, His Honour Robert Frederick, (Derek); a County Court Judge, Northern Ireland, 1997–2012; *b* 10 June 1947; *s* of Fred and Peggy Rodgers; *m* 1973, Kathleen Mary Colling; one *s* one *d. Educ:* Royal Belfast Academical Instn; Queen's Univ., Belfast (LLB 1970). J. C. Taylor & Co., solicitors, 1970–89; a Dep. District Judge, 1986–89; a District Judge, 1989–97. Parole Comr for Northern Ireland (formerly Life Sentence Review Comr), 2002–. Mem., Legal Adv. Cttee, C of I, 2002–. Chancellor, Diocese of Connor, 2007–. *Recreations:* travel, reading, music, Rugby, sailing. *Clubs:* Ulster Reform; Carrickfergus Sailing; Ballymena Rugby Football.

RODHAM, Ven. Morris; Archdeacon of Warwick, and Archdeacon Missioner, Diocese of Coventry, since 2010; *b* 1959. *Educ:* Hatfield Coll., Durham (BA 1981); St John's Coll., Durham (PGCE 1985); Trinity Coll., Bristol (MA 1993). Ordained deacon, 1993, priest, 1994; Asst Curate, St Mark, New Milverton, 1993–97; Vicar, St Mary's, Leamington Priors, 1997–2010; Rural Dean, Warwick and Leamington, 2006–09. *Address:* c/o Cathedral and Diocesan Offices, 1 Hill Top, Coventry CV1 5AB. *T:* (024) 7652 1337.

RODHOUSE, Prof. Paul Gregory Kenneth, PhD, DSc; FLS; British Antarctic Survey Emeritus Fellow, since 2013; *b* Bromley, Kent, 13 Feb. 1951; *s* of Kenneth Frederick Rodhouse and Eileen Frances Rodhouse; *m* 1991, Laura Matthews; two *s* one *d. Educ:* St Mary's Coll., Southampton; Westfield Coll., Univ. of London (BSc Hons 1972); Univ. of Southampton (MSc 1973; PhD 1977; DSc 1995). Cambridge and London Galapagos Is Expedn, 1972; Res. Scientist, University Coll., Galway/NUI, 1977–82; Res. Associate and Lectr, SUNY at Stony Brook, 1982–84; British Antarctic Survey: Res. Scientist, 1985–2000; Hd, Biol Scis Div. and Mem. Bd, 2000–10; Student Registrar, 2010–13; Principal Scientist, S Georgia Govt Lab. at King Edward Point, 2001–13. Hon. Prof., Univ. of Aberdeen, 2001–. Mem., Innovation and Strategy Bd, NERC, 2010–13. Pres., Cephalopod Internat. Adv. Council, 1997–2000. Chair, Scientific Cttee for Antarctic Res. prog. on evolution in the Antarctic, 1999–2004. Sen. Mem., St Edmund's Coll., Cambridge, 2003–. Trustee (formerly Patron), Gilbert White's House and Garden and Oates Collection, 2010–. FLS 1988. *Publications:* (with M. Drummond) The Yachtsman's Naturalist, 1980; (ed jtly) Squid Recruitment Dynamics, 1998; (with P. R. Boyle) Cephalopods: ecology and fisheries, 2005; contrib. papers to learned jls. *Recreations:* yachting, painting, natural history, angling, photography. *Address:* British Antarctic Survey, High Cross, Madingley Road, Cambridge CB3 0ET. *E:* p.rodhouse@bas.ac.uk.

RODLEY, Sir Nigel (Simon), KBE 1998; PhD; Professor of Law, 1994–2015, now Emeritus, and Chair, Human Rights Centre, since 2003, University of Essex; *b* 1 Dec. 1941; *s* of John Peter Rodley (*né* Hans Israel Rosenfeld) and Rachel Rodley (*née* Kantorowitz); *m* 1967, Lyn Bates. *Educ:* Clifton Coll.; Univ. of Leeds (LLB 1963); Columbia Univ. (LLM 1965); New York Univ. (LLM 1970); Univ. of Essex (PhD 1993). Asst Prof. of Law, Dalhousie Univ., 1965–68; Associate Economic Affairs Officer, UN HQ, NY, 1968–69; Vis. Lectr in Pol Sci., New Sch. for Social Res., NY, 1969–72; Res. Fellow, NY Univ. Center for Internat. Studies, 1970–72; Founder and Hd, Legal Office, Amnesty Internat., 1973–90; Vis. Lectr in Law, 1973–90, Res. Fellow, 1983, LSE; Reader in Law, Univ. of Essex, 1990–94. Dist. Vis. Scholar, Grad. Sch. of Internat. Studies, Univ. of Denver, 2002. Special Rapporteur on Torture, UN Commn on Human Rights, 1993–2001; Member: Council, Justice, 1997–; UN Human Rights Cttee, 2001– (Vice-Chm., 2003–04, 2009–10; Chm., 2013–14); Internat. Ind. Gp of Eminent Persons, Sri Lankan Commn of Inquiry, 2007–08; Foreign Sec.'s Adv. Gp on Human Rights, 2010–; Bahrain Ind. Commn of Inquiry, 2011. Pres., Internat. Commn of Jurists, 2013– (Comr, 2003–; Exec. Cttee, 2004–06). Trustee, Stephen Roth Inst. for the Study of Anti-Semitism and Racism, Tel Aviv Univ., 2002–. Patron: Peace Brigades Internat., 2007–; The Rights Practice, 2009; Coram Children's Legal Centre, 2011–; Freedom from Torture (formerly Med. Foundn for the Care of Victims of Torture), 2013– (Trustee, 2003–13); REDRESS, 2013–. Hon. FFFLM 2008. Hon. LLD Dalhousie, 2000. Goler T. Butcher Human Rights Medal, Amer. Soc. of Internat. Law, 2005. Co-Ed. in Chief, Israel Law Review, 2010–; Member: Editl Review Bd, Human Rights Qly, 1994–; Editl Cttee, British Yearbook of Internat. Law, 2000–. *Publications:* (ed jtly) International Law in the Western Hemisphere, 1974; (jtly) Enhancing Global Human Rights, 1979; The Treatment of Prisoners under International Law, 1987, 3rd edn 2009 (Chinese edn 2006); (ed) To Loose the Bands of Wickedness: international intervention in defence of human rights, 1992; (ed jtly) International Responses to Traumatic Stress, 1996; (ed jtly) Routledge Handbook of International Human Rights Law, 2013; numerous articles in learned jls and contribs to books. *Recreations:* music, theatre, cinema, crosswords, walking. *Address:* School of Law, University of Essex, Wivenhoe Park, Colchester CO4 3SQ. *T:* (01206) 872562; (home) Lord Nelson House, Ferry Road, Fingringhoe, Colchester CO5 7BX. *T:* (01206) 728111.

RODNEY, family name of **Baron Rodney.**

RODNEY, 11th Baron *cr* 1782; **John George Brydges Rodney;** Bt 1764; *b* 5 July 1999; *o s* of 10th Baron Rodney and of Jane, *d* of Hamilton Rowan Blakeney; *S* father, 2011. *Heir: kinsman* Nicholas Simon Harley Rodney, *b* 20 Dec. 1947.

RODNEY, Philip Emanuel; Chairman, Burness Paull LLP, since 2012 (Chairman, Burness LLP, 2005–12); *b* Glasgow, 21 Aug. 1953; *s* of Peter Rodney and Joan Rodney; *m* 1993, Cherie Lisus; three *s*. *Educ:* Giffnock Primary Sch.; High Sch., Glasgow; Univ. of Strathclyde (LLB). Partner: Alexander Stone & Co., 1979–98; Burness, 1998–2004. Chm. of Govs, Glasgow Sch. of Art, 2010–13. *Recreations:* music, cars, travel. *Address:* Burness Paull LLP, 120 Bothwell Street, Glasgow G2 7JL. *T:* (0141) 273 6760. *E:* philip.rodney@burnesspaull.com.

RODRIGUES, Christopher John, CBE 2007; Chairman: VisitBritain, since 2007; Almeida Theatre, since 2008; British Bobsleigh & Skeleton Association Ltd, since 2013; Openwork Ltd, since 2014; *b* 24 Oct. 1949; *s* of late Alfred John Rodrigues and of Joyce Margaret Rodrigues (*née* Farron-Smith); *m* 1976, Priscilla Purcell Young; one *s* one *d*. *Educ:* University College Sch.; Jesus Coll., Cambridge (BA Econs and Hist.; Pres., Cambridge Univ. Boat Club, 1971; rowing Blue, 1970 and 1971); Harvard Business Sch. (Baker Scholar; MBA 1976). With Spillers Foods, London, 1971–72; Foster Turner & Benson, London, 1972–74; McKinsey & Co., London, 1976–79; American Express, NY and London, 1979–88; Thos Cook Gp, 1988–95 (Chief Exec., 1992–95); Gp Chief Exec., Bradford & Bingley Bldg Soc., subseq. plc, 1996–2004; Chief Exec., Visa Internat., San Francisco, 2004–06. Chm., Internat. Personal Finance, 2007–15; non-executive Director: Energis PLC, 1997–2002; Hilton Gp, 2003–06; Ladbrokes plc, 2006–13. Non-exec. Dir, FSA, 1997–2003. Exec. Cttee Mem., World Travel and Tourism Council, 2007–. Mem. Council (formerly Exec. Cttee), 1994–2004, 2010–, Trustee, 2012–, Nat. Trust. Chm., Windsor Leadership Trust, later Windsor Leadership, 2007–15. FRSA 1994. Steward, Henley Royal Regatta, 1998–. *Recreations:* cooking, ski-ing, rowing, shooting, opera, ballet. *Address:* VisitBritain, 20 Great Smith Street, SW1P 3BT. *T:* (020) 7578 1298. *Clubs:* Leander Rowing (former Chm.) (Henley); Hawks (Cambridge); Century (Harvard); Brook (NY).

RODRÍGUEZ IGLESIAS, Gil Carlos; Professor of International Public Law, Madrid Complutense University, since 2003; *b* 26 May 1946; *m* 1972, Teresa Díez Gutiérrez; two *d*. *Educ:* Oviedo Univ. (LLL 1968); Madrid Autonomous Univ. (doctorate 1975). Internat. law asst, then Lectr, Oviedo, Freiburg, Madrid Autonomous and Madrid Complutense Univs, 1969–82; Professor: Madrid Complutense Univ., 1982–83; Granada Univ., 1983–2003 (on leave 1986–2003); Judge, EC Court of Justice, 1986–2003; Pres., Court of Justice of Eur. Communities, 1994–2003. Dir, Real Instituto Elcano, Madrid, 2005–12. Hon. Bencher: Gray's Inn, 1995; King's Inns, Dublin, 1997. Hon. Dr: Univ. of Turin, 1996; Univ. of Babes-Bolyai' Cluj-Napoca, Romania, 1996; Univ. of Saarbrücken, Germany, 1997; Univ. of Oviedo, 2001; St Clement of Ohrid Univ. of Sofia, 2002; Univ. of Cádiz, 2010; Univ. of Granada, 2012; Hon. Dip. Romanian Acad., 2002. Walter-Hallstein Prize, City of Frankfurt, Johann-Wolfgang-Goethe Univ. of Frankfurt, and Dresdner Bank, 2003. Encomienda de la Orden de Isabel la Católica (Spain), 1976; Cruz de Honor de la Orden de San Raimundo de Peñafort (Spain), 1986; Gran Cruz, Orden del Mérito Civil (Spain), 1999; Grand Cross: Order of the Phoenix (Greece), 2001; Nat. Order of Star (Romania), 2002; Order of Merit (Luxembourg), 2004; Order of Isabel la Católica (Spain), 2005; Grande Ufficiale, Ordine al Merito (Italy), 2002. *Publications:* El régimen jurídico de los monopolios de Estado en la Comunidad Económica Europea, 1976; various articles and studies on EC law and internat. law. *Address:* Faculty of Law, Madrid Complutense University, 28040 Madrid, Spain.

RODRÍGUEZ-MÚNERA, (José) Mauricio; Ambassador of Colombia to the Court of St James's, 2009–13; *b* Bogotá, 5 March 1958; *s* of Jorge Rodríguez and Cecilia Múnera; *m* 2009, Sugey Pinzón-Alonso; two *s*. *Educ:* Colegio de Estudios Superiores de Administration, Bogota (BA Business Admin). Founder and Dir, Portafolio newspaper, 1993–2007; journalist for Caracol Radio, El Tiempo, El Espectador and Poder Magazine, 2007–09. Professor, Universidad de Los Andes, Bogota, 1982–2009; Professor, 1982–2009, Pres., 2007–09, Colegio de Estudios Superiores de Administration, Bogota. *Publications:* Brujulas Empresariales, I, 2004, II, 2005, III, 2007; Brujulas Curiosas, 2006; Geografía Económica de Colombia, 2006; Perfiles Empresariales, 2007. *Recreations:* reading, writing, enjoying art and classical music.

RODRÍGUEZ-POSE, Prof. Andrés, PhD; Professor of Economic Geography, London School of Economics and Political Science, since 2004; *b* Madrid, 9 June 1966; *s* of José Luis Rodríguez and Josefina Pose; *m* 1997, Leticia Verdú; one *s* one *d*. *Educ:* Complutense Univ. of Madrid (BA Geog. and Hist. 1989; PhD *summa cum laude* Geog. 1993); Universidad Nacional de Educación a Distancia (LLB Law 1991); Inst. of European Studies, Brussels (MSc dist. Eur. Studies 1991); European University Inst., Florence (PhD with dist. Soc. and Pol Scis 1996). Res. Dir, Cabinet for Planning and Spatial Develt, Galician Regl Govt, 1994–95; Lectr, 1995–2000, Sen. Lectr, 2000–02, Reader, 2002–04, in Econ. Geog., LSE. Vis. Prof. on Growth and Cohesion, College of Europe, Bruges, 2004–; Professorial Res. Fellow, Social Scis, Instituto Madrileño de Estudios Avanzados, 2009–; Leverhulme Trust Major Res. Fellow, 2009–. Vice Pres., Eur. Regl Sci. Assoc., 2012– (Sec., 2001–06). Member, Board of Trustees: Internat. Centre for Advanced Econ. and Soc. Studies, Madrid, 2005–; Madrid Inst. for Advanced Studies, 2006–; Enterprise LSE Ltd, 2006–. Man. Ed., Envmt and Planning C: Govt and Policy, 2008–. Gill Meml Award, RGS, 2001. *Publications:* Reestructuración socioeconómica y desequilibrios regionales en la Unión Europea, 1995; The Dynamics of Regional Growth in Europe: social and political factors, 1998; The European Union: economy, society, and polity, 2002 (L'Unione Europea: economia, politica e società, 2003); (jtly) Local and Regional Development, 2006; (jtly) Handbook of Local and Regional Development, 2010; more than 70 articles in learned jls. *Recreations:* reading, spending time with family and friends, swimming, listening to music (especially classical, R&B, rock, disco, funk). *Address:* Department of Geography and Environment, London School of Economics, Houghton Street, WC2A 2AE. *T:* (020) 7955 7971, *Fax:* (020) 7955 7412. *E:* a.rodriguez-pose@lse.ac.uk.

RODRÍGUEZ ZAPATERO, José Luis; Prime Minister of Spain, 2004–11; Member, Council of State, Spain, since 2012; *b* 4 Aug. 1960; *m*; two *d*. *Educ:* Univ. of León (Law Degree). Mem. (PSOE) for León, Congress of Deputies, 1986–2011. Sec. Gen., Socialist Fedn of León, 1988–2000; Pres., Socialist Parly Gp, Congress of Deputies, 2000–04; Vice-Pres., Socialist Internat., 2003. Mem., PSOE, 1979–, Sec. Gen., 2000–12.

RODWAY, Susan Caroline; QC 2002; two *s* two *d*. *Educ:* Cheltenham Ladies' Coll.; King's Coll., London (BA Hons); City Univ. (Dip. in Law). Accredited Mediator, 2000. Called to the Bar, Middle and Inner Temple, 1981, Bencher, 2009. Lay Mem., Clinical Standards Cttee, Guy's and St Thomas's NHS Trust, 1998–2001. Dep. Chm., NHS Tribunals, 2000–04. Mem., Professional Negligence Cttee, 2001–, and Personal Injuries Cttee, Bar Assoc. *Publications:* (contrib.) Application of Neural Networks in Clinical Practice, 2000; numerous articles and lectures. *Recreations:* motorcycling, riding. *Address:* 39 Essex Street, WC2R 3AT. *E:* susan.rodway@39essex.com.

RODWELL, His Honour Daniel Alfred Hunter, QC 1982; a Circuit Judge, 1986–2002; *b* 3 Jan. 1936; *s* of late Brig. R. M. Rodwell, AFC, and Nellie Barbara Rodwell (*née* D'Costa); *m* 1967, Veronica Ann Cecil; two *s* one *d*. *Educ:* Munro Coll., Jamaica; Worcester Coll., Oxford, 1956–59 (BA Law). National service, 1954–56; 2/Lieut 1st West Yorks, PWO, 1955; TA, 1956–67: Captain and Adjt 3 PWO, 1964–67. Called to Bar, Inner Temple, 1960. A Deputy Circuit Judge, 1977 and 2002–05; a Recorder, 1980–86. *Recreations:* gardening, sailing. *Address:* The Old Surgery, 16 West Street, Buckingham MK18 1HP.

RODWELL, Dr Warwick James, OBE 2009; FSA, FSAScot, FRHistS; consultant archaeologist and architectural historian; *b* 24 Oct. 1946; *s* of late George and Olive Rodwell; *m* 1st, 1972, Kirsty Gomer (marr. diss. 1983); 2nd, 1984, Christine Bensted (marr. diss. 1999); 3rd, 2004, Diane Marie Gibbs. *Educ:* Southend High Sch. for Boys; Univ. of Nottingham (teaching cert. and dip. 1968); Univ. of London (BA Hons 1972; DLit 1998); Worcester Coll., Oxford (DPhil 1976; DLitt 1992); Univ. of Birmingham (MA 1979). FSAScot 1965; FSA 1977; FRHistS 1992. Res. Asst, MPBW, 1968–69; Dir, Cttee for Rescue Archaeol. in Avon, Glos and Somerset, 1975–81. Vis. Prof. in Archaeol., Univ. of Reading, 2002–. Consultant Archaeologist: Glastonbury Abbey, 1976–2005; Bristol Cath., 1976–2010; Wells Cath., 1977–2014; Lichfield Cath., 1982–2009; Westminster Abbey, 2004–. Directed major res. projs and/or excavations at Westminster Abbey, Dorchester Abbey, Lichfield Cath., Wells Cath. and parish churches at Barton-upon-Humber, Hadstock, Kellington and Rivenhall; directed res. and excavation campaigns in Jersey at Mont Orgueil Castle, Elizabeth Castle, Les Ecréhous Priory, St Lawrence Ch, St Helier Ch, Fishermen's Chapel and Hamptonne Farm. Member: Council for the Care of Churches, 1976–86; Cathedrals Adv. Commn, 1981–90; Cathedrals Fabric Commn for England, 1991–96; Member, Fabric Advisory Committee: Salisbury Cath., 1987–2006; Exeter Cath., 1999–2006. Mem., Coll. of Westminster Abbey, 2008–. Pres., Bristol and Gloucester Archaeol. Soc., 1999–2000. Trustee, Bath Archaeol. Trust, 1976–2005. Hon. Mem., La Société Jersiaise, 1998. Hon. BSc Loughborough, 2009. Frend Medal, Soc. of Antiquaries, 1988. *Publications:* Small Towns of Roman Britain (with T. Rowley), 1975; Historic Churches: a wasting asset, 1977; Temples, Churches and Religion in Roman Britain, 1980; Archaeology of the English Church, 1981, 3rd edn 2005; (with J. Bentley) Our Christian Heritage, 1984; (with K. Rodwell) Rivenhall: investigations of a villa, church and village, vol. 1 1985, vol. 2 1993; The Fishermen's Chapel, Jersey, 1990; Origins and Early Development of Witham, Essex, 1993; Les Ecréhous, Jersey, 1996; (with M. Paton and O. Finch) La Hougue Bie, Jersey, 1999; Archaeology of Wells Cathedral, 2001; Westminster Abbey Chapter House and Pyx Chamber, 2002; Church Archaeology, 2005; Mont Orgueil Castle, Jersey, 2006; (with G. Leighton) Architectural Records of Wells by John Carter 1784–1808, 2006; Dorchester Abbey, Oxfordshire, 2009; Jersey's Houses, Castles and Churches, 2009; (with R. Mortimer) Westminster Abbey Chapter House, 2010; The Lantern Tower of Westminster Abbey, 1060–2010, 2010; St Peter's, Barton-upon-Humber: a parish church and its community, 2011; The Archaeology of Churches, 2012; The Coronation Chair and Stone of Scone, 2013; numerous contribs to learned jls and multi-author vols. *Recreations:* visiting historic buildings, horology, bibliophilia, family history. *Address:* 2c Little Cloister, Westminster Abbey, SW1P 3PA.

ROE, Anthony Maitland, DPhil; CChem, FRSC; Executive Secretary, Council of Science and Technology Institutes, 1987–94; *b* 13 Dec. 1929; *s* of late Percy Alex Roe and Flora Sara Roe (*née* Kisch); *m* 1958, Maureen (*d* 2008), *d* of late William James Curtayne and of Kathleen (*née* Wigfull); two *s* one *d*. *Educ:* Harrow Sch.; Oriel Coll., Oxford (BA, MA, DPhil). ARIC 1955; FRSC, CChem 1976. Commnd Intell. Corps, 1955–57. Univ. of Rochester, NY, 1957–59; Sen. Chemist, Smith Kline & French Res. Inst., 1959–65; Hd of Chemistry Gp, Smith Kline & French Labs Ltd, 1965–78; Dir of Chemistry, Smith Kline & French Res. Ltd, 1978–86. Royal Society of Chemistry: Mem. Council, 1982–85, 1987–91; Vice-Pres., Perkin Div., 1986–88; Chm., Heterocyclic Gp, 1986–88; Chm., 'Chemistry in Britain' Management Cttee, 1987–91. Founder Cttee Mem., Soc. for Drug Res., 1966–77; Member: Bd for Science, BTEC, 1985–88; Parly and Scientific Cttee, 1987–94. Chm., Welwyn Hatfield CAB, 1996–2000. Member: Council, Liberal Jewish Synagogue, St John's Wood, 1976–86; Cttee of Maccabaeans, 1986–; Cttee, London Soc. of Jews and Christians, 2010–. *Publications:* research papers, patents and reviews in the field of organic and medicinal chemistry. *Recreations:* travel, walking, good food and wine. *Address:* 10 Lodge Drive, Hatfield, Herts AL9 5HN. *T:* (01707) 265075.

ROE, Chang Hee; Senior Advisor, Federation of Korean Industries, 1998–2003; *b* 25 Feb. 1938; *m* 1963, Chung Ja Lee; one *s* one *d*. *Educ:* Seoul Nat. Univ., Korea (BA Econ 1960). Joined Min. of Foreign Affairs, 1960: Instructor ROK Air Force Acad., 1962–66; Dir of Legal Affairs, 1968–69; First Sec., Korean Embassy, Canada, 1969–72; Private Sec. to Minister of Foreign Affairs, 1972–73; Dir, Treaties Div., 1973–75; Counsellor, Sweden, 1975–78; Dep. Dir-Gen., American Affairs Bureau, 1978–80; Dir-Gen., Treaties Bureau, 1980–82; Minister and Dep. Chief of Mission, USA, 1982–85; Ambassador to Nigeria, 1985–88; Sen. Protocol Sec. to Pres., 1988–91; Ambassador and Perm. Rep. to UN, 1991–92; Vice Minister of Foreign Affairs, 1992–93; Ambassador to UK, 1993–96; Ambassador at Large, 1996–98. Guest Prof., Hanseo Univ., Korea, 1998–2001. Gov., Asia Europe Foundn, 2001–05. *Recreations:* golf, ski-ing. *Address:* Hanyang Apt 62–606, Apkujong-dong, Kangnam-gu, Seoul 135–110, Korea.

ROE, David John, CBE 2001; organisation and leadership consultant, since 2011; Director, Innovation Capability (formerly Public Sector Innovation), Department for Business, Innovation and Skills, 2009–11; *b* 26 Nov. 1958; *s* of Malcolm Roe and late Pauline Roe (*née* Baker); partner, Alison Mary Sharpe; one *s*. *Educ:* Selwyn Coll., Cambridge (BA 1981); Queen Mary Coll., London (MA 1983); Roffey Park Inst. (MSc 2012). Export Credits Guarantee Dept, 1983–85; DTI, 1985–92; HM Treasury, 1992–2000: Hd, Internat. Financial Instns, 1994–97; Hd, Financial Regulatory Reform, 1997–2000; on secondment to Charities Aid Foundn, 2001–02; Prime Minister's Strategy Unit, 2002–03; Department for Culture, Media and Sport: Hd, Strategy, Policy and Delivery, 2003–05; Dir, Strategy, 2005–07; Dir, Change, 2007–08; Dir, Corporate Services, 2008–09. UK Alternate Dir (pt-time), EBRD, 1995–97. Parent Gov., Fielding Primary Sch., 2005–12. *Recreations:* playing the saxophone, watching Brentford Football Club, being at the seaside, books, football management, golf.

ROE, Geoffrey Eric, FRAeS; Director, Air Tanker Ltd, 2000–03 (Chairman, 2002–03); *b* 20 July 1944; *s* of Herbert William Roe and Florence Roe (*née* Gordon); *m* 1968, Elizabeth Anne Ponton; one *s* one *d*. *Educ:* Tottenham Grammar Sch. FRAeS 1996. Min. of Aviation, 1963; Finance (R&D) Br., 1963–67; Asst Private Sec. to Sir Ronald Melville, 1967–69; Exports and Internat. Relations Div., Min. of Technology, 1969–74; Guided Weapons Contracts Branch, 1974–76; seconded British Aerospace, 1976–78; Rocket Motor Exec., 1978–81; Asst Dir Contracts (Air), 1981–86; Dir of Contracts (Underwater Weapons), 1986–89; Head, Material Co-ord. (Naval), 1989–90; Principal Dir, Navy and Nuclear Contracts, 1990–91; Director-General: Defence Contracts, MoD, 1991–95; Commercial, MoD, 1995; Aircraft Systems 2, 1995–96. Man. Dir, FR Aviation Gp (formerly FR Aviation Ltd), 1997–2002; Director: Cobham plc, 1997–2002; FR Aviation Services Ltd, 2000–02; FBS Ltd, 2000–02; FBH Ltd, 2000–02. Chm., Nat. Jet Systems, Australia, and Nat. Air Support, Australia, 2000–02. Dir, SBAC, 1998–2000. Mem., Light Aircraft Assoc., 1990–. *Recreations:* ski-ing, sailing, flying and maintaining a homebuilt aircraft (Jodel D18). *Address:* Pond Barton, Norton St Philip, Bath BA2 7NE.

ROE, Prof. Howard Stanley James, DSc; Director, Southampton Oceanography Centre, NERC and the University of Southampton, 1999–2005; Professor, University of Southampton, 2000–05, now Emeritus; *b* 23 May 1943; *s* of Eric James Roe and Freda Mary Roe (*née* Perkins); *m* 1970, Heather Anne Snelling; one *s* two *d*. *Educ:* Bedford Sch.; University Coll. London (BSc 1st Cl. Hons Zool. 1965; DSc Biol Oceanography 1998). Natural Environment Research Council: Scientific Officer, Whale Res. Unit, 1965–68; transferred to Biol. Dept, Nat. Inst. Oceanography, 1968; Project Co-ordinator for develt of

Southampton Oceanography Centre, 1989–95; Hd, George Deacon Div., Inst. Oceanographic Scis, later Southampton Oceanography Centre, 1993–99 (Dep. Dir, 1997–99). Public Orator, Univ. of Southampton, 2008–10. Chairman: NERC Project Bd, RRS James Cook, 2002–07; Partnership for Observing the Global Ocean, 2003–05; DEFRA Science Audit of CEFAS, 2005–06. Member: Council for Ocean Policy Studies, Ship and Ocean Foundn, Japan, 2003–; Natural Scis Adv. Gp, English Nature, 2003–05; Exec. Cttee, Sargasso Sea Alliance, 2010–14 (Mem. Bd, 2011–14); Search and Evaluation Cttee, Inst. for Basic Sci., Korea, 2014–; Chair, Sargasso Sea Commn, 2014–. Non-exec. Mem., Marine Sci. Co-ordination Cttee, DEFRA, 2009–13. Chm., Ext. Rev. Cttee, Seoul Nat. Univ., 2002–. Mem., Challenger Soc. for Marine Sci. FIMarEST, 2003. POGO Award, 2008. *Publications:* (ed jtly) Of Seas and Ships and Scientists, 2010; contrib. numerous papers and reports to jls, etc, dealing with whale biology, biological oceanography and develt of sampling technol., conservation and biology of the Sargasso Sea. *Recreations:* fishing, gardening, travel, amateur dramatics. *Address:* National Oceanography Centre Southampton, Empress Dock, Southampton SO14 3ZH; Barton Mere, Barton Court Avenue, New Milton, Hants BH25 7HD. *T:* (01425) 622092. *Clubs:* Christchurch Angling; Ringwood Fly Dressers.

ROE, James Kenneth; Chairman, New Star Investment Trust, 2005–09; Director, Jupiter International (formerly Jupiter Tyndall) Group, 1993–2000; Member, Monopolies and Mergers Commission, 1993–99; *b* 28 Feb. 1935; *s* of late Kenneth Alfred Roe and Zirphie Norah Roe (*née* Luke); *m* 1958, Marion Audrey Keyte (*see* Dame M. A. Roe); one *s* two *d*. *Educ:* King's Sch., Bruton. National Service commn, RN, 1953–55. Joined N. M. Rothschild & Sons, 1955; Director, 1970–92. Chm., China Investment Trust, 1993–98; Dep. Chm., Innovations Gp (formerly Kleeneze Holdings), 1985–96; Director: Rothschild Trust Corp., 1970–95; Jupiter European Investment Trust, 1990–2000; GAM Selection Inc., 1992–2005; Ronson (formerly Halkin Holdings), 1993–98 (Chm., 1993–97); Microvitec, 1993–97; JP Morgan Fleming (formerly Fleming) Income and Capital Investment Trust, 1995–2006; Whitehall Fund Managers Ltd, 1998–2000; Principle Capital Investment Trust, 2005–09. FRSA 1991–2009; FInstD 1993. *Recreations:* reading, theatre. *Clubs:* Brooks's, MCC.
See also P. M. Roe.

ROE, Dame Marion (Audrey), DBE 2004; *b* 15 July 1936; *d* of William Keyte and Grace Mary (*née* Bocking); *m* 1958, James Kenneth Roe, *qv*; one *s* two *d*. *Educ:* Bromley High Sch. (GPDST); Croydon High Sch. (GPDST); English Sch. of Languages, Vevey, Switzerland. Member: London Adv. Cttee, IBA, 1978–81; Gatwick Airport Consultative Cttee, 1979–81; SE Thames RHA, 1980–83. Member (C): Bromley Borough Council, 1975–78; for Ilford N, GLC, 1977–86 (Cons. Dep. Chief Whip, 1978–82). Contested (C) Barking, 1979; MP (C) Broxbourne, 1983–2005. Parly Private Secretary to: Parly Under-Secs of State for Transport, 1985; Minister of State for Transport, 1986; Sec. of State for Transport, 1987; Parly Under Sec. of State, DoE, 1987–88. Member, Select Committee: on Agriculture, 1983–85; on Social Services, 1988–89; on Procedure, 1990–92; on Sittings of the House, 1991–92; Chairman: Select Cttee on Health, 1992–97 (Mem., 1988–89, 2000–01); H of C Admin. Cttee, 1997–2005 (Mem., 1991–97); Mem., Speaker's Panel of Chairmen, 1997–2005. Vice Chairman: All-Party Fairs and Showgrounds Gp, 1992–2005 (Jt Chm., 1989–92); All-Party Parly Garden Club, 1995–2005; All-Party Gp on Alcohol Misuse, 1997–2005; All-Party Gp on Domestic Violence, 1999–2005; Chairman: All-Party Hospice Gp, 1992–2005 (Sec., 1990–92); Jt Chm., All-Party Gp on Breast Cancer, 1997–2005; Member: H of C Liaison Cttee, 1992–2005; H of C Finance and Services Cttee, 1997–2005; UNICEF Parly Adv. Cttee, 2002–05; Chairman: Cons. Back bench Horticulture and Markets Sub-Cttee, 1989–97 (Sec., 1983–85); Cons. Back bench Social Security Cttee, 1990–97 (Vice-Chm., 1988–90); Vice-Chairman: Cons. Back bench Environment Cttee, 1990–97; Cons. Parly Health Cttee, 1997–99; 1922 Cttee, 2001–05 (Mem. Exec., 1992–94; Sec., 1997–2001); Sec., Cons. Back bench Horticulture Cttee, 1983–85; Jt Sec., Cons. Back bench Party Orgn Cttee, 1985; Vice-Chm., British-Canadian Parly Gp, 1997–2005 (Sec., 1991–97); Mem., Adv. Cttee on Women's Employment, Dept of Employment, 1989–92; Substitute Mem., UK Delegn to Parly Assemblies of Council of Europe and WEU, 1989–92; Mem., Exec. Cttee, UK Br., CPA, 1997–2005 (Vice Chm., 2002–03); Inter-Parliamentary Union: Mem. Exec. Cttee, British Gp, 1997–98, 2001–05 (Vice-Chm., 1998–2001); Mem., Internat. Panel on Prohibition of Female Genital Mutilation, 2002–05. Chm., Nat. Council for Child Health and Well-being (formerly Child Health Gp), 2001–; Vice-Pres., Women's Nationwide Cancer Control Campaign, 1985–87, 1988–2001; Patron: UN Women UK (formerly UK Nat. Cttee for UN Develt Fund for Women), 2004– (Mem., 1985–87); Hospice of Hope, Romania, Serbia and Moldova, 2005–; Gov., Research into Ageing Trust, 1988–97; Managing Trustee, Parly Contributory Pension Fund, 1990–97; Mem., Internat. Women's Forum, 1992–2005; Trustee, Nat. Benevolent Fund for the Aged, 1999– (Chm., 2010–). Vice-President: Capel Manor Horticultural and Envmtl Centre, 1994– (Chm., Trust Fund, 1989–94). Hoddesdon Soc., 2005–. Pres., Broxbourne Parly Cons Assoc., 2013– (Pres., Women's Section, 1983–2015; Patron, 2006–13). Mem. Council, Wine Guild of the UK, 2007–. Hon. Life Mem., Showmen's Guild of GB, 2005–. Fellow, Industry and Parlt Trust, 1990. Freeman: City of London, 1981; Borough of Broxbourne, 2005; Liveryman, Gardeners' Co., 1993–. Hon. MIHort 1993. *Recreations:* family, theatre, ballet, opera, travel.
See also P. M. Roe.

ROE, Prof. Nicholas Hugh, DPhil; Professor of English Literature, University of St Andrews, since 1996; *b* Fareham, 14 Dec. 1955; *s* of Dennis Roe and Stella Mary Roe; *m* 1990, Susan Jane Stabler; one *s*. *Educ:* Royal Grammar Sch., High Wycombe; Trinity Coll., Oxford (BA 1978; DPhil 1985). Lectr in English, QUB, 1982–85; University of St Andrews: Lectr in English, 1985–93; Reader, 1993–96; Founder and Dir, St Andrews Poetry Festival, 1986–92. Visiting Professor: Univ. of São Paulo, 1988; Victoria Univ., Wellington, NZ, 2011, 2012; Leverhulme Res. Fellow, 1993–94; Joan Nordell Fellow, Harvard Univ., 2009. Director: Coleridge Summer Conf., 1994–2010; Wordsworth Summer Conf., 2010–; Trustee: Keats-Shelley Meml Assoc., 1997–2015; Wordsworth Conf. Foundn, 2007–; Wordsworth Trust, 2011–; Chm., Keats Foundn, 2011–. Hon. FEA 2006; FRSE 2009. Editor: Romanticism, 1995–; Keats-Shelley Review, 2008–15. *Publications:* (ed jtly) Coleridge's Imagination, 1986; Wordsworth and Coleridge: the radical years, 1988; (ed) William Wordsworth: selected poetry, 1992; The Politics of Nature, 1992, 2nd edn 2002; (ed) Keats and History, 1995; (ed) Selected Poems of John Keats, 1995; John Keats and the Culture of Dissent, 1997; (ed) Samuel Taylor Coleridge and the Sciences of Life, 2002; (ed) Leigh Hunt: life, poetry, politics, 2003; Fiery Heart: the first life of Leigh Hunt, 2005; (ed) Romanticism: an Oxford guide, 2005; (ed) English Romantic Writers and the West Country, 2010; John Keats: a new life, 2012. *Recreations:* walking, aircraft, Malta, railways. *Address:* School of English, University of St Andrews, St Andrews, Fife KY16 9AR. *T:* (01334) 462666. *E:* nhr@st-and.ac.uk.

ROE, Philippa Marion, (Mrs Stephen Couttie); Member (C), Westminster City Council, since 2006 (Leader, since 2012); *b* 25 Sept. 1962; *d* of James Kenneth Roe, *qv* and Dame Marion Audrey Roe, *qv*; *m* 2002, Stephen Couttie; one *s* one *d*. *Educ:* Roedean Sch.; St Andrews Univ. (BSc Hons). Co-Founder, Wearne Public Relations, 1987–90; Chief Exec., Cornerstone Communications, 1990–92; Proprietor and CEO, PR Consultants, 1992–99; Associate Dir, J. Henry Schroder, 1999–2000; Dir, Citigroup Securitisation Div., 2000–06. Westminster City Council: Member: Children's Services Overview and Scrutiny Cttee, 2006–07; Planning and City Develt Cttee, 2006–07; Sch. Govs Appt Cttee, 2007–08; Resources and Corp. Services Overview and Scrutiny Cttee, 2007–08; Dep. Cabinet Mem., Children's Services, 2007–08; Cabinet Member: for Housing, 2008–11; for Strategic Finance, 2011–. Conservative Party: Hd, Educn Team, Private Finance Panel, 1997–99; Hd, Treasury Team, James Cttee, 2004–05; Chm., Public Sector Efficiency subgp, Econ. Competitive Policy Gp, 2006–07; Advr on Benefit Caps to DWP, 2011–. Deputy Leader: LGA, 2014– (Mem. Exec., Cons. Gp, 2013–); London Councils, 2014– (Lead, Public Sector Reform and Devolution, 2014–). Chairman: Westminster Health and Wellbeing Bd, 2012–13; West End Partnership, 2013–. Member: London Crime Reduction Bd, 2012–14; Bd, Royal Parks, 2012–; Bd, London Local Enterprise Partnership, 2014–; London Infrastructure Delivery Bd, 2014–. Non-exec. Sen. Advr, FTI Consulting, 2014–. Mem. Council, Imperial Coll. London, 2006–14 (Chm. Audit Cttee, 2006–14). Vice Chm., London Events, MacMillan Cancer Support, 2004–; Patron, Breast Cancer Haven, 2004–. *Recreations:* ski-ing, travelling, reading, ancient history, antiquities, opera. *Address:* Westminster City Council, Westminster City Hall, 64 Victoria Street, SW1E 6QP.

ROE, Thomas Idris; QC 2014; *b* St Albans, 3 June 1972; *s* of Philip Roe and Joy Roe; *m* 2002, Helen Berry; three *s* one *d* (and one *s* decd). *Educ:* St Albans Sch.; Downing Coll., Cambridge (BA 1994). FCIArb 2010. Called to the Bar, Middle Temple, 1995; in practice as barrister, 1996–; Jun. Counsel to the Crown, 2010–14. *Publications:* (with M. Happold) Settlement of Investment Disputes under the Energy Charter Treaty, 2011; (contrib.) International Investment Law: sources of rights and obligations, 2012; various contribs to Cambridge Law Jl, Modern Law Rev., New Law Jl. *Recreations:* family, reading, classical music, travel, foreign languages. *Address:* 3 Hare Court, Temple, EC4Y 7BJ. *T:* (020) 7415 7800, *Fax:* (020) 7415 7873. *E:* thomasroe@3harecourt.com.

ROE, William Deas, CBE 2010; Chairman: Highlands and Islands Enterprise, 2004–12; Skills Development Scotland, 2008–10; *b* Perth, Scotland, 9 July 1947. *Educ:* Edinburgh Univ. (BSc). Chm., Rocket Sci. UK Ltd, 2004–09. Scotland Comr, UK Commn for Employment and Skills, 2008–12. Non-exec. Dir, Deptl Bd, DWP, 2011–15. Chair, British Council Scotland, 2015–. FRSA. DUniv Open, 2009. *Recreations:* sailing, ski-ing, hill-walking, visual arts, music, travel, restoring a garden. *Address:* Duirinish Lodge, Duirinish, Wester Ross IV40 8BE. *T:* 07771 930880. *E:* willyroe@gmail.com.

ROEBUCK, Roy Delville; barrister-at-law; *b* Manchester, 25 Sept. 1929; *m* 1957, Dr Mary Ogilvy Adams (*d* 1995); one *s*. *Educ:* various newspapers; Inns of Court Sch. of Law; Univ. of Leicester (LLM 1997; MA 2000). Called to the Bar, Gray's Inn, 1974. Served RAF (National Service), 1948–50 (wireless operator, FEAF). Journalist, Stockport Advertiser, Northern Daily Telegraph, Yorkshire Evening News, Manchester Evening Chronicle, News Chronicle, Daily Express, Daily Mirror and Daily Herald, and Asst Ed., Forward, 1950–66; freelance journalist, 1966–; columnist, London Evening News, 1968–70. Contested (Lab): Altrincham and Sale, 1964 and Feb. 1965; Leek, Feb. 1974. MP (Lab) Harrow East, 1966–70; Member, Select Committee: on Estimates, 1968–70; on Parly Comr, 1968–70; aide to Rt Hon. George Wigg, Paymaster-Gen., 1966–67, to Lord Wigg, Pres. of Betting Office Licensees Assoc., 1975–83. Founder Mem., Labour Common Market Safeguards Cttee, 1967. Member: Islington CHC, 1988–92; Bd of Governors, Moorfields Eye Hospital, 1984–88. Fellow, Atlantic Council, 1993–. Governor, Thornhill Sch., Islington, 1986–88. *Recreations:* tennis, ski-ing, music, reading Hansard and the public prints. *Address:* 12 Brooksby Street, N1 1HA. *T:* (020) 7607 7057. *Clubs:* Royal Automobile, Victory Services, Union Jack.

ROEG, Nicolas Jack, CBE 1996; film director; *b* 15 Aug. 1928; *s* of Jack Roeg and Gertrude Silk; *m* 1st, 1957, Susan (marr. diss.), *d* of Major F. W. Stephen, MC; four *s*; 2nd, Theresa Russell (marr. diss. 2004); two *s*; 3rd, 2005, Harriett, *d* of Kenneth Harper. *Educ:* Mercers' Sch. Fellow, BFI, 1994–. Original story of Prize of Arms; Cinematographer: The Caretaker, 1963; Masque of the Red Death, 1964; Nothing But the Best, 1964; A Funny Thing Happened on the Way to the Forum, 1966; Fahrenheit 451, 1966; Far From the Madding Crowd, 1967; Petulia, 1968, etc; 2nd Unit Director and Cinematographer: Lawrence of Arabia, 1962; Judith, 1965; Co-Dir, Performance, 1968; Director: Walkabout, 1970; Don't Look Now, 1972; The Man who Fell to Earth, 1975; Bad Timing, 1979; Eureka, 1983; Insignificance, 1985; Castaway, 1986; Track 29, 1987; Aria, 1987; Sweet Bird of Youth, 1989; Witches, 1990; Cold Heaven, 1991; Heart of Darkness, 1993; Two Deaths, Hotel Paradise, Full Body Massage, 1995; Samson and Delilah, 1996; (also writer) The Sound of Claudia Schiffer, 2000; Puffball, 2007; Exec. Producer, Without You I'm Nothing, 1989; writer of screenplays: Ivanhoe, Kiss of Life, 1999; Night Train, 2001; (with Andrew Hislop) History Play, 2004–05. Hon. Prof. of Film Studies, Univ. of Exeter, 2007–. Hon. DLitt Hull, 1995; Hon. DFA Brooklyn Coll., City Univ. of NY, 2003. *Publications:* The World is Ever Changing, 2013. *Address:* c/o Independent, 7a Pindock Mews, W9 2PY.

ROFE, Christopher Henry; Chief Executive Officer, Royal Institution of Great Britain, since 2009; *b* London, 16 Jan. 1965; *s* of Brian Henry Rofe and Margaret Anne Rofe; *m* 1991, Julie; one *d* (one *s* decd). *Educ:* Royal Shrewsbury Sch.; Loughborough Univ. (BSc Hons Recreation Mgt 1987); Kingston Univ. (MBA 1997). Visitor Ops Manager, Science Mus., 1993–98; Dep. Dir Ops, New Millennium Experience Co. (The Dome), 1999–2001; Gen. Manager, Bourne Leisure, 2001–03; Dir of Ops, BM, 2003–08. Mem., Grocers' Co. *Recreations:* golf, football, sailing. *Address:* Banstead, Surrey. *T:* 07764 761372. *E:* chris.rofe@btinternet.com. *Club:* Royal Automobile.

ROFF, Derek Michael, OBE 1972; HM Diplomatic Service, retired; *b* 1 Aug. 1932; *m* 1957, Diana Susette Barrow; three *s*. *Educ:* Royal Grammar Sch., Guildford; St Edmund Hall, Oxford (BA). National Service with The Cameronians (Scottish Rifles) and King's African Rifles, 1952–54. ICI Ltd, 1958–67; entered Foreign Office, 1967; Consul (Economic), Frankfurt, 1968; First Sec., UK Delegn to the European Communities, Brussels, 1970; Consul (Economic), Düsseldorf, 1973; First Sec., FCO, 1977; Counsellor, FCO, 1981–92. Regl Dir, BESO, 1993–97. Mem., Internat. Cttee, Leonard Cheshire, 1997–2005.

ROFFE, Melvyn Westley; Principal, George Watson's College, Edinburgh, since 2014; *b* Derby, 15 June 1964; *s* of Brian Roffe and Vera Roffe (*née* Hickinbotham); *m* 1988, Catherine Stratford; one *s* one *d*. *Educ:* Noel-Baker Sch., Derby; Univ. of York (BA Eng. and Related Lit. 1985); Univ. of Durham (PGCE 1986). English Master, Oundle Sch., 1986–93; Monmouth School: Hd of English, 1993–97; Dir of Studies, 1997–2001; Headmaster, Old Swinford Hosp., Stourbridge, 2001–07; Principal, Wymondham Coll., 2007–14. Chairman: State Boarding Schs' Assoc., 2004–06; Boarding Schs' Assoc., 2008–09. Chm., Lay Adv. Panel, 2001–06, Lay Trustee, 2001–06, Coll. of Optometrists. Member: Corp., City Coll., Norwich, 2009–13; Merchants' Co., City of Edinburgh, 2015–; Adv. Cttee, Duke of Edinburgh's Award in Scotland, 2015–. Trustee: Thetford Learning Trust, 2010–13; ESU Scotland, 2014–. Hon. Pres., Norwich and Norfolk ESU, 2011–14. FRSA 2001. Hon. FCOptom 2008. Mem., E Northants DC, 1991–93; Mayor of Oundle, 1993. Contested (Lib Dem) Corby, 1992. *Recreations:* travel, cultural pursuits, historic transport, observing politics. *Address:* George Watson's College, Colinton Road, Edinburgh EH10 5EG. *T:* (0131) 446 6000. *E:* melvynroffe@hotmail.com. *Club:* National Liberal.

ROGAN, family name of **Baron Rogan**.

ROGAN, Baron *cr* 1999 (Life Peer), of Lower Iveagh in the county of Down; **Dennis Robert David Rogan;** Leader, Ulster Unionist Party in House of Lords, since 2001; President, Ulster Unionist Party, since 2004 (Chairman, 1996–2001; Hon. Secretary, 2001–04); *b* 30 June 1942; *s* of Robert Henderson Rogan and Florence Rogan; *m* 1968, Lorna Elizabeth Colgan; two *s*. *Educ:* Wallace High Sch., Lisburn; Belfast Inst. of Technol.; Open Univ. (BA). Moygashel Ltd, 1960–69; Wm Ewart & Co., 1969–72; Lamont Holdings plc, 1972–78; Chairman: (exec.) Associated Processors Ltd, 1985–; Stakeholder Communications Ltd, 2005–; Stakeholder Events Ltd, 2005–; Dep. Chm., Ind. News & Media (NI) Ltd, 2000–08.

Member, International Advisory Board: Ind. Newspapers, 2001–08; Parker Green Internat., 2008–. Chm., Lisburn Unit of Mgt, Eastern Health Bd, 1984–85. Chairman: Ulster Young Unionist Council, 1968–69; S Belfast UU Constituency Assoc., 1992–96. Member: UK Br., CPA, 1999–; IPU, 2002–. Gov., Westminster Foundn for Democracy, 2005–08. Mem., Council, RFCA (NI), 2002–. Patron, Somme Assoc., 2000–. Hon. Col, 40 (Ulster) Signals Regt, 2009–10. *Recreations:* Rugby football, oriental carpets, shooting, gardening. *Address:* 31 Notting Hill, Belfast BT9 5NS. *T:* (028) 9066 2468. *Clubs:* Army and Navy; Ulster Reform (Belfast).

ROGAN, Rev. Canon John; Chaplain of St Mark's, Lord Mayor's Chapel, Bristol, 1999–2008; Canon Residentiary, 1983–93, and Chancellor, 1989–93, Bristol Cathedral (Precentor, 1983–89), Canon Emeritus since 1993; *b* 20 May 1928; *s* of William and Jane Rogan; *m* 1953, Dorothy Margaret Williams; one *s* one *d*. *Educ:* Manchester Central High School; St John's Coll., Univ. of Durham. BA 1949, MA 1951; DipTheol with distinction, 1954; BPhil 1981. Education Officer, RAF, 1949–52. Asst Curate, St Michael and All Angels, Ashton-under-Lyne, 1954–57; Chaplain, Sheffield Industrial Mission, 1957–61; Secretary, Church of England Industrial Cttee, 1961–66; Asst Secretary, Board for Social Responsibility, 1962–66; Vicar of Leigh, Lancs, 1966–78; Sec., Diocesan Bd for Social Responsibility, 1967–74, Chm. 1974–78; Rural Dean of Leigh, 1971–78; Hon. Canon of Manchester, 1975–78; Provost, St Paul's Cathedral, Dundee, 1978–83; Bishop's Adviser in Social Responsibility, dio. Bristol, 1983–93. *Publications:* (ed jtly) Principles of Church Reform: Thomas Arnold, 1962; (ed) Bristol Cathedral: history and architecture, 2000; Reading Roman Inscriptions, 2006; Roman Provincial Administration, 2011; Mysterious Deaths, 2012. *Recreations:* music, reading. *Address:* 84 Concorde Drive, Bristol BS10 6PX.

ROGÉ, Pascal; pianist; *b* Paris, 6 April 1951; two *s*. *Educ:* Paris Conservatoire. Débuts in Paris and London, 1969. Soloist with leading orchestras worldwide. Specialist in music of Ravel, Poulenc, Debussy and Satie. Piano duo with wife, Ami Rogé. Numerous recordings. *Address:* c/o Clarion/Seven Muses, 47 Whitehall Park, N19 3TW.

ROGERS, family name of **Barons Lisvane** and **Rogers of Riverside**.

ROGERS OF RIVERSIDE, Baron *cr* 1996 (Life Peer), of Chelsea in the Royal Borough of Kensington and Chelsea; **Richard George Rogers,** CH 2008; Kt 1991; RA 1984 (ARA 1978); RDI 2014; RIBA; architect; Chairman, Rogers Stirk Harbour + Partners LLP (formerly Richard Rogers Architects Ltd), UK, Sydney and Shanghai; Director, River Cafe Restaurant, London; *b* 23 July 1933; *s* of Dada Geiringer and Nino Rogers; *m* 1st, 1961, Su Rogers; three *s*; 2nd, 1973, Ruth Elias (*see* Lady Rogers of Riverside); one *s* (and one *s* decd). *Educ:* Architectural Assoc. (AA Dipl.); Yale Univ. (MArch; Fulbright and Yale Scholar). Reith Lectr, 1995. Winner of numerous internat. competitions incl. for Centre Pompidou, Paris, 1971–77; Lloyd's HQ, City of London, 1978. Major internat. work includes: *masterplanning:* River Arno, Florence, 1983; Royal Docks, London, 1984–86; Potsdamer Platz, Berlin, 1991; Shanghai, 1992; Shanghai Pu Dong District, 1994; Parc BIT, Mallorca, 1994; South Bank, 1994–95; Dunkirk, 1998; E Manchester, 1999; Greenwich Peninsula, 2000; Bankside, 2000–05; Singapore, 2001; Almada, Portugal, 2002; Woolston Shipyard, Southampton, 2003–05; Wembley, London, 2003–06; Granada, Spain, 2004–; Wood Wharf, London, 2004–08; Valladolid Alta Velocidad, Spain, 2005–08; *buildings:* PA Technology, Cambridge, 1975–83; Centre Pompidou, Paris, 1977; IRCAM, Paris, 1977; Fleetguard Manufacturing Centre, Quimper, France, 1981; PA Technology, Princeton, NJ, 1984; Patscentre, Princeton, 1985; Linn Products, Glasgow, 1987; Inmos Microprocessor Factory, Newport, 1987; Billingsgate Securities Market, London, 1988; Thames Wharf Studios and Thames Reach Housing, 1989; Marseille Airport, 1992; Reuters Data Centre, London, 1992; Europier, Terminal 1, Heathrow Airport, 1993; Kabuki-Cho, Tokyo, 1993; Channel 4 HQ, London, 1994; European Court of Human Rights, Strasbourg, 1995; Thames Valley Univ., Slough, 1996; VR Techno offices and lab., Gifu, Japan, 1998; Bordeaux Law Courts, 1998; Amano Res. Labs, Gifu, Japan, 1999; Daimler Chrysler, Berlin, 1999; Law Courts, Bordeaux, 1999; Millennium Dome, Greenwich, 1999; 88 Wood Street, London, 2000; Ashford Retail Designer Outlet, 2000; Lloyd's Register of Shipping, London, 2000; Montevetro Residential, London, 2000; Broadwick Street, London, 2002; Minami Yamashiro Sch., Kyoto, 2003; First Base Housing, 2004; Paddington Waterside, London, 2004; Nat. Assembly for Wales, Cardiff, 2005; Terminal 4, Barajas Airport, Madrid, 2005 (Stirling Prize, 2006); Paddington Basin, London, 2005; Mossbourne Community Acad., Hackney, 2005; Law Courts, Antwerp, 2005; Birmingham City Library, 2005; Roppongi GRIPS campus, Tokyo, 2005; Hesperia Hotel and Conference Centre, Barcelona, 2006; R9 Station, Kaohsiung, Taiwan, 2007; Ching Fu HQ, Kaohsiung, Taiwan, 2007; Terminal 5, Heathrow Airport, 2008; Cambridge Station area redevelt, 2008; Jacob Javits Convention Center, NY, 2008; Bodegas Protos, Penafiel, 2008; Maggie's Centre, London, 2008 (Stirling Prize, RIBA, 2009); 300 New Jersey Avenue, Washington DC, 2009; Campus Palmas Atlas/HQ for Abengoa, Seville, 2009; Las Arenas, Barcelona, 2011; One Hyde Park, Knightsbridge, 2011; NEO Bankside, London, 2012; Up at the O_2, London, 2012; 8 Chifley Sq., Sydney, 2013; Nuovo Centro Civico, Scandicci, Italy, 2013; World Conservation and Exhibns Centre, British Mus., 2014. *Current projects include:* The Leadenhall Building, London; Bullring, Barcelona; The Berkeley Hotel, London; Capodichino Tube Station, Naples; Tower 3 on World Trade Centre site, NY; Future of Paris Agglomeration; Port Authority Bus Terminal and Tower, NY; Extension to British Mus., London; 1201 K Street, Washington DC; P7 - Campus de la Justicia de Madrid; Santa Maria del Pianto Underground Station, Naples; Oxley Woods Housing, Milton Keynes (Manser Medal, 2008); White City Health Centre, London; 360 Residential, London; Sewoon Sang Ga, Seoul; Heron Quays, Canary Wharf; Parc1, Yeouido, Seoul; Canary Riverside South; Chiswick Business Park; BBVA Bancomer HQ, Mexico City; Barangaroo Masterplan, Sydney; Lok Wo Sha residential, Hong Kong; Beirut Grand Hotel. *Exhibitions worldwide include:* Royal Acad.; Mus. of Modern Art, NY; Louisiana Mus., Copenhagen; Richard Rogers + Architects touring exhibn, Paris 2007, London 2008, Madrid, Barcelona 2009, Taipei 2010, Singapore 2011. Teaching posts include: AA, London; Cambridge Univ.; Yale; UCLA. Chairman: Nat. Housing Tenants Resource Centre; Architecture Foundn, 1991–2001; Tate Gall. Trust, 1984–88; Govt Urban Task Force, 1998–2001; Vice-Chm., Arts Council of England, 1994–97; Mem., UN Architects' Cttee; Mem., Urban Strategies Adv. Council, Barcelona; Mem., Internat. Business Adv. Council for London, 2008–; UK Business Ambassador, 2008–; Trustee: London First; UK Bd, Médecins du Monde. Hon. Mem., Royal Inst. of Architects, Scotland, 1999; Hon. FAIA 1986. Hon. Dr RCA. Royal Gold Medal for Arch., 1985; Thomas Jefferson Meml Foundn Medal in Architecture, 1999; Praemium Imperiale, 2000; Pritzker Prize, 2007. Chevalier de la Légion d'Honneur, France, 1986. Subject of several television documentaries and jl articles on architecture. *Publications:* Richard Rogers + Architects, 1985; A+U: Richard Rogers 1978–1988, 1988; Architecture: a modern view, 1990; (jtly) A New London, 1992; Cities for a Small Planet (Reith Lectures), 1997; Richard Rogers: the complete works, vol. 1, 1999, vol. 2, 2001, vol. 3, 2006; (with Anne Power) Cities for a Small Country, 2000; Richard Rogers + Architects: from the house to the city, 2010; *relevant publications:* Richard Rogers, a biography, by Bryan Appleyard, 1986; Richard Rogers, by Kenneth Powell, 1994; The Architecture of Richard Rogers, by Deyan Sudjic, 1994; Richard Rogers Partnership, by Richard Burdett, 1995; Richard Rogers: architect of the future, by Kenneth Powell, 2006. *Recreations:* friends, art, architecture, travel, food. *Address:* (office) Thames Wharf, Rainville Road, W6 9HA. *T:* (020) 7385 1235.

See also P. W. Rogers.

ROGERS OF RIVERSIDE, Lady; Ruth Rogers, MBE 2010; Chef and owner, River Cafe Restaurant, since 1987; *b* 2 July 1948; *d* of Frederick and Sylvia Elias; *m* 1973, Richard George Rogers (*see* Baron Rogers of Riverside); one *s* (and one *s* decd), and three step *s*. *Educ:* Bennington Coll., NY; London Coll. of Printing (BA Hons Design). Penguin Books, 1970–73; Richard Rogers & Partners, 1973–87. *Publications:* with Rose Gray: River Cafe Cook Book, 1995; River Cafe Cook Book Two, 1997; Italian Kitchen, 1998; River Cafe Cook Book Green, 2000; River Cafe Cook Book Easy, 2003; River Cafe Two Easy, 2005; River Cafe Pocket Books, 2006; River Cafe Classic Italian Cookbook, 2009. *Address:* River Cafe, Thames Wharf, Rainville Road, W6 9HA. *T:* (020) 7386 4200.

ROGERS, Alan James, MA; freelance journalist; Headmaster, Wellington School, Somerset, 1990–2006; Principal, Lodge International School, Kuching, Sarawak, Malaysia, 2007–09; *b* 30 March 1946; *s* of William James Albert Rogers and Beatrice Gwendolyn Rogers (*née* Evans); *m* 1968, Sheila Follett; one *s* two *d*. *Educ:* Humphry Davy Grammar Sch., Penzance; Jesus Coll., Oxford (MA; PGCE). Asst Master, Pangbourne Coll., 1969–73; Head of Geography and Geology, Arnold Sch., Blackpool, 1973–78; Head of Geography, Wellington Coll., 1978–82; Second Master and Dep. Headmaster, Wellington Sch., Som, 1982–90. *Publications:* frequent contribs to Malaysian Nature Soc. columnist, Borneo Sunday Post; articles on geographical educn in UK and Commonwealth jls and in various books and newspapers. *Recreations:* alpine and rainforest environments, hockey, house restoration.

ROGERS, Prof. Alex David, PhD; Professor of Conservation Biology, University of Oxford, since 2010; Fellow of Somerville College, Oxford, since 2010; *b* Walthamstow, London, 21 Jan. 1968; *s* of David Rogers and Anne Rogers; *m* 1996, Candida Michaela Reed; two *d*. *Educ:* St Edmund Campion Sch., Hornchurch; Univ. of Liverpool (BSc Hons 1st Cl. Marine Biol. 1989; PhD 1993). Res. Fellow, Marine Biol Assoc. of UK, Plymouth, 1992–97; NERC Advanced Res. Fellow, Univ. of Southampton, 1997–2001; Principal Investigator in Biodiversity Res., British Antarctic Survey, 2001–06; Sen. Res. Fellow, 2006–09, Reader, 2009–10, Inst. of Zool., Zool Soc. of London. Scientific Dir, Internat. Prog. on State of the Ocean, 2006–. Zoological Society of London: Conservation Fellowship, 2011; Marsh Award for Marine and Freshwater Conservation, 2013. *Publications:* (jtly) Photographic Guide to the Sea and Shore Life of Britain and North-West Europe, 2001; (ed jtly) Antarctic Ecology: from genes to ecosystems part 1, 2007; (ed jtly) Antarctic Ecology: from genes to ecosystems part 2: evolution, diversity and functional ecology, 2007; (ed jtly) Antarctic Ecosystems: an extreme environment in a changing world, 2012; over 92 papers in jls; 20 chapters in books; 60 reports and policy communications. *Recreations:* writing about science and policy, walking, reading science fiction and fantasy, collecting books on marine biology and zoology (antiquarian), home brewing, allotment growing. *Address:* Department of Zoology, University of Oxford, Tinbergen Building, South Parks Road, Oxford OX1 3PS. *T:* (01865) 271104, *Fax:* (01865) 310447. *E:* alex.rogers@zoo.ox.ac.uk.

ROGERS, Alice; *see* Rogers, F. A.

ROGERS, Allan Ralph, FGS; *b* 24 Oct. 1932; *s* of John Henry Rogers and Madeleine Rogers (*née* Smith); *m* 1955, Ceridwen James; one *s* three *d*. *Educ:* University College of Swansea (BSc Hons Geology). Geologist, UK, Canada, USA, Australia, 1956–63; Teacher, 1963–65; Tutor-organiser, WEA, 1965–70, District Sec., 1970–79. Vis. Prof., Univ. of S Wales (formerly Univ. of Glamorgan), 1997–. MP (Lab) Rhondda, 1983–2001. Opposition spokesman: on defence, 1987–92; on foreign affairs, 1992–94. Mem., Intelligence and Security Cttee, 1994–2001. European Parliament: Mem. (Lab) SE Wales, 1979–84; Vice-Pres., 1979–82. Non-exec. Dir, Buy As You View, 2001–. Bd Mem., British Geol Survey, 2001–05. Chm., Earth Sci. Educn Forum, 2002–. *Recreation:* all sports. *Address:* 2 Dilwyn Avenue, Hengoed, Caerphilly CF82 7AG. *Clubs:* Workmen's (Treorchy); Penallta Rugby Football (Pres.).

ROGERS, Anthony Gordon, GBS 2011; QC (Hong Kong) 1984; JP; arbitrator, mediator, independent executor and expert witness; *b* 16 Feb. 1946; *s* of late Gordon Victor Rogers and Olga Elena Rogers; *m* 1970, Barbara Ann Zimmern; one *s* two *d*. *Educ:* Beaumont Coll. Called to the Bar, Gray's Inn, 1969; practised at the Bar: London, 1970–76; Hong Kong, 1976–93; Judge of the High Court, 1993–97, Judge of the Court of Appeal, 1997–2000, Vice-Pres. of the Court of Appeal, 2000–11, Hong Kong; Judge of Court of Appeal, Brunei Darussalam, 2010–11. Chm., Hong Kong Bar Assoc., 1990, 1991. Mem., Basic Law Consultative Cttee, 1985–90; Chm., Standing Cttee on Company Law Reform, 1994–2004. JP Hong Kong 1988. Dir, 1992–2010, Sec., 1995–, Hong Kong China Rowing Assoc. *Recreations:* rowing, golf, music, keeping the family happy. *Address:* 9C Jonsim Place, 228 Queen's Road East, Hong Kong. *T:* 92882910. *Clubs:* Thames Rowing, Sloane; Hong Kong, Hong Kong Country, Shek-O, Lion Rock Rowing (Hong Kong).

ROGERS, Brett, OBE 2014; Director, Photographers' Gallery, London, since 2005; *b* 22 Dec. 1954; *d* of Bob and Jerry Rogers; *m* 1982, Alan Lowery (marr. diss. 2007); one *s* one *d*. *Educ:* Univ. of Sydney (BA Hons 1976); Courtauld Inst. of Art, Univ. of London (MA 1981). Exhibns Officer, 1976–78, Hd of Exhibns, 1978–80, Australian Gall. Dirs Council; Exhibns Officer, 1982–95, Hd of Exhibns and Dep. Dir, 1996–2005, Fine Arts Dept, British Council. Vis. Fellow, UAL, 2014–. *Publications:* Madame Yevonde: Be Original or Die, 1998; Reality Check: recent developments in British photography, 2003; To be continued……aspects of recent British and Finnish photography, 2005. *Recreations:* visual arts, theatre, swimming. *Address:* Photographers' Gallery, 16–18 Ramillies Street, W1F 7LW. *T:* (020) 7087 9310. *E:* Brett.rogers@tpg.org.uk.

ROGERS, Catherine W.; *see* Wyn-Rogers.

ROGERS, Christopher; *see* Rogers, L. C. G.

ROGERS, Dafydd Harries; theatre producer; *b* London, 5 May 1969; *s* of Mac and Maggie Rogers; *m* 2002, Colleen Brown; one *s* one *d*. *Educ:* St Paul's Sch., Barnes; King's Coll. London (BD Hons Theol.). Productions include: Art, Wyndham's, 1996, transf. NY, 1998; Rebecca, UK tour, 2001; The Play What I Wrote, Wyndham's, 2001; Heroes, Wyndham's, 2005; Equus, Gielgud, 2007, transf. NY, 2009; God of Carnage, Gielgud, 2008, transf. NY, 2009; Noël Coward's Brief Encounter, Cinema Haymarket, 2008, transf. NY, 2009; Calendar Girls, Chichester, 2008, transf. Noël Coward, 2009; Deathtrap, Noël Coward, 2010; The Full Monty, Sheffield and UK tour, 2013. *Recreations:* circus, capoeira, sculling. *Address:* Wyndham's Theatre, 32–36 Charing Cross Road, Leicester Square, WC2H 0DA. *T:* (020) 7292 0390. *E:* dafydd@davidpughltd.com.

ROGERS, Dr David Andrew; Director, Strategy and Constitution, Scottish Government, since 2012. *Educ:* St Peter's Coll., Oxford (MA); Sidney Sussex Coll., Cambridge (PhD 1988). Post-doctoral Res. Fellow, Univ. of Oxford, 1988–89; geologist, oil industry, 1989–93; Scottish Office, 1993–99; Scottish Exec., later Scottish Govt, 1999–. *Address:* Scottish Government, St Andrew's House, Regent Road, Edinburgh EH1 3DG. *T:* (0131) 244 5210. *E:* david.rogers@scotland.gsi.gov.uk.

ROGERS, Ven. David Arthur; Archdeacon of Craven, 1977–86; *b* 12 March 1921; *s* of Rev. Canon Thomas Godfrey Rogers and Doris Mary Cleaver Rogers (*née* Steele); *m* 1951, Joan Malkin; one *s* three *d*. *Educ:* Saint Edward's School, Oxford (scholar); Christ's College, Cambridge (exhibitioner). BA 1947, MA 1952. War service with Green Howards and RAC, 1940–45; Christ's Coll. and Ridley Hall, Cambridge, 1945–49; Asst Curate, St George's, Stockport, 1949–53; Rector, St Peter's, Levenshulme, Manchester, 1953–59; Vicar of

Sedbergh, Cautley and Garsdale, 1959–79; Rural Dean of Sedbergh and then of Ewecross, 1959–77; Hon. Canon of Bradford Cathedral, 1967. *Address:* 24 Towns End Road, Sharnbrook, Bedford MK44 1HY. *T:* (01234) 782650.

ROGERS, Dr David P., FRMetS; President and Chair of the Board, Health and Climate Foundation, since 2007; *b* 20 March 1957. *Educ:* UEA (BSc Hons); Univ. of Southampton (PhD). Navigating Officer, British MN; res. appts, Desert Res. Inst., Univ. of Nevada; Scripps Institution of Oceanography, University of California, San Diego: res. scientist; Associate Dir, Calif Space Inst.; Dir, Physical Oceanography Res. Div. and Dir, Jt Inst. for Marine Observations, 1989–2000; Dir, Office of Weather and Air Quality Res. and Associate Dir of Res., Nat. Oceanographic and Atmospheric Admin, USA, 2000–03; Vice Pres., Meteorol and Oceanographic Services, Sci. Applications Internat. Corp., Virginia, 2003–04; Chief Exec., Met Office, 2004–05. *E:* drogers@hc-foundation.org.

ROGERS, Prof. (Frances) Alice, PhD; Professor of Mathematics, King's College London, since 2007; *b* 13 Sept. 1947; *d* of John George Monroe and Jane Monroe (*née* Reynolds); *m* 1970, Richard Ian Rogers (*d* 2009); one *s* one *d*. *Educ:* Cranborne Chase Sch.; New Hall, Cambridge (BA Maths 1968); Hughes Hall, Cambridge (PGCE 1969); Imperial Coll., London (PhD 1981). Secondary sch. teacher, 1969–76; SERC Res. Fellow, Imperial Coll., London, 1981–83; Department of Mathematics, King's College London: Res. Associate, 1983–84; SERC Adv. Res. Fellow, 1984–89; Royal Soc. Univ. Res. Fellow, 1989–94; Lectr, 1994–96; Reader, 1996–2007. Mem., Adv. Cttee on Maths Educn, 2007–11. Trustee and Educn Sec., LMS, 2012–. FKC 2015. *Publications:* Supermanifolds: theory and applications, 2007; articles on mathematical physics in scientific jls. *Recreations:* gardening, history, hills, choral singing. *Address:* Department of Mathematics, King's College London, Strand, WC2R 2LS. *E:* alice.rogers@kcl.ac.uk.

ROGERS, (George) Stuart L.; *see* Lawson-Rogers.

ROGERS, Hayley; Parliamentary Counsel, since 2007; Project Lead, Good Law initiative, since 2013; *b* 16 July 1967; *d* of Peter Jordan and Ann Catherine Jordan (*née* Newman); *m* 1990, Steven Alexander Rogers. *Educ:* Univ. of Reading (LLB 1988); Coll. of Law, Guildford. Articled clerk, then solicitor, Boys and Maughan Solicitors, Margate, 1989–93; Asst Parly Counsel, 1993–98; Sen. Asst Parly Counsel, 1998–2002; Dep. Parly Counsel, 2002–07; Head Drafter, Tax Law Rewrite Project, HM Revenue and Customs, 2005–07. Associate Res. Fellow, Inst. of Advanced Legal Studies, 2013–. *Recreations:* walking, painting, gardening. *Address:* Parliamentary Counsel Office, 1 Horse Guards Road, SW1A 2HQ. *E:* hayley.rogers@cabinetoffice.gov.uk.

ROGERS, Ian Paul; QC 2014; *b* Newport, S Wales, 2 Jan. 1973; *s* of late Neil Rogers and of Denise Rogers. *Educ:* Hertford Coll., Oxford (BA 1st Cl. Hons 1994); Eur. Inst., Florence (LLM Comparative Eur. and Internat. Law 2007). Called to the Bar, Gray's Inn, 1995. Member: Attorney Gen.'s A Panel of Treasury Counsel, until 2014; Welsh Govt A Panel of Treasury Counsel, until 2014. Mem., RFU Judiciary, 2014–. *Publications:* (contrib.) Oliver & Dingeman's Employer's Liability Cases, 2003; contribs to jls incl. Solicitors' Jl, Legal Week, Eur. Human Rights Law Rev. *Recreations:* hiking, travel, theatre, cinema. *Address:* Monckton Chambers, 182 Raymond Buildings, Gray's Inn, WC1R 5NR. *T:* (020) 7405 7211. *E:* irogers@monckton.com.

ROGERS, Prof. Jane Rosalind, FRSL; novelist; Professor of Writing, Sheffield Hallam University, since 2005; *b* London, 21 July 1952; *d* of Andrew Walton Rogers and Margaret Kathleen Rogers (*née* Farmer); *m* 1981, Michael Harris; one *s* one *d*. *Educ:* Oxford High Sch. for Girls; New Hall, Cambridge (BA Hons English 1974); Univ. of Leicester (PGCE 1976). Writer of novels, scripts and short stories, 1981–. Lectr (pt-time), Sheffield Hallam Univ., 1987–. Teacher of writing: Arvon Foundn; British Council, Open Coll. of the Arts, 2010–12; mentor, Gold Dust; writer, teacher and project co-ordinator, Radio Mifumi, Uganda, 2010. Scriptwriter: *television:* Dawn and the Candidate (play), 1989 (Samuel Beckett Award for best first television drama, 1989); Mr Wroe's Virgins (series), 1993; *radio:* adaptations: Diary of a Provincial Lady, 1999; Shirley, 2002; Lorna Doone, 2004; The Age of Innocence, 2008; The Custom of the Country, 2010; The Chrysalids, 2012; The Testament of Jessie Lamb, 2013; *plays*: Island, 2002; The Inland Sea, 2004; Meanwood, 2005; Dear Writer, 2008; Red Enters the Eye, 2011. FRSL 1994. *Publications: fiction:* Separate Tracks, 1983; Her Living Image (Somerset Maugham Award), 1984; The Ice is Singing, 1987; Mr Wroe's Virgins, 1991; Promised Lands, 1995 (Writers' Guild Best Fiction Book award, 1996); Island, 1999; The Voyage Home, 2004; The Testament of Jessie Lamb, 2011 (Arthur C. Clarke Award, 2012); Hitting Trees with Sticks (collected stories), 2012; *non-fiction:* (ed) The Good Fiction Guide, 2001, 2nd edn 2005. *Recreations:* walking, reading. *Address:* c/o Charles Walker, United Agents, 12–26 Lexington Street, W1F 0LE. *T:* (020) 3214 0800. *E:* jane.rogers@btinternet.com, CWalker@unitedagents.co.uk. *W:* www.janerogers.org.

ROGERS, Very Rev. John; Dean of Llandaff, 1993–99, now Emeritus; *b* 27 Nov. 1934; *s* of William Harold and Annie Mary Rogers; *m* 1972, Pamela Mary Goddard (*d* 2003); one *s* one *d*. *Educ:* Jones' W Monmouth Sch., Pontypool; St David's Coll., Lampeter (BA 1955); Oriel Coll., Oxford (BA 1957; MA 1960); St Stephen's House, Oxford, 1957–59. Ordained deacon, 1959, priest, 1960; Assistant Curate: St Martin's, Roath (dio. of Llandaff), 1959–63; St Sidwell's, Lodge, with Holy Redeemer, Ruimveldt, Guyana, 1963–67; Vicar: Holy Redeemer, Ruimveldt, Guyana, 1967–69; Wismar and Lower Demerara River Missions, 1969–71; Caldicot, 1971–77; Monmouth, 1977–84; Rector, Ebbw Vale, 1984–93. Rural Dean: Monmouth, 1981–84; Blaenau Gwent, 1986–93; Canon of St Woolos Cathedral, 1988–93. *Recreations:* gardening, fencing, reading. *Address:* Fron Lodge, Llandovery SA20 0LJ. *T:* (01550) 720089.

ROGERS, Prof. (John) Michael, DPhil; FSA; FBA 1988; Khalili Professor of Islamic Art, School of Oriental and African Studies, University of London, 1991–2000, now Emeritus; Hon. Curator, Nasser D. Khalili Collection of Islamic Art, Nour Foundation, since 2001; *b* 25 Jan. 1935. *Educ:* Ulverston Grammar Sch.; Corpus Christi Coll., Oxford (MA, DPhil). FSA 1974. Robinson Sen. Student, Oriel Coll., Oxford, 1958–61; Tutor in Philosophy, Pembroke and Wadham Colls, Oxford, 1961–65; Asst, then Associate, Prof. of Islamic Art and Archaeol., Center for Arabic Studies, Amer. Univ. in Cairo, 1965–77; Dep. Keeper, Dept of Oriental Antiquities, BM, 1977–91. Vis. Sen. Res. Fellow, Merton Coll., Oxford, 1971–72; Vis. Res. Fellow, New Coll., Oxford, 1998; Slade Prof. of Fine Art, Oxford Univ., 1991–92. Pres., British Inst. of Persian Studies, 1993–96. Corresp. Mem., Deutsches Archäologisches Inst., Berlin, 1988. Order of the Egyptian Republic, 2nd cl., 1969. *Publications:* The Spread of Islam, 1976; Islamic Art and Design 1500–1700, 1983; (with R. M. Ward) Süleyman the Magnificent, 1988; Mughal Painting, 1993, 2nd edn 2006; Empire of the Sultans: Ottoman art in the Khalili collection, 1995; (with M. B. Piotrovsky) Heaven on Earth: art from Islamic lands, 2004; Sinan, 2006; (with M. Bayani) Tale and Image: Persian paintings in the Khalili Collection, vol. II, 2014; numerous articles on hist. and archaeol. of Islamic Turkey, Egypt, Syria, Iran and Central Asia. *Recreations:* walking, music, botany. *Address:* The Nour Foundation, Unit 24, Victoria Industrial Estate, W3 6UU. *Club:* Beefsteak.

ROGERS, His Honour John Michael Thomas; QC 1978; a Circuit Judge, 1998–2010; *m* 2006, Mrs Angela Victoria Galaud (*née* Ginders); one step *s* one step *d*, and one *d* from a former marriage. *Educ:* Rydal Sch.; Birkenhead Sch.; Fitzwilliam House, Cambridge (MA, LLB). Called to Bar, Gray's Inn, 1963, Bencher 1991. A Recorder, 1976–98. Chancellor, Dio. of St Asaph, 1982–2010. Leader, Wales and Chester Circuit, 1990–92. *Recreations:* farming, gardening. *Clubs:* Reform; Pragmatist's (Wirral); Barbarians Rugby Football.

ROGERS, Air Chief Marshal Sir John (Robson), KCB 1982; CBE 1971; FRAeS; Executive Chairman, RAC Motor Sports Association, 1989–98; *b* 11 Jan. 1928; *s* of B. R. Rogers; *m* 1955, Gytha Elspeth Campbell; two *s* two *d*. *Educ:* Brentwood Sch.; No 1 Radio Sch., Cranwell; Royal Air Force Coll., Cranwell. OC 56(F) Sqdn, 1960–61; Gp Captain, 1967; OC RAF Coningsby, 1967–69; Air Commodore, 1971; Dir of Operational Requirements (RAF), 1971–73; Dep. Comdt, RAF Coll., 1973–75; RCDS, 1976; Air Vice-Marshal, 1977; Dir-Gen. of Organisation, RAF, 1977–79; AOC Training Units, RAF Support Comd, 1979–81; Air Mem. for Supply and Organisation, MoD, 1981–83; Controller Aircraft, MoD PE, 1983–86, retired. Director: British Car Auctions, 1986–90; First Technology Gp, 1986–93. Pres., Internat. Historic Commn, Fedn Internat. de l'Automobile, 1995–2004. Chm., Children's Fire and Burn Trust, 2000–04. FRAeS 1983. *Recreation:* motor racing. *Address:* c/o Lloyds Bank, 27 High Street, Colchester, Essex. *Clubs:* Royal Automobile (Vice-Chm., 1990–98; Life Vice Pres., 1999), Royal Air Force.

ROGERS, Prof. (Leonard) Christopher (Gordon), PhD; Professor of Statistical Science, University of Cambridge, since 2002. *Educ:* St John's Coll., Cambridge (BA 1975; PhD 1980). Lecturer: Univ. of Warwick, 1980–83; Univ. Coll. of Swansea, 1983–85; Univ. of Cambridge, 1985–91; Fellow of St John's Coll., Cambridge, 1985–91; Prof. of Math. Statistics, QMW, 1991–94; Prof. of Probability, Univ. of Bath, 1994–2002. *Publications:* (with David Williams) Diffusions, Markov Processes, and Martingales, vol. 1, Foundations, 1979, vol. 2, Itô calculus, 1987; articles in learned jls. *Address:* Department of Pure Mathematics and Mathematical Statistics, Centre for Mathematical Sciences, Wilberforce Road, Cambridge CB3 0WB.

ROGERS, Malcolm Austin, CBE 2004; DPhil; FSA; Ann and Graham Gund Director, Museum of Fine Arts, Boston, Mass, 1994–2015; *b* 3 Oct. 1948; *s* of late James Eric Rogers and Frances Anne (*née* Elsey). *Educ:* Oakham School; Magdalen College, Oxford (Open Exhibnr); Christ Church, Oxford (Senior Scholar). Violet Vaughan Morgan Prize, 1967; BA (Eng. Lang. and Lit. 1st cl.), 1969; MA 1973; DPhil 1976. National Portrait Gallery: Asst Keeper, 1974–83; Dep. Keeper, 1983–85; Keeper, 1985–94; Dep. Dir, 1983–94. Trustee, Assoc. of Art Mus. Dirs, 2010–14. Mem., Amer. Acad. Arts and Scis, 2011. Humanitas Vis. Prof. in Museums, Galleries and Libraries, Univ. of Oxford, 2012. Freeman, City of London, 1992; Liveryman, Girdlers' Co., 1992. Hon. DFA Emmanuel Coll., Boston, 2011; Hon. DHL Boston Architectural Coll., 2014. Excellency Award, Foundn for Italian Art and Culture, 2010; Award of Merit, British Assoc., 2012. Chevalier de l'Ordre des Arts et des Lettres (France), 2007; Commendatore al Merito della Repubblica Italiana, 2009; Encomienda de la Orden de Isabel la Católica (Spain), 2010. *Publications:* Dictionary of British Portraiture, 4 vols (ed jtly), 1979–81; Museums and Galleries of London, 1983, 3rd edn 1991; William Dobson, 1983; John and John Baptist Closterman: a catalogue of their works, 1983; Elizabeth II: portraits of sixty years, 1986; Camera Portraits, 1989; Montacute House, 1991; (with Sir David Piper) Companion Guide to London, 1992; (ed) The English Face, by Sir David Piper, 1992; Master Drawings from the National Portrait Gallery, 1993; articles and reviews in Burlington Magazine, Apollo, TLS. *Recreations:* food and wine, opera, travel. *Address:* Russell Court, Lower Green, Broadway, Worcs WR12 7BU. *T:* (01386) 854828. *Clubs:* Beefsteak; Algonquin (Hon. Mem.), Wednesday Evening Club of 1777, Thursday Evening (Boston).

ROGERS, Mark Nicholas; His Honour Judge Mark Rogers; a Circuit Judge, since 2009; a Deputy High Court Judge (Queen's Bench and Family Divisions), since 2011; Nominated Judge, Court of Protection, since 2011; *b* High Wycombe, 10 Dec. 1955; *s* of late Leslie Paul and Mabel Rogers; *m* 1979, Valerie Ann Haynes; one *s* one *d*. *Educ:* Royal Grammar Sch., High Wycombe; Brasenose Coll., Oxford (BA); Poly. of Central London. Called to the Bar, Middle Temple, 1980; in practice as barrister, 1980–2006; Dep. Dist Judge, 2000–06, Dist Judge, 2007–09; Recorder, 2001–09. *Recreations:* music, watching men's and women's cricket, theatre, food and drink. *Address:* Leicester Combined Court, 90 Wellington Street, Leicester LE1 6HG. *T:* (0116) 222 5800.

ROGERS, Martin John Wyndham, OBE 2000; Director: Fellowships in Religious Education for Europe, since 2001; International Association for Science and Religion in Schools, since 2010; *b* 9 April 1931; *s* of late John Frederick Rogers and Grace Mary Rogers; *m* 1957, Jane Cook; two *s* one *d*. *Educ:* Oundle Sch.; Heidelberg Univ.; Trinity Hall, Cambridge (MA); MA Oxon 1995. Henry Wiggin & Co., 1953–55; Westminster School: Asst Master, 1955–60; Sen. Chemistry Master, 1960–64; Housemaster, 1964–66; Under Master and Master of the Queen's Scholars, 1967–71; Headmaster of Malvern Coll., 1971–82; Chief Master, King Edward's Sch., Birmingham, Headmaster of the Schs of King Edward VIth in Birmingham, 1982–91; Dir, Farmington Inst. for Christian Studies, 1991–2001. Seconded as Nuffield Research Fellow (O-level Chemistry Project), 1962–64; Salter's Company Fellow, Dept of Chemical Engrg and Chemical Technology, Imperial Coll., London, 1969; Associate Fellow, Manchester, subseq. Harris Manchester, Coll., Oxford, 1991–2001. Chairman: Curriculum Cttee of HMC, GSA and IAPS, 1979–86; HMC, 1987; Mem. Council, GPDST, 1991–93. Chm., European Council, Nat. Assocs of Ind. Schs, 1994–97. Co-Dir, Sci. and Religion in Schs Project, 2001–11. Mem. Council, Birmingham Univ., 1985–92. Governor: Oundle Sch., 1988–2001; Westonbirt Sch., 1991–97; Elmhurst Ballet Sch., 1991–95; English Coll., Prague, 1991–2005. Chm., Millwood Educn Trust, 2001–04; Trustee: Sandford St Martin Trust, 1994–2003; Smallpeice Trust, 2000–02. FRSA. *Publications:* John Dalton and the Atomic Theory, 1965; Chemistry and Energy, 1968; Gas Syringe Experiments, 1970; (co-author) Chemistry: facts, patterns and principles, 1972; Editor: Foreground Chemistry Series, 1968; Farmington Papers, 1993–2001; Science and Religion in Schools, 2006. *Address:* Eastwards, 24 Millwood End, Long Hanborough, Oxon OX29 8BX. *T:* (01993) 883930. *Club:* East India, Devonshire, Sports and Public Schools.

ROGERS, Michael; *see* Rogers, J. M.

ROGERS, Nigel David; free-lance singer, conductor and teacher; Professor of Singing, Royal College of Music, 1978–2000; *b* 21 March 1935; *m* 1961, Frederica Bement Lord (*d* 1992); one *d*; *m* 1999, Lina Zilinskyte; one *d*. *Educ:* Wellington Grammar Sch.; King's Coll., Cambridge (MA). Studied in Italy and Germany. Professional singer, 1961–; began singing career in Munich with group Studio der frühen Musik. Is a leading specialist in field of Baroque music, and has made over 70 recordings from Monteverdi to Schubert; gives concerts, recitals, lectures and master classes in many parts of world; most acclaimed role in opera as Monteverdi's Orfeo. Formed vocal ensemble Chiaroscuro, to perform vast repertory of Italian Baroque music, 1979, later extended to include Chiaroscuro Chamber Ensemble and Chiaroscuro Baroque Orch. Has lectured and taught at Schola Cantorum Basiliensis, Basle, Switzerland. Hon. RCM 1981. *Publications:* chapter on Voice, Companion to Baroque Music (ed J. A. Sadie), 1991; articles on early Baroque performance practice in various periodicals in different countries. *Address:* Wellington House, 13 Victoria Road, Deal, Kent CT14 7AS. *T:* and *Fax:* (01304) 379249.

ROGERS, Parry; *see* Rogers, T. G. P.

ROGERS, Patricia Maureen S.; *see* Shepheard Rogers.

ROGERS, Sir Peter, Kt 2009; Chairman, New West End Company, since 2013; *b* Wolverhampton, Sept. 1949. *Educ:* Wednesfield Grammar Sch. Accountancy and financial roles with local authorities; joined Westminster CC, 1996, Chief Exec., 2000–08; Chief Exec., London Develt Agency, 2008–11. Advr to Mayor of London for Regeneration, Growth and Enterprise, 2011–12. Mem. Bd, Housing Corp., 2004–08. Non-exec. Dir, Liberata UK Ltd, 2012– (Chm., CapacityGRID, 2012–). Dir, Rogers' Performance Mgt

Consultancy, 2008–. Chm., PeopleToo, 2011–. Dir, Regents Park Open Air Th., 2010–. *Address:* New West End Company, 3rd Floor, Morley House, 320 Upper Regent Street, W1B 3BE.

ROGERS, Peter Brian, CBE 2001; Chief Executive, Independent Television Commission, 1996–2000; *b* 8 April 1941; *s* of late William Patrick Rogers and Margaret Elizabeth Rogers; *m* 1966, Jean Mary Bailey (*d* 2014); one *s* two *d. Educ:* De La Salle Grammar Sch., Liverpool; Manchester Univ. (1st Cl. Hons BAEcon; Cobden Prize); London Sch. of Econs and Pol Science, London Univ. (MSc Econs). Tax Officer, Inland Revenue, 1959–67; Res. Associate, Manchester Univ., 1967–68; Econ. Adviser, HM Treasury, 1968–73; Sen. Econ. Adviser, Central Policy Review Staff, Cabinet Office, 1973–74; Dir of Econ. Planning, Tyne and Wear CC (on secondment from Central Govt), 1974–76; Sen. Econ. Adviser, DoE, 1976–79; Dep. Chief Exec., Housing Corp., 1979–82; Dir of Finance, IBA, 1982–90; Dep. Chief Exec. and Dir of Finance, ITC, 1991–96. Dir, Channel Four Television Co., 1982–92. Trustee and Hon. Treas., Lakeland Arts Trust, 2006–13. *Address:* Thorphinsty House, Cartmel Fell, Grange over Sands, Cumbria LA11 6NF. *T:* (01539) 552515. *E:* pbrogers@btinternet.com.

ROGERS, Peter Lloyd, CBE 2011; Chief Executive, Babcock International plc, since 2003; *b* Rugby, 29 Dec. 1947; *s* of Arnold Rogers and Ivy Rogers; *m* 2006, Stephanie Corrigan. *Educ:* Wymondham Coll.; Manchester Univ. (LLB Hons 1968). FCA 1971. Ford Motor Co., 1972–84; Director: Imagination Ltd, 1984–85; Sperry UK, 1985–86; Courtaulds plc, 1996–98; Dep. Chief Exec., Acordis Gp, 1998–2000; Chief Operating Officer, Babcock Internat. plc, 2000–03. Non-exec. Dir, Galliford Try plc, 2008–. *Recreations:* golf, scuba diving, reading. *Address:* Babcock International plc, 33 Wigmore Street, W1U 1QX. *T:* (020) 7355 5300, *Fax:* (020) 7355 5360. *E:* peter.rogers@babcockinternational.com.

ROGERS, Peter Richard; Master of Costs Office (Costs Judge) (formerly Taxing Master), Supreme Court, 1992–2009; Deputy Costs Judge, 2009–13; *b* 2 April 1939; *s* of Denis Roynan Rogers and Lucy Gwynneth (*née* Hopwood); *m* 1966, Adrienne Winifred Haylock. *Educ:* Bristol Univ. (LLB Hons). Solicitor of the Supreme Court. Articled Clerk, then solicitor, Turner Kenneth Brown (formerly Kenneth Brown Baker Baker) (solicitors), 1961–92; Partner, 1968–92; Dep. Supreme Court Taxing Master, 1991–92. Mem., London No 13 Legal Aid Cttee, 1980–92. Consulting Ed., Greenslade on Costs, 1995–99 and 2010–13 (Gen. Ed., 1999–2010); Jt Editor, Costs Law Reports, 1997–2013. *Recreations:* weather, steam and other railways, environmental concerns. *Address:* 15 Knole Road, Sevenoaks, Kent TN13 3XH.

ROGERS, Peter Standing; JP; Member (C) North Wales, National Assembly for Wales, 1999–2003; *b* 2 Jan. 1940; *s* of late Harold Rogers and of Joan Thomas; *m* 1973, Margaret Roberts; two *s. Educ:* Prenton Secondary Sch., Birkenhead; Cheshire Sch. of Agriculture. Farm Manager, 1962–65; Sales Manager, Ciba Geigy UK, 1965; self-employed farmer, 1965–. Mem. (Ind) Isle of Anglesey CC, 2004–. Contested: (C) Ynys Môn, Nat. Assembly for Wales, 2003; (Ind) Ynys Môn, 2005, 2010. JP Ynys Môn, 1990; High Sheriff, Gwynedd, 2008. *Recreations:* sports, all rural activities. *Address:* Bodrida, Brynsiencyn, Anglesey LL61 6NZ. *Clubs:* Old Birkonians (Birkenhead); Welsh Crawshays Rugby.

ROGERS, Peter William, CBE 2007; Eur Ing, FREng; director of property companies; Founding Partner, Lipton Rogers Developments, since 2013; *b* 25 Oct. 1946; *s* of Dr Nino Rogers and Dada (*née* Geiringer); *m* 1971, Hélène Tombazis (marr. diss.); one *s* one *d*; *m* 1988, Barbara Peters; two *s. Educ:* Portsmouth Poly. (BSc). CEng 1975, FREng 2005; MICE 1975; Eur Ing 1989. Various construction industry appts, UK, USA, France, Holland and ME, 1970–84; Dir, Stanhope Plc (formerly Stanhope Properties Plc), 1985–2013, resp. for construction of Broadgate, 1985–91. Advr on arts projects, incl., Nat. Gall., Glyndebourne Opera House, Royal Opera House, Tate Modern, Royal Academy, Serpentine Gall. and RSC, 1986–. Non-exec. Dir, Firstbase, 2006– (Exec. Dir, 2004–06). Mem., Construction Industry Sector Gp, NEDO, 1988–92. Mem., Foresight Panel, DTI, 1994–95 and 2000–01. Advr, Heritage Lottery Fund, 1995–2000. Advr to Mayor of London, and Chm., Olympic Orbit, 2010–12. Dir, Reading Construction Forum, 1994–99; Chairman: Strategic Forum for Construction, 2002–06 (Chm., 2012 Task Gp, 2005–12); Constructing Excellence, 2003–08; DCLG (formerly ODPM) Steering Cttee for Sustainable Bldgs, 2005–07; UK Green Bldg Council, 2006–14; Mem., Bldgs Steering Cttee, Courtauld Inst. of Art, 2014–. Trustee and Founder Chm., Buildings Strategy Cttee, V&A Mus., 1999–2008; Trustee, Serpentine Gall., 2010–11. Visitor, Ashmolean Mus., 2007–09. FRSA 2001. Hon. FRIBA 2004. *Recreations:* theatre, ballet, art, music, travel, sailing, ski-ing. *Address:* Lipton Rogers Developments LLP, 33 Cavendish Square, W1G 0DT. *T:* (020) 3757 0566. *E:* rogers@liptonrogers.com. *Club:* Royal Yachting Association.

See also Baron Rogers of Riverside.

ROGERS, Philip John, MBE 1990; FREng, FInstP; Optical Design Consultant, VNF Ltd, since 2006; *b* 4 Oct. 1942; *s* of late John William Rogers and Lilian (*née* Fleet); *m* 1979, Wendy Joan Cross; one *s* two *d. Educ:* Burnley Grammar Sch.; North London Poly. (HNC Applied Physics 1965). CPhys 1990; CEng 1993. Optical Designer, Hilger & Watts, London, 1960–66; Pilkington PE, subseq. Pilkington Optronics, then Thales Optics Ltd: Optical Designer, 1966–69; Chief Optical Designer, 1969–2005; Chief Optics Engr, 3 sites, Pilkington Optronics Gp, 1994–2000. Visiting Professor: Cranfield Univ., 2007–13; Glyndwr Univ., 2012–; lecturing activities incl. OU TV broadcast, 1977. Mem., Thomson Coll., Paris, 1992–98. FInstP 1992; FREng 1998; Fellow: Internat. Soc. for Optical Engrg, 1991 (Dir, Bd, 1995–97); Optical Soc. of America, 1998. *Publications:* (contrib.) Electro Optical Displays, 1992; (contrib.) Optical Society of America Handbook of Optics, Vol. 1, 1995; conf. procs papers; contrib. 6 articles in jls; 27 patents covering infrared, night vision, avionic, visual and miscellaneous optics. *Recreations:* listening to music, armchair astronomy, reading (history and science particularly), messing about on computers. *Address:* 24 Cilgant Eglwys Wen, Bodelwyddan, Denbighshire LL18 5US. *T:* (01745) 582498.

ROGERS, Raymond Thomas, CPhys, FInstP; Managing Director, Dragon Health International (formerly Ray Rogers Associates), 1997–2008; *b* 19 Oct. 1940; *s* of late Thomas Kenneth Rogers and of Mary Esther Rogers (*née* Walsh); *m* 1964, Carmel Anne Saunders; two *s* one *d. Educ:* Gunnersbury Grammar Sch.; Birmingham Univ. (BSc). CPhys, FInstP 1962. Basic Med. Physicist, London Hosp., 1962–66; Sen. Med. Physicist, Westminster Hosp., 1966–70; Department of Health and Social Security, later Department of Health: PSO, Scientific and Tech. Br., 1970; Supt Engr, then Dir 1984; Asst Sec., Health Inf. Br., 1984–91; Under Sec., and Exec. Dir Information Mgt Gp, 1991–97. FRSA 1997. *Publications:* contribs to scientific jls and books. *Recreations:* trekking, opera, science, peace. *Address:* 7 Pilgrims View, Ash Green, Surrey GU12 6HU. *T:* (01252) 650138.

ROGERS, Ruth; *see* Rogers of Riverside, Lady.

ROGERS, Sheila; equality, diversity and human rights consultant in public and voluntary sectors, since 2005; *b* 29 March 1947; *d* of Charles Rogers and Peggy Baird; *m* (marr. diss.); one *d. Educ:* Univ. of Winnipeg (BA 1976); Univ. of Manitoba (LLB 1979); CIPFA (AdvDip 1999). Legal Aid Manitoba, 1980–86, Dep. Dir, 1986; Equal Opportunities Commn for NI, 1989–98, Dir of Finance and Admin, 1993–98; Chief Exec., Commn for Racial Equality for NI, 1998–99; Dir of Race Unit, 1999–2002, and Asst Chief Exec., 2000–01, Equality Commn for NI; Commission for Racial Equality (on secondment): Hd, Community Policy and Progs, 2002–04; Dir, Strategy and Delivery, 2004; Chief Exec., 2004–05. Trustee, Dance Resource Base NI, 2009–. *Publications:* (contrib.) Equal Opportunities: women's working lives, 1993; (contrib.) Workplace Equality: an international perspective on legislation, policy and practice, 2002. *E:* rogers.sheila@gmail.com.

ROGERS, (Thomas Gordon) Parry, CBE 1991; Director, The Plessey Co. plc, 1976–86; *b* 7 Aug. 1924; *s* of late Victor Francis Rogers and Ella (*née* May); *m* 1st, 1947, Pamela Mary (*née* Greene) (marr. diss. 1973); one *s* seven *d*; 2nd, 1973, Patricia Juliet (*née* Curtis); one *s* one *d. Educ:* West Hartlepool Grammar Sch.; St Edmund Hall, Oxford (MA). Served RAC and RAEC, 1944–47. Procter & Gamble Ltd, 1948–54; Mars Ltd, 1954–56; Hardy Spicer Ltd, 1956–61 (Dir, 1957–61); IBM United Kingdom Ltd, 1961–74 (Dir, 1964–74); The Plessey Co. plc, 1974–86; Chairman: Percom Ltd, 1984–94; ECCTIS 2000 Ltd, 1989–97; Director: MSL Gp Internat. Ltd, 1970–78; ICL plc, 1977–79; Hobsons Publishing plc, 1985–90; Butler Cox plc, 1985–91; Norman Broadbent Internat. Ltd, 1985–90; Ocean Group plc, 1988–94; Future Perfect (Counselling) Ltd, 1986–92; PRIMA Europe Ltd, 1987–93; BNB Resources plc, 1990–94. Chm., Plessey Pension Trust, 1978–86; Trustee, BNB Resources Pension Trust, 1991–94. Chairman: BTEC, 1986–94; SW London Coll. HEC, 1989–91; IT Skills Agency, 1984–96; Salisbury HA, 1986–90; Commn on Charitable Fundraising, NCSS, 1970–76; Member: Employment Appeal Tribunal, 1978–87; Standing Cttee on Pay Comparability, 1980–81; Nat. Steering Gp, Trng and Vocational Educn Initiative, MSC, 1983–86; CBI/BIM Panel on Mgt Educn, 1968–78; CBI Employment Policy Cttee, 1980–86; Rev. Team, Children and Young Persons Benefits, DHSS, 1984–85; Oxford Univ. Appts Cttee, 1972–87; Member Council: CRAC, 1965–94; ISCO, 1988–95; Inst. of Manpower Studies, 1970–86; Indust. Participation Assoc., 1972–86; Inst. of Dirs, 1980–95 (Chm., 1985–88; Vice Pres., 1988–95); Inst. of Personnel Management, 1954– (Pres., 1975–77); EEF, 1980–86; Econ. League, 1982–86; E Europe Trade Council, 1982–85. Governor: Ashridge Management Coll., 1985–94; Warminster Sch., 1989–99; St Mary's Sch., Shaftesbury, 1991–94. Patron, Dorset Chamber Orch. Freeman, City of London, 1987; Mem., Information Technologists' Co., 1987–. CCIPD; CCMI. *Publications:* The Recruitment and Training of Graduates, 1970; contribs on management subjects to newspapers and jls. *Recreations:* birdwatching, tennis, photography, listening to music. *Address:* St Edward's Chantry, Bimport, Shaftesbury, Dorset SP7 8BA. *T:* (01747) 852789.

ROGERSON, Rt Rev. Barry; Bishop of Bristol, 1985–2002; an Assistant Bishop, Diocese of Bath and Wells, since 2003; *b* 25 July 1936; *s* of Eric and Olive Rogerson; *m* 1961, Olga May Gibson; two *d. Educ:* Magnus Grammar School; Leeds Univ. (BA Theology); Wells Theol Coll. Midland Bank Ltd, 1952–57; Curate: St Hilda's, South Shields, 1962–65; St Nicholas', Bishopwearmouth, Sunderland, 1965–67; Lecturer, Lichfield Theological Coll., 1967–71, Vice-Principal, 1971–72; Lectr, Salisbury and Wells Theol Coll., 1972–75; Vicar, St Thomas', Wednesfield, 1975–79; Team Rector, Wednesfield Team Ministry, 1979; Bishop Suffragan of Wolverhampton, 1979–85. Chm., ABM (formerly ACCM), 1987–93; Mem. Central Cttee, WCC, 1991–2002 (Mem., Faith and Order Commn, 1987–98); Pres., CTBI, 1999–2002. Chm., Melanesian Mission, 1979–2002. Hon. Freeman, City and County of Bristol, 2003. Hon. LLD Bristol, 1993; Hon. DLitt UWE, 2003. *Recreations:* cinema, stained glass windows. *Address:* Flat 2, 30 Albert Road, Clevedon, N Somerset BS21 7RR. *E:* barry.rogerson@blueyonder.co.uk.

ROGERSON, Daniel John; *b* 23 July 1975; *s* of Stephen John Rogerson and Patricia Anne Rogerson (*née* Jones); *m* 1999, Heidi Lee Purser; two *s* one *d. Educ:* St Mary's Sch., Bodmin; Bodmin Coll.; Univ. of Wales, Aberystwyth (BSc Econ Pols 1996). Local govt officer, Bedford BC, 1996–98; admin. officer, De Montfort Univ., 1998–2002. Mem., Bedford BC, 1999–2002. MP (Lib Dem) N Cornwall, 2005–15; contested (Lib Dem) same seat, 2015. Parly Under-Sec. of State, DEFRA, 2013–15. *Recreations:* listening to blues music, reading, travel. *Club:* Camelford Liberal.

ROGERSON, Nicolas; Chairman, AIGIS Blast Protection Ltd, 2001–12; *b* 21 May 1943; *s* of late Hugh and Olivia Rogerson; *m* 1998, Hon. Caroline Elizabeth Tamara Le Bas (*d* 2001), *er d* of Baron Gilbert, PC; *m* 2009, Dinah Vivien Verey, *née* Nicolson. *Educ:* Cheam Sch.; Winchester Coll.; Magdalene Coll., Cambridge. Investors Chronicle, 1964–65; Executive, Angel Court Consultants, 1966–68; formed Dewe Rogerson, 1969; Chief Exec., Dewe Rogerson Gp, 1969–99; Chm., Dewe Rogerson Internat., 1985–99. Appeals Chm., King George's Fund for Sailors. *Recreations:* sailing, ski-ing, fly fishing, field sports, languages and European history. *Clubs:* Beefsteak; Royal Yacht Squadron.

ROGERSON, Paul, CBE 2007; DL; Chief Executive, Leeds City Council, 1999–2010; Consultant, Walton & Co., Planning Lawyers, Leeds, since 2010; *b* 10 June 1948; *s* of late John Rogerson and Hilda Rogerson (*née* Hepworth); *m* 1971, Eileen Kane; four *s* two *d. Educ:* De La Salle Coll., Sheffield; Manchester Univ. (LLB, MA Econ). Called to the Bar, Gray's Inn, 1971; Lectr, Univ. of Leeds, 1969–75; Principal Legal Officer: Barnsley MBC, 1975–78; Kirklees MDC, 1978–89; Asst Dir/Chief Legal Officer, 1989–95, Exec. Dir, 1995–99, Leeds CC. Dir, Northern Gas Networks, 2014–. Vis. Prof., Univ. of Louisville, USA, 1972–73. Trustee and Chair: Lineham Farm Children's Centre, 2010–; Heart Research UK, 2012–; Unipol Student Homes, 2014–. Governor and Vice Chair: Leeds Cathedral Choir Sch., 2010–; Leeds Trinity Univ., 2013–. DL W Yorks, 2010. Jt Gen. Ed., Local Govt Law Reports, 1999–2001. *Recreations:* family, friends, travel. *Address:* 12 Oakwood Lane, Leeds LS8 2JQ. *T:* (0113) 368 9146.

ROGERSON, Philip Graham; Chairman: Bunzl, since 2010; De La Rue, since 2012 (non-executive Director, since 2012); *b* 1 Jan. 1945; *s* of Henry and Florence Rogerson; *m* 1968, Susan Janet Kershaw; one *s* two *d. Educ:* William Hulme's Grammar Sch., Manchester. FCA 1968. Dearden, Harper, Miller & Co., Chartered Accountants, 1962–67; Hill Samuel & Co. Ltd, 1967–69; Thomas Tilling Ltd, 1969–71; Steetley Ltd, 1971–72; J. W. Chafer Ltd, 1972–78; with ICI plc, 1978–92 (General Manager, Finance, 1989–92); British Gas, later BG plc: Man. Dir, Finance, 1992–94; Exec. Dir, 1994–98; Dep. Chm., 1996–98. Non-executive Chairman: Pipeline Integrity Internat., 1998–2002; Bertram Gp Ltd, 1999–2001; United Engineering Forgings Ltd, 1999–2001; KBC Advanced Technologies plc, 1999–2004; Viridian Gp plc, 1999–2005 (Dep. Chm., 1998); Project Telecom plc, 2000–03; Aggreko, 2002–12 (Dep. Chm., 1997–2002); Thus Gp plc, 2004–08; Carillion, 2005–14 (Dep. Chm., 2004–05); Northgate plc, 2007–09 (non-exec. Dir, 2003–07); non-executive Director: Leeds Permanent Bldg Soc., then Halifax Bldg Soc., now Halifax plc, 1994–98; Limit plc, 1997–2000; Internat. Public Relations, 1997–98; Wates City of London Properties, 1998–2001; British Biotech, 1999–2003; Octopus Capital plc, 2000–01; CopperEye Ltd, 2001–03; Celltech Gp plc, 2003–04; Davis Service Gp, 2004–10. Chm. Adv. Bd, NE London Commng Support Unit, 2013–. Chm., Central YMCA, 2011–. Trustee, Changing Faces, 1997–2011. *Recreations:* golf, tennis, theatre.

ROGG, Lionel; organist and composer; Professor of Organ and Improvisation, Geneva Conservatoire de Musique, 1961–2002; Professor of Improvisation, Royal Academy of Music, 2004–09; *b* 1936; *m* Claudine Effront; three *s. Educ:* Conservatoire de Musique, Geneva (1st prize for piano and organ). Concerts or organ recitals on the five continents. Records include: 3 versions of complete organ works of J. S. Bach (Grand Prix du Disque, 1970, for The Art of the Fugue); works by Buxtehude (complete organ works; Deutscher Schallplatten Preis, 1980), Couperin, Grigny, Handel, Mozart, Liszt, Reger; transcriptions and own compositions. *Compositions:* Acclamations, 1964; Chorale Preludes, 1971; Partita, 1975; Variations on Psalm 91, 1983; Cantata "Geburt der Venus", 1984; Introduction, Ricerare and Toccata, 1985; Two Etudes, 1986; Monodies, 1986; Psalm 92, 1986; Piece for Clarinette,

1986; Face-à-face for two pianos, 1987; Organ Concerto, 1991. DèsL Univ. de Genève, 1989. *Publications:* Eléments de Contrepoint, 1969. *Address:* 38A route de Troinex, 1234 Vessy-Genève, Switzerland. *E:* lrogg@vtxnet.ch.

ROH, Tae Woo, Hon. GCMG 1989; President of Republic of Korea, 1988–93; *b* 4 Dec. 1932; *m* 1959, Kim-Ok-Sook; one *s* one *d. Educ:* Korean Military Academy; Republic of Korea War College. Commander, Capital Security, 1978, Defence Security, 1980; retd as Army General; Minister of State for Nat. Security and Foreign Affairs, 1981; Minister of Sports, and of Home Affairs, 1982; President: Seoul Olympic Organizing Cttee, 1983; Asian Games Organizing Cttee, 1983; Korean Olympic Cttee, 1984. Mem., Nat. Assembly and Pres., Ruling Democratic Justice Party, 1985. Hon. Dr George Washington Univ., 1989. Order of Nat. Security Merit (Sam Il Medal) (Korea), 1967; Grand Order of Mugunghwa (Korea), 1988; foreign decorations, incl. France, Germany, Kenya, Paraguay. *Publications:* Widaehan pot'ongsaram ui shidae (A great era of the ordinary people), 1987, trans. Japanese, 1988; Korea: a nation transformed, 1990. *Recreations:* tennis, swimming, golf, music, reading.

ROITH, Oscar, CB 1987; FREng, FIMechE; Deputy Chairman, British Maritime Technology, 1997–2002 (Director, 1987–2002); Chief Engineer and Scientist, Department of Trade and Industry, 1982–87; *b* London, 14 May 1927; *s* of late Leon Roith and Leah Roith; *m* 1950, Irene Bullock; one *d. Educ:* Gonville and Caius Coll., Cambridge (minor schol.; Mech. Scis Tripos; MA). FIMechE 1967; FREng (FEng 1983); Eur Ing 1988. Research Dept, Courtaulds, 1948; Distillers Co. Ltd: Central Engrg Dept, 1952; Engrg Manager, Hull Works, 1962; Works Manager, 1968, Works Gen. Manager, 1969, BP Chemicals, Hull; General Manager: Engrg and Technical, BP Chemicals, 1974; Engrg Dept, BP Trading, 1977; Chief Exec. (Engrg), BP Internat., 1981. Dir, Trueland Ltd, 1987–2004. Mem., Yorks and Humberside Economic Planning Council, 1972–74. Comr, Royal Commn for Exhibition of 1851, 1988–98. Chm., Mech. and Electrical Engrg Requirements Bd, 1981–82; Member: Mech. Engrg and Machine Tools Requirements Bd, 1977–81; (non-exec.) Res. Cttee. British Gas, 1987–96; ACORD, 1982–87; ACARD, 1982–87; Process Plant EDC, NEDO, 1979–82; SERC, 1982–87; NERC, 1982–87; Bd (part-time), LRT, 1988–95; Chm., Res. Adv. Gp, PCFC, 1989–92. Pres., IMechE, 1987–88 (Dep. Pres., 1985–87; Mem. Council, 1981–92; Mem., Process Engrg Gp Cttee, 1962–68); Dep. Chm. Council, Foundn for Science and Technol., 1988–95; Hon. Sec., Mech. Engrg, Council of Fellowship of Engrg, 1988–91. Hon. Prof., Dept of Mgt Sci., Univ. of Stirling, 1992–95; Hon. Fellow, Univ. of Brighton, 1992. Governor: Brighton Polytechnic, 1988–91; ICSTM, 1990–98. CCMI; FRSA. Hon. DSc West of England, 1993. *Recreations:* cricket, gardening, walking. *Address:* 20 Wraymill House, Wraymill Park, Batts Hill, Reigate, Surrey RH2 0LJ. *T:* (01737) 779633. *Club:* Athenæum.

ROITT, Prof. Ivan Maurice, FRS 1983; Emeritus Professor of Immunology, University College London, 1992–2009; Professor, 1969–92, and Head of Department of Immunology, 1969–92, and of Rheumatology Research, 1984–92, University College and Middlesex School of Medicine (formerly Middlesex Hospital Medical School); Chief Scientist, NALIA Systems Ltd, since 2005; Hon. Director, Middlesex University Centre for Investigative and Diagnostic Oncology, since 2009; *b* 30 Sept. 1927; *e s* of Harry Roitt; *m* 1953, Margaret Auralie Louise, *d* of F. Haigh; three *d. Educ:* King Edward's Sch., Birmingham; Balliol Coll., Oxford (exhibnr; BSc 1950; MA 1953; DPhil 1953; DSc 1968; Hon. Fellow 2004). FRCPath 1973. Res. Fellow, 1953, Reader in Immunopathol., 1965–68, Middlesex Hosp. Med. Sch. Chm., WHO Cttee on Immunol Control of Fertility, 1976–79; Mem., Biol. Sub-Cttee, UGC. Mem., Harrow Borough Council, 1963–65; Chm., Harrow Central Lib. Assoc., 1965–67. Vis. Prof., Middx Univ., 2006. Florey Meml Lectr, Adelaide Univ., 1982. Trustee, RSocMed, 2010–. Hon. FRCP 1995. Hon. Dr Middx, 2007. (Jtly) Van Meter Prize, Amer. Thyroid Assoc., 1957; Gairdner Foundn Award, Toronto, 1964. *Publications:* Essential Immunology, 1971, 12th edn 2011; (jtly) Immunology of Oral Diseases, 1979; (jtly) Immunology, 1985, 8th edn 2013; (jtly) Current Opinion in Immunology (series), 1989–93; (jtly) Clinical Immunology, 1991; Slide Atlas of Essential Immunology, 1992; (with Peter J. Delves) Encyclopedia of Immunology, 1992, 2nd edn 2000; (ed jtly) Medical Microbiology, 1993, 5th edn 2013; 283 contribs to learned scientific jls. *Recreations:* tennis, golf, clarinet (modest), piano (very modest), banjo (subliminal), the contemporary novel, models of public debate. *Address:* Department of Biomedical Sciences, Middlesex University, Hatchcroft Building, Room H115, The Burroughs, Hendon, NW4 4BT.

ROJO, Tamara; ballerina; Artistic Director, English National Ballet, since 2012; *d* of Pablo Rojo and Sara Diez. *Educ:* Centro de Danza de Victor Ullate; Conservatorio Profesional de Danza Mariemma, Madrid (Bachelor of Dance and Choreog.); Univ. Rey Juan Carlos (Master of Scenic Arts). Compañía de Danza Victor Ullate, 1991–96; Guest Dancer, Scottish Ballet, 1996–97; Principal, English Nat. Ballet, 1997–2000; Principal Dancer, Royal Ballet, 2000–12. Guest Dancer: Birmingham Royal Ballet; Kirov Ballet; La Scala Ballet; Nat. Ballet of China; English Nat. Ballet; Tokyo Ballet; New Nat. Tokyo Ballet; Mikhailovsky Ballet; Royal Swedish Ballet; Nat. Ballet of Finland; Ballet Nat. de Cuba; Deutsche Oper Ballet Berlin; Ballet de La Opera de Niza; Ente Publico Arena di Verona; Scottish Ballet; Ballet Victor Ullate, Madrid. Resident Guest Teacher, Royal Ballet Sch. Advr, Superior Counsel of Artistic Studies, Spain. Member, Board: Dance UK; Arts Council East. Patron, DanceEast Acad., Norwich. Grand Prix Femme, Concours Internat. de Danse de Paris, 1994; Best Dancer of Year, Italian Critics, 1996; Award for Outstanding Achievements in Dance, Barclay's Th. Awards, 2000; Best Female Dancer of Year 2001, Critic's Circle Dance Awards, 2002; Leonid Massine Premio al Valore, 2004; Internat. Medal for the Arts, Madrid, Interpretation Award, Villa de Madrid, 2007; Prince of Asturias Arts Award, Benois de la Danse Award, 2008; Dancer Revelation of Year Award, The Times; Possitano Dance Award. Medalla de Oro al Mérito en las Bellas Artes (Spain), 2002. *Address:* c/o English National Ballet, Markova House, 39 Jay Mews, SW7 2ES. *W:* www.tamara-rojo.com.

ROKISON, Dr Abigail; Lecturer in Shakespeare and Theatre, Shakespeare Institute, University of Birmingham, since 2013; *b* Epsom, 23 Sept. 1975; *d* of Kenneth Stuart Rokison, *qv*; *m* 2015, Andrew Woodall. *Educ:* Croydon High Sch.; LAMDA (Dip. Acting 1996); Open Univ. (BA Hons 1st Cl. Humanities with Lit. 2001); King's Coll. London (MA Shakespeare Text and Playhouse (Dist.) 2002); Trinity Hall, Cambridge (PhD 2006). Actor, 1992–2000; Lectr in Eng. and Drama, Faculty of Educn, Univ. of Cambridge, 2006–12; Fellow, and Dir, Studies in Eng. and Drama, Homerton Coll., Cambridge, 2006–12. Chm., Trustees, British Shakespeare Assoc., 2008–10. *Publications:* Shakespearean Verse Speaking, 2010 (Shakespeare's Globe Book Award, 2012); Shakespeare for Young People: productions, versions and adaptations, 2013; articles in Shakespeare Jl, Literature Compass. *Recreations:* theatre, ballet, music, singing, cooking. *Address:* Shakespeare Institute, Church Street, Stratford-upon-Avon CV37 6HP. *T:* (0121) 414 9511. *E:* a.rokison@bham.ac.uk.

ROKISON, Kenneth Stuart; QC 1976; a Judge of the Courts of Appeal of Jersey and Guernsey, 2000–07; a former Deputy High Court Judge; *b* 13 April 1937; *s* of late Frank Edward and late Kitty Winifred Rokison; *m* 1973, Rosalind Julia (*née* Mitchell); one *s* two *d. Educ:* Whitgift School, Croydon; Magdalene College, Cambridge (BA 1960). Called to the Bar, Gray's Inn, 1961, Bencher, 1985–2003. A Recorder, 1989–94. *Recreations:* theatre, tennis, charity bicycle rides. *Address:* Ashcroft Farm, Gadbrook, Betchworth, Surrey RH3 7AH. *T:* (01306) 611244.

See also A. Rokison.

ROLAND, Prof. Martin Oliver, CBE 2003; DM; FRCP, FRCGP; FMedSci; Professor of Health Services Research, University of Cambridge, since 2009; Professorial Fellow and Chairman, Art Committee, Murray Edwards College, Cambridge, since 2014; *b* 7 Aug. 1951; *s* of Peter Ernest Roland and Margaret Eileen Roland; *m* 1st, 1971, Gillian Chapman; one *s*; 2nd, 1979, Rosalind Thorburn; two *s* one *d. Educ:* Rugby Sch.; Merton Coll., Oxford (BA 1972; BM BCh 1975; DM 1989). MRCP 1978, FRCP 2001; FRCGP 1994. Lectr in Gen. Practice, St Thomas's Hosp. Med. Sch., 1979–83; Dir of Studies in Gen. Practice, Cambridge Univ. Sch. of Clinical Medicine, 1987–92; Prof. of General Practice, Univ. of Manchester, 1992–2009; Director: Nat. Primary Care Res. and Develt Centre, 1999–2009; NIHR Sch. for Primary Care Res., 2006–09. Mem., MRC Health Services Research Bd, 1992–96 (Chm. and Mem. MRC Council, 1994–96). FMedSci 2000. *Publications:* contribs on gen. practice, hosp. referrals, back pain, quality of care and out of hours care. *Recreations:* walking, opera, contemporary women's art. *Address:* Cambridge Centre for Health Services Research, Institute of Public Health, University of Cambridge, Forvie Site, Robinson Way, Cambridge CB2 0SR. *T:* (01223) 330320.

ROLFE; *see* Neville-Rolfe.

ROLFE, Mervyn James, CBE 2000; DL; Chairman, ESEP Ltd, 1999–2014; *b* 31 July 1947; *s* of late Raymond Rolfe and Margaret Rolfe; *m* 1977, Christine Margaret Tyrell; one *s. Educ:* Buckhaven High Sch., Fife; Dundee Univ. (MEd Hons); Abertay Dundee Univ. (MSc). FSAScot 1993. Civil servant, MSC, 1977–83; Co-ordinator, Dundee Resources Centre for Unemployed, 1983–87. Tayside Regional Council: Councillor, 1986–96; Convener of Educn, 1986–94; Depute Leader, 1990–94; Opposition Leader, 1994–96; Dundee City Council: Mem., 1995–2003; Convener of Econ. Develt and Depute Leader, 1999–2003; Lord Provost and Lord-Lieut of Dundee, 1996–99. Chief Exec., Dundee and Tayside Chamber of Commerce and Industry, 2002–06; Dir, Scottish Enterprise Tayside, 1992–96, 1999–2003. Convenor, Scottish Police Services Authy, 2007–08. Lectr in Econs and Mgt, Univ. of Abertay, Dundee, 2008–13. Member: General Teaching Council Scotland, 1986–96; Exec., COSLA, 1990–96. Mem. Court, Dundee Univ., 1986–2000. Vice Chm. of Govs, HM Frigate Unicorn Preservation Soc., 1998–2014; Hon. Col, 2 (City of Dundee) Signals Sqn, TA, 2003–10. Hon. Fellow, Univ. of Abertay Dundee, 1999. FRSA 1992. JP 1988–2008, DL 1999, Dundee. OStJ 1997. *Recreations:* reading, music, local history. *Address:* 17 Mains Terrace, Dundee DD4 7BX. *T:* (01382) 450073.

ROLFE, Richard B.; *see* Boggis-Rolfe.

ROLFE, William David Ian, PhD; FRSE, FGS, FMA; Keeper of Geology, National Museums of Scotland, 1986–96; *b* 24 Jan. 1936; *s* of late William Ambrose Rolfe and Greta Olwen Jones; *m* 1960, Julia Mary Margaret, *d* of late Capt. G. H. G. S. Rayer, OBE; two *d. Educ:* Royal Liberty Grammar Sch., Romford; Birmingham Univ. (BSc 1957; PhD 1960). FGS 1960; FMA 1972; FRSE 1983. Demonstrator in Geol., UC of N Staffs, 1960; Fulbright Schol., and Asst Curator, Mus. of Comparative Zool., Harvard Coll., Cambridge, Mass, 1961–62; Geol. Curator, Univ. Lectr, then Sen. Lectr in Geol., Hunterian Mus., Univ. of Glasgow, 1962–81; Dep. Dir, 1981–86. Vis. Scientist, Field Mus. of Natural Hist., Chicago, 1981. Mem., Trng Awards Cttee, NERC, 1980–83. President: Palaeontol Assoc., 1992–94 (Vice-Pres., 1974–76); Soc. Hist. Natural Hist., 1996–99 (Vice-Pres., 1987). Geological Society of Glasgow: Ed., Scottish Jl of Geol., 1967–72; Pres., 1973–76; Geological Society: Editl Chm., Journal, 1973–76; Chm., Conservation Cttee, 1980–85; Murchison Fund, 1978; Tyrrell Res. Fund, 1982; Coke Medal, 1984; Edinburgh Geological Society: Pres., 1989–91; Clough Medal, 1997. FRSA 1985. *Publications:* (ed) Phylogeny and Evolution of Crustacea, 1963; Treatise on Invertebrate Paleontology, part R, 1969; Geological Howlers, 1980; papers on fossil phyllocarid crustaceans and palaeontol., esp. other arthropods, and hist. of 18th century natural sci. illustration. *Recreations:* visual arts, walking, music. *Address:* 4A Randolph Crescent, Edinburgh EH3 7TH. *T:* (0131) 226 2094.

ROLLAND, Lawrence Anderson Lyon, PPRIBA; PPRIAS; FRSE; Senior Partner, Hurd Rolland Partnership (formerly L. A. Rolland & Partners and Robert Hurd and Partners), 1959–97; President of Royal Institute of British Architects, 1985–87; *b* 6 Nov. 1937; *s* of Lawrence Anderson Rolland and Winifred Anne Lyon; *m* 1960, Mairi Melville; two *s* two *d. Educ:* George Watson's Boys' College, Edinburgh; Duncan of Jordanstone College of Art. Diploma of Art (Architecture) 1959. ARIBA 1960; FRIAS 1965 (Pres., RIAS, 1979–81); FRSE 1989. Founder Mem., Scottish Construction Industry Group, 1979–81; Mem., Bldg EDC, NEDC, 1982–88. Mem. Bd, Architects' Registration Bd, 1996–2004 (Chm., Qualifications Adv. Gp, 2000–04). Architect for: The Queen's Hall, concert hall, Edinburgh; restoration and redesign of Bank of Scotland Head Office (original Architect, Sibbald, Reid & Crighton, 1805 and later, Bryce, 1870); much housing in Fife's royal burghs; British Golf Museum, St Andrews; General Accident Life Assurance, York; redesign, Council Chamber, GMC. Chairman: RIBA Educn Trust Fund, 1996–2003; RIBA Educn Funds Cttee, 1996–2003; Gen. Trustee, Church of Scotland, 1979– (Chm., Adv. Cttee on Artistic Matters, 1975–81); Mem. of Council and Bd, Nat. Trust for Scotland, 2005–11. Chm. Bd of Govs, Duncan of Jordanstone Coll. of Art, 1993–94; Chm. Court, Univ. of Dundee, 1997–2004 (Mem., 1993–2009; Chancellor's Assessor, 2005–10). FRSA 1988. Hon. LLD Dundee, 2004. Winner of more than 20 awards and commendations from Saltire Soc., Stone Fedn, Concrete Soc., Civic Trust, Europa Nostra, RIBA, and Times Conservation Award. *Recreations:* music, fishing, food, wine, cars. *Address:* Blinkbonny Cottage, Newburn, nr Upper Largo, Leven, Fife KY8 6JF. *T:* (01333) 360383.

ROLLINS, Marva; Headteacher, Raynham Primary School, Edmonton, since 2000; *b* St Andrews, Barbados, 14 Dec. 1951; *d* of Franklyn and Myrtle Hurst; *m* (marr. diss.); three *s*; partner, Eric Parke. *Educ:* Poly. of N London (BEd 1986); Open Univ. (MA Educn 1990). Comptometer operator, 1968–72; class teacher, Kensington, Salisbury and Sandringham Primary Schs, Newham, 1986–92; Dep. Headteacher, Cleves Primary Sch., Newham, 1992–95; Headteacher, Godwin Jun. Sch., Newham, 1995–2000. Lecturer (pt-time): Newham Coll., 1990–95; Inst. of Educn, Univ. of London, 2003– (Vis. Fellow, 2011–). Educn Advr, Barbadian Overseas Nationals Orgn, 1998–2004. Founder Member: Sickle Cell Soc., 1979; E London Black Women Orgn, 1979–; Newham African Caribbean Assoc., 1984–. Keynote speaker and trainer in educn leadership and personal develt. Hon. Licentiate, Coll. of Preceptors, 1996. Windrush Educn Champion, 2004. *Recreations:* travelling, reading, walking. *Address:* Raynham Primary School, Raynham Avenue, Edmonton, N18 2JQ. *T:* (020) 8807 4726, *Fax:* (020) 8807 8013. *E:* Headteacher@raynham.enfield.sch.uk.

ROLLINSON, Timothy John Denis, CBE 2012; Director-General and Deputy Chairman, Forestry Commission, 2004–13; *b* 6 Nov. 1953; *s* of William Edward Denis Rollinson and Ida Frances Rollinson (*née* Marshall); *m* 1st, 1975 (marr. diss.); one *s* two *d*; 2nd, 2013, Frances Isabel Smith. *Educ:* Chigwell Sch.; Edinburgh Univ. (BSc Hons). MICFor 1978, FICFor 1995; FIAgrE 2004; CEnv 2005. Forestry Commission: District Officer: Kent, 1976–78; New Forest, 1978–81; Head of: Growth and Yield Studies, 1981–88; Land Use Planning, 1988–90; Parly and Policy Div., 1990–93; Sec., 1994–97; Chief Conservator, England, 1997–2000; Head of Policy and Practice Div., 2000–03; Dir, Forestry Gp, 2003–04. Chairman: Forest Res. Co-ordination Cttee, 2000–04; Global Partnership on Forest Landscape Restoration, 2002–; Pres., Inst. of Chartered Foresters, 2000–02. Trustee: Royal Botanic Gardens, Edinburgh, 2009–; Woodland Trust, 2013–. Patron, Tree Aid, 2008–. CCMI 2006. *Publications:* Thinning Control in British Woodlands, 1985; articles in forestry jls. *Recreations:* golf, food. *Clubs:* Craigmillar Park Golf (Edinburgh); Dunbar Golf.

ROLLO, family name of **Lord Rollo**.

ROLLO, 14th Lord *cr* 1651; **David Eric Howard Rollo;** Baron Dunning 1869; *b* 31 March 1943; *s* of 13th Lord Rollo and Suzanne Hatton; *S* father, 1997; *m* 1971, Felicity Anne Christian, *o d* of Lt-Comdr J. B. Lamb; three *s*. *Educ:* Eton. Late Captain Grenadier Guards. *Heir: s* Master of Rollo, *qv*. *Address:* Pitcairns House, Dunning, Perthshire PH2 9BX. *Clubs:* Cavalry and Guards, Turf.

ROLLO, Master of; Hon. James David William Rollo; *b* 8 Jan. 1972; *s* and *heir* of Lord Rollo, *qv*; *m* 2001, Sophie Sara, *d* of Hubert de Castella; one *s* three *d*. *Educ:* Eton; Edinburgh Univ.

ROLLO, Prof. James Maxwell Cree, CMG 1998; Director, InterAnalysis Ltd, since 2008; Professor of European Economic Integration, University of Sussex, and Co-Director, Sussex European Institute, 1999–2011, now Professor Emeritus; *b* 20 Jan. 1946; *s* of late James Maxwell Cree Rollo and Alice Mary (*née* Killen); *m* 1st, 1970, Sonia Ann Halliwell (marr. diss. 2008); one *s* one *d*; 2nd, 2008, Rachel Ann Thompson. *Educ:* Gourock High Sch.; Greenock High Sch.; Glasgow Univ. (BSc); London School of Economics (MSc Econ). Asst Economist, 1968–75, Economic Advr, 1975–79, MAFF; Economic Advr, FCO, 1979–81; Sen. Economic Advr, ODA, 1981–84; Dep. Head, Economic Advrs, FCO, 1984–89; Dir, Internat. Econs Programme, RIIA, 1989–93; Chief Economic Advr, FCO, 1993–98. Dir, ESRC Res. Prog., One Europe or Several?, 2001–03. Special Prof., Univ. of Nottingham, 1996–99. Trustee, Mus. of Migration and Diversity, Spitalfields, 2001–. FAcSS (AcSS 2009). Ed., Jl of Common Market Studies, 2003–10. *Publications:* The New Eastern Europe: Western responses, 1990; (with John Flemming) Trade, Payments and Adjustment in Central and Eastern Europe, 1992; articles in learned jls. *Recreation:* having fun. *Address:* InterAnalysis Ltd, Sussex Innovation Centre, University of Sussex, Brighton BN1 9SB. *T:* (01273) 234642. *E:* j.rollo@sussex.ac.uk.

ROLLS, Prof. Edmund Thomson, DPhil, DSc; Director, Oxford Centre for Computational Neuroscience, since 2008; Professor of Computational Neuroscience, University of Warwick, since 2013; *b* 4 June 1945; *s* of Eric Fergus Rolls and May Martin Rolls (*née* Thomson); *m* 1969, Barbara Jean Simons (marr. diss. 1983); two *d*. *Educ:* Hardye's Sch., Dorchester; Jesus Coll., Cambridge (BA Preclinical Medicine 1967; MA); Queen's Coll., Oxford (Thomas Hardy Schol.); Magdalen Coll., Oxford (DPhil 1971); DSc Oxon 1986. Fellow by Exam., Magdalen Coll., Oxford, 1969–73; Lectr in Exptl Psychol., 1973–96, Prof. of Exptl Psychol., 1996–2008, Oxford Univ.; Fellow and Tutor in Psychol., Corpus Christi Coll., Oxford, 1973–2008. Principal Res. Fellow, Univ. of Warwick, 2008–13. Associate Dir, MRC Oxford IRC for Cognitive Neurosci., 1990–2003. Member: Soc. for Neurosci.; Physiological Soc.; Exptl Psychol. Soc. Secretary: Eur. Brain and Behaviour Soc., 1973–76; Council, Eur. Neurosci. Assoc., 1985–88; Membre d'Honneur, Société Française de Neurologie, 1994; Mem., Academia Europaea. Canadian Commonwealth Fellow, 1980–81. Hon. DSc Toyama, 2005. Spearman Medal, BPsS, 1977. *Publications:* The Brain and Reward, 1975; (with B. J. Rolls) Thirst, 1982; (with A. Treves) Neural Networks and Brain Function, 1998; (jtly) Introduction to Connectionist Modelling of Cognitive Processes, 1998; The Brain and Emotion, 1999; (with G. Deco) Computational Neuroscience of Vision, 2002; Emotion Explained, 2005; Memory, Attention and Decision-Making, 2008; (with G. Deco) The Noisy Brain: stochastic dynamics as a principle of brain function, 2010; Neuroculture: on the implications of brain science, 2012; Emotion and Decision-Making Explained, 2014; over 530 scientific papers. *Recreations:* yachting, windsurfing, music, including opera. *W:* www.oxcns.org.

ROMAIN, Rabbi Dr Jonathan Anidjar, MBE 2004; Minister, Maidenhead Synagogue, since 1980; Chairman, Assembly of Rabbis, 2007–09; *b* 24 Aug. 1954; *s* of Daniel and Gabrielle Romain; *m* 1981, Sybil Sheridan; four *s*. *Educ:* University Coll. London (BA Hons); Univ. of Leicester (PhD 1990). Semicha/Rabbinic Ordination, Leo Baeck Coll., London. Chaplain, Jewish Police Assoc., 2003–. Chm., Accord Coalition, 2009–; Member, Board: CCJ, 1989–; Three Faiths Forum, 2005–. Patron, Dignity in Dying, 2012–. *Publications:* Signs and Wonders, 1985; The Jews of England, 1988; Faith and Practice, 1991; Tradition and Change, 1995; Till Faith us to Part, 1996; Renewing the Vision, 1996; Your God Shall Be My God, 2000; (ed) Reform Judaism and Modernity, 2004; God, Doubt and Dawkins, 2008; Really Useful Prayers, 2009; (ed) Great Reform Lives, 2010; (ed) A Passion for Judaism, 2011; Royal Jews, 2013; (ed) Assisted Dying—Rabbinic Responses, 2014. *Recreations:* tennis, completing a never-ending family tree, preaching what I think I ought to practise. *Address:* Grenfell Lodge, Ray Park Road, Maidenhead, Berks SL6 8QX. *T:* (01628) 673012.

ROMAINE, Prof. Suzanne, PhD; Merton Professor of English Language, and Fellow of Merton College, Oxford University, since 1984. *Educ:* Bryn Mawr Coll., Penn (AB); Edinburgh Univ. (MLitt); PhD Birmingham Univ. Lectr in Linguistics, Birmingham Univ., 1979–84. Fellow, Finnish Acad. of Sci. and Letters, Helsinki, 2010. PhD *hc*: Tromsø 1998; Uppsala 1999. *Publications:* Socio-historical Linguistics: its status and methodology, 1982; Sociolinguistic Variation in Speech Communities, 1982; Language of Children and Adolescents, 1984; Pidgin and Creole Languages, 1988; Bilingualism, 1989; (ed) Language in Australia, 1991; Language Education and Development, 1992; Language in Society: introduction to sociolinguistics, 1994; (ed) Cambridge History of the English Language, vol. IV, 1998; Communicating Gender, 1999; (with D. Nettle) Vanishing Voices, 2000. *Address:* Merton College, Oxford OX1 4JD.

ROMAN, Stephan, CMG 2011; Regional Director, South Asia, British Council, since 2011; *b* 29 March 1953; *s* of Victor and Muriel Roman; *m* 1986, Dorcas Pearmaine; one *s* two *d*. *Educ:* St Peter's Coll., Oxford (BA Hons Mod. Hist. 1974, MA); Univ. of Sheffield (MA Librarianship and Inf. Studies 1976). Libraries, Arts and Mus Dept, Coventry CC, 1974–78; British Council: Sudan and Yemen, 1979–82; Saudi Arabia and Gulf, 1983–86; Indonesia, 1986–91; Dir, Information Services, 1992–2001; Regl Dir, SE Europe, 2001–05; Regl Dir, W Europe and N America, 2005–11. Order of Merit (Romania), 2004. *Publications:* The Development of Islamic Library Collections in Western Europe and North America, 1990. *Recreations:* history, philosophy, current affairs. *Address:* British Council, Tariq bin Zaid Street (near Rashid Hospital), PO Box 1636, Dubai, UAE.

ROMAN, Stephen Thomas B.; *see* Braviner Roman.

ROMANIUK, Paula Shane; *see* Pryke, P. S.

ROMANOW, Hon. Roy John, OC 2003; PC (Can.) 2003; QC (Sask.); Senior Fellow in Public Policy, Department of Political Studies, University of Saskatchewan, Canada, since 2001; Senior Policy Fellow, Saskatchewan Institute of Public Policy, University of Regina, since 2001; *b* 1939; *s* of Mike and Tekla Romanow; *m* 1967, Eleanore Boykowich. *Educ:* Univ. of Saskatchewan (Arts and Law degrees). First elected to Saskatchewan Legislative Assembly, 1967; MLA (NDP) Saskatoon-Riversdale, 1967–82, 1986–2001; Dep. Premier, 1971–82; Attorney General, 1971–82; Minister of Intergovtl Affairs, 1979–82; Opposition House Leader for NDP Caucus, 1986; Leader, Saskatchewan NDP, 1987–2001; Premier, Saskatchewan, 1991–2001. Hd, Commn on Future of Health Care in Canada, 2001–02; Mem., Security Intelligence Rev. Cttee, 2003–08. Vis. Fellow, Sch. of Policy Studies, Queen's Univ., 2001–. *Publications:* (jtly) Canada Notwithstanding, 1984. *Address:* c/o Department of Political Studies, University of Saskatchewan, 9 Campus Drive, 919 Arts Building, Saskatoon, SK S7N 5A5, Canada.

ROMEO, Antonia; Director General, Economic and Domestic Affairs Secretariat, Cabinet Office, since 2015; *b* London, 20 Oct. 1974; *d* of Prof. Peter Rice-Evans and Prof. Catherine Rice-Evans; *m* 1999, John Romeo; two *s* one *d*. *Educ:* N London Collegiate Sch.; Westminster Sch.; Brasenose Coll., Oxford (MA PPE 1996); London Sch. of Econs and Pol Sci. (MSc Econs 2000). Strategy Consultant, Oliver Wyman and Co., 1996–99; Lord Chancellor's Department, then Department for Constitutional Affairs, later Ministry of Justice: economist, 2000–04; Hd of Inf., Rights Div., Constitution Directorate, 2004–06; Principal Private Sec. to Lord Chancellor and Sec. of State for Constitutional Affairs, then for Justice, 2006–08; Dir, FCO, 2008–10; Exec. Dir, Governance Reform, Cabinet Office, 2010–11; Dir Gen., Transforming Justice, 2011–13, Criminal Justice, 2013–15, MoJ. *Recreations:* theatre, karaoke, cards, Lego. *Address:* Cabinet Office, 70 Whitehall, SW1A 2AS. *Clubs:* Athenæum, Kit Cat.

ROMEO, Lyn; Chief Social Worker for Adults, Department of Health, since 2013; *b* Griffith, NSW, 8 Sept. 1955; *d* of Domenico and Mary Romeo. *Educ:* Univ. of NSW (BSW 1978); Univ. of Leeds (MBA 1995). Hosp. Social Worker, St Vincent's Hosp., Sydney, 1977–79; Residential Social Worker, Leeds CC, 1980–81; Bradford Metropolitan District Council: Social Worker, 1981–86; Social Work Team Leader, 1986–90; Area Social Services Manager, 1990–92; Principal Care Manager, 1992–2000; Area Manager, 2000–02; Social Services Inspector, DoH, 2002–05; Asst Dir, Adult Social Care, London Bor. of Camden, 2005–13. *Recreations:* hill walking, cycling, dancing, theatre. *Address:* Department of Health, Richmond House, 79 Whitehall, SW1A 2NS. *E:* chiefsocialworkerforadults@dh.gsi.gov.uk.

ROMETTY, Virginia M., (Ginni); President, Chief Executive Officer and Chairman, IBM Corporation, since 2012. *Educ:* Northwestern Univ. (BSc Computer Sci. and Electrical Engrg). Joined IBM Corporation, 1981; posts include: Gen. Manager, Global Services, Americas; Gen. Manager, Global Insce and Financial Services Sector; Sen. Vice Pres., Global Business Services; Sen. Vice Pres. and Gp Exec., Sales, Mktg and Strategy. Mem., Council on Foreign Relations. Member: Bd of Trustees, Northwestern Univ.; Bd of Managers, Memorial Sloan-Kettering Cancer Center. *Address:* IBM Corporation, 1 New Orchard Road, Armonk, NY 10504–1722, USA.

ROMINGER, Rev. Roberta Carol Sears; General Secretary, United Reformed Church, 2008–14; Pastor, Mercer Island United Church of Christ, Washington, USA, since 2015; *b* USA, 30 Aug. 1955; *d* of Robert Alden Sears and Janet Carol Sears (*née* Graef); *m* 1990, Rev. Dale Rominger. *Educ:* Univ. of California, Berkeley (BA 1977); Pacific Sch. of Religion, Berkeley (MDiv 1982). Ordained Minister, 1982; Minister: Tombstone Community Church, United Church of Christ, Arizona, 1982–85; York Rd URC, Woking, 1985–90; Worplesdon URC, Guildford, 1987–90; Wideopen URC, Newcastle upon Tyne, 1991–98; Kingston Park Ecumenical Church, Newcastle upon Tyne, 1993–98; Moderator, Thames North Synod, URC, 1998–2008. *Recreation:* playing the cello.

ROMNEY, 8th Earl of, *cr* 1801; **Julian Charles Marsham;** Bt 1663; Baron of Romney, 1716; Viscount Marsham, 1801; *b* 28 March 1948; *s* of late Col Peter William Marsham, MBE and Hersey Marsham (*née* Coke); *S* cousin, 2004; *m* 1975, Catriona Ann Stewart (*see* Countess of Romney); two *s* one *d*. *Educ:* Eton. High Sheriff, Norfolk, 2007. *Heir: s* Viscount Marsham, *qv*.

ROMNEY, Countess of; Catriona Ann Marsham; Vice Lord-Lieutenant of Norfolk, since 2012; *b* Edinburgh, 10 March 1954; *d* of Lt-Col Sir Robert (Christie) Stewart, *qv*; *m* 1975, Julian Charles Marsham (*see* Earl of Romney); two *s* one *d*. Trustee, Westacre Arts Foundn; Dir, Fine Art Commns. Former Chair, Gayton Parish Council. Chair, NSPCC, W Norfolk, and involved with other local organisations and charities. DL Norfolk, 2005. *Recreations:* gardening, cooking, walking, grandchildren. *Address:* Wensum Farm, West Rudham, King's Lynn, Norfolk PE31 8SZ. *T:* (01485) 528432. *E:* ciciromney@icloud.com.

ROMNEY, Daphne Irene; QC 2009; *b* London, 29 July 1955; *d* of Dr David Romney and Olga Romney (*née* Lempert). *Educ:* Camden Sch. for Girls; Newnham Coll., Cambridge (BA 1978). Called to the Bar, Inner Temple, 1979; in practice as barrister specialising in employment law. Chm., Employment Law Bar Assoc., 2007–09. Trustee, Save-A-Child, 2009–. *Recreations:* watching Arsenal, gym and pilates, cooking, eating, travel. *Address:* Cloisters, 1 Pump Court, EC4Y 7AA. *T:* (020) 7827 4000, *Fax:* (020) 7827 4100. *E:* dr@cloisters.com.

ROMNEY, (Willard) Mitt; Executive Partner and Group Chairman, Solamere Capital, since 2012; *b* Detroit, 12 March 1947; *s* of George and Lenore Romney; *m* 1969, Ann Davies; five *s*. *Educ:* Brigham Young Univ. (BA 1971); Harvard Univ. (JD, MBA 1975). Consultant, Boston Consulting Gp, 1975–77; Consultant, 1977–78, Vice-Pres., 1978–84, Bain & Co.; Man. Partner and CEO, Bain Capital Inc., 1984–99; interim CEO, Bain & Co., 1990–92; Pres. and CEO, Salt Lake Organizing Cttee, 2002 Winter Olympics, 1999–2002; Gov., Massachusetts, 2003–07. Dir, Marriott Internat. Inc., 1993–2002, 2009–11, 2012–. Republican Candidate for Presidency of USA, 2012. *Publications:* Turnaround: crisis, leadership and the Olympic Games (with T. Robinson), 2004; No Apology: the case for American greatness, 2010.

RONALDSHAY, Earl of; Robin Lawrence Dundas; Director: Fine Art Commissions Ltd, since 1997; Zetland Estates Ltd (formerly Dundas Estates Ltd), since 1999; *b* 5 March 1965; *s* and *heir* of Marquess of Zetland, *qv*; *m* 1997, Heather, *d* of late Robert Hoffman, Maryland, USA and of Mrs Richard Cazenove, Cottesbrooke, Northants; four *d* (incl. twins). *Educ:* Harrow; Royal Agricl Coll., Cirencester. Director: Catterick Racecourse Co., 1988–2006; Redcar Racecourse Ltd (formerly Redcar Race Co.), 1989–2006; Zetland Estates (Shetland) Ltd, 2004–10; Man. Dir, Musks Ltd, 1993–99. Dir, Stronghill Develts Ltd, 2004–11. Member: Richmond Burgage Pastures Cttee, 2000– (Chm., 2005–); Yorks Cttee, CLA, 2001–05. Chm., Yorks HHA, 2008–13 (Treas., 2000–05; Dep. Chm., 2005–08). Trustee, Trebetherick Estate Club, 1995–. Chm., Aske Parish Meeting, 1998–. *Club:* Slainte Mhah.

RONAYNE, Prof. Jarlath, AM 2002; PhD; FRSC, FTSE; Tan Sri Jeffrey Cheah Distinguished Professor, Sunway University (formerly University College), Malaysia, since 2009 (Academic Director, 2004–06; Vice-Chancellor, 2006–09; Director, Manchester Business School Centre, 2010–14); Senior Associate, Ronayne Francis International, Melbourne, since 2005; International Academic Director, Le Cordon Bleu, London, since 2012; *b* 3 Sept. 1938; *s* of late Michael Ronayne and Anne Ronayne (*née* Kenny); *m* 1st, 1965, Rosalind Hickman (decd); two *s*; 2nd, 1995, Margaret Francis. *Educ:* Trinity Coll., Dublin (BA 1965; MA 1968; Hon. Fellow 1997); St John's Coll., Cambridge (PhD 1968). FRSC 1988; FTSE 1995. Lecturer: Dept of Applied Sci., Wolverhampton Poly., 1968–70; Dept of Sci. and Technol. Policy, Manchester Univ., 1970–74; Sen. Lectr, then Dir, Sci. Policy Res. Centre, Sch. of Sci., Griffith Univ., Brisbane, 1974–77; University of New South Wales: Prof. of Hist. and Philosophy of Sci., 1977–91; Hd of Dept of Hist. and Philosophy of Sci., 1977–83; Dean, Faculty of Arts, 1983–84; Pro-Vice-Chancellor, 1984–88; Dep. Vice-Chancellor, 1988–91; Prof. Emeritus, 1991; Vice-Chancellor and Pres., 1991–2003, Distinguished Professorial Fellow, 2004–08, Victoria Univ. of Technol., later Victoria Univ. Hon. Prof., Shanghai Inst. Tourism, 1993; Vis. Prof., Dept of Chem., TCD, 2010–; Visiting Fellow: Oriel Coll., Oxford, 1999; Wolfson Coll., Cambridge, 2004; President's Guest, St John's Coll., Cambridge, 2004. Member: Internat. Council on Sci. Policy Studies, 1984–; Exec. Cttee, Australian Higher Educn Industrial Assoc., 1996–99; Bd, Communications Law Centre, Sydney, 1996–2003; Standing Cttee on Internat. Matters, AVCC, 1998– (Leader, AVCC Delegn to India, 1998); Bd Dirs, Sunway Univ. (formerly Coll.) Sdn Bhd, 2004–.

Consultant to Commonwealth Dept of Employment, Educn and Youth Affairs, 1998. Mem., Victorian Educn Ministry Delegns to SE Asia and S America, 1998. Member Board: Melba Conservatorium of Music, Melbourne, 1995–; Playbox Theatre Co., Melb., 2000–03; Member: Academic Adv. Bd, Hong Kong Inst. of Technol., 2003–. Dir of Admissions (Australia), RCSI, 2003–13. Hon. Consul for Ireland in Victoria, 2002–09. Manoel de Vilhena Award, Malta, 1999. *Publications:* Guide to World Science: Australia and New Zealand, 1975; (jtly) Science, Technology and Public Policy, 1979; Science in Government: a review of the principles and practice of science policy, 1983; Science and Technology in Australasia, Antarctica and Pacific Islands, 1989; First Fleet to Federation: Irish supremacy in colonial Australia, 2001, republd as The Irish in Australia: rogues and reformers, First Fleet to Federation, 2003; contrib. numerous jl articles in chemistry and sci. policy, and book chapters in chemistry, hist. of sci. and sci. policy, and Irish history. *Recreations:* reading, especially Irish history. *Address:* PO Box 656, Williamstown, Vic 3016, Australia.

RONEY, Joanne Lucille, OBE 2009; FCIH; Chief Executive, Wakefield Council, since 2008; *b* 13 Sept. 1961; *d* of John William Roney and Grace (*née* Darnley). *Educ:* Univ. of Birmingham (MBA Public Admin 1996). Housing, Birmingham CC, 1977–89; Regl Dir, Sanctuary Housing Assoc., 1989–91; Dir of Housing, Kirklees MBC, 1991–99; Exec. Dir for Housing and Direct Services Orgn, 1999–2005, Exec. Dir for Neighbourhoods and Community Care, 2005–08, Sheffield CC. FCIH 2000 (Chm. Policy Bd, 2000–06). *Recreations:* travel, reading, music. *Address:* Wakefield Council, Town Hall, Wakefield WF1 2HQ.

RONEY, Peter John; Director, UK and European Pensions, Cambridge Associates LLC, since 2012; *b* 12 Oct. 1949. *Educ:* Durham Univ. (BA Hons Pol. and Econs). Investment Manager, Derbys CC; Chief Investment Officer, S Yorks CC; CEO, Combined Actuarial Performance Services Ltd; Man. Dir, Halifax Financial Services Ltd; Chief Exec., Save & Prosper Gp Ltd, 1996–98; Man. Dir, Consumer Financial Services, Great Universal Stores PLC, 1998–2000; with Cambridge Associates, 2001–: Man. Dir, Cambridge Associates Asia, Singapore, 2008–09; Co-Dir of Res., Cambridge Associates LLC, 2009–12.

RONSON, Dame Gail, DBE 2004; Board Member, since 1992, and Deputy President, since 2010, Jewish Care (Deputy Chairman, 2002–10); Director, Royal Opera House, 2001–14 (Ambassador, since 2014); President, Royal National Institute of Blind People, since 2012; *b* 3 July 1946; *d* of Joseph and Marie Cohen; *m* 1967, Gerald Maurice Ronson, *qv*; four *d*. *Educ:* Clarke's Coll. Co-Chm., St Mary's Hosp. Save the Baby Fund, 1985–96; Vice-Pres., Assoc. for Res. into Stammering in Childhood, 1991–. Jt Chm., Council for a Beautiful Israel, 1987–94. Trustee: Ronson Foundns, 1980–95; Royal Opera House Trust, 1985–; Home Farm Develt Trust, 1991–94; Gerald Ronson Foundn, 2005– (Dep. Chm., 2005–). *Recreation:* opera and ballet lover. *Address:* Heron House, 4 Bentinck Street, W1U 2EF. *T:* (020) 7486 4477, *Fax:* (020) 7487 2970. *E:* gailronson@heron.co.uk.

RONSON, Gerald Maurice, CBE 2012; Chief Executive: Heron Corporation PLC; Heron International PLC; Chairman and Chief Executive, Snax 24 Corporation Ltd; Chairman: Ronson Capital Partners; Rontec; *b* 27 May 1939; *s* of Henry and Sarah Ronson; *m* 1967, Gail (*see* Dame G. Ronson); four *d*. Chief Executive: Heron Corp. PLC, 1976– (Chm., 1978–93); Heron International PLC, 1983– (Chm., 1983–93). Chm. Trustees, Gerald Ronson Foundn, 2005–. Ambassador of Druse community on Mount Carmel. Hon DCL Northumbria, 2009; Hon. PhD Hebrew Univ. of Jerusalem, 2014. Encomienda de Numero of the Order of Civil Merit (Spain), 2009. *Recreation:* work. *Address:* Heron House, 4 Bentinck Street, W1U 2EF. *T:* (020) 7486 4477.

ROOCROFT, Amanda Jane; soprano; *b* 9 Feb. 1966; *d* of Roger Roocroft and Valerie Roocroft (*née* Metcalfe); *m* 1999; three *s*. *Educ:* Southlands High Sch.; Runshaw Tertiary Coll.; Royal Northern Coll. of Music. Début as Sophie in Der Rosenkavalier, WNO, 1990; has sung at Glyndebourne, Royal Opera House, English Nat. Opera, Bayerische Staatsoper, BBC Promenade Concerts, Edinburgh Internat. Fest.; rôles include: Fiordiligi in Così fan Tutte; Donna Elvira in Don Giovanni; Pamina in Die Zauberflöte; Giulietta in I Capuleti e I Montecchi; Mimi in La Bohème; Amelia in Simon Boccanegra; Jenifer in The Midsummer Marriage; Eva in Die Meistersinger; Desdemona in Otello; Tatyana in Eugene Onegin; Marschallin in Der Rosenkavalier; Duchess of Argyll in Powder Her Face; title rôles: in Katya Kabanova; in Jenufa; in The Merry Widow. Hon. DMus Manchester, 2003. *Address:* c/o Askonas Holt Ltd, Lincoln House, 300 High Holborn, WC1V 7JH.

ROOK, Peter Francis Grosvenor; QC 1991; **His Honour Judge Rook;** a Senior Circuit Judge, Central Criminal Court, since 2005; *b* 19 Sept. 1949; *s* of Dr Arthur James Rook and Frances Jane Elizabeth Rook (*née* Knott); *m* 1978, Susanna Marian Tewson; one *s* two *d*. *Educ:* Charterhouse; Trinity College, Cambridge (Open Exhibnr; MA Hist.); Bristol Univ. (Dip. Soc. Studies). Called to the Bar, Gray's Inn, 1973, Bencher, 2000; 2nd Standing Counsel to Inland Revenue at Central Criminal Court and Inner London Courts, 1981, 1st Standing Counsel, 1989; Asst Recorder, 1990–95; a Recorder, 1995–2005; Hd of Chambers, 18 Red Lion Court, 2002–05. Chm., Criminal Bar Assoc. of England and Wales, 2002–03 (Dir of Educn, 2003–05). Course Dir, Serious Sexual Offences Seminar, Judicial Studies Bd, 2006–09. *Publications:* Rook and Ward on Sexual Offences, 1990, 4th edn 2010. *Recreations:* tennis, squash, cricket, theatre, growing tropical plants. *Address:* Central Criminal Court, Old Bailey, EC4M 7EH. *Clubs:* MCC; Coolhurst Lawn Tennis and Squash.

ROOKE, His Honour Giles Hugh, TD 1963; QC 1979; DL; a Circuit Judge, 1981–2001; Resident Judge, Canterbury, 1995–2001; *b* 28 Oct. 1930; *s* of late Charles Eustace Rooke, CMG, and Irene Phyllis Rooke; *m* 1968, Anne Bernadette Seymour, *d* of His Honour John Perrett; three *s* one *d* (and one *s* decd). *Educ:* Stowe; Exeter Coll., Oxford (MA). Kent Yeomanry, 1951–61, Kent and County of London Yeomanry, 1961–65 (TA), Major. Called to Bar, Lincoln's Inn, 1957; practised SE Circuit, 1957–81; a Recorder of the Crown Court, 1975–81. Hon. Recorder of Margate, 1980–2001. Mem. Council, Univ. of Kent at Canterbury, 1997–2003; Hon. Sen. Fellow, Univ. of Kent at Canterbury Law Sch., 1999–2002. Hon. Burgess, Margate, 2001. DL Kent, 2001. *Address:* St Stephen's Cottage, Bridge, Canterbury CT4 5AH. *T:* (01227) 830298. *Club:* Army and Navy.

ROOKE, Rt Rev. Patrick William; *see* Tuam, Killala and Achonry, Bishop of.

ROOKER, Baron *cr* 2001 (Life Peer), of Perry Barr in the County of West Midlands; **Jeffrey William Rooker;** PC 1999; CEng; Chairman: Food Standards Agency, 2009–13; National Environmental Board, since 2014; *b* 5 June 1941; *m* 1st, 1972, Angela Edwards (*d* 2003); 2nd, 2010, Helen M. Hughes. *Educ:* Handsworth Tech. Sch.; Handsworth Tech. Coll.; Warwick Univ. (MA); Aston Univ. (BScEng). CEng, FIET; MCMI. Apprentice toolmaker, King's Heath Engrg Co. Ltd, Birmingham, 1957–63; student apprentice, BLMC, 1963–64; Asst to Works Manager, Geo. Salter & Co., West Bromwich, 1964–65, Assembly Manager, 1965–67; Prodn Manager, Rola Celestion Ltd, Thames Ditton and Ipswich, 1967–70; Industrial Relations and Safety Officer, Metro-Cammell, Birmingham, 1971; Lectr, Lanchester Polytechnic, Coventry, 1972–74. MP (Lab) Birmingham, Perry Barr, Feb. 1974–2001. Opposition spokesman on social services, 1979–80, on social security, 1980–83, on treasury and economic affairs, 1983–84, on housing, 1984–87, on local government, 1987–88, on health and social services, 1990–92, on higher educn, 1992–93; Dep. Shadow Leader of H of C, 1994–97; Minister of State: MAFF, 1997–99; DSS, 1999–2001; Home Office, 2001–02; for Housing, Planning and Regeneration, ODPM, 2002–05; NI Office, 2005–06; DEFRA, 2006–08. Mem., Public Accounts Cttee, 1989–91. Chair, Labour Campaign for Electoral Reform, 1989–95. Mem. Council, Instn of Prodn Engrs, 1975–81. Lay Gov., Aston Univ., 2008–10. Chair, Motor Sports Trng Trust, 2012–. Trustee and Gov., James Brindley Sch., Birmingham, 2015–. Hon. DSc Aston, 2001; DUniv UCE, 2002. *Address:* House of Lords, SW1A 0PW. *T:* (020) 7219 6469.

ROOKES, Caroline Mary, CBE 2010; Chief Executive, Money Advice Service, since 2013; *b* 28 Oct. 1954; *d* of late James Harold Hartley and Mary Irene Hartley; *m* 1975, John William Rookes (marr. diss. 1986); partner, Michael Pearce. *Educ:* Fleetwood Grammar Sch.; Downer Grammar Sch.; Univ. of Lancaster (BA Hons English 1975). Civil Service, 1975–2013: various postings in DHSS, subseq. DSS; Inland Revenue, then HM Revenue and Customs: Head, Review of Analytical Services, 1999; Dir of Charities, 2000; Head, Share Scheme, 2000–02; Director: Savings, Pensions, Share Schemes, 2002–05; Individuals, 2005; Department for Work and Pensions: Dir, Private Pensions, Retirement Planning and Older People, 2005–07; Dir, Workplace Pension Reform, later Private Pensions, 2007–13. Trustee, Pension Scheme: Nat. Employment Savings Trust; Civil Service Sports Council. *Recreations:* opera, fell walking, friends, family, good food and wine, all things Italian. *Address:* (office) Holborn Centre, 120 Holborn, EC1N 2TD. *T:* (020) 7943 0401. *E:* caroline.rookes@moneyadviceservice.org.uk.

ROOKS, Robert John; *b* 20 Nov. 1948; *s* of Ronald Sidney Rooks and Daisy Rooks; *m* 1970, Elizabeth Lewis; one *s* one *d*. *Educ:* Hardye's Sch., Dorchester; Liverpool Univ. (BEng Hons). Spacecraft Design Engr, BAC, 1970–72; Ministry of Defence: Admin. Trainee, Chief Exec. Dockyards, 1972–73; Adjutant Gen. Secretariat, 1973–74; Size, Shape and Cost of RAF Prog., Defence Secretariat, 1974–75; Private Sec. to Chief of Defence Procurement, 1975–78; Fighting Vehicles and Engrg, Equipment Secretariat, 1978–80; RAF Ops, Defence Secretariat, 1980–83; Mgt Services Orgn, 1983–85; Finance Mgt and Planning, 1985–88, Head, 1988–90, Controller Aircraft Secretariat; Head of: Adjutant Gen. Secretariat 2, 1990–93; Civilian Mgt (Personnel) 1, 1993–97; Dir of Orgn and Mgt, 1998–99; Comd Sec., RAF PTC, 1999–2003; Fellow, Weatherhead Center for Internat. Affairs, Harvard Univ., 2003–04; Dir Gen., Security and Safety, MoD, 2004; Dir, Business Resilience, MoD. *Recreations:* sailing, travel, IT. *Club:* Royal Air Force.

ROOLEY, Anthony; lutenist; Artistic Director, The Consort of Musicke, since 1969; *b* 10 June 1944; *s* of Madge and Henry Rooley; *m* 1967, Carla Morris; three *d*; one *s* by Emma Kirkby (*see* Dame Emma Kirkby); *m* 2014, Evelyn Tubb. *Educ:* Royal Acad. of Music. LRAM (Performers). Recitals in Europe, USA, Middle East, Japan, S America, New Zealand, Australia; radio and TV in UK, Europe and USA; numerous recordings, British and German. Vis. Prof., York Univ., 1998–; Vis. Prof., 1999–2007, Prof., 2007–, Dir, Advanced Vocal Ensemble Studies Practical Masters Prog., 2010–, Lectr in performance, repertoire and presentation, 2007–, Schola Cantorum Basiliensis, Basle, Switzerland; Vis. Orpheus Scholar, Florida State Univ., Tallahassee, 2003–05, 2007–. Hon. FRAM 1990. *Publications:* Penguin Book of Early Music, 1982; Performance—revealing the Orpheus within, 1990. *Recreations:* food, wine, gardening, philosophy. *Address:* Bwlch y Ddinas, Llansawel, Llandeilo, Carmarthenshire SA19 7PQ.

ROOM, Maxine, CBE 2012; Principal and Chief Executive Officer, LeSoCo (formerly Lewisham College), 2009–14; *b* London, 21 Jan. 1956; *d* of Arthur and Vera Johnson; *m* (marr. diss.); one *d*. *Educ:* Skinners' Co. Sch. for Girls; Bath Coll. of Higher Educn (Cert Ed 1978); Bristol Univ. (BEd Hons 1979; MEd 1992). Joined Bridgwater Coll., Somerset, as Lectr, 1979; various posts, 1979–95, incl. Hd, Care, Public Services, Complementary Therapies; Filton College, Bristol: Team Leader, Care and Child Care, 1995–97; Dir, Progs and Planning, 1997–98; Dir, Curriculum, 1998–2001; Vice Principal, Curriculum, 2001–03; Principal and Chief Executive Officer: Swansea Coll., 2003–07; Leeds Park Lane Coll., 2007–09. Board Member: Northern Ballet; Women's Leadership Network; Helena Kennedy Foundn. Gov., South Bank Univ. MInstD 2007. *Recreations:* gym junkie, travelling.

ROONEY, Dougie; energy consultant, since 2011; National Officer, responsible for Energy and Utilities, AEEU, later Amicus, then Unite the Union, 1997–2010; President, Trades Union Congress, 2010–11; *b* Edinburgh, 12 Oct. 1947. *Educ:* Balgreen Primary Sch., Edinburgh; Tynecastle Secondary Sch., Edinburgh. Ferranti: apprenticeship as mechanical fitter; craftsman, 1970 and Shop Steward for AEU, 1970, Sen. Shop Steward, 1974–85; Divl Organiser, AEU, 1985–97. Mem., Gen. Council, TUC, 1998–. *Recreations:* walking, golf. *Address:* 41 Baberton Mains Lea, Edinburgh EH14 3HB. *T:* 07531 911666. *E:* dougie.rooney@gmail.com.

ROONEY, Fiona; *see* Fox, F.

ROONEY, Michael John, RA 1991 (ARA 1990); Head of Painting, Royal Academy Schools, 1991–95; *b* 5 March 1944; *s* of Elisabeth and John Rooney; *m* 1st, 1967, Patricia Anne Lavender (marr. diss. 1984); one *s* one *d*; 2nd, 1988, Alexandra Grascher, Vienna; one *s*. *Educ:* primary and secondary schools; Sutton Sch. of Art; Wimbledon Sch. of Art (NDD); Royal Coll. of Art (MA RCA, ARCA); British Sch. at Rome (Austin Abbey Major Award). Part-time lectr, various art colls; artist-in-residence, Towner Art Gall., Eastbourne, 1983; one man exhibns in Holland, Austria, London, Edinburgh and other UK locations; jt exhibns in Chicago, NY, Portland (Oregon), and throughout Europe and UK; commissions include: painting for FT Centenary, 1988; London Transport Poster, 1990; tapestry for TSB Ltd, Birmingham, 1991; work in public collections: Sussex; Cumbria; Birmingham; Punta del Este, Uruguay; London; Govt Art Collection. Chm., Soc. of Painters in Tempera. Prizes include: Calouste Gulbenkian Printmakers' Award, 1984; John Player Portrait Award, Nat. Portrait Gallery, 1985; RA Summer Exhibn Awards, 1986, 1988, 1989; Chichester Arts Prize, 1995. *Recreations:* cooking, travel. *Club:* Chelsea Arts.

ROONEY, Terence Henry; *b* 11 Nov. 1950; *s* of Eric and Frances Rooney; *m* 1969, Susanne Chapman; one *s* two *d*. *Educ:* Buttershaw Comprehensive Sch.; Bradford Coll. Formerly: commercial insurance broker; Welfare Rights Advice Worker, Bierley Community Centre. Councillor, Bradford City, 1983–91 (Dep. Leader, 1990). MP (Lab) Bradford N, Nov. 1990–2010; contested (Lab) Bradford E, 2010.

ROOSE-EVANS, James Humphrey; freelance theatre director and author; non-stipendiary Anglican priest; Founder and Artistic Director, Frontier Theatre Productions Ltd, since 2014; *b* 11 Nov. 1927; *s* of Jack Roose-Evans and Catharina Primrose Morgan. *Educ:* St Benet's Hall, Oxford (MA). Started career in repertory, as an actor; Artistic Dir, Maddermarket Theatre, Norwich, 1954–55 (dir. English première of The Language of Flowers, 1955); Faculty of Juilliard Sch. of Music, NY, 1955–56; on staff of RADA, 1956–; founded Hampstead Theatre, 1959; Resident Dir, Belgrade Theatre, Coventry, 1961; Founder and Artistic Dir, Frontiers Productions, 2013–. Regularly tours USA, lecturing and leading workshops. Productions directed include: *Hampstead Theatre*: The Square, 1963; The Little Clay Cart (also adapted), 1964; Adventures in the Skin Trade, world première, The Two Character Play, world première, Letters from an Eastern Front (also adapted), 1966; An Evening with Malcolm Muggeridge (also devised), 1966; *West End*: Cider with Rosie (also adapted), 1963; Private Lives, 1963; An Ideal Husband, 1966; The Happy Apple, 1967; 84 Charing Cross Road (also adapted), 1981, NY 1982 (awards for Best Play and Best Dir, 2001), tour 2004, Salisbury Playhouse, 2015; Seven Year Itch, 1986; The Best of Friends, 1988 (also prod Comédie des Champs-Elysées, Paris, 1989), Hampstead and tour, 2006; Temptation, 1990; Irving (also jt author with Barry Turner), 1995; Legend of Pericles, 1996; *other productions:* Venus Observed, Chichester, 1992; Pericles, 2000, Macbeth, 2001, Ludlow Fest. Author, Re: Joyce!, West End, 1991; The Bargain, Th. Royal, Bath and tour, 2007. Consultant, Theatre Mus. Founder and Chm., Bleddfa Trust-Centre for Caring and the Arts, subseq. Bleddfa Centre for Creative

Spirit, Powys, 1974–; Bleddfa Lect., 2007. Columnist (Something Extra), Woman, 1986–88. Trng at Glasshampton Monastery, Worcs; ordained priest, 1981. *Publications:* adaptation of The Little Clay Cart, by King Sudraka, 1965; Directing a Play, 1968; Experimental Theatre, 1970, 4th rev. edn, 1988; London Theatre, 1977; play version of 84 Charing Cross Road, by Helene Hanff, 1983; Inner Journey, Outer Journey, 1987, rev. edn 1998 (US as The Inner Stage, 1990); (introd and ed) Darling Ma: the letters of Joyce Grenfell, 1988; The Tale of Beatrix Potter, 1988; (with Maureen Lipman) Re:Joyce!, 1988; (introd and ed) The Time of My Life: wartime journals of Joyce Grenfell, 1989; (trans.) Obey, On the Edge of Midnight, 1989; Passages of the Soul: ritual today, 1994; Cider with Rosie (stage adaptation), 1994; One Foot on the Stage (biog. of Richard Wilson), 1996; Eminently Victorian: the story of Augustus Hare (play), 1996; Loving without Tears (stage adaptation of Molly Keane novel), 1996; The Christ Mouse, 2004; (devised and ed) The Cook-a-Story Book, 2005; What is Spirituality?, 2005; Holy Theatre, 2005; Opening Doors and Windows: a memoir in four acts, 2009; Finding Silence: 52 meditations for daily living, 2009; *for children:* The Adventures of Odd and Elsewhere, 1971; The Secret of the Seven Bright Shiners, 1972; Odd and the Great Bear, 1973; Elsewhere and the Gathering of the Clowns, 1974; The Return of the Great Bear, 1975; The Secret of Tippity-Witchit, 1975; The Lost Treasure of Wales, 1977. *Recreations:* gardening, writing. *Address:* c/o Sheil Land Associates, 52 Doughty Street, WC1N 2LF. *W:* www.jamesrooseevans.co.uk. *Club:* Garrick.

ROOT, Jane; Founder and Chief Executive, Nutopia, since 2010; *b* 18 May 1957; *e d* of James William Root and Kathleen Root; *m* 2003, Ray Hill; one *d*. *Educ:* Sussex Univ.; London Coll. of Printing. Manager, Cinema of Women (Film Distribn Co.), 1981–83; freelance journalist and film critic, 1981–83; Lectr in Film Studies, UEA, 1981–84; Researcher, Open the Box, Beat Productions, 1983; Co-Creator, The Media Show, 1986; Jt Founder and Jt Man. Dir, Wall to Wall Television, 1987–96; Head of Independent Commng Gp, BBC, 1997–98; Controller, BBC2, 1999–2004; Discovery Channel: Exec. Vice-Pres., 2004–06; Gen. Manager, 2004–07; Pres., 2006–07. Theme Leader, Connecting With Audiences, BBC, 2001. Mem., Exec. Cttee, Edinburgh TV Fest. (Chair, 1995). *Publications:* Pictures of Women: sexuality, 1981; Open the Box: about television, 1983. *Address:* 4209 Thornapple Street, Chevy Chase, MD 20815–5116, USA.

ROOTES, family name of **Baron Rootes**.

ROOTES, 3rd Baron *cr* 1959; **Nicholas Geoffrey Rootes;** author and copy-writer; business owner, Nick Rootes Associates; *b* 12 July 1951; *s* of 2nd Baron Rootes and of Marian, *d* of Lt-Col H. R. Hayter, DSO and *widow* of Wing Comdr J. H. Slater, AFC; *S* father, 1992; *m* 1976, Dorothy Anne Burn-Forti (*née* Wood); one step *s* one step *d*. *Educ:* Harrow Sch. Trustee, Rootes Charitable Trust, 1992–; Patron, Assoc. of Rootes Car Clubs, 1993–. *Publications:* The Drinker's Companion, 1987; Doing a Dyson, 1996. *Recreations:* ski-ing, fly-fishing. *Heir: cousin* William Brian Rootes [*b* 8 Nov. 1944; *m* 1969, Alicia, *y d* of Frederick Graham Roberts, OBE; two *d*]. *Address:* 26 Solent Landing, Beach Road, Bembridge, Isle of Wight PO35 5NZ. *Club:* Ski of Great Britain.

ROOTS, Guy Robert Godfrey; QC 1989; *b* 26 Aug. 1946; *s* of late William Lloyd Roots, QC and Elizabeth Colquhoun Gow (*née* Gray); *m* 1975, Caroline (*née* Clarkson); three *s*. *Educ:* Winchester College; Brasenose College, Oxford (MA). Called to the Bar, Middle Temple, 1969, Harmsworth Scholar, 1970, Bencher, 2000. Asst Boundary Comr, 2011–12. Chm., Planning and Envmt Bar Assoc., 2000–04. Fellow, Soc. of Advanced Legal Studies, 1998–. Liveryman, Drapers' Co., 1972. General Editor: Ryde on Rating and the Council Tax, 1986–; Tottel's Compulsory Purchase and Compensation Service, 1999–. *Publications:* Law of Compulsory Purchase and Compensation, 2011. *Recreations:* sailing, fishing, ski-ing, photography, woodworking. *Address:* Francis Taylor Building, Temple, EC4Y 7BY. *T:* (020) 7353 8415. *E:* clerks@ftb.eu.com. *Club:* Itchenor Sailing.

ROOTS, Paul John; Director of Industrial Relations, Ford Motor Co. Ltd, 1981–86, retired; *b* 16 Oct. 1929; *s* of John Earl and Helen Roots; *m* 1950, Anna Theresa Pateman; two *s* two *d*. *Educ:* Dormers Wells Sch.; London Sch. of Economics; Open Univ. BA Hons 1993; Cert. in Personnel Admin. CCIPD; CCMI. RN, 1947–54: service in Korean War. Personnel Officer, Brush Gp, 1955; Labour Officer, UKAEA, 1956, Labour Manager, 1959; Ford Motor Co. Ltd: Personnel Manager, Halewood, 1962; Forward Planning Manager, 1966; Labour Relations Manager, 1969; Dir of Employee Relations, 1974. Vice-Pres., IPM, 1981–83. Chairman: CBI Health and Safety Policy Cttee, 1984–; CBI Health and Safety Consultative Cttee, 1984–; Member: Council of Management, CBI Educn Foundn, 1981–; CBI Working Party on the Employment of Disabled People, 1981–; CBI Employment Policy Cttee, 1983–; CBI Council, 1984–; Engrg Industry Training Bd, 1985–. *Publications:* (jtly) Communication in Practice, 1981; (jtly) Corporate Personnel Management, 1986; Financial Incentives for Employees, 1988; articles in personnel management jls. *Recreations:* riding, theatre, music.

ROOTS, William; Chief Executive and Director of Finance, City of Westminster, 1994–2000; *b* 12 April 1946; *s* of William Roots and Violet (*née* Frost); *m* 1st, 1963, Norma Jane Smith (marr. diss.); one *s* one *d*; 2nd, 1980, Susan Grace Sharratt; two *s*. *Educ:* Wandsworth Sch. Sun Life Assce Soc., 1962–64; joined GLC as trainee, 1964; Hd of Budget, 1980; London Borough of Southwark: Head of: Exchequer, 1980–81; Finance, 1982; Director of Finance: London Borough of Bexley, 1982–90; City of Westminster, 1990–94. Mem., CIPFA 1970. *Recreations:* sport (esp. Rugby), relaxing with friends, films. *E:* bill@roots88.fsnet.co.uk.

ROP, Anton; Honorary Vice-President and Director, European Investment Bank since 2013 (Vice-President, 2010–13); *b* 27 Dec. 1960. *Educ:* Univ. of Ljubljana (MA). Asst Dir, Slovene Inst. for Macroecon. Analysis and Develt, 1985–92. Former Mem., Nat. Assembly, Slovenia (Lib Dem, until 2007, Soc Dem, 2007–10); State Sec., Min. of Econ. Relations and Develt, 1993–96; Minister of Labour, Family and Social Affairs, 1996–2000, of Finance, 2000–02; Prime Minister, 2002–04. Former Leader, Parly Gp, Liberal Democratic Party, until 2005. *Address:* c/o European Investment Bank, 100 boulevard Konrad Adenauer, 2950 Luxembourg.

ROPER, family name of **Baron Roper**.

ROPER, Baron *cr* 2000 (Life Peer), of Thorney Island in the City of Westminster; **John Francis Hodgess Roper;** PC 2005; *b* 10 Sept. 1935; *e s* of late Rev. Frederick Mabor Hodgess Roper and Ellen Frances (*née* Brockway); *m* 1959, (Valerie) Hope (*d* 2003), *er d* of late Rt Hon. L. John Edwards, PC, OBE, MP, and late Mrs D. M. Edwards; one *d*. *Educ:* William Hulme's Grammar Sch., Manchester; Reading Sch.; Magdalen Coll., Oxford; Univ. of Chicago. Nat. Service, commnd RNVR, 1954–56; studied PPE, Oxford, 1956–59 (Pres. UN Student Assoc., 1957; organised Univ. referendum on Nuclear Disarmament); Harkness Fellow, Commonwealth Fund, 1959–61; Research Fellow in Economic Statistics, Univ. of Manchester, 1961; Asst Lectr in Econs, 1962–64, Lectr 1964–70, Faculty Tutor 1968–70; RIIA: Editor of International Affairs, 1983–88; Head of Internat. Security Programme, 1985–88, and 1989–90; Dir of Studies, 1988–89; Associate Fellow, 1996–99; Hd, WEU Inst. for Security Studies, Paris, 1990–95. Vis. Prof., Coll. of Europe, Bruges, 1997–2000; Hon. Prof., Inst. for German Studies, Univ. of Birmingham, 1999–2007. Contested: (Lab) High Peak (Derbys), 1964; (SDP) Worsley, 1983. MP (Lab and Co-op 1970–81, SDP 1981–83) Farnworth, 1970–83; PPS to Minister of State, DoI, 1978–79; opposition front bench spokesman on defence, 1979–81; Social Democrat Chief Whip, 1981–83; Lib Dem Chief Whip, H of L, 2001–05. Mem., H of L, 2000–15. Principal Dep. Chm. of Cttees and Chm., Select Cttee on the EU, H of L, 2008–12. Vice-Chairman: Anglo-German Parly Gp, 1974–83; Anglo-Benelux Parly Gp, 1979–83; Chm., British-Atlantic Gp of Young Politicians, 1974–75. Council of Europe: Consultant, 1965–66; Mem., Consultative Assembly, 1973–80; Chm., Cttee on Culture and Educn, 1979–80; Mem., WEU Assembly, 1973–80; Chm., Cttee on Defence Questions and Armaments, WEU, 1977–80. Hon. Treasurer, Fabian Soc., 1976–81; Chairman: Labour Cttee for Europe, 1976–80; GB/East Europe Centre, 1987–90; Council on Christian Approaches to Defence and Disarmament, 1983–89; Mem., Internat. Commn on the Balkans, 1995–96. Research Adviser (part-time), DEA in NW, 1967–69. Director: Co-op. Wholesale Soc., 1969–74; Co-op Insurance Soc., 1973–74. Pres., Gen. Council, UNA, 1972–78; Mem. Council, Inst. for Fiscal Studies, 1975–90; Mem. Gen. Adv. Council, IBA, 1974–79. Vice-Pres., Manchester Statistical Soc., 1971–. Trustee, Hist. of Parlt Trust, 1974–84. *Publications:* Towards Regional Co-operatives, 1967; The Teaching of Economics at University Level, 1970; The Future of British Defence Policy, 1985; (ed with Karl Kaiser) British-German Defence Co-operation, 1988; (ed with Yves Boyer) Franco-British Defence Co-operation, 1988; (ed with Nicole Gnesotto) Western Europe and the Gulf, 1992; (ed with Nanette Gantz) Towards a New Partnership, 1993; (ed with Laurence Martin) Towards a Common Defence Policy, 1995. *Recreations:* reading, travel. *Club:* Oxford and Cambridge.

See also Sir J. C. Jenkins, Rev. G. E. H. Roper.

ROPER, Brian Anthony; Chief Executive, 2002–09, and Vice Chancellor, 2004–09, London Metropolitan University; *b* 15 Dec. 1949; *s* of Harold Herbert Albert Roper and Elizabeth Roper (*née* Rooney); *m* 1971, Margaret Patricia Jones; one *s* one *d*. *Educ:* UWIST (BSc Hons Econs 1971); Univ. of Manchester (MA Econs 1973); Swansea Metropolitan Univ. (DipAD 2012). Tutor in Econs, UWIST, 1971–72; Lectr in Econs, Teesside Poly., 1973–75; Sen. Lectr, then Principal Lectr, Leicester Poly., 1975–80; Hd, Sch. of Econs, Dean, Faculty of Social Scis and Asst Dir, Resources, Newcastle upon Tyne Poly., 1980–90; Dep. Vice Chancellor Acad. Affairs and Dep. Chief Exec., Oxford Poly., subseq. Oxford Brookes Univ., 1991–94; Vice-Chancellor and Chief Exec., Univ. of N London, 1994–2002. DUniv Chelyabinsk State, Russia, 2001; Hon. DLitt Pennsylvania, 2004; Hon. DTech Nizhni Novgorod, Russia, 2007. *Publications:* contrib. Econ. Theory and Policy, Higher Educn Policy and Mgt; contrib. haiku to Blythe Spirit, poetry to Cardiff Women's Aid Anthology, and theatre reviews to New Welsh Rev., Buzz Mag. *Recreations:* thoughtful art, observing nature, haiku, haibun. *Club:* Porthcawl Rugby Football.

ROPER, Rev. Geoffrey Edward Hodgess; Associate General Secretary (Free Churches), and Secretary, Free Churches Group, Churches Together in England, 2001–05; Company Secretary, Council for World Mission (UK), 2011–15; *b* 24 April 1940; *y s* of late Rev. Frederick Mabor Hodgess Roper and Ellen Frances (*née* Brockway); *m* 1967, Janice Wakeham; one *s* one *d*. *Educ:* Christ's Hosp.; Magdalen Coll., Oxford (PPE); Mansfield Coll., Oxford (Theol.); MA Oxon. Ordained 1965; Minister: Trinity Congregational Church, Ifield, Crawley, 1965–71; Streatham Congregational Church, 1971–78 (URC from 1972); Seaford URC, 1978–85; Christ Church, Chelmsford, 1985–95; Gen. Sec., Free Church Fed. Council, later Free Churches' Council, 1996–2001; various tasks in connection with Council for World Mission, 2005–15; Cataloguing Asst (LMS archives), SOAS, 2006–07. Sec., URC Deployment Cttee, 1978–84; Convenor, URC Maintenance of Ministry Sub-Cttee, 2005–09; URC Ecumenical Officer: Sussex East, 1979–85; Essex, 1986–95; Dir, URC Ministers Pension Fund, 2005–09. Vice-Chm., Churches Main Cttee, 2004–05. Sec., Gen. Body of Dissenting Ministers and Deputies of the Three Denominations, 1998–2005. Chm., Churches Cttee for Hospital Chaplaincy, 2001–04; Mem., Eastbourne CHC, 1980–85 (Vice-Chm., 1983–84). British Isles Mem., Exec. Cttee, Leuenberg Doctrinal Conversations of Reformed and Lutheran Churches in Europe, 1987–94. Chair, King's Cross Develt Forum, 2006–10. Director: Highway Trust, 1977–94; Farthing Trust, 1985–95; British and Internat. Sailors' Soc., 1999–2006. Secretary: Lumen United Reformed Church, 2009–14; Chair, United Reformed Church History Soc., 2012–; Vice-Pres., Friends of Dr Williams's Library, 2014– (Chm. of Cttee, 1991–2005; Sec., 2005–14); Compliance Project Analyst, Turn2us (Elizabeth Finn Care), 2014–15. Trustee: St George's Chapel, Heathrow Airport, 1999–2005; Congregational Fund, 2007– (Chair, 2014–); Project for Seniors and Lifelong Ministry, 2008–13. Pres., Mansfield Coll. Assoc., 2005–08. Hon. Treas., Soc. for Ecumenical Studies, 2012–15. Green gown volunteer, Westminster Abbey, 2009–. *Recreations:* church and family history, cycling. *Address:* 25 Witley Court, Coram Street, WC1N 1HD.

See also Baron Roper.

ROPER, Prof. Lyndal Anne, PhD; FBA 2011; Regius Professor of History, University of Oxford, since 2011; Fellow of Oriel College, Oxford, since 2011; *b* Melbourne, 1956; *m* 2002, Prof. E. Nicholas R. Stargardt; one *s*, and one step *s*. *Educ:* Univ. of Melbourne (BA Hons Hist. with Philos. 1978); Univ. of London (PhD 1985). Jun. Res. Fellow, Merton Coll., Oxford, 1983–86; Lectr, KCL, 1986–87; Royal Holloway and Bedford New College, later Royal Holloway, University of London: Lectr in Hist., 1987–93; Reader in Hist., 1993–99; Prof. of Early Mod. Hist., 1999–2002; Lectr, 2002–04, Prof., 2004–11, Univ. of Oxford; Fellow and Tutor, Balliol Coll., Oxford, 2002–11. FAHA 2007. Jt Editor, Past & Present, 2000–12. *Publications:* The Holy Household, 1989 (German 1995); Oedipus and the Devil, 1993; Witch Craze: terror and fantasy in Baroque Germany, 2005; The Witch in the Western Imagination, 2011; Imagination, 2012. *Address:* Oriel College, Oxford OX1 4EW.

ROPER, Martyn Keith, OBE 2013; HM Diplomatic Service; Minister and Deputy Head of Mission, Beijing, from July 2015; *b* Halifax, W Yorks, 8 June 1965; *s* of Keith Roper and Sandra Heaton (*née* Parsisson); *m* 1989, Elisabeth Melanie Harman; one *s* one *d*. *Educ:* Heath Grammar Sch.; Hull Univ.; Open Univ. (BSc Hons 1999). Joined FCO, 1984; Middle East Dept, 1984–86; Tehran, 1986–87; Maputo, 1988–90; Vice Consul, Kuwait, 1990; Third Sec., Karachi, 1991–93; Second, then First Sec., FCO, 1994–98; First Sec., UK Delegn to OECD, 1999–2003; Dep. Hd, UN Dept, FCO, 2004–07; Dep. Hd of Mission, Brasilia, 2007–10; Ambassador to Algeria, 2010–14. *Recreations:* cycling, tennis, keeping fit, reading. *Address:* c/o Foreign and Commonwealth Office, King Charles Street, SW1A 2AH.

ROPER, Michael, CB 1992; FRHistS; Keeper of Public Records, 1988–92; *b* 19 Aug. 1932; *s* of Jack Roper and Mona Roper (*née* Nettleton); *m* 1957, Joan Barbara Earnshaw; one *s* one *d*. *Educ:* Heath Grammar Sch., Halifax; Univ. of Manchester (BA, MA; Langton Fellow). Registered Mem., Soc. of Archivists, 1987. Public Record Office: Asst Keeper, 1959–70; Principal Asst Keeper, 1970–82; Records Admin Officer, 1982–85; Dep. Keeper of Public Records, 1985–88. Lectr (part time) in Archive Studies, UCL, 1972–87, Hon. Res. Fellow, 1988–; Dist. Visitor, Univ. of BC, 1994; Vis. Prof., Surugadai Univ., Japan, 1999. Sec., Adv. Council on Public Records, 1963–68; Vice-President: Soc. of Archivists, 1992– (Vice-Chm., 1983–84; Chm., 1985–86; Pres., 1989–92); British Records Soc., 1988–; RHistS, 1989–93 (Hon. Treas., 1974–80); Sec.-Gen., Internat. Council on Archives, 1988–92 (Sec. for Standardization, 1984–88; Hon. Mem., 1992); Hon. Sec., Assoc. of Commonwealth Archivists and Records Managers, 1996–2000. Chairman: Voices from the Past, 1992–95; English Record Collections, 1994–. Ext. Examr, Nat. Univ. of Ireland, 1982–86, Univ. of Liverpool, 1986–89, Univ. of London, 1988–93. Chm., Judy Segal Trust, 1990–98; Hon. Treasurer, Bethlem Art & Hist. Collections Trust, 1995–2007. Hon. DLitt Bradford, 1991. *Publications:* Yorkshire Fines 1300–1314, 1965; Records of the Foreign Office 1782–1939, 1969; (with J. A. Keene) Planning, Equipping and Staffing a Document Reprographic Service, 1984; Guidelines for the Preservation of Microforms, 1986; Directory of National Standards Relating to Archives Administration and Records Management, 1986; Planning, Equipping and Staffing an Archival Preservation and Conservation Service, 1989; Geresye to Jersey: the record endures, 1991; Records of the War Office and Related Departments 1660–1964, 1998;

Records of the Foreign Office 1782–1968, 2002; (with C. Kitching) Yorkshire Fines 1314–1326, 2006; contribs to learned jls. *Recreations:* listening to music, choral singing, local history. *Address:* Sherwood House, Vicarage Road, Roxwell, Chelmsford, Essex CM1 4NY. *T:* (01245) 249033. *E:* MRoper3784@aol.com.

ROPER, Prof. Stephen Nicholas, PhD; Professor of Enterprise, since 2008, and Director, Enterprise Research Centre, since 2013, Warwick Business School, University of Warwick; *b* Hong Kong, 27 June 1960; *s* of Norman Roper and Gillian Roper; *m* 1981, Marjorie Roberts; two *d*. *Educ:* Durham Univ. (BA Hons Econs 1981); St Peter's Coll., Oxford (MPhil 1983); London Sch. of Econs and Pol Sci. (PhD 1987). Res. Officer, then Sen. Res. Officer, 1986–98, Asst Dir, 1998–2003, NI Econ. Res. Centre; Prof. of Business Innovation, Aston Business Sch., 2003–07. FAcSS (AcSS 2010); FRSA 2012. *Publications:* Entrepreneurship: a global perspective, 2012; papers in Res. Policy, Technovation, Regl Studies, Industry and Innovation. *Recreations:* phillumeny, wood-turning, hoarding Japanese design. *Address:* Warwick Business School, University of Warwick, Coventry CV4 7AL. *T:* (024) 7652 2501. *E:* stephen.roper@wbs.ac.uk.

ROPER, Prof. Warren Richard, FRS 1989; FRSNZ 1984; Professor of Chemistry, University of Auckland, New Zealand, 1984–2007, now Emeritus; *b* 27 Nov. 1938; *m* 1961, Judith Delcie Catherine Miller; two *s* one *d*. *Educ:* Nelson Coll., Nelson, NZ; Univ. of Canterbury, Christchurch, NZ (MSc, PhD). FNZIC. Postdoctoral Res. Associate, Univ. of N Carolina, 1963–65; Lectr in Chemistry, Univ. of Auckland, 1966. Vis. Lectr, Univ. of Bristol, 1972; Pacific W Coast Inorganic Lectr, 1982; Brotherton Vis. Res. Prof., Univ. of Leeds, 1983; Visiting Professor: Univ. de Rennes, 1984, 1985; Stanford Univ., 1988; Sydney Univ., 2001. Mellor Lectr, NZ Inst. of Chemistry, 1985; Centenary Lectr and Medallist, RSC, 1988; Glenn T. Seaborg Lectr, Univ. of Calif., Berkeley, 1995; Gordon Stone Lectr, Univ. of Bristol, 2003; Arthur D. Little Lectr, MIT, 2005. Fellow, Japan Soc. for Promotion of Science, 1992. Hon. DSc Canterbury, 1999. RSC Award in Organometallic Chemistry, 1983; ICI Medal, NZ Inst. of Chemistry, 1984; Hector Medal, Royal Soc. of NZ, 1991; 12th Inorganic Award, Royal Australian Inst. of Chemistry, 1992; Dwyer Medallist, Univ. of NSW, 2000. *Publications:* 220 sci. papers in internat. jls. *Recreations:* music, espec. opera, walking. *Address:* 26 Beulah Avenue, Rothesay Bay, Auckland 0630, New Zealand. *T:* (9) 4786940.

ROPER-CURZON, family name of **Baron Teynham**.

ROPNER, Sir John (Bruce Woollacott), 2nd Bt *cr* 1952; *b* 16 April 1937; *s* of Sir Leonard Ropner, 1st Bt, MC, TD, and Esmé (*d* 1996), *y d* of late Bruce Robertson; *S* father, 1977; *m* 1st, 1961, Anne Melicent (marr. diss. 1970), *d* of late Sir Ralph Delmé-Radcliffe; two *d* (and one *d* decd); 2nd, 1970, Auriol (marr. diss. 1993; she *m* 1997, Marquess of Linlithgow, *qv*), *d* of late Captain Graham Lawrie Mackeson-Sandbach, Caerllo, Llangernyw; one *s* two *d*; 3rd, 1996, Diana Nicola, *d* of Peter Agnew. *Educ:* Eton; St Paul's School, USA. High Sheriff, N Yorks, 1991. *Recreation:* field sports. *Heir: s* Henry John William Ropner, *b* 24 Oct. 1981. *Address:* Thorp Perrow, Bedale, Yorks DL8 2PR.

See also Viscount Knutsford.

ROPNER, Sir Robert (Clinton), 5th Bt *cr* 1904; Director and Chairman, HR & F Management Services, 2004–10; *b* 6 Feb. 1949; *s* of Sir Robert Douglas Ropner, 4th Bt and Patricia Kathleen (*née* Scofield); *S* father, 2004; *m* 1978, Diana Felicia Abbott; one *s* one *d* (twins). *Educ:* Harrow. FCA 1977. Global Funds Reporting Manager, Invesco Europe Ltd, 1999–2002. *Recreations:* motoring, ski-ing, gardening. *Heir: s* Christopher Guy Ropner, *b* 18 Jan. 1979. *Address:* 152 Bishops Road, SW6 7JG. *T:* (020) 7736 7482. *E:* robert.ropner@btinternet.com.

ROQUES, (David) John (Seymour); Senior Partner and Chief Executive, Deloitte & Touche (formerly Touche Ross & Co.), 1990–99; *b* 14 Oct. 1938; *s* of late Frank Davy Seymour Roques and of Marjorie Mabel Hudson; *m* 1963, Elizabeth Anne Mallender; two *s* one *d*. *Educ:* St Albans Sch. Mem., Inst. of Chartered Accountants of Scotland, 1962. Touche Ross & Co., later Deloitte & Touche: Partner, 1967; Partner in charge, Midlands region, 1973; Partner in charge, Scottish region, 1978; Partner in charge, London office, 1984; Man. Partner, 1990. Chm., Portman Bldg Soc., 1999–2006 (Dir, 1995–2006). Non-executive Director: British Nuclear Fuels, 1990–2000; BBA Aviation plc, 1999–2010; Premier Farnell plc, 1999–2008; Chubb plc, 2003; Henderson Gp plc (formerly HHG plc), 2004–09. Member: Financial Reporting Review Panel, 1991–94; Financial Reporting Council, 1996–2001. Gov., Health Foundn, 2001–05. *Recreations:* Rugby football, racing, opera, gardening, golf. *Address:* High Down, Cokes Lane, Chalfont St Giles, Bucks HP8 4TQ. *Clubs:* Brooks's, MCC; Harewood Downs Golf.

RORKE, Prof. John, CBE 1979; PhD; FRSE; FIMechE; Professor of Mechanical Engineering, 1980–88, and Vice-Principal, 1984–88, Heriot-Watt University, now Professor Emeritus; *b* 2 Sept. 1923; *s* of John and Janet Rorke; *m* 1948, Jane Craig Buchanan; two *d*. *Educ:* Dumbarton Acad.; Univ. of Strathclyde (BSc, PhD). Lectr, Strathclyde Univ., 1946–51; Asst to Engrg Dir, Alexander Stephen & Sons Ltd, 1951–56; Technical Manager, subseq. Gen. Man., and Engrg Dir, Wm Denny & Bros Ltd, 1956–63; Tech. Dir, subseq. Sales Dir, Man. Dir, and Chm., Brown Bros & Co. Ltd (subsid. of Vickers Ltd), 1963–78; Man. Dir, Vickers Offshore Engrg Gp, 1978; Dir of Planning, Vickers Ltd, 1979–80. Chairman: Orkney Water Test Centre Ltd, 1987–94; Environment and Resource Technology Ltd, 1991–94. Pres., Instn of Engineers and Shipbuilders in Scotland, 1985–87. Hon. DEng Heriot-Watt, 1994. *Recreations:* golf, bridge. *Address:* Flat 23 Lyle Court, 25 Barnton Grove, Edinburgh EH4 6EZ. *T:* (0131) 339 3116. *Club:* Bruntsfield Links Golfing Society (Edinburgh).

ROSBOROUGH, Dr Linda; Director, Marine Scotland, Scottish Government, since 2012; *b* Coleraine, NI; *d* of John and Elaine Rosborough; *m* Paul Stollard; two *s*. *Educ:* Coleraine High Sch.; Nottingham Univ. (BSc; PhD). Lectr, Leeds Poly.; Advr, Envmt Cttee, H of C; NI Office; Scottish Govt. *Address:* Marine Scotland, Scottish Government, Victoria Quay, Leith Docks, Edinburgh EH6 6QQ.

ROSCOE, Alexis Fayrer; *see* Brett-Holt, A. F.

ROSCOE, Gareth; *see* Roscoe, J. G.

ROSCOE, Dr Ingrid Mary, FSA; Lord-Lieutenant, West Yorkshire, since 2004 (Vice Lord-Lieutenant, 2001–04); *b* 27 May 1944; *d* of late Dr Arthur Allen and Else (*née* Markenstam) and adopted *d* of late Brig. Kenneth Hargreaves; *m* 1963, John Richard Marshall Roscoe; one *s* two *d*. *Educ:* St Helen's, Northwood; Univ. of Leeds (BA; PhD 1990). FSA 1998. Res. Fellow, Huntington Library, 1988; Lectr in Sculpture Hist., Univ. of Leeds, 1990–96. Co. Rep., NACF, 1972–93; Ed., Ch Monuments Jl, 1993–2000. Mem., Exec. Cttee, Walpole Soc., 2000–05. Chm. Trustees, 1996–03, High Steward, 2000–08, Selby Abbey; Trustee: Martin House Children's Hospice, 1989–98; York Minster, 2005–11; Yorkshire Sculpture Park, 2006–; Founding Trustee, Hepworth Wakefield Charitable Trust, 2006–; President: Calderdale Community Foundn, 2004–; Safe Anchor Trust, 2006–; Leeds Philharmonic Chorus, 2008–; Great Northern Art Show, 2008–; ABF W Yorks; RBL W Yorks; W Yorks Scouts, 2012–; Together Women Project, 2013–. Patron: Nat. Mining Mus., 2004–; Yorks Volunteers Regtl Assoc., 2004–; Yorks Historic Churches, 2004–; W Yorks, Prince's Trust, 2005–; Nat. Heritage Trng Acad., Yorks and Humber, 2009–; Yorks Archaeol Soc.; W Riding Woodcarvers, 2010–; Huddersfield Choral Soc., 2013–. Mem. Council, Huddersfield Univ., 2010–. Hon. Col, Leeds Univ. OTC, 2007–14; Pres., Yorks RFCA, 2011–14. Hon. DCL: Huddersfield, 2007; Leeds, 2010; Hon. LLD Leeds Metropolitan, 2008; Hon. DLitt Bradford, 2010. DStJ 2012 (OStJ 2006). *Publications:* (contrib.) The Royal Exchange, 1997; (jtly and Ed. in Chief) A Biographical Dictionary of British Sculptors, 2009; (contrib.) Durham Cathedral, 2014; contrib. articles to Apollo, Gazette des Beaux-Arts, Grove Dictionary of Art, Walpole Soc. Jl, Oxford DNB, etc. *Recreations:* the arts, British history, Shakespeare's plays, walking, grandchildren. *Address:* Church House, Nun Monkton, York YO26 8EW. *T:* (01423) 339145.

ROSCOE, James Paul; Communications Secretary to the Queen, Buckingham Palace, since 2013 (Head of News and Deputy Press Secretary, 2012–13); *b* Bangor, Gwynedd, 29 June 1976; *s* of Meurig W. Roscoe and Eleri A. Roscoe; *m* 2008, Clemency Burton-Hill; one *s*. *Educ:* Diocesan Coll., Cape Town; Durham Univ. (BA Hons). Joined FCO, 2000; FCO, 2001–03; COS to Regl Co-ordinator, Coalition Provisional Authy, Basra, Iraq, 2003–04; Second Sec., Sierra Leone, 2004–06; Chief Press Officer, Foreign Affairs and Defence, Prime Minister's Office, 2006–09 (on secondment); First Sec., UK Mission to UN, 2009–12. *Recreations:* hiking, cricket, opera, music, reading. *Address:* Press Office, Buckingham Palace, SW1A 1AA. *Clubs:* Travellers, Hurlingham.

ROSCOE, (John) Gareth; barrister; Legal Adviser, Competition Commission, 2002–04 and 2005–07; Lawyer, Department for Work and Pensions, 2004–05; *b* 28 Jan. 1948; *s* of late John Roscoe and Ann (*née* Jones); *m* 1st, 1970, Helen Jane Taylor (marr. diss. 1979; she *d* 2012); one *d*; 2nd, 1980, Alexis Fayrer Brett-Holt, *qv*; one *s* one *d*. *Educ:* Manchester Warehousemen and Clerks' Orphan Schools (now Cheadle Hulme Sch.); Stretford Tech. Coll.; London Sch. of Economics and Political Science (LLB); Univ. of Leicester (LLM 2003). Called to the Bar, Gray's Inn, 1972; in practice, 1972–75; Legal Asst 1975–79, Sen. Legal Asst 1979, DoE; Law Officers' Dept, Attorney-General's Chambers, 1979–83; Asst Solicitor, 1983–87, Dep. Solicitor, 1987–89, DoE; Dir, BBC Enterprises Ltd, 1989–96; Legal Advr to the BBC, 1989–98; Company Sec., BBC Worldwide Ltd, 1996–98; Consultant Advr, DTI, 1999–2001. Non-executive Director: Optimum NHS Trust, 1995–97; King's Coll. Hosp. NHS Trust, 2001–04. Mem., Gen. Council of the Bar, 1987–90. Member: Adv. Cttee, Centre for Communications and Information Law, UCL, 1991–98; Legal Cttee, EBU, 1989–98. Trustee and Dir, Anglia Care Trust, 2009– (Chm., 2011–14). *Recreations:* music, gardening and the company of friends.

ROSE, family name of **Baron Rose of Monewden**.

ROSE OF MONEWDEN, Baron *cr* 2014 (Life Peer), of Monewden in the County of Suffolk; **Stuart Alan Ransom Rose,** Kt 2008; Chairman: Ocado, since 2013 (non-executive Director, since 2013); Fat Face, since 2013; Oasis Healthcare Group, since 2013; *b* 17 March 1949; *s* of Harry Ransom Rose and late Margaret Ransom Rose; *m* 1973, Jennifer Cook (marr. diss. 2010); one *s* one *d*. *Educ:* St Joseph's Convent, Dar-es-Salaam; Bootham Sch., York. With Marks and Spencer plc, 1971–89, Commercial Exec., Europe; Chief Executive: Multiples, Burton Gp plc, 1989–97; Argos plc, 1998; Booker plc, 1998–2000; Iceland Group plc, 2000; Arcadia plc, 2000–02; Chief Exec., 2004–10, Exec. Chm., 2008–10, Marks and Spencer plc. Non-executive Director: Land Securities, 2003–13; Woolworths Hldgs, 2011–; RM2 Internat., 2014–; Member: Eur. Adv. Cttee, Bridgepoint Capital, 2010–. Chairman: British Fashion Council, 2003–08; BITC, 2008–10; Blue Inc., 2012–14; Dressipi, 2012–. Retail Advr, HSBC, 2013–. Chm., Healing Foundn, 2011–. Trustee, RA, 2013–. *Recreation:* wine. *Address:* 146–148 Freston Road, W10 6TR. *Club:* Groucho.

ROSE, Alan Douglas, AO 1994; Consultant, HWL Ebsworth Lawyers, since 2011; *b* 3 May 1944; *s* of late Willfred Allen Rose and Hazel Agnes Rose (*née* Heinemann-Mirre); *m* 1966, Helen Elizabeth Haigh; two *d*. *Educ:* Univ. of Queensland (BA 1966; LLB Hons 1969); LSE, Univ. of London (LLM 1979). Barrister, Supreme Court of Queensland, 1973; Dep. Sec., Dept of Prime Minister and Cabinet, 1982–86; Sec. to Aust. Dept of Community Services, 1986–87; Associate Sec. and Sec. to Aust. Attorney-Gen. Dept, 1987–94; Pres., Aust. Law Reform Commn, 1994–99; Gen. Counsel, Phillips Fox Lawyers, 1999–2002; Consultant, DLA Phillips Fox Lawyers (formerly Phillips Fox Lawyers), 2002–11; Chm., Defence Honours and Awards Tribunal, 2011–14. *Publications:* articles in legal jls and works on public admin. *Recreations:* surfing, ski-ing, reading, travelling. *Address:* PO Box 3296, Manuka, ACT 2603, Australia.

ROSE, Alison Mary; a District Judge (Magistrates' Courts), since 2002; *b* 31 May 1958; *d* of late Brian Henry Rose and of José Gwendoline Rose (*née* Rixon). *Educ:* Univ. of Exeter (LLB Hons 1979). Articled clerk, John H. Rosen & Co., 1980–82; admitted solicitor, 1983; Asst Solicitor, Rosen Hudson & Co., 1983–88; Partner, Hudson Freeman Berg, 1988–2000; Asst Solicitor, Farrell Matthews & Weir, 2000–02; Dep. Dist Judge (Magistrates' Courts), W Midlands, 1999–2002. *Address:* Thames Magistrates' Court, 58 Bow Road, E3 4DJ. *T:* (020) 8271 1219.

ROSE, Anthea Lorrainne, (Mrs H. D. Rose); Chief Executive, Association of Chartered Certified Accountants (formerly Chartered Association of Certified Accountants), 1993–2003; *d* of Philip Brown and Muriel (*née* Seftor); *m* 1971, Hannan David Rose. *Educ:* St Hugh's Coll., Oxford (MA Mod. Hist.). Administrator, Open Univ., 1968–69; Personnel Officer, Beecham Pharmaceuticals, 1969–71; Administrator, Univ. of Kent, 1971–77; Chartered Association of Certified Accountants, later Association of Chartered Certified Accountants, 1977–2003: Under Sec., 1982–88; Dep. Chief Exec., 1988–93. Man. Dir, Everywhere Associates Ltd, 2004–09. Vis. Prof., Oxford Brookes Univ., 2002–07. Lay Mem., Nursing & Midwifery Council, 2006–07. Hon. DBA Kingston, 2002. *Recreations:* travel, food, wine.

ROSE, Sir (Arthur) James, Kt 2007; CBE 1996; education consultant; President, National Foundation for Educational Research, since 2008; President, CfBT Education Committee, since 2015 (Trustee, since 2010; Chair, 2010–15); *m* 1960, Pauline; one *d*. *Educ:* Kesteven College; Leicester University. HM Chief Inspector for Primary Educn, DES, subseq. DFE, 1986–92; Dep. Dir of Inspection, 1992–94, Dir of Inspection, 1994–99, OFSTED. Leader: review of teaching of reading, DFES, 2006–; review of Primary Curriculum, DFES, 2008–; Ind. Review on Identifying and Teaching Children and Young People with Dyslexia and Literacy Difficulties, 2009. Chair, Dyslexia-Specific Learning Difficulties Trust, 2014–. Hon. DLaws Leicester, 2009; Hon. DEd Beds, 2009.

ROSE, Aubrey, CBE 1997 (OBE 1986); Deputy Chairman, Commission for Racial Equality, 1995 (Commissioner, 1991–95); *b* 1 Nov. 1926; *s* of Solomon Rosenberg and Esther Rosenberg (*née* Kurtz); *m* 1954, Sheila Ray Glassman (*d* 2007); one *s* one *d* (and one *s* decd). *Educ:* at various grammar schs incl. Central Foundn Sch., London. Admitted as solicitor, 1952; Sen. Partner, 1971–95. Chm., Legal Cttee, CRE, 1993–95. Founder Mem. and Treas., Commonwealth Human Rights Initiative, 1990–2003. Dep. Chm., British Caribbean Assoc., 1990–; Jt Chm., Indian-Jewish Assoc., 1996–2003 (Pres., 2008–). Sen. Vice-Pres., Bd of Deputies of British Jews, 1991–97; Chm., Jewish Wkg Gp on Envmt, 1991–; Jt Patron, New Assembly of Churches, 1993–. Trustee, Project Fullemploy, 1994–. Pres., Royal British Nurses' Assoc., 2009–. FRSA 1993. Freeman, City of London, 1965. DUniv N London, 2000. *Publications:* Judaism and Ecology, 1992; Jewish Communities of the Commonwealth, 1993; Journey into Immortality, 1997; Brief Encounters of a Legal Kind, 1997; The Rainbow Never Ends, 2005; Letters to My Wife: a tribute to Sheila Rose, 2007; Arich Handler: modern Jewish hero, 2010; Sea Olympics, 2013; Beyond the Rainbow, 2014. *Recreations:* gardening, walking, various sports, writing, reading, lecturing, listening to music. *Address:* 14 Pagitts Grove, Hadley Wood, Herts EN4 0NT. *T:* (020) 8449 2166.

ROSE, Barry Michael, OBE 1998; FRSCM; FRAM; Master of the Music, St Albans Abbey, 1988–97; *b* 24 May 1934; *s* of late Stanley George Rose and Gladys Mildred Rose; *m* 1965, Elizabeth Mary Ware; one *s* two *d. Educ:* Sir George Monoux Grammar Sch., Walthamstow; Royal Acad. of Music (ARAM). FRSCM 1973; FRAM 1989. First Organist and Master of the Choristers, new Guildford Cathedral, 1960–74; Sub-Organist, St Paul's Cath., 1974–77; Master of the Choir, 1977–84; Master of the Choirs, The King's School, Canterbury, 1985–88. Music Adviser to Head of Religious Broadcasting, BBC, 1970–90. Hon. FRCO 2003; Hon. FGCM 2004. Hon. DMus City, 1991; MUniv Surrey, 1992. *Recreation:* collecting and restoring vintage fountain-pens. *Address:* Level Crossing, Milking Lane, Draycott, Somerset BS27 3TL. *T:* and *Fax:* (01934) 744838. *E:* brose80648@aol.com. *W:* www.barryrose.co.uk.

ROSE, Brian; HM Diplomatic Service, retired; *b* 26 Jan. 1930; *s* of Edwin and Emily Rose; *m* 1952, Audrey Barnes; one *d. Educ:* Canford Sch., Dorset. Intelligence Corps, 1948–50. Min. of Food, 1950–54; CRO, 1954; Peshawar, 1955–56; Ottawa, 1958–61; Kingston, Jamaica, 1962–65; Rome, 1966; Zagreb, 1966–68; Zomba, Malawi, 1968–71; FCO, 1971–74; Düsseldorf, 1974–77; E Berlin, 1977–78; Zürich, 1978–82; Consul-Gen., Stuttgart, 1982–85; Commercial and Econ. Counsellor, Helsinki, 1985–88. *Recreations:* tennis, music.

ROSE, Major Charles Frederick, CBE 1988 (MBE 1968); CEng, FICE; independent consultant in railway engineering and safety, 1989–98; *b* 9 July 1926; *s* of Charles James Rose and Ida Marguerite Chollet; *m* 1956, Huguette Primerose Lecoultre; one *s* one *d. Educ:* Xaverian Coll., Brighton; Royal School of Military Engineering, 1951–52 and 1957–59. Student engineer, Southern Railway Co., 1942–46; commnd RE, 1947; service with mil. railways, Palestine and Egypt, 1947–51; with a Field Sqdn in Germany, 1952–53; Engr SO, Korea, 1953–54; Instructor: Mons Officer Cadet Sch., 1954–57; Transportation Centre, Longmoor, 1959–62; OC a Field Sqdn, Germany, 1962–64; Instr, Royal Sch. of Mil. Engrg, 1964–66; Engr, RE road construction project, Thailand, 1966–68; Inspecting Officer of Railways, MoT, 1968–82; Chief Inspecting Officer of Railways, Dept of Transport, 1982–88. Chm., Anglo-French Channel Tunnel Safety Authy, 1987–89; Mem., Intergovtl Commn for Channel Tunnel, 1987–89. MInstRE 2000. *Recreations:* walking, foreign travel, music. *Address:* 13 Home Farm Road, Busbridge, Godalming, Surrey GU7 1TX. *T:* (01483) 416429.

ROSE, Rt Hon. Sir Christopher (Dudley Roger), Kt 1985; PC 1992; Chief Surveillance Commissioner, 2006–15; a Lord Justice of Appeal, 1992–2006; *b* 10 Feb. 1937; *s* of late Roger and Hilda Rose, Morecambe; *m* 1964, Judith, *d* of late George and Charlotte Brand, Didsbury; one *s* one *d. Educ:* Morecambe Grammar Sch.; Repton; Leeds Univ. (LLB and Hughes Prize, 1957); Wadham Coll., Oxford (1st cl. hons BCL 1959, Eldon Scholar 1959; Hon. Fellow, 1993). Lectr in Law, Wadham Coll., Oxford, 1959–60; called to Bar, Middle Temple, 1960 (Bencher, 1983; Treas., 2002); Bigelow Teaching Fellow, Law Sch., Univ. of Chicago, 1960–61; Harmsworth Scholar, 1961; joined Northern Circuit, 1961; QC 1974; a Recorder, 1978–85; a Judge of the High Court, QBD, 1985–92; Presiding Judge, Northern Circuit, 1987–90. Vice-Pres., Court of Appeal (Criminal Div.), 1997–2006. Chm., Criminal Justice Consultative Council, 1994–2000. Mem., Senate of Inns of Court and Bar, 1983–85. UK Trustee, Harold G. Fox Foundn, 1995–2005. Hon. LLD Leeds, 2008. *Recreations:* playing the piano, listening to music, travel. *Club:* Garrick.

ROSE, Sir Clive (Martin), GCMG 1981 (KCMG 1976; CMG 1967); HM Diplomatic Service, retired; *b* 15 Sept. 1921; *s* of late Rt Rev. Alfred Carey Wollaston Rose and Lois Juliet (*née* Garton); *m* 1946, Elisabeth Mackenzie (*d* 2006), *d* of late Rev. Cyril Lewis, Gilston; two *s* three *d. Educ:* Marlborough College; Christ Church, Oxford (MA). Rifle Bde, 1941–46 (Maj.; despatches): served in Europe, 1944–45; India, 1945; Iraq, 1945–46. CRO, 1948; Office of Deputy High Comr, Madras, 1948–49; Foreign Office, 1950–53; UK High Commn, Germany, 1953–54; British Embassy, Bonn, 1955; FO, 1956–59; 1st Sec. and HM Consul, Montevideo, 1959–62; FO, 1962–65; Commercial Counsellor, Paris, 1965–67; Imp. Defence Coll., 1968; Counsellor, British Embassy, Washington, 1969–71; Asst Under-Sec. of State, FCO, 1971–73; Ambassador and Head, British Delegn to Negotiations on Mutual Reduction of Forces and Armaments and Associated Measures in Central Europe (MBFR), Vienna, 1973–76; Dep. Secretary, Cabinet Office, 1976–79; Ambassador and UK Permanent Rep. on North Atlantic Council, 1979–82. Lectr to RCDS, 1979–87 (Mem., Adv. Bd, 1985–91). Consultant, Control Risks Gp, 1983–95; Dir, Control Risks Information Services Ltd, 1986–93 (Chm., 1991–93). Pres., Emergency Planning Assoc. (formerly Assoc. of Civil Defence and Emergency Planning Officers), 1987–93; Vice-Patron, RUSI, 1993–2001 (Chm. Council, 1983–86; Vice-Pres., 1986–93). Vice-Patron, Suffolk Preservation Soc., 2007– (Chm., 1985–88; Vice-Pres., 1988–2007). FRSA 1982; Hon. FICD 1989. *Publications:* Campaigns Against Western Defence: NATO's adversaries and critics, 1985, 2nd edn 1986; The Soviet Propaganda Network, 1988; The Unending Quest: a search for ancestors, 1996; Alice Owen: the life, marriages and times of a Tudor lady, 2006; (ed) Lavenham Remembers, 2006; Fanfare for Lavenham (epic poem), 2007; contrib. to FCO Occasional Papers. *Recreations:* reading, history. *Address:* Chimney House, Lavenham, Sudbury, Suffolk CO10 9QT.

ROSE, David Edward; independent film and television producer; *b* 22 Nov. 1924; *s* of Alvan Edward Rose and Gladys Frances Rose; *m* 1st, 1952, Valerie Edwards (*d* 1966); three *s* three *d*; 2nd, 1966, Sarah Reid (marr. diss. 1988); one *d*, and one step *s* one step *d* adopted; 3rd, 2001, Karin Bamborough. *Educ:* Kingswood Sch., Bath; Guildhall Sch. of Music and Drama. Repertory Theatre, 1952; Ballets Jooss, and Sadler's Wells Theatre Ballet, 1954; BBC Television, 1954–81 (in production and direction; Head of Television Training, 1969; Head of Regional Television Drama, 1971–81); Sen. Commng Editor (Fiction), 1981–88, Hd of Drama, 1988–90, Channel Four TV. Member: BAFTA; Eur. Film Acad. Fellow: BAFTA, 1999; BFI, 2010. Prix Italia TV Award (for film Medico), 1959; BAFTA Producer and Director's Award, (for Z Cars (prod original series)), 1963; BFI Award (for Film on Four and work of new writers and directors), 1985; Desmond Davies Award, BAFTA, 1987; Prix Roberto Rossellini (for Channel Four Television), Cannes Film Fest., 1987; Critics Circle Special Film Award, 1987; Gold Medal, RTS, 1988.

ROSE, Dinah Gwen Lison; QC 2006; barrister; *b* 16 July 1965; *d* of Michael and Susan Rose; *m* 1991, Peter Kessler; two *d. Educ:* City of London Sch. for Girls; Magdalen Coll., Oxford (BA Hons Mod. Hist. 1987); City Univ. (Dip. Law 1988). Called to the Bar, Gray's Inn, 1989, Bencher, 2009; in practice as barrister, 1989–, specialising in public and employment law and human rights. *Address:* Blackstone Chambers, Blackstone House, Temple, EC4Y 9BW. *T:* (020) 7583 1770, *Fax:* (020) 7822 7350. *E:* dinahrose@blackstonechambers.com.

ROSE, Prof. Francis Dennis, LLD, DCL; Professor of Maritime and Commercial Law, University of Southampton, since 2012; *b* 11 Jan. 1950; *s* of Francis Joseph Rose and late Catherine Mary Rose; *m* 1974, Lynda Kathryn Banks; one *s* two *d. Educ:* Farnborough Grammar Sch.; Magdalen Coll., Oxford (BA 1972, BCL 1973, MA 1975; DCL 2007); UCL (PhD 1986); MA 1992, LLD 2006, Cantab. Called to the Bar, Gray's Inn, 1983; barrister; Associate Mem., Quadrant Chambers (formerly 2, then 4, Essex Court Chambers). Lecturer in Law: Liverpool Univ., 1973–75; Cardiff Law Sch., UWIST, 1975–77; UCL, 1977–85; Sen. Lectr, UCL, 1985–89; Lectr in Law, Univ. of Cambridge and Fellow, St John's Coll., Cambridge, 1989–92; Prof. of Commercial and Common Law, Univ. of Buckingham, 1993–99; Prof. of Commercial Law, Univ. of Bristol, 2000–12. Visiting Professor: UCL, 1992–94; Univ. of Natal, 1996; Internat. Maritime Law Inst., Malta, 2001–07; Univ. of Auckland, 2002; Tulane Univ., 2005; Univ. of Queensland, 2007; Robert S. Campbell Vis. Fellow, Magdalen Coll., Oxford, 2012–13. Convener, Restitution Section, SLS (formerly SPTL), 1983–2008 (Mem. Council, 1986–99; Sections Sec., 1990–96). Associate Ed., Current Legal Problems, 1983–85; Ed., 1983–87, Gen. Ed., 1987–, Lloyd's Maritime and Commercial Law Qly; Gen. Ed., Restitution Law Review, 1993–; Ed.-in-Chief, Company, Financial and Insolvency Law Review, 1997–99. Editl Dir, Mansfield Press, 1993–2000; Ed., Internat. Maritime and Commercial Yearbook, 2002–. *Publications:* The Modern Law of Pilotage, 1984; Kennedy and Rose, The Law of Salvage, 5th edn 1985 (jtly) and 8th edn 2013; (ed) New Foundations for Insurance Law, 1987; (ed) International Commercial and Maritime Arbitration, 1987; (ed) Restitution and the Conflict of Laws, 1995; (ed) Consensus Ad Idem, 1996; (ed) Failure of Contracts: contractual, restitutionary and proprietary consequences, 1997; General Average: law and practice, 1997, 2nd edn 2005; (ed) Restitution and Banking Law, 1998; (ed jtly) Lessons of the Swaps Litigation, 2000; (ed jtly) Restitution and Equity, vol. I, Resulting Trusts and Equitable Compensation, 2000; (ed) Lex Mercatoria, 2000; (ed) Restitution and Insolvency, 2000; Marine Insurance: law and practice, 2004, 2nd edn 2012; contribs to legal jls and books. *Recreations:* family, music, photography, collecting. *Address:* Faculty of Law, University of Southampton, Highfield, Southampton SO17 1BJ. *T:* (023) 8059 3708. *E:* Francis.Rose@soton.ac.uk.

ROSE, Graham Hunt; a Master of the Senior Courts (formerly Supreme Court), Queen's Bench Division, 1992–2010; *b* 15 July 1937; *er s* of late William Edward Hunt Rose and Mary Musgrave Rose (*née* Kent); *m* 1st, 1962, Malvinia Ann Saunders (marr. diss. 1988); three *s*; 2nd, 2009, Sara Margaret Gibbon (*née* Comer). *Educ:* Canford Sch.; University Coll., Oxford (MA). Nat. Service, RA, 1955–57: commnd 1956; active service, 1957. Called to the Bar, Inner Temple, 1961; practised at the Bar, 1961–92, Western Circuit. Jt Editor, Civil Procedure (formerly Supreme Court Practice), 1992–2010. *Publications:* Revision of The Queen's Bench Guide, 2014. *Recreations:* most ball games, walking, gardening, birdwatching. *Address:* c/o Royal Courts of Justice, Strand, WC2A 2LL. *Clubs:* Travellers; Parkstone Golf.

ROSE, Prof. Harold Bertram; Emeritus Professor of Finance, London Business School (formerly London Graduate School of Business Studies), since 1996 (Esmée Fairbairn Chair, 1965–75; Visiting Professor of Finance, since 1975); *b* 9 Aug. 1923; *s* of late Isaac Rose and Rose Rose (*née* Barnett); *m* 1st, 1949, Valerie Frances Anne Chubb (marr. diss. 1974); three *s* one *d*; 2nd, 1974, Diana Mary Campbell Scarlett; one *s* one *d. Educ:* Davenant Foundn Sch.; LSE (BCom). Served with RA in Britain, India and Burma, 1942–46 (Captain). Head of Econ. Intell. Dept, Prudential Assce Co., Ltd, 1948–58; Sen. Lectr, then Reader, in Economics, LSE, 1958–65; Member: Council, Consumers' Assoc., 1958–63; Central Adv. Council on Primary Educn (Plowden Cttee), 1963–65; Business Studies Cttee, SSRC, 1967–68, and Univ. Grants Cttee, 1968–69; Reserve Pension Bd, 1973–75; HM Treasury Inquiry into Value of Pensions, 1980; Special Adviser to: H of C Treasury and Civil Service Cttee, 1980–81; DoI, 1980–81. Gp Economic Advr, Barclays Bank, 1975–88. Director: Economist Newspaper, 1969–71; Abbey National Building Soc., 1975–83. Mem., Retail Prices Adv. Cttee, 1985–89. Trustee, IEA, 1975–98 (Chm., 1995–98); Trustee, Inst. for Study of Civil Soc., 2000–06 (Treas., 2000–04). Gov., The Hall Sch., 1987–95. *Publications:* The Economic Background to Investment, 1960; Disclosure in Company Accounts, 1963; Management Education in the 1970s, 1970; various papers in econ. and financial jls. *Address:* 33 Dartmouth Park Avenue, NW5 1JL. *T:* (020) 7485 7315. *E:* harold@hbrose.co.uk. *Club:* Reform.

ROSE, Gen. Sir (Hugh) Michael, KCB 1994; CBE 1986; DSO 1995; QGM 1981; DL; Adjutant General, 1995–97; Aide de Camp General to the Queen, 1995–97; *b* 5 Jan. 1940; *s* of late Lt-Col Hugh Vincent Rose, IA and Mrs Barbara Phoebe Masters (*née* Allcard); *m* 1968, Angela Raye Shaw; two *s. Educ:* Cheltenham College; St Edmund Hall, Oxford (2nd Cl. Hons PPE; Hon. Fellow, 1995); Staff College; RCDS. Commissioned Gloucestershire Regt, TAVR, 1959; RAFVR, 1962; Coldstream Guards, 1964; served Germany, Aden, Malaysia, Gulf States, Dhofar, N Ireland (despatches), Falkland Is (despatches); BM 16 Para. Bde, 1973–75; CO 22 SAS Regt, 1979–82; Comd 39 Inf. Bde, 1983–85; Comdt, Sch. of Infantry, 1987–88; DSF, 1988–89; GOC NE Dist and Comdr 2nd Inf. Div., 1989–91; Comdt, Staff Coll., 1991–93; Comdr, UK Field Army and Insp. Gen. of TA, 1993–94; Comdr, UN Protection Force, Bosnia-Herzegovina, 1994–95; Dep. C-in-C, Land Comd, 1995. Col, Coldstream Guards, 1999–2009. Hon. Col, Oxford Univ. OTC, 1995–2000. DL Somerset, 2003. Hon. DLitt Nottingham, 1999. Freeman, City of London, 1998; Liveryman, Drapers' Co., 1998. Comdr, Legion of Honour (France), 1995. *Publications:* Fighting for Peace, 1998; Washington's War, 2007. *Recreations:* sailing, ski-ing. *Address:* c/o Regimental HQ Coldstream Guards, Wellington Barracks, Birdcage Walk, SW1E 6HQ. *Clubs:* Pratt's, Cavalry and Guards.

ROSE, Prof. Jacqueline Susan, PhD; FBA 2006; Professor of Humanities, Birkbeck Institute for the Humanities, Birkbeck, University of London, since 2015; *b* 19 May 1949; *d* of Leslie David Stone and Lynn Rose; one *d. Educ:* St Hilda's Coll., Oxford (BA Hons English 1971); Paris-Sorbonne (MA Comparative and Gen. Lit. 1972); PhD London 1979. Lectr, 1976–88, Sen. Lectr, 1988–91, Reader, 1991–92, in English, Univ. of Sussex; Prof. of English, QMUL, 1992–2014; Diane Middlebrook/Carl Djerassi Prof. of Gender Studies, Univ. of Cambridge, 2014. Writer and presenter, TV prog., Dangerous Liaisons: Israel and America, 2002. Co-founder, Independent Jewish Voices, 2007. *Publications:* The Case of Peter Pan, or, The Impossibility of Children's Fiction, 1984, 2nd edn 1993; Sexuality in the Field of Vision, 1986, 2nd edn 2005; The Haunting of Sylvia Plath, 1991, 2nd edn 1996; Why War?: psychoanalysis, politics and the return to Melanie Klein, 1993; States of Fantasy, 1995; Albertine (novel), 2001; On Not Being Able to Sleep: psychoanalysis in the modern world, 2003; The Question of Zion, 2005; The Last Resistance, 2007; Conversations with Jacqueline Rose, 2010; The Jacqueline Rose Reader, 2011; Proust Among the Nations: from Dreyfus to the Middle East, 2011; Women in Dark Times, 2014. *Address:* Birkbeck Institute for the Humanities, Birkbeck, University of London, Malet Street, WC1E 7HX. *T:* (020) 7631 6153. *E:* j.rose@bbk.ac.uk.

ROSE, Sir James; *see* Rose, Sir A. J.

ROSE, Jeffrey David, CBE 1991; Chairman of the Royal Automobile Club, 1981–98 (Deputy Chairman, 1979–81); *b* 2 July 1931; *s* of late Samuel and Daisy Rose; *m* 1st, 1958, Joyce (*née* Clompus) (marr. diss. 1999); one *s* two *d*; 2nd, 1999, Helga Maria Wiederschwinger Dusauzay (marr. diss. 2001). *Educ:* Southend High Sch.; London Sch. of Econs and Pol Science. Nat. Service, RA, 1950–52 (Lieut). Chm., RAC Motoring Services, 1980–98; Vice Chm., British Road Fedn, 1982–98; Vice President: Fédn Internationale de l'Automobile, 1983–93 and 1994–96 (Hon. Vice Pres., 1996–); Inst. of the Motor Industry, 1992–98; RAC Motor Sports Council, 1994–98; Chm., Commonwealth Motoring Conf., 1988–98; Member: Council, Inst. of Advanced Motorists, 1987–94; Adv. Council, Prince's Youth Business Trust, 1992–2000. Chm., Trustees, Brain and Spine Foundn, 1995–2005; Trustee, Brooklands Mus., 1991–2001. FIMI 1989. Liveryman, Worshipful Co. of Coachmakers and Coach Harness Makers, 1981– (Master, 2006–07). *Recreations:* dining, music. *Address:* Albany, Piccadilly, W1J 0AX. *Clubs:* Royal Automobile (Vice-Pres., 1998-), Brooks's, MCC; Automobile de France.

ROSE, Sir John (Edward Victor), Kt 2003; FRAeS, FIMechE; Deputy Chairman, Rothschild Group, since 2011; *b* 9 Oct. 1952; *s* of (Wentworth) Victor Rose and late Doris Rose (*née* Bridge); *m* 1979, Emma Felicity Granville; two *s* one *d. Educ:* Charterhouse Sch.; Univ. of St Andrews (MA Hons Psychology). FRAeS 1993. Rolls-Royce, 1984–2011: Board

Mem., 1992–2011; Chief Exec., 1996–2011. Hon. FREng 2009. Commander, Légion d'Honneur (France), 2008; Public Service Star (Singapore), 2008. *Recreations:* ski-ing, sailing, scuba-diving, te nnis, theatre, arts. *Clubs:* Hurlingham, Travellers.

ROSE, Maj. Gen. John Gordon, CB 2009; MBE 1991; Director General, Intelligence Collection, Ministry of Defence, 2006–09; *b* 30 May 1955; *s* of Charles and Yvonne Rose; *m* 1982, Mandie Jones; one *s. Educ:* Kitale Primary Sch., Kenya; Lenana Sch., Kenya; Dollar Acad. Royal Marines: joined, 1974, young officer trng; Troop Comdr 40 Commando, 1975–76; Ops Officer, Desert Regt, Sultan of Oman Land Forces (on secondment), 1976–78; Instructor, SNCO Tactics Wing (Army) and RM Officers Trng, 1979–82; Adjutant 40 Commando, 1982–83; SO HQ 3 Commando Bde, 1984–87; Army staff course, Camberley, 1988; COS Logistics HQ UK Mobile Force, 1989–90; Company Comdr 42 Commando, 1990–92; SO Directorate of Naval Staff Duties, MoD, 1992–93; COS 3 Commando Bde, 1994–96; Staff of C-in-C Fleet, 1996; Asst Dir, Middle East, MoD, 1997–98; CO 40 Commando, 1999–2000; Dir, Intelligence Ops, MoD Defence Intelligence Staff, 2000–03; Chief of Defence Staff Liaison Officer, Pentagon, 2003; hcsc, 2004; Comdr 3 Commando Bde, 2004–06. Rep. Col Comdt, RM, 2009–12. Project Dir, African Union/UN Inf. Support Team for Somalia, 2012–13. *Recreations:* golf, photography, motor bike touring. *Address:* c/o Royal Marines Secretary, Whale Island, Portsmouth PO1 3LS.

ROSE, John Raymond; Clerk of Standing Committees, House of Commons, 1987–91; *b* 22 April 1934; *s* of late Arthur Raymond Rose and Edith Mary Rose, Merstham, Surrey and Minehead, Somerset; *m* 1st, 1961, Vivienne (marr. diss. 1991), *d* of late Charles Dillon Seabrooke, IoW; one *s* one *d*; 2nd, 1991, Dr Betty Webb, *d* of late Ernest Julian Webb, Statesville, NC, USA. *Educ:* Marlborough; Trinity Hall, Cambridge (Major Scholar in Classics; Law Tripos 1st Cl. Hons, Pts I and II). 2nd Lieut DCLI, Belize and Jamaica, 1953–55. Clerk's Department, House of Commons, 1958–91: Clerk of Select Cttees on Estimates (Sub-Cttee), Public Accounts, Violence in the Family, Race Relations, Abortion, European Community Secondary Legislation, Foreign Affairs, 1959–87. Vis. Kenan Prof., 1981, Adjunct Prof., 1991–, Meredith Coll., NC, USA. Fellow, Industry and Parlt Trust, 1987. Freeman, City of London, 1959; Liveryman, Salters' Co., 1959. *Recreations:* travel, walking, cycling, gardening, bridge. *Address:* 1612 Oberlin Road, Raleigh, NC 27608, USA. *T:* (919) 8283443; 4 St James's Square, Bath BA1 2TR. *T:* (01225) 481115. *E:* johnrrose34@hotmail.com.

ROSE, Jonathan Lee; His Honour Judge Rose; a Circuit Judge, since 2008; *b* Leeds, 29 Oct. 1958; *s* of Malcolm and Shirley Rose; *m* 1990, Philippa, *d* of Eric and Pearl Green; one *s* one *d. Educ:* Roundhay Sch., Leeds; Preston Poly. (BA Hons); Keble Coll., Oxford. Called to the Bar, Middle Temple, 1981; barrister, N Eastern Circuit, 1983–2008; Recorder, 2000–08. Legal Mem., Mental Health Rev. Tribunal, 2002–08. Vice Pres., 2005–06, Pres., 2006–11, United Hebrew Congregation, Leeds. *Publications:* Innocents: how justice failed Stefan Kisko and Lesley Molseed, 1997. *Recreations:* music, scuba diving, cycling, natural history, history. *Address:* Bradford Combined Court Centre, Exchange Square, Bradford BD1 1JA. *T:* (01274) 840274, *Fax:* (01274) 840275.

ROSE, Ven. Judith; *see* Rose, Ven. K. J.

ROSE, Judith Ann; *see* Goffe, J. A.

ROSE, Sir Julian (Day), 4th Bt *cr* 1909, of Hardwick House, and 5th Bt *cr* 1872, of Montreal; President, International Coalition to Protect the Polish Countryside, since 2000; *b* 3 March 1947; 3rd and *o* surv. *s* of Sir Charles Henry Rose, 3rd Bt and of Phoebe, *d* of 2nd Baron Phillimore (*d* 1947); *S* father, 1966, and cousin, Sir Francis Cyril Rose, 4th Bt, 1979; *m* 1976, Elizabeth Goode Johnson, Columbus, Ohio, USA (marr. diss. 2002); one *s* one *d. Educ:* Stanbridge School. Actor/asst dir, Players' Theatre of New England, 1973–79; Co-founder, Inst. for Creative Develt, Antwerp, 1978–83. Co-ordinator, Organic Farming practice, Hardwick Estate, 1975–. Chm., Assoc. of Rural Businesses in Oxfordshire, 1995–; Member: Council, Soil Assoc., 1984–96; Agricl Panel, Intermediate Technology Develt Gp, 1984–87; Bd, UK Register of Organic Food Standards, Food From Britain, 1987–90; BBC Rural and Agricl Affairs Adv. Cttee, 1991–93; Adv. Cttee, Food and Farming, Univ. of W London (formerly Thames Valley Univ.), 1994–; Agricl and Rural Economy Cttee, CLA, 1999–2002. Rural Economy Advr, SE of England Develt Agency, 1999–. Pres., Internat. Coalition to Protect the Polish Countryside, 2004–; Patron: Family Farmers Assoc., 2004–; Natural Food Finders, 2009–; Bees Action Network, 2010–. Trustee: SAFE Alliance, 1995–; Dartington Trust, 1996–2000. Agricl Correspondent, Environment Now, 1989–90; Presenter, Letter from Poland, Farming Today, BBC Radio 4, 2007–08. Chair, The Future of Agriculture, St George's House consultation, 1999–. Food Award, 1986, Best Dairy Produce, 1998, Soil Assoc. *Publications:* (contrib.) Town and Country, 1999; Changing Course for Life: local solutions to global problems, 2009; Back to our Roots, Resurgence, 2010; In Defence of Life: essays on a radical reworking of green wisdom, 2013; contrib. Fourth World Rev. *Heir: s* Lawrence Michael Rose, *b* 6 Oct. 1986. *Address:* Hardwick House, Whitchurch-on-Thames, Oxfordshire RG8 7RB. *W:* www.changingcourseforlife.info.

ROSE, Ven. (Kathleen) Judith; Archdeacon of Tonbridge, 1996–2002; *b* 14 June 1937; *d* of Cuthbert Arthur Rose and Margaret Rose; *m* 1991, David Ernest Gwyer (*d* 2000); two step *d. Educ:* Sexey's Grammar Sch., Blackford; Seale Hayne Agricl Coll. (NDD 1960); St Michael's House Theol Coll., Oxford (DipTh 1966); London Bible Coll. (BD(Hons)). Agriculture, 1953–64; Parish Worker, Rodbourne Cheney Parish Church, 1966–71; ordained deaconess, 1976, deacon, 1987, priest, 1994; Parish Worker, then Deaconess, St George's Church, Leeds, 1973–81; Chaplain, Bradford Cathedral, 1981–85; Minister responsible for St Paul's Parkwood, Gillingham, 1986–90; Chaplain to Bishop of Rochester, 1990–95. Rural Dean of Gillingham, 1988–90. *Publications:* Sunday Learning for All Ages, 1982; (contrib.) Women in Ministry, 1991; (contrib.) Women Priests: the first years, 1996; (contrib.) A Time and A Season, 2000; (contrib.) Voices of this Calling, 2002; Sow in Tears, Reap in Joy, 2007. *Recreations:* gardening, walking, home-making. *Address:* 47 Hill Lea Gardens, Cheddar, Somerset BS27 3JH.

ROSE, Martin Tristram; Senior Consultant, Middle East and North Africa, British Council, since 2014; *b* 3 Dec. 1954; *s* of Geoffrey Rose and Jocelyn Rose (*née* Briggs); *m* 1984, Georgina Benson; one *s* three *d. Educ:* Bradfield Coll.; Magdalen Coll., Oxford (BA Hons Mod. Hist. 1976; MA 1984); St Antony's Coll., Oxford (MPhil Mod. Mid. Eastern Studies 1984). Sub-ed., The Egyptian Gazette, 1976–78; Sales exec., later ELT Sales, Macmillan Press, S Africa and Mid East, 1979–82; Mid East Dept, Mellon Bank NA, 1984–88; British Council, 1988–: Asst Rep., Baghdad, 1989–90; Asst Dir, Rome and founding Dir, Pontignano Conf., 1991–96; Hd, Eur. Series, London, 1996–99; Dir, Brussels and Cultural Counsellor, HM Embassies, Belgium and Luxembourg, 1999–2002; Dir, Counterpoint, 2002–06; Dir, Canada, and Cultural Counsellor, High Commn, Ottawa, 2006–10; Dir, Morocco, and Cultural Attaché, HM Embassy Rabat, 2010–14. Shaikh Zaki Badawi Meml Lect., Assoc. of Muslim Social Scientists UK, 2009. Vis. Fellow, Prince Waleed bin Talal Centre for Islamic Studies, Cambridge Univ., 2014–. Trustee, BAX British-Arab Exchanges, 2014–. Fellow, Royal Canadian Geographical Soc., 2009. *Publications:* (with N. Wadham-Smith) Mutuality, Trust and Cultural Relations, 2004; (with M. Leonard) British Public Diplomacy in an Age of Schisms, 2005; The Affair of the Emerods, 2009; (ed with A. Hussey) The Challenge of North Africa, 2014; Education in North Africa, 2014. *Recreations:* history, literature, language, memory, Middle East, gravestones. *Address:* 20 Beeches Close, Saffron Walden, Essex CB11 4BT. *T:* 07880 932604. *E:* martin.rose@magd.oxon.org.

ROSE, Martyn Craig; Chairman: English National Opera, 2013–15; DanceEast, 2010–13; Floreat Education, since 2013; *b* Llandrindod Wells, 27 May 1948; *s* of Charles Rose and Margaret Rose; *m* 1990, Philippa Savill; one *s* one *d. Educ:* Malvern Coll.; Inns of Court Sch. of Law. Called to the Bar, Inner Temple, 1972. Chairman: Cherry Blossom Ltd, 1977–; Grangers Internat. Ltd, 1977–; Macaw Soft Drinks, 1990–2005; Minster Sound Radio plc, 1992–2000; Frost and Reed Ltd, 1993–; Publishing Technology plc, 2005–; Dir, Dentons Pension Mgt Ltd, 2000–. Chm., Society Network Foundn, 2011–14 (Chm., Britain's Personal Best, 2013–14). Trustee, Cystic Fibrosis Trust, 2004–14. Gov., Orwell Park Sch., 2001–. *Recreations:* Wimbledon, golf, shooting, performing arts both classical and modern, fine art collecting and dealing, struggling to beat my son at tennis. *Address:* 7 Trebeck Street, W1J 7LU. *T:* (020) 7408 0792, *Fax:* (020) 7408 0783. *E:* mcr@martynrose.com.

ROSE, Gen. Sir Michael; *see* Rose, Gen. Sir H. M.

ROSE, Norman John, FRICS, FCIArb; Member, Upper Tribunal (Lands Chamber) (formerly Lands Tribunal), 1998–2013; *b* 22 Oct. 1943; *s* of late Jack Rose and Margaret Rose (*née* de Groot); *m* 1968, Helena de Mesquita; three *s. Educ:* Christ's Coll., Finchley; Coll. of Estate Management (BSc (Est. Man.); Valuation Prize). FRICS 1976; FCIArb 1977. Gerald Eve & Co., 1964–71; Partner, de Groot Collis, 1971–91; Dir of Valuation, Chesterton, 1992–98. *Address:* c/o Upper Tribunal (Lands Chamber), 43–45 Bedford Square, WC1B 3AS.

ROSE, Paul (Bernard); HM Coroner, London Southern District, 1988–2002; *b* 26 Dec. 1935; *s* of Arthur and Norah Rose; *m* 1957, Eve Marie-Thérèse; two *s* one *d. Educ:* Bury Gram. Sch.; Manchester Univ.; Gray's Inn. LLB (Hons) Manch., 1956; Barrister-at-Law, 1957. Legal and Secretarial Dept, Co-op. Union Ltd, 1957–60; Lectureship, Dept of Liberal Studies, Royal Coll. of Advanced Technology, Salford, 1961–63; Barrister-at-Law, 1963–88; Asst Recorder (formerly Dep. Circuit Judge), 1974–88; Immigration Adjudicator (part-time), Hatton Cross, 1987– (Special Adjudicator, 1993–). MP (Lab) Manchester, Blackley, 1964–79; PPS to Minister of Transport, 1967–68; Opposition Front Bench Spokesman, Dept of Employment, 1970–72. Chairman: Parly Labour Home Office Group, 1968–70; Parly Labour Employment Group, 1974–79; Campaign for Democracy in Ulster, 1965–73. Delegate to Council of Europe and WEU, 1968–69; Vice-Chm., Labour Cttee for Europe, 1977–79. Mem., Campaign for Electoral Reform, 1975–. Founder Mem., SDP (Brent Area Sec., 1981–82). Chm., NW Regional Sports Council, 1966–68. Member: Coroners' Soc. (Pres., SE Coroners Soc., 1996–97); Medico-Legal Soc. AIL. *Publications:* Handbook to Industrial and Provident Societies Act, 1960; Guide to Weights and Measures Act 1963, 1965; The Manchester Martyrs, 1970; Backbencher's Dilemma, 1981; The Moonies Unmasked, 1981; (jt) A History of the Fenian Movement in Britain, 1982; contrib. to many periodicals on political and legal topics. *Recreations:* sport, theatre, languages, travel, computers. *Address:* Lynnden, 70 Amersham Road, Chalfont St Peter, Bucks SL9 0PB.

ROSE, Paul Telfer; QC 2002; fee-paid Employment Judge, since 2003; *b* 18 Nov. 1958; 3rd *s* of late Ian Alexander Rose and of Pamela Margaret Rose (*née* Paisley); *m* 1986, Sara Jane Herbert; three *s* one *d. Educ:* University Coll. Sch., Hampstead; Reading Univ. (LLB 1980). Called to the Bar, Gray's Inn, 1981; in practice as barrister, specialising in employment law and personal injury law, 1983–. Fee-paid Judge, Employment Tribunals, 2003–. *Recreations:* travel, Rugby, cricket, golf, walking with friends and family. *Address:* Old Square Chambers, 10–11 Bedford Row, WC1R 4BU. *T:* (020) 7269 0300. *E:* roseqc@oldsquarechambers.co.uk.

ROSE, Prof. Richard, FBA 1992; Director, Centre for the Study of Public Policy, University of Strathclyde and University of Aberdeen (formerly at University of Strathclyde, then at University of Aberdeen), since 1976; Professor of Politics, University of Strathclyde, since 2012; *b* 9 April 1933; *o s* of late Charles Imse and Mary C. Rose, St Louis, Mo, USA; *m* 1956, Rosemary J., *o d* of late James Kenny, Whitstable, Kent; two *s* one *d. Educ:* Clayton High Sch., Mo; Johns Hopkins Univ., BA (Double distinction, Phi Beta Kappa) comparative drama, 1953; London Sch. of Economics, 1953–54; Oxford University, 1957–60, DPhil (Lincoln and Nuffield Colls). Political public relations, Mississippi Valley, 1954–55; Reporter, St Louis Post-Dispatch, 1955–57; Lecturer in Govt, Univ. of Manchester, 1961–66; Prof. of Politics and Public Policy, Strathclyde Univ., 1966–2005; Sen. Fellow, Oxford Internet Inst., 2003–05; Sixth Century Prof. of Politics and Public Policy, Univ. of Aberdeen, 2005–11. Consultant Psephologist, The Times, Independent Television, Daily Telegraph, STV, UTV etc., 1964–. American SSRC Fellow, Stanford Univ., 1967; Vis. Lectr in Political Sociology, Cambridge Univ., 1967; Dir, ISSC European Summer Sch., 1973. Sec., Cttee on Political Sociology, Internat. Sociological Assoc., 1970–85; Founding Mem., European Consortium for Political Res., 1970; Member: US/UK Fulbright Commn, 1971–75; Eisenhower Fellowship Programme, 1971. Guggenheim Foundn Fellow, 1974; Visiting Scholar: Woodrow Wilson Internat. Centre, Washington DC, 1974; Brookings Inst., Washington DC, 1976; Amer. Enterprise Inst., Washington, 1980; Fiscal Affairs Dept, IMF, Washington, 1984; Visiting Professor: European Univ. Inst., Florence, 1977–78, 2011–; Central European Univ., Prague, 1992–95; Instituto Ortega y Gasset, Madrid, 2000; Visitor, Japan Foundn, 1984; Hinkley Prof., Johns Hopkins Univ., 1987; Vis. Fellow, Wissenschaftszentrum, Berlin, 1988–90, 2006–11, 2015–; Research Associate: UN Eur. Centre for Social Welfare Policy and Res., 1992–; Centre for Study of Democracy, Univ. of Westminster, 1998–2000; Fellow, Max-Planck Transformation Process Gp, Berlin, 1996; Wei Lun Prof., Chinese Univ. of Hong Kong, 2000. Ransone Lectr, Univ. of Alabama, 1990. Consultant Chm., NI Constitutional Convention, 1976; Mem., Home Office Working Party on Electoral Register, 1975–77. Co-Founder: British Politics Gp, 1974; Global Barometer Survey Network, 2001–05; Convenor, Work Gp on UK Politics, Political Studies Assoc., 1976–88; Mem. Council, Internat. Political Science Assoc., 1976–82; Keynote Speaker, Aust. Inst. of Political Science, Canberra, 1978; Steering Cttee, World Values Study, 1995; Transparency Internat. Res. Adv. Cttee, 1998–. Technical Consultant: OECD; World Bank; Internat. Inst. for Democracy and Electoral Assistance, Stockholm; Council of Europe; Dir, ESRC (formerly SSRC) Res. Programme, Growth of Govt, 1982–86; UNDP Cons. to Pres. of Colombia, 1990; Scientific Advr, Paul Lazarsfeld Soc., Vienna, 1991–. Mem. Council, Scottish Opera Ltd, 1992–. Hon. Vice-Pres., Political Studies Assoc., UK, 1986. Editor, Jl of Public Policy, 1985–2012. Foreign Member: Finnish Acad. of Science and Letters, 1985; Amer. Acad. of Arts and Scis, 1994. Hon. Dr: Orebru, 2005; European Univ. Inst., 2010. Amex Internat. Econs Prize, 1992; Lasswell Prize for Public Policy, Policy Studies Orgn, USA, 1999; Lifetime Achievement Award, UK Pol Studies Assoc., 2000; Lifetime Achievement Award, Council for Comparative Study of Electoral Systems, 2008; Dogan Foundn Award, Eur. Consortium for Pol Res., 2009; Sir Isaiah Berlin Lifetime Achievement Award, Pol Studies Assoc. of the UK, 2010. Subject of prog. in Man of Action series, BBC Radio 3, 1974. *Publications:* The British General Election of 1959 (with D. E. Butler), 1960; Must Labour Lose? (with Mark Abrams), 1960; Politics in England, 1964, 5th edn 1989; (ed) Studies in British Politics, 1966, 3rd edn 1976; Influencing Voters, 1967; (ed) Policy Making in Britain, 1969; People in Politics, 1970; (ed, with M. Dogan) European Politics, 1971; Governing Without Consensus: an Irish perspective, 1971; (with T. Mackie) International Almanack of Electoral History, 1974, 3rd edn 1991; (ed) Electoral Behavior: a comparative handbook, 1974; (ed) Lessons from America, 1974; The Problem of Party Government, 1974; (ed) The Management of Urban Change in Britain and Germany, 1974; Northern Ireland: a time of choice, 1976; Managing Presidential Objectives, 1976; (ed) The Dynamics of Public Policy, 1976; (ed, with D. Kavanagh) New Trends in British Politics, 1977; (ed with J. Wiatr) Comparing Public Policies, 1977; What is Governing?: Purpose and Policy in Washington, 1978; (ed, with G. Hermet and A. Rouquié) Elections without Choice, 1978; (with B. G. Peters) Can

Government Go Bankrupt?, 1978; (ed with W. B. Gwyn) Britain: progress and decline, 1980; Do Parties Make a Difference?, 1980, 2nd edn 1984; (ed) Challenge to Governance, 1980; (ed) Electoral Participation, 1980; (ed with E. Suleiman) Presidents and Prime Ministers, 1980; Understanding the United Kingdom, 1982; (with I. McAllister) United Kingdom Facts, 1982; (ed with P. Madgwick) The Territorial Dimension in United Kingdom Politics, 1982; (ed with E. Page) Fiscal Stress in Cities, 1982; Understanding Big Government, 1984; (with I. McAllister) The Nationwide Competition for Votes, 1984; Public Employment in Western Nations, 1985; (with I. McAllister) Voters Begin to Choose, 1986; (with D. Van Mechelen) Patterns of Parliamentary Legislation, 1986; (ed with R. Shiratori) The Welfare State East and West, 1986; Ministers and Ministries, 1987; (with T. Karran) Taxation by Political Inertia, 1987; The Post-Modern President: the White House meets the world, 1988, 2nd edn 1991; Ordinary People in Public Policy, 1989; (with I. McAllister) The Loyalty of Voters: a lifetime learning model, 1990; Lesson-Drawing in Public Policy: a guide to learning across time and space, 1993; (with P. L. Davies) Inheritance in Public Policy: change without choice in Britain, 1994; What is Europe?, 1996; (with S. White and I. McAllister) How Russia Votes, 1997; (with W. Mishler and C. Haerpfer) Democracy and Its Alternatives, 1998; (ed jtly) A Society Transformed?: Hungary in time-space perspective, 1999; International Encyclopedia of Elections, 2000; The Prime Minister in a Shrinking World, 2001; (with Neil Munro) Elections Without Order: Russia's challenge to Vladimir Putin, 2002; (with Neil Munro) Elections and Parties in New European Democracies, 2003; Learning from Comparative Public Policy, 2005; (with W. Mishler and Neil Munro) Russia Transformed, 2006; Understanding Post-Communist Transformation, 2009; (with Neil Munro) Parties and Elections in New European Democracies, 2009; (jtly) Popular Support for an Undemocratic Regime, 2011; Representing Europeans: a pragmatic approach, 2013; Learning about Politics in Time and Space: a memoir, 2014; (with C. Peiffer) Paying Bribes for Public Services, 2015; numerous contribs to academic journals in Europe and America; trans. into eighteen foreign languages; broadcasts on comparative politics and public policy. *Recreations:* architecture, textiles, music, writing. *Address:* 1 East Abercromby Street, Helensburgh, Scotland G84 7SP. *T:* (01436) 672164. *W:* www.profrose.eu. *Clubs:* Reform; Cosmos (Washington, DC).

ROSE, Prof. Steven Peter Russell, PhD; Professor of Biology and Director, Brain and Behaviour Research Group, Open University, 1969–2006, now Emeritus Professor; *b* 4 July 1938; *s* of Lionel Sydney Rose and Ruth Rose (*née* Waxman); *m* 1961, Hilary Ann Chantler; two *s*. *Educ:* Haberdashers' Aske's Sch., Hampstead; King's Coll., Cambridge (BA); Inst. of Psychiatry, Univ. of London (PhD). FRSB (FIBiol 1970). Beit Meml and Guinness Res. Fellow, New Coll., Oxford, 1961–63; NIH Res. Fellow, Istituto Superiore di Sanità, Rome, 1963–64; MRC Res. Staff, Dept of Biochem., Imperial Coll., London, 1964–69. Vis. Sen. Res. Fellow, ANU, 1977; Vis. Schol., Harvard Univ., 1980; Distinguished Res. Prof., Univ. of Minn, 1992; Osher Fellow, Exploratorium, San Francisco, 1993; Vis. Prof., UCL, 1999–; Jt Gresham Prof. of Physic, 1999–2002. FRSA 1980. Anokhin Medal, Russia, 1990; Sechenov Medal, Russia, 1992; Ariens Kappers Medal, Netherlands Royal Acad. of Sci., Amsterdam, 1999; Biochem. Soc. Prize, 2002; Edinburgh Medal, 2004; Lifetime Award for Outstanding Contributions to Neuroscience, British Neurosci. Assoc., 2012. *Publications:* The Chemistry of Life, 1966, 4th edn 1999; (with Hilary Rose) Science and Society, 1969; The Conscious Brain, 1973; No Fire No Thunder, 1984; (jtly) Not in our Genes, 1984; The Making of Memory, 1992, new edn 2003 (Science Book Prize, COPUS, 1993); Lifelines, 1997; (ed) From Brains to Consciousness?, 1998; (ed with Hilary Rose) Alas, Poor Darwin, 2000; The 21st Century Brain: explaining, mending and manipulating the mind, 2005; (with Hilary Rose) Genes, Cells and Brains: the Promethean promises of the new biosciences, 2012; numerous edited books, res. papers and scholarly articles. *Address:* Department of Life, Health and Chemical Sciences, The Open University, Milton Keynes MK7 6AA.

ROSE, Hon. Dame Vivien (Judith), DBE 2013; **Hon. Mrs Justice Rose;** a Judge of the High Court, Chancery Division, since 2013; a President, Upper Tribunal (Tax and Chancery Chamber), since 2015; *b* London, 13 April 1960; *d* of late Eric Rose and of Jacqueline Rose (*née* Sugarman); *m* 2002, Dr Bernard Joseph Bulkin. *Educ:* Kingsbury High Sch.; Newnham Coll., Cambridge (BA Law 1982); Brasenose Coll., Oxford (BCL 1983). Called to the Bar, Gray's Inn, 1984, Bencher, 2013; in practice as a barrister, Monckton Chambers, Gray's Inn, 1985–95; Standing Counsel to Dir Gen. of Fair Trading, 1992–95; Advr, Legal Dept, HM Treasury, 1996–2002, apptd to Sen. Civil Service, 2000; Dir, Operational and Internat. Humanitarian Law, MoD, 2002–05; Dep. Counsel, Office of Counsel to the Speaker of the H of C, 2005–08; Chm., Competition Appeal Tribunal, 2005–13; Judge, First-tier Tribunal, Charity Jurisdiction, 2005–13, Envmt Jurisdiction, 2010–13; a Recorder, 2009–13; a Dep. High Court Judge, Chancery Div., 2012–13. *Publications:* (ed) Bellamy and Child, 4th edn, Common Market Law of Competition, 1993; (ed with Hon. Mr Justice Roth) Bellamy and Child, 6th edn, European Community Law of Competition, 2007; (ed with David Bailey) Bellamy and Child, 7th edn, European Union Law of Competition, 2013. *Recreations:* theatre and cinema, choral singing. *Address:* Royal Courts of Justice, 7 Rolls Building, Fetter Lane, EC4A 1NL.

ROSEBERY, 7th Earl of, *cr* 1703; **Neil Archibald Primrose;** DL; Bt 1651; Viscount of Rosebery, Baron Primrose and Dalmeny, 1700; Viscount of Inverkeithing, Baron Dalmeny and Primrose, 1703; Baron Rosebery (UK), 1828; Earl of Midlothian, Viscount Mentmore, Baron Epsom, 1911; *b* 11 Feb. 1929; *o* surv. *s* of 6th Earl of Rosebery, KT, PC, DSO, MC, and Eva Isabel Marian (Eva Countess of Rosebery, DBE) (*d* 1987), *d* of 2nd Baron Aberdare; *S* father, 1974; *m* 1955, Alison Mary Deirdre, *d* of late Ronald William Reid, MS, FRCS; one *s* four *d*. *Educ:* Stowe; New Coll., Oxford. DL Midlothian, 1960. *Heir:* *s* Lord Dalmeny, *qv*. *Address:* Dalmeny House, South Queensferry, West Lothian EH30 9TQ.

ROSEN, Alan Peter; Headteacher, Aylesbury High School, since 2005 (Deputy Headteacher, 1995–2005); *b* Edgware, Middx, 27 June 1955; *s* of M. and R. Rosen; *m* 1977, Janet; one *s* one *d*. *Educ:* Haberdashers' Aske's Sch., Elstree; Univ. of Wales, Aberystwyth (BSc Hons Maths and Computer Sci. 1976; PGCE 1977); Hatfield Poly. (MEd Classroom Processes 1989). NPQH 2001. Teacher, Hatfield Sch., Hatfield, 1977–83; Hd of IT, Astley Cooper Sch., Hemel Hempstead, 1983–89; Curriculum Manager, Maths, Sci. and Technol., Westfield Sch., Watford, 1989–95. *Recreations:* World Challenge Expedition Leader, orienteering—national and international competitor, controller (referee) of 1999 World Championships and 2005 World Cup. *Address:* c/o Aylesbury High School, Walton Road, Aylesbury, Bucks HP21 7SX. *T:* (01296) 388222, *Fax:* (01296) 388200. *E:* secretary@ahs.bucks.sch.uk.

ROSEN, Howard John, CBE 2003; Founder and Principal, Howard Rosen Solicitors, since 1989; Managing Director, Rosetrust AG, since 1993; *b* London, 14 April 1955; *s* of Leonard Sidney Rosen and Betty Clarissa Rosen; *m* 1985, Michelle Anne Oberman; two *s*. *Educ:* Braintcroft Primary Sch.; City of London Sch.; Exeter Coll., Oxford (BA Juris. 1978; MA). Admitted solicitor, 1980; Asst Solicitor, Tarlo Lyons & Aukin, 1980; UK Counsel, United Leasing plc, 1980–82; European Gen. Counsel, Equilease Gp, 1982–88. Chm., Rail Wkg Gp, 1995–; Corresp., UNIDROIT, 2001–. Pres., British-Swiss Chamber of Commerce, 1998–2003 (Hon. Life Councillor, 2013); Pres., Council of British Chamber of Commerce in Europe, 2005–12 (Chm., Public Affairs Commn, 2006–). Member: Law Soc. of England and Wales; Internat. Bar Assoc.; Soc. of Trust and Estate Practitioners; MInstD. *Publications:* (ed) Leasing Law in the European Union, 1994; contribs to Asset Finance and Leasing Digest, Leasing World, Internat. Financial Law Rev., UK Law Soc. Gazette, Private Client Business, Uniform Law Rev., Trust and Trustees, Railways of the World, Eur. Rev. of Private Law. *Recreations:* ski-ing, singing, football, aquarist. *Address:* Howard Rosen Solicitors, Baarerstrasse 98, PO Box 2258, 6302 Zug, Switzerland. *T:* (41) 7602888, *Fax:* (41) 7602909. *E:* howard.rosen@legalease.ch. *Club:* Baur au Lac (Zurich).

ROSEN, Rabbi Jeremy, PhD; Professor of Jewish Studies, Faculty for Comparative Study of Religions, Wilrijk, Belgium, since 1991 (President, 1994–2015); Scholar in Residence, Jewish Community Center, New York, since 2008; Rabbi, Persian Jewish Community, New York, since 2009; *b* 11 Sept. 1942; *s* of Rabbi Kopul Rosen and Bella Rosen; *m* 1st, 1971, Vera Giuditta Zippel (marr. diss. 1987); two *s* two *d*; 2nd, 1988, Suzanne Kaszirer. *Educ:* Carmel Coll.; Pembroke Coll., Cambridge (MA); Mir Academy, Jerusalem. Minister, Bulawayo Hebrew Congregation, Rhodesia, 1966; Minister, Giffnock Hebrew Congregation, Scotland, 1968–71; Headmaster, 1971–84, Principal, 1983–84, Carmel Coll.; Minister, Western Synagogue, subseq. (following amalgamation in 1990 with Marble Arch Synagogue) Marble Arch Western Synagogue, 1985–93; Principal, Yakar Study Centre, London, 1999–2007. Chief Rabbi's Rep. on Inter-Faith Affairs, 1987–91. Mem. Bd, Centre Européen Juif d'Information, Brussels, 1991–97. Trustee, Yakar Educn Foundn, 1990–2000. *Publications:* Exploding Myths that Jews Believe, 2001; Understanding Judaism, 2003; Beyond the Pulpit, 2005; Kabbalah, 2005; Right or Right: how to reconcile religion with rationality, 2013. *Address:* 1965 Broadway, Apt 30e, New York, NY 10023, USA. *T:* (212) 7217502. *E:* jeremyrosen@msn.com. *W:* www.jeremyrosen.com.

ROSEN, Prof. Michael, CBE 1990; FRCA; FRCOG; FRCS; Consultant Anaesthetist, South Glamorgan Health Authority, since 1961; Hon. Professor, University of Wales College of Medicine, 1986–93; President, College of Anaesthetists, 1988–91 (Dean of the Faculty of Anaesthetists, Royal College of Surgeons, 1988); *b* 17 Oct. 1927; *s* of Israel Rosen and Lily Hyman; *m* 1955, Sally Cohen; two *s* one *d*. *Educ:* Dundee High Sch. (Dux, 1944); St Andrews Univ. (MB ChB 1949). FRCA (FFARCS 1957); FRCOG 1989; FRCS 1994. House appts, Bolton, Portsmouth and Bradford, 1949–52; served RAMC, 1952–54; Registrar Anaesthetist, Royal Victoria Infirmary, Newcastle upon Tyne, 1954–57; Sen. Registrar, Cardiff, 1957–60; Fellow, Case Western Reserve Univ., Ohio, 1960–61. Member: GMC, 1989–; Clinical Standards Adv. Gp, 1991–94. Mem. Bd, College (formerly Faculty) of Anaesthetists, RCS, 1978–94; Pres., Assoc. of Anaesthetists of GB and Ire, 1986–88 (Mem. Council, 1972–91; formerly Sec. and Treasurer); Founder Academician, European Acad. of Anaesthesiol., 1972 (Treas., 1985–91; Hon. Mem., 1996); Chairman: Obstetric Anaesthesia Cttee, World Fedn of Socs of Anaesthesia, 1980–88; World Fedn of Socs of Anaesthesia Foundn, 2000–04; Exec. Officer and Treas., World Fedn of Socs of Anesthesiologists, 1992–2000. Hon. Mem., French and Australian Socs of Anaesthetists; Hon. FFARCSI 1990; Hon. Fellow, Acad. of Medicine, Malaysia, 1989. Hon. LLD Dundee, 1996. Sir Ivan Magill Gold Medal, Assoc. of Anaesthetists, 1993. *Publications:* Percutaneous Cannulation of Great Veins, 1981, 2nd edn 1992; Obstetric Anaesthesia and Analgesia: safer practice, 1982; Patient-Controlled Analgesia, 1984; Tracheal Intubation, 1985; Awareness and Pain in General Anaesthesia, 1987; Ambulatory Anaesthesia, 1991; Quality Measures for the Emergency Services, 2001; Current Usage of Patient-Controlled Analgesia, 2009. *Recreations:* family, reading, opera, bridge, exercise. *Address:* 45 Hollybush Road, Cardiff CF23 6TZ. *T:* and *Fax:* (029) 2075 3893. *E:* rosen@mrosen.plus.com.

ROSEN, Michael Wayne, PhD; FRSL; poet and author; Children's Laureate, 2007–09; BBC Radio presenter, since 1989; *b* 7 May 1946; *s* of Harold Rosen and Connie Ruby Isakofsky; *m* 1st, 1976, Susanna Steele (marr. diss. 1987); one *s* (and one *s* decd); 2nd, 1987, Geraldine Clark (marr. diss. 1997); one *s*, and two step *d*; 3rd, 2003, Emma-Louise Williams; one *s* one *d*. *Educ:* Wadham Coll., Oxford (BA); Reading Univ. (MA); Univ. of N London (PhD 1997). BBC general trainee, 1969–73; freelance, 1973–, incl. BBC Radio 4, World Service, Radio 3; Word of Mouth, Radio 4, 1998–; On Being Selfish, Radio 4, 2004; Dons and Dragons, Radio 4, 2006; The People in the Playground Revisited, Radio 4, 2008. Guest Dir, Brighton Fest., 2013. Prof. of Children's Lit., Goldsmiths, Univ. of London, 2013–. Film, Under the Cranes, 2011. FEA 2006. DUniv Open, 2005; Hon. DLitt: Exeter, 2007; Tavistock and Portman NHS Foundn Trust/UEL, 2008. Sunday Times NUS Drama Fest. Award for Best New Play, 1968; Glenfiddich Award for Best Radio Programme on subject of food, 1996; Eleanor Farjeon Award for Distinguished Services to Children's Literature, 1997; Sony Radio Acad. Short Form Award for On Saying Goodbye, 2003. Chevalier, Ordre des Arts et des Lettres (France), 2008. *Publications:* include: Backbone, 1968; Mind Your Own Business, 1974; Quick, Let's Get Out of Here, 1983; Don't put Mustard in the Custard, 1985; The Hypnotiser, 1988; We're Going on a Bear Hunt, 1989 (Smarties Award for Best Children's Book of Year, 1990); You Wait Till I'm Older Than You, 1996; Michael Rosen's Book of Nonsense, 1997; (ed) Classic Poetry, 1998; Rover, 1999; Centrally Heated Knickers, 2000; Shakespeare, His Work and His World, 2001; Carrying the Elephant, 2002; Oww!, 2003; This Is Not My Nose, 2004; Howler, 2004; Michael Rosen's Sad Book, 2004 (Exceptional Award, English Assoc.); Shakespeare's Romeo and Juliet, 2004; Totally Wonderful Miss Plumberry, 2006; Mustard, Custard, Grumble Belly and Gravy, 2006; Fighters for Life, 2007; Selected Poems, 2007; What's so Special about Shakespeare?, 2007; What's so Special about Dickens?, 2007; The Bear in the Cave, 2007; Dear Mother Goose, 2008; Tiny Little Fly, 2010; Even My Ears Are Smiling, 2011; Fantastic Mr Dahl, 2012; Alphabetical, 2013; Good Ideas: how to be your child's (and your own) best teacher, 2014; A Great Big Cuddle: poems for the very young, 2015; Uncle Gobb and the Dread Shed, 2015. *Recreations:* Arsenal Football Club, politics, general arts. *Address:* c/o United Agents, 12–26 Lexington Street, W1F 0LE.

ROSEN, Miriam Catherine, CB 2012; Executive Director, 2009–10, HM Chief Inspector, 2011, Office for Standards in Education, Children's Services and Skills; Consultant, Ark Schools, 2012–15; *b* Manchester, 24 July 1949; *d* of late Charles Bescoby and Bessie Bescoby; *m* 1976, David Leon Rosen. *Educ:* Friends' Sch., Ackworth; Bangor Univ. (BSc Hons 1970); Univ. of Bath (PGCE 1973); Thames Poly. (Postgrad. Cert. Physics for Teachers). VSO teacher, Kenya, 1970–72; Science Teacher, Wheatley Park Sch., 1973–76; Hd of Biology, St Paul's Way Sch., 1976–79; Hd of Biology, then Actg Hd of Sci., Haverstock Sch., 1980–86; Hd, Sci. Faculty, Morecambe High Sch., 1986–89; Sci. Adv. Teacher, Lancs, 1989–90; HMI, DES, then Ofsted, 1991–2010; Dir, Educn, Ofsted, 2004–09. *Recreations:* running, orienteering, theatre, natural history. *Address:* 27 Beech Road, Halton, Lancaster LA2 6QQ. *T:* (01524) 811553. *Club:* Thames Hare and Hounds.

ROSEN, Murray Hilary; QC 1993; a Recorder, since 2000; a Deputy High Court Judge, Chancery Division, since 2014; arbitrator and mediator; *b* 26 Aug. 1953; *s* of Joseph and Mercia Rosen; *m* 1975, Lesley Samuels; one *s* three *d*. *Educ:* St Paul's Sch.; Trinity Coll., Cambridge (MA). FCIArb 1999. Called to the Bar, Inner Temple, 1976; Mem., Lincoln's Inn *ad eundem*, Bencher, 2004; Head of Chambers, 11 Stone Buildings, 2000–04; admitted Solicitor, 2006; Partner, Herbert Smith Freehills (formerly Herbert Smith), 2006–14 (Hd, Advocacy Unit, 2006–13). Panel Arbitrator, Sports Resolution, 1997–; Panel Deemster, Isle of Man, 2012–. Accredited mediator (ADR Gp, 1989, CEDR, 2013). Chairman: Bar Sports Law Gp, 1998–2001; British Assoc. for Sport and Law, 2003–06. *Recreations:* books, arts, sports. *Address:* 4 New Square, Lincoln's Inn, WC2A 3RJ.

ROSENBAUM, Martin George; Executive Producer, BBC Political Programmes, since 2004; specialist in freedom of information and data journalism; *b* London, 29 July 1959; *s* of Laurie Rosenbaum and Olga Rosenbaum (*née* Kochan); *m* 1992, Jane Ashley; two *s* one *d*. *Educ:* University College Sch., London; King's Coll., Cambridge (BA Maths, Philos. 1981); Univ. of Warwick (MA Philos. 1982); Green Coll., Oxford (Reuters Fellow 2004). Social action campaigner, 1983–90; freelance journalist and author, 1990–98; Radio Producer, BBC News, 1998–2003. Mem., ESRC, 2012–. *Publications:* From Soapbox to Soundbite: party political campaigning in Britain since 1945, 1997; Britain and Europe: the choices we face, 2001. *Address:* BBC Political Programmes Department, 4 Millbank, SW1P 3JQ. *T:* (020) 7973 6132. *E:* martin.rosenbaum@bbc.co.uk.

ROSENBERG, Michael Anthony; a District Judge (Magistrates' Courts) (formerly Provincial Stipendiary Magistrate), South Yorkshire, 1993–2011; *b* 6 March 1943; *s* of late Harry Rosenberg and Gertrude Rosenberg (*née* Silver); *m* 1969, Gillian Anne Wolff; two *s*. *Educ:* Hymers Coll., Hull; Law Soc. Joined Myer Wolff & Co., Hull, 1961: articled clerk, 1963–68; qualified as solicitor, 1969; Asst Solicitor, 1970–73; Jt Sen. Partner, 1973–93. *Recreations:* sport, gardening, music, humour. *Address:* The Old School House, Main Road, Scalby, Gilberdyke, E Yorks HU15 2UU.

ROSENBERG, Pierre Max; Officier de la Légion d'honneur, 2005; Member, Académie française, since 1995; President-Director, Louvre Museum, Paris, 1994–2001; *b* Paris, 13 April 1936; *s* of Charles Rosenberg and Gertrude (*née* Nassauer); *m* 1981, Béatrice de Rothschild; one *d*. *Educ:* Lycée Charlemagne, Paris; Law Faculty, Paris (Licence); Louvre Sch., Paris (Dip.). Chief Curator, Dept of Paintings, Louvre Mus., 1982–94. Member: Hist. of French Art Soc. (Pres., 1982–84); French Hist. of Art Cttee (Pres., 1984–96). *Publications:* Chardin, 1979, 2nd edn 1999; Peyron, 1983; Watteau, 1984; Fragonard, 1987; La Hyre, 1988; Les frères Le Nain, 1993; Poussin, 1994; Watteau: catalogue raisonné des dessins, 1996; Georges de la Tour, 1997; exhibn catalogues. *Address:* 35 rue de Vaugirard, 75006 Paris, France.

ROSENBERG, Richard Morris; Chairman and Chief Executive Officer, BankAmerica Corporation and Bank of America NT&SA, 1990–96; *b* 21 April 1930; *s* of Charles Rosenberg and Betty (*née* Peck); *m* 1956, Barbara C. Cohen; two *s*. *Educ:* Suffolk Univ. (BS 1956); Golden Gate Univ. (MBA 1962; LLB 1966). Served from Ensign to Lieut, USNR, 1953–59. Publicity Assistant, Crocker-Anglo Bank, San Francisco, 1959–62; Wells Fargo Bank: Banking Services Officer, 1962–65; Asst Vice Pres., 1965–68; Vice Pres., Marketing Dept, 1968; Vice Pres., Dir of Marketing, 1969; Sen. Vice Pres., Marketing and Advertising Div., 1970–75; Exec. Vice Pres., 1975–80; Vice Chm., 1980–83; Vice Chm., Crocker Nat. Corp., 1983–85; Pres., Chief Op. Officer and Dir, Seafirst Corp., 1986–87; Pres. and Chief Op. Officer, Seattle-First Nat. Bank, 1985–87; Vice Chm., BankAmerica Corp., 1987–90. Mem. Bd, Forbes.com, 2003–. Past Director: Airborne Express; Northrop Corp.; SBC Communications; past Chm., Mastercard Internat. Director: Buck Inst. for Age Res.; Health Care Property Investors Inc.; San Francisco Symphony; Naval War Coll. Foundn; Chairman: UCSF Foundn; Exec. Council, Univ. of Calif Med. Center. Mem., Bd of Trustees, CIT. Mem., State Bar of Calif. Jewish. *Recreation:* avid reader of history. *Address:* BankAmerica Corporation, 555 California Street CA5–705–11–01, San Francisco, CA 94104, USA. *T:* (415) 9537963. *Club:* St Francis Yacht (San Francisco).

ROSENBLATT, Ian Isaac; Founder and Senior Partner, Rosenblatt Solicitors, since 1989; Co-Founder, Redleaf Communications, since 2000; *b* Liverpool, 2 Nov. 1959; *s* of Eliot and Ruth Rosenblatt; *m* 2007, Emma Kane; two *s* one *d*, and one step *s* one step *d*. *Educ:* Liverpool Coll.; London Sch. of Econs and Pol Sci. (LLB Hons). Articled clerk, Collyer-Bristow, 1981–83; admitted Solicitor, 1983; Sheridans, 1983–89 (Partner, 1985). Hon. Co-Treas., Royal Philharmonic Soc., 2008–. Founder: Rosenblatt Recital Series, 1999–; Branscombe Fest., 2013–. Trustee, Susan Chilcott Scholarship, 2007–. Owner, Les Aldrich Music Shop, 2013–. *Recreations:* opera, art, family, working in Les Aldrich. *Address:* 9–13 St Andrew Street, EC4A 3AF. *T:* (020) 7955 1462. *E:* ianr@rosenblatt-law.co.uk.

ROSENCRANTZ, Claudia Emma, (Mrs Daniel Abineri); Chief Executive Officer, Jamie Oliver Media Group, since 2015; *b* 23 June 1959; *d* of late Alfred Rosenkranz and Leonore (*née* Meyer); *m* 1998, Daniel Abineri; one *d*. *Educ:* Queen's Coll., London; French Inst., London. Picture editor and journalist, The Telegraph Sunday Mag., Sunday Mag., and Elle, 1979–86; TV Researcher, LWT, An Audience with Victoria Wood, Dame Edna Experience, 1986; Producer: Dame Edna Experience, 1989; Incredibly Strange Film Shows, A Late Lunch with Les, An Audience with Jackie Mason, A Night on Mount Etna, 1990 (Golden Rose of Montreux, 1991); Dame Edna's Hollywood, Edna Time, Tantrums and Tiaras; Creator and Producer, Dame Edna's Neighbourhood Watch, 1992; Exec. Producer, Don't Forget Your Toothbrush, 1994; Exec. Producer, BBC, 1994–95; Controller of Entertainment, ITV Network, 1995–2006; Director of Programming: Living TV, 2006–11; FTN, 2006–07; Dir of Television, Living TV Gp (formerly Virgin Media TV), 2007–11; Dir of Progs, Fresh One Prodns, 2012–15. Responsible for commissioning over 600 progs a year, incl. Who Wants to be a Millionaire (Best Light Entertainment Prog., BAFTA, 1999 and 2000), Popstars (Silver Rose of Montreux, 2001), Pop Idol (Best Entertainment Prog., TRIC Awards, 2002; Lew Grade Award for Entertainment Prog. or Series, BAFTA 2002), I'm a Celebrity… Get Me Out of Here! (BAFTA 2003), Ant and Dec's Saturday Night Takeaway, The X Factor, Hell's Kitchen, Dancing on Ice, TV Burp, Dating in the Dark (Best Multi-Channel Prog., RTS Award, 2009). FRTS 2004. Woman of the Year, 2003. *Address:* Fresh One Productions, 19–21 Nile Street, N1 7LL.

ROSENFELD, Alfred John, CB 1981; Deputy Secretary, 1979–82, and Principal Finance Officer, 1976–82, Department of Transport; *b* 27 Feb. 1922; *s* of late Ernest Rosenfeld and late Annie Jeanette Rosenfeld (*née* Samson); *m* 1955, Mary Elisabeth (*née* Prudence); two *s* one *d*. *Educ:* Leyton County High Sch. Entered Public Trustee Office, 1938. Served War, Fleet Air Arm, 1942–46. Min. of Civil Aviation, 1947 (later, Min. of Transport, and Dept of Environment); Private Sec. to Jt Parliamentary Sec., 1958–59; Asst Sec., 1967; Under-Sec., 1972. Special Advr to Envmt Cttee, H of C, 1983–96. Mem., Shoreham Port Authority, 1983–92 (Dep. Chm., 1984–89; Chm., 1990–92). *Recreations:* chess, bridge, gardening, cherishing grandchildren. *Address:* 33 Elmfield Road, Chingford, E4 7HT. *T:* (020) 8529 8160.

ROSENKRANZ, Franklin Daniel, (Danny); Chief Executive, BOC Group plc, 1996–99; Chairman, 4C Associates, since 2010; *b* 28 May 1945; *s* of Manfred and Hendel Rosenkranz; *m* 1990, Catherine Ann Eisenklam. *Educ:* UMIST (BSc Chem. Engrg 1967); Univ. of Waterloo, Canada (MASc 1969); Manchester Business Sch. (DipBA 1970). Plessey Radar, 1970–73; BOC, later BOC Group plc: Monitoring Manager, 1973–74; Business Manager, Industrial, Sparklets, 1974–76; UK Manager, 1976–78, Gen. Manager, 1978–81, BOC Sub Ocean Services; Business Develt Dir, 1982–83, Man. Dir, 1983–90, Edwards High Vacuum; Chief Exec., Vacuum Technology and Distribution Services, 1990–94; Man. Dir, 1994–96; Dir, 1994–99. Non-exec. Dir, 3i, 2000–07. *Recreations:* reading, music, theatre, sport, gardening.

ROSENTHAL, Jim; presenter, ITV Sport, 1980–2012; lead presenter, Box Nation, since 2011; *b* 6 Nov. 1947; *s* of late Albi and Maud Rosenthal; *m* 1987, Chrissy (*née* Smith); one *s*. *Educ:* Magdalen College Sch., Oxford. Oxford Mail and Times, 1968–72; BBC Radio Birmingham, 1972–76; BBC Radio Sports Unit, 1976–80; presenter: Sport on Two; Sports Report; World Cup, and Wimbledon, 1978; host, FA Cup draw, 2008–12; award-winning Formula One coverage, ITV Sport, 1997–2005; Rugby World Cup, 1999, 2003 and 2007; ITV Boxing and World Cup, 2006 and 2010; eight football World Cups; Five Europa League coverage, 2010–12; presenter: Rugby World Cup, OSN Sports, Dubai, 2011, 2015; British Lions tests, Australia, OSN, 2013; Matchday Live Football League Files (series), MUTV. Dir, Oxford United FC, 2011–12. Sports Presenter of the Year, TRIC, 1990, RTS, 1997, 1999. *Recreation:* still trying to drag my body round football and cricket pitches! *Address:* Saxons Productions, 714 Balmoral, 2 Praed Street, W2 1JL. *E:* Jim.Rosenthal@btinternet.com. *Clubs:* Lord's Taverners; Oxford United Football; NY.

ROSENTHAL, Maureen Diane, (Mrs J. M. Rosenthal); *see* Lipman, M. D.

ROSENTHAL, Sir Norman Leon, Kt 2007; freelance curator and art consultant; Exhibitions Secretary, Royal Academy of Arts, 1977–2008; *b* 8 Nov. 1944; *s* of Paul Rosenthal and Kate Zucker; *m* 1989, Manuela Beatriz Mena Marques, *d* of Francisco Mena and Manuela Marques de Mena, Madrid; two *d*. *Educ:* Westminster City Grammar School; University of Leicester. BA Hons History. Librarian, Thomas Agnew & Sons, 1966–68; Exhibitions Officer, Brighton Museum and Art Gallery, 1970–71; Exhibition Organiser, ICA, 1974–76; organiser of many exhibns including: Art into Society, ICA, 1974; A New Spirit in Painting, RA, 1981; Zeitgeist, West Berlin, 1982; German Art of the Twentieth Century, RA, London and Staatsgalerie, Stuttgart, 1985–86; Italian Art of the Twentieth Century, RA, 1989; Metropolis, Berlin, 1991; American Art in the Twentieth Century, Martin-Gropius Bau, Berlin, and RA, 1993; at Royal Academy: Charlotte Salomon, 1998; Apocalypse, 2000; Frank Auerbach, The Genius of Rome 1592–1628, Botticelli's Dante, 2001; Paris: capital of the arts 1900–1968, Return of the Buddha, The Galleries Show, The Aztecs, 2002; Masterpieces from Dresden, Kirchner: expressionism and the city, 2003; Illuminating the Renaissance: the triumph of Flemish manuscript painting in Europe, The Art of Philip Guston 1913–1980, 2004; Turks: a journey of a thousand years 600–1600, Edvard Munch by Himself, China: the three emperors 1662–1795, 2005; Jacob van Ruisdael: master of landscape, Modigliani and His Models, USA Today: new American art from the Saatchi Gallery, 2006; Georg Baselitz Retrospective, 2007; Empire State: New York Art Now, PalaExpo, Rome, 2013; Anish Kapoor, Martin-Gropius Bau, Berlin, 2013. TV and radio broadcasts on contemporary art. Member: Opera Bd, Royal Opera House, 1994–98; Bd, Palazzo Grassi, Venice, 1995; Comité Scientifique, Réunion des Musées Nationaux, Paris, 2005; Trustee, Thyssen Bornemisza Foundn, 2002–12; Baltic Centre for Contemporary Art, Gateshead, 2004–. Hon. Fellow RCA, 1987. Hon. DLitt: Southampton, 2003; Leicester, 2006. German British Forum Award, 2003. Cavaliere Ufficiale, Order of Merit (Italy), 1992; Cross, Order of Merit (Germany), 1993; Officier, l'Ordre des Arts et des Lettres (France), 2003 (Chevalier, 1987); Order of Aztec Eagle (Mexico), 2006. *Publications:* The History of the Saatchi Gallery, 2011; Jeff Koons: conversations with Sir Norman Rosenthal, 2014; contribs to exhibn catalogues. *Recreations:* classical and contemporary music, particularly opera.

ROSER, Air Vice-Marshal Phillip Wycliffe, CB 2003; MBE 1983; Senior Directing Staff, Royal College of Defence Studies, 1999–2003, retired; *b* 11 July 1948; *s* of George Alfred Roser and Margaret Elizabeth Roser; *m* 1974, Andrea Jean Dobbin; one *s* one *d*. *Educ:* Thetford Grammar Sch.; RAF Coll., Cranwell; RAF Staff Coll., Bracknell. Qualified Weapons Instructor, 1974; Fighter Pilot, Lightning, Phantom, Tornado F3, 1970–94; on staff, MoD, 1979–83; MA to Minister for Armed Forces, MoD, 1983–85; OC 111(F) Sqdn, 1985–87; Operational Staff, Strike Comd, 1987–91; OC RAF Leeming, N Yorks, 1992–94; UK Liaison Officer, HQ US European Comd, Stuttgart, 1994–95; rcds 1996; Air Ops Staff, NATO, Sarajevo, 1996–97; NATO Staff, Heidelberg and Ramstein, Germany, 1997–98; Dep. UK Mil. Rep., HQ NATO, Brussels, 1998–99. Trustee, RAF Benevolent Fund, 2000–03. *Recreations:* golf, hill-walking, home maintenance, gardening, photography, woodwork. *Address:* c/o Lloyds Bank, Cox's and King's Branch, 8–10 Waterloo Place, SW1Y 4BE. *Club:* Royal Air Force (Chm., 2000–03).

ROSEVEARE, Nicholas William, MBE 1997; Chief Executive, Mines Advisory Group (MAG), since 2011; *b* Washington, DC, 3 May 1961; *s* of Robert William Roseveare, *qv*; *m* 1999, Caroline Mary Allison; two *s*. *Educ:* Bedford Sch., Bedford; Univ. of Newcastle upon Tyne (BA Hons Combined Arts 1982). Performing arts mgt, 1982–88; Oxfam: various internat. positions, Sudan, Ethiopia, Mozambique, 1988–2004; Humanitarian Dir, 2004–08; Chief Exec., British Overseas NGOs in Development, 2008–11. *Recreations:* hill walking, theatre, film, poetry, France. *Address:* MAG, Suite 3A, 11 Peter Street, Manchester M2 5QR.

ROSEVEARE, Robert William, CBE 1977; Secretary, 1967–83, and Managing Director, Policy Co-ordination, 1973–83, British Steel Corporation; *b* Mandalay, Burma, 23 Aug. 1924; *s* of W. L., (Bill), Roseveare, MC and Marjory Roseveare; *m* 1954, Patricia Elizabeth, *d* of Guy L. Thompson, FRCS, Scarborough; one *s* three *d*. *Educ:* Gresham's Sch., Holt; University Coll., Oxford (Naval short course, 1943); St John's Coll., Cambridge (BA 1948). Served in Fleet Air Arm (Observer), 1943–46. Entered Home Civil Service, 1949. Asst Private Sec. to Minister of Fuel and Power, 1952–54; Cabinet Office, 1958–60; British Embassy, Washington, 1960–62; Asst Sec., Ministry of Power, 1964; seconded to Organising Cttee for British Steel Corporation, 1966; left Civil Service, 1971; Dir, 1969–71, Man. Dir, Corporate Admin, 1971–73, BSC. Mem. Council, CBI, 1969–83. Non-exec. Dir, Community Industry Ltd, 1983–91. Member: St Albans Bishops Council, 1983–85; Exec. Cttee, Hereford Diocesan Bd of Finance, 1986–95. Churchwarden, St John's, Harpenden, 1971–76. *Recreations:* hill-walking, bird-watching, music. *Address:* 38 Denehurst Court, Shrewsbury Road, Church Stretton, Shropshire SY6 6EQ. *T:* (01694) 723233.

See also N. W. Roseveare.

ROSEWARN, John; Secretary, Royal Institution of Naval Architects, 1989–97; *b* 14 Jan. 1940; *s* of Ernest and Frances Beatrice Rosewarn; *m* 1963, Josephine Rita Mullis; two *s*. *Educ:* Westminster City Sch. Royal Institution of Naval Architects, 1958–97: Administrator, 1958–65; Chief Clerk, 1965–75; Asst Sec., 1975–84; Sen. Asst Sec., 1984–89. Freeman, City of London, 1976. *Recreations:* sailing, DIY, reading. *Address:* Little Fisher Farm, South Mundham, Chichester, West Sussex PO20 1ND.

ROSEWELL, Bridget Clare, OBE 2013; Senior Adviser, Volterra Partners, since 2014 (Chairman, 2011–14); *b* 19 Sept. 1951; *d* of Geoffrey Noel Mills and Helen Handescombe Mills; divorced; one *s* one *d*. *Educ:* Wimbledon High Sch.; St Hugh's Coll., Oxford (MA, MPhil). Tutor and Lectr in Econs, St Hilda's and Oriel Colls, Oxford, 1976–84; Dep. Dir, Econs, CBI, 1984–86; Chief European Economist, Wharton Econometric Forecasting Associates (WEFA), 1986–88; Founder and Chm., Business Strategies Ltd, 1988–2000; Chm., Volterra Consulting, 1999–2011. Consultant Chief Economist, GLA, 2002–08. Non-executive Director: Britannia Building Soc., 1999–; DWP, 2003–05; Network Rail, 2011–; Ulster Bank Gp, 2012–; Atom Bank, 2014–. Member: Forum UK, 1990–; Internat. Women's Forum, 1990–. FRSA 1991; FICE 2013. *Publications:* Reinventing London, 2013; pamphlets and contribs on econs to press and econ. jls. *Recreations:* hill walking, picture framing, yoga, curiosity. *Address:* Volterra Partners LLP, 56-58 Putney High Street, SW15 1SF. *T:* (020) 8878 6333, *Fax:* (020) 8878 6685. *E:* brosewell@volterra.co.uk.

ROSIER, Rt Rev. Stanley Bruce, AM 1987; Rector of St Oswald's, Parkside, Diocese of Adelaide, 1987–94, retired; *b* 18 Nov. 1928; *s* of S. C. and A. Rosier; *m* 1954, Faith Margaret Alice Norwood (*d* 2006); one *s* three *d*. *Educ:* Univ. of WA; Christ Church, Oxford. Asst Curate, Ecclesall, Dio. of Sheffield, 1954; Rector of: Wyalkatchem, Dio. of Perth, 1957; Kellerberrin Dio. of Perth, 1964; Auxiliary Bishop in Diocese of Perth, Western Australia, 1967–70; Bishop of Willochra, 1970–87. *Recreation:* natural history. *Address:* 5A Fowlers Road, Glenunga, SA 5064, Australia. *T:* (8) 83382019.

ROSIN, (Richard) David, FRCS, FRCSE; Consultant in General Surgery and Surgical Oncology, St Mary's Hospital, London, 1979–2007, now Honorary; Honorary Consultant, Imperial College School of Medicine, since 2007; Professor of Surgery, University of the West Indies, Cavehill Campus, Barbados, since 2008; *b* 29 April 1942; *s* of late Isadore Rowland Rosin and Muriel Ena Rosin (*née* Wolff); *m* 1971, Michele Shirley Moreton (marr. diss. 2009); one *s* two *d*. *Educ:* St George's Jesuit Coll., Zimbabwe; Westminster Hosp. Sch. of Medicine, Univ. of London (MB, MS); DHMSA 2003. Westminster Hospital: House Physician, subseq. House Surg., 1966–67; Sen. House Officer in Clin. Pathology, 1968, Surgical Rotation,

1969–71; Sen. Registrar, 1975–79; Ship's Surg., P & O Lines, 1967; Sen. House Officer, Birmingham Accident Hosp., 1969; Registrar: Sutton Hosp., Surrey, 1971–73; St Helier's Hosp., Carshalton, 1973–74; Clin. Asst, St Mark's Hosp., London, 1974–75; Sen. Registrar, Kingston Hosp., 1975–77; Vis. Lectr, Univ. of Hong Kong, 1978–79; Clin. Dir of Surgery, St Charles' Hosp., 1990–92; Chm., Div. of Surgery, St Mary's Hosp., London, 1992–96. Consultant Surg., King Edward VII's Hosp. for Officers, 1995–96. Chm. DTI Cttee, Operating Room of Year 2010, 1995–2000. Regl Advr, NW Thames Region, RCSE, 1990–; Member: Council, RCS, 1994–2006 (Vice-Pres., 2004–05; Sen. Vice-Pres., 2005–06; Penrose-May Tutor, 1985–90; Hunterian Prof., 1987; Lectures: Arris and Gale, 1978; Arnott, 1991; Gordon Gordon Taylor, 2005; Vicary, 2006; Stanford Cade, 2006; Zachary Cope, 2008); RSM, 1975 (Pres., Clin. Section, 1982–83, Surgery Section, 1992–93; Mem. Council, 2002–); Surgical Res. Soc., 1980; British Assoc. of Surgical Oncology, 1980 (Hon. Sec., 1983–86, Vice Pres., 2000–01, Pres., 2002–03); British Soc. of Gastroenterology, 1980; Melanoma Study Gp, 1988 (Hon. Sec., 1986–89, Pres., 1989–92); Soc. of Minimally Invasive Gen. Surgs, 1991 (Founder and Hon. Sec.); Hunterian Soc., 1994; Internat. Coll. of Surgs, 1992–. Chm., Intercollegiate Bd of Surgical Examinations, 2003–. First Pres., Caribbean Soc. Endoscopic Surgeons, 2013–. Fellow: Assoc. of Surgs of GB and Ire., 1975; Assoc. of Endoscopic Surgs of GB and Ire. (Mem. Council, 1995–); Assoc. of Upper Gastro-Intestinal Surgs of GB and Ire., 1997. Mem. Council, Marie Curie Foundn, 1984–92. Sir Ernest Finch Meml Lectr, Sheffield, 2000; G. B. Ong Lectr, Hong Kong Coll. of Surgeons, 2007; British Jl of Surgery Lectr, 2008; Moynihan Lectr, 2012. Freeman, City of London, 1972; Liveryman: Soc. of Apothecaries, 1971; Co. of Barber Surgeons, 1978. Series Ed., Minimal Access textbooks, 1993–; Editor-in-Chief: Internat. Jl of Surgery, 2007–; Internat. Jl of Surgical Case Reports, 2011–. *Publications:* (ed jtly) Cancer of the Bile Ducts and Pancreas, 1989; (ed jtly) Head and Neck Oncology for the General Surgeon, 1991; (ed jtly) Diagnosis and Management of Melanoma in Clinical Practice, 1992; (ed) Minimal Access Medicine and Surgery: principles and practice, 1993; (ed) Minimal Access General Surgery, 1994; (ed) Minimal Access Surgical Oncology, 1995; (co-ed) Minimal Access Thoracic Surgery, 1998; papers in jls and contribs to books. *Recreations:* all sport, particularly golf; opera, music, theatre, history of medicine and surgery, travelling. *Address:* 302 Westcliffe, 1 South Wharf Road, W2 1JB. *T:* (020) 7087 4260; Middle Earth, Richmond, St Joseph, Barbados, West Indies; Queen Elizabeth Hospital, Martindales Road, Bridgetown, Barbados, West Indies. *E:* rdavidrosin@gmail.com, david.rosin@cavehill.uwi.edu. *Clubs:* Garrick, MCC, Royal Society of Medicine; New Zealand Golf (Weybridge); Barbados Cricket Assoc., Barbados Gold, Barbados Turf, Barbados Golf.

ROSINDELL, Andrew; MP (C) Romford, since 2001; *b* Romford, 17 March 1966; *s* of Frederick William Rosindell and Eileen Rosina Rosindell (*née* Clark). *Educ:* Rise Park Jun. and Infant Sch.; Marshalls Park Secondary Sch. Researcher and freelance journalist, and Res. Asst to Vivian Bendall, MP, 1986–97; Dir, 1997–99, Internat. Dir, 1999–2005, Eur. Foundn. Mem., London Accident Prevention Council, 1990–95. Mem. (C) Havering BC, 1990–2002 (Vice-Chm., Housing Cttee, 1996–97; Hon. Alderman, 2007–); Chm., N Romford Community Area Forum, 1998–2002. Contested (C): Glasgow Provan, 1992; Thurrock, 1997. An Opposition Whip, 2005–07; Shadow Home Affairs Minister and spokesman on Animal Welfare, 2007–10; Member: Deregulation and Regulatory Reform Select Cttee, 2001–05; Constitutional Affairs Select Cttee, 2004–05; Foreign Affairs Select Cttee, 2010–; Jt Cttee on Statutory Instruments, 2002–04; NI Grand Cttee, 2006–07; All Party Parliamentary Groups: Secretary: Falkland Is, 2001–; S Pacific Is, 2009–; Belize, 2010–; Jt Chm., British-Swiss, 2010–; Vice-Chairman: Iceland, 2005–; Bermuda, 2005–; Channel Is, 2006–; Madagascar, 2007–; British Indian Ocean Territory (Chagos Is), 2008–; Gibraltar, 2010– (Sec., 2001–02); Queen's Diamond Jubilee, 2010–; Vice Chm. and Sec., Cayman Is, 2010–; Chairman: Montserrat, 2005–; British-Manx (formerly Anglo-Manx), 2005–; Greyhound, 2006–; St George's Day, 2007–; Flags and Heraldry, 2008–; Australia/NZ, 2010– (Sec., 2001–10); Zoos and Aquariums, 2010– (Sec., 2007–10); Canada, 2010– (Sec., 2008–10); British Overseas Territory, 2010–; Turks and Caicos Is, 2010–; Mauritius, 2010–; Pitcairn Is, 2010–; Liechtenstein, 2010– (Sec., 2005–10); Central America, 2011– (Sec., 2010–11); Founding Chm., Polar Regs (Arctic and Antarctic), 2011–14; Co-Chairman: Mongolia, 2010–; St Lucia, 2012–; Treasurer: Danish, 2005– (Jt Treas., 2001–05); Botswana, 2010–; Mem., Panel of Chairs, 2010–. Member: Commonwealth Parly Assoc., 2001– (Mem. Exec. Cttee, 2010–); Inter-Parly Union, 2001– (Mem. Exec. Cttee, 2010–); British-American Parly Gp, 2001–; Adv. Bd, Commonwealth Exchange, 2013–. Fellow, Industry and Parlt Trust India Fellowship, 2009; Mem., British-Irish Parly Assembly, 2010–. Armed Forces Parly Scheme (RM), 2002–03, (RAF), 2005–07, (Army), 2009–13. Chairman: Royal Soc. of St George, Houses of Parlt Br., 2009–; Palace of Westminster Philatelic Soc., 2010–. Sec., Cons. 92 Gp, 2003–06; Mem., No Turning Back Gp. Parly Advr, Guild of Travel and Tourism, 2008–. Joined Cons. Party and Young Conservatives, 1981; Chairman: Romford YC, 1983–84 (Pres., 2006–); Gtr London YC, 1987–88; Nat. YC, 1993–94; Eur. YC, 1993–97; Vice-Pres., Conservative Future, 2013–; Conservative Party: Mem., Nat. Union Exec. Cttee, 1986–88 and 1992–94; Vice-Chm., 2004–05; Pres., Gibraltar Br., 2004–; Chm., Romford Cons. Assoc., 1998–2001. Chm., Cons. Friends of Gibraltar, 2002–, of Australia and NZ, 2010–; Pres., Cons. Friends of Taiwan, 2011–; Member: Cons. Middle East Council, 2005–; Cons. Friends of Israel, 2001–, India, 2005–, America, 2008–; Pres., Cons. Commonwealth Assoc., 2013. Chairman: Internat. Young Democrat Union, 1998–2002; UK-Norfolk Island Friendship Gp, 2009–; Zimbabwe-Rhodesia Relief Fund, 2010–. Pres., Caribbean Young Democrat Union, 2001–; Co-Pres., British-Middle E and N Africa Council, 2012–. Vice-Pres., Constitutional Monarchy Assoc. Member: Council, Freedom Assoc., 2005–; Flag Inst., 2008–; Bd of Govs, Westminster Foundn for Democracy, 2010–; Council, Canada UK Colloquium, 2010–; Hon. Bd Mem., Iman Foundn, 2011–. Pres., Romford Sqdn ATC, 2002–; Hon. Member: HMS Antrim Assoc., 2008–; Romford Lions Club, 2008– (Vice-Pres., 2010–); Burma Star (SW Essex Br.), 2010–; Romford Cons. and Constitutional Club, 2001–; Falkland Is Assoc., 2001–; Vice President: Romford and Dist Scout Assoc., 1995–; Romford RBL Band and Corps of Drums, 2010–; Romford Rotary Club, 2010–; Flag Inst., 2014–. Member: Salvation Army, Romford Citadel, 1973–82; St Edward the Confessor Ch, Romford Market, 1988–; St Alban Protomartyr Ch, Romford, 2001–. Member: RAFA; RBL; Essex Wildlife Trust, 2007–; British Overseas Territories Conservation Forum, 2003–; Trustee, Friends of British Overseas Territories, 2014–. Governor: Bower Park Sch., Romford, 1989–90; Dame Tipping C of E Sch., Havering-atte-Bower, 1990–2002. Vice-Pres., Romford FC; Hon. Mem., Havering-atte-Bower CC. Trustee, Retired Greyhound Trust, 2010–. Patron: Justice for Dogs; Remus Meml Horse Sanctuary, 2005–; Assoc. of British Counties, 2007–; Lennox Children's Cancer Fund, 2009–; Romford Cons. Business and Enterprise Club, 2012–; British Monarchist Soc., 2013–. Hon. Member: Staffs Bull Terrier Club; E Anglian Staffs Bull Terrier Club; Romford Lions, 2007. Freeman, City of London, 2003. *Publications:* (jtly) Defending Our Great Heritage, 1993. *Recreations:* Staffordshire bull terriers, travel, philately, history. *Address:* House of Commons, SW1A 0AA. *T:* (020) 7219 8475; (constituency office) 85 Western Road, Romford, Essex RM1 3LS. *T:* (01708) 766700, (home) (01708) 761186. *E:* andrew@rosindell.com, andrew.rosindell.mp@parliament.uk. *Clubs:* Romford Conservative and Constitutional; Romford Golf (Hon.).

ROSLING, Derek Norman, CBE 1988; FCA; Vice-Chairman, Hanson PLC, 1973–93; *b* 21 Nov. 1930; *s* of Norman and Jean Rosling; *m* 1st (marr. diss. 1982); two *s* one *d*; 2nd, 2000, Julia Catherine Crookston; one step *s*. *Educ:* Shrewsbury Sch. ACA 1955, FCA 1962. Professional practice, 1956–65; Hanson PLC, 1965–94. *Recreations:* golf, sailing, theatre. *Address:* South Hayes, Grove Road, Lymington, Hants SO41 3RN. *T:* (01590) 670201. *Clubs:* Royal Yacht Squadron (Cowes); Royal Southampton Yacht; Brokenhurst Manor Golf; Royal Lymington Yacht.

ROSOFF, Margaret Jill, (Meg); writer, since 2003; *b* Boston, USA, 16 Oct. 1956; *d* of late Dr Chester Rosoff and of Lois Friedman (*née* Goldman); *m* 1990, (David) Paul Hamlyn; one *d*. *Educ:* Harvard Univ. (BA 1979); St Martin's Coll. of Art (Adv. Sculpture course 1978). Editorial Asst, People mag., 1980–82; Copywriter: New York Times, 1982–85; Backer & Spielvogel, 1985–89; Dep. Press Sec., NY State, Democratic presidential campaign, 1988; Copywriter: Young & Rubicam, 1990–93; Ogilvy & Mather, 1994–97; J. Walter Thompson, 1998–2003. *Publications:* How I Live Now, 2004 (filmed, 2013); Meet Wild Boars, 2005; Just In Case, 2006; What I Was, 2007; Jumpy Jack and Googily, 2007; Wild Boars Cook, 2008; The Bride's Farewell, 2009; Vamoose, 2010; There Is No Dog, 2011; Moose Baby, 2012; Picture Me Gone, 2013. *Recreations:* horse riding, misplacing things. *Address:* 140 Aberdeen Park, N5 2BA. *T:* (020) 7226 2353. *E:* meg@megrosoff.co.uk.

ROSPIGLIOSI, family name of **Earl of Newburgh**.

ROSS, Rt Hon. Lord; Donald MacArthur Ross; PC 1985; a Senator of the College of Justice, Scotland, and Lord of Session, 1977–97; Lord Justice-Clerk and President of the Second Division of the Court of Session, 1985–97; Lord High Commissioner, General Assembly, Church of Scotland, 1990 and 1991; *b* 29 March 1927; *s* of late John Ross, solicitor, Dundee; *m* 1958, Dorothy Margaret (*d* 2004), *d* of late William Annand, Kirriemuir; two *d*. *Educ:* Dundee High School; Edinburgh University. MA (Edinburgh) 1947; LLB with distinction (Edinburgh) 1951. National Service with The Black Watch (RHR), 2nd Lt, 1947–49. Territorial Service, 1949–58, Captain. Advocate, 1952; QC (Scotland) 1964; Vice-Dean, Faculty of Advocates of Scotland, 1967–73; Dean, 1973–76; Sheriff Principal of Ayr and Bute, 1972–73. Dep. Chm., Boundary Commn for Scotland, 1977–85. Member: Scottish Cttee of Council on Tribunals, 1970–76; Cttee on Privacy, 1970; Parole Bd for Scotland, 1997–2002; Chm., Judicial Studies Cttee, Scotland, 1997–2001. Mem. Court, Heriot-Watt Univ., 1978–90 (Chm., 1984–90). FRSE 1988 (Mem. Council, 1997–99, Vice Pres., 1999–2002). Hon. LLD: Edinburgh, 1987; Dundee, 1991; Abertay Dundee, 1994; Aberdeen, 1998. DUniv Heriot-Watt, 1988. Bicentenary Medal, RSE, 2004. *Recreations:* gardening, walking, travelling. *Address:* 7/1 Tipperlinn Road, Edinburgh EH10 5ET. *T:* (0131) 447 6771. *E:* RosD33@aol.com. *Club:* New (Edinburgh).

ROSS, Rear Adm. Alastair Boyd, CB 1999; CBE 1995; Clerk to Worshipful Company of Drapers, 2000–12; *b* 29 Jan. 1947; *s* of Joseph Charles Patrick Ross and Shirley Carlile (*née* Stoddart); *m* 1977, Heather Judy Currie; two *d*. *Educ:* Radley Coll.; BRNC, Dartmouth. Joined RN, 1965; commnd 1968; specialised in aviation; flew as Anti-Submarine Warfare helicopter observer, 1970–80; commanded: HMS Brinton, 1977–79; HMS Falmouth, 1983–85; HMS Edinburgh, 1988–89; RCDS 1990; Capt., HMS Osprey, 1991–93; Comdr, NATO Standing Naval Force, Mediterranean (Adriatic Ops), 1993–94; Dir Overseas (ME and Africa), MoD, 1994–96; Asst Dir Ops, Internat. Mil. Staff, NATO HQ, 1996–99. Mem., RNSA, 1984–. Trustee, Portman Estate, 2011–. Freeman, City of London, 2004; Liveryman, Drapers' Co., 2008. Honorary Fellow: Univ. of Wales, Bangor, 2005; QMUL, 2009. *Recreations:* sailing, golf. *Address:* Barn Cottage, Vosporth Hill, Crantock, Newquay, Cornwall TR8 5RQ. *Clubs:* Farmers, Royal Navy of 1765 and 1785, Pratt's.

ROSS, Alastair Ian; Member (DemU) East Antrim, Northern Ireland Assembly, since May 2007; *b* Belfast, 4 March 1981; *s* of Ian and Jennifer Ross; *m* 2010, Shakheera Lee. *Educ:* Friends Grammar Sch., Lisburn; Univ. of Dundee (MA Political Sci.); Queen's Univ., Belfast (MA Irish Politics). Policy Officer, DUP, 2005; Parly researcher for Sammy Wilson, MP, 2005–07. Northern Ireland Assembly: Chm., Cttee for Standards, 2010–14; Private Sec. to Minister for Enterprise, Trade and Investment, 2011–14; Chair, Justice Cttee, 2014–. Mem., NI Policing Bd, 2010–11. *Recreations:* hockey, travel. *Address:* c/o DUP Constituency Office, 31 Lancasterian Street, Carrickfergus BT38 7AB. *T:* (028) 9332 9980. *E:* office@alastairross.org.

ROSS, Alexander, (Sandy); freelance television producer; media consultant; Managing Director, Murrayfield Media Ltd, since 2007; *b* 17 April 1948; *s* of late Alexander Coutts Ross and Charlotte Edwards (*née* Robertson); *m* 1992, Alison Joyce Fraser; two *s* one *d*. *Educ:* Edinburgh Univ. (LLB); Moray House Coll., Edinburgh (Pres., Students' Union, 1977–78; Cert. Youth and Community Work). Articled Solicitor, 1971; Solicitor, 1971–73; Lectr in Law, Paisley Coll., 1975–77; Researcher and Producer, Granada Television, 1978–86; Scottish Television: Controller Entertainment, 1986–97; Dep. Chief Exec., Scottish TV Enterprises, 1997–98; Controller Regional Production, Scottish TV and Grampian TV, Scottish Media Gp, 1998–2000; Controller, 2000; Man. Dir, 2000–04; Man. Dir, Internat. Develt Div., 2004–07. Councillor, Edinburgh Corp., 1971–74; Mem., Edinburgh DC, 1974–78. Dir, Assembly Th., 2004–; Chm., Salford Conf. on Television from Nations and Regions, 2005–. Associate, Adam Smith Coll., Fife, 2010–; Rector's Assessor, Edinburgh Univ., 2015–. Mem., BAFTA, 1990 (Mem., Scotland Cttee, 2004–; Chm., 2004–08, Vice-Chm., 2008–10, BAFTA Scotland). *Recreations:* golf, theatre, music, reading, curling, ski-ing (but never doing the Vallée Blanche run again!). *Address:* 10 Campbell Avenue, Edinburgh EH12 6DS. *T:* (0131) 539 1192, 07803 970107. *E:* sandy.ross@murrayfieldmedia.com. *Clubs:* Oyster (Edinburgh); Haunted Major Golf Society (N Berwick) (Correspondent, 2002–); Glen Golf, Prestonfield Golf, Edinburgh Corporation Golf (Capt., 2012–14); East Linton Curling.

ROSS, Amanda; Joint Managing Director, Cactus TV, since 1994; *b* 4 Aug. 1962; *m* 1990, Simon Ross; two *s*. *Educ:* Univ. of Birmingham (BA Hons Drama and Theatre Arts). Freelance TV producer and presenter, 1984–94; Founder, with Simon Ross, Cactus TV, 1994; programmes produced include: The Roux Scholarship; Roux Legacy; Madhur Jaffrey's Curry Nation; Richard and Judy Live, 2001– (numerous awards incl. Bookseller Expanding Mkt Award, 2007, for Richard and Judy Summer Read; RTS Award for Best Campaign, Lost for Words Season, Channel 4, 2008); Saturday Kitchen Live, 2006– (Best TV Cookery Show, Olive mag., 2007); The TV Book Club; Galaxy Nat. Book Awards; ITV Crime Thriller Season; Ten Mile Menu; Munch Box; Weekend; Spring Kitchen; Christmas Kitchen; Music and Entertainment Specials; numerous cookery series and chat shows. Opened Cactus Kitchens Cookery Sch. with Michel Roux Jr, 2013. Member: BAFTA; RTS. Trustee: Kidscape, 1993–2014 (Ambassador, 2014–); UK Adv. Bd, Room to Read, 2008–14; Ambassador: Wellbeing of Women, 2010–; Nat. Literary Trust, 2010–. Award for Outstanding Contribution to Bookselling, Bookseller, 2009. *Publications:* (ed) Richard and Judy Wine Guide, 2005; Saturday Kitchen Cookbook, 2007, 2013; Saturday Kitchen: best bites, 2008; Saturday Kitchen at Home, 2010; Saturday Kitchen Cooking Bible, 2013; Saturday Kitchen Suppers, 2014. *Recreations:* my two boys, my dog Lulu. *Address:* c/o Cactus, 1 St Luke's Avenue, Clapham, SW4 7LG. *T:* (020) 7091 4900. *Clubs:* Bluebird, Hospital.

ROSS, Lt-Col Sir Andrew (Charles Paterson), 3rd Bt *cr* 1960, of Whetstone, Middlesex; RM; *b* 18 June 1966; *s* of Sir James Keith Ross, 2nd Bt, RD, FRCS, FRCSE and of Jacqueline Annella Ross (*née* Clarke); *S* father, 2003; *m* 1997, Surg. Comdr Sarah Joanne Murray, RN; one *s* one *d*. *Educ:* Sherborne; Plymouth Poly. (BSc). Joined RM, 1988; left RM 2007. Risk and Assce Manager, Royal Dutch Shell. *Recreations:* sailing, hill walking, Telemark ski-ing, Rugby coaching. *Heir:* *s* James Ross, *b* 21 May 1999.

ROSS, Anthony Lee, (Tony); author and illustrator; *b* 10 Aug. 1938; *s* of Eric Turle Lee Ross and Effie Ross (*née* Griffiths); *m* 1st, 1961, Carole D'Arcy (marr. diss. 1971); 2nd, 1971, Joan Spokes (marr. diss. 1976); 3rd, 1979, Zoe Goodwin; partner, Wendy Finney. *Educ:*

Helsby Grammar Sch.; Liverpool Art Sch. (NDD, ATD). Advertising work, 1962–65; Sen. Lectr, Manchester Poly., 1965–86; children's author, illustrator and film-maker, 1972–; TV animated films: Towser, 1985; Horrid Henry, 2006; Little Princess, 2007; books published in UK, Europe, USA, Japan, Australia, Korea and S America. *Publications: picture books include:* Towser (series), 1984; I'm Coming to Get You, 1984; I Want My Potty (series), 1986; Oscar Got The Blame, 1987; Super Dooper Jezebel, 1988; I Want a Cat, 1989; A Fairy Tale, 1991; Don't Do That, 1991; Through the Looking Glass, 1992, and Alice's Adventures in Wonderland, 1993, abridged from Lewis Carroll; The Shop of Ghosts, from G. K. Chesterton, 1994; Three Little Kittens and Other Favourite Nursery Rhymes, 2007; My First Nursery Collection, 2009; My Favourite Fairy Tales, 2010; I Want To Do It By Myself, 2010; *books illustrated include:* Eric Morecambe, The Reluctant Vampire, 1982; Willis Hall, Vampire Park, 1983; Michael Palin, Limericks, 1985; Roald Dahl, Fantastic Mr Fox, 1988; Simon Brett, How to be a Little Sod, 1992; Michael Morpurgo, Red Eyes at Night, 1998; Oscar Wilde, The Picture of Dorian Gray, 2000; Jeanne Willis, Flabby Cat and Slobby Dog, 2009; David Walliams, Billionaire Boy, 2010; Jeanne Willis, I'm Going to a Party, 2011; Gervase Phinn, Who Am I?, 2011; series: Ian Whybrow, Little Wolf, 1985; Jeanne Willis, Dr Xargle, 1988; Richmal Crompton, Meet Just William, 1999; Astrid Lindgren, Pippi Longstocking, 2000; Francesca Simon, Horrid Henry, 2003. *Recreations:* sailing, gentle sports, keeping unfit. *Address:* c/o Andersen Press, 20 Vauxhall Bridge Road, SW1V 2SA. *Club:* Chelsea Arts.

ROSS, Candice Kathleen; *see* Atherton, C. K.

ROSS, Cathryn Elizabeth; Chief Executive, Ofwat, since 2013; *b* Davyhulme, Manchester, 15 April 1972; *d* of David Henderson Ross and Pamela Jean Ross; *m* 1999, Piotr Jasinski. *Educ:* Altrincham Grammar Sch. for Girls; University Coll. London (BScEcon Economics); London Sch. of Economics and Pol Sci. (MSc Econ. Eur. Studies). Res. Asst, Regulatory Policy Inst., Oxford, 1997–2000; Econ. Advr, Oftel, 2000–01; Hd, Competition Econs, Office of the Rail Regulator, 2001–03; Dir, Remedies and Business Analysis, Competition Commn, 2003–08; Executive Director: Mkts and Econs, Ofwat, 2008–11; Railway Mkts and Econs, Office of Rail Regulation, 2011–13. *Publications:* several articles in Communist Economies and Economic Transformation. *Recreations:* golf, gardening, crosswords, classical music, jazz. *Address:* Ofwat, Centre City Tower, 7 Hill Street, Birmingham B5 4UA. *T:* (0121) 644 7500, *Fax:* (0121) 644 7559. *E:* cathryn.ross@ofwat.gsi.gov.uk. *Club:* Frilford Heath Golf.

ROSS, David Peter John; Chairman: David Ross Foundation, since 2007; David Ross Education Trust, since 2007; Co-Founder, 1991, and Deputy Chairman, 2003–08, The Carphone Warehouse (Chief Operating Officer, 1996–2003); *b* 10 July 1965; *s* of late John Malcolm Thomas and of Linda Susan Ross; one *s*. *Educ:* Uppingham Sch.; Univ. of Nottingham (BA Hons Law 1987). Chartered accountant; with Arthur Andersen, 1988–91; Finance Dir, Carphone Warehouse plc, 1991–96. Non-exec. Chairman: Nat. Express Gp, 2001–08; Gondola Hldgs plc, 2005–06; non-executive Director: Big Yellow Self Storage, 2000–08; Wembley Nat. Stadium Ltd, 2002–07; Trinity Mirror plc, 2004–07; Cosalt plc, 2005– (Chm., 2005–08, 2009–). Mem., Audit Cttee, Home Office, 2004–07. Mem. Council, Sport England, 2001–05. Dir, LOCOG, 2008; Member, Board: BOA, 2011–; London Legacy Develt Corp., 2012–. Trustee: Uppingham Sch., 2001–; NPG, 2006–; Member, Council: Serpentine Gall., 2008–; Univ. of Nottingham, 2009–. Founder, Nevill Holt Opera, 2013–. Liveryman, Co. of Chartered Accountants. *Recreations:* opera, sport, shooting. *Address:* Nuffield House, 41–46 Piccadilly, W1J 0DS. *T:* (020) 7534 1547, *Fax:* (020) 7534 1560. *E:* eci@kandahar.co.uk. *Clubs:* Royal Automobile, Carlton.

ROSS, Donald Grant, OBE 2005; Lord Lieutenant of Dunbartonshire, 2007–08; *b* 24 June 1946; *s* of John Sutherland Ross and Catherine Grant Ross; *m* 1974, Doreen Colina; two *s* one *d*. *Educ:* High Sch. of Glasgow; King Edward VI Grammar Sch., Chelmsford; Army Staff Coll., Camberley. Commnd Argyll and Sutherland Highlanders, 1967; i/c British Contingent, Multi-nat. Force and Observers, Sinai, 1987–88; i/c 3/51 Highland Volunteers, 1988–90; COS British Rear Combat Zone, Germany, 1990–93; Comdr, Recruiting and Liaison Staff, Scotland, 1993–96; retd 1996; Comdt, Garelochhead Trng Area, 1996. Member: Exec. Cttee, Erskine Hosp., 1997–2008; C of S Cttee on Chaplains to the Armed Forces, 1996–99. Comdt, Argyll and Sutherland Highlanders Army Cadets, 1998–2003; Hon. Pres., Lennox and Argyll Boys' Bde, 2007–08. Chairman: Grangemouth Br., RBL, 2002; Argyll and Sutherland Highlanders Regtl Assoc., 2011; Hon. Pres., Dunbartonshire Br., SSAFA, 2007–08. Trustee, Tullochan Trust, 2007–08. *Recreations:* sailing, hill-walking, gardening. *Address:* Cruachan, Shore Road, Cove, Helensburgh, Dunbartonshire G84 0NX. *T:* (01436) 842555, *Fax:* (01436) 810369. *E:* donaldanddoreen@hotmail.com.

ROSS, Rt Hon. Donald MacArthur; *see* Ross, Rt Hon. Lord.

ROSS, Prof. Douglas Alan, DPhil; FRS 2005; Professor of Physics, University of Southampton, 1993–2013, now Emeritus; *b* 9 May 1948; *s* of late Arnold Ross and of Odette Ross; *m* 1973, Jacqueline Nahoum; two *s*. *Educ:* New Coll., Oxford (MA 1969; DPhil 1972). Postdoctoral Fellow: Imperial Coll., London, 1972–74; Rijksuniversiteit Utrecht, 1974–76; Fellow, CERN, 1976–78; Sen. Res. Fellow, CIT, 1978–80; Lectr, Univ. of Southampton, 1980–93. *Publications:* (with J. R. Forshaw) Quantum Chromodynamics and the Pomeron, 1997. *Recreations:* singing in choir (bass), learning modern languages, playing clarinet. *Address:* 242 Hill Lane, Southampton SO15 7NT. *T:* (023) 8078 7711. *E:* doug@soton.ac.uk.

ROSS, Duncan Alexander, CBE 1993; CEng, FIET; Chairman, Southern Electric plc (formerly Southern Electricity Board), 1984–93, retired; *b* 25 Sept. 1928; *s* of William Duncan Ross and Mary Ross; *m* 1958, Mary Buchanan Clarke Parsons; one *s* one *d*. *Educ:* Dingwall Academy; Glasgow Univ. (BSc Elec. Engrg). Various engineering posts, South of Scotland Electricity Board, 1952–57; engineering, commercial and management posts, Midlands Electricity Board, 1957–72; Area Manager, South Staffs Area, 1972–75, Chief Engineer, 1975–77; Dep. Chm., 1977–81, Chm., 1981–84, South Wales Electricity Bd. Mem., Electricity Council, 1981–90. CCMI. *Recreations:* golf, ski-ing. *Address:* Winterfold, Dovers Orchard, Hoo Lane, Chipping Campden, Glos GL55 6AZ. *T:* (01386) 841797.

ROSS, Ernest; *b* Dundee, July 1942; *m*; two *s* one *d*. *Educ:* St John's Jun. Secondary Sch. Quality Control Engineer, Timex Ltd. Mem., MSF (formerly AUEW (TASS)). MP (Lab) Dundee W, 1979–2005. Mem., Select Cttee on Foreign Affairs, 1997–99; Chm., All-Party Poverty Gp, 1997–2005. Chm. Bd of Govs, Westminster Foundn for Democracy, 1997–2002. Mem. Bd, Claverhouse Gp, 2002–. Mem. Council, Al-Maktoum Coll. (formerly Al-Maktoum Inst.), 2001–.

ROSS, Prof. Graham Garland, PhD; FRS 1991; Professor of Theoretical Physics, Oxford University, 1992–2011, now Emeritus; Fellow of Wadham College, Oxford, 1983–2011, now Emeritus. *Educ:* Aberdeen Univ. (BSc); Durham Univ. (PhD); MA Oxon. Rutherford Atlas Res. Fellow, Pembroke Coll., Oxford, 1981–83; Lectr, 1983–90, Reader and SERC Sen. Res. Fellow in Theoretical Physics, 1990–92, Oxford Univ. *Address:* Rudolf Peierls Centre for Theoretical Physics, 1 Keble Road, Oxford OX1 3RH. *T:* (01865) 273999; Woodcock Cottage, Lincombe Lane, Boars Hill, Oxford OX1 5DX.

ROSS, Hilary Anne, (Mrs C. M. Hix); Partner, since 2011, Sector Group Head of Retail, Food and Hospitality, since 2012, and Executive Partner for London, since 2015, DWF LLP; *b* Kilwining, Scotland, 25 April 1969; *d* of David Stewart Ross and Amy Urquhart Ross (*née* McCreadie); *m* 2002, Christopher Martin Hix; one *s*. *Educ:* Winton Primary Sch.; Ardrossan Acad.; Glasgow Univ. (LLB; Dip. Legal Studies). Admitted solicitor: Scotland, 1993; England and Wales, 1994. Trainee, Hughes Dowdall, 1992–94; Associate: McKenna & Co., 1994–96; Sonnenschein Nath & Rosenthal, 1996–98; Partner: Berwin Leighton Paisner, 1998–2008; Bond Pearce, 2008–12. Mem. Cttee, Food Law Gp, 1998–. Chm., Eur. Food Law Assoc. (UK), 2008–11. *Recreation:* walking. *Address:* DWF LLP, 20 Fenchurch Street, EC3M 3BY. *T:* (020) 7645 9587, *Fax:* (020) 7645 9501. *E:* hilary.ross@dwf.co.uk.

ROSS, Hugh Robert; Director, Hehir-Ross Partnership Ltd, since 2011; consultant, since 2011; *b* 21 April 1953; *s* of Robert James Ross and Marion Bertha Ross (*née* Maidment); *m* 1981, Margaret Catherine Hehir; one *s* one *d*. *Educ:* Univ. of Durham (BA Pol. and Sociol.); London Business Sch. (MBA). Fellow, IHSM, 1987. Admin. Trainee, NHS, 1976–78; Asst Adminr, Princess Margaret Hosp., Swindon, 1978–80; Asst Adminr, 1980–81, Patient Services Officer, 1981–83, Westminster Hosp.; Dep. Adminr, 1983–84, Dir of Operational Services, 1984–86, St Bartholomew's Hosp.; Unit General Manager: City Unit, Coventry, 1986–90; Leicester Gen. Hosp., 1990–92; Chief Executive: Leicester Gen. Hosp. NHS Trust, 1993–95; Utd Bristol Healthcare NHS Trust, 1995–2002; Prog. Dir, Bristol Health Services Plan, 2002–04; Chief Exec., Cardiff and Vale NHS Trust, 2004–09; Dir, NHS Wales Health Strategy Unit, 2009–11. Mem. Bd, HEFCE, 2011–. *Recreations:* Southampton FC, golf, travel, real ale, rock music. *Address:* 40 Alma Road, Clifton, Bristol BS8 2DB. *T:* (0117) 974 4987.

ROSS, Ian; *see* Ross, W. J.

ROSS, James Hood, OBE 2011; Deputy Chairman, National Grid Transco plc, 2002–04 (Chairman, National Grid Group plc, 1999–2002); *b* 13 Sept. 1938; *s* of Thomas Desmond Ross and Lettice Ferrier Ross (*née* Hood); *m* 1964, Sara Blanche Vivian Purcell; one *s* two *d*. *Educ:* Sherborne Sch.; Jesus Coll., Oxford (BA Hons Modern Hist.); Manchester Business Sch. (Dip. with distinction). British Petroleum, 1962–92: Gen. Manager, Corporate Planning, 1981–85; Chief Exec., BP Oil Internat., 1986–88; Chm. and Chief Exec., BP America, 1988–92; a Man Dir, BP, 1991–92; Chief Exec. and Dep. Chm., Cable and Wireless, 1992–96; Chm., Littlewoods Orgn, 1996–2002. Non-executive Director: McGraw Hill; Datacard; Schneider Electric; Prudential, 2004–11. Chm., Leadership Foundn for Higher Educn, 2003–10; Mem., Marshall Commn, 2005–10. Hon. LLD: Manchester, 2001; Liverpool, 2001. *Recreations:* gardening, travel, swimming, golf.

ROSS, Jane Angharad; *see* Watts, Jane A.

ROSS, John Alexander, CBE 1993; DL; FRAgS; Chairman, Dumfries and Galloway NHS Board, 2001–08; Lord-Lieutenant for Dumfries and Galloway (District of Wigtown), since 2015 (Vice Lord-Lieutenant, 2014–15); *b* 19 Feb. 1945; *m* 1967, Alison Jean Darling; two *s* one *d*. *Educ:* Mahaar Primary Sch., Stranraer; George Watson's Coll., Edinburgh. FRAgS 1993. National Farmers' Union of Scotland: Convener, Hill Farming Sub-cttee, 1984–90; Wigtown Area Pres., 1985–86; Convener, Livestock Cttee, 1987–90; Vice-Pres., 1986–90; Pres., 1990–96. Comr, Meat & Livestock Commn, 1996–2002; Chm., Scotch Quality Beef and Lamb Assoc. Ltd, 1997–2000. Bd Dir, 1996–2007, Chm. Regl Bd, Scotland, 2007–12, NFU Mutual Insurance Soc. Dir, Animal Diseases Res. Assoc., 1986–2012; Chairman: Moredun Res. Inst., 2002–04; Moredun Res. Foundn, 2004–12; Care Farming Scotland, 2011–. Chairman: Dumfries and Galloway Health Bd, 1997–2000; Dumfries and Galloway Primary Care NHS Trust 2000–01; Nat. Prog. Bd for Prisoners' Healthcare, 2009–11; Care Farming Scotland, 2012–. Comr, Northern Lighthouse Bd, 2008–. Chm., Stranraer Sch. Council, 1980–89. Session Clerk, Portpatrick Parish Church, 1975–80; Elder, C of S. DL Wigtown, 2010. Hon. Fellow, Scottish Agricl Coll., 2010. Hon. DVetMed and Surgery Glasgow, 2013. *Recreations:* golf, curling. *Address:* Auchenree Cottage, Portpatrick, Stranraer DG9 8TN. *T:* (01776) 810259. *Club:* Farmers.

ROSS, John Graffin; QC 2001; a Recorder, since 1994; *b* 9 March 1947; *er s* of late James Ross, MRCVS and of Eileen Ross; *m* 1973, Elizabeth Patricia Alexandra Layland. *Educ:* Umtali Boys' High Sch., Southern Rhodesia; University Coll. of Rhodesia and Nyasaland (LLB (ext.) London Univ.); University College London (LLM). Called to the Bar, Inner Temple, 1971, Bencher, 2006; Asst Recorder, 1990–94; Hd of Chambers, 1 Chancery Lane, 2007–. Legal Assessor, RCVS, 2007–. Chairman: Professional Negligence Bar Assoc., 2011–13 (Vice-Chm., 2009–11; Mem. Cttee, 2006–13); Cttee, London Common Law and Commercial Bar Assoc., 2006–11. *Publications:* (contrib.) Pittaway and Hammerton, Professional Negligence Cases, 1998. *Recreations:* music, bridge, riding, golf, ski-ing. *Address:* c/o 1 Chancery Lane, WC2A 1LF. *T:* 0845 634 6666. *Clubs:* Denham Golf; Valderrama (Golf).

ROSS, Jonathan Steven, OBE 2005; broadcaster; *b* 17 Nov. 1960; *m* 1988, Jane Goldman; one *s* two *d*. *Educ:* Sch. of Slavonic and E European Studies, Univ. of London (BA History). Formerly researcher, Channel 4; founding co-Producer, Channel X. Television includes: chat shows: The Last Resort (deviser and associate producer with Alan Marke), 1987; One Hour with Jonathan Ross, 1990; Tonight with Jonathan Ross, 1990; The Late Jonathan Ross, 1996; Friday Night with Jonathan Ross, 2001–10; The Jonathan Ross Show, 2011–; presenter: The Incredibly Strange Film Show, 1988–89; Jonathan Ross Presents; For One Week Only, 1991; Gag Tag; In Search Of...; The Big Big Talent Show; Film 1999–2010; Secret Map of Hollywood, 2005; Pinewood: 80 Years of Movie Magic, 2015; panel games: (host) It's Only TV... But I Like It, 1999–2002; (team mem.) They Think It's All Over, 1999–2006. Radio presenter, 1987–. Gov., BFI, 2014–. *Publications:* Why Do I Say These Things?, 2008; (jtly) Turf, 2011. *Address:* c/o Off the Kerb Productions, Hammer House, 113–117 Wardour Street, W1F 0UN.

ROSS, Kenneth Alexander; Sheriff of South Strathclyde, Dumfries and Galloway at Dumfries, 2000–14; President, Law Society of Scotland, 1994–95 (Vice-President, 1993–94); *b* 21 April 1949; *s* of Alexander Cree Ross and Mary Hamilton Ross (*née* M'Lauchlan); *m* 1972, Morag Laidlaw; one *s* one *d*. *Educ:* Hutchesons' GS, Glasgow; Edinburgh Univ. (LLB (Hons) 1971). Pres., Edinburgh Univ. Union, 1970–71. Partner, M'Gowans, later Gillespie, Gifford & Brown, solicitors, Dumfries, 1975–97. Temp. Sheriff, 1987–97; Sheriff of Lothian and Borders at Linlithgow, 1997–2000. Member: Scottish Legal Aid Bd, 2004–09; Judicial Appointments Bd for Scotland, 2008–12. Mem. Council, Law Soc. of Scotland, 1987–96. Contested (C): Kilmarnock, Feb. 1974; Galloway, Oct. 1974. *Recreations:* gardening, golf, beekeeping, curling. *Address:* Slate Row, Auchencairn, Castle Douglas, Kirkcudbrightshire DG7 1QL; 70 Orchard Brae Avenue, Edinburgh EH4 2GA.

ROSS, Leslie Samuel, CB 2006; Managing Director, Business International, Invest Northern Ireland, 2002–05; advisor on economic development, since 2005; *b* 5 July 1944; *s* of Herbert Ross and late Gretta Ross; *m* 1969, Violet Johnston; one *s* one *d*. *Educ:* Portora Royal Sch.; Open Univ. (BA Hons). Dep. Chief Exec. and other sen. positions, 1982–2000, Chief Exec., 2000–02, Industrial Develt Bd, NI. *Recreations:* sport, gardening, travel. *Address:* 5 Belmont Drive, Belfast BT4 2BL.

ROSS, Lt-Col Sir Malcolm; *see* Ross, Lt-Col Sir W. H. M.

ROSS, Margaret Beryl C.; *see* Clunies Ross.

ROSS, Michael David, CBE 2001; Chief Executive, Scottish Widows plc (formerly Managing Director, then Group Chief Executive, Scottish Widows' Fund and Life Assurance Society), 1991–2003; Joint Deputy Group Chief Executive, Lloyds TSB Group plc, 2000–03; *b* 9 July 1946; *s* of Patrick James Forrest Ross and Emily Janet; *m* 1973, Pamela Marquis Speakman. *Educ:* Daniel Stewart's Coll., Edinburgh. FFA 1969–2012. Joined Scottish Widows', 1964, as Trainee Actuary; Asst Gen. Manager, 1986–88; Actuary, 1988; Gen. Manager, 1988–90; Dep. Man. Dir, 1990–91. Non-executive Director: Phoenix Life, 2005–;

mform Ltd, 2005–10; Principle Insce Hldgs Ltd (formerly British Islamic Insce Hldgs), 2006–11. Chm., Scottish Financial Enterprise, 1999–2004 (Dep. Chm., 1998). Mem., Investment Cttee, 2005–, Audit and Risk Mgt Cttee, 2008–, Nat. Trust for Scotland. Association of British Insurers: Chm., 2001–03; Chm., Customer Impact Panel, 2006–11. CCMI (CBIM 1991). *Publications:* contrib. Trans. Faculty of Actuaries. *Recreations:* golf, ski-ing, gardening. *Clubs:* Caledonian; Mortonhall Golf.

ROSS, Moira; Head of Entertainment, Wall to Wall, since 2012; *b* Wallasey, Merseyside; *d* of Keith Ross and Eileen Ross. *Educ:* Royal Scottish Acad. of Music and Drama (BA Hons Drama Studies); Drama Studio, London. ABC: Sen. Producer, Dancing with the Stars, 2007–08; Co-Exec. Producer, Dance War, 2008; BBC: Executive Producer: Last Choir Standing, 2008; Eurovision: Your Country Needs You, Tonight's the Night, 2009; So You Think You Can Dance, 2010; Strictly Come Dancing, 2010–11; Editor of Format Entertainment, 2011; Wall to Wall: Exec. Producer, The Voice UK, 2012–. *Recreations:* theatre, concerts. *Address:* Wall to Wall Television, 85 Gray's Inn Road, WC1X 8TX. *E:* moira.ross@walltowall.co.uk. *Club:* Soho House.

ROSS, Nicholas David, (Nick Ross); broadcaster and journalist; *b* 7 Aug. 1947; *s* of late John Caryl Ross and of Joy Dorothy Ross; *m* 1985, Sarah Caplin; three *s*. *Educ:* Wallington County Grammar Sch.; Queen's Univ., Belfast (BA Hons Psychol). Broadcaster, BBC N Ireland, 1971–72; Radio 4: reporter, Today, World at One, 1972–75; presenter, The World Tonight, Newsdesk, 1972–74, World at One, 1982, Call Nick Ross, 1986–97, Gulf News, 1991, The Commission, 1998–2005, documentaries, 2005–; producer and dir, TV documentaries, 1979–81; presenter, BBC TV: Man Alive, Man Alive Debates, Out of Court, 1975–82; Breakfast Time, Fair Comment, Star Memories, 60 Minutes, 1982–85; Watchdog, 1985–86; Crimewatch UK, 1984–2007; Westminster with Nick Ross, 1994–97; political party confs, 1996; Campaign Roadshow, 1997; So You Think You're A Good Driver, 1999–2002; The Syndicate, 2000; Nick Ross debates, 2000; The Truth About Crime with Nick Ross, 2009; ind. TV incl. A Week in Politics, Ch 4, 1986–88, Crime Museum, 2008. Member: COPUS, 1991–96; Cttee on the Ethics of Gene Therapy, DoH, 1991–93; Gene Therapy Adv. Cttee, DoH, 1993–96; Wider Working Gp on Health of the Nation, DoH, 1992–; Nuffield Council on Bioethics, 1999–2005; NHS Action Team, 2000–01; RCP Cttee on Ethics in Medicine, 2004–14; Acad. of Med. Scis inquiry into use of non-human primates in res., 2005–06. Member: Nat. Bd for Crime Prevention, 1993–96; Crime Prevention Agency, 1996–99; Property Crime Task Force, 1999–2002; Victim Support Adv. Bd, 1991–2008; Crime Concern Adv. Bd, 1991–2003. President: SANEline, 1990–2010; Tacade, 1996–2011; Healthwatch, 1990–; London Accident Prevention Council, 2007–; Vice-President: Patients' Assoc., 1991–93; IAM, 2010– (Mem. Council, 2002–10); Chm., Adv. Bd, Wales Cancer Bank, 2010– (Vice-Chm., 2008–10); Vice-Chm., Nat. Road Safety Campaign, RoSPA, 1990–93. Chm., Evidence Matters, 2015–. Chm., Rhône-Poulenc, then Aventis, Prize for Sci. Books, 1993, 2006. Guest Dir, Cheltenham Sci. Festival, 2008. Trustee: UK Stem Cell Foundn, 2005–; Crimestoppers, 2007–; Sense About Science, 2008–; Dfuse, 2011–. Chm., Jill Dando Inst. of Crime Sci., UCL, 2000–. Vis. Prof. and Hon. Fellow, UCL, 2006. Ambassador, WWF, 2000–11. Pres., Kensington Soc., 2011–. Patron of various charities. FRSA 1994; FRSocMed 1998. Hon. Fellow, Acad. of Experimental Criminology, 2007; Hon. FRCP, 2015. DUniv QUB, 2002. *Publications:* Crime: how to solve it and why so much of what we're told is wrong, 2014. *Recreations:* ski-ing, scuba diving, influencing public policy. *Address:* PO Box 999, London, W2 4XT. *E:* nick@nickross.com. *W:* www.nickross.com.

ROSS, Peter Michael; His Honour Judge Peter Ross; a Circuit Judge, since 2004; *b* 24 June 1955; *s* of Michael and Colleen Ross; *m* 1979, Julie Anna Ibbetson; two *s* one *d*. *Educ:* John Hampden GS, High Wycombe; Venerable English Coll., Gregorian Univ., Rome (PhB 1975); Coll. of Law. Admitted solicitor, 1980; called to the Bar, Inner Temple, 2000. Articles of clerkship, Allan Janes & Co., 1976–79; Court Clerk, High Wycombe Magistrates' Court, 1979–81; Thames Valley Police: Asst Prosecuting Solicitor, 1981–82; Sen. Prosecuting Solicitor, 1982–84; Principal Prosecuting Solicitor, 1984–86; Sen. Crown Prosecutor, 1986–87, Br. Crown Prosecutor, 1987–90, CPS Aylesbury; Br. Crown Prosecutor, N London CPS, 1990–93; Asst Chief Crown Prosecutor (Ops), CPS London, 1993–96; Dir, Office for Supervision of Solicitors, 1996–99; an Asst Recorder, 1999–2000; a Recorder, 2000–04. *Recreations:* shooting, smallholding, gardening, fishing, hedgelaying.

ROSS, Prof. Richard Lawrence; freelance writer and screenwriter, since 2007; Research Professor, Norwegian Film School, 2001–07; Head of Diploma Course and Deputy to Director, National Film and Television School, 1998–2000; *b* 22 Dec. 1935; *s* of Lawrence Sebley Ross and Muriel Ross; *m* 1957, Phyllis Ellen Hamilton; one *s* one *d*. *Educ:* Westland High School, Hokitika, NZ; Canterbury University College, NZ. Exchange Telegraph, 1958–60; Visnews Ltd, 1960–65; BBC TV News, 1965–80; Prof. of Film and TV, then of Film, RCA, 1980–89; Co-Chm. (with Milos Forman) Grad. Film Dept, Columbia Univ., NY, 1989–90; Chm., Grad. Film Dept, NY Univ., 1990–92; Sen. Lectr in Film, 1995–96, Hd, Curriculum Planning, 1996–98, Nat. Film and TV Sch. Hon. Prof. of Film, Hochschule für Fernsehen und Film, Munich, 1992–2004; Visiting Professor: Jerusalem Film and TV Sch., 1992–2005; Deutsche Film- und Fernsehakad., Berlin, 1993–2003. Consultant Dir, Film Educn, 1986–89; Dir, Nat. Youth Film Foundn, 1988–89. Consultant: Univ. Sains, Penang, Malaysia, 1984–86; Calouste Gulbenkian Foundn, Lisbon, 1983–85. Chm., Educn Cttee, British Film Year, 1985–86; Exec. Mem., Centre Internat. de Liaison des Ecoles de Cinéma et de Télévision, 1990–95 (Chm., Short Film Project, 1990–95; Hon. Mem., 2004). Fellow in Fine Arts, Trent Polytechnic, 1970–72. Fellow, RCA, 1981–89. *Publications:* Strategy for Story-Telling (2 vols), 1992; Triangle (The Creative Partnership), vol. 1, 1998, vol. 2, 2001, vol. 3, 2002; Training the Trainers (11 manuals for film educn teachers), 2007. *Recreations:* walking in London, eating in France, talking and drinking anywhere. *E:* dickross@dircon.co.uk.

ROSS, Richard Y.; *see* Younger-Ross.

ROSS, Sir Robert; *see* Ross, Sir W. R. A.

ROSS, Lt-Gen. Sir Robert (Jeremy), (Sir Robin), KCB 1994 (CB 1992); OBE 1978; Chairman, SSAFA Forces Help, 2000–10; *b* 28 Nov. 1939; *s* of Gerald and Margaret Ross; *m* 1965, Sara (*née* Curtis); one *s* one *d*. *Educ:* Wellington Coll.; Corpus Christi Coll., Cambridge (MPhil). Entered RM, 1957; Commando and Sea Service, 1959–69; Army Staff Coll., 1970; Commando Service, 1971–78; Instr, Army Staff Coll., 1978–79; CO 40 Commando RM, 1979–81; RCDS 1982; MoD, 1984–86; Comdr 3 Commando Bde, 1986–88; Maj.-Gen. RM Trng, Reserve and Special Forces, 1988–90; Maj.-Gen. RM Commando Forces, 1990–93; CGRM, 1993–96. Liveryman, Plaisterers' Co., 1996. Comdr, Legion of Merit (USA), 1993. *Recreation:* fishing.

ROSS, Sandy; *see* Ross, Alexander.

ROSS, Sophie, (Mrs R. P. Ross); *see* Mirman, S.

ROSS, Tessa Sarah, CBE 2010; consultant, National Theatre, since 2015 (Chief Executive, 2014–15); *b* 26 July 1961; *d* of E. Leonard Ross and Sharon F. Ross (*née* Kingsley), MBE; *m* 1987, Mark Scantlebury; two *s* one *d*. *Educ:* Somerville Coll., Oxford (BA Hons Oriental Studies (Chinese)). Literary Agent, Anthony Shiel Associates, 1986–88; Script Editor, BBC Scotland, 1988–89; Hd of Develt, British Screen Finance, 1990–93; Independent Commng Exec., 1993–97, Hd of Independent Commng, 1997–2000, BBC TV Drama; Channel 4: Hd of Drama, 2000–03; Hd of FilmFour, 2003–05; Hd of FilmFour and Drama, then Controller, Film and Drama, 2005–14. Outstanding British Contribn to Cinema Award, BAFTA, 2013. *Address:* National Theatre, South Bank, SE1 9PX. *Club:* Union.

ROSS, Timothy David M.; *see* Melville-Ross.

ROSS, Victor; Chairman, Reader's Digest Association Ltd, 1978–84; *b* 1 Oct. 1919; *s* of Valentin and Eva Rosenfeld; *m* 1st, 1944, Romola Wallace; two *s*; 2nd, 1970, Hildegard Peiser. *Educ:* schs in Austria, Germany and France; London Sch. of Economics. Served in Army, 1942–45. Journalist and writer, 1945–55; joined Reader's Digest, 1955; Man. Dir and Chief Exec., 1972–81. Dir, Folio Soc., 1985–89. Pres., Assoc. of Mail Order Publishers, 1979–80, 1983–84; Mem., Data Protection Tribunal, 1985–95. Hon. Fellow, Inst. of Direct Marketing, 1995. Mackintosh Medal for Advertising, Advertising Assoc., 1989. *Publications:* A Stranger in my Midst, 1948; Tightrope, 1952; Basic British, 1956. *Recreations:* collecting books, fishing.

ROSS, Lt-Col Sir (Walter Hugh) Malcolm, GCVO 2005 (CVO 1994; KCVO 1999); OBE 1988; Lord-Lieutenant, Stewartry of Kirkcudbright (Dumfries and Galloway Region), since 2006; *b* 27 Oct. 1943; *s* of Col Walter John Macdonald Ross, CB, OBE, MC, TD and Josephine May (*née* Cross); *m* 1969, Susie, *d* of Gen. Sir (James) Michael Gow, GCB; one *s* two *d*. *Educ:* Eton Coll.; Royal Military Acad., Sandhurst. Served in Scots Guards, 1964–87; Asst Comptroller, 1987–91, Comptroller, 1991–2006, Lord Chamberlain's Office; Management Auditor, The Royal Household, 1987–89; Master, Household of the Prince of Wales and Duchess of Cornwall, 2006–08. Sec., Central Chancery of the Orders of Knighthood, 1989–91. Chm., Westminster Gp plc, 2007–. An Extra Equerry to the Queen, 1988–. Mem., Queen's Body Guard for Scotland, Royal Company of Archers, 1981– (Brigadier, 2003; Ensign, 2012). Stewartry of Kirkcudbright (Dumfries and Galloway): DL 2003; JP 2006. Freeman, City of London, 1994. Prior, Order of St John, Scotland, 2009– (KStJ 2009; CStJ 2007). *Address:* Netherhall, Bridge of Dee, Castle Douglas, Kirkcudbrightshire DG7 2AA. *Clubs:* Pratt's; New (Edinburgh).

See also Sir W. R. A. Ross.

ROSS, Sir (Walter) Robert (Alexander), KCVO 2012 (CVO 2006); FRICS; Secretary and Keeper of the Records, Duchy of Cornwall, 1997–2013; *b* 27 Feb. 1950; *s* of Col Walter John Macdonald Ross, CB, OBE, MC, TD and Josephine May Ross (*née* Cross); *m* 1985, Ingrid Wieser; one *s* one *d*. *Educ:* Eton Coll.; Royal Agricl Coll., Cirencester. FRICS 1982. Chartered Surveyor, Buccleuch Estates Ltd, Selkirk, 1972–73; joined Savills, 1973: Partner, 1982–86; Dir, 1986–97. *Club:* Boodle's.

ROSS, William; *b* 4 Feb. 1936; *m* 1974, Christine; three *s* one *d*. MP (UU) Londonderry, Feb. 1974–83, Londonderry East, 1983–2001 (resigned seat Dec. 1985 in protest against Anglo-Irish Agreement; re-elected Jan. 1986); contested (UU) Londonderry E, 2001. *Recreations:* fishing, shooting. *Address:* Hillquarter, Turmeel, Dungiven, Northern Ireland BT47 4SL. *T:* (028) 7774 1428.

ROSS, William John, (Ian), OBE 2007; Chairman, Scottish Natural Heritage, since 2014; *b* Inverness, 6 March 1957; *m* 1987, Dr Lindsey Crum; one *s* one *d*. *Educ:* Fortrose Acad.; Univ. of Aberdeen (BSc Hons Forestry). FICFor 2001. Forest Officer, Forestry Commn, 1979–82; Scottish School of Forestry: Lectr, 1982–88; Sen. Lectr, 1988–95; pt-time Lectr, 1995–2014. Mem., Highland Council, 1999–2012 (Chairman: Sustainable Develt, 2001–07; Planning, Envmt and Develt, 2008–12; Vice-Convenor, Northern Jt Police Bd, 2007–12). Mem. Bd, Scottish Police Authy, 2012–. FRSA. *Recreations:* family, reading, cycling, Rotary Club, travel. *Address:* Scottish Natural Heritage, Great Glenn House, Leachkin Road, Inverness IV3 8NW. *T:* (01463) 725002. *E:* ian.ross@snh.gov.uk.

ROSS RUSSELL, Graham; Founder Chairman, Securities Institute, 1992–2000; *b* 3 Jan. 1933; *s* of Robert Ross Russell and Elizabeth Ross Russell (*née* Hendry); *m* 1963, Jean Margaret Symington; three *s* one *d*. *Educ:* Loretto; Trinity Hall, Cambridge (MA; Hon. Fellow, 2001); Harvard Business School (MBA; Frank Knox Fellow, 1958–60). Sub Lieut, RNVR, 1951–53 (Mediterranean Fleet). Merchant banking: Morgan Grenfell & Co. and Baring Brothers, 1956–58; Philip Hill Higginson Erlanger, 1960–63; Stockbroker, Laurence Prust & Co., 1963–90, Partner, 1965; Chm., Laurence Prust & Co. Ltd, 1986–88. Chairman: Braham Miller Group, 1981–84; C. C. F. Hldgs, 1988–90; EMAP, 1990–94 (Dir, 1970–94); Tunnel Services Ltd, 1991–2002; F & C Capital and Income (formerly F & C Pep and Isa) Investment Trust plc, 1993–2005; Advent, then Foresight 3, Venture Capital Trust plc, 1996–2014; Enterprise Panel, 1997–2011; UK Business Incubation, 1997–2011; non-executive Director: UK Select Investment Trust (formerly Investment Trust of Guernsey) plc, 1995–2013; Fordath, 1971–84; Foster Braithwaite, 1988–96; Nasdaq (Europe) (formerly EASDAQ) SA, 1995–98 (Pres., 2000–01, Mem., Market Authy, 1999–2003); Barloworld plc, 1998–2003; Bamboo Investments plc, 2000–06; Barloworld Ltd, 2001–03. Dir, SIB, 1989–93; Mem. Council, Internat. Stock Exchange, subseq. London Stock Exchange, 1973–91 (Dep. Chm., 1984–88; Chairman: Pre-emption Gp, 1987–2000; Rev. Cttee on Initial Public Offers, 1989–90). Comr, Public Works Loan Bd, 1980–95; Chm., Domestic Promotions Cttee, British Invisible Exports Council, 1987–91. Chm. Trustees, F & C Asset Mgt Pension Fund, 2004–07; Mem., Investment Cttee, RBK&C Pension Fund, 2004–14. Trustee, NESTA, 2001–07. Mem. Council, Crown Agents Foundn, 1997–2002. Chm. Govs, Sutton's Hosp., Charterhouse, 1996–2006. Pres., Trinity Hall Assoc., 1994–95. Co-founder, retirementreinvented.com website, 2009. Hon. FCSI 2000. FRSA 1989. *Publications:* occasional articles in esoteric financial and fiscal jls. *Recreations:* tennis, golf, reading. *Address:* 30 Ladbroke Square, W11 3NB. *T:* (020) 7727 5017. *Clubs:* Athenæum; Hawks (Cambridge); Woodpeckers (Oxford and Cambridge).

ROSS-WAWRZYNSKI, Dame Dana, DBE 2013; Executive Headteacher (formerly Headmistress), Altrincham Grammar School for Girls, since 1999; Chief Executive Officer, Bright Futures Educational Trust, since 2011; *b* 24 March 1951; *d* of Richard and Pauline Ross; *m* 1974, Jack Wawrzynski; two *s*. *Educ:* Glasgow Univ. (BSc Hons 1975); Strathclyde Univ. (MSc 1976); Manchester Univ. (NPQH 1999). Teacher, Loreto Sixth Form Coll., Manchester, 1977–81; Hd of Lower Sch. Sci., Central High Sch. for Boys, Manchester, 1981–82; Hd of Sci., St Joseph's High Sch. for Girls, Manchester, 1982–84; Dep. Headteacher, Abraham Moss High Sch. and N Manchester Coll., 1984–90; Dep. Headteacher, All Hallows High Sch., Macclesfield, 1990–98. Educnl expert consultant, Centre for Social Justice, 2012–14. Chair, Review of Headteachers' Standards in England, DFE, 2014–15. Mem. Bd, Ofqual, 2013–. *Publications:* sex educn booklet, papers. *Recreations:* classical music, hill walking, reading, ski-ing. *Address:* Bright Futures Educational Trust, Lodge House, Cavendish Road, Bowdon, Altrincham, Cheshire WA14 2NJ. *T:* (0161) 941 5681.

ROSSANT, Dr Janet, FRS 2000; FRSC; Professor, Department of Molecular Genetics (formerly Department of Molecular and Medical Genetics), since 1988, University Professor, since 2001, University of Toronto; Chief of Research, Hospital for Sick Children, Toronto, since 2005; *b* 13 July 1950; *d* of Leslie and Doris Rossant; *m* 1977, Alex Bain; one *s* (one *d* decd). *Educ:* St Hugh's Coll., Oxford (BA, MA 1972); Darwin Coll., Cambridge (PhD 1976). Beit Meml Fellow, Univ. of Oxford, 1975–77; Asst Prof., 1977–82, Associate Prof., 1982–85, Brock Univ., St Catharines, Ont.; Associate Prof., Univ. of Toronto, 1985–88; Sen. Scientist, 1985–2005, and Co-head, 1998, Prog. in Develt and Fetal Health, Samuel Lunenfeld Res. Inst., Toronto. FRSC 1996. For. Associate, NAS, USA, 2008. Hon. LLD: Dalhousie, 2005; Acadia, 2013; Windsor, 2014; Hon. DSc British Columbia, 2014. *Publications:* (with R. A. Pedersen) Experimental Approaches to Mammalian Development, 1986; (with P. L. M. Tam)

Mouse Development, 2002; contrib. numerous articles to peer-reviewed jls. *Recreations:* walking, cooking, theatre. *Address:* Hospital for Sick Children, 555 University Avenue, Toronto, ON M5G 1X8, Canada.

ROSSDALE, Rt Rev. David Douglas James; Bishop Suffragan of Grimsby, 2000–13; an Assistant Bishop, Diocese of Lincoln, since 2013; *b* 22 May 1953; *m* 1982, Karen; two *s*. *Educ:* St John's Sch., Leatherhead; King's Coll., London; Westminster Coll., Oxford (MA 1990); Roehampton Inst. (MSc 2000); King's Coll., London (MSc 2010). Ordained deacon, 1981, priest, 1982; Curate, Upminster, 1981–86; Vicar: St Luke, Moulsham, 1986–90; Cookham, 1990–2000; Area Dean of Maidenhead, 1994–2000. Hon. Canon, Christ Church, Oxford, 1999–2000; Canon and Preb., Lincoln Cathedral, 2000–; Mem., Gen. Synod, 2010–13. Non-exec. Dir, Reach2 Ltd, 2013–. Vice Chair, Nat. Soc., 2010–13. Trustee and Treas., Sons and Friends of the Clergy, 2007–; Trustee, Blue Cross, 2015–. Gov., Wellington Coll., 2004–10. *Recreations:* travel, cookery, DIY, microlights. *Address:* Home Farm, Fen Lane, East Keal, Spilsby, Lincs PE23 4AY. *T:* (01790) 752163. *Club:* Farmers.

ROSSDALE, Peter Daniel, OBE 1996; PhD; FRCVS; Editor, 1980–2010, Editor Emeritus, 2011, Equine Veterinary Journal, Editor-in-Chief, Equine Veterinary Education, 1979–2003, and Chairman, Equine Veterinary Journal Ltd, 1985–2005; *b* 8 Sept. 1927; *s* of George and Kate Rossdale; *m* 1st, 1954, Jillian Ruth Clifton (*d* 1999); two *s* one *d*; 2nd, 2003, Mary Annette Sharkey (*née* Lawrence). *Educ:* Egerton House; Stowe Sch.; Trinity Coll., Cambridge (MA, PhD 1985); RVC. FRCVS 1967. Founding Partner, Rossdale and Partners, Newmarket, 1959–2002, now Consultant. Dir, Romney Publications Ltd, 2010–. British Equine Veterinary Association: Treas., 1960–65; Pres., 1976–77; Chm., BEVA Trust, 1978–82; Chm., 1980–84, Treas., 1984–90, Internat. Equine Reproduction Symposia Cttee; Member: Veterinary Adv. Cttee, Wellcome Trust, 1975–79; Sci. Adv. Cttee, Animal Health Trust, 1978–90; Veterinary Adv. Cttee, Horserace Betting Levy Bd, 1983–96; Chm., Internat. Veterinary Perinatology Soc., 1992–95. Mem., 1957–2003, Hon. Mem., 2003–, Neonatal Soc. (Vickers Lecture); Frank Milne Lecture, American Assoc. of Equine Practitioners, 2004. FACVSc 1973; Dip. of Equine Stud Medicine, 1986. Hon. FRVC 2010. Dr *hc* Berne, 1987; Edinburgh, 2001; Sydney, 2007. William Hunting Prize, Vet. Record, 1973; George Fleming Prize, British Vet. Jl, 1974; John Henry Steel Meml Medal, RCVS, 1978; Hochmoor Prize, Tierklinik Hochmoor, 1987; Equestrian Award, Animal Health Trust, 1992; Dalrymple Champneys Award, BVA, 1996; Duke of Devonshire Award, 2004; Merial Lifetime Achievement Award, World Equine Veterinary Assoc., 2008. *Publications:* (jtly) The Practice of Equine Stud Medicine, 1974, revd edn 1980; (jtly) The Horse's Health from A–Z, 1974, revd edn 1998; The Horse from Conception to Maturity, 1975, revd edn 2003; Inside the Horse, 1975; Seeing Equine Practice, 1976; Horse Ailments Explained, 1979; Horse Breeding, 1981 (trans. French, Japanese, German, Swedish); (ed) Veterinary Notes for Horse Owners, 1987; (ed jtly) Equine Medical Veterinary Encyclopedia, 2010; (contrib. and ed jtly) The History of Veterinary Practice in Newmarket 1831–2011, 2011; (with Julie Galliard) The Power of Whitby, 2013; Canon George Austen Remembered in a Personal Perspective of Today, 2015; contrib. peer reviewed jls inc. Vet. Rec., EVJ, Jl Reprod. Fert., Res. Vet. Sci., Lancet, Nature, etc and jls of educn. *Recreations:* contract bridge, music, opera, horseracing and breeding, photography, travel. *T:* (01638) 663639. *E:* pd.rossdale@btinternet.com.

ROSSE, 7th Earl of, *cr* 1806; **(William) Brendan Parsons;** Bt 1677; Baron Oxmantown 1792; *b* 21 Oct. 1936; *s* of 6th Earl of Rosse, KBE, and Anne (*d* 1992), *o d* of Lt-Col Leonard Messel, OBE; *S* father, 1979; *m* 1966, Alison Margaret, *er d* of Major J. D. Cooke-Hurle, Startforth Hall, Barnard Castle, Co. Durham; two *s* one *d*. *Educ:* Aiglon Coll., Switzerland; Grenoble Univ.; Christ Church, Oxford (MA 1964). 2nd Lieut, Irish Guards, 1955–57. UN Official 1963–80, appointed successively to Ghana, Dahomey, Mid-West Africa, Algeria, as first UN Volunteer Field Dir (in Iran) and UN Disaster Relief Co-ordinator (in Bangladesh). Govt of Ireland: Mem., Adv. Council on Develt Co-operation, 1984–89; Dir, Agency for Personal Service Overseas, 1986–90. Founder and Dir, Birr Scientific and Heritage Foundn (resp. for creation of Ireland's Historic Science Centre), 1985–; Director: Historic Irish Tourist Houses and Gardens Assoc., 1980–91; Lorne House Trust, 1993–2001; Trustee, The Tree Register, 1989–. Lord of the Manor: Womersley, Yorks; Newtown, Parsonstown and Roscomroe, Ireland. FRAS; FTCD 2014; Hon. FIEI. Hon. LLD Dublin, 2005. *Heir: s* Lord Oxmantown, *qv*. *Address:* (home) Birr Castle, Co. Offaly, Ireland. *T:* (57) 912 0023.

See also Earl of Snowdon.

ROSSEINSKY, Prof. Matthew Jonathan, DPhil; FRS 2008; FRSC; Professor of Inorganic Chemistry, since 1999, and Royal Society Research Professor, since 2013, University of Liverpool; *m*; three *c*. *Educ:* St John's Coll., Oxford (BA Hons Chem. 1987); Merton Coll., Oxford (DPhil 1990). FRSC 1997. Postdoctoral mem., tech. staff, A T & T Bell Labs, Murray Hill, NJ, 1990–92; Lectr, Dept of Chem., Univ. of Oxford, 1992–99. De Gennes Prize in Materials Chem., RSC, 2009; Hughes Medal, Royal Soc., 2011. *Publications:* contribs to jls incl. Applied Physics Letters, Jl Amer. Chem. Soc., Science, Advanced Materials, Chem. of Materials, Nature, Nature Materials. *Address:* Department of Chemistry, University of Liverpool, Liverpool L69 7ZX.

ROSSER, family name of **Baron Rosser**.

ROSSER, Baron *cr* 2004 (Life Peer), of Ickenham in the London Borough of Hillingdon; **Richard Andrew Rosser;** JP; General Secretary, Transport Salaried Staffs' Association, 1989–2004; *b* 5 Oct. 1944; *s* of Gordon William Rosser and Kathleen Mary (*née* Moon); *m* 1973, Sheena Margaret (*née* Denoon); two *s* one *d*. *Educ:* St Nicholas Grammar Sch., Northwood. BScEcon London (external degree), 1970. CMILT (MCIT 1968). Clerk, London Transport, 1962–65; PA to Operating Man. (Railways), LTE, 1965–66; joined full staff of TSSA, 1966: Res. Officer, 1966–74; Asst, London Midland Div. Sec., 1974–76; Finance and Organising Officer, 1976–77; London Midland Region Div. Sec., 1977–82; Asst Gen. Sec., 1982–89. Non-exec. Dir, Nat. Offender Mgt Bd (formerly Correctional Services Bd), 2000–09; non-exec. Chm., National Offender Management Service (formerly Prison Service) Audit Cttee, 2003–09. Councillor, London Bor. of Hillingdon, 1971–78 (Chm., Finance Cttee, 1974–78); contested (Lab) Croydon Central, Feb. 1974. Mem., NEC, Labour Party, 1988–98; Vice-Chair, 1996–97, Chair, 1997–98, Labour Party. House of Lords: an Opposition Whip, 2010–11; opposition front bench spokesperson on defence, 2011–; Mem., opposition front bench team, Home Office, 2011–, Transport, 2011–. Mem. General Council, TUC, 2000–04. Hon. Vice-Pres., Ryman Isthmian Football League, 2008–; Vice-Pres., Level Playing Field (formerly Nat. Assoc. of Disabled Supporters) (Football), 2009–. JP Middlesex, 1978 (Chm., Uxbridge Bench, 1996–2000). *Recreations:* walking, music, reading The Guardian, and watching non-league football. *Address:* House of Lords, SW1A 0PW.

ROSSI, Sir Hugh (Alexis Louis), Kt 1983; farmer and arboriculturist, Dordogne, since 1991; consultant in environmental law with Simmons and Simmons, solicitors, 1991–97; *b* 21 June 1927; *m* 1955, Philomena Elizabeth Jennings; one *s* three *d* (and one *d* decd). *Educ:* Finchley Catholic Gram. Sch.; King's Coll., Univ. of London (LLB; FKC 1986). Solicitor with Hons, 1950. Member: Hornsey BC, 1956–65; Haringey Council, 1965–68; Middlesex CC, 1961–65. MP (C) Hornsey, 1966–83, Hornsey and Wood Green, 1983–92; Govt Whip, Oct. 1970–April 1972; Europe Whip, Oct. 1971–1973; a Lord Comr, HM Treasury, 1972–74; Parly Under-Sec. of State, DoE, 1974; opposition spokesman on housing and land, 1974–79; Minister of State: NI Office, 1979–81; for Social Security and the Disabled, DHSS, 1981–83. Chm., Select Cttee on the Environment, 1983–92. Dep. Leader, UK Delegn to Council of Europe and WEU, 1972–73 (Mem., 1970–73). Non-exec. Dir, Iveco NV, 1989–2003; Consultant, Wimpey Environmental Ltd, 1993–95. Vice President: (UK), Adv. Cttee on Protection of the Seas, 1992–2002; Nat. Soc. for Clean Air, 1985–. Chairman: UNA (UK), 1992–96; Italian Hosp., London, 1988–89, Italian Hosp. Fund, 1990–2002; Assoc. of Papal Orders in GB of Pius IX, St Gregory and St Sylvester, 1989–99; Historic Chapels Trust, 1992–2002 (Hon. Pres., 2002–14); Trustee, Trusthouse Charitable Foundn (formerly Mem., Forte Council), 1992–. Pres., KCL Assoc., 2004–06 (Vice Pres., 2003). Hon. FCIWEM 1990; Hon. Fellow, Inst. Wastes Management, 1993. Knight of Holy Sepulchre, 1966; KCSG 1985. *Publications:* Guide to the Rent Act, 1974; Guide to Community Land Act, 1975; Guide to Rent (Agriculture) Act, 1976; Guide to Landlord and Tenant Act, 1987; Guide to Local Government Acts 1987 and 1988, 1988. *Club:* Athenæum.

ROSSINGTON, (Timothy) David; Finance Director, Department for Culture, Media and Sport, since 2015; *b* 9 Feb. 1958; *s* of late Peter Gilman Rossington and of Freda Elizabeth (*née* Moseley); one *s* one *d*. *Educ:* Balliol Coll., Oxford (BA 1980); Kennedy Sch. of Govt, Harvard (Masters Public Policy 1982); Birkbeck Coll., London (MSc Econ 1985). Joined Civil Service, 1982; Private Sec. to Lord Belstead, 1986; seconded to UK Repn, Brussels, and EC, 1988–91; Private Sec. to Minister of Agriculture, 1991–93; Hd of Div., MAFF, 1993–2000 (Project Dir, IT system to trace cattle in GB, 1996–99); e-Business Dir, DEFRA, 2000–04 (Ops Dir in Cumbria during foot and mouth outbreak, 2001); Dir, Efficiency Team, OGC, 2004–07; Department for Communities and Local Government: Dir, Local Democracy, 2007–08; Acting Dir Gen., Communities, 2008–09; Dir, Strategy, Performance and Delivery, 2009–10; Acting Dir Gen., Finance and Corporate Services, 2010–11; Finance Dir, 2011–15. ACMA 2013. *Recreations:* hill walking, gardening, music, history, running. *Address:* Department for Culture, Media and Sport, SW1A 2BQ. *T:* (020) 7211 2089. *E:* david.rossington@culture.gov.uk.

ROSSITER, Ann Helen; Executive Director, Society of College, National and University Libraries, since 2010; *b* 18 May 1966; *d* of Charles and Averil Rossiter. *Educ:* Birkbeck Coll., Univ. of London (BA Philosophy). Researcher, BBC Political Res. Unit, 1988–90; Asst Producer, BBC/C4, 1990–92; Researcher: John Denham, MP, 1992–94; Glenda Jackson, MP, 1994–96; Consultant, 1996–99, Dir, 1999–2001, Fishburn Hedges; Dir, Lexington Communications, 2001–02; Dir of Res. and Dep. Dir, 2003–05, Dir, 2005–08, Social Mkt Foundn; Special Adviser: to Sec. of State for Innovation, Univs and Skills, 2008–09; to Sec. of State for Communities and Local Govt, 2009–10. FRSA. *Publications:* The Future of the Private Finance Initiative, 2004; Choice; the evidence, 2004; News Broadcasting in the Digital Age, 2005; Road User Charging: a map, 2007; The Future of Healthcare, 2007; (contrib.) Public Matters: the renewal of the public realm, ed Patrick Diamond, 2007. *Recreations:* exploring Cornwall, contemporary art, bending the ear of politicians, gardening, serial music, film. *Address:* Society of College, National and University Libraries, 94 Euston Street, NW1 2HA. *T:* (020) 7387 0317.

ROSSITER, Rt Rev. (Anthony) Francis, OSB; Abbot President of the English Benedictine Congregation, 1985–2001 (Second Assistant, 1976–85); *b* 26 April 1931; *s* of Leslie and Winifred Rossiter. *Educ:* St Benedict's, Ealing; Sant Anselmo, Rome (LCL). Priest, 1955; Second Master, St Benedict's School, 1960–67; Abbot of Ealing, 1967–91; Vicar for Religious, Archdiocese of Westminster, 1969–88; Pres., Conf. of Major Religious Superiors of England and Wales, 1970–74; Pro-Primate, Benedictine Confedn, 1995–96 (Mem., Abbot Primate's Council, 1988–98). Hon. DD St Vincent Coll., Pa, 1988. *Address:* Ealing Abbey, W5 2DY. *T:* (020) 8862 2100.

ROSSLYN, 7th Earl of, *cr* 1801; **Peter St Clair-Erskine,** CVO 2014; QPM 2009; Bt 1666; Baron Loughborough, 1795; Master of the Household to the Prince of Wales and the Duchess of Cornwall, since 2014; *b* 31 March 1958; *s* of 6th Earl of Rosslyn, and of Athenais de Mortemart, *o d* of late Duc de Vivonne; *S* father, 1977; *m* 1982, Helen, *e d* of Mr and Mrs C. R. Watters, Christ's Hospital, Sussex; two *s* two *d*. *Educ:* Eton; Bristol Univ. (BA); Univ. of Cambridge (MSt). Metropolitan Police, 1980–94; Thames Valley Police, 1994–2000; a Comdr, Metropolitan Police, 2000–; Comdr, Royalty and Diplomatic Protection Dept, 2003–14. Elected Mem., H of L, 1999. Mem., Queen's Body Guard for Scotland, Royal Company of Archers, 2005–. Dir, A. G. Carrick, 2014–. Trustee, Dunimarle Museum. Commandeur, Légion d'Honneur (France), 2014. *Heir: s* Lord Loughborough, *qv*. *Address:* House of Lords, SW1A 0PW. *Club:* White's.

ROSSMORE, 7th Baron *cr* 1796; **William Warner Westenra;** *b* 14 Feb. 1931; *o s* of 6th Baron Rossmore and Dolores Cecil (*d* 1981), *d* of late Lieut-Col James Alban Wilson, DSO, West Burton, Yorks; *S* father, 1958; *m* 1982, Valerie Marion, *d* of Brian Tobin; one *s*. *Educ:* Eton; Trinity Coll., Cambridge (BA). 2nd Lieut, Somerset LI. Co-founder, Coolemine Therapeutic Community, Dublin, 1973. *Recreations:* drawing, painting. *Heir: s* Hon. Benedict William Westenra, *b* 6 March 1983. *Address:* Rossmore Park, Co. Monaghan, Eire. *T:* 81947.

ROSSOR, Prof. Martin Neil, MD, FRCP, FMedSci; Professor of Neurology, since 1998, and Chairman, Division of Neurology, 2002–12, Institute of Neurology, University College London; Hon. Consultant Neurologist: St Mary's Hospital, London, 1986–2010; National Hospital for Neurology and Neurosurgery, since 1998; *b* 24 April 1950; *s* of late Bruce Rossor and of Eileen Rossor; *m* 1973, Eve Lipstein; two *s* one *d*. *Educ:* Watford Boys' Grammar Sch.; Jesus Coll., Cambridge (MA, MD); King's College Hosp. Med. Sch. (MB BChir). FRCP 1990. Clinical Scientist, MRC Neurochemical Pharmacology Unit, 1978–82; Registrar, 1982–83, Sen. Registrar, 1983–86, Nat. Hosp. for Nervous Diseases and King's Coll. Hosp.; Clinical Dir, Medical Specialities, St Mary's Hosp., 1989–92; Sen. Lectr, Inst. of Neurology, 1992–98; Clin. Dir for Neurology, Nat. Hosp. for Neurology and Neurosurgery, 1994–98; NIHR Nat. Dir for Dementia Res., 2014–. Director: NIHR Clin. Res. Network for Dementia and Neurodegenerative Diseases, 2005–14; NIHR Queen Sq. Dementia Biomedical Res. Unit, 2012–. Pres., Assoc. of British Neurologists, 2011–13. FMedSci 2002. Liveryman, Soc. of Apothecaries, 1978– (Mem., Ct of Assistants, 1999–). Ed., Jl of Neurology, Neurosurgery and Psychiatry, 2004–09. *Publications:* Unusual Dementias, 1992; (with J. Growdon) Dementia, 1998, 2nd edn 2007; (with C. Clarke, R. Howard and S. Shorvon) Neurology: a Queen Square textbook, 2009; papers on Alzheimer's disease and related dementias. *Recreations:* English literature, equestrian sports, sailing. *Address:* The National Hospital for Neurology and Neurosurgery, Queen Square, WC1N 3BG. *T:* (020) 3448 4773. *Club:* Athenæum.

ROSSWALL, Prof. Thomas; Professor, Swedish University of Agricultural Sciences, 2000–09, now Emeritus; Chairman: Mistra Urban Futures, since 2014; Mistra Centre on Evidence-based Environmental Management, since 2011; *b* 20 Dec. 1941; *s* of Axel Rosswall and Britta (*née* Lindroth). *Educ:* Univ. of Uppsala (BSc 1966). Asst, Dept of Biochemistry, Univ. of Uppsala, 1967–70; Res. Asst, Dept of Microbiol., Swedish Univ. of Agricl Scis, 1970–76; Programme Officer, Swedish Council for Planning and Co-ordination of Research, 1976–80; Researcher, 1980–82, Asst Prof., 1982–84, Associate Prof., 1984, Dept of Microbiol., Swedish Univ. of Agricl Research; Prof., Dept of Water and Envmtl Studies, Univ. of Linköping, 1984–92; Exec. Dir, Internat. Geosphere-Biosphere Prog., 1987–94; Rector, Swedish Univ. of Agricl Scis, 1994–2000. Prof., Stockholm Univ., 1992–2000; Dir, Internat. Secretariat, System for Analysis, Res. and Trng, Washington, 1992–93; Dir, Internat. Foundn for Science, Stockholm, 2000–01; Exec. Dir, Internat. Council for Sci., 2002–09. Chair, Consultative Gp on Internat. Agricultural Res., Res. (formerly Challenge) Prog. on Climate Change, Agriculture and Food Security, 2009–14. MAE 1989; Fellow: Royal Swedish Acad. of Scis, 1989; Royal Swedish Acad. of Agric. and Forestry, 1995; Royal Acad. of Arts and Scis of Uppsala, 1999; World Acad. of Arts and Scis, 2005; Associate Fellow,

World Acad. of Scis (formerly Third World Acad. of Sci., then Acad. of Scis for the Developing World), 2002. *Publications:* edited: Systems Analysis in Northern Coniferous Forests, 1971; (jtly) IBP Tundra Biome Procs 4th International Meeting on Biological Productivity of Tundra, 1971; Modern Methods in the Study of Microbial Ecology, 1973; (jtly) Structure and Function of Tundra Ecosystems, 1975; Nitrogen Cycling in West African Ecosystems, 1980; (jtly) Terrestrial Nitrogen Cycles: processes, ecosystems strategies and management impacts, 1981; (jtly) Nitrogen Cycling in South-East Asian Wet Monsoonal Ecosystems, 1981; (jtly) The Nitrogen Cycle, 1982; (jtly) Nitrogen Cycling in Ecosystems of Latin America and the Caribbean, 1982; (jtly) Scales and Global Change: spatial and temporal variability of biospheric and geospheric processes, 1988; (jtly) Ecology of Arable Land: the role of organism in carbon and nitrogen cycling, 1989; 100 papers in scientific jls. *Address:* 57 chemin du Belvédère, 06530 Le Tignet, France. *T:* (6) 30487798. *E:* thomas.rosswall@gmail.com.

ROST, Peter Lewis; energy consultant, retired; *b* 19 Sept. 1930; *s* of Frederick Rosenstiel and Elisabeth Merz; *m* 1961, Hilary Mayo; two *s* two *d. Educ:* various primary schs; Aylesbury Grammar Sch. National Service, RAF, 1948–50; Birmingham Univ. (BA Hons Geog.), 1950–53. Investment Analyst and Financial Journalist with Investors Chronicle, 1953–58; firstly Investment Advisor, 1958, and then, 1962, Mem. London Stock Exchange, resigned 1977. MP (C) Derbys SE, 1970–83, Erewash, 1983–92. Secretary: Cons. Parly Trade and Industry Cttee, 1972–73; Cons. Parly Energy Cttee, 1974–77; Select Cttee on Energy, 1979–92. Treasurer, Anglo-German Parly Gp, 1974–92; Jt Chm., Alternative and Complementary Medicine Parly Gp, 1989–92. Chairman: Major Energy Users' Council, 1992–95; Utility Buyers' Forum, 1995–98; Vice-Pres., Combined Heat and Power Assoc. (Hon. Life Mem.). FRGS (Mem. Council, 1980–83); Fellow, Industry and Parlt Trust, 1987; Companion, Inst. of Energy, 1992. Freeman, City of London. Grand Cross, Order of Merit, Germany, 1979. *Publications:* Weimar to Westminster (autobiog.), 2010; papers on energy. *Recreations:* tennis, ski-ing, gardening, antique map collecting. *Address:* Norcott Court, Berkhamsted, Herts HP4 1LE. *T:* (01442) 866123, 07818 007236, *Fax:* (01442) 865901; 629 Chemin de la Gipiere, 83440 Montauroux, Var, France. *T:* 494477067.

ROSTRON, Martin Keith; Principal, Greenhead College, Huddersfield, 2002–13; educational adviser, Alkemygold Ltd (Alps), since 2013; *b* 10 Sept. 1953; *s* of Harold and Lucy Rostron; *m* 1976, Linda Potts; two *s* one *d. Educ:* Liverpool Univ. (BA Hons English 1974; PGCE 1977). Teacher: Knutsford High Sch., 1977–84; Priestley Coll., Warrington, 1984–91; Vice Principal, Greenhead Coll. (Sixth Form Coll.), 1991–2002. FRSA 2005. *Recreations:* walking, reading, cookery, classical music, watching sport, travel, visits to children and grandson overseas.

ROTH, Prof. Klaus Friedrich, FRS 1960; Emeritus Professor, University of London; Hon. Research Fellow, Department of Mathematics, University College London, since 1996; *b* 29 Oct. 1925; *s* of late Dr Franz Roth and Mathilde Roth; *m* 1955, Melek Khairy, BSc, PhD (*d* 2002). *Educ:* St Paul's Sch.; Peterhouse, Cambridge (BA 1945; Hon. Fellow, 1989); University College, London (MSc 1948; PhD 1950; Fellow, 1979). Asst Master, Gordonstoun School, 1945–46. Member of Dept of Mathematics, University College, London, 1948–66; title of Professor in the University of London conferred 1961; Prof. of Pure Maths (Theory of Numbers), 1966–88, Vis. Prof. in Dept of Maths, 1988–96, Fellow, 1999, Imperial College, London. Visiting Lecturer, 1956–57, Vis. Prof., 1965–66, at Mass Inst. of Techn., USA. Foreign Hon. Mem., Amer. Acad. of Arts and Scis, 1966. Hon. FRSE 1993. Fields Medal awarded at International Congress of Mathematicians, 1958; De Morgan Medal, London Math. Soc., 1983; Sylvester Medal, Royal Soc., 1991. *Publications:* papers in various mathematical jls. *Recreations:* chess, cinema, ballroom dancing.

ROTH, Martin, PhD; Director, Victoria and Albert Museum, since 2011; *b* Stuttgart, 16 Jan. 1955; *m* 1996, Dr Harriet Roth; one *s* two *d. Educ:* Eberhard Karls Univ. (PhD 1987). Postdoctoral res., La Maison des Sciences de l'Homme, École des hautes études en sciences sociales, 1988; Curator, German Historical Mus., Berlin, 1989–91; Dir, German Hygiene Mus., Dresden, 1991–2000; Dir Gen., Dresden State Art Collections, Dresden, 2001–11. Dir, Thematic Exhibns, Worldwide Project and Global Dialogue Confs, German World Fair Expo 2000, Hannover, 1996–2001. President: German Mus Assoc., 1995–2003; Cultural Foundn of Federal State of Saxony, 1996–2003; Member, Advisory Board: Prussian Cultural Heritage Foundn/Nat. Mus Berlin, 2003–; German Ministry of Foreign Affairs, 2005–12. Member: Council, RCA, 2011–; Court, Imperial Coll. London, 2012–. Trustee: Arts and Music, Dresden Foundn, 2012–; British Council, 2013–; Musées des Arts Décoratifs, Paris, 2014–. Chevalier, Ordre des Arts et des Lettres (France), 2007; Order of Dannebrog (Denmark), 2010. *Publications:* (jtly) Kunst-Transfer: Thesen und Visionen zur Restitution von Kunstwerken, München und Berlin, 2009; (ed jtly) Zukunft seit 1560: Von der Kunstkammer zu den Staatlichen Kunstsammlungen Dresden, 2010; (ed jtly) Im Sog Der Kunst: Museen Neu Denken, 2012. *Address:* Victoria and Albert Museum, Cromwell Road, SW7 2RL.

ROTH, Hon. Sir Peter Marcel, Kt 2009; **Hon. Mr Justice Roth;** a Judge of the High Court of Justice, Chancery Division, since 2009; President, Competition Appeal Tribunal, since 2013; *b* 19 Dec. 1952; *s* of Stephen Jeffery Roth and Eva Marta Roth; *m* 2010, Tessa Margaret Fras; one *d*, and one step *s* one step *d. Educ:* St Paul's Sch.; New Coll., Oxford (Open Schol.; BA 1974; MA 1986); Law Sch., Univ. of Pennsylvania (Thouron Fellow; LLM 1977). Called to the Bar, Middle Temple, 1977 (Harmsworth Schol.), Bencher, 2008; in practice at the Bar, 1979–2009; QC 1997; Recorder, 2000–09; Deputy High Court Judge, 2008–09. Vis. Associate Prof., Law Sch., Univ. of Pennsylvania, 1987; Vis. Prof., KCL, 2003–09. Jt Chair, Bench and Bar Cttee, United Jewish Israel Appeal, 1997–2003. Chair, Competition Law Assoc., 2003–09. Chm., Lawyers' Adv. Cttee, Peace Brigades Internat. UK, 2007–. Trustee: British Inst. of Internat. and Comparative Law, 2006–09; New Coll. Develt Fund, 2014–. Chair, Insurance Wkg Party, Terrence Higgins Trust, 1989–94. Gov., Tel Aviv Univ., 2006–09. *Publications:* (Gen. Ed.) Bellamy & Child's European Community Law of Competition, 5th edn 2001, 6th edn 2008; articles in legal jls. *Recreations:* travel, music. *Address:* Competition Appeal Tribunal, Victoria House, Bloomsbury Place, WC1A 2EB.

ROTHERAM, Steven Philip; MP (Lab) Liverpool Walton, since 2010; *b* 4 Nov. 1961; *s* of Harry and Dorothy Rotheram; *m* 1989, Sandra; one *s* two *d. Educ:* Ruffwood Comprehensive Sch.; Kirkby Further Educn Coll.; Liverpool John Moores Univ. (MA Urban Renaissance). Work in construction sector, 1978–89; instructor, 1989–2001; Director: SIP Property Develt LLP, 2006–; SPR Consultants. Dir, Liverpool Inst. for Performing Arts, 2004–10. Mem. (Lab) Liverpool CC, 2002–11 (Lord Mayor, 2008). *Address:* House of Commons, SW1A 0AA.

ROTHERMERE, 4th Viscount *cr* 1919, of Hemsted, co. Kent; **Jonathan Harold Esmond Vere Harmsworth;** Bt 1910; Baron 1914; Chairman, Daily Mail and General Trust plc, since 1998; *b* 3 Dec. 1967; *s* of 3rd Viscount Rothermere and his 1st wife, Patricia Evelyn Beverley (*née* Matthews; *d* 1992); *S* father, 1998; *m* 1993, Claudia, *d* of T. J. Clemence; two *s* three *d. Heir: s* Hon. Vere Richard Jonathan Harold Harmsworth, *b* 20 Oct. 1994. *Address:* (office) Northcliffe House, 2 Derry Street, W8 5TT.

ROTHERWICK, 3rd Baron *cr* 1939, of Tylney, Southampton; **Herbert Robin Cayzer;** 6th Bt *cr* 1904, of Gartmore and 3rd Bt *cr* 1924, of Tylney; *b* 12 March 1954; *s* of 2nd Baron Rotherwick and Sarah-Jane (*d* 1978), *o d* of Sir Michael Nial Slade, 6th Bt; *S* father, 1996; *S* kinsman, Sir James Cayzer, 5th Bt, 2012; *m* 1st, 1982, Sara Jane (marr. diss. 1994), *o d* of Robert James McAlpine; two *s* one *d*; 2nd, 2000, Tania, *d* of Christopher Fox; one *s* one *d* (and one *s* decd). *Educ:* Harrow; RAC, Cirencester. Lieut, Life Guards. Elected Mem., H of L, 1999; Opposition Whip, H of L, 2001–05; Opposition spokesperson for Educn and Skills, Work and Pensions, 2001–03, for DEFRA, 2003–05. Mem., Council of Europe, 2000–01. Fellow, Industry and Parlt Trust, 2005. Mem., Armed Forces Parly Scheme, 2010–12. Pres., Gen. Aviation Awareness Council, 1997–. Director: PFA (Ulair) Ltd, 1999–2003; Cayzer Continuation PCC Ltd, 2004–; Cornbury Estates Co. Ltd, 2006–; Light Aircraft Assoc. Ltd, 2008–; Cornbury Maintenance Co. Ltd, 2012–; Bygone Engrg Ltd, 2013–14. Chm., Air Touring Ltd, 2006–10. *Heir: s* Hon. Herbert Robin Cayzer, *b* 10 July 1989. *Address:* Cornbury Park, Charlbury, Oxford OX7 3EH.

ROTHES, 22nd Earl of, *cr* before 1457; **James Malcolm David Leslie;** Lord Leslie 1445; Baron Ballenbreich 1457; *b* 4 June 1958; *s* of 21st Earl of Rothes and of Marigold, *o d* of Sir David Evans Bevan, 1st Bt; *S* father, 2005. *Educ:* Eton. Graduated Parnham House, 1990. *Heir: b* Hon. Alexander John Leslie [*b* 18 Feb. 1962; *m* 1st, 1990, Tina Gordon (marr. diss.); 2nd, 2008, Mrs Francesca Clare MacManaway (marr. diss.); 3rd, 2014, Miranda Grant]. *Address:* Littlecroft, West Milton, Bridport, Dorset DT6 3SL.

ROTHNIE, Iain Andrew; Partner, Real Estate, Herbert Smith LLP, international law firm, 2008–11; *b* 14 Nov. 1955; *s* of late Norman George Rothnie and Margaret Venables Rothnie; *m* 2003, Julie Fewtrell. *Educ:* Reading Sch.; Pembroke Coll., Cambridge (BA 1978). Admitted solicitor, 1981; Herbert Smith: Partner, 1988–; Hd, Real Estate, 2000–02; Exec. Partner, subseq. Chief Operating Officer, 2002–06; Global Hd, Real Estate, 2006–08. *Recreations:* travel, art, theatre.

ROTHSCHILD, family name of **Baron Rothschild**.

ROTHSCHILD, 4th Baron *cr* 1885; **Nathaniel Charles Jacob Rothschild,** Bt 1847; OM 2002; GBE 1998; Chairman, RIT Capital Partners plc, since 1988; President, Five Arrows Ltd, since 2010 (Chairman, 1980–2010); *b* 29 April 1936; *e s* of 3rd Baron Rothschild, GBE, GM, FRS and Barbara, *o d* of St John Hutchinson, KC; *S* father, 1990; *m* 1961, Serena Mary, *er d* of late Sir Philip Gordon Dunn, 2nd Bt; one *s* three *d. Educ:* Eton; Christ Church, Oxford (BA 1st cl. hons History; Hon. Student, 2006). Chairman: Bd of Trustees, Nat. Gallery, 1985–91; Nat. Heritage Meml Fund, 1992–98, administering Heritage Lottery Fund, 1995–98. Dep. Chm., BSkyB Gp plc, 2003–08. Fellow, Ashmolean Mus., Oxford, 2006; Hon. Fellow, Courtauld Inst. of Art, 2008; Hon. FKC 2002; Hon. FBA 1998; Hon. FRIBA 1998; Hon. FRAM 2002. Hon. PhD Hebrew Univ. of Jerusalem, 1992; Hon. DLitt: Newcastle, 1998; Warwick 2003; Hon. LLD Exeter, 1998; DUniv Keele, 2000; Hon. DCL Oxon, 2002; Hon. DSc (Econs) London, 2004. Hon. Fellow, City of Jerusalem, 1992. Weizmann Award for Humanities and Scis, 1997; J. Paul Getty Medal, 2014. Comdr, Order of Henry the Navigator (Portugal), 1985. *Heir: s* Hon. Nathaniel Philip Victor James Rothschild, *qv. Address:* The Pavilion, Eythrope, Aylesbury, Bucks HP18 0HS. *T:* (01296) 748337.

See also E. Rothschild, Hon. H. M. Rothschild.

ROTHSCHILD, Emma, CMG 2000; Knowles Professor of History, since 2008, and Affiliated Professor, Harvard Law School, since 2013, Harvard University (Professor of History, 2007–08); Co-Director, Joint Centre for History and Economics, Magdalene College and King's College (formerly at King's College), Cambridge, since 1991, and Harvard University, since 2007; Fellow, Magdalene College, Cambridge, since 2010; *b* 16 May 1948; *d* of 3rd Baron Rothschild, GBE, GM, FRS and of Lady Rothschild, MBE (*née* Teresa Mayor); *m* 1991, Prof. Amartya Kumar Sen, *qv. Educ:* Somerville Coll., Oxford (MA; Hon. Fellow, 2012); Massachusetts Inst. of Technology (Kennedy Schol. in Econs). Associate Professor: of Humanities, MIT, 1978–80; of Science, Technology and Society, MIT, 1979–88; Dir de Recherches Invité, Ecole des Hautes Etudes en Sciences Sociales, Paris, 1981–82. Fellow, King's College, Cambridge, 1988–2010; Hon. Prof. of Hist. and Econs, Univ. of Cambridge, 2010–. Mem., OECD Gp of Experts on Science and Technology in the New Socio-Economic Context, 1976–80; OECD Sci. Examiner, Aust., 1984–85. Member: Govg Bd, Stockholm Internat. Peace Res. Inst., 1983–93; Govg Bd, Stockholm Envmt Inst., 1989–93; Bd, Olof Palme Meml Fund (Stockholm), 1986–2007; Royal Commn on Environmental Pollution, 1986–94; Bd, British Council, 1993–98; Bd, UN Foundn, 1998–; Council for Sci. and Technol., 1998–2001; Chairman: UN Res. Inst. for Social Develt, 1999–2005; Kennedy Meml Trust, 2000–09. Internat. Mem. (formerly Foreign Mem.), Amer. Philosophical Soc., 2002. Hon. DLitt Edinburgh, 2013. *Publications:* Paradise Lost: the Decline of the Auto-Industrial Age, 1973; Economic Sentiments, 2001; The Inner Life of Empires: an eighteenth-century history, 2011; articles in learned and other jls. *Address:* Department of History, Harvard University, 1730 Cambridge Street, Cambridge, MA 02138, USA.

ROTHSCHILD, Baron Eric Alain Robert David de; Chairman, Rothschild Bank AG, since 2000; Partner, Rothschild et Compagnie Banque, since 1982; *b* NY, 3 Oct. 1940; French nationality; *m* 1983, Maria Béatrice Caracciolo di Forino; two *s* one *d. Educ:* Ecole Polytechnique Fédérale, Zürich (Engr 1963). Chairman: Paris Orléans, 1974; Soc. du Château Rieussec, 1999; Managing Partner: Soc. Civile de Château Lafite Rothschild, 1974; Soc. Civile de Duhart Milon Rothschild, 1975; Partner, Rothschild et Cie Gestion, 1998; Board Member: N. M. Rothschild & Sons (London), 1978; SIACI, 1983; Los Vascos, 1993; Christie's France, 1994. Chairman: Fondation de Rothschild, 1982; Centre de Documentation Juive Contemporaine, 1984; Mémorial du Martyr Juif Inconnu, 1984; Fondation Casip-Cojasor, 1988; Fondation Nat. des Arts Graphiques et Plastiques, 1989; Fondation Rothschild, 1993; Rothschild Private Mgt Ltd, 2003; Vice Chm., Fondation pour la Mémoire de la Shoah, 2001; Bd Mem., Alliance Israélite Universelle, 1994. *Address:* (office) 3 rue de Messine, 75008 Paris, France. *T:* (1) 40744006, *Fax:* (1) 40749816.

ROTHSCHILD, Sir Evelyn de, Kt 1989; Chairman, E. L. Rothschild Ltd; *b* 29 Aug. 1931; *s* of late Anthony Gustav de Rothschild; *m* 1973, Victoria Schott (marr. diss. 2000); two *s* one *d*; *m* 2000, Lynn Forester. *Educ:* Harrow; Trinity Coll., Cambridge. Chm., N. M. Rothschild and Sons Ltd, 1976–2003. Chairman: Economist Newspaper, 1972–89; St Mary's Hosp. Med. Sch., London, 1977–88; United Racecourses Ltd, 1977–94; former Chm., Concordia BV. Chm., British Merchant Banking and Securities Houses Assoc. (formerly Accepting Houses Cttee), 1985–89. Gov., LSE, 1968–. Chairman: ERANDA Foundn, 1967–; Cambridge Business Sch. Appeal; Hon. Life Pres., Norwood and Ravenswood Children's Charity. *Recreations:* art, racing.

ROTHSCHILD, Hon. Hannah Mary; director and author; *b* London, 22 May 1962; *d* of 4th Baron Rothschild, *qv*; three *d. Educ:* St Paul's Girls' Sch.; Marlborough Coll.; St Hilda's Coll., Oxford (BA Mod. Hist.). Freelance TV and film dir, producer and script writer, profiles and interviews for Vanity Fair, Vogue, House & Gardens, W mag., Independent, The Times, 1985–; Sen. Editor, Harpers Bazaar, 2012–. *Television* includes: Keeping up with the Medici (dir and writer), 1998; The Jazz Baroness (dir and writer), 2009; Hi Society: The Wonderful World of Nicky Haslam (dir, prod. and writer), 2009; Mandelson - The Real PM? (dir and prod.), 2010; *film:* Eddie Loves Mary (dir and writer), 2002. Vice Pres., Hay Literary Fest., 2000–; Trustee: Rothschild Foundn, 2008–; Nat. Gall., 2009– (Chm. Trustees, 2015–); Waddesdon Manor, 2010–; Tate Gall., 2013–. *Publications:* The Baroness: the search for Nica, the rebellious Rothschild, 2012; The Improbability of Love, 2015. *Recreations:* art, film, books, charity. *E:* hannah@hannahrothschild.co.uk.

See also Hon. N. P. V. J. Rothschild.

ROTHSCHILD, Hon. Nathaniel Philip Victor James; Chairman, JNR Ltd, since 2002; *b* London, 12 July 1971; only *s* and heir of 4th Baron Rothschild, *qv. Educ:* Eton Coll.; Wadham Coll., Oxford (BA Hist.). Co-Chm., Atticus Capital LP, 1996–2009; Founder, Co-

Chm. and non-exec. Dir, Vallar plc, later Bumi plc, 2009–12; Director: RIT Capital Partners plc, 2002–10; Rothschild Foundn. Non-exec. Dir, Barrick Gold Corp., 2010–13. Mem., Internat. Adv. Council, Brookings Inst. Mem., Belfer Center for Sci. and Internat. Affairs, Harvard Univ. *Recreations:* ski-ing, horseracing. *Address:* Riedweg 11A, Klosters 7250, Switzerland. *Club:* White's.

ROTHSCHILD AGIUS, Kate Juliette de; Trustee, Wallace Collection, since 2013; *b* London, 11 July 1949; *d* of late Edmund Leopold de Rothschild, CBE, TD and Elizabeth Edith de Rothschild; *m* 1971, Marcus Ambrose Paul Agius, *qv*; two *d. Educ:* Courtauld Inst. of Art, Univ. of London (BA Hons 1971). Curatorial asst, Fogg Art Mus., Cambridge, Mass, 1971–72; intern, Sotheby's, London, 1972–74; dealer (sole trader) in master drawings, 1974–2007; Chm., Patrons of BM, 2008–13. Member, vetting committees: Grosvenor Hse Antiques Fair, London, 1990–; Fine Art and Antique Dealers Fair, NY, 1996–. *Recreations:* visiting museums and galleries, visiting gardens, looking after Exbury Gardens, travel, being with my family. *Address:* 25 Chelsea Square, SW3 6LF. *T:* (020) 7351 7868, *Fax:* (020) 7351 7475. *E:* kate@katederothschild.co.uk.

ROTHWELL, Margaret Irene, CMG 1992; HM Diplomatic Service, retired; Ambassador to Côte d'Ivoire, 1990–97, and concurrently to the Republic of Niger, the People's Democratic Republic of Burkina and Liberia; *b* 25 Aug. 1938; *d* of Harry Rothwell and Martha (*née* Goedecke). *Educ:* Southampton Grammar School for Girls; Lady Margaret Hall, Oxford (BA LitHum). Foreign Office, 1961; Third, later Second Secretary, UK Delegn to Council of Europe, Strasbourg, 1964; FO, 1966; Second Sec. (Private Sec. to Special Representative in Africa), Nairobi, 1967; Second, later First Sec., Washington, 1968; FCO, 1972; First Sec. and Head of Chancery, Helsinki, 1976; FCO, 1980; Counsellor and Hd of Trng Dept, FCO, 1981–83; Counsellor, Consul-Gen. and Head of Chancery, Jakarta, 1984–87; Overseas Inspectorate, FCO, 1987–90. Reviewer, Quinquennial Review of the Marshall Aid Commemoration Commn, 1998; UK Rep., Jt US/UK Commn on Student Travel Exchanges, 1998; voluntary work for Govt of Rwanda, 2001. Mem. Cttee and Ed., Password, 2007–. Lay Rep., Council of Inns of Court, 2004–12. Vice-Chm., 1993–2007, Mem. Cttee and Ed., Password, 2007–, FCO Assoc. Chm., Ampfield Parish Council, 1993–. Trustee, Pimpernel Trust, 2007–. Hon. LLD Southampton, 1994. *Recreations:* travel, gardening, cooking, tennis. *Address:* Hill House, Knapp, Ampfield, Romsey, Hants SO51 9BT.

ROTHWELL, Dame Nancy (Jane), DBE 2005; DL; PhD, DSc; FMedSci; FRS 2004; FRSB; Professor of Physiology, since 1994, and President and Vice-Chancellor, since 2010, University of Manchester (Vice President for Research, 2004–07; Deputy President and Deputy Vice-Chancellor, 2007–10). *Educ:* Univ. of London (BSc, PhD, DSc). Royal Soc. Res. Fellow, 1987, then Reader in Physiol Scis, and formerly Res. and Graduate Dean for Biol Scis, Univ. of Manchester. Chm., MRC Neurosci. and Mental Health Bd, 2002–04; Member, Council: MRC, 2000–04; BBSRC, 2005–08; Cancer Res. UK, 2002–08; NESTA, 2002–06; Council for Sci. and Technol., 2011– (Co-Chm., 2012–); Mem., Greater Manchester Local Enterprise Partnership Bd, 2011–. Chm., Wellcome Trust Public Engagement Strategy Gp, 2005–08. President: British Neurosci. Assoc., 2000–03; Soc. of Biology (formerly Bioscis Fedn), 2008–14. Mem. Council, Royal Soc., 2013–. Royal Instn Christmas Lectures, 1998. FMedSci 1999; Hon. FRCP 2006; FRSA. DL Gtr Manchester, 2010. *Publications:* over 250 research papers and several books. *Address:* Office of the President and Vice-Chancellor, University of Manchester, Oxford Road, Manchester M13 9PL.

ROUCH, Ven. Peter Bradford; Archdeacon of Bournemouth, since 2011; *b* Rochester, 22 April 1966; *s* of Victor Maurice Rouch and Esmée Edith May Rouch; *m* 1994, Tracey Michelle Hemmerdinger; two *d. Educ:* Sir Joseph Williamson's Math. Sch., Rochester; Brasenose Coll., Oxford (BA Hons Zool. 1987); Peterhouse, Cambridge (MA 1998); Univ. of Manchester (PhD 2005). Ordained deacon, 1999, priest, 2000; Asst Curate, St John the Evangelist, East Dulwich, 1999–2002; Junior Res. Fellow, St Stephen's House, Oxford, 2002–04; Chaplain, St John's Coll., Oxford, 2003–04; Priest-in-charge, Church of the Apostles', Manchester, with St Cuthbert, Miles Platting, 2005–11. *Address:* Glebe House, 22 Bellflower Way, Chandlers Ford, Hants SO53 4HN. *T:* (023) 8026 0955. *E:* peter.rouch@winchester.anglican.org.

ROUCH, Peter Christopher; QC 1996; *b* 15 June 1947; *s* of Rupert Trevelyan Rouch and Doris Linda Rouch; *m* 1980, Carol Sandra Francis; one *s* one *d. Educ:* UCW, Aberystwyth (LLB). Called to the Bar, Gray's Inn, 1972. *Recreations:* golf, ski-ing, fishing, cinema, music. *Address:* Church View, 9 Mayals Road, Mayals, Swansea SA3 5BT; 20 Archery Close, W2 2BE.

ROUGIER, Maj.-Gen. Charles Jeremy, CB 1986; FICE; Director, Royal Horticultural Society's Garden, Rosemoor, 1988–95; *b* 23 Feb. 1933; *s* of late Lt-Col and Mrs C. L. Rougier; *m* 1964, Judith Cawood Ellis (*d* 2013); three *s* one *d. Educ:* Marlborough Coll.; Pembroke Coll., Cambridge (MA). FICE 1986. Aden, 1960; Instructor, RMA Sandhurst, 1961–62; psc 1963; MA to MGO, 1964–66; comd 11 Engineer Sqn, Commonwealth Bde, 1966–68; jssc 1968; Company Comd, RMA Sandhurst, 1969–70; Directing Staff, Staff Coll., Camberley, 1970–72; CO 21 Engineer Regt, BAOR, 1972–74; Staff of Chief of Defence Staff, 1974–77; Commandant, Royal Sch. of Military Engineering, 1977–79; RCDS 1980; COS, Headquarters Northern Ireland, 1981; Asst Chief of General Staff (Trng), 1982–83; Dir of Army Training, 1983–84; Chm., Review of Officer Training and Educn Study, 1985; Engr-in-Chief (Army), 1985–88, retd. Col Comdt, RE, 1987–92. Mem. (part-time), Lord Chancellor's Panel of Ind. Inspectors, 1988–2003. Gold Veitch Meml Medal, RHS, 1995. *Recreations:* hill walking, DIY, gardening. *Address:* c/o Lloyds Bank plc, PO Box 99 BX1 1LT.

ROULSTONE, Brig. Joan Margaret; Director, Women (Army), 1992–94; Aide-de-Camp to the Queen, 1992–95; *b* 7 Nov. 1945; *d* of Eric Laurie Frank Tyler and Jessie Tyler (*née* Louise); *m* 1971, Peter John Roulstone. *Educ:* seven schools worldwide. Commnd, WRAC, 1964; UK and BAOR, 1965–78; resigned 1978, reinstated, 1980; UK, 1980–86; Corps Recruiting and Liaison Officer, WRAC, 1986–87; Chief G1/G4 NE Dist and 2nd Inf. Div., 1988–89; Comd WRAC, UKLF, 1990–92. *Address:* c/o Barclays Bank, Priestpopple, Hexham, Northumberland NE46 1PE.

ROUND, Prof. Nicholas Grenville, FBA 1996; Hughes Professor of Hispanic Studies, University of Sheffield, 1994–2003, now Emeritus; *b* 6 June 1938; *s* of Isaac Eric Round and Laura Christabel (*née* Poole); *m* 1966, Ann Le Vin; one *d. Educ:* Boyton CP Sch., Cornwall; Launceston Coll.; Pembroke Coll., Oxford. BA (1st cl. Hons, Spanish and French) 1959; MA 1963; DPhil 1967. MITI 1990. Lecturer in Spanish, Queen's Univ. of Belfast, 1962–71, Reader, 1971–72; Warden, Alanbrooke Hall, QUB, 1970–72; Stevenson Prof. of Hispanic Studies, Glasgow Univ., 1972–94. Mem., Exec. Cttee, Strathclyde Region Labour Party, 1986–94; Chm., Cornwall Labour Party, 2007–10. Trustee, Morrab Library, Penzance, 2011–. Pres., Assoc. Internat. de Galdosistas, 1999–2001. Officer, Order of Isabel the Catholic (Spain), 1990. *Publications:* Unamuno: Abel Sánchez: a critical guide, 1974; The Greatest Man Uncrowned: a study of the fall of Alvaro de Luna, 1986; trans., Tirso de Molina, Damned for Despair, 1986; (ed) Re-reading Unamuno, 1989; On Reasoning and Realism: three easy pieces, 1991; Libro llamado Fedrón, 1993; (ed) Translation Studies in Hispanic Contexts, 1998; (ed) New Galdós Studies, 2003; contribs to: Mod. Lang. Review, Bulletin Hispanic Studies, Proc. Royal Irish Academy, etc. *Recreations:* reading, music, all aspects of Cornwall. *Address:* 10 King's Road, Penzance, Cornwall TR18 4LG. *Club:* (Hon. Life Mem.) Students' Union (Belfast).

ROUNDS, Helen; *see* Edwards, Helen.

ROUNTREE, His Honour Peter Charles Robert; a Circuit Judge, 1986–2001; *b* 28 April 1936; *s* of late Francis Robert George Rountree, MBE and Mary Felicity Patricia Rountree, MBE (*née* Wilson); *m* 1st, 1968, Nicola Mary (*née* Norman-Butler) (marr. diss. 1996); one *s*, and one step *d*; 2nd, 2004, Shirley Murray (*née* Arbuthnot); one step *s* one step *d. Educ:* Uppingham School; St John's College, Cambridge (MA). Called to the Bar, Inner Temple, 1961; a Recorder, April–July 1986. *Recreations:* sailing, golf, tennis. *Clubs:* Boodle's, Pratt's, Royal Yacht Squadron; Rye Golf, New Zealand Golf.

ROUQUIER, Prof. Raphaël Alexis Marcel, PhD; Professor of Mathematics, University of California, Los Angeles, since 2012; *b* Etampes, France, 9 Dec. 1969; *s* of Pierre Rouquier and Danièle Rouquier (*née* Raynaud); *m* 2003, Dr Meredith Cohen. *Educ:* Lycée Saint-Louis, Paris; Ecole Normale Supérieure, Paris; Université Paris 7 (PhD 1992). Chargé de Recherches, 1992–2002, Dir de Recherches, 2002–05, CNRS; Prof. of Representation Theory, Univ. of Leeds, 2005–06; Waynflete Prof. of Pure Maths, Univ. of Oxford, 2007–12; Fellow of Magdalen Coll., Oxford, 2007–12. *Address:* Department of Mathematics, University of California, Los Angeles, CA 90095–1555, USA.

ROURKE, Josephine Frances; Artistic Director, Donmar Warehouse, since 2012; *b* Salford, Gtr Manchester, 3 Sept. 1976; *d* of Sean Rourke and Vivienne Rourke (*née* Perrin). *Educ:* St Patrick's RC High Sch.; Eccles Coll. of Further Educn; New Hall, Cambridge (BA Hons English 1998). Trainee Resident Asst Dir, Donmar Warehouse, 2000–01; Trainee Associate Dir, Royal Court Theatre, 2002–03; Associate Dir, Sheffield Theatres, 2005–06; Artistic Dir, Bush Theatre, 2007–11. *Productions include:* King John, RSC, 2006; Men Should Weep, NT, 2010; Much Ado About Nothing, Wyndham's, 2011; Donmar Warehouse: The Recruiting Officer, Berenice, The Physicists, 2012; The Weir, Coriolanus, 2013; Privacy, City of Angels, 2014; The Vote, 2015; Dir, The Machine, Manchester Internat. Film Fest., 2013. Non-exec. Mem. Bd, Channel 4, 2012–. *Recreations:* cooking, walking and reading, rarely at the same time. *Address:* c/o Fay Davies, The Agency (London) Ltd, 24 Pottery Lane, Holland Park, W11 4LZ.

ROUS, family name of **Earl of Stradbroke**.

ROUS, Matthew James; HM Diplomatic Service; Consul-General, Guangzhou, China, since 2014; *b* 29 June 1964; *s* of Ronald Frank Rous and Florence Mary (*née* Woodward); *m* 1989, Beryl Ann Scott; one *s* two *d. Educ:* Burnt Mill Sch., Harlow; Churchill Coll., Cambridge (BA 1986; MA 1989). Chugai Pharmaceutical Co. Ltd, Tokyo, 1986–88; Asahi Shimbun European Gen. Bureau, London, 1989–91; joined HM Diplomatic Service, 1991; Project Officer, Know How Fund Prog., FCO, 1991–92; First Secretary: (Chancery), Beijing, 1994–97; (Commercial), Tokyo, 1998–2001; Dep. Hd of Mission and Consul-Gen., Brussels, 2002–05; Dep. Hd of Mission, 2005–10 and Consul-Gen., 2008–10, Jakarta; Hd, Progs Dept and Portfolio Dir, Inf. and Technol. Directorate, FCO, 2010–13; Interim Hd of Mission, Baku, 2013. *Recreations:* globetrotting, stargazing, family history, playing the bassoon badly. *Address:* c/o Foreign and Commonwealth Office, King Charles Street, SW1A 2AH.

ROUSE, Jonathan Mark; Director-General, Social Care, Local Government and Care Partnerships, Department of Health, since 2013; *b* 23 May 1968; *s* of James Clement Rouse and Barbara Jean Rouse (*née* Fowler); *m* 1991, Heulwen Mary Evans. *Educ:* Univ. of Manchester (LLB); Univ. of Nottingham (MBA Finance Dist.); Univ. of N London (MA Dist.). Principal Policy Officer, Ealing BC, 1992–93; Policy Analyst, Energy Saving Trust, 1993–94; Private Sec. to Housing Minister, 1994–95; Policy and Communications Manager, English Partnerships, 1995–98; Sec., Govt Urban Task Force, 1998–99; Chief Executive: CABE, 2000–04; Housing Corp., 2004–07; London Borough of Croydon, 2007–13. Non-exec. Dir, English Partnerships, 2004–07. Trustee, Homeless Internat., 2005–08. Hon. RIBA 2001; Hon. RTPI 2002. DUniv Oxford Brookes, 2003. *Recreations:* tennis, golf, hiking. *Address:* Department of Health, Richmond House, Whitehall, SW1A 2NS. *Club:* Queen's Park Rangers Football.

ROUSE, Justin Clive Douglas; QC 2015; a Recorder, since 2004; *b* Horndean, Hants, 21 May 1958; *s* of Lt Comdr D. Malcolm Rouse, MBE and Patricia Eileen Rouse; *m* 1989, Hilary Jane Brader; one *s* four *d. Educ:* Ryde Sch.; City of London Poly. (BA Hons Law); Inns of Court Sch. of Law. Called to the Bar, Lincoln's Inn, 1982; in practice as barrister, specialising in criminal law, 1983–. Advocacy trainer, Lincoln's Inn, 2005–. Mem., Criminal Bar Assoc. *Recreations:* fishing, countryside, family, Rugby coach, school governor, travel, reading, gardening. *Address:* 9 Bedford Row, WC1R 4AZ. *T:* (020) 7484 2727, *Fax:* (020) 7489 2828. *E:* justin.rouse@9bedfordrow.co.uk. *Club:* Amersham and Chiltern Rugby Football.

ROUSE, Ruth Elizabeth; Permanent Secretary, Ministry of Education and Human Resource Development, Grenada, since 2013; *b* 30 Jan. 1963. *Educ:* German Foundn for Internat. Develt, Berlin (Dip. Internat. Relns and Econ. Co-operation 1987); Diplomatic Acad. of London, PCL, (Post-Grad. Prog. in Diplomacy, Practice, Procedures, Dynamics 1989); Carleton Univ., Canada (BA French and Spanish 1996); Univ. of Westminster, London (MA Diplomatic Studies 2002). Ministry of Foreign Affairs, Grenada: Desk Officer (Africa and ME Affairs), Political and Economic Affairs Div., 1982–83; Protocol Officer, Protocol and Consular Div., 1983–90; Second Sec. (Protocol, Culture and Develt), Orgn of Eastern Caribbean States, High Commn, Ottawa, 1990–96; Chief of Protocol, 1996–99; High Comr in UK, 1999–2004; High Comr (non resident) to S Africa, 2000–05; Ambassador Designate to France, 2001–04; Perm. Rep. of Grenada to the UN, New York, 2004–07; High Comr for Grenada in UK, 2008–13 and (non-resident) to S Africa, 2012–13. Perm Rep., IMO, 2000–04, 2011–13. Mem., Nat. Celebrations Cttee, Grenada, 1996; Mem. Council, Royal Commonwealth Soc., 2010–13. Governor: Commonwealth Inst., 1999–2004; Commonwealth Foundn, 1999–2004, 2008–13; Advr, Commonwealth Business Council, 2010–13. Independence Award for Exemplary Public Service, 1998. *Recreations:* reading, travelling, Caribbean cooking, tennis, designing (art), photography, meeting people of different cultures, communications (radio/television), music (piano). *E:* ruth_elizabeth43@yahoo.com, ruthelizabethrouse@gmail.com. *Clubs:* Royal Over-Seas League, Women in Diplomatic Service; Commonwealth Countries League.

ROUSSEAU, Prof. George Sebastian, PhD; Professor, Faculty of History, 2003–15, and Co-Director, Centre for the History of Childhood, 2003–14, University of Oxford; *b* 23 Feb. 1941; *s* of Hyman Victoire Rousseau and Esther (*née* Zacuto). *Educ:* Amherst Coll., USA (BA 1962); Princeton Univ. (MA 1964; PhD 1966). Princeton University: Osgood Fellow in English Lit., 1965–66; Woodrow Wilson Dissertation Fellow, 1966; Instructor, then Asst Prof., Harvard Univ., 1966–68; University of California, Los Angeles: Asst Prof. of English, 1968–69; Associate Prof., 1969–76; Prof., 1976–94; Regius Prof. of English Lit. and Dir, Thomas Reid Inst., Aberdeen Univ., 1994–98; Res. Prof. of English, De Montfort Univ., 1999–2003. Fulbright Res. Prof., W Germany, 1970; Cambridge University: Hon. Fellow, Wolfson Coll., 1974–75; Overseas Fellow, 1979; Vis. Fellow Commoner, Trinity Coll., 1982; Sen. Fulbright Res. Schol., Sir Thomas Browne Inst., Netherlands, 1983; Vis. Exchange Prof., King's Coll., Cambridge, 1984; Clark Liby Prof., Univ. of Calif, 1985–86; Sen. Fellow, NEH, 1986–87; Vis. Fellow and Waynflete Lectr, Magdalen Coll., Oxford, 1993–94. Book reviewer, NY Times (Sunday), 1967–82. FRSocMed 1967; FRSA 1973. Dr *hc* Bucharest, 2007. *Publications:* (with M. Hope Nicolson) This Long Disease My Life: Alexander Pope and the sciences, 1968; (with N. Rudenstine) English Poetic Satire, 1969; (ed jtly) The Augustan Milieu: essays presented to Louis A. Landa, 1970; (ed jtly) Tobias Smollett: bicentennial essays presented to Lewis M. Knapp, 1971; (ed) Organic Form: the life of an idea, 1972; Goldsmith: the critical heritage, 1974; (with R. Porter) The Ferment of Knowledge: studies in the historiography of science, 1980; The Letters and Private Papers of Sir John Hill, 1981; Tobias Smollett: essays of two decades, 1982; (ed) Science and the Imagination: the Berkeley Conference, 1987; (with R. Porter) Sexual Underworlds of the Enlightenment, 1987; (with P. Rogers) The Enduring Legacy: Alexander Pope Tercentenary Essays, 1988; (with R. Porter) Exoticism in the Enlightenment, 1990; The Languages of Psyche: mind and body in enlightenment thought, 1990; Perilous Enlightenment: pre- and post-modern discourses - sexual, historical, 1991; Enlightenment Crossings: pre- and post-modern discourses - anthropological, 1991; Enlightenment Borders: pre- and post-modern discourses - medical, scientific, 1991; (jtly) Hysteria Before Freud, 1993; (with Roy Porter) Gout: the patrician malady, 1998; Framing and Imagining Disease in Cultural History, 2003; Yourcenar: a biography, 2004; Nervous Acts: essays on literature, culture and sensibility, 2004; Children and Sexuality: the Greeks to the Great War, 2007; The Notorious Sir John Hill: the man destroyed by ambition in the era of celebrity, 2012; Rachmaninoff's Cape: a nostalgia memoir, 2015; contrib. numerous articles to learned jls and mags. *Recreations:* chamber music, opera, walking, travel. *Address:* Magdalen College, Oxford OX1 4AU. *E:* george.rousseau@ntlworld.com.

ROUT, Leslie; Director General, National Kidney Research Fund and Kidney Foundation, 1992–97; *b* 5 Dec. 1936; *s* of James Rout and Ada Elizabeth Rout; *m* 1957, Josephine Goodley; one *s* one *d*. *Educ:* Queens, Wisbech. Police cadet, 1952–54; Nat. Service, 1954–56; Police Service, 1956–89: served in all depts; attained rank of Comdr Ops; awarded 6 commendations. FCMI. *Recreations:* music, history, travel.

ROUT, Owen Howard, FCIB; Executive Director (UK Operations), Barclays PLC and Barclays Bank PLC, 1987–90; Chairman: Barclays Financial Services Ltd, 1988–90; Starmin plc, 1990–93 (Deputy Chairman, 1993–94); *b* 16 April 1930; *s* of Frederick Owen and Marion Rout; *m* 1954, Jean (*née* Greetham); two *d*. *Educ:* Grey High Sch., Port Elizabeth, SA. ACIS. Dir, Barclays Bank UK Ltd, 1977–87; Gen. Man., Barclays PLC and Barclays Bank PLC, 1982–87. Chairman: Barclays Insurance Services Co. Ltd, 1982–85; Barclays Insurance Brokers International Ltd, 1982–85; Mercantile Gp, 1989–92; Director: Spreadeagle Insurance Co. Ltd, 1983–85; Baric Ltd, 1982–84; Albaraka Internat. Bank, 1990–93. Chartered Institute of Bankers: Mem. Council, 1985–90; Treas., 1986–90. Mem., Supervisory Bd, Banking World Magazine, 1986–90. Mem., Bd of Govs, Anglia Polytechnic Univ., 1993–2001. *Recreations:* watching sport—Rugby and cricket, playing golf, listening to music, gardening. *Club:* Aldeburgh Golf.

ROUTH, Donald Thomas; Under Secretary, Department of the Environment, 1978–90; *b* 22 May 1936; *s* of Thomas and Flora Routh; *m* 1961, Janet Hilda Allum. *Educ:* Leeds Modern Sch. Entered WO, Northern Comd, York, as Exec. Officer, 1954; Nat. Service, RN, 1954–56; Higher Exec. Officer, Comd Secretariat, Kenya, 1961–64; Asst Principal, Min. of Housing and Local Govt, 1964–66; Asst Private Sec. to Minister, 1966–67; Principal, 1967; on loan to Civil Service Selection Bd, 1971; Asst Sec., DoE, 1972; Under Sec., 1978; Regional Dir, West Midlands, 1978–81; Hd of Construction Industries Directorate, 1981–85; Dir of Senior Staff Management, 1985–86; Controller, The Crown Suppliers, 1986.

ROUTLEDGE, (Katherine) Patricia, CBE 2004 (OBE 1993); actress; *b* 17 Feb. 1929; *d* of Isaac Edgar Routledge and Catherine (*née* Perry). *Educ:* Birkenhead High Sch.; Univ. of Liverpool (BA Hons 1951); Bristol Old Vic Theatre Sch. *Theatre* appearances include: A Midsummer's Night Dream, Liverpool Playhouse, 1952; The Duenna, Westminster, 1954; musical version, The Comedy of Errors, Arts, 1956; The Love Doctor, Piccadilly, 1959; revue, Out of My Mind, Lyric, Hammersmith, 1961; Little Mary Sunshine, Comedy, 1962; Virtue in Danger, Mermaid, transf. Strand, 1963; How's the World Treating You?, Hampstead Theatre Club, 1965, New Arts, transf. Wyndham's, Comedy and Broadway, 1966 (Whitbread Award); Darling of the Day, George Abbott, NY, 1967 (Antoinette Perry Award); The Caucasian Chalk Circle, The Country Wife, and The Magistrate, Chichester Fest., transf. Cambridge Th., 1969; Cowardy Custard, Mermaid, 1972; Dandy Dick, Chichester Fest., transf. Garrick, 1973; 1600 Pennsylvania Avenue, Mark Hellinger, NY, 1976; Pirates of Penzance, NY, 1980; Noises Off, Savoy, 1981; When the Wind Blows, Whitehall, 1983; Richard III, RSC, 1984–85; Candide, Old Vic, 1988–89 (Laurence Olivier Award); Come for the Ride (one-woman show), Playhouse, nat. tour, 1989; Carousel, NT, 1992; The Corn is Green, Greenwich and tour, 1992; The Rivals, Chichester, transf. Albery, 1994; Beatrix, Chichester, 1996, tour and transf. Greenwich, 1997; The Importance of Being Earnest, Chichester, transf. Haymarket, 1999, Australian tour, Savoy, 2001; Wild Orchids, Chichester, 2002; The Solid Gold Cadillac, Garrick, 2004; The Best of Friends, Hampstead, 2006; Facing the Music, Menier Chocolate Factory, 2006, nat. tour, 2007–14; Office Suite, Chichester, 2007; Crown Matrimonial, nat. tour, 2008; Admission: One Shilling, Nat. Gall., 2009, nat. and Eur. tour, 2010–14, Australian tour, 2014; An Ideal Husband, Chichester, 2014; *television* appearances include: A Visit from Miss Protheroe, 1978; Doris and Doreen, 1978; A Woman of No Importance, 1982; Victoria Wood As Seen on TV, 1983–86; Marjorie and Men, 1985; A Lady of Letters, 1988; Keeping Up Appearances (5 series), 1990–95 (Best Actress, British Comedy Awards, 1991); Hildegard of Bingen, 1994; Hetty Wainthropp Investigates (4 series), 1995–98; Miss Fozzard finds her Feet, 1998; Anybody's Nightmare, 2001; many radio plays. Hon. DLitt: Liverpool, 1999; Lancaster, 2008. Grand Order of Water Rats Award, 1991; Variety Club of GB Award, 1993; 60th Anniv. Award, BBC, 1996. *Address:* c/o Penny Wesson Management, 26 King Henry's Road, NW3 3RP.

ROUTLEDGE, Air Vice-Marshal Martin John, CB 2009; independent consultant; Chairman, London Luton Airport Consultative Committee, since 2009; Assistant Chief of Staff Reserves, Headquarters Air Command, since 2010; *b* 22 Nov. 1954; *s* of James Routledge and Pamela Routledge (*née* Bangor-Ward); *m* 1981, Annette Powell; one *s* one *d*. *Educ:* St John's Sch., Episkopi; Glyn Sch.; Portsmouth Poly. (BSc Elec. Engrg); RAF Coll., Cranwell. Joined RAF, 1972; front-line service as navigator on Phantoms, 1977–89; commanded 29 (F) Sqdn equipped with Tornadoes, 1995–97; Comdr, British Air Forces Italy, 1999; Dep. Principal SO to Chief of Defence Staff, 1999–2001; AO Scotland and Comdr RAF Leuchars, 2001–03; staff duties, MoD, 2003–05; Nat. Mil. Rep. to SHAPE, 2006; COS Strategy, Policy and Plans, HQ Air Command, High Wycombe, 2007–09. RAF Vice-Pres., CCF Assoc., 2010–. *Recreations:* conservation and the environment, watching wildlife, ornithology, walking, fighting the lawn, enjoying wine. *Club:* Royal Air Force.

ROUTLEDGE, Patricia; *see* Routledge, K. P.

ROUX, Michel Albert; Chef Patron, Le Gavroche, since 1991; *b* Kent, 23 May 1960; *s* of Albert and Monique Roux; *m* 1990, Gisele Malbos; one *d*. *Educ:* Highfield Sch. Apprenticeship in Paris, under Maître Pâtissier, Hellegouarche, 1976–79; commis chef de cuisine, with Alain Chapel at Mionay, 1980–82; mil. service, kitchens of Elysée Palace, Paris, 1982–83; sous chef, Gavvers Restaurant, London, 1983–84; commis de cuisine: Tante Claire, London, 1984; Mandarin Oriental, Hong Kong, 1984; Chef, Roux Restaurants, London, 1985–90. TV presenter: MasterChef: the professionals, 2008–13; Michel Roux's Service, 2010; Great British Food Revival, 2010–11; Michel Roux on Escoffier, 2012; Food & Drink, 2013; Patisserie, 2013; First Class Cooks, 2015. *Publications:* Le Gavroche Cookbook, 2001; The Marathon Chef, 2003; Matching Food and Wine, 2005; Vin de Constance, 2006; Michel Roux: a life in the kitchen, 2009; Cooking with the Master Chef, 2010. *Recreations:* running marathons, Manchester United supporter, Harlequins Rugby Club supporter. *Address:* Le Gavroche, 43 Upper Brook Street, W1K 7QR. *T:* (020) 7408 0881, *Fax:* (020) 7491 4387. *E:* bookings@le.gavroche.com.

ROUX, Michel André, Hon. OBE 2002; former Chef de cuisine; *b* 19 April 1941; *s* of late Henry Roux and Germaine Triger; *m* 1984, Robyn (Margaret Joyce); one *s* two *d* by previous marr. *Educ:* Ecole Primaire, Saint Mande; Brevet de Maîtrise (Pâtisserie). Apprenticeship, Pâtisserie Loyal, Paris, 1955–57; Commis Pâtissier-Cuisinier, British Embassy, Paris, 1957–59; Commis de Cuisine with Miss Cécile de Rothschild, Paris, 1959–60; Military service, 1960–62, at Versailles and Colomb Bechar, Sahara; Chef with Miss Cécile de Rothschild, 1962–67; came to England, 1967; restaurants opened: Le Gavroche, 1967; Le Poulbot, 1969; Waterside Inn, 1972; Gavvers, 1981. Mem., UK Br., Académie Culinaire de France, 1984–. TV series, At Home with the Roux Brothers, 1988. Numerous French and British prizes and awards, including: Médaille d'Or, Cuisiniers Français, 1972; Restaurateur of the Year, Caterer & Hotelkeeper, 1985; Personnalité de l'Année, Gastronomie dans le Monde, Paris, 1985; Culinary Trophy, Assoc. of Maîtres-Pâtissiers La Saint Michel, 1986; (with Albert Roux) Men of the Year (Radar), 1989; (with Albert Roux) Lifetime Achievement Award, Restaurant Magazine, 2006. Chevalier, National Order of Merit (France), 1987; Officer, Order of Agricultural Merit (France), 1987; Chevalier, Order of Arts and of Letters (France), 1990; Chevalier, Legion of Honour (France), 2004. *Publications:* Desserts: a lifelong passion, 1994; Sauces, 1996, rev. edn 2009; Life is a Menu (autobiog.), 2000; Only the Best, 2002; Eggs, 2006; Pastry, 2008; Desserts, 2011; Michel Roux: The Collection, 2012; The Essence of French Cooking, 2014; with Albert Roux: New Classic Cuisine, 1983 (French edn 1985); The Roux Brothers on Pâtisserie, 1986; At Home with the Roux Brothers, 1988; French Country Cooking, 1989, rev. edn 2010; Cooking for Two, 1991. *Recreations:* shooting, walking, ski-ing. *Address:* Chalet Venus, Appartement 4, 10 Chemin du Mont Paisible, 3963 Crans Montana, Switzerland.

ROVE, Rev. Sir Ikan, KBE 2005; Spiritual Authority of the Christian Fellowship Church, Solomon Islands, since 1990; *b* 13 Sept. 1942; *s* of late Silas Eto (Founder and Holy Mama, Christian Fellowship Ch) and Mary Nanasabe; *m* 1981, Marama Elesi Lupaqula; four *s* one *d*. Began church work at age 14; ordained minister, 1960; succeeded father to take control of tasks and responsibilities, Christian Fellowship Ch, 1983. Encourages and engages rural community participation in socio-econ. develt. *Address:* Christian Fellowship Church, Duvaha Village, PO Box 974, Honiara, Solomon Islands. *E:* ocksi@hotmail.com.

ROWALLAN, 4th Baron *cr* 1911; **John Polson Cameron Corbett;** Director: Rowallan Holdings, 1991–2013; Rowallan Activity Centre Ltd, 1991–2013; Rowallan Asset Management, since 2002; Rowallan Investments, since 2011; *b* 8 March 1947; *s* of 3rd Baron Rowallan and of his 1st wife, Eleanor Mary Boyle; *S* father, 1993; *m* 1st, 1971, Jane Green (marr. diss. 1983); one *s* one *d*; 2nd, 1984, Sandrew Bryson (marr. diss. 1994); one *s* one *d*; 3rd, 1995, Claire Dinning; one step *s* one step *d*. *Educ:* Cothill House; Eton Coll.; RAC, Cirencester. Chartered Surveyor, 1972–; farmer, 1975–2014. British Show Jumping Association: Area Rep., 1982–2007; Judge, 1982–; Dir, 1998–2008, 2010–11; Jumping Judge, 2000–, Internat. Show Jumping Judge, 2003–, FEI; Show Jumping Judge, London Olympics, 2012. Commentator at equestrian events. Contested (C): Glasgow, Garscadden, Oct. 1974; Kilmarnock, 1979. Former Member All Party Groups on: Mental Health; Clinical Depression; Arts and Heritage; Alternative Medicine; Racing and Bloodstock; Rwanda and Genocide; Conservation; Advertising; Epilepsy; introduced Mental Health (Amendment) Act 1998 to H of L. Chairman: Diamond Resorts and Hotels Ltd; Scotia Exploration Ltd. Mem., Greenway Cttee. Dir, SANE, 1996–2007. Patron, Depression Alliance, 1998–. Chm., Fenwick and Lochgoin Covenanters Trust, 1977–. *Recreations:* commentating, ski-ing, travel, humanitarian projects. *Heir: s* Hon. Jason William Polson Cameron Corbett [*b* 21 April 1972; *m* 2000, Anna, *d* of Chris Smedley; two *s*]. *Address:* Meiklemosside House, Fenwick, Ayrshire KA3 6AY. *T:* (01560) 600667.

ROWAN, David; Editor, Wired magazine, since 2008; *b* 8 April 1965; *s* of Nigel Rowan and Iris Rowan; *m* 1995, Sarah Harris; two *s* one *d*. *Educ:* Haberdashers' Aske's Sch. for Boys; Gonville and Caius Coll., Cambridge (BA Hist. 1988). Trainee journalist, The Times, 1988–89; The Guardian, 1990–2000: Editor: EG and Education magazines, 1990–93; Outlook, Saturday section, 1993–94; Comment and letters, 1994–97; Analysis page, 1997–98; The Editor magazine, 1998–99; Guardian Unlimited websites, 1999–2000; freelance journalist and broadcaster, 2000–06: columnist, The Times; interviewer for Evening Standard; magazine writer, Sunday Times and Telegraph; film maker, Channel 4 News and More4 News; Editor, The Jewish Chronicle, 2006–08. *Publications:* A Glossary for the Nineties, 1998. *Recreations:* cycling past traffic, crashing into deadlines, collecting inspiring conferences. *Address:* Wired, 13 Hanover Square, W1S 1HN. *T:* (020) 7499 9080.

ROWAN, Patricia Adrienne, (Mrs Ivan Rowan); journalist; Editor, The Times Educational Supplement, 1989–97; *d* of late Henry Matthew Talintyre and Gladys Talintyre; *m* 1960, Ivan Settle Harris Rowan; one *s*. *Educ:* Harrow County Grammar School for Girls. Time & Tide, 1952–56; Sunday Express, 1956–57; Daily Sketch, 1957–58; News Chronicle, 1958–60; Granada Television, 1961–62; Sunday Times, 1962–66; TES, 1972–97. Mem. Bd of Trustees, Nat. Children's Bureau, 1997–2003; Trustee, Stroud Valleys Project, 2001–10 (Chm., 2002–09). Hon. Fellow, Inst. of Educn, London Univ., 1997. Hon. FRSA 1989. *Publications:* What Sort of Life?, 1980; (contrib.) Education—the Wasted Years?, 1988. *Recreations:* cookery, gardening. *Club:* Reform.

See also D. G. Talintyre.

ROWAN-ROBINSON, Prof. (Geoffrey) Michael, PhD; FInstP; Professor of Astrophysics, Blackett Laboratory, 1993–2012, now Emeritus, and Head, Astrophysics Group, 1993–2007, Imperial College, University of London; *b* 9 July 1942; *s* of John Christopher Rowan-Robinson and Audrey Christine (*née* Wynne); *m* 1978, Mary Lewin (*née* Tubb); one *d*, and two step *s*. *Educ:* Eshton Hall Sch., Gargrave, Yorks; Pembroke Coll., Cambridge (BA 1963); Royal Holloway Coll., London (PhD 1969). FInstP 1992. Queen Mary, later Queen Mary and Westfield College, London: Asst Lectr in Maths, QMC, 1967–69; Lectr, 1969–78; Reader in Astronomy, 1978–87; Prof. of Astrophysics, 1987–93. Royal Soc. and Academia dei Lincei Vis. Res. Fellow, Univ. of Bologna, 1969, 1971, 1976; Vis. Res. Fellow, Univ. of Calif, Berkeley, 1978–79. Member: Exec. Cttee, IAU Commn 47 on Cosmology, 1976–79; Sci. Team for Infrared Astronomical Satellite, 1977–84; Astronomy Wkg Gp, ESA, 1985–88; Space Sci. Prog. Bd, BNSC, 1988–91. Chairman, Time Allocation Committee: Isaac Newton Gp, 1988–91; Eur. Southern Observatory, 2011; Member, Time Allocation Committee: ESA's Infrared Space Observatory mission, 1993–96; Hubble Space Telescope, 1995 and 2000. Co-investigator: Herschel-SWIRE, 1993–2008; Planck-HFI, 1993–2013; Infrared Space Observatory Photometer, ESA, 1996–99; Principal Investigator, European Large Area ISO Survey, 1995–2000. Chm., Res. Assessment Panel for Astronomy, PPARC, 1994–97. Mem., RAS, 1965– (Pres., 2006–08). Mem., Scientists for Global Responsibility, 1992–; Vice-Chm., Scientists Against Nuclear Arms, 1988–92. Chm., Hornsey Lab. Party, 1971–72. Governor: Creighton Comp. Sch., 1971–78; Fortismere Comp. Sch., 1985–88. Chm., Southwold and Reydon Soc., 2012–15. Hon. DSc Sussex, 2008. Daiwa Adrian Prize, Daiwa Anglo-Japanese Foundn, 2004; Hoyle Medal, Inst. of Physics, 2008. *Publications:* Cosmology, 1977, 4th edn 2004; Cosmic Landscape, 1979; The Cosmological Distance Ladder, 1985; Fire and Ice: the nuclear winter, 1985; Our Universe: an armchair guide, 1990; Ripples in the Cosmos, 1993; Nine Numbers of the Cosmos, 1999; Night Vision, 2013; numerous research papers in astronomical jls, articles and book reviews. *Recreations:* poetry, politics, going to the theatre, music, especially Liszt, golf. *Address:* Astrophysics Group, Blackett Laboratory, Imperial College, Prince Consort Road, SW7 2AZ. *T:* (home) (01502) 725223.

ROWBOTHAM, Prof. Sheila; writer; *b* 27 Feb. 1943; *d* of Lancelot and Jean Rowbotham; one *s* with Paul Atkinson. *Educ:* Hunmanby Hall Sch.; St Hilda's Coll., Oxford (BA Hons Hist. 1964); Chelsea Coll., London Univ. Lectr in Liberal Studies, Chelsea Coll. of Advanced Technol. and Tower Hamlets Coll. of Further Educn, 1964–68; Extra-mural Lectr, WEA, 1968–80; Vis. Prof. in Women's Studies, Univ. of Amsterdam, 1981–83; Res. Officer, Industry and Employment Dept, GLC, 1983–86; Course Tutor, MA Women's Studies, Univ. of Kent, 1987–89; Res. Advr, World Inst. for Develt and Econ. Res., Helsinki, UN Univ., 1987–91; Sociology Department, Manchester University: Simon Res. Fellow, 1993–94; Sen. Res. Fellow, 1995–2000; Sen. Lectr, 2000–01; Reader, 2001–03; Prof. of Gender and Labour History, 2003–08; Simon Res. Prof., 2008–11; Hon. Fellow, 2011. Writer-in-residence, Eccles Centre for Amer. Studies, British Liby, 2012. Hon. Fellow, Bristol, 2011. FRSA. Hon. DSSc N London, 1994; Hon. DLitt Sheffield, 2010. *Publications:* Women, Resistance and Revolution, 1973; Woman's Consciousness, Man's World, 1973; Hidden from History, 1973; Socialism and the New Life, 1977; A New World for Women: Stella Browne, Socialist Feminist, 1977; (jtly) Beyond the Fragments: Feminism and the Making of Socialism, 1980; Dreams and Dilemmas: collected writings, 1983; Friends of Alice Wheeldon, 1986; The Past is Before Us: feminism in action since the 1960s, 1989; Women in Movement: feminism and social action, 1993; Homeworkers Worldwide, 1993; A Century of Women, 1999; Threads Through Time, 1999; Promise of a Dream, 2000; Edward Carpenter: a life of liberty and love, 2008; Dreamers of a New Day: women who invented the twentieth century, 2010; *edited jointly:* Dutiful Daughters: women talk about their lives, 1977; Dignity and Daily Bread: new forms of economic organisation among poor women, 1994; Women Encounter Technology, 1995; Women Resist Globalization, 2001; Looking at Class, 2001. *Recreations:* cinema, reading, swimming. *Address:* 16 Montgomery Street, Bristol BS3 4SE.

ROWE, Prof. Adrian Harold Redfern; Professor of Conservative Dentistry, University of London, at Guy's Hospital, 1971–91, now Professor Emeritus; Dean of Dental Studies, 1985–89, Dean of Dental Sch., 1989–91, and Head of Department of Conservative Dental Surgery, 1967–91, United Medical and Dental Schools of Guy's and St Thomas' Hospitals (Hon. Fellow, 1997); *b* 30 Dec. 1925; *y s* of late Harold Ridges Rowe and Emma Eliza (*née* Matthews), Lymington, Hants; *m* 1951, Patricia Mary Flett; three *s*. *Educ:* King Edward VI Sch., Southampton; Guy's Hosp. Dental Sch., London Univ. (BDS 1948, distinguished in Surgery, Op. Dental Surgery, Dental Surgery and Orthodontics; distinguished in Dental Anatomy, 2nd BDS, 1946); MDS London, 1965. FDSRCS 1954; MCCDRCS 1989. Nat. Service, RADC, 1949–50. Guy's Hospital Dental School: part-time practice and teaching, 1950–63; Sen. Lectr, 1963–67; Hon. Consultant, 1966–; Univ. Reader, 1967–71; London University: Chm., Bd of Studies in Dentistry, 1980–83; Mem., Senate, 1981–83. Member: Lewisham and N Southwark DHA, 1986–90; Special HA, 1986–90. Member: Dental Sub-Cttee, UGC, 1974–83; Council, Medical Defence Union, 1977–96; Specialist Adv. Cttee in Restorative Dentistry, 1979–85; Bd, Faculty in Dental Surgery, RCS, 1980–93 (Vice Dean, 1987); Faculty Advr for SE Thames reg., RCS, 1983–89; President: British Endodontic Soc., 1964 (Hon. Mem., 1974); British Soc. for Restorative Dentistry, 1978 (Hon. Mem., 1991). Past examiner in dental surgery in Univs of Belfast, Birmingham, Cardiff, Colombo, Dublin, Dundee, Edinburgh, Lagos, London, Malaysia, Malta, Manchester, Nairobi, Newcastle and Singapore; Statutory Exam. of GDC; Examr for Licence and Fellowship exams of RCS and for Fellowship of RCSI. Dir, Medical Sickness Annuity and Life Assce Soc., 1987–95. Governor: UMDS of Guy's and St Thomas' Hosps, 1985–91; Eastman Dental Hosp., 1986–90. First Pres., GKT Dental Alumni Assoc., 2003–05. Governor: Walmer Sci. Coll., 1997–2008; Kingsdown and Ringwood C of E Primary Sch., 1997–2009. Church Warden, St Nicholas Church, Ringwould, 1995–2013. Freeman, City of London, 1990; Liveryman, Soc. of Apothecaries, 1995–. Hon. FKC 1998. Colyer Gold Medal, Faculty of Dental Surgery, RCS, 1993. Ed., Jl of Endodontics, 1961–64. *Publications:* (Ed. in Chief) Companion to Dental Studies, vol. I: Book I, Anatomy, Biochemistry and Physiology, 1982; Book II, Dental Anatomy and Embryology, 1981; vol. II, Clinical Methods, Medicine, Pathology and Pharmacology, 1988; vol. III, Clinical Dentistry, 1986; papers on endodontics and medico-legal subjects in British and foreign dental jls. *Recreations:* DIY, gardening, wood turning, river and ocean cruising. *Address:* Manor Lodge, Manor Mews, Ringwould, Deal, Kent CT14 8HT. *T:* (01304) 375487. *E:* profrowe@btopenworld.com.

See also O. J. T. Rowe.

ROWE, Bridget; Senior Partner, African Strategic, since 2007; Founder Partner, Chartwell Political; *b* 16 March 1950; *d* of late Peter and Myrtle Rowe; *m*; one *s*. *Educ:* St Michael's School, Limpsfield. Editor, Look Now, 1971–76; Editor, Woman's World, 1976–81; Asst Editor, The Sun, 1981–82; Editor: Sunday Magazine, 1982–86; Woman's Own, 1986–90; TV Times, 1990–91; Sunday Mirror, 1991–92; Editor, 1992–96, Man. Dir, 1995–98, The People; Man. Dir, 1995–98, and Editor, 1997–98, Sunday Mirror; Dir of Communications, Nat. Magazines, 1998–99; Content Dir, Yava, 2000–01; Hd of Communications, Europe of Freedom and Democracy Gp, Eur. Parlt, 2009–10. Judge, Press Awards. *Recreations:* football, shopping.

ROWE, Crispin; Headmaster, St Paul's School, São Paulo, Brazil, 2008–14; *b* 28 May 1955; *s* of Peter Whitmill Rowe, *qv*; *m* 1977, Jillian Highton (*d* 2008); two *s* one *d*. *Educ:* Univ. of Newcastle upon Tyne (BA Hons; PGCE). Assistant Teacher: Watford Boys' Grammar Sch., 1978–80; Royal Grammar Sch., Newcastle upon Tyne, 1980–92; Dep. Hd, 1992–2004, Headmaster, 2004–08, King Edward's Sch., Bath. *Recreations:* sport, running, golf, music.

ROWE, Dr Dorothy; psychologist and writer, since 1962; *b* Newcastle, NSW, 17 Dec. 1930; *d* of John Thomas Conn and Ella Barbara Conn; *m* 1956, Edward Rowe (marr. diss. 1964); one *s*. *Educ:* Sydney Univ. (BA, DipED, Dip. Clin. Psychol); Sheffield Univ. (PhD 1971). Principal Psychologist, Dept of Clin. Psychol., N Lincs HA, 1972–86. Visiting Professor: Middlesex Univ., 2001–08; London Metropolitan Univ., 2008–; Sunderland Univ., 2009–10. *Publications:* The Experience of Depression, 1978, reissued as Choosing Not Losing, 1988; The Construction of Life and Death, 1982, reissued as The Courage to Live, 1991; Depression: the way out of your prison, 1983, 3rd edn 2003; Living with the Bomb: can we live without enemies?, 1985, reissued 2015; Beyond Fear, 1987, 3rd edn 2007; The Successful Self, 1988; The Depression Handbook, 1990, reissued as Breaking the Bonds, 1991; Wanting Everything, 1991; Time on our Side, 1994; Dorothy Rowe's Guide to Life, 1995; The Real Meaning of Money, 1997; Friends and Enemies, 2000; My Dearest Enemy, My Dangerous Friend, 2007; What Should I Believe?, 2008; Why We Lie, 2010. *Recreation:* looking at the sea. *Address:* c/o Edward Rowe, PO Box 992, Spit Junction, NSW 2088, Australia. *W:* www.dorothyrowe.com.au.

ROWE, Jennifer, (Mrs J. Ellis), CB 2013; Chief Executive, UK Supreme Court, 2009–15; *b* 2 Oct. 1955; *d* of Caryl Rowe and Beryl Rose Florence Rowe; *m* 1993, John Richard Ellis. *Educ:* Sir James Smith's Sch., Camelford; King's Coll., London (BA Hons Hist. 1977); Coll. of Law, Lancaster Gate; Birkbeck Coll., London (MSc Policy Admin 1984). Principal Private Sec. to Lord Chancellor, 1990–93; Principal Estabt and Finance Officer, Serious Fraud Office, 1993–95; Lord Chancellor's Department: Hd, Criminal Policy, 1995–97; Principal Private Sec. to Lord Chancellor, 1997–99; Dir, Corporate Services, 1999–2002; Dir, Finance and Corporate Affairs, 2002–03; Sec., Butterfield Rev., 2003; Dir, Policy Admin, Attorney General's Office, 2004–08. Nat. Treas., Civil Service Retirement Fellowship, 2013–. Trustee, RBL, 2005–13. Adv. Editor, Civil Procedure (The White Book), 2009–. Mem., Council of Reference, Westminster Abbey Inst., 2013–. Chm., Friends of Lanteglos Ch, 2011–. Mem., Girls' Cricket Bd, Chance to Shine, 2012–14. Trustee, RN and RM Charity, 2014–. *Recreations:* reading, theatre, opera, gardening, cricket. *E:* jenny-rowe@outlook.com. *Clubs:* Royal Over-Seas League, Middlesex CC, Surrey CC.

ROWE, Judith May; QC 2003; **Her Honour Judge Rowe;** a Circuit Judge, since 2012; a Deputy High Court Judge, Family Division, since 2005; *b* 7 Aug. 1957; *d* of David and Eileen Rowe; *m* 1989, Bill Waite; two *d*. *Educ:* Rednock Sch., Dursley; UCL (LLB Hons). Called to the Bar: Gray's Inn, 1979, Bencher, 2007; Lincoln's Inn, 1988. Recorder, 1999–2012. *Recreations:* ski-ing, scuba diving, gardening. *Address:* Clerkenwell and Shoreditch County Court, 29–41Gee Street, EC1V 3RE.

ROWE, Kerry; *see* Rowe, R. K.

ROWE, Owen John Tressider, MA; retired; *b* 30 July 1922; *e s* of late Harold Ridges Rowe and Emma E. Rowe (*née* Matthews), Lymington, Hampshire; *m* 1946, Marcelle Ljufliny Hyde-Johnson (*d* 1986); one *s* one *d*. *Educ:* King Edward VI School, Southampton; Exeter College, Oxford (Scholar; 1st Cl. Hons Classical Hon. Mods, 1942; BA 1st Cl. Hons Lit Hum 1947; MA). Served War of 1939–45, Lieut in Roy. Hampshire Regt, 1942–45. Assistant Master: Royal Grammar School, Lancaster, 1948–50; Charterhouse, 1950–60 (Head of Classical Dept); Officer Comdg Charterhouse CCF, 1954–60; Headmaster: Giggleswick School, 1961–70; Epsom College, 1970–82; Head of Classics, St John's Sch., Leatherhead, 1982–87. Governor: Welbeck Coll., 1964–82; Rosebery Sch., Epsom, 1972–97; St John's Sch., Leatherhead, 1988–94. *Recreations:* Rotary, gardening, charitable activities work. *Address:* 8 Pine Hill, Epsom KT18 7BG. *Club:* Rotary (Epsom).

See also A. H. R. Rowe.

ROWE, Rear-Adm. Sir Patrick (Barton), KCVO 2002 (LVO 1975); CBE 1990; Deputy Master and Chairman of the Board, Trinity House, 1996–2002; Chairman, General Lighthouse Authority, 1996–2002; *b* 14 April 1939; *e s* of Captain G. B. Rowe, DSC, RN and Doreen Rowe (*née* Robarts), Liphook, Hants; *m* 1964, Alexandra, *e d* of Alexander Mellor, OBE; one *s* one *d*. *Educ:* Wellington College; RNC Dartmouth. Served Far East Fleet, 1960–65; specialised in Navigation, 1966; navigation appts, 1966–70; Comd, HMS Soberton, 1970–71; Army Staff Coll., 1972; Navigation Officer, HM Yacht Britannia, 1973–75; Comd, HMS Antelope, 1977–79; Naval Staff appts, 1979–82; Comd, HMS Keren, 1983; Comd, HMS Liverpool, 1983–85; RN Presentation Team, 1985–86; Commodore, Clyde, 1986–88; RCDS 1989; Mil. Deputy, Defence Export Services, 1990–92; Clerk to the Worshipful Co. of Leathersellers, 1993–96. Liveryman: Shipwrights' Co., 1993–2008; Leathersellers' Co., 1996–2014. *Recreations:* sailing, travel, DIY. *Address:* Juniper Cottage, Meonstoke, Southampton, Hampshire SO32 3NA. *Clubs:* Army and Navy; Royal Yacht Squadron.

ROWE, Prof. Peter John, PhD, LLD; Professor of Law, 1995–2014, now Emeritus, and Head of School of Law, 1995–2000 and 2003–05, Lancaster University; *s* of late Major Dennis Rowe and Anne Rowe; *m* 1970, Anne Murland, *d* of D. A. White, OBE and J. C. White; one *s* one *d*. *Educ:* Methodist Coll., Belfast; Queen's Univ. Belfast (LLB; LLD 2011); University College London (LLM); Univ. of Liverpool (PhD). Called to the Bar, Lincoln's Inn, 1979. Appts at Anglia Poly., 1970–77 and Lancashire Poly., 1977–79; University of Liverpool, 1979–95: Prof. of Law, 1988–95; Head of Dept of Law, 1988–93. Dir of Legal Studies, Cayman Islands Law Sch., 1982–84; Sir Ninian Stephen Vis. Scholar, Faculty of Law, Univ. of Melbourne, 2003. Chm., Ind. Tribunal Service, subseq. Tribunals Service, 1988–2008. Chm., UK Gp, Internat. Soc. for Mil. Law and Law of War, 1990–98. Mem., Governing Body, St Martin's Coll., Lancaster, 2005–07. *Publications:* (with S. Knapp) Evidence and Procedure in the Magistrates' Court, 1983, 3rd edn 1989; (ed with C. Whelan) Military Intervention in Democratic Societies, 1985; Defence: the legal implications, military law and the laws of war, 1987; (ed) The Gulf War 1990–91, in International and English Law, 1993; (ed jtly) The Permanent International Criminal Court, 2004; The Impact of Human Rights Law on Armed Forces, 2006; contrib. on Armed Conflict and Emergency vol. 3 and on Legal Position of the Armed Forces to vol. 3 (ii), Halsbury's Laws of England, 5th edn, 2011; articles in learned jls. *Recreations:* sailing, hill-walking. *Address:* c/o Lancaster University Law School, Lancaster LA1 4YN.

ROWE, Peter Whitmill, MA; Schoolteacher at Kent College, Canterbury, 1983–90, retired; *b* 12 Feb. 1928; British; *s* of Gerald Whitmill Rowe, chartered accountant, one-time General Manager of Morris Commercial Cars Ltd; *m* 1952, Bridget Ann Moyle; two *s* one *d*. *Educ:* Bishop's Stortford College; St John's College, Cambridge. BA 1950; MA (Hons) 1956. VI Form History Master, Brentwood School, Essex, 1951–54; Senior History Master, Repton School, Derbys, 1954–57; Headmaster: Bishop's Stortford Coll., Herts, 1957–70; Cranbrook Sch., Kent, 1970–81; teacher, Williston-Northampton Sch., Mass, USA, 1981–83. JP Bishop's Stortford, 1968–70, Cranbrook, 1971–81. *Recreations:* literature, music, woodland restoration, golf.

See also C. Rowe.

ROWE, Prof. (Ronald) Kerry, PhD, DEng; FRS 2013; FRSC; FREng; Professor, since 2000, and Canada Research Chair in Geotechnical and Geoenvironmental Engineering, since 2010, Queen's University, Kingston; *b* Australia, 1951; *s* of Ronald Rowe and Alma Rowe; *m* 1973, Kathryn; two *s* one *d*. *Educ:* Fort Street Boys High Sch., Sydney; Univ. of Sydney (BSc 1973; BE Hons I 1975; PhD 1979; DEng 1993). CPEng 1978; PEng 1980. Cadet Engr, 1971–74, Civil Engr, 1975–78, Dept of Construction, Australian Govt; University of Western Ontario: Asst Prof., 1979–82; Associate Prof., 1982–86; Prof., 1986–2000; Associate Dean (Res. and Graduate Affairs), Faculty of Engrg Sci., 1988–89; NSERC Steacie Fellow, 1989–91; Chair, Dept of Civil and Envmtl Engrg, 1992–2000; Vice-Principal (Res.), Queen's Univ., Kingston, 2000–10. Killam Fellow, 2012–14. Adjunct Professor: Dept of Civil Engrg, Royal Military Coll., Canada, 2008–; Dept of Civil Engrg, Monash Univ., 2011–. Fellow, Canadian Acad. of Engrg, 2001; FRSC 2001; FREng 2010. *Publications:* (jtly) Clayey Barrier Systems for Waste Disposal Facilities, 1995; (ed) Geotechnical and Geoenvironmental Engineering Handbook, 2001; (jtly) Barrier Systems for Waste Disposal Facilities, 2004; 14 book chapters; approx. 290 papers in jls; over 280 conf. papers. *Recreations:* canoeing, ski-ing. *Address:* Department of Civil Engineering, Queen's University, Kingston, ON K7L 3N6, Canada. *T:* (613) 5333113, *Fax:* (613) 5332128. *E:* kerry@civil.queensu.ca.

ROWE, Prof. William Walton, PhD; FBA 2011; Anniversary Professor of Poetics, and Director, Contemporary Poetics Research Centre, Birkbeck, University of London. *Educ:* Pembroke Coll., Cambridge (BA 1965); Univ. of London (PhD). Teacher: Univ. of Lambayeque, Peru; Univ. of Liverpool; Univ. of San Marcos, Peru; Univ. Católica, Peru; Univ. Iberoamericana, Mexico; Univ. Autónoma de Barcelona; Personal Chair in Latin Amer. Cultural Studies, KCL. Founding Ed., Jl Latin Amer. Cultural Studies: Travesia (Mem., Adv. Bd). Hon. Dr Católica, Peru, 2012. Congressional Medal of Honour (Peru), 2010. *Publications:* Juan Rulfo: el llano en llamas, 1987; (with V. Schelling) Memory and Modernity: popular culture in Latin America, 1991; Ensayos arguedianos, 1996; Hacia una poética radical: ensayos de hermenéutica cultural, 1996; Siete ensayos sobre poesia latinoamericana, 2003; Ensayos vallejianos, 2006; Three Modern Lyric Poets: Harwood, Torrance and MacSweeney, 2009; Cesar Vallejo: el acto y la palabra, 2010; (ed jtly) Huellas del mito prehispánico en la literatura latinoamericana, 2010. *Address:* Department of Iberian and Latin American Studies, Birkbeck, University of London, 43 Gordon Square, WC1H 0PD.

ROWE-BEDDOE, family name of **Baron Rowe-Beddoe**.

ROWE-BEDDOE, Baron *cr* 2006 (Life Peer), of Kilgetty in the County of Dyfed; **David Sydney Rowe-Beddoe,** Kt 2000; DL; Chairman: Wales Millennium Centre, 2001–10, now Life President; Cardiff International Airport Ltd, 2013–15; Deputy Chairman, Toye & Co. plc, 2003–14; *b* 19 Dec. 1937; *s* of late Sydney Rowe-Beddoe and Dolan Rowe-Beddoe (*née* Evans); *m* 1st, 1962, Malinda Collison (marr. diss. 1982); three *d*; 2nd, 1984, Madeleine Harrison. *Educ:* Cathedral Sch., Llandaff; Stowe Sch.; St John's Coll., Cambridge (MA); Harvard Univ. Grad. Sch. of Business Admin (PMD). Served RN, Sub-Lt, RNVR, 1956–58, Lieut, RNR, 1958–66. Thomas de la Rue & Company, 1961–76: Chief Executive, 1971–76; Exec. Dir, De la Rue Co. plc, 1974–76; Revlon Inc., NY, 1976–81; President: Latin America and Caribbean, 1976–77; Europe, ME and Africa, 1977–81; Pres. and Chief Exec. Officer, Ges. für Trendanalysen, 1981–87; Pres., Morgan Stanley-GFTA Ltd, 1983–91; Director: Development Securities plc, 1994–2000; EHC International Ltd and subsidiaries, 2001–13; Newport Networks Gp plc, 2004–09; Bd Mem., Hafren Power Ltd, 2012–; Chairman: Victoria Capital (UK) Ltd, 2004–07; GFTA - Euro/Dollar Technol. Co. Ltd (formerly GFTA Analytics Ltd), 2005–13; European Property Advisors Ltd, 2010– (Dir, 2010–). Member: Select Cttee on the EU, Sub-cttee B (Internal Mkt), H of L, 2007–12; Admin and Works Cttee, H of L, 2009–14; Econ. Affairs Cttee, H of L, 2012–15. Chairman: Welsh Development Agency, 1993–2001; Develt Bd for Rural Wales, 1994–98; N Wales Econ. Forum, 1996–2001; Mid Wales Partnership, 1996–2001; SE Wales Econ. Forum, 1999–2001; Cardiff Business Club, 2002–06 (Pres., 2006–); Member: Welsh Economic Council, 1994–96; UK Regl Policy Forum, 1999–2002; Dep. Chm., UK Statistics Authy, 2008–12. Chm., Rep. Body, Church in Wales, 2002–12; Pres., Welsh Centre for Internat. Affairs, 1999–2005. Director: Welsh Internat. Film Fest. Ltd, 1998–2000; Cardiff Internat. Festival of Musical Theatre Ltd, 2000–04; City of London Sinfonia, 2000–03; President: Celtic Film Festival, 2000; Llangollen Internat. Musical Eisteddfod, 2000–05; Johnian Soc., Cambridge Univ., 2007. Mem., Prince of Wales' Cttee, 1994–97; Patron: Prince's Trust Bro, 1997–; Menuhin Competition, 2008; Chm., Aloud Charity, 2012–; Trustee, Jeremy Winston Meml Fund, 2012–. Pro-Chancellor, Univ. of S Wales (formerly Glamorgan Univ.), 2007–. Pres., RWCMD (formerly WCMD), 2004– (Gov., 1993–2004; Chm., 2000–04). Freeman, City of London, 1993; Liveryman, 1993–, Mem. Ct of Assts, 2002–, Broderers' Co. DL Gwent, 2003. FRSA 1993. Hon. Fellow: Univ. of Wales Coll. Newport, 1998; Cardiff Univ., 1999; UWIC, 2002; Aberystwyth Univ., 2008. DUniv Glamorgan, 1997; Hon. DScEcon Wales, 2004. Order of Rising Sun, Gold Rays with Neck Ribbon (Japan), 2008. *Recreations:* music, theatre, country pursuits. *Clubs:* Garrick; Cardiff and County; Brook (New York).

ROWE-HAM, Sir David (Kenneth), GBE 1986; chartered accountant, since 1962; Lord Mayor of London, 1986–87; Consultant to Touche Ross & Co., 1984–93; *b* 19 Dec. 1935; *o s* of late Kenneth Henry and Muriel Phyllis Rowe-Ham; *m* Sandra Celia (*née* Nicholls), *widow* of Ian Glover; three *s*. *Educ:* Dragon School; Charterhouse. FCA. Commnd 3rd King's Own Hussars. Mem., Stock Exchange, 1964–84; Sen. Partner, Smith Keen Cutler, 1972–82. Chairman: Asset Trust plc, 1982–89; Jersey General Investment Trust Ltd, 1988–89; Olayan Europe Ltd, 1989–; Brewin Dolphin Hldgs PLC, 1992–2003; APTA Healthcare PLC, 1994–96; Coral Products PLC, 1995–2006; Peninsular S Asia Investment Co. (formerly BNP Paribas South Asia Investment Co.) Ltd, 1995–2008; Arden Partners PLC, 2006–10; Jt Chm., Gradus Group PLC, 1995–97; Regional Dir (London), Lloyds Bank plc, 1985–91; Director: W. Canning plc, 1981–86; Savoy Theatre Ltd, 1986–98; Williams PLC, 1992–2000; CLS Hldgs plc, 1994–99; Chubb plc, 2000–03; Hikma Pharmaceuticals plc, 2005–14. Pres., Crown Agents Foundn, 1996–2002. Chm., Adv. Panel, Guinness Flight Unit Trust Managers Ltd, 1987–99. Alderman, City of London, Ward of Bridge and Bridge Without, 1976–2004; Sheriff, City of London, 1984–85; HM Lieut, City of London, 1987–2004. Liveryman: Worshipful Co. of Chartered Accountants in England and Wales (Master, 1985–86); Worshipful Co. of Wheelwrights; Hon. Mem., Worshipful Co. of Launderers. Mem. Ct, 1981–86, Chancellor, 1986–87, City Univ. Gov., Royal Shakespeare Co., 1988–2003; former Trustee, Friends of D'Oyly Carte. Pres., Black Country Mus. Develt Trust, 1989–2010. Chm., Birmingham Municipal Bank, 1970–72; Mem., Birmingham CC, 1965–72. Chm., Political Council, Junior Carlton Club, 1977; Dep. Chm., Political Cttee, Carlton Club, 1977–79; Chm., 1900 Club, 2003–08. Mem., Pilgrims. JP City of London, 1976 (Chief Magistrate, 1986–87; Supp. List, 1994–). Hon. DLitt City Univ., 1986. KJStJ 1986. Commandeur de l'Ordre Mérite, France, 1984; Commander, Order of the Lion, Malaŵi, 1985; Order of the Aztec Eagle (Cl. II), Mexico, 1985; Order of King Abdul Aziz (Cl. 1), 1987; Grand Officer, Order of Wissam Alouite, Morocco, 1987; Order of Diego Losada, Caracas, Venezuela, 1987; Pedro Ernesto Medal, Rio de Janeiro, 1987. *Recreation:* theatre. *Address:* 140 Piccadilly, W1J 7NS. *Club:* Garrick.

ROWELL, Anthony Aylett, CMG 1992; Founding Member, Advisory Council, and Senior Adviser (formerly Consultant), Good Governance Group (G3 UK), since 2007; *b* 10 Jan. 1937; *s* of Geoffrey William and Violet Ella Aylett Rowell; *m* 1st, 1965, Bridget Jane Reekie (marr. diss. 1985); one *s* one *d*; 2nd, 1985, Caroline Anne Edgcumbe. *Educ:* Marlborough. With British American Tobacco, 1959–65; HM Diplomatic Service, 1966–93: 2nd Sec., Lusaka, 1968–69; 1st Secretary: FCO, 1969; Bucharest, 1970–73; FCO, 1974–78; Nicosia, 1979–80; FCO, 1981–85; Counsellor: Nairobi, 1985–90; Pretoria, 1990–93. Pol Advr (Southern Africa), Racal Radio Group UK, 1993; Dir, Racal Electronics SA Ltd, 1994; Pol Advr (Southern Africa), Racal Electronics PLC, 1996–97; Consultant (Africa), Kroll Associates, 1998–2005. *Recreations:* badminton, mountain and dog walking, international politics, photography, fine wines, cooking. *Address:* Bracken Cottage, Devauden, Monmouthshire NP16 6NS. *E:* anthonyrowell@g3.eu. *Club:* Muthaiga Country (Nairobi).

ROWELL, Rt Rev. Dr (Douglas) Geoffrey; Bishop of Gibraltar in Europe, 2001–13; an Honorary Assistant Bishop: Diocese of Chichester, since 2014; Diocese of Portsmouth, since 2015; *b* 13 Feb. 1943; *s* of late Cecil Victor Rowell and Kate (*née* Hunter). *Educ:* Eggars Grammar Sch., Alton, Hants; Winchester Coll.; Corpus Christi Coll., Cambridge (MA, PhD); MA, DPhil, DD Oxon; Cuddesdon Theol Coll. Ordained deacon, 1968, priest 1969; Hastings Rashdall Student and Asst Chaplain, New Coll., Oxford, 1968–72; Hon. Asst Curate, St Andrew's, Headington, 1968–71; University of Oxford: Fellow, Chaplain and Tutor in Theology, Keble Coll., 1972–94 (Emeritus Fellow, 1994–); Lectr in Theology, 1977–94; Leader, expedn to Ethiopia, 1974; Pro-Proctor, 1980–81; Suffragan Bishop of Basingstoke, 1994–2001. Canon, Chichester Cathedral, 1981–2002; Vis. Canon-Theologian, St James' Episcopal Cathedral, Chicago, 1988. Member: C of E Liturgical Commn, 1981–91; C of E Doctrine Commn, 1991–96, 1998–2005 (Consultant, 1996–98); Inter-Anglican Standing Commn on Ecumenical Relations, 2000–08 (Vice-Chm., 2003–08); Anglican Co-Chm., Anglican-Oriental Orthodox Jt Doctrinal Commn, 2001–15 (Consultant, 2015–; Mem., Anglican-Oriental Orthodox Internat. Forum, 1985, 1989, 1993, 1996); Chm., Churches Funerals Gp (formerly Churches Gp on Funeral Services in Cemeteries and Crematoria), 1997–2012. Examining Chaplain to: Bp of Leicester, 1979–90; Bp of Winchester, 1991–93. Hon. Dir, Archbp's Exam. in Theol., 1985–2001; Conservator, Mirfield Cert. in Pastoral Theol., 1987–94; Member: Theol Colls Assessment Gp, 1993; Notaries Qualifications Bd, 2014. Gov., SPCK, 1984–94, 1997–2004 (Vice-Pres., 1994–). Member: Council of Almoners, Christ's Hosp., 1979–89; Council of Mgt, St Stephen's Hse, Oxford, 1986– (Chm., 2003–13); Governor: Pusey Hse, Oxford, 1979– (Pres., Govs, 1996–2009); Eggar's Sch., Alton, 1994–98; Chm. Council, Hse of St Gregory and St Macrina, Oxford, 1987–94. Vis. Prof., UC, Chichester (formerly Chichester Inst. of Higher Educn), 1996–2003. Chairman: Nikaean Ecumenical Trust, 2002–; Philip Usher Meml Fund, 2002–. Trustee, Scott Holland Lectureship, 1979–2015 (Chm., 1992–2015); Louise Ward Haskin Lectr, St Paul's, Washington, 1995. Hon. Consultant, Nat. Funerals Coll., 1995–2001. Contrib., Credo column, The Times, 1992–. Mem., Internat. Editl Bd, Mortality, 1995–; Jt Ed., Internat. Jl for Study of the Christian Church, 2001–. FRSA 1989–2015. Hon. DD Nashotah House, Wisconsin, 1996. *Publications:* Hell and the Victorians: a study of the 19th century theological controversies concerning eternal punishment and the future life, 1974; (ed with B. E. Juel Jensen) Rock-Hewn Churches of Eastern Tigray, 1976; The Liturgy of Christian Burial: an historical introduction, 1977; The Vision Glorious: themes and personalities of the Catholic Revival in Anglicanism, 1983; (ed) Tradition Renewed: the Oxford Movement Conference Papers, 1986; (ed and contrib.) To the Church of England, by G. Bennett, 1988; (ed with M. Dudley) Confession and Absolution, 1990; (ed) The English Religious Tradition and the Genius of Anglicanism, 1992; (ed with M. Dudley) The Oil of Gladness: anointing in the Church, 1993; The Club of Nobody's Friends 1800–2000, 2000; (contrib.) History of the University of Oxford: Nineteenth Century Oxford, pt 2, 2000; (with J. Chilcott-Monk) Flesh, Bone, Wood: entering into the mysteries of the cross, 2001; (ed jtly) Love's Redeeming Work: the Anglican quest for holiness, 2001; (with J. Chilcott-Monk) Come, Lord Jesus!: daily readings for Advent, Christmas and Epiphany, 2002; (ed jtly and contrib.) The Gestures of God: explorations in sacramentality, 2004; (contrib.) Glory Descending: Michael Ramsey and his writings, 2005; (contrib.) Death Our Future, 2008; (ed) John Henry Newman: essays on miracles, 2010; (contrib.) Christ and Culture, 2010; (contrib.) Boundless Grandeur: the wisdom and witness of A. M. Donald Allchin, 2015; (contrib.) Oxford Handbook of the Oxford Movement, 2015; contributor to various books on theol subjects, to Oxford DNB, and Oxford Dict. of the Christian Church (3rd edn); articles in Jl Theol Studies, English Hist. Rev., Jl Ecclesiastical Hist., Church Hist., Anglican and Episcopal Hist., Internationale Cardinal-Newman Studien, Studia Urbania, etc. *Recreations:* travel in remote places, reading, music, examining graduate theses. *Address:* 2 Roman Wharf, Fishbourne Road, Fishbourne, Chichester, W Sussex PO19 3RZ. *T:* (01243) 789867. *E:* geoffrey.rowell@btconnect.com.

ROWELL, Jack, OBE 1998; Chairman: Turleigh Ltd, since 1995; Ukrainian Food Products plc, since 2005; *s* of late Edwin Cecil Rowell and Monica Mary Rowell (*née* Day); *m* 1969, Susan, *d* of Alan Cooper; two *s*. *Educ:* West Hartlepool Grammar Sch.; St Edmund Hall, Oxford (MA). FCA 1964. With Procter & Gamble to 1976; Finance Dir, then Chief Exec., Lucas Ingredients, Bristol, 1976–88; Chief Exec., Golden Wonder, 1988–92; Exec. Dir, Dalgety, 1993–94; Chairman: Lyon Seafoods Ltd, 1994–2003; Marlar Bennetts Internat. Ltd, 1994–99; Dolphin Computer Services Ltd, 1994–99; OSI Ltd, 1995–99; Pilgrim Foods Ltd, 1995–2004; Celsis plc, 1997–98, 2000–09 (Dir, 1995; Chief Exec., 1998–2000); Coppice Ltd, 2002–04; Dir, Oliver Ashworth Gp, 1997–98. Played for Gosforth RFC, later Newcastle Gosforth (Captain, later coach; Cup winners, 1976); coach, Bath RFC, 1977–94: Cup winners 8 times, League winners 5 times, Middlesex Sevens winners, 1994; Manager, England RFU Team, 1994–97; Dir, 1998–2000, Man. Dir, 2000–02, Bristol Rugby Ltd; Dir, 2002–07, Pres., 2007–09, Bath RFC (Chm. of Trustees, Bath Rugby, 2010–14). Advr, Sch. of Mgt, Univ. of Bath, 2009–14. Member: Bd, Sport England, 2006–09; Council, Prince's Trust (SW), 2008–13. Hon. LLD Bath, 1994.

ROWELL, Prof. John Martin, DPhil; FRS 1989; Professor, School of Materials, Arizona State University, 2002, now Distinguished Visiting Professor; *b* 27 June 1935; *s* of Frank L. and P. E. Rowell; *m* 1959, Judith A. Harte (*d* 2002); two *s* one *d*. *Educ:* Wadham Coll., Oxford (BSc, MA; DPhil 1961). Bell Telephone Labs, 1961–84; Bell Communications Research, 1984–89; Conductus Inc., 1989–95; Prof., Materials Res. Inst., Northwestern Univ., 1997. Chm., Sci. Adv. Bd, Hypres Inc. Member: Acad. of Scis, 1994; Acad. of Engrg, 1995. Fellow, Amer. Physical Soc., 1974. Fritz London Meml Low Temperature Physics Prize, 1978. *Publications:* about 100 pubns in jls. *Address:* 102 Exeter Drive, Berkeley Heights, NJ 07922–1726, USA. *T:* (908) 4646994.

ROWEN, Paul John; Director: Corinya (Uganda) Ltd, since 2004; Rochdale Reform Building Company, since 2010; Transport and Urban Transit Publishing, since 2014; Director, since 2010, and Vice Chairman, since 2014, Light Rapid Transit Association; *b* 11 May 1955. *Educ:* Bishop Henshaw RC Meml High Sch., Rochdale; Univ. of Nottingham (BSc 1976); PGCE 1977; NPQH 2004. Teacher of sci., Kimberley Comprehensive Sch., Nottingham, 1977–80; Hd of Chemistry, St Albans RC High Sch., Oldham, 1980–86; Hd of Sci., Our Lady's RC High Sch., Oldham, 1986–90; Dep. Headteacher, Yorkshire Martyrs Catholic Coll., Bradford, 1990–2005. Ind. consultant on educn and govt, 2010–. Mem. (Lib Dem), Rochdale MBC, 1983–2006. Contested (Lib Dem) Rochdale, 2001. MP (Lib Dem) Rochdale, 2005–10; contested (Lib Dem) same seat, 2010. Mem. Bd, Transport Focus (formerly Passenger Focus), 2013–. Gov., St Cuthbert's RC High Sch., Rochdale, 2000–. Trustee, Arthritis Research UK, 2009–. *Address:* c/o 144 Drake Street, Rochdale OL16 1PZ. *Club:* Rotary (Rochdale).

ROWLAND, Barry Alan; Corporate Director of Local Services, Northumberland County Council, since 2012; *b* Co. Durham, 9 Aug. 1961; *m* 1985, Lynne; four *c*. *Educ:* Univ. of Durham Business Sch. (MBA 1997). Newcastle City Council: mgt trainee, 1979–82; Dist Inspector, 1982–85; Mgt Services Officer, 1985–86; Principal Ops Manager, 1986–89; Gen. Manager, Building Services, 1989–94; Divl Dir, 1994–95; Exec. Dir, 1995–2002; Dir, Strategic Change, 2002–03; Dep. Chief Exec., 2003–09; Chief Exec., 2009–12.

ROWLAND, Rev. Prof. Christopher Charles; Dean Ireland's Professor of the Exegesis of Holy Scripture, University of Oxford, 1991–2014, now Emeritus; Fellow of Queen's College, Oxford, 1991–2014; *b* Doncaster, 21 May 1947; *s* of late Eric Rowland and Frances Mary Lawson; *m* 1969, Catherine Rogers; three *s* one *d*. *Educ:* Doncaster Grammar Sch.; Christ's Coll., Cambridge; Ridley Hall, Cambridge; BA 1969, PhD 1975, Cantab. Ordained deacon, 1975, priest 1976. Lectr in Religious Studies, Univ. of Newcastle upon Tyne, 1974–79; Curate: St James', Benwell, 1975–78; All Saints', Gosforth, 1978–79; Asst Lectr in Divinity, 1983–85, Lectr in Divinity, 1985–91, Univ. of Cambridge; Fellow and Dean, Jesus Coll., Cambridge, 1979–91. Canon Theologian, Liverpool Cathedral, 2005–14. *Address:* Queen's College, Oxford OX1 4AW.

ROWLAND, Sir David; *see* Rowland, Sir J. D.

ROWLAND, Sir Geoffrey (Robert), Kt 2009; Bailiff of Guernsey, 2005–12; President, Court of Appeal of Guernsey, 2005–12; a Judge of the Court of Appeal of Jersey, 2005–12; *b* 5 Jan. 1948; *s* of late Percy George Rowland and Muriel Florence (*née* Maunder); *m* 1972, Diana Janet Caryl; two *s*. *Educ:* Elizabeth Coll., Guernsey; Univ. of Southampton; Univ. of Caen. Called to the Bar, Gray's Inn, 1970, Hon. Bencher, 2008; called to the Guernsey Bar, 1971; QC (Guernsey) 1993. In private practice as advocate, Guernsey, 1971–91; Sen. Partner, Collas Day and Rowland, 1984–91; Solicitor General for Guernsey, 1992–99; Attorney-General for Guernsey, 1999–2002; HM Receiver General for Guernsey, 1999–2002; Dep. Bailiff of Guernsey, 2002–05. Vice-Chm., Guernsey Financial Services Commn, 1988–92. Chairman: Guernsey Press Co. Ltd, 1990–92; TSB Foundn for CI, 1990–92. Chm., Guernsey Commonwealth Games Assoc. Appeal Bd, 2012–. President: Guernsey, Western Br., RBL, 2012–; Guernsey Bn, Boys' Bde, 2012–; Comr, Guernsey Youth Commn, 2014–. Trustee, Wessex Med. Trust, 2012–. Patron: Guernsey FC, 2011–; Bailiwick of Guernsey, BRCS, 2012–. Provincial Grand Master, Guernsey and Alderney, United Grand Lodge of Freemasons of England, 2000–07. Hon. Fellow, Soc. for Advanced Legal Studies, 2001–. Hon. LLD: Bournemouth, 2006; Southampton, 2009. *Recreations:* ski-ing, reading history, international travel. *Address:* Armorica, L'Ancresse, Guernsey, CI GY3 5JR. *T:* (01481) 247494. *E:* gdrowland@cwgsy.net. *Clubs:* United (Guernsey); Royal Guernsey Golf (Hon. Mem.).

ROWLAND, Sir (John) David, Kt 1997; Hon. Fellow, Templeton College, later Green Templeton College, Oxford, 2003 (President, 1998–2003); Chairman and Chief Executive, National Westminster Bank plc, 1999–2000 (Joint Deputy Chairman, 1998–99); *b* 10 Aug. 1933; *s* of Cyril Arthur Rowland and Eileen Mary Rowland; *m* 1st, 1957, Giulia Powell (marr. diss. 1991); one *s* one *d*; 2nd, 1991, Diana Louise Matthews (*née* Dickie). *Educ:* St Paul's School; Trinity College, Cambridge (MA Natural Sciences). Joined Matthews Wrightson and Co., 1956, Dir, 1965; Dir, Matthews Wrightson Holdings, 1972; Dep. Chm., 1978–81, Chm., 1981–87, Stewart Wrightson Holdings plc; Dep. Chm., Willis Faber plc, 1987–88; Chief Exec., 1988–92, Chm., 1989–92, Sedgwick Gp plc; Chm. of Lloyd's, 1993–97. Chm., Westminster Insurance Agencies, 1981–88; Dir, Sedgwick Lloyd's Underwriting Agencies, 1988–92. Director: Project Fullemploy, 1973–88; Fullemploy Gp Ltd, 1989–90; non-executive Director: Royal London Mutual Insurance Soc., 1985–86; S. G. Warburg Gp, 1992–95; Somerset House Ltd, 1997–2003; NatWest Gp, 1998–2000. Mem. Council, Lloyd's, 1987–90; Mem., President's Cttee, Business in the Community, 1986–92 (Mem., City of London section, 1983–86). Vice-Pres., British Insurance Brokers' Assoc. (formerly British Insurance and Investment Brokers' Assoc.), 1980–88; Member of Council: Industrial Soc., 1983–88; Contemporary Applied Arts, subseq. British Crafts Centre, 1985–92; Council of Industry and Higher Educn, 1990–92. Chm. Develt Bd, Th. Royal Bury St Edmunds, 2003–07. Member: Council, Templeton Coll. (Oxford Centre for Management Studies), 1980–2003 (Chm., 1985–92); Governing Bd, City Res. Project, 1991–92; Governor: Coll. of Insurance, 1983–85; St Paul's Schs, 1991–2007 (Dep. Chm., St Paul's Sch., 2001–07). Trustee, Suffolk Foundn. Hon. FIA 2000; Hon. Fellow, Cardiff Univ., 1999. Hon. MA Oxford, 1993; Hon. DPhil London Guildhall, 1996; Hon. DSc City, 1997. Lloyd's Gold Medal, 1996. *Recreations:* family, admiring my wife's garden, golf, running slowly. *Address:* 44 Boss House, SE1 2PS; The Manor House, Honey Hill, Bury St Edmunds, Suffolk IP33 1RT. *T:* (01284) 703075. *Clubs:* Brooks's, MCC; Royal and Ancient Golf (St Andrews), Royal St George's (Sandwich), Royal Worlington and Newmarket Golf.

ROWLAND, John Peter; QC 1996; Partner, Clayton Utz, Sydney, since 2011; *b* 17 Jan. 1952; *s* of Peter Rowland and Marion Rowland (*née* Guppy); *m* 1979, Juliet Hathaway; three *s* two *d*. *Educ:* Univ. of Western Australia (BEc Hons); King's Coll., London (LLB Hons). Pilot Officer, RAAF (Reserves), 1970–72; Sen. Tutor and Lectr in Econs, Univ. of Western Australia, 1973–74; Lectr in Economics, WA Inst. of Technology, 1974–75; called to the Bar, Middle Temple, 1979; admitted to practice, NSW, 2001, Victoria, 2001. *Recreations:* cricket, walking, ski-ing. *Address:* Clayton Utz, PO Box H3, Australia Square, Sydney, NSW 1215, Australia. *Club:* Theberton Cricket.

ROWLAND, Mark; an Upper Tribunal Judge (Administrative Appeals Chamber) (formerly a Social Security Commissioner and Child Support Commissioner), since 1993; *b* 20 July 1953; *s* of late Sqdn Leader Bernard Rowland and Elizabeth Rowland (*née* Cuerden); *m* 1977, Eileen Cleary; two *d*. *Educ:* Ampleforth Coll.; Univ. of Warwick (LLB Hons). Called to the Bar, Gray's Inn, 1975; Welfare rights adviser, CPAG, 1975–78; private practice at the Bar, 1979–93; part-time Chm., social security, medical and disability appeal tribunals, 1988–93; Dep. Social Security Comr, 1992–93; Chairman: registered homes tribunal, 1995–2002; care standards tribunal, 2002–08; Mem., Tribunal Procedure Cttee, 2008–15. *Publications:* (ed jtly) Rights Guide to Non-means-tested Benefits, 2nd edn 1978, 14th edn 1991; The Industrial Injuries Scheme, 1983; Medical and Disability Appeal Tribunals: the Legislation, 1993, 3rd edn 1998; (ed jtly) Social Security Legislation, 2000, 16th edn 2015. *Recreations:* railways, military history, social history. *Address:* Upper Tribunal, Administrative Appeals Chamber, 5th Floor, Rolls Building, 7 Rolls Buildings, Fetter Lane, EC4A 1NL.

ROWLAND, Rev. Mgr Phelim Christopher; Rector, St Mary's, Holly Place, Hampstead, since 2006; *b* 9 Dec. 1949; *s* of Hugh and Ann Rowland. *Educ:* Tyburn Sch.; St George's Sch., London; Campion House; St Edmund's Coll., Ware. Ordained priest, 1975; Asst Priest, Holy Trinity, Brook Green, Hammersmith, 1975–79; commnd RN Chaplaincy Service, 1979–86: served in various estabts, incl. BRNC Dartmouth; served in Falkland Is, 1982; transf. RAChD, 1986: served Germany, NI, Cyprus, Bosnia, Kosovo and RMA Sandhurst; Principal RC Chaplain and VG for HM Land Forces, 2002–06. QHC 2004–06. Gov., St Edmund's Coll., Ware, 2001–. *Recreations:* cinema, military history. *Address:* 4 Holly Place, Hampstead, NW3 6QU. *T:* (020) 7435 6678. *Club:* Army and Navy.

ROWLAND, His Honour Robert Todd; QC 1969; County Court Judge of Northern Ireland, 1974–90; President, Lands Tribunal for Northern Ireland, 1983–90; part-time Chairman, Value Added Tax Tribunals, 1990–94; *b* 12 Jan. 1922; *yr s* of late Lt-Col Charles Rowland and Jean Rowland; *m* 1952, Kathleen (*d* 1991), *er d* of late H. J. Busby, Lambourn, Berks; two *s*. *Educ:* Crossley and Porter Sch., Halifax, Yorks; Ballyclare High Sch.; Queen's Univ. of Belfast (LLB 1948). Called to Bar of N Ireland, 1949; Mem., Bar Council, 1967–72. Served 2nd Punjab Regt, IA, in India, Assam, Burma, Thailand, Malaya, 1942–46. Counsel to Attorney-Gen. for N Ireland, 1966–69; Sen. Crown Prosecutor for Co. Tyrone, 1969–72; Vice-Pres., VAT Tribunal for N Ireland, 1972–74. Served on County Court Rules Cttee, 1965–72; Chairman: War Pensions Appeal Tribunal, 1962–72; Commn of Inquiry into Housing Contracts, 1978; Member: Bd of Governors, Strathearn Sch., 1969–89; Legal Adv. Cttee, Gen. Synod of Church of Ireland, 1975–89. Chancellor, dioceses of Armagh, and Down and Dromore, 1978–89. *Recreations:* fly-fishing, golf, hill-walking. *Address:* The Periwinkle, 25 Back Lane, South Luffenham, Oakham, Rutland LE15 8NQ. *Club:* Flyfishers'.

ROWLAND, Robin James Leslie; Executive Chairman, Yo! Sushi, since 2014 (Chief Executive Officer, 2000–14); *b* London, 9 March 1961; *s* of late Christopher Rowland and of Leslie Rowland; *m* 1997, Fiona Gillespie; two *s* one *d*. *Educ:* St Dunstan's Coll., London; Univ. of Kent (BA Hons American Studies); Univ. of S Carolina. Area Manager, Whitbread Inns, 1984–88; Old Orleans Ops Manager, Grand Metropolitan, 1988–92; Retail Dir, Scottish & Newcastle, 1992–95; Gp Franchise Dir, The Restaurant Gp, 1995–99; Ops Dir, Yo! Sushi, 1999–2000. Non-executive Director: Marston's plc, 2010–; Tortilla, 2012–; Caffe Nero, 2012–; Masterfoods (Gulf), 2014–. *Recreations:* ski-ing, sailing, mountain biking, family trekking. *Address:* Yo! Sushi, 95 Farringdon Road, EC1R 3BT. *T:* (020) 7841 0700. *E:* robin@yosushi.com.

ROWLAND-JONES, Prof. Sarah Louise, (Mrs R. T. Walton), DM; FRCP, FMedSci; Professor of Immunology, since 2000, and MRC Research Professor, since 2008, University of Oxford; Research Student, Christ Church, Oxford, since 1997; *b* 8 Nov. 1959; *d* of Timothy Louis Rowland-Jones and Kathleen Norah Rowland-Jones; *m* 1988, Prof. Robert Thompson Walton; one *d*. *Educ:* Girton Coll., Cambridge (BA 1st Cl. Hons 1980; MA 1984); Green Coll., Oxford (BM BCh 1983; DM 1995). MRCP 1986, FRCP 1999. Postgrad. med. trng in gen. medicine and infectious diseases, Oxford, London (St George's and Brompton Hosps) and Sheffield, 1983–89; Molecular Immunology Group, Oxford: MRC Trng Fellow, 1989–92; MRC clinician scientist, 1992–95; MRC Sen. Fellow, 1995–2000; Dir, Oxford Centre for Tropical Medicine, 2001–04; Dir of Res., MRC Labs, The Gambia, 2004–08. Hon. Consultant in Infectious Diseases, Churchill Hosp., Oxford, 1995–. FMedSci 2000. Elizabeth Glaser Scientist Award, Paediatric Aids Foundation, 1997. *Publications:* (ed with A. J. McMichael) Lymphocytes: a practical approach, 2000; contrib. papers to Nature, Nature Medicine, Immunity, The Lancet, Jl Exptl Medicine, Jl Immunology, Jl Virology, etc. *Recreations:* scuba diving, travel, gardening, collecting art deco, good wine and good company. *Address:* Nuffield Department of Medicine, Weatherall Institute of Molecular Medicine, John Radcliffe Hospital, Headington, Oxford OX3 9DS. *T:* (01865) 222316; 53 Jack Straw's Lane, Headington, Oxford OX3 0DW.

ROWLANDS, family name of **Baron Rowlands**.

ROWLANDS, Baron *cr* 2004 (Life Peer), of Merthyr Tydfil and of Rhymney in the County of Mid-Glamorgan; **Edward Rowlands,** CBE 2002; *b* 23 Jan. 1940; *e s* of W. S. Rowlands; *m* 1968, Janice Williams (*d* 2004), Kidwelly, Carmarthenshire; two *s* one *d*. *Educ:* Rhondda Grammar Sch.; Wirral Grammar Sch.; King's Coll., London. BA Hons History (London) 1962. Research Asst, History of Parliament Trust, 1963–65; Lectr in Modern History and Govt, Welsh Coll. of Adv. Technology, 1965–66. MP (Lab): Cardiff North, 1966–70; Merthyr Tydfil, April 1972–1983, Merthyr Tydfil and Rhymney, 1983–2001. Parliamentary Under-Secretary of State: Welsh Office, 1969–70, 1974–75; FCO, 1975–76; Minister of State, FCO, 1976–79; Opposition spokesman on energy, 1980–87; Mem., Select Cttee on Foreign Affairs, 1987–2001; Chm., Jt Cttee (inquiring into strategic export controls) of Select Cttees on Defence, Internat. Develt, and Trade and Industry, 1999–2001. Trustee, History of Parliament Trust, 1991– (Chm., 1993–2001). Member: Governing Body, Commonwealth Inst., 1980–92; Academic Council, Wilton Park, 1983–92. A Booker Prize Judge, 1984. *Publications:* various articles. *Recreations:* music, golf. *Address:* 110 Duncan House, Dolphin Square, Pimlico, SW1V 3PW. *T:* (020) 7798 5647; House of Lords, SW1A 0PW; 42 Station Road, Kidwelly, Carms SA17 4UT.

ROWLANDS, Prof. Brian James, MD; Professor of Gastrointestinal Surgery, Queen's Medical Centre and University of Nottingham, 1997–2009, now Emeritus Professor of Surgery; *b* 18 March 1945; *s* of Arthur Leslie Rowlands and Lilian Grace Allan; *m* 1971, Judith Thomas (*d* 2008); one *d*; partner, Kalliope Valassiadou; one *d*. *Educ:* Wirral Grammar Sch. for Boys; Guy's Hosp., Univ. of London (MB BS 1968); Univ. of Sheffield (MD 1978). Surgical trng, Sheffield Hosps, 1971–77; Associate Prof. of Surgery, Univ. of Texas Health Sci. Center, Houston, 1977–86; Prof. of Surgery and Hd, Dept of Surgery, QUB, and Consultant Surgeon, Royal Victoria Hosp., Belfast, 1986–97. Pres., Assoc. of Surgeons of GB and Ireland, 2007–08. Dir of Professional Affairs, E Midlands Strategic HA, 2009–, Vice-Chm., Dir of Professional Affairs Forum, RCS, 2009–. *Publications:* Critical Care for Post Graduate Trainees, 2005; ABC of Tubes, Drains, Lines and Frames, 2008; numerous peer-reviewed contribs on surgical clinical practice, res., educn and trng. *Recreations:* the mountains and the sea, anything Greek, music and theatre. *Address:* Section of Surgery, Queen's Medical Centre/University Hospital, Nottingham NG7 2UH. *T:* (0115) 823 1149, *Fax:* (0115) 823 1160. *E:* bjr.surgery@nottingham.ac.uk; 96 Station Road, Cropston, Leicester LE7 7HE.

ROWLANDS, Christopher John, FCA; Chief Operating Officer and Deputy Chairman, Apace Media plc, 2006–07; *b* 29 Aug. 1951; *s* of late Wilfrid John Rowlands and of Margaretta (*née* Roberts); *m* 1978, Alison Mary Kelly; twin *d*. *Educ:* Roundhay Sch., Leeds; Gonville and Caius Coll., Cambridge (MA Econ). FCA 1975. Peat Marwick Mitchell: articled clerk, 1973–75; CA, 1975; Manager, 1981; seconded as Partner, Zambia, 1981–83; Sen. Manager, London, 1983–85; Asda Group plc: Controller, business planning, Asda Stores, 1985–86; Divl Dir, Gp Finance, 1986–88; Dep. Man. Dir and Finance Dir, Asda Gp/Property Develt and Investment cos, 1988–92; Gp Finance Dir, 1992–93, Chief Exec., 1993–97, HTV Gp plc; Chief Exec., The Television Corporation, 1998–2001. Non-executive Director: iTouch plc, 2002–05; Standard Life (formerly Deutsche) Equity Investment Trust plc, 2003–12; Bristol & London plc, 2003–04. Mem. Council, ITVA, 1993–97 (Chm., Engrg Policy Gp, 1993–96). CCMI (CIMgt 1995); FRSA 1995. *Recreations:* family, theatre, church, reading, ski-ing, tennis, travel.

ROWLANDS, Rev. Chancellor John Henry Lewis; Team Rector, Rectorial Benefice of Whitchurch, since 2001 (Vicar, 1997–2001); Chaplain of Whitchurch Hospital, since 1997; Chancellor, Llandaff Cathedral, since 2002; *b* 16 Nov. 1947; *s* of William Lewis and Elizabeth Mary Rowlands; *m* 1976, Catryn Meryl Parry Edwards; one *s* two *d*. *Educ:* Queen Elizabeth Grammar Sch., Carmarthen; St David's University Coll., Lampeter (BA); Magdalene Coll., Cambridge (MA); Durham Univ. (MLitt); Wescott House, Cambridge. Ordained deacon, 1972, priest, 1973 (St David's Cathedral); Curate, Rectorial Benefice of Aberystwyth, 1972–76; Chaplain, St David's University Coll., Lampeter, 1976–79; Youth Chaplain, dio. of St David's, 1976–79; Dir, Academic Studies, St Michael's Coll., Llandaff, 1979–84, Sub-Warden, 1984–88, Warden, 1988–97. Lectr, Faculty of Theology, University Coll., Cardiff, later Univ. of Wales Coll. of Cardiff, then Univ. of Wales, Cardiff, 1979–97, Asst Dean, 1981–83; Dean, Faculty of Divinity: Univ. of Wales, 1991–95; Univ. of Wales, Cardiff, 1993–97. Diocesan Dir of Ordinands, Dio. Llandaff, 1985–88; Examng Chaplain to Archbishop of Wales, 1987–91; Sec., Doctrinal Commn of the Church in Wales, 1987–94. Hon. Canon, 1990–97, Residentiary Canon, 1997–2002, Llandaff Cathedral. Chaplain, Whitchurch Br., RBL, 1997–. Pres., Diwinyddiaeth (Soc. of Theol. Grads, Univ. of Wales), 1989–92. Member: (*ex officio*) Governing Body of the Church in Wales, 1988–97; Court, Univ. of Wales, 1988–94; Court, Univ. of Wales Coll. of Cardiff, 1988–97; Academic Bd, Univ. of Wales, 1991–94; Council, Llandaff Cathedral Sch., 1991–. Fellow, Woodard Corp., 1993. *Publications:* (ed) Essays on the Kingdom of God, 1986; Church, State and Society 1827–45, 1989; Doing Theology, 1996. *Recreations:* beachcombing, auctioneering, antique markets. *Address:* The Rectory, 6 Penlline Road, Whitchurch, Cardiff CF14 2AD. *T:* and *Fax:* (029) 2062 6072. *E:* rector@beneficeofwhitchurch.org.uk.

ROWLANDS, John Kendall, FSA; Keeper, Department of Prints and Drawings, British Museum, 1981–91; *b* 18 Sept. 1931; *s* of Arthur and Margaret Rowlands; *m* 1st, 1957, Else A. H. Bachmann (marr. diss. 1981); one *s* two *d*; 2nd, 1982, Lorna Jane Lowe; one *d*. *Educ:* Chester Cathedral Choir Sch.; King's Sch., Chester; Gonville and Caius Coll., Cambridge (MA Cantab 1959); MA Oxon. FSA 1976. Asst Keeper, Dept of Art, City Mus. and Art Gall., Birmingham, 1956–60; Editor, Clarendon Press, Oxford, 1960–65; Asst Keeper, 1965–74, Dep. Keeper, 1974–81, Dept of Prints and Drawings, British Museum. Mem. Adv. Cttee, Collected Works of Erasmus, 1979. Collaborated on film, Following the Trail of a Lost Collection, Amsterdam, 1995. *Publications:* David Cox Centenary Exhibition Catalogue, 1959; Graphic Work of Albrecht Dürer, 1971; Bosch, 1975; Rubens: drawings and sketches…, 1977; Urs Graf, 1977; Hercules Segers, 1979; Bosch, the Garden of Earthly Delights, 1979; German Drawings from a Private Collection, 1984; Master Drawings and Watercolours in the British Museum: from Fra Angelico to Henry Moore, 1984; The Paintings of Hans Holbein the Younger, 1985; The Age of Dürer and Holbein, 1988; Drawings by German Artists in the British Museum: 15th century, and 16th century by artists born before 1530, 1993; contribs to specialist journals, Festschriften. *Recreation:* music making. *Address:* Brant House, Brant Broughton, Lincs LN5 0SL. *T:* (01400) 272184. *Club:* Beefsteak.

ROWLANDS, Marc Humphreys; QC 2012; *b* Den Haag, Netherlands, 8 Nov. 1967; *s* of Paul Rowlands and Alison Rowlands; *m* 1996, Amanda Jane Dixon; three *s* two *d*. *Educ:* Marlborough Coll.; Magdalen Coll., Oxford (BA). Called to the Bar, Gray's Inn, 1990. *Recreations:* French bureaucracy, child psychology, sexual politics. *Address:* Keating Chambers, 15 Essex Street, WC2R 3AA. *T:* (020) 7544 2600. *E:* mrowlands@keatingchambers.com.

ROWLANDS, Rhys Price; His Honour Judge Rowlands; a Circuit Judge, since 2010; Resident Judge, North Wales, since 2014; *b* Bangor, N Wales; *s* of Emyr Price Rowlands and Aileen Price Rowlands; *m* 1989, Kären Jayne Woolley; two *d*. *Educ:* Brynhyfryd Sch., Ruthin; University Coll. London (LLB Hons); Univ. of Wales, Cardiff (MSc). Admitted solicitor, 1982; in practice as a solicitor, 1982–86; called to the Bar, Gray's Inn, 1986; in practice as a barrister, 1986–2010; Recorder, 2000–10. Hon. Recorder, Caernarfon, 2015. *Recreations:* tennis, hill walking, gardening, local history. *Address:* Mold Crown Court, Mold CH7 1AE. *T:* (01352) 707300. *E:* HHJudgeRhys.Rowlands@judiciary.gsi.gov.uk.

ROWLATT, Amanda, (Mrs T. Heymann), CBE 2011; Chief Analyst and Strategy Director, Department for Transport, since 2014; *b* 21 Dec. 1962; *d* of Charles Rowlatt and Penelope Anne Rowlatt, *qv*; *m* 1995, Tim Heymann; two *s* one *d*. *Educ:* University Coll., Oxford (MA Maths); St Antony's Coll., Oxford (MPhil Econs). Economist, FCO and ODA, 1987–91; Econ. Advr, HM Treasury, 1991–98; Chief Economist: ONS, 1998–2002; Competition Commn, 2002–05; Dir, Internat. Finance and Europe (formerly Europe, Trade and Internat. Financial Instns), DFID, 2005–08; Associate, Oxera, 2007–08; Chief Economist and Dir for Families and Child Poverty, DWP, 2008–11; Chief Analyst, BIS, 2011–14 (interim Dir Gen., Econs and Mkts, 2013). Vice Chair, Care Internat. UK, 2003–05. Mem. Council, REconS, 2003–08. Board Member: VSO UK, 2011–; Central and NW London NHS Foundn Trust, 2014–. Governor: Richmond Adult Community College, 2010–; NIESR, 2014–.

ROWLATT, Penelope Anne, PhD; economist; *b* 17 May 1936; *d* of Theodore Alexander Maurice Ionides and Anne Joyce Ionides (*née* Cooke); *m* 1961, Charles Rowlatt; one *s* three *d*. *Educ:* King Alfred Sch.; Somerville Coll., Oxford (BA 1959); Imperial Coll., London (PhD 1963); London Sch. of Economics (MSc 1973); University Coll. London (MPhil 2010). Chief Economist, Economic Models Gp of Cos, 1975–76; Economist, NIESR, 1976–78; Economic Advr, HM Treasury, 1978–86; Sen. Economic Advr, Dept of Energy, 1986–88; Director: Nat. Economic Res. Associates, 1988–98; Europe Economics, 1998–2001. Publisher, Medicine Today, 2000–03. Member: Retail Prices Adv. Cttee, 1991–94; Royal Commn on Envmtl Pollution, 1996–2000; Steering Gp, Performance and Innovation Unit Project, Cabinet Office, 1999; Better Regulation Commn (formerly Task Force), 2000–07. Treas., REconS, 1999–2008. *Publications:* Group Theory and Elementary Particles, 1966; Inflation, 1992; papers in learned jls on nuclear physics, economics and philosophy. *Recreations:* walking, sailing, bridge, eating and drinking, debating current affairs with friends. *Address:* 10 Hampstead Hill Gardens, NW3 2PL.

See also A. Rowlatt.

ROWLEY, (John) James; QC 2006; a Recorder, since 2002; *b* 24 June 1964; *s* of late John Rowley and of Gillian E. M. Rowley; *m* 1990, Clare Louise Brown; three *s*. *Educ:* Stonyhurst Coll.; Emmanuel Coll., Cambridge (BA Hons Classics 1985); Dip. Law. Called to the Bar, Lincoln's Inn, 1987 (Hardwicke Scholar); in practice as a barrister, Manchester, 1987– and London, 2004–; Counsel to Royal Liverpool Children's Inq., 2000–01. Chm., Personal Injuries Bar Assoc., 2010–12. *Publications:* (contrib.) Personal Injuries Handbook, 1997, 3rd edn 2007; contrib. articles to Jl Personal Injuries Litigation. *Recreations:* cricketer, gardener, cook. *Address:* Byrom Street Chambers, 12 Byrom Street, Manchester M3 4PP. *T:* (0161) 829 2100.

ROWLEY, Karl John; QC 2013; a Recorder, since 2009; *b* Stoke-on-Trent, 16 Oct. 1969; s of John Rowley and Noreen Rowley; *m* 1994, Georgina Roberts. *Educ:* Oriel Coll., Oxford (BA Phil. and Theol.; DipLaw 1993). Called to the Bar, Middle Temple, 1994; in practice as a barrister, specialising in family law: Regent Chambers, 1995–97; Young St Chambers, 1997–2005, St John's Bldgs, 2005–. *Recreations:* walking, reading, cycling, fishing. *Address:* St John's Buildings, 24a–28 St John Street, Manchester M3 4DJ. *T:* (0161) 214 1500. *E:* clerks@stjohnsbuildings.co.uk.

ROWLEY, Keith Nigel; QC 2001; *s* of James and late Eva Rowley; *m* 1986, Chantal Anna Mackenzie; one *s* one *d*. *Educ:* King's Coll., London (LLB). Called to the Bar, Gray's Inn, 1979; Bencher, Lincoln's Inn, 2008; in practice at Chancery Bar, 1980–. Judge, First-tier Tribunal (formerly Chm., Consumer Credit Appeals Tribunal), 2008–. *Recreations:* classical music, gardening, theatre, wine. *Address:* Radcliffe Chambers, 11 New Square, Lincoln's Inn, WC2A 3QB. *T:* (020) 7831 0081. *Club:* Hurlingham.

ROWLEY, Sir Richard (Charles), 8th Bt *cr* 1836, of Hill House, Berkshire, and 9th Bt *cr* 1786, of Tendring Hall, Suffolk; *b* 14 Aug. 1959; *s* of Sir Charles Robert Rowley, 7th and 8th Bt and of Astrid Pennington Cleife, *d* of Sir Arthur Massey, CBE; *S* father, 2008; *m* 1st, 1989, Elizabeth Alison (marr. diss. 1999), *d* of late Henry Bellingham; two *s*; 2nd, 2013, Mrs Louise Gilks. *Educ:* Exeter Coll., Oxford (BA Metallurgy and Material Scis 1982); Open Univ. (BSc Psychol. 2005); Nottingham Univ. (MSc Occupational Psychol. 2006). Director: CMC Consultants Ltd, 2009–; Mansley Gp Hldgs Ltd, 2015. *Heir: s* Joshua Andrew Rowley, *b* 5 Dec. 1989. *Address:* 21 Tedworth Square, SW3 4DR; Naseby Hall, Northants NN6 6DP.

ROWLEY-CONWY, family name of **Baron Langford**.

ROWLING, Joanne Kathleen, OBE 2000; FRSL; writer; *b* 31 July 1965; *d* of Peter John Rowling and late Anne Rowling; *m* 1st, 1992 (marr. diss.); one *d*; 2nd, 2001, Dr Neil Murray; one *s* one *d*. *Educ:* Univ. of Exeter (BA 1986). FRSL 2002. Author of the Year, British Book Awards, 2000. Chevalier de la Légion d'Honneur (France), 2009. *Publications:* Harry Potter and the Philosopher's Stone, 1997 (Smarties Prize, 1997; filmed, 2001); Harry Potter and the Chamber of Secrets, 1998 (Smarties Prize, 1998; Children's Book Award, Scottish Arts Council, 1999; filmed, 2002); Harry Potter and the Prisoner of Azkaban, 1999 (Smarties Prize, 1999; Whitbread Children's Book of the Year, 2000; filmed, 2004); Harry Potter and the Goblet of Fire, 2000 (WH Smith Children's Book of the Year, Children's Book Award, Scottish Arts Council, 2001; filmed, 2005); Harry Potter and the Order of the Phoenix, 2003 (filmed, 2007); Harry Potter and the Half-Blood Prince, 2005 (filmed, 2009); Harry Potter and the Deathly Hallows, 2007 (Part 1 filmed, 2010; Part 2 filmed 2011); The Tales of Beedle the Bard, 2008; The Casual Vacancy, 2012; (as Robert Galbraith) The Cuckoo's Calling, 2013; The Silkworm, 2014; Very Good Lives, 2015. *Address:* c/o Neil Blair, The Blair Partnership, Middlesex House, 4th Floor, 34–42 Cleveland Street, W1T 4JE.

ROWLING, Sir John (Reginald), Kt 2003; educational consultant; Headteacher, Nunthorpe School, Middlesbrough, 1984–2003; *b* 8 Jan. 1941; *m* 1977, Sheila Elizabeth; one *s* one *d*. *Educ:* Durham Univ. (BSc Maths 1962; MSc Applied Maths 1963). Teacher, Royal GS, Newcastle, 1963–74; teacher, later Dep. Head, Hirst High Sch., Ashington, 1974–84. Vis. Prof., St Mary's UC, Twickenham, 2008–. Dir, PiXL Club, 2009–. *Publications:* Heading Towards Excellence, 2002, 2nd edn 2003; Changing Towards Excellence, 2003; Climbing Towards Excellence, 2006. *Recreations:* golf, photography, walking, gardening. *Address:* Cromwell House, 38 College Square, Stokesley TS9 5DW. *T:* (01642) 712095. *E:* therowlings@hotmail.com.

ROWLINSON, Sir John (Shipley), Kt 2000; DPhil; FRS 1970; FREng, FRSC, FIChemE; Dr Lee's Professor of Physical Chemistry, Oxford University, 1974–93, now Emeritus; Fellow of Exeter College, Oxford, 1974–93, now Emeritus Fellow; *b* 12 May 1926; *er s* of late Frank Rowlinson and Winifred (*née* Jones); *m* 1952, Nancy Gaskell (*d* 2012); one *s* one *d*. *Educ:* Rossall School (Scholar); Trinity College, Oxford (Millard Scholar; BSc, MA, DPhil; Hon. Fellow, 1992). Research Associate, Univ. of Wisconsin, USA, 1950–51; ICI Research Fellow, Lecturer, and Senior Lecturer in Chemistry, University of Manchester, 1951–60; Prof. of Chemical Technology, London Univ. (Imperial Coll.), 1961–73. Mary Upson Prof. of Engrg, 1988, Andrew D. White Prof.-at-large, 1990–96, Cornell Univ. Lectures: Liversidge, Chem. Soc., 1978; von Hofmann, Gesell. Deutscher Chem., 1980; Faraday, 1983, Lennard-Jones, 1985, Priestley, 2004, RSC; Guggenheim, Reading Univ., 1986; T. W. Leland, Rice Univ., Houston, Texas, 1990; Rossini, IUPAC, 1992; Dreyfus, Dartmouth Coll., 1993; Birch, ANU, 1994. Pres., Faraday Div., Chem. Soc., 1979–81; Hon. Treas., Faraday Society, 1968–71; Vice-Pres., Royal Instn of GB, 1974–76, 1993–95; Physical Sec. and Vice-Pres., Royal Soc., 1994–99. Member, Sale Borough Council, 1956–59. FREng (FEng 1976). Hon. FCGI 1987. Hon. For. Mem., Amer. Acad. of Arts and Scis, 1994. Meldola Medal, Roy. Inst. of Chemistry, 1954; Marlow Medal, Faraday Soc., 1957; Leverhulme Medal, Royal Soc., 1993; Edelstein Award, ACS, 2008. *Publications:* Liquids and Liquid Mixtures, 1959, (jtly) 3rd edn, 1982; The Perfect Gas, 1963; Physics of Simple Liquids (ed jtly), 1968; (trans. jtly) The Metric System, 1969; (jtly) Thermodynamics for Chemical Engineers, 1975; (jtly) Molecular Theory of Capillarity, 1982; (ed) J. D. van der Waals, On the Continuity of the Gaseous and Liquid States, 1988; (jtly) Record of the Royal Society 1940–1989, 1993; (jtly) Van der Waals and Molecular Science, 1996; Cohesion: a scientific history of intermolecular forces, 2002; (ed jtly) Chemistry at Oxford: a history from 1600 to 2005, 2009; James Dewar: a ruthless chemist, 2012; papers in scientific journals. *Address:* 12 Pullens Field, Headington, Oxford OX3 0BU. *T:* (01865) 767507; Physical and Theoretical Chemistry Laboratory, South Parks Road, Oxford OX1 3QZ. *T:* (01865) 275157. *Club:* Alpine.

ROWNTREE, Timothy John; Director, Organisation Conjointe de Coopération en Matière d'Armement, since 2013; *b* 13 Sept. 1956; *s* of George Arthur and Cicely Beryl Rowntree; *m* 1982, Susan Margaret Jones; two *d*. *Educ:* Strensall Primary Sch.; Joseph Rowntree Secondary Modern Sch.; Univ. of Bradford (BTech Hons Electrical Engrg); King's Coll., London (MA Internat. Studies 2009). Systems Analyst, Army Electro Magnetic Compatibility Agency, Blandford, 1980–84; Sen. Engr, RAE, Farnborough, 1984–87; Attack and Identification System Manager, NATO Eur. Fighter Aircraft Mgt Agency, Munich, 1987–92; Head, RAF Signal Engrg Labs, RAF Henlow, 1992–96; Head, Tornado Mission Systems Support Authy, 1996–99, Dep. Tornado Integrated Project Team Leader, 1999–2001, RAF Wyton; Lynx Helicopter Integrated Project Team Leader, Yeovilton, 2001–04; Dep. Ops Dir, Air Systems, Defence Procurement Agency, Bristol, 2004–07; Dir Air Support, Defence Equipment and Support, MoD, 2007–13. *Recreations:* more than I can fit in my busy lifestyle, involving family, friends and the family dog, including walking, gardening, theatre, music, boating, fishing, vintage motorcycles and tractors. *Address:* Organisation Conjointe de Coopération en Matière d'Armement EA, Godesberger Allee 140, 53175 Bonn, Germany. *Club:* Royal Air Force.

ROWSELL, Edmund Charles P.; *see* Penning-Rowsell.

ROWSON, John Anthony; Director, Royal & Sun Alliance Insurance Group, 1996–2000; *b* 6 May 1930; *s* of Thomas Herbert Rowson and Hilda Elizabeth Rowson; *m* 1st, 1955, Elizabeth Mary (*née* Fiddes) (marr. diss. 1980); two *s* one *d*; 2nd, 1989, Molly Lesley (*née* Newman). *Educ:* Beckenham Grammar Sch.; College of Law. Admitted Solicitor, 1959. Partner, Herbert Smith, 1960, Sen. Partner, 1988–93. Director: Glaxo Trustees Ltd, 1992–96 (Chm., 1994–96); Royal Insurance Holdings, 1994–96. Master, Solicitors' Co., and Pres., City of London Law Soc., 1992–93. FRSA 1992. *Recreations:* tennis, golf, ski-ing, music. *Address:* 112 Rivermead Court, Ranelagh Gardens, SW6 3SB. *Clubs:* Athenæum, Royal Automobile; Hurlingham; Royal Mid Surrey Golf.

ROWSON, Martin George Edmund; cartoonist, illustrator, writer, poetaster and broadcaster; *b* 15 Feb. 1959; adopted *s* of late K. E. K. Rowson, MD, PhD; *m* 1987, Anna Victoria Clarke; one *s* one *d*. *Educ:* Merchant Taylors' Sch., Northwood; Pembroke Coll., Cambridge (BA 1982). Cartoons contributed regularly to: New Statesman, 1982–84, 1985–86, 1995–98; One Two Testing/Making Music, 1983–91; Chartist, 1985–; Financial Weekly, 1985–90; Today, 1986–92; Sunday Today, 1986–87; Guardian, 1987–89, 1991–93, 1994–; Sunday Correspondent, 1989–91; Independent, 1989–; Time Out, 1990–2002; Sunday Tribune, 1991–2000; Independent on Sunday, 1991–; European, 1991–92; Modern Review, 1993–95; Tribune, 1994–; Daily Mirror, 1995–; Observer, 1996–98; Scotsman, 1998–2009; TES, 1998–2005; Irish Times, 1999–2000; Daily Express, 1999–2001; Red Pepper, 1999–; Erotic Review, 1999–; Index on Censorship, 2000–; The Times, 2001–05; Scotland on Sunday, 2002–04; New Humanist, 2002–; Spectator, 2007–; Morning Star, 2007–. Book reviews, Independent on Sunday, 1994–; Cult Books Expert, Mark Radcliffe Show, Radio 1, 1996–97; columnist, Tribune, 1998–, Dir, Tribune Publications, 2000–04. Chm., British Cartoonists' Assoc., 2000. Vice-Pres., Zool Soc. of London, 2002–05, 2009–10 (Council Mem., 1991–2005, 2007–11). Chm., Ken Sprague Trust, 2004–; Trustee, Cartoon Mus., 2003–; Rep. Gov., Powell-Cotton Mus., 2007–. Hon. Associate, Nat. Secular Soc.; Dist. Supporter, British Humanist Assoc., 2009– (Trustee, 2011–); Trustee, People's Trust for Endangered Species, 2013–. Cartoonist Laureate to Mayor of London (in return for 1 pint of London Pride Ale per annum), 2001–. Political Cartoonist of the Year, 2000, 2003, Caricaturist of the Year, 2011, Cartoon Arts' Trust; Political Cartoon of the Year, 2002, 2007, Political Cartoonist of the Year, 2010, Political Cartoon Soc. Premio Satira Politica Award, Italy, 2007. Hon. DLitt Westminster, 2007. *Publications:* Scenes from the Lives of the Great Socialists, 1983 (with Kevin Killane); Lower than Vermin: an anatomy of Thatcher's Britain, 1986; The Waste Land, 1990; (with Anna Clarke) The Nodland Express, 1994; (with Chris Scarre) Imperial Exits, 1995; (with Will Self) Sweet Smell of Psychosis, 1996; The Life and Opinions of Tristram Shandy, Gentleman, 1996; (with John Sweeney) Purple Homicide, 1997; Mugshots, 2005; Snatches, 2006; Stuff, 2007; The Dog Allusion, 2008; Fuck: the human odyssey, 2008; Giving Offence, 2009; The Limerickiad: vol. I: from Gilgamesh to Shakespeare, 2011; vol. II: John Donne to Jane Austen, 2012; vol. III, Byron to Baudelaire, 2013; Gulliver's Travels, 2012; The Coalition Book, 2014. *Recreations:* cooking, drinking, ranting, atheism, zoos, collecting taxidermy. *Address:* 46 Vicar's Hill, SE13 7JL. *T:* (020) 8244 7576, *Fax:* (020) 8244 7577. *E:* martin.rowson1@ntlworld.com. *Clubs:* Soho House, Chelsea Arts, Academy; Zoological.

ROWTHORN, Prof. Robert Eric; Professor of Economics, Cambridge University, 1991–2006, now Emeritus; Fellow, King's College, Cambridge, since 1991; *b* 20 Aug. 1939; *s* of Eric William Rowthorn and Eileen Rowthorn; *m* 1981, Amanda Jane Wharton; one *s* one *d*. *Educ:* Newport High Sch. for Boys; Jesus Coll., Oxford (BA, BPhil, MA). University of Cambridge: Res. Fellow, Churchill Coll., 1964–65; College Lectr, King's Coll., 1965–66; Asst Lectr, 1966–71; Lectr, 1971–82; Reader in Economics, 1982–91. *Publications:* International Big Business, 1971; Capitalism, Conflict and Inflation, 1980; (with J. Wells) De-industrialisation and Foreign Trade, 1987; (with N. Wayne) Northern Ireland: the political economy of conflict, 1988; (ed jtly) The Role of the State in Economic Change, 1995; (ed jtly) Democracy and Efficiency in the Economic Enterprise, 1996; (ed jtly) Transnational Corporations and the Global Economy, 1998; (ed with Antony Dnes) The Law and Economics of Marriage and Divorce, 2002. *Recreations:* swimming, reading, scuba-diving. *Address:* King's College, Cambridge CB2 1ST.

ROXBEE COX, Philip Ardagh, (Philip Ardagh); children's author, poet, reviewer and commentator; *b* Shortlands, Kent, 11 Sept. 1961; *s* of Hon. Christopher Withers Roxbee Cox and Rosemary Joyce Roxbee Cox (*née* Ardagh); *m* 1994, Dr Héloïse Jeanne-Marie Coffey; one *s*. Literary prize judge for: Guardian Children's Book Award, 2003; Roald Dahl Funny Prize, 2010; Young Minds Book Award, 2010. Writer, Secret Undercover Vets on Ice (interactive drama), BBC Radio 7, 2004; Co-writer, The Gift (short film), 2013. On-line writer in residence, Booktrust, 2014–15; Patron: Stratford-upon-Avon Literary Fest., 2013–; Northern Children's Book Fest., 2015. *Publications:* over 100 books, primarily for children, including: The Hieroglyphs Handbook, 1999; The Eddie Dickens Trilogy: Awful End, 2000 (Luchs Prize, 2002; Deutschen Jugendliteraturpreis, 2003), Dreadful Acts, 2001, Terrible Times, 2002; The Further Adventures of Eddie Dickens: Dubious Deeds, 2003, Horrendous Habits, 2005, Final Curtain, 2006; Unlikely Exploits: The Fall of Fergal, 2002, Heir of Mystery, 2003, The Rise of the House of McNally, 2004; The Green Men of Gressingham, 2002, The Red Dragons of Gressingham, 2008; Grubtown Tales: Stinking Rich and Just Plain Stinky (Roald Dahl Funny Prize), 2009, The Year that it Rained Cows, 2009, The Far From

Great Escape, 2009, The Wrong End of the Dog, 2010, Trick Eggs and Rubber Chickens, 2010, Splash, Crash and Loads of Cash, 2010, The Great Pasta Disaster, 2010, When Bunnies Turn Bad, 2011; (with Sir Paul McCartney and G. Dunbar) High in the Clouds, 2005; Philip Ardagh's Book of Absolutely Useless Lists for Every Day of the Year, 2007; Philip Ardagh's Book of Howlers, Blunders and Random Mistakery, 2009; The Henry's House non-fiction series, 2009–; Philip Ardagh's Book of Kings, Queens, Emperors and Rotten Wart-Nosed Commoners, 2011; The Grunts in Trouble, 2012; The Grunts all at Sea, 2013; The Grunts in a Jam, 2014; The Grunts on the Run, 2015; The Black Knight of Gressingham, 2015; for adults: The Not-So-Very-Nice Goings-on at Victoria Lodge: without illustrations by the author, 2004; The Silly Side of Sherlock Holmes: a brand new adventure using a bunch of old pictures, 2005; The Scandalous Life of the Lawless Sisters: criminally illustrated with what was to hand, 2008. *Recreations:* general beard maintenance, ducking through doorways, visiting historical and archaeological sites, Sherlock Holmes. *Address:* c/o Faber & Faber, Bloomsbury House, 74–77 Great Russell Street, WC1B 3DA.

ROXBURGH, Charles Fergusson; Director General, Financial Services, HM Treasury, since 2013; *b* London, 25 Oct. 1959; *s* of Robert Roxburgh and Muriel Smith; *m* 1987, Karen Elizabeth Pierce, *qv*; two *s*. *Educ:* Stowe Sch., Buckingham; Trinity Coll., Cambridge (BA 1981); Harvard Business Sch. (MBA 1986). Associate, Arthur Andersen, 1981–84; McKinsey & Company, 1986–2013: Co-Hd, Global Strategy Practice, 1999–2003; Hd, UK Financial Instns Practice, 2003–05; Co-Hd, Corporate and Investment Banking Practice, 2005–09; Dir, McKinsey Global Inst., 2009–13. Chm., Financial Services Trade and Investment Bd, 2013–. *Publications:* (jtly) The Emerging Equity Gap, 2012. *Recreations:* spending time with family, music, history. *Address:* HM Treasury, One Horse Guards Road, SW1A 2HQ. *E:* charles.roxburgh@hmtreasury.gsi.gov.uk. *Clubs:* Royal Automobile, Tuesday.

ROXBURGH, Iain Edge; consultant in local governance and public service management, since 2001; *b* 4 Nov. 1943; *s* of John and Irene Roxburgh; *m* 1965, Tessa Breddy; two *s*. *Educ:* William Hulme's Grammar Sch., Manchester; Imperial Coll., London (BSc Eng, MSc, DIC). ACGI; CEng; MICE. Civil Engineer and transport planner, 1965–80; Greater London Council: Dep. Head of Personnel Services, 1981–83; Dir of Admin, 1983–85; Dep. Sec., AMA, 1985–89; Chief Exec. and Town Clerk, Coventry City Council, 1989–2001. Dir, Warwick Research Consortium, 2003–08. Sen. Res. Associate, 2003–13, Associate Fellow, 2006–13, Warwick Business Sch. Mem. Bd and Vice Chm., New Local Govt Network, 2013– (Chm., 2007–13). *Recreations:* photography, motor cycling, walking, ski-ing, golf. *Address:* Hill Rise, Leys Lane, Meriden, Coventry CV7 7LQ. *T:* (01676) 522496, 07971 780616.

ROXBURGH, Prof. Ian Walter; Professor of Mathematics and Astronomy, 1987–2001, Research Professor of Astronomy, 2001–11, Queen Mary, University of London (formerly Queen Mary College, later Queen Mary and Westfield College, University of London), now Emeritus Professor of Astronomy and Mathematics; *b* 31 Aug. 1939; *s* of Walter McRonald Roxburgh and Kathleen Joyce (*née* Prescott); *m* 1960, Diana Patricia (*née* Dunn); two *s* one *d*. *Educ:* King Edward VII Grammar Sch., Sheffield; Univ. of Nottingham (BSc Mathematics 1st Cl. Hons); Univ. of Cambridge (PhD); Elected Res. Fellow, Churchill Coll., Cambridge, 1963; Asst Lectr, Mathematics, 1963–64, Lectr, 1964–66, KCL; Reader in Astronomy, Univ. of Sussex, 1966–67; Queen Mary, later Queen Mary and Westfield College, London University: Prof. of Applied Maths, 1967–87; Hd, Dept of Applied Maths, 1978–84; Dir, Astronomy Unit, 1983–2001; Hd, Sch. of Math. Scis, 1984–95; Pro-Principal, 1987. Chm., Cttee of Heads of Univ. Depts of Maths and Stats, 1988–93. Chercheur associé, Observatoire de Paris, 2000–09. ESA scientist on COROT mission. Contested: (L) Walthamstow W, 1970; (SDP) Ilford N, 1983. *Publications:* (ed jtly) Physical Processes in Astrophysics, 1993; (ed jtly) Convection in Astrophysics, 2007; articles in Monthly Notices RAS, Astrophys. Jl, Astronomy and Astrophysics, Jl Geophysical Res., Phil. Trans Royal Soc., Gen. Relativity and Gravitation, Jl Physics A., Foundations of Physics, Nature, Solar Physics, Brit. Jl for the Philosophy of Science. *Recreations:* politics, economics, philosophy. *Address:* 37 Leicester Road, Wanstead, E11 2DW. *T:* (020) 8989 7117.

ROXBURGH, Karen Elizabeth; *see* Pierce, K. E.

ROXBURGHE, 10th Duke of, *cr* 1707; **Guy David Innes-Ker;** Baron Roxburghe 1600; Earl of Roxburghe, Baron Ker of Cessford and Cavertoun, 1616; Bt (NS) 1625; Viscount Broxmouth, Earl of Kelso, Marquis of Bowmont and Cessford, 1707; Earl Innes (UK), 1837; *b* 18 Nov. 1954; *s* of 9th Duke of Roxburghe, and Margaret Elisabeth (*d* 1983) (who *m* 1976, Jocelyn Olaf Hambro, MC), *d* of late Frederick Bradshaw McConnel; *S* father, 1974; *m* 1st, 1977, Lady Jane Meriel Grosvenor (*see* Lady J. M. Dawnay) (marr. diss. 1990); two *s* one *d*; 2nd, 1992, Virginia, *d* of David Wynn-Williams; one *s* one *d*. *Educ:* Eton; RMA Sandhurst (Sword of Honour, June 1974); Magdalene Coll., Cambridge (BA (Land Economy) 1980; MA 1984). Commnd into Royal Horse Guards/1st Dragoons, 1974; RARO 1977. Mem., Jockey Club. Mem., Fishmongers' Co.; Freeman of City of London, 1983. *Recreations:* shooting, fishing, golf, racing, ski-ing. *Heir:* *s* Marquis of Bowmont and Cessford, *qv*. *Address:* Floors Castle, Kelso TD5 7RW. *T:* (01573) 224288. *Clubs:* Turf, White's.
See also Viscount Grimston.

ROY, Frank; *b* 29 Aug. 1958; *s* of James Roy and Esther McMahon; *m* 1977, Ellen Foy; one *s* one *d*. *Educ:* St Joseph's High Sch.; Our Lady's High Sch., Motherwell; Motherwell Coll. (HNC Mktg); Glasgow Caledonian Univ. (BA Consumer and Mgt Studies 1994). Steelworker, Ravenscraig Steelworks, Motherwell, 1977–91; PA to Helen Liddell, MP, 1994–97. MP (Lab) Motherwell and Wishaw, 1997–2015; contested (Lab) same seat, 2015. An Asst Govt Whip, 2005–06; a Lord Comr, HM Treasury (Govt Whip), 2006–10; an Opposition Whip, 2010. *Recreations:* gardening, reading, football.

ROY, Lindsay Allan, CBE 2004; *b* 19 Jan. 1949; *s* of John and Margaret Roy; *m* 1972, Irene Patterson; two *s* one *d*. *Educ:* Univ. of Edinburgh (BSc 1970). Principal Teacher of Mod. Studies, Queen Anne High Sch., 1974–83; Asst Rector, Kirkcaldy High Sch., 1983–86; Depute Rector, Glenwood High Sch., 1986–89; Rector, Inverkeithing High Sch., 1990–2008; Rector, Kirkcaldy High Sch., 2008. Associate Assessor, HM Inspectorate of Educn, 1996–2008. Pres., Headteachers' Assoc. of Scotland, 2004–05; Member: Jt Adv. Cttee, Scottish Credit and Qualifications Framework, 2003–07; Nat. Qualifications Steering Gp, 2003–08. Chm., Curriculum and Student Affairs Cttee, Lauder Coll., 1997–2006. Exec. Mem., Internat. Confederation of Principals, 2006–10. MP (Lab) Glenrothes, Nov. 2008–2015. FRSA 2004. *Recreations:* angling, mountain biking.

ROY, Paul David; Founding Partner, NewSmith LLP (formerly NewSmith Capital Partners LLP), 2003–15; *b* 8 May 1947; *s* of Vernon Alfred Roy and Elsie Florence Roy; *m* 1985, Susan Mary Elkies; five *s* one *d*. *Educ:* Trinity Sch., Croydon; Liverpool Univ. (BA Hons Econs). Partner: Morton Bros (Stockbrokers), 1974–77; Kemp-Gee & Co., 1977–87; Jt Man. Dir, Citicorp Scrimgeour Vickers, 1987–89; Man. Dir, Smith New Court (UK), 1989–95; Chief Exec., Smith New Court plc, 1995; Merrill Lynch & Co.: Man. Dir Equities, Europe, Middle East and Africa, 1995–98; Sen. Vice-Pres. and Head of Global Equities, 1998–2001; Exec. Vice-Pres. and Co-Pres., Investment Banking and Global Markets, 2001–03. Chairman: New River Retail Ltd, 2009–; NewSmith Asset Mgt LLP, 2011–. Chm., British Horseracing Authy, 2007–13; Mem. Bd, Horserace Betting Levy Bd, 2008–13. *Recreations:* art, golf, tennis, fishing, watching school matches.

ROY, Sheila; Group Director of Healthcare Services, Westminster Health Care, 2000–05; *b* 27 Feb. 1948; *d* of late Bertie and of Dorothy Atkinson; *m* 1970, Robert Neil Roy. *Educ:* BA Open Univ.; RGN; DN (London); Cert Ed Leeds Univ.; RNT; PMD Harvard Business Sch. Milton Keynes Health Authority: Dir, Nursing Studies, 1983–86; Actg Chief Nursing Officer and Dir, Nursing Studies, Feb.–May 1986; Dist Nursing Advr and Dir, Nurse Educn, Hillingdon HA, 1986–88; Dir of Nursing Management and Res., NW Thames RHA, 1988–91; Dir, Newchurch & Co., 1991–96; owner, Sheila Roy & Associates, 1996–2000. Non-exec. Dir, Meditech Gp Ltd, 1996–2001. Participant in Prosavin gene therapy trial for Parkinson's disease, 2011–. *Recreations:* gardening, writing, painting.

ROYALL OF BLAISDON, Baroness *cr* 2004 (Life Peer), of Blaisdon in the County of Gloucestershire; **Janet Anne Royall;** PC 2008; *b* 20 Aug. 1955; *d* of Basil Oscar Royall and Myra Jessie (*née* Albutt); *m* 1980, Stuart Henry James Hercock (*d* 2010); two *s* one *d*. *Educ:* Westfield Coll., Univ. of London (BA Hons). Flower importer, Covent Garden, 1978; Gen. Sec., British Labour Gp, European Parlt, 1979–85; Policy Advr/PA, 1985–92, Researcher/Press Officer, 1992–95, to Rt Hon. Neil Kinnock, MP; Mem., Cabinet of Mr Kinnock as Comr, then Vice-Pres., EC, 1995–2001; Parly Co-ordinator, Directorate Gen., Press and Communication, EC, 2001–03; Hd, EC Office in Wales, 2003–05. A Baroness in Waiting (Govt Whip), 2005–08; Captain of the Hon. Corps of Gentlemen at Arms (Govt Chief Whip in H of L), 2008; Leader of the House of Lords, 2008–10; Chancellor of the Duchy of Lancaster, 2009–10; Shadow Leader of the House of Lords, 2010–15. Vice Pres., Party of Eur. Socialists, 2012–. Pro-Chancellor, Univ. of Bath, 2014–. *Recreations:* reading, gardening, cooking, swimming. *Address:* House of Lords, SW1A 0PW.

ROYCE, Felicity Ann Hope; *see* Harvey, F. A. H.

ROYCE, Hon. Sir (Roger) John, Kt 2002; a Judge of the High Court, Queen's Bench Division, 2002–14; a Presiding Judge, Western Circuit, 2006–10; *b* 27 Aug. 1944; *s* of late J. Roger Royce and Margaret A. Royce (*née* Sibbald); *m* 1979, Gillian Wendy Adderley (marr. diss. 2013); two *s* one *d*; *m* 2013, Mary Teresa Pringle. *Educ:* The Leys Sch., Cambridge; Trinity Hall, Cambridge (BA). Qualified as Solicitor, 1969; called to the Bar, Gray's Inn, 1970, Bencher, 1997; a Recorder, 1986–2002; QC 1987; a Dep. High Ct Judge, QBD, 1993–2002; Leader, Western Circuit, 1998–2001. Master, St Stephen's Ringers, 2002. Cambridge Hockey Blue, 1965, 1966; Captain Somerset Hockey, 1976; Austrian qualified ski instructor. Commandeur, Commanderie de Bordeaux (Bristol). Hon. LLD UWE, 2005. *Recreations:* cricket, ski-ing, golf, collecting corkscrews. *Clubs:* Hawks (Cambridge); St Enodoc Golf.

ROYDEN, Sir Christopher (John), 5th Bt *cr* 1905; *b* 26 Feb. 1937; *s* of Sir John Ledward Royden, 4th Bt, and Dolores Catherine (*d* 1994), *d* of late Cecil J. G. Coward; *S* father, 1976; *m* 1961, Diana Bridget, *d* of Lt-Col J. H. Goodhart, MC; two *s* (one *d* decd). *Educ:* Winchester Coll.; Christ Church, Oxford (MA). Duncan Fox & Co. Ltd, 1960–71; Spencer Thornton & Co., 1971–88: Partner, 1974–86; Dir, 1986–88; Associate Dir, Gerrard Vivian Gray Ltd, 1988–96. *Recreations:* fishing, shooting, gardening. *Heir:* *s* John Michael Joseph Royden [*b* 17 March 1965; *m* 1989, Lucilla, *d* of J. R. Stourton; two *d*]. *Address:* Bridge House, Ablington, Bibury, Cirencester, Glos GL7 5NY. *Club:* Boodle's.

ROYLE, Catherine Jane; HM Diplomatic Service; Political Adviser, NATO, since 2015; *b* 17 Aug. 1963; *d* of Peter and Anne Royle; *m* 1991, Dr Marcelo Camprubi; two *s*. *Educ:* Somerville Coll., Oxford (MA 1985; Hon. Fellow 2007); Univ. of Wales, Aberystwyth (MScEcon 1990). Joined FCO, 1986; Third, then Second Sec., Chile, 1988–91; First Sec., FCO, 1992–97; First Sec., Dublin, 1997–2001; Policy Advr on European Constitution, FCO, 2001–03; Dep. Hd of Mission, Buenos Aires, 2003–06; Ambassador to Venezuela, 2007–10; Dep. Ambassador, Afghanistan, 2010–12; Hd of Secretariat, Internat. Police Co-ordination Bd, Afghanistan, 2012–13; Sen. Advr to Minister of Interior, Afghanistan, 2013–14. *Recreations:* reading, riding, sailing, cinema, politics, travelling.

ROYLE, Rev. Canon Roger Michael; freelance broadcaster and writer, since 1979; Hon. Canon and Chaplain, Southwark Cathedral, 1993–99; *b* 30 Jan. 1939; *s* of Reginald and Agnes Royle. *Educ:* St Edmund's Sch., Canterbury; King's Coll. London (AKC 2nd Class Hons). Curate, St Mary's, Portsea, Portsmouth, 1962–65; Sen. Curate, St Peter's, Morden, 1965–68; Succentor, Southwark Cathedral, 1968–71; Warden of Dorney Parish, Eton Coll. Project, 1971–74; Conduct, Eton Coll., 1974–79; Chaplain, Lord Mayor Treloar Coll., 1990–92; permission to officiate, dio. Southwark, 1999–. Hon. Chaplain, Entertainment Artistes' Benevolent Fund. Radio broadcasts incl. Sunday Half Hour, Radio 2, 1991–2007. MA Lambeth, 1990. Hon. Fellow, Harris Manchester Coll., Oxford, 2006. *Publications:* A Few Blocks from Broadway, 1987; Royle Exchange, 1989; To Have and to Hold, 1990; Picking up the Pieces, 1990; Mother Teresa: her life in pictures, 1992; Between Friends, 2001. *Recreations:* theatre, music, patience, cooking.

ROYLE, Timothy Lancelot Fanshawe, FCIM; Chairman, Cotswold Assistance, since 2005; *b* 24 April 1931; *s* of Sir Lancelot Carrington Royle, KBE, and Barbara Rachel Royle; *m* 1958, Margaret Jill Stedeford; two *s* one *d*. *Educ:* Harrow; Mons Mil. Acad. FCIM (FInstM 1977). Commnd 15th/19th King's Royal Hussars, 1949, Inns of Court Regt, TA, 1951–63. Joined Hogg Robinson Gp, 1951; Man. Dir, 1980–81. Chairman: Control Risks Group, 1972–91; Berry Palmer & Lyle, 1984–91; Hemotex Holdings, 1991–93; Director: Imperio Reinsurance Co. (UK), 1989–97; Imperio Holdings Ltd, 1995–97. Mem., Insce Brokers Regulatory Council, 1989–94. Member: Church Assembly of C of E, 1965–70; Gen. Synod of C of E, 1985–2005; Church Comr, 1966–83. Director: Christian Weekly Newspapers, 1975–2002 (Chm., 1979–97); Lindley Educn Trust, 1970–2002 (Chm., 1970–98); Wellmarine Reinsurance Brokers, 1976–2002. Trustee: Ridley Hall, Cambridge, 1976–2003; Wycliffe Hall, Oxford, 1976–2003; Charinco, 1977–2002; Charishare, 1977–2002; Intercontinental Church Soc., 1977–2001. Reader, Church of England, 1958–. Freeman, City of London, 1976; Founder Member: Marketors' Co., 1977; Insurers' Co., 1979. Councillor (C) Cotswold DC, 1999–2007 (Chm. Council, 2001–04). *Recreations:* country pursuits, ski-ing, old age. *Address:* The Well House, Donnington, Moreton-in-Marsh, Glos GL56 0XZ. *Clubs:* Cavalry and Guards, MCC; St Moritz Tobogganing (St Moritz).

ROYSTON, Viscount; Philip Alexander Joseph Yorke; *b* 3 Dec. 2009; *s* and *heir* of Earl of Hardwicke, *qv*.

ROZARIO, Patricia Maria, OBE 2001; soprano; *b* Bombay; *m* Mark Troop; two *c*. *Educ:* Guildhall Sch. of Music (Gold Medal); Nat. Opera studio. Performances include: Sophie, Werther, Opera North, 1985; Pamina, Magic Flute, Kent Opera; Ilia, Idomeneo, Glyndebourne, 1985; Zerlina, Don Giovanni, Aix-en-Provence; première, Miriam, Golem, 1989; première, Belisa, The Nightingale's to Blame; première, Another America: Fire & Earth, Linbruy Studio, Royal Opera Hse; Tancredi and Clorinda, ENO; works written for her, incl. by Arvo Pärt, Roxanna Panufnik and John Tavener; numerous concerts and recitals in UK and worldwide. Recordings include Schubert songs, Tavener's Akhmatova songs. Prof. of Voice, RCM, 2006–. Co-Dir, Chamber Music Co. Co-Founder, Giving Voice Soc., 2009. FRCM 2014.

ROZENBERG, Joshua Rufus; legal journalist and commentator; *b* 30 May 1950; *s* of late Zigmund and Beatrice Rozenberg; *m* 1974, Melanie Phillips, *qv*; one *s* one *d*. *Educ:* Latymer Upper Sch., Hammersmith; Wadham Coll., Oxford (MA 1976). Solicitor's articled clerk, 1972; admitted Solicitor, 1976; trainee journalist, BBC, 1975; Legal Affairs Correspondent, 1985–97, Legal and Constitutional Affairs Correspondent, 1997–2000, BBC News; Legal

Editor, Daily Telegraph, 2000–08. Hon. Bencher, Gray's Inn, 2003. Hon. LLD: Hertfordshire, 1999; Nottingham Trent, 2012; Lincoln, 2014; Univ. of Law, 2014. *Publications:* Your Rights and the Law (with Nicola Watkins), 1986; The Case for the Crown, 1987; The Search for Justice, 1994; Trial of Strength, 1997; Privacy and the Press, 2004. *Recreations:* reading, writing and wrestling with computers. *Address:* BCM Rozenberg, WC1N 3XX. *E:* joshua@rozenberg.net. *Club:* Garrick.

ROZENBERG, Melanie; *see* Phillips, Melanie.

ROZENTAL, Andrés; President: Rozental y Asociados, since 1997; Mexican Council on International Affairs, since 2001; Chairman, ArcelorMittal Mexico (formerly Mittal Steel Mexico), since 2000; Retired Eminent Ambassador of Mexico; *b* 27 April 1945; *s* of Leonid Rozental and Neoma Gutman; *m* 1971, Vivian Holzer; two *d*. *Educ:* Univ. of Bordeaux (Dip. French 1962); Univ. of the Americas (BA 1965); Univ. of Pennsylvania (MA 1966). Joined Foreign Service, 1967; Alternate Perm. Rep. to OAS, Washington, 1971–74; Counsellor, London, 1974–76; Prin. Advr to the Minister, 1977–79; Dir-Gen. of Diplomatic Service, 1979; Dir-Gen. for N American Affairs, 1979–82; Ambassador: to UN, Geneva, 1982–83; to Sweden, 1983–88; Sen. Vice-Pres., Banco Nacional de México, 1988; Dep. Foreign Minister, 1988–94; Amb. to Court of St James's, 1995–97; Amb. at Large, Mexico, 2000–01. Member, non-executive Board: ArcelorMittal Brazil, 2007–; Ocean Wilson Hldgs, Wilson Sons Brazil, 2010–; HSBC Bank Mexico, 2013–; Mem., Strategy Cttee for Mexico, Airbus Gp, 2006– (formerly Mem., non-exec. Bd, EADS Mexico); Member, Advisory Board: Kansas City Southern de Mexico, 2009–14. Sen. Non-resident Fellow, Brookings Instn, 2007–14. Member: Internat. Bd of Governors, 2002–, Operating Bd, 2011–, Centre for Internat. Governance Innovation, Canada. Gov., Internat. Develt Res. Centre, Canada, 2007–12. Trustee, Migration Policy Inst., 2008–. Orders include: Polar Star (Sweden), 1983; Civil Merit (Spain), 1991; Order of Merit (France), 1993. *Publications:* (jtly) Paradoxes of a World in Transition, 1993; (jtly) The United Nations Today: a Mexican vision, 1994; Mexican Foreign Policy in the Modern Age, 1994; (jtly) Foreign Ministries: change and adaptation, 1997; (jtly) Mexico under Fox, 2004; (jtly) Canada Among Nations, 2009–2010: as others see us, 2009; (jtly) The Obama Administration and the Americas: agenda for change, 2010; (ed jtly) Canada Among Nations, 2011–2012: Canada and Mexico's unfinished agenda, 2012; (contrib.) The End of Nostalgia: Mexico confronts the challenges of global competition, 2013; (contrib.) Oxford Handbook of Modern Diplomacy, 2013. *Recreations:* swimming, sailing, hiking. *Address:* (home) Virreyes 1360, Col. Lomas de Chapultepec, 11000 México DF, México. *T:* (55) 52025347. *E:* mexconsult@gmail.com.

ROZHDESTVENSKY, Gennadi Nikolaevich, Hon. CBE 2014; Founder, Artistic Director and Chief Conductor, State Symphony Orchestra of Ministry of Culture, Russia (New Symphony Orchestra), 1983–92; Chief Conductor, Royal Stockholm Philharmonic Orchestra, 1991–95; Professor of Conducting, Moscow State Conservatoire, since 1965; *b* 4 May 1931; *m* Victoria Postnikova, concert pianist. Studied piano at Moscow Conservatoire; started conducting at 18. Bolshoi Theatre: Asst Conductor, 1951; Conductor, 1956–60; Principal Conductor, 1965–70; Artistic Dir, 2000–01. Chief Conductor, USSR Radio and Television Symphony Orchestra, 1960–74; Chief Conductor: Stockholm Philharmonic Orchestra, 1974–77; BBC Symphony Orchestra, 1978–81; Moscow Chamber Opera, 1974–83; Vienna Symphony Orchestra, 1981–83. Guest conductor, Europe, Israel, America, Far East, Australia. Lenin Prize, 1970; People's Artist, USSR, 1972; Order of Red Banner of Labour, 1981. *Recreation:* music. *Address:* c/o Rayfield Allied, Southbank House, Black Prince Road, SE1 7SJ. *Club:* Athenæum.

RUANE, Caitríona; Member (SF) South Down, Northern Ireland Assembly, since 2003; *b* 19 July 1962; *d* of Michael Ruane and Nuala Gilmartin; *m* Brian McAteer; two *d*. *Educ:* St Angela's Nat. Sch., Mayo; St Joseph's Secondary Sch., Mayo. Former professional tennis player; human rights and develt worker, US aid foundn, Central America, 1983–87; Latin Amer. Project Officer, Trocaire, Dublin, 1987–88; Co-ordinator, Human Rights Centre, Centre for Res. and Documentation, Belfast, 1988–96; Dir, Féile an Phobail, W Belfast, 1997–2001. Minister for Educn, NI, 2007–11. Northern Ireland Assembly: Equality spokesperson, 2003–07; SF Chief Whip, 2011–; Member: Assembly Commn, 2011–; N/S Interparly Exec., 2012–. Mem., NI Policing Bd. Contested (SF) S Down, 2010. *Address:* Northern Ireland Assembly, Parliament Buildings, Belfast BT4 3XX.

RUANE, Christopher Shaun; *b* 18 July 1958; *s* of late Michael Ruane, labourer, and of Esther Ruane, dinner lady; *m* 1994, Gill, *d* of late Joe and of Phyl Roberts; two *d*. *Educ:* Blessed Edward Jones Comp. Sch., Rhyl; UCW Aberystwyth (BSc); Liverpool Univ. (PGCE). Teacher, Ysgol Mair RC Primary Sch., Rhyl, 1982–97 (Dep. Hd, 1991–97). Mem. (Lab) Rhyl Town Council, 1988–98. Contested (Lab) Clwyd NW, 1992. MP (Lab) Vale of Clwyd, 1997–2015; contested (Lab) same seat, 2015. PPS to Sec. of State for Wales, 2002–07, to Minister of State, DWP, 2007–08, to Minister for Housing, DCLG, 2008, to Foreign Sec., 2009–10, to Shadow Home Sec., 2010–11, to Shadow Chancellor, 2011; an Opposition Whip, 2011–13. Mem., Welsh Affairs Select Cttee, 1999–2002; Vice-Chm., 2007–08, Chm., 2008–15, PLP Welsh Regl Gp. Chairman: N Wales Gp of Labour MPs, 2002–15; All Party Gp on Heart Disease, 2002–15; All Party Gp on Irish in Britain, 2011–15.

RUAUX, Her Honour Gillian Doreen, (Mrs W. D. Partington); a Circuit Judge, 1993–2006; *b* 25 March 1945; *d* of late Charles Edward Ruaux and Denise Maud Ruaux (*née* Le Page); *m* 1968, William Derek Partington; one *d*. *Educ:* Bolton Sch.; Univ. of Manchester (LLB Hons, LLM). Called to the Bar, Gray's Inn, 1968; practised at the Bar, Manchester, 1968–93. *Recreations:* theatre, opera, horse-racing, cookery.

RUBBIA, Prof. Carlo; physicist; Senior Physicist, European Organisation for Nuclear Research, since 1993 (Director-General, 1989–93); Professor of Physics, University of Pavia, since 1997; Scientific Director, Institute for Advanced Sustainability Studies, Potsdam, since 2010; *b* 31 March 1934; *s* of Silvio and Bice Rubbia; *m* Marisa; one *s* one *d*. *Educ:* Scuola Normale Superiore, Pisa; Univ. of Pisa (Dr 1957). Research Fellow, Columbia Univ., 1958–59; Lectr, Univ. of Rome, 1960–61; CERN, 1960– (head of team investigating fundamental particles on proton-antiproton collider); scientist, Fermi Nat. Accelerator Lab., USA, 1969–73; Higgins Prof. of Physics, Harvard Univ., 1971–88. Pres., Agency for New Technology, Energy and the Envmt, Rome, 1999–2005; Mem., EU Adv. Gp on Energy and Climate Change, 2007–; Special Advr for Energy to Sec. Gen., ECLAC, 2009–. Member: Papal Acad. of Science, 1985–; Amer. Acad. of Arts and Sciences, 1985; Accademia dei XL; Accademia dei Lincei; European Acad. of Sciences; Ateneo Veneto; Foreign Member: Royal Soc.; Soviet Acad. of Scis, 1988; US Nat. Acad. of Scis; Polish Acad. of Scis. Senator for Life, Italian Senate, 2013. Hon. Doctorates: Boston, Chicago, Geneva, Genoa, Northwestern, Udine, Carnegie-Mellon, Loyola, Sofia, Moscow, Chile, Padova, Madrid, Rio de Janeiro, La Plata and Oxford Universities. Gold Medal, Italian Physical Soc., 1983; Lorenzo il Magnifico Prize for Sciences, 1983; Achille de Gasperi Prize for Sciences, 1984; Nobel Prize for Physics (jtly), 1984; Leslie Prize for exceptional achievements, 1986. Knight Grand Cross, Italy, 1985; Officer, Legion of Honour, France, 1989; Order of Merit (Poland), 1993. *Publications:* papers on nuclear physics: weak force quanta (W–, W+ and Z particles, intermediate vector bosons); proton-antiproton collision; sixth quark. *Address:* CERN, 1211 Geneva 23, Switzerland.

RUBEN, Prof. David-Hillel; Hon. Research Fellow, Birkbeck, University of London, 2011–13, now Professor Emeritus; Visiting Professor, King's College London, 2011–13, now Professor Emeritus; *b* 25 July 1943; *s* of Blair S. Ruben and Sylvia G. Ruben; *m* 1968, Eira (*née* Karlinsky); one *s* two *d*. *Educ:* Dartmouth Coll. (BA); Harvard Univ. (PhD). Tutor in Philosophy, Univ. of Edinburgh, 1969; Lecturer in Philosophy: Univ. of Glasgow, 1970–75; Univ. of Essex, 1975–79; Lectr, 1979–82, Sen. Lectr, 1982–84, City Univ.; Prof. of Philosophy, LSE, 1984–98; Director: Jews' Coll., London, later London Sch. of Jewish Studies, 1998–99; NY Univ. in London, 1999–2011; London Dir and Regl Dir for UK and Ireland, Arcadia Univ. in London, 2012–13; part-time Professor of Philosophy: SOAS, London, 2000–04; Birkbeck, Univ. of London, 2004–11; Prof. of Philosophy, Oxford Brookes Univ., 2013–14. Phi Beta Kappa, 1964. *Publications:* Marxism and Materialism, 1977, 2nd edn 1979; Metaphysics of the Social World, 1985; Explaining Explanation, 1990; (ed) Explanation, 1994; Action and its Explanation, 2003; articles in phil. jls.

RUBENS, Prof. Robert David, MD; FRCP; Professor of Clinical Oncology, Guy's, King's and St Thomas' School of Medicine of King's College London (formerly United Medical and Dental Schools of Guy's and St Thomas' Hospitals), University of London, 1985–2003; Consultant Physician in Medical Oncology, Guy's Hospital, 1975–2003; *b* 11 June 1943; *s* of Joel Rubens and Dinah Rubens (*née* Hasseck); *m* 1970, Margaret Chamberlin; two *d*. *Educ:* King's Coll., London (BSc); St George's Hosp. Med. Sch. (MB, BS); MD London. FRCP 1984. House and Registrar appts, St George's, Brompton, Hammersmith and Royal Marsden Hosps, 1968–72; Clin. Res. Fellow, ICRF Labs, 1972–74; Dir, ICRF Clinical Oncology Unit, Guy's Hosp., 1985–97. Chm., EORTC Breast Cancer Co-op. Gp, 1991–94. Examr, RCP, 1987–93. Pres., Assurance Medical Soc., 2003–05. Editor-in-Chief, Cancer Treatment Reviews, 1993–2001. *Publications:* A Short Textbook of Clinical Oncology, 1980; Bone Metastases: diagnosis and treatment, 1991; Cancer and the Skeleton, 2000; ed and contrib. books and papers on cancer and other med. subjects. *Recreations:* golf, bridge. *Address:* 5 Currie Hill Close, Wimbledon, SW19 7DX. *Club:* Royal Wimbledon Golf.

RUBENSTEIN, Alan Martin, FFA; Chief Executive, Pension Protection Fund, since 2009; *b* Edinburgh, 3 Sept. 1956; *m* 1980, Beverley Glass; two *d*. *Educ:* Heriot-Watt Univ. (BSc Hons). FFA 1984. Scottish Widows, 1978–91; Dir, Barclays de Zoete Wedd, 1991–94; Chief Exec., Lucas Varity Fund Mgt Ltd, 1995–97; Managing Director: Morgan Stanley, 1997–2006; Lehman Bros, 2006–08. Mem., Takeover Panel, 2000–03. Mem., Supervisory Bd, Robeco Groep NV, 2014–. Investment Advr, British Coal Staff Superannuation Scheme, 2013–. Vice-Chm., Nat. Assoc. of Pension Funds, 2000–02. Member, Council: Faculty of Actuaries, 2004–09; Inst. and Faculty of Actuaries, 2012–. Gov., Pensions Policy Inst., 2011–.

RUBERY, Dr Eileen Doris, CB 1998; Senior Research Fellow and Registrar of the Roll, Girton College, Cambridge, 2000–13 (Visiting Senior Fellow, 1997–2000); Tutor in Art History, Institute of Continuing Education, University of Cambridge, since 2004; *b* 16 May 1943; *d* of James and Doris McDonnell; *m* 1969, Philip Huson Rubery; one *d*. *Educ:* Westcliff High Sch. for Girls; Sheffield Univ. Med. Sch. (MB ChB Hons); PhD Cambridge 1973; MA Art Hist. London Univ. 2004. FRCR 1976; FRCPath 1986; FFPH (FFPHM 1993). Royal Infirmary, Sheffield, 1966–67; MRC Res. Fellow, Dept of Biochem., Cambridge, 1967–71; Meres' Sen. Student, St John's Coll., Cambridge, 1971–73; Addenbrooke's Hospital, Cambridge: Registrar in Radiotherapy and Oncology, 1973–76; Sen. Registrar, 1976–78; Wellcome Sen. Clinical Res. Fellow, 1978–83; Hon. Consultant, 1978–83; Sen. Res. Fellow and Dir of Med. Studies, Girton Coll., 1981–83; SMO (Toxicology), DHSS, 1983–88; Department of Health: PMO, 1988–89; SPMO and Hd of Med. Div., Communicable Disease and Immunisation, 1989–91; SPMO and Hd of Health Promotion Med. Div., 1991–95; Under Sec. and Hd of Health Aspects of Envmtl and Food Div., 1995–97; Under Sec. and Hd of Protection of Health Div., 1996–99. Lectr in Public Policy, 1997–2004, Course Dir, Masters in Community Enterprise, 1997–2001, Sen. Associate, 2004–09, Judge Business Sch. (formerly Judge Inst. of Mgt Studies), Cambridge Univ. Advr to Food Standards Agency and other public sector bodies on public health and public policy issues, 2000–07. Mem., Professional Conduct Cttee, 2000–06, Professional Performance Cttee, 2003–06, GMC. QHP, 1993–96. *Publications:* (ed) Indications for Iodine Prophylaxis following a Nuclear Accident, 1990; (ed) Medicine: a degree course guide, 1974–83; papers on art history, especially on Byzantine Rome, the consequences of longevity, public health, food safety, health promotion, professionals and public sector incl. policy making, the management of uncertainty and leadership in community enterprise, in professional jls. *Recreations:* visiting Rome, reading Proust, Byzantine and Medieval art, opera, Wagner, Ruskin. *E:* edr1001@cam.ac.uk.

RUBERY, Prof. Jill Christine, PhD; FBA 2006; Director, European Work and Employment Centre, since 1994, Professor of Comparative Employment Systems, since 1995, and a Deputy Dean, 2007–12, Manchester Business School, University of Manchester (formerly University of Manchester Institute of Science and Technology); *b* 4 Nov. 1951; *d* of late Austin Rubery and Gladys Mary Rubery (*née* Clueit); *m* 1974, Andrew Wilson; one *d*. *Educ:* Wintringham Grammar Sch., Grimsby; Newnham Coll., Cambridge (BA 1973, MA 1976); New Hall, Cambridge (PhD 1987). Res. Asst, Queen Elizabeth House, Oxford, 1973–75; Jun. Res. Officer, Res. Officer, then Sen. Res. Officer, Dept of Applied Econs, Univ. of Cambridge, 1978–89; Fellow and Dir of Studies in Econs, New Hall, Cambridge, 1977–89, Emeritus Fellow, 2006; Lectr, then Sen. Lectr, Manchester Sch. of Mgt, UMIST, 1989–95. Vis. Associate Prof., Univ. of Notre Dame, 1989; Visiting Fellow: Wissenschaftszentrum für Sozialforschung, Berlin, 1993; Inst. Industrial Relns, Univ. of Calif, Berkeley, 2002. Member: Bd of Arbitrators, ACAS, 1989–; Adv. Forum on Employment Regulations, DTI, 2005–09; High-Level Expert Gp on Social Investment, EC, 2012–. Co-ordinator, expert gp on gender and employment, EC, 1991–96, 2000–03 and 2004–07. *Publications:* (jtly) Labour Market Structure, Industrial Organisation and Low Pay, 1982; (ed) Women and Recession, 1988; (jtly) Women and European Employment, 1988; (ed) Equal Pay in Europe, 1988; (ed jtly) International Integration and Labour Market Organisation, 1992; (ed with F. Wilkinson) Employer Strategy and the Labour Market, 1994; (ed jtly) Occupation and Skills, 1994; (jtly) Women's Employment in Europe: trends and prospects, 1999; (jtly) Managing Employment Change: the new realities of work, 2002; (with D. Grimshaw) The Organization of Employment: an international perspective, 2003; (ed jtly) Systems of Production: markets, organizations and performance, 2003; (jtly) Fragmenting Work: blurring organisational boundaries and disordering hierarchies, 2005; (ed jtly) European Employment Models in Flux, 2009; (ed jtly) Welfare States and Life Transitions, 2010; contribs to jls in econs, mgt, industrial relns and sociology. *Recreations:* cooking, holidays, reading. *Address:* Manchester Business School, University of Manchester, Booth Street West, Manchester M15 6PB. *T:* (0161) 306 3406, *Fax:* (0161) 306 3505. *E:* Jill.Rubery@manchester.ac.uk.

RUBERY, His Honour Reginald John; a Circuit Judge, 1995–2010; Member, Parole Board for England and Wales, since 2010; *b* 13 July 1937; *s* of Reginald Arthur Rubery and Phyllis Margaret (*née* Payne); *m* 1st, 1961, Diana Wilcock Holgate (marr. diss.); one *s*; 2nd, 1974, Frances Camille Murphy; one step *d*. *Educ:* Wadham House, Hale, Cheshire; King's Sch., Worcester. Admitted Solicitor, 1963; Partner: Whitworths, Manchester, 1966–72; Taylor Kirkman & Mainprice, 1972–78; County Court and Dist Registrar, then District Judge, 1978–95; Asst Recorder, 1987–91; a Recorder, 1991–95; Judge, St Helena Court of Appeal, 1997–2012; Justice of Appeal, Falkland Is, British Indian Ocean Territory, British Antarctic Territory. Chm. (pt-time) Immigration Appeal Tribunal, 1998–2005; Tribunal Judge (formerly Mem., Mental Health Review Tribunal), 2001–10. Mem., Manchester City Council, 1968–71. Hon. Sec., Manchester Law Soc., 1974–78. *Recreations:* golf, swimming, gardening. *Address:* Birkby, Charnes Road, Ashley, Market Drayton, Shropshire TF9 4LQ. *Club:* Lansdowne.

RUBIDGE, Caroline Janet Pamela; *see* Wright, C. J. P.

RUBIN, Sir Peter (Charles), Kt 2010; DM; FRCP; Professor of Therapeutics, University of Nottingham, 1987–2014 (Dean, Faculty of Medicine and Health Sciences, 1997–2003); *b* 21 Nov. 1948; *s* of late Woolf Rubin and Enis Rubin; *m* 1976, Dr Fiona Logan (marr. diss. 2006); one *s* one *d*. *Educ:* Redruth Grammar Sch.; Emmanuel Coll., Cambridge (MA; Hon. Fellow 2011); Exeter Coll., Oxford (DM 1980). FRCP 1989. Jun. hosp. posts, Stoke on Trent, 1974–77; American Heart Assoc. Fellow, Stanford Med. Center, 1977–79; Sen. Registrar (Medicine and Clinical Pharmacology), Glasgow, 1979–82; Wellcome Trust Sen. Fellow in Clinical Sci., Glasgow, 1982–87; University of Nottingham: Chairman: Dept of Medicine, 1991–97; Veterinary Sch. Project Bd, 2002–06. Mem., Nottingham HA, 1998–2002; Chairman: Specialist Adv. Cttee in Clinical Pharmacol. and Therapeutics, RCP, 1992–95; Steering Cttee, MAGPIE trial, MRC, 1998–2004; GMC Educn Cttee, 2002–08; Postgrad. Med. Educn and Trng Bd, 2005–08; GMC, 2009–14; Co-Chm., Dental Jt Implementation Gp, 2005–09; Member: Physiol Medicine and Infections Grants Cttee, MRC, 1992–96; Bd, HEFCE, 2003–09. Hon. FRCGP 2006; Hon. FRCPE 2009; Hon. FRCPI 2012; Hon. FRCP Thailand 2015. Hon. DSc: Lincoln, 2004; Exeter, 2011; Hon. DM Plymouth, 2012. *Publications:* Lecture Notes on Clinical Pharmacology, 1981, 7th edn 2006; Prescribing in Pregnancy, 1987, 4th edn 2007; Hypertension in Pregnancy, 1988, 2nd edn 2000. *Recreations:* sport, walking, music, photography. *E:* peter.rubin@nottingham.ac.uk. *Clubs:* Oxford and Cambridge; Redruth.

RUBIN, Robert E(dward); Counselor, Centerview Partners LLC, since 2010; Chairman of the Executive Committee, Citigroup, 1999–2009; Secretary of the United States Treasury, 1995–99; *b* 29 Aug. 1938; *s* of Alexander Rubin and Sylvia Rubin (*née* Seiderman); *m* 1963, Judith Leah Oxenberg; two *s*. *Educ:* Harvard (AB *summa cum laude* 1960); LSE, London Univ.; Yale Univ. (LLB 1964). Admitted to NY Bar, 1965; Associate, Cleary, Gottlieb, Steen & Hamilton, 1964–66; Goldman, Sach & Co.: Associate, 1966–70; Partner, 1971; Mem. Mgt Cttee, 1980; Vice Chair and Co-Chief Operating Officer, 1987–90; Sen. Partner and Co-Chair, 1990–93; Asst to the Pres. on econ. policy and Head, Nat. Econ. Council, Exec. Office of US President, 1993–95. Chm., Local Initiatives Support Corp., 1999–; Co-Chm., Council on Foreign Relations, 2007–. Member, Board of Directors: Chicago Bd of Options Exchange, Inc., 1972–76; NY Futures Exchange, 1979–85; Center for Nat. Policy, 1982–93 (Vice Chair, 1984); NY Stock Exchange, Inc., 1991–93 (Mem., Regulatory Adv. Cttee, 1988–90); NYC Partnership Inc., 1991–93 (also Partner). Member: Adv. Cttee on Tender Offers, 1983, Adv. Cttee on Market Oversight and Financial Services, 1991–93, Securities and Exchange Commn; NY Adv. Cttee on Internat. Capital Markets, Federal Reserve Bank, 1989–93; Mayor's Council of Econ. Advrs, 1990. Trustee: Amer. Ballet Theatre Foundn, 1969–93; Mt Sinai Hosp., 1977 (Vice-Chm., 1986); Collegiate Sch., 1978–84; Station WNET-TV, 1985–93; Carnegie Corp., NY, 1990–93; Harvard Mgt Co. Inc., 1990–93; Mem., Harvard Corp., 2002–. Hon. DHL Yeshiva, 1996. Nat. Assoc. of Christians and Jews Award, 1977; Dist. Leadership in Govt Award, Columbia Business Sch., 1996; Finance Minister of the Year Award, Euromoney mag., 1996. *Publications:* (with J. Weisberg) In an Uncertain World (memoirs), 2003. *Recreation:* fly fishing. *Clubs:* Harvard, Links (New York); Century Country (Purchase).

RUBIN, Stephen Charles; QC 2000; a Recorder, since 2004; *b* 14 March 1955; *s* of late Joseph Rubin and of Shirley Rubin (*née* Dank); *m* 1985, Jayne Anne Purdy; two *s* two *d*. *Educ:* Merchant Taylors' Sch., Northwood; Brasenose Coll., Oxford (Open Exhibnr; MA Jurisp.). Called to the Bar, Middle Temple, 1977, Bencher, 2014; in practice at the Bar, 1979–. Member: Professional Conduct and Complaints Cttee, Bar Council, 1994–99; Cttee, London Common Law and Commercial Bar Assoc., 2001–04; Chm., Bar Disciplinary Tribunal, 2013–; Hon. Mem. Bd, UK Law Students' Assoc., 2011–. *Recreations:* contemporary art, tennis, ski-ing, golf. *Address:* Fountain Court Chambers, Temple, EC4Y 9DH.

RUBINS, Jack, FIPA; Chairman, Osprey Communications plc, 1993–2002 (non-executive Chairman, 1999–2000; Chief Executive, 1993–95); *b* 4 Aug. 1931; *m* 1962, Ruth Davids; three *s*. *Educ:* Northern Polytechnic (Architecture). Chm. and Chief Exec., DFS Dorland Advertising, 1976–87; Chm. and Chief Exec., McCann Erickson Gp UK, 1990–91; Chm., SMS Communications, 1991–93. *Recreations:* philately, golf. *Address:* 8 Portman Hall, Old Redding, Harrow Weald, Middx HA3 6SH.

RUBINSTEIN, Mark Gabriel; Theatre Producer and General Manager, since 2000; Director, Mark Rubinstein Ltd, since 2000; *b* London, 6 May 1961; *s* of Hilary and Helge Rubinstein; *m* 1987, Sue Johnston; one *s* one *d*. *Educ:* Latymer Upper Sch., Hammersmith; Kingsway Princeton Coll., London; Univ. of Sussex (BA Hons Soc. Anthropol. and Cognitive Studies 1985). Finance Dir, Royal Court Th., 1989–95; Gen. Manager, Inst. of Contemp. Arts, 1995–96; Sen. Producer, Bill Kenwright Ltd, 1996–99; Producer, Old Vic Productions Ltd, 1999–2002; ind. theatre producer, 2002–. Productions as Producer or General Manager include: Jesus Hopped the A Train, 2002; Sexual Perversity in Chicago, 2003; By the Bog of Cuts, 2004; Otherwise Engaged, 2005; Whose Life is it Anyway, 2005; Bent, 2006; Sunday in the Park with George, 2006; Desperately Seeking Susan, 2007; Tintin, 2007; The Drowsy Chaperone, 2007; Glengarry Glen Ross, 2007; La Clique, 2008–10; Isango Portobello prodn of The Magic Flute, 2008; transfer of NT's War Horse, 2009 (UK tour, 2014–15); The Mysteries, 2009; La Soirée, 2010–; Butley, 2011; Fela! Eur. tour, 2011; Curious Incident of the Dog in the Night, 2013; The Drowned Man, 2013–14; A Doll's House, 2013; Jeeves and Wooster in Perfect Nonsense, 2013–; ONCE, 2014–15; Beautiful—The Carole King Musical, 2015–. Trustee: Soc. of London Theatre, 2004–10, 2011– (Chm., Finance Cttee; Pres., 2011–14; Vice Pres., 2015–); Theatre Develt Fund, 2004–10, 2011–; Complicite, 2006–13; Theatre Investment Fund, 2007–; Mousetrap Foundn for the Arts, 2007–11; League of Ind. Producers, 2012–. *Recreations:* paragliding (pilot level, recreational and competing in club competitions), cycling. *Address:* Mark Rubinstein Ltd, 25 Short Street, SE1 8LJ. *T:* (020) 7021 0787, *Fax:* 0870 705 9731. *E:* info@mrluk.com.

RUCKER, (Belinda) Christian, MBE 2010; Founder, The White Company, since 1994; *b* 6 Nov. 1968; *d* of Anthony Rucker and Rosemary Calcutt; *m* 1995, Nicholas Charles Tyrwhitt Wheeler, *qv*; one *s* three *d*. *Educ:* Combe Bank Sch., Sevenoaks. Various asst roles, Condé Nast Pubns, 1987–90; PR Asst, Clarins UK Ltd, 1991; Asst Health and Beauty Asst, Harpers & Queen magazine, 1992–94. *Recreation:* looking after four children in every spare moment! *Address:* The White Company, 1 Derry Street, W8 5HY.

RUCKER, His Honour Jeffrey Hamilton; a Circuit Judge, 1988–2007; a Resident Judge, Truro Crown Court, 2001–07; *b* 19 Dec. 1942; *s* of late Charles Edward Sigismund Rucker and Nancy Winifred Hodgson; *m* 1965, Caroline Mary Salkeld; three *s*. *Educ:* St Aubyn's, Rottingdean; Charterhouse. Called to the Bar, Middle Temple, 1967; a Recorder, 1984; a Circuit Judge, assigned to SE Circuit, 1988, transf. W Circuit, 2001. Legal Mem., Mental Health Rev. Tribunals, 1995–. Mem. Council of Govs, UMDS of Guy's and St Thomas', 1991–98. *Recreations:* sailing, ski-ing, music.

RUDD, Rt Hon. Amber; PC 2015; MP (C) Hastings and Rye, since 2010; Secretary of State, Department of Energy and Climate Change, since 2015; *b* London, 16 Aug. 1963; *m* 1991, Adrian Anthony Gill, *qv* (marr. diss.); one *s* one *d*. *Educ:* Queen's Coll., London; Edinburgh Univ. (MA Hons Hist. 1986). With J P Morgan, London and NY, 1986–87; Director: Lawnstone Ltd, 1988–97; MacArthur & Co., 1997–99; CEO, Investors Noticeboard Ltd, 1999–2001; Consultant, I-Search Ltd, 2001–03; Man. Dir and Sen. Consultant, Lawnstone Ltd, 2003–10. Columnist, Corporate Financier, 2003–10. Contested (C) Liverpool Garston, 2005. PPS to Chancellor of Exchequer, 2012–13; an Asst Govt Whip, 2013–14; Parly Under-Sec. of State, DECC, 2014–15. Mem., Envmt, Food and Rural Affairs Select Cttee, 2010–12. *Address:* House of Commons, SW1A 0AA.

RUDD, Prof. Anthony George, CBE 2013; FRCP; Professor of Stroke Medicine, King's College London, since 2010; Consultant Stroke Physician, Guy's and St Thomas' NHS Foundation Trust (formerly St Thomas' Hospital, then Guy's and St Thomas' Hospital Trust), since 1988; *b* Bolton, Lancs, 15 June 1954; *s* of Jack Rudd and Erica Rudd; *m* 1979, Lynne Simpson; three *s* one *d*. *Educ:* Haberdashers' Aske's Sch., Elstree; Jesus Coll., Cambridge (BA 1975; MB 1979); King's Coll. Med. Sch. (BChir 1978). FRCP 1994. Registrar, Hammersmith Hosp., 1982–83; Lectr, Geriatric Medicine, St George's Hosp. Med. Sch., 1983–88; London Stroke Clin. Dir, 2010–; Nat. Clin. Dir for Stroke, NHS England, 2013–. Pres., British Assoc. of Stroke Physicians, 2004–06; Trustee, Stroke Assoc., 2005–14 (Hon. Vice Pres., 2014–). *Publications:* A Strategy for Stroke Services and Research, 1996; Stroke at Your Fingertips, 2000, 2nd edn 2004; Measuring the Quality of Health Care, 2001; A Practical Guide to Stroke Care, 2011; articles in jls on stroke epidemiology, recovery, treatment and quality improvement. *Recreations:* flute playing, cooking, gardening, family. *Address:* Stroke Unit, St Thomas' Hospital, Westminster Bridge Road, SE1 7EH. *T:* (020) 7188 2515. *E:* anthony.rudd@kcl.ac.uk.

RUDD, Sir (Anthony) Nigel (Russell), Kt 1996; DL; Chairman: Heathrow (SP) Ltd (formerly BAA), since 2007; BBA Aviation plc, since 2014 (non-executive Director, since 2013); *b* 31 Dec. 1946; *m* 1969, Lesley Elizabeth (*née* Hodgkinson); two *s* one *d*. *Educ:* Bemrose Grammar Sch., Derby. FCA. Qualified Chartered Accountant 1968; Divl Finance Dir, London & Northern Group, 1970–77; Chairman: C. Price & Son Ltd, 1977–82; Williams Holdings (later Williams plc), 1982–2000; Dep. Chm., Raine Industries, 1992–94 (non-exec. Chm., 1986–92); non-executive Chairman: Pendragon PLC, 1989–10; East Midlands Electricity, 1994–97 (Dir, 1990–97); Pilkington plc, 1995–2006 (Dir, 1994–2006); Kidde, 2000–03; The Boots Co. plc, subseq. Alliance Boots plc, 2003–07 (non-exec. Dir, 1999–2007; Dep. Chm., 2001–03); Invensys plc, 2009–14; Meggitt plc, 2015–; Aquarius Platinum, 2015–; Dep. Chm., Barclays Bank plc, 2004–09 (non-exec. Dir, 1996–2009). Chm., UK Business Angels Assoc., 2012–. Member: European Round Table of Industrialists 1996–2001; Council, CBI, 1999–. Chancellor, Loughborough Univ., 2010–. Freeman, City of London; Mem., Chartered Accountants' Co. DL Derbys, 1996. Hon. DTech Loughborough, 1998; DUniv Derby, 1998. *Recreations:* golf, ski-ing, theatre, field sports. *Clubs:* Brooks's, Royal Automobile.

RUDD, Dominic; international mountain leader, since 2009; *b* 4 Oct. 1958; *s* of William Rudd and Primrose (*née* Saddler Phillips; now Lady Lewis, widow of Adm. Sir Andrew Lewis, KCB); *m* 2004, Helena Clayton; two *s* by a previous marriage. *Educ:* Bedford Sch. Midshipman, RN, 1976–77; Officer, RM, 1977–89. Partner, Holley, Hextall & Associates, 1989–99; Manager for Wales, 1999–2001, Dir of Ops, 2001–07, RSPCA; CEO, Samaritans, 2007–09; interim CEO, Switchback, 2012. *Recreations:* rock climbing, Alpine mountaineering. *E:* dominic_rudd@hotmail.com.

RUDD, Hon. Kevin Michael; Senior Fellow, John F. Kennedy School of Government and Visiting Fellow, Institute of Politics, Harvard University, since 2014; Prime Minister of Australia, 2007–10 and 2013; *b* Nambour, Qld, 21 Sept. 1957; *s* of Bert and Margaret Rudd; *m* 1981, Thérèse Rein; two *s* one *d*. *Educ:* Marist Coll., Ashgrove; Nambour State High Sch.; Australian Nat. Univ. (BA 1st cl. Hons Asian Studies 1981). Diplomat, Aust. Dept of Foreign Affairs, 1981–88: served Stockholm, later First Sec., Beijing; Counsellor, 1988; COS to Hon. Wayne Goss, Leader of the Opposition, later Premier, of Qld, 1988–91; Dir-Gen., Office of the Cabinet, Qld, 1991–95; Sen. China Consultant, KPMG Australia, 1996–98. Contested (ALP) Griffith, Qld, 1996. MP (ALP) Griffith, Qld, 1998–2013. Chm., Parly ALP Cttee on Nat. Security and Trade, 1998; Shadow Minister: for Foreign Affairs, 2001–06; for Internat. Security, 2003–06; for Trade, 2005–06; Leader of the Opposition, Australia, 2006–07; Minister for Foreign Affairs, 2010–12. Leader, ALP, 2006–10 and 2013. *Publications:* articles on Chinese politics, Chinese foreign policy, Australia-Asia relations and globalisation.

RUDD, Sir Nigel; *see* Rudd, Sir A. N. R.

RUDD, His Honour Norman Julian Peter Joseph; a Circuit Judge, 1988–2004; *b* 12 May 1943; *s* of Norman Arthur Rudd and Winifred Rudd; *m* 1968, Judith Margaret Pottinger; three *s*. *Educ:* Paston Sch., N Walsham, Norfolk; University Coll. London (LLB, LLM). Called to the Bar, Inner Temple, 1969; Asst Recorder, 1982–87, Head of Chambers, 1982–87; a Recorder, 1987. Trustee, New Forest Commoning Trust, 1993– (Chm., 1993–98, 2012–); Chm., Northern Commoners Assoc. (New Forest), 1999–. *Recreation:* farming.

RUDD, Roland Dacre; Chairman, RLM Finsbury, since 2011; *b* London, 24 April 1961; *s* of Anthony Rudd and Ethne Rudd; *m* 1991, Sophie Alice Yarde Hale; two *s* one *d*. *Educ:* Millfield Sch.; Regent's Park Coll., Oxford (BA Hons Philos. and Theol. 1985; Hon. Fellow). Pres., Oxford Union, 1985. Policy Coordinator for David Owen, MP, 1985; Employment Corresp., The Times, 1985–89; Dep. City Ed., Sunday Correspondent, 1989–91; Financial and Political Writer, FT, 1991–94; Sen. Partner, Finsbury Ltd, 1994–2011. Founding Chm., Business for New Europe, 2006–; Mem. Bd, Breakingviews, 1999–; non-exec. Dir, Exec. Cttee of the Army Bd, 2009–. Chm., Corporate Adv. Gp, Tate, 2005–; Trustee, Royal Opera House, 2011; Corporate Partnerships Bd, Great Ormond Street Hosp., 2011. Vis. Fellow, Centre for Corporate Reputation, Univ. of Oxford, 2008–. *Recreations:* Chelsea Football Club, Wagner, modern art. *Address:* RLM Finsbury, Tenter House, 45 Moorfields, EC2Y 9AE. *T:* (020) 7073 6356, *Fax:* (020) 7374 4133.

RUDDOCK, Rev. Canon Bruce; *see* Ruddock, Rev. Canon R. B.

RUDDOCK, Joan Elizabeth, CBE 2004 (OBE 1995); Parliamentary Boundary Commissioner for Northern Ireland, 2003–08; Independent Assessor for Public Appointments, 2004–09; *b* 22 May 1948; *d* of Robert John Boyle and Bertha Irene Boyle (*née* Johnston); *m* 1968, Alvin Ruddock. *Educ:* Trinity Coll., Dublin (BA 1970); Univ. of Ulster (Postgrad. DMS 1977); Open Univ. (BSc 1st Cl. Hons 2002). FCIM 1997. Mktg Manager, Conf. Div., FT, London, 1972–74; Redevelt Team Leader, NI Housing Exec., 1975–76; Corp. Finance Exec., NI Develt Agency, 1976–79; Mgt Consultant, Coopers & Lybrand, 1979–82; Sen. Exec., Industrial Develt Bd NI, 1982–84; Advr to European Pres. and Dir of Res., AVX Ltd, 1984–86; Gen. Manager, European Special Products Div., 1986–90; Man. Dir, Educational Company Ltd, 1990–99. Director: LEDU, 1984–98; Investment Belfast Ltd, 2000–06. Ind. Bd Mem., Dept of Agric. and Rural Develt, 2006–10. Chm., Belfast City Hosp. HSS Trust, 1999–2007; Dep. Chm., Gtr Village Regeneration Trust, 2000–06; Member: NIHEC, 1998–2005; Central Investment Trust for Charities, 1998–2004.

RUDDOCK, Rt Hon. Dame Joan (Mary), DBE 2012; PC 2010; *b* 28 Dec. 1943; *d* of Ken and Eileen Anthony; *m* 1st, 1963, Keith Ruddock (*d* 1996); 2nd, 2010, Frank Doran, *qv*. *Educ:* Pontypool Grammar Sch. for Girls; Imperial Coll., Univ. of London (BSc; ARCS). Worked for Shelter, national campaign for the homeless, 1968–73; Dir, Oxford Housing Aid Centre, 1973–77; Special Programmes Officer with unemployed young people, MSC, 1977–79; Organiser, CAB, Reading, 1979–86. Chairperson, CND, 1981–85, a Vice Chairperson, 1985–86. MP (Lab) Lewisham, Deptford, 1987–2015. Opposition spokesperson: on transport, 1989–92; on home affairs, 1992–94; on envmtl protection, 1994–97; Parliamentary Under-Secretary of State: for Women, DSS, 1997–98; DEFRA, 2007–08; DECC, 2008–09; Minister of State, DECC, 2009–10. Active in politics and pressure groups, and mem. of anti-racist concerns, throughout working life. Bd Mem., Trinity Laban, 2005–14. Hon. Fellow: Goldsmiths Coll., Univ. of London, 1996; Laban Centre, 1996; Hon. Companion, Trinity Laban, 2014. Frank Cousins' Peace Award, TGWU, 1984. *Publications:* CND Scrapbook, 1987; co-author of pubns on housing; (contrib.): The CND Story, 1983; Voices for One World, 1988. *Recreations:* music, travel, gardening.

RUDDOCK, Sir Paul (Martin), Kt 2012; FSA; Chief Executive and Co-Founder, Lansdowne Partners Ltd, 1998–2013; *b* 28 Aug. 1958; *s* of William Frederick Ruddock and Mary Eileen Ruddock; *m* 1991, Jill Ann Shaw; two *d. Educ:* King Edward's Sch., Birmingham; Mansfield Coll., Oxford (BA 1st Cl. Law 1980, MA 1984; Bancroft Fellow, 2008). Goldman Sachs, 1980–84; Man. Dir, Hd of Internat., Schroder & Co. Inc., 1984–98. Dir, Alternative Investment Mgt Assoc., 2009–12. Trustee: V&A Mus., 2002– (Chm., 2007–15; Chm., Finance Cttee, 2002–07; Chm., Develt Cttee, 2002–07; Mem., Collections Cttee, 2002–); Burlington Mag. Foundn, 2005–12; Metropolitan Mus. of Art, NY, 2011–; Chm., Gilbert Trust for the Arts, 2009–. FSA 2010; Life Fellow, Metropolitan Mus. of Art, 2014. *Recreations:* tennis, mountain walking, medieval art, theatre.

RUDDOCK, Air Marshal Peter William David, CB 2011; CBE 2001; FRAeS; FCMI; Business Development Director, Lockheed Martin UK, since 2011; *b* 5 Feb. 1954; *s* of William Ruddock and Evelyn (*née* Besanson); *m* 2001, Joanna Elizabeth Milford; one *s* one *d. Educ:* Grosvenor High Sch., Belfast. Joined RAF, 1974; Fighter Pilot, Qualified Weapons Instructor, to 1990; Advanced Staff Coll., Bracknell, 1990; Wing Comdr, MoD, 1991–93; OC Ops Wg, RAF Coningsby (Display Pilot, Battle of Britain Meml Flight), 1993–96; Gp Capt., MoD, 1996–99; Station Comdr, RAF Coningsby, 1999–2000; Air Cdre Defence Ops, HQ 1 Gp, 2000–02; Dir of Air Staff, 2002–04; Air Sec., 2004–06; Dir Gen., Saudi Armed Forces Project, 2006–11. Mem., Ascent Bd, 2014. Officer, American Legion of Merit, 2003. FRAeS 2004. FCMI 2011. *Recreations:* golf, sailing, equestrian activities, most sports, military history. *Address:* Lockheed Martin UK, Cunard House, 15 Regent Street, SW1Y 4LR. *Club:* Royal Air Force.

RUDDOCK, Rev. Canon (Reginald) Bruce; Residentiary Canon and Precentor of Peterborough Cathedral, since 2004 (Diocesan Liturgical Officer, Peterborough, 2004–11); Chaplain to the Queen, since 2008; *b* 17 Dec. 1955; *s* of Reginald and Hilary Ruddock; *m* 1983, Vivien Chrismas. *Educ:* Hurstpierpoint Coll., Sussex; Guildhall Sch. of Music and Drama (AGSM); Chichester Theol Coll.; Southampton Univ. (Cert. Theol.). Ordained deacon, 1983, priest, 1984; Asst Curate, St Mary's, Felpham with St Nicholas, Middleton-on-Sea, 1983–86; Priest-in-Charge, St Wilfrid's Church, Parish of St Mary, Portsea, 1986–88; Vicar, St Michael's, Barnes, 1988–95; Dir, Anglican Centre in Rome, and Archbishop of Canterbury's Counsellor for Vatican Affairs, 1995–99; Residentiary Canon, Worcester Cathedral, 1999–2004. Hon. Canon, Amer. Cathedral, Paris, 1996. *Recreations:* music, cricket, art, theatre, visiting Italy and Ireland. *Address:* Cathedral Office, Minster Precincts, Peterborough, Cambs PE1 1XS. *T:* (01733) 355310.

RUDENSTINE, Neil Leon; Chairman, ARTstor, since 2001; President Emeritus, Harvard University, since 2001; *b* 21 Jan. 1935; *s* of Harry Rudenstine and Mae Esperito Rudenstine; *m* 1960, Angelica Zander; one *s* two *d. Educ:* Princeton Univ. (BA 1956); New Coll., Oxford (BA 1959; MA 1963; Hon. Fellow, 1992); Harvard Univ. (PhD 1964). Instructor, English and American Lit. and Lang., Harvard Univ., 1964–66, Asst Prof. 1966–68; Princeton University: Associate Prof., English Dept, 1968–73; Dean of Students, 1968–72; Prof. of English, 1973–88; Dean of College, 1972–77; Provost, 1977–88, Provost Emeritus, 1988–; Exec. Vice-Pres., Andrew W. Mellon Foundn, 1988–91; Pres., and Prof. of English and Amer. Lit. and Lang., Harvard Univ., 1991–2001. Chair, Rockefeller Archive Center; Vice Chair, J. Paul Getty Trust; Mem. Bd, Barnes Foundn. Hon. Fellow, Emmanuel Coll., Cambridge, 1991. Hon. DPhil: Princeton, 1989; Yale, 1992. Hon. DCL: Harvard, 1992; Oxford, 1998. *Publications:* Sidney's Poetic Development, 1967; (ed with George Rousseau) English Poetic Satire: Wyatt to Byron, 1972; (with William Bowen) In Pursuit of the PhD, 1992; Pointing Our Thoughts, 2001; The House of Barnes, 2012; Ideas of Order, 2014. *Address:* 41 Armour Road, Princeton, NJ 08540, USA.

RUDERS, Poul; full-time composer, since 1991; *b* Ringsted, Denmark, 27 March 1949; *s* of late Poul Ruders and Inge Ruders; *m* 1995, Annette Gerlach. *Educ:* Royal Danish Conservatory (Organist's degree 1975). Self-taught composer. Guest Prof., Yale Music Sch., 1991; Distinguished Internat. Vis. Prof. of Composition, RAM, London, 2002–04. Composer in Residence, Aspen Music Fest., Colorado, 2003. Principal *compositions:* Symphony No 1, 1989; Solar Trilogy, 1992–95; Listening Earth, 2002; Final Nightshade, 2003; *operas:* The Handmaid's Tale, 1996–98; Kafka's Trial, 2001–03; Selma Jezková (formerly Dancer in the Dark), 2007–08. *Publications:* Tundra (orch.), 1990; Violin Concerto No 2, 1991; Anima (2nd 'cello concerto), 1993; Symphony No 2, 1997; Oboe Concerto, 1998; Horn Trio, 1998; Fairytale (orch.), 1999; Paganini Variations (2nd guitar concerto), 2000; The Handmaid's Tale, vocal score 2002, full score 2003; Kafka's Trial, 2004; *relevant publication:* Acoustical Canvases: the music of Poul Ruders, by Per Erland Rasmussen, 2007. *Recreations:* reading, DIY activities. *Address:* c/o Edition Wilhelm Hansen, 1 Bornholmsgade, 1266 Copenhagen K, Denmark. *T:* 33117888. *E:* ewh@ewh.dk. *W:* www.PoulRuders.net.

RUDGE, Sir Alan (Walter), Kt 2000; CBE 1995 (OBE 1987); PhD; FRS 1992; FREng; Chairman, ERA Technology Ltd, 1997–2003; President, ERA Foundation, since 2013 (Chairman, 2001–12); President, MSI Cellular (Celtel), 2002–04 (Chief Executive Officer, 2001–02); *b* 17 Oct. 1937; *s* of Walter Thomas Rudge and Emma (*née* McFayden); *m* 1969, Jennifer Joan Minott; one *s* one *d. Educ:* Hugh Myddelton Sch.; London Polytechnic; Univ. of Birmingham (PhD ElecEng). FIET, FIEEE; FREng (FEng 1984). Res. Engr, Illinois Inst. of Technol. Res. Inst., 1968–71; Lectr, Electronic and Elec. Engrg Dept, Univ. of Birmingham, 1971–74; Engrg Adviser, Illinois Inst. of Technol. Res. Inst., 1974–79; Man. Dir, Era Technology Ltd, 1979–86; BT (formerly British Telecom): Dir, Research and Technology, 1987–89; Group Technology and Develt Dir, 1989–90; Mem. Main Bd, 1989–97; Man. Dir, Develt and Procurement, 1990–95; Dep. Gp Man. Dir, 1995–96; Dep. Chief Exec., 1996–97; Chm., WS Atkins plc, 1997–2001. Non-executive Director and Member Board: British Maritime Technology Ltd, 1984–89; Ricardo Consulting Engrs PLC, 1985–89; BT&D Technologies Ltd, 1987–93; Telecom Securicor Cellular Radio, 1989–90; MCI (USA), 1995–96; LucasVarity plc, 1997–99; GEC, subseq. Marconi, plc, 1997–2002; GUS plc, 1997–2006; MSI Cellular Investment Hldgs BV, 1998–2002; non-exec. Chm., Metapath Software Internat. Inc., 1999–2000; Sen. Ind. Dir, Experian plc, 2006–14 (Dep. Chm., 2011–14). Vis. Prof., Queen Mary and Westfield Coll. (formerly QMC), Univ. of London, 1985–. Pres., AIRTO, 1986. Pres., IEE, 1993–94 (Vice Chm., 1989–91; Dep. Pres., 1991; Mem., Electronics Divl Bd, 1980–89, Chm., 1984; Faraday Medal, 1991); Chairman: Learned Soc. Bd, 1989–91; EPSRC, 1994–99; Senate, Engrg Council, 1996–99; Member: Systems and Electronics Bd, MoD Defence Scientific Adv. Council, 1981–87; CBI Res. and Technol. Cttee, 1980–86; ACOST, 1987–90; Council, DRA, then DERA, MoD, 1991–96; Council for Sci. and Technology, 1993–97. Chairman: Bd of Trustees, British Retinitis Pigmentosa Soc., 1996–2011 (Trustee, 1996–2012); Bd of Mgt, Royal Commn for Exhibn of 1851, 2001–12 (Mem., 1997–2012); Trustee, Civitas, 2015–. Member, Council: QMW, 1991–93; Royal Instn, 1992–95. Pro-Chancellor, Univ. of Surrey, 2002–07. Freeman, City of London; Liveryman, Engineers' Co., 1998–. Hon. FIEE 2000. Hon. Fellow, UCL, 1998. Hon. DEng: Birmingham, 1991; Bradford, Portsmouth, 1994; Nottingham Trent, 1995; Hon. DSc: Strathclyde, 1992; Bath, Loughborough, 1995; Westminster, 1996; DUniv Surrey, 1994. Duncan Davies Meml Medal, R&D Soc., 1998; Founder's Medal, IEEE, 1998; Millennium Medal, IEEE, 2000; President's Medal, RAEng, 2009; 1851 Royal Commn Medal, Royal Commn for Exhibn of 1851, 2012. *Publications:* The Handbook of Antenna Design, vol. 1 1982, vol. 2 1983; papers in sci. and tech. jls on antennas, microwaves and satellite communications. *Recreations:* sailing, cycling, reading. *Address:* ERA Foundation, Cleeve Road, Leatherhead, Surrey KT22 7SA. *Clubs:* Athenæum, Royal Automobile, Royal Ocean Racing; Royal Southampton Yacht, Royal Southern Yacht.

RUDGE, Christopher John, CBE 2012; FRCS; Honorary Professor, Queen Mary, University of London, since 2012; Chairman, UK Donation Ethics Committee, since 2014; *b* 1 Oct. 1948; *s* of Ben Rudge, DFC and Joan Rudge; *m* 1973, Elizabeth Mary Jameson; two *s. Educ:* Guy's Hosp. Medical Sch. (BSc 1969, MB BS 1972). FRCS 1976. Consultant Transplant Surgeon: Guy's Hosp., London, 1981–85; St Peter's Hosps, London, 1985–95; Royal London Hosp., 1995–2001, (part-time) 2001–11; Med. Dir, UK Transplant, 2001–05; Man. and Transplant Dir, UK Transplant, 2005–08; Nat. Clinical Dir for Transplantation, DoH, 2008–11. Patron: Live Life Then Give Life, 2012–; British Kidney Patients Assoc., 2013–. Gov., Tonbridge School, 2007–. *Recreations:* Rugby Union, music, gardening, travel, cricket. *Address:* Pennis Farm, Fawkham, Kent DA3 8LZ. *T:* and *Fax:* (01474) 707522. *E:* cjrudge@btinternet.com. *Clubs:* MCC, Kent County Cricket.

RUDIN, Toni Richard Perrott; Secretary, Magistrates' Association, 1986–93; *b* 13 Oct. 1934; *s* of Richard William Rudin and Sarah Rowena Mary Rudin (*née* Perrott); *m* 1958, Heather Jean (*née* Farley); one *s* three *d. Educ:* Bootham Sch.; Millfield Sch.; RMA Sandhurst; Army Staff Coll.; Univ. of London; Coll. of Law, Guildford. Commissioned Royal Artillery, 1954; served BAOR, Cyprus (1957–60), UK; MoD, 1967–69; Battery Comdr and 2 i/c 26th Field Regt, RA, BAOR, 1969–72; MoD, 1972–75; retired, 1975. Solicitor, 1978; private practice as solicitor, 1978–80; Press and Public Relations, Law Soc., 1980–86. Mem., Chartered Accountants Disciplinary Cttees, 1989–94. Pt-time Legal Chm., Pensions Appeal Tribunals, 1994–2007. Gen. Comr of Income Tax, 1995–97. Mem. Cttee, Rutland and Leics Army Benevolent Fund, 1997–2001. *Recreations:* 19th century history, house renovation, France, woodwork, bridge. *Address:* 2 Chapel Walk, Adderley Street, Uppingham, Rutland LE15 9NE. *T:* (01572) 822999. *Club:* Army and Navy.

RUDKIN, David; *see* Rudkin, J. D.

RUDKIN, Duncan Hugh; Chief Executive and Registrar, General Pharmaceutical Council, since 2010; *b* 2 Aug. 1966; *s* of Philip Rudkin and Peggy Rudkin (*née* Watts). *Educ:* Queen's Coll., Oxford (BA Mod. Langs 1989). Solicitor, City of London; General Dental Council: Dir, Legal Services, 1998; Dir, Professional Standards, 2001–06; Dep. Chief Exec., 2005–06; Chief Exec. and Registrar, 2006–09. Trustee, St Catherine's Hospice, Crawley. *Address:* General Phamaceutical Council, 25 Canada Square, E14 5LQ.

RUDKIN, (James) David; dramatist and screenwriter; *b* 29 June 1936; *s* of David Jonathan Rudkin and Anne Alice Martin; *m* 1967, Alexandra Margaret Thompson; one *s* two *d* (and one *s* decd). *Educ:* King Edward's Sch., Birmingham; St Catherine's Coll., Oxford (MA). Judith E. Wilson Fellow, Cambridge Univ., 1984; Vis. Prof., Middlesex Univ., 2004–; Hon. Prof., Aberystwyth Univ. (formerly Univ. of Wales), 2006–. *Screenplays:* Testimony, 1987; December Bride, 1991; The Woodlanders, 1996; *opera libretti:* Broken Strings, 1992; (with Jonathan Harvey) Inquest of Love, 1993; Black Feather Rising, 2008; *radio plays:* The LoveSong of Alfred J. Hitchcock, 1993; The Haunting of Mahler, 1994; The Giant's Cause…, 2005; Macedonia, 2015. *Publications:* plays: Afore Night Come, 1963, 2nd edn 2000; (trans.) Moses and Aaron (opera libretto), 1965; (trans.) The Persians, 1965; The Grace of Todd (orig. opera libretto), 1969; Cries from Casement as his Bones are Brought to Dublin (radio), 1974; Penda's Fen (film), 1975; Burglars (for children), 1976; (trans.) Hecuba, 1976; Ashes, 1978; (trans.) Hippolytus, 1980; The Sons of Light, 1981; The Triumph of Death, 1981; (trans.) Peer Gynt, 1983; The Saxon Shore, 1986; (trans.) When We Dead Waken, 1989; (trans.) Rosmersholm, 1990; Vampyr (monograph), 2005; Red Sun, 2011; Merlin Unchained, 2011; The LoveSong of Alfred J. Hitchcock (stage version), 2014; articles, reviews etc. for Encounter, Drama, Tempo, Theatre Res. Internat. *Recreations:* piano, geology, anthropology, languages (now mainly Celtic), cliff-walking, bridge. *Address:* c/o Casarotto Ramsay Ltd, Waverley House, 7–12 Noel Street, W1F 8GQ. *T:* (020) 7287 4450, *Fax:* (020) 7287 9128.

RUDLAND, Margaret Florence; Headmistress, Godolphin and Latymer School, 1986–2008; recruitment consultant, since 2010; *b* 15 June 1945; *d* of Ernest George and Florence Hilda Rudland. *Educ:* Sweyne School, Rayleigh; Bedford College, Univ. of London (BSc); Inst. of Education (PGCE). Asst Mathematics Mistress, Godolphin and Latymer Sch., 1967–70; VSO, Ilorin, Nigeria, 1970–71; Asst Maths Mistress, Clapham County Sch., 1971–72; Asst Maths Mistress and Head of Dept, St Paul's Girls' Sch., 1972–83; Deputy Headmistress, Norwich High Sch., GPDST, 1983–85. Pres., GSA, 1996 (Chm., Educn Cttee, 1993–94). Member: UCAS Bd, 2002–06; Gen. Teaching Council, 2002–06. Member Council: Nightingale Fund, 1989–2011 (Chm., 1998–2011); UCL, 1998–2006; Mem. Bd, Assoc. of Governing Bodies of Ind. Schs, 2009–. Governor: St Margaret's Sch., Bushey, 1997–2012; Merchant Taylors' Sch., Northwood, 2000–12; Redcliffe Sch., 2001–09; Glendower Prep. Sch., 2003–12; St Mary's, Ascot, 2003–13; British Sch. of Paris, 2007–; English Coll., Prague, 2008–; ESU, 2008–10; Headington Sch., 2009–; St Swithun's Sch., 2011–; Channing Sch., 2011–14. *Recreations:* opera, cinema, travel. *Address:* 3 Langham Place, Chiswick, W4 2QL.

RUDLAND, Martin William; His Honour Judge Rudland; a Circuit Judge, Northern Circuit, since 2002; *b* 13 March 1955; *s* of late Maurice Rudland and Patricia Rudland (*née* Crossley); *m* 1st, 1980, Norma Jane Lee (marr. diss. 1989); two *s*; 3rd, 1997, Linda Sturgess Jackson (*née* Potter); one step *s* one step *d. Educ:* Rowlinson Sch., Sheffield; Sheffield Univ. (LLB Hons 1976). Called to the Bar, Middle Temple, 1977 (Harmsworth Schol. 1977); in practice at the Bar, North Eastern Circuit, 1977–2002; Circuit Jun., 1985; Asst Recorder, 1992–96; a Recorder, 1996–2002. *Recreations:* books, music, cinema, travel. *Address:* Manchester Crown Court, Courts of Justice, Crown Square, Manchester M3 3FL.

RUDMAN, Michael Edward; theatre director and producer; Artistic Director, Sheffield Theatres (Crucible and Lyceum), 1992–94; *b* Tyler, Texas, 14 Feb. 1939; *s* of M. B. Rudman and Josephine Davis; *m* 1963, Veronica Anne Bennett (marr. diss. 1981); two *d*; *m* 1983, Felicity Kendal, *qv* (marr. diss. 1994); one *s. Educ:* St Mark's Sch., Texas; Oberlin Coll. (BA *cum laude* Govt); St Edmund Hall, Oxford (MA). Pres., OUDS, 1963–64. Asst Dir and Associate Producer, Nottingham Playhouse and Newcastle Playhouse, 1964–68; Asst Dir, RSC, 1968; Artistic Director: Traverse Theatre Club, 1970–73; Hampstead Theatre, 1973–78 (Theatre won Evening Standard Award for Special Achievement, 1978); Associate Dir, Nat. Theatre, 1979–88; Dir, Lyttelton Theatre (National), 1979–81; Dir, Chichester Festival Theatre, 1990. Mem., Bd of Dirs, Hampstead Theatre, 1979–89. *Plays directed* include: *Nottingham Playhouse:* Changing Gear, Measure for Measure, A Man for All Seasons, 1965; Julius Caesar, She Stoops to Conquer, Who's Afraid of Virginia Woolf, Death of a Salesman, 1966; Long Day's Journey into Night, 1967; Lily in Little India, 1968; *RSC Theatregoround:* The Fox and the Fly, 1968; *Traverse Theatre:* Curtains (transf. Open Space, 1971), Straight Up (transf. Piccadilly, 1971), A Game called Arthur (transf. Theatre Upstairs, 1971), Stand for my Father, (with Mike Wearing) A Triple Bill of David Halliwell plays, 1970; The Looneys, Pantagleize, 1971; Caravaggio Buddy, Tell Charlie Thanks for the Truss, The Relapse, 1972; *Hampstead Theatre:* Ride across Lake Constance (transf. Mayfair), A Nightingale in Bloomsbury Square, 1973; The Black and White Minstrels, The Show-off, The Connection, The Looneys, 1974; Alphabetical Order (transf. Mayfair), 1975; Clouds, 1977 (transf. Duke of York's, 1978); Cakewalk, Beyond a Joke, Gloo-Joo (transf. Criterion), 1978; Making it

Better (transf. Criterion), 1992; Benchmark (also co-writer), 2002; Berlin Hanover Express, 2009; *National Theatre:* For Services Rendered (televised, 1980), Death of a Salesman, 1979; Thee and Me, The Browning Version/Harlequinade, Measure for Measure, 1980; The Second Mrs Tanqueray, 1981; Brighton Beach Memoirs (transf. Aldwych), The Magistrate, 1986; Six Characters in Search of an Author, Fathers and Sons, Ting Tang Mine, Waiting for Godot, 1987; *Chichester:* The Merry Wives of Windsor, Rumours, 1990; Mansfield Park, 1996; The Admirable Crichton, 1997; Tallulah!, 1997; Our Betters, 1997; *Sheffield:* A Midsummer Night's Dream, 1992; Donkeys' Years, (with Robert Delamere) Jane Eyre, Hamlet, Mansfield Park, 1993; The Grapes of Wrath, 1994; *West End:* Donkeys' Years, Globe, 1976; Taking Steps, Lyric, 1980; Camelot, 1982; The Winslow Boy, 1983; The Dragon's Tail, Apollo, 1985; Exclusive, Strand, 1989; Fallen Angels, Apollo, 2000; A Man for all Seasons, Th. Royal, Haymarket, 2005; Mrs Warren's Profession, Comedy, 2010; *Gate Theatre, Dublin:* The Heiress, 1997; *New York:* The Changing Room, 1973 (Drama Desk Award); Hamlet, 1976; Death of a Salesman, 1984 (Tony Award for Best Revival); Measure for Measure, 1993; Have you spoken to any Jews lately?, 1995; The Old Masters, 2011; Chin-Chin, UK tour, 2013. *Publications:* I Joke Too Much: the theatre director's tale, 2014. *Address:* c/o Helen Mumby, MLR, 44 South Molton Street, W1K 5RT. *T:* (020) 7493 2444. *Clubs:* Royal Automobile; Royal Mid-Surrey Golf, Liphook Golf.

RUDWICK, Prof. Martin John Spencer, PhD, ScD; FBA 2008; Professor of History, University of California, San Diego, 1988–98, now Emeritus; Affiliated Research Scholar, History and Philosophy of Science, University of Cambridge, since 1998; *b* 26 March 1932; *er s* of Joseph Spencer Rudwick and Olivia Grace Rudwick (*née* Western); *m* 1st, 1965, Gillian Yendell (marr. diss. 1972); 2nd, 1974, Tricia MacColl (marr. diss. 1995). *Educ:* Harrow Sch.; Trinity Coll., Cambridge (BA 1953; PhD 1958; ScD 1976). University of Cambridge: Demonstrator, 1955–59; Sen. Asst in Res., 1960–65; Lectr, in Geol., 1965–67, in Hist. of Sci., 1967–74; Fellow, Trinity Coll., 1956–60, Corpus Christi Coll., 1962–74, Cambridge; Prof. of Hist. and Social Aspects of the Natural Scis, Vrije Univ., Amsterdam, 1974–80; Fellow-Commoner, Trinity Coll., Cambridge, 1983–85; Prof. of Hist., and Hist. of Sci., Princeton Univ., 1985–87. Vis. Fellow, Clare Hall, Cambridge, 1994–95. Visiting Professor of History of Science: Princeton Univ., 1981; Hebrew Univ., Jerusalem, 1982; Mem., Inst. for Advanced Study, Princeton, 1982–84; Maître de Recherche Associé, École des Mines de Paris, 1985; Vis. Prof. of Hist. of Scis Rijksuniversiteit Utrecht, 1993. Guggenheim Foundn Fellow, 1994–95. Tarner Lectr, Trinity Coll., Cambridge, 1994–97. Mem., Doctrine Commn, C of E, 1982–85. Mem., Acad. Internat. d'Histoire des Scis, 1980–; Pres., Hist. of Earth Scis Soc., 2005–06. Scientific Medal, Zool Soc. of London, 1973; Hist. of Geol. Award, Geol Soc. of America, 1987; Friedman Medal, Geol Soc. of London, 1988; Founder's Medal, Soc. for Hist. of Natural Hist., 1988; Bernal Prize, Soc. for Social Studies of Sci., 1999; Sarton Medal, Hist. of Sci. Soc., 2007; Prix Wegmann, Soc. Géologique de France, 2008; Levinson Prize, Hist. of Sci. Soc., 2012. *Publications:* Living and Fossil Brachiopods, 1970; The Meaning of Fossils, 1972, 2nd edn 1985; The Great Devonian Controversy, 1985; Scenes from Deep Time, 1992; Georges Cuvier, 1997; The New Science of Geology, 2004; Lyell and Darwin Geologists, 2005; Bursting the Limits of Time, 2005; Worlds before Adam, 2008; Earth's Deep History, 2014; contrib. articles to learned jls on paleontology and hist. of earth scis. *Recreations:* early music, hill walking, wood-turning, vernacular architecture. *Address:* Moat House, 2 Welsh Street, Bishop's Castle, Shropshire SY9 5BT.

RUF, Beatrix; Director, Stedelijk Museum, Amsterdam, since 2014; *b* Singen, 14 Feb. 1960; *d* of Helmuth Ruf and Ruth Ruf. *Educ:* Konservatorium der Stadt Wien (MA 1987); Univ. of Zurich (Lic.phil 1991). Curatorial Asst, Haus für konstruktive und konkrete Kunst Zürich, 1992; freelance curator and publishing, 1993; Curator: Zeiträume für Kunst, Dresden, 1993–95; Kunstmuseum, Canton of Thurgau, Warth, 1994–98; Director and Chief Curator: Kunsthaus Glarus, 1998–2001; Kunsthalle Zürich, Zurich, 2001–14. Art expert, Ringier Collection, Zürich, 1995–; Artistic Dir, Shed im Eisenwerk, Frauenfeld, 1995–98. Teaching position: Hochschule für Theater und Performance, Bern, 1995–99; Kunsthistorisches Institut, Univ. of Zurich, 2000; Curatorial Advr, Postgrad. Prog. in Curating MAS, 2009–12, Mentor, MA Fine Arts, 2013–, Zürcher Hochschule der Künste; Mentor, Universität St Gallen, 2006–14. Vis. Curator, MacDonald Art Centre, Guelph and Toronto, 1997; Curator/Moderator, Engadin Art Talks, 2010–; Curatorial Educn Advr, deAppel Art Center, Amsterdam. Member: Art Commn, Swiss Re, 1999–; Bd, Graphische Gesellschaft der Schweiz, 1999–; Bd of Dirs, JRP|Ringier, 2004–; Cultural Adv. Bd, CERN, Geneva, 2011–; Prog. Cttee, Bundeskunsthalle, Bonn; Supervisory Bd, MuMoK, Museum Moderne Kunst, Vienna. Expert, Core Gp Think Tank for a Mus. of the 21st Century, LUMA Foundn, 2006–. Jury mem. in numerous commns incl. Preis der Nationalgalerie Berlin; Vincent, Stedlijk Mus. Amsterdam; Beck's Futures, ICA London. *Publications:* (ed) Peter Zimmermann, 1997; (ed) Roland Herzog, Balsam, 1998; (ed) Jeroen de Rijke and Willem de Rooij, 2004; (ed) Eva Rothschild, 2004; (ed) Richard Prince, Jokes and Cartoons, 2006; (ed) Laura Owens, 2006; (ed) Bekanntmachungen, 2006; (ed) Daria Martin, 2006; (ed jtly) Valentin Carron, 2007; (ed) Blasted Allegories: works from the Ringier Collection, 2008; (ed) Josh Smith, 2009; (ed jtly) Seth Price, 2010; (ed jtly) Mark Morrisroe, 2010; (ed jtly) Tris Vonna Michell, 2010; (ed jtly) Helen Marten, 2013; (ed jtly) Engadin Art Talks, 2013; contrib. and ed exhibn catalogues. *Address:* Stedelijk Museum, Postbus 75082, 1070 AB Amsterdam, Netherlands. *T:* 205732911, *Fax:* 206752716. *E:* info@stedelijk.nl.

RUFFLES, Philip Charles, CBE 2001; RDI 1997; FRS 1998; FREng, FRAeS, FIMechE; Technical Advisor, Rolls-Royce plc, 2001–04; *b* 14 Oct. 1939; *s* of Charles Richard Ruffles and Emily Edith Ruffles; *m* 1967, Jane Connor; two *d.* *Educ:* Sevenoaks Sch.; Bristol Univ. (BSc 1st Cl. Mech. Engrg 1961). FRAeS 1985; FREng (FEng 1988); FIMechE 1989. Rolls-Royce: trainee, 1961–63; technical appts, 1963–77; Chief Engr, RB211, 1977–81; Head of Engrg, Small Engines, 1981–84; Dir, Technol. & Design Engrg, 1984–89; Technical Dir, 1989–91; Dir of Engrg, Aerospace Gp, 1991–96; Dir, Engrg and Technol., 1997–2001. Non-exec. Dir, Domino Printing Science plc, 2002–14. Member: Defence Scientific Adv. Council, 1990–93; Technol. Foresight Defence and Aerospace Panel, 1994–97; LINK Bd (OST), 1995–98; Council for Central Lab. of Res. Councils, 1998–2004; Council for Sci. and Technol., 2007–10. Member Council: Royal Acad. Engrg, 1994–97, 2002–05; RAeS, 1995–2004; Royal Soc., 2010. FRSA 1998. Liveryman, Engineers' Co., 1998. Hon. FIC 2002. Hon. DEng: Bristol, 1995; Birmingham, 1998; Sheffield, 1999; Hon. DSc City, 1998. Ackroyd Stuart Prize, 1987, Gold Medal, 1996, RAeS; MacRobert Award, 1996, Prince Philip Medal, 2001, Royal Acad. of Engrg; James Clayton Prize, IMechE, 1998; Duncan Davies Meml Medal, R & D Soc., 2000; François-Xavier Bagnoud Aerospace Prize, Univ. of Michigan, 2001; R. Tom Sawyer Award, ASME, 2002; Premio Internazionale Barsanti e Matteucci, 2002; Glazebrook Medal, Inst. of Physics, 2011. *Publications:* contrib. to numerous learned jls on engrg and technol. topics. *Recreations:* Rugby, D-I-Y. *Address:* 5 Ford Lane, Allestree, Derby DE22 2EX.

RUFFLEY, David Laurie; *b* 18 April 1962; *s* of J. L. Ruffley, solicitor. *Educ:* Queens' Coll., Cambridge (Exhibnr, 1981, Foundn Scholar, 1983; Histl Tripos pt 1, Law Tripos pt 2, BA 1985, MA 1988). Articled clerk and Solicitor with Coward Chance, then Clifford Chance, 1985–91; Special Advr to Sec. of State for Educn and Science, 1991–92, to Home Sec., 1992–93, to Chancellor of the Exchequer, 1993–96. MP (C) Bury St Edmunds, 1997–2015. An Opposition Whip, 2004–05; Shadow Minister: for Work and Pensions, 2005–07; for Police Reform, 2007–10. Member: Select Cttee on Public Admin, 1997–99; Select Cttee on Treasury Affairs, 1998–2004 and 2010–15; Exec., 1922 Cttee, 2003–04; Secretary: Cons. Backbench Finance Cttee, 1999–2003; Parly Gp on Wholesale Financial Mkts and Services, 2010–15; Dep. Chm., Cons. Backbench Econ. Affairs Gp, 2010–15. US State Dept Internat. Visitor, res. prog. on econ. develt and trade, 2003; Fellow, British-American Project, 2002. *Recreation:* golf. *E:* druffley62@gmail.com. *Club:* Pratt's.

RUGBY, 3rd Baron *cr* 1947, of Rugby, Co. Warwick; **Robert Charles Maffey;** farmer; *b* 4 May 1951; *s* of 2nd Baron Rugby and of Margaret Helen, *d* of late Harold Bindley; *S* father, 1990; *m* 1974, Anne Penelope, *yr d* of late David Hale; two *s.* *Educ:* Brickwall House Sch., Northiam. *Recreations:* shooting, woodwork and metal work. *Heir:* *s* Hon. Timothy James Howard Maffey, *b* 23 July 1975.

RUGG, Prof. Michael Derek, PhD; Distinguished Professor of Behavioral and Brain Sciences, since 2011 and Director, Center for Vital Longevity, since 2014, University of Texas, Dallas (Co-Director, 2011–14); *b* 23 Sept. 1954; *s* of Derek and Brenda Rugg; *m* 1976, Elizabeth Jackson; one *s.* *Educ:* Univ. of Leicester (BSc Psychol; PhD 1979). FRSE 1996. Res. Fellow, Dept of Psychology, Univ. of York, 1978–79; University of St Andrews: Lectr in Psychology, 1979–88; Reader, 1988–92; Prof., 1992–98; Head, Sch. of Psychology, 1992–94; Prof. of Cognitive Neurosci. and Wellcome Trust Principal Res. Fellow, UCL, 1998–2003; Prof. of Neurobiol. and Behavior, 2003–10, Dir, Center for Neurobiol. of Learning and Memory, 2004–10, Univ. of Calif, Irvine. Hon. Res. Fellow, Inst. of Neurology, 1994–98. Member: DoH Wkg Gp on Organophosphates, 1998–99; Govt Ind. Expert Gp on Mobile Phones, 1999–2000; Prog. mgt cttee, mobile telecomm. and health res. prog., 2000–03 and 2005–; Adv. gp on non-ionising radiation, NRPB, 2001–03; Cognition Perception Study Section, 2007–11 (Chm., 2009–11), Neurobiology of Learning and Memory Study Section, 2014–, NIH. FAAAS 2009; Fellow, Assoc. for Psychol Sci., 2009. *Publications:* (ed with A. D. Milner) Neuropsychology of Consciousness, 1991; (ed with M. G. H. Coles) Electrophysiology of Mind, 1995; (ed) Cognitive Neuroscience, 1996; over 200 articles in cognitive neuroscience and related fields in learned jls. *Recreations:* rock climbing, ski-ing, 20th century novels and visual arts, music. *Address:* Center for Vital Longevity, University of Texas at Dallas, 1600 Viceroy Drive, Suite 800, Texas 7235, USA.

RUGGLES-BRISE, Sir Timothy (Edward), 3rd Bt *cr* 1935, of Spains Hall, Finchingfield; owner, Spains Hall estate, since 1966; Partner, Spains Hall hospitality business, wedding venue and conference centre, since 2011 (proprietor, 2006–11); *b* 11 April 1945; *s* of Guy Edward Ruggles-Brise, TD and Elizabeth Ruggles-Brise (*née* Knox); *S* uncle, 2007; *m* 1975, Rosemary Elizabeth (*née* Craig); three *s* two *d.* *Educ:* Eton Coll.; Regent St Polytechnic; RAC Cirencester. DipCE; DipAgr; CDipAF. CEng, MICE, now retired. 1964–78: Sen. Engr, Livesey & Henderson then Rendel Palmer & Tritton; civil engrg consultant. Sen. Partner, Whitehouse Farms Partnership, 1974–2001; estab. and Sen. Partner, Spains Hall Forest Nursery, 1979–2008. Chm., Forestry Gp, Horticultural Trades Assoc., and E Anglian Br., Timber Growers Assoc., 1993–97. Jt Master, East Essex Foxhounds, 1980–83. Mem., Finchingfield PCC; Churchwarden, St John the Baptist, Finchingfield. Master, Armourers' and Brasiers' Co., 2011–12; Chm., Armourers' and Brasiers' Gauntlet Trust. *Recreations:* country pursuits, food and wine. *Heir:* *s* Archibald Edward Ruggles-Brise [*b* 9 Dec. 1979; *m* 2007, Anna French]. *Address:* Spains Hall, Finchingfield, Braintree, Essex CM7 4NJ. *T:* (01371) 810232. *E:* tim@rugglesbrise.co.uk. *Club:* Essex.

RUGMAN, Jonathan Anthony; Foreign Affairs Correspondent, Channel 4 News, since 2008; *b* London, 15 Nov. 1965; *s* of Roderick and Wendy Rugman; *m* 1995, Rachel Lewis; two *s* one *d.* *Educ:* Bradfield Coll.; Kent Sch., Connecticut; Churchill Coll., Cambridge (BA Hons English Lit. 1988). Turkey corresp., BBC World Service, 1991–92; Istanbul corresp., Guardian and Observer, 1993–96; reporter, File on 4, BBC Radio 4, 1996–98; associate producer, Lion Television, 1997–98; ITN Channel 4 News: Business corresp., 1999–2003; Washington corresp., 2003–06; Diplomatic corresp., 2006–08. Retail Business Award, 1999, Best Broadcast, 2000, 2001, Business Journalist of Year Awards; Business Broadcaster of Year, Harold Wincott Foundn, 2000; Midlands Current Affairs Award, RTS, 2000; British Envmt Award, 2006; Foreign Press Assoc. Award, 2009. *Publications:* Ataturk's Children: Turkey and the Kurds, 1996. *Recreations:* bicycling, music. *Address:* ITN Channel 4 News, 200 Gray's Inn Road, WC1X 8XZ. *T:* (020) 7430 4606. *E:* jonathan.rugman@itn.co.uk. *Club:* West London Trades Union.

RUHFUS, Dr Jürgen, Officer's Cross, Order of Merit, Federal Republic of Germany, 1983; Hon. KBE 1978; State Secretary, Federal Foreign Office, Germany, 1984–87; *b* 4 Aug. 1930; three *d.* *Educ:* Universities of Munich, Münster and Denver, USA. Joined Federal Foreign Office, Bonn, 1955; Consulate General: Geneva, 1956–57; Dakar, 1958–59; Embassy, Athens, 1960–63; Dep. Spokesman of Federal Foreign Office, 1964, Official Spokesman, 1966; Ambassador to Kenya, 1970–73; Asst Under-Secretary, Federal Foreign Office, 1973–76; Adviser on Foreign Policy and Defence Affairs to Federal Chancellor Helmut Schmidt, 1976–80; Ambassador to UK, 1980–83; Head of Political Directorate-General (dealing with Third World and other overseas countries), Federal Foreign Office, Dec. 1983–June 1984; Ambassador to USA, 1987–92; Chm., Deutsch-Englische Ges., 1993–98; Mem., Supervisory Bd, Adam Opel AG, 1993–2001. *Recreations:* golf, tennis, ski-ing, shooting. *Address:* Ettenhausener Strasse 23a, 53229 Bonn, Germany.

RUHNAU, Heinz; consultant in strategic planning, since 1991; Professor of Business Administration, Technical University, Dresden, 1990; *b* Danzig, 5 March 1929; *m* Edith Loers; three *d.* *Educ:* Dip. in Business Administration, 1954. Asst to Chm., IG-Metall, Frankfurt; Regional Dir, IG-Metall, Hamburg, 1956–65; Mem., Senate of Free Hanseatic City of Hamburg (responsible for security and city admin.), 1965–73; Mem., Exec. Bd, COOP, 1973; State Sec., Ministry of Transport, 1974–82; CEO, Deutsche Lufthansa, 1982–91. Chairman: IATA, 1985; Assoc. of European Airlines, 1988. Federal Grand Cross of Merit, 1980, with Star, 1989, FRG; Officer, Légion d'Honneur (France), 1989; Cross of Merit (Spain), 1990. *Address:* Elsa Brändström Straße 213, 53227 Bonn, Germany.

RUIZ, Cristina; Editor-at-Large, The Art Newspaper; *b* 16 Oct. 1971; *d* of Grazia and Domenico Ruiz. *Educ:* University Coll. London (BA Hons Ancient and Medieval Hist.); Courtauld Inst. of Art (MA Classical Art). Mem., British Drawings and Watercolours Dept, Christie's, London, 1994–95; The Art Newspaper: joined as staff reporter, 1995; Dep. Editor, 2000–03; Editor, 2003–08; Features Editor, 2009. *Recreations:* trash television, scuba-diving. *Address:* The Art Newspaper, 70 South Lambeth Road, SW8 1RL. *T:* (020) 7735 3331.

RULE, Brian Francis; Director General of Information Technology Systems, Ministry of Defence, 1985–94; Chairman, Emeritus Plus Ltd, 1994–98; *b* 20 Dec. 1938; *s* of late Sydney John Rule and Josephine Rule, Pen-y-ffordd, near Chester; *m* 1993, Irene M. Rees, Pembs. *Educ:* Daniel Owen Sch., Mold; Loughborough Univ. of Technology (MSc). Engineer, de Havilland Aircraft Co., 1955–59; Res. Assistant, Loughborough Univ., 1963–65; Lectr, Univ. of Glasgow, 1965–67; University of Aberdeen: Lectr, 1967–70; Sen. Lectr, 1970–72; Dir of Computing, 1972–78; Dir, Honeywell Information Systems Ltd, 1978–79; Dir of Scientific Services, NERC, 1979–85. *Publications:* various papers in scientific jls. *Recreations:* Boxer dogs, antique clocks. *Address:* c/o Lloyds Bank, 14 Castle Street, Cirencester, Glos GL7 1QJ.

RULE, David Stephen; Executive Director, Prudential Policy, Bank of England, since 2014; *b* Poole, Dorset, 1 Jan. 1967; *s* of Dennis and Mary Rule; *m* 1997, Michelle Gillam; two *s* one *d.* *Educ:* Balliol Coll., Oxford (BA Modern Hist.); Univ. of Toronto (MA Pol Sci.); Queens' Coll., Cambridge (MPhil Econs 1996). Bank of England, 1990–2007; FSA, 2009–13; Bank of England, 2013–. *Address:* Bank of England, Threadneedle Street, EC2R 8AH. *E:* david.rule@bankofengland.co.uk.

RUMALSHAH, Rt Rev. Munawar Kenneth, (Mano); Bishop of Peshawar, 1994–98 and 2003–10, now Bishop Emeritus; Coordinator, Church of Pakistan, since 2013; *b* 16 June 1941; *s* of Ven. Inayat and Mrs Akhtar Rumalshah; *m* 1st, 1966, Rosalind Andrews; two *d*; 2nd, 1984, Sheila Benita Biswas; one *d*. *Educ:* Punjab Univ. (BSc 1960); Serampur Univ. (BD 1965); Karachi Univ. (MA 1968); Cambridge Univ. (PGCE 1986). Ordained deacon, 1965, priest, 1966; Curate: Holy Trinity Cathedral, Karachi, 1965–69; St Edmund Roundhay, Leeds, 1970–73; Area Sec., and Asst Home Sec., CMS, 1973–78; Educn Sec., BCC, 1978–81; Priest-in-charge, St George, Southall, 1981–88; Presbyter, St John's Cathedral, and Lectr, Edwarde's Coll., Peshawar, 1989–94; Gen. Sec., USPG, 1998–2003, and an Asst Bp, Southwark Dio., 1999–2003; Bishop in Residence, St John the Divine Episcopal Cath., NY, 2007. Member: Archbp of Canterbury's Commn on Urban Priority Areas, 1984–86; Archbp of Canterbury's Anglican Communion Fund, 2008–10. Ramsden Preacher, Cambridge Univ., 2003; Vis. Prof., Gen. Theol Seminary of Episcopal Church, NY, 2007–; Hon. Vis. Fellow, Yale Divinity Sch., Yale Univ., 2012–13. Jt Ed., Lambeth Conf., 1998. *Publications:* Focus on Pakistan, 1989, 4th edn 1999; Being a Christian in Pakistan, 1998. *Recreations:* watching cricket, music, reading, travel. *Address:* Diocesan Centre, 1 Sir Syed Road, Peshawar 25000, Khyber Pukhtunkhwa, Pakistan. *T:* (91) 5279094.

RUMBELOW, His Honour (Arthur) Anthony; QC 1990; a Circuit Judge, 2002–14; a Deputy High Court Judge (Family Division), 2000–14; Designated Family Judge, Northampton County Court, 2013–14; *b* Salford, Lancs, 9 Sept. 1943; *er s* of Arthur Rumbelow and Theresa (*née* Lucketti); *m* 1st; three *d*; 2nd, 2010, Vivienne Ashworth (*née* Fletcher); one *d*. *Educ:* Salford Grammar Sch.; Queens' Coll., Cambridge (Squire Schol.; BA 1966). Called to the Bar, Middle Temple, 1967 (Harmsworth Exhibnr, Astbury Schol.). Recorder, 1988–2002; Sen. Judge, British Sovereign Bases, Cyprus, 2008–13. Chairman: Medical Appeal Tribunal, 1988–2002; Mental Health Rev. Tribunal, 2000–13. Mem., Parole Bd, 2010–. Mem., Rochdale MBC, 1982–84. *Recreations:* wine, theatre, gardening.

RUMBELOW, (Roger) Martin, CEng; director and consultant, since 1996; *b* 3 June 1937; *s* of Leonard Rumbelow and Phyllis (*née* Perkins); *m* 1965, Marjorie Elizabeth Glover. *Educ:* Cardiff High Sch.; Bristol Univ. (BSc); Cranfield Inst. of Technol. (MSc). CEng 1966. National Service, RAF Pilot, 1955–57. British Aircraft Corporation, 1958–74: Dep. Prodn Controller, 1967–73; Concorde Manufg Project Manager, 1973–74; Department of Trade and Industry, 1974–96: Principal, 1974–78; Asst Sec., 1978–86; Under Sec., 1987–96; Services Management Div., 1987–92; Head, Electronics and Engrg Div., 1992–96. Chm. and Dir, KPRA Ltd, 2001–. Dir and Trustee, Florestan Trust, 2006–12. *Recreations:* singing, opera, theatre, tennis. *Club:* Royal Air Force.

RUMBLE, Peter William, CB 1984; Chief Executive, Historic Buildings and Monuments Commission, (English Heritage), 1983–89; Director-General, Union of European Historic Houses Associations, 1991–94; *b* 28 April 1929; *s* of Arthur Victor Rumble and Dorothy Emily (*née* Sadler); *m* 1953, Joyce Audrey Stephenson (*d* 2010); one *s* one *d*. *Educ:* Harwich County High Sch.; Oriel Coll., Oxford (MA). Entered Civil Service, 1952; HM Inspector of Taxes, 1952; Principal, Min. of Housing and Local Govt, 1963; Asst Sec., 1972, Under Sec., 1977, DoE. Member: Architectural Heritage Fund, 1984–98 (Vice-Chm., 1992–98); Cttee, Southern Region, NT, 1990–96; Churches Conservation Trust (formerly Redundant Churches Fund), 1991–99; Rep., Church Heritage Forum, 1997–99. Trustee, Amer. Friends of English Heritage, 1988–94. *Recreations:* music, pottery. *Address:* 11 Hillside Road, Cheam, Surrey SM2 6ET. *T:* (020) 8643 1752.

RUMBLES, Michael John; Member (Lib Dem) West Aberdeenshire and Kincardine, Scottish Parliament, 1999–2011; *b* 10 June 1956; *s* of Samuel and Joan Rumbles; *m* 1985, Pauline Sillars; two *s*. *Educ:* Univ. of Wales (MSc Econ). Commissioned RAEC, 1979–94 (Major); Team Leader in Business Management, Aberdeen Coll., 1995–99. Contested (Lib Dem) W Aberdeenshire and Kincardine, Scottish Parlt, 2011. *Recreations:* family, hill walking.

RUMBOLD, Sir Henry (John Sebastian), 11th Bt *cr* 1779; Partner, Dawson Cornwell, 1991–2004; *b* 24 Dec. 1947; *s* of Sir Horace Anthony Claude Rumbold, 10th Bt, KCMG, KCVO, CB, and Felicity Ann Rumbold (*née* Bailey); *S* father, 1983; *m* 1978, Frances Ann (*née* Hawkes, formerly wife of Julian Berry). *Educ:* Eton College; College of William and Mary, Virginia, USA (BA). Articled Stileman, Neate and Topping, 1975–77; admitted solicitor, 1977; asst solicitor, Stileman, Neate and Topping, 1977–79; Partner, 1979–81; joined Stephenson Harwood, 1981, Partner, 1982–91. *Recreations:* shooting, reading. *Heir: cousin* Charles Anton Rumbold [*b* 7 Feb. 1959; *m* 1987, Susan, *er d* of J. M. Tucker; one *d*]. *Address:* 19 Hollywood Road, SW10 9HT. *T:* (020) 7352 9148; Hatch House, Tisbury, Wilts SP3 6PA. *T:* (01747) 870622. *Clubs:* Boodle's, Groucho.

RUMFITT, Nigel John; QC 1994; *b* 6 March 1950; *s* of late Alan Regan Rumfitt and Dorothy Rumfitt (*née* Ackroyd); *m* 1984, Dorothy Pamela Pouncey. *Educ:* Leeds Modern Sch.; Pembroke Coll., Oxford (MA, BCL). Teaching Associate, Northwestern Univ. Sch. of Law, Chicago, 1972–73; called to the Bar, Middle Temple, 1974, Bencher, 2008; Asst Recorder, 1991–95; Recorder, 1995–2010. *Recreations:* ski-ing, travel, sailing, Francophilia. *Address:* 7 Bedford Row, WC1R 4BS. *T:* (020) 7242 3555.

RUMSFELD, Hon. Donald Henry; Secretary of Defense, USA, 1975–77 and 2001–06; *b* Chicago, 9 July 1932; *s* of George Donald Rumsfeld and Jeannette Rumsfeld (*née* Husted); *m* 1954, Joyce Pierson; one *s* two *d*. *Educ:* New Trier High Sch., Ill; Princeton Univ. (AB 1954). Served US Navy, 1954–57. Admin. Asst, US House of Reps, 1957–59; investment broker, A. G. Becker & Co., Chicago, 1960–62. Mem., House of Reps, 1963–69; Dir, Office of Econ. Opportunity, and Asst to US Pres., 1969–70; Dir, Econ. Stabilization Prog., and Counsellor to the Pres., 1971–72; US Ambassador and Perm. Rep. to NATO, 1973–74; Chief of Staff, White House, and Asst to the Pres., 1974–75. Pres. and CEO, then Chm., G. D. Searle & Co., Ill, 1977–83 and 1984–85; special envoy to ME, 1983–84; Sen. Advr, William Blair & Co., 1985–90; Chm. and CEO, General Instrument Corp., Chicago, 1990–93; in private business, 1996–97; Chm., Gilead Sciences Inc., Calif, 1997–2000. US Presidential Medal of Freedom, 1977. *Publications:* Known and Unknown: a memoir, 2011.

RUNACRES, Mark Alastair; India Adviser, Confederation of British Industry, since 2009; Chairman, British Business Group, Delhi, since 2014 (Secretary, 2008–14); *b* 19 May 1959; *s* of John and Coral Runacres; *m* 1989, Shawn Reid; two *s* one *d*. *Educ:* St John's Coll., Cambridge (BA Hons). Entered FCO, 1981; FCO, 1981–83; New Delhi, 1983–86; Trade Relations Dept, 1986–88, and News Dept, 1988–90, FCO; First Sec. (Chancery), Paris, 1991–95; SE Asia Dept, FCO, 1995–97; Dir, Trade for S Asia and Africa, DTI, 1997–99 (on secondment); Counsellor (Economic and Social Affairs), UKMIS to UN, NY, 1999–2002; Minister and Dep. High Comr, New Delhi, 2002–06; on sabbatical from FCO, 2006–11; Sen. Vis. Fellow, Energy and Resources Inst., New Delhi, 2006–08. Director: Business and Community Foundn (Delhi), 2006–; Sheffield Haworth (India) Private Ltd, 2007–; Action for a Global Climate Community, 2008–10; SQN Partners, 2009–; Canta Consultants, 2011–; Mass1 Engagement, 2011–; non-executive Director: Mind Tree Ltd, 2006–12; G4S (India) Ltd, 2006–15; Elara Capital (India) Pvt. Ltd, 2007–; Religare Capital Markets Europe, 2009–; Religare Capital Markets Ltd, 2012–; non-exec. Chm., A4e India Pvt Ltd, 2012–14; Advisory Board: Avian Media Pvt. Ltd, 2008–; Public Affairs Asia, 2008–; Liqvid eLearning Services Pvt. Ltd, 2011–12; Mem. Bd, FCO Prosperity Fund, India, 2011–15. *Address:* Farm House 25, Kapashera Estate, Kapashera Village, New Delhi 110037, India. *E:* mark.runacres@cbi.org.uk. *Clubs:* Royal Over-Seas League, MCC; Delhi Gymkhana.

RUNCIE, Hon. James Robert; writer; freelance director, since 2000; *b* Cambridge, 7 May 1959; *s* of Baron Runcie, MC, PC and late Angela Rosalind Runcie (*née* Turner); *m* 1985, Marilyn Imrie; one *d* and one step *d*. *Educ:* Marlborough Coll.; Trinity Hall, Cambridge (BA 1981); Bristol Old Vic Th. Sch. Producer and dir, BBC, 1985–2000; Artistic Dir, Bath Lit. Fest., 2010–13; Hd of Literature and Spoken Word, Southbank Centre, 2012–15. *Publications:* The Discovery of Chocolate, 2001; The Colour of Heaven, 2002; Canvey Island, 2006; East Fortune, 2009; The Grantchester Mysteries: Sidney Chambers and the Shadow of Death, 2012; Sidney Chambers and the Perils of the Night, 2013; Sidney Chambers and the Problem of Evil, 2014; Sidney Chambers and the Forgiveness of Sins, 2015. *Recreations:* diligent indolence, the fortunes of Manchester City Football Club. *Address:* c/o David Godwin Associates, 55 Monmouth Street, WC2H 9DG. *T:* (020) 7240 9992. *E:* David@DavidGodwinAssociates.co.uk. *Club:* Athenæum.

RUNCIMAN, family name of **Viscount Runciman of Doxford**.

RUNCIMAN OF DOXFORD, 3rd Viscount *cr* 1937; **Walter Garrison Runciman, (Garry),** CBE 1987; FBA 1975; Bt 1906; Baron Runciman, 1933, of Shoreston; President, British Academy, 2001–05; Fellow, Trinity College, Cambridge, since 1971; *b* 10 Nov. 1934; *o s* of 2nd Viscount Runciman of Doxford, OBE, AFC, AE and Katherine Schuyler (*d* 1993), *y d* of late William R. Garrison, New York; *S* father, 1989; *m* 1963, Ruth (*see* Viscountess Runciman of Doxford); one *s* two *d*. *Educ:* Eton (Oppidan Schol.); Trinity Coll., Cambridge (Schol.; Fellow, 1959–63, 1971–). National Service, 1953–55 (2/Lt, Grenadier Guards); Harkness Fellow, 1958–60; part-time Reader in Sociology, Univ. of Sussex, 1967–69; Vis. Prof., Harvard Univ., 1970; Vis. Fellow, Nuffield Coll., Oxford, 1979–87 (Hon. Fellow, 1998). Lectures: Radcliffe-Brown, British Acad., 1986; Spencer, Oxford Univ., 1986; Chorley, London Univ., 1993; ESRC, 1993; T. H. Marshall, Southampton Univ., 1994; British Acad., 1998; Walters, Univ. of Bath, 2006. Chairman: Walter Runciman plc, 1976–90; Runciman Investments Ltd, 1990–2012; Andrew Weir & Co. Ltd, 1991–2005. Treas., Child Poverty Action Gp, 1972–97; Member: SSRC, 1974–79; Securities and Investments Board, 1986–97 (a Dep. Chm., 1990–97); British Library Bd, 1999–2002; Dep. Chm., FSA, 1997–98. Pres., Gen. Council of British Shipping, 1986–87 (Vice-Pres., 1985–86). Chm., Royal Commn on Criminal Justice, 1991–93. Hon. Foreign Mem., Amer. Acad. of Arts and Sciences, 1986. Hon. DSc (SocScis) Edinburgh, 1992; DUniv York, 1994; Hon. DLitt Oxford, 2000; Hon. DSc (Soc Sci) London, 2007; Hon. DCL Newcastle, 2012. *Publications:* Plato's Later Epistemology, 1962; Social Science and Political Theory, 1963, 2nd edn 1969; Relative Deprivation and Social Justice, 1966, 2nd edn 1972; Sociology in its Place, and other essays, 1970; A Critique of Max Weber's Philosophy of Social Science, 1972; A Treatise on Social Theory: vol. I, 1983, vol. II, 1989, vol. III, 1997; Confessions of a Reluctant Theorist, 1989; The Social Animal, 1998; The Theory of Cultural and Social Selection, 2009; Great Books, Bad Arguments, 2010; Very Different But Much the Same, 2015; articles in academic jls. *Heir: s* Prof. David Walter Runciman [*b* 1 March 1967; *m* 1997, Beatrice, (Bee), *yr d* of A. N. Wilson, *qv* and Katherine Duncan-Jones, *qv*; two *s* one *d*]. *Address:* 44 Clifton Hill, NW8 0QG. *Club:* Brooks's.

RUNCIMAN OF DOXFORD, Viscountess; Ruth Runciman, DBE 1998 (OBE 1991); Chairman, Central and North West London NHS Foundation Trust (formerly Central and North West London Mental Health NHS Trust), 2001–13; *b* 9 Jan. 1936; *o d* of Joseph Hellmann and Dr Ellen Hellmann; *m* 1st, 1959, Denis Mack Smith, *qv* (marr. diss. 1962); 2nd, 1963, Viscount Runciman of Doxford, *qv*; one *s* two *d*. *Educ:* Roedean Sch., Johannesburg; Witwatersrand Univ. (BA 1956); Girton Coll., Cambridge (BA 1958; Hon. Fellow, 2001). Chairman: Mental Health Act Commn, 1994–98; Ind. Inquiry into Misuse of Drugs Act 1971, 1997–2000; Member: Adv. Council on Misuse of Drugs, 1974–95; Press Complaints Commn, 1998–2001 (Mem., Charter Compliance Panel, 2004–06). Council Mem., Nat. Assoc. of CAB, 1978–83; Outreach advice worker, Kensington CAB, 1988–2000; Chairman: Nat. AIDS Trust, 2000–06 (Trustee, 1989–93); UK Drug Policy Commn, 2007–13; Adv. Cttee, Miscarriages of Justice Support Service; Dep. Chm., Prison Reform Trust, 1981–. Trustee: Prince's Trust Volunteers, 1989–94; Mental Health Foundn, 1990–96; Pilgrim Trust, 1999–2011; Sainsbury Centre for Mental Health, 2001–03. Dir, ENO, 1978–83. Hon. Fellow, Univ. of Central Lancs, 2000. Hon. LLD De Montfort, 1997. *Address:* 44 Clifton Hill, NW8 0QG.

RUNCORN, Ven. Jacqueline Ann; *see* Searle, Ven. J. A.

RUNDELL, Richard John; His Honour Judge Rundell; a Circuit Judge, since 2001; *b* 29 July 1948; *s* of Norman Henry Rundell and Pamela Anne Rundell; *m* 1969, Yvonne Doreen Lipinski; two *s*. *Educ:* Chelmsford Tech. High Sch.; Mid Essex Tech. Coll., Chelmsford (LLB London). Called to the Bar, Gray's Inn, 1971; barrister in practice, S Eastern Circuit, 1972–2001; a Recorder, 1996–2001. *Recreations:* cricket, choral music, opera, gardening. *Address:* c/o Midland Circuit, Regional Director's Office, PO Box 11772, 6th Floor, Temple Court, Bull Street, Birmingham B4 6WF. *T:* (0121) 681 3206.

RUNDLE, Hon. Anthony Maxwell, AO 2010; Treasurer, 1993–98, and Premier, 1996–98, Tasmania; *b* 5 March 1939; *s* of M. J. Rundle; *m* Caroline Watt; two *d*. *Educ:* Launceston Church Grammar Sch. Journalist, Australian Associated Press, London, 1961–62; Eric White & Associates Public Relns, London, 1963–68; journalist, Tasmanian TV, 1979. MHA (L) Braddon, Tasmania, 1986–2002; Govt Whip, 1986; Speaker, House of Assembly, 1988–89; Shadow Minister for Tourism and for Transport, 1989–92; Minister: for Forests and for Mines, 1992–93; assisting Premier on Econ. Develt, 1992–93; for Public Sector Mgt, 1993–96; for Finance, 1993–95; for Employment and for Racing and Gaming, 1993–95; assisting Premier on State Develt and Resources, 1993–96; for Energy, 1995–96; Leader of the Opposition, 1998–99; Shadow Minister: for Energy, 1998–2002; for Tourism, for Nat. Parks & Public Lands, and for Planning & Inland Fisheries, 1999–2001; for Small Business, 2001; for Planning, 2001–02. Chairman: Port Devonport Authy, 1982–87; Australian Fisheries Mgt Authy, 2004–09. *Recreations:* golf, Asia. *Address:* 8a Reid Road, Wongaling Beach, Qld 4852, Australia.

RUPERT'S LAND, Bishop of, since 2000; **Rt Rev. Donald David Phillips;** *m* Nancy. *Educ:* Univ. of Western Ontario (BSc 1976, MSc 1979); Huron Coll., Univ. of Western Ontario (MDiv 1981; Hon. DD 2002). Ordained deacon, 1981, priest, 1981; incumbent, Lac La Biche, Alberta, 1981–84; Priest in charge, St Thomas Ch, Fort McMurray and St Paul's Ch, Fort Chipewyan, Alberta, 1984–87; incumbent, St Michael and All Angels, Moose Jaw, Sask, 1987–92; Ministries Develt Co-ordinator, 1992–96, Exec. Officer, 1997–2000, Dio. Qu'Appelle. Hon. Asst, Parish of St Matthew, Regina, Sask, 1992–2000. *Address:* (office) 935 Nesbitt Bay, Winnipeg, MB R3T 1W6, Canada. *T:* (204) 9924212, *Fax:* (204) 9924219. *E:* dphillips@rupertsland.anglican.ca.

RUSBRIDGE, Brian John, CBE 1984; exhibition and training consultant, since 1998; *b* 10 Sept. 1922; *s* of late Arthur John and Leonora Rusbridge, Appleton, Berks; *m* 1951, Joyce, *d* of late Joseph Young Elliott, Darlington; two *s*. *Educ:* Willowfield Sch., Eastbourne; Univ. of Oxford Dept of Social and Admin. Studies (Dip. Social Admin.). Served War of 1939–45, Lieut RNVR. Personnel Manager, Imperial Chemical Industries (Teesside), 1949; British Railways Board: Dir of Industrial Relations, 1963; Divisional Manager, London, 1970; Dir, LACSAB (advising on human relations for Local Govt in UK), 1973–87. Ed., Municipal Year Book, 1987–94; Dir, Newman Books Ltd, 1991–94. Dir, Assoc. of Exhibition Organisers, 1992–98. Freeman, City of London, 1976. CCIPD; CMILT. FRSA. *Recreations:* walking, travel, local politics. *Address:* 19 Beauchamp Road, East Molesey, Surrey KT8 0PA. *T:* (020) 8979 4952.

RUSBRIDGE, Christopher Anthony; Director, Digital Curation Centre, University of Edinburgh, 2005–10; consultant in data curation, digital preservation and project evaluation, 2010–13; *b* 25 Feb. 1946; *s* of Charles Edward Rusbridge and Elma May Rusbridge; *m* 1973, Sheila Margaret Stuart; one *s* two *d*. *Educ:* Imperial Coll., Univ. of London (BSc; ARCS). Programmer and Manager, ICT/ICL, 1967–74; Asst Dir, ADP, S Australian Public Service Hosps Dept, 1974–75; Programming Services Manager, 1975–83, Acad. Computing Services Manager, 1983–92, SA Inst. of Technol., then Univ. of S Australia; Dir, IT Services, Univ. of Dundee, 1992–94; Liby IT Co-ordinator, Univ. of S Australia, 1994; Dir, Jt Inf. Systems Cttee Electronic Libraries Prog., Univ. of Warwick, 1995–2000; Dir, Inf. Services, Glasgow Univ., 2000–05. *Recreations:* walking, music, photography.

RUSBRIDGER, Alan Charles; Principal, Lady Margaret Hall, Oxford, since 2015; *b* 29 Dec. 1953; *s* of late G. H. Rusbridger and B. E. Rusbridger (*née* Wickham); *m* 1982, Hon. Lindsay Mackie, *d* of Baron Mackie of Benshie, CBE, DSO, DFC; two *d*. *Educ:* Cranleigh Sch.; Magdalene Coll., Cambridge (MA). Reporter, Cambridge Evening News, 1976–79; reporter, columnist and feature writer, The Guardian, 1979–86; TV Critic, The Observer, 1986–87; Washington Corresp., London Daily News, 1987; Editor, Weekend Guardian, 1988–89; The Guardian: Features Editor, 1989–93; Dep. Editor, 1993–95; Editor, 1995–2015; Exec. Ed., The Observer, 1997–2015. Director: Guardian Newspapers Ltd, 1994–2015; Guardian Media Gp, 1999–2015. Vis. Fellow, Nuffield Coll., Oxford, 2004–12; Vis. Prof., QMC, London Univ.; Hon. Prof. of Journalism, Cardiff Univ., 2013 Mem., The Scott Trust, 1997– (Chm, 2016–). Chairman: Photographer's Gall., 2001–04; NYO of GB, 2004–12. Co-author (with Ronan Bennett), Fields of Gold, BBC TV, 2002. Editor of the Year: Granada TV What the Papers Say Awards, 1996 and 2001; Newspaper Focus Awards, 1996; Nat. Newspaper Editor, Newspaper Industry Awards, 1996; Freedom of the Press Award, London Press Club, 1998; Judges Award, Granada TV What the Papers Say, 2005; Goldsmith Career Award, Harvard Univ., 2012; Media Soc. Award, 2012; Burton Benjamin Award, Cttee for Protection of Journalists, 2012; Pulitzer Prize for Public Service, 2014; European Press Prize, 2014; Ortega y Gasset Award, 2014; Liberty Human Rights Award, 2014; Right Livelihood Award, 2014. *Publications: for children:* Coldest Day at the Zoo, 2004; Wildest Day at the Zoo, 2004; Play it Again, 2013. *Recreations:* chamber music, piano-playing, photography, golf. *Address:* Lady Margaret Hall, Oxford OX2 6QA. *Clubs:* Soho House; Broadway Golf.

RUSE, David John; Tri-borough Director of Libraries and Archives, Westminster City Council, Royal Borough of Kensington and Chelsea and London Borough of Hammersmith and Fulham, 2011–13; *b* 24 Aug. 1951; *s* of Ronald Frank and Betty Irene Ruse; *m* 1975, Carole Anne Lawton; two *d*. *Educ:* Birmingham Coll. of Commerce. MCLIP (ALA 1973). Bath Municipal Libraries, 1969–70; Asst Librarian, London Borough of Havering, 1972–77; Branch Librarian, London Borough of Barking and Dagenham, 1977–81; Asst Dir, Library Assoc., 1981–89; Head, Planning and Review, Berks CC, 1989–93; Westminster City Council: Asst Dir, Leisure and Libraries, 1993–99; Asst Dir, Lifetime, then Lifelong Learning, later Dir of Libraries and Culture, 1999–2011. Member: Bd, Lifelong Learning UK, 2005–08; Adv. Council on Libraries, 2006–10. *Publications:* chapters in various librarianship books; various articles in professional library press. *Recreations:* social history of railways, reading, music, countryside matters. *E:* david.ruse@btinternet.com.

RUSEDSKI, Gregory; professional tennis player, retired 2007; media commentator; *b* Montreal, 6 Sept. 1973; *s* of Tom and Helen Rusedski; *m* 1999, Lucy Connor; one *s* one *d*. *Educ:* Lower Canada Coll. Mem., British Davis Cup Team, 1995–2007. Winner of 15 career titles including: singles: Newport, Rhode Is., 1993, 2004, 2005; Paris Indoor Open, 1998; Compaq Grand Slam Cup, 1999; Vienna Indoor Open, 1999; Sybase Open, San Jose, 2001; Indianapolis Open, 2002; Auckland, 2002. Recorded world record serve of 149 mph, 1998. LTA Talent Ambassador, 2007–. Sports Personality of the Year, BBC, 1997. *Recreations:* golf, chess, Arsenal Football Club, cinema, James Bond. *Address:* PO Box 31369, SW11 3GH. *E:* sharon@park54.fsnet.co.uk.

RUSH, Ann Patricia; consultant, Archam, since 2002; *b* 17 March 1948; *d* of Peter Deshaw and Hanni Adele Gray; *m* 1969, Charles Anthony Rush; one *s* one *d*. *Educ:* Ursuline Convent; LSE (MSc). The Observer, 1966–68; RABI, 1969–76; CR Associates, 1974–89; Dep. Dir, 1990–92, Dir, Migraine Trust, 1992–2002. Trustee, Neurological Alliance, 1999–2001. *Publications:* Migraine, 1996. *Recreations:* family, reading, sailing. *E:* chanrush@live.co.uk.

RUSH, Geoffrey Roy, AC 2014; actor; *b* Toowoomba, Qld, 6 July 1951; *s* of Roy Baden Rush and Merle Kiehne (*née* Bischof); *m* 1988, Jane Menelaus; one *s* one *d*. *Educ:* Everton Park High Sch., Brisbane; Univ. of Queensland (BA); Jacques Lecoq Sch. of Mime, Movement and Th., Paris. Stage début in Wrong Side of the Moon, 1971; Mem., Qld Th. Co., 1971–74; Mem., Lighthouse State Th. Co., SA, 1982–83; Dir, Magpie Th., SA, 1984–86; Associate Artist, Qld Arts Council, 2003–. *Theatre* includes: The Diary of a Madman, 1989; The Government Inspector, 1991; Uncle Vanya, The Importance of Being Earnest, 1992; Oleanna, 1993; Hamlet, 1994; The Alchemist, 1996; The Marriage of Figaro, 1998; The Small Poppies, 2000; Exit the King, 2007 (Tony Award for Best Actor in a Play, 2009); also dir numerous prodns. *Films* include: Hoodwink, 1981; Twelfth Night, 1987; Children of the Revolution, Shine, 1996 (Academy, Golden Globe, BAFTA and Aust. Film Inst. Awards for Best Actor); Oscar and Lucinda (voice), 1997; Les Misérables, Elizabeth, Shakespeare in Love (BAFTA Award for Best Supporting Actor), 1998; Mystery Men, House on Haunted Hill, 1999; The Tailor of Panama, Lantana, Quills, 2001; Swimming Upstream, 2002; The Banger Sisters, Frida, Ned Kelly, Intolerable Cruelty, Pirates of the Caribbean: The Curse of the Black Pearl, Finding Nemo (voice), 2003; The Life and Death of Peter Sellers, 2004 (Golden Globe, Screen Actors and Emmy Awards, 2005); Munich, Pirates of the Caribbean: Dead Man's Chest, 2006; Pirates of the Caribbean: At World's End, Elizabeth: The Golden Age, 2007; The King's Speech (BAFTA Award for Best Supporting Actor), 2011; Pirates of the Caribbean: On Stranger Tides, 2011; The Book Thief, The Best Offer, 2014; *television* includes: Menotti, 1981; Mercury, 1996; Frontier, 1997. Inaugural Pres., Australian Acad. of Cinema and Television Arts, 2011–. Australian of the Year, Nat. Australia Day Council, 2012. Centenary Medal (Australia), 2001. *Publications:* (jtly) The Popular Mechanicals (play), 1992; (adapted with J. Clarke) Aristophanes' Frogs; (trans. jtly) The Government Inspector; (trans. jtly) Exit the King, 2008. *Address:* c/o Shanahan Management, PO Box 1509, Darlinghurst, NSW 1300, Australia.

RUSHDIE, Sir (Ahmed) Salman, Kt 2007; FRSL; writer; *b* 19 June 1947; *s* of Anis Ahmed Rushdie and Negin Rushdie (*née* Butt); *m* 1976, Clarissa Luard (marr. diss. 1987); one *s*; *m* 1988, Marianne Wiggins (marr. diss. 1993); *m* 1997, Elizabeth West (marr. diss. 2002); one *s*; *m* 2004, Padma Lakshmi (marr. diss. 2007). *Educ:* Cathedral Sch., Bombay; Rugby Sch.; King's Coll., Cambridge (MA (Hons) History). Hon. Prof., MIT, 1993; Dist. Fellow in Lit., UEA, 1995. Pres., PEN America Center, 2004–. Hon. DLitt Bard Coll., 1995; Hon. Dr: Amherst, Tromsø, 1997; Torino, UEA, Liège, Free Univ. of Berlin, 1999; Sorbonne, Albion Coll., 2003. Arts Council Literature Bursary Award; Kurt Tucholsky Prize, Sweden, 1992; Prix Colette, Switzerland, 1993; Austrian State Prize for European Literature, 1994; EU Aristeion Prize for Literature, 1996; London Internat. Writers' Award, 2002; PEN Pinter Prize for British Writers, 2014. Freedom of Mexico City, 1999. Commandeur, Ordre des Arts et des Lettres (France), 1999. *Films for TV:* The Painter and the Pest, 1985; The Riddle of Midnight, 1988. *Publications:* Grimus, 1975; Midnight's Children, 1981 (Booker Prize for Fiction, 1981; James Tait Black Meml Book Prize; ESU Literary Award; Booker of Bookers Prize, 1993; Best of the Booker award, 2008) (adapted for stage, 2003, for film, 2012); Shame, 1983 (Prix du Meilleur Livre Etranger, 1984); The Jaguar Smile: a Nicaraguan journey, 1987; The Satanic Verses, 1988 (Whitbread Novel Award; German Author of the Year Award, 1989); Haroun and the Sea of Stories, 1990 (Writers' Guild Award); Imaginary Homelands (essays), 1991; The Wizard of Oz, 1992; East, West, 1994; The Moor's Last Sigh (Whitbread Novel Award; British Book Awards Author of the Year), 1995; (ed with Elizabeth West) The Vintage Book of Indian Writing, 1947–97, 1997; The Ground Beneath Her Feet, 1999; Fury, 2001; Step Across This Line: collected non-fiction 1992–2002, 2002; Shalimar the Clown, 2005; The Enchantress of Florence, 2008; Luka and the Fire of Life, 2010; Two Years, Eight Months and Twenty-Eight Nights, 2015; Joseph Anton, 2012; contribs to many journals. *Address:* c/o Wylie Agency (UK) Ltd, 17 Bedford Square, WC1B 3JA.

RUSHFORTH, Philip Christopher; Director of Music, Chester Cathedral, since 2007; *b* Chester, 31 Dec. 1972; *s* of Christopher and Gillian Rushforth; *m* 2001, Louise Walker; two *s* one *d*. *Educ:* Abbey Gate Coll., Chester; Trinity Coll., Cambridge (BA 1994; MA 1998). ARCO 1993. Asst Organist, Southwell Minster, 1994–2002; Asst Dir of Music, Chester Cath., 2002–07. *Recreations:* Olympic class ships, horology, biography. *Address:* Chester Cathedral Office, 12 Abbey Square, Chester CH1 2HU. *T:* (01244) 500974. *E:* philip.rushforth@chestercathedral.com.

RUSHTON, Ian Lawton, FIA, FCII; Chairman, Hackney Empire Ltd, 1994–2004; Vice Chairman, Royal Insurance Holdings plc, 1991–93 (Group Chief Executive, 1989–91); *b* 8 Sept. 1931; *s* of Arthur John and Mabel Lilian Rushton; *m* 1st, 1956, Julia Frankland (decd); one *d*; 2nd, 1986, Anita Spencer; one step *s* one step *d*. *Educ:* Rock Ferry High Sch., Birkenhead; King's Coll., London (BSc Mathematics). FIA 1959; FCII 1961. Served RAF, 1953–56 (Flt-Lieut). Royal Insurance, 1956–93: Dep. Gen. Man. (UK), 1972; Exec. Vice Pres., Royal US, 1980; Gen. Man. Royal UK, 1983; Exec. Dir and Gp Gen. Man., Royal Insurance plc, 1986. Chairman: Fire Protection Assoc., 1983–87; Assoc. of British Insurers, 1991–93; Vice Pres., Inst. of Actuaries, 1986–89. FRSA. *Recreations:* wine, theatre, music. *Address:* Flat 136, 4 Whitehall Court, SW1A 2EP.

RUSHTON, Prof. Julian Gordon, DPhil; West Riding Professor of Music, University of Leeds, 1982–2002, now Emeritus; *b* 22 May 1941; *s* of Prof. William A. H. Rushton and Marjorie Rushton; *m* 1968, Virginia S. M. Jones (marr. diss. 2000); two *s*. *Educ:* Trinity Coll., Cambridge (BA 1963; BMus 1965; MA 1967); Magdalen Coll., Oxford (DPhil 1970). Lecturer in Music: UEA, 1968–74; and Fellow, King's Coll., Cambridge, 1974–81. Chm., Editl Bd, Musica Britannica, 1993–. Pres., Royal Musical Assoc., 1994–99. Corresp. Mem., Amer. Musicol Soc., 2000; Dir-at-large, Internat. Musicol Soc., 2007–. MAE 2010. *Publications:* Berlioz: Huit Scènes de Faust, 1970; La Damnation de Faust, vol. 1, 1979, vol. 2, 1986; W. A. Mozart: Don Giovanni, 1981, 2nd edn 1990; The Musical Language of Berlioz, 1983; Classical Music: a concise history, 1986; Berlioz: Choral Music I, 1991; W. A. Mozart: Idomeneo, 1993; Berlioz: Roméo et Juliette, 1994; Elgar: Enigma Variations, 1999; The Music of Berlioz, 2001; Potter: Symphony in G minor, 2001; (ed with D. M. Grimley) The Cambridge Companion to Elgar, 2004; Mozart: an extraordinary life, 2005; Mozart (Master Musicians series), 2006; (ed with R. Cowgill) Europe, Empire, and Spectacle in Nineteenth-Century British Music, 2006; (ed with J. P. E. Harper-Scott) Elgar Studies, 2007; (ed) Let Beauty Awake: Elgar, Vaughan Williams, and literature, 2010; Elgar Complete Edition: music for string orchestra, 2011; Elgar Complete Edition: songs with orchestra, 2012; Vaughan Williams: Serenade (1898) for small orchestra, 2012: Vaughan Williams: Bucolic Suite, 2012; contrib. to Music & Letters, Music Analysis, Cambridge Opera Jl, Musical Times, Elgar Soc. Jl, Early Music, Jl Amer. Musicological Soc. *Recreations:* literature, walking, gardening, preserving. *Address:* School of Music, University of Leeds, Leeds LS2 9JT. *E:* j.g.rushton@leeds.ac.uk; 362 Leymoor Road, Golcar, Huddersfield HD7 4QF.

RUSHTON, Prof. Neil, MD; FRCS; FIMMM; Professor of Orthopaedics, University of Cambridge, 2003–10, now Emeritus; Fellow of Magdalene College, Cambridge, 1984, now Emeritus (Life Fellow, 2010); *b* 16 Dec. 1945; *s* of John Allen Rushton and Iris Rushton; *m* 1971, Sheila Margaret Johnson; two *s* one *d*. *Educ:* Middlesex Hosp., London (MB BS 1970); Magdalene Coll., Cambridge (MA 1979; MD 1984). LRCP 1970; MRCS 1970, FRCS 1975; FIMMM 2008. Pre-Registration Sen. House Officer, Orsett Hosp., 1971–75; Registrar in Trauma and Orthopaedics, Royal Northern, Royal Free and Heatherwood Hosps, 1975–77; University of Cambridge: Sen. Registrar Orthopaedics, 1977–79; Clinical Lectr in Surgery, Cambridge and Black Notley, 1979–83; Lectr in Surgery, 1983–2000; Sen. Lectr, 2000–01, Reader, 2001–03, in Orthopaedics; Hon. Consultant in Orthopaedics, Addenbrooke's Hosp., 1983–. Dep. Ed. (Res.), Jl of Bone and Joint Surgery, 1996–2006; Ed., British Orthopaedic News, 2002–06. *Publications:* Surgical Exposures of the Limbs, 1984; Classification of Limb Fractures in Adults, 2002; chapters in 8 books; articles on biocompatibility of materials used in orthopaedics, tissue engrg bone and cartilage, fractures of the proximal femur and the bone response to arthroplasty, in Jl of Bone and Joint Surgery, Acta Orthopaedica Scandinavica, Biomaterials and Jl of Materials Sci.: Materials in Medicine. *Recreations:* sailing, ski-ing, scuba diving, music, cycling, wine. *Address:* 37 Bentley Road, Cambridge CB2 8AW. *T:* (01223) 353624. *E:* nr10000@cam.ac.uk. *Club:* Athenæum.

RUSHTON, Ven. Samantha Jayne; Archdeacon of Cleveland, since 2015; *b* 1965; *m* Peter Rushton; two *s*. *Educ:* St Hilda's Coll., Oxford (BA 1987); Trinity Coll., Bristol (BA 2005). Mgt Consultant, Lloyds TSB; ordained deacon, 2005, priest, 2006; Curate: St Michael, Highworth, 2005–08; St Leonard, Broad Blunsdon, 2005–08; St Paul, Chippenham with Hardenhuish and Langley Burrell, 2008–15; St Michael, Kington St Michael, 2008–15; Advr for Licensed Ministry, 2008–15, Warden of Readers, 2011–15, Diocese of Bristol; Area Dean, Chippenham, 2013–15. *Address:* 48 Langbaurgh Road, Hutton Rudby, Yarm TS15 0HL.

RUSHWORTH, Dr (Frank) Derek; Headmaster, Holland Park School, London, 1971–85; *b* 15 Sept. 1920; *s* of late Frank and Elizabeth Rushworth, Huddersfield; *m* 1941, Hamidah Begum, *d* of late Justice S. Akhlaque Hussain, Lahore, and Edith (*née* Bayliss), Oxford; two *d* (and one *d* decd). *Educ:* Huddersfield Coll.; St Edmund Hall, Oxford (Schol.; BA 1942, MA 1946); Doctorate of Univ. of Paris (Lettres), 1947. Served 6th Rajputana Rifles, Indian Army, 1942–45 (Major); began teaching, 1947; Head of Modern Languages: Tottenham Grammar Sch., 1953; Holland Park Sch., 1958; Head of Shoreditch Sch., London, 1965. Chairman: Associated Examining Board, French Committee, 1964–74; Schools Council, 16+ Examination Feasibility Study (French), 1971–75; Pres., London Head Teachers' Assoc., 1985. Governor, Holland Park Sch., 1990–95. *Publications:* Our French Neighbours, 1963, 2nd edn 1966; French text-books and language-laboratory books; articles in French Studies, Modern Languages, also educnl jls. *Recreation:* photography. *Address:* 25c Lambolle Road, NW3 4HS. *T:* (020) 7794 3691.

RUSKELL, Mark Christopher; Director, Ruskell Communications, since 2011; *b* 14 May 1972; *s* of David and Brenda Ruskell; *m* 1999, Melinda McEwen; two *s*. *Educ:* Edinburgh Acad.; Stevenson Coll., Edinburgh; Univ. of Stirling (BSc Hons Envmtl Sci. with Biol.); Scottish Agricl Coll., Univ. of Aberdeen (MSc Sustainable Agric.). Develt Worker, Falkirk Voluntary Action Resource Centre, 1997–2000; Regeneration Officer, Midlothian Council, 2000–02; Project Officer, Soil Assoc., 2002–03; Communications Manager, Scottish Renewables Forum, 2008–10. MSP (Green) Scotland and Mid Fife, 2003–07. Dir, LETSlink Scotland, 1996–99. Mem. (Green) Stirling Council, 2012–. Contested (Green) Stirling, 2001, 2010, 2015. *Recreations:* cycling, growing and cooking food.

RUSSELL; *see* Hamilton-Russell, family name of Viscount Boyne.

RUSSELL, family name of **Duke of Bedford**, **Earl Russell**, and **Barons Ampthill**, **de Clifford** and **Russell of Liverpoolde Clifford** and **Russell of Liverpool**.

RUSSELL, 7th Earl *cr* 1861; **John Francis Russell;** Viscount Amberley 1861; *b* 19 Nov. 1971; *yr s* of 5th Earl Russell, FBA and Elizabeth Franklyn Russell (*née* Sanders); *S* brother, 2014; *m* 2002, Jane Elizabeth Swann; one *d*. *Heir:* none.

RUSSELL OF LIVERPOOL, 3rd Baron *cr* 1919; **Simon Gordon Jared Russell;** *b* 30 Aug. 1952; *s* of Captain Hon. Langley Gordon Haslingden Russell, MC (*d* 1975) (*o s* of 2nd Baron), and of Kiloran Margaret, *d* of late Hon. Sir Arthur Jared Palmer Howard, KBE, CVO; *S* grandfather, 1981; *m* 1984, Dr Gilda Albano, *y d* of late Signor F. Albano and of Signora Maria Caputo-Albano; two *s* one *d*. *Educ:* Charterhouse; Trinity Coll., Cambridge; INSEAD, Fontainebleau, France. Elected Mem., H of L, 2014. *Heir: s* Hon. Edward Charles Stanley Russell, *b* 2 Sept. 1985.

RUSSELL, Alan Keith, OBE 2000; DPhil; President, Dresden Trust, since 2014 (Chairman, 1993–2014); charity administrator, consultant and writer; *b* 22 Oct. 1932; *s* of late Keith Russell and Gertrude Ann Russell; *m* 1959, Philippa Margaret Stoneham (*see* Dame P. M. Russell); two *s* one *d*. *Educ:* Ardingly Coll.; Lincoln Coll., Oxford (BA; MA Econ and Pol Sci. 1956); Nuffield Coll., Oxford (DPhil 1962); Oxford Brookes Univ. (Cert. in Architectural Hist., 1997; Dip. in Historic Conservation, 1998). Colonial Office, ODM, FCO, 1959–69, 1972–75; CS Coll., 1969–71; Dir, Inter University Council for Higher Educn Overseas, 1980–81; sen. official, Commn of EC, 1976–79, 1981–86, 1988–89; Fellow, Lincoln Coll., Oxford and Sen. Res. Associate, Queen Elizabeth House, 1986–88; manager, Civic Improvement Trust, 1990–92. Vice Pres., British-German Assoc., 2012–13. Medal of Honour, City of Dresden, 2006; Erich Kästner Prize, Presseclub, Dresden, 2006. Order of Merit (FRG), 1997, 2006; Mem., Order of St Henry, 2015. *Publications:* (ed) The Economic and Social History of Mauritius, 1962; Liberal Landslide: the General Election of 1906, 1973; (contrib.) Edwardian Radicalism, 1974; The Unclosed Eye (poems), 1987, 2013; The Year the Cotton Broke (poems), 1987, 2015; (ed and contrib.) Dresden: a city reborn, 1999; (ed and contrib.) Why Dresden?, 2000; (ed and contrib.) Kulturelle Beziehungen zwischen Sachsen und Grossbritannien, 2002; (contrib.) Firestorm: the bombing of Dresden, 2006; (contrib.) When Stones Bring Warmth to the Soul, 2012; The Dresden Trust: a Trust for our time, 2014; An Englishman Speaks Out, 2015; Trittsteine zur Freundschaft, 2015; articles on: Dresden, Saxony and Germany; conservation; internat. relations and development; historic conservation. *Recreations:* conservation and town planning, German and European history, services for the mentally handicapped. *Address:* Dresden House, 30 Stirling Road, Chichester, W Sussex PO19 7DS.

RUSSELL, Sir (Alastair) Muir, KCB 2001; FRSE; FInstP; Chairman, Judicial Appointments Board for Scotland, since 2008; *b* 9 Jan. 1949; *s* of Thomas Russell and Anne Muir; *m* 1983, Eileen Alison Mackay, *qv*. *Educ:* High Sch. of Glasgow; Univ. of Glasgow (BSc Nat. Phil.). FInstP 2003. Joined Scottish Office, 1970; seconded as Sec. to Scottish Development Agency, 1975–76; Asst Sec., 1981; Principal Private Sec. to Sec. of State for Scotland, 1981–83; Under Sec., 1990; seconded to Cabinet Office, 1990–92; Under Sec. (Housing), Scottish Office Envmt Dept, 1992–95; Dep. Sec., 1995; Sec. and Hd of Dept, Scottish Office Agric., Envmt and Fisheries Dept, 1995–98; Permanent Under-Sec. of State, Scottish Office, 1998–99; Permanent Sec., Scottish Exec., 1999–2003; Principal and Vice-Chancellor, Univ. of Glasgow, 2003–09. Non-exec. Director: Stagecoach Hldgs, 1992–95; National House-Building Council, 2012– (Chm., Scottish Cttee, 2012–; Chm., Audit Cttee, 2014–). Dir, UCAS, 2005–09; Member, Council: ACU, 2006–10; RSE, 2012–; Convener, Universities Scotland, 2006–08; Mem. Bd, Univs Superannuation Scheme, 2007–09. Council Mem., Edinburgh Festival Soc., 2004–09; Chm., Dunedin Consort, 2009–. Mem. Bd, Moredun Res. Inst., 2009–. Chm., Royal Botanic Garden, Edinburgh, 2011–. Gov., Glasgow Sch. of Art, 2009– (Vice Chair, 2011–). Freeman, City of London, 2006. DL Glasgow, 2004–09. FRSE 2000; CCMI (CIMgt 2001). Hon. FRCPSGlas 2005. Hon. LLD Strathclyde, 2000; DUniv Glasgow, 2001; Dhc Edinburgh, 2009. *Recreations:* music, food, wine. *E:* muir.russell@btinternet.com. *Club:* New (Edinburgh).

RUSSELL, (Albert) Muir (Galloway), CBE 1989; QC (Scot.) 1965; Sheriff of Grampian, Highland and Islands (formerly Aberdeen, Kincardine and Banff) at Aberdeen and Stonehaven, 1971–91; *b* 26 Oct. 1925; *s* of Hon. Lord Russell; *m* 1954, Margaret Winifred, *o d* of T. McW. Millar, FRCSE, Edinburgh; two *s* two *d*. *Educ:* Edinburgh Academy; Wellington College; Brasenose College, Oxford (BA (Hons) 1949); LLB Edinburgh, 1951. Lieut, Scots Guards, 1944–47. Member of Faculty of Advocates, 1951–. *Recreation:* golf. *Address:* Tulloch House, Aultbea, Ross-shire IV22 2JB. *T:* (01445) 731325.

RUSSELL, Hon. Dame Alison Hunter, DBE 2014; **Hon. Ms Justice Russell;** a Judge of the High Court of Justice, Family Division, since 2014; *b* Harrogate, 17 June 1958; *d* of Alexander Law Macpherson Russell and Margaret Erskine Russell; partner, Julian Francis. *Educ:* Wellington Sch., Ayr; Poly. of South Bank (BA Hons 1982). Called to the Bar, Gray's Inn, 1983, Bencher, 2014; in practice as barrister specialising in family law, human rights and internat. family law, 1983–2014; a Recorder, 2004–14; QC 2008; a Dep. High Court Judge, 2011–14. Mem., Family Justice Council, 2009–14. *Recreations:* Spain, Handel, reading, cooking and, most of all, playing with my niece and nephews, Bessie, Vincent and Felix. *Address:* Royal Courts of Justice, Strand, WC2A 2LL.

RUSSELL, Andrew Victor Manson; Chief Executive (formerly Executive Director), Association for Spina Bifida and Hydrocephalus, 1991–2009; *b* 7 Dec. 1949; *s* of Manson McCausland Russell and Margaret Ivy Russell; *m* 1974, Susan Elizabeth Aykroyd; one *s* one *d*. *Educ:* Dartington Hall; Fitzwilliam Coll., Cambridge Univ. (MA). NSMHC, 1974–85; General Manager, Eastern Div., Royal MENCAP Soc., 1985–91. Member: Ethics and Governance Council, UK Biobank, 2008–; Bd, UK Clinical Res. Collaboration, 2009–13. *Recreations:* sailing, music.

RUSSELL, Rt Rev. Anthony John, DPhil; FRAgS; Bishop of Ely, 2000–10; an Honorary Assistant Bishop, Diocese of Oxford, since 2010; *b* 25 Jan. 1943; *s* of Michael John William and Beryl Margaret Russell; *m* 1967, Sheila Alexandra, *d* of Alexander Scott and Elizabeth Carlisle Ronald; two *s* two *d*. *Educ:* Uppingham Sch.; Univ. of Durham (BA); Trinity Coll., Oxford (DPhil; Hon. Fellow 2011); Cuddesdon Coll., Oxford. Deacon 1970, Priest 1971; Curate, Hilborough Group of Parishes, 1970–73; Rector, Preston on Stour, Atherstone on Stour and Whitchurch, 1973–88; Chaplain, Arthur Rank Centre (Nat. Agricl Centre), 1973–82, Director, 1983–88; Canon Theologian, Coventry Cathedral, 1977–88; Chaplain to the Queen, 1983–88; Area Bp of Dorchester, 1988–2000. Entered H of L, 2007. Hulsean Preacher, Cambridge Univ., 2004; Univ. Select Preacher, Oxford Univ., 2011. Mem., Gen. Synod, 1980–88. Royal Agricultural Society: Chaplain, 1982–91; Vice-Pres., 1991–2002; Vice-Patron, 2002; Pres., 2004–05; Hon. Chaplain, RABI, 1983–2002. ARAgS 2003, FRAgS 2008. Comr, Rural Develt Commn, 1991–99. Trustee, Rural Housing Trust, 1983–2006. President: Woodard Corp., 2003–; E of England Agricultural Soc., 2007–08. Gov., Radley Coll., 2003–. Visitor, Jesus Coll., St John's Coll., and Peterhouse, Cambridge, 2000–10. Hon. Fellow: St Edmund's Coll., Cambridge, 2000; Wolfson Coll., Cambridge, 2001; St Chad's Coll., Durham, 2007. *Publications:* Groups and Teams in the Countryside (ed), 1975; The Village in Myth and Reality, 1980; The Clerical Profession, 1980; The Country Parish, 1986; The Country Parson, 1993.

RUSSELL, His Honour Anthony Patrick; QC 1999. a Circuit Judge, 2004–15; a Senior Circuit Judge and Resident Judge, Lancashire Crown Courts, 2006–15; *b* 11 April 1951; *s* of late Dr Michael Hibberd Russell and Pamela Russell (*née* Eyre). *Educ:* King's Sch., Chester; Pembroke Coll., Oxford (MA). Called to the Bar, Middle Temple, 1974, Bencher, 2008; in practice at the Bar, Northern Circuit, 1974–2004; Junior, Northern Circuit, 1977; Standing Counsel to Inland Revenue, 1994–96; a Recorder, 1993–96, 2001–04; Hon. Recorder of Preston, 2006–15; Recorder, Preston Guild, 2012. Mem., Gen. Council of the Bar, 1987–94. Hon. Fellow, Univ. of Central Lancs, 2013. Hon. FGCM 2001 (Vice-Pres., 2005–). Hon. Burgess, City of Preston, 2012. *Recreations:* music, especially singing, the countryside, family history. *Address:* c/o Law Courts, Openshaw Place, Ringway, Preston PR1 2LL. *T:* (01772) 844700. *Club:* Oxford and Cambridge.

RUSSELL, Sir (Arthur) Mervyn, 8th Bt *cr* 1812, of Swallowfield, Berkshire; *b* 7 Feb. 1923; *s* of Sir Arthur Edward Ian Montagu Russell, 6th Bt, MBE, and his 2nd wife, Cornélie, *d* of Maj. Jacques de Bruijn, Amsterdam; *S* half brother, 1993, but his name does not appear on the Official Roll of the Baronetage; *m* 1st, 1945, Ruth Holloway (marr. diss.); one *s*; 2nd, 1956, Kathleen Joyce Searle (*d* 2005); one *s*. *Heir: s* Stephen Charles Russell [*b* 12 Jan. 1949; *m* 1974, Dale Frances Markstein; one *d*].

RUSSELL, Ven. Brian Kenneth, PhD; Senior Chaplain, St Edmund's, Oslo, since 2014 (with oversight of the Anglican Church in Norway); Archdeacon of Aston, 2005–14, now Archdeacon Emeritus; *b* 1 Aug. 1950; *s* of William George Russell and Joan Russell; *m* 1976, Pamela Jean Gillard; one *s* one *d*. *Educ:* Bristol Grammar Sch.; Trinity Hall, Cambridge (BA 1973, MA 1976); Cuddesdon Coll., Oxford; Birmingham Univ. (MA 1977; PhD 1983). Ordained deacon, 1976, priest, 1977; Curate, St Matthew, Redhill, 1976–79; Priest-in-charge, St John, Kirk Merrington, and Dir of Studies, NE Ordination Course, 1979–83; Dir of Studies and Lectr in Christian Doctrine, Lincoln Theol Coll., 1983–86; Sec. to Cttee for Theol Educn, and Selection Sec., ACCM, subseq. ABM, 1986–93; Bishop's Dir for Ministries, Dio. Birmingham, 1993–2005. Hon. Canon, Birmingham Cathedral, 1999–. Mem., Bishops' Inspections Wkg Pty, 2003–08. Gov., Queen's Foundn for Theol Educn, Birmingham, 1994–2013. *Publications:* (ed jtly) Leaders for the 21st Century, 1993; (ed) Formation in a Changing Church, 1999; articles on theol educn in Theology and British Jl of Theol Educn, and reviews in Theology. *Recreations:* theatre, literature, National Hunt racing, links with Nordic and Baltic Churches. *Address:* Harald Hårfagres Gate 2, Apartment 512, 0363 Oslo, Norway. *T:* (47) 22692214. *E:* B-Russell5@sky.com.

RUSSELL, Sir Charles (Dominic), 4th Bt *cr* 1916, of Littleworth Corner, Burnham, co. Buckingham; antiquarian bookseller, trading as Russell Rare Books, since 1978; *b* 28 May 1956; *o s* of Sir Charles Ian Russell, 3rd Bt and Rosemary Lavender Russell (*née* Prestige) (*d* 1996); *S* father, 1997; *m* 1st, 1986, Sarah Chandor (marr. diss. 1995); one *s*; 2nd, 2005, Wandee Ruanrakrao. *Educ:* Worth Sch. *Heir: s* Charles William Russell, *b* 8 Sept. 1988. *Club:* Chelsea Arts.

RUSSELL, Christine Margaret; JP; *b* 25 March 1945; *d* of John Alfred William Carr and Phyllis Carr; *m* 1971, Dr James Russell (marr. diss. 1991); one *s* one *d*. *Educ:* Spalding High Sch.; London Sch. of Librarianship (ALA). PA to Brian Simpson, MEP, 1992–94. Mem. (Lab) Chester CC, 1980–97 (Chair, Develt). Co-ordinator, Mind Advocacy Scheme, 1995–97. MP (Lab) City of Chester, 1997–2010; contested (Lab) same seat, 2010. Chair of Govs, West Cheshire Coll., 2012–. JP 1980. DLit Chester, 2011. *Recreations:* film, visual arts, walking, football. *E:* russellcm@hotmail.co.uk.

RUSSELL, Christopher; *see* Russell, R. C. G.

RUSSELL, Clare Nancy; Lord-Lieutenant for Banffshire, since 2002 (Vice Lord-Lieutenant, 1998–2002); estate owner and rural land manager, Ballindalloch, since 1979; *b* 4 Aug. 1944; *d* of Sir Ewan Macpherson-Grant, 6th Bt, and Lady Macpherson-Grant; *m* 1967, Oliver Henry Russell; two *s* one *d*. *Educ:* in Scotland. Professional florist, Head Decorator, Constance Spry, 1962–65; Sec. to Fourth Clerk at the Table, H of C, 1965–67; Dir, Craigo Farms Ltd, 1970–; living at Ballindalloch, 1978–; opened Ballindalloch Castle to public, 1993. Mem., Moray Health Council, 1986–91. Mem. Council, NT for Scotland, 1985–88; Dist Organiser, Moray and Banff, 1980–93; Mem. Exec. Cttee, 1987–93, Scotland's Garden Scheme. Chm., Queen Mary's Clothing Guild, 1990–93 (started Queen Mary's Clothing Guild in Scotland, 1986). Mem. Bd, Children's Hospice Assoc., Scotland, 1995–2002. Sunday Sch. teacher, Inveraven Ch, 1982–94. DL Banffshire, 1991–98. JP Aberdeenshire, 2003–07. Hon. MUniv Aberdeen, 2010. *Publications:* Favourite Recipes, Dried Flowers and Pot Pourri from Ballindalloch Castle, 1993; Favourite Puddings from Ballindalloch Castle, 1995; Favourite First Courses from Ballindalloch Castle, 1996; Favourite Recipes from Ballindalloch Castle, 1998; I Love Food, 2004; I Love Banffshire, 2009; I Love Food 2, 2012. *Recreations:* dog-handling, gardening, flower arranging, piano, tapestry, knitting, cooking, historic houses, antiques. *Address:* Ballindalloch Castle, Banffshire AB37 9AX. *T:* (01807) 500206. *Club:* Sloane.

RUSSELL, Dan Chapman; Sheriff of South Strathclyde, Dumfries and Galloway at Hamilton, 1992–2004; *b* 25 Dec. 1939; *s* of William Morris Russell and Isabella Ritchie Stein Scott; *m* 1969, Janet McNeil; three *d*. *Educ:* Airdrie Acad.; Glasgow Univ. (MA 1960; LLB 1963). Qualified as Solicitor, 1963; in private practice, 1963–92; Partner, Bell, Russell & Co., Solicitors, Airdrie, 1965–92; Temp. Sheriff, 1976–78 and 1985–92. Reporter, Airdrie Children's Panel, 1972–75. Mem. Council, Law Soc. of Scotland, 1975–84; Dean, Airdrie Soc. of Solicitors, 1986–88. *Recreations:* golf, bridge, walking.

RUSSELL, David Norman; Chief Executive Officer, Education and Training Foundation, since 2014; *b* Aberdeen, 6 May 1973; *s* of Norman George Fisher Russell and Margaret Jane Russell (*née* Dawson); *m* 2003, Zoe Elisabeth James; three *s*. *Educ:* Crieff Primary Sch.; Crieff High Sch.; St Andrews Univ. (MA Hons Ancient Hist. and Philosophy); Moray Hse Inst. of Educn (PGCE (Sec.)). Department for Children, Schools and Families, later Department for Education: Deputy Director: Adult Skills, 2004–08; Academies, 2008–09; Director: Apprenticeships, 2009–10; Curriculum and Behaviour Policy, 2010–11; Closing the Gap, 2012–14. *Recreations:* music, running and learning. *Address:* Education and Training Foundation, 157–197 Buckingham Palace Road, SW1W 9SP. *E:* david.russell@etfoundation.co.uk.

RUSSELL, Prof. Donald Andrew Frank Moore, FBA 1971; Fellow, St John's College, Oxford, 1948–88, now Emeritus; Professor of Classical Literature, Oxford, 1985–88; *b* 13 Oct. 1920; *s* of Samuel Charles Russell (schoolmaster) and Laura Moore; *m* 1967, Joycelyne Gledhill Dickinson (*d* 1993). *Educ:* King's College Sch., Wimbledon; Balliol Coll., Oxford (MA 1946); DLitt Oxon 1985. Served War: Army (R Signals and Intelligence Corps), 1941–45. Craven Scholar, 1946; Lectr, Christ Church, Oxford, 1947; St John's College, Oxford: Tutor, 1948–84; Dean, 1957–64; Tutor for Admissions, 1968–72; Reader in Class. Lit., Oxford Univ., 1978–85. Paddison Vis. Prof., Univ. of N Carolina at Chapel Hill, 1985; Vis. Prof. of Classics, Stanford Univ., 1989, 1991. Co-editor, Classical Quarterly, 1965–70. *Publications:* Commentary on Longinus, On the Sublime, 1964; Ancient Literary Criticism (with M. Winterbottom), 1972; Plutarch, 1972; (with N. G. Wilson) Menander Rhetor, 1981; Criticism in Antiquity, 1981; Greek Declamation, 1984; (ed) Antonine Literature, 1990; Commentary on Dio Chrysostom, Orations, 7, 12, 36, 1992; (trans.) Plutarch: selected essays and dialogues, 1993; (trans.) Libanius, Imaginary Speeches, 1996; (trans. and ed) Quintilian, 2001; (ed with D. Konstan) Heraclitus: Homeric problems, 2005; (trans. and ed with H. G. Nesselrath and others) Plutarch: on the daimonion of Socrates, 2010; (ed with R. Hunter) Plutarch: how to study poetry, 2011; (trans. and ed with H. G. Nesselrath and others) Synesius: *de insomniis*, 2014; articles and reviews in classical periodicals. *Address:* 35 Belsyre Court, Oxford OX2 6HU. *T:* (01865) 556135.

RUSSELL, Eileen Alison, (Lady Russell); *see* Mackay, E. A.

RUSSELL, Sir George, Kt 1992; CBE 1985; Deputy Chairman: Granada plc, 2002–04; ITV plc, 2004–09; *b* 25 Oct. 1935; *s* of William H. Russell and Frances A. Russell; *m* 1959, Dorothy Brown; three *d. Educ:* Gateshead Grammar Sch.; Durham Univ. (BA Hons). ICI, 1958–67 (graduate trainee, Commercial Res. Officer, Sales Rep., and Product Sales Man.); Vice President and General Manager: Welland Chemical Co. of Canada Ltd, 1968; St Clair Chemical Co. Ltd, 1968; Man. Dir, Alcan UK Ltd, 1976; Asst Man. Dir, 1977–81, Man. Dir, 1981–82, Alcan Aluminium (UK) Ltd; Man. Dir and Chief Exec., British Alcan Aluminium, 1982–86; Chief Exec., 1986–92, Chm., 1989–93, non-exec. Chm., 1993–97, Marley plc; Dir, 1992–2001, Chm., 1993–2001, 3i Gp plc; Chm., Camelot Gp plc, 1995–2002. Chairman: Luxfer Holdings Ltd, 1976–78; Alcan UK Ltd, 1978–82; Northern Develt Co., 1994–99; Director: Alcan Aluminiumwerke GmbH, Frankfurt, 1977–82; Northern Rock plc (formerly Bldg Soc.), 1985–2006; Alcan Aluminium Ltd, 1987–2000; Taylor Woodrow, 1992–2004; British Alcan plc, 1997–2001. Chairman: ITN, 1987–88; IBA, 1988–92 (Mem., 1979–86); ITC, 1991–96; Cable Authy, 1989–90; Dep. Chm., Channel Four TV, 1987–88. Visiting Professor, Univ. of Newcastle upon Tyne, 1978. Chm., IPPR North Commn on Public Sector Reform in NE, 2007–09; Member: Board, Northern Sinfonia Orchestra, 1977–80; Northern Industrial Development Board, 1977–80; Washington Development Corporation, 1978–80; Board, Civil Service Pay Research Unit, 1980–81; Megaw Inquiry into Civil Service Pay, 1981; Widdicombe Cttee of Inquiry into Conduct of Local Authority Business, 1985. Dir, 2002–08, Chm., 2011–, Wildfowl and Wetlands Trust. Trustee, Beamish Develt Trust, 1985–90. Dir, Digital Theatre, 2011–. Hon. DEng Newcastle upon Tyne, 1985; Hon. DBA Northumbria, 1992; Hon. LLD: Sunderland, 1995; Durham, 1997. *Recreations:* tennis, bird watching. *Club:* Garrick.

RUSSELL, George Thomas, FIA; Deputy Government Actuary (Director of Actuarial Operations), since 2009; *b* Glasgow, 11 Feb. 1962; *s* of John and Anne Russell; *m* 1988, Pamela McLachlan; one *s. Educ:* Hermitage Acad., Helensburgh; Strathallan Sch., Perthshire; Churchill Coll., Cambridge (BA 1983; MA 1987). FIA 1990. Actuarial Trainee, Coopers & Lybrand, 1983–84; Actuarial Trainee, then Consulting Actuary, Bacon & Woodrow, 1984–94; Government Actuary's Department: Actuary, 1994–99, Chief Actuary, 1999–2009, Pensions Policy, Demography and Stats Div.; Mem., Mgt Bd, 2008–. Hon. Treas., Inst. of Actuaries, 2005–08. *Recreations:* France, opera, cycling. *Address:* Government Actuary's Department, Finlaison House, 15–17 Furnival Street, EC4A 1AB. *T:* (020) 7211 2666, *Fax:* (020) 7211 2630. *E:* george.russell@gad.gov.uk. *Club:* Caledonian.

RUSSELL, Gerald Francis Morris, MD; FRCP, FRCPE, Hon. FRCPsych; Professor of Psychiatry, Institute of Psychiatry, University of London, and Physician, Bethlem Royal and Maudsley Hospital, 1979–93, now Professor Emeritus; Consultant Psychiatrist, Eating Disorders Unit, The Priory Hospital Hayes Grove, 1993–2014 (Director, 1993–2001); *b* Grammont, Belgium, 12 Jan. 1928; 2nd *s* of late Maj. Daniel George Russell, MC, and late Berthe Marie Russell (*née* De Boe); *m* 1950, Margaret Taylor, MB, ChB; three *s. Educ:* Collège St Jan Berchmans, Brussels; George Watson's Coll., Edinburgh (Dux); Univ. of Edinburgh (Mouat Schol. in Practice of Physic). MD (with commendation), 1957; DPM; FRCPE 1967; FRCP 1969; FRCPsych 1971. Hon. FRCPsych 1994. RAMC Regimental Med. Off., Queen's Bays, 1951–53; Neurological Registrar, Northern Gen. Hosp., Edin., 1954–56; MRC Clinical Res. Fellow, 1956–58; Inst. of Psychiatry, Maudsley Hospital: 1st Asst, 1959–60; Senior Lectr, 1961–70; Dean, 1966–70; Bethlem Royal and Maudsley Hospital: Physician, 1961–70; Mem. Bd of Governors, 1966–70; Mem., Special Health Authority, 1979–90; Prof. of Psychiatry, Royal Free Hosp. Sch. of Medicine, 1971–79. Chairman: Educn Cttee, Royal Medico-Psychological Assoc., 1970 (Mem. Council, 1966–71); Sect. on Eating Disorders, World Psychiatric Assoc., 1989–99; Assoc. of Univ. Teachers of Psychiatry, 1991–94; Sec. of Sect. of Psychiatry, Roy. Soc. Med., 1966–68 (Pres., 1998–99); Special Interest Gp on Eating Disorders, RCPsych, 1995–99; Mem., European Soc. for Clinical Investigation, 1968–72; Pres., Soc. for Psychosomatic Res., 1989–91. Corresp. Fellow, Amer. Psychiatric Assoc., 1967–2000. Member Editorial Boards: British Jl of Psychiatry, 1966–71; Psychological Medicine, 1970–2000; Jl Neurology, Neurosurgery and Psychiatry, 1971–75; Medical Education, 1975–84; Internat. Jl of Eating Disorders, 1981–2002. Mem., 1942 Club, 1978–. *Publications:* contrib. to Psychiatrie der Gegenwart, vol. 3, 1975; (ed jtly with L. Hersov and contrib.) Handbook of Psychiatry, vol. 4, The Neuroses and Personality Disorders, 1984; (contrib. and ed jtly) Anorexia Nervosa and Bulimic Disorders: current perspectives, 1985; (contrib.) Oxford Textbook of Medicine, 2nd edn, 1987; (contrib.) Handbook of Treatment for Eating Disorders, 2nd edn, 1997; (contrib.) New Oxford Textbook of Psychiatry, 2000, 2nd edn 2009; articles in med. jls on psychiatry, bulimia nervosa, anorexia nervosa, dyslexia, education and neurology. *Recreations:* art galleries, language, photography.

RUSSELL, Gerald William, FCA; President, Institute of Chartered Accountants in England and Wales, 2010–11 (Deputy President, 2009–10); *b* Twickenham, 21 May 1950; *s* of late Cyril and Elizabeth Russell; *m* 1976, Tessa (*d* 2009); one *s* four *d. Educ:* Ampleforth Coll. FCA 1973. With Ernst & Whinney, later Ernst & Young, 1969–2008: Partner, 1983–88; Man. Partner, S Reg., 1988–98; Man. Partner, London, 1998–2006; retd 2008. *Recreations:* sailing, golf, classic cars. *Address:* The White House, Castle Road, Weybridge, Surrey KT13 9QN. *T:* (01932) 84498. *E:* gwrussell1@gmail.com. *Clubs:* Aldeburgh Yacht, Aldeburgh Golf.

RUSSELL, Graham; *see* Russell, R. G. G.

RUSSELL, Graham R.; *see* Ross Russell.

RUSSELL, Ven. (Harold) Ian (Lyle); Archdeacon of Coventry, 1989–2000; Chaplain to the Queen, 1997–2004; *b* 17 Oct. 1934; *s* of Percy Harold and Emma Rebecca Russell; *m* 1961, Barbara Lillian Dixon; two *s* one *d. Educ:* Epsom College; London Coll. of Divinity (BD, ALCD). Shell Petroleum Co., 1951–53; RAF, Jan. 1953; RAF Regt, Nov. 1953–1956; London Coll. of Divinity, 1956–60; ordained, 1960; Curate of Iver, Bucks, 1960–63; Curate-in-charge of St Luke's, Lodge Moor, Parish of Fulwood, Sheffield, 1963–67; Vicar: St John's, Chapeltown, Sheffield, 1967–75; St Jude's, Mapperley, Nottingham, 1975–89. *Recreations:* walking, photography, sport, gardening. *Address:* 5 Old Acres, Woodborough, Nottingham NG14 6ES. *T:* (0115) 965 3543.

RUSSELL, Prof. Ian John, FRS 1989; Professor of Neurobiology, University of Brighton, since 2011; *b* 19 June 1943; *s* of Philip William George Russell and Joan Lillian Russell; *m* 1968, Janice Marion Russell (marr. diss. 2006); one *s* one *d. Educ:* Chatham Technical Sch.; Queen Mary Coll., London (BSc Zoology); Univ. of British Columbia (NATO Student; MSc Zool.); Univ. of Cambridge (SRC Student; Trinity Hall Res. Student; PhD Zool.). Res. Fellowship, Magdalene Coll., Cambridge, 1969–71; SRC Res. Fellowship, Cambridge, 1969–71; Royal Soc. Exchange Fellowship, King Gustav V Res. Inst., Stockholm, 1970–71; University of Sussex: Lectr in Neurobiology, 1971–79; Reader in Neurobiology, 1979–80 and 1982–87; Prof. of Neurobiol., 1987–2011. MRC Sen. Res. Fellow, 1980–82, 1995–98. Award of Merit, Assoc. for Res. in Otolaryngology, 2010. *Publications:* on the neurobiology of hearing, in learned jls. *Recreations:* hockey, windsurfing, reading, music, gardening, walking. *Address:* Little Ivy Cottage, Waldron, Heathfield, East Sussex TN21 0QX. *T:* (01435) 813382.

RUSSELL, Ian Simon MacGregor, CBE 2007; CA; Chairman: Remploy Ltd, since 2007; Johnston Press, since 2009 (non-executive Director, 2007–09); *b* 16 Jan. 1953; *s* of James MacGregor Russell and Christine Russell (*née* Clark); *m* 1975, Fiona Brown; one *s* one *d. Educ:* George Heriot's Sch., Edinburgh; Univ. of Edinburgh (BCom). Mem., ICAS, 1977. Auditor, Thomson McLintock, 1974–78; accountant, Mars Ltd, 1978–81; Controller, Pentos plc, 1981–83; Finance Dir, HSBC, 1983–90; Financial Controller, Tomkins plc, 1990–94; Finance Dir, 1994–99, Dep. Chief Exec., 1999–2001, Chief Exec., 2001–06, Scottish Power plc. Chm., Seeing is Believing Network, BITC. Chm., Russell Commn, 2004–05.

RUSSELL, Jack; *see* Russell, R. C.

RUSSELL, Jenni Cecily; newspaper columnist, since 2002; *b* Johannesburg, 16 July 1960; *d* of Martin Russell and Dr Margo Russell (*née* Phillips); *m* 1988, Stephen Lambert, *qv*; one *s* one *d. Educ:* City of Norwich Sch.; Maru-a-Pula Sch., Botswana; Wymondham Coll., Norfolk; St Catharine's Coll., Cambridge (BA Hons Hist. 1982). News trainee, 1985–87, Producer, World Service, 1987–88, BBC; Producer, 1989–92, Sen. Producer, 1992–94, Channel 4 News; Dep. Ed., Current Affairs, BBC Radio, 1994–97; Ed., The World Tonight, BBC Radio 4, 1997–2001; columnist on politics and social policy: Guardian, 2002–; Sunday Times, 2009–; Evening Standard, 2011–. Mem., Adv. Council, Demos, 2009–. Fellow, Young Foundn, 2006–. FRSA 2011. Orwell Prize for political journalism, 2011. *Recreations:* piano, ski-ing, entertaining friends. *E:* jennirussell01@gmail.com. *T:* 07711 032155.

RUSSELL, Jeremy Jonathan; QC 1994; *b* 18 Dec. 1950; *s* of Sidney Thomas Russell and Maud Eugenie Russell; *m* 1987, Gillian Elizabeth Giles; one *s* one *d. Educ:* Watford Boys' GS; City of London Poly. (BA); LSE (LLM). Lectr in Law, City of London Poly., 1973–80; called to the Bar, Middle Temple, 1975; in practice, 1977–. Lloyd's Salvage Arbitrator, 2000–05, 2009–. CEDR accredited mediator, 2001. *Recreations:* reading, gliding, classic cars. *Address:* Quadrant Chambers, Quadrant House, 10 Fleet Street, EC4Y 1AU.

RUSSELL, John Harry; Chairman and Chief Executive, Duport plc, 1981–86; *b* 21 Feb. 1926; *s* of Joseph Harry Russell and Nellie Annie Russell; *m* 1951, Iris Mary Cooke; one *s* one *d. Educ:* Halesowen Grammar Sch. FCA. War Service, RN. Joseph Lucas Ltd, 1948–52; Vono Ltd (Duport Gp Co.), 1952–59; Standard Motors Ltd, 1959–61; rejoined Duport Gp, 1961: Man. Dir, Duport Foundries Ltd, 1964; Dir, Duport Parent Bd, 1966; Chm., Burman & Sons Ltd (formerly part of Duport), 1968–72; Chief Exec., Duport Engrg Div., 1972–73; Dep. Gp Man. Dir, 1973–75; Gp Man. Dir, 1975–80, Dep. Chm., 1976–81, Duport plc. Chm., Blagg plc, 1994–95; non-exec. Dir, Birmingham Local Bd, Barclays Bank Ltd, 1976–88. Chm., Black Country Museum Trust Ltd, 1988–99. CBIM. Liveryman, Worshipful Co. of Glaziers and Freeman and Citizen of London, 1976. *Recreations:* reading, music, antiques. *Address:* 442 Bromsgrove Road, Hunnington, Halesowen, West Midlands B62 0JL.

RUSSELL, Mark Francis; Chief Executive, Shareholder Executive, Department for Business, Innovation and Skills, since 2013; *b* Manchester, 22 May 1960; *s* of Arthur Russell and Mary Russell; *m* 1991, Emma Wright; three *d. Educ:* Ampleforth Coll.; Univ. of Stirling (BA Hons Econs and Mgt Scis 1982); Cranfield Sch. of Mgt (MBA 1987). Associate, A. T. Kearney, 1982–85; Exec., Lazard Brothers & Co., 1985–86; Manager, Robert Fleming & Co., 1987–89; Dir, Coopers & Lybrand, later PricewaterhouseCoopers, 1989–2000; Partner, KPMG, 2000–04; Dir, 2004–07, Dep. Chief Exec., 2007–13, Shareholder Executive, BERR, later BIS. Non-executive Director: Working Links (Employment) Ltd, 2005–12; Eurostar Internat. Ltd, 2010–; London & Continental Railways, 2010–; BP World, 2014–. *Recreations:* cycling, photography, italic handwriting. *Address:* Shareholder Executive, Department for Business, Innovation and Skills, 1 Victoria Street, SW1H 0ET. *T:* (020) 7215 6897.

RUSSELL, Canon Mark Kenneth; Chief Executive, Church Army, since 2006 (Member, Board, since 2006); *b* 25 June 1974; *s* of Kenneth and Elizabeth Russell. *Educ:* Portadown Coll.; Queen's Univ., Belfast (LLB 1995). Proj. Exec., W. D. Irwin & Sons Ltd, 1995–97; Youth Pastor, Lurgan Methodist Ch, 1997–2000; Youth Minister, Christ Ch, Chorleywood, 2000–06. Member: Conf. of Methodist Ch in Ireland, 1996–98; Gen. Synod of C of E, 2005–11; Archbishops' Council, 2005–11; Marylebone Project Bd, 2006– (Chm., 2010–); Council, Evangelical Alliance, 2007–12; Coll. of Evangelists, 2008–; Mission and Public Affairs Council, C of E, 2011–; ACEVO, 2012–; Council of Reference for Youth for Christ, 2012–; Archbp's Task Gp, 2014–. Hon. Canon, Worcester Cath., 2011–. Gov., Talbot Special Sch., Sheffield, 2012–. Member: Christians on the Left (formerly Christian Socialist Movement), 2008–; Amnesty Internat. *Recreations:* theatre, cinema, supporter of Tottenham Hotspur FC. *Address:* Church Army, Wilson Carlile Centre, 50 Cavendish Street, Sheffield S3 7RZ. *T:* 0300 123 2113. *E:* ceo@churcharmy.org.uk.

RUSSELL, Sir Mervyn; *see* Russell, Sir (Arthur) M.

RUSSELL, Michael William; Member (SNP) Argyll and Bute, Scottish Parliament, since 2011 (Scotland South, 1999–2003 and 2007–11); Professor in Scottish Culture and Governance (part-time), University of Glasgow, since 2015; *b* 9 Aug. 1953; *s* of late Thomas Stevenson Russell and Jean Marjorie Russell (*née* Haynes); *m* 1980, Cathleen Ann Macaskill; one *s. Educ:* Marr Coll., Troon; Edinburgh Univ. (MA 1974). Creative Producer, Church of Scotland, 1974–77; Dir, Cinema Sgire, Western Isles Islands Council, 1977–81; Founder and Dir, Celtic Film and Television Fest., 1981–83; Exec. Dir, Network Scotland Ltd, 1983–91; Dir, Eala Bhan Ltd, 1991–2009; Chief Exec., SNP, 1994–99. Scottish Parliament: Opposition front bench spokesman for Parlt, 1999–2000, for children, educn and culture, 2000–03; Minister for Envmt, 2007–09, for Culture, External Affairs and Constitution, 2009; Cabinet Sec. for Educn and Lifelong Learning, 2009–14. Contested (SNP): Clydesdale, 1987; Cunninghame South, Scottish Parlt, 2003. Culture columnist, The Herald, 1999–2006; political columnist, Holyrood Mag., 2003–07; columnist, TES Scotland, 2004–07. FRSA 2007. *Publications:* (ed) Glasgow: the book, 1990; (ed) Edinburgh: a celebration, 1992; A Poem of Remote Lives: the enigma of Werner Kissling, 1997; In Waiting: travels in the shadow of Edwin Muir, 1998; A Different Country, 2002; (ed) Stop the World, 2004; (with Dennis MacLeod) Grasping the Thistle, 2006; The Next Big Thing, 2007; (with Iain McKie) The Price of Innocence, 2007. *Recreations:* cooking, tending my garden. *Address:* Scottish Parliament, Edinburgh EH99 1SP; Feorlean, Glendaruel, Argyll PA22 3AH.

RUSSELL, Muir; *see* Russell, A. M. G.

RUSSELL, Sir Muir; *see* Russell, Sir Alastair M.

RUSSELL, Ven. Norman Atkinson; Archdeacon of Berkshire, 1998–2013; *b* 7 Aug. 1943; *s* of Norman Gerald Russell and Olive Muriel Russell (*née* Williamson); *m* 1974, Victoria Christine Jasinska; two *s. Educ:* Royal Belfast Academical Instn; Churchill Coll., Cambridge (BA 1965; MA 1969); London Coll. of Divinity (BD London 1970). Articled Clerk, Coopers & Lybrand, 1966–67; ordained deacon, 1970, priest, 1971; Curate: Christ Church with Emmanuel, Clifton, Bristol, 1970–74; Christ Church, Cockfosters, and pt-time Chaplain, Middx Poly., 1974–77; Rector, Harwell with Chilton, 1977–84; Priest in Charge: St James, Gerrards Cross, 1984–88; St James, Fulmer, 1985–88; Rector, Gerrards Cross and Fulmer, 1988–98; RD, Amersham, 1996–98. Vice-Chm., Ecumenical Council for Corporate Responsibility, 1999–2002. Member: Gen. Synod, C of E, 2002–10; Archbishops' Council, C of E, 2005–10. Prolocutor, Lower House of the Convocation of Canterbury, 2005–10. *Publications:* Censorship, 1972. *Recreations:* downland walking, watching Rugby football. *Address:* 47a Theobalds Way, Camberley, Surrey GU16 9RF. *T:* (01276) 64110.

RUSSELL, Pam; *see* Ayres, P.

RUSSELL, Paul Anthony Wellington; QC 2011; *b* London, 4 Dec. 1961; *s* of Anthony Russell, MRCOG, MRCS and Jilly Russell (*née* Pengilley); *m* 1989, Sara Young; two *d. Educ:* Taunton Sch.; Durham Univ. (BA Hons Law). Called to the Bar, Middle Temple, 1984.

Recreations: family, golf, Rugby Union, Cornwall, Youth Offending Team of London Borough of Wandsworth. *Address:* 12 King's Bench Walk, Temple, EC4Y 7EL. *T:* (020) 7583 0811. *E:* russell@12kbw.co.uk. *Clubs:* Wimbledon Park Golf, Rosslyn Park Rugby Football.

RUSSELL, Prof. Philip St John, DPhil; FRS 2005; Alfried Krupp von Bohlen und Halbach Professor, Institute for Optics, Information and Photonics, University of Erlangen-Nuremberg, since 2005; a Director, Max-Planck Institute for Science of Light, Erlangen, Germany, since 2009; *b* 25 March 1953; *s* of Edward Augustine Russell and Emily Frances Russell (*née* Stevenson); *m* 1981, Alison Rosemary Bennett; two *s*. *Educ:* Royal Belfast Academical Instn; Magdalen Coll., Oxford (BA 1976; MA, DPhil 1979). Hayward Jun. Res. Fellow, Oriel Coll., Oxford, 1978–81; Alexander von Humboldt Fellow, Technische Universität Hamburg-Harburg, 1981–83; World Trade Vis. Scientist, IBM TJ Watson Res. Center, NY, 1983, 1985; Professeur Associé, Univ. de Nice, 1985, 1986; Lectr, then Reader, Univ. of Southampton, 1986–89, 1991–96; Reader, Univ. of Kent, 1989–90; Prof. of Physics, Univ. of Bath, 1996–2009. Chief Tech. Officer and Founder, BlazePhotonics Ltd, 2000–04. Fellow, Optical Soc. of America, 2000 (Joseph Fraunhofer Award, Robert M. Burley Prize, 2000). Wolfson Res. Merit Award, Royal Soc., 2004–05; Dist. Lectr, IEEE Lasers and Electro-Optics Soc., 2004–06. Applied Optics Div. Prize, 2002, Thomas Young Prize, 2005, Inst. of Physics; Körber Prize for Eur. Sci., 2005. *Publications:* approaching 600 papers in learned jls and scientific confs. *Recreations:* classical and jazz piano playing, music composition and improvisation, art, reading. *Address:* Max-Planck Institute for Science of Light, Guenther-Scharowsky-Strasse 1, 91058 Erlangen, Germany. *E:* philip.russell@mpl.mpg.de.

RUSSELL, Dame Philippa (Margaret), DBE 2009 (CBE 2001; OBE 1998); Chair, Standing Commission on Carers, Department of Health, 2007–14; *b* Sheffield, 4 Feb. 1938; *d* of Garth Rivers Stoneham, FRCOG and Nancy Wooler Stoneham (*née* Leslie); *m* 1959, Dr Alan Keith Russell, *qv*; two *s* one *d*. *Educ:* Barrow-in-Furness Grammar Sch. for Girls; St Hilda's Coll., Oxford (BA Modern Hist.). Develt Officer, Council for Children's Welfare, 1968–76; Dir, Council for Disabled Children, 1976–2003; Disability Policy Advr, Nat. Children's Bureau, 2003–07; Disability Advr, DFES, 2003–05. Member: Nat. Disability Council, 1996–2000; Disability Rights Task Force, 1997–99. Trustee: Family Fund, 1998–2004; Mental Health Foundn, 2001–07; Nat. Develt Team for Inclusion, 2008–; Chair of Trustees, MOVE, 2000–. Hon. FRCPCH 1993; Hon. FRCPsych 2012; Hon. Fellow, Univ. of Central Lancs, 1988. Hon. Dr: York, 1998; Lincoln, 2013. Rose Fitzgerald Kennedy Centenary Internat. Award, 1990; Lifetime Achievement Award, RADAR, 2005. *Publications:* The Wheelchair Child, 1978 (Oddfellows Prize, Oddfellows Friendly Soc., 1979) (trans. 8 langs); articles and contribs on disabled children, family support, disability, social care and carers issues. *Recreations:* music, reading, the family. *Address:* c/o National Children's Bureau, 8 Wakley Street, EC1V 7QE. *T:* (020) 7843 9708. *E:* prussell@ncb.org.uk.

RUSSELL, Robert Charles, (Jack), MBE 1996; cricketer; international artist; *b* 15 Aug. 1963; *s* of late Derek John Russell and of Jennifer Russell; *m* 1985, Aileen Ann Dunn; two *s* three *d*. *Educ:* Uplands Co. Primary Sch.; Archway Comprehensive Sch. Played for Glos CCC, 1981–2004; internat. début, England *v* Pakistan, 1987; played 54 Test Matches and 40 One-day Internationals; world record (11) for dismissals in a Test Match, England *v* SA, Johannesburg, 1995; record for dismissals (27) in a Test series for England, England *v* SA, 1995–96; retd from internat. cricket, 1998. Opened Jack Russell Gall., Chipping Sodbury, 1992; paintings sold and displayed in museums and collections worldwide; commissions include: We Will Remember Them, for RRF, in Tower of London; The Ten Field Marshals of the British Army, for Army Benevolent Fund, in Nat. Army Museum; Cricket World Cup Final, 1999, Australia *v* Pakistan, for NatWest Bank; Ashes Series 2005; Legal London series; portraits include: Duke of Edinburgh; Duke of Kent; Eric Clapton; Sir Norman Wisdom. *Publications:* A Cricketer's Art: sketches by Jack Russell, 1988; (illustr.) Sketches of a Season, 1989; Jack Russell's Sketch Book, 1996; Jack Russell: unleashed (autobiog.), 1997; The Art of Jack Russell: a collection of paintings, 1999; New Horizons: a collection of paintings, 2006; Eighteen Counties: a collection of cricket paintings and sketches, 2013. *Address:* Jack Russell Gallery, 41 High Street, Chipping Sodbury, S Glos BS37 6BA. *T:* (01454) 329583, *Fax:* (01454) 329683.

RUSSELL, Sir Robert Edward, (Sir Bob), Kt 2012; *b* 31 March 1946; *s* of late Ewart Russell and Muriel Russell (*née* Sawdy); *m* 1967, Audrey Blandon; twin *s* one *d* (and one *d* decd). *Educ:* Myland Primary Sch., Colchester; St Helena Secondary Modern Sch., Colchester; NE Essex Technical Coll. Reporter, Essex County Standard and Colchester Gazette, 1963–66; News Editor, Braintree & Witham Times, 1966–68; Editor, Maldon & Burnham Standard, 1968–69; Sub-Editor, London Evening News, 1969–72; Sub-Editor, London Evening Standard, 1972–73; Press Officer, Post Office Telecommunications, subseq. British Telecom (Eastern Reg.), 1973–85; Publicity Officer, Univ. of Essex, 1986–97. Mem., Colchester BC, 1971–2002 (Lab 1971–81, SDP 1981–88, Lib Dem 1988–2002) (Mayor, 1986–87). MP (Lib Dem) Colchester, 1997–2015; contested (Lib Dem) same seat, 2015. *Recreation:* promoting the interests of the town of Colchester. *Club:* Colchester Gala Bingo.

RUSSELL, Prof. (Robert) Graham (Goodwin), PhD, DM; FRCP, FRCPath, FMedSci; FRS 2008; Professor of Musculoskeletal Pharmacology, Nuffield Department of Orthopaedics, Rheumatology and Musculoskeletal Sciences (formerly Nuffield Department of Orthopaedic Surgery), University of Oxford, since 2006 (Norman Collisson Professor of Musculoskeletal Science, 2000–06); Fellow of St Peter's College, Oxford, 2001–07, now Emeritus; Professor of Musculoskeletal Pharmacology, Mellanby Centre for Bone Research, University of Sheffield Medical School, since 2009; *b* 16 Feb. 1941; *s* of Charles Chambers Russell and Mary (*née* Goodwin); *m* 1960, Diana Mary (*née* Allfrey); one *s* three *d*. *Educ:* Clare Coll., Cambridge (BA 1962; MA 1966; MB BChir 1971); PhD Leeds 1967; DM Oxon 1975. MRCP 1974, FRCP 1981; MRCPath 1974, FRCPath 1986. MRC Unit, Leeds, 1962–65; Res. Fellow, Swiss Res. Inst., Davos, 1965–67; Med. Student, Clinical Sch., Oxford Univ., 1967–71; House Officer posts, Radcliffe Infirmary, Oxford, 1972–73; Med. Res. Fellow, St Peter's Coll., Oxford, 1973–76; Sen. Lectr, 1976–77, Prof. and Head of Dept of Human Metabolism and Clin. Biochemistry, 1977–2000, Sheffield Univ.; Dir, Botnar Res. Centre (Oxford Univ. Inst. of Musculoskeletal Scis), 2002–07; Head, Nuffield Dept of Orthopaedic Surgery, Oxford Univ., 2003–06. Sen. Lectr, Univ. Bern, 1970–71; Asst Prof. of Medicine, Harvard Med. Sch., 1974–75. Chm., Nat. Osteoporosis Soc., 2000–02 (Kohn Award, 2000). President: Internat. Bone and Mineral Soc., 1998–2001 (Gaillard Award, 2007); Paget's Assoc., 2009–. FMedSci 2001. Hon. MD Sheffield, 2003. John B. Johnson Award, Paget's Foundn, USA, 1997; Neuman Award, Amer. Soc. of Bone and Mineral Metabolism, 2000; Dent Award, Bone Res. Soc. UK, 2013; Rodan Award, Amer. Soc. of Bone and Mineral Metabolism, 2014; Horton Award, Eur. Soc. Calcified Tissues, 2015. *Publications:* contribs to learned jls and books. *Recreations:* fishing, ski-ing, nature, third generation. *Address:* Oxford University Institute of Musculoskeletal Sciences, Botnar Research Centre, Nuffield Department of Orthopaedics, Rheumatology and Musculoskeletal Sciences, Nuffield Orthopaedic Centre, Windmill Road, Headington, Oxford OX3 7LD; 20 Feilden Grove, Headington, Oxford OX3 0DU. *E:* graham.russell@ndorms.ox.ac.uk.

RUSSELL, (Ronald) Christopher (Gordon), FRCS; Consultant Surgeon: Middlesex Hospital, 1975–2005; King Edward VII Hospital, since 1985; *b* 15 May 1940; *s* of Rognvald Gordon Russell, OBE and Doris Isa Russell (*née* Troup); *m* 1965, Mary Ruth Pitcher; two *s* (and one *s* decd). *Educ:* Epsom College; Middlesex Hosp. Med. Sch. (MB BS, MS). Sen. Lectr in Surgery, St Mary's Hosp., 1973–75. Medical Advr, Nuffield Hosps, 1988–2003; Civilian Medical Advr, RN, 2002–08. Member Council: Med. Defence Union, 1996–; RCS, 1999–2008 (Chm., Ct of Examnrs, 1997–99; Vice-Pres., 2006–08); Pres., Assoc. of Upper Gastrointestinal Surgeons, 1998–2000; Pres., Assoc. of Surgeons of GB and Ire., 2001–02. Chm., Jt Cttee on Inter-Collegiate Examinations, 2000–04. Chm., British Jl of Surgery Soc. Ltd, 1996–04; Associate Editor, 1978, Co-Editor, 1986–91, British Jl of Surgery; Gen. Editor, Operative Surgery, 1986–. Hon. FRCPSGlas 2005; Hon. FRCSI 2009; Hon. FFGDP(UK) 2009. Cheselden Medal, RCS, 2009. *Publications:* (ed) Recent Advances in Surgery, vol. XI 1982, vol. XII 1985, vol. XIII 1991; (ed jtly) Bailey & Love Textbook of Surgery, 1991–2005; numerous contribs to surgical and gastroenterological jls. *Recreation:* travel. *Address:* Grey Roofs, 34 West Common, Gerrards Cross SL9 7RE. *T:* (01753) 882264. *Club:* Royal Society of Medicine.

RUSSELL, Sally Joy; *see* Feldman, S. J.

RUSSELL, Stephen George; Chief Executive, The Boots Co., 2000–03; *b* 13 March 1945; *s* of Llandel and Olive Russell; *m* 1969, Elizabeth Jane Brook; one *s* one *d*. *Educ:* Tiffin Sch., Kingston upon Thames; Trinity Hall, Cambridge (BA Hons Classics). Joined Boots 1967; Dir of Merchandise, Boots The Chemists, 1988–92; Managing Dir, Do It All Ltd, 1992–95; Man. Dir, Boots The Chemists, 1995–2000; Jt Gp Man. Dir, Boots Co., 1997–2000. Non-executive Director: Woolwich plc, 1998–2000; Barclays Bank plc, 2000–09; Business Control Solutions Gp, 2005– (Chm., 2007–); Network Rail Ltd, 2007–12. Trustee, Tommy's the Baby Charity, 2003–. Mem. Council, Nottingham Univ., 2003–. *Recreations:* sport, classical music, opera, reading. *Club:* Hawks (Cambridge).

RUSSELL, Thomas, CMG 1980 CBE 1970 (OBE 1963); HM Overseas Civil Service, retired; Representative of the Cayman Islands in UK, 1982–2000; *b* 27 May 1920; *s* of late Thomas Russell, OBE, MC and Margaret Thomson Russell; *m* 1951, Andrée Irma Désfossés (*d* 1989); (one *s* decd). *Educ:* Hawick High Sch.; St Andrews Univ.; Peterhouse, Cambridge. MA St Andrews; Dip. Anthrop. Cantab. War Service, Cameronians (Scottish Rifles), 1941; 5th Bn (Scottish), Parachute Regt, 1943: served in N Africa and Italy; POW, 1944; Captain 1945; OC Parachute Trng Company, 1946. Cambridge Univ., 1946–47. Colonial Admin. Service, 1948; District Comr, British Solomon Is Protectorate, 1948; Asst Sec., Western Pacific High Commn, Fiji, 1951; District Comr, British Solomon Is Protectorate, 1954–56; seconded Colonial Office, 1956–57; Admin. Officer Class A, 1956; Dep. Financial Sec., 1962; Financial Sec., 1965; Chief Sec. to W Pacific High Commn, 1970–74; Governor of the Cayman Islands, 1974–81. Member Council: Pacific Islands Soc. of UK and Ire., 1986–2000 (Chm., 1982–86); Royal Commonwealth Ex Services League (formerly British Commonwealth Ex Services League), 1982– (Chm., Welfare Cttee, 1993–2005; Vice Pres., 2012–); Chm., Dependent Territories Assoc., 1997–98. FRAI. *Publications:* I Have The Honour To Be, 2003. *Recreations:* anthropology, archæology. *Address:* Hassendean, Gattonside, Melrose TD6 9NA. *Club:* Caledonian.

RUSSELL, William Martin, (Willy); author, since 1971; *b* 23 Aug. 1947; *s* of William and Margery Russell; *m* 1969, Ann Seagroatt; one *s* two *d*. *Educ:* St Katharine's Coll. of Educn, Liverpool, 1970–73 (Cert. of Educn). Ladies' Hairdresser, 1963–69; Teacher, 1973–74; Fellow in Creative Writing, Manchester Polytechnic, 1977–78. Founder Mem., and Dir, Quintet Films; Hon. Dir, Liverpool Playhouse. *Theatre:* Blind Scouse (3 short plays), 1971–72; When the Reds (adaptation), 1972; John, Paul, George, Ringo and Bert (musical), 1974; Breezeblock Park, 1975; One for the Road, 1976; Stags and Hens, 1978; Educating Rita, 1979; Blood Brothers (musical), 1983; Our Day Out (musical), 1983; Shirley Valentine, 1986; *television plays:* King of the Castle, 1972; Death of a Young, Young Man, 1972; Break In (for schools), 1974; Our Day Out, 1976; Lies (for schools), 1977; Daughters of Albion, 1978; Boy with Transistor Radio (for schools), 1979; One Summer (series), 1980; *radio play:* I Read the News Today (for schools), 1976; *screenplays:* Band on the Run, 1979 (not released); Educating Rita, 1981; Shirley Valentine, 1988; Dancing Through the Dark, 1989. Hon. MA Open Univ., 1983; Hon. DLit Liverpool, 1990. *Publications:* Breezeblock Park, 1978; One for the Road, 1980, rev. edn 1985; Educating Rita, 1981; Our Day Out, 1984; Stags and Hens, 1985; Blood Brothers, 1985 (also pubd as short non-musical version for schools, 1984); Shirley Valentine, 1989; The Wrong Boy (novel), 2000; several other plays included in general collections of plays; songs and poetry. *Recreations:* playing the guitar, composing songs, gardening, cooking. *Address:* c/o Casarotto Company Ltd, Waverley House, 7–12 Noel Street, W1F 8GQ. *T:* (020) 7287 4450. *Club:* Athenæum (Liverpool).

RUSSELL BEALE, Simon; *see* Beale.

RUSSELL-COBB, Piers Andrew Conrad; Founder, Media Fund Ltd, since 1991; *b* Geneva, 14 Oct. 1953; *s* of Trevor Russell-Cobb and Nancy Florence Russell-Cobb (*née* Stanley-Hughes); *m* 1982, Sophia Melissa Jane, *d* of Sir Robin Chichester-Clark, *qv*; two *s*. *Educ:* Westminster Sch.; New Coll., Oxford (BA 1975; MA 1980). Chatto, Bodley Head and Cape Services, 1975–77; writer and screenwriter, NY and LA; Exec. Ed., Marshall Editions, 1978; Internat. Mktg Manager, Thames and Hudson Ltd, 1979–87; Publicity and Promotions Dir, Reed Publishing Gp, 1987–90; Asst Dir, Ansbacher Media Ltd, 1990–91; Publisher, City Limits magazine, 1991. Owner, Arcadia Books Ltd, 2012–. Ambassador, 2010–, Mem., Develt Cttee, 2011–14, RADA. Trustee, Music in Country Churches, 2000–11. Liveryman: Merchant Taylors' Co., 1990; Stationers' and Newspaper Makers' Co., 2009. *Publications:* Great Chefs of France (with Quentin Crewe), 1978; contrib. publishing and media mags; cookery book reviewer. *Recreations:* reading, music, fishing, food and drink. *Address:* Media Fund Ltd, 139 Highlever Road, W10 6PH. *T:* (020) 8960 4967. *E:* prc@mediafund.co.uk. *Clubs:* Academy, Blacks, Beefsteak, Century, Groucho.

RUSSELL FLINT, Simon Coleridge; QC 2003; a Recorder of the Crown Court, since 2000; *b* 8 Oct. 1957; *s* of late Francis Murray Russell Flint and of Susan Mary Russell Flint (*née* Sumner); *m* 1983, Jacqueline Ann Verden; one *s* one *d*. *Educ:* Cranleigh Sch.; Polytechnic of Central London (BA Hons Law); Inns of Court Sch. of Law. Called to the Bar, Inner Temple, 1980; Asst Recorder, 1998–2000; Hd of Chambers, 2009–. A Chm., Police Discipline Appeals Tribunal, 2003–. Chm., Kent Bar Mess, 2004. Gov., St George's Sch., Wrotham, 1996–. *Recreations:* tennis, ski-ing, Liverpool Football Club, armchair sport. *Address:* 23 Essex Street, WC2R 3AA. *T:* (020) 7413 0353, *Fax:* (020) 7413 0374. *E:* srf@23es.com.

RUSSELL-JONES, Maj. Gen. (Peter) John, OBE 1988; Army Adviser to BAE Systems, since 2001; *b* 31 May 1948; *s* of Peter Rathbone Russell-Jones and Margaret Silis Russell-Jones; *m* 1976, Stella Margaret Barrett; one *s* one *d*. *Educ:* Wellington Coll.; RMCS (BScEng Hons 1972). Commnd RE, 1968; Regtl duty, 1972–79; Army Staff Coll., 1979–80; MA to Master Gen. of the Ordnance, 1986–88; CO 23 Engr Regt, 1988–90; Col, Defence Policy, MoD, 1990–91; Comdt, Royal Mil. Sch. of Engrg, 1992–95; rcds, 1995; Dir, Internat. Orgns, MoD, 1996–97; ACDS, Operational Requirements (Land Systems), MoD, 1997–99; Capability Manager (Manoeuvre), MoD, 1999–2001. *Recreations:* travel, rock and roll, family, golf. *Address:* Regimental HQ RE, Brompton Barracks, Chatham, Kent ME4 4UG.

RUSSELL-SMITH, Penelope, CVO 2007 (LVO 2000); voluntary worker, since 2007; Deputy Superintendent Registrar, Gloucestershire, since 2013; *b* 22 Oct. 1956; *d* of late Denham William Russell-Smith and of Barbara Cynthia Russell-Smith. *Educ:* Sherborne Sch. for Girls; Girton Coll., Cambridge (MA). Dep. Editor, Whitaker's Almanack, 1980–81; Editor of Navy and Army publications, MoD, 1982–84; MoD Press Office (incl. Falkland Is, 1986), 1984–88; Chief Press Officer, Dept of Transport, 1988–90; EU Desk, News Dept, FCO, 1990–93; Asst Press Sec., 1993–97, Dep. Press Sec., 1997–2000, Press Sec., 2000–02, Communications and Press Sec., 2002–07, to the Queen; Dir of External Relations, AQ

Research, 2007–08. Trustee, RBL Poppy Factory, 2008–10; Volunteer: Nat. Trust, 2009–; RVS (formerly WRVS), 2010–14. *Address:* Tree House, 2 Hetton Gardens, Charlton Kings, Glos GL53 8HU.

RUSSEN, Jonathan Huw Sinclair; QC 2010; barrister; *b* Newport, S Wales, 26 Feb. 1963; *s* of Peter John Sinclair Russen and Ruth Cecilia Russen (*née* Warren); *m* 1990, Gaynor Jacqueline Couch; one *s* one *d*. *Educ:* St Julian's Comp. Sch., Newport; University Coll. of Wales, Aberystwyth (LLB 1984); Sidney Sussex Coll., Cambridge (LLM 1985). Called to the Bar, Lincoln's Inn, 1986; in practice as barrister at Chancery Bar, 1988–. Mem., British Assoc. for Shooting and Conservation. *Publications:* Financial Services: a litigator's guide, 2006. *Recreations:* my dogs, cycling, Rugby (especially Welsh hegemony thereof). *Address:* Maitland Chambers, 7 Stone Buildings, Lincoln's Inn, WC2A 3SZ.

RUSSILL, Patrick Joseph; Director of Music, London Oratory, since 1999; Head of Choral Conducting (formerly Choral Direction and Church Music), since 1997, and Professor of Organ, since 1999, Royal Academy of Music; *b* 9 Sept. 1953; *e s* of John Leonard Russill and Vera Mary Russill (*née* Clarke); *m* 1979, Jane Mary Rogers; two *s* three *d*. *Educ:* Shaftesbury Grammar Sch.; New Coll., Oxford (Organ Schol.; BA 1st Cl. Hons 1975; MA). ARCO 1971. Asst Organist, 1976–77, Organist, 1977–99, London Oratory; Dir, Oxford Chamber Choir, 1976–79; organist for Papal Mass, Wembley Stadium, 1982; Prof. of Acad. Studies, 1982–87, Hd of Ch Music, 1987–97, RAM; Director: London Oratory Jun. Choir, 1984–2003; Europa Singers of London, 1985–89. RFH recital début, 1986; appearances as organist and conductor in UK, Europe, Near East and Asia; has made recordings. Visiting Lecturer: St George's Coll., Jerusalem, 1994–95; Malmö Coll. of Music, Sweden, 1994; Sibelius Acad., Helsinki, 2013; Vis. Lectr, 1999, Vis. Prof. of Choral Conducting, 2001–, Leipzig Hochschule für Musik und Theater. External Examiner: UEA, 1991–97; Univ. of Leeds, 2003–05; Univ. of Sheffield, 2013; Ext. Moderator, Archbps' Cert., Guild of Ch Musicians, 1997–2002; Chief Examr, RCO, 2005–; Adjudicator, Llangollen Internat. Eisteddfod, 2008–11. Mem. Council, RCO, 1996–2009. Trustee: Ch Music Soc., 1990–; Organists Charitable Trust (formerly Organists' Benevolent League), 1994–; Nicholas Danby Trust, 1998–. Organ restoration consultant, incl. St Dominic's Priory, London, 1992, Ely Cathedral, 1997–2001. Vice-Pres., Herbert Howells Soc., 2007– (Hon. Patron, 1993–2007). Hon. Mem., Cathedral Organists' Assoc., 2012. Hon. RAM 1993 (Hon. ARAM 1989); Hon. FGCM 1997; Hon. FRCO 2002. *Publications:* (musical ed.) The Catholic Hymn Book, 1998; (contrib.) The Cambridge Companion to the Organ, 1998; Geschichte der Kirchenmusik, 2011; (ed) Sweelinck and Howells choral works; contrib. articles and reviews in Gramophone, Musical Times, Organists' Rev., Choir and Organ, British Inst. Organ Studies Jl, RCO Year Book. *Recreations:* family photography, rural open air. *Address:* 65 Sandford Avenue, Wood Green, N22 5EJ.

RUSSON, David, CPhys, FInstP; Deputy Chief Executive, British Library, 1996–2001; *b* 12 June 1944; *s* of Thomas Charles Russon and Violet Russon (*née* Jarvis); *m* 1967, Kathleen Mary Gregory; one *s* two *d*. *Educ:* Wellington Grammar Sch.; University College London (BSc); Univ. of York. CPhys, FInstP 2000. Various appts, Office for Scientific and Technical Information, DES, 1969–74; British Library: R & D Dept, 1974–75; Lending Div., 1975–85; Dir, Document Supply Centre, 1985–88; Dir Gen., Sci., Technol. and Industry, later Boston Spa, 1988–96; Mem., British Liby Bd, 1988–2001. Pres., Internat. Council for Scientific and Technical Information, 1995–2001 (Vice Pres., 1992–95). FCLIP. *Publications:* contribs to professional jls of library and inf. science. *Recreations:* golf, bridge, village tennis and badminton. *Address:* March House, Tollerton, York YO61 1QQ. *T:* (01347) 838253.

RUST, Prof. John Neville, PhD; CPsychol; FSS, FBPsS; Director, Psychometrics Centre, University of Cambridge, since 2008; Senior Member, Darwin College, Cambridge, since 2009; *b* Scunthorpe, 25 Nov. 1943; *s* of John Cyprian Walcot Rust and Frances Mary Rust; *m* 1979, Prof. Susan Esther Golombok, *qv*; one *s*, and one *d* by a previous partner. *Educ:* Cirencester Grammar Sch.; Birkbeck Coll., Univ. of London (BSc 1st Cl. Hons Psychol., Statistics and Computer Sci. 1970; MA Philos. 1976); Inst. of Psychiatry, Univ. of London (PhD 1974). CPsychol 1982. University of London: Researcher and Lectr, Inst. of Psychiatry, 1972–76; Institute of Education: Lectr, then Sen. Lectr in Psychometrics, 1976–91; Hd, Dept of Child Develt and Educnl Psychol., 1984–87; Senator for Faculty of Educn, 1983–87; Sen. Lectr, then Reader in Psychometrics, Goldsmiths Coll., 1991–2002; Prof. of Psychometrics, City Univ., London, 2002–05; Dir, Psychometrics Centre, Cambridge Assessment, 2005–08. Visiting Academic: Univ. of Jos, 1979 and 1980; De La Salle Univ., Manila, 1986. Fellow, Amer. Acad. of Assessment Psychol., 1993. Freeman, City of London, 1986. Founder Editor, Philosophical Psychology, 1988. Author of and UK standardisations of psychometric tests. FSS 1976; FBPsS 1985. *Publications:* Modern Psychometrics (with S. E. Golombok), 1989, 3rd edn 2009; articles in learned jls. *Recreations:* astrophysics, promoting diversity and multiculturalism, genealogy, internet, cooking, films. *Address:* Psychometrics Centre, University of Cambridge, 17 Mill Lane, Cambridge CB2 1RX. *T:* (01223) 769483. *E:* jnr24@cam.ac.uk.

RUST, Nicholas John; Chief Executive, British Horseracing Authority, since 2015; *b* Wallsend, Tyne and Wear, 14 June 1967; *s* of John Oubridge Rust and Carole Margaret Rust; *m* 1993, Margarita Victoria Shoebridge; one *s*. *Educ:* Berwick upon Tweed Co. High Sch. Ladbrokes plc: Trainee Shop Manager, 1987–88; Shop Manager, 1988–89; District Supervisor, 1990–94; Area Manager, 1994–97; Regl Controller, 1997–98; Mktg Dir, 1998–99; Commercial Dir, eGaming, 2000–02; Managing Director: Sky Bet-BSkyB, 2002–07; Coral, 2007–10; Retail, Ladbrokes plc, 2010–14. Mem., Bookmakers' Cttee, Horserace Betting Levy Bd, 2007–10 and 2011–14. Mem., Mensa 2008. *Recreations:* golf, philately, racehorse ownership. *Address:* British Horseracing Authority, 75 High Holborn, WC1V 6LS. *T:* (020) 7152 0000. *E:* nrust@britishhorseracing.com.

RUST, Susan Esther; *see* Golombok, S. E.

RUTHERFORD, Adam David, PhD; Video Editor, Nature, 2002–13; *b* 16 Jan. 1975; *m* 2011, Georgia Murray; one *s* one *d*. *Educ:* Ipswich Sch.; University Coll. London (BSc 1997); Inst. of Child Health, Univ. of London (PhD Genetics 2001). Presenter, BBC Television: The Cell, 2009; The Gene Code, 2011; Horizon (episode), 2012; The Beauty of Anatomy, 2014; presenter, Radio 4 and World Service progs. Journalist, various publications incl. The Guardian. *Publications:* Creation: the origin and future of life, 2013. *Recreations:* cricket, cinema, eating and drinking. *E:* adam.rutherford@gmail.com. *Club:* Celeriac XI Cricket (Founder Mem.).

RUTHERFORD, Prof. Alfred William, (Bill), PhD; FRS 2014; Professor of Biochemistry of Solar Energy, Imperial College London, since 2011; *b* Morpeth, Northumberland, 2 Jan. 1955; *s* of Stanley Rutherford and Patricia Rutherford; *m* 1980, Agnes Vega (separated 2003); one *d*. *Educ:* King Edward VI Grammar Sch. for Boys, Morpeth; Univ. of Liverpool (BSc Hons Biochem. 1976); University Coll. London (PhD Microbiol. (Biophys) 1979). Post Grad. Student, Dept of Botany and Microbiol., UCL, 1976–79; Post Doctoral Associate, Dept of Biophys and Physiol., Univ. of Illinois, Urbana, 1979–81; CEN Saclay, then CEA Saclay: Post Doctoral Fellow, 1982–83, Gp Leader, 1985–2011, Dépt de Biologie, Service de Biophysique; Dir, Res. Unit 1290, Service de Bioénergétique, CNRS, 1992–96; Hd, Service de Bioénergétique, Dept Biologie Joliot-Curie; Dir, Nat. Res. Prog. on 'Photosynthèse Membranaire', 2000–04; Hd, Lab. of Biophys of Oxidative Stress Service de Bioénergétique, Dept Biologie Cellulaire et Moleculaire, 2001–07; Hd, Lab. of Molecular Bioenergetics and Photosynthesis, Inst. of Biol. and Technol. Saclay, 2007–11; Directeur de Recherche, CNRS, 2ème classe, 1988–92, 1ère classe, 1992–2009, Classe Exceptionelle, 2009–11 (en détachement, 2011–). Vis. Res. Scientist, Solar Energy Lab., RIKEN, Saitama, Japan, 1982, 1983; Vis. Prof. of Chem., 2005, Vis. Res. Fellow, 2006, 2007, 2008, ANU; Vis. Prof., QMC, 2007–11. Lectures: Craig Lect. of Chem., ANU, 2005; Total, Eur. Bioenergetics Conf., Dublin, 2008; Drummond, QMC, 2011; Sir Hans Krebs, Univ. of Sheffield, 2014. Mem., EMBO, 2001. Hon. Dr Uppsala, 2013. Silver Medal, CNRS, 2001; Wolfson Merit Award, Royal Soc., 2011. *Publications:* over 180 articles in learned jls; over 50 other articles and chapters. *Recreations:* musician: guitar, harmonica, vocals; genre: rock, blues, Americana, singer-songwriter; bands: Baskerville Willy (CD No Ordinary Hound, 2012, www.baskervillewilly.com), Baskervilles Blues Band (CD Elementary, 1997). *Address:* Department of Life Sciences, Sir Ernst Chain Building, Imperial College London, South Kensington Campus, SW7 2AZ. *E:* a.rutherford@imperial.ac.uk.

RUTHERFORD, Andrew; His Honour Judge Rutherford; DL; a Circuit Judge, since 1995; *b* 25 March 1948; *s* of late Robert Mark Rutherford and Alison Wellington (*née* Clark); *m* 1994, Lucy Elizabeth Bosworth; two *d*. *Educ:* Clifton Coll.; Exeter Univ. (LLB). Called to the Bar, Middle Temple, 1970; Asst Recorder, 1990–93; Recorder, 1993–95. Chm., Fees Adv. Commn, 2006–11, Legal Aid Commn, 2011–, Gen. Synod of C of E. DL Somerset, 2000. *Address:* c/o Bristol Civil Justice Centre, Redcliffe Street, Bristol BS1 6GR. *Club:* Bath and County.

RUTHERFORD, Derek Thomas Jones, CBE 1994; FCA; financial and management accounting consultant, 1990–96; *b* 9 April 1930; *s* of late Sydney Watson Rutherford and Elsie Rutherford; *m* 1956, Kathleen Robinson; one *s* four *d*. *Educ:* Doncaster Grammar School. Practising accountant and auditor, 1955–59; Company Sec./Accountant, P. Platt & Sons, 1959–61; Retail Accountant, MacFisheries, 1961–63; Factory Management Accountant, then Company Systems Manager, T. Wall & Son (Ice Cream), 1963–70; Dir of Finance, Alfa-Laval Co., 1970–74; Group Financial Dir, Oxley Printing Group, 1974; HMSO: Chief Accountant, Publications Group, 1975–76; Dir, Management Accounting Project, 1976–77; Dir of Finance and Planning Div., 1977–83; Principal Estabt and Finance Officer, 1983–84; Comr for Admin and Finance, Forestry Commn, 1984–90. *Recreations:* reading, gardening, home computing. *Address:* 3 Berkeley Gardens, Bury St Edmunds, Suffolk IP33 3JW. *T:* (01284) 767279. *Club:* Royal Air Force.

RUTHERFORD, Frederick John; District Judge (Magistrates' Courts), Humberside, since 2001; *b* Kelso, 6 Aug. 1954; *s* of late Frederick George Rutherford and Isabella Rutherford; *m* 1997, Jayne Louise Curry; one *s* two *d*. *Educ:* Heckmondwike Grammar Sch.; Leicester Univ. (LLB Hons). Articled Clerk, 1976–78, Asst Solicitor, 1978–80, Partner, 1980–89, Inesons, Solicitors, Cleckheaton; Partner, Jordans, Solicitors, Dewsbury, 1989–2000. *Recreations:* reading, walking, gardening, fly fishing.

RUTHERFORD, Jessica Marianne Fernande, FSA; Head of Libraries and Museums, and Director of the Royal Pavilion (Brighton and Hove), 1996–2005; *b* 7 Feb. 1949; *d* of Raymond Denys Rutherford and Simone Genvieve (*née* Michaud); *m* 2004, Nigel Pittman. *Educ:* Brighton and Hove High Sch.; Manchester Univ. (BA Hons Hist. of Art); Sussex Univ. (PGCE). V&A Mus., 1974; Royal Pavilion, Art Gallery and Museums, Brighton: Keeper of Decorative Art, 1974–85; Principal Keeper, Royal Pavilion, 1985–87; Asst Dir (Collections), 1987–92; Head of Mus and Dir, Royal Pavilion, 1992–96. Member: Steering Cttee, Nat. Report on Mus. Educn, Dept of Nat. Heritage, 1994–97; Bd, SE Museums Agency, 2001–02; Libraries, Museums & Archives Expert Panel, Heritage Lottery Fund, 2002–05 (Advr, Heritage Lottery Fund, 2005–). Decorative Arts Society: Sec., 1975–85; Trustee, 1992–2004; Mem. Council, Charleston Trust, 1992–2005; Sec. to Trustees and Governors, Friends of Royal Pavilion, Art Gall. and Museums, 1992–2004. Sussex University: Mem. Council, 1995–2001; Mem. Ct, 2002–; Dir, Gardner Arts Centre, 1996–98; Trustee, The Barlow Collection, 1996–2001. FRSA 1998. Hon. DLit Sussex, 2005. *Publications:* Art Nouveau, Art Deco and the Thirties: the furniture collections at Brighton Museum, 1983; (jtly) Art Nouveau, Art Deco and the Thirties: the ceramic, glass and metalwork collections at Brighton Museum, 1986; The Royal Pavilion: the palace of George IV, 1995; A Prince's Passion: the life of the Royal Pavilion, 2003; *chapters in:* James Tissot, 1984; The Crace Firm of Royal Decorators 1768–1900, 1990; Country House Lighting, 1992; articles and reviews for learned jls. *Recreations:* Spain, ceramics (Raku), horses. *Address:* 24 Clifton Hill, Brighton, E Sussex BN1 3HQ. *T:* (01273) 326718.

RUTHERFORD, John Alexander; Chief Executive, Sea Fish Industry Authority, 2002–10; Chairman, Fasfa Ltd, since 2012 (Director, since 2011); *b* 5 Dec. 1948; *s* of John and Pamela Gordon Rutherford; *m* 1970, Judith Ann Lodge; three *s*. *Educ:* Univ. of Birmingham (BCom). FCA 1972. Accountant, Cooper Bros & Co., 1969–72; Mgt Accountant, Procter & Gamble Ltd, 1972–75; Finance Dir, West of England Farmers Ltd, 1986–91; West Midland Farmers Ltd, subseq. WMF Ltd: Finance Dir, 1991–96; Man. Dir, 1996–99; Dep. Man. Dir, Countrywide Farmers, 1999–2001. Chm., Biggar Little Fest., 2011–. Treas., S Charlton PCC, 2013–. *Recreation:* classic sports cars. *Address:* 4 Taylors Field, Alnwick NE66 2JN. *T:* (01665) 579316. *Clubs:* Farmers; Morgan Sports Car.

RUTHERFORD, Thomas, CBE 1982; Chairman, North Eastern Electricity Board, 1977–89, retired; *b* 4 June 1924; *s* of Thomas and Catherine Rutherford; *m* 1950, Joyce Foreman; one *s* one *d*. *Educ:* Tynemouth High Sch.; King's Coll., Durham Univ. BSc(Hons); CEng, FIET. Engrg Trainee, subseq. Research Engr, A Reyrolle & Co. Ltd, Hebburn-on-Tyne, 1943–49; North Eastern Electricity Bd: various engrg and commercial appts, 1949–61; Personal Asst to Chm., 1961–63; Area Commercial Engr, then Area Engr, Tees Area, 1964–69; Dep. Commercial Man., 1969–70; Commercial Man., 1970–72; Chief Engr, 1972–73; Dep. Chm., 1973–75; Chm., SE Electricity Board, 1975–77. *Address:* 76 Beach Road, Tynemouth, Northumberland NE30 2QW. *T:* (0191) 257 1775.

RUTHERFORD-JONES, Maj. Gen. David John, CB 2010; Clerk to the Trustees and Chief Executive, Morden College, since 2011; *b* Steamer Point, Aden, 11 Aug. 1958; *s* of Arthur and Penelope Rutherford-Jones; *m* 1985, Sarah Jane McNish; one *s* one *d*. *Educ:* Lancing Coll.; RMA Sandhurst. Commnd 15th/19th Hussars, 1977; COS 1st Mechanized Bde, 1993–95; Balkan Planning, HQ Allied Powers Europe, 1995–97; Comd Light Dragoons, 1997–2000; COS 3rd UK Div., 2000; Comd 20 Armoured Bde, Kosovo and Iraq, 2001–04; Dir Land Studies, UK Defence Acad., 2004–05; Dir RAC, 2005–07; Comdt, RMA Sandhurst, 2007–09; Military Secretary, 2009–11. Hon. Col, Corps of Army Music, 2009–12. Light Dragoons: Trustee, 1999– (Chm. Trustees, 2013–); Col, 2013–. Trustee: RAC Benevolent Fund, 2010–13; Blind Veterans UK (formerly St Dunstan's), 2011–; Chm., Hodson's Horse Meml Trust, 2012–. Fellow, Wellington Coll., 2009–12; Gov., Lancing Coll., 2011–. Cdre, Army Sailing, 2007–11; Chm., Services Telemark Skiing, 2007–11. Mem. Cttee, Grand Military Gold Cup, Sandown, 2011–13. Founder and Chm., Augustdorf Lunch Club, 2013–; Co-Founder and Co-Chair, CRAFT (Salcombe), 2013–. *Recreations:* sailing, ski-ing, fishing, reading, walking, Newcastle United FC. *Address:* 19 St Germans Place, SE3 0PW.

RUTHVEN; *see* Hore-Ruthven, family name of Earl of Gowrie.

RUTHVEN OF CANBERRA, Viscount; Patrick Leo Brer Hore-Ruthven; IT Consultant, Lloyds Banking Group, 2010; *b* 4 Feb. 1964; *s* and *heir* of 2nd Earl of Gowrie, *qv*; *m* 1990, Julie Goldsmith; one *s*. *Heir:* *s* Hon. Heathcote Patrick Cornelius Hore-Ruthven, *b* 28 May 1990.

RUTHVEN, Prof. Kenneth Borthwick Howard, PhD; FAcSS; Professor of Education, University of Cambridge, since 2005; Fellow, Hughes Hall, Cambridge, since 1983; *b* 1 Feb. 1952. *Educ:* Corpus Christi Coll., Oxford (BA Hons Maths 1973, MA 1977); Moray House Coll., Edinburgh (PGCE 1974); Univ. of Edinburgh (DipEd 1974); Univ. of Stirling (PhD Educn 1980); MA Cantab 1983. Teacher of Maths and Computing, 1974–83: Broughton High Sch., Edinburgh; Brighton Hove & Sussex Sixth Form Coll.; Hills Road Sixth Form Coll., Cambridge; Lectr, 1983–98, Reader, 1998–2005, in Educn, Univ. of Cambridge. Mem., British Soc. for Res. into Learning Maths, 1983– (Chm., 2006–08). Trustee, Sch. Mathematics Proj., 1996– (Dep. Chm., 2004–05, Chm., 2006–, of Trustees). Adv. Editor, Educnl Studies in Maths, 2001– (Ed., 1994–95, Ed.-in-Chief, 1996–2000). FAcSS (AcSS 2011). *Publications:* Society and the New Technology, 1983; The Maths Factory, 1989; Learning from Computers: mathematics education and technology, 1993; The Didactical Challenge of Symbolic Calculators: turning a computational device into a mathematical instrument, 2005; Mathematical Knowledge in Teaching, 2011; around 75 res. papers in peer-reviewed jls. *Address:* University of Cambridge Faculty of Education, 184 Hills Road, Cambridge CB2 8PQ. *T:* (01223) 767600, *Fax:* (01223) 767602. *E:* kr18@cam.ac.uk.

RUTHVEN, Hon. Malise Walter Maitland Knox Hore, PhD; writer; *b* 14 May 1942; *s* of late Major Hon. Alexander Hardinge Patrick Hore-Ruthven and Pamela Margaret Hore-Ruthven (*née* Fletcher); *m* 1967, Ianthe Hodgkinson; two *d. Educ:* Eton Coll.; Trinity Coll., Cambridge (BA Eng. Lit. 1964; MA 1994; PhD Social and Pol Scis 2000). Writer and ed., BBC External Services, 1966–70, 1976–86; Lectr, Dept of Divinity with Religious Studies, Univ. of Aberdeen, 1994–99. Visiting Professor: Dartmouth Coll., NH, 1989–90; UCSD, 1990–91, 1999–2000; Colorado Coll., Colorado Springs, 2000–01. *Publications:* Torture: the grand conspiracy, 1978; Islam in the World, 1984, 3rd edn, 2006; Traveller Through Time: a photographic journey with Freya Stark, 1986; The Divine Supermarket, 1989, repr. 2012; A Satanic Affair: Salman Rushdie and the wrath of Islam, 1990; Islam: a very short introduction, 1997, 2nd edn 2000; A Fury for God: the Islamist attack on America, 2002; Fundamentalism: the search for meaning, 2004; Encounters with Islam: on religion, politics and modernity, 2012; (with Gerard Wilkinson) Children of Time: the Aga Khan and the Ismailis, 2016. *Recreation:* walking. *Address:* Hameau Travers, St Jacques de Néhou, 50390, France. *T:* (02) 33013849. *E:* maliseruthven@gmail.com.

See also Earl of Gowrie.

RUTLAND, 11th Duke of, *cr* 1703; **David Charles Robert Manners;** Marquess of Granby 1703; Earl of Rutland 1525; Baron Manners of Haddon 1679; Baron Roos of Belvoir 1896; *b* 8 May 1959; *er s* of 10th Duke of Rutland, CBE and of Frances Helen (*née* Sweeny); *S* father, 1999; *m* 1992, Emma, *d* of John Watkins; two *s* three *d*. Mem. Civilian Cttee, ATC Sqdn, Grantham. Mem., HHA (Chm., E Midlands Area, 1995–99). President: Notts Rifle Assoc.; Ex-Aircrew Assoc., Grantham and Dist Br.; Vice Pres., Buckminster Gliding Club, 2006–; Patron, Grantham to Nottingham Canal Preservation Trust. Freeman, City of London; Liveryman, Gunsmiths' Co. *Recreations:* shooting, fishing, flying when I can. *Heir: s* Marquis of Granby, *qv*. *Address:* Belvoir Castle, Grantham, Lincs NG32 1PE. *T:* (01476) 870246. *Clubs:* Turf, Annabel's.

RUTLEDGE, Kelvin Albert; QC 2013; *b* London, 14 April 1955; *s* of William Horace Sidney Rutledge and Dorothy Bessie Rutledge; one *s* two *d. Educ:* Mayflower Comp. Sch., Billericay; Univ. of Essex (LLB Hons); King's Coll. London (LLM). Called to the Bar, Middle Temple, 1989; in practice as a barrister, Cornerstone Barristers, 1990–. Vis. Fellow, Univ. of Essex, 1998–. Mem., Sheringham Soc. *Recreations:* angling, photography, cooking, reading history. *Address:* Cornerstone Barristers, 2–3 Gray's Inn Square, WC1R 5JH. *T:* (020) 7242 4986. *E:* kelvinr@cornerstonebarristers.com. *Club:* Amwell Magna Fly Fishing.

RUTLEY, David Henry; MP (C) Macclesfield, since 2010; *b* Gravesend, Kent, 7 March 1961; *s* of John Rutley and Birthe Rutley; *m* 1994, Rachel Faber; two *s* two *d. Educ:* Lewes Priory Sch.; London Sch. of Econs and Pol Sci. (BSc Econ 1985); Harvard Business Sch. (MBA 1989). Business Develt Dir, PepsiCo Internat., 1991–94; Special Advr to Cabinet Office, MAFF, HM Treasury, 1994–96; Dir, Business Effectiveness, Safeway Stores, 1996–2000; Dir, Financial Services and Dir, E-commerce, Asda Stores, 2000–05; Sales and Mktg Dir, Halifax Gen. Insce, 2005–07; Business Consultant, 2008–09, Mktg Dir, 2009–10, Barclays Bank. Contested (C) St Albans, 1997. Parliamentary Private Secretary: to Minister for Immigration, 2010–12; to Minister for Policing and Criminal Justice, 2012–14; to Minister for Europe, 2014–15; to Sec. of State for Work and Pensions, 2015–. Mem., Treasury Select Cttee, 2010; Sec., All Party Parly Gp on National Parks, 2012– (Vice-Chm., 2010–12); Co-Chm., All Party Parly Gp on Mountaineering, 2010–. *Recreations:* family, walking in the Peak District, mountaineering, church. *Address:* House of Commons, SW1A 0AA. *T:* (020) 7219 7106. *E:* david.rutley.mp@parliament.uk.

RUTNAM, Philip McDougall; Permanent Secretary, Department for Transport, since 2012; *b* Orpington, 19 June 1965; *s* of Michael Donald Rutnam and Helen McDougall Rutnam (*née* Halliday); *m* 1996, Anna Frances Longman; one *s* two *d. Educ:* Dulwich Coll.; Trinity Hall, Cambridge (BA Hons Histl Tripos 1986); Harvard Univ. (Kennedy Scholar). Various posts, HM Treasury, 1987–2002, on secondment to Morgan Stanley Asia Ltd, Hong Kong, 1995–97; Dir, Regulatory Policy, Oftel, 2002–03; Partner, Competition and Mkts, 2003–07, Mem. Bd, 2007–09, Ofcom; Dir Gen., Business, then Business and Skills, BERR, later BIS, 2009–12, Actg Perm. Sec., BIS, 2010. *Recreations:* running, cycling, ski-ing, taking family up mountains, arts. *Address:* c/o Department for Transport, Great Minster House, 33 Horseferry Road, SW1P 4DR.

RUTOVITZ, Jeanne Elisabeth; *see* Bell, J. E.

RUTTER, Barrie Thomas, OBE 2015; Founder and Artistic Director, Northern Broadsides Theatre Co., since 1992; *b* 12 Dec. 1946; *s* of Edward and Annie Rutter; one *d*; *m* 1978, Carol Chillington (marr. diss. 1997); two *d* (one *s* decd). *Educ:* Newton Hall, Hull; Royal Scottish Acad. of Music and Drama; Nat. Youth Th. Professional actor, 1968–, mostly in theatre, but occasional TV, film and radio; *theatre* includes: Napoleon, in Animal Farm, 1984, and Silenus, in The Trackers of Oxyrhynchus, 1990, NT; Northern Broadsides Theatre Co., director: Richard III (also title rôle), 1992; A Midsummer Night's Dream (Shakespeare's Globe, Tyrone Guthrie Award for Best Production), 1995; Antony and Cleopatra (also title rôle), 1995; Samson Agonistes (also title rôle), 1998; King Lear (also title rôle), 1999; Alcestis (Ted Hughes' final play), 2000; Antigone, 2003; The Merchant of Venice (Shylock), 2004; Sweet William (Fat Jack), Comedy of Errors (Egeon), 2005; Wars of the Roses (also edited and acted, Duke of York), 2006; The Tempest (Prospero), 2007; Othello, 2009; Medea (Creon), 2010; Rutherford & Son (acted), 2013; A Chorus of Disapproval (acted), Harold Pinter Th., 2012. Hon. DLitt: Hull, 2001; Bradford, 2005; Huddersfield, 2006. TMA Award for best dir, 1995; Overall Winner, Creative Briton Awards, Arts & Business/Prudential, 2000; Sam Wanamaker Award, Shakespeare's Globe, 2003; Pragnell Shakespeare Award, 2010. *Recreations:* food and drink, sport, poetry. *Address:* Northern Broadsides, Dean Clough, Halifax HX3 5AX. *T:* (01422) 369704, *Fax:* (01422) 383175. *E:* rutter@northern-broadsides.co.uk.

RUTTER, Dr (James) Michael, CBE 2002; Consultant, JMR Consultancy, since 2002; Director of Veterinary Medicines, 1989–2002, and Chief Executive, Veterinary Medicines Directorate, 1990–2002, Department for Environment, Food and Rural Affairs (formerly Ministry of Agriculture, Fisheries and Food); *b* 20 Aug. 1941; *s* of late James and Lily Rutter; *m* 1967, Jacqueline Patricia Watson; one *d. Educ:* Kendal Grammar Sch.; Univ. of Edinburgh (BVM&S 1964; BSc 1965; PhD 1967). MRCVS 1964. Res. Schol., 1964–67, Res. Asst, 1967–69, Univ. of Edinburgh; Institute for Research on Animal Diseases, later Institute for Animal Health: Vet. Res. Officer, 1969–73; Principal Vet. Res. Officer, 1973–84 (on secondment to DES, 1975–78); Head: Dept of Microbiol., 1984–89; Compton Lab., 1986–89. Expert Consultant: ODA; FAO; WHO. Member: Cttee for Vet. Medicinal Products, EC, 1991–99; Mgt Bd, MAFF, 1992–99; Mgt Bd, Eur. Medicines Evaluation Agency, 1996–2002; Assessor, Animal Medicines Trng Regulatory Authy, 2007–. Chm., Poultry Res. Cttee, DEFRA/British Poultry Council, 2008–. Dir, 2004–13, Sec., 2006–13, Vet. Benevolent Fund; Pres., Vet. Res. Club, 2007–08. FRSocMed 1985. *Publications:* Perinatal Ill Health in Calves, 1973; Pasteurella and Pasteurellosis, 1989; contrib. numerous papers to scientific jls. *Recreations:* gardening, outdoor sports, theatre, ballet, music.

RUTTER, Jill Kathleen; Programme Director, Institute for Government, since 2011; *b* 30 Oct. 1956; *d* of Derek John Rutter and June Kathleen Rutter. *Educ:* Somerville Coll., Oxford (BA PPE 1978). HM Treasury, 1978–97; BP plc, 1998–2004; Dir, Strategy and Sustainable Develt, DEFRA, 2004–09; Whitehall Fellow, Inst. for Govt, 2009–11. Harkness Fellow, Grad. Sch. of Public Policy, Univ. of Calif, Berkeley, 1988–89. *Address:* Institute for Government, 2 Carlton Gardens, SW1Y 5AA. *E:* jill.rutter@instituteforgovernment.org.uk.

RUTTER, John Milford, CBE 2007; composer and conductor; *b* 24 Sept. 1945; *s* of Laurence Frederick and Joan Mary Rutter (*née* Milford); *m* 1980, JoAnne Redden; one *s* (and one *s* decd), and one step *d. Educ:* Highgate Sch.; Clare Coll., Cambridge (MA, MusB; Hon. Fellow, 2001). Fellow and Director of Music, Clare Coll., Cambridge, 1975–79; Founder and Director, Cambridge Singers, 1981–. Hon. Freeman, Barbers' Co., 2008. Hon. FGCM 1988; Hon. Fellow, Westminster Choir Coll., Princeton, 1980; Hon. Bencher, Middle Temple, 2008. Hon. Life Mem., RPO, 2012. DMus Lambeth, 1996; Hon. Dr: Anglia Ruskin, 2004; Leicester, 2005; Hull, 2008; Durham, 2012; DUniv Open, 2014. Medal, RCO, 2014. *Publications:* compositions include choral and orchestral works, anthems and carols, 1969–. *Address:* c/o Oxford University Press, Great Clarendon Street, Oxford OX2 6DP.

RUTTER, Michael; *see* Rutter, J. M.

RUTTER, Sir Michael (Llewellyn), Kt 1992; CBE 1985; MD; FRCP, FRCPsych, FMedSci; FRS 1987; Professor of Child Psychiatry, 1973–98, Professor of Developmental Psychopathology, since 1998, Institute of Psychiatry, Psychology and Neuroscience, King's College London (formerly Institute of Psychiatry, University of London); *b* 15 Aug. 1933; *s* of Llewellyn Charles Rutter and Winifred Olive Rutter; *m* 1958, Marjorie Heys; one *s* two *d. Educ:* Moorestown Friends' Sch., USA; Wolverhampton Grammar Sch.; Bootham Sch., York; Birmingham Univ. Med. Sch. (MB ChB 1955, MD Hons 1963). MRCS 1955; LRCP 1955, MRCP 1958, FRCP 1972; FRCPsych 1971. Training in paediatrics, neurology and internal medicine, 1955–58; Maudsley Hosp., 1958–61; Nuffield Med. Travelling Fellow, Albert Einstein Coll. of Medicine, NY, 1961–62; Mem., Sci. Staff, MRC Social Psych. Res. Unit, 1962–65; University of London Institute of Psychiatry: Sen. Lectr, then Reader, 1966–73; Hon. Dir, MRC Child Psychiatry Unit, 1984–98; Dir, Social, Genetic and Develtl Psychiatry Res. Centre, 1994–98. Fellow, Center for Advanced Study in Behavioral Scis, Stanford, Calif, 1979–80. Lectures: Goulstonian, RCP, 1973; Salmon, NY Acad. of Medicine, 1979; Adolf Meyer, Amer. Psych. Assoc., 1985; Maudsley, RCPsych, 1986. Pres., Soc. for Res. in Child Develt, 1999–2001 (Pres.-elect, 1997–99). Gov., 1996–2003, Dep. Chm., 1999–2003, Wellcome Trust; Trustee: Nuffield Foundn, 1992–; Jacobs Foundn, 1998–2004; Novartis Foundn, 1999–; One Plus One, 2001–. Founding Mem., Acad. Europaea, 1988; Founder FMedSci 1998; Foreign Associate Member: Inst. of Medicine, Nat. Acad. of Scis, USA, 1988; US Nat. Acad. of Educn, 1990; Foreign Hon. Mem., Amer. Acad. of Arts and Scis, 1989. FKC 1998. Hon. Prof., Amsterdam Univ., 2001. Hon. FBPsS 1978; Hon. Fellow: Amer. Acad. of Pediatrics, 1981; RSocMed 1996; Hon. FRCPCH 1996; Hon. FBA 2002. Hon. DSSc Univ. of Leiden, 1985; Hon. Dr Leuven, 1990; Hon. DSc: Birmingham, 1990; Chicago, 1991; Minnesota, 1993; Ghent, 1994; Warwick, 1999; E Anglia, 2000; Oxon, 2005; St Andrews, 2013; Sussex, 2014; Hon. MD Edinburgh, 1990; Hon. DPsych Jyväskylä, Finland, 1996; DUniv: N London, 2000; York, 2005. Numerous awards, UK and USA. *Publications:* Children of Sick Parents, 1966; (jtly) A Neuropsychiatric Study in Childhood, 1970; (ed jtly) Education, Health and Behaviour, 1970; (ed) Infantile Autism, 1971; Maternal Deprivation Reassessed, 1972, 2nd edn 1981; (ed jtly) The Child with Delayed Speech, 1972; Helping Troubled Children, 1975; (jtly) Cycles of Disadvantage, 1976; (ed jtly) Child Psychiatry, 1977, 2nd edn as Child and Adolescent Psychiatry, 1985, 4th edn, 2002; (ed jtly) Autism, 1978; Changing Youth in a Changing Society, 1979; (jtly) Fifteen Thousand Hours: secondary schools and their effects on children, 1979; (ed) Scientific Foundations of Developmental Psychiatry, 1981; A Measure of Our Values: goals and dilemmas in the upbringing of children, 1983; (jtly) Lead Versus Health, 1983; (jtly) Juvenile Delinquency, 1983; (ed) Developmental Neuropsychiatry, 1983; (ed jtly) Stress, Coping and Development, 1983; (ed jtly) Depression in Young People, 1986; (jtly) Treatment of Autistic Children, 1987; (ed jtly) Language Development and Disorders, 1987; (jtly) Parenting Breakdown: the making and breaking of inter-generational links, 1988; (ed jtly) Assessment and Diagnosis in Child Psychopathology, 1988; (ed) Studies of Psychosocial Risk: the power of longitudinal data, 1988; (ed jtly) Straight and Devious Pathways from Childhood to Adulthood, 1990; (ed jtly) Biological Risk Factors for Psychosocial Disorders, 1991; (jtly) Developing Minds: challenge and continuity across the life span, 1993; (ed jtly) Development Through Life: a handbook for clinicians, 1994; (ed jtly) Stress, Risk and Resilience in Children and Adolescents: processes, mechanisms and interventions, 1994; (ed jtly) Psychosocial Disorders in Young People, 1995; (jtly) Behavioural Genetics, 3rd edn, 1997; (jtly) Antisocial Behaviour by Young People, 1998; (jtly) Sex Differences in Antisocial Behaviour: conduct disorder, delinquency and violence in the Dunedin longitudinal study, 2001; (ed jtly) Ethnicity and Causal Mechanisms, 2005; Genes and Behaviour, 2006; Genetic Effects on Environmental Vulnerability to Disease, 2008; (ed jtly) Policy and Practice Implications from the English and Romanian Adoptees Study, 2009; (ed jtly) Gene-environment Interactions in Developmental Psychopathology, 2011. *Recreations:* fell walking, tennis, wine tasting, theatre, family. *Address:* 190 Court Lane, Dulwich, SE21 7ED. *Club:* Royal Society of Medicine.

RUTTER, Trevor John, CBE 1990 (OBE 1976); Assistant Director General, British Council, 1990–91, retired; *b* 26 Jan. 1934; *s* of Alfred Rutter and Agnes Rutter (*née* Purslow); *m* 1959, Josephine Henson (*d* 2009); one *s. Educ:* Monmouth Sch.; Brasenose Coll., Oxford (BA). National Service, Army, 1955–57. British Council, Indonesia, W Germany (Munich), London, 1959–66; First Secretary, Foreign Office, 1967; British Council, 1968–91: Representative: Singapore, 1968–71; Thailand, 1971–75; various appointments, London, 1975–85, including: Head, Home Div., 1980; Asst Dir Gen., 1981–85; Rep. in W Germany, 1986–90. *Address:* 7 Grove Mews, Totnes, Devon TQ9 5GT.

RUTTLE, (Henry) Stephen (Mayo); QC 1997; *b* 6 Feb. 1953; *s* of His Honour Henry Samuel Jacob Ruttle and Joyce Mayo Ruttle (*née* Moriarty); *m* 1985, Fiona Jane Mitchell-Innes; two *s* two *d. Educ:* Westminster Sch. (Queen's Schol.); Queens' Coll., Cambridge (BA Hons Eng. Lit. and Law). Called to the Bar, Gray's Inn, 1976, Bencher, 2004; in practice at the Bar, 1976–; practising as commercial and community mediator, 2000– (CEDR accredited mediator, 1998); Chm. of Trustees, Wandsworth Mediation Service, 2005–. A Lieut Bailiff of Guernsey, 2008–. Fellow, Internat. Acad. of Mediators, 2005–. *Recreations:* Church, fly-fishing, the countryside, mountains, oak furniture. *Address:* Brick Court Chambers, 7–8 Essex Street, WC2R 3LD. *T:* (020) 7379 3550, *T:* (020) 7520 9871. *Club:* Flyfishers'.

RYAN, Prof. Alan James, FBA 1986; Professor of Politics, University of Oxford, 1997–2010, now Emeritus; Fellow, New College, Oxford, 1969–2010 (Warden, 1996–2009; Senior Research Fellow in Politics, 2009–10; Hon. Fellow, 2010); *b* 9 May 1940; *s* of James William Ryan and Ivy Ryan; *m* 1971, Kathleen Alyson Lane; one *d. Educ:* Christ's Hospital; Balliol Coll., Oxford (Hon. Fellow, 2004). Lectr in Politics, Univ. of Keele, 1963–66, Univ. of Essex, 1966–69; Lectr in Politics, 1969–78, Reader, 1978–87, Univ. of Oxford; Prof. of Politics, Princeton Univ., 1988–96; Dir, Rothermere Amer. Inst., Univ. of Oxford, 1999–2002. Visiting Professor in Politics: City University of New York, 1967–68; Univs of Texas, 1972, California, 1977, the Witwatersrand, 1978; Vis. Schol., Princeton Univ., 2009–14; William H. Bonsall Vis. Prof. of Philosophy, Stanford Univ., 2014–15; Vis. Fellow, ANU, 1974, 1979; Mellon Fellow, Inst. for Advanced Study, Princeton, 1991–92; Fellow, Center for Advanced Study, Stanford, 2002–03; de Carle Lectr, Univ. of Otago, 1983. Official Mem., CNAA, 1975–80. Delegate, Oxford Univ. Press, 1983–87. *Publications:* The Philosophy of John Stuart Mill, 1970, 2nd edn 1987; The Philosophy of the Social Sciences, 1970; J. S. Mill, 1975; Property and Political Theory, 1984; (ed jtly) The Blackwell Encyclopaedia of Political Thought, 1987; Property, 1987; Bertrand Russell: a political life, 1988; John Dewey and the High Tide of American Liberalism, 1995; Liberal Anxieties and Liberal Education, 1998; The Making of Modern Liberalism, 2012; On Politics, 2012; On Machiavelli, 2014; On Aristotle, 2014; On Tocqueville, 2014; On Marx, 2014. *Recreations:* dinghy sailing, long train journeys. *Address:* 21 Cunliffe Close, Oxford, OX2 7BJ. *Club:* Oxford and Cambridge.

RYAN, Prof. Anthony John, OBE 2006; PhD, DSc; Professor of Physical Chemistry, since 1997, and Pro Vice Chancellor (Faculty of Science), since 2008, University of Sheffield (ICI Professor of Physical Chemistry, 2002–08); *b* 20 March 1962; *s* of Anthony Ryan and Margaret Ryan; *m* 1990, Angela Potts; two *d. Educ:* Univ. of Manchester (BSc Hons 1983; PhD 1988); DSc UMIST 2004. Lectr, 1985–88 and 1990–94, Sen. Lectr, 1994–95, Reader, 1995–97, in Polymer Sci. and Technol., UMIST; NATO Res. Fellow, Univ. of Minnesota, 1988–89; Hd, Chemistry Dept, Univ. of Sheffield, 1998–2003. Christmas Lectr, Royal Instn, 2002. *Publications:* Polymer Processing: structure development, 1998; Emerging Themes in Polymer Science, 2000; Project Sunshine: how science can use the sun to fuel and feed the world, 2013; (with S. Mckevitt) The Solar Revolution: One World, One Solution: providing the energy and food for 10 billion people, 2014. *Recreations:* road and mountain biking, eating, drinking and being merry. *Address:* Faculty of Science, University of Sheffield, Sheffield S10 2TN. *T:* (0114) 222 9760, *Fax:* (0114) 222 9774.

RYAN, David, CBE 2003; Area Director Designate, Crime, London Region, HM Courts Service, 2004–05; *b* 7 Dec. 1948; *s* of Christopher and Ellen Ryan; *m* 1971, Anna Maria Scumaci; one *s* one *d. Educ:* City Grammar Sch., Lincoln. Personnel and Finance Officer, Midland and Oxford Circuit, 1987–92; Courts Administrator, Winchester, 1992–97; Circuit Administrator: Western Circuit, 1997–2003; S Eastern Circuit, 2003–04. *Recreations:* supporting Aston Villa and spectating sports generally, drinking the odd glass of red wine, holidays in Calabria. *Address:* 1 The Paddocks, Ampfield, Romsey, Hants SO51 9BG. *E:* daveandanna123@gmail.com. *Club:* Hampshire Cricket.

RYAN, Maj.-Gen. Denis Edgar, CB 1987; Director of Army Education, 1984–87; *b* 18 June 1928; *s* of late Reginald Arthur Ryan and Amelia (*née* Smith); *m* 1955, Jean Mary Bentley; one *s* one *d. Educ:* Sir William Borlase School, Marlow; King's College, London (LLB). Commissioned RAEC, 1950; served BAOR, 1950–54; Instr, RMA Sandhurst, 1954–56; Adjt, Army Sch. of Educn, 1957–59; Staff Coll., 1960; served in Cyprus, Kenya and UK, 1961–67; CAES, HQ 4 Div., BAOR, 1968–70; Cabinet Office, 1970–72; TDA, Staff Coll., 1972–75; Col GS MoD, 1976–78; Chief Education Officer: HQ SE Dist, 1978–79; HQ BAOR, 1979–82; Comd, Education, UK, 1982–84. Col Comdt, RAEC, 1990–92; Dep. Col Comdt, AGC, 1992–93. *Recreations:* cricket, tennis, Rugby, music, theatre.

RYAN, Sir Derek (Gerald), 4th Bt *cr* 1919, of Hintlesham, Suffolk; architect; *b* 25 March 1954; *s* of Sir Derek Gerald Ryan, 3rd Bt and of Penelope Anne Hawkings; *S* father, 1990; *m* 1st (marr. diss.); 2nd, 1997, Roberta Tonn (marr. diss. 2000). *Educ:* Univ. of California at Berkeley (BAED 1977). Washington State Architect License #4296, 1984; NCARB Certificate #32,269, 1984; Idaho State Architect License #AR-2623. NBBJ architects and planners, Seattle, WA, 1980–99; Williams Partners Architects (formerly Jeffrey Charles Williams Architects), Ketchum, ID, 1999–. *Recreations:* ski-ing, guitar. *Heir: cousin* Barry Desmond Ryan [*b* 30 June 1943; *m* 1976, Evodia Massemola; one *s* one *d*]. *Address:* PO Box 6966, Ketchum, ID 83340, USA. *T:* (208) 7204153. *E:* derek@williams-partners.com.

RYAN, Gerard Charles; QC 1981; a Recorder of the Crown Court, 1984–98; *b* 16 Dec. 1931; *er s* of Frederick Charles Ryan, Hove, and Louie Violet Ryan (*née* Ball); *m* 1960, Sheila Morag Clark Cameron, *qv*; two *s. Educ:* Clayesmore Sch.; Brighton Coll.; Pembroke Coll., Cambridge (Exhibnr; MA); Inchbald Sch. of Design (Dip. Garden Design 2003). Served RA, 1955–57 (Lieut). Called to the Bar, Middle Temple, 1955, Bencher, 1988; Harmsworth Scholar, 1956; in practice at Common Law Bar, 1957–65, at Parly Bar and Planning and Envmt Bar, 1965–2001. Chm., Tribunal of Inquiry into Loscoe (Derbyshire) gas explosion, 1986–87. Chairman: Soc. of Sussex Downsmen, 1977–80; Murray Downland Trust, 1993–2001 (Jt Founder, 1993). *Publications:* (with A. O. B. Harris) Outline of the Law of Common Land, 1967. *Recreations:* conservation, growing trees and other plants, walking. *Address:* Bayleaves, Bepton, Midhurst, Sussex GU29 9RB.

RYAN, Rt Hon. Joan (Marie); PC 2007; MP (Lab) Enfield North, 1997–2010 and since 2015; consultant in communications and strategy; Advisor, Global Tamil Forum, since 2012 (Chief Executive Officer, 2010–12); *b* 8 Sept. 1955; *d* of late Michael Joseph Ryan and Dolores Marie Ryan (*née* Joyce); *m* 1998, Martin Hegarty; one *s* one *d*, and one step *s* one step *d. Educ:* City of Liverpool Coll. of Higher Educn (BA Hons 1979); South Bank Poly. (MSc 1983); Avery Hill Coll. (PGCE 1984). Sociology, Soc. Sci., Religious Studies and Eur. Politics Teacher, and Hd of Year, Hurlingham and Chelsea Secondary Sch., Fulham, 1984–89; Head of Pastoral Educn, Hawksmoor Sixth Form Coll., Fulham, 1989–94; Head of Humanities, William Morris Acad., Hammersmith, 1994–97. Mem. (Lab) Barnet LBC, 1990–98. Contested (Lab) Enfield N, 2010. An Asst Govt Whip, 2002–03; a Lord Comr of HM Treasury (Govt Whip), 2003–06; Parly Under-Sec. of State, Home Office, 2006–07; Special Rep. to Cyprus, 2007–10. Dir, Labour No 2 AV, 2010–12. Chair, Riders for Health, 2010–. Oral history interviewer, Imperial War Mus., 1984–86. *Recreations:* visiting historic buildings, cinema, learning to sail. *Address:* House of Commons, SW1A 0AA.

RYAN, Matthew Richard Goolden; director and teacher; *b* London, 26 Jan. 1965; *s* of Brian Tyler and late Veronica Foley; partner, Ian Stephenson. *Educ:* Wanstead High Sch.; Sylvia Young Theatre Sch. Actor, theatre, film, TV and radio, 1974–90; theatre includes Peter Pan, Ardele, Cause Célèbre, Forty Years On, West End; Close of Play, NT. Resident/Associate Director, Les Misérables, Miss Saigon, Cameron Mackintosh Ltd, and Aspects of Love, Really Useful Group Ltd, 1988–99; Director: Miss Saigon, Aust. premiere, Netherlands premiere, 1st UK tour; Les Misérables, Australia, Asia, South African premiere, 2nd UK tour; Is There Life After High School?, Bridewell, 2001; Royal Academy of Music, 1999–: They Shoot Horses, Don't They?, Company, Cabaret, Sweeney Todd, Grand Hotel, Assassins, Promises Promises, A Doll's Life, Lady in the Dark, A Little Night Music, Sunday in the Park with George, Jane Eyre, A Man of No Importance, A Catered Affair (Eur. premiere); Mountview Academy of Theatre Arts, 2000–15: Sweet Charity, Carousel, Oklahoma!, Nine, Songs for a New World, The York Realist, The Rink, Hello Again, A Winter's Tale, Pal Joey; Stage Entertainment, Netherlands, 2006–09: My Fair Lady (John Kraaijkamp Award for Best Dir), Evita, La Cage aux Folles; London School of Musical Theatre, 2009–14: Violet, American Idiot, Carnival, Rent, The Wild Party, Bernarda Alba (Eur. premiere); William Finn's Elegies, Liverpool Inst. of Performing Art, 2011; The Importance of Being Earnest, English Th., Frankfurt, 2011; Dogfight, Southwark Playhouse, 2014. Devised/directed entertainments for Philip Quast, Clare Burt and Frances Ruffelle. Hon. Mem., RAM, 2014. *Recreations:* theatre, reading, classic Hollywood cinema, Broadway musicals, cooking and entertaining. *E:* mryanlondon@aol.com.

RYAN, Michael James, CBE 2005; Vice President and General Manager, Bombardier Aerospace, Belfast, Aerostructures and Engineering Services, since 2000; *b* 14 Aug. 1959; *s* of Patrick and Maeve Ryan; *m* 1986, Mary Gibson; two *s* one *d. Educ:* Queen's Univ., Belfast (BSc Hons Aeronautical Engrg). CEng 1992; FRAeS 2003. Joined Short Brothers, 1981: Develt Engr, 1981–84; Prodn Engr, 1985–87; Prodn Engrg Manager, 1988–89; Bombardier Aerospace: Ops Manager, 1990–93; Dir of Manufg, 1993–97; Procurement Dir, 1997–99; Gen. Manager Procurement, Montreal, 1999–2000. Chm., Maydown Precision Engrg, 2000–. Mem., Econ. Adv. Gp to Minister for Enterprise, Trade and Investment, NI, 2011–. Council Mem., SBAC, 2000–09; Mem. Council and Operating Bd, ADS, 2009–. Chm., W Belfast/Gtr Shankhill Employers' Forum, 2005–; Member: Bd, BITC, NI, 2000– (Chm., 2005–09); Bd, Centre for Competitiveness, 2000–13; Aerospace Growth Partnership, 2011–. Pres. NI Br., RAeS, 2004–05. *Recreations:* keeping fit, reading, music, art, travel. *Address:* Bombardier Aerostructures and Engineering Services, Belfast, Airport Road, Belfast BT3 9DZ. *T:* (028) 9073 3553, *Fax:* (028) 9073 3143. *E:* michael.ryan@aero.bombardier.com.

RYAN, Peter James, QPM 1991; management consultant; Principal Security Advisor: International Olympic Committee, 2000–15; Athens 2004 Olympic Games, 2002–04, Turin, 2006, Beijing, 2008, Vancouver, 2010, London, 2012, Sochi, 2014; *b* 18 May 1944; *s* of late Lawrence Joseph Ryan and of Margaret Jane (*née* Stephenson); *m* 1985, Adrienne Margaret Butterworth; two *d. Educ:* Newman Coll., Preston; Univ. of Lancaster (BA Hons); Preston Poly. (DMS); Open Univ. (MSc). FIPM 1994. Lancs Constabulary, 1963–83; Metropolitan Police, 1983–84; Asst Chief Constable, N Yorks Police, 1984–88; Dep. Chief Constable, Durham Constabulary, 1988–90; Chief Constable, Norfolk, 1990–93; Nat. Dir of Police Trng and Comdt Police Staff Coll., 1993–96; Comr of Police for NSW, 1996–2002. Dir for Infrastructure and Resilience, Hyder Consulting, 2006–08; CEO, Crystal Professional Development, 2009–10. Advr, Bd, Canadian Centre for Emergency Preparedness, 2002–04; Member, Advisory Board: UN/WHO Pandemics and Mass Gatherings, 2010–; Internat. Centre for Sports Security, 2010–. Sec., 1991–92, Chm., 1992–93, Personnel & Trng Cttee, ACPO. Mem., BTEC, 1985–88. Vis. Fellow, UEA Sch. of Educn, 1993–96; Grad., FBI Nat. Exec. Inst., 1994. Pres., Assoc. of Eur. Police Colls, 1996; Vice Pres., Police Mutual Assurance Soc., 1994–96. Asst Dir Gen., St John Ambulance, 1995. FCMI (FIMgt 1980); FCIPD 1990; MAICD 2002. FRSA 1992. Hon. LLD Macquarie, 2000. OStJ 1995. *Publications:* (with Sue Williams) The Inside Story (autobiog.), 2002. *Recreations:* occasional golf, reading. *Address:* St Mary's Cottage, St Mary's Road, Shoreham by Sea, W Sussex BN93 5ZA. *Club:* Royal Sydney Yacht Squadron.

RYAN, Sheila Morag Clark, (Mrs G. C. Ryan); *see* Cameron, S. M. C.

RYAN, Prof. Terence John, DM; FRCP; Clinical Professor of Dermatology, Oxford University, 1992–97, now Emeritus Professor; Fellow, Green College, 1979–97, now Emeritus Fellow; *b* 24 July 1932; *s* of Gerald John Ryan and Kathleen May (*née* Knight); *m* 1968, Trudie Anne Merry; one *s* one *d. Educ:* numerous schs including: Michael Hall (Rudolf Steiner); Brickwall Sch., Northiam; Worcester Coll., Oxford (BM, BCh 1957; DM 1977). FRCP 1975. Capt. RAMC, 1955–60: Officer i/c Dept of Dermatol. and ENT Surgery, Colchester Mil. Hosp.; Radcliffe Infirmary, Oxford: Hse Officer, 1958; Registrar and Sen. Registrar in Dermatol., 1962–68; Lectr and Sen. Lectr, Inst. of Dermatol., London Univ., 1967–71; Dept of Dermatol., RPMS, 1968–71; Lectr in Dermatology, Oxford Univ., 1971–92. Cons. Dermatologist, 1969–97, Hon. Cons., 1997–, Oxon HA. Vis. Prof., Brookes Univ., Oxford, 1991–; Adjunct Professor: Jefferson Univ., Philadelphia, 1988–; Univ. of Limerick, 2007–; Univ. of Minneapolis, 2012–; Hon. Prof., Nanjing, 2003–. Med. Advr, St Francis Leprosy Guild, 1987–2012; Advr, Morbidity Control, Global Alliance to Eliminate Lymphatic Filariasis, 2003–. Promoter, Sine Lepra and Healthy Skin for All programmes, Internat. League of Dermatologists, 1987–2002; Dir, Fuel Initiatives Resources Strategies Technologies, 1998–; Chm., Skin Care for All Taskforce, 2008–. Pres., Section of Dermatol., RSocMed, 1990. Mem., Internat. Cttee of Dermatol., 1987–2002; Pres., Internat. Soc. for Dermatol., 1994–99 (Hon. Pres., 1999; Chm., Skin Care for All: Community Dermatol. Task Force, 2010–); Chm., Internat. Foundn for Dermatol., 1997–2002. Trustee: Oxford Internat. Biomedical Centre, 1999–; Arts Dyslexia Trust, 1999–2012; British Skin Foundn, 1999. Hon. Mem., various foreign nat. socs of dermatol. Hon. DM Martin Luther Univ., Halle-Wittenberg, 2007; Hon. DSc Hull, 2013. Gold Medal: Eur. Tissue Repair Soc., 1995; Brit. Assoc. Dermatology, 1997; Curatorium Angiologiae Internationalis, 2002; Brazilian Acad. Medicine, 2003. KStJ 1984 (County Surgeon Comr, then Comdr, SJAB, Oxon). *Publications:* (contrib.) Oxford Textbook of Medicine, 3rd edn 1995 to 5th edn 2002; (contrib.) White Paper Wounds and Lymphoedema, 2010; contrib. textbooks of dermatology and numerous in field of blood supply and lymphatics, dermatology and internat. dermatological policy. *Recreations:* painting water-colours, flowers, piano playing, foreign travel. *Address:* Brook House, Brook Street, Great Bedwyn, Wilts SN8 3LZ.

RYAN, Prof. William Francis, DPhil; FSA; FBA 2000; Librarian, 1976–2002, Emeritus Professor, 2003, and Hon. Fellow, since 2003, Warburg Institute, and Professor of Russian Studies, School of Advanced Study, 2000–02, University of London; *b* 13 April 1937; *s* of William Gerard Ryan and Marjorie Ellen Ryan; *m* 1st, 1963, Marina Guterman (marr. diss. 1970); two *d*; 2nd, 1986, Janet Margaret Hartley; one *s* one *d. Educ:* Bromley GS for Boys; Oriel Coll., Oxford (MA; DPhil 1970). FSA 1972. Editor, Clarendon Press, Oxford, 1963–65; Asst Curator, Mus. of Hist. of Science, Oxford, 1965–67; Lectr in Russian Lang. and Lit., SSEES, London Univ., 1967–76. President: Folklore Soc., 2005–08; Hakluyt Soc., 2008–11. Dhc Russian Acad. of Scis, 2007. *Publications:* (with Peter Norman) The Penguin Russian Dictionary, 1995; The Bathhouse at Midnight: an historical survey of magic and divination in Russia, Stroud and University Park PA, 1999. *Address:* Warburg Institute, Woburn Square, WC1H 0AB. *E:* will.ryan.home@gmail.com.

RYCROFT, Matthew John, CBE 2003; HM Diplomatic Service; Permanent Representative and Ambassador to the United Nations, New York, since 2015; *b* 16 June 1968; *s* of Prof. Michael John Rycroft, *qv*; *m* 1997, Alison Emma Victoria Semple; three *d. Educ:* Merton Coll., Oxford (BA Maths and Philos. 1989). Joined FCO, 1989; Third Sec., Geneva, 1990; Third, then Second, Sec. (Chancery), Paris, 1991–95; First Sec., FCO, 1995–98; First Sec. (Political), Washington, 1998–2002; Private Sec. for Foreign Affairs to the Prime Minister, 2002–04; Ambassador to Bosnia and Herzegovina, 2005–08; Dir, EU, later Europe, FCO, 2008–11; Chief Operating Officer, FCO, 2011–14. *Address:* c/o Foreign and Commonwealth Office, King Charles Street, SW1A 2AH. *E:* matthew.rycroft@fco.gov.uk.

RYCROFT, Prof. Michael John, PhD; Proprietor, Cambridge Atmospheric, Environmental and Space Activities and Research Consultancy, since 1998; Professor, International Space University, France, since 1995 (part-time, since 1998); *b* 15 July 1938; *s* of late John Lambert Rycroft and Molly Elizabeth Rycroft (*née* Riglen); *m* 1967, Mary Cheeseright; three *s. Educ:* Merchant Taylors' School, Northwood; Imperial Coll., London (BSc Hons Physics); Churchill Coll., Cambridge (PhD Met. Physics). CPhys, MInstP; CMath, FIMA; CSci; FRAS. Lectr, Dept of Physics, Univ. of Southampton, 1966–79; Head,

Atmospheric Scis Div., NERC British Antarctic Survey, Cambridge, 1979–90; Prof. of Aerospace, 1990–94, Hd, Coll. of Aeronautics, 1990–92, Cranfield Inst. of Technol., subseq. Cranfield Univ. Visiting Professor: Dept of Physics, Univ. of Houston, 1974–75; Cranfield Univ., 1995–; De Montfort Univ., 1998–2003; Vis. Sen. Fellow, Univ. of Bath, 2005–. Gen. Sec., Eur. Geophysical Soc., 1996–2003. Mem., Internat. Acad. of Astronautics, 1986; MAE 2000. Editor-in-Chief, Jl of Atmospheric and Solar-Terrestrial Physics, 1989–99; Man. Editor, Surveys in Geophysics, 2001–. Hon. DSc De Montfort, 1998. *Publications:* (with D. Shapland) Spacelab: research in Earth orbit, 1984; (ed) Cambridge Encyclopedia of Space, 1990; (with G. Genta) Space, the Final Frontier?, 2003; (with V. Y. Trakhtengerts) Whistler and Alfvén Mode Cyclotron Masers in Space, 2008; 250 pubns on atmospheric and space sci. and related fields. *Recreations:* music, gardening, wining and dining. *Address:* Bassett Mead, 35 Millington Road, Cambridge CB3 9HW. *T:* (01223) 353839, *Fax:* (01223) 303839. *E:* michaelrycroft@btinternet.com.

See also M. J. Rycroft.

RYCROFT, Philip John, CB 2014; DPhil; Director General, Deputy Prime Minister's Office, Cabinet Office, since 2012; *b* 22 May 1961; *s* of John and Shirley Rycroft; *m* 1989, Kate Richards; two *s*. *Educ:* Leys Sch., Cambridge; Wadham Coll., Oxford (MA; DPhil 1988). Scottish Office: Res. Div., Agric. Dept, 1989–90; Private Sec. to Scottish Office Agric. and Fisheries Minister, 1990–91; Principal: European Support Unit, Industry Dept, 1992–94; Fisheries Gp, Fisheries Policy Branch, 1994; Cabinet of Sir Leon Brittan, EC, 1995–97; Scottish Office: Hd, Agricl Policy Co-ordination and Rural Develt Div. and IT Support Div., Agric., Envmt and Fisheries Dept, 1997–98; Hd, Mgt Gp Support Staff Unit, 1998–99; Dep. Hd, Scottish Exec. Policy Unit, 1999–2000; Public Affairs Manager, Scottish & Newcastle plc, 2000–02; Hd, Schs Gp, Scottish Exec. Educn Dept, 2002–06; Hd of Scottish Exec. Enterprise, Transport and Lifelong Learning Dept, 2006–07; Dir-Gen., Educn, Scottish Exec., later Scottish Govt, 2007–09; Dir-Gen., Business and Innovation, DIUS, later Dir-Gen., Innovation and Enterprise, and Chief Exec., Better Regulation Exec., BIS, 2009–11; Dir, Corporate Affairs, Hutchison Whampoa Ltd, 2011–12. *Recreations:* hill-walking, woodwork, triathlon. *Address:* Cabinet Office, 70 Whitehall, SW1A 2AS.

RYCROFT, Sir Richard (John), 8th Bt *cr* 1784, of Calton, Yorkshire; *b* 15 June 1946; *s* of Cdre Henry Richard Rycroft, OBE, DSC, RN, 4th *s* of 5th Bt, and Penelope Gwendoline Rycroft (*née* Evans-Lombe); *S* cousin, 1999. *Educ:* Sherborne. Lifeboat Operations Manager, Burnham-on-Crouch RNLI Lifeboat, 2006–. *Recreations:* sailing, classic boats and cars, jazz music, Burmese cats. *Heir: cousin* Francis Edward Rycroft [*b* 4 Aug. 1950; *m* 1975, Cherry Willmott; one *s* one *d*]. *Club:* Royal Corinthian Yacht.

RYDER, family name of **Earl of Harrowby** and of **Baron Ryder of Wensum**.

RYDER OF WENSUM, Baron *cr* 1997 (Life Peer), of Wensum in the co. of Norfolk; **Richard Andrew Ryder,** OBE 1981; PC 1990; Chairman, Child Bereavement UK, since 2013; *b* 4 Feb. 1949; *s* of Richard Stephen Ryder, JP, DL, and Margaret MacKenzie; *m* 1981, Caroline Mary, CVO, MBE, *o d* of Sir David Stephens; one *d* (one *s* decd). *Educ:* Radley; Magdalene Coll., Cambridge (BA Hons History, 1971). Journalist. Chm., Eastern Counties Radio, 1997–2001; Vice-Chm., Bd of Govs, BBC, 2002–04 (Acting Chm., 2004). Dir, Great Bradley Farms Co. and other businesses, 2002–. Political Secretary: to Leader of the Opposition, 1975–79; to Prime Minister, 1979–81. Contested (C) Gateshead E, Feb. and Oct., 1974. MP (C) Mid Norfolk, 1983–97. Parliamentary Private Secretary: to Financial Sec. to the Treasury, 1984; to Sec. of State for Foreign and Commonwealth Affairs, 1984–86; an Asst Govt Whip, 1986–88; Parly Under-Sec. of State, MAFF, 1988–89; Econ. Sec. to HM Treasury, 1989–90; Paymaster General, 1990; Parly Sec. to HM Treasury and Govt Chief Whip, 1990–95. Chm., Cons. Foreign and Commonwealth Council, 1984–89. Chm., UCanDoIT, 2011–14. Chm., Bd of Mgt, Inst. of Cancer Res., 2005–13. *Address:* House of Lords, SW1A 0PW.

See also C. B. Stephens.

RYDER, Edward Alexander, CB 1992; HM Chief Inspector of Nuclear Installations, Health and Safety Executive, 1985–91; Joint Chairman and Head of UK Delegation, Channel Tunnel Safety Authority, 1992–97; *b* 9 Nov. 1931; *s* of Alexander Harry and Gwendoline Gladys Ryder; *m* 1956, Janet (*d* 2005); one *s* one *d*. *Educ:* Cheltenham Grammar School; Bristol University (BSc). CPhys; FInstP. Flying Officer, RAF, 1953–55; Engineer, GEC Applied Electronics Labs, 1955–57; Control Engineer, Hawker Siddeley Nuclear Power Co., 1957–61; Sen. Engineer, CEGB, 1961–71; Principal Inspector, then Superintending Inspector, HM Nuclear Installations Inspectorate, 1971–80; Head of Hazardous Installations Policy Branch, 1980–85, Head of Nuclear Installations Policy Branch, 1985, HSE. Sec., Adv. Cttee on Major Hazards, 1980–85. Chairman: HSC Working Gp on Ionising Radiations, 1987–91; IAEA Nuclear Safety Standards Adv. Gp, 1988–93; Mem., Intergovtl Commn for Channel Tunnel, 1992–97. Organiser, Shiplake and Dunsden Area, RBL Poppy Appeal, 1996–2003. Mem., Shiplake Parish Council, 1999–2011 (Vice-Chm., 2000–03 and 2007–11; Chm., 2003–05). *Recreations:* golf—or is it nature study, concertgoing, bridge. *Address:* Pinewood, Baskerville Lane, Lower Shiplake, Henley on Thames, Oxon RG9 3JY.

RYDER, Rt Hon. Sir Ernest (Nigel), Kt 2004; PC 2013; TD 1996; **Rt Hon. Lord Justice Ryder;** DL; a Lord Justice of Appeal, since 2013; Senior President of Tribunals, since 2015; *b* 9 Dec. 1957; *s* of Dr John Buckley Ryder, TD and Constance Ryder; *m* 1990, Janette Lynn Martin; one *d*. *Educ:* Bolton Sch.; Peterhouse, Cambridge (MA 1983). Merchant banker, Grindley Brandt & Co., 1979; called to the Bar, Gray's Inn, 1981, Bencher, 2004; QC 1997; Asst Recorder, 1997–2000; a Recorder, 2000–04; a Dep. High Court Judge, 2001–04; a Judge of the High Ct of Justice, Family Div., 2004–13; Presiding Judge, Northern Circuit, 2009–13; Judge in Charge of Modernisation of Family Justice, 2011–13. Counsel, N Wales Tribunal of Inquiry, 1996–99. Asst Boundary Comr, 2000–04. Commnd Duke of Lancaster's Own Yeomanry, 1981; Sqdn Leader, 1990; Sqdn Leader, Royal Mercian and Lancastrian Yeomanry, 1992. Chancellor, Univ. of Bolton, 2014–. Trustee, Nuffield Foundn, 2014–. DL Greater Manchester, 2009. FRSA 2010. Hon. LLD Bolton, 2013. *Recreations:* listening, walking. *Address:* Royal Courts of Justice, Strand, WC2A 2LL.

RYDER, Janet; Member (Plaid Cymru) North Wales, National Assembly for Wales, 1999–2011; *b* Sunderland, 21 June 1955; *m* 1977, Peter Ryder (marr. diss. 2005); two *s* one *d*. *Educ:* Northern Counties Coll. of Educn (Teacher's Cert. (Dist.)); Open Univ. (BA Hist./Arts). Teacher: Little Weighton Co. Primary Sch., E Riding of Yorks, 1980–83; St Bede's Catholic Primary Sch., Hull, 1987–88; Coleford Primary Sch., Hull (i/c Religious and Moral Educn), 1988–89; Bransholme Youth Club, Hull. Member: N Wales Fire Authy, 1995–99; Bd, Denbighshire Voluntary Services Council, 1995–99. Mem., voluntary gps, incl. Strategic Planning Gp for People with a Learning Difficulty. Member (Plaid Cymru): Rhuthun Town Council, 1992–2003 (Mayor, 1998–2000); Denbighshire CC, 1994–99 (mem., various cttees; Chairman: Children and Families Sub-cttee, 1995–98; Denbigh Early Years Partnership, 1996–98; Denbigh Plan Partnership). National Assembly for Wales: Plaid Cymru spokesperson on local govt, planning, housing, envmt and transport, 1999–2001, on local govt and finance, 2001–03, on educn and life-long learning, 2003–09. Mem., Nat. Exec., Plaid Cymru, 1993–99, 2006–10.

RYDER, John; QC 2000; a Recorder, since 2000; *m* 1989, Carolyn Espley; one *d*. *Educ:* Monmouth Sch. Called to the Bar, Inner Temple, 1980; Asst Recorder, 1997–2000. *Recreations:* riding, ski-ing, opera. *Address:* 21 College Hill, EC4R 2RP. *Club:* Travellers.

RYDER, Michael, CMG 2007; HM Diplomatic Service, retired; Chairman, Peace Direct, since 2013; Director, Avera Consulting Ltd, since 2012; *b* Manchester, 13 Nov. 1953; *s* of Bill and Vera Ryder; *m* Dr Frances Klemperer; one *s* one *d*. *Educ:* Marple Hall Grammar Sch. for Boys; Trinity Hall, Cambridge (BA 1976). Harkness Fellow, Johns Hopkins Univ., 1977–79; history supervisor, Cambridge Univ., 1979–82; Lectr, Osaka Gakuin Univ., 1982–84; entered FCO, 1984; various posts, FCO, 1984–97; Hd, Security Policy Dept, FCO, 1997; Special Rep. for Internat. Drug Issues, 1998–2003; Hd, Iraq Inquiry Unit, FCO and Dep. Sec., Butler Inquiry into Intelligence on Weapons of Mass Destruction in Iraq, 2003–04; Minister and Dep. Hd of Mission, Kabul, 2006–07; UK Sen. Civilian Rep. in Helmand, 2008; UK Special Envoy to Republic of Mali, 2009; Special Rep. for Sudan, 2010–12. Non-exec. Dir, Knowledge Unlatched, 2013–. *Publications:* contrib. articles to Histl Jl, Notes and Queries. *Recreations:* mountain walking, reading.

RYDER, Dr Peter, CB 1994; FRMets; consultant in environmental information services, since 1996; General Secretary, Royal Meteorological Society, 2001–06; *b* 10 March 1942; *s* of Percival Henry Sussex Ryder and Bridget (*née* McCormack); *m* 1965, Jacqueline Doris Sylvia Rigby; two *s* one *d*. *Educ:* Yorebridge Grammar Sch., Askrigg; Univ. of Leeds (BSc 1963; PhD 1966). FRMets 2004. Research Asst, Physics Dept, Univ. of Leeds, 1966–67; Meteorological Office, 1967–96: Asst Dir, Cloud Physics Res., 1976–82; Asst Dir, Systems Develt, 1982–84; Dep. Dir, Observational Services, 1984–88; Dep. Dir, Forecasting Services, 1988–89; Dir of Services, 1989–90; Dep. Chief Exec. and Dir of Ops, then Man. Dir (Ops), 1990–96. Royal Meteorological Society: Mem. Council, 1980–83; Mem., Qly Jl Editing Cttee, 1981–84. Chairman: Thames Regl Flood Defence Cttee, EA, 2003–09 (Mem., 1997–2003); EuroGOOS, 2003–08; Scientific Adv. Panel, Marine Protected Areas, DEFRA, 2009–12. William Gaskell Meml Medal, RMetS, 1981; L. G. Groves Meml Prize for Meteorology, MoD, 1982. *Publications:* papers in learned jls on experimental atmospheric physics and meteorology. *Recreations:* gardening, fishing, photography, grandchildren. *Address:* 8 Sherring Close, Bracknell, Berks RG42 2LD.

RYDER, Dr Richard Hood Jack Dudley; author, campaigner; *b* 3 July 1940; *s* of late Major D. C. D. Ryder, JP, Rempstone Hall, and Vera Mary (*née* Cook); *m* 1974, Audrey Jane Smith (marr. diss. 1999); one *s* one *d*. *Educ:* Sherborne Sch.; Cambridge Univ. (MA; PhD 1993); Edinburgh Univ. (DCP); Columbia Univ., NY (Fellow). AFBPsS; FZS. Sen. Clinical Psychologist, Warneford Hosp., Oxford, 1967–84; Principal Clin. Psychologist, St James Hosp., Portsmouth, 1983–84. Chm., Oxford Div. of Clin. Psych., 1981–83. Member: Oxford Regional Adolescent Service, 1971–84; DHSS Health Adv. Service, 1977–78. Dir, Radon Control Ltd, 1990; Chm., Animal Books and Media Ltd, 2012–. Royal Society for Prevention of Cruelty to Animals: Mem. Council, 1972– (Chm., 1977–79 and 2002–03; Vice Chm., 1990–91); Dep. Treas., 2000–01; Chairman: Political Cttee, 1979–80; Animal Experimentation Adv. Cttee, 1983–85; Public Relns and Campaign Cttee, 1990–91; Scientific Cttee, 1992–; Internat. Cttee, 1999–. Dep. Chm., Cttee on Welfare of Animals in Psychology, BPsS, 2001–. Political Consultant, 1991–93, Dir, 1993–97, Political Animal Lobby Ltd. Founder Mem., Gen. Election Co-ordinating Cttee on Animal Protection, 1978; Founder, Eurogroup for Animal Welfare, 1979; Pres., British Union for Abolition of Vivisection, 1980; Prog. Organiser, 1984–91, Dir of Animal Welfare Studies, 1997–2000, IFAW; UK Delegate, Eurogroup, 1980, 2002. Chm., Liberal Animal Welfare Gp, 1981–88; Member: Liberal Party Council, 1983–87; Liberal Party Policy Panels on defence, health, home affairs, Eur. affairs, foreign affairs, environment, 1981–88; contested (L): Buckingham, 1983; Teignbridge, 1987. Pres., Lib Dems Animal Protection Gp, 1989–91. Chairman: Teignbridge NSPCC, 1984–87; Teignbridge Home Start, 1987–89; Strategic Animal Welfare Panel, RSPCA, 2009. Mellon Prof., Dept of Philosophy, Tulane Univ., New Orleans, 1996. Broadcaster and writer on psychological, ethical, political and animal protection subjects. Trustee, NT, 2001–04. Mem. Cttee, British Conifer Soc., 2005–11 (Chm., 2008–10). Co-founder of business, Psychoprofiles, 2005. FRSA 1992. *Publications:* Speciesism, 1970; Victims of Science, 1975, 2nd edn 1984; (ed) Animal Rights—a Symposium, 1979; Animal Revolution: changing attitudes to speciesism, 1989, 2nd edn 2000; Painism, 1990; (ed) Animal Welfare and the Environment, 1992; The Political Animal, 1998; Painism: a modern morality, 2001; The Calcrafts of Rempstone Hall, 2005; Putting Morality Back into Politics, 2006; Nelson, Hitler and Diana, 2009; Speciesism, Painism and Happiness: a morality for the twenty-first century, 2011; The Black Pimpernel, 2013. *Recreations:* trees, opera, philosophy. *Address:* 11 The Imperial, Exeter EX4 4AJ. *T:* (01392) 426727. *Club:* National Liberal.

RYDSTRÖM, Marilyn, OBE 2009; Director General, People's Dispensary for Sick Animals, 1999–2008; *b* 24 Oct. 1947; *d* of Kenneth Oberg and Averil Irene Oberg (*née* Harding); *m* 1985, Björn Lennart Rydström. *Educ:* Guildford Co. Tech. Coll.; Bedford Coll., London Univ. (BSc Hons Sociol.). Churchill Fellow, 1984. Probation Officer, Surrey Probation Service, 1971–72; Social Worker, Surrey CC, 1972–74; Sen. Social Worker, Borough of Hillingdon, 1974–77; Hd of Community Projects, Capital Radio Plc, 1977–87; Dir, Fundraising, RNID, 1987–89; Consultant, Chapter One Ketchum Fundraising, 1989–92; Mktg/Commercial Dir, Stowe Sch., 1992–95; Dir, Client Services, Guide Dogs for the Blind, 1995–99. Mem., Crime Prevention Adv. Cttee, NACRO, 1979–83. Member: Grants Cttee, Help a London Child, 1977–84; Mgt Cttee, Piccadilly Advice Centre, 1978–82; Mgt Cttee, Alone in London, 1979–82. The Prince's Trust: Member: NW London Cttee, 1982–90 (Chm., 1987–90); Council, 1986–88; Strategy Gp for London, 1989–90. Member: Lord Chancellor's Adv. Cttee to appoint Shropshire JPs, 2010–12; Lord Chancellor's West Mercia Adv. Cttee, 2012–13; Shropshire Adv. Sub-Cttee, 2012–13. Founding Trustee and Mem., Mgt Cttee, Artsline, 1983–85; Director and Trustee: Severn Hospice Ltd, 2007–; Marine Conservation Soc., 2010–14. CCMI 2007. *Publications:* various articles/features of social/health interest in women's press. *Recreations:* marine biology and marine conservation, scuba diving, wildlife photography. *E:* marilynrydstrom@aol.com.

RYKWERT, Prof. Joseph, CBE 2014; MA (Cantab), DrRCA; Paul Philippe Cret Professor of Architecture, University of Pennsylvania, 1988–98, now Emeritus; *b* 5 April 1926; *s* of Szymon Rykwert and Elizabeth Melup; *m* 1st, 1960 (marr. diss. 1967); 2nd, 1972, Anne-Marie Sandersley; one *s* one *d*. *Educ:* Charterhouse; Bartlett Sch. of Architecture; Architectural Assoc. (Hon. Fellow 2013). Lectr, Hochschule für Gestaltung, Ulm, 1958; Librarian and Tutor, Royal Coll. of Art, 1961–67; Prof. of Art, Univ. of Essex, 1967–80; Lectr on Arch., 1980–85, Reader, 1985–88, Univ. of Cambridge. Bollingen Fellow, 1966; Inst. for Arch. and Urban Studies, NY, 1969–71; Sen. Fellow, Council of Humanities, Princeton Univ., 1971; Visiting Professor: Institut d'Urbanisme, Univ. of Paris, 1974–76; Princeton Univ., 1977; Andrew Mellon Vis. Prof., Cooper Union, NY, 1977; Slade Prof. of Fine Art, Cambridge Univ., 1979–80; Vis. Fellow, Darwin Coll., Cambridge, 1979–80; Mem., Trinity Hall, Cambridge, 1980–; Sen. Fellow, Center for the Advanced Studies in the Visual Arts. Nat. Gall. of Art, Washington; Vis. Prof., Univ. of Louvain, 1981–84; George Lurcy Vis. Prof., Columbia, 1986; Sen. Schol., Getty Res. Inst. in Hist. of Art and Humanities, 1992–93; British Acad. Vis. Prof., Univ. of Bath, 1998–99. Pres., Comité Internat. des Critiques d'Architecture, 1996–. Mem. Commn, Venice Biennale, 1974–78. Consultant, Min. of Urban Develt and Ecology, Republic of Mexico, 1986–88. Co-ed., RES (Anthropology and Aesthetics), 1981–. Member: Accademia Clementina, 1992; Accademia di S Luca, 1993; Polish Acad. of Arts and Scis, 1998. Hon. FRA 2011. Hon. DSc: Edinburgh, 1995; Bath, 2000; Hon. Dr: Córdoba, Argentina, 1998; Rome, 2005; Toronto, 2005; Trieste 2008. Alfred Jurzykowski Foundn Award, 1990; Medalla de Oro en las Bellas Artes, Spain, 2009; Royal Gold Medal, RIBA, 2014. Chevalier des Arts et des Lettres, 1984. *Publications:* The Golden House, 1947; (ed) The Ten Books of Architecture, by L. B. Alberti (annotated edn of Leoni trans. of 1756), 1955, new translation from Latin, as On the Art of Building in Ten Books,

1988; The Idea of a Town, 1963, 3rd edn 1988; Church Building, 1966; On Adam's House in Paradise, 1972, 2nd edn 1982; (ed) Parole nel Vuoto, by A. Loos, 1972; The First Moderns, 1980; The Necessity of Artifice, 1981; (with Anne Rykwert) The Brothers Adam, 1985; The Dancing Column, 1996; The Seduction of Place, 2000, 2nd edn 2004; The Judicious Eye, 2008; contrib. Arch. Rev., Burlington Mag., Lotus. *Recreation:* rare. *Address:* 26A Wedderburn Road, NW3 5QG. *Club:* Savile.

RYLANCE, His Honour John Randolph Trevor; a Circuit Judge, 2003–14; a Deputy Circuit Judge, since 2014; *b* 26 Feb. 1944; *s* of late Dr Ralph Curzon Rylance and Margaret Joan Clare Rylance (*née* Chambers); *m* 1974, Philippa Anne Bailey; two *d*. *Educ:* Shrewsbury Sch. Called to the Bar, Lincoln's Inn, 1968; Parly Res. Asst to Sir Edward Gardner, QC, MP, 1971–73; Asst Recorder, 1989–93; a Recorder, 1993–2003. Gov., Fulham Cross Sch., 1977–88. Mem. Exec. Cttee, Fulham Soc., 1988–2012. Trustee, Fulham Palace Trust, 1991–2012 (Chm., 1996–2011). *Address:* 28 Doneraile Street, SW6 6EN. *Club:* Hurlingham.

RYLANCE, Prof. Richard William, PhD; Professor of English, University of Exeter, since 2003; Chief Executive, Arts and Humanities Research Council, since 2009 (on secondment); Chairman, Executive, Research Councils UK, since 2011; *b* Manchester, 30 Jan. 1954; *s* of John and Doreen Rylance; *m*; one *d*. *Educ:* Bury Grammar Sch., Lancs; Univ. of Leicester (BA 1st Cl. English; PGCE 1981; PhD 1990). Lectr, Principal Lectr, Prof. and Dean, Anglia Poly. Univ., 1985–2002; Hd of English, 2005, Hd, Sch. of Arts, Languages and Literatures, 2005–09, Univ. of Exeter. Chair: Council for Coll. and Univ. English, 2000–03; Sub-panel for English, RAE 2008. *Publications:* Roland Barthes, 1994; Victorian Psychology and British Culture 1850–1880, 2000; contribs to jls and acad. books. *Recreations:* long distance hill walking, scuba diving, music, Manchester City Football Club. *Address:* Arts and Humanities Research Council, Polaris House, North Star Avenue, Swindon SN2 1FL. *T:* (01793) 416012, *Fax:* (01793) 416001. *E:* r.rylance@ahrc.ac.uk.

RYLAND, His Honour Timothy Richard Godfrey Fetherstonhaugh; a Circuit Judge, 1988–2008; a Judge at Central London Civil Trial Centre (formerly Central London County Court), 1994–2008; *b* 13 June 1938; *s* of late Richard Desmond Fetherstonhaugh Ryland and Frances Katharine Vernon Ryland; *m* 1991, Jean Margaret Muirhead. *Educ:* St Andrew's Coll.; TCD (BA (Moderatorship), LLB). Called to Bar, Gray's Inn, 1961. Dep. Circuit Judge, 1978; a Recorder, 1983–88. *Recreations:* opera, wine. *Clubs:* Lansdowne; Kildare Street and University (Dublin).

RYLANDS, Rt Rev. Mark James; *see* Shrewsbury, Bishop Suffragan of.

RYLE, Evelyn Margaret; consultant and author; *b* 26 March 1947; *d* of Paul McConnell Cassidy and Emily Margaret Cassidy (*née* Wright); *m* 1975, Anthony E. Ryle, OBE; one *s* one *d*. *Educ:* King's Park Sch., Glasgow; Univ. of Glasgow (MA Hons; Dip. Management Studies). Dexion-Comino Internat., 1969; commnd WRAF; Flight Lieut, accountant officer, 1973; financial systems analyst: Dexion Gp, 1975; Southern Electricity, 1976; Departments of Trade and Industry, 1977–96; British Steel Corp. Finance; Commercial Relations and Exports; Consumer Affairs; Vehicles Div.; Dep. Dir, IT Services, 1987; Head, Educn and Trng Policy, 1990; seconded to Design Council as Dir-Gen., 1993; Dir, Business Competitiveness, Govt Office for London, 1995–96; Mem., CSSB Panel of Chairs, 1996–99. Mem., Finance Cttee, 1996–2002 (Chair, 2001–02), Mem., Exec., 1999–2002, Charter 88. Mem. Cttee, Romantic Novelists' Assoc., 2003–11 (Hon. Treasurer, 2004–08; Hon. Sec., 2008–11; Vice Pres., 2014). *Recreations:* family, reading, music, gardening, needlework, walking. *E:* eryle@btinternet.com. *Club:* Royal Air Force.

RYLEY, John Hamilton; Head, Sky News, since 2006; *b* Chelmsford, 21 Dec. 1961; *s* of late Ted Ryley and of Wanda Ryley; *m* 1987, Harriet Constable; one *s* two *d*. *Educ:* Eastbourne Coll.; Durham Univ. (BA); Wharton Sch. of Business, Philadelphia (AMP). Freelance radio journalist, 1985–87; news trainee, BBC, 1987–89; news producer, 1990–92, prog. ed., 1992–95, News at Ten, ITN; Exec. Producer, 1995–2000, Exec. Ed., 2000–06, Sky News; producer, Sky Gen. Election results, Budget progs and breaking news specials. Mem. Bd, Nat. Council for Training of Journalists. Mem. Bd, Media Trust. Individual Achievement Award, Broadcast Digital Awards, for launching campaign for televised leaders debates, 2010. *Recreations:* cricket, cycling, fishing. *Address:* c/o Sky News, Isleworth, Middx TW7 5ED. *E:* john.ryley@BskyB.com.

RYMAN, John; *b* 7 Nov. 1930. *Educ:* Leighton Park; Pembroke College, Oxford. Inns of Court Regt (TA), 1948–51. Called to the Bar, Middle Temple, 1957. Harmsworth Law Scholar. MP (Lab): Blyth, Oct. 1974–1983; Blyth Valley, 1983–87. Mem. Council, Assoc. of the Clergy, 1976. *Recreation:* horses.

RYMER, Rear Adm. Alan Robert; Director, Lune Consulting Ltd, since 2012; *b* Southport, 2 April 1958; *s* of Robert Rymer and Muriel Rymer; *m* 1979, Janis Taylor; two *d*. *Educ:* King George V Grammar Sch., Southport; BRNC; Royal Naval Engrg Coll., Manadon (BSc Hons Mechanical Engrg 1979); Manchester Business Sch. (Chartered Mgt Inst. Strategic Direction and Leadership prog.). CEng 1994. HMS Blake, 1979; HMS Torquay, 1980–81; HMS Leander, 1981–83; HMS Sultan, 1983–86; HM Yacht Britannia, 1986–88; HMS Active, 1988–90; RN Staff Coll., Greenwich, 1991; Asst Defence Attaché, Bonn, 1992–94; HMS Marlborough, 1995–97; Naval Manning Agency, 1997–99; MoD, London, 1999–2000; CSO Engrg, 2000–03; Dir Naval Officer Appts (Engr), 2003; Dir of Ops, Warship Support Agency, 2003–05; Dir Naval Personnel, 2006–07; CO HMS Sultan and Comdt, Defence Coll. of Electro-Mechanical Engrg, 2007–10; Dir, Trng and Educn, MoD, 2010–12. Chm., C of E Soldiers', Sailors' and Airmen's Clubs Housing Assoc., 2014–; non-exec. Dir, SE Coast Ambulance Service NHS Foundn Trust, 2015–. Vice Pres., Inst. of Marine Engrg, Sci. and Technol., 2008–13. Pres., Selsey RNLI Lifeboat Stn, 2012–. *Recreations:* family, golf, River Lune, guitar. *E:* al.rymer@hotmail.com. *Club:* Goodwood.

S

SAAKASHVILI, Mikheil; Governor, Odessa Region, Ukraine, since 2015; President of Georgia, 2004–13; *b* 21 Dec. 1967; *s* of Nokoloz Saakashvili and Giuli Alasania; *m* Sandra Elizabeth Roelofs; two *s*. *Educ:* Nat. Law Center, George Washington Univ.; Columbia Univ. (LLM); Internat. Inst. of Human Rights, France (Dip.); Dept of Internat. Law, Kiev State Univ. (law degree). Hd, Dept of Ethnic Relns, Georgian Cttee for Human Rights and Ethnic Relns, 1992–94; Foreign Lawyer, Patterson, Belknap, Webb & Tyler, NY, 1994–95; MP, Georgia, 1995–98; Chm., Cttee for Const., Legal Affairs and Rule of Law, Parlt of Georgia, 1995–98; Co-Chm., Council of Justice, Georgia, 1998; Vice-Pres., Parly Assembly of Council of Europe, 2000; Minister of Justice, 2000–01; Chm., Tbilisi City Council, 2002–03. Chm., Majority Faction of Union of Citizens, Parlt of Georgia, 1998.

SAATCHI, family name of **Baron Saatchi**.

SAATCHI, Baron *cr* 1996 (Life Peer), of Staplefield in the county of West Sussex; **Maurice Saatchi;** Partner, M & C Saatchi plc, since 1995; *b* 21 June 1946; *s* of late Daisy and Nathan Saatchi; *m* 1984, Josephine Hart (*d* 2011); one *s*, and one step *s*. *Educ:* London School of Economics and Political Science (1st class BSc Econ). Co-Founder of Saatchi & Saatchi Co., 1970, Chm., 1985–94. Chm., Finsbury Food Gp (formerly Megalomedia) PLC, 1995–2008. Opposition spokesman, H of L, on Treasury affairs, 1999–2003, on Cabinet Office affairs, 2001–03. Co-Chm., Conservative Party, 2003–05. A Trustee, Victoria and Albert Mus., 1988–96; Member: Council, RCA, 1997–2000; Westminster Abbey Inst.; Director: Centre for Policy Studies, 1999– (Chm., 2009–); Garden Mus. (formerly Mus. of Garden History), 2001–. Mem. Bd, Cons. Party Foundn. Governor, LSE, 1996–. *Publications:* The Science of Politics, 2001; *pamphlets:* The War of Independence, 1999; Happiness Can't Buy Money, 1999; The Bad Samaritan, 2000; Poor People! Stop Paying Tax!, 2001; If This is Conservatism, I am a Conservative, 2005; In Praise of Ideology, 2006; Sleeping Beauty, 2007. *Address:* (office) 36 Golden Square, W1F 9EE. *T:* (020) 7543 4510.
See also C. Saatchi.

SAATCHI, Charles; Founder, Saatchi & Saatchi Co., 1970–93; Partner, M & C Saatchi plc, 1995–2006; *b* 9 June 1943; *m* 2003, Nigella Lucy Lawson, *qv* (marr. diss. 2013). *Educ:* Christ's Coll., Finchley. Founder, The Saatchi Gallery, 1985. *Publications:* My Name is Charles Saatchi and I am an Artoholic, 2009; Be The Worst You Can Be: life's too long for patience & virtue, 2012; Babble, 2013. *Address:* Saatchi Gallery, Duke of York's HQ, King's Road, SW3 4RY.

SABAPATHY, Paul Chandrasekharan, CBE 2004 (OBE 1995); Lord Lieutenant of West Midlands, 2007–15; *b* Madras, 26 Sept. 1942; *s* of John and Catherine Sabapathy; *m* 1969, Win White; one *s* one *d*. *Educ:* Lawrence Sch., Lovedale, India; Madras Christian Coll. (BSc Phys 1963); Aston Univ., Birmingham (MSc Industrial Admin 1968). ACMA 1994. IMI plc: Accountant, Eley Ltd, 1968–72; Cost Accountant, Enots Ltd, 1972–74; Finance Dir, IMI Refiners Ltd, 1974–88; IMI Gp Corporate Services Manager, 1988–92; Asst Man. Dir, IMI Titanium Ltd, 1992–96. Member Board: Black Country Develt Corp., 1987–89; Birmingham Heartland Develt Corp., 1992–98; Pres., Walsall Chamber of Commerce, 1988; Chm., W Midlands Industrial Develt Adv. Bd, 1997–2002. Chief Exec., N Birmingham Community NHS Trust, 1996–2000; Member Board: Nat. Blood Authy, 2000–05; N Birmingham PCT, 2001–03; Chairman: E Birmingham PCT, 2004–06; Birmingham E and N PCT, 2006–11; Vice Chm., NHS Confederation PCT Network, 2007–11. Trustee: New Walsall Art Gall., 1997–2003; Refugee Council, 2002–03; Bournville Village Trust, 2006–. Chm., Birmingham City Univ., 2002–09; Dep. Chm., Cttee of Univ. Chairmen, 2004–05. FRSA; FRSocMed 2006. *Recreations:* travelling, gardening.

SABBEN-CLARE, James Paley; Headmaster, Winchester College, 1985–2000; *b* 9 Sept. 1941; *s* of late Ernest Sabben-Clare and Rosamond Dorothy Mary Scott; *m* 1969, Geraldine Mary Borton, LLB; one *s* one *d*. *Educ:* Winchester College (Scholar); New College, Oxford (Scholar; 1st Class Classical Hon. Mods and Greats, 1964; MA). Asst Master, Marlborough College, 1964–68; Vis. Fellow, All Souls College, Oxford, 1967–68; Winchester College, 1968–2000: Head of Classics Dept, 1969–79; Second Master, 1979–85. Chm., HMC, 1999. Governor: Oundle Sch., 2001–09; British Sch., Paris, 2001–13; Gordonstoun Sch., 2002–06. Member, Advisory Board: Global Educn Mgt Systems (GEMS), 2003–07; VT Educn and Skills, 2004–06. Academic Consultant, Prince's Teaching Inst., 2006–. Trustee: Bournemouth SO Endowment Trust, 2009–12; Dorset Historic Churches Trust, 2009–. *Publications:* Caesar and Roman Politics, 1971, 2nd edn 1981; Fables from Aesop, 1976; The Culture of Athens, 1978, 2nd edn 1980; Winchester College, 1981, 2nd edn 1988; (contrib.) Winchester: history and literature, 1992; contribs to educnl and classical jls. *Recreations:* Italian opera, mountains, furniture making, living in Dorset. *Address:* Sandy Hill Barn, Corfe Castle, Dorset BH20 5JF. *T:* (01929) 481080.
See also R. M. Sabben-Clare.

SABBEN-CLARE, Rebecca Mary; QC 2012; *b* Winchester, 13 June 1971; *d* of James Paley Sabben-Clare, *qv*; *m* 2008, William Howard; one *s* one *d*. *Educ:* St Swithun's Sch., Winchester; Winchester Coll.; New Coll., Oxford (BA). Called to the Bar, Gray's Inn, 1993; in practice as a barrister, 1993–. *Recreations:* scuba diving, cooking, building sandcastles. *Address:* 7 King's Bench Walk, Temple, EC4Y 7DS. *T:* (020) 7910 8300, *Fax:* (020) 7910 8400. *E:* rsabbenclare@7kbw.co.uk.

SABIN, Paul Robert; DL; Chairman, Veolia Water Southeast (formerly Folkestone and Dover Water Company), 2007–12 (non-executive Director, since 1998); Chief Executive, Leeds Castle Foundation and Leeds Castle (Enterprises) Ltd, 1998–2003; *b* 29 March 1943; *s* of Robert Reginald and Dorothy Maude Sabin; *m* 1965, Vivien Furnival; one *s* two *d*. *Educ:* Oldbury Grammar Sch. DMS Aston Univ.; CPFA (IPFA 1966). West Bromwich CBC, 1959–69; Redditch Develt Corp., 1969–81, Chief Finance Officer, 1975–81; City of Birmingham, 1981–86: City Treas., 1982–86; Dep. Chief Exec., 1984–86; Chief Exec., Kent CC, 1986–97. Hon. Citizen, City of Baltimore, Md, USA, 1985. Kent Ambassador, 2002–. DL Kent, 2001. *Recreations:* fine books, music.

SABINE, Peter Aubrey, DSc; FRSE; FIMMM; CEng, CGeol, CSci, FGS; Deputy Director (Chief Scientific Officer, Chief Geologist), British Geological Survey (formerly Institute of Geological Sciences), 1977–84; *b* 29 Dec. 1924; *s* of late Bernard Robert and Edith Lucy Sabine; *m* 1946, Peggy Willis Lambert, MSc, FBCS, CITP, FRSA, FSS; one *s*. *Educ:* Brockley County Sch.; Chelsea Polytechnic; Royal Coll. of Science, Imperial Coll., London (BSc, ARCS (1st Cl. Geol.; Watts Medal) 1945); PhD 1951, DSc 1970, London. FRSE 1964. Represented Youth of Empire, Westminster Abbey Empire Youth Service, 1940. Apptd Geological Survey of Gt Britain as Geologist, 1945; Geological Museum, 1946–50; in charge Petrographical Dept, Geol Survey and Museum, 1950, Chief Petrographer, 1959; Asst Dir, S England and Wales, 1970; Chief Geochemist, 1977; Dep. Dir, 1977–84. Sec., Geol Soc. of London, 1959–66, Vice-Pres., 1966–67, 1982–84 (Lyell Fund, 1955; Sen. Fellow, 1994); International Union of Geological Sciences: Mem. Commn on Systematics of Igneous Rocks, 1969–2002; Mem. Commn on Systematics in Petrology, 1980–96 (Chm., 1984–92; Vice-Chm., 1992–96); Chief UK Deleg., 1980–84; Mem. Council, 1980–92; Member Council: Geologists' Assoc., 1966–70 (Life Mem., 1991); Mineralogical Soc., 1950–53; Instn of Mining and Metallurgy, 1976–80; Mineral Industry Res. Orgn, 1983–86; Member: DTI Chem. and Mineral Research Requirements Bd, 1973–82; Minerals, Metals Extraction and Reclamation Cttee, 1981–84; EEC Cttees on minerals and geochemistry; Cttee of Dirs of W European Geol Surveys, 1978–84; Chm., Sub-Cttee on geochem. and cosmochem. of British Nat. Cttee for Geology, 1977–86. Royal Institution: Visitor, 1979–82; Mem., Audit Cttee, 1987–90 (Chm., 1989–90). Life Fellow, Mineralogical Soc., 1999 (Mem., 1945; Mem. Council, 1950–53); FMSA 1959 (Sen. Fellow, 2003); FBCartS 1996. FRSA. *Publications:* Chemical Analysis of Igneous Rocks (with E. M. Guppy), 1956; (with D. S. Sutherland) Petrography of British Igneous Rocks, 1982; (jtly) Classification of Igneous Rocks, 1989, 2nd edn 2002 (trans. Chinese and Russian); numerous scientific contribs in Mem. Geol. Surv., Qly Jl Geol. Soc., Mineral. Mag., Phil. Trans Roy. Soc., etc. *Recreations:* gardening, genealogy. *Address:* Malmsmead, 12 Orchehill Avenue, Gerrards Cross, Bucks SL9 8PX. *T:* (01753) 891529. *Clubs:* Athenæum; Geological Society (Sen. Hon. Mem.); Royal Scots (Edinburgh); Probus (Hon. Life Mem.).

SABOURIAN, Prof. Hamid, PhD; FBA 2013; Professor of Economics and Game Theory, University of Cambridge, since 2005; Fellow, King's College, Cambridge, since 1985; *b* Tehran, 1 Jan. 1959; *s* of Eynollah Sabourian and Nosrat Zaman Sabourian (*née* Dashti); *m* 1998, Elisa May Sampson; one *s* three *d*. *Educ:* Safinia Primary Sch., Tehran; Alborz High Sch., Tehran; Clifton Coll., Bristol; King's Coll., Cambridge (BA 1st Cl. Econs 1980; MA Econs 1984; PhD 1987); London Sch. of Econs and Pol Sci. (MSc Math. Econs 1981). Asst Lectr, 1987–90, Lectr, 1990–2002, Reader, 2002–05, Univ. of Cambridge; Prof. of Econs, Birkbeck, Univ. of London, 2005–07; Chm., Faculty of Econs, Univ. of Cambridge, 2007–11. Visiting Professor: UCLA, 1992; Eur. Univ. Inst., Florence, 1995–96; NY Univ., 1999; Cowles Foundn, Yale Univ., 1999; CV Star Center, NY Univ., 2001, 2003; Birkbeck, Univ. of London, 2001–04, 2007–11; Univ. Carlos III Madrid, 2013 (Banco Santander Chair of Excellence, 2013); Singapore Mgt Univ., 2013; Fung Vis. Prof., Hong Kong Univ. of Sci. and Technol., 2011–14; Vis. Lectr, LSE, 1996. Fellow, Soc. for Advancement of Econ. Theory, 2011; Keynes Fellow, Univ. of Cambridge, 2011. Associate Ed., Jl Econ. Theory, 2004–13; Mem., Editl Bd, Econ. Theory, 2009–. *Publications:* contribs to jls incl. Econometrica, Jl Econ. Theory, Games and Econ. Behavior, Econ. Jl, Eur. Econ. Jl, Jl Math. Econs, Math. Social Scis. *Recreations:* tennis, ski-ing, football. *Address:* Faculty of Economics, University of Cambridge, Sidgwick Avenue, Cambridge CB3 9DD. *T:* (01223) 335248, *Fax:* (01223) 335475. *E:* hs102@cam.ac.uk.

SACHRAJDA, Prof. Christopher Tadeusz Czeslaw, PhD; FRS 1996; Professor of Physics, University of Southampton, since 1990; *b* 15 Nov. 1949; *s* of Czeslaw Sachrajda and Hanna Teresa Sachrajda (*née* Grabowska); *m* 1974, Irena Czyzewska; two *s* one *d*. *Educ:* Finchley GS; Univ. of Sussex (BSc); Imperial Coll. of Sci. and Technol. (PhD 1974). CPhys, FInstP 1989. Harkness Fellow, Stanford Linear Accelerator Center, Stanford Univ., 1974–76; Fellow and Staff Mem., CERN, 1976–79 (Scientific Associate, 1986–87, 1995–96 and 2002); Department of Physics, University of Southampton: Lectr, 1979–86; Sen. Lectr, 1986–88; Reader, 1988–89; Hd of Dept of Physics and Astronomy, 1997–99. Sen. Fellow, SERC and PPARC, 1991–96; Fellow, Winchester Coll., 2010–. Mem. Council, PPARC, 1998–2004. *Publications:* numerous research and review articles on theory of elementary particles. *Recreations:* family, tennis, philately (early Polish), walking. *Address:* School of Physics and Astronomy, University of Southampton, Southampton SO17 1BJ. *T:* (023) 8059 2105. *E:* cts@phys.soton.ac.uk; (home) 20 Radway Road, Southampton SO15 7PW. *Club:* Portswood Lawn Tennis (Southampton).

SACHS, Andrew; actor and writer; *b* 7 April 1930; *s* of Hans and Katharina Sachs; *m* 1962, Melody Good; two *s* one *d*. *Educ:* Zinnowwald Sch., Berlin; William Ellis Sch., London. Nat. service, RAC, 1949–51. Started acting career in rep., 1948–49, 1951–56; *theatre* includes: as actor: Whitehall farces, 1958–61; A Voyage Round My Father, Haymarket, 1971; Habeas Corpus, Lyric, 1973; Jumpers, Aldwych, 1985; Kafka's Dick, Royal Court, 1986; Wild Oats, RNT, 1995; Enoch Arden, Steinway Hall, London, NY, 1998 and arts fests, 1998–; Life After Fawlty (tour), 2001; pantomimes, UK and Canada; writer, Made in Heaven, Chichester Fest., 1975; *television* includes: as actor: The Tempest, 1979; History of Mr Polly (serial), 1979; series: Fawlty Towers, 1975, 1979; Every Silver Lining, 1993; Jack of Hearts, 1999; Attachments, 2000, 2001; Single Voices, 2002; Coronation Street, 2009; Going Postal, 2010; Spies of Warsaw, 2012; commentaries for TV documentaries; as actor and co-writer of series: The Galactic Garden, 1984; When in Spain, 1987; Berliners, 1988; *radio* includes: as actor, Heart of a Dog, 1988 (Sony Best Actor Award, 1989); as writer: numerous plays and series, incl. The Revenge, 1978 (Ondas Prize, Radio Barcelona, 1979); audio-cassettes (Talkies Award, for best actor, 1999); *films:* Nicholas Nickleby, 1946; Hitler - the Last Ten Days, 1972; Taxandria, 1989; Mystery of Edwin Drood, 1992; Nowhere in Africa, 2003; Speer and Hitler: The Devil's Architect, 2005; Quartet, 2013. *Publications:* I Know Nothing! (autobiog.), 2014. *Address:* c/o Lynda Ronan Personal Management, Hunters House, 1 Redcliffe Road, SW10 9NR.

SACKLER, Dame Jillian (Lesley), DBE 2005; President, AMS Foundation for the Arts, Sciences and Humanities, since 1980; *b* 17 Nov. 1948; *d* of Kenneth Herbert Tully and Doris Queenie Gillman Smith; *m* 1980, Arthur Mitchell Sackler (*d* 1987). *Educ:* Bromley Girls' High Sch.; New York Univ. Bd Mem., US Cttee for UNICEF, 1988–97. Chm., Cttee,

Edinburgh Internat. Fest., 1985–90; Member: Vis. Cttee for Art Mus of Harvard Univ., 1983–; Bd, Metropolitan Opera, NY, 1986–2001; President's Circle, NAS, 1989–; Nat. Bd, Smithsonian Instn, 1989–; Bd, New York City Ballet, 1992–2001; Trustee: RA, 1988–; Council, Nat. Gall. of Art, Washington, 1986–94; American Film Inst., 1986–; Tufts Univ., 1986–98; Foundn for NIH, 2000–. Patron and Hon. Dir, Arthur M. Sackler Mus. of Art and Archaeol., Peking Univ., 1994–. Dame with Crown, Order of Malta, 1994. *Address:* 660 Park Avenue, New York, NY 10065, USA. *T:* (212) 5178880, *Fax:* (212) 6282879. *Clubs:* Queen's; Pilgrims, Cosmopolitan, Town Tennis (New York).

SACKLER, Dame Theresa (Elizabeth), DBE 2012; philanthropist; Board Member, Purdue Pharma Inc., Stamford, Connecticut, since 1993; *b* Werrington, Staffs, 14 Sept. 1949; *d* of Maj. William Daniel Rowling and Margaret Mary Cecilia Rowling (*née* McKimmie); *m* 1980, Dr Mortimer David Sackler, Hon. KBE (*d* 2010); one *s* two *d*. *Educ:* Holt Hill Convent, Wirral, Cheshire; Maria Assumpta Coll. of Educn, London (Cert Ed 1971). Teacher, Sion Convent, Notting Hill, 1971–79. Dir, Sackler Trust, 2009–; Trustee: Dr Mortimer and Theresa Sackler Foundn, 1988–; Capital City Acad., Brent, N London; Dulwich Picture Gall., 2002–13; Tate Foundn; V&A Mus., 2011–. Mem., Chancellor's Ct of Benefactors, Univ. of Oxford. Hon. FRCA 2012. Prince of Wales Medal for Arts Philanthropy, 2011. Chevalier, Légion d'Honneur (France), 1999. *Recreations:* travel, gardens, natural history, arts. *Address:* 95 Eaton Square, SW1W 9AQ. *Clubs:* Eagle Ski (Gstaad); Gstaad Yacht.

SACKS, family name of **Baron Sacks**.

SACKS, Baron *cr* 2009 (Life Peer), of Aldgate in the City of London; **Jonathan Henry Sacks,** Kt 2005; PhD; Chief Rabbi of the United Hebrew Congregations of the Commonwealth, 1991–2013; Professor of Law, Ethics and the Bible, King's College London, since 2013; *b* 8 March 1948; *s* of late Louis David Sacks and Louisa (*née* Frumkin); *m* 1970, Elaine (*née* Taylor); one *s* two *d*. *Educ:* Christ's Coll., Finchley; Gonville and Caius Coll., Cambridge (MA 1972; Hon. Fellow, 1993); New Coll., Oxford; PhD London, 1981. Rabbinic Ordination: Jews' Coll., London, 1976; Yeshivat Etz Hayyim, London, 1976. Lectr in Moral Philosophy, Middlesex Polytechnic, 1971–73; Jews' College, London: Lectr in Jewish Philosophy, 1973–76; Lectr on the Talmud and in Phil., 1976–82; apptd (first) Sir Immanuel (later Lord) Jakobovits Prof. of Modern Jewish Thought, 1982–90; Dir, Rabbinic Faculty, 1983–90; Principal, 1984–90; Rabbi: Golders Green Synagogue, 1978–82; Marble Arch Synagogue, 1983–90. Member (Univ. of London): Bd of Phil., 1985–90; Bd of Studies in Oriental Languages and Literature, 1985–90; Bd of Studies in Theology and Religious Studies, 1986–90. Member: Theol. and Religious Studies Bd, CNAA, 1984–87; Central Religious Adv. Cttee, BBC and IBA, 1987–90. Visiting Professor: Univ. of Essex, 1989–90; Hebrew Univ. in Jerusalem, 1999–; KCL, 1999–. BBC Reith Lectr, 1990. Associate Pres., Conf. of European Rabbis, 2000–13. Editor, L'Eylah: A Journal of Judaism Today, 1984–90. Freeman, City of London and London Bor. of Barnet, 2006. FKC 1993. Hon. Bencher, Inner Temple, 2001. DD Lambeth, 2001; Hon. DD: Cantab, 1993; Heythrop Coll., London, 2006; DUniv Middlesex, 1993; Hon. PhD: Haifa, 1996; Glasgow, 2001; Hon. LLD Liverpool, 1997; Hon. Dr: Yeshiva, NY, 1997; St Andrews, 1998; Bar-Ilan, Leeds Metropolitan, 2004; Roehampton, 2009; Basel, 2010; Ben Gurion, Aberdeen, 2011; Salford, 2013; Liverpool Hope, 2013. Jerusalem Prize, 1995; Grawemayer Award, 2003; Guardian of Zion Award, Israel, 2014; Katz Prize, Israel, 2014; Creativity Award, Moment Mag., 2015. *Publications:* Torah Studies, 1986; (ed) Tradition and Transition: essays presented to Sir Immanuel Jakobovits, 1986; Traditional Alternatives, 1989; Tradition in an Untraditional Age, 1990; The Persistence of Faith, 1991; Argument for the Sake of Heaven, 1991; (ed) Orthodoxy Confronts Modernity, 1991; Crisis and Covenant, 1992; One People? Tradition, Modernity and Jewish Unity, 1993; Will we have Jewish grandchildren?, 1994; Faith in the Future, 1995; Community of Faith, 1996; The Politics of Hope, 1997; Morals and Markets, 1999; Celebrating Life, 2000; Radical Then, Radical Now, 2001; The Dignity of Difference, 2002, 2nd edn 2003; The Passover Haggadah, 2003; From Optimism to Hope, 2004; To Heal a Fractured World, 2005; The Authorised Daily Prayer Book, 4th edn (new trans. and commentary), 2007; The Home We Build Together: recreating society, 2007; Future Tense: a vision for Jews and Judaism in the global culture, 2009; Covenant and Conversation: a weekly reading of the Jewish Bible, Genesis, 2009, Exodus, 2010, Leviticus, 2015; The Great Partnership, 2011; Koren Sacks Yom Kippur Mahzor (trans. and commentary), 2011; Koren Sacks Rosh Hashana Mahzor (trans. and commentary), 2012; Koren Sacks Pesach Mahzor, 2013; Not in God's Name, 2015; The Koren Succot Mahzor (trans. and commentary), 2015; articles, booklets and book reviews.

SACKS, Hon. Charlotte Mary; *see* Hogg, Hon. C. M.

SACKUR, Stephen John; Presenter, HARDtalk, BBC World News, since 2005; *b* 9 Jan. 1964; *s* of Robert Neil Humphrys Sackur and Sallie Caley; *m* 1992, Zina Sabbagh; two *s* one *d*. *Educ:* Emmanuel Coll., Cambridge (BA Hons Hist. 1985). Reporter, Hebden Bridge Times, 1981–82; Henry Fellow, Harvard Univ., 1985–86; BBC: Producer, Current Affairs, 1986–89; Foreign Affairs Corresp., 1989–92; ME Corresp., Cairo, 1992–95; Jerusalem Corresp., 1995–97; Washington Corresp., 1997–2002; Europe Corresp., 2002–05. *Publications:* On the Basra Road, 1991. *Recreations:* books, films, sports, family adventures. *Address:* c/o BBC World News, BBC Broadcasting House, Portland Place, W1A 1AA.

SACKVILLE, family name of **Earl De La Warr**.

SACKVILLE, 7th Baron *cr* 1876; **Robert Bertrand Sackville-West;** DL; *b* 10 July 1958; *s* of Hugh Rosslyn Inigo Sackville-West, MC and Bridget Eleanor (*née* Cunliffe); *S* uncle, 2004; *m* 1st, 1985, Catherine Dorothea Bennett (marr. diss. 1992); 2nd, 1994, Margot Jane MacAndrew; one *s* two *d*. DL Kent, 2014. *Publications:* Inheritance: the story of Knole and the Sackvilles, 2010; The Disinherited, 2014. *Heir: s* Hon. Arthur Sackville-West, *b* 25 Feb. 2000.

SACKVILLE, Hon. Thomas Geoffrey, (Tom); Chief Executive, International Federation of Health Plans (formerly International Federation of Health Funds), since 1998; *b* 26 Oct. 1950; 2nd *s* of 10th Earl De La Warr (*d* 1988) and of Anne Rachel, *o d* of Geoffrey Devas, MC, Hunton Court, Maidstone; *m* 1979, Catherine Theresa, *d* of Brig. James Windsor Lewis; one *s* one *d*. *Educ:* St Aubyn's, Rottingdean, Sussex; Eton Coll.; Lincoln Coll., Oxford (BA). Deltec Banking Corp., New York, 1971–74; Grindlays Bank Ltd, London, 1974–77; Internat. Bullion and Metal Brokers (London) Ltd, 1978–83. MP (C) Bolton West, 1983–97; contested (C) same seat, 1997. PPS to Minister of State at the Treasury, 1985, to Minister for Social Security, 1987–88; an Asst Govt Whip, 1988–90; a Lord Comr of HM Treasury (Govt Whip), 1990–92; Parliamentary Under-Secretary of State: DoH, 1992–95; Home Office, 1995–97. Sec., All-Party Cttee on Drug Misuse, 1984–88. Consultant, Smith Sq. Partners LLP, 2014–. Chm., Family Survival Trust, 2007–. *Address:* (office) 83 Victoria Street, SW1H 0HW. *E:* tom@ifhp.com.

SACKVILLE-WEST, family name of **Baron Sackville**.

SACRANIE, Sir Iqbal (Abdul Karim Mussa), Kt 2005; OBE 1999; Secretary General, The Muslim Council of Britain, 2002–06; Chairman, Muslim Aid, 2008–12 (Trustee, since 1995); *b* 6 Sept. 1951; *s* of Abdul Karim Mussa and Mariam Mussa; *m* 1976, Yasmin; three *s* two *d*. *Educ:* Kennington Coll.; Walbrook Coll. Fellow, Inst. of Financial Accountants, 1978; MInstAM 1978. Man. Dir, Global Traders and Exporters Ltd (family business). Chm., Muslim Council of Britain Charitable Foundn, 2000–12; Chm. Bd of Trustees, Memon Assoc. UK, 1998–; Dep. Pres., World Memon Org., 2002–14; Vice Pres., Assoc. of Family Welfare, 1998–; Member: Inner Cities Religious Council, 1992–2001; Rev. of Coroners' System, 2001–03; Higher Council, Islamic Educnl Scientific and Cultural Org., 2001–; Race Equality Adv. Panel, 2003–05; Bd, World Islamic Economic Forum, 2005–15. Chairman Board of Trustees: Balham Mosque, 1986–; Al Risalla Sch. Trust, 2002–. Patron, Commn on Multi-Faith Britain, 2013–. Hon. DLaws Leeds Metropolitan, 2006. Award for Excellence, Muslim News, 2000; Award for commitment and dedication to community work, Memon Assoc. UK, 2001. *Publications:* joint author and contributor: Need for Reform, 1992; Election 1997 and British Muslims, 1997; The Quest for Sanity, 2003; contrib. to Muslim News, News Internat., Daily Jang, Nation, Asian News and other ethnic media. *Recreations:* golf, cricket, volleyball. *T:* (020) 8974 2780, *Fax:* (020) 8974 2781. *E:* raheena@glotex.co.uk.

SADDLER, Joan Angela, OBE 2007; Associate Director, Patients and Communities, NHS Confederation, since 2013; *b* Leeds, 11 May 1962; *d* of Ashton Saddler and Bronte Saddler; one *s*. *Educ:* Jacob Krammer Coll. of Art, Leeds (Student Award 1979; Adv. Dip. Design 1981); Middlesex Poly. (Cultural Studies specialising in Race, Culture and Women's Liberation Movement); Southbank Univ. (Cert. Mgt 2000; Dip. Mgt 2006); INSEAD (Strategic Change Mgt 2006). Company Dir and Chief Exec., Haringey Women's Forum, 1997–2004; Dir, Direct Development Consultancy Ltd, 2007–; Nat. Dir, Patient and Public Affairs, DoH, 2008–13. Non-exec. Dir, Haringey Healthcare Trust, 1998–2000; Chm. Bd, Walthamstow Forest (formerly Walthamstow, Leyton and Leytonstone) PCT, 2001–08. Member: Equality and Diversity Council, DoH, 2009–; Nat. Commissioning a Patient-Led NHS Expert Panel, 2005; Independent Inquiry into Access to Healthcare for People with Learning Disabilities, 2007–08. Mem. Bd, Adventist Develt Relief Agency UK, 2001–. Ambassador, Mary Seacole Meml Statue Appeal, 2014–. Black and Minority Ethnic Leader Award, Health Service Jl, 2014. *Publications:* contribs to Health Service Jl and Nursing Standard. *Recreations:* music (Mem., London Adventist Chorale, winner of Sainsbury's Choir of the Year, 1994), art and design (designer, Where are we now? exhibn, London's Living Room, City Hall, 2001), reading, black history.

SADEQUE, Shahwar; educational and ICT consultant, since 1996; Managing Director, TriEs Ltd, since 2004; a Governor, BBC, 1990–95; *b* 31 Aug. 1942; *d* of late Ali Imam and of Akhtar Imam; *m* 1962, Pharhad Sadeque (*d* 2010); one *s* one *d*. *Educ:* Dhaka Univ., Bangladesh (BSc 1st Cl. Hons Physics); Bedford Coll., London (MPhil Physics); Kingston Poly. (MSc Inf. Technol.). Computer Programmer with BARIC Services Ltd, 1969–73; Teacher, Nonsuch High Sch., Sutton, 1974–84; research in computer integrated manufacture incorporating vision systems and artificial intelligence, Kingston Univ. (formerly Poly.), 1985–92. Associate Hosp. Manager, SW London and St George's Mental Health NHS Trust, 2004–. Member: Commn for Racial Equality, 1989–93; VAT Tribunals (England and Wales), 1991–2009; (pt-time) Income and Corporation Tax Tribunals, 1992–2009; (pt-time) First-tier Tax Tribunal, 2009–14; SCAA, 1993–97; NCET, 1994–97; Metropolitan Police Cttee, 1995–2000; Cttee on Ethical Issues in Medicine, RCP, 1998–2007; Wkg Gp on operational and ethical guidelines (tissue collections), MRC, 1998–2001; Good Practice in Consent Adv. Gp, DoH, 2000–01; Wkg Pty on Healthcare-related Res. in Developing Countries, Nuffield Council on Bioethics, 2000–02; Patient Inf. Adv. Gp, DoH, 2001–04; Patient and Carer Network, RCP, 2004–07; Lord Chancellor's Adv. Council on Public Records, subseq. on Nat. Records and Archives, 1999–2004. Foreign and Commonwealth Office: Member: Panel 2000, 1998; Marshall Aid Commemoration Commn, 1998–2004; Special Rep. of Sec. of State, FCO, 1998–. Vice-Chm., Immigration Adv. Service, 2000–07. Member: Bd, Waltham Forest HAT, 1991–2002; Council, C&G, 1995–2011; Bd of Govs, Kingston Univ., 1995–2002; Panel of Ind. Persons, UCL, 2003–. Gov., Res. into Ageing, 1998–2001; Trustee, Windsor Leadership Trust, 1998–2005. FRSA 1994–2000. Hon. FCGI 2008. *Publications:* papers (jointly): Education and Ethnic Minorities, 1988; Manufacturing—towards the 21st Century, 1988; A Knowledge-Based System for Sensor Interaction and Real-Time Component Control, 1988. *Recreations:* collecting thimbles and perfume bottles, cooking Indian-style, passion for keeping up-to-date with current affairs. *E:* shahwar.sadeque@btinternet.com.

SADGROVE, Very Rev. Michael; DL; Dean of Durham, 2003–15; *b* 13 April 1950; *s* of late Ralph Sadgrove and of Doreen Sadgrove; *m* 1974, (Elizabeth) Jennifer Suddes; one *s* three *d*. *Educ:* UCS; Balliol Coll., Oxford (BA (Maths and Philosophy) 1971; BA (Theology) 1973; MA 1975); Trinity Coll., Bristol. Ordained, deacon, 1975, priest, 1976; Lectr in OT studies, 1977–82, Vice-Principal, 1980–82, Salisbury and Wells Theol College; Vicar, Alnwick, Northumberland, 1982–87; Canon Residentiary and Vice-Provost, Coventry Cathedral, 1987–95; Provost, subseq. Dean, Sheffield, 1995–2003. Bishops' Sen. Inspector of Theol Educn, 1997–2010. Member: General Synod, 2003–10; Council for Ministry, 2005–10. Chm., Ethics Adv. Cttee, Univ. of Durham, 2004–14; Durham DAC, 2005–10; Mem., Cathedrals Fabric Commn for England, 1996–2006. Chm., Sheffield Common Purpose, 1996–99. Mem. Council, Univ. of Durham, 2003–15; Rector, St Chad's Coll., Durham, 2009– (Visitor, 2003–09). President: St Cuthbert's Hospice, Durham, 2003–15; MUSICON, Univ. of Durham, 2003–15. Hon. Pres., Durham City Trust, 2010–15. FRSA 1997. DL Durham, 2011. *Publications:* A Picture of Faith, 1995; The Eight Words of Jesus, 2006; Wisdom and Ministry, 2008; I Will Trust in You: a companion to the evening psalms, 2009; Lost Sons: God's long search for humanity, 2012; Landscapes of Faith, 2013; (with P. Nixon) Durham Cathedral: a pilgrimage in photographs, 2013; contributor to: Studia Biblica, 1978; Reflecting the Word, 1989; Lion Handbook of the World's Religions, 1982, 2nd edn 1994; Rethinking Marriage, 1993; Coventry's First Cathedral, 1994; The Care Guide, 1995; Calling Time, 2000; Creative Chords, 2001; Dreaming Spires?, 2006; Treasures of Durham University Library, 2007; On Being Human, 2009; Reconciling People: Coventry Cathedral at fifty, 2011; Durham Cathedral: history, language, culture, 2015; articles and reviews in theol jls. *Recreations:* music, arts, literature, history, culture and landscapes of north-east of England, travels in Burgundy, European issues, photography. *Address:* Burswell House, Church Street, Haydon Bridge, Northumberland NE47 6JG. *E:* sadgrove@yahoo.co.uk. *Club:* Royal Over-Seas League.

SADLER, Ven. Anthony Graham; Archdeacon of Walsall, 1997–2004, now Emeritus; *b* 1 April 1936; *s* of Frank and Hannah Sadler; unmarried. *Educ:* Bishop Vesey's Grammar Sch.; The Queen's Coll., Oxford (MA); Lichfield Theol Coll. Ordained deacon, 1962, priest, 1963; Asst Curate, St Chad, Burton upon Trent, 1962–65; Vicar: All Saints, Rangemore and St Mary, Dunstall, 1965–72; St Nicholas, Abbots Bromley, 1972–79; St Michael, Pelsall, 1979–90; Rural Dean of Walsall, 1982–90; Priest-in-charge of Uttoxeter, Bramshall, Gratwich, Marchington Kingstone, Marchington Woodlands, Checkley, Stramshall and Leigh, and Leader of the Uttoxeter Area of Ministry Develt, 1990–97; Rector of Uttoxeter, 1997. Prebendary of Whittington, 1987–97, Hon. Canon, 1997–, Lichfield Cathedral. Hon. Chaplain, Oswestry Sch., 2007–. *Recreations:* music, painting. *Address:* Llidiart Newydd, Llanrhaeadr-ym-Mochnant, Oswestry, Powys SY10 0ED. *T:* (01691) 780276.

SADLER, Joan; Principal, Cheltenham Ladies' College, 1979–87; *b* 1 July 1927; *d* of Thomas Harold Sadler and Florence May Sadler. *Educ:* Cambridgeshire High Sch.; Univ. of Bristol (BA Hons (History); DipEd; MEd 1998); Univ. of Glos (PhD 2006). Downe House, Cold Ash, Newbury, Berks: Asst History teacher, 1950–56; Head of History Dept, 1956–58; Heriots Wood School, Stanmore, Middx: Head of History Dept, 1958–68; Sen. Mistress, 1966–68; Headmistress, Howell's School, Denbigh, 1968–79. Chairman: Boarding Schools' Assoc., 1983–85; Independent Schools' Curriculum Cttee, 1986; Trustee: Central Bureau for Educnl Visits and Exchanges; Common Entrance Examination for Girls' Schools. Hon. Freewoman: City of London; Drapers' Co., 1979. FRSA. *Recreations:* music, theatre, travel, reading.

SADLER, John Stephen, CBE 1982; Chairman, Argent Group PLC, 1997–2001; *b* 6 May 1930; *s* of late Bernard and Phyllis Sadler; *m* 1952, Ella (*née* McCleery); three *s*. *Educ:* Reading Sch.; Corpus Christi Coll., Oxford (MA 1st cl. PPE). Board of Trade, 1952–54; Treasury, 1954–56; Board of Trade, 1956–60; British Trade Commissioner, Lagos, Nigeria, 1960–64; Board of Trade, 1964–66. John Lewis Partnership Ltd, 1966–89: Finance Dir, 1971–87; Dep. Chm., 1984–89. Chairman: Water Res. Centre, subseq. WRC, 1989–93; West End Bd, Royal & Sun Alliance (formerly Sun Alliance) Insurance Gp, 1991–2001; UK Bd, Australian Mutual Provident Soc. and London Life, 1991–96; Pearl Gp PLC, 1994–96; Dir, Debenham Tewson & Chinnock Hldgs plc, 1987–2000. Dir, IMRO, 1987–94; Chm., Authorised Conveyancing Practitioners Bd, 1991–93; Mem., Monopolies and Mergers Commn, 1973–85. Special Advr, Ofgem, 1996–2001. Trustee, British Telecommunications Staff Superannuation Scheme, 1983–98. *Publications:* report of enquiry into cross media promotion. *Recreation:* boating. *Address:* Riverlea, The Warren, Caversham, Reading RG4 7TQ. *Clubs:* Oriental, Leander.

SADLER, Kevin Ian; Development Director, HM Courts and Tribunals Service, Ministry of Justice, since 2015; *b* 18 March 1962; *s* of Colin and Brenda Sadler; *m* 2004, Gillian (*née* Hazlehurst); two *d*. *Educ:* Leicester Polytechnic (BA Hons Law). DSS, 1984–93; Cabinet Office, 1993–95; DSS, subseq. DWP, 1995–2002; Dir, Tribunals, Unified Admin and Magistrates' Courts, LCD, subseq. DCA, 2002–05; Dir, Corporate Mgt, then Change Dir, DCA, subseq. MoJ, 2005–08; Strategic Planning and Performance Dir, MoJ, 2008–09; Chief Exec., Tribunals Service, MoJ, 2009–11; Dir of Civil, Family and Tribunals, HM Courts and Tribunals Service, MoJ, 2011. *Address:* Ministry of Justice, 102 Petty France, SW1H 9AJ. *T:* (020) 3334 3400, *Fax:* 0870 739 4486.

SADLER, Prof. Peter John, DPhil; FRS 2005; FRSE; Professor of Chemistry, University of Warwick, since 2007 (Head, Department of Chemistry, 2007–10); *b* 6 April 1946; *s* of Alfred George and Louisa Elsie Sadler; *m* 1972, Dr Tessa Elizabeth Halstead; two *s* one *d*. *Educ:* City of Norwich Sch.; Magdalen Coll., Oxford (MA 1972; DPhil Chemistry 1972). CChem, FRSC 1987; CSci 2004. MRC Res. Fellow, Univ. of Cambridge and NIMR, Mill Hill, 1971–73; Birkbeck College, London: Lectr in Chemistry, 1973–85; Reader in Biol Inorganic Chemistry, 1985–91; Prof. of Chemistry, 1991–96; Crum Brown Prof. of Chemistry, Univ. of Edinburgh, 1996–2007. Mok Hing Yiu Dist. Vis. Prof. in Chem., Univ. of Hong Kong, 2012–. EPSRC Recognising Inspirational Scientists and Engrs Fellow, 2014. FRSE 1999. *Publications:* res. papers in jls, inc. Jl of ACS, Angewandte Chemie, Inorganic Chemistry, Chemical Communications, Dalton Transactions, Nature Structural Biology, Science, Jl of Medicinal Chemistry, Procs of NAS, Nature Communications, Amer. Chem. Soc. Chem. Biol., Chem. Sci. *Recreations:* gardening, amateur dramatics and musical theatre, playing clarinet, guitar and piano. *Address:* Department of Chemistry, University of Warwick, Gibbet Hill Road, Coventry CV4 7AL. *T:* (024) 7652 3818, *Fax:* (024) 7652 3819.

SAEED, Saleh, OBE 2013; Chief Executive, Disasters Emergency Committee, since 2012; *b* Yafa, Yemen, 15 Jan. 1967; *s* of Saeed Abubakr Yafai and Razina Mohammed; *m* 1991, Roqaya Ahmed; two *s* three *d*. *Educ:* Univ. of Wolverhampton (BA Hons Business Enterprise 1991). Mktg and Fundraising Dir, Islamic Relief Worldwide, 1991–2000; Develt Manager, Sandwell HA, 2000–02; Policy and Communications Officer, W Midlands Regl Authy, 2002; Project Manager, Sandwell Council, 2002–07; Digital Inclusion Manager, Black Country Consortium, 2007–08; CEO, Islamic Relief Worldwide, 2008–12. *Recreations:* football, cycling. *Address:* Disasters Emergency Committee, 43 Chalton Street, NW1 1DU. *T:* (020) 7387 2000. *E:* info@dec.org.uk.

SAFFMAN, Andrew Maurice; His Honour Judge Saffman; a Circuit Judge, since 2013; *b* Leeds, 8 Feb. 1953; *s* of Leonard Saffman and Rita Saffman; *m* 1980, Andrea Jacqueline Spital; two *s* one *d*. *Educ:* Carmel Coll., Wallingford; Roundhay Grammar Sch., Leeds; Univ. of Leeds (LLB Hons 1974). Admitted solicitor, 1977; private practice, 1977–2001; a Dep. Dist Judge, 1995–2001; a Dist Judge, 2001–13. *Recreations:* cycling, running, ski-ing, travel, walking. *Address:* Leeds Combined Court Centre, 1 Oxford Row, Leeds, W Yorks LS1 3BG.

SAGE, Stephen Paul; management consultant, since 2011; *b* 3 June 1953; *s* of late Ivor John Sage and Kathleen Gwendoline Sage (*née* Jeffrey); *m* 1982, Anne Jennifer Mickleburgh; two *s* one *d*. *Educ:* Bristol Grammar Sch.; Peterhouse, Cambridge (BA Hons Classics 1974; MA). MCIPS 1993. John Henderson Sports, 1976–78; Crown Agents, 1978–80; Department of the Environment, 1980–93: Private Sec. to Housing Minister, 1984–85; Controller, Merseyside Task Force, 1989–93; Chief Exec., The Buying Agency, 1993–2000; Chief Exec., FCO Services, FCO, 2000–06; Dir, Trading Fund Programme, FCO, 2006–08; Dir, Stephen Sage Consulting Ltd, 2008–11. Member: Cttee, Pierhead Housing Assoc., 1994–2000; Cttee, Wirral and N Cheshire Prostate Cancer Support Gp, 2015–. Trustee, Lancs W and Wigan (formerly Lancs W) Groundwork Trust, 2005–08. Captain, The Buying Agency Golf Soc., 2011–14. *Recreations:* reading, music, Alfa Romeos, tennis, golf. *E:* sage247@hotmail.co.uk. *Clubs:* Bristol City Football; Oaks at Mollington Golf (Seniors Sec., 2015–).

SAGGERSON, Alan David; His Honour Judge Saggerson; a Circuit Judge, since 2009; *b* Newcastle upon Tyne, 24 Dec. 1956; *s* of Graeme and Margaret Saggerson. *Educ:* Wilmslow Grammar Sch.; Hertford Coll., Oxford (BCL, MA Juris.); Inns of Court Sch. of Law. Called to the Bar, Lincoln's Inn, 1981, Bencher, 2007; Recorder, 2003–09. Member, Editorial Board: Internat. Travel Law Jl, 2002–; Travel Law Qly, 2009–. Chm., Travel and Tourism Lawyers' Assoc., 1997–2009. Trustee, St Giles Organ Project, 2009–. *Publications:* Travel Law and Litigation, 1998, 4th edn 2008; Package Travel Cases and Materials, 2008. *Recreations:* classical pipe organs (playing, listening, restoring), choral music. *Address:* Woolwich Crown Court, 2 Belmarsh Road, SE28 0EY.

SAGOVSKY, Rev. Canon Nicholas, PhD; Whitelands Professorial Fellow, Roehampton University, since 2011; *b* 13 Aug. 1947; *s* of Vladimir Sagovsky and Hilary Douglas Sagovsky (*née* Taylor); *m* 1974, Ruth Scott; one *s* one *d*. *Educ:* Oundle Sch.; Corpus Christi Coll., Oxford (BA (English Lang. and Lit.) 1969); St John's Coll., Nottingham and Nottingham Univ. (BA (Theol.) 1973); St Edmund's Coll., Cambridge (PhD 1981). Ordained deacon, 1974, priest, 1975; Curate: St Gabriel's, Heaton, 1974–77; Gt St Mary's, Cambridge, 1981–82; Vice Principal, Edinburgh Theol Coll., 1982–86; Dean, Clare Coll., Cambridge, 1986–97; William Leech Prof. of Applied Christian Theol., Newcastle Univ., 1997–2002; Liverpool Prof. of Theol. and Public Life, Liverpool Hope UC, 2002–04; Canon Theologian, 2004–11, Sub-Dean, 2010–11, Westminster Abbey. Hon. Prof., Durham Univ., 1997–2000; Vis. Prof., Liverpool Hope Univ. (formerly University Coll.), 2004–. Mem., ARCIC, 1992–. *Publications:* Between Two Worlds: George Tyrrell's relationship to the thought of Matthew Arnold, 1983; On God's Side: a life of George Tyrrell, 1990; Ecumenism, Christian Origins and the Practice of Communion, 2000; Christian Tradition and the Practice of Justice, 2008. *Recreations:* rough gardening and other Northumbrian pursuits. *Address:* c/o Chapter Office, Dean's Yard, Westminster Abbey, SW1P 3PA. *T:* (020) 7654 4808.

SAHOTA, Onkar Singh; JP; Member (Lab) Ealing and Hillingdon, London Assembly, Greater London Authority, since 2012; *s* of Pargat Singh and Parminder Kaur; one *s* two *d*. *Educ:* Sheffield Univ. Med Sch. (MB ChB 1983); London Business Sch. (MBA 1999). MRCS, LRCP 1984; DRCOG 1988; MRCGP 1989. Specialisation in family medicine, St Mary's Hosp. Med. Sch., London; hse surgeon, Royal Hallamshire Hosp., Sheffield, 1984; hse physician, Milton Keynes Gen. Hosp., 1985; gen. practice vocational trng scheme, 1986–89; GP, 1989–; est. own practice, Hanwell and Southall, 1994. Consultant, DFID and World Bank health projects, 1999–2003. Chm. and Mem., Southall and W Ealing PCG, 2001–05; Mem., Ealing PCT, 2005–12; Dir, Family Health Practices Gp, 2008–. Greater London Authority: Chair, Health Cttee, 2014–; Member: Transport Cttee, 2014–; Economy Cttee, 2014–. JP Middx 1999. *Address:* Greater London Authority, City Hall, Queen's Walk, SE1 2AA.

SAÏD, Wafic Rida; businessman, entrepreneur and philanthropist; Founder and Chairman, Saïd Foundation (formerly Karim Rida Saïd Foundation), since 1982; Founder, 1987, and Chairman, Investment Committee, since 2012, Saïd Holdings Ltd (Chairman of the Board, 1987–2012); *b* Damascus, 21 Dec. 1939; *s* of Dr Rida Saïd and Kheire Mamiche Saïd; *m* 1969, Rosemary Thompson; one *s* one *d* (and one *s* decd). *Educ:* Coll. de Notre-Dame de Jamhour, Lebanon. Inst. of Bankers. Started investment banking career at Union Bank of Switzerland, Geneva, 1968; estd consultancy business for design and construction projects, Saudi Arabia, 1969; Co-Founder, Sagitta Asset Mgt Ltd, 1995. Mem., Bd, Banque Libano-Française, 2005–. Benefactor and Founder Trustee, Saïd Business Sch. Foundn, 1998; Mem., Ct of Benefactors, Univ. of Oxford, 1992–. Hon. Fellow, Trinity Coll., Oxford, 2004. Ambassador of St Vincent and the Grenadines to UNESCO, 1996–, to the Holy See, 2012–. Grand Commandeur: Ordre de Mérite du Cèdre (Lebanon); Ordre Chérifien (Morocco). *Recreations:* architecture, art, music. *Clubs:* Royal Automobile; Monaco Yacht; Cercle de l'Union Interalliée (Paris); Eagle (Gstaad).

SAINI, Pushpinder Singh; QC 2008; barrister; *b* Nairobi, 26 Feb. 1968; *s* of late Surrinder Jit Singh Saini and Janak Dulari; *m* 1996, Gemma White; one *s* one *d*. *Educ:* Dormers Wells High Sch., Southall; Corpus Christi Coll., Oxford (MA, BCL). Called to the Bar, Gray's Inn, 1991, Bencher, 2012; barrister, Blackstone Chambers, 1992–. *Address:* Blackstone Chambers, Temple, EC4Y 9BW. *T:* (020) 7583 1770.

SAINSBURY, family name of **Barons Sainsbury of Preston Candover** and **Sainsbury of Turville**.

SAINSBURY OF PRESTON CANDOVER, Baron *cr* 1989 (Life Peer), of Preston Candover in the county of Hampshire; **John Davan Sainsbury,** KG 1992; Kt 1980; President, J Sainsbury plc, since 1992 (Vice-Chairman, 1967–69; Chairman, 1969–92; Director, 1958–92); *b* 2 Nov. 1927; *e s* of Baron Sainsbury; *m* 1963, Anya Linden, *qv*; two *s* one *d*. *Educ:* Stowe School; Worcester College, Oxford (Hon. Fellow 1982). Director: Royal Opera House, Covent Garden, 1969–85 (Chm., 1987–91; Hon. Vice Pres., 2009–); Rambert Sch. of Ballet and Contemporary Dance, 2003–05; Chairman: Friends of Covent Garden, 1969–81; Benesh Inst. of Choreology, 1986–87; Bd of Trustees, Dulwich Picture Gall., 1994–2000 (Patron, 2004–); Govs, Royal Ballet, 1995–2003 (Gov., 1987–2003); Trustees, Royal Opera House Endowment Fund, 2001–05; Rambert Sch. Trust, 2005–10 (Chm., Develt Cttee, 2002–03, Steering Cttee, 2005–09); Gov., Royal Ballet Sch., 1965–76, and 1987–91. Director: The Economist, 1972–80; Royal Opera House Trust, 1974–84 and 1987–97; Jt Hon. Treas., European Movt, 1972–75; Pres., British Retail Consortium, 1993–97 (Mem. Council, Retail Consortium, 1975–79); Member: Nat. Cttee for Electoral Reform, 1976–85; President's Cttee, CBI, 1982–84; Jt Parly Scrutiny Cttee on Draft Charities Bill, 2004–05; Bd, Centre for Policy Studies, 2009–12. Contemporary Arts Society: Hon. Sec., 1965–71; Vice Chm., 1971–74; Vice Pres., 1984–96; Vice Patron, 1998–2006; Patron, Sir Harold Hillier Gardens and Arboretum, 2005–; Trustee: Nat. Gall., 1976–83; Westminster Abbey Trust, 1977–83; Tate Gall., 1982–83; Rhodes Trust, 1984–98; Saïd Business Sch. Foundn, 2003–15. Visitor, Ashmolean Mus., 2003–15. Dir, Friends of the Nelson Mandela Children's Fund, 1996–2000. Pres., Sparsholt Coll., Hants, 1993–2000. Hon. Bencher, Inner Temple, 1985. Hon. Fellow, British Sch. at Rome, 2002. Hon. DScEcon London, 1985; Hon. DLitt South Bank, 1992; Hon. LLD Bristol, 1993; Hon. DEconSc Cape Town, 2000. Albert Medal, RSA, 1989; Hadrian Award, World Monuments Fund, 2000; Prince of Wales Medal for Arts Philanthropy, 2008; Sheldon Medal, Univ. of Oxford, 2010; Gjergj Kastrioti-Skenderbeg Presidential Award, Albania, 2014. *Address:* c/o 33 Holborn, EC1N 2HT. *T:* (020) 7695 6000. *Clubs:* Garrick, Beefsteak.

See also Rt Hon. Sir T. A. D. Sainsbury.

SAINSBURY OF PRESTON CANDOVER, Lady; *see* Linden, Anya.

SAINSBURY OF TURVILLE, Baron *cr* 1997 (Life Peer), of Turville in the co. of Buckinghamshire; **David John Sainsbury;** Chancellor, University of Cambridge, since 2011; *b* 24 Oct. 1940; *s* of Sir Robert Sainsbury and Lisa Ingeborg (*née* Van den Bergh); *m* 1973, Susan Carroll Reid (CBE 2010); three *d*. *Educ:* King's Coll., Cambridge (BA); Columbia Univ., NY (MBA). Joined J. Sainsbury, 1963; Finance Dir, 1973–90; Dep. Chm., 1988–92; Chm., 1992–98; Chief Exec., 1992–97. Parly Under-Sec. of State, DTI, 1998–2006. Member: Cttee of Review of the Post Office (Carter Cttee), 1975–77; IPPR Commn on Public Policy and British Business, 1995–97. Founder, Gatsby Charitable Foundn, 1967. Trustee, Social Democratic Party, 1982–90; Mem. Governing Body, London Business Sch., 1985–98 (Chm., 1991–98); Chairman: Transition Bd, Univ. for Industry, 1998–99; Inst. for Govt, 2009–. Hon. FREng (Hon. FEng 1994); Hon. FRS 2008; Hon. FMedSci 2008. Hon. doctorates from Cambridge, Oxford, Manchester, Imperial Coll. London and Rockefeller Univ. Andrew Carnegie Medal of Philanthropy (on behalf of Sainsbury family), Carnegie Inst., 2003. *Publications:* Government and Industry: a new partnership, 1981; (with Christopher Smallwood) Wealth Creation and Jobs, 1987; A Race to the Top: a review of Government's science and innovation policies, 2007; Progressive Capitalism: how to achieve economic growth, liberty and social justice, 2013.

SAINSBURY, Alexander John; Founder, and Director, Raven Row, since 2008; *b* London, 17 Jan. 1968; *s* of Rt Hon. Sir Timothy Alan Davan Sainsbury, *qv*; *m* 2003, Elinor Jansz; two *s*. *Educ:* Eton Coll.; New York Univ. Rear Window, contemp. art exhibns collective, 1993–95; Dir, 38 Langham St Art Gall., 2001–03. Settlor Trustee, Glass-House Trust, 1994–; Co-founder Trustee: Peer, 1998–2003; MayDay Rooms, 2013–; Founder, A Space, Children's Centre, Hackney, 1997 (Mem., Steering Gp, 1997–); Founder and Chair of Bd, Glass-House Community Led Design, 1999–2011. *Publications:* (ed) Francesco Lo Savio, 2001. *Recreations:* cinema, travelling, architecture. *Address:* Sainsbury Family Charitable Trusts, The Peak, 5 Wilton Road, SW1V 1AP. *T:* (020) 7410 0330, *Fax:* (020) 7410 0332. *E:* info@ravenrow.org.

SAINSBURY, Prof. (Richard) Mark, FBA 1998; Professor of Philosophy, University of Texas at Austin, since 2002; *b* 2 July 1943; *s* of late Richard Eric Sainsbury and Freda Margaret Sainsbury (*née* Horne); *m* 1st, 1970, Gillian McNeill Rind (marr. diss. 2000); one *s* one *d*; 2nd, 2000, Victoria Goodman. *Educ:* Sherborne Sch.; Corpus Christi Coll., Oxford (MA, DPhil). Lecturer in Philosophy: Magdalen Coll., Oxford, 1968–70; St Hilda's Coll., Oxford, 1970–73; Brasenose Coll., Oxford, 1973–75; Univ. of Essex, 1975–78; Bedford Coll., Univ. of London, 1978–84; King's College London: Lectr in Philosophy, 1984–87; Reader in Philosophy, 1987–89; Stebbing Prof. of Philosophy, 1989–2008. Leverhulme Sen. Res. Fellow, 2000–02. Editor of Mind, 1990–2000. *Publications:* Russell, 1979; Paradoxes, 1988, 3rd edn 2009; Logical Forms, 1991, 2nd edn 2000; Departing From Frege, 2002; Reference Without Referents, 2005; Fiction and Fictionalism, 2009; (with Michael Tye) Seven Puzzles of Thought and How to Solve Them: an originalist theory of concepts, 2012. *Recreation:* baking bread. *Address:* Department of Philosophy, University of Texas, Austin, TX 78712, USA. *E:* marksainsbury@austin.utexas.edu.

SAINSBURY, Rt Rev. Dr Roger Frederick; Chairman, Churches Together in England Urban Mission Group, 2011–13; an Assistant Bishop, diocese of Bath and Wells, since 2003; *b* 2 Oct. 1936; *s* of Frederick William Sainsbury and Lillian Maude Sainsbury; *m* 1960, Jennifer Marguerite Carey. *Educ:* High Wycombe Royal Grammar School; Jesus Coll., Cambridge

(MA); Clifton Theological Coll.; Seabury-Western Theol Seminary (DMin). Curate, Christ Church, Spitalfields, 1960–63; Missioner, Shrewsbury House, Liverpool, 1963–74; Warden, Mayflower Family Centre, Canning Town, 1974–81; Priest-in-Charge, St Luke, Victoria Dock, 1978–81; Vicar of Walsall, 1981–87; Rector, Walsall Team Ministry, 1987–88; Archdeacon of West Ham, 1988–91; Area Bp of Barking, 1991–2002. Alderman, London Borough of Newham, 1976–78. Moderator, Churches' Commn for Racial Justice, 1999–2003; Chairman: Frontier Youth Trustees, 1987–92; Barking Area Church Leaders Gp, 1994–2002; Urban Bishops Panel, 1996–2001; London Churches Gp, 1998–2002; Nat. Youth Agency, 2002–08; Trustees, Children in Distress, 1998–2000; Centre for Youth Ministry, 2004–07; UK Urban Congress Exec., 2005–; Co-Chair, Urban Mission Develt Adv. Project, 2004–10. Member: Coll. of Preachers, 2002–; Coll. of Evangelists, 2003–. Pres., Frontier Youth Trust, 2002–. Trustee, Evangelical Coalition for Urban Mission, 2002–. Tutor, Trinity Coll., Bristol, 2006–09. Mem., Friends of Sedgewick Mus., 2005–. *Publications:* From a Mersey Wall, 1970; Justice on the Agenda, 1985; Lifestyle, 1986; Rooted and Grounded in Love, 1988; God of New Beginnings, 1990; Barking Mad Letters, 1999; Young People as Prophets, 2006; Ten Commandments for Today, 2013. *Recreations:* geology, art, gardening. *Address:* (home) Abbey Lodge, Battery Lane, Portishead, Bristol BS20 7JD.

SAINSBURY, Rt Hon. Sir Timothy (Alan Davan), Kt 1995; PC 1992; *b* 11 June 1932; *y s* of Baron Sainsbury; *m* 1961, Susan Mary Mitchell; two *s* two *d*. *Educ:* Eton; Worcester Coll., Oxford (MA; Hon. Fellow 1982). Dir, J. Sainsbury, 1962–83; non-exec. Dir, J. Sainsbury plc, 1995–99; Chairman: Pendennis Shipyard (Hldgs) Ltd, 1999–2007; Marlborough Tiles Ltd, 1999–. Chm., Council for the Unit for Retail Planning Information Ltd, 1974–79. MP (C) Hove, Nov. 1973–1997. PPS to Sec. of State for the Environment, 1979–83, to Sec. of State for Defence, 1983; a Govt Whip, 1983–87; Parly Under-Sec. of State for Defence Procurement, 1987–89; Parly Under-Sec. of State, FCO, 1989–90; Minister of State, DTI, 1990–94 (Minister for Trade, 1990–92, for Industry, 1992–94). Pres., Cons. Friends of Israel, 1997–2005 (Parly Chm., 1994–97). Chm., Somerset House Ltd, then Somerset House Trust, 1997–2002. Mem. Council, RSA, 1981–83. Visitor, Ashmolean Mus., Oxford, 2000–06; Trustee, V&A Mus., 2004–11; Chm., V&A Foundn, 2012–. Hon. FRIBA 1994; Hon. FRICS 1994.

See also P. Frankopan, Baron Sainsbury of Preston Candover, A. J. Sainsbury, Rt Hon. S. A. Woodward.

SAINT, Prof. Andrew John; General Editor, Survey of London, since 2006; *b* 30 Nov. 1946; *s* of late Arthur James Maxwell Saint and Elisabeth Yvetta Saint (*née* Butterfield); three *d*. *Educ:* Christ's Hosp.; Balliol Coll., Oxford. Part-time Lectr, Univ. of Essex, 1971–74; Architectural Editor, Survey of London, 1974–86; Historian, London Div., English Heritage, 1986–95; Prof. of Architecture, Univ. of Cambridge, 1995–2006. Hon. FRIBA 1993. *Publications:* Richard Norman Shaw, 1976, 2nd edn 2010; The Image of the Architect, 1983; Towards a Social Architecture, 1987; (ed with D. Keene and A. Burns) St Paul's: the cathedral church of London 604–2004, 2004; Architect and Engineer: a study in sibling rivalry, 2007. *Address:* Survey of London, c/o English Heritage, 138–142 Holborn, EC1N 2ST. *T:* (020) 7973 3638. *E:* ajs61@cam.ac.uk; (home) 14 Denny Crescent, SE11 4UY. *T:* (020) 7735 3863.

ST ALBANS, 14th Duke of, *cr* 1684; **Murray de Vere Beauclerk;** Earl of Burford, Baron of Heddington, 1676; Baron Vere of Hanworth, 1750; Hereditary Grand Falconer of England; Hereditary Registrar, Court of Chancery; Partner, Burford & Partners LLP (formerly Burford & Co.), chartered accountants, 1981–2015; *b* 19 Jan. 1939; *s* of 13th Duke of St Albans, OBE and Nathalie Chatham, *d* of P. F. Walker (later Mrs Nathalie C. Eldrid, *d* 1985); *S* father, 1988; *m* 1st, 1963, Rosemary Frances Scoones (marr. diss. 1974); one *s* one *d*; 2nd, 1974, Cynthia Theresa Mary (marr. diss. 2002; she *d* 2002), *d* of late Lt-Col W. J. H. Howard, DSO and formerly wife of Sir Anthony Robin Maurice Hooper, 2nd Bt; 3rd, 2002, Gillian Anita, *d* of late Lt-Col C. G. R. Northam and *widow* of Philip Nesfield Roberts. *Educ:* Tonbridge. Chartered Accountant, 1962. Gov.-Gen., Royal Stuart Soc., 1989–. Pres., Beaufort Opera, 1991–; Patron, Bestwood Male Voice Choir, 2001–. Liveryman, Drapers' Co., 1971–. *Heir: s* Earl of Burford, *qv*. *Address:* 16 Ovington Street, SW3 2JB.

See also D. C. S. Smellie.

ST ALBANS, Bishop of, since 2009; **Rt Rev. Alan Gregory Clayton Smith,** PhD; *b* 14 Feb. 1957; *s* of late Frank Eric Smith and of Rosemary Clayton Smith (*née* Barker). *Educ:* Trowbridge Grammar Sch.; Univ. of Birmingham (BA Theol. 1978; MA 1979; Hon. DD 2010); Wycliffe Hall, Oxford; Univ. of Wales, Bangor (PhD 2002). Ordained deacon, 1981, priest, 1982; Assistant Curate: St Lawrence, Pudsey, 1981–82; St Lawrence and St Paul, Pudsey, 1982–84; Chaplain, Lee Abbey Community, Devon, 1984–90; Diocesan Missioner, Lichfield, 1990–97; Team Vicar, St Matthew's, Walsall, 1990–97; Archdeacon, Stoke-upon-Trent, 1997–2001; Bishop Suffragan of Shrewsbury, 2001–09. Hon. Canon, Lichfield Cathedral, 1997–2009. Entered H of L, 2013. Chm., Shropshire Strategic Partnership, 2005–09. *Publications:* Growing Up in Multifaith Britain, 2007; God-Shaped Mission, 2008; The Reflective Leader, 2011; Saints and Pilgrims in the Diocese of St Albans, 2013. *Recreations:* classical music, travel, ski-ing. *Address:* Abbey Gate House, Abbey Mill Lane, St Albans AL3 4HD. *T:* (01727) 853305, *Fax:* (01727) 846715. *E:* bishop@stalbans.anglican.org.

ST ALBANS, Dean of; *see* John, Very Rev. J. P. H.

ST ALBANS, Archdeacon of; *see* Smith, Ven. J. P.

ST ALDWYN, 3rd Earl *cr* 1915; **Michael Henry Hicks Beach;** Bt 1619; Viscount St Aldwyn 1906; Viscount Quenington 1915; *b* 7 Feb. 1950; *s* of 2nd Earl St Aldwyn, GBE, TD, PC and Diana Mary Christian Smyly (*d* 1992), *o d* of Henry C. G. Mills; S father, 1992; *m* 1st, 1982, Gilda Maria, *o d* of Barão Saavedra, Copacabana, Rio de Janeiro (marr. diss. 2005); two *d*; 2nd, 2005, Louise Wigan (marr. diss. 2014). *Educ:* Eton; Christ Church, Oxford (MA). *Heir: b* Hon. David Seymour Hicks Beach [*b* 25 May 1955; *m* 1993, Kate, *d* of Michael Henriques; one *s* two *d*]. *Address:* The Mill House, Coln St Aldwyns, Cirencester, Glos GL7 5AJ. *T:* (01285) 750226.

ST ANDREWS, Earl of; George Philip Nicholas Windsor; *b* 26 June 1962; *s* of HRH the Duke of Kent and HRH the Duchess of Kent; *m* 1988, Sylvana Tomaselli; one *s* two *d*. *Educ:* Eton (King's Scholar); Downing College, Cambridge. Attached to FCO (UN, NY and Budapest), 1987–88. Specialist, Christie's (Books and Manuscripts Dept), 1996–98. Trustee: GB-Sasakawa Foundn, 1995– (Chm., 2005–); SOS Children's Villages UK, 1999–; Golden Web Foundn, 2003–12 (Chm., 2006–12); Prince George Galitzine Meml Library, 2005–; Global EHealth Foundn, 2013–; Mem., Adv. Bd, Next Century Foundn, 2012–. Patron: Assoc. for Internat. Cancer Res., 1995–; Princess Margarita of Romania Trust, 1997–; Welsh Sinfonia, 2011–; Friends of Mongolia and Inner Asia Studies Unit, Univ. of Cambridge, 2012–; Centre for Islamic Finance, Univ. of Bolton, 2013–. *Heir: s* Lord Downpatrick, *qv*. *Address:* York House, St James's Palace, SW1A 1BQ.

See under Royal Family.

ST ANDREWS AND EDINBURGH, Archbishop of, (RC), since 2013; **Most Rev. Leo Cushley;** *b* Wester Moffat, 18 June 1961; *s* of William Cushley and Eileen Cushley (*née* Kane). *Educ:* St Mary's Coll., Blairs; Gregorian Univ., Rome (BPhil; BTh; DCnL 1997); Pontifical Liturgical Inst., Rome (Licence in Liturgy). Ordained priest, 1985; Asst Priest, Cath. Church of Our Lady of Good Aid, Motherwell, 1987–88; Curate, St Serf's Parish, Airdrie and Chaplain, St Margaret's High Sch., Airdrie, 1988–92; Curate, St Aidan's Parish, Wishaw, 1992–93; Chaplain: St Aidan's High Sch., Wishaw, 1992–93; Our Lady's High Sch., Motherwell, 1992–93; entered Dip. Service of Holy See, 1997; Secretary, Apostolic Nunciature in Burundi, 1997–2001, in Portugal, 2001–04, in S Africa, 2007–09; Holy See Perm. Observer Mission to the UN, New York; Hd, English-lang. section, Vatican Secretariat of State, 2009–13; Prelate of the Ante-camera, 2012. *Recreations:* hill-walking, music, films, books. *Address:* Archdiocesan Offices, 100 Strathearn Road, Edinburgh EH9 1BB.

ST ANDREWS, DUNKELD AND DUNBLANE, Bishop of, since 2005; **Most Rev. David Robert Chillingworth;** Primus of the Scottish Episcopal Church, since 2009; *b* 23 June 1951; *s* of David Andrew Richard Chillingworth and Sheila Margaret (*née* Bateman); *m* 1975, Alison Penney; two *s* one *d*. *Educ:* Portora Royal Sch., Enniskillen; Royal Belfast Academical Instn; Trinity Coll., Dublin (BA Classics 1973); Oriel Coll., Oxford (BA Theol. 1975, MA 1981); Ripon Coll., Cuddesdon. Ordained deacon, 1976, priest, 1977; Curate-Asst, Holy Trinity, Joanmount, 1976–79; C of I Youth Officer, 1979–83; Curate-Asst, Bangor Abbey, 1983–86; Rector, Seagoe Parish Ch, Portadown, 1986–2005; Dean of Dromore, 1995–2002; Archdeacon of Dromore, 2002–05. Hon. DD South, Sewanee, Tenn, 2014. *Recreations:* music, reading, cycling, sailing, travel. *Address:* Diocesan Office, 28 Balhousie Street, Perth PH1 5HJ. *T:* (01738) 580426. *E:* bishop@standrews.anglican.org. *W:* www.bishopdavid.net.

ST ANDREWS, DUNKELD AND DUNBLANE, Dean of; *see* Rathband, Very Rev. K. W.

ST ASAPH, Bishop of, since 2009; **Rt Rev. Gregory Kenneth Cameron;** *b* Tredegar, Monmouthshire, 6 June 1959; *s* of Kenneth Hughes Cameron and Irene Cameron; *m* 1995, Clare Margaret Lee; three *s*. *Educ:* Croesyceiliog Grammar, later Comprehensive Sch., Torfaen; Lincoln Coll., Oxford (MA 1984; Hon. Fellow 2010); Downing Coll., Cambridge (MA 1986); St Michael and All Angels Theol Coll., Llandaff (Dip. in Pastoral Studies 1983); Univ. of Wales Coll., Cardiff (MPhil 1990; LLM 1997). Ordained deacon, 1983, priest, 1984; Asst Curate, Parish of St Paul, Newport, 1983–86; Asst Priest/Team Vicar, Rectorial Benefice of Llanmartin, 1986–88; Chaplain and Hd of Religious Studies, Wycliffe Coll., Stonehouse, Glos, 1988–94 (Asst Housemaster, Haywardsfield, 1991–94); Dir, Bloxham Project, Oxford, 1994–2000; Chaplain to the Archbishop of Wales, 2000–03; Dep. Sec. Gen. and Dir of Ecumenical Affairs and Studies, Anglican Consultative Council, 2003–09. Anglican Co-Chair, Anglican Oriental Orthodox Internat. Commn, 2015–. Hon. Canon, Monmouth, 2003–09. Tutor, St Michael's Theol Coll., Llandaff, 1986–89; Lectr in Old Testament, Univ. Coll., Cardiff, 1986–89; Res. Fellow, 1998, Hon. Res. Fellow, 1999–, Centre for Law and Religion, Cardiff Univ. JP Glos, 1992–98. Hon. DD Episcopal Divinity Sch., Cambridge, Mass, 2007. *Publications:* (contrib.) Render Unto Caesar, 1999; (jtly) Christian Character, 2001; (contrib.) Faithful Discipleship, 2001; (ed jtly) Anglican-Lutheran Agreements, 2004; (co-ed) Mary, Grace and Hope in Christ: study guide, 2006; (contrib.) An Anglican Covenant, 2008; (contrib.) Faith in Action, 2008; (contrib.) Companion to the Anglican Communion, 2013. *Recreations:* art, ancient history, calligraphy, classical and film music, egyptology, heraldry, liturgy, reading, travel, world history. *Address:* Esgobty, Llanelwy, St Asaph LL17 0TW. *T:* (01745) 583503. *E:* bishop.stasaph@churchinwales.org.uk.

ST ASAPH, Dean of; *see* Williams, Very Rev. N. H.

ST ASAPH, Archdeacon of; *see* Lomas, Ven. J. D. P.

ST AUBIN de TERÁN, Lisa Gioconda; writer; *b* London, 2 Oct. 1953; *d* of Cuthbert Jan Alwin Rynveld Carew and late Joan Mary St Aubin; *m* 1st, 1970, Jaime Terán (marr. diss. 1981); one *d*; 2nd, 1982, George Mann Macbeth (marr. diss. 1989; he *d* 1992); one *s*; 3rd, 1989, Robbie Charles Duff-Scott (marr. diss. 2004); one *d*; partner, Mees van Deth. *Educ:* James Allen's Girls' Sch., Dulwich. Sugar farmer and plantation manager, Venezuelan Andes, 1971–78. Founder, Teran Foundn, 2004; voluntary worker, Community Coll. of Tourism and Agriculture, Teran Foundn, Mossuril Dist, N Mozambique, 2005–. Writer of 3 film screenplays. John Llewellyn Rhys Prize, 1983; Eric Gregory Award for Poetry, 1983. *Publications:* Keepers of the House, 1982 (Somerset Maugham Award, 1983); The Slow Train to Milan, 1983; The Tiger, 1984; High Place (poetry), 1985; The Bay of Silence, 1986; Black Idol, 1987; Indiscreet Journeys, 1989; The Marble Mountain (short stories), 1989; Off the Rails: memoirs of a train addict, 1989; Joanna, 1990; Venice: the four seasons (essays), 1992; Nocturne, 1992; A Valley in Italy: confessions of a house addict, 1994; Distant Landscapes, 1995; The Hacienda (memoirs), 1997; The Palace, 1997; (ed) The Virago Book of Wanderlust and Dreams, 1998; Southpaw (short stories), 1999; Memory Maps (memoirs), 2001; Otto, 2005; Mozambican Mysteries, 2007. *Address:* Caixa Postal 81, Ilha de Moçambique, Provincia de Nampula, Mozambique.

ST AUBYN, family name of **Baron St Levan**.

ST AUBYN, Edward; writer; *b* London, 14 Jan. 1960; one *s* one *d*. *Educ:* Westminster Sch.; Keble Coll., Oxford. *Publications:* Patrick Melrose novels: Never Mind (Betty Trask Award), 1992; Bad News, 1992; Some Hope, 1994; Mother's Milk, 2006 (Prix Femina Etranger, 2007; South Bank Show Award for Literature, 2007; filmed, 2012); At Last, 2011; other novels: On the Edge, 1998; A Clue to the Exit, 2000; Lost for Words, 2014 (Bollinger Everyman Wodehouse Prize, 2014). *Address:* c/o Aitken Alexander Associates Ltd, 291 Gray's Inn Road, WC1X 8EB. *T:* (020) 7373 8672. *E:* reception@aitkenalexander.co.uk.

ST AUBYN, Nicholas Francis; *b* 19 Nov. 1955; *yr s* of late Hon. Piers St Aubyn, MC, and Mary St Aubyn (*née* Bailey-Southwell); *m* 1980, Jane Mary, *d* of late William Frederick Brooks; two *s* three *d*. *Educ:* Eton Coll.; Trinity Coll., Oxford (MA PPE). With J. P. Morgan, 1977–86; Kleinwort Benson, 1986–87; American Internat. Gp, 1987–89; Gemini Clothescare, 1989–93; Chm., Fitzroy Gp, 1993. Contested (C) Truro, March 1987, gen. elecn 1987 and 1992. MP (C) Guildford, 1997–2001; contested same seat, 2001. Mem., Select Cttee on Educn and Employment, 1997–2001. Chm. Trustees, Arab-British Centre, 2005–13. Director: Project Trust, 2001–08; Zebra Housing Assoc., 2001–. MInstD. *Publications:* Custom of the County, 2010. *Recreations:* riding, shooting, swimming, sailing. *Address:* 66 Westminster Gardens, SW1P 4JG. *T:* (020) 7828 2804. *Club:* Brooks's.

See also Baron St Levan.

ST AUBYN, Sir William M.; *see* Molesworth-St Aubyn.

ST CLAIR, family name of **Lord Sinclair**.

ST CLAIR, William Linn, FBA 1992; FRSL; author; Senior Research Fellow: School of Advanced Study, University of London, since 2006; Centre for History and Economics, University of Cambridge, since 2007; Chairman, Open Book Publishers, since 2008; *b* 7 Dec. 1937; *s* of late Joseph and Susan St Clair, Falkirk; two *d*. *Educ:* Edinburgh Acad.; St John's Coll., Oxford. FRSL 1973. Admiralty and MoD, 1961–66; First Sec., FCO, 1966–69; transferred to HM Treasury, 1969, Under Sec., 1990–92; Consultant to OECD, 1992–95, to EC, 1997. Visiting Fellow: All Souls Coll., Oxford, 1981–82; Huntington Library, Calif, 1985; Fellow: All Souls Coll., Oxford, 1992–96; Trinity Coll., Cambridge, 1998–2006. Member: Cttee, London Liby, 1996–2000; Council, British Acad., 1996–2000. Internat. Pres., Byron Soc. Thalassa Forum award for culture, Greece, 2000. *Publications:* Lord Elgin and the Marbles, 1967, 3rd edn 1998; That Greece Might Still Be Free, 1972 (Heinemann prize), rev. edn 2008; Trelawny, 1978; Policy Evaluation: a guide for managers, 1988; The Godwins and the Shelleys, 1989 (Time Life prize and Macmillan silver pen); Executive Agencies: a guide to setting targets and measuring performance, 1992; (ed with Irmgard Maassen) Conduct Literature for Women 1500–1640, 2000; Conduct Literature for Women 1640–1710, 2002; (ed with Peter France) Mapping Lives: the uses of biography, 2002; The

Reading Nation in the Romantic Period, 2004; The Political Economy of Reading, 2005, rev. edn 2012; The Grand Slave Emporium: Cape Coast Castle and the British slave trade, 2006; The Door of No Return, 2007. *Recreations:* old books, Scottish hills. *Address:* 52 Eaton Place, SW1X 8AL. *Clubs:* Athenæum, PEN.

ST CLAIR-ERSKINE, family name of **Earl of Rosslyn**.

ST CLAIR-FORD, Sir Robin (Sam), 9th Bt *cr* 1793, of Ember Court, Surrey; *b* 6 June 1941; *s* of Lt-Comdr Drummond St Clair-Ford, RN, 2nd brother of 6th Bt and Nora Elizabeth Astley (*née* Maberly, later Buckley); *S* brother, 2012; *m* 1980, Alison Frances, *yr d* of late William Greenfield Carnegie Dickson; two *s*. *Educ:* Pangbourne Coll.; RMA Sandhurst. *Heir: s* (William) Sam St Clair-Ford [*b* 24 Jan. 1982; *m* 2011, Kate Esther Anne, *d* of Brian Henderson].

ST CYRES, Viscount; Thomas Stafford Northcote; *b* 5 Aug. 1985; *s* and *heir* of Earl of Iddesleigh, *qv*. *Educ:* Oratory Sch., Reading; Univ. of Exeter (BA Hons 2009; MA Classics and Ancient History 2010). *Recreations:* cricket, Real tennis, cooking, shooting, Rugby, music, opera, fundraising. *Address:* Hayne Barton, Newton St Cyres, Exeter, Devon EX5 5AH. *Clubs:* MCC, Tennis and Rackets Assoc.

ST DAVIDS, 4th Viscount *cr* 1918; **Rhodri Colwyn Philipps;** Baron Strange of Knokin, 1299; Baron Hungerford, 1426; Baron de Moleyns, 1445; Bt 1621; Baron St Davids, 1908; *b* 16 Sept. 1966; *s* of 3rd Viscount St Davids and Augusta Victoria Correa Larrain, *d* of late Don Estanislao Correa Ugarte; *S* father, 2009; *m* 2003, Sarah Louise, *o d* of late Dr Peter Butcher. *Educ:* Worth. *Heir: b* Hon. Roland Augusto Jestyn Estanislao Philipps [*b* 9 April 1970; *m* 1997, Jane Amber Robinson (marr. diss. 2004); two *d*].

ST DAVIDS, Bishop of, since 2008; **Rt Rev. (John) Wyn Evans,** FSA, FRHistS; *b* 4 Oct. 1946; *o s* of late Ven. David Eifion Evans and Iris Elizabeth (*née* Gravelle); *m* 1997, Diane Katherine, *d* of George and Kathleen Baker. *Educ:* Ardwyn Grammar Sch., Aberystwyth; University Coll., Cardiff (BA); St Michael's Theol Coll., Llandaff (BD); Jesus Coll., Oxford. FSA 1989; FRHistS 1994. Deacon 1971, priest 1972; Curate, St Davids, 1971–75; Minor Canon, St Davids Cathedral, 1972–75; grad. student, Jesus Coll., Oxford, 1975–77, permission to officiate Oxford diocese, 1975–77; Diocesan Adviser on Archives, St Davids, 1976–83; Rector, Llanfallteg with Castell Dwyran and Clunderwen with Henllan Amgoed and Llangan, 1977–82; Exam. Chaplain to Bishop of St Davids, 1977; Diocesan Warden of Ordinands, 1978–83; Chaplain and Lectr, Trinity Coll., Carmarthen, 1982–90; Diocesan Dir of Educn, 1982–92; Hon. Canon, St Davids Cathedral, 1988–90, Canon (4th Cursal), 1990–94; Dean of Chapel, Trinity Coll., Carmarthen, 1990–94; Head, Dept of Theology and Religious Studies, 1991–94; Dean and Precentor, St Davids Cathedral, 1994–2008; Rector, Rectorial Benefice of Dewisland, 2001–08. Visitor, Univ. of Wales Trinity St David, 2010–. Chairman: Deans of the Church in Wales, 2001–08; Cathedral Libraries and Archives Assoc., 2001–07; Member: St Davids Diocesan Adv. Cttee, 1994– (Chm., 2006–08); Cathedrals and Churches Commn, Church in Wales, 1995–; Exec., Friends of Friendless Churches, 1995–2006 (Episcopal Patron, 2009–); Rep. Body, Church in Wales, 1999–2004. Mem. Governing Body, Trinity Coll., Carmarthen, 1994–2006; Member Court: Nat. Liby of Wales, 1998–2006; Univ. of Wales Cardiff, 2002–09. Mem., Cambrian Archaeological Assoc., 1972– (Pres., 2010–11). Mem., Gorsedd of Bards (White Robe), 1997–. Hon. Fellow, Univ. of Wales, Lampeter, 2006. *Publications:* (with Roger Worsley) St Davids Cathedral 1181–1981, 1981; (ed jtly) St David of Wales, Cult, Church and Nation, 2007; contribs to jls, including Jl Welsh Ecclesiastical History, Carmarthen Antiquary, Diwinyddiaeth. *Recreations:* reading, music, antiquities. *Address:* Llys Esgob, Abergwili, Carmarthen SA31 2JG. *T:* (01264) 236597, *Fax:* (01267) 243381. *Club:* Oxford and Cambridge.

ST DAVIDS, Dean of; *see* Lean, Very Rev. D. J. R.

ST DAVIDS, Archdeacon of; *see* Wight, Ven. D. M.

ST EDMUNDSBURY, Dean of; *see* Ward, Very Rev. F. E. F.

ST EDMUNDSBURY AND IPSWICH, Bishop of, since 2015; **Rt Rev. Martin Alan Seeley;** an Honorary Assistant Bishop, Diocese of Ely, since 2015; *b* 29 May 1954; *s* of Alan and Joyce Seeley; *m* 1st, 1980, Cynthia McLean (marr. diss. 1989); 2nd, 1999, Rev. Jutta Brueck; one *s* one *d*. *Educ:* Jesus Coll., Cambridge (BA 1976, MA 1979); Ripon Coll., Cuddesdon, Oxford; Union Theol Seminary, NYC (STM 1978). Ordained deacon 1978, priest 1979; Curate: Bottesford with Ashby, Scunthorpe, 1978–80; Ch of the Epiphany, NYC, 1980–85; Asst Dir, Trinity Inst., Wall St, NYC, 1981–85; Exec. Dir, Thompson Center, St Louis, Mo, 1985–90; Sec. for Contg Ministerial Educn and Selection Sec., ABM, Gen. Synod of C of E, 1990–96; Vicar, Isle of Dogs, 1996–2006; Principal, Westcott House, Cambridge, 2006–15. Pres., Cambridge Theological Fedn, 2012–15. Hon. Canon, Ely Cathedral, 2007. *Recreations:* cooking, playing tenor saxophone, cinema. *Address:* Bishop's House, 4 Park Road, Ipswich, Suffolk IP1 4ST. *T:* (01473) 252829. *E:* bishop@cofesuffolk.org.

ST GEORGE, Sir John (Avenel Bligh), 10th Bt *cr* 1766 (Ire.), of Athlone, co. Westmeath; *b* 18 March 1940; *s* of Sir George Bligh St George, 9th Bt and Mary Somerville St George (*née* Sutcliffe); *S* father, 1995; *m* (marr. diss.); two *d*; *m* 1981, Linda, *d* of Robert Perry; two *s*. *Heir: s* Robert Alexander Bligh St George [*b* 17 Aug. 1983; *m* 2014, Alison]. *Address:* 6 Challin Street, SE20 8LW.

ST GEORGE-HYSLOP, Prof. Peter Henry, MD; FRCPC; FRS 2004; FRSC 2002; FMedSci; Professor of Experimental Neuroscience, University of Cambridge, since 2007; University Professor, since 2003, Director, Tanz Centre for Research in Neurodegenerative Diseases, since 1995, University of Toronto; Consultant in Neurology, University Health Network, since 1990; *b* 10 July 1953; *s* of Noel St George-Hyslop and Daphne Bower Hyslop (*née* Tinker); *m* 1985, Veronika Andrea Fried; three *d*. *Educ:* Wellington Sch., Somerset; Univ. of Ottawa (MD *primum cum laude* 1976); Univ. of Toronto; Harvard Univ. FRCPC 1989. Instructor, Dept of Neurology, Harvard Med. Sch., 1987–90; Asst Prof., 1990–95, Prof., 1995–2003, Dept of Medicine, Univ. of Toronto. Dir, Toronto Western Hospital Res. Inst., 2004–. FMedSci 2009. *Publications:* more than 300 peer-reviewed scientific articles and 20 book chapters. *Recreation:* vintage sports car racing. *Address:* Cambridge Institute for Medical Research, Cambridge Biomedical Campus, Wellcome Trust/MRC Building, Addenbrooke's Hospital, Hills Road, Cambridge CB2 0XY. *E:* phs22@cam.ac.uk; Tanz Centre for Research in Neurodegenerative Diseases, University of Toronto, Krembil Discovery Tower, KD 6–417, 60 Leonard Avenue, Toronto, ON M5T 2S8, Canada. *T:* (416) 978 7461, *Fax:* (416) 978 1878. *E:* CRND.secr@utoronto.ca.

ST GERMANS, 10th Earl of, *cr* 1815; **Peregrine Nicholas Eliot;** Baron Eliot 1784; *b* 2 Jan. 1941; *o s* of 9th Earl of St Germans, and Helen Mary (*d* 1951), *d* of late Lieut-Col Charles Walter Villiers, CBE, DSO, and Lady Kathleen Villiers; *S* father, 1988; *m* 1st, 1964, Hon. Jacquetta Jean Frederika Lampson (marr. diss. 1989), *d* of 1st Baron Killearn and Jacqueline Aldine Lesley (*née* Castellani); two *s* (and one *s* decd); 2nd, 1992, Elizabeth Mary Williams (marr. diss. 1996); 3rd, 2005, Catherine Elizabeth Wilson. *Educ:* Eton. *Recreation:* mucking about. *Heir: g s* Lord Eliot, *qv*. *Address:* Port Eliot House, St Germans, Cornwall PL12 5ND. *Clubs:* Pratt's; Cornish Club 1768.

ST GERMANS, Bishop Suffragan of, since 2013; **Rt Rev. Dr Christopher David Goldsmith;** *b* 1954; *m* Ellen. *Educ:* Dartford Grammar Sch.; York Univ. (BA 1976; DPhil 1979); N Thames Ministerial Trng Course. Worked in oil and gas industry; ordained deacon, 2000, priest, 2001; non-stipendiary Minister, Pitsea with Nevendon, Essex, 2000–04; Vicar, Christ Church, Warley and St Mary the Virgin, Gt Warley, Essex, 2004–13; Warden of the Readers, Dio. of Truro, 2013–. *Address:* Lis Escop, Truro TR3 6QQ.

ST HELENA, Bishop of, since 2011; **Rt Rev. Dr Richard David Fenwick;** *b* 3 Dec. 1943; *s* of Ethel May and William Samuel Fenwick; *m* 1975, Dr Jane Elizabeth Hughes; one *s* one *d*. *Educ:* Glantâf Secondary Modern Sch.; Monkton House; Canton High Sch., Cardiff; Univ. of Wales, Lampeter (BA, MA, PhD); Trinity Coll., Dublin (MusB, MA); Fitzwilliam Coll., Cambridge; Ridley Hall, Cambridge. FLCM; FTCL. Ordained deacon, 1968, priest, 1969; Assistant Curate: Skewen, 1968–72; Penarth with Lavernock, 1972–74; Priest-Vicar, Succentor and Sacrist of Rochester Cathedral, 1974–78; Minor Canon, 1978–83, Succentor, 1979–83, Warden of the Coll. of Minor Canons, 1981–83, St Paul's Cathedral; Vicar, St Martin's, Ruislip, 1983–90; Priest-Vicar of Westminster Abbey, 1983–90; Canon Residentiary and Precentor, 1990–97, Sub-Dean, 1996–97, Guildford Cathedral; Dean of Monmouth, 1997–2011. Chm., Liturgical Commn of the Church in Wales, 1998–2011. Warden, Guild of Church Musicians, 1998–2011. Liveryman, Musicians' Co.; Hon. Liveryman, Co. of Gold and Silver Wyre Drawers. Hon. FVCM, 1990; Hon. FGCM, 2004. OStJ 2001. Hon. DLitt Central Sch. of Religion, 2011. Hon. Archbishop of Wales's Award in Church Music, 2012. *Publications:* contribs to various musical and theol jls. *Recreations:* travel, reading, music. *Address:* Bishopsholme, St Helena, South Atlantic Ocean, STHL 1ZZ. *T:* 24471.

ST HELENS, 2nd Baron *cr* 1964; **Richard Francis Hughes-Young;** *b* 4 Nov. 1945; *s* of 1st Baron St Helens, MC, and Elizabeth Agnes (*d* 1956), *y d* of late Captain Richard Blakiston-Houston; *S* father, 1980; *m* 1983, Mrs Emma R. Talbot-Smith; one *s* one *d*. *Educ:* Nautical College, Pangbourne. *Heir: s* Henry Thomas Hughes-Young, *b* 7 March 1986.

ST JOHN, family name of **Earl of Orkney, Viscount Bolingbroke** and **Baron St John of Bletso**.

ST JOHN, Lord; Michael John Paulet; *b* 31 Aug. 1999; *s* and *heir* of Earl of Wiltshire, *qv*.

ST JOHN OF BLETSO, 21st Baron *cr* 1558; **Anthony Tudor St John;** Bt 1660; *b* 16 May 1957; *s* of 20th Baron St John of Bletso, TD, and of Katharine, *d* of late A. G. von Berg; *S* father, 1978; *m* 1994, Dr Helen Westlake (marr. diss. 2012); two *s* two *d*. *Educ:* Diocesan College, Cape Town; Univ. of Cape Town (BSocSc 1977, BA (Law) 1978); Univ. of S Africa (BProc 1982); London Univ. (LLM 1983). Solicitor. Financial consultant to Smith New Court plc, later Merrill Lynch, London, 1989–2008; Man. Dir, Globix Corp., 1998–2002; Consultant to Globix Europe, 2002–05. Non-executive Chairman: Estate & General (IOM Ltd), 1994–; Spiritel plc, 2004–10; Equest Balkan Properties plc, 2005–08; non-executive Director: Regal Petroleum plc, 2003–10; Albion Ventures VCT, 2007–; Obtala Resources plc, 2009–. Strategic Adviser: 2e2 Gp plc, 2007–; Chayton Atlas Agriculture (formerly Chayton Capital), 2008–11. Chm., Governing Bd, Certification Internat., 1995–. An Extra Lord-in-Waiting to the Queen, 1998–. Cross-bencher in House of Lords, specific interests foreign affairs, envmtl protection, sport, financial services, Africa, IT. Vice Chm., Parly South Africa Gp; Member: EU Select Cttee A on Trade, Finance and Foreign Affairs, 1996–99, 2001–; EU Sub Cttee B, 2003–08; H of L Information Cttee, 2009–; H of L Select Cttee on Communications, 2009–; Exec. Cttee, All Party Africa Gp; elected Mem., H of L, 1999. Trustee: Tusk; M'Afrika Tikkun; Citizens online, 2000–; Coexistence Trust; Alexandra Rose charities (Chm., 2010–); Christel House, 2010–; Life Neurological Research Trust; Helen Feather Memorial Trust. *Recreations:* golf, tennis and ski-ing; bridge. *Heir: s* Hon. Oliver Beauchamp St John, *b* 11 July 1995. *Address:* c/o House of Lords, SW1A 0AA. *Clubs:* Alfred's, Hurlingham; Royal Cape Golf, Sunningdale Golf.

ST JOHN, Rt Rev. Andrew Reginald; Rector, Church of the Transfiguration, New York, since 2005; *b* 16 Feb. 1944; *s* of Reginald and Leila St John. *Educ:* Wesley Coll., Melbourne; Melbourne Univ. (LLB 1966); Trinity Coll., Melbourne (ThSchol 1971); Gen. Theol Seminary, New York (STM 1984). Barrister and solicitor, Supreme Court of Victoria, 1967. Ordained priest, 1972; Precentor, St Paul's Cathedral, Melbourne, 1975–78; Vicar: St Mary's, E Chadstone, 1978–84; Holy Trinity, Kew, 1984–95; an Asst Bp, dio. of Melbourne (Bp of the Western Region), 1995–2001. Hon. DD Gen. Theol Seminary, NY, 1995. *Recreations:* reading, gardening, opera. *Address:* 1 East 29th Street, New York, NY 10016, USA. *T:* (212) 6843275. *Clubs:* Melbourne, Melbourne Cricket (Melbourne); Players (NY).

ST JOHN, Lauren; author and journalist, since 1987; *b* 21 Dec. 1966; *d* of Errol Antonie Kendall and Margaret May Dutton Kendall. *Educ:* Roosevelt High Sch., Harare, Zimbabwe; Harare Poly. (Dip. Journalism). Sub-editor, Resident Abroad magazine, 1987; journalist, Today's Golfer, 1988–89; Golf Correspondent, Sunday Times, 1994–98. Mem., Assoc. of Golf Writers, 1989–. *Publications:* Shooting at Clouds: inside the European golf tour, 1991; Seve: the biography, 1993, 2nd edn 1997; Out of Bounds: inside professional golf, 1995; Greg Norman: the biography, 1998; Walkin' After Midnight: a journey to the heart of Nashville, 2000; Hardcore Troubadour: the life and near death of Steve Earle, 2002; Rainbow's End: a memoir of childhood, war and an African farm, 2007; The Obituary Writer, 2013; Race the Wind, 2013; Rendezvous in Russia, 2013; Fire Storm, 2014; The Glory, 2015; *for children:* The White Giraffe, 2006; Dolphin Song, 2007; The Last Leopard, 2008; The Elephant's Tale, 2009; Dead Man's Cove, 2010; Kidnap in the Caribbean, 2011; The One Dollar Horse, 2012; Kentucky Thriller, 2012; articles in Sunday Times. *Recreations:* music, painting, music, horse riding, saving wildlife.

ST JOHN, Oliver Beauchamp, CEng, FRAeS; Chief Scientist, Civil Aviation Authority, 1978–82; *b* 22 Jan. 1922; 2nd *s* of late Harold and Ella Margaret St John; *m* 1945, Eileen (*née* Morris); three *s*. *Educ:* Monkton Combe Sch.; Queens' Coll., Cambridge (MA); London Univ. (External) (BSc). Metropolitan Vickers, Manchester, 1939; Royal Aircraft Estabt, Farnborough, from 1946, on automatic control of fixed-wing aircraft and helicopters; Supt, Blind Landing Experimental Unit, RAE, Bedford, 1966; Director of Technical Research & Development, CAA, 1969–78. Queen's Commendation for Valuable Services in the Air, 1956. *Publications:* A Gallimaufry of Goffering: a history of early ironing implements, 1982. *Recreations:* mountaineering, early music, family history research. *Address:* The Old Stables, Manor Farm Lane, East Hagbourne OX11 9ND. *T:* (01235) 818437.

See also P. R. T. St John.

ST JOHN, Peter Rowland Tudor; Partner, Caruso St John Architects, since 1991; *b* 27 June 1959; *s* of Oliver St John, *qv*; *m* 1988, Siw Thomas; two *s* one *d*. *Educ:* University Coll. London (BSc Hons); AA Dip. Hons 1984. Major projects include: New Art Gall., Walsall, 2000; extn to Hallfield Sch., Paddington, 2005; Gagosian Gall., King's Cross, 2005; extn to V&A Mus. of Childhood, 2006; Millbank Project, Tate Britain, 2006–13; Chiswick House Gardens Café, 2010; Nottingham Contemporary, 2010. Sen. Lectr, Poly. of N London, 1990–97; Course Tutor, Grad. Sch. of Design, Harvard Univ., 2005–06. Visiting Professor: Acad. of Architecture, Mendrisio, 1999–2001; Dept of Architecture and Civil Engrg, Univ. of Bath, 2001–04; Cass Sch. of Architecture, 2012–; Guest Prof., ETH Zurich, 2007–09. Hon. DDes Wolverhampton, 2001. *Recreations:* woodlands, swimming. *Address:* Caruso St John Architects, 1 Coate Street, E2 9AG.

ST JOHN-MILDMAY, Sir Walter (John Hugh), 11th Bt *cr* 1772, of Farley, Southampton; *b* 3 Sept. 1935; *s* of Michael Paulet St John-Mildmay (*d* 1993), *ggs* of Sir Henry Paulet St John-Mildmay, 3rd Bt, and Joan Elizabeth (*née* Stockley; *d* 1977); *S* kinsman, Rev. Sir (Aubrey) Neville St John-Mildmay, 10th Bt, who *d* 1955, after which Btcy was dormant until revived, 1998. *Educ:* Wycliffe Coll.; Emmanuel Coll., Cambridge (BA 1958); Hammersmith Coll. of Art and Building; RAC Cirencester. *Heir: b* Michael Hugh Paulet St John-Mildmay [*b* 28 Sept. 1937; *m* 1965, Mrs Crystal Margaret Ludlow; two *s* one *d*]. *Address:* 11 The Empire, Grand Parade, Bath BA2 4DF.

ST JOHN PARKER, Michael, MA, MSc; FSA; Headmaster, Abingdon School, Oxfordshire, 1975–2001; *b* 21 July 1941; *s* of Rev. Canon J. W. Parker; *m* 1965, Annette Monica Ugle; two *s* two *d*. *Educ:* Stamford Sch.; King's Coll., Cambridge (MA); Kellogg Coll., Oxford (MSc). Asst Master: Sevenoaks Sch., 1962–63; King's Sch., Canterbury, 1963–69; Winchester Coll., 1969–75; Head of History Dept, Winchester Coll., 1970–75. Schoolmaster Student, Christ Church, Oxford, 1984. Member: Council, Hansard Soc., 1972–2003 (Exec. Cttee, 2001–03); Marsh Cttee on Politics and Industry, 1978–79. Chm., Midland Div., HMC, 1984; Member: Exec. Cttee, Assoc. of Governing Bodies of Ind. Schs, 2002–08; Council, Nat. Trust, 2008– (Member: Stowe Adv. Cttee, 2002–; Governance Rev. Cttee, 2014–15). Governor: St Helen's Sch., 1975–83; Christ Church Cathedral Sch., 1981–2013; Cokethorpe Sch., 1985–2009 (Chm., 1990–2009; Gov. Emeritus, 2010); Josca's Sch., 1988–98; Hatherop Castle Sch., 2002–14 (Chm., 2003–14); Walsall Acad. (formerly Walsall City Acad.), 2003–; Midhurst Rother Coll., 2008–15. Fellow, Winchester Coll., 2006–13. Chm., Cambridge Soc. of Oxfordshire, 2003–. Dir, Bampton Classical Opera, 2005–. Master, Civic Guild of Old Mercers, 2004–05; Liveryman, 2006, Hon. Archivist, 2007–, Masons' Co. FSA 2011. Contrib. Ed., Attain mag., 2007–. *Publications:* The British Revolution—Social and Economic History 1750–1970, 1972; The Martlet and the Griffen, 1997; various pamphlets and articles, incl. contribs to Oxford DNB. *Recreations:* old buildings, music, books, gardens. *Address:* Exeter House, Cheapside, Bampton, Oxfordshire OX18 2JL. *Clubs:* Athenæum; Leander.

ST JOHN-STEVENS, Philip Simeon; His Honour Judge St John-Stevens; a Circuit Judge, since 2009; *b* Herts, 10 March 1960; *s* of late Terence Stevens and of Betty Stevens; *m* 1990, Kathryn Jane Nightingale; two *s*. *Educ:* University Coll. Cardiff (LLB Hons). Called to the Bar, Inner Temple, 1985; Attorney Gen. of Montserrat, BWI, 2002. *Recreations:* golf, cricket, cycling. *Address:* Maidstone Combined Courts, Law Courts, Maidstone ME16 8EQ. *Club:* Rye Golf.

ST JOHNSTON, Colin David; Director, Ocean Transport and Trading Ltd, 1974–88; *b* 6 Sept. 1934; *s* of Hal and Sheilagh St Johnston; *m* 1958, Valerie Paget; three *s* one *d*. *Educ:* Shrewsbury Sch.; Lincoln Coll., Oxford. Booker McConnell Ltd, 1958–70; Ocean Transport and Trading Ltd, 1970–88: Dep. Gp Chief Exec., 1985–88; Man. Dir, Ocean Cory, 1976–85; non-exec. Dir, FMC plc, 1981–83; Man. Dir, PRO NED, 1989–95. Mem. Council: Royal Commonwealth Society for the Blind, 1967–95; Industrial Soc., 1981–96; Trustee, Frances Mary Buss Foundn, 1981–95; Governor: Camden Sch., 1974–96; Arnold House Sch., 1993–2005 (Chm., 1995–2004). FRSA. *Recreations:* music, Real and lawn tennis. *Address:* 30 Fitzroy Road, NW1 8TY. *T:* (020) 7722 5932. *Club:* MCC.

See also R. D. St Johnston.

ST JOHNSTON, Prof. (Robert) Daniel, PhD; FRS 2005; Professor of Developmental Genetics, since 2003, and Director, Gurdon Institute, since 2009, University of Cambridge; Bye Fellow, Peterhouse, Cambridge, since 1995; Wellcome Trust Principal Fellow, Wellcome Trust/Cancer Research UK Institute of Cancer and Developmental Biology, since 1997; *b* 24 April 1960; *s* of Colin St Johnston, *qv*; partner, Bénédicte Sanson; one *s* one *d*. *Educ:* Christ's Coll., Cambridge (BA 1st cl. (Natural Scis) 1981); Harvard Univ. (PhD (Cellular and Develtl Biol.) 1988). EMBO Post-doctoral Fellow, Max-Planck Inst., Tübingen, Germany, 1988–91; Wellcome Trust Sen. Fellow, Wellcome/CRC Inst. of Cancer and Develtl Biol., and Dept of Genetics, Cambridge Univ., 1991–97. Loeb Fellow, Woods Hole Marine Biol. Lab., 1982; Fellow, EMBO, 1997 (Gold Medal, 2000). Mem. Editl Adv. Bd, Development, 1999–. *Publications:* numerous papers in jls on anterior-posterior axis formation in Drosophila, how cells become polarized, and mechanism of messenger RNA localization. *Recreations:* cryptic crosswords, hill walking, cooking. *Address:* Wellcome Trust/Cancer Research UK Gurdon Institute, Tennis Court Road, Cambridge CB2 1QN. *T:* (01223) 334127.

ST LEGER, family name of **Viscount Doneraile**.

ST LEVAN, 5th Baron *cr* 1887; **James Piers Southwell St Aubyn;** Bt 1866; *b* 6 June 1950; *s* of Hon. Oliver Piers St Aubyn, MC (*d* 2006), *s* of 3rd Baron St Levan, and Mary Bailey Southwell (*d* 1987); *S* uncle, 2013; *m* 1981, Mary Caroline, *y d* of Peter Ward Bennett, OBE; two *s* two *d*. *Educ:* Eton; Magdalen Coll., Oxford. *Heir: s* Hon. Hugh James St Aubyn, *b* 14 June 1983.

See also N. F. St Aubyn.

ST OSWALD, 6th Baron *cr* 1885, of Nostell, co. York; **Charles Rowland Andrew Winn;** DL; landowner; *b* 22 July 1959; *s* of 5th Baron St Oswald and of Charlotte Denise Eileen Winn, *d* of Wilfred Haig Loyd; *S* father, 1999; *m* 1985, Louise Alexandra, *yr d* of Stewart Mackenzie Scott; one *s* one *d*. *Educ:* New Sch., King's Langley. DL W Yorks, 2004. *Recreations:* shooting, walking. *Heir: s* Hon. Rowland Charles Sebastian Henry Winn, *b* 15 April 1986. *Address:* Nostell Priory Estate Office, Doncaster Road, Nostell, Wakefield, W Yorkshire WF4 1AB. *T:* (01924) 862221.

ST PATRICK'S, Dublin, Dean of; *see* Stacey, Very Rev. V. G.

ST PAUL'S, Dean of; *see* Ison, Very Rev. D. J.

ST VINCENT, 8th Viscount *cr* 1801; **Edward Robert James Jervis;** *b* 12 May 1951; *er s* of 7th Viscount St Vincent and Phillida (*née* Logan); *S* father, 2006; *m* 1977, Victoria Margaret (*d* 2015), *o d* of Wilton Joseph Oldham; one *s* one *d*. *Educ:* Radley. *Heir: s* Hon. James Richard Anthony Jervis, *b* 1982.

SAINTY, Sir John Christopher, KCB 1986; Clerk of the Parliaments, 1983–90, retired; *b* 31 Dec. 1934; *s* of late Christopher Lawrence Sainty and Nancy Lee Sainty (*née* Miller); *m* 1965, (Elizabeth) Frances Sherlock; three *s*. *Educ:* Winchester Coll.; New Coll., Oxford (MA). FSA; FRHistS. Clerk, Parlt Office, House of Lords, 1959; seconded as Private Sec. to Leader of House and Chief Whip, House of Lords, 1963; Clerk of Journals, House of Lords, 1965; Res. Asst and Editor, Inst. of Historical Research, 1970; Reading Clerk, House of Lords, 1974. Mem., Royal Commn on Historical MSS, 1991–2002. Institute of Historical Research: Sen. Res. Fellow, 1994; Hon. Fellow, 2000–. *Publications:* Treasury Officials 1660–1870, 1972; Officials of the Secretaries of State 1660–1782, 1973; Officials of the Boards of Trade 1660–1870, 1974; Admiralty Officials 1660–1870, 1975; Home Office Officials, 1782–1870, 1975; Colonial Office Officials 1794–1870, 1976; (with D. Dewar) Divisions in the House of Lords: an analytical list 1685–1857, 1976; Officers of the Exchequer, 1983; A List of English Law Officers, King's Counsel and Holders of Patents of Precedence, 1987; The Judges of England 1272–1990, 1993; (with R. O. Bucholz) Officials of the Royal Household 1660–1837, vol. 1 1997, vol. 2 1998; Peerage Creations 1649–1800, 1998; articles in Eng. Hist. Rev., Bull. Inst. Hist. Research. *Address:* 94 Ramillies Road, W4 1JA. *T:* (020) 8747 0988. *Club:* Brooks's.

SAKER; *see* Gordon-Saker.

SAKMANN, Prof. Bert, MD; Scientific Director, 2010–11, and Group Leader, Digital Neuroanatomy, since 2010, Max Planck Florida Institute; *b* Stuttgart, 12 June 1942; *m* 1970, Dr Christiane Wülfert; two *s* one *d*. *Educ:* Univ. of Tübingen; Univ. of Munich; University Hosp., Munich; Univ. of Göttingen (MD). Research Asst, Max-Planck-Institut für Psychiatrie, Munich, 1969–70; British Council Fellow, Dept of Biophysics, UCL, 1971–73; Max-Planck-Institut für biophysikalische Chemie, University of Göttingen: Res. Asst, 1974–79; Res. Associate, Membrane Biology Gp, 1979–82; Head, Membrane Physiology Unit, 1983–85; Dir 1985–87, Prof. 1987–89, Dept of Cell Physiology; Dir, Dept of Cell Physiology, Max-Planck-Institut für medizinische Forschung, Heidelberg, 1989–2008; Prof. of Physiology, Medical Faculty, Univ. of Heidelberg, 1990–2007; Gp Leader, Max-Planck-Institut für Neurobiologie, Martinsried, 2008–10. Lectures: Yale, 1982; Washington Univ., Seattle, 1986, 1990; Univ. of Miami, 1989; Liverpool Univ., 1990; Univ. of Rochester, NY, 1991. Foreign Member: Royal Soc., 1994; Nat. Acad., USA, 1993. Numerous prizes and awards; (jtly) Nobel Prize for Physiology, 1991. *Publications:* (contrib.) The Visual System: neurophysiology, biophysics and their clinical applications, 1972; (contrib.) Advances in Pharmacology and Therapeutics, 1978; (contrib. and ed with E. Neher) Single Channel Recording, 1983; (contrib.) Membrane Control of Cellular Activity, 1986; (contrib.) Calcium and Ion Channel Modulation, 1988; (contrib.) Neuromuscular Junction, 1989; numerous articles in jls incl. Annual Rev. Physiol., Jl Physiol., Nature, Proc. Nat. Acad. Scis, Pflügers Archiv, Jl Exptl Physiol., Neuron, FEBS Lett., Science, Eur. Jl Biochem., Proc. Royal Soc., Jl Cell Biol. *Recreations:* tennis, ski-ing, music, reading. *Address:* Max Planck Florida Institute, 1 Max Planck Way, Jupiter, FL 33458, USA.

SAKO, Prof. Mari, PhD; Professor of Management Studies, University of Oxford, since 1997; Fellow, New College, Oxford, since 2007; *b* Japan, 12 June 1960; *d* of Kanzo Sako and Akemi Sako; *m* 1983, Sumantra Chakrabarti (*see* Sir S. Chakrabarti); one *d*. *Educ:* Lady Margaret Hall, Oxford (BA Hons); London Sch. of Econs (MSc); PhD London 1990. Researcher, Technical Change Centre, London, 1984–86; London School of Economics and Political Science: Lectr in Modern Japanese Business, 1987–92; Lectr in Industrial Relns, 1992–94; Reader, 1994–97; Fellow, Templeton Coll., Oxford, 1997–2007. Fellow, Japanese Soc. for Promotion of Sci., Kyoto Univ., 1992; Japan Foundn Fellow, Tokyo Univ., 1997. *Publications:* (with R. Dore) How the Japanese Learn to Work, 1989, rev. edn 1998; Prices, Quality and Trust: inter-firm relations in Britain and Japan, 1992; (ed with H. Sato) Japanese Labour and Management in Transition, 1997; (jtly) Are Skills the Answer?, 1998; Shifting Boundaries of the Firm, 2006. *Recreation:* music. *Address:* Saïd Business School, University of Oxford, Park End Street, Oxford OX1 1HP. *T:* (01865) 288925.

SAKORA, Hon. Sir Bernard Berekia, KBE 2013 (CBE 2005); CSM; Judge, Supreme Court of Papua New Guinea, since 1992; *b* Tufi, Northern Province, PNG, 19 Nov. 1947; *s* of Korimaga and Gandai Sakora; *m* 1975, Roslyn Gay Cunningham; three *s* one *d*. *Educ:* Boys' Grammar Sch., Ipswich, Qld, Australia; Univ. of Papua New Guinea (LLB); University Coll. London (LLM). Barrister and solicitor, Supreme Court of PNG; Legal Officer, Crown Solicitor's Office, 1974–75; Sen. Legal Officer and Dep. State Solicitor, 1975–76; Principal Legal Officer and Asst Sec. for Justice, 1977–79; Dep. Sec., 1979–81; Sen. Lectr, Law Faculty, Univ. of PNG, 1982–92. Chm., Law Reform Commn, 1985–87. Chancellor, Anglican Ch of PNG, 2010–. *Recreations:* reading, watching Rugby and cricket on TV, swimming. *Address:* c/o Judges Chambers, Supreme Court, PO Box 7018, Boroko, National Capital District, Papua New Guinea. *T:* 3245734, 3232922, *Fax:* 3250425. *E:* sakora@pngjudiciary.gov.pg.

SALAS, Dame Margaret Laurence, (Dame Laurie), DBE 1988; QSO 1982; *b* 8 Feb. 1922; *d* of Sir James Lawrence Hay, OBE and late Davidina Mertel (*née* Gunn); *m* 1946, Dr John Reuben Salas, FRCSE, FRACS (*d* 2014); two *s* four *d*. *Educ:* Christchurch; Univ. of New Zealand (BA). Teacher, audiometrist in Med. practice. National Council of Women of NZ: legislative and parly work; Nat. Sec., 1976–80; Nat. Vice-Pres., 1982–86, now Hon. Life Mem.; Vice-Convener, Internat. Council, Women's Cttee on Develt, 1985–94; Nat. Sec., Women's Internat. League for Peace and Freedom, 1985–90; Pres., UNA, NZ, 1988–92, now Hon. Life Mem.; Vice-Pres., World Fedn of UNAs, 1993–2000; Hon. Life Mem., UNIFEM. Member: Public Adv. Cttee, Disarmament and Arms Control, 1987–96; Nat. Cons. Cttee on Disarmament (Chair, 1979–90); Adv. Cttee, External Aid and Develt, 1986–88; Educn Cttee, Alcoholic Liquor Adv. Council, 1976–81; Nat. Review Cttee on Social Studies, Educn Dept; Cttee, SCF, 1970–76; Nat. Commn, UN Internat. Year of the Child, 1978–80; UN Internat. Year of Peace, Aotearoa Cttee (Vice-Chair, 1986); NZ Cttee, Council for Security and Co-operation in Asia and Pacific, 1994–2007. Hon. Vice-Pres., NZ Inst. of Internat. Affairs, 1994–. Pres., Wellington Branch, NZ Fedn of Univ. Women, 1970–72; repr. NZ, overseas meetings. Patron: Peace Foundn, NZ; UNIFEM, NZ. Silver Jubilee Medal, 1977; NZ Commemoration Medal, 1990. *Publications:* Disarmament, 1982. *Recreations:* choral and classical music, enjoying extended family.

See also Sir D. R. Hay.

SALEM, Bridget Anne; *see* O'Connor, B. A.

SALES, (Donald) John; gardens consultant; Chief Gardens Adviser, then Head of Gardens, The National Trust, 1974–98; *b* 1 May 1933; *s* of Frederic Donald Sales and Alice Elizabeth (*née* Burrell); *m* 1958, Lyn Thompson; three *s*. *Educ:* Westminster City Sch.; Kent Horticultural Coll.; Royal Botanic Gardens, Kew. MHort (RHS) 1957. Lectr in Horticulture, Writtle Agricl Coll., Chelmsford, 1958–70 (Fellow, 1998); Horticulturist (Asst to Gardens Advr), NT, 1971–74. Vice-President: Garden History Soc., 2004–; RHS, 2008–. Medal of Honour, Internat. Castles Inst., 1991; VMH, RHS, 1992; Inst. of Horticulture Award for Outstanding Services to Horticulture, 1996. *Publications:* West Country Gardens, 1980; A Year in the Garden, 2001; contrib. articles in Country Life. *Recreations:* gardening, photography, walking, music, ballet, the arts generally. *Address:* Covertside, Perrott's Brook, Cirencester, Glos GL7 7BW. *T:* (01285) 831537.

SALES, Rt Hon. Sir Philip James, Kt 2008; PC 2014; **Rt Hon. Lord Justice Sales;** a Lord Justice of Appeal, since 2014; *b* 11 Feb. 1962; *s* of Peter and Janet Sales; *m* 1988, Miranda Wolpert; one *s* one *d*. *Educ:* Royal Grammar Sch., Guildford; Churchill Coll., Cambridge (BA 1983); Worcester Coll., Oxford (BCL 1984). Called to the Bar, Lincoln's Inn, 1985; barrister, 1986–2008; First Treasury Jun. Counsel (Common Law), 1997–2006; Asst Recorder, 1999–2001; Recorder, 2001–08; Dep. High Court Judge, 2004–08; QC 2006; First Treasury Counsel (Common Law), 2006–08; a Judge of the High Court of Justice, Chancery Div., 2008–14. Mem., Panel of Chairmen, Competition Appeal Tribunal, 2008–; Dep. Chm., Boundary Commn for England, 2009–14; Vice-Pres., Investigatory Powers Tribunal, 2014–15. *Publications:* (Asst Ed) Halsbury's Laws of England, Vol. I (I), Administrative Law, 4th edn 1989; articles in Cambridge Law Jl, Oxford Jl of Legal Studies, Law Qly Rev., Public Law, Judicial Rev. *Recreations:* theatre, film, reading. *Address:* Royal Courts of Justice, Strand, WC2A 2LL.

SALFORD, Bishop of, (RC), since 1997; **Rt Rev. Terence John Brain;** *b* 19 Dec. 1938; *s* of Reginald John Brain and Mary Cooney. *Educ:* Cotton Coll., North Staffordshire; St Mary's Coll., Oscott, Birmingham. Ordained priest, 1964; Asst Priest, St Gregory's, Longton, 1964–65; mem. of staff, Cotton Coll., 1965–69; Hosp. Chaplain, St Patrick's, Birmingham, 1969–71; Archbishop's Secretary, Birmingham, 1971–82; Parish Priest: Bucknall, Stoke-on-Trent, 1982–88; St Austin's, Stafford, 1988–91; Auxiliary Bishop of Birmingham, 1991–97. RC Bishop for Prisons, 1994–2013. Chm., RC Bishops' Social Welfare Cttee, 1992–2002. Episcopal Advr, Nat. Council of Lay Assocs, 1993–2006. Trustee, Caritas Social Action Network, 2002– (Chm. of Trustees, 2007–14). *Recreations:* crossword puzzles, water colour painting. *Address:* Wardley Hall, Worsley, Manchester M28 2ND.

SALFORD, Archdeacon of; *see* Sharples, Ven. D. J.

SALISBURY, 7th Marquess of, *cr* 1789; **Robert Michael James Gascoyne-Cecil,** KCVO 2012; PC 1994; DL; Baron Cecil, 1603; Viscount Cranborne, 1604; Earl of Salisbury, 1605; Baron Gascoyne-Cecil (Life Peer), 1999; *b* 30 Sept. 1946; *s* of 6th Marquess of Salisbury and of Marjorie Olein, (Molly), *d* of Captain Hon. Valentine Wyndham-Quin, RN; *S* father, 2003; *m* 1970, Hannah Ann, *er d* of Lt-Col William Joseph Stirling of Keir; two *s* three *d. Educ:* Eton; Oxford. MP (C) Dorset South, 1979–87. Summoned to the Upper House of Parliament, 1992, as Baron Cecil, of Essendon in the County of Rutland; Parly Under-Sec. of State for Defence, MoD, 1992–94; Lord Privy Seal and Leader of H of L, 1994–97; Leader of the Opposition, H of L, 1997–98. Chairman: Comparative Clinical Sci. Foundn, 2004–; Friends of Lambeth Palace Liby, 2008–; Thames Diamond Jubilee Foundn, 2011–14; President: Friends of BL, 2005–; Game and Wildlife Conservation Trust, 2008–. Chm. Council, RVC, 1998–2007; Chancellor, Univ. of Herts, 2005–. Mem., Bd of Trustees, Hunterian Collection, 2014–. Governor, The Charterhouse, 2009–. Chm., Ct of Patrons, Thrombosis Res. Inst., 2010–. DL Herts, 2007. *Heir: s* Viscount Cranborne, *qv. Address:* 2 Swan Walk, SW3 4JJ.

SALISBURY, Bishop of, since 2011; **Rt Rev. Nicholas Roderick Holtam;** *b* 8 Aug. 1954; *s* of late Sydney Holtam and Kathleen (*née* Freeberne); *m* 1981, Helen Harris; three *s* one *d. Educ:* Latymer Grammar Sch., Edmonton; Collingwood Coll., Univ. of Durham (BA Geog.; MA Theol.); King's Coll. London (BD, AKC; FKC 2005); Westcott House, Cambridge. Ordained deacon, 1979, priest, 1980; Asst Curate, St Dunstan and All Saints, Stepney, 1979–82; Tutor, Lincoln Theol Coll., 1983–87; Vicar, Christ Church and St John with St Luke, Isle of Dogs, 1988–95; Vicar, St Martin-in-the-Fields, 1995–2011. Took seat in H of L, 2014. Hon. DCL Durham, 2005. *Publications:* A Room With a View: ministry with the world at your door, 2008; The Art of Worship, 2011. *Recreations:* walking, cycling, reading, writing. *Address:* South Canonry, 71 The Close, Salisbury SP1 2ER. *T:* (01722) 334031. *E:* bishop.salisbury@salisbury.anglican.org.

SALISBURY, Dean of; *see* Osborne, Very Rev. J.

SALISBURY, David Maxwell, CB 2001; FRCP, FRCPCH, FFPH; Director of Immunisation, Department of Health, 2004–13; Associate Fellow, Centre on Global Health Security, Chatham House, since 2013; *b* 10 Aug. 1946; *s* of Dr Steven Salisbury and Judith Grace Vivien Salisbury; *m* 1974, Anne Harvey; one *s* one *d. Educ:* Epsom Coll.; Royal London Hosp., Univ. of London (MB BS 1969). FRCP 1992; FRCPCH 1997; FFPH (FFPHM 1998). Sir William Coxen Res. Fellow, Dept of Paediatrics, Univ. of Oxford, 1973–75; Paediatric Registrar, John Radcliffe Hosp., Oxford, 1976–77; Sen. Registrar, Great Ormond Street Hosp. for Children, 1977–85; Consultant Paediatrician, New Cross Hosp., Wolverhampton, 1985–86; PMO, DoH, 1986–2004. Vis. Prof., Dept of Infectious Disease Epidemiology, Imperial Coll., London, 2007–. Chairman: Strategic Adv. Gp of Experts on Immunization, WHO, 2005–10; Commn for Certification of Poliomyelitis Eradication, European Region, WHO, 2007–; Mem., WHO Global Commn for Certification of Poliomyelitis Eradication. Chm. Bd, Jenner Vaccine Foundn, 2012–. Freeman, City of London, 1980; Liveryman, Soc. of Apothecaries, 1980–. *Publications:* contrib. jls and textbooks on immunisation, infectious disease, paediatrics and neonatology. *Recreations:* destructive gardening (lawns, logs and hedges), sailing. *Address:* Dobsons, Brightwell-cum-Sotwell, Wallingford OX10 0RH. *T:* (01491) 837209.

SALISBURY, David Murray; Chairman, Dimensional Fund Advisors Ltd, London, 2002–14 (Director, Dimensional Fund Advisors Inc., 1991–96); *b* 18 Feb. 1952; *s* of late Norman Salisbury and of Isobel Sutherland Murray; *m* 1977, Lynneth Mary Jones; two *d. Educ:* Harrow Sch.; Trinity Coll., Oxford (MA). Joined J. Henry Schroder Wagg & Co. Ltd, 1974; Exec. Vice Pres., 1984–86, Chief Exec., 1986–96, Schroder Capital Management International Inc.; Jt Chief Exec., 1996–97, Chm., 1998–2000, Schroder Investment Management Ltd; Dir, Schroders PLC, 1998–2001; Chief Exec., Schroders, 2000–01. Gov., Harrow Sch., 1996–99, 2002–06. *Recreations:* tennis, ski-ing. *Address:* The Dutch House, West Green, Hartley Wintney, Hants RG27 8JN.

SALISBURY, John; *see* Caute, J. D.

SALISBURY, Sir Robert (William), Kt 1998; educational consultant, Northern Ireland; consultant to Department for Education and Skills, since 2001; Director of Partnerships, University of Nottingham, 1999–2004; *b* 21 Oct. 1941; *s* of Ernest Arthur Salisbury and Vera Ellen Salisbury; *m* 1975, Rosemary D'Arcy (former Principal, Drumragh Coll., Omagh, NI, now nat. educnl consultant); three *s. Educ:* Henry Mellish Sch., Nottingham; Kesteven Trng Coll., Lincs (Teacher's Cert.); Nottingham Univ. (CFPS); Loughborough Univ. (MA). Geography teacher, Holgate Sch., Hucknall, Notts, 1962–64; study in Europe, 1964–66; Second in English, Kimberley Comp. Sch., Notts, 1973–77; Head of Humanities and of 6th Form, Gedling Comp. Sch., Notts, 1977–83; Dep. Head, Alderman White Comp. Sch., Notts, 1983–89; Headteacher, Garibaldi Sch., Mansfield, 1989–99. Vis. Prof., Sch. of Educn, Nottingham Univ., 1998. Chairman: Educnl Funding Rev., Dept of Educn, NI, 2012–13; Further Educn Colls Rev., NI, 2013–14. Chief Examr, JMB/NEAB, 1979–90; tutor, Professional Qualification for Headship, 2000–; Co-Leader, Nat. Coll. of Sch. Leadership (Trainee Heads Scheme), 2000–. Formerly Ind. Chm., NE Lincs Educn Action Zone, 1998–99. Chm., Sherwood Partnership, 1998–2002; Vice-Chair, Integrated Educn Fund, NI, 2003–05. Associate Advr, Industrial Soc., 1992–; Mem. Adv. Council, Carlton Television, 2000–02; Educational Advisor: Centre for British Teaching, 1996–; CfBT Educn Trust, 2003–; QUB, 2006–. Regl Chairman: Teaching Awards Trust, 1998–; Literacy and Numeracy Task Force, NI, 2008–; Chairman, Trustees: Fathers Direct, 1998–2005; Sherwood Coalfield Develt Trust, 1999–2003. Patron, Drugs Abuse Resistance Educn, 2002–. Nat. and internat. speaker, 1992–. FRSA 1998. *Publications:* Series Ed., Humanities textbooks, 1988; Marketing for Schools Guide, 1993; (contrib.) A River Never Sleeps, 2010; Days with Dog and Gun, 2012; A Wolf's Tale (for children), 2013; contrib. numerous articles on educational issues, also on fishing and country matters to Irish Anglers Digest, Irish Shooter's Digest, Australian Hunter; freelance articles for The Times and TES. *Recreations:* trout and salmon fishing, travel, gardening and creating a wildlife area. *Address:* The Fod, 46 Drumconnelly Road, Omagh, Co. Tyrone BT78 1RT.

SALJE, Prof. Ekhard Karl Hermann, PhD; FRS 1996; FInstP, FGS; Professor of Mineralogy and Petrology, Cambridge University, 1994–2014, now Emeritus (Professor of Mineral Physics, 1992–94; Head of Department of Earth Sciences, 1998–2008); President, Clare Hall, Cambridge, 2001–08; *b* Hanover, Germany, 26 Oct. 1946; *s* of Gerhard Salje and Hildegard (*née* Drechsler); *m* 1980, Elisabeth Démaret; one *s* four *d. Educ:* Univ. of Hanover (PhD 1971); MA Cantab 1986. FInstP 1996; FGS 1997. University of Hanover: Lectr in Physics, 1972–75; Habilitation in Crystallography, 1975; Prof. of Crystallography, 1978–86; Hd, Dept of Crystallography and Petrology, 1983–86; Mem., Senate, 1980–82; Lectr, Cambridge Univ., 1987–92; Fellow, Darwin Coll., Cambridge, 1987–2001, Hon. Fellow, 2002. Programme Dir, Cambridge-MIT Inst., 2001–03; Chairman: Cambridge Envmtl Initiative, 2003–08; Mgt Cttee, Isaac Newton Inst., Cambridge, 2007–08. Chm., Eur. Network on Mineral Transformations, 1997–2001; Mem., Royal Soc. Cttee on Nuclear Waste, 2002. Associate Prof. of Physics, Univ. of Paris, 1981; Prof. invité in Physics, Grenoble Univ., 1990–91, 2011; Mombushu Vis. Prof., Nagoya, Japan, 1996; Visiting Professor: Le Mans Univ., France, 1998, 2000; Bilbao Univ., Spain, 1999; Leipzig, 2008; Max Planck Inst., Leipzig, 2009; Univ. of Paris, 2009; Ulam Scholar, Center for Nonlinear Studies, Los Alamos Nat. Lab, 2010; Hon. Prof., Xi'ou Jintong Univ., China, 2012. Advr to British, French, German and EU scientific orgns incl. to Max Planck Soc., 1998–2010. Member: Wissenschaftsrat and German Sci. Foundn, 2006–12; Steering Cttee, Eur. Academies Adv. Council, 2006–08; Pres., Alexander von Humboldt Assoc., 2004–08. Member Board: Univ. of Hamburg, 2000–08; Max Planck Inst. of Maths, Leipzig, 2001–10; Univ. of Wurzburg, 2011–. Fellow, Leopoldina German Acad. of Natural Sci., 1994; For. Mem., Royal Soc. for Scis and Arts, Barcelona, 2010. Schlumberger Medal, 1988; G. Werner Medal, 1995, Agricola Medal, 2006, Mineralogical Soc., Germany; Humboldt Prize, Humboldt Foundn, Germany, 1999; Ernst Ising Prize for Physics, Univ. of Hamburg, 2002; Gold Medal for Internat. Relns, Univ. of Hamburg, 2002. Chevalier, Ordre des Palmes Académiques (France), 2003. FRSA 1996. Cross, Order of Merit (Germany), 2007. *Publications:* Physical Properties and Thermodynamic Behaviour of Minerals, 1987; Phase Transitions in ferroelastic and co-elastic crystals, 1991; Application of Landau Theory for the Analysis of Phase Transitions in Minerals, 1992; numerous res. papers in solid state physics, crystallography and mineralogy. *Recreations:* painting, music. *Address:* 59 Glisson Road, Cambridge CB1 2HG.

SALLON, Christopher Robert Anthony; QC 1994; a Recorder, since 1996; *b* 3 May 1948; *s* of late Alexander and Alice Sallon; *m* 1971, Jacqueline Gould; two *s.* Called to the Bar: Gray's Inn, 1973, Bencher, 2002; Eastern Caribbean, 1994; Trinidad and Tobago, 2008. Bar Council: South Eastern Circuit Rep., 1992–94; Member: Professional Conduct Cttee, 1992–93; Public Affairs Cttee, 1994–97; Dir, Public Affairs, 1995–98. Fellow, American Bd of Criminal Lawyers, 1997. Member, Board: Counsel Magazine, 1995–2005; Nat. Campaign for the Arts, 2005–. *Recreations:* swimming, cycling, music. *Address:* Doughty Street Chambers, 53–54 Doughty Street, WC1N 2LS. *T:* (020) 7404 1313. *Club:* Garrick.

SALMON, Maj. Gen. Andrew, CMG 2009; OBE 2004; Deputy Chief of Staff Force Readiness, Supreme Headquarters Allied Powers Europe, 2010–13; *b* Wellington, Shropshire, 2 July 1959; *s* of Gordon John Grant Salmon and Margaret Salmon; *m* 1986, Elizabeth Jane Bolt; one *s* two *d. Educ:* Royal Grammar Sch., Guildford; Godalming Sixth Form Coll.; Univ. of Warwick (BA Hons Mod. Hist. 1980); King's Coll. London (MA Defence Studies 1993). Joined RM, 1977; Troop Comdr, 40 Cdo, 1981–83; OC RM, Ice Patrol Ship, 1984; Jun. Div., Staff Coll., 1985; Platoon Comdr, RMA, 1985–87; Batch Officer, Officer Trng Wing, 1987–88; Company Comdr, 45 Cdo, 1989–91; HQ Cdo Forces, 1992; psc 1993; Special Forces Requirements, MoD, 1994–95; HQ RM, 1995–97; COS Secretariat, MoD, 1997–99; CO, 42 Cdo, 2000–01; Dir Balkans, MoD, 2001–03; Dir Plans, Coalition Mil. Adv. Trng Team, Iraq, 2003; RCDS 2004; ACOS Plans and Resources, Fleet Comd, 2004–06; HCSC 2006; Comdt, Cdo Trng Centre, RM, 2006–08; Comdr, Multi Nat. Div. (SE), Iraq, 2008–09; Comdr UK Amphibious Forces, 2008–10; Comdt Gen., RM and Capt. of Deal Castle, 2009–10. Special Advr, Human Security Study Gp, 2004–. Vis. Sen. Fellow, 2008–, Mem., Adv. Bd, Security in Transition prog., 2011–, LSE. Practitioners' Adv. Bd, Jl of Global Policy, 2010–. Vice President: RNRU, 2006–; RNLTA, 2007–; Pres., C Group, 2008–. QCVS 2000. Bronze Star (USA), 2006. *Recreations:* music, walking, cycling, swimming, mountains, ski-ing, tennis.

SALMON, Charles Nathan; QC 1996; *b* 5 May 1950; *s* of His Honour Judge Cyril Salmon, QC and of Patrice Salmon; *m* 1981, Vanessa Clewes; one *s. Educ:* Carmel Coll.; University Coll. London (LLB Hons 1971). Travelled through Asia and SE Asia, 1971–73, worked as rubber tapper in Malaysia; called to the Bar, Middle Temple, 1972; volunteer, ME war, 1973; in practice as barrister, 1974–; exclusively defending in substantial white collar fraud, 1996–. *Recreations:* reading about Middle East history, 2nd World War and Italian Risorgimento, travel, collecting 18th century Japanese woodcuts and contemporary European paintings. *Address:* 25 Bedford Row, WC1R 4HD. *T:* (020) 7067 1500, *Fax:* (020) 7067 1507.

SALMON, Christopher Keith; Executive Director, Markets, Bank of England, since 2014; *b* Stroud, 29 Aug. 1968; *s* of Tony and Jean Salmon; *m* 1999, Gina Hunt. *Educ:* Bristol Univ. (BSc Econs 1990); London Sch. of Econs and Pol Sci. (MSc Econometrics and Math. Econs 1991). Bank of England: various positions, Monetary Analysis Directorate, 1991–2000; IMF, 2000–02 (on secondment); Internat. Finance Div., 2002–04, Hd, 2004–06; Governor's Private Sec., 2006–09; Hd, Sterling Mkts Div., 2009–11; Exec. Dir, Banking Services and Chief Cashier, 2011–14. *Recreations:* running, tennis, family. *Address:* Bank of England, Threadneedle Street, EC2R 8AH. *T:* (020) 7601 3345.

SALMON, Michael John; Vice Chancellor, Anglia Polytechnic University, 1992–95, now Emeritus Professor; Partner, Salmons Reach Consultancy, since 2008; Chairman, Postgraduate Medical Institute, Anglia Ruskin University, 2009–13; *b* 22 June 1936; *o s* of Arthur and May Salmon; *m* 1st, 1958, Angela Cookson (marr. diss. 1973); one *s*; 2nd, 1973, Daphne Bird (*d* 1996); one *s*; 3rd, 1998, Sheila Frances Sisto (*see* S. F. Salmon). *Educ:* Roundhay Sch., Leeds; Leeds Univ.; Leicester Univ. Served RAF, 1957–62; commnd 1957. Teaching posts: Letchworth Coll. of Technology, 1962–65; Leeds Coll. of Technology, 1965–68; Barking Regional Coll., 1968–71; Head of Dept, NE London Poly., 1971–77; Dep. Dir, Chelmer Inst., 1977–83; Dir, Essex Inst., 1983–89; Director: Anglia HEC, 1989–91; Anglia Poly., 1991–92. Member: CNAA, 1970–92; IBA Educn Adv. Council, 1973–81; Electricity Industry Trng Council, 1971–74; PCFC, 1989–93; CBI (Eastern Region) Council, 1990–93; Gen. Optical Council, 1999– (Vice-Chm., 2002–05). Dir, Essex TEC, 1990–93. Member: Court, Essex Univ., 1987–2006; Acad. Cttee, RCM, 1994–2000; Governor: Norwich Sch. of Art and Design, 1996–2001 (Chm. Govs, 1998–2001); King Edward VI GS, Chelmsford, 1995–2001. Director: Proshare, 1991–93; Mid-Essex NHS Hosp. Trust, 1993–95; Chm., Essex Rivers Healthcare NHS Trust, 1995–2005. Mem., Disciplinary Cttee, Royal Pharmaceutical Soc., 2005–11. Chm., Tendring Community Develt Forum, 1998–2001. Vice Patron, Helen Rollason Cancer Appeal, 2001–. Mem., Spectacle Makers' Co., 2005–. FCMI (FBIM 1983); FRSA 1984. Hon. Fellow: Limburg Poly., Netherlands, 1993; Fachhochschule für Wirtschaft, Berlin, 1994.

SALMON, Nicholas; Director, Playful Productions, since 2010; *b* London, 21 Nov. 1947; *s* of Brian Salmon and Annette Salmon (*née* Mackay); partner, Janey Sargent; two *s* one *d. Educ:* Wellington Coll.; Jesus Coll., Cambridge (BA 1969). Chief Executive Officer: Churchill Th., 1983–91; (pt-time) Stage One (formerly Th. Investment Fund), 1989–2012; Th. of Comedy, 1991–96; Act Prodns, 1997–2010. Productions include: Sweeney Todd, Adelphi Th., 2012; The Audience, Gielgud Th., 2012, Apollo Th., transf. NY, 2015; Wolf Hall and Bring Up the Bodies, Aldwych Th., 2014; Wolf Hall Parts I and II, NY, 2015; Shrek the Musical, UK tour, 2015; American Buffalo, Wyndham's Th., 2015. Pres., Soc. of London Th., 1993–96. *Recreations:* films, theatre, photography, cooking. *Address:* Playful Productions, 4th Floor, 41–44 Great Queen Street, WC2B 5AD. *T:* (020) 7811 4600. *E:* annie@playfuluk.com. *Club:* Garrick.

SALMON, Nicholas Robin, FREng, FIMechE; Chairman: South East Water, since 2015; Acal plc, since 2015; *b* 13 June 1952; *s* of Keneth Salmon and Winifred Elsie Salmon (*née* Martin); *m* 1976, Deirdre Ann Thompson Hardy; two *d. Educ:* Bristol Univ. (BSc (Hons) Mech. Engrg 1973). Grad. trainee, 1969–74, Project Engr, 1974–77, CEGB; Project Manager, China Light and Power Co. Ltd (Hong Kong), 1977–88; Dir and Gen. Manager, Power Station Projects Div., GEC Turbine Generators Ltd, 1988–89; Dep. Man. Dir, Power Stn Projects Div. and Gas Turbine and Diesel Div., GEC Alsthom, 1989–93; Chief Exec., Babcock Internat. Gp plc, 1993–97; Man. Dir, Power Generation Div., GEC Alsthom, 1997–99; Exec. Vice Pres., ABB ALSTOM, subseq. ALSTOM Power, then ALSTOM, 1999–2004; Chief Exec., Cookson Gp, 2004–12. Non-executive Director: United Utilities Gp plc, 2005–14 (Sen. Ind. Dir, 2007–14); Interserve plc, 2014–; Sen. Ind. Dir, Elementis plc, 2014–. FREng (FEng 1995). *Recreations:* sailing, ski-ing, bridge. *Club:* Royal Hong Kong Yacht.

SALMON, Paul Raymond, FRCPE, FRCP; independent consultant Physician and Gastroenterologist, 1989–2004; *b* 11 July 1936; *s* of late Harold William Salmon and Blanche Percy Salmon (*née* Piper); *m* 1st, 1962 (marr. diss. 1980); one *s* one *d*; 2nd, 1984, Diana Frances Lawrence. *Educ:* Epsom Coll.; Middx Hosp. Sch. of Medicine, Univ. of London (BSc Hons Anatomy 1958). MRCS 1961; MRCPE 1966, FRCPE 1977; MRCP 1967, FRCP 1978. House Physician and House Surgeon, 1962, Casualty MO, 1963–64, Middlesex Hosp.; House Physician, London Chest Hosp., 1963; Sen. House Physician, Ipswich and E Suffolk Hosp., 1964–65; Med. Registrar, Princess Margaret Hosp., Swindon, 1965–66; Res. Registrar in Gastroenterology, Bristol Royal Infirmary, 1967–68; Lectr in Medicine, 1969–73, Sen. Lectr in Medicine, 1974–79, Univ. of Bristol; Hon. Sen. Registrar, United Bristol Hosps, 1969–73; Hon. Consultant Physician, Bristol Health Dist, 1974–79; Consultant Physician, UCH, and Sen. Clin. Lectr in Gastroenterology, Sch. of Medicine, UCL, 1978–89; Consultant Physician, Middlesex Hosp., 1985–89. Annual Foundn Lectr, British Soc. for Digestive Endoscopy, 1979; Poona Orator, Indian Gastroenterology Soc., 1984. FDS Examr, RCS, 1982–88. Pres., Eur. Laser Assoc., 1981–85; Member: British Soc. of Gastroenterology, 1969–2004; Chelsea Clin. Soc., 1986– (Mem. Council, 2000–04); Independent Doctors Forum, 1989–. FRSocMed 1986. Freeman, City of London, 1985; Liveryman: Co. of Farriers, 1986; Soc. of Apothecaries, 1993. Privilegiate *hc*, 1996, Fellow, 2008, St Hilda's Coll., Oxford. Several teaching films (Dip., Marburg Film Fest., 1977, Silver Award, BMA Film Competition, 1983). *Publications:* Fibreoptic Endoscopy, 1974; (ed) Topics in Modern Gastroenterology, 1976; (jtly) Radiological Atlas of Biliary and Pancreatic Disease, 1978; (ed) Ranitidine, 1982; (ed) Advances in Gastrointestinal Endoscopy, 1984; (ed) Key Developments in Gastroenterology, 1988; 200 contribs to books, scientific papers and review articles. *Recreations:* golf, music, reproducing pianos, ski-ing, travel, angling. *Address:* 2d Melbury Road, W14 8LP. *T:* (020) 7602 3311. *E:* paulsalmon@btinternet.com. *Clubs:* Athenæum; Sunningdale Golf.

SALMON, Peter; Director, BBC England, since 2013 (Director, BBC North, 2009–13); *b* 15 May 1956; *s* of Patrick and Doreen Salmon; three *s*; *m* 2001, Sarah Jane Abigail Lancashire, *qv*; one *s*. *Educ:* Univ. of Warwick (BA English and European Lit.). VSO, 1977; Min. of Overseas Develt, 1978; Chatham News, 1979–81; BBC, 1981–93: Series Producer, Crimewatch UK; Editor, Nature; Exec. Producer, 999, and The Wrong Trousers; Head of TV Features, BBC Bristol; Controller of Factual Programmes, Channel 4, 1993–96; Dir of Programmes, Granada TV, 1996–97; Controller, BBC 1, 1997–2000; Dir of Sport, BBC, 2000–05; Chief Exec., Television Corp., 2005–06; Chief Creative Officer, BBC Vision Prodns, 2006–09. *Recreations:* music, football, cycling, museums. *Address:* BBC Quay House, MediaCity UK, Salford M50 2QH.

SALMON, Sarah Jane Abigail; *see* Lancashire, S. J. A.

SALMON, Prof. Sheila Frances, FRSocMed; Chairman, Mid Essex Hospitals NHS Trust, since 2010; *b* Middlesex, 1952; *d* of Edward and Daisy Patterson; *m* 1st, 1971, Francisco Sisto (marr. diss. 1989); two *s* one *d*; 2nd, 1998, Michael John Salmon, *qv*. *Educ:* Walpole Grammar Sch.; Univ. of Surrey (MSc; Postgrad. Cert. Educn of Adults 1989; Postgrad. Dip. Professional Educn 1993); Royal Coll. of Midwives; Inst. of Leadership and Mgt (Postgrad. Cert. Exec. Coaching and Leadership Mentoring 2007). Nat. Nursery Exam. Bd 1971; RM 1974; ADM 1987; RMT 1989. Trained in Kensington, Chelsea and Hammersmith Hosps, 1969–72, Plymouth Hosps, 1972–74; Clin. Practice Midwifery, Women's and Children's Services, 1975–87; Clin. Tutor, Obstetrics and Family Health Midwifery, Essex, Kent, London and Surrey, 1987–90; Sen. Midwife Teacher, 1990–92, Hd of Dept, Postgrad. and Professional Studies, 1992–94, S Essex Coll. of Nursing and Midwifery; Associate Dean, Faculty of Health and Social Work, 1994–95, Exec. Dean and Dir of Health Strategy, 1995–2006, Anglia Ruskin Univ. (formerly Anglia Poly. Univ.); Chairman: Essex Ambulance Service NHS Trust, 2005–06; NHS NE Essex, 2006–10. Lead Visitor, Nursing and Midwifery Council, 2002–06. Lay Partner, GMC (formerly PMETB), 2008–. Equality and Diversity Ambassador, 2010–. Founder, Salmons Reach Consultancy, 2006. Non-exec. Dir and Trustee, Essex Air Ambulance Charity, 2002–06. FRSocMed 2007. *Publications:* contribs to British Jl Midwifery, Adult Educn, Internat. Congress of Midwives Triennial Conf. Procs. *Recreations:* travel, family, fundraising charity events. *Address:* Barberries, 10 Russell Lane, Danbury, Essex CM3 4NZ. *T:* (01245) 223734, 07940 512374. *E:* sheila.salmon@gmail.com, sheila.salmon@meht.nhs.uk.

SALMOND, Rt Hon. Alexander Elliot Anderson; PC 2007; MP (SNP) Gordon, since 2015; Member (SNP) Aberdeenshire East, Scottish Parliament, since 2011 (Gordon, 2007–11); *b* 31 Dec. 1954; *s* of Robert F. F. Salmond and late Mary S. Milne; *m* 1981, Moira F. McGlashan. *Educ:* Linlithgow Acad.; St Andrews Univ. (MA Hons). Govt Econ. Service, 1980; Asst Agricl and Fisheries Economist, DAFS, 1978–80; Energy Economist, Royal Bank of Scotland plc, 1980–87. Scottish National Party: Mem. Nat. Exec., 1981–; Vice-Chair (Publicity), 1985–87; Sen. Vice-Convener (Dep. Leader) (formerly Sen. Vice-Chair), 1987–90; Leader, 1990–2000 and 2004–14. MP (SNP) Banff and Buchan, 1987–2010. SNP parly spokesperson on energy, treasury and fishing, 1987–88, on economy, energy, environment and poll tax, 1988–97, on constitution and fishing, 1997–2005; on foreign affairs, 2015–. Mem. (SNP) Banff & Buchan, Scottish Parlt, 1999–2001; Ldr of the Opposition, 1999–2000; First Minister, 2007–14. Vis. Prof of Economics, Univ. of Strathclyde, 2003–. *Publications:* The Dream Shall Never Die: 100 days that changed Scotland forever (autobiog.), 2015; articles and conference papers on oil and gas economics; contribs to Scottish Government Yearbook, Fraser of Allander Economic Commentary, Petroleum Review, Opec Bulletin, etc. *Address:* Scottish Parliament, Edinburgh EH99 1SP; 84 North Street, Inverurie, Aberdeenshire AB51 4QX; House of Commons, SW1A 0AA.

SALMOND, Dame Anne; *see* Salmond, Dame M. A.

SALMOND, Prof. George Peacock Copland, PhD; ScD; FRSB; FRSE; Professor of Molecular Microbiology, since 1996 and Deputy Head, Department of Biochemistry, since 2010, University of Cambridge; Fellow, Wolfson College, Cambridge, since 2000; *b* 15 Nov. 1952; *s* of John Brown Salmond and Joan Tennant Lambie Salmond (*née* Copland); *m* 1975, Christina Brown Adamson (marr. diss. 1985); partner, Carolyn Ann Alderson; one *d*. *Educ:* Whitburn Primary Sch.; Bathgate Acad.; Whitburn Acad.; Univ. of Strathclyde (BSc 1st cl. Hons Microbiology); Univ. of Warwick (PhD Bacterial Genetics); MA, ScD 2006, Cantab. FRSB (FSB 2009); FRSE 2012. Postdoctoral Res. Fellow, Dept of Molecular Biology, Univ. of Edinburgh, 1977–80; Lectr in Microbiology, Biological Lab., Univ. of Kent at Canterbury, 1980–83; Lectr in Microbiology, 1983–89, Sen. Lectr, 1989–93, Prof., 1993–96, Dept of Biological Scis, Univ. of Warwick. Biotechnology and Biological Sciences Research Council: Member: Plants and Microbial Scis Cttee, 1999–2002; Integration Panel, BBSRC Inst. Sci. Quality Assessment, 2001; Cross Cttee Gp on Antimicrobial Res., 2001; Sequencing Panel, 2002–; Plant and Microbial Metabolomics Initiative Sift Panel, 2002; Res. Cttee B, 2009–10; Chairman: Plant and Microbial Scis Cttee 'Natural Products Biology' Steering Gp, 2000–02; Res. Equipment Initiative Cttee, 2002–04; Mem., Plant Panel, 2002, Integration Panel, 2002, and Chm., Plant Panel for Scottish Res. Insts, 2002, Quality of Sci. Assessment Panels, Scottish Exec. Envmt and Rural Affairs Dept; Member: Adv. Bd, NSC Technologies, USA, 1996–2000; Panel for Jt Res. Councils Equipment Initiative, 2001; Pathogen Sequencing Adv. Gp, Wellcome Trust Sanger Inst., 2002–06; Scottish Science Adv. Council, 2010–. Mem., Internat. Expert Rev. Panel (Medicine), Linnaeus Res. Centres, Swedish Res. Council, 2013–14. Society for General Microbiology: Mem. Council, 1997–2001, 2004–09; Convener, Physiol., Biochem. and Molecular Genetics Gp Cttee, 2002–07; Internat. Sec., 2004–09; Colworth Prize Lect., 2011. Member Council: Fedn of Eur. Microbiol Socs, 2004–09; Sci. Unions Cttee, Royal Soc., 2005–09. Member, Governing Body: Wolfson Coll., Cambridge, 2000–; Scottish Crop Res. Inst., 2003–11 (Sci. Cttee, 2006–11); Member: Governing Council, Dir and Trustee, John Innes Centre, Norwich, 2003–10; Governing Bd and Adv. Cttee on Sci., James Hutton Inst., 2011–14. UK Sen. Ed., Jl of Molecular Microbiology and Biotechnology, 1998–2008; Member Editorial Board: Molecular Microbiology, 1988–97; Molecular Plant Pathology-On Line, 1996–99; Microbiology, 1999–2000; Molecular Plant Pathology, 1999–2002; Associate Editor: European Jl of Plant Pathology, 1992–98; Molecular Plant-Microbe Interactions, 1993–98; Editl Adv. Panel, Future Microbiology, 2006–. Member: Biochem. Soc.; Genetics Soc.; Amer. Soc. of Microbiol.; Soc. for Industrial Microbiol., USA; Soc. for Applied Microbiol.; British Soc. for Antimicrobial Chemotherapy; British Soc. for Plant Pathology (Vice-Pres., 2009; Pres. Elect, 2009–10; Pres., 2011–12). Founding Fellow, Inst. of Contemp. Scotland, 2001; Fellow: Cambridge Phil Soc.; Amer. Acad. Microbiol., 2013. FRSA 2001. Hon. DSc Strathclyde, 2010. *Publications:* many res. articles on molecular microbiology, incl. studies on bacterial cell div., molecular phytopathology, antibiotics, quorum sensing, bacterial virulence, protein secretion, gas vesicles, bacterial viruses, anti-viral abortive infection and toxin-antitoxin systems in learned jls. *Recreations:* philosophy, poetry, comedy. *Address:* Department of Biochemistry, University of Cambridge, Tennis Court Road, Cambridge CB2 1QW. *T:* (01223) 333650.

SALMOND, Dame (Mary) Anne, DBE 1995 (CBE 1988); PhD; FRSNZ; Distinguished Professor, University of Auckland, since 2001 (Professor of Social Anthropology and Maori Studies, 1992–2001; Pro Vice-Chancellor (Equal Opportunity), 1997–2006); *b* 16 Nov. 1945; *d* of Jack Thorpe and Joyce Thorpe; *m* 1971, Jeremy Salmond; two *s* one *d*. *Educ:* Univ. of Auckland (BA 1966; MA 1st cl. 1966); Univ. of Pennsylvania (PhD 1972). FRSNZ 1990. Post-grad. Schol., Univ. of Auckland, 1968; Fulbright Schol., 1969; Nuffield Fellow, 1980–81; Capt. James Cook Fellow, RSNZ, 1987; Caird Fellow, Nat. Maritime Mus., 2004. Cecil H. and Ida Green Vis. Prof., UBC, 2013. Henry Myers Lectr, RAI, 1996. Chm., NZ Historic Places Trust, 2002–07. Corresp. FBA 2008. Founding Fellow, NZ Acad. of the Humanities, 2007. Foreign Associate, NAS, 2009. Elsdon Best Meml Gold Medal, Polynesian Soc., 1976; Wattie Book of Year Awards, 1977, 1981, 1991; Nat. Book Award (non-fiction), 1991, 2004; Ernest Scott Prize, Melbourne Univ., 1992, 1997; NZ Prime Minister's Award for Literary Achievement, 2004; Kea World Class New Zealander, 2011; New Zealander of Year, Kiwibank, 2013. *Publications:* Hui: a study of Maori ceremonial gatherings, 1975, 7th edn 1994; Amiria: the life story of a Maori woman, 1976, 3rd edn 1994; Eruera: the teachings of a Maori Elder, 1980; Two Worlds: first meetings between Maori and Europeans 1642–1772, 1991, 2nd edn 1993; Between Worlds: early Maori-European exchanges 1773–1815, 1997; The Trial of the Cannibal Dog: Captain Cook in the South Seas, 2003; Aphrodite's Island: the European discovery of Tahiti, 2009; Bligh: William Bligh in the South Seas, 2011. *Recreations:* ecological restoration, reading, family and friends. *Address:* 14 Glen Road, Devonport, Auckland, New Zealand. *T:* (9) 4452573.

SALOLAINEN, Pertti Edvard; Grand Cross, Order of the Lion of Finland, 1994; MP (C) Helsinki, Parliament of Finland, since 2007; Hon. Minister, since 2004; *b* 19 Oct. 1940; *s* of Edvard Paavali Salolainen and Ella Elisabet Salolainen; *m* 1964, Anja Sonninen (*d* 2005); one *s* one *d*. *Educ:* Helsinki Sch. of Economics (MSc Econ 1969). TV newsreader and editor, then producer, 1962–66, London Correspondent, 1966–69, Finnish Broadcasting Co.; London Editor, BBC Finnish Sect., 1966; Head of Dept, Finnish Employers' Confedn, 1969–89. Ambassador of Finland to UK 1996–2004. MP (C), Helsinki, 1970–96; Minister for Foreign Trade, Finland, 1987–95; Dep. Prime Minister of Finland, 1991–95; Ministerial Chm., Finland-EU membership negotiations, 1991–95; Chm., Foreign Affairs Cttee, 2007–. Leader, Conservative Party of Finland, 1991–94. Hon. Founder, WWF Finland, 1972 (Pres., 2006). Major, Mil. Reserve. Freeman, City of London, 1998. Liveryman: Co. of Hackney Carriage Drivers; Co. of Horners. Internat. Conservation Award, WWF, 1990. Grand Cross, Nordstjerna Order (Sweden), 1996; Grand Cross, nat. orders of Germany, Austria, Hungary and Estonia. *Recreations:* nature conservation, nature photography, tennis. *Address:* Parliament of Finland, 00100 Helsinki, Finland. *Clubs:* Athenæum, Travellers.

SALOMON, Eve Coulter; Chairman, Regulatory Board, Royal Institution of Chartered Surveyors, since 2009; *b* Tokyo, 22 April 1957; *d* of Ernest Salomon and Ruth Salomon (*née* Coulter); *m* 1st, 1983, Stephen Moss (marr. diss. 2002); one *s* one *d*; 2nd, 2004, Stephen Charles Whittle, *qv*. *Educ:* Univ. of Bath (BSc Hons Sociol. 1978); City of London Poly. (Law Soc. Finals 1981). Admitted solicitor, 1983; solicitor: Bulcraigs, 1981–87; Colyer-Bristow, 1987–92; Sen. Advertising and Sponsorship Officer, 1992–96, Dep. Sec. to the Commn, 1996–98, ITC; Dir, Legal Services and Sec., Radio Authy, 1998–2003. Dir, Salomon Whittle Ltd, 2004–. Member: Gambling Commn, 2004–11; Press Complaints Commn, 2004–10. Chm., Internet Watch Foundn, 2009–12. Chm. Trustees, Horniman Mus. and Gardens, 2014–. FRSA. *Publications:* Guidelines on Broadcasting Regulation, 2006, 2nd edn 2009. *Recreations:* friends and family, music. *Address:* 4 Carmarthen Place, SE1 3TS. *T:* (020) 7407 2016. *E:* eve.salomon@btopenworld.com.

SALOMONSEN, Victor Erik Stanhope; His Honour Judge Salomonsen; a Circuit Judge, since 2008; *b* Guildford, 26 Jan. 1951; *s* of Victor and Kathleen Salomonsen; *m* 1976, Frances Mary Douthwaite; three *d*. *Educ:* Queen's Coll., Taunton; Queen's Coll., Oxford (BA 1972; MA 1978). Admitted Solicitor, 1973; Partner, Bond Pearce LLP, 1979–2008; Asst Recorder, 1996–2000; Recorder, 2000–08. *Recreations:* sailing, choral music, walking. *Address:* Exeter Crown Court, Southernhay Gardens, Exeter, Devon EX1 1UH. *Club:* Royal Cruising.

SALONEN, Esa-Pekka; conductor and composer; Principal Conductor and Artistic Adviser, Philharmonia Orchestra, London, since 2008; *b* 30 June 1958; *s* of Raimo Salonen and Pia Salonen; *m* 1991, Jane Price; one *s* two *d*. *Educ:* Sibelius Acad., Helsinki. Principal Conductor, Swedish Radio Symphony Orch., 1985–95; Principal Guest Conductor, Philharmonia Orch., 1985–94; Music Dir, Los Angeles Philharmonic Orch., 1992–2009, now Conductor Laureate. Artistic Dir, Helsinki Fest., 1995–96; Co-founder and Artistic Dir, Baltic Sea Fest., 2003–. Mem., Royal Swedish Music Acad., 1991; FRCM 1995. Hon. Dr: Hong Kong Acad. of Performing Arts, 2009; S Calif, 2010; Hon. DMus RAM, 2011. Opera Award, 1995, Conductor Award, 1997, Royal Philharmonic Soc.; numerous record and composition awards. Pro Finlandia Medal (Finland), 1992; Litteris et Artibus Medal (Sweden), 1996; Helsinki Medal (Finland), 2005. Officier de l'ordre des Arts et des Lettres (France), 1998. *Compositions include:* Saxophone Concerto, 1980; Floof, 1982; Giro, 1982–97; YTA I, 1982, II, 1985 and III, 1986; MIMO II, 1992; LA Variations, 1996; Gambit, 1998; Five Images after Sappho, 1999; Mania, 2000; Concert Etude, 2000; Two Songs to Poems of Ann Jäderlund, 2000; Dichotomie, 2000; Foreign Bodies, 2001; Insomnia, 2002; Wing on Wing, 2004; Piano Concerto, 2007; Homunculus (string quartet), 2008; Violin Concerto, 2009; Nyx, 2011; Dona Nobis Pacem, 2011. *Address:* c/o Philharmonia Orchestra, 6th Floor, The Tower Building, 11 York Road, SE1 7NX. *T:* (020) 7921 3900.

SALOP, Archdeacon of; *see* Thomas, Ven. P. W.

SALSBURY, Peter Leslie; Independent Management Consultant, P&S Salsbury Ltd, since 2002; Chairman: TR Property Investment Trust, 2004–13 (Director, 1997–2013); Molten Consulting Group, since 2011; *b* 20 June 1949; *s* of Joseph Leslie Salsbury and Sylvia Olive (*née* Cook); *m* 1987, Susan Elizabeth Gosling; one *s* from previous *m*. *Educ:* Bancroft's Sch.; London Sch. of Econs (BSc Econ). Joined Marks & Spencer, 1970: mgt trainee in stores, 1970–73; merchandiser, Head Office, 1973–76; Merchandise Manager, 1976–82; Exec.,

1982–85; Sen. Exec., 1985–86; Divisional Director: Homeware Gp, 1986–88; Ladieswear Gp, 1988–90; Dir, Personnel, 1990–93, and Store Ops, 1993–94; Man. Dir, 1994–98; Chief Exec., 1998–2000. Consultant Dir, Praesta LLP (formerly The Change Partnership), 2002–12. Non-exec. Dir, NORWEB plc, 1992–95; Dep. Chm. and Sen. Ind. Dir, Highway Insurance plc, 2006–09. Mem., Govt Better Regulation Task Force, 1997–99. Member Council: Inst. of Employment Studies, 1995–2005; C&G, 1997–2009. *Address:* TR Property Investment Trust, 11 Hanover Street, W1S 1YQ.

SALT, Christine Anne, (Chrys), MBE 2014; poet, writer; Artistic Director: The Bakehouse, Galloway, since 2005; BIG LIT Literature Festival, since 2011; *b* Birmingham, 15 May 1944; *d* of Frederick Arthur Salt and Joyce Winifred Salt; *m* 1997, Richard Macfarlane; two *s* one *d* by a previous marriage. *Educ:* Erdington Grammar Sch.; Birmingham Th. Sch.; Birmingham Rep. Th. Freelance writer and performer, 1962–2015; Parly Res. Asst, 1970–82; Tutor, London Actors Centre, 1982–2015; Artistic Dir, Bare Boards and Passion Th. Co., 1995–2006. Mem., London Actors Centre, 1981–. *Publications:* (ed) Of Whole Heart Cometh Hope, 1983; (with J. Layzell) Here We Go! Women's Memories of the 1984/85 Miners' Strike, 1985; (with M. Wilson) We Are of One Blood: memories of the first 60 years of the Woodcraft Folk, 1985; (with E. Bennett) College Lives, 1986; Inside Out, 1989; Daffodils at Christmas, 1998; Make Acting Work, 1997, 2nd rev. edn 2003; The Methuen Book of Contemporary Monologues for Men, 2003; The Methuen Book of Contemporary Monologues for Women, 2003; Collateral Damage, 2004; The Methuen Book of Modern Monologues for Men, 2004; The Methuen Book of Modern Monologues for Women, 2004; The Methuen Book of Classical Monologues for Men, 2005; The Methuen Book of Classical Monologues for Women, 2005; Greedy for Mulberries, 2009; (ed with J. Hudson) Adrian: Scotland celebrates Adrian Mitchell, 2009; Old Times, 2009; Grass, 2012; Home Front/Front Line, 2013; Weaver of Grass, 2014; Dancing on a Rock, 2015. *Recreations:* theatre, travel, family, cinema, art, books, politics. *Address:* 149 Chamberlayne Road, NW10 3NT. *T:* 07891 803027; The Bakehouse, 44 High Street, Gatehouse of Fleet, Kirkcudbrightshire DG7 2NP. *W:* www.chryssalt.com.

SALT, Rt Rev. John William, OGS; Bishop of St Helena, 1999–2011; an Honorary Assistant Bishop, Diocese of Norwich, since 2011; *b* 30 Oct. 1941; *s* of William Edward and Jenny Salt. *Educ:* Kelham Theol Coll.; London Univ. (DipTh). Ordained deacon, 1966, priest, 1967; Curate, St Matthew's, Barrow-in-Furness, 1966–69; dio. of Lesotho, 1970–77; dio. of Kimberley and Kuruman, 1977–89; Dean of Zululand, 1989–99. *Recreations:* music, walking, reading. *Address:* Palmers, 5 Common Place, Walsingham, Norfolk NR22 6BW. *T:* (01328) 820823.

SALT, Sir Michael; *see* Salt, Sir T. M. J.

SALT, Sir Patrick (Macdonnell), 7th Bt *cr* 1869, of Saltaire, Yorkshire; *b* 25 Sept. 1932; *s* of Sir John Salt, 4th Bt and Stella Houlton Jackson (*d* 1974); *S* brother, 1991; *m* 1976, Ann Elizabeth Mary Kilham Roberts, *widow* of Denys Kilham Roberts, OBE. *Educ:* Summer Fields, Oxford; Stowe Sch. Dir, Cassidy Davis Members Agency Ltd, 1983–92. *Recreation:* fishing. *Heir: cousin* Daniel Alexander Salt [*b* 15 Aug. 1943; *m* 1968, Merchide, *d* of Dr Ahmad Emami; two *d*]. *Address:* Hillwatering Farmhouse, Langham, Bury St Edmunds, Suffolk IP31 3ED. *T:* (01359) 259367.

SALT, Sir (Thomas) Michael (John), 4th Bt *cr* 1899; *b* 7 Nov. 1946; *s* of Lt-Col Sir Thomas Henry Salt, 3rd Bt, and Meriel Sophia Wilmot, *d* of late Capt. Berkeley C. W. Williams and Hon. Mrs Williams, Herringston, Dorchester; *S* father, 1965; *m* 1971, Caroline, *er d* of Henry Hildyard; two *d*. *Educ:* Eton. *Recreations:* cricket, shooting. *Heir: b* Anthony William David Salt [*b* 5 Feb. 1950; *m* 1978, Olivia Anne, *yr d* of Martin Morgan Hudson; two *s*]. *Address:* Shillingstone House, Shillingstone, Blandford Forum, Dorset DT11 0QR.

SALTER, family name of **Baroness Wheatcroft**.

SALTER, Ian George; Consultant, Deutsche Bank Private Wealth Management, 2008–10; *b* Hobart, Tasmania, 7 March 1943; *s* of Desmond and Diane Salter. *Educ:* Hutchins Sch., Hobart, Tasmania. AASA. Member: Hobart Stock Exchange, 1965–69; London Stock Exchange, 1970–2000; Principal, Strauss Turnbull, subseq. Société Générale Strauss Turnbull (Investment Advisers Ltd), then SG (formerly Socgen) Investment Management Ltd, 1978–2003, Man. Dir, 2001–03; Dir, Tilney Private Wealth Mgt (formerly Tilney Investment Mgt), 2003–07; Chm., EmdexTrade, subseq. CCH International plc, 2001–09; non-executive Director: Plus Markets Gp plc, 2007–09; Pan Hldgs, 2008–12. Mem., Stock Exchange Council, 1980–91, subseq. London Stock Exchange Bd, 1991–2004, a Dep. Chm., 1990–2004. DTI Inspector, 1984–87. Mem., Bd, British Youth Opera, 1998–2000. *Recreations:* opera, travel, gardening. *Address:* Flat 2, 34 St Leonards Terrace, SW3 4QQ.

SALTER, Martin John; National Campaigns Co-ordinator, Angling Trust, since 2011; *b* 19 April 1954; *s* of Raymond and Naomi Salter. *Educ:* Univ. of Sussex. Co-ordinator, Reading Centre for Unemployed, 1986; Regl Manager, Co-operative Home Services Housing Assoc., 1987–96. Mem., Reading BC, 1984–96 (Dep. Leader, 1987–96). Contested (Lab) Reading E, 1987. MP (Lab) Reading W, 1997–2010.

SALTER, Rebecca Margaret, RA 2014; artist, since 1981; *b* Middleton-on-Sea, 24 Feb. 1955; *d* of Rev. Samuel Salter and Margaret Salter; *m* 1991, Geoffrey Winston. *Educ:* Pate's Grammar Sch. for Girls, Cheltenham; Bristol Poly. (BA 1977); Kyoto City Univ. of Arts, Japan. Freelance work, 1981–96; Associate Lectr, 1996–, Res. Fellow, 2002–11, Camberwell Coll. of Arts, Univ. of the Arts, London. *Solo exhibitions* include: Inner Eye, 2004, The Unquiet Gaze, 2007, and 2011, Howard Scott Gall., NY; Bliss of Solitude, 2006, Pale Remembered, 2009, Drawn, 2011, Beyond, 2013, Beardsmore Gall., London; into the light of things: Rebecca Salter 1981–2011, Yale Center for British Art, Conn, 2011; *work in collections* including: Tate Gall.; BM; V&A Mus.; British Council; Govt Art Collection; Cambridge Inst. for Med. Res.; Frechen Kunstverein, Germany; Graphotek, Stadtbucherei, Stuttgart; Yale Center for British Art, New Haven, Conn; Yale Univ. Art Gall.; Liby of Congress, Washington. *Publications:* Japanese Woodblock Printing, 2001, 2nd edn 2013; Japanese Popular Prints, 2006. *Recreations:* outdoor swimming, cookery, things Japanese, dogs. *Address:* c/o Royal Academy of Arts, Piccadilly, W1S 3ET. *T:* (020) 7300 8000. *E:* info@rebeccasalter.com.

SALTER, Richard Stanley; QC 1995; a Recorder, since 2000; a Deputy High Court Judge, Queen's Bench Division, since 2010; *b* 2 Oct. 1951; *s* of late Stanley James Salter and Betty Maud Salter (*née* Topsom); *m* 1991, Shona Virginia Playfair Cannon. *Educ:* Harrow County Sch. for Boys; Balliol Coll., Oxford (MA); Inns of Court Sch. of Law. Called to the Bar, Inner Temple, 1975, Bencher, 1991; pupil to Sir Henry Brooke, 1975–76; in practice at Commercial Bar, 1976–; an Asst Recorder, 1997–2000. Chm., London Common Law and Commercial Bar Assoc., 2004–05 (Mem. Cttee, 1986–2001; Vice-Chm., 2002–03). Member: Council of Legal Educn, 1990–96; Advocacy Studies Bd, 1996–2000; (ex-officio) 2004–05, (elected) 2006–08, (nominated) 2009–13, Bar Council; Chairman: Bd of Examnrs for Bar Vocational Course, 1992–93; Scholarships Cttee, Inner Temple, 2002–09; Bar Council Legal Services Cttee, 2010–13. Vis. Fellow in Financial Law, Oxford Univ. Faculty of Law, 2013–. Gov., Inns of Court Sch. of Law, 1996–2001; Member: Adv. Bd, City Univ. Inst. of Law, 2001–07; Develt Bd, Centre for Commercial Law Studies, 2012–. Mem. Bd, English Touring Opera Ltd, 2015–. Freeman, Musicians' Co., 2013. Trustee, Oxford Univ. Law Foundn, 2011–. Consulting Ed., All England Commercial Cases, 1999–; Legislation Ed., Encyclopedia of Insurance Law, 2001–04. Dist. Friend of Oxford Award, 2014. *Publications:* (contrib.) Banks, Liability and Risk, 1991, 3rd edn 2001; (contrib.) Banks and Remedies, 1992, 2nd edn 1999; Guarantee and Indemnity, Halsbury's Laws of England, Vol. 20, 4th edn 1993; (ed) Legal Decisions Affecting Bankers, vols 12–14, 2001. *Recreations:* books, music, theatre, cricket. *Address:* 3 Verulam Buildings, Gray's Inn, WC1R 5NT. *T:* (020) 7831 8441. *Clubs:* Savile; Shoscombe Village Cricket.

SALTHOUSE, Edward Charles, PhD; CEng, FIET; Master of University College, Durham University, 1979–98; *b* 27 Dec. 1935; *s* of Edward Salthouse, MBE, and Mrs Salthouse (*née* Boyd); *m* 1961, Denise Kathleen Margot Reid; two *s*. *Educ:* Campbell Coll., Belfast; Queen's University of Belfast (BSc, PhD). Lecturer in Electrical Engrg, Univ. of Bristol, 1962–67; University of Durham: Reader in Elec. Engrg Science, 1967–79; Chairman, Board of Studies in Engrg Science, 1976–79; Dean, Faculty of Science, 1982–85; First Chm., School of Applied Science and Engrg, 1985–87; Pro-Vice-Chancellor, 1985–88. Sec., Scottish Industrial Heritage Soc., 1998–2008. *Publications:* papers on electrical insulation in Proc. IEE and other appropriate jls. *Recreations:* industrial archaeology, photography. *Address:* Shieldaig, Hume, Kelso TD5 7TR.

SALTOUN, Lady (20th in line), *cr* 1445, of Abernethy (by some reckonings 21st in line); **Flora Marjory Fraser;** Chief of the name of Fraser; *b* 18 Oct. 1930; *d* of 19th Lord Saltoun, MC, and Dorothy (*d* 1985), *e d* of Sir Charles Welby, 5th Bt; *S* father, 1979; *m* 1956, Captain Alexander Ramsay of Mar, Grenadier Guards retd (*d* 2000), *o s* of late Adm. Hon. Sir Alexander Ramsay, GCVO, KCB, DSO, and The Lady Patricia Ramsay, CI, VA, CD; three *d*. Elected Mem., H of L, 1999–2014. *Heiress: d* Hon. Katharine Ingrid Mary Isabel Fraser [*b* 11 Oct. 1957; *m* 1980, Captain Mark Malise Nicolson, Irish Guards; one *s* two *d*].

SALUSBURY-TRELAWNY, Sir John William Richard; *see* Trelawny, Sir J. W. R. S.

SALVAGE, Jane Elizabeth; author, nursing and health consultant; *b* 6 Aug. 1953; *d* of Robert Salvage and Patricia Grutchfield; *m* 1995, Nareman Taha Wahab. *Educ:* Newnham Coll., Cambridge (BA Hons); Royal Holloway and Bedford New Coll., London (MSc). RGN 1978; Staff Nurse, London Hosp., 1978–80; worked on British nursing jls, and Ed., Sen. Nurse, 1980–88; Dir, Nursing Develt Prog., King's Fund, London, 1988–91; Regl Advr for Nursing and Midwifery, European Reg., WHO, 1991–95; Editor, 1996–97, Editor-in-Chief, 1997–99, Nursing Times; Nursing Dir, Emap Healthcare, 2000–02; Ed., Nursing and Midwifery Council Review, 2011–12. Mem. Bd, Geneva Initiative on Psychiatry, 2001–04. Jt Lead, Support Office, Prime Minister's Commn on the Future of Nursing and Midwifery in England, 2009–10; Ind. Advr and report author, Willis Commn on Nursing Educn, 2012; Policy Advr, All-Party Parly Gp on Global Health, 2012–. Associate, Newnham Coll., Cambridge, 1993–2004 (Hon. Associate, 2012–); Visiting Professor: Sheffield Univ., 1999–2004; Florence Nightingale Sch. of Nursing and Midwifery, KCL, 2007–13; Vis. Prof. and Writer-in-Residence, Kingston Univ. and St George's, Univ. of London, 2013–. Trustee, Queen's Nursing Inst., 2011–14. First Hon. Mem., Romanian Nurses Assoc., 1992. FRCN 2012. Hon. Fellow, Queen's Nursing Inst., 2009. Hon. LLD Sheffield, 1996; Hon. DSc Kingston and St George's, 2011. *Publications:* The Politics of Nursing, 1985; (ed) Models for Nursing, Vol. 1 1986, Vol. 2 1990; Nurses at Risk, 1988, 2nd edn 1999; (ed) Nurse Practitioners, 1991; (ed) Nursing in Action, 1993; (ed) Nursing Development Units, 1995; (ed) Nursing in Europe, 1997; Now More Than Ever: nurses, midwives and primary health care—past and present, 2010; Skyros: island of dreams, 2011; contrib. numerous articles. *Recreations:* friendship, travel, reading, swimming, cooking and eating, walking, theatre, watching football, cloudspotting. *Address:* 18 Leicester Road, Lewes, E Sussex BN7 1SX. *W:* www.janesalvage.com.

SALVESEN, (Charles) Hugh, PhD; Ambassador to Uruguay, 2005–08; *b* 10 Sept. 1955; *s* of late John and Eelin Salvesen; *m* 1983, Emilie Maria Ingenhousz (marr. diss. 2012); two *s* (one *d* decd). *Educ:* Loretto Sch., Musselburgh; Christ's Coll., Cambridge (MA, PhD). Joined Diplomatic Service, 1982; FCO, 1982–84; First Sec., BMG, Berlin, 1984–85; Bonn, 1985–88; FCO, 1988–93; Argentina, 1993–96; Dep. High Comr, NZ, 1996–2000; Dep. Hd, Econ. Policy Dept, FCO, 2000–02; Hd, Mgt Consultancy, FCO, 2002–05. Trustee, Drumduan Trust.

SALVIDGE, Paul; Member, Consumer Panel, Financial Services Authority, 2000–06; *b* 22 Aug. 1946; *s* of Herbert Stephen and Winifred Alice Elisabeth Salvidge; *m* 1972, Heather Margaret (*née* Johnson); one *d*. *Educ:* Cardiff High School; Birmingham Univ. (LLB). Ministry of Power, 1967; Dept of Trade and Industry, 1972–2000: Asst Secretary, 1982; Under Sec., 1989; Dir, Employment Relations, 1998–2000; Acting Legal Services Ombudsman, 2002–03. Dir, Saffron Walden Mus. Soc. Ltd.

SALWAY, Francis William; Chairman, Town and Country Housing Group, since 2012; *b* 5 Oct. 1957; *m* 1985, Sarah Peplow; one *s* one *d*. *Educ:* Rugby Sch.; Christ's Coll., Cambridge (BA 1979; MA 1983). Richard Ellis, 1979–82; Abacus Develts Ltd, 1982–85; Coll. of Estate Management, 1985–86; Standard Life, 1986–2000; Land Securities Gp plc, 2000–12: Dir, 2001–12; Chief Operating Officer, 2003–04; Chief Exec., 2004–12. Non-executive Director: Next plc, 2010–; Investment Property Databank, 2012; Cadogan Gp Ltd, 2012–. Vis. Prof., LSE, 2012–. Chm., Property Adv. Gp, TfL, 2015–. Chairman: The London Community Foundn, 2012–; Crossrail 2 Funding Taskforce, London First, 2013–14. Pres., British Property Fedn, 2008–09. *Publications:* Depreciation of Commercial Property, 1986. *Recreations:* walking, swimming, allotment.

SALZ, Sir Anthony (Michael Vaughan), Kt 2013; Executive Vice Chairman, N. M. Rothschild & Sons Ltd, since 2006; *b* 30 June 1950; *s* of Michael H. Salz and Veronica Edith Dorothea Elizabeth Salz (*née* Hall); *m* 1975, Sally Ruth Hagger; one *s* two *d*. *Educ:* Summer Fields Sch., Oxford; Radley Coll.; Exeter Univ. (LLB Hons). Admitted Solicitor, 1974; Kenneth Brown Baker Baker, 1972–75; joined Freshfields, 1975, Partner, 1980, Sen. Partner, 1996–2000; seconded to Davis Polk & Wardwell, NY, 1977–78; Jt Sen. Partner, Freshfields Bruckhaus Deringer, 2000–06. Chm., Bloomsbury Publishing plc, 2013–. Vice-Chm., Bd of Govs, BBC, 2004–06. Ind. Rev. of Barclays business practices, 2013. Advr, Teach First, Business Leaders Council, 2012–. Dir, Forward Inst., 2014–. Member: Tate Gall. Corporate Adv. Gp, 1997– (Chm., 1997–2002); Adv. Bd, Sch. of Business and Econs, Univ. of Exeter, 2003–; Adv. Panel, Swiss Re Centre for Global Dialogue, 2006–11; Adv. Bd, Financial Services Knowledge Transfer Network, 2010–; lead non-exec. Bd Mem., DfE, 2010–12. Director: Tate Foundn, 2000–; Habitat for Humanity GB, 2004–10; Royal Opera Hse Covent Gdn Foundn, 2008–; Scott Trust, 2009–. Trustee: Eden Trust, 2002– (Chm., 2009–15); Paul Hamlyn Foundn, 2005–; Conran Foundn, 2007–; Media Standards Trust, 2008–; SHINE: Support and Help in Educn, 2008–10; Reprieve, 2011–; High Street Fund, 2011–13. Chairman: London Higher Skills Bd, 2008–10; Ind. Commn on Youth Crime and Antisocial Behaviour, 2008–; Co-Chm., Educn and Employers Taskforce, 2009–10. Gov., Wellington Acad., 2008–. FRSA 1996. Hon. LLD: Exeter, 2003; Coll. of Law, 2008. *Publications:* contrib. to various legal books and jls. *Recreations:* golf, fly-fishing, watching sports (including Southampton FC), tennis, walking, theatre, contemporary art. *Address:* Rothschild, New Court, St Swithin's Lane, EC4N 8AL. *Clubs:* Walbrook, MCC; Berkshire Golf, Trevose Golf.

SALZEDO, Simon Lopez; QC 2011; *b* London, 4 Jan. 1968; *s* of Maurice Salzedo and Marion Leighton; *m* 1992, Catherine Jane Dundon; two *s* two *d*. *Educ:* Trinity Sch., Croydon; Lowlands Sixth Form Coll., Harrow; Keble Coll., Oxford (BA PPE 1990); City Univ. (DipLaw 1994). ACA 1993, FCA 2011. Tax consultant, Price Waterhouse, 1990–93; called to the Bar, Lincoln's Inn, 1995; in practice as a barrister, Brick Court Chambers, 1995–.

Publications: (with R. D. Lord) Guide to the Arbitration Act 1996, 1996; (with C. Hollander) Conflicts of Interest, 2000, 4th edn 2011. *Address:* Brick Court Chambers, 7–8 Essex Street, WC2R 3LD. *T:* (020) 7379 3550.

SAMAAN, Alice Thomas; Ambassador of Bahrain to the Court of St James's, 2011–15, to Republic of Ireland, 2012–15, and to the Netherlands, 2014–15; *b* Manama, Bahrain. *Educ:* British Lebanese Trng Coll., Beirut; BBC Broadcasting Hse, London (Dip. Radio Prodn and Directing); Dip. Hosp. Admin, London; Dip. Supervisory Mgt, Bahrain; Univ. of Southern Calif (Dip. Trng of Trainers). Teacher, Amer. Mission Sch., Bahrain; producer, presenter and dir of radio progs for religious radio stn, Beirut, Lebanon; Hd, Overseas and Local Trng, Min. of Health, Bahrain; Internat. Prog. Officer in Bahrain and Oman, UNICEF; ed., producer and presenter of news, Bahrain Radio and TV Stn. Mem., Shura Council (Second Dep. Chm.; Mem., Adv. Council, 2000–02; Mem., Services Cttee (Vice Chm.); Mem., Ad-hoc Cttee for women and children). Member: Exec. Bd, American Mission Hosp.; Bd of Dirs, Al-Raja Sch. Member: Supreme Council for Vocational Trng, Bahrain; Bd, Coll. of Health Scis, Min. of Health, Bahrain; Exec. Cttee, Nat. Prog. for Mother and Child Care, Oman. *Clubs:* Mark's, Mosimann's.

SAMANI, Prof. Sir Nilesh (Jayantilal), Kt 2015; DL; MD; FRCP, FMedSci; Professor of Cardiology, University of Leicester, since 1997; Hon. Consultant Cardiologist, Glenfield Hospital, Leicester, since 1993; *b* Nanyuki, Kenya, 19 July 1956; *s* of Jayantilal and Kantaben Samani; *m* 1984, Varsha Raja; two *s*. *Educ:* Lenana Sch., Nairobi; Charles Keene Coll., Leicester; Univ. of Leicester (BSc 1978; MB ChB 1981; MD 1994). FRCP 1994. HO, Medicine and Surgery, 1981–82; SHO, Medicine, 1982–85; University of Leicester: MRC Clin. Trainee Fellow, 1985–88; Lectr in Medicine, 1988–93; Sen. Lectr in Cardiol., 1993–97. FMedSci 2002. DL Leics, 2010. *Publications:* contribs to jls incl. Nature, Nature Genetics, Lancet, New England Jl Medicine. *Recreations:* sports, reading, family. *Address:* Department of Cardiovascular Sciences, University of Leicester, BHF Cardiovascular Research Centre, Glenfield Hospital, Leicester LE3 9QP. *T:* (0116) 204 4758, *Fax:* (0116) 287 5792. *E:* njs@le.ac.uk.

SAMARAWEERA, Hon. Mangala Pinsiri; MP Matara, since 1989 (Freedom, 1989–2007; United Nat., since 2007); Minister of Foreign Affairs, Telecommunications and Information Technology, Sri Lanka, since 2015; *b* Matara; *s* of Mahanama and Khema Samaraweera. *Educ:* Royal Coll., Colombo; Central Sch. of Art and Design (BA Hons Fashion and Textile Design). Minister: of Posts and Telecommunications, 1994–2000; of Urban Develt and Housing, 2000–01; Chief Opposition Whip, 2001–04; Minister: of Ports, Aviation and Media, 2004–07; of Foreign Affairs, 2005–07. *Address:* Ministry of Foreign Affairs, Republic Building, Colombo 01, Sri Lanka. *T:* 0777576495.

SAMBLES, Prof. (John) Roy, PhD; FRS 2002; CPhys, FInstP; Professor of Physics, Exeter University, since 1991; *b* 14 Oct. 1945; *s* of Charles Henry Sambles and Georgina (*née* Deeble); *m* 1966, Sandra Elizabeth Sloman; two *s* one *d*. *Educ:* Callington Grammar Sch., Cornwall; Imperial Coll., London Univ. (BSc 1st Cl. Hons Physics 1967; ARCS; PhD 1970; DIC). CPhys 1988; FInstP 1988. Fellow, Imperial Coll., London, 1970–72; Exeter University: Lectr in Physics, 1972–85; Sen. Lectr, 1985–88; Reader, 1988–91. Mem., EPSRC, 2008–14. Pres., Inst. of Physics, 2015–. George Gray Medal, British Liquid Crystal Soc., 1998; Thomas Young Medal and Prize, 2003, Faraday Medal, 2012, Inst. of Physics. *Publications:* numerous papers in learned scientific jls, incl. works on liquid crystals, melting, electron microscopy, resistivity of thin samples, spin waves in metals, molecular electronics, surface plasmons, structural colour in nature, microwave metasurfaces and acoustic metamaterials. *Recreations:* writing poetry, local Methodist preacher. *Address:* School of Physics, University of Exeter, Exeter, Devon EX4 4QL. *T:* (01392) 264103.

SAMBROOK, Prof. Joseph Frank, PhD; FRS 1985; FAA; Distinguished Fellow, Peter MacCallum Cancer Institute, Melbourne, since 2003 (Director of Research, 1995–2000; Director, Familial Cancer Centre, 2000–05); Executive Scientific Director, Australian Stem Cell Centre, 2006–07 and 2009–11; *b* 1 March 1939; *s* of Thomas Sambrook and Ethel Gertrude (*née* Lightfoot); *m* 1st, 1960, Thelma McGrady (marr. diss. 1984); two *s* one *d*; 2nd, 1986, Mary-Jane Gething; one *d*. *Educ:* Liverpool Univ. (BSc 1962); Australian Nat. Univ. (PhD 1965). FAA 2000. Res. Fellow, John Curtin Sch. of Med. Res., ANU, 1965–66; Postdoctoral Fellow, MRC Lab. of Molecular Biol., 1966–67; Jun. Fellow, Salk Inst. for Biol Studies, 1967–69; Sen. Staff Investigator, 1969–77, Asst Dir, 1977–85, Cold Spring Harbor Lab.; Prof. and Chm., Dept of Biochemistry, Southwestern Medical Center, Dallas, 1985–91; Dir, McDermott Center for Human Growth and Develt, Southwestern Med. Sch., Dallas, 1991–94. Hon. DSc: Watson Sch. of Biol Scis, 2007; Liverpool, 2007. *Publications:* contribs to learned jls. *Recreation:* music. *Address:* Peter MacCallum Cancer Institute, St Andrews Place, East Melbourne, Vic 3002, Australia. *T:* (3) 96561356, *Fax:* (3) 96561411; PO Box 3254, East Melbourne, Vic 3002, Australia.

SAMBROOK, Prof. Richard Jeremy; Professor of Journalism, and Director, Centre for Journalism, Cardiff University, since 2012; *b* 24 April 1956; *s* of Michael Sambrook and Joan Sambrook (*née* Hartridge); *m* 1987, Susan Fisher; one *s* one *d*. *Educ:* Maidstone Sch. for Boys; Reading Univ. (BA); Birkbeck Coll., London Univ. (MSc). Trainee journalist, Thomson Newspapers, 1977–80; joined BBC, 1980: Radio News, 1980–84; TV News, 1984–87; Dep. Ed., Nine O'Clock News, 1988–92; News Editor, BBC News, 1992–96; Head, Newsgathering, 1996–99; Dep. Dir, 1999–2001, Dir, 2001–04, BBC News; Dir, BBC Global News, 2004–10; Global Vice Chm., Edelman, 2010–12. Vis. Fellow, Reuters Inst. for the Study of Journalism, 2010–. FRTS 1992; FRSA. *Recreations:* walking, golf, music. *Address:* Cardiff School of Journalism, Media and Cultural Studies, Cardiff University, Bute Building, King Edward VII Avenue, Cardiff CF10 3NB.

SAMEK, Charles Stephen; QC 2009; *b* London, 4 July 1965; only *s* of Major Herbert Samek, OBE, REME, and Terry Samek (*née* Nash); *m* 2005, Maria Pierfederici; one *s* one *d*. *Educ:* St Paul's Sch., Barnes; Oriel Coll., Oxford (MA Lit. Hum.); City Univ. (DipLaw). Called to the Bar, Middle Temple, 1989 (Astbury Schol., 1988); in practice as barrister, specialising in commercial litigation, civil fraud and internat. arbitration and private internat. law, 1989–; Mem., Inner Temple (ad eundem), 1997. Member: Commercial Bar Assoc., 1993–; Chancery Bar Assoc., 2007–; Internat. Bar Assoc., 2009–; British-Italian Law Assoc., 2009–; Commercial Fraud Lawyers Assoc., 2010–. Mem., Lord Mayor's Big Curry Cttee, ABF The Soldiers' Charity (formerly ABF), 2009–13. Freeman, City of London, 2012; Liveryman, Feltmakers' Co., 2012. *Recreations:* opera, ballet, chess, watching Arsenal FC, ski-ing, wine. *Address:* Littleton Chambers, 3 King's Bench Walk, Temple, EC4Y 7HR. *T:* (020) 7797 8600. *E:* clerks@littletonchambers.co.uk. *Club:* Athenæum.

SAMMONS, Prof. Pamela, PhD; Professor of Education, University of Oxford, since 2009; Senior Research Fellow, Jesus College, Oxford, since 2010; *b* 6 April 1956; *d* of Albert Edward Henry Sammons and Violet Ruth Sammons; *m* 1st, 1984, David Michael Greet (*d* 2003); two *d*; 2nd, 2011, John Allen Lerwill. *Educ:* Nower Hill High Sch.; Harrow County Girls' Sch.; Univ. of Bristol (BSocSci Geog. with Econs); CNAA (PhD 1986). Sen. Res. Officer, Res. and Stats Br., ILEA, 1981–90; Res. Fellow, Centre for Educnl Res., LSE, 1990–93; Institute of Education, London: Sen. Researcher, 1993–98; Reader in Educn, 1998; Prof. of Educn, and Co-ordinating Dir, Internat. Sch. Effectiveness and Improvement Centre, 1999–2004; Prof. of Educn, Univ. of Nottingham, 2004–09. *Publications:* (jtly) School Matters: the junior years, 1988; (jtly) Forging Links: effective schools and effective departments, 1997; School Effectiveness: coming of age in the 21st century, 1999; (jtly) Teachers Matter, 2007; (jtly) Methodological Advances in Educational Effectiveness Research, 2010; (jtly) Early Childhood Matters, 2010; (jtly) Successful School Leadership, 2011; (ed jtly) School Effectiveness and Improvement Research, Policy and Practice: challenging the orthodoxy?, 2012; (jtly) Effective Classroom Practice, 2014; many articles, etc in area of school effectiveness. *Recreations:* walking, visiting museums and art galleries. *Address:* Department of Education, University of Oxford, 15 Norham Gardens, Oxford OX2 6PY. *E:* pamela.sammons@education.ox.ac.uk.

SAMMUT ALESSI, Charles; *see* Alessi, C.

SAMPAIO, Jorge Fernando Branco de, Hon. GCMG 2002; Hon. GCVO 1993; Special Envoy of the UN Secretary-General to Stop Tuberculosis, 2006–13; High Representative of the UN Secretary-General for the Alliance of Civilisations, 2007–13; Counsellor of State, Portugal, since 2006; *b* Lisbon, 18 Sept. 1939; *s* of António Arnaldo de Carvalho Sampaio and Fernanda Bensaúde Branco de Sampaio; *m* Maria José Ritta; one *s* one *d*. *Educ:* Law Sch., Univ. of Lisbon. Practised as a lawyer, specialising in defending political prisoners. Sec. of State for External Co-operation, 1975; MP, Lisbon, 1979–84; Speaker, Socialist Parly Gp, 1987–88; Mem., Council of State, 1989–92; Mayor of Lisbon, 1989–95; Pres. of Portugal, 1996–2006. Founder, Intervenção Socialista, 1975; joined Socialist Party, 1978: Mem., Nat. Secretariat, 1979–92; Dir, Internat. Dept, 1986–87; Sec. Gen., 1989–92. Mem., European Human Rights Commn, Council of Europe, 1979–84. Mem. Bd, Carnegie Corp., NY. Numerous decorations, including: Grand Officer, Order of Prince Henry (Portugal), 1983; Grand Collar: Order of Southern Cross (Brazil), 1997; Orders of the Tower and Sword, of Valour, Loyalty, Merit, and of Liberty (Portugal), 2006; Collar: Order of Charles III (Spain), 1996; Order of Isabel la Católica (Spain), 2000; Grand Cross: Order of Orange Nassau (Netherlands), 1990; Order of White Eagle (Poland), 1997; Order of Merit (Germany), 1998; Légion d'Honneur (France), 1999. *Publications:* A Festa de um Sonho, 1991; A Look on Portugal, 1995; Os Portugueses, vols I-IX, 1997–2005; Com os Portugueses: dez anos na Presidência da República, 2005; numerous articles on political issues. *Recreations:* music, golf. *Address:* Casa do Regalo, Tapada das Necessidades, 1350–213 Lisbon, Portugal.

SAMPRAS, Peter; tennis player; *b* 12 Aug. 1971; *s* of Sam and Georgia Sampras; *m* 2000, Bridgette Wilson; two *s*. Professional tennis player, 1988–2003; won US Open, 1990 (youngest winner), 1993, 1995, 1996, 1999, 2002; Australian Open, 1994, 1997; Wimbledon, 1993, 1994, 1995, 1997, 1998, 1999, 2000; ATP World Champion, 1991, 1994, 1996, 1997, 1999; Davis Cup player. Co-Founder, Pure Sports Mgt LLC, 2007. Member: American Cancer Soc. Public Awareness Council; Board, Tim and Tom Gullikson Foundation; Founder, Aces for Charity Fund. *Publications:* (with Peter Bodo) A Champion's Mind: lessons from a life in tennis, 2008. *Recreations:* golf, basketball, Formula 1 racing. *Address:* c/o 200 ATP Tour Boulevard, Ponte Vedra Beach, FL 32082, USA. *T:* (904) 2858000.

SAMPSON, Adam; Chief Ombudsman, Office for Legal Complaints, 2009–14; *b* 13 June 1960; *s* of Derek and Janet Sampson; *m* 2000, Siobhan Grey; one *s* one *d*. *Educ:* Brasenose Coll., Oxford (BA; MSc). Jun. Dean, Brasenose Coll., Oxford, 1986–87; Probation Officer, Tottenham, 1987–89; Dep. Dir, Prison Reform Trust, 1989–94; Asst Prisons Ombudsman, Home Office, 1994–97; CEO, RAPt, 1998–2002; Dir, then Chief Exec., Shelter, 2003–09. *Publications:* Acts of Abuse, 1993. *Recreation:* sleeping.

SAMPSON, Sir Colin, Kt 1993; CBE 1988; QPM 1978; DL; HM Chief Inspector of Constabulary for Scotland, 1991–93; *b* 26 May 1929; *s* of James and Nellie Sampson; *m* 1953, Kathleen Stones; two *s*. *Educ:* Stanley Sch., Wakefield; Wakefield Technical Coll.; Univ. of Leeds (Criminology). Joined Police Force, 1949; served mainly in the CID (incl. training of detectives), at Dewsbury, Skipton, Doncaster, Goole, Wakefield, Huddersfield, Rotherham, Barnsley; Comdt, Home Office Detective Trng Sch., Wakefield, 1971–72; Asst Chief Constable, West Yorks, 1973; Dep. Chief Constable, Notts, 1976; Chief Constable, W Yorks, 1983–89; HM Inspector of Constabulary, 1989–90 (for NE England, 1990). Advr on police matters to govt of Namibia, 1989–93. Vice Pres., Yorkshire Soc., 1983–. Freeman, City of London, 1990. DL West Yorks, 1994. DUniv Bradford, 1988; Hon. LLD Leeds, 1990. KStJ 1998. *Recreations:* choral music, walking, gardening. *Address:* 5 Peacock Green, Morley, Leeds LS27 8GY.

SAMPSON, Prof. Fiona Ruth, FRSL; poet and writer; Professor of Poetry and Director, Roehampton Poetry Centre, University of Roehampton, since 2013; Editor, Poem, since 2013; *b* London, 7 Oct. 1963; *d* of Aylwin Arthur Sampson and Pamela Mary Sampson. *Educ:* Penglais Comprehensive Sch.; Pates Grammar Sch. for Girls; Royal Acad. of Music (Foundn Schol.; John Waterhouse Prize); Manchester Coll., Oxford (Newdigate Prize; MA PPE 1992); Catholic Univ. of Nijmegen (PhD 2001). ARCM 1980. Writing residencies in health and social care, incl. Isle of Wight HA, Dyfed Probation Service, Age Concern Swindon, Addenbrooke's Hosp., Cambridge, 1992–2005. Founder Dir, Aberystwyth Internat. Poetry Fest., 1995–99; Dir, Stephen Spender Meml Trust, 1999–2001; Founder Ed., Orient Express, 2002–05; Ed., Poetry Review, 2005–12. Visiting Research Fellow: Univ. of Sussex, 2000–03; Inst. of English Studies, Sch. of Advanced Study, Univ. of London, 2011, 2012–13; Inst. of Musical Res., Univ. of London, 2012–15; AHRC Fellow in Creative and Performing Arts, Oxford Brookes Univ., 2002–05; Fellow in Creativity, Univ. of Warwick, 2007–08; Dist. Writer, 2009–13, Prof. of Poetry, 2013, Kingston Univ.; Writer's Fellowship: Hawthornden Castle, 2001; Fundación Valparaiso, 2002; Heinrich Böll Hse, 2005; Estonian Writers' Union Hse, 2009; Arts Council of England Grant, 2012; Keats-Shelley Mus., Rome, 2015. FRSL 2009; FEA 2009. FRSA 2013. Member, Board: Poetry Translation Centre, 2006–; Wasafiri, 2008–. Mem., Council, RSL, 2011–. Judge: Foyle Young Poets, 2003; IMPAC Award, Irish Times, 2006; Ind. Foreign Fiction Prize, 2009; Forward Prizes, Soc. of Authors Eric Gregory Awards, 2011; Griffin Prizes, Canada, 2012; Cholmondeley Awards, Soc. of Authors, 2012–; T. S. Eliot Prize, 2015; Ondaatje Prize, 2015; Roehampton Prize, 2015 (Chm. Judges). Southern Arts Writer's Award, 1993; Oppenheimer-John Downes Award, 1998; Writer's Award, Arts Council of Wales, 1999; Kathleen Blundell Trust Award, 2002; Zlaten Prsten Prize, Macedonia, 2003; Charles Angoff Award, USA, 2006; Cholmondeley Award, Soc. of Authors, 2009. *Publications:* (ed jtly) The Self on the Page, 1998 (Hebrew edn 2002); The Healing Word, 1999; Folding the Real, 2001 (Romanian edn 2004); Patuvachki Knevnik, 2004; (trans.) Evening Brings Everything Back, by Jaan Kaplinski, 2004; (ed jtly) A Fine Line: new poetry from Central and Eastern Europe, 2004; (ed) Creative Writing in Health and Social Care, 2004; (jtly) Writing: self and reflexivity, 2005; The Distance Between Us, 2005 (Romanian and Macedonian edns 2005, Albanian edn 2006, Bulgarian edn 2009); (trans.) Day, by Amir Or, 2006; On Listening, 2007; Selected Poems in Hebrew Translation, 2007; Common Prayer, 2007; Zweimal sieben Gedichte, 2009; Poetry Writing, 2009; (ed) A Century of Poetry Review, 2009 (Special Commendation, Poetry Book Soc.); Poljupci I Molitva, 2010; Rough Music, 2010; (trans. jtly) Selected Poems, by Jaan Kaplinski, 2011; Music Lessons, 2011; (ed) Percy Bysshe Shelley, 2011 (On-line Choice, Poetry Book Soc.); Beyond the Lyric, 2012; Coleshill, 2013 (Recommendation, Poetry Book Soc.); Night Fugue: selected poems, 2013; Revenant (Chinese trans.), 2014; Volta, 2015; Preskochiti, 2015; Pryvyd, 2015. *Recreations:* string chamber music, English parish churches, Balkan train journeys. *Address:* Department of English and Creative Writing, Digby Stuart College, University of Roehampton, Roehampton Lane, SW15 5PU. *E:* Fiona.Sampson@roehampton.ac.uk.

SAMPSON, James; His Honour Judge Sampson; a Circuit Judge, since 2010; *b* Driffield, 15 Sept. 1962; *s* of James and Mary Sampson; *m* 1987, Helen Hewitt; one *s* two *d*. *Educ:* Bransholme High Sch.; Univ. of Nottingham; Inns of Court Sch. of Law. Called to the Bar,

Inner Temple, 1985; in practice as barrister specialising in crime; Recorder, 2003–10. *Recreations:* cycling, swimming, running, ski-ing. *Clubs:* Barracuda Triathlon, City of Hull Athletic.

SAMPSON, Nicholas Alexander, MA; Headmaster, Cranbrook School, Sydney, since 2012; *b* 27 Aug. 1958; *s* of Charles and Patricia Sampson; *m* 1981, Nancy Threlfall (marr. diss. 2014); two *d*. *Educ:* Gillingham Grammar Sch.; Howard Sch., Kent; Selwyn Coll., Cambridge (MA); Westminster Coll., Oxford (PGCE). Teacher of English and Housemaster, Wells Cathedral Sch., 1984–94; Headmaster, Sutton Valence Sch., 1994–2000; Principal, Geelong Grammar Sch., Australia, 2001–04; Master, Marlborough Coll., 2004–12. Member: Bd, Assoc. of Ind. Schs of Vic, 2003–04; Council, Marcus Oldham Coll., 2001–04; Council, Janet Clarke Hall, 2002–04. Governor: King's Sch., Rochester, 2006–12; St Andrew's Sch., Pangbourne, 2006–12; Swindon Acad., 2007–12; Marlborough Coll., Malaysia, 2012–. *Recreations:* family, literature, history, sport. *Address:* Cranbrook School, 5 Victoria Road, Bellevue Hill, NSW 2023, Australia. *Club:* Athenæum.

SAMS, Craig Lynn; Co-founder, 2007, and Executive Chairman, Carbon Gold Ltd; Director, Soil Association Certification Ltd (Chairman, 2007); President, Green & Black's, since 1999; *b* 17 July 1944; *s* of Kenneth Sams and Margaret Sams; *m* 1991, Josephine Fairley, *qv*; one *s* one *d* by a previous marriage. *Educ:* Wharton Sch., Univ. of Pennsylvania (BSc Econs). Co-founded Whole Earth Foods, 1967; estabd Ceres Bakery, 1972 (Chm.); co-founded Green & Black's Chocolate, 1991, created Maya Gold Chocolate, 1993; Director: Judges Bakery Ltd, 2004–13; Duchy Originals Ltd, 2009–; Gusto Organic Ltd. Hon. Treas., 1990–2001, Chm., 2001–07, Soil Assoc. Co-Publisher, Seed: the jl of organic living, 1972–77. Mem., Guild of Food Writers. FRSA. *Publications:* About Macrobiotics, 1972; The Macrobiotic Brown Rice Cookbook, 1993; The Little Food Book, 2003; (with Jo Fairley) Sweet Dreams: the story of Green & Black's, 2008. *Recreations:* allotment gardening, orchardist, cliff walking, propcycling. *Address:* 106 High Street, Hastings, E Sussex TN34 3ES. *T:* (01424) 430016. *E:* craig@craigsams.com. *Club:* Groucho.

SAMS, Jeremy Charles; composer, translator, director; *b* 12 Jan. 1957; *s* of late Eric Sams and Enid Sams (*née* Tidmarsh); one *s*. *Educ:* Magdalene Coll., Cambridge (BA); Guildhall Sch. of Music. Freelance pianist, 1977–82; director: *theatre* includes: Entertaining Mr Sloane, Greenwich, 1992; Wind in the Willows, Tokyo, 1993, Old Vic, 1995; Neville's Island, Apollo, 1994; Wild Oats, RNT, 1995; Passion, Queen's, 1996; Marat/Sade, RNT, 1997; Enter the Guardsman, Donmar, 1997; Two Pianos, Four Hands, Birmingham Rep., and Comedy, 1999; Spend! Spend! Spend!, Piccadilly, 1999; Noises Off, RNT, 2000, transf. Piccadilly and NY, 2001; What the Butler Saw, Theatre Royal, Bath, and tour, 2001; Benefactors, Albery, and tour, 2002; The Water Babies, Chichester, 2003; Little Britain, UK tour, 2005; Donkeys' Years, Comedy, 2006; The Sound of Music, Palladium, 2006, UK tour, 2009; 13 The Musical, Broadway, 2008; The King and I, Royal Albert Hall, 2009; Educating Rita, Menier Chocolate Factory, transf. Trafalgar Studios, 2010; The Wizard of Oz, Palladium, 2011, Toronto, 2013, US tour, 2013; *opera:* The Reluctant King, Opera North, 1994; (libretto) The Enchanted Island, Metropolitan Opera, NY, 2012; La Périchole (also trans.), Garsington, 2012; Peter Grimes, Grange Park, 2014; *translations* include: The Rehearsal, Almeida and Garrick, 1991 (Time Out Award), Minerva, Chichester (also dir), 2015; Becket, Theatre Royal Haymarket, 1991; The Miser, NT; Les Parents Terribles, RNT and NY, 1990; Mary Stuart, RNT, 1996; Merry Widow, Royal Opera, 1997; A Fool and His Money, Nottingham Playhouse and Birmingham Rep., 1998; Colombe, Salisbury Playhouse, 1999; Twilight of the Gods (The Rhinegold, The Valkyrie, Siegfried), 2001, Così fan tutte, 2002, and The Magic Flute, Macbeth, Figaro's Wedding, La Bohème, in repertory, ENO; Scapino, Chichester, 2005; Arms and the Cow, Opera North, 2006; Don Giovanni, ENO, 2010; Die Fledermaus, Metropolitan Opera, NY, 2014; Exit the King (Ionesco), Ustinov. Th., Bath, 2014; Rise and Fall of the City of Mahagonny, Royal Opera, 2015; *adaptations* include: Waiting in the Wings, NY, 1999; Chitty Chitty Bang Bang, Palladium, 2002, transf. NY; Amour, NY, 2002; A Damsel in Distress, Chichester, 2015; composer of numerous scores: *theatre* includes: Kean, Old Vic, 1990; for RSC: Temptation, The Tempest, Measure for Measure, Merry Wives of Windsor, Midsummer Night's Dream; for RNT: Ghetto (also lyrics); Wind in the Willows (also lyrics); Arcadia; Honour, 2003; *television:* Persuasion, 1996 (BAFTA Award for Original TV Music); Have Your Cake, 1997; *films:* The Mother, 2003; Enduring Love (Ivor Novello Award), 2004; Hyde Park on Hudson, 2013; Le Weekend, 2013. Hon. FRAM 2013. DUniv Birmingham City, 2013. *Publications:* (ed) Wild Oats, 1995; *translations:* Molière, The Miser, 1991; Anouilh, The Rehearsal, 1991; Cocteau, Les Parents Terribles, 1995; Schiller, Mary Stuart, 1996; Anouilh, Becket, 1997; Lehár, The Merry Widow, 2000; Antigone, 2002; Eric Emmanuel Schmitt, Plays: 1, 2002; Enigma Variations, 2003. *Address:* c/o The Agency, 24 Pottery Lane, W11 4LZ.

SAMSON, Polly; writer and lyricist; *b* London, 29 April 1962; *d* of Lance Samson and Esther Cheo Ying; *m* 1994, David Jon Gilmour, *qv*; three *s* one *d*. *Educ:* Newton Abbot Grammar Sch. Publicity Dir, Jonathan Cape, 1986–89; journalist and columnist, Sunday Times, 1990–93. *Publications:* Lying in Bed, 1999; Out of the Picture, 2000; Perfect Lives, 2010; The Kindness, 2015. *Recreations:* music, books, dogs. *Address:* 8 Medina Terrace, Brighton BN3 2WL. *T:* 07768 018009. *E:* polly@pollysamson.com. *Club:* Groucho.

SAMSON, Prof. Thomas James, (Jim), PhD; FBA 2000; Professor of Music, Royal Holloway, University of London, 2002–11, now Emeritus; *b* 6 July 1946; *s* of Edward Samson and Matilda Jayne (*née* Smyth). *Educ:* Queen's Univ., Belfast (BMus); UC, Cardiff, (MMus; PhD 1972). LRAM 1972. Res. Fellow in Humanities, Univ. of Leicester, 1972–73; University of Exeter: Lectr in Music, 1973–87; Reader in Musicology, 1987–92; Prof. of Musicology, 1992–94; Stanley Hugh Badock Prof. of Music, Univ. of Bristol, 1994–2002. Vis. Prof., Univ. of Trondheim, 2004–07. Ed.-in-Chief, Grove Music Online Revisions, Eastern Europe, 2012–. Order of Merit, Ministry of Culture (Poland), 1990. *Publications:* Music in Transition: a study of tonal expansion and early atonality 1900–1920, 1977, 3rd edn 1993; The Music of Szymanowski, 1980; The Music of Chopin, 1985, 2nd edn 1994 (trans. German 1991); (ed) Chopin Studies, 1988; (ed) The Late Romantic Era: Vol. VII, Man and Music, 1991; Chopin: the Four Ballades, 1992 (trans. Polish 2012); (ed) The Cambridge Companion to Chopin, 1992; (ed with J. Rink) Chopin Studies 2, 1994; Master Musicians Chopin, 1996 (trans. Japanese 2012); (ed) The Cambridge History of Nineteenth-Century Music, 2002; (ed with Bennett Zon) Nineteenth Century Music: selected proceedings of the Tenth International Conference, 2002; Virtuosity and the Musical Work: the Transcendental Studies of Liszt, 2003 (Royal Philharmonic Bk Prize, 2004); The Complete Chopin: a new critical edition, Ballades, 2006 (Internat. Piano Award, 2009); (ed with P. J. E. Harper-Scott) Introduction to Music Studies, 2008 (trans. Korean 2014); Music in the Balkans, 2013; (ed with M. Milin) Serbian Music: Yugoslav contexts, 2014. *Recreation:* astronomy. *Address:* 81 Gainsborough Road, Kew, Richmond TW9 2ET; 19 Odos Kyknou, Kallithea, 21060 Drepano, Nafplio, Greece.

SAMSON-BARRY, Hilary Alice; executive coach; Director, Koru Leadership Ltd, since 2012; *b* 16 Aug. 1958; *d* of Dr Mattanja Erasmus Richard Samson and Dr Margaret Noel Samson (*née* Williams); *m* 1989, Desmond Neville Barry; one *s* one *d*. *Educ:* Sch. of St Mary and St Anne, Abbots Bromley; Ellesmere Coll.; Univ. of Exeter (BA Hons (Econs and Geog.) 1980); Cranfield Univ. (MBA 1986). Personnel Manager, Securiguard Services Ltd, 1980–85; Mgt Consultant, Towers Perrin, 1986–91; Project Manager, London Implementation Gp, DoH, 1992–95; Dir, Camden and Islington HA, 1995–96; Head: Health Develt, NHS London Region, 1997–2000; Policy Integration and Health, GLA, 2000–01; Dir, Productivity and Diversity, Women and Equality Unit, Cabinet Office and DTI, 2001–04; Hd of Children, Families and Maternity, DoH, 2004; Dir, Turning Point, 2010. Trustee, Scope. Gov., Francis Combe Sch. and Community Coll., 2003. Hon. DSc Greenwich, 2001. *Recreations:* family, horse riding, community, personal development. *Address:* Highclere, 34 Abbots Road, Abbots Langley, Herts WD5 0AZ. *E:* HSamsonBarry@aol.com.

SAMSOVA, Galina; producer, teacher; *b* Stalingrad, 1937; *d* of a Byelorussian; *m* 1st, Alexander Ursuliak; 2nd, André Prokovsky. *Educ:* the Ballet Sch., Kiev (pupil of N. Verekundova). Joined Kiev Ballet, 1956 and became a soloist; Canadian Ballet, 1961; created chief rôle in Cendrillon, Paris 1963 (Gold Medal for best danseuse of Paris Festival). Ballerina, Festival Ballet, 1964–73; headed the group of André Prokovsky, The New London Ballet, (disbanded in 1977, revived for 3 new productions, The Theatre Royal, York, 1979); a Principal Dancer, Sadler's Wells Royal Ballet, subseq. Birmingham Royal Ballet, 1980–91; Artistic Dir, Scottish Ballet, 1991–97; has danced principal rôles in Sleeping Beauty, Nutcracker, Giselle, Swan Lake, Anna Karenina, and other classical ballets; danced in Europe, Far East and USA. Produced: Sequence from Paquita, Sadler's Wells, 1980; (with Peter Wright) Swan Lake, Sadler's Wells, 1983, Covent Garden, 1991, Royal Swedish Ballet, 2001; Giselle, London City Ballet, 1986, Birmingham Royal Ballet, 2013; Les Sylphides, Birmingham Royal Ballet, 1992; Sleeping Beauty, Scottish Ballet, 1994, Tulsa Ballet, USA, 2000; Swan Lake, Scottish Ballet, 1995, Rome Opera House, 2003, NBA Ballet Co., Japan, 2006.

SAMUEL, family name of **Viscounts Bearsted** and **Samuel**.

SAMUEL, 5th Viscount *cr* 1937, of Mount Carmel and of Toxteth, Liverpool; **Jonathan Herbert Samuel;** *b* 17 Dec. 1965; *s* of 4th Viscount Samuel (who had succeeded to the title in Oct. 2014) and Nonni Esther Samuel (*née* Gordon); *S* father, Nov. 2014; *m* 1995, Bridget Elizabeth, *d* of late Prof. Michael Mahoney, Princeton, USA; two *d*. *Heir: half-b* Hon. Benjamin Angus Samuel, *b* 29 Dec. 1983.

SAMUEL, Andrew; *see* Samuel, M. A.

SAMUEL, Gillian Patricia; Director (formerly General Manager) of Corporate Communications, P&O Nedlloyd Ltd, 1998–2005; *b* 19 Oct. 1945; *d* of Harry Martin Samuel and Kathleen Joyce Samuel (*née* Drake). *Educ:* Edmonton Co. Grammar Sch.; Exeter Univ. (BA Hons Hist.). Current Affairs Gp, BBC TV, 1968–70; Plessey Co., 1970–72; Department of: Nat. Savings, 1972–75; Industry, later DTI, 1975–87; Dir of Information, Dept of Transport, 1987–92; Press Sec. and Chief of Information, 1992–97, Sen. Advr, Internal Communications Develt, 1997–98, MoD. JP E Dorset, 2008–15. *Recreations:* golf, walking, choral singing, modern jazz.

SAMUEL, Sir John (Michael Glen), 5th Bt *cr* 1898; Chartered Engineer, Business Development, Renewable Energy Dynamics Technology Ltd, since 2009; *b* 25 Jan. 1944; *o s* of Sir John Oliver Cecil Samuel, 4th Bt, and Charlotte Mary, *d* of late R. H. Hoyt, Calgary, Canada; *S* father, 1962; *m* 1st, 1966, Antoinette Sandra, *d* of late Captain Antony Hewitt, RE, 2nd SAS Regt, and Mrs K. A. H. Casson, Frith Farm, Wolverton, Hants; two *s*; 2nd, 1982, Mrs Elizabeth Ann Molinari, *y d* of late Major R. G. Curry, Bournemouth, Dorset. *Educ:* Radley; London Univ. Director: Enfield Automotive, 1967–70; Advanced Vehicle Systems Ltd, 1971–78; Chairman: Electric Auto Corp. (USA), 1978–83; Synergy Management Services Ltd, 1983–; Founder and Tech. Dir, RE-Fuel Technol. Ltd, 2001–09 (Chm., 2008). *Recreation:* motor racing. *Heir: s* Anthony John Fulton Samuel [*b* 13 Oct. 1972; *m* 2004, Gemma Chloe Rose Gubbins; three *s*].

SAMUEL, Dr (Marcus) Andrew; Chief Executive, Oil and Gas Authority, since 2015; *b* Lusaka, Zambia, 7 July 1969; *s* of Marcus, (Jimmy), Samuel and Heather Samuel; *m* 1999, Sue Entwistle; two *s*. *Educ:* Stowe Sch.; Sidney Sussex Coll., Cambridge (BA Hons Nat. Scis 1990); Birkbeck Coll., Univ. of London (PhD 1993). Postdoctoral Fellowship, Birkbeck Coll., Univ. of London; BG Group: UK-based geologist, 1994–99; Sen. Geologist, BG Egypt and Rashpetco JV Cairo, 1999–2002; UK Exploration Manager, 2003–06; North Sea High Pressure, High Temperature Asset Manager, 2006–08; Dep. Asset Gen. Manager, Trinidad and Tobago, 2008–10; Pres. and Gen. Manager, Appalachia shale gas Jt Venture, BG Gp and EXCO, 2010–12; Man. Dir, Europe Exploration and Prodn, BG Gp, 2012–14. *Publications:* articles in Jl of Amer. Assoc. of Petroleum Geologists, Marine and Petroleum Geol. and Jl of Geol Soc. *Recreations:* keen on variety of sports and outdoor pursuits including hiking, surfing, yoga, sailing, loves travel. *Address:* Oil and Gas Authority, Atholl House, 86–88 Guild Street, Aberdeen AB11 6AR. *T:* (01224) 254050. *E:* andy.samuel@oga.gsi.gov.uk.

SAMUEL, Martin; Chief Sports Writer, Daily Mail, since 2009; *b* 25 July 1964; *s* of Arthur Samuel and Rita Samuel; *m* 1994, Deborah Edmead; three *s*. *Educ:* Fairlop Jun. Sch.; Ilford Co. High Sch. Hayters Sports Agency, 1982–84; The People, 1984–87; The Sun, 1987–97, Chief Football Writer, 1994–97; The Express: Football Editor, 1997–2000; Chief Sports Writer and Columnist, 2000–02; Chief Sports Writer, News of the World, 2002–07; Columnist, 2002–09, Chief Football Corresp., 2007–09, The Times. Sports Writer of the Year: What the Papers Say, 2002, 2005, 2006; Sports Journalists' Assoc., 2005, 2006, 2007, 2010; British Press Awards, 2008. *Address:* Daily Mail, Northcliffe House, 2 Derry Street, W8 5TT.

SAMUELS; *see* Turner-Samuels.

SAMUELS, Rev. Canon Christopher William John; Rector of St Mary without-the-walls, Handbridge, Chester, 1983–2005; Chaplain to the Queen, 2001–12; *b* 8 Oct. 1942; *s* of John Bernard Boniface Samuels and Ethel Samuels (*née* Bamford); *m* 1967, Sarah Parry (*née* Irving); one *s* one *d*. *Educ:* Denstone Coll., Uttoxeter; KCL (AKC 1966); St Boniface, Warminster. Ordained deacon, 1967, priest, 1968; Curate, St Thomas, Kirkholt, Rochdale, 1967–72; Priest i/c, St Thomas, Parkside, Houghton Regis, 1972–76; Rector, St Helen's, Tarporley, 1976–83; Rural Dean of Chester, 1997–2005. Hon. Canon, Chester Cathedral, 1997–2005, now Emeritus. Nat. Chaplain, Dunkirk Veterans' Assoc., 1996–2000. Chm. of Trustees, Children in Distress, 2007–. Chm. of Govs, King's Sch., Chester, 2002–05. Freeman, City of London, 1996. Paul Harris Fellow, Rotary Club, 1997. *Recreations:* book collecting, Scottish islands, travel. *Address:* 14 Gardd Eithin, Northop Hall, Mold, Flintshire CH7 6GJ. *T:* (01244) 297490. *Club:* Rotary (Chester) (Pres., 2014–).

SAMUELS, Jeffrey Keith; QC 2009; a Recorder, since 2012; *b* Manchester, 9 July 1965; *s* of Michael and Brenda Samuels; *m* 2000, Andrea Cowen; three *s* one *d*. *Educ:* Leeds Univ. (LLB Hons); Inns of Court Sch. of Law. Called to the Bar, Middle Temple, 1988; in practice as barrister specialising in crime. *Address:* St Johns Buildings, 24a–28 St John Street, Manchester M3 4DJ. *T:* (0161) 214 1500, *Fax:* (0161) 835 3929. *E:* jeffrey.samuels@stjohnsbuildings.co.uk.

SAMUELS, His Honour John Edward Anthony; QC 1981; a Circuit Judge, 1997–2006; a Deputy Circuit Judge, 2006–10; Chairman, Criminal Justice Alliance, since 2012; *b* 15 Aug. 1940; *s* of late Albert Edward Samuels, solicitor, Reigate, Surrey, and Sadie Beatrice Samuels; *m* 1967, Maxine (*née* Robertson), JP; two *s*. *Educ:* Charterhouse; Perugia; Queens' Coll., Cambridge (MA). Commnd, Queen's Royal Regt (TA), 1959; Lieut, Queen's Royal Surrey Regt (TA), 1961–67. Chairman, Cambridge Univ. United Nations Assoc., 1962. Called to Bar, Lincoln's Inn, 1964 (Mansfield Schol., 1963; Bencher, 1990); South Eastern Circuit; a Dep. High Court Judge, 1981–97; a Recorder, 1985–97. Asst Parly Boundary Comr, 1992–95. Judicial Mem., Parole Bd, 2005–. Mem. Bd (rep. England and Wales), Internat. Assoc. of Drug Treatment Cts, 2007–. Member: Senate of the Inns of Court and the Bar,

1983–86; Bar Council, 1992–97; Council of Legal Educn, 1983–90; Chm., Jt Regulations Cttee, Inns' Council and Bar Council, 1987–90. Mem. Cttee, Council of HM Circuit Judges, 2001–12 (Chm., Criminal Sub-Cttee, 2002–06; Representative of retired judiciary, 2006–12). Co-opted Mem., ILEA Education Cttee, 1964–67; Jt Chm., ILEA Disciplinary Tribunals, 1977–87; Alternate Chm., Burnham Cttee, 1981–87; Lay Chm., NHS Complaints Panels, 1996–97; Dep. Chm., Disciplinary Cttee, RPSGB, 2006–10; Mem., Criminal Injuries Compensation Appeal Panel, 1997; Mem., Nat. Sentencer Probation Forum (representing Crown Court judges), 2004–12. Member: Richmond, Twickenham and Roehampton HA, 1982–86; Kingston and Richmond FPC, 1982–86. Vice-Pres., Assoc. of Members of Ind. Monitoring Bds, 2015–. Trustee: Richmond Parish Lands Charity, 1986–96 (Chairman: Educn Cttee, 1987–89; Property Cttee, 1987–95); Prisoners' Educn Trust, 2000– (Chm., 2006–12; Pres., 2012–); Centre for Crime and Justice Studies, 2002–13; Howard League for Penal Reform, 2007– (Chm. Legal Cttee, 2009–). Vice-Pres., Unlock (Nat. Assoc. for Reformed Offenders), 2006–. Vis. Prof., Nottingham Law Sch., 2012–. Occasional broadcaster. FRSA 2012. *Publications:* Action Pack: counsel's guide to chambers' administration, 1986, 2nd edn 1988; contributor to Halsbury's Laws of England, 4th edn. *Recreations:* conservation, restoration, serendipity. *Address:* c/o Treasury Office, Lincoln's Inn, WC2A 3TL. *T:* (020) 7405 1393. *Club:* Garrick.

SAMUELSON, Sir James Francis, 6th Bt *cr* 1884, of Bodicote, Banbury, Oxfordshire; *b* Hartfield, Sussex, 20 Dec. 1956; *er s* of Sir (Bernard) Michael (Francis) Samuelson, 5th Bt, and of Janet Amy, *yr d* of Lt-Comdr L. G. Elkington; *S* father, 2008; *m* 1987, Caroline Anne Woodley; two *d. Educ:* Hailsham Sch. *Heir: b* Edward Bernard Samuelson, *b* 30 June 1967. *Address:* Brookside, Kings Court Road, Gillingham, Dorset SP8 4LD. *T:* (01747) 833772.

SAMUELSON, Sir Sydney (Wylie), Kt 1995; CBE 1978; first British Film Commissioner, 1991–97; President, 1990–95, Senior Consultant, 1998–2000, Samuelson Group PLC (Chairman and Chief Executive, 1966–90); *b* 7 Dec. 1925; 2nd *s* of G. B. and Marjorie Samuelson; *m* 1949, Doris (*née* Magen); three *s. Educ:* Irene Avenue Council Sch., Lancing, Sussex. Served RAF, 1943–47. From age 14, career devoted to various aspects of British film industry: cinema projectionist, 1939–41; asst film editor, 1942–43; asst film cameraman, cameraman and dir of documentary films and television, 1947–59; founded Samuelson Gp, company to service film, TV and, later, audio-visual prodn organisations, supplying cameras and other technical equipment, with purchase of first camera, 1954; continued filming as technician on locations throughout world until 1959, when activities concentrated on developing the company. Mem., BAFTA, 1965– (Vice-Chm. Film, 1971–73; Chm. of Council, 1973–76; Trustee, 1974–2009; Chm., Bd of Mgt, 1976–2001; Mem., Business Bd, 1994–2001; Michael Balcon Award, 1985; Fellow, 1993); Chm., BAFTA-Shell UK Venture, 1988–91; Member: BECTU History Project, 1995–2002; Exec. Cttee, Cinema and Television Veterans, 1978– (Pres., 1980–81); Council and Exec. Cttee, Cinema and TV Benevolent Fund, 1969–92 (Trustee, 1982–89; Pres., 1983–86). Pres., Projected Picture Trust, 2002–. Hon. Mem., Brit. Soc. of Cinematographers (Governor, 1969–79; 1st Vice-Pres., 1976–77; award for Outstanding Contribution to Film Industry, 1967; special award for services to UK film prodn sector as British Film Comr, 1997); Associate Mem., Amer. Soc. of Cinematographers, 1981–96; Hon. Life Mem., BECTU, 1990 (Mem., ACTT, 1947); Fellow, BFI, 1997; Hon. Life Fellow, BKSTS - The Moving Image Soc., 1995 (Patron, 1997–; Award of Merit, 2003; Lifetime Achievement Award, 2015); Hon. Mem., Guild of British Camera Technicians (Trustee, 1993–). Hon. Technical Advr, Royal Naval Film Corp.; Member: Adv. Bd, Northern Media Sch., 1996–2001; Assoc. of Film Comrs Internat., 1999–. Pres., UK Friends of Akim (Israel Assoc. for Mentally Handicapped); Vice Pres., Muscular Dystrophy UK (formerly Muscular Dystrophy Campaign); Patron, Young Persons Concert Foundn. Dr (*hc*) Sheffield Hallam, 1996. Britannica Award for Television News Film, BBC Sportsview, 1961; Award of Merit, Guild of Film Prodn Execs, 1986; Lifetime achievement award, Birmingham Internat. Film and TV Festival, 1997; Howard Dutch Horton Award, Assoc. of Film Comrs Internat., 1997; Friese Greene Award for outstanding career in cinema and television, 2011. *Recreations:* listening to music, vintage motoring, veteran jogging (finished a mere 13,006 places behind the winner, London Marathon 1982). *Address:* 31 West Heath Avenue, NW11 7QJ. *T:* (020) 8455 6696, *Fax:* (020) 8458 1957.

SAMUELSSON, Prof. Bengt Ingemar; Professor of Medical and Physiological Chemistry, Karolinska Institutet, Stockholm, 1972–99, now Emeritus; Chairman, Nobel Foundation, Stockholm, 1993–2005; *b* Halmstad, Sweden, 21 May 1934; *s* of Anders and Stina Samuelsson; *m* 1958, Inga Karin Bergstein; one *s* one *d* (and one *d* decd). *Educ:* Karolinska Institutet (DMedSci 1960, MD 1961). Res. Fellow, Harvard Univ., 1961–62; Asst Prof. of Med. Chemistry, Karolinska Inst., 1961–66; Prof., Royal Vet. Coll., Stockholm, 1967–72; Chm., Dept of Chemistry, 1973–83, Dean of Med. Faculty, 1978–83, Pres., 1983–95, Karolinska Inst., Stockholm. Vis. Prof., Harvard, 1976; T. Y. Shen Vis. Prof. in Med. Chem., MIT, 1977; Walker-Ames Prof., Washington Univ., 1987. Lectures include: Shirley Johnson Meml, Philadelphia, 1977; Sixth Annual Marrs McLean, Houston, 1978; Harvey, NY, 1979; Lane Medical, Stanford Univ., 1981; Eighth Annual Sci. in Med., Univ. of Washington, 1981; Arthur C. Corcoran Meml, Cleveland, Ohio, 1981; Kober, Assoc. of Amer. Physicians, 1982; Brown-Razor, Rice Univ., Houston, 1984; Solomon A. Berson Meml, Mount Sinai Sch. of Medicine, NY, 1984; Angelo Minich, Venice, 1988; Hans Neurath, Univ. of Washington, 1990; Dunham, Harvard Med. Sch., 1990; First Fogarty Internat., NIH, 1992. Member: Nobel Assembly, Karolinska Inst., 1972–99 (Chm., 1990); Nobel Cttee for Physiol. or Medicine, 1984–89 (Chm., 1987–89); Swedish Govt Res. Adv. Bd, 1985–88; Nat. Commn on Health Policy, 1987–90; ESTA, 1995–97. Member: Royal Swedish Acad. of Scis, 1981–; Mediterranean Acad., Catania, 1982–; US Nat. Acad. of Scis, 1984; French Acad. of Scis, 1989; Royal Soc., 1990; Royal Nat. Acad. of Medicine, Spain, 1991; Hon. Prof., Bethune Univ. of Med. Scis, China, 1986; Hon. Member: Amer. Soc. of Biological Chemists, 1976; Assoc. of American Physicians, 1982; Swedish Med. Assoc., 1982; Italian Pharmacological Soc., 1985; Acad. Nac. de Medicina de Buenos Aires, 1986; Internat. Soc. of Haematology, 1986; Spanish Soc. of Allergology and Clinical Immunology, 1989; Foreign Hon. Member: Amer. Acad. of Arts and Scis, 1982–; Internat. Acad. of Science, ICSD; Founding Mem., Academia Europaea, 1988. Hon. DSc: Chicago, 1978; Illinois, 1983; DUniv: Rio de Janeiro, 1986; Buenos Aires, 1986; Complutense, Madrid, 1991; Milan, 1993; Louisiana State, 1993; Uppsala, 2007. Nobel Prize in Physiology or Medicine (jtly), 1982; numerous awards and prizes. *Publications:* papers on biochemistry of prostaglandins, thromboxanes and leukotrienes. *Address:* Department of Medical Biochemistry and Biophysics, Karolinska Institutet, 17177 Stockholm, Sweden. *T:* (8) 52487600.

SAMWORTH, Sir David (Chetwode), Kt 2009; CBE 1985; DL; President, Samworth Brothers (Holdings) Ltd (formerly Gorran Foods Ltd), since 2005 (Director since 1981; Chairman, 1984–2005); *b* 25 June 1935; *s* of Frank and Phyllis Samworth; *m* 1969, Rosemary Grace Cadell; one *s* three *d. Educ:* Uppingham Sch. Chm., Pork Farms Ltd, 1968–81; Dir, Northern Foods Ltd, 1978–81. Non-executive Director: Imperial Gp, 1983–85; Thorntons plc, 1988–93. Chm., Meat and Livestock Commn, 1980–84. Member: Leicester No 3 HMC, 1970–74; Trent RHA, 1974–78, 1980–84. President: RASE, 2000–01; Leics Agricl Soc., 1996–99; Young Enterprise, Leics, 2001–04. Pres., Coll. of Canons, Leicester Cathedral, 2013–. Chm. Trustees, Uppingham Sch., 1995–99. DL Leics, 1984, High Sheriff, Leics, 1997. Hon. LLD Leicester, 2012. *Recreation:* fishing. *Address:* Samworth Brothers (Holdings) Ltd, Chetwode House, Samworth Way, Melton Mowbray, Leics LE13 1GA.

SANDARS, Christopher Thomas; Director General (Central Budget) (formerly Assistant Under-Secretary of State (General Finance)), Ministry of Defence, 1997–2002; *b* 6 March 1942; *s* of late Vice-Adm. Sir Thomas Sandars, KBE, CB and Lady Sandars; *m* 1966, Elizabeth Anne Yielder; three *s* one *d. Educ:* Oundle Sch.; Corpus Christi Coll., Cambridge (Trevelyan Schol.; Foundation Schol.). Joined MoD, 1964; Asst Private Sec. to Minister of State, 1967–69; Central Policy Review Staff, Cabinet Office, 1971–74; Private Sec. to Minister of State, 1975–77; Hd, General Finance Div. 1, 1977–80; Hd, Defence Secretariat 13, 1980–84; RCDS, 1985; Hd, Secretariat 9 (Air), 1986–90; Asst Under-Sec. of State, MoD, 1990–95; Fellow, Center for Internat. Affairs, Harvard Univ., 1995–96. *Publications:* America's Overseas Garrisons: the leasehold empire, 2000. *Recreations:* painting, gardening, theatre. *Address:* 10 Crescent Grove, SW4 7AH.

SANDARS, Nancy Katharine, FBA 1984; FSA; archaeologist; *b* 29 June 1914; *d* of Edward Carew Sandars and Gertrude Annie Sandars (*née* Phipps). *Educ:* at home; Wychwood School, Oxford; Inst. of Archaeology, Univ. of London (Diploma 1949); St Hugh's College, Oxford (BLitt 1957). Archaeological research and travel in Europe, 1949–69; British School at Athens, 1954–55; Elizabeth Wordsworth Studentship, St Hugh's College, Oxford, 1958–61; travelled in Middle East, 1957, 1958, 1962, 1966; conferences, lectures (Prague, Sofia, McGill Univ.); excavations in British Isles and Greece. *Publications:* Bronze Age Cultures in France, 1957; The Epic of Gilgamesh, an English version, 1960, rev. edn 1972; Prehistoric Art in Europe, 1967, rev. edn 1985; Poems of Heaven and Hell from Ancient Mesopotamia, 1971; The Sea-Peoples: warriors of the ancient Mediterranean, 1978; Grandmother's Steps: poems, 2001; articles on David Jones, painter and poet. *Recreations:* walking, translating, looking at pictures. *Address:* The Manor House, Little Tew, Chipping Norton, Oxford OX7 4JF. *Club:* University Women's.

SANDBACH, Antoinette; *see* Mackeson-Sandbach.

SANDBERG, family name of **Baron Sandberg**.

SANDBERG, Baron *cr* 1997 (Life Peer), of Passfield in the co. of Hampshire; **Michael Graham Ruddock Sandberg,** Kt 1986; CBE 1982 (OBE 1977); Chairman: The Hongkong and Shanghai Banking Corporation, 1977–86; The British Bank of the Middle East, 1980–86; *b* 31 May 1927; *s* of Gerald Arthur Clifford Sandberg and Ethel Marion Sandberg; *m* 1954, Carmel Mary Roseleen Donnelly; two *s* two *d. Educ:* St Edward's Sch., Oxford. 6th Lancers (Indian Army) and First King's Dragoon Guards, 1945. Joined The Hongkong and Shanghai Banking Corp., 1949. Director: Winsor Properties Hldgs Ltd, HK; Winsor Industrial Corp. Ltd, HK; Green Island Cement Hldgs Ltd, HK; New World Develt Co. Ltd, HK. Mem. Exec. Council, Hong Kong, 1978–86. Mem., H of L, 1997–2015. Steward, Royal Hong Kong Jockey Club, 1972–86, Chm., 1981–86; Treasurer, Univ. of Hong Kong, 1977–86. FCIB (FIB 1977; Vice Pres. 1984–87); FRSA 1983. Freeman, City of London, 1988. Hon. LLD: Hong Kong, 1984; Pepperdine, 1986. *Publications:* The Sandberg Watch Collection, 1998. *Recreations:* horse racing, bridge, cricket, horology. *Address:* Field House, Wheatsheaf Enclosure, Liphook, Hants GU30 7EJ. *Clubs:* White's, Garrick, MCC; Surrey CC (Pres. 1988), Hampshire CC.

SANDBY-THOMAS, Rachel Mary, CB 2012; Director General, Enterprise and Skills and Legal Services (formerly Legal Business and Skills), Department for Business, Innovation and Skills, since 2012; *b* 25 May 1963; *d* of Dr Paul and Mary Sandby-Thomas; *m* 1999, Richard Gough; two *s. Educ:* St Catharine's Coll., Cambridge (BA Law (double 1st) 1985). Admitted solicitor, 1989; Linklaters & Paines, 1987–92; Legal Adviser: Legal Advrs, HM Treasury, 1993–95; Legal Advrs, Cabinet Office, 1995–97; Attorney General's Chambers, 1997–99; DoH, 1999–2004; Legal Advrs, Cabinet Office, 2004; Dir, Legal Services B, DTI, 2004–07; Dir, Tax Law Gp, HMRC, 2007–08; Solicitor and Dir Gen., Legal Services, then Dir Gen., Legal, People and Communications, BERR, later BIS, 2008–12. *Recreations:* reading, socialising, family. *Address:* Department for Business, Innovation and Skills, 1 Victoria Street, SW1H 0ET. *T:* (020) 7215 3039. *E:* Rachel.Sandby-Thomas@bis.gsi.gov.uk.

SANDELL, Terence, (Terry), OBE 1991; consultant and researcher, since 2010; Director, Cultural Futures LLP, since 2010; Senior Associate, St Antony's College, Oxford, since 2010; Head, EU-Eastern Partnership Cultural Programme, Kyiv, since 2015; *b* 8 Sept. 1948; *s* of James William Sandell and Helen Elizabeth McCombie; *m* 1984, Kate Ling; two *s. Educ:* Watford Grammar Sch. for Boys; Univ. of Nottingham (BA Hons); Univ. of Edinburgh; City Univ. (MA with Dist.). VSO, Berber, N Sudan, 1970–72. Joined British Council, 1974: Asst Rep. Dir, Omdurman Centre, Sudan, 1974–78; Regional Officer, Soviet Union and Mongolia, London, 1978–81; 1st Sec. (Cultural), British Embassy, Moscow, 1981–83; Asst Rep., Vienna, 1983–86, Rep. 1986–89; Projects Manager, Soviet Union, London, 1989; Dir, Soviet Union/CIS, and Cultural Counsellor, British Embassy, Moscow, 1989–92; attachment to Dept of Arts Policy and Management, City Univ., 1992–93; Consultant, Arts Policy Develt, British Council, 1993–94; Dir, Visiting Arts Office of GB and NI, subseq. Visiting Arts, 1994–2005; Dir, Ukraine, British Council, and Cultural Counsellor, British Embassy, Kyiv, 2005–08; Special Advr (Arts), British Council, 2008–10. Chairman, Council of Europe Review of Cultural Policy: Russian Fedn, 1995–96 and 2011–13; Romania, 1998–99; Georgia, 2000–02; Azerbaijan, 2000–02; Armenia, 2003; Ukraine, 2005–07; Co-Dir, Nat. Cultural Policy Review of Russian Fedn, 2011–13; Sen. Expert, EU Eastern Partnership Culture Prog., 2011–14. Dir, British-Ukrainian Soc., 2008–14. Trustee, Academia Rossica, 2000–. Hon. Doktor Nauk Ukrainian Acad. of Pedagog. Scis, 2008. *Recreations:* appreciation of beauty, cultures and people, thinking, walking, l'art de vivre. *E:* terry.sandell@gmail.com.

SANDER, Her Honour Audrey Olga Helen; a Circuit Judge, 1995–2003; *b* 10 Nov. 1936; *d* of Ernest Sander and Marian Sander; *m* 1963, Prof. Adrian Gale; one *s* two *d. Educ:* St Paul's Girls' Sch.; Somerville Coll., Oxford (MA Jurisprudence). Called to the Bar, Gray's Inn, 1960; in practice at the Bar, 1960–77; Editl Asst, Legal Action Gp, 1978–83; admitted solicitor, 1986; practised as solicitor, 1986–95 (at Gill Akaster, 1989–95); Asst Recorder, 1990–94; Recorder, 1994–95. Legal Mem., Mental Health Rev. Tribunals, 1992–2011; Mem., Parole Bd of England and Wales, 2000–06. Civil and Family Mediator. *Address:* c/o Clerksroom, Equity House, Blackbrook Park Avenue, Taunton, Som TA1 2PX.

SANDERS, Adrian Mark; *b* 25 April 1959; *s* of late John Sanders and Helen Sanders; *m* 1992, Alison Nortcliffe. *Educ:* Torquay Boys' Grammar Sch. Vice Pres., Nat. League of Young Liberals, 1985. Campaigns Officer, Assoc. of Liberal Councillors, 1986–89; Parly Officer, Lib Dem Whips' Office, 1989–90; Res. Officer, Assoc. of Lib Dem Councillors, 1990–92; Project Officer, Paddy Ashdown, MP, 1992–93; Policy Officer, NCVO, 1993–94; Grants Advr, Southern Assoc. of Voluntary Action Gps for Europe, 1994. Mem. (L) Torbay BC, 1984–86. Contested (Lib Dem): Torbay, 1992; Devon and Plymouth East, EP elecn, 1994. MP (Lib Dem) Torbay, 1997–2015; contested (Lib Dem) same seat, 2015. Lib Dem spokesman: on local govt and housing (on housing, 1997–2001, and on local govt, 1999–2001); on tourism, 2001–05; a Lib Dem Whip, 1997–2001; Lib Dem Dep. Chief Whip, 2006–10. Member: DCMS Select Cttee, 2005–15; Transport Select Cttee, 2012–15; Chairs Panel, 2014–15. Chm., All Pty Diabetes Gp, 1997–2015; Pres., Parly Diabetes Global Network, 2013–15. Vice Pres., League Against Cruel Sports, 2013–.

SANDERS, Prof. Dale, PhD, ScD; FRS 2001; Director, John Innes Centre, since 2010; *b* 13 May 1953; *s* of Leslie G. D. Sanders and Daphne M. Sanders; *m* 1983, Marcelle Mékiès (*d* 2005); three *d. Educ:* Hemel Hempstead Grammar Sch.; Univ. of York (BA); Darwin Coll., Cambridge (PhD 1978, ScD 1993). James Hudson Brown Res. Fellow, 1978–79, Post-doctoral Res. Associate, 1979–83, Sch. of Medicine, Yale Univ.; Department of Biology,

University of York: Lectr, 1983–89; Reader, 1989–92; Prof., 1992–2010; Hd of Dept, 2004–10; Hon. Vis. Prof., 2010–. Hon. Prof., UEA, 2010–. Nuffield Foundn Sci. Res. Fellow, 1989–90; Royal Soc./Leverhulme Trust Sen. Res. Fellow, 1997–98. President's Medal, Soc. for Exptl Biol., 1987; Körber Eur. Sci. Award, 2001. *Publications:* numerous refereed articles in learned jls. *Recreations:* early music, literature, talking and walking with family and friends, cooking. *Address:* John Innes Centre, Norwich Research Park, Colney, Norwich NR4 7UH. *T:* (01603) 450000.

SANDERS, Prof. David John, PhD; FBA 2005; Professor of Government, since 1993, and Regius Professor of Political Science, since 2014, University of Essex; *b* 19 Dec. 1950; *s* of John Sanders and Nora Sanders; *m* 2001, Gillian Wills; three *s* one *d. Educ:* John Port Sch., Etwall; Loughborough Univ. (BSc); Univ. of Essex (MA; PhD). University of Essex: Lectr, 1975–88, Sen. Lectr, 1988–90, Reader, 1990–93, in Government; Pro Vice Chancellor for Res., 1997–2001 and 2011–15. Vis. Prof., Univ. of Wisconsin-Madison, 1981–82. *Publications:* Patterns of Political Instability, 1981; Lawmaking and Co-operation in International Politics, 1986; Losing an Empire, Finding a Role, 1990; (jtly) On Message, 1997; Political Choice in Britain, 2004; Performance Politics, 2009; Affluence, Austerity and Electoral Change in Britain, 2013; The Political Integration of Ethnic Minorities in Britain, 2013; over 70 articles in learned jls. *Recreations:* playing folk music in pubs, walking. *Address:* Department of Government, University of Essex, Wivenhoe Park, Colchester CO4 3SQ. *T:* (01206) 872759. *E:* sanders@essex.ac.uk.

SANDERS, Donald Neil, AO 1994; CB 1983; Chief Executive, 1987–92 and Managing Director, 1991–92, Commonwealth Bank of Australia; *b* Sydney, 21 June 1927; *s* of L. G. and R. M. Sanders; *m* 1952, Betty Elaine, *d* of W. B. and E. M. Constance; four *s* one *d. Educ:* Wollongong High Sch.; Univ. of Sydney (BEc). Commonwealth Bank of Australia, 1943–60; Australian Treasury, 1956; Bank of England, 1960; Reserve Bank of Australia, 1960–87: Supt, Credit Policy Div., Banking Dept, 1964–66; Dep. Manager: Banking Dept, 1966–67; Res. Dept, 1967–70; Aust. Embassy, Washington DC, 1968; Chief Manager: Securities Markets Dept, 1970–72; Banking and Finance Dept, 1972–74; Adviser and Chief Manager, Banking and Finance Dept, 1974–75; Dep. Governor and Dep. Chm., 1975–87; Man. Dir, Commonwealth Banking Corp., 1987–91. Chm., H-G Ventures Ltd, 1995–2000; Director: Queensland Investment Corp., 1992–98; Lend Lease Corp. Ltd, 1992–99; Australian Chamber Orch. Ltd, 1993–99; MLC Ltd, 1994–99 (Chm., 1998–99). *Address:* 106 Blaxland Road, Wentworth Falls, NSW 2782, Australia.

SANDERS, Prof. Ed Parish, FBA 1989; Arts and Sciences Professor of Religion, Duke University, 1990–2005; *b* 18 April 1937; *s* of Mildred Sanders (*née* Parish) and Eula Thomas Sanders; *m* 1st, 1963, Becky Jill Hall (marr. diss. 1978); one *d*; 2nd, 1996, Rebecca N. Gray. *Educ:* Texas Wesleyan College (BA); Southern Methodist Univ. (BD); Union Theological Seminary, NY (ThD). Asst Prof. of Religious Studies, McMaster Univ., 1966–70, Associate Prof., 1970–74, Prof., 1974–88; Dean Ireland's Prof. of Exegesis of Holy Scripture, Oxford Univ., 1984–89. Visiting Professor: Jewish Theol. Seminary, 1980; Chair of Judeo-Christian Studies, Tulane Univ., 1980; Walter G. Mason Dist. Vis. Prof., Coll. of William and Mary in Virginia, 1981; Vis. Fellow Commoner, Trinity Coll., Cambridge, 1982; Kraft-Hiatt Vis. Prof., Brandeis Univ., 1999. Donnellan Lectr, TCD, 1982. Fellow, Amer. Acad. of Arts and Scis, 2003. *Publications:* The Tendencies of the Synoptic Tradition, 1969; Paul and Palestinian Judaism, 1977, 2nd edn 1981; (ed) Jewish and Christian Self-Definition, vol. I, The Shaping of Christianity in the Second and Third Centuries, 1980, vol. II, Aspects of Judaism in the Graeco-Roman Period, 1981, vol. III, Self-Definition in the Graeco-Roman World, 1982; Paul, The Law and the Jewish People, 1983; Jesus and Judaism, 1985, 3rd edn 1987; (ed) Jesus, The Gospels and the Church, 1987; (with Margaret Davies) Studying the Synoptic Gospels, 1989; Jewish Law from Jesus to the Mishnah, 1990; Paul, 1991; Judaism: practice and belief 63 BCE to 66 BCE, 1992; The Historical Figure of Jesus, 1993; Paul: a very short introduction, 2001; articles in NT Studies, Jl of Biblical Literature, Harvard Theol. Review, Jewish Quarterly Review.

SANDERS, Prof. Jeremy Keith Morris, CBE 2014; FRS 1995; Professor, Department of Chemistry, 1996–2015, and Pro-Vice-Chancellor for Institutional Affairs, 2011–15, University of Cambridge; Fellow of Selwyn College, Cambridge, since 1976; *b* 3 May 1948; *s* of Sidney Sanders and Sylvia (*née* Rutman); *m* 1972, Louise Elliott; one *s* one *d. Educ:* Imperial Coll., London (BSc, ARCS Chem. 1969); PhD 1972, MA 1974, ScD 2001, Cantab. FRSC, CChem. Junior Res. Fellow, Christ's Coll., Cambridge, 1972; NATO/EMBO Fellow, Stanford Univ., 1972–73; Cambridge University: Demonstrator, 1973–78; Lectr in Chemistry, 1978–92; Reader in Chemistry and Asst Hd, Dept of Chemistry, 1992–96; Dep. Hd, 1998–2000, Hd, 2000–06, Dept of Chem.; Dep. Vice-Chancellor, 2006–10; Hd, Sch. of Physical Scis, 2009–11; Mem. Council, 1999–2002; Chm., Allocations Cttee, 1999–2000; Chm., Bd of Mgt, Cambridge Prog. for Industry, 2003–07. Chm., Chem. sub-panel, 2008 RAE, 2004–08. Trustee, Cambridge Foundn, 2007–13; Dep. Chm., NW Cambridge Syndicate, 2011–15; Syndic, Fitzwilliam Mus., 2012–14. Pres., Bürgenstock Conf., Switzerland, 2011. FRSA 1997. Associate Ed., New Jl of Chemistry, 1998–2000; Chm. Editl Bd, Chem. Soc. Reviews, 2000–02; Ed.-in-Chief, Royal Soc. Open Sci., 2016–. Pfizer Awards, Pfizer plc, 1984, 1988; Royal Society of Chemistry: Meldola Medal, 1975; Hickinbottom Award, 1981; Josef Loschmidt Prize, 1994; Pedler Lect. and Medal, 1996; Fellow, Japan Soc. for the Promotion of Science, 2002; Izatt-Christensen Award for Macrocyclic Chemistry, USA, 2003; Davy Medal, Royal Soc., 2009. *Publications:* (with B. K. Hunter) Modern NMR Spectroscopy, 1987, 2nd edn 1993; contribs to chem. and biochem. jls. *Recreations:* family, cooking, music. *Address:* University Chemical Laboratory, Lensfield Road, Cambridge CB2 1EW. *T:* (01223) 336411, *Fax:* (01223) 336017. *Club:* Athenæum.

SANDERS, Rear-Adm. Jeremy Thomas, CB 1994; OBE 1982; Commander British Forces, Gibraltar, 1992–94; *b* 23 Nov. 1942; *s* of late Thomas Sanders and Pauline (*née* Woodfield-Smith); *m* 1st, 1966, Judith Rosemary Jones (*d* 2003); two *d*; 2nd, 2005, Jane Elizabeth Cambrook. *Educ:* Norwood Sch., Exeter; Pangbourne Coll. BRNC, Dartmouth, 1960; appts include: Lieut i/c HMS Chilcompton and Kellington, 1968–69; long communications course, HMS Mercury, 1970; Lt Comdr on staff of Flag Officer, Submarines, 1974–76; Comdr i/c HMS Salisbury, 1977–78; ndc 1979; SO Ops to Flag Officer, 1st Flotilla, 1981–83; Capt., 8th Frigate Sqdn and i/c HMS Andromeda, 1985–87; Dir, Maritime Tactical Sch., 1987–89; Chief Naval Signal Officer, 1989–90; Dir, Naval Warfare, 1990–92. Trustee: Falkland Islands Memorial Chapel, 2003–12 (Chm., 2006–12); RN Submarine Mus., 2004–06. JP S Hants 1997–2006 (Dep. Chm. Bench, 2003, 2004). *Recreations:* countryside, family and travel. *Clubs:* MCC, Anchorites; Exeter Flotilla.

SANDERS, John Leslie Yorath; HM Diplomatic Service, retired; *b* 5 May 1929; *s* of late Reginald Yorath Sanders and Gladys Elizabeth Sanders (*née* Blything); *m* 1953, Brigit Mary Lucine Altounyan (*d* 1999); one *s* two *d. Educ:* Dulwich Coll. Prep. Sch.; Cranleigh School. Higher Dip. in Furniture Prodn and Design, London Coll. of Furniture, 1982. Nat. Service in HM Forces (RA), 1948–50; entered HM Foreign Service, 1950; FO, 1950–52; MECAS, Lebanon, 1953; Damascus, 1954–55; Bahrain, 1955–56; Vice-Consul, Basra, 1956–60; Oriental Sec., Rabat, 1960–63; FO, 1964–67; 1st Sec., Beirut, 1968–70; 1st Sec. and Head of Chancery, Mexico City, 1970–73; Counsellor, Khartoum, 1973–75; Counsellor, Beirut, 1975–76; Dir of Res., FCO, 1976–78; Ambassador to Panama, 1978–80. *Publications:* contrib. to Archaeologia Aeliana. *Recreations:* genealogy, music.

SANDERS, Michael David, FRCS, FRCP, FRCOphth; Consultant Ophthalmologist, National Hospital for Neurology and Neurosurgery, 1969–99; *b* 19 Sept. 1935; *s* of Norris Manley Sanders and Gertrude Florence Sanders (*née* Hayley); *m* 1969, Thalia Margaret Garlick; one *s* one *d. Educ:* Tonbridge Sch.; Guy's Hosp., Univ. of London (MB BS). DO RCS/RCP; FRCS 1967; FRCP 1977; FRCOphth 1990 (Hon. FRCOphth 2001). Guy's Hosp., 1954–60; Moorfields Eye Hosp., 1964–67; Univ. of California, San Francisco, 1967–68; Consultant Ophthalmologist, St Thomas' Hosp., 1972–96. Civilian Consultant, RAF, 1975–2000; Dep. Hospitaller, St John Ophthalmic Hosp., Jerusalem, 1992. Visiting Professor: Mayo Clinic, 1979; Univ. of New South Wales, 1982; NY Eye and Ear Infirmary, 1995. Lectures: Middlemore, Birmingham and Midlands Eye Hosp., 1985; Percival J. Hay Meml, N of England Ophthalmol Soc., 1986; Ida Mann, Oxford Univ., 1987; Sir Stewart Duke Elder, Ophthalmol. Soc. UK, 1987; Lettsomian, Med. Soc. London, 1988; Sir William Bowman, RCOphth, 1996; Montgomery, Irish Coll. of Ophthalmologists, 1997. Trustee, Frost Charitable Trust, 1974–96 (Chm., 1996–); Med. Advr, Iris Fund for Prevention of Blindness, 1982–97 (Mem. Council, 1997–2003); Pres., Internat. Neuro-Ophthalmology Soc., 1990– (Mem. Council, 1974–97); Mem. Council, Gift of Sight, 2009–. Chm., Friends of Chawton Ch, 2003–. *Publications:* Topics in Neuro-Ophthalmology, 1978; Computerised Tomography in Neuro-Ophthalmology, 1982; Common Problems in Neuro-Ophthalmology, 1997. *Recreations:* golf, collecting. *Address:* Chawton Lodge, Chawton, near Alton, Hants GU34 1SL. *T:* (01420) 86681. *Clubs:* Royal Air Force; Hankley Common Golf (Farnham).

SANDERS, Neil John Tait; His Honour Judge Sanders; a Circuit Judge, since 2010; *b* Suva, Fiji, 17 April 1953; *s* of Sir Robert (Tait) Sanders, *qv*; *m* 1984, Frances Ann Spencer; two *s* one *d. Educ:* Fettes Coll., Edinburgh; Pembroke Coll., Cambridge (BA 1974); Coll. of Law. Called to the Bar, Inner Temple, 1975; a Recorder, 2001–10. *Recreations:* golf, sailing, tennis, theatre, music. *Address:* Snaresbrook Crown Court, 75 Hollybush Hill, Snaresbrook, E11 1QW. *Clubs:* Royal Solent Yacht, Yarmouth Sailing, Clapham Common All Weather Tennis.

SANDERS, Nicholas John, CB 1998; PhD; Higher Education Adviser, Department for Education and Skills, 2004–05; *b* 14 Sept. 1946; *s* of Ivor and Mollie Sanders; *m* 1971, Alison Ruth Carter; one *s* one *d. Educ:* King Edward's Sch., Birmingham; Magdalene Coll., Cambridge (MA, PhD). Joined DES, 1971, subseq. Dept for Educn, then DFEE, then DFES; Principal Private Sec. to Sec. of State, 1974–75; Private Sec. to Prime Minister, 1978–81; Prin. Finance Officer, 1989–93; Hd, Teachers Br., 1993–95; Dir, Teachers, Funding and Curriculum, 1995–99; Dir for Higher Education, 1999–2003. Mem. Council, Univ. of Warwick, 2004–10 and 2011–14. Hon. LLD Manchester, 2004.

SANDERS, Nicholas Paul Martin; a District Judge (Magistrates' Courts), Manchester, since 2013 (Merseyside, 2004–13, Cheshire, 2007–13); *b* 25 Feb. 1958; *s* of late Oswald Sanders and Betty Sanders (*née* Hooper); *m* 1981, Alexandra (*née* Langham); two *d. Educ:* Exeter Sch.; Britannia Royal Naval Coll.; Univ. of Exeter (LLB Hons). RN officer, 1976–89. Called to the Bar, Middle Temple, 1987; admitted solicitor, 1990; Solicitor: Linford Brown, Exmouth, 1989–94; Rundle Walker, Exeter, 1994–2001; Sen. Magistrate and HM Coroner, Falkland Is and British Antarctic Territory, 2001–04; Sen. Magistrate, Ascension Is., 2004–06. Dep. Chm., Adv. Cttee on Conscientious Objectors, 2014–. Reader, C of E, 2013–. *Recreations:* English canals, motor cycles, association croquet. *Address:* c/o Manchester City Magistrates' Court, Crown Square, Manchester M60 1PR.

SANDERS, Maj. Gen. Patrick Nicholas Yardley Monrad, CBE 2012 (OBE 2004); DSO 2008; General Officer Commanding 3rd (UK) Division, since 2015; *b* Tidworth, Hants, 6 April 1966; *s* of John Sanders and Marianne Sanders (*née* Monrad); *m* 1992, Fiona Bullen; one *s. Educ:* Worth Abbey; RMA Sandhurst; Cranfield Univ. (MA Defence Technol.). Commnd 3RGJ, 1986; acsc 1997–99; COS 1st Mech. Bde, 2001–03; CO 2RGJ, then 4 Rifles, 2004–07; Col Army Strategy, 2008–09; Comd 20 Armoured Bde, 2009–12; CDS Liaison Officer to Chm. Jt Chiefs of Staff, 2012; Hd, Overseas Ops, 2012–13; ACDS (Ops), 2013–15. Dep. Col, Rifles, 2012–; Hon. Col, Manchester Univ. OTC, 2013–; Col Comdt, Small Arms Sch. Corps, 2014–. Pres., Army Rifle Assoc., 2013–. *Publications:* articles in RUSI Jl, BAR and Defence Acad. Yearbook. *Recreations:* ski-ing, jagd, Spurs, whisky, cycling, sailing, golf. *Address:* c/o Regimental Headquarters The Rifles, Peninsula Barracks, Romsey Road, Winchester, Hants SO23 8TS. *T:* (01962) 828527.

SANDERS, Peter Basil, CBE 1993; Chief Executive, Commission for Racial Equality, 1988–93 (Director, 1977–88); *b* 9 June 1938; *s* of Basil Alfred Horace Sanders and Ellen May Sanders (*née* Cockrell); *m* 1st, 1961, Janet Valerie (*née* Child) (marr. diss. 1984); two *s* one *d*; 2nd, 1988, Anita Jackson. *Educ:* Queen Elizabeth's Grammar Sch., Barnet; Wadham Coll., Oxford (MA, DPhil). Administrative Officer, Basutoland, 1961–66; Research in Oxford for DPhil, 1966–70; Officer, Min. of Defence, 1971–73; Race Relations Bd: Principal Conciliation Officer, 1973–74; Dep. Chief Officer, 1974–77. Chm., Stop Stansted Expansion, 2004–. *Publications:* Lithoko: Sotho Praise-Poems (ed jtly and trans. with an Introd. and Notes), 1974; Moshoeshoe, Chief of the Sotho, 1975; The Simple Annals: the history of an Essex and East End family, 1989; (ed jtly) Race Relations in Britain: a developing agenda, 1998; The Last of the Queen's Men: a Lesotho experience, 2000; (with C. Murray) Medicine Murder in Colonial Lesotho: the anatomy of a moral crisis, 2005; 'Throwing Down White Man': Cape rule and misrule in colonial Lesotho, 1871–1884, 2011. *Address:* 31D Church Street, Saffron Walden, Essex CB10 1JW. *T:* (01799) 520411.

SANDERS, Sir Robert (Tait), KBE 1980; CMG 1974; HMOCS; Secretary to the Cabinet, Government of Fiji, 1970–79; Treaties Adviser, Government of Fiji, 1985–87; *b* 2 Feb. 1925; *s* of late A. S. W. Sanders and Charlotte McCulloch; *m* 1951, Barbara, *d* of G. Sutcliffe; two *s* (and one *s* decd). *Educ:* Canmore Public Sch., Dunfermline; Dunfermline High Sch.; Fettes Coll., Edinburgh; Cambridge Univ. (Major Open Classical Schol., Pembroke Coll., 1943; John Stewart of Rannoch Schol. in Latin and Greek, 1947; 1st cl. Hons, Pts I and II of Classical Tripos); London Sch. of Economics, 1949–50; SOAS, 1949–50. Served War, 1943–46: Lieut, 1st Bn the Royal Scots, India and Malaya. Sir Arthur Thomson Travelling Schol., 1948; Sir William Browne Medal for Latin Epigram, 1948; MA (Cantab) 1951. Joined HM Overseas Civil Service, Fiji, as Dist Officer, 1950; Sec. to Govt of Tonga, 1956–58; Sec., Coconut Commn of Enquiry, 1963; MLC, Fiji, 1963–64; Sec. for Natural Resources, 1965–67; Actg Sec. Fijian Affairs, and Actg Chm. Native Lands and Fisheries Commn, 1967; MEC, Fiji, 1967; Sec. to Chief Minister and to Council of Ministers, 1967; apptd Sec. to Cabinet, 1970, also Sec. for Foreign Affairs, 1970–74, Sec. for Home Affairs, 1972–74 and Sec. for Information, 1975–76. Fiji Independence Medal, 1970; 25th Anniversary of Fiji's Independence Medal, 1995. *Publications:* Interlude in Fiji, 1963; Fiji Treaty List, 1987; articles in Corona, jl of HMOCS. *Recreations:* languages, travel, golf, music. *Address:* 6 Park Manor, Crieff PH7 4LJ. *Club:* Royal Scots (Edinburgh).

See also N. J. T. Sanders.

SANDERS, His Honour Roger Benedict; a Circuit Judge, 1987–2005; Resident Judge, Harrow Crown Court, 1999–2005; *b* 1 Oct. 1940; *s* of late Maurice and Lilian Sanders; *m* 1st, 1969, Susan Brenner (marr. diss. 1992); two *s* (one *d* decd); 2nd, 1998, Dee Connolly, *e d* of John and Mary Connolly. *Educ:* Highgate School. Co-founder, Inner Temple Debating Soc., 1961, Chm. 1962. Called to the Bar, Inner Temple, 1965; South Eastern Circuit. Metropolitan Stipendiary Magistrate, 1980–87; a Recorder, 1986–87. A Chm., Inner London Juvenile Courts, 1980–87; Chm., Legal Cttee, Inner London Juvenile Panel, 1983–86; First Chm., No 1 (London S) Regional Duty Solicitor Cttee, 1984–85; Chm., NW London Adv.

Cttee (Magistrates), 2008–10 (Dep. Chm., 2004–08); Member: Inner London Magistrates' Training Panel, 1983–87; Mental Health Review Tribunal, 1990–2000, 2006–10; Middx Probation Cttee, 1999–2001; Restorative Justice Panel, 2003–05; occasional facilitator and assessor for intermediaries and professional witnesses, City Law Sch., City Univ. London, 2007–. Hon. Pres., Middx Br., Magistrates' Assoc., 2009–10. Chairman, Walker School Assoc. (Southgate), 1976, 1977; Schools' Debating Assoc. Judge, 1976–93. Mem., Haringey Schools Liaison Group, 1979. Hon. Fellow, Univ. of E London, 1993. *Recreations:* painting, writing, travel.

SANDERS, Sir Ronald (Michael), KCMG 2002 (CMG 1997); KCN 2001; Hon. AM 2012; international consultant and writer; Senior Ambassador with Ministerial rank, Antigua and Barbuda, 1999–2004; High Commissioner for Antigua and Barbuda in London, 1984–87 and 1995–2004; non-resident Ambassador to France and Germany, 1996–2004; *b* Guyana, 26 Jan. 1948; *m* 1975, Susan Indrani (*née* Ramphal). *Educ:* Sacred Heart RC Sch., Guyana; Boston Univ., USA; Sussex Univ., UK. Gen. Man., Guyana Broadcasting Service, 1973–76; Communication Cons. to Pres., Caribbean Develt Bank, Barbados, 1977; Cons. to Govt of Antigua, 1977–81; Advr to For. Minister of Antigua and Barbuda, 1981–82; Dep. Perm. Rep. to UN, 1982–83; Ambassador to UNESCO and EEC, 1983–87, to FRG, 1986–87; Vis. Fellow, Oxford Univ., 1988–89; Ambassador to WTO, 2000–04. Director: Swiss Amer. Nat. Bank, Antigua, 1990–97; Guyana Telephone and Telegraph Co., 1991–97; Innovative Communications Corp., USA, 1998–2008; US Virgin Islands Telephone Co., 2003–08; Belize Telephone Ltd, 2004–05; consultant, Internat. Relns, Atlantic Tele Network, USA, 1989–97; Advr to Commonwealth Secretariat and World Bank on Small States, 2002. Dep. Chm., 2002–03, Chm., 2003–04, Caribbean Financial Action Task Force. Member: Inter-Govtl Council, Internat. Prog. for Develt of Communications, UNESCO, 1983–87; Exec. Bd, UNESCO, 1985–87; RIIA, 1987–; Internat. Inst. of Communications, 1984–2009; Caribbean Adv. Bd to FCO, 2007–08; and Rapporteur, Eminent Persons Gp advising Commonwealth Hds of Govt on reform of Commonwealth, 2010–11; Friends of Democratic Charter, 2011–. Sen. Res. Fellow, Inst. of Commonwealth Studies, Univ. of London, 2012–; Sen. Associate Fellow, Massey Coll., Univ. of Toronto, 2015–. Hon. DLitt W Indies, 2014. *Publications:* Broadcasting in Guyana, 1977; Antigua and Barbuda: transition, trial, triumph, 1984; (ed) Inseparable Humanity—an anthology of reflections of Shridath Ramphal, Commonwealth Secretary-General, 1988; (ed) Antigua Vision, Caribbean Reality: perspectives of Prime Minister Lester B. Bird, 2002; Crumbled Small: the Commonwealth Caribbean in world politics, 2005; contrib. chapters in several books; several contribs to internat. jls on the Commonwealth, the Caribbean, and the Small States, also political commentaries in weekly leading newspapers in Caribbean and on internet news websites. *Recreations:* reading, cinema. *Clubs:* Royal Automobile, St James's.

SANDERS, Prof. Roy, FRCS; consultant plastic surgeon, 1974–2006; former Consultant: Mount Vernon Centre for Plastic Surgery; BUPA Hospital Harpenden; BUPA Hospital Bushey; Humana Hospital; Bishops Wood Hospital, Northwood; *b* 20 Aug. 1937; *s* of Leslie John Sanders and Marguerite Alice (*née* Knight); *m* 1st, 1961, Ann Ruth Costar (marr. diss.); two *s* one *d*; 2nd, 1984, Fleur Annette Chandler, Baroness von Balajthy (*d* 2011). *Educ:* Hertford Grammar Sch.; Charing Cross Hosp. Med. Sch. (BSc Hons Anatomy, MB, BS). LRCP 1962; FRCS 1967. Various hosp. appts; Sen. Lectr in Plastic Surgery, London Univ. and Hon. Cons. Plastic Surgeon, Mt Vernon Centre for Plastic Surgery, 1972–74; Cons. Plastic Surgeon, St Andrew's Hosp., Billericay and St Bart's Hosp., 1974–76; Hon. Sen. Lectr, London Univ., 1976–93; Hd, Service Dept, Plastic Maxillo-Facial and Oral Surgery, Mt Vernon Hosp., 1986–2003; Hon. Prof., UCL, 1993–. Sec., Brit. Assoc. Aesthetic Plastic Surgeons, 1984–87; Pres., Brit. Assoc. Plastic Surgeons, 1993 (Sec., 1987–90); Mem. Senate, RCS, 1994–96. OC Light Cavalry, HAC, 1996–2004. *Publications:* scientific pubns in med. jls and textbooks. *Recreations:* equestrian pursuits, watercolour painting, books. *Address:* 77 Harley Street, W1G 8QN. *T:* (020) 7935 7417; Upper Rye Farmhouse, Moreton-in-Marsh, Glos GL56 9AB. *T:* (01608) 650542. *Clubs:* Garrick, Honourable Artillery Company.

SANDERS, Sebastian; Stable Jockey to Sir Mark Prescott, since 1997; *b* 25 Sept. 1971; *s* of Kevin Sanders and Jean Sanders (now Cooper); *m* 1998, Leona Robertson; one *d*. *Educ:* Lakeside Sch., Tamworth, Staffs. Champion Apprentice, 1995; winner: July Cup, on Compton Place, 1997; Irish 2000 Guineas, on Bachelor Duke, 2004; Preis von Europa, on Albanova, 2004; Nunthorpe, on Bahamian Pirate, 2004; French Prix de Diane Hermes, on Confidential Lady, 2006; Oaks, on Look Here, 2008. (Jt) Champion Flat Jockey, 2007. *Recreations:* golf, scuba diving.

SANDERS, Prof. Thomas Andrew Bruce, PhD, DSc; Professor of Nutrition and Dietetics, 1994–2014, now Emeritus, and Head, Diabetes and Nutritional Sciences Division, 2010–14, School of Medicine, King's College London; *b* Eastbourne, 29 Dec. 1949; *s* of John Bruce Sanders and Annie Sanders; *m* 1973, Linda Marie Fassbender; one *s* one *d*. *Educ:* Eastbourne Coll.; Queen Elizabeth Coll., Univ. of London (BSc Nutrition 1971; PhD 1977; DSc 1996). Registered Public Health Nutritionist 2001. Prog. Associate, UNICEF, 1971–73; Res. Asst, Kingston Hosp., 1973–77; Queen Elizabeth College: Rank Prize Funds Fellow, 1977–79; Res. Fellow, 1979–82; Lectr in Nutrition, 1982–84; King's College London: Lectr in Nutrition, 1984–91; Reader, 1991–94; Head: Dept of Nutrition and Dietetics, 1995–2001; Div. of Nutritional Scis, Sch. of Biomed. and Health Scis, 2003–10. Member: UK Scientific Adv. Cttee on Novel Foods and Processes, 1994–2001; UK Scientific Adv. Cttee, Jt Health Claims Initiative, 2001–08; WHO/FAO Expert consultation on role of fats and fatty acids in human nutrition, 2008. Hon. Nutritional Dir, HEART UK, 2005–. Scientific Gov., 2000–, Trustee, 2005–14, British Nutrition Foundn. MRSocMed 1986, FRSocMed 2014; Member: Nutrition Soc., 1971; Internat. Atherosclerosis Soc., 1983; British Atherosclerosis Soc., 1993; Biochemical Soc., 1994; Amer. Heart Assoc., 1995; Assoc. for Nutrition, 2012; Amer. Soc. for Nutrition, 2012. FHEA 2007; Fellow, Assoc. for Nutrition, 2013. *Publications:* The Vegetarian's Healthy Diet Book, 1986; The Food Revolution, 1991; You Don't Have to Diet!, 1994; Dietary Fats, 1994, 2nd edn 1999; Foods that Harm, Foods that Heal, 1999; The Molecular Basis of Human Nutrition, 2003; over 250 articles in scientific jls. *Recreations:* theatre, opera, cinema, walking, surfing, sailing, diving, watching wildlife, travel. *Address:* School of Medicine, King's College London, Room 4.72 Franklin Wilkins Building, 150 Stamford Street, SE1 9NH. *T:* (020) 7848 4273, *Fax:* (020) 7848 4171. *E:* tom.sanders@kcl.ac.uk.

SANDERS, William George, CB 1991; CEng, FRINA; RCNC; Head of Royal Corps of Naval Constructors, 1986–91; Director General, Submarines, Ministry of Defence (PE), 1985–91; *b* 22 Jan. 1936; *s* of George and Alice Irene Sanders; *m* 1956, Marina Charlotte Burford; two *s* one *d*. *Educ:* Public Secondary Sch., Plymouth; Devonport Dockyard Tech. Coll.; RN Coll., Greenwich. Asst Constructor, Ship Dept, Admiralty, 1961–68; FNCO Western Fleet, 1968–70; Constructor, Ship Dept, MoD (Navy), 1970–77; Principal Naval Overseer, Scotland, 1977–79; Marconi Space and Defence Systems, 1979–81; Project Director, Type 23, 1981–83; DG Future Material Projects (Naval), MoD (PE), 1983–85. *Recreations:* golf, painting, gardening. *Address:* 12 New Lawns, Melksham, Wilts SN12 7UB.

SANDERSON, family name of **Baron Sanderson of Bowden**.

SANDERSON OF AYOT; 2nd Baron *cr* 1960, title disclaimed by the heir, Dr Alan Lindsay Sanderson, 1971.

SANDERSON OF BOWDEN, Baron *cr* 1985 (Life Peer), of Melrose in the District of Ettrick and Lauderdale; **Charles Russell Sanderson,** Kt 1981; Chairman, Clydesdale Bank PLC, 1998–2004 (Director, 1986–87 and since 1994; Deputy Chairman, 1996–98); Vice Lord-Lieutenant, Borders Region (Roxburgh, Ettrick and Lauderdale), 2003–08; *b* 30 April 1933; *s* of Charles Plummer Sanderson and Martha Evelyn Gardiner; *m* 1958, Frances Elizabeth Macaulay; one *s* two *d* (and one *s* decd). *Educ:* St Mary's Sch., Melrose; Trinity Coll., Glenalmond; Scottish Coll. of Textiles, Galashiels; Bradford Coll. (now Bradford Univ.). Commnd Royal Signals, 1952; served: 51 (Highland) Inf. Div. Signal Regt TA, 1953–56, KOSB TA, 1956–58. Partner, Chas P. Sanderson, Wool and Yarn Merchants, Melrose, 1958–87; Chairman: Edinburgh Financial Trust (formerly Yorkshire & Lancashire Investment Trust), 1983–87; Shires Investment Trust, 1984–87; Hawick Cashmere Co., 1991–; Scottish Mortgage & Trust, 1993–2003 (Mem. Bd, 1991–); Scottish Pride plc, 1994–97; Director: United Auctions, 1992–99; Edinburgh Woollen Mills, 1993–97; Watson & Philip, 1993–99; Morrison Construction Group, 1995–2000; Nat. Australia Gp Europe, 1998–2004; Develica Deutschland plc, 2006–; Accsys Technologies plc, 2007–. Minister of State, Scottish Office, 1987–90. Chairman, Roxburgh, Selkirk and Peebles Cons. and Unionist Assoc., 1970–73; Scottish Conservative Unionist Association: Chm. Central and Southern Area, 1974–75; Vice-Pres. 1975–77; Pres. 1977–79; Vice-Chm. Nat. Union of Cons Assocs, 1979–81 (Mem. Exec. Cttee, 1975–); Chm. Exec. Cttee, Nat. Union of Cons. Assocs, 1981–86; Member: Cons. Party Policy Cttee, 1979–86; Standing Adv. Cttee of Parly Candidates, 1979–86 (Vice-Chm. with responsibility for Europe, 1980–81); Chm., Scottish Cons. Party, 1990–93. Chm., Scottish Peers Assoc., 1998–2000. Pres., RHASS, 2002–03. Deacon, Galashiels Manufrs Corp., 1976; Chm., Eildon Housing Assoc., 1978–82. Chm., Abbotsford Trust, 2008–. Mem. Court, Napier Univ., 1994–2001; Governor, St Mary's Sch., Melrose, 1977–87 (Chm., 1998–2004); Mem. Council, Trinity Coll., Glenalmond, 1982–2000 (Chm., 1994–2000). Comr, Gen. Assembly of Ch of Scotland, 1972. Mem. Court, Framework Knitters' Co., 2000– (Master, 2005–06). DL Roxburgh, Ettrick and Lauderdale, 1990. *Recreations:* golf, fishing, amateur operatics (Past Pres., Producer and Mem. Melrose Amateur Operatic Soc.). *Address:* Becketts Field, Bowden, Melrose, Roxburgh TD6 0ST. *T:* (01835) 822736. *Clubs:* Caledonian; Hon. Co. of Edinburgh Golfers (Muirfield).

SANDERSON, Prof. Alexis Godfrey James Slater; Spalding Professor of Eastern Religions and Ethics, University of Oxford, 1992–2015; Fellow of All Souls College, Oxford, since 1992; *b* 28 June 1948; *e s* of J. J. Sanderson, Houghton-le-Spring. *Educ:* Royal Masonic Sch., Watford; Balliol Coll., Oxford (BA 1971). Oxford University: Domus Sen. Schol., Merton Coll., 1971–74; Platnauer Jun. Res. Fellow, Brasenose Coll., 1974–77; Univ. Lectr in Sanskrit, 1977–92; Fellow of Wolfson Coll., 1977–92, Fellow Emeritus, 1992. Petra Kappert Fellow, Centre for Study of Manuscript Cultures, Hamburg Univ., 2012; Vis. Prof., Kyoto Univ., 2012. *Address:* All Souls College, Oxford OX1 4AL.

SANDERSON, Bryan Kaye, CBE 1999; Chairman, Florence Nightingale Foundation, since 2008; *b* 14 Oct. 1940; *s* of Eric and Anne Sanderson; *m* 1966, Sirkka Kärki; one *s* one *d*. *Educ:* Dame Allan's Sch., Newcastle upon Tyne; LSE (BSc Econ.); Dip. Business Studies, IMEDE Lausanne, 1973. VSO Peru, 1962–64; British Petroleum, 1964; Sen. BP rep., SE Asia and China, 1984–87; Chief Exec. Officer, BP Nutrition, 1987–90; CEO, BP Chemicals, then Chief Exec., BP Amoco Chemicals, 1990–2000; Man. Dir, British Petroleum, then BP Amoco, 1992–2000. Chairman: BUPA, 2001–06; Standard Chartered plc, 2003–06 (non-exec. Dir, 2002–06); Northern Rock plc, 2007–08; non-executive Director: Corus (formerly British Steel), 1994–2001; Six Continents plc, 2001–03; Sunderland FC plc, 1997–2006 (Chm., 1998–2004); Argus Media Ltd, 2012–; Chm., Sunderland Area Regeneration Co., 2001–09. Chm., LSC, 2000–04. Mem., DTI Co. Law Steering Gp, 1998–2001. Mem., Cttee of Mgt, King's Fund, 1999–2006. Chm., Home Renaissance Foundn, 2006–. Dir, Durham CCC, 2005–. Gov., LSE, 1997– (Vice-Chm. Govs, 1998–2003). Trustee, Economist, 2006–. Hon. FIChemE 2002. Hon. DBA: Sunderland, 1998; York, 1999. *Recreations:* reading, golf, walking, gardening. *Address:* 40 Netherhall Gardens, Hampstead, NW3 5TP. *T:* (020) 7794 2488.

SANDERSON, Charles Denis; HM Diplomatic Service, retired; Fellow, St Peter's College, Oxford, 1985–96, now Emeritus; *b* 18 Dec. 1934; *s* of Norman and Elsie Sanderson; *m* 1960, Mary Joyce Gillow; one *s* two *d*. *Educ:* Bishopshalt Sch., Hillingdon, Middx; Pembroke Coll., Oxford (MA). National Service, 1953–55; Oxford, 1955–58; British Petroleum Co. Ltd, 1958–64; Second, later First Secretary, Commonwealth Relations Office, 1964–67; First Sec., Kingston, and concurrently, Haiti, 1967–70; Acting Consul, Port au Prince, 1969; First Sec., Head of Chancery and Consul, Panama, 1970–73; First Sec., FCO, 1973–75; Consul (Commercial), British Trade Development Office, New York, 1975–77; Dep. Consul General and Director Industrial Development, New York, 1977–79; Counsellor, Caracas, 1979–84; Hd, W Indian and Atlantic Dept, FCO, 1984–85. Domestic Bursar, 1985–92, Bursar, 1992–96, St Peter's Coll., Oxford. *Address:* Reskajeage Farm, Gwithian, Hayle, Cornwall TR27 5EF. *T:* (01209) 712512.

SANDERSON, Eric Fenton; Chairman: MWB Group Holdings PLC (formerly Marylebone Warwick Balfour plc), 2005–12 (non-executive Director, 2002–12); Schroder UK Mid Cap Fund plc, since 2014 (non-executive Director, 2011–14); *b* 14 Oct. 1951; *s* of Francis Kirton Sanderson and Margarita Shand (*née* Fenton); *m* 1975, Patricia Ann Shaw; three *d*. *Educ:* Morgan Acad., Dundee; Univ. of Dundee (LLB); Harvard Business Sch. (AMP). FCIBS (MCIBS 1991). Touche Ross & Co., CA, 1973–76; CA 1976; British Linen Bank Group Ltd, 1976–97: Corporate Finance Div., 1976–84; Dir, British Linen Bank and Head, Corporate Finance Div., 1984–89; Chief Exec., 1989–97; Chief Exec., Bank of Scotland Treasury Services PLC, 1997–99; Chm., Kwik-Fit Insurance Services Ltd, 2002–03 (Dir, 1999–2002; Man. Dir, 2000–01). Non-executive Director: MyTravel Group (formerly Airtours) plc, 1987–2004 (Dep. Chm., 2001–02; Chm., 2002–04); DLR Ltd, 1999–2001 (Chm., Quality Panel, 2001–05); First Milk Ltd, 2006–12; MWB Malmaison Hldgs Ltd, 2012 (Chm., 2012); MWB Business Exchange plc, 2012; Black Rock Gtr Eur. Investment Trust plc, 2013–. Mem., BRB, 1991–94. Graduates Assessor and Mem. Court, Univ. of Dundee, 2005– (Chm. Court, 2010–). *Recreations:* tennis, photography, gardening. *E:* ericsanderson@blueyonder.co.uk. *Club:* New (Edinburgh).

SANDERSON, Sir Frank (Linton), 3rd Bt *cr* 1920, of Malling Deanery, South Malling, Sussex; OBE 2005; *b* 21 Nov. 1933; *s* of Sir Bryan Sanderson, 2nd Bt and Annette Korab Laskowska (*d* 1967); *S* father, 1992; *m* 1961, Margaret Ann, *o d* of late John Cleveland Maxwell, New York, USA; two *s* three *d* (incl. twin *d*). *Educ:* Stowe; Univ. of Salamanca. RNVR, 1950–65. J. H. Minet & Co. Ltd, 1956–93 (Dir, 1985); Dir, Knott Hotels Co. of London, 1965–75; Dir and Chm., Humber Fertilisers plc, 1972–88. Underwriting Mem. of Lloyd's, 1957–88. Mem., Chichester Dio. Synod, 1980–93. Chm., Thiepval Project, 1999–2006. Master, Worshipful Co. of Curriers, 1993–94. *Heir: s* David Frank Sanderson [*b* 26 Feb. 1962; *m* 1990, Fiona Jane Ure; one *d*]. *Address:* Grandturzel Farm, Fontridge Lane, Burwash, Etchingham, East Sussex TN19 7DE. *Clubs:* Naval, City of London, Farmers.

SANDERSON, Lt-Gen. John Murray, AC 1994 (AO 1991; AM 1985); ActionAid Australia Ambassador for Cambodia, 2006–12; Chairman, Indigenous Implementation Board, Department of Indigenous Affairs, Western Australia, 2008–11; Governor of Western Australia, 2000–05; *b* 4 Nov. 1940; *s* of John Edward, (Jack), Sanderson and (Dorothy) Jean Sanderson; *m* 1962, Viva Lorraine; one *s* two *d*. *Educ:* Bunbury High Sch., WA; Royal Mil. Coll., Duntroon; Royal Melbourne Inst. of Technol. (Fellow 1964). Australian Army: Comdr of Sqdn, Vietnam, 1970–71; Sen. Instructor, Sch. of Mil. Engrg, 1972; Instructor, Staff Coll., Camberley, UK, 1976–78; Comdr, 1st Field Engrg Regt, 1979–80; MA to CGS, 1982; Dir of Army Plans, 1982–85; Comdr, 1st Bde, 1986–88; Chief of Staff, Land HQ, 1989; Asst Chief, Defence Forces Develt, 1989–91; Mil. Comdr, UN Transitional Authy, Cambodia, 1992–93; Comdr, Jt Forces Aust., 1993–95; CGS, 1995–97; Chief of Aust. Army, 1997–98.

Adjunct Professor: Murdoch Univ., 2006–; Griffith Univ., 2006–. Mem. Bd, Australian Centre for Christianity and Culture, 2007–. Fellow, Aust. Inst. of Internat. Affairs, 2008. Hon. FIEAust 2000. Comdr, Legion of Merit, USA, 1997; Grand Cross, Royal Cambodian Order, 2006.

SANDERSON, Kerry Gaye, AO 2004; Governor of Western Australia, since 2014; *b* Perth, WA, 21 Dec. 1950; *d* of late Stanley Thomas Smith and Valma June Smith; *m* 1972, Lancelot John Sanderson (*d* 2007); two *s*. *Educ:* Univ. of Western Australia (BSc, BEc). FCILT. Treasury, WA, 1971–87, incl. Dir, Econ. and Financial Policy, 1980–87; Dep. Dir Gen., Transport, WA, 1987–91; CEO, Fremantle Ports, 1991–2008. Dir, AWB Ltd, 1995–2005. Mem. Bd, Australian Trade Commn, 2005–06. Pres., Ports Australia, 2007–08; Agent Gen. for WA in London, 2008–11. Chm., State Emergency Mgt Cttee, WA, 2012–14. Co-Chair, First Murdoch Commn, 2013. Adjunct Prof., Curtin Univ., 2013–14. Chm., Gold Corp., 2012–14; Ind. non-exec. Dir, Atlas Iron Ltd, 2012–14; non-executive Director: Downer EDI Ltd, 2012–14; St John of God Healthcare, 2012–14; Internat. Centre for Radio-Astronomy Res., 2013–14; Mem. Bd, Rio Tinto WA Future Fund, 2002–08; Trustee, Fremantle Hosp. Med. Res. Foundn, 1998–2008; Director: Senses Foundn, 2012–14; Paraplegic Benefit Fund, 2012–14. FAIM; FAICD. Hon. LittD WA, 2005. Centenary Medal, 2001. Telstra Businesswoman of Year, WA, 1996. *Recreations:* hiking, swimming.

SANDERSON, Dr Michael David; Chairman, Third Wave Enterprise Ltd, since 2006; *b* 7 June 1943; *s* of Arthur Joseph Sanderson and Betty (*née* Potter); *m* 1967, Mariana Welly Madinaveitia; one *s* one *d*. *Educ:* Strode's Sch., Egham; Univ. of Reading (BSc Hons Chem. 1964); Univ. of Leeds (PhD 1968). With Wilkinson Sword: Research Scientist, 1968–71; Technical Manager, 1971–73; Technical Dir, 1973–79; Internat. Marketing Dir, 1979–82; Engrg Dir, AMF Legg, 1982–84; with Lansing Bagnall: Export Dir, 1984–87; Gp Dir, UK Market, 1987–89; Jt Man. Dir, Lansing Linde, 1989–90; Man. Dir, AWD Bedford, 1990–91; Chief Executive: BSI, 1991–93; Nat. Assoc. of Goldsmiths and Sec. Gen., Internat. Confedn of Jewellers, 1994–95; Engrg and Marine Trng Authy, subseq. Sci., Engrg and Manufacturing Technologies Alliance, 1995–2004; Man. Dir, Technical Qualifications Validation Ltd, 2005–07. Pres., Inst. of Supervision and Mgt, 1995–99; Chairman: Action for Engrg, Task Force 3, 1995–96; Output Standards Adv. Cttee, Engrg Professors Council, 2000–05; Res. Div., Inst. of Continuing Professional Develt, 2004–06; Nat. Chm., Women into Sci. and Engrg Campaign, 2001–03; Dep. Nat. Chm., Inst. Materials Management, 1991–93; Member Council: Inst. of Materials, 1993–96; Inst. of Logistics, 1988–94; Inst. of Quality Assurance, 1997–2001; Foundn for Sci. and Technol., 2000–04; Dir, Engrg and Technol. Bd, 2001–02. Consultant, Engrg Council, 2005–. Mem., Benchmarking Forum, Amer. Soc. for Trng and Develt, 1999–2004. Trustee: Enterprise Education Trust (formerly Understanding Industry, subseq. Business Dynamics), 1998–; Scottish Council of NTOs, 1999–2004; EdExcel Foundn, 2001–04; Sci., Engrg Technol. and Math. Network, 1999–2004; E Midlands Leadership Centre, 2004–. Chm. and Trustee, Young Electronic Designer of the Year Award, 2002–05; Trustee, Nat. Exam. Bd for Occupational Health and Safety, 2005–. Member Court: Cranfield Univ., 1996–2005; Imperial Coll. London, 2002–; City Univ., 2004–. Mem., Editorial Bd, TQM Magazine, 1993–. Chm., Childs Hill Allotment Soc., 2006–07 (Dep. Chm., 2005–06). Freeman: City of London, 1995; City of Glasgow, 2001; Incorp. of Hammermen of City of Glasgow, 2001; Freeman, 1994–96, Liveryman, 1996–, Mem. Court, 2000–, Master, 2008–09, Clockmakers' Co.; Freeman, 2002–03, Liveryman, 2003–, Engrs Co. Hon. FIET (Hon. FIIE 2003). *Publications:* contribs to learned jls on surface chemistry, thin surface films, materials management, quality and general management topics. *Recreation:* books. *Address:* 31 Murray Mews, NW1 9RH. *T:* (020) 7284 3155, *Fax:* (020) 7267 9453. *Clubs:* Athenæum, Carlton.

SANDERSON, Rev. Canon Peter Oliver; Supply Priest, Diocese of the Rio Grande, New Mexico, since 2010; *b* 26 Jan. 1929; *s* of Harold and Doris Sanderson; *m* 1956, Doreen Gibson; one *s* one *d* (and one *s* decd). *Educ:* St Chad's College, Durham Univ. (BA, DipTh). Asst Curate, Houghton-le-Spring, Durham Diocese, 1954–59; Rector, Linstead and St Thomas Ye Vale, Jamaica, 1959–63; Chaplain, RAF, 1963–67; Vicar, Winksley-cum-Grantley and Aldfield-with-Studley, Ripon, 1967–74; Vicar, St Aidan, Leeds, 1974–84; Provost of St Paul's Cathedral, Dundee, 1984–91; Vicar, All Saints' Episcopal Ch, Storm Lake, Iowa, 1991–2000; Interim Dean, Trinity Cathedral, Davenport, Iowa, 2005–06; Interim Priest-in-Charge, Lincoln County, Dio. of the Rio Grande, New Mexico, 2008–10. Hon. Canon, St Paul's Cath., Desmoines, Iowa, 2004–. *Recreations:* gardening, music, reading.

SANDERSON, Roy, OBE 1983; National Secretary, Federation of Professional Associations Section, Amalgamated Engineering and Electrical Union, 1992–93; *b* 15 Feb. 1931; *s* of George and Lillian Sanderson; *m* 1951, Jean (*née* Booth); two *s* (and one *s* decd). *Educ:* Carfield Sch., Sheffield. Electrical, Electronic Telecommunication & Plumbing Union: Convenor, Lucas Aerospace, Hemel Hempstead, 1952–67; Asst Educn Officer, 1967–69; Nat. Officer, 1969–87; Nat. Sec., Electrical and Engrg Staff Assoc., 1987–92. Non-exec. Dir, UKAEA, 1987–96. Member: Armed Forces Pay Review Body, 1987–95; Economic and Social Cttee, EU, 1990–98; Industrial Tribunals, 1992–99; Employment Appeal Tribunal, 1995–2002. *Recreations:* golf, snooker; supporter of Watford Football Club.

SANDERSON, Theresa Ione, (Tessa), CBE 2004 (OBE 1998; MBE 1985); Head of Talent Development for 2012, Newham Council, 2005–12; former athlete; *b* 14 March 1956; *m* 2010, Densign White. *Educ:* Wards Bridge Comprehensive Sch., Wednesfield, Wolverhampton; Bilston Coll. of Further Educn. Javelin thrower; represented GB, 1974–96: Olympic Games: Gold Medal, Los Angeles, 1984 (Olympic record); finalist, Barcelona, 1992; competitor, Atlanta, 1996 (record 6th Olympic Games); Gold Medal, Commonwealth Games, 1978, 1986, 1990; Silver Medal, European Championships, 1978; Gold Medal, World Cup, Cuba, 1992. Set UK record, javelin, 1976 and 1983; UK record, heptathlon, 1981. Sports presenter, Sky News, 1989–92; presenter of own Sunday radio show for Colourful Radio. Mem., 1998–2005, Vice-Chm., 1999–2005, Sport England; Mem., Sports Honours Cttee, 2005–; Ambassador for London 2012, 2005–12. Founder: Tessa Sanderson Foundn and Acad., 2009–; Newham Classic 10K, 2009–. Patron, Disabled Olympics. Hon. MA Birmingham. *Publications:* Tessa: my life in athletics (autobiog.), 1985.

SANDFORD, 3rd Baron *cr* 1945, of Banbury; **James John Mowbray Edmondson;** elementary school counsellor, since 1981; President, Surrey School Counsellors Association, British Columbia, 2001–07; *b* Winchester, England, 1 July 1949; *er s* of 2nd Baron Sandford, DSC and Catharine Mary, *d* of Rev. Oswald Andrew Hunt; *S* father, 2009; *m* 1st, 1973, Ellen Sarah Shapiro (marr. diss. 1985); one *d*; 2nd, 1985, Linda, *d* of Mick and Betty Wheeler, Nova Scotia; one *s*. *Educ:* York Univ., UK (BA Hons Political Sci.); Univ. of British Columbia (MEd Counselling Psychol.). Elementary sch. teacher, 1974–81. Pres., Vancouver-Kensington NDP, 2005–11. Pres., Vancouver Folk Song Soc., 1988–92. Member: singing and recording gp, Three Strong Winds, 1989–99; singing gp, Lemon Gin with Lyn Pinkerton, 2005–. *Heir: s* Hon. Devon John Wheeler Edmondson, *b* 15 April 1986. *Address:* 404–908 West 7th, Vancouver, BC V5Z 1C3, Canada. *T:* (778) 2290594. *E:* jimedmondson@telus.net.

SANDFORD, Arthur; DL; Chairman, Trent Strategic Health Authority, 2002–06; *b* 12 May 1941; *s* of Arthur and Lilian Sandford; *m* 1963, Kathleen Entwistle; two *d*. *Educ:* Queen Elizabeth's Grammar Sch., Blackburn; University Coll., London (LLB Hons (Upper 2nd Class)). Preston County Borough Council: Articled Clerk to Town Clerk, 1962–65; Asst Solicitor, 1965–66; Sen. Asst Solicitor, 1966–68; Asst Solicitor, Hants CC, 1969–70; Nottinghamshire County Council: Second Asst Clerk, 1970–72; First Asst Clerk, 1972–74; Dep. Dir of Admin, 1973–75; Dir of Admin, 1975–77; Dep. Clerk and County Sec., 1977–78; Clerk and Chief Exec., 1978–89; Chief Executive: Football League, 1990–92; Manchester CC, 1992–98. Chm., Christie Hosp. NHS Trust, 1999–2002. Consultant: Pannone & Partners, 1998–2002; Amey plc, 1998–2002. DL Notts, 1990. *Recreations:* watching sport, gardening, golf. *Address:* 4 Wentworth Way, Edwalton, Nottingham NG12 4DJ. *T:* (0115) 914 9854.

SANDHURST, 6th Baron; *see* Mansfield, G. R. J.

SANDIFORD, Rt Hon. Sir Lloyd Erskine, KA 1999; PC (Barbados); PC 1989; JP; Ambassador of Barbados to the People's Republic of China, since 2009; Prime Minister of Barbados, 1987–94; *b* 24 March 1937; *s* of Cyril and Eunice Sandiford; *m* 1963, Angelita P. Ricketts; one *s* two *d*. *Educ:* Coleridge/Parry Sec. Sch.; Harrison Coll.; Univ. of WI, Jamaica (BA Hons English); Univ. of Manchester (MAEcon). Assistant Master: Modern High Sch., Barbados, 1956–57; Kingston Coll., Jamaica, 1960–61; Asst Master, 1963–64, Sen. Graduate Master, 1964–66, Harrison Coll., Barbados; part-time Tutor and Lectr, Univ. of the WI, Barbados, 1963–65; Asst Tutor, Barbados Community Coll., 1976–86. Democratic Labour Party, Barbados: Mem., 1964–; Asst Sec., 1966–67; Gen. Sec., 1967–68; (first) Vice-Pres., 1972–74; Pres., 1974–75; Vice-Pres., 1975–76; Founder, Acad. of Politics. Member: Senate, 1967–71; House of Assembly, St Michael South, 1971–99; Personal Asst to the Prime Minister, 1966–67; Minister: of Educn, 1967–71; of Educn, Youth Affairs, Community Develt and Sport, 1971–75; of Health and Welfare, 1975–76; Dep. Leader of Opposition, 1978–86; Dep. Prime Minister and Minister of Educn and Culture, 1986–87; Minister: for Civil Service, 1987–94; of Finance and Economic Affairs, 1987–93; of Economic Affairs, 1993–94; of Tourism and Internat. Transport, 1994. Dist. Fellow, Univ. of WI, Barbados. Order of the Liberator (Venezuela), 1987. *Publications:* Books of Speeches 1987–1994; The Essence of Economics, 1997; Politics and Society in Barbados and the Caribbean, 2000; Fighting for the Just Society: an autobiographical note, 2011; *poems:* Ode to the Environment; When She Leaves You; (contrib.) Business, Government and Society, ed Monya Anyadike-Danes. *Address:* Hillvista, Porters, St James, Barbados, West Indies.

SANDIFORD, Peter, OBE 1992; Director, Spain, British Council, 1999–2003; *b* 23 May 1947; *s* of Jack Sandiford and Joan Mary Sandiford; *m* 1st, 1970, Yvonne Kay Haffenden (marr. diss. 2005); one *s* one *d*; 2nd, 2006, Victoria Francesca Cornwell-García. *Educ:* Watford Grammar Sch. for Boys; University College London (BSc Hons Anthropology 1969). VSO Volunteer, Malawi, 1965–66; Archaeologist, MPBW, 1969–70; British Council: Asst Dir, Singapore, 1971–75; Regl Dir, Munich, 1975–82; Dir, Mgt Services Dept, London, 1982–86; Dir, Israel, 1986–94; Regl Dir, East and Southern Europe, 1994–96, Americas, 1996–98, London. *Recreations:* amateur radio, sailing, hiking.

SANDILANDS, family name of **Baron Torphichen.**

SANDIS, Alexandros C.; Director, Diplomatic Office of the Prime Minister, Athens (with rank of Ambassador), 2004–09; *b* Alexandria, Egypt, 29 Aug. 1947; *s* of Constantinos and Maria Sandis; *m* 1969, Anastasia Tsagarakis; one *s* one *d*. *Educ:* Univ. of Athens (BA Pol and Econ. Scis). Joined Ministry of Foreign Affairs, Athens, 1971: Attaché, 1971–73; 2nd Sec., New Delhi, 1973–77; Counsellor, Nicosia, 1977–83; Counsellor, Perm. Delegn to EC, Brussels, 1983–88; Dir, EU Affairs Dept, Athens, 1989–91; Ambassador to: Zimbabwe, 1991–93; Cyprus, 1993–97; Italy, 1997–2000; UK, 2000–03. Greek Govt Rep. at Cyprus Talks, 1997–2001. Grand Cross: Order of Makarios III (Cyprus), 1993; Norwegian Order of Merit (Norway), 2004; Order of the Phoenix (Greece), 2005; Order of the Honour in Gold, First Class (Austria), 2007; Comdr, Order of Greek Orthodox Patriarchate of Alexandria, 1995; Grand Comdr, Order of Dannebrog (Denmark), 2006. *Recreations:* history, music, theatre, football.

SANDIS, Aristidis C.; Ambassador of Greece to the Court of St James's, 2010–12; Permanent Representative to the International Maritime Organization, since 2010; *b* Alexandria, Egypt, 1 Dec. 1951; *s* of Constantinos and Maria Sandis; *m* Ekaterini Simopoulou; three *d*. *Educ:* Univ. of Athens (Public Law and Pol Scis degree 1973). Joined Greek Diplomatic Service as Attaché, 1974; 2nd Pol Directorate, Min. of For. Affairs, 1974–76; Second Sec., Bonn, 1976–80; Consul of Greece, Cape Town, 1981–87; Minister-Counsellor, Moscow, 1987–91; Hd, Diplomatic Cabinet of Dep. Minister of For. Affairs, Min. of For. Affairs, 1991–93; Dep. Perm. Rep. to OSCE, Vienna, 1993–96; Ambassador to Jordan, 1996–99; Hd, A6 Directorate for Arab Countries and Middle East, Min. of For. Affairs, 1999–2001; Perm. Rep. to OSCE, Vienna, 2001–05; Ambassador to Rep. of SA, and concurrently to Botswana, Lesotho, Mozambique, Namibia and Swaziland, 2005–09; Sec. Gen., Min. of For. Affairs, 2009. Grand Cross, Order of Phoenix (Greece), 2007 (Grand Comdr, 1999); Cross, 1st Cl., Order of Merit (Germany), 1981; Grand Cordon, Order of Independence (Jordan), 1999; Comdr, Order of Cedar (Lebanon), 2001.

See also Alexandros C. Sandis.

SANDISON, Alexander, (Alec), FCCA; charity governance and management consultant, 1994–2010; *b* 24 May 1943; *s* of late Alexander and Mary Sandison; *m* Judy Hamilton (*née* Evans). *Educ:* Cambs High Sch.; Trinity Sch. of John Whitgift, Croydon. FCCA 1975 (ACCA 1970). Commercial Union Assce Co., 1962–63; John Mowlem PLC, 1964–71 (Gp Financial Accountant, 1970–71); Chief Accountant: and Co. Sec., J. E. Freeman & Co., 1972–73; Wings Ltd, 1973–78; Divl Financial Dir, Doulton Glass Inds, 1978–80; Sec. for Finance and Corporate Controller, RICS, 1980–90; Chief Exec., Surveyors Holdings Ltd, 1985–89; Chm., Imaginor Systems Ltd, 1989–90; Director: Cruse-Bereavement Care, 1990–91; Finance and Admin, Prince's Trust and Royal Jubilee Trusts, 1992–94; Co. Sec., Who Cares? Trust, 1995–2008. Mem. Charities Panel, Chartered Assoc. of Certified Accountants, 1998–2012. Trustee: Chartered Certified Accountants Benevolent Fund, 1999–; Islington Volunteer Centre, 1999–2002; Charity Appointments, 2002–; Dystonia Soc., 2012–; Co-Founder, SpeakersBank, 2002–05. Chm., Finance Cttee, Lutheran Council of GB, 2010–11 (Mem., 1998–2011). Chm., LCGB Trading Ltd, 2008–12. *Publications:* People to People: course notes, 1985; Watton-at-Stone Village Guide, 1989; contribs to learned jls, brainteasers and poetry. *Recreations:* family, voluntary social work; reading, writing; avoiding involvement with and conversations about sport.

SANDISON, Craig Robert Kindness; QC (Scot.) 2009; *b* Falkirk, 30 May 1966; *s* of George Edward Grant Sandison and Margaret Sandison (*née* Kindness). *Educ:* Queens' Coll., Cambridge (Schol.; LLM 1990); Magdalene Coll., Cambridge (PhD 1994). Advocate, 1996, specialising in commercial law. *Recreation:* international affairs. *Address:* 29 Northumberland Street, Edinburgh EH3 6LR. *T:* (0131) 226 2881. *E:* crks@cantab.net.

SANDISON, James Sinclair, FCA; freelance financial and management consultant, 1998–2000; *b* 22 June 1936; *s* of William Robert Sandison and Evelyn Gladys Sandison; *m* 1978, Jeannette Avery Keeble; one *s* one *d*. *Educ:* John Lyon Sch., Harrow. FCA 1958. Nat. Service, 2nd Lt, 1958–60. Franklin, Wild & Co., 1953–58; Touche Ross & Co., 1960–62; British Relay Wireless and Television Ltd, 1962–66; joined Dexion Gp, 1966: Gp Controller, 1975–76; Finance Dir, Dexion Ltd, 1977–91; Royal Society for Encouragement of Arts, Manufactures and Commerce: Dir of Finance and Admin, 1991–96; Acting Dir, 1996–97. Treas., London Soc., 2005–08. FRSA 1998. *Recreations:* tennis, silent and world cinema, film noir, London, European history, British and European Art 1850–1950. *Address:* 33 Montagu Road, Highcliffe, Christchurch, Dorset BH23 5JT.

SANDLE, Prof. Michael Leonard, DFA; RA; FRBS 1994; sculptor; Professor of Sculpture, Akademie der Bildenden Künste, Karlsruhe, Germany, 1980–99; *b* 18 May 1936; *s* of Charles Edward Sandle and Dorothy Gwendoline Gladys (*née* Vernon); *m* 1971, Cynthia Dora Koppel (marriage annulled 1974); *m* 1988, Demelza Spargo (marriage annulled 2004); one *s* one *d*. *Educ:* Douglas High Sch., IOM; Douglas Sch. of Art and Technol.; Slade Sch. of Fine Art (DFA 1959). ARA 1982, RA 1989, resigned 1997, rejoined 2004. Studied painting and printmaking, Slade Sch. of Fine Art, 1956–59; changed to sculpture, 1962; various teaching posts in Britain, 1961–70, including Lectr, Coventry Coll. of Art, 1964–68; resident in Canada, 1970–73; Vis. Prof., Univ. of Calgary, Alberta, 1970–71; Vis. Associate Prof., Univ. of Victoria, BC, 1972–73; Lectr in Sculpture, Fachhochschule für Gestaltung, Pforzheim, W Germany, 1973–77, Prof., 1977–80. Sen. Res. Fellow, De Montfort Univ., 1996–2001; Fellow, Kenneth Armitage Foundn, 2004–06. Has participated in exhibns in GB and internationally, 1957–, including: V Biennale, Paris, 1966; Documenta IV, Kassel, W Germany, 1968 and Documenta VI, 1977. Work in public collections, including: Arts Council of GB, Tate Gall.; Australian Nat. Gall., Canberra; Met. Mus., NY; Stzüki Mus., Lodz; Nat. Gall., Warsaw; Wilhelm Lehmbruck Mus., Duisburg, W Germany. Designed: Malta Siege Bell Meml, Valetta, 1992; Seafarers Meml, for Internat. Maritime Orgn's HQ, London, 2001. Nobutaka Shikanai Special Prize, Utsukushi-Ga-Hara Open-Air Mus., Japan, 1986; Henry Hering Meml Medal, Nat. Sculpture Soc. of Amer., 1995. *Address:* c/o The Royal British Society of Sculptors, 108 Brompton Road, SW7 3RA.

SANDLER, Ronald Arnon, Hon. CBE 2004; Chairman: Ironshore Inc., since 2007; Towry, since 2014; Centaur Media, since 2015; *b* 5 March 1952; *s* of Bernard Maurice Sandler and Carla Sandler; *m* 1977, Susan Lee; two *s*. *Educ:* Milton Sch., Bulawayo; Queens' Coll., Cambridge (MA); Stanford Univ., USA (MBA). Boston Consulting Gp Inc., 1976–84, Dir 1983–84; Sen. Vice Pres., Booz Allen & Hamilton Inc., 1984–88; Chm., Chalcon Ltd, 1989–93; Chm. and Chief Exec., Martin Bierbaum Gp plc, 1990–93; Chief Executive: Exco plc, 1993–94; Lloyd's of London, 1995–99; Chief Operating Officer, NatWest Gp, 1999–2000. Chairman: Computacenter plc, 2001–08; Kyte Gp, 2000–08; Oxygen Gp plc, 2004–08; Paternoster Ltd, 2006–11; Northern Rock plc, 2008–12; Phoenix Gp (formerly Pearl), 2009–12; non-executive Director: Greenalls Gp plc, 1998–2000; Fortis, 2004–09. Pres., CIB, 2004–05. Mem., Partnership Council, Herbert Smith, 2001–06. Chm., Personal Finance Educn Gp, 2003–08. Trustee, Royal Opera House, 1999–2001. Hon. DSc City, 2012. *Recreations:* golf, ski-ing, guitar playing, fly fishing. *Address:* 5 Southside, Wimbledon, SW19 4TG. *T:* (020) 8946 1179. *Clubs:* MCC; Sunningdale; Lloyd's Fly Fishing.

SANDON, Viscount; Dudley Anthony Hugo Coventry Ryder; *b* 5 Sept. 1981; *s* and *heir* of Earl of Harrowby, *qv*. *Educ:* Eton Coll.; Edinburgh Univ. (MA). *Address:* Sandon Estate Office, Sandon, Stafford ST18 0DA.

SANDON, Henry George, MBE 2008; antiques expert and broadcaster; *b* London, 4 Aug. 1928; *s* of Augusto Sandon and Clara Sandon; *m* 1956, Barbara Sophia (*d* 2013); three *s*. *Educ:* High Wycombe Royal Grammar Sch.; Guildhall Sch. of Music. FLCM; ARCM. Music Master, Worcester Royal Grammar Sch., 1953–59; Curator, Royal Worcester Porcelain, and Dyson Perrins Mus., subseq. Museum of Royal Worcester, 1966–83, Patron, 1999–. Lay Clerk, Worcester Cathedral, 1953–82. Regular expert, BBC Antiques Roadshow, 1978–. Mem., Cttee of Mgt, Choir Benevolent Fund; Chm., Commemorative Collectors' Soc.; President: Pershore, St John's Ambulance; City of Worcester Decorative and Fine Arts Soc. Mem., Claines, Worcester Br., RBL. Freedom, City of London, 2006. Hon. MA Worcester, 2009. Police Long Service (Specials) Medal. *Publications:* British Pottery and Porcelain, 1969, 1980; Worcester Porcelain 1751–1793, 1969, 2nd edn 1974; Coffee Pots and Teapots, 1973; Royal Worcester Porcelain, 1973, 3rd edn 1978; Flight and Barr Worcester Porcelain, 1978; Sandon Guide to Worcester Figures, 1987; Living with the Past (autobiog.), 1997. *Recreation:* giving pots a good home and love. *Address:* c/o Museum of Royal Worcester, Severn Street, Worcester WR1 2ND. *T:* (01905) 21247.

SANDON, Susan; Managing Director, Cornerstone Division, Penguin Random House UK, since 2007 (Deputy Managing Director, 2003–07); *b* Camberley, Surrey, 4 June 1959; *d* of Frederick Donald Peace Weaver and Doris Lilian Weaver; one *s*; partner, Richard Hamilton Cable. *Educ:* Frimley and Camberley Grammar Sch.; Broadmoor Sch. of Nursing (RMN); Univ. of Sussex (BA 1st Cl. Hons); Univ. of E Anglia (MA). Headline, 1987–89; Publicity Manager, then Mktg Dir, Virago Press, 1989–92; Publicity Dir, Penguin, 1992–95; Gp Publicity and Mktg Dir, Random House, 1995–2003. *Recreation:* reading. *Address:* Penguin Random House UK, 20 Vauxhall Bridge Road, SW1V 2SA. *T:* (020) 7840 8622. *E:* ssandon@penguinrandomhouse.co.uk.

SANDS, Catherine K.; *see* Knight-Sands.

SANDS, John Robert; Chairman: Invesco English and International Trust, 2006–10 (Director, 2004–10); Wear Inns Ltd, since 2006; *b* 8 Oct. 1947; *s* of John Sands and Jane Caroline Sands (*née* Reay); *m* 1969, Susan Elizabeth McCulloch; two *s* two *d*. J. W. Cameron & Co. Ltd: Trng and Develt Manager, 1980–81; Tied Trade Dir, 1981–84; Trade Dir, 1984–85; Managing Director: Cameron Inns, 1985–88; and CEO, Tollemache & Cobbold Breweries Ltd, 1988–89; Brent Walker Inns and Retail, 1989–91; Man. Dir, 1991–96, Chief Exec., 1996–2002, Exec. Chm., 2002–04, Pubmaster Ltd. Non-exec. Chm., Admiral Taverns, 2014–. Non-exec. Dir, Jennings Brothers, 2004–07. *Recreations:* ski-ing, keep fit, playing guitar and banjo, playing mahjong, watching Newcastle United FC.

SANDS, Jonathan Peter, OBE 2011; Chairman, Elmwood Design, brand design consultancy, since 1989; *b* 27 March 1961; *s* of Peter and Viveanne Sands; *m* 1983, Carolyn Fletcher; two *s* one *d*. *Educ:* Normanton Boys' Sch.; Stockport Coll. of Technol. Council Mem., Design Council, 2000–10. Former Mem., Arts Council Yorkshire. Regular speaker at internat. confs on design worldwide. FRSA (Council Mem., 1997–2000). Hon. DSc Huddersfield, 2002. *Publications:* regular contribs to design jls and media. *Recreation:* long-suffering Derby County supporter. *Address:* Elmwood, 105 Water Lane, Leeds LS11 5WD. *Clubs:* Groucho; Harrogate Golf, Gullane Golf.

SANDS, Peter Alexander; Group Chief Executive Officer, Standard Chartered plc, 2006–15 (Group Finance Director, 2002–06); *b* 8 Jan. 1962; *s* of Martin and Susan Sands; *m* 1989, Mary Elizabeth, (Betsy), Tobin; one *s* three *d*. *Educ:* Brasenose Coll., Oxford (BA PPE); Kennedy Sch. of Govt, Harvard Univ. (MPA). Asst Desk Officer for Afghanistan and Pakistan, and Desk Officer for Libya, FCO, 1984–86; McKinsey & Co.: Associate, 1988–96; Principal, 1996–2000; Dir, 2000–02. Lead non-exec. Dir, DoH. *Recreations:* reading, music, riding, football.

SANDS, Prof. Philippe Joseph; QC 2003; Professor of Laws, and Director, Centre on International Courts and Tribunals, University College London, since 2002; *b* 17 Oct. 1960; *s* of Alan Sands and Ruth (*née* Buchholz); *m* 1993, Natalia Schiffrin; one *s* two *d*. *Educ:* Corpus Christi Coll., Cambridge (BA 1982; LLM 1983). Res. Fellow, St Catharine's Coll., Cambridge, 1984–88; called to the Bar, Middle Temple, 1985, Bencher, 2009; Lectr, Faculty of Law, KCL, 1988–92; Lectr, then Reader, subseq. Prof. of Internat. Law, SOAS, 1993–2001. *Publications:* Chernobyl: law and communication, 1988; (ed and contrib.) Greening International Law, 1993; Principles of International Environmental Law, 1995, 3rd edn 2012; Manual of International Courts and Tribunals, 1999, 2nd edn 2010; (jtly) Bowett's Law of International Institutions, 6th edn 2009; From Nuremburg to The Hague, 2003; Lawless World, 2005; Torture Team: deception, cruelty and the compromise of law, 2008. *Address:* Matrix Chambers, Gray's Inn, WC1R 5LN. *T:* (020) 7404 3447, *Fax:* (020) 7404 3448. *E:* philippesands@matrixlaw.co.uk.

SANDS, Sir Roger (Blakemore), KCB 2006; Clerk and Chief Executive of the House of Commons, 2003–06; *b* 6 May 1942; *s* of late Thomas Blakemore Sands and Edith Malyon (Betty) Sands (*née* Waldram); *m* 1966, Jennifer Ann Cattell; one *d* (and one *d* decd). *Educ:* University Coll. Sch., Hampstead; Oriel Coll., Oxford (scholar; MA LitHum). A Clerk, House of Commons, 1965–2006; Sec. to H of C Commn and Clerk to H of C (Services) Cttee, 1985–87; Clerk of Overseas Office, 1987–91; Clerk of Select Cttees and Registrar of Members' Interests, 1991–94; Clerk of Public Bills, 1994–97; Clerk of Legislation, 1998–2001; Clerk Asst, 2001–02. Chm., Study of Parlt Group, 1993–95. Chm., Standards Cttee, Mid Sussex DC, 2007–12; ind. advr on standards matters, 2012–. Ind. Mem., UK Public Affairs Council, 2010–14. *Recreations:* listening to music, walking, incompetent golf. *Address:* No 4 (Ashurst Suite), Woodbury House, Lewes Road, East Grinstead, W Sussex RH19 3UD. *T:* (01342) 302245. *Club:* Holtye Golf.

SANDS SMITH, David, CBE 2002; development administrator; *b* 19 April 1943; *s* of late Arthur S. Smith and Eileen Annie Smith; *m* 1966, Veronica Harris; one *s* one *d*. *Educ:* Brighton Coll. of Technology, Dept of Technical Co-operation, 1963–71. 2nd Sec., British High Commn, Kuala Lumpur, 1971–75; Overseas Development Administration: Principal: European Community Dept, 1975–80; Zimbabwe Desk, 1980–85; Asst Head, 1985–88, Head, 1988–90, European Community Dept; Head, British Develt Div. in Eastern Africa, 1990–93; UK Perm. Rep., FAO, World Food Programme and IFAD, 1993–97; Head: Procurement, Appts and NGOs Dept, DFID, 1997–99; Develt Policy Dept, DFID, 1999–2001. Consultant to FAO, 2003–06. Trustee, Sightsavers Internat., 2006–11.

SANDWICH, 11th Earl of, *cr* 1660; **John Edward Hollister Montagu;** Viscount Hinchingbrooke and Baron Montagu of St Neots, 1660; editor and researcher; *b* 11 April 1943; *er s* of (Alexander) Victor (Edward Paulet) Montagu (who disclaimed his peerages for life) and Rosemary Peto; *S* father, 1995; *m* 1968, Caroline, *o d* of late Canon P. E. C. Hayman, Beaminster, Dorset; two *s* one *d*. *Educ:* Eton; Trinity College, Cambridge. Inf. Officer, 1974–85, Res. Officer, 1985–86, Mem., Bd, 1999–2004, Christian Aid; Editor, Save the Children Fund, 1987–92; Consultant, CARE Britain, 1987–93; Mem. Council, Anti-Slavery Internat., 1997–2006. Chm., Britain Afghanistan Trust, 1995–2000; Trustee, TSW Telethon Trust, 1987–91; Gov. Beaminster Sch., 1996–2004. Pres., Earl of Sandwich, 2001–. Jt Administrator, Mapperton Estate, 1982–. Crossbencher, H of L, 1995–; elected Mem., H of L, 1999; Member: Information Cttee, 2001–04; Constitution Cttee, 2004–06; Ind. Asylum Commn, 2006–08; EU Sub-Cttee E, 2009–13; EU Select Cttee, 2010–15; EU Sub-Cttee C, 2013–. Mem., Adv. Panel, British Coll., Kathmandu, 2012–. Pres., Samuel Pepys Club, 1985–. *Publications:* The Book of the World, 1971; Prospects for Africa's Children, 1990; Children at Crisis Point, 1992; (ed jtly) Hinch: a celebration of Viscount Hinchingbrooke, MP 1906–1995, 1997; (ed) Rosemary Peto Illustrated Letters, 2009; Sandwich Man, 2015. *Heir: s* Viscount Hinchingbrooke, *qv*. *Address:* House of Lords, SW1A 0PW.

SANDYS, Laura Jane; Chair, European Movement, since 2015; *b* 5 June 1964; *d* of Baron Duncan-Sandys, CH, PC and of Marie-Claire (*née* Schmitt); *m* 2007, Dr Randolph Kent. *Educ:* Univ. of Cambridge (MSt Internat. Relns). Founded and sold two companies specialising in communications and mktg, 1993–99; led Parly Unit, Consumers' Assoc., 1986–87; former Sen. Research Associate, Centre for Defence Studies, KCL; former journalist and commentator. Vis. Sen. Fellow, KCL; Mem., Carbon Capture and Storage Adv. Gp, Imperial Coll. London. MP (C) S Thanet, 2010–15. PPS to Minister for Energy and Climate Change, 2012–13. Member: Energy and Climate Change Select Cttee, 2010–12; Jt Cttee on Draft H of L Reform Bill, 2011–12; Eur. Main Team; Chairman: All-Party Parly Gp for Epilepsy; All-Party Gp for Civic Voice; Vice Chm., All-Party Parly Gp for Carers. Co-Founder, Powerful Women Gp; Founder, Food Foundn. Former Chm., OpenDemocracy.net; former Dep. Chm., Civic Trust; former Trustee, Open Univ.

SANÉ, Pierre Gabriel; Founder and President, Imagine Africa Institute, since 2010; *b* 7 May 1948; *s* of Nicolas Sané and Therese Carvalho; *m* 1981, Ndeye Sow; one *s* one *d*. *Educ:* London Sch. of Econs and Pol Sci. (MSc in Public Admin and Public Policy); Ecole Supérieure de Commerce, Bordeaux (MBA); Carleton Univ., Canada (doctoral studies in pol scis). Regl Dir, Internat. Develt Research Centre, Ottawa, Canada, 1978–92; Sec.-Gen., Amnesty Internat., 1992–2001; Asst Dir-Gen. for Social and Human Scis, UNESCO, 2001–10. *Address:* Imagine Africa Institute, 01 Place de l'Independance, Dakar, Senegal.

SANGHERA, Jasvinder, CBE 2013; Founder and Chief Executive Officer, Karma Nirvana, since 1993; *b* Derby, 28 Sept. 1965; *d* of Chanan Singh and Jagir Kaur; marr. diss. 1998; one *s* two *d*. *Educ:* Littleover Sch., Derby; Univ. of Derby (BA 1st Cl. Hons Social and Cultural Studies). Non-exec. Dir, Derby PCT, 1998–2006. Ind. Mem., Derbys Police Authy, 2003–07. Expert witness to courts on forced marriages and honour-based violence, 2009–. Mem., RSA. Hon. Mem., Rotary Amber Valley, 2014. Paul Harris Fellow, Rotary Internat., 2014. Hon. Dr Derby, 2010. Women of the Year Window to the World Award, 2007. *Publications:* Shame (autobiog.), 2007; Daughters of Shame, 2009; Shame Travels, 2011. *Address:* PO Box 515, Leeds LS6 9DW.

SANGSTER, Nigel; QC 1998; a Recorder, since 2000; *s* of Dr H. B. Singh and Irene Singh (*née* Carlisle), JP. *Educ:* Repton; Leeds Univ. (LLB Hons). Called to the Bar, Middle Temple, 1976, Bencher, 2008; criminal defence barrister specialising in fraud cases; Head of Chambers, St Pauls Chambers, Leeds, 1995–2005; joined 25 Bedford Row, 2005. Member: Bar Council, 1994–2004; Criminal Bar Assoc. *Address:* 25 Bedford Row, WC1R 4HD. *T:* (020) 7067 1500. *E:* mail@nigelsangster.qc.com.

SANIN POSADA, Noemi; Ambassador of Colombia to the Court of St James's, 1994–95 and 2008–09; *b* Bogotá, 10 June 1949; *d* of Jaime Sanin Echeverri and Noemi Posada de Sanin; one *d*. *Educ:* Univ. Javeriana, Bogota; postgrad. studies in financial and commercial law. Pres., Colmena, Colombia, 1980–84; Minister of Communications, 1984–86; Pres., Corp. Financiera Colombiana, 1988–90; Ambassador to Venezuela, 1990–91; Minister of Foreign Relns, 1991–94; Fellow, Harvard Univ., 1999–2001; Ambassador to Spain, 2002–08. Presidential candidate, 1998, 2002, 2010. Mem., Peace Commn, Colombia. Hon. Dr: Soka Gakkai Univ. of Japan; Autonoma of Bucaramanga, Colombia. Gran Cruz Extraordinaria, Orden de Boyacá (Colombia); holds numerous foreign decorations, including: Orden de Isabel la Católica, Orden Civil al Merito (Spain); Orden del Sol, 1st Cl. (Peru); Orden de Cruceiro del Sur, 1st Cl. (Brazil). *Recreations:* walking, reading.

SANKEY, John Anthony, CMG 1983; PhD; HM Diplomatic Service, retired; Secretary General, Society of London Art Dealers, 1991–96; *b* 8 June 1930; *m* 1958, Gwendoline Putman; two *s* two *d*. *Educ:* Cardinal Vaughan Sch., Kensington; Peterhouse, Cambridge (Classical Tripos Parts 1 and 2, Class 1; MA); Univ. of Leeds (PhD 2002). 1st (Singapore) Regt, RA (2nd Lieut), 1952. Colonial Office, 1953–61; UK Mission to United Nations, 1961–64; Foreign Office, 1964–68; Guyana, 1968–71; Singapore, 1971–73; NATO Defence Coll., Rome, 1973; Malta, 1973–75; The Hague, 1975–79 (Gov., British Sch. in the Netherlands); FCO, 1979–82; High Comr, Tanzania, 1982–85; UK Perm. Rep. to UN Office, Geneva, 1985–90. Leader, British Govt Delegn to Internat. Red Cross Conf., 1986. Dir, Internat. Art and Antiques Loss Register Ltd, 1993–96. Chm., Tanzania Develt Trust, 1997–2004; Legacies Officer, St Francis Leprosy Guild, 2005–. Sir Evelyn Wrench Lectr,

ESU, 1990. KCHS 2003 (KHS 1996). *Publications:* (contrib.) The United Kingdom—the United Nations, 1990; The Conscience of the World, 1995; (ed) Thomas Brock, Forgotten Sculptor of the Victoria Memorial: a memoir by Frederick Brock, 2012. *Address:* 108 Lancaster Gate, W2 3NW.

SANKEY, Vernon Louis; Chairman, Firmenich SA, 2008–13 (Director, since 2005); *b* 9 May 1949; *s* of late Edward Sankey and Marguerite Elizabeth Louise (*née* van Maurik); *m* 1976, Elizabeth, *d* of Tom Knights; three *s* one *d* (of whom one *s* one *d* are twins). *Educ:* Harrow School; Oriel Coll., Oxford (MA Mod. Langs). Joined Reckitt & Colman, 1971: Mgt Trainee, 1971–74; Asst Manager, Finance and Planning, 1974–76; Dir, Planning and Develt, Europe, 1976–78; General Manager, Denmark, 1978–80; PA to Chm. and Chief Exec., 1980–81; Man. Dir, France, 1981–85; Man. Dir, Colman's of Norwich, 1985–89; Chm. and Chief Exec. Officer, Reckitt & Colman Inc., USA, 1989–92; Chief Exec., 1992–99. Chairman: The Really Effective Develt Co. Ltd, 2000–05; Thomson Travel Gp, 2000; Gala Gp Holdings, 2000–03; Photo-Me Internat. plc, 2005–07 (Dir and Dep. Chm., 2000–05); Dep. Chm., Beltpacker plc, 2000–04; non-executive Director: Pearson, 1993–2006; Allied Zurich plc, 1998–2000; Zurich Allied AG, 1998–2000; Zurich Financial Services AG, 2000–12; Cofra AG, 2001–07; Taylor Woodrow plc, 2004–07; Zurich Insurance Co. AG, 2004–12; Atos SE (formerly Atos Origin SA), 2005–; Vividas plc, 2005–07. Member: Internat. Adv. Bd, Korn/Ferry Internat., 1994–2005; Adv. Bd, Proudfoot UK, 2000–06; Adv. Bd, GLP LLP, 2005–. Mem. Bd, Grocery Manufacturers of Amer., 1995–99. Member: Listed Cos Adv. Cttee, London Stock Exchange, 1997–99; Bd, Food Standards Agency, 2000–05. FRSA 2000. *Recreations:* fitness, tennis. *Address:* c/o Corporate Affairs, Atos SE, River Ouest, Quai Voltaire, 95877 Bezons, France. *Club:* Leander (Henley).

SANKEY, William Patrick F.; *see* Filmer-Sankey.

SANSOM, Bruce Edward; freelance ballet coach, repetiteur and teacher; *b* 8 Sept. 1963; *s* of Dr Bernard Sansom and Prudence Sansom. *Educ:* Royal Ballet Sch. Joined Royal Ballet Co., 1982; Soloist, 1985; Principal Dancer, 1987–2000; also danced with San Francisco Ballet Co., 1991–92 season; has danced principal rôles in all major ballets, incl. La Fille Mal Gardée, Swan Lake, Giselle, The Nutcracker, Manon, Sleeping Beauty, La Bayadère, Cinderella, The Dream, Romeo and Juliet, Scènes de Ballet, Manon; leading rôles created for him in a number of ballets including Galanteries, Still Life at the Penguin Café, Pursuit, Piano, Prince of the Pagodas, Tombeaux; Dir, Central Sch. of Ballet, 2006–09; Ballet Master and Asst to Artistic Dir, San Francisco Ballet, 2009–13. Time Out Award for performances with Royal Ballet, 1990. *Recreations:* opera, contemporary art, Parson Jack Russell terriers, shooting.

SANT, Hon. Dr Alfred; Member (Lab) Malta, European Parliament, since 2014; *b* 28 Feb. 1948; *s* of Joseph and Josephine Sant; one *d*. *Educ:* Univ. of Malta (BSc, MSc); Inst. Internat. d'Admin Publique, Paris (Dip.); Boston Univ. (MBA); Harvard Univ. (DBA). Res. Fellow, Harvard Business Sch. First Sec., Malta Mission to EEC, Brussels, 1970–75; Man. Dir, Medina Consulting Gp, 1979–80; Dep. Chm., Malta Develt Corp., 1980–82. MP (Lab) Malta, 1987–2013; Leader, Labour Party, 1992–2008; Prime Minister of Malta, 1996–98; Leader of Opposition, 1998–2008. *Publications:* Malta's European Challenge, 1995; Memoires: confessions of a European Maltese, 2003; Malta and the euro, 2012; *novels:* L-Ewwel Weraq tal-Bajtar, 1968; Silg fuq Kemmuna, 1982; Bejgħ u Xiri, 1984; La Bidu, La Tmiem, 2001; L-Għalqa tal-Iskarjota, 2009 (The Iscariot Field, 2011); Bħal f'Dizzjunarju, 2011; George Bush in Malta, 2013; *dramas:* Min hu Evelyn Costa?, 1982; Fid-Dell tal-Katidral, 1994; Qabel Tiftaħ l-Inkjesta - u drammi oħra, 1999. *Recreations:* listening to classical music, walking. *Address:* 18A Victory Street, B'Kara, Malta.

SANTANA CARLOS, António Nunes; Ambassador of Portugal to the Court of St James's, 2006–10; *b* Lisbon, 20 March 1945; *s* of Victor Santana Carlos and Maria N. C. Santana Carlos; *m* 1982, Maria Pena Escudeiro; one *s*. *Educ:* Univ. of Lisbon (Soc. and Pol Scis). Joined Foreign Service, 1971, Attaché of Embassy; Third Sec., 1973–74; Second Sec., Tokyo, 1974–76; Hd, Cipher Dept, Foreign Office, 1976–79; First Sec., Dept of Internat. Econ. Orgns, Foreign Office, 1979–82; Perm. Mission of Portugal in Geneva, 1982–86; Minister Counsellor, Portuguese Embassy, Luanda, 1986–90; Dir, Multilateral Affairs Dept, Foreign Office, 1990–93; Minister Plenipotentiary and Dep.-Dir Gen. of Pol and Econ. Affairs, 1993–94; Dir, Office of Econ. Affairs, 1994, Chargé de Mission to the Minister of Foreign Affairs for promotion of Expo 98, Lisbon World Exhibn, 1995; Sen. Rep. to Sino-Portuguese Jt Liaison Gp and Pres., Interministerial Commn on Macau, 1996–2000; rank of Ambassador, 2000; Chargé de Mission to Minister of Foreign Affairs for East Timor Affairs, 2000; Dir-Gen. of Foreign Policy (Pol Dir), 2000–02; Ambassador to the People's Republic of China, 2002–06. Grand Cross, Order of Christ (Portugal); Grand Cross, Order of Merit (Portugal); Grand Officer, Order of Infante Dom Henrique (Portugal); Grand Officer, Order of Wissan Alouite (Morocco); Knight, Order of Rio Branco (Brazil). *Recreations:* golf, sailing, cinema. *Address:* c/o Portuguese Embassy, 11 Belgrave Square, SW1X 8PP. *Clubs:* Athenæum, Travellers, Royal Automobile; Royal Mid-Surrey Golf.

SANTER, Jacques; Chairman, CLT-UFA, since 2004; Member of the Board, RTL Group, since 2004; Chairman, UniCredit International Bank, Luxembourg, since 2005; *b* 18 May 1937; *m* Danièle Binot; two *s*. *Educ:* Athénée de Luxembourg; Paris Univ.; Strasbourg Univ.; Inst. d'Etudes Politiques, Paris. DenD. Advocate, Luxembourg Court of Appeal, 1961–65; Attaché, Office of Minister of Labour and Social Security, 1963–65; Govt Attaché, 1965–66; Christian Socialist Party: Parly Sec., 1966–72; Sec.-Gen., 1972–74; Pres., 1974–82; Sec. of State for Cultural and Social Affairs, 1972–74; Mem., Chamber of Deputies, 1974–79; MEP, 1975–79 (a Vice-Pres., 1975–77); Minister of Finance, Labour and Social Security, Luxembourg, 1979–84; Prime Minister of Luxembourg, 1984–95; Pres. of Govt, Minister of State and Minister of Finance, 1984–89; Minister for Cultural Affairs, 1989–94; Pres., EC, 1995–99; MEP (EPP), 1999–2004.

SANTER, Rt Rev. Mark; Bishop of Birmingham, 1987–2002; an Hon. Assistant Bishop: Diocese of Worcester, since 2002; Diocese of Birmingham, since 2003; *b* 29 Dec. 1936; *s* of late Rev. Canon Eric Arthur Robert Santer and Phyllis Clare Barlow; *m* 1st, 1964, Henriette Cornelia Weststrate (*d* 1994); one *s* two *d*; 2nd, 1997, Sabine Böhmig Bird. *Educ:* Marlborough Coll.; Queens' Coll., Cambridge (MA; Hon. Fellow, 1991); Westcott House, Cambridge. Deacon, 1963; priest 1964; Asst Curate, Cuddesdon, 1963–67; Tutor, Cuddesdon Theological Coll., 1963–67; Fellow and Dean of Clare Coll., Cambridge, 1967–72 (and Tutor, 1968–72; Hon. Fellow, 1987); Univ. Asst Lectr in Divinity, 1968–72; Principal of Westcott House, Cambridge, 1973–81; Hon. Canon of Winchester Cathedral, 1978–81; Area Bishop of Kensington, 1981–87. Co-Chm., Anglican Roman Catholic Internat. Commn, 1983–98. Hon. DD Birmingham, 1998; DD Lambeth, 1999; DUniv UCE, 2002. *Publications:* (contrib.) The Phenomenon of Christian Belief, 1970; (with M. F. Wiles) Documents in Early Christian Thought, 1975; Their Lord and Ours, 1982; (contrib.) The Church and the State, 1984; (contrib.) Dropping the Bomb, 1985; contrib. Jl of Theological Studies, Ecclesiology, Theology. *Address:* 81 Clarence Road, Birmingham B13 9UH. *T:* (0121) 441 2194.

SANTOMARCO, family name of **Baroness King of Bow**.

SANTOS-NEVES, Carlos Augusto Rego; Consul-General for Brazil in Porto, 2010; *b* Rio de Janeiro, 26 Jan. 1944; *m* Mary Joan Hershberger; two *s* one *d*. *Educ:* Colégio Pedro II, Rio de Janeiro; Inst. Rio Branco (Brazilian Diplomatic Acad.) (*summa cum laude;* doctorate); Fundação Getúlio Vargas (MBA Finance); Columbia Univ. (postgrad. pol sci.). Ministry of External Affairs, Brazil: Asst to Foreign Minister, 1977–79; COS to Sec. Gen., 1985–88; Consul Gen., NY, 1988–92; Ambassador: to Mexico, 1992–96; (non-resident) to Belize, 1995–96; to Canada, 1996–99; Sec., Policy Planning, 1999–2001; Consul Gen., Houston, 2001–03; Ambassador: to Russian Fedn, 2003–08; (non-resident) to Belarus, Georgia, Turkmenistan and Uzbekistan, 2003–08 and Kazakhstan, 2003–06; to the Court of St James's, 2008–10. Order of Rio Branco, Order of the Navy, Order of the Army, Order of the Air Force (Brazil); holds numerous foreign decorations incl. Chevalier, Légion d'Honneur, Ordre du Mérite (France); Simon Bolívar, Orden de Francisco de Miranda (Venezuela).

SANTS, Sir Hector (William Hepburn), Kt 2013; Chief Adviser to Abu Dhabi Global Market, since 2014; *b* 15 Dec. 1955; *s* of Hector John Sants and late Elsie Ann Watt Sants (*née* Hepburn); *m* 1987, Caroline Jane Mackenzie; three *s*. *Educ:* Clifton Coll.; Corpus Christi Coll., Oxford (MA PPP). Phillips & Drew, stockbrokers: joined as grad. trainee res., 1977; Partner, 1984–89; Hd, European Equities, Union Bank of Switzerland, 1989–97; Hd, Internat. Equities, Donaldson, Lufkin and Jenrette, 1997–2000; European Chief Exec., Credit Suisse First Boston, 2001–04; Man. Dir, Wholesale and Instnl Mkts, 2004–07, Chief Exec., 2007–12, FSA; Hd of Compliance and Govt Affairs, and Mem., Gp Exec. Cttee, Barclays Bank, 2013–14. Non-executive Director: London Stock Exchange, 1996–2001; LCH.Clearnet, 2003–04. Mem., Interim Financial Policy Cttee, Bank of England, 2011–12. Chm., Archbp's Task Gp on credit and savings, 2014–. Chm. Bd, Saïd Business Sch., Oxford Univ., 2010–13 (Mem., Adv. Bd, 2001–10); Mem. Bd, Nuffield Orthopaedic Centre, 2002–07.

SAPERSTEIN, Rabbi Prof. Marc Eli, PhD; Professor of Jewish History and Homiletics, Leo Baeck College, London, since 2011 (Principal, 2006–11); *b* 5 Sept. 1944; *s* of Harold Irving Saperstein and Marcia Belle Saperstein (*née* Rosenblum); *m* 2007, Tamar de Vries Winter; two *d* from former marriage. *Educ:* Harvard Coll. (AB English Lit. 1966); Hebrew Univ. of Jerusalem (MA Jewish Hist. 1971); Hebrew Union Coll.-Jewish Inst. of Religion, NY (MA 1972); Harvard Grad. Sch. of Arts and Scis (PhD Jewish Hist., Lit. and Thought 1977). Ordained Rabbi, 1972; Lectr on Hebrew Lit., Harvard Faculty of Arts and Scis, 1977–79; Asst Prof. of Jewish Studies, 1979–83, Associate Prof. of Jewish Studies, 1983–86, Harvard Divinity Sch.; Goldstein Prof. of Jewish Hist. and Thought, Washington Univ. in St Louis, 1986–97; Charles E. Smith Prof. of Jewish Hist. and Dir of Prog. in Judaic Studies, George Washington Univ., 1997–2006. Visiting Professor: Columbia Univ., 1980; Univ. of Pennsylvania, 1995; Revel Grad. Sch., Yeshiva Univ., 2002; KCL, 2009–; Harvard, 2012; Yale, 2013; Visiting Fellow: Inst. for Advanced Studies, Jerusalem, 1989; Center for Advanced Judaic Studies, Univ. of Pennsylvania, 1995–96; Centre for Jewish-Christian Relns, Cambridge, 2002; Harvard Center for Jewish Studies, 2005. Mem. Bd of Dirs, Assoc. for Jewish Studies, 1983–99; Vice Pres., Amer. Acad. for Jewish Res., 2004–06. Book Rev. Ed., Assoc. for Jewish Studies Rev., 1997–2002. *Publications:* Decoding the Rabbis: a thirteenth-century commentary on the Aggadah, 1980; Jewish Preaching 1200–1800, 1980; Moments of Crisis in Jewish-Christian Relations, 1989; Your Voice Like a Ram's Horn: themes and texts in traditional Jewish preaching, 1996; Exile in Amsterdam: Saul Levi Morteira's sermons to a congregation of New Jews, 2005; Jewish Preaching in Times of War 1800–2001, 2008; editor: Essential Papers on Messianic Movements and Personalities in Jewish History, 1992; Harold I. Saperstein: Witness from the Pulpit: topical sermons 1933–1980, 2000; Leadership and Conflict: tensions in medieval and early modern Jewish history and culture, 2014; articles and reviews on Jewish hist., lit. and thought. *Recreation:* classical piano. *Address:* Leo Baeck College, 80 East End Road, N3 2SY. *T:* (020) 8349 5600. *E:* msaper@gwu.edu.

SAPHIR, Nicholas Peter George; Chairman: OMSCo, The Organic Milk Suppliers Co-operative, since 2003; Epicore Health Ltd, since 2014; *b* 30 Nov. 1944; *s* of Emanuel Saphir and Ann (*née* Belikoff); *m* 1971, Ena Bodin; one *s*. *Educ:* City of London Sch.; Manchester Univ. (LLB Hons). Called to the Bar, Lincoln's Inn, 1967. Chm., Hunter Saphir, 1987–97; Director: Bodin & Nielsen Ltd, 1975–; Albert Fisher Gp PLC, 1993–97; City Food Centres Ltd, 2011–; Chairman: Coressence, 2006–14; New Israel Fund, 2009–14; non-executive Director: Dairy Crest Ltd, 1987–93; San Miguel SA (Argentina), 1993–98, 2001–07. Chairman: CCAHC, 1980–83; Agricultural Forum, 2001–04; Rural Revival, 2004–07; Founder Chm., Food From Britain, 1983–87; Mem., Food and Drink EDC, 1984–87; Chm., British Israel Chamber of Commerce, 1991–94. Pres., Fresh Produce Consortium, 1997–2000. *Recreation:* sailing. *Address:* Combe Manor Farm, Coombe Lane, Wadhurst, E Sussex TN5 6NU. *T:* (01892) 785111, *Fax:* (01892) 785222. *Clubs:* Farmers; Royal Cinque Ports Yacht.

SAPIN, Michel Marie; Deputy (Soc.) for Indre, National Assembly, France, since 2007; Minister of Finance, France, since 2014; *b* 9 April 1952; *m* 1982, Yolande Millan; three *s*. *Educ:* Ecole Normale Supérieure de la rue d'Ulm (MA Hist., post-grad. degree Geog.); Institut d'Etudes Politiques de Paris; Ecole Nationale d'Administration. Joined Socialist Party, 1975; National Assembly: Socialist Deputy of the Indre, 1981–86, of Hauts-de-Seine, 1986–91; Sec., 1983–84; Vice-Pres., 1984–85, 1988; Vice-Chm., Socialist Gp, 1987–88; Pres., Commn of Law, 1988–91. Minister-Delegate of Justice, 1991–92; Minister of the Economy and Finance, 1992–93, for the Civil Service and Admin. Reform, 2000–02; Minister of Labour, Employment and Social Dialogue, 2012–14. Mem., Monetary Policy Council, Bank of France, 1994–95. City Cllr, Nanterre, 1989–94; Regl Cllr, Ile de France, 1992–94; Gen. Cllr of the Indre, 1998–2004; Pres., 1998–2000, 2004–07, Vice-Pres., 2000–01, Centre Regl Council. Mayor, Argenton-sur-Creuse (Indre), 1995–2014. First Vice-Pres., Assoc. of Regions of France, 1998–2000. *Address:* 9 bis rue Dupertuis, 36200 Argenton-sur-Creuse, France.

SAPNARA, Khatun; Her Honour Judge Sapnara; a Circuit Judge, since 2014; *b* Sylhet, Bangladesh, 29 April 1967; *d* of Mimbor Ali and Sufia Khanam; *m* 2000, Simon Stanley, JP; two *s*. *Educ:* Chadwell Heath Sch., Essex; London Sch. of Econs and Pol Sci. (LLB Hons); Inns of Court Sch. of Law. Called to the Bar, Middle Temple, 1990; in practice as barrister, specialising in family law, 1990–2014; a Recorder, 2006–14. Mem., Family Justice Council, 2004–10. Chair, Ashiana Network, 2003–14. Mem. Bd, Rights of Women, 2009–14. Gov., Chadwell Heath Sch., 1992–2008. *Publications:* (contrib.) Re-Rooted Lives, 2007; (contrib.) Forced Marriage: social justice and human rights, 2011. *Recreations:* foreign travel, cooking and world cuisine, antique Indian textiles. *Address:* East London Family Court, 11 Westferry Circus, Canary Wharf, E14 8RP. *E:* HHJudge.sapnara@judiciary.gsi.gov.uk.

SARDAR, Ziauddin; writer, critic, broadcaster; Director, Center for Postnormal Policy and Futures Studies, East West University, Chicago, since 2014; *b* 31 Oct. 1951; *s* of late Salahuddin Sardar and of Hamida Bagum; *m* 1978, Saliha Basit; two *s* one *d*. *Educ:* Brooke House Sec. Sch., London; City Univ., London (BSc Hons 1974, MSc Inf. Sci. 1975). Inf. Consultant, Hajj Res. Centre, King Abdul Aziz Univ., Jeddah, 1975–79; Reporter, LWT, 1981–83; Dir, Centre for Policy and Future Studies, East West Univ., Chicago, 1985–88; Advr to Dep. Prime Minister of Malaysia, 1988–97. Member: Commn for Equality and Human Rights, 2006–09; Interim Nat. Security Forum, 2009–. Prof. of Law and Society, Middlesex Univ., 2011–14. Editor, Futures, 1997–2012; Co-editor: Third Text, 1999–2006; Critical Muslim, 2012–. *Publications:* Science, Technology and Development in the Muslim World, 1977; (jtly) Hajj Studies, 1978; Muhammad: aspects of his biography, 1978; Science Policy and Developing Countries, 1978; Islam: outline of a classification scheme, 1979; The Future of Muslim Civilization, 1979, 1987; Science and Technology in the Middle East, 1982; (ed) Touch of Midas: science values and environment in Islam and the West, 1984, 1999; Islamic Futures: the shape of ideas to come, 1986; (ed) The Revenge of Athena: science, exploitation and the Third World, 1988; Information and the Muslim World: a strategy for the twenty-first century, 1988; (ed) Building Information Systems in the Islamic World, 1988;

(ed) An Early Crescent, 1989; Explorations in Islamic Science, 1989; (jtly) Distorted Imagination: lessons from the Rushdie affair, 1990; (jtly) Christian-Muslim Relations: yesterday, today, tomorrow, 1991; (ed) How We Know, 1991; Introducing Islam, 1992; Barbaric Others, 1993; (ed jtly) Muslim Minorities in the West, 1995; (ed jtly) Cyberfutures, 1996; Postmodernism and the Other, 1998; (ed) Futures Studies; Orientalism, 1999; Introducing Muhammad, 1999; Introducing Mathematics, 1999; The Consumption of Kuala Lumpur, 2000; Thomas Kuhn and the Science Wars, 2000; Introducing Media Studies, 2000; Introducing Chaos, 2001; Introducing Cultural Studies, 2001; (jtly) Introducing Learning and Memory, 2002; Introducing Science, 2002; Aliens R Us, 2002; The A to Z of Postmodern Life, 2002; (jtly) Why Do People Hate America?, 2002; (ed jtly) The "Third Text" Reader on Art, Culture and Theory, 2002; (jtly) The No-Nonsense Guide to Islam, 2003; Islam, Postmodernism and other Futures, 2003; Desperately Seeking Paradise, 2004; (jtly) American Dream, Global Nightmare, 2004; (jtly) What is British?, 2004; American Terminator: myths, movies and global power, 2004; How Do We Know?: reading Ziauddin Sardar on Islam, science and cultural relations, 2005; What Do Muslims Believe?, 2006; Balti Britain: a journey through the British Asian experience, 2008; (jtly) Will America Change?, 2008; Reading the Qur'an, 2011; Muhammad: all that matters, 2012; (ed jtly) Muslims in Britain: making social and political space, 2012; Future: all that matters, 2013; Mecca: the Sacred City, 2014. *Recreation:* smoking Havana cigars. *E:* zsardar51@gmail.com. *Club:* Athenæum.

SARGEANT, Carl; Member (Lab) Alyn and Deeside, National Assembly for Wales, since 2003; Minister for Natural Resources, since 2014; *b* 1968; *s* of Malcolm and Sylvia Sargeant; *m* Bernie; one *s* one *d*. Trained industrial fire fighter; quality and envmtl auditor; process operator, manufacturing co., N Wales. Mem. (Lab) Connah's Quay Town Council. National Assembly for Wales: Chief Whip and Dep. Business Minister, 2007; Minister for Local Govt and Communities (formerly Social Justice and Local Govt), 2009–13; Minister for Housing and Regeneration, 2013–14. Gov., Deeside Coll. *Address:* (office) 70 High Street Connah's Quay, Deeside, Flintshire CH5 4DD; National Assembly for Wales, Cardiff CF99 1NA.

SARGEANT, Rt Rev. Frank Pilkington; an Hon. Assistant Bishop, Diocese of Manchester, since 1999, and Diocese of Liverpool, since 2007; *b* 12 Sept. 1932; *s* of John Stanley and Grace Sargeant; *m* 1958, Sally Jeanette McDermott; three *s* two *d*. *Educ:* Boston Grammar School; Durham Univ., St John's Coll. and Cranmer Hall (BA, Dip Theol); Nottingham Univ. (Diploma in Adult Education). National Service Commission, RA (20th Field Regt), 1955–57. Assistant Curate: Gainsborough Parish Church, 1958–62; Grimsby Parish Church, and Priest-in-Charge of St Martin's, Grimsby, 1962–67; Vicar of North Hykeham and Rector of South Hykeham, 1967–73; Residentiary Canon, Bradford Cathedral, 1973–77; Archdeacon of Bradford, 1977–84; Bishop Suffragan of Stockport, 1984–94; head of the Archbishop of Canterbury's staff (with title of Bishop at Lambeth), 1994–99, and Asst Bishop, dio. of Canterbury, 1995–99; retired 1999. Hon. Asst Bishop, Dio. in Europe, 1999–2008. Pres., Actors' Church Union, 1995–2007; Chm., Retired Clergy Assoc., 2003–07. *Publications:* A Complete Parish Priest: Peter Green 1871–1961, 2011; Dispatches from the Home Front, 2015. *Address:* 32 Brotherton Drive, Trinity Gardens, Salford M3 6BH. *T:* (0161) 839 7045. *E:* franksargeant68@outlook.com.

SARGENT, Anthony; *see* Sargent, D. A.

SARGENT, Dick; *see* Sargent, J. R.

SARGENT, (Donald) Anthony, CBE 2013; General Director, Sage Gateshead (formerly Music Centre Gateshead) and North Music Trust, 2000–15; *b* 18 Dec. 1949; *s* of Sir Donald Sargent, KBE, CB and Mary (*née* Raven); *m* 1st, 1978, Sara Gilford (marr. diss.); 2nd, 1986, Caroline Gant; one *d*. *Educ:* King's Sch., Canterbury; Oriel Coll., Oxford (Open Exhibnr; MA Hons PPE); Magdalen Coll., Oxford (Choral Schol.); Christ Church, Oxford (Choral Schol.). Various prodn and presentation posts, BBC Radio and TV, 1974–86 (Manager, BBC Concert Planning, 1982–86); Artistic Projects Dir, S Bank Centre, London, 1986–89; Hd of Arts, Birmingham CC, 1989–99; Partnerships and Prog. Develt Manager, BBC Music Live, 1999–2000. Chairman: NewcastleGateshead Cultural Venues, 2009–12; Fest. of the NE, 2011–13. Mem. Bd, Internat. Soc. for Performing Arts, 2005– (Chm., 2013–Jan. 2016). Freeman, Bor. of Gateshead, 2015. FRSA 1999. Hon. Fellow: Birmingham Conservatoire, 1999; Sunderland Univ., 2005. Hon. DMus Newcastle, 2015. Hotspur Award, Northumbrian Assoc., 2008. *Publications:* contrib. miscellaneous periodical and professional articles. *Recreations:* problem solving, fresh air, laughing. *Address:* 6 Winchester Terrace, Summerhill Square, Newcastle upon Tyne NE4 6EH.

SARGENT, Prof. John Reid, PhD; FRSE; Professor of Biological Science, University of Stirling, 1986–2001, now Emeritus; Director, Natural Environment Research Council Unit of Aquatic Biochemistry, University of Stirling, 1986–98; *b* 12 Oct. 1936; *s* of Alex and Annie Sargent; *m* 1961, Elizabeth Jean Buchan; two *d*. *Educ:* Buckie High Sch.; Robert Gordon's Coll., Aberdeen; Aberdeen Univ. (BSc 1st Cl. Hons, PhD). FRSE 1986. Res. Fellow, Middlesex Hosp. Med. Sch., 1961–64; Lectr, Biochem. Dept, Univ. of Aberdeen, 1964–69; PSO, then SPSO, then Dir, NERC Inst. of Marine Biochem., 1970–85; Stirling University: Head of Dept of Biol Science, 1985–89; Head of Sch. of Natural Scis, 1989–93. Bond Gold Medal, Amer. Oil Chemists' Soc., 1971. *Publications:* numerous research pubns in biochem. and marine biol., esp. on marine lipids and polyunsaturated fatty acids. *Recreations:* walking, talking. *Address:* 2 Hopeward Court, Dalgety Bay, Fife KY11 9TF; c/o Institute of Aquaculture, Faculty of Natural Sciences, University of Stirling, Stirling FK9 4LA. *T:* (01786) 473171.

SARGENT, John Richard, (Dick); *b* 22 March 1925; *s* of John Philip Sargent and Ruth (*née* Taunton); *m* 1st, 1949, Anne Elizabeth Haigh (marr. diss. 1980; *d* 2012); one *s* two *d*; 2nd, 1980, Hester Mary Campbell (*d* 2004). *Educ:* Dragon Sch., Oxford; Rugby Sch.; Christ Church, Oxford (MA). Fellow and Lectr in Econs, Worcester Coll., Oxford, 1951–62; Econ. Consultant, HM Treasury and DEA, 1963–65; Prof. of Econs, Univ. of Warwick, 1965–73 (Pro-Vice-Chancellor, 1971–72), Hon. Prof., 1974–81 and 2007–. Vis. Prof. of Econs, LSE, 1981–82; Gp Economic Adviser, Midland Bank Ltd, 1974–84; Houblon-Norman Res. Fellow, Bank of England, 1984–85. Member: Doctors and Dentists Rev. Body, 1972–75; Armed Forces Pay Rev. Body, 1972–86; Channel Tunnel Adv. Gp, 1974–75; SSRC, 1980–85; Pharmacists Review Panel, 1986–; Pres., Société Universitaire Européenne de Recherches Financières, 1985–88. Editor, Midland Bank Rev., 1974–84. *Publications:* British Transport Policy, 1958; (ed with R. C. O. Matthews) Contemporary Problems of Economic Policy, 1983; To Full Employment: the Keynesian Experience and After, 2007; articles in various economic jls, and in vols of conf. papers etc. *Recreation:* work. *Address:* 38 The Leys, Chipping Norton, Oxon OX7 5HH. *T:* (01608) 641773. *Club:* Reform.

SARGENT, Robert John; independent consulting hydrologist, since 2012; *b* Hove, Sussex, 17 Oct. 1952; *s* of Reginald and Patricia Sargent; *m* 1978, Elizabeth Mutch; two *d*. *Educ:* Hove Grammar Sch.; Univ. of Lancaster (BA 1974); Internat. Mgt Coll. (MBA 1985). CSci 2005; CEnv 2005. Chief Hydrologist, Forth River Bd, 1975–96; Hd, Envmtl Services, SEPA, 1996–2003; Principal Hydrologist, Marcus Hodges Envmt, 2003–04; Dir, Water Envmt, Hyder Consulting, 2005–11; Water Envmt Dir, Envmtl Gain Ltd, 2011–12. *Publications:* book chapters; contrib. papers to learned jls. *Recreations:* running, cycling, gardening and plant propagation. *Address:* Brook House, Mead Lane, Wanstrow, Som BA4 4TF. *E:* bobjsargent@msn.com.

SARGENT, Prof. Roger William Herbert, FREng; Courtaulds Professor of Chemical Engineering, Imperial College, 1966–92, now Emeritus; Senior Research Fellow, Imperial College, since 1992; *b* 14 Oct. 1926; *s* of Herbert Alfred Sargent and May Elizabeth (*née* Gill); *m* 1951, Shirley Jane Levesque (*née* Spooner); two *s*. *Educ:* Bedford Sch.; Imperial Coll., London (FIC 1994). BSc, ACGI, PhD, DScEng, DIC; FIChemE, FIMA; FREng (FEng 1976). Design Engineer, Société l'Air Liquide, Paris, 1951–58; Imperial College: Sen. Lectr, 1958–62; Prof. of Chem. Engrg, 1962–66; Dean, City and Guilds Coll., 1973–76; Head of Dept of Chem. Engrg and Chem. Technology, 1975–88; Dir of Interdisciplinary Res. Centre in Process Systems Engrg, 1989–92. Member: Engrg and Technol. Adv. Cttee, British Council, 1976–89 (Chm., 1984–89); Technol. Subcttee, UGC, 1984–88. Pres., Instn of Chem. Engrs, 1973–74; For. Associate, US Nat. Acad. of Engrg, 1993. FRSA 1988. Hon. FCGI 1977. *Dhc:* Institut Nat. Polytechnique de Lorraine, 1987; Univ. de Liège, 1996; Hon. DSc Edinburgh, 1993. *Publications:* contribs to: Trans Instn Chem. Engrs, Computers and Chemical Engrg, Jl of Optimization Theory and Applications, SIAM Jl of Optimization, Mathematical Programming, Internat. Jl of Control, etc. *Address:* Mulberry Cottage, 291A Sheen Road, Richmond, Surrey TW10 5AW. *T:* (020) 8876 9623.

SARGENT, Prof. Thomas John, PhD; Senior Fellow, Hoover Institution, Stanford University, since 1987; William R. Berkley Professor of Economics and Business, Leonard W. Stern School of Business, New York University, since 2002; *b* Pasadena, Calif, 19 July 1943; *s* of Charles R. Sargent; *m* Carolyn. *Educ:* Univ. of Calif, Berkeley (BA Econs 1964); Harvard Univ. (PhD Econs 1968). First Lieut, then Captain, US Army, 1968–69. Associate Prof. of Econs, Univ. of Pennsylvania, 1970–71; Associate Prof. of Econs, 1971–75, Prof. of Econs, 1975–87, Univ. of Minnesota; David Rockefeller Prof. of Econs, Univ. of Chicago, 1991–98; Donald Lucas Prof. of Econs, Stanford Univ., 1998–2002. Res. Associate, Nat. Bureau of Econ. Res., 1970–73, 1979–. Advr, Fed. Reserve Bank of Minneapolis, 1971–87. President: Soc. for Econ. Dynamics and Control, 1989–92; Amer. Econ. Assoc., 2007. Fellow: Econometric Soc., 1976 (Pres., 2005); NAS, 1983; Amer. Acad. Arts and Scis, 1983. Corresp. FBA, 2011. Mary Elizabeth Morgan Prize for Excellence in Econs, Univ. of Chicago, 1979; Erwin Nemmers Prize for Econs, Northwestern Univ., 1996; (jtly) Nobel Prize in Econ. Scis, 2011; NAS Award for Scientific Reviewing, 2011. *Publications:* (with N. Wallace) Rational Expectations and the Theory of Economic Policy, 1975, 3rd edn 2013; Macroeconomic Theory, 1979, 2nd edn 1987; (ed with R. Lucas) Rational Expectations and Econometric Practice, 1981; (ed) Energy, Foresight and Strategy, 1985; Rational Expectations and Inflation, 1986, 3rd edn 2013; Dynamic Macroeconomic Theory, 1987; Bounded Rationality in Macroeconomics, 1993; The Conquest of American Inflation, 1999; (with F. Velde) The Big Problem of Small Change, 2002; (with L. Ljungqvist) Recursive Macroeconomic Theory, 2004, 3rd edn 2012; (with L. P. Hansen) Robustness, 2008; (with L. P. Hansen) Recursive Models of Dynamic Linear Economies, 2013. *Address:* Department of Economics, New York University, 19 W Fourth Street, New York, NY 10012–1119, USA.

SARIN, Arun, Hon. KBE 2010; Chief Executive, Vodafone plc, 2003–08; *b* 21 Oct. 1954; *s* of Lt Col Krishan Sarin and Romilla Sarin; *m* 1980, Rummi Anand; one *s* one *d*. *Educ:* Indian Inst. of Technol., Kharagpur (BS Engrg); Univ. of California, Berkeley (MS Engrg; MBA). Various positions, Pacific Telesis Gp Inc., 1984–94; Vice Pres., Human Resources, Corporate Strategy and Develt, AirTouch Communications, 1994–95; Pres. and Chief Exec., AirTouch Internat., 1995–97; Pres. and Chief Operating Officer, AirTouch Communications, 1997–99; Chief Executive Officer: US/Asia Pacific Reg., Vodafone AirTouch, 1999–2000; Infospace, 2000; Accel-KKR Telecom, 2001–03. Non-executive Director: Cisco Systems Inc., 1998–2003 and 2009–; Bank of England, 2005–09; Safeway Inc., 2009–; Aricent Inc., 2010–; Devicespace, 2013–; Sen. Advr, KKR, 2009–. *Recreations:* golf, tennis, running.

SARK, Seigneur of; *see* Beaumont, J. M.

SARKAR, Bidesh; Founder and Chief Executive Officer, ed4work, since 2015; *b* Leicester, 1 June 1969; *s* of Bibhuti Kumar Sarkar and Jharna Sarkar; *m* 1995, Emma Louise; two *s* one *d*. *Educ:* Univ. of Sussex (BSc Hons Maths and Econs); INSEAD (MBA). ACA 1994. Kimberly-Clark Europe, 1997–2005, Divl Finance Dir, 2003–05; Gp Finance Dir, Plan Internat., 2005–07; Chief Financial Officer, British Council, 2007–13. Dir and Chm., Pinkham Way Alliance, 2011–. Gov., Hollickwood Primary Sch., N London, 2010–. *Recreations:* running (London Marathon, 2009), yoga, cycling.

SARKIS, Angela Marie, CBE 2000; Member, Youth Justice Board, since 2009; *b* 6 Jan. 1955; *d* of Rupert Sadler and Hazel Sadler (*née* McDonald); *m* 1980, Edward Tacvor Sarkis; one *s* one *d*. *Educ:* Cottesmore Sch., Nottingham; Clarendon Coll. of Further Educn, Nottingham; Leeds Univ. (BA Theol./Sociol.); Leicester Univ. (Dip. Social Work and CQSW). Probation Officer, Middx Probation Service, 1979–89; Unit Manager, Brent Family Services Unit, 1989–91; Asst Dir, Intermediate Treatment Fund, 1991–93; Dir, DIVERT Trust, 1993–96; Chief Exec., Church Urban Fund, 1996–2001; a Governor, BBC, 2002–06; Nat. Sec., YMCA England, 2006–08; Chief Exec., Nurture Group Network, 2009–11. Advr, Social Exclusion Unit, Cabinet Office, 1997–; Mem., H of L Appts Commn, 2000–08; a Civil Service Comr, 2012–. Mem. Council, Howard League for Penal Reform, 1998–. Member: Housing and Neighbourhood Cttee, Joseph Rowntree Foundn, 1997–; Bd, Capacitybuilders, 2008–11. Mem. Council, Evangelical Alliance, 1995–99; Vice-Pres., African and Caribbean Evangelical Alliance, 1996; Mem., Leadership Team, Brentwater Evangelical Ch, NW2, 1990–94. Mem. Cttee, Assoc. Charitable Foundns, 1995–99; Trustee: BBC Children in Need, 1995–2002; Inst. Citizenship Studies, 1995–97; Notting Hill Housing Trust, 1995–97. Trustee: Single Homeless Housing Project, NW10, 1980–87; Learie Constantine Youth Club, NW2, 1980–90; Single Mothers Project, NW10, 1984–90; Tavistock Youth Club, NW10, 1985–90. *Recreations:* gardening, family, singing.

SARKOZY DE NAGY-BOCSA, Nicolas Paul Stéphane; Grand Croix de la Légion d'Honneur, 2007; Hon. GCB 2008; President of the French Republic, 2007–12; Member, Constitutional Council of France, 2012–13; *b* 28 Jan. 1955; *s* of Pal Sarkozy de Nagy-Bocsa and Andrée (*née* Mallah); *m* 1996, Cécilia Ciganer-Albeniz (marr. diss. 2007); one *s*, and two *s* from previous marriage; *m* 2008, Carla Bruni; one *d*. *Educ:* Maîtrise de droit privé, 1978; Cours St-Louis de Monceau; Inst d'Études Politiques, Paris (Cert d'aptitude à la profession d'avocat, 1981); Univ. Paris X-Nanterre. Lawyer, 1981–87. Neuilly-sur-Seine: Municipal Councillor, 1977–83; Mayor, 1983–2002; Dep. Mayor, 2002; Conseil Général des Hauts-de-Seine: Mem., 1985–88 and 2004; Vice-Pres., 1986–88; Pres., 2004–07; Deputy (RPR) Hauts-de-Seine, 1988, re-elected 1993, 1995, 1997, 2002. Minister: of the Budget, 1993–95; of Communication, 1994–95; of the Interior, Interior Security and Local Freedom, 2002–04; of State, and Minister of the Economy, Finance and Industry, 2004; of the Interior and Regional Develt, 2005–07. Rassemblement pour la République: Nat. Sec., 1988–92; Dep. Sec.-Gen., 1990–93; Mem., Political Office, 1993; Sec. Gen., then interim Pres., 1998–99; Pres., Deptl Cttee, Hauts-de-Seine, 2000; Pres., UMP, later Les Républicains, 2004–07 and 2014–. *Publications:* Georges Mandel: le moine de la politique, 1994; (with M. Denisot) Au bout de la passion, l'équilibre, 1995; Libre, 2001; La République, les Réligions, l'Espérance, 2004; Témoignage, 2006; Ensemble, 2007. *Address:* 77 rue de Miromesnil, 75008 Paris, France.

SARMADI, Morteza; Deputy Foreign Minister, Iran, since 2013; *b* July 1954; *m* 1982, Fatemeh Hosseini; four *d*. *Educ:* Sharif Univ. (BS Metallurgy); Tehran Univ. (Internat. Relns). Joined Ministry of Foreign Affairs, Tehran, 1981: Dir Gen., Press and Inf., 1982–89; Deputy Foreign Minister: for Communication, 1989–97; Eur. and American and CIS Countries' Affairs, 1997–2000; Iranian Ambassador to UK, 2000–04; Dep. Foreign Minister for

European and American Affairs, Iran, 2004–05; Advr to Foreign Minister for Political and Internat. Studies, 2005–08; Sec. Gen. (formerly Exec. Dir), Indian Ocean Rim Assoc. for Regl Co-operation, 2008–11. Special Rep. to Caspian Sea Legal Regime; Sen. Mem., Delegn for Iran and Iraq Peace Negotiation. Has participated in numerous confs internationally. Trustee Member: Islamic Thought Foundn; Islamic Republic News Agency; Islamic High Council of Propagation Policy; Inst. for Political and Internat. Studies. *Recreations:* reading, watching TV, swimming, spending time with the family.

SARNAK, Prof. Peter, PhD; FRS 2002; Eugene Higgins Professor of Mathematics, since 2002, and Professor, Institute for Advanced Study, since 2007, Princeton University; *b* Johannesburg, 18 Dec. 1953. *Educ:* Univ. of Witwatersrand (BSc 1975); Stanford Univ. (PhD 1980). Asst Prof., 1980–83, Associate Prof., 1983–84, Prof., 2001–05, Courant Inst. of Math. Scis, NY Univ.; Associate Prof., 1984–87, Prof., 1987–91, Stanford Univ.; Princeton University: Prof., 1991–; H. Fine Prof., 1995–96; Chm., Dept of Maths, 1996–99; Mem., Inst. for Advanced Study, 1999–2002 and 2005–07. *Publications:* Some Applications of Modular Forms, 1990; (jtly) Extremal Riemann Surfaces, 1997; (ed jtly) Random Matrices, Frobenius Eigenvalues and Monodromy, 1998; articles in jls. *Address:* Department of Mathematics, Princeton University, Fine Hall, Washington Road, Princeton, NJ 08544–1000, USA.

SAROOP, Narindar, CBE 1982; Senior Adviser, Gow & Partners, 2005–07; *b* 14 Aug. 1929; *e s* of late Chaudhri Ram Saroop, Ismaila, Rohtak, India and Shyam Devi; *m* 1st, 1952, Ravi Gill (marr. diss. 1967), *o* surv. *c* of the Sardar and Sardarni of Premgarh, India; one *d* (and one *s* one *d* decd); 2nd, 1969, Stephanie Denise, *yr d* of Alexander and Cynthia Amie Cronopulo, Zakynthos, Greece. *Educ:* Aitchison Coll. for Punjab Chiefs, Lahore; Indian Military Acad., Dehra Dun. Served as regular officer, 2nd Royal Lancers (Gardner's Horse) and Queen Victoria's Own The Poona Horse; retired, 1954. Management Trainee, Yule Catto, 1954; senior executive and Dir of subsidiaries of various multinationals, to 1976; Hon. Administrator, Oxfam Relief Project, 1964; Director: Devi Grays Insurance Ltd, 1981–84; Capital Plant International Ltd, 1982–86. Adviser: Develt, Clarkson Puckle Gp, 1976–87; Banque Belge, 1987–91; Cancer Relief Macmillan Fund, 1992–95; Nat. Grid plc, 1993; Coutts & Co., 1995–98. Mem., BBC Adv. Council on Asian Programmes, 1977–81. Pres., Indian Welfare Soc., 1983–92. Member Council: Freedom Assoc., 1978–86; Internat. Social Services, 1981–91; Inst. of Directors, 1983–93; Founder Mem., Tory Asians for Representation Gp, 1984–85; Mem. Adv. Council, Efficiency in Local Govt, 1984. Contested (C) Greenwich, 1979 (first Asian Tory Parliamentary candidate this century); Founder and 1st Chm., UK Anglo Asian Cons. Soc., 1976–79, 1985–86; Vice Chm., Cons. Party Internat. Office, 1990–92. Councillor (C), Kensington and Chelsea, 1974–82; initiated Borough Community Relations Cttee (Chm., 1975–77, 1980–82); Chm., Working Party on Employment, 1978; Founder and Chm., Durbar Club, 1981–2014. Mem., V & A Mus. Appeal Cttee, 1994–95. Patron, Conservative World, 2003–05. Hon. Mem., Clan Moncreiffe, 2000. *Publications:* In Defence of Freedom (jtly), 1978; A Squire of Hindoostan, 1983; The Last Indian (autobiog.), 2005. *Recreation:* keeping fools, boredom and socialism at bay. *Clubs:* Beefsteak, Cavalry and Guards, Pratt's; Puffin's (Edinburgh); Imperial Delhi Gymkhana; Royal Bombay Yacht, Royal Calcutta Golf.

SAROOSHI, Prof. Dan, PhD; Professor of Public International Law, University of Oxford, since 2006; Senior Research Fellow, Queen's College, Oxford, since 2012 (Fellow, 2003); barrister, since 2005; *b* 3 March 1968; *s* of R. and R. Sarooshi; *m* 1997, Mary Huddleston; two *s*. *Educ:* Univ. of New South Wales (LLB/BComm 1991); King's Coll., London (LLM 1992); London Sch. of Econs (PhD 1997). Lectr, Sen. Lectr then Reader in Public Internat. Law, UCL, 1997–2003; Lectr, then Herbert Smith Reader in Public Internat. Law, Univ. of Oxford, 2003–06. Emile Noël Fellow, Sch. of Law, New York Univ., 2002. Of Counsel, Tite & Lewis, in assoc. with Ernst & Young, 2001–04; called to the Bar, Middle Temple, 2005; barrister, Essex Court Chambers, 2006–. Member: List of Panellists, World Trade Orgn Dispute Settlement, 2006–; Attorney-Gen.'s Panel (A) of Public Internat. Law Counsel, 2013–. Mem., Exec. Council, Amer. Soc. of Internat. Law, 2008–11. Hon. MA Oxon, 2003. *Publications:* The United Nations and the Development of Collective Security: the delegation by the United Nations Security Council of its Chapter VII powers, 1999 (Guggenheim Book Prize, Swiss Guggenheim Foundn, 1999; Book Prize, Amer. Soc. of Internat. Law, 2001); (ed with M. Fitzmaurice) Issues of State Responsibility before International Judicial Institutions, 2004; International Organizations and their Exercise of Sovereign Powers, 2005 (Myres S. McDougal Book Prize, Amer. Soc. for the Policy Scis, 2006; Book Prize, Amer. Soc. of Internat. Law, 2006). *Recreations:* opera, jazz. *Address:* Essex Court Chambers, 24 Lincoln's Inn Fields, WC2A 3EG. *T:* (020) 7813 8000. *E:* Dan.Sarooshi@law.ox.ac.uk.

SARUM, Archdeacon of; *see* Jeans, Ven. A. P.

SARWAR, Anas; *b* Glasgow, 14 March 1983; *s* of Mohammad Sarwar, *qv*; *m* 2006, Furheen Ashrif; two *s*. *Educ:* Hutchesons' Grammar Sch.; Sch. of Dentistry, Univ. of Glasgow (BDS Dentistry 2005). NHS Dentist, 2005–10. MP (Lab) Glasgow Central, 2010–15; contested (Lab) same seat, 2015. Mem., Internat. Develt Select Cttee, 2010–12. *Recreations:* current affairs, sport, reading, travelling, spending time with family.

SARWAR, Mohammad; Governor of Punjab, Pakistan, 2013–15; *b* 18 Aug. 1952; *s* of Mohammed and Rashida Abdullah Sarwar; *m* 1976, Perveen Sarwar; three *s* one *d*. *Educ:* Government Coll., Faisalabad (FSC; BA). Shopkeeper, 1976–83; Dir, United Wholesale Ltd, 1983–97. Member (Lab): Glasgow DC, 1992–96; Glasgow CC, 1995–97. MP (Lab) Glasgow Govan, 1997–2005, Glasgow Central, 2005–10. First ethnic minority MP in Scotland; first Muslim MP in Britain. *Recreation:* relaxing with family and friends.

See also A. Sarwar.

SASSOON, family name of **Baron Sassoon**.

SASSOON, Baron *cr* 2010 (Life Peer), of Ashley Park in the County of Surrey; **James Meyer Sassoon,** Kt 2008; FCA; Executive Director, Jardine Matheson Holdings, since 2013; *b* 11 Sept. 1955; *s* of Hugh Meyer Sassoon and Marion Julia Sassoon (*née* Schiff); *m* 1981, Sarah Caroline Ray Barnes, *d* of Sir (Ernest) John Ward Barnes; one *s* two *d*. *Educ:* Eton Coll.; Christ Church, Oxford (MA). ACA 1980, FCA 1991. Thomson McLintock & Co., 1977–86; SG Warburg & Co. Ltd, 1987–95 (Dir, 1991–95); Warburg Dillon Read, subseq. UBS Warburg: Man. Dir, 1995–2002; Vice Chm., Investment Banking, 2000–02; Man. Dir, Finance, Regulation and Industry, 2002–06, Chancellor's Rep. for Promotion of City, 2006–08, HM Treasury. Pres., Financial Action Task Force, 2007–08. Author of The Tripartite Review, 2009. Mem., Econ. Recovery Cttee, Shadow Cabinet, 2009–10; Commercial Sec. to HM Treasury, 2010–13. Director: Partnerships UK, 2002–06; Nuclear Liabilities Fund, 2008–10. Dir, Hackney Business Venture, subseq. HBV Enterprise, 2000–02. Director: Dairy Farm Internat. Hldgs, 2013–; Hongkong Land Hldgs, 2013–; Mandarin Oriental Internat., 2013–; Jardine Lloyd Thompson, 2013–. Chairman: ifs Sch. of Finance, 2009–10; Merchants Trust, 2010 (Dir, 2006–10); China-Britain Business Council, 2013–; Member: Adv. Bd, Resolution Foundn, 2007–10; Global Adv. Bd, Mitsubishi UFJ Financial Gp, 2013–; Cttee, Hong Kong Assoc., 2013–. Trustee: Gerald Coke Handel Foundn, 2001–10; Nat. Gall. Trust, 2002–09; British Mus., 2009–10 and 2013–. Governor, Ashdown House Sch., 2001–06. *Publications:* articles in art and financial jls. *Recreations:* travel, the arts, watching sport. *Address:* Jardine Matheson Holdings, 3 Lombard Street, EC3V 9AQ. *Club:* MCC.

See also A. D. Sassoon.

SASSOON, Adrian David; dealer in 18th century French porcelain and contemporary British studio ceramics, glass and silver, since 1992; *b* 1 Feb. 1961; *s* of Hugh Meyer Sassoon and Marion Julia Sassoon (*née* Schiff). *Educ:* Sunningdale Sch.; Eton Coll.; Inchbald Sch. of Design, London; Christie's, London (fine arts diploma). Asst Curator of Decorative Arts, J. Paul Getty Mus., Malibu, 1980–84; ind. researcher, 1984–87; Dir, Alexander & Berendt Ltd, London, 1987–92; private dealer and art advr, 1992–. Trustee: UK Friends of Hermitage Mus., St Petersburg, 2006–; Wallace Collection, 2007–; The Silver Trust, 2013–. Mem. Council, Furniture History Soc., 2010–13. *Publications:* Decorative Arts: a handbook catalogue of the collection of the J. Paul Getty Museum (with Gillian Wilson), 1986; Catalogue of Vincennes and Sèvres Porcelain in the J. Paul Getty Museum, Malibu, 1991; Vincennes and Sèvres Porcelain from a European Private Collector, 2001; Jewels by JAR, 2013. *Recreations:* museums, beaches. *E:* email@adriansassoon.com. *Clubs:* Brooks's; Lyford Cay (Nassau).

See also Baron Sassoon.

SASSOON, Prof. Donald, PhD; Professor of Comparative European History, Queen Mary, University of London, 1997–2012, now Emeritus; *b* 25 Nov. 1946; *s* of Joseph Isaac Sassoon and Doris Sassoon (*née* Bardak); *m* 1973, Anne Showstack (marr. diss. 1987); one *d*. *Educ:* schools in Paris, Milan and Tunbridge Wells; University Coll. London (BSc Econ 1969); Pennsylvania State Univ. (MA 1971); Birkbeck Coll., Univ. of London (PhD 1977). Lectr in Hist., 1979–89, Reader in Hist., 1989–97, Westfield Coll., then QMW, Univ. of London. Nuffield Social Sci. Fellow, 1997–98; Vis. Prof., Univ. of Trento, 1999; Leverhulme Maj. Res. Fellow, 2000–03; Sen. Res. Fellow, New York Univ., 2001; Samuel Wood Brooks Vis. Prof. of English Lit., Univ. of Qld, 2009. Mem., Comité Scientifique (formerly Comité d'Orientation), Maison de l'Histoire de France, 2011–12. Literary Ed., Political Qly, 2000–. *Publications:* The Strategy of the Italian Communist Party, 1981; Contemporary Italy: politics, economy and society since 1945, 1986, 2nd edn 1997; One Hundred Years of Socialism: the West European Left in the Twentieth Century, 1996 (Deutscher Meml Prize 1997); Mona Lisa: the history of the world's most famous painting, 2001; Leonardo and the Mona Lisa Story, 2006; The Culture of the Europeans, 2006 (Premio Alassio Internazionale, 2009); Mussolini and the Rise of Fascism, 2007; contribs to jls. *Recreations:* travel, classical music, country walking. *Address:* School of History, Queen Mary, University of London, Mile End Road, E1 4NS. *E:* d.sassoon@qmul.ac.uk.

SATCHELL, Keith; Group Chief Executive, Friends Provident plc (formerly Friends Provident Life Office), 1997–2007; *b* 3 June 1951; *s* of Dennis Joseph Satchell and Joan Betty Satchell; *m* 1972, Hazel Burston; two *s* one *d*. *Educ:* Univ. of Aston (BSc). FIA 1976. With Duncan C. Fraser, 1972–75; UK Provident, 1975–86; Friends Provident, 1986–2007: Gen. Manager, 1987–97; Dir, 1992–2007. Chairman: ABI, 2005–07; Rothesay Life, 2007–; Barnett Waddingham, 2007–. *Recreations:* soccer, golf, ski-ing, theatre.

SATCHWELL, Sir Kevin (Joseph), Kt 2001; Headmaster, Thomas Telford School, since 1991; *b* 6 March 1951; *e s* of late Joseph and Pauline Satchwell; *m* 1975, Maria Bernadette Grimes; one *s* one *d*. *Educ:* Wodensborough High Sch.; Wednesbury Boys' High Sch.; Shoreditch Coll. of Technology (Cert Ed London Univ. 1973); Open Univ. (BA 1977; AdvDip Educn Mgt 1978). Teacher, Cantril High Sch., Liverpool, 1973–79; Dep. Head, Brookfield Sch., Liverpool, 1979–87; Headteacher, Moseley Park Sch., Wolverhampton, 1987–90. Dir, London Qualifications, 2003–05. Member: NCET, 1994–96; City Technology Colls Principals' Forum, 1991 (Chm., 1997); Chm., W Midlands Consortium for School Centred Initial Teacher Trng, 1993–. Trustee: Edge Foundn, 2010–; Baker Dearing Educnl Trust, 2014–. *Recreations:* family, football coaching, tennis, golf. *Address:* Thomas Telford School, Old Park, Telford TF3 4NW. *T:* (01952) 200000.

SATOW, Rear-Adm. Derek Graham, CB 1977; *b* 13 June 1923; *y s* of late Graham F. H. Satow, OBE, and Evelyn M. Satow (*née* Moore); *m* 1944, Patricia E. A. Penaliggon (*d* 2014); two *d*. *Educ:* Oakley Hall Sch.; Haileybury Coll.; Royal Naval Engineering Coll. CEng, FIMechE, FIMarEST. Sea trng, HMS Belfast, 1941; HMS Ceylon, 1945–46; RNC, Greenwich, 1946–48; HMS Duke of York, 1948–49; RAE Farnborough, 1949–51; HMS Newcastle, 1951–53 (despatches, 1953); Naval Ordnance and Weapons Dept, Admiralty, 1953–59; Dir of Engineering, RNEC, 1959–62; HMS Tiger, 1962–64; Asst and Dep. Dir of Marine Engineering, MoD, 1964–67; IDC, 1968; Captain, RNEC, 1969–71; Dir, Naval Officer Appointments (Eng), MoD, 1971–73; Chief Staff Officer, Technical, later Engineering, to C-in-C Fleet, 1974–76; Dep. Dir-Gen., Ships, MoD, 1976–79; Chief Naval Engr Officer, 1977–79. Comdr, 1955; Captain, 1964; Rear-Adm., 1973. Arctic Star, 2013; Ushakov Medal (Russia), 2014.

SATSANGI, Prof. Jyoti, (Jack), DPhil; FRCP, FRCPE, FMedSci; FRSE; Professor of Gastro-enterology, University of Edinburgh, since 2000; Honorary Consultant Physician, Western General Hospital, Edinburgh, since 2000; *b* Yorks, 8 May 1963; *s* of Prem Nath Satsangi and Nirmal Satsangi; *m* 2008, Patricia Moore; one *s* one *d*. *Educ:* Brentwood Sch.; St Thomas's Hosp. Med. Sch., London (BSc 1984; MB BS (Dist.) 1987); Worcester Coll., Oxford (DPhil 1996). MRCP 1990, FRCP 2005; FRCPE 2002. Hse Physician, St Thomas's Hosp., London, 1987–88; SHO, Oxford Radcliffe Hosps., 1988–90; University of Oxford: Registrar in Medicine, Nuffield Dept of Medicine, 1990–92; MRC Clinical Fellow, 1992–96; MRC Clinician Scientist and Hon. Consultant Physician, 1997–2000. FMedSci 2009; FRSE 2010. *Publications:* articles in many jls incl. Nature, Nature Genetics, Lancet, New England Jl. *Recreations:* tennis, running, cycling, reading to my children. *Address:* 9 Cluny Place, Edinburgh EH10 4RH. *E:* j.satsangi@ed.ac.uk.

SATTERTHWAITE, Christopher James; Group Chief Executive, Chime Communications plc, since 2003; *b* 21 May 1956; *s* of Col Richard George Satterthwaite and Rosemary Ann Satterthwaite; *m* 1988, Teresa Mary Bailey; two *s* one *d*. *Educ:* Ampleforth Coll.; Lincoln Coll., Oxford (MA Mod. Hist.). Graduate trainee, H. J. Heinz, 1978–81; IMP Ltd, 1981–98, Chief Exec., 1990–98; Chief Executive: HHCL Ltd, 1998–2000; Bell Pottinger Ltd, 2000–02. Chm., Roundhouse, 2010–; Sen. Ind. Dir, Centaur Media, 2011–. *Recreations:* Parson Woodforde Society, marathon running, bombology. *Address:* Tuesley Manor, Tuesley Lane, Godalming, Surrey GU7 1UD. *T:* (01483) 429336. *E:* csatterthwaite@chime.plc.uk.

SATYANAND, Rt Hon. Sir Anand, GNZM 2009 (PCNZM 2006; DCNZM 2005); QSO 2007; Governor-General of New Zealand, 2006–11; Chairman, Commonwealth Foundation, since 2013; *b* 22 July 1944; *s* of Dr Mutyala Satyanand and Tara Satyanand; *m* 1970, Susan Jean Sharpe; one *s* two *d*. *Educ:* Univ. of Auckland (LLB). Barrister and solicitor, 1970–82; Dist Court Judge with Jury Trial Warrant, 1982–2005; Parly Ombudsman, 1995–2005. Registrar, Pecuniary Interests of MPs, 2005. Chairman: Confidential Forum for Former In Patients of Psychiatric Hosps, 2005–06; Aegis Study of Govt Information Sharing, 2013–; Patron, Transparency Internat. NZ 2012–13. Hon. LLD Auckland, 2006. KStJ 2006. *Publications:* contrib. jls and legal pubns on legal educn, trial skills enhancement and ombudsman studies. *Recreations:* reading, writing, sport, sporting administration. *Address:* PO Box 9062, Marion Square, Wellington 6141, New Zealand. *T:* (2) 1586409. *E:* anand.satyanand@gmail.com. *Clubs:* Wellington, Royal Commonwealth (Wellington); Northern (Auckland).

SAUER, Fernand Edmond; Honorary Director General, European Commission, since 2006; *b* 14 Dec. 1947; *s* of Ferdinand Sauer and Emilie Scherer Sauer; *m* 1971, Pamela Sheppard; one *s* two *d*. *Educ:* Univ. of Strasbourg (pharmacist, 1971); Paris II Univ. (Masters in European Law, 1977). Hosp. Pharmacist, Reunion Island, 1972–73; Pharmaceutical Insp., Health Min.,

France, 1974–79; European Commission: Adminr, 1979–85; Head of Pharmaceuticals, 1986–94; Exec. Dir, Eur. Agency for the Evaluation of Medicinal Products, 1994–2000; Dir, Public Health Policy, DG for Health and Consumer Protection, EC, 2000–05. Member: Faculty of Pharmacy, London Univ., 1996–; High Council for Public Health (France), 2007–11. Mem., French Acad. of Pharmacy, 2000. Hon. Fellow, RPSGB, 1996. Chevalier de l'Ordre du Mérite (France), 1990; Chevalier de la Légion d'Honneur (France), 1998. *Publications:* various articles and publications on pharmaceutical regulation. *Recreation:* jogging. *Address:* 12 avenue de la Marne, 13260 Cassis, France.

SAUL, Berrick; *see* Saul, S. B.

SAUL, Christopher Francis Irving; Senior Partner, Slaughter and May, since 2008; *b* Carlisle, 1955; *s* of Irving and Greta Saul; *m* 1985, Anne Cartier; one *s* one *d. Educ:* Tiffin Sch.; St Catherine's Coll., Oxford (BA Juris.). Joined Slaughter and May, 1977; Partner, 1986–. *Recreations:* motor cars, contemporary music, reading, cinema. *E:* christopher.saul@slaughterandmay.com.

SAUL, Hon. David John; JP; PhD; financial consultant; President, Fidelity International Bermuda Ltd, 1984–99, retired; Premier of Bermuda, 1995–97; *b* 27 Nov. 1939; *s* of late John Saul and Sarah Saul; *m* 1963, Christine Hall; one *s* one *d. Educ:* Queen's Univ., Canada (BA); Univ. of Toronto (MEd, PhD); Nottingham Univ. (CertEd); Loughborough Univ. of Tech. (DipEd). Perm. Sec. for Educn, 1972–76, Financial Sec., 1976–81, Bermuda Govt; Chief Admin. Officer, Edmund Gibbons Ltd, 1982–84; MP (United Bermuda Party) Devonshire South, 1989–97; Minister of Finance, Bermuda, 1989–95. Pres., Fidelity Internat. Ltd, 1984–95; Exec. Vice Pres., Fidelity Investments, Worldwide, 1990–95; Director: Fidelity Internat. Ltd, 1984–; Lombard Odier (Bermuda) Ltd, 1995–2010. Director: Bermuda Monetary Authority, 1987–89, 1998–99; Bermuda Track and Field Assoc., 1987–; London Steamship Owners Mutual Assoc., 1989–2010; Odyssey Marine Exploration Inc., 2001–. Trustee, Bermuda Underwater Exploration Inst., 1992–99 (Life Trustee, 1999). Hon. BSc 2009, DUniv 2012, Loughborough. *Recreations:* running, scuba, fishing, kayaking, stalking, collecting Bermuda stamps, Bermuda currency notes, and sea shells, carving old cedar roots. *Address:* Rocky Ledge, 18 Devonshire Bay Road, Devonshire DV 07, Bermuda. *T:* 2367338. *E:* davidjsaul@aol.com. *Clubs:* Explorers (New York); Mid Ocean, Royal Hamilton Amateur Dinghy (Bermuda).

SAUL, Prof. Nigel Edward, DPhil; FSA, FRHistS, FHA; Professor of Medieval History, Royal Holloway, University of London, since 1997; *b* 20 June 1952; *s* of Edward Thomas Saul and Marion Saul (*née* Duffy); *m* 1983, Jane Melanie Nichols; one *s* one *d. Educ:* King Edward VI Sch., Stratford-upon-Avon; Hertford Coll., Oxford (BA 1974; MA, DPhil 1978). FRHistS 1984; FSA 1988; FHA 2012. Royal Holloway, University of London: Lectr in Medieval Hist., 1978–88; Reader in Medieval Hist., 1988–97; Hd, Dept of History, 2002–05. Vice-Pres., Monumental Brass Soc., 2002– (Pres., 1995–2002). Lectures: Bond Meml, St George's Chapel, Windsor, 2008; Cantilupe, Hereford Cathedral, 2011. Trustee, Victoria County History, 2009–. Series Editor, Hambledon and London Books, 1998–2007; Mem., Editorial Adv. Bd, History Today, 1987–. *Publications:* Knights and Esquires: the Gloucestershire gentry in the fourteenth century, 1981; Scenes from Provincial Life: knightly families in Sussex 1280–1400, 1986; (ed and contrib.) Historical Atlas of Britain: prehistoric to medieval, 1994; Richard II, 1997; (ed and contrib.) Oxford Illustrated History of Medieval England, 1997; Companion to Medieval England 1066–1400, 2000; (ed) Fourteenth Century England, vol. I, 2000; Death, Art and Memory: the Cobham family and their monuments 1300–1500, 2001; The Three Richards, 2005; (ed) St George's Chapel, Windsor, in the Fourteenth Century, 2005; Fourteenth Century England, vol. V, 2008; English Church Monuments in the Middle Ages: history and representation, 2009; (ed jtly) St George's Chapel, Windsor: history and heritage, 2010; For Honour and Fame: chivalry in England, 1066–1500, 2011; articles in learned jls. *Recreations:* visiting country churches, lepidoptera, gardening. *Address:* Gresham House, Egham Hill, Egham, Surrey TW20 0ER. *E:* n.saul@rhul.ac.uk.

SAUL, Roger John; Owner: Sharpham Park, since 2004; Kilver Court Designer Village and Gardens, since 2008; *b* 25 July 1950; *s* of Michael and Joan Saul; *m* 1977, Monty Cameron; three *s. Educ:* Kingswood Sch., Bath; Westminster Coll., London. Founded Mulberry Co., 1971 (Queen's Award to Industry for Export, 1979, 1989 and 1996); Chm. and Chief Exec., 1971–2002; Pres., 2002–03; launched Mulberry at Home, 1991; opened Charlton House Hotel and Mulberry Restaurant, 1997 (Michelin Star, annually, 1997–2003); launched Sharpham Park (rare breed meat) and Spelt Flour (bread, pasta and cereal range), 2005; built first organic spelt flour mill in UK, 2006; created Feastival, eco/sustainability event, 2009; curated Eco Car event, London, 2010; creator and CEO, Kilver Court Designer Outlet Village, 2011–. Chm., London Designer Collections, 1976–80; Dir, Monty's, 2004–09. Dir, EV Cup, 2011–. Trustee and Chm., Bottletop, 2003–09. Mem., RHS. Gov., Kingswood Sch., 2006–10. Classic Designer of Year, British Fashion Council, 1992. *Publications:* Mulberry at Home, 1992; Spelt Cookbook, 2014; Spelt Recipe Book, 2015. *Recreations:* gardening, tennis, tai chi, historic car racing (Mem., Vintage Sports Car Club; winner: Brooklands Trophy, 2006; Porto GP, Irish GP, Donnington Legends, 2006; Brighton Speed Trials Pre '59 Trophy, 2007), 6m yacht racing, Tai Chi. *Address:* Kilver Court, Shepton Mallet, Somerset BA4 5NF. *Club:* Blacks.

SAUL, Prof. (Samuel) Berrick, CBE 1992; PhD; Executive Chairman, Universities and Colleges Admissions Service, 1993–97; Vice Chancellor, University of York, 1979–93; *b* 20 Oct. 1924; *s* of Ernest Saul and Maud Eaton; *m* 1953, Sheila Stenton; one *s* one *d. Educ:* West Bromwich Grammar Sch.; Birmingham Univ. (BCom 1949, PhD 1953). National Service, 1944–47 (Lieut Sherwood Foresters). Lectr in Econ. History, Liverpool Univ., 1951–63; Edinburgh University: Prof. of Econ. History, 1963–78; Dean, Faculty of Social Sciences, 1970–75; Vice Principal, 1975–77; Actg Principal, 1978. Rockefeller Fellow, Univ. of Calif (Berkeley), and Columbia Univ., 1959; Ford Fellow, Stanford Univ., 1969–70. Vis. Prof., Harvard Univ., 1973. Chairman: Central Council for Educn and Trng in Social Work, 1986–93; Standing Conf. on Univ. Entrance, 1986–93; Vice-Chm., Commonwealth Scholarship Commn, 1993–2000. Hon. LLD York, Toronto, 1981; Hon. Dr *hc* Edinburgh, 1986; DUniv York, 1994. *Publications:* Studies in British Overseas Trade 1870–1914, 1960; The Myth of the Great Depression, 1969; Technological Change: the US and Britain in the 19th Century, 1970; (with A. S. Milward) The Economic Development of Continental Europe 1780–1870, 1973; (with A. S. Milward) The Development of the Economies of Continental Europe 1850–1914, 1977. *Recreations:* travel, music. *Address:* 3 The Spinney, Elston, Newark, Notts NG23 5PE. *T:* (01636) 526844.

SAULL, Rear-Adm. (Keith) Michael, CB 1982; Chairman, New Zealand Ports Authority, 1984–88; *b* 24 Aug. 1927; *s* of Harold Vincent Saull and Margaret Saull; *m* 1952, Linfield Mabel (*née* Barnsdale) (*d* 2010); two *s* one *d. Educ:* Altrincham Grammar Sch.; HMS Conway. Royal Navy, 1945–50; transferred to Royal New Zealand Navy, 1951; commanded HMNZ Ships: Kaniere, Taranaki, Canterbury, 1956–71; Naval Attaché, Washington DC, 1972–75; RCDS 1976; Commodore, Auckland, 1978; Chief of Naval Staff, RNZN, 1980–83. Vice Patron, Royal NZ Coastguard Fedn, 1987–2000.

SAULTER, Paul Reginald; Managing Director, 1989–2012, Hon. Chairman, since 2012, Heritage of Industry (formerly Cornwall of Mine) Ltd; *b* 27 Aug. 1935; *s* of Alfred Walter Saulter and Mabel Elizabeth Oliver. *Educ:* Truro Sch.; University Coll., Oxford (MA). Admin. Asst, Nat. Council of Social Service, 1960–63; Sen. Asst and Principal, CEGB, 1963–65; Dep. Head, Overseas Div., BEAMA, 1965–69; Dir, Internat. Affairs, ABCC, 1969–73; Sec.-Gen., British Chamber of Commerce in France, 1973–81; Chief Executive: Manchester Chamber of Commerce and Industry, 1981–85; Assoc. of Exhibn Organisers, 1985–86; Administrator, St Paul's, Knightsbridge, 1987–95. Mgt consultant, 1986–89; Exhibn Advr, London Chamber of Commerce, 1986–88. Secretary: For. Trade Working Gp, ORGALIME, 1967–69; Council of British Chambers of Commerce in Continental Europe, 1977–80; Member: Export Promotion Cttee, CBI, 1983–86; Bd, Eur. Fedn of Assocs of Industrial and Technical Heritage, 1999–2014 (Vice-Pres., 2002–11; Pres., 2011–13). Member: RHS; Trevithick Soc., 1986–; Assoc. for Industrial Archaeology; Newcomen Soc., 1995– (Mem. Council, 1995–98, 1999–2002). Trustee: Kirkaldy Testing Mus. Southwark Ltd, 2014–; A4Altruistic, 2015–. *Recreations:* walking, music, theatre, researching Cornish mining history, industrial archaeology. *Address:* Rye, Sussex.

SAUMAREZ, family name of **Baron de Saumarez**.

SAUMAREZ SMITH, Dr Charles Robert, CBE 2008; FSA; Secretary and Chief Executive, Royal Academy of Arts, since 2007; *b* 28 May 1954; *s* of late William Hanbury Saumarez Smith, OBE and of Alice Elizabeth Harness Saumarez Smith (*née* Raven); *m* 1979, Romilly Le Quesne Savage; two *s. Educ:* Marlborough Coll.; King's Coll., Cambridge (BA 1st cl. History of Art 1976; MA 1978); Henry Fellow, Harvard, 1977; Warburg Inst. (PhD 1986). FSA 1997. Christie's Res. Fellow in Applied Arts, Christ's Coll., Cambridge, 1979–82 (Hon. Fellow, 2002); Asst Keeper with resp. for V&A/RCA MA course in history of design, 1982–90, Head of Res., 1990–94, V & A; Dir, NPG, 1994–2002; Slade Prof., Univ. of Oxford, 2001–02; Dir, National Gallery, 2002–07. Vis. Fellow, Yale Center for British Art, 1983; Benno Forman Fellow, Winterthur Mus., 1988; South Square Fellow, RCA, 1990; Vis. Prof., QMUL, 2007–. Member, Executive Committee: Design History Soc., 1985–89; Soc. of Architectural Historians, 1987–90; Assoc. of Art Historians, 1990–94; London Library, 1992–96; Member, Advisory Council: Paul Mellon Centre for British Studies, 1995–99; Warburg Inst., 1997–2003; Inst. of Historical Research, 1999–2003; Sch. of Advanced Study, 2003–07; Mem. Council, Museums Assoc., 1998–2001 (Vice-Pres., 2002–04; Pres., 2004–06). Gov., Univ. of the Arts, London (formerly London Inst.), 2001–13. Trustee: Soane Monuments Trust, 1988–2006; Charleston, 1993–; Prince's Drawing Sch., 2003–; Public Catalogue Foundn, 2003–. FRSA 1995. Hon. Fellow, RCA, 1991; Hon. FRIBA 2000. Hon. DLitt: UEA, 2001; Westminster, 2002; London, 2003; Sussex, 2003; Essex, 2005. *Publications:* The Building of Castle Howard, 1990 (Alice Davis Hitchcock Medallion); Eighteenth Century Decoration, 1993; The National Portrait Gallery, 1997; The National Gallery: a short history, 2009; The Company of Artists: the origins of the Royal Academy of Arts in London, 2012; New Annals of The Club, 2014. *Address:* Royal Academy of Arts, Burlington House, Piccadilly, W1J 0BD. *T:* (020) 7300 8020. *E:* chiefexecutive@royalacademy.org.uk.

SAUNDERS, Alison Margaret, CB 2013; Director of Public Prosecutions, since 2013; *b* Aberdeen, 14 Feb. 1961; *d* of Hugh Colin Brown and Margaret Bennett Brown; *m* 1986, Neil Saunders; two *s. Educ:* St Teilo's Church in Wales Sch., Cardiff; Runshaw 6th Form Coll., Leyland, Lancs; Univ. of Leeds (LLM Hons). Called to the Bar, Inner Temple, 1983; Lloyd's of London, 1984–86; Crown Prosecution Service: joined, 1986; Policy Directorate, 1991; London, 1997; Dep. Chief Crown Prosecutor London, 1999–2002; Chief Crown Prosecutor Sussex, 2002–04; Dep. Legal Sec., Attorney Gen.'s Office, 2004–06; Hd, Organised Crime Div., CPS, 2006–10; Chief Crown Prosecutor for London, 2010–13. Gov., Eastbourne Coll., 2009–. *Recreations:* cooking, theatre, reading, family. *Address:* Crown Prosecution Service, Rose Court, 2 Southwark Bridge Road, SE1 9HS. *T:* (020) 3357 0000. *E:* privateoffice@cps.gsi.gov.uk.

SAUNDERS, Andrew William, CB 1998; Director, Communications-Electronics Security Group, 1991–98; *b* 26 Oct. 1940; *s* of late Joseph and Winifred Saunders; *m* 1964, Josephine Sharkey; one *s* two *d. Educ:* Wolverhampton Grammar Sch.; Christ Church, Oxford (MA). Joined Civil Service, GCHQ, 1963: Principal, 1968; Asst Sec., 1978; Counsellor, Washington, 1983–86 (on secondment); Under Sec., 1991. *Recreations:* outdoor pleasures and practicalities, genealogy, history. *Address:* c/o Barclays Bank PLC, 128 High Street, Cheltenham, Glos GL50 1EL.

SAUNDERS, Ann Loreille, MBE 2002; PhD; FSA; historian; Lecturer in History of London, University of Connecticut Programme, City University, London, 1982–2007; *b* 23 May 1930; *d* of George and Joan Cox-Johnson; *m* 1960, Bruce Kemp Saunders; one *s* (and one *d* decd). *Educ:* Henrietta Barnett Sch., London; Queen's Coll., London; UCL (BA); Leicester Univ. (PhD 1965). FSA 1975. Asst, City of York Art Gall., 1951–52; Dep. Librarian, Lambeth Palace, 1952–55; Temp. Asst Keeper, BM, 1955–56; Borough Archivist, Marylebone Public Library, 1956–63; freelance writing, lecturing and editing, 1965–; Lectr in Hist. of London, Richmond Coll., London, 1979–94; Fellow and Hon. Res. Fellow, UCL, 1992–. Mem. Council, Soc. of Antiquaries of London, 1989–91; President: Camden History Soc., 1984–89; St Marylebone Soc., 1985–89; Regent's Park DFAS, 1989–95. Governor, Bedford Coll., 1982–85. Asst to Hon. Editor, Jl of British Archaeol Assoc., 1963–75; Honorary Editor: Costume Soc., 1967–2008; London Topographical Soc., 1975–2015. *Publications:* Regent's Park: a study of the development of the area from 1066 to the present day, 1969, 2nd edn 1981; (ed) Arthur Mee's London North of the Thames, 1972; (ed) Arthur Mee's London: the City and Westminster, 1975; The Art and Architecture of London: an illustrated guide (Specialist Guide Book of the Year Award, London Tourist Bd), 1984, 3rd edn 1992; (ed and contrib.) The Royal Exchange, 1997; St Paul's: the story of the cathedral, 2001, 2nd edn as St Paul's: 1,400 years at the heart of London, 2012; (jtly) The History of the Merchant Taylors' Company, 2004; (ed) The London County Council Bomb Damage Maps, 2005; Historic Views of London: photographs from the collection of B. E. C. Howarth-Loomes, 2008; contribs to Burlington Mag., London Jl, Geographical Mag., Dome, LAMAS, etc. *Recreations:* reading, walking, embroidery, cooking, studying London, going to exhibitions and theatres, visiting churches. *Address:* 3 Meadway Gate, NW11 7LA. *T:* (020) 8455 2171.

SAUNDERS, Sir Bruce (Joshua), KBE 2012 (OBE 2003); Managing Director, BJS Group of Companies, since 1980; *b* Port Pirie, SA, 20 Dec. 1941; *s* of Edward Hugh Saunders and Grace Olive Saunders; *m* 1966, Keithie Wilma Blum, OBE; three *d. Educ:* Sch. Leaving Cert. Trained as chef, William Angliss Trade Sch., Melbourne; managed: catering facilities, Sydney, 1961–66; Hotel Rarotonga, Cook Is, 1966–68; family business of A. J. and G. Blum, Solomon Is, 1968. Member: Tourist Authy, 1972–75; Govt of Solomon Is Think Tank, 1996–98; Civil Society Network, 2000–04; Vice Chm., Solomon Is Chamber of Commerce, 1998–2013 (Exec. Mem.); Mem. Bd, Central Bank of Solomon Is, 2005–07; Mem. Bd, Pacific Is Private Sector Orgn, 2012–. Proj. Manager to Trustee Bd, Solomon Scouts and Coastwatchers Memorial, 2009–; Trustee, Blue Light Police Youth Assoc., 2012–. Mem., Baha'i World Faith, 1956–. *Recreations:* tennis, squash, reading, community service reading. *T:* 7496448. *E:* bruce@bjs.com.sb. *Club:* Rotary (Honiara) (Paul Harris Fellow).

SAUNDERS, Christopher John, MA; Headmaster, Lancing College, 1993–98; *b* 7 May 1940; *s* of R. H. Saunders and G. S. Saunders (*née* Harris); *m* 1973, Cynthia Elizabeth Stiles; one *s* one *d. Educ:* Lancing Coll.; Fitzwilliam Coll., Cambridge (MA); PGCE Wadham Coll., Oxford. Assistant Master, Bradfield College, 1964–80 (Housemaster, 1972–80); Headmaster, Eastbourne Coll., 1981–93. Life Vice-Pres., FA, 2012 (Vice-Pres., 2002–12). *Recreations:* music, bridge, theatre, gardening, soccer (Oxford Blue 1963), cricket (Oxford Blue 1964), golf, people. *Address:* Folly Bottom, Scottalls Lane, Hampstead Norreys, Thatcham, Berks RG18 0RT. *T:* (01635) 200222. *Clubs:* MCC; Hawks (Cambridge).

SAUNDERS, David, DPhil; FIIC, FSA; Keeper of Conservation and Scientific Research (formerly Conservation, Documentation and Science), British Museum, 2005–15, now Honorary Research Fellow; *b* 10 Oct. 1959; *s* of Morris and Gwen Saunders; *m* 1984, Alison

Hesketh. *Educ:* Harrow Co. Sch. for Boys; Univ. of York (BSc Chem. 1981; DPhil Chem. 1984). FIIC 1993. Post-doctoral Researcher, Univ. of Bristol, 1984–85; Scientist, Nat. Gall., London, 1985–2005. Vice Pres., Internat. Inst. for Conservation, 2013– (Dir, Pubns, 2003–09). FSA 2013. Editor: Studies in Conservation, 1990–2009; BM Technical Res. Bulletin, 2007–. *Publications:* 100 articles incl. in Nat. Gall. Technical Bulletin, Studies in Conservation and Jl of Chemical Soc. *Recreations:* cooking for friends, Italian and Scandinavian cities, hill-walking, orienteering, selected opera, other people's museums. *Address:* British Museum, Great Russell Street, WC1B 3DG.

SAUNDERS, Air Vice-Marshal David John, CBE 1986; FIMechE; FRAeS; FCILT; Advisor, Airinmar Group, 2011–12 (Director of Logistics, 1997–99; Senior Vice President, 1999–2011); *b* 12 June 1943; *s* of John Saunders and Nina Saunders (*née* Mabberley); *m* 1966, Elizabeth Jane Cairns; one *s* one *d*. *Educ:* Commonweal Grammar Sch.; RAF College; Cranfield Inst. of Technology. BSc, MSc; CEng, FRAeS 1993; FCILT (FILog 1997). Joined RAF 1961; management appts, 1966–85; Station Comdr, RAF Sealand, 1983; ADC to HM the Queen, 1984–86; Command Mechanical Engineer, HQ RAF Germany, 1986; Dir of Engineering Policy (RAF), MoD, 1989–91; ACDS (Logistics), 1991–93; Hd of RAF Mobility Study, 1993; AO Engrg and Supply, 1993–97. Director: Airinmar Gp Ltd, 2000–11; Airinmar UK Ltd, 2000–11; Airinmar Inc., 2000–11. *Recreations:* rowing, off-road cycling, horse riding, season ticket holder Swindon Town FC. *Address:* The Hermitage, 150 Above Town, Dartmouth, Devon TQ6 9RH. *Club:* Royal Air Force.

SAUNDERS, David John; Senior Advisor, Financial Conduct Authority, since 2014; Special Advisor, Europe Economics, since 2014; *b* 4 Aug. 1953; *s* of James and Margaret Saunders; *m* 1975, Elizabeth Jean Hdgson; two *s* two *d*. *Educ:* Royal Grammar Sch., Guildford; Kingston Poly. (BSc Chemistry and Business Studies); Aston Univ. (PhD Applied Business Studies 1978). Joined DTI, 1978; Private Sec. to Sec. of State, 1981–82, to Parly Under Sec. of State, 1982–84; seconded to OFT, 1984–87; British Steel privatisation, 1987–88; Export Promotion, 1988–95; Sec., BOTB, 1990–95; Director: Nuclear Power Privatisation Team, 1995–96; Oil and Gas Directorate, 1996–98; Regl Dir, Govt Office for SE, 1998–2002; Dir, Business Support, DTI, 2002–04; Dir, Consumer and Competition Policy, DTI, later BERR, 2004–09; Chief Exec., Competition Commn, 2009–14. *Recreations:* swimming, cycling, diving, photography, ballet, music. *Address:* Financial Conduct Authority, 25 The North Colonnade, Canary Wharf, E14 5HS. *T:* (020) 7066 9668. *Club:* Reform.

SAUNDERS, David William, CB 1989; Counsel to the Chairman of Committees, House of Lords, 1999–2005; *b* 4 Nov. 1936; *s* of William Ernest Saunders and Lilian Grace (*née* Ward); *m* 1963, Margaret Susan Rose Bartholomew. *Educ:* Hornchurch Grammar Sch.; Worcester Coll., Oxford (MA). Admitted solicitor, 1964. Joined Office of Parly Counsel, 1970; Dep. Parly Counsel, 1978–80; Parly Counsel, 1980–94 and 1996–99; Second Parly Counsel, 1994–96; with Law Commn, 1972–74, 1986–87. *Recreations:* golf, bridge. *Address:* Highfields, High Wych, Sawbridgeworth, Herts CM21 0HX. *T:* (01279) 724736. *Club:* Oxford and Cambridge.

SAUNDERS, Ernest Walter, MA; President, Stambridge Management (formerly Associates), 1992; *b* 21 Oct. 1935; *m* 1963, Carole Ann Stephings; two *s* one *d*. *Educ:* Emmanuel Coll., Cambridge (MA). Man. Dir, Beecham Products Internat., and Dir, Beecham Products, 1966–73; Chm., European Div., Great Universal Stores, 1973–77; Pres., Nestlé Nutrition SA, and Mem. Worldwide Management Cttee, Nestlé SA, Vevey, Switzerland, 1977–81; Chm., Beechnut Corp., USA, 1977–81; Chief Exec., 1981–87, Chm., 1986–87, Arthur Guinness & Sons plc, later Guinness PLC; Chairman: Arthur Guinness Son & Co. (Great Britain), 1982–87; Guinness Brewing Worldwide, 1982–87. Dir, Brewers' Soc., 1983. Dir, Queens Park Rangers Football & Athletic Club, 1983. *Recreations:* ski-ing, tennis, football.

SAUNDERS, Dr Frances Carolyn, CB 2011; CEng, FREng; CPhys, FInstP; Chief Executive, Defence Science and Technology Laboratory, Ministry of Defence, 2006–12; *b* Cambridge, 28 June 1954; *d* of Archibald John Christopher Reger, MBE and Joyce Anne Reger (*née* Wood); *m* 1977, Martin Vernon Saunders. *Educ:* Portsmouth High Sch.; Nottingham Univ. (BSc, PhD 1984). CPhys, FInstP 1999; CEng, FREng 2011. Electronics engr, British Leyland, 1975–78; Res. Scientist, RSRE, 1978–92; Hd, Tech. Policy, Defence Res. Agency, 1992–95; rcds 1995; Director: Defence Test and Evaluation Orgn, 1995–97; Centre for Defence Analysis, DERA, 1997–2000; Res. Councils, OST, DTI, 2000–03; Tech./Ops Dir, DSTL, 2003–06. Non-executive Director: Becatech Systems Ltd, 2013–14; Sentinor Ltd, 2014–. Mem., UK Space Agency Steering Bd, 2015–. Mem., REF 2014 Physics Panel, 2012–14. Pres., Inst. of Physics, 2013–15; Trustee, Engrg Develt Trust, 2012–. Mem. Council, Cranfield Univ., 2008–. *Recreations:* cycling, walking, music, playing guitar, travel. *E:* francessaunders@hotmail.com.

SAUNDERS, Jennifer; actress, writer; *b* 6 July 1958; *m* Adrian Edmondson; three *d*. *Educ:* Central Sch. of Speech and Drama. *Theatre:* An Evening with French and Saunders (nat. tour), 1989; Me and Mamie O'Rourke, Strand, 1993; French and Saunders Live - 2000, Apollo Hammersmith, 2000; French and Saunders: Still Alive (nat. tour), 2008; writer, Viva Forever!, Piccadilly Th., 2012; *television:* actor and co-writer: Ab Fab The Last Shout, 1996; Mirrorball, 2000; actor: The Boy in the Dress, 2014; *series:* The Comic Strip Presents…, 1982–90; Girls on Top, 1985–87; French and Saunders (5 series); Absolutely Fabulous, 1992–96, 2001–03, 2011 (Emmy Award, 1993; BAFTA Award, 2012); Jam and Jerusalem, 2006, 2008, 2009; The Life and Times of Vivienne Vyle, 2007; (actor) Let Them Eat Cake, 1999; (documentary) Jennifer Saunders: Back in the Saddle, 2012; (actor) Five Go To Rehab, 2012; (actor) Blandings, 2013–14; *films:* The Supergrass, 1984; Muppet Treasure Island, 1996; In the Bleak Midwinter, 1996; Fanny and Elvis, 1999. Fellow, BAFTA, 2009. *Publications:* (with Dawn French) A Feast of French and Saunders, 1992; Absolutely Fabulous: the scripts, 1993; Absolutely Fabulous: Continuity, 2001; Bonkers: my life in laughs, 2013. *Address:* c/o United Agents, 12–26 Lexington Street, W1F 0LE.

SAUNDERS, Hon. Sir John Henry Boulton, Kt 2007; **Hon. Mr Justice Saunders;** a Judge of the High Court of Justice, Queen's Bench Division, since 2007; *b* 15 March 1949; *s* of Kathleen Mary Saunders and Henry G. B. Saunders; *m* 1975, Susan Mary Chick; one *s* two *d*. *Educ:* Uppingham School; Magdalen College, Oxford (BA). Called to the Bar, Gray's Inn, 1972; a Recorder, 1990–2004; QC 1991; a Senior Circuit Judge, 2004–07; Recorder of Birmingham, 2004–07. Mem., Sentencing Council for England and Wales, 2013–. Hon. DLaws Birmingham, 2008. *Publications:* (ed) Paterson's Licensing Acts, 2004–. *Recreation:* music. *Address:* Royal Courts of Justice, Strand, WC2A 2LL.

SAUNDERS, Prof. Kenneth Barrett, MD, DSc; FRCP; Professor of Medicine, St George's Hospital Medical School, 1980–95, now Emeritus; *b* 16 March 1936; *s* of Harold N. Saunders and Winifred F. Saunders (*née* Gadge); *m* 1961, Philippa Mary Harrison; one *s* one *d*. *Educ:* Kingswood Sch., Bath; Trinity Hall, Cambridge (MB BChir 1961; MA 1966; MD 1966); St Thomas's Hosp. Med. Sch.; DSc London 1995. FRCP 1978. Sen. Lectr, then Reader in Medicine, Middx Hosp. Med. Sch., 1972–80; Dean, Fac. of Medicine, London Univ., 1990–94. Member: GMC, 1992–95; Jt Planning and Adv. Cttee, 1990–94; Jt Cttee on Higher Med. Trng, 1990–94. Hon. Consultant Physician to the Army, 1994–97. Chm., Assoc. of Clinical Profs of Medicine, 1993–95. Royal College of Physicians: Tudor Edwards Lectr, 1987; Procensor, 1986–87; Censor, 1987–88. Member: Governing Body, BPMF, 1990–96; Council, Sch. of Pharmacy, London Univ., 1990–96. Vice-Pres., Hellenic Soc., 2005– (Hon. Treas., 1998–2005). *Publications:* Clinical Physiology of the Lung, 1977; various papers on respiratory science and medicine, and on Homer. *Recreations:* English, classical and Egyptian literature, gardening, golf. *Address:* 77 Lee Road, Blackheath, SE3 9EN. *T:* (020) 8852 8138. *Clubs:* Royal Automobile, Academy, Royal Society of Medicine; Royal Blackheath Golf.

SAUNDERS, Matthew John, MBE 1998; FSA; Secretary, Ancient Monuments Society, since 1977; *b* 12 April 1953; *s* of John William Saunders and Joyce Mary Saunders. *Educ:* Latymer Sch., Edmonton; Corpus Christi Coll., Cambridge (MA Hist. and Hist. of Architecture 1974). FSA 1980. Editorial Asst, Whitaker's Almanack, 1975; Sec., SAVE Britain's Heritage, 1976–77; Asst Sec., Ancient Monuments Soc., 1976. Sec., Jt Cttee of Nat. Amenity Socs, 1982–2005; Dir, Friends of Friendless Churches, 1993–; Trustee: Historic Chapels Trust, 1993–95; Heritage Lottery Fund, 2005–11 (Member: Places of Worship Adv. Cttee, 1995–98; Historic Bldgs and Land Panel, 1999–2005); Mem., Fabric Adv. Cttee, St Paul's Cathedral, 2001–03. Pres., Men of the Stones, 2015– (Vice Pres., 2000–15); Vice President: Ecclesiological Soc., 1994–; Enfield Preservation Soc., 1999–. IHBC 1998. *Publications:* (contrib.) Railway Architecture, 1979; (contrib.) The Architectural Outsiders, 1985; The Historic Home Owner's Companion, 1987; (contrib.) Concerning Buildings, 1996; Saving Churches: the first 50 years of the Friends of Friendless Churches, 2010. *Recreations:* music, travel, photography, good food. *Address:* (office) St Ann's Vestry Hall, 2 Church Entry, EC4V 5HB. *T:* (020) 7236 3934.

SAUNDERS, Michael Potter; Managing Director, Bibendum Wine Ltd, since 2006 (Joint Managing Director, 2001–06); Chief Executive, Bibendum PLB Group, since 2014; *b* Bath, 20 Aug. 1963; *s* of Peter Saunders and Didi Saunders; *m* 1992, Katherina Peyton-Jones; two *s* one *d*. *Educ:* Eton Coll. Bibendum Wine Ltd, 1982–, Sales Dir, 1989–2001. *Recreations:* golf, ski-ing. *Address:* Bibendum Wine Ltd, 113 Regents Park Road, NW1 8UR. *T:* (020) 7449 4049. *E:* msaunders@bibendum-plb.com. *Club:* White's.

SAUNDERS, Nigel James, MD; FRCOG; Consultant Obstetrician, Southampton University Hospitals, 1992; *b* 9 May 1955; *s* of Peter St John and Eileen Saunders; *m* 1988, Deborah Sanderson; three *d*. *Educ:* Manchester Grammar Sch.; Manchester Univ. (MB ChB; MD 1989). FRCSE 1983; FRCOG 1983. Lectr in Obstetrics and Gynaecol., Sheffield Univ., 1985–89; Consultant and Sen. Lectr, St Mary's Med. Sch., Paddington, 1989–92; Med Dir, Southampton Univ. Hosps NHS Trust, 2001–07. *Publications:* articles and editorials relating to labour ward mgt and minimally invasive surgery in BMJ, Lancet. *Recreations:* cycling, reading, songwriting, blues guitar. *Address:* Ridgemount House, Romsey Road, Romsey, Hants SO51 6AE. *E:* nigelsaunders@gmail.com.

SAUNDERS, Peter Gordon; Editor, The Birmingham Post, 1986–90; *b* 1 July 1940; *s* of late Gordon and Winifred Saunders; *m* 1964, Teresa Geraldine Metcalf; two *d*. *Educ:* Newport High Sch. for Boys, Gwent; London Sch. of Econs and Pol Science (BScEcon 1961). Reporter, Gloucestershire Echo, 1961–63; Sports Reporter, Sunderland Echo, 1963–64; Sub-Editor: Yorkshire Post, 1964; The Birmingham Post, 1964–69; Lectr in Journalism, Cardiff Coll. of Commerce, 1969–70; The Birmingham Post, 1971–90: successively Dep. Chief Sub-Editor, Chief Sub-Editor, Asst Editor, Exec. Editor; media consultant, 1991–2005. *Recreations:* Rugby Union, reading, rhythm and blues, golf. *Address:* 3 Carpenter Close, Langstone, Newport, South Wales NP18 2LF. *T:* and *Fax:* (01633) 411688. *E:* petesaund@sky.com. *Club:* Newport High School Old Boys.

SAUNDERS, Prof. Philippa Tansy Kemp, PhD; FMedSci; Professorial Fellow and Programme Leader, MRC Centre for Reproductive Health, since 2011 (Director, 2011–12), and Dean, Postgraduate Research, College of Medicine and Veterinary Medicine, since 2012, University of Edinburgh; *b* London, 2 Aug. 1955; *d* of late Christopher and of Hazel Saunders; *m* 1989, William Byers; one *s* one *d*. *Educ:* Bristol Univ. (BSc Hons); Darwin Coll., Cambridge (PhD 1982). Postdoctoral Associate, Univ. of Florida, 1981–84; Res. Associate, Inst. of Zool., Zool Soc. of London, 1984–87; University of Edinburgh: Res. Fellow, Dept of Obstetrics and Gynaecol., 1987–89; Prog. Leader, MRC Human Reproductive Scis Unit, 1989–2011; granted tenured post with MRC, 1993; Hon. Res. Fellow, 1998–2005; Hon. Prof., 2005–11; Hd, Centre for Reproductive Biol., 2007–11. *Publications:* contribs to learned jls related to field of reproductive health. *Recreations:* jogging, pilates, theatre, city breaks. *Address:* MRC Centre for Reproductive Health, Queen's Medical Research Institute, 47 Little France Crescent, Edinburgh EH16 4TJ. *T:* (0131) 242 6388, *Fax:* (0131) 242 6441. *E:* p.saunders@ed.ac.uk.

SAUNDERS, Raymond; Secretary, British Museum (Natural History), 1976–87; *b* 24 July 1933; *s* of late Herbert Charles Saunders and Doris May (*née* Kirkham-Jones); *m* 1959, Shirley Marion (*née* Stringer); two *s*. *Educ:* Poole Grammar Sch. WO, 1950; Air Min., 1956; Min. of Land and Natural Resources, 1966; Land Commn, 1967; Treasury, 1968; CSD, 1969. *Recreations:* reading biographies, gardening, sport (now as spectator). *Address:* High Trees, 24 Landguard Manor Road, Shanklin, Isle of Wight PO37 7HZ.

SAUNDERS, Richard; Partnership Consultant, Christ's Hospital, 1993–96; *b* 4 July 1937; *s* of late Edward E. Saunders and Betty Saunders; *m* 1st, 1961, Suzannah Rhodes-Cooke (marr. diss.); one *s*; 2nd, 1970, Alison Fiddes. *Educ:* St Edmund's Sch., Hindhead; Uppingham. FRICS 1965. National Service, commnd The Life Guards, 1958–60. Jun. Partner, Richard Ellis, Chartered Surveyors, 1966–69; formed Richard Saunders & Partners, 1969; Baker Harris Saunders, 1977; Chm., Baker Harris Saunders Group, 1986–92; Director: Herring Baker Harris, 1992–93; (non-exec.) Herring Baker Harris Gp, 1992–93. Chm., City Br., RICS, 1979–80; Pres., Associated Owners of City Properties, 1985–87; Member: Council, British Property Fedn, 1974–90 (Hon. Treas., 1974–85); Bd, Gen. Practice Finance Corp., 1984–89. Chairman: Barbican Residential Cttee, 1979–81; Barbican Centre Cttee, 1983–86; Metropolitan Public Gardens Assoc., 1984–90; Governor: Bridewell Royal Hosp. and King Edward's Sch., Witley, 1976–93; St Edmund's Sch., Hindhead, 1979–93 (Chm., 1979–87); (also Almoner), Christ's Hosp., 1980–93; Royal Star and Garter Home, 1984–2007. Mem., Court of Common Council, Corp. of London, 1975–2000; Deputy for Ward of Candlewick, 1983–2000; Liveryman: Clothworkers' Co., 1960– (Warden, 1989; Master, 2001–02); Co. of Chartered Surveyors, 1979–93; Church Warden, St Lawrence Jewry-by-Guildhall, 1984–2004; Sheriff, City of London, 1987–88. *Recreations:* instant gardening, music, golf, tennis. *Address:* The Old Rectory, Bagendon, Cirencester, Glos GL7 7DU. *Club:* MCC.

SAUNDERS, Steven Michael; Creative Director and Founding Partner, Fabled Studio, since 2011; *b* Reading, 28 June 1982; *s* of Michael Trevor and Susan Saunders; partner, Carolyn Sophie Kelly. *Educ:* Arts Inst., Bournemouth (BA Hons 3D Design 2004). Jun. designer, GMP Design Associates, 2004–07; middle weight designer, United Designers, 2007; Sen. Interior Designer, David Collins Studio, 2007–11. *Publications:* Room: inside contemporary interiors, 2014. *Recreation:* sharpening knives and pretending to be a chef! *Address:* Fabled Studio, 4th Floor, 57 Hatton Gardens, EC1N 8HP. *T:* (020) 7269 9900. *E:* steven@fabledstudio.com.

SAUNDERS, Prof. William Philip, PhD; Professor of Endodontology, University of Dundee, 2000–13, now Emeritus; Hon. Consultant in Restorative Dentistry: Greater Glasgow Health Board, 1988–2000; Tayside Health Board, 2000–13; Dean, Dental Faculty, Royal College of Surgeons Edinburgh, since 2014; *b* 12 Oct. 1948; *s* of late William Walton Saunders and of Elva Doreen Saunders; *m* 2009, Jennifer Anne, *d* of Alexander Birrell Wilkinson, *qv*; one *s* one *d* from a previous marriage. *Educ:* RAF Changi Grammar Sch., Singapore; Maidstone Grammar Sch.; Royal Dental Hosp. of London (BDS 1970); Univ. of Dundee (PhD 1986). FDSRCSE 1982; FDSRCPSGlas 1993; MRD 1994; FDSRCS *ad hominem* 2001; FCDSHK. Dental Officer, RAF, 1971–75; gen. dental practice, 1975–81; Lectr, Dept of Conservative Dentistry, Univ. of Dundee, 1981–88; University of Glasgow:

Sen. Lectr in Clinical Practice, 1988–93; Personal Chair in Clinical Practice, 1993–95; Personal Chair in Endodontology, 1995–2000; Dean and Hd of Dept, Univ. of Dundee Dental Sch., 2000–11. Postgrad. Dental Hosp. Tutor, Glasgow Dental Hosp., 1992–95. Chairman: Council of Heads and Deans of Dental Schs, later Dental Schs Council, 2008–11; Dental Cttee, NHS Educn for Scotland, 2013–. Pres., British Endodontic Soc., 1997–98; Chm., Assoc. of Consultants and Specialists in Restorative Dentistry, 1999–2002; Mem., Dental Council, 2000–, Chm., Speciality Adv. Bd in Restorative Dentistry, 2006–12, RCSE. Chm. Educn Cttee, 1996–2009, Congress Pres., 2007–09, Eur. Soc. of Endodontology. FHEA (ILTM 2000). DSc (ad hominem) Aberdeen, 2011. *Publications:* chapters in textbooks; res. papers on endodontics and applied dental materials. *Recreations:* ornithology (a lapsed bird ringer), natural history, golf (badly), Scottish art. *Address:* University of Dundee Dental School, Park Place, Dundee DD1 4HN. *T:* (01382) 635977, *Fax:* (01382) 225163. *E:* w.p.saunders@dundee.ac.uk. *Clubs:* Royal Air Force; New (Edinburgh).

SAUNDERS WATSON, Comdr (Leslie) Michael (Macdonald), CBE 1993; RN (retired); Chairman: British Library Board, 1990–93; Kettering General Hospital NHS Trust, 1993–99; *b* 9 Oct. 1934; *s* of Captain L. S. Saunders, DSO, RN (retd), and Elizabeth Saunders (*née* Culme-Seymour); *m* 1958, Georgina Elizabeth Laetitia, *d* of Adm. Sir William Davis, GCB, DSO; two *s* one *d*. *Educ:* Eton; BRNC, Dartmouth. Joined Royal Navy, 1951; specialised in Communications (Jackson Everett Prize); Comdr 1969; retired, 1971, on succession to Rockingham Castle Estate. Pres., Historic Houses Assoc., 1982–88 (Dep. Pres., 1978–82; Chm., Tax and Parly Cttee, 1975–82); Chairman: Northamptonshire Assoc. Youth Clubs, 1977–91 (Pres., 1997–2008); Heritage Educn Year, 1977; Corby Community Adv. Gp, 1979–86; Ironstone Royalty Owners Assoc., 1979–91; Nat. Curriculum History Wkg Gp, 1988–90; Heritage Educn Trust, 1988–99; Modern Records Centre Adv. Cttee, Warwick Univ., 1993–98; Public Affairs Cttee, ICOMOS UK, 1994–98; Friends of British Library, 1994–2000; Vice-Chm., Northamptonshire Small Industries Cttee, 1974–79; Member: British Heritage Cttee, BTA, 1978–88; Northamptonshire Enterprise Agency, 1986–90; Country Landowners' Association: Member: Taxation Cttee, 1975–90; Exec. Cttee, 1977–82, 1987–92; Legal and Land Use Cttee, 1982–87; F and GP Cttee, 1994–98; Chairman: Northamptonshire Branch, 1981–84; Game Fair Local Cttee, 1997. Director: Lamport Hall Preservation Trust, 1978–91; English Sinfonia, 1981–2000. Trustee: Royal Botanic Gdns, Kew, 1983–91 (Chm., Bldgs and Design Cttee, 1985–91); Nat. Heritage Meml Fund, 1987–96. Chm., Governors Lodge Park Comprehensive Sch., 1977–82; Trustee, Oakham Sch., 1975–77. FSA 2001; FRSA 1986. High Sheriff, 1978–79, DL 1979–2009, Northamptonshire. Hon. DLitt: Warwick, 1991; Leicester, 1997. *Publications:* I Am Given A Castle: a memoir, 2008. *Recreations:* sailing, music, gardening, painting. *Address:* The Manor House, Ashley Road, Stoke Albany, Market Harborough, Leicestershire LE16 8PL.

SAUVAIN, Stephen John; QC 1995; *b* 1949; *s* of Alan Sauvain and Norah Sauvain; *m* 1980, Christine McLean; two *s*, and one step *s*. *Educ:* King Edward VII Grammar Sch., King's Lynn; Sidney Sussex Coll., Cambridge (MA, LLB). Lectr in Law, Univ. of Manchester, 1971–78; called to the Bar, Lincoln's Inn, 1977; in practice as barrister, 1978–. *Publications:* Highway Law, 1988, 5th edn 2013; (ed) Encyclopedia of Highway Law and Practice. *Address:* Kings Chambers, 36 Young Street, Manchester M3 3FT. *T:* (0161) 832 9082; Francis Taylor Building, Temple, EC4Y 7BY.

SAUVEN, John Bernard; Executive Director, Greenpeace, since 2007; *b* London, 6 Sept. 1954; *s* of late Maurice Oswald Sauven and of Helen Mary Orpin; *m* 1990, Janet Helene Convery; two *s*. *Educ:* University Coll., Cardiff (BSc Econ). Actg Gen. Sec., CND, 1989; Campaign and Communications Dir, Greenpeace, 2001–07. *Recreations:* photography, poetry, sailing. *Address:* Greenpeace, Canonbury Villas, N1 2PN. *T:* 07929 638296. *E:* john.sauven@greenpeace.org.

SAVAGE, Caroline Le Quesne; *see* Lucas, C.

SAVAGE, Francis Joseph, CMG 1996; LVO 1986; OBE 1989; HM Diplomatic Service, retired; Adviser to Foreign and Commonwealth Office, since 2003; *b* Preston, Lancs, 8 Feb. 1943; *s* of Francis Fitzgerald Savage and late Mona May Savage (*née* Parsons); *m* 1966, Veronica Mary McAleenan; two *s*. *Educ:* Holy Cross Convent, Broadstairs; St Stephen's Sch., Welling, Kent; NW Kent Coll., Dartford. Joined FO, 1961; served in: Cairo, 1967–70; Washington, 1971–73; Vice-Consul, Aden, 1973–74; FCO, 1974–78; Vice-Consul, then Consul (Commercial), Düsseldorf, 1978–82; Consul, Peking, 1982–86; First Sec. (Consular), Lagos, and Consul for Benin, 1987–90; First Sec., FCO, 1990–93; Counsellor, FCO, 1993; Governor: Montserrat, 1993–97; British Virgin Islands, 1998–2002. Member: Catenian Assoc., 1991–; Montserrat Nat. Trust, 1993–97; Montserrat Cricket Assoc., 1993–97; London Soc. of Ragamuffins, 2002– (Pres., 2008–09). Trustee: Virgin Islands Search and Rescue, UK, 2002–; Montserrat Foundn, 2008–. Chm., Friends of the BVI, 2005–. Montserrat Badge of Honour, 2001. KCSG 2002. *Recreations:* cricket, volcano watching, hurricane dodging, travel, meeting people. *Address:* FS Associates, 19 Cleeve Park Gardens, Sidcup, Kent DA14 4JL. *Clubs:* Royal Over-Seas League; Peking Cricket; Royal British Virgin Islands Yacht (Life Mem.).

SAVAGE, Gary John, MA, PhD; Head Master, Alleyn's School, since 2010; *b* Oulton Broad, Suffolk, 5 Dec. 1970; *s* of Keith Savage and Doreen Savage; *m* 1992, Natalie Watts. *Educ:* Bungay High Sch.; Sidney Sussex Coll., Cambridge (BA Hist. 1992; PhD 2005). Eton College: Asst Master, 1996–2000; Hd of Hist., 2000–02; Master-in-Coll., 2002–06; Under Master, Westminster Sch., 2006–10. Chm., London Div., HMC, 2014–15. Trustee, Dulwich Picture Gall., 2014–. Gov., Notting Hill Prep. Sch., 2004–14. FRSA. *Publications:* (contrib.) Cultures of Power in Europe During the Long Eighteenth Century, 2007. *Recreations:* German, Ipswich Town FC, the Arts. *Address:* Alleyn's School, Townley Road, Dulwich, SE22 8SU. *T:* (020) 8557 1500. *E:* headmaster@alleyns.org.uk.

SAVAGE, Prof. Michael, PhD; FBA 2007; Martin White Professor of Sociology, London School of Economics and Political Science, since 2014 (Professor of Sociology, 2012–14); *b* 20 June 1959; *s* of Dennis Savage and Margaret Savage; one *s*. *Educ:* Univ. of York (BA 1980); Univ. of Lancaster (MA 1981; PhD 1984). Res. Asst, Univ. of Lancaster, 1984–85; Res. Fellow in Urban Studies, 1985–87, British Acad. Post-doctoral Res. Fellow, 1988–89, Univ. of Sussex; Temp. Lectr, Univ. of Surrey, 1987–88; Keele University: Lectr, 1989–93; Sen. Lectr, 1993–94; Reader, 1994–95; University of Manchester: Prof. of Sociol., 1995–2010; Hd, Dept of Sociol., 1999–2001; Dir, ESRC Centre for Res. on Socio-Cultural Change, 2003–10 (Vis. Fellow, 2010–); University of York: Prof. of Sociol., 2010–12; Hd of Dept, 2011–12; Vis. Prof., 2012–. Visiting Professor: Univ. of N Carolina at Chapel Hill, 1995–96; Sciences Po, Paris, 2004; Adjunct Prof., Bergen, 2010–11. FAcSS (AcSS 2003). Managing Ed., Sociol. Rev., 2001–07. *Publications:* (jtly) Localities, Class and Gender, 1985; The Dynamics of Working-class Politics: Labour movement in Preston, 1880–1940, 1987; (ed jtly) Gender and Bureaucracy, 1992; (jtly) Property, Bureaucracy and Culture: middle class formation in contemporary Britain, 1992; (with A. Wardle) Urban Sociology, Capitalism and Modernity, 1993, 2nd edn (with K. Ward) 2003 (trans. Portuguese, Arabic, Chinese, 2003); (with A. Miles) The Remaking of the British Working Class 1840–1940, 1993; (ed jtly) Social Change and the Middle Classes, 1995; (jtly) Gender, Organisations and Careers, 1997; Class Analysis and Social Transformation, 2000; (ed jtly) Renewing Class Analysis, 2000; (jtly) Globalisation and Belonging, 2004; (ed jtly) Rethinking Class, Identities, Cultures and Lifestyles, 2004; (ed jtly) Remembering Elites, 2008; (ed jtly) Networked Urbanism, 2008; (jtly) Culture, Class Distinction, 2009; Identities and Social Change in Britain since 1940, 2010; contribs to jls incl. Sociol., Cultural Sociol., Contemp. British Hist., Sociol Rev., British Jl Sociol. *Address:* Department of Sociology, London School of Economics and Political Science, Houghton Street, WC2A 2AE.

SAVAGE, Prof. (Richard) Nigel, PhD; Chairman, Savage Hutchinson Consulting Ltd, since 2014; Chief Executive, 1996–2013, President, 2013–14, now Emeritus President, University of Law (formerly College of Law of England and Wales); *b* 27 May 1950; *s* of Jack and Joan Savage; *m* 1st, 1976, Linda Jane Sherwin (marr. diss. 2006); two *s*; 2nd, 2010, Sarah Hutchinson. *Educ:* Edward Cludd Sch., Southwell; Newark Tech. Coll.; Manchester Poly. (BA 1st cl. 1972); Univ. of Sheffield (LLM 1974); Univ. of Strathclyde (PhD 1980). Lectr, Univ. of Strathclyde, 1974–83; Principal Lectr, Nottingham Poly., 1983–85; Prof., 1985–96, and Dean and Founding Man. Dir, 1989–96, Nottingham Law Sch. Mem., HEFCE, 2002–09. Consultant, Nat. Centre for Citizenship and the Law, 2014–. *Publications:* Business Law, 1987, 2nd edn (with R. Bradgate) 1993; (with R. Bradgate) Commercial Law, 1991; articles in business and legal jls. *Recreation:* cricket. *Address:* 14 Nantwich Road, Tarporley, Cheshire CW6 9UW. *Club:* Reform.

SAVAGE, Thomas Hixon, CBE 1990; Chairman: North American Trust Co., 1992–95; A. G. Simpson Automotive Inc., 1996–2000; *b* Belfast, 21 Nov. 1928; *s* of Thomas Hixon Savage and Martha Foy Turkington; *m* 1st, 1950, Annie Gloria Ethel Gilmore (marr. diss. 1975); one *s* two *d*; 2nd, 1976, Evelyn Phyllis Chapman. *Educ:* Belfast High Sch.; Indian Army Officers' Trng Coll.; Univ. of Toronto Dept of Extension (Indust. Management). Supervisor, Methods & Standards, W. J. Gage, 1953–58; Manager, Process Engrg, Hallmark Greeting Cards, 1958–63; Manager, Ops Improvemts, Union Carbide (Canada) 1963–68; ITT Canada Ltd: Dir, Ops Staffs, 1968–73; Chm. and Pres., 1973–93; Sen. Officer (Canada), ITT Corp., NY, 1984–93. Dir, Samuel Manu-Tech Inc., 1994–2010. Chm., Abbey Life Insurance Co., Canada; formerly Chief Industrial Engineer: Dunlop Canada; Electric Reduction Co.; Dir, Acklands; Mem. Adv. Bd, Accenture (formerly Andersen Consulting). Former Mem., Policy Cttee, Business Council on Nat. Issues; Business Co-Chm., Canadian Labour Market & Productivity Center, 1990. Director: Nat. Retinitis Pigmentosa Eye Res. Foundn, Canada; Ireland Fund of Canada, 1979–95 (Chm., 1996–98). Mem., Bd of Trustees, 1995–99, Heritage Gov., 2000–05, Royal Ontario Mus. Chairman: Bd of Govs, West Park Hosp., 1991–94; Adv. Bd, Canadian Inst. of Management, 1971 (Life Mem.); Adv. Bd, Boys' and Girls' Clubs of Canada; NI Partnership in Canada. *Recreation:* golf. *Address:* 15 Prince William Way, Barrie, ON L4N 0Y9, Canada. *Clubs:* Ontario (Toronto); Lambton Golf and Country (Islington).

SAVAGE, (Thomas) William, CMG 1993; HM Diplomatic Service, retired; Senior Duty Officer, Cabinet Office, 1996–2001; *b* Knockloughrim, Co. Derry, 21 Nov. 1937; *s* of late Hugh Murray Savage and Anna Mary Savage (*née* Whyte); *m* 1966, Gloria Jean Matthews; three *d*. *Educ:* Sullivan Upper Sch., Holywood, Co. Down; Queen's Univ., Belfast (BA (Hons), DipEd); LSE. Vice-Pres. and Sec., 1961–64, Pres., 1964–66, Nat. Union of Students; journalist, ITN, 1967; joined Diplomatic Service, 1968; Dar es Salaam, 1970–73; First Sec., FCO, 1973; Counsellor, on loan to Cabinet Office, 1981; Counsellor, FCO, 1984–93. *Recreations:* amateur drama, golf, topiary. *Clubs:* Royal Over-Seas League; Wimbledon Park Golf, Tanganyika Golfing Society.

SAVAGE, Wendy Diane, FRCOG; Senior Lecturer in Obstetrics and Gynaecology, St Bartholomew's and the Royal London School of Medicine and Dentistry, Queen Mary and Westfield College (formerly London Hospital Medical College), University of London, 1977–2000; *b* 12 April 1935; *d* of William George Edwards and Anne (*née* Smith); *m* 1960, Miguel Babatunde Richard Savage (marr. diss. 1973); two *s* two *d*. *Educ:* Croydon High School for Girls; Girton Coll., Cambridge (BA); London Hosp. Med. Coll. (MB BCh); London Sch. of Hygiene and Tropical Medicine (MSc (Public Health) 1997). MRCOG 1971, FRCOG 1985. Res. Fellow, Harvard Univ., 1963–64; MO, Nigeria, 1964–67; Registrar: Surgery and Obst. and Gynaec., Kenya, 1967–69; Obst. and Gynaec., Royal Free Hosp., 1969–71; venereology, abortion work, family planning, Islington, 1971–73; Specialist in obst. and gynaec., family planning and venereology, Gisborne, NZ, 1973–76; Lectr, London Hosp., 1976–77. Queen Mary, University of London: Hon. Sen. Clinical Lectr, Wolfson Inst. of Preventive Medicine, Bart's and The London Sch. of Medicine and Dentistry, 2002–05; Hon. Sen. Res. Fellow, Centre for Envmtl and Preventative Medicine and Dentistry, 2005–. Hon. Vis. Prof., Middx Univ., 1991–. Contract as Hon. Cons. suspended for alleged incompetence, April 1985 - reinstated by unanimous vote of DHA after exoneration by HM61/112 Enquiry, July 1986. Mem., GMC, 1989–2005. Public Gov., Camden and Islington NHS Foundn Trust, 2012–. Pres., Keep Our NHS Public, 2013–. Hon. DSc Greenwich, 2001. Lifetime Achievement Award in Sexual Health, Brook/FPA, 2013. *Publications:* Hysterectomy, 1982; (with Fran Reader) Coping with Caesarean Section and other difficult births, 1983; A Savage Enquiry - who controls childbirth?, 1986; (jtly) Caesarean Birth in Britain, 1993; (jtly) Birth and Power, 2008; papers on abortion, sexually transmitted disease, ultrasound, sex in pregnancy, cervical cytology, medical education. *Recreations:* playing piano duets, reading, fell-walking. *Address:* Flat 11, Galileo Apartments, 48 Featherstone Street, EC1Y 8RT. *E:* wd.savage@qmul.ac.uk, wdsavage@doctors.org.uk.

SAVAGE, William; *see* Savage, T. W.

SAVAGE-SMITH, Prof. Emilie, PhD; FBA 2010; former Professor of the History of Islamic Science, University of Oxford; Archivist, St Cross College, Oxford (former Fellow). Sen. Res. Consultant, Bodleian Liby. Co-Pres., Soc. for Hist. of Medieval Technol. and Sci. Former Mem. Council, British Inst. for Study of Iraq (formerly British Sch. of Archaeol. in Iraq). *Publications:* Science, Tools and Magic, Pt I (with F. Maddison), Body and Spirit, Mapping the Universe, Pt II, Mundane Worlds, 1997; (with E. Edson) Medieval Views of the Cosmos, 2004; A Descriptive Catalogue of Oriental Manuscripts at St John's College, Oxford, 2005; (with P. Pormann) Medieval Islamic Medicine, 2007; A New Catalogue of Arabic Manuscripts in the Bodleian Library, University of Oxford, Vol. 1: Medicine, 2011. *Address:* c/o Oriental Institute, University of Oxford, Pusey Lane, Oxford OX1 2LE.

SAVARESE, Signora Fernando; *see* Elvin, Violetta.

SAVERNAKE, Viscount; Thomas James Brudenell-Bruce; *b* 11 Feb. 1982; *s* and *heir* of Earl of Cardigan, *qv*. *Educ:* Radley Coll.; Univ. of Edinburgh.

SAVIĆ, Prof. Dragan, PhD; FREng, FICE; Professor of Hydroinformatics, since 2001, and Head of Engineering, since 2010, University of Exeter; *b* Belgrade, 22 April 1960; *s* of Aleksander and Danica Savić; *m* 2006, Alison; one *s* one *d*. *Educ:* Univ. of Belgrade (Dip. Ing. 1983; MSc Civil Engrg 1987); Univ. of Manitoba (PhD Civil Engrg). CEng, FREng 2013; FCIWEM. Hydraulic Engineer: Energoprojekt, Belgrade, Yugoslavia, 1983–90; KGS Gp, Winnipeg, Canada, 1990–91; Lecturer: Univ. of Novi Sad, Yugoslavia, 1991–95; Univ. of Exeter, 1995–2001. Visiting Professor: Harbin Inst. of Technol., China; Tech. Univ. of Bari, Italy; UNESCO-IHE, Delft, Netherlands; Univ. of Novi Sad; Univ. of Belgrade. Ed.-in-Chief, Internat. Water Assoc. Jl Hydroinformatics. *Publications:* Water Distribution Modeling, 2001; Advanced Water Distribution Modeling and Management, 2003; Water Distribution Systems, 2011. *Recreation:* running. *Address:* Engineering Department, College of Engineering, Mathematics and Physical Sciences, University of Exeter, Harrison Building, Exeter EX4 4QF. *T:* (01392) 723637, *Fax:* (01392) 217965. *E:* d.savic@exeter.ac.uk.

SAVIDGE, Malcolm Kemp; Senior Fellow in Nuclear Non-Proliferation and Disarmament, David Davies Memorial Institute of International Studies, and Honorary Departmental Fellow in International Politics, Aberystwyth University, since 2009; *b* 9 May 1946; *s* of late David Gordon Madgwick Savidge and Jean Kirkpatrick Savidge (*née* Kemp). *Educ:* Wallington County Grammar Sch., Surrey; Aberdeen Univ. (MA); Aberdeen Coll. of Educn (Teaching Cert.). Production Control and Computer Asst, Bryans Electronics Ltd, 1970–71; Teacher: Greenwood Dale Secondary Sch., Nottingham, 1971; Peterhead Acad., 1972–73; Teacher of Maths, Kincorth Acad., Aberdeen, 1973–97. Mem. (Lab) Aberdeen City Council, 1980–96 (Dep. Leader, 1994–96). Contested (Lab) Kincardine and Deeside, Nov. 1991 and 1992. MP (Lab) Aberdeen N, 1997–2005. Convener, All Party Parly Gp on Global Security and Non-Proliferation, 2000–05. Parly Consultant, Oxford Res. Gp, 2005–08. Advr, British American Security Inf. Council, 2011– (Mem. Bd, 2005–11). Vice-President: UNA (UK), 2003–; One World Trust, 2005–; Hon. Pres., UNA-Scotland, 2008–12. Governor: Robert Gordon's Inst. of Technol., 1980–88; Aberdeen Coll. of Educn, 1980–87. Member: IISS; RIIA; RUSI. Hon. Fellow, Robert Gordon Univ., 1997. *Recreation:* exploring "life, the Universe and everything". *Address:* Flat 1, 5 Ridgeway Road, Redhill, Surrey RH1 6PQ. *E:* mksavidge@aol.com.

SAVILE, family name of **Earl of Mexborough**.

SAVILE, 4th Baron *cr* 1888; **John Anthony Thornhill Lumley-Savile;** *b* 10 Jan. 1947; *s* of late Hon. Henry Leoline Thornhill Lumley-Savile and of Presiley June, *o d* of Geoffrey Herbert Elliot Inchbald; *S* uncle, 2008; *m* 1986, Barbara Ann Holmes, *d* of Anthony Henry Toms. *Educ:* Aiglon Coll., Switzerland. *Heir: half b* Hon. James George Augustus Lumley-Savile [*b* 30 April 1975; *m* 2005, Stephanie, *d* of Dr A. Barba Mendoza].

SAVILL, Sir John Stewart, Kt 2008; PhD; FRCP, FRCPE, FMedSci; FRS 2013; FRSE; Chief Executive and Deputy Chairman, Medical Research Council, 2010–March 2016; Professor of Experimental Medicine, since 2005, and Vice-Principal and Head of College of Medicine and Veterinary Medicine, since 2002, University of Edinburgh (Professor of Medicine, 1998–2005); Hon. Consultant Physician in Renal and General Medicine, Royal Infirmary of Edinburgh, since 1998; *b* 25 April 1957; *s* of Peter Edward Savill and Jean Elizabeth Savill (*née* Garland); *m* 1979, Barbara Campbell; two *s*. *Educ:* St Catherine's Coll., Oxford (BA 1st cl. Hons Physiol Scis 1978); Sheffield Univ. Med. Sch. (MB ChB Hons 1981; Hon. MD 2010); Royal Postgrad. Med. Sch., London (PhD 1989). MRCP 1984, FRCP 1994; FRCPE 2000; FRSE 2005. Jun. med. posts in Sheffield, Nottingham and London, 1981–85; Department of Medicine, Royal Postgraduate Medical School, Hammersmith Hospital: Registrar in Renal Medicine, 1985–86; MRC Training Fellow, 1986–89; Sen. Registrar in Renal Medicine 1989–90; Wellcome Trust Sen. Res. Fellow in Clin. Sci., Hon. Sen. Lectr and Consultant Physician, 1990–93; Prof. in Medicine and Hd, Div. of Renal and Inflammatory Disease, 1993–98, Hd of Sch., 1997–98, Sch. of Med. and Surgical Scis, Univ. of Nottingham Faculty of Medicine and Health Scis; Dir, Univ. of Edinburgh/MRC Centre for Inflammation Res., 2000–02; Chief Scientist, Scottish Govt Health Directorates, 2008–10. Mem., MRC, 2002–08 (Chair: Physiol Med. and Infections Bd, 2002–04; Physiol Systems and Clinical Scis Bd, 2004–07). Chm., Progs and Chairs Cttee, British Heart Foundn, 2007–10. Non-exec. Dir, NHS Lothian, 2002–10. Gov., Health Foundn, 2002–10. Founder FMedSci 1998 (Chm., Wkg Party on Career Structure and Prospects for Clinical Scientists in UK, 1999–2000); Fellow, Amer. Soc. of Nephrology, 2004. Hon. FRCSE 2012. Presidential Award, Soc. of Leukocyte Biology of USA, 1989, 1990; Milne-Muehrcke Award, Nat. Kidney Foundn, USA, 1992; Lifetime Achievement Award, European Cell Death Orgn, 2004. *Publications:* papers on cell death in inflammation. *Recreations:* hockey, cricket, real ale. *Address:* College of Medicine and Veterinary Medicine, University of Edinburgh, Queen's Medical Research Institute, Edinburgh EH16 4TJ. *T:* (0131) 242 9313. *Club:* Wollaton Cricket (Pres., 2011–).

SAVILL, Mark Ashley; His Honour Judge Savill; a Circuit Judge, since 2015; *b* Eastbourne, E Sussex, 17 May 1969; *s* of Brian and Claire Savill; *m* 1997, Rachel; one *s* one *d*. *Educ:* Eton; Durham Univ. (BA Hons Law). Called to the Bar, Inner Temple, 1993; in practice as barrister: Fenners Chambers, Cambridge, 1993–94; Deans Court Chambers, Manchester, 1994–2015. Fee-paid Judge, Mental Health Rev. Tribunal, 2004–; First Jun. Counsel to Rosemary Nelson Inquiry, 2005–10. Lead Asst Parly Boundary Comr, NW Reg., 2011–12. *Recreations:* golf, yoga. *Address:* Bradford Combined Court Centre, Drake Street, Bradford, W Yorks BD1 1JA. *T:* (01274) 840274, *Fax:* (01264) 347975. *E:* HHJ.Savill@judiciary.gsi.gov.uk. *Clubs:* MCC; Bradford; Hale Golf; Bar Golfing Society.

SAVILL, Peter David; Chairman, British Horseracing Board, 1998–2004; *b* 30 July 1947; *s* of late Harry and Betty Savill; *m* 1996, Ruth Pinder; two *s* four *d*. *Educ:* Ampleforth Coll.; Downing Coll., Cambridge (LLB 1969). Trainee, Doyle Dane Bernbach, Advertising Agency, 1969–70; Special Projects Manager, Admaster Corp., 1970–71; Asst to Chm., Barclay Securities, 1971–75; President: P & D International, 1975–91; International Voyager Publications, 1980–91; Shorex International, 1991–95; Chm., North South Net, 1985–98. Chm., Plumpton Racecourse, 1998–. Director: Horserace Totalisator Bd, 1998–2002; Horserace Betting Levy Bd, 1998–99; Attheraces, 2001–04. *Recreations:* cricket, golf, horse racing, sport. *Clubs:* Residence (Dublin); K; Gleneagles.

SAVILL, Dame Rosalind (Joy), DBE 2009 (CBE 2000); FBA 2006; FSA; Director, The Wallace Collection, 1992–2011, now Curator Emeritus; *b* 12 May 1951; *d* of late Dr Guy Savill and Lorna (*née* Williams); one *d*. *Educ:* Wycombe Abbey Sch.; Châtelard Sch., sur-Montreux; Univ. of Leeds (BA Hons 1972); Study Centre, London (Dip in Fine and Decorative Arts 1973). Ceramics Dept, V&A Mus., 1973–74; The Wallace Collection: Museum Asst, 1974–78; Asst to Dir, 1978–92. Guest Scholar, J. Paul Getty Mus., 1985. Mem. Council, Attingham Trust, 1980–92; Member: Nat. Trust Arts Panel, 1995–; Art Adv. Cttee, Nat. Mus and Galls of Wales, 1997–2003; Museums and Collections Adv. Cttee, English Heritage, 1998–2003; Accreditation Panel, MLA (formerly Registration Cttee, Museums and Galls Commn), 1999–2007; Adv. Cttee, Royal Mint, 1999–2007; Expert Panel, NHMF, 2006–13; Academic Cttee, Waddesdon Manor, 2012–. Conseiller d'Administration, Sèvres: Cité de la Céramique, 2010–12. Trustee: Somerset House Trust, 1997–2004; Campaign for Museums, 1999–2008; Samuel Courtauld Trust, 2008–; Holburne Museum, Bath, 2003–07; Buccleuch Living Heritage Trust, 2009–; Hertford House Trust, 2012–; Royal Collection Trust, 2012–. Pres., French Porcelain Soc., 1999– (Chm., 1988–94). Governor: Camden Sch. for Girls, 1996–2009; Alpha Plus Schs, 2012– (non-exec. Dir, Alpha Plus Hldgs, 2012–). Vis. Prof., Univ. of Arts, London, 2008–11; Professorial Res. Fellow, History of the Decorative Arts, Univ. of Buckingham, 2011–. FSA 1990; FRSA 1990. Hon. PhD Bucks and Chiltern UC, 2005; Hon. DLitt Buckingham, 2013. Officier, l'Ordre des Arts et des Lettres (France), 2013. Nat. Art Collections Award for Scholarship, 1990; European Woman of Achievement Arts and Media Award, EUW, 2005; Iris Foundn Award for Outstanding Contribution to Decorative Arts, Bard Graduate Center, NY, 2014. *Publications:* The Wallace Collection Catalogue of Sèvres Porcelain, 3 vols, 1988; (contrib.) Treasure Houses of Britain, 1985; Boughton House, 1992; Versailles: tables royales, 1993; articles in Apollo, Burlington Mag., Antologia di Belle Arti, J. Paul Getty Mus. Jl, Ars Ceramica, Antique Collector, French Porcelain Soc. Jl. *Recreations:* music, birds, wildlife, Sèvres patrons and collectors.

SAVILLE, family name of **Baron Saville of Newdigate**.

SAVILLE OF NEWDIGATE, Baron *cr* 1997 (Life Peer), of Newdigate in the co. of Surrey; **Mark Oliver Saville,** Kt 1985; PC 1994; a Justice of the Supreme Court of the United Kingdom, 2009–10 (a Lord of Appeal in Ordinary, 1997–2009); *b* 20 March 1936; *s* of Kenneth Vivian Saville and Olivia Sarah Frances Gray; *m* 1961, Jill Gray; two *s*. *Educ:* St Paul's Primary Sch., Hastings; Rye Grammar Sch.; Brasenose Coll., Oxford (BA, BCL; Hon. Fellow, 1998). Nat. Service, 2nd Lieut Royal Sussex Regt, 1954–56; Oxford Univ., 1956–60 (Vinerian Schol. 1960); called to Bar, Middle Temple, 1962 (Bencher, 1983); QC 1975; Judge of the High Court, QBD, 1985–93; a Lord Justice of Appeal, 1994–97. Chm., Bloody Sunday Inquiry Tribunal, 1998–2010. Hon. LLD: London Guildhall, 1997; Nottingham Trent, 2008. *Recreations:* sailing, flying, computers. *Address:* House of Lords, SW1A 0PW. *Club:* Garrick.

SAVILLE, Clive Howard; Chief Executive, UKCOSA: Council for International Education, 1997–2004; *b* 7 July 1943; *m* 1967, Camille Kathleen Burke. *Educ:* Bishop Gore Grammar Sch., Swansea; University Coll., Swansea (BA). Joined DES as Asst Principal, 1965; Cabinet Office, 1975; Private Sec. to Leader of H of C and Lord Pres. of Council, 1975–77; Grade 3, DES, then DFE, later DFEE, 1987–97. Member: Exec. Cttee, Nat. Literary Trust, 1997–2007; British Accreditation Council for Ind. Further and Higher Educn, 1998–2004; Adv. Panel, Office of Immigration Services Comr, 2001–05. Governor: Morley Coll., 1999–2002; UCL Hosps Foundn Trust, 2004–09. *E:* savilleclive@aol.com.

SAVILLE, Jenny, RA 2007; painter; *b* Cambridge, 1970. *Educ:* Glasgow Sch. of Art (BA 1992). Lectr, Slade Sch. of Fine Arts, London, 2000–06. *Solo exhibitions* include: Place McGill Gall., NY, 1996; Gagosian Gall., NY, 1999, 2003; Gagosian Gall., Beverly Hills, 2002; Univ. of Massachusetts, 2004; Museo d'Arte Contemporanea, Rome, 2005; Gagosian Gall., London, 2010, 2014; Modern Art Oxford, 2012, 2014; *group exhibitions* include: RA, London, 1990, 1997; Saatchi Gall., London, 1994; McLellan Galls, Glasgow, 1995; NPG, 2000; Kunsthalle Emden, 2002; 50th Biennale di Venezia, 2003; Frist Center for Arts, Nashville, 2009; Gagosian Gall., London, 2010.

SAVILLE, John Donald William; HM Diplomatic Service; Ambassador to Venezuela, since 2014; *b* 29 June 1960; *s* of Donald and Elizabeth Saville; *m* 1992, Fabiola Moreno de Alboran; one *d*. *Educ:* Hitchin Boys' Grammar Sch.; Jesus Coll., Oxford (MA). Joined FCO, 1981; Third, then Second Sec., Jakarta, 1982–85; FCO, 1985–88; Second, then First Sec., Warsaw, 1988–91; First Secretary: FCO, 1991–95; Vienna, 1995–98; Hd, Commonwealth and Burma Section, SE Asia Dept, FCO, 1998–2000; Dep. Hd of Mission, Havana, 2000–03; Hd, Weapons of Mass Destruction Review Unit (Butler Review of Iraq Intelligence), FCO, 2004; High Comr, Brunei, 2005–09; Counsellor, FCO, 2009; Hd, Foreign Policy Climate Change Adaptation Proj., FCO, 2009–10; Dir, Asia, 2010–14, Acting Man. Dir, 2013–14, UKTI. *Recreations:* fishing, pulling sofas from the River Wandle, jungle trekking. *Address:* c/o Foreign and Commonwealth Office, King Charles Street, SW1A 2AH. *Clubs:* Travellers, Royal Geographical Society.

SAVILLE, Peter Andrew, RDI 2011; designer; *b* 9 Oct. 1955; *s* of Lionel Stuart Saville and Dorothy Mabel Saville (*née* Foley). *Educ:* St Ambrose Coll., Altrincham; Manchester Poly. (BA 1st Cl. Hons Graphic Design 1978). Founding Partner, Factory Records, 1979, created album covers for Joy Division and New Order, etc; Art Dir, Dindisc Records, 1979–82; founded Peter Saville Associates design studio, 1983; Partner, Pentagram, 1990–92; Art Dir, Frankfurt Balkind, LA, 1993–94; founded: The Apartment, with Meiré and Meiré, advertising and design agency, 1995; with Nick Knight, SHOWstudio.com, 1999; Consultant Creative Dir to Manchester CC, 2004–. Vis. Prof., Univ. of the Arts, London, 2008. *Exhibitions* include: major retrospective, Design Mus., London, 2003, transf. Tokyo and Manchester; ESTATE, Migros Mus., Zurich, 2005. MInstD. Hon. DArts Manchester Metropolitan, 2005. *Publications:* Designed by Peter Saville, 2003; (jtly) Peter Saville Estate, 2007. *E:* mail@petersavillestudio.com. *Club:* Groucho.

SAVILLE ROBERTS, Elizabeth; MP (Plaid Cymru) Dwyfor Meirionnydd, since 2015; *b* London, 16 Dec. 1964; *d* of Nicholas and Nancy Saville; *m* 1994, Dewi Wyn Roberts; twin *d*. *Educ:* Univ. of Wales, Aberystwyth (BA Hons Celtic Studies 1987); Bi-lingual Postgrad. Cert. for Personal Assts 1988; NCTJ 1991; Coleg Meirion-Dwyfor, Dolgellau (PGCE 1996). Sec., French and Russian Depts, QMC, 1988–89; staff reporter, Retail Newsagent, 1989–90; news reporter, Herald Newspapers, 1990–92; Lectr, 1993–2001, Hd, Canolfan Sgiliaithth, 2001–12, Coleg Meirion-Dwyfor; Dir of Bilingualism, Grŵp Llandrillo, Menai, 2012–14. Mem. (Plaid Cymru) Gwynedd CC, 2004–15. *Recreations:* horse riding, hill walking, art, history, poetry. *Address:* Angorfa, Heol Meurig, Dolgellau, Gwynedd LL40 1LN. *T:* (01341) 422661. *E:* liz.savilleroberts.mp@parliament.uk.

SAVORY, Sir Michael Berry, Kt 2006; Managing Partner, Muckleburgh Collection, since 1989; Lord Mayor of London, 2004–05; *b* 10 Jan. 1943; *s* of late Claude Berry Savory and Irene Anne Parker; *m* 1992, Fiona Anne Macrae; two *d*. *Educ:* Whitestones, Bulawayo, Zimbabwe; Harrow Sch. Partner, Foster & Braithwaite Stockbrokers, 1967–89; Chm., BT Batsford, 1981–90; Dir, Terrafix, 1985–90. Chairman: HSBC Bank plc Stockbroker Services, 2001–05; ProShare, 2003–05. Chief Exec., Young Enterprise, 2006–09. Mem. Council, SSAFA-Forces Help, 1972–2006; Treas., Royal Nat. Mission to Deep Sea Fishermen, 1985–2006; Trustee: Hull Fishermen's Widows and Orphans Trust, 1985–2006; John Rice Charity, 1991–2003; Adm. Arthur Phillip Meml Trust, 1996–; Lord Mayor's 800th Anniversary Trust, 2000–; Britain-Australia Bicentennial Trust, 2001–14; John Carpenter Trust, 2002–. Hon. FCSI. Hon. Col, London Regt, TA, 2007–11. Churchwarden, St Margaret, Lothbury, 1987–2003; Freeman, City of London, 1964; Corporation of London: Mem., Court of Common Council, 1981–96; Alderman, 1996–2013; Sheriff, 2001–02; Freeman, Co. of Goldsmiths, 1984; Liveryman: Co. of Poulters (Master, 1996); Co. of Clockmakers (Master, 1998); Co. of Information Technologists, 2004. *Recreation:* military vehicle collection. *Address:* Muckleburgh House, Kelling, Norfolk NR25 7EG. *T:* (01263) 588159. *E:* mbsavory@aol.com.

SAVOURS; *see* Campbell-Savours, family name of Baron Campbell-Savours.

SAVULESCU, Prof. Julian, PhD; Uehiro Professor of Practical Ethics, since 2002, Director, Oxford Uehito Centre for Practical Ethics, since 2003, and Director, Oxford Centre for Neuroethics, since 2009, University of Oxford; Fellow of St Cross College, Oxford, since 2002; *b* 22 Dec. 1963; *s* of Radu Ion and Valda Jean Savulescu. *Educ:* Monash Univ., Australia (BMedSci 1st cl. Hons 1985; MB BS 1st cl. Hons 1988; PhD 1994). Sir Robert Menzies Med. Scholar, Oxford Univ., 1994–97; Clinical Ethicist, Oxford Radcliffe Hosps, 1995–97; Logan Res. Fellow, Monash Univ., 1997–98; Director: Bioethics Prog., Centre for Study of Health and Society, Univ. of Melbourne, 1998–2002; Ethics of Genetics Prog., Murdoch Children's Res. Inst., Royal Children's Hosp., Melbourne, 1998–2002. Louis Matheson Vis. Prof., Monash Univ., 2010–. Chm., Dept of Human Services, Victoria Ethics Cttee, 1998–2002. Editor: Jl of Med. Ethics, 2001–04, 2011–; Jl of Practical Ethics, 2013–. *Publications:* (jtly) Medical Ethics and Law: the core curriculum, 2003; over 240 articles in BMJ, Lancet, Australasian Jl of Philosophy, Bioethics, Jl of Med. Ethics, American Jl of Bioethics, Med. Jl of Australia, Philosophy, Psychiatry and Psychology and New Scientist. *Recreations:* ski-ing, surfing, cycling, swimming, roller blading, film, wine. *Address:* Oxford Uehiro Centre for Practical Ethics, Littlegate House, St Ebbe's Street, Oxford OX1 1PT. *T:* (01865) 286888, *Fax:* (01865) 286886. *E:* ethics@philosophy.ox.ac.uk.

SAWATZKY, Prof. George Albert, PhD; FRS 2008; FRS(Can); Professor of Applied and Solid State Physics, University of Groningen, since 1985; Professor of Physics and Chemistry of Nanostructured Materials, University of British Columbia, since 2001. *Educ:* Univ. of Manitoba (PhD). University of Groningen: NRC postdoctoral res. in solid state physics, 1969–71; Associate Prof., Physical Chem. Dept, 1971–79; Prof. of Physical Chem., 1979–85; Dir, Materials Sci. Centre, 1986–97. Member: Sci. Adv. Cttee, Eur. Synchrotron Radiation

Facility, Grenoble, 1997–98; Sci. Technol. Adv. Cttee, Synchrotron Radiation Facility of China, 1998; Dutch Forum for Technol. and Sci., 1999–2002; Adv. Bd, Dutch Res. Sch. of Theoretical Physics, Utrecht Univ., 1999. Mem., Royal Dutch Acad. of Scis, 1991; Associate Mem., Canadian Inst. for Advanced Res., 1998. FRS(Can) 2002. NWO-Spinoza Award, Netherlands Orgn for Scientific Res., 1996; Nieuwsblad van het Noorden Prize, 1997; Henry Marshall Tory Medal, Royal Soc. of Canada, 2007. *Address:* Department of Physics and Astronomy, University of British Columbia, 6224 Agricultural Road, Vancouver, BC V6T 1Z1, Canada.

SAWER, Dr David Peter; composer; Professor of Composition, Royal Academy of Music, since 2008; *b* Stockport, 14 Sept. 1961; *s* of Brian and Mavis Sawer; civil partnership 2008, Jesus Jimenez Jimenez. *Educ:* Ipswich Sch.; Univ. of York (BA Hons; DPhil 1988); Staatliche Hochschule für Musik Rheinland, Köln. DAAD Schol., 1984–85; Fulbright-Chester-Schirmer Fellow in Composition, 1992–93. *Publications: compositions:* Cat's-eye, 1986; Songs of Love and War, 1990; Byrnan Wood, 1992; Trumpet Concerto, 1994; Hollywood Extra, 1996; Tiroirs, 1996; the greatest happiness principle, 1997; From Morning to Midnight, 2001; Piano Concerto, 2002; Rebus, 2004; Skin Deep, 2008; Rumpelstiltskin, 2009; Flesh and Blood, 2011; The Lighthouse Keepers, 2013; Bronze and Iron, 2013; Coachman Chronos, 2014. *Address:* c/o Allied Artists, Southbank House, Black Prince Road, SE1 7SJ. *T:* (020) 7589 6243.

SAWERS, David Richard Hall; environmental campaigner and writer; *b* 23 April 1931; *s* of late Edward and Madeline Sawers; unmarried. *Educ:* Westminster Sch.; Christ Church, Oxford (MA). Research Asst to Prof. J. Jewkes, Oxford Univ., 1954–58; Journalist, The Economist, 1959–64; Vis. Fellow, Princeton Univ., 1964–65; Econ. Adviser, Min. of Aviation and of Technology, 1966–68; Sen. Econ. Adviser, Min. of Technology, Aviation Supply, and DTI, 1968–72; Under-Sec., Depts of Industry, Trade and Prices and Consumer Protection, 1972–76; Under-Sec., Depts of Environment and Transport, 1976–83; Principal Res. Fellow, Technical Change Centre, 1984–86. Chairman: Forum of Arun Dist Amenity Gps, 1998–; E Preston and Kingston Preservation Soc., 2000–. *Publications:* (with John Jewkes and Richard Stillerman) The Sources of Invention, 1958; (with Ronald Miller) The Technical Development of Modern Aviation, 1968; Competition in the Air, 1987; Should the Taxpayer Support the Arts, 1993; (contrib.) Markets and the Media, 1996; (contrib.) Does the Past Have a Future?: the political economy of heritage, 1998; articles in daily press and journals. *Recreations:* listening to music, watching ballet and opera, looking at pictures, gardening. *Address:* 10 Seaview Avenue, East Preston, Littlehampton BN16 1PP. *T:* (01903) 779134.

SAWERS, Sir (Robert) John, GCMG 2015 (KCMG 2007; CMG 1996); Chairman, Macro Advisory Partners, since 2015; *b* 26 July 1955; *s* of Colin Simon Hawkesley Sawers and Daphne Anne Sawers; *m* 1981, Avril Helen Shelley Lamb; two *s* one *d*. *Educ:* Beechen Cliff Sch., Bath; Univ. of Nottingham (BSc Hons Physics and Philosophy). FCO 1977; served Sana'a, 1980; Damascus, 1982; FCO, 1984; Pretoria/Cape Town, 1988; Head, EU Presidency Unit, 1991; Principal Private Sec. to Sec. of State for Foreign and Commonwealth Affairs, 1993–95; Career Develt Attachment, Harvard Univ., 1995–96; Counsellor, Washington, 1996–99; For. Affairs Private Sec. to the Prime Minister, 1999–2001; Ambassador to Egypt, 2001–03; Special Rep. for Iraq, 2003; Political Dir, FCO, 2003–07; UK Perm. Rep. to UN, 2007–09; Chief, Secret Intelligence Service (MI6), 2009–14. Non-exec. Dir, BP, 2015–. Gov., Ditchley Foundn. *Recreations:* sport, the arts.

SAWFORD, Andrew; *b* Desborough, Northants, 15 March 1976; *s* of Philip Andrew Sawford, *qv*; *m* 2000, Joanna Veevers; one *s* one *d*. *Educ:* Durham Univ. (BA Hist. 1997). Worked for Philip Hope, MP, H of C, 1997; work in business and public service; Dir, Connect Public Affairs, 2003–07; Chief Exec., Local Govt Information Unit, 2008–12. Mem. (Lab) Dartford BC, 1999–2003. MP (Lab) Corby, Nov. 2012–2015; contested (Lab) same seat, 2015. Shadow Minister for Local Govt, 2013–15. Mem., Communities and Local Govt Select Cttee, 2012–13; All Party Parly Gps on steel making, local govt and local growth, 2012–15.

SAWFORD, Philip Andrew; *b* 26 June 1950; *s* of John and Audrey Sawford; *m* 1971, Rosemary Stokes; two *s*. *Educ:* Ruskin Coll., Oxford (Dip. Soc.); Univ. of Leicester (BA Hons). Manager, training orgn, Wellingborough, 1985–97 and 2007–09; Northamptonshire Enterprise Ltd, 2009–10. Member (Lab): Desborough Town Council, 1977–97; Kettering BC, 1979–83, 1986–97, 1991–97 (Leader). Contested (Lab): Wellingborough, 1992; Kettering, 2005, 2010. MP (Lab) Kettering, 1997–2005. *Recreations:* playing guitar, reading. *Address:* 46 Federation Avenue, Desborough, Northants NN14 2NX.
See also A. Sawford.

SAWYER, Baron *cr* 1998 (Life Peer), of Darlington in the co. of Durham; **Lawrence Sawyer, (Tom);** *b* 12 May 1943. *Educ:* Eastbourne Sch., Darlington; Darlington Tech. Sch. Dep. Gen. Sec., NUPE, later UNISON, 1981–94; Gen. Sec., Labour Party, 1994–98. Mem., NEC, Labour Party, 1981–94 and 1999–2001; Chm., Labour Party, 1990–91. Non-exec. Chm., Reed Health Gp, 2001–03; Chairman: Royal Mail Partnership Bd, 2001–07; Norlife, 2004–; non-exec. Dir, Investors in People UK, 1998–2005. Chairman: Notting Hill Housing Gp, 1998–2005; Supervisory Bd, Thompsons, Solicitors, 2001–11; Union Insurance (formerly Union Income Benefit), 2003–. Vis. Prof., Cranfield Sch. of Mgt, 1999–2013. Chancellor, Univ. of Teesside, 2005–. *Address:* House of Lords, SW1A 0PW.

SAWYER, Anthony Charles, CB 1999; fiscal expert, International Monetary Fund, 1999–2007 (expert missions to Bulgaria, Egypt, Jordan, Kenya, Kyrgyzstan, Nigeria, Pakistan, Romania, Tajikistan, Tanzania and the Philippines); *b* 3 Aug. 1939; *s* of Charles Bertram and Elizabeth Sawyer; *m* 1962, Kathleen Josephine McGill; two *s* one *d*. *Educ:* Redhill Tech. Coll., Surrey. Nat. Service, RA, 1960. Underwriter, Northern Assurance Group, 1962; Customs and Excise, 1964–99: Collector, Edinburgh, 1984; Dep. Dir, 1988; Comr, 1991–99; Director: Outfield, 1991–94; Enforcement, 1994–99. Dir, Customs Annuity and Benevolent Fund, 1998–2004. Non-exec. Dir, Retail Banking Bd, Royal Bank of Scotland, 1994–97; fiscal adviser: Kyrgyzstan, 2000; Egypt, 2003; Ethiopia, 2004. FRSA 1994; FCMI (FIMgt 1996); FInstD 1997; FRMetS 2001. *Recreations:* walking, cricket, poetry. *Clubs:* National Liberal; Royal Scots (Edinburgh).

SAWYER, Rt Hon. Dame Joan (Augusta), DBE 1997; PC 2004; President, Bahamas Court of Appeal, 2001–10; *b* 26 Nov. 1940; *m* 1962, Geoffrey Sawyer (*d* 2004); one *s*. *Educ:* London Univ. (LLB 1973). Clerk, 1958–68; HEO (Public Service), 1968–73; called to the Bar, Gray's Inn, 1973; Asst Crown Counsel, 1973–78; acting Stipendiary and Circuit Magistrate, 1978; Sen. Counsel, 1979–83; acting Dir, Legal Affairs, 1983; Counsel, Central Bank of the Bahamas, 1984–88; Justice, 1988–95, Sen. Justice, 1995–96, Supreme Court of Bahamas; Chief Justice of the Bahamas, 1996–2001. *Publications:* articles in Bahamian Review. *Recreations:* reading, sewing, serious theatre, gardening, embroidering. *Address:* PO Box N-1733, Nassau, Bahamas. *T:* 3943055.

SAWYER, Miranda Caroline; freelance journalist and broadcaster; *b* Bristol, 7 Jan. 1967; *d* of Richard and Jennifer Sawyer; *m* 2007, Michael Smiley; one *s* one *d*. *Educ:* Cheadle Hulme Sch., Cheadle Hulme; Pembroke Coll., Oxford (BA Juris.). Writer: Smash Hits, 1988–90; Select, 1990–95; The Face, 1994–98; columnist, Time Out, 1993–96; Feature Writer, 1993–, Radio Critic, 2005–, The Observer; presenter, The Culture Show, BBC TV, 2008–. Member: Council, Tate Members, 2008– (Dep. Chm.); Bd, South London Gallery. Writer of the Year, PPA, 1993; Record of the Day Award for Music Journalism, 2012. *Publications:* Park and Ride, 1999. *Recreations:* reading, writing, pop music, contemporary art, contemporary theatre, second-hand shops, outdoor swimming pools, chatting, tweeting, fannying about. *E:* mail@mirandasawyer.com.

SAWYER, Priti; *see* Patel, P.

SAWYERS, Bridget Truus; Director, Bridget Sawyers Ltd, since 2002; *b* Dover, 31 May 1965; *d* of David Sawyers and Truus Sawyers. *Educ:* Kingston Poly. (BA Hons Arch. 1986); Poly. of Central London, later Univ. of Westminster (DipArch 1986; RIBA Pt III 1991; MA Urban Design 1995). Architect, Building Design Partnership, 1989–96; Sen. Officer, Architecture, Arts Council of England, 1996–2000; Hd, Regions, CABE, 2000–02; Chief Exec., Architecture Centre Network, 2009–12. Dir, Project Compass CIC, 2013–. Mem., Nat. Panel, Civic Trust Awards, 2011–15; Prize Manager, Queen Elizabeth Prize for Engrg, 2013–14. Academician, Acad. of Urbanism, 2012–14. *Publications:* (ed jtly) International Architecture Centres, 2003; contribs to architecture and public art publns. *Recreations:* visual arts, architecture, art in the public realm, travel, Wicks Vintners wine tasting, growing vegetables. *Address:* 19 Windmill House, Windmill Walk, SE1 8LX. *T:* (020) 7928 7131. *E:* bridgetsawyerslimited@gmail.com.

SAXBEE, Rt Rev. John Charles, PhD; Bishop of Lincoln, 2001–11; Assistant Bishop, Diocese of St David's, since 2011; *b* 7 Jan. 1946; *s* of Charles Albert Saxbee and Florence Violet Saxbee (*née* Harris); *m* 1965, Jacqueline Margaret Carol Skym; one *d*. *Educ:* Cotham Grammar Sch., Bristol; Bristol Univ. (BA 1968); Durham Univ. (DipTh 1969; PhD 1976); Cranmer Hall, Durham. Ordained deacon, 1972, priest, 1973; Asst Curate, Emmanuel with St Paul, Plymouth, 1972–77; Vicar of St Philip, Weston Mill, Plymouth, 1977–81; Team Vicar, Central Exeter Team Ministry, 1981–87; Dir, SW Ministry Training Course, 1981–92; Priest-in-Charge of Holy Trinity, Wistanstow with St Michael, Cwm Head and St Margaret, Acton Scott, 1992–94; Archdeacon of Ludlow, 1992–2001, Bishop Suffragan of Ludlow, 1994–2001. Prebendary: of Exeter Cathedral, 1988–92; of Hereford Cathedral, 1992–2001. Chm., C of E Bd of Educn, 2008–11. Pres., Modern Churchpeople's Union, 1997–2011; Chm., Rural Theology Assoc., 2011–14. Religious Advr, Central TV, 1997–2006. Member: Exec., Springboard, 1998–2004; Coll. of Evangelists, 1999–2012. Hon. Dr Bishop Grosseteste UC Lincoln, 2010. *Publications:* Liberal Evangelism: a flexible response to the decade, 1994; No Faith in Religion: some variations on a theme, 2009; Waymarkers: a route map through Lent to Easter, 2013. *Recreations:* televised sport, most kinds of music. *Address:* 22 Shelley Road, Priory Park, Haverfordwest, Dyfed SA61 1RX.

SAXBY, Oliver Charles John; QC 2013; *b* London, 10 Nov. 1969; *s* of Marygold Saxby (now Turner) and step *s* of late Dr Colin Turner; *m* 1996, Rebecca Helen Leighton; one *d*. *Educ:* Eton Coll.; Univ. of Southampton (LLB (Hons) Law). Called to the Bar, Inner Temple, 1992; in practice as a criminal barrister, 1992–. Chm., Kent Bar Mess, 2013– (Jun., 2001–03); Sec., Bar Golfing Soc., 2004–07; Capt., Inner Temple Golfing Soc., 2012. *Recreations:* football, golf, ski-ing, shooting, fishing, opera. *Address:* 6 Pump Court, Temple, EC4Y 7AR. *T:* (020) 7797 8400, *Fax:* (020) 7797 8401. *E:* oliversaxby@aol.com. *Clubs:* Garrick; Rye Golf, Royal St George's Golf; Eton Ramblers, Band of Brothers.

SAXBY, Sir Robin (Keith), Kt 2002; FRS 2015; FREng; CEng; angel investor and advisor to UK HQ technology start ups; Chairman, Arolla Partners Ltd, since 2008; *b* 4 Feb. 1947; *s* of Keith William Saxby and Mary Saxby; *m* 1970, Patricia Susan Bell; one *s* one *d*. *Educ:* Univ. of Liverpool (BEng Electronics 1968). CEng 2002. R&D engr, Rank Bush Murphy, 1968–72; Sen. Engr, Pye TMC, 1972–73; Sales Engr, then System Strategy Manager, Europe, Motorola Semiconductors, 1973–84; Chief Exec., Henderson Security Systems, 1984–86; Man. Dir, ES2 Ltd, 1986–91; Chief Exec. and Chm., 1991–2001, Chm., 2001–06, Emeritus Chm., 2006–07, Advanced RISC Machines Ltd, later ARM Hldgs plc. Non-exec. Dir, Glotel, 1999–2007. Vis. Prof., Dept of Electronics, Univ. of Liverpool. Pres., IET, 2006–07. FREng 2002. FRSA; CCMI. Hon. FIET. Hon. DEng Liverpool, 2000; Hon. DTech: Loughborough, 2001; Anglia Ruskin, 2010; Nottingham Trent, 2012; DU: Essex, 2003; York, 2009. Faraday Medal, IET, 2002; Global Semiconductor Alliance Leadership Award, 2012. *Publications:* (contrib.) Electronic Engineers' Reference Book, 1983; Microcomputer Handbook, 1985; (contrib.) Advances in Information Technology, 1998. *Recreations:* tennis, ski-ing, music, swimming, astronomy, genealogy, old technology, bird watching, music, painting.

SAXON, Prof. David Harold, OBE 2005; DPhil, DSc; CPhys, FInstP; FRAS; FRSE; Kelvin Professor of Physics, 1990–2008, now Professor Emeritus, Dean, Physical Sciences, 2002–08, University of Glasgow; *b* 27 Oct. 1945; *s* of late Rev. Canon Eric Saxon and Ruth (*née* Higginbottom); *m* 1968, Margaret Flitcroft; one *s* one *d*. *Educ:* Manchester Grammar Sch.; Balliol Coll., Oxford (MA, DSc); Jesus Coll., Oxford (DPhil). CPhys 1985; FInstP 1985; FRSE 1993; FRAS 2004. Jun. Res. Fellow, Jesus Coll., Oxford, 1968–70; Res. Officer, Nuclear Physics Dept, Oxford, 1969–70; Res. Associate, Columbia Univ., NY, 1970–73; Rutherford Appleton Laboratory, Oxford: Res. Associate, 1974–75; SSO, 1975–76; PSO, 1976–89; Grade 6, 1989–90; Glasgow University: Hd, Dept of Physics and Astronomy, 1996–2001; Vice-Dean, Physical Scis, 2000–02. Member, SERC Committees: Particle Physics Experiment Selection Panel, 1989–92; Particle Physics, 1991–94 (Chm., 1992–94); Nuclear Physics Bd, 1992–93; Particles, Space & Astronomy Bd, 1993–94. Member Council: PPARC, 1997–2001 (Chairman: Particle Physics Cttee, 1994–95; Public Understanding of Sci. Panel, 1997–2001); CCLRC, 2000–01, 2005–07 (Chm., Particle Physics Users Adv. Cttee, 1998–2004). Chairman: 27th Internat. Conf. on High Energy Physics, 1994; Scottish Univs Summer Schs in Physics, 1997–2003; Member: Scientific Policy Cttee, 1993–98, External Rev. Cttee, 2001–02, CERN, Geneva; Physics Res. Cttee, Deutsches Elektronen Synchrotron, Hamburg, 1993–99; MRC Scientific Adv. Gp on Technology, 1999; MRC Discipline Hopping Panel, 2000–01 and 2006–08; Eur. Cttee on Future Accelerators, 2003–05; Commn C11, Internat. Union of Pure and Applied Physics, 2006–08; Chm., STFC CALICE Oversight Cttee, 2006–08. Member: Physics Panel, 1996 RAE, HEFC; Physics Benchmarking Panel, QAA, 2000–01; Res. Exchange Panel, British Council, 2006–08. Mem. Council, 2001–04, Res. Convener, 2002–05, RSE; Chm., Inst. of Physics in Scotland, 2003–05. Mem., Scientific Adv. Panel, Univ. Trento, Italy, 2001–05. FRSA 1997. *Recreations:* staying close to home, visiting grandchildren. *Address:* c/o Miss V. Flood, School of Physics and Astronomy, University of Glasgow, Glasgow G12 8QQ. *T:* (01788) 832225.
See also R. G. Saxon.

SAXON, Richard Gilbert, CBE 2001; Client Adviser for construction projects, Consultancy for the Built Environment, since 2005; *b* 14 April 1942; *s* of late Rev. Canon Eric Saxon and Ruth Saxon (*née* Higginbottom); *m* 1968, Elizabeth Anne Tatton. *Educ:* Manchester Grammar Sch.; Univ. of Liverpool (BArch 1st cl. Hons 1965; MCD 1966). RIBA 1970; FRICS 2013. Joined Building Design Partnership, 1966: Partner, 1977–2005; Mem., Mgt Gp, 1984–86; Project Dir, J. P. Morgan HQ, AELTC Masterplan, Adam Opel HQ, 1986–93; Chm., London Office, 1993–99; Practice Chm., 1996–2002; Dir, Strategic Marketing, 1999–2005. Non-exec. Dir, BLP Insurance, 2013–Sept. 2016. BIM Ambassador for Growth, 2012–13. Consultant to EC Harris LLP, 2007–10. Pres., British Council for Offices, 1995–96; Vice-Pres., RIBA, 2002–08. Chairman: Reading Construction Forum, 1999–2002; Be (Collaborating for the Built Environment), 2002–04; City Architecture Forum, 2005–; Jt Contracts Tribunal, 2015–; Member: Exec. Bd, Construction Industry Council, 2006–14; Ind. Dispute Avoidance Panel for the London Olympics, 2008–12; Res. Reference Gp, CABE, 2008–11; Cross-Cutting Issues Gp, Low-Carbon Construction Innovation and Growth Team, 2010. Mem., Bldg Cttee, Univ. of Cambridge, 2004–Dec. 2016. MCIM

1990. FRSA 1987. Liveryman, Co. of Chartered Architects, 1988 (Master, 2005–06). *Publications:* Atrium Buildings: development and design, 1983, 2nd edn 1986 (also USA, Japan, Russia); The Atrium Comes of Age, 1993 (also USA, Japan); Be Valuable, 2005; City Architecture: redesigning the City of London 1991–2011, 2011; Growth through BIM, 2013; BIM for Construction Clients, 2015; articles in Building Res. and Inf., Architects Jl, Building Design and Building, RIBA Jl, Architecture Today, Public Service Review. *Recreations:* travel, early music, theatre, film, birds, enjoying London. *Address:* Consultancy for the Built Environment, 9 Whistlers Avenue, SW11 3TS. *T:* (020) 7585 1976. *E:* Richard@saxoncbe.com. *W:* www.saxoncbe.com.

See also D. H. Saxon.

SAXTON, Jonathon Hugh Christopher, (Joe); Driver of Ideas, nfpSynergy, since 2003 (Head, Not for Profit, Future Foundation, 2000–03); *b* Bristol, 6 Feb. 1962; *s* of Hugh Michael Saxton and Barbara Bevil Saxton; *m* 1990, Julie Margaret Evans; two *s* one *d*. *Educ:* Leigh Prim. Sch.; Downsend Sch.; Bedales Sch.; Robinson Coll., Cambridge (BA Nat. Sci. 1984); Univ. of E Anglia (MA Develt Studies 1986); Henley Management Coll. (MBA 1995). Co-ordinator, Harambee Centre, Cambridge, 1986–88; Fundraising Dept, Oxfam, Oxford, 1988–91; Account Dir and Dep. Client Services Dir, Brann Ltd, Cirencester, 1991–96; Dir of Communications, RNID, 1997–2000. Trustee: RSPCA, 1994–2001; Inst. of Fundraising, 2002–08 (Chm., 2005–08); Chm. and Co-founder, CharityComms, 2007–13; Chm., People & Planet, 2005–. *Publications:* It's Competition, but not as we know it?, 1997; What are Charities For?, 1998; Polishing the Diamond, 2002; Mission Impossible, 2004; The 21st Century Volunteer, 2005; The 21st Century Donor, 2007. *Recreations:* DIY, reading, sports training with my kids, fell walking, kayaking, snuggling with my wife. *Address:* nfpSynergy, 2–6 Tenter Ground, Spitalfields, E1 7NH. *T:* (020) 7426 8888. *E:* joe.saxton@nfpsynergy.net.

SAXTON, Prof. Robert Louis Alfred, DMus; FGS; Professor of Composition, Oxford University, since 2008 (University Lecturer, 1999–2008); Tutor and Fellow in Music, Worcester College, Oxford, since 1999; Director, University of York Music Press, since 2004; *b* 8 Oct. 1953; *s* of Jean Augusta Saxton (*née* Infield) and late Ian Sanders Saxton; *m* 2005, Teresa Cahill, *qv*. *Educ:* Bryanston Sch.; St Catharine's Coll., Cambridge (MA); Worcester Coll., Oxford (BMus; DMus 1992). FGS (FGSM 1987). Lectr, Bristol Univ., 1984–85; Fulbright Arts award, 1985; Vis. Fellow, Princeton Univ., 1986; Head of Composition: GSMD, 1990–98; RAM, 1998–99; Vis. Fellow in Composition, Bristol Univ., 1995–2001. Artistic Dir, Opera Lab, 1994–2000; Associate Dir, Performing Arts Labs, 1998–2001; Pres., Brunel Ensemble, 1995–. Hon. Pres., Assoc. of English Singers and Speakers, 1997–. Dir, South Bank Centre, 1998– (Mem., Site Develt Bd, 1997–). Patron, Bristol Univ. Music Soc., 1997–2008; Trustee, Mendelssohn/Boise Foundn, 2010– (Trustee, Mendelssohn Scholarship, 2012–). Advr, Orchestra Europa, 2006–. Finalist, BBC Young Composers' Comp., 1973; First Prize, Gaudeamus Music Fest., Holland, 1975; early works at ISCM Fest., Bonn, 1977, Royan Fest., 1977; later works, majority recorded, include: The Ring of Eternity, 1983; Concerto for Orchestra, 1984; The Circles of Light, 1985; The Child of Light (carol), 1985; The Sentinel of the Rainbow, 1984; Viola Concerto, 1986; Night Dance, 1986–87; I Will Awake the Dawn, 1987; In the Beginning, 1987; Elijah's Violin, 1988; Chacony, 1988; Music to celebrate the Resurrection of Christ, 1988; Violin Concerto, Leeds Fest., 1990; Caritas (opera with libretto by Arnold Wesker), 1990–91; Paraphrase on Mozart's Idomeneo, 1991; At the Round Earth's Imagined Corners (anthem), 1992; 'Cello Concerto, 1992; Psalm—a song of ascents, 1992; O Sing unto the Lord a new song (anthem), 1993; Fantazia, 1993; Canticum Luminis, 1994; A Yardstick to the Stars, 1994; Ring, Time, 1994; Songs, Dances, Ellipses, 1997; Prayer before Sleep, 1997; Music for St Catharine, 1998; Miniature Dance for a Marionette Rabbi, 1999; Sonata for solo 'cello on a theme of Sir William Walton, 1999; The Dialogue of Zion and God, 2000; Alternative Canticles, 2002; Five Motets, 2003; Was It Winter? (carol), 2005; Song Without Words, 2005; There and Back, 2005; O Living Love (anthem), 2007; The Beach in Winter: Scratby (for Tess), 2008; The Wandering Jew (radio opera), 2010; String Quartet No 3, 2011; Hortus Musicae, 2012; Time and the Seasons, 2013; Shakespeare Scenes, 2012–13; Sonata for brass band on a Prelude of Gibbons, 2014; Vexilla Regis, 2014; Chorale Prelude: Wo Gott zum Haus, 2014; The Legend of King Herla, 2015; works commissioned by: Fires of London, London Sinfonietta, BBC, LSO, ECO, Aldeburgh Fest., Cheltenham Fest., Opera North, LPO, RPO, City of London Fest./St Paul's Cathedral, Leeds Fest. *Publications:* contributor to: Composition-Performance-Reception, 1998; Cambridge Companion to the Orchestra, 2003; Composing Music for Worship, 2003; all compositions; contribs TLS, Musical Times, etc. *Recreations:* theatre, cinema, studying history, reading philosophy. *Address:* c/o Music Sales, 14/15 Berners Street, W1T 3LJ. *T:* (020) 7612 7400; University of York Music Press, Department of Music, University of York, Heslington, York YO10 5DD. *T:* (01904) 432434, *Fax:* (01904) 432450. *E:* lizwebbmanagement@gmail.com. *W:* www.robertsaxton.net.

SAYCE, Lucy Elizabeth, (Liz), OBE 2009; Chief Executive, Disability Rights UK (formerly Royal Association for Disability and Rehabilitation, then Royal Association for Disability Rights), since 2007; *b* 12 Jan. 1954; *d* of late Dr Richard Sayce and Dr Olive Sayce; partner, Dr Rachel Perkins. *Educ:* Kent Univ. (BA English and French 1976); Bedford Coll., London Univ. (MSc Soc. Work and Soc. Policy, CQSW, 1985). Policy Dir, Mind, 1990–98; Director: Lambeth, Southwark and Lewisham Health Action Zone, 1998–2000; Policy and Communications, Disability Rights Commn, 2000–07. Harkness Fellow, Washington, 1995–96. Member: Mental Health Task Force, 1994; Disability Rights Task Force, 1997–99; Commn for Health Improvement Investigation Team, N Lakeland NHS Trust, 2000; Mental Health Media Adv. Gp, 2002–07; NICE Cttee on Confidential Inquiries, 2003–04; DWP Images of Disability Steering Gp, 2003–05; EU Steering Gp on Anti-Discrimination Campaigns, 2003–06; Healthcare Commn Expert Ref. Gp, 2005–07; Disability Cttee, Equality and Human Rights Commn, 2007–10; UK Commn for Employment and Skills, 2007–. FRSA. Trustee, Stonewall, 2005–11. *Publications:* From Psychiatric Patient to Citizen, 2000; contrib. numerous chapters; papers in disability and mental health jls, reports pubd by Mind, Research and Develt for Psychiatry. *Recreation:* walking the Thames and other waterways. *Address:* Disability Rights UK, CAN Mezzanine, 49–51 East Road, N1 6AH. *T:* (020) 7250 8178. *E:* liz.sayce@disabilityrightsuk.org.

SAYE AND SELE, 21st Baron *cr* 1447 and 1603; **Nathaniel Thomas Allen Fiennes;** DL; *b* 22 Sept. 1920; *s* of Ivo Murray Twisleton-Wykeham-Fiennes, 20th Baron Saye and Sele, OBE, MC, and Hersey Cecilia Hester, *d* of late Captain Sir Thomas Dacres Butler, KCVO; *S* father, 1968; *m* 1958, Mariette Helena, DL, *d* of Maj.-Gen. Sir Guy Salisbury-Jones, GCVO, CMG, CBE, MC; two *s* one *d* (and two *s* decd). *Educ:* Eton; New College, Oxford. Served with Rifle Brigade, 1941–49 (despatches twice). Chartered Surveyor. Partner in firm of Laws and Fiennes. Regl Dir, Lloyds Bank, 1982–90. Trustee, Ernest Cook Trust, 1960–95 (Chm. Trustees, 1965–92). DL Oxfordshire, 1979. Fellow, Winchester Coll., 1967–83. *Heir: s* Hon. Martin Guy Fiennes [*b* 27 Feb. 1961; *m* 1996, Pauline Kang Chai Lian, *o d* of Kang Tiong Lam; three *s*]. *Address:* Broughton Castle, Banbury, Oxon OX15 5EB. *T:* (01295) 262624.

SAYEED, Jonathan; Chairman, Ranelagh International Ltd, since 2005; *b* 20 March 1948; *m* 1980, Nicola Anne Parkes Power; two *s*. *Educ:* Britannia Royal Naval Coll., Dartmouth; Royal Naval Engrg Coll., Manadon. Chairman, Ranelagh Ltd, 1992–96; Trng Div., Corporate Services Group plc, 1996–97. MP (C) Bristol E, 1983–92; contested (C) same seat, 1992; MP (C) Mid Bedfordshire, 1997–2005. PPS to Paymaster General and Minister of State for NI, 1991–92; Opposition frontbench spokesman on the environment, 2001–03. Vice-Chm., 1987–91, Chm., 1991–92, Cons. Backbench Shipping and Shipbuilding Cttee; Dep. Chm., All Party Maritime Group, 1987–92; Member: Environment Select Cttee, 1987–92; Defence Select Cttee, 1988–91; Chairman's Panel, 1999–2001, 2003–05. Pres., Bristol E Cons. Assoc., 1995–. Pres., Bristol West Indian Cricket Club, 1986–. Mem., RNSA. *Recreations:* golf, yachting, riding, classical music, architecture. *Clubs:* Carlton; Royal Thames Yacht; Highgate Golf.

SAYER, John Raymond Keer, MA; Research Fellow, Department of Educational Studies, University of Oxford, since 1991; *b* 8 Aug. 1931; *s* of Arthur and Hilda Sayer; *m* 1955, Ilserose (*née* Heyd); one *s* one *d*. *Educ:* Maidstone Grammar Sch.; Brasenose Coll., Oxford (Open Scholar; MA). Taught languages, 1955–63; Dep. Head, Nailsea Sch., Somerset, 1963–67; Headmaster, Minehead Sch., Somerset, 1967–73; Principal, Banbury Sch., 1973–84; Vis. Fellow, Univ. of London Inst. of Educn, 1985–92 (Dir, Educn Management Unit, 1987–90); Dir, E. C. Tempus Projects: Developing Schs for Democracy in Europe, Oxford Univ., 1991–2000; Co-Dir, European Sch. of Educnl Mgt, 1991–96; Dir, Developing Services for Teaching in Europe, 1997–2012. Chairman: Reform of Assessment at Sixteen-Plus, 1972–75; External Relations Cttee, Headmasters' Assoc., 1974–77; Secondary Heads Association: Mem. Exec., 1978–86; Press and Publications Officer, 1978–79, 1982–84; Pres., 1979–80. Chm., Jt Council of Heads, 1981; Member: Exec., UCCA, 1975–84; Schools Panel, CBI, 1975–82; Heads Panel, TUC, 1975–80; National Adv. Council on Educn for Industry and Commerce, 1974–77; Adv. Cttee on Supply and Educn of Teachers, 1982–85. Hon. Sec., 1990–94, Vice-Chm., 1994–2000, Chm., 2000–02, GTC (England and Wales) Trust. Trustee and Mem. Exec., Education 2000, 1983–89 (Hon. Sec., 1987–89); Trustee, English Trust for European Educn, 2006–11 (Patron, 2012–). Mem. Exec., Schools Curriculum Award, 1986–91. Hon. Prof., Russian Fedn Min. of Educn (Perm State Humanitarian-Pedagogical Univ.), 1998–. *Publications:* (ed) The School as a Centre of Enquiry, 1975; (ed) Staffing our Secondary Schools, 1980; (ed) Teacher Training and Special Educational Needs, 1985; What Future for Secondary Schools?, 1985; Secondary schools for All?, 1987, 2nd edn 1994; (ed) Management and the Psychology of Schooling, 1988; Schools and External Relations, 1989; Managing Schools, 1989; Towards the General Teaching Council, 1989; The Future Governance of Education, 1993; Developing Schools for Democracy in Europe, 1995; (ed) Developing Teaching for Special Needs in Russia, 1999; (ed with K. Van der Wolf) Opening Schools to All, 1999; (ed with J. Vanderhoeven) School Choice, Equity and Social Exclusion, 2000; (ed with J. Vanderhoeven) Reflection for Action, 2000; The General Teaching Council, 2000; (ed) Opening Windows to Change, 2002; Jean Racine: life and legend, 2006; (ed with L. Erler) Schools for the Future Europe, 2012; Wolf Graf Baudissin: life and legacy, 2015. *Recreation:* postal history. *Address:* 8 Northmoor Road, Oxford OX2 6UP. *T:* (01865) 556932.

SAYER, Robert; Senior Partner, Sayer Moore & Co., since 1983; President, Law Society, 1999–2000 (Vice-President, 1995–96 and 1998–99); *b* 16 Jan. 1952; *s* of Kenneth Albert Ernest Sayer and Ellen Sayer; *m* 1997, Cathy Hunt. *Educ:* Salvatorian Coll., Harrow Weald, Middx; Swansea Univ. (BA Hons). Admitted Solicitor, 1979. Law Society: Dep. Vice Pres., 1997–98; Treas., 1997–99. Hon. Mem., Inst. of Advanced Legal Studies, 2000. *Publications:* numerous articles in legal jls. *Recreations:* sailing, walking. *Address:* (office) 190 Horn Lane, W3 6PL. *T:* (020) 8993 7571. *Club:* Naval and Military.

SAYER, Roger Martin; Organist and Director of Music, Temple Church, London, since 2013; *b* Portsmouth, 1 May 1961; *s* of Dennis and Barbara Sayer; one *s* one *d*. *Educ:* Royal Coll. of Music (Dip. RCM 1st Cl.; ARCM). FTCL; LRAM. Organist, Woodford Parish Church, 1981–89; Rochester Cathedral: Asst Organist, 1989–94; Dir of Music, 1994–2008; Organist, 2008–13. London Symphony Chorus: Accompanist, 2005–; Deputy Chorus Dir, 2012–. *Recreations:* travel, aircraft, cats, football. *Address:* 2 King's Bench Walk, 1st Floor, Temple, EC4Y 7DE. *E:* roger@templechurch.com.

SAYER, Susan Joscelyn, CBE 2013 (OBE 2000); Vice President, United Response, since 2015 (Co-founder and Chief Executive, 1972–2014); Chair, Campaign to Protect Rural England, since 2014; *b* Chichester, W Sussex, 7 Feb. 1947; *d* of Charles Edmund Johnson and Joscelyn Fay Johnson; *m* 1972, Richard John Sayer (marr. diss. 2000); two *s*. *Educ:* Hollington Park Sch.; Seaford Coll.; Reading Univ. (BSc Hons Chem. Physics 1969). Chair, ACEVO (formerly ACENVO), 1991–94; Chair, Mem. Bd, and Mem. Develt Cttee, Southern Housing Gp, 1994–99. Ambassador and Hon. Sen. Vis. Fellow, Faculty of Mgt, Cass Business Sch., City Univ., 2006–. Non-exec. Dir, Hounslow and Richmond Community Healthcare NHS Trust, 2013–. Member, Board: Council for Professions Supplementary to Medicine, 1999–2001; Nat. Care Standards Commn, 2001–04. Mem. Bd, Silver Line, 2012–. Vice Chair: Bath Univ. Students' Union, 2009–11; Seaford Coll., 2010–. Trustee: NCVO, 1996–99; Save the Children, 1998–2004; Trustee and Vice Chair, Prostate Cancer UK, 2002–12. Outstanding Achievement, Charity, Finance Charity Awards, 2003; Lifetime Achievement, Charity Times UK Charity Awards, 2004. *Publications:* Playing Safe: a parents' guide to keeping children safe, 1989. *Recreations:* family, countryside, walking, theatre, cinema. *Address:* c/o Campaign to Protect Rural England, 5–11 Lavington Street, SE1 0NZ. *T:* (020) 8788 6464, 07785 273047. *E:* susayercbe@gmail.com.

SAYERS, Michael Patrick; QC 1988; a Recorder of the Crown Court, 1986–2005; *b* 28 March 1940; *s* of Major Herbert James Michael Sayers, RA (killed on active service, 1943) and late Joan Sheilah de Courcy Holroyd (*née* Stephenson); *m* 1976, Mrs Moussie Brougham (*née* Hallstrom); one *s* one *d*, and one step *s*. *Educ:* Harrow School; Fitzwilliam College, Cambridge (Evelyn Rothschild Scholar; MA). Called to the Bar, Inner Temple, 1970, Bencher, 1994; Junior, Central Criminal Court Bar Mess, 1975–78; Supplementary Prosecuting Counsel to the Crown, Central Criminal Court, 1977–88; a Dep. Circuit Judge, 1981–82; Asst Recorder, 1982–86. Mem. Cttee, Barristers' Benevolent Assoc., 1991–2007. Vice-Pres., Harrow Assoc., 1999– (Chm., 1992–97). Hon. Sec., Anglo-Swedish Council, 2006–. *Recreations:* shooting, stalking, theatre, Sweden. *Address:* 26 King's Quay, Chelsea Harbour, SW10 0UX. *T:* (020) 7351 6003. *Clubs:* Garrick, Pratt's; Swinley Forest Golf.

SAYLE, Alexei David; actor, comedian, writer; *b* 7 Aug. 1952; *s* of Joseph Henry Sayle and Malka Sayle; *m* 1974, Linda Rawsthorn. *Educ:* Alsop GS, Liverpool; Southport Coll. of Art; Chelsea Sch. of Art (DipAD); Garnett Coll. (CertEd). Compère: Comedy Store Club, 1979–80; Comic Strip Club, 1980–81; live stand-up comedy, Soho Th., Edinburgh Fringe and nat. tour, 2013; *television series:* Young Ones, 1982–84; Alexei Sayle's Stuff (also writer), 1988–89, 1991; The Gravy Train, 1990; All New Alexei Sayle Show (also writer), 1994–95; Alexei Sayle's Merry-go-round, 1998; Arabian Nights, 2000; Alexei Sayle's Liverpool, 2008; *films include:* Gorky Park, 1983; Indiana Jones and the Last Crusade, 1989; Swing, 1998. Columnist: Independent; Daily Telegraph; formerly on Observer, Time Out, Car, Sunday Mirror. Hon. Prof., Thames Valley Univ., 1995. *Publications:* Train to Hell, 1982; Geoffrey the Tube Train and the Fat Comedian, 1987; Great Bus Journeys of the World, 1988; Barcelona Plates (short stories), 2000; The Dog Catcher (short stories), 2001; Overtaken (novel), 2003; The Weeping Women Hotel (novel), 2006; Mister Roberts (novel), 2008; Stalin Ate My Homework (memoir), 2010. *Recreation:* walking. *Address:* c/o Cassie Mayer, 5 Old Garden House, The Lanterns, Bridge Lane, SW11 3AD. *T:* (020) 7350 0880. *Club:* Chelsea Arts.

SCACCHI, Greta; actress. *Films* include: Heat and Dust, 1983; The Coca Cola Kid, 1985; Burke & Wills; Defence of the Realm, 1986; Good Morning Babylon, 1987; A Man in Love, 1988; White Mischief, 1988; Love and Fear (Les Trois Soeurs), 1990; Presumed Innocent, 1990; Fires Within, 1991; Shattered, 1991; Turtle Beach, 1992; The Player, 1992; Salt on our

Skin; The Browning Version, 1994; Jefferson in Paris, 1994; Country Life, 1994; Emma, 1996; The Serpent's Kiss; The Red Violin, 1999; Cotton Mary, 1999; Tom's Midnight Garden, 2000; Beyond the Sea, 2004; Shoot on Sight, 2007; Brideshead Revisited, 2008; The Falling, 2015; *television:* The Ebony Tower, 1984; Dr Fischer of Geneva; Waterfront (Best Actress, Penguin and Golden Logie Awards, Australia); Rasputin (Emmy for best-supporting actress), 1996; The Odyssey, 1997; Macbeth, 1997; Daniel Deronda, 2002; Miss Austen Regrets, 2008; *radio:* Life and Fate, 2011; *stage:* Cider with Rosie, Phoenix Arts, Leicester, 1982; Times Like These, Bristol Old Vic, 1985; Airbase, Oxford Playhouse, 1986; Uncle Vanya, Vaudeville, 1988; The Doll's House, Fest. of Perth, 1991; Miss Julie, 1992, Simpatico, 1996, Sydney Theatre Co.; The Guardsman, Albery, 2000; The True Life Fiction of Mata Hari Palace Theatre, Watford, 2002; Private Lives, Th. Royal, Bath, 2005; The Deep Blue Sea, Vaudeville, 2008; Bette and Joan, Arts Th., 2011; The Glass Menagerie, W Yorkshire Playhouse, 2015. *Address:* c/o Conway van Gelder Grant Ltd, 8–12 Broadwick Street, W1F 8HW.

SCADDING, Dr John William, OBE 2015; FRCP; Consultant Neurologist, National Hospital for Neurology and Neurosurgery, 1982–2008, now Honorary Consultant Emeritus (Medical Director, 1993–96); *b* 17 June 1948; *s* of late Prof. John Guyett Scadding, FRCP. *Educ:* University College London and UCH Med. Sch. (BSc 1st Cl. Hons, MB BS, MD). Jun. hosp. posts at UCH, Hammersmith, Brompton, Royal Free and National Hosps, 1972–82; Res. Fellow, UCL and Royal Free Hosp. Sch. of Medicine, 1978–80. Hon. Sen. Lectr, Inst. of Neurology, 1982–2008. Consultant Neurologist, Whittington Hosp., 1982–2003; Hon. Neurologist: St Luke's Hosp. for the Clergy, 1983–2002; Royal Soc. of Musicians, 1996–2008; Civilian Consultant Adviser, MoD, 1983–; Civilian Consultant Neurologist to RN, 1993–2003, to RAF, 1997–2003. Royal Society of Medicine: Associate Dean, 2002–06; Dean, 2006–08; Emeritus Dean, 2008–; Vice Pres., 2010–12. Chm., RSocMed Press, 2008–. Trustee: Royal Hosp. for Neurodisability, 2004–; Cure Parkinson's Trust, 2008–11 (Chm., Res. Cttee, 2009–); CORDA, 2009–14; Chm. and Trustee, Neuro-disability Res. Trust, 2012–13. Gov., Yehudi Menuhin Sch., 2011–. RSM Medal, 2013. *Publications:* research papers on mechanisms of pain in neurological disease; contribs to learned jls. *Recreations:* music (pianist), mountain walking. *Address:* National Hospital for Neurology and Neurosurgery, Queen Square, WC1N 3BG. *T:* (020) 7837 3611.

SCALES, Neil, OBE 2005; Director-General, Department of Transport and Main Roads, Australia, since 2013; *b* 24 June 1956; *s* of Gordon and Joyce Scales; *m* 1983, June Bradley; one *s* one *d*. *Educ:* Sunderland Poly. (BSc 1981; MSc 1984; DMS 1986); Open Univ. (MBA 1991). Apprentice, Sunderland Corp. Transport, 1972–76; engrg posts, Tyne & Wear PTE, 1976–86; Chief Engr, 1986–88, Dir of Engrg, 1988–90, Greater Manchester Buses; Man. Dir, Northern Counties, 1990–96; Greater Manchester PTE, 1996; consultant, private sector, 1997–99; Dir of Customer Services, 1999, CEO and Dir Gen., 1999–2012, Merseytravel; CEO, TransLink Authy, Australia, 2012–13. Hon. Fellow, Liverpool John Moores Univ., 2011. *Recreations:* Sunderland FC, tutoring with Open University. *Clubs:* Reform; Brisbane.

SCALES, Prunella, (Prunella Margaret Rumney West), CBE 1992; actress; *d* of John Richardson Illingworth and Catherine Scales; *m* 1963, Timothy Lancaster West, *qv*; two *s*. *Educ:* Moira House, Eastbourne; Old Vic Theatre School, London; Herbert Berghof Studio, New York (with Uta Hagen). Repertory in Huddersfield, Salisbury, Oxford, Bristol Old Vic, etc; seasons at Stratford-on-Avon and Chichester Festival Theatre; plays on London stage include: The Promise, 1967; Hay Fever, 1968; It's a Two-Foot-Six-Inches-Above-The-Ground-World, 1970; The Wolf, 1975; Breezeblock Park, 1978; Make and Break, 1980; An Evening with Queen Victoria, 1980; The Merchant of Venice, 1981; Quartermaine's Terms, 1981; Big in Brazil, 1984; When We Are Married, 1986; Single Spies (double bill), 1988; The School for Scandal, 1990; Long Day's Journey into Night, 1991; Mother Tongue, 1992; The Birthday Party, 1999; A Day in the Death of Joe Egg, 2001; A Woman of No Importance, 2003; Carrie's War, 2009; regional theatre: Happy Days, Leeds, 1993; The Matchmaker, Chichester, 1993; Staying On, nat. tour, 1997; The Cherry Orchard, Oxford Playhouse, 2000; Gertrude's Secret, Apollo Th. and nat. tour, 2006–08; *films include:* Howard's End, 1992; Second Best, 1993; Wolf, 1994; An Awfully Big Adventure, 1994; An Ideal Husband, 1999; Ghost of Greville Lodge, 2001; *television:* Fawlty Towers (series), 1975, 1978; Grand Duo, The Merry Wives of Windsor, 1982; Mapp and Lucia (series), 1985–86; Absurd Person Singular, 1985; The Index Has Gone Fishing, What the Butler Saw, 1987; After Henry (series), 1988, 1990; The Rector's Wife, Fair Game, 1994; Dalziel & Pascoe, 1996; Signs and Wonders, Lord of Misrule, Breaking the Code, 1997; Midsomer Murders, 2001; Looking for Victoria, 2003; Casualty, 2004; Where the Heart Is, 2005; Great Canal Journeys, 2014–15; frequent broadcasts, readings, poetry recitals and fringe productions. Has directed plays at Bristol Old Vic, Arts Theatre, Cambridge, Billingham Forum, Almost Free Theatre, London, Nottingham Playhouse, Palace Theatre, Watford, W Yorks Playhouse, Leeds, Nat. Theatre of WA, Perth, and taught at several drama schools. Pres., CPRE, 1997–2002. Hon DLitt: Bradford, 1995; East Anglia, 1996. *Publications:* (with Timothy West) So You Want to be an Actor?, 2005. *Recreation:* gardening. *Address:* c/o Conway van Gelder Grant Ltd, 3rd Floor, 8–12 Broadwick Street, W1F 8HW.

See also S. A. J. West.

SCALES, Sheila Lesley, (Mrs Roger Harris); Director, Early Years, Extended Schools and Special Educational Needs Group (formerly Sure Start Extended Schools and Childcare Group), Department for Children, Schools and Families (formerly Department for Education and Skills), 2006–09; *b* Leeds, 22 Aug. 1949; *d* of Lesley and Hilda Scales; *m* 1973, Dr Roger Harris; three *s* one *d*. *Educ:* New Hall, Cambridge (BA 1970). Joined DES, 1970; Private Sec. to Perm. Under-Sec. of State, DES, 1973–75; Develt Planner, Kiribati, 1977–79; various posts, DES, then DfE, later DfEE, 1979–97; Asst Chief Exec., Surrey CC, 1997–98; Dep. Dir, Standards and Effectiveness Unit, DfEE, then DfES, 1998–2001; on secondment to Ofsted, 2001–02; Dep. Dir, Improving Behaviour and Attendance, 2002–04, Dir, Local Transformation Gp, 2004–06, DfES. Gov., City Acad., Hackney, 2008–; Advr, East End CAB, 2010–. *T:* 07850 169467.

SCALIA, Antonin Gregory; Associate Justice, United States Supreme Court, since 1986; *b* 11 March 1936; *s* of S. Eugene Scalia and Catherine Louise (*née* Panaro); *m* 1960, Maureen McCarthy; five *s* four *d*. *Educ:* Georgetown Univ. (AB 1957); Fribourg Univ., Switzerland; Harvard (LLB 1960; Sheldon Fellow, 1960–61). Admitted to Ohio Bar, 1962, to Virginia Bar, 1970. Associate, Jones, Day, Cockley & Reavis, Cleveland, 1961–67; Associate Prof., 1967–70, Prof., 1970–74, Univ. of Virginia Law Sch.; Gen. Counsel, Office of Telecommunications, Exec. Office of Pres., 1971–72; Chm., Admin. Conf. US, Washington, 1972–74; Asst Attorney Gen., US Office of Legal Counsel, Justice Dept, 1974–77; Prof., Law Sch., Chicago Univ., 1977–82; Judge, US Court Appeals (DC Circuit), 1982–86. American Bar Association: Mem. Council, 1974–77, Chm., 1981–82, Section Admin. Law; Chm., Conf. Section, 1982–83. Jt Editor, Regulation Magazine, 1979–82. *Publications:* (jtly) A Matter of Interpretation: Federal Courts and the law, 1997; (with Bryan A. Garner) Making Your Case: the art of persuading judges, 2008. *Address:* US Supreme Court, 1 First Street NE, Washington, DC 20543–0001, USA.

SCALLY, Dr Gabriel John, FFPH; Director, WHO Collaborating Centre for Healthy Urban Environments, University of the West of England, 2012–14; *b* 24 Sept. 1954; *s* of Bernard Gabriel Scally and Maureen Scally (*née* Hopkins); *m* 1990, Rona Margaret Campbell; two *d*. *Educ:* St Mary's Grammar Sch., Belfast; Queen's Univ., Belfast (MB, BCh, BAO 1978); London Sch. of Hygiene and Tropical Medicine, Univ. of London (MSc 1982). MFPHM 1984, FFPH (FFPHM 1991); MFPHMI 1992; MRCGP 1993; FRCP 2004. Trainee in Gen. Practice, 1980–81; Sen. Tutor, Dept of Community Medicine, QUB, 1984–86; Consultant in Public Health Medicine, 1986–88, Chief Admin. MO and Dir of Public Health, 1989–93, Eastern Health and Social Services Bd, Belfast; Regional Director of Public Health: SE Thames RHA, 1993–94; South and West RHA, 1994–96; SW Region, DoH, 1996–2012. Member: NI Bd for Nursing, Health Visiting and Midwifery, 1988–93; Council, BMA, 1985–86, 1988–89 (Chm., Jun. Mems Forum, 1988–89); GMC, 1989–99. Hon. DSc UWE, 2012. *Publications:* papers on med. res. and health policy in med. jls. *Recreations:* sailing, traditional and contemporary Irish music, London Irish RFC. *Address:* 11 Dowry Square, Bristol BS8 4SH. *T:* (0117) 926 8510.

SCAMPION, John, CBE 2001; DL; Chairman, Determinations Panel, Pensions Regulator, 2005–13; *b* 22 Aug. 1941; *s* of John William and Rosa Mary Scampion; *m* 1995, Jennifer Mary Reeves; two *s*, and two step *d*. *Educ:* Queen Elizabeth's Grammar Sch., Alford, Lincs; Downing Coll., Cambridge (MA). Admitted solicitor, 1966; Town Clerk and Chief Exec., Solihull MBC, 1977–95; Social Fund Comr for GB and NI, 1995–2000; Comr for Immigration Services, 2000–05; Chm., Immigration Adv. Service, 2007–11. Tribunal Judge (formerly Mem.), Criminal Injuries Compensation Tribunal (formerly Appeals Panel), 1997–2012; Mem., Healthcare Commn (formerly Commn for Health Audit and Improvement), 2003–09. Vice Chm., Stratford-upon-Avon Soc., 2013–. Trustee, Arts in Minds Foundn, Worcester, 2015. FRSocMed 2008. DL W Midlands, 1992. *Recreations:* theatre-going, directing plays - occasionally, watching football, reading, hill walking, music listening. *Address:* 1 Olivers Lock, Stratford-upon-Avon, Warwicks CV37 6PS.

SCANLAN, Dorothy, (Mrs Charles Denis Scanlan); *see* Quick, Dorothy.

SCANLAN, Prof. John Oliver, (Sean), PhD, DSc; FIEEE, FIET, FIMA, FIEI; Professor of Electronic Engineering, University College Dublin, 1973–2002, now Emeritus; President, Royal Irish Academy, 1993–96; *b* 20 Sept. 1937; *s* of John and Hannah Scanlan; *m* 1961, Ann Weadock. *Educ:* University Coll. Dublin (BE, ME); Leeds Univ. (PhD); NUI (DSc). FIMA 1971; FIET (FIEE 1972); FIEEE 1976; FIEI 1980. Lectr, 1963–68, Prof. of Electronic Engrg, 1968–73, Univ. of Leeds. Dir, Telecom Eireann, 1984–97. MRIA 1977 (Sec., 1981–89). Editor, Internat. Jl of Circuit Theory and Applications, 1973–2005. *Publications:* Analysis and Synthesis of Tunnel Diode Circuits, 1966; Circuit Theory, vol. I, 1970, (with R. Levy) vol. II, 1973; numerous contribs to learned jls. *Recreations:* golf, music. *Address:* School of Electrical, Electronic and Communications Engineering, University College Dublin, Belfield, Dublin 4, Ireland.

SCANLAN, Michael; Consultant, Russells Gibson McCaffrey (formerly Russells), Solicitors, Glasgow, 2011–13 (Senior Partner, 1982–2011); *b* 6 June 1946; *s* of William Scanlan and Agnes (Nancy) Scanlan; *m* 1971, Margaret Denvir (OBE 2006); one *s*. *Educ:* St Aloysius Coll., Glasgow; Glasgow Univ. Apprentice, T. F. Russell & Co., 1965–71; admitted solicitor, 1971; Asst, 1971–73, Partner, 1973–82, T. F. Russell & Co., subseq. Russells. Lectr in Evidence and Procedure, Strathclyde Univ., 1979–85. Ext. Examr in Evidence and Procedure, Glasgow Univ., 1982–85. Temp. Sheriff, 1986–96. Pres., Law Soc. of Scotland, 1999–2000 (Vice-Pres., 1998–99). Member: Judicial Appts Bd for Scotland, 2002–08; Scottish Cttee, Administrative Justice and Tribunals Council, 2009–13. *Recreations:* golf, reading, music. *Address:* 43a Watermill Avenue, Lenzie, Glasgow G66 5EL.

SCANLAN, Sean; *see* Scanlan, J. O.

SCANLON, Mary Elizabeth; Member (C) Highlands and Islands, Scottish Parliament, 1999–2006 and since 2007; *b* 25 May 1947; *d* of John Charles Campbell and Anne Campbell (*née* O'Donnell); *m* 1970, James Scanlon; one *s* one *d*. *Educ:* Univ. of Dundee (MA Econ/Pol 1982). Civil Service Administrator; Lecturer: Dundee Inst. of Technology, 1982–85; Perth Coll., 1985–88; Lectr in Econs, Dundee Coll. of Technology, 1988–94; Lectr in Econs and Business Studies, Inverness Coll., 1994–99. Contested (C) Moray, Scottish Parlt, April 2006. *Recreations:* hill walking, swimming, gardening. *Address:* 5 Broughton Place, Edinburgh EH1 3RL; (constituency office) 14A Ardross Street, Inverness IV3 5NS.

SCARBOROUGH, Vernon Marcus; HM Diplomatic Service, retired; Deputy High Commissioner, Tarawa, Republic of Kiribati, 2000–04; *b* 11 Feb. 1940; *s* of George Arthur Scarborough and Sarah Florence Scarborough (*née* Patey); *m* 1966, Jennifer Bernadette Keane; three *d*. *Educ:* Brockley County Grammar Sch.; Westminster Coll. Passport Office, FO, 1958–61, CRO 1961; served Dacca, Karachi, Brussels (Vice Consul, 1969–71), Bathurst, later Banjul, FCO, Muscat, Lagos and El Salvador; Kuala Lumpur, 1983–86 (First Sec., 1983); FCO, 1986; Chargé d'Affaires, San Salvador, 1987–90; Dep. Consul Gen. and Trade Comr, Auckland, 1990–94; Dep. High Comr, Suva, Tuvalu, Nauru and Ambassador to Palau, Federated States of Micronesia and Marshall Is, 1995–2000. Mem. Council, Pacific Is Soc. of UK, 2004–. *Recreations:* photography, antiques, grandchildren. *Address:* Broadoaks, 29 Erica Way, Copthorne, W Sussex RH10 3XG. *Clubs:* Fiji, Defence, Returned Servicemen's and Ex-Servicemen's Association (Suva).

SCARBROUGH, 13th Earl of, *cr* 1690; **Richard Osbert Lumley;** DL; Viscount Lumley (Ire.), 1628; Baron Lumley, 1681; Viscount Lumley, 1690; *b* 18 May 1973; *s* of 12th Earl of Scarbrough, and of Lady Elizabeth Ramsay, LVO, *d* of 16th Earl of Dalhousie, KT, GCVO, GBE, MC; S father, 2004; *m* 2007, Mrs Henrietta Elfrida Helen Scherman (*née* Boyson). DL S Yorks, 2011. *Heir:* *b* Hon. Thomas Henry Lumley, *b* 6 Feb. 1980.

SCARD, Dennis Leslie; General Secretary, Musicians' Union, 1990–2000; *b* 8 May 1943; *s* of late Charles Leslie Scard and Doris Annie (*née* Farmer); *m* 1st (marr. diss.); two *s*; 2nd, 1993, Linda Perry. *Educ:* Lascelles Co. Secondary Sch.; Trinity Coll. of Music, London (Hon. Fellow, 1997). Professional horn player, 1962–85, performed with leading symphony and chamber orchestras. Part-time instrumental teacher, London Borough of Hillingdon, 1974–85. Musicians' Union: Chm., Central London Br., 1972–85; Mem., Exec. Cttee, 1979–85; full-time Official, Birmingham, 1985–90. Mem., TUC Gen. Council, 1990–2001. Bd Mem., 2002–, Dep. Chm., 2003–06, Chm., 2007–11, Shoreham Port Authy. Worker Rep., BIS (formerly DTI, then BERR) Central Arbitration Cttee, 2002–14; Lay Mem., Employment Tribunal Service, 2005–13. Mem. Bd, Trinity Coll. of Music, 1998–2006. Trustee, Performances (Birmingham) Ltd (Symphony Hall and Town Hall Birmingham), 1996–. Chair, Henry Wood Accommodation Trust (formerly Music Students Hostel Trust), 2003–. *Recreations:* music, walking, theatre, lawn bowls. *Address:* 6 Cranborne Avenue, Meads, Eastbourne BN20 7TS. *T:* (01323) 648364.

SCARDINO, Dame Marjorie (Morris), DBE 2002; DJur; Chief Executive, Pearson plc, 1997–2012; *b* 25 Jan. 1947; *d* of Robert Weldon and Beth Morris (*née* Lamb); adopted dual American-British nationality, 2002; *m* 1974, Albert James Scardino; two *s* one *d*. *Educ:* Baylor Univ. (BA); Univ. of San Francisco (DJur). Partner, Brannen Wessels & Searcy, 1976–85; Pres., Economist Newspaper Gp Inc., 1985–93; Chief Exec., Economist Gp, 1993–97. Non-executive Director: Nokia, 2001–13 (Vice Chm., 2007–13); Twitter, 2013–. Trustee: Carter Center, 2003–; MacArthur Foundn, 2005– (Chm., 2012–); Oxfam, 2010–. Fellow, Amer. Acad. of Arts and Scis, 2010.

SCARFE, Gerald Anthony, CBE 2008; RDI 1989; artist; *b* 1 June 1936; *m* Jane Asher, *qv*; two *s* one *d*. *Educ:* scattered (due to chronic asthma as a child). Punch, 1960; Private Eye, 1961; Daily Mail, 1966; Sunday Times, 1967–; cover artist to illustrator, Time Magazine, 1967; animation and film directing for BBC, 1969–; artist, New Yorker, 1993–. Has taken part in exhibitions: Grosvenor Gall., 1969 and 1970; Pavilion d'Humour, Montreal, 1967 and 1971; Expo '70, Osaka, 1970; six sculptures of British Character, Millennium Dome, 2000.

One-man exhibitions of sculptures and lithographs: Waddell Gall., New York, 1968 and 1970; Grosvenor Gall., 1969; Vincent Price Gall., Chicago, 1969; National Portrait Gall., 1971; retrospective exhibn, Royal Festival Hall, 1983; drawings: Langton Gall., 1986; Chris Beetles Gall., 1989; Gerald Scarfe Meets Walt Disney, MOMI, 1997; Gerald Scarfe, The Art of Hercules, Z Gall., NY, 1997; Nat. Portrait Gall., 1998, 2003; Cleveland Gall., 1998; Millennium Galls, Sheffield, 2005; Fine Arts Soc., London, 2005; Portcullis House, Westminster, 2008–09; Halle, 2009; Hanover, 2010; Cesky Krumlov, Czech Republic, 2012; Prague, 2013; Milk Snatcher, Bowes Mus., Co. Durham, 2015; perm. display, Scarfes Bar, Rosewood, London, 2014–. Animated film for BBC, Long Drawn Out Trip, 1973 (prizewinner, Zagreb); title sequence of TV series: Yes Minister, 1980; Yes Prime Minister, 1986; New Yes Prime Minister, 2013; Dir, Scarfe by Scarfe, BBC (BAFTA Award, 1987); Designer and Dir, animated sequences in film, The Wall, 1982; designer: Who's A Lucky Boy?, Royal Exchange, Manchester, 1984; Orpheus in the Underworld, ENO, 1985; Born Again, Chichester, 1990; The Magic Flute, Los Angeles, 1993, Houston, Texas, 1997, Seattle, 1999, San Francisco, 2007, Los Angeles, 2009; An Absolute Turkey, Globe, 1994 (Olivier Award for best costumes); Mind Millie For Me, Haymarket, 1996; Fantastic Mr Fox, Los Angeles Opera, 1998; The Nutcracker, English Nat. Ballet, 2002; production designer, Hercules (Walt Disney film), 1995–97; costume designer, Peter and the Wolf, Holiday on Ice and world tour, 2000; animation sequence, Miss Saigon, UK and internat. tour, 2004; animation, The Wall by Roger Waters, internat. tour, 2011. Hon. DLitt Kent, 2003; Hon. DArts Liverpool, 2005; Hon. LLD Dundee, 2007. *Publications:* Gerald Scarfe's People, 1966; Indecent Exposure (ltd edn), 1973; Expletive Deleted: the life and times of Richard Nixon (ltd edn), 1974; Gerald Scarfe, 1982; Father Kissmass and Mother Claws, 1985; Scarfe by Scarfe (autobiog.), 1986 (televised, 1987); Scarfe's Seven Deadly Sins, 1988; Scarfe's Line of Attack, 1988; Scarfeland: a lost world of fabulous beasts and monsters, 1989; Scarfe on Stage, 1992; Scarfeface, 1993; Hades: the truth at last, 1997; Heroes and Villains, 2003; Gerald Scarfe: drawing blood - 40 years of Scarfe uncensored, 2005; Monsters: how George Bush saved the world and other tall stories, 2008; The Making of Pink Floyd The Wall, 2011. *Recreations:* drawing, painting and sculpting. *Address:* c/o 24 Cale Street, SW3 3QU.

SCARFE, Jane; *see* Asher, J.

SCARGILL, Arthur; General Secretary, Socialist Labour Party; Honorary President, National Union of Mineworkers, since 2002 (General Secretary, 1992; President, 1981–2002); *b* 11 Jan. 1938; *oc* of Harold and Alice Scargill; *m* 1961, Anne, *d* of Elliott Harper; one *d*. *Educ:* Worsbrough Dale School; White Cross Secondary School; Leeds Univ. Miner, Woolley Colliery, 1953; Mem., NUM branch cttee, 1960; Woolley branch deleg. to Yorks NUM Council, 1964; Mem., Nat. Exec., 1972, Pres., 1973, Yorks NUM. Mem., TUC Gen. Council, 1986–88. Member: Young Communists' League, 1955–62; Co-op Party, 1963; Labour Party, 1966–95; Socialist Labour Party, 1996; CND. Contested (Socialist Lab): Newport East, 1997; Hartlepool, 2001; London, Eur. Parlt, 2009. *Address:* c/o Socialist Labour Party, 9 Victoria Road, Barnsley, S Yorks S70 2BB.

SCARLETT, family name of **Baron Abinger**.

SCARLETT, Sir John (McLeod), KCMG 2007 (CMG 2001); OBE 1987; Senior Adviser, Morgan Stanley, since 2010; Chairman, Strategy Advisory Council, Statoil ASA, since 2012; Chairman, Bletchley Park Trust, since 2012; Chief, Secret Intelligence Service, 2004–09; *b* 18 Aug. 1948; *s* of late Dr James Henri Stuart Scarlett and Clara Dunlop Scarlett; *m* 1970, Gwenda Mary Rachel Stilliard; one *s* three *d* (and one *s* decd). *Educ:* Epsom Coll.; Magdalen Coll., Oxford (MA). Secret Intelligence Service, 1971–2001: Nairobi, 1973–74; lang. student, 1974–75; Second, later First, Sec., Moscow, 1976–77; First Secretary: London, 1977–84; Paris, 1984–88; London, 1988–91; Counsellor: Moscow, 1991–94; London, 1994–2001 (Dir of Security and Public Affairs, 1999–2001); Chm., Jt Intelligence Cttee, and Intelligence Co-ordinator, then Head of Intelligence and Security Secretariat, Cabinet Office, 2001–04. Advr, Swiss Re Zurich, 2010–; Dir, Times Newspaper Hldgs, 2010–. Sen. Associate Fellow, RUSI, 2010–. Trustee: Imperial War Mus., 2010–; Friends of the French Inst., UK, 2012–. Officier, Légion d'Honneur (France), 2011. *Recreations:* family, history. *Club:* Oxford and Cambridge.

SCARLETT, Liam; Artist in Residence, Royal Ballet, since 2012; *b* Ipswich, 8 April 1986; *s* of Laurence Stephen and Deborah Frances Scarlett. *Educ:* Royal Ballet Sch. Artist, 2005–07, First Artist, 2007–12, Royal Ballet; has worked with NYC Ballet, San Francisco Ballet, American Ballet Th., Miami City Ballet, K-Ballet, Ballet Boyz, English Nat. Ballet. *Recreations:* theatre, ballet, cinema, art, poetry, family, cooking, reading. *Address:* Royal Ballet, Royal Opera House, Covent Garden, WC2E 9DD. *T:* (020) 7212 9685. *E:* liam.scarlett@roh.org.uk.

SCARONI, Paolo, Cavaliere del Lavoro, 2004; Chief Executive, Eni, 2005–14; Deputy Chairman, Rothschild Group, since 2014; *b* 28 Nov. 1946; *s* of Bruno and Clementina Boniver Scaroni; *m* 1974, Francesca (*née* Zanconato); two *s* one *d*. *Educ:* Luigi Bocconi Commercial Univ., Milan (Dr Econs 1969); Columbia Univ., NY (MBA). Chevron, 1968–71; Associate, McKinsey & Co., 1972–73; Saint-Gobain, 1973–85: Financial Dir, Italy, 1973–78; General Delegate: Venezuela, Colombia, Ecuador, and Peru, 1978–81; Italy, 1981–84; Pres., Flat Glass Div. (world-wide), France, 1984–85; Exec. Vice-Pres., Techint, Italy, 1985–96; Pilkington plc: Pres., Automotive Products Worldwide, 1996–98; Gp Chief Exec., 1997–2002; Dep. Chm., 2002; Chief Exec., Enel SpA, 2002–05. Non-executive Director: Burmah Castrol plc, 1998–2000; BAE SYSTEMS, 2000–04; Alliance UniChem, 2003–06 (Chm., 2005–06); London Stock Exchange Gp, 2007–14 (Dep. Chm., 2010–14); Generali, 2007–; Mem., Supervisory Bd, ABN AMRO Bank NV, 2003. Mem., Bd of Overseers, Columbia Business Sch., 1996–. Commandeur, Légion d'Honneur (France), 2013 (Officier, 2007). *Publications:* (jtly) Professione Manager, 1985. *Recreations:* reading, ski-ing, golf. *Address:* Rothschild Group, New Court, St Swithin's Lane, EC4N 8AL. *Club:* Royal Automobile.

SCARRATT, Richard John; His Honour Judge Scarratt; a Circuit Judge, since 2009; a Deputy High Court Judge, since 2014; Designated Family Judge for Kent, since 2014; *b* Leicester, 21 Aug. 1955; *s* of late Richard Geoffrey Lawrence Scarratt and June Scarratt (*née* Beck); *m* 1989, Sarah Jane May; three *s*. *Educ:* Ryde Sch., IoW; Birmingham Univ. (LLB Hons 1978); Inns of Court Sch. of Law. Called to the Bar, Lincoln's Inn, 1979; Dep. Dist Judge, Principal Registry of Family Div., 2003–09; Recorder, Western Circuit, 2005–09. *Recreations:* family, sailing, ski-ing, gardening, music, keeping busy. *Address:* The Law Courts, Chaucer Road, Canterbury, Kent CT1 1ZA. *T:* (01227) 819283, *Fax:* (01227) 819283. *E:* HHJudge.scarratt@judiciary.gsi.gov.uk. *Clubs:* Hurlingham; Rock Sailing (Cornwall).

SCARSDALE, 4th Viscount *cr* 1911; **Peter Ghislain Nathaniel Curzon;** Bt (Scot.) 1636, (Eng.) 1641; Baron Scarsdale 1761; *b* 6 March 1949; *s* of 3rd Viscount Scarsdale and his 1st wife, Solange Yvonne Palmyre Ghislaine Curzon (*née* Hanse); *S* father, 2000; *m* 1st, 1983, Mrs Karen Osborne (marr. diss. 1996); one *d*; 2nd, 1996, Michelle Reynolds. *Educ:* Ampleforth. *Heir:* *b* Hon. David James Nathaniel Curzon [*b* 3 Feb. 1958; *m* 1981, Ruth Linton (*d* 2010); one *s* one *d*].

SCHAFF, Alistair Graham; QC 1999; *b* 25 Sept. 1959; *s* of John Schaff and Barbara Schaff (*née* Williams); *m* 1991, (Marie) Leona Burley; one *s* one *d*. *Educ:* Bishop's Stortford Coll.; Magdalene Coll., Cambridge (MA 1st Cl. Jt Hons History and Law). Called to the Bar, Inner Temple, 1983; in practice at the Bar, 1983–. *Recreations:* family life, foreign travel, history, spectator sport. *Address:* 7 King's Bench Walk, Temple, EC4Y 7DS. *T:* (020) 7583 0404.

SCHALLER, George Beals; Senior Conservationist, Wildlife Conservation Society, New York, since 2008; Vice President, Panthera, New York, since 2008; *b* 26 May 1933; *m* 1957, Kay Morgan; two *s*. *Educ:* Univ. of Alaska (BA, BS 1955); Univ. of Wisconsin (PhD 1962). Fellow, Center for Advanced Study in the Behavioral Sciences, Stanford Univ., 1962–63; Res. Associate, Johns Hopkins Univ., 1963–66; Wildlife Conservation (formerly NY Zoological) Society, 1966–: Dir of Internat. Progs, 1972–88; Dir for Sci., 1988–2001; Vice Pres., 2001–08. *Publications:* The Mountain Gorilla, 1963; The Year of the Gorilla, 1964; The Deer and the Tiger, 1967; The Serengeti Lion, 1972; Serengeti: a kingdom of predators, 1972; Golden Shadows, Flying Hooves, 1973; Mountain Monarchs: wild sheep and goats of the Himalaya, 1977; Stones of Silence, 1980; (with Chinese co-authors) The Giant Pandas of Wolong, 1985; The Last Panda, 1993; Tibet's Hidden Wilderness, 1997; Wildlife of the Tibetan Steppe, 1998; (ed jtly) Antelopes, Deer and Relatives, 2000; A Naturalist and other Beasts, 2007; Tibet Wild, 2012. *Recreations:* watching wildlife, photography. *Address:* Wildlife Conservation Society, 2300 Southern Boulevard, Bronx, NY 10460, USA; Panthera, 8 West 40th Street, 18th Floor, New York, NY 10018, USA.

SCHALLY, Dr Andrew Victor; Distinguished Medical Research Scientist, Veterans Affairs Department, and Chief of Endocrine, Polypeptide and Cancer Institute, Veterans Affairs Medical Center, Miami, since 2006; Professor, University of Miami, Miller School of Medicine, since 2006; *b* Wilno, Poland, 30 Nov. 1926; US Citizen (formerly Canadian Citizen); *s* of Casimir and Maria Schally; *m* 1st, 1956, Margaret White (marr. diss.); one *s* one *d*; 2nd, 1976, Ana Maria Comaru (*d* 2004); 3rd, 2011, Maria Rasmussen. *Educ:* Bridge of Allan, Scotland (Higher Learning Cert.); London (studied chemistry); McGill Univ., Montreal, Canada (BSc Biochem., 1955; PhD Biochem., 1957). Res. Assistant: Dept of Biochem., Nat. Inst. for Med. Res., MRC, Mill Hill, 1949–52; Endocrine Unit, Allan Meml Inst. for Psych., McGill Univ., Montreal, 1952–57; Baylor University Coll. of Medicine, Texas Med. Center: Res. Associate, Dept of Physiol., 1957–60; Asst Prof. of Physiol., Dept of Physiol., and Asst Prof. of Biochem., Dept of Biochem., 1960–62; Chief, Endocrine, Polypeptide and Cancer Inst., Veterans Admin Hosp., then Veterans Affairs Med. Center, New Orleans, 1962–2006, Sen. Med. Investigator, 1973–99; Tulane University School of Medicine, New Orleans: Associate Prof., 1962–67; Prof. of Medicine, 1967–2006; Head, Section of Experimental Medicine, 1978–2006. Member: Endocrine Soc., USA; AAAS; Soc. of Biol Chemists; Amer. Physiol Soc.; Soc. for Experimental Biol. and Med.; Amer. Assoc. for Cancer Res.; Amer. Soc. for Reproductive Medicine; Internat. Brain Res. Org.; Nat. Acad. of Medicine, Mexico; Nat. Acad. of Medicine, Brazil; Nat. Acad. of Medicine, Venezuela; Nat. Acad. of Scis (US); Hungarian Acad. of Scis; Acad. of Scis, Russia, 1991; Acad. of Medicine, Poland, 1995; Royal Acad. of Medicine, Spain, 2004. Hon. Member: Chilean Endocrine Soc.; Mexican Soc. of Nutrition and Endocrinol.; Acad. of Med. Sciences of Cataluna and Baleares; Endocrine Soc. of Madrid; Polish Soc. of Internal Med.; Endocrine Soc. of Ecuador; Endocrine Soc. of Peru. Member, Editorial Board: Life Sciences, 1980–; Peptides, 1980–; The Prostate, 1985–. Dr *hc* State Univ. of Rio de Janeiro, 1977; Rosario, Argentina, 1979; Univ. Peruana Cayetano Heredia, Lima, 1979; Univ. Nat. de San Marcos, Lima, 1979; MD *hc*: Tulane, 1978; Cadiz, 1979; Univ. Villareal-Lima, 1979; Copernicus Med. Acad., Cracow, 1979; Chile, 1979; Buenos Aires, 1980; Salamanca, 1981; Complutense Univ., Madrid, 1984; Pécs Univ., 1986; Autónoma, Madrid, 1994; Alcalá, Madrid, 1996; Malaga, 2002; Milan, 2005; Hon. DSc McGill, 1979; Hon. Dr Université René Descartes, Paris, 1987; Hon. Dr rer. nat. Regensburg Univ., 1992; Hon. Dr Nat. Sci. Salzburg, 1997; Hon. Dr: Federal Univ. Porto Alegre, Brazil, 1998; Univ. Nacional Autónoma de México, 2001; Rio de Janeiro, 2003; Athens, 2003; Szeged, 2012; Debrecen, 2012. Nobel Prize in Physiology or Medicine, 1977. Veterans Administration: William S. Middleton Award, 1970; Exceptional Service Award and Medal, 1978. Van Meter Prize, Amer. Thyroid Assoc., 1969; Ayerst-Squibb Award, US Endocrine Soc., 1970; Charles Mickle Award, Faculty of Med., Univ. of Toronto, 1974; Gairdner Foundn Internat. Award, Toronto, 1974; Edward T. Tyler Award, 1975; Borden Award, Assoc. of Amer. Med. Colls, 1975; Albert Lasker Basic Med. Res. Award, 1975; Spanish Pharmaceutical Soc., 1977; Laude Award, 1978; Heath Meml Award from M. D. Anderson Tumour Inst., 1989. Chevalier, Légion d'Honneur (France), 2004. *Publications:* (compiled and ed with William Locke) The Hypothalamus and Pituitary in Health and Disease, 1972; over 2400 other pubns (papers, revs, books, abstracts). *Address:* Research Service (151), Veterans Administration Medical Center, 1201 NW 16th Street, Miami, FL 33125, USA. *T:* (305) 5753477.

SCHAMA, Prof. Simon Michael, CBE 2001; University Professor, Department of History, Columbia University, since 1997; writer, New Yorker (art critic, 1995–98); *b* 13 Feb. 1945; *s* of Arthur Osias Schama and Gertrude Steinberg Schama; *m* 1983, Virginia Papaioannou; one *s* one *d*. *Educ:* Christ's Coll., Cambridge (BA 1966; MA 1969; Hon. Fellow, 1995). Fellow and Dir of Studies in History, Christ's Coll., Cambridge, 1966–76; Fellow and Tutor in Modern History, Brasenose Coll., Oxford, 1976–80; Mellon Prof. of History, 1980–90, and Kenan Prof., 1990–93, Harvard Univ.; Old Dominion Foundation Prof. in the Humanities, Columbia Univ., 1993–96. Writer and presenter: A History of Britain, BBC TV Series, 2000, 2001, 2002; Simon Schama's Power of Art, BBC2, 2006; The American Future: A History, 2008; Simon Schama's John Donne, BBC2, 2009; Simon Schama on Obama's America, BBC2, 2010; Simon Schama's Shakespeare, BBC2, 2012; The Story of the Jews, BBC2, 2013; Schama on Rembrandt, BBC2, 2014; The Face of Britain, 2015. Corresp. FBA 2015. *Publications:* Patriots and Liberators: revolution in the Netherlands 1780–1813, 1978; Two Rothschilds and the Land of Israel, 1979; The Embarrassment of Riches: an interpretation of Dutch culture in the Golden Age, 1987; Citizens: a chronicle of the French Revolution, 1989; Dead Certainties (Unwarranted Speculations), 1991; Landscape and Memory, 1995; Rembrandt's Eyes, 1999; A History of Britain, vol. 1, 3000 BC–AD 1603, 2000, vol. 2, The British Wars 1603–1776, 2001, vol. 3, The Fate of Empire 1776–2000, 2002; Hang-Ups: essays on painting (mostly), 2004; Rough Crossings, 2005; Power of Art, 2006; The American Future: a history, 2008; Scribble, Scribble, Scribble: writings on ice cream, Obama, Churchill and my mother, 2010; The Story of the Jews: finding the words (1000 BCE–1492 CE), 2013; The Face of Britain: the nation through its portraits, 2015. *Recreations:* Bordeaux wine, gardening, Brazilian music. *Address:* Department of History, Fayerweather Hall, Columbia University, New York, NY 10027, USA. *T:* (212) 8544593. *Club:* Century (New York).

SCHAPIRA, Prof. Anthony Henry Vernon, MD; DSc; FRCP, FMedSci; Chairman and Professor of Neurology, University Department of Clinical Neurosciences, Institute of Neurology, University College London, and Professor of Neurology, National Hospital for Neurology and Neurosurgery, Queen Square, and Royal Free Hospital, London, since 1990; Vice-Dean, University College London Medical School and Director of Royal Free Campus, since 2009; *b* 3 Sept. 1954; *s* of Markus and Constance Schapira; *m* 2003, Laura Jean Johnson; one *d*. *Educ:* Bradford Grammar Sch.; Westminster Med. Sch., London Univ. (BSc Hons, AKC; MB BS, MD, DSc). MRCP, FRCP 1992; FMedSci 1999. House Physician to Chief Physician to the Queen, 1979; med. trng, Hammersmith and Whittington Hosps, Nat. Hosp. for Neurology and Neurosurgery and St Thomas' Hosp., 1980–84; trng in neurology, Royal Free Hosp. and Nat. Hosp. for Neurology and Neurosurgery, 1983–88; Wellcome Res. Fellow, 1985–87; Sen. Lectr and Consultant in Neurology, Royal Free Hosp. and UC Med. Sch., and Inst. of Neurology, London, 1988–90; Consultant Neurologist, Royal Free Hosp. and Nat. Hosp. for Neurology and Neurosurgery, 1988–. Sen. Investigator, NIHR, 2012–. Hon. Prof. of Neurology, Mount Sinai Med. Sch., NY, 1995; Visiting Professor: Harvard, 2009; Yale, 2010. Non-executive Director: Royal Free London Foundn Trust, 2009–; Office of the Public Guardian, MoJ, 2012–. Member: Movement Disorders Soc., 1992–; Harveian Soc., 1994–. Co-Ed.-in-Chief, 2006–12, Ed.-in-Chief, 2012–, Eur. Jl of Neurology. Queen

Square Prize, Inst. of Neurology, 1986; Graham Bull Prize for Clinical Sci., RCP, 1995; European Prize for Clinical Sci., Eur. Soc. Clin. Sci., 1998; Buckston Browne Medal, Harveian Soc., 1995; Opprecht Prize, Neurol. Soc. Switzerland, 1999; Duchenne Prize, German Neurol. Soc., 2005. *Publications:* (ed jtly) Mitochondrial Disorders in Neurology, 1994, 2nd edn 2002; Mitochondria: DNA, protein and disease, 1994; (ed jtly) Muscle Diseases, 1999; (ed jtly) Clinical Cases in Neurology, 2001; (ed) Mitochondrial Function and Dysfunction, 2002; Treatment of Parkinson's Disease, 2005; Understanding Parkinson's Disease, 2005; Neurology and Clinical Neuroscience, 2007; Parkinsonian Disorders, 2008. *Recreations:* chess (Yorkshire champion, 1966), European history, international affairs. *Address:* University Department of Clinical Neurosciences, University College London, Rowland Hill Street, NW3 2PF. *T:* (020) 7830 2012, *Fax:* (020) 7472 6829. *E:* anthony.schapira@nhs.net. *Club:* Athenæum.

SCHARPING, Rudolf; Founder and Managing Partner, RSBK GmbH, since 2004; *b* Niederelbert, Westerwald, 2 Dec. 1947. *Educ:* Univ. of Bonn. State Chm. and Nat. Dep. Chm., Jusos (Young Socialists), 1966; joined SPD, 1966; Rhineland-Palatinate: Mem., State Parlt, 1975–94; Leader, SPD, 1985–91; Leader of Opposition, 1985–91; Minister-Pres., 1991–94; Mem., Bundestag, 1994–2005; Leader of Opposition, 1994–98; Minister of Defence, 1998–2002; Dep. Chm., SPD, 1995–2003 (Chm., 1993–95); Pres., SDP of Europe, 1994–2001. Vis. Prof., Fletcher Sch., Tufts Univ., USA, 2004–06. Pres., Fedn of German Cyclists, 2005–. *Address:* RSBK GmbH, Schweizer Strasse 1, 60594 Frankfurt am Main, Germany.

SCHÄUBLE, Dr Wolfgang; Member of Bundestag, since 1972; Federal Minister of Finance, since 2009; Deputy Chairman, CDU/CSU Parliamentary Group, Germany, 2002–05 (Chairman, 1991–2000); *b* 18 Sept. 1942; *s* of Karl Schäuble and Gertrud (*née* Göhring); *m* 1969, Ingeborg Hensle; one *s* three *d*. *Educ:* Univ. of Freiburg; Univ. of Hamburg (Dr jur 1971). Tax Revenue Dept, State of Baden-Württemberg, 1971–72; solicitor, 1978–84; Parly Sec., CDU/CSU, 1981–84; Federal Minister with special responsibility and Head of Federal Chancellery, 1984–89; Federal Minister of the Interior, 1989–91 and 2005–09. Chm., 1998–2000, Mem. Governing Bd, 2000–, CDU, Germany. Chairman: CDU Cttee on Sports, 1976–84; Working Gp, European Border Regions, 1979–82. Grosskreuz des Verdienstordens der Bundesrepublik Deutschland, 1990; Internationaler Karlspreis zu Aachen, 2012. *Publications:* Der Vertrag, 1991; Und der Zukunft zugewandt, 1994; Mitten im Leben, 2000; Scheitert der Westen?, 2003; Braucht unsere Gesellschaft Religion 2, 2009; Zukunft mit Maß, 2009. *Recreation:* classical music. *Address:* (office) c/o Deutscher Bundestag, Platz der Republik 1, 11011 Berlin, Germany. *E:* wolfgang.schaeuble@bundestag.de. *W:* www.wolfgang-schaeuble.de.

SCHAUFUSS, Peter; ballet dancer, producer, choreographer, director; *b* 26 April 1950; *s* of late Frank Schaufuss and Mona Vangsaae, former solo dancers with Royal Danish Ballet. *Educ:* Royal Danish Ballet School. Apprentice, Royal Danish Ballet, 1965; soloist, Nat. Ballet of Canada, 1967–68; Royal Danish Ballet, 1969–70; Principal, London Festival Ballet, 1970–74; NY City Ballet, 1974–77; Principal, National Ballet of Canada, 1977–83; Artistic Dir, London Fest. Ballet, later English Nat. Ballet, 1984–90; Dir of Ballet, Deutsche Oper, Berlin, 1990–93; Ballet Dir, Royal Danish Ballet, 1994–95; Founder Dir, Peter Schaufuss Ballet, 1997–. Guest appearances in Austria, Canada, Denmark, France, Germany, Greece, Israel, Italy, Japan, Norway, S America, Turkey, UK, USA, USSR; Presenter, Dancer, BBC, 1984; numerous TV appearances. Roles created for him in: Phantom of the Opera; Orpheus; Verdi Variations; The Steadfast Tin Soldier; Rhapsodie Espagnole. Produced ballets: La Sylphide (London Fest. Ballet, Stuttgart Ballet, Roland Petit's Ballet de Marseille, Deutsche Oper Berlin, Teatro Comunale, Florence, Vienna State Opera, Opernhaus Zurich, Teatro dell' Opera di Roma, Hessisches Staatstheater, Wiesbaden, Ballet du Rhin, Royal Danish Ballet, Ballet West); Napoli (Nat. Ballet of Canada, Teatro San Carlo, English Nat. Ballet); Folktale (Deutsche Oper Berlin); Dances from Napoli (London Fest. Ballet); Bournonville (Aterballetto); The Nutcracker (English Nat. Ballet, Deutsche Oper, Berlin); Giselle, Sleeping Beauty, Swan Lake, Tchaikovsky Trilogy (Deutsche Oper, Berlin). Staging for Ashton's Romeo and Juliet, and prod. and choreog. Hamlet, Royal Danish Ballet, 1996; produced and/or choreographed, for Peter Schaufuss Ballet, new versions of: Swan Lake, Sleeping Beauty, The Nutcracker, 1997; Hamlet, Romeo and Juliet, 1998; The King, Manden der Onskede Sig en Havudsigt, 1999; Midnight Express, The Three Presents, 2000; Hans Christian Andersen, 2001; Satisfaction, 2007; Divas, 2008; Marilyn. Solo award, 2nd Internat. Ballet Competition, Moscow, 1973; Star of the Year, Munich Abendzeitung, 1978; Evening Standard and SWET ballet award, 1979; Manchester Evening News theatre award, 1986; Lakerolprisen, Copenhagen, 1988; Berlin Co. award, Berlinerzeitung, 1991; Edinburgh Festival Critics' Prize, 1991. Knight of the Dannebrog (Denmark), 1988; Officier de l'Ordre de la Couronne (Belgium), 1995. *Recreation:* boxing. *Address:* c/o Peter Schaufuss Ballet, Middelfartvej 61–63 Hal L., 5462 Vissenbjerg, Denmark.

SCHEEL, Walter; Grand Cross First Class of Order of Merit of Federal Republic of Germany; President of the Federal Republic of Germany, 1974–79; *b* 8 July 1919; *m* 1942, Eva Kronenberg (*d* 1966); one *s*; *m* 1969, Dr Mildred Wirtz (*d* 1985); one *s* two *d*; *m* 1988, Barbara Wiese. *Educ:* Real Gymnasium, Solingen. Served in German Air Force, War of 1939–45. Founder and Partner, Interfinanz, and Intermarket, 1946–61. Mem. of Bundestag, 1953–74; Federal Minister for Economic Co-operation, 1961–Oct. 1966, Vice-President of Bundestag, 1967–69; Vice-Chancellor and Foreign Minister, 1969–74. Mem., Landtag North Rhine Westphalia, 1950–54; Mem. European Parlt, 1958–61 (Vice-Chm., Liberal Gp; Chm., Cttee on Co-operation with Developing Countries). Free Democratic Party: Mem., 1946; Mem. Exec. Cttee for North Rhine/Westphalia, 1953–74; Mem. Federal Exec., 1956–74; Chm., 1968–74; Hon. Pres., 1979. Member, Supervisory Board: Thyssen AG, 1979–99; Thyssen Stahl, 1983–99. Hon. Chm., Deutsche Investitions- und Entwicklungs GmbH, 1998–. Holds numerous hon. degrees and foreign decorations. *Publications:* Konturen einer neuen Welt, 1965; Formeln deutscher Politik, 1968; Warum Mitbestimmung und wie - eine Diskussion, 1970; Reden und Interviews, 1969–79; Vom Recht des anderen, 1977; Die Zukunft der Freiheit, 1979; Wen schmerzt noch Deutschlands Teilung?, 1986. *Address:* Persönliches Büro, Spreeweg 1, 10557 Berlin, Germany.

SCHEER, Hon. Andrew James; MP (C) Regina-Qu'Appelle, since 2004; Speaker, House of Commons, Canada, since 2011; *b* Ottawa, 20 May 1979; *s* of James Scheer and Mary Scheer (*née* Enright); *m* 2003, Jillian Ryan; two *s* two *d*. *Educ:* Immaculata High Sch., Ottawa; Univ. of Ottawa (BA Hist.). Canadian Accredited Insce Broker Level 1. Insce agent, Regina, Saskatchewan, 2003–04. Dep. Speaker, H of C, Canada, 2008–11. Saskatchewan Centennial Medal, 2005. *Recreations:* Roman history, golf, tennis. *Address:* House of Commons, Ottawa, ON K1A 0A6, Canada. *T:* (613) 9924593, *Fax:* (613) 9954253; (office) 984 Albert Street, Regina, SK S4R 2P7, Canada. *T:* (306) 7904727, *Fax:* (306) 7904728.

SCHELLING, Prof. Thomas Crombie, PhD; Distinguished University Professor, University of Maryland, 1990–2005; *b* 14 April 1921; *s* of John M. Schelling and Zelda Ayres Schelling; *m* 1st, 1947, Corinne Saposs (marr. diss. 1991); four *s*; 2nd, 1991, Alice Coleman. *Educ:* Univ. of Calif, Berkeley (AB 1944); Harvard Univ. (PhD 1951). US Bureau of the Budget, 1945–46; ECA, Europe, 1948–51; White House and Exec. Office of the President, 1951–53; Associate Prof., then Prof. of Econs, Yale Univ., 1953–58; RAND Corp., 1958–59; Prof. of Econs, 1959–90, Lucius N. Littauer Prof. of Political Econ., 1969–90, now Emeritus, Harvard Univ. NAS Award, 1993; (jtly) Nobel Prize for Econs, 2005. *Publications:* National Income Behavior, 1951; International Economics, 1958; The Strategy of Conflict, 1960; (with Morton H. Halperin) Strategy and Arms Control, 1961; Arms and Influence, 1966; Micromotives and Macrobehavior, 1978; Thinking Through the Energy Problem, 1979; Choice and Consequence, 1984; Strategies of Commitment, 2006. *Recreation:* hiking. *Address:* 8300 Burdetate Road, Bethesda, MD 20817, USA. *T:* (301) 3209411, *Fax:* (301) 3206698. *E:* tschelli@umd.edu.

SCHELLNHUBER, Prof. Hans Joachim, (John), Hon. CBE 2004; PhD; Director, Potsdam Institute for Climate Impact Research, and Professor for Theoretical Physics, Potsdam University, since 1993; Distinguished Science Advisor, Tyndall Centre for Climate Change Research, 2005–09; *b* 7 June 1950; *s* of Gottlieb and Erika Schellnhuber; *m* 1981, Petra (*d* 2001); *m* 2003, Margret Boysen; one *s*. *Educ:* Regensburg Univ. (MSc; PhD); Univ. of California, Santa Barbara and Santa Cruz; Oldenburg Univ. (Habitation). Heisenberg Fellow, 1987–89; Prof. for Theoretical Physics, Oldenburg Univ., 1989–93; Res. Dir, Tyndall Centre for Climate Change Res., and Prof. for Envmtl Scis, UEA, 2001–05. Vis. Prof. of Physics, Oxford Univ., 2005–09. Mem., German Adv. Council on Global Change, 1992– (Chm.); Chm., Global Change Adv. Gp, EC, 2002–06; Chief Govt Advr on Climate to German EU/G8 Presidency, 2007; Mem., High-Level Adv. Gp on Energy and Climate to Pres. EU Commn, 2007–11. Scientific Mem., Max Planck Soc., 2002–. Member: NAS, 2005; German Nat. Acad. (formerly German Acad. of Scis) Leopoldina, 2007. Wolfson Res. Merit Award, Royal Soc., 2002; German Envmt Prize, Deutsche Bundesstiftung Umwelt, 2007; Envmt Prize, Bundesdeutsche Arbeitskreis für Umweltbewusstes Mgt, 2008. Order of Merit: State of Brandenburg, 2008; FRG, 2011. *Publications:* author or editor of about 40 books on complex systems theory and environmental analysis; over 200 articles in Nature, Science, Physical Rev. Letters, etc. *Recreations:* Romanesque art, philosophy of science, reading about history, mountain hiking. *Address:* Potsdam Institute for Climate Impact Research, PO Box 601203, 14412 Potsdam, Germany. *T:* (331) 2882501, *Fax:* (331) 2882600. *E:* director@pik-potsdam.de.

SCHIEMANN, Rt Hon. Sir Konrad Hermann Theodor, Kt 1986; PC 1995; a Judge of the Court of Justice of the European Union (formerly European Communities), 2004–12; *b* 15 Sept. 1937; *s* of Helmuth and Beate Schiemann; *m* 1965, Elisabeth Hanna Eleonore Holroyd-Reece; one *d*. *Educ:* King Edward's Sch., Birmingham; Freiburg Univ.; Pembroke Coll., Cambridge (Schol.; MA, LLB; Hon. Fellow, 1998). Served Lancs Fusiliers, 1956–58 (commnd, 1957). Called to Bar, Inner Temple, 1962 (Bencher, 1985; Reader, 2002; Treas., 2003); Junior Counsel to the Crown, Common Law, 1978–80; QC 1980; a Recorder of the Crown Court, 1985–86; a Justice of the High Court, QBD, 1986–95; a Lord Justice of Appeal, 1995–2004. Chairman of panels conducting Examinations in Public of: North-East Hants and Mid Hants Structure Plans, 1979; Merseyside Structure Plan, 1980; Oxfordshire Structure Plan, 1984. Mem., Parole Bd, 1990–92 (Vice-Chm., 1991–92). Member, Advisory Board: Centre for Eur. Legal Studies, Cambridge Univ., 1996–; Eur. Law Rev., 2007–. Mem. Council of Mgt, British Inst. of Internat. and Comparative Law, 2000–06. Patron, Busoga Trust, 1999– (Chm., 1989–99); Trustee, St John's, Smith Square, 1990–2004 (Chm., 1994–2004). Dir, Acad. of Ancient Music, 2001–04; Gov., English Nat. Ballet, 1995–2001. *Publications:* contrib. English and German legal books and jls. *Recreations:* music, reading. *Address:* 1 Temple Gardens, EC4Y 9BB. *Club:* Athenæum.

SCHIFF, Sir András, Kt 2014; concert pianist and conductor; *b* Budapest, 21 Dec. 1953; *s* of Odon Schiff and Klara Schiff (*née* Csengeri); *m* 1987, Yuuko Shiokawa. *Educ:* Franz Liszt Academy of Music, Budapest; with Prof. Pal Kadosa, Ferenc Rados and Gyorgy Kurtag; private study with George Malcolm. Artistic Dir, September Chamber Music Fest., Mondsee, Austria, 1989–98; Co-founder, Ittinger Pfingstkonzerte, Switzerland, 1995; Founder, Homage to Palladio Fest., Vicenza, Italy, 1998; Artist in Residence, Kunstfest, Weimar, 2004–. Hon. Prof., Music Schs in Budapest, Detmold and Munich; Supernumerary Fellow, Balliol Coll., Oxford, 2009. Concerts as soloist with orchestras including: NY Philharmonic, Chicago Symphony, Vienna Phil., Concertgebouw, Orch. de Paris, London Phil., London Symph., Philharmonia, Royal Phil., Israel Phil., Philadelphia, Washington Nat. Symph., Hallé; orchestras conducted include: Baltimore Symphony, Chamber Orch. of Europe, City of Birmingham Symphony, Danish Radio, LA Philharmonic, Philadelphia and Philharmonia; major festival performances include: Salzburg, Lucerne, Edinburgh, Aldeburgh, Tanglewood, Feldkirch Schubertiade, Lucerne. Created Cappella Andrea Barca orch., 1999. Recordings include: extensive Bach repertoire (Grammy Award for recording of English Suites, 1990); all Mozart Piano Sonatas; all Mozart Piano Concertos; all Schubert Sonatas; all Bartok Piano Concertos; all Beethoven Piano Concertos; Lieder records with Peter Schreier, Robert Holl and Cecilia Bartoli. Hon. Member: Beethoven House, Bonn, 2006; Vienna Konzerthaus, 2012. Prizewinner, Tchaikovsky competition, Moscow, 1974 and Leeds comp., 1975; Liszt Prize, 1977; Premio, Accademia Chigiana, Siena, 1987; Wiener Flotenuhr, 1989; Bartok Prize, 1991; Instrumentalist of the Year, Internat. Classical Music Awards, 1993; Claudio Arrau Meml Medal, 1994; Instrumentalist of the Year, Royal Philharmonic Soc., 1994; Kossuth Prize, 1996; Deutsche Schallplattenkrik, 1996; Leonie Sonnings Music Prize, Copenhagen, 1997; Palladio d'Oro, Citta di Vicenza, 2003; Musikfest Preis, Bremen, 2003; Abbiati Prize, Italian Critics' Assoc., 2007; Bach Prize, RAM, 2007; Wigmore Hall Medal, 2008; Ruhr Piano Fest. Prize, 2009; Schumann Prize, City of Zwickau, 2011; Golden Mozart-Medaille, Internat. Stiftung Mozarteum, 2012; Gold Medal, Royal Philharmonic Soc., 2013. Order of Merit (FRG), 2012. *Recreations:* literature, languages, soccer, theatre, art, cinema. *Address:* c/o Askonas Holt Ltd, Lincoln House, 300 High Holborn, WC1V 7JH.

SCHIFF, Heinrich; conductor; 'cellist; *b* Gmunden, Austria, 18 Nov. 1951. Studied with Tobias Kühne and André Navarra; attended Hans Swarowsky's conducting class. Joined professional orchestras, 1986; Chief Conductor and Guest Conductor of numerous orchestras in Austria, Finland, Germany, Holland, Sweden, Switzerland, UK, USA; also opera director. Artistic Dir, Northern Sinfonia, 1990–96; Principal Conductor: Musikkollegium, Winterthur, 1995–2001; Copenhagen Philharmonic Orchestra, 1996–99; Chief Conductor, Vienna Chamber Orch., 2005–08. Numerous recordings. *Address:* Künstlersekretariat Astrid Schoerke, Grazer Strasse 30, 30519 Hannover, Germany.

SCHIFFRIN, Prof. David Jorge, PhD; FRSC; Brunner Professor of Physical Chemistry, University of Liverpool, 1990–2004, now Emeritus, and Senior Fellow, since 2004; *b* 8 Jan. 1939; *s* of Bernardo Schiffrin and Berta Kurlat Schiffrin; *m* 1965, Margery Watson; one *s* one *d*. *Educ:* Univ. of Buenos Aires (BSc); Univ. of Birmingham (PhD). FRSC 1997. Lectr in Physical Chemistry, Univ. of Buenos Aires, 1966; Asst Technical Manager, CIABASA, Buenos Aires, 1967–68; Lectr in Physical Chemistry, Chemistry Dept, Univ. of Southampton, 1968–72; Head of Applied Electrochemistry Div., Nat. Inst. of Technology, Buenos Aires, 1972–77; Asst Technical Manager, R. Kurlat, Buenos Aires, 1977–79; Manager and Dir, Wolfson Centre for Electrochemical Science, 1979–90, Sen. Lectr, Chemistry Dept, 1988–90, Univ. of Southampton. Mem., Dept of Energy Adv. Cttee on impact of hydrogen on greenhouse gas abatement, 1990–91 and 2002. Project assessor for numerous internat. organisations. Vis. Prof., Helsinki Univ. of Technol., 2004–08. Chm., EU Marie Curie Chem. Panel, 2009 (Vice Chm., 2005–08); Ind. Observer, EU Marie Curie Fellowship Prog., 2011. Foreign Mem., Finnish Soc. of Scis and Letters, 1996; Mem., Internat. Selection Cttee, Fellowship Panel, Finnish Acad. of Scis, 2006. Electrochemistry Medal and Prize, RSC, 2001; RAICES Prize for Internat. Collaborations, Min. of Sci., Argentina, 2013. Member: Editorial Bd, Jl of Electroanalytical Chemistry, 1997–; Adv. Editl Bd, Physical Chemistry Chemical Physics, 2005–. *Publications:* over 259 articles in jls; chapters in books; over 170 conf. papers. *Recreations:* hill walking, music, photography. *Address:* Chemistry Department, University of Liverpool, Liverpool L69 7ZD. *T:* (0151) 794 3574.

SCHILD, Geoffrey Christopher, CBE 1993; PhD, DSc; FRCPath, FRCPE, FMedSci; FRSB; Director, National Institute for Biological Standards and Control, 1985–2002; Chief Scientific Officer, InB:Biotechnologies Inc., USA, 2006–09; *b* 28 Nov. 1935; *s* of Christopher and Georgina Schild; *m* 1961, Tora Madland; two *s* one *d*. *Educ:* High Storrs Sch., Sheffield; Univ. of Reading (BSc Hons 1954; DSc 1993); Univ. of Sheffield (PhD 1963). FRSB (FIBiol 1978); FRCPath 1993; FRCPE 1998. Hon. FRCP 1995. Res. Fellow 1961–63, Lectr in Virology 1963–67, Univ. of Sheffield; National Institute for Medical Research: Mem., Scientific Staff of MRC, 1967–75; Dir, World Influenza Centre, 1970–75; Hd, Div. of Virology, Nat. Inst. for Biol Standards, 1975–85; Dir, MRC Directed Prog. of AIDS Res., 1987–95. Professional Affairs Officer, Soc. for Gen. Microbiol., 2002–06. Chm., WHO Steering Cttee on Biomed. Res. on AIDS, 1987–90; Member: WHO Scientific Adv. Gp on Vaccine Develt, 1991–93; Strategic Planning Task Force, Internat. Children's Vaccine Initiative, 1996; Bd, UK Health Protection Agency, 2003–08. Mem. Bd, Internat. Assoc. for Biologicals, 1979–. Chm., Steering Cttee, Acad. Med. Scis Forum on safety assessment of medicinal products, 2004–; Founding Mem., Bd Mem. and Actg Chm., Internat. Soc. for Influenza and other Respiratory Viruses, 2006–. Vis. Prof., Haukeland Hosp., Univ. of Bergen, Norway, 2001–04; Mem. Council, RVC, Univ. of London, 2005–06. Vice Chm. Bd of Trustees, UNDP Internat. Vaccine Inst., Seoul, 1995–96. Freeman, City of London, 1989. FMedSci 2001. Hon. DSc Sheffield, 2002. *Publications:* Influenza, the Virus and the Disease, 1975, 2nd edn 1985; some 300 original res. papers on virology in learned jls. *Recreations:* hill walking, music, Scandinavian ecology and ornithology. *E:* the.schilds@btinternet.com.

SCHILLING, Keith; Co-Founder and Senior Partner, Schillings International LLP (formerly Schilling, Gleadow and Lom, later Schilling and Lom), since 1984; *b* Orpington, 25 July 1956; *s* of Sidney and Violet Schilling; *m*; marr. diss.; two *s*. *Educ:* City of London Poly. (MA Eur. Business Law 1982). Articled Wright Webb Syrett; admitted as solicitor, 1981; specialises in libel, privacy and family law; landmark decisions include first-time recovery of 50% of assets by wife in big money divorce (Lambert v Lambert, 2002), re-introduction to English law of John Doe injunction (J. K. Rowling v persons unknown, 2003), first-time establishment of right of privacy in English law (Naomi Campbell v Mirror Gp Newspapers, 2004), first-time use of video link in libel trial (Roman Polanski v Vanity Fair, 2005); Solicitor-Advocate (Higher Civil Courts, England and Wales), 2008–. Lectr on legal topics. *Publications:* contrib. articles to legal jls. *Recreations:* reading, trekking, sailing, climbing, sports. *Address:* Schillings International LLP, 41 Bedford Square, Bloomsbury, WC1B 3HX. *T:* (020) 7034 9000, *Fax:* (020) 7034 9200. *E:* legal@schillings.co.uk. *Clubs:* Groucho, Soho House.

SCHINDLER, Prof. David William, DPhil; FRS 2001; FRSC 1983; Killam Memorial Professor of Ecology, University of Alberta, 1989–2013, now Emeritus. *Educ:* N Dakota State Univ. (BSc 1962); St Catherine's Coll., Oxford (Rhodes Schol.; DPhil 1966). Asst Prof., Trent Univ., 1966–68; Prog. Leader, then Res. Scientist, Experimental Limnology Prog., Freshwater Inst., and Founder and Dir, Experimental Lakes Project, Dept of Fisheries and Oceans, Canada, 1968–89. Adjunct Prof., Univ. of Manitoba, 1971–89. *Publications:* contrib. learned jls. *Address:* Department of Biological Sciences, University of Alberta, Edmonton, AB T6G 2E9, Canada.

SCHLAGMAN, Richard Edward; Chairman and Publisher, Phaidon Press Ltd, 1990–2012; *b* 11 Nov. 1953; *s* of Jack Schlagman and late Shirley Schlagman (*née* Goldston); partner, Mia Hägg; two *s*. *Educ:* University Coll. Sch., Hampstead; Brunel Univ. Co-Founder, Jt Chm., and Man. Dir, Interstate Electronics Ltd, 1973–86; purchased Bush from Rank Orgn, renamed IEL Bush Radio Ltd, 1981, floated on London Stock Exchange, 1984; sold as Bush Radio Plc, 1986; acquired Phaidon Press Ltd, 1990; President: Phaidon Press Inc., 1998–2012; Phaidon SARL, 1999–2012; Phaidon Verlag, 2000–12; Phaidon KK, 2004–12; Owner and Publisher, Cahiers du cinéma, 2009– (acquired from Le Monde, 2009). Mem., Exec. Cttee, Patrons of New Art, Tate Gall., 1994–97. Mem., Judd Foundn, Marfa, Texas, 1999–2009 (Pres., 1999–2001); Jury Mem., City of Ascona Concert Hall Architecture Comp., 2004. Member: Glyndebourne Fest. Soc.; Freunde der Bayreuther Festspiele; Freunde der Salzburger Festspiele. Patron: Bayreuther Festspiele; Salzburger Festspiele; Salzburger Osterfestspiele; Schubertiade. FRSA 1994. *Recreations:* music, art, architecture. *Address:* Piazza Grande 26, 6600 Locarno, Switzerland. *T:* (91) 7596000. *Club:* Chelsea Arts.

SCHLESINGER, David Adam; Founder and Managing Director, Tripod Advisors, since 2012; *b* 15 April 1960; *s* of Ernest Carl and Gabriella Pintus Schlesinger; *m* 1987, Rachel Shiu-Ping Wong. *Educ:* Oberlin Coll. (BA 1982); Harvard Univ. (AM 1986). Freelance journalist, 1986–87; Reuters: correspondent, Hong Kong, 1987–89; Bureau Chief: Taiwan, 1989–91; China, 1991–94; Ed., Greater China, 1994–95; Financial Ed., 1995–97, Man. Ed., 1997–2000, Ed., 2000–03, Americas; Global Man. Ed., News, 2003–06; Ed.-in-Chief, News, 2006–11. Board Mem., Internat. News Safety Inst., 2005–11. Hon. Pres., Internat. Network of Street Papers, 2009–14. Chairman: Danenberg Oberlin-in-London Prog., 2008–11 (Dir, 2007–08); Thomson Reuters China, 2011–12; Poseidon Research Ltd, 2012–14; Director: Thomson Reuters Foundn (formerly Reuters Foundn), 2008–11; Cttee to Protect Journalists, 2009–; ChinaWeb, 2011–12; Index on Censorship, 2012–. Hon. Fellow, Reuters Inst. for Journalism, Oxford, 2012–. *Address:* D. A. Schlesinger Ltd, 30/F Entertainment Building, 30 Queen's Road Central, Hong Kong. *T:* 28248727. *E:* das@daschlesinger.com. *Clubs:* Blacks; Frontline; Foreign Correspondents (Hong Kong).

SCHLUTER, Prof. Dolph, PhD; FRS 1999; FRSC 2001; Professor of Zoology, University of British Columbia, since 1996 (Director, Biodiversity Research Centre, 2003–07); *b* 22 May 1955; *s* of Antoine Schluter and Magdalena Schluter; *m* 1993, Andrea Lawson; one *d*. *Educ:* Univ. of Guelph, Ont (BSc Wildlife Biol. 1977); Univ. of Michigan (PhD Ecol. and Evolution 1983). NSERC Postdoctoral Fellow, Zool. Dept, UBC and Univ. of Calif, Davis, 1983–85; Zoology Department, University of British Columbia: NSERC Univ. Res. Fellow, 1985–89; Asst Prof., 1989–91; Associate Prof., 1991–96. E. W. R. Steacie Meml Fellow, NSERC, 1993; Izaak Walton Killam Meml Faculty Res. Fellow, UBC, 1996; Scholar-in-Residence, Peter Wall Inst. of Advanced Studies, UBC, 1999; Canada Res. Chair, 2001–; Guggenheim Fellow, 2003–04; Killam Sen. Res. Fellow, Canada Council, 2011–13. Pres., American Soc. of Naturalists, 2013 (Vice-Pres., 1999; President's Award, 1997); Pres., Soc. for Study of Evolution, 2005. Foreign Mem., Amer. Acad. of Arts and Scis, 2012. Charles A. McDowell Medal, 1995, Killam Res. Prize, 2008, Killam Mentoring Award, 2010, UBC; Rosenblatt Award, Scripps Inst. of Oceanography, 2006; Sewall Wright Award, Amer. Soc. of Naturalists, 2007; Darwin-Wallace Medal, Linnean Soc., 2014. *Publications:* (ed with R. Ricklefs) Species Diversity in Ecological Communities: historical and geographical perspectives, 1993; The Ecology of Adaptive Radiation, 2000; (with M. C. Whitlock) The Analysis of Biological Data, 2008; (ed jtly) Speciation and Patterns of Diversity, 2009; contrib. chapters in books; contrib. numerous articles to Science, Nature, Evolution, American Naturalist, Ecology, Proc. Royal Soc., Philosophical Trans Royal Soc. *Address:* Zoology Department, University of British Columbia, 6270 University Boulevard, Vancouver, BC V6T 1Z4, Canada. *T:* (604) 8222387, *Fax:* (604) 8222416. *E:* schluter@zoology.ubc.ca.

SCHMIDHUBER, Peter Michael; Member, Commission of the European Communities, 1987–94; attorney in Munich; *b* 15 Dec. 1931; *s* of Jakob Schmidhuber and Anna (*née* Mandlmayr); *m* 1960, Elisabeth Schweigart; one *d*. *Educ:* Univ. of Munich (MA Econs 1955). Qualified as lawyer, 1960. Mem. Bd, Deutsche Bundesbank, 1995–. Member: Bundestag, 1965–69 and 1972–78; Bundesrat, Bavarian Parliament, 1978–87 (Bavarian Minister of State for Federal Affairs). Mem., CSU. *Address:* Wiesengrund 1b, 81243 Munich, Germany.

SCHMIDT, Benno Charles, Jr; Chairman of the Board of Trustees, City University of New York, since 2003 (Vice Chairman, 1999–2003); Chairman, Avenues: The World School, since 2011; *b* 20 March 1942; *s* of Benno Charles Schmidt and Martha Chastain; *m* 2001, Anne McMillen; one *s* two *d* from previous marriage. *Educ:* Yale Univ. (BA 1963; LLB 1966). Mem., DC Bar, 1968; Law Clerk to Chief Justice Earl Warren, 1966–67; Special Asst AG, Office of Legal Counsel, US Dept of Justice, Washington, 1967–69; Harlan Fiske Stone Prof. of Constitutional Law, Columbia Univ., 1969–86, Dean of Law School, 1984–86; Professor of Law, and President, Yale Univ., 1986–92; Pres. and Chief Exec., The Edison Project, 1992–98; Chm. Bd, 1998–2007, Vice-Chm., 2007–, Edison Schs, later Edison Learning. Hon. Bencher, Gray's Inn, 1988. Hon. degrees: LLD Princeton, 1986; DLitt Johns Hopkins, 1987; LLD Harvard, 1987. Hon. AM, 1989. *Publications:* Freedom of the Press Versus Public Access, 1974; (with A. M. Bickel) The Judiciary and Responsible Government 1910–1921, 1985. *Address:* City University of New York, 585 East 80th Street, New York, NY 10028, USA.

SCHMIDT, Prof. Brian Paul, AC 2013; PhD; FRS 2012; FAA; Australian Research Council Australian Laureate Fellow, since 2009, and Distinguished Professor, since 2010, Research School of Astronomy and Astrophysics, Australian National University; *b* Missoula, Montana, USA, 24 Feb. 1967; *s* of Dana C. Schmidt and Donna P. Pentz; *m* Jennifer Gordon; two *s*. *Educ:* Univ. of Arizona (BS Astronomy and Physics 1989); Harvard Univ. (AM Astronomy 1992; PhD 1993). FAA 2008. CFA Postdoctoral Fellow, Harvard Smithsonian Center for Astrophysics, 1993–94; Australian National University: Postdoctoral Fellow, 1995–96; Lectr in Introductory Astrophysics, 1996–98; Res. Fellow, 1997–99; Fellow, 1999–2002; Lectr in Observational Astronomy, 1999; ARC Professorial Fellow, 2003–05; Lectr in Observational Cosmol., 2004–; ARC Fedn Fellow, 2005–09. Non-exec. Dir, Astronomy Australia Ltd, 2007–. Member: Anglo Australian Telescope Bd, 2004–08; Australia Telescope Steering Cttee, 2010–; Adv. Cttee, Australia Astronomical Observatory, 2010–; Adv. Bd, Questacon, 2012–. Member, Council: Astronomical Soc. of Australia, 2001–03; Australian Acad. Sci., 2012– (Mem., Nat. Cttee of Astronomy, 2010–). Vigneron and grape grower, Maipenrai Vineyard and Winery. Fellow: Japanese Soc. for Promotion of Sci., 1999; NAS, USA, 2008. Hon. DLitt Macquarie, 2012; Dr *hc* Chile, 2012; Hon. Dr Arizona, 2012. Pawsey Medal, Australian Acad. Sci., 2001; Vainu Bappu Medal, Astronomical Soc. India, 2002; (jtly) Shaw Prize, Shaw Foundn, 2006; (jtly) Gruber Prize for Cosmol., Gruber Foundn, 2007; Peter Baume Award, ANU, 2010; (jtly) Nobel Prize in Physics, 2011; Dirac Medal, Univ. of NSW, 2012. *Address:* Research School of Astronomy and Astrophysics, Mount Stromlo Observatory, Australian National University, Cotter Road, Weston, ACT 2611, Australia.

SCHMIDT, Helmut H. W.; Chancellor, Federal Republic of Germany, 1974–82; Member of Bundestag, Federal Republic of Germany, 1953–61, and 1965–87; Publisher, Die Zeit, since 1983; *b* 23 Dec. 1918; *s* of Gustav Lentfält Schmidt and Ludovica Schmidt; *m* 1942, Hannelore Glaser (*d* 2010); one *d*. *Educ:* Univ. of Hamburg. Diplom-Volkswirt, 1949. Manager of Transport Administration, State of Hamburg, 1949–53; Social Democratic Party: Member, 1946–; Mem. Federal Executive, 1958–83; Chm., Parly Gp, 1967–69; Vice-Chm. of Party, 1968–84; Senator (Minister) for Domestic Affairs in Hamburg, 1961–65; Minister of Defence, 1969–72; Minister of Finance and Economics, 1972; Minister of Finance, 1972–74. Hon. LLD: Newberry Coll., S Carolina, 1973; Johns Hopkins Univ., 1976; Cambridge, 1976; Hon. DCL Oxford, 1979; Hon. Doctorate: Harvard, 1979; Sorbonne, 1981; Georgetown, 1986; Scranton, Pennsylvania, 1987; Bergamo, 1989; Keio, Tokyo, 1991; Nat. Chung-Hsing, Taipei, 1992; Potsdam, Haifa, 2000. Athinai Prize for Man and Mankind, Onassis Foundn, Greece, 1986. *Publications:* Defence or Retaliation, 1962; Beiträge, 1967; Balance of Power, 1971; Auf dem Fundament des Godesberger Programms, 1973; Bundestagsreden, 1975; Kontinuität und Konzentration, 1975; Als Christ in der politischen Entscheidung, 1976; (with Willy Brandt) Deutschland 1976—Zwei Sozialdemokraten im Gespräch, 1976; Der Kurs heisst Frieden, 1979; Freiheit verantworten, 1980; Pflicht zur Menschlichkeit, 1981; A Grand Strategy for the West, 1985; Menschen und Mächte, 1987 (trans. as Men and Powers, 1989); Die Deutschen und ihre Nachbarn, 1990; Handeln für Deutschland, 1993; Das Jahr der Entscheidung, 1994; Weggefährten, 1996; Jahrhundertwende, 1998; Allgemeine Erklärung der Menschenpflichten, 1998; Globalisierung, 1998; Auf der Suche nach einer öffentlichen Moral, 1998; Die Selbstbehauptung Europas, 2000; Hand aufs Herz, 2002; Die Mächte der Zukunft, 2004; Auf dem Weg zur deutschen Einheit, 2005; (with Frank Sieren) Nachbar China, 2007; Ausser Dienst, 2008; (with Fritz Stern) Unser Jahrhundert: ein gespräch, 2010; Religion in der Verantwortung, 2011; (with Peer Steinbrück) Zug um Zug, 2012; Ein Letzer Besuch: begegnungen mit der weltmacht China, 2013. *Recreations:* sailing, chess, playing the organ. *Address:* c/o Deutscher Bundestag, Platz der Republik 1, 11011 Berlin, Germany.

SCHMIDT, Prof. Michael Norton, OBE 2006; FRSL; Professor of Poetry, Glasgow University, 2006–15; Founder, and Editorial and Managing Director, Carcanet Press Ltd, since 1969; Writer in Residence, St John's College, Cambridge, 2012–15; *b* 2 March 1947; *s* of Carl Bernhardt Schmidt and Elizabeth Norton Schmidt (*née* Hill); *m* 1979, Claire Harman (marr. diss. 1989); two *s* one *d*; civil partnership 2010, Angel Garcia-Gomez. *Educ:* Harvard Univ.; Wadham Coll., Oxford (BA 1969; MA); Univ. of Cambridge (MA 2015). Manchester University: Gulbenkian Fellow of Poetry, 1970–73; Special Lectr, Poetry, 1973–92; Sen. Lectr in Poetry, 1992–98; Dir, Writing Sch., 1998–2005, and Prof. of English, 2000–05, Manchester Metropolitan Univ. Founder and Ed., PN Rev. (formerly Poetry Nation), 1971–; Poetry Ed., Grand Street (NY), 1998–2000. FRSL 1994. Hon. Dr Bolton, 2006. *Publications: criticism:* Fifty Modern British Poets: an introduction, 1979; Fifty English Poets 1300–1900: an introduction, 1979; Reading Modern Poetry, 1989; Lives of the Poets, 1998; The Story of Poetry: from Caedmon to Caxton, 2001; The Story of Poetry: from Skelton to Dryden, 2002; The First Poets: lives of the ancient Greek poets, 2004; The Story of Poetry: from Pope to Burns, 2007; The Novel: a biography, 2014; *translations:* (with E. Kissam) Flower and Song: Aztec poetry, 1977; On Poets and Others, by Octavio Paz, 1986; *poetry anthologies* include: Eleven British Poets, 1980; The Harvill Book of 20th Century Poetry in English, 1999; The Great Modern Poets, 2006; Five American Poets, 2010; New Poetries V, 2011; *fiction:* The Colonist, 1983; The Dresden Gate, 1988; *poetry* includes: New and Selected Poems, 1997; The Resurrection and the Body, 2007; Collected Poems, 2009; The Stories of My Life, 2013. *Address:* Carcanet Press Ltd, Alliance House, 30 Cross Street, Manchester M2 7AQ. *Club:* Savile.

SCHMIDT-GARRÉ, Philomene Korinna Kornelia; *see* Magers, P. K. K.

SCHOFIELD, Prof. Andrew Noel, MA, PhD (Cantab); FRS 1992; FREng, FICE; Professor of Engineering, Cambridge University, 1974–98, now Professor Emeritus; Fellow of Churchill College, Cambridge, 1963–66 and since 1974; *b* 1 Nov. 1930; *s* of late Rev. John Noel Schofield and Winifred Jane Mary (*née* Eyles); *m* 1961, Margaret Eileen Green; two *s* two *d*. *Educ:* Mill Hill Sch.; Christ's Coll., Cambridge. John Winbolt Prize, 1954. Asst Engr, in Malawi, with Scott Wilson Kirkpatrick and Partners, 1951. Cambridge Univ.: Demonstrator, 1955, Lectr, 1959, Dept of Engrg. Research Fellow, California Inst. of Technology, 1963–64. Univ. of Manchester Inst. of Science and Technology: Prof. of Civil Engrg, 1968; Head of Dept of Civil and Structural Engrg, 1973. Chm., Andrew N. Schofield & Associates Ltd, 1984–2000. Rankine Lecture, ICE British Geotechnical Soc., 1980. Chm., Tech. Cttee on Centrifuge Testing, Internat. Soc. for Soil Mech. and Foundn Engrg, 1982–85. FREng (FEng 1986). James Alfred Ewing Medal, ICE, 1993. US Army Award, Civilian Service 1979. *Publications:* (with C. P. Wroth) Critical State Soil Mechanics, 1968; (ed with W. H. Craig and R. G. James and contrib.) Centrifuges in Soil Mechanics, 1988; (ed with J. R. Gronow and R. K. Jain and contrib.) Land Disposal of Hazardous Waste, 1988; Disturbed Soil Properties and Geotechnical Design, 2005; papers on soil mechanics and civil engrg. *Address:* 9 Little St Mary's Lane, Cambridge CB2 1RR. *T:* (01223) 314536. *E:* ans10@cam.ac.uk.

SCHOFIELD, Prof. Christopher Joseph, DPhil; FRS 2013; FRSC; Professor of Chemistry, since 1998 and Head of Organic Chemistry, since 2011, University of Oxford; Fellow of Hertford College, Oxford, since 1990; *b* Barnston, 17 June 1960; *s* of Anthony Schofield and Bridget Ann Schofield (*née* Smith); *m* 1987, Pauline Poh Lin Tan; three *s* one *d*. *Educ:* Barnston Co. Primary Sch.; St Anselm's Coll., Birkenhead; Univ. of Manchester Inst. of Sci. and Technol. (BSc 1st Cl. 1982); St John's Coll., Oxford (DPhil 1985). FRSC 2005. Deptl Demonstrator, 1985–90, Lectr, 1990–98, Univ. of Oxford. Jeremy Knowles Award, RSC, 2011. *Publications:* articles in scientific jls. *Recreations:* sport, 'gardening'. *Address:* Chemistry Research Laboratory, Department of Chemistry, University of Oxford, Mansfield Road, Oxford OX1 3TA. *T:* (01865) 265725. *E:* christopher.schofield@chem.ox.ac.uk; Rivendell, Old Boars Hill, Oxford OX1 5JJ.

SCHOFIELD, Derek; a Recorder, 2000–15; Consultant, Schofield and Associates, since 2010; *b* 20 Feb. 1945; *s* of John Schofield and Ethelena Schofield (*née* Calverley); *m* 1st, 1967, Judith Danson (marr. diss.); one *s* one *d*; 2nd, 1983, Anne Wangeci Kariuki; one *s* one *d*. *Educ:* Morecambe Grammar Sch.; NAJCA Dip. in Magisterial Law, 1966; Mediation Trng Inst. Internat. (Cert. Professional Mediation 2012). English Magisterial Service, 1961–74; called to the Bar, Gray's Inn, 1970; Kenya: Resident Magistrate, 1974–78; Sen. Resident Magistrate, 1978–82; Puisne Judge, 1982–87; Judge of Grand Court, Cayman Islands, 1988–96; Chief Justice of Gibraltar, 1996–2009; Asst Recorder, 1997–2000. *Recreations:* travel, reading.

SCHOFIELD, John Allen, PhD; FSA; archaeologist and architectural historian, since 2008; Curator, Architecture, Museum of London, 1998–2008; *b* 23 Aug. 1948; *s* of Jack and Edna Schofield. *Educ:* Christ Church Coll., Oxford (BA 1970); Univ. of Edinburgh (MPhil 1974); Royal Holloway Coll., Univ. of London (PhD 1989). FSA 1981; MCIfA (MIFA 1983). Museum of London: Field Officer, Dept of Urban Archaeol., 1977–87; Actg Chief Urban Archaeologist, 1987–90; Hd of Pubns, Archaeol. Service, 1991–98. Archaeol. Advr, Dio. of London, 1985–2007. Cathedral Archaeologist, St Paul's Cathedral, 1990–. Chm., Assoc. of Diocesan and Cathedral Archaeologists, 2000–06; Hon. Sec., City of London Archaeol. Trust, 1990–. Reviews Ed., Trans, 2002–, Chm., Pubns Cttee, 2005–, Series Ed., Special Papers, 2013–15, London and Middx Archaeol. Soc.; Series Ed., Studies in the Archaeology of Medieval Europe, 2003–13. *Publications:* Building of London from the Conquest to the Great Fire, 1984, 3rd edn 1999; The London Surveys of Ralph Treswell, 1987; (with A. Vince) Medieval Towns, 1994, 2nd edn 2003; Medieval London Houses, 1995, rev. edn 2003; (ed with C. Maloney) Archaeology in the City of London 1907–91: a guide to records of excavations by the Museum of London, 1998; (ed with A. Saunders) Tudor London: a map and a view, 2001; (with R. Lea) Holy Trinity Priory Aldgate, City of London, 2005; London 1100–1600: the archaeology of a capital city, 2011; St Paul's Cathedral Before Wren, 2011. *Recreations:* travel, jazz. *Address:* 2 Carthew Villas, W6 0BS.

SCHOFIELD, Kenneth Douglas, CBE 1996; Executive Director, European Golf Tour, Professional Golfers' Association, (PGA European Tour), 1975–2004, now Consultant; *b* 3 Feb. 1946; *s* of late Douglas Joseph and Jessie Schofield (*née* Gray); *m* 1968, Evelyn May Sharp; two *d*. *Educ:* Auchterarder High Sch. Associate, Savings Bank Inst., 1966. Joined Trustee Savings Bank, Perth, 1962, Br. Manager, Dunblane, 1969–71; Media and PR Exec. to Dir-Gen., PGA Tournament, 1971–74; Sec., PGA European Tour, 1975. Order of Merit, Royal Spanish Golf Fedn, 1993; Christer Lindberg Award, PGA of Europe, 2002. *Publications:* Pro Golf: the official PGA European Tour Media Guide, 1972–1975. *Recreations:* golf, cricket, soccer, walking. *Address:* European Tour, Wentworth Drive, Virginia Water, Surrey GU25 4LX. *T:* (01344) 840452. *Clubs:* Caledonian; Wentworth Golf; Crieff Golf; Auchterarder Golf; Royal and Ancient Golf (St Andrews).

SCHOFIELD, Prof. Malcolm, FBA 1997; Professor of Ancient Philosophy, University of Cambridge, 1998–2009, now Emeritus; Fellow, St John's College, Cambridge, since 1972; *b* 19 April 1942; *er s* of Harry Schofield and Ethel Schofield (*née* Greenwood); *m* 1970, Elizabeth Milburn (*d* 2005); one *s*. *Educ:* St Albans Sch.; St John's Coll., Cambridge; Balliol Coll., Oxford. Asst Prof. of Classics, Cornell Univ., 1967–69; Dyson Res. Fellow in Greek Culture, Balliol Coll., Oxford, 1970–72; Cambridge University: Lectr in Classics, 1972–89; Reader in Ancient Philosophy, 1989–98; Dir of Research, Faculty of Classics, 2009–11; Mem., Gen. Bd, 1991–94 and 1999–2003; Chm. Council, Sch. of Arts and Humanities, 1993–94; Chm. Faculty Bd of Classics, 1997–98, 2009–10; Mem., Univ. Council, 1997–2003; Chm., Liby Syndicate, 1998–2003; St John's College: Praelector, 1975–76, 1977–80, 2006–11; Dean, 1979–82; Tutor, 1982–89; Pres., 1991–95; Fellows' Steward, 2014–. Chm., Benchmarking Gp for Classics and Ancient History, QAA, 1999–2000. Editor, Phronesis, 1987–92. Hon. Sec., Classical Assoc., 1989–2003 (Pres., 2006–07); Pres., Soc. for Promotion of Hellenic Studies, 2008–11. Carlyle Lectr, Univ. of Oxford, 2012; J. H. Gray Lectr, Univ. of Cambridge, 2015. Chm. Council, British Sch. at Athens, 2010–. Hon. Citizen, Rhodes, 1992. *Publications:* (ed jtly) Articles on Aristotle, 4 vols, 1975–79; (ed jtly) Doubt and Dogmatism, 1980; An Essay on Anaxagoras, 1980; (ed with M. Nussbaum) Language and Logos, 1982; (ed jtly) Science and Speculation, 1982; (with G. S. Kirk and J. E. Raven) The Presocratic Philosophers, 2nd edn, 1983; (ed with G. Striker) The Norms of Nature, 1986; The Stoic Idea of the City, 1991; (ed with A. Laks) Justice and Generosity, 1995; Saving the City, 1999; (ed jtly) The Cambridge History of Hellenistic Philosophy, 1999; (ed with C. J. Rowe) The Cambridge History of Greek and Roman Political Thought, 2000; Plato: political philosophy, 2006; (ed with T. Griffith) Plato: Gorgias, Menexenus, Protagoras, 2010; (ed) Aristotle, Plato and Pythagoreanism in the First Century BC, 2013. *Address:* St John's College, Cambridge CB2 1TP. *T:* (01223) 338644.

SCHOFIELD, Michael, CBE 1999; Chairman, Dorset Community NHS Trust, 1996–2001; *b* 30 Jan. 1941; *s* of Edward Ronald Schofield and Edna Schofield (*née* Davies); *m* 1st, 1971, Patricia Ann Connell (marr. diss. 1982); two *s*; 2nd, 1989, Angela Rosemary Tym. *Educ:* Manchester Grammar Sch.; Exeter Coll., Oxford (BA Mod. Hist. 1962); Manchester Univ. (Dip. Social Admin). Asst House Gov., General Infirmary, Leeds, 1969–72; Asst Sec., United Liverpool Hosps, 1972–74; Dep. Dist Administrator, Liverpool Central and Southern NHS Dist, 1974–76; Area Administrator, 1976–86, and Chief Exec., 1985–86, Rochdale HA; Dir, Health Services Mgt Unit, Univ. of Manchester, 1987–95; Chm., Bradford Community NHS Trust, 1992–96. Vis. Prof., Bournemouth Univ., 1999–2007. Mem., EOC, 1997–2000. Chm., Nat. Assoc. of Health Authorities and Trusts, 1995–97. Pres., IHSM, 1990–91; Mem. Council, RPSGB, 1999–2007. *Publications:* (jtly) The Future Healthcare Workforce, First Report, 1996, Second Report, 1999, Final Report, 2002. *Recreations:* golf, music, gardening. *Address:* 8 Gravel Lane, Charlton Marshall, Blandford Forum, Dorset DT11 9NS. *T:* (01258) 450588. *Clubs:* Ashley Wood Golf, Ferndown Golf (Dorset).

SCHOFIELD, Naomi Wendy; *see* Climer, N. W.

SCHOFIELD, Neill. DoE, 1970–78; Dept of Energy, 1978–82; Department of Employment, later Department for Education and Employment, 1982–96: Director: Business and Enterprise, 1990–92; Quality Assurance, 1992–93; Training, Infrastructure and Employers Div., 1994–96. *Recreations:* walking, German language, history and culture, politics.

SCHOFIELD, Peter Hugh Gordon; Director General, Neighbourhoods Group, Department for Communities and Local Government, since 2012; *b* Redhill, 27 April 1969; *s* of John Michael Stuart Schofield and Bridget Merrilyn Schofield; *m* 2001, Sarah-Louise Prime; two *s* one *d*. *Educ:* Whitgift Sch.; Gonville and Caius Coll., Cambridge (BA 1991; MA 1994). HM Treasury: Public Enterprises Team, 1991–93; Educn Team, 1993–94; Privatisation Team, 1994–96; Private Sec. to Chief Sec., 1996–98; Hd of Public Enterprises, 1998–2002; Investment Exec., London Buy-out Team, 3i Gp plc, 2002–04 (on secondment); Dir, Shareholder Exec., 2004–08 (Mem. Bd, 2009–12); Dir, Enterprise and Growth Unit, HM Treasury, 2008–12. Non-executive Director: Partnerships UK, 2006–15; Local Partnerships, 2011–. *Address:* Department for Communities and Local Government, 2 Marsham Street, SW1P 4DF. *T:* 0303 444 2747.

SCHOFIELD, Dr Roger Snowden, LittD; FRHistS; FBA 1988; FSS; Senior Research Associate, Cambridge Group for the History of Population and Social Structure, Economic and Social Research Council, 1994–98 (Director, 1974–94); Fellow of Clare College, Cambridge, since 1969; *b* 26 Aug. 1937; *s* of Ronald Snowden Schofield and Muriel Grace Braime; *m*; one *d*. *Educ:* Leighton Park Sch., Reading; Clare Coll., Cambridge (BA (History); PhD 1963); LittD Cantab 2005. FRHistS 1970; FSS 1987. Hon. Reader in Historical Demography, Univ. of Cambridge, 1991–98. Vis. Prof., Div. of Humanities and Social Scis, CIT, 1992–94. Member: Computing Cttee, SSRC, 1970–75; Stats Cttee, SSRC, 1974–78; Software Provision Cttee, UK Computer Bd, 1977–79. Mem., Population Investigation Cttee, 1976–97 (Treas., 1981–85; Pres., 1982–87); British Society for Population Studies: Mem., Council, 1979–87; Treas., 1981–85; Pres., 1985–87. *Publications:* (with E. A. Wrigley) The Population History of England 1541–1871: a reconstruction, 1981, repr. with introd. essay, 1993; (ed with John Walter) Famine, Disease, and the Social Order in Early Modern Society, 1989; (jtly) English Population History from Family Reconstitution 1580–1837, 1997; Taxation under the early Tudors, 2004; contrib. to Population Studies, Jl of Interdisciplinary Hist., Jl of Family Hist. *Address:* Clare College, Cambridge CB2 1TL. *T:* (01223) 333189.

SCHOLAR, Sir Michael (Charles), KCB 1999 (CB 1991); President, St John's College, Oxford, 2001–12; Pro-Vice-Chancellor, University of Oxford, 2005–12; *b* 3 Jan. 1942; *s* of Richard Herbert Scholar and Mary Blodwen Scholar; *m* 1964, Angela Mary (*née* Sweet); three *s* (one *d* decd). *Educ:* St Olave's Grammar School, Bermondsey; St John's College, Cambridge (PhD, MA; Hon. Fellow, 1999). ARCO. Teaching asst, Univ. of California at Berkeley, 1964–65; Loeb Fellow, Harvard Univ., 1967; Asst Lectr in Philosophy, Leicester Univ., 1968; Fellow, St John's College, Cambridge, 1969; HM Treasury, 1969; Private Sec. to Chief Sec., 1974–76; Barclays Bank International, 1979–81; Private Sec. to Prime Minister, 1981–83; Under Secretary, HM Treasury, 1983–87, Dep. Sec., 1987–93; Permanent Secretary: Welsh Office, 1993–96; DTI, 1996–2001. Chm., UK Statistics Authy, 2008–12. Non-exec. Dir, Legal & Gen. Investment Mgt (Hldgs), 2002–07. Chm., Civil Service Sports Council, 1998–2001 (Chm., Staff Pension Fund, 2006–12); Mem., Council of Mgt, NIESR, 2001–05. Chm., Benton Fletcher Trust, 2004–11. Fellow: Univ. of Wales, Aberystwyth, 1996; Cardiff Univ., 2003. Freeman: Merchant Taylors' Co., 2012; City of London, 2013. Hon. Dr Glamorgan, 1999. *Recreations:* playing the piano and organ, making long journeys by foot. *Address:* 9 Stanley Road, Oxford OX4 1QY.

See also T. W. Scholar.

SCHOLAR, Thomas Whinfield; Prime Minister's Adviser on European and Global Issues, since 2013; *b* 17 Dec. 1968; *s* of Sir Michael Charles Scholar, *qv*. *Educ:* Trinity Hall, Cambridge (MA); LSE (MSc). HM Treasury, 1992–2007: Principal Private Sec. to Chancellor of the Exchequer, 1997–2001; UK Exec. Dir, IMF and World Bank, and Minister (Econ.), British Embassy, Washington, 2001–07; Chief of Staff and Principal Private Sec. to the Prime Minister, 2007–08; Man. Dir, Internat. and Finance Directorate, 2008–09, Second Perm. Sec., 2009–13, HM Treasury. *Address:* Cabinet Office, 70 Whitehall, SW1A 2AS.

SCHOLEFIELD, Susan Margaret, CMG 1999; JP; Secretary and Chief Legal Officer, London School of Economics and Political Science, since 2012; Chairman, Competition Service, since 2013; *b* 9 May 1955; *d* of John and Millicent Scholefield; *m* 1977 (marr. diss. 1981); one *s*. *Educ:* Blackheath High Sch.; Somerville Coll., Oxford (MA); Univ. of Calif, Berkeley (MA). Joined MoD, 1981; on secondment to Ecole Nationale d'Admin, Paris, 1985–86; Principal, MoD, 1986–92 (Private Sec. to Chief of Defence Procurement, 1990–92); Asst Sec., Efficiency Unit, Cabinet Office (on secondment), 1992–95; Head, Balkans Secretariat, MoD, 1995–98; Asst Sec., NI Office (on secondment), 1998–2000; Under Sec., 2000, Finance and Exec. Dir, 2000–02, Defence Procurement Agency, MoD; Head, Civil Contingencies Secretariat, Cabinet Office (on secondment), 2002–04; Comd Sec., Permt Jt HQ, Northwood, MoD, 2004–07; Dir Gen. for Equalities, 2007, for Cohesion and Resilience, 2007–08, DCLG; Dir Gen. for HR and Corporate Services, MoD, 2008–12. JP Kent, 2014. *Recreations:* reading, music, theatre, gardening. *Address:* c/o Competition Service, Victoria House, Bloomsbury Place, WC1A 2EB.

SCHOLES, Hon. Gordon Glen Denton, AO 1993; MHR for Corio (Victoria), Australia, 1967–93; *b* 7 June 1931; *s* of Glen Scholes and Mary Scholes; *m* 1957, Della Kathleen Robinson; two *d*. *Educ:* various schs. Loco-engine driver, Victorian Railways, 1949–67. Councillor, Geelong City, 1965–67; Pres., Geelong Trades Hall Council, 1965–66. House of Representatives: Chm. cttees, 1973–75; Speaker, 1975–76; Shadow Minister for Defence, 1977–83; Minister for Defence, 1983–84; Minister for Territories, 1984–87. Amateur Boxing Champion (Heavyweight), Vic, 1949. *Recreations:* golf, reading. *Address:* 20 Stephen Street, Newtown, Vic 3220, Australia.

SCHOLES, Mary Elizabeth, (Mrs A. I. M. Haggart), OBE 1983; SRN; Chief Area Nursing Officer, Tayside Health Board, 1973–83; *b* 8 April 1924; *d* of late John Neville Carpenter Scholes and Margaret Elizabeth (*née* Hines); *m* 1983, Most Rev. Alastair Iain Macdonald Haggart (*d* 1998). *Educ:* Wyggeston Grammar Sch. for Girls, Leicester; Leicester Royal Infirmary and Children's Hosp. (SRN 1946); Guy's Hosp., London (CMB Pt I Cert. 1947); Royal Coll. of Nursing, London (Nursing Admin (Hosp.) Cert. 1962). Leicester Royal Infirmary and Children's Hospital: Staff Nurse, 1947–48; Night Sister, 1948–50; Ward Sister, 1950–56; Night Supt, 1956–58; Asst Matron, 1958–61; Asst Matron, Memorial/Brook Gen. Hosp., London, 1962–64; Matron, Dundee Royal Infirm. and Matron Designate, Ninewells Hosp., Dundee, 1964–68; Chief Nursing Officer, Bd of Mgt for Dundee Gen. Hosps and Bd of Mgt for Ninewells and Associated Hosps, 1968–73. Pres., Scottish Assoc. of Nurse Administrators, 1973–77. Member: Scottish Bd, Royal Coll. of Nursing, 1965–70; Gen. Nursing Council for Scotland, 1966–70, 1979–; Standing Nursing and Midwifery Cttee, Scotland, 1971–74 (Vice-Chm., 1973–74); UK Central Council for Nursing, Midwifery and Health Visiting, 1980–84; Mgt Cttee, State Hosp., Carstairs, 1983–92; Scottish Hosp. Endowments Res. Trust, 1986–96; Chm., Scottish National Bd for Nursing, Midwifery and Health Visiting, 1980–84. *Recreations:* travel, music. *Address:* 14/2 St Margaret's Place, Edinburgh EH9 1AY. *Club:* Royal Over-Seas League.

SCHOLES, Prof. Myron Samuel, PhD; Chairman, Platinum Grove Asset Management (formerly Oak Hill Platinum Partners), 1999–2009; Frank E. Buck Professor of Finance, Graduate Business School, Stanford University, 1983–95, now Emeritus; *b* 1 July 1941; *m*; two *d*; *m* 1998, Jan Blaustein. *Educ:* McMaster Univ.; Univ. of Chicago. Instr, Univ. of Chicago Business Sch., 1967–68; Asst Prof., 1968–72, Associate Prof., 1972–73, MIT Mgt Sch.; University of Chicago: Associate Prof., 1973–75; Prof., 1975–79; Dir, Center for Res. in Security Prices, 1975–81; Edward Eagle Brown Prof. of Finance, 1979–82; Prof. of Law,

1983–87, and Sen. Res. Fellow, Hoover Inst., 1988–93, Stanford Univ. Man. Dir, Salomon Bros, 1991–93; Partner, Long-Term Capital Management, 1994–98; Man. Partner, Oak Hill Capital Mgt, 1999–2005; Chm., Bd of Economic Advrs, Sterling Stamos Capital Mgt. (Jtly) Nobel Prize for Economics, 1997. *Publications:* (jtly) Taxes and Business Strategy: a planning approach, 1992.

SCHOLEY, Sir David (Gerald), Kt 1987; CBE 1976; Senior Advisor, UBS Investment Bank (formerly SBC Warburg, then Warburg Dillon Read, later UBS Warburg), since 1997; Chairman, UBS Pension Trustee Company, since 2004; *b* 28 June 1935; *s* of Dudley and Lois Scholey; *m* 1960, Alexandra Beatrix, *d* of Hon. George and Fiorenza Drew, Canada; one *s* one *d. Educ:* Wellington Coll., Berks; Christ Church, Oxford (Hon. Student, 2003). Nat Service, RAC, 9th Queen's Royal Lancers, 1953–55; TA Yorks Dragoons, 1955–57; 3/4 CLY (Sharpshooters), 1957–61; Metropolitan Special Constabulary (Thames Div.), 1961–65. Thompson Graham & Co. (Lloyd's brokers), 1956–58; Dale & Co. (Insce brokers), Canada, 1958–59; Guinness Mahon & Co., 1959–64; joined S. G. Warburg & Co., 1965, Dir, 1967–95, Dep. Chm., 1977, Jt Chm., 1980–84, Chm., 1985–95; Chm., SBC Warburg, July–Nov. 1995; Sen. Advr, IFC, Washington, 1996–2005. Director: Mercury Securities, 1969–86 (Chm., 1984–86); Orion Insurance Co., 1963–87; Stewart Wrightson Holdings Ltd, 1972–81; Union Discount Co. of London, 1976–81; Bank of England, 1981–98; British Telecom, 1986–94; Chubb Corp. (USA), 1991–2008; General Electric Co., 1992–95; J. Sainsbury, 1996–2000; Vodafone Group, 1998–2005; Close Bros, 1999–2006 (Chm., 1999–2006); G3 Good Governance Gp Ltd, 2012–13; Cranemere Gp, 2014–; Anglo-American: non-exec. Dir, 1999–2005; Member: Remuneration Cttee, 1999–2002 (Chm., 1999–2000); Nomination Cttee, 1999–2005; Safety and Sustainable Develt Cttee, 2003–05; Advisor: Vice Chief of Defence Staff, MoD, 1997–2001; Capgemini Financial Services UK, 2005–10; Longreach Gp, 2006–; MDM Bank (Moscow), 2008–12; Senior Adviser: FSA, 2010–13; Good Governance Gp G3, 2013–. Mem., Export Guarantees Adv. Council, 1970–75 (Dep. Chm. 1974–75); Chm., Construction Exports Adv. Bd, 1975–78; Member: Inst. Internat. d'Etudes Bancaires, 1976–94 (Pres., 1988); Cttee on Finance for Industry, NEDO, 1980–87; Council, IISS, 1984–93 (Hon. Treas., 1984–90); Industry and Commerce Gp, 1989–95, Lord Mayor's Appeal Cttee, 2002–03, SCF; President's Cttee, BITC, 1988–91; Ford Foundn Adv. Gp on UN Financing, 1992–93; London First, 1993–96; Bd of Banking Supervision, 1996–98; Mitsubishi Internat. Adv. Cttee, 2001–07; Sultanate of Oman Financial Adv. Gp, 2002–06; Fitch Internat. Services Adv. Cttee, 2002–07; Develt Bd, Christ Church, Oxford, 2002–15. Dir, INSEAD, 1989–2005 (Chairman: UK Council, 1994–97; Internat. Council, 1995–2003 (Hon. Chm., 2005); Hon. Alumnus, 2000). Gov., BBC, 1994–2000; Dir, LSO, 2012– (Mem. Adv. Council, 1998–2004); Advisor: BBC Philharmonic Orch., 2006–13; Royal Opera House Muscat, 2011–. Trustee: Glyndebourne Arts Trust, 1989–2002; Nat. Portrait Gallery, 1992–2005 (Chm., 2001–05). Governor: Wellington Coll., 1978–88, 1996–2004 (Vice-Pres., 1998–2004); NIESR, 1984–2014; LSE, 1993–96. FRSA. Dist. Friend of Oxford Univ., 2011. Hon. DLitt London Guildhall, 1993; Hon. DSc UMIST, 1999. *Address:* (office) 1 Finsbury Avenue, EC2M 2PP.

SCHOLEY, Dr Keith Douglas; Director: Wild Horizons Ltd, since 2008; Big Cat Ltd, since 2008; Silverback Films Ltd, since 2013; *b* 24 June 1957; *s* of Douglas and Jeannie Scholey; *m* 1985, Elizabeth Sara Potter; two *s. Educ:* Reed's Sch., Surrey; Univ. of Bristol (BSc Hons; PhD 1982). Postgrad. res., Bristol Univ., 1978–81; joined BBC, 1982: researcher, 1982–85; TV asst producer, 1985–88; TV producer, 1989–93; editor, TV series, Wildlife on One and Wildlife specials, 1993–98; Head, Natural Hist. Unit, 1998–2002; Controller: Specialist Factual, 2002–06; Factual Production, 2006; Controller, Content Prodn and Dep. Chief Creative Officer, BBC Vision Studios, 2006–08. Hon. DSc Bristol, 2001. *Recreations:* flying (private pilot's licence), scuba diving, sailing, photography. *Address:* 59 Cotham Hill, Cotham, Bristol BS6 6JR.

SCHOLL, Andreas; countertenor; *b* Germany, 1967. *Educ:* Schola Cantorum Basiliensis, Switzerland (Dip. in Ancient Music). Former chorister, Kiedricher Chorbuben, Germany. Début internat. recital, Théâtre de Grévin, Paris, 1993; opera début in Handel's Rodelinda, Glyndebourne, 1998; appears regularly in recitals and concerts at all major European venues, and in N America. Teacher, Schola Cantorum Basiliensis, 2000–. Composes and records pop music; prizewinning recordings include works by Vivaldi and Caldara, and English folk and lute songs. *Address:* c/o HarrisonParrott Ltd, 5–6 Albion Court, Albion Place, W6 0QT.

SCHOLL, Prof. Anthony James, DPhil; Kuwait Professor of Number Theory and Algebra, University of Cambridge, since 2001; *b* 18 Dec. 1955; *s* of late William Howard Scholl and Barbara Russell Beilby; *m* 1st, 1980, Caroline Somerville-Large (marr. diss. 2000); three *s*; 2nd, 2002, Gülsin Onay. *Educ:* Worth Sch., Sussex; Christ Church, Oxford (MA, MSc; DPhil 1980). University of Oxford: SRC Res. Fellow, 1980–81; Jun. Lectr, 1981–84; University of Durham: Lectr, 1984–89; Prof. of Pure Mathematics, 1989–2001. Mem., Inst. for Advanced Study, Princeton, 1989–90; Prof. Associé, Univ. Paris-Sud, 1992; Leverhulme Trust Res. Fellow, 2001–02. *Recreation:* music (listening, playing and composing). *Address:* Department of Pure Mathematics and Mathematical Statistics, Centre for Mathematical Sciences, Wilberforce Road, Cambridge CB3 0WB. *T:* (01223) 765889. *E:* a.j.scholl@dpmms.cam.ac.uk.

SCHOLTE, Nicholas Paul; Chief Executive, NHS Business Services Authority, since 2006; *b* 6 May 1959; *s* of Christiaan and Sylvia Joyce Scholte; one *s* one *d* by Iris Esters (*d* 2003); *m* 2006, Claire Louise Emmerson, BEM. *Educ:* Chesterfield Grammar Sch.; Manchester Univ. (BA Hons Politics). Law Society: Exec. Officer, 1981–85; Sen. Exec. Officer, 1985–86; Finance Manager, 1986–89; Legal Aid Board: Gp Manager (NE), 1990–96; Business Systems Dir, 1996–99; Chief Exec., Prescription Pricing Authy, 1999–2006. Non-exec. Dir, Supporta plc, 2005–10. *Recreations:* sailing, ballet, literature, football. *Address:* NHS Business Services Authority, Stella House, Goldcrest Way, Newburn Riverside, Newcastle upon Tyne NE15 8NY. *T:* (0191) 203 5209.

SCHOLZ, Prof. Dr Rupert; Professor of Public Law, Institut für Politik und öffentliches Recht, University of Munich, 1981–2005, now Emeritus; Of Counsel, Gleiss Lutz, since 2005; *b* 23 May 1937; *s* of Ernst and Gisela Scholz (*née* Merdas); *m* 1971, Dr Helga Scholz-Hoppe. *Educ:* Abitur, Berlin; studied law and economics, Berlin and Heidelberg; Dr Jur., Univ. of Munich. Prof., Univ. of Munich, taught in Munich, Berlin, Regensburg, Augsburg; Public Law Chair, Berlin and Munich, 1978. Senator of Justice, Land Berlin, 1981; Acting Senator for Federal Affairs; Mem., Bundesrat, 1982; Mem., N Atlantic Assembly, 1982; Senator for Federal Affairs, Land Berlin, 1983; MHR, Berlin, and Senator for Justice and Federal Affairs, 1985; Federal Minister of Defence, FRG, 1988–89; Mem. (CDU), German Bundestag, 1990–2002. *Publications:* numerous papers in jurisp., German policy, foreign policy, economic policy. *Address:* Gleiss Lutz, Friedrichstrasse 71, 10112 Berlin, Germany.

SCHÖNBERGER, Viktor M.; *see* Mayer-Schönberger.

SCHOPPER, Prof. Herwig Franz; Professor of Physics, University of Hamburg, 1973–89, now Emeritus; *b* 28 Feb. 1924; *s* of Franz Schopper and Margarete Hartmann; *m* 1949, Dora Klara Ingeborg (*née* Stieler); one *s* one *d. Educ:* Univ. of Hamburg. Dip. Phys. 1949, Dr rer. nat. 1951. Asst Prof. and Univ. Lectr, Univ. of Erlangen, 1954–57; Prof., Univ. of Mainz, 1957–60; Prof., Univ. of Karlsruhe and Dir of Inst. for Nuclear Physics, 1961–73; Chm., Scientific Council, Kerforschungszentrum, Karlsruhe, 1967–69; Chm., Deutsches Elektronen Synchrotron particle physics Lab., Hamburg, 1973–80; European Organisation for Nuclear Research (CERN): Res. Associate, 1966–67; Head, Dept of particle physics and Mem., Directorate for experimental prog., 1970–73; Chm., Intersecting Storage Ring Cttee, 1973–76; Mem., Sci. Policy Cttee, 1979–80; Dir-Gen., 1981–88. Chm., Assoc. of German Nat. Research Centres, 1978–80; Mem., Scientific Council, IN2P3, Paris; Advr, UNESCO, 1994–2009; Chm., Scientific Bd, Internat. Basic Sci. Prog., UNESCO, 2003–12. President: German Physical Soc., 1992–94; European Physical Soc., 1995–97; Internat. Council, Centre of Res. for Synchrotron Radiation in Jordan, 1999–2008; Council, Synchrotron-light for Exptl Sci. and Applications in Middle East, 2003–08. Member: Akad. der Wissenschaften Leopoldina, Halle; Joachim Jungius Gesellschaft, Hamburg; Sudetendeutsche Akad. der Wissenschaft, 1979; Acad. Scientiarium et Artium, Vienna, 1993; Portuguese Acad. of Scis; Bd of Trustees, Cyprus Inst., 2002– (Chm., Scientific Council, 2002–); MAE 1992; Corresp. Mem., Bavarian Acad. of Scis, 1981; Hon. Member: Hungarian Acad. of Scis, 1995; Eur. Physical Soc., 2011; Deutsche Physikalische Gesellschaft, 2013. Fellow, APS, 2006; Foreign FInstP 1996. Dr *hc*: Univ. of Erlangen, 1982; Univ. of Moscow, 1989; Univ. of Geneva, 1989; Univ. of London, 1989; Jt Inst. of Nuclear Res., Dubna, 1998; Inst. of High Energy Physics, Russia, 1999. Physics Award, Göttinger Akad. der Wissenschaft, 1957; Carus Medal, Akad. Leopoldina, 1958; Ritter von Gerstner Medal, 1978; Sudetendeutscher Kulturpreis, 1984; Golden Plate Award, Amer. Acad. of Achievement, 1984; Gold Medal, Weizmann Inst., 1987; Wilhelm Exner Medal, Gewerbeverein, Austria, 1991; Purkyne Meml Medal, Czech Acad. of Scis, 1994; 650 Years Jubilee Medal, Charles Univ., Prague, 1998; Tate Medal, Amer. Inst. Physics, 2004; Einstein Gold Medal, UNESCO, 2004; Bohr Gold Medal, UNESCO-Denmark, 2005; Medal of Honour, Portuguese Minister for Higher Educn and Res., 2009; Medal of Honour, Lanskroun, Czech Republic, 2010; Physics Medal, First Grade, Czech Physical Soc., 2010. Grosses Bundesverdienstkreuz (FRG), 1989; Friendship Order of Russian Pres., 1996; Grand Cordon, Order of Independence (Jordan), 2003; Grosses Verdienstkreuz (Cyprus), 2012; Goldene Ehrenmedal, Deutsches Elektronen-Synchrotron, 2013. Editor, data on Nuclear and Particle Physics, Elementary Particles, Nuclei and Atoms in Springer Materials: The Landoldt Börnstein Database. *Publications:* Weak Interactions and Nuclear Beta Decay, 1966; (ed) Investigation of Nuclear Structure by Scattering Processes, 1975; Matter—Antimatter, 1989; (ed) Advances of Accelerator Physics and Technologies, 1993; (ed with M. Jacob) Large Facilities in Physics, 1995; LEP - The Lord of the Collider Rings at CERN, 2009; (ed with L. Di Lella) 60 Years of Experiments and Discoveries at CERN, 2015; papers on elementary particle physics, high energy accelerators, relation of science and society. *Recreations:* music, gardening. *Address:* c/o CERN, 1211 Geneva 23, Switzerland. *T:* (22) 7675350.

SCHORI, Most Rev. Katharine J.; *see* Jefferts Schori.

SCHREIBER, family name of **Baron Marlesford**.

SCHREMPP, Jürgen E.; Chairman, Board of Management, DaimlerChrysler AG, 2000–05 (Joint Chairman, 1998–2000); *b* 15 Sept. 1944; *m* 2000, Lydia Deininger; one *s* one *d*, and two *s* from previous marriage. *Educ:* Univ. for Applied Scis, Offenburg. Apprentice motor mechanic, Mercedes-Benz Dealership, Freiburg, 1961–64; joined Daimler-Benz AG, 1967; Mercedes-Benz of South Africa: Manager, Service Div., 1974–80; Mem., Bd of Mgt, 1980–82, 1984–87; Vice Pres., 1984; Pres., 1985–87, now non-exec. Chm.; Pres., Euclid Inc., USA (subsidiary of Daimler-Benz AG), 1982–84; Daimler-Benz Board of Management: Dep. Mem., 1987–89; Mem., 1989–95; Chm., 1998; Pres. and CEO, Daimler-Benz Aerospace AG, 1989–95. Non-executive Director: Sasol Ltd, 1997– (Lead Ind. Dir, 2008–); Vodafone Gp plc, 2000; Cie Financière Richemont SA, 2003–; Jonah Capital (Pty) Ltd. Partner, Cie Financière Rupert, 2006–. Mem., President's Internat. Investment Council, SA. Chm., Southern Africa Initiative of German Business. Cross, Order of Merit (Germany); Order of Good Hope (SA). *Address:* PO Box 200651, 80006 Munich, Germany.

SCHREUDER, Prof. Deryck Marshall, DPhil; FAHA; FRHistS; historian and educationalist; Emeritus Professor, Macquarie University and University of Western Sydney, 1998, and University of Western Australia, 2004; Visiting Professor, Faculty of Education and Social Work (formerly College of Humanities and Social Sciences), University of Sydney, since 2004; Adjunct Professor, Australian National University, since 2005; *b* 19 Jan. 1942; *s* of Pieter Jurian and Jean Margaret Schreuder; *m* 1965, Patricia Anne Pote; three *s. Educ:* Llewellin High Sch., Zambia; Univ. of Rhodes, S Africa (BA Hons; Beit Meml Hist. Prize, 1963); DPhil Oxon 1964. FAHA 1985; FRHistS 1988. Rhodes Schol. from Central Africa, 1964–67; Kennedy Fellow of Modern Hist., New Coll., Oxford, 1967–69; Prof. of Hist., and Hd of Dept, Trent Univ., Ontario, 1970–79; Challis Prof. of Hist., Univ. of Sydney, 1980–93 (Dep. Chm., Acad. Bd, 1984–85); on secondment as Associate Dir, Humanities Res. Centre, ANU, 1992–93; Dep. Vice-Chancellor (Acad.), Macquarie Univ., 1993–95; Vice-Chancellor, Univ. of Western Sydney, 1995–98; Vice-Chancellor, and Principal, subseq. Pres., Univ. of WA, 1998–2004. Res. Fellow, Res. Sch. of Social Scis, ANU, 1976–77. Pres., Aust. Vice-Chancellors' Cttee, 2002–03; Chm., Aust. Univs Quality Agency, 2004–09; Member: Aust. Res. Grants Cttee, 1986–92; Commn on Commonwealth Studies, 1995–97; Dir, Aust. Scholarship Foundn, 2008–. President: Aust. Hist. Assoc., 1985–86; Aust. Acad. Humanities, 1992–95 (Vice-Pres., 1989–90). Associate Ed., Oxford DNB, 1995–2000. Hon. LLD Rhodes, 2004. Centenary Medal (Australia), 2001. *Publications:* Gladstone and Kruger: Liberal Government and Colonial Home Rule (1880–85), 1969; The Scramble for Southern Africa (1877–95): the politics of partition reappraisal, 1981, 2nd edn 2010; (jtly) The Rise of Colonial Nationalism: Australia, New Zealand, Canada and South Africa first assert their nationality 1880–1914, 1988; (ed jtly) The Commonwealth and Australia in World Affairs, 1990; (ed jtly) History and Social Change: the G. A. Wood Memorial Lectures 1949–91, 1991; (ed) Imperialisms, 1991; A Letter from Sydney: history and the post-Colonial society (J. M. Ward Memorial Lecture), 1991; (ed jtly) History at Sydney, 1992; (ed) The Humanities and the Creative Nation, 1995; (ed jtly) Africa Today, 1997; (ed jtly) The State and the People: Australian federation 1870–1901, 2002; (ed jtly) Sir Graham Bower's Secret History of the Jameson Raid and the South African Crisis 1895–1902, 2002; Who Killed Newman?: the ideal of a university and its enemies, 2007; (ed jtly) Australia's Empire, 2008, in The Oxford History of the British Empire Companion Series; (ed) Universities for a New World: making a global network in higher education, 1913–2013, 2013; chapters in major scholarly volumes incl. Cambridge History of Australia, 2014. *Recreations:* writing history, travel, voluntary work in the community, bike riding. *Address:* Faculty of Education and Social Work, University of Sydney, Sydney, NSW 2006, Australia.

SCHREYER, Rt Hon. Edward Richard, CC 1979; CMM 1979; CD 1979; OM 2000; PC (Can.) 1984; High Commissioner for Canada in Australia, and concurrently Ambassador to Vanuatu, 1984–88; *b* Beausejour, Man, 21 Dec. 1935; *s* of John and Elizabeth Schreyer, a pioneer family of the district; *m* 1960, Lily, *d* of Jacob Schulz, MP; two *s* two *d. Educ:* Beausejour, Manitoba; United Coll., Winnipeg; St John's Coll., Winnipeg, Univ. of Manitoba (BA, BEd, MA). While at university served as 2nd Lieut, COTC, Royal Canadian Armored Corps, 1954–55. Member, Legislative Assembly of Manitoba, 1958; re-elected, 1959 and 1962; MP: for Springfield, 1965; for Selkirk, 1968; chosen as Leader of New Democratic Party in Manitoba, 1969, and resigned seat in House of Commons; MLA for Rossmere and Premier of Manitoba, 1969–77; Minister of: Dominion-Provincial Relns, 1969–77; Hydro, 1971–77; Finance, 1972–74; re-elected MLA, 1977; Governor-Gen. and C-in-C of Canada, 1979–84. Prof. of Political Science and Internat. Relns, St John's Coll., Univ. of Manitoba, 1962–65. Distinguished Vis. Prof., Univ. of Winnipeg, 1989–90; Vis. Prof., Simon Fraser Univ., Vancouver, 1991; Distinguished Fellow, Inst. for Integrated Energy Systems, Univ. of Victoria, 1992–94; Univ. of BC, 1995–96. Director: Perfect Pacific Investments, 1989–; China International Trade and Investment Corp., Canada, 1991–; Saskatchewan Energy Conservation and Develt Authy, 1993–96; Alternate Fuel Systems Inc.

(Calgary), 1994–; Cephalon Oil & Gas Resource Corp. (Calgary), 1994–95. Chancellor, Brandon Univ., 2002–08. Chm., Canadian Shield Foundn, 1984–; Member: Internat. Assoc. of Energy Economists; CPA; IPU. Hon. LLD: Manitoba, 1979; Mount Allison, 1983; McGill, 1984; Simon Fraser, 1984; Lakehead, 1985; Hon. Dr Sci. Sociale Ottawa, 1980. *Recreations:* reading, golf, sculpting, woodworking. *Address:* 250 Wellington Center, Unit 401, Winnipeg, MB R3M 0B3, Canada. *T:* (204) 9897580, *Fax:* (204) 9897581. *Clubs:* Rideau (Ottawa); York, Upper Canada (Toronto).

SCHREYER, Michaele, PhD; Member, European Commission, 1999–2004; *b* Cologne, 9 Aug. 1951. *Educ:* Univ. of Cologne (Dip. Econs and Sociology 1976); Univ. of Berlin (PhD 1983). Res. Asst, Inst. for Public Finances and Social Policy, Free Univ. of Berlin, 1977–82; Green Party Advr, Bundestag, 1983–87; Researcher, Inst. for Econ. Res., 1987–88. Mem., Green Party, 1987–; Minister for Urban Develt and Envmtl Protection, State Govt (Senate) of Berlin, 1989–90; Mem., State Parlt of Berlin (Green Party), 1991–99 (Chair, Green Party Gp, 1998–99). Vice-Pres., European Movt, Germany, 2006–. Lectr on European Politics, Free Univ. of Berlin and Univ. of Bonn, 2004–. Mem., Adv. Council, Transparency Internat., Germany, 2005–; Co-Chair, Supervisory Bd, Heinrich Böll Stiftung, Germany, 2009–. Member, Foundation Council: European Univ. Viadrina Frankfurt (Oder), 2008–; Georg-August Univ. Göttingen, 2009–.

SCHRIEFFER, Prof. John Robert, PhD; University Professor, Florida State University, 1992 (Chief Scientist, National High Magnetic Field Laboratory, 1992–2004); University Eminent Scholar Professor, State of Florida University System, 1995; *b* Oak Park, Ill, 31 May 1931; *s* of John Henry Schrieffer and Louise Anderson; *m* 1960, Anne Grete Thomsen (*d* 2013); one *s* two *d. Educ:* MIT (BS); Univ. of Illinois (MS, PhD). Nat. Sci. Foundn Fellow, Univ. of Birmingham, and Niels Bohr Inst. for Theoretical Physics, Copenhagen, 1957–58; Asst Prof., Univ. of Chicago, 1957–59; Asst Prof., Univ. of Illinois, 1959–60, Associate Prof., 1960–62; Univ. of Pennsylvania: Mem. Faculty, 1962–79; Mary Amanda Wood Prof. of Physics, 1964–79; University of California, Santa Barbara: Prof. of Physics, 1980–91; Chancellor's Prof., 1984–91; Dir, Inst. for Theoretical Physics, 1984–89. Guggenheim Fellow, Copenhagen, 1967. Member: Nat. Acad. Scis; Amer. Acad. of Arts and Scis; Amer. Philos. Soc.; Amer. Phys Soc. (Vice-Pres., 1994; Pres.-elect, 1995; Pres., 1996); Danish Royal Acad. Sci.; Acad. of Sci. of USSR, 1989. Hon. ScD: Technische Hochschule, Munich, 1968; Univ. of Geneva, 1968; Univ. of Pennsylvania, 1973; Illinois Univ., 1974; Univ. of Cincinnati, 1977; Hon. DSc Tel-Aviv Univ., 1987. Buckley Prize, Amer. Phys Soc., 1968; Comstock Prize, Nat. Acad. Scis, 1968; (jtly) Nobel Prize for Physics, 1972; John Ericsson Medal, Amer. Soc. of Swedish Engineers, 1976; Nat. Medal of Science, USA, 1985. *Publications:* Theory of Superconductivity, 1964; articles on solid state physics and chemistry. *Recreations:* painting, gardening, wood working. *Address:* NHMFL/FSU, 1800 E Paul Dirac Drive, Tallahassee, FL 32310, USA.

SCHROCK, Prof. Richard Royce, PhD; Frederick G. Keyes Professor of Chemistry, Massachusetts Institute of Technology, since 1989; *b* Berne, Indiana, 4 Jan. 1945; *s* of late Noah J. Schrock and Martha A. Schrock (*nee* Habegger); *m* 1971, Nancy F. Carlson; two *s. Educ:* Mission Bay High Sch.; Univ. of Calif, Riverside (AB 1967); Harvard Univ. (PhD 1971). Postdoctoral Fellow, Univ. of Cambridge, 1971; Res. Chemist, Central Res. and Develt Dept, E. I. duPont de Nemours and Co., Wilmington, Delaware, 1972–75; joined MIT, 1975, Prof., 1980–89. Foreign Mem., Royal Soc., 2008. (Jtly) Nobel Prize for Chemistry, 2005. *Publications:* articles in jls. *Address:* Department of Chemistry, Massachusetts Institute of Technology, 77 Massachusetts Avenue, Cambridge, MA 02139–4307, USA.

SCHRÖDER, Gerhard; Member, Bundestag, 1980–86 and 1998–2005; Chancellor, Federal Republic of Germany, 1998–2005; Chairman, Social Democratic Party, Germany, 1999–2004; *b* Mossenberg, 7 April 1944; *m* 1997, Doris Köpf. *Educ:* Univ. of Göttingen. Apprentice retailer, 1959–61; qualified as lawyer, 1976; in practice, Hannover, 1978–90 and 2005–. Joined SPD, 1963; Mem. for Lower Saxony Landtag, 1986–98; Chm., SPD Gp, 1986–90; Prime Minister, Lower Saxony, 1990–98. Sozialdemokratische Partei Deutschlands: Chm., Young Socialists, Göttingen, 1969–70; Nat. Chm., Young Socialists, 1978–80; Member: Exec. Cttee, Hannover, 1977 (constituency Chm., 1983–93); Party Council, 1979–2005; NEC, 1986–2005; Presiding Council, 1989–2005; Chm., Lower Saxony Br., 1994–98. Advr, Ringier AG, 2005–; Chm., Shareholders' Cttee, Nord Stream AG, 2006–; Mem., Eur. Adv. Council, Rothschild Gp, 2006–; Dir, TNK-BP, 2009–11. Hon. Chairman: German Near and Middle East Assoc.; Emirati-German Friendship Soc. Patron, Gesicht Zeigen. *Publications:* Entscheidungen: mein leben in der politik, 2007; Klare Worte, 2014. *Address:* Deutscher Bundestag, Platz der Republik 1, 11011 Berlin, Germany.

SCHRÖDER, Prof. Martin, PhD, DIC; FRSC; FRSE; Vice President, and Dean, Faculty of Engineering and Physical Sciences, University of Manchester, since 2015; *b* Taplow, Berks, 14 April 1954; *s* of Herman and Edith Schröder; *m* 1985, Dr Leena-Kreet Kore; one *s. Educ:* Univ. of Sheffield (BSc Special Hons in Chem. 1975); Imperial Coll. of Sci., Technol. and Medicine (PhD 1978; DIC). FRSC 1994. Royal Soc./Swiss Nat. Foundn Postdoctoral Fellow, Laboratorium für Organische Chemie, ETH, Zürich, 1978–79; Postdoctoral Res. Asst, Univ. Chem. Labs, Univ. of Cambridge, 1980–82; Department of Chemistry, University of Edinburgh: Sen. Demonstrator, 1982–83; Lectr, 1983–91; Reader in Inorganic Chem., 1991–94; Personal Chair in Inorganic Chem., 1994–95; University of Nottingham: Prof. of Inorganic Chem., 1995–2015; Hd, Sch. of Chem., 1999–2005; Exec. Dean, Faculty of Sci., 2011–15. Vis. Prof., Lash Miller Labs, Univ. of Toronto, 1990; Mellor Vis. Prof., Dept of Chem., Univ. of Dunedin, NZ, 1995; Vis. Prof., Sch. of Chem., Univ. Louis Pasteur, Strasbourg, 2004. Support Res. Fellow, RSE, 1991–92; Leverhulme Trust Sen. Res. Fellow, 2005–06. Member: Rev. Panel for Commonwealth Scholarships, 2001–06; Strategic Adv. Team for EPSRC Chem. Prog., 2002–04; Inorganic and Physical Rev. Panel for Sci. Foundn Ireland, 2003; Sen. Jury, Review Panel, Inst. Universitaire de France, 2011–12, 2014–. Royal Society of Chemistry: Member: Dalton Div., Standing Cttee on Confs, 1997–99 (Chm., 1999–2001); Dalton Council, 1998–2001; Nat. Organising Cttee of Annual Conf., 1999–2002; Chm., Macrocyclic and Supramolecular Chem. Subject Gp, 2000–05. FRSE 1994. Hon. Dr Chem., Tech. Univ. of Tallinn, 2005. Royal Society of Chemistry: Corday Morgan Medal and Prize, 1989; Tilden Lectr and Medal, 2001–02; Award for Chem. of Transition Metals, 2003; Award for Chem. of Noble Metals and their Compounds, 2008; Wolfson Merit Award, Royal Soc., 2005–10. *Publications:* 470 publications, patents and book chapters. *Recreations:* opera, music, travel. *Address:* Faculty of Engineering and Physical Sciences, University of Manchester, Oxford Road, Manchester M13 9PL.

SCHRODER, Dr Timothy Bruno, FSA; freelance lecturer, curator and advisor; *b* Ascot, Berks, 12 Aug. 1953; *s* of John and Joan Schroder; *m* 1987, Ellen Laskey; one *s* three *d. Educ:* St Edward's Sch., Oxford; Christ Church, Oxford (BA Philosophy and Theol.; MA; DLitt 2013). Technical Asst, 1976–80, Dir, Silver Dept, 1981–84, Christie's; Curator, Decorative Arts, Los Angeles Co. Mus. of Art, 1984–89; Dir, Partridge Fine Arts, 1991–96; Keeper, Gilbert Collection, 1996–2000; Consultant Curator, V&A Mus., 2000–09. Chm., Prostate Cancer Res. Centre, 2008–. Chm., Silver Soc., 2011–. Trustee: Silver Trust, 2012–; Wallace Collection, 2013–. Liveryman, Goldsmiths' Co., 1993 (Prime Warden, 2015–16). FSA 1997. *Publications:* English Domestic Silver, 1988; The Gilbert Collection of Gold and Silver, 1988; Renaissance Silver from the Schroder Collection, 2007; (ed) Treasures of the English Church: a thousand years of sacred gold and silver, 2008; British and Continental Gold and Silver in the Ashmolean Museum, 2009; The Zilkha Collection, 2012; contrib. articles to jls incl. Apollo, Burlington Mag., Silver Soc. Jl. *Recreations:* running, punning, Beethoven. *Address:* 32 Steeles Road, NW3 4RE. *T:* 020 7722 5937. *E:* tim@schroder.uk.com. *Club:* Brooks's.

SCHROEDER, Dominic Sebastian; HM Diplomatic Service; Ambassador to Denmark, from Aug. 2016; *b* London, 13 Nov. 1965; *s* of Hermann Schroeder and Isobel Schroeder (*née* Allen); *m* 1997, Susan Caroline Kerr; one *s* one *d. Educ:* Highgate Wood Sch.; St Anne's Coll., Oxford (BA Mod. Hist.). Asst Desk Officer, NATO, FCO, 1988–89; Third, then Second Sec., Kinshasa, 1989–91; Asst Desk Officer, Middle E Peace Process, FCO, 1992–93; Second Sec., UK Mission to the UN, NY, 1993; Sen. Press Officer, News Dept, 1994–96, Hd, Iran Section, 1996–97, FCO; Chargé d'Affaires (temp.), Tehran, 1997; First Sec. and Hd, Commercial Section, Berlin, 1997–2001; Dep. Hd, Eastern Dept, 2001–04, Hd, Common Foreign and Security Policy, 2004–06, FCO; Counsellor, EU/Econ., 2006–10 and Dep. Hd of Mission, 2009–10, Berlin; Hd of Mission, Bratislava, 2011; Hd of Delegation to OSCE (with personal rank of Ambassador), Vienna, 2011–15. *Address:* c/o Foreign and Commonwealth Office, King Charles Street, SW1A 2AH.

SCHUBERT, Sir Sydney, Kt 1985; Chief Executive, Daikyo Group Australia, 1988–2000; *b* 22 March 1928; *s* of Wilhelm F. Schubert and Mary A. Price; *m* 1961, Maureen Kistle (*d* 2005); two *d. Educ:* Univ. of Queensland; Univ. of Durham. Queensland Government: Civil Engr, 1950; Dep. Chief Engr, Main Roads Dept, 1965–69; Chief Engr Dept, 1969–72; Dep. Co-ordinator Gen., 1972–76, Co-ordinator Gen. and Permanent Head, 1982–88, Dir Gen., 1987–88, Premier's Dept. Director: Jupiters, 1988–92 (Dep. Chm., 1990–92); Coffey Internat., 1990–96; APN Hldgs, 1992–; Victoria Hotels Pty Ltd (Christchurch), 1990–; Premier Hotels Pty Ltd (Christchurch), 1990–; Christchurch Casinos Pty Ltd, 1992–. Chancellor, Bond Univ., 1987–89. Mem., Gt Barrier Reef Marine Park Authy, 1978–88; Deputy Chairman: Brisbane Exposition and S Bank Redevelt Authy, 1984–88; Qld Cultural Centre Trust, 1986–88. Member: Bd of Management, Graduate Sch. of Management, Univ. of Queensland, 1985–88; Exec. Council, Australia Japan Assoc. Qld, 1988–90. Eisenhower Fellow, Aust., 1972. FIE(Aust); Hon. Fellow, Aust. Instn of Engrs. DUniv James Cook, 2006. Queensland Greats Award, 2012. *Recreation:* golf. *Address:* 118 Crescent Road, Hamilton, Brisbane, Qld 4007, Australia. *Clubs:* Queensland, Royal Queensland Golf.

SCHÜELEIN-STEEL, Danielle Fernande Dominique, (Danielle Steel); writer; *b* 14 Aug. 1947; *d* of John and Norma Schüelein-Steel; *m* Claude-Eric Lazard; one *d*; *m* John Traina (marr. diss.); one *s* four *d* (and one *s* decd). *Educ:* Lycée Français, NYC; Parsons Sch. of Design, NY; New York Univ. Vice-Pres. of Public Relations and New Business, Supergirls Ltd, 1968–71; copywriter, Grey Advertising Agency, 1973–74. Officier, Ordre des Arts et des Lettres (France), 2002. *Publications: fiction:* Going Home, 1973; Passion's Promise, 1977; Now and Forever, 1978; The Promise, 1978; Season of Passion, 1980; Summer's End, 1980; The Ring, 1980; To Love Again, 1981; Palomino, 1981; Loving, 1981; Remembrance, 1981; A Perfect Stranger, 1982; Once in a Lifetime, 1982; Crossings, 1982; Changes, 1983; Thurston House, 1983; Full Circle, 1984; Secrets, 1985; Family Album, 1985; Wanderlust, 1986; Fine Things, 1987; Kaleidoscope, 1987; Zoya, 1988; Star, 1989; Daddy, 1989; Message from Nam, 1990; Heartbeat, 1991; No Greater Love, 1991; Jewels, 1992; Mixed Blessings, 1992; Vanished, 1993; Accident, 1994; The Gift, 1994; Wings, 1994; Lightning, 1995; Five Days in Paris, 1995; Malice, 1996; Silent Honor, 1996; The Ranch, 1997; The Ghost, 1997; Special Delivery, 1997; The Long Road Home, 1998; The Klone and I, 1998; Mirror Image, 1998; Bittersweet, 1999; Granny Dan, 1999; Irresistible Forces, 1999; The Wedding, 2000; The House on Hope Street, 2000; Journey, 2000; Lone Eagle, 2001; Leap of Faith, 2001; The Kiss, 2002; The Cottage, 2003; Sunset in St Tropez, 2002; Answered Prayers, 2002; Dating Game, 2003; Johnny Angel, 2003; Safe Harbour, 2003; Ransom, 2004; Second Chance, 2004; Echoes, 2004; Impossible, 2005; Miracle, 2005; Toxic Bachelors, 2005; The House, 2006; Coming Out, 2006; HRH, 2006; Sisters, 2007; Bungalow 2, 2007; Amazing Grace, 2007; Rogue, 2008; Honor Thyself, 2008; A Good Woman, 2008; One Day at a Time, 2009; Matters of the Heart, 2009; Southern Lights, 2009; Big Girl, 2010; Family Ties, 2010; Legacy, 2010; 44 Charles Street, 2011; Happy Birthday, 2011; Hotel Vendome, 2011; Betrayal, 2012; Friends Forever, 2012; The Sins of the Mother, 2012; Until the End of Time, 2013; First Sight, 2013; Winners, 2013; Power Play, 2014; Pegasus, 2014; A Perfect Life, 2014; Prodigal Son, 2015; *non-fiction:* (contrib.) Having a Baby, 1984; His Bright Light: the story of Nick Traina, 1998; A Gift of Hope, 2012; Pure Joy, 2013; *poetry:* Love, 1981; several children's books incl. Pretty Minnie in Paris, 2014. *Address:* c/o Morton Janklow and Associates, 1540 Broadway, New York, NY 10036, USA.

SCHULTZ, Prof. Wolfram, MD; FRS 2009; Wellcome Trust Principal Research Fellow, and Professor of Neuroscience, University of Cambridge, since 2001; Fellow, Churchill College, Cambridge, since 2004; *b* 27 Aug. 1944; *s* of Robert and Herta Schultz; *m* 1972, Gerda Baumann; two *s* one *d. Educ:* Heidelberg (MD 1972); Univ. of Fribourg (Habilitation 1981). Postdoctoral work, 1973–77: MPI, Goettingen; NY State Univ., Buffalo, NY; Karolinska Inst., Stockholm; Asst, Associate, then full Prof. of Neurophysiology, Univ. of Fribourg, 1977–2001. Vis. Prof., Tamagawa Univ., Japan, 2001–; Vis. Res. Associate, CIT, 2004–. Sabbaticals: Univ. of Cambridge, 1993; Tokyo Metropolitan Inst. for Neurosci., 1997; Moore Fellow, CIT, Pasadena, 2005. Ellermann Prize, Swiss Socs for Neurology, Neurosurgery and Neuropathology, Bern, 1984; (jtly) Theodore-Ott Prize, Swiss Acad. of Medical Scis, 1997; Golden Brain Award, Minerva Foundn, Berkeley, Calif, 2002; (jtly) Ipsen Prize for Neuronal Plasticity, 2005; Eur. Jl of Neurosci. Award, Fedn of Eur. Neurosci. Socs, 2010; (jtly) Zülch Prize, Gertrud Reemtsma Foundn, 2013. *Publications:* articles in learned jls. *Recreations:* sailing, scuba diving, snowboarding. *Address:* Department of Physiology, Development and Neuroscience, University of Cambridge, Downing Street, Cambridge CB2 3DY. *T:* (01223) 333779. *E:* ws234@cam.ac.uk.

SCHUMACHER, Diana Catherine Brett, OBE 2011; Director, Work Structuring Ltd, since 2002; *b* 8 April 1941; *d* of Clarence Edward Brett Binns and Phyllis Mary Brett Binns; *m* 1966, Christian Schumacher; two *d. Educ:* St Hilda's Coll., Oxford (MA Mod. Hist.). British Council, 1964–66; Internat. Survey Res., Univ. of Chicago, 1969–73; Partner, Schumacher Projects Consultancy, 1979–2002; Co-Founder, Green Books, 1986. Founder Mem. and Trustee, Schumacher Soc., 1978– (Pres., 1991–2000); Advr, Schumacher Coll., 1991–93; Founder Mem., Schumacher Inst., 2005. Member: Exec. Cttee, Green Alliance, 1982–92; Mgt Bd, Centre for Internat. Peacebuilding, 1985–; Founder Member and Trustee: Gandhi Foundn, 1983–98; New Econs Foundn, 1986–98; Founder Member: Envmtl Law Foundn, 1987– (Vice Chm., 1987–95; Life Vice-Pres., 1995–); SPES Forum, 2005–; Trustee: India Develt Gp, 1980–2005; Ecological Action Gp for Europe, 1984– (Vice Pres., 2005–); Themba Trust, 2005–. Patron: UK Social Investment Forum; Green Network; Peace Child Internat.; Tree Aid; Member: PRASEG; Soil Assoc. Gov., St Stephen's C of E and Middle Sch., S Godstone, 1970–90. FRSA. *Publications:* (jtly) Going Solar, 1977, 2nd edn 1979; (jtly) Solar Flatplate Collectors for Developing Countries, 1979; Energy: crisis or opportunity, 1985; Our Human Shelter Within the Global Shelter, 1987; Ten Principles for an Organic Energy Policy, 1992; Small is Manageable: from theory to practice, 2003; Small is Beautiful in the 21st Century: the legacy of E. F. Schumacher, 2011; *contributions to:* Habitat un ambiente per Vivere, 1994; This I Believe, 1997; Cuba Verde, 1999; The Council of Europe as the Conscience of Europe, 1999; Spirituality as a Public Good, 2007; contribs to jls incl. European Business Review, Resurgence, etc. *Recreations:* walking, the arts, organic gardening and food, making incomprehensible lists. *Address:* Church House, Godstone, Surrey RH9 8BW. *Club:* Royal Over-Seas League.

SCHUMACHER, Michael; professional racing driver, 1983–2006 and 2010–12; *b* 3 Jan. 1969; *s* of Rolf and late Elisabeth Schumacher; *m* 1995, Corinna Betsch; one *s* one *d.* Formula 3, 1983–90; European and World Champion, 1990; Formula 1, 1991–2006; Jordan-Ford team, 1991; Benetton-Ford team, 1991–95; Ferrari team, 1996–2006; Mercedes GP,

2010–12; Drivers' World Champion, 1994, 1995, 2000, 2001, 2002, 2003, 2004. *Publications:* (jtly) Formula for Success, 1996; (jtly) Michael Schumacher: driving force, 2003. *Address:* The MS Office, Avenue du Mont-Blanc 14B, 1196 Gland, Switzerland.

SCHÜSSEL, Dr Wolfgang; MP (People's Party), Austria, 1979–2011; Chancellor of Austria, 2000–07; *b* Vienna, 7 June 1945; *m*; two *c*. *Educ:* Vienna Univ. (DJur). Sec., Austrian People's Party, 1968–75; Sec.-Gen., Austrian Econ. Fedn, 1975–89. Minister of Econ. Affairs, Austria, 1989–95; Vice-Chancellor and Minister of Foreign Affairs, 1996–2000. Chm., 1995–2006, Leader, Parly Gp, 2006–08, Austrian People's Party. Mem., Bd of Trustees, Bertelsmann Foundn, 2007–.

SCHWAB, Dr Klaus, Hon. KCMG 2006; Founder and Executive Chairman, World Economic Forum, since 1971; *b* 30 March 1938; *s* of Eugen and Erika Schwab; *m* 1971, Hilde Stoll; one *s* one *d*. *Educ:* Humanistisches Gymnasium, Ravensburg; Swiss Fed. Inst. of Technology (Dip. ing 1962; Dr ing 1966); Univ. of Fribourg (Lic.ès.sc.écon 1963; Dr rer. pol. 1967); John F. Kennedy Sch. of Govt, Harvard (MPA 1967). Experience on shop floor of several cos, 1958–62; Asst to Dir Gen. of German Machine-building Assoc., Frankfurt, 1963–65; Mem., Managing Bd, Sulzer Escher Wyss AG, Zurich, 1967–70. Prof., Geneva Univ., 1973–2003. Co-founder and Mem. Foundn Bd, Schwab Foundn for Social Entrepreneurship, Geneva, 1998–. Trustee, Peres Center for Peace, Tel Aviv, 1997–; Mem. Adv. Bd, Foreign Policy, Washington, 1997–. Mem. Vis. Cttee, JFK Sch. of Govt, Harvard Univ., 1996–; Hon. Prof., Ben-Gurion Univ. of the Negev, Israel, 2003–; Mem. President's Council, Univ. of Tokyo, 2006–. Mem. Bd, Lucerne Fest., 2007–. Freedom, City of London, 2006. Twelve hon. doctorates. Grand Cross, Nat. Order of Merit (Germany), 1995; Knight, Légion d'Honneur (France), 1997; Golden Grand Cross, Nat. Order (Austria), 1997; Medal of Freedom (Slovenia), 1997; Comdr's Cross with Star, Nat. Order (Poland), 2002; Decoration of 1st Degree for Outstanding Giving (Jordan), 2005; Comdr's Cross (Lithuania), 2008. *Publications:* Global Competitiveness Report (annually), 1979–; numerous articles. *Recreations:* cross-country ski marathon, high mountain climbing. *Address:* (office) World Economic Forum, 91–93 route de la Capite, 1223 Cologny, Switzerland. *T:* (22) 8691212, *Fax:* (22) 7862744. *E:* contact@weforum.org.

SCHWARTE, Maria; *see* Adebowale, M.

SCHWARTZ, Prof. Steven, AM 2013; PhD; Chief Executive Officer, Council for the Humanities, Arts and Social Sciences, Australia, since 2013; *b* New York, 5 Nov. 1946; *s* of Robert and Frances Schwartz; *m* 2001, Claire Mary Farrugia; one *s* three *d* (and one *s* decd). *Educ:* Brooklyn Coll., City Univ. of New York (BA); Syracuse Univ., New York (MSc, PhD). FASSA 1991; FAICD 2001; FAIM 2001. Res. Scientist, Dept of Psychiatry, Community and Public Health, Med. Br., Univ. of Texas, 1975–79; Sen. Lectr, Dept of Psychology, Univ. of Western Australia, Perth, 1978–79; University of Queensland: Prof. and Hd, Dept of Psychology, 1980–90; Pres., Academic Bd, 1991–93; Exec. Dean, Faculty of Medicine and Dentistry, Univ. of WA, 1994–95; Vice-Chancellor and Pres., Murdoch Univ., 1996–2001; Vice-Chancellor and Principal, Brunel Univ., 2002–05; Vice-Chancellor and Pres., Macquarie Univ., Sydney, 2006–12. Royal Soc. Anglo-Australian Exchange Fellow, ICRF Labs, London, 1988. Leader, Admissions to Higher Educn Review, 2003–04; Mem. and Sen. Fellow, Adv. Bd, Centre for Ind. Studies, 1997–; Member: Bd, Council for Internat. Educn Exchange, 1997–2009; Nat. Panel, Student Aptitude Test for Tertiary Admission, Aust. Govt, 2007–; Bd, Univs Australia, 2009–12; Internat. Adv. Cttee, Zhejiang Univ., 2014–; Adv. Bd, Acquire Educn, 2015–; Chm., Bologna Process Steering Gp, Dept of Educn, Employment and Workplace Relns, 2007–12. Mem., London Production Industries Commn, 2004–05; Director: Australia-America Fulbright Commn, 2007– (Chm., 2011–); Teach for Australia, 2013–; NSW Library Foundn, 2013–. Sen. Advr, Nous Gp, 2012–. Gov., Richmond, Amer. Internat. Univ. in London, 2004–05; Australian Govt Rep., Council, Univ. of South Pacific, 2007–. Mem. Adv. Council, Reform, 2004–. Oliver Smithies Fellow, Balliol Coll., Oxford, 2013; Hon. Sen. Fellow, Univ. of Melbourne, 2014–. *Publications:* (jtly) Psychopathology of Childhood, 1981, 2nd edn 1995; Measuring Reading Competence, 1984; Classic Studies in Psychology, 1986 (trans. German 1991); (with T. Griffin) Medical Thinking: the psychology of medical judgement and decision-making, 1986; Pavlov's Heirs, 1987; Classic Studies in Abnormal Psychology, 1993; Abnormal Psychology, 2000; *edited:* (jtly) Human Judgement and Decision Processes, 1975; (jtly) Human Judgement and Decision Processes in Applied Settings, 1977; Language and Cognition in Schizophrenia, 1978; Case Studies in Abnormal Psychology, 1992; contrib. books and learned jls. *Recreations:* bushwalking, reading, writing. *Address:* Council for the Humanities, Arts and Social Sciences, PO Box 12226, Melbourne Franklin Street Post Shop, A'Beckett Street, Melbourne, Vic 8006, Australia; Apartment 802, 45 Bowman Street, Pyrmont, Sydney, NSW 2009, Australia.

SCHWARTZMAN, Arnold Martin, OBE 2002; RDI 2006; President, Arnold Schwartzman Productions, Los Angeles, since 1985; *b* London, 6 Jan. 1936; *s* of David and Rose Schwartzman; *m* 1st, 1958, Marilyn Bild (marr. diss. 1979); one *d*; 2nd, 1980, Isolde Weghofer. *Educ:* Shoreham Grammar Sch.; Thanet Sch. of Art and Crafts, Margate; Canterbury Coll. of Art (NDD 1955). Served Royal Sussex Regt, Germany and Korea, 1955–57. Graphic Designer: Southern TV, Southampton, 1959–60; Associated-Rediffusion Television, London, 1960–66; Concept Planning Executive, Erwin Wasey Advertising, London, 1966–69; Dir, Conran Design Gp, 1969; Principal, Arnold Schwartzman Prodns, London, 1970–78; Design Dir, Saul Bass & Associates, LA, 1978–79; Producer/Dir, Genocide, 1981 (Acad. Award for Best Documentary Feature); Dir of Design, 1984 Los Angeles Olympic Games, 1982; Creative Dir, Voices and Visions, 2011–12. Other documentary feature films as prod. and dir include: Building a Dream, 1989; Echoes that Remain, 1991; Liberation, 1994. Muralist, London Time and Golden Age of Transportation, Cunard's Queen Elizabeth, 2010; designer, UN Peace Bell Meml, Korean War Meml Mus., Seoul, 2013. Exhibn, Schwartzman's Six Decades of Graphic Art and Film, CG Showroom, W Hollywood, 2015. First Co-Chm., 1997–98, Chm. Bd, 1999–2000, Gov., 2000–, BAFTA/LA; Chm. Documentary Exec. Cttee, Acad. of Motion Picture Arts and Scis, 2000–01. Mem., Bd of Govs, Univ. for the Creative Arts, 2008–. Patron: UK Nat. Defence Medal Campaign, 2010–; Margate Clock Tower Time Ball Restoration Project, 2014–; Margate Sch., 2015. Mem., AGI, 1974–. FRSA 1998. *Publications:* Airshipwreck (with Len Deighton), 1978; Graven Images, 1993; Phono-Graphics, 1993; Liberation, 1994; Designage, 1998; It's a Great Wall (with Michael Webb), 2000; Flicks: how the movies began, 2000; Deco Landmarks, 2005; London Art Deco, 2007; Griffith Observatory 80th Anniversary: a celebration of its architectural splendour, 2015. *Recreations:* cinema, photography. *Address:* 317½ North Sycamore Avenue, Los Angeles, CA 90036, USA. *T:* (323) 9381481. *E:* arnold@schwartzmandesign.com.

SCHWARZ, Cheryl Lynn; *see* Studer, C. L.

SCHWARZ, Gerard; conductor; Music Director: Seattle Symphony Orchestra, 1985–2011, now Conductor Laureate; Royal Liverpool Philharmonic Orchestra, 2001–06; *b* NJ, 19 Aug. 1947; *m* 1984, Jody Greitzer; two *s* two *d*. *Educ:* Juilliard Sch., NYC. Conductor, 1966–; Music Director: Erick Hawkins Dance Co., 1967–72; SoHo Ensemble, 1969–75; Eliot Field Dance Co., NYC, 1972–78; NY Chamber SO, 1977–2002; LA Chamber Orch., 1976–86; Music Advr, 1983–84, Principal Conductor, 1984–85, Seattle SO. Estabd Music Today, 1981, Music Dir, 1981–89; Music Advr, Mostly Mozart Fest., NYC, 1982–84 (Music Dir, 1984–2001); Artistic Advr, Tokyo Bunkamura's Orchard Hall, 1994–97; operatic conducting début with Washington Opera, 1982, with Seattle Opera, 1986. Guest Conductor with major orchestras in N America, Europe, Australia and Japan. Has made numerous recordings. Hon. DMus: Juilliard Sch.; Puget Sound; Hon. DFA: Farleigh Dickinson; Seattle. Ditson Conductor's Award, Columbia Univ., 1989; Conductor of Year, Musical America Internat. Directory of Performing Arts, 1994. *Address:* c/o Seattle Symphony Orchestra, 200 University Street, Seattle, WA 98101, USA.

SCHWARZ, Michael Robert; Solicitor, Partner, since 1995, and Member, Bindmans LLP; *b* 16 July 1963. *Educ:* Lancaster Royal Grammar Sch.; Hertford Coll., Oxford (BA Juris.); Coll. of Europe, Bruges (Dip. Adv. European Legal Studies). Admitted as solicitor, 1992; Bindmans LLP, specialising in criminal and human rights law, 1990–. Vis. Lectr, Univ. of Westminster, 2007–12. Chm., Trustees, Sheila McKecknie Foundn, 2013–. *Publications:* (jtly) The Law of Public Order and Protest, 2010. *Recreation:* species survival. *Address:* Bindmans LLP, 236 Gray's Inn Road, WC1X 8HB. *T:* (020) 7833 4433, *Fax:* (020) 7837 9792. *E:* m.schwarz@bindmans.com.

SCHWARZENEGGER, Arnold Alois; actor; Governor of California, 2003–11; Co-founder, Chair and Governor Downey Professor of State and Global Policy, Schwarzenegger Institute for State and Global Policy, University of Southern California, since 2012; *b* Graz, Austria, 30 July 1947; *s* of late Gustav Schwarzenegger and Aurelia Schwarzenegger (*née* Jedrny); arrived in USA 1968, naturalized citizen of USA, 1983; *m* 1986, Maria Owings Shriver (marr. diss. 2011); two *s* two *d*; one *s* by Mildred Baena. *Educ:* Univ. of Wisconsin-Superior (BA 1980). Weightlifter and bodybuilder, 1965–75; Jun. Mr Europe, 1965; Best Built Man of Europe, 1966; Mr Europe, 1966; Internat. Powerlifting Champion, 1966; Mr Universe, Nat. Amateur Body Builders' Assoc., (amateur) 1967, (professional) 1968, 1969, 1970; German Powerlifting Champion, 1968; Mr International, 1968, Mr Universe (amateur), 1969, Mr Olympia, annually, 1970–75, 1980, Internat. Fedn of Body Building; Mr World, 1970. *Films include:* Stay Hungry, 1976; Pumping Iron, 1977; The Villain, 1979; The Jayne Mansfield Story, 1980; Conan the Barbarian, 1982; Conan the Destroyer, 1983; The Terminator, 1984; Commando, 1985; Raw Deal, 1986; Predator, Running Man, 1987; Red Heat, Twins, 1988; Total Recall, Kindergarten Cop, 1990; Terminator 2: Judgement Day, 1991; The Last Action Hero (also prod.), 1993; True Lies, Junior, 1994; Jingle All the Way, Eraser, 1996; Batman and Robin, With Wings of Eagles, 1997; End of Days, 1999; The Sixth Day (also prod.), 2000; Collateral Damage, 2002; Terminator 3: Rise of the Machines, 2003; The Expendables 2, 2012; The Last Stand, 2013; Sabotage, 2014; Terminator Genysis, Maggie, 2015. Chm., US President's Council on Physical Fitness and Sports, 1990–93. *Publications:* (jtly) Arnold: the education of a bodybuilder, 1977; Arnold's Bodyshaping for Women, 1979; Arnold's Bodybuilding for Men, 1981; Arnold's Encyclopedia of Modern Bodybuilding, 1985, 2nd edn 1998; (jtly) Arnold's Fitness for Kids, 1993; Total Recall (memoir), 2012.

SCHWEBEL, Stephen Myron; President, Administrative Tribunal, World Bank, since 2010 (Member, since 2007); international arbitrator; *b* 10 March 1929; *s* of Victor Schwebel and Pauline Pfeffer Schwebel; *m* 1972, Louise Killander; two *d*. *Educ:* Harvard Coll. (BA); Trinity Coll., Cambridge (Frank Knox Meml Fellow; Hon. Fellow, 2005); Yale Law Sch. (LLB). Attorney, White & Case, 1954–59; Asst Prof. of Law, Harvard Law Sch., 1959–61; Asst Legal Advr, State Dept, 1961–66; Exec. Dir, Amer. Soc. of Internat. Law, 1967–73; Dep. Legal Advr, State Dept, 1973–81; Judge, 1981–2000, Pres., 1997–2000, Internat. Court of Justice. Pres., Admin. Tribunal, IMF, 1993–2010. Burling Prof. of Internat. Law, Sch. of Advanced Internat. Studies, Johns Hopkins Univ., 1967–81. Member: UN Internat. Law Commn, 1977–81; Panel of Arbitrators, ICSID, 2001–; Perm. Court of Arbitration, The Hague, 2006–. Hon. Bencher, Gray's Inn, 1998. Weill Medal, NY Univ. Sch. of Law, 1992; Medal of Merit, Yale Law Sch., 1997; Manley O. Hudson Medal, Amer. Soc. of Internat. Law, 2000. *Publications:* The Secretary-General of the United Nations, 1952; International Arbitration: three salient problems, 1987; Justice in International Law, 1994; Justice in International Law: further selected writings, 2011. *Recreations:* music, walking. *Address:* (office) Suite 3432, 399 Park Avenue, New York, NY 10022, USA. *T:* (212) 7151135; Cady Brook Farm, PO Box 356, South Woodstock, VT 05071, USA. *T:* (802) 4571358. *Clubs:* Athenæum; Harvard (New York); Cosmos, Metropolitan (Washington).

SCHWEITZER, Louis; Chairman, Renault, 1992–2009, now Hon. Chairman (Chief Executive Officer, 1992–2005); Special Representative of Minister of Foreign Affairs to Japan, since 2012; Chairman, Council of Foreign Affairs, since 2013; General Commissioner for Investment, since 2014; *b* Geneva, 8 July 1942; *s* of late Pierre-Paul Schweitzer; *m* 1972, Agnès Schmitz; two *d*. *Educ:* Institut d'Etudes Politiques, Paris; Faculté de Droit, Paris; Ecole Nationale d'Administration, Paris. Inspectorate of Finance, 1970–74; special assignment, later Dep. Dir, Min. of Budget, 1974–81; Chief of Staff: to Minister of Budget, 1981–83; of Industry and Research, 1983; to Prime Minister, 1984–86; Régie Renault: Vice-Pres. for Finance and Planning, 1986–90; Chief Finance Officer, 1988–90; Exec. Vice-Pres., 1989–90; Pres. and Chief Operating Officer, 1990–92. Prof., Inst d'Etudes Politiques de Paris, 1982–86. Director: Inst Français des Relations Internats, 1989–; BNP, 1993–2013; Philips, 1997–2008; EDF, 1999–2008; Volvo, 2001–12 (Chm., 2010–12); Veolia Environnement, 2003–; L'Oréal, 2005–; BPI France, 2014–; non-exec. Chm., AstraZeneca, 2005–12. Chm., Supervisory Bd, Le Monde, 2008–10. Chm., Haute Autorité de Lutte contre les Discriminations et pour l'Égalité, 2005–10; Pres., France Initiative, 2011–. Grand Officier: Ordre National du Mérite (France), 2007 (Officier, 1992, Comdr, 2002); Légion d'Honneur (France), 2013 (Officier, 1998; Comdr, 2005). *Address:* General Commissariat for Investment, 32 rue de Babylone, 75007, Paris, France.

SCHWEITZER, Prof. Miguel; Dean, Finisterrae University Law School, since 2003; Senior Partner, Schweitzer & Co., law firm, since 1970; *b* 22 July 1940; *s* of Miguel Schweitzer and Cora Walters; *m*; three *s* two *d*. *Educ:* The Grange School, Santiago (preparatory and secondary schooling); Law School, Univ. of Chile (law degree). Doctorate in Penal Law, Rome, 1964–65; Professor of Penal Law: Law Sch., Univ. of Chile, 1966; High Sch. of Carabineros (Police), 1968, 1970 and from 1974; Director, Dept of Penal Sciences, Univ. of Chile, 1974–76; Chile's Alternate Representative with the Chilean Delegn to UN, 1975, 1976, 1978; Ambassador on special missions, 1975–80; Chilean Delegate to OAS, 1976–78; Ambassador to UK, 1980–83; Minister for Foreign Affairs, Chile, 1983. *Publications:* El Error de Derecho en Materia Penal (Chile), 1964; Sull elemento soggettivo nel reato di bancarotta del l'imprenditore (Rome), 1965; Prospectus for a Course on the Special Part of Penal Law (USA), 1969. *Recreations:* music, reading, golf, tennis, Rugby. *Address:* Floor 15, Miraflores 178, Santiago, Chile. *E:* msw@schweitzer.cl. *Clubs:* Union; Prince of Wales Country (Santiago); Marbella Country.

SCICLUNA, Martin Anthony; Chairman: Great Portland Estates, since 2009 (Director, since 2008); RSA Insurance Group, since 2013; *b* 20 Nov. 1950; *s* of late William Scicluna and Miriam Scicluna; *m* 1979 (marr. diss. 2000); two *s* one *d*. *Educ:* Berkhamsted Sch., Herts; Univ. of Leeds (BCom). Joined Deloitte & Touche (formerly Touche Ross & Co.), 1973; Partner, 1982–2008; Head, London Audit, 1990–95; Mem., Bd of Partners, 1991–2007; Chm., 1995–2007; Mem. Bd Dirs and Governance Cttee, 1999–2007, Managing Partner, Global Strategic Clients, 2001–03, Deloitte Touche Tohmatsu. Dir, Lloyds Banking Gp, 2008–13 (Chm., Audit Cttee, 2009–13); non-exec. Dir, Worldpay, 2013– (Chm., Audit Cttee, 2013–). Mem., Financial Services Trade and Investment Bd, 2013–15. Chm., Accounting and Reporting Working Gp, and Mem., Steering Gp, Company Law Review, 1999–2001. Chm., London Soc. Chartered Accountants in England and Wales, 1989–90; Institute of Chartered Accountants in England and Wales: Mem. Council, 1990–95; Chm., Auditing Cttee, 1990–95. Chm., Chairmen's Business Forum, Leeds Univ. Bus. Sch., 2002–06; Mem. Council, Leeds Univ., 2008–11. Trustee, Understanding Industry,

1999–2003; Mem. Bd of Trustees, WellBeing, 2000–03. Vice Patron, businessdynamics, 2003–06. Member: Sailability Develt Bd, RYA, 2000–03; Adv. Council, Cancer Res. UK (formerly CRC), 1999–2003; Finance Cttee, V&A Mus., 2007–08. Governor: NIESR, 2002–; Berkhamsted Sch., 2008–. Freeman, City of London, 1993. Hon. LLD Leeds, 2008. *Recreations:* Arsenal FC, tennis, gardening, wine. *Address:* Parkways, Little Heath Lane, Potten End, Herts HP4 2RX.

SCICLUNA, Martin Leonard Andrew; Director General, Today Public Policy Institute, since 2007; Chairman, National Commission for Further and Higher Education, Malta, since 2013; Council Member for Life, Din l-Art Helwa (National Trust of Malta) (Council Member, 1996–2014; Executive President, 2001–05; Vice-President, 2005–13); *b* 16 Nov. 1935; *s* of Richard Hugh Scicluna and Victoria Mary (*née* Amato-Gauci); *m* 1st, 1960, Anna Judith Brennand (marr. diss. 1988); one *s*; 2nd, 1989, Loraine Jean Birnie; two step *d*. *Educ:* St Edward's Coll., Cottonera, Malta; RMA, Sandhurst. Royal Malta Artillery, 1953–65 (commnd 1955); transferred to RA, 1965–74 (Army Staff Coll., 1965). Joined Civil Service, MoD, 1974; Principal: Naval Personnel Div., 1974–76; Naval and Army Defence Secretariats, 1976–80; Asst Sec., 1980; Hd, Air Force Logistics Secretariat, 1980–83; Dep. Chief, Public Relns, 1983–85; Hd, Gen. Staff Secretariat, 1985–89; RCDS, 1989; Hd, Manpower Resources and Progs, 1990–91; Hd, Resources and Progs (Management Planning), 1991; Asst Under Sec. of State (Adjt Gen.), MoD, 1992; on secondment to FCO, UK delegn to NATO, 1993–95; Ambassador of Malta to NATO, 1996; Advr on Defence Policy to the PM of Malta, 1996–99; Dir of Finance and Infrastructure, PricewaterhouseCoopers, Malta, 1999–2002. Advr on Illegal Immigration to Minister of Home Affairs and Nat Security (formerly of Justice and Home Affairs), Malta, 2005–13. Director: HSBC Cares for Heritage Fund, 2007–10; HSBC Malta Heritage Foundn, 2010–14. 1992–93: Chm. of Comrs, Duke of York's Royal Mil. Coll.; Comr, Royal Hosp., Chelsea; Commissioner: Queen Victoria Sch., Dunblane; Welbeck Coll., Notts; Chm., of Trustees, Army Welfare Fund; Trustee: Nat. Army Mus.; Army Benevolent Fund. Member: Council, 2003–09, Bd, 2009–12, Europa Nostra; Cttee of Guarantee of Malta's Cultural Heritage, 2003–05; Nat. Commn for Sustainable Develt, 2003–08; Bd, Internat. Nat. Trusts Orgn, 2005–12; Pres., European Network of Nat. Heritage Orgns, 2003–04; Chm., ESU Malta, 2009–11 (Mem. Cttee, ESU Malta, 2011–). Chm. Bd of Govs, St Edward's Coll., 2000–05; Trustee, Lady Strickland's Trust for St Edward's Coll., 2000–14. *Recreations:* painting, theatre, watching sport, other sedentary pursuits. *Address:* c/o Barclays Bank plc, 212 Regent Street, W1A 4BP; Dar San Martin, Triq Il-Bali Guarena, Qrendi QRD 1350, Malta. *T:* 21689532.

SCLATER, Prof. John George, PhD; FRS 1982; Professor of Marine Geophysics, Scripps Institution of Oceanography, University of California at San Diego, since 1991; *b* 17 June 1940; *s* of John George Sclater and Margaret Bennett Glen; *m* 1st, 1968, Fredrica Rose Felcyn; two *s*; 2nd, 1985, Paula Ann Edwards (marr. diss. 1991); 3rd, 1992, Naila Gloria Cortez; one *d*. *Educ:* Carlekemp Priory School; Stonyhurst College; Edinburgh Univ. (BSc); Cambridge Univ. (PhD 1966). Research Scientist, Scripps Instn of Oceanography, 1965; Massachusetts Institute of Technology: Associate Prof., 1972; Professor, 1977; Dir, Jt Prog. in Oceanography and Oceanographic Engrg with Woods Hole Oceanographic Instn, 1981; Prof., Dept of Geol Scis, and Associate Dir, Inst. for Geophysics, 1983–91, Shell Dist. Prof., 1983–88, Univ. of Texas at Austin. Guggenheim Fellow, 1998–99. Fellow Geological Soc. of America; Fellow Amer. Geophysical Union; Mem., US Nat. Acad. of Scis, 1989. Rosenstiel Award in Oceanography, Rosenstiel Sch., Univ. of Miami, 1979; Bucher Medal, Amer. Geophysical Union, 1985. *Recreations:* running, swimming, golf. *Address:* Scripps Institution of Oceanography, 9500 Gilman Drive, La Jolla, CA 92093–0220, USA.

SCLATER, John Richard, CVO 1999; Managing Partner, Sutton Hall Farms, since 2002; Chairman, Sclater Estates Ltd (formerly Berner, Nicol & Co. Ltd), 2002–04 and since 2005 (Director, 1968–2004); *b* 14 July 1940; *s* of late Arthur William Sclater and Alice Sclater (*née* Collett); *m* 1st, 1967, Nicola Mary Gloria Cropper (marr. diss.); one *s* (one *d* decd); 2nd, 1985, Grizel Elizabeth Catherine Dawson, MBE. *Educ:* Charterhouse; Gonville and Caius Coll., Cambridge (schol., 1st Cl. Hons History Tripos, BA, MA); Commonwealth Fellow, 1962–64; Yale Univ. (MA 1963); Harvard Univ. (MBA 1968). Glyn, Mills & Co., 1964–70; Dir, Williams, Glyn & Co., 1970–76; Chief Exec., Nordic Bank, 1976–85 (Chm., 1985); Dir, 1985–87, Jt Dep. Chm., 1987, Guinness Peat Gp PLC; Dir and Dep. Chm., 1985–87, Chm., 1987, Guinness Mahon & Co. Ltd; Chairman: Foreign & Colonial Investment Trust PLC, 1985–2002 (Dir, 1981–2002); Graphite (formerly Foreign & Colonial) Enterprise Trust Plc, 1986–2009; Foreign & Colonial Ventures Ltd, 1989–98; Berisford plc, 1990–2000 (Dir, 1986–2000); Hill Samuel Bank Ltd, 1992–96 (Dir, 1990–96; Vice-Chm., 1990–92); Graphite (formerly Foreign & Colonial) Private Equity Trust PLC, 1994–2002; Union (formerly Union Discount Co. of London) plc, 1996 (Dir, 1981–96, Dep. Chm., 1986–96); Biotech Growth Trust plc (formerly Reabourne Merlin, then Finsbury, Life Scis Investment Trust, subseq. Finsbury Emerging Biotechnol. Trust plc), 1997–2012; Argent Gp Europe Ltd, 1998–2012; Pres., Equitable Life Assce Soc., 1994–2001 (Dir, 1985–2002); Deputy Chairman: Yamaichi International (Europe) Ltd, 1985–97; Millennium & Copthorne Hotels PLC, 1996–2007; Grosvenor Gp Ltd (formerly Grosvenor Estate Hldgs), 1999–2005 (Dir, 1989–); Director: James Cropper PLC, 1972–2008; Holker Estates Co. Ltd, 1974–2013; F & C Group (Hldgs) Ltd, 1989–2001; Fuel Tech (Europe), 1990–98; Angerstein Underwriting Trust PLC, 1995–96; Wates Group Ltd, 1999–2004; Member, London Bd of Halifax Building Soc., 1983–90. Trustee, Grosvenor Estate, 1973–2005. Mem., City Taxation Cttee, 1973–76. Chm., Assoc. of Consortium Banks, 1980–82. Mem., City Adv. Gp, CBI, 1988–99. Mem. Council, Duchy of Lancaster, 1987–2000. First Church Estates Comr, 1999–2001; Mem., Archbishops' Council and Gen. Synod, C of E, 1999–2001. Governor: Internat. Students House, 1976–99; Brambletye Sch. Trust, 1976–2006. Freeman, City of London, 1992; Liveryman, Goldsmiths' Co., 1992–. *Recreation:* country pursuits. *Address:* Sutton Hall, Barcombe, near Lewes, Sussex BN8 5EB. *T:* (01273) 400450, *Fax:* (01273) 401086. *Clubs:* Brooks's; University Pitt (Cambridge); Sussex.

SCLATER-BOOTH, family name of **Baron Basing**.

SCOBIE, James Timothy Norman; QC 2010; *b* Dhekelia, Cyprus, 7 Sept. 1960; *s* of Col F. H., (Jim), Scobie and Goodeth Scobie; *m* 1995, Sophie; two *d*. *Educ:* Eton Coll.; Univ. of Exeter (BA Gen. Hons 1982); City Univ. (DipLaw 1983). Called to the Bar, Gray's Inn, 1984; in practice as a barrister, specialising in crime, Francis Taylor Bldg, 1985–91, Garden Court Chambers, 1991–. *Recreations:* follower of all sports, especially cricket and football, lifelong supporter of Manchester United Football Club. *Address:* Garden Court Chambers, 57–60 Lincoln's Inn Fields, WC2A 3LJ. *Clubs:* MCC (Mem., 1979–); Surrey County Cricket (Internat. Mem.); Old Etonian Association Football (Sec.).

SCOBIE, Kenneth Charles, CA; Chairman, Chemring, 1997–2010; *b* 29 July 1938; *s* of Charles Scobie and Shena (*née* Melrose); *m* 1973, Adela Jane Hollebone; one *s* one *d*. *Educ:* Daniel Stewart's Coll., Edinburgh; Edinburgh Univ. CA 1961. Romanes-Munro, CA, 1956–61; BMC (Scotland) Ltd, 1961–63; Rolls-Royce Ltd, 1963–66; Robson Morrow & Co., 1966–70; Black & Decker, 1971–72; Vavasseur South Africa Ltd, 1972–76; H. C. Sleigh Ltd, 1979–83; Blackwood Hodge plc, 1984–90; Dep. Chm. and Chief Exec., Brent Walker Group, 1991–93; Chairman: Lovells Confectionery Ltd, 1991–98; William Hill Group, 1992–93; Allied Leisure, 1994–2000; Dep. Chm., Addis, 1993–94; Dir, Postern Exec. Gp, 1991–97. Non-exec. Director: Albrighton plc, 1990–93; Gartmore Venture Capital, 1993–98. Chm. Exec. Bd, Scottish Rugby Union, 2000–03. CCMI (CBIM 1987). *Recreations:* sport, Bridge. *Address:* Path Hill House, Path Hill, Goring Heath, Oxon RG8 7RE. *T:* (0118) 9842417. *Clubs:* London Scottish Football (Pres., 1997–2001); Huntercombe Golf; Durban (S Africa).

SCOBLE, Christopher Lawrence; Assistant Under-Secretary of State, Home Office, 1988–95; *b* 21 Nov. 1943; *s* of Victor Arthur Oliphant Scoble and Mabel Crouch; *m* 1st, 1972, Florence Hunter (*d* 2001); one *s* one *d*; 2nd, 2012, Sheelagh Hunter. *Educ:* Kent Coll., Canterbury; Corpus Christi Coll., Oxford. Asst Principal, Home Office, 1965; Private Sec. to Minister of State, Welsh Office, 1969–70; Home Office: Principal, 1970; Sec. to Adv. Council on the Penal System, 1976–78; Asst Sec., 1978; Asst Under-Sec. of State, Broadcasting and Miscellaneous Dept, 1988–91, Establishment Dept, 1991–94, Police Dept, 1994–95. Vice-Chm., Media Policy Cttee, Council of Europe, 1985–87. CS (Nuffield and Leverhulme) Travelling Fellowship, 1987–88. *Publications:* Fisherman's Friend: a life of Stephen Reynolds, 2000; (ed) A Poor Man's House, by Stephen Reynolds, 2001; Colin Blythe: lament for a legend, 2005; Letters from Bishopsbourne: three writers in an English village, 2010; Under Shrub Hill: a Chestfield childhood, 2012. *Address:* The School House, Church Lane, Sturminster Newton, Dorset DT10 1DH. *T:* (01258) 473491.

SCOBLE, Malcolm John, PhD, DSc; Scientific Associate, Entomology Department, Natural History Museum, since 2010 (Keeper of Entomology, 2006–10); *b* Buckfastleigh, Devon, 6 July 1950; *s* of George Luis Evan, (Dick), Scoble and Edith Maud, (Babs), Scoble; *m* 1982, Theresa Jean Smuts. *Educ:* Kelly Coll., Tavistock; Portsmouth Poly. (BSc Zool., London ext., 1972; MPhil 1974); Rhodes Univ. (PhD 1982); DSc London 2002. MRSB (MIBiol 1982); CBiol 1982; FLS 1995; FRES 1987. Res. Asst, Portsmouth Poly., 1972–74; Professional Officer, then Sen. Professional Officer in Entomol., Transvaal Mus., Pretoria, 1975–82; Asst Curator/Actg Curator, Hope Entomological Collections, University Mus., Univ. of Oxford, 1982–85; Res. Entomologist, 1985–2002, Associate Keeper, 2002–06, Natural Hist. Mus. Member Council: Systematics Assoc., 1986–89; Brit. Entomol and Natural Hist. Soc., 1997–98 (Vice Pres., 1994–95, 1996–97; Pres., 1995–96); Mem. Council, 1995–98, 2007–, Zoological Sec., 2009–12, Scientific Sec., 2012–, Linnean Soc. of London (Vice-Pres., 1997–98, 2009–10, 2011–12, 2013–14); Mem. Adv. Bd, Centre for Arts and Humanities, Natural History Mus., 2011–. Karl Jordan Medal, Amer. Lepidopterists' Soc., 2002. *Publications:* The Lepidoptera: form, function and diversity, 1992; (ed) A taxonomic catalogue to the Geometridae of the world (Insecta: Lepidoptera), 1999; (ed) ENHSIN: the European natural history specimen information network, 2003; (ed jtly) Digital Imaging of Biological Type Specimens: a manual of best practice, 2005; articles in learned jls on Lepidoptera taxonomy (incl. Linnaeus's butterflies), natural history museum resources and information access, biodiversity informatics, esp. internet-based taxonomy. *Recreations:* natural history, music, theatre, Devon. *Address:* Holybrook, Grange Road, Buckfast, Buckfastleigh, Devon TQ11 0EH. *T:* (01364) 643274. *E:* m.scoble@nhm.ac.uk.

SCOLES, Prof. Giacinto, FRS 1997; Donner Professor of Science, Princeton University, 1987–2008, now Emeritus; Professor of Biophysics and Condensed Matter, International School for Advanced Studies, Trieste, since 2004; Distinguished Adjunct Professor of Biology, Temple University, Philadelphia, since 2008; *b* 2 April 1935; *m* 1964, Giok-Lan Lim; one *d*. *Educ:* Univ. of Genova (DChem 1959; Libera docenza 1968). Asst Prof., 1960–61 and 1964–68, Associate Prof., 1968–71, Physics Dept, Univ. of Genova; Res. Associate, Kamerlingh-Onnes Lab., Univ. of Leiden, 1961–64; Prof. of Chemistry and Physics, Univ. of Waterloo, Canada, 1971–86. Sen. Consultant for Nanotechnol., UNIDO Internat. Center for Sci. and High Technol., Trieste. Hon. DPhys Genova, 1996; Hon. DSc Waterloo, Canada, 2000. Peter Debye Award, ACS, 2002; Benjamin Franklin Medal, Franklin Inst., 2006. *Publications:* Atomic and Molecular Beam Methods, vol. 1, 1988, vol. 2, 1992; The Chemical Physics of Atomic and Molecular Clusters, 1990; contribs to learned jls. *Address:* Biology Department, Temple University, Biology Life Sciences Building, Room 449A, N 12th Street, Philadelphia, PA 19122, USA; International School for Advanced Studies, Via Beirut 2–4, Trieste 34151, Italy.

SCOONES, Andrew Geoffry; Director, Building Centre, 2005–13; *b* Shrewsbury, 1 Oct. 1959; *s* of Kenneth Geoffry Scoones and Anne Elizabeth Scoones; *m* 1990, Kwee; one *s* one *d*. *Educ:* Univ. of Leeds (BA Hons Eng. and French); Birkbeck Coll., London (MSc Computer Sci.). Manager, Building Centre Trust, 1994–. Dir, Italian Wine Club. Hon. FRIBA 2008. *Publications:* Renewable Energy in the Built Environment, 2003; Prefabulous Homes, 2005. *Recreations:* tennis, Italian wine, gardening.

SCOPELITIS, Anastase; Ambassador Emeritus, Greece, since 2012; *b* Port Said, 1944; *s* of Evangelos Scopelitis and late Rhodesia Scopelitis (*née* Antoniadis); *m* 1971, Hélène Lolos; three *s*. *Educ:* Univ. of Athens (Master in Politics and Econs). Lectr in Public Finance, Univ. of Athens, 1969–71; Ministry of Foreign Affairs: Attaché, 1971; Third Sec., Cairo, 1973; Second Sec., 1976–79, First Sec., 1979, London; Dep. Hd of Mission, The Hague, 1980; Second Counsellor, 1982; First Counsellor, 1985; Hd, EC Ext. Relns and EC New Policies Units, 1987; European Correspondent and Actg Dir of European Political Cooperation, 1989; Minister Plenipotentiary 2nd Cl. and Dir of European Political Cooperation, 1991; Minister and Dep. Hd of Mission, London, 1993, Minister Plenipotentiary 1st Cl., 1994; Ambassador to Denmark, 1996–99; Dir Gen. for Political Affairs and Political Dir, 1999, promoted to Ambassador, 2001; Sec. Gen., 2002–03; Ambassador to Court of St James's and Permanent Rep. to IMO, 2003–06; Special Advr to Minister of Foreign Affairs, Greece, 2006–12. Hd, Working Gp for 2009 Greek Chair of Global Forum on Migration and Develt, Athens, 2008–10. Grand Cross, Order of Phoenix (Greece), 2003. Commander: Order of Merit (Egypt), 1976; Order of Oranje-Nassau (Netherlands), 1987; Grand Cross: Order of White Star (Estonia), 1999; Order of Dannebrog (Denmark), 1999; Order of Merit (Germany), 2001; Order of Leopold II (Belgium), 2001; Order of Infante Dom Henrique (Portugal), 2002; Order of Merit (Italy), 2003; Order of Merit (Cyprus), 2003; Grand Cross, Order of Phoenix (Greece), 2003. *Address:* 6 Panagouli Street, 190 09 Rafina, Greece.

SCOREY, David William John; QC 2015; *b* Manchester, 27 Oct. 1973; *m* 2004, Katie Renwick; two *s* one *d*. *Educ:* St John's Coll., Oxford (BA Juris.); Leiden Univ. (LLM EU Law). Called to the Bar, Lincoln's Inn, 1997; Mem., Essex Court Chambers, in practice at commercial and revenue bars, 1998–. Consultant Ed., De Voil Indirect Tax Intelligence, 2015–. *Publications:* (with Tim Eicke) Human Rights Damages, 2001; (jtly) The Bermuda Form: interpretation and dispute resolution of excess liability insurance, 2011. *Recreations:* wine, reading, Dorset. *Address:* Essex Court Chambers, 24 Lincoln's Inn Fields, WC2A 3EG. *T:* (020) 7813 8000, *Fax:* (020) 7813 8080. *E:* dscorey@essexcourt.com. *Club:* Garrick.

SCORSESE, Martin; American film director; *b* 17 Nov. 1942; *s* of Charles Scorsese and Catherine (*née* Cappa); *m* 1st, 1965, Laraine Marie Brennan (marr. diss.); one *d*; 2nd, Julia Cameron (marr. diss.); one *d*; 3rd, 1979, Isabella Rosellini (marr. diss. 1983); 4th, 1985, Barbara DeFina; *m* 1999, Helen Morris; one *d*. *Educ:* Univ. of New York (BS 1964; MA 1966). Faculty Asst, 1963–66, Lectr, 1968–70, Dept of Film, Univ. of New York; dir and writer of documentaries, incl. No Direction Home - Bob Dylan, 2005; George Harrison: living in the material world, 2011. *Films* include: Who's That Knocking At My Door? (also writer), 1968; Mean Streets (also co-writer), 1973; Alice Doesn't Live Here Any More, 1974; Taxi Driver (Palme d'Or, Cannes Film Fest.), 1976; New York, New York, 1977; The Last Waltz (also actor), 1978; Raging Bull, 1980; After Hours, 1985 (Best Dir Award, Cannes Film Fest., 1986); The Color of Money, 1986; acted in 'Round Midnight, 1986; The Last Temptation of Christ, 1988; Goodfellas, 1990; Cape Fear, 1992; The Age of Innocence, 1993; Bringing out the Dead, 1999; Gangs of New York, 2002; The Aviator, 2005; The Departed,

2006 (Acad. Award, Best Dir, 2007); Shine a Light, 2008; Shutter Island, 2010; Hugo, 2011; The Wolf of Wall Street, 2014; producer: Mad Dog and Glory, 1993; Naked in New York, 1994; Casino, 1996; Kundun, 1998; The Young Victoria, 2009. Fellow, BAFTA, 2012.

SCOTFORD, Garth Barrie, OBE 1994; QFSM 1982; County Manager, Berkshire County Council, 1993–96; *b* 28 Oct. 1943; *s* of Albert Edward Scotford and Louisa Emily Jane Scotford (*née* Leach); *m* 1st, 1964, Gillian Avril Patricia Constable (*d* 1999); one *s* two *d*; 2nd, 2000, Caroline Susan James. *Educ:* Reading Grammar Sch. Joined Fire Service, 1961: served in Reading, Liverpool, Hants and Gtr Manchester; Chief Fire Officer, Berks, 1984–93, retd. FIFireE 1977 (Pres., 1985). *Recreations:* opera, bridge. *Address:* 9 Tarbenian Way, Brigadoon, WA 6069, Australia. *T:* (8) 387649.
See also J. E. Scotford.

SCOTFORD, John Edward, CBE 1993; Treasurer, Hampshire County Council, 1983–97; *b* 15 Aug. 1939; *s* of Albert and Louisa Scotford; *m* 1st, 1962, Marjorie Clare Wells (marr. diss. 2001); one *s*; 2nd, 2001, Alison Cawley. *Educ:* Reading Grammar Sch. CPFA. Reading County Borough Council, 1955–62; Coventry County Borough Council, 1962–65; Hampshire CC, 1965–97; Dep. County Treasurer, 1977–83. Public Works Loan Comr, 1992–96. Pres., CIPFA, 1996–97. Freeman, City of London, 1995. *Address:* Manor House Barn, Petherton Park, North Petherton, Bridgwater, Somerset TA7 0DT.
See also G. B. Scotford.

SCOTHERN, Mark Francis; freelance psychotherapist, since 2010; *b* 2 July 1960; *s* of late Norman Scothern and of Joan Scothern; *m* 1998, Caroline Fiske. *Educ:* Austin Friars Sch., Carlisle; MBA Warwick Univ. Business Sch., 2000. Co-ordinator, Thamesdown Housing Link, 1984–88; Policy Officer, CHAR (Housing Campaign for Single People), 1988–91; Dir, Crisis (formerly Crisis at Christmas), 1991–96; Develt Man., Shelter, 1997–98; Associate, Rho Delta, mgt consultancy, 1998–99; Director: Derby CVS, 1999–2005; Cornwall Foundn of Promise, 2006–07; Psychotherapist: Cornwall PCT, 2007–08; Outlook South West, 2008–10. *Recreations:* film, contemporary music, food, biographies, cycling.

SCOTLAND OF ASTHAL, Baroness *cr* 1997 (Life Peer), of Asthal in the co. of Oxfordshire; **Patricia Janet Scotland;** PC 2001; QC 1991; *b* 19 Aug. 1955; *m* 1985, Richard Mawhinney; two *s*. *Educ:* London Univ. (LLB). Called to the Bar, Middle Temple, 1977, Bencher, 1997; Mem., Antigua Bar; a Recorder, 2000. Parly Under-Sec. of State, FCO, 1999–2001; Parly Sec., LCD, 2001–03; Minister of State (Minister for Criminal Justice System and Law Reform, subseq. for Criminal Justice and Offender Mgt), Home Office, 2003–07; Attorney General, 2007–10; Shadow Attorney Gen., 2010–11. Former Mem., Commn for Racial Equality; Mem., Millennium Commn, 1994–99; Chm., National Catholic Safeguarding Commn, 2011–12. Chancellor, Univ. of Greenwich, 2014–. *Address:* House of Lords, SW1A 0PW.

SCOTLAND, Alastair Duncan, OBE 2012; FRCSE, FRCP, FRCGP, FFPH; Medical Director, National Clinical Assessment Service, 2005–11; *b* 19 Aug. 1951; *s* of James Scotland and Jean (*née* Cowan). *Educ:* Glasgow High Sch.; Aberdeen Grammar Sch.; Aberdeen Univ. (MB ChB 1975). FRCSE 1980; MFPHM 1987, FFPH (FFPHM 1993); FRCP 1999; FRCGP 2008. House Surgeon/House Physician, Aberdeen Royal Infirmary, 1975–76; training prog. in surgery specialising in plastic surgery, Aberdeen, Inverness, Dundee and Perth Hosps, 1976–83; training prog. in public health medicine, SE and NW Thames RHAs, 1983–88; Consultant in Public Health Medicine, then Regl MO, NE Thames RHA, 1988–94; Trust Unit Med. Dir, N Thames RHA, 1994–96; Dir of Med. Educn and Res. and Postgrad. Clinical Tutor, Chelsea and Westminster Hosp., 1996–2001; Chief Exec. and Med. Dir, Nat. Clin. Assessment Authy, NHS, 2001–05. Associate Consultant, Edgecumbe Gp, Bristol, 2011–. Hon. Senior Lecturer in Public Health Medicine: ICSM, 2000–01; KCL Sch. of Medicine (formerly GKT), 2001–; Vis. Prof. in Public Health, KCL Sch. of Medicine (formerly GKT), 2004–. Advr, Med. Educn, Training and Staffing, London Implementation Gp, 1993–95; Chairman: Clinical Disputes Forum for England and Wales, 1996–2002; Health of Health Professional Staff Wkg Gp, 2007–10; Member: Ministerial Gp on Jun. Doctors' Hours of Work, 1990–95; Jt Cttee, Funding of Postgrad. Med. and Dental Educn in NHS, 1991–96; CMO's Cttee on Specialist Med. Training, 1992–95; Jt Cttee, NHS Consultant Appointment Procedures, 1992–94. FRSocMed 1981. FRSA 1992. Member Editorial Boards: Hospital Medicine, 1989–2008; Clinical Risk, 2000–12. *Publications:* (with L. Swift) Disciplining and Dismissing Doctors in the NHS, 1995; (ed) Clinical Governance One Year On, 2000; (contrib.) Clinical Negligence, 4th edn 2008; orig. papers on medical professional and public health issues. *Recreations:* theatre, music, antique conservation and restoration. *Address:* Cobham, Surrey. *Club:* Reform.

SCOTT; *see* Hepburne Scott, family name of Lord Polwarth.

SCOTT; *see* Montagu Douglas Scott, family name of Duke of Buccleuch.

SCOTT; *see* Stedman-Scott.

SCOTT, family name of **Earl of Eldon, Baron Scott of Foscote** and **Baroness Scott of Needham Market**.

SCOTT OF BYBROOK, Baroness *cr* 2015 (Life Peer), of Upper Wraxall in the County of Wiltshire; **Jane Antoinette Scott,** OBE 2010; Member (C) and Leader, Wiltshire Council, since 2009. *Educ:* Lancs Coll. of Agric. Mem. (C), Wilts CC, 1997–2009 (Leader, 2003–09). *Address:* House of Lords, SW1A 0PW.

SCOTT OF FOSCOTE, Baron *cr* 2000 (Life Peer), of Foscote in the county of Buckinghamshire; **Richard Rashleigh Folliott Scott,** Kt 1983; PC 1991; a Lord of Appeal in Ordinary, 2000–09; *b* 2 Oct. 1934; *s* of Lt-Col C. W. F. Scott, 2/9th Gurkha Rifles and Katharine Scott (*née* Rashleigh); *m* 1959, Rima Elisa, *d* of Salvador Ripoll and Blanca Korsi de Ripoll, Panama City; two *s* two *d*. *Educ:* Michaelhouse Sch., Natal; Univ. of Cape Town (BA); Trinity Coll., Cambridge (BA, LLB). Bigelow Fellow, Univ. of Chicago, 1958–59. Called to Bar, Inner Temple, 1959, Bencher, 1981. In practice, Chancery Bar, 1960–83; QC 1975; Attorney Gen., 1980–83, Vice-Chancellor, 1987–91, Duchy and County Palatine of Lancaster; Judge of the High Court of Justice, Chancery Div., 1983–91; a Lord Justice of Appeal, 1991–94; Vice-Chancellor, Supreme Court, 1994–2000; Head of Civil Justice, 1995–2000; a non-permanent Judge, Hong Kong Court of Final Appeal, 2003–11. Inquiry into defence related exports to Iraq and related prosecutions, 1992–96. Chm. of the Bar, 1982–83 (Vice-Chm., 1981–82). Editor-in-Chief, Supreme Court Practice, 1996–2000. Member, House of Lords Select Committee: on EU, 2002–05 (Chm., Sub-Cttee E (Law and Instns), 2009–14); for Privileges, 2010–14; on Merits of Statutory Instruments, 2009–14. Hon. Member: Amer. Bar Assoc., 1983; Canadian Bar Assoc., 1983. Hon. LLD: Birmingham, 1996; Buckingham, 1999. *Publications:* articles in legal jls. *Recreations:* hunting, tennis, bridge, twelve grandchildren, formerly Rugby (Cambridge Blue, 1957). *Address:* House of Lords, SW1A 0PW. *Club:* Hawks (Cambridge).

SCOTT OF NEEDHAM MARKET, Baroness *cr* 2000 (Life Peer), of Needham Market in the co. of Suffolk; **Rosalind Carol Scott;** President, Liberal Democrat Party, 2009–10; *b* 10 Aug. 1957; *d* of Kenneth Vincent and Carol Jane Leadbeater; *m* 1st (marr. diss.); one *s* one *d*; 2nd, 2008, Mark Valladares. *Educ:* Whitby Grammar Sch.; Univ. of East Anglia. Member (Lib Dem) Mid Suffolk DC, 1991–94; Suffolk CC, 1993–2005 (Gp Leader, 1997–2000). Member: UK delegn to EU Cttee of the Regions, 1998–2002; Commn for Integrated Transport, 2001–07. Chm., Transport Cttee, LGA, 2002–04 (Vice-Chair, 1996–2002). Mem., H of L Appts Commn, 2010–. Contested (Lib Dem) Eastern Region, EP elecns, 1999. Non-executive Director: Entrust, 2000–07; Anglia TV, 2002–05; Lloyds Register, 2004–08. Chm., English Volunteer Develt Council, 2011–; Mem. Bd, Harwich Haven Authy, 2013–. *Recreations:* walking, travel, genealogy. *Address:* House of Lords, SW1A 0PW.

SCOTT, Hon. Lady; Margaret Elizabeth Scott; a Senator of the College of Justice in Scotland, since 2012; partner, Frank Richard Crowe, *qv*; one *s*. *Educ:* Univ. of Edinburgh (LLB Hons); Univ. of Strathclyde (DipLP). Admitted: solicitor, 1989; to Faculty of Advocates, 1991; QC (Scot.) 2002; pt-time Sheriff, 2003–12. *Address:* Court of Session, Parliament House, Parliament Square, Edinburgh EH1 1RQ.

SCOTT, Alan James, CVO 1986; CBE 1982; Governor, Cayman Islands, 1987–92; *b* 14 Jan. 1934; *er s* of Rev. Harold James Scott and Mary Phyllis Barbara Scott; *m* 1st, 1958, Mary Elizabeth Ireland (*d* 1969); one *s* two *d*; 2nd, 1971, Joan Hall; one step *s* two step *d*. *Educ:* King's Sch., Ely; Selwyn Coll., Cambridge. Suffolk Regt, Italy and Germany, 1952–54. HMOCS, 1958–87: Fiji: Dist Officer, 1958; Estabts Officer, 1960; Registry of Univ. of S Pacific, 1968; Controller, Organisation and Estabts, 1969; Hong Kong: Asst Financial Sec., 1971; Prin. Asst Financial Sec., 1972; Sec. for CS, 1973; MLC, 1976–85; Sec. for Housing, and Chm. Hong Kong Housing Authy, 1977; Sec. for Information, 1980; Sec. for Transport, 1982; Dep. Chief Sec., 1985–87. President: Fiji AAA, 1964–69; Hong Kong AAA, 1978–87. *Recreations:* dilatory travel, writing. *Address:* 6 Home Farm, Iwerne Minster, Dorset DT11 8LB.

SCOTT, Hon. Alexander; *see* Scott, Hon. W. A.

SCOTT, Allan; *see* Shiach, A. G.

SCOTT, Prof. Andrew, DPhil; Professor of Economics, since 2005, and Deputy Dean, since 2010, London Business School; Fellow, All Souls College, Oxford, since 2011; *b* London, 12 May 1965; *s* of John Scott and Ray Scott (*née* Palmer); two *s* one *d*. *Educ:* Trinity Coll., Oxford (BA 1987); London Sch. of Econs and Pol Sci. (MSc 1991); All Souls Coll., Oxford (DPhil 1994). Prize Fellow, All Souls Coll., Oxford, 1991–98; Res. Officer, LSE, 1991–94; Lectr, Oxford Univ., 1994–96; Associate Prof. of Econs, London Business Sch., 1996–2005. Vis. Asst Prof., Harvard Univ., 1996. Econ. Advr to Prime Minister of Mauritius, 2005–. Ed., Econ. Jl, 2003–10. Non-exec. Dir, FSA, 2009–13. *Publications:* (with Ramon Marimon) Computational Methods for Dynamic Economies, 1999; (with David Miles) Macroeconomics, 2001, 3rd edn 2012. *Recreations:* film, music, football, Irish literature. *Address:* Department of Economics, London Business School, Sussex Place, Regents Park, NW1 4SA. *T:* (020) 7000 8416. *E:* ascott@london.edu.

SCOTT, Andrew John, CBE 2006; FMA; CEng; Director, National Railway Museum, 1994–2009; Acting Director, National Museum of Science and Industry, 2009–10; *b* 3 June 1949; *s* of late Cyril John Scott and of Gertrude Ethel (*née* Miller); *m* 1972, Margaret Anne Benyon, JP, MA. *Educ:* Bablake Sch., Coventry; Univ. of Newcastle upon Tyne (BSc Civil Engrg 1970; MSc Mining Engrg 1971). CEng, MICE 1976. AMA 1987, FMA 1993. Practising civil engr, 1972–84; Actg Dir, W Yorks Transport Mus., 1984–86; Keeper of Technol., Bradford City Museums, 1986–87; Dir, London Transport Mus., 1988–94. Member: North Eastern Locomotive Preservation Gp, 1967– (Pres., 2009–); Bd, N Yorks Moors Historical Railway Trust, 2010–; Bd, N Yorks Moors Nat. Park Authy, 2012–; Council Member: Assoc. of Ind. Museums, 1991–2003; Internat. Assoc. of Transport Museums, 1992–2011 (Vice Pres., 1999–2011); Vice Chairman: Assoc. of British Transport and Engrg Museums, 1992–; Ffestiniog Railway Heritage Ltd, 2010–. Dir, York Tourism Bureau, 1995–2008 (Chm., 1999–2008). Trustee: Friends of Nat. Railway Mus., 1994–; York Civic Trust, 2013– (Chm., 2015–). Pres., London Underground Railway Soc., 1995–96. *Publications:* North Eastern Renaissance, 1991; (with C. Divall) Making Histories in Transport Museums, 2001; contrib. to railway and museological jls and books. *Recreations:* travel, railways, ecclesiastical architecture. *Address:* 14 New Walk Terrace, York YO10 4BG.

SCOTT, Anthony Douglas, TD 1972; chartered accountant in public practice, 1988–2005; *b* 6 Nov. 1933; *o s* of Douglas Ernest and Mary Gladys Scott; *m* 1962, Irene Robson; one *s* one *d*. *Educ:* Gateshead Central Technical Secondary Sch. Articled to Middleton & Middleton, also J. Stanley Armstrong, Chartered Accountants, Newcastle upon Tyne, 1952–57; National Service, WO Selection Bd, 1957–59; Accountant with Commercial Plastics Ltd, 1959; joined ICI Ltd (Agricl Div), 1961; seconded by ICI to Hargreaves Fertilisers Ltd, as Chief Accountant, 1966; ICI Ltd (Nobel Div) as Asst Chief Acct, 1970; seconded by ICI to MoD as Dir-Gen. Internal Audit, 1972–74. Dir of Consumer Credit, Office of Fair Trading, 1974–80. Chief Exec. and Dir, CoSIRA, 1981–88. Chm., Teesside Soc. of Chartered Accts, 1969–70; Mem. Cttee, London Chartered Accountants, 1974–79. Chm., Jt Working Party on Students' Societies (ICAE&W), 1979–80. Mem., Smaller Firms Council, CBI, 1983–86. TA (17th (later 4th) Bn Para. Regt (9 DLI) TA, 44 Para. Bde (TA) and 6th (V) Bn Royal Anglian Regt), 1959–91, Major. *Publications:* Accountants Digests on Consumer Credit Act 1974, 1980; Accountants Digest on Estate Agents Act 1979, 1982. *Recreations:* antiquary, walking, gardening. *Address:* 9 The Foresters, Harpenden, Herts AL5 2FB. *T:* (01582) 763067.

SCOTT, Sir Anthony (Percy), 3rd Bt *cr* 1913; *b* 1 May 1937; *s* of Sir Douglas Winchester Scott, 2nd Bt, and of Elizabeth Joyce, *d* of W. N. C. Grant; *S* father, 1984; *m* 1962, Caroline Theresa Anne, *er d* of Edward Bacon; two *s* one *d*. *Educ:* Harrow; Christ Church, Oxford. Called to the Bar, Inner Temple, 1960. *Recreation:* racing. *Heir: s* Henry Douglas Edward Scott [*b* 26 March 1964; *m* 1993, Carole Ruth Maddick]. *Address:* Chateau La Coste, 81140 Larroque, France.

SCOTT, Brough; *see* Scott, J. B.

SCOTT, Dame Catherine Margaret Mary; *see* Scott, Dame M.

SCOTT, Charles Thomas, FCA; Chairman, William Hill, 2004–10; *b* 22 Feb. 1949. FCA 1979. Binder Hamlyn, 1967–72; ITEL Internat. Corp., 1972–77; IMS Internat. Inc., 1978–89; Saatchi & Saatchi Co. plc, later Cordiant plc, 1990–97: Chief Exec., 1993–95; Chm., 1995–97; Chm., Cordiant Communications Group plc, 1997–2003. *Recreations:* golf, tennis, sport in general.

SCOTT, Christina Martha Elena; Governor of Anguilla, since 2013; *b* London; *d* of Preb. Allan G. Scott and Elena Delcheva-Scott. *Educ:* Francis Holland Sch., Clarence Gate; Christ Church, Oxford (BA (Hons) PPE). Various graduate develt posts with Civil Service, 1996–99; Office of the Dir Gen., Envmt, EC, 1999–2000; Hd, EU Enlargement Team, DfT, 2000–01; Asst Dir, Eur. Secretariat, Cabinet Office, 2001–03; Asst Dir, Corporate and Private Finance Team, HM Treasury, 2003–04; Dep. Dir, West Midlands and SW Div., 2004–05, Principal Private Sec. to Sec. of State, 2005–06, DfT; Private Sec. to the Prime Minister, 10 Downing St, 2006–09; Dir, Civil Contingencies Secretariat, Cabinet Office, 2009–13. *Recreations:* cycling along canal paths, good food with friends, opera, travel, cooking. *Address:* Government House, Old Ta, PO Box 60, The Valley, AI-2640, Anguilla.

SCOTT, Prof. Clive, DPhil; FBA 1994; Professor of European Literature, University of East Anglia, 1991–2007, now Emeritus; *b* 13 Nov. 1943; *s* of Jesse Scott and Nesta Vera Scott (*née* Morton); *m* 1st, 1965, Elizabeth Anne (*née* Drabble) (marr. diss.); one *s* one *d*; 2nd, 1984, Marie-Noëlle Guillot; two *s*. *Educ:* St John's Coll., Oxford (MA, MPhil, DPhil). University of East Anglia: Asst Lectr, 1967–70; Lectr, 1970–88; Reader, 1988–91; Hd, Sch. of Literature and Creative Writing, 2004–05. Clark Lectr, Trinity Coll., Cambridge, 2010. Pres., Modern

Humanities Res. Assoc., 2014. Officier, Ordre des Palmes Académiques (France), 2008. *Publications:* French Verse-Art: a study, 1980; Anthologie Eluard, 1983; A Question of Syllables: essays in nineteenth-century French verse, 1986; The Riches of Rhyme: studies in French verse, 1988; Vers Libre: the emergence of free verse in France 1886–1914, 1990; Reading the Rhythm: the poetics of French free verse 1910–1930, 1993; The Poetics of French Verse: studies in reading, 1998; The Spoken Image: photography and language, 1999; Translating Baudelaire, 2000; Channel Crossings: French and English poetry in dialogue 1550–2000, 2002 (R. H. Gapper Book Prize, Soc. for French Studies, 2004); Translating Rimbaud's Illuminations, 2006; Street Photography: from Atget to Cartier-Bresson, 2007; Translating the Perception of Text: literary translation and phenomenology, 2012 (R. H. Gapper Book Prize, Soc. for French Studies, 2013); Literary Translation and the Rediscovery of Reading, 2012; Translating Apollinaire, 2014. *Address:* School of Literature, Drama and Creative Writing, University of East Anglia, Norwich NR4 7TJ. *T:* (01603) 592135.

SCOTT, Craig Alexander Leslie; QC (Scot.) 2012; Sheriff Principal of Glasgow and Strathkelvin, since 2011; *b* Edinburgh, 10 May 1961; *s* of Leslie Scott and Evelyn Scott (*née* Thomson); *m* 1987, Elizabeth Nicola Annand (*d* 2013); two *s* one *d*. *Educ:* Royal High Prep. Sch., Edinburgh; George Watson's Coll., Edinburgh; Aberdeen Univ. (LLB, DipLP). Trainee and Qualified Asst, Biggart, Baillie & Gifford, WS, 1982–85; pupil of Malcolm G. Thomson and Donald R. Findlay, 1985–86; admitted Faculty of Advocates, 1986; Standing Jun. Counsel, Scottish Office Envmt Dept, 1993–94 and 1997–99; Advocate Depute, 1994–97; Temp. Sheriff, 1997–99; Sheriff of Glasgow and Strathkelvin, 1999–2011. *Recreations:* golf, walking, music. *Address:* Sheriff Principal's Chambers, Sheriff Court of Glasgow and Strathkelvin, 1 Carlton Place, Glasgow G5 9DA. *Clubs:* New (Edinburgh); Luffness New Golf.

SCOTT, Prof. Dana Stewart, FBA 1976; Hillman University Professor of Computer Science, Philosophy and Mathematical Logic, Carnegie Mellon University, 1981–2003, now Emeritus; *b* Berkeley, Calif, 11 Oct. 1932; *m* 1959, Irene Schreier; one *d*. *Educ:* Univ. of Calif, Berkeley (BA); Princeton Univ. (PhD). Instructor, Univ. of Chicago, 1958–60; Asst Prof., Univ. of Calif, Berkeley, 1960–63; Associate Prof. and Prof., Stanford Univ., 1963–69; Prof., Princeton, 1969–72; Prof. of Mathematical Logic, Oxford Univ., 1972–81. Visiting Professor: Amsterdam, 1968–69; Linz, 1992–93; Institut Mittag-Leffler, Sweden, 2001; Vis. Scholar, Univ. of Calif, Berkeley. Guggenheim Fellow, 1978–79; Humbolt Stiftung Sen. Vis. Scientist, Munich, 2003. Winchester Lectr, Univ. of Oxford, 2010. Member: US Nat. Acad. of Scis, 1988; Amer. Assoc. for Advancement of Sci.; Amer. Acad. of Arts and Scis; Amer. Math. Soc.; Assoc. for Computing Machinery; Finnish Acad. of Scis and Letters; NY Acad. of Scis; MAE. Hon. Fellow, Merton Coll., Oxford, 2014. Hon. Dr: Rijksuniversiteit Utrecht, 1986; Tech. Univ. of Darmstadt, 1995; Edinburgh, 1995; Ljubljana, 2003; St Andrews, 2014. Leny P. Steele Prize, Amer. Math. Soc., 1972; Harold Pender Award, Univ. of Pennsylvania, 1990; Rolf Schock Prize in Logic and Philosophy, Royal Acad. of Scis, 1997; Bolzano Medal for Merit, Czech Acad. of Scis, 2001; Gold Medal, Sobolev Inst. of Maths, 2009. *Publications:* papers on logic and mathematics in technical jls. *Address:* 1149 Shattuck Avenue, Berkeley, CA 94707–2609, USA.

SCOTT, David Gidley; Registrar of the High Court in Bankruptcy, 1984–96; *b* 3 Jan. 1924; *s* of late Bernard Wardlaw Habershon Scott, FRIBA and Florence May Scott; *m* 1948, Elinor Anne, *d* of late Major Alan Garthwaite, DSO, MC, and Mrs Garthwaite; two *s* two *d*. *Educ:* Sutton Valence School (scholarship); St John's College, Cambridge (exhibnr, MA, LLM). Army service, 1942–47, Royal Engineers; Assault RE European theatre, 1944–45 (wounded); Acting Major, Palestine. Called to the Bar, Lincoln's Inn, 1951; practised Chancery Bar, 1951–84. *Recreation:* choral singing. *Address:* 45 Benslow Lane, Hitchin, Herts SG4 9RE. *T:* (01462) 434391.

SCOTT, David Gordon Islay, MD; FRCP, FRCPE; Consultant Rheumatologist, Norfolk and Norwich University Hospital NHS Trust, 1988–2011, now Honorary Consultant; *b* Elgin, 8 July 1948; *s* of late Gordon Islay Scott and Mora Joan Scott (*née* Craig); *m* 1976, Daphne Bellworthy, (Dee); three *s*. *Educ:* Trinity Coll., Glenalmond; Univ. of Bristol Med. Sch. (MB ChB 1973; MD 1982). MRCP 1977, FRCP 1994; FRCPE 2007. Lectr in Rheumatol., Univ. of Birmingham, 1981–88. Hon. Sen. Lectr in Rheumatol., Royal London Hosp. Med. Sch., 1988–96; Hon. Sen. Lectr in Rheumatol., 1995–98, Hon. Prof., Norwich Medical Sch. (formerly Sch. of Medicine, Health Policy and Practice), 1998–, UEA. Pres., British Soc. for Rheumatol., 2002–04; Chief Med. Advr, Nat. Rheumatoid Arthritis Soc., 2007–; Patient Involvement Officer, RCP, 2007–11; Clinical Dir, Norfolk and Suffolk Comp. Local Res. Network, 2007–11; Secondary Care Rep., Gt Yarmouth and Waveney CCG, 2012–. *Publications:* contrib. chapters in medical textbooks on clinical aspects, epidemiology and outcome of systemic vasculitis; over 250 reviews, editorials and papers. *Recreations:* hockey—(ex) player, now watching, running—marathons/half marathons (Great North Run x 14 so far). *Address:* Department of Rheumatology, Norfolk and Norwich University Hospital, Colney Lane, Norwich NR4 7UY. *T:* (01603) 286766, *Fax:* (01603) 287004. *E:* David.Scott@nnuh.nhs.uk.

SCOTT, David Maxwell, FREng; FRSE; Director, Engineering Excellence Group, Laing O'Rourke, since 2012; *b* Glasgow, 11 March 1956; *s* of Archibald and Grietje Scott; *m* 1984, Marion Mapstone; two *c*. *Educ:* Bearsden Acad.; Edinburgh Univ. (BSc 1977). FREng 2014. Engr, Arup Hong Kong, 1984–98; Associate Dir, then Dir, Arup NY, 1998–2009; Americas Building Practice Leader, Arup, 2010–12. Chm., Council on Tall Buildings and Urban Habitat, 2006–09. FRSE 2010. Hon. AIA 2009. *Recreations:* walking, sailing, bad golf, theatre, food, fun and family. *Address:* Laing O'Rourke, Bridge Place, Admirals Park, Dartford, Kent DA2 6SN. *T:* 07771 885996. *E:* davidscott@laingorourke.com. *Club:* Caledonian.

SCOTT, Sir David (Richard Alexander), Kt 2013; CBE 2006; FCA; business consultant; Chief Executive, Digital UK (formerly SwitchCo) Ltd, 2008–13 (Director, 2005–13); *b* 25 Aug. 1954; *s* of R. I. M. Scott, OBE and Daphne Scott (*née* Alexander); *m* 1981, Moy Barraclough; one *s* one *d*. *Educ:* Wellington Coll. FCA 1979. Chartered Accountant, Peat Marwick Mitchell & Co., 1972–81; Channel Four Television, subseq. Channel Four Television Corporation: Controller of Finance, 1981–88; Dir of Finance, 1988–97; Man. Dir, 1997–2005; Dep. Chief Exec., 2002–05; Consultant, 2005–08. Dir, Digital Television Gp Ltd, 2006–. FRTS 2004. *Recreations:* sailing, walking, film, opera, bridge, ballet. *Address:* 25 Moreton Place, Pimlico, SW1V 2NL. *Clubs:* Boodle's; Guards' Polo, Royal Thames Yacht.

SCOTT, Dermot; *see* Scott, W. D.

SCOTT, Sir Dominic James M.; *see* Maxwell Scott.

SCOTT, Douglas Keith, (Doug Scott), CBE 1994; *b* Nottingham, 29 May 1941; *s* of George Douglas Scott and Edith Joyce Scott; *m* 1st, 1962, Janice Elaine Brook (marr. diss. 1988); one *s* two *d*; 2nd, 1993, Sharavati, (Sharu), Prabhu (marr. diss. 2003); two *s*; 3rd, 2007, Patricia Lang. *Educ:* Cottesmore Secondary Modern Sch.; Mundella Grammar Sch., Nottingham; Loughborough Teachers' Trng Coll. (Teaching Certificate). Began climbing age of 12; first ascent, Tarso Teiroko, Tibesti Mts, Sahara, 1965; first ascents, Cilo Dag Mts, SE Turkey, 1966; first ascent, S face Koh-i-Bandaka (6837 m), Hindu Kush, Afghanistan, 1967; first British ascent, Salathé Wall, El Capitan, Yosemite, 1971; 1972: Spring, Mem., European Mt Everest Expedn to SW face; Summer, first ascent, E Pillar of Mt Asgard, Baffin Island Expedn; Autumn, Mem., British Mt Everest Expedn to SW face; first ascent, Changabang (6864 m), 1974; first ascent, SE spur, Pic Lenin (7189 m), 1974; reached summit of Mt Everest, via SW face, with Dougal Haston, as Members, British Everest Expedn, 24th Sept. 1975 (first Britons on summit); first Alpine ascent of S face, Mt McKinley (6226 m), via new route, British Direct, with Dougal Haston, 1976; first ascent, East Face Direct, Mt Kenya, 1976; first ascent, Ogre (7330 m), Karakoram Mountains, 1977; first ascent, N Ridge route, Kangchenjunga (8593 m), without oxygen, 1979; first ascent, N Summit, Kussum Kangguru, 1979; first ascent, N Face, Nuptse, 1979; Alpine style, Kangchungtse (7640 m), 1980; first ascent Shivling E Pillar, 13-day Alpine Style push, 1981; Chamlang (7366 m) North Face to Central Summit, with Rheinhold Messner, 1981; first ascent, Pungpa Ri (7445 m), 1982; first ascent Shishapangma South Face (8046 m), 1982; first ascent, Lobsang Spire (Karakoram), and ascent Broad Peak (8047 m), 1983; Mt Baruntse (7143 m), first ascent, East Summit Mt Chamlang (7287 m), and traverse over unclimbed central summit Chamlang, Makalu SE Ridge, Alpine Style, to within 100 m of summit, 1984; first Alpine style ascent, Diran (7260 m), 1985; first ascent of rock climbs in S India, 1986; first ascent of rock climbs, Wadi Rum, Jordan, 1987; Mt Jitchu Drake (Bhutan) (6793 m), South face first ascent of peak, Alpine style, 1988; first ascent, Indian Arete Latok III, 1990; first ascent, Hanging Glacier Peak South (6294 m), via South Ridge, 1991; first British ascent of Chimtarga (5482 m), Fanskiye Mountains, Tadzhikistan, 1992; first ascent, Central Mazeno Peaks (6970 m) of Nanga Parbat, 1992; first ascent, Mt Pelagic (2000 m), Tierra del Fuego, 1993; first ascent Carstensz Pyramid North Face, 1995; first ascent, Chombu East (5745 m), NE Sikkim, 1996; first ascent Drohmo Central summit (6855 m), via South pillar, Alpine style, with Roger Mear, 1998; first ascent, Targo Ri (6650 m), Central Tibet, 2000. Pres., Alpine Climbing Gp, 1976–82; Vice-Pres., British Mountaineering Council, 1994–97. Hon. MA: Nottingham, 1991; Loughborough, 1993; Hon. MEd Nottingham Trent, 1995; Hon. Dr Derby, 2007. *Publications:* Big Wall Climbing, 1974; (with Alex MacIntyre) Shishapangma, Tibet, 1984; Himalayan Climber, 1992; contrib. to Alpine Jl, Amer. Alpine Jl, Mountain Magazine and Himal Magazine. *Recreations:* rock climbing, photography, organic gardening. *Address:* Stewart Hill Cottage, Hesket Newmarket, Wigton CA7 8HX. *T:* (01768) 484841, 07752 251256, (office) (01768) 484842. *E:* dougscott25@hotmail.com. *Clubs:* Alpine (Pres., 1999–2001); Alpine Climbing Group; Nottingham Climbers'.

SCOTT, Edward McM.; *see* McMillan-Scott.

SCOTT, Eleanor Roberta; Member (Green) Highlands and Islands, Scottish Parliament, 2003–07; *b* 23 July 1951; *d* of late William Ettles and Roberta Ettles (*née* Reid); *m* 1977, David Scott (marr. diss. 1995); one *s* one *d*; partner, Robert McKay Gibson, *qv*. *Educ:* Bearsden Acad.; Glasgow Univ. (MB ChB 1974). Jun. doctor posts, 1974–80; Clin. Med. Officer, Community Paediatrics, Inverness, 1980–87; Sen. Clin. Med. Officer, Community Paediatrics, Dingwall, Ross-shire, 1987–2003. *Recreations:* traditional music, gardening. *Address:* Tir Nan Oran, 8 Culcairn Road, Evanton IV16 9YT. *T:* (01349) 830388. *E:* eleanorsco@googlemail.com.

SCOTT, Emma Jane; Managing Director, Freesat, since 2007; *b* 21 May 1968; *d* of Michael Bryan Scott and late Jennifer Scott (*née* Birtwistle); *m* 2003, James Tatam (marr. diss. 2010); two *d*. *Educ:* Hatfield Sch.; Univ. of Hull (BA Hons Pols and Legislative Studies); Bradford Management Sch. (MBA with distinction). Researcher to Austin Mitchell, MP, 1989 and 1990–91; Strategy Analyst, Optus Communications, Sydney, 1992–95; Cogent Consulting, Nortel, 1996; BBC: Sen. Advr, Corporate Strategy, 1997; Hd, Dir Gen.'s Office, 1999–2004; Freeview Launch Dir, 2002–03; Hd, Partnership Strategy, 2005; Freesat Launch Dir, 2006. Mem., Adv. Panel, RTS, 2010– (Vice Chm.); Trustee, Bd, Ovarian Cancer Action, 2010–. FRSA. *Recreation:* baking and books with my children. *Address:* Freesat, 23–24 Newman Street, W1T 1PJ.

SCOTT, Finlay McMillan, CBE 2009; TD 1984; Chief Executive and Registrar, General Medical Council, 1994–2009; *b* 25 May 1947; *s* of Finlay McMillan Scott and Anne Cameron Robertson Coutts Scott; *m* 1st, 1969, Eileen Frances Marshall (marr. diss. 2001); one *s* one *d*; 2nd, 2002, Prof. Elizabeth Susan Perkins. *Educ:* Greenock High Sch.; Open Univ. (BA Hons; LLB Hons); Durham Univ. (MSc). Department of Education and Science, subseq. Department for Education, 1975–94: Head of Pensions Br. and Controller, Darlington, 1983–86; Head of Inf. Systems Br., 1986–90; on secondment: to UFC, 1990–93; to PCFC, 1992–93; to HEFCE, 1992–94; Under Sec., 1990–94. Lt-Col, RAOC, 1989–93, RLC, 1993–95, RARO, 1995–, TA. Member: NIHEC, 1993–2001; Medical Workforce Standing Adv. Cttee, 1996–2001; Postgrad. Med. Educn and Trng Bd, 2003–10. Governor: London Guildhall Univ., 1996–2002; London Metropolitan Univ., 2003–09. *Recreations:* horse riding, learning to be a farmer. *E:* finlayscott@kilnfarm.org.

SCOTT, Sir (George) Peter, Kt 2007; Professor of Higher Education Studies, Institute of Education, University College London (formerly Institute of Education, University of London), since 2011; *b* 1 Aug. 1946; *s* of George Edward Grey Scott and Evelyn Mary Scott (*née* Robb); *m* 1968, Cherill Andrea Williams; one *d*. *Educ:* Merton Coll., Oxford (BA 1st cl. Hons Modern History 1967). Journalist: TES, 1967–69; The Times, 1969–71; Dep. Editor, THES, 1971–73; Vis. Scholar (Harkness Fellow), Grad. Sch. of Public Policy, Univ. of Calif at Berkeley, 1973–74; leader writer, The Times, 1974–76; Editor, THES, 1976–92; Prof. of Education, 1992–97, Pro-Vice-Chancellor, 1996–97, Univ. of Leeds; Vice-Chancellor, Kingston Univ., 1998–2010. Mem. Bd, HEFCE, 2000–06. Chm. Council, Univ. of Glos, 2011–. Hon. Fellow, UMIST, 1992. Hon. LLD Bath, 1992; Hon. DLitt: CNAA, 1992; Grand Valley State Univ., 1999; St George's, Univ. of London, 2012; Leicester, 2013; Hon. PhD Anglia Polytech. Univ., 1998. *Publications:* The Crisis of the University, 1986; Knowledge and Nation, 1990; The New Production of Knowledge, 1994; The Meanings of Mass Higher Education, 1995; Governing Universities, 1996; Re-thinking Science, Knowledge and the Public in an age of uncertainty, 2001; (with C. Callender) Browne and Beyond: the reform of English higher education, 2013; (with L. Engwall) Trust in Universities, 2013. *Address:* UCL Institute of Education, 20 Bedford Way, WC1H 0AL. *T:* (020) 7612 6048.

SCOTT, Dr Graham Alexander; Deputy Chief Medical Officer, Scottish Home and Health Department, 1975–89; *b* 26 Nov. 1927; *s* of Alexander Scott and Jessie Scott; *m* 1951, Helena Patricia Margaret Cavanagh (*d* 2009); two *s* one *d*. *Educ:* Daniel Stewart's Coll., Edinburgh; Edinburgh Univ. (MB, ChB). FRCPE, FFPH, DPH. RAAMC, 1951–56 (Dep. Asst Dir, Army Health, 1st Commonwealth Div., Korea, 1953–54). Sen. Asst MO, Stirling CC, 1957–62, Dep. County MO, 1962–65; Scottish Home and Health Department: MO, 1965–68; SMO, 1968–74; PMO, 1974–75. Consultant in Public Health Medicine, Borders Health Board, 1990–93. QHP 1987–90. *Recreations:* gardening, walking. *Address:* 56 High Road, Auchtermuchty, Cupar, Fife KY14 7BE.

SCOTT, Prof. Hamish Marshall, PhD; FBA 2006; FRSE, FSAScot; Professor of International History, 2000–06, Wardlaw Professor of International History, 2006–09, University of St Andrews, now Emeritus; Honorary Senior Research Fellow, School of Humanities (History) (formerly Department of History), University of Glasgow, since 2009; *b* 12 July 1946; *s* of James Donaldson Scott and Elizabeth Levack Scott (*née* Dalrymple); *m* 2005, Julia M. H. Smith. *Educ:* George Heriot's Sch., Edinburgh; Univ. of Edinburgh (MA 1968); London Sch. of Econs (PhD 1978). Lectr, Univ. of Birmingham, 1970–78; Lectr, then Sen. Lectr, Univ. of St Andrews, 1979–2000. Pres., Royal Philosophical Soc. of Glasgow, 2012–14. FRSE 2008; FSAScot 2010. MAE 2009. *Publications:* (with D. McKay) The Rise of the Great Powers 1648–1815, 1983; British Foreign Policy in the Age of the American Revolution, 1990; (ed) Enlightened Absolutism: reform and reformers in later eighteenth-century Europe, 1990; (ed) The European Nobilities in the Seventeenth and Eighteenth Centuries, 2 vols, 1995, 2nd edn 2007; (ed jtly) Royal and Republican Sovereignty in Early

Modern Europe: essays in memory of Ragnhild Hatton, 1997; The Emergence of the Eastern Powers 1756–1775, 2001; The Birth of a Great Power System 1740–1815, 2006; (ed jtly) Cultures of Power in Europe during the Long Eighteenth Century, 2007; (ed) The Oxford Handbook of Early Modern European History, 2 vols, 2015; contrib. to learned jls and collected vols. *Recreations:* music, sport, hill-walking, cooking. *Address:* School of Humanities (History), University of Glasgow, 2 University Gardens, Glasgow G12 0QB. *E:* Hamish.Scott@glasgow.ac.uk.

SCOTT, Hilary; independent development consultant; *b* 9 June 1954; *d* of Stephen and late June Scott; civil partnership 2007, Linda Charlton. *Educ:* Camden Sch. for Girls; Poly. of Central London (BA Hons Social Sci. 1978); Poly. of South Bank (MSc Sociol. of Health and Illness 1986); DipHSM 1983. Nat. Admin. Trainee, NHS, 1978–81; Asst House Gov., St Stephen's Hosp., 1981–83; Dep. Administrator, Brook Gen. Hosp., 1983–86; Outpatient and Diagnostic Services Manager, Northwick Park Hosp., 1986–89; Chief Exec., Enfield & Haringey FHSA, 1989–93; Project Dir, City and E London Family and Community Health Services, 1993–95; Chief Exec., Tower Hamlets Health Care NHS Trust, 1995–99; Dep. Health Service Ombudsman, 1999–2003; Complaints and Clin. Negligence Prog. Manager, DoH, 2003–04. Chm., Action on Elder Abuse, 2004–07; Trustee, Action against Medical Accidents, 2010–. Vice Chm., Gwynedd Cttee, North Wales Community Health Council, 2012–13. Middlesex University Business School: Vis. Prof., 2002–07; Associate Prof., 2007–10; Vis. Prof., 2010–; Vis. Sen. Fellow, Birmingham Univ., 2004–. Mem. Ct of Govs, Univ. of Westminster, 2002–09. FIHM 1997. *Recreations:* family, friends, gardening, sewing, Welsh learner at Bangor University, 2011–.

SCOTT, Prof. Ian Richard, PhD; Barber Professor of Law, 1978–2000, Professor of Law (personal chair), 2001–05, University of Birmingham, Emeritus Professor, since 2006; *b* 8 Jan. 1940; *s* of Ernest and Edith Scott; *m* 1971, Ecce Cole; two *d*. *Educ:* Geelong Coll.; Queen's Coll., Univ. of Melbourne (LLB); King's Coll., Univ. of London (PhD). Barrister and Solicitor, Supreme Court of Victoria; called to Bar, Gray's Inn, 1995. Dir, Inst. of Judicial Admin, 1975–82. Exec. Dir, Victoria Law Foundn, 1982–84; Dean, Faculty of Law, Univ. of Birmingham, 1985–94. Member: Lord Chancellor's Civil Justice Review Body, 1985–88; Policy Adv. Gp, NHS Litigation Authy, 1996–2000; Alternative Dispute Resolution sub-cttee, Civil Justice Council, 1998–2002; Chm., N Yorks Magistrates' Courts Inquiry, 1989. Non-exec. Dir, Royal Orthopaedic Hosp. NHS Trust, 1995–2000. Hon. Bencher, Gray's Inn, 1988. Life Mem., Aust. Inst. of Judicial Admin, 1990. An Ed., 1989–2006, Gen. Ed., 2007–, Civil Procedure (the White Book). *Recreation:* law. *Address:* School of Law, University of Birmingham, Birmingham B15 2TT.

SCOTT, Irene Elizabeth; *see* Gray, I. E.

SCOTT, Prof. James, FRCP; FRS 1997; Professor of Medicine, since 1997 and Deputy Principal for Research, since 2000, Imperial College London (Deputy Vice-Principal, 1997–2000); Director, Imperial College Genetics and Genomics Research Institute, 2000; *b* 13 Sept. 1946; *s* of Robert Bentham Scott and Iris Olive Scott (*née* Hill); *m* 1976, Diane Marylin Lowe; two *s* one *d*. *Educ:* London Univ. (BSc 1968); London Hosp. Med. Coll. (MB, BS 1971; MSc Biochem. 1978). MRCP 1974, FRCP 1986. House Officer: London Hosp., 1971–72; Hereford Co. Hosp., 1972; Sen. House Officer, Midland Centre for Neurosurgery and Neurol., and Queen Elizabeth Hosp., Birmingham, 1972–73; Registrar in Medicine: General Hosp., Birmingham, 1973–74; Acad. Dept of Medicine, Royal Free Hosp., 1975–76; MRC Res. Fellow and Hon. Sen. Registrar, RPMS and Hammersmith Hosp., 1977–80; European Molecular Biol. Fellow, Dept of Biochem., Univ. of Calif, San Francisco, 1980–83; MRC Clinical Scientist and Hon. Consultant Physician, MRC Clinical Res. Centre and Northwick Park Hosp., 1983–91; Prof. and Chm. of Medicine, RPMS, 1992–97; Dir of Medicine and Chief of Service Med. Cardiology, Hammersmith Hosps NHS Trust, 1994–97; Hon. Consultant Physician, Hammersmith Hosp., 1992–; Hon. Dir, MRC Molecular Medicine Gp, 1992–. Member: RCP Res. Cttee, 1988–91; Assoc. of Physicians of GB and Ireland, 1987; European Molecular Biol. Orgn, 1993–; RSocMed Adv. Cttee, 1999–; Chm., N Thames Higher Merit Award Adv. Cttee, 1996–2000. Lectures include: Humphrey Davy Rolleston, RCP, 1989; Simms, RCP, 1995; Pfizer, Clin. Res. Inst., Montreal; Guest, Japan Atherosclerosis Soc., 1992; Dolan Boyd Pritchett Meml, Perelman Sch. of Medicine, Univ. of Pennsylvania, 2008; Crisps/Cas 9 Technol., St Hilda's Coll., Oxford, 2015. Founder FMedSci 1998. Graham Bull Prize, RCP, 1989; Squibb Bristol Myers Award for Cardiovascular Res., 1993. *Publications:* numerous on molecular medicine, molecular genetics, atherosclerosis, RNA modification, RNA editing and gene expression. *Recreations:* family and friends, the twentieth century novel, British Impressionists and modern painting, long distance running, swimming. *Address:* National Heart and Lung Institute, Imperial College London, Hammersmith Campus, W12 0HS.

SCOTT, James Alexander, OBE 1987; FCA; Partner, Binder Hamlyn, Chartered Accountants, 1969–98; Chairman, Schroder Exempt Property Unit Trust, 2010–12 (Director, 1994–2012); *b* 30 April 1940; *s* of Douglas McPherson Scott and Mabel Mary (*née* Skepper); *m* 1965, Annette Goslett; three *s* two *d*. *Educ:* Uppingham Sch.; Magdalene Coll., Cambridge (Schol.; MA); London Business Sch. (MSc). Joined Binder Hamlyn, 1961; Man. Partner, London Region, 1980–88; Nat. Man. Partner, 1988–89. Dir, Vestey Group Ltd, 1992–. Chm. Trustees, Lonmin Superannuation Scheme, 2000–09; Trustee, Western Utd Gp Pension Scheme, 2009–. Mem., Agricl Wages Bd for England and Wales, 1971–86; Sec., Review Bd for Govt Contracts, 1969–98; Member: NHS Pharmacists Remuneration Review Panel, 1982; Restrictive Practices Court, 1993–2000. DTI Inspector, Atlantic Computers plc, 1990. *Recreations:* walking, golf, tennis, ski-ing. *Clubs:* Berkshire Golf; St Enodoc Golf.

SCOTT, James Archibald, CB 1988; LVO 1961; FRSE; Deputy Spokesman on trade and industry, Scottish National Party, 1997–99; *b* 5 March 1932; *s* of late James Scott, MBE, and Agnes Bone Howie; *m* 1957, Elizabeth Agnes Joyce Buchan-Hepburn; three *s* one *d*. *Educ:* Dollar Acad.; Queen's Univ. of Ont.; Univ. of St Andrews (MA Hons). FRSE 1993. RAF aircrew, 1954–56. Asst Principal, CRO, 1956; served in New Delhi, 1958–62, and UK Mission to UN, New York, 1962–65; transf. to Scottish Office, 1965; Private Sec. to Sec. of State for Scotland, 1969–71; Asst Sec., Scottish Office, 1971; Under-Sec., Scottish Economic Planning Dept, later Industry Dept for Scotland, 1976–84; Sec., Scottish Educn Dept, 1984–87; Sec., Industry Dept for Scotland, 1987–90; Chief Exec., SDA, 1990–91; Exec. Dir, Scottish Financial Enterprise, 1991–94. Non-exec. Director: Scottish Power plc, 1992–96; Dumyat Investment Trust plc, 1995–2000. Fellow, SCOTVEC, 1990. Chevalier, Ordre National du Mérite (France), 1995. *Recreations:* travel, golf. *Address:* 38 Queen's Crescent, Edinburgh EH9 2BA. *T:* (0131) 667 8417.

SCOTT, Prof. James Floyd, PhD; FRS 2008; Professor of Physics, and Research Director, Department of Physics, Cavendish Laboratory, University of Cambridge, since 2009; *b* 4 May 1942; *s* of William Burgess Scott and Isabel Miles; *m* 1982, Galina Alexeevna Dergilyova; one *d*. *Educ:* Harvard (AB 1963); Ohio State Univ. (PhD 1966). Prof. (Physics) and Asst Vice Chancellor, Univ. of Colorado, 1971–92; Professor and Dean: RMIT, Melbourne, 1992–95; Univ. of New South Wales, 1995–99. Chm. Bd, 1986–90, Dir, 1986–99, Symetrix Corp., USA; Prof. of Ferroics, 1999–2009, Symetrix Professor of Ferroics, 1999–2004, Univ. of Cambridge. Fellow, APS, 1974. Mem., Acad. of Scis, Slovenia, 2011. Humboldt Prize, Germany, 1997; Monkasho Prize, Japan, 2001; Gold Medal, Materials Res. Soc., 2008; Jozef Stefan Gold Medal, Slovenia, 2009. *Publications:* Ferroelectric Memories, 2000; over 700 articles in learned jls. *Recreations:* travel, gardening. *Address:* Thorndyke, Huntingdon Road, Cambridge CB3 0LG. *T:* (01223) 277793, *Fax:* (01223) 333450. *E:* jfs32@hermes.cam.ac.uk.

SCOTT, Sir James (Jervoise), 3rd Bt *cr* 1962, of Rotherfield Park, Alton, Hants; DL; farmer and landowner; *b* 12 Oct. 1952; *e s* of Lt-Col Sir James Walter Scott, 2nd Bt, and Anne Constantia (*née* Austin); *S* father, 1993; *m* 1982, Judy Evelyn, *d* of Brian Trafford and Hon. Mrs Trafford; one *s* one *d*. *Educ:* Eton; Trinity Coll., Cambridge (MA). Agricultural journalist, 1977–88. Mem., Hampshire CC, 2001–05. High Sheriff, Hants, 2004–05. DL Hants, 2013. *Recreation:* shooting. *Heir: s* Arthur Jervoise Trafford Scott [*b* 2 Feb. 1984; *m* 2011, Emily Helen Wahlberg, *d* of David George Fossett Thompson, *qv*; one *s*]. *Address:* Estate Office, Rotherfield Park, East Tisted, Alton, Hampshire GU34 3QN. *T:* (01420) 588207. *Clubs:* White's, Travellers.

SCOTT, Jane Elizabeth, (Mrs Justin Byam Shaw); UK Director, Professional Boards Forum, since 2009; *b* Theydon Bois, 21 Aug. 1960; *d* of Dr Sydney Scott and Dr Margaret Scott (*née* Barrie); *m* 1991, Justin Byam Shaw; one *s* (and one *s* decd). *Educ:* City of London Sch. for Girls; Trinity Coll., Oxford (BA Modern Langs 1983; MA); London Business Sch. (MBA 1996). Mktg Manager, 1986–91, Mktg Dir, 1991–92, Wolff Olins; ind. mgt consultant, 1992–2008. Founder Mem., Steering Cttee, 30% Club, 2010–; compiler, BoardWatch reports, 2011–. Vice Pres., Muscular Dystrophy UK (formerly Muscular Dystrophy Campaign), 2009–. Trustee, Felix Byam Shaw Foundn, 2014–. Gov., Byam Shaw Sch. of Art, 1994–99. *Recreations:* tennis, yoga, ski-ing, student drama. *E:* jane@boardsforum.co.uk, jane@byamshaw.com. *Clubs:* Holland Park Lawn Tennis, Dragon School Ski.

SCOTT, Janet Howard; *see* Darbyshire, J. H.

SCOTT, Janys Margaret; QC (Scot.) 2007; Advocate, since 1992; part-time Sheriff, since 2005; *b* Radcliffe, 28 Aug. 1953; *d* of John and Dylys Allen; *m* 1974, Dr Kevin F. Scott; two *s* one *d*. *Educ:* Newnham Coll., Cambridge (BA 1974). Articled clerk, Oxford, 1974–76; Asst Lectr, Sulaimaniyah Univ., Iraq, 1976–78; Solicitor, Oxford, 1978–86, Edinburgh, 1987–91. Hon. Lectr, Dundee Univ., 1989–94. Convener, Scottish Child Law Centre, 1992–97; Chairman: Stepfamily Scotland, 1998–2002; Scottish Legal Gp, Brit. Assoc. for Adoption and Fostering, 2004–10; Advocates Family Law Assoc., 2013–; UK Deleg., Family and Succession Cttee (formerly CCBE Family and Succession Working Gp), 2012–. Vice-Pres. (part-time), Sheriffs' Assoc., 2014–. *Publications:* Education Law in Scotland, 2003. *Recreations:* growing vegetables, cooking, reading. *Address:* Westwater Advocates, Parliament House, Edinburgh EH1 1RF.

SCOTT, Jean Grant, (Mrs Donald Macleod); Chairman, Independent Schools Council, 2001–06; Headmistress, South Hampstead High School GDST, 1993–2001; *b* 7 Oct. 1940; *d* of Dr Duncan W. D. MacLaren and Etta M. MacLaren (*née* Speirs); *m* 1st, 1964, John Scott (*d* 1979); two *s*; 2nd, 2000, Donald Macleod. *Educ:* George Watson's Ladies' Coll., Edinburgh; Wellington Sch., Ayr; Univ. of Glasgow (BSc Hons Zool.); Univ. of London Inst. of Educn (PGCE). Research Biologist: Glaxo Labs Ltd, 1962–65; ICI, Alderley Edge, 1966–67; part-time Lectr in Biol., Newcastle-under-Lyme Coll. of FE, 1969–70; Teacher of Biology: (part-time) Dr Challoner's High Sch., 1970–76; Northgate Grammar Sch., Ipswich, 1976–77; Hd of Biol. and Sen. Mistress, Ipswich High Sch. (GPDST), 1977–86; Headmistress, St George's Sch. for Girls, Edinburgh, 1986–93. Trustee, American Sch. in London, 1997–2005. Governor: Central Sch. of Speech and Drama, 1998–2006; Downe Hse Sch., 2001–10; Haileybury Coll., 2001–; Haileybury Almaty Sch., Kazakhstan, 2008–; Haileybury Astana Sch., Kazakhstan, 2011–; Edge Grove Sch., Aldenham, 2011– (Chm., 2014–). *Recreations:* concerts, theatre, film, swimming, ski-ing, golf, loch fishing, travel abroad. *Address:* 3 Merton Rise, NW3 3EN.

SCOTT, Prof. Joanne, FBA 2013; FRSE; Professor of European Law, University College London, since 2005; *b* Edinburgh, 17 Dec. 1965; *d* of Terence Scott and Jean Isabella Scott (*née* Meikle); partner, Ferguson Morton Murray. *Educ:* Madras Coll., St Andrews; Univ. of Aberdeen (LLB 1987); European University Inst., Florence (LLM 1989). Lectr, Univ. of Kent at Canterbury, 1988–93; Lectr, 1994–98, Reader, 1998–2000, QMW, then QMUL; Lectr, 2000–02, Reader, 2002–05, Law Faculty, Univ. of Cambridge; Fellow, Clare Coll., Cambridge, 2000–05. Visiting Professor: Columbia Law Sch., 2002–03; Harvard Law Sch., 2005–06. Mem., Royal Commn on Envmtl Pollution, 2009–11. Leverhulme Major Res. Fellow, 2009–12. FRSE 2012. *Publications:* EC Environmental Law, 1997; (ed with G. de Burca) Constitutional Change in the EU: from uniformity to flexibility, 2000; (ed with G. de Burca) The EU and the WTO: legal and constitutional aspects, 2001; European Regional Development Policy: confusing quantity with quality, 2005; (ed with G. de Burca) Law and New Approaches to Governance in the EU and US, 2006; Commentary on the Sanitary and Phytosanitary Measures Agreement, 2007; articles in jls incl. Eur. Jl of Internat. Law, Amer. Jl of Comparative Law, Common Mkt Law Rev., Eur. Law Jl. *Recreations:* walking, birdwatching, travelling, opera. *Address:* Faculty of Laws, University College London, Endsleigh Gardens, WC1H 0EG. *T:* (020) 7699 1408. *E:* joanne.scott@ucl.ac.uk.

SCOTT, Sir John; *see* Scott, Sir P. J. and Scott, Sir W. J.

SCOTT, John; *see* Scott, W. J. G.

SCOTT, Prof. John Anthony Gerard, FRCP; Professor of Vaccine Epidemiology, and Director, Vaccine Centre, London School of Hygiene and Tropical Medicine, since 2013; Wellcome Trust Senior Research Fellow in Clinical Science, Kenya Medical Research Institute-Wellcome Trust Research Programme, Kenya, since 2008; *b* Liverpool, 6 Nov. 1962; *s* of John Scott and Mary Scott (*née* McCabe); *m* 1985, Louise M. M. Leahy; two *s* two *d*. *Educ:* Churchill Coll., Cambridge (BA Psychol. 1984); Merton Coll., Oxford (BM BCh 1987); London Sch. of Hygiene and Tropical Medicine, Univ. of London (MSc Epidemiol. 1993). MRCP 1990, FRCP 2004; DTM&H 1991. Clin. trng, in Medicine, Newcastle, 1988–90, in Infectious Diseases, Northwick Park Hosp., 1991–92; Wellcome Trust Res. Trng Fellow, 1992–96, Tropical Res. Fellow, 1998–2000, Career Develt Fellow, 2001–07, Kenya Med. Res. Inst. - Wellcome Trust Res. Prog., Kilifi, Kenya and Univ. of Oxford; Co-Dir, Kilifi Health and Demographic Surveillance System, 2000–; Prof. of Epidemiol., Univ. of Oxford, 2010–12. Vis. Prof., Univ. of Oxford, 2013–. Associate, Johns Hopkins Sch. of Public Health, 2011–14. Hon. Consultant Physician, Oxford Univ. Hosps Trust, 2000–. Mem., Jt Cttee on Vaccination and Immunisation, 2013–. FMedSci 2013. *Publications:* (contrib.) Oxford Textbook of Medicine, 5th edn 2010, 6th edn 2012; (contrib.) Principles of Medicine in Africa, 3rd edn 2004, 4th edn 2011; contrib. res. papers on infectious disease epidemiol., pneumococcal disease and vaccines. *Recreations:* hiking, mountain biking, swimming, photography. *Address:* Department of Infectious Disease Epidemiology, London School of Hygiene and Tropical Medicine, Keppel Street, WC1E 7HT. *T:* (020) 7927 2827. *E:* anthony.scott@lshtm.ac.uk.

SCOTT, (John) Brough; Founding Director, Racing Post, 1986–2007; journalist and broadcaster; *b* 12 Dec. 1942; *s* of Mason Hogarth Scott and Irene Florence Scott, Broadway, Worcs; *m* 1973, Susan Eleanor MacInnes; two *s* two *d*. *Educ:* Radley College; Corpus Christi, Oxford (BA History). Amateur, then professional, Nat. Hunt jockey, 1962–71 (100 winners, incl. Imperial Cup and Mandarin Chase). ITV presenter, sports programmes and documentaries, 1971–; chief racing presenter, ITV, 1979–85; chief presenter, Channel 4 Racing, 1985–2001. Evening Standard sports correspondent, 1972–74; sports journalist: Sunday Times, 1974–90, 1993–94; The Independent on Sunday, 1990–92; Sports Writer, Sunday Telegraph, 1995–2008. Vice-Pres., Jockeys' Assoc., 1969–71; Trustee, Injured Jockeys Fund, 1978– (Chm., 2007–); Trustee, Moorcroft Racehorse Welfare Centre, 2003–. Lord Derby Award, 1978 (racing journalist of the year); Clive Graham Trophy, 1982; Sports

Feature Writer of the Year, 1985, 1991, 1992. *Publications:* World of Flat Racing, 1983; On and Off the Rails, 1984; Front Runners, 1991; Up Front—Willie Carson, 1994; Racing Certainties, 1995; Galloper Jack, 2003; Of Horses and Heroes, 2008; (ed) McCoy, 2010; Warrior, 2011; Henry Cecil: trainer of genius, 2013. *Recreation:* making bonfires. *Address:* Meadow House, Coneyhurst Lane, Ewhurst, Surrey GU6 7PL. *T:* (01483) 277379, 07860 258881.

SCOTT, Prof. John Donald, PhD; FRS 2003; Edwin G. Krebs-Speights Professor of Cell Signaling and Cancer Biology, Department of Pharmacology, University of Washington, since 2008; Investigator, Howard Hughes Medical Institute, 2004 (Associate Investigator, 1997–2003); *b* 13 April 1958; *m* Shonnie; one *s* one *d. Educ:* Heriot-Watt Univ., Edinburgh (BSc Hons (Biochem.) 1980); Univ. of Aberdeen (PhD Biochem.). Med. Endowments Hon. Scholar, Univ. of Aberdeen, 1980–83; NIH Postdoctoral Fellow, Dept of Pharmacol., 1983–86, Res. Asst Prof., Dept of Biochem., 1986–88, Univ. of Washington, Seattle; Sen. Associate, Howard Hughes Med. Inst., 1986–88; Asst Prof., Dept of Physiol. and Biophysics, Univ. of Calif, Irvine, 1988–89; Asst Scientist, 1990–92, Scientist, 1993–96, Sen. Scientist, 1997–2008, Vollum Inst., Oregon Health and Sciences Univ. Consultant, ICOS Corp., Seattle, 1992–2000; Scientific Adv. Bd, Upstate Biotechnology, Lake Placid, 1995–; Trellis Bioscience Inc., Mountain View, 2003–. Member NIH Study Section: Med. Biochem., 1993–96; Biochem., 1998–2002. Member: Biochemical Soc., 1981–; Amer. Soc. for Biochem. and Molecular Biol., 1990– (Mem. Program Cttee, 2000–); Endocrine Soc., 1997– (Ernst Oppenheimer Award, 2001); Amer. Soc. for Pharmacol. and Experimental Therapeutics, 1997– (Mem., 1999–2001, Chm., 2001–, John Jacob Abel Award Selection Cttee; John J. Abel Award in Pharmacol., 1996). Mem. Editl Bd, Jl of Biological Chemistry, 1993–98; Review Ed., Biochemical Jl, 2002–. D'Agrosa Meml Lecture, St Louis Univ., 2001. Discovery Award, Med. Res. Foundn, 2003. *Publications:* many articles in learned jls. *Address:* Department of Pharmacology, University of Washington, 1959 Pacific Avenue NE, Box 357750, Seattle, WA 98195, USA. *T:* (206) 6163340, *Fax:* (206) 6163386. *E:* scottjdw@u.washington.edu.

SCOTT, Rev. Prof. John Fraser, AO 1990; Associate Priest, St George's, Malvern, since 1992; *b* 10 Oct. 1928; *s* of Douglas Fraser Scott and Cecilia Louise Scott; *m* 1956, Dorothea Elizabeth Paton Scott; one *s* three *d. Educ:* Bristol Grammar Sch.; Trinity Coll., Cambridge (MA); Melbourne Coll. of Divinity (BD 1994). FIS. Research Asst, Univ. of Sheffield, 1950–53; Asst, Univ. of Aberdeen, 1953–55; Lectr in Biometry, Univ. of Oxford, 1955–65; University of Sussex: Reader in Statistics, 1965–67; Prof. of Applied Statistics, 1967–77; Pro-Vice-Chancellor, 1971–77; Vice-Chancellor, La Trobe Univ., Melbourne, 1977–90. Adv. Prof., E China Normal Univ., 1988. Visiting Consultant in Statistics: Nigeria, 1961, 1965; Sweden, 1969; Kuwait, 1973, 1976; Iraq, 1973; Malaysia, 1976. Reader, Church of England, 1971–77; Examining Chaplain to Bp of Chichester, 1974–77; Diocesan Lay Reader, Anglican Dio. of Melbourne, 1977–90; ordained deacon, then priest, 1990; Asst Curate, St George's, E Ivanhoe, 1990–91. Chairman: Jt Cttee on Univ. Statistics, 1978–86; Cttee of Review of Student Finances, 1983; Aust. Univs Industrial Assoc., 1986–88; AVCC, 1986–88 (Dep. Chm., 1986, Chm., Wkg Party on Attrition, 1981–86); Council for Chaplains in Tertiary Instns, 1990–94; Member: Grad. Careers Council of Aust., 1980–86; Council, 1986–89, Exec. Cttee, 1986–88, ACU; ABC Victorian State Adv. Cttee, 1978–81; Ethics Cttee, Victorian State Dept of Health, 1990–2004; Pres., Victorian State Libraries Bd, 1990–96. Dir, La Trobe Univ. Credit Union, 2001–05. Chieftain, Ringwood Highland Games, 2003. Editor, Applied Statistics, 1971–76; Mem., Editl Bd, The Statistician, 1987–. DUniv La Trobe, 1990. *Publications:* The Comparability of Grade Standards in Mathematics, 1975; Report of Committee of Review of Student Finances, 1983; papers in JRSS, Lancet, BMJ, Chemistry and Industry, Statistician, etc. *Recreations:* wine, women and song; canals. *Address:* 1/18 Riversdale Road, Hawthorn, Victoria 3122, Australia. *T:* (3) 98191862. *Club:* Melbourne.

SCOTT, Sir John (Hamilton), KCVO 2011; Lord-Lieutenant for Shetland, 1994–2011; farming in Bressay and Noss; *b* 30 Nov. 1936; *s* of Dr Thomas Gilbert Scott and Elizabeth M. B. Scott; *m* 1965, Wendy Ronald; one *s* one *d. Educ:* Bryanston; Cambridge Univ.; Guy's Hosp., London. Shepherd, Scrabster, Caithness, 1961–64. Chm., Woolgrowers of Shetland Ltd, 1981–. Pres., Shetland NFU, 1976; Chairman: Shetland Crofting, Farming and Wildlife Adv. Gp, 1984–95; Shetland Arts Trust, 1993–98; Sail Shetland Ltd, 1997–2002; Belmont Trust, 1997–; Member: Nature Conservancy Council Cttee for Scotland, 1984–91; NE Regl Bd, Nature Conservancy Council for Scotland, 1991–92, Scottish Natural Heritage, 1992–97. Trustee, Shetland Charitable Trust, 1994–2011. *Recreations:* mountain climbing, Up-Helly-Aa, music. *Address:* Keldabister Banks, Bressay, Shetland ZE2 9EL. *T:* (01595) 820281. *E:* scott.gardie@virgin.net. *Club:* Alpine.

See also T. H. Scott.

SCOTT, (John) Michael, CMG 2003; independent rural livelihoods consultant, since 2003; *b* 18 Feb. 1943; *s* of late Harold Scott and Joan Winifred Scott (*née* Holroyd); *m* 1967, Pauline Rachel Wright; one *d. Educ:* Boston Grammar Sch., Lincs; Royal Veterinary Coll., London Univ. (BVetMed 1967); Royal (Dick) Sch. of Vet. Studies, Univ. of Edinburgh. MRCVS 1967. Vet. Surgeon, Whittle, Taylor and Chesworth, Rochdale, 1967–69; Vet. Officer, Govt of Botswana, Mahalapye and Francistown, 1969–71; Veterinary Investigation Officer (funded as UK Government Technical Co-operation Officer): Ethiopia, 1972–77; El Salvador, 1977–79; Overseas Development Administration: Animal Health and Prodn Advr, 1979–82; Sen. Animal Health and Prodn Advr, 1982–86; Sen. Natural Resources Advr, Fiji, 1987–90; Hd, Natural Resources Policy and Adv. Dept, 1990–97; Department for International Development: Hd, Rural Livelihoods Dept, 1997–2003; Chief Natural Resources Advr, 2002–03; Sen. Rural Livelihoods Advr, Southern Africa, 2003–04, Bangladesh, 2004–07; short-term consultancies, 2007–09; Natural Resource Mgt Advr, DFID/Danida, Cambodia, 2009–10; short assignments, DFID, 2011–14; Sen. Mgt Team, BRACED, 2014–. *Publications:* contrib. learned jls on animal trypanosomiasis and fascioliasis. *Recreations:* international affairs, running, cricket, ornithology, wildlife. *Address:* 63 Oxford Road, Wokingham, Berks RG41 2YH. *T:* (0118) 978 6603. *E:* jm.vets@btinternet.com.

SCOTT, Prof. John Peter, CBE 2013; PhD; FBA 2007; sociologist; Professor of Sociology, 2008–13, and Pro Vice-Chancellor (Research), 2010–13, University of Plymouth; *b* 8 April 1949; *s* of Philip Charles Scott and Phyllis Scott (*née* Bridges); *m* 1971, Gillian Wheatley; one *s* one *d. Educ:* Kingston Coll. of Technol. (BScSoc London 1971); London Sch. of Econs; Univ. of Strathclyde (PhD 1976). Lectr in Sociol., Univ. of Strathclyde, 1972–76; University of Leicester: Lectr, 1976, Reader, 1987–91, in Sociol.; Prof. of Sociol., 1991–94; Prof. of Sociol., Univ. of Essex, 1994–2008. Adjunct Prof., Bergen Univ., Norway, 1997–2005; Hon. Prof., Univ. of Copenhagen, 2012–; Hon. Vis. Prof., Exeter Univ., 2014–. British Sociological Association: Mem., 1970–; Chm., 1992–93; Pres., 2000–02; Hon. Vice Pres., 2002–. FAcSS (AcSS 2003); FRSA 2005. Dist. Services to British Sociology Award, British Sociological Assoc., 2014. Editor: Network, 1984–87; Sociology Review, 1986–2002; European Societies, 2006–10. *Publications:* Corporations, Classes and Capitalism, 1979, 2nd edn 1985; The Anatomy of Scottish Capital, 1980; The Upper Classes: property and privilege in Britain, 1982; (with C. Griff) Directors of Industry, 1984; (ed jtly) Networks of Corporate Power, 1985; Capitalist Property and Financial Power, 1986; A Matter of Record: documentary sources in social research, 1990; (ed) The Sociology of Elites, three vols, 1990; Who Rules Britain?, 1991; Social Network Analysis, 1992, 3rd edn 2013; (ed jtly) Reviewing Sociology, 1993; (with M. Nakata and H. Hasegawa) Kigyo to kanri no kokusai hikaku (An International Study of Enterprise and Administration), 1993; Poverty and Wealth: citizenship, deprivation and privilege, 1994; (ed) Power, three vols, 1994; Sociological Theory: contemporary debates, 1995, 2nd edn 2012; Stratification and Power: structures of class, status and domination, 1996; (ed) Class, four vols, 1996; Corporate Business and Capitalist Classes, 1997; (with Masao Watanabe and John Westergaard) Kaikyu genron no genzai igirisu to Nihon (Debates on Class in Contemporary Britain and Japan), 1998; (with James Fulcher) Sociology, 1999, 4th edn 2011; (with José López) Social Structure, 2000; (ed jtly) Renewing Class Analysis, 2000; Power, 2001; (ed) Social Networks: critical concept, four vols, 2002; (ed jtly) Rethinking Class: culture, identities, and lifestyle, 2004; (ed jtly) Models and Methods in Social Network Analysis, 2005; (ed with G. Marshall) Oxford Dictionary of Sociology, 3rd edn 2005; Social Theory: central issues in sociology, 2006; (ed) Documentary Research, four vols, 2006; (ed) Sociology: the key concepts, 2006; (ed) Fifty Key Sociologists: the formative theorists, 2007; (ed) Fifty Key Sociologists: the contemporary theorists, 2007; (ed with P. Carrington) The Sage Handbook of Social Network Analysis, 2011; Conceptualising The Social World, 2011; (ed with G. Murray) Financial Elites and Transnational Business, 2012; What is Social Network Analysis?, 2012; (with G. Letherby and M. Williams) Objectivity and Subjectivity in Social Research, 2013; (with R. Bromley) Envisioning Sociology: Victor Branford, Patrick Geddes and the quest for social reconstruction, 2013; (ed with A. Nilsen) C. Wright Mills and the Sociological Imagination, 2013; contribs to many learned jls inc. British Jl of Sociol., Sociol Rev., Sociology, Sociol Analysis and Theory, etc. *Recreations:* listening to music, reading. *E:* johnscottcbe@gmail.com.

SCOTT, Jonathan Willoughby; Senior Partner, Herbert Smith Freehills (formerly Herbert Smith) LLP, 2010–15. *Educ:* St Catharine's Coll., Cambridge (BA 1978). Herbert Smith, later Herbert Smith Freehills: joined as trainee, 1979; Partner, 1988–2015; Head: Brussels office, 1989; EU and Competition Practice, until 2007. Mem., Gambling Commn, 2015–.

SCOTT, Judith Margaret, CEng, FBCS; Chief Executive, British Computer Society, 1995–2002; *b* 4 Oct. 1942; *d* of Robert Wright and Marjorie Wood; *m* 1972, Gordon Robert Scott; two *d. Educ:* St Andrews Univ. (BSc Hons); Cambridge Univ. (Dip. Computer Sci.). Various posts, Computel Systems Ltd (Canada), 1968–79; seconded to Computer/Communications Policy Task Force, Govt of Canada, 1971–72; Manager, Product Mktg, Gandalf Data Inc. (Canada), 1979–82; Dir Corporate Planning, Gandalf Technologies Inc. (Canada), 1982–87; Man. Dir, Gandalf Digital Communications Ltd, UK, 1987–95. Mem., PPARC, 2001–06. Vice Pres., Reading Univ., 2007. DUniv Staffs, 2002. *Recreation:* orchid growing. *Address:* 4 Crescent Road, Wokingham, Berks RG40 2DB.

SCOTT, Sir Kenneth (Bertram Adam), KCVO 1990; CMG 1980; an Extra Equerry to the Queen, since 1996; *b* 23 Jan. 1931; *s* of late Adam Scott, OBE, and Lena Kaye; *m* 1st, 1966, Gabrielle Justine (*d* 1977), *d* of R. W. Smart, Christchurch, New Zealand; one *s* one *d*; 2nd, 1990, Esme Walker, CBE (*d* 2010); one step *s. Educ:* George Watson's Coll., Edinburgh; Edinburgh Univ. MA Hons 1952. Foreign Office, 1954; served in Moscow, Bonn, Washington and Vientiane; Counsellor and Head of Chancery, Moscow, 1971; Sen. Officers' War Course, RNC, Greenwich, 1973; Dep. Head, Personnel Ops Dept, FCO, 1973; Counsellor and Head of Chancery, Washington, 1975; Head of E European and Soviet Dept, FCO, 1977; Minister and Dep. UK Perm. Rep. to NATO, 1979–82; Ambassador to Yugoslavia, 1982–85; Asst Private Sec. to the Queen, 1985–90; Dep. Private Sec. to the Queen, 1990–96. Vice-Chm., Provisional Election Commn for Bosnia and Herzogovina, Sarajevo, 1996. Trustee: Hopetoun House Preservation Trust, 1998–2007; Develt Trust, Edinburgh Univ., 1999–2007. Gov., George Watson's Coll., 1997–2002. *Publications:* St James's Palace: a history, 2010; Lords of Dalkeith, 2014. *Address:* 13 Clinton Road, Edinburgh EH9 2AW. *Clubs:* Royal Over-Seas League (Vice Chm., 2000–02; Vice-Pres., 2002–); New (Edinburgh).

SCOTT, Lee; *b* 6 April 1956; *s* of late Sidney and Renne Scott; *m* 1987, Estelle Dombey; two *s* three *d. Educ:* Clarks Coll., Ilford; Coll. for Distributive Trades, London. Worked for: Scott & Fishell (Leather Goods); Selfridges, 1975–80; Tatung, 1980–82; Toshiba, 1982–84; ITT, 1984–86; NFR Office Furniture, 1986–88; Campaign Dir, Utd Jewish Israel Appeal, 1988–98; Scott Associates (consultancy working with charities), 1998–2005. Contested (C) Waveney, 2001. MP (C) Ilford N, 2005–15; contested (C) same seat, 2015. *Recreations:* music, travel, football (Leyton Orient supporter), tennis.

SCOTT, Linda Valerie; *see* Agran, L. V.

SCOTT, Malcolm Charles Norman; QC (Scot.) 1991; *b* 8 Sept. 1951; *s* of James Raymond Scott and Marjorie Stewart Simpson. *Educ:* Trinity Coll., Glenalmond; Gonville and Caius Coll., Cambridge (BA 1972); Glasgow Univ. (LLB 1975). Advocate 1978. Dir, Mid Wynd International Investment Trust plc, 1990–. *Recreations:* fishing, ski-ing, hill walking. *Club:* New (Edinburgh).

SCOTT, Dame Margaret, (Dame Catherine Margaret Mary Denton), AC 2005; DBE 1981 (OBE 1977); Founding Director of the Australian Ballet School, 1964–90, retired; *b* 26 April 1922; *d* of John and Marjorie Douglas-Scott; *m* 1953, Derek Ashworth Denton, *qv*; two *s. Educ:* Parktown Convent, Johannesburg, S Africa; Graduate Dip. in Visual and Performing Arts, RMIT, 2000. Sadler's Wells Ballet, London, 1940–43; Principal: Ballet Rambert, London and Australia, 1944–49; National Ballet, Australia, 1949–50; Ballet Rambert, and John Cranko Group, London, 1951–53; private ballet teaching, Australia, 1953–61; planned and prepared the founding of the Aust. Ballet Sch., 1962–64. Hon. Life Mem., Australian Ballet Foundn, 1988. Hon. LLD Melbourne, 1989; Hon. DEd RMIT, 2001. Life Time Achievement Award: Green Room Awards Assoc., 1998; Aust. Dance Awards, 1998; JC Williamson Award, Live Performance Australia, 2007. *Recreations:* music, theatre, garden. *Address:* 816 Orrong Road, Toorak, Melbourne, Vic 3142, Australia. *T:* (3) 98272640.

SCOTT, Margaret Elizabeth; *see* Scott, Hon. Lady.

SCOTT, Matthew Paul Noy; composer and musician; Head of Music, National Theatre, since 2006; *b* 19 Sept. 1956; *s* of David and Elizabeth Scott. *Educ:* Eton Coll.; Epsom Coll.; City Univ./Guildhall Sch. of Music and Drama (BSc 1979). Freelance composer, 1979–; Tutor, RADA, 1984–; Lectr, Univ. of Reading, 1996–2000; Lectr, 1996–2013, Prof. of Composition, 2013–, Univ. of Southampton (Mem. of Senate, 2015–); Associate Artist, Birmingham Rep Th., 1997–; Associate Composer, Chichester Fest. Th., 2006–. Many theatre and television credits as composer incl. Drop the Dead Donkey, 1990; films including: Lord of Misrule, 1996; The Landgirls (co-composer), 1998. *Publications:* A New Orpheus, 1985; *composition:* Four Bars of Agit, 1983. *Recreations:* architecture, surrealism, surrealist architecture, stationery and gadgets, detecting scepticism in others and comparing. *Address:* Music Department, National Theatre, SE1 9PX. *T:* (020) 7452 3390. *E:* mscott@nationaltheatre.org.uk.

SCOTT, Michael; *see* Scott, J. M.

SCOTT, Prof. Michael, PhD; DL; Vice-Chancellor, Glyndŵr University, 2008–15. *Educ:* Univ. of Wales, Lampeter; Univ. of Nottingham; De Montfort Univ. (PhD). Prof. of English and Hd, Sch. of Humanities, Sunderland Poly., until 1989; Pro Vice-Chancellor, De Montfort Univ., 1989–2008. Formerly Vis. Prof of English, Georgetown Univ. (Centennial Award for Dist. Teaching and Scholarship, 1989). Dir, UK Nat. Commn for UNESCO, 2005–09; Chm., UNESCO Cymru. Formerly: Mem., Broadcasting Council for Wales; Chm., N Wales Film Commn. Mem. Council, CBI. Vice-Chair, Clwyd Th., Cymru. FRSA; FHEA. DL Clwyd, 2008. *Publications:* Antony and Cleopatra, 1983; Renaissance Drama and a Modern Audience, 1985; (ed) Harold Pinter, The Birthday Party, The Caretaker and The Homecoming, 1986; Shakespeare and the Modern Dramatist, 1993; (ed jtly) Talking Shakespeare, 2001.

SCOTT, Maj.-Gen. Michael Ian Eldon, CB 1997; CBE 1987; DSO 1982; author; Complaints Commissioner, Bar Council, 1997–2006; *b* 3 March 1941; *s* of Col Eric Scott and Rose-Anne Scott; *m* 1968, Veronica Daniell; one *s* one *d*. *Educ:* Bradfield Coll. Commnd Scots Guards, 1960; Regtl service in UK, E Africa, N Ireland, BAOR; Staff Coll., Camberley, 1974; 2nd MA to CGS, 1975; COS Task Force Delta, 1979; Armed Forces Staff Coll., USA, 1981; CO, 2nd Bn Scots Guards, London, Falklands War and Cyprus, 1981–84; Comd 8th Inf. Bde, N Ireland, 1984–86; RCDS 1987; Dep. Mil. Sec., 1988–93; GOC Scotland and Gov., Edinburgh Castle, 1993–95; Mil. Sec., 1995–97. Pres., Third Guards Club, 1999–. *Publications:* (with David Rooney) In Love and War: the lives of Sir Harry and Lady Smith, 2008; Scapegoats: thirteen victims of military injustice, 2013. *Recreations:* travel, visual arts. *Clubs:* Pratt's, Garrick.

SCOTT, Sir Oliver (Christopher Anderson), 3rd Bt *cr* 1909 of Yews, Westmorland; Radiobiologist, Richard Dimbleby Cancer Research Department, St Thomas' Hospital, 1982–88; Radiobiologist, 1954–66, Director, 1966–69, British Empire Cancer Campaign Research Unit in Radiobiology; *b* 6 Nov. 1922; *s* of Sir Samuel H. Scott, 2nd Bt and Nancy Lilian (*née* Anderson); *S* father, 1960; *m* 1951, Phoebe Ann Tolhurst; one *s* two *d*. *Educ:* Charterhouse; King's College, Cambridge. Clinical training at St Thomas' Hosp., 1943–46; MRCS, LRCP, 1946; MB, BCh, Cambridge, 1946; MD Cambridge, 1976; Surgeon-Lieutenant RNVR, 1947–49. Dir, Provincial Insurance Co., 1955–64. Hon. Consultant, Inst. of Cancer Res., Sutton, 1974–82. Pres., Section of Oncology, RSM, 1987–88. Mem. Council, Cancer Res. Campaign, 1978–91. Mem., BIR, 1999. Hon. FRCR 1998. High Sheriff of Westmorland, 1966. *Publications:* contributions to scientific books and journals. *Recreations:* music, walking. *Heir:* *s* Christopher James Scott [*b* 16 Jan. 1955; *m* 1988, Emma, *o d* of Michael Boxhall; two *s* two *d*]. *Address:* 31 Kensington Square, W8 5HH. *T:* (020) 7937 8556. *Club:* Brooks's.

SCOTT, Paul Henderson, CMG 1974; writer; HM Diplomatic Service, retired 1980; *b* 7 Nov. 1920; *s* of Alan Scott and Catherine Scott (*née* Henderson), Edinburgh; *m* 1st, 1953, Beatrice Celia Sharpe (marr. diss. 2010); one *s* one *d*; 2nd, 2010, Laura Florentini. *Educ:* Royal High School, Edinburgh; Edinburgh University (MA, MLitt). HM Forces, 1941–47 (Major RA). Foreign Office, 1947–53; First Secretary, Warsaw, 1953–55; First Secretary, La Paz, 1955–59; Foreign Office, 1959–62; Counsellor, Havana, 1962–64; Canadian National Defence College, 1964–65; British Deputy Commissioner General for Montreal Exhibition, 1965–67; Counsellor and Consul-General, Vienna, 1968–71; Head of British Govt Office, 1971, Consul-Gen., 1974–75, Montreal; Research Associate, IISS, 1975–76; Asst Under Sec., FO (negotiator on behalf of EEC Presidency for negotiations with USSR, Poland and East Germany), 1977; Minister and Consul-General, Milan, 1977–80. Chairman: Adv. Council for the Arts in Scotland, 1981–98; Steering Cttee for a Scottish Nat. Theatre, 1988–; Mem., Constitutional Steering Cttee, which drew up A Claim of Right for Scotland, published 1988; Pres., Saltire Soc., 1996–2002 (Dep. Chm., 1981–95; Hon. Pres., 2004; Vice-Convenor, 2005–11); Member: Council, Nat. Trust for Scotland, 1981–87; Assoc. for Scottish Literary Studies, 1981–; Scots Language Soc., 1981–; Cockburn Assoc., 1982–; Council, Edinburgh Internat. Fest., 1984–87; Chm., Friends of Dictionary of Older Scottish Tongue, 1984–2002; President: Andrew Fletcher Soc., 1988–96; Scottish Centre, PEN Internat., 1992–97. Scottish National Party: Mem., NEC, 1989–97; spokesman on educn and the arts, 1991–97; Vice-Pres., 1992–97; dep. spokesman on Europe and external affairs, 1997–99; contested (SNP): Eastwood, 1992; Lothians, Scottish Parlt, 1999. Convener, Scottish Centre for Econ. and Social Res., 1990–95. Rector, Dundee Univ., 1989–92. Hon. Fellow, Glasgow Univ., 1996. Grosse Goldene Ehrenzeichen, Austria, 1969. *Publications:* 1707: The Union of Scotland and England, 1979; (ed with A. C. Davis) The Age of MacDiarmid, 1980; Walter Scott and Scotland, 1981; (ed) Walter Scott's Letters of Malachi Malagrowther, 1981; (ed) Andrew Fletcher's United and Separate Parliaments, 1982; John Galt, 1985; In Bed with an Elephant, 1985; (ed with George Bruce) A Scottish Postbag, 1986; The Thinking Nation, 1989; Towards Independence, 1991; Andrew Fletcher and the Treaty of Union, 1992; Scotland in Europe: a dialogue with a sceptical friend, 1992; (ed) Scotland: a concise cultural history, 1993; Defoe in Edinburgh and Other Papers, 1995; (ed) Scotland's Ruine: Lockhart of Carnwath's Memoirs, 1995; Scotland: an unwon cause, 1997; Still in Bed with an Elephant, 1998; The Boasted Advantages, 1999; A Twentieth Century Life (autobiog.), 2002; Scotland Resurgent, 2003; (ed) The Saltoun Papers, 2003; (ed) Spirits of the Age: Scottish self-portraits, 2005; The Union of 1707: why and how, 2006; The Age of Liberation, 2008; The New Scotland: a 21st century sequel, 2008; (ed) A Nation Again, 2008; Scotland: a creative past, an independent future, 2013. *Address:* 33 Drumsheugh Gardens, Edinburgh EH3 7RN. *T:* (0131) 225 1038. *Club:* New (Edinburgh).

SCOTT, Sir Peter; *see* Scott, Sir G. P.

SCOTT, Peter Anthony; Managing Director, Peel Holdings plc, 1985–2007 (non-executive Director, 2007–12); *b* 24 April 1947; *s* of Barclay and Doris Scott; *m* 1969, Lynne Smithies; one *s* one *d*. *Educ:* Heywood Grammar Sch.; Littleborough High Sch.; Manchester Poly. ACCA 1979. Financial Accountant: Fothergill & Harvey Ltd, 1962–75; Crane Fruehauf Trailers (Oldham) Ltd, 1975–77; Co. Sec., 1977–81, Financial Dir, 1981–85, Peel Hldgs plc. *Address:* 6 Bowling Green Way, Bamford, Rochdale, Lancs OL11 5QQ.

SCOTT, Peter Denys John, CBE 2008; QC 1978; Chairman, City Panel on Takeovers and Mergers, 2000–10; *b* 19 April 1935; *s* of John Ernest Dudley Scott and Joan G. Steinberg. *Educ:* Monroe High Sch., Rochester, NY, USA; Balliol Coll., Oxford (MA). Second Lieut, RHA, Lieut (TA), National Service, 1955. Called to the Bar, Middle Temple (Harmsworth Scholar), 1960, Bencher, 1984; Standing Counsel: to Dir, Gen. of Fair Trading, 1973–78; to Dept of Employment, 1974–78. Member: Home Sec.'s Cttee on Prison Disciplinary System, 1984; Interception of Communications Tribunal, 1986–2002; Lord Chancellor's Adv. Cttee on Legal Educn and Conduct, 1991–94; Investigatory Powers Tribunal, 2000–10; Investigatory Powers Guernsey Tribunal, 2006–; conducted Attorney Gen.'s rev. of Northern Irish judicial proceedings, 2006–07; Chm., Appeal Bd, Inst. of Actuaries, 1995–2001; a Judicial Tribunal Chm., City Disputes Panel, 1997–. Vice-Chm., Senate of the Inns of Court and the Bar, 1985–86; Chm., General Council of the Bar, 1987; Mem., Senate and Bar Council, 1981–87; Chm., London Common Law Bar Assoc., 1983–85. Hon. Mem., Canadian Bar Assoc., 1987. Mem. Adv. Council, Centre for Commercial Law Studies, QMW, 1990–2006; former Chm., Dame Colet House and Tower Hamlets Law Centre. Chm., Bd of Trustees, Nat. Gall., 2000–08. Chairman: N Kensington Amenity Trust, 1981–85; Kensington Housing Trust, 1999–2002. *Recreations:* gardening, theatre. *Address:* 4 Eldon Road, W8 5PU. *T:* (020) 7937 3301, *Fax:* (020) 7376 1169; Château Bellegarde, 32140 Masseube, France. *T:* (5) 62660027, *Fax:* (5) 62661683.

SCOTT, Air Vice-Marshal Peter John, CB 2003; CEng, FIMechE; Air Officer Logistics and Communications Information Systems, HQ Strike Command, 1998–2004; *b* 4 April 1949; *s* of John and Kathleen Scott; *m* 1973, Carolyn Frances, (Chips), Barrett; one *d*. *Educ:* Bromley Grammar Sch.; RAF Coll. Cranwell (BSc Hons 1971); Cranfield Inst. of Technol. (MSc 1979). Joined RAF, 1967; 96C Entry Cranwell, tours at Chivenor, Honington, Abingdon; OC Engineering and Supply Wing, RAF Germany Wildenrath, 1985–87; OC Engineering Wing, Falkland Islands, 1987–88; rcds 1995; Station Comdr and AO Wales, RAF St Athan, and ADC to the Queen, 1995–97. Patron, Univ. of Wales Air Sqn, 2004–09. *Recreations:* golf, model railways, hill walking. *Address:* Princes Risborough. *Clubs:* Royal Air Force; Ellesborough Golf (Capt., 2012–13).

SCOTT, Sir (Philip) John, KBE 1987; FRCP; FRACP; FRSNZ; Professor of Medicine, University of Auckland, 1975–97, now Emeritus; *b* 26 June 1931; *s* of Horace McD. Scott and Doris A. Scott (*née* Ruddock); *m* 1st, 1956, Elizabeth Jane MacMillan (*d* 2002); one *s* three *d*; 2nd, 2003, Margaret Fernie Wann (*d* 2007); 3rd, 2011, Alison Rhona Roberton. *Educ:* Univ. of Otago (BMedSci; MB, ChB); Univ. of Birmingham (MD). Qual. in medicine, Dunedin, 1955; hosp. and gen. practice experience, Auckland, 1956–58; postgrad. trng, RPMS, London, 1959–60; Queen Elizabeth Hosp. and Univ. of Birmingham, 1960–62; Med. Res. Fellowships, Auckland, 1962–68; Sen. Lectr, Univ. of Otago, based on Auckland Hosp., 1969–72; University of Auckland: Sen. Lectr, 1970–72; Associate Prof., 1973–75; Hd, Dept of Medicine, the Univ.'s Sch. of Medicine, 1979–87. Pres., Royal Soc. of NZ, 1998–2000. Res. interests in lipoprotein metabolism, arterial disease, human nutrition, med. econs and educn, professional ethics. *Publications:* (first author/co-author) articles in sci./med. jls and in press, on aspects of coronary artery disease, atherosclerosis, lipoprotein metabolism, human nutrition, ethical issues, medical history and educn, health service orgn. *Recreations:* music, pottery, gardening. *Address:* 64 Temple Street, Meadowbank, Auckland 1072, New Zealand. *T:* (9) 5215384.

SCOTT, Primrose Smith; Head of Quality Review, Institute of Chartered Accountants of Scotland, 1999–2002; Senior Partner, The McCabe Partnership (formerly Primrose McCabe & Co.), 1987–99; *b* 21 Sept. 1940. *Educ:* Ayr Acad. Trained with Stewart Gilmour, Ayr; qualified as CA, 1963; joined Romanes & Munro, Edinburgh, 1964; progressed through manager ranks to Partner, Deloitte Haskins & Sells, 1981–87; set up own practice, Linlithgow, 1987; moved practice to Edinburgh, 1997. Dep. Chm., Dunfermline Building Soc., 1998–2006; non-exec. Dir, Northern Venture Trust PLC, 1995–2010; Dir, Ecosse Unique Ltd, 2004–. Pres., Institute of Chartered Accountants of Scotland, 1994–95. Trustee, New Lanark Conservation Trust, 2002–06. Comr, Queen Victoria Sch., Dunblane, 1998–2006. Hon. Treas., Hospitality Industry Trust Scotland, 1994–2002; Treasurer: Age Scotland (formerly Age Concern Scotland), 2004–14; Borders Youth Th., 2007–14. Fellow, SCOTVEC, 1994. *Recreation:* walking dogs in Scottish Borders. *Address:* The Cleugh, Redpath, Earlston, Berwicks TD4 6AD. *T:* (01896) 849042.

SCOTT, Richard John Dinwoodie; Sheriff of Lothian and Borders at Edinburgh, 1986–2004; *b* 28 May 1939; *s* of late Prof. Richard Scott and Mary Ellen Maclachlan; *m* 1969, Josephine Moretta Blake; two *d*. *Educ:* Edinburgh Academy; Univ. of Edinburgh (MA, LLB) (Vans Dunlop Schol. in Evidence and Pleading, 1963). Lektor in English, British Centre, Sweden, 1960–61; Tutor, Faculty of Law, Univ. of Edinburgh, 1964–72; admitted to Faculty of Advocates, 1965; Standing Jun. Counsel to Min. of Defence (Air) in Scotland, 1968–77. Sheriff of Grampian, Highland and Islands, at Aberdeen and Stonehaven, 1977–86. Mem., Parole Bd for Scotland, 2003–09. Convenor, Additional Support Needs Tribunals for Scotland, 2005–10. Chm., Scottish Assoc. for Study of Delinquency, 1996–2001 (Chm., Aberdeen Branch, 1978–86, Edinburgh Branch, 1993–96); Mem., Working Party on Offenders aged 16–18, 1991–93; Chm., Grampian Victim Support Scheme, 1983–86; Pres., Sheriffs' Assoc., 2002–04 (Mem. Council, 1979–82 and 1994–2004; Vice-Pres., 2001–02); Mem., Sheriff Court Rules Council, 1995–98. Chm., Birthlink, 2008–14. Hon. Lectr, Univ. of Aberdeen, 1980–86. *Publications:* various articles in legal jls. *Recreations:* golf, curling, traditional music of Scotland. *Address:* c/o Sheriff Court House, 27 Chambers Street, Edinburgh EH1 1LB.

SCOTT, Sir Ridley, Kt 2003; film director and producer; *b* S Shields, 30 Nov. 1937. *Educ:* Royal Coll. of Art. *Films include:* director: The Duellists, 1976; Alien, 1978; Black Rain, 1989; director and producer: Blade Runner, 1980; Someone to Watch over Me, 1987; Thelma and Louise, 1991; 1492: Conquest of Paradise, 1992; White Squall, 1996; GI Jane, 1997; Gladiator, 2000; Hannibal, 2001; Black Hawk Down, 2002; Matchstick Men, 2003; Kingdom of Heaven, 2005; A Good Year, 2006; American Gangster, 2007; Body of Lies, 2008; Robin Hood, 2010; Prometheus, 2012; Life in a Day (documentary), 2011; The Grey, 2012; The Counsellor, 2013; Exodus, 2014; The Martian, 2015; prod., Child 44, 2015; *for television:* Churchill - The Gathering Storm, 2002; Gettysburg (drama documentary), 2011. *Address:* Scott Free, 42–44 Beak Street, W1F 9RH. *T:* (020) 7437 3163.

SCOTT, Robert Avisson, CBE 2002; *b* 6 Jan. 1942; *s* of Robert Milligan Scott and Phyllis Winifred Scott; *m* 1979, Joanne Rose Adams; two *d*. *Educ:* Scots Coll., Wellington, NZ. Associate: Australian Insce Inst.; Insce Inst. NZ; FCIBS 2004. South British Insce Co. Ltd, later NZI Corp. Ltd, then General Accident plc, subseq. CGU plc, then CGNU plc, 1959–2001: Asst Gen. Manager, NZ, 1981–83; Australia: Asst Gen. Manager, 1983–85; Gen. Manager, 1985–87; Chief Gen. Manager, 1987–90; Dep. Gen. Manager, UK, 1990–91, Gen. Manager, 1991–94; Dep. Chief Exec., 1994–96; Gp Chief Exec., 1996–2001. Hon. FCII 2005. *Recreations:* sporting interests, walking, do it yourself. *Address:* 51 Great Pulteney Street, Bath, Som BA2 4DP. *T:* (01225) 313308.

SCOTT, Sir Robert (David Hillyer), Kt 1994; Chairman, South London Business Council (formerly South London Economic Development Alliance), 1999–2014; *b* 22 Jan. 1944; *s* of Sir David Aubrey Scott, GCMG; *m* 1st, 1972, Su Dalgleish (marr. diss. 1995); two *s* one *d*; 2nd, 1995, Alicia Tomalino; two step *d*. *Educ:* Haileybury; Merton Coll., Oxford (Pres., OUDS, 1965–66). Actor, 1966–67; Administrator: 69 Theatre Co., Manchester, 1968–74; Royal Exchange Theatre Trust, 1974–77; Man. Dir, Manchester Theatres Ltd, 1978–96; Chairman: Manchester Olympic Bid Cttee, 1985–93; Manchester Commonwealth Games Bid Cttee, 1993–95; Chief Exec., Greenwich Millennium Trust, 1995–2001; Chief Exec., 2000–03, Chm., 2003–05, Internat. Ambassador, 2005–09, Liverpool Culture Co. Chm., EC Panel for choosing and monitoring European Capitals of Culture, 2008–11. Mem., Central Manchester Devclt Corp., 1988–96. Special Projects Dir, Apollo Leisure Gp, 1994–99. Chairman: Cornerhouse Manchester, 1984–95; Granada Foundn, 1993–; Piccadilly Radio, 1993–2001; Tour East London, 1998–2001; City Bars and Restaurants, 1999–2003; Greenwich Theatre, 1999–2008; Bexley Heritage Trust, 1999–2007; Greenwich Peninsula Partnership, 2001–08; Trinity Laban, 2005–12; City Screen Ltd, 2006–12. Director: Royal Exchange Theatre, 1976–94; Hallé Concerts Soc., 1989–94; White Horse Fast Ferries, 1998–2002; London First, 1999–2003. Mem. Cttee, Whitworth Art Gall., 1989–95. DL Greater Manchester, 1988–97. Hon. RNCM 1990. Hon. Fellow: Manchester Poly., 1987; UMIST, 1989; Liverpool John Moores Univ., 2003. Hon. MA: Manchester, 1988; Salford, 1991; Hon. LLD Greenwich, 2003; Hon. DArts Leeds Metropolitan, 2010. Officier de l'Ordre des Arts et des Lettres (France), 1991. *Publications:* The Biggest Room in the World, 1976. *Recreations:* food, travel, talking, sport, theatre. *Address:* 62 Crooms Hill, Greenwich, SE10 8HG.

SCOTT, Robert William Lowry, OBE 2005; FRICS; JP; Lord Lieutenant of County Tyrone, since 2009; *b* Oakham, Rutland, 17 June 1951; *s* of Robert Irwin Maddin Scott and Margaret Sylvia Daphne (*née* Alexander); *m* 1978, Marie-Christine Cormerais; two *d*. *Educ:* Wellington Coll., Berks; Royal Agricl Coll., Cirencester. FRICS 1988. Agent and Factor, Abercorn Estates, 1977–2013. Dir, Balcas Ltd, 2005–15. Chairman: Forestry and Timber Assoc., 2002–04; Pro Silva Ireland, 2004–07; Tyrone Electric Ltd, 2014–; Dep. Chm., Confedn of Forest Industries (UK) Ltd, 2004–05. Trustee, Scottish Forestry Trust, 2002–12

(Chm., 2010–12). Hon. Col, 152 (N Irish) Regt RLC, 2014–. JP 1990, Sheriff 1992, Co. Tyrone. *Recreations:* silviculture, ski-ing. *Address:* Ballyrenan, Newtownstewart, Co. Tyrone, Northern Ireland BT78 4HB.

SCOTT, Prof. Roger Davidson, PhD; CPhys, FInstP; FRSE; Director, Scottish Universities Research and Reactor Centre, 1991–98; Professor of Nuclear Science, University of Glasgow, 1994–98; *b* 17 Dec. 1941; *s* of Alexander N. Scott and Jessie H. Scott (*née* Davidson); *m* 1965, Marion S. McCluckie; two *s* one *d. Educ:* Anderson Inst., Lerwick; Univ. of Edinburgh (BSc 1st Cl. Hons Physics; PhD Nuclear Physics). University Demonstrator, Univ. of Edinburgh, 1965–68; Lectr, 1968–88, Depute Dir, 1988–91, Scottish Univs Res. and Reactor Centre. Non-exec. Dir, Nuclear Decommissioning Authy, 2004–08. FRSE 1995. *Publications:* articles on nuclear physics and envmtl radioactivity; contribs to learned jls. *Recreations:* watching football, walking wife and dogs, home maintenance. *Address:* 6 Downfield Gardens, Bothwell, Glasgow G71 8UW. *T:* (01698) 854121.

SCOTT, Sheila Margaret, OBE 2007; Chief Executive, National Care Association (formerly National Care Homes Association), since 1993; *b* 18 Dec. 1948; *d* of G. W. Brownlow and late Audrey Brownlow (*née* Louth); *m* 1973, A. L. Scott (marr. diss. 1996); one *s* one *d. Educ:* Wisbech High Sch.; Addenbrooke's Hosp., Cambridge (RGN 1971). Sister, Springdene Gp, N London, 1975–83; care home proprietor, N London, 1983–88; with Nat. Care Homes Assoc. (later Nat. Care Assoc.), 1988–; Office Manager/Company Sec., 1988–93; on secondment to DoH, 1992–93. *Recreations:* travel, cinema, cycling, gardening. *Address:* 1 Westwater Crescent, Hampton Vale, Peterborough PE7 8LT. *E:* sheilamscott@hotmail.com.

SCOTT, Sionaidh D.; *see* Douglas-Scott.

SCOTT, Prof. Sophie Kerttu, PhD; FMedSci; Wellcome Trust Senior Fellow, Institute of Cognitive Neuroscience, University College London, since 2005; *b* London, 16 Nov. 1966; *d* of Colin Mountford Scott and Christine Winnifred Scott; partner, Dr Tom Manly; one *s. Educ:* Westholme Sch., Blackburn; Queen Elizabeth's Grammar Sch., Blackburn; Poly. of Central London (BSc Hons Life Scis 1990); University Coll. London (PhD Cognitive Sci. 1994). SO, MRC Applied Psychol. Unit, Cambridge, 1995–98; University College London: Res. Fellow, 1998–2001; Wellcome Trust Career Develt Fellow, 2001–05. FMedSci 2012. *Publications:* over 90 papers. *Recreation:* watching and performing stand-up comedy. *Address:* Institute of Cognitive Neuroscience, University College London, 17 Queen Square, WC1N 3AR. *T:* (020) 7679 1144. *E:* sophie.scott@ucl.ac.uk.

SCOTT, Prof. Stephen Basil Cuthbert, CBE 2014; PhD; FRCP, FRCPsych; Professor of Child Health and Behaviour, and Director, National Academy for Parenting Research, King's College London, since 2007; Consultant Child and Adolescent Psychiatrist, Maudsley Hospital; *b* Cambridge, 28 Sept. 1951; *s* of John and Eleanor Scott; *m* 1990, Penelope Susan Titman; three *s. Educ:* Leys Sch., Cambridge; King's Coll., Cambridge (MB BChir 1980; PhD). MRCP 1988; MRCPsych 1990. Hd, Nat. Adoption and Fostering Clinic and Nat. Conduct Problems Clinic, Maudsley Hosp., London, 1995–. Chair, NICE Guideline on Antisocial Behaviour, 2012. Chair, Assoc. for Child and Adolescent Mental Health, 2015. *Publications:* (with R. Goodman) Child and Adolescent Psychiatry, 1997, 3rd edn 2012 (trans. 7 langs); Fostering Changes, 2000, 2nd edn 2005. *Recreations:* cycling in Provence, tennis, ski-ing. *Address:* Box P85, Children's Department, Institute of Psychiatry, Psychology and Neuroscience, King's College London, De Crespigny Park, SE5 8AF. *T:* (020) 7848 0746. *E:* Stephen.Scott@kcl.ac.uk.

SCOTT, Tavish Hamilton; farmer; Member (Lib Dem) Shetland Islands, Scottish Parliament, since 2011 (Shetland, 1999–2011); *b* 6 May 1966; *s* of Sir John Hamilton Scott, *qv*; *m* 2008, Kirsten Campbell; one *s*; two *s* one *d* by a former marriage. *Educ:* Napier Coll., Edinburgh (BA Hons Business Studies). Research Asst to J. R. Wallace, MP, 1989–90; Press Officer, Scottish Lib Dem Party, 1990–92. Mem. (Lib Dem) Shetland Islands Council, 1994–99. Scottish Executive: Dep. Minister for Parlt, 2000–01, for Parly Business and for Finance and Public Services, 2003–05; Minister for Transport, 2005–07; Opposition front bench spokesman on finance and sustainable growth, Scottish Parlt, 2007–08. Leader, Scottish Lib Dems, 2008–11. Chm., Lerwick Harbour Trust, 1997–99. *Recreations:* football, golf, cinema, reading, current affairs, Up Helly Aa. *Address:* Scottish Parliament, Edinburgh EH99 1SP. *T:* (0131) 348 6296.

SCOTT, Timothy John Whittaker; QC 1995; a Recorder, since 1999; *b* 19 July 1949; *s* of late John Dick Scott and Helen Scott (*née* Whittaker); *m*; one *s* two *d. Educ:* Westminster Sch. (Queen's Schol.); New Coll., Oxford (Exhibnr; MA). Journalist, 1970–72; called to the Bar, Gray's Inn, 1975; Asst Recorder, 1995–99. *Publications:* articles on family law topics in specialist jls. *Recreations:* fishing, reading, travel. *Address:* 29 Bedford Row, WC1R 4HE. *T:* (020) 7404 1044. *Club:* Garrick.

SCOTT, Sir (Walter) John, 5th Bt *cr* 1907, of Beauclerc, Bywell St Andrew, Northumberland; countryside campaigner, farmer, author, columnist and broadcaster, snuff manufacturer; *b* 24 Feb. 1948; *s* of Sir Walter Scott, 4th Bt and Diana Mary (*d* 1985), *d* of J. R. Owen; *S* father, 1992; *m* 1st, 1969, Lowell Patria (marr. diss. 1971), *d* of late Gp Capt. Pat Vaughan Goddard, Auckland, NZ; one *d*; 2nd, 1977, Mary Gavin, *d* of Alexander Fairly Anderson, Gartocharn, Dunbartonshire; one *s* one *d*. Chm., Sir Walter Scott's Fine Border Snuff. Chm., N Pennine Hunt, 2008– (Jt Master, 2009–); President: Union of Country Sports Workers, 2000–; Tay Valley Wildfowlers' Assoc., 2001–; Gamekeepers Welfare Trust, 2009–; Newcastle upon Tyne Wildfowlers' Assoc., 2009–; Member Board: Heather Trust, 2004–; Eur. Squirrel Fedn, 2004–; Patron: Sporting Lucas Terrier Assoc., 2004–; Nat. Orgn of Beaters and Pickers Up, 2007–; Wildlife Ark Trust, 2008–; Centenary Patron, British Assoc. for Shooting and Conservation, 2008–. Writer and co-presenter, Clarissa and the Countryman, TV series, 2000–03. Founder Mem., Cholmondeley Coursing Club, 1995. *Publications:* (jtly) Clarissa and the Countryman, 2000; (jtly) Clarissa and the Countryman Sally Forth, 2001; (jtly) A Sunday Roast, 2002; (jtly) The Game Cookbook, 2004; (jtly) A Greener Life, 2005; A Book of Britain, 2010. *Recreation:* field sports. *Heir: s* Walter Samuel Scott, *b* 6 Dec. 1984. *Address:* The Hermitage Farmhouse, Newcastleton, Roxburghshire TD9 0LY. *Club:* Pratt's.

SCOTT, Hon. (William) Alexander, CBE 2013; JP; MP (PLP) Warwick South East, 1993–2012; Premier of Bermuda, 2003–06; *b* 12 June 1940; *s* of Willard Alexander Scott and Edith Lucille Scott; *m* 1972, Olga Lawrence; one *s* one *d. Educ:* Temple Univ., Philadelphia (BA Fine Arts). Graphic designer and design consultant; owner, Scotts Crafts Ltd, 1964–97. Founding Mem. and former Chm., Big Brothers. Mem., Pitt Commn, 1978. Mem. (PLP), 1985–93, and Leader of the Opposition, 1989–93, Senate, Bermuda; Minister of Works and Engrg, 1998–2003. JP Bermuda, 1985.

SCOTT, (William) Dermot; Head, European Parliament Office for the United Kingdom, 2002–09; *b* 19 Sept. 1943; *s* of Rev. Dr Eric Scott and Bee Scott (*née* Knight); *m* 1970, Susan Burdon Davies; one *s* one *d. Educ:* Campbell Coll., Belfast; Trinity Coll., Dublin (BA Mod., MSc Econ); Sch. of Public Admin, Dublin. Institute of Public Administration, Dublin, 1967–79; European Parlt Office in Ireland, 1979–98; Hd, European Parlt Office in Scotland, 1998–2002. Life Member: NUJ; Irish Inst. of Internat. and European Affairs. Mem., Royal Dublin Soc. (Mem. Council, 2012–). Silver Medal, Fondation du Mérite européen, 2011. *Publications:* Caisléan Eireannacha, 1972; (contrib.) Ireland and EU Membership Evaluated, 1991; Ireland's Contribution to the European Union, 1994; Ireland and the IGC, 1996; (ed) Europe is Our Story: towards a new narrative for the European Union, 2014; numerous articles on European affairs. *Recreations:* trout fishing, putting on recitals, looking at ruins. *Address:* 29 Wellington Road, Ballsbridge, Dublin 4, Ireland. *T:* (1) 6684652. *Clubs:* Reform; Kildare Street and University (Dublin).

SCOTT, (William) John (Graham); Member (C) Ayr, Scottish Parliament, since March 2000; *b* 7 June 1951; *s* of William Scott and Elizabeth Haddow Scott; *m* 1975, Charity Nadine Mary Bousfield (*d* 2000); one *s* one *d. Educ:* Barrhill Primary Sch.; George Watson's Coll.; Edinburgh Univ. (BSc Civil Engrg 1973). Farming in family partnership, 1973–; Partner, family catering business, 1985–2000. Founder Dir, Ayrshire Country Lamb Ltd, 1988–93; created Ayrshire Farmers' Mkts, 1999 (Chm., 1999–). Convenor, Hill Farming Cttee, NFU Scotland, 1993–99; Chairman: S of Scotland Regl Wool Cttee, 1996–2000; Ayrshire and Arran Farming Wildlife Adv. Gp, 1993–99. Scottish Parliament: Cons. Shadow Cabinet Sec. for Rural Affairs and Envmt, 2007; Dep. Presiding Officer, 2011–; Member: Transport and Envmt Cttee, 2001–03; Corporate Body, 2003–07; Vice-Chm., Petitions Cttee, 2003–07 (Mem., 2000–01); Vice Chm., Rural Affairs and Envmt Cttee, 2007–. Chm., Hill Sheep and Native Woodland Project, Scottish Agricl Coll., 1999–. Founder Chm., Scottish Assoc. of Farmers' Markets, 2001–05. JP Girvan, 1997–99. Elder, Ballantrae Ch, 1985–. *Recreations:* curling, geology, bridge. *Address:* Scottish Parliament, Edinburgh EH99 1SP. *T:* (0131) 348 5664, *Fax:* (0131) 348 5617; (constituency office) 17 Wellington Square, Ayr KA7 1EZ. *T:* (01292) 286251, *Fax:* (01292) 280480.

SCOTT, Rev. Preb. William Sievwright, CVO 2014; Sub-Dean of Her Majesty's Chapels Royal, Deputy Clerk of the Closet, Sub-Almoner and Domestic Chaplain to the Queen, 2007–15; a Chaplain to the Queen, 2003–15; an Extra Chaplain to the Queen, since 2015; *b* 1 Feb. 1946; *s* of David Anderson Harper Scott and Amelia Scott (*née* Sievwright). *Educ:* Harris Acad., Dundee; Edinburgh Theol Coll. Ordained deacon 1970, priest 1971; Curate: St Ninian's, Glasgow, 1971–73; St Francis, Bridgwater, 1973–77; Rector: Shepton Beauchamp, Barrington, Puckington and Stocklinch, 1977–82; Woolavington and Cossington, 1982–84; Chaplain, Community of All Hallow's, Ditchingham, 1984–91; Vicar, St Mary's, Bourne St, SW1, 1991–2002; Area Dean, Westminster (St Margaret), 1997–2004; Preb., St Paul's Cathedral, 2000–15, now Preb. Emeritus; Chaplain of the Queen's Chapel of the Savoy and of the Royal Victorian Order, 2002–07. Chaplain, Priory of Our Lady of Walsingham, 1991–2007. *Recreations:* music making and listening, reading novels and poetry, conducting retreats. *Address:* 13 Kylestrome House, Cundy Street, SW1W 9JT. *Club:* National Liberal.

SCOTT, William Wootton, CB 1990; Under Secretary, Industry Department for Scotland, 1985–90; *b* 20 May 1930; *s* of Dr Archibald C. Scott and Barbara R. Scott; *m* 1958, Margaret Chandler, SRN; three *s* one *d. Educ:* Kilmarnock Academy; Dollar Academy; Glasgow Univ. (MA, 1st Cl. Hons History). National Service in Royal Artillery, 1952–54. Assistant Principal, 1954, Principal, 1958, Min. of Transport and Civil Aviation; Principal Private Sec. to Minister of Transport, 1965–66; Asst Sec., 1966; Regional Controller (Housing and Planning), Northern Regional Office of DoE, 1971–74; joined Scottish Development Dept, 1974, Under Sec., 1978. *Publications:* occasional historical notes. *Recreations:* music, gardening, reading. *Address:* Steindaf, Hardgate, Castle Douglas, Kirkcudbrightshire DG7 3LD. *T:* (01556) 660200.

SCOTT CATO, Molly; Member (Green) South West Region, European Parliament, since 2014; *b* Wrexham, 21 May 1963; *d* of David Brian Curtis and Mary Curtis (*née* French); *m* 1987, Raymond Alexander Scott (marr. diss.); two *s* one *d. Educ:* Bath High Sch.; Oxford Univ. (MA PPE); Univ. of Wales, Aberystwyth (PhD 2001). Desk ed., OUP, 1988; Lectr, Mgt Sch., 2001–12, Dir, Cardiff Inst. for Cooperative Studies, 2008–12, Univ. of Wales Inst., Cardiff, later Cardiff Metropolitan Univ.; Prof. of Green Economics, Univ. of Roehampton, 2012–14. Mem. (Green) Stroud DC, 2011–14 (Leader, Green Gp, 2012–14). *Publications:* The Pit and the Pendulum, 2004; Market Schmarket, 2006; Green Economics: theory, policy and practice, 2009; Environment and Economy, 2011; The Bioregional Economy, 2012. *Recreations:* choral singing, basket-making, bodging. *Address:* European Parliament, 60 Rue Wiertz, Brussels 1047, Belgium. *E:* molly.scottcato@europarl.europa.eu.

SCOTT-GALL, Anthony Robert Gall; His Honour Judge Scott-Gall; a Circuit Judge, since 1996; *b* 30 March 1946; *s* of Robert and Daphne Scott-Gall; *m* 1973, Caroline Anne Scott; one *s* one *d. Educ:* Stowe Sch.; New Coll., Oxford (BA). Called to the Bar, Middle Temple, 1971; Recorder, 1993. *Recreations:* cricket, Rugby football, gardening, travel, ornithology, history, music, five grandchildren and the dog. *Address:* 3 Temple Gardens, Temple, EC4Y 9AU. *T:* (020) 7353 3102. *Clubs:* Richmond Football; Armadillos Cricket.

SCOTT-KERR, William Andrew; Publisher, Transworld Publishers Ltd, since 2005; *b* Stoke on Trent, 27 April 1964; *s* of Robert James Scott-Kerr and Ann Alexandra (*née* Sagar); *m* 1995, Joanna Frank (marr. diss. 2010); three *s. Educ:* Sedbergh Sch.; Southampton Univ. (BA English and Hist. 1985). Bookseller, Hatchards Booksellers, 1985–87; Fiction Buyer, Pan Bookshop, 1987–88; Jun. Ed. to Editl Dir, Pan Macmillan Ltd, 1988–94; Editl Dir, Transworld Publishers Ltd, 1994–2005. *Recreations:* photography, music, walking, cinema. *Address:* Transworld Publishers Ltd, 61–63 Uxbridge Road, W5 5SA. *T:* (020) 8579 2652. *E:* b.scott-kerr@transworld-publishers.co.uk.

SCOTT-LEE, Sir Paul (Joseph), Kt 2007; QPM 1997; DL; Chief Constable, West Midlands Police, 2002–09; *b* 25 July 1953; *s* of Hubert George Scott-Lee and Decima Florence Scott-Lee (*née* Hancorn); *m* 1975, Rosemary Susan Hargreaves. *Educ:* Whitley Abbey Comprehensive Sch., Coventry; Police Staff Coll., Bramshill. Joined Warwickshire and Coventry Constabulary from Cadet Corps, 1972; Sergeant to Chief Inspector, W Midlands Police, 1978–88; Superintendent to Chief Superintendent, Northants Police, 1988–92; Asst Chief Constable, Kent Co. Constabulary, 1992–94; Dep. Chief Constable, 1994–98, Chief Constable, 1998–2002, Suffolk Police. Ind. Assessor, Leveson Inquiry into culture, practice and ethics of the press, 2011–. Trustee, Police Arboretum Meml Trust, 2014–. Patron, St Paul's Community Trust, Balsall Heath, Birmingham, 2010–. DL W Midlands, 2003. Hon. DLaws Wolverhampton, 2009. *Recreations:* fly fishing, golf, reading.

SCOTT-MANDERSON, Marcus Charles William; QC 2006; *b* 10 Feb. 1956; *s* of late Dr William Scott-Manderson, MB ChB, MRCGP and of Pamela Scott-Manderson; *m* 2003, Melinda Penelope Tillard. *Educ:* Harrow Sch.; Christ Church, Oxford (BCL, MA); Hague Acad. of Internat. Law; Glasgow Univ. Called to the Bar, Lincoln's Inn, 1980; in practice, specialising in internat. cases relating to children. *Recreations:* archaeology, travel. *Address:* 4 Paper Buildings, Temple, EC4Y 7EX. *T:* (020) 7583 0816. *Club:* Lansdowne.

SCOTT-MONCRIEFF, Lucy Ann, CBE 2014; a Mental Health Tribunal Judge, since 2008; Managing Director, Scott-Moncrieff and Associates Ltd, since 2011; *b* England, 26 March 1954; *d* of late William Scott-Moncrieff and (Dora) Rosemary Scott-Moncrieff (*née* Knollys); two *s* by John Dowie. *Educ:* St Mary's, Calne; Guildford Tech. Coll.; Univ. of Kent (BA 1975). Admitted as solicitor, 1978; Asst Solicitor, Offenbach and Co. and Bradbury's, 1979–86; Partner, Offenbach's, 1986–87; Partner, Scott-Moncrieff Harbour and Sinclair, 1987–2011. Mental Health Act Comr, 1987–89; Postcomm Comr, 2008–11; Comr, Judicial Appts Commn, 2014–. Law Society of England and Wales: Mem. Council, 2002–; Vice Pres., 2011–12; Pres., 2012–13; Chair, Equality, Diversity and Inclusion Cttee. Chair, Adv. Panel, UK Admin. Justice Inst.; Co-Chair, Access to Justice and Legal Aid Cttee, Internat. Bar Assoc. Mem., QC Appts Panel, 2005–11. Hon. LLD Kent, 2009. *Publications:* contribs to New Law Jl, Jl Forensic Psychiatry, Jl Mental Health Law. *Recreations:* gardening, reading, ignoring housework, enthusing about new ways of doing things (not housework). *E:* lscottmoncrieff@scomo.com.

SCOTT THOMAS, Dame Kristin, DBE 2015 (OBE 2003); actress; *b* 24 May 1960; *m* 1981, François Olivennes (marr. diss.); two *s* one *d*. *Educ:* Cheltenham Ladies' Coll.; Central Sch. of Speech and Drama; École Nationale des Arts et Technique de Théâtre, Paris. *Theatre includes:* Bérénice, Paris, 2001; The Three Sisters, 2003, As You Desire Me, 2005, Playhouse Th.; The Seagull, Royal Court, 2007 (Best Actress, Laurence Olivier Award, 2008); Betrayal, Comedy Th., 2011; Old Times, Harold Pinter Th., 2013; Electra, Old Vic, 2014; The Audience, Apollo Th., 2015. *Films include:* Under the Cherry Moon, 1986; A Handful of Dust, 1988; Bitter Moon, 1992; Four Weddings and a Funeral, 1994; Angels and Insects, 1995 (Best Actress Award, BAFTA); Richard III, The Confessional, Mission Impossible, 1996; The English Patient, 1997; The Horse Whisperer, 1998; Random Hearts, 1999; Up at the Villa, Play, 2000; Gosford Park, Life as a House, 2002; Petites Coupures, 2003; Man to Man, The Adventures of Arsène Lupin, Keeping Mum, 2005; The Walker, 2007; Il y a longtemps que je t'aime, Easy Virtue, 2008; Nowhere Boy, 2009; Partir, 2010; Sarah's Key, 2011; The Woman in the Fifth, Bel Ami, Salmon Fishing in the Yemen, In Your Hands, 2012; In the House, Only God Forgives, 2013; The Invisible Woman, Before the Winter Chill, My Old Lady, 2014; Suite Française, 2015. *Television includes:* The Tenth Man, 1988; Endless Game, Framed, 1990; Titmuss Regained, 1991; Look At It This Way, 1992; Body and Soul, 1994.

SCOTT WHYTE, Stuart; *see* Whyte, J. S. S.

SCOULLER, (John) Alan; Head of Industrial Relations, Midland Bank Group, 1975–88; Visiting Professor in Industrial Relations, Kingston University (formerly Kingston Polytechnic), 1988–95; Senior Visiting Fellow, City University Business School, 1989–92; *b* 23 Sept. 1929; *e s* of late Charles James Scouller and Mary Helena Scouller; *m* 1954, Angela Geneste Ambrose; two *s* five *d*. *Educ:* John Fisher Sch., Purley. Army service, Queen's Own Royal W Kent Regt, 1948–58 (Captain). Joined Unilever as management trainee, 1958; Personnel Man., Wall's Ice Cream, 1959–62; Domestos, 1963–66; Holpak, 1966–68; Commercial Plastics and Holpak, 1968–69; left Unilever to join Commn on Industrial Relations, 1969; Dir of Industrial Relations until 1973, full-time Comr, 1973–74. Member: Employment Appeal Tribunal, 1976–2000; Educn Commn, RC Dio. of Westminster, 1990–2006. Gov., John Henry Newman RC Sch., Stevenage, 1984–2004. FIPD. Chm., Letchworth Garden City Heritage Foundn, 2004–09 (Gov., 1995–2009). KSG 1996. *Recreations:* reading political biographies, walking, listening to music, looking after grandchildren, cricket. *Address:* Walnut Cottage, 33 Field Lane, Letchworth Garden City, Herts SG6 3LD. *T:* (01462) 682781.

SCOURSE, Rear-Adm. Frederick Peter, CB 1997; MBE 1972; FREng, FIET; Acting Controller of the Navy, 1996–97; *b* 23 June 1944; *s* of late Frederick David John Scourse and Margaret Elaine Scourse; *m* 1967, Nicolette Jean Somerville West; one *s*. *Educ:* Wells Cathedral Sch.; RN Coll., Dartmouth; Churchill Coll., Cambridge (MA Mech Sci., Elect. Sci.). Served HM Ships: Dido, 1963–64; Warspite, 1969–72; Renown, 1974–77; MoD (PE), 1979–82; NDC, 1982–83; MoD (PE), 1983–89; Dir-Gen., Surface Weapons (Navy), 1989–94; Dir-Gen., Surface Ships, 1994–97. Nuclear Weapons Safety Advr, MoD, 1997–2003. Industry Advr, Churchill Coll., Cambridge, 1998–2007. Dir, Wild Trout Trust, 2002–04; Sec., Five Valleys Trust, 2004–. Vice Chm., Regular Forces Employment Assoc., 1998–2002. FREng 2000. *Recreations:* fly fishing, singing. *Address:* Valley View, 278a Turleigh, Bradford on Avon BA15 2HH.

SCOWCROFT, Gen. Brent, Hon. KBE 1993; President: Forum for International Policy, since 1993; Scowcroft Group, since 1993; *b* 19 March 1925; *s* of James Scowcroft and Lucile (*née* Ballantyne); *m* 1951, Marian (Jackie) Horner (*d* 1995); one *d*. *Educ:* Ogden City Schs; US Mil. Acad.; Columbia Univ. (MA 1953; PhD 1967); Lafayette Coll.; Georgetown Univ. Joined Army 1943; qualified pilot 1948; Prof. of Russian History, US Mil. Acad., 1953–57; service in Washington, Yugoslavia, Colorado, Western Hemisphere Region; with Jt Chiefs of Staff, 1970; MA to President, 1972–73; Dep. Asst, 1973–75, and Asst 1975–77 and 1989–93, to successive Presidents, for Nat. Security Affairs; retired from mil. service, 1975; Dir, Council on Foreign Relations, 1983–89; served on major US cttees, commns and bds, 1977–89. Vice-Chm., Kissinger Associates, 1982–89. Chm., CSIS/Pacific Forum, 1993–; Co-Chm., Blue Ribbon Commn on America's Nuclear Future, 2010–12. Mem. Bd of Visitors, USAF Acad., 1993–99. US Medal of Freedom, 1991; numerous Service medals and awards. *Recreation:* ski-ing.

SCRAFTON, Douglas, CMG 1998; Member, St Blaise Town Council, since 2007; Member (Lib Dem), Cornwall Council, since 2013; *b* 14 July 1949; *s* of late Douglas Scrafton and Irene Hilda Kirk (formerly Scrafton, *née* Hammett); *m* 1975, Carolyn Patricia Collison; one *s* one *d*. HM Diplomatic Service, 1967–2001: Mem., UK Delegn (later UK Perm. Repn) to EC, 1970–73; Kampala, 1973–74; Mbabane, 1975–77; FCO, 1977–80; Jedda, 1980–82; British Liaison Office, Riyadh, 1982–84; Cairo, 1984–85; FCO, 1985–87; on loan to Cabinet Office, 1987–88; Ottawa, 1989–92; FCO, 1992–94; Ambassador: to Yemen Republic, 1995–97; to Democratic Republic of the Congo, 1998–2000; Foreign Sec.'s Special Rep. for the Great Lakes region, 2000–01. Volunteer, CAB, 2003–10. *Recreations:* photography, reading, gardening, beekeeping. *Address:* Reynards Rest, The Mount, Par, Cornwall PL24 2BZ.

SCRASE-DICKINS, Mark Frederick Hakon, CMG 1991; DL; HM Diplomatic Service, retired; *b* 31 May 1936; *s* of late Alwyne Rory Macnamara Scrase-Dickins and Ingeborg Oscara Frederika Scrase-Dickins; *m* 1969, Martina Viviane Bayley; one *s* one *d* (and one *d* decd). *Educ:* Eton Coll.; RMA, Sandhurst. Commnd Rifle Bde (later Royal Green Jackets), 1956; Malaya, 1956–57 (despatches); ADC to GOC Ghana Army, 1958–59; ADC to Chief of Imperial Gen. Staff, 1959–60; SE Asia, 1962–65; Army Staff Coll., 1967; Hong Kong, 1968–70; transferred to FCO, 1973; Vientiane, 1975; Muscat, 1976; Counsellor: Jakarta, 1983; Riyadh, 1990. Pres., St John Ambulance Sussex, 2005–11. Chm. Trustees, John Bodley Trust, 2004–; Trustee, Lodge Hill Trust, 2006–11. High Sheriff, 2003–04, DL 2004, West Sussex. OStJ 2013 (SBStJ 2008). *Recreation:* field sports. *Address:* Coolhurst Grange, Horsham, West Sussex RH13 6LE. *T:* (01403) 252416. *Clubs:* White's, Special Forces.

SCREECH, Rev. Prof. Michael Andrew, FBA 1981; FRSL; Fellow and Chaplain, All Souls College, Oxford, 2001–03, now Emeritus Fellow (Senior Research Fellow, 1984–93); Assistant Curate (non-stipendiary), St Giles with St Philip, and St James with St Margaret, Oxford, 1993–2006; *b* 2 May 1926; 3rd *s* of Richard John Screech, MM and Nellie Screech (*née* Maunder); *m* 1956, Anne (*née* Reeve); three *s*. *Educ:* Sutton High Sch., Plymouth; University Coll. London (BA (1st cl. Hons) 1950; Fellow, 1982); University of Montpellier, France; Oxford Ministry Course; DLitt Birmingham, 1959; DLit London, 1982; DLitt Oxon 1990. Other Rank, Intelligence Corps (mainly Far East), 1944–48. Asst, UCL, 1950–51; Birmingham Univ.: Lectr, 1951–58; Sen. Lectr, 1959–61; UCL: Reader, 1961–66; Personal Chair of French, 1966–71; Fielden Prof. of French Language and Lit., London Univ., 1971–84; Extraordinary Fellow, 1993–2001, Hon. Fellow, 2001, Wolfson Coll., Oxford. Ordained deacon, 1993, priest, 1994. Visiting Professor: Univ. of Western Ontario, 1964–65; Univ. of New York, Albany, 1968–69; Johnson Prof., Inst. for Research in the Humanities, Madison, Wisconsin, 1978–79; Vis. Fellow, All Souls, Oxford, 1981; Edmund Campion Lectr, Regina, 1985; Wiley Vis. Prof., N Carolina, 1986; Professeur, Collège de France, 1989; Prof. Associé, Paris IV (Sorbonne), 1990; Leverhulme Emeritus Fellow, 1995–98. Member: Cttee, Warburg Inst., 1970–84; Comité d'Humanisme et Renaissance, 1971–; Comité de parrainage des Classiques de l'Humanisme, 1988–; Corresponding Member: Société Historique de Genève, 1988; Acad. des Inscriptions et Belles Lettres, Paris, 2000. Hon. DLitt Exeter, 1993; Hon. Dr: Geneva, 1998; Neuchâtel, 2009. Chevalier dans l'Ordre National du Mérite, 1983; Médaille de la Ville de Tours, 1984; Chevalier, Légion d'Honneur, 1992. *Publications:* The Rabelaisian Marriage, 1958, rev. edn trans. French, 1992; L'Evangélisme de Rabelais, 1959, rev. edn trans. English, 1992; Tiers Livre de Pantagruel, 1964; Les épistres et évangiles de Lefèvre d'Etaples, 1964; (with John Jollife) Les Regrets et autres oeuvres poëtiques (Du Bellay), 1966; Marot évangélique, 1967; (with R. M. Calder) Gargantua, 1970; La Pantagrueline Prognostication, 1975; Rabelais, 1980, rev. edn trans. French, 1992; Ecstasy and the Praise of Folly, 1981, rev. edn trans. French, 1991; Montaigne and Melancholy, 1983, rev. edn trans. French, 1992; (prefaces) Erasmus' Annotations on the New Testament (ed Anne Reeve): The Gospels, 1986, Acts, Romans, I and II Corinthians, 1990, Galatians—Revelation, 1993; (ed trans.) Montaigne, An Apology for Raymond Sebond, 1987; (with Stephen Rawles *et al.*) A New Rabelais Bibliography: editions before 1626, 1987; (ed trans.) The Essays of Montaigne, 1991; Some Renaissance Studies, ed. M. Heath, 1992; Clément Marot: a Renaissance poet discovers the Gospel, 1994; Monumental Inscriptions in All Souls College, Oxford, 1997; Laughter at the Foot of the Cross, 1998; Montaigne's Copy of Lucretius, 1998; (ed trans.) Rabelais, Gargantua and Pantagruel, 2006; *edited reprints:* Le Nouveau Testament de Lefèvre d'Etaples, 1970; F. de Billon: Le Fort inexpugnable de l'Honneur du Sexe Féminin, 1970; Opuscules d'Amour par Héroët et autres divins poëtes, 1970; Amyot: Les œuvres morales et meslées de Plutarque, 1971; Warden Mocket of All Souls: Doctrina et Politia Ecclesiae Anglicanae, 1995. *Recreation:* walking. *Address:* 5 Swanston-field, Whitchurch-on-Thames, Reading RG8 7HP. *T:* (0118) 984 2513. *Clubs:* Athenæum; Pangbourne Working Men's.

SCREECH, Rt Rev. Royden; Bishop Suffragan of St Germans, 2000–11; *b* 15 May 1953; *s* of Raymond Kenneth Screech and Gladys Beryl Screech; *m* 1988, Angela May Waring; no *c*. *Educ:* Cotham Grammar Sch.; King's Coll. London (BD 1974, AKC 1974); St Augustine's Coll., Canterbury. Ordained deacon, 1976, priest, 1977; Curate, St Catherine, Hatcham, 1976–80; Vicar, St Antony, Nunhead, 1980–87; Priest-in-charge, St Silas, Nunhead, 1982–87; Rural Dean, Camberwell, 1984–87; Vicar, St Edward, New Addington, 1987–94; Selection Sec., 1994–97, Sen. Selection Sec., 1997–2000, ABM, subseq. Ministry Div., Archbishops' Council. *Recreations:* opera, holidays in Italy, Coronation Street.

SCRIVEN, Baron *cr* 2014 (Life Peer), of Hunters Bar in the City of Sheffield; **Paul James Scriven;** Managing Partner, Scriven Consulting; *b* 7 Feb. 1966. Former NHS manager. Mem. (Lib Dem) Sheffield CC, 2000–12 (Leader, 2008–11). Contested (Lib Dem) Sheffield Central, 2010.

SCRIVEN, Rt Rev. Henry William; Mission Director for Latin America, Church Mission Society, since 2009; an Honorary Assistant Bishop: Diocese of Oxford, since 2010; Diocese of Winchester, since 2013; *b* 30 Aug. 1951; *s* of late William Hamilton Scriven and Jeanne Mary Edwards; *m* 1975, Catherine Rose Ware; one *s* one *d*. *Educ:* Repton Sch.; Sheffield Univ. (BA Hons); St John's Theol Coll., Nottingham. Ordained deacon, 1975, priest, 1976; Asst Curate, Holy Trinity, Wealdstone, Harrow, 1975–79; Missionary with S American Missionary Soc., N Argentina, 1979–82; Educn Associate Rector, Christ Church, Little Rock, Arkansas, 1982–83; Missionary, S American Missionary Soc., Spain, 1984–90; Chaplain, British Embassy Church of St George, Madrid, 1990–95; Suffragan Bp of Gibraltar in Europe, 1995–2002; Asst Bp of Pittsburgh, USA, 2002–08. *Recreations:* reading, walking, cycling, music. *Address:* 16 East St Helen Street, Abingdon, Oxon OX14 5EA. *T:* (01235) 536607; (office) Church Mission Society, Watlington Road, Oxford OX4 6BZ. *T:* (01865) 787500. *E:* henry.scriven@cms-uk.org.

SCRIVEN, Pamela; QC 1992; a Recorder, since 1996; *b* 5 April 1948; *d* of Maurice Scriven and Evelyn Scriven (*née* Stickney); *m* 1973; two *s*. *Educ:* University College London (LLB Hons). Called to the Bar, Inner Temple, 1970 (Bencher, 1995). Chm., Family Law Bar Assoc., 1999–2001. *Address:* 1 King's Bench Walk, Temple, EC4Y 7DB. *T:* (020) 7583 6266.

SCRIVENER, Christiane; Commandeur de la Légion d'Honneur, 2001 (Officier, 1995); Médiateur, Société Générale, since 1996; Member, Commission of the European Communities, 1989–95; *b* 1 Sept. 1925; *m* 1944, Pierre Scrivener; one *s* decd. *Educ:* Lycée de Grenoble; Faculté de lettres et de droit de Paris. Dip. Psychol.; Dip. Harvard Business Sch. Directeur Général: l'Assoc. pour l'organisation des Stages en France, 1958–69; l'Assoc. pour l'organisation des missions de coopération technique, 1961–69; l'Agence pour la coopération technique industrielle et économique, 1969–76; Sec. d'Etat à la Consommation, 1976–78; Pres., la Commission chargée d'étudier les problèmes éthiques de la publicité, 1978; Sec. Gen. Adj. du parti républicain, 1978–79; Mem., Parlement européen (UDF), 1978–89; Mem., Conseil d'admin des Assurances Générales de France, 1986–89. Alumni Achievement Award (Harvard Business Sch.), 1976. Officier, Polonia Restituta, 1968; Médaille d'Or du Mérite Européen, 1990; Grand Croix de l'Ordre de Léopold II (Belgium), 1995; Grand Croix de Mérite du Grand Duché de Luxembourg, 1996. *Publications:* L'Europe, une bataille pour l'avenir, 1984; (pour les enfants) L'histoire du Petit Troll, 1986. *Recreations:* ski-ing, tennis, classical music. *Address:* 21 avenue Robert-Schumann, 92100 Boulogne-Billancourt, France.

SCRIVER, Prof. Charles Robert, CC 1997 (OC 1986); GOQ 1997; FRS 1991; FRSC 1973; Alva Professor of Human Genetics, 1994–2002, Professor of Pediatrics, Faculty of Medicine, and Professor of Biology, Faculty of Science, 1969–2002, McGill University, Montreal, now Professor Emeritus; *b* 7 Nov. 1930; *s* of Walter DeMoulpied Scriver and Jessie Marion (*née* Boyd); *m* 1956, Esther Katharine Peirce; two *s* two *d*. *Educ:* McGill Univ., Montreal (BA *cum laude* 1951, MD, CM *cum laude* 1955). Intern, Royal Victoria Hosp., Montreal, 1955–56; Resident: Royal Victoria and Montreal Children's Hosps, 1956–57; Children's Med. Center, Boston, 1957–58; McLaughlin Travelling Fellow, UCL, 1958–60; Chief Resident in Pediatrics, Montreal Children's Hosp., 1960–61; Asst, Associate Prof., Pediatrics, 1961–69, Markle Schol., 1962–67, McGill Univ. Rutherford Lectr, RSCan, 1983. Associate, 1968–95, Dist. Scientist, 1995–, MRC; Dir, MRC Gp (Med. Genetics), 1982–94; Associate Dir, Can. Genetic Diseases Networks (Centers of Excellence), 1989–98. President: Can. Soc. Clinical Investigation, 1974–75; Soc. Pediatric Res., 1975–76; Amer. Soc. Human Genetics, 1986–87; Amer. Pediatric Soc., 1994–95. FAAAS 1992; Member: Amer. Soc. Clinical Investigation; Assoc. Amer. Physicians; Hon. Member: Brit. Paediatric Assoc.; RCPI; Soc. Française de Pédiatrie. Hon. DSc: Manitoba, 1992; Glasgow, 1993; Montreal, 1993; Utrecht, 1999; UBC, 2002; Western Ontario, 2007; McGill, 2007. Wood Gold Medal, McGill Univ., 1955; Mead Johnson Award, 1968, Borden Award 1973, Amer. Acad. Pediatrics; Borden Award, Nutrition Soc. Can., 1969; Allan Award, 1978, Excellence in Human Genetics Educn Award, 2001, Amer. Soc. Human Genetics; G. Malcolm Brown Award, Can. Soc. Clin. Invest., 1979; Gairdner Internat. Award, Gairdner Foundn, 1979; McLaughlin Medal, RSC, 1981; Ross Award, Can. Pediatric Soc., 1990; Award of Excellence, Genetic Soc. of Canada, 1992; Prix du Québec (Wilder Penfield), 1995; Lifetime Achievement Award in Genetics, Birth Defects Foundn, 1997; Querci Prize, Italy, 2001; McGill Alumni Global Lifetime Achievement Award, 2009; Folling Award, Eur. Phenylketonuria Gp, 2010; Pollin Prize, Columbia Univ. and NY Presbyterian Hosp., 2010; Howland Medal, Amer. Pediatric Soc., 2010. *Publications:* (jtly) Amino Acid Metabolism and its Disorders, 1973; (ed) The Metabolic Basis of Inherited Disease, 6th edn 1986, 7th edn as The Metabolic and Molecular Bases of Inherited Disease, 1995, 8th edn 2001; numerous res. pubns. *Recreations:* history, music, photography, literature. *Address:* 232 Strathearn N, Montreal West, QC H4X 1Y2, Canada. *E:* charles.scriver@sympatico.ca; (home) 232 Strathearn N, Montreal West, QC H4X 1Y2, Canada. *T:* (514) 4860742.

SCRUTON, Prof. Roger Vernon, FBA 2008; FRSL; writer and philosopher; *b* 27 Feb. 1944; *s* of John Scruton and Beryl C. Haynes; *m* 1st, 1973, Danielle Laffitte (marr. diss. 1979); 2nd, 1996, Sophie Jeffreys; one *s* one *d*. *Educ:* Jesus Coll., Cambridge (MA, PhD). FRSL 2004.

Called to the Bar, Inner Temple, 1978; Bencher, 2015. Res. Fellow, Peterhouse, 1969–71; Lectr in Philosophy, Birkbeck Coll., London, 1971–79, Reader, 1979–85, Prof. of Aesthetics, 1985–92; Prof. of Philosophy, Boston Univ., Mass, 1992–95. Res. Prof., Inst. of Psychological Scis, Arlington, Va, 2007–09; Sen. Res. Fellow, Blackfriars Hall, Oxford, 2008–; Vis. Prof. in Philosophy, Univ. of Oxford, 2010–; Professorial Fellow in Moral Philosophy, Univ. of St Andrews, 2011–14. Founder and Dir, The Claridge Press, 1987–. Medal for Merit (1st Cl.) (Czech Republic), 1998. Editor, Salisbury Review, 1982–2000. *Publications:* Art and Imagination, 1974, 2nd edn 1982; The Aesthetics of Architecture, 1979; The Meaning of Conservatism, 1980, 3rd edn 2001; From Descartes to Wittgenstein, 1981, 2nd edn 1995; Fortnight's Anger (novel), 1981; The Politics of Culture, 1981; Kant, 1982; A Dictionary of Political Thought, 1982, 2nd edn 1996; The Aesthetic Understanding, 1983; (with Baroness Cox) Peace Studies: A Critical Survey, 1984; Thinkers of the New Left, 1985; (jtly) Education and Indoctrination, 1985; Sexual Desire, 1986; Spinoza, 1986; A Land held Hostage, 1987; Untimely Tracts, 1987; The Philosopher on Dover Beach (essays), 1990; Francesca (novel), 1991; A Dove Descending and Other Stories, 1991; (ed) Conservative Texts: an anthology, 1992; Xanthippic Dialogues (novel), 1993; Modern Philosophy, 1994; The Classical Vernacular, 1994; An Intelligent Person's Guide to Philosophy, 1996; The Aesthetics of Music, 1997; On Hunting, 1998; (ed with Anthony Barnett) Town and Country, 1998; An Intelligent Person's Guide to Modern Culture, 1998; Animal Rights and Wrongs, 2000; England: an elegy, 2000; The West and the Rest: globalisation and the terrorist threat, 2002; Death-devoted Heart: sex and the sacred in Wagner's Tristan and Isolde, 2004; News from Somewhere, 2004; Gentle Regrets, 2005; A Political Philosophy, 2006; Culture Counts, 2008; Beauty, 2009; The Uses of Pessimism and the Danger of False Hope, 2010; Green Philosophy: how to think seriously about the planet, 2012; The Face of God, 2012; Our Church: a personal history of the Church of England, 2012; Notes from Underground (novel), 2014; The Soul of the World, 2014; How to be a Conservative, 2014; The Disappeared (novel), 2015; contribs to The Times, Guardian, etc. *Recreations:* music, architecture, literature, hunting. *Address:* Sunday Hill Farm, Brinkworth, Wilts SN15 5AS.
See also E. Hodder.

SCRYMGEOUR, family name of **Earl of Dundee**.

SCRYMGEOUR, Lord; Henry David Wedderburn of that Ilk; *b* 20 June 1982; *s* and *heir* of 12th Earl of Dundee, *qv*; *m* 2005, Eloise, *d* of Ludovic van der Heyden, Fontainebleau; one *s*. *Heir: s* Tassilo Alexander Robert Scrymgeour, Master of Scrymgeour, *b* 16 Dec. 2005.

SCUDAMORE, Prof. James Marfell, CB 2004; consultant, since 2004; Professor of Livestock and Veterinary Public Health, University of Liverpool, since 2004; *b* 24 March 1944; *s* of Leonard John Scudamore and Joan Kathleen Scudamore; *m* 1968, Alison Ceridwen Foulkes. *Educ:* Chester City Grammar Sch.; Liverpool Univ. (BVSc 1967; BSc 1st cl. Hons 1968). Qualified as vet. surg., 1967; Dist Vet. Officer, Kenya, 1968–71; Vet. Res. Officer, Kenya, 1971–74; joined MAFF, 1974: Vet. Investigation Service, 1974–80; Divl Vet. Officer, Tolworth, 1980–84, Taunton, 1984–87; Regl Vet. Officer, S Scotland, 1987–90; Asst Chief Vet. Officer, Edinburgh, 1990–96, Tolworth (Meat Hygiene), 1996–97; Chief Vet. Officer, 1997–2004, and Dir Gen., Animal Health and Welfare, 2001–04, MAFF, subseq. DEFRA. *Recreations:* reading, swimming, gardening. *Address:* 56 Horseshoe Lane East, Guildford, Surrey GU1 2TL. *T:* (01483) 572706.

SCUDAMORE, Peter Michael, MBE 1990; National Hunt jockey, 1979–93; Assistant Trainer at Arlary House Stables, Kinross, since 2007; *b* 13 June 1958; *s* of late Michael and Mary Scudamore; two *s*. *Educ:* Belmont Abbey, Hereford. Champion Jockey, 1981–82 and annually, 1986–93; rode for British Jump Jockeys; winners in Australia, Belgium, Germany, New Zealand, Norway; Leading Jockey, Ritz Club Charity Trophy, Cheltenham Festival, 1986; leading jockey, Cheltenham, 1986, 1987; set new record for number of winners ridden in career, 1989, for number in one season (221), 1989; rode 1,500th winner, 1992; record 1,678 wins on retirement. Asst Trainer at Bromsash, Herefordshire, with son, Michael Scudamore, 2003–06. Racing journalist, Daily Mail, 1993–; Commentator for Nat. Hunt racing, Grandstand, BBC TV, 1993–2012. *Publications:* Scu: the autobiography of a champion, 1993. *Recreations:* golf, watching sport. *E:* p.scu13@googlemail.com.

SCUDAMORE, Richard Craig; Chief Executive, Premier League (formerly Football Association Premier League), since 1999; *b* 11 Aug. 1959; *s* of late Kenneth Ronald Scudamore and of Enid Doreen Scudamore (*née* Selman); *m* 1999, Catherine Joanne Ramsey; three *s* two *d*. *Educ:* Kingsfield Sch., Bristol; Nottingham Univ. Regl Dir, BT Yellow Pages, ITT World Directories, 1981–89; Man. Dir, Newspaper and Media Sales Ltd, Ingersoll Publications, 1989–90; Thomson Corporation: Newspaper Gp Sales and Mktg Dir, 1991–94; Asst, then Man. Dir, Scotsman Publications, 1994–95; Sen. Vice Pres., N America, 1995–98; Chief Exec. and Dir, Football League Ltd, 1998–99. *Recreations:* golf, music, children, and of course football. *Address:* Premier League, 30 Gloucester Place, W1U 8PL. *T:* (020) 7864 9103.

SCULLY, Prof. Crispian Michael, CBE 2000; MD, PhD; FDSRCPSGlas, FFDRCSI, FDSRCS, FDSRCSE, FRCPath, FMedSci, FHEA; Emeritus Professor, UCL Eastman Dental Institute, University of London, since 2008; Professor of Oral Medicine, Pathology and Microbiology, University of London, since 1993; Professor of Oral Medicine, University of Bristol, 2010–12; *b* 24 May 1945; *s* of Patrick and Rosaleen Scully; *m* Zoitsa Boucoumani; one *d*. *Educ:* Univ. of London (BSc, BDS, PhD); Univ. of Glasgow; Univ. of Bristol (MD, MDS). MRCS; LRCP; LDS RCS; FDSRCPSGlas 1979; FFDRCSI 1983; FDSRCS 1988; FDSRCSE 1998; FRCPath 1998. MRC Research Fellow, Guy's Hosp., 1975–78; Lectr, 1979–81, Sen. Lectr, 1981–82, Univ. of Glasgow; Prof. of Stomatology, 1982–93, and Dean, 1982–92, Univ. of Bristol; Dean and Dir of Studies and Res., UCL Eastman Dental Inst., 1993–2008; Fellow, UCL, 2008. Hon. Consultant: Inst. of Dental Surgery, later UCL Eastman Dental Inst., London Univ. and UCL Hosps NHS Foundn Trust, 1993–; Great Ormond St Hosp., 1998–; Nuffield Orthopaedic Centre, Oxford, 1998–2002; John Radcliffe Hosp., Oxford, 1998–2002. Clinical Dir, UC London Hosps NHS Trust, 1995–96. Visiting Professor: Middx Univ., 1998–; UWE, 1998–; Univ. of Edinburgh, 2006–08; Univ. of Athens, 2008–; Adjunct Prof., Univ. of Helsinki, 2005–08. Consultant Adviser in Dental Research, DHSS, 1986–98. Member: GDC, 1984–94, 2000–03; Adv. Council for Misuse of Drugs, 1985–89; Chm., Central Examining Bd for Dental Hygienists, 1989–94; Member: Medicines Control Agency Cttee on Dental and Surgical Materials, 1990–93; Standing Dental Adv. Cttee, 1992–99; Adv. Cttee on Infected Health Care Workers, 1991–2002; Expert Adv. Cttee on Antimicrobial Resistance, 2001–02. Chm. Jt Adv. Cttee, Additional Dental Specialities, 1993–99. Pres., Eur. Assoc. for Oral Medicine, 2002–04 (Sec.-Gen., 1993–2002; Vice-Pres., 2000–02; Past Pres., 2004–06); Sec.-Gen., Internat. Acad. of Oral Oncology, 2005–08 (Vice-Pres., 2007–09). Founder FMedSci 1998; FHEA 2005. Founder, Internat. Fedn of Oral Medicine, 1998. Hon. DSc Athens, 2006; Hon. DMed Pretoria, 2008; Hon. DChD Granada, 2009; Hon. Dr Helsinki, 2010. *Publications:* Medical Problems in Dentistry, 1982, 7th edn 2014; (jtly) Multiple Choice Questions in Dentistry, 1985; Handbook for Hospital Dental Surgeons, 1985; (jtly) Slide Interpretation in Oral Disease, 1986; Dental Surgery Assistants' Handbook, 1988; Colour Atlas of Stomatology, 1988, 2nd edn 1996; Colour Aids to Oral Medicine, 1988, 3rd edn 1998; The Dental Patient, 1988; The Mouth and Perioral Tissues, 1989; Patient Care: a dental surgeon's guide, 1989; (jtly) Occupational Hazards in Dentistry, 1990; (jtly) Clinic Virology in Oral Medicine and Dentistry, 1992; (jtly) Medicine and Surgery for Dentistry, 1993, 2nd edn 1999; (jtly) Colour Atlas of Oral Diseases in Children and Adolescents, 1993, 2nd edn 2001; (jtly) Colour Atlas of Oral Pathology, 1995; (jtly) Oxford Handbook of Dental Patient Care, 1998, 2nd edn 2005; Handbook of Oral Disease, 1999; (jtly) Dermatology of the Lips, 2000; ABC of Oral Health, 2000; (jtly) Patologia e Medicina del Cavo Orale, 2001; (jtly) Periodontal Manifestations of Systemic Disease, 2002; (jtly) Oxford Handbook of Applied Dental Sciences, 2003; (jtly) Orofacial Disease: a guide for the dental clinical team, 2003; Oral and Maxillofacial Medicine, 2004, 2nd edn 2008; (jtly) Atlas of Oral and Maxillofacial Diseases, 2004, 2nd edn 2010; (jtly) Key Topics in Human Disease, 2005; (jtly) Culturally Sensitive Oral Health Care, 2006; (jtly) Oral Medicine—Update for the Dental Practitioner, 2006; (jtly) Medicina y Patologia Oral, 2006; (jtly) Special Care Dentistry: handbook of oral health care, 2007; (jtly) Applied Medicine and Surgery in Dentistry, 2010; (jtly) Common Medical Conditions, 2010; (jtly) Dental Nursing, 2011; Genetics in Dentistry and Oral Diseases, 2011; 1000 contribs to learned jls. *Recreations:* music, ski-ing, cycling, walking, windsurfing, sailing. *Address:* UCL Eastman Dental Institute, 256 Gray's Inn Road, WC1X 8LD. *T:* (020) 3456 1170.

SCULLY, Hugh; television presenter and producer; Founder and Chairman, Fine Art Productions, since 1988; *b* Bradford on Avon, Wilts, 5 March 1943; *s* of Wing Comdr Hugh Scully and Edith Scully; *m* 1966, Barbara Dean, Lusaka; two *s*. *Educ:* British mil. schs, Malta and Egypt; Prior Park Coll., Bath. Artists liaison, Steinway & Sons, 1960–61; Paris sabbatical, 1962–63; freelance presenter and reporter, BBC Plymouth, 1963–78; Chm., Talking About Antiques, BBC Radio 4, 1968–78; Presenter: Collectors World, BBC 2, 1970–72; Nationwide, BBC 1, 1977–84; Antiques Roadshow, BBC 1, 1980–99; The Story of English Furniture, BBC 2, 1993; Melodies for You, BBC Radio 2, 1996–99; Britain's Finest Stately Homes, ITV, 2003; Executive Producer: The Falklands War, Channel 4, 1992; Thatcher: the Downing Street Years, BBC 1, 1993; The Gulf War, BBC 1, 1995. *Recreations:* music, fine claret and long lingering lunches in France. *E:* hugh.scully@btinternet.com. *Clubs:* Athenæum; Royal Cornwall Yacht.

SCULLY, Paul Stuart; MP (C) Sutton and Cheam, since 2015; *b* Rugby, 29 April 1968; *s* of Basil and Joan Scully; *m* 1990, Emma; one *s* one *d*. *Educ:* Bedford Sch.; Univ. of Reading. Political Assistant: office of Andrew Pelling, MP, 2005–07; office of Shailesh Vara, MP, 2007–09; office of Alok Sharma, MP, 2010–12; Partner, Nudge Factory Ltd, 2011–. Mem. (C) Sutton LBC, 2006–10 (Leader of Opposition, 2006–10). *Address:* (office) Donnington House, 2a Sutton Court Road, Sutton, Surrey SM1 4SY. *T:* (020) 8642 3791. *E:* info@scully.org.

SCULLY, Sean Paul, RA 2013; artist; *b* Dublin, 30 June 1945; *s* of John Anthony Scully and Holly Scully; *m* 1st, 1978, Catherine Lee (marr. diss.); (one *s* decd); *m* 2nd, 2007, Liliane Tomasko; one *s*. *Educ:* Croydon Coll. of Art; Newcastle Univ.; Harvard Univ. Became American citizen, 1983. Lecturer: Harvard Univ., 1972–73; Chelsea Sch. of Art, and Goldsmiths' Sch. of Art, 1973–75; Princeton Univ., 1978–83; Parsons Sch. of Design, NY, 1983–; Prof. of Painting, Acad. of Fine Arts, Munich, 2002–07. *Solo exhibitions* include: Rowan Gall., London, 1973, 1975, 1977, 1979, 1981; Tortue Gall., Calif, 1975–76; Nadin Gall., NY, 1979; Mus. für (Sub-) Kultur, Berlin, 1981; retrospective, Ikon Gall., Birmingham, and tour, 1981; David McKee Gall., NY, 1983, 1985–87; Art Inst. of Chicago, 1988; University Art Mus., Univ. of Calif at Berkeley, 1988; Paintings and Works on Paper 1982–88, Whitechapel Art Gall., Neubachhaus, Munich, Palacio Velázquez, Madrid, 1989; Waddington Gall., 1992, 1995; The Catherine Paintings, Mus. of Modern Art, Fort Worth, 1993, Palais de Beaux-Arts, Belgium, 1995, Galerie Nat. de Jeu de Paume, Paris, 1996; Haus der Kunst, Munich, 2001; Abbot Hall Gall., Cumbria, 2005; Timothy Taylor Gall., London, 2004, 2006, 2009, 2010, 2012, 2014; Fundacio Joan Miro, Barcelona, 2007; Ingleby Gall., Carlow Centre for Contemp. Art, Leeds Art Gall., Künstammlungen Chemnitz, 2010; Chazen Mus. of Art, Madison, 2011; Granada Palacio Carlos V, Athens Benaki Mus., Kunstmuseum Bern, 2012; Galleria Nazionale d'Arte Moderna, Rome 2013; Triptychs, Pallant House Gall., Chichester, 2013–14; *works in public collections* include: Mus. of Modern Art, NY; Tate Gall.; V & A Mus.; Aust. Nat. Gall., Canberra; Art Gall. of NSW, Sydney; Guggenheim Mus., NY; Centro de Arte Reina Sofia, Madrid. *Address:* c/o Timothy Taylor Gallery, 15 Carlos Place, W1K 2EX; c/o Neo Neo Inc., 447 West 17th Street, New York, NY 10011, USA.

SEABECK, Alison Jane; *b* 20 Jan. 1954; *d* of late Michael John Ward and of Lilian Ward (*née* Lomas); *m* 1975 (marr. diss. 2007); two *d*; *m* 2012, Rt Hon. Wyvill Richard Nicolls Raynsford, (Rt Hon. Nick), *qv*. *Educ:* North East London Polytechnic. Parly Asst to Rt Hon. Roy Hattersley, MP, 1987–92; Advr to Rt Hon. Nick Raynsford, MP, 1992–2005. MP (Lab) Plymouth Devonport, 2005–10, Plymouth, Moor View, 2010–15; contested (Lab) same seat, 2015. PPS to Minister of State for Europe, 2006–07; an Asst Govt Whip, 2007–08; PPS to Sec. of State for Transport, 2008–09; Shadow Minister for Housing, 2010–11; Shadow Defence Minister, 2010–15. Member: Select Cttee for Communities and Local Govt, 2005–06; Regulatory Reform Select Cttee, 2005–07; Chairman: Select Cttee for SW, 2009–10; All Party Gp for Local Govt, 2006–10. *Recreations:* reading, walking, swimming, gardening.

SEABORN, Hugh Richard, CVO 2014; Chief Executive Officer, Cadogan Estates Ltd, since 2008; *b* 24 May 1962; *s* of Richard Anthony Seaborn and Wendy Nora Seaborn (*née* Punt); *m* 2000, Michaela Louise Scanlon; three *s*. *Educ:* Pocklington Sch.; Newcastle upon Tyne Poly. (BSc 1984). FRICS 1999. Landmark Property Consultants, Cape Town, 1985–88; Richard Ellis Fleetwood-Bird, Gaborone, 1988–91; Dir and Hd, Investment Mgt Dept, Richard Ellis, 1991–2000; CEO and Agent to Trustees, The Portman Estate, 2000–08. Mem. Council and Audit Cttee, Duchy of Lancaster, 2005–13. Chairman: Westminster Property Owners Assoc., 2008 (Dep. Chm., 2006–08); Estate Business Gp, 2012–; Knightsbridge Business Gp, 2015–. Non-exec. Dir, TR Property Investment Trust, 2007–. *Recreations:* family, cycling, fly fishing. *Address:* (office) 18 Cadogan Gardens, SW3 2RP. *T:* (020) 7730 4567. *Club:* Sloane.

SEABROOK, Graeme; Director (non-executive): P. Cleland Enterprises Ltd, Australia, 1997–2003; Country Road Ltd, 1997–2003; *b* 1 May 1939; *s* of Norman and Amy Winifred Seabrook; *m* 1967, Lorraine Ellen Ludlow; one *s* one *d*. G. J. Coles & Co. (later Coles Myer), Australia, 1955; Chief Gen. Manager, G. J. Coles, 1982; acquisition of Myer, 1985; Man. Dir, Discount Stores Group, 1985; Jt Man. Dir, Coles Myer, 1987, resigned 1988; joined Dairy Farm International, Hong Kong and seconded to Kwik Save Group, 1988: Man. Dir, 1988–93, Chief Exec., 1989–93, non-exec. Dir, 1993–96; Man. Dir, Dairy Farm Internat., Hong Kong, 1993–96. Non-exec. Dir, Woolworths Hldgs Ltd, S Africa, 1997–2000. *Recreations:* lawn bowls, photography.

SEABROOK, Peter John, MBE 2005; VMH; consultant horticulturist, since 1971; *b* 2 Nov. 1935; *s* of Robert Henry Seabrook and Emma Mary Seabrook (*née* Cottey); *m* 1960, Margaret Ruth Risbey; one *s* one *d*. *Educ:* King Edward VI Grammar Sch., Chelmsford; Essex Inst. of Agric., Writtle (Dip. Hort, MHort). Cramphorn Ltd, 1952–66; Bord Na Mona, 1966–70; Gardening Corresp., Sun, 1977–; Director: Wm Strike Ltd, 1972–95; Roger Harvey Ltd, 1981–99. TV presenter: WGBH TV, Boston, USA, 1975–97; Pebble Mill At One, 1975–86; Gardeners' World, 1976–79; Chelsea Flower Show, (annually) 1976–89; Gardeners' Direct Line, 1982–90; Peter Seabrook's Gardening Week, 1996. Hon. Fellow, Writtle Coll., 1997. Pearson Meml Medal, Horticultural Trades Assoc., 1985; Associate of Honour, 1996, VMH 2003, RHS. *Publications:* Shrubs for Your Garden, 1973, 10th edn 1991; Plants for Your Home, 1975; Complete Vegetable Gardener, 1976, 4th edn 1981; Book of the Garden, 1979, 2nd edn 1984; Good Plant Guide, 1981; Good Food Gardening, 1983; Shrubs for Everyone, 1997. *Recreation:* gardening. *Address:* (office) 212A Baddow Road, Chelmsford, Essex CM2 9QR. *T:* (01245) 354870. *Club:* Farmers.

SEABROOK, Robert John; QC 1983; a Recorder, 1985–2007; a Deputy High Court Judge, 1991–2010; *b* 6 Oct. 1941; *s* of late Alan Thomas Pertwee Seabrook, MBE and Mary Seabrook (*née* Parker); *m* 1965, Liv Karin Djupvik, Bergen, Norway (marr. diss. 2008); two *s* one *d*. *Educ:* St George's Coll., Salisbury, Southern Rhodesia; University Coll., London (LLB). Called to the Bar, Middle Temple, 1964, Bencher, 1990, Treas., 2007. Leader, SE Circuit, 1989–92; Chm., Bar Council, 1994. Member: Criminal Justice Consultative Council, 1995–2003; Interception of Communications Tribunal, 1996–2000; Investigatory Powers Tribunal, 2000–; Regulation of Investigatory Powers Tribunal for Guernsey, 2006–. Member: Brighton Fest. Cttee, 1976–86; Court, Univ. of Sussex, 1988–93. Vice Pres., Brighton Coll., 2005– (Gov., 1993–2004; Chm. of Govs, 1998–2004). Liveryman, Curriers' Co., 1972– (Master, 1995–96). *Recreations:* travel, walking, listening to music, wine. *Address:* (chambers) 1 Crown Office Row, Temple, EC4Y 7HH. *T:* (020) 7797 7500. *Clubs:* Athenæum, Les Six.

SEAFIELD, 13th Earl of, *cr* 1701; **Ian Derek Francis Ogilvie-Grant;** Viscount Seafield, Baron Ogilvy of Cullen, 1698; Viscount Reidhaven, Baron Ogilvy of Deskford and Cullen, 1701; *b* 20 March 1939; *s* of Countess of Seafield (12th in line), and Derek Studley-Herbert (who assumed by deed poll, 1939, the additional surnames of Ogilvie-Grant; he *d* 1960); *S* mother, 1969; *m* 1st, 1960, Mary Dawn Mackenzie (marr. diss. 1971), *er d* of Henry Illingworth; two *s*; 2nd, 1971, Leila, *d* of Mahmoud Refaat, Cairo. *Educ:* Eton. *Recreations:* shooting, fishing, tennis. *Heir: s* Viscount Reidhaven, *qv*. *Address:* Old Cullen, Cullen, Banffshire AB56 4XW. *T:* (01542) 840221. *Club:* White's.

SEAFORD, 6th Baron *cr* 1826, of Seaford, co. Sussex; **Colin Humphrey Felton Ellis;** *b* 19 April 1946; *o s* of Major William Felton Ellis and Edwina (*née* Bond); *S* to Seaford Barony of cousin, 9th Baron Howard de Walden, 1999; *m* 1st, 1971, Susan Magill (marr. diss. 1992); two *s* two *d*; 2nd, 1993, Penelope Mary Bastin. *Educ:* Sherborne; RAC, Cirencester (MRAC 1968). MRICS (ARICS 1970). *Heir: s* Hon. Benjamin Felton Thomas Ellis, *b* 17 Dec. 1976. *Address:* Bush Farm, West Knoyle, Warminster, Wilts BA12 6AE.

SEAFORD, Very Rev. John Nicholas Shtetinin; Dean of Jersey and Rector of St Helier, 1993–2005; *b* 12 Sept. 1939; *s* of Nicholas Shtetinin Seaford and Kathleen Dorothy (*née* Longbotham); *m* 1967, Helen Marian Webster; two *s* one *d*. *Educ:* Radley Coll.; St Chad's Coll., Durham Univ. (BA 1967; DipTh 1968). Ordained deacon, 1968, priest, 1969; Assistant Curate: St Mark, Bush Hill Park, Enfield, 1968–71; St Luke, Winchester, 1971–73; Vicar: Chilworth and North Baddesley, 1973–78; Highcliffe and Hinton Admiral, 1978–93. Hon. Canon, Winchester Cathedral, 1993–2005, now Canon Emeritus. Vice Chm., Adv. Cttee for the Care of Churches, Dio. of Salisbury, 2014–. Chaplain, HM Prison La Moye, Jersey, 2003–05. Religious Broadcasting Advr, Channel TV, 1993–2005. Mem., States of Jersey, 1993–2005. *Recreation:* walking.

SEAGA, Most Hon. Edward Philip George; PC 1982; ON 2002; Pro-Chancellor, University of Technology, Jamaica, since 2008; Distinguished Fellow, University of the West Indies, 2005; Leader of the Jamaica Labour Party, 1974–2005; *b* 28 May 1930; *s* of late Philip Seaga and of Erna (*née* Maxwell); *m* 1965, Marie Elizabeth (marr. diss. 1995) (*née* Constantine) (Miss Jamaica, 1964); two *s* one *d*; *m* Carla Frances Vendryes, MPA; one *d*. *Educ:* Wolmers Boys' Sch., Kingston, Jamaica; Harvard Univ., USA (BA Social Science, 1952). Did field research in connection with Inst. of Social and Econ. Res., University Coll. of the West Indies (now Univ. of the WI), Jamaica, on develt of the child, and revival spirit cults, by living in rural villages and urban slums; proposed estabt of Unesco Internat. Fund for Promotion of Culture, 1971, and was founding mem. of its Administrative Council. Nominated to Upper House (Legislative Council), 1959 (youngest mem. in its history); Asst Sec., Jamaica Labour Party, 1960–62; MP for Western Kingston, 1962–2005; Minister of Develt and Social Welfare, 1962–67; Minister of Finance and Planning, 1967–72, and 1980–89; Leader of Opposition, 1974–80, 1989–2004; Prime Minister, 1980–89. Director: Consulting Services Ltd, to 1979; Capital Finance Co. Ltd, to 1979. Hon. LLD: Miami, 1981; Tampa, 1982; S Carolina, 1983; Boston, 1983; Hartford, 1987. Grand Collar, and Golden Mercury Internat. Award, Venezuela, 1981; Grand Cross, Order of Merit of Fed. Rep. of Germany, 1982. Gold Key Award, Avenue of the Americas, NYC, 1981; Environment Leadership Award, UN, 1987; Golden Star Caribbean Award Man of the Year, 1988. Religion Anglican. *Publications:* The Development of the Child; Revival Spirit Cults; Edward Seaga: my life and leadership (autobiog.), vol. 1, 1930–1980, 2009, vol. 2, 1980–2008, 2010. *Recreations:* classical music, reading, sport. *Address:* University of Technology, Jamaica, 237 Old Hope Road, Kingston 6, Jamaica. *Clubs:* Kingston Cricket, Jamaica Gun (Jamaica).

SEAGER, family name of **Baron Leighton of Saint Mellons**.

SEAGER BERRY, Thomas Henry Seager; Deputy Costs Judge, 2005–08; Master (Costs Judge) of the Supreme Court Costs (formerly Taxing) Office, 1991–2005; *b* 29 Jan. 1940; *s* of late Thomas Geoffrey Seager Berry, CBE and Ann Josephine Seager Berry; *m* 2002, Agnes Christine Thomson. *Educ:* Shrewsbury Sch. Admitted solicitor, 1964; Sherwood & Co., 1964–69 (Partner, 1966–69); Partner, Boodle Hatfield, 1969–91. Pres., London Solicitors Litigation Assoc., 1982–84; Mem. Cttee, Media Soc., 1985–91; Mem. Council, Feathers Clubs Assoc., 1986–2007. Liveryman, Merchant Taylors' Co., 1967. *Publications:* Longman's Litigation Practice, 1988. *Recreations:* tennis, gardening, wine-tasting, walking. *Clubs:* Hurlingham, MCC.

SEAGROATT, Hon. Conrad; a Judge of the Court of First Instance of the High Court (formerly a Judge of the High Court), Hong Kong, 1995–2003; a Recorder of the Crown Court, 1980–2004; Deputy High Court Judge, Hong Kong, since 2011; *s* of late E. G. Seagroatt, Solicitor of the Supreme Court and Immigration Appeals Adjudicator, and of Gray's Inn, and of Barbara C. Seagroatt; *m* Cornelia Mary Anne Verdegaal; five *d*. *Educ:* Solihull Sch., Warwicks; Pembroke Coll., Oxford (MA Hons Modern History). Admitted Solicitor of the Supreme Court, 1967; called to the Bar, Gray's Inn, 1970, Bencher, 1991; QC 1983; Dep. High Court Judge, 1993–2004; Judge i/c of Hong Kong Personal Injury List, 1998–2003. Member: Senate of the Inns of Court and the Bar, 1980–83; Criminal Injuries Compensation Bd, 1986–94. Mem., Hong Kong Chief Justice's Wkg Party on Civil Reform Process, 2000–03. Mem., Editl Adv. Bd, Hong Kong Court Forms, 2000–03; Adv. Ed., Hong Kong Civil Procedure, (The White Book), 2000–03. *Publications:* (contrib.) The Reform of the Civil Process in Hong Kong, 1999; contrib. Hong Kong Law Jl. *Recreations:* running, fairweather ski-ing.

SEAGROVE, Jennifer Ann; actress, since 1979; Trustee, Born Free, since 2002; Founding Trustee, Mane Chance Sanctuary, since 2011; *b* 4 July 1957; *d* of late Derek and Pauline Seagrove; *m* 1984, Madhav Sharma (marr. diss. 1988); partner, William Kenwright, *qv*. *Educ:* St Hilary's Sch., Godalming; Queen Anne's Sch., Caversham; Kirby Lodge, Cambridge; Bristol Old Vic Theatre Sch. *Theatre* includes: Jane Eyre, Chichester, 1986; King Lear in New York, Chichester, 1992; Present Laughter, Globe, 1993; The Miracle Worker, Comedy, 1994; Dead Guilty, Apollo, 1995; Hurlyburly, Queen's, 1997; Brief Encounter, Lyric, 2000; The Female Odd Couple, Apollo, 2001; The Constant Wife, Apollo, 2002; The Secret Rapture, Lyric, 2003; The Night of the Iguana, Lyric, 2005; The Letter, Wyndhams, 2007; Absurd Person Singular, Garrick, 2007; Pack of Lies, UK tour, 2009; A Daughter's a Daughter, Trafalgar Studios, 2009; Bedroom Farce, Duke of Yorks, 2010; The Country Girl, Apollo, 2010; Volcano, UK tour and Vaudeville, 2012; The Governess, UK tour, 2013; Fallen Angels, UK tour, 2014; Brief Encounter on air, 2015; *films* include: Local Hero, 1982; A Shocking Accident, 1982; Savage Islands, 1982; Appointment with Death, 1987; A Chorus of Disapproval, 1988; The Guardian, 1989; Miss Beatty's Children, 1992; Don't Go Breaking My Heart, 1997; Zoe, 1999; (short film) Pranks, 2011; *television* includes: The Woman in White, 1982; A Woman of Substance, 1984; Diana, 1984; Judge John Deed, 2000–07; Lewis, 2012; Endeavour, 2013; Camp X, 2014. Founder, Springing Dog Prodns, film prodn co., 2008–. FRSA. Michael Elliott Award for Best Actress, 2006. *Recreations:* dog walking, tennis, running, cycling, promoting organic farming and animal welfare, trying to save the planet! *Address:* c/o Gavin Denton Jones, Creative Artists Management, 55–59 Shaftesbury Avenue, W1D 6LD. *T:* (020) 7292 0600.

SEAL, Dr Barry Herbert; Chairman: U Can Recycling CiC, since 2010; Age UK Leeds, since 2013; *b* 28 Oct. 1937; *s* of Herbert Seal and Rose Anne Seal; *m* 1963, Frances Catherine Wilkinson; one *s* one *d*. *Educ:* Heath Grammar Sch., Halifax; Univ. of Bradford (MSc, PhD); European Business Sch., Fontainebleau. CEng. Served RAF, 1955–58. Trained as Chem. Engr, ICI Ltd, 1958–64; Div. Chem. Engr, Murex Ltd, 1964–68; Sen. Engr, BOC Internat., 1968–71; Principal Lectr in Systems, Huddersfield Polytechnic, 1971–79. Contested (Lab) Harrogate, Oct. 1974; Leader, Bradford MDC Labour Gp, 1976–79. MEP (Lab) Yorks W, 1979–99. European Parliament: Leader, British Lab. Gp, 1988–89; Chm., Econ., Monetary and Industrial Policy Cttee, 1984–87; Pres., delegn to USA, 1998–99. Chairman: N Kirklees PCT, 2002–07; Bradford District Care Trust, 2007–12. Hon. Freeman, Borough of Calderdale, 2000. *Publications:* papers on computer and microprocessor applications. *Recreations:* walking, reading, films, bridge. *Address:* Brookfields Farm, Brookfields Road, Wyke, Bradford, West Yorks BD12 9LU. *E:* barryseal@sky.com.

SEAL, (Karl) Russell, OBE 2013; Joint Managing Director, British Petroleum Co. plc, 1991–97; *b* 14 April 1942; *m* 1966, Pauline Hilarie (*née* Edwards); three *s*. *Educ:* Keele Univ. Joined BP, 1964; NY, 1970–72; Rotterdam, 1976–78; Asst Gen. Manager, Gp Corporate Planning, 1978–80; Chief Exec., Mktg and Refining, Singapore, Malaysia, and Hong Kong, and Sen. Rep., SE Asia, 1980–84; Gen. Manager, BP Oil Trading & Supply Dept, 1984; Chief Exec. and Man. Dir, BP Oil, 1988–95. Non-executive Director: Commonwealth Develt Corp., 1996–2001; Blue Circle plc, 1996–2001. Sen. Exec. Prog., Stanford Univ., 1984. Pro-Chancellor and Chm. Council, Exeter Univ., 2005–12. *Recreations:* jogging, walking, golf.

SEAL, Richard Godfrey, FRCO; FRSCM; Organist of Salisbury Cathedral, 1968–97; *b* 4 Dec. 1935; *s* of late William Godfrey Seal and of Shelagh Seal (*née* Bagshaw); *m* 1975, Dr Sarah Helen Hamilton; two *s*. *Educ:* New Coll. Choir Sch., Oxford; Cranleigh Sch., Surrey; Christ's Coll., Cambridge (MA). FRCO 1958; FRSCM 1987; FGCM 2008. Assistant Organist: Kingsway Hall, London, 1957–58; St Bartholomew the Great, London, 1960–61; Chichester Cathedral (and Dir of Music, Prebendal Sch.), Sussex, 1961–68. DMus Lambeth, 1992. *Address:* The Bield, Flamstone Street, Bishopstone, Salisbury, Wilts SP5 4BZ. *Club:* Crudgemens (Godalming).

SEAL, Russell; *see* Seal, K. R.

SEALE, Sir (Clarence) David, Kt 2000; JP; Chairman and Managing Director, R. L. Seale & Co., since 1969; *b* 11 Dec. 1937; *m* 1961, Margaret Anne Farmer; one *s* three *d*. *Educ:* Harrison Coll., Barbados. Airline Clerk, 1956–62; Gen. Manager, R. L. Seale & Co., 1962–69. JP Bridgetown, 1978. *Recreation:* horse racing. *Address:* Hopefield Manor, Hopefield, Christ Church, Barbados. *T:* 4280065. *Club:* Barbados Turf (Bridgetown).

SEALE, Sir John Henry, 5th Bt *cr* 1838; RIBA; *b* 3 March 1921; *s* of Sir John Seale, 4th Bt; *S* father, 1964; *m* 1953, Ray Josephine (*d* 2009), *d* of Robert Gordon Charters, MC, Christchurch, New Zealand; one *s* one *d*. *Educ:* Eton; Christ Church, Oxford. Served War of 1939–45: Royal Artillery, North Africa and Italy; Captain, 1945. ARIBA 1951. *Heir: s* John Robert Charters Seale [*b* 17 Aug. 1954; *m* 1996, Michelle, *d* of K. W. Taylor]. *Address:* Slade, Kingsbridge, Devon TQ7 4BL.

SEALEY, Barry Edward, CBE 1990; Director, Archangel Informal Investments Ltd, 2000–11 (Chairman, 2005–07); *b* 3 Feb. 1936; *s* of Edward Sealey and Queenie Katherine Sealey (*née* Hill); *m* 1960, Helen Martyn; one *s* one *d*. *Educ:* Dursley GS; St John's Coll., Cambridge (BA 1958; MA 1991); Harvard Business Sch. (PMD 1968). Christian Salvesen plc, 1958–90: Dir, 1969–90; Man. Dir, 1981–89; Chm., Optos plc (formerly Besca Ltd), 1992–2006. Director: Scottish American Investment Co. plc, 1983–2001; Morago Ltd, 1989–2011; Queen's Hall (Edinburgh) Ltd, 1990–99; Caledonian Brewing Co. Ltd, 1990–2004; Wilson Byard plc, 1992–2003; Interface Graphics Ltd, 1992–99; Stagecoach Hldgs plc, 1992–2001; Scottish Equitable Policy Holders Trust Ltd, 1993–2006; Scottish Equitable, 1993–99; ESI Investors Ltd, 1999–2008; Northern 3 VCT plc, 2001–07; CXR Biosciences Ltd, 2001–09 (Chm., 2001–07); Scottish Health Innovations Ltd, 2002–07 (Chm., 2002–07); Lab 901 Ltd, 2002–08 (Chm., 2002–08); Dundas Commercial Property (Gen. Partner), Ltd, 2002–11; Earlsgate Hldgs Ltd, 2004–06; Indigo Lighthouse Gp, 2004–14 (Chm., 2004–14); EZD Ltd, 2005–09; Landmark Trustee Co. Ltd, 2006–11. Chairman: Edinburgh Healthcare NHS Trust, 1993–99; Lothian Univ. Hosps NHS Trust, 1999–2002; Dir, Lothian Health Bd, 1999–2001. Mem. Council and Policy Cttee, Industrial Soc., 1990–2001. Dep. Chm. of Court, Napier Poly., subseq. Univ., 1987–98. *Recreations:* walking, music. *Address:* Flat 5, 2 The Cedars, Colinton Road, Edinburgh EH13 0PL. *T:* (0131) 441 2802. *E:* bes@morago.co.uk. *Club:* New (Edinburgh).

SEALY, Sir Austin (Llewellyn), Kt 2015; Managing Partner, A. Sealy & Co., international business consultancy and management services, since 1996; *b* 17 Sept. 1939; *s* of Kenneth Llewellyn Sealy and Gerdsene Elaine Sealy (*née* Crawford); *m* 1964, Rita Anita Pilgrim; three *s*. *Educ:* St Mary's Boys' Sch., Barbados; Harrison Coll., Barbados. Banker, 1958–93: Sen. Mgt Official with Barclays Bank PLC in Caribbean; High Comr for Barbados in UK, and Ambassador to Israel, 1993–94. Pres., Nat. Olympic Cttee of Barbados, 1982–96; Hon. Treas., Commonwealth Games Fedn, 1986–; Member: IOC, 1994–; Exec. Council, Assoc. of Nat. Olympic Cttees, 1995–2002. Silver Crown of Merit (Barbados), 1985; Merit Award, Assoc. of Nat. Olympic Cttees, 2012. *Recreations:* cricket, tennis, golf. *Address:* Crestview, 35 Highgate Gardens, St Michael, Barbados. *T:* 4272256; A. Sealy & Co., Leamington House, 4th Avenue, Belleville, St Michael, Barbados. *E:* austinsealy@sealygroup.com.

SEALY, Prof. Leonard Sedgwick, PhD; S. J. Berwin Professor of Corporate Law, University of Cambridge, 1991–97, now Emeritus; Life Fellow, Gonville and Caius College, Cambridge, since 1997 (Fellow, 1959–97); *b* 22 July 1930; *s* of Alfred Desmond Sealy and Mary Louise Sealy, Hamilton, NZ; *m* 1960, Beryl Mary Edwards; one *s* two *d*. *Educ:* Stratford High Sch.; Auckland Univ. (MA, LLM); Gonville and Caius Coll., Cambridge (PhD). Barrister and solicitor, NZ, 1953; in practice at NZ Bar, 1953–55 and 1958–59. Faculty of Law, University of Cambridge: Asst Lectr, 1959–61; Lectr, 1961–91; Tutor, 1961–70, Sen. Tutor, 1970–75, Gonville and Caius Coll. Gen. Ed., British Co. Law and Practice, 1989–2014. *Publications:* Cases and Materials in Company Law, 1971, 11th edn (with S. Worthington) 2015; Company Law and Commercial Reality, 1984; Disqualification and Personal Liability of Directors, 1986, 5th edn 2000; (with D. Milman) Guide to the 1986 Insolvency Legislation, 1987, (with D. Milman and P. Bailey) 18th edn as Annotated Guide to the Insolvency Legislation, 2015; (with R. Hooley) Cases and Materials in Commercial Law, 1994, 4th edn 2008; Cases/Company Law, 10th edn (with S. Worthington) 2014; Insolvency, 17th edn 2014; (ed with A. G. Guest *et al.*) Benjamin's Sale of Goods, 1974, 7th edn 2006; (General Editor): British Company Law and Practice, 1989; International Corporate Procedures, 1992–2005; Commonwealth Editor, Gore-Browne on Companies, 1997–2005. *Address:* Gonville and Caius College, Cambridge CB2 1TA. *T:* (01223) 332400.

SEAMAN, Christopher; international conductor; Music Director, Rochester Philharmonic Orchestra, New York, 1998–2011, now Conductor Laureate for Life; *b* 7 March 1942; *s* of late Albert Edward Seaman and Ethel Margery Seaman (*née* Chambers). *Educ:* Canterbury Cathedral Choir Sch.; The King's Sch., Canterbury; King's Coll., Cambridge. MA, double first cl. Hons in Music; ARCM, ARCO. Principal Timpanist, London Philharmonic Orch., 1964–68 (Mem., LPO Bd of Dirs, 1965–68); Asst Conductor, 1968–70, Principal Conductor, 1971–77, BBC Scottish Symphony Orchestra; Principal Conductor and Artistic Dir, Northern Sinfonia Orch., 1974–79; Principal Guest Conductor, Utrecht Symphony Orch., 1979–83; Principal Conductor, BBC Robert Mayer concerts, 1978–87; Conductor-in-Residence, Baltimore SO, 1987–98; Music Dir, Naples Phil. Orch., Florida, 1993–2004; also works widely as a guest conductor, and appears in America, Holland, France, Germany, Belgium, Italy, Norway, Spain, Portugal, Czechoslovakia, Israel, Hong Kong, Japan, Australia, New Zealand and all parts of UK. FGS (FGSM 1972). Hon. DMus Rochester, NY, 2009. *Recreations:* people, reading, walking, theology. *Address:* 25 Westfield Drive, Glasgow G52 2SG.

SEAMMEN, Diana Jill; *see* Hansen, D. J.

SEAR, Prof. John William, PhD; Professor of Anaesthetics, University of Oxford, 2002–10, now Emeritus; Fellow, Green Templeton College (formerly Green College), Oxford, 1982–2010, now Emeritus; *b* 3 Sept. 1947; *e s* of late Lionel and Ethel Alice Moore, and adoptive *s* of late Frederick Carl William Sear; *m* 1978, Yvonne Margaret Begley; three *s*. *Educ:* Enfield Grammar Sch.; London Hosp. Med. Coll. (BSc, MBBS); Univ. of Bristol (PhD); MA Oxford. FFARCS, FANZCA. Posts in London Hosp., 1972–75; Registrar in Anaesthetics, Royal Devon & Exeter Hosp. and United Bristol Hosps, 1975–77; University of Bristol: MRC Res. Training Fellow and Hon. Sen. Registrar, 1977–80; Lectr in Anaesthetics, 1980–81; University of Oxford: Clin. Reader in Anaesthetics, 1982–2002; Dir of Clinical Studies, 1995–98; Vice Warden, Green Coll., Oxford, 2002–07. Hon. Consultant Anaesthetist, Oxford Radcliffe Hosp. NHS Trust, 1982–2010; non-exec. Dir, Nuffield Orthopaedic Centre NHS Trust, 1993–2002. Member, Editorial Board: British Jl of Anaesthesia, 1989–2009; Jl of Clinical Anesthesia, USA, 1989–; Anesthesia and Analgesia, 2006–; Current Anaesthesiology Reports, 2014–. Hon. Fellow, Colleges of Medicine, S Africa, 2009. *Publications:* papers in learned jls. *Recreations:* sport, music, writing. *Address:* 6 Whites Forge, Appleton, Abingdon, Oxon OX13 5LG. *T:* (01865) 863144.

SEARBY, Richard Henry, AO 2006; QC (Aust.) 1971; Deputy Chairman, Times Newspapers Holdings Ltd, since 1981; *b* 23 July 1931; *s* of late Henry and Mary Searby; *m* 1962, Caroline (*née* McAdam) (*d* 2014); three *s*. *Educ:* Geelong Grammar Sch., Corio, Vic; Corpus Christi Coll., Oxford Univ. (MA Hons). Called to Bar, Inner Temple, London, 1956; admitted Barrister and Solicitor, Victoria, Aust., 1956; called to Victorian Bar, 1957; Associate to late Rt Hon. Sir Owen Dixon, Chief Justice of Aust., 1956–59; commenced practice, Victorian Bar, 1959; Independent Lectr in Law relating to Executors and Trustees, Univ. of Melbourne, 1961–72. Director: Equity Trustees Executors & Agency Co. Ltd, 1975–2000 (Chm., 1980–2000); CRA Ltd, then Rio Tinto Ltd, 1977–97; Rio Tinto PLC, 1995–97; Shell Australia Ltd, 1977–98; News Corp. Ltd, 1977–92 (Chm., 1981–91; Dep. Chm., 1991–92); News Ltd, 1977–92 (Chm., 1981–92); News International plc, 1980–92 (Chm., 1981–89); South China Morning Post Ltd, 1986–92 (Chm., 1987–92); Reuters Founders Share Co. Ltd, 1987–93; BRL Hardy Ltd, 1992–2003; Amrad Corp. Ltd, 1992–2001; Tandem Australian Ltd, 1992–98; Woodside Petroleum Ltd, 1998–2004; Chairman: Bowater Trust, 2006–09; Hearing Co-operative Res. Centre Ltd, 2007–. Member Council: Nat. Library of Australia, 1992–95; Mus. of Victoria, 1993–98. President: Medico-Legal Soc. of Vic, 1986–87; Aust. Inst. of Internat. Affairs, 1993–97. Chancellor, Deakin Univ., 1997–2005. Chm., Geelong Grammar Sch., 1983–89. Hon. LLD Deakin, 2005. *Publications:* (jtly) report on Conciliation and Arbitration Act, 1981. *Recreations:* reading, music, tennis, fishing. *Address:* 23A Hampden Road, Armadale, Vic 3143, Australia. *Club:* Melbourne (Melbourne).

SEARBY, Maj. Gen. Robin Vincent, CB 2002; Arab affairs and security consultant, since 2007; Prime Minister's Counter Terrorism Adviser for North Africa and the Sahel, 2009–12; *b* 20 July 1947; *s* of late John Henry Searby and Eva Searby; *m* 1976, Caroline Angela Beamish; one *s* two *d*. *Educ:* Leasam House; RMA Sandhurst. Commissioned 9th/12th Royal Lancers, 1968; Directing Staff, Camberley, 1984–87; CO, 9th/12th Royal Lancers, 1987–89; COS to HQ Dir, RAC, 1989–91; Comdr, Armoured 1st (Br) Corps, 1991–93; Comdr, British Forces Bosnia-Hercegovina, 1993; Pres., Regular Commissions Bd, 1994; Chief, Jt Ops (Bosnia), HQ Allied Forces Southern Europe, 1995; GOC 5th Div., 1996–2000; Sen. British Loan Service Officer, Sultanate of Oman, 2000–04; UK Defence Co-ordinator for Libya, 2004–10. Hon. Col, 9th/12th Lancers, 2003–08; Hon. Chm., London Central, SSAFA, 2012–. Distinguished Service Medal for Gallantry, Sultanate of Oman, 1975; QCVS 1994. *Recreations:* walking, country sports, reading. *Clubs:* Cavalry and Guards, Beefsteak.

SEARLE, Prof. Geoffrey Russell, PhD; FBA 2005; FRHistS; Professor of Modern British History, University of East Anglia, 1993–2001, now Emeritus; *b* 3 Oct. 1940; *s* of George William, (Bill), Searle and Winifred Alice Searle (*née* Chapman); *m* 1994, Barbara Elisabeth Caroline Rahn. *Educ:* St Dunstan's Coll., Catford; Peterhouse, Cambridge (BA 1962; PhD 1966). FRHistS 1977. Lectr in Hist., 1962–81, Sen. Lectr, 1981–93, Univ. of East Anglia. *Publications:* The Quest for National Efficiency 1899–1914, 1971; Eugenics and Politics in Britain 1900–1914, 1976; Corruption in British Politics 1895–1930, 1987; The Liberal Party: triumph and disintegration 1886–1929, 1992, 2nd edn 2001; Entrepreneurial Politics in Mid-Victorian Britain, 1993; Country Before Party 1885–1987, 1995; Morality and the Market in Victorian Britain, 1998; A New England?: peace and war 1886–1918, 2004; Miles Edmund Cotman, 2014. *Recreations:* music, art, literature, supporter of local football team. *Address:* School of History, University of East Anglia, Norwich, Norfolk NR4 7TJ.

SEARLE, Ven. Jacqueline Ann, (Mrs D. C. Runcorn); Archdeacon of Gloucester, and Canon Residentiary, Gloucester Cathedral, since 2012; *b* Redhill, 26 Sept. 1960; *d* of Alan John Searle and Joan Mary Searle; *m* 1992, David Charles Runcorn; two *s*. *Educ:* Talbot Heath, Bournemouth; Whitelands Coll., Roehampton (BEd); Trinity Coll., Bristol (DipTh; MA Applied Theol.). Teacher: Gt Walstead, Sussex, 1982–85; Sheen Mt Primary Sch., E Sheen, 1985–89; ordained deacon, 1992, priest, 1994; Assistant Curate: Roxeth Team, Harrow, 1992–94; St Stephen's, Ealing, 1994–96; Tutor in Applied Theology, and Dean of Women, Trinity Coll., Bristol, 1996–2003; Vicar, St Peter's, Littleover, 2003–12; Dean of Women's Ministry, Dio. of Derby, 2006–10; Rural Dean, Derby South, 2010–12. Hon. Canon, Derby Cath., 2011–12. Trustee, SPCK, 2009–13. Associate Trainer, Bridge Builders, 2010–. Governor: Elmlea Infants' Sch., Bristol, 2000–03; St Peter's C of E/Voluntary Aided Jun. Sch., Littleover, 2003–12. *Address:* 9 College Green, Gloucester GL1 2LX. *T:* (office) (01452) 835583.

SEARS, David; *see* Sears, R. D. M.

SEARS, Hon. Raymond Arthur William; Judge of the Court of First Instance of the High Court (formerly a Judge of the Supreme Court), Hong Kong, 1986–99; Commissioner of the Supreme Court of Brunei Darussalam, 1987–99; *b* 10 March 1933; *s* of William Arthur and Lillian Sears; *m* 1960 (marr. diss. 1981); one *s* one *d*. *Educ:* Epsom Coll.; Jesus Coll., Cambridge. BA 1956. Lieut RA (TA) Airborne, 1953. Called to Bar, Gray's Inn, 1957. QC 1975; Recorder of the Crown Court, 1977–86. Vice-Chm., Judges' Forum, Internat. Bar Assoc., 1993. Dir, South China Financial Hldgs Ltd (formerly South China Brokerage Ltd), 2000–. *Recreations:* watching horse-racing, music. *Address:* 3A Ewan Court, 54–56 Kennedy Road, Hong Kong. *Clubs:* Hong Kong, Hong Kong Jockey (Hong Kong); Sydney Turf (Sydney).

SEARS, (Robert) David (Murray); QC 2003; barrister; *b* 13 Dec. 1957; *s* of Robert Murray and Janet Leslie Sears; *m* 1984, Victoria Morlock (marr. diss. 2007); one *s* one *d*. *Educ:* Eton Coll.; Trinity Coll., Oxford (MA Jurisprudence 1979). Called to the Bar, Middle Temple, 1984; in practice, specialising in professional negligence and construction law, 1985–. *Recreations:* sailing, motorcycling, supporting Ipswich Town FC, working with heavy horses (Suffolk Punches). *Address:* Crown Office Chambers, 2 Crown Office Row, Temple, EC4Y 7HJ. *E:* sears@crownofficechambers.com. *Clubs:* Leander (Henley-on-Thames); Vincent's (Oxford).

SEATON, Andrew James; Executive Director, British Chamber of Commerce in Hong Kong, since 2015; *b* 20 April 1954; *s* of Albert William Seaton and Joan Seaton (*née* Mackenzie); *m* 1983, Helen Elizabeth Pott; three *s*. *Educ:* Royal Grammar Sch., Guildford; Univ. of Leeds (BA Hons); Beijing Univ. Joined FCO, 1977; Third, later Second, Sec., Dakar, 1979–81; Hd, China Trade Unit, British Trade Commn, Hong Kong, 1982–86; FCO, 1987–92; Asst Hd, Aid Policy Dept, ODA, 1992–95; Trade Counsellor, British Trade Commn, Hong Kong, 1995–97; Dep. Consul-Gen., Hong Kong, 1997–2000; Hd, China Hong Kong Dept, FCO, 2000–03; Consul-General: Chicago, 2003–07; Hong Kong, 2008–12; FCO, 2012–13. *Recreations:* family, wine, walking. *Address:* British Chamber of Commerce, 1201 Emperor Group Centre, 288 Hennessy Road, Hong Kong.

See also J. A. Seaton.

SEATON, Prof. Anthony, CBE 1997; MD; FRCP, FRCPE, FMedSci; Professor of Environmental and Occupational Medicine, Aberdeen University, 1988–2003, now Emeritus; Hon. Consultant, Institute of Occupational Medicine, Edinburgh, since 2003; *b* 20 Aug. 1938; *s* of late Douglas Ronald Seaton and Julia Seaton; *m* 1962, Jillian Margaret Duke; two *s*. *Educ:* Rossall Sch.; King's Coll., Cambridge (BA, MB, MD); Liverpool Univ. FRCP 1977; FFOM 1982; FRCPE 1985. Jun. med. posts, Liverpool and Stoke-on-Trent, 1962–69; Asst Prof. of Medicine, W Virginia Univ., 1969–71; Consultant Chest Physician, Cardiff, 1971–77; Dir, Inst. of Occupational Medicine, Edinburgh, 1978–90. Chairman: Expert Panel on Air Quality Standards, DoE, 1992–2002; Res. Adv. Cttee, NERC, 2006–08; Member: Cttee on Med. Effects of Air Pollution, DoH, 1992–2003; Wkg Gp on Nanotechnol., Royal Soc./Royal Acad. Engrg, 2003–04; Industrial Injuries Adv. Council, 2013–; EU Scientific Cttee on Occupational Exposure Limits, 2015–. Lectures: Tudor Edwards, RCP, 1996; Baylis, PPP, 1997; Warner, British Occupational Hygiene Soc., 1998; Hunter, FOM, 2000; Gehrmann, Amer. Coll. of Occupational and Envmtl Medicine, 2001; Thackrah, SOM, 2010. President: British Thoracic Soc., 1999; Harveian Soc., 2007. Founder FMedSci 1998. Editor, Thorax, 1977–81. Hon. DSc Aberdeen, 2007. Medal, British Thoracic Soc., 2006. *Publications:* jointly: Occupational Lung Diseases, 1975, 3rd edn 1995; Crofton and Douglas's Respiratory Diseases, 1989, 2nd edn 2000; Practical Occupational Medicine, 1994, 2nd edn 2004; papers in med. literature and essays in Scottish Review. *Recreations:* opera, painting, sculpture. *Address:* 8 Avon Grove, Cramond, Edinburgh EH4 6RF. *T:* (0131) 336 5113. *Club:* St Andrew Boat.

SEATON, Prof. Jean Ann; Professor of Media History, University of Westminster, since 2002; Official Historian of the BBC, since 2003; Director, Orwell Prize for Political Writing and Journalism, since 2007; *b* 6 March 1947; *d* of late Albert William Seaton and Joan Seaton (*née* MacKenzie); *m* 1977, Benjamin John Pimlott (*d* 2004); three *s*. *Educ:* Grey Coat Hosp. for Girls; Univ. of Leicester (BSc); Univ. of Essex (MA). Lecturer: Holloway Prison for Women, 1971; Birkbeck Coll., Univ. of London, 1972–73; Oxford Poly., 1973–74; Sen. Lectr, 1974–90, Hd of Dept, 1990–96, South Bank Poly., later Univ.; Reader, 1996–2002, Hd, Grad. Prog., 1998–2001, Westminster Univ. British Acad. Thank-Offering to Britain Res. Fellow, 1981–82; Vis. Fellow, Griffiths Univ., Australia, 1982–83; Leverhulme Res. Fellow, 2008–09. Ed., Political Qly, 2003–. *Publications:* Power Without Responsibility: the press and broadcasting in Britain (with James Curran), 1981, 7th edn as Power Without Responsibility: press, broadcasting and the internet in Britain, 2009; The Media in British Politics, 1984; The Media of Conflict, 1995; Harlots and Prerogatives: the media and politics, 2000; What Can be Done?: making the media and politics better, 2005; Carnage and the Media, 2005; Pinkoes and Traitors: the BBC and the nation 1974–1987, 2015; numerous articles. *Recreations:* books, art, suppers, sons. *Address:* 9 Milner Place, Islington, N1 1TN. *T:* (020) 7609 1793. *E:* j.seaton@theorwellprize.co.uk. *Club:* Frontline.

See also A. J. Seaton.

SEATON, Prof. Nigel Anthony, PhD; CEng, FREng; FIChemE; Principal and Vice-Chancellor, Abertay University (formerly University of Abertay Dundee), since 2012; *b* Falkirk, 27 Aug. 1960; *s* of Denis and Daphne Seaton; *m* 1985, Roxana Jiménez Eguiluz; three *s*. *Educ:* Linlithgow Primary Sch.; Linlithgow Acad.; Univ. of Edinburgh (BSc Chem. Engrg 1982); Univ. of Pennsylvania (MSE 1984; PhD 1986). CEng 1995; FIChemE 2000; FREng 2012. Research Engineer: Atkins R&D, 1986–87; BP, 1987–89; Lectr, Univ. of Cambridge, 1989–97; University of Edinburgh: Prof. of Interfacial Engrg, 1997–2008; Head: Div. of Engrg, 1999–2002; Inst. for Materials and Processes, 2002–03; Dean, Undergrad. Studies, 2003–07; Asst Principal, 2007–08; Dep. Vice-Chancellor (Acad. Develt), 2008–09, Sen. Dep. Vice-Chancellor, 2009–12, Univ. of Surrey. *Publications:* res. papers. *Recreations:* family, walking, cycling, travel. *Address:* Abertay University, Dundee DD1 1HG. *T:* (01382) 308016. *E:* n.seaton@abertay.ac.uk.

SEAWARD, Colin Hugh, CBE 1987; HM Diplomatic Service, retired; *b* 16 Sept. 1926; *s* of late Sydney W. Seaward and Molly W. Seaward; *m* 1st, 1949, Jean Bugler (decd); three *s* one *d*; 2nd, 1973, Judith Margaret Hinkley; two *d*. *Educ:* RNC, Dartmouth. Served Royal Navy, 1944–65. Joined HM Diplomatic Service, 1965; served: Accra, 1965; Bathurst (Banjul), 1966; FO, 1968; Rio de Janeiro, 1971; Prague, 1972; FCO, 1973; RNC, Greenwich (sowc), 1976; Counsellor (Econ. and Comm.), Islamabad, 1977–80; Consul-General, Rio de Janeiro, 1980–86, retd; re-employed in FCO, 1987–91. Sec., Anglo-Brazilian Soc., 1992–95 (Hon. Sec., 1986–91). Freeman, City of London, 1987. Hon. Citizen, State of Rio de Janeiro, 1984. *Address:* 7 Darent Close, Chipstead, Sevenoaks TN13 2RX.

SEAWARD, Tracey; film producer, since 1992; *b* Hull, 5 March 1964; partner, Mark Tildesley. Films: producer: Nora, 2000; Dirty Pretty Things, 2002 ((jtly) Best Brit. Film, BIFA, Best Film, Evening Standard Brit. Film Awards, 2003); The Queen, 2006 ((jtly) Best Film, BAFTA Awards, 2007); Chéri, 2009; Tamara Drewe, 2010; Philomena, 2013; co-producer: The Good Thief, 2002; Millions, 2004 ((jtly) Christopher Award, 2006); The Constant Gardener, 2005; Eastern Promises, 2007; War Horse, 2012 ((jtly) Christopher Award, 2011); Producer, Opening Ceremony, London Olympic Games 2012. Member: BAFTA; Acad. for Motion Picture Arts and Scis; Eur. Film Acad. Hon. DLitt Hull, 2008. Envy Producer Award, Sky Women in Film and TV Awards, 2012. *Address:* c/o Sue Greenleaves, Independent Talent, 40 Whitfield Street, W1T 2RH. *T:* (020) 7636 6565. *E:* suegreenleaves@independenttalent.com. *Club:* Groucho.

SEAWRIGHT, Prof. Paul, PhD; FRPS; Head, Belfast School of Art, University of Ulster, since 2012; *b* Belfast, 20 Aug. 1965; *s* of William J. Seawright and Isobel Seawright; *m* 1988, Sarah Homan; three *s*. *Educ:* W Surrey Coll. of Art and Design (BA 1st Cl. Hons Film and Photography 1988); Univ. of Wales, Newport (PhD 2006). FRPS 2006. Lectr in Art and Design, Univ. of Ulster, 1991–94; University of Wales College, Newport, later University of Wales, Newport: Lectr in Photography, 1994–96; Hd of Res. - Art and Design, 1996–2002;

Dean, Sch. of Art and Design, 2002–06; Prof. of Photography, Univ. of Ulster, 2007–12. Artworks in collections incl. Tate, Irish MOMA, Internat. Center of Photography, NY, Govt Art Collection, San Francisco MOMA, Imperial War Mus., Ulster Mus. Mem. Bd, Arts Council, NI, 2007–. Vice-Pres., Royal Ulster Acad., 2012–. Hon. Fellow, Cardiff Metropolitan Univ., 2008. FRSA. *Publications:* Inside Information, 1995; The Forest, 2001; Hidden, 2003; Invisible Cities, 2007; Volunteer, 2013; Things Left Unsaid, 2014. *Address:* University of Ulster, Belfast School of Art, York Street, Belfast BT15 1LE. *E:* p.seawright@ulster.ac.uk.

SEBAG-MONTEFIORE, Charles Adam Laurie; Trustee, National Gallery, since 2012; *b* London, 25 Oct. 1949; *s* of late Denzil Sebag-Montefiore and Ruth Sebag-Montefiore (*née* Magnus); *m* 1979, Pamela Mary Diana Tennant; one *s* two *d. Educ:* Eton Coll.; Univ. of St Andrews (MA). FCA 1974; FSA 1995. With Touche Ross & Co., 1971–76: articled clerk, 1971; Tax Supervisor, 1976; Partner, Grieveson Grant and Co., 1981–86; Dir, Kleinwort Benson Securities Ltd, 1986–94; Dep. Chm., Harvill Press Ltd, 1994–2002. Director: Euclidian plc, 1994–99; Elderstreet Corporate Finance Ltd, 1997–99; IDJ Ltd, 1999–2004; Govett European Enhanced Investment Trust plc, 1999–2004 (Chm., 2003–04); Kiln plc, 2001–06; Ludgate Investments Ltd, 2004–13 (non-exec. Dir, 2013–); Chm., Community Careline Services Ltd, 2001–02; non-exec. Dep. Chm., West 175 Media Gp, 2001–06 (Dir, 2000–06); non-executive director: Hightex Gp plc, 2006–14; Scholium Gp plc, 2014–; Trustee, HSBC Common Funds for Growth and Income, 1994–2002. Chm., Projects Cttee, 1977–86, Trustee, 2000–11, Nat. Art Collections Fund; Chm., London Historic House Mus Trust, 1992–2009 (Trustee, 1987–2009); Trustee: Samuel Courtauld Trust, 1992–2007; Nat. Manuscripts Conservation Trust, 2000–; Montefiore Endowment, 2004–07; Oxford Centre for Hebrew and Jewish Studies, 2004–; Strawberry Hill Trust, 2004–07; Wordsworth Trust, 2013–; Harewood House Trust, 2014–; Hon. Treasurer: Friends of Nat. Libraries, 1990–; Friends of BL, 1990–95; Friends of Lambeth Palace Liby, 1990–; London Liby, 1991–2003; Walpole Soc., 1992–; Gov., Patrons, Nat. Gall. of Scotland, 1992–2010; Treas., Roxburghe Club, 2002–; Jt Sec., Soc. of Dilettanti, 2002–. FRSA 1980; FSA 1995. Liveryman, Spectacle Makers' Co., 1973. *Publications:* The British as Art Collectors: from the Tudors to the present (jtly), 2012; A Dynasty of Dealers: John Smith and successors 1801–1924, 2013; (ed) Brooks's 1764–2014: the story of a Whig club, 2013. *Recreations:* reading, visiting bookshops and picture galleries, opera. *Address:* 21 Hazlewell Road, SW15 6LT. *T:* (020) 8789 5999. *E:* csmontefiore@gmail.com. *Clubs:* Brooks's, Beefsteak, Roxburghe.

SEBAG-MONTEFIORE, Rupert Owen, FRICS; FAAV; Head of Global Residential, Savills (UK) Ltd, since 2012; *b* London, 11 Nov. 1953; *s* of late Stephen Sebag-Montefiore and of April Sebag-Montefiore (*née* Jaffe); *m* 1979, Charlotte Anne Sain-Ley-Berry; one *s* two *d. Educ:* Wellington Coll., Berks; Magdalene Coll., Cambridge (BA 1975; MA); Reading Univ. (BSc Surveying). Dir, Savills plc, 1995–; Chm. and Chief Exec., Savills (L&P) Ltd, 2000–12. Non-executive Director: Bournemouth Univ., 1999–2007; Fastcrop plc, 2001–08; Adventis plc, 2004–06; Pigeon Land, 2012–; Penhurst Properties Ltd, 2013–. Chairman: Develt Council, Regent's Park Open Air Th., 2009–11; Investment Cttee, Winchester Coll., 2009–; Investment Gp, Christ Church, Oxford, 2012–. *Recreations:* riding, tennis, walking, tree-planting, hobby farming, opera, theatre, books. *Address:* Savills (UK) Ltd, 33 Margaret Street, W1G 0JD. *T:* (020) 7499 8644.

See also S. J. Sebag-Montefiore.

SEBAG-MONTEFIORE, Simon Jonathan, FRSL; writer; historian; novelist; *b* London, 1965; *s* of late Dr Stephen Sebag-Montefiore and of April Jaffe; *m* 1998, Santa Palmer-Tomkinson; one *s* one *d. Educ:* Harrow Sch.; Gonville and Caius Coll., Cambridge (BA Hist. 1987, PhD 2013). Presenter, TV series: Jerusalem: the making of a Holy City, 2011; Rome: a history of the Eternal City, 2012; Byzantium: a tale of three cities, 2013. *Publications:* Catherine the Great and Potemkin, 2000; Stalin: the Court of the Red Tsar, 2003 (History Book of the Year, British Book Awards, 2004); Young Stalin, 2007 (Costa Biography Prize, LA Times Book Prize in Biography, Bruno Kreisky Prize for Political Lit., 2007; Le Grand Prix de la Biographie Politique, 2008); Heroes: great men and women for an unheroic age, 2007; Monsters: history's most evil men and women, 2008; Jerusalem: the biography, 2011; Titans of History, 2012; *novels:* King's Parade, 1991; My Affair With Stalin, 1997; Sashenka, 2008; One Night in Winter, 2013. *Address:* c/o Georgina Capel, Georgina Capel Associates Ltd, 29 Wardour Street, W1D 6PS. *T:* (020) 7734 2414. *W:* www.simonsebagmontefiore.com. *Club:* Literary Society.

See also R. O. Sebag-Montefiore.

SEBAN, Alain Pierre; Chevalier de la Légion d'Honneur, 2011; Chairman, Director and Chief Executive Officer, Centre national d'Art et de Culture Georges Pompidou, since 2007; *b* Toulouse, 15 July 1964; *s* of Roger Seban and Andrée Moure. *Educ:* Pamiers High Sch.; Pierre de Fermat High Sch., Toulouse; Ecole Polytechnique; Institut d'études politiques de Paris; Ecole nationale de la statistique et de l'administration économique; Ecole nationale d'admin. Jun. Judge, 1991, Master of the Roll, 1994, Conseil d'Etat, France; Mem., Picq Cttee on responsibility and orgn of the State, 1993–94; Sec. Gen., Cttee for creation of a Nat. Inst. of Hist. of Art, 1994–95; Personal Advr to Cabinet Minister of Culture, 1995–97; Legal Advr to Assoc. for creation of Quai Branly Mus., 1997–2002; Special Personal Advr to Minister of Foreign Affairs, 2002; Dir of Media, Prime Minister's Office, 2002–05; Personal Advr for Educn and Culture to Pres. of the Republic of France, 2005–07. Professor: Ecole Polytechnique, 1993; Ecole nationale d'admin, 1996–99. Chairman, Board: Bibliothèque publique d'information, 2007–; Institut de recherche et de coordination acoustique-musique, 2007–; Centre Pompidou-Metz, 2010–. Comdr, Ordre des Arts et des Lettres (France), 2002. *Publications:* (contrib.) Bilan de la France 1981–93, 1993. *Recreations:* art, opera, literature. *Address:* Centre national d'Art et de Culture Georges Pompidou, 4 rue Brantôme, 75003 Paris, France. *T:* (1) 44784960. *E:* alain.seban@centrepompidou.fr.

SEBASTIAN, Sir Cuthbert (Montraville), GCMG 1996; OBE 1970; MD; Governor-General, St Christopher and Nevis, 1996–2013; *b* 22 Oct. 1921. *Educ:* Mount Allison Univ., Canada (BSc 1953); Dalhousie Univ., Canada (MD, CM 1958). Pharmacist and Lab. Technician, Cunningham Hosp., St Kitts, 1942–43; RAF, 1944–45; Captain Surg., St Kitts Nevis Defence Force, 1958–80; Medical Superintendent: Cunningham Hosp., 1966; Joseph N. France Gen. Hosp., 1967–80; CMO, St Christopher and Nevis, 1980–83; private medical practitioner, 1983–95. Hon. FRCS 2000; Hon. FRCSE 2002. Hon. LLD Dalhousie, 1998. *Publications:* 100 Years of Medicine in St Kitts, 2001. *Recreations:* farming, reading, dancing. *Address:* #6 Cayon Street, Basseterre, St Kitts, West Indies. *T:* 4652315. *Club:* Rotary of St Kitts.

SEBASTIAN, Timothy; freelance writer, broadcaster and consultant; *b* 13 March 1952; *s* of late Peter Sebastian, CBE and Pegitha Saunders; *m* 1977, Diane Buscombe (marr. diss. 1995); one *s* two *d. Educ:* Westminster School; New College, Oxford. BA (Hons) Mod. Lang. BBC Eastern Europe correspondent, 1979–82; BBC TV News: Europe correspondent, 1982–84; Moscow correspondent, 1984–85; Washington correspondent, 1986–89. Presenter, Hardtalk, BBC TV, 1997–2004. Fellow Commoner, Corpus Christi Coll., Cambridge, 2015–16. Chairman: Doha Debates, 2004–12; New Arab Debates, 2011–. TV journalist of the year, 1982, Interviewer of the Year, 2000, 2001, RTS; Richard Dimbleby Award, BAFTA, 1982. *Publications:* Nice Promises, 1985; I Spy in Russia, 1986; *novels:* The Spy in Question, 1988; Spy Shadow, 1989; Saviour's Gate, 1990; Exit Berlin, 1992; Last Rights, 1993; Special Relations, 1994; War Dance, 1995; Ultra, 1997.

SEBBA, Anne Marietta; biographer and journalist; *b* London, 31 Dec. 1951; *d* of Eric Rubinstein, MBE and Joan Rubinstein; *m* 1975, Mark Jonathan Sebba; one *s* two *d. Educ:* King's Coll. London (BA Hons Hist. 1972). Trainee, BBC World Service, 1972; Foreign Corresp., London and Rome, Reuters, 1972–78. Mem. Exec. and Mem., Writers in Prison Cttee, PEN, 1993–2003; Chm., Mgt Cttee, Soc. of Authors, 2012–14. *Publications:* Samplers: five centuries of a gentle craft, 1980; Enid Bagnold, 1986, 3rd edn 2013; Laura Ashley: a life by design, 1990, 3rd edn 2013; Battling for News: the rise of the woman reporter, 1994, 4th edn as Battling for News from the Risorgimento to Tiananmen, 2013; Mother Teresa Beyond the Image, 1997; The Exiled Collector: William Bankes and the making of an English country house, 2004, 3rd edn 2013; Jennie Churchill, Winston's American Mother, 2007, 5th edn 2011; That Woman: the life of Wallis Simpson, Duchess of Windsor, 2011. *Recreations:* cooking, grandchildren, learning Greek. *Address:* c/o Clare Alexander, Aitken Alexander Associates, 291 Gray's Inn Road, WC1X 8EB. *E:* anne@annesebba.com.

SEBER, Andrew James, CBE 2004; consultant in leadership, education and public services, since 2006; *b* 18 Sept. 1950; *s* of Philip George Seber and Helen Kathleen Seber (*née* Medhurst); *m* 1972, Sally Elizabeth Tyrrill; one *s* one *d. Educ:* East Barnet Grammar Sch.; Hertford Coll., Oxford (MA Biochemistry); Univ. of York; Middlesex Poly. (PGCE dist. 1977). Science Teacher: City of Leeds Sch., 1973–74; Hayes Manor Sch., 1974–79; Education Officer: Ealing LBC, 1979–81; Bucks CC, 1981–83; Hants CC, 1983–98; City Educn Officer, Portsmouth CC, 1998; County Educn Officer, Hants CC, 1998–2005; Dir, Andrew Seber Ltd Consultancy, 2006–13. Director: Southern Careers Ltd, 1996–2005; South Central Connexions, 2001–05; Chm., Hants and Portsmouth Learning Partnership, 2002–04; Advr, Service Children's Educn, 2000–02; Mem., local LSC, 2001–05. Mem. and Vice-Pres., Nat. Council, Soc. of Educn Officers, 2000–02; Pres., Confedn of Educn Service Managers, 2002–04. Mem., Governing Council, 2006–12, and Chm., Strategy Cttee, 2007–12, Nat. Coll. for Sch. Leadership; Observer, Bd, Training and Develt Agency for Schs, 2007–12. Member: Educn Adv. Cttee, St John Ambulance, 2013–; Cttee, Oxford Educn Soc., 2014–. Trustee, Helena Kennedy Foundn, 2014–. *Publications:* contribs to educnl jls. *Recreations:* university of the third age, biochemistry, genetics, guitar, ukulele, cycling, rambling, grandsons. *E:* andrewseber@yahoo.co.uk.

SEBRIGHT, Sir Rufus Hugo Giles, 16th Bt *cr* 1626, of Besford, Worcestershire; *b* 31 July 1978; *s* of Sir Peter Giles Vivian Sebright, 15th Bt and his 1st wife, Regina Maria (*née* Clarebrough); *S* father, 2003, but his name does not appear on the Official Roll of the Baronetage.

SECCOMBE, family name of **Baroness Seccombe**.

SECCOMBE, Baroness *cr* 1991 (Life Peer), of Kineton in the County of Warwickshire; **Joan Anna Dalziel Seccombe,** DBE 1984; an Extra Baroness in Waiting to the Queen, since 2004; *b* 3 May 1930; *d* of Robert John Owen and Olive Barlow Owen; *m* 1950, Henry Lawrence Seccombe (*d* 2008); two *s. Educ:* St Martin's Sch., Solihull. Member: Heart of England Tourist Bd, 1977–81 (Chm., Marketing Sub-Cttee, 1979–81); Women's Nat. Commn, 1984–90; Chm., Lord Chancellor's Adv. Cttee, 1975–93. Mem. Exec., 1975–97, Vice-Chm., 1984–87, Chm., 1987–88, Nat. Union of Cons. and Unionist Assocs; Chairman: W Midlands Area Cons. Women's Cttee, 1975–78; Cons. Women's Nat. Cttee, 1981–84; Cons. Party Social Affairs Forum, 1985–87; Dep. Chm., W Midlands Area Cons. Council, 1979–81; Vice-Chm., with special responsibility for women, Cons. Party, 1987–97. Mem., W Midlands CC, 1977–81 (Chm., Trading Standards Cttee, 1979–81). House of Lords: An Opposition Whip, 1997–2001; Dep. Opposition Chief Whip, 2001–10; Cons. Party Whip, 2010–. Governor, 1988–2001, Dep. Chm., 1994–2001, Nuffield Hosps; Chm. Trustees, Nuffield Hosps Pension Scheme, 1992–2000. Pres., Govs of St Martin's Sch., Solihull, 1990–2011 (Patron, 2011–). Patron, W Midlands Youth Ballet, 1998–2010. JP Solihull, 1968–2000 (Chm., 1981–84). *Recreations:* family, canvassing (especially for the family!), enjoying each day. *Address:* House of Lords, SW1A 0PW. *Club:* St Enodoc Golf (Pres., 1992–).

SECKER-WALKER, Prof. Lorna Margaret, PhD; Professor of Cancer Cytogenetics, Royal Free Hospital School of Medicine, 1993–97, Emeritus since 1997; *b* 17 Nov. 1933; *d* of late William Elmer Lea and Margaret Violet Lea (*née* Rees); *m* 1957, David Secker-Walker; one *s* three *d. Educ:* numerous schs; St Anne's Coll., Oxford (BA 1955; MA 1959); Inst. of Orthopaedics, London Univ. (PhD 1961). FRCPath 1996. Res. Fellow, MRC Unit for bone seeking isotopes, Oxford, 1955–56; Post-grad. Scholarship, Louvain Univ., Belgium, 1956–57; Royal Marsden Hospital, 1967–84; Non-clinical Lectr in cytogenetics of leukaemia; Gordon Jacobs, MRC and Leukaemia Res. Fund Fellowships; Royal Free Hospital School of Medicine: Lectr, 1984–85; Sen. Lectr, 1985–93. Member Editorial Board: Acta Haematologica, 1988–2000; Cancer Genetics and Cytogenetics, 1987–97; Leukemia, 1994–2001. Chm., UK Cancer Cytogenetics Gp, 1988–97; Dir, Leukaemia Res. Fund Leukaemia Cytogenetics Gp and UK Cancer Cytogenetics Gp Karyotype Database in Acute Lymphoblastic Leukaemia, 1992–97; Mem. Fac., European Sch. of Haematol., 1986–95. Advr to MRC on cytogenetics of leukaemia, 1985–97. Member: Brit. Soc. Haematol., 1975–97; Internat. Soc. Hematol., 1976–97; Genetical Soc., 1976–97; RSocMed, 1984–; Assoc. of Clin. Cytogeneticists, 1984–97; Amer. Soc. Hematol., 1994–97; European Haematol. Assoc., 1994–97; European Soc. Human Genetics, 1994–97. *Publications:* Chromosomes and Genes in Acute Lymphoblastic Leukemia, 1997; chapters in: Postgraduate Haematology, 3rd edn 1989, 4th edn 1998; Haematological Oncology, 1994; over 100 articles in scientific and med. jls. *Recreations:* theatre, opera, travel, jigsaw puzzles, Sudoku. *Address:* 18 Pavilion Court, Frognal Rise, NW3 6PZ. *T:* (020) 7722 6467.

SECKERSON, Edward Stuart; music critic, writer and broadcaster; *s* of William Douglas Seckerson and Daphne Lilian (*née* Beard). *Educ:* Spender Park Sch.; private studies music and drama. BBC Gramophone Liby, 1966–69; Marketing Assistant, Decca Record Co., 1969–72; professional actor, 1972–80; music journalist, 1980–; contributor to: music mags incl. Classical Music, Hi-Fi News & Record Rev., BBC Music Mag., Gramophone; newspapers: The Guardian; The Times; Chief Music Critic, Sunday Correspondent, 1989–90; Chief Classical Music Critic, Independent, 1991–2012. Founder, ArtsPod audio podcasts, 2010. Presenter, Singular Sensations, Charing Cross Theatre, 2013. Radio and TV: contrib. BBC Radio 2, 3, 4 and World Service; commentator, Cardiff Singer of the World, BBC TV, 1991, 1993, 1995, 1997, 2004, 2007. Founder Mem., theartsdesk.com, 2009–. *Publications:* Mahler: his life and times, 1984; Viva Voce: conversations with Michael Tilson Thomas, 1994. *Recreations:* music, literature, cinema, theatre. *W:* www.edwardseckerson.biz.

SECOMBES, Prof. Christopher John, PhD, DSc; FRSE; FRSB; Regius Professor of Natural History, University of Aberdeen, since 2014 (Established Professor of Zoology, 2004–14); *b* London, 1 April 1956; *s* of Alfred Robert Secombes and Joan Helena Secombes; *m* 1982, Karen Ruth Misseldine; two *s* one *d. Educ:* Longdean Sch., Hemel Hempstead; Univ. of Leeds (BSc 1977); Univ. of Hull (PhD 1981); Univ. of Aberdeen (DSc 1997). FRSB (FIBiol 1998). University of Aberdeen: Lectr, 1984–91; Sen. Lectr, 1991–97; Personal Chair, 1997; Head: Dept of Zoology, 2001–02; Scottish Fish Immunol. Res. Centre, 2001–; Sch. of Biol Scis, 2002–11; Chairman: Genetically Modified Organisms Cttee, 2002–; DSc Cttee, 2012–. Adjunct Prof., Univ. of Tromso, 2003–06. Member: Marine Scis Peer Rev. Cttee, NERC, 2001–03; BBSRC Panel of Experts, 2014–. Mem., Exec. Cttee, 1990–2009, Pres., 2003–06, Internat. Soc. for Develtl and Comparative Immunol.; Life Mem., Internat. Soc. of Fish and Shellfish Immunol., 2013. Chm., Aquaculture grant round, Norwegian Res. Council, 2009–11, 2013–14; Mem., Sci. Adv. Bd, Sea Lice Res. Center, Bergen, 2013–. Ed.,

Fish and Shellfish Immunol., 1995–; Member: Editl Bd, Veterinary Immunol. and Immunopathol., 2001–; Editl Adv. Bd, Molecular Immunol., 2009–. FRSE 2007. Hon. DSc Hull, 2014. Alexander Ninian Bruce Prize, RSE, 2007. *Publications:* over 400 res. papers and articles in jls. *Address:* School of Biological Sciences, University of Aberdeen, Zoology Building, Tillydrone Avenue, Aberdeen AB24 2TZ. *T:* (01224) 272872, *Fax:* (01224) 272396. *E:* c.secombes@abdn.ac.uk.

SECONDÉ, Sir Reginald (Louis), KCMG 1981 (CMG 1972); CVO 1968 (MVO 1957); HM Diplomatic Service, retired; Ambassador to Venezuela, 1979–82; *b* 28 July 1922; *s* of late Lt-Col Emile Charles Secondé and Doreen Secondé (*née* Sutherland); *m* 1951, Catherine Penelope (*d* 2004), *d* of late Thomas Ralph Sneyd-Kynnersley, OBE, MC and late Alice Sneyd-Kynnersley; one *s* two *d*. *Educ:* Beaumont; King's Coll., Cambridge. Served, 1941–47, in Coldstream Guards: N Africa and Italy (despatches); Major. Entered Diplomatic Service, 1949; UK Delegn to the UN, New York, 1951–55; British Embassy: Lisbon, 1955–57; Cambodia, 1957–59; FO, 1959–62; British Embassy, Warsaw, 1962–64; First Secretary and later Political Counsellor, Rio de Janeiro, 1964–69; Head of S European Dept, FCO, 1969–72; Royal Coll. of Defence Studies, 1972–73; Ambassador to Chile, 1973–76, to Romania, 1977–79. *Address:* Stowlangtoft Hall, Stowlangtoft, Bury St Edmunds, Suffolk IP31 3JY. *T:* (01359) 230927. *Club:* Cavalry and Guards.

SECRETAN, Lance Hilary Kenyon; corporate adviser, executive coach, author and keynote speaker; Founder and President, The Secretan Center Inc., since 1972; Founder, The Higher Ground Community; President, Thaler Resources Ltd, since 1981; *b* Amersham, 1 Aug. 1939; *s* of late Kenyon Secretan and Marie-Therese Secretan (*née* Haffenden); *m* 1st, 1961, Gloria Christina (marr. diss. 1990; she *d* 2000); two *d* (and one *d* decd); 2nd, 1993, Patricia Edith Sheppard (*d* 2014). *Educ:* Los Cocos, Argentina; Italia Conti, London; St Peters, Bournemouth; Univ. of Waterloo, Canada; Univ. of Southern California (MA in International Relations, *cum laude*, 1980); LSE (PhD in International Relations 1984). Emigrated to Canada, 1959; Sales Manager, J. J. Little and Ives, Toronto, 1959–60; Analyst, Toronto Stock Exchange, 1960; Sales Manager, Office Overload Co. Ltd, 1960–67; Man. Dir, Manpower Ltd Gp of Cos, UK, Ireland, Middle East and Africa, 1967–81. Prof. of Entrepreneurship, McMaster Univ., 1981–82; Vis. Prof., York Univ., Toronto, 1983–84; Special Goodwill Ambassador for Canada, UNEP, 1989–93; Chm. Adv. Bd, 1997 Special Olympics World Winter Games. Internat. Caring Award, US Senate, 1999; McFeely Award, Internat. Mgt Council, 2002. *Publications:* How to be an Effective Secretary, 1972; From Guns to Butter, 1983; Managerial Moxie, 1986, rev. edn 1993; The State of Small Business in Ontario, 1986; The Masterclass, 1988; The Way of the Tiger, 1989; The Personal Masterclass, 1992; Living the Moment, 1992; Reclaiming Higher Ground, 1996; Inspirational Leadership, 1999; Spirit@Work Cards, 2002; !Inspire! What Great Leaders Do, 2004; One: the art and practice of conscious leadership, 2006; The Spark, the Flame, and the Torch, 2010. *Recreations:* life, music, ski-ing, Mother Earth. *T:* (Canada) (519) 9275213. *E:* info@secretan.com. *Club:* Mensa.

SEDAT, Elizabeth Helen, (Mrs J. W. Sedat); *see* Blackburn, E. H.

SEDCOLE, Cecil Frazer, FCA; a Vice Chairman, Unilever PLC, 1982–85; *b* 15 March 1927; *s* of late William John Sedcole and Georgina Irene Kathleen Bluett (*née* Moffatt); *m* 1962, Jennifer Bennett Riggall; one *s* one *d*. *Educ:* Uppingham Sch., Rutland. FCA 1952; CBIM 1982. Joined Unilever Group of Cos, 1952: Dir, Birds Eye Foods, 1960–66; Vice-Chairman: Langnese-Iglo, Germany, 1966–67; Frozen Products Gp, Rotterdam, 1967–71; Dir, Unilever PLC and Unilever NV, 1974–85; Chm., UAC International, 1976–79; Mem., 1971–75, Chm., 1979–85, Overseas Cttee, Unilever; Dir, Tate & Lyle, 1982–90; Dep. Chm., Reed International, 1985–87. Mem., BOTB, 1982–86; Mem. Bd, Commonwealth Develt Corp., 1984–88. Trustee, Leverhulme Trust, 1982–97. Governor: Bedales Sch., 1983–90; Queen Elizabeth's Foundn for Disabled People, 1993–2002. *Recreation:* golf. *Address:* The Old Manor House, Hay Street, Marshfield, S Glos SN14 8NL. *Club:* Royal Air Force.

SEDGMAN, Francis Arthur, AM 1980; Lawn Tennis Champion: Australia, 1949, 1950; USA, 1951, 1952; Wimbledon, 1952; Italy, 1952; Asia, 1952; Professional Tennis Player, since 1953; *b* Victoria, Australia, 29 Oct. 1927; *m* 1952, Jean Margaret Spence; four *d*. *Educ:* Box Hill High School, Vic, Australia. First played in the Australian Davis Cup team, 1949; also played in winning Australian Davis Cup team, 1950, 1951, 1952. With John Bromwich, won Wimbledon doubles title, 1948; with Kenneth McGregor, won the Australian, French, Wimbledon and American doubles titles in the same year (1951), the only pair ever to do so; with Kenneth McGregor also won Australian, French and Wimbledon doubles titles, 1952; with Doris Hart, won French, Wimbledon and US mixed doubles titles, 1952. Last male player to win three titles at Wimbledon in one year, 1952. Director of many private companies. USA Hall of Fame, 1987; Australian Hall of Fame, 1988. *Publications:* Winning Tennis, 1955; Game, Sedge and Match, 2015. *Recreations:* golfing, racing. *Clubs:* All England Lawn Tennis and Croquet, Queen's; Melbourne Cricket (Melbourne); Kooyong Tennis; Grace Park Tennis; Carbine (Melbourne); Mornington Racing (Life Mem.).

SEDGMORE, Lynne, CBE 2004; Executive Director, 157 Group, since 2008; *b* 23 Oct. 1955; *d* of Mansel Sedgmore and Vera Sedgmore; *m* 1975, John Capper; one *d*, and two step *d*. *Educ:* Clayton Hall Grammar Sch.; Univ. of Kent (BA Hons); Madeley Coll. (PGCE 1980); Univ. of Surrey (MSc 1995). Lectr in further educn colls, 1979–86; Hd of Dept, Hackney Coll., 1986–88; Croydon College: Dir of Mktg, 1988–90; Hd, Croydon Business Sch., 1990–94; Vice Principal, 1994–98; Principal, Guildford Coll., 1998–2004; Chief Exec., Centre for Excellence in Leadership, 2004–08. Non-exec. Dir of several Bds; Dir, Talent Foundn, 2008–. MCIM 1989; MInstD 1998; FRSA 2002. *Publications:* Marketing for College Managers, 1992. *Recreations:* comparative religion, grandchildren, travel to Far East/India. *T:* (office) 07855 395313.

SEDGWICK, (Ian) Peter; Chairman, Schroders, 2000–02 (Deputy Chairman, 1995–2000); *b* 13 Oct. 1935; *m* 1956, Verna Mary Churchward; one *s* one *d*. National Westminster Bank, 1952–59; Ottoman Bank, 1959–69; J. Henry Schroder Wagg & Co., 1969–89; Chief Exec., Schroder Investment Management, 1985–95; Chm., Schroders plc, 1987–2002; Pres. and CEO, Schroders Inc., NY, 1996–2000; Chm., Schroder & Co. Inc., NY, 1996–2000; Vice Pres., Equitable Life Assurance Soc., 1995–2001. Dir, Frimley Park Hosp. Trust, 1992–96; Vice-Pres., Queen Elizabeth's Foundn for disabled people, 2010– (Chm., 2006–10). Mem., Global Adv. Bd, J. E. Robert Property Co., Washington, 2002–06. *Recreations:* golf, theatre, grandchildren.

SEDGWICK, Rev. Canon Peter Humphrey, PhD; Principal, St Michael's College, Llandaff, 2004–14; Metropolitan Canon, Province of Wales, Llandaff Cathedral, since 2006; *b* 13 Dec. 1948; *s* of Oliver George Humphrey Sedgwick and Cathleen Winifred Sedgwick; *m* 1st, 1973, Helena Elizabeth Cole (marr. diss. 1995); one *s* two *d*; 2nd, 1996, Rev. Janet Gould. *Educ:* Trinity Hall, Cambridge (BA (Hist.) 1970; BA (Theol.) 1973); Durham Univ. (PhD 1983). Ordained deacon, 1974, priest, 1975; Curate, St Dunstan's, Stepney, 1974–77; Priest-in-charge, St Lawrence, Pittington, Durham, 1977–79; Lectr in Theol., Birmingham Univ., 1979–82; Theol Consultant, NE Churches, 1982–88; Lectr in Theol., Hull Univ., 1988–94; Fellow, Center for Theol Inquiry, Princeton, 1991; Vice Principal, Westcott House, Cambridge, 1994–95; Policy Officer (Home Affairs), C of E Bd for Social Responsibility, 1996–2004; Ministry Officer, 2006–14, Permission to officiate, 2014–, Church in Wales. Vis. Schol., Faculty of Divinity, Univ. of Cambridge, 2011; Alan Richardson Fellow, Dept of Theol., Durham Univ., 2014. Member: Anglican-Roman Catholic Internat. Commn, 2011–; English Anglican-Roman Catholic Cttee, 2014–; Chm., Church in Wales Standing Doctrinal Commn, 2013–. Moderator, Church and Society, CTBI, 2007–10. Trustee, William Temple Foundn, Manchester, 2015–. *Publications:* Mission Impossible?: a theology of the local church, 1990; The Enterprise Culture, 1992; (ed) The Weight of Glory: the future of liberal theology, 1992; (ed) God in the City, 1996; The Market Economy and Christian Ethics, 1999; (ed) The Future of Criminal Justice, 2002; (with A. Britton) Economic Theory and Christian Belief, 2003 (trans. German 2009); (ed) Rethinking Sentencing, 2004. *Recreations:* gardening, walking, dogs. *Address:* Church House, Grand Avenue, Ely, Cardiff CF5 4HX. *T:* (029) 2067 9833. *E:* peter.sedgwick2@btinternet.com.

SEDGWICK, Peter Norman; Vice-President, and Member of Management Committee, European Investment Bank, 2000–06; Director, European Investment Fund, 2002–06; Chairman, 3i Infrastructure plc, since 2007; *b* 4 Dec. 1943; *s* of late Norman Victor Sedgwick and Lorna Clara (*née* Burton); *m* 1984, Catherine Jane, *d* of Mr and Mrs B. D. T. Saunders; two *s* two *d*. *Educ:* Westminster Cathedral Choir Sch.; Downside; Lincoln Coll., Oxford (MA PPE, BPhilEcon). HM Treasury: Economic Asst, 1969; Economic Adviser, 1971; Sen. Economic Adviser, 1977; Under Sec., 1984; Hd of Internat. Finance Gp, 1990–94; Hd of Educn, Trng and Employment Gp, 1994–95; Dep. Dir, Public Services (formerly Public Spending) Directorate, 1995–99. Chm. 1979–84, Mem. Develt Cttee 1984–93, London Symphony Chorus; Trustee, London Symphony Chorus Endowment Fund, 1993–; Trustee and Dir, Dyslexia Action, 2007–11 (Chm., Governance Cttee, 2007–11); Chm., Bowel Cancer UK, 2013–. *Recreations:* singing, walking, gardening. *Address:* 20 Skeena Hill, SW18 5PL.

SEDLEY, Prof. David Neil, PhD; FBA 1994; Laurence Professor of Ancient Philosophy, University of Cambridge, 2000–14, now Emeritus; Fellow, Christ's College, Cambridge, since 1976; *b* 30 May 1947; *s* of William Sedley and Rachel Sedley (*née* Seifert); *m* 1973, Beverley Anne Dobbs; two *s* one *d*. *Educ:* Westminster Sch.; Trinity Coll., Oxford (BA Lit. Hum. 1969; MA 1973; Hon. Fellow 2003); University Coll. London (PhD 1974). Dyson Jun. Res. Fellow in Greek Culture, Balliol Coll., Oxford, 1973–75; University of Cambridge: Asst Lectr in Classics, 1975–78; Lectr, 1978–89; Reader in Ancient Philosophy, 1989–96; Prof. of Ancient Philosophy, 1996–2000. Townsend Lectr, Cornell Univ., 2001; Sather Prof., Univ. of California, Berkeley, 2004. Foreign Hon. Mem., Amer. Acad. of Arts and Scis, 1998. Editor: Classical Qly, 1986–92; Oxford Studies in Ancient Philosophy, 1998–2007. *Publications:* (with A. A. Long) The Hellenistic Philosophers, 2 vols, 1987; Lucretius and the Transformation of Greek Wisdom, 1998; (ed) The Cambridge Companion to Greek and Roman Philosophy, 2003; Plato's Cratylus, 2003; The Midwife of Platonism: text and subtext in Plato's Theaetetus, 2004; Creationism and its Critics in Antiquity, 2007; articles in classical and philosophical jls and collaborative vols. *Recreations:* cinema, vegetable growing. *Address:* Christ's College, Cambridge CB2 3BU. *T:* (01223) 334910; 97 Hills Road, Cambridge CB2 1PG. *T:* (01223) 368845.

See also Rt Hon. Sir S. J. Sedley.

SEDLEY, Rt Hon. Sir Stephen (John), Kt 1992; PC 1999; a Lord Justice of Appeal, 1999–2011; *b* 9 Oct. 1939; *s* of William and Rachel Sedley; *m* 1st, 1968, Ann Tate (marr. diss. 1995); one *s* two *d*; 2nd, 1996, Teresa, (Tia) (*née* Chaddock). *Educ:* Mill Hill Sch. (entrance schol.); Queens' Coll., Cambridge (open schol./exhibnr; BA Hons 1961). Musician, translator, 1961–64; called to the Bar, Inner Temple, 1964, Bencher, 1989; QC 1983; a Judge of the High Court of Justice, QBD, 1992–99; Pres., Nat. Reference Tribunals for the Coalmining Industry, 1983–88. Chm., Sex Discrimination Cttee, Bar Council, 1992–95; Mem., Judicial Cttee, Privy Council, 2000–13. President: British Inst. of Human Rights, 2000–12; British Tinnitus Assoc., 2006–. *Ad hoc* judge, European Court of Human Rights, 2000. Vis. Professorial Fellow, Warwick Univ., 1981; Vis. Fellow, 1987, Vis. Prof., 1997, Osgoode Hall Law Sch., Canada; Distinguished Visitor, Hong Kong Univ., 1992; Hon. Professor: Univ. of Wales, Cardiff, 1993–; Univ. of Warwick, 1994–; Vis. Fellow, Victoria Univ. of Wellington, NZ, 1998; Judicial Visitor, UCL, 1999–; Vis. Prof., Univ. of Oxford, 2011–15. Lectures: Bernard Simons Meml, 1994; Paul Sieghart Meml, 1995; Radcliffe (with Lord Nolan), 1996; Laskin, 1997; Hamlyn, 1998; Lord Morris of Borth-y-Gest, 1999; MacDermott, 2001; Atkin, 2001; Pilgrim Fathers, 2002; Leicester Univ., 2004; Holdsworth, 2005; Blackstone, 2006; Mishcon, 2007. A Dir, Public Law Project, 1989–93; Hon. Vice-Pres., Administrative Law Bar Assoc., 1992–. Mem., Internat. Commn on Mercenaries, Angola, 1976. Chm., British Council Adv. Cttee on Governance, 2002–05. Sec., Haldane Soc., 1964–69. Hon. Fellow: Inst. for Advanced Legal Studies, 1997; Mansfield Coll., Oxford, 2012. Hon. Dr N London, 1996; Hon. LLD: Nottingham Trent, 1997; Bristol, 1999; Warwick, 1999; Durham, 2001; Hull, 2002; Southampton, 2003; Exeter, 2004; Essex, 2007. *Publications:* (trans.) From Burgos Jail, by Marcos Ana and Vidal de Nicolas, 1964; (ed) Seeds of Love (anthology), 1967; Whose Child? (report of inquiry into death of Tyra Henry), 1987; (ed) A Spark in the Ashes: writings of John Warr, 1992; (with Lord Nolan) The Making and Remaking of the British Constitution (Radcliffe Lectures), 1997; Freedom, Law and Justice (Hamlyn Lectures), 1999; Ashes and Sparks, 2011; contributed: Orwell: inside the myth, 1984; Civil Liberty, 1984; Police, the Constitution and the Community, 1986; Challenging Decisions, 1986; Public Interest Law, 1987; Civil Liberties in Conflict, 1988; Law in East and West, 1988; Citizenship, 1991; Administrative Law and Government Action, 1994; Frontiers of Legal Scholarship, 1995; Law Society and Economy, 1997; Human Rights for the 1990s, 1997; The Golden Metwand and the Crooked Cord (essays for Sir William Wade), 1998; Freedom of Expression and Freedom of Information (essays for Sir David Williams), 2000; Judicial Review in International Perspective (essays for Lord Slynn of Hadley), 2000; Discriminating Lawyers, 2000; The New Brain Sciences, 2004; Le Conseil d'Etat et le Code Civil, 2004; Liber amicorum (essays for Luzius Wildhaber), 2007; A Simple Common Lawyer (essays for Michael Taggart), 2009; Lions Under The Throne, 2015; contrib. DNB: Missing Persons; Oxford DNB; London Review of Books, Public Law, Modern Law Review, Jl of Law and Soc., Civil Justice Qly, Law Qly Review, Industrial Law Jl, Eur. Human Rights Law Rev., NI Law Qly, Jl of Legal Ethics, Aust. Jl of Administrative Law. *Recreations:* carpentry, music, cycling, walking, changing the world. *Address:* c/o Cloisters, Temple, EC4Y 7AA.

See also D. N. Sedley.

SEDWILL, Mark Philip, CMG 2008; Permanent Secretary, Home Office, since 2013; *b* 21 Oct. 1964; *s* of late Edward Peter Sedwill and of Mary June Sedwill; *m* 1999, Sarah-Jane Lakeman; one *d*. *Educ:* Univ. of St Andrews (BSc Hons); St Edmund Hall, Oxford (MPhil). Joined FCO, 1989; Second Secretary: Security Coordination Dept, FCO, 1989–91; Cairo, 1991–94; First Secretary: Resource Mgt Dept, 1994–96, ME Dept, attached to UN Special Commn, 1996–98, FCO; Nicosia, 1998–2000; Press Sec., FCO, 2000; Private Sec. to Sec. of State for Foreign and Commonwealth Affairs, 2000–02; Dep. High Comr, Islamabad, 2003–05; Dep. Dir, Middle East and N Africa, FCO, 2005; Director: UK Visas, 2006–08; Internat. Gp, UK Border Agency, 2008–09; Ambassador to Afghanistan, 2009–10; NATO Sen. Civilian Rep. in Afghanistan, 2010–11; UK Special Rep. for Afghanistan and Pakistan, 2011–13; Dir Gen., Political, FCO, 2012–13. UK Dir, American Acad. of Overseas Studies, 1987. FInstD 2011. FRGS 2010. DSM (USA) 2011; MSM (NATO) 2011. *Recreations:* golf, squash, scuba diving, windsurfing, hill-walking, history, family and friends. *Address:* Home Office, 2 Marsham Street, SW1P 4DF. *Clubs:* Special Forces; Kate Kennedy (St Andrews); Vincent's (Oxford).

SEED, Rev. Michael Joseph Steven Wayne, SA; STD; Chaplain of Westminster Cathedral, 1985–2008; *b* Manchester, 16 June 1957; *né* Godwin; adopted *s* of late Joseph Seed and Lillian Seed (*née* Ramsden). *Educ:* St Mary's Coll., Aberystwyth; St Joseph's Coll., Cork; Missionary Inst., Mill Hill; Washington Theol Inst., Md; Catholic Univ. of America, Washington (MDiv.

1984); Heythrop Coll.; Pontifical Lateran Univ., Rome (STL 1987; STD 1989); Polish Univ., London (PhD 1991). Entered Franciscan Friars of the Atonement, 1979; final profession, 1985; ordained deacon, 1985, priest, 1986; Chaplain, Westminster Hosp., 1986–90; Officiating Chaplain to the Forces, Wellington Barracks, 1990–2000. Sec., Ecumenical Commn (formerly Ecumenical Officer), Archdio. of Westminster, 1988–2008 (on sabbatical, 2009). Hon. Prof., Polish Univ., London, 1991. Chaplain: Soc. of Useless Information, 1998; St Mary's Sch., Ascot, 2010–11. For. Corresp. Academician, Historical Inst. of Dom Luiz I (Portugal), 1998. Mem., Zwingli Soc., Zurich, 2009–. Freeman, City of London, 2005. Hon. Chaplain: Internat. Cttee for the Promotion of Human Dignity, Rome (formerly Eur. Parlt), 2009–; to Archbishop of Cardiff, 2013–. Cross of Merit in Gold (Poland), 1988; Order of Orthodox Hospitallers (Cyprus), 1988; Ecclesiastical Kt Comdr of Grace, Sacred and Mil. Constantinian Order of St George (Naples), 1989; Knight of Justice with Grand Cross, Military Order of the Collar of St Agatha of Paternò, 2001 (Titular Abbot of Brontë, 2007–); Cross Pro Ecclesia et Pontifice (Holy See), 2004; Three Faiths Forum Interfaith Gold Medallion, 2006. *Publications:* I Will See You in Heaven, 1991; (contrib.) Sons and Mothers, 1996; (contrib.) Faith, Hope and Chastity, 1999; Will I See You in Heaven?, 1999; Assurance, 2000; Letters from the Heart, 2000; (contrib.) Catholic Lives, 2001; The Gift of Assurance, 2003; Nobody's Child (autobiog.), 2007; Thinking of Becoming a Catholic?, 2007; (contrib.) C4 x 25, 2007; Sinners and Saints (memoir), 2009; contribs to various publications. *Recreations:* politicians, pizza, Zwingliana. *Address:* c/o The Friary, 47 Francis Street, SW1P 1QR. *Clubs:* Beefsteak, Nicolson Toynbee.

SEED, Nigel John; QC 2000; **His Honour Judge Seed;** a Circuit Judge, since 2010; *b* 30 Jan. 1951; *s* of late Thomas Robinson Seed and of Joan Hall Seed (*née* Evison). *Educ:* Ellesmere Port Grammar Sch. for Boys; St Chad's Coll., Durham (BA 1972). Called to the Bar, Inner Temple, 1978, Bencher, 2008; Mem., Western Circuit, 1981–2010; Asst Recorder, 1995–2000; Recorder, 2000–10. Special Adjudicator, Immigration and Asylum Appeals, 1997–98. Chancellor: Dio. of Leicester, 1989–2002; Dio. of London, 2002–; Deputy Chancellor: Dio. of Salisbury, 1992–97; Dio. of Norwich, 1992–98. Freeman, City of London, 2009. *Recreations:* walking, cooking, eating and drinking. *Address:* Inner London Crown Court, Sessions House, Newington Causeway, SE1 6AZ. *Club:* Athenæum.

SEED, Ven. Richard Murray Crosland; Residentiary Canon and Prebendary, York Minster, since 2011; *b* 9 May 1949; *s* of Denis Briggs Seed and Mary Crosland Seed (*née* Barrett); *m* 1974, Jane Margaret Berry; one *s* three *d*. *Educ:* St Philip's Sch., Burley-in-Wharfedale; Edinburgh Theol Coll.; Leeds Univ. (MA). Deacon 1972, priest 1973; Asst Curate, Christ Church, Skipton, 1972–75, Baildon, 1975–77, Dio. of Bradford; Team Vicar, Kidlington, Oxford, 1977–80; Chaplain, HM Detention Centre, Campsfield House, 1977–80; Vicar of Boston Spa, Dio. of York, 1980–99; Priest-in-charge: Clifford, 1989–99; Thorp Arch with Walton, 1998–99; Archdeacon of York, 1999–2012, now Archdeacon Emeritus; Priest-in-charge, St Mary, Bishophill Junior, 2000–04; Rector, Holy Trinity, Micklegate, 2000–12. Mem., Gen. Synod of C of E, 2000–10. Chairman: Diocesan Redundant Churches Cttee, 1999–; Diocesan Pastoral Cttee, Dio. of York, 2003–. Founder Chm., 1980–2012, Chaplain, 1980–99, Martin House Hospice for Children. Life Mem., Friends of Mount Athos. *Publications:* (contrib.) Appointed for Growth, 1994. *Recreations:* swimming, travel, Byzantine studies, monastic spirituality, walking dogs. *Address:* Mill Cottage, Main Street, Allerston, Pickering, N Yorks YO18 7PG.

SEEISO, HRH Prince Seeiso Bereng; High Commissioner of Lesotho to the United Kingdom, 2005–11; *b* 16 April 1966; *s* of HM King Bereng Seeiso; *m* HRH Princess Mabereng Seeiso; two *s* one *d*. *Educ:* Gilling Castle; Ampleforth Coll.; Nat. Univ. of Lesotho; Birmingham Univ.; Guyana. Principal Chief, Matsieng, 1991. Member: Senate, 1992–; Nat. Constituent Assembly, 1993–. Patron, Sentebale. *Recreations:* horse-riding, theatre, reading, football, Rugby.

SEEL, Derek, FDSRCS; FRCS; FRCA; Dental Postgraduate Dean, University of Bristol, 1986–98; *b* 2 April 1932; *s* of William Alfred and Olive Seel; *m* 1960, Gillian Henderson. *Educ:* Stockport Sch.; Manchester Univ. Inst. of Dental Surgery (BDS). MOrthRCS; FRCS 1994; FRCA 1995. General dental practice, 1956–62; orthodontic trainee, 1962–68; Lectr in Orthodontics, Bristol Univ., 1967–69; Consultant Orthodontist, Univ. of Wales Coll. of Medicine, 1969–94; Consultant in Orthodontics, Welsh RHA, 1969–94. Dean, Faculty of Dental Surgery, RCS, 1990–92. LRPS 1991. Hon. Diploma in Gen. Dental Practice, RCS 1994. C. F. Ballard Medal, Consultant Orthodontists' Gp, 1992; Colyer Gold Medal, RCS, 1994. *Recreations:* golf, music, reading, photography. *Address:* 20 Blenheim Road, Bristol BS6 7JP. *T:* (0117) 973 6635. *E:* seelderek@gmail.com.

SEELEIB-KAISER, Prof. Martin, Dr phil; Barnett Professor of Comparative Social Policy and Politics, since 2013, and Head, Department of Social Policy and Intervention, since 2011, University of Oxford; Fellow of St Cross College, Oxford, since 2013; *b* 13 Feb. 1964. *Educ:* Ludwig-Maximilians Univ. (MA Politics 1989; Dr phil Politics 1992); Univ. of Bremen (Habil. Politics 2000). Res. Fellow, Univ. of Bremen, 1993–99; Deutscher Akademischer Austauschdienst Associate Prof. of Pol Sci. and Sociol., Duke Univ., 1999–2002; Sen. Res. Fellow, Univ. of Bremen, 2002–04; Interim Prof. of Social Policy, Univ. of Bielefeld, 2003–04; University of Oxford: Lectr, 2004–06; Reader, 2006–09; Prof. of Comparative Social Policy and Politics, 2009–12; Fellow, Green Coll., subseq. Green Templeton Coll., Oxford, 2004–13. *Publications:* The Dual Transformation of the German Welfare State, 2004; (jtly) Party Politics and Social Welfare, 2008; (ed) Welfare State Transformations: comparative perspectives, 2008; (ed jtly) The Age of Dualization, 2012. *Address:* Department of Social Policy and Intervention, University of Oxford, Barnett House, 32 Wellington Square, Oxford OX1 2ER. *E:* martin.seeleib@spi.ox.ac.uk.

SEELEY, Rt Rev. Martin Alan; *see* St Edmundsbury and Ipswich, Bishop of.

SEELY, family name of **Baron Mottistone**.

SEELY, Sir Nigel (Edward), 5th Bt *cr* 1896; *b* 28 July 1923; *s* of Sir Victor Basil John Seely, 4th Bt and Sybil Helen, *d* of late Sills Clifford Gibbons; *S* father, 1980; *m* 1949, Loraine (marr. diss.; she *d* 2007), *d* of late W. W. Lindley-Travis; three *d*; *m* 1984, Trudi Pacter, *d* of Sydney Pacter. *Educ:* Stowe. Formerly with Dorland International. *Heir: nephew* William Victor Conway Seely, *b* 16 Sept. 1983. *Address:* 3 Craven Hill Mews, W2 3DY. *Clubs:* Buck's; Royal Solent.

SEENEY, Leslie Elon Sidney, OBE 1978; Director General (formerly General Secretary), National Chamber of Trade, 1971–87; *b* 19 Jan. 1922; *s* of Sidney Leonard and Daisy Seeney, Forest Hill; *m* 1947, Marjory Doreen Greenwood, Spalding (*d* 2008); one *s*. *Educ:* St Matthews, Camberwell. RAFVR, 1941–46 (Flt Lt, Pilot). Man. Dir, family manufg business (clothing), 1946–63, with other interests in insce and advertising. Mem., West Lewisham Chamber of Commerce, 1951, subseq. Sec. and Chm.; Delegate to Nat. Chamber of Trade, 1960; joined NCT staff, 1966. Mem., Home Office Standing Cttee on Crime Prevention, 1971–87. Council Member: (founding) Retail Consortium, 1971–87; Assoc. for Prevention of Theft from Shops, 1976–87. Fellow, Soc. of Assoc. Executives, 1970. *Publications:* various articles. *Recreations:* genealogy, travel, photography.

SEEYAVE, Sir René (Sow Choung), Kt 1985; CBE 1979; Chairman: Altima Group, since 2004; Innodis (formerly Mauritius Farms, then Happy World Foods) Ltd, 1974–2013; *b* 15 March 1935; *s* of late Antoine Seeyave, CBE and Lam Tung Ying; *m* 1961, Thérèse How Hong; one *s* four *d*. *Educ:* Royal College, Port Louis, Mauritius. Gp Man. Dir, 1968–86, Gp Chm., 1986–2004, Happy World Ltd. Chm., Electricity Adv. Cttee, 1972–76. Vice Chairman: Mauritius Employers' Fedn, 1972; Mauritius Broadcasting Corp., 1980–81. Director: Mauritius Development Investment Trust Ltd, 1968–2000; Swan Insurance Co. Ltd, 1969–2003; Mauritius Marine Authority, 1980–95. Mauritius Res. Council, 1997–2000; Vice-Chm. Council, Univ. of Mauritius, 1985–87. Chm., Sui Loong Elders Centre, 1997–. Hon. Pres., Heen Foh Soc., 1991–. *Address:* Altima Ltd, Level 10, Ebène Heights, 34 Ebène Cybercity, Ebène, Mauritius. *T:* 4016363, *Fax:* 4542828. *E:* sir.rene@altima.mu. *Clubs:* Royal Over-Seas League; Mauritius Gymkhana, Port Louis City.

SEFI, Michael Richard, LVO 2013; FCA; FRPSL; Keeper of the Royal Philatelic Collection, since 2003 (Deputy Keeper, 1996–2002); *b* 11 Dec. 1943; *s* of Antony Michael Sefi and Judith Sefi (*née* Hull); *m* 1968, Harriet Mary Davidson; one *s* two *d*. *Educ:* Downside Sch. Chartered Accountant 1970; FCA 1975. Partner, Mann Judd, then Touche Ross, 1975–83; Dir, Noble Lowndes Personal Financial Services Ltd, then Noble Lowndes & Partners Ltd, 1983–92. FRPSL 1990 (Council Mem., 1990–2005); Pres., GB Philatelic Soc., 1998–2000 and 2012–14. Fellow, Royal. Philatelic Soc. of Canada, 2012. Signatory, Roll of Distinguished Philatelists, 2012. *Publications:* contrib. to London Philatelist, GB Jl, Crosspost. *Recreations:* philately, ski-ing, diving, naval history. *Address:* Royal Philatelic Collection, Buckingham Palace, SW1A 1AA. *E:* michael.sefi@royal.gsx.gov.uk. *Club:* Army and Navy.

SEFTON, Dr Allan Douglas; Director, Rail Safety, and HM Chief Inspector of Railways, Health and Safety Executive, 2001–05; *b* 15 April 1945; *s* of James and Alice Sefton; *m* 1968, Jennifer Elizabeth Pratt; two *s*. *Educ:* UCNW, Bangor (BSc; PhD 1970). FIOSH 1990. Trainee, HM Insp. of Factories, Dept of Employment, Scotland, 1969–73; HM Insp. of Factories, Dept of Employment and HSE, Scotland, 1973–81; Health and Safety Executive: HM Insp., Hazardous Substances Div., 1981–86; Principal Insp., Field Ops Div., 1986–87; Hd, Hazardous Installation Nat. Interest Gp, 1987–90; Dir, W and N Yorks, 1990–92; Dir of Ops, 1992–96, Hd, 1996–2000, Off-shore Safety Div.; Dir, Scotland, 2000–01. Non-exec. Dir, Angel Trains Gp, 2006–12. *Publications:* Getting Started at Fly Fishing for Trout, 2013. *Recreations:* fishing, game shooting. *Address:* 4 Barnfield, Common Lane, Hemingford Abbots, Cambs PE28 9AX.

SEGAL, Prof. Anthony Walter, MD; PhD, DSc; FRCP, FMedSci; FRS 1998; Charles Dent Professor of Medicine, University College London, since 1986; *b* 24 Feb. 1944; *s* of late Cyril Segal and Doreen (*née* Hayden); *m* 1966, Barbara Miller; three *d*. *Educ:* Univ. of Cape Town (MB, ChB; MD 1974); PhD 1979, DSc 1984, London. FRCP 1987. Internship, Groote Schuur Hosp., SA, 1968–69; Sen. House Officer, Registrar and Sen. Registrar in Medicine, Hammersmith Hosp., 1970–76; Registrar and Clinical Scientist, Northwick Park Hosp. and Clinical Res. Centre, 1971–79; Wellcome Trust Sen. Clinical Fellow, UCL, 1979–86; Hon. Consultant Physician, UCH, 1979–. Fellow, UCL, 2002. Founder FMedSci 1998. *Publications:* contribs on biochemistry, cell biology, immunology and gastroenterology. *Recreations:* golf, sculpture, painting, theatre, music, dining. *Address:* Rayne Building, Centre for Molecular Medicine, 5 University Street, WC1E 6JJ. *T:* (020) 7679 6175. *Clubs:* Garrick; Highgate Golf.

SEGAL, Graeme Bryce, DPhil; FRS 1982; Senior Research Fellow, All Souls College, Oxford, 1999–2009, now Emeritus; *b* 21 Dec. 1941; *s* of Reuben Segal and Iza Joan Harris; *m* 1962, Desley Rae Cheetham (marr. diss. 1972); partner, 1978–2000, Helen Elizabeth Phillips; partner, 2002–, Marina Sarah Warner (*see* Dame M. S. Warner). *Educ:* Sydney Grammar School; Univ. of Sydney (BSc 1962); Univ. of Cambridge; Univ. of Oxford (MA, DPhil 1967). Oxford University: Junior Res. Fellow, Worcester Coll., 1964–66; Junior Lectr in Mathematics, 1965–66; Fellow, St Catherine's Coll., 1966–90; Reader in Maths, 1978–89; Prof. of Maths, 1989–90; Lowndean Prof. of Astronomy and Geometry, and Fellow, St John's Coll., Cambridge, 1990–99. Mem., Inst. for Advanced Study, Princeton, 1969–70. Pres., LMS, 2011–13. Editor, Topology, 1970–90. *Publications:* (with A. Pressley) Loop Groups, 1986; articles in learned jls. *Address:* c/o All Souls College, Oxford OX1 4AL. *E:* graeme.segal@all-souls.ox.ac.uk; 1 Beechcroft Road, Oxford OX2 7AY. *T:* (01865) 558016.

SEGAL, Michael Giles, PhD; consultant; Director, Strategy and Evidence Group, Department for Environment, Food and Rural Affairs, 2009–11; *b* 31 July 1950; *s* of late Paul and Hanna Maria Segal; *m* 1972, Agnes Henderson; one *s* (and one *s* decd). *Educ:* St Paul's Sch.; King's Coll., Cambridge (BA 1972; PhD 1975). MRSC, 1983–2011. Res. Officer, CEGB, 1978–88; Civil Servant: MAFF, 1988–99, variously Hd, Food Safety (Radiation) Unit, Hd, Radiological Safety Div. and Chief Nuclear Inspector, and Hd, Radiological Safety and Nutrition Div.; Dir of Corporate Strategy and Sec. to the Bd, Food Standards Agency, 2000–01; Department for Environment, Food and Rural Affairs: Hd, Livestock Strategy Div., 2001–04; Dir, Food Chain Analysis and Farming Regulation, 2004–06; Dir, Sustainable Farming Strategy, 2006–07; Dir, Food and Farming Gp, 2007–09. *Publications:* approx. 70 articles in learned jls, conf. procs, etc. *Recreations:* sports—cricket, badminton, ski-ing and scuba diving, photography (incl. underwater), dancing, travel.

SEGAL, Michael John; District Judge (formerly Registrar), Principal Registry, Family Division, 1985–2010; *b* 20 Sept. 1937; *s* of Abraham Charles Segal and Iris Muriel (*née* Parsons); *m* 1963, Barbara Gina Fluxman; one *d*. *Educ:* Strode's Sch., Egham; Birkbeck, Univ. of London (BA 2014). Served 7th RTR, 1955–56. Called to the Bar, Middle Temple, 1962. Practised at Bar, Midland and Oxford Circuit, 1962–84. Mem., Civil and Family Cttee, Judicial Studies Bd, 1990–94. Editor, Family Div. section, Butterworth's Cost Service, 1987–2008; Jt Editor, Supreme Court Practice, 1991–94; contributor: Protecting Children Update, 2003–; Education Law Update, 2006–. FLS 2004. *Publications:* Costs Advocacy, 2002; contribs to New Law Jl, Family Law. *Recreation:* living in the past. *Address:* 28 Grange Road, N6 4AP. *T:* (020) 8348 0680. *Clubs:* Garrick, Savage.

SEGAL, Prof. Naomi Dinah, PhD; Professorial Fellow, School of Arts, Birkbeck, University of London, since 2011; *b* 6 Oct. 1949; *d* of Prof. Judah Benzion Segal, MC, FBA and Leah Segal (*née* Seidemann); marr. diss.; one *d* one *s*. *Educ:* Newnham Coll., Cambridge (BA 1972); King's Coll. London (PhD 1978). Fellow, Tutor and Lectr, Queens' Coll., Cambridge, 1980–86; Fellow, Tutor and Lectr, St John's Coll., Cambridge, 1986–93; Prof. of French Studies, Univ. of Reading, 1993–2004; Dir, Inst. of Germanic & Romance Studies, Sch. of Advanced Study, Univ. of London, 2004–11. Convenor, Panel 5, Advanced Res., and Mem. Bd, AHRB, then AHRC, 1999–2005; UK Rep., Standing Cttee for Humanities, ESF, 2005–11. Chair or Mem., nat. and internat. panels, incl. AHRC, Humanities in European Res. Area, IUF, RAE, and in Bulgaria, Latvia, Czech Republic. Academic Associate, British Psychoanalytic Soc., 2012–. MAE 2013. Chevalier, l'Ordre des Palmes académiques, 2005. *Publications:* The Banal Object, 1981; The Unintended Reader, 1986; Narcissus and Echo, 1988; (ed jtly) Freud in Exile, 1988; The Adulteress's Child, 1992; (ed jtly) Scarlet Letters: fictions of adultery from antiquity to the 1990s, 1997; André Gide: pederasty and pedagogy, 1998; (ed jtly) Coming Out of Feminism, 1998; Le Désir à l'œuvre, 2000; (ed jtly) Indeterminate Bodies, 2003; Consensuality, 2009; (ed jtly) When familiar meanings dissolve…: essays in French studies in memory of Malcolm Bowie (1943–2007), 2011; (ed jtly) Vicissitudes: histories and destinies of psychoanalysts, 2013; (ed jtly) From Literature to Cultural Literacy, 2014; (ed jtly) Opera, Exoticism and Visual Culture, 2015; numerous articles. *Recreation:* friendship. *Address:* School of Arts, Birkbeck, University of London, 43 Gordon Square, WC1H 0PD. *E:* n.segal@bbk.ac.uk.

SEGAL, Oliver Leon; QC 2011; *b* London, 18 April 1963; *s* of Ronald and Susan Segal; *m* 1992, Lesley Mitchell; one *s* one *d*. *Educ:* Corpus Christi Coll., Oxford (MA Lit.Hum. 1985). Called to the Bar, Middle Temple, 1992. *Publications:* Partnership Bidding at Bridge, 1991. *Recreations:* meditation, bridge. *Address:* Old Square Chambers, 10–11 Bedford Row, WC1R 4PU. *E:* segal@oldsquare.co.uk.

SEGALL, Anne Celia, (Mrs D. H. Evans); freelance journalist; Economics Correspondent, Daily Telegraph, 1985–2001; *b* 20 April 1948; *d* of John Segall and Marsha (*née* Greenberg); *m* 1973, David Howard Evans, *qv*; two *s*. *Educ:* St Paul's Girls' Sch., London; St Hilda's Coll., Oxford (BA Hons PPE 1969). Banking correspondent: Investors' Chronicle, 1971–76; The Economist, 1976–80; Daily Telegraph, 1981–85. Wincott Award for Financial Journalism, 1975. *Recreations:* swimming, reading, theatre. *Address:* 24 Pembroke Gardens, W8 6HU.

SEGAR, Christopher Michael John, CMG 2004; HM Diplomatic Service, retired; Programme Manager (formerly Energy Analyst), Europe, Middle East and North Africa, International Energy Agency, Paris, 2008–15; *b* 25 Nov. 1950; *s* of Cyril John Segar and Margery (*née* Angliss). *Educ:* Sevenoaks Sch.; Sidney Sussex Coll., Cambridge (BA Hons). VSO, Cameroun, 1969; joined FCO, 1973; MECAS, 1974–76; Third, later Second Sec., Dubai, 1976–79; FCO, 1979–84; Head of Chancery and Consul, Luanda, 1984–87; UK Delegn to OECD, Paris, 1987–90; Dep. Head of Mission and Consul Gen., Baghdad, 1990–91; on secondment to MoD, 1991–94; Commercial Counsellor: Riyadh, 1994–97; Peking, 1997–2001; Head of Aviation, Maritime, Sci. and Energy Dept, subseq. Aviation, Maritime and Energy Dept, FCO, 2001–03; Head of British Office, Baghdad, 2003–04. Dep. Dir, Centre for Studies in Security and Diplomacy, Univ. of Birmingham, 2006–08. Chm., Arab-British Centre, 2006–10; Trustee, Foundn for Relief and Reconciliation in the Middle East (formerly Foundn for Reconciliation in the Middle East), 2006– (Chm. Trustees, 2005–06). *Recreations:* music, travel. *Club:* Royal Over-Seas League.

SEGARS, Joanne, OBE 2003; Chief Executive, National Association of Pension Funds, since 2006 (Director of Policy, 2005–06); *b* 5 Dec. 1964; *d* of Terry and Jean Segars; partner, David Coats. *Educ:* Liverpool Poly. (BA Hons Econs 1986); Univ. of Warwick (MA Industrial Relns 1987). Sen. Policy Officer (Pensions), TUC, 1987–2001; Hd, Pensions and Savings, ABI, 2001–05. Mem. Bd, Occupational Pensions Regulatory Authy, 1987–2002. Mem. Council and Gov., Pensions Policy Inst., 2001–; Chm., Shadow Scheme Adv. Bd, Local Govt Pension Scheme, 2013–. Dir, PensionsEurope (formerly Eur. Fedn of Retirement Provision), 2007– (Chm., 2012–). *Recreations:* travel, photography. *Address:* National Association of Pension Funds, Cheapside House, 138 Cheapside, EC2V 6AE. *T:* (020) 7601 1700, *Fax:* (020) 7601 1799. *E:* napf@napf.co.uk.

SEGHATCHIAN, Tanya; film and television producer; *b* 17 April 1968. *Educ:* Gonville and Caius Coll., Cambridge (BA 1st Cl. Hons Hist. 1990). Researcher, then Producer, South Bank Show and BBC Documentary Features and Music and Arts, 1990–95; Script Editor, BBC Drama, 1995–96; Hd of Develt, Heyday Films, 1997–2001; Film Producer, 2001–07: Harry Potter and the Philosopher's Stone, 2001; Harry Potter and the Chamber of Secrets, 2002; Harry Potter and the Prisoner of Azkaban, 2004; My Summer of Love, 2004; Harry Potter and the Goblet of Fire, 2005; Angel, 2007. Head: Develt Fund, 2007–10, Film Fund, 2010–11, UK Film Council; Film Fund, BFI, 2011. Prof., Manchester Univ., 2014–. Mem. Bd, Almeida Th., 2015–; Trustee: BAFTA, 2013–15; Literature Prize Foundn, 2013–.

SEIF EL NASR, Hatem; Assistant Minister for European Affairs and Security and Strategic Organizations in Europe, Egyptian Ministry of Foreign Affairs, since 2013; *b* Cairo, 30 July 1957; *s* of Nevine Adly Yassine; one *s* one *d*. *Educ:* Cairo Univ. (BA Econs and Political Scis). Cabinet, Dep. Prime Minister and Minister of Foreign Affairs, Cairo, 1979–82; Mem., Egyptian Perm. Mission to UN, 1982–86; Cabinet, Dr Boutrous Boutrous-Ghali, Minister of State for Foreign Affairs, 1986–88; Pol Counsellor, Egyptian Embassy, Washington, 1988–93; Hd, UN Dept, Ministry of Foreign Affairs, 1993–96; Minister Plenipotentiary, Dep. Chief of Mission, Egyptian Embassy, Paris, 1996–2000; Ambassador of Egypt: to Brazil, 2000–01; to Lebanon, 2001–02; to France, 2002–06; Asst Minister of Foreign Affairs for the Americas and the Orgn of American States, 2006–08; Ambassador of Egypt to the Court of St James's, 2008–12; Perm. Rep. of Egypt to IMO, 2010–12. *E:* hatemseifelnasr@gmail.com.

SEIFTER, Pavel, PhD; Ambassador of the Czech Republic to the Court of St James's, 1997–2003; Distinguished Visiting Fellow, Civil Society and Human Security Research Unit, Department of International Development (formerly Centre for the Study of Global Governance, then LSE Global Governance), London School of Economics and Political Science, since 2003; *b* 27 May 1938; *s* of Karel and Anna Seifter; *m* 1st, 1966, Jana Macenauerová; one *d*; 2nd, 1986, Lenka Urbanová; 3rd, 1999, Lesley Chamberlain. *Educ:* Charles Univ., Prague (Hist., Czech Lang. and Lit. degree 1961; PhD Hist. 1968); Centre Universitaire Européen, Nancy, France (postgrad. study). Lectr in Hist., Charles Univ., Prague, 1964–68; translator, window cleaner, editor of dissident histl publications, 1969–89; Deputy Director: Inst. of Contemporary Hist., Prague, 1990–91; Inst. of Internat. Relns, Prague, 1991–92; Dir, Foreign Policy Dept, Office of Pres. of Czech Republic, 1993–97. Visiting Fellow: CISAC, Stanford Univ., 1992; Uppsala Univ., 1992.

SEIKEN, Jason; Chief Content Officer and Editor in Chief, Telegraph Media Group, 2013–15; *b* Michigan, USA; *s* of Arnold and Ione Seiken; *m* 2005, Juyoung Seo; one *s* one *d*. *Educ:* Union Coll., NY (BA Pol Sci.); Stanford Univ. Reporter, 1983–86, Ed., City and West Edns, 1986–93, Quincy Patriot Ledger; Ed. in Chief, washingtonpost.com, 1994–97; Vice President: AOL, 1997–2001; AOL Europe, 2001–06; Sen. Vice Pres. and Gen. Manager, Public Broadcasting Service Digital, 2006–13. *E:* seikenj@gmail.com.

SEITLER, Jonathan Simon; QC 2003; barrister; *b* 11 June 1961; *s* of Benjamin and Sandra Seitler; *m* 2012, Fiona Fishman; one *s* one *d* from a previous marriage. *Educ:* Stand Grammar Sch., Whitefield, Manchester; Pembroke Coll., Oxford (BA Hons PPE); City Univ., London (Dip Law). Called to the Bar, Inner Temple, 1985; in practice, specialising in law of property and related professional negligence. *Publications:* Property Finance Negligence: claims against solicitors and valuers, 1995; Commercial Property Disputes: law and practice, 1999; Leases: covenants and consents, 2009. *Address:* Wilberforce Chambers, 8 New Square, Lincoln's Inn, WC2A 3QP. *T:* (020) 7306 0102. *E:* JSeitler@wilberforce.co.uk.

SEITZ, Raymond George Hardenbergh; Chairman, Sun-Times Media Group, 2006–09; *b* Hawaii, 8 Dec. 1940; *s* of Maj.-Gen. John Francis Regis Seitz and Helen Johnson Hardenbergh; one *s* one *d*; *m* 1985. *Educ:* Yale University (BA History 1963). Joined Foreign Service, Dept of State, 1966; served Montreal, Nairobi, Bukavu, Zaire, 1966–72; Staff Officer, later Director, Secretariat Staff, Washington, Special Asst to Dir Gen., Foreign Service, 1972–75; Political Officer, London, 1975–79; Dep. Exec. Sec., Washington, 1979–81; Senior Dep. Asst Sec., Public Affairs, Washington, 1981–82; Exec. Asst to Secretary George P. Shultz, Washington, 1982–84; Minister and Dep. Chief of Mission, US Embassy, London, 1984–89; Asst Sec. for European and Canadian Affairs, State Dept, Washington, 1989–91; Ambassador to UK, 1991–94; a Sen. Man. Dir, 1995–96, Vice Chm., 1996–2003, Lehman Brothers. Trustee: Nat. Gall., 1996–2001; Royal Acad., 1996. Gov., Ditchley Foundn, 1995. Benjamin Franklin Medal, RSA, 1996. Kt Comdr's Cross (Germany), 1991. *Publications:* Over Here (memoir), 1998. *Address:* PO Box 22, 159 Norris Road, Orford, NH 03777, USA.

SEKERS, David Nicholas Oliver, OBE 1986; FMA, FSA; consultant for heritage, museums and charities; *b* 29 Sept. 1943; *s* of Sir Nicholas Sekers, MBE and Lady Sekers; *m* 1965, Simone, *er d* of late Moran Caplat, CBE; one *d*. *Educ:* Eton; Worcester College, Oxford (BA). Dir, Gladstone Pottery Museum (Museum of the Year 1976), 1973–78; Museum Dir, Quarry Bank Mill (Museum of the Year 1984), 1978–89; Dir, Southern Reg., 1989–98, Dir of the Regions, 1998–2001, Nat. Trust; Specialist Advr, DCMS Select Cttee, 2005–. FSA 2010. *Publications:* The Potteries, 2009; (ed) The Diary of Hannah Lightbody 1786–1790, 2009; A Lady of Cotton: Hannah Greg, mistress of Quarry Bank Mill, 2013. *Recreations:* growing vegetables, fell-walking. *Address:* Cross House, Henstridge BA8 0QZ. *Club:* Garrick.

SEKIMIZU, Koji; Secretary-General, International Maritime Organization, since 2012; *b* Yokohama, Japan, 3 Dec. 1952; *m* 1976, Chiho; one *s* one *d*. *Educ:* Elementary and secondary schs, Yokohama; Osaka Univ. (BEng 1975; MEng 1977). Ministry of Transport, Japan: ship inspector, 1977; Chief Officer in charge of IMO regulations, Safety Planning Section, Ship Bureau, 1979; Shipbuilding Res. Assoc. of Japan, 1980; Dep. Dir, Envmt Div., Min. of Transport, 1982–84; Dep. Dir, Second Internat. Orgns Div., Econ. Affairs Bureau, Min. of Foreign Affairs, 1984–86; Dep. Dir, Safety Standards Div., Maritime Technol. and Safety Bureau, 1986–89; International Maritime Organization: Tech. Officer, Sub-Div. for Technol., 1989–92, Hd, Technol. Section, 1992–97, Maritime Safety Div.; Sen. Dep. Dir, 1997–2000, Dir, 2000–04, Marine Envmt Div.; Dir, Maritime Safety Div., 2004–11. Chancellor, World Maritime Univ., 2012; Chm., Governing Bd, Internat. Maritime Law Inst., 2012. Mem., Japan Soc. of Naval Architects, 1975–; Councillor, Alumni Soc. of Naval Architects of Osaka Univ. (Kousi Zosen Kai), 1985–. *Recreations:* plays golf, playing guitar and composing songs. *Address:* International Maritime Organization, 4 Albert Embankment, SE1 7SR. *T:* (020) 7735 7611, *Fax:* (020) 7587 3210. *E:* secretary-general@imo.org.

SELBORNE, 4th Earl of, *cr* 1882; **John Roundell Palmer,** GBE 2011 (KBE 1987); FRS 1991; DL; Baron Selborne, 1872; Viscount Wolmer, 1882; Chairman, Foundation for Science and Technology, since 2006 (Vice-Chairman, 1994–2006); *b* 24 March 1940; *er s* of William Matthew, Viscount Wolmer (killed on active service, 1942), and Priscilla (who *m* 1948, Hon. Peter Legh, later 4th Baron Newton (*d* 1992); she *m* 1994, Frederick Fryer; she *d* 2010), *d* of late Captain John Egerton-Warburton; *S* grandfather, 1971; *m* 1969, Joanna Van Antwerp, PhD, *yr d* of late Evan Maitland James; three *s* one *d*. *Educ:* Eton; Christ Church, Oxford (MA). Chm., AFRC, 1983–90 (Mem., 1975–90; Vice-Chm., 1980–83); Vice-Chm., Apple and Pear Devel Council, 1969–73; Mem., Hops Mkting Bd, 1972–82 (Chm., 1978–82); Pres., British Crop Protection Council, 1977–80; Chm., SE Regl Panel, MAFF, 1979–83. Member: Royal Commn on Environmental Pollution, 1993–98; Govt Panel on Sustainable Develt, 1994–97. Chm., UK Chemical Stakeholder Forum, 2000–04. Chairman: H of L Select Cttee on Sci. and Technol., 1993–97 and 2014–; Sub-Cttee D (Agric. and Food), H of L Select Cttee on European Communities, 1991–93; Sub-Cttee D (Agric., Food, Envmt and Consumer Affairs), H of L Select Cttee on EU, 1999–2003; elected Mem., H of L, 1999; Pres., Parly and Scientific Cttee, 1997–2000. Director: Agricl Mortgage Corp., 1990–2002 (Chm., 1995–2002); Lloyds Bank, 1994–95; Lloyds TSB Gp, 1995–2004. Chm., Jt Nature Conservation Cttee, 1991–97. President: South of England Agric. Soc., 1984; RASE, 1988; Royal Bath & West Agricl Soc., 1995; RGS (with IBG), 1997–2000; Vice-Pres., RSPB, 1996–2007; Chm., Trustees, Royal Botanic Gdns, Kew, 2003–09 (Trustee, 1993–98). Chancellor, Southampton Univ., 1996–2006. Treas., Bridewell Royal Hosp. (King Edward's Sch., Witley), 1972–83. Mem., Hampshire County Council, 1967–74. FRSB (FIBiol 1984); FRAgS 1986; FLS, 1994. Master, Mercers' Co., 1989–90. JP Hants 1971–78; DL Hants 1982. Hon. LLD Bristol, 1989; Hon. DSc: Cranfield, 1991; UEA, 1996; Southampton, 1996; Birmingham 2000. *Heir: s* Viscount Wolmer, *qv*. *Address:* Temple Manor, Selborne, Alton, Hants GU34 3LR. *T:* (01420) 473646. *Club:* Travellers.

SELBOURNE, David Maurice; author; *b* 4 June 1937; *s* of Hugh Selbourne, MD and Sulamith Amiel; *m* 1963, Hazel Savage; one *s* one *d*. *Educ:* Manchester Grammar Sch.; Balliol Coll., Oxford (Winter Williams Law Schol., Hon. Exhibnr, Paton Studentship, Jenkins Law Prize, BA Hons, MA). Called to the Bar, Inner Temple, 1960. British Commonwealth Fellow, Univ. of Chicago, 1959; Tutor, Ruskin Coll., Oxford, 1966–86 (Mem. Governing Body, 1973–75). Freelance journalist, 1975–: New Society, New Statesman, Spectator, Independent, Guardian, Tribune, The Times, Sunday Times, Daily Telegraph, Sunday Telegraph, India Today (Delhi), Sunday (Calcutta), *etc*. Member: Chief Minister's Cttee on Human Rights in Sri Lanka, Madras, 1984; Steering Cttee on Ethnic Violence, Dutch Inst. of Human Rights, 1984–85. Vis. Fellow, Europa Inst., Univ. of Leiden, 1964; Aneurin Bevan Meml Fellow, Govt of India, 1975–76; Indian Council of Social Sci. Res. Fellow, New Delhi, 1979–80. Lectures: The Times-Dillon's, LSE, 1994; Geraldine Aves Meml, H of C, 1994; Spectator Debates, 2010; Visiting Lectures, 1975–2005: RIIA; Inst. Commonwealth Studies, Oxford; Jawaharlal Nehru Univ., New Delhi; Aligarh Muslim Univ.; Czech Underground Univ., Prague and Bratislava, 1987, 1989; Berkeley; UCSD; Notre Dame Univ., Indiana, *etc*. Mem., Accademia Rubiconia, Savignano, Italy, 1993. *Plays* performed, 1968–83: Traverse Th., Edinburgh; Everyman Th., Liverpool; Northcott Th., Exeter; Crucible Th., Sheffield; Soho Th., London; People's Th., Calcutta, *etc*. Officer, Order of Merit of the Italian Republic, 2001. *Publications:* The Play of William Cooper and Edmund Dew-Nevett, 1968; The Two-backed Beast, 1969; Samson, 1971; The Damned, 1971; An Eye to China, 1975, 2nd edn 1978; An Eye to India, 1977; Through the Indian Looking-Glass, 1982; The Making of A Midsummer Night's Dream, 1982, 3rd edn 2010; (ed) In Theory and in Practice, 1985; Against Socialist Illusion, 1985; Left Behind: journeys into British politics, 1987; (ed) A Doctor's Life: the diaries of Hugh Selbourne, MD 1960–64, 1989, 2nd edn 2009; Death of the Dark Hero: Eastern Europe 1987–1990, 1990, 2nd edn 2009; The Spirit of the Age, 1993; Not an Englishman: conversations with Lord Goodman, 1993; The Principle of Duty: an essay on the foundations of the civic order, 1994, 4th edn 2009; Moral Evasion, 1998; The City of Light, 1997, 2nd edn 1998, other edns in translation, incl. Catalan, Chinese, French, German, Hebrew, Hungarian, Korean, Norwegian, Polish, Portuguese and Spanish, 1997–2002; The Losing Battle with Islam, 2005; contribs to learned jls, incl. Bull. Concerned Asian Scholars, Critique, Electoral Studies, Hist. Workshop Jl, Monthly Review, Social Scientist and Third World Qly. *Recreations:* listening to music, reading, walking, talking. *Address:* c/o Christopher Sinclair-Stevenson, 3 South Terrace, SW7 2TB. *Club:* Oxford and Cambridge.

SELBY, 6th Viscount *cr* 1905, of the City of Carlisle; **Christopher Rolf Thomas Gully;** *b* 18 Oct. 1993; *s* of 5th Viscount Selby and of his 1st wife, Charlotte Cathrine Brege; *S* father, 2001. *Educ:* Glenalmond Coll. *Heir: great-uncle* Hon. James Edward Hugh Grey Gully [*b* 17 March 1945; *m* 1971, Fiona Margaret Mackenzie (*d* 2012); two *s*].

SELBY, Bishop Suffragan of, since 2014; **Rt Rev. Dr John Bromilow Thomson;** *b* Edinburgh, 1 July 1959; *s* of David and Betty Thomson; *m* 1986, Susan Clare Wade; two *d*. *Educ:* Edinburgh Acad.; Haberdashers' Aske's Sch., Elstree; Univ. of York (BA Hons Hist. 1981); Wycliffe Hall, Oxford (MA Theol. 1991); Univ. of Nottingham (PhD Theol. 2001). Ordained deacon, 1985, priest, 1986; Asst Curate and Youth Chaplain, All Saints, Ecclesall, Sheffield, 1985–89; Tutor, St Paul's Coll., Grahamstown, SA, 1989–92; Asst Lectr, Rhodes Univ., Grahamstown, SA, 1991–92; Vicar, St Mary, Wheatley, Doncaster, 1993–2001; Dir of Ministry, Dio. of Sheffield, 2001–14. *Publications:* The Ecclesiology of Stanley Hauerwas: a Christian theology of liberation, 2003; Church on Edge? Practising Christian Ministry Today, 2004; Doxa: a discipleship course, 2007; Living Holiness: Stanley Hauerwas and the church, 2010; Sharing Friendship: exploring Anglican character, vocation, witness and ministry, 2015. *Recreations:* cycling, choral singing, walking, reading, gardening, cooking. *Address:* Bishop's House, York Road, Barlby, Selby YO8 5JP. *T:* (01757) 429982. *E:* bishopofselby@yorkdiocese.org.

SELBY, Dona Pamela; consultant on fundraising and market research, since 2009; *d* of Donald and Sybil Davis; *m* 1981, Peter Selby. *Educ:* Bexleyheath Technical High Sch. Royal Mail: Marketing Asst, 1971–76; Marketing Exec., 1976–81; Marketing Manager, 1981–86; Sen. Corporate Manager, WWF, 1989–92; Great Ormond Street Hospital Children's Charity: Head of Commercial and Direct Marketing, then Dir of Fundraising, 1992–2001; Exec. Dir, 2001–06; Dir of Fundraising, Jeans for Genes, 2006–08; Exec. Fundraiser, 2007–08, Trustee, 2008–, Orchid Cancer Appeal. *Recreations:* keep fit, travel, motor racing. *E:* dona.selby21@gmail.com.

SELBY, Prof. Peter John, CBE 2001; MD, DSc; FMedSci; Professor of Cancer Medicine, and Consultant Physician, St James's University Hospital, Leeds, 1988–2010; *b* 10 July 1950; *s* of Joseph Selby and Dorothy Selby (*née* Cross); *m* 1972, Catherine Elisabeth, *d* of Peter Thomas; one *s* one *d*. *Educ:* Lydney Grammar Sch.; Christ's Coll., Cambridge (MA; MB BChir; MD 1980); Univ. of Leeds (DSc 2011). FRCP 1990; FRCR 1994. Registrar, Fellow and Sen. Lectr (Consultant), Royal Marsden Hosp. and Inst. Cancer Res., 1977–88; Director: Cancer Res. UK Clinical Centre (formerly ICRF Cancer Medicine Res. Unit), Leeds, 1993–; Clin. Res., ICRF, 1997–2001; Lead Clinician, then Clin. Dir, Leeds Cancer Centre, 1997–2005. Dir, Nat. Cancer Res. Network, 2001–05; Foundn Dir, Leeds Inst. of Molecular Med. and Cancer Res., 2003–06; Jt Dir, UK Clinical Res. Network, 2005–10; Sen. Investigator, NIHR, 2010–. President: British Oncol Assoc., 1992–94; Assoc. of Cancer Physicians, 2008–; Eur. Cancer Concord, 2014– (Mem., Steering Gp, 2013–); Mem. Council, Res. Strategy Cttee. Trustee, CRUK, 2012–. FMedSci 1998. Pfizer Prize for Excellence in Oncology, British Oncol Soc., 2008. *Publications:* Hodgkin's Disease, 1987; Confronting Cancer: Care and Prevention, 1993; Cancer in Adolescents, 1995; Malignant Lymphomas, 2000; Cell and Molecular Biology of Cancer, 2005; Problem Solving in Oncology, 2007; Problem Solving in Acute Oncology, 2014; Problem Solving for Older Cancer Patients, 2015. *Recreations:* reading, music, watching sport. *Address:* 17 Park Lane, Roundhay, Leeds LS8 2EX.

SELBY, Rt Rev. Peter Stephen Maurice, PhD; Bishop of Worcester, 1997–2007; *b* 7 Dec. 1941. *Educ:* St John's Coll., Oxford (BA 1964; MA 1967); Episcopal Theol Sch., Cambridge, Mass (BD 1966); Bishops' Coll., Cheshunt; PhD London, 1975. Asst Curate, Queensbury, 1966–68; Associate Dir of Training, Southwark, 1969–73; Asst Curate, Limpsfield with Titsey, 1969–77; Vice-Principal, Southwark Ordination Course, 1970–72; Asst Missioner, Dio. Southwark, 1973–77; Canon Residentiary, Newcastle Cathedral, 1977–84; Diocesan Missioner, Dio. Newcastle, 1977–84; Suffragan Bishop, 1984–91, Area Bishop, 1991–92, of Kingston-upon-Thames; William Leech Professorial Fellow in Applied Christian Theol., Univ. of Durham, 1992–97; Bishop to HM Prisons, 2001–07; Hon. Asst Bishop, dios of Durham and Newcastle, 1992–97, dio. of Portsmouth, 2008–11, dio. of Southwark, 2011–. Interim Co-Dir, St Paul's Inst., 2012–14. Visitor Gen., Community of Sisters of the Church, 1991–2001. Vis. Prof., Dept of Theol. and Religious Studies and Internat. Centre for Prison Studies, KCL, 2008–; Hon. Prof., Univ. of Worcester, 1998–. Charles Gore Lectr, Westminster Abbey, 2006; Eric Symes Abbott Lectr, Westminster Abbey and Keble Coll., Oxford, 2012; Hugh Price Hughes Lectr, 2013. Mem., Doctrine Commn, 1991–2003. Pres., Nat. Council for Ind. Monitoring Bds, 2008–13. President: Modern Churchpeople's Union, 1990–96; Soc. for Study of Theology, 2003–04. Hon. DD Birmingham, 2007. *Publications:* Look for the Living, 1976; Liberating God, 1983; BeLonging, 1991; Rescue, 1995; Grace and Mortgage, 1997; An Idol Unmasked, 2014.

SELDON, Sir Anthony (Francis), Kt 2014; PhD; FRHistS; Vice-Chancellor, University of Buckingham, since 2015; *b* 2 Aug. 1953; *s* of late Arthur Seldon, CBE and (Audrey) Marjorie Seldon (*née* Willett); *m* 1982, Joanna Pappworth; one *s* two *d*. *Educ:* Tonbridge Sch.; Worcester Coll., Oxford (MA 1980); London School of Economics (PhD 1981); KCL (PGCE 1983); MBA Poly. of Central London 1989. FRHistS 1992. Res. Fellow and Tutor, London School of Economics, 1980–81; Consultant Historian, Rio Tinto Zinc, 1981–83; Head of Politics, Whitgift Sch., 1983–86; Co-founder, 1987, and first Dir, 1987–89, Inst. of Contemporary British History; Head of History and Gen. Studies, Tonbridge Sch., 1989–92; Dep. Headmaster, 1993–97, acting Headmaster, 1997, St Dunstan's Coll.; Headmaster, Brighton Coll., 1997–2005; Master, Wellington Coll., 2006–15; Exec. Head, Wellington Acad., 2013–15. Prof. of Educn, Coll. of Teachers, 2009–. Member: Bd, RSC, 2012–; Social Integration Commn, 2014–. FRSA 1990; FKC 2013. Hon. DLitt Buckingham, 2013. Series Ed., Making Contemporary Britain, 1988. Co-founder: Contemporary Record, 1987 (Ed., 1987–95); Modern Hist. Rev., 1988 (Ed., 1989–92); Twentieth Century British Hist., 1989 (Consulting Ed., 1989–91); Contemp. European Hist., 1989 (Consulting Ed., 1989–90). Hon. DLitt Brighton, 2004. *Publications:* Churchill's Indian Summer, 1981; (jtly) By Word of Mouth, 1983; (ed) Contemporary History, 1987; (ed jtly) Ruling Performance, 1987; (ed) Political Parties since 1945, 1988; (ed jtly) Thatcher Effect, 1989; (jtly) Politics UK, 1991; (ed jtly) Conservative Century, 1994; (ed jtly) Major Effect, 1994; (ed jtly) The Heath Government 1970–74, 1996; (ed jtly) Contemporary History Handbook, 1996; (ed jtly) Ideas That Shaped Postwar Britain, 1996; (ed) How Tory Governments Fall: the Conservative Party in power since 1783, 1996; Major: a political biography, 1997; 10 Downing Street: the illustrated history, 1999; (jtly) Britain under Thatcher, 1999; (jtly) The Powers Behind the Prime Minister, 1999; The Foreign Office: an illustrated history of the place and the people, 2000; (ed) The Blair Effect, 2001; (jtly) A New Conservative Century?, 2001; Public and Private Education, 2001; Brave New City, 2002; Partnership not Paternalism, 2002; Blair: the biography, 2004; (ed jtly) Governing or New Labour, 2004; (jtly) The Conservative Party: an illustrated history, 2004; (ed jtly) Recovering Power: the Conservatives in Opposition since 1867, 2005; (ed) The Blair Effect 2, 2001–05: a wasted term?, 2005; Blair Unbound: 2001–07, 2007; (ed) Blair's Britain 1997–2007, 2007; Autonomy Lost, Autonomy Regained, 2009; Trust: how we lost it and how to get it back, 2009; An End to Factory Schools: an education manifesto 2010–2020, 2010; (jtly) Brown At 10, 2010; Why Schools? Why Universities?, 2011; The Politics of Optimism, 2011; The Great War and Public Schools, 2013; (jtly) The Architecture of Diplomacy, 2014; Schools United, 2014; Beyond Happiness, 2015; (ed jtly) The Coalition Effect 2010–2015, 2015; (jtly) Cameron at 10: the inside story 2010–15, 2015. *Recreations:* drama, sport, writing, walking, running. *Address:* University of Buckingham, Hunter Street, Buckingham MK18 1EG. *Club:* East India.

SELF, Deborah Jane; *see* Orr, D. J.

SELF, William Woodard; writer, since 1990; Professor of Contemporary Thought, Brunel University, since 2012; *b* 26 Sept. 1961; *s* of late Prof. Peter John Otter Self and of Elaine Self (*née* Rosenbloom); *m* 1st, 1989, Katharine Sylvia Chancellor (marr. diss. 1997); one *s* one *d*; 2nd, 1997, Deborah Jane Orr, *qv*; two *s*. *Educ:* Exeter Coll., Oxford (BA Hons). Freelance cartoonist, 1982–88; Publishing Dir, Cathedral Publishing, 1988–90; contributing editor, London Evening Standard mag., 1993–95; columnist: Observer, 1995–97; The Times, 1998–99; Independent on Sunday, 1999–2001; London Evening Standard, 2002–09; New Statesman, 2009–. *Publications:* The Quantity Theory of Insanity, 1991; Cock & Bull, 1992; My Idea of Fun, 1993; Grey Area, 1994; Junk Mail, 1995; The Sweet Smell of Psychosis, 1996; Great Apes, 1997; Tough Tough Toys for Tough Tough Boys, 1998; Sore Sites, 2000; How the Dead Live, 2000; Perfidious Man, 2000; Feeding Frenzy, 2001; Dorian, 2002; Dr Mukti and Other Tales of Woe, 2004; The Book of Dave, 2006; PsychoGeography, 2007; The Butt, 2008; Liver, 2008; Psycho Too, 2009; Walking to Hollywood, 2010; Umbrella, 2012; Shark, 2014. *Recreation:* walking. *Address:* The Wylie Agency, 17 Bedford Square, WC1B 3JA. *T:* (020) 7908 5900.

SELINGER, Hon. Gregory F.; MLA (NDP) Saint-Boniface, Manitoba, since 1999; Premier of Manitoba, since 2009; *b* Regina, Saskatchewan, 16 Feb. 1951; *s* of late Margaret E. Crawford; *m* 1976, Claudette Toupin; two *s*. *Educ:* Univ. of Manitoba (Bachelor Social Work); Queen's Univ. (MPA); London Sch. of Econs and Pol Sci. (PhD). Associate Prof., Faculty of Social Work, Univ. of Manitoba, 1984–99. Former Mem., St Boniface CC (Chm., Finance and Admin Cttee). Legislative Assembly of Manitoba: Minister: of Finance, 1999–2009; responsible for Francophone Affairs (formerly French Lang. Services), 1999–; charged with admin of Crown Corporations Public Rev. and Accountability Act, 1999–2009; charged with admin of Manitoba Hydro Act, 1999–2002, 2006–09; responsible for Civil Service, 2001–09; charged with admin of Liquor Control Act, 2002–03, 2007–08; charged with admin of Manitoba Lotteries Corp. Act, 2007–08; resp. for Skills Strategy; of Federal-Provincial Relns; Pres., Exec. Council, 2009–. Former Board Member: St Boniface Hosp.; St Boniface Mus.; former Pres., Old St Boniface Residents' Assoc. Coach, YMCA. *Recreations:* cycling, fishing, outdoor activities. *Address:* Office of the Premier of Manitoba, 212–450 Broadway, Winnipeg, MB R3C 0V8, Canada. *T:* (204) 9453714, *Fax:* (204) 9491484. *E:* premier@leg.gov.mb.ca.

SELKIRK, Earldom of (*cr* 1646); title disclaimed by 11th Earl (*see under* Selkirk of Douglas, Baron).

SELKIRK OF DOUGLAS, Baron *cr* 1997 (Life Peer), of Cramond in the City of Edinburgh; **James Alexander Douglas-Hamilton;** PC 1996; QC (Scot.) 1996; Lord High Commissioner, General Assembly, Church of Scotland, 2012 and 2013; *b* 31 July 1942; 2nd *s* of 14th Duke of Hamilton, and *b* of 15th Duke of Hamilton; disclaimed Earldom of Selkirk, 1994, prior to succession being determined in his favour, 1996; *m* 1974, Hon. Priscilla Susan Buchan, *d* of 2nd Baron Tweedsmuir, CBE, CD, and late Baroness Tweedsmuir of Belhelvie, PC; four *s* (incl. twins). *Educ:* Eton College; Balliol Coll., Oxford (MA, Mod. History; Oxford Boxing Blue, 1961; Pres., Oxford Univ. Cons. Assoc., 1963; Pres., Oxford Union Soc., 1964); Edinburgh Univ. (LLB, Scots Law). Cameronian Officer, 6th/7th Bn of Cameronians (Scottish Rifles), 1961–66; 2nd Bn of Lowland Vols, 1971–74, Capt., 1973. Advocate at Scots Bar and Interim Procurator Fiscal Depute, 1968–74. Town Councillor, Murrayfield-Cramond, Edinburgh, 1972–74. MP (C) Edinburgh West, Oct. 1974–1997; contested (C) same seat, 1997. Scottish Conservative Whip, 1977; a Lord Comr of HM Treasury, and Govt Whip for Scottish Cons. Mems, 1979–81; PPS to Foreign Office Minister, 1983–86, to Sec. of State for Scotland, 1986–87; Parly Under-Sec. of State for Home Affairs and the Envmt, 1987–92, for Educn and Housing, 1992–95, Scottish Office; Minister of State for Home Affairs and Health, Scottish Office, 1995–97. MSP (C) Lothians, 1999–2007. Scottish Parliament: Business Manager and Chief Whip, Conservative Gp, 1999–2001; spokesman on home affairs, 2000–03, on education, 2003–07. Captain Cameronian Co., 2 Bn Low Vols RARO, 1972–92. Hon. Air Cdre, No 2 (City of Edinburgh) Maritime HQ Unit, 1994–99; Hon. Air Cdre, 603 (City of Edinburgh) Sqn, RAAF, 1999–2015; Pres., Internat. Rescue Corps, 1995. Hon. Pres., Scottish Amateur Boxing Assoc., 1975–99; President: Royal Commonwealth Soc. in Scotland, 1979–87; Scottish Council, UNA, 1981–87. Chm., Scottish Adv. Cttee, Skillforce, 2009–. Mem. Royal Co. of Archers, Queen's Body Guard for Scotland. Patron, Hope and Homes for Children, 2002– (Chm., Edinburgh Support Gp, 2002–07); President: Scottish Veterans Garden City Assoc. Inc., 2003–; Trefoil House Charity, 2008–. *Publications:* Motive for a Mission: The Story Behind Hess's Flight to Britain, 1971; The Air Battle for Malta: the diaries of a fighter pilot, 1981, 2nd edn 1990; Roof of the World: man's first flight over Everest, 1983; The Truth About Rudolf Hess, 1993; After You, Prime Minister, 2009. *Recreations:* golf, forestry, modern history. *Heir: (to Earldom of Selkirk): s* Hon. John Andrew Douglas-Hamilton, Master of Selkirk, *b* 8 Feb. 1978. *Address:* House of Lords, SW1A 0PW. *Clubs:* Sloane; Royal Scot (Hon. Mem.) (Edinburgh); Hon. Company of Edinburgh Golfers.

See also Duke of Hamilton.

SELL, Rev. Prof. Alan Philip Frederick, DD, DLitt, PhD; FSA, FRHistS; philosopher-theologian and ecumenist; *b* 15 Nov. 1935; *s* of Arthur Philip Sell and Freda Marion Sell (*née* Bushen); British and Canadian citizen; *m* 1959, Dr Karen Elisabeth Lloyd; one *s* two *d*. *Educ:* Pewley Sch., Guildford; Univ. of Manchester (Cert Biblical Knowledge 1954; BA 1957; BD 1959; MA 1961; DD 1998); Univ. of Nottingham (PhD 1967; DLitt 2006). LTCL 1981, FTCL 1983; LGSM (Public Speaking) 1981, LGSM (Speech and Drama) 1982; LLAM 1982; FRHistS 1980. FSA, 1981–2000, 2009. Ordained, Congregational Ch, 1959; Minister: Sedbergh and Dent, 1959–64; Angel St, Worcester with Hallow and Ombersley, 1964–68; Lectr, Sen. Lectr, then Prin. Lectr, 1968–83, Coll. Counsellor, 1970–83, W Midlands Coll. of Higher Educn; Tutor, Open Univ., 1970–73; Theol Sec., World Alliance of Reformed Churches (Presbyterian and Congregational), Geneva, 1983–87; Chair of Christian Thought, Univ. of Calgary, 1988–92; Prof. of Christian Doctrine and Philosophy of Religion, United Theol Coll., Aberystwyth, 1992–2001. Service with Presbyterian Church of Wales, 1992–2001. Visiting Professor: Acadia Divinity Coll., 1996–2006; Phillips Theol Seminary, 1998; Hon. Prof., Sárospatak Theol. Acad., Hungary, 1996; Hon. Vis. Prof., Univ. of Chester, 2013–. External examiner at numerous univs. Lectures include: Simpson, Acadia, 1989; Staley, Union Coll., Ky, 1991; Congregational, London, 1991; Alfred Stocks, Liverpool, 1993; Ingram, Memphis, 1996; Davies, Wales, 2001; Protestant Dissenting Deputies, 2001; Christianity and Culture, St Francis Xavier Univ., 2003; Didsbury, Manchester, 2006. Dist. Fellow, Acadia Divinity Coll., 2005. Hon. Res. Fellow, Univ. of Wales Trinity St David, 2012–. Chairman: World Church and Mission Dept, 1980–83, and Dir of Auxiliary Trng, 1978–83, W Midlands Province, URC; Worcester Council of Churches, 1967–68; Pres., Worcester and Dist Free Church Fed. Council, 1966–67. Member: Exec. Cttee, and County Sec. for Youth and Educn, Worcs Congregational Union; Doctrine and Worship Cttee, URC, 1980–83, 1993–96, 2004–07; Doctrine Cttee, Presbyterian Church of Wales, 1993–2001. Founder: Eighteenth Century Studies Gp, Univ. of Calgary, 1988; Centre for Study of British Christian Thought, United Theol Coll., Aberystwyth, 1993; Assoc. of Denominational Historical Socs and Cognate Libraries, 1993 (Convener, 1993–2001); Pres., Sub Rosa, 2009–12. Vice-Pres., Friends of Dr Williams's Liby, 1983; Chm., Friends of the Congregational Liby, 2006–12 (Pres., 2013–). Member: Soc. for the Study of Theol., 1969 (Mem. Cttee, 1984–87); Mercersburg Soc., 1985–; Canadian Theol Soc., 1988–; Amer. Theol Soc., 1990; Chapels Soc., 1992–; Historical Societies: Congregational, 1962–; Scottish Church, 1972–; Strict Baptist, 1972–; Unitarian, 1972–; United Reformed, 1972–; Friends, 1974–; Baptist, 1975–; Wesley, 1975–; Presbyterian Ch of Wales, 1976–. Member: Yorks Rural Churches Commission, 1961–62; Sedbergh Rural DC, 1962–64. Hon. DD: Ursinus Coll., USA, 1988; Acadia, Canada, 2002; Hon. DTheol: Debrecen, Hungary, 1995; Cluj, Romania, 2003. *Publications:* Congregationalism at Worplesdon, 1822–1972, 1972; Alfred Dye, Minister of the Gospel, 1974; Robert Mackintosh, Theologian of Integrity, 1977; God Our Father, 1980; The Great Debate: Calvinism, Arminianism and Salvation, 1983; Church Discipline, 1983; Responding to Baptism: Eucharist and ministry, 1984; Church Planting: a study of Westmorland Nonconformity, 1986; Theology in Turmoil: the roots, course and significance of the Conservative-Liberal debate in modern theology, 1986; Saints: Visible, Orderly and Catholic: the Congregational idea of the Church, 1986; Defending and Declaring the Faith: some Scottish examples 1860–1920, 1987; The Philosophy of Religion 1875–1980, 1988; Aspects of Christian Integrity, 1990; Dissenting Thought and the Life of the Churches: studies in an English tradition, 1990; Rhetoric and Reality: theological reflections upon Congregationalism and its heirs, 1991; A Reformed, Evangelical, Catholic Theology: the contribution of the World Alliance of Reformed Churches 1875–1982, 1991; Conservation and Exploration in

Christian Theology, 1992; Commemorations: studies in Christian thought and history, 1993; Philosophical Idealism and Christian Belief, 1995; John Locke and the Eighteenth-Century Divines, 1997; Mill and Religion: contemporary responses to Three Essays on Religion, 1997; Christ Our Saviour, 2000; The Spirit Our Life, 2000; Reminiscence, Reflection, Reassurance, 2001; Confessing and Commending the Faith: historic witness and Apologetic Method, 2002; Philosophy, Dissent and Nonconformity 1689–1920, 2004; Mill on God: the pervasiveness and elusiveness of Mill's religious thought, 2004; Testimony and Tradition: studies in reformed and dissenting thought, 2005; Enlightenment, Ecumenism, Evangel: theological themes and thinkers 1550–2000, 2005; Nonconformist Theology in the Twentieth Century, 2006; Hinterland Theology: a stimulus to theological construction, 2008; Four Philosophical Anglicans, 2010; Convinced, Concise and Christian: the thought of Huw Parri Owen, 2011; Christ and Controversy: the person of Christ in nonconformist thought and ecclesial experience, 1600–2000, 2012; Philosophy, History and Theology: selected reviews 1975–2011, 2012; Confessing the Faith Yesterday and Today: essays reformed, dissenting and Catholic, 2013; The Theological Education of the Ministry: soundings in the British reformed and dissenting traditions, 2013; Content and Method in Christian Theology: a case study of the thought of Nels Ferré, 2014; One Ministry, Many Ministers: a case study from the reformed tradition, 2014; *edited:* Reformed and Disciples of Christ in Dialogue, 1985; Reformed Theology and the Jewish People, 1986; (jtly) Baptism, Peace and the State in the Reformed and Mennonite Traditions, 1991; Protestant Nonconformists and the West Midlands of England, 1996; P. T. Forsyth: theologian for a new millennium, 2000; (jtly) Protestant Nonconformity in the Twentieth Century, 2003; The Bible in Church, Academy and Culture: essays in honor of John Tudno Williams, 2011; The Great Ejectment of 1662: its antecedents, aftermath and ecumenical significance, 2012; *novel:* (as Isaac Owen) A Land of Pure Delight: Elijah Morgan and the Saints of Bethel, 2009; *Festschrift:* Ecumenical and Eclectic, ed Anna M. Robbins, 2007; Series Editor: Philosophy and Christian Thought 1700–1900, 1998–2000; Studies in Christian History and Thought, 2004–; Christian Doctrines in Historical Perspective, 2004–; Protestant Nonconformist Texts, 4 vols, 2006–07; dictionary articles, and articles and reviews in theol, philosophical and historical jls. *Recreations:* music (piano, organ, clarinet, saxophone), dissenting and university history, British dance bands 1930–50. *E:* alan@theolsing.co.uk.

SELLA, Prof. Andrea, DPhil; Professor of Chemistry, University College London, since 2012; *b* Milan, 20 Feb. 1961. *Educ:* Trinity Coll., Univ. of Toronto (BSc Chem. 1984; MSc Chem. 1986); Balliol Coll., Oxford (DPhil Inorganic Chem. 1990). Lectr, 1990–96, Sen. Lectr, 1996–2012, in Inorganic Chemistry, UCL. EPSRC Sen. Media Fellow, 2007–12. Founder and Mem., Gillespie Sci. Club, 2006–. Columnist, Classic Kit series, Chemistry World, 2007–. Contrib./consultant on TV progs incl. Secret Life of Chaos, 2010, Chemistry: A Volatile History, 2010, The Story of Science, 2010, Everything and Nothing, 2011, Order and Disorder, 2012; consultant and contributor, Elemental Economics, BBC World Service, 2014–. Michael Faraday Prize, Royal Soc., 2014. *Publications:* articles in acad. jls. *Recreation:* playing. *Address:* Department of Chemistry, University College London, 20 Gordon Street, WC1H 0AJ. *E:* a.sella@ucl.ac.uk. *Club:* Cycling (Hackney).

SELLAPAN, Ramanathan, (S R Nathan); President, Republic of Singapore, 1999–2011; *b* 3 July 1924; *s* of V. Sellapan and Madam Abirami; *m* 1958, Urmila, (Umi), Nandey; one *s* one *d*. *Educ:* Anglo-Chinese Primary and Middle Sch.; Rangoon Rd Afternoon Sch.; Victoria Sch.; Univ. of Malaya in Singapore (Dip. Social Studies with Dist. 1954). Clerical Service, Johore Govt (Malaya), 1945–55; Almoner, Medical Dept, Gen. Hosp., Singapore, 1955–56; Seamen's Welfare Officer, Min. of Labour, 1956–62; Asst Dir, 1962–63, Dir, 1964–66, Labour Res. Unit; Ministry of Foreign Affairs, Singapore: Asst Sec., 1966; Principal Asst Sec., 1966–67; Dep. Sec., 1967–71; Perm. Sec. (Actg), Min. of Home Affairs, 1971; Dir, Security and Intelligence Div., MoD, 1971–79; First Perm. Sec., Min. of Foreign Affairs, 1979–82; Exec. Chm., Straits Times Press, 1982–88; High Comr to Malaysia, 1988–90; Ambassador to USA, 1990–96; Ambassador-at-Large, Min. of Foreign Affairs, 1996–99; Dir, Inst. of Defence and Strategic Studies, Nanyang Technol Univ., 1996–99. Chm., Mitsubishi Singapore Heavy Industries (Pte) Ltd, 1973–86; Director: Singapore Nat. Oil Co. (Pte), 1980–88; Singapore Mint Pte, 1983–88; Singapore Press Hldgs, 1984–88; Marshall Cavendish, London, 1985–88; Singapore Internat. Media Pte, 1996–99. Chm., Hindu Endowments Bd, 1983–88; Mem. Bd of Trustees, NTUC Res. Unit, 1983–88; Founding Mem. and Trustee, Singapore Indian Develt Assoc., 1997–99. Pro-Chancellor, National Univ. of Singapore, 1996–99. Mem., Bd of Govs, CS Coll., 1997–99. Public Service Star (Singapore), 1964; Public Admin Medal (Silver) (Singapore), 1967; PJG (Meritorious Service Medal) (Singapore), 1974; Pravasi Bharatiya Samman (India), 2012; Order of Temasek (1st Class) (Singapore), 2013. *Publications:* Why Am I Here?, 2010; Winning Against the Odds, 2011; An Unexpected Journey: path to the presidency, 2012; 50 Stories From My Life, 2013; S R Nathan In Conversation, 2015. *Recreations:* walking, reading. *Address:* Katong Post Office, Box No 205, Singapore 91437.

SELLAR, Irvine; Founder and Chairman, Sellar Property Group, since 1991. Founder, Irvine Sellars Fashion Gp, 1966–81; Property Chief Exec., 1984–91. *Recreations:* judo, tennis. *Clubs:* Queen's, Annabel's, Mark's.

SELLAR, W(illiam) David H(amilton), MVO 2014; Islay Herald Extraordinary, since 2014 (Lord Lyon King of Arms and Secretary of the Order of the Thistle, 2008–14); *b* Burnside, Rutherglen, 27 Feb. 1941; *s* of William and Esther Sellar; *m* 1981, Susan Bonar (*née* Sainsbury); three *s*, and one step *s*. *Educ:* Kelvinside Acad.; Fettes Coll.; Univ. of Oxford (BA Hons Hist.); Univ. of Edinburgh (LLB). Legal Assessor, Scottish Land Court, 1967–68; Lectr, Sen. Lectr and Hon. Fellow, Faculty of Law, Univ. of Edinburgh, 1968–. Mem., Ancient Monuments Bd for Scotland, 1991–98. Sec., Co. of Scottish Hist. Ltd, 1972–77; Literary Dir, Stair Soc., 1979–84; Pres., Scottish Soc. for Northern Studies, 1984–87; Chm. Council, Scottish Hist. Soc., 1998–2001; Vice-Pres., Soc. of Antiquaries of Scotland, 1999–2002. Bute Pursuivant of Arms, 2001–08. *Publications:* articles and contribs on genealogy, history, law and legal history. *Recreations:* genealogy, golf, island hopping, numismatics. *Address:* The Court of the Lord Lyon, HM New Register House, Edinburgh EH1 3YT. *T:* (0131) 556 7255, *Fax:* (0131) 557 2148.

SELLARS, John Ernest, CBE 1994; Chief Executive, Business and Technology (formerly Business and Technician) Education Council, 1983–94; *b* 5 Feb. 1936; *s* of late Ernest Buttle Sellars and Edna Grace Sellars; *m* 1958, Dorothy Beatrice (*née* Morrison); three *d*. *Educ:* Wintringham Grammar Sch., Grimsby; Manchester Univ. (BSc, MSc). Research Engineer, English Electric (GW) Ltd, 1958–61; Lectr, Royal College of Advanced Technology (now Univ. of Salford), 1961–67; Head of Mathematics, Lanchester College of Technology, Coventry, 1967–71; Head of Computer Science, Lanchester Polytechnic, Coventry/Rugby, 1971–74; Chief Officer, Business Educn Council, 1974–83. Member: Bd, Nat. Adv. Body for Public Sector Higher Educn, 1982–88; BBC School Broadcasting Council for UK, 1982–87; City Technology Colls Trust, 1989–94; Engrg and Technol. Adv. Cttee, British Council, 1990–95; Engrg Council, 1994–95 (Mem., Standing Cttee for Engrg Profession, 1994–95); British Accreditation Council for Ind., Further and Higher Educn, 1999–2002. Mem. Exec. Cttee, RoSPA, 1994–2002. Governor, London Guildhall Univ., 1994–2000. Trustee, Gatsby Technical Educn Projects, 1999–2005. Hon. FCP 1989. DUniv Sheffield Hallam, 1994; Hon. DTech London Guildhall, 2001. *Publications:* papers on mathematics, computer science and business educn. *Recreation:* walking. *Clubs:* Reform, MCC.

SELLARS, Peter; American opera and theatre director; *b* 27 Sept. 1957. *Educ:* Phillips Acad., Mass; Harvard Univ. (BA 1980). Artistic Director: Boston Shakespeare Co., 1983–84; American Nat. Theater at Kennedy Center for the Performing Arts, 1984; LA Fest., 1990, 1993. Prof. of World Arts and Cultures, UCLA. *Productions* include: Armida, Monadnock Music Fest., 1981; The Mikado, Lyric Opera of Chicago, 1983; Così fan tutte, Castle Hill Fest., Mass, 1984; The Electrification of the Soviet Union, Glyndebourne Touring Opera, 1987; Nixon in China, Houston, 1987, ENO, 2000; Die Zauberflöte, Glyndebourne, 1990; The Death of Klinghoffer, Théâtre Royal de la Monnaie, Brussels, 1991; The Persians, Edinburgh Fest., 1993; Pelléas and Mélisande, Amsterdam, 1993; The Merchant of Venice, Barbican, 1994; Mathis der Maler, Royal Opera House, 1995; Theodora, Glyndebourne, 1996; The Rake's Progress, 1996, El Niño, 2000, L'Amour de Loin, 2001, Châtelet, Paris; Idomeneo, Glyndebourne, 2003; Tristan und Isolde, Opéra Nat. de Paris, 2005; Dr Atomic, San Francisco, 2005; Zaïde, Barbican, 2006; Othello, NY, 2009; Desdemona, Barbican, 2012; The Gospel According to the Other Mary, Coliseum, 2014; The Indian Queen, Coliseum, 2015.

SELLARS, Wendy Jane; *see* Lloyd, W. J.

SELLERS, Ann H.; *see* Henderson-Sellers.

SELLERS, Basil Alfred, AM 2003; Chairman, Sellers Group, since 1987; *b* 19 June 1935; *s* of William Alfred Sellers and Irene Ethel Sellers (*née* Freemantle); *m* 2nd, 1980, Gillian Clare Heinrich; two *s* one *d* from previous marr. *Educ:* King's College, Adelaide, SA. Clerk, State Bank of SA, 1952; Clerk, Cutten & Harvey, Adelaide, 1954–69 (Investment Advr, 1969); owner, Devon Homes, SA, 1970; bought Ralph Symonds Ltd, 1975 (Man. Dir); Chm., Gestetner plc, 1987–94. *Recreations:* cricket, art, music. *Address:* 43 William Street, Double Bay, NSW 2028, Australia. *Clubs:* MCC, Cricketers'; University (Australia).

See also E. Sellers.

SELLERS, Elizabeth, (Libby); Founder and Director, Gallery Libby Sellers, since 2007; *b* Adelaide, Australia, 1972; *d* of Basil Alfred Sellers, *qv* and Beverley Maizie Daw (*née* Addicott). *Educ:* Badminton Sch., Bristol; Univ. of East Anglia (BA Hons Hist. of Art 1994); Central St Martins (MA Journalism 1996); Royal Coll. of Art (MA Hist. of Design 1998). Asst Curator, Glasgow 1999, City of Architecture and Design, 1998; Partner, Restructure Ltd, 1999–2001; Curator, Design Mus., London, 2001–07. Patron, Rambert Dance Co., 2010–. *Publications:* Why What How: collecting design in a contemporary market, 2010. *E:* gallery@libbysellers.com.

SELLERS, Geoffrey Bernard, CB 1991; Parliamentary Counsel, 1987–2010; *b* 5 June 1947; *s* of late Bernard Whittaker Sellers and Elsie (*née* Coop); *m* 1971, Susan Margaret Faulconbridge (*d* 1995); two *s* two *d*. *Educ:* Manchester Grammar Sch. (Scholar); Magdalen Coll., Oxford (Mackinnon Scholar; BCL 1st Cl. Hons; MA). Called to the Bar, Gray's Inn, 1971 (Macaskie Scholar). Legal Assistant: Law Commn, 1971; Commn on Industrial Relations, 1971–74; Office of Parly Counsel, 1974–2010; with Law Commn, 1982–85, and 1991–93; with Inland Revenue, 1996–99. *Address:* 53 Canonbury Road, N1 2DG.

See also J. M. Sellers.

SELLERS, John Marsland, CB 2005; Parliamentary Counsel, 1998–2010; *b* 15 July 1951; *s* of late Bernard Whittaker Sellers and Elsie (*née* Coop); *m* 1975, Patricia Susan Burns; two *s*. *Educ:* Manchester Grammar Sch.; Magdalen Coll., Oxford (BA, BCL). Lecturer: Lincoln Coll., Oxford, 1973–75; LSE, 1975–77; Articled Clerk, 1977–80, Solicitor, 1980–83, Freshfields; Asst Parly Counsel, 1983–88; Sen. Asst Parly Counsel, 1988–91; Dep. Parly Counsel, 1991–98; on secondment to Law Commn, 1998–2001, to Tax Law Rewrite Project, 2007–09, to Law Commn, 2010. *Address:* Crestover, Horsell Rise, Woking, Surrey GU21 4BA. *T:* (01483) 770559.

See also G. B. Sellers.

SELLERS, Libby; *see* Sellers, E.

SELLERS, Philip Edward, CBE 2001; Director C4MA, Climate Change Capital, 2007–13; *b* 20 March 1937; *s* of George Edward and Helen Sellers; *m* 1962, Brenda Anne Bell; two *s*. *Educ:* Ernest Bailey Grammar School, Matlock; CIPFA. Local Govt, 1953–72; Controller of Audit, British Gas Corp., 1972–76; Finance Dir, North Thames Gas, 1976–80; Dir of Finance and Planning, British Rail Board, 1980–84; Board Mem. for Corporate Finance and Planning, Post Office, 1984–89. Mem., Postel Property Cttee, 1992–94; non-exec. Dir, Postel Investment Management, 1994–95; Trustee, Post Office Pension Funds, 1985–99; Chm., Audit Cttee, DTI, 1994–2003; Chm., Nuclear Decommng Prog. Bd, DTI, 2003–05. Non-executive Chairman: CSL Group, 1989–93; ICL Outsourcing Ltd (formerly CFM Group Ltd, then ICL/CFM), 1989–99; Pegasus Group plc, 1992–2000; Inner City Enterprises, 1992–98; Powerleague Soccer Centres Ltd (formerly Powerplay Supersoccer Ltd), 1995–99; Workplace Technologies plc, 1995–99; Alexander Mann Associates Ltd, 1997–2000; Dep. Chm., Powerleague Ltd, 1999–2001; non-exec. Dir, Etam Gp, 1991–98; Advr, Nomura Asset Mgt, 2002–07. UK rep., IFAC Public Sector Cttee, 1987–90; Philip Sellers Communications and Consultancy, 1989–2010. Mem., NCC Impact Adv. Bd, 1989–92. Pres., CIPFA, 1985–86; Chm., Nationalised Industries Finance Panel, 1986–89. Non-exec. Dir, London Festival Orch., 1994–98. *Recreations:* tennis, ski-ing. *Address:* Magnolia, School Lane, Seer Green, Bucks HP9 2QJ.

SELLIER, Robert Hugh, FICE; Chief Executive, Y. J. Lovell, 1991–95; *b* 15 Nov. 1933; *s* of Major Philip Joseph Sellier and Lorna Geraldine Sellier (*née* Luxton); *m* 1st, 1963, Cynthia Ann Dwelly (*d* 1985); one *d*; 2nd, 1987, Gillian Dalley (*née* Clark). *Educ:* St Joseph's Coll., Oxford; King's Coll., Durham Univ. (BScCivEng). FCIHT. Man. Dir, New Ideal Homes, 1972–74; Dep. Man. Dir, Cementation International, 1974–79; Man. Dir, Cementation Construction, 1979–83; Chm., Cementation Gp of Companies, 1983–86; Gp Man. Dir, George Wimpey, 1986–91. Non-exec. Dir, Hyder plc, 1993–2000. *Recreations:* ski-ing, shooting, scuba, flying. *Address:* Mullions, 4 Trulls Hatch, Argos Hill, Rotherfield, Crowborough, E Sussex TN6 3QL. *T:* (01892) 853752.

SELLS, (Edward) Andrew (Perronet), FCA; Chairman, Natural England, since 2014; *b* 30 Nov. 1948; *s* of Sir David Perronet Sells and Beryl Cecilia Sells (*née* Charrington); *m* 1st, 1997, Kate Hatch (marr. diss.); one *s* one *d*; 2nd, 2015, Marina, (Mini), Dumas, *d* of late Allan Heyman, QC and Anne-Marie Castenschiold, of Denmark. *Educ:* St Peter's, Seaford; Wellington Coll.; London Business Sch. (MSc 1988). FCA 1972. With Schroders Gp, 1972–82; Man. Dir, venture capital funds, 1983–2000, incl. Man. Dir, Sovereign Capital Ltd, 1990–2000. Chairman: Linden plc, 1992–2007; Westerleigh Gp, 1992–2003; Garden Centre Gp (Wyevale), 2009–13. Advr on Work Prog. to Minister of State, DWP, 2013–15 (Chair, Best Practice Gp, 2013–15). Trustee: RHS, 2003–10 (Hon. Treas., 2008–10); Policy Exchange, 2007–13; Open Europe, 2011–13. Co-Treas., No2AV Campaign, 2011. *Recreations:* cricket, travel, trees. *Address:* Sandy Farm, Sopworth, Chippenham, Wilts SN14 6PP.

See also O. M. Sells.

SELLS, Oliver Matthew; QC 1995; a Recorder of the Central Criminal Court, since 2008 (Crown Court, 1991–2008); *b* 29 Sept. 1950; *s* of Sir David Perronet Sells and Beryl Cecilia Sells (*née* Charrington); *m* 1986, Lucinda Jane, *d* of late Gerard William Mackworth-Young and Lady Eve Mackworth-Young; one *s* one *d*. *Educ:* St Peter's, Seaford; Wellington Coll.; Coll. of Law, London. Mem., Hon. Soc. of Inner Temple, 1969–; called to the Bar, Inner Temple, 1972, Bencher, 1996; SE Circuit, 1974–; Supplementary Counsel to the Crown, 1981–86. Chm., SE Circuit Liaison Cttee, 1998–2007. Member: Gen. Council of the Bar, 1977–80 and 1986–91; Commonwealth Law Assoc. (Legal Advr, 2008–); Chair: Symposium on Economic Crime, Cambridge Univ., 2008–; Open Europe, 2008. Mem. Council,

Conservative Policy Forum, 2011–. Hon. Mem., Amer. Bar Assoc.; Dir, Music for Charity. Trustee, Breckland Soc. *Recreations:* mediaeval wall paintings, travel, dendrology. *Address:* 5 Paper Buildings, Temple, EC4Y 7HB. *T:* (020) 7583 6117. *Clubs:* Boodle's, MCC; Norfolk (Norwich); Royal West Norfolk Golf.

See also E. A. P. Sells.

SELLS, Robert Anthony, FRCS, FRCSE; Consultant Surgeon, Royal Liverpool University Hospital (formerly Liverpool Royal Infirmary), 1970–2005; *b* 13 April 1938; *s* of late Rev. William Blyth Sells and Eleanor Mary Sells; *m* 1st, 1964, Elizabeth Lucy Schryver (marr. diss. 1976); two *s* one *d*; 2nd, 1977, Pauline Gilchrist Muir; two *s*. *Educ:* Christ's Hosp. Sch., Horsham; Guy's Hosp. Med. Sch., Univ. of London (MB BS). FRCS 1966; FRCSE 1966. Lecturer, Department of Surgery: Guy's Hosp. Med. Sch., 1966–67; Univ. of Cambridge, 1967–69; MRC Travelling Schol., Univ. of Harvard, 1969–70; Dir of Transplantation, 1970–97, Dir of Surgery, 1997–99, Royal Liverpool Univ. Hosp.; Hon. Prof. of Surgery and Immunology, Univ. of Liverpool, 1998–. Vis. Professor: Detroit Univ., 1977; Adelaide Univ., 1984; Minnesota Univ., 1984–85; London Univ., 1998. Gen. Sec. and Pres., British Transplantation Society, 1978–86; Mem. Council, Chm. of Ethics Cttee and Vice Pres., The Transplantation Soc., 1986–94; Vice Pres., Inst. of Med. Ethics, 1986–2007; Co-Founder and Chm., Internat. Forum for Transplant Ethics, 1995–; Pres., Liverpool Med. Instn, 1997–98 (Mem., 1972–). Expert Witness, 1982–. Principal Conductor and Musical Dir, Crosby SO, 1982–2014, now Conductor Laureate; Founder and Dir, Vale of Clwyd Singers, 2010–; Hon. Pres., Aberwheeler Show, 1995. Hon. Fellow, Amer. Soc. of Transplant Surgeons, 1978–. Liveryman, Livery Co. of Wales (formerly Welsh Livery Guild), 2009–. *Publications:* (ed jtly) Transplantation Today, 1983; (ed jtly) Organ Transplantation: Current Clinical and Immunological Concepts, 1989; papers on transplantation and bioethics in med. jls. *Recreations:* collecting Victorian pickle jars, orchestral and choral conducting. *Address:* Cil Llwyn, Llandyrnog, Denbighshire LL16 4HY. *T:* (01745) 710296. *Clubs:* Moynihan Chirurgical Travelling (Pres., 2000–01), Twenty (Liverpool); Cheshire Pitt.

SELLWOOD, Philip Henry George; Chief Executive, Energy Saving Trust, since 2003; *b* 10 Jan. 1954; *s* of Albert Edward Sellwood and Irene Sellwood; *m* 1977, Lynn Ann Harris (marr. diss. 2005); one *s* one *d*; partner, Susan Hollis; one *d*. *Educ:* Nottingham Univ. (BEd); Univ. of Westminster (MBA Dist.). Marks & Spencer plc, 1977–2000: Commercial Exec.; Dir, Gp Strategy, 1998–2000; Man. Dir, Thresher Gp, 2000–02. Non-executive Director: Veos plc, 1999–2002; Marks & Spencer Financial Services, 1998–2001; Criminal Records Bureau, 2000–03; Local Govt Improvement and Develt (formerly Improvement and Develt Agency), 2002–; Renewable Energy Assurance Ltd, 2013–. Dir, Low Carbon Vehicle Partnership, 2005– (Dep. Chair, 2013); Member: Adv. Bd, Nat. Consumer Council, 2003–09; Sustainable Bldgs Task Force, 2004–05; UK Energy Res. Council, 2005–; LGA Climate Commn, 2007–09. Trustee, Ellen Macarthur Foundn, 2009–. FCMI; FRSA. *Recreations:* reading, wine, cricket, the arts. *Address:* The Beach House, 30 Val Prinseps Road, Pevensey Bay, E Sussex BN24 6JG. *T:* (01323) 762064, 07831 829888. *E:* philip_sellwood@hotmail.com.

SELOUS, Andrew Edmund Armstrong; MP (C) South West Bedfordshire, since 2001; Parliamentary Under-Secretary of State, Ministry of Justice, and an Assistant Government Whip, since 2014; *b* 27 April 1962; *s* of late Gerald M. B. Selous, OBE, VRD, and Miranda Selous (*née* Casey); *m* 1993, Harriet Marston; three *d*. *Educ:* London Sch. of Econs (BSc Econ). ACII 1993. Great Lakes Re (UK) PLC, 1991–2001. Served TA, HAC and RRF, 1981–94. *Recreation:* family life. *Address:* House of Commons, SW1A 0AA. *Clubs:* Leighton Buzzard Conservative, Dunstable Conservative.

SELSDON, 3rd Baron *cr* 1932, of Croydon; **Malcolm McEacharn Mitchell-Thomson;** Bt 1900; banker; Exploitant Vini-Viticole, Provence, France, since 1987; *b* 27 Oct. 1937; *s* of 2nd Baron Selsdon (3rd Bt, *cr* 1900), DSC; *S* father, 1963; *m* 1st, 1965, Patricia Anne (marr. diss.), *d* of Donald Smith; one *s*; 2nd, 1995, Gabrielle Tesseron (*née* Williams). *Educ:* Winchester College. Sub-Lieut, RNVR. Deleg. to Council of Europe and WEU, 1972–78. C. T. Bowring Gp, 1972–76; Midland Bank Group, 1976–90: EEC Advr, 1979–85; Public Finance Advr, 1985–90. Dir of various companies. Chm., Committee for Middle East Trade (COMET), 1979–86; Member: BOTB, 1983–86; E European Trade Council, 1985–87. Pres., British Exporters Assoc., 1990–98. Elected Mem., H of L, 1999. Chm., Greater London and SE Regional Council for Sport and Recreation, 1977–83. *Recreations:* rackets, squash, tennis, lawn tennis, ski-ing, sailing. *Heir: s* Hon. Callum Malcolm McEacharn Mitchell-Thomson [*b* 7 Nov. 1969; *m* 1999, Vanessa, *d* of Stefan Glasmacher; one *s* one *d*]. *Address:* c/o House of Lords, SW1A 0PW. *Club:* MCC.

SELTEN, Prof. Reinhard J., PhD; Professor of Economics, University of Bonn, 1984–96, now Emeritus; Research Co-ordinator, Laboratory for Experimental Research in Economics, University of Bonn, since 1984; *b* 5 Oct. 1930; *s* of Adolf Selten and Käthe Selten; *m* 1959, Elisabeth. *Educ:* Univ. of Frankfurt (Dip. Maths; PhD Maths 1961). Asst posts in econs, Frankfurt, 1975–67; Vis. Prof., Schs of Business Admin, Univ. of Calif., Berkeley, 1967–68; privat docent, econs, Frankfurt, 1968–69; Professor of Economics: Berlin, 1969–72; Bielefeld, 1972–84. Fellow: Econometric Soc.; European Economic Assoc. Hon. PhD (Economics): Bielefeld, 1989; Frankfurt, 1991; Graz, 1996; Breslau, 1996; UEA, 1997; Hon. Dr: Ecole Normale Supérieure de Cachan, Paris, 1998; Innsbruck, 2000; Chinese Univ. of Hong Kong, 2003; Osnabrück, 2006. (Jtly) Nobel Prize in Economics, 1994. Bundesverdienstkreuz am Band mit Stern (Germany); Verdienstorden für Wissenschaft und Kunst (Germany), 2006. *Publications:* Preispolitik der Mehrproduktenunternehmung in der Statischen Theorie, 1970; (with T. H. Marschak) General Equilibrium with Price Making Firms, 1974; Models of Strategic Rationality, 1988; (with John C. Harsanyi) A General Theory of Equilibrium Selection in Games, 1988. *Recreation:* hiking. *Address:* Laboratory for Experimental Research in Economics, University of Bonn, Adenauerallee 24-42, 53113 Bonn, Germany.

SELVANAYAGAM, Rev. Dr Israel; Professor of Religions, Gurukul Lutheran Theological College, since 2010; *b* 10 March 1951; *s* of Samuel and Nallathai Selvanayagam; *m* 1977, Gnana Leelal; two *d*. *Educ:* Kerala Univ. (MA); Serampore Coll. (BD 1978; DTh 1990); Tamilnadu Theol Seminary. Probationer in church ministry, Kanyakumari dio., Ch of S India, 1969–73; ministerial training, 1973–77; on staff of Tamilnadu Theol Seminary, Madurai, S India, teaching religions, mission and inter-faith dialogue with special responsibilities in lay theol educn, prog. on dialogue and editing Tamil theol books, 1977–96; ordained deacon, 1980, presbyter, 1981; World Ch Tutor, World Ch in Britain Partnership, Wesley Coll., Bristol, 1996–2000; Principal, United Coll. of the Ascension, Birmingham, 2001–06; Interfaith Consultant, Heartlands Team of Elmdon Circuit, Birmingham Dist of Methodist Ch, 2006; Principal, United Theol Coll., Bangalore, 2008–09. Advr for Inter-faith Dialogue, WCC, 1991–98. *Publications:* A Dialogue on Dialogue, 1995; The Dynamics of Hindu Religious Traditions, 1996; Gospel and Culture in Tamilnadu, 1996; Vedic Sacrifice, 1996; A Second Call: ministry and mission in a multifaith milieu, 2000; (ed) Moving Forms of Theology, 2002; Relating to People of Other Faiths, 2004; Being Evangelical and Dialogical: healthy balance in a multifaith context, 2012; (jtly) Glimpses of Life through the Bible (booklets), 2012–; The Last Week of Jesus (in Tamil), 2015; contribs to learned jls incl. Asian Jl Theol., Current Dialogue. *Recreations:* music, composing Tamil songs, swimming, early morning fast walking 6 days a week.

SELVARATNAM, Vasanti Emily Indrani, (Mrs P. Capewell); QC 2001; a Recorder, since 2000; *b* 9 April 1961; *d* of late George H. Selvaratnam and Wendy L. Selvaratnam (*née* Fairclough); *m* 1989, Phillip Capewell; one *s*. *Educ:* King's Coll., London (AKC 1982; LLB Hons 1982, LLM 1st Cl. 1984); Inns of Court Sch. of Law. Called to the Bar, Middle Temple, 1983, Bencher, 2011; in practice as barrister, specialising in commercial and shipping law, 1985–; Asst Recorder, Western Circuit, 1999–2000. *Recreations:* fine dining, foreign travel, horse riding. *Address:* (chambers) Stone Chambers, 4 Field Court, Gray's Inn, WC1R 5EF. *T:* (020) 7440 6900. *Clubs:* Royal Automobile; Phyllis Court (Henley-on-Thames).

SELVEY, Michael Walter William; Cricket Correspondent, The Guardian, since 1987; *b* 25 April 1948; *s* of late Walter Edwin Selvey and Edith Milly Selvey; *m* 1st, 1970, Mary Evans (marr. diss. 1991); one *d*; 2nd, 1992, Sarah (*née* Taylor); two *s* one *d* (triplets). *Educ:* Battersea Grammar Sch.; Univ. of Manchester (BSc Geog.); Emmanuel Coll., Cambridge (Cert Ed). Professional cricketer: Middlesex, 1972–82; Glamorgan, 1983–84 (Capt.); played 3 Tests for England: two *v* West Indies, 1976; one *v* India, 1977. Journalist, Guardian, 1985–. *Publications:* The Ashes Surrendered, 1989. *Recreations:* golf, fitness, cooking, real ale, crosswords, garden, children, guitar. *Address:* c/o The Guardian, Kings Place, 90 York Way, N1 9AG. *Club:* Woburn Golf and Country.

SELWAY, Mark Wayne; Chief Executive, IMI plc, since 2014; *b* Adelaide, Australia, 2 June 1959; *s* of Vernon and Dawn Selway; *m* 1985, Catherine Piper; twin *s* one *d*. *Educ:* Westminster Sch., Adelaide. Pres., Britax Rainsfords Inc., USA, 1989–94; Board Member: Britax Rear Vision Systems, 1995–96; Britax Internat. Plc, 1996–2000; Shefenacker Internat. AG, 2000–01; Chief Executive: Weir Group plc, 2001–09; Boral Ltd, 2010–13. Non-exec. Dir, Lend Lease, 2008–10. Mem., Efficient Govt Adv. Bd, Scottish Enterprise, 2003–06. *Address:* IMI plc, Lakeside, Solihull Parkway, Birmingham Business Park, Birmingham B37 7XZ.

SELWOOD, His Honour Maj.-Gen. David Henry Deering; a Circuit Judge, 1992–2004; Resident Judge, Portsmouth Crown Court, 1996–2004; *b* 27 June 1934; *s* of late Comdr George Deering Selwood, RN, and Enid Marguerite Selwood (*née* Rowlinson); *m* 1973, Barbara Dorothea (*née* Hütter); three *s* one *d*. *Educ:* Kelly Coll., Tavistock; University College of the South-West; Law Society's School of Law. Articled to G. C. Aldhouse, Esq., Plymouth, 1952–57; admitted Solicitor 1957; National Service, RASC 2/Lieut, 1957–59; private practice, Plymouth, 1959–61; TA 4 Devons, Lieut, 1959–61; commnd Army Legal Services Staff List, 1961; service on legal staffs, MoD, Headquarters: BAOR, MELF, FARELF, UKLF, Land Forces Cyprus, 1961–85; Brig., Legal, HQ BAOR, 1986–90; Dir of Army Legal Services, MoD, 1990–92. Asst Recorder, SE Circuit, 1980, Recorder, 1985–92. Dep. Col Comdt, AGC, 1996–2003. Hon. Advocate, US Court of Military Appeals, 1972. *Publications:* (jtly) Criminal Law and Psychiatry, 1987; (ed jtly) Crown Court Index, 1996–2004.

SELWOOD, Prof. Sara Michel, PhD; independent cultural analyst, since 2008; *b* 3 Aug. 1953; *d* of Maurice David Selwood and Cordelia Selwood; *m* 1994, Russell Southwood. *Educ:* Putney High Sch.; Univ. of Newcastle (BA 1st cl. Hons Fine Arts 1974); Univ. of Essex (MPhil Hist. and Theory of Art 1979); Univ. of Westminster (PhD 2005). Director: AIR Gall., London, 1986–89; Art & Society, London, 1989–91; Res. Fellow, 1991–95, Hd of Cultural Prog., 1995–98, Policy Studies Inst.; Quintin Hogg Res. Fellow, then Principal Lectr, Sch. of Media, Arts and Design, Univ. of Westminster, 1998–2005; Prof. of Cultural Policy and Mgt, 2005–08, Hon. Prof., 2010–, City Univ. Hon. Prof., Inst. of Archaeology, UCL, 2009–. Trustee, NPG, 2002–10; Bd Mem., MLA, 2006–07; Chm., Portrait Trust, 2012–. Editor, Cultural Trends, 1996–. *Publications:* The Benefits of Public Art: the polemics of permanent art in public places, 1995; The UK Cultural Sector: profile and policy issues, 2001; frequent contribs to learned jls incl. Cultural Trends. *Recreations:* food, films, biology, visiting museums and galleries, travel. *Address:* 54 Walnut Tree Walk, SE11 6DN. *E:* s.selwood@city.ac.uk.

SEMKEN, John Douglas, CB 1980; MC 1944; Legal Adviser to the Home Office, 1977–83; *b* 9 Jan. 1921; *s* of Wm R. Semken and Mrs B. R. Semken (*née* Craymer); *m* 1952, Edna Margaret, *yr d* of T. R. Poole; three *s*. *Educ:* St Albans Sch.; Pembroke Coll., Oxford (MA, BCL). Solicitor's articled clerk, 1938–39. Commnd in Sherwood Rangers Yeo., 1940; 1st Lieut 1941, Captain 1942, Major 1944; 8th Armd Bde, N Africa, 1942–43; Normandy beaches to Germany, 1944. Called to Bar, Lincoln's Inn, 1949; practised at Chancery Bar, 1949–54; joined Legal Adviser's Br., Home Office, 1954; Mem., Criminal Law Revision Cttee, 1980–83. Silver Star Medal (USA), 1944. *Address:* 4 Mariner's Court, Victoria Road, Aldeburgh IP15 5EH. *T:* (01728) 453754.

SEMMENS, Victor William; Partner, Eversheds Solicitors, until 2002 (Chairman, 1989–96; Director of International Business, 1998–2002); *b* 10 Oct. 1941; *s* of Ronald William Semmens and Cecile Maude Semmens; *m* 1964, Valerie Elizabeth Norton; two *s*. *Educ:* Blundell's. Qualified Solicitor, 1964; Partner, Wells & Hind, subseq. Eversheds, Nottingham, 1968–2002. Various non-exec. directorships, 2002–. Chm., Nottingham Library, Bromley House, 2002–. *Recreations:* golf, tennis, ski-ing, bowls. *Address:* 12 Park Valley, Nottingham NG7 1BQ.

SEMPER, Very Rev. Colin (Douglas); Canon of Westminster, 1987–97; House for Duty Priest, Parish of Frensham, 2003–06; *b* 5 Feb. 1938; *s* of William Frederick and Dorothy Anne Semper; *m* 1962, Janet Louise Greaves (*d* 2011); two *s*. *Educ:* Lincoln School; Keble College, Oxford (BA); Westcott House, Cambridge. Curate of Holy Trinity with St Mary, Guildford, 1963–66; Recruitment and Selection Sec., ACCM, 1966–69; Head of Religious Programmes, BBC Radio, and Deputy Head of Religious Broadcasting, BBC, 1969–82; Provost of Coventry Cathedral, 1982–87. Hon. Chaplain, 1985–, Freeman, 1991, Liveryman, 1991–, Feltmakers' Co. *Recreations:* travel, reading modern novels, canals, golf. *Address:* 9 St Marys Cottages, Frensham, Surrey GU10 3EA. *E:* colin.semper@btinternet.com.

SEMPILL, family name of **Baron Sempill**.

SEMPILL, 21st Baron *cr* 1489; **James William Stuart Whitemore Sempill;** Marketing Consultant, since 2006; Director, Panalba.Ltd, 2009–11; Scottish heritage tour guide, since 2012; *b* 25 Feb. 1949; *s* of Lady Sempill (20th in line), and Lt-Col Stuart Whitemore Chant-Sempill (*d* 1991); *S* mother, 1995; *m* 1977, Josephine Ann Edith, *e d* of J. Norman Rees, Kelso; one *s* one *d*. *Educ:* The Oratory School; St Clare's Hall, London (BA Hons History, 1971); Hertford Coll., Oxford. Gallaher Ltd, 1972–80; PA to Man. Dir, Sentinel Engineering Pty Ltd, Johannesburg, 1980–81; Manager, TWS Public Relations Company, Johannesburg, 1981–83; investment manager, Alan Clarke and Partners, 1982–83; Marketing Manager, S African Breweries, 1983–86; Account Director: Bates Wells (Pty), 1986; Partnership in Advertising, Johannesburg, 1988–90; Client Service Dir, Ogilvy & Mather, Cape Town, 1990–92; Trade Marketing Dir, 1993–95, Dir, Special Projects, 1995, Scottish & Newcastle; Sales and Marketing Manager, Angus Distillers plc, 2001–03; Dir of Marketing, Caledonian Brewing Co. Ltd, Edinburgh, 2003–06. Chm., Edinburgh N and Leith Cons. Assoc., 1999–2001. Contested (C) Edinburgh N and Leith, Scottish Parly elecn, 1999; Prosp. Scottish Parly Cand. (C) Edinburgh Central, 2006–07. Member: Standing Council of Scottish Chiefs, 1996– (Vice-Convenor, 2005–11); Bd, American Scottish Foundn, 2011–. Moderator, High Constabulary of Port of Leith, 2015–16. *Heir: s* Master of Sempill, *qv*.

SEMPILL, Master of; Hon. Francis Henry William Forbes Sempill; Investment Manager and Head of Client Service (formerly Investment Manager), Walter Scott & Partners Ltd, Edinburgh, since 2001; *b* 4 Jan. 1979; *s* and *heir* of Baron Sempill, *qv*; *m* 2010, Robin Anna, *er d* of Donald Strathairn, Aberfeldy; one *s* one *d*. *Educ:* Western Province Prep. Sch., Cape Town; Merchiston Castle Sch., Edinburgh; Napier Univ., Edinburgh. *Recreations:* cricket, golf, travel. *Address:* Kevock Bank House, Kevock Road, Lasswade EH18 1HX.

SEMPLE, Andrew Greenlees; *b* 16 Jan. 1934; *s* of late William Hugh Semple and Madeline, *d* of late E. H. Wood, Malvern, Worcs; *m* 1st, 1961, Janet Elizabeth Whates (*d* 1993); one *s* one *d*; 2nd, 2000, Susan Lucy Jacobs. *Educ:* Winchester Coll.; St John's Coll., Cambridge (MA). Entered Min. of Transport and Civil Aviation, 1957; Private Sec. to Permanent Sec., 1960–62; Principal, 1962; Asst Sec., 1970; Private Sec. to successive Secs of State for the Environment, 1972–74; Under Sec., DoE, 1976; Principal Finance Officer, PSA, DoE, 1980–83; Sec., Water Authorities Assoc., 1983–87; Man. Dir, Anglian Water Authority, 1987–89; Gp Man. Dir, 1989–90, Vice-Chm., 1990–92, Anglian Water plc. Mem., Bd, Eureau, 1983–92. Chm., Huntingdonshire Enterprise Agency, 1990–2001. Governor: Huntingdonshire Regl Coll., 1992–2002; Kimbolton Sch., 2001–08. Trustee, Plumstead Almshouses, 2001–13. Hon. Mem., IWO (AWO, 1988). FCIWEM 1994. *Recreations:* reading, gardens, watching cricket. *Address:* 14 Druce Road, SE21 7DW. *T:* (020) 8693 8202. *Club:* Surrey CC.

SEMPLE, Sir John (Laughlin), KCB 2000 (CB 1993); Head of Northern Ireland Civil Service, 1997–2000; Director, Northern Ireland Affairs for Royal Mail Group (known as Consignia, 2001–02), 2001–06; *b* 10 Aug. 1940; *s* of late James E. Semple and Violet E. G. Semple; *m* 1970, Maureen Anne Kerr; two *s* one *d*. *Educ:* Campbell Coll., Belfast; Corpus Christi Coll., Cambridge (MA); BScEcon London. Joined Home CS as Asst Principal, Min. of Aviation, 1961; transf. to NI CS, 1962; Asst Principal, Mins of Health and Local Govt, Finance, and Health and Social Services, 1962–65; Dep. Principal, Min. of Health and Social Services, 1965; Principal: Min. of Finance, 1968; Min. of Community Relations, 1970–72; Asst Sec. (Planning), Min. of Develt, 1972; Asst Sec. (Housing), DoE, 1977–79; Under Sec. (Housing), DoE for N Ireland, 1979–83; Under Sec., 1983–88, Permanent Sec., 1988–97, Dept of Finance and Personnel for NI; Second Perm. Under-Sec. of State, NI Office, 1998–99; Sec. to Exec. Cttee, NI Assembly, 1999–2000. *Recreations:* golf, gardening, reading.

SEMPLE, Margaret Olivia, (Maggie), OBE 2000; Chief Executive and Director, The Experience Corps, since 2001; owner, Maggie Semple Ltd, since 2010; *b* 30 July 1954; *d* of Robert Henry Semple and Olivia Victorine Semple. *Educ:* Shelborne High Sch. for Girls; Worcester Coll. of Higher Educn (BEd); Univ. of London (Advanced Dip.); Univ. of Sussex (MA). Teacher, Hd of Performing Arts, Inspector, ILEA, 1975–88; Dir, Educn and Trng, Arts Council of GB, 1989–97; Dir, Learning Experience, New Millennium Experience Co., 1997–2001. Civil Service Comr, Cabinet Office, 2001–07. Non-executive Director: HM Court Service, 2007–08; Criminal Cases Rev. Commn, 2011–. Member: DfES Nat. Curriculum PE Working Gp, 1989–90; DfES Widening Participation Cttee, 1995–97; DfES Lifelong Learning Cttee, 2001–02; DfES e-learning Task Gp, 2002–03. Fellow, British American Project, 1992; Expert: EC Cttee, 1994–97; European Cultural Centre, Delphi, 1997–2000; Council of Europe Young People's Cttee, 1998–2000. Member: Commonwealth Inst. Educn Cttee, 1992–94; All Souls Educn Gp, All Souls Coll., Oxford, 1994–; TTA, 2000–03; Women's Liby, 2000–04; De Montfort Univ., 2000–; Inst. of Educn, London, 2003–11; Adv. Bd, Arts Council London, 2003–06; Council, C&G, 2006–; Pres., Laban Guild, 1994–2000; Chairman: Nat. Youth Music Th., 2002–12; Nat. Res. and Develt Centre, 2004–11; Wolfson Welcome Dana Centre, 2004–11. Ext. Examr, Liverpool Inst. for Performing Arts, 1997–2000. Trustee: Barnardo's, 1997–2000; RSA, 1998–2003 (Council Mem., 1992–98); Rambert Dance Th., 1998–2006; Roundhouse Trust, 2000–06; Arts Educnl Schs Trust, 2000–10; Nat. Mus of Sci. and Ind., 2003–11; Balance Foundn for Unclaimed Assets, 2004–07; British Library, 2007–15. Mem. Bd, South Bank Arts Centre, 2011–. Sen. Associate, King's Fund, 2001–04. Governor: Brit Sch., 2000–; Sadler's Wells Th., 2005–11. Mem. Bd, South Bank Univ., 2011–12. FCGI 2005. Hon. DEd De Montfort, 2000. *Recreations:* being an entrepreneur, reading. *Address:* The Experience Corps Ltd, 4 Goodwins Court, WC2N 4LL. *E:* maggie.semple@experience-corps.co.uk.

SEMPLE, Maj. Gen. Richard James, CBE 2014; Director Information, Army Headquarters, since 2015; *b* Plymouth, 26 Aug. 1964; *s* of William John Semple and Judith Mary Semple; *m* 1992, Hilary Wylie; one *s* one *d*. *Educ:* Sir Roger Manwood's Sch., Sandwich; Hatfield Poly. (BSc); RMA Sandhurst; Cranfield Univ. (MBA). Commnd RE, 1986; CO 32 Engr Regt, 2003–06; DACOS Commnd Battlespace Management HQ Land Forces, 2006–08; ACOS J6 PJHQ, 2008–11; Brig. Gen. Staff, 2011–13; Dir Gen. Logistic Support and Equipment, 2013–15. *Recreations:* walking, running, ski-ing, field sports. *E:* richardsemple@live.co.uk.

SEMPLE, Prof. Stephen John Greenhill, MD, FRCP; Senior Research Investigator, Department of Respiratory Medicine, Imperial College London, 2000–06; Professor Emeritus of Medicine, Imperial College London, 2006; *b* 4 Aug. 1926; *s* of late John Edward Stewart and Janet Semple; *m* 1961, Penelope Ann, *y d* of Sir Geoffrey Aldington, KBE, CMG; three *s*. *Educ:* Westminster; London Univ. MB, BS, 1950, MD 1952, FRCP 1968. Research Asst, St Thomas' Hosp. Med. Sch., 1952; Jun. Med. Specialist, RAMC, Malaya, 1953–55; Instr, Med. Sch., Univ. of Pennsylvania, USA, 1957–59; St Thomas' Hospital Medical School: Lectr, 1959; Sen. Lectr, 1961; Reader, 1965; Prof. in Medicine, 1969; Prof. of Medicine, The Middlesex Hosp. Medical Sch., 1970–87; Prof. of Medicine and Hd, Dept of Medicine, UCL, 1987–91, now Prof. Emeritus. Vis. Prof. of Medicine, Imperial Coll. Sch. of Medicine (at Charing Cross Hosp.), 1991–2000, now Emeritus Prof. Hon. Consultant Physician, Hammersmith Hosps NHS Trust, 1991–2005. Jt Course Leader for respiratory section, Life Support Systems, for 1st year med. students, Imperial College London, 2010–. British Thoracic Soc. Medal, 2009. *Publications:* Disorders of Respiration, 1972; articles in: Lancet, Jl Physiol. (London), Jl Applied Physiol. *Recreations:* tennis, music. *Address:* White Lodge, 3 Claremont Park Road, Esher, Surrey KT10 9LT. *T:* (01372) 465057. *Club:* Queen's.

SEN, Prof. Amartya Kumar, Bharat Ratna, 1999; Hon. CH 2000; FBA 1977; Professor of Economics and Philosophy and Lamont University Professor, Harvard University, 1988–98 and since 2004 (Emeritus Professor, 1998–2003); *b* 3 Nov. 1933; *s* of late Dr Ashutosh Sen, Dhaka, and of Amita Sen, Santiniketan, India; *m* 1st, 1960, Nabaneeta Dev (marr. diss. 1975); two *d*; 2nd, 1978, Eva Colorni (*d* 1985); one *s* one *d*; 3rd, 1991, Emma Rothschild, *qv*. *Educ:* Calcutta Univ.; Trinity Coll., Cambridge (MA, PhD; Hon. Fellow, 1991). Prof. of Economics, Jadavpur Univ., Calcutta, 1956–58; Trinity Coll., Cambridge: Prize Fellow, 1957–61; Staff Fellow, 1961–63; Professor of Economics: Delhi Univ., 1963–71 (Chm., Dept of Economics, 1966–68, Hon. Prof., 1971–); LSE, 1971–77; Oxford Univ., 1977–80; Fellow, Nuffield College, Oxford, 1977–80 (Associate Mem., 1980–89; Hon. Fellow, 1998); Drummond Prof. of Political Economy, and Fellow, All Souls Coll., Oxford, 1980–88 (Distinguished Fellow, 2005); Sen. Fellow, Harvard Soc. of Fellows, 1989–98; Master, Trinity Coll., Cambridge, 1998–2004; Chancellor and Chm. Bd of Governors, Nalanda Univ., 2012–15. Hon. Dir, Agricultural Economics Research Centre, Delhi, 1966–68 and 1969–71. Res. Advr, World Inst. for Develt Econ. Res., Helsinki, Finland, 1985–93; Special Advr to Sec. Gen. of UN, 2001–. Visiting Professor: MIT, 1960–61; Univ. of Calif at Berkeley, 1964–65; Harvard Univ., 1968–69; Andrew D. White Professor-at-large, Cornell Univ., 1978–84. Chm., UN Expert Gp Meeting on Role of Advanced Skill and Technology, New York, 1967. President: Develt Studies Assoc., 1980–82; Econometric Soc., 1984 (Fellow 1968–, Vice-Pres. 1982–83); Internat. Economic Assoc., 1986–89 (Hon. Pres., 1989); Indian Econ. Assoc., 1989; Amer. Econ. Assoc., 1994; Soc. for Social Choice and Welfare, 1993–94; Vice-Pres., Royal Economic Soc., 1988– (Mem. Council, 1977–87); Hon. Advr, Oxfam, 2002– (Hon. Pres., 2000–02); Trustee: Inst. for Advanced Study, Princeton, 1987–94; British Mus., 2010–. Member: Accademia Nazionale dei Lincei; Amer. Philos. Assoc.; Foreign Hon. Mem., Amer. Acad. of Arts and Sciences, 1981; Hon. Mem., Amer. Econ. Assoc., 1981. Hon. FRSE; Hon. FMedSci; Hon. Fellow: Inst. of Social Studies, The Hague, 1982; LSE, 1984; IDS, Sussex Univ., 1984; SOAS, London Univ., 1998; Darwin Coll., Cambridge, 1998; LSHTM; St Edmund's Coll., Cambridge, 2004; Frances Perkins Fellow, Amer. Acad. of Political and Social Sci., 2003. Hon. DLitt: Saskatchewan, 1980; Visva-Bharati, 1983; Georgetown, 1989; Jadavpur, Kalyani, 1990; Williams Coll., City of London Poly., 1991; New Sch. for Social Res., NY, 1992; Calcutta, 1993; Syracuse, 1994; Oxford, 1996; Bard Coll., 1997; Leicester, Kingston, Columbia, Chhatrapati Shahu Ji Maharaj, 1998; UEA, Nottingham, Heriot-Watt, 1999; Allahabad, Assam, Strathclyde, Kerala, 2000; Mumbai, 2002; N Bengal, 2002; Cambridge, 2009; Hon. DHumLit: Oberlin Coll., 1993; Wesleyan, 1995; McGill, 1998; Mass, Lowell, 2006; Hon. DSc: Bath, 1984; Edinburgh, 1995; Dhaka, 1999; Assam Agricl, Birmingham, London, 2000; Sussex, 2003; Michigan, 2006; Hon. DSocSc: Chinese Univ. of HK, 1999; Yale, 2003; DU: Essex, 1984; Rabindra Bharati, 1998; Dr *hc*: Caen, 1987; Bologna, 1988; Univ. Catholique de Louvain, 1989; Athens Univ. of Econs and Business, 1991; Valencia, Zurich, 1994; Antwerp, 1995; Stockholm, 1996; Kiel, 1997; Padua, 1998; Athens, Méditerranée (Marseille), Delhi, 1999; Tech. Univ. of Lisbon, Univ. Jaume I de Castellón, Spain, 2001; Tokyo, Clark Univ. (Worcester, USA), Southampton, 2002; Univ. Pierre Mendès France, Grenoble, 2002; Santa Clara Univ., Calif, 2002; Bidhan Chandra Krishi Viswavidyalaya, 2003; Ritsumeikan, Japan, 2003; York, 2004; Koç, Turkey, 2004; Rhodes, S Africa, 2004; York, Canada, 2004; Rovira I Virgili, Tarrogona, 2004; Simmons Coll., Boston, 2005; Göttingen, 2005; Hon. LLD: Tulane, 1990; Queen's Univ., Kingston, Ont., 1993; Harvard, 2000; Mount Holyoke Coll., USA, 2003; Toronto, 2004; Connecticut, 2006; Hon. Dr Ph Jawaharlal Nehru, 1998; Hon. DSc Econs: London, 2000; Cape Town, 2006; Laurea *hc*: Florence, 2000; Turin, 2004; Pavia, 2005; DUniv Open, 2002; Hon. DCL Durham, 2002. Mahalanobis Prize, 1976; Frank E. Seidman Dist. Award in Pol Econ., 1986; Agnelli Internat. Prize, 1990; Alan Shawn Feinstein World Hunger Award, 1990; Jean Mayer Global Citizenship Award, 1993; Indira Gandhi Gold Medal Award, Asiatic Soc., 1994; Edinburgh Medal, 1997; Catalonia Internat. Prize, 1997; Nobel Prize for Economics, 1998; Leontief Prize, 2000; Ayrton Senna Grand Prix of Journalism, 2002; Medal of Distinction, Barnard Coll., USA, 2005; Silver Banner, Florence, 2005; George C. Marshall Award, USA, 2005. Eisenhower Medal, USA, 2000; Presidency of Italian Republic Medal, 2000. Grand Cross, Order of Scientific Merit (Brazil), 2000. *Publications:* Choice of Techniques, 1960, 3rd edn 1968; Growth Economics, 1970; Collective Choice and Social Welfare, 1971; On Economic Inequality, 1973; Employment, Technology and Development, 1975; Poverty and Famines: an essay on entitlement and deprivation, 1981; (ed with Bernard Williams) Utilitarianism and Beyond, 1982; Choice, Welfare and Measurement, 1982; Resources, Values and Development, 1984; Commodities and Capabilities, 1985; On Ethics and Economics, 1987; The Standard of Living, 1987; (with Jean Drèze) Hunger and Public Action, 1989; (ed with Jean Drèze) The Political Economy of Hunger, 3 vols, 1990–91; Inequality Re-examined, 1992; (with Jean Drèze) India: economic development and social opportunity, 1995; Development as Freedom, 1999 (Bruno-Kreisky Award for Political Book of the Year, 2001; European Economics Book Prize, 2002); Rationality and Freedom, 2002; The Argumentative Indian, 2005; Identity and Violence: the illusion of destiny, 2006; The Idea of Justice, 2009; (with Jean Drèze) An Uncertain Glory: India and its contradictions, 2013; articles in various jls in economics, philosophy, political science, decision theory, demography and law. *Address:* Harvard University, University Hall, Cambridge, MA 02138, USA.

SEN, Emma; *see* Rothschild, Emma.

SEN, Ranendra, (Ronen); Director, Tata Motors Ltd, 2010–12; Ambassador for India to the United States of America, 2004–09; *b* 9 April 1944; *s* of late Satyendra Mohan Sen and Shrimati Suniti Rani; *m* 1970, Kalpana Chowdhury; one *d*. *Educ:* Calcutta Univ. (BA Hons). Joined Indian Foreign Service, 1966; served: Moscow, 1968–71; San Francisco, 1972–74; Dhaka, 1974–77; Dep. Sec., Min. of External Affairs, 1977; Dep. Sec., Dept of Atomic Energy, and Sec., Atomic Energy Commn, 1978–80; Counsellor, then Minister, Moscow, 1981–84; Jt Sec., Min. of External Affairs, 1984–85; Jt Sec. to Prime Minister of India, 1986–91; Ambassador: to Mexico, 1991–92; to Russia, 1992–98; to Germany, 1998–2002; High Comr in UK, 2002–04. *Recreations:* music, reading, travel. *Clubs:* Delhi Gymkhana; Cosmos (Washington).

SENEWIRATNE, Kshenuka Dhireni; Permanent Secretary, Ministry of External Affairs, Sri Lanka, since 2014; *b* 20 July 1960; *d* of late Deutram de Silva and of Githa de Silva; *m* 1998, Surendra Senewiratne. *Educ:* Univ. of Salford (BSc Econs 1982); Corpus Christi Coll., Oxford (Chevening Schol.; Foreign Affairs Study Prog.); Univ. of Colombo (MA Internat. Relns 1992). Asst Dir, Bureau of the Minister of Foreign Affairs, Min. of Foreign Affairs, Sri Lanka, 1985–88; diplomatic posting, Perm. Mission of Sri Lanka to the UN, NY, 1988–90; Ministry of Foreign Affairs: Deputy Director: Publicity Div., 1990–91; UN and Multilateral Affairs Div., 1991–93; diplomatic posting, Brussels, 1993–96; Ministry of Foreign Affairs: Dir, UN and Multilateral Div., 1997–98; Dir, 1998–2001, Actg Dir Gen., 2001–02, Econ. Affairs Div.; Dep. High Comr, London, 2002–04; Additional Dir Gen., Econ. Affairs Div., Min. of Foreign Affairs, 2004–05; High Comr in UK, 2005–08; Dir Gen. for Europe and CIS, Min. of Foreign Affairs, Sri Lanka, 2008–09; Ambassador and Perm. Rep. to UN Office at Geneva, and Consul Gen. in Switzerland, 2009–11; Additional Sec., Min. of Foreign Affairs. *Recreations:* reading, cycling, music, travelling. *Address:* c/o Ministry of External Affairs, Republic Building, Colombo 1, Sri Lanka.

SENIOR, Gary; Partner, Baker & McKenzie, London, since 1992 (Managing Partner, 2003–13; Member, Executive Committee, since 2013; Chairman, Global Executive Committee, Europe, Middle East and Africa Region, since 2014); *b* Leeds, 23 May 1962; *s* of Harry Fern Senior and Anne Senior; *m* 1988, Sarah Gibson; one *s* one *d*. *Educ:* Cross Green Sch., Leeds; Durham Univ. (BA Law). Admitted as solicitor, 1986; Baker & McKenzie: articled clerk, 1984; Associate, 1986; Chm., Global Policy Cttee, 2011–13. *Recreations:* chess, Leeds United, family, cricket, history. *Address:* Baker & McKenzie, 100 New Bridge Street, EC4V 6JA. *T:* (020) 7919 1890. *E:* gary.senior@bakermckenzie.com. *Club:* MCC.

SENNITT, His Honour John Stuart; a Circuit Judge, 1994–2007; *b* Cambridge, 5 March 1935; *s* of late Stuart Osland Sennitt and Nora Kathleen Sennitt; *m* 1966, Janet Ann; one *s* two *d*. *Educ:* Culford Sch., Bury St Edmunds; St Catharine's Coll., Cambridge (MA, LLB). Admitted Solicitor, 1961; Partner, Wild, Hewitson & Shaw, Cambridge, 1963–83; County Court Registrar, then Dist Judge, 1983–94; Asst Recorder, 1988–92; a Recorder, 1992–94. *Address:* c/o Cambridge County Court, 197 East Road, Cambridge CB1 1BA.

SENTAMU, Most Rev. and Rt Hon. John Tucker Mugabi; *see* York, Archbishop of.

SENTANCE, Dr Andrew William, CBE 2012; Senior Economic Adviser, PricewaterhouseCoopers LLP, since 2011; Professorial Fellow (part-time), University of Warwick, since 2006; *b* 17 Sept. 1958; *s* of William Thomas Wulfram Sentance and Lillian Sentance (*née* Bointon); *m* 1985, Anne Margaret Penfold; one *s* one *d*. *Educ:* Eltham Coll., London; Clare Coll., Cambridge (BA Hons, MA); London Sch. of Econs (MSc Econ; PhD 1988). Manager, Petrocell Ltd, 1980–81; with NCB, 1982–83; Confederation of British Industry: Head, Econ. Policy, 1986–89; Dir, Econ. Affairs, 1989–93; London Business School: Sen. Res. Fellow, 1994–95; Dir, Centre for Economic Forecasting, 1995–98; British Airways: Chief Economist, 1998–2006; Head of Envmtl Affairs, 2003–06; Mem., Monetary Policy Cttee, Bank of England, 2006–11. Chief Economic Advr, British Retail Consortium, 1995–98. Member: HM Treasury Panel of Independent Forecasters, 1992–93; various statistical adv. cttees, 1988–99. Comr, Commn for Integrated Transport, 2006–10. Vis. Prof. of Econs, Royal Holloway, Univ. of London, 1998–; Vis. Prof., Cranfield Univ., 2001–08.

Fellow, Soc. of Business Economists (Mem. Council, 1991–2003; Chm., 1995–2000; Dep. Chm., 2000–03; Vice Pres., 2013–). Trustee: Anglo-German Foundn, 2001–09; British Airways Pension Funds, 2002–06; BuildIT Internat., 2012–. Ed., London Business Sch. Econ. Outlook, 1994–98. *Publications:* Rediscovering Growth: after the crisis, 2013; numerous articles in books and jls on current economic issues. *Recreations:* playing piano, guitar and organ, listening to music. *E:* andrew.w.sentance@pwc.com.

SEOKA, Rt Rev. Johannes Thomas; *see* Pretoria, Bishop of.

SEPHTON, Craig Gardner; QC 2001; a Recorder, since 2002; a Deputy High Court Judge, since 2010; *b* 7 Dec. 1957; *s* of Bruce and Betty Sephton; *m* 1st, 1985, Colette (marr. diss.); three *s*; 2nd, 2008, Tanya Anne Mackenzie. *Educ:* Ecclesbourne Sch., Duffield; Lincoln Coll., Oxford (MA, BCL). Called to the Bar, Middle Temple, 1981. Hd of Chambers, Deans Court Chambers, 2013–. Sometimes Treas., Personal Injuries Bar Assoc.; Treas., Northern Circuit, 2010–. *Recreations:* swimming, mountaineering, music, cycling. *Address:* 24 St John Street, Manchester M3 4DF. *T:* (0161) 214 6000.

SEPHTON, Prof. Mark Andrew, PhD; Professor of Organic Geochemistry and Meteoritics, Imperial College London, since 2007; *b* St Helens, Merseyside, 1966; *m* 1996, Sarah Victoria Rogers: two *s* one *d*. *Educ:* Univ. of Durham (BSc Hons 1991); Univ. of Newcastle (MSc 1992); Open Univ. (PhD 1997). Post Doctoral Researcher, Netherlands Inst. for Sea Res. and Univ. of Utrecht, 1996–98; Post Doctoral Researcher, 1998–2000, Lectr, 2000–05, Open Univ.; Reader, Imperial Coll. London, 2005–07. Chm., Space Exploration Adv. Cttee, UK Space Agency, 2013–. Asteroid 7552 named 'Sephton' by IAU, 2006. *Publications:* (with I. Gilmour) An Introduction to Astrobiology, 2004, 2nd edn (with I. Gilmour and D. A. Rothery) 2011; over 150 scientific articles. *Recreations:* running, hillwalking. *Address:* Department of Earth Science and Engineering, South Kensington Campus, Imperial College London, SW7 2AZ. *T:* (020) 7594 6542. *E:* m.a.sephton@imperial.ac.uk.

SEPÚLVEDA-AMOR, Bernardo, Hon. GCMG 1985; Judge, 2006–15, and Vice President, 2012–15, International Court of Justice, The Hague; *b* 14 Dec. 1941; *s* of Bernardo Sepúlveda and Margarita Amor; *m* 1970, Ana Yturbe; three *s*. *Educ:* Univ. of Mexico (Law Degree *magna cum laude*, 1964); Queens' Coll., Cambridge (LLB 1966; Hon. Fellow, 1990). Prof. of Internat. Law, El Colegio de México, 1967–81; Dep. Dir Gen. for Legal Affairs to Secretary of the Presidency, 1968–70; Asst Sec. for Internat. Affairs, Min. of the Treasury, 1976–80; Principal Advisor on Internat. Affairs to the Minister of Planning and Budget, 1981; Ambassador to USA, 1982; Minister of Foreign Relations, Mexico, 1982–88; Ambassador to UK, 1989–93; Foreign Affairs Advr to Pres. of Mexico, 1993. Mem., UN Internat. Law Commn, 1996–2006. Bencher, Middle Temple, 2011. Ind. Mem., Bd of Dirs, Empresas ICA, 2015–. Dr *hc* Univ. of San Diego, Calif, 1982; Univ. of Leningrad, 1987. Principe de Asturias Prize, Spain, 1984; Simón Bolívar Prize, UNESCO, 1985. Grand Cross, Order of: Civil Merit (Spain), 1979; Isabel the Catholic (Spain), 1983; Southern Cross (Brazil), 1983; Boyacá (Colombia), 1984; Merit (FRG), 1984; Liberator San Martín (Argentina), 1984; Vasco Núñez de Balboa (Panama), 1984; Manuel Amador Guerrero (Panama), 1985; Christ (Portugal), 1985; Crown (Belgium), 1985; Quetzal (Guatemala), 1986; Prince Henry the Navigator (Portugal), 1986; Sun (Peru), 1987; Rio Branco (Brazil), 1988; Grand Officier, Nat. Order of Legion of Honour (France), 1985; also orders and decorations from Korea, Venezuela, Poland, Yugoslavia, Greece, Japan, Egypt and Jamaica. *Publications:* The United Nations: dilemma at 25, 1970; Foreign Investment in Mexico, 1973; Transnational Corporations in Mexico, 1974; articles on internat. law in prof. jls. *Recreations:* reading, music. *Clubs:* Brooks's, Travellers.

SERAFÍN, David; *see* Michael, I. D. L.

SERGEANT, Emma; artist; *b* 9 Dec. 1959; *d* of Sir Patrick John Rushton Sergeant, *qv*; *m* 2001, Count Adam Zamoyski. *Educ:* Channing Sch.; Camden High Sch.; Camberwell Sch. of Arts and Crafts; Slade Sch. of Fine Art. Commnd by NPG to paint portraits of Lord David Cecil and Lord Olivier, 1981; Official Royal Tour Artist to Prince of Wales: Egypt and Morocco, 1995; Ukraine and Central Asian Republics of Turkmenistan, Kazakhstan, Kyrgyzstan and Uzbekistan, 1996. Exhibitions include: Drinks at Milapote: friends and family, 1984, Afghanistan, in aid of UNICEF, 1986, Faces from Four Continents, 1988, Orpheus and the Underworld, 1994, Agnew's, London; Retour en Afghanistan, in aid of Médecins du Monde, Mona Bismarck Foundn, Paris, 1987; Gods, Newhouse Gall., NY, and Agnew's, London, 1996; Dolphins, 1998, From the Sea, 1999, Shades of Grey, 2004, Fine Art Soc.; Scenes from a Hittite Court, Prince's Foundn, 2001; portrait commissions include: the Duke of York, Sir Christopher Cockerell, Lord Carrington, Imran Khan, Lord Todd, Sir William Deacon, Paul Dacre, Padraic Fallon, Lord Rothermere, Trudie Styler, Earl of Radnor, Sir Rocco Forte, Jeremy Paxman, Michael Portillo, Jerry Hall. NPG Award, 1981. *Recreation:* horses. *Address:* Fine Art Society plc, 148 New Bond Street, W1S 2JT. *T:* (020) 7629 5116. *E:* art@faslondon.com.

SERGEANT, John; broadcaster and journalist; Chief Political Correspondent, BBC, 1988–2000; Political Editor, ITN, 2000–03; *b* 14 April 1944; *s* of Ernest Sergeant and late Olive Sergeant (then Stevens); *m* 1969, Mary Smithies; two *s*. *Educ:* Millfield Sch., Street; Magdalen Coll., Oxford (BA Hons PPE). Appeared in On the Margin, BBC TV, 1966–67; Reporter, Liverpool Daily Post and Echo, 1967–70; BBC: Reporter, 1970–81: reported from 25 countries, incl. conflicts in Vietnam, Cyprus, Israel, Lebanon, Rhodesia and NI; acting Corresp., Dublin, Paris and Washington; Presenter, current affairs progs, Radio 4, incl. Today, World at One, PM; Political Corresp., 1981–88; Lobby Chm., 2000–01. Mem., Hansard Soc. Commn on Communication of Parly Democracy, 2004–05. Has appeared on numerous TV and radio progs, incl. Have I Got News for You, Room 101, Call My Bluff, News Quiz, Quote Unquote, Strictly Come Dancing, One Show, Argumental, QI, John Sergeant on the Tourist Trail, John Sergeant on Tracks of Empire, Britain's Flying Past: the Spitfire, Britain's Flying Past: the Sea King, Britain's Flying Past: the Lancaster, Britain's First Photo Album, Sergeant on Spike, Royal Greenwich, Barging Round Britain, etc.; regular contributor to BBC One Show; UK theatre tour, An Audience with John Sergeant, 2003–09. Pres., Johnson Soc., 2003–04. Hon. DLitt: Teesside, 2010; Lincoln, 2013. Most Memorable TV Broadcast award, BPG, 1991; Best Individual TV Contributor, Voice of the Listener and Viewer, 1999. *Publications:* Give Me Ten Seconds (memoirs), 2001; Maggie: her fatal legacy, 2005; (with David Bartley) Barging Round Britain, 2015. *Recreations:* sailing, listening to classical music. *Address:* c/o Anita Land Ltd, 10 Wyndham Place, W1H 2PU.

SERGEANT, Sir Patrick (John Rushton), Kt 1984; City Editor, Daily Mail, 1960–84; Founder, 1969, and Chairman, 1985–92, Euromoney Publications (Managing Director, 1969–85); *b* 17 March 1924; *s* of George and Rene Sergeant; *m* 1952, Gillian Anne Wilks, Cape Town; two *d*. *Educ:* Beaumont Coll. Served as Lieut, RNVR, 1945. Asst City Editor, News Chronicle, 1948; Dep. City Editor, Daily Mail, 1953. Director: Associated Newspapers Group, 1971–83; Daily Mail General Trust, 1983–2004; (non-exec.) Euromoney Institutional Investor plc (formerly Euromoney Publications), 1992–. Domus Fellow, St Catherine's Coll., Oxford, 1988. Freeman, City of London, 1987. Wincott Award, Financial Journalist of the Year, 1979. *Publications:* Another Road to Samarkand, 1955; Money Matters, 1967; Inflation Fighters Handbook, 1976. *Recreations:* tennis, swimming, talking. *Address:* One The Grove, Highgate Village, N6 6JU. *T:* (020) 8340 1245. *Clubs:* Royal Automobile, Garrick; All England Lawn Tennis and Croquet, Queen's.

See also E. Sergeant.

SERHAL, Paul; Medical Director, Centre for Reproductive and Genetic Health (formerly Assisted Conception Unit), since 1990; Consultant in Reproductive Medicine, since 1990; *b* Lebanon, 18 Sept. 1954; *s* of Farid Serhal and Lili Serhal; *m* Claude; one *s* two *d*. *Educ:* MB BS. MRCOG. University College Hospital, London: Clin. Res. Fellow in Reproductive Medicine, Dept of Obstetrics and Gynaecol., 1985–87; Clin. Lectr and Sen. Registrar, 1987–90. Grand Officer, Nat. Order of the Cedar (Lebanon). *Publications:* (ed with Caroline Overton) Good Clinical Practice in Assisted Reproduction, 2004; contrib. learned jls incl. Lancet, Jl for Sterility and Fertility and Human Reproduction. *Recreations:* horse riding, sailing. *Address:* Centre for Reproductive and Genetic Health, 230–232 Great Portland Street, W1W 5QS. *T:* (020) 7837 2905, *Fax:* (020) 7278 5152. *E:* info@crgh.co.uk.

SERJEANT, Graham Roger, CMG 1981; MD; FRCP; Chairman, Sickle Cell Trust of Jamaica, since 1986; *b* 26 Oct. 1938; *s* of Ewart Egbert and Violet Elizabeth Serjeant; *m* 1965, Beryl Elizabeth, *d* of late Ivor Edward King, CB, CBE. *Educ:* Sibford Sch., Banbury; Bootham Sch., York; Clare Coll., Cambridge (BA 1960, MA 1965); London Hosp. Med. Sch.; Makerere Coll., Kampala. MB BChir 1963, MD 1971, Cantab. MRCP 1966, FRCP 1977. House Physician: London Hosp., 1963–64; Royal United Hosp., Bath, 1965–66; RPMS, 1966; Med. Registrar, University Hosp. of WI, 1966–67; Wellcome Res. Fellow, Dept of Medicine, Univ. of WI, 1967–71; Medical Research Council: Mem., Scientific Staff, Abnormal Haemoglobin Unit, Cambridge, 1971–72; Epidemiology Res. Unit, Jamaica, 1972–74; Dir, MRC Labs, Jamaica, 1974–99. Hon. Prof. of Clin. Epidemiology, Univ. of WI, 1981–99, now Emeritus. Pres., Caribbean Orgn of Sickle Cell Assocs, 1997–2000. Gold Musgrave Medal, Inst. of Jamaica, 1995; Pelican Award, Univ. of WI, 1995; Vice-Chancellor's Award for Excellence, 1999. Dist. Res. Award, Caribbean Health Res. Council, 1999. Hon. CD (Jamaica), 1996; Commander, Mérite Congolais, 2005. *Publications:* The Clinical Features of Sickle Cell Disease, 1974; Sickle Cell Disease, 1985, 3rd edn 2001; Guide to Sickle Cell Disease, 2001; approx. 400 papers on the nat. hist. of sickle cell disease, in med. jls. *Recreations:* theatre, art, Greek peasant life, travel. *Address:* Sickle Cell Trust, 14 Milverton Crescent, Kingston 6, Jamaica, WI. *T:* 9272300, *Fax:* 9700074. *E:* grserjeant@cwjamaica.com.

SERJEANT, William Ronald, FRHistS; County Archivist, Suffolk, 1974–82, retired; Vice-President, Society of Archivists, since 1988 (President, 1982–88); Hon. Archivist to British Association for Local History, 1982–2011; *b* 5 March 1921; *s* of Frederick William and Louisa (*née* Wood); *m* 1961, Ruth Kneale (*née* Bridson); one *s*. *Educ:* Univ. of Manchester (BA Hons History); Univ. of Liverpool (Dip. Archive Admin. and Study of Records). Archivist/Librarian: Univ. of Sheffield, Sheffield City Library, Liverpool Record Office, 1952–56; Librarian/Archivist, Manx Nat. Library and Archives, Dep. Dir, Manx Mus. and Nat. Trust, 1957–62; County Archivist, Notts, 1962–70; Jt County Bor. and County Archivist, Ipswich and E Suffolk, 1970–74. Hon. Archivist: to Lord de Saumarez, 1982–2007; to Lord Tollemache, 1983–2013. Member: Lord Chancellor's Adv. Council on Public Records, 1982–88; Suffolk Heraldry Soc., 1982–; Member, Executive Committee: Suffolk Local History Council, 1970–2001; Ipswich Film Soc., 1974–; Council Member: Suffolk Inst. of Archeology and History, 1970–90; Suffolk Records Soc., 1970–; British Records Soc., 1974–2001; Ipswich Building Preservation Trust, 1988–2009; British Assoc. for Local History, 1994–97 (Mem. Publications Cttee, 1982– (Chm., 1988–92)); Trustee, 1983–2005, Patron, 2005–, Leiston Long Shop (formerly Steam) Museum. Editor: Jl of the Manx Museum, 1957–62; The Suffolk Review, 1970–82; The Blazon (Suffolk Heraldry Soc.), 1984–88. *Publications:* The History of Tuxford Grammar School, 1969; (ed) Index to the Probate Records of the Court of the Archdeacon of Suffolk 1444–1700, 1979–80; (ed) Index to the Probate Records of the Court of the Archdeacon of Sudbury 1354–1700, 1984; articles in county and other local history periodicals. *Recreations:* walking, participation in local historical and heraldic studies and activities, theatre and cinema going; any gaps filled by reading novels. *Address:* 23 Dalton Road, Ipswich, Suffolk IP1 2HT. *T:* (01473) 221219.

SERMON, (Thomas) Richard, MBE 2010; FCIS; Chairman, Gryphon Corporate Counsel, since 1996; *b* 25 Feb. 1947; *s* of Eric Thomas Sermon and Marjorie Hilda (*née* Parsons); *m* 1970, Rosemary Diane, *yr d* of Thomas Smith; one *s* one *d*. *Educ:* Nottingham High Sch. FCIS 1972. Crest Hotels, 1969–74; Good Relations Gp, 1974–79; Co-founder and Chief Exec., 1979–87, Chm., 1987–90, 1996–2000, Shandwick Consultants; Man. Dir, Shandwick Consulting Gp, 1987–88; Chief Executive: Shandwick Europe, 1988–90; Shandwick International, 1990–96; public relns advr, Goldman Sachs Internat., 1992–96. Director: Gryphon Partners (formerly Wrightson Wood Associates), 1994–; Jardine Lloyd Thompson Gp, 1996–2005; Newmond, 1997–2000; MoD Defence Storage and Distributions Agency, 1999; Mgt Bd, Defence Acad. of UK, 2007–; China Eastsea Business Software Ltd, 2008–; Appointed Mem., PPP, 1993–98. Mem., Nat. Adv. Council on Employment of People with Disabilities, 1994–98. Mem. Council, C & G, 1993– (Mem. Exec. Cttee, 1999–; Hon. Mem., 1999; Jt Hon. Sec., 2005–). Vice-President: RADAR, 1987–; Providence Row, 1999–; Mem. Exec. Cttee, Fedn of London Youth Clubs (formerly London Fedn of Clubs for Young People), 1994– (Hon. Treas., 1995–96; Chm., 1996–2008; Dep. Chm., 2008–). Dir, City of London Sinfonia, 1995–2001. Chm., The Home Improvement Trust, 1997–. Freeman, City of London, 1968; Sheriff, City of London, 2010–11; Member, Court of Assistants: Wheelwrights' Co., 1990– (Master, 2000–01); Chartered Secretaries and Administrators' Co., 1991– (Master, 2006–07). Hon. FCGI 2004. *Address:* Friars Well, Roundtown, Aynho, Banbury, Oxon OX17 3BG. *T:* (01869) 810284. *Clubs:* City of London, City Livery, Walbrook.

SEROTA, His Honour Daniel; QC 1989; a Circuit Judge, 1999–2015; *b* 27 Sept. 1945; *s* of Louis and N'eema Serota; *m* 1970; two *d*. *Educ:* Carmel Coll.; Jesus Coll., Oxford (MA). Called to the Bar, Lincoln's Inn, 1969; a Recorder, 1989–99. Consulting Ed., Civil Practice Law Reports.

SEROTA, Sir Nicholas (Andrew), CH 2013; Kt 1999; Director of the Tate Gallery, since 1988; *b* 27 April 1946; *s* of Stanley Serota and Beatrice Serota (Baroness Serota, DBE); *m* 1st, 1973, Angela Beveridge (marr. diss. 1995); two *d*; 2nd, 1997, Teresa Gleadowe; two step *d*. *Educ:* Haberdashers' Aske's Sch., Hampstead and Elstree; Christ's Coll., Cambridge (BA; Hon. Fellow, 2002); Courtauld Inst. of Art, London (MA). Regional Art Officer and Exhibn Organiser, Arts Council of GB, 1970–73; Dir, Museum of Modern Art, Oxford, 1973–76; Dir, Whitechapel Art Gallery, 1976–88. Mem. Bd, Olympic Delivery Authy, 2006–12. Chm., Visual Arts Adv. Cttee, British Council, 1992–98 (Mem., 1976–98); Comr, Commn for Architecture and the Built Envmt, 1999–2006. Trustee: Public Art Develt Trust, 1983–87; Architecture Foundn, 1991–99; Little Sparta Trust, 1995–2007; Chinati Foundn, 1999–. Sen. FRCA 1996. Hon. Fellow: QMC 1988; Goldsmiths' Coll., Univ. of London, 1994. Hon. FRIBA 1992. Hon. DLitt: Keele, 1994; South Bank, 1996; Surrey, 1997; Exeter, 2000; London Inst., 2001; Hon. Dr Arts: City of London Polytechnic, 1990; Plymouth, 1993; DU Essex, 2002. Officier de l'Ordre des Arts et des Lettres (France), 2003; Légion d'Honneur (France), 2012. *Publications:* Experience or Interpretation: the dilemma of museums of modern art, 1996. *Address:* Tate, Millbank, SW1P 4RG. *T:* (020) 7887 8003.

SERRA, Davide; Founding Partner and Chief Executive, Algebris Investments LLP, since 2006; *b* Genoa, 19 Jan. 1971; *m* 1998; two *s* two *d*. *Educ:* Bocconi Univ. (BA Hons Econs and Finance *cum laude* 1994); Univ. Catholique de Louvain and NHH, Norway (Community of Eur. Mgt Schs Master 1995). Sen. Financial Analyst, UBS, Italy, 1995–2000; Co-Hd, Eur. Banks, Morgan Stanley Internat. Ltd, London, 2001–06. Mem., Industry Partnership, WEF. Designated Young Global Leader, 2010. *Recreations:* climbing, mountaineering, off-piste ski-ing in the Alps and mountains, sailing. *Address:* Algebris Investments LLP, 7 Clifford Street, W1S 2FT. *T:* (020) 7851 1740, *Fax:* (020) 7851 1769. *E:* info@algebris.com. *Club:* Ambrosetti (Italy).

SERRANO-QUEVEDO, Rafael; Founder and Chief Executive, Prime Investors Capital Ltd, since 2009; *b* Madrid, 9 Aug. 1966; *s* of Ramon Serrano-Garcia and Cristina Serrano-Quevedo; *m* 2009, Marije Visser; one *s* one *d.* *Educ:* London Business Sch. (Postgrad. Cert. Finance and Investment Portfolio); Univ. of Oxford (Dip. Business and Mgt); Faculty of Law, Univ. of Madrid (MA Hons). Investment Banker, Capital Mkts and Internat. Fund Mgt, JP Morgan, 1991–99; Man. Dir, Focus Investment Gp, Europe, 2000–09. Prime Investors Capital Ltd projects include restoration and development of Bvlgari Hotel and Residences, Knightsbridge and of Admiralty Arch, Westminster. *Recreations:* arts, opera, classical music, history, property, hotels, tennis, charity work. *Address:* 4 Elm Park Road, SW3 6BB. *T:* (020) 3178 4660. *E:* rserrano@primeinvestors.com. *Clubs:* Arts, Queen's; Travellers (Paris).

SERVICE, Louisa Anne, OBE 1997; Joint Chairman: The Hemming Group (formerly The Municipal Group) of Companies, 1976–2011 (non-executive Director, since 2011); Hemming Publishing Ltd, 1987–2011; *d* of late Henry Harold Hemming, OBE, MC, and Alice Louisa Weaver, OBE; *m* 1959, Alastair Stanley Douglas Service, CBE, MVO (marr. diss. 1984; he *d* 2013); one *s* one *d.* *Educ:* private and state schs, Canada, USA and Britain; Ecole des Sciences Politiques, Paris; St Hilda's Coll., Oxford (BA and MA, PPE). Export Dir, Ladybird Appliances Ltd, 1957–59; Municipal Journal Ltd and associated cos: Financial Dir, 1966; Dep. Chm., 1974; Chm., Merchant Printers Ltd, 1975–80; Dir, Brintex Ltd, 1965–; Dir, Glass's Information Services Ltd, 1971, Dep. Chm. 1976–81, Chm., 1982–95. Member: Dept of Trade Consumer Credit Act Appeals Panel, 1981–2006; Cttee of Magistrates, 1985–88; FIMBRA Appeals Panel, 1988–92; Solicitors Complaints Bureau, 1992–93. JP Inner London Juvenile Courts, 1969–2001; Chm., Hackney Youth Court, 1975–82, Westminster Juvenile Ct, 1982–88, Hammersmith and Fulham Juvenile Court, 1988–94, Camden Youth and Family Proceedings Ct, 1994–2002; JP Inner London (5) PSD, 1980–; Chairman: Exec. Cttee, Inner London Juvenile Courts, 1977–79; Inner London Juvenile Liaison Cttee, 1986–88 (Mem., 1980–86); Member: working party on re-org. of London Juvenile Courts, 1975; Inner London Family Proceedings Courts, 1991–2002; Inner London Youth Courts, 1992–2002; Inner London Magistrates' Cts Cttee, 1995–2001; Vice-Chm., Paddington Probation Hostel, 1976–86. Corresp. mem., SDP Policy Gp on Citizens' Rights, 1982–89. Mem., St Hilda's Coll. Develt Adv. Cttee, 1996–2012; Dir, 1997–, Chm., 2001–06, Jacqueline du Pré Music Building Ltd. Dir, Opera Circus Ltd, 2000–04. Chm. Council, Mayer-Lismann Opera Workshop, 1976–91; Hon. Sec., Women's India Assoc. of UK, 1967–74. Dir, Arts Club Ltd, 1981–84; Member Council: Friends of Covent Garden, 1982–2005; Haydn-Mozart Soc., 1988–93; Chm., Youth & Music, 1990–2001 (Dir, 1988–90); Mem., E-SU Music Cttee, 1984–91, 1997–2001. Mem. Adv. Bd, Rudolf Kempe Soc., 2000–03. Trustee, Performing Arts Labs, 1996–99. Pres., Commonwealth Countries League, 2009–14, now Patron (Vice Pres., 1994–2009; Trustee, Educn Fund, 1994–2004). Judge, Historical Dagger, Crime Writers' Assoc., 2013–. Distinguished Friend of Oxford, Oxford Univ., 2012. *Publications:* articles on a variety of subjects. *Recreations:* travel, and attractive and witty people including my family. *Address:* c/o Hemming Group, 32 Vauxhall Bridge Road, SW1V 2SS. *T:* (020) 7973 6404. *Club:* Athenæum (Member: Gen. Cttee, 2003–09; Exec. Cttee, 2004–09; Talk Dinner Cttee, 2010–; Music Cttee, 2014–).
See also J. H. Hemming.

SERVICE, Prof. Robert John, PhD; FBA 1998; Professor of Russian History, Oxford University, 2002–13, now Emeritus; Fellow, St Antony's College, Oxford, 1998–2014, now Emeritus; *b* 29 Oct. 1947; *s* of Matthew Service and Janet Service (*née* Redpath); *m* 1975, Adele Biagi; two *s* two *d.* *Educ:* Northampton Town and County Grammar Sch. for Boys; King's Coll., Cambridge (Douton Open Schol. in Classics; BA 1970; MA 1971); Univ. of Essex (MA Govt and Politics 1971; PhD 1977). British Council Exchange Res. Student, Leningrad, 1973–74; Lectr in Russian Studies, Univ. of Keele, 1975–84; School of Slavonic and East European Studies, University of London: Lectr in Hist., 1984–87; Reader in Soviet Hist. and Politics, 1987–91; Prof. of Russian Hist. and Politics, 1991–98; Chairman: Hist. Dept, 1987–90; Acad. Assembly, 1990–92; Grad. Studies, 1993–97; Oxford University: Dir, Grad. Studies in Russian and E European Studies, 2000–02; Dean, St Antony's Coll., 2003. *Publications:* The Bolshevik Party in Revolution, 1979; Lenin: a political life, Vol. 1 1985, Vol. 2 1991, Vol. 3 1995; The Russian Revolution 1900–1927, 1986, 3rd rev. edn 1999; A History of Twentieth-Century Russia, 1997; Lenin: a biography, 2000; Russia: experiment with a people, from 1991 to the present, 2002; A History of Modern Russia from Nicholas II to Putin, 2003; Stalin: a biography, 2004; Comrades: Communism, a world history, 2007; Trotsky: a biography, 2009; Spies and Commissars, 2011; The End of the Cold War: 1985–1991, 2015. *Recreations:* walking, bicycling, singing. *Address:* 6 Braydon Road, N16 6QB. *T:* (020) 8809 1800; St Antony's College, Oxford OX2 6JF. *T:* (01865) 284747.

SERWOTKA, Mark Henryk; General Secretary, Public and Commercial Services Union, since 2002 (General Secretary elect, 2001–02); *b* 26 April 1963; *s* of Henryk Josef Serwotka and Audrey Phylis Serwotka; *m* 2001, Ruth Louise Cockroft; one *s* one *d.* *Educ:* St Margaret's RC Primary Sch., Aberdare; Bishop Hedley RC Comprehensive Sch., Merthyr Tydfil. Admin Officer, DHSS, subseq. DSS, 1980–2001. *Recreations:* sport (golf, football), reading, walking. *Address:* (office) 160 Falcon Road, SW11 2LN; 132 Portnalls Road, Chipstead, Coulsdon, Surrey CR5 3DX. *T:* (01737) 554545.

SESHADRI, Prof. Conjeevaram Srirangachari, PhD; FRS 1988; Director, Chennai Mathematical Institute (formerly Dean, School of Mathematics, SPIC Science Foundation, then SPIC Mathematic Institute), 1989–2010, now Director Emeritus; *b* 29 Feb. 1932; *s* of C. Srirangachari and Chudamani; *m* 1962, Sundari; two *s.* *Educ:* Loyola College, Madras (BA Hons Maths Madras Univ. 1953); PhD Bombay Univ. 1958. Tata Institute of Fundamental Research: Student, 1953; Reader, 1961; Professor, 1963; Senior Professor, 1975–84; Sen. Prof., Inst. of Math. Scis, Madras, 1984–89. *Publications:* Fibres Vectorials sur les courtes algébriques, Asterisque, 96, 1982; Introduction to the Theory of Standard Monomials, 1985. *Recreation:* south Indian classical music. *Address:* Chennai Mathematical Institute, Plot H1, SIPCOT IT Park, Padur PO, Siruseri 603103, India.

SESHMI, Uanu, MBE 2008; Co-Founder, and Creative Director, since 2008, From Boyhood to Manhood Foundation (Director, 1996–2008); male therapist, since 2009; *b* Kingston, Jamaica, 8 Dec. 1959; one *d.* Graphic designer; creator and author of Calling the Shots curriculum concept, anti-knife and gun educn and information resource. Anne Frank Award, Anne Frank Trust UK, 2007. *Recreations:* yoga, meditation, nutrition, jazz, drumming. *E:* uanu_seshmi@yahoo.co.uk.

SESSIONS, John; *see* Marshall, J. G.

SETCH, Terence Frank, RA 2009; RWA; professional artist (painter), since 1960; *b* London, 11 March 1936; *s* of Frank Arthur Setch and Florence Beatrice Setch; *m* 1967, Dianne Shaw; one *d.* *Educ:* Sutton and Cheam Sch. of Art; Slade Sch. of Fine Art; University Coll. London (DFA 1959). Lectr, Leicester Coll. of Art, 1960–64; Principal Lectr in Painting, Cardiff Coll. of Art, 1964–2001. Vis. Lectr, Emily Carr Coll. of Art, Vancouver, 1981; Artist in Residence, Victorian Coll. of the Arts, Melbourne. External Examiner BA: Slade Sch. of Fine Art, UCL, 1989–92; Faculty of Art, Univ. of Reading, 1989–92. Artist Advr, Derek Williams Trust Cttee, Nat. Mus. of Wales, 1996–2005. *Solo exhibitions include:* Grabowski Gall., 1967, 1968, 1970, 1973; Serpentine Gall., 1980; Nigel Greenwood Gall., 1982, 1985, 1987; Welsh Arts Council, Nat. Mus. of Wales, Cardiff, Camden Arts Centre, Talbot Rice Arts Centre, 1992; RWA, Univ. of Wales Inst., Howard Gdns Gall., Glynn Vivian Art Gall., 2001; Collins Gall., Glasgow, 2002; Art Space Gall., Islington, 2008–10; Cork St Gall., 2012; Flowers Gall., 2014. Elected to Faculty of Painting, British Sch. at Rome, 1987; RWA 2002. *Relevant publications:* Terry Setch, by Paul Moorhouse, 1992; Terry Setch: a retrospective (essays), by Michael Tooby and Martin Holman, 2001; Terry Setch, by Martin Holman, 2009. *Recreations:* watching films, listening to music. *E:* setch@terrysetch.co.uk. *Clubs:* Chelsea Arts, Arts.

SETCHELL, Sir Marcus (Edward), KCVO 2014 (CVO 2004); FRCSE, FRCS, FRCOG; Surgeon-Gynaecologist to the Queen, 1990–2014; Consultant Obstetrician and Gynaecologist: London Clinic, 1975–2014; Portland Hospital, 1980–2014; *b* 4 Oct. 1943; *s* of late Eric Hedley Setchell and Barbara Mary (*née* Whitworth); *m* 1973, Dr Sarah French; two *s* two *d.* *Educ:* Felsted Sch.; Gonville and Caius Coll., Cambridge (MA, MB BChir); St Bartholomew's Hosp. Consultant Obstetrician and Gynaecologist: St Bartholomew's and Homerton Hosps, 1975–2000, now Hon. Consultant; Whittington Hosp. NHS Trust, 2000–08; Consultant Gynaecologist: King Edward VII Hosp. (formerly King Edward VII Hosp. for Officers), 1982–2014 (Chm. Med. Cttee, 1998–2005); St Luke's Hosp. for Clergy, 1983–2009. Advr in Gynaecology, Nat. Patient Safety Agency, 2003–06. Convener, Scientific Meetings, 1989–92, Mem. Council, 1994–2000, Chm., Consumers' Forum, 1995–98, RCOG; Mem., Council, 1990–94, Pres., Section of Obstetrics and Gynaecology, 1994–95, RSocMed. Chm. of Govs, Voluntary Hosp. of St Bartholomew, 2007–. Pres., WellBeing of Women, 2014– (Trustee, 2004–11). *Publications:* (with R. J. Lilford) Multiple Choice Questions in Obstetrics and Gynaecology, 1985, 3rd edn 1996, 4th edn (with B. Thilaganathan) 2001; (contrib.) Ten Teachers in Obstetrics and Gynaecology, 13th edn 1980 to 16th edn 1995; (with E. E. Philipp) Scientific Foundations of Obstetrics and Gynaecology, 1991; (with C. N. Hudson Shaw) Shaw's Textbook of Operative Gynaecology, 5th edn, 2001 to 7th edn (with J. H. Shepherd) 2012. *Recreations:* tennis, ski-ing, gardening, walking. *Address:* 64 Wood Vale, N10 3DN. *T:* (020) 8444 5266. *Clubs:* Royal Society of Medicine, St Albans Medical, Garrick; All England Lawn Tennis.

SETH, Vikram, Hon. CBE 2001; writer; *b* 20 June 1952; *s* of Premnath and Leila Seth. *Educ:* Doon Sch., Dehra Dun, India; Tonbridge Sch., Kent; Corpus Christi Coll., Oxford (MA Hons PPE; Hon. Fellow 1994); Stanford Univ., Calif (MA Econs); Nanjing Univ., China. Sen. Editor, Stanford Univ. Press, 1985–86. Trustee, British Mus., 2004–08. Officier, Ordre des Arts et des Lettres (France), 2010 (Chevalier, 2001); Padma Shri (India), 2007. *Publications:* Mappings (poems), 1982; From Heaven Lake: travels through Sinkiang and Tibet, 1983; The Humble Administrator's Garden (poems), 1985; The Golden Gate (novel in verse), 1986; All You Who Sleep Tonight (poems), 1990; Three Chinese Poets: translations of Wang Wei, Li Bai and Du Fu, 1992; Beastly Tales From Here and There (fables in verse), 1992; A Suitable Boy (novel), 1992; Arion and the Dolphin (libretto), 1994; An Equal Music (novel), 1999; Two Lives (memoir), 2005; The Rivered Earth (libretti), 2011; Summer Requiem (poems), 2015. *Recreations:* music, Chinese calligraphy, swimming. *Address:* c/o David Godwin Associates, 55 Monmouth Street, WC2H 9DG.

SETHIA, Anjum; *see* Anand, A.

SETHIA, Babulal, FRCS, FRCP; Consultant Cardiac Surgeon, Royal Brompton Hospital, since 1999; President, Royal Society of Medicine, since 2014; *b* Edinburgh, 9 Feb. 1951; *s* of Babulal and Joan Sethia; *m* 1978, Nicola Jane Austin; one *s* three *d.* *Educ:* Rugby Sch.; St Thomas's Hosp. Med. Sch., London Univ. (BSc 1972; MB BS 1975). FRCS 1981; FRCP 2014. Surgical Registrar, Bournemouth and Southampton Hosps, 1976–80; Registrar, then Sen. Registrar, Cardiac Surgery, Glasgow Royal Infirmary, 1980–85; Sen. Registrar, Hosp. for Sick Children, Great Ormond St, London, 1985–87; Consultant Cardiac Surgeon, Birmingham Univ. and Children's Hosp., 1987–99. Hon. Sen. Lectr, Imperial Coll. London, 2012–. *Publications:* contribs on congenital heart surgery to internat. jls. *Recreations:* classical music, opera, wine. *Address:* Royal Society of Medicine, 1 Wimpole Street, W1G 0AE. *T:* (020) 7290 2902. *E:* B.Sethia@rsm.ac.uk.

ŠETINC, Marjan; Ambassador of Slovenia to Poland, 2009–14; *b* 15 May 1949; *s* of late Martin Šetinc and Ana Šetinc; *m* 1973, Marta Bartol; one *s* one *d.* *Educ:* Atlantic Coll., S Wales; Univ. of Ljubljana (BA Psychol.); London Sch. of Econs (MSc). Researcher, TUC of Slovenia, 1974–80; Sen. Researcher, Educnl Res. Inst., Ljubljana, 1980–92. MP (Liberal Democracy) Brezice, Slovenia, 1992–96; Mem., Culture and Educn, Sci. and Technol. and Foreign Affairs Select Cttees; Chm., EU Affairs Select Cttee. Rep. of Slovenia, OSCE Parly Delegn, IPU Delegn and Delegn to EU Parlt; Chm., Parly delegns to various bilateral confs; Ambassador to UK and to Ireland, 1998–2002; Dir Gen., Develt Co-operation, 2002–06, Ambassador Responsible for Relns with Multi-Lateral Econ. Orgns, 2006–09, Min. of Foreign Affairs. Member: Gen. Assembly for Slovenia, Internat. Assoc. for Evaluation of Educnl Achievement, 1989–96; Exec. Cttee, Eur. Educnl Res. Assoc., 1996–2001; Nat. Stats Council, 1996–2000. Mem., London Diplomatic Assoc., 1998–2002. Vice-Pres., Slovene Assoc. for Internat. Relns 2015–. Founder Ed., Theory and Res. in Educn jl (formerly School Field), 1989–. *Publications:* Social Conflicts and Strikes, 1975; Public Opinion on Political Decision-Making, 1980; The Averageachieving Curriculum: comparative assessment of pre-university mathematics in Slovenia, 1991; (jtly) Knowledge for Entering the 21st Century, Maths and Natural Sciences: comparison of the achievements of school children aged 14 to 15, in 45 countries, 1997; (jtly) Slovenian International Development Cooperation 2002–04, 2005; contrib. numerous articles and papers to scientific jls. *Recreations:* tennis, mountain walking, chess. *Address:* Mestni trg 17, 1000 Ljubljana, Slovenia.

SETON, Sir Charles Wallace, 13th Bt *cr* 1683 (NS), of Pitmedden, Aberdeenshire; *b* 25 Aug. 1948; *s* of Charles Wallace Seton (*d* 1975) and of Joyce (*née* Perdunn); *S* uncle, 1998, but his name does not appear on the Official Roll of the Baronetage; *m* 1st, 1974, Rebecca (marr. diss. 1994), *d* of Robert Lowery; one *d*; 2nd, 2000, Cindy, *d* of Billy Lee Smith. *Heir: b* Bruce Anthony Seton [*b* 29 April 1957; *m* 1991, Paula Harper; one *s* one *d*].

SETON, Sir Iain (Bruce), 13th Bt *cr* 1663 (NS), of Abercorn; *b* 27 Aug. 1942; *s* of Sir (Christopher) Bruce Seton, 12th Bt and Joyce Vivien (*d* 2005), *d* of late O. G. Barnard; *S* father, 1988; *m* 1963, Margaret Ann, *d* of Walter Charles Faulkner; one *s* one *d.* *Educ:* Colchester and Chadacre. Farming until 1972; mining, 1972–2004. *Heir: s* Laurence Bruce Seton [*b* 1 July 1968; *m* 1990, Rachel, *d* of Jeffery Woods; one *s* two *d*]. *Address:* 16 Radiata Drive, Albany, WA 6330, Australia. *T:* (8) 98415667.

SETTRINGTON, Lord; Charles Henry Gordon-Lennox; *b* 20 Dec. 1994; *s* and *heir* of Earl of March and Kinrara, *qv.*

SEVER, (Eric) John; *b* 1 April 1943; *s* of Eric and Clara Sever; *m* Patricia; one *d.* *Educ:* Sparkhill Commercial School. Travel Executive with tour operator, 1970–77. MP (Lab) Birmingham, Ladywood, Aug. 1977–1983; PPS to the Solicitor General, 1978–79. Contested (Lab) Meriden, 1983. *Recreations:* theatre, cinema, reading. *Address:* 16 The Chase, Sutton Coldfield, West Midlands B76 1JS.

SEVERIN, Prof. Dorothy Virginia Sherman, Hon. OBE 2003; PhD; FSA; Gilmour Professor of Spanish, University of Liverpool, 1982–2008, now Professor Emerita; *b* 24 March 1942; *d* of Wilbur B. and Virginia L. Sherman; marr. diss.; one *d.* *Educ:* Harvard Univ. AB 1963; AM 1964; PhD 1967. FSA 1989. Teaching Fellow and Tutor, Harvard Univ., 1964–66; Vis. Lectr, Univ. of W Indies, 1967–68; Asst Prof., Vassar Coll., 1968; Lectr, Westfield Coll., London Univ., 1969–82; Pro-Vice-Chancellor, Univ. of Liverpool, 1989–92. Member: NI Higher Educn Council, 1993–2001; Res. Panel, British Acad. Humanities Res. Council,

1994–96; Iberian sub-panel, 2008 RAE, HEFCE, 2005–08; Peer Review Coll., AHRC, 2006–09. Vis. Associate Prof., Harvard Univ., 1982; Visiting Professor: Columbia Univ., 1985; Yale Univ., 1985; Univ. of Calif, Berkeley, 1996. Past Pres., British Br., Internat. Courtly Lit. Soc.; Member: Cttee, Asociación Hispánica de Literatura Medieval, 1997–99; Cttee, Asociación Internacional de Hispanistas, 2004–10; Cttee, Convivio, 2004–09; Trustee, 1979–2013, Hon. Treas., 2009–13, MHRA. Corresp. Mem. for UK, Real Academia Española, 2009–. Editor, Bulletin of Hispanic Studies, 1982–2008; Mem. Editl Bd, Hispanic Rev., Celestinesca, Boletín de Real Academia Española. *Publications:* (ed) de Rojas, La Celestina, 1969; Memory in La Celestina, 1970; (ed) Diego de San Pedro, La pasión trobada, 1973; (ed) La Lengua de Erasmo romançada por muy elegante estilo, 1975; The Cancionero de Martínez de Burgos, 1976; (ed with K. Whinnom) Diego de San Pedro, Poesía (Obras completas III), 1979; (ed with Angus MacKay) Cosas sacadas de la Historia del rey Juan el Segundo, 1982; (ed) Celestina, trans. James Mabbe (Eng./Spanish text), 1987; (ed) Celestina (Spanish edn), 1987; Tragicomedy and Novelistic Discourse in Celestina, 1989; Cancionero de Oñate-Castañeda, 1990; ADMYTE: The Paris Cancioneros, 1993, 2nd edn 1999 (PN2 with M. Garcia, PN9, PN13 with F. Maguire); Witchcraft in Celestina, 1995; Animals in Celestina, 1999; Two Spanish Songbooks: The Colombina (LB3) and Egerton (SV2), 2000; Del manuscrito a la imprenta en la época de Isabel la Católica, 2004; Religious Parody and the Spanish Sentimental Romance, 2005; An Electronic Corpus of 15th Century Castilian Cancionero Manuscripts, 2007; Religious Piety and Religious Parody: lives of Christ in late fifteenth-century Castile, 2013; contribs to learned jls incl. Hispanic Rev., Romance Philology, Medium Aevum, MLR and THES. *Address:* Department of Modern Languages and Cultures, Cypress Building, The University, Chatham Street, Liverpool L69 7ZR.

SEVERIN, (Giles) Timothy; author, traveller and historian; *b* 25 Sept. 1940; *s* of Maurice Watkins and Inge Severin; *m* 1966, Dorothy Virginia Sherman (marr. diss. 1979); one *d*. *Educ:* Tonbridge School; Keble Coll., Oxford. MA, BLitt. Commonwealth Fellow, USA, 1964–66. Expeditions: led motorcycle team along Marco Polo route, 1961; R Mississippi by canoe and launch, 1965; Brendan Voyage from W Ireland to N America, 1977; Sindbad Voyage from Oman to China, 1980–81; Jason Voyage from Iolkos to Colchis, 1984; Ulysses Voyage from Troy to Ithaca, 1985; first Crusade route by horse to Jerusalem, 1987–88; travels by horse in Mongolia, 1990; N Pacific voyage by bamboo sailing raft, 1993; Moluccan Islands voyage by traditional sailing prahu, 1996; Pacific and Indonesian island travels, 1998; Caribbean rim travels, 2000. Hon. DLitt Dublin, 1997; Hon. LLD NUI, 2003. Founders Medal, RGS; Livingstone Medal, RSGS; Sykes Medal, RSAA. *Publications:* Tracking Marco Polo, 1964; Explorers of the Mississippi, 1967; The Golden Antilles, 1970; The African Adventure, 1973; Vanishing Primitive Man, 1973; The Oriental Adventure, 1976; The Brendan Voyage, 1978; The Sindbad Voyage, 1982; The Jason Voyage, 1985; The Ulysses Voyage, 1987; Crusader, 1989; In Search of Genghis Khan, 1991; The China Voyage, 1994; The Spice Islands Voyage, 1997; In Search of Moby Dick, 1999; Seeking Robinson Crusoe, 2002; *fiction:* Viking trilogy: Odinn's Child; Sworn Brothers; King's Man, 2005; Pirate series: Corsair, 2007; Buccaneer, 2008; Sea Robber, 2009; Privateer, 2014; Saxon trilogy: The Book of Dreams, 2012; The Emperor's Elephant, 2013; The Pope's Assassin, 2015. *Address:* Timoleague, Co. Cork, Eire. *E:* severin.tim@gmail.com.

SEVERN, Viscount; James Alexander Philip Theo Mountbatten-Windsor; *b* 17 Dec. 2007; *s* of TRH the Earl and Countess of Wessex.
See under Royal Family.

SEVERNE, Air Vice-Marshal Sir John (de Milt), KCVO 1988 (LVO 1961); OBE 1968; AFC 1955; Extra Equerry to the Queen, since 1984; *b* 15 Aug. 1925; *s* of late Dr A. de M. Severne, Wateringbury, Kent; *m* 1951, Katharine Veronica, *d* of late Captain V. E. Kemball, RN (Retd); three *d*. *Educ:* Marlborough. Joined RAF, 1944; Flying Instr, Cranwell, 1948; Staff Instr and PA to Comdt CFS, 1950–53; Flt Comdr No 98 Sqdn, Germany, 1954–55; Sqdn Comdr No 26 Sqdn, Germany, 1956–57; Air Min., 1958; Equerry to Duke of Edinburgh, 1958–61; psa 1962; Chief Instr No 226 Operational Conversion Unit (Lightning), 1963–65; jssc 1965; Jt HQ, ME Comd, Aden, and Air Adviser to the South Arabian Govt, 1966–67; DS, JSSC, 1968; Gp Captain Organisation, HQ Strike Comd, 1968–70; Stn Comdr, RAF Kinloss, 1971–72; RCDS 1973; Comdt, Central Flying School, RAF, 1974–76; Air Cdre Flying Trng, HQ RAF Support Comd, 1976–78; Comdr, Southern Maritime Air Region, Central Sub-Area Eastern Atlantic Comd, and Plymouth Sub-Area Channel Comd, 1978–80; retd 1980; recalled as Captain of the Queen's Flight, 1982–89. ADC to The Queen, 1972–73. Hon. Air Cdre, No 3 (Co. of Devon) Maritime HQ Unit, RAuxAF, 1990–95. President: SW Area Council, RAFA, 1981–95; Queen's Flight Assoc., 1990–2000; CFS Assoc., 1993–98; Taunton and dist Br., ESU, 1996–2009. Pres., RAF Equitation Assoc., 1976–79 (Chm. 1973); Chm., Combined Services Equitation Assoc., 1977–79 (Vice-Chm., 1976). Won King's Cup Air Race, British Air Racing Champion, 1960. DL Somerset, 1991–2001. *Publications:* Silvered Wings (memoirs), 2007. *Address:* Ashley House, Alhampton, Shepton Mallet, Somerset BA4 6PY. *Club:* Royal Air Force.

SEVILLE, Prof. Jonathan Peter Kyle, PhD; CEng, FREng, FIChemE; Dean, Faculty of Engineering and Physical Sciences, University of Surrey, since 2011; *b* 5 Feb. 1956; *s* of Peter Linton Seville and Joan Kathleen Seville (*née* Monks); *m* 1984, Elizabeth Jane Pope; two *d*. *Educ:* Gonville and Caius Coll., Cambridge (BA 1979, MA 1983; MEng 1994); Univ. of Surrey (PhD 1987). FIChemE 1997; FREng 2004. Chemical engr, Courtaulds Ltd, 1979–81; Lectr, 1984–91, Sen. Lectr, 1991–94, Univ. of Surrey; Prof. of Chemical Engrg, 1994–2008, Hd, Dept of Chemical Engrg, 1998–2008, Univ. of Birmingham; Dean of Engrg, Univ. of Warwick, 2008–11. Visiting Professor: Univ. of BC, 1989; Tech. Univ. of Denmark, 1997. Ed.-in-Chief, Powder Technol., 1995–2014. Mem. Council, 2003–10, 2015–, Dep. Pres., 2015–16, IChemE; Mem. Bd, Engrg Council, 2013–. *Publications:* (ed jtly) Gas Cleaning at High Temperatures, 1993; (jtly) Processing of Particulate Solids, 1997; (ed) Gas Cleaning in Demanding Applications, 1997; (ed jtly) Granulation, 2007. *Recreation:* theatre. *Address:* 33 Franklin Court, Wormley, Godalming, Surrey GU8 5US. *E:* j.p.k.seville@surrey.ac.uk.

SEWARD, Dame Margaret (Helen Elizabeth), DBE 1999 (CBE 1994); Chief Dental Officer, Department of Health, 2000–02; *b* 5 Aug. 1935; *d* of Dr Eric Oldershaw and Gwen Oldershaw; adopted, 1938, by John Hutton Mitchell and Marion Findlay Mitchell; *m* 1962, Prof. Gordon Seward, CBE; one *s* one *d*. *Educ:* Latymer Sch., Edmonton; London Hosp. Med. Coll. Dental Sch. (BDS Hons 1959; MDS 1970). FDSRCS 1962; MCCDRCS 1989. Dental practice: Highlands Hosp., 1962–64; Cheshunt Community Clinic, 1969–75; Royal London Hosp., 1980–94. Sen. Res. Fellow, BPMF, Univ. of London, 1975–77. Member: GDC, 1976–99; Bd, Faculty of Dental Surgery, RCS, 1980–94 (Vice-Dean, 1990). President: Section of Odontology, RSM, 1991; BDA, 1993–94; GDC, 1949–99. Editor: Brit. Dental Jl, 1979–92; Internat. Dental Jl, 1990–2000. Dir, Teamwork Project, DoH, 1991–95; Ind. Dir, Quality Assessment Agency, 1997–2000. Chm., Communication Cttee, FDI, 1984–89. Hon. Pres., Women in Dentistry, 1989–92; Hon. Member: Amer. Dental Assoc., 1992; Amer. Coll. of Dentists, 1994. Chm. Govs, Latymer Sch., 1984–94. Hon. FDSRCSE 1995; Hon. Fellow, QMW, 1997. Hon. DDSc: Newcastle, 1995; Sheffield, 2002; Hon. DDS Birmingham, 1995; Hon. DSc: Portsmouth 2005; Plymouth 2011. List of Honour, FDI World Dental Federation, 2008. *Publications:* Disturbances Associated with the Eruption of the Primary Dentition, 1969; Provision of Dental Care by Women Dentists in England and Wales, 1975, 2nd survey 1985; Better Opportunities for Women Dentists, 2001; Open Wide: memoir of the dental dame, 2009; numerous articles in learned jls, UK and internationally. *Recreations:* cooking, entertaining, house-work! *Address:* 1 Wimpole Street, W1G 0AE. *Club:* Royal Society of Medicine.

SEWEL, family name of **Baron Sewel**.

SEWEL, Baron *cr* 1995 (Life Peer), of Gilcomstoun in the District of the City of Aberdeen; **John Buttifant Sewel,** CBE 1984; PhD; *b* 15 Jan. 1946; *s* of late Leonard Buttifant Sewel and of Hilda Ivy Sewel (*née* Brown); *m* 2005, Jennifer Ann (*née* Lindsay). *Educ:* Hanson Boys' Grammar Sch., Bradford; Univ. of Durham (BA 1967); UC, Swansea (MSc (Econ) 1970); Univ. of Aberdeen (PhD 1977). Res. Asst, Dept of Sociology and Anthropology, UC, Swansea, 1967–69; University of Aberdeen: Res. Fellow, Dept of Politics, 1969–72, Depts of Educn and Political Economy, 1972–75; Lectr, 1975; Sen. Lectr, 1988; Prof., Regl Centre for Study of Econ. and Social Policy, 1991–97; Dean: Econ. and Social Scis, 1988–95; Social Scis and Law, 1995–96; Vice-Principal, 1994–96 and 1999–2001; Sen. Vice-Principal, 2001–04. Mem., City of Aberdeen DC, 1974–84 (Leader, 1977–80). Mem., H of L, 1995–2015. Parly Under-Sec. of State, Scottish Office, 1997–99. Chm. of Cttees and Principal Dep. Speaker, H of L, 2012–15. Mem., NATO Parly Assembly, 2000–12. Pres., COSLA, 1982–84. Member: Accounts Commn for Scotland, 1987–96; Scottish Constitutional Commn, 1994–95. Hon. LLD: Aberdeen, 2008; Swansea, 2012. *Publications:* Colliery Closure and Social Change, 1975; Education and Migration, 1976; (with F. W. Bealey) The Politics of Independence: a study of a Scottish town, 1981; (jtly) The Rural Community and the Small School, 1983; articles and chapters on sociology and politics. *Recreations:* hill walking, ski-ing, watching cricket.

SEWELL, Prof. Herbert Fitzgerald, PhD; FRCP, FRCPGlas, FRCPath, FMedSci; Professor of Immunology, and Consultant Immunologist, Faculty of Medicine, University of Nottingham, since 1990; *b* 19 May 1949; *s* of late Wilfred Sewell and Maud Sewell; two *s*. *Educ:* King Edward's Grammar Sch., Aston, Birmingham; Univ. of Birmingham (BDS 1973, MSc 1975, PhD 1978); Univ. of Leicester (MB ChB 1983). MRCPath 1980, FRCPath 1992; MRCPGlas 1987, FRCPGlas 1989; FRCP 1998. Jun. dental posts, Birmingham Dental and Gen. Hosp., 1974–75; MRC Student and Res. Fellow, Dept Exptl Pathol., Univ. of Birmingham, 1974–78; jun. med. posts, East Birmingham Hosp., 1983–84; Consultant Immunologist, Glasgow Royal Infirmary, 1984–85; Sen. Lectr and Hon. Consultant, Dept of Pathology, Univ. of Aberdeen, 1985–90; Pro-Vice-Chancellor Res., Univ. of Nottingham, 2002–07. Chm., Jt Commn on Immunology and Allergy, RCP and RCPath, 1994–98; Member: UK Xenotransplantation Interim Regulatory Authy, 1997–2001; UK Medicines Commn, 1998–2004; Nuffield Council on Bioethics, 2002–06; Medical Research Council: Council Mem., 2004–11; Member: Clinical Trng and Career Develt Panel, 1998–2001; subgp on Inflammatory Bowel Disease and Autism, Strategy Develt Gp, 1998–2000. Founder FMedSci 1998. Hon. DDS Birmingham 2001; Hon. DSc West Indies, 2003. *Publications:* (ed jtly) Essential Immunology for Surgeons, 2011; papers on mechanisms in allergy and on basic and clinical immunology, auto-antibodies (immuno-biomarkers) used in early detection and diagnosis of human solid cancers, such as lung (clinical test, Early CDT-Lung), breast and colorectal tumours. *Recreations:* road jogging, Chinese and African cultural studies, sampling rums of the world. *Address:* A Floor West Block, Queen's Medical Centre, Notts NG7 2UH. *T:* (0115) 823 0001, *Fax:* (0115) 823 0759. *E:* herb.sewell@nottingham.ac.uk.

SEWELL, James Reid, OBE 2001; FSA; City Archivist (formerly Deputy Keeper of Records), Corporation of London, 1984–2003; *b* 12 April 1944; *s* of late James Campbell Sewell and Iris Eveleen Sewell (*née* Reid). *Educ:* High Sch., Glasgow; Univ. of Glasgow (MA Hons Hist.); University Coll. London (Dip. Archive Admin). FSA 1979. Asst Archivist, Durham Co. Record Office, 1967–70; Asst Dep. Keeper, Corp. of London Records Office, 1970–84. Chm. and Pres., Section of Municipal Archives, Internat. Council on Archives, 1992–2000 (Mem. Cttee, 1986–92). Chm., Morley Coll. Ceramic Circle, subseq. London Ceramic Circle at Morley Coll., 2010–15. Fellow, Guildhall Wine Acad., 1993. *Publications:* (with W. A. L. Seaman) The Russian Journal of Lady Londonderry 1836–37, 1973; The Artillery Ground and Fields in Finsbury, 1977; contrib. articles to various professional jls. *Recreations:* tennis, orchid growing, wine. *Address:* 120 Addiscombe Road, Croydon, Surrey CR0 5PQ. *T:* (020) 8656 4046. *Club:* Shirley Park Lawn Tennis (Hon. Sec., 1983–98).

SEWELL, Rufus Frederick; actor; *b* 29 Oct. 1967; *s* of late Bill Sewell and of Jo Sewell; *m* 1999, Yasmin Abdallah (*see* Y. Sewell) (marr. diss.); partner, Amy Gardener; one *s*. *Theatre includes:* As You Like It, The Government Inspector, The Seagull, Crucible, Sheffield, 1989; Royal Hunt of the Sun, Comedians, Compass, 1989; Pride and Prejudice, Royal Exchange, Manchester, 1991; Making It Better, Hampstead and Criterion, 1992; Arcadia, NT, 1993; Translations, Plymouth Th., NY, 1995; Rat in the Skull, Duke of York's, 1995; Macbeth, Queen's, 1999; Luther, NT, 2001; Rock 'n' Roll, Royal Court, 2006 (Best Actor: London Evening Standard Th. Awards, 2006; Critics' Circle Th. Awards, 2006; Laurence Olivier Awards, 2007); Old Times, Harold Pinter Th., 2013; Closer, Donmar, 2015. *Films include:* Twenty-One, 1991; Dirty Weekend, 1993; A Man of No Importance, 1994; Carrington, Victory, 1995; Hamlet, 1997; Dark City, The Woodlanders, At Sachem Farm, Martha Meet Frank Daniel and Laurence, Illuminata, 1998; The Honest Courtesan, In a Savage Land, 1999; Bless the Child, A Knight's Tale, 2001; Extreme Ops, 2003; The Legend of Zorro, 2005; Tristan & Isolde, The Holiday, 2006; The Illusionist, Amazing Grace, 2007; All Things to All Men, 2013; The Sea, 2014; Hercules 3D, 2014. *Television includes:* The Last Romantics, 1991; Gone to Seed, 1992; Dirty Something, 1993; Citizen Locke, Middlemarch, 1994; Cold Comfort Farm, Henry IV, 1995; Arabian Nights, 2000; She-Creature, 2001; Helen of Troy, 2003; Charles II: The Power and the Passion, 2003; The Pillars of the Earth, 2010; Zen, 2011; Parade's End, Restless, 2012; Killing Jesus, 2015. *Address:* c/o Julian Belfrage Associates, 3rd Floor, 9 Argyll Street, W1F 7TG.

SEWELL, Thomas Robert McKie; HM Diplomatic Service, retired; Contributing Editor, Informa Group Publishing plc, since 1991; international grains consultant; *b* 18 Aug. 1921; *s* of late O. B. Fane Sewell and Frances M. Sewell (*née* Sharp); *m* 1955, Jennifer Mary Sandeman (decd); one *d* (and one *d* decd). *Educ:* Eastbourne Coll.; Trinity Coll., Oxford (Schol., Heath Harrison Prize, MA); Lausanne and Stockholm Univs (Schol.). HM Forces, 1940–46 (despatches), Indian Armoured Corps (paratrooper); Major. Entered Foreign Service, 1949; Second Sec., Moscow, 1950–52; FO, 1952–55; First Sec., 1954; Madrid, 1955–59; Lima, 1959–61; Chargé d'Affaires, 1960; FO, 1961–63; Counsellor and Head of Chancery, Moscow, 1964–66; Diplomatic Service Rep. at IDC, 1966; Head of Associated States, West Indies and Swaziland Depts, Commonwealth Office, 1967–68; accompanied Sec. of State to Swazi Independence Celebrations, 1968; Head of N American and Caribbean Dept, FCO, 1968–70; Asst Sec., MAFF, 1970–81; UK Rep. to Internat. Wheat Council, 1972–81. Chm., World Grain Conf., Brussels, 1984–92. Contested: (C) Greater Manchester Central, EP elecn, 1984; (Referendum) Weston-super-Mare, 1997. Vis. Fellow, Hubert H. Humphrey Inst. of Public Affairs and Dept of Agricl and Applied Econs, Univ. of Minnesota, 1985; Leverhulme Res. Fellow, 2003. Chm., 1987–2001, Pres., 2001–, Training the Teachers of Tomorrow Trust. *Publications:* Famine and Surplus (with John de Courcy Ling), 1985; The World Grain Trade, 1992; Grain-Carriage by Sea, 1998, 2nd edn 2002 (trans. Japanese 2002); The Global Grain Market, 2000, 2nd edn 2004; What Did You Do in the Cold War, Daddy?, 2006. *Recreations:* international trail riding, inland waterways cruising. *Clubs:* Farmers, Airborne.

SEWELL, Maj.-Gen. Timothy Patrick T.; *see* Toyne Sewell.

SEWELL, Yasmin; Founder and Director, Yasmin Sewell Ltd, since 2008; *b* Sydney, 22 Jan. 1976; *d* of Robert Abdallah and Joyce Abdallah; *m* 1999, Rufus Frederick Sewell, *qv* (marr. diss.); *m* 2012, Kyle Robinson; one *s*. *Educ:* St Catherine's Sch., Waverly. Founder and Dir, Yasmin Cho Boutique, London, 1998–2001; Buying Dir, Browns, London, 2005–08; Chief

Creative Consultant, Liberty, London, 2008–09. Young Australian of the Year Award, 2012. *Publications:* (contrib.) Pattern, 2013. *Address:* Yasmin Sewell Ltd, 123 Clifton Street, EC2A 4LD. *T:* (020) 7613 2766. *E:* you@yasminsewell.com.

SEXTON, David Howard; Literary Editor, since 1997, and Lead Film Reviewer, since 2010, London Evening Standard (formerly Evening Standard); *b* 2 Aug. 1958; *s* of late Richard Herbert Sexton and of Margaret Laura Sexton (*née* Page); *m* 1988, Emma Crichton-Miller (marr. diss. 1997); one *d* by Catherine Bennett. *Educ:* Colchester Royal Grammar Sch.; Trinity Coll., Cambridge (BA 1980). Literary Ed., Sunday Correspondent, 1990–91; columnist, TLS, 1991–97; radio critic, Sunday Telegraph, 1991–2007. Critic of the Year, British Press Awards, 2015. *Publications:* The Strange World of Thomas Harris, 2001. *Recreations:* food, wine, books, trees, France. *Address:* Evening Standard, Northcliffe House, 2 Derry Street, W8 5EE. *E:* David.Sexton@standard.co.uk; Saint Caprais, 82110 Bouloc, France.

SEYCHELLES, Bishop of the, since 2009; **Rt Rev. James Richard Wong Yin Song;** *b* Rodrigues Island, Mauritius, 13 Jan. 1960; *s* of Maxime and Louisa Wong Yin Song; *m* 1982, Doreen Kuin Fong; one *s* one *d*. *Educ:* St Paul's Theol Coll., Mauritius; Selly Oak Colls, Birmingham. Ordained deacon and priest, 1983; Canon, St James Cathedral, Mauritius, 2002; Archdeacon of Mauritius, 2003. *Address:* Bishop's House, Bel Eau, PO Box 44, Victoria, Mahé, Seychelles. *T:* (office) 323879, 322508, (mobile) 777780. *E:* bp.james.wong@gmail.com.

SEYFRIED HERBERT, family name of **Baron Herbert**.

SEYMOUR, family name of **Duke of Somerset,** and **Marquess of Hertford**.

SEYMOUR, Lord; Sebastian Edward Seymour; *b* 3 Feb. 1982; *s* and *heir* of 19th Duke of Somerset, *qv*; *m* 2006, Arlette Lafayeedney (marr. diss. 2013). *Educ:* Marlborough Coll.; RAC Cirencester. MRICS. *Recreations:* Middle East and African business, politics, travel, food and wine, sports. *Address:* The Estate Office, Shadrack, Berry Pomeroy, Totnes, Devon TQ9 6NJ.

SEYMOUR, Anya; *see* Hindmarch, A.

SEYMOUR, Prof. Carol Anne, (Mrs Carol Seymour-Richards), PhD; FRCP, FRCPath, FFFLM; Professor of Clinical Biochemistry and Metabolic Medicine, St George's Hospital Medical School, 1991–2004, now Emeritus; Medico-legal Adviser, Medical Protection Society, since 2003; *b* 19 March 1945; *d* of Raymond and Erica Seymour; *m* 1987, Prof. Peter Richards (*d* 2011). *Educ:* Badminton Sch.; St Anne's Coll., Oxford (MA, BM BCh); RPMS (MSc, PhD); Holborn Coll., Univ. of Wolverhampton (Postgrad. DipLaw 1998); Inns of Court Sch. of Law (Postgrad. DipLS 2001). MRCP 1972, FRCP 1985; FRCPath 1993; FFFLM 2006. Lectr in Medicine and Hon. Consultant Physician, Univ. of Cambridge Sch. of Clinical Medicine/Addenbrooke's Hosp., 1977–91; Fellow, and Dir of Med. Studies, Trinity Coll., Cambridge, 1981–91. Dir of Med. Advice to Parly and Health Service Comr, 1997–2003; Royal College of Physicians: Academic Registrar, 1987–91; Examiner for MRCP, 1991–; Mem. Council, 1996–2000, 2003–05; Examiner for MRCPath, RCPath, 1993–2005; Mem., GMC, 1987–91 (Lead Performance Assessor, 1999–2003). Vice Pres., Faculty of Forensic and Legal Medicine, 2014–. Called to the Bar, Gray's Inn, 2001. *Publications:* (contrib.) Oxford Textbook of Medicine, 1983, 3rd edn 1995; Clinical Clerking, 1984, (jtly) 3rd edn 2003; many articles on liver disease and metabolic aspects of clinical medicine. *Recreations:* music (clarinet and organ), walking, cycling. *Address:* Barefords, 78 Commercial End, Swaffham Bulbeck, Cambs CB25 0NE. *T:* (01223) 812007. *E:* carol.seymour@mps.org.uk.

SEYMOUR, David, CB 2005; Independent Reviewer, Justice and Security (Northern Ireland) Act 2007, since 2014; Legal Adviser to the Home Office and Northern Ireland Office, 2000–12; *b* 24 Jan. 1951; *s* of late Graham Seymour and Betty (*née* Watson); *m* 1972, Elisabeth Huitson; one *s* two *d*. *Educ:* Trinity Sch., Croydon; Queen's Coll., Oxford (Open Exhibn; BA Jurisprudence 1972; MA 1977); Fitzwilliam Coll., Cambridge (LLB 1974). Law clerk, Rosenfeld, Meyer & Susman (Attorneys), Beverly Hills, Calif, 1972–73; called to the Bar: Gray's Inn (Holt Schol.), 1975, Bencher, 2001; NI, 1997; pupillage, 1975–76; Legal Advr's Br., Home Office, 1976–97; Principal Asst Legal Advr, 1994; Dep. Legal Advr, 1996; Legal Sec. to the Law Officers, 1997–2000. Vis. Lectr in European Human Rights Law, Univ. of Conn Sch. of Law, 1986. Mem., Review of Criminal Justice System in NI, 1998–2000. Master of Estates and Mem., Mgt Cttee, Gray's Inn, 2012–14. Governor: Trinity Sch., Croydon, 2010– (Chm. Govs, 2015–); Court, Whitgift Foundn, 2015–. Chm., Reigate Squash Club, 2007–11. *Recreations:* watching cricket, gardening, walking, golf. *Address:* c/o Home Office, 2 Marsham Street, SW1P 4DF. *Clubs:* MCC; Reigate Heath Golf.

SEYMOUR, Jill; Member (UK Ind) West Midlands Region, European Parliament, since 2014; *b* Cosford, Shropshire, 8 May 1958; *m* Brian Seymour; one *s*. PR exec., Aga-Rayburn; sales exec., American Express and Thomson Internat. Contested (UK Ind) Wrekin, 2015. *Address:* European Parliament, 60 Rue Wiertz, 1047 Brussels, Belgium.

SEYMOUR, Sir Julian (Roger), Kt 2014; CBE 2001; *b* 19 March 1945; *s* of Evelyn Roger Seymour and Rosemary Evelyn Seymour (*née* Flower); *m* 1984, Diana Elizabeth Griffith; one *s* one *d*. *Educ:* Eton. Director: Collett, Dickinson, Pearce Ltd, 1969–79; Robert Fox Ltd, 1980–85; Dir, Corporate Finance, Lowe Gp PLC, 1985–91; Dir, Lady Thatcher's Private Office, 1991–2000. Non-executive Director: Chime Communications PLC, 1990–2007; Vanderbilt Homes, 2014–. Comr, English Heritage, 1992–98; Chm., Margaret Thatcher Archive Trust, 2005–. *Recreations:* gardening, shooting. *Address:* 37 Surrey Lane, SW11 3PA.

SEYMOUR, Prof. Leonard William, PhD; Professor of Gene Therapies, University of Oxford, since 2002 (Head, Department of Clinical Pharmacology, 2009–10); *b* 4 Sept. 1958; *s* of Percy and Daisy Seymour. *Educ:* Plymouth Coll.; Univ. of Manchester (BSc Hons 1980); Keele Univ. (PhD 1985). Lectr, 1993–99, Reader in Molecular Therapy, 1999–2002, CRC Inst. for Cancer Studies, Univ. of Birmingham. Pres. (first), British Soc. for Gene Therapy, 2004–09; Gen. Sec., European Soc. for Gene and Cell Therapy, 2009–14. Co-founding Scientist: Hybrid Systems Ltd, 1998; Oxford Genetics Ltd, 2010. *Publications:* over 100 primary scientific papers in fields of gene therapy and virotherapy of cancer. *Recreations:* all forms of music, playing keyboard, hill walking and trekking through remote areas. *Address:* Department of Oncology, University of Oxford, Old Road Campus Research Building, Old Road Campus, off Roosevelt Drive, Headington, Oxford OX3 7DQ. *T:* (01865) 617020.

SEYMOUR, Lynn, CBE 1976; ballerina; *b* Wainwright, Alberta, 8 March 1939. *Educ:* Vancouver; Sadler's Wells Ballet School. Joined Sadler's Wells Ballet Company, 1957; Deutsche Oper, Berlin, 1966; Artistic Director: Ballet of Bavarian State Opera, Munich, 1979–80; Greek National Opera Ballet, 2006–07; has danced with Royal Ballet, English Nat. Ballet, Berliner Ballet, and Adventures in Motion Pictures. *Roles created:* Adolescent, in The Burrow, Royal Opera House, 1958; Bride, in Le Baiser de la Fée, 1960; Girl, in The Invitation, 1960; Young Girl, in Les Deux Pigeons, 1961; Principal, in Symphony, 1963; Principal, in Images of Love, 1964; Juliet, in Romeo and Juliet, 1964; Albertine, BBC TV, 1966; Concerto, 1966; Anastasia, 1966; Flowers, 1972; Side Show, 1972; A Month in the Country, 1976; Five Brahms Waltzes in the manner of Isadora Duncan, 1976; mother, in Fourth Symphony, 1977; Mary Vetsera, in Mayerling, 1978; Take Five, 1978. *Choreography for:* Rashomon, for Royal Ballet Touring Co., 1976; The Court of Love, for SWRB, 1977; Intimate Letters, 1978 and Mac and Polly, for Commonwealth Dance Gala, 1979; Boreas, and Tattoo, for Bavarian State Opera Ballet, 1980; Wolfi, for Ballet Rambert, 1987; Bastet, for SWRB, 1988. A Time to Dance (film), 1986.

SEYMOUR, Sir Michael Patrick Culme-, 6th Bt *cr* 1809, of Highmount, co. Limerick and Friery Park, Devonshire; consultant, entrepreneur, photographer; Partner, Competitive Capital Ltd, Singapore, since 2009; *b* 28 April 1962; *s* of Major Mark Charles Culme-Seymour and of his 3rd wife, Patricia June, *d* of Charles Reid-Graham; *S* cousin, 1999; *m* 1st, 1986, Karin Fleig (marr. diss. 2007); two *s*; 2nd, 2008, Christin Kaufmann; one *d*. Regl Vice-Pres., Asia, Pacific and India, Swisscargo, 1998–2003; CEO, Asia, Pacific and EMEA, DHL Global Mail, 2003–08; Owner: MCS Lifestyle Photography, Singapore, 2008–; Fischer Road Express Asia Pte Ltd, Singapore, 2012–. *Heir:* *s* Michael Culme-Seymour, *b* 5 Oct. 1986. *E:* mcslifestyle@gmail.com.

SEYMOUR, His Honour Richard William; QC 1991; a Senior Circuit Judge, 2000–15; *b* 4 May 1950; *e s* of late Albert Percy and Vera Maud Seymour; *m* 1971, Clare Veronica, BSS, MSc, *d* of Stanley Victor Peskett; one *s* one *d*. *Educ:* Brentwood Sch.; Royal Belfast Academical Instn; Christ's Coll., Cambridge (schol.; BA 1971; MA 1975). Holker Jun. Exhibn, 1970, Holker Sen. Schol., 1972, Gray's Inn; called to the Bar, Gray's Inn, 1972. Asst Recorder, 1991–95; Recorder, 1995–2000; a Judge of the Technology and Construction Court, 2000–05; assigned to Queen's Bench Div. of High Court, 2005–15. Pres., Mental Health Review Tribunals, 2000. Gov., Anglia Ruskin Univ., 2011–. *Publications:* (ed jtly) Kemp and Kemp, The Quantum of Damages, 4th edn 1975; legal chapters in: Willis and Willis, Practice and Procedure for the Quantity Surveyor, 8th edn 1980; Willis and George, The Architect in Practice, 6th edn 1981; with Clare Seymour: Courtroom Skills for Social Workers, 2007; Courtroom and Report Writing Skills for Social Workers, 2011; Practical Child Law for Social Workers, 2013. *Recreations:* archaeology, walking, foreign travel.

SEYMOUR, Richard William; Founder and Director, Seymour Powell, since 1984; *b* 1 May 1953; *s* of Bertram Seymour and Annie Irene (*née* Sherwood); *m* 1980, Anne Margaret Hart; one *s* one *d*. *Educ:* Central Sch. of Art & Design (BA); Royal Coll. of Art (MA; Sen. Fellow, 2005). Advertising Creative Dir, Blazelynn Advertising, London, 1978–81; film prodn designer, with Anton Furst, later Seymour Furst, 1981–83; freelance designer working on advertising and new product develt projects, 1982–83; Founder, with D. Powell, Seymour Powell (product and transportation design consultancy), 1984 (clients incl. Nokia, Ford, Aqualisa). Vis. Prof. of Product and Transportation Design, RCA, 1995–. Trustee, Design Mus., London, 1994–. Contrib. to TV progs and children's progs featuring design and future thinking. Pres., D&AD, 1999 (Mem., Exec. Cttee, 1997–). FRSA 1993; FCSD 1993. Hon. DDes Centre of Creative Studies, Michigan, 2002. Awards include: Best Overall Design and Product Design (for Norton F1 motorcycle), Design Week Awards, 1990; Silver Awards (for Technophone Cellular Phone), 1991, and (for MuZ Scorpion motorcycle), 1993, and President's Award (for outstanding contribn to design), 1995, D&AD; Product Design Award, BBC Design Awards, 1994; Design Effectiveness Award, Design Business Assoc. (for SEB appliances), 1995, 2002, 2003; Special Commendation, Prince Philip Designers Prize, 1997; Janus award, France, 2002; Gerald Frewer Meml Trophy, Inst. of Engrg Designers, 2003; Star Pack Award, 2003; Best Corporate Film, Golden Camera Awards: for Samsung European Premium Design, 2003; for Unilever, 2005; Lifetime Achievement Award, FX Mag., 2010. *Publications:* (with M. Palin) The Mirrorstone (Smarties Design Award, Hatchard's Top Ten Author's Award), 1986. *Recreations:* Early English music, cello, motorcycling. *Address:* Seymour Powell, The Factory, 265 Merton Road, SW18 5JS. *T:* (020) 7381 6433. *Clubs:* Bluebird, Chelsea Arts.

SEYMOUR, Urmila; *see* Banerjee, U.

SEYMOUR-JACKSON, Ralph; Chief Executive Officer, Student Loans Company Limited, 2003–10; *b* 11 May 1963; *s* of Alan and Arabella Seymour-Jackson; *m* 1993, Angela Fenn; one *s* one *d*. *Educ:* Wadham Coll., Oxford (BA Maths 1984). FIA 1991. Pilot, RAF, 1980–88; Actuary, Norwich Union, 1988–92; Chief Exec., Scoplife Insce Co., Athens, 1992–96; Scottish Provident Institution (Mutual Life Insurer): Gp Corporate Develt and Mktg Manager, Gp Hd Office, Edinburgh, 1996–98; Hd, UK Ops, 1998–2000; IT Dir, Abbey National Finance and Investment Services, 2001–03. *Recreations:* skydiving, cooking, children.

SEYMOUR-RICHARDS, Carol Anne; *see* Seymour, C. A.

SEYS LLEWELLYN, Anthony John, QC 2003; **His Honour Judge Seys Llewellyn;** a Senior Circuit Judge and Designated Civil Judge for Wales, since 2008; *b* 24 April 1949; *s* of late His Honour John Desmond Seys-Llewellyn and Hilda Elaine (*née* Porcher); *m* 1975, Helen Mary Manson; two *s* two *d*. *Educ:* King's Sch., Chester; Jesus Coll., Oxford (1st cl. Hons Law 1970; BCL 1st cl. Hons 1971). Called to the Bar, Gray's Inn, 1972 (scholarships; Bencher, 2006); Recorder of the Crown Court, Wales and Chester Circuit, 1990–2008. Asst Comr, Parly Boundary Commns for England and Wales, 1991–2008. *Recreations:* sports including rowing (now viewed from river banks), art, music, family man. *Address:* Cardiff Civil Justice Centre, 2 Park Street, Cardiff CF10 1ET.

SHACKERLEY, Very Rev. Dr (Albert) Paul; Dean of Brecon, since 2014; *b* Tredegar, S Wales, 16 Aug. 1956. *Educ:* Chichester Theol Coll.; King's Coll. London (MA 1997); Sheffield Univ. (PhD 2007). Served Royal Army Medical Corps, 1977–80; Church Army Officer, 1980–97; ordained deacon, 1993, priest, 1994; Asst Curate, All Souls, Harlesden, 1993–96; Priest-in-charge, 1996–98, Vicar, 1998–2002, All Saints, Chelmsford; Canon Residentiary, 2002–09, Vice-Dean, 2005–10, Hon. Canon, 2010–14, Sheffield Cathedral; Vicar, Doncaster Minster, 2010–14. *Address:* The Deanery, Cathedral Close, Brecon LD3 9DP.

SHACKLE, Prof. Christopher, PhD; FBA 1990; Professor of Modern Languages of South Asia, University of London, 1985–2007, now Emeritus; *b* 4 March 1942; *s* of late Francis Mark Shackle and Diana Margaret Shackle (*née* Harrington, subseq. Thomas); *m* 1st, 1964, Emma Margaret Richmond (marr. diss.); one *s* two *d*; 2nd, 1988, Shahrukh Husain; one *s* one *d*. *Educ:* Haileybury and ISC; Merton College, Oxford (BA 1963); St Antony's College, Oxford (DipSocAnthrop 1965; BLitt 1966); PhD London, 1972. School of Oriental and African Studies, University of London: Fellow in Indian Studies, 1966; Lectr in Urdu and Panjabi, 1969; Reader in Modern Languages of South Asia, 1979; Pro-Dir for Academic Affairs, 1997–2002 (Acting Dir, Jan.–April 2001); Pro-Dir, 2002–03; Res. Prof., 2007–08. British Academy: Mem. Council, 1995–96, 2001–04; Chm., Sect. H3 Oriental and African Studies, 1999–2003. Medal, Royal Asiatic Soc., 2006. Sitara-i-Imtiaz (Pakistan), 2005. *Publications:* Teach Yourself Punjabi, 1972; (with D. J. Matthews) An Anthology of Classical Urdu Love Lyrics, 1972; The Siraiki Language of Central Pakistan, 1976; Catalogue of the Panjabi and Sindhi Manuscripts in the India Office Library, 1977; A Guru Nanak Glossary, 1981; An Introduction to the Sacred Language of the Sikhs, 1983; The Sikhs, 1984; (with D. J. Matthews and S. Husain) Urdu Literature, 1985; (with R. Snell) Hindi and Urdu since 1800, 1990; (with Z. Moir) Ismaili Hymns from South Asia, 1992; (with R. Snell) The Indian Narrative, 1992; (with S. Sperl) Qasida Poetry in Islamic Asia and Africa, 1996; (with J. Majeed) Hali's Musaddas, 1997; (with N. Awde) Treasury of Indian Love Poetry, 1999; (with G. Singh and A. Mandair) Sikh Religion, Culture and Ethnicity, 2001; (with D. Arnold) SOAS Since the Sixties, 2003; (with A. Mandair) Teachings of the Sikh Gurus, 2005; (with L. Lewisohn) Attar and the Persian Sufi Tradition, 2006 (Internat. Book of the Year Award, Iran, 2008); (trans.) Mazhar ul Islam, The Season of Love, Bitter Almonds and Delayed Rains, 2006; (ed and trans.) Bulleh Shah, Sufi Lyrics, 2015; numerous articles.

SHACKLETON, family name of **Baroness Shackleton of Belgravia.**

SHACKLETON OF BELGRAVIA, Baroness *cr* 2010 (Life Peer), of Belgravia in the City of Westminster; **Fiona Sara Shackleton,** LVO 2006; Personal Solicitor to Prince William of Wales and Prince Harry of Wales, since 1996; Partner, Payne Hicks Beach, since 2001; *b* 26 May 1956; *d* of late Jonathan Philip Charkham, CBE and Moira Elizabeth Frances Charkham; *m* 1985, Ian Ridgeway Shackleton; two *d. Educ:* Francis Holland Sch.; Benenden Sch.; Univ. of Exeter (LLB 1977). Articled Clerk, Herbert Smith, 1978–80; admitted solicitor, 1980; Partner, Brecher & Co., 1981–84; Farrer & Co., 1984–2000 (Partner, 1987–2000); Personal Solicitor to Prince of Wales, 1996–2005. Inaugural Mem., Internat. Acad. of Matrimonial Lawyers, 1986–. Mem., Adv. Council, LPO, 2013–. Trustee, Endowment Fund, ROH, 2013–. Gov., Benenden Sch., 1986–2007. Hon. LLD Exeter, 2010. *Publications:* (with Olivia Timbs) The Divorce Handbook, 1992. *Recreations:* listening to music, particularly opera, cooking, calligraphy, bridge. *Address:* 10 New Square, Lincoln's Inn, WC2A 3QG. *T:* (020) 7465 4300.

SHACKLETON, Margaret; Headteacher, Sutton Coldfield Grammar School for Girls, since 2010; *b* Solihull, 1 Sept. 1969; *d* of Anne Corkery; *m* 1999, Paul Shackleton. *Educ:* Univ. of East Anglia (BA Hons; PGCE). NPQH 2010. Teacher of Hist. and Eng., and Hd of Year, Acle High Sch., 1993–96; Hd of Hist., Pingle Sch., 1997–2001; Asst Headteacher, George Spencer Technology Coll., 2001–07; Dep. Headteacher, Sutton Coldfield Grammar Sch. for Girls, 2007–10. *Recreations:* reading, cinema, walking with Paul and our dogs, watching 'The West Wing', avoiding spending time in the kitchen. *Address:* Sutton Coldfield Grammar School for Girls, Jockey Road, Sutton Coldfield, W Midlands B73 5PT. *T:* (0121) 354 1479. *E:* msh@suttcold.bham.sch.uk.

SHADBOLT, Sir Nigel (Richard), Kt 2013; PhD; CEng, FREng; CPsychol; Professor of Artificial Intelligence, since 2000, and Head, Web and Internet Science Group, since 2011, University of Southampton (Deputy Head, School of Electronics and Computer Science, 2000–11); Chairman and Co-Founder, Open Data Institute, London, since 2012; *b* 9 April 1956; *s* of Douglas William Robert and Audrey Shadbolt; *m* 1992, Beverly Saunders; one *s* one *d. Educ:* Univ. of Newcastle upon Tyne (BA 1st cl. Hons Philosophy and Psychol.); Univ. of Edinburgh (PhD Artificial Intelligence 1983). CPsychol 1990; CITP 2004; CEng 2005, FREng 2006. Res. Fellow, Univ. of Edinburgh, 1982–83; University of Nottingham: Lectr, 1983–90; Reader, 1990–92; Allan Standen Prof. of Intelligent Systems, 1992–99. Chief Technol. Officer, 2006–10, Chief Scientific Officer, 2010–11, Garlik Ltd. UK Information Advr, 2009–10; Chairman: Local Public Data Panel, DCLG, 2010–; MiData Prog., BIS, 2011–. Member: Public Sector Transparency Bd, 2010–; Sci. Adv. Bd, Home Office, 2010–; Res. Sector Transparency Bd, DoH, 2012–; Health and Social Care Transparency Panel; Inf. Economy Council, BIS, 2013–. Dir, World Wide Web Foundn, 2009–13; Dir and Trustee, Web Science Trust, 2009–. FBCS 2002 (Vice Pres., 2003–05; Dep. Pres., 2005–06; Pres., 2006–07). Hon. DSc Nottingham, 2011. *Publications:* (jtly) POP-11 Programming for Artificial Intelligence, 1987; Research and Development in Expert Systems VI, 1989; (jtly) Advances in Knowledge Acquisition, 1996; (jtly) Knowledge Engineering and Management, 2000; (jtly) The Spy in the Coffee Machine: the end of privacy as we know it, 2008; over 500 articles on facets of artificial intelligence, psychology, web science, open data and computing. *Recreations:* my family, sailing, reading, collecting - ranging from space memorabilia to fossils! *Address:* Electronics and Computer Science, University of Southampton, Southampton SO17 1BJ. *E:* nrs@ecs.soton.ac.uk.

SHAFER, Prof. Byron Edwin, PhD; Glenn B. and Cleone Orr Hawkins Professor of Political Science, University of Wisconsin, Madison, since 2001; *b* 8 Jan. 1947; *s* of Byron Henry Shafer and Doris Marguerite (*née* Von Bergen); *m* 1981, Wanda K. Green; one *s. Educ:* Yale Univ. (BA Magna Cum Laude, Deptl Hons in Pol Sci. with Excep. Dist. 1968); Univ. of California at Berkeley (PhD Pol Sci. 1979). Resident Scholar, Russell Sage Foundn, USA, 1977–84; Associate Prof. of Pol Sci., Florida State Univ., 1984–85; Andrew W. Mellon Prof. of American Govt, Univ. of Oxford, 1985–2001; Fellow, 1985–2001, now Emeritus, and Actg Warden, 2000–01, Nuffield Coll., Oxford. John G. Winant Vis. Prof. of American Govt, Univ. of Oxford, 2015. Editor, The Forum: a Jl of Applied Res. in Contemporary Politics, 2007–. Hon. MA Oxford, 1985. E. E. Schattschneider Prize, 1980, Franklin L. Burdette Prize, 1990, Jack L. Walker Award, 1997, Amer. Pol Sci. Assoc.; V. O. Key Award, Southern Pol Sci. Assoc., 2007. *Publications:* Presidential Politics, 1980; Quiet Revolution: the struggle for the Democratic Party and the shaping of post-reform politics, 1983; Bifurcated Politics: evolution and reform in the National Party Convention, 1988; Is America Different?, 1991; The End of Realignment?: interpreting American electoral eras, 1991; The Two Majorities: the issue context of modern American politics, 1995; Postwar Politics in the G-7, 1996; Present Discontents: American politics in the very late twentieth century, 1997; Partisan Approaches to Postwar American Politics, 1998; Contesting Democracy: substance and structure in American political history 1775–2000, 2001; The State of American Politics, 2002; The Two Majorities and the Puzzle of Modern American Politics, 2003; The End of Southern Exceptionalism, 2006; The American Public Mind: the issue structure of mass politics in the postwar United States, 2010; The American Political Landscape, 2014; articles in learned jls. *Recreations:* furniture restoration, gardening, livestock management. *Address:* Department of Political Science, University of Wisconsin, 110 North Hall, 1050 Bascom Mall, Madison, WI 53706, USA.

SHAFFER, Elinor Sophia, PhD; FBA 1995; Senior Research Fellow, School of Advanced Study, Institute of Modern Languages Research (formerly Institute of Germanic Studies, then Institute of Germanic and Romance Studies), University of London, since 1998 (Fellow, 1997–98); *b* 6 April 1935; *d* of Vernon Cecil Stoneman and Helene Dorothy Stoneman (*née* Nieschlag); *m* 1964, Brian M. Shaffer; two *s. Educ:* Chicago Univ. (BA 1954); St Hilda's Coll., Oxford (BA 1958; MA 1962); PhD Columbia Univ., NY, 1966; MA Cantab 1968. Fellow, Columbia Univ., 1961–63; Instr, Dept of English, Univ. of Calif, Berkeley, 1963–64; Res. Fellow, Clare Hall, Cambridge, 1968–71; Lectr, 1971–77, Reader in English and Comparative Lit., 1977–97, UEA. Visiting Professor: Brown Univ., 1983–84; Zurich Univ., 1986; Stanford Univ., 1988; Vis. Lectr, Free Univ., Berlin, 1979; Study Fellow, ACLS, 1971; Leverhulme Fellowship, 1976; Research Fellow: Humanities Res. Centre, ANU, 1982; Humanities Res. Inst., Univ. of Calif, 1991; Dist. Fellow, Eur. Humanities Res. Centre, Oxford, 1995–; Vis. Fellow, All Souls Coll., Oxford, 1996; Hon. Prof., UCL, 2013–. Editor: Comparative Criticism, 1979–2004; inaugural issue (with A. Brady), 2004, special issue on reception studies, 2006, Comparative Critical Studies; Series Editor, The Reception of British and Irish Authors in Europe (contrib. preface or introduction to all vols), 1997–. Hon. Dr Bucharest, 2013. *Publications:* 'Kubla Khan' and The Fall of Jerusalem: the mythological school in Biblical criticism and secular literature 1770–1880, 1975; Erewhons of the Eye: Samuel Butler as painter, photographer and art critic, 1988; The Third Culture: literature and science, 1998; (ed jtly and introd.) The Reception of S. T. Coleridge in Europe, 2007; (ed jtly and introd.) The Reception of Charles Darwin in Europe, vols III and IV, 2013; (ed jtly and introd.) The Reception of George Eliot in Europe; (with J. T. Leerssen) Comparative Critical Studies in Britain 1800 to the Present, 2015; Coleridge's Literary Theory, 2015; *chapters in:* The Coleridge Connection, 1990; Romanticism and the Sciences, 1990; Aesthetic Illusion: theoretical and historical approaches, 1990; Reflecting Senses: perception and appearance in literature, culture and the arts, 1994; Milton, the Metaphysicals and Romanticism, 1994; Apocalypse Theory and the Ends of the World, 1995; Boydell's Shakespeare Gallery, 1996; Transports: imaginative geographies 1600–1830, 1996; (contrib.) Oxford Encyclopedia of Aesthetics, 1998, 2nd edn 2014; The Cambridge History of Literary Criticism, vol. V, Romanticism, 2000; Coleridge and the Science of Life, 2001; Mapping Lives: the uses of biography, 2001; Goethe in the English-speaking World, 2002; (contrib.) Oxford Companion to Photography, 2003; Anglo-German Affinities and Antipathies in the Nineteenth Century, 2004; Samuel Butler: Victorian against the grain, 2007; Oxford Handbook of Coleridge, 2008; contrib. to Oxford DNB; catalogues for exhibns about Samuel Butler, 1989, 2002; many lectures, reviews and contribs to learned jls. *Recreations:* theatre, travelling, photography, wine. *Address:* 9 Cranmer Road, Cambridge CB3 9BL.

SHAFFER, Sir Peter (Levin), Kt 2001; CBE 1987; FRSL; playwright; *b* 15 May 1926; *s* of Jack Shaffer and Reka Shaffer (*née* Fredman). *Educ:* St Paul's School, London; Trinity College, Cambridge. Literary Critic, Truth, 1956–57; Music Critic, Time and Tide, 1961–62. Cameron Mackintosh Vis. Prof. of Contemporary Theatre, and Fellow, St Catherine's Coll., Oxford Univ., 1994. Mem., European Acad. of Yuste (Cervantes Seat), 1998. Hon. DLitt St Andrews, 1999. Hamburg Shakespeare Prize, 1989; William Inge Award for Distinguished Achievement in the American Theatre, 1992. *Stage Plays:* Five Finger Exercise, prod. Comedy, London, 1958–60, NY, 1960–61 (Evening Standard Drama Award, 1958; NY Drama Critics Circle Award (best foreign play), 1959–60); (double bill) The Private Ear (filmed 1966) and The Public Eye, produced, Globe, London, 1962, NY, 1963 (filmed 1972); It's About Cinderella (with Joan Littlewood and Theatre Workshop) prod. Wyndham's Theatre, Christmas, 1963; The Royal Hunt of the Sun, Nat. Theatre, Chichester Festival, 1964, The Old Vic, and Queen's Theatres, 1964–67, NY, 1965–66 (filmed 1969), Nat. Theatre, 2006; Black Comedy, Nat. Theatre, Chichester Fest., 1965, The Old Vic and Queen's Theatres, 1965–67; as double bill with White Lies, NY, 1967, Shaw, 1976; The White Liars, Lyric, 1968; The Battle of Shrivings, Lyric, 1970; Equus, Nat. Theatre, 1973, NY, 1974, Albery Theatre, 1976 (NY Drama Critics' and Antoinette Perry Awards) (filmed 1977), Gielgud, 2007, NY, 2008; Amadeus, Nat. Theatre, 1979 (Evening Standard Drama Award, Plays and Players Award, London Theatre Critics Award), NY, 1980 (Antoinette Perry Award, Drama Desk Award), Her Majesty's, 1981 (filmed 1984, Acad. Award, Golden Globe Award, Los Angeles Film Critics Assoc. Award, Premi David di Donatello, 1985), Old Vic, 1998, NY, 1999, Wilton's Music Hall, 2006, Chichester Festival Th., 2014; Yonadab, Nat. Theatre, 1985; Lettice and Lovage, Globe, 1987, Barrymore Theatre, NY, 1990 (Evening Standard Drama Award for Best Comedy, 1988); The Gift of the Gorgon, Barbican, 1992, transf. Wyndhams, 1993; Whom Do I Have the Honour of Addressing?, Chichester, 1996. Plays produced on television and sound include: The Salt Land (ITV), 1955; Balance of Terror (BBC TV), 1957; Whom Do I Have the Honour of Addressing? (radio), 1989, etc. *Recreations:* music, architecture. *Address:* c/o Macnaughton Lord Representation, 44 South Molton Street, W1K 5RT. *T:* (020) 7499 1411. *Club:* Garrick.

SHAFIK, Dame Nemat, (Minouche), DBE 2015; DPhil; a Deputy Governor and Member, Monetary Policy Committee, Bank of England, since 2014; *b* 13 Aug. 1962; *d* of Dr Talaat Shafik and Maissa Hamza; *m* 2002, Dr Raffael Jovine; one *s* one *d*, and three step *c. Educ:* Univ. of Massachusetts, Amherst (BA *summa cum laude* Pols and Econs 1983); London Sch. of Econs (MSc Econs 1986); St Antony's Coll., Oxford (DPhil Econs 1989). World Bank: joined 1990, as economist in Res. Dept; Country Economist, Central Europe, 1992–94; Dir, Private Sector and Finance, ME and N Africa, 1997–99; Vice-Pres., Private Sector and Infrastructure, 1999–2004; Dir Gen., Country (formerly Regl) Progs, 2004–08, Perm. Sec., 2008–11, DFID; Dep. Man. Dir, IMF, 2011–14. Adjunct Prof., Econs, Georgetown Univ., 1989–94; Vis. Associate Prof., Wharton Business Sch., Univ. of Pennsylvania, 1996. Non-exec. Dir, Mgt Bd, DFID, 2002–04. Chairman: Consultative Gp to Assist the Poorest, 1999–2004; Infodev, 1999–2004; Global Water and Sanitation Prog., 1999–2004; Private Participation in Infrastructure Adv. Facility, 1999–2004; Treas., Our Place DC, 2001–04; Bd Mem., Operating Council, Global Alliance for Workers and Communities, 1999–2003. Bd Mem., Middle East Jl, 1996–2002. Woman of the Year, GG2, 2009. *Publications:* Reviving Private Investment in Developing Countries, 1992; Globalization Regionalism and Growth, 1996; Challenges Facing Middle Eastern and North African Countries: alternative futures, 1998; Prospects for Middle East and North African Economies: from boom to bust and back?, 1998; articles in Jl of Develt Economics, Oxford Economic Papers, World Develt, Columbia Jl of World Business, Middle East Jl. *Address:* Bank of England, Threadneedle Street, EC2R 8AH.

SHAFTESBURY, 12th Earl of, *cr* 1672; **Nicholas Edmund Anthony Ashley-Cooper;** Bt 1622; Baron Ashley 1661; Baron Cooper 1672; *b* 3 June 1979; *yr s* of 10th Earl of Shaftesbury and of Christina Eva (*née* Montan); *S* brother, 2005; *m* 2010, Dinah Streifeneder; one *s* two *d. Heir: s* Anthony Francis Wolfgang Ashley-Cooper, Lord Ashley, *b* 24 Jan. 2011.

SHAGARI, Alhaji Shehu Usman Aliyu, GCFR 2000; President of Nigeria and Commander-in-Chief of the Armed Forces, 1979–83; *b* Feb. 1925; *s* of Magaji Aliyu; *m* 1946; two *s* three *d* (and one *s* decd). *Educ:* Middle Sch., Sokoto; Barewa Coll., Kaduna; Teacher Trng Coll., Zaria. Teacher of science, Sokoto Middle Sch., 1945–50; Headmaster, Argungu Sen. Primary Sch., 1951–52; Sen. Visiting Teacher, Sokoto Prov., 1953–58. Entered politics as Mem. Federal Parlt, 1954–58; Parly Sec. to Prime Minister, 1958–59; Federal Minister: Economic Develt, 1959–60; Establishments, 1960–62; Internal Affairs, 1962–65; Works, 1965–66; Sec., Sokoto Prov. Educnl Develt Fund, 1966–68; State Comr for Educn, Sokoto Province, 1968–70; Fed. Comr for Econ. Develt and Reconstruction, 1970–71; for Finance, 1971–75. Mem., Constituent Assembly, Oct. 1977–83; Mem., Nat. Party of Nigeria. *Publications:* (poetry) Wakar Nijeriya, 1948; Dun Fodia, 1978; (collected speeches) My Vision of Nigeria, 1981. *Recreations:* Hausa poetry, reading, farming, indoor games.

SHAH, Akhil; QC 2010; *b* Nairobi, Nov. 1965; *s* of Jayu Shah and Sibylle Shah; *m* 1993, Sarah Anderson; one *s* one *d. Educ:* Haberdashers' Aske's Sch., Elstree; St John's Coll., Cambridge (BA 1989). Called to the Bar, Inner Temple, 1990; in practice as a barrister, specialising in commercial law, 1990–. *Publications:* (jtly) Carriage by Air, 2000; (contrib.) Bullen and Leake and Jacobs Precedents of Pleading, 15th edn 2004 to 17th edn 2012. *Recreations:* cricket, tennis, travel, music. *Address:* Fountain Court, Temple, EC4Y 9DH. *T:* (020) 7583 3335. *Club:* MCC.

SHAH, Bharat Chimanlal; Chairman: Nijjar Holdings Ltd, since 2010; Alderbrooke Ltd, since 2015; *b* Jinja, Uganda, 8 Dec. 1953; *s* of Chimanlal Shankerlal Shah and Lalitaben Chimanlal Shah; *m* 1982, Asha Bharat Shah; one *s* one *d. Educ:* FCCA 1987. Eastman Kodak Company, 1973–2001: Finance Dir, EMEA Reg., Kodak Consumer Imaging, 1992–95; Chm. and Man. Dir, Kodak Processing Cos, 1995–97; Man. Dir, UK, Ire., Nordic and Baltics, Kodak Consumer Imaging, 1997–2000; CEO, EMEA Reg., Kodak Consumer Imaging, and Vice Pres., Eastman Kodak Co., 2000–01. Founder and Chairman: ABS/BCS Business Consultants Ltd, 2001–; Smart-Sal Ltd, 2012–. Chairman: Picdar Gp, 2002–05; West Bromwich Building Soc. Staff Retirement Scheme, 2006–; Sure Gp, 2008–10; non-executive Director: West Bromwich Building Soc., 2004–10; Places for People Gp Ltd, 2010–; Vice Pres., EMEA, SVP Worldwide, 2006. Dep. Chm., Audit Commn, 2007–15. Ind. Mem., Remuneration Cttee, ACCA, 2005–06. Trustee, Paul Strickland Scanner Centre, 2010–14. *Recreations:* family, dining out, tennis, gym, travelling.

SHAH, Dipesh Jayantilal, OBE 2007; Chairman, ANHD International Advisory Services, since 2007; a Crown Estate Commissioner, since 2011; *b* 11 May 1953; *s* of Jayantilal S. Shah and Sumati J. Shah; *m* 1983, Annie Therese Duchesne; one *s* one *d. Educ:* Warwick Univ. (BA Hons Econs); Birkbeck Coll., London (MSc Distn Econs); Harvard Business Sch. (Prog. for Mgt Develt); Templeton Coll., Oxford (Strategic Leadership Prog.). Various roles in planning, Shell-Mex and BP, 1974–75; BP plc, 1976–2002: Chief Economist, BP Oil UK, 1977–79; Commercial Dir, Natural Resources, NZ, 1985–87; Man. Dir and CEO, BP Solar

Internat., 1991–97; Chief Exec., Forties Pipeline System, and Gen. Manager, Grangemouth, 1998–99; Global Hd, Acquisitions and Divestments, 2000–02; Chief Exec., and Bd Mem., UKAEA, 2003–06. Non-exec. Chm., IT Power Ltd, 2002–05; Chairman: Viridian Gp plc, 2005–06 (non-exec. Dir, 2003–04); Hg Capital Renewable Power Partners LLP, 2002–08; Jetion Holdings Ltd, 2007–08; non-executive Director: Babcock Internat. Gp plc, 1999–2009; Kemble Gp of Cos, 2007–14; Thames Water Gp of Cos, 2007–15; Lloyd's of London Franchise Bd, 2008–10; JKX Oil and Gas plc, 2008– (Sen. Ind. Dir, 2012–); Cannacord Genuity Inc. (formerly Canaccord Financial Inc.), 2012–; non-exec. Dir and Sen. Ind. Dir, Equus Petroleum plc, 2013–. Mem., Renewable Energy Adv. Cttee, DTI, 1994–2002. Bd Advr, Crown Estate, 2009–10. Chm., European Photovoltanics Industry Assoc., Brussels, 1992–97; Mem., UK Panel, European Awards for Envmt, 2000. Mem. Bd and Chm., Investment Cttee, EU Marguerite Fund, 2010–. Trustee, British Youth Opera, 2010–. Gov., Merchant Taylors' Sch., 2009–. MInstD; FRSA. *Recreations:* sports, travel (with family), reading. *Club:* Harvard Business School Alumni (London).

SHAH, Monisha; Managing Director, Hogerty Hill Ltd, since 2010; Chair, Rose Bruford College of Theatre and Performance, since 2015; *b* Bombay, India, 11 Sept. 1969; *d* of Amrit Shamji Shah and Rekha Shah (*née* Pavagadhi); partner, Mark Young; one *s*. *Educ:* Univ. of Bombay (BA Pol Sci. 1989); Sch. of Oriental and African Studies, Univ. of London (MSc Politics of Asia and Africa 1991); London Business Sch. (MBA 2002). Dir, BBC World India, 2001–10. BBC Worldwide Bd Rep., Radio Mid-Day West, India, 2006–10; Dir, Emerging Markets, 2005–08, Dir, Developed and Emerging Markets, EMEA, 2008–10, BBC Worldwide; Dir, Worldwide Media, India, 2008–10. Trustee: Tate, 2007–; Nat. Gall., 2013–15; non-executive Director: Tate Enterprises, 2008–; Next MediaWorks plc, 2011–; Cambridge Imaging Systems, 2015–. Young Global Leader, World Econ. Forum, 2009. *Recreations:* Manchester United FC, travelling, cooking for friends and family, walking the dogs, collecting contemporary Indian art, watching copious amounts of television, reading (anything). *Address:* Hogerty Hill, Lunghurst Road, Woldingham, Caterham, Surrey CR3 7HE. *E:* hogerty.hill@live.co.uk.

SHAH, Naseem Akhter; MP (Lab) Bradford West, since 2015; *b* 13 Nov. 1973; *d* of Zoora Shah; two *s* one *d*. Carer for children with disabilities; advocate for women with disabilities and their carers; work for Samaritans; work with NHS in commng services; Chm., Sharing Voices Bradford, mental health charity, 2012. *Address:* House of Commons, SW1A 0AA.

SHAH, Navin; Member (Lab) Brent and Harrow, London Assembly, Greater London Authority, since 2008; *b* Ahmedabad, India; *m* Rekha; one *s* one *d*. *Educ:* Acad. of Architects, Bombay; University Coll. London. Formerly in private practice as architect and develt planner. Mem. (Lab) Harrow LBC, 1994–2014 (Leader, 2004–06). *Address:* Greater London Authority, City Hall, Queen's Walk, SE1 2AA.

SHAH, Samir, OBE 2000; DPhil; Chief Executive, Juniper, since 2006 (Managing Director, 1998–2006); *b* 29 Jan. 1952; *s* of Amrit Shah and Uma Bakaya (*née* Chaudhary); *m* 1983, Belkis Bhegani; one *s*. *Educ:* Latymer Upper Sch.; Univ. of Hull (BSc Hons 1973); St Catherine's Coll., Oxford (DPhil 1978). Sen. Res. Officer, Home Office, 1978–79; London Weekend Television, 1979–87: Producer, Eastern Eye, 1982–84; Editor: Credo, 1984–86; The London Programme, 1986–87; British Broadcasting Corporation, 1987–98: Head: Current Affairs, TV, 1987–94; Political Programming, TV and Radio, 1994–98. Non-exec. Dir, BBC, 2007–10. Special Prof., Centre for Study of Post Conflict Cultures, Univ. of Nottingham, 2006–. Chairman: Runnymede Trust, 1999–2009; Screen West Midlands, 2009–11; Geffrye Mus., 2014–; Trustee: Med. Foundn for Victims of Torture, 2004–06; V&A Mus., 2005– (Dep. Chair, 2013–); Reprieve, 2014–; BAFTA, 2015–. FRTS 2002; FRSA 2008. *Recreations:* Manchester United, movies, music. *Address:* Juniper, 52 Lant Street, SE1 1RB. *T:* (020) 7407 9292. *Clubs:* Groucho, Chelsea Arts.

SHAIKH, Dr Abdul Hafeez; General Partner, New Silk Route Partners LLC, New York, 2006–10 and since 2013; *b* Jacobabad, 26 Dec. 1954; *s* of Abdul Nabi Shaikh and Afroze Nabi Shaikh; *m* Nadene Nichols; three *d*. *Educ:* Boston Univ. (PhD Econs). Country Hd, Saudi Arabia, World Bank; Minister for Finance, Planning and Develt, Sindh, 2000–02; Mem. (Pakistan People), Senate of Pakistan; Chm., Senate Cttee on WTO; Federal Minister for Investment and Privatization, 2003–06; Mem., Senate of Pakistan, 2010–13; Advr to Prime Minister of Pakistan on Finance, Revenue, Econ. Affairs, Stats, and Planning and Develt, 2010; Minister for Finance, Revenue, Econ. Affairs, Stats, and Planning and Develt, 2010–13.

SHAKER, Mohamed Ibrahim, PhD; Order of the Arab Republic of Egypt (Second Grade), 1976; Order of Merit (Egypt) (First Grade), 1983; Chairman, Egyptian Council for Foreign Affairs, 1999–2003 and since 2009 (Vice Chairman, 2003–09; Chairman of Trustees: Sawiris Foundation for Social Development, since 2001; Magdi Yacoub Foundation for Heart Research, since 2008; National Centre for Middle East Studies; *b* 16 Oct. 1933; *s* of Mahmoud Shaker and Zeinab Wasef; *m* 1960, Mona El Kony; one *s* one *d*. *Educ:* Cairo Univ. (Lic. en Droit); Inst. of Internat. Studies, Geneva (PhD). Representative of Dir-Gen. of IAEA to UN, New York, 1982–83; Amb. and Dep. Perm. Rep. of Egypt to UN, New York, 1984–86; Amb. to Austria, 1986–88; Hd of Dept of W Europe, Min. of For. Affairs, Cairo, 1988; Ambassador of the Arab Republic of Egypt to UK, 1988–97. President: Third Review Conf. of the Parties to the Treaty on Non-Proliferation of Nuclear Weapons, Geneva, 1985; UN Conf. for the Promotion of Internat. Co-operation in the Peaceful Uses of Nuclear Energy, Geneva, 1987; Member: UN Sec. General's Adv. Bd on Disarmament, 1993–98 (Chm., 1995); Core Gp of Prog. for Promotion of Non-Proliferation of Nuclear Weapons, 1987–97; Court on Values, Arab Rep. of Egypt, 2004–06. Advr, Regl Information Technol. and Software Engrg Centre, Cairo, 1997–. *Publications:* The Nuclear Non-Proliferation Treaty: origin and implementation 1959–1979, 1980; The Evolving Regime of Nuclear Non-proliferation, 2006; several articles. *Recreations:* tennis, music. *Address:* 9 Aziz Osman Street, Zamalek, Cairo, Egypt; Regional Information Technology and Software Engineering Centre, 11A Hassan Sabry Street, Zamalek, Cairo, Egypt; Egyptian Council for Foreign Affairs, Osman Towers No 2, 12th Floor, Kornish El Nile, Maadi, Cairo, Egypt; Magdi Yacoub Foundation, 22 Montazah Street, Zamalek, Cairo, Egypt. *Clubs:* Royal Automobile; Guizera Sporting (Cairo).

SHAKERLEY, Sir Nicholas Simon Adam, 7th Bt *cr* 1838, of Somerford Park, Cheshire; *b* 20 Dec. 1963; *s* of Sir Geoffrey Adam Shakerley, 6th Bt and Virginia Elizabeth (*née* Maskell); *S* father, 2012. *Heir:* *b* Jonathan Peter Shakerley [*b* 1966; *m* 1995, Meii-Jung, (Sonia) Sung; two *d*].

SHAKESPEARE, John William Richmond, CMG 1985; LVO 1968; HM Diplomatic Service, retired; *b* 11 June 1930; *s* of late Dr W. G. Shakespeare; *m* 1955, Lalage Ann, *d* of late S. P. B. Mais; three *s* one *d*. *Educ:* Winchester; Trinity Coll., Oxford (Scholar, MA). 2nd Lieut Irish Guards, 1949–50. Lectr in English, Ecole Normale Supérieure, Paris, 1953–54; on editorial staff, Times Educational Supplement, 1955–56 and Times, 1956–59; entered Diplomatic Service, 1959; Private Sec. to Ambassador in Paris, 1959–61; FO, 1961–63; 1st Sec., Phnom-Penh, 1963–64; 1st Sec., Office of Pol Adviser to C-in-C Far East, Singapore, 1964–66; Dir of British Information Service in Brazil, 1966–69; FCO, 1969–73; Counsellor and Consul-Gen., Buenos Aires, 1973–75; Chargé d'Affaires, Buenos Aires, 1976–77; Head of Mexico and Caribbean Dept, FCO, 1977–79; Counsellor, Lisbon, 1979–83; Ambassador to Peru, 1983–87, to Kingdom of Morocco, 1987–90. Mem., Sensitivity Review Unit, FCO, 1991–2002. Chm., Morgan Grenfell Latin American Cos Trust, 1994–2000; Latin Amer. Consultant, Clyde & Co., 1991–2002. Chm., Anglo-Portuguese Soc., 1994–97; Mem., Exec. Cttee, S Atlantic Council, 1998–2013. Hon. Vice Pres., Anglo-Peruvian Soc., 1991–. Officer, Order of Southern Cross (Brazil), 1968; Commander, Alaouite Order (Morocco), 1990. *Recreations:* gardening, music (light), travel. *Address:* Townsend Wood, Sutton Mandeville, Salisbury SP3 5ND. *Club:* Garrick.

See also N. W. R. Shakespeare.

SHAKESPEARE, Nicholas William Richmond; novelist and biographer; *b* 3 March 1957; *s* of J. W. R. Shakespeare, *qv*; *m* 1999, Gillian Johnson; two *s*. *Educ:* Dragon Sch., Oxford; Winchester Coll.; Magdalene Coll., Cambridge (MA English). BBC TV, 1980–84; Dep. Arts and Literary Editor, The Times, 1985–87; Literary Editor: London Daily News, 1987–88; Daily Telegraph, 1988–91; Sunday Telegraph, 1989–91; film critic, Illustrated London News, 1989; Chief book reviewer, Daily Telegraph, 2009–. Associate Mem., Exeter Coll., Oxford, 2012–. Work for TV includes: writer and narrator: The Evelyn Waugh Trilogy; Mario Vargas Llosa; Iquitos; For the Sake of the Children (Christopher Award, USA); Return to the Sacred Ice; In the Footsteps of Bruce Chatwin; The Private Dirk Bogarde (BAFTA and RTS awards, 2001); presenter, Cover to Cover. FRSL 1999. Borges Lect., Anglo-Argentine Soc., 2010. *Publications:* The Men who would be King, 1984; Londoners, 1986; The Vision of Elena Silves, 1989 (Somerset Maugham Award, Betty Trask Award, 1990); The High Flyer, 1993; The Dancer Upstairs, 1995 (American Liby Assoc. Award, 1997; adapted for film, 2002); Bruce Chatwin, 1999; Snowleg, 2004; In Tasmania, 2004 (Tasmania Book Prize, 2007); Secrets of the Sea, 2007; Inheritance, 2010; (ed with Elizabeth Chatwin) Under the Sun: the letters of Bruce Chatwin, 2010; Priscilla: the hidden life of an Englishwoman in wartime France, 2013; Stories from Other Places, 2015. *Recreations:* travelling, drawing. *Address:* Miles Cottage, Sutton Mandeville, Wilts SP3 5LX. *Club:* Beefsteak.

SHAKESPEARE, Stephan; Co-Founder, 2000, and Chief Executive Officer, YouGov plc; Founder, PoliticsHome.com; Owner, ConservativeHome.com; *b* Mönchengladbach, 9 April 1957; *s* of Karl-Heinz Kukowski and Lina Kukowski; *m* 1984, Rosamund Shakespeare; two *d*. *Educ:* Christ's Hospital, Horsham; St Peter's Coll., Oxford (BA Eng. Lang. and Lit.). Chm., Data Strategy Bd, BIS. Trustee, NPG, 2012–. *Recreations:* art, music, Arsenal. *Address:* YouGov plc, 50 Featherstone Street, EC1Y 8RT. *E:* Stephan.Shakespeare@YouGov.com.

SHAKESPEARE, Sir Thomas William, 3rd Bt *cr* 1942, of Lakenham, City of Norwich; (known professionally as Dr Tom Shakespeare); Senior Lecturer, University of East Anglia, since 2013; *b* 11 May 1966; *er s* of Sir William Geoffrey Shakespeare, 2nd Bt and of Susan Mary Shakespeare (*née* Raffel); *S* father, 1996; one *d* by Lucy Ann Broadhead; one *s* by Judy Brown; *m* 2002, Caroline Emily (*née* Bowditch) (marr. diss. 2008). *Educ:* Pembroke Coll., Cambridge (BA (Hons) 1987); King's Coll., Cambridge (PhD 1994). Printer, Cambridge Free Press, 1987–88; Administrator, The Works Theatre Co-operative, 1988–89; Lectr, Univ. of Sunderland, 1993–95; Res. Fellow, Univ. of Leeds, 1996–99; Newcastle University: Dir of Outreach, 1999–2005; Res. Fellow, Policy, Ethics and Life Scis Res. Inst., 2005–08; NESTA Fellow, 2005–08; Consultant, 2008–10, Tech. Officer, 2010–13, WHO. Mem., Working Party on the ethics of res. on genes and behaviour, 2000–02, Mem. Council, 2014–, Nuffield Council on Bioethics. Vice-Chair, Gateshead Voluntary Orgns Council, 1993–96; Chair, Northern Disability Arts Forum, 1993–95. Vice-Chm., Northern Arts Bd, 1998–99 (Mem., 1995–99 and 2000–02); Member: Tyneside Cinema Bd, 1995–97; Arts Council England, 2004–10 (Chm., NE Regl Arts Council, 2004–10). Trustee, Equal Lives, 2013–. *Publications:* (jtly) The Sexual Politics of Disability, 1996; The Disability Reader, 1998; (jtly) Exploring Disability, 1999; Help, 2000; (jtly) Disability and Postmodernism, 2002; (jtly) Genetic Politics, 2002; Disability Rights and Wrongs, 2006; Disability Rights and Wrongs Revisited, 2013; Disability Research Today, 2015; various articles in academic jls. *Recreations:* arts and culture, gardening, cooking. *Heir:* *b* James Douglas Geoffrey Shakespeare [*b* 12 Feb. 1971; *m* 1996, Alison (*née* Lusby)]. *Address:* 511 Earlham Road, Norwich NR4 7HN; Medical School, University of East Anglia, Earlham Road, Norwich, Norfolk NR4 7TJ.

SHALIT, Jonathan Sigmund, OBE 2014; Chairman: ROAR Global, since 2009; Cole Kitchenn, since 2010; *b* London, 17 April 1962; *s* of David Manuel Shalit and Sophie Shalit, JP (*née* Gestetner); *m* 2010, Katrina; two step *d*. *Educ:* City of London Sch. Account Manager, Saatchi and Saatchi Gp, 1981–87; Managing Director: ROAR Global (formerly Shalit Global), 1994–; FAB, 1997–2004. Vis. Prof., 2012, Hon. Prof., 2014, Henley Sch. of Business. Trustee: REGAIN the Trust for Sports Tetraplegics, 1992–2010; Chicken Shed Theatre Co., 1996–; Variety Club of GB, 2005– (Vice-Pres., 2005–). Freeman, City of London, 1987; Liveryman, Coachmakers' and Coach Harness Makers' Co., 1987. Mem., BAFTA. *Recreations:* sailing, music, theatre, family, television, film. *Address:* ROAR Global, ROAR House, 46 Charlotte Street, W1T 2GS. *E:* jonathan@roarglobal.com. *Clubs:* Annabel's, Ivy, Royal Automobile, Groucho, Soho House, 5 Hertford St, Arts.

SHALLICE, Prof. Timothy, PhD; FRS 1996; FBA 2013; Professor of Psychology, University College London, 1990–2005, now Emeritus (Director, Institute of Cognitive Neuroscience, 1996–2004); *b* 11 July 1940; *s* of Sidney Edgar Shallice and Doris Dronsfield Shallice; *m* 1987, Maria Anna Tallandini. *Educ:* St John's Coll., Cambridge (BA 1961); University Coll. London (PhD 1965; Fellow, 2010). Asst Lectr in Psychol., Univ. of Manchester, 1964–65; Lectr in Psychol., UCL, 1966–72; Sen. Res. Fellow in Neuropsychol., Inst. Neurology, London, 1972–77; Scientist, MRC Applied Psychol. Unit, 1978–90. Prof. of Cognitive Neurosci., Scuola Internazionale Superiore di Studi Avanzati, Trieste, 1994–2010. MAE 1996. Founder FMedSci 1998. Hon. Dr: Univ. Libre de Bruxelles, 1992; London Guildhall, 1999; Trinity Coll., Dublin, 2005. President's Award, BPsS, 1991; Mind and Brain Prize, Univ. Torino, 2013; British Acad. Medal, 2013. *Publications:* From Neuropsychology to Mental Structure, 1988; (with D. Plaut) Connectionist Modelling in Cognitive Neuropsychology, 1994; (with R. Cooper) The Organisation of Mind, 2011. *Recreations:* e-mail chess, mountain walking, cinema, theatre. *Address:* Institute of Cognitive Neuroscience, University College London, Gower Street, WC1E 6BT.

SHAND, His Honour John Alexander Ogilvie; DL; a Circuit Judge, 1988–2005; *b* 6 Nov. 1942; *s* of late Alexander Shand and Marguerite Marie Shand; *m* 1st, 1965, Patricia Margaret (*née* Toynbee) (marr. diss.); two *s* one *d*; 2nd, 1990, Valerie Jean (*née* Bond). *Educ:* Nottingham High Sch.; Queens' Coll., Cambridge (MA, LLB; Chancellor's Medal for Law 1965); Centre for Reformation and Early Modern Studies, Univ. of Birmingham (MA 2008). Called to the Bar, Middle Temple, 1965 (Harmsworth Scholarship); practised on Midland and Oxford Circuit (Birmingham), 1965–71 and 1973–81 (Dep. Circuit Judge, 1979); a Recorder, 1981–88. Chm. of Industrial Tribunals (Birmingham Reg.), 1981–88. Fellow and Tutor, Queens' Coll., Cambridge, 1971–73. Chancellor: Dio. Southwell, 1981–2004; Dio. Lichfield, 1989–2005 (Licensed Reader, 2014–). Mem., House of Laity, Gen. Synod of C of E, 2010–. DL Staffs, 1998. *Publications:* (with P. G. Stein) Legal Values in Western Society, 1974; contrib. various articles in Cambridge Law Jl. *Address:* c/o Stafford Combined Court Centre, Victoria Square, Stafford ST16 2QQ. *T:* (01785) 610801.

SHAND, Lesley Munro, (Mrs T. G. Reid); QC (Scot.) 2005; *b* 9 Feb. 1960; *d* of Alexander Dewar Shand and Isabella Shand (*née* Irving); *m* 1988, Thomas Graham Reid; two *s* one *d*. *Educ:* Lenzie Acad.; Edinburgh Univ. (LLB Hons; DipLP). Admitted solicitor, 1985; in practice, 1985–89; Advocate, 1990–. *Recreations:* reading, cycling, walking. *Address:* Faculty of Advocates, Parliament House, Edinburgh EH1 1RQ. *T:* (0131) 226 5071. *E:* lesley.shand@advocates.org.uk.

SHAND, William Stewart, MD; FRCS, FRCSE; Hon. Consulting Surgeon to St Bartholomew's Hospital and The Royal London Hospital, since 1997; *b* 12 Oct. 1936; *s* of William Paterson Shand and Annabella Kirkland Stewart Shand (*née* Waddell); *m* 1972, (Anne) Caroline Dashwood (*née* Charvet) (*d* 2005); two *s*, and one step *s* two step *d*. *Educ:* Repton

Sch.; St John's Coll., Cambridge (BA 1958, MA 1962; MB BChir 1962; MD 1970); Medical Coll. of St Bartholomew's Hosp. LRCP; MRCS; FRCS 1970; FRCSE 1970. Consultant Surgeon: St Bartholomew's, Hackney and Homerton Hosps, London, 1973–96; King Edward VII's Hosp. for Officers, London, 1995–97. Hon. Consultant Surgeon: St Luke's Hosp. for the Clergy, London, 1982–97; St Mark's Hosp. for Diseases of Colon and Rectum, London, 1986–96. Senior Fellow: Assoc. of Surgeons of GB and Ireland, 2001–; Assoc. of Coloproctology of GB and Ireland, 2001–. Penrose May Tutor, 1980–85, Penrose May Teacher, 1985–, RCS. Member: Ct of Examrs, RCS, 1985–91; Bd of Examrs, RCSE, 1986–96; Examiner: Professional and Linguistic Assessment Bd for GMC, 1983–98; Univ. of London, 1990–96; Univ. of Liverpool, 1991–96. FRSocMed 1967. Fellow: Hunterian Soc., 1971–; Harveian Soc. of London, 1972–. Vice-Pres., Phyllis Tuckwell Hospice, Farnham, 2001– (Trustee, 1995–2000). Governor: Med. Coll. of St Bartholomew's Hosp., 1987–96; Sutton's Hosp. in Charterhouse, 1989–2009; BPMF, 1991–96. Member: Ct of Assts, Soc. of Apothecaries, 1990 (Master, 2004–05); Ct of Assts, Barbers' Co., 1992 (Master, 2001–02); Travelling Surgical Soc. of GB and NI, 1982 (Pres., 1994–97). Member: Cambridge Med. Graduates' Club, subseq. Cambridge Graduates' Med. Soc. (Pres., 1993–2006); Hon. Med. Panel, Artists' Gen. Benevolent Instn, 1979–. Chm., Homerton Hosp. Art Work Cttee, 1988–92; Hon. Curator of Ceramics, RCS, 1980–. Reader, C of E, 1996–. NACF Award, 1992. *Publications:* (jtly) The Art of Dying: the story of two sculptors' residency in a hospice, 1989; contribs to books and articles in jls on surgery, colorectal disease, chronic inflammatory bowel disease in children and oncology. *Recreations:* maker of stained glass windows, water-colour painting, ski-ing, dry-fly fishing, walking. *Address:* Fennel Cottage, 25 Station Road, Nassington, Peterborough PE8 6QB. *T:* (01780) 782933.

SHANKS, Duncan Faichney, RSA 1990 (ARSA 1972); RGI 1982; RSW 1987; artist; *b* 30 Aug. 1937; *s* of Duncan Faichney Shanks and Elizabeth Clark; *m* 1966, Una Brown Gordon. *Educ:* Glasgow School of Art; DA (Post Diploma) 1960. Travelling scholarship to Italy, 1961; part-time teacher, Glasgow Sch. of Art, 1963–79; full-time artist, 1979–. *Recreation:* classical and contemporary music.

SHANKS, Ian Alexander, OBE 2012; PhD; FRS 1984; FREng; FRSE; Vice President, Physical and Engineering Sciences (formerly Head of Engineering Sciences), Unilever plc, 2001–03; *b* 22 June 1948; *s* of Alexander and Isabella Affleck (*née* Beaton); *m* 1971, Janice Smillie Coulter; one *d*. *Educ:* Dumbarton Acad.; Glasgow Univ. (BSc); Glasgow Coll. of Technology (PhD). CEng, MIEE 1983, FIET (FIEE 1990); FREng (FEng 1992). Projects Manager, Scottish Colorfoto Labs, 1970–72; Research Student, Portsmouth Polytechnic, 1972–73 (liquid crystal displays); RSRE, Malvern, 1973–82 (displays and L-B films); Unilever Research, 1982, Principal Scientist, 1984–86 (electronic biosensors); Chief Scientist, THORN EMI plc, 1986–94; Divl Sci. Advr, Unilever Res., 1994–2000. Vis. Prof. of Electrical and Electronic Engrg, Univ. of Glasgow, 1985–. Chm., Inter-Agency Cttee for Marine Sci. and Technol., 1991–93; Member: Opto-electronics Cttee, Rank Prize Funds, 1985–; Science Consultative Gp, BBC, 1989–91; ABRC, 1990–93; Sci. Adv. Gp, NPL, 1998–2007 (Chair, 2008–14); Sci. Adv. Bd, Inst. of Nanotechnology, 2001–06; Strategic Adv. Bd, Photonics Explorer, 2009–. A Vice-Pres. and Mem. Council, Royal Soc., 1989–91; Vice-Pres., Industrial Trust, 1999–; Pres., Assoc. for Science Educn, Scotland, 2007–08. Founder and Chm., Optoelectronics Coll., 2006–. FRSA 1993; FRSE 2000. Hon. Fellow, Inst. of Nanotechnology, 2005. Hon. DEng Glasgow, 2002. Paterson Medal and Prize, Inst. of Physics, 1984; Best Paper Award, Soc. for Inf. Display, 1983. *Publications:* numerous sci. and tech. papers; numerous patents. *Recreations:* music, horology, Art Deco sculpture. *Address:* 23 Reres Road, Broughty Ferry, Dundee DD5 2QA.

SHANKS, Murray George; His Honour Judge Shanks; a Circuit Judge, since 2009; *b* Windsor, 19 June 1960; *s* of Paul and Maggie Shanks. *Educ:* Worth Abbey; Trinity Coll., Cambridge (BA 1983). Called to the Bar, Middle Temple, 1984; Acting High Court Judge: Belize, 2000; Eastern Caribbean Supreme Court, 2003–05; Recorder, 2004–09; Dep. Chm., Information Tribunal, 2007–10. *Publications:* (contrib.) Information Rights, 2004, 2nd edn 2007. *E:* HHJudge.Shanks@judiciary.gsi.gov.uk. *Clubs:* Groucho, Soho House.

SHANKS, Prof. Robert Gray, (Robin), CBE 1997; MD, DSc; FRCP, FRCPI, FRCPE, FACP; Whitla Professor of Therapeutics and Pharmacology, 1977–98, now Emeritus, and Pro-Vice-Chancellor, 1991–98, Queen's University, Belfast; *b* 4 April 1934; *s* of Robert Shanks and Mary Anne Shanks (*née* Gray); *m* 1st, 1960, Denise Isabelle Sheila Woods (*d* 1998); four *d*; 2nd, 2000, Mary Carson; one step *s* one step *d*. *Educ:* Queen's Univ., Belfast (MD; DSc). FRCPE 1977; FRCP 1987; FRCPI 1987; FACP 1998. MRIA. RMO, Royal Victoria Hosp., Belfast, 1958–59; Res. Fellow, Medical Coll. of Georgia, 1959–60; Lectr in Physiology, QUB, 1960–62; Pharmacologist, ICI, 1962–66; Queen's University, Belfast: Sen. Lectr, Therapeutics and Pharmacology, 1967–72; Prof., Clinical Pharmacology, 1972–77; Dean, Faculty of Medicine, 1986–91; Consultant Physician, Belfast City and Royal Victoria Hosps, 1967–98. Hon. LLD QUB, 1999. *Publications:* papers in scientific jls. *Recreations:* golf, gardening, cooking. *Address:* Whitla Lodge, 15 Lenamore Park, Lisburn, Northern Ireland BT28 3NJ. *Club:* Royal County Down Golf.

SHANKS, Sharon; *see* Heal, S.

SHANNON, 10th Earl of, *cr* 1756 (Ire.); **Richard Henry John Boyle;** Viscount Boyle, Baron Castle Martyr, 1756; Baron Carleton (GB), 1786; *b* 19 Jan. 1960; *s* of 9th Earl of Shannon and Susan Margaret (*née* Hogg); S father, 2013. *Heir: cousin* Robert Francis Boyle [*b* 15 Aug. 1930; *m* 1956, Janet Eleanor Ashley Cooper; two *s* one *d*]. *Address:* Edington House, Edington, Bridgwater, Somerset TA7 9JS.

SHANNON, Alan David, CB 2012; Permanent Secretary, Department for Employment and Learning, Northern Ireland, 2010–13; Chair, Northern Ireland Federation of Housing Associations, since 2014; *b* 11 Jan. 1949; *s* of Samuel and Florence Shannon; *m* 1972, Christine Montgomery; one *s* two *d*. *Educ:* Belfast Royal Acad.; Queen's Univ., Belfast (BA Hons 1971). Joined NI Civil Service as Asst Principal, 1971; Min. of Agriculture (NI), 1971–82; Cabinet, British Mem. of European Court of Auditors, Luxembourg, 1982–85; Hd of Efficiency Scrutiny, Health Service, NI Dept of Finance and Personnel, 1985–86; Northern Ireland Office: Hd of Police Div., 1986–90; Hd of Probation, Juveniles and Compensation Div., 1990–92; Chief Exec., NI Prison Service, 1992–98; Principal Estabt and Finance Officer, NI Office, 1998–99; Permanent Secretary: Dept of Higher and Further Educn, Training and Employment, subseq. Dept for Employment and Learning, NI, 1999–2003; Dept for Social Develt, NI, 2003–10. *Recreations:* tennis, golf, local history, music.

SHANNON, David William Francis, PhD; Chief Scientist, Department of Environment, Food and Rural Affairs (formerly Ministry of Agriculture, Fisheries and Food), 1986–2001; *b* 16 Aug. 1941; *s* of late William Francis Shannon and Elizabeth (*née* Gibson); *m* 1967, Rosamond (*née* Bond); one *s* one *d*. *Educ:* Wallace High Sch., Lisburn, NI; Queen's Univ., Belfast (BAgr, PhD); DMS Napier Coll., Edinburgh, 1976. Poultry Res. Centre, ARC, Edinburgh, 1967; study leave; Dept of Animal Science, Univ. of Alberta, Edmonton, 1973–74; Hd of Nutrition Sect., Poultry Res. Centre, AFRC, 1977, Dir, 1978. Member: AFRC, 1986–94; BBSRC, 1995–2001; NERC, 1995–2001; Pres., UK Br., World's Poultry Science Assoc., 1986–90. Chm., Exec. Council, CAB Internat., 1988–91. Director: The Perry Foundn, 2002–; David Shannon Ltd, 2002–11. Mem. Court, Cranfield Univ., 1996–2001. FRSA 1996. *Publications:* contribs to learned jls on poultry science and animal nutrition. *Recreations:* golf, bridge. *Address:* 4 Old Court, Ashtead, Surrey KT21 2TS. *T:* (01372) 813096.

SHANNON, James; *see* Shannon, R. J.

SHANNON, Keith; HM Diplomatic Service; Deputy Director, Eastern Europe and Central Asia Directorate, Foreign and Commonwealth Office, since 2014; *b* Edinburgh, 17 Sept. 1966; *s* of Andrew Graeme Shannon and Catherine Lavin Shannon (*née* Sutherland); *m* 2002, Catherine Maria Levesley. *Educ:* Craigmount High Sch., Edinburgh; Univ. of St Andrews (MA Hons Modern Hist. with Internat. Relns). Entered HM Diplomatic Service, 1988; Asst Desk Officer, EC Dept (Internal), FCO, 1989–90; Desk Officer, Latin America Dept, FCO, 1990–91; Third Sec. (Aid/Commercial), Maputo, 1991–94; Second Sec. (Technol.), Paris, 1995–99; Head of Section: Drugs and Internat. Crime Dept, FCO, 1999–2002; Financial Planning and Performance Dept, FCO, 2002–03; Dep. Hd of Mission and Consul, Vilnius, 2004–08; Ambassador to Moldova, 2009–13; Dep. Dir, Foreign Policy, Nat. Security Secretariat, Cabinet Office (on secondment), 2013. *Recreations:* travel, literature, history, sport (especially football, cricket and golf), rock music. *Address:* c/o Foreign and Commonwealth Office, King Charles Street, SW1A 2AH. *E:* Keith.Shannon@fco.gov.uk.

SHANNON, (Richard) James; MP (DemU) Strangford, since 2010; *b* Omagh, 25 March 1955; *s* of Richard James Shannon and Mona Rebecca Rhoda Shannon; *m* 1987, Sandra George; three *s*. *Educ:* Ballywalter Primary Sch.; Coleraine Academical Instn. Served UDR, 1974–75 and 1976–77; 102 Light Air Defence Regt, RA, 1978–89. Ards Borough Council: Mem. (DemU), 1985–2010; Mayor, 1991–92; Alderman, 1997–2010. Mem., NI Forum, 1996–98; Mem. (DemU) Strangford, NI Assembly, 1998–2010. GSM (NI) 1974. *Recreations:* field sports, football, Ulster-Scots language and culture. *Address:* (office) 34a Frances Street, Newtownards, Co. Down BT23 7DN. *T:* (028) 9182 7990.

SHANT, Nirmal Kanta; QC 2006; **Her Honour Judge Shant;** a Circuit Judge, since 2015; *b* 2 July 1962; *d* of Chaman Lal Shant and Santosh Lakhanpal; *m* 1992, Narinder Sharma; two *d*. *Educ:* Univ. of Leicester (LLB Hons 1983); Council of Legal Educn. Called to the Bar, Gray's Inn, 1984, Bencher, 2010; in practice as a barrister specialising in criminal law; a Recorder, 2001–15. *Recreations:* tennis, theatre, reading, cooking.

SHAPCOTT, Jo A.; poet; *b* 24 March 1953; *d* of Frank William Gordon Shapcott and Josephine Cann; *m* 1995, Simon Andrew James Hainault Mundy. *Educ:* Cavendish Sch., Hemel Hempstead; TCD (BA 1st cl. Hons, MA); Bristol Univ. (DipEd); Harvard Univ. (Harkness Fellowship). Lectr in English, Rolle Coll., Exmouth, 1981–84; Educn Officer, South Bank Centre, 1986–92. Judith E. Wilson Vis. Fellow, Cambridge Univ., 1991; Penguin Writers' Fellow, BL, 1996–97; Northern Arts Literary Fellow, 1998–2000; Visiting Professor: Newcastle Univ., 2000–; Univ. of the Arts, London (formerly London Inst.), 2003–; Royal Literary Fund Fellow, Oxford Brookes Univ., 2003–05. Mem., Yr Academi Cymreig (Welsh Acad.). FRSL. First Prize, Nat. Poetry Competition, 1985, 1991; Queen's Gold Medal for Poetry, 2011. *Publications: poetry:* Electroplating the Baby, 1988 (Commonwealth Poetry Prize); Phrase Book, 1992; (ed with Matthew Sweeney) Emergency Kit: poems for strange times, 1996; Motherland, 1996; Penguin Modern Poets 12, 1997; My Life Asleep, 1998 (Forward Poetry Prize); (ed with Don Paterson) Last Words: poetry for the new century, 1999; Her Book: poems 1988–1998, 2000; Tender Taxes, 2002; The Transformers, 2007; Of Mutability, 2010 (Costa Book of the Year, 2010); *essay collection:* (ed with Linda Anderson) Elizabeth Bishop: poet of the periphery, 2002. *Address:* c/o Faber & Faber, Bloomsbury House, 74–77 Great Russell Street, WC1B 3DA.

SHAPER, Prof. (Andrew) Gerald, FRCP; FRCPath; FFPH; Professor of Clinical Epidemiology and Head of Department of Primary Care and Population Sciences, Royal Free Hospital School of Medicine, University of London, 1975–92, now Professor Emeritus, University College Medical School, Royal Free Campus; *b* 9 Aug. 1927; *s* of Jack and Molly Shaper; *m* 1952, Lorna June Clarke; one *s*. *Educ:* Univ. of Cape Town (MB ChB); DTM&H with Milne Medal (Liverpool). Ho. Phys./Surg., Harare, 1952; SHO, Trop. Diseases Unit, Sefton Gen. Hosp., Liverpool, and Res. Asst, Liverpool Sch. of Trop. Med., 1953–54; Registrar: Clatterbridge Gen. Hosp., 1954–55; Hammersmith Hosp. and Post Grad. Med. Sch., 1955–56; Lectr, Sen. Lectr, Reader in Medicine and Prof. of Cardiovascular Disease, Makerere Univ. Med. Sch., Kampala, 1957–69; Mem. Sci. Staff, MRC Social Medicine Unit, LSHTM, 1970–75; Hon. Cons. Phys. (Cardiology), UCH, 1975–87; Hon. Consultant in Community Medicine, subseq. Public Health Medicine, Hampstead HA, 1975–92. RCP Milroy Lectr, 1972; Pickering Lectr, British Hypertension Soc., 1993. Chm., Jt Wkg Party of RCP and Brit. Cardiac Soc. on Prevention of Coronary Heart Disease, 1976; Member: DHSS Cttee on Med. Aspects of Water Quality, 1978–84; DHSS Cttee on Med. Aspects of Food Policy, 1979–83; Chairman: MRC Health Services Res. Panel, 1981–86; Heads of Academic Depts of Public Health (formerly Community) Medicine, 1987–90; Vice-Chm., Nat. Heart Forum, 1995–98; Member: WHO Expert Adv. Panel on Cardiovascular Disease, 1975–; DHSS Central Health Monitoring Unit Steering Gp, 1989–91. Elected Mem., Commonwealth Caribbean MRC, 1986–98. Alwyn Smith Prize Medal, FPHM, 1991. *Publications:* (ed) Medicine in a Tropical Environment, 1972; (ed) Cardiovascular Disease in the Tropics, 1974; Coronary Heart Disease: risks and reasons, 1988. *Recreations:* walking, second-hand/antiquarian books, theatre, golf. *Address:* 12 Greenholme Farm, Leather Bank, Burley in Wharfdale, Ilkley, W Yorks LS29 7HP. *T:* (01943) 865675. *E:* agshaper@wentworth.u-net.com.

SHAPIRO, Dr Bernard Jack, OC 1999; Principal and Vice-Chancellor, McGill University, Montreal, 1994–2002, now Emeritus; first Ethics Commissioner of Canada, 2004–07; *b* 8 June 1935; *s* of Maxwell Shapiro and Mary Tafler; *m* 1957, Dr Phyllis Schwartz (*d* 2004); one *s* one *d*. *Educ:* McGill Univ. (Schol.; BA Hons Econs and Pol Sci. 1956); Harvard Univ. (MAT Social Sci.; EdD Measurement and Stats 1967). Vice-Pres., William Barbara Corp., 1956–61; Res. Fellow, Educnl Testing Service, 1963; Res. Asst/Associate, Educnl Res. Council of America, 1965–67; Boston University: Asst Prof., 1967–71; Associate Prof., 1971–76; Chm., Dept of Humanistic and Behavioral Studies, 1971–74; Associate, Sch. of Educn, 1974–76; University of Western Ontario: Dean, Faculty of Educn and Prof. of Educn, 1976–78; Vice-Pres. (Academic) and Provost, 1978–80; Dir, Ont Inst. for Studies in Educn, 1980–86; Deputy Minister, Ontario: of Educn, 1986–89; of Skills Develt, 1988–89; Dep. Sec. of Cabinet, Ont, 1989–90; Deputy Minister: and Sec., Mgt Bd, 1990–91; of Colls and Univs, 1991–93; Prof. of Educn and Public Policy, Univ. of Toronto, 1992–94. Co-Chm., Nat. Adv. Cttee on Educn Stats, 1987–89. Chm., Governing Bd, OECD Centre for Educnl Res. and Innovation, 1984–86. President: Canadian Soc. for Study of Educn, 1983–84; Social Sci. Fedn of Canada, 1985–86; Conf. of Rectors and Principals of Quebec Univs, 1997–99. Hon. LLD: McGill, 1988; Toronto, 1994; Ottawa, 1995; Yeshiva, 1996; McMaster, 1997; Montreal, 1998; Edinburgh, 2000; Glasgow, 2001; Bishop's, 2001.

See also H. T. Shapiro.

SHAPIRO, Dr Harold Tafler; Professor of Economics and Public Affairs, Woodrow Wilson School, and President Emeritus, Princeton University, since 2001; *b* Montreal, 8 June 1935; *s* of Maxwell Shapiro and Mary Tafler; *m* Vivian; four *d*. *Educ:* McGill Univ. (Lieut Governor's Medal; BA 1956); Graduate Sch., Princeton (PhD Econ 1964). University of Michigan: Asst Prof. of Economics, 1964; Associate Prof., 1967; Prof., 1970–88; Vice-Pres. for Acad. Affairs and Chm., Cttee on Budget Admin, 1977; President, 1980–88; President, Princeton Univ., 1988–2001. Dir, Nat. Bureau of Economic Research. Member: Conference Board Inc.; Govt-Univ.-Industry Res. Round-table; Inst. of Medicine, Nat. Acad. of Scis; Council of Advrs to Pres. Bush on Sci. and Technology, 1990–92; Bd, Robert Wood Johnson Med. Sch., 2000–; Bd, DeVry Inst., 2001–; Bd, Hastings Center, 2001–; Bd of Dirs, Reading is Fundamental, 2001–04; Knight Foundn Cttee on Intercollegiate Athletics, 2004–; Merck

Vaccine Adv. Bd, 2004–; Stem Cell Inst. of NJ Jt Bd Managers, 2005–; Adv. Cttee, Human Embryonic Stem Cell Res., 2006–; Cttee on America's Energy Future, NAS, 2007–. Mem., Amer. Philosophical Soc.; Fellow, Amer. Acad. of Arts and Scis. Trustee: Alfred P. Sloan Foundn; Univs Res. Assoc.; Univ. of Pa Med. Center; Educnl Testing Service; Amer. Jewish Cttee, 2002–; Princeton Healthcare Systems, 2006–; Univ. of Med. and Dentistry of NJ, 2006–. William D. Carey Lectureship Award, 2006. *Publications:* (ed jtly) Universities and their Leadership, 1998; A Larger Sense of Purpose: higher education and society, 2005; (ed jtly) Belmont Revisited: ethical principles for research with human subjects, 2005. *Address:* Woodrow Wilson School, Princeton University, 359 Wallace Hall, Princeton, NJ 08544, USA.

See also B. J. Shapiro.

SHAPIRO, Leonard Melvyn, MD; FRCP, FACC; Consultant Cardiologist, with special interest in non-coronary intervention and valve disease, Papworth Hospital, Cambridge, since 1988; *b* 9 March 1951; *s* of Joseph and Stella Shapiro. *Educ:* Manchester Univ. (BSc 1st Cl.; MB ChB Hons 1976). MD 1981; FRCP 1994; FACC 1994. Senior Registrar: Brompton Hosp., 1982–84; Nat. Heart Hosp., 1984–88. Medical Advr, FA, 1997–. Founding Pres., British Soc. of Echocardiography, 1994–96. *Publications:* (jtly) A Colour Atlas of Hypertension, 1985, 2nd edn 1992; (jtly) A Colour Atlas of Angina Pectoris, 1986; (jtly) A Colour Atlas of Heart Failure, 1987, 2nd edn 1995; (jtly) A Colour Atlas of Physical Signs in Cardiovascular Disease, 1988; (jtly) A Colour Atlas of Palpitations and Syncope, 1990; (jtly) A Colour Atlas of Congenital Heart Disease in the Adult, 1990; A Colour Atlas of Coronary Atherosclerosis, 1992, 2nd edn 1993; (jtly) Mitral Valve Disease Diagnosis and Treatment, 1995; (jtly) An Atlas of Cardiac Ultrasound, 1998. *Recreations:* sport, triathlon. *Address:* Papworth Hospital, Cambridge CB23 3RE. *T:* (01480) 364353, *Fax:* (01480) 831035. *E:* sec@lmshapiro.com. *W:* www.lmshapiro.com.

SHAPLAND, Prof. Joanna Mary, DPhil; Professor of Criminal Justice, since 1993 and Edward Bramley Professor of Criminal Justice, since 2013, University of Sheffield; *b* 17 Feb. 1950; *d* of late Brig. John C. C. Shapland and Mary W. Shapland (*née* Martin, then Moberly); *m* 1978, Dr John Patrick George Mailer; one *s*. *Educ:* Croydon High Sch.; St Hilda's Coll., Oxford (BA 1971); Darwin Coll., Cambridge (Dip. Criminol. 1972); Wolfson Coll., Oxford (DPhil 1975). CPsychol 1989; Chartered Forensic Psychologist, 1993. Home Office Res. Fellow in Criminology, KCL, 1975–78; Res. Fellow, Centre for Criminol. Res., Oxford Univ., 1978–88; Jun. Res. Fellow, 1979–83, Res. Fellow, 1983–88, Wolfson Coll., Oxford; Sheffield University: Sen. Res. Fellow, Centre for Criminol. and Socio-Legal Studies, 1988–89; Lectr, 1989–91, Sen. Lectr, 1991–93, Dept of Law; Director: Inst. for the Study of the Legal Profession, 1993–2005; Centre for Criminological Res., 2005–10 and 2014–; Hd, Sch. of Law, 2009–13. Chm., Restorative Justice Forum (Scotland), 2014–. Cons. Expert, Select Cttee on Victim and Criminal and Social Policy, Council of Europe, 1982–87; Ind. Assessor, Review of Criminal Justice in NI, 1998–2000. Co-Ed., 1989–2002, Exec. Ed., 2002–, Internat. Review of Victimology; Ed., British Jl of Criminology, 1990–98. Outstanding Achievement Award, British Soc. of Criminology, 2013. *Publications:* Between Conviction and Sentence: the process of mitigation, 1981; *jointly:* Victims in the Criminal Justice System, 1985; Policing by the Public, 1988; Developing Vocational Legal Training for the Bar, 1990; Violent Crime in Small Shops, 1993; Arson in Schools, 1993; Drug Usage and Drugs Prevention, 1993; Organising UK Professions: continuity and change, 1994; Studying for the Bar, 1995; Starting Practice, 1995; Pupillage and the Vocational Course, 1995; Milton Keynes Criminal Justice Audit: the detailed report, 1996; Professional Bodies' Communications with Members and Clients, 1996; Affording Civil Justice, 1998; Good Practice in Pupillage, 1998; Social Control and Policing: the public/private divide, 1999; A Civil Justice Audit, 2002; The Informal Economy: threat and opportunity in the City, 2003; Evaluation of Statutory Time Limit Pilot Scheme in the Youth Court, 2003; The Junior Bar in 2002, 2003; Restorative Justice in Practice, 2006; Justice, Community and Civil Society, 2008; Urban Crime Prevention, Surveillance and Restorative Justice, 2009; Restorative Justice in Practice: evaluating what works for victims and offenders, 2011; (ed) Getting By or Getting Rich?: the formal, informal and criminal economies in a globalised world, 2013. *Recreations:* gardening, music, tapestry. *Address:* School of Law, University of Sheffield, Bartolomé House, Winter Street, Sheffield S3 7ND. *T:* (0114) 222 6712.

SHAPPS, Rt Hon. Grant; PC 2010; MP (C) Welwyn Hatfield, since 2005; Minister of State: Department for International Development, since 2015; Foreign and Commonwealth Office, since 2015; *b* 14 Sept. 1968; *s* of Tony and Beryl Shapps; *m* 1997, Belinda Goldstone; two *s* one *d* (of whom one *s* one *d* are twins). *Educ:* Watford Grammar Sch.; Cassio Coll., Watford (business and finance); Manchester Polytech. (HND Business and Finance). Founded Printhouse Corp. (design, web and print co.), 1990, Chm., 2000–. Contested (C) Welwyn Hatfield, 2001. Shadow Housing Minister, 2007–10; Minister of State, DCLG, 2010–12; Minister of State (Minister without Portfolio), Cabinet Office, 2012–15. Mem., Public Admin Select Cttee, 2005–07. Vice Chm. (Campaigning), 2005–07, Chm., 2012–15, Cons. Party. *Recreation:* private pilot with IMC and night qualifications. *Address:* House of Commons, SW1A 0AA. *T:* (020) 7219 8497, *Fax:* (020) 7219 0659. *E:* grant@shapps.com.

SHAPS, Simon; Chairman, MercuryMedia, 2010–14; Managing Director, International Content and Production, Core Media Group, 2013–14; *b* 10 Sept. 1956; *m*. *Educ:* Magdalene Coll., Cambridge (BA 1979). Researcher, Thames TV, 1982–83; London Weekend Television: researcher, 1983–90; Head of Current Affairs, 1990–93; Controller, Factual Progs, 1993–96; Dir of Progs, 1996–97; Dir of Progs, Granada TV, 1997–2000; Managing Director: Granada Prodns, 2000; Granada Broadband, 2000–01; Man. Dir, then Chief Exec., Granada Content, 2001–04; Chief Exec., Granada, 2004–05; Dir of Television, ITV, 2005–08; Chm., A Brand Apart TV, 2009–13. Chm., Nat. Film and TV Sch., 2009–13.

SHARIF, Mohammad Nawaz; Prime Minister of Pakistan, 1990–93, 1997–99 and since 2013; Leader, Pakistan Muslim League; *b* 25 Dec. 1949; *m* Kalsoom Nawaz Sharif; two *s* two *d*. *Educ:* St Anthony Sch., Lahore; Government Coll., Lahore; University Law Coll., Lahore. Finance Minister, Govt of Punjab, 1981–85; Chief Minister, Punjab, 1985–90; Leader of the Opposition, Nat. Assembly of Pakistan, 1993–97. *Recreations:* sports, especially cricket.

SHARKEY, family name of **Baron Sharkey**.

SHARKEY, Baron *cr* 2010 (Life Peer), of Niton Undercliff in the County of the Isle of Wight; **John Kevin Sharkey;** Director, Sharkey Associates Ltd; *b* 24 Sept. 1947; *m* Astrid; three *d*. Jt Man. Dir, Saatchi & Saatchi UK; Dep. Chm., Saatchi Internat.; Chief Operating Officer, Blue Arrow plc; Chm., BDDP Hldgs Ltd; Co-Chm. and Proprietor, Bainsfair Sharkey Trott, 1990–97; Co-Chm., BDDP GGT, 1997–98. Chairman: Highland Partners Europe; Ad-Air. Advr on Strategic Communications, Leader of Lib Dems, 2008; Chm., Lib Dem Gen. Election Campaign, 2010. Mem., Hansard Soc., 2004– (Hon., Treas., 2007–10). Gov., Inst. for Govt, 2013–. *Address:* House of Lords, SW1A 0PW.

SHARKEY, Annette, CBE 2004; Chief Operating Officer, Technology, Department for Work and Pensions, since 2015; *b* 4 May 1963; *d* of David Richard Willacy and Edith Willacy; *m* Peter Francis Sharkey. *Educ:* Preston Poly. (HND Business Studies (Dist.)). Joined DHSS, 1984; various information technol. and business change roles until 1999 (incl. secondment to Australian DSS, 1992–93); Lord Chancellor's Department, subseq. Department for Constitutional Affairs: IT Dir, Court Service, 1999–2002; Chief Inf. Officer, 2002–06; Interim Dir, Criminal Justice IT, 2003–04; Home Office: Chief Inf. Officer, Identity and Passport Service, 2006–08; Chief Inf. Officer, 2008–10; on sabbatical, 2010–15. Dir, MTC Educn and Glasstastik, 2011–. Mem., Contemporary Glass Soc., 2011–. Mem. Cttee, Newton Residents Assoc., 2012–. FBCS 2010. *Recreations:* glass artist, travel, sailing, golf. *E:* annette@farmpdn.com.

SHARLAND, Andrew James; Partner, Clintons, since 1990; *b* Chandlers Ford, Hants, 24 Nov. 1963; *s* of Ian James and Margaret Sharland; *m* 2005, Corinna Anne; two *d*. *Educ:* Winchester Coll.; Jesus Coll., Cambridge (BA 1985). Called to the Bar, Lincoln's Inn, 1986; admitted as solicitor, 1988; Partner, D. M. Landsman & Co., 1988–90. *Recreations:* contemporary music, analogue synthesizers, football, yoga. *Address:* Clintons, 55 Drury Lane, WC2B 5RZ. *T:* (020) 7379 6080, *Fax:* (020) 7240 9310. *E:* asharland@clintons.co.uk.

SHARLAND, (Edward) John; HM Diplomatic Service, retired; High Commissioner, the Seychelles, 1992–95; *b* 25 Dec. 1937; *s* of late William Rex Sharland and Phyllis Eileen Sharland (*née* Pitts); *m* 1970, Susan Mary Rodway Millard; four *d*. *Educ:* Monmouth Sch.; Jesus Coll., Oxford. BA Hons History; MA. FO, 1961–62; Bangkok, 1962–67; Far Eastern Dept, FCO, 1967–69; Dep. Perm. Rep. to UNIDO and Dep. Resident Rep. to IAEA, Vienna, 1969–72; Bangkok, 1972–75; Montevideo, 1976–79; Cultural Relations Dept, FCO, 1979–82; Consul-Gen., Perth, 1982–87; Consul-Gen., Cleveland, 1987–89; High Comr, PNG, 1989–91. *Recreations:* bridge, stamp collecting.

SHARLAND, Susan Margaret, (Mrs D. Woodwark), PhD; Chief Executive, Transport Research Foundation and TRL Ltd, 2001–13; *b* 26 Aug. 1961; *d* of Ian and Margaret Sharland; *m* 2005, Dr David Woodwark. *Educ:* St Swithun's Sch., Winchester; New Hall, Cambridge (BA (Maths) 1983); Imperial Coll., London (PhD 1988). Res. Scientist/Dept Manager, UKAEA, 1983–96; Gen. Manager, AEA Technology plc, 1996–98; Man. Dir, AEA Technology Consulting/Engineering Software, 1998–2001. Non-executive Director: MGM Assurance, 2003–09; HR Wallingford Gp Ltd, 2008–; LUC Ltd, 2013–; Transport Systems Catapult Ltd, 2014–; non-executive Advisory Director: CEFAS, 2010–; Vehicle Certification Agency, 2013–. *Recreations:* gardening, travelling, walking, gym. *E:* susan.sharland@icloud.com.

SHARMA, Alok; MP (C) Reading West, since 2010; *b* 7 Sept. 1967; *m*; two *d*. *Educ:* Blue Coat Sch., Reading; Salford Univ. (BSc Applied Physics with Electronics 1988). CA. Accountancy and corporate finance advr. *Address:* House of Commons, SW1A 0AA.

SHARMA, Kamalesh; Commonwealth Secretary-General, since 2008; *m* Babli; one *s* one *d*. *Educ:* Modern Sch. and St Stephen's Coll., Delhi; King's Coll., Cambridge (Eng. Lit.). Lectr in English, Delhi Univ.; Indian Foreign Service, 1965–2002: Hd of Divs, Technical Co-opn, Econ. Relns, Internat. Orgns and Policy Planning, Min. of External Affairs; Oil Sector and Develt Assistance from Europe, Treasury; served in Bonn, Hong Kong, Saudi Arabia and Turkey; Ambassador: to GDR; to Republics of Kazakhstan and Kyrgyzstan; Ambassador and Perm. Rep. of India to the UN, Geneva, 1988–90, NY, 1997–2002; Special Rep. of Sec.-Gen. of the UN to E Timor, as Under-Sec.-Gen., 2002–04; High Comr for India in the UK, 2004–08. Formerly Mem. Bd, Internat. Peace Acad., NY. Chancellor, QUB, 2009–15, now Chancellor Emeritus. Gov., Ditchley Foundn. Fellow, Weatherhead Center for Internat. Affairs, Harvard Univ. Hon. Dr: Middx; London; De Montfort; Nat. Univ. of Rwanda; Glasgow, 2014. Medal, Foreign Policy Assoc., USA, 2001. *Publications:* (ed) Imagining Tomorrow: rethinking the global challenge, 1999; (ed) Mille Fleurs: poetry from around the world, 2000. *Recreations:* literature, religious and mystical traditions, cosmology, development, global affairs, human society, cricket, Indian classical music, jazz. *Address:* Commonwealth Secretariat, Marlborough House, Pall Mall, SW1Y 5HX. *Clubs:* Athenaeum, Beefsteak, Travellers, Royal Automobile.

SHARMA, Murari Raj; Ambassador of Nepal to the Court of St James's, 2007–09; *b* Dingla, Bhojpur, Nepal, 16 April 1951; *s* of Dina Raj Adhikari and Padma K. Adhikari; *m* 1989, Nila Koirala Adhikari; two *s*. *Educ:* Univ. of Pittsburgh (MPIA 1983); Tribhuvan Univ. (MA Econs 1975; MCom 1978; BL 1990). Asst Lectr, Tribhuvan Univ., 1974–76; Jt Accounts Officer, Nat. Commercial Bank, Nepal, 1976–77; Officer, Nepal Food Corp., 1977–78; Section Officer, Min. of Finance, 1978–83; Under Sec., Min. of Gen. Admin., 1983–88; Under Sec., Min. of Home, 1988–90; Jt Sec. (Dir-Gen.), Ministries of Finance and of Foreign Affairs, 1991–97; Foreign Sec., 1997–2000; Ambassador of Nepal to the UN, NY, 2000–04; Mem., Adv. Cttee on Admin. and Budgetary Questions, UN, 2004–06. Consultant, Admin. Reform Commn, 1991; Convener, High-level Foreign Policy Rev. Cttee of Nepal, 2006. Columnist, República, Nepal, 2011–. Educnl consultant, 2012–. Gorkha Dakshin Bahu (Nepal), 1999. *Publications:* Murari Adhikari's Short Stories, 2000; (jtly) Reinventing the United Nations, 2007; (jtly) United Nations International Civil Service, 2009; papers and articles on topical issues in reputed daily newspapers, weekly magazines and e-magazines. *Recreations:* reading, writing, travel, volleyball, tennis. *Address:* 110/49 Janasahayog Marg, New Baneshwar, Kathmandu–34, Nepal. *T:* 4474048. *E:* murari.sharma@gmail.com. *Club:* Lions (Dingla, Bhojpur).

SHARMA, Surinder Mohan; JP; National Director (formerly Director General), Equality and Human Rights, Department of Health, 2004–12; *s* of Daulat Ram Sharma and Raksha Vati Sharma; *m* 1976, Vijay; one *s* one *d*. *Educ:* Univ. of Kent, Canterbury (BA Hons Law). Joined CRE, 1978; work at BBC TV; Corporate Equal Opportunities Manager, Littlewoods, until 2000; Dir, Diversity, Ford of Europe, 2000–04. Diversity and Inclusion Consultant, 2005–08, Mem., Diversity and Inclusion Global Adv. Council, 2008–12, Novartis Internat. AG, Basel. Member: EOC, 2000–07; Diversity Panel, MoD, 2008–; Ind. Advr for BIS, Diversity and Equality Council, 2011–; Chm., NHS and Social Care Black and Minority Ethnic Networks. Board Member: Race for Health, 2006–12; Race for Opportunity Campaign, 2008–12; Chm., Leicester Racial Equality Council. Mem., Leicester CC, 1983–91 (Hon. Alderman, 2013); Ind. Person, Leicestershire CC, 2013. Shadow Gov., Leics Partnership NHS Trust, 2012–. Trustee: Nat. Space Centre, 2003–; UNICEF UK, 2013–. JP Leicester, 1983. Hon. Professor: Wolverhampton, 2010; Manchester Univ. Business Sch., 2013. Mem. Council, Aston Univ., 2012– (Mem., Audit Cttee, 2012–; Chair, Ethics Sub Cttee, 2012–). Hon. Dr Central England, 2006; Hon. DLitt De Montfort, 2007. *Recreations:* gardening, holidays, playing cricket.

SHARMA, Virendra; MP (Lab) Ealing and Southall, since July 2007; *b* 5 April 1947; *s* of Dr Lekh Raj Sharma and R. P. Sharma; *m* 1968, Nirmala; one *s* one *d*. *Educ:* London Sch. of Econs (MA 1979). Started working life as bus conductor; subseq. in voluntary sector; Day Services Manager for people with learning disabilities, Hillingdon, 1996–2007. Mem. (Lab) Ealing BC, 1982–2010. Member: Jt Cttee on Human Rights, 2007–15; Health Select Cttee, 2010–15; Internat. Develt Cttee, 2015–. Chm., Indo-British All Party Parly Gp. Nat. Ethnic Minorities Officer, Lab Party, 1986–92. *Recreations:* reading, walking. *Address:* House of Commons, SW1A 0AA. *T:* (020) 7219 6080. *E:* sharmav@parliament.uk.

SHARMAN, family name of **Baron Sharman**.

SHARMAN, Baron *cr* 1999 (Life Peer), of Redlynch in the county of Wiltshire; **Colin Morven Sharman,** OBE 1979; FCA; Chairman, Aviva plc, 2006–12; *b* 19 Feb. 1943; *s* of late Col Terence John Sharman and of Audrey Emmiline Sharman (*née* Newman); *m* 1966, Angela M. Timmins; one *s* one *d*. *Educ:* Bishop Wordsworth's Sch., Salisbury. FCA 1977. Qualified as Chartered Accountant with Woolgar Hennel & Co., 1965; joined Peat Marwick Mitchell, later KPMG Peat Marwick, then KPMG, 1966; Manager, Frankfurt office, 1970–72; The Hague, 1972–81 (Partner 1973, Partner i/c, 1975); London, 1981–99; Sen. Partner (Nat. Mkting and Industry Gps), 1987–90; Sen. Mgt Consultancy Partner, 1989–91;

Sen. Regl Partner (London and SE), 1990–93; Sen. Partner, 1994–98; Chm., KPMG International, 1997–99. Chm., Aegis Gp plc, 2000–08 (Dep. Chm., 1999–2000); Chm., then Dep. Chm., Securicor plc, later Group 4 Securicor, 2003–05; non-executive Director: BG Gp plc, 2000–11; Reed Elsevier plc, 2001–11; Supervisory Dir, ABN Amro NV, 2003–07; Chm., Le Gavroche Restaurant. Mem., H of L, 1999–2015. Conducted review of audit and accountability for Central Govt (report published, 2001). Pres., GamCare, 2011–. Chm., Salisbury Cath. Council, 2010–. Mem., Industrial Soc. CCMI. Liveryman, Co. of Gunmakers, 1992 (Master, 2010–11). *Publications:* (jtly) Living Culture, 2001. *Recreations:* fishing, shooting, sailing, opera, wine and food. *Clubs:* Reform, Flyfishers'; Royal Yacht Squadron.

SHARMAN, Maj.-Gen. Alan George, CBE 2002; CEng, FIMechE; non-executive Director: MIRA Ltd, since 2006; Aspire Defence Holdings Ltd, since 2006; *b* 14 May 1942; *s* of late Major Frederick Sharman and Margaret (*née* Watkins); *m* 1st, 1967, Caroline Anne Lister (marr. diss.); one *d*; 2nd, 1977, Juanita Jane Lawson; one *s* one *d*. *Educ:* Hutton Grammar Sch.; Welbeck Coll.; RMA, Sandhurst; Reading Tech. Coll.; Army Staff Coll. CEng, FIMechE 1989. Commnd REME, 1962; served Aden and Oman, 1963; Elec. and Mech. Engr, The Life Guards, Singapore, 1967–68; psc, 1974–75; Signals Res. and Develt Establishment, 1976–77; Comd Allied Comd Europe Mobile Force (Land) Workshop, 1978–79; Mil. Sec's Dept, MoD, 1979–80; REME Combat Develt, 1981–83; Comdr Maintenance, 1 (Br) Corps Troops, 1984; Col Elec. and Mech. Engr 7, 1985–87; Project Manager, Logistic Vehicles, MoD (PE), 1987–89; Dir Elec. and Mech. Engr (Orgn and Trng), 1990–91; Prog. Dir, Tank Systems, MoD (PE), 1991–95; Dir Gen. Land Systems, MoD (PE), 1995–96. Dir Gen., Defence Manufrs Assoc., 1997–2007. Member: DTI Defence and Aerospace Cttee, 1998–2002; Defence Industries Council, 1997–2007; Vice Pres., Eurodefense UK, 2012–. Col Comdt, REME, 1996–2002; Pres., Bordon Br., REME Assoc., 1998–. Chm., Auto. Div., IMechE, 1996. *Recreations:* yachting, gardening, travel, family, military history. *Address:* c/o Regimental HQ REME, MoD Lyneham, Lyneham, Chippenham SN15 9HB. *Clubs:* Army and Navy; Royal Southern Yacht (Southampton) (Dir, 2012–).

SHARMAN, Evelyn Janet, (Jane), CBE 1998; *b* 5 July 1943; *d* of Kenneth Blair Austin Dobson and Evelyn Barbara Dobson (*née* Phillips); *m* 1972, John Matthew Reid Sharman; two *s*. *Educ:* St Andrews Univ. (MA 1st Cl. Hons Mod. and Med. History); Bryn Mawr Coll., USA. Asst Principal, MPBW then DoE, 1968–72; Principal, DoE, 1972–85 (incl. secondment to Cabinet Office and Royal Commn on Envmtl Pollution); English Heritage: Head, Ancient Monuments Div., 1985–89; Actg Dir of Conservation, 1989–91; Dir of Conservation, 1991–96; Acting Chief Exec., 1996–97. Sec., Historic Buildings Council, 1981–84. Chm., Architectural Heritage Fund, 2001–07. Trustee: Chatham Historic Dockyard Trust, 1997–2008; Royal Artillery Museums, 1998–2009; Bexley Heritage Trust, 2001–13; Greenwich Foundn for Old Royal Naval Coll., 2002–10. *Recreations:* reading, travelling.

SHARMAN, Mark Brian; Chairman, S3Media Ltd, since 2009; *b* 2 Jan. 1950; *s* of Stanley Sharman and Beryl Sharman; *m* 1981, Patricia; two *s*. *Educ:* John Port Grammar Sch., Etwall, Derby. Reporter, Derby Evening Telegraph, 1967–71; Sports Sub-Editor, Birmingham Evening Mail, 1971–76; Asst Producer, ATV Birmingham, 1976–77; Prog. Ed., Sport, LWT, 1977–81; Controller of News and Sport, TVS, Southampton, 1981–88; Man. Dir, Chrysalis Television, 1988–92; Dir of Progs, London News Network, 1992–94; Dep. Man. Dir, Sky Sports, 1994–98; Controller of Sport, Channel 4, 1998–2000; Dir of Broadcasting, 2000–03, Dep. Man. Dir, 2003–04, Sky Networks, BSkyB Ltd; Dir (formerly Controller), Sport, 2005–08, and Dir, News, 2007–08, ITV.

SHARMAN, Peter William, CBE 1984; Director, 1974–95 and Chief General Manager, 1975–84, Norwich Union Insurance Group; *b* 1 June 1924; *s* of William Charles Sharman and Olive Mabel (*née* Burl); *m* 1946, Eileen Barbara Crix; one *s* two *d*. *Educ:* Northgate Grammar Sch., Ipswich; Edinburgh Univ. MA 1950; FIA 1956. War service as Pilot, RAF. Joined Norwich Union Insce Gp, 1950; Gen. Man. and Actuary, 1969. Chairman: Life Offices' Assoc., 1977–78; British Insurance Assoc., 1982–83. *Recreation:* golf. *Address:* 28B Eaton Road, Norwich NR4 6PZ. *T:* (01603) 451230.

SHARP, family name of **Baroness Sharp of Guildford**.

SHARP OF GUILDFORD, Baroness *cr* 1998 (Life Peer), of Guildford in the co. of Surrey; **Margaret Lucy Sharp;** *b* 21 Nov. 1938; *d* of Osmund and Sydney Mary Ellen Hailstone; *m* 1962, Thomas Sharp, *qv*; two *d*. *Educ:* Tonbridge Girls' Grammar Sch.; Newnham Coll., Cambridge (BA 1960; MA 1962; Associate Fellow, 2007–10). Asst Principal, Bd of Trade and HM Treasury, 1960–63; Lectr in Economics, LSE, 1963–72; (pt-time) Guest Fellow, Brookings Instn, Washington, DC, 1973–76; Econ. Advr, NEDO, 1977–81; Res. Fellow, Sussex European Res. Centre, 1981–84, Sen. Fellow, Sci. Policy Res. Unit, 1984–99, Vis. Fellow, 1999–, Univ. of Sussex. Mem., Lib Dem Federal Policy Cttee, 1992–2003. Contested: (SDP/Alliance) Guildford, 1983 and 1987; (Lib Dem) Guildford, 1992 and 1997. Lib Dem front bench spokesman on educn, H of L, 2000–09. Mem., Corp., Guildford Coll. for Further and Higher Educn, 2005–13 (Chm., Curriculum Standards Cttee, 2008–13); Gov., Weyfield Community Primary Sch., 2005–; Chm., Colleges in their Communities Commn, NIACE/Assoc. of Colleges/157 Gp, 2010–12. Chm., Age Concern Surrey, 2004–08; Patron, Surrey Law Centre, 2010–14. Trustee, Transformation Trust, 2009–. Hon. FCGI 2004. Hon. Fellow, Birkbeck Coll., London, 2006. Hon. Liveryman, Plumbers' Co., 2013. Hon. LLD Sussex, 2005. *Publications:* The State, the Enterprise and the Individual, 1974; The New Biotechnology: European Governments in search of a strategy, 1985; (ed) Europe and the New Technologies, 1985; (with Geoffrey Shepherd) Managing Change in British Industry, 1986; (ed with Peter Holmes) Strategies for New Technologies, 1987; (with Claire Shearman) European Technological Collaboration, 1987; (ed jtly) Technology and the Future of Europe, 1992; (with John Peterson) Technology Policy in the European Union, 1998; many articles in learned jls dealing with science and technology policy. *Recreations:* reading, walking, theatre. *Address:* House of Lords, SW1A 0PW. *T:* (020) 7219 3121. *E:* sharpm@parliament.uk.

SHARP, Sir Adrian, 4th Bt *cr* 1922, of Warden Court, Maidstone, Kent; *b* 17 Sept. 1951; *s* of Sir Edward Herbert Sharp, 3rd Bt and of Beryl Kathleen, *d* of Leonard Simmons-Green; *S* father, 1986; *m* 1st, 1976, Hazel Patricia Bothwell (marr. diss. 1986), *o d* of James Trevor Wallace; 2nd, 1994, Denise, *o d* of Percy Edward Roberts; one *s*. *Heir:* *s* Hayden Sean Sharp, *b* 27 Aug. 1994. *Address:* 33 Calder Crescent, Whitby, ON L1N 6M2, Canada.

SHARP, Ann Elizabeth; *see* Hussey, A. E.

SHARP, Christopher Francis; QC 1999; a Recorder, since 2005; a Deputy High Court Judge, Family Division, since 2011; *b* 17 Sept. 1952; *s* of late (Charles Vyvyan) Peter Sharp and (Lilian) Corona Sharp (*née* Bradshaw); *m* 1978, Sarah Margot Cripps, LLB, JP; one *s* one *d*. *Educ:* Canford Sch., Dorset; Worcester Coll., Oxford (MA). Called to the Bar, Inner Temple, 1975; Mem., Western Circuit; founder mem., St John's Chambers, Bristol, 1978 (Dep. Hd, 1988–2000, Hd of Chambers, 2000–08). Founder Chm., Bristol Family Law Bar Assoc., 1990–96. Vis. Fellow, Faculty of Law, UWE, 2003–. Mem. Adv. Council, Worcester Coll., Oxford, 2006–15. Trustee, Quartet Community Foundn, 2011– (Mem. Cttee, 2010). *Publications:* articles in legal jls. *Recreations:* walking, ski-ing, Real tennis, Dorset. *Address:* St John's Chambers, 101 Victoria Street, Temple, Bristol BS1 6PU. *Clubs:* Bar Yacht, Bristol and Bath Tennis.

SHARP, Howard; QC (Jersey) 2010; Solicitor General for Jersey, 2010–15; *b* Cambridge, 19 Dec. 1975; *s* of John and Barbara Sharp; partner, Caroline Dutot. *Educ:* Warwick Univ. (BA Hons Hist.); Coll. of Law, London (CPE, BVC). Called to the Bar, Inner Temple, 2001; in practice as barrister, specialising in crime, internat. money laundering and corruption, 2001–08; Crown Advocate, Jersey, 2008–10. *Recreation:* scuba diving.

SHARP, Isobel Nicol, CBE 2009; Partner, Deloitte (formerly Deloitte & Touche) LLP, 2002–12; President, Institute of Chartered Accountants of Scotland, 2007–08; *d* of late Alexander and of Catherine Sharp. *Educ:* Kirkcaldy High Sch.; Univ. of Edinburgh (BSc 1976). CA 1980; ACIS 1986. Member: Financial Reporting Rev. Panel, 1994–99; Accounting Standards Bd, 2000–05; Ind. Parly Standards Authy, 2009–13; non-executive Member: Audit and Assurance Bd, Scottish Parlt Corporate Body, 2014–; HM Passport Office, 2014–. Hon. Prof., Edinburgh Univ. Business Sch., 2008– (Mem., Internat. Adv. Bd). Non-executive Director: Green Investment Bank plc, 2012–; Winton Capital Ltd, 2013–. *Publications:* Stock Exchange Reporting, 1994; Financial Statements for Smaller Companies, 1997, 4th edn 2002; Financial Statements for UK Listed Groups, 2004, 9th edn as Annual Report Disclosures for UK Listed Groups, 2012; Financial Statements for UK Unlisted Groups, 2007, 3rd edn 2010.

SHARP, James Lyall; HM Diplomatic Service; Director, Migration, Foreign and Commonwealth Office, since 2013; *b* 12 April 1960; *s* of Sir Richard Lyall Sharp, KCVO, CB; *m* 1992, Sara Essam El-Gammal; two *s*. *Educ:* Queen Elizabeth's Boys' Sch., Barnet; Durham Univ. (BA Hons Modern Middle Eastern Studies 1982). Customer Relations, British Aerospace, Riyadh, 1983–86; entered FCO, 1987; S America Dept, 1987–88; lang. trng, 1988–89, 2nd Sec., Chancery/Inf., 1989–92, Cairo; Hd of Section, Eastern Dept, 1992–95, Hong Kong Dept, 1995–96, FCO; 1st Sec., OSCE, Vienna, 1996–98; Hd of Section, NE Asia and Pacific Dept, FCO, 1998–2000; Dep. Hd, Security Policy Dept, FCO, 2000–01; lang. trng, 2002; Ambassador to Kazakhstan, 2002–05; Hd, Western Mediterranean/Justice and Home Affairs Gp, FCO, 2006–08; Regl Dir Asia-Pacific, UK Border Agency, Hong Kong, 2008–12. *Address:* c/o Foreign and Commonwealth Office, King Charles Street, SW1A 2AH.

SHARP, Sir Leslie, Kt 1996; QPM 1986; Chief Constable of Strathclyde Police, 1991–95; *b* 14 May 1936; *s* of George James Sharp and Lily Mabel (*née* Moys); *m* 1st, 1956, Maureen (*née* Tyson) (decd); two *d*; 2nd, 1985, Audrey (*née* Sidwell); two *d*. *Educ:* University Coll. London (LLB). MRC, 1952–54; Nat. Service, Middx Regt, 1954–56; Metropolitan Police, 1956–80; Asst Chief Constable, 1980–83, Dep. Chief Constable, 1983–88, W Midlands Police; Chief Constable, Cumbria Constab., 1988–91. Hon. LLD Strathclyde, 1995. *Recreations:* home computing, genealogy.

SHARP, Dr Lindsay Gerard; museum consultant, since 2005; Director, National Museum of Science & Industry, 2000–05; *b* 22 Aug. 1947; *s* of late Clifford Douglas Sharp and Olive Dora Sharp; *m* 1st, 1968, Margaret Mary Sommi (marr. diss. 1979); one *s*; 2nd, 1981, Robyn Catherine Peterson; one *d*. *Educ:* Wadham Coll., Oxford (BA 1st cl. Hons 1969); Queen's Coll., Oxford (DPhil 1976). Clifford Norton Res. Fellow, Queen's Coll., Oxford, 1972–75; Asst Keeper, Pictorial Collection, Science Mus., 1976–78; Dep. Dir, then Dir, Mus. of Applied Arts and Scis, Sydney, 1978–88; Director: Entertainment and Leisure, Merlin Internat. Properties, Sydney, 1988–90; The Earth Exchange, Sydney, 1990–93; consultant, Asia and Australasia, 1990–93; Sen. Mus. Consultant and Dep. Dir, Mus. of Creativity Project, Milken Family Foundn, Santa Monica, 1993–96; Pres. and CEO, Royal Ontario Mus., Toronto, 1996–2000. *Recreations:* reading, garden design, music, opera, film, wine collection, travel, cultural and architectural history, bio-diversity, sustainability and cultural diversity issues.

SHARP, Michael John Todkill; Chief Executive Officer, Debenhams plc, since 2011; *b* Stamford, Lincs, 22 March 1957; *s* of Sqdn Leader Joseph Todkill Sharp and Doreen Mary Sharp; *m* 1985, Elaine Agnes Walsh; five *d*. *Educ:* St Bartholomew Sch., Eynsham; Oxford Coll. of Further Educn. Sears Hldgs, 1976–81; Littlewoods Orgn, 1982–85; Burton Gp, 1985–92; Buying and Merchandising Dir, Topshop/Topman, 1992–96; Man. Dir, Principles and Racing Green, 1996–97; Chief Operating Officer, 2003–08, Dep. Chief Exec., 2008–11, Debenhams plc. Hon. Prof. in Fashion Business, Glasgow Caledonian Univ., 2013. *Recreations:* tennis, swimming, electric guitar. *Address:* Debenhams plc, 10 Brock Street, Regent's Place, NW1 3FG. *Club:* Essex.

SHARP, Peter Marjoribanks; health, social care and education consultant, since 2015; *b* Aberdeen, 12 March 1955; *s* of Harold Sharp and Isobel Sharp; *m* 1987, Lindsey May Darking; two *d*. *Educ:* Kings Norton Grammar Sch.; Poly. of Central London (BSc Life Scis 1977); Southlands Coll., London (PGCE 1978); Inst. of Educn, Univ. of London (DipEd 1983; MA Child Develt 1986); Tavistock Clinic (Cert Ed Psych. 1987). CPsychol 1991; CSci 2007; AFBPsS 2010. Teacher, Langdon Sch., 1978–80; Hd of Sci., Park High Sch., 1980–86; Psychologist, 1988–90, Sen. Psychologist, 1990–92, Divisional Sen. Psychologist, 1992–94, Asst Principal Educnl Psychologist, 1994–97, Hants; Principal Educnl Psychologist, Southampton CC, 1997–2002; Mouchel: Principal Consultant, 2002–05; Director: Children's Services, 2005–07; Learning, 2007–09; Wellbeing, 2009–13; Chief Exec., Centre for Workforce Intelligence, 2010–13; Hd, Wellbeing, Cordis Bright, 2013–15. *Publications:* (jtly) Anger Management, 1998, 2nd edn 2009; (contrib.) Clinical Counselling in Schools, 2000; Nurturing Emotional Literacy, 2001. *Recreations:* family, photography, Francophile, reading, trustee, travel, social media @Peter_M_Sharp. *T:* (020) 7330 9170, 07818 567202. *E:* petersharp12@gmail.com.

SHARP, Prof. Phillip Allen, PhD; Institute Professor, David H. Koch Institute for Integrative Cancer Research (formerly Center for Cancer Research), Massachusetts Institute of Technology, since 1999 (Salvador E. Luria Professor, 1992–99); *b* 6 June 1944; *s* of Joseph W. Sharp and Katherin (*née* Colvin); *m* 1964, Ann Christine Holcombe; three *d*. *Educ:* Union Coll., Barbourville, Ky (BA 1966); Univ. of Illinois (PhD 1969). NIH Postdoctoral Fellow, CIT, 1969–71; Sen. Res. Investigator, Cold Spring Harbor Lab., NY, 1972–74; Massachusetts Institute of Technology: Associate Prof., 1974–79; Prof. of Biol., 1979–86; Class of '41 Prof., 1986–87; John D. MacArthur Prof., 1987–92; Associate Dir, 1982–85, Dir, 1985–91, Center for Cancer Res.; Hd, Dept of Biol., 1991–99; Dir, McGovern Inst., 2000–04. Co-founder, and Mem. Director Bd, 1978–2009; Chm., Scientific Bd, 1987–2002, Biogen IDEC (formerly Biogen, Inc.); Co-founder, and Mem., Scientific and Director Bds, Alnylam Pharmaceuticals Inc., 2002–. Chm., General Motors Cancer Res. Foundn Awards Assembly, 1994–2006. Member: Cttee on Sci., Engrg and Public Policy, 1992–95; President's Cttee of Advrs on Sci. and Technol., 1994–97; Scientific Cttee, Ludwig Inst. for Cancer Res., 1998–; Bd of Scientific Govs, Scripps Res. Inst., 1999–; Bd of Advrs, Polaris Venture Partners, 2002–; Adv. Bd, Verastem, 2010–; Bd of Dirs, Syros Pharmaceuticals, 2012–. Advr, Longwood Fund, 2010–. Mem., Alfred P. Sloan Foundn, 1995–2004; Mem. Bd of Trustees, Massachusetts Gen. Hosp., 2002–11. Member: American Acad. of Arts and Scis, 1983; NAS, 1983; Inst. of Medicine, NAS, 1991; American Philosophical Soc., 1991 (Benjamin Franklin Medal, 1999). FAAAS 1987 (Pres., 2013–14). Hon. FRSE 2002. Hon. Mem., NAS, Republic of Korea, 2004; Foreign Mem., Royal Soc., 2011. Hon. Dr: Union Coll., Ky, 1991; Univ. of Ky, 1994; Bowdoin Coll., Maine, 1995; Univ. of Tel Aviv, 1996; Albright Coll., Penn, 1996; Univ. of Glasgow, 1998; Thomas Moore Coll., Ky, 1999; Uppsala Univ., 1999; Univ. of Buenos Aires, 1999; Northern Ky Univ., 2001; Rippon College, Wis, 2006. Alfred P. Sloan Jr Prize for Cancer Res., Gen. Motors Res. Foundn, 1986; Gairdner Foundn Internat. Award, Canada, 1986; Albert Lasker Basic Med. Res. Award, 1988; Nobel Prize in Physiology or Medicine, 1993; Nat. Medal of Sci., 2004; Double Helix Medal for Sci. Res., Cold Spring Harbor Lab.,

NY, 2006; Othmer Gold Medal, Chemical Heritage Foundn, 2015. *Publications:* numerous scientific articles in jls and other pubns. *Address:* The Koch Institute, Room 76–461A, Massachusetts Institute of Technology, 77 Massachusetts Avenue, Cambridge, MA 02139–4307, USA. *T:* (617) 2536421.

SHARP, Robin; *see* Sharp, Sir S. C. R.

SHARP, Robin John Alfred, CB 1993; Director, Global Environment, Department of the Environment, 1994–95; *b* 30 July 1935; *s* of Robert Arthur Sharp and Yona Maud (*née* Brazier); *m* 1963, Anne Elizabeth Davison. *Educ:* Brentwood Sch.; Brasenose Coll., Oxford (MA); Wesley House, Cambridge (BA). Methodist Minister, West Mersea, 1960–62; Theol Colls Sec., SCM, 1962–65; Minister, Paddington, 1965–66. Principal, Min. of Housing and Local Govt and DoE, 1966–72; Asst Sec., 1972; Special Advr to Chancellor of Duchy of Lancaster, Cabinet Office, 1972; Department of the Environment: Road Safety Div., 1972–75; Housing Div., 1975–81; Under Sec., 1981; Public Housing and Right to Buy, 1981–86; Local Govt, 1986–91; Dir of Rural Affairs, 1991–94. Chairman: European Sustainable Use Gp, IUCN, 1997–2007, now Emeritus; New Renaissance Gp, 1997–2002; Brent Fairtrade Network, 2012–; Kilburn Locality Patient Participation Gp, NHS Brent Commng Gp, 2012–; Brent Patient Voice, 2014–; Vice Pres., BTCV, 1997–2007. Trustee, Fauna and Flora Internat., 1995–2004 (Company Sec., 2000–04). Harry Messel Award for Conservation Leadership, IUCN Species Survival Commn, 2006. *Publications:* (jtly) Preparing for the Ministry of the 1970s, 1964; (jtly) Worship in a United Church, 1964; (contrib.) British Environmental Policy and Europe, 1998; (jtly) Freshwater Fisheries in Central and Eastern Europe, 2004; (contrib.) Recreational Hunting: conservation and livelihoods, 2009; (contrib.) Silent Summer: the state of the nation's wildlife, 2010; (contrib.) Transitional Environmental Support Systems Design: global solutions, 2013. *Recreations:* bird-watching, walking, concert-going, travel. *Address:* 30 Windermere Avenue, NW6 6LN. *T:* (020) 8969 0381.

SHARP, Dr Roy Martin; Chief Executive, Tertiary Education Commission, 2008–11; *b* 3 April 1946; *s* of Leonard and Freda Sharp; *m* 1971, Beverley Davison; two *s* one *d*. *Educ:* Dame Allan's Sch., Newcastle-on-Tyne; St Peter's Coll., Oxford (MA; DPhil). Dist. FIPENZ (FIPENZ 1992). University of Auckland: Lectr, 1973–75; Sen. Lectr, 1975–89; Prof., 1989–97; Dean of Engrg, 1992–97; Asst Vice-Chancellor, 1993–94; Dep. Vice-Chancellor, 1995–96; Dep. Vice-Chancellor, Victoria Univ. of Wellington, 1997–2003; Vice-Chancellor, Univ. of Canterbury, NZ, 2003–08. *Recreations:* walking, music.

SHARP, Sir Sheridan (Christopher Robin), 4th Bt *cr* 1920, of Heckmondwike, co. York, (known as **Mr Robin Sharp**); *b* 25 April 1936; *s* of Reginald Sharp (*d* 1969), 3rd *s* of Sir Milton Sheridan Sharp, 1st Bt and Doris Eve (*née* Faulder; *d* 1985); *S* cousin, 1996; *m* 1st, 1958, Sheila Aileen Moodie (marr. diss. 1967); 2nd, 1969, Anna Maria, *d* of N. H. Saverio Rossi, Rome; one *s* one *d*. *Educ:* Rugby Sch. News Ed., United Press, Montreal, 1956–58; Reuters, London, 1959–60; Correspondent, Australian Broadcasting Corp., 1961–71; Head of Public Affairs, Oxfam, 1973–77; Dir of Information, Soc. for Internat. Develt, Rome, 1978–81; Sec. Gen., World Food Assembly, 1983–86; Internat. Inst. for Envmt and Develt, 1986–92; Dir of Res., Right Livelihood Award, 1993–2003. FRSA. *Publications:* Whose Right to Work?, 1976; Europe and the World Without, 1977; Burkina Faso: new life for the Sahel?, 1990; Senegal: a state of change, 1994; All About Elcombe: the intimate history of a Cotswold hamlet, 2003. *Heir:* *s* Fabian Alexander Sebastian Sharp [*b* 5 Nov. 1973; *m* 2006, Marcia Debbie Gordon, *d* of Wentworth Williams].

SHARP, Dr Sonia, CPsychol; Deputy Secretary, Early Child and School Education Group, Department of Education and Early Childhood Development, State Government of Victoria, Australia, since 2013; *b* Sheffield, 22 Oct. 1961; *d* of Dr Mike Sharp and Beryl Sharp; partner, Edwin; two *d*. *Educ:* Univ. of Aston in Birmingham (BSc Hons, PGCE); Univ. of Sheffield (MSc; PhD 1998). CPsychol 1990. NPQH 2001. Teaching posts in Derbys, Leeds and Barnsley, 1984–88; Educational Psychologist: Barnsley, 1989–94; Lincs, 1994–97; Chief Educnl Psychologist, Bucks, 1997–99; Asst Dir of Educn, Birmingham CC, 1999–2003; Dep. Chief Exec., Educn Leeds, 2003–05; Dir of Children's Services, Rotherham MBC, 2005–08; Exec. Dir, Children and Young People's Services, Sheffield CC, 2008–12; Dep. Sec., Early Childhood Develt Gp, Dept of Educn and Early Childhood Develt, Vic, 2012–13. Chm., Yorks and Humber Br., Assoc. of Dirs of Children's Services, 2007–09. British Psychological Society: Chm., Div. of Child and Educnl Psychol., 1996–98; Associate Fellow, 1998. *Publications:* (with D. A. Thompson) Improving Schools: establishing and integrating whole school behaviour policies, 1994; (ed with P. K. Smith) How to Tackle Bullying in your School, 1994; (with H. Covie) Peer Counselling in Schools, 1996; (with H. Covie) Supporting and Counselling Children in Distress, 1998; (jtly) Bullying Behaviour: a long term perspective, 2002. *Recreations:* walking, fell-running, dance.

SHARP, Thomas, (Tom), CBE 1987; retired; General Manager, Names' Interests, Lloyd's of London, 1987–91; *b* 19 June 1931; *s* of late William Douglas Sharp and Margaret Sharp (*née* Tout); *m* 1962, Margaret Lucy Hailstone (*see* Baroness Sharp of Guildford); two *d*. *Educ:* Brown Sch., Toronto; Abbotsholme Sch., Derbys; Jesus Coll., Oxford. BoT and DTI (with short interval HM Treasury), 1954–73; Counsellor (Commercial), British Embassy, Washington, 1973–76; Dept of Trade, 1976–79; Dept of Industry, 1979–83; DTI, 1983–87. Member (Lib Dem): Surrey CC, 1989–2005 (Chm., Social Services Cttee, 1993–95); Guildford BC, 1991–99. Chm., Guildford CAB, 2004–07. *Publications:* (ed jtly) Just a Larger Family: letters of Marie Williamson from the Canadian Home Front, 1940–1944, 2011. *Address:* 96 London Road, Guildford, Surrey GU1 1TH. *T:* (01483) 572669. *E:* tomsharp96@ntlworld.com.

SHARP, Rt Hon. Dame Victoria (Madeleine), DBE 2009; PC 2013; **Rt Hon. Lady Justice Sharp;** a Lady Justice of Appeal, since 2013; *b* 8 Feb. 1956; *d* of Lord Sharp of Grimsdyke, CBE and of Marion (*née* Freedman); *m* 1986; three *s* one *d*. *Educ:* N London Collegiate Sch.; Univ. of Bristol (LLB). Called to the Bar, Inner Temple, 1979, Bencher, 2009; a Recorder, 1998–2008; a Judge of the High Ct of Justice, QBD, 2009–13; a Presiding Judge, Western Circuit, 2012–13. QC 2001.

SHARPE, Prof. David Thomas, OBE 1986; FRCS; Consultant Plastic Surgeon, Bradford Royal Infirmary, 1985–2014; Director, Plastic Surgery and Burns Research Unit, 1986–2014, and Professor in Plastic and Reconstructive Surgery, 1996–2014, University of Bradford; *b* 14 Jan. 1946; *s* of Albert Edward Sharpe and Grace Emily Sharpe; *m* 1st, 1971, Patricia Lilian Meredith (marr. diss. 2002); one *s* two *d*; 2nd, 2004, Tracey Louise Bowman. *Educ:* Grammar School for Boys, Gravesend; Downing Coll., Cambridge (MA); Clin. Med. Sch., Oxford (MB BChir); FRCS 1975. Ho. Surg., Radcliffe Inf., Oxford, 1970–71; Senior House Officer: Plastic Surgery, Churchill Hosp., Oxford, 1971–72; Accident Service, Radcliffe Inf., 1972; Pathology, Radcliffe Inf., 1972–73; Gen. Surgery, Royal United Hosp., Bath, 1973–75; Plastic Surgery, Welsh Plastic Surgery Unit, Chepstow, 1976; Registrar, Plastic Surgery: Chepstow, 1976–78; Canniesburn Hosp., Glasgow, 1978–80; Sen. Registrar, Plastic Surgery, Leeds and Bradford, 1980–84; Visiting Consultant Plastic Surgeon: Yorkshire Clinic, Bradford, 1985; BUPA Hosp., Elland, W Yorks, 1985–2011; Cromwell Hosp., London, 1985–2006. Chm., Breast Special Interest Gp, British Assoc. of Plastic Surgeons, 1997. Pres., British Assoc. of Aesthetic Plastic Surgeons, 1997–99. Chm., Yorks Air Ambulance, 2001–03. Inventor and designer of med. equipment and surgical instruments and devices; exhibitor, Design Council, London, 1987. British Design Award, 1988; Prince of Wales Award for Innovation and Production, 1988. *Publications:* chapters, leading articles and papers on plastic surgery topics, major burn disaster management, tissue expansion and breast reconstruction. *Recreations:* painting, shooting, flying. *Address:* Danby Low Mill, near Middleham, N Yorks DL8 4PX. *T:* (01969) 625795. *E:* profsharpe@hotmail.com.

SHARPE, John Herbert S.; *see* Subak-Sharpe.

SHARPE, Malcolm David; His Honour Judge Sharpe; a Circuit Judge, since 2014; Designated Family Judge, Mid and West Wales, since 2014; *b* Liverpool, 6 July 1966; *s* of Barrie Ronald Walter Sharpe and Joan Sharpe (*née* Waters); *m* 2006, Stephanie Phyllis Davidson; one *s*. *Educ:* St Edward's Coll., Liverpool; Univ. of Sheffield (LLB); Queen's Univ., Belfast (LLM); Inns of Court Sch. of Law. Called to the Bar, Lincoln's Inn, 1989; a Recorder, 2010–14. *Publications:* (contrib.) Child Care Management Practice, 2010, 3rd edn 2015. *Recreations:* football, cycling, technology. *Address:* c/o Swansea Civil Justice Centre, Caravella House, Quay West, Quay Parade, Swansea SA1 1SP.

SHARPE, Prof. Richard, PhD; FBA 2003; FSA, FRHistS; Professor of Diplomatic, University of Oxford, since 1998, and Fellow, Wadham College, Oxford, since 1990; *b* 17 Feb. 1954; *s* of John Maden Sharpe and Dorothy Sharpe (*née* Lord). *Educ:* St Peter's Sch., York; Trinity Coll., Cambridge (BA, MA, PhD). FRHistS 1988; FSA 1990. Asst Warden, YHA Lakeland Reg., 1973; Asst Editor, Dictionary of Medieval Latin from British Sources, 1981–90; University of Oxford: Reader in Diplomatic, 1990–98; Sen. Tutor, Wadham Coll., Oxford, 1997–2000; Jun. Proctor, 2000–01. O'Donnell Lectr in Celtic Studies, Oxford, 2004, Univ. of Wales, 2007. Res. Assoc., Sch. of Celtic Studies, Dublin Inst. of Adv. Studies, 1988–2010; Mem., Sch. of Historical Studies, IAS, Princeton, 1997. Mem., Oxford CC, 1987–95. Mem., Commn internat. de diplomatique, 2008–. Member: Oxford Archaeol Adv. Cttee, 1987–2000 (Chm., 1995–2000); Council, Oxford Historical Soc., 1990–; Pres., Surtees Soc., 2002–. Gen. Editor, Corpus of British Medieval Library Catalogues, 1990–. *Publications:* Raasay: a study in island history, vol. 1 1977, vol. 2 1978, 2nd edn 1982; (with M. Lapidge) A Bibliography of Celtic-Latin Literature 400–1200, 1985; (contrib. with D. R. Howlett) Dictionary of Medieval Latin from British Sources, fasc. III 1986, fasc. IV 1989, fasc. V 1997; Medieval Irish Saints' Lives, 1991; (with J. Blair) Pastoral Care before the Parish, 1992; Adomnán of Iona: Life of St Columba, 1995; (with R. G. Eales) Canterbury and the Norman Conquest, 1995; (jtly) English Benedictine Libraries, 1996; A Handlist of the Latin Writers of Great Britain and Ireland before 1540, 1997; (with A. T. Thacker) Local Saints and Local Churches in the Early Medieval West, 2002; Titulus: identifying Medieval Latin texts, 2003; Norman Rule in Cumbria 1092–1136, 2006; Roderick O'Flaherty's Letters, 2013; (with R. Easting) Peter of Cornwall's Book of Revelations, 2013; contribs to books and learned jls. *Recreations:* exploring Britain, working out, piano. *Address:* Old Indian Institute, Broad Street, Oxford OX1 3BD. *E:* richard.sharpe@history.ox.ac.uk.

SHARPE, Robert James, FRCO; Director of Music, York Minster, since 2008; *b* 14 Nov. 1971; *s* of Nigel and Carole Sharpe; *m* 1998, Mary, (Polly), Proctor; one *s* one *d*. *Educ:* Lincoln Christ's Hosp. Sch.; Exeter Coll., Oxford (Organ Schol.; BA Music 1994; MA 1998). FRCO 1993. Asst Organist, Lichfield Cathedral, 1994–2002. Asst Conductor, Birmingham Bach Choir, 1996–2002; Dir of Music, Truro Cath., 2002–08; Conductor, Three Spires Singers and Orch., 2002–08. FRSA. Hon. FGCM 2008. Cornish Gorsedd Cornwhylen Cross, 2008. *Recreations:* wine, food, furniture, interior design, architecture, technology, people. *Address:* 1 Minster Court, York YO1 7JJ. *E:* robert@robertsharpe.org.uk.

SHARPE, Rosemary Helen, CMG 2011; HM Diplomatic Service; Counsellor, Foreign and Commonwealth Office, since 2003; *b* 11 March 1956. *Educ:* Lady Margaret Hall, Oxford (BA Juris. 1974). Second Secretary: FCO, 1982–85; (Inf.), New Delhi, 1985–87; First Secretary: UK Repn, Brussels, 1987–88; FCO, 1988–91; (Econ.), Berlin, 1991–96; FCO, 1996–2000; Counsellor, Madrid, 2000–03.

SHARPE, Samuel John; Chief Financial Officer, Save the Children UK, since 2014; *b* London, 4 May 1962; *s* of Anthony John Sharpe and late Monica Margaret Sharpe (*née* Vincent); *m* 1997, Tansy Stephané-Jessop; two *s*. *Educ:* University Coll., Oxford (BA Classics 1985); Birkbeck Coll., Univ. of London (MSc Econs 1988). CPFA 2008. Various posts, ODA, 1985–97; Department for International Development: India, 1997–2000; South Africa, 2000–04; Policy Div., 2004–07; Finance Dir, 2007–10; Hd of India Office, 2010–14. *Address:* Save the Children UK, 1 St John's Lane, EC1M 4AR.

SHARPE, Thomas Anthony Edward; QC 1994; *b* 21 Dec. 1949; *e s* of late James Sharpe, MC, Maxwelltown, Dumfriesshire and Lydia de Gegg, Donauwörth, Germany; *m* 1988, Phillis M. Rogers, *y d* of late W. P. Rogers and Mrs M. Rogers, Warlingham, Surrey; one *s* one *d*; one *s* one *d* by previous marriage. *Educ:* Trinity Hall, Cambridge (MA). Called to the Bar: Lincoln's Inn, 1976 (Bencher, 2004); St Kitts and Nevis, 2002; Fellow in Law, Wolfson and Nuffield Coll., Oxford, 1979–88; in practice at the Bar, 1987–. Comr, Commn of Inquiry into Maladministration, St Kitts and Nevis, 2009–. Exec. Dir (part-time), Inst. for Fiscal Studies, 1981–87. Member: Adv. Bd, Centre for Competition Policy, UEA, 2005– (Chm., 2012–); Editl Bds, European Competition Jl and Concurrences, 2005–. Chm., New London Orch., 1998–2000; Trustee, Help Musicians UK (formerly Musicians' Benevolent Fund), 1999–; Mem. Council, LPO, 2014–. FRSA. *Publications:* monographs and articles in law jls on competition law, utility regulation and EC law. *Recreations:* music, travel, history, wine, grandchildren. *Address:* 1 Essex Court, Temple, EC4Y 9AR. *T:* (020) 7583 2000, *Fax:* (020) 7583 0118. *Clubs:* Reform, Beefsteak.

SHARPE, Prof. William Forsyth; STANCO 25 Professor of Finance, Stanford University, 1995–99, now Emeritus (Timken Professor of Finance, 1970–89; Professor of Finance, 1993–95); *b* 16 June 1934; *s* of Russell Thornley Sharpe and Evelyn Jillson Maloy; *m* 1st, 1954, Roberta Ruth Branton; one *s* one *d*; 2nd, 1986, Kathryn Peck. *Educ:* UCLA (AB 1955; MA 1956; PhD 1961). Economist, Rand Corp., 1957–61; University of Washington: Asst Prof. of Economics, 1961–63; Associate Prof., 1963–67; Prof., 1967–68; Prof., Univ. of California, Irvine, 1968–70. Pres., William F. Sharpe Associates, 1986–92. Chm., Financial Engines Inc., 1996–2003. Hon. DHumLit De Paul, 1997; Dr *hc* Alicante, 2003; Dr Econs *hc* Vienna, 2004; Hon. DSc(Econ) London Business Sch., 2008. Graham and Dodd Award, 1972, 1973, 1986, 1988, 1998, 2007, 2010, Nicholas Molodovsky Award, 1989, Financial Analysts Fedn; (jtly) Nobel Prize in Economics, 1990; UCLA Medal, 1998. *Publications:* Economics of Computers, 1969; Portfolio Theory and Capital Markets, 1970; Investments, 1978, 6th edn 1999; Fundamentals of Investments, 1989, 3rd edn 2000; Investors and Markets, 2007. *Recreations:* sailing, opera, music. *Address:* Graduate School of Business, Stanford University, Stanford, CA 94305–5015, USA. *T:* (650) 7254876.

SHARPLES, family name of **Baroness Sharples**.

SHARPLES, Baroness *cr* 1973 (Life Peer); **Pamela Sharples;** Director, TVS, 1981–90 and 1991–93; *b* 11 Feb. 1923; *o d* of late Lt-Comdr K. W. Newall and Violet (who *m* 2nd, Lord Claud Hamilton, GCVO, CMG, DSO); *m* 1st, 1946, Major R. C. Sharples, MC, Welsh Guards (later Sir Richard Sharples, KCMG, OBE, MC, assassinated 1973); two *s* two *d*; 2nd, 1977, Patrick D. de Laszlo (*d* 1980); 3rd, 1983, Robert Douglas Swan (*d* 1995). *Educ:* Southover Manor, Lewes; Florence. WAAF, 1941–46. Mem., Review Body on Armed Forces Pay, 1979–81. Trustee, Wessex Med. Trust, 1997–. *Address:* 60 Westminster Gardens, SW1P 4JG. *T:* (020) 7821 1875.

See also Hon. C. J. Sharples.

SHARPLES, Adam John, CB 2007; Chairman, Ixion Group, since 2012; *b* 1 Feb. 1954; *s* of Frederick Sharples and Margaret (*née* Robertson); *m* 1982, Barbara Bleiman; one *s* one *d*. *Educ:* Corpus Christi Coll., Oxford (BA PPE 1975); Queen Mary Coll., London Univ. (MSc Econs 1977). Economist, Labour Party, 1978–83; Head of Res., NUPE, 1983–88; HM Treasury: Principal, 1988; Head: Tax Policy Team, 1992–96; Transport Team, 1996–97; Public Enterprise Partnerships Team, 1997–98; Dep. Dir, Public Services Directorate, then Dir, Public Spending, 1998–2003; Dir, Internat., Bd of Inland Revenue, 2003–04; Dir Gen., Work, Welfare and Equality Gp, 2004–09, Employment, 2009–11, DWP; Dir of Policy, Which?, 2012. FRSA 2000. *Recreations:* family, football, guitar, cooking. *Address:* Ixion, Halford House, Coval Lane, Chelmsford, Essex CM1 1TD.

SHARPLES, Hon. Christopher John; Director: Unigestion (UK) Ltd, since 2000; Wheatley Associates, since 2010; *b* 24 May 1947; *s* of Sir Richard Sharples, KCMG, OBE, MC and of Baroness Sharples, *qv*; *m* 1st, 1975, Sharon Joanne (marr. diss. 2009), *d* of late Robert Sweeny, DFC and Joanne Sweeny; one *s* two *d*; 2nd, 2010, Gaynor Malet, *d* of late Major Rhydian Llewellyn MC and of Lady Honor Llewellyn. MCSI (MSI 1992). VSO, India, 1965–66; C. Czarnikow Ltd (commodity brokers), 1968–72; Co-founder and Dir, Inter-Commodities Ltd, 1972 (renamed GNI Ltd, 1984; Chm., 1994–96); Director: GNI Holdings Ltd, 1984–2000; GNI Wallace Ltd, 1986–97; Founder Director and Chairman: ICV Ltd, 1981–98; Intercom Data Systems (renamed RoyalBlue Ltd), 1982–90; Chairman: GH Asset Management Ltd, 1991–94; Datastream Internat. Ltd, 1996–98; Lombard Street Research, 1997–2000; Membertrack Ltd, 1999–2000; Director: Gerrard Vivian Gray, 1994–98; Hiscox Dedicated Insurance Fund, 1995–96; Digital River Inc., 1998–2000; Grandeye Ltd, 2004–08; Seeker Wireless Ltd, 2006–12. Member: Adv. Panel to SIB, 1986–87; City Panel on Takeovers and Mergers, 1991–95; Association of Futures Brokers and Dealers, 1987–92: Chairman: Rules Cttee, 1987–91; F and GP Cttee, 1987–91; Chm., Securities and Futures Authority, 1991–95 (Chairman: Exec. Cttee, 1991–95; Capital Rules Cttee, 1991–95; Finance Cttee, 1991–95). International Petroleum Exchange: Dir, 1981–87; Dep. Chm., 1986–87; Mem., Public Relns Cttee, 1981–87; Member: Public Relns Cttee, London Commodity Exchange, 1983–96; Clearing Cttee, LIFFE, 1982–87; Taxation Cttee, British Fedn of Commodity Assocs, 1985–87; London Markets Adv. Gp on Regulation, 1986–87. Chm., Air Sqdn, 1998–2005; Chm., Yacht Squadron Racing Ltd, 2014–. Mem., Younger Brethren, Trinity House, 2014–. *Recreations:* sailing, flying. *Address:* 39 Rose Square, SW3 6RS. *Clubs:* Pratt's, White's; Royal Yacht Squadron (Cdre, 2013–); Royal Bermuda Yacht.

SHARPLES, Ven. David John; Archdeacon of Salford, since 2009; *b* Manchester, 17 March 1958; *s* of Eric and Jean Sharples; *m* 1982, Elaine Maria Cottrell; two *s*. *Educ:* King's Coll., London (BD 1981; AKC 1981); Coll. of the Resurrection, Mirfield. Ordained deacon 1982, priest 1983; Asst Curate, St Mary the Virgin, Prestwich, 1982–87; Vicar, St Anne's, Royton, 1987–2002; Area Dean, Tandle, 1994–2002; Dir of Ordinands, Dio. of Manchester, 2002–. Chaplain, Dr Kershaw's Hospice, 1989–2002. Hon. Canon, Manchester Cathedral, 2006–. *Recreation:* Manchester City FC. *Address:* c/o Bishopscourt, Bury New Road, Manchester M7 4LE. *T:* (0161) 708 9366.

SHARPLES, Sir James, Kt 1996; QPM 1989; DL; Chief Constable, Merseyside Police, 1989–98. Lancashire Constabulary, 1964–74; Greater Manchester Police, 1974–82; Asst Chief Constable, 1982–85, Dep. Chief Constable, 1985–88, Avon and Somerset Constabulary; Dep. Chief Constable, Merseyside Police, 1988–89. Mem., ESRC, 1996–98. Non-exec. Chm., Countess of Chester NHS Trust, 2005–12 (non-exec. Dir, 2001–12). DL Merseyside, 1997.

SHARPLES, Hon. Sir Pita Russell, KNZM 2015; CBE 1990; PhD; Director, Tū Māori Mai Ltd, consultancy business; *b* Waipawa, NZ, 20 July 1941; *s* of Paul Massey Sharples and Ruiha Karani Niania; *m* 1990, Arapera Wikitoria Hineamaru; three *s* two *d*. *Educ:* Waituna W Primary Sch.; Takapo Primary Sch.; Waipukurau Dist High Sch.; Te Aute Coll.; Auckland Teachers' Coll. (Dip. Teaching 1966); Univ. of Auckland (BA 1967; MA; PhD Anthropol. and Linguistics 1977). Prof. of Educn, Auckland Univ. MP (Māori Party) Tāmaki Makaurau, New Zealand, 2005–14; Minister of Māori Affairs, 2008–14; Associate Minister of Educn and Corrections, 2008–14. Founding CEO, Race Relns Office. Estabd Māori Taskforce. Co-Leader, Māori Party, 2004–13. Tohunga Huarewa, Takitimu Māori Performing Arts Sch. and Massey Univ., 2001. *Publications:* contrib. articles and papers on educn, race relns, Māori culture and lang., Māori hist. and the justice system of NZ. *Recreations:* Rugby, Māori fighting arts, Māori performing arts. *Address:* 52 San Marino Drive, Western Heights, West Auckland 0612, New Zealand. *T:* 212446950. *E:* drpitasharples@gmail.com.

SHARPLESS, Prof. K. Barry, PhD; W. M. Keck Professor of Chemistry, The Scripps Research Institute, since 1990, and Skaggs Institute for Chemical Biology, La Jolla, California, since 1996; *b* 28 April 1941; *m* 1965, Jan Dueser; two *s* one *d*. *Educ:* Dartmouth Coll. (BA 1963); Stanford Univ. (PhD 1968). Postdoctoral Associate: Stanford Univ., 1968; Harvard Univ., 1969; Chemistry Faculty, MIT, 1970–77; Stanford Univ., 1977–80; Prof., 1980–90, Arthur C. Cope Prof., 1987–90, Chemistry Faculty, MIT. Fellow: Nat. Sci. Foundn, 1963; NIH, 1968; Foundation Fellow: A. P. Sloan, 1973; Camille and Henry Dreyfus, 1973; Sherman Fairchild, CIT, 1987; Simon Guggenheim, 1987. FAAAS 1984; Fellow: American Acad. Arts and Sci., 1984; NAS, 1985 (Chemical Scis Award, 2000); Hon. MRSC 1998. Honorary Doctorate: Dartmouth Coll., 1995; Royal Inst. of Technology, Stockholm, 1995; Technical Univ., Munich, 1995; Catholic Univ. of Louvain, 1996; Wesleyan Univ., 1999. Janssen Prize, 1986; Chemical Pioneer Award, Amer. Inst. of Chemists, 1988; Prelog Medal, ETH, Zurich, 1988; Scheele Medal, Swedish Acad. of Pharm. Scis, 1991; Tetrahedron Prize, 1993; King Faisal Prize for Sci., 1995; Microbial Chemistry Medal, Kitasato Inst., Tokyo, 1997; Harvey Sci. and Tech. Prize, Israel Inst. of Tech., 1998; Chirality Medal, Italian Chemical Soc., 2000; (jtly) Nobel Prize for Chemistry, 2001; Wolf Prize in Scis, Israel, 2001; Rhône Poulenc Medal, UK, 2001; Benjamin Franklin Medal, 2001, John Scott Prize and Medal, 2001, Philadelphia. American Chemical Society: Award for Creative Work in Organic Synthesis, 1983; Arthur C. Cope Scholar, 1986; Arthur C. Cope Award, 1992; Roger Adams Award in Organic Chemistry, 1997. *Address:* The Scripps Research Institute, 10550 North Torrey Pines Road, La Jolla, CA 92037, USA. *T:* (858) 784 7505, *Fax:* (858) 784 7562. *E:* sharples@scripps.edu.

SHARPLEY, Ven. Roger Ernest Dion; Archdeacon of Hackney and Vicar of Guild Church of St Andrew, Holborn, 1981–92; *b* 19 Dec. 1928; *s* of Frederick Charles and Doris Irene Sharpley; unmarried. *Educ:* Dulwich College; Christ Church, Oxford (MA); St Stephen's House, Oxford. Deacon, 1954; Priest, 1955; Curate of St Columba, Southwick, 1954–60; Vicar of All Saints', Middlesbrough, 1960–81; Curate-in-charge, St Hilda with St Peter, Middlesbrough, 1964–72; RD of Middlesbrough, 1970–81; Canon and Prebendary of York Minster, 1974–81; Priest-in-charge, St Aidan, Middlesbrough, 1979–81. Chaplain, Grey Coll., Durham Univ., 1996–98. *Address:* 2 Hill Meadows, High Shincliffe, Durham DH1 2PE. *T:* (0191) 386 1908.

SHARPLING, Drusilla Hope, CBE 2007; HM Inspector of Constabulary, since 2009; *b* London, 7 Aug. 1955; *d* of James and Dulcie Sharpling; one *s*. *Educ:* City of London Sch. for Girls; Birmingham Univ. (LLB). Called to the Bar; various roles, incl. Hd of Casework and Crown Prosecutor, CPS, 1987–99; Associate, Penningtons, 1999–2002; Chief Crown Prosecutor, London Area, CPS, 2002–09. Mem., Ind. Panel Inquiry into Child Sexual Abuse, 2014–. *Recreation:* music. *Address:* HM Inspectorate of Constabulary, 4th Floor, 5 St Philips Place, Birmingham B3 2PW.

SHARPSTON, Eleanor Veronica Elizabeth; QC 1999; Advocate General, Court of Justice of the European Union (formerly Communities), since 2006; Fellow in Law, King's College, Cambridge, 1992–2010, Emeritus Fellow, 2011; *b* 13 July 1955; *d* of late Charles Sharpston and Pauline Sharpston (*née* Bryant); *m* 1991, David John Lyon (*d* 2000). *Educ:* St Paul's Girls' Sch. (Schol.); Bedales Sch. (Schol.); Konservatorium der Stadt Wien, Vienna; King's Coll., Cambridge (BA 1st Cl. Hons 1976; Schol. 1976; MA 1979); Corpus Christi Coll., Oxford (Squash Blue, 1978; Rowing Blue, 1978, 1979, 1980; Pres., Oxford Univ. Women's Boat Club, 1978–79 and 1979–80; Hon. Fellow, 2010); Inns of Court Sch. of Law. Called to the Bar: Middle Temple, 1980 (Bencher, 2005); Republic of Ireland, 1986; Gibraltar, 1999; Hong Kong, 2001; in practice as barrister, specialising in EU and ECHR law, Brussels, 1981–87, London, 1990–2005; référendaire (judicial asst) to Advocate Gen. (later Judge) Sir Gordon Slynn at Court of Justice of EC, Luxembourg, 1987–90; Lectr and Dir of Eur. Legal Studies, UCL, 1990–92; Univ. Lectr, 1992–98, Affiliated Lectr, 1998–2006, Sen. Fellow, Centre for Eur. Legal Studies, 1998–2005, Yorke Dist. Vis. Fellow, 2006–, Cambridge. Hon. Prof., Riga Grad. Sch. of Law, 2011–. Hon. LLD: Glasgow, 2010; Nottingham Trent, 2011; Stockholm, 2014. *Publications:* Interim and Substantive Relief in Claims Under Community Law, 1993; contrib. articles to Eur. Law Rev., Common Market Law Rev. and other books and jls on EU law. *Recreations:* theatre, classical music, European literature, sailing square riggers, karate, ski-ing, squash. *Address:* Court of Justice of the European Union, L-2925 Luxembourg. *T:* 43032215. *Clubs:* Athenæum; Leander (Henley); Remenham (Henley).

SHARRATT, Steven, OBE 2009; Group Chief Executive, Bio Group Ltd, since 2006; *b* Nottingham, 20 Aug. 1964; *s* of late Ian Sharratt and of Brenda Sharratt; *m* 1989, Sarah Mason; one *s* one *d*. *Educ:* Univ. of Kent (BA Hons Law); Chester Coll. of Law. Articled Clerk and Solicitor, Edge & Ellison, 1987–90; Solicitor, BP plc, 1990–91; Dir, Neville Gp and Subsidiaries, 1991–92; Solicitor, Gepp and Sons, 1992–94; Partner, Connolly Sharratt, 1994–97; Partner and Consultant, Taylor Vinters, 1997–2002; Gp Man. Dir, Chameleon Gp, 2000–02. Non-exec. Chm., Cambridge Recycling Services Ltd, 2002–06. Chm., Business Challenge Panel, BIS, 2011–; Member: Small Business Investment Taskforce, DTI, 2004–07; Admin. Burdens Adv. Bd, HMRC, 2006–; Climate Change Taskforce, 2007; Adv. Council, BASE, 2010–; Bd, Green Economy Pathfinder, New Anglia Local Enterprise Partnership, 2011–; Employment Sector Champion, Red Tape Challenge, 2011–. Confederation of British Industry: Chairman: Small and Medium Enterprises Council, 2006–08; Eastern Reg., 2008–10 (Vice Chm., 2010–11); Climate Change Bd, 2008–; Climate Change Policy Cttee, 2013–; Mem., Mayday (formerly Envmtl) Leadership Gp, 2008–12, Regl Leadership Team, 2009–12, BITC. Founder, Mayday East of England (formerly Carbon Coalition), 2008–12; Founder and Co-Chair, East of England Space 4 Ideas Forum, 2010–12. Mem., Adv. Gp, Prince of Wales Mayday Network, 2007–10; Chm., Prince's Trust, Suffolk, 2009–11. FRSA 2008. *Recreations:* my children, playing rock guitar, game shooting, zero emission fast cars and motorcycles (still searching), Manchester United FC, enjoying wonderful Suffolk produce from land and the coast. *Address:* Bio Group Ltd, The Barn, Fordham House Estate, Cambs CB7 5LL. *T:* 08446 330 100. *E:* Steve.Sharratt@biogroup.co.uk.

SHARROCK, Jonathan Owen; Director, London and Olympics, since 2011, and Director, High Speed Two Strategy and Engagement, since 2013, Department for Transport; *b* Reading, 28 Oct. 1971; *s* of Colin Sharrock and Lesley Sharrock; *m* 2002, Tracey Pennyfather; two *d*. *Educ:* Reading Sch.; Bristol Univ. (BA Hons 1st Cl. Pols and French 1994). Eur. fast-stream, 1994–99, Policy Manager, Rough Sleepers Unit, 1999–2001, DoE, later DETR; desk officer, Eur. Secretariat, Cabinet Office, 2001–03; Department for Transport: Hd, Airspace Div., 2003; Hd, Airports Policy Div., 2004–07; Hd, Aviation Security, 2007–09; Dir, London and Road Demand Mgt, 2009–11. *Recreations:* my family, gardening, road running, Europe. *Address:* Department for Transport, Great Minster House, 33 Horseferry Road, SW1P 4DR. *T:* (020) 7944 4080. *E:* jonathan.sharrock@dft.gsi.gov.uk. *Club:* Collingwood Athletic.

SHATTOCK, David John, CBE 1995; QPM 1985; Personal Advisor to Prime Minister of Mauritius, 1998–2000; Chief Constable, Avon and Somerset Constabulary, 1989–98; *b* 25 Jan. 1936; *s* of Herbert John Shattock and Lucy Margaret Shattock; *m* 1973, Freda Thums; three *s*. *Educ:* Sir Richard Huish's Sch., Taunton. Joined as Constable, final post Asst Chief Constable, Somerset and Bath, later Avon and Somerset Constabulary, 1956–82; Deputy Chief Constable: Wilts Constab., 1983–85; Dyfed-Powys Police, 1985–86; Chief Constable, Dyfed-Powys Police, 1986–89. Hon. MA Bristol, 1998; Hon. LLD UWE, 1999. OStJ 1989. *Recreations:* racket sports, particularly badminton, antique restoration, keeping fit, horse riding. *Club:* Bristol Savages (Bristol).

SHAUGHNESSY, family name of **Baron Shaughnessy**.

SHAUGHNESSY, 5th Baron *cr* 1916, of Montreal and of Ashford, Limerick; **Charles George Patrick Shaughnessy;** actor; *b* 9 Feb. 1955; *s* of late Capt. Alfred James Shaughnessy and of Jean Margaret (*née* Lodge); *S* cousin, 2007; *m* 1983, Susan Rachael, *d* of Sydney Fallender; two *d*. *Educ:* Eton; Magdalene Coll., Cambridge (BA Hons Law 1977); Central Sch. of Speech and Drama. Theatre includes Salisbury Repertory, 1981–83 and stage appearances in USA; television in UK and USA incl. Days of Our Lives (series), 1984–91; The Nanny (series), 1992–99; also many film credits. Co-Founder, Bus Stop 31 Prodns, 2005. *Heir:* *b* David James Bradford Shaughnessy [*b* 3 March 1957; *m* 1985, Anne-Marie, *d* of Thomas Schoettle; three *d*]. *Address:* 3631 Barry Avenue, Los Angeles, CA 90066, USA. *E:* chucker22@mac.com.

SHAVE, Alan William, CVO 1994; OBE 1991; HM Diplomatic Service, retired; businessman; *b* 3 Nov. 1936; *s* of late William Alfred Shave and Emily Shave; *m* 1961, Lidia Donoso Bertolotto; one *s* one *d*. *Educ:* George Green's Grammar Sch., Poplar. Cert., Nat. Council of Journalists. Journalist, E London Advertiser, 1953–57; Nat. Service, RAF, 1957–59; Journalist: Greenock Telegraph, 1960; Bristol Evening World, 1961; Asst Information Officer, COI, 1961; joined CRO, 1961; Salisbury, Rhodesia, 1961–62; Dar es Salaam, 1962–64; Sydney, 1964–66; La Paz, 1966–70; FCO, 1970–72; Santiago, 1972–76; Consul (Commercial): Barcelona, 1977–81; Milan, 1981–84; First Sec., FCO, 1984–88; Dep. Hd of Mission and Consul, La Paz, 1988–92; Governor of Anguilla, 1992–95. Representative: for Bolivia, BESO, 1996–2005; for Bolivia, British Consultancy Charitable Trust, 2005–13; for La Paz, PUM Netherlands Sen. Experts, 2006–10; for Bolivia, Confedn of European Sen. Expert Services, 2006–10. *Recreations:* cycling, ornithology, travel. *Address:* Casilla 3–35183, San Miguel (Calacoto), La Paz, Bolivia. *E:* awshave@gmail.com.

SHAW; *see* Byam Shaw.

SHAW, family name of **Barons Craigmyle** and **Shaw of Northstead**.

SHAW OF NORTHSTEAD, Baron *cr* 1994 (Life Peer), of Liversedge in the County of West Yorkshire; **Michael Norman Shaw,** Kt 1982; JP; DL; *b* 9 Oct. 1920; *e s* of late Norman Shaw; *m* 1951, Joan Mary Louise, *o d* of Sir Alfred L. Mowat, 2nd Bt; three *s*. *Educ:* Sedbergh. Chartered Accountant. MP (L and C) Brighouse and Spenborough, March 1960–Oct. 1964; MP (C) Scarborough and Whitby, 1966–74, Scarborough, 1974–92. Mem., H of L, 1994–2015. Mem., UK Delegn to European Parlt, 1974–79. FCA. JP Dewsbury, 1953; DL W Yorks, 1977. *Address:* Duxbury Hall, Liversedge, W Yorkshire WF15 7NR. *T:* (01924) 402270. *Club:* Carlton.

SHAW, Rt Rev. (Alexander) Martin; Bishop of Argyll and the Isles, 2004–09; an Honorary Assistant Bishop, Diocese of Exeter, since 2010; *b* 22 Sept. 1944; *s* of James D. D. Shaw, MBE and Jean Shaw; *m* 1971, Elspeth Longden; one *s* one *d* (and one *s* decd). *Educ:* Trinity Coll., Glenalmond; KCL (AKC 1967); Glasgow Univ. (Dip. Social Psych. 1969). Ordained deacon, 1968, priest, 1969; Curate: St Oswald's, Glasgow, 1968–70; Old St Paul's, Edinburgh, 1970–75; Chaplain, King's Coll., Cambridge, 1975–77; Principal, Inst. of Christian Studies, All Saints, Margaret St, W1, 1977–78; Rector, Holy Trinity, Dunoon, 1978–81; Succentor, Exeter Cathedral, 1981–83; Diocesan Missioner, Exeter Dio., 1983–89; Res. Canon, Precentor and Sub-Dean, St Edmundsbury Cathedral, 1989–2004; Temp. Dean, King's Coll., Cambridge, 2002. Broadcaster on radio and television; writer of poetry; singer (baritone), song recitals and oratorios. *Publications:* First Light, 2001; My Father's Arms, song cycle for soprano and string trio, 2002; Christ's Winter Pilgrimage, 2006. *Recreations:* walking, movies, photography, opera, reading, avoiding gardening. *Address:* 11 Russell Terrace, Exeter EX4 4HX. *E:* amartinshaw@gmail.com.

SHAW, Andrew Jeremy; a District Judge (Magistrates' Courts), since 2004; *b* 2 Feb. 1956; *s* of late Geoffrey James Shaw and of Noelle Shaw; *m* 2004, Miriam Jane Taylor; one *s*. *Educ:* Bromsgrove Sch.; Berkhamsted Sch.; Staffordshire Univ. (BA Hons Law). Admitted solicitor, 1981; joined Walker Smith & Way, 1981; Partner and Hd of Criminal Dept; Higher Courts Advocate (Criminal), 1999–2004. *Recreations:* golf, ski-ing, mountaineering.

SHAW, Angela Brigid L.; *see* Lansbury, A. B.

SHAW, Antony Michael Ninian; QC 1994; a Recorder, 2000–07; *b* 4 Oct. 1948; *s* of Harold Anthony Shaw and Edith Beatrice Sandbach (*née* Holmes); *m* 1983, Louise Göta Faugust (*d* 2006); one *s* two *d*. *Educ:* King's Sch., Canterbury; Trinity Coll., Oxford (Schol.; BA Juris. 1969). Researcher in Law, Bedford Coll., London, 1972–74; called to the Bar, Middle Temple, 1975 (Astbury Scholar, 1975; Bencher 2003); an Asst Recorder, 1997–2000. Head of Chambers, 4 Brick Court, 1988–99. Major cases: Guinness; Eagle Trust; Polly Peck; BCCI; Butte Mining; Alliance; VHS; Holbein; VHP; Operation Aloof (insider trading); Operation Amazon (carbon credits/tax relief); Innospec 2 (corruption); LIBOR. Vice Chm., Fees and Legal Aid Cttee, 1995–97, Chm., Remuneration Cttee, 2010–11, Gen. Council of the Bar. Gov., Internat. Students House, 1999–2003. *Publications:* contrib. Halsbury's Laws of England, 1977; (ed jtly) Archbold: Criminal Pleading, Evidence and Practice, 1991–; (Dep. Ed.) Fraud: Criminal Law and Procedure, 2010–; contrib. various law jls and Practical Law. *Recreations:* history, most literature. *Address:* 18 Red Lion Court, EC4A 3EB. *T:* (020) 7520 6000.

SHAW, Prof. Bernard Leslie, FRS 1978; FRSC; Professor of Chemistry, 1971–94, Research Professor, 1995– 2005, now Emeritus Professor, University of Leeds; *b* Springhead, Yorks, 28 March 1930; *s* of Thomas Shaw and Vera Shaw (*née* Dale); *m* 1951, Mary Elizabeth Neild; two *s* (and one *s* decd). *Educ:* Hulme Grammar Sch., Oldham; Univ. of Manchester (BSc 1st cl. Hons Chem.; PhD). Sen. DSIR Fellow, Torry Research Station, Aberdeen, 1953–55; Scientific Officer, CDEE, Porton, 1955–56; Technical Officer, ICI Ltd, Akers Research Labs, Welwyn, 1956–61; Lectr, Reader, and Prof., Univ. of Leeds, 1962–. Consultant for large-scale petrochemical industry, USA. Visiting Professor: Univ. of Western Ontario, 1969; Carnegie Mellon Univ., 1969; ANU, 1983; Univ. of Auckland, 1986; Univ. of Strasbourg, 1993. Liversidge Lectr, 1987–88, Ludwig Mond Lectr, 1992–93, Sir Edward Frankland Prize Lectr, 1996, RSC. Member: Royal Soc. Cttees; RSC Cttees; SERC (formerly SRC) Chem. Cttee, 1975–78, 1981–84 (and Inorganic Panel, 1977–78, Co-operative Grants Panel, 1982–84); Tilden Lectr and Prizewinner, 1975; Chem. Soc. Medal and Prize for Transition Metal Chem., 1975; Premo Calabria Prize for Sci., 2001. *Publications:* Transition Metal Hydrides, 1967; (with N. Tucker) Organotransition Metal Chemistry, and Related Aspects of Homogeneous Catalysis, 1973; over 400 original papers and reviews in chem. jls, several patents. *Recreations:* pottery, music, walking, gardening. *Address:* Department of Chemistry, The University of Leeds, Leeds LS2 9JT. *T:* (0113) 343 6465.

SHAW, Brian Hamilton; Director and Chief Executive, Britannic Group plc (formerly Britannic Assurance plc), 1997–2001; *b* 26 April 1942; *s* of late Dennis Hamilton Shaw and Peggy Shaw (later Dolan). *Educ:* King Edward's Sch., Birmingham. FIA 1966. Nat. Farmers' Union Mutual Insurance Soc., 1960–63; joined Britannic Assurance, 1963: Dir and Gen. Manager, 1979–86; Dir, Gen. Manager and Actuary, 1986–97. *Recreation:* sports. *Address:* 15 Saturn Way, Stratford on Avon CV37 7NE. *T:* (01789) 299202. *Club:* Royal Automobile.

SHAW, Carolyn Janet; Headmistress, Roedean School, 2003–08; *b* 24 April 1947; *d* of Norman and Mary Carey; *m* 1974, Dr Charles Drury Shaw; one *s* one *d*. *Educ:* Goldsmiths' Coll., Univ. of London (BA Hons 1970); Liverpool Univ. (PGCE 1971). English Teacher, La Sainte Union Convent, Bath, 1972–74; Head of English, Mount Saint Agnes Acad., Bermuda, 1974–77; English Teacher and Univ. Advr, Cheltenham Ladies' Coll., 1989–96; Headmistress, St Mary's Sch., Calne, 1996–2003. Chm. Govs, Amberley C of E First Sch., 2010–. Hon. Treas., Chichester Singers, 2011–. Trustee, Southern Pro Musica, 2012–. *Recreations:* reading, gardening, music, travel.

SHAW, Sir Charles (de Vere), 8th Bt *cr* 1821, of Bushy Park, Dublin; Chief Executive Officer, Leadership Dynamics Oman LLC; *b* 1 March 1957; *s* of John Frederick de Vere Shaw, *yr s* of 6th Bt and of Penelope Ann Shaw (*née* Milbank, now Mills); *S* uncle, 2002; *m* 1985, Sonia (*née* Eden) (marr. diss. 2013); one *s* one *d*. *Educ:* Michaelhouse, Natal; RMA Sandhurst. Officer, 5th Royal Inniskilling Dragoon Guards, 1976–87 (Major, retd). Dir, Safetynet plc, 1987–94; Gp Man. Dir, Morgan Lovell plc, 1994–2000; CEO, IntelliSpace, 2001–05. Country Dir and Chm., TQ Oman, 2013–. Non-executive Director: Shaw Travel Co. Ltd, 2002–10; Interiors Gp, 2008–13; Hurley Palmer Flatt, 2008–12. Expedition leader: Geographic North Pole, Aconcagua, Kilimanjaro, Himalayas, South China Seas. FRGS 2003. *Recreations:* shooting, fishing, photography, active Rugby supporter, cycling. *Heir: s* Robert Jonathan de Vere Shaw, *b* 7 Aug. 1988. *Address:* Bondoni, PO Box 34, PC 104, CPU Al Bahjah, Seeb, Sultanate of Oman. *T:* 24514101, 93227010. *E:* charles@leadershipdynamics.co.uk. *Club:* Army and Navy.

SHAW, Prof. Charles Timothy, CEng; Professor of Mining, Imperial College, London, 1980–2000, now Emeritus (Head of Department of Mineral Resources Engineering, 1980–85; Dean, Royal School of Mines, 1991–95); *b* 4 Oct. 1934; *s* of Charles John and Constance Olive Shaw (*née* Scotton); *m* 1962, Tuulike Raili Linari-Linholm (*d* 2009); one *s* two *d*. *Educ:* Univ. of Witwatersrand (BSc (Mining) 1956); McGill Univ. (MSc(Applied) (Mineral Exploration) 1959). Mine Manager's, Mine Overseer's and Mine Surveyor's Certs of SA; Chartered Engineer. Johannesburg Consolidated Investment Co. Ltd (JCI): numerous positions at various levels, 1960–67; Head of Computer Div., 1967–70; Manager, 1970–72 (as such an appointed dir of 14 cos incl. Consolidated Murchison Ltd and Alternate Dir of 9 cos); Consulting Engr, Consolidated Murchison Ltd, Randfontein Estates Gold Mining Co. (Wits.) Ltd and Shangani Mining Corp. (Zimbabwe), 1972–74; Consulting Engr and Alternate Dir, Rustenburg Platinum Mines Ltd, 1974–76; Chief Consulting Engr and Alternate Dir, Johannesburg Consolidated Investment Co. Ltd, also Man. Dir, Western Areas Gold Mining Co. Ltd, 1976–77; Associate Prof., Virginia Polytechnic Inst. and State Univ., 1977–80. Rep. for JCI on Technical Adv. Cttee of SA Chamber of Mines, 1974–77; Alternate Mem. for Gold Producers Cttee, 1976–77. Sec. Gen., Soc. of Mining Professors, 1990–2005; Member Council: IMM, 1981–88; IMinE, 1989– (Pres., S Counties Br., 1988–89). Hon. Prof., Inst. of Archaeol., London. Hon. PhD Miskolc, Hungary, 1995; Hon. Dr Moscow State Mining Univ., 1999. *Publications:* (with J. R. Lucas) The Coal Industry: Industry Guides for Accountants, Auditors and Financial Executives, 1980; papers both in technical literature and in house at Johannesburg Consolidated Investment Co. Ltd. *Recreations:* golf, mining history. *Address:* Department of Earth Science and Engineering, Imperial College, SW7 2AZ.

SHAW, Prof. Christopher Edward Dennistoun, MD; FRCP, FRACP; Professor of Neurology and Neurogenetics, King's College London, since 2004; *b* 27 March 1960; *s* of Roger and Helen Shaw; *m* 1988, Pinar Bagci; one *s* one *d*. *Educ:* Burnside High Sch.; Otago Medical Sch. (MB ChB 1984); MD 1997. FRACP 1993; FRCP 2000. Med. trng, Northland Hosp., 1985, and Wellington Hosp., 1986–92; Wellcome Trust-HRCNZ Res. Fellow, Univ. of Cambridge, 1992–95; Institute of Psychiatry, King's College London: Lectr, 1995–98; Sen. Lectr, 1998–2004; Dir, Maurice Wohl Clinical Neuroscience Inst., 2013–. FMedSci 2010. *Publications:* 70 scientific articles; res. interest includes genetic and molecular basis of motor neuron disorders, use of cloning technologies in discovery of novel therapies. *Recreations:* house building, watching old films, dancing with family, slow meals with extended family, holidays in Turkey. *Address:* Clinical Neuroscience PO 41, Institute of Psychiatry, Psychology and Neuroscience, King's College London, De Crespigny Park, SE5 8AF. *T:* (020) 7848 5180, *Fax:* (020) 7848 0988. *E:* Chris.shaw@kcl.ac.uk.

SHAW, Christopher Thomas; Editorial Director, ITN Productions, since 2011; *b* 19 June 1957; *s* of John Denis Bolton Shaw and Isabel Shaw (*née* Löewe); *m* 2001, Martha Catherine Kearney, *qv*. *Educ:* Westminster Sch.; Balliol Coll., Oxford (BA Hons Modern Hist.). Independent Radio News, 1980–85; ITN, 1985–89; Sen. Prog. Ed., Sky News, 1989–91; Foreign Ed., Channel 4 News, 1991–93; Programme Ed., News At Ten, 1993–95; Exec. Producer, ITN Factual, 1995–96; Ed., Channel 5 News, 1996–98; Controller, News, Current Affairs and Documentaries, Channel 5, 1998–2000; Sen. Programme Controller, Five (formerly Channel 5), 2000–10. Dir, Edinburgh TV Fest., 2006–. FRTS 2008. *Recreations:* travel, watching football, archaeology. *Address:* c/o ITN, 200 Gray's Inn Road, WC1X 8XZ.

SHAW, David, PhD; Executive Director, International Badminton Federation, 1992–98; *b* 19 Oct. 1936; *s* of Thomas Young Boyd Shaw and Elizabeth Shaw; *m* 1961, Margaret Esmé Bagnall; one *s* one *d*. *Educ:* Univ. of Birmingham (BA (Hons) Geography); Univ. of Sussex (Adv. Dip. Educnl Technology); Univ. of Leicester (PhD 2003); Univ. of London (MA 2009). Education Officer in Royal Air Force, final rank Sqn Ldr, 1960–76; Training Adviser to North Western Provincial Councils, 1976–78; Gen. Sec., British Amateur Athletic Bd, 1978–81; Gen. Sec., ITCA, then Dir, ITV Assoc., 1981–92. Represented Great Britain in Athletics (3000 metres steeplechase), 1958; British Universities Cross-Country Champion, 1959. *Recreations:* reading, walking, theological research. *Club:* Royal Air Force.

SHAW, Prof. David Aitken, CBE 1989; FRCP, FRCPE; Professor of Clinical Neurology, University of Newcastle upon Tyne, 1976–89, now Emeritus; *b* 11 April 1924; *s* of John James McIntosh Shaw and Mina Draper; *m* 1960, Jill Parry; one *s* two *d*. *Educ:* Edinburgh Academy; Edinburgh Univ. MB ChB (Edin) 1951; FRCPE 1968; FRCP (Lond.) 1976. Served in RNVR, 1943–46, demobilised in rank of Lieut. Jun. hospital appts, Edinburgh Royal Infirmary, 1951–57; Lectr, Inst. of Neurology, Univ. of London, 1957–64; Mayo Foundation Res. Fellow, 1962–63; University of Newcastle upon Tyne: Sen. Lectr, 1964–76; Public Orator, 1976–79; Dean of Medicine, 1981–89. Hon. FRCSLT (Hon. FCST 1988). *Publications:* (with N. E. F. Cartlidge) Head Injury, 1981; chapters in books and scientific articles in medical jls. *Recreations:* golf, fishing. *Address:* 5 Little Dene, Lodore Road, High West Jesmond, Newcastle upon Tyne NE2 3NZ. *T:* (0191) 285 2029.

SHAW, Maj. Gen. David Anthony Hirst, CBE 2012; Director: Unicorn ARC Ltd, since 2012; AFV Estates Ltd, since 2012; Red Lion Foods, since 2013; *b* Ceylon, 19 Feb. 1957; *m* 1985, Verity Jane Negus; two *s*. *Educ:* Haileybury, Hertford; RMA Sandhurst; Cranfield Univ. (MDA). Dip. CIM. Commnd RA, 1976; served 3 Regt RHA and 40 Regt, RA; CO 40 Regt RA, 1995–98; Comdr, 15 NE Bde, 2002–04; COS, Regl Forces, HQ Land Comd, 2004–07; Dir, Army Media and Communication, 2007–09; Mil. Advr to Royal Mil. Tattoo, 2009–12; GOC 2nd Div. and Gov., Edinburgh Castle, 2010–12. Vis. Prof., Robert Gordon Univ., Aberdeen, 2010–. HM Comr, Queen Victoria Sch., 2009–. Trustee, Scottish Nat. War Meml, 2009–12; Chm. Trustees, AF&V Launchpad, 2013–. FCIPD 2006; CIPR 2008. *Recreations:* painting, sailing, ski-ing. *Clubs:* Royal Scots; Royal Artillery Yacht, Bembridge Sailing.

SHAW, David Lawrence, FCA; chartered accountant; Founder, Chairman and Director, Sabrelance Ltd, corporate finance advisers, since 1983; *b* 14 Nov. 1950; *m* 1986, Dr Lesley Brown; one *s* one *d*. *Educ:* King's Sch., Wimbledon; City of London Polytechnic. FCA 1974. Coopers & Lybrand, 1971–79; County Bank, 1979–83. Chairman: RRI PLC, 1994–2000; 2020 Strategy Ltd, 1997–; Dep. Chm., The Adscene Group PLC, 1986–99; Dir, Nettec plc, 2003–05. Mem., Political, Communications and Marketing Cttee, Quoted Cos Alliance (formerly City Gp for Smaller Quoted Cos), 1997–2006. Mem., Royal Borough of Kingston upon Thames Council, 1974–78. Contested (C) Leigh, 1979; MP (C) Dover, 1987–97; contested (C) same seat, 1997; contested (C) Kingston and Surbiton, 2001. Chm., Bow Gp, 1983–84 (Founder, Transatlantic Conf., 1982); Mem., Social Security Select Cttee, 1991–97; Jt Chm., All Party Cttee on Dolphins, 1989–97; Chm., Cons. Backbench Smaller Businesses Cttee, 1990–97 (Sec., 1987–90); Vice Chm., Cons. Backbench Finance Cttee, 1991–97 (Hon. Sec., 1990–91). Vice-Chm., Kingston and Malden Cons. Assoc., 1979–86. Director: Business Council for Internat. Understanding (Europe) Ltd, 2002–; Internat. Trade and Investment Center, 2010–. Mem., Bd of Sen. Advrs, Center for Global Econ. Growth, Washington DC, 2005–. Founder and Dir, David Shaw Charitable Trust, 1994–. Vice-Pres., Inst. of Patentees and Inventors, 1996–. *Address:* 66 Richborne Terrace, SW8 1AX.

SHAW, David Lewis, OBE 2014; FRICS; Head, Regent Street Portfolio, The Crown Estate, since 2002; Chairman, The Pollen Estate, since 2015; *b* Cheadle, Cheshire, 20 July 1947; *s* of Joseph Lewis Shaw and Sarah Eirwen Mary Shaw (*née* Jenkins); *m* 1972, Heather Anne Johnson; two *s*. *Educ:* Wellington Sch.; Bristol Tech. Coll. FRICS 1981. Dir, Arrowcroft Investments Ltd, 1971–79; Partner, Richard Main & Co., 1979–82; Dir, Crouch Gp plc, 1982–84; Dir, Shearwater Hldgs, Rosehaugh Gp, 1984–92; Man. Dir, Burton Property Trust, 1992–95; Dir, Mgt Bd, Burton Gp, 1995–99; Property Dir, Servus Hldgs, Nomura Gp, 1999–2001. Dir, New West End Co., 2002–. Dir and Trustee, Orpheus Foundn Trust, 2007–. *Recreations:* walking, classical music, gadgets. *Address:* 9 Hamilton House, Vicarage Gate, W8 4HL. *T:* 07900 901135. *E:* dls.user@gmail.com.

SHAW, Dr Dennis Frederick, CBE 1974; Fellow, 1957, Professorial Fellow, 1977, Emeritus Fellow, 1992, Keble College, Oxford; Keeper of Scientific Books, Bodleian Library, Oxford, 1975–91; *b* 20 April 1924; 2nd *s* of Albert Shaw and Lily (*née* Hill), Teddington; *m* 1949, Joan Irene, *er d* of Sidney and Maud Chandler; one *s* three *d*. *Educ:* Harrow County Sch.; Christ Church, Oxford. BA 1945, MA 1950, DPhil 1950. FPhysS 1947; FInstP 1971, CPhys; FZS. Jun. Sci. Officer, MAP, 1944–46; DSIR Res. Student, 1946–49; Res. Officer in Physics, Clarendon Lab., Oxford, 1950–57, Sen. Res. Officer 1957–64; Univ. Lectr in Physics, Oxford, 1964–75. Vis. Prof. of Physics and Brown Foundn Fellow, Univ. of the South, Tennessee, 1974. Hon. Mem., Internat. Assoc. of Technol Univ. Libraries, 1992 (Sec., 1983–85; Pres., 1986–90); International Federation of Library Associations: Chm., Cttee for Sci. and Technol. Libys, 1987–91 (Mem., 1985–87); Finance Officer, Special Libraries Div., 1991–93; Mem., Press Cttee, ICSU, 1991–2002. Mem., Oxford City Council, 1963–67; Chm., Oxford City Civil Emergency Cttee, 1966–67; Member: Home Office Sci. Adv. Council, 1966–78; Home Defence Sci. Adv. Cttee, 1978–95; Hebdomadal Council, 1980–89; Chairman: Oxford Univ. Delegacy for Educnl Studies, 1969–73; Home Office Police Equipment Cttee, 1969–70; Home Office Police Sci. Develt Cttee, 1971–74. Member:

Amer. Phys. Soc., 1957; NY Acad. of Scis, 1981–2009. Gov., Christ's Hosp., 1980– (Almoner, 1980–98). Freeman, City of London, 1997. *Publications:* An Introduction to Electronics, 1962, 2nd edn 1970; A Review of Oxford University Science Libraries, 1977, 2nd edn 1981; (ed) Information Sources in Physics, 1985, 3rd edn 1994; (ed jtly) Electronic Publishing in Science, 1996; papers in sci. jls and chapters in books. *Recreations:* gardening, enjoying music. *Address:* Keble College, Oxford OX1 3PG. *T:* (01865) 272727. *Club:* Oxford and Cambridge.

SHAW, Donald, WS, NP; Partner, CMS Cameron McKenna, since 2014; *b* 14 Jan. 1956; *s* of D. B. Shaw, DSC, BL, NP and P. E. Shaw; *m* Susan; two *d. Educ:* Univ. of Aberdeen (LLB 1977). NP 1982; WS 1984. Dundas & Wilson: joined 1979; Partner, 1985–2014; Real Estate Industry Leader, 2003–06; Man. Partner, 2006–12. Leader Real Estate Law, Andersen Worldwide, 1998–2002. Dir, Four Quarter Develts Ltd, 2014–. Fellow, Soc. for Advanced Legal Studies, 1999. *Recreations:* history, music, travel, family, wine. *Address:* CMS Cameron McKenna LLP, Mitre House, 160 Aldersgate Street, EC1A 4DD. *E:* donald.shaw@cms-cmck.com.

SHAW, Rev. Prof. Douglas William David, OBE 2009; Professor of Divinity, 1979–91, and Principal, St Mary's College, 1986–92, University of St Andrews; *b* 25 June 1928; *s* of William David Shaw and Nansie Smart. *Educ:* Edinburgh Acad.; Loretto; Ashbury Coll., Ottawa; Univs of Cambridge and Edinburgh. MA (Cantab), BD (Edin.), LLB (Edin.). WS. Practised law as Partner of Davidson and Syme, WS, Edinburgh, 1953–57. Ordained Minister of Church of Scotland, 1960; Asst Minister, St George's West Church, Edinburgh, 1960–63; Official Observer of World Alliance of Reformed Churches at Second Vatican Council, Rome, 1962. University of Edinburgh: Dean, Faculty of Divinity, and Principal, New College, 1974–78; Lectr in Divinity, 1963–79; Dean, Faculty of Divinity, Univ. of St Andrews, 1983–86. Croall Lectr, New Coll., Edinburgh, 1983; Alexander Robertson Lectr, Univ. of Glasgow, 1991–92. Editor, Theology in Scotland, 1994–2002. Hon. DD: Glasgow, 1991; St Andrews, 2005. *Publications:* Who is God? 1968, 2nd edn 1970; The Dissuaders, 1978; trans. from German: F. Heyer: The Catholic Church from 1648 to 1870, 1969; (ed) In Divers Manners—a St Mary's Miscellany, 1990; Dimensions—Literary and Theological, 1992; various articles in theological jls. *Recreations:* squash (Scottish Amateur Champion, 1950–51–52), golf. *Address:* 4/13 Succoth Court, Edinburgh EH12 6BZ. *T:* (0131) 337 2130. *W:* www.dwdshaw.co.uk. *Clubs:* New (Edinburgh); Royal and Ancient (St Andrews); Edinburgh Sports.

SHAW of Chapelverna, Very Rev. Duncan; Representer of Clan Shaw of Argyll and the Isles (MacGilleChainnich of Dalriada); *b* 27 Jan. 1925; *e s* of Neil Shaw (Mac Gille Chainnich), master carpenter, and Mary Thompson Borthwick; *m* 1st, 1955, Ilse (*d* 1989), *d* of Robert Peiter and Luise Else Mattig, Dusseldorf; one *s* two *d;* 2nd, 1991, Prof. Anna Libera, DrPhil, Dr hab., *d* of Maestro Luigi Dallapiccola and Dr Laura Coen Luzzatto, Florence. *Educ:* Univ. of Edinburgh (PhD). Served REME, TA(WR), 1943–47 (Warrant Officer, cl. I 1946). Minister of parish: of St Margaret, Dumbiedykes, Edinburgh, 1951–59, of Craigentinny, Edinburgh, 1959–97. Scottish Rep. of Aktion Sühnezeichen, Berlin, 1966–71; Chm. of Bd, St Andrew Press, 1967–74; Editorial Dir, 1974–2000, Man Dir, 2000–, Edina Press, Edinburgh; Chm., IMS Trust and Instant Muscle (Scotland) plc, 1988–92; Dir, Instant Muscle plc, London, 1988–95. Dir, Centre for Theological Exploration Inc. USA, 1989–95. Trustee: Nat. Museum of Antiquities of Scotland, 1974–85; Edinburgh Old Town Charitable Trust, 1989–2005; Luigi and Laura Dallapiccola Foundn, 1997–. Pres., Scottish Record Soc., 1998–2014 (Treas., 1964–97); Founder and Chm. of Council, Scottish Soc. for Reformation History, 1980–2000. University of Edinburgh: Sec. of Gen. Council, 1965–93; Sen. Hume Brown Prizeman for Scottish History, 1965; Visiting Fellow, Inst. for Advanced Studies in the Humanities, 1975; part-time Lectr in Theological German, Faculty of Divinity, 1975–81; Sec., Gen. Council Trust, 1982–90; Dr *hc* 1990. Guest Prof., Lancaster Theolog. Seminary and Vis. Lectr, Princeton Theolog. Seminary, USA, 1967; Hastie Lectr in Divinity, Univ. of Glasgow, 1968–71; Visiting Lecturer: Univ. of Munich, 1980; Univ. of Heidelberg, 1983; McGill Univ., Montreal, 1984; Univ. of Mainz, 1991; St Andrew's Coll., Laurenburg, USA, 1999. Member of Advisory Committee: Christian Peace Conf., Prague, 1960–68; Conf. of European Churches, 1970–86 (acted as Gen. Sec., 1971). Hon. Mem., United Church of Berlin Brandenburg, 1969; Mem. of Cons. Cttee, Selly Oak Colls, Birmingham, 1976–87; Moderator, Presbytery of Edinburgh, 1978; Moderator, Gen. Assembly of Church of Scotland, 1987–88. Freeman, City of London, 1990; Liveryman, Scriveners' Co., 1990. JP 1974–2007; Chm., City of Edinburgh Justices Cttee, 1984–87; Burgess and Freeman, City of Edinburgh, 2007. KStJ 1983 (Mem., Chapter Gen., 1984–93, Chancellor of Scotland, 1986–92, Order of St John). ThDr *hc* Comenius Faculty of Theology, Charles Univ., Prague, 1969. Patriarchal Cross, 1978, for Hierarchs, 1988, Romanian Orthodox Church; Bundesverdienstkreuz, 1st cl. (Germany), 1980; Com. al Merito Melitense (SMO Malta), 1987; Order of St Sergius, 1987, Order of St Vladimir, 1997, Russian Orthodox Church. *Publications:* The General Assemblies of the Church of Scotland 1560–1600: their Origins and Development, 1964; (contrib. and ed) Reformation and Revolution: Essays presented to Principal Emeritus Hugh Watt, 1967; Inauguration of Ministers in Scotland 1560–1600, 1968; (contrib. and ed) John Knox: A Quartercentenary Reappraisal, 1975; Knox and Mary, Queen of Scots, 1980; (contrib. foreword and supervised translation) Zwingli's Thought: New Perspectives (by G. W. Locher), 1981; (contrib. and ed with I. B. Cowan) The Renaissance and Reformation in Scotland: Essays in Honour of Gordon Donaldson, 1983; A Voice in the Wilderness, 1995; Valedictory Address, 1997; (contrib.) Die Zürcher Reformation: Ausstrahlungen und Rückwirkungen, 2001; (ed) Acts and Proceedings of the General Assemblies of the Church of Scotland 1560–1618, 3 vols, 2004; Renaissance and Zwinglian Influence in 16th Century Scotland, 2012; The Clan Shaw of Argyll and the Isles, 2015; contrib. Oxford DNB; contribs to learned jls. *Address:* 4 Sydney Terrace, Edinburgh EH7 6SL. *T:* (0131) 669 9155; 12 Castelnau Gardens, Arundel Terrace, SW13 8DU. *T:* (020) 8746 3087. *Club:* Royal Scots (Edinburgh).

SHAW, Elizabeth Angela; Chair, Members Allowance Panel, South Somerset District Council, 2003–10; *b* 5 June 1946; *d* of John Edward Comben and Irene (*née* Thomson); *m* 1st, 1970, Graham Shaw (marr. diss. 1985); two *s* one *d;* 2nd, 1993, Adrian Carter. *Educ:* Sydenham High Sch.; Open Univ. (BA 2003). Executive Officer: Home Office, 1965–68; FCO, 1968–70; DSS, 1970–72; Department of Health and Social Security: HEO (Develt), 1972–77; Principal, 1977–84; Asst Sec., 1984–87; Dir of Finance, Planning and Marketing, Civil Service Coll., 1987–90; Head of Staff Develt, DoH, 1990–91; Exec. Dir, Charity Commn, 1991–96. Chair: COMPAID Trust, 1997–99; St Michael's Fellowship, 1997–99; Dir, Musikansky Theatre Co., 1998–2003. Chair, Spectra Musica chamber choir, 2011–. *Recreations:* music, literature, walking, riding, family.

SHAW, Fiona Mary, Hon. CBE 2001; actress; *b* 10 July 1958; *d* of Dr Denis Joseph Wilson and Mary Teresa Wilson (*née* Flynn), MSc; adopted Shaw as stage name. *Educ:* University Coll. Cork (BA); Royal Acad. of Dramatic Art (Hons Dip.; Bancroft Gold medal; Tree Prize; Ronson Award). *Theatre* includes: The Rivals, 1983; RSC, 1985–88: Philistines; As You Like It; Les Liaisons Dangereuses; Mephisto; Much Ado About Nothing; The Merchant of Venice; Hyde Park; The Taming of the Shrew; New Inn; Electra (title rôle); Mary Stuart, Greenwich, 1988; As You Like It, Old Vic, 1989; The Good Person of Sichuan, NT, 1989; Hedda Gabler (title rôle), Dublin and Playhouse, 1991; Machinal, NT (Best Actress, Evening Standard Awards), 1993; Footfalls, Garrick, 1994; Richard II, The Way of the World, RNT, 1995; The Waste Land, Brussels and Dublin Fests, NY (Drama Desk Award), 1996, Wilton's Music Hall, London, 1997, Adelaide, 1998; The Prime of Miss Jean Brodie, RNT, 1998; Medea, Abbey Th., Dublin, 2000, Queen's (Best Actress, Evening Standard Awards), 2001, NY 2002; The PowerBook, NT, 2002; The Seagull, Edinburgh, 2004; My Life as a Fairy Tale, NY, 2005; Julius Caesar, Barbican, 2005; Woman and Scarecrow, Royal Ct, 2006; Happy Days, NT, 2007; Mother Courage and Her Children, NT, 2009; The Waste Land, Wilton's Music Hall, 2009; London Assurance, NT, 2010; John Gabriel Borkman, Abbey Th., Dublin, 2010, NY, 2011; Scenes from an Execution, NT, 2012; The Rime of the Ancient Mariner, Old Vic Tunnels, 2012; Testament of Mary, NY, 2013, Barbican, 2014; Director: Riders to the Sea, London Coliseum, 2008; Elegy for Young Lovers, Young Vic, 2010; The Marriage of Figaro, ENO, 2011; The Rape of Lucretia, Glyndebourne, 2013, 2015. *Films* include: My Left Foot, 1988; The Mountains of the Moon, 1988; Three Men and a Little Lady, 1990; London Kills Me, 1991; Super Mario Brothers, 1993; Undercover Blues, 1993; Jane Eyre, 1994; Anna Karenina, 1996; The Butcher Boy, 1996; The Avengers, 1997; The Last September, 2000; Harry Potter and the Philosopher's Stone, 2001; Harry Potter and the Chamber of Secrets, 2002; The Triumph of Love, 2004; The Black Dahlia, 2006; Catch and Release, 2007; Fracture, 2007; Harry Potter and the Order of the Phoenix, 2007; Dorian Gray, 2009; Harry Potter and the Deathly Hallows, Pt 1, 2010; The Tree of Life, 2011; *television* includes: Fireworks for Elspeth, 1983; Persuasion, 1994; The Waste Land, 1995; Gormenghast, 2000; Mind Games, 2000; True Blood, 2011; Marple: Greenshaw's Folly, 2013; Lumen, 2015; (documentary) The British Face, 2011. Hon. Prof. of Drama, TCD, 1997. Hon. LLD NUI, 1996; DUniv Open, 1998; Hon. DLitt: TCD, 2001; Ulster, 2004. London Theatre Critics' Award, 1989, 1992; Best Actress, Olivier Awards, 1989, 1994. Officier, Ordre des Arts et des Lettres (France), 2003. *Publications:* contributor to: Players of Shakespeare, 1987; Clamorous Voices, 1988; Conversations with Actresses, 1990. *Recreations:* travel, reading, walking, thinking, painting. *Address:* c/o Independent Talent Group Ltd, 40 Whitfield Street, W1T 2RH.

SHAW, Howard; *see* Shaw, J. H.

SHAW, Sir John (Calman), (Jack), Kt 1995; CBE 1989; CA; FRSE; Governor, Bank of Scotland, 1999–2001 (non-executive Director, 1990–2001; Deputy Governor, 1991–99); *b* 10 July 1932; *m* 1960, Shirley Botterill; three *d. Educ:* Strathallan Sch.; Edinburgh Univ. BL; JDipMA. National Service, RAF, 1955–57. Partner in Graham, Smart & Annan (later Deloitte, Haskins & Sells), 1960, Sen. Edinburgh Partner, 1980–87. Pres., Inst. of Chartered Accountants of Scotland, 1983–84. Johnstone Smith Prof. of Accountancy (pt-time appt), Glasgow Univ., 1977–82. Chairman: Scottish American Investment Co. PLC (formerly Trust), 1991–2001 (Dir, 1986–2003); US Smaller Cos Investment Trust, 1991–99 (Dir, 2000); TR European Growth Trust PLC, 1998–2002 (Dir, 1992); Director: Scottish Metropolitan Property plc, 1994–2000; Scottish Mortgage and Trust PLC, 1982–2001; Templeton Emerging Markets Investment Trust plc, 1994–2003. Chairman: SHEFC, 1992–98; Scottish Financial Enterprise, 1995–99 (Exec. Dir, 1986–90); Scottish Science Trust, 1998–2002; Edinburgh Technology Fund, 1999–2001; Member: Bd, Scottish Enterprise, 1990–98; Financial Reporting Council, 1990–96. Chm., David Hume Inst., 1995–2002. Dep. Chm., Edinburgh Fest. Soc., 1991–2000. Mem. Court, Univ. of Edinburgh, 1998–2003. Dr *hc* Edinburgh, 1998; Hon. LLD: Glasgow, 1998; Abertay Dundee, 1998; St Andrews, 1999; Hon. DEd Napier, 1999. Receiver General, The Priory of Scotland of Most Venerable Order of St John, 1992–2002; KStJ 1992. *Publications:* (ed) Bogie on Group Accounts (3rd edn), 1973; The Audit Report, 1980; (jtly) Information Disclosure and the Multinational Corporation, 1984; numerous articles in accountancy and res. jls. *Recreations:* opera, theatre, walking. *Club:* New (Edinburgh).

SHAW, John Campbell; Managing Director: Amberton Shaw, 1997–2004; Stannifer Group Holdings, 1998–2004; *b* 2 Aug. 1949; *s* of late John C. B. Shaw and of May B. Shaw; *m;* two *d. Educ:* Grosvenor High Sch., Belfast; QUB (BSc Hons in Urban Geography); Heriot-Watt Univ. (MSc in Town & Country Planning). Lanarkshire CC, 1973–75; Motherwell DC, 1975–78; East Kilbride Development Corporation, 1978–95: Head of Planning, 1982; Tech. Dir, 1986; Man. Dir, 1990–95; Bd Mem., Lanarkshire Develt Agency, 1991–95. Director: Ramoyle Gp, 2008–10; Total Retail Concepts, 2010–15; Shaw Sandison Ltd, 2010–. *Recreation:* sport.

SHAW, John Frederick, CB 1996; Director of Corporate Affairs, National Health Service Executive, 1993–96; *b* 7 Dec. 1936; *s* of James Herbert and Barbara Shaw; *m* 1964, Ann Rodden; two *s* one *d. Educ:* Loretto Sch., Musselburgh; Worcester Coll., Oxford (MA). National Service, 2/Lieut KOYLI, 1955–57. Church Comrs, 1960–62; Industrial Christian Fellowship, 1962–63; HQ Staff, VSO, 1963–73; Principal (Direct Entry), DHSS, 1973, Asst Sec. 1978; Under Sec., DHSS, then DoH, 1987–93. Chairman: REACH, 1988–92; Nat. Family Mediation, 1996–2001; Rickmansworth Waterways Trust, 1997–2006; UK Transplant Support Services Authority, 1998–2001; Nat. Centre for Volunteering, 1999–2004 (Trustee, 1996–2004, Chm. Trustees, 1998–2004); Member Council: Patients' Assoc., 1996–99 (Vice-Chm., 1996–98); British Assoc. of Day Surgery, 1998–2005; Lay Mem., 1996–2003, Associate Mem., 2003–06, GMC; Lay Mem., Jt Cttee on Postgrad. Training for General Practice, 1997–2005. Mem. Cttee, Watford and Three Rivers Refugee Partnership, 2007–16. *Recreations:* church activities, singing, gardening. *Address:* Hyde House, West Hyde, Rickmansworth, Herts WD3 9XH.

SHAW, (John) Howard; QC 2011; arbitrator, since 2013; *b* Oldham, 6 Sept. 1948; *s* of Arthur Shaw and Edith Shaw; *m* 1972, Mary; two *s. Educ:* Hulme Grammar Sch., Oldham; Univ. of London (LLB). Called to the Bar, Inner Temple, 1973, Ire., 1998; Hd of Chambers, 3 Dr Johnson's Bldg, 1990–96. Qualified collaborative lawyer, 2009. MCIArb 2013. *Recreations:* theatre, travel, reading, walking the dogs, watching the tortoises, sport. *Address:* 29 Bedford Row, WC1R 4HE. *T:* (020) 7404 1044. *Fax:* (020) 7831 0626. *E:* hshaw@29br.co.uk. *Club:* Wimbledon Village.

SHAW, Jonathan Rowland; *b* 3 June 1966; *s* of Alan James Shaw and Lesbia Virginia Percival Shaw; *m* 1990, Susan Lesley Gurmin; one *s* one *d. Educ:* Vinters Boys' Sch., Maidstone; Bromley Coll., Kent (Cert. in Social Services). Social Worker, Kent Social Services, 1990–97. MP (Lab) Chatham and Aylesford, 1997–2010; contested (Lab) same seat, 2010. An Asst Govt Whip, 2006–07; Minister for the SE, 2007–10; Parly Under-Sec. of State, DEFRA, 2007–08, DWP, 2008–10. *Recreations:* walking, cooking, reading.

SHAW, Prof. Josephine, LLD; AcSS; Salvesen Professor of European Institutions, since 2005 and Director, Institute for Advanced Studies in the Humanities, since 2014, University of Edinburgh; *b* Shipley, W Yorks, 17 Sept. 1961; *d* of Robert Shaw and Freda Shaw (*née* Baxter); partner, 2001, Alf Thomas; one *s. Educ:* Bradford Girls' Grammar Sch.; Trinity Coll., Cambridge (BA 1982); Université Libre de Bruxelles (Licence en droit européen 1983); Univ. of Edinburgh (LLD 2008). Lectr in Law, Univ. of Exeter, 1984–90; Lectr, then Sen. Lectr in Law, Keele Univ., 1990–95; Professor of European Law: Univ. of Leeds, 1995–2001; Univ. of Manchester, 2001–04. Vis. Prof., Harvard Law Sch., 1998. AcSS 2005. FRSA 2001. *Publications:* The Transformation of Citizenship in the European Union, 2007; (jtly) Economic and Social Law and Policy in the European Union, 2007. *Recreations:* music, galleries, photography, Blipfoto. *Address:* Institute for Advanced Studies in the Humanities, University of Edinburgh, Hope Park Square, Meadow Lane, Edinburgh EH8 9NW. *T:* (0131) 650 9587. *E:* jo.shaw@ed.ac.uk.

SHAW, Prof. Kenneth Martin, MD, FRCP; consultant physician; Visiting Professor of Medicine, Portsmouth University, 1996–2008, now Emeritus; *b* 20 April 1943; *s* of late Frank Shaw and Gwen (*née* Mosson); *m* 1968, Phyllis Dixon; two *s. Educ:* City of Norwich Sch.; Downing Coll., Cambridge (BA 1965, MA 1969; BChir 1968, MB 1969; MD 1979);

University Coll. Hosp., London. FRCP 1985. MRC Res. Fellow, Dept of Clin. Pharmacol., UCH Med. Sch., 1971–72; Sen. Registrar, 1973–77, Resident Asst Physician, 1977–78, UCH, London; Portsmouth and SE Hants Health Dist, later Portsmouth Hosps NHS Trust: Associate Clin. Dir, Medicine, and Dir, 1979, Clin. Dir, then Hd of Service, 1979–2008, Dept of Diabetes and Endocrinol.; Sen. Consultant Physician, 1979–2008; Hon. Consultant, 2008–; Postgrad. Clin. Tutor, Univ. of Southampton, 1983–90; Dir, R&D, Portsmouth Hosps NHS Trust, and R&D Support Unit and Portsmouth R&D Consortium, Sch. of Postgrad. Medicine, Univ. of Portsmouth (at Queen Alexandra Hosp.), 1995–2008; Clin. Lead (Diabetes/Metabolic and Endocrine), Hants and IoW Comprehensive Local Res. Network, 2008–09. Arnold Bloom Lect., Diabetes UK, 2011. Editor-in-Chief, Practical Diabetes Internat., 1992–. External Examiner: Sch. of Medicine, Univ. of Cardiff, 2008–11; Coll. of Medicine, Univ. of Leicester, 2012–; Mem. Adv. Bd, Inst. of Diabetes for Older People, Univ. of Bedfordshire, 2008–13; Ext. Consultant Reviewer, Standards of Acute Medical Care, Univ. Hosp. Southampton NHS Foundn Trust, 2014–15. Royal College of Physicians: Hon. Sec., Jt Specialty Cttee for Endocrinol. and Diabetes, 2001–08 (Mem., 1998–2009); Mem., Adv. Panel for Service Rev. Visits, 2000–08; Diabetes UK (formerly British Diabetic Association): Mem., Med. Adv. Cttee, 1982–86; Vice Chm., Specialist Care Cttee, 1998–2002; Mem., 2002–, Mem. Exec., 2006–11, Professional Adv. Council; Chm., Professional Support and Develt Cttee, 2006–11; Chm., Wessex Diabetes and Endocrinol. Assoc., 1989–96; Mem., Med. Panel (Diabetes), DVLA, 2005–15; Ind. Specialist Consultant (Diabetes), CAA, 2010–; Member: Healthcare Professionals' Wkg Party, EMEA, 2013–; Transparency of Doctors' Interests Wkg Gp, RCP/BMA, 2014–. Member: Eur. Assoc. for Study of Diabetes, 1980–; Amer. Diabetes Assoc., 1995–2008; Internat. Diabetes Fedn, 1995–; Founding Mem. and Trustee, Assoc. of British Clin. Diabetologists, 1996– (Hon. Treas., 1996–2006; Hon. Chm., 2006–08; Hon. Trustee, Diabetes Care Trust (formerly Charitable Trust), 1996–). Hon. Trustee, Solent Diabetes Charitable Trust, 2007–13. FRSocMed 1972; Scientific FZS 1974. Mem., Harveian Med. Soc. of London, 1969–. UK Hosp. Diabetes Team Award, 1998. *Publications:* Complications of Diabetes, 1996, 3rd edn 2012; contrib. chapters in books; contrib. numerous rev. articles and peer-reviewed original scientific articles. *Recreations:* golf, opera. *Address:* Castle Acre, Hospital Lane, Portchester, Hants PO16 9QP. *W:* www.profkenshaw.com.

SHAW, Prof. Malcolm Nathan; QC 2002; PhD; Sir Robert Jennings Professor of International Law, University of Leicester, 1994–2011, now Professor Emeritus; Senior Fellow, Lauterpacht Centre for International Law, University of Cambridge, since 2010; *b* 8 July 1947; *s* of late Benjamin Shaw, CBE, and Paulette Shaw; *m* 1974, Judith Freeman; one *s* two *d*. *Educ:* Liverpool Univ. (LLB Hons); Hebrew Univ., Jerusalem (LLM with distinction); Keele Univ. (PhD). Called to the Bar, Gray's Inn, 1988; Lectr, then Principal Lectr, Liverpool Poly., 1972–81; Sen. Lectr and Reader in Law, 1981–89, Founder, Human Rights Centre, 1983, Essex Univ.; Ironsides, Ray and Vials Prof. of Law, Leicester Univ., 1989–94. Hebrew University of Jerusalem: Forcheimer Vis. Prof., 1986–87; Lady Davis Vis. Prof., 2009; Dist. Vis. Prof., 2013–14; Vis. Fellow, Lauterpacht Res. Centre for Internat. Law, Cambridge Univ., 2000–01 and 2005; Vis. Prof., Univ. of Paris Ouest, Nanterre-La Défense, 2009. Hersch Lauterpacht Meml Lectr, Univ. of Cambridge, 2010. Mem., Law Assessment Panel, 1996 and 2001 RAE, HEFCE. Trustee, British Inst. of Internat. and Comparative Law, 2010–. Associate Mem., Institut de Droit Internat. *Publications:* International Law, 1977, 7th edn 2014 (trans. Polish, Hungarian, Chinese, Portuguese); Title to Territory in Africa, 1986; contrib. British Yr Book of Internat. Law, Finnish Yr Book of Internat. Law, Internat. and Comparative Law Qly, European Jl of Internat. Law, Collected Courses of Xiamen Acad., China. *Recreations:* reading, listening to music, watching TV, maps. *Address:* 50 Carisbrooke Road, Leicester LE2 3PB. *E:* shawmalcolm@hotmail.com; Essex Court Chambers, 24 Lincoln's Inn Fields, WC2A 3EG. *T:* (020) 7813 8000, *Fax:* (020) 7813 8080. *E:* mshaw@essexcourt.net.

SHAW, Mark Richard; QC 2002; *b* 6 June 1962; *s* of Dennis Ronald Shaw and Jill Merilyn Shaw; *m* 1991, Elisabetta Ladisa. *Educ:* St Peter's Sch., Bournemouth; Durham Univ. (BA 1984); Gonville and Caius Coll., Cambridge (LLM 1985). Called to the Bar, Inner Temple, 1987; in practice, specialising in public law, human rights, professional discipline/regulation and mediation; Jun. Counsel to the Crown, Common Law, 1992–2002; Special Advocate, 1998–. CEDR Accredited Mediator, 2008. Fellow, Internat. Acad. of Trial Lawyers, 2008–. Member: Cttee, Constitutional and Admin. Law Bar Assoc., 1995–98; Adv. Bd, Judicial Rev., 1996–; Cttee, Assoc. of Regulatory and Disciplinary Lawyers, 2009–12. *Publications:* (jtly) Immigration and Nationality, in Halsbury's Laws of England: vol. 4, 1992; (contrib.) Human Rights Law and Practice, 1999, and Supplement, 2000. *Recreations:* golf, scuba diving, running, wine, travel (especially in Italy). *Address:* Blackstone Chambers, Temple, EC4Y 9BW. *T:* (020) 7583 1770. *Clubs:* Athenæum; Royal St George's Golf.

SHAW, Dr Mark Robert, FRSE; Keeper of Geology and Zoology, 1996–2005, now Hon. Research Associate, National Museums of Scotland; *b* 11 May 1945; *s* of William Shaw and Mabel Courtenay Shaw (*née* Bower); *m* 1970, Francesca Dennis Wilkinson; two *d*. *Educ:* Dartington Hall Sch.; Oriel Coll., Oxford (BA 1968; MA, DPhil 1972). FRSE 2004. Res. Assistant, Manchester Univ., 1973–76; Univ. Res. Fellow, Reading Univ., 1977–80; Asst Keeper, Dept of Natural History, 1980–83, Keeper of Natural History, 1983–96, Royal Scottish Mus., subseq. Nat. Museums of Scotland. *Publications:* contribs (mainly on parasitic wasps) to entomological jls. *Recreations:* field entomology, family life. *Address:* 48 St Albans Road, Edinburgh EH9 2LU. *T:* (0131) 667 0577.

SHAW, Martin; actor; *b* 21 Jan. 1945; two *s* one *d*. *Educ:* Great Barr Sch., Birmingham; LAMDA. *Stage* includes: appearances at Royal Court and National Theatre; West End: Are You Lonesome Tonight, Phoenix, 1985; The Big Knife, Albery, 1987; Other People's Money, Lyric 1990; Betrayal, 1991; An Ideal Husband, Globe, 1992, Haymarket, 1996 (Best Actor Award, NY Drama Desk, 1996), 1997, transf. Gielgud, and Albery, 1998, Haymarket, and Lyric, 1999; Rough Justice, Apollo, 1994; A Man for All Seasons, Haymarket, 2006; The Country Girl, Apollo, 2010; Twelve Angry Men, Garrick, 2013; *television* includes, 1968–: The Professionals; The Chief, 1994; title rôle in Rhodes, 1996; The Scarlet Pimpernel, 1999; Always and Everyone, later A & E, 1999–2002; Judge John Deed, 2001–07; Death in Holy Orders, 2003; The Murder Room, 2004; Cranford, 2007; Inspector George Gently, 2007–. Hon. Bencher, Gray's Inn. *Recreation:* flies own antique biplane.

SHAW, Rt Rev. Martin; *see* Shaw, Rt Rev. A. M.

SHAW, Group Captain Mary Michal, RRC 1981; Director and Matron-in-Chief, Princess Mary's Royal Air Force Nursing Service, and Deputy Director, Defence Nursing Services, 1985–88; *b* 7 April 1933; *d* of Ven. Archdeacon Thorndike Shaw and Violet Rosario Shaw. *Educ:* Wokingham Grammar School for Girls. SRN 1955, Royal Berkshire Hosp., Reading; SCM 1957, Central Middlesex Hosp., London and Battle Hosp., Reading; PMRAFNS, 1963–88; QHNS, 1985–88. OStJ 1974. *Recreations:* gardening, home crafts.

SHAW, Michael Hewitt, CMG 1990; foreign affairs adviser and consultant; HM Diplomatic Service, retired; *b* 5 Jan. 1935; *s* of late Donald Shaw and Marion (*née* Hewitt); *m* 1963, Elizabeth Rance; three *d* (and one *d* decd). *Educ:* Sedbergh; Clare College, Cambridge (MA); UCL (MA 1992). HM Forces, 1953–55. HMOCS Tanganyika, 1959–62; joined Diplomatic Service, 1963; served The Hague, FCO and Vientiane, 1964–68; First Sec., FCO, 1968–72, Valletta, 1972–76, FCO, 1976–82, Brussels, 1982–84; Counsellor, Brussels, 1984–86, FCO, 1986–95. Chm., Lynchmere Soc., 2007–12. *Recreations:* cricket, theatre, travel, historical research, preservation of the countryside. *Address:* The Close, Marley Common, Haslemere, Surrey GU27 3PT. *E:* michael@mhshaw.co.uk. *Clubs:* Army and Navy, MCC; Ashton Lacrosse.

See also R. O. Shaw.

SHAW, Sir Neil (McGowan), Kt 1994; Chairman: Tate & Lyle PLC, London, 1986–98 (Director, 1975–98; Chief Executive, 1986–92); Tate & Lyle Holdings, 1981–98; Tate & Lyle Industries, 1981–98; Tunnel Refineries, 1982–98 (Director, 1981–98); Vice-Chairman: Redpath Industries, 1981–98 (Director, 1972–98); A. E. Staley Manufacturing Co., 1988–98; *b* 31 May 1929; *s* of late Harold LeRoy Shaw and Fabiola Marie Shaw; *m* 1952, Audrey Robinson (marr. diss.); two *s* three *d*; *m* 1985, Elizabeth Fern Mudge-Massey. *Educ:* Knowlton High Sch.; Lower Canada Coll., Canada. Trust Officer, Crown Trust Co., Montreal, 1947–54; Exec. Asst, Redpath Industries, 1954–58; Merchandising Manager, 1958–63, Vice Pres. and Gen. Manager, 1967–72, Canada & Dominion Sugar Co., Toronto; Export Sales Manager, Tate & Lyle PLC, 1963–68; Pres., Redpath Industries Ltd, 1972–80; Gp Man. Dir, Tate & Lyle PLC, 1980–86. Director: Americare Corp. 1980–96; Alcantara, 1983–98; Canadian Imperial Bank of Commerce (Toronto), 1986–2000; United Biscuits (Hldgs), 1988–97; M & G Investment Income Trust, 1991–95; Medcan (Toronto), 2001–10. Non-executive Director: Texaco Canada Inc., 1974–89; Smiths Industries, 1986–96; Scottish and Newcastle Breweries, 1986–92. Dir, World Sugar Res. Orgn, 1982–97 (Chm., 1994–96); Gov., World Food and Agro Forum, 1988–96. Chairman: BITC, 1991–94; Assoc. of Lloyd's Members, 1992–94; E London Partnership, 1989–91; Member: Food Assoc., 1989–95; Church Urban Fund Council, 1989–91; Canadian Univs Soc. of GB, 1989–2001; Adv. Council, PYBT, 1990–98; Listed Cos Adv. Cttee, Stock Exchange, 1991–97; Chm. and Dir, Federal Security Agency, Toronto, 2008–. Trustee, Royal Botanic Gardens, Kew, 1990–98 (Chm., Trustees and Friends, 1994–2000). Dir, Inst. of Dirs, 1986–97. Dir and Gov., United World Coll. of Atlantic, 1997–2000. Gov., Montreal Gen. Hosp. Jt Chm., Percent Club, 1992–97. CIMgt, 1981–98; Fellow, Inst. of Grocery Distribn, 1989–2000 (Mem., British N American Cttee, 1991–97). Hon. Fellow, RHBNC, 1995. Hon. LLD E London, 1997. *Recreations:* dogs, golfing.

SHAW, Nicola Jane; QC 2012; *b* Bishop's Stortford; *d* of Michael John Shaw and Christine Shaw. *Educ:* Pembroke Coll., Oxford (BA Hons Juris.; BCL). Called to the Bar, Inner Temple, 1995; Attorney Gen.'s Panel of Jun. Counsel to the Crown, C Panel, 2001, B Panel, 2006. *Recreations:* parties, screenwriting, applied philosophy, downhill ski-ing, modern American literature, cooking, racquet sports, creative retreats, sailing, karaoke, restaurants, theatre. *Address:* Gray's Inn Tax Chambers, 36 Queen Street, EC4R 1BN. *T:* (020) 7242 2642, *Fax:* (020) 7831 9017. *E:* ns@taxbar.com.

SHAW, Peter Alan, PhD, DCL; CB 2000; Partner, Praesta Partners, since 2005; *b* 31 May 1949; *s* of late Frank Shaw and Ursula Lister Shaw (*née* Dyson); *m* 1975, Frances Willcox; two *s* one *d*. *Educ:* Bridlington Sch.; Durham Univ. (BSc Geography; DCL 2015); Bradford Univ. (MSc Traffic Eng. and Planning); Regent Coll., Univ. of British Columbia (Master in Christian Studies); Chester Univ. (PhD Leadership Develt 2011). FCIHT. Department of Education and Science, subseq. Department for Education, then Department for Education and Employment, then Department for Education and Skills, 1972–2003: Private Sec. to Perm. Sec., 1975–76; Principal Private Sec. to Sec. of State, 1979–81; Asst Sec., 1981–91; on loan to HM Treasury, 1985–86; Press Sec. to DES Sec. of State, 1988–89; Grade 3, 1991–98; on loan to Depts of the Envmt and Transport as Regl Dir, Northern Reg., 1991–93; Dir of Estabts and Personnel, 1993–94; Dir of Services (personnel, analytical and inf. systems), 1994–95; Leader, Sen. Mgt Review, 1995; Dir, Sch. Places, Buildings and Governance, 1995–97; Dir, Finance, 1997–98; Grade 2, 1998–2003; Director-General: Finance and Analytical Services, 1998–2000; Employment, Equality and Internat. Relations, 2000–01; Youth Policy, 2001–03; Partner, Change Partnership, 2003–05. Hon. Visiting Professor: Educn Dept, Univ. of Durham, 1997–2000; of Leadership Develt, Newcastle Univ. Business Sch., 2008–; Univ. of Chester Business Faculty, 2011–; Vis. Lectr, Regent Coll., UBC, 2008–. Trustee, Christian Assoc. of Business Execs, 2005–11. Member: Council, St John's Coll., Durham Univ., 1993–2008 (Hon. Fellow, 2009–14, now Hon. Professorial Fellow); Ct, Univ. of Newcastle upon Tyne, 2005–12; Governing Body, Godalming Sixth Form Coll., 1996–2008; Chm. of Trustees, Friends of Regent Coll., UBC, 2010–. Anglican Lay Reader, 1972–, Chm. of Selectors for Lay Readers in Trng, 1999–, Mem., Ministerial Adv. Council, 1999–2004, dio. of Guildford. FRSA. *Publications:* Mirroring Jesus as Leader, 2004; Conversation Matters, 2005; The Vs of Leadership: vision, values, value added and vitality, 2006; Finding Your Future: the second time around, 2006; (with Robin Linnecar) Business Coaching: achieving practical results through effective engagement, 2007; Making Difficult Decisions: how to be decisive and get the business done, 2008; Deciding Well: a Christian perspective on making decisions as a leader, 2009; Raise Your Game: how to succeed at work, 2009; Effective Christian Leaders in the Global Workplace, 2010; Defining Moments, 2010; (with Alan Smith) The Reflective Leader, 2011; Thriving in Your Work, 2011; Getting the Balance Right, 2012; (with Graham Shaw) Leading in Demanding Times, 2013; (with Colin Shaw) The Emerging Leader: stepping up in leadership, 2013; 100 Great Personal Impact Ideas, 2013; Celebrating Your Senses, 2014; 100 Great Coaching Ideas, 2014; Sustaining Leadership, 2014; 100 Great Team Effectiveness Ideas, 2015; Wake up and Dream, 2015; The Reluctant Leader, 2016; articles on exec. coaching, leadership and spirituality. *Recreations:* long-distance walking (completed 20 UK long distance walks), travelling, bus rides with grandchildren. *Address:* Praesta Partners, 43 Berkeley Square, W1J 5AP. *T:* (020) 7907 2473. *E:* peter.shaw@praesta.com.

SHAW, Dr Richard Oliver; Interim Chief Executive, South Downs National Park Authority, 2009–12; *b* 20 Jan. 1949; *s* of Donald Smethurst Shaw and Marion Clarissa Shaw; *m* 1983, Poorna Charles; three *s*. *Educ:* Sedbergh Sch.; Univ. of Sussex (BA 1st cl. Hons); Univ. of Exeter (PGCE 1973); UCL (PhD 1981). Teacher: Lycée el Hourriya, Algeria, 1971–72; Rishi Valley Sch., India, 1974–76; Sen. Educn Officer, then Field Dir, PNG, VSO, 1976–81; Head Teacher, Pahadi Sch., India, 1981–87; teacher, ILEA, 1987–88; Hd, Rural Affairs, then Hd, Global Atmosphere, DoE, 1988–97; Dir for the Envmt, Surrey CC, 1997–2001; Chief Executive: Oxfordshire CC, 2001–04; Surrey CC, 2005–09. Non-exec. Dir, Surrey and Sussex Healthcare NHS Trust, 2012–. Chm., UK Local Govt Alliance for Internat. Develt, 2009–; Associate, Nat. Sch. of Govt, 2009–. Mem. Council, Univ. of Surrey, 2005–09 (Mem., Audit Cttee, 2006–09). *Publications:* English lang. school textbooks for India. *Recreations:* tennis, PADI Master scuba diver, travel, family, music.

See also M. H. Shaw.

SHAW, Prof. Richard Wright, CBE 1997; Vice-Chancellor and Principal, University of Paisley, 1992–2001 (Principal, Paisley College, 1987–92); *b* 22 Sept. 1941; *s* of late George Beeley Shaw and Bella Shaw; *m* 1965, Susan Angela Birchley; two *s*. *Educ:* Lancaster Royal Grammar Sch.; Sidney Sussex Coll., Cambridge (MA). Leeds University: Asst Lectr in Management, 1964–66; Lectr in Econs, 1966–69; Stirling University: Lectr in Econs, 1969–75; Sen. Lectr, 1975–84; Head of Dept of Econs, 1982–84; Paisley College: Head, Dept of Econs and Management and Prof., 1984–86; Vice Principal, 1986–87. Convenor, Cttee of Scottish Higher Educn Principals, 1996–98. Member: Scottish Economic Council, 1995–98; Scottish Business Forum, 1998–99; Chm., Lead Scotland, 2001–07. Fellow, SCOTVEC, 1995; FRSA. DUniv: Glasgow, 2001; West of Scotland, 2008. *Publications:* (with C. J. Sutton) Industry and Competition, 1976; articles in Jl Industrial Econs, Scottish Jl Pol Econ., Managerial and Decision Econs. *Recreations:* walking, listening to music, sketching and painting. *Address:* Drumbarns, 18 Old Doune Road, Dunblane, Perthshire FK15 9AG.

SHAW, Prof. Robert Wayne, CBE 2002; MD; FRCSE, FRCOG; Professor of Obstetrics and Gynaecology, Nottingham University, 2002–12, now Emeritus; *b* 25 June 1946; *s* of Arthur Stanley Shaw and Margery Maude Shaw (*née* Griffiths); *m* 1980, Mary Philomena McGovern; one *s* one *d*. *Educ:* Priory Grammar Sch., Shrewsbury; Birmingham Univ. Med. Sch. (MB ChB 1969; MD 1975). FRCSE 1978; MRCOG 1977, FRCOG 1993. Lectr, 1975–79, and Sen. Lectr, 1979–81, in Obstetrics and Gynaecology, Birmingham Univ.; Sen. Lectr, Edinburgh Univ., 1981–83; Prof., Royal Free Hosp. Sch. of Medicine, 1983–92; Prof. and Head of Acad. Dept of Obstetrics and Gynaecology, Univ. of Wales Coll. of Medicine, 1992–2001; Postgrad. Dean, Med. and Dental Educn, Eastern Deanery, Univ. of Cambridge, 2001–02. Vice-Pres., 1995–98, Pres., 1998–2001, RCOG. Chm. Bd, Nat. Collaborating Centre for Women's and Children's Health (producing clinical guidelines for NICE), 2007–. Founder FMedSci 1998; FRCPI 2000; FACOG 2000. Hon. FFSRH (Hon. FFFP 2002); Hon. Fellow, Finnish Gynaecological Soc., 1992. *Publications:* (ed jtly) Gynaecology, 1992, 4th edn, 2010; (ed) Endometriosis: current management, 1995; (ed jtly) Atlas of Endometriosis, 3rd edn 2008; over 320 articles on gynaecological reproductive medicine. *Recreations:* sailing, hill walking. *Address:* Grosvenor House, Weaverlake Drive, Yoxall, Staffs DE13 8AD. *Club:* Athenæum.

SHAW, Prof. Rory James Swanton, MD; FRCP; Medical Director, Healthcare UK, since 2013; *b* 5 Jan. 1954; *s* of late Dr James Brian Shaw, OBE and of Irma Valerie Shaw, JP; *m* 1991, Sarah Margaret Foulkes (*d* 2011); two *d*. *Educ:* Bedford Sch.; St Bartholomew's Hosp. Med. Sch. (BSc 1974; MB BS 1977); MD 1985, MBA 1995, London. MRCP 1979, FRCP 1993. Sen. Lectr, St Mary's Hosp. Med. Sch., Imperial Coll., and Consultant Physician in Respiratory Medicine, 1989–97; Prof. of Respiratory Med., Imperial Coll. Sch. of Med., 1997–; Medical Director: Hammersmith Hosps NHS Trust, 1998–2006; Royal Berkshire NHS Foundn Trust, 2007–09; NW London Hosps NHS Trust, 2009–13. Chm., Nat. Patient Safety Agency, 2001–03; non-exec. Dir, NHS Litigation Authy, 2007–15. *Publications:* (jtly) Management Essentials for Doctors, 2011; articles on tuberculosis and asthma in learned jls. *Address:* Healthcare UK, UK Trade and Investment, 1 Victoria Street, SW1H 0ET.

SHAW, Stephen Arthur, CBE 2004; PhD; Independent Assessor of Complaints, Crown Prosecution Service, since 2013; Independent Complaints Assessor, Department for Transport, since 2013; *b* 26 March 1953; *s* of late Walter Arthur Shaw and Gwendolyn Primrose Shaw (*née* Cottrell); *m* 1977, Christine Elizabeth Robinson; partner, Jane Angela Skinner; two *s*. *Educ:* Rutlish Sch., Merton; Univ. of Warwick (BA 1974); Univ. of Leeds (MA 1976); Univ. of Kent (PhD 1979). Lectr in Further Educn, Mid-Kent Coll. of Technology, 1977–79; Researcher, NACRO, 1979–80; Research Officer, Home Office, 1980–81; Dir, Prison Reform Trust, 1981–99; Prisons Ombudsman, 1999–2001; Prisons and Probation Ombudsman, 2001–10; Chief Exec., Office of the Health Professions Adjudicator, 2010–12. Chair, Ind. Adv. Panel on Non-Compliance Mgt, 2013–14, Lead Reviewer, Ind. Review into Welfare in Detention of Vulnerable Persons, 2015, Home Office. Dir, Procordia Ltd, 2012–; Associate, Verita Consultants LLP, 2013–. Mem., Disciplinary Panel, Nat. Fedn of Property Professionals, 2012–. *Publications:* numerous contribs to books and jls. *Recreations:* family, sport, gardening, collecting antiques, watching Fulham FC. *E:* stephen.shaw999@gmail.com.

SHAW, Sir Thomas Joshua B.; *see* Best-Shaw.

SHAW, Prof. Timothy Milton, PhD; Professor and Graduate Program Director, PhD in Global Governance and Human Security, University of Massachusetts Boston, since 2012; *b* 27 Jan. 1945; *s* of Arnold and Margaret Shaw; *m* 1983, Jane Little Parpart; one *s* one *d*, and two step *d*. *Educ:* Univ. of Sussex (BA 1967); Univ. of East Africa (MA Internat. Relns 1969); Princeton Univ. (MA Politics 1971, PhD Politics 1975). Teaching Fellow, Dept Political Sci., Makerere UC, Kampala, 1968–70; Dalhousie University, Canada, 1971–2001: Asst Prof., then Assoc. and Full Prof. of Political Sci.; Dir, Centre for African Studies, 1977–78, 1983–89; Exec. Dir, Pearson Inst. for Internat. Develt, 1985–88; Prof. in Internat. Develt Studies, 1990–2000; Dir, Centre for Foreign Policy Studies, 1993–2000; Dir, Inst. of Commonwealth Studies and Prof. of Commonwealth Governance and Develt, Sch. of Advanced Study, Univ. of London, 2001–06; Dir and Prof., Inst. of Internat. Relns, Univ. of West Indies, 2007–11. Vis. Lectr, Univ. of Zambia, 1973–74; Vis. Assoc. Prof., Carleton Univ., 1978–80; Vis. Sen. Lectr, Univ. of Ife, Nigeria, 1979–80; Visiting Professor: Univ. of Zimbabwe, 1989; Univs of Stellenbosch and Western Cape, South Africa, 1998–; Aalborg Univ., Denmark, 2000–01 and 2012; Makerere Univ. Business Sch., 2006–; Bank of Uganda Vis. Prof., Mbarara Univ. of Sci. and Tech., 2000–. Hon. DLitt St Andrews, 2014. *Publications:* Commonwealth, 2008; *edited jointly and contributed*: Africa's Challenge to International Relations Theory, 2001; Crises of Governance in Asia and Africa, 2001; Theories of New Regionalism, 2003; Twisting Arms and Flexing Muscles: humanitarian intervention and peacebuilding in perspective, 2005; The Political Economy of Regions and Regionalisms, 2005; The Diplomacies of Small States, 2009, 2nd edn 2013; Inter-American Cooperation at a Crossroads, 2011; Africa and International Relations in the Twenty-First Century: still challenging theory?, 2011; Ashgate Research Companion to Regionalisms, 2011; Rethinking Development Challenges for Public Policy: insights from contemporary Africa, 2012; Comparative Regionalisms for Development in the 21st Century, 2013. *Recreations:* jogging, swimming, tennis, cycling, travelling, cooking. *Address:* 318 Selby Avenue, Ottawa, ON K1Z 6R1, Canada.

SHAW, Prof. William V., MD; Professor of Biochemistry, 1974–97, of Chemical Microbiology, 1997–98, Leicester University, now Professor Emeritus; *b* Philadelphia, Pennsylvania, 13 May 1933. *Educ:* Williams Coll., Williamstown, Mass (BA Chemistry 1955); Columbia Univ., New York (MD 1959). Diplomate: Amer. Bd of Med. Examrs, 1960; Amer. Bd of Internal Med., 1968 (Examiner, 1970). Appts, Presbyterian Hosp., New York, Nat. Heart Inst., Bethesda, Maryland, and Columbia Univ., New York, until 1966; Asst Prof. of Medicine, Columbia Univ., New York, 1966–68; University of Miami School of Medicine, Miami, Florida: Associate Prof. of Medicine and Biochemistry, 1968–73; Chief, Infectious Diseases, 1971–74; Prof. of Medicine, 1973–74. Hon. Prof. of Biochemistry, Univ. of Glasgow, 1998–2001. Founder, 1998, Chief Scientific Officer, 1998–2000, Sen. Consultant, 2000–, PanTherix Ltd. Vis. Scientist, MRC Lab. of Molecular Biology, Cambridge, Eng., 1972–74. Member: MRC Cell Biology and Disorders Bd, 1976–80 (Bd Chm. and Mem. Council, 1978–80); Science Council, Celltech Ltd, 1980–89 (Chm., 1983–89); Lister Inst. Sci. Adv. Cttee, 1981–85 (Chm., 1997–2000); AFRC, 1990–94. Member: Amer. Soc. for Clinical Investigation, 1971; Infectious Disease Soc. of Amer., 1969; Amer. Soc. of Biol Chemists; Biochem. Soc. (UK); Amer. Soc. for Microbiology; Soc. for Gen. Microbiology (UK). *Publications:* contribs to professional works and jls in microbial biochemistry and molecular enzymology. *Address:* PO Box 83, Sunset, ME 04683, USA. *T:* (207) 3482588, *Fax:* (207) 3482717. *E:* wvshaw33@gmail.com.

SHAW STEWART, Sir Ludovic (Houston), 12th Bt *cr* 1667 (NS), of Greenock and Blackhall, Renfrewshire; *b* 12 Nov. 1986; *s* of Sir Houston Shaw-Stewart, 11th Bt, MC, TD and of Lucinda Victoria (*née* Fletcher, later Hon. Mrs Christopher Chetwode); *S* father, 2004. *Educ:* Belhaven; Eton; Edinburgh Univ. *Recreation:* finding silver linings of clouds and promptly unthreading them.

SHAWCROSS, Conrad, RA 2013; artist; sculptor; *b* London, 26 April 1977; *s* of Hon. William (Hartley Hume) Shawcross, *qv* and Dame Marina (Sarah) Warner, *qv*; *m* 2013, Carolina Mazzolari. *Educ:* Westminster Sch.; Chelsea Sch. of Art (Foundn 1996); Ruskin Sch. of Drawing and Fine Art, Oxford (BA Hons Fine Art 1999); Slade Sch. of Art, University Coll. London (MFA Fine Art 2001). *Solo exhibitions* include: Sci. Mus., 2011–12; Victoria Miro Gall., 2011; Nat. Gall. and Royal Opera House, 2012; Palais de Tokyo, Paris, 2013; Roundhouse, 2013; *group exhibitions* include: Mus. of Old and New Art, Tasmania, 2011, 2014; KW Inst. for Contemp. Art, Berlin, 2012; Grand Palais, Paris, 2013. *Recreation:* trapeze. *E:* studio@conradshawcross.com.

SHAWCROSS, His Honour Roger Michael; a Circuit Judge, 1993–2008; Deputy Designated Family Judge, Hampshire and Isle of Wight, 2006–08; *b* 27 March 1941; *s* of Michael and Friedel Shawcross; *m* 1969, Sarah Broom; one *s* one *d*. *Educ:* Radley Coll.; Christ Church, Oxford (MA). Called to the Bar, Gray's Inn, 1967; a Recorder, 1985–93; Res. Judge, Newport, IoW, 1994–99. Member: Ancillary Relief Adv. Cttee, Family Justice Council, 1994–2005; Family Appeals Review Gp, 1998–2005; Magistrates' Area Trng Cttee (Hants and IoW), 2005–08; Chm., Hants and IoW Family Justice Council, 2006–08. *Recreations:* growing vegetables, reading, history, music, cinema, travel, admiring my wife's gardening skills, playing golf.

SHAWCROSS, Valerie, CBE 2002; Member (Lab) Lambeth and Southwark, London Assembly, since 2000; *b* 1958; *d* of Alfred and Florence Shawcross; *m* 1st, 1983, Alan Frank Neil Parker, *qv* (marr. diss. 2002); 2nd, 2005, Michael John Anteney. *Educ:* Univ. of Liverpool (BA Hons Pol Theory and Instns 1980); Inst. of Education, Univ. of London (MA Educn 1986). Sabbatical Officer, Liverpool Univ. Guild of Undergraduates, 1980–81; UK Council for Overseas Students' Affairs, 1981–84; ILEA, 1984–86; World Univ. Service (UK), 1986; Commonwealth Secretariat, 1987–91; freelance appointments, 1992–: NFWI, Labour Party, Westminster Foundn for Democracy, Body Shop Internat., Public Policy Unit, Infolog, Commonwealth Local Govt Forum. Mem. (Lab), Croydon LBC, 1994–2000 (Chair of Educn, 1995, Dep. Leader, 1997, Leader, 1997–2000). Mem., Labour Party, 1979–. London Assembly, Greater London Authority: Dep. Leader and Whip, Labour Gp, 2012–; Chm., Transport Cttee, 2008–11, 2013–14 and 2015–16. Chm., London Fire and Emergency Planning Authy, 2000–08 (Mem., 2013–); Mem., Metropolitan Police Authy, 2009–12. Contested (Lab) Bermondsey and Old Southwark, 2010. Volunteer, N Africa and Middle East Prog., Nat. Democratic Inst., USA, 2014. *Recreation:* poetry. *Address:* Greater London Authority, City Hall, Queen's Walk, SE1 2AA. *T:* (020) 7983 4371. *E:* valerie.shawcross@london.gov.uk.

SHAWCROSS, Hon. Mrs William; *see* Polizzi, Hon. Olga.

SHAWCROSS, Hon. William (Hartley Hume), CVO 2011; writer and broadcaster; Chairman, Charity Commission, since 2012; *b* 28 May 1946; *s* of Baron Shawcross, GBE, PC, QC; *m* 1st, 1971, Marina Sarah Warner (*see* Dame M. S. Warner); one *s*; 2nd, 1981, Michal Levin; one *d*; 3rd, 1993, Hon. Olga Polizzi, *qv*. *Educ:* Eton; University Coll., Oxford. Chm., Article 19, Internat. Centre on Censorship, 1986–96; Mem. Bd, Internat. Crisis Gp, 1995–2006; Member: Informal Adv. Gp, High Comr for Refugees, 1996–2001; BBC Govs World Service Consultative Gp, 1997–2004; Council, Disasters Emergency Cttee, 1998–2002; Exec. Cttee, Anglo-Israel Assoc., 2011–12. Presenter and Assoc. Producer, Queen and Country, BBC TV, 2002. Mem. Bd, Henry Jackson Soc., 2011–12. Patron, Weiner Liby, 2007–12. *Publications:* Dubcek, 1970; Crime and Compromise, 1974; Sideshow: Kissinger, Nixon and the destruction of Cambodia, 1979; The Quality of Mercy: Cambodia, holocaust and modern memory, 1984; The Shah's Last Ride, 1989; Kowtow: a plea on behalf of Hong Kong, 1989; Murdoch, 1992; Cambodia's New Deal, 1994; Deliver Us from Evil, 2000; Queen and Country, 2002; Allies, 2003; Queen Elizabeth, the Queen Mother: the official biography, 2009; Justice and the Enemy: Nuremberg, 9/11 and the trial of Khalid Sheikh Mohammed, 2012; Counting One's Blessings: the selected letters of Queen Elizabeth, the Queen Mother, 2012. *Recreations:* walking, sailing. *Address:* c/o Janklow and Nesbit, 13a Hillgate Street, W8 7SP. *E:* william.shawcross@gmail.com. *Clubs:* Special Forces, Beefsteak; Royal Yacht Squadron, St Mawes Sailing.

See also C. Shawcross.

SHAWE-TAYLOR, Desmond Philip, LVO 2011; Surveyor of the Queen's Pictures, since 2005; *b* 30 Sept. 1955; *s* of late Brian Newton Shawe-Taylor and Jocelyn Cecilia Shawe-Taylor; *m* 1987, Rosemary Gillian North; two *s* one *d*. *Educ:* Shrewsbury Sch.; University Coll., Oxford; Courtauld Inst. of Art, London. Lectr, History of Art Dept, Nottingham Univ., 1979–96; Dir, Dulwich Picture Gall., 1996–2005. *Publications:* Genial Company: the theme of genius in eighteenth-century British portraiture, 1987; The Georgians: eighteenth-century portraiture and society, 1990; Dramatic Art: theatrical paintings from the Garrick Club, 1997; Rembrandt to Gainsborough: masterpieces from Dulwich Picture Gallery, 1999; Shakespeare in Art, 2003; Bruegel to Rubens: masters of Flemish painting, 2007; The Conversation Piece: scenes of fashionable life, 2009; Dutch Landscapes, 2010; The First Georgians: art and monarchy 1714–1760, 2014. *Recreation:* playing the piano. *Address:* Flat 1, 20 Tregothnan Road, SW9 9JX. *T:* 07710 376667.

SHAWYER, Eric Francis, CBE 1998; FICS; Chairman, E. A. Gibson Shipbrokers Ltd, 1988–2000; Chairman, Baltic Exchange, 1996–98 (Director, 1991–98); *b* 17 July 1932; *m* 1956, Joyce Patricia Henley; one *s* one *d*. Joined E. A. Gibson Shipbrokers, 1948; Dir, 1963–; Man. Dir, 1969–98. Chairman: Worldscale Assoc. (London) Ltd, 1979–96; London Tanker Brokers Panel Ltd, 1990–96; Director: Maersk Air Ltd, 1994–2003; Maersk Air Hldg Ltd, 1994–2003; Corda, 2003–14. Trustee: Old Royal Naval Coll. Chapel Fund, 2005–; Wellington Trust, 2009–. Gov., George Green's Sch., 2000–13. FICS 1994 (Pres., 1996). Freeman, City of London, 1980; Liveryman, Co. of Shipwrights, 1981 (Mem., Ct of Assts); Freeman: Co. of Watermen and Lightermen, 1989; Co. of Master Mariners, 2009. *Address:* Souvenir, Woodlands Road, Bromley, Kent BR1 2AE.

SHAWYER, Peter Michael, FCA; Chairman: British International Ltd, since 2006; Ingenious Media plc, since 2007; *b* 11 Sept. 1950; *s* of Edward William Francis Shawyer and Marjorie Josephine Shawyer; *m* 1979, Margot Bishop; one *s* one *d*. *Educ:* Enfield GS; Univ. of Sheffield (BA Hons). FCA 1975. Touche Ross & Co., subseq. Deloitte & Touche, 1972–2004: admitted Partner, 1982; Tax Partner, 1982–84; Group Partner, a Tax Group, 1984–93; Partner in charge of Tax Dept, 1993–95; Partner in charge of London Office, 1995–99; Man. Partner, 1999–2004; Mem. Bd, Deloitte & Touche, UK. Non-executive Director and Member, Audit Committee: HSBC Bank, 2004–14; HSBC France, 2005–14. *Recreation:* golf. *Address:* c/o Janice Aminoff, Deloitte, Stonecutter Court, 1 Stonecutter Street, EC4A 4TR. *Clubs:* Hadley Wood Golf; Brocket Hall Golf.

SHCHASNY, Uladzimir; Chairman, National Commission of Republic of Belarus for UNESCO, since 2001; Ambassador at Large, Ministry of Foreign Affairs, Belarus, since 2001; *b* 25 Nov. 1948; *s* of Ryhor and Nadzeya Shchasny; *m* 1972, Lyudmila Kazakova (marr. diss. 1993). *Educ:* Minsk State Linguistic Univ. (grad. 1972). Interpreter for USSR Min. of Geology, Pakistan, 1969–70, 1972–74; Lectr, Minsk State Inst. of Foreign Languages, 1975–77; Translation Service, UN Secretariat, NY, 1978–82; joined Min. of Foreign Affairs, Belarus, 1983; Press Dept and Dept of Internat. Orgns, 1983–91; Asst to Minister for Foreign Affairs, 1991–92; Dir, Dept of Bilateral Co-operation, 1992–93; Chargé d'Affaires, 1993–94, Counsellor Minister, 1994–95, Lithuania; Ambassador of the Republic of Belarus to the UK and to the Republic of Ireland, 1995–2000; Dir, Dept of Bilateral Relations with CIS Countries, Min. of For. Affairs, 2000–01; Belarus Rep., Exec. Bd, UNESCO, 2001–05, 2009–. Frantsysk Skaryna Medal (Belarus), 2009. *Publications:* Artists of Paris School from Belarus, 2010; numerous translations of works of English and Urdu writers into Belarusian; articles in Belarusian jls. *Recreation:* antique map collecting. *Address:* Ministry of Foreign Affairs, ul. Lenina 19, Minsk, Belarus.

SHEADER, Timothy; Artistic Director, Open Air Theatre, Regent's Park, since 2008; *b* Scarborough, 23 Nov. 1971; *s* of Harry and Carol Sheader. *Educ:* Univs of Birmingham and Limoges (LLB Law with French). Freelance theatre dir, until 2008, working at RSC, West End and regl theatres. *Recreations:* dance, yoga, voluntary work. *Address:* Regent's Park Open Air Theatre, Inner Circle, Regent's Park, NW1 4NU.

SHEAR, Graham Julian; Partner, Corporate and Commercial Disputes, Berwin Leighton Paisner LLP, since 2009 (Head of Corporates and Private Wealth Group, since 2010); *b* London, 19 June 1963; *s* of Ronald and Frula Shear; *m* 1991, Dalya Freedman; three *s*. *Educ:* Seaford Coll., Sussex; City of London Sch. for Boys; Poly. of N London (LLB Hons); Lancaster Gate Coll. of Law. Admitted Solicitor, 1989; joined Teacher Stern Selby, subseq. Teacher Stern as trainee solicitor, 1986; specialised in commercial entertainment and music law, 1986–91; Litigation Dept, 1991–2009; Man. Partner, 2001–09; founder, Media and Reputation Protection practice gp, 1999; established Sports practice gp, 2000. Mem., Law Panel, The Times, 2008–. *Publications:* contrib. The Times Law Supplement. *Recreations:* contemporary and modern art, Latin music and culture, especially Cuban, lifelong fan of West Ham United FC. *Address:* Berwin Leighton Paisner LLP, Adelaide House, London Bridge, EC4R 9HA. *T:* (020) 3400 4191, *Fax:* (020) 3400 1111. *E:* graham.shear@blplaw.com. *Clubs:* Soho House, Ivy.

SHEARD, Rodney Kilner; Senior Principal, Populous (formerly HOK sport architecture), 1999; *b* 11 Sept. 1951; *s* of Saville Kilner Sheard and Margaret Helen Sheard; *m* 1989, Catherine Elisabeth Nouqueret; two *s*. *Educ:* Queensland Univ. of Technol. (DipArch 1975). RIBA 1977; ARAIA 1979. Partner, LOBB Architectural Practice, 1981; changed from partnership to co., 1993; merged with HOK, 1999. *Architect for:* Alfred McAlpine Stadium, Huddersfield, 1996; Millennium Stadium, Cardiff, 1998; Telstra Stadium (Sydney Olympic Stadium), 2000; Ascot Racecourse, 2006; Emirates Stadium, 2006; Wembley Stadium, 2007; Wimbledon Centre Court, 2009; London Olympic Stadium, 2012. Initiator of concept 'Generations of Stadia'. FRSA. Hon. DSc Luton, 2002. *Publications:* Stadia: a design and development guide, 1998 (jtly); Sport Architecture, 2000; numerous articles in sports jls. *Recreations:* flyfishing, tennis, sailing. *Address:* Populous, 14 Blades Court, 121 Deodar Road, Putney, SW15 2NU. *T:* (020) 8874 7666, *Fax:* (020) 8874 7470. *E:* rod.sheard@populous.com. *Club:* Royal Automobile.

SHEARER, Alan, OBE 2001; DL; football commentator, BBC Television; *b* 13 Aug. 1970; *s* of Alan Shearer and Anne Shearer (*née* Collins); *m* Lainya; one *s* two *d*. *Educ:* Gosforth High Sch. Professional footballer, scoring 409 goals, with: Southampton FC, 1988–92; Blackburn Rovers, 1992–96; Newcastle United FC, 1996–2006, Captain, 1997–2006; played for England, 1992–2000, Captain, 1996–2000 (63 caps; 30 goals). Manager, Newcastle United FC, 2009. DL Northumberland, 2009. *Publications:* The Story So Far (autobiog.), 1998.

SHEARER, Anthony Presley; Chairman, Abbey Protection, since 2007; *b* 24 Oct. 1948; *s* of Francis and Judy Shearer; *m* 1st, 1972, Jenny Dixon (marr. diss. 2007); two *d*; 2nd, 2007, Pam Mapes. *Educ:* Rugby Sch. FCA 1971. Partner, Deloitte Haskins & Sells, 1967–88; Commercial Dir, Harland & Wolff, 1987; Chief Operating Officer, M&G Gp, 1988–96; Dep. Chief Exec., Old Mutual Internat., 1997–2000; consultant to Old Mutual and other cos, 2000–02; Singer & Friedlander Group plc: Gp Finance Dir, and Chief Operating Officer, 2003–05; Chief Exec., 2004–05. Chairman: Uruguay Mineral Exploration, 2002–09; Caxton FX, 2006–11; Jerrold, 2006–07; UK Wealth Management, 2007–11; Gees Haulage, 2008–11; Updata, 2009–; Triple Plate Junction, 2010–; Orosur Mining Inc., 2012–; Director: Wogen, 2005–09, 2010–; Harvard Internat. (formerly Alba plc), 2008–12; Sanctuary Partners, 2010–. *Recreations:* ski-ing, tennis, rock 'n roll, Elvis Presley. *Address:* Apt 103, 8 Kew Bridge Road TW8 0FG. *T:* (020) 8560 5849. *E:* tony@tonyshearer.com. *Clubs:* Brooks's, Hurlingham.

SHEARLOCK, Very Rev. David John; Dean and Rector of St Mary's Cathedral, Truro, 1982–97, now Dean Emeritus; *b* 1 July 1932; *s* of Arthur John Shearlock and Honora Frances Hawkins; *m* 1959, Jean Margaret Marr; one *s* one *d*. *Educ:* Univ. of Birmingham (BA); Westcott House, Cambridge. Assistant Curate: Guisborough, Yorks, 1957–60; Christchurch Priory, Hants, 1960–64; Vicar: Kingsclere, 1964–71; Romsey Abbey, 1971–82; Diocesan Director of Ordinands (Winchester), 1977–82; Hon. Canon of Winchester, 1978–82. Chm., Beaminster Arts Festival, 1998–2003. FRSA 1991; FRGS 1992; ARSCM 1998. *Publications:* The Practice of Preaching, 1990; When Words Fail: God and the world of beauty, 1996. *Address:* 3 The Tanyard, Shadrack Street, Beaminster, Dorset DT8 3BG. *T:* (01308) 863170. *E:* dshearlock@toucansurf.com.

SHEARMAN, Prof. Clifford Paul, FRCS; Professor of Vascular Surgery, University of Southampton, since 1999; Consultant Vascular Surgeon, since 1994, and Associate Medical Director, since 2008, University Hospital Southampton NHS Foundation Trust (formerly Southampton University Hospitals NHS Trust); *b* Ramsgate, 28 April 1955; *s* of Douglas Shearman and Dorothy Shearman; *m* 1982, Susan Mary Robinson; one *s* two *d*. *Educ:* Worthing High Sch. for Boys; Guy's Hosp. Med. Sch., London (BSc 1st Cl. Hons 1976; MB BS 1979; MS 1989). FRCS 1983. Sen. Lectr, and Hon. Consultant Vascular Surgeon, Queen Elizabeth Hosp., Birmingham, 1990–94; Sen. Lectr, Southampton Univ. Hosps NHS Trust, 1994–99; Head, Postgrad. Sch. of Surgery, Wessex Deanery, 2007–12. President: Vascular Soc. of GB and Ire., 2009–10; Soc. of Academic and Res. Surgery, 2013–; Chair, Vascular Surgery Specialist Adv. Cttee, 2012–; Dir, Professional Affairs, Assoc. of Surgeons of GB and Ire., 2011–12; Council, RCS, 2015–. *Publications:* (jtly) MCQs in Surgery, 1994; (jtly) Chronic Wound Healing, 1999; (jtly) Vascular Surgery, 1999; Management of Diabetic Foot Complications, 2015. *Recreations:* running, long distance walking in the UK, Shakespearean theatre, art, live music. *Address:* Department of Vascular Surgery, Mail Point 46, University Hospital Southampton, Southampton SO16 6YD. *T:* (023) 8079 4519. *E:* cps@soton.ac.uk.

SHEARMAN, Donald Norman; *b* 6 Feb. 1926; *s* of late S. F. Shearman, Sydney; *m* 1952, Stuart Fay, *d* of late Chap. F. H. Bashford; three *s* three *d*. *Educ:* Fort St and Orange High Schools; St John's Theological College, Morpeth, NSW. Served War of 1939–45: air crew, 1944–46. Theological College, 1948–50. Deacon, 1950; Priest, 1951. Curate: of Dubbo, 1950–52; of Forbes, and Warden of St John's Hostel, 1953–56; Rector of Coonabarabran, 1957–59; Director of Promotion and Adult Christian Education, 1959–62; Canon, All Saints Cathedral, Bathurst, 1962; Archdeacon of Mildura and Rector of St Margaret's, 1963; Bishop of Rockhampton, 1963–71; Chairman, Australian Board of Missions, Sydney, 1971–73; Bishop of Grafton, 1973–85; Asst Bishop, dio. of Brisbane, 1989–91; resigned Holy Orders, 2003. *Address:* PO Box 241, Deception Bay, Qld 4508, Australia.

SHEARMAN, Martin James, CVO 2003; HM Diplomatic Service; UK Mission to the United Nations, New York (with rank of Ambassador), since 2013; *b* 7 Feb. 1965; *s* of John Christopher Shearman and Barbara Wendy Shearman; *m* 1996, Miriam Elizabeth Pyburn; two *s*. *Educ:* Skinners' Sch., Tunbridge Wells; Trinity Coll., Oxford (BA Hons). Joined FCO, 1989; Third, then Second Sec., FCO, 1989–91; Second, then First, Sec., Tokyo, 1993–96; on secondment to DTI, 1996–98, to Cabinet Office, 1998; NATO Secretariat, 1999; FCO, 1999–2003; Dep. High Comr, Abuja, 2003–06; Hd, Common Foreign and Security Policy Gp, Europe Directorate, FCO, 2006–08; High Comr, Uganda, 2008–12.

SHEARS, Philip Peter; QC 1996; a Recorder, since 1990; *b* 10 May 1947; *m* 1990, Sarah; two *s* one *d* by previous marriage. *Educ:* Leys Sch., Cambridge; Nottingham Univ. (LLB); St Edmund's Coll., Cambridge (LLB). Called to the Bar, Middle Temple, 1972; Mem., Midland Circuit. Liveryman, Fletchers' Co., 2011–. *Recreations:* sailing, France. *Address:* 7 Bedford Row, WC1R 4BS. *T:* (020) 7242 3555. *Clubs:* Royal London Yacht (Trustee; former Cdre); Bar Yacht.

SHEBBEARE, Sir Thomas Andrew, (Sir Tom), KCVO 2003 (CVO 1996); Chairman: Virgin StartUp, since 2013; Virgin Money Giving, since 2012 (Director, since 2008); Spring Films Ltd, since 2012; Royal Parks Foundation, since 2014; *b* 25 Jan. 1952; *s* of late Robert Austin Shebbeare and Frances Dare Graham; *m* 1976, Cynthia Jane Cottrell; one *s* one *d*. *Educ:* Malvern Coll.; Univ. of Exeter (BA Politics). World University Service (UK), 1973–75; Gen. Sec., British Youth Council, 1975–80; Administrator, Council of Europe, 1980–85; Exec. Dir, European Youth Foundn, 1985–88; Exec. Dir, The Prince's Trust and Sec., The Royal Jubilee Trusts, 1988–99; Chief Exec., The Prince's Trust, 1999–2004; Dir of Charities to the Prince of Wales, then Dir, The Prince's Charities, 2004–11. Director: CIM Asset Mgt, 2007–; Delphis-Eco Ltd, 2011–. Trustee: Nations Trust (S Africa), 1995–2008; Sentebale—The Princes' Fund for Lesotho, 2005–09; Turquoise Mountain Foundn (Kabul), 2005–; Prince's Charities Foundn (China), 2009–; Dir, Gifts in Kind UK, 1994–2011. Fellow, Green Templeton Coll., Oxford, 2012. Hon. LLD Exeter, 2005. *Recreations:* family, cooking, garden, food and drink. *E:* tom@shebbeare.com.

SHECHTMAN, Prof. Daniel, PhD; Philip Tobias Professor of Materials Science, since 1989, and Distinguished Professor, since 1998, Technion-Israel Institute of Technology; Professor of Materials Science and Engineering, Iowa State University, since 2004; Senior Chemist, Materials Chemistry and Biomolecular Materials, Ames Laboratory, Iowa, since 2004; *b* Tel Aviv, British Mandate of Palestine, 24 Jan. 1941; *m* Tzipora; one *s* three *d*. *Educ:* Technion-Israel Inst. of Technol. (BSc Mech. Engrg 1966; MSc Materials Engrg 1968; PhD 1972). Nat. Res. Council postdoctoral res. associate, Aerospace Res. Labs, Wright Patterson AFB, Ohio, 1972–75; Department of Materials Engineering, Technion-Israel Institute of Technology: Lectr, 1975–77; Sen. Lectr, 1977–84; Associate Prof., 1984–86; Prof., 1986–98; on sabbatical at Johns Hopkins Univ., 1981–83, at Nat. Inst. Standards Technol., Md, 1992–94. Visiting Professor: Dept of Materials Engrg, 1981–89, Physics and Astronomy, 1989–97, Johns Hopkins Univ.; Univ. of Maryland, Baltimore, 1997–2004; Tohoku Univ., Japan, 2006–. Member: Israel Acad. Scis, 1996; NAE, USA, 2000; Eur. Acad. Scis, 2004. Hon. Dr Ben Gurion, 2002. Awards include: Internat. Award for New Materials, Amer. Physical Soc., 1988; Rothschild Prize in Engrg, Rothschild Prizes Foundn, 1990; Weizmann Sci. Award, Weizmann Inst., 1993; Israel Prize in Physics, 1998; Wolf Prize in Physics, Wolf Foundn, 1999; Gregori Aminoff Prize, Royal Swedish Acad. of Scis, 2000; EMET Prize in Chem., AMN Foundn, Israel, 2002; 25th Anniv. Award, Eur. Materials Res. Soc., 2008; Nobel Prize in Chem., 2011. *Publications:* contribs to jls incl. Nature, Jl de Physique, Jl Materials Res., Jl Materials Sci., Materials Sci. Forum. *Address:* Department of Materials Science and Engineering, Technion-Israel Institute of Technology, Technion City, Haifa 32000, Israel; College of Engineering, Iowa State University, 342 Spedding, Ames, IA 50011–3020, USA.

SHEDDEN, Alfred Charles, OBE 2008; Chairman, Centre for Confidence and Wellbeing Ltd, since 2005; *b* 30 June 1944; *s* of Alfred Henry Shedden and Jane Murray Shedden; *m* 1st, 1968, Rosalyn Terris; one *s*; 2nd, 1979, Irene McIntyre; one *d*. *Educ:* Aberdeen Univ. (MA, LLB). Mem., Law Soc. of Scotland. McGrigor Donald: apprentice, 1967; Partner, 1971; Managing Partner, 1985–92; Sen. Partner, 1993–2000. Chm., Halladale Gp plc, 2001–07; Vice-Chm., Glasgow Housing Assoc. Ltd, 2003–09; non-executive Director: Standard Life Assurance Co., 1992–99; Scottish Financial Enterprise, 1988–99; Martin Currie Japan Investment Trust plc, 1996–2005; Scottish Metropolitan Property plc, 1998–2000; Burn Stewart Distillers plc, 2000–03; Iomart Group plc, 2000–11; Murray Internat. Trust plc, 2000–14; Equitable Life Assurance Soc., 2002–09. Mem., Scottish FEFC, 1999–2005. Gov., Glasgow Sch. of Art, 2002–10. *Recreations:* contemporary Scottish art, wine, travel, being a grandfather. *Address:* 17 Beaumont Gate, Glasgow G12 9ED. *T:* (0141) 339 4979, 07810 553672.

SHEDDEN, Rev. John, CBE 1998; Minister, Fuengirola, Costa del Sol, 2005–08; *b* 23 June 1943; *s* of Robert Blair Arnott Shedden and Grace Roberts (*née* Henderson); *m* 1965, Jeannie Lillian Gilling; one *s* one *d*. *Educ:* Johnstone High Sch.; Univ. of St Andrews (BD Hons; Dip. in Pastoral and Social Studies). Asst Minister, Paisley Abbey, 1970–72; ordained 1971; Parish Minister, Thornhill, Dumfries, 1972–75; Social Welfare Officer, Salisbury, Rhodesia, 1975–76; Chaplain, RN, 1977–84; Minister, St Mark's, Moose Jaw, Sask., 1984–86; Chaplain, RAF, 1986–98; Principal Chaplain, Church of Scotland and Free Churches, RAF, 1994–98; Minister: Hawick Wilton with Teviothead, 1998–2001; Glenorchy Innishael with Strathfillan, 2001–05. QHC 1994–98. *Recreations:* hill-walking, D-I-Y, reading, radio.

SHEEHAN, family name of Baroness Sheehan.

SHEEHAN, Baroness *cr* 2015 (Life Peer), of Wimbledon in the London Borough of Merton and of Tooting in the London Borough of Wandsworth; **Shaista Ahmad, (Shas) Sheehan;** *m* Patrick Sheehan; three *c*. *Educ:* Rosa Bassett Grammar Sch.; University Coll. London (BSc Hons 1978); Imperial Coll. London (MSc Dist. Envmtl Technol. 1990). Teacher, auxiliary nurse at New Cross Hosp. and sen. planner and buyer in advertising, 1981–2005; Hd of Office and Sen. Caseworker for Susan Kramer, MP, 2005–08; charity worker, Wimbledon Guild Daycentre and Faith in Action project for homeless people, 2010–. Mem. (Lib Dem), Richmond upon Thames LBC, 2006–10. Contested (Lib Dem) Wimbledon, 2010. *Address:* House of Lords, SW1A 0PW.

SHEEHAN, Albert Vincent; Sheriff of Tayside, Central and Fife, 1983–2005; *b* 23 Aug. 1936; *s* of Richard Greig Sheehan and May Moffat; *m* 1965, Edna Georgina Scott Hastings (*d* 2000); two *d*. *Educ:* Bo'ness Acad.; Edinburgh Univ. (MA 1957; LLB 1959). Admitted as solicitor, 1959. 2nd Lieut, 1st Bn The Royal Scots (The Royal Regt), 1960; Captain, Directorate of Army Legal Services, 1961. Depute Procurator Fiscal, Hamilton, 1961–71; Sen. Depute Procurator Fiscal, Glasgow, 1971–74; Depute Crown Agent for Scotland, 1974–79; Asst Solicitor, Scottish Law Commn, 1979–81; Sheriff of Lothian and Borders, 1981–83. Leverhulme Fellow, 1971. *Publications:* Criminal Procedure in Scotland and France, 1975; Criminal Procedure, 1990, 2nd edn 2003. *Recreations:* naval history, travel, legal history.

See also W. A. Sheehan.

SHEEHAN, Prof. Antony; President, Church Health Center, Memphis, Tennessee, since 2013; *b* 10 Sept. 1964; *s* of late Thomas Sheehan and Mary Kerr Sheehan; *m* 2001, Andrea Coleman; one *s* one *d*. *Educ:* Manchester Metropolitan Univ. (BEd Hons 1992); Nottingham Univ. (MPhil 1998); RN 1986. Nurse Manager; Chief Exec., Nat. Inst. for Mental Health in England, 2001–03; Dir Gen. for Care Services, 2003–06, for Health and Care Partnerships, 2006–07, DoH; Prof. of Health and Social Care Strategy, Univ. of Central Lancs, 2006; Chief Exec., Leics Partnership NHS Trust, 2007–13. Chm., Internat. Initiative for Mental Health Leadership, 2005–08. Patron, AS-IT (IT consultancy for people with Asperger Syndrome), 2007–09. Hon. DSc Wolverhampton, 2003; DUniv Staffordshire, 2006. *Publications:* more than 50 articles and book chapters. *Recreations:* walking (with two very big labradors), Manchester United, travel (in particular the USA), goalkeepers' gloves (and other paraphernalia), coffee (especially latte).

SHEEHAN, Gerald; Chief Executive (Deputy Master and Comptroller), Royal Mint, 2001–06; *b* 20 March 1950; *s* of Edmund and Morfydd Sheehan; *m* 1987, Jacqueline Marian; two *s* one *d*. *Educ:* Univ. of Nottingham (BSc Hons); Univ. of Sheffield (MSc); Harvard Business Sch. (AMP). ASW Holdings plc, 1981–2001: Bd Mem., 1996–2001; Ops Dir, 1999–2001. Mem. Business Leaders Gp, Prince's Trust. *Recreations:* squash, boating, fishing.

SHEEHAN, Gen. John Joseph, USMC; Senior Vice President for Europe, Africa, Middle East and Southwest Asia, Bechtel Group Inc., 2001; Supreme Allied Commander, Atlantic and Commander-in-Chief, US Atlantic Command, 1994–97; *b* 23 Aug. 1940; *s* of John J. Sheehan and Ellen Sheehan; *m* Margaret M. Sullivan; one *s* three *d. Educ:* Boston Coll. (BA English 1962); Georgetown Univ. (MA Govt 1985). Joined USMC, 1960; various postings, incl. Vietnam; Amphibious Warfare Sch., 1969–70; Airborne Corps, 1970–71; 2nd Marine Div., 1971–73; Naval War Coll., 1974–75; HQ USMC, 1975–78; 1st Marine Air Wing, 1978–79; Nat. War Coll., 1979–80; 1st Marine Bde, 1980–83; Jt Staff, 1983–84; Office of Sec. of Defense, 1984–86; 2nd Marine Div., 1986–88; 4th Marine Exped. Bde, 1988–89; HQ USMC, 1989–91; US Naval Forces Central Comd, 1991; US Atlantic Comd, 1991–93; Jt Staff, 1993–94. Joined Bechtel Gp Inc., 1998. Numerous gallantry and other Service awards. Grand Cross, Norwegian Order of Merit, 1996. *Publications:* contribs to Joint Forces Qly. *Recreations:* golf, tennis, gardening. *Clubs:* Military Order of the Carabao, Ancient and Honorable Artillery Company of Massachusetts.

SHEEHAN, Malcolm Peter; QC 2015; *b* London, 28 July 1968; *s* of John and Mary Josephine Sheehan; partner, Alexis Roberts. *Educ:* All Saints' High Sch.; Oriel Coll., Oxford (BA 1st Cl. Hons Modern Hist. 1989; MA 1993). Called to the Bar, Lincoln's Inn, 1993; in practice as barrister, 1993–. Judicial Asst to Court of Appeal, 1997; Judge (pt-time) of First-tier Tribunal (Property Chamber), 2009–. Mem., Attorney Gen.'s Panel of Jun. Counsel to the Crown, 2006–15. *Publications:* contributor: Civil Practitioner's Guide to the Human Rights Act 1998, 1999; Halsbury's Laws of England, 4th edn reissue, Appeals; Butterworth's Civil Court Precedents, 2009–; Kluwer International Product Law Manual, 2011. *Recreations:* tennis, swimming, theatre, running, cycling. *Address:* Henderson Chambers, 2 Harcourt Buildings, Temple, EC4Y 9DB. *T:* (020) 7583 9020, *Fax:* (020) 7583 2686. *E:* msheehan@hendersonchambers.co.uk.

SHEEHAN, Wendy Anne; Sheriff of Lothian and Borders at Edinburgh, since 2014; *b* Glasgow, 26 Dec. 1968; *d* of Albert Vincent Sheehan, *qv. Educ:* St George's Sch. for Girls; Univ. of Aberdeen (LLB 1989; DLP 1990). Accredited Family Law Mediator 1996; Accredited Family Law Specialist 1998. Admitted solicitor, 1991; Solicitor, Russel + Aitken, 1990–96; Associate, Balfour & Manson, 1996–2000; Partner, Mowat Hall Dick, 2000–06; Hd, Family Law, Pagan Osborne, 2006–08; Dir, Sheehan Kelsey Oswald Solicitors, accredited family law specialists, 2008–11; Sheriff of Glasgow and Strathkelvin at Glasgow, 2011–14. Chm., Lothian, Couple Counselling, 1996–2005; former Convenor, CALM; Sec., Family Law Arbitration Gp, Scotland. *Publications:* (contrib.) Butterworths Family Law Service; (contrib.) Butterworths Elderly Client Service; (contrib.) The Art of Family Law. *Recreations:* Director of Licketyspit Ltd (early years theatre company), scuba diving, water ski-ing, art, cinema. *Address:* Edinburgh Sheriff Court, 27 Chambers Street, Edinburgh EH1 1LB. *T:* (0131) 225 2525. *E:* sheriffwsheehan@scotcourts.gov.uk.

SHEEHY, Rev. Jeremy Patrick, DPhil; Rector, Swinton and Pendlebury, since 2006; *b* 31 Oct. 1956; *s* of Eric Sheehy and late Noreen Patricia Sheehy. *Educ:* Trinity Sch. of John Whitgift; Bristol Grammar Sch.; King Edward's Sch., Birmingham; Magdalen Coll., Oxford (BA (Jurisprudence Cl. 1)); St Stephen's House, Oxford (BA (Theol. Cl. 1)); MA 1981, DPhil 1990, Oxon. Ordained deacon 1981; priest 1982; Assistant Curate: St Barnabas, Erdington, 1981–83; St Gregory, Small Heath, 1983–84; Dean of Divinity, Chaplain and Fellow, New Coll., Oxford, 1984–90; Vicar, St Margaret, Leytonstone, 1990–96; Priest in charge, St Andrew, Leytonstone, 1993–96; Principal, St Stephen's House, Oxford, 1996–2006. Area Dean, Eccles, 2011–13. Chm., Oxford Partnership for Theol Educn and Trng, 1999–2001. Examining Chaplain to Bishop of Manchester, 2008–. Vis. Lectr, Nashotah House, Wis, USA, 2006. Guardian, Shrine of Our Lady of Walsingham, 1997–. Gov., Quainton Hall Sch., Harrow, 1998–2007. Hon. DD: Grad. Theol Foundn, Indiana, 2004; Nashotah House, Wisconsin, 2009. *Recreations:* hill-walking, cooking. *Address:* St Peter's Rectory, Vicarage Road, Swinton, Manchester M27 0WA. *T:* (0161) 794 1578.

SHEEHY, Sir Patrick, Kt 1991; Chairman, B.A.T. Industries, 1982–95; *b* 2 Sept. 1930; *s* of Sir John Francis Sheehy, CSI and Jean Newton Simpson; *m* 1964, Jill Patricia Tindall; one *s* one *d. Educ:* St Ignatius Coll., Riverview, Australia; Ampleforth Coll., Yorks. Served Irish Guards, 1948–50; rank on leaving 2nd Lieut. Joined British-American Tobacco Co., 1950, apptd to Gold Coast (Ghana), 1951–53; Reg. Sales Manager, Nigeria, 1953–54; Ethiopian Tobacco Monopoly, 1954–57; Marketing Dir, Jamaica, 1957; Barbados, 1961; Marketing Advr, London, 1962; Gen. Man., Holland, 1967–70; Mem., Gp Bd, 1970; Mem., Chm.'s Policy Cttee, and Chm., Tobacco Div. Bd, 1975; Dep. Chm., 1976–81, Vice-Chm., 1981–82, B.A.T. Industries; Chm., British-American Tobacco Co., 1976–82. Chairman: Marlborough Underwriting Agency, 1996; Perpetual Income and Growth Investment Trust plc, 2005–09; Director: BP, 1993–98; EFG Private Bank; Cluff Mining; Sherritt Internat., 1995–2012; ASDA Property Co., 1995–2004; Sherritt Power, 1997–2005. Chairman: Council of Internat. Advrs, Swiss Bank Corp., 1985–97; European Round Table Industrialists, 1986–96; Council, RIIA, 1986–96; S London Business Initiative, 1986–96; Mem., Action Cttee for Europe, 1985–95. Chm., Inquiry into Police Responsibilities and Rewards, 1992–93. Director: The Spectator Ltd, 1993; Celtic Football Club plc, 1997. Co-founder, Franco-British Colloque, 1994; Chm., Appeal to save Royal Commonwealth Soc. Library, 1994. Ordem Nacional do Cruzeiro do Sul (Brazil), 1993; Chevalier, Légion d'Honneur (France), 1997. *Address:* 11 Eldon Road, W8 5PU. *T:* (020) 7937 6250.

SHEEN, Michael Christopher, OBE 2009; actor; *b* Newport, S Wales, 5 Feb. 1969; *s* of Meyrick and Irene Sheen; one *d* by Kate Beckinsale. *Educ:* Glan Afan Comprehensive Sch., Port Talbot; Royal Acad. of Dramatic Art. *Theatre* includes: When She Danced, Globe, 1991; Romeo and Juliet, Manchester Royal Exchange, 1992; Don't Fool with Love, Donmar Warehouse, 1993; Peer Gynt, Oslo, Tokyo and Barbican, 1994; Charley's Aunt, Manchester Royal Exchange, 1994; The Seagull, Theatre Royal, Bath, 1995; The Homecoming, NT, 1997; Henry V, RSC, Stratford, 1997; Amadeus, Old Vic, trans. NY, 1998; Look Back in Anger, NT, 1999; Caligula, Donmar Warehouse, 2003 (Evening Standard and London Th. Critics Awards for Best Actor); The UN Inspector, NT, 2005; Frost/Nixon, Gielgud, 2006; The Passion (also dir), NT of Wales, 2011 ((jtly) Theatre UK Award for Best Dir), filmed version as The Gospel of Us, 2012; Hamlet, Young Vic, 2011; *films* include: Othello, 1995; Mary Reilly, 1996; Wilde, 1997; The Four Feathers, Heartlands, Bright Young Things, Underworld, Timeline, 2003; Laws of Attraction, 2004; Kingdom of Heaven, 2005; Underworld: Evolution, The Queen, Dead Long Enough, Blood Diamonds, 2006; Music Within, 2007; Frost/Nixon, 2008; Underworld: the Rise of the Lycans, The Damned United, My Last Five Girlfriends, The Twilight Saga: New Moon, 2009; Unthinkable, Tron: Legacy, 2010; Midnight in Paris, The Twilight Saga: Breaking Dawn, Resistance, 2011; Kill the Messenger, Far from the Madding Crowd, 2015; *television* includes: Gallowglass, 1993; The Deal, 2003; Dirty Filthy Love, 2004; H. G. Wells: War with the World, Kenneth Williams: Fantabulosa!, 2006 (RTS Award for Best Actor), Ancient Rome: the Rise and Fall of an Empire, 2006; 30 Rock, The Special Relationship, 2010; Masters of Sex, 2013–. Variety Award, BIFA, 2008; BAFTA Britannia Award for British Artist of Year, 2010. *Address:* c/o Roxanne Vacca Management, 61 Judd Street, WC1H 9QT.

SHEEPSHANKS, David Richard, CBE 2013; DL; Chairman: St George's Park (formerly National Football Centre), Football Association, since 2008; UK Community Foundations, since 2013; *b* London, 30 Oct. 1952; *s* of Robin Sheepshanks and Lilias Sheepshanks; *m* 1978, Mona Ullbin; one *s* one *d. Educ:* Eton Coll. Chm. and Man. Dir, Starfish Ltd, 1980–89; Chm., Suffolk Foods Ltd, 1990–2004. Chairman: Ipswich Town FC, 1995–2009; Football League, 1996–98. Regl Chm., Coutts Bank, 2009–. Chm., Suffolk Foundn, 2005–13. DL Suffolk, 2005. Hon. DCL UEA, 2004. *Recreations:* playing golf, swimming, gardening, flower arranging, watching football, cricket and golf. *Address:* The White Lodge, Eyke, Woodbridge, Suffolk IP12 2RP. *T:* (01394) 461540. *E:* dsheep@whitelodge.biz. *Clubs:* White's, George, MCC.

SHEERMAN, Barry John; MP (Lab) Huddersfield, since 1983 (Huddersfield East, 1979–83); *b* 17 Aug. 1940; *s* of late Albert William Sheerman and Florence Sheerman (*née* Pike); *m* 1965 Pamela Elizabeth (*née* Brenchley); one *s* three *d. Educ:* Hampton Grammar Sch.; LSE (BSc (Econs) Hons; MSc Hons). Lectr, Univ. Coll. of Swansea, 1966–79. Visiting Professor: of Social Enterprise, Huddersfield Univ.; Inst. of Educn, London Univ. Chairman: Policy Connect, 1995–; Urban Mines. An opposition front bench spokesman on: employment, dealing with training, small business and tourism, 1983–88; home affairs, dealing with police, prisons, crime prevention, drugs, civil defence and fire services, 1988–92; disabled people's rights, 1992–94. Mem., Public Accounts Cttee, 1981–83; Co-Chm., Educn and Employment Select Cttee, 1999–2001 (Chm., Sub-Cttee on Educn, 1999–2001); Chm., Select Cttee on Educn and Skills, 2001–10; Chairman: Parly Adv. Council on Transport Safety, 1981–; Labour Campaign for Criminal Justice, 1989–92; Labour Party Commn on Sch.-to-Work; Co-Chm., Parly Manufg Industry Gp, 1993–; Vice-Chm., Parly Univ. Gp, 1994–2012. Chm., Parly Gps for Sustainable Waste Mgt, 1995–, and for Manufg, Design and Innovation, 1999–; Chm., Cross-Party Adv. Gp on Preparation for EMU, 1998–, on European Economic Reform, 2005–. Mem., Sec. of State for Trade and Industry's Manufg Task Force, 1999–2002. Chairman: World Bank Business Partnerships for Develt Cttee, 2001–03; Global Road Safety Partnership, 2001–. Chm., John Clive Trust. FRSA; FRGS 1989; FCGI 2005. Hon. Dr: Kingston, 2007; Bradford, 2007. *Publications:* (jtly) Harold Laski: a life on the Left, 1993; pamphlets on education and training, tourism, and justice. *Address:* House of Commons, SW1A 0AA. *W:* www.twitter.com/bsheermanmp.

SHEFFIELD, Bishop of, since 2009; **Rt Rev. Dr Steven John Lindsey Croft;** *b* 29 May 1957; *s* of James and Marian Croft; *m* 1978, Ann Christine Baker; two *s* two *d. Educ:* Worcester Coll., Oxford (BA Hons 1980, MA 1983); St John's Coll., Durham (PhD 1984). Ordained deacon, 1983, priest, 1984; Curate, St Andrew's, Enfield, 1983–87; Vicar, St George's, Ovenden, Halifax, 1987–96; Mission Consultant, Dio. Wakefield, 1993–96; Priest-in-charge, St Augustine, Halifax, 1994–96; Warden, Cranmer Hall, St John's Coll., Durham, 1996–2004; Archbishop's Missioner, and Team Leader, Fresh Expressions, 2004–09. Took seat in H of L, 2013. *Publications:* The Identity of the Individual in the Psalms, 1987; Growing New Christians, 1993; Making New Disciples, 1994; (jtly) Emmaus, The Way of Faith, vols 1–6, 1996, vols 7–8, 1998; Man to Man: friendship and faith, 1999; Ministry in Three Dimensions: ordination and leadership in the local church, 1999; (jtly) Travelling Well, 2000; The Lord is Risen, 2001; Missionary Journeys, Missionary Church, 2001; Transforming Communities: re-imagining the Church for the 21st century, 2002; (jtly) Learning for Ministry: making the most of study and training, 2005; Moving On in a Mission-Shaped Church, 2005; The Advent Calendar, 2006; (ed) The Future of the Parish System, 2006; (ed) Mission-shaped Questions, 2008; Jesus' People: what the church should do next, 2009; (ed) Fresh Expressions in the Sacramental Tradition, 2010; Exploring God's Mercy, 2010; Exploring God's Love, 2011; (jtly) Women and Men in Scripture and the Church: a guide to key issues, 2013. *Recreations:* walking, cooking, films. *Address:* Bishopscroft, Snaithing Lane, Sheffield S10 3LG. *T:* (0114) 230 2170, *Fax:* (0114) 263 0110. *E:* bishop@bishopofsheffield.org.uk.

SHEFFIELD, Dean of; *see* Bradley, Very Rev. P. E.

SHEFFIELD AND ROTHERHAM, Archdeacon of; *see* Chamberlain, Ven. M. L.

SHEFFIELD, Graham Edward, CBE 2010; Director, Arts, British Council, since 2011; *b* 12 Feb. 1952; *s* of Gordon and Jacqueline Sheffield; *m* 1979, Ann Roberta Morton; two *s. Educ:* Tonbridge Sch.; Edinburgh Univ. (BMus Hons 1975). Producer, then Sen. Producer, Music Dept, BBC Radio 3, 1976–90; Music Dir, South Bank Centre, 1990–95; Artistic Dir, Barbican Centre, 1995–2010; CEO, W Kowloon Cultural Dist Authy, Hong Kong, 2010–11. Dir, City Arts and Culture Forum, 2007–10; Consultant, Luminato Fest., Toronto, 2007–10; Advr, Arts and Creative Economy, British Council, 2009–10. Mem. Council, Arts Council England (London), 2002–08. Mem. Council, 1999–, Chm., 2006–10, Royal Philharmonic Soc.; Chairman: Internat. Soc. for Performing Arts, 2004–06 (Sec., 2000–01; Chm.-elect, 2002–03; Internat. Citation of Merit, 2015); Help Musicians UK, 2014–. Trustee, Rambert, 2014–. Hon. FGSM 2010. Hon. DArts City, 2004. Chevalier, Tastevin de Bourgogne, 2005. Chevalier, Ordre des Arts et des Lettres (France), 2005. *Recreations:* piano, golf, ski-ing, travel, fine wine. *Address:* 107 Breton House, Barbican, EC2Y 8PQ. *Club:* MCC.

SHEFFIELD, (John) Julian (Lionel George); DL; Chairman, North Hampshire Medical Fund, 2002–09; *b* 28 Aug. 1938; *s* of late John Vincent Sheffield, CBE and Anne Margaret, *d* of Sir Lionel Faudel-Phillips, 3rd Bt; *m* 1961, Carolyn Alexander Abel Smith; three *s* one *d. Educ:* Eton Coll.; Christ's Coll., Cambridge. Joined Portals Ltd, 1962; Dir, 1969–95, Chm., 1979–95, Portals Hldgs, then Portals Gp. Director: Norcros, 1974–96 (Chm., 1989–93); Tex Hldgs, 1985–93; Guardian Royal Exchange, 1981–99 (Dep. Chm., 1988–99); Newbury Racecourse, 1988–2005; Inspec, 1994–99. Chm., Axa UK Gp Pension Scheme, 1993–2008. Mem., Economic and Commercial Cttee, EEF, 1974–90. Member: Council, St John's Sch., Leatherhead, 1966–96; Bd of Govs, N Foreland Lodge, 1987–97 (Chm., 1992–97). Trustee: Henry Smith's, subseq. Henry Smith Charity, 1971–2007 (Chm., 1997–2007); Winchester Cathedral Trust, 1984–2014; Hosp. of St Cross and Almshouse of Noble Poverty, 1996–2010 (Chm., 2005–06). High Sheriff, 1998, DL 2001, Hants. *Recreations:* outdoor sports, collecting. *Address:* Spring Pond, Laverstoke, Whitchurch, Hants RG28 7PD. *T:* (01256) 895130. *Clubs:* White's, MCC.

SHEFFIELD, Sir Reginald (Adrian Berkeley), 8th Bt *cr* 1755; DL; Director, Normanby Estate Co. Ltd, since 1983, and other companies; *b* 9 May 1946; *s* of Edmund Charles Reginald Sheffield, JP, DL (*d* 1977) and Nancie Miriel Denise (*d* 1997), *d* of Edward Roland Soames; *S* uncle, 1977; *m* 1st, 1969, Annabel Lucy Veronica Jones (*see* Viscountess Astor) (marr. diss. 1975); two *d*; 2nd, 1977, Victoria Penelope, *d* of late R. C. Walker, DFC; one *s* two *d. Educ:* Eton. Member of Stock Exchange, 1973–75. Vice-Chm., S Humberside Business Advice Centre Ltd, 1984–2010. Pres., S Humberside CPRE, 1985–96; Member: Cttee, Lincs Br., CLA, 1987–99; Taxation Cttee, CLA, 1989–95; Central Transport Consultative Cttee (NE Reg.), 1988–94; Rail Users Consultative Cttee for NE England, 1994–97. Mem. (C) for Ermine Ward, Humberside County Council, 1985–93. Chm., Brigg and Goole Cons. Assoc., 2007–09. Pres., Scunthorpe United Football Club, 1982–94. Pres., Scunthorpe and Dist, Victim Support Scheme, 1989–2003; Vice-Pres., Victim Support Humber, 2003–08. DL Humberside, now Lincs, 1985. *Heir: s* Robert Charles Berkeley Sheffield, *b* 1 Sept. 1984. *Address:* Estate Office, Normanby, Scunthorpe, N Lincs DN15 9HS. *E:* norestate@btconnect.com. *Clubs:* Beefsteak, White's, Pratt's; Lincolnshire (Sleaford).

SHEGOG, Rev. Preb. Eric Marshall; Director of Communications, Church of England, 1990–97; *b* 23 July 1937; *s* of late George Marshall Shegog and Helen (*née* Whitefoot); *m* 1961, Anne Thomas; two *s* one *d. Educ:* Leigh Grammar School; College of St Mark and St John; Whitelands College; Lichfield Theol College; City Univ. (MA). CertEd London; DipTh London. Asst Master, Holy Trinity Primary Sch., Wimbledon, 1960–64; Asst Curate, All Saints, Benhilton, 1965–68; Asst Youth Adviser, Dio. of Southwark, 1968–70; Vicar, St Michael and All Angels, Abbey Wood, 1970–75; Town Centre Chaplain, Sunderland, 1976–83; Head of Religious Broadcasting, IBA, 1984–90; Dir of Communications, 1997–2000 and Acting Gen. Sec., 1999–2000, Dio. of London; Communications Advr, Dio.

of Europe, 2000–02; Prebendary, St Paul's Cathedral, 1997–2000, now Emeritus. Chairman: BBC Adv. Cttee for NE, 1980–83; Mgt Cttee, Churches TV Centre, 1997–2007; Dir, World Assoc. for Christian Communication, 1990–93 (Vice-Chm., Eur. Region, 1990–93). Chm., Age Concern Sunderland, 1980–83. *Publications:* (jtly) Religious Television: controversies and conclusions, 1990; (jtly) Religious Broadcasting in the 90s, 1991; (contrib.) Elvy, Opportunities and Limitations in Religious Broadcasting, 1991; (contrib.) The Communication of Values, 1993. *Recreations:* gardening, opera. *Address:* The Coach House, 7A High Street, Clophill, Beds MK45 4AB. *T:* (01525) 864868.

SHEHADIE, Sir Nicholas (Michael), AC 1990; Kt 1976; OBE 1971; Managing Director, Nicholas Shehadie Pty Ltd, 1959; *b* 15 Nov. 1926; *s* of Michael and Hannah Shehadie; *m* 1957, Marie Roslyn Bashir (*see* Hon. Prof. Dame Marie Bashir); one *s* two *d*. *Educ:* Sydney. Elected Alderman, City of Sydney, Dec. 1962; Dep. Lord Mayor, Sept. 1969–73; Lord Mayor of Sydney, Sept. 1973–75. Chm., Special Broadcasting Services, to 2000. Rugby Union career: Captained NSW and Australia; played 30 Internationals and 6 overseas tours; Mem., Barbarians'. Chm., Sydney Cricket Ground, 1990–2001. *Publications:* A Life Worth Living (autobiog.), 2003. *Recreations:* Rugby, surfing, horse racing, bowls. *Club:* Randwick Rugby.

SHEIKH, Baron *cr* 2006 (Life Peer), of Cornhill in the City of London; **Mohamed Iltaf Sheikh;** Chairman, Macmillan Sheikh plc, 2010–14; *b* 13 June 1941; *s* of late Mohamed Abdullah Sheikh and Kalsum Ara Sheikh; *m* 1986, Shaida Begum, *d* of Mohamed Lateef Thantrey; one *d* from previous *m*. *Educ:* Mbale Secondary Sch., Uganda; Holborn Coll.; City of London Coll. ACII 1966, FCII 1968; FPC 1998. With Sun Alliance Insurance Co., 1962–66; Household and General Insurance Co., 1966–69; Guardian Royal Exchange, 1969–78; Camberford Law plc, 1978–2008. Dir, BIBA (Regl Chm., 1998–2002). Pres., Insce Inst. of Croydon, 1981–82 (Chm., Life and Pensions Gp, 1989–90). Member: Nat. Council, Chartered Insce Inst., 1985–87; Cttee, FIMBRA, 1991, 1996. Chairman: Sheikh Abdullah Foundn, 2003–; Conservative Muslim Forum, 2003–14 (Pres., 2014–); Conservative Ethnic Diversity Council, 2005–. Freeman, City of London, 1995. Hon. Fellow, BICSc. *Recreations:* walking, countryside, keeping fit, travelling. *Address:* House of Lords, SW1A 0PW. *Club:* Carlton.

SHEIKH, Prof. Aziz, OBE 2014; MD; FRCP, FRCPE, FRCGP, FFPH, FRSE; Professor of Primary Care Research and Development, since 2003, and Co-Director, Centre for Population Health Sciences, since 2012, University of Edinburgh; *b* Karachi, 15 Dec. 1968; *s* of Hafeez Sheikh and Kausar Sheikh; *m* 1991, Dr Sangeeta Dhami; three *s* one *d*. *Educ:* Bancroft's Sch., Woodford Green; University Coll. London (BSc Hons Physiol. 1990; MB BS Medicine 1993; Imperial Coll., London (MD 2001); London Sch. of Hygiene and Tropical Medicine, Univ. of London (MSc Epidemiol. 2002). DRCOG 1995; DCH 1996; MRCP 1996, FRCP 2006; MRCGP 1997, FRCGP 2004; FRCPE 2013; FFPH 2015. Imperial College of Science, Technology and Medicine, London: London Acad. Trng Scheme, 1997–98; Clin. Res. Fellow, 1998–99; NHS R&D Nat. Primary Care Trng Fellow, 1999–2002; NHS/PPP Nat. Primary Care Post-Doctoral Researcher, St George's Hosp. Med. Sch., London, 2002–03. Harkness Fellow in Health Care Policy and Practice, Brigham and Women's Hosp., Boston, 2013–14. Hon. Consultant in Paediatric Allergy, Royal Hosp. for Sick Children, Edinburgh, 2008–. Visiting Professor: Care and Public Health Res. Inst., Faculty of Medicine, Univ. of Maastricht, 2009–; Univ. of Birmingham, 2011–; Barts and The London Sch. of Medicine and Dentistry, QMUL, 2012–; of Medicine, Harvard Med. Sch., Boston, 2014–. FRSE 2015. *Publications:* (ed with A. R. Gatrad) Caring for Muslim Patients, 2000, 2nd edn 2007; (ed with A. R. Harnden) Key Topics in Child Health Promotion, 2002; (ed jtly) Basic Skills in Statistics: a guide for healthcare professionals, 2004; (ed with A. R. Gatrad) Palliative Care for South Asians: Muslims, Hindus and Sikhs, 2006; (ed jtly) Caring for Hindu Patients, 2008; (ed with B. Hurwitz) Health Care Errors and Patient Safety, 2009; (jtly) Landmarks in Allergy, 2013; (ed jtly) Healthcare Improvement and Safety at a Glance, 2014; over 650 articles in learned internat. jls incl. Lancet, BMJ, PLOS Medicine, Jl of Allergy and Clin. Immunol., Thorax, Allergy and Jl of Amer. Med. Informatics Assoc. *Recreations:* table tennis, travelling, reading. *Address:* Centre for Population Health Sciences, University of Edinburgh, Medical School, Doorway 3, Teviot Place, Edinburgh EH8 9AG. *T:* (0131) 651 4151, *Fax:* (0131) 650 9119. *E:* aziz.sheikh@ed.ac.uk.

SHEIKH, Saira Kabir; QC 2014; *b* Kensington, 29 July 1969; *d* of Salim Kabir Sheikh and Latifa Kabir Sheikh; *m* 1996, Paul David Jennings; one *s* one *d*. *Educ:* St Swithun's Sch., Winchester; Kinnaird Coll., Lahore (BA); Univ. of the Punjab (LLB); University Coll. London (LLM); Lewis and Clark North Western Sch. of Law, Portland, Oregon (LLM). Advocate, Lahore High Court, 1995; called to the Bar, Inner Temple, 2000; in practice as barrister, 2002–. *Recreations:* travel, reading. *Address:* Francis Taylor Building, Temple, EC4Y 7BY. *T:* (020) 7353 8415, *Fax:* (020) 7353 7622. *E:* clerks@ftb.eu.com.

SHEIKH, Tasmina; *see* Ahmed-Sheikh.

SHEIKHOLESLAMI, Prof. (Ali) Reza, PhD; Soudavar Professor of Persian Studies, Oxford University, 1990–2006; Fellow, Wadham College, Oxford, 1990–2006; *b* 21 July 1941; *s* of Ali Soltani Sheikholeslami and Shah-Zadeh Mansouri; *m* 1996, Scheherezade Vigeh. *Educ:* Columbia Univ., NY (BA); Northwestern Univ. (MA); UCLA (PhD). Asst Prof. of Pol Sci., Univ. of Washington, Seattle, 1975–85; Res. Fellow, Harvard Univ., 1987–88; Iranian Fellow, St Antony's Coll., Oxford, 1988–90. *Publications:* Political Economy of Saudi Arabia, 1984; The Structure of Central Authority in Qajar Iran 1876–1896, 1996; articles on 19th and 20th Century Persia in jls and book chapters. *Recreations:* reading, travelling. *Address:* Wadham College, Oxford OX1 3PN. *T:* (01865) 278200.

SHEIL, Brenda Margaret Hale, (Lady Sheil); barrister; Member, Radio Authority, 1994–99; *o d* of late Rev. Forde Patterson and Elizabeth Bell Patterson (*née* Irwin); *m* 1979, John Joseph Sheil (*see* Rt Hon. Sir J. J. Sheil); one *s*. *Educ:* Armagh Girls' High Sch.; Trinity Coll., Dublin (BA (Mod) Legal Science; LLB 1966; MA 1990). Called to the Bar, NI, 1976, Ireland, 1995; Government Service (Legal): Min. of Home Affairs, NI, 1967–72; NI Office, 1972–79; Head, Legal Div., NI Court Service, Lord Chancellor's Dept, 1979–80. Chm. (part time), Industrial Tribunals, 1984–87. Member: Secretariat of Anglo-Irish Law Commn, 1973–74; Ind. Commn for Police Complaints, 1988–90. Mem., Gen. Consumer Council, NI, 1985–88. Mem., Standing Cttee, Gen. Synod of Church of Ireland, 1988–2011 (Lay Hon. Sec., 1999–2011); Lay Rep., Ch of Ireland, ACC, 1994–2000; Lay Canon, St Patrick's Cathedral, Armagh, 2008–. Governor, Royal Sch., Armagh, 1992–; Trustee, Irish Sch. of Ecumenics Trust, 2004–. *Recreations:* horses (Hon. Sec., Tynan and Armagh Hunt, 1973–), gardening, travel, golf. *Address:* Bar Library, Royal Courts of Justice, Belfast BT1 3JF.

SHEIL, Rt Hon. Sir John (Joseph), Kt 1989; PC 2005; a Surveillance Commissioner, since 2010; a Lord Justice of Appeal, Supreme Court of Judicature, Northern Ireland, 2004–06; *b* 19 June 1938; *yr* twin *s* of late Hon. Mr Justice (Charles Leo) Sheil and Elizabeth Josephine Sheil (*née* Cassidy); *m* 1979, Brenda Margaret Hale Patterson (*see* B. M. H. Sheil); one *s*. *Educ:* Clongowes Wood Coll.; Queen's Univ. Belfast (LLB); Trinity Coll., Dublin (MA). Called to Bar: NI, 1964 (Bencher 1988), QC 1975; Gray's Inn, 1974 (Hon. Bencher, 1996); Ireland, 1976. A Judge of the High Court, NI, 1989–2004. Chairman: Mental Health Rev. Tribunal, 1985–87; Fair Employment Appeals Bd, 1986–89; Mem., Standing Adv. Commn on Human Rights, 1981–83. Mem., NI Cttee, British Council, 2002–06. Senator, QUB, 1987–99. Hon. Bencher, Middle Temple, 2005. *Recreations:* theatre, golf, travel. *Address:* c/o Royal Courts of Justice, Belfast BT1 3JY.

SHEINWALD, Sir Nigel (Elton), GCMG 2011 (KCMG 2001; CMG 1999); HM Diplomatic Service, retired; Ambassador to the United States of America, 2007–12; *b* 26 June 1953; *s* of late Leonard and Joyce Sheinwald; *m* 1980, Dr Julia Dunne; three *s*. *Educ:* Harrow Co. Sch. for Boys; Balliol Coll., Oxford (BA Classics 1976; Hon. Fellow 2014). Joined HM Diplomatic Service, 1976; Japan Desk, FCO, 1976–77; Russian lang. trng, 1977–78; Third, later Second Sec., Moscow, 1978–79; Rhodesia/Zimbabwe Dept, FCO, 1979–81; E European and Soviet Dept, FCO, 1981–83; First Sec., Washington, 1983–87; Deputy Head: Policy Planning Staff, FCO, 1987–89; European Community Dept (Internal), FCO, 1989–92; Counsellor and Hd of Chancery, UK Perm. Rep. to EU, Brussels, 1993–95; Hd of News Dept, FCO, 1995–98; Dir, EU, FCO, 1998–2000; Ambassador and UK Perm. Rep. to EU, Brussels, 2000–03; Foreign Policy and Defence Advr to the Prime Minister, 2003–07. Prime Minister's Special Envoy on intelligence and law enforcement data sharing, 2014–. Non-executive Director: Royal Dutch Shell, 2012–; Innovia Gp, 2015–; Sen. Advr, Universal Music Gp, 2012–. Vis. Prof., 2012–, Mem., Governing Council, 2014–, KCL. Member: Adv. Bd, Centre for European Reform, 2012–; Business for New Europe, 2012–; British American Business, 2012–; Governing Council, Ditchley Foundn, 2012–; Campaign for British Influence in Europe, 2014–; UK-US Fulbright Commn, 2015–. Hon. Bencher, Middle Temple, 2011. *Recreations:* theatre, music. *Address:* c/o Department of War Studies, King's College London, Strand, WC2R 2LS.

SHEKERDEMIAN, Marcia Anna-Maria; QC 2015; *b* London, 16 Nov. 1963; *d* of Hrant and Loretta Shekerdemian; *m* 1993, Roland Higgs (*d* 2009); one *s* one *d*. *Educ:* Notting Hill and Ealing High Sch.; Trinity Hall, Cambridge (BA 1986). Called to the Bar, Middle Temple, 1987; in practice as a barrister, 11 Stone Bldgs, 1989–; a Dep. Registrar of High Court in Bankruptcy, 2002–. *Recreations:* theatre, cinema, fashion, listening to live music, cooking, family life. *Address:* 11 Stone Buildings, Lincoln's Inn, WC2A 3TG. *T:* (020) 7831 6381. *E:* shekerdemian@11sb.com. *Club:* Athenæum.

SHELBROOKE, Alec Edward; MP (C) Elmet and Rothwell, since 2010; *b* 10 Jan. 1976; *s* of Derek and Patricia Shelbrooke; *m* 2011, Susan Spencer. *Educ:* St George's C of E Comp. Sch., Gravesend; Brunel Univ. (BEng Hons 1998). Project mgt, Univ. of Leeds, 1999–2010. Mem. (C), Leeds CC, 2004–10. Contested (C) Wakefield, 2005. *Address:* House of Commons, SW1A 0AA.

SHELDON, family name of **Baron Sheldon**.

SHELDON, Baron *cr* 2001 (Life Peer), of Ashton-under-Lyne in the County of Greater Manchester; **Robert Edward Sheldon;** PC 1977; *b* 13 Sept. 1923; *m* 1st, 1945, Eileen Shamash (*d* 1969); one *s* one *d*; 2nd, 1971, Mary Shield. *Educ:* Elementary and Grammar Schools; Engineering Apprenticeship; Technical Colleges in Stockport, Burnley and Salford; WhSch 1944. Engineering diplomas; external graduate, London University. Contested (Lab) Withington, Manchester, 1959; MP (Lab) Ashton-under-Lyne, 1964–2001. Chm., Labour Parly Economic Affairs and Finance Group, 1967–68; Opposition front bench spokesman on Civil Service and Machinery of Govt, also on Treasury matters, 1970–74; Minister of State, CSD, March–Oct. 1974; Minister of State, HM Treasury, Oct. 1974–June 1975; Financial Sec. to the Treasury, 1975–79; Opposition front bench spokesman on Treasury matters, 1981–83; Chairman: Public Accounts Cttee, 1983–97 (Mem., 1965–70, 1975–79); Standards and Privileges Cttee, 1997–2001; Liaison Cttee, 1997–2001; Public Accounts Commn, 1997–2001; Dep. Chm., All Party Arts and Heritage Gp, 1997–2001; Member: Public Expenditure Cttee (Chm. Gen. Sub-Cttee), 1972–74; Select Cttee on Treasury and Civil Service, 1979–81 (Chm., Sub-Cttee); Econ. Affairs Cttee, 2003–07. Mem., Fulton Cttee on the Civil Service, 1966–68. Chm., NW Gp of Labour MPs, 1970–74. Mem., H of L, 2001–15. *Address:* 2 Ryder Street, SW1Y 6QA.

SHELDON, Clive David; QC 2011; *b* London, 13 Oct. 1966; *s* of Jack Cecil Sheldon and Jacqueline Sheldon (*née* Anisfeld); *m* 1993, Jean Horowitz; one *s* two *d*. *Educ:* Latymer Sch., Edmonton; Gonville and Caius Coll., Cambridge (BA 1989); Univ. of Pennsylvania (LLM). Called to the Bar, Inner Temple, 1991; in practice as barrister specialising in public and employment law; Lectr (pt-time) in Labour Law, 1991–92; Mem., NY State Bar, 1992–; Associate, Cleary, Gottlieb, Steen & Hamilton, NY, 1992–94; barrister, 11 King's Bench Walk Chambers, 1995–. Mem., Complaints Cttee, Bar Standards Bd, 2010–12. Co-Chm., Masorti Judaism (formerly Assembly of Masorti Synagogues), 2012–15 (Vice Chm., 2011–12); Mem. Council, Jewish Leadership Council, 2013–15; Chm., New Israel Fund, 2015–. Vice Chm., Govs, Akiva Sch., 2008–10. *Recreations:* cycling, swimming. *Address:* 11 King's Bench Walk Chambers, Temple, EC4Y 7EQ. *T:* (020) 7632 8500, *Fax:* (020) 7583 9123. *E:* sheldon@11kbw.com.

SHELDON, David Henry; QC (Scot.) 2013; *b* Dundee, 22 April 1965; *s* of Henry Duncan, (Harry), Sheldon and Muriel Sheldon. *Educ:* High Sch. of Dundee; Univ. of Aberdeen (LLB 1st Cl. Hons; DipLP). University of Edinburgh: Lectr in Law, 1990–98; Associate Dean, 1994–98; Advocate, 1998–2013. *Publications:* Scots Criminal Law (with R. A. A. McCall Smith), 1992, 2nd edn 1997; Evidence: cases and materials, 1996, 2nd edn 2002; (contrib.) Stair Memorial Encyclopaedia of Scots Law, 1995–; (contrib.) Court of Session Procedure, 2002–; articles in legal jls incl. Criminal Law Rev., Scots Law Times, Edinburgh Law Rev. *Recreations:* cycling, running, rock climbing, choral singing, music. *Address:* Advocates Library, Parliament House, Edinburgh EH1 1RF. *T:* 07780 483910. *E:* david.sheldon@compasschambers.com. *Club:* Edinburgh Road.

SHELDON, John Denby, OBE 2000; Joint General Secretary, Public and Commercial Services (formerly Public Services, Tax and Commerce) Union, 1996–2000; *b* 31 Jan. 1941; *s* of Frank and Doreen Sheldon; *m* 1976; two *s*. *Educ:* Wingate County Primary Sch.; West Leeds High Sch.; Oxford Univ. Diploma in Social Studies. Post Office Engineer, 1957–68; student, Ruskin Coll., 1968–70; full time Trade Union Official, Instn of Professional Civil Servants, 1970–72; Civil Service Union: National Officer, 1972–78; Deputy Gen. Sec., 1978–82; Gen. Sec., 1982–88; Dep. Gen. Sec., 1988–93, Gen. Sec., 1993–96, Nat. Union of Civil and Public Servants. *Recreations:* cricket, Rugby League as spectator, family. *Address:* 20 Clifton Park Road, Caversham, Reading, Berks RG4 7PD.

SHELDON, Peter, OBE 2010; FCA; Chairman: BATM Advanced Communications Ltd, 1999–2014 (Director, 1998–99); Kardan NV, since 2012; *b* 11 June 1941; *s* of Izydor Schuldenfrei and Regina Schuldenfrei; surname changed to Sheldon by Deed Poll, 1964; *m* 1965, Judith Marion Grunberger; two *s* one *d*. *Educ:* Kilburn Grammar Sch. FCA 1969. Partner: Alfred N. Emanuel & Co., Chartered Accountants, 1963–70; Bright, Grahame Murray, Chartered Accountants, 1970–71; Director: UDS Gp Plc, 1971–83; Hambros Bank, 1983–85; World of Leather Plc, 1985–97; Geo Interactive Media Gp Ltd, 1996–98. Chairman: Stirling Gp Plc, 1990–94; BATM Advanced Technologies Ltd, 1999–2014; Video Domain Technologies Ltd, 2001–07; Dir, Kindertec Ltd, 1994–2000. Pres., United Synagogue, 1999–2005. JP Haringey, 1979–90 and 1997–2011. *Recreations:* theatre, travel, walking, grandchildren. *Address:* Flat 8, Denver Court, 132 Hendon Lane, N3 3RH. *T:* (020) 8346 5155.

SHELDON, Richard Michael; QC 1996; a Deputy High Court Judge, 2003–15; *b* 29 Sept. 1955; *s* of Ralph Maurice Sheldon and Ady Sheldon (*née* Jaudel); *m* 1983, Helen Mary Lake; two *s* one *d*. *Educ:* Maidenhead Grammar Sch.; Jesus Coll., Cambridge (MA). Called to the Bar, Gray's Inn, 1979, Bencher, 2004. Vis. Prof., Nottingham Trent Univ. *Publications:* Gen.

Ed., Cross-Border Insolvency, 3rd edn, 2012, 4th edn, 2015; contrib. Halsbury's Laws of England. *Recreations:* music, bassoon. *Address:* 3/4 South Square, Gray's Inn, WC1R 5HP. *T:* (020) 7696 9900.

SHELDRAKE, Prof. Philip Farnsworth; Senior Research Fellow, Westcott House Cambridge Theological Federation, since 2010; Moulsdale Fellow, St Chad's College, University of Durham, since 2003; Professor and Director, Institute for the Study of Contemporary Spirituality (formerly Professor of Christian Spirituality), Oblate School of Theology, San Antonio, Texas, since 2013; *b* 22 Nov. 1946; *s* of Archibald Douglas Farnsworth Sheldrake, MC and Ann Mary Sheldrake (*née* Fitzgibbon). *Educ:* Heythrop Pontifical Athenaeum (Phil. Bac. 1969); Campion Hall, Oxford (MA 1976; BD 1995; DD 2015); Univ. of London (PGDPT 1977; MTh 1977). Dir, Inst. of Spirituality, Heythrop Coll., London, 1983–92; Dir of Pastoral Studies, Westcott House, Cambridge, 1992–97; Sen. Res. Fellow, Queen's Foundn, Birmingham, 1997–98; Academic Dir and Vice-Principal, Sarum Coll., Salisbury, 1998–2003; William Leech Professorial Fellow in Applied Christian Theol., Univ. of Durham, 2003–08. Hon. Prof. of Theol., Univ. of Wales, Lampeter, later Univ. of Wales Trinity St David, 1998–2013; Hon. Res. Fellow, Centre for Study of Cities and Regions, Univ. of Durham, 2008–13. Sen. Mem., St Edmund's Coll., Cambridge, 1993–; Hulsean Lectr, Univ. of Cambridge, 1999–2000. Visiting Professor: Univ. of Notre Dame, Indiana, 1995–2010; Boston Univ., 2002; Boston Coll., Chestnut Hill, 2005–; Bellarmine Univ., 2012; Joseph Vis. Prof., Boston Coll., 2008–09; Veale Prof., Milltown Inst., Dublin, 2010–11. FRSA 1998; FRHistS 2005. *Publications:* Images of Holiness, 1987; Spirituality and History, 1991, 2nd edn 1996; Befriending our Desires, 1994, 2nd edn 2001; Living Between Worlds: place and journey in Celtic Christianity, 1995; Spirituality and Theology, 1998; Love Took My Hand: the spirituality of George Herbert, 2000; Spaces for the Sacred: place, memory, identity, 2001; (ed) New Dictionary of Christian Spirituality, 2005; A Brief History of Spirituality, 2006, 2nd edn as Spirituality: a brief history, 2013; Heaven in Ordinary: George Herbert and his writings, 2009; Explorations in Spirituality, 2010; Spirituality: a very short introduction, 2012; A Spiritual City: theology, spirituality and the urban, 2014; Spirituality: a guide for the perplexed, 2014. *Recreations:* music, art, contemporary literature, international affairs, wine (Mem., Wine Soc.), travel, history and culture of Italy, family and friends. *Address:* Westcott House, Jesus Lane, Cambridge CB5 8BP. *T:* (01223) 741000. *E:* ps220@cam.ac.uk.

SHELDRICK, Dame Daphne (Marjorie), DBE 2006 (MBE 1989); Chairman, David Sheldrick Wildlife Trust, since 1977; *b* 14 June 1934; *d* of Bryan and Marjorie Jenkins; *m* 1960, David Leslie William Sheldrick (*d* 1977); two *d. Educ:* Nakuru Primary Sch.; Kenya Girls' High Sch., Nairobi. Wildlife conservation, 1955–, initially alongside David Sheldrick, founder Warden of Tsavo Nat. Park, then as Chairman of David Sheldrick Wildlife Trust, estabd in his memory; she is a recognised internat. authy on rearing of wild creatures and first person to perfect milk formula and necessary husbandry for infant milk-dependent elephants and rhinos. Hon. DVMS Glasgow, 2000. Global 500 Roll of Honour, UNEP, 1992; Lifetime Achievement Award: BBC, 2002; Jackson Hole Film Fest., 2013. Mem., Burning Spear (Kenya), 2002. *Publications:* The Orphans of Tsavo, 1966; The Tsavo Story, 1973; My Four Footed Family, 1970; An Elephant Called Eleanor, 1980; An African Love Story (memoir), 2012. *Recreation:* nature. *Address:* Box 15555, 00503 Mbagathi, Nairobi, Kenya. *T:* (20) 891996, (20) 890125, (20) 890335, *Fax:* (20) 890053. *E:* RC-H@africaonline.co.ke.

SHELDRICK, Prof. George Michael, PhD; FRS 2001; Professor of Structural Chemistry (formerly of Inorganic Chemistry), University of Göttingen, 1978–2011, now Emeritus; *b* 17 Nov. 1942; *s* of George and Elizabeth M. Sheldrick; *m* 1968, Katherine E. Herford; two *s* two *d. Educ:* Huddersfield New Coll.; Jesus Coll., Cambridge (MA; PhD 1966). University of Cambridge: Demonstrator, 1966–71, Lectr, 1971–78, Dept of Inorganic, Organic and Theoretical Chm.; Fellow, Jesus Coll., 1966–78. Mem., Akademie der Wissenschaften zu Göttingen, 1989. Mineral Sheldrickite named after him, 1996. Meldola Medal, 1970, Corday-Morgan Medal, 1978, Award for Structural Chem., 1981, RSC; Leibniz Prize, Deutsche Forschungsgemeinschaft, 1987; Patterson Prize, Amer. Crystallographic Assoc., 1993; Carl-Hermann Medal, Deutsche Ges. für Kristallographie, 1999; Hodgkin Prize, British Crystallographic Assoc., 2004; Perutz Prize, Eur. Crystallographic Assoc., 2004; Gregori Aminoff Prize, Royal Swedish Acad. of Sci., 2009; Ewald Prize, Internat. Union of Crystallography, 2011. *Publications:* numerous papers in scientific jls. *Recreations:* tennis, chess. *Address:* Institut für Anorganische Chemie, Tammannstrasse 4, 37077 Göttingen, Germany. *T:* (551) 3933021. *E:* gsheldr@shelx.uni-ac.gwdg.de.

SHELFORD, William Thomas Cornelius; DL; *b* 27 Jan. 1943; *s* of late Cornelius William Shelford and Helen Beatrice Hilda (*née* Schuster); *m* 1971, Annette Heap Holt; two *s* one *d. Educ:* Eton Coll.; Christ Church, Oxford (MA Jurisprudence). Partner, 1970–2002, Sen. Partner, 1990–2002, Cameron Markby Hewitt, later Cameron McKenna; Consultant, CMS Cameron McKenna, 2002–07. Chm. Govs, 2004–14, Chm. Trustees, 2014–, Chailey Heritage Foundn (formerly Sch.). Vice Chm., Friends of the Keep, E Sussex archival services, 2014–. High Sheriff 2009–10, DL 2011, E Sussex. *Recreations:* gardening, walking, ski-ing, golf. *Club:* City of London.

SHELLAM, Fiona Juliet; *see* Stanley, F. J.

SHELLARD, Dr Dominic Marcus; Vice-Chancellor and Chief Executive, De Montfort University, since 2010; *b* Farnborough, Kent, 24 April 1966; *s* of Marcus Reginald Shellard and Christine Jean Shellard; civil partnership 2010, John Walker. *Educ:* Crofton Infants and Jun. Sch.; Dulwich Coll.; St Peter's Coll., Oxford (MA English and German 1989; DPhil English Lit. 1993). Researcher for Ann Clwyd, MP, Shadow Sec. of State for Nat. Heritage, 1993; Lectr in English, Univ. of Salford, 1993–96; University of Sheffield: Lectr in English Lit., 1996–99; Reader in English Lit., 1999–2003; Prof. of English Lit., 2003–10; Hd, Sch. of English, 2004–07; Pro-Vice-Chancellor for Ext. Affairs, 2008–10. *Publications:* Harold Hobson: the complete catalogue 1922–1988, 1995; Harold Hobson: witness and judge, 1995; Shakespeare: a writer's life, 1998; British Theatre Since the War, 2000; (ed) British Theatre in the 1950s, 2000; Kenneth Tynan: a life, 2003; (with S. Nicholson) The Lord Chamberlain Regrets… A History of British Theatre Censorship, 2004; An Economic Impact Study of UK Theatre, 2004; (with W. McDonnell) A Social Impact Study of UK Theatre, 2006; Kenneth Tynan: theatre writings, 2007; (ed) The Golden Generation: new light on British theatre 1945–1968, 2008. *Recreations:* supporting QPR, reading, current affairs, convivial meals, travelling, going to the theatre, attending sports events. *Address:* Vice-Chancellor's Office, Trinity House, De Montfort University, The Gateway, Leicester LE1 9BH. *T:* (0116) 250 6091/6081, *Fax:* (0116) 250 6092. *E:* vc@dmu.ac.uk.

SHELLARD, Maj.-Gen. Michael Francis Linton, CBE 1989; Comptroller, Royal Artillery Institution, 2001–08; *b* 19 Aug. 1937; *s* of Norman Shellard and Stella (*née* Linton); *m* 1960, Jean Mary Yates; one *s* one *d. Educ:* Queen's Coll., Taunton; RMA, Sandhurst. Commnd, RA, 1957; Staff Coll., Camberley, 1969; NDC, Latimer, 1974; GSO1 MO4, MoD, 1975–76; CO 22 AD Regt, 1977–79; Col, 1983; Brig., 1985; Comd 1st Artillery Bde and Dortmund Garrison, 1985–88; Comdr Artillery, 1st British Corps, 1990–92. Dir, NATO Area, Short Brothers plc, 1992–94; Chief Exec., Regular Forces Employment Assoc., 1994–2001. Col Comdt, RA, 1993–2002; Hon. Col 22nd Regt, RA, 1993–2000. Chairman: RA Historical Affairs Cttee, 1994–2002; RA Historical Trust, 1994–2002. Dir, RA Museums Ltd, 1997–2004. Mem., Army Benevolent Fund Grants Cttee, 2002–14. Chm., Confedn of British Service and Ex-Service Orgns, 2003–06. Chm., Andover Talking Newspaper, 2014–. Gov., Queen's Coll., Taunton, 1989–2012. *Recreations:* golf, gardening, Hawk Conservancy Trust, Samaritans. *Address:* c/o HSBC, High Street, Amesbury, Wilts SP4 7DN. *Club:* Army and Navy (Chm., 2000–03; Trustee, 2004–15).

SHELLEY, David Richard; Chief Executive, Little, Brown Book Group and Orion Publishing Group, since 2015; *b* Dusseldorf, 1976; *s* of Alan and Jennifer Shelley; civil partnership, 2005, Chris Gardner. *Educ:* Priory Sch., Lewes; Varndean Coll., Brighton; New Coll., Oxford (BA English). Editor, 1997–99, Publisher, 2000–05, Allison & Busby; Editl Dir, Little, Brown, 2005–07; Publisher, Sphere, 2007–09; Dep. Publisher, Hachette Book Gp, 2009–10; Publisher, Little, Brown Book Gp, 2010–15. *Recreations:* hiking, swimming, reading, gardening. *Address:* Hachette, Carmelite House, 50 Victoria Embankment, EC4Y 0DZ. *T:* (020) 3122 6942. *E:* david.shelley@hachette.co.uk.

SHELLEY, Howard Gordon, OBE 2009; concert pianist and conductor; *b* 9 March 1950; *s* of Frederick Gordon Shelley and Katharine Anne Taylor; *m* 1975, Hilary Mary Pauline Macnamara; one *s*, and one step *s. Educ:* Highgate Sch.; Royal College of Music (ARCM Hons 1966; Foundn Schol. 1967–71); Boise Schol. 1971–72; ARCO 1967. Studied with Vera Yelverton, Harold Craxton, Kendall Taylor, Lamar Crowson and Ilona Kabos. Recital début, Wigmore Hall, 1971; televised Henry Wood Prom début, 1972; conducting début, London Symphony Orch., Barbican, 1985; Associate Conductor, 1990–92, Principal Guest Conductor, 1992–98, Conductor Laureate, 2014–, London Mozart Players; Music Dir and Principal Conductor, Uppsala Chamber Orch., Sweden, 2000–03. Internat. solo career extending over five continents; performed world's first complete exposition of solo piano works of Rachmaninov, Wigmore Hall, 1983; soloist, 100th anniv. of Henry Wood Proms, 1995. Discography of over 150 recordings includes: Rachmaninov solo works (8 vols), Rachmaninov two-piano works, Rachmaninov Complete Piano Concertos, Mozart, Hummel (9 vols) and Mendelssohn Piano Concertos, and contribs to Hyperion's Romantic Piano series, including Concertos by Moscheles, Herz, Hiller and Kalkbrenner; Chopin, Schumann recitals, Schubert recital on fortepiano, piano concertos of Alwyn, Gershwin, Tippett, Vaughan Williams, Howard Ferguson, Szymanowski, Korngold, Rubbra, Carwithen, Balakirev, Messiaen and Peter Dickinson; Mozart and Schubert symphonies (conductor); Haydn's London and Cycle of Spohr symphonies; complete Clementi sonatas (6 double CD vols); 4 CDs of complete works of Beethoven for piano and orch. (conductor/soloist). 2 piano partnership with Hilary Macnamara, 1976–. Presenter, conductor and pianist, TV documentary on Ravel (Gold Medal, NY Fests Awards), 1998. Chappell Gold Medal and Peter Morrison Prize, 1968, Dannreuther Concerto Prize, 1971, RCM; Silver Medal, Co. of Musicians, 1971. *Address:* c/o Caroline Baird Artists, Stable Cottage, High Street, Culham, Oxon OX14 4NA. *E:* caroline@carolinebairdartists.co.uk.

SHELLEY, James Edward, CBE 1991; Secretary to Church Commissioners, 1985–92; *b* 1932; *s* of Vice-Adm. Richard Shelley and Eve Cecil; *m* 1956, Judy Grubb; two *s* two *d. Educ:* Eton; University College, Oxford (MA). Joined Church Commissioners' staff, 1954; Under Secretary General, 1976–81; Assets Secretary, 1981–85. Dir, Save & Prosper, 1987–94. *Recreation:* country pursuits. *Address:* Mays Farm House, Digweeds Lane, Ramsdell, Tadley, Hants RG26 5RE. *T:* (01256) 850770.

SHELLEY, Sir John (Richard), 11th Bt *cr* 1611; (professionally Dr J. R. Shelley); general medical practitioner; farmer; *b* 18 Jan. 1943; *s* of John Shelley (*d* 1974), and Dorothy, *d* of Arthur Irvine Ingram; *S* grandfather, 1976; *m* 1965, Clare, *d* of late Claud Bicknell, OBE; two *d. Educ:* King's Sch., Bruton; Trinity Coll., Cambridge (BA 1964, MA 1967); St Mary's Hosp., London Univ. MB, BChir 1967; DObstRCOG 1969; MRCGP 1978; Exeter Univ. (MA Theol. 2009). Mem., Exeter Diocesan Synod for South Molton Deanery, 1976–79, for Cadbury Deanery, 2002– (Lay Chair, 2007–); Mem., Gen. Synod, C of E, 2009–. Member: CLA; NFU. *Heir: b* Thomas Henry Shelley [*b* 3 Feb. 1945; *m* 1st, 1970, Katherine Mary Holton (marr. diss. 1992); three *d*; 2nd, 1994, Linda Joyce Wallis (*née* Poole)]. *Address:* Shobrooke Park, Crediton, Devon EX17 1DG.

SHELTON, Gen. (Henry) Hugh; Chairman, Joint Chiefs of Staff, USA, 1997–2001; *b* 2 Jan. 1942; *s* of late Hugh Shelton and of Sarah Shelton (*née* Laughlin); *m* 1963, Carolyn L. Johnson; three *s. Educ:* N Carolina State Univ. (BS Textiles 1963); Auburn Univ., Alabama (MS Pol Sci.); Harvard Univ.; Air Comd and Staff Coll., Alabama; Nat. War Coll., Washington. Entered US Army, 1963: active duty assignments in US, Hawaii and Vietnam (2 tours), 1963–87; Dep. Dir for Ops, Nat. Mil. Comd Center, Jt Chiefs of Staff, Washington, 1987–88; Chief, Current Ops, Jt Chiefs of Staff, 1988–89; Assistant Division Commander, 101st Airborne Division (Air Assault): Fort Campbell, Kentucky, 1989–90; Operations Desert Shield and Desert Storm, Saudi Arabia, 1990–91; Fort Campbell, March–May 1991; Commanding General: 82nd Airborne Div., Fort Bragg, NC, 1991–93; XVIII Airborne Corps and Fort Bragg, 1993–96 (i/c Jt Task Force, Operation Uphold Democracy, Haiti, 1994); Lt-Gen. 1993; Gen. 1996; C-in-C, US Special Ops Comd, MacDill Air Force Base, Fla, 1996–97. Mem., Council on Foreign Relns, 1998–. Mem., Assoc. of US Army, 1983–. Gov., American Red Cross, 1998–. Purple Heart, 1967; Bronze Star Medal: (with V device), 1967; (with three Oak Leaf Clusters), 1968, 1969, 1991; MSM (with two Oak Leaf Clusters), 1979, 1982, 1983; Legion of Merit (with Oak Leaf Cluster), 1985, 1991; DSM 1994; Defense DSM (with two Oak Leaf Clusters), 1989, 1994, 1997. *Publications:* Without Hesitation: the odyssey of an American warrior, 2010; contrib. to Harvard Internat. Rev., Armed Forces Jl, Nat. Defense, Special Warfare, Jt Force Qly, Qly Mil. Rev. *Recreations:* jogging, woodworking, reading, playing guitar. *Address:* c/o The Pentagon, Room 2E872, Washington, DC 20318–9999, USA. *T:* (703) 6979121.

SHELVEY, (Elsie) Miriam; a District Judge (Magistrates' Court) (formerly Provincial Stipendiary Magistrate), Greater Manchester, since 1999; *b* 23 Aug. 1955; *d* of Francis James Dunn and Edith Elsie Dunn; *m* 1977, Peter Anthony Shelvey; one *d. Educ:* Liverpool Univ. (LLB). Admitted Solicitor, 1979; Partner, Silverman Livermore, 1980–99. *Recreation:* gardening. *Address:* Liverpool City Magistrates' Court, 107 Dale Street, Liverpool L2 2JQ. *T:* (0151) 243 5597.

SHENG, Prof. Morgan Hwa-Tze, PhD; FRS 2007; Vice President, Neuroscience and Molecular Biology, Genentech Inc., since 2008; *b* London; *m*; one *s* one *d. Educ:* Corpus Christi Coll., Oxford (BA Physiol. 1979); Guy's Hosp. Med. Sch., Univ. of London (MB BS 1982); Harvard Univ. (PhD Molecular Genetics 1990). MRCP. Internship and residency in gen. medicine, London, 1982–86; Postdoctoral Fellow in Neurosci., UCSF, 1990–94; Asst Prof., 1994–98, Associate Prof., 1998–2001, Dept of Neurobiol., Massachusetts Gen. Hosp. and Harvard Med. Sch., Boston; Asst Investigator, then Associate Investigator, Howard Hughes Med. Inst., Mass Gen. Hosp., 1994–2001; Massachusetts Institute of Technology: Principal Investigator, RIKEN-MIT Neurosci. Res. Center, 2001–08; Investigator, Howard Hughes Med. Inst., 2001–08; Menicon Prof. of Neurosci., Picower Inst. for Learning and Memory, Dept of Brain and Cognitive Scis and Dept of Biol., 2001–08. FAAAS. Member: Soc. for Neurosci.; Amer. Soc. for Cell Biol.; Soc. Chinese Bioscientists of America. *Publications:* contribs to jls incl. Cell, Neuron, Jl Neurosci. *Address:* Genentech Inc., 1 DNA Way, South San Francisco, CA 94080–4990, USA.

SHENKIN, Prof. Alan, PhD; FRCP, FRCPath, FRCPGlas; Professor of Clinical Chemistry, University of Liverpool, 1990–2007, now Emeritus; Hon. Consultant and Clinical Director, Royal Liverpool and Broadgreen University Hospitals NHS Trust, 1990–2007 (Director of Research and Development, 1998–2004); *b* 3 Sept. 1943; *m* 1967, Leonna Estelle Delmonte; one *s* two *d. Educ:* Hutchesons' Boys' Grammar Sch.; Univ. of Glasgow (BSc Hons 1965; MB ChB 1969; PhD 1974). FRCPath 1990; FRCPGlas 1990; FRCP 1993. Lectr in Biochem.,

Univ. of Glasgow, 1970–74; Sen. Registrar in Clinical Biochem., Glasgow Royal Infirmary, 1974–78; Royal Soc. Eur. Exchange Fellow, Karolinska Inst., Stockholm, 1976–77; Consultant in Clinical Biochem., Glasgow Royal Infirmary, 1978–90. Chm., Specialty Adv. Cttee on Chemical Pathology, RCPath, 1995–98; Chairman: Royal Med. Colls Intercollegiate Gp on Nutrition, 1996–2006; Sub-Cttee on Metabolic Medicine, Jt Cttee on Higher Med. Trng, 2001–04. Pres., Assoc. Clinical Biochemists, 2000–03; Hon. Treas., Eur. Soc. Parenteral and Enteral Nutrition, 1988–92 (Vice-Pres., 2002–03; Hon. Mem., 2010); Scientific Vice-Pres., British Nutrition Foundn, 2005–10 (Hon. Pres., 2010–). Hon. Associate, British Dietetic Assoc., 1989; Hon. Member: Czechoslovakian Med. Soc., 1990; Czechoslovakian Soc. for Parenteral and Enteral Nutrition, 1990; Assoc. for Clin. Biochem., 2007. Trustee, Alkaptonuria Soc., 2006–. Trustee and Mem. Council, Royal Philosophical Soc., 2013–. 650th Anniversary Jubilee Medal, Charles Univ., 1998. *Publications:* contrib. res. papers, book chapters and reviews on trace elements and vitamins in health and disease, nutritional support, metabolic response to illness, and role of laboratory in assessing nutritional status. *Recreations:* golf, word games, malt whisky, travel. *Address:* 9/3 Barcapel Avenue, Newton Mearns, Glasgow G77 6QJ. *Club:* Glasgow Golf.

SHENNAN, Robert Duncan James; Controller, BBC Asian Network, since 2004, and BBC Radio 2 and 6 Music, since 2009; Director of Music, BBC, since 2014; *b* 18 March 1962; *s* of Joseph and Margaret Shennan; *m* 1987, Joanne Margaret Melford; two *s* one *d*. *Educ:* Lancaster Royal Grammar Sch.; Corpus Christi Coll., Cambridge (BA Hons English Lit. 1984). Journalist, Hereward Radio, 1984–87; BBC: Radio Sport: Producer, 1987–90; Asst Editor, 1990–92; Editor, 1992–94; Head, 1994–97; Head of Sport (TV and Radio), 1997–2000; Controller: BBC Radio Five Live, 2000–08; Five Live Sports Extra, 2002–08; Dir of Radio, Channel 4, 2008–09. *Recreations:* sport, music, my children. *Address:* BBC, Western House, 99 Great Portland Street, W1A 1AA; Fairbanks, 30 Amersham Road, High Wycombe, Bucks HP13 6QU. *T:* (01494) 459216.

SHENNAN, Prof. Stephen James, PhD; FBA 2006; Professor of Theoretical Archaeology, University College London, since 1996 (Director, Institute of Archaeology, 2005–14); *b* 9 May 1949; *s* of James Francis Shennan and Martha Shennan (*née* Elias); *m* 2006, Lúcia Nagib; one *s* one *d* from former marriage. *Educ:* Becket Sch., Nottingham; Fitzwilliam Coll., Cambridge (BA 1971, MA 1974; PhD 1977). University of Southampton: Lectr in Archaeol., 1978–90; Reader, 1990–95; Prof. of Archaeol., 1995–96. MAE 2013. Rivers Meml Medal, RAI, 2010. *Publications:* (ed with C. Renfrew) Ranking, Resource and Exchange, 1982; (jtly) Prehistoric Europe, 1984; The East Hampshire Survey, 1985; Quantifying Archaeology, 1988, 2nd edn 1997; (ed) Archaeological approaches to Cultural Identity, 1989; (with C. W. Beck) Amber in Prehistoric Britain, 1991; Bronze Age Copper Producers of the Eastern Alps, 1995; (ed with J. Steele) The Archaeology of Human Ancestry: power, sex and tradition, 1996; Genes, Memes and Human History: Darwinian archaeology and cultural evolution, 2002; (ed jtly) The Explanation of Culture Change, 2004; (ed jtly) The Evolution of Cultural Diversity: a phylogenetic approach, 2005; (ed jtly) Mapping Our Ancestors: phylogenetic methods in anthropology and prehistory, 2006; (ed jtly) A Future for Archaeology: the past in the present, 2006; (ed) Pattern and Process in Cultural Evolution, 2009; (ed jtly) Innovation in Cultural Systems: contributions from evolutionary anthropology, 2010; (ed jtly) The Origins and Spread of Domestic Animals in Southwest Asia and Europe, 2013; monographs; contrib. numerous acad. papers. *Recreations:* rock climbing, walking, classical music (especially opera), cinema. *Address:* Institute of Archaeology, University College London, 31–34 Gordon Square, WC1H 0PY. *T:* (020) 7679 4739, *Fax:* (020) 7387 2572. *E:* s.shennan@ucl.ac.uk.

SHENTON, Caroline, DPhil; FSA, FRHistS; Director, Parliamentary Archives Accommodation Programme, since 2014 (Director, Parliamentary Archives, 2008–14); *b* Evesham, Worcs, 16 Nov. 1965; *d* of Peter Shenton and Gillian Shenton; *m* 1994, Mark Purcell. *Educ:* Univ. of St Andrews (MA (Hons) Medieval Hist. 1989); Worcester Coll., Oxford (DPhil 1996); University Coll. London (Dip. Archives and Records Mgt 1997). Registered Archivist 2000. FSA 2007; FRHistS 2009. PR Account Exec., Lindy Beveridge Public Relns, 1989–90; Archive Cataloguer, 1993–96, Sen. Archivist, 1996–99, PRO; Asst Clerk of the Records, Parly Archives, 1999–2008. Hon. Teaching Fellow, Centre for Archive and Information Studies, Univ. of Dundee, 2011–. Member: Lindley Liby and Arts Cttee, RHS, 2011–; Cttee, Section of Archives of Parliaments and Political Parties, Internat. Council on Archives, 2012–. Trustee, H of L Collection Trust, 2008–. *Publications:* Victoria Tower Treasures from the Parliamentary Archives (ed jtly), 2010; The Day Parliament Burned Down, 2012 (Political Book of the Year, Paddy Power and Total Politics Political Book Awards, 2013); historical and inf. mgt articles in learned jls. *Recreations:* historical research, Italian language and culture, early music, Twitter, foreign travel. *Address:* Parliamentary Archives, Houses of Parliament, SW1A 0PW. *T:* (020) 7219 3074. *E:* shentonc@parliament.uk.

SHEPHARD OF NORTHWOLD, Baroness *cr* 2005 (Life Peer), of Northwold in the county of Norfolk; **Gillian Patricia Shephard;** PC 1992; JP; DL; *b* 22 Jan. 1940; *d* of Reginald and Bertha Watts; *m* 1975, Thomas Shephard; two step *s*. *Educ:* North Walsham High Sch. for Girls; St Hilda's Coll., Oxford (MA Mod. Langs; Hon. Fellow, 1991). Educn Officer and Schools Inspector, 1963–75; Lectr, Cambridge Univ. Extra-Mural Bd, 1965–87. Councillor, Norfolk CC, 1977–89 (Chm. of Social Services Cttee, 1978–83, of Educn Cttee, 1983–85); Chairman: W Norfolk and Wisbech HA, 1981–85; Norwich HA, 1985–87; Co-Chm., Women's Nat. Commn, 1990–91. MP (C) SW Norfolk, 1987–2005. PPS to Economic Sec. to the Treasury, 1988–89; Parly Under Sec. of State, DSS, 1989–90; Minister of State, HM Treasury, 1990–92; Sec. of State for Employment and Minister for Women, 1992–93; Minister of Agric., Fisheries and Food, 1993–94; Sec. of State for Educn, later Educn and Employment, 1994–97; Shadow Leader, H of C, 1997; Opposition front bench spokesman on the envmt, transport and the regions, 1997–99. Mem., Procedure Cttee, H of L, 2007–09. Dep. Chm., Cons. Party, 1991–92 and 2002–03; Chm., Assoc. of Conservative Peers, 2007–12. Member: Cttee on Standards in Public Life, 2003–08; Jt Cttee on Reform of H of L, 2011–12; Pres., Video Standards Council, 2006–14; Dep. Chm., Commn on Social Mobility, 2013–. Vice Pres., Hansard Soc., 1997–2004. Mem., Franco-British Council, 1997–2006; Chairman: Cons. Friends of Israel, 1997–2001; E of England Bio-Fuels Forum, 2004–12; Franco-British Soc., 2005–11; Patron, WEA, 2006–. Comr, Fawcett Soc., 2005–. Mem. Council, 2000–06, Mem., Bd of Continuing Educn, 2005–, Univ. of Oxford; Chairman, Council: RVC, 2008–12; Inst. of Educn, Univ. of London, 2010–. Gov., NIESR, 2014–. President: Royal Norfolk Agricl Assoc., 2000–01; Norfolk Assoc. of Local Councils, 2008–14; Chm., Oxford Univ. Soc., 2007– (Pres., Norfolk Br., 2007–); Vice Patron, Norfolk Community Foundn, 2006–. JP Norwich, 1973; DL Norfolk, 2003. FRVC 2012. Hon. Fellow, QMUL, 2008. Chevalier, Légion d'Honneur (France), 2009. *Publications:* The Future of Local Government, 1999; Shephard's Watch, 2000; Knapton Remembered, 2007; Knapton: 20th century village voices, 2011; The Real Iron Lady: working with Margaret Thatcher, 2013. *Recreations:* music, gardening, France. *Address:* House of Lords, SW1A 0PW.

See also N. Shephard.

SHEPHARD, Jonathan; Chief Executive, Autism West Midlands, 2010–March 2016; *b* 20 March 1949; twin *s* of Grey and Mollie Shephard; *m* 1985, Penelope Guest (marr. diss. 2000); two *s* one *d* (triplets). *Educ:* Sir Thomas Rich's Sch., Gloucester; St Catherine's Coll., Oxford (BA (English) 1971; BA (Law) 1973; Chancellor's English Essay Prize, Matthew Arnold Meml Prize). Called to the Bar, Inner Temple, 1977; with Which?, 1979–94: Financial Researcher, 1979–83, Financial Res. Manager, 1983–86; Editor: Holiday Which?, 1986–90; Health Which?, 1988–90; Project Dir, 1990–92; Dir of Mgt Inf., 1992–94; Mktg Dir, 1994–95, Man. Dir, 1995–97, Newhall Gp; Man. Dir, Southern Magazines, 1997–2002; Gen. Sec., subseq. Chief Exec., Independent Schs Council, 2004–08; Chief Exec., PPA, 2008–09. Director: Audit Bureau of Circulations, 2008–09; Advertising Standards Bd of Finance, 2008–09; Copyright Licensing Agency, 2008–09; Eur. Fedn of Mag. Publishers, 2008–09; Internat. Fedn of Periodical Press, 2008–09; Publishers Licensing Soc., 2008–09; Press Standards Bd of Finance, 2008–09. Dir and Trustee, Autism Alliance, 2011–March 2016; Dir, SPARC Autism, 2013–; Trustee, Success in Shortage Subjects, 2007–. *Publications:* (ed) Which? Book of Tax, 1986. *Recreations:* music, architecture, writing novels. *Address:* (until March 2016) Autism West Midlands, Regent Court, George Road, Edgbaston B15 1NU.

SHEPHARD, Prof. Neil, PhD; FBA 2006; Professor of Economics and of Statistics, since 2013, and Chair, Department of Statistics, since 2015, Harvard University; *b* 8 Oct. 1964; *s* of Dr Thomas F. Shephard (who *m* 1975, Gillian Watts (*see* Baroness Shephard of Northwold)) and late Tydfil Shephard; *m* 1998, Dr Heather Bell; two *d*. *Educ:* Univ. of York (BA Hons Econs and Stats 1986); London Sch. of Economics (MSc Stats 1987; PhD 1990). Lectr, LSE, 1988–93; Gatsby Res. Fellow in Econometrics, 1991–93, Official Fellow in Econs, 1993–2006, Professorial Fellow, 2006–13, Nuffield Coll., Oxford; Titular Prof. of Econs, 1999–2006, Prof. of Econs, 2006–13, Res. Dir, Oxford-Man Inst., 2007–11, Univ. of Oxford. Fellow, Econometric Soc., 2004. Hon. DEcon, Aarhus Univ., 2009. Richard Stone Prize, Soc. for Applied Econometrics, 2012. *Publications:* scientific papers in Econometrica, Rev. of Econ. Studies, Jl of Amer. Stat. Assoc., Biometrika, etc. *Recreations:* reading, cricket, family. *Address:* Department of Economics, Harvard University, Littauer Center, 1802 Cambridge Street, Cambridge, MA 02138, USA. *E:* shephard@fas.harvard.edu.

SHEPHARD, Capt. Samuel John, GC 2014; Officer, Royal Marines, since 2011; *b* Craigavon, 20 July 1987; *s* of John Shephard, MBE and Grace Shephard; partner, Victoria Gass. *Educ:* Royal Sch., Armagh; Queen's Univ., Belfast (BSc Marine Biol.; MSc Fisheries and Aquaculture). Royal Marines: Officer-in-Comd 5 Troop, Bravo Co., 40 Cdo (Herrick 17); Second-in-Comd, Bravo Co., 40 Cdo; Flag Lieut to First Sea Lord. *Address:* c/o Royal Marines Secretary, Whale Island, Portsmouth PO2 8ER.

SHEPHEARD ROGERS, Patricia Maureen; Mathematics Educator: Open University, since 1972; National Centre for Excellence in the Teaching of Mathematics, since 2010; *b* Colchester, 18 May 1947; *d* of Maj. Gen. Joseph Kenneth Shepheard, CB, DSO, OBE and Maureen E. H. Shepheard (*née* Bowen-Colthurst); *m* 1969, David Rogers (marr. diss. 2004); two *s*. *Educ:* New Hall, Cambridge (BA Hons 1968); Inst. of Educn, London Univ. (PGCE); Univ. of Greenwich (DMS). Lecturer in Mathematics: West Kent Coll., 1968–69; Univ. of Lagos Coll. of Educn, 1969–71; King's Coll., Lagos, 1971–72; Foreman Christian Coll., Univ. of Punjab, 1975–78; Founder and Dir, Computer Materials Prog., Centre for World Develt Educn, 1979–85; broadcaster and newspaper columnist, S Korea, 1985–89; develt educn researcher and writer, 1981–90; Chief Executive: Council for Educn in World Citizenship, 1990–99; Pestalozzi Internat. Village, 1999–2005; Jubilee Debt Campaign, 2005–08. Director: RIIA, 2007–10 (Mem., 1990–); UN Assoc.-UK, 2007–12; British Humanist Assoc., 2008– (Vice Chair, 2010–). Leader of occasional CPD for rural maths teachers with AKRA, Pakistan, 2010–. *Publications:* Sand Harvest, 1985; Let's Visit South Korea, 1988. *Address:* 27 River Court, Upper Ground, SE1 9PE. *T:* (020) 7928 3667. *E:* trisha_rogers@yahoo.com.

SHEPHERD, family name of **Baron Shepherd**.

SHEPHERD, 3rd Baron *cr* 1946, of Spalding, co. Lincoln; **Graeme George Shepherd;** Founder, 1986, and Chairman, Anglo Sterling Ltd; Director, Star Material Solutions Ltd, Hong Kong, since 2005; *b* 6 Jan. 1949; *er s* of 2nd Baron Shepherd, PC and Allison (*née* Redmond); *S* father, 2001; *m* 1971, Eleanor Philomena (marr. diss. 2002), *d* of Patrick Glynn; one *s*; *m* 2005, Evelyn Cortes; two *s*. *Heir: s* Hon. Patrick Malcolm Shepherd [*b* 10 July 1980; *m* 2007, Laura, *d* of Tim Street; one *s* one *d*]. *Clubs:* Oriental; Hong Kong, Shek O Golf and Country (Hong Kong).

SHEPHERD, Alan Arthur, CBE 1984; PhD; FREng, FInstP; Director, Ferranti plc, 1981–94; *b* 6 Sept. 1927; *s* of Arthur and Hannah Shepherd; *m* 1953, Edith Hudson; two *d*. *Educ:* Univ. of Manchester (BSc, MSc, PhD). FREng (FEng 1986). Lectr, Physics Dept, Univ. of Keele, 1950–54; Ferranti Ltd: Chief Engineer, Electronic Components Div., 1954–67; Gen. Manager, Instrument Dept, 1967–70; Gen. Manager, Electronic Components Div., 1970–78; Man. Dir, Ferranti Electronics, 1978–87; Dep. Man. Dir, Ops, Ferranti, then Ferranti Internat. Signal plc, 1987–89; Chm., Ferranti California Group of Cos, 1978–87. Hon. Fellow, UMIST, 1988. J. J. Thomson Medal, IEE, 1985. *Publications:* The Physics of Semiconductors, 1957. *Recreations:* golf, swimming, photography. *Address:* 9 Rossett Beck, Harrogate HG2 9NT. *T:* (01423) 547012. *Club:* St James's (Manchester).

SHEPHERD, Rev. Canon Anthony Michael; Vicar, St Peter's, Harrogate, 1987–2015; Chaplain to the Queen, since 2009; *b* Broadstairs, 8 July 1950; *s* of Alfred Shepherd and Betty Shepherd; *m* 1978, Ann Elisabeth Gilbert-Trujols; one *s* one *d*. *Educ:* Chatham House Grammar Sch., Ramsgate; Emmanuel Coll., Cambridge (BA 1972; MA 1976). Ordained deacon, 1974, priest, 1975; Curate, Folkestone Parish Church, 1974–79; Bishop's Chaplain, Dio. of Ripon, 1979–87. Hon. Canon, Ripon Cathedral, 1989. *Recreations:* golf, old postcards. *Address:* 3 Heatherdale, Summerbridge, Harrogate, N Yorks HG3 4BQ. *E:* ashepherd@talktalk.net.

SHEPHERD, Sir Colin (Ryley), Kt 1996; Director of Parliamentary Studies, Centre for Political and Diplomatic Studies, 1999–2010; *b* 13 Jan. 1938; *s* of late T. C. R. Shepherd, MBE; *m* 1966, Louise, *d* of late Lt-Col E. A. M. Cleveland, MC; three *s*. *Educ:* Oundle; Caius Coll., Cambridge; McGill Univ., Montreal. RCN, 1960–63; Dir, Haigh Engineering Co. Ltd, 1963–2010. MP (C) Hereford, Oct. 1974–1997; contested (C) same seat, 1997. PPS to Sec. of State for Wales, 1987–90. Jt Sec., Cons. Parly Agr. Fish. and Food Cttee, 1975–79, Vice-Chm., 1979–87, 1991–92; Member: Select Cttee on H of C Services, 1979–92; Select Cttee on H of C Finance and Services, 1993–97; Sec., Cons. Parly Hort. Sub-Cttee, 1976–87; Chairman: Library Sub-Cttee, 1983–91; Catering Cttee, 1991–97. Chm., UK Br., CPA, 1991–94 (Mem. Exec. Cttee, 1986–97; Treas., 1991–93, Chm., 1993–96, Internat. Exec. Cttee). Council Mem., RCVS, 1983–99 (Hon. ARCVS 2001); Governor, Commonwealth Inst., 1989–97; Chm., Trustees, Friends of the Commonwealth Foundn, 1998–2014. Fellow, Industry and Parlt Trust, 1985. *Address:* Manor House, Ganarew, Monmouth NP25 3SU. *T:* (01600) 890220.

SHEPHERD, David; *see* Shepherd, R. D.

SHEPHERD, Prof. James, PhD; FRCPath, FRCPGlas, FMedSci; FRSE; Professor, and Head of Department of Pathological Biochemistry, University of Glasgow and Glasgow Royal Infirmary, 1988–2006, now Professor Emeritus; *b* 8 April 1944; *s* of James Bell Shepherd and Margaret McCrum Shepherd (*née* Camick); *m* 1969, Janet Bulloch Kelly; one *s* one *d*. *Educ:* Hamilton Acad.; Glasgow Univ. (BSc Hons 1965; MB ChB Hons 1968; PhD 1972). MRCPath 1982, FRCPath 1994; FRCPGlas 1990. Lectr in Biochemistry, Univ. of Glasgow, 1969–72; Lectr, 1973–77, Sen. Lectr and Hon. Consultant, 1977–88, Dept of Pathological Biochemistry, Univ. of Glasgow and Glasgow Royal Infirmary; Clin. Dir, Labs, Glasgow Royal Infirmary, 1993–2004. Asst Prof. of Medicine, Methodist Hosp., Houston, Texas, 1976–77; Vis. Prof. of Medicine, Cantonal Hosp., Geneva, 1984. Dir, W Scotland Coronary Prevention Study, 1989–96; Chairman: European Atherosclerosis Soc., 1993–96 (Chm., Congress, 2001); Prospective Study of Pravastatin in the Elderly at Risk, 1997–2002; Mem., Exec. Cttee, Treating to New Targets Study, 2001–06; UK Principal Investigator:

Justification for the Use of Statins in Primary Prevention, 2005–08; JUPITER (Mem., Internat. Cttee). Mem., Internat. Atherosclerosis Soc., 1977–. FRSE 1996; Founder FMedSci, 1998. *Publications:* (jtly) Lipoproteins in Coronary Heart Disease, 1986; (jtly) Atherosclerosis: developments, complications and treatment, 1987; Lipoprotein Metabolism, 1987; (ed jtly) Coronary Risks Revisited, 1989; (ed jtly) Human Plasma Lipoproteins, 1989; (ed jtly) Preventive Cardiology, 1991; (ed jtly) Lipoproteins and the Pathogenesis of Atherosclerosis, 1991; (ed jtly) Cardiovascular Disease: current perspectives on the Asian-Pacific region, 1994; (jtly) Clinical Biochemistry, 1995, 4th edn 2008; (jtly) Lipoproteins in Health and Disease, 1999; (jtly) Statins in Perspective, 1999, 2nd edn 2004; (jtly) Atherosclerosis Annual, 2001; Lipids and Atherosclerosis Annual, 2003. *Recreations:* travel, walking, art appraisal. *Address:* (home) 17 Barriedale Avenue, Hamilton ML3 9DB. *T:* (01698) 428259.

SHEPHERD, James Rodney; Under-Secretary, Department of Trade and Industry (formerly Department of Industry), 1980–89, retired; *b* 27 Nov. 1935; *s* of Richard James Shepherd and Winifred Mary Shepherd. *Educ:* Blundell's; Magdalen Coll., Oxford (PPE; Diploma in Statistics). National Inst. of Economic and Social Res., 1960–64; Consultant to OECD, 1964; HM Treasury, 1965–80 (Under-Sec., 1975–80). *Publications:* articles in technical jls.

SHEPHERD, Sir John (Alan), KCVO 2000; CMG 1989; Director, Global Leadership Foundation, since 2007; *b* 27 April 1943; *s* of William (Mathieson) Shepherd and (Elsie) Rae Shepherd; *m* 1st, 1969, Jessica Mary Nichols (*d* 2011); one *d*; 2nd, 2015, Alison Mairi Sephton (*née* Forsyth). *Educ:* Charterhouse; Selwyn Coll., Cambridge (MA); Stanford Univ., Calif (MA). Merchant Navy, 1961; HM Diplomatic Service, 1965–2003: CO, 1965–66; MECAS, Lebanon, 1966–68; 3rd Sec., Amman, 1968–70; 2nd Sec., Rome, 1970–73; 1st Secretary: FCO, 1973–76; The Hague, 1977–80; First Sec., 1980–82, Counsellor and Hd of Chancery, 1982–84, Office of UK Rep. to EEC, Brussels; Head of European Community Dept (External), FCO, 1985–87; Ambassador to Bahrain, 1988–91; Minister, Bonn, 1991–96; Dir, Middle East and North Africa, FCO, 1996–97; Dep. Under-Sec. of State, FCO, 1997–2000; Ambassador to Italy, 2000–03; Sec.-Gen., Global Leadership Foundn, 2003–06. Chm., Norbert Brainin Foundn, 2003–; Deputy Chairman: Trustees, Prince's Sch. of Traditional Arts, 2004–10; Bahrain Soc., 2009–. *Recreations:* hills, birds, tennis. *Club:* Oxford and Cambridge.

SHEPHERD, Prof. John Graham, CBE 2010; PhD; FRS 1999; CMath, FIMA; Professorial Research Fellow in Earth System Science, University of Southampton, since 2006 (Professor of Marine Sciences, 1994–2006); *b* 24 Aug. 1946; *s* of Ian Alastair Shepherd and Eileen Alice Mary Shepherd; *m* 1968, Deborah Mary Powney; two *s*. *Educ:* Pembroke Coll., Cambridge (MA); Cavendish Lab., Cambridge (PhD 1971). FIMA 1989; CMath 1991. Res. Officer, CEGB, 1970–74; MAFF Fisheries Lab., Lowestoft, 1974–94, Dep. Dir and Hd, Fish Stock Mgt Div., 1989–94; Director: Southampton Oceanography Centre, NERC, 1994–99; Earth System Modelling Initiative, Univ. of Southampton, 1999–2006. Vis. Sen. Res. Associate, Lamont-Doherty Geol Observatory, Columbia Univ., NY, 1978–79. Pres., Challenger Soc., 2000–02. *Publications:* numerous professional articles on marine science, climate change, fish stock assessment and fishery mgt. *Recreations:* rowing, music, walking, beekeeping. *Address:* National Oceanography Centre, European Way, Southampton SO14 3ZH. *T:* (023) 8059 6256. *Club:* Lowestoft Rowing.

SHEPHERD, Prof. John Henry, FRCS, FRCOG, FACOG; Professor of Surgical Gynaecology, Barts and the London School of Medicine and Dentistry, Queen Mary University of London (formerly St Bartholomew's and the Royal London Hospital School of Medicine and Dentistry, then Barts and the London, Queen Mary's School of Medicine and Dentistry), 1999–2008, now Emeritus; Consultant Surgeon and Gynaecological Oncologist, Royal Marsden Hospital, London, since 1983; *b* 11 July 1948; *s* of late Dr Henry Robert Shepherd, DSC and of Mimika Matarki; *m* 1972, Alison Brandram Adams; one *s* two *d*. *Educ:* Blundell's Sch., Tiverton; St Bartholomew's Hosp. Med. Coll. (MB BS 1971). LRCP 1971; FRCS 1976; MRCOG 1978 (Gold Medal), FRCOG 1996; FACOG 1981. Fellow in Gynaecol Oncology, Univ. of S Florida, Tampa, 1979–81; Sen. Registrar, Queen Charlotte's Hosp., 1978–79; Consultant Surgeon and Gynaecological Oncologist, St Bartholomew's Hosp., 1981–2008; Consultant Surgeon, Chelsea Hosp. for Women, 1983–84; Consultant: London Clinic, 1994–; King Edward VII Hosp., London, 1995–. Hunterian Prof., RCS, 2006–07. *Publications:* (jtly) Gynaecological Oncology, 1985, 2nd edn 1990; (jtly) Ovarian Cancer, 2002; (jtly) Gynaecological Surgery, 2013; numerous articles on gynaecol cancer and pelvic surgery. *Recreations:* sailing (offshore ocean racing), ski-ing, opera. *Address:* London Clinic Consulting Rooms, 5 Devonshire Place, W1G 6HE. *T:* (020) 7935 4444, *Fax:* (020) 7935 6224. *Clubs:* MCC, Royal Ocean Racing.

SHEPHERD, Prof. Jonathan Paul, CBE 2008; PhD, DDSc; FDSRCS, FMedSci; FLSW; Professor of Oral and Maxillofacial Surgery, Cardiff University (formerly University of Wales College of Medicine, later Wales College of Medicine, Cardiff University), since 1991; Vice Dean, Cardiff University, since 2004; *b* 25 Sept. 1949; *s* of Paul Richard Shepherd and Heather Mary Shepherd (*née* Gifford); *m* 1980, Daphne Elizabeth Bird; three *s* one *d*. *Educ:* Bideford Grammar Sch.; King's Coll. London (BDS); Wolfson Coll., Oxford (MSc); PhD Bristol 1988; DDSc Wales 2000. FDSRCS 1977; FRCEM (FFAEM 2001). House Surgeon: KCH, 1974; Queen Victoria Hosp., E Grinstead, 1974–75; Registrar, Royal Infirmary, Oxford, 1975–80; Res. Fellow, Univ. of Oxford, 1978–79; Sen. Registrar in Oral and Maxillofacial Surgery, Yorks RHA, and Hon. Lectr, Univ. of Leeds, 1980–83; Sen. Lectr in Oral and Maxillofacial Surgery, 1983–88, Reader, 1988–91, Univ. of Bristol; Hd, Dept of Oral Surgery, Medicine and Pathol., UWCM, Cardiff Univ., 1991–2004. Hon. Consultant Oral and Maxillofacial Surgeon: Bristol and Weston HA, 1983–91; Cardiff and Vale Univ. Health Bd (formerly University Hosp. of Wales/Cardiff and Vale NHS Trust), 1991–. King James IV Prof., RCSE, 2006–08; Bradlaw Orator, RCS, 2014. Chm., WHO Violent Crime Task Gp, 1996–; author of reports for Home Office on violence prevention, 2010, and hate violence, 2011, for Cabinet Office on effectiveness, 2014; Member: Council, Acad. of Med. Scis, 2011–14; Sci. Adv. Council, Home Office, 2012–; What Works Council, Cabinet Office, 2013–; Public Services Leadership Bd, Welsh Govt, 2014–. Dir, Violence and Society Res. Gp, 1996–. Trustee: Victim Support, 1998–2006 (Vice Chair, 2000–03); Hunterian Mus., RCS, 2013–. Mem. Governing Body, Church in Wales, 2014–. FMedSci 2002; FLSW 2011. Hon. FDSRCSE 1996; Hon. FFPH 2001; Hon. FRCPsych 2008; Hon. FFGDP 2008; Hon. FRCS 2012. Hon. Dr Odontol. Malmö, 2005. Stockholm Criminology Prize, 2008; Colyer Gold Medal, RCS, 2014; Down Surgery Prize, BAOMS, 2014. *Publications:* Slide Interpretation in Oral Diseases and the Oral Manifestations of Systemic Diseases, 1986; Violence in Healthcare, 1994, 2nd edn 2001; contributions: on decision-making and cost effectiveness in surgery and anaesthesia to surgery, dentistry, anaesthesia and clin. decision-making jls; on psycho-social causes and sequelae and epidemiol. of violence to med. and social sci. jls; on the effectiveness and orgn of res. for public services and social policy; series of randomised controlled expts in epidemiol., psychiatry and emergency medicine jls; res. discoveries to BMJ and Lancet editls; policy guidelines for medical Royal Colls. *Recreations:* industrial archaeology (Mem., Trevithick Soc.), walking, 19th century history. *Address:* School of Dentistry, Cardiff University, Heath Park, Cardiff CF14 4XY. *T:* and *Fax:* (029) 2074 4215. *E:* shepherdjp@cardiff.ac.uk.

SHEPHERD, Louise Claire; Chief Executive, Alder Hey Children's NHS Foundation Trust, since 2008; *b* Derby, 26 Aug. 1964; *d* of Leslie Reginald and Joan Kirk; *m* 1991, Keith Andrew Shepherd; one *s* one *d*. *Educ:* Clare Coll., Cambridge (BA Hons 1985; MA); Warwick Business Sch. (MBA 1997); Inst. of Public Finance and Accountancy (CPFA 1989). Trainee accountant, Dudley MBC, 1985–89; Sen. Manager, KPMG, 1989–93; Dir, Business Develt, Birmingham Heartlands and Solihull NHS Trust, 1993–97; Finance Dir, Countess of Chester NHS Foundn Trust, 1997–2003; Chief Exec., Liverpool Women's NHS Foundn Trust, 2003–08. Trustee, Royal Liverpool Philharmonic Soc., 2004–10. *Recreations:* favourite challenges: playing the violin, climbing the Scottish Munros, following Derby County FC, bringing up two children. *Address:* Alder Hey Children's NHS Foundation Trust, Eaton Road, West Derby, Liverpool L12 2AP. *T:* (0151) 252 5412. *E:* louise.shepherd@alderhey.nhs.uk.

SHEPHERD, Sister Margaret Ann; Member, Religious Congregation (RC) of Our Lady of Sion, and Province Leader of UK/Ireland Province, 2005–08; Secretary, Bishops' Committee for Catholic Jewish Relations, Catholic Bishops' Conference of England and Wales, since 2011; Director, Sion Centre for Dialogue and Encounter, since 2013; *b* 26 April 1944; *d* of Alfred and Alice Shepherd. *Educ:* Maria Assumpta Coll. of Educn (DipEd); Open Univ. (BA); Leo Baeck Coll. (Dip. Jewish Studies 1980); King's Coll., London (MTh Biblical Studies). Teacher of English (part time) during noviciate period; teacher, English and religious studies: Our Lady of Sion Boarding Sch., Shropshire, 1969–70; Our Lady of Sion Sen. Sch., Worthing, 1970–77; full time rabbinical studies, 1977–80; Study Centre for Christian Jewish Relations: Team Mem., 1980–86; Dir, 1986–89; Council of Christians and Jews: Educn Officer, 1989–93; Dep. Dir, 1993–98; Dir, 1999–2003; Mem. Exec. Bd, Internat. CCJ, 2002–08; State Coordinator for Mississippi, 2008–, and Texas, 2010–, Lifelines. Trustee, Ammerdown Centre, 2005–. Gov., St Mary's Sch., Battersea, 2009–11. *Publications:* contributor: Dialogue with a Difference, ed Tony Bayfield and Marcus Braybrooke, 1992; Splashes of Godlight, ed Terence Copley, 1997; The Holocaust and the Christian World, 2000; Jews and Christians: making theological space for each other, 2000; He Kissed Him and They Wept: towards a theology of Jewish-Catholic partnership, ed Tony Bayfield, Sidney Brichto and Eugene Fisher, 2002; Public Life and the Place of the Church, ed Michael Brierley, 2006; The Legacy of John Paul II, ed Gerald O'Collins and Michael A. Hayes, 2008; contrib. to The Month. *Recreations:* visiting art galleries and exhibitions, music, painting, poetry, browsing in second hand bookshops, spending time with friends. *Address:* 35 Gilbert Close, Shooters Hill Road, SE18 4PT. *T:* (020) 8319 1930. *E:* margaretashepherd@gmail.com.

SHEPHERD, Nicholas José, FRICS; Chairman, Property Income Trust for Charities, since 2013; *b* London, 29 Nov. 1958; *s* of Ian Shepherd and Sylvia Shepherd; *m* 1984, Deborah Weller; one *s* two *d*. *Educ:* Royal Grammar Sch., High Wycombe; Sidney Sussex Coll., Cambridge (BA Geog. 1980). FRICS 1990. Drivers Jonas, later Drivers Jonas Deloitte, 1984–2012; Partner, 1988–2012; Managing Partner, 2001–11; Mem. Exec. Bd, 2010–12, Vice Chm., 2012–13, Deloitte LLP; Consultant, Deloitte Real Estate, 2013. Non-executive Director: Riverside Capital, 2013–; Innovation City (London) Ltd, 2013–; McKay Securities plc, 2015–. Surveyor to Skinners' Co., 1991–2014. Mem., Surveyors' Assoc. *Recreations:* golf, horse riding, ski-ing, walking. *Address:* Hanger Lodge, Frensham Lane, Churt, Surrey GU10 2QG. *T:* 07771 798852. *E:* nick.shepherd999@gmail.com. *Club:* Liphook Golf.

SHEPHERD, Philip Alexander; QC 2003; a Recorder of the Crown Court, since 2000; *b* 1 May 1950; *s* of John and Eve Shepherd; *m* 1984 (marr. diss. 2013); two *s*; *m* 2014, Francesca Kate Liebling; one *s*. *Educ:* St George's Coll., Weybridge; Monash Univ., Melbourne; LSE (BSc Econ). Called to the Bar, Gray's Inn, 1975; barrister specialising in commercial litigation and aviation law. MCIArb 1997; Member: Commercial Bar Assoc.; British-Italian Law Assoc.; Internat. Bar Assoc.; Internat. Cttee, Bar Council. *Recreations:* Rugby, theatre, opera. *Address:* 24 Old Buildings, Lincoln's Inn, WC2A 3UP. *T:* (020) 7691 2424, *Fax:* (020) 7405 1360. *E:* philip.shepherd@xxiv.co.uk. *Club:* Royal Automobile.

SHEPHERD, Sir Richard (Charles Scrimgeour), Kt 2013; *b* 6 Dec. 1942; *s* of late Alfred Reginald Shepherd and Davida Sophia Wallace. *Educ:* LSE; Johns Hopkins Univ. (Sch. of Advanced Internat. Studies). Director: Shepherd Foods (London) Ltd, 1970–; Partridges of Sloane Street Ltd, 1972–. Mem., SE Econ. Planning Council, 1970–74. Underwriting Mem. of Lloyds, 1974–94. MP (C) Aldridge-Brownhills, 1979–2015. Member: Treasury and Civil Service Select Cttee, 1979–83; Modernisation Select Cttee, 1997–2010; Jt Cttee on Human Rights, 2001–15; Secretary: Cons. Parly Industry Cttee, 1980–81; Cons. Parly European Cttee, 1980–81. Parly Co-Vice Chm., Campaign for Freedom of Inf., 1989–2015. Sponsor, Liberty, 2001–14. Mem., Court of Govs, LSE, 1996–. Backbencher of the Year, Spectator, 1987; Special Award, Campaign for Freedom of Information, 1988; Parliamentarian of the Year, Spectator, 1995. *Recreations:* book collecting; searching for the Home Service on the wireless. *Clubs:* Garrick, Beefsteak, Pratt's, Chelsea Arts.

SHEPHERD, (Richard) David, CBE 2008 (OBE 1980); artist; *b* 25 April 1931; *s* of Raymond Oxley Shepherd and Margaret Joyce Shepherd (*née* Williamson); *m* 1957, Avril Shirley Gaywood; four *d*. *Educ:* Stowe. Art trng under Robin Goodwin, 1950–53; started career as aviation artist (Founder Mem., Soc. of Aviation Artists). Exhibited, RA, 1956; began painting African wild life, 1960. First London one-man show, 1962; painted 15 ft reredos of Christ for army garrison church, Bordon, 1964; 2nd London exhibn, 1965; Johannesburg exhibns, 1966 and 1969; 3rd London exhibn, 1971; exhibn, Tryon Gall., London, 1978; exhibn, Rountree Tryon Galls, 2014. Painted: HE Dr Kaunda, President of Zambia, 1967; HM the Queen Mother for King's Regt, 1969; HE Sheikh Zayed of Abu Dhabi, 1970; HH Shaikh Khalifa Bin Sulman Al Khalifa, Prime Minister of Bahrain, 2001. Auctioned 5 wildlife paintings in USA and raised sufficient to purchase Bell Jet Ranger helicopter to combat game poaching in Zambia, 1971; painted Tiger Fire, for Operation Tiger, 1973; presented with 1896 steam locomotive by Pres. Kenneth Kaunda of Zambia (its return to Britain subject of BBC TV documentary, Last Train to Mulobezi); purchased 2 main line steam locomotives from BR, 1967 (92203 Black Prince, 75209 The Green Knight); Founder Chm., E Somerset Railway. BBC made 50-minute colour life documentary, The Man Who Loves Giants, 1970; series, In Search of Wildlife, in which he is shown tracking down and painting endangered species, Thames TV, 1988. Established The David Shepherd Conservation, subseq. Wildlife, Foundn, 1984. Mem. of Honour, World Wildlife Fund, 1979. FRGS 1989; FRSA 1986. Freeman, City of London, 2004. Hon. DFA, Pratt Inst., New York, for services to wildlife conservation, 1971; Hon. DSc Hatfield Polytechnic, 1990. OStJ 1996. Order of the Golden Ark, Netherlands, for services to wildlife conservation (Zambia, Operation Tiger, etc), 1973. *Publications:* Artist in Africa, 1967; (autobiog.) The Man who Loves Giants, 1975; Paintings of Africa and India, 1978; A Brush with Steam, 1983; David Shepherd: the man and his paintings, 1985; An Artist in Conversation, 1992; David Shepherd: my painting life, 1995; Painting with David Shepherd, 2004. *Recreations:* driving steam engines, raising money for wildlife. *Address:* Brooklands Farm, Hammerwood, East Grinstead, West Sussex RH19 3QA. *T:* (01342) 302480. *E:* david@davidshepherdartist.co.uk.

SHEPHERD, Richard Thorley, FRCPath, FFFLM; Senior Lecturer in Forensic Medicine and Head of Forensic Medicine Unit, St George's Hospital Medical School, 1996–2010; Hon. Consultant, Forensic Pathology, Royal Liverpool Hospital, since 2007; *b* 20 Sept. 1952; *s* of George and Lucy Shepherd; *m* 1st, 1978, Jane Caroline Malcolm (marr. diss. 2007); one *s* one *d*; 2nd, 2008, Linda Evelyn Teebay. *Educ:* University Coll. London (BSc Hons); St George's Hosp. Med. Sch. (MB BS 1977). DMJ 1984; MRCPath 1987, FRCPath 1997; FFFLM 2006. Lectr in Forensic Medicine, St George's Hosp. Med. Sch., 1981–86; Lectr in Forensic Medicine, 1986–88, Sen. Lectr, 1988–96, UMDS of Guy's and St Thomas' Hosps. Visiting Professor: City Univ., 2007–13; Chester Univ., 2013–. Civilian Consultant to RAF, 2006–12. Asst Ed., Medico-Legal Jl, 1986–97. President: Sect. of Clin. Forensic and Legal Medicine, RSocMed, 2003–05; British Assoc. in Forensic Medicine, 2004–06. Member:

Tribunal Service, Criminal Injuries Compensation (formerly Criminal Injuries Compensation Appeals Panel), 2000–10; Ind. Adv. Panel on Non-Compliance Mgt, UK Border Agency, Home Office, 2013–14. Expert Advisor: Bloody Sunday Inquiry, 1998–2002; Operation Paget (inquiry into the death of Diana, Princess of Wales), 2004–08; Attorney Gen.'s Rev. concerning reopening of inquest into death of Dr David Kelly, 2010–11; Ind. Pathology Expert, Hillsborough Stadium Disaster Inquests, 2013–; Member: Ministerial Ind. Adv. Gp on Deaths in Custody, 2009–; Restraint Adv. Bd (formerly Accreditation Panel), 2010–12; Bd, Faculty of Forensic and Legal Medicine, RCP, 2010–14; Ind Review into Self-Inflicted Deaths in Custody of 18–24 year-olds (Harris Review), MoJ, 2014–15. Presenter, TV series: Death Detective, 2006; Autopsy (4 series), 2014–15. *Publications:* Simpson's Forensic Medicine, 12th edn 2003; (contrib.) A Physician's Guide to Clinical Forensic Medicine, 2000, 3rd edn 2011; (contrib.) Fire Toxicity, 2011. *Recreation:* flying light aircraft. *Address:* Forensic Pathology Unit, Royal Liverpool Hospital, Liverpool L69 3GA. *Clubs:* Athenæum, Lansdowne.

SHEPHERD-BARRON, Prof. Nicholas Ian, PhD; FRS 2006; Professor of Geometry, King's College London, since 2013; *b* 17 March 1955; *s* of late John Adrian Shepherd-Barron, OBE and (Jane Patricia) Caroline Shepherd-Barron; *m* 1988, Michelle Stern; one *d. Educ:* Winchester; Jesus Coll., Cambridge (BA 1976); Warwick Univ. (PhD 1981). Asst Prof., Columbia Univ., NY, 1982–86; Asst, then Associate, Prof., Univ. of Illinois, Chicago, 1986–93; University of Cambridge: Lectr, 1990–97; Reader, 1997–2000; Prof. of Algebraic Geometry, 2000–13; Fellow, Trinity Coll., Cambridge, 1990–. *Publications:* papers in mathematical jls. *Recreation:* learning the piano. *Address:* Department of Mathematics, Strand, King's College London, WC2R 2LS. *T:* (020) 7848 7126. *E:* nicholas.shepherd-barron@kcl.ac.uk.

SHEPLEY, Christopher John, CBE 2002; Principal, Chris Shepley Planning Consultancy; *b* 27 Dec. 1944; *s* of George Frederick Shepley and Florence Mildred Shepley (*née* Jepson); *m* 1st, 1967, Jennifer Webber (marr. diss. 1992); one *s* one *d*; 2nd, 1998, Janet Winifred Molyneux. *Educ:* Stockport Grammar Sch.; LSE (BA Hons Geography); Univ. of Manchester (DipTP). MRTPI. Manchester City Council, 1966–73; Greater Manchester County Council, 1973–85 (Dep. County Planning Officer, 1984–85); Plymouth City Council: City Planning Officer, 1985–92; Dir of Develt, 1992–94; Chief Planning Inspector and Chief Exec., Planning Inspectorate Agency, DoE, then DETR, then DTLR, then ODPM and Welsh Office, then Nat. Assembly for Wales, 1994–2002. Mem., Architecture Adv. Gp, Arts Council England (formerly Arts Council of England), 1992–2003. Chm., Bath Festivals Trust, 2003–06; Trustee, Theatres Trust, 2003–12. Chm., Nat. Retail Planning Forum, 2013–. Pres., RTPI, 1989. Honorary Visiting Professor: Univ. of Manchester Dept of Planning and Landscape, 1990–94; Univ. of Westminster, 2007–. Hon. DSc West of England, 2001. *Publications:* The Grotton Papers, 1979; (contrib.) Plymouth: a maritime city in transition, 1990; Grotton Revisited, 2010; articles in planning and local govt jls. *Recreations:* music, watching sport, travel, walking. *Address:* Greenleas, Perrymead, Bath BA2 5AX. *T:* (01225) 834499.

SHEPPARD, Andy; jazz saxophonist and composer; *b* 20 Jan. 1957; *s* of Philip Charles Sheppard and Irene Sheppard (*née* Rhymes); *m* Rebecca Sian, *d* of Rod Allerton (marr. diss.); one *s* one *d*; *m* 2013, Sara Da Costa. *Educ:* Bishop Wordsworth Grammar Sch. Performances with bands incl. Urban Sax, In Co Motion, Big Co Motion, Inclassifiable, Moving Image (tours of UK, Europe, world). Composer for TV, film, theatre and dance. Recordings incl. Introductions in the Dark, Soft on the Inside, In Co Motion, Rhythm Method, Inclassifiable, Songs with Legs, Moving Image, Delivery Suite, Learning to Wave, Nocturnal Tourist, Music for a New Crossing, PS, Deep River, The Lost Chords find Paolo Fresu, On the Edge of a Perfect Moment, Movements in Colour, Trio Libero, Surrounded by Sea. *Address:* c/o Serious Ltd, 51 Kingsway Place, Sans Walk, EC1R 0LU.

SHEPPARD, Audley William; QC 2015; Partner, Clifford Chance LLP, since 1995; *b* Hastings, NZ, 19 Aug. 1960; *s* of William Searle Sheppard and Joyce Marion Sheppard (*née* Audley); *m* 1997, Amanda Caroline Carter; one *s* one *d. Educ:* Hereworth Sch., Havelock North, NZ; Lindisfarne Coll., Hastings, NZ; Victoria Univ. of Wellington (LLB Hons 1983; BCA 1984); Sidney Sussex Coll., Cambridge (LLM 1986). With Bell Gully, NZ, 1984–85; admitted as barrister and solicitor, NZ, 1985; joined Coward Chance, subseq. Clifford Chance LLP, 1986; admitted as solicitor, England and Wales, 1990. Vice Pres., London Court of Internat. Arbitration, 2012–. Vis. Prof., Sch. of Internat. Arbitration, QMUL, 2011–. Co-Chair, Arbitration Cttee, Internat. Bar Assoc., 2006–08. *Recreation:* family. *Address:* Clifford Chance LLP, 10 Upper Bank Street, Canary Wharf, E14 5JJ. *T:* (020) 7006 1000, *Fax:* (020) 7006 5555. *E:* audley.sheppard@cliffordchance.com. *Club:* Roehampton.

SHEPPARD, Francis Henry Wollaston; General Editor, Survey of London, 1954–82, retired; *b* 10 Sept. 1921; *s* of late Leslie Alfred Sheppard; *m* 1st, 1949, Pamela Gordon Davies (*d* 1954); one *s* one *d*; 2nd, 1957, Elizabeth Fleur Lees (*d* 2014); one *d. Educ:* Bradfield; King's Coll., Cambridge (MA); PhD London. FRHistS. Asst Archivist, West Sussex CC, Chichester, 1947–48; Asst Keeper, London Museum, 1948–53. Mayor of Henley on Thames, 1970–71; Pres., Henley Symphony Orchestra, 1973–76. Visiting Fellow, Leicester Univ., 1977–78; Alice Davis Hitchcock Medallion of Soc. of Architectural Historians of Gt Britain, 1964. *Publications:* Local Government in St Marylebone 1688–1835, 1958; London 1808–1870: The Infernal Wen, 1971; Brakspear's Brewery, Henley on Thames, 1779–1979, 1979; The Treasury of London's Past, 1991; London: a history, 1998; (ed) Survey of London, Vols XXVI–XLI, 1956–83. *Address:* 10 Albion Place, West Street, Henley on Thames, Oxon RG9 2DT. *T:* (01491) 574658.

SHEPPARD, Maurice Raymond, RWS; painter; President, Royal Society of Painters in Water-Colours, 1984–87; *b* 25 Feb. 1947; *s* of late Wilfred Ernest Sheppard and of Florence Hilda (*née* Morris). *Educ:* Loughborough; Kingston upon Thames (Dip AD Hons 1970); Royal College of Art (MA 1973). ARWS 1974, RWS 1977, Vice-Pres., 1978–83, Trustee, 1983–95, Hon. Retired Mem., 2002; NEAC 2000. One man exhibitions: New Grafton Gallery, 1979; Christopher Wood Gall., 1989; inaugural exhibn of L'Institut Européen de l'Aquarelle, Brussels, 1986; Casgliad Maurice Sheppard Collection, Nat. Library of Wales, 2007; works in: Royal Library, Windsor; BM; Contemporary Art Soc. for Wales; V&A; Nat. Museum of Wales; Beecroft Museum and Art Gallery, Southend; Birmingham City Mus. and Art Gallery; Glynn Vivian Mus., Swansea; Towner Art Gall., Eastbourne; Nat. Library of Wales; Tullie House, Carlisle; Topsham Mus., Devon; watercolour: The Golden Valley (for film, Shadowlands, 1993). British Instn Award, 1971; David Murray Landscape Award, 1972; Geoffrey Crawshay Meml Travelling Schol., Univ. of Wales, 1973. *Publications:* articles and essays in jls and catalogues; *relevant publication:* Maurice Sheppard, RWS, by Felicity Owen (Old Watercolour Society Club, vol. 59, 1984). *Recreations:* cycling, a small garden, the pursuit of quiet. *Address:* 33 St Martins Park, Haverfordwest, Pembrokeshire SA61 2HP. *T:* (01437) 762659.

SHEPPARD, Prof. Michael Charles, PhD; FRCP; Professor of Medicine, University of Birmingham, since 1986 (William Withering Professor of Medicine, 2000–08; Provost and Vice-Principal, 2008–13); *b* 24 Jan. 1947; *s* of Kenneth Alfred and Eileen Maude Sheppard; *m* 1973, Judith Elaine James; two *s* one *d. Educ:* Univ. of Cape Town (MB, ChB; PhD 1979). MRCP 1974, FRCP 1985. University of Birmingham: Wellcome Trust Sen. Lectr, Dept of Medicine, 1982–86; Hd, Dept of Medicine, 1992–2006; Vice Dean, 2000–07, Dean and Hd, 2007, Med. Sch.; Pro-Vice-Chancellor, 2007–08; Hon. Consultant Physician, Queen Elizabeth Hosp., Birmingham, 1982–. Pres., Assoc. of Physicians of GB and Ireland, 2009–10. Founder FMedSci, 1998. *Publications:* numerous contribs to learned jls and works on clinical and experimental endocrinology. *Recreations:* coastal walking, sport, glass and porcelain collecting. *Address:* University of Birmingham, Edgbaston, Birmingham B15 2TT. *T:* (0121) 414 5938. *Club:* Edgbaston Priory (Birmingham).

SHEPPARD, Maj.-Gen. Peter John, CB 1995; CBE 1991 (OBE 1982); Controller (Chief Executive), Soldiers, Sailors, Airmen and Families Association—Forces Help, 1996–2004; *b* 15 Aug. 1942; *s* of Kenneth Wescombe Sheppard and Margaret Sheppard; *m* 1964, Sheila Elizabeth Bell; one *s* one *d. Educ:* Welbeck Coll.; RMA Sandhurst; RMCS (BScEng 1st Class Hons London Univ.). Commnd Royal Engineers, 1962; Staff Coll., 1974 (psc); British Embassy, Washington, 1975; OC 29 Field Sqn, 1977 (despatches 1978); GSO1 Mil. Ops, MoD, 1980; CO 35 Engineer Regt, 1982; ACOS, HQ 1st (BR) Corps, 1984; Comdr Corps RE, 1st (BR) Corps, 1986; Dir, Army Plans and Programmes, MoD, 1989; COS HQ BAOR, 1991; Dir Gen. Logistic Policy (Army), MoD, 1993; COS HQ QMG, 1994. Special Advr, H of C Defence Select Cttee, 1997–2001. Dir, Army Charitable Adv. Co., 2004–08. Chairman: RE Officers Widows Soc., 2000–06; REACH Volunteering, 2009–12. Chm., ABF the Soldiers Charity (formerly Army Benevolent Fund), 2011– (Trustee, 2006–). Gov., Royal Sch., Hampstead, 1997–2004 (Chm., Bd of Govs, 1999–2004). *Publications:* contribs to RE Jl, NATO's 16 Nations, Officer mag. *Recreations:* golf, philately, travel. *Address:* c/o Lloyds, 3 Allendale Place, Tynemouth, Tyne and Wear NE30 4RA. *Club:* Army and Navy.

SHEPPARD, Thomas; MP (SNP) Edinburgh East, since 2015; *b* Coleraine, NI, 6 March 1959; partner, Catherine Louise Burton; two step *d. Educ:* Aberdeen Univ. (MA Sociol. and Politics 1982). Vice Pres., NUS, 1982–84; work in PR and campaigns: Capa Ltd, 1984–86; Camden LBC, 1986–88; Islington LBC, 1988–93; Edinburgh DC, 1993–94; Asst Gen. Sec., Labour Party in Scotland, 1994–97; Dir, Stand Comedy Club, 1998–2015. Mem. (Lab) Hackney LBC, 1986–94 (Dep. Leader, 1990–94). *Address:* House of Commons, SW1A 0AA. *E:* tommy.sheppard.mp@parliament.uk.

SHEPPERSON, Prof. George Albert, CBE 1989; William Robertson Professor of Commonwealth and American History, University of Edinburgh, 1963–86, now Emeritus; *b* 7 Jan. 1922; *s* of late Albert Edward Shepperson and Bertha Agnes (*née* Jennings); *m* 1952, Joyce Irene (*née* Cooper) (*d* 2006); one *d. Educ:* King's Sch., Peterborough; St John's Coll., Cambridge (Schol.; 1st Class Hons: English Tripos, Pt I, 1942; Historical Tripos, Pt II, 1947); 1st Cl. CertEd (Cantab), 1948. Served War, commnd Northamptonshire Regt, seconded to KAR, 1942–46. Edinburgh University: Lectr in Imperial and American History, 1948, Sen. Lectr, 1960, Reader, 1961; Dean of Faculty of Arts, 1974–77. Visiting Professor: Roosevelt and Chicago Univs, 1959; Makerere Coll., Uganda, 1962; Dalhousie Univ., 1968–69; Rhode Is Coll., 1984; Vis. Scholar, W. E. B. DuBois Inst. for Afro-American Res., Harvard Univ., 1986–87; Lectures: Herskovits Meml, Northwestern Univ., 1966 and 1972; Livingstone Centenary, RGS, 1973; Soc. of the Cincinnati, State of Virginia, 1976; Sarah Tryphena Phillips, in Amer. Lit. and Hist., British Acad., 1979; Rhodes Commem., Rhodes Univ., 1981; Alan Graham Meml, Queen's Univ., Belfast, 1992. Chairman: British Assoc. for American Studies, 1971–74; Mungo Park Bicentenary Cttee, 1971; David Livingstone Documentation Project, 1973–89; Commonwealth Inst., Scotland, 1973–89; Mem., Marshall Aid Commemoration Commn, 1976–88. Hon. Life Mem., 2011, Hd of Roll of Honour, 2011, Soc. of Malaŵi. FEIS 1990. DUniv: York, 1987; Edinburgh, 1991; Hon. DLitt Malaŵi, 2002. Jt Editor, Oxford Studies in African Affairs, 1969–85. Dist. Africanist Award, African Studies Assoc. UK, 2008. *Publications:* Independent African: John Chilembwe, 1958, 6th edn 2000; David Livingstone and the Rovuma, 1964; many articles and chapters in learned jls, collaborative vols and encycs. *Recreations:* reading, music. *Address:* 15 Farleigh Fields, Orton Wistow, Peterborough PE2 6YB. *T:* (01733) 238772.

SHER, Sir Antony, KBE 2000; actor, writer, artist; *b* 14 June 1949; *s* of late Emmanuel and Margery Sher; civil partnership 2005, Gregory Doran, *qv. Educ:* Sea Point Boys' Junior and High Schools, Cape Town; Webber-Douglas Acad. of Dramatic Art, London, 1969–71. Repertory seasons at Liverpool Everyman, Nottingham Playhouse and Royal Lyceum, Edinburgh; John, Paul, George, Ringo and Bert; Teeth and Smiles; Goose-Pimples; Torch Song Trilogy, Albery, 1985; National Theatre: True West; The Trial, The Resistible Rise of Arturo Ui, 1991; Uncle Vanya, 1992; Stanley, 1996 (also NY, 1997); Primo, 2004 (also Cape Town, and NY, 2005); Royal Shakespeare Co.: Associate Artist, 1982–; Richard III, Merchant of Venice, Twelfth Night, King Lear, The Revenger's Tragedy, Molière, Tartuffe, Hello and Goodbye, Maydays, Red Noses, Singer, Tamburlaine the Great, Travesties, Cyrano de Bergerac, The Winter's Tale, Macbeth, The Roman Actor, The Malcontent, Othello, (co-prodn with Baxter Th., Cape Town) The Tempest, (dir) Breakfast with Mugabe, Henry IV Parts 1 and 2; Death of a Salesman; Titus Andronicus, Johannesburg and RNT, 1995; Mahler's Conversion, Aldwych, 2001; (also writer) I.D., Almeida, 2003; Kean, Apollo, 2007; An Enemy of the People, Sheffield Crucible, 2010; Broken Glass, Tricycle Th., 2010, transf. Vaudeville, 2011; Travelling Light, NT, 2012; Hysteria, Theatre Royal, Bath, 2012, Hampstead Th., 2013; The Captain of Köpenick, NT, 2013; *films:* Shadey, 1986; The Young Poisoner's Handbook, 1995; Alive and Kicking, 1996; Mrs Brown, 1997; Shakespeare in Love, 1999; Churchill the Hollywood Years, 2004; *television series:* The History Man, 1980; The Jury, 2002; *television films:* The Land of Dreams, 1990; Genghis Cohen, 1994; Macbeth, 2001; Home, 2003; Primo, 2007; God on Trial, 2008. Art exhibitions: Barbican, 1985; NT, 1996, 2009; London Jewish Cultural Centre, 2007; Sheffield Crucible Th., 2010; Coventry Herbert Gall., 2010. Hon. DLitt: Liverpool, 1998; Exeter, 2003; Warwick, 2007; Cape Town, 2010. Best Actor Awards: Drama Magazine, 1984; Laurence Olivier, 1985, 1997; Evening Standard, 1985; TMA, 1995; Evening Standard Peter Sellers Film Award, 1998; Best Solo Performance Awards, NY Drama Desk and Outer Critics Circle, 2006; Best Shakespearean Performance, Critics Circle, 2014. *Publications:* Year of the King, 1985; Middlepost (novel), 1988; Characters (paintings and drawings), 1989; Changing Step (TV filmscript), 1989; The Indoor Boy (novel), 1991; Cheap Lives (novel), 1995; (with Greg Doran) Woza Shakespeare!, 1996; The Feast (novel), 1998; Beside Myself (memoir), 2001; I.D. (stageplay), 2003; Primo (stageplay), 2005; Primo Time, 2005; The Giant (stageplay), 2007; Year of the Fat Knight: the Falstaff diaries, 2015. *Address:* c/o Paul Lyon-Maris, Independent Talent Group Ltd, 40 Whitfield Street, W1T 2RH. *T:* (020) 7636 6565.

SHER, Samuel Julius, (Jules); QC 1981; a Deputy High Court Judge, Chancery Division and Commercial Court, 1989–2010; *b* 22 Oct. 1941; *s* of Philip and Isa Phyllis Sher; *m* 1965, Sandra Maris; one *s* two *d. Educ:* Athlone High Sch., Johannesburg; Univ. of the Witwatersrand (BComm, LLB); New Coll., Oxford (BCL). Called to the Bar, Inner Temple, 1968, Bencher, 1988; Hd of Chambers, Wilberforce Chambers, 2006–10. Special Advr to Attorney-Gen. of Singapore on Mgt of Complex Disputes, 2012–. Mem., Ethics Cttee, Tate, 2007–. Qualified Mediator, 2012; Arbitrator, Wilberforce Chambers, 2014–. *Recreation:* tennis. *Address:* 12 Constable Close, NW11 6TY. *T:* (020) 8455 2753.

See also V. H. Sher.

SHER, Victor Herman, (Harold), CA (SA); Executive Chairman, Amalgamated Metal Corporation Plc, since 2015 (Chief Executive, 1992–2015); *b* 13 Jan. 1947; *s* of Philip Sher and Isa Phyllis Sher; *m* 1979, Molly Sher; one *s* three *d. Educ:* King Edward VII Sch., Johannesburg; Univ. of the Witwatersrand, Johannesburg (BComm). Chartered Accountant, Fuller, Jenks Beechcroft, 1972–73; Amalgamated Metal Corporation: Taxation Manager, 1973; Finance Manager, 1977; Dir of Corporate Finance, 1978; Dir of Corporate Treasury,

1981; Finance Dir, 1983; Finance and Trading Dir, 1986; Gp Man. Dir, 1988–92. Chm. of Trustees, Amalgamated Metal Corp. Pension Scheme, 1983–91 (Trustee, 1978). *Recreation:* golf.

See also S. J. Sher.

SHERATON, Kenneth Frederick; a District Judge (Magistrates' Courts) for Cambridgeshire, since 2006; *b* 23 July 1955; *s* of Antony and Marian G. Sheraton; *m* 2003, Jayne Claire, *d* of Peter and Audrey Bustin; one *s* one *d* from a previous marriage. *Educ:* Kingsbury County Grammar Sch.; Bristol Poly. (Dip Magisterial Law 1980); Inns of Court Sch. of Law. Called to the Bar, Gray's Inn, 1983; admitted solicitor, 1991. Magistrates' Court Clerk, then Principal Court Clerk, 1976–90; Solicitor, Messrs Hodders, London, 1990–2000; freelance solicitor, 2000–06. Committee Member: Central and S Middx Law Soc., 1994–96; London Criminal Courts Solicitors Assoc., 2003–06. *Recreations:* most sports, watching Queens Park Rangers Football Club, travel, walking. *Address:* c/o Peterborough Magistrates' Court, The Court House, Bridge Street, Peterborough PE1 1ED. *T:* 0845 310 0575, *Fax:* (01733) 313749. *E:* districtjudge.sheraton@judiciary.gsi.gov.uk.

SHERBOK, Dan C.; *see* Cohn-Sherbok.

SHERBORNE, Bishop Suffragan of; *no new appointment at time of going to press.*

SHERBORNE, Archdeacon of; *see* Taylor, Ven. P. S.

SHERBORNE, Montague; QC 1993; *b* 2 Dec. 1930; *s* of Abraham and Rose Sherborne; *m* 1963, Josephine Valerie Jay; two *s* one *d. Educ:* East Ham Grammar Sch.; New Coll., Oxford (BA Hons PPE); London Univ. (PGCE). Teaching, E London, 1954–58; called to the Bar, Middle Temple, 1960 (Harmsworth Schol.). *Recreations:* bridge, my grandchildren. *Address:* 47 Shirehall Park, NW4 2QN.

SHERBOURNE OF DIDSBURY, Baron *cr* 2013 (Life Peer), of Didsbury in the City of Manchester; **Stephen Ashley Sherbourne,** Kt 2006; CBE 1988; *b* 15 Oct. 1945; *s* of late Jack and Blanche Sherbourne. *Educ:* Burnage Grammar Sch., Manchester; St Edmund Hall, Oxford (MA PPE). Hill Samuel, 1968–70; Conservative Research Dept, 1970–75: Head of Economic Section, 1973–74; Asst Dir, 1974–75; Head of Rt Hon. Edward Heath's Office, 1975–76; Gallaher, 1978–82; Special Adviser to Rt Hon. Patrick Jenkin, (then) Sec. of State for Industry, 1982–83; Political Sec. to the Prime Minister, 1983–88; Sen. Corporate Communications Consultant, Lowe Bell Communications, 1988–92; Man. Dir, Lowe Bell Consultants, subseq. Bell Pottinger Consultants, 1992–99; Chm., Lowe Bell Political, subseq. Bell Pottinger Public Affairs, 1994–2001; Dir, Chime Communications plc, 2001–03; Chief of Staff to Leader of the Opposition, 2003–05. Director: Newscounter, 2007–10; Smithfield Consultants, 2006–; Trufflenet, 2010–14; Chm., Interel Consulting UK, 2012–13. Mem., Policy Adv. Bd, Social Mkt Foundn, 2007–. Trustee, China Oxford Scholarship Fund, 2006–11. *Recreations:* cinema, tennis, music, theatre. *Address:* House of Lords, SW1A 0PW. *E:* sherbournes@parliament.uk. *Clubs:* Reform, Beefsteak.

SHERCLIFF, Simon, OBE 2004; HM Diplomatic Service; Deputy High Commissioner, Abuja, since 2014; *b* 23 Dec. 1972; *s* of Robin Frank Shercliff and Judith Shercliff; *m* 2002, Emma Louise Cole; one *s* one *d. Educ:* High Ham Primary Sch.; Wells Cathedral Sch.; St Catharine's Coll., Cambridge (BA Hons Nat. Scis 1995). Chemistry teacher, VSO, Tanzania, 1995–97; FCO, 1998; Pol Officer, Tehran, 2000–03; Private Sec. to Prime Minister's Special Rep. for Iraq, Baghdad, 2003–04; Press Officer, FCO, 2004–06; Actg Press Sec. for Foreign Sec. and Dir Commns, 2006; Pol Officer, Kabul, 2007–08; First Sec., Washington, 2006–11; Dep. Hd, S Asia Dept, 2011–12, Hd, Counter-Terrorism Dept, 2012–14, FCO. Trustee, Orphans in the Wild charity, Tanzania, 2005–. *Recreations:* biking, running and outdoor pursuits, cricket, Rugby, mountains, Tanzania, gardening. *Address:* c/o Foreign and Commonwealth Office, King Charles Street, SW1A 2AH. *T:* (020) 7008 4970, (Nigeria) (9) 462 2203. *E:* simon.shercliff@fco.gov.uk. *Clubs:* Hawks, Vann (Cambridge); 1890; Incogniti Cricket.

SHERFIELD, 3rd Baron *cr* 1964, of Sherfield-on-Loddon, Southampton; **Dwight William Makins;** *b* 2 March 1951; *yr s* of 1st Baron Sherfield, GCB, GCMG, FRS and Alice Brooks (*d* 1985), *e d* of Hon. Dwight Davis; *S* brother, 2006; *m* 1st, 1983, Penelope Massy Collier (marr. diss.); 2nd, 2010, Jennifer Rolls. *Educ:* Winchester; Christ Church, Oxford (MA). Man. Dir, John Govett & Co. Ltd, 1984–88; Chairman: Cadiz Inc., 1992–2002; Greenway plc, 1997–99. *Recreation:* National Hunt racing. *Heir:* none. *Club:* Boodle's.

SHERGOLD, Peter Roger, AC 2007 (AM 1996); PhD; Chancellor and Chairman, Board of Trustees, University of Western Sydney, since 2011; *b* 27 Sept. 1946; *s* of Archibald Amos Shergold and Kathleen Dora Shergold; *m* Carol Green; one *d. Educ:* Univ. of Hull (BA 1967); Univ. of Illinois (MA 1968); LSE (PhD 1976). Hd, Dept of Econ. Hist., Univ. of NSW, 1985–87; Dir, Office of Multicultural Affairs, 1987–90; Chief Executive Officer: Aboriginal and Torres Strait Islander Commn, 1991–94; Comcare Australia, 1994–95; Comr, Public Service and Merit Protection Commn, 1995–98; Secretary: Dept of Employment, Workplace Relns and Small Business, 1998–2002; Dept of Educn, Sci. and Trng, 2002–03; Dept of the Prime Minister and Cabinet, 2003–08. Macquarie Gp Foundn Prof. (formerly Chief. Exec.), Centre for Social Impact, Univ. of NSW, 2008–12. Sen. Vis. Fellow, Singapore Civil Service Coll., 2008–. Director: AMP Ltd, 2008–; AMP Life Ltd, 2008–; Corrs Chambers Westgarth, 2009–; Veda Gp, 2013–; Chm., QuintessenceLabs, 2008–. Chairman: Australian Rural Leadership Foundn, 2008–11; Nat. Centre for Vocational Educn Res., 2009–; NSW Public Service Commn Adv. Bd, 2011–; Aged Care Sector Cttee, 2014–15; Tertiary Educn Quality Standards Agency Adv. Council, 2014–15; Opal Aged Care, 2014–; Higher Educn Standards Panel, 2015–; Member: Prime Minister's Indigenous Adv. Council, 2013–; Council, State Library of NSW, 2015–. Director: Nat. Centre for Indigenous Excellence, 2008–12; Sir John Monash Foundn, 2009–14; Public Sector Renewal Bd, Qld, 2011–15; Chair, Ethics Cttee, Fundraising Inst. of Australia, 2009–11; Dep. Chair, Sydney Writers' Fest., 2011–. FASSA 2005. Centenary Medal, Australia, 2003. *Publications:* Working Class Life, 1982. *Recreations:* history, tennis, ski-ing. *T:* (2) 96787848. *E:* p.shergold@uws.edu.au. *Club:* Commonwealth (Canberra).

SHERIDAN, Christopher Julian; Chairman, Yorkshire Building Society, 2001–06 (non-executive Director, 1995–2006); *b* 18 Feb. 1943; *s* of late Mark Sheridan and Olive Maud Sheridan (*née* Hobbs); *m* 1972, Diane Virginia (*née* Wadey); one *d. Educ:* Berkhamsted School. Joined Samuel Montagu & Co., 1962; Dir, 1974; Managing Dir, 1981; Chief Exec., 1984–94; Dep. Chm., 1988–94. Mem., Internat. Exec. Cttee, Lovells (formerly Lovell White Durrant), 1996–2006. Non-executive Director: Hanover Acceptances Ltd, 1995–; Prudential Bache International Bank, 1996–2004; Minerva plc, 1996–2008; Willmott Dixon Ltd, 1999–2003; Standard Bank Ltd, 1999–; Alpha Bank London, 2004–; Willmott Dixon Hldgs Ltd, 2008–; Dep. Chm., Inspace plc, 2005–08. Mem., Adv. Bd, Alexander Proudfoot, 2010–12. *Recreations:* theatre, travel, tennis.

SHERIDAN, Prof. Desmond John, MD, PhD; FRCP; Professor of Clinical Cardiology, Imperial College London Faculty of Medicine (formerly St Mary's Hospital School of Medicine), 1985–2009, now Emeritus; Consultant Cardiologist: St Mary's Hospital, 1985–2009 (Head of Academic Cardiology, 1985–2006); The Royal Brompton Hospital, 2006–09; *b* 10 Feb. 1948; *s* of Bernard Sheridan and Maureen Sheridan (*née* Kelly); *m* 1971, Jacqueline Hirschfeld; two *s. Educ:* Patrician Coll., Ballyfin; Trinity Coll. Dublin (MB, BAO, BCh 1971; MD 1974); Univ. of Newcastle upon Tyne (PhD 1982). MRCP 1974, FRCP 1987; LRPS 2013. British-American Fellow, Washington Univ., St Louis, 1978–79; Sen. Lectr in Cardiology, Univ. of Wales Coll. of Medicine, 1981–85; Consultant Cardiologist, UCH, Cardiff, 1981–85; Clinical Dean, ICSM, 1998–2001. Member: Nat. Forum for Prevention of Coronary Heart Disease, 1991–98; Physiology, Medicine and Infections Bd, MRC, 1997–2001. Principal Advr, Cardiovascular Science, Global R&D, Pfizer, 2002–05. John Banks Medal and Travelling Fellow, 1974. *Publications:* (contrib.) Early Arrhythmias from Myocardial Ischaemia, 1982; (contrib.) Autonomic Failure, 1988; (contrib.) Clinical Aspects of Cardiac Arrhythmias, 1989; (contrib.) Cerebrovascular Ischaemia: investigation and management, 1996; Left Ventricular Hypertrophy, 1998; Innovation in the Biopharmaceutical Industry, 2007; Medical Science in the 21st Century: sunset or new dawn, 2012; peer reviewed articles relating to disturbances in heart rhythm and normal and abnormal growth of heart muscle. *Recreations:* country walking, making furniture, letter writing, photography. *Address:* Brackenwood, Holne, Newton Abbot, Devon TQ13 7RU. *E:* d.sheridan@imperial.ac.uk.

SHERIDAN, Francis Anthony; His Honour Judge Sheridan; a Circuit Judge, since 2009; Resident Judge, Aylesbury and Amersham Crown Courts, since 2014; *b* Belfast, 24 Jan. 1957; *s* of Maurice Joseph Sheridan and Kathleen Sheridan (*née* O'Hare); *m* 1987, Colette Maggs; three *s* two *d. Educ:* Chelmer Inst. of Higher Educn (BA Hons; BL). Called to the Bar: Inner Temple, 1980; Ireland, 1991; NI, 1994; Recorder, 2005–09. Gov., Chesham Prep. Sch., 2001–14 (Chm., 2010–14). Hon. Recorder of Aylesbury, 2011–. *Publications:* (contrib.) Inns of Court Advocacy Manual, 1987; (contrib.) Criminal Plea Bargains in the English and Polish Administration, 2011. *Recreations:* farming, power boating, gardening, sub-aqua diving. *Address:* Aylesbury Crown Court, County Hall, 38 Market Square, Aylesbury HP20 1XD.

SHERIDAN, James; *b* 24 Nov. 1952; *s* of Frank and Annie Sheridan; *m* 1977, Jean McDowell; one *s* one *d. Educ:* St Pius Secondary Sch., Drumchapel, Glasgow. Worked in manufacturing industry since leaving school, 1967; full-time Trade Union Official, TGWU, 1998–99. MP (Lab) W Renfrewshire, 2001–05, Paisley and Renfrewshire N, 2005–15; contested (Lab) same seat, 2015. *Recreations:* leisure activities, current affairs.

SHERIDAN, Prof. Lionel Astor, PhD, LLD; Professor of Law, University College, Cardiff, 1971–88 (Acting Principal, 1980 and 1987); retired; *b* 21 July 1927; *s* of Stanley Frederick and Anne Agnes Sheridan; *m* 1948, Margaret Helen (*née* Béghin); one *s* (one *d* decd). *Educ:* Whitgift Sch., Croydon; University College London (LLB 1947; LLD 1969); Queen's Univ., Belfast (PhD 1953). Called to the Bar, Lincoln's Inn, 1948. Part-time Lectr, Univ. of Nottingham, 1949; Lectr, QUB, 1949–56; Prof. of Law, Univ. of Singapore (formerly Univ. of Malaya in Singapore), 1956–63; Prof. of Comparative Law, QUB, 1963–71. Hon. LLD Univ. of Singapore, 1963. *Publications:* Fraud in Equity, 1957; Constitutional Protection, 1963; Rights in Security, 1974; Injunctions and Similar Orders, 1999; *jointly:* The Cy-près Doctrine, 1959; Constitution of Malaysia, 1961, 5th edn 2004; Malaya, Singapore, The Borneo Territories, 1961; Equity, 1969, 3rd edn 1987; Survey of the Land Law of Northern Ireland, 1971; The Modern Law of Charities, 1971, 4th edn 1992; The Law of Trusts, 10th edn 1974, 12th edn 1993; The Comparative Law of Trusts in the Commonwealth and the Irish Republic, 1976; Digest of the English Law of Trusts, 1979; papers in jls. *Recreations:* reading, theatre-going. *Address:* 9 Warwick House, Westgate Street, Cardiff CF10 1DH. *Club:* Athenæum.

SHERIDAN, Susan Elizabeth; *see* Norman, S. E.

SHERIDAN, Tommy; Member for Glasgow, Scottish Parliament, 1999–2007 (Scot Socialist, 1999–2006, Solidarity Group, 2006–07); Co-Convenor, Solidarity (Scotland), since 2006; *b* 1964; *m* 2000, Gail; one *d. Educ:* Lourdes Secondary Sch., Glasgow; Univ. of Stirling. Former Columnist: Daily Record; Sunday Herald; Scottish Socialist Voice. Mem. (Scot Mil Lab) Glasgow Council, 1992–2007. Nat. Convenor, Scottish Socialist Party, 1999–2004. Contested: (Scot Mil Lab) Glasgow Pollok, 1992; (Solidarity) Glasgow NE, Nov. 2009; (Trade Unionist and Socialist Coalition) Glasgow NE, 2010. Contested (No2EU) Scotland, Eur. Parlt, 2009. Pres., Anti-Poll Tax Fedn, 1989–92. *Publications:* (jtly) A Time to Rage, 1994; (with Alan McCombes) Imagine, 2000. *Address:* 2005 Paisley Road West, Glasgow G52 3TD.

SHERINGHAM, Prof. Michael Hugh Tempest, PhD; FBA 2010; Marshal Foch Professor of French Literature, University of Oxford, since 2004; Fellow, All Souls College, Oxford, since 2004; *b* 2 June 1948; *s* of late John Guy Tempest Sheringham and Yvette Agnès (*née* Habib); *m* 1974, Priscilla Monique Duhamel; one *s* one *d. Educ:* Wallingford County Grammar Sch.; Univ. of Kent at Canterbury (BA 1970; PhD 1993); MA Oxon 2004. Lectr in French, NUI, 1973–74; University of Kent at Canterbury: Lectr, 1974–87; Sen. Lectr, 1987–92; Prof. of French Lit., 1992–95; Prof. of French, Royal Holloway, Univ. of London, 1995–2004; Associate Dir, Inst. of Romance Studies, Univ. of London, 1999–2003. Visiting Professor: Univ. Paris VII, 1995–96; Univ. Paris IV Sorbonne, 2002; Collège de France, 2006; ENS Ulm, 2007; Pajus Dist. Vis. Prof., Univ. of Calif, Berkeley, 2006. Lectures: Roy Knight Meml, Univ. of Wales, Swansea, 2002; Saintsbury, Univ. of Edinburgh, 2005; Vinaver Meml, Univ. of Manchester, 2006; Kent Inst. for Advanced Studies in Humanities, Univ. of Kent, 2009; AA Files, Architectural Assoc., 2009. Gen. Ed., Cambridge Studies in French, 1996–2001. Pres., Soc. for French Studies, 2002–04. Leverhulme Res. Fellow, 2009–10; Fellow, Camargo Foundn, 2010. Officier, Ordre des Palmes académiques (France), 2006 (Chevalier, 1998). *Publications:* André Breton: a bibliography, 1971; Samuel Beckett: Molloy, 1986; French Autobiography: devices and desires, 1993; (ed) Parisian Fields, 1996; (ed with J. Gratton) The Art of the Project, 2005; Everyday Life: theories and practices from Surrealism to the present, 2006 (trans. French 2013); contribs to learned jls and collective works. *Address:* All Souls College, Oxford OX1 4AL. *T:* (01865) 279347. *E:* michael.sheringham@all-souls.ox.ac.uk.

SHERLOCK, family name of **Baroness Parminter**.

SHERLOCK, Baroness *cr* 2010 (Life Peer), of Durham in the County of Durham; **Maeve Christina Mary Sherlock,** OBE 2000; an Opposition Whip, and Opposition Spokesperson on Work and Pensions, House of Lords, since 2013; *b* 10 Nov. 1960; *d* of William and Roisin Sherlock. *Educ:* Our Lady's Convent, Abingdon; Univ. of Liverpool (BA Hons Sociol. 1984); Open Univ. (MBA 1997); Durham Univ. (MA 2007). Treas., Univ. of Liverpool Guild, 1984–85; National Union of Students: Exec. Officer, 1985–86; Treas., 1986–88; Pres., 1988–90; Dep. Dir, 1990–91, Dir, 1991–97, UKCOSA; Dir, NCOPF, 1997–2000; Advr to the Chancellor of the Exchequer, 2000–03; Chief Exec., British Refugee Council, 2003–06. Chair: Nat. Student Forum, 2008–10; Chapel Street Gp, 2011–. Member: Adv. Bd on Naturalisation and Integration, 2004–; Nat. Refugee Integration Forum, 2006–; Equality and Human Rights Commn, 2007–10. Non-executive Director: Financial Ombudsman Service, 2008–; Child Maintenance and Enforcement Commn, 2008–10. Mem., Exec. Bd, Eur. Assoc. for Internat. Educn, 1994–97. Dir, Endsleigh Insce, 1986–90. Member: Court, Univ. of Warwick, 1993–95; Assembly, Greenwich Univ., 1995–97; Mem. Council and Dir, St John's Coll., Durham Univ., 2008–; Gov., Sheffield Hallam Univ., 1997–2000. Trustee: Nat. Family and Parenting Inst., 1999–2000; Demos, 2004–07. Hon. Fellow, St Chad's Coll., Durham, 2006. DUniv Sheffield Hallam, 2000. *Recreations:* politics, theology, music, books, cooking. *Address:* c/o House of Lords, SW1A 0PW.

SHERLOCK, Barry; *see* Sherlock, E. B. O.

SHERLOCK, David Christopher, CBE 2006; FCGI; Director, Beyond Standards Ltd, since 2007; Chair, Prospects College of Advanced Technology, since 2013; *b* 6 Nov. 1943; *s* of Frank Ernest Sherlock and Emily Edna (*née* Johnson); *m* 1st, 1970, Jean Earl; 2nd, 1976, Cynthia Mary (*née* Hood); one *s* one *d*. *Educ:* Rutlish Sch., Merton; Newcastle upon Tyne College of Art and Industrial Design; Univ. of Nottingham (BA, MPhil). Nottingham Coll. of Art, 1966–70; Trent Polytechnic, 1970–74; Dep. Dir, Nat. College of Art and Design, Dublin, 1975–80; Principal, Winchester Sch. of Art, 1980–87; Exec. Chm., Hampshire Consortium for Art, Design and Architecture, 1985–87; Head of Central Saint Martin's Coll. of Art and Design and Asst Rector, London Inst., 1988–91; Dir of Develt, RCA, 1991–93; Sen. Inspector, Art, Design and Performing Arts, and for SE England, FEFCE, 1993–97; Chief Inspector and Chief Exec., Training Standards Council, 1997–2001; Chief Inspector of Adult Learning and Chief Exec., Adult Learning Inspectorate, 2000–07. Chm., GTA England, 2009–13. City and Guilds of London Institute: Mem., Fellowship Adv. Cttee for Educn, Health and Social Care, 2010–; Chm., Quality and Standards Cttee, 2015–; Professional Lead, Rev. of Professionalism in Further Educn, 2012. Mem., QCA, 2006–09. Pres., NIACE, 2006–12 (Life Mem., 2012); Vice Chm., Inst. for FE, 2013–. Chm., Nat. Skills Acad. for Social Care, 2008–12. FRSA. Award for Services to Lifelong Learning, Assoc. of Coll. Mgt, 2007. *Publications:* (with N. Perry) Quality Improvement in Adult Vocational Education and Training: transforming skills for the global economy, 2008; (contrib.) Further Education: coming of age, 2015. *Recreations:* sailing, mountain biking. *Address:* Poplar Farm, West Tytherley, Salisbury SP5 1NR.

SHERLOCK, (Edward) Barry (Orton), CBE 1991; Chairman, Life Assurance and Unit Trust Regulatory Organisation, 1986–96; *b* 10 Feb. 1932; *s* of Victor Edward and Irene Octavia Sherlock; *m* 1955, Lucy Trerice Willey; two *d*. *Educ:* Merchant Taylors' School; Pembroke College, Cambridge (MA 1st cl. Hons Maths). Joined Equitable Life Assurance Society, 1956; qualified actuary, 1958; Asst Actuary, 1962; Asst Gen. Manager, 1968; Gen. Manager and Actuary, 1972–91; Dir, 1972–94. Director: USS Ltd, 1978–96 (Dep. Chm., 1993–96); M & G Group, 1994–96; Medical Defence Union Ltd, 1994–96. Institute of Actuaries: Hon. Sec., 1978–80; Vice-Pres., 1981–84. Chairman: Life Offices' Assoc., 1985; Life Insurance Council, Assoc. of British Insurers, 1985–86. Trustee, Harvest Help, 1993–96. *Recreations:* music, gardening.

SHERLOCK, Neil Roger, CBE 2015; Partner and Head of Reputational Strategy, PricewaterhouseCoopers, since 2013; *b* Windlesham, Surrey, 13 Aug. 1963; *s* of Roger Sherlock and late Susan Sherlock; *m* 1994, Kathryn Jane, (Kate), Parminter (*see* Baroness Parminter); two *d*. *Educ:* Esher Co. Grammar Sch.; Esher Coll.; Christ Church, Oxford (BA 1st Cl. Hons PPE 1984; Pres., Oxford Union Soc., 1985). Peat Marwick Mitchell, later KPMG Peat Marwick, then KPMG, 1985–2011; Partner, Public Affairs, KPMG, 1999–2011; Vice Chm., KPMG Foundn, 2000–11; Special Advr and Dir of Govt Relns for the Dep. Prime Minister, 2012–13. Contested (Lib Dem) SW Surrey, 1992, 1997. Speechwriter for Rt Hon. Paddy Ashdown, MP, 1988–99, Rt Hon. Charles Kennedy, MP, 2001, Rt Hon. Sir Menzies Campbell, MP, 2006–07; Hd, Communications, leadership campaign of Nick Clegg, MP, 2007; Advr, TV Debates for Nick Clegg, MP, 2010. Member: Armed Forces' Pay Review Body, 2001–07; Commn of Inquiry into Future of Civil Society, 2008–10; Panel on Fair Access to the Professions, 2009. Chairman: Enterprise Europe, 1995–2001; Working Families, 2009–11; Trustee: CentreForum, 2003–11; Heart of the City, 2005–11; HTI, 2007–10; Demos, 2008–11 and 2014–; PwC Foundn, 2014–; Member: Bd of Govs, Inst. for Govt, 2009–11; Speakers' Adv. Council on Public Engagement, 2010–11; Women's Justice Taskforce, Prison Reform Trust, 2010–11. Pres., SW Surrey Lib Dems, 2007–. *Publications:* (ed with Neal Lawson) The Progressive Century: the future of the Centre-Left in Britain, 2001. *Recreations:* cricket, golf, football, reading, theatre. *Address:* The Corner House, Grosvenor Road, Godalming, Surrey GU7 1PA. *Clubs:* National Liberal; Godalming Cricket.

SHERLOCK, Sir Nigel, KCVO 2014; OBE 2003; JP; Lord-Lieutenant, County of Tyne and Wear, 2000–15; *b* 12 Jan. 1940; *s* of late Horace Sherlock and Dorothea Sherlock (*née* Robinson); *m* 1966, Helen Diana Frances Sigmund; two *s* one *d*. *Educ:* Barnard Castle Sch.; Univ. of Nottingham (BA Law). Chief Exec., 1993–2002, Chm., 2002–05, Wise Speke; Director: Ockham Hldgs, 1993–98; Brewin Dolphin Holdings plc, 1998–2002; Brewin Dolphin Securities, 1998–2005; non-executive Director: London Stock Exchange, 1995–2001; Skipton Bldg Soc., 1998–2007. Mem. Bd, Assoc. of Private Client Investment Managers and Stockbrokers, 1993–2003 (non-exec. Dep. Chm., 1995–2003). Mem. Council, NE Regl Chamber of Commerce, 1997–2004 (Pres., 2000–01). Member: Council, Nat. Assoc. of Pension Funds, 1988–90; C of E Pension Bd, 1998–2009. Member: Bishop's Council, Dio. Newcastle, 1975–94; Financial Adv. Cttee, Dean and Chapter of Durham Cathedral, 1997–; Chairman: Council, Newcastle Cathedral, 2002–05 (Hon. Lay Canon, 2007–10, now Emeritus Lay Canon); Crown Nominations Commn for appt of Archbp of York, 2005. Patron, Northumbrian Coalition Against Crime, 2001– (Vice-Patron, 1995–2001). Founder Mem., Community Foundn of Tyne and Wear, 1988 (Vice-Pres., 2001–). Member: Council, 1984–2002 (Pro Chancellor and Chm., 1993–2002), Court, 2002–09 (Emeritus Mem., 2009), Univ. of Newcastle upon Tyne; Council, St John's Coll., Univ. of Durham, 1984–95 (Hon. Fellow, 1997); Bd of Govs, Royal GS, Newcastle upon Tyne, 1998–2006 (Chm., 2000–05). Member: Bd, N Music Trust, 2000–05 (Chm., Fundraising Cttee, 2000–05); Bd, Northern Sinfonia Orchestral Soc., 1974–95 (Chm., 1990–95); Northern Sinfonia Develt Trust, 1980–2001 (Trustee, 1980–2001; Chm., 1981–2001). Pres., Northumberland Co. Scouts, 2000–12 (Mem. Council, 1980–98, Chm., 1990–97; Silver Wolf, 2007). Co-Pres., RFCA, N of England, 2001–. Jt Pres., St John Ambulance, Northumbria, 2001–12. Trustee: Bede Monastery Mus. Trust, 1980–90 (Chm., 1985–90); William Leech Charity, 1990–. Hon. Brother, Trinity House, Newcastle upon Tyne, 1995–. CCMI (CIMgt 2000). Tyne and Wear: High Sheriff, 1990–91, DL, 1995–2000, JP 2001. Hon. Colonel: Royal Marines Reserve Tyne, 2003–12; Northumbrian Univs OTC, 2003–08. Freeman: City of London, 2000; City of Newcastle, 1985; Liveryman, Scriveners' Co. of Newcastle, 1985–. Hon. DCL: Newcastle, 2002; Northumbria, 2006. KStJ 2002. *Recreations:* family, the countryside, listening to music, theatre. *Address:* 14 North Avenue, Gosforth, Newcastle upon Tyne NE3 4DS. *T:* (0191) 285 4379. *Clubs:* Brooks's; Northern Counties (Newcastle upon Tyne).

SHERMAN, Prof. Lawrence William, PhD; Wolfson Professor of Criminology, since 2009, Director, Cambridge Police Executive Programme, since 2007, Director, Jerry Lee Centre of Experimental Criminology, since 2008, and Director, Institute of Criminology, since 2012, University of Cambridge; Fellow of Darwin College, Cambridge, since 2009; *b* 25 Oct. 1949; *s* of Donald L. and Margaret H. Sherman; *m* 1st, 1973, Eva Fass (marr. diss. 2010); one *s* one *d*; 2nd, 2010, Heather Strang. *Educ:* Denison Univ. (BA High Hons Political Sci. 1970); Univ. of Chicago (MA Social Sci. 1970); Darwin Coll., Cambridge (Dip. Criminol. 1973); Yale Univ. (PhD Sociol. 1976); Univ. of Pennsylvania (MA Hons 1999); Univ. of Cambridge (MA Hons 2009). Sloan Foundn Urban Fellow, Office of the Mayor, NYC, 1970–71; Prog. Res. Analyst, NYC Police Dept, 1971–72; Ford Foundn Fellow, Cambridge Univ., 1972–73; Associate-in-Res., Yale Univ., 1974–76; Asst to Associate Prof. of Criminal Justice, SUNY at Albany, 1976–82; University of Maryland, College Park: Associate Prof., 1982–84; Prof., 1984–98; Dist. Univ. Prof., 1998–99 and 2010–; Chair, Dept of Criminol. and Criminal Justice, 1995–99; University of Pennsylvania: Albert M. Greenfield Prof. of Human Relns, 1999–2007; Prof. of Sociol., 1999–2009; Director: Fels Inst. of Govt, 1999–2005; Jerry Lee Center of Criminol., 2000–10; Prof. of Criminol., 2003–09. Seth Boyden Dist. Vis. Prof., Rutgers Univ., 1987; Adjunct Prof., Regulatory Institutions Network, ANU, 1994–. Dir of Res., Police Foundn, Washington, 1979–85; Pres., Crime Control Inst., Washington, 1985–95; Scientific Dir, Reintegrative Shaming Experiments, Australian Fed. Police, 1995–2000; Co-Dir, Justice Res. Consortium, UK, 2001–; Co-Dir, Mid-Career Trng Prog. Phase IV, Nat. Police Acad. of India, 2010–12; non-exec. Dir, Coll. of Policing, 2013–. Mem., Adv. Bd, HM Inspectorate of Constabulary, 2014–. Co-Chm., Jury, Stockholm Prize in Criminol., 2006–. Founding Pres., Acad. Exptl Criminol., 1998 (Fellow 1999; McCord Award, 2006); President: Internat. Soc. of Criminol., 2000–05; Amer. Soc. of Criminol., 2001–02 (Fellow 1994; Sutherland Prize, 1999); Amer. Acad. Political and Social Sci., 2001–05 (Sellin Fellow, 2009); Hon. Pres., British Soc. of Evidence-Based Policing, 2010–. FRSA 2007 (Life Fellow 2011). Hon. PhD (Social Sci.) Stockholm, 2013. Beccaria Medal, German Soc. of Criminol., 2009; Boruch Award, Campbell Collaboration, 2010; Benjamin Franklin Medal, RSA, 2011. *Publications:* Scandal and Reform: controlling police corruption, 1978; Policing Domestic Violence: experiments and dilemmas, 1992; (jtly) Preventing Crime: what works, what doesn't, what's promising, 1997; (ed jtly) Evidence-Based Crime Prevention, 2002; (with Heather Strang) Restorative Justice: the evidence, 2007; contribs to learned jls incl. Amer. Sociol. Rev., Criminology, Jl Amer. Med. Assoc. *Recreations:* running, walking, rowing, swimming, performing in rock band The Hot Spots. *Address:* Institute of Criminology, University of Cambridge, Sidgwick Avenue, Cambridge CB3 9DA. *Club:* Cosmos (Washington).

SHERR, Prof. Avrom Hirsh, PhD; Woolf Professor of Legal Education, Institute of Advanced Legal Studies, University of London, 1995–2014, now Emeritus Professor (Director, 2004–12, on sabbatical, 2012–14); *b* 28 March 1949; *s* of Louis Julian Sherr and Charlotte Maissel; *m* 1974, Lorraine Isaacs; three *s* one *d*. *Educ:* Carmel Coll. (Sch. Bursary); London Sch. of Econs (LLB 1971); Sch. of Law, Univ. of Warwick (PhD 1992). Admitted solicitor, 1974, Coward Chance; University of Warwick: Lectr in Law, Sch. of Law, 1974–90; Dir, Legal Practice, 1976–90; University of Liverpool: Alsop-Wilkinson Prof. of Law, 1990–95; Dir, Centre for Business and Professional Law, 1991–95; Associate Dean, 2010–12, Dep. Dean, 2011–12, Sch. of Advanced Study, Univ. of London. Vis. Professor: Sch. of Law, Univ. of San Francisco, 1981; Sch. of Law, UCLA, 1984–85; Univ. of Essex, 1995–2000; Penn State Dickinson Sch. of Law, 2004–05; summer schools: Sch. of Law, Univ. of Bridgeport, 1984; New York Law Sch., 1985; Law Sch., Touro Coll., 1987; William Mitchell Law Sch., 1987, 1988; Hon. Prof., UCL, 1995–; Vis. Fellow, Law Sch., LSE, 2013–14. Adviser to: Amer. Bar Assoc., Central and Eastern Eur. Law Initiative on legal competence in Eastern Europe, 2003; EC on changes to the system of legal aid in Turkey, 2004; British Council and British Embassy on judicial corruption in Bulgaria, 2006; British Council, Santiago and Public Defender Office, Chile on monitoring professional competence, 2006–08; Korean Legal Aid Corp. on develt of legal aid, 2009; People's Republic of China, China-EU Access to Justice Workshop, 2015; Chairman: Adv. Bd and Strategy Cttee, UK Centre for Legal Educn, 2007–11; Adv. Panel, Office of the Adjudicator for Higher Educn, 2009–13; Advice Quality Standard Cttee, 2012–. Member: Exec. Cttee, Law Centres Fedn, 1979–83; Ethnic Minorities Adv. Cttee, Judicial Studies Bd, 1991–94; Lord Chancellor's Adv. Cttee on Legal Educn and Conduct, 1995–2000; Exec. Cttee, Soc. of Advanced Legal Studies, 1997–; Consumer Adv. Bd, Legal Services Complaints Comr, 2005–11. Law Society of England and Wales: Member: Internat. Human Rights Gp, 1987–90; Trng Contracts Cttee, 1992–94; Equal Opportunities Cttee, 1994–2002; Ethics Forum, 2004. Gov., Heythrop Coll., Univ. of London, 2002–07. Chm., Hamlyn Trust, 2009–; Trustee, Jewish Law Pubn Fund, 1990–2011. Chm., London Jewish Chaplaincy Bd, 2001. Minister, Coventry Hebrew Congregation, 1976–90; Hon. Minister, Wembley United Synagogue, 1986–87. Chm., Ner Yisrael Community, 2005–07 (Gabay, 2002–05). Founder Ed., Internat. Jl of Legal Profession, 1993–. *Publications:* Client Interviewing for Lawyers: an analysis and guide, 1986, 2nd edn as Client Care for Lawyers: an analysis and guide, 1999; Freedom of Protest, Public Order and the Law, 1989; (jtly) Transaction Criteria: quality assurance standards in legal aid, 1992; Advocacy, 1993; (jtly) Lawyers—The Quality Agenda, 2 vols, 1994; (ed with I. Manley) Advising Clients with AIDS/HIV—A Guide for Lawyers, 1998; (jtly) Willing Blindness?: OSS complaints handling procedures, 2000; (jtly) Quality and Cost, Final Report on the Contracting of Civil, Non-Family Advice and Assistance Pilot, 2001; (jtly) Where Science Meets Law: an inquiry into training and qualification for patent agents and trade mark attorneys, 2003; The Other Side of the Mountain: an evaluation of the Overberg Access to Justice programme in South Africa, 2003; (jtly) The Regulation of Private English Language Teaching Institutions, 2004; (ed) Legal Aid, vol. 27 (3), in Halsbury's Laws of England, 4th edn, 2006 issue; (jtly) Evaluation of the Public Defender Service in England and Wales, 2007; Religion and Human Rights: redressing the balance, 2007; (jtly) Effectiveness of Online Dispute Resolution in the County Court, 2009; Decline of Legal Aid, Litigants in Person and Independence of the Judiciary, 2010; Policing the Conflict in South Africa: Tony Mathews and the Pietermaritzburg Conference, 2011; The Legal Education and Training Review, 2013; numerous articles on legal profession, legal ethics, legal services and legal aid in learned jls. *Recreations:* wadi walking in Eilat mountains, tennis, scuba diving, entertaining grandchildren Zac and Lilia. *Address:* Institute of Advanced Legal Studies, Charles Clore House, 17 Russell Square, WC1B 5DR. *T:* (020) 7862 5859, *Fax:* (020) 7862 5850. *Clubs:* Ner Yisrael Kiddush, Templars Lawn Tennis.

SHERRARD, Charles Isaac; QC 2012; *b* London, 17 Feb. 1965; *s* of Barry Sherrard and Jean Sherrard; *m* 1991, Sara Melanie Tropp; one *s* two *d*. *Educ:* University College Sch., Hampstead; Univ. of East Anglia (LLB Hons). Called to the Bar, Middle Temple, 1986; in practice as a barrister, 1986–. *Recreations:* Hertfordshire League tennis player, Middlesex League cricketer, regular golfer. *Address:* 8 Sunnyfield, NW7 4RG. *T:* 07590 530243. *E:* charlie@sherrard.co.uk. *Club:* MAL Cricket.

SHERRARD, Simon Patrick; DL; Chairman, Bibby Line Group Ltd, 1999–2015; *b* 22 Sept. 1947; *s* of Patrick Sherrard and Angela Beatrice Sherrard (*née* Stacey); *m* 1975, Sara Anne Stancliffe; one *s* three *d*. *Educ:* Eton Coll. Samuel Montagu & Co. Ltd, 1968–74; Jardine Matheson & Co. Ltd, 1974–85; Man. Dir, Bibby Line Group Ltd, 1985–99; Mem., PLA, 2000–09 (Chm., 2001–09). Chairman: Abacus Syndicates Ltd, 1999–2002 (Dir, 1997–2002); A & P Group, 2002–09; Johnson Service Gp plc, 2004–08 (Dir, 2000–08); Cooke Bros (Tattenhall) Ltd, 2005 (Dir, 1991–2005). Dir and Trustee, Lloyds Register, 2005–08 (Dep. Chm., 2002–05); Pres., Chamber of Shipping, 2000–01; UK Rep. on Exec. Cttee, Internat. Chamber of Shipping, 1993–2001 (Vice Chm., 1999–2001). Elder Brother, Corp. of Trinity House, 2001–. Mem. Adv. Bd, Liverpool Business Sch., 1996–2001; Member Council: Liverpool Sch. of Tropical Medicine, 1998–2007 (Dep. Chm., 2002–07); Mission to Seafarers, 1999–2015; White Ensign Assoc., 2004–; RNLI, 2006–. Chm., Cornwall MS Therapy Centre Ltd, 2009–. Trustee: Royal Liverpool Philharmonic Hall Diamond Jubilee Foundn, 1996–2005; Plymouth Marine Lab., 2012–; Nat. Maritime Mus., Cornwall, 2014–. Liveryman, Co. of Shipwrights, 1993– (Prime Warden, 2010); Freeman, Co. of Watermen and Lightermen, 2002–. High Sheriff, Cheshire, 2004; DL Cornwall, 2014. *Recreations:* golf, tennis, breeding rare sheep. *E:* simon@sherrard1.demon.co.uk. *Clubs:* Boodle's, Beefsteak, MCC.

SHERRATT, Antoinette; *see* Mackeson-Sandbach, A.

SHERRATT, Brian Walter, OBE 1995; PhD; JP; researcher in political science, since 2010; Headmaster, Great Barr School, 1984–2005; *b* 28 May 1942; *er s* of Walter Eric Sherratt and Violet Florence Sherratt (*née* Cox-Smith); *m* 1966, (Pauline) Brenda Hargreaves; two *s* two *d*. *Educ:* Univ. of Leeds (BA Hons 1964, PGCE 1965); Inst. of Educn, Univ. of London (AcDipEd 1973, MA 1976); Univ. of Birmingham (PhD 2004). Asst Master, Normanton GS, 1965–67; Hd, Religious Studies Dept, Selby GS, 1967–70; Avery Hill College of Education:

Sen. Lectr in Religious Studies and Warden, 1970–73 (Sen. Warden, 1972–73); Warden, Mile End Teachers' Centre, 1971–73; concurrently Asst Master, Kidbrooke Sch., London, 1970–71; Sen. Master, 1973–76, Dep. Headmaster, 1976–79, Sandown Court Sch., Tunbridge Wells; Headmaster and Warden, Kirk Hallam Sch. and Community Centre, Ilkeston, Derbys, 1979–84. Mem. Court, 1986–90, Hon. Lectr, Sch. of Educn, 1988–, Univ. of Birmingham; Mem., Academic Adv. Council, Univ. of Buckingham, 2005–; Visiting Lecturer: Univ. of Bristol, 2001–02; Univ. of Asmara, 2001–02. Member: Centre for Policy Studies, 1994–; Politeia, 1995–; Civitas, 2000–; Educn Commn, 2003–05. Chairman: Eco-Schs Adv. Panel, 1997–2001; Green Code for Schs Adv. Panel, 1998–2001; non-executive Director: Going for Green, 1994–98 (Mem., Organising Cttee, 1994–96); Envmtl Campaigns, 1998–2005 (Trustee, Pension Fund, 1999–2005; Mem., Resources Cttee, 2002–03, Audit Cttee, 2003–05; Vice-Chm., 2003–05; Chm., Devolution Cttee, 2004–05). Founder, Sherratt Sch. Leadership Lab. website, 2012. Chm., Nottingham Park Estate Ltd, 2008–11 (Dir, 2005–11). Mem., Magistrates' Assoc., 2006–; Magistrate Trng Observer, Nottingham Bench, 2008–12. Mem., T. S. Eliot Soc., 2012– FCMI (FIMgt 1984); FRSA 1984. Freeman: City of London, 2012; Liveryman, Educators' Co., 2013– (Freeman, Guild of Educators, 2003). JP Notts, 2006. Queen Mother's Birthday Award for the Envmt, 1999; Best Thesis Award, British Educnl Leadership Mgt and Admin Soc., 2005; George Cadbury Prize in Educn, 2005. *Publications:* Gods and Men: a survey of world religions, 1971; Local Education Authorities Project, 1988; Opting for Freedom: a stronger policy on grant-maintained schools, 1994; Grant-Maintained Status: considering the options, 1994; (jtly) A Structured Approach to School and Staff Development: from theory to practice, 1996; (jtly) Headteacher Appraisal, 1997; (jtly) Radical Educational Policies and Conservative Secretaries of State, 1997; (jtly) Policy, Leadership and Professional Knowledge in Education, 1999; Educational Leadership: effective use of resources in pursuit of leadership aims, 2008; contrib. to TES, etc. *Recreations:* opera, buildings, reading, antiques. *Address:* Oakhurst, 17 Lenton Road, The Park, Nottingham NG7 1DQ. *E:* brian.sherratt@ntlworld.com. *W:* www.briansherratt.org, www.twitter.com/BrianSherratt. *Club:* Athenaeum.

SHERRATT, Prof. David John, PhD; FRS 1992; FRSE; Professor of Biochemistry, University of Oxford, since 2010; Fellow, Linacre College, Oxford, since 1994; *b* 14 June 1945; *m* 1st, 1968, Susan Bates (marr. diss. 1992); one *s* two *d*; 2nd, 1992, Dr Lidia Kamilla Arciszewska; one *d*. *Educ:* Manchester Univ. (BSc 1st Cl. Biochem. 1966); Edinburgh Univ. (PhD Molecular Biol. 1969). FRSE 1984. Post-doctoral Fellow, Univ. of California, 1969–71; Lectr in Microbial Genetics, Univ. of Sussex, 1971–80; Prof. of Genetics, Inst. of Genetics, Glasgow Univ., 1980–93; Iveagh Prof. of Microbiol., 1994–2010, and Hd, Microbiol. Unit, Univ. of Oxford. Mem., EMBO, 1983. *Publications:* scientific papers and reviews; editor of several jls. *Recreation:* variety of outdoor pursuits. *Address:* Linacre College, Oxford OX1 3JA.

SHERRIFF, Paula Michelle; MP (Lab) Dewsbury, since 2015; *b* Alexandria, Scotland. Victim support rôle, Police Service, 1993–2003; community healthcare, NHS, 2003–13; private healthcare sector, 2013–15. Chair, Pontefract Business Forum. Mem. (Lab) Wakefield Council, 2012–15. *Address:* House of Commons, SW1A 0AA. *E:* paula.sherriff.mp@parliament.uk.

SHERRINGTON, Prof. David, PhD; FRS 1994; FInstP; Wykeham Professor of Physics, University of Oxford, 1989–2008, now Emeritus; Fellow, New College, Oxford, 1989–2008, now Emeritus (Sub-Warden, 2006–07); *b* 29 Oct. 1941; *s* of James Arthur and Elfreda Sherrington; *m* 1966, Margaret Gee-Clough; one *s* one *d*. *Educ:* St Mary's Coll.; Univ. of Manchester (BSc 1st Cl. Hons Physics, 1962; PhD Theoretical Physics, 1966). FInstP 1974. Asst Lectr in Theoretical Physics, 1964–67, Lectr, 1967–69, Univ. of Manchester; Asst Res. Physicist, UCSD, 1967–69, Lectr in Theor. Solid State Phys, 1969–74, Reader in Theor. Solid State Phys, 1974–83, Prof. of Phys, 1983–89, Imperial Coll., Univ. of London; Cadre Supérieur, Inst Laue Langevin, Grenoble, France, 1977–79; Ulam Scholar, Los Alamos Nat. Lab., USA, 1995–96. Bakerian Lect., Royal Soc., 2001; Scott Lectures, Cambridge, 2008. Delegate, OUP, 2001–06. MAE 2012. Fellow: Amer. Physical Soc., 1985; Eur. Acad. of Scis. Editor, Advances in Physics, 1984–; Hon. Editor, Jl of Physics A: Mathematical and General, 1989–93. Hon. MA Oxford, 1989. Dirac Medal and Prize, Inst. of Physics, 2007; Blaise Pascal Medal in Physics, Eur. Acad. of Scis, 2010. *Publications:* (ed jtly) Phase Transitions in Soft Condensed Matter, 1990; (ed jtly) Spontaneous Formation of Space-Time Structures and Criticality, 1991; (ed jtly) Phase Transitions and Relaxation in Systems with Competing Energy Scales, 1993; (ed jtly) Physics of Biomaterials: fluctuations, self-assembly and evolution, 1995; (ed jtly) Dynamical properties of unconventional magnetic systems, 1998; (ed jtly) Stealing the Gold, 2004; papers in learned jls. *Recreations:* wine tasting, travel, theatre, walking, ski-ing, gardening. *Address:* c/o Rudolf Peierls Centre for Theoretical Physics, 1 Keble Road, Oxford OX1 3NP.

SHERRINGTON, Rt Rev. John Francis; Auxiliary Bishop of Westminster, (RC), since 2011; Titular Bishop of Hilta, since 2011; *b* Leicester, 5 Jan. 1958; *s* of Frank and Catherine Sherrington. *Educ:* Wyggeston Boys' Grammar Sch., Leicester; Queens' Coll., Cambridge (BA Maths 1980); All Hallows Coll., Dublin; Gregorian Univ., Rome (STL 1990). Arthur Andersen Mgt Consultants, London, 1980–82; ordained priest, 1987; Asst Priest, St Anne's, Ratcliffe on Trent, 1987–88; Lecturer in Moral Theology, Director of Studies and Formation Director: All Hallows Coll., Dublin, 1990–98; St John's Seminary, Wonersh, 1998–2004; Parish Priest: Our Lady of Lourdes, Derby, 2004–09; Good Shepherd Parish, Nottingham, 2009; Mem., Bishop's Council and Episcopal Vicar for Derbyshire, 2008–11. Chairman: Marriage and Family Life Commn, Archdio. of Nottingham, 2008–11; Educn Commn, Archdio. of Westminster, 2011–. Member: Bioethics Cttee, British Assoc. Sovereign Mil. Order of Malta, 2004–12; Bishops' Conf. Healthcare Ref. Gp, 2005; Internat. Methodist Roman-Catholic Dialogue, 2011–; Mem., 2004–11, Co-Chair, 2011–14, British Methodist-Roman Catholic Cttee; Bishops' Conf. Dept for Catholic Educn and Formation, 2011–14; Catholic Bishops' Conf. Dept for Christian Responsibility and Citizenship, 2014–. Trustee and Mem., Mgt Cttee, Catholic Educn Service of Eng. and Wales, 2012–14; Trustee, CAFOD, 2015–. Pres., Nat. Bd of Religious Inspectors and Advrs, 2011–14. *Address:* Archbishop's House, Ambrosden Avenue, SW1P 1QJ. *T:* (020) 7798 9075. *E:* johnsherrington@rcdow.org.uk.

SHERRINGTON, Patrick Philip; Regional Managing Partner, Asia and Middle East, since 2013, and Member, International Management Committee, since 2010, Hogan Lovells International LLP; *b* Portsmouth, 1 Nov. 1951; *s* of John Sherrington and Peggy Sherrington; *m* 1976, (Sheila) Joy Smallman; two *s* one *d*. *Educ:* St John's Coll., Southsea; Univ. of Exeter (LLB); Univ. of Illinois (LLM). Teaching Fellow, Univ. of Illinois Coll. of Law, 1975–76; Vis. Asst Prof. of Law, Depaul Univ., Chicago, 1976–77; admitted solicitor, England, 1980, Hong Kong, 1987, and Australia, 1990; Lovell White & King, then Lovell White Durrant, later Lovells, subseq. Hogan Lovells Internat. LLP: Partner, 1985–; seconded to Hong Kong office, 1989–96; Mem., Internat. Exec., 2000–10; Global Hd of Dispute Resolution, 2000–13. Member: Council, Law Soc. of Hong Kong, 1990–96 (Vice Pres., 1993–96); Council, Inter Pacific Bar Assoc., 1991–96, 2005–09. Chm., Pacific Rim Adv. Council, 2008–10; Mem. Bd, CEDR, 2002–. Chm. Council, Wycombe Abbey Sch., 2010–. *Recreations:* family first, keeping busy and staying relevant, education, art, opera, sport, Chelsea FC. *Address:* Hogan Lovells International LLP, 11th Floor, One Pacific Place, 88 Queensway, Hong Kong. *T:* 22190888, *Fax:* 22190222. *E:* patrick.sherrington@hoganlovells.com; 12 St James's Gardens, W11 4RD. *Clubs:* Carlton, Reform, Arts; Hong Kong, Hong Kong Jockey.

SHERRINGTON, Air Vice-Marshal Terence Brian, CB 1997; OBE 1984; Director Welfare, RAF Benevolent Fund, 1998–2006; *b* 30 Sept. 1942; *s* of Thomas and Edna Sherrington; *m* 1969, Anne Everall; one *s* one *d*. *Educ:* Ottershaw Sch.; Westminster Technical Coll. Commnd RAF, 1963; served Aden, Sharjah, Germany and UK, 1963–78; RAF Staff College, 1979; MoD, 1980–81; OC Admin Wing, RAF Leuchars, 1981–83; OC, RAF Hereford, 1983–85; RCDS, 1986; Sen. Officer Admin, HQ 11 Gp, 1987–88; Dir of Personnel (Ground), MoD, 1988–91; AOA and AOC Support Units, RAF Support Comd, 1992–93; Head, RAF Admin. Br., 1992–97; AO Admin and AOC Directly Administered Units, Strike Comd, 1994–97. Mem. Council, Wycombe Abbey Sch., 1998–; Gov., Duke of Kent Sch., 2003–08. Freeman, City of London, 2002; Liveryman, Tallow Chandlers' Co., 2002. *Recreations:* fishing, golf, Rugby. *Address:* c/o Lloyds, Shipston-on-Stour Branch, PO Box 99 BX1 1LT. *Club:* Royal Air Force.

SHERRY, Prof. Norman, FRSL; writer; Mitchell Distinguished Professor of Literature, Trinity University, San Antonio, Texas, 1983; *b* 6 July 1935; *m* 1st, 1960, Sylvia Brunt (marr. diss. 1990); 2nd, 1990, Carmen Flores (marr. diss. 1996); one *s* one *d*. *Educ:* Univ. of Durham (BA Eng Lit); Univ. of Singapore (PhD). FRSL 1986. Lectr, Univ. of Singapore, 1961–66; Lectr and Sen. Lectr, Univ. of Liverpool, 1966–70; Prof. of English, 1970–83, Hd, Dept of English, 1980–83, Univ. of Lancaster. Exchange Prof., Univ. of Texas, Austin, 1977–78; Vis. Prof., Univ. of Sierra Leone, 1980; Vis. Res. Fellow, Merton Coll., Oxford, 1996. Hon. Res. Fellow, UCL, 1973; Fellow, Humanities Research Center, N Carolina, 1982; Guggenheim Fellow, 1989–90. Mem., Academic Adv. Council, UC, later Univ. of Buckingham, 1976. Pres., Conrad Soc. of GB, 1972–74. UK Ed., Conradiana, 1970–72. *Publications:* Conrad's Eastern World, 1966, 2005; The Novels of Jane Austen, 1966; Charlotte and Emily Bronte, 1969; Conrad's Western World, 1971, 2005; Conrad and his World, 1972; (ed) Conrad: the Critical Heritage, 1973; (ed) An Outpost of Progress and Heart of Darkness, 1973; (ed) Lord Jim, 1974; (ed) Nostromo, 1974; (ed) The Secret Agent, 1974; (ed) The Nigger of Narcissus, Typhoon, Falk and Other Stories, 1975; (ed) Joseph Conrad: a commemoration, 1976; The Life of Graham Greene, vol. I, 1904–1939, 1989, vol. II, 1939–1955, 1994, vol. III, 1955–1991, 2004 (Edgar Allan Poe Award, Britannica Book of the Year, 1990); contribs to Review of English Studies, Notes & Queries, Modern Language Review, TLS, Observer, The Daily Telegraph, The Guardian, Oxford Magazine, Academic American Encyclopedia. *Recreations:* reading, writing, jogging, body building. *Club:* Savile.

SHERSTON-BAKER, Sir Robert (George Humphrey), 7th Bt *cr* 1796, of Dunstable House, Richmond, Surrey; *b* 3 April 1951; *o s* of Sir Humphrey Sherston-Baker, 6th Bt and Margaret Alice (*m* 2nd, Sir Ronald Leach, GBE; she *d* 1994), *o d* of Henry William Binns; *S* father, 1990; *m* 1991, Vanessa, *y d* of C. E. A. Baird; one *s* one *d*. *Heir: s* David Arbuthnot George Sherston-Baker; *b* 24 Nov. 1992.

SHERVAL, Rear-Adm. David Robert, CB 1989; CEng; FIMechE; FIMarEST; Chief Surveyor and Deputy General Manager, The Salvage Association, 1990–98; *b* 4 July 1933; *s* of William Robert Sherval (HMS Hood, 1941), and Florence Margaret Sherval (*née* Luke); *m* 1961, Patricia Ann Phillips; one *s* one *d*. *Educ:* Portsmouth Southern Grammar School. Artificer Apprentice, 1950; BRNC Dartmouth, 1951; Training: at sea, HM Ships Devonshire, Forth and Glasgow, 1951–52 and 1955; RNEC, 1952–54, 1956; served: HM Ships Eagle, Tiger, Hampshire, HM Dockyard Gibraltar and HMY Britannia, 1957–68; BRNC, 1968–70; HMS Juno, 1970–72; NDC, 1972–73; Naval Plans, MoD, 1973–75; Staff of FO Sea Training, 1975–76; Naval Op. Requirements, MoD, 1976–77; NATO Defence Coll., Rome, 1979; ACOS (Intell.) to SACLANT, 1979–82; Fleet Marine Engineer Officer, 1982–84; Dir, Naval Logistic Planning, 1984–85; ADC to the Queen, 1985; CSO (Engrg) to C-in-C Fleet, 1985–87; Dir Gen. Ship Refitting, 1987–89. *Recreation:* music.

SHERWIN, Deborah Ann; Her Honour Judge Sherwin; a Circuit Judge, since 2014; *d* of William Anthony and Dinah June Sherwin; *m* 1981, Stephen John Ashurst, *qv*; one *s* one *d*. *Educ:* Wycombe High Sch.; Exeter Univ. (LLB Hons). Called to the Bar, Inner Temple, 1979; in practice as barrister, 1980–2014; Asst Recorder, 1995–98, Recorder, 1998–2014. *Recreations:* relaxing with family, walking, running, cycling, ski-ing. *Address:* The Law Courts, Quayside, Newcastle upon Tyne NE1 3LA. *T:* (0191) 201 2000.

SHERWIN, Glynn George; Chairman and non-executive Director, Sheffield International Venues Ltd, since 2005; Head of Corporate Finance, Sheffield City Council, 1998–2001; *b* 27 Feb. 1948; *s* of George Sherwin and Lilian Sherwin (*née* Billingham); *m* 1969, Janet Heather Broomhead Ferguson; one *s* two *d*. *Educ:* Firth Park Grammar Sch., Sheffield; Chesterfield Coll. of Technol. CPFA (Hons Final) 1971. Various posts, Sheffield CBC, 1966–74; Sheffield City Council: Principal Accountant, 1974–79; Chief Develt Officer, 1979–88; Asst City Treas., 1988–94; Dep. City Treas., 1994–98. Project Examr, 1978–83, Sen. Project Examr, 1983–86, Chartered Inst. Public Finance and Accountancy. Non-executive Director: MFH Engrg (Hldgs) Ltd, 2006–; Quoit Assets Ltd, 2006–. Dir, Sheffield Carers Centre, 2009–. Mem., Bd of Govs, Sheffield City Trust Ltd, 2003–. *Recreations:* keep fit, reading, cinema, theatre, walking.

SHERWIN, Hon. Dame Sarah Jane; *see* Asplin, Hon. Dame S. J.

SHERWOOD, Bishop Suffragan of, since 2006; **Rt Rev. Anthony Porter;** *b* 10 Feb. 1952; *s* of Sydney and Valerie Porter; *m* 1974, Lucille Joyce Roberts; two *s* two *d*. *Educ:* Don Valley High Sch.; Gravesend Sch. for Boys; Hertford Coll., Oxford (BA English 1974, MA); Ridley Hall, Cambridge (BA Theol. 1977). Ordained deacon, 1977, priest, 1978; Curate: Edgware, 1977–80; St Mary, Haughton, 1980–83; Priest-in-charge, Christ Ch, Bacup, 1983–87; Vicar, 1987–91, Rector, 1991–2006, Holy Trinity, Rusholme. Mem., Coll. of Evangelists, 2009–. Archbishops' Sport Ambassador, 2014–. *Publications:* Chips, 1979; Super Jack, 1983; Mission Countdown, 1986; Prince of Thieves, 2006; Seed Scattering, 2013. *Recreation:* sport. *Address:* Jubilee House, Westgate, Southwell, Notts NG25 0JH. *T:* (01636) 819133, *Fax:* (01636) 819085. *E:* bishopsherwood@southwell.anglican.org.

SHERWOOD, Antony; *see* Sherwood, R. A. F.

SHERWOOD, James Blair; Founder and President, Sea Containers Group, Bermuda and London, 1965–2005; Founder, 1976, and Chairman Emeritus, 2011, Belmond Ltd (formerly Orient-Express Hotels) (Chairman, 1987–2007; Director, 2007–11); Proprietor: Capannelle Wine Resort Srl (formerly Capannelle Vineyards), Tuscany, since 1997; Panorama Farms, Tulbagh, CP, South Africa, since 2014; *b* 8 Aug. 1933; *s* of William Earl Sherwood and Florence Balph Sherwood; *m* 1977, Shirley Angela Masser Cross; two step *s*. *Educ:* Yale Univ. (BA Economics 1955). Lieut US Naval Reserve, Far East service, afloat and ashore, 1955–59. Manager, French Ports, later Asst General Freight Traffic Manager, United States Lines Co., Le Havre and NY, 1959–62; Gen. Manager, Container Transport Internat. Inc., NY and Paris, 1963–64. In partnership with Mark Birley, established Harry's Bar Club in London, 1979. Restored, and brought into regular service, the Venice Simplon-Orient-Express, 1982. Dir, Save Venice Inc., 2000–. Non-exec. Dir, Casuarina Shipping Pte Ltd, Singapore, 2011–. Trustee: Solomon R. Guggenheim Foundn, 1989–; Oxford Philomusica, 2009–. Mem. Internat. Council, Yale Univ., 2002–. Hon. Citizen of Venice, 1995; Grand Master, Nat. Order of the Southern Cross (Brazil), 2004; Comdr, Chevaliers de Tastevin, 2005. *Publications:* James Sherwood's Discriminating Guide to London, 1975, 2nd edn 1977; Orient-Express, a personal journey, 2012. *Recreations:* sailing, tennis, ski-ing. *Address:* Hinton Manor, Hinton Waldrist, Oxon SN7 8SA. *T:* (01865) 820260. *Clubs:* Garrick, Hurlingham, Pilgrims, Mark's, Walbrook.

SHERWOOD, (Robert) Antony (Frank), CMG 1981; Assistant Director-General, British Council, 1977–81, retired; *b* 29 May 1923; *s* of Frank Henry Sherwood and Mollie Sherwood (*née* Moore); *m* 1953, Margaret Elizabeth Simpson; two *s* two *d*. *Educ:* Christ's Hospital; St John's Coll., Oxford (BA 1949, MA 1953). War service, RAF, 1942–46. Apptd to British Council, 1949; served in Turkey, Nigeria (twice), Syria, Uganda, Somalia and at HQ. Help the Aged: Vice-Chm., Internat. Cttee, 1982–88, Chm., 1988–92; Trustee, 1988–94; Mem. Council and Exec. Cttee, HelpAge Internat., 1983–93; Hon. PRO, Surrey Voluntary Service Council, 1982–88. Vice-Chm., Management Cttee, Guildford Inst. of Univ. of Surrey, 1993–97 (Chm., Finance Cttee, 1988–93). *Publications:* (ed) Directory of Statutory and Voluntary Health, Social and Welfare Services in Surrey, 1987; Looking Back: all the world's a stage, recollections of my first fifty years, 2009; Looking Back: one man in his time, more recollections 1975–2011, 2011. *Recreations:* travel, genealogy and family history, reading. *Address:* 18 Rivermount Gardens, Guildford, Surrey GU2 4DN. *T:* (01483) 538277. *E:* asherwood18@hotmail.co.uk.

SHERWOOD, Prof. Thomas, FRCP, FRCR; Professor of Radiology, 1978–94, Clinical Dean, 1984–96, University of Cambridge, now Professor Emeritus; Fellow of Girton College, Cambridge, since 1982; *b* 25 Sept. 1934; *m* 1961, Margaret Gooch; two *s* one *d*. *Educ:* Frensham Heights Sch.; Guy's Hospital, London. MA; DCH. Consultant Radiologist, Hammersmith Hospital and St Peter's Hospitals, 1969–77. Chm. Govs, Frensham Heights Sch., 1996–2000. Ombudsman, The Lancet, 1996–2001. *Publications:* Uroradiology, 1980; Roads to Radiology, 1983; Blow the Wind Southerly, 1988; papers in medical and radiological jls, 1964–. *Recreations:* music, reading and writing. *Address:* 19 Clarendon Street, Cambridge CB1 1JU.

SHESTOPAL, Dawn Angela, (Mrs N. J. Shestopal); *see* Freedman, Her Honour D. A.

SHETTY, Rajeev Rama; His Honour Judge Shetty; a Circuit Judge, since 2014; *b* London, 30 March 1973; *s* of Rama Bogu Shetty and Mahabando Shetty; *m* 2001, Dr Emma Jayne Watts; one *s* one *d*. *Educ:* Univ. of Southampton (LLB Hons). Called to the Bar, Inner Temple, 1996; barrister, 9 Gough Square, 1999–2014; a Recorder, 2009–14. Attorney Gen.'s List of Criminal Advocates Panel, 2002–07; Legal Assessor to GMC, 2010–14; Dir, Bar Mutual Indemnity Fund, 2011–14. Treas., Herts and Beds Bar Mess, 2005–12. *Publications:* (contrib.) APIL Guide to Evidence, 2012; (contrib.) APIL Guide to Industrial Disease Claims, 2013; (contrib.) APIL Guide to Road Traffic Accidents, 2013. *Recreations:* golf, football, films, greyhounds. *Address:* Chester Crown Court, The Castle, Chester, Cheshire CH1 2AN. *E:* HisHonourJudge.Shetty@judiciary.gsi.gov.uk. *Club:* Woking Golf.

SHETTY, Salil; Secretary General, Amnesty International, since 2010; *b* Bombay, 3 Feb. 1961; *s* of V. T. Rajashekar and Hamlatha Shetty; *m* 1984, Bina Rani; one *s* one *d*. *Educ:* Bangalore Univ.; Indian Inst. of Management, Ahmedabad (MBA); London Sch. of Econs and Pol Sci. (MSc). ActionAid: joined 1985; postings to Africa and India; CEO, 1998–2003; Dir, UN Millennium Campaign, 2003–10. Strategic Planning Gp, Amnesty Internat. *Address:* Office of Secretary General, International Secretariat, Amnesty International, Peter Benenson House, 1 Easton Street, WC1X 0DW. *T:* (020) 7413 5500, *Fax:* (020) 7413 5727. *E:* secgen@amnesty.org.

SHEWRY, Prof. Peter Robert, CBiol, FRSB; Professor of Crops and Health, University of Reading, since 2012; Distinguished Research Fellow, Rothamsted Research, since 2012 (Associate Director, 2003–12); *b* 19 March 1948; *s* of late Robert Thomas Shewry and Mary Helen Shewry; *m* 1969, Rosemary Willsdon; one *s* one *d*. *Educ:* Bristol Univ. (BSc, PhD, DSc). Postdoctoral Res. Fellow, Westfield Coll., Univ. of London, 1972; Rothamsted Experimental Station: Res. Scientist, 1974; Head of Biochem. Dept, 1986; Dir, Long Ashton Res. Stn and Prof. of Agricl Scis, Univ. of Bristol, 1989–2003. Dr *hc*: Swedish Univ. of Agricultural Scis, Uppsala, 2007; Budapest Univ. of Technol. and Econs, 2012. Rank Prize for Nutrition (with Donald D. Kasarda), 2002. *Publications:* (ed with Steven Gutteridge) Plant Protein Engineering, 1992; (ed) Barley: genetics, biochemistry, molecular biology and biotechnology, 1992; (ed with A. K. Stobart) Seed Storage Compounds, 1993; (ed jtly) Protein Phosphorylation in Plants, 1996; (ed jtly) Engineering Crop Plants for Industrial End Uses, 1998; (ed with R. Casey) Seed Proteins, 1999; (ed with A. S. Tatham) Wheat Gluten, 2000; (ed jtly) Biotechnology of Cereals, 2001; (ed with G. Lookhart) Wheat Gluten Protein Analysis, 2003; (ed jtly) Elastomeric Proteins, 2003; (ed with E. N. C. Mills) Plant Protein Allergies, 2004; (ed with K. Khan) Wheat Chemistry and Technology, 4th edn, 2009; (ed with H. Jones) Transgenic Wheat, Barley and Oats: production and characterisation protocols, 2009; (ed with J. Ward) Healthgrain Methods: analysis of bioactive components in small grain cereals, 2009; (ed with S. Ullrich) Barley Chemistry and Technology, 2nd edn, 2014; numerous papers in sci. jls on plant genetics, biochem. and molecular biol. *Address:* Rothamsted Research, Harpenden, Herts AL5 2JQ. *T:* (01582) 763133.

SHI JIUYONG; a Judge, International Court of Justice, 1994–2010 (Vice-President, 2000–03; President, 2003–06); *b* 9 Oct. 1926; *m* 1956, Zhang Guoying; one *s*. *Educ:* St John's Univ., Shanghai (BA Govt and Public Law 1948); Columbia Univ., NY (MA Internat. Law 1951). Legal Advr, Min. of Foreign Affairs, People's Republic of China, 1980–93; Prof. of Internat. Law, Foreign Affairs Coll., Beijing, 1984–93. Hon. Prof. of Internat. Law, East China Coll. of Law and Political Sci., 2001–. Pres., Xiamen Acad. of Internat. Law, 2005–. Honorary President: Chinese Soc. of Internat. Law, Beijing, 2006–; Coll. of Internat. Law, Univ. of Foreign Relations, Beijing, 2007–. Mem., 1987–93, Chm., 1990, Internat. Law Commn, UN.

SHIACH, Allan George; film writer (as Allan Scott) and producer; Chairman: Macallan-Glenlivet plc, 1980–96; Rafford Films Ltd, since 1983; *b* Elgin; *er s* of late Gordon Leslie Shiach, WS and Lucy Sybil (*née* De Freitas); *m* 1966, Kathleen Swarbreck; two *s* one *d*. *Educ:* Gordonstoun Sch.; L'Ecole des Roches; McGill Univ. (BA). Writer of TV and radio drama, 1965–72; screenwriter and co-writer of films, including: Don't Look Now, 1975; Joseph Andrews, 1977; Martin's Day, 1980; D.A.R.Y.L., 1984; Castaway, 1985; A Shadow on the Sun, 1987; The Witches, 1989; Cold Heaven, 1990; Two Deaths, 1994; In Love and War, 1996; The Preacher's Wife, 1996; Regeneration, 1997; also Producer or Exec. Producer: Cold Heaven, 1991; Shallow Grave, 1994; Two Deaths, 1995; True Blue, 1996; Grizzly Falls, 1999; The Match, 1999; The Fourth Angel, 2001; (co-prod. and co-writer) Priscilla Queen of the Desert - The Musical, Palace Th., 2009–12, NY, 2011–, Brazil, 2012–, Milan, 2012–; Rome, 2013–; UK and US tours, 2013; (co-writer and script consultant) Kon Tiki, 2013. Dir, Scottish Media Group plc (formerly Scottish Television plc), 1993–2006. Mem., BBC Broadcasting Council (Scotland), 1987–90; Chairman: Writers' Guild of GB, 1989 and 1990; Scottish Film Council, 1991–97; Scottish Film Prodn Fund, 1992–97; Scottish Screen, 1997–98; Governor, BFI, 1993–2000. Mem., Amer. Acad. of Motion Picture Arts & Scis, 1991–. Mem. Council, Scotch Whisky Assoc., 1983–96. Liveryman, Distillers' Co., 1989–. Hon. DA Napier Univ., Edinburgh, 2007; Dr *hc* Aberdeen, 2009. *Recreations:* writing, cooking, tennis. *Address:* Rafford Films Ltd, Amadeus House, 27b Floral Street, WC2E 9DP. *Clubs:* Savile, Garrick.

SHIACH, Gordon; Sheriff of Lothian and Borders, at Edinburgh, 1984–97, also at Peebles, 1996–97; *b* 1935; *o s* of late Dr John Shiach, FDS, QHDS; *m* 1962; one *d* (and one *d* decd). *Educ:* Lathallan Sch.; Gordonstoun Sch.; Edinburgh Univ. (MA, LLB 1959); Open Univ. (BA Hons 1979); Rose Bruford Coll. (BA Hons in Opera Studies 2006; DipHE Theatre Studies 2012). Admitted to Faculty of Advocates, 1960; practised as Advocate, 1960–72; Tutor, Dept of Evidence and Pleading, Univ. of Edinburgh, 1963–66; Clerk to Rules Council of Court of Session, 1963–72; Standing Jun. Counsel in Scotland to Post Office, 1969–72; Sheriff of: Fife and Kinross, later Tayside, Central and Fife, at Dunfermline, 1972–79; Lothian and Borders at Linlithgow, 1979–84; Hon. Sheriff at Elgin, 1986–. Mental Welfare Comr for Scotland, 2001–05. Member: Council, Sheriffs' Assoc., 1989–95 (Pres., 1993–95); Bd, Lothian Family Conciliation Service, 1989–93; Standing Cttee on Criminal Procedure, 1989–93; Parole Bd for Scotland, 1990–99 (Vice-Chm., 1995–99); Council, Faculty of Advocates, 1993–95; Shrieval Training Gp, 1994–95; Review Gp on Social Work Nat. Standards for Throughcare, 1994–95. Chairman: The Scottish Soc., 1992–93; Edinburgh Sir Walter Scott Club, 1995–98. FSAScot 1998. *Recreations:* hill-walking, swimming, music, art, theatre, film. *Club:* New (Edinburgh).

SHIELDS, Baroness *cr* 2014 (Life Peer), of Maida Vale in the City of Westminster; **Joanna Shields,** OBE 2014; Parliamentary Under-Secretary of State, Department for Culture, Media and Sport, since 2015; *b* 12 July 1962; holds dual US/UK nationality; *m* Andrew Stevenson; one *s*. *Educ:* Pennsylvania State Univ.; George Washington Univ. (MBA). Man. Dir, Europe, RealNetworks International, 2001–03; Man. Dir, EMEA, Google Inc., 2005–07; CEO, Bebo Inc., 2007–08; Vice Pres., Aol, 2007–09; Vice Pres. and Man. Dir, EMEA, Facebook, 2010–12; Chief Exec., 2012–14, Chm., 2014–15, Tech City UK. Non-exec. Dir, London Stock Exchange Gp 2014–. UK Business Ambassador for Digital Industries, 2012–. Trustee, American Sch. in London, 2013–.

SHIELDS, Elizabeth Lois; Lecturer, Medieval Studies Department, University of York, since 1995; *b* 27 Feb. 1928; *d* of Thomas Henry Teare and Dorothy Emma Elizabeth Roberts-Lawrence; *m* 1961, David Cathro Shields. *Educ:* Whyteleafe Girls' Grammar School; UCL (BA Hons Classics); Avery Hill College of Education (Cert Ed); MA York 1988. Asst Teacher, St Philomena's Sch., Carshalton, 1954–59; Head of Department: Jersey Coll. for Girls, 1959–61; Whyteleafe Girls' Grammar Sch., 1961–62; Trowbridge Girls' High Sch., 1962–64; St Swithun's, Winchester, 1964–65; Queen Ethelburga's, Harrogate, 1967–69; Malton Sch., N Yorks, 1976–86; Univ. of York (on secondment), 1985–86 (Medieval Studies). Mem., Ryedale DC, 1980– (Chm., 1989–2007; Chm., Community Services Cttee; Chm., Overview and Scrutiny Cttee, 2007); Mem. (Lib Dem) N Yorks CC, 2013– (Chm., Young People and Children Overview and Scrutiny Cttee, 2013–). Contested (L) Howden, 1979, Ryedale, 1983, 1992; MP (L) Ryedale, May 1986–87. Lib Dem spokesman on envmt, Yorks and Humberside Reg., 1989–; Chm., Yorks and Humberside Lib Dem Candidates' Assoc., 1992–97; President: Lib Dems in Ryedale Constituency, 1995–; Yorks and Humberside Lib Dem Regl Party, 1998–. Chm., Ryedale Housing Assoc., 1990–91; President: Ryedale Motor Neurone Disease Assoc., 1990–; Ryedale Cats' Protection League, 1991–2002. *Publications:* A Year to Remember, 1996. *Recreations:* gardening, music, travel, Arsenal FC supporter 2004–. *Address:* Firby Hall, Kirkham Abbey, Westow, York YO60 7LH. *T:* (01653) 618474. *Club:* National Liberal.

SHIELDS, (Robert) Michael (Coverdale), CBE 2002; Deputy Chairman and Trustee, Manufacturing Institute, since 2006; *b* 23 Jan. 1943; *s* of Thomas and Dorothy Shields; *m* 1965, Dorothy Jean Dennison; two *s* one *d*. *Educ:* Durham Johnston Grammar Tech. Sch.; Durham Univ. (BSc Hons); Newcastle Univ. (DipTP). MRTPI. Planning Departments: Newcastle upon Tyne, 1964–65; Durham CC, 1965–69; Nottingham, 1969–73; Dep. Dir of Planning, Leeds City Council, 1973–78; City Tech. Services Officer and Dep. Chief Exec., Salford City Council, 1978–83; Chief Executive: Trafford BC, 1983–87; Trafford Park Develt Corp., 1987–98; Northwest (formerly NW Regl) Develt Agency, 1998–2003; Manchester Knowledge Capital, 2003–05; Principal, URC Associates, 2003–11; Associate, AMION Consulting, 2004–11. Chm., Liverpool Land Develt Co., 2005–08 (Dep. Chm., 2004–05); non-exec. Dep. Chm., Merseycare NHS Trust, 2009–12. Non-exec. Dir, Innvotec North West Trust Ltd, 1998–2001. Chm., United Utilities Trust Fund, 2005–09. Salford University: Pro Chancellor, 1993–99; Chm. Council, 1997–99 (Dep. Chm., 1999–2003). Mem. Bd, Altrincham Forward, 2011–14; Chm., AltrinchamTown Centre Neighbourhood Business Plan Forum Working Gp, 2013–. Gov., Altrincham Grammar Sch., 1988–98 (Chm., 1988–93). Hon. DSc Salford, 2000; Hon. DLit UMIST, 2004; Hon. LLD Manchester, 2004. Howorth Medal for Enterprise and Innovation, RSA, 2004. *Recreations:* family, books. *Address:* 42 Crescent Road, Hale, Altrincham, Cheshire WA15 9NA. *E:* mike.shields@urca.co.uk.

SHIFFNER, Sir Henry David, 8th Bt *cr* 1818; company director; *b* 2 Feb. 1930; *s* of Major Sir Henry Shiffner, 7th Bt, and Margaret Mary (*d* 1987), *er d* of late Sir Ernest Gowers, GCB, GBE; *S* father, 1941; *m* 1st, 1949, Dorothy Jackson (marr. diss. 1956); one *d* (and one *d* decd); 2nd, 1957, Beryl (marr. diss. 1970), *d* of George Milburn, Saltdean, Sussex; (one *d* decd); 3rd, 1970, Joaquina Ramos Lopez. *Educ:* Rugby; Trinity Hall, Cambridge. *Heir: cousin* Michael George Edward Shiffner [*b* 5 March 1963; *m* 1996, Suzanne E. Buss (marr. diss. 2007); one *d*].

SHIFFNER, Rear-Adm. John Robert, CB 1995; DL; Consultant, Newton Industrial Consultants, 2002–07; *b* 30 Aug. 1941; *s* of late Captain John Scarlett Shiffner, RN and Margaret Harriet Shiffner (*née* Tullis); *m* 1969, Rosemary Tilly; two *s* one *d*. *Educ:* Sedbergh Sch.; BRNC Dartmouth; RNEC Manadon; RNC Greenwich (BSc). CEng, FIMarEST. Joined RN, 1959; served in HM Ships Centaur, Glamorgan, Andromeda, Zulu; Staff Marine Engineer Officer, CBNS Washington, 1980; RCDS 1983; MoD Procurement Executive: Project Manager, Type 42 Destroyer/Aircraft Carrier, 1984–86; Dir, Mechanical Engineering, 1987–88; Captain, Britannia RNC, Dartmouth, 1989–91; ADC to the Queen, 1989–91; COS to C-in-C Naval Home Comd, 1991–93; Dir Gen. Fleet Support (Equipment and Systems), MoD, 1993–95. Director: MSI-Defence Systems Ltd, 1996–2001; GEC Marine, 1996–98; Marconi Electronic Systems, 1997–99; Internat. Festival of the Sea Ltd, 2000–02. Chairman: Britannia Assoc., 2004–07; Dartmouth RNLI, 2007–. DL Devon, 2005. *Recreations:* golf, sailing, country pursuits, garden taming, picture restoration. *Address:* Higher Redlap, Dartmouth, S Devon TQ6 0JR. *Club:* Royal Yacht Squadron (Cowes).

SHIGEHARA, Kumiharu; President, International Economic Policy Studies Association (formerly Head, International Economic Policy Studies Group), since 2001; *b* 5 Feb. 1939; *s* of Seizaburo Shigehara and Rutsu (*née* Tanabe); *m* 1965, Akiko Yoshizawa; one *s* one *d*. *Educ:* Law Sch., Univ. of Tokyo (Hozumi Hon. Award, 1960). Joined Bank of Japan, 1962; joined OECD, 1970: Principal Administrator, 1971–72; Hd, Monetary Div., 1972–74; Councillor on policy planning, and Advr on Internat. Finance, Bank of Japan, 1974–80; Dep. Dir, Gen. Econs Br., OECD, 1980–82; Manager of Res., Inst. for Monetary and Econ. Studies, Bank of Japan, 1982–87, Dep. Dir, 1987; Dir, Gen. Econs Br., OECD, 1987–89; Dir, Inst. for Monetary and Econ. Studies, Bank of Japan, 1989–92; Hd, Econs Dept and Chief Economist, OECD, 1992–97; Dep. Sec.-Gen., OECD, 1997–99. Hon. Dr Econs Liège, 1998. *Publications:* The Role of Monetary Policy in Demand Management (with Niels Thygesen), 1975; Stable Economic Growth and Monetary Policy, 1991; New Trends in Monetary Theory and Policy, 1992; (with Paul Atkinson) Surveillance by International Institutions: lessons from the global financial and economic crisis, 2011; Japan at the OECD and the OECD in Japan, 2014; The Limits of Surveillance and Financial Market Failure, 2014. *Recreations:* art, hiking, classical music. *E:* office.shigehara@online.fr.

SHILLER, Prof. Robert James, PhD; Professor of Economics, since 1982, and Sterling Professor of Economics, since 2013, Yale University; *b* Detroit, Michigan, 29 March 1946; *s* of Benjamin P. Shiller and Ruth R. Shiller (*née* Radzvill); *m* 1976, Virginia M. Faulstich; two *s*. *Educ:* Southfield High Sch., Michigan; Univ. of Michigan (BA 1967); Massachusetts Inst. of Technol. (SM 1968; PhD 1972). Asst Prof., Univ. of Minnesota, 1972–74; Associate Prof., Univ. of Pennsylvania, 1974–80; Vis. Schol., Harvard Univ. and Nat. Bureau of Econ. Res., 1980–81; Vis. Prof., Dept of Econs, MIT, 1981–82. Member: Amer. Acad. of Arts and Scis;

Amer. Philosophical Soc. (Jtly) Nobel Prize in Econs, 2013. *Publications:* Market Volatility, 1989; Macro Markets, 1993; Irrational Exuberance, 2000, 2nd edn 2005; The New Financial Order, 2003; Subprime Solution, 2008; Animal Spirits, 2009; Finance and the Good Society, 2012. *Address:* Cowles Foundation for Research in Economics, Yale University, 30 Hillhouse Avenue, New Haven CT 06520–8281, USA. *T:* (203) 4323708, *Fax:* (203) 4326167. *E:* robert.shiller@yale.edu.

SHILLING, Elizabeth Mary; *see* Carter, E. M.

SHILLING, (Hugh) David (V.); artist, designer; President, David Shilling, since 1976; *b* 27 June 1954; *s* of late Ronald and Gertrude Shilling. *Educ:* Colet Court; St Paul's Sch., Hammersmith. Founded David Shilling, 1976. Sen. Consultant on design, ITC, UNCTAD and GATT, 1990. One person shows in UK and worldwide, 1979–, including: NT and Crafts Council, 1979; Ulster, Worthing, Plymouth, Leeds, Cheltenham, Durham, Salisbury, Chester and Edinburgh Museums; LA Co. Mus., 1982; Moscow, 1989; Sotheby's, Stockholm, 1992; Salama-Caro Gall., London, 1993; Rio de Janeiro, 1993; Manila, 1994; Brit. Embassy, Paris, 1995; British Council, Cologne, 1995, and Delhi and Bombay, 1996; War Child/Pavarotti, Modena, 1995; Royal Shakespeare Theatre, Stratford upon Avon, 1996; Dubai, 1999; Hatworks Mus., Stockport, 2001; Nat. Horseracing Mus., Newmarket, 2001; Internat. Mus. of the Horse, Lexington, Ky, 2002; Newmarket Racecourse, 2002; Nat. Mus. of Scotland Dumfries, 2003; Musée Chapeau, Lyon, 2004–05; Ferrero Gall., Nice, 2004, 2005; Regent's Park, London, 2005; Holdenby, Northampton, 2006; Museu da Chapeleria, Portugal, 2008; rue Princesse Caroline, Monaco, 2009; Beijing, 2009; Decoh Exhibn, Monaco, 2010; work in permanent collections: Metropolitan Mus., NY, LA Co. Mus., Philadelphia Mus. of Art, Musée des Arts Décoratifs, Paris, V&A Mus. Pres. for Life, Valdivia, Ecuador, 1993. Freeman, Gold and Silver Wyre Drawers, 1975. *Publications:* Thinking Rich, 1986. *Address:* 2 rue Basse, Monaco, MC 98000. *T:* 97770137. *Clubs:* City Livery; City Livery Yacht.

SHILSON, Stuart James, LVO 2004; *b* 12 Feb. 1966. *Educ:* St Paul's Sch.; Balliol Coll., Oxford (BA 1st Cl. Hons 1988, MSc 1989); St John's Coll., Cambridge (MPhil 1990). Called to the Bar, Middle Temple, 1992; in practice at the Bar, 1992–97; McKinsey & Co., 1997–2001; Sen. Civil Servant, Cabinet Office, 1999–2000 (on leave of absence); Asst Pvte Sec. to the Queen, 2001–04, and Asst Keeper of the Queen's Archives, 2002–04; rejoined McKinsey & Co., 2005. FRGS 1989; FRSA 1996.

SHILSTON, David Thomas; Technical Director for Engineering Geology, Atkins Ltd, since 2004; President, Geological Society of London, 2012–14; *b* Staines, 1954; *s* of Michael Shilston, CEng, MICE; *m* Pauline, *d* of Dr Eric Meek; one *s* one *d*. *Educ:* King's College Sch., Wimbledon; Univ. of Nottingham (BSc Geol. 1975); St John's Coll., Cambridge (Post-grad. Cert. Prehistoric Archaeol. 1976); Imperial Coll. London (MSc and DIC Engrg Geol. 1980). Affiliate ICE 1976; FGS 1981; MIGeol 1983; CGeol 1990; Affiliate, Instn of Field Archaeologists, 1991; CSci 2005. Student engr, Sir William Halcrow & Partners, 1972–73; Geologist, Nuttall Geotechnical Services Ltd, 1976–79; Engrg Geologist, Soil Mechanics Ltd, 1980–88; Sen. Engrg Geologist, Principal Engrg Geologist, then Chief Engrg Geologist, Atkins Ltd, 1988–2004. Ground Engrg Advr, UK Register of Ground Engrg Professionals, 2011. FRSA 1996. *Publications:* contrib. articles to tech. jls, conf. procs and tech. pubns. *Recreations:* hill walking, archaeology, rural and urban landscapes (ancient and modern). *Address:* Atkins Ltd, Woodcote Grove, Ashley Road, Epsom KT18 5BW. *T:* (01372) 754409.

SHILTON, Peter, OBE 1991 (MBE 1986); footballer; *b* 18 Sept. 1949; *s* of Les and May Shilton; *m* 1970, Sue. *Educ:* King Richard III Sch., Leicester. Goalkeeper; started playing, 1964, for Leicester City; scored a goal, 1967; Stoke City, 1974; Nottingham Forest, 1977; Southampton, 1982; Derby County, 1987; Plymouth Argyle, 1992–95 (player-manager); Leyton Orient, 1996; 1,000 League appearances (record), 1996; first played for England, 1970; 125 England caps (record); final appearance, World Cup, 1990. PFA Footballer of the Year, 1978. *Publications:* Peter Shilton: the autobiography, 2004.

SHIMMON, Ross Michael, OBE 2000; Secretary General, International Federation of Library Associations and Institutions, 1999–2004; *b* 10 Jan. 1942; *s* of late John Ross Shimmon and Eileen Margaret Shimmon; *m* 1967, Patricia, *d* of late Ronald George Hayward, CBE; one *s* two *d*. *Educ:* St John's Coll., Southsea; Poly. of North London; Coll. of Librarianship, Wales. FLA 1972; Hon. FCLIP (Hon. FLA 2000). Liby Assistant, Portsmouth City Libraries, 1960; Asst Librarian, 1962, Area Librarian, Havant, 1964, Hants County Liby; Lectr, Southampton Coll. of Technol., 1964; Librarian (Tech. Assistant), London Bor. of Bexley, 1966; Professional Assistant to Library Advisers, DES, 1968; Lectr, Coll. of Librarianship, Wales, 1970; Services Librarian, Preston Poly., 1975; Head, Liby Studies Dept, Admin. Coll. of PNG, 1979; Library Association: Sec. for Manpower and Educn, 1984; Dir, Professional Practice, 1988; Chief Exec., 1992–99. Member: Adv. Council, 1992–99, Adv. Cttee, 1994–99, British Council; BookAid Internat. Council, 1994–99; Adv. Cttee, Liby and Inf. Stats Unit, Univ. of Loughborough, 1997–99; Cttee on Freedom of Access to Information and Freedom of Expression, IFLA, 1998–99; Adv. Council on Libraries, 1999; Design Gp, Museums, Libraries and Archives Council, 1999. President: Eur. Bureau of Liby, Inf. and Documentation Assocs, 1992–95; Internat. Cttee of Blue Shield, 2003. Hon. Mem. PNG Liby Assoc., 1983; Hon. Life Mem., Liby and Inf. Assoc. of S Africa, 2007. Hon. Fellow, Univ. of Central Lancs, 2002. Trustee, Faversham Activity for Health (formerly Activity for Health), 2005–11 (Chm. Trustees, 2009–11). Member: Adv. Cttee, Internat. Jl on Recorded Information, 2001–03; Editl Adv. Bd, Information Develt, 2005–07; Ed., The Colonel, 2004–14. *Publications:* Reader in Library Management, 1976; conf. papers and contribs to liby jls. *Recreations:* cricket, photography, railways (prototype and model). *Address:* 7 Nobel Court, Faversham, Kent ME13 7SD. *E:* pandrshimmon@btinternet.com.

SHIMOMURA, Dr Osamu; Senior Scientist, Marine Biological Laboratory, Woods Hole, Massachusetts, 1982–2001; Adjunct Professor, Boston University Medical School, 1982–2001, now Professor Emeritus; *b* Fukuchiyama, Japan, 27 Aug. 1928; *s* of Chikara and Yukie Shimomura; *m* 1960, Akemi Okubo; one *s* one *d*. *Educ:* Nagasaki Coll. of Pharmacy (BS 1951; MS Organic Chem. 1958); Nagoya Univ. (PhD 1960). Res. Biochemist, Princeton Univ., 1960–63 and 1965–82; Associate Prof., Water Sci. Inst., Nagoya Univ., 1963–65. Pearse Prize, Royal Microscopical Soc., 2004; Asahi Prize, Asahi shimbun newspaper, 2006; (jtly) Nobel Prize in Chem., 2008. Order of Culture (Japan), 2008. *Publications:* Bioluminescence: chemical principles and methods, 2006; contrib. papers in Cell Comp. Physiol., Nature. *Address:* c/o Marine Biological Laboratory, 7 MBL Street, Woods Hole, MA 02543, USA.

SHIN, Prof. Hyun Song, DPhil; FBA 2005; Economic Adviser and Head of Research, Bank for International Settlements, since 2014; *b* 9 Aug. 1959. *Educ:* Magdalen Coll., Oxford (BA 1985); Nuffield Coll., Oxford (MPhil 1987); DPhil Oxon 1988. Lectr in Econs, Univ. of Oxford and Fellow, University Coll., Oxford, 1990–94; Prof. of Econs, Univ. of Southampton, 1994–96; Lectr in Public Econs, Univ. of Oxford and Fellow, Nuffield Coll., Oxford, 1996–2000; Prof. of Finance, LSE, 2000–05; Prof. of Econs, Princeton Univ., 2005–14. *Publications:* articles in learned jls. *Address:* Bank for International Settlements, Centralbahnplatz 2, 4051 Basel, Switzerland.

SHINDLER, Nicola; television executive producer; Founder and Chief Executive, Red Production Company, since 1998; *b* Rochdale, 8 Oct. 1968. *Educ:* Bury Grammar Sch.; Gonville and Caius Coll., Cambridge (BA 1990). Began career at Granada TV; script editor, Cracker, 1993; BBC, until 1998. Television series: prod., Queer as Folk, 1999; executive producer: Bob and Rose, 2001; Linda Green, 2001–02; Clocking Off, 2000–02; Conviction, 2004; Mine All Mine, 2004; Casanova, 2005; New Street Law, 2006–07; Single Father, 2010; Exile, 2011; Bedlam, 2011–12; Scott and Bailey, 2011–; Love Life, 2012; The Syndicate, 2012; Last Tango in Halifax, 2012–; Happy Valley, 2014. *Address:* Red Production Company, MediaCityUK, Level 2, White, Salford M50 2NT.

SHINE, Prof. Keith Peter, PhD; FRS 2009; Regius Professor of Meteorology and Climate Science, University of Reading, since 2013; *b* Birmingham, 19 April 1958; *s* of Isaac and Sylvia Shine; two *s*. *Educ:* Halesowen Grammar Sch.; Imperial Coll. London (BSc Physics; ARCS); Univ. of Edinburgh (PhD Meteorol. 1981). Research scientist: Univ. of Liverpool, 1981–83; Univ. of Oxford, 1983–88; University of Reading: res. scientist, 1988–90; Lectr, 1990–94; Reader, 1994–98; Prof. of Physical Meteorology, 1998–2013. Lead Author, Sci. Assessment of Intergovtl Panel on Climate Change, 1990, 1995. *Publications:* contrib. papers to learned jls with h-index of 45. *Recreations:* season ticket holder, Reading FC, fan of McCartney, Monet and MASH. *Address:* Department of Meteorology, University of Reading, Earley Gate, Reading RG6 6BB. *T:* (0118) 378 8405, *Fax:* (0118) 378 8905. *E:* k.p.shine@reading.ac.uk.

SHINE, Stephen Frank, OBE 2011; Chairman: Anesco Ltd, since 2012; UKDN Waterflow Ltd, 2013–15; Chief Executive Officer, SSLS Ltd, since 2012; *b* Raynes Park, London, 20 March 1957; *s* of Dennis Arthur Shine and Sheila Mary Shine; *m* 1981, Janice Margaret Nolan; one *s* two *d*. *Educ:* South Thames Coll. (HNC Electrical Engrg); Croydon Coll. (DMS); DipM, MCIM; Southbank Univ. (MBA). Various positions incl. apprentice electrician, Principal Engr and Engrg Dir, London Electricity Bd, subseq. LEB, then London Electricity plc, 1973–95; Managing Director: London Electricity Contracting, 1995–2000; 24seven Utility Services Ltd, 2000–05; CEO, SGB Ltd, Harsco Corp., 2005–07; Chief Operating Officer, Thames Water Ltd, 2007–12. Non-exec. Dir, Veolia Water Outsourcing Ltd, 2012–14. Trustee, Canal and River Trust, 2012–. FInstD 2011; MCMI; MIET. *Recreations:* shooting, fishing, golf. *Address:* Surrey. *T:* 07739 923481. *E:* Steve@theShines.net.

SHINER, Janice, CB 2005; Chairman, National Youth Agency, 2009–12. PGCE. Private sector advertising; human resource and communication mgt in various cos incl. WH Smith and Chase Manhattan Bank; Vice-Pres. Human Resources, Chase Manhattan, 1987; Vice Principal, Yeovil Coll., 1989–93; Sen. Inspector, 1993–97, Dir of Educn and Instns, 1997–99, FEFC; Principal, Leicester Coll., 1999–2002; Dir Gen. for Lifelong Learning, DfES, 2002–05; Chief Exec., Tertiary Educn Commn, NZ, 2005–08.

SHINER, Prof. Philip Joseph; Head of Strategic Litigation, Public Interest Lawyers (International), since 2014 (Principal, Public Interest Lawyers Ltd, 1999–2014); Professor in Practice Law, Middlesex University, since 2014; *b* Coventry, 25 Dec. 1956; *s* of Peter and Patricia Shiner; two *s* three *d*. *Educ:* Univ. of Birmingham (LLB 1978); Coll. of Law; Univ. of Warwick (LLM (by res.) 1985). Articled clerk, Needham and James, 1979–81; Solicitor: Robin Thompson and Partners, 1981–82; Small Heath Community Law Centre, 1982–84; Birmingham Council Estates Project, 1985–89; Thompsons, 1989–90; Community develt worker, Barnardo's, 1990–92; Solicitor, Birkenhead Resource Unit, 1992–95; Partner, Tyndallwoods, Solicitors, 1995–99. Hon. Prof. of Law, London Metropolitan Univ., 2005–13; Hon. Res. Fellow, Sch. of Law, Univ. of Warwick, 1999–2004; Vis. Fellow, Sch. of Law, LSE, 2005–13. Hon. LLD Kent, 2012. *Publications:* (ed with A. Williams) The Iraq War and International Law, 2008; contrib. Eur. Human Rights Law Rev., Local Econ., Judicial Rev., Mineral Planning, Legal Action Jl, Planning, Local Govt Chronicle. *Recreations:* running, cycling, contemporary music, comedy, hill walking, current affairs, religious affairs. *Address:* Public Interest Lawyers (International), 8 Hylton Street, Birmingham B18 6HN. *T:* (0121) 515 5069, *Fax:* (0121) 515 5129. *E:* phil_shiner@publicinterestlawyers.co.uk.

SHINGLES, Godfrey Stephen, (Geoff), CBE 1987; CEng, FIET; FBCS; Chairman, Imagination Technologies (formerly VideoLogic) Group PLC, 1995–2015; *b* 9 April 1939; *s* of Sidney and Winifred Shingles; *m*; two *s*; *m* 1997, Frances Margaret Mercer; one *d*. *Educ:* Paston Sch., N Walsham; Leeds Univ. (BSc). Digital UK, 1965–94; Chm., Digital Equipment Co. Ltd, 1991–94 (Man. Dir, 1983–91; Chief Exec., 1991–93). Vice-Pres., Digital Equipment Corp., 1981–92. Chm. and CEO, Celebrus Technologies Ltd (formerly Speed-Trap Hldgs Ltd), 2007–15 (non-exec. Dir, 2004–07); non-exec. Chm., Sarantel, 2006–14. FInstD. Freeman, City of London. *Recreations:* sailing, cricket, Rugby, golf, ski-ing. *Clubs:* Royal Ocean Racing, MCC.

SHINKWIN, Kevin; Parliamentary and Campaigns Director, Wine and Spirit Trade Association, since 2013. *Educ:* Univ. of Hull (BA British Politics and Legislative Studies). Campaigning work with charities incl. RNID; Parly Affairs Manager, Macmillan Cancer Support, until 2005; Campaigns Manager, CRUK, 2005; Leader, Public Affairs Team, RBL. *Address:* House of Lords, SW1A 0PW.

[Created a Baron (Life Peer) 2015 but title not yet gazetted at time of going to press.]

SHINNER, Thomas Patrick James; Director of Strategy, Department for Education, since 2014; *b* Aylesbury, 18 Oct. 1985; *s* of Patrick and Stephanie Shinner. *Educ:* Dr Challoner's Grammar Sch., Amersham; Magdalen Coll., Oxford (MA Modern Hist. 2007). With McKinsey & Co., 2006–13; on sabbatical as Teacher of Hist., Dr Challoner's GS, 2009–11; Sen. Policy Advr to Sec. of State for Educn, 2013. Lieut, RNR, 2004–. *Recreations:* sailing, ski-ing, running, walking, school governor (secondary). *E:* tom.shinner@education.gsi.gov.uk.

SHINWELL, Sir Adrian; *see* Shinwell, Sir M. A.

SHINWELL, Anne Hilary; *see* Middle, A. H.

SHINWELL, Sir (Maurice) Adrian, Kt 1996; NP; solicitor; Senior Partner, Kerr Barrie (formerly Kerr, Barrie & Duncan), Glasgow, since 1991; *b* 27 Feb. 1951; *s* of late Maurice Shinwell and Andrina (*née* Alexander); *m* 1973, Lesley McLean; one *s* one *d* (and one *s* decd). *Educ:* Hutchesons' Boys' Grammar Sch.; Glasgow Univ. (LLB). NP 1976. MCIArb 1999–2008 (ACIArb 1990). Admitted solicitor, 1975; Solicitor-Mediator, 1994–2004. Mem., Children's Panel, 1973–77. Part-time Tutor, Law Faculty, Glasgow Univ., 1980–84. Dir, Digital Animations Gp plc, 2002–07. Dir, Nat. Th. of Scotland, 2007–15. Scottish Conservative & Unionist Association: Mem., 1975–2014; Mem., Scottish Council, 1982–98; Chairman: Eastwood Assoc., 1982–85; Cumbernauld & Kilsyth Assoc., 1989–91; Scottish Cons. Candidates' Bd, 1997–2000; Vice-Pres., 1989–92; Pres., 1992–94; Member: Gen. Purposes Cttee, 1993–98; Scottish Exec. and Scottish Council, 1998–2000. Mem., Central Adv. Cttee on Justices of the Peace, 1996–99; Vice Chm., JP Adv. Cttee, E Renfrewshire, 2000–06. Dir, St Leonards Sch., St Andrews, 2000–03. DL Renfrewshire, 1999–2012. *T:* (office) (0141) 221 6844. *E:* mas@kerrbarrie.com.

SHIPLEE, Howard John, CBE 2012; Director General, Universal Credit, Department of Work and Pensions, 2013–14; *b* Liverpool, 21 Oct. 1946; *s* of William James Shiplee and Dorothy Elizabeth Shiplee; *m* 1968, Barbara Joan Callaghan; one *s* one *d*. *Educ:* Liverpool Coll. of Building (OND; HND Building 1966); Univ. of Liverpool (Postgrad. Dip. 1967). FCIOB 2002; FICE 2008. Engrg and mgt roles with Sir Alfred McAlpine, Cementation Construction, John Howard and Co., and Shell UK, 1968–75; sen. mgt roles, Middle East Construction Co., Qatar, 1975–84; Gen. Manager, Al Qahtari Gp, Saudi Arabia, 1984–86; Divl Dir, Boris Construction, 1986–88; Amec Construction: N Reg. Ops Dir, 1988–92; Proj. Dir, Manchester Airport Terminal 2, 1992–95; Proj. Dir, British-Chinese-Japanese Jt Venture, Hong Kong Airport, 1995–99; London Dir of Construction, Capitaland, 1999–2001; Dir of Carillion Bldg/Proj. Dir, GCHQ, 2001–02; Prog. Dir, Network Rail-Thameslink, 2002–04; Dir, High-Point Rendel, 2004–06 (Redevelt Chief Exec., Ascot

Racecourse, 2004–06); Dir, Construction, Olympic Delivery Authy, 2006–11; Exec. Dir, Laing O'Rourke plc, 2011–13. Non-exec. Dir, HSE, 2012–14. *Recreations:* home, horticulture, vehicle renovation, labradors.

SHIPLEY, family name of **Baron Shipley**.

SHIPLEY, Baron *cr* 2010 (Life Peer), of Gosforth in the County of Tyne and Wear; **John Warren Shipley,** OBE 1995; Member (Lib Dem) Newcastle upon Tyne City Council, 1975–2003 and 2004–12 (Leader, 2006–10; Opposition Leader, 1988–98); *b* 5 July 1946; *m* 1969, Margaret Pattison; one *s* one *d*. *Educ:* University Coll., London (BA Hist. 1969). Brand mgt, Procter & Gamble Ltd, 1969–71; with Open Univ., 1971–2005 (Regl Dir, North and EU, 1997–2005). Mem., Tyne and Wear Passenger Transport Authy, 2004–06. Mem. Bd, One North East, 2005–12. Contested: (Lib) Blyth, Feb. and Oct. 1974, Hexham, 1979; (Lib/SDP) Newcastle N, 1983 and 1987. Mem., Select Cttee on Econ. Affairs, H of L, 2010–15. Dep. Chm., Ind. Adv. Panel, Regl Growth Fund, 2012–15. Chm., Prince's Trust NE, 2011–12. *Address:* House of Lords, SW1A 0PW.

SHIPLEY, Debra Ann; writer and lecturer; *b* 22 June 1957. *Educ:* Oxford Poly. (BA Hons); MA London. Writer and lecturer, history, critical studies and architecture. MP (Lab) Stourbridge, 1997–2005. Chm., Drinkaware, 2007. *Publications:* 17 books on subjects including architecture, museums, heritage, travel. *Recreations:* walking, reading, cooking.

SHIPLEY, Rt Hon. Dame Jennifer (Mary), DNZM 2009 (DCNZM 2003); PC 1998; Managing Director, Jenny Shipley New Zealand Ltd, since 2002; Chairman, Seniors Money International Ltd, since 2007; Prime Minister of New Zealand, 1997–99; *b* 4 Feb. 1952; *d* of Rev. Len Robson and Adele Robson; *m* 1973, Burton Shipley; one *s* one *d*. *Educ:* Marlborough Coll., NZ; Christchurch Coll. of Educn (Dip. Teaching). Primary Sch. Teacher, 1972–77; farmer in partnership, 1973–88. MP (Nat.) Ashburton, then Rakaia, NZ, 1987–2002; MEC, NZ, 1990–99; Minister: of Social Welfare, 1990–93; of Women's Affairs, 1990–99; of Health, 1993–96; of State Services, of Transport, i/c Accident Rehabilitation and Compensation Insurance, for State Owned Enterprises, and i/c Radio NZ, 1996–97; i/c Security Intelligence Service, 1997–99; Chair, Security and Intelligence Cttee, 1997–99; Leader of the Opposition, 1999–2001. Chm., Mainzeal Property and Construction Ltd, 2004–13; Director: Richina Pacific, 2004–; Momentum, 2005–; China Construction Bank, 2007. *Recreations:* gardening, walking, water sports. *Address:* Seniors Money International Ltd, 87 Hurstmere Road, Takapuna, Auckland, New Zealand.

SHIPLEY DALTON, Duncan Edward; Member (UU) Antrim South, Northern Ireland Assembly, 1998–2003; barrister-at-law; *b* 7 Nov. 1970; *s* of Kenneth Shipley and Susan Iris Dalton, BSc, MA, PhD. *Educ:* Carisbrooke, Isle of Wight; Univ. of Essex (LLB Hons); Queen's Univ., Belfast (CPLS 1996); BL Inn of Court of NI 1996. Called to the Bar, N Ireland, 1996. 7th (City of Belfast) Bn, Royal Irish Regt, 1994–98. *Recreations:* reading (history and politics), karate, computers.

SHIPPERLEY, (Reginald) Stephen; Executive Chairman, Connells Group, since 2008 (Chief Executive, 1989); *b* 31 Oct. 1958; *s* of Reginald Scott Shipperley and Elizabeth May Shipperley; *m* Janet Frances; three *d*. *Educ:* Brill Primary Sch.; Aylesbury Grammar Sch. Connells Estate Agents, 1977–; Founding Dir, 2000, non-exec. Dir, 2006–10, Rightmove plc. *Recreations:* cricket (player and spectator), all other sports as spectator, golf.

SHIPSTER, Michael David, CMG 2003; OBE 1990; HM Diplomatic Service, retired; international consultant, since 2013; *b* 17 March 1951; *s* of late Col John Neville Shipster, CBE, DSO and Cornelia Margaretha Shipster (*née* Arends); *m* 1974, Jackie, *d* of late Norman Mann, SA Springbok cricketer; one *s* two *d*. *Educ:* Ratcliffe Coll., Leicester; St Edmund Hall, Oxford (MA 1972); Sch. of Develt Studies, UEA (MA 1977). Nuffield Fellow, ODI, in Botswana, 1972–74; worked for Botswana Develt Corp., 1972–75; joined HM Diplomatic Service, 1977: Second Sec., FCO, 1977–79; Army Sch. of Languages, Beaconsfield, 1979–80; First Sec. (Econ.), Moscow, 1981–83; FCO, 1983–86; First Secretary: New Delhi, 1986–89; Lusaka, 1990; Consul (Political), Johannesburg, 1991–94; Counsellor: FCO, 1994–2004; Washington, 2004–06. Chm., Jt Adv. Gp for Overseas Business Risk (formerly Security Inf. for Business), UK Trade and Industry and FCO, 2011–13. Dir, Internat., Rolls-Royce, 2008–13. Trustee, Riders for Health, 2014–. *Recreations:* music, military history, messing about on bikes and boats. *Address:* Carman's House, Compton, Winchester, Hants SO21 2AR. *Clubs:* Vincent's (Oxford); Royal Naval Sailing Association, Royal Cruising.

SHIPTON, Alyn Graham, PhD; Presenter, Jazz Record Requests, BBC Radio 3, since 2012; *b* Guildford, 24 Nov. 1953; *s* of Donald Shipton and Catherine Mary Shipton (*née* O'Donnell); *m* 1977, Siobhan Fraser; one *s* two *d*. *Educ:* Farnham Grammar Sch.; St Edmund Hall, Oxford (BA 1975); Oxford Brookes Univ. (PhD 2004). Sch. Books Editor, Macmillan, 1975–81; Publisher, Grove's Dictionaries of Music, 1981–87; Reference Publisher, Blackwell, 1987–95, Dir, NCC Blackwell Publishing, 1991–95. Presenter, BBC Radio 3, 1989–. Lectr in Music, Oxford Brookes Univ., 2003–04; Lectr in Jazz Hist., 2008–, Res. Fellow, 2013–, RAM; Lectr in Jazz, City Univ., London, 2012–13. Hon. ARAM 2012. *Publications:* (with Danny Barker) A Life in Jazz, 1986; Fats Waller: his life and times, 1988, 2nd edn 2002; (with Alan Groves) The Glass Enclosure: the life of Bud Powell, 1993; Making Music, vols 1–6, 1993; (with Doc Cheatham) I Guess I'll Get The Papers and Go Home, 1996; Groovin' High: the life of Dizzy Gillespie, 1999; (with Danny Barker) Buddy Bolden and the Last Days of Storyville, 2000; A New History of Jazz, 2001, 2nd edn 2007; Jazz Makers, 2002; Handful of Keys, 2004; (with George Shearing) Lullaby of Birdland, 2004; Out of the Long Dark, 2006; I Feel a Song Coming On, 2009; Hi-De-Ho: life of Cab Calloway, 2010; Nilsson, 2013; (with Chris Barber) Jazz Me Blues, 2013. *Recreations:* gardening, living and travelling in France, art, music, Co-Leader of Buck Clayton Legacy Band (jazz). *Address:* c/o BBC Radio 3, Broadcasting House, Portland Place, W1A 1AA. *E:* alyn.shipton@bbc.co.uk.

SHIRAKAWA, Prof. Hideki, PhD; Professor, Institute of Materials Science, University of Tsukuba, 1982–2000, now Emeritus; *b* Tokyo, Aug. 1936; *s* of Hatsutarou and Fuyuno Shirakawa; *m* 1966, Chiyoko Shibuya; two *s*. *Educ:* Tokyo Inst. of Technol. (PhD 1966). Res. Associate, Tokyo Inst. of Technol., 1966–79; Associate Prof., Inst. of Materials Sci., Univ. of Tsukuba, 1979–82. Pioneered work on conductive polymers. (Jtly) Nobel Prize for Chemistry, 2000. Order of Culture (Japan), 2000. *Address:* c/o Institute of Materials Science, University of Tsukuba, Sakura-mura, Ibaraki 305, Japan.

SHIRE, Rabbi Dr Michael Jonathan; Dean, Shoolman Graduate School of Jewish Education, Hebrew College, Boston, since 2011; *b* 15 Dec. 1957; *s* of Dr Heinz Shire and Ruth Shire; *m* 1991, Rabbi Marcia Plumb; one *s* one *d*. *Educ:* George Dixon Sch., Birmingham; University Coll. London (BA Hons 1981); Hebrew Union Coll., USA (MA 1983; PhD 1996); Leo Baeck Coll. (MA 1995). Dir of Educn, Temple Beth Hillel, Calif, 1983–88; Dep. Dir, 1988–90, Dir, 1990–2002, Centre for Jewish Educn; Vice-Principal, Leo Baeck Coll. - Centre for Jewish Educn, later Leo Baeck Coll., 2002–11. Ordained, 1996. *Publications:* The Illuminated Haggadah, 1998; L'Chaim, 2000; The Jewish Prophet, 2002; Mazal-Tov, 2003. *Recreations:* theatre, contemporary architecture, the men's movement, modern fiction. *Address:* Hebrew College, 160 Herrick Road, Newton Centre, MA 02459, USA. *T:* (617) 6784951.

SHIRLEY, family name of **Earl Ferrers**.

SHIRLEY, Malcolm Christopher, CEng; Secretary, Royal Commission for the Exhibition of 1851, 2002–10; *b* 10 April 1945; *s* of late Leonard Noel Shirley and Edith Florence Shirley (*née* Bullen); *m* 1970, Lucilla Rose Geary Dyer; three *s*. *Educ:* Churcher's Coll., Petersfield; BRNC Dartmouth; RNEC Plymouth (BSc 1969). CEng 1973; FIMarEST (FIMarE 1981). Royal Navy: served HMS Manxman, HMS Triumph, HMS Zulu, HMS Rapid, HMS Eastbourne, 1970–74; Sen. Engr, HM Yacht Britannia, 1975–77; RNSC Greenwich, 1977; Staff, Dir Gen. Ships, 1977–79; HMS Coventry, 1980–82; Asst Naval Attaché, Paris, 1982–84; staff appts, MoD Naval Staff, 1984–86, 1990–92; Nat. Rep. SHAPE, NATO, 1992–94; Cdre, 1994; Naval Manpower Study Leader, 1994–95; CO HMS Sultan, 1995–98. Dir Gen., Engrg Council, 1998–2001. Member: RNSA, 1967; Assoc. of Cape Horners, 1974. Hon. FRCA 2009. Freeman, City of London, 1999; Liveryman, Engineers' Co., 1999 (Asst, 2002). *Recreations:* sailing, music. *Address:* Greyhound Cottage, Freshford, Bath BA2 7TT. *T:* (01225) 722424. *Clubs:* Royal Yacht Squadron, Royal London Yacht.

SHIRLEY, Martin William, CBE 2010; PhD; FRSB; CBiol; Director, Institute for Animal Health, 2006–10; *b* Leighton Buzzard, 8 Dec. 1949; *s* of William Shirley and Pamela Shirley; *m* 1992, Fiona Clare Dunsdon; one *s* one *d*, and one step *s* one step *d*. *Educ:* Cedars Sch., Leighton Buzzard; Brunel Univ. (BSc 1974; PhD 1977). MIBiol 1974, FRSB (FSB 2009); CBiol 1994. Houghton Poultry Research Station: Technician, 1967–74; Res. Scientist, 1974–92; Institute for Animal Health: Principal Scientist, 1992–2003; Hd, Molecular Biol., 2003–04; Dep. Dir, 2004–06. Visiting Professor: Liverpool Univ., 2002; Guangdong Acad. of Agricultural Scis, 2003. Hon. Prof., RVC, 2007. Trustee: Houghton Trust, 1996–2014; British Egg Mktg Bd Trust, 2011–; Chairman: Chicken (formerly Poultry) Tech. Adv. Cttee, 2011–, Duck Tech. Adv. Cttee, 2013–, Red Tractor. Hon. Fellow, Liverpool Sch. of Tropical Medicine, 2003; Hon. Associate, RCVS, 2010. Tom Newman Meml Medal Internat. Award for Poultry Sci., British Poultry Council, 1989; Res. Medal, Royal Agricl Soc. of England, 2004. *Publications:* over 200 articles on biology of avian coccidial parasites, *Eimeria* spp. and coccidiosis. *Recreations:* computing, photography, learning about wine, a daily Codeword, golf, spending time with grandchildren, Ava, Lucas and Serennah. *Address:* 48 Vineyard Way, Buckden, St Neots, Cambs PE19 5SR. *Clubs:* Farmers; Brampton Park Golf; Hunstanton Golf.

SHIRLEY, Dame (Vera) Stephanie, (Steve), DBE 2000 (OBE 1980); CEng, FREng; FBCS CITP; philanthropist; UK Ambassador for Philanthropy, 2009–10; *b* 16 Sept. 1933; *d* of late Arnold Buchthal and Mrs Margaret Brook (formerly Buchthal, *née* Schick); name changed to Brook on naturalisation, 1951; *m* 1959, Derek George Millington Shirley; (one *s* decd). *Educ:* Sir John Cass Coll., London. BSc (Spec.) London 1956. FBCS CITP 2003 (FBCS 1971); CEng 1990. PO Res. Stn, Dollis Hill, 1951–59; CDL (subsid. of ICL), 1959–62; F International Group, later F.I. Group, 1962–93 (Founder and Chief Exec., 1962–87; Settlor Xansa Employee (formerly FI Shareholders') Trust, 1981); Life Pres., Xansa (formerly F.I. Gp plc), 1993; Director: AEA Technology Plc, 1992–2000; Tandem Computers Inc., 1992–97; John Lewis Partnership plc, 1999–2001; European Adv. Bd, Korn/Ferry Internat., 2001–04; CSR Adv. Bd, Steria, 2008. Member: Computer, Systems and Electronics Requirements Bd, 1979–81; Electronics and Avionics Requirements Bd, 1981–83; Open Tech, MSC, 1983–86; Council, Industrial Soc., 1984–90; NCVQ, 1986–89; Strategy Bd, Oxford Internet Inst., 2000–11. Pres., British Computer Soc., 1989–90; Vice Pres., C&G, 2000–05. Consulting Editor on information processing, J. Wiley & Sons, 1978–87. Member: Council, Duke of Edinburgh's Seventh Commonwealth Study Conf., 1991–92; British–N American Cttee, 1992–2001. Chm., Women of Influence, 1993. President: Autistica (formerly Nat. Alliance for Autism Res. (UK), then Autism Speaks), 2009 (Founder, 2006); Autism Cymru, 2012– (Founder, 2001); Trustee: Help The Aged, 1987–90; Nat. Alliance for Autism Res. (USA), 2004–06. Patron: Disablement Income Gp, 1989–2001; Centre for Tomorrow's Co., 1997–; Fellow, Oxford Univ. Ct of Benefactors, 2001–; Companion, Guild of Cambridge Benefactors, 2006–. Founder: The Kingwood Trust, 1993; The Shirley Foundn, 1996; Prior's Court Foundn, 1998. Master, Information Technologists' Co., 1992 (Liveryman, 1992); Freeman, City of London, 1987. CCMI (CBIM 1984); FREng 2001. Hon. FCGI 1989. Hon. Fellow: Manchester Metropolitan Univ. (formerly Poly.), 1989; Staffordshire Univ. (formerly Poly.), 1991; Sheffield Hallam Univ., 1992; IMCB, 1999; Birkbeck, 2002; Murray Edwards Coll. (formerly New Hall), Cambridge, 2002; Foundn Fellow, Balliol Coll., Oxford, 2001. Hon. DSc: Buckingham, 1991; Aston, 1993; Nottingham Trent, 1994; Southampton Inst., 1994; Southampton, 2003; Brunel, 2005; Lincoln, 2014; Hon. DTech: Loughborough, 1991; Kingston, 1995; DUniv: Leeds Metropolitan, 1993; Derby, 1997; London Guildhall, 1998; Stirling, 2000; Hon. DLitt de Montfort, 1993; Hon. DBA: West of England, 1995; City, 2000; Hon. Dr: Edinburgh, 2003; Open, 2009; Strathclyde, 2014; Hon. LLD: Leicester, 2005; Bath, 2006; St Andrews, 2011; University Campus Suffolk, 2012. Recognition of Information Technology Achievement Award, 1985; Gold Medal, Inst. of Mgt, 1991; Mountbatten Medal, IEE, 1999; Beacon Prize for Startups, Beacon Fellowship Charitable Trust, 2003; Lifetime Achievement Award, BCS, 2004; Philanthropist of Year, Spears Wealth Mgt Awards, 2010; Lifetime Achievement Award, Jewish Care, 2014. US Nat. Women's Hall of Fame, 1995. *Publications:* Let IT Go (memoir), 2012. *Recreation:* wishful thinking. *Address:* 47 Thames House, Phyllis Court Drive, Henley-on-Thames, Oxon RG9 2NA. *T:* (01491) 579004, *Fax:* (01491) 574995. *E:* steve@steveshirley.com. *Club:* Royal Society of Medicine.

SHIRRAS, Ven. Edward Scott; Priest-in-charge, Marcham with Garford, diocese of Oxford, 2002–09; *b* 23 April 1937; *s* of Edward Shirras and Alice Emma Shirras (*née* Morten); *m* 1962, Pamela Susan Mackenzie; two *s* two *d*. *Educ:* Sevenoaks School; St Andrews Univ. (BSc); Union Coll., Schenectady, NY, USA; Clifton Theol Coll., Bristol. Curate: Christ Church, Surbiton Hill, 1963–66; Jesmond Parish Church, Newcastle upon Tyne, 1966–68; Church Pastoral Aid Society: Youth Sec., 1968–71; Publications Sec., 1971–74; Asst Gen. Sec., 1974–75; Vicar of Christ Church, Roxeth, dio. London, 1975–85; Area Dean of Harrow, 1982–85; Archdeacon of Northolt, 1985–92; Vicar, Christ Church, Winchester, 1992–2001. *Recreations:* transport photography (Scottish), Aberdeen FC. *Address:* 4 Culham Close, Abingdon, Oxon OX14 2AS. *T:* (01235) 553129. *E:* epshirras@aol.com.

SHIRREFF, Gen. Sir (Alexander) Richard (David), KCB 2010; CBE 2001; Director, Strategia Worldwide Ltd, since 2014; *b* 21 Oct. 1955; *s* of Alexander David Shirreff, MC and Dione Hilary Shirreff (*née* Wood-White); *m* 1980, Sarah-Jane Patrick; one *s* one *d*. *Educ:* Oundle Sch.; Exeter Coll., Oxford (BA, MA Mod. Hist.). Commnd 14th/20th King's Hussars, 1978; sc 1986–87; COS HQ 33 Armoured Bde, 1988–89; MA to C-in-C BAOR and Comdr Northern Army Gp, 1992–94; Comdg King's Royal Hussars, 1994–96; Col, Army Plans, MoD, 1996–98; Comdr 7th Armoured Bde, 1999–2000; Principal SO to CDS, 2000–02; rcds 2003; COS HQ Land Comd, 2003–05; GOC 3rd (UK) Div., 2005–07; Comdr Allied Rapid Reaction Corps, 2007–11; Dep. Supreme Allied Comdr Europe, 2011–14. Hon. Colonel: Oxford Univ. OTC, 2007–13; Royal Wessex Yeomanry, 2010–15; Col, King's Royal Hussars, 2013–. *Recreations:* ski-ing, game shooting, history, reading. *Address:* c/o Home HQ (South), King's Royal Hussars, Peninsula Barracks, Winchester, Hants SO23 8TS. *T:* (01962) 828539. *Clubs:* Cavalry and Guards, Pitt.

SHIRREFS, Richard; Executive Vice-President, RHJ International SA, 2006; *b* 7 May 1955; *s* of William R. and Patricia W. Shirrefs; *m* (marr. diss.); one *s*. *Educ:* Univ. of Birmingham (BSc Hons 1977). ACCA 1981, FCCA 1986. Financial analyst, Tube Investments, 1977–79; Mgt Accountant, El Paso, Paris, 1979–83; Analyst, 1983–86, Finance Dir, Aftermarket Div., 1986–90, Gp Controller, 1990–93, Bendix Europe; Finance and Logistics Dir, Catteau

(Tesco), 1993–96; Chief Financial Officer, 1996–2001, Chief Exec., 2002–04, Eurotunnel. Non-executive Director: D&M Hldgs Inc., 2007–08; Columbia Music Entertainment Inc., 2007–10; Shaklee Global Gp Inc., 2007; Phoenix Resort KK, 2007–12.

SHIVJI, Rebecca; *see* Stubbs, R.

SHLAIM, Prof. Avi, PhD; FBA 2006; Professor of International Relations, University of Oxford, 1996–2011; Fellow, St Antony's College, Oxford, 1987–2011, now Emeritus; *b* Baghdad, 31 Oct. 1945; *s* of Joseph and Aida Shlaim; *m* 1973, Gwyneth Daniel; one *d*. *Educ:* Jesus Coll., Cambridge (BA Hist. 1969); London Sch. of Econs (MSc(Econ.) Internat. Relns 1970); Reading Univ. (PhD Politics 1980). Lectr, 1970–86, Reader in Politics, 1986–87, Univ. of Reading; University of Oxford: Alastair Buchan Reader in Internat. Relns, 1987–96; Dir, Grad. Studies in Internat. Relns, 1993–95 and 1998–2001; Dir, Middle E Centre, 2007–08, Sub-Warden, 2008–10, St Antony's Coll., Oxford. Fellow, Woodrow Wilson Internat. Center for Scholars, Washington, 1980–81; British Acad. Res. Reader, 1995–97; British Acad. Res. Prof., 2003–06. Sir Percy Sykes Meml Medal, RSAA, 2011. *Publications:* (jtly) British Foreign Secretaries since 1945, 1977; The United States and the Berlin Blockade 1948–49: a study in crisis decision-making, 1983; Collusion across the Jordan: King Abdullah, the Zionist Movement, and the partition of Palestine, 1988; The Politics of Partition, 1990; War and Peace in the Middle East: a concise history, 1995; (ed jtly) The Cold War and the Middle East, 1997; The Iron Wall: Israel and the Arab world, 2000, rev. edn 2014; (ed jtly) The War for Palestine: rewriting the history of 1948, 2001; Lion of Jordan: the life of King Hussein in war and peace, 2007; Israel and Palestine: reappraisals, revisions, refutations, 2009; (ed jtly) The 1967 Arab-Israeli War: origins and consequences, 2012. *Recreation:* walking and talking. *Address:* St Antony's College, Oxford OX2 6JF. *T:* (01865) 274460. *E:* avi.shlaim@sant.ox.ac.uk.

SHOCK, Sir Maurice, Kt 1988; Rector, Lincoln College, Oxford, 1987–94, Hon. Fellow, 1995; *b* 15 April 1926; *o s* of Alfred and Ellen Shock; *m* 1947, Dorothy Donald (*d* 1998); one *s* three *d*. *Educ:* King Edward's Sch., Birmingham; Balliol Coll., Oxford (MA); St Antony's Coll., Oxford. Served Intell. Corps, 1945–48. Lectr in Politics, Christ Church and Trinity Coll., Oxford, 1955–56; Fellow and Praelector in Politics, University Coll., Oxford, 1956–77, Hon. Fellow, 1986; Estates Bursar, 1959–74; Vice-Chancellor, Leicester Univ., 1977–87. Sen. Treasurer, Oxford Union Soc., 1954–72 (Trustee, 1988–); Member: Franks Commn of Inquiry into the University of Oxford, 1964–66; Hebdomadal Council, Oxford Univ., 1969–75; Chairman: Univ. Authorities Panel, 1980–85; CVCP, 1985–87. Vis. Prof. of Govt, Pomona Coll., 1961–62, 1968–69. Member: ESRC, 1981–85; GMC, 1989–94; RAND Health Bd, 2000; a Governing Trustee, 1980–2003, Chm., 1988–2003, Nuffield Trust. Trustee, Age Concern, Oxon, 2000–. Hon. Vice-Pres., Political Studies Assoc., 1989. Review Panel on Machinery of Government of Jersey, 1999–2000. Hon. FRCP 1989. Hon. LLD Leicester, 1987. *Publications:* The Liberal Tradition; articles on politics and recent history. *Recreations:* gardening, theatre. *Address:* 4 Cunliffe Close, Oxford OX2 7BL.

SHOEBRIDGE, Michele Indianna; Interim Chief Operating Officer, University of the West of Scotland, since 2015; Director, Academic Services, University of Exeter, 2006–15; *b* 7 Nov. 1954; *d* of Charles William Shoebridge and Maisie Indianna Shoebridge (*née* Wissenden); one *d*. *Educ:* Maidstone Tech. High Sch. for Girls; Univ. of Birmingham (BA Hons Medieval and Mod. Hist. 1976); City of Birmingham Poly. (Postgrad. DipLib 1977); Wolverhampton Univ. (MA 1982). University of Birmingham: various posts, University Library, 1979–95, Information Services, 1995–2002; Dir, Inf. Services, 2002–06. *Publications:* Women in Sport: a select bibliography, 1988; Union Catalogue of Periodicals in Sport and Recreation, 1988; Information Sources in Sport and Leisure, 1991; (jtly) A History of the Birmingham Athletic Institute, 1992; articles in jls on aspects of inf. mgt, teaching and learning. *Recreations:* family, cinema, travel.

SHONE, Carole Gibson; *see* Mundell, C. G.

SHONE, Very Rev. John Terence; Team Vicar, Cullercoats Team, Marden St Hilda, Diocese of Newcastle, 1989–2000; retired; *b* 15 May 1935; *s* of late Arthur Shone and E. B. Shone; *m* 1st, 1958, Ursula Ruth Buss (marr. diss.); three *s*; 2nd, 1987, Annette Simmons (*d* 2011), *d* of late William Caterer and Ada Caterer. *Educ:* St Dunstan's College; Selwyn Coll., Cambridge (BA 1958, MA 1962); Lincoln Theological Coll.; Newcastle Univ. (MA 1992). Deacon 1960, priest 1961, London; Curate, St Pancras Parish Church, 1960–62; Chaplain, St Andrew's Cathedral, Aberdeen, 1962–65; Chaplain to Anglican Students, Aberdeen, 1962–68; Lectr, Aberdeen Coll. of Education, 1965–68; Exam. Chaplain to Bishop of Aberdeen, 1966–68; Vicar, St Andrew and St Luke, Grimsby, 1968–69; Rector, St Saviour, Bridge of Allan, 1969–86; Chaplain, Stirling Univ., 1969–80; Priest i/c, St John's, Alloa, 1977–85, and St James', Dollar, 1981–86; Canon, St Ninian's Cathedral, Perth, 1980–82; Dean, 1982–89, Dean Emeritus, 2000, United Dio. of St Andrews, Dunkeld and Dunblane; Diocesan R & D Officer, 1986–89. *Address:* Carnoch Croft, 33d Grange Road, Alloa, Clackmannanshire FK10 1LR. *T:* (01259) 721388, 07983 407551. *E:* j.shone267@btinternet.com.

SHONE, Richard Noel; Editor, The Burlington Magazine, 2003–15; *b* Doncaster, 8 May 1949; *s* of Dr Godfrey Noel Shone and Eleanor May Shone (*née* Clough). *Educ:* Wrekin Coll.; Clare Coll., Cambridge (BA 1971). Associate Ed., The Burlington Mag., 1979–2003. Exhibition Curator: Portraits by Duncan Grant, Arts Council, 1969; Duncan Grant: designer, 1980; Portraits by Walter Sickert, 1990; Sickert (co-selector), RA and Van Gogh Mus., Amsterdam, 1992–93; Head First, Arts Council tour, 1998–99; The Art of Bloomsbury, Tate Gall., London, Huntington Liby, San Marino, Calif, Yale Center for British Art, New Haven, Conn, 1999–2000. Mem., Adv. Cttee, Govt Art Collection, 1990–94. Member: Charleston Trust, 1981–2011; Jury, Turner Prize, 1988. *Publications:* Bloomsbury Portraits: Vanessa Bell, Duncan Grant and their circle, 1976, 2nd edn 1993; The Century of Change: British painting since 1900, 1977; The Post-Impressionists, 1980; Walter Sickert, 1988; Rodrigo Moynihan, 1988; Alfred Sisley, 1992; Damien Hirst, 2001; (ed jtly) The Books that Shaped Art History, 2013; numerous catalogue introductions. *Address:* 87 High Street, Hastings, E Sussex TN34 3ES. *Club:* Cranium.

SHONIBARE, Yinka, MBE 2004; RA 2013; visual artist, since 1991; *b* London, 9 Aug. 1962; *s* of Olatunji Shonibare and Laide Shonibare; one *s*. *Educ:* Redrice Sch.; Byam Shaw Sch. of Art; Goldsmiths Coll. (MA 1991; Hon. Fellow 2003). *Exhibitions include:* Sensation, RA, 1997; Documenta 11, Kassel, 2002; Nelson's Ship in a Bottle, Fourth Plinth, Trafalgar Square, 2010, Nat. Maritime Mus., 2013. Estabd Guest Projects, experimental project space, 2009–. FRSA 2010. Hon. Dr: Huron, 2007; RCA, 2010. Wollaston Award, RA, 2010. *Recreations:* opera, cinema, music, museums. *Address:* Sunbury House, 1 Andrews Road, E8 4QL. *T:* (020) 7249 1409. *E:* info@guestprojects.com. *Clubs:* Arts, Shoreditch House, Black's.

SHOOTER, Adrian, CBE 2010; FREng; FIMechE; Chairman: Vivarail Ltd, since 2012; Global Travel Ventures, since 2014; *b* London, 22 Nov. 1948; *s* of late Prof. Reginald Arthur Shooter, CBE and Jean Shooter (*née* Wallace); *m* 1st, 1970, Diana Crombie (marr. diss. 2002); one *s* one *d*; 2nd, 2006, Barbara Harding. *Educ:* Epsom Coll.; N Staffs Poly. (HND Mech. Engrg 1970). With British Railways, 1970–96: engrg grad. trainee, 1970–71; engrg mgt posts, 1971–84; Area Manager, St Pancras, 1984–87; Man. Dir, Red Star Parcels, 1987–89; Dir, Parcels Business, 1989–93; Man. Dir, 1993–2001, Chm., 2002–11, Chiltern Rlys. Chm., Oxon Local Enterprise Partnership, 2012–. Non-executive Director: Railway Safety and Standards Bd, 2004–11; Wabtec UK Ltd, 2012–14. Chm., W Midlands Regl Council, CBI, 2011–13. Hon. Dr: Staffs, 2002; Birmingham, 2013. *Recreations:* restoring and driving vintage cars, running steam railways, helping develop communities. *E:* shooter.adrian@gmail.com.

SHOOTER, Prof. Eric Manvers, FRS 1988; Professor of Neurobiology, Stanford University, 1975–2004, now Emeritus; *b* 18 April 1924; adopted US nationality, 1991; *s* of Fred and Pattie Shooter; *m* 1949, Elaine Staley Arnold; one *d*. *Educ:* Gonville and Caius Coll., Cambridge (BA 1945; MA 1950; PhD 1950; ScD 1986); DSc London 1964. Senior Scientist, Brewing Industry Research Foundn, 1950–53; Lectr in Biochem., University Coll. London, 1953–63; Stanford University: Associate Prof. of Genetics, 1963–68; Prof. of Genetics and Prof. of Biochem., 1968–75; Chm. of Neurobiol., 1975–87. Macy Faculty Scholar, Univ. of Geneva, 1974–75. Member: Inst. of Medicine, Nat. Acad. of Scis, USA, 1989; Nat. Acad. of Scis, 2000; Amer. Philos. Soc., 2002. Fellow: American Acad. of Arts and Scis, 1993; AAAS, 1998. Wakeman Award, 1988; Ralph W. Gerard Prize in Neuroscience, 1995; Bristol-Myers Squibb Award for Dist. Achievement in Neurosci. Res., 1997. *Publications:* (associate editor) Annual Review of Neuroscience, vols 6–24, 1983–2001; numerous papers in sci jls. *Address:* Department of Neurobiology, Stanford University School of Medicine, Stanford, CA 94305–5125, USA. *T:* (650) 8518373.

SHOOTER, Michael Stanhope, CBE 2005; FRCPsych; President: Royal College of Psychiatrists, 2002–05; British Association for Counselling and Psychotherapy, 2012–15; *b* 19 Sept. 1944; *s* of Arnold Shooter and Audrey Frances Shooter (*née* Stanhope); *m* 1967, Mary Davies; three *s* one *d*. *Educ:* Lady Manners Sch., Bakewell; St Catharine's Coll., Cambridge (MA Hist./Law); Clare Coll., Cambridge (MB BChir). FRCPsych 1994. Consultant: Child and Adolescent Psychiatry, S Glamorgan, 1982–94; and Clinical Dir, Child Psychiatry Service, Gwent Healthcare NHS Trust, 1994–2002. Dir of Public Educn, 1994–2002, Registrar, 1997–2002, RCPsych. Chairman: Young Minds, 2006–09; Children in Wales, 2006–12; Mental Health Foundn, 2008–11. *Publications:* contrib. books and jls on all aspects of psychiatry and paediatric liaison in UK, USA and elsewhere. *Recreations:* horse-racing, poetry, late-night cards in isolated country pubs. *Address:* Royal College of Psychiatrists, 21 Prescot Street, E1 8BB. *E:* mshooter@rcpsych.ac.uk; Ty Boda, Upper Llanover, Abergavenny, Gwent NP7 9EP. *Club:* East India.

SHORE OF STEPNEY, Lady; *see* Shore, E. C.

SHORE, Andrew; freelance operatic baritone, since 1979; *b* Oldham, Lancs, 30 Sept. 1952; *s* of Frank and Edith Shore; *m* 1976, Fiona Mary Macdonald; three *d*. *Educ:* Counthill Grammar Sch., Oldham; Bristol Univ. (BA Theol. 1974); Royal Northern Coll. of Music; London Opera Centre. Débuts: Kent Opera, 1979; ENO, 1987; Glyndebourne Fest. Opera, 1988; Royal Opera, Covent Gdn, 1992; Paris Opera, 1995; Metropolitan Opera, NY, 2006; Bayreuth Fest., Germany, 2006; La Scala, Milan, 2009; rôles include: title rôles in Falstaff, Don Pasquale, Gianni Schicchi, King Priam, Wozzeck, Jakob Lenz; Papageno in Die Zauberflöte; Bartolo in Barbiere di Siviglia; Dulcamara in L'Elisir d'amore; Leporello in Don Giovanni; Alberich in Der Ring des Nibelungen; Pooh Bah in The Mikado; Major-General in The Pirates of Penzance; Beckmesser in Die Meistersinger. Hon. DMus Bristol, 2014. *Recreations:* theatre, art galleries, country-walking, fine wine, model railways. *Address:* c/o Ingpen & Williams Ltd, 7 St George's Court, 131 Putney Bridge Road, SW15 2PA. *T:* (020) 8874 3222. *E:* jg@ingpen.co.uk. *Club:* Two Brydges.

SHORE, Dr Elizabeth Catherine, CB 1980; Chairman, St Ives University of the Third Age, 2004–07; *b* 19 Aug. 1927; *d* of Edward Murray Wrong and Rosalind Grace Smith; *m* 1948, Peter David Shore (later Baron Shore of Stepney, PC; he *d* 2001); one *s* two *d* (and one *s* decd). *Educ:* Newnham Coll., Cambridge; St Bartholomew's Hospital; BA Hons Open 1999. MRCP, FRCP; MRCS, FFCM, DRCOG. Joined Medical Civil Service, 1962; Dep. Chief Medical Officer, DHSS, 1977–85. Dean of Postgrad. Medicine, NW Thames Reg., 1985–93; Assoc. Dean of Postgrad. Med. Educn, N Thames Reg., 1993–95. Hon. Sen. Lectr, Charing Cross and Westminster Med. Sch., 1993–97. Mem., GMC, 1989–94 (Member: Standards Cttee, 1989–91; Professional Conduct Cttee, 1991–93; Educnl Cttee, 1992–93; Prelim. Proceeding Cttee, 1993). Pres., Med. Women's Fedn, 1990–92 (Chm., Careers Cttee, 1989–95); Chair: BMA Career Progress Cttee, 1994–96; BMA Working Party on Exodus of Doctors, 1996–97. Mem. Council, PSI, 1992–2001; Chm., Mgt Cttee, St Ives Archive Centre, 2005–07. Trustee, Child Accident Prevention Trust, 1985–91 (Chm., Council and Professional Cttee, 1985–90). Editor, Medical Woman, 1992–98. *Recreations:* reading, cookery, swimming in rough seas. *Address:* 3 Barnaloft, St Ives, Cornwall TR26 1NJ.

SHORE, Prof. Paul Raymond, PhD; FREng; Head, Engineering Measurement Division, National Physical Laboratory, since 2015; McKeown Professor of Ultra Precision Technologies, Cranfield University, since 2003 (Head, Precision Engineering Centre, 2003–15); *b* Chester, 5 Oct. 1962; *s* of John Shore and Eileen Shore (*née* Walker); *m* 1993, Siân Jones; one *s* two *d*. *Educ:* Liverpool Poly. (HND Mech. Engrg 1984); Cranfield Inst. of Technol. (MSc Machine Design 1986); Cranfield Univ. (PhD Ultra Precision Engrg 1995). FREng 2009. Process Develt Manager, Cranfield Unit for Precision Engrg, 1988–95; Sen. Engr, SKF (Netherlands), 1996–97; Tech. Develt Manager, Lidköping Machine Tools, 1997–2000; Gp Tech. Manager, SKF (Sweden), 2000–03. Pres., Eur. Soc. for Precision Engrg and Nanotechnol., 2011–13. *Publications:* contribs to jls incl. Wear, Advanced Engrg Materials, Key Engrg Materials, Ingenia. *Recreations:* classic motorcycling, football. *Address:* 29 The Mount, Aspley Guise, Beds MK17 8DZ. *T:* (01908) 582944. *E:* shores29@btinternet.com. *Club:* Brickhill Rangers Association Football.

SHORLEY, Deborah Catherine, FCLIP; Director of Library Services, Imperial College London, 2007–12; President, Chartered Institute of Library and Information Professionals, 2005–06; *b* 28 May 1950; *d* of Dennis Randall and Monica (*née* Wilson); *m* 1976, Christopher Shorley (*d* 2007). *Educ:* Univ. of Durham (BA Hons French 1972); Queen's Univ., Belfast (DLIS 1977). FCLIP 2004. Librarian: Central Liby, Belfast, 1977–80; Ulster Polytechnic, subseq. Univ. of Ulster, 1980–2000; Univ. of Sussex, 2000–07. *Publications:* (ed with M. Jubb) The Future of Scholarly Communication, 2013; articles on liby and information issues to professional jls. *E:* dshorley@gmail.com.

SHORROCK, (John) Michael; QC 1988; a Recorder of the Crown Court, since 1982; *b* 25 May 1943; *s* of late James Godby Shorrock and Mary Patricia Shorrock (*née* Lings); *m* 1971, Marianne (*née* Mills); two *d*. *Educ:* Clifton College, Bristol; Pembroke College, Cambridge. MA. Called to the Bar, Inner Temple, 1966, Bencher, 1995; practising on Northern Circuit, 1966–: Junior, 1968; Sec., Exec. Cttee, 1981–85. Member: Criminal Injuries Compensation Bd, 1995–2000; Criminal Injuries Compensation Appeals Panel, 1996–2008; Tribunal Judge, Social Entitlement Chamber, Criminal Injuries Compensation, 2008–. Gov., William Hulme's Grammar Sch., 1999–2005. *Recreations:* walking, gardening, opera, theatre, cinema. *Address:* 2 Harcourt Buildings, Temple, EC4Y 9DB. *T:* (020) 7353 2112; St Johns Buildings, 24a–28 St John Street, Manchester M3 4DJ. *T:* (0161) 214 1500.

SHORROCK, Philip Geoffrey; His Honour Judge Shorrock; a Circuit Judge, since 2009; *b* 28 June 1956; *s* of Geoffrey and Jean Shorrock. *Educ:* King's Sch., Canterbury; Clare Coll., Cambridge (BA Hons Law 1977). Called to the Bar, Middle Temple, 1978, Bencher, 2005; in practice as barrister, 1978–2009; Recorder, 2002–09. *Recreations:* the turf, cricket, soccer, good food, drink and company. *Address:* Woolwich Crown Court, 2 Belmarsh Road, SE28 0EY. *T:* (020) 8321 7000. *Clubs:* Garrick, XII.

SHORT, Alan; *see* Short, C. A.

SHORT, Andrew John; QC 2010; *b* Sidcup, 30 March 1967; *s* of John Short and Shirley Short; *m* 1998, Frances Louise Tomlinson; one *d*. *Educ:* Dartford Grammar Sch.; Bristol Univ. (LLB Hons). Called to the Bar, Gray's Inn, 1990; in practice as barrister, specialising in employment, discrimination and pensions law. *Publications:* Disability Discrimination: law and practice, 1996. *Recreations:* triathlon, Arsenal, food (all aspects). *Address:* Outer Temple Chambers, The Outer Temple, 222 Strand, WC2R 1BA. *T:* (020) 7353 6381. *E:* andrew.short@outertemple.com. *Club:* East London Triathletes.

SHORT, Bernard David, CBE 1995; Head of Further Education Support Unit, Department for Education and Employment (formerly Department for Education), 1993–96; *b* 9 June 1935; *s* of late Bernard Charles and of Ethel Florence Short; *m* 1960, Susan Yvonne Taylor; two *s* one *d*. *Educ:* St Edmund Hall, Oxford (MA). Served The Royal Scots, 1953–56 (commnd 1954). Taught at Ingiliz Erkek Lisesi, Istanbul, Turkey, 1960–63; Lectr, Univ. of Kyushu, Japan, 1963–65; Asst Lectr, Garretts Green Technical Coll., Birmingham, 1966–67; Lectr, Bournville Coll. of Further Educn, Birmingham, 1967–71; Sen. Lectr, Henley Coll. of Further Educn, Coventry, 1971–73; Head, Dept of Gen. Studies, Bournville Coll., Birmingham, 1973–76; HM Inspectorate of Schools, 1976–93: Inspector, 1976; Staff Inspector, 1984; Chief Inspector, Further Education, 1986. Chm. of Govs, Bournville Coll., Birmingham, 2000–06. FRSA 1991. *Publications:* A Guide to Stress in English, 1967; Humour, 1970. *Recreations:* music, gardening, boats.

SHORT, Prof. (Charles) Alan, RIBA; Professor of Architecture, University of Cambridge, since 2001 (Head, Department of Architecture, 2001–04); Fellow, Clare Hall, Cambridge, since 2002; Principal, Short & Associates, since 1997; *b* 23 March 1955; *s* of C. R. and D. H. Short; *m* 2003, Slaine Catherine Campbell; one *d*. *Educ:* Trinity Coll., Cambridge (MA, DipArch). RIBA 1981. Exchange Fellow, Harvard Grad. Sch. of Design, 1979–80; Partner: Edward Cullinan Architects, 1980–86; Peake Short and Partners, 1986–92; Short Ford & Associates, 1992–97; Dean, Faculty of Art and Design, De Montfort Univ., 1997–2001. FRSA 1998. George Collins Fellowship, Soc. of Architectural Historians, USA, 2014; Geddes Fellow, Univ. of Edinburgh, 2014. Major projects include: Simonds Farsons Cisk Brewery, Malta (High Architecture, Low Energy Award, Architecture Today jl, 1994); Queen's Building, Leicester (Green Building of the Year Award, Independent/RIBA, 1995); Coventry Univ. Library (Public Building of Year award, Building mag., 2001); Poole Arts Centre, Dorset, 2002 (Project of Year Award, CIBSE, 2003); Lichfield Garrick Theatre, 2003 (Project of Year Award, CIBSE, 2004); new SSEES for UCL, 2005 (RIBA Award, 2006; Envmtl Initiative of the Year Award, CIBSE, 2006; Public Building of the Year, BDA, 2006); Braunstone Integrated Health and Social Care Centre, 2005. FRSA. President's Award for Res., 2007, President's Commendation for Res., 2009, RIBA. Mem., Editl Bd, Bldg Res. and Inf., 2011–. Global Sustainability Film Award, tv/e, 2013. *Publications:* Geometry and Atmosphere, 2011; contribs to res. and professional jls, UK, China, USA, Italy and Germany. *Recreations:* restoration of family home and gardens in Lincolnshire, historical and contemporary landscape. *Address:* Department of Architecture, University of Cambridge, 1–4 Scroope Terrace, Trumpington Road, Cambridge CB2 1PX. *T:* (01223) 332958, *Fax:* (01223) 307443. *E:* cas64@cam.ac.uk. *Clubs:* Chelsea Arts, Oxford and Cambridge.

SHORT, Rt Hon. Clare; PC 1997; *b* 15 Feb. 1946; *d* of late Frank Short and Joan Short; *m* 1981, Alexander Ward Lyon (*d* 1993), sometime MP for York; one *s* by previous marriage. *Educ:* Keele Univ.; Leeds Univ. (BA Hons Political Sci.). Home Office, 1970–75; Dir, All Faiths for One Race, Birmingham, 1976–78; Dir, Youth Aid and the Unemployment Unit, 1979–83. MP Birmingham, Ladywood, 1983–2010 (Lab, 1983–2006, Ind, 2006–10). Chm., All Party Parly Gp on Race Relations, 1985–86; Mem., Home Affairs Select Cttee, 1983–85; front bench spokesperson on employment, 1985–88, on social security, 1989–91, on envmtl protection, 1993, on women, 1993–95, on transport, 1995–96, on overseas develt, 1996–97; Sec. of State for Internat. Develt, 1997–2003. Mem., Labour Party NEC, 1988–98. Chair, Extractive Industries Transparency Initiative, 2011–. Sen. Policy Advr, Cities Alliance, 2006–. *Publications:* Talking Blues: a study of young West Indians' views of policing, 1978; Handbook of Immigration Law, 1978; Dear Clare … this is what women think about Page 3, 1991; An Honourable Deception?: New Labour, Iraq and the misuse of power, 2004. *Recreations:* family and friends, swimming. *W:* www.clareshort.co.uk.

SHORT, Maj. Gen. James Henderson Terry, CB 2005; OBE 1994; Director, Joint Warfare Centre (formerly Joint Headquarters North), Norway, 2002–05; Director, AugMentor UK, 2006–13; *b* 20 March 1950; *s* of Frederick Gordon Terry Short and Verona Margaret Terry Short (*née* Peters); *m* 1975, Claire Elizabeth Hedley (*née* Hooper); two *s*. *Educ:* Wellington Coll., Berks; RMCS, Shrivenham (BSc Hons Applied Sci.). Regtl Service, 9th/12th Royal Lancers, 1970–82; army staff course, 1982–83; Cabinet Office Assessments Staff, 1984–85; MA to Comdr 1 (BR) Corps, 1985–87; Directing Staff, Staff Coll., Camberley, 1988–90; Procurement Exec., MoD, 1991–92; CO 9th/12th Royal Lancers, 1992–94; Comdr 39 Infantry Bde, Belfast, 1995–97; Dir, RAC, 1997–2000; Special Advr to Macedonian Govt, 2000–02. Col, 9th/12th Royal Lancers, 2008–. Chm., Jesse May Trust, 2008–. FCMI (FIMgt 1997). *Recreations:* sailing, ski-ing, tennis, windsurfing. *Address:* 11 Tansy Lane, Portishead, N Somerset BS20 7JL. *T:* (01275) 848991. *E:* jhtshort@hotmail.com. *Club:* Cavalry and Guards.

SHORT, Dr Mary Elizabeth; Headmistress, St Helen's School, Northwood, since 2011; *b* Gillingham, Kent, 2 Oct. 1958; *d* of Alexander Short and Joyce Short; *m* 2005, David Dyke. *Educ:* Chatham Grammar Sch. for Girls; University Coll. London (BA Hons Hist.); Inst. of Educn, Univ. of London (PGCE); St John's Coll., Cambridge (PhD 1986). Teacher of History and Politics, City of London Sch., 1987–95; Hd of Hist., St Paul's Girls' Sch., 1995–2004; Dep. Hd, Pastoral, Haberdashers' Aske's Sch. for Girls, 2004–11. *Recreations:* walking, reading, history, pottering - gardening, cooking, drawing. *Address:* St Helen's School, Eastbury Road, Northwood, Middx HA6 3AS. *T:* (01923) 843209, *Fax:* (01923) 843201. *E:* headmistress@sthn.co.uk.

SHORT, Nigel David, MBE 1999; professional chess player, commentator, coach and writer; *b* 1 June 1965; *s* of David Malcolm Short and Jean Short (*née* Gaskell); *m* 1987, Rhea Argyro, *d* of Nikolaos Karageorgiou; one *s* one *d*. *Educ:* Bolton Sch. British chess champion: 1979 (equal first), 1984, 1987, 1998; English Chess Champion, 1991; internat. master 1980; grandmaster 1984; world championship candidate, 1985–93 (finalist, 1992, defeating Anatoly Karpov in semi-final); Commonwealth Champion, 2004, 2006, 2008; EU Champion, 2006; Canadian Open Champion, 2013. Formed Professional Chess Assoc. with Garry Kasparov, 1993, Pres., 2005–08. Chess columnist: Sunday Telegraph, 1996–2005; The Guardian, 2005–06; New in Chess, 2011–. Chess Coach, Islamic Republic of Iran, 2006–07. Hon. ScD Bolton, 2010. *Recreations:* olive farming, cricket, swimming, guitar.

SHORT, Norma Ann; *see* Winstone, N. A.

SHORT, Peter, BA; financial management consultant, 1995–2009; *b* 21 June 1945; *s* of Christopher John Grewcock Short and Isabella Short; *m* 1967, Eileen Short (*née* Makin); one *s* one *d*. *Educ:* South Shields Grammar Sch.; Univ. of Exeter (2nd Cl. Hons, Div. 1, Modern Economic History). IPFA, 1971–2009 (1st place Final, 1970). Local Govt Accountant with Manchester City Council, 1967–73; Leeds City Council, 1973–78; Dir of Finance, South Tyneside MDC, 1978–83; City Treas. and Dep. Chief Exec., Manchester CC, 1983–89; Dir of Finance, Greater Manchester Buses Ltd, 1989–93; Man. Dir, Gtr Manchester Buses South Ltd, 1993–95. *Recreations:* reading, walking, avoiding household maintenance, reminiscing about walking the Pennine Way. *Address:* 2 Netherwood Road, Northenden, Manchester M22 4BQ.

SHORT, Robin; *see* Short, W. R.

SHORT, Prof. Roger Valentine, AM 2004; FRCOG; FRS 1974; FRSE; FRCVS; FAA; Hon. Professorial Fellow, Faculty of Medicine, University of Melbourne, since 2006; *b* 31 July 1930; *s* of F. A. and M. C. Short, Weybridge, Surrey; *m* 1st, 1958, Dr Mary Bowen Wilson (marr. diss. 1981); one *s* three *d*; 2nd, 1982, Prof. Marilyn Bernice Renfree; two *d*. *Educ:* Sherborne Sch.; Univs of Bristol (BVSc, MRCVS), Wisconsin (MSc) and Cambridge (PhD, ScD). FRSE 1974; FRCVS 1976; FAA 1984; FRCOG 1991. Mem., ARC Unit of Reproductive Physiology and Biochemistry, Cambridge, 1956–72; Fellow, Magdalene Coll., Cambridge, 1962–72; Lectr, then Reader, Dept of Veterinary Clinical Studies, Cambridge, 1961–72; Dir, MRC Unit of Reproductive Biology, Edinburgh, 1972–82; Prof. of Reproductive Biology, Monash Univ., Australia, 1982–95; Wexler Professorial Fellow, Dept of Perinatal Medicine, subseq. Obstetrics and Gynaecol., Univ. of Melbourne, 1996–2005. Hon. Prof., Univ. of Edinburgh, 1976–82. Chm., Bd of Dirs, Family Health Internat., NC, USA, 1984–90. Fellow, American Acad. of Arts and Scis. Hon. DSc: Guelph, 1988; Bristol, 1997; Edinburgh, 2002. *Publications:* (ed, with C. R. Austin) Reproduction in Mammals, vols 1–8, 1972–80, 2nd edn vols 1–5, 1982–86; (ed, with D. T. Baird) Contraceptives of the Future, 1976; (with M. Potts) Ever Since Adam and Eve, 1999; contrib. Jl Endocrinology, Jl Reproduction and Fertility, Jl Zoology, Lancet, Nature. *Recreations:* gardening, wildlife, history of biology, elephants. *Address:* The Dean's Ganglion, Level 4, 766 Elizabeth Street, University of Melbourne, Vic 3010, Australia.

SHORT, Maj.-Gen. William Robert, (Robin), CB 1999; Operations Director, PHC Ltd, 1999–2007; *b* 30 March 1942; *s* of Dr Andrew Galbraith Short and Dr Helen Greig Short (*née* Dunlop); *m* 1st, 1967, Annette Pamela Barrow (*d* 2012); three *s*; 2nd, 2013, Sylvia Nina Quayle, OBE. *Educ:* Glasgow High Sch.; Glasgow Univ. (MB ChB). RMO, 1 Black Watch, RHR, 1969–72; 19 Field Ambulance, RAMC, 1972–73; RAMC Trng Centre, 1973–76; Army Staff Coll., 1976–77 (psc); SO2, Med. HQ 1 (BR) Corps, 1978–81; CO, 3 Armd Field Ambulance, RAMC, 1981–84; Chief Instr, RAMC Trng Centre, 1984–86; Comdr Med. 1 Armd Div., 1986–88; Col, Ops and Plans, 1988–91, Dir Med. Ops and Logistics, 1991–94, Defence Med. Services Directorate; Comdr, Med. HQ Land Comd, 1994–96; DGAMS, 1996–99. Chm., RAMC Assoc., 1999–2005. QHP, 1996–99. CStJ 1997 (OStJ 1971). *Recreations:* running a smallholding, collecting cigarette cards (cartophily).

SHORTER, Hugo Benedict; HM Diplomatic Service; Ambassador to Lebanon, since 2015; *b* 11 Aug. 1966; *s* of Gervase Shorter and Charmian Shorter (*née* Stopford-Adams); *m* 2001, Laura Mercedes Lindon; two *s* one *d*. *Educ:* Lycée Molière, Rio de Janeiro; Queen's Coll., Oxford (BA 1988); Ecole Nat. d'Admin, Paris. Entered HM Diplomatic Service, 1990; FCO, 1990–92; Second Sec., on attachment to Ecole Nat. d'Admin, Paris, 1992–93; Second, later First, Sec., UK Delegn to NATO, 1994–98; FCO, 1998; Private Sec to Minister of State, FCO, 2000–01; Dep. Hd, NE Asia and Pacific Dept, FCO, 2001–04; Dep. Hd of Mission, Brasilia, 2004–07; Counsellor (Global Issues), later Minister-Counsellor (Europe and Global Issues), Paris, 2007–12; Hd, Europe Directorate - External, FCO, 2012–15. *Recreations:* reading, travel, sailing. *Address:* Foreign and Commonwealth Office, King Charles Street, SW1A 2AH. *E:* hugo.shorter@fco.gov.uk.

SHORTIS, Maj.-Gen. Colin Terry, CB 1988; CBE 1980 (OBE 1977; MBE 1974); General Officer Commanding North West District, 1986–89; *b* 18 Jan. 1934; *s* of late Tom Richardson Shortis and Marna Evelyn Shortis (*née* Kenworthy); *m* 1st, 1957, Sylvia Mary (*d* 2006), *o d* of H. C. A. Jenkinson; two *s* two *d*; 2nd, 2009, Sylvia Dawn, *d* of G. A. Payne. *Educ:* Bedford School. Enlisted Army 1951; 2nd Lieut Royal Fusiliers, 1953; transf. to Dorset Regt, 1955; served Hong Kong, Korea, Suez Canal Zone, Sudan, BAOR, Aden, Singapore and British Guiana, 1953–63; Instructor, Sch. of Infantry, 1964–65; Staff Coll., 1966; Co. Comdr, 1st Devonshire and Dorset, 1967–73; served Malta, NI, Belize, Cyprus, BAOR, CO 1974–77; Directing Staff, Staff Coll., 1977; Comdr, 8 Infantry Brigade, 1978–80; RCDS 1981; Comdr, British Mil. Adv. and Training Team, Zimbabwe, 1982–83; Dir of Infantry, 1983–86. Col Comdt, The Prince of Wales Div., 1983–88; Col, Devonshire and Dorset Regt, 1984–90. *Recreation:* sailing. *Address:* Hart House, 52 Fore Street, Topsham, Exeter EX3 0HW. *Club:* Army and Navy.

SHORTRIDGE, Sir Jon Deacon, KCB 2002; Permanent Secretary, Welsh Office, then National Assembly for Wales, later Welsh Assembly Government, 1999–2008; *b* 10 April 1947; *s* of late Eric Creber Deacon Shortridge and Audrey Joan Shortridge (*née* Hunt); *m* 1972, Diana Jean Gordon; one *s* one *d*. *Educ:* Chichester High Sch.; St Edmund Hall, Oxford (MA; Hon. Fellow 2012); Edinburgh Univ. (MSc). Min. of Housing, then Countryside Commn, subseq. DoE, 1969–75; Shropshire County Planning Dept, 1975–84; Welsh Office: Principal, 1984–88, Pvte Sec. to Sec. of State for Wales, 1987–88; Asst Sec., 1988–92; G3, 1992–97; Dir of Economic Affairs, 1997–99; Perm. Sec., 1999; Interim Permanent Sec., DIUS, then BIS, 2009. Mem., UK Statistics Authy, 2010–12; Adv. Mem., Commn for Local Govt in England, 2012–. Chair: Audit Cttee (formerly Audit Panel), Cardiff CC, 2009–; Audit Cttee, Parly and Health Service Ombudsman, 2010– (Mem., Unitary Bd (formerly Adv. Bd), 2012–); Audit Cttee, Commn for Local Govt in England, 2012–; Member: Audit and Scrutiny Cttee, Oxford Univ., 2012–; Audit Cttee, Royal Soc., 2014–. Chair, Community Service Volunteers, 2010–. Mem. Council, Cardiff Univ., 2008–12. Chancellor and Chm., Glyndŵr Univ., 2012–. Hon. Fellow: Aberystwyth Univ., 2008; Univ. of Wales Inst., Cardiff, 2008; Glyndwyr Univ., 2011. DUniv Glamorgan, 2010. *Recreations:* gardening, tennis, walking, modern history. *Address:* Ebor House, 31 Kennedy Road, Shrewsbury, Shropshire SY3 7AB. *Club:* Oxford and Cambridge.

SHORVON, Prof. Simon David, MD; FRCP; Professor in Clinical Neurology, Institute of Neurology, University College London, since 1995; Hon. Consultant Neurologist, National Hospital for Neurology and Neurosurgery (formerly for Nervous Diseases), since 1983; *b* 17 June 1948; *s* of late Hyam Joseph Shorvon, DPM and of Mary Barbara Shorvon (*née* Bensusan Butt), MRCPsych; *m* 1st, 1984, Penelope Farmer (marr. diss.); 2nd, 1999, Dr Lynne Soon Li Low; one *s*. *Educ:* City of London Sch.; Trinity Coll., Cambridge (BA 1970; MB BChir 1974; MA 1974; MD 1983); St Thomas' Hosp. Med. Sch. MRCP 1975, FRCP 1990. Jun. med. and academic appts, Oxford, Manchester, KCH, Maudsley Hosp., and Nat. Hosp. for Nervous Diseases, 1973–83; Vis. Scientist, Univ. of Virginia, 1981; Sen. Lectr, 1983–92, Reader in Neurology, 1992–95, Chm., Dept of Clin. Neurology, 1998–2002, Inst. of Neurology, UCL; Dir, Nat. Neurosci. Inst., Singapore, 2000–03. Med. Dir, Nat. Soc. for Epilepsy, 1989–98. Member: Med. Panel, DVLA, 1987–; Disability Living Allowance Bd, 1994–96; Chm., Med. Commn, Nat. Hosp. for Neurology and Neurosurgery, 2010–. Harveian Librarian and Mem. Council, RCP, 2012–. Mem., Exec. Cttee, Internat. League Against Epilepsy (Vice-Pres., 1993–). Mem., editl bds, internat. learned jls; Guarantor, Brain, 1998–; Ed.-in-Chief, Epilepsia, 1999–. Eur. Epileptology Award, Internat. League against Epilepsy, 2008; Lennox Award, Amer. Epilepsy Soc., 2010; T. S. Shrinivasan Award, 2010. *Publications:* Neurological Emergencies, 1989; Status Epilepticus: its clinical form and treatment in children and adults, 1994; (ed jtly) Magnetic Resonance Scanning and Epilepsy, 1994; (ed jtly) Epilepsy, 2nd edn 1995; Clinical Epilepsy, 1995; (ed jtly) The Treatment of Epilepsy, 1996, 4th edn 2015; Handbook of Epilepsy Treatment, 2000, 4th edn 2016; (ed jtly) Neurology: a Queen Square textbook, 2009, 2nd edn 2015; International League Against Epilepsy 1909–2009: a centenary history, 2009; The Causes of Epilepsy, 2011; The Beginning of the End of the Falling Sickness, 2012; Oxford Textbook of Epilepsy and Epileptic Seizures, 2013; The National Hospital, Queen Square, 2016; contribs to epilepsy, epidemiology and clin. neurology in learned jls. *Recreations:* the liberal arts, human rights and political freedom.

Address: UCL Institute of Neurology, Box 5, National Hospital for Neurology and Neurosurgery, Queen Square, WC1N 3BG. *T:* (020) 3448 3422. *E:* s.shorvon@ucl.ac.uk. *Club:* Athenæum.

SHOSTAK, Raymond Jon, Hon. CBE 2005; Lead Executive, Core Assets Group, 2011–13; *b* 2 July 1949; *s* of late Jerome M. Shostak and Alma (*née* Stern); *m* 1980, Gill Rivaz; one *s* one *d. Educ:* Nanuet Jun. Sen. High Sch.; Syracuse Univ. (BA Hons); Univ. of Southern Calif (MSc). Teacher: Isbell Jun. High Sch., Santa Paula, Calif, 1971–73; Leggatts Sch., Watford, Herts, 1973–74; Dep. Warden, 1974, Warden, 1975–83, SW Herts Teachers' Centre, Herts CC; Sen. Staff Inspector, Notts CC Adv. Inspection Service, 1983–86; Asst Dir of Educn and Chief Advr, W Sussex CC, 1989–96; Ofsted Inspector, 1993–99; Head, Pupil Performance Team, Sch. Effectiveness Div., DFEE, 1996–97; Dir of Educn, 1997–2001, Dir, Children, Schs and Families Service, 2001–03, Herts CC; Strategic Advr, Children's Services, Improvement and Develt Agency, 2003; Dir, Public Services, HM Treasury, 2003–07; Head, Prime Minister's Delivery Unit, 2007–10. Internat. advr to govts, 2013–. Non-exec. Dir, Nat. Audit Office, 2015–. Dir, Herts TEC, 1997–2001; Board Member: QCA, 2001–03; Herts Learning and Skills Council, 2001–03; Chm., Wallenberg Centre for Improvement in Educn, Univ. of Cambridge, 1998–2001. Mem., Eastern Region NHS Children's Task Force, 2001–03. Sec., Soc. of Chief Inspectors and Advrs, 1992–96. Chm. Trustees, Consortium of Voluntary Adoption Agencies, 2014–; Trustee, Early Intervention Foundn. Vis. Fellow (part-time), Sussex Univ., 1996–99; Norham Fellow, Oxford Univ., 2014–. FRSA 1993. *Recreations:* family, ski-ing, tennis, photography, woodturning.

SHOTT, Ian Dermot, CBE 2009; CEng, FREng, FIChemE, FRSC; Managing Partner, Shott Trinova, since 2011; Chairman: KFS Ltd, since 2011; Industrial Biotechnology Innovation Centre, since 2013; BPE Design Support Ltd, since 2014; *b* Tanga, Tanganyika, 26 Feb. 1957; *s* of Albert Shott and Mary Shott (*née* White); *m* 1985, Nicole Sara Poirier; one *s* one *d. Educ:* King Edward VI Grammar Sch., Southampton; Imperial Coll., London (BScEng Hons Chem. Engrg); INSEAD (Adv. Mktg Dip.). CEng 1984; FIChemE 2003; FRSC 2007; FREng 2008. Gen. Manager, Zeneca, 1990–93; Sen. Vice Pres., Lonza, 1993–98; Chief Operating Officer and Pres., Chirex, 1998–2000; Pres., Rhodia Chirex, 2000–03; Founder and CEO, Ian Shott Enterprises Ltd, subseq. Excelsyn, 2003–10; CEO, Shott Consulting Ltd, 2011–13. Chairman: Gap Technologies Ltd, 2011–13; GXPi Ltd, 2011–13. Chairman: Pharmaceutical and Specialty Cluster, 2001–04; RTC North, 2002–05; Centre of Excellence for Life Scis, 2006–12; UK Innovation and Growth Team for Industrial Biotechnol., 2007–10; Industrial Biotechnol. Leadership Forum, 2010–13; Dep. Chm., NE Process Industry Cluster, 2004–05; Member: Ministerial Adv. Gp on Manuf. Strategy, 2008–10; Governing Bd, InnovateUK (formerly Technology Strategy Bd), 2011– (Chm., Catapult Cttee, 2014–); Chemistry Growth Partnership, Govt Industrial Strategy, 2013–; Specialist Advr to Sci. and Technol. Cttee, H of L, 2013–14; Chm., Strategic Adv. Bd (Chem. Engrg), Imperial Coll. London, 2014–. Vis. Prof., Newcastle Univ., 2004– (Mem. Council, 2004–12; Hon. Prof. 2007); Hon. Prof., Sustainable Process Technol., Nottingham Univ., 2014– (Chm., Strategic Adv. Bd, Synthetic Biol. Res. Centre). Pres., IChemE, 2009–10. Royal Academy of Engineering: Mem., Policy Cttee, 2010–13; Chairman: Enterprise Fellowship Cttee, 2010–13; Enterprise Hub Cttee, 2013–; Enterprise Cttee, 2014–. Hon. DSc Nottingham, 2010. *Recreations:* motoring, squash, ski-ing, golf, food and wine.

SHOTT, Nicholas Roland; Vice Chairman, European Investment Banking and Head, UK Investment Banking, Lazard, since 2009; *b* Surrey, 22 Sept. 1951; *s* of Roland and Madeline Shott; *m* 2007, Melanie Sarah Hutton; two *s*; one *d* from previous marriage. *Educ:* Haileybury and ISC. Joined Beaverbrook Newspapers Ltd as exec., 1971; Gen. Manager, Evening Standard, 1981; Dir, Express Newspapers, 1981–87; Man. Dir, Express Newspapers (North), 1983; Chief Exec., Sunday Correspondent, 1987–90; Lazard: banker, 1991–; Dir, 1993–96; Man. Dir, 1996. Hd of Inquiry into viability of local TV for Sec. of State, DCMS, 2010. MCSI (MSI 1992). *Recreations:* shooting, walking, sailing/boating, opera. *Address:* Lazard, 50 Stratton Street, W1J 8LL. *E:* nicholas.shott@lazard.com. *Clubs:* Thirty, Annabel's, Mark's, Harry's Bar.

SHOTTER, Very Rev. Edward Frank; Dean of Rochester, 1989–2003, now Dean Emeritus; *b* 29 June 1933; *s* of late Frank Edward Shotter and Minnetta Shotter (*née* Gaskill); *m* 1978, Jane Edgcumbe; two *s* one *d. Educ:* Humberstone Foundation School, Clee; Durham Univ. School of Architecture; St David's Coll., Lampeter, Univ. of Wales (BA 1958); St Stephen's House, Oxford. Deacon 1960, priest 1961; Curate of St Peter, Plymouth, 1960–62; Intercollegiate Sec., SCM, London, 1962–66; Dir of Studies, London Medical Group, 1963–89; Dir, Inst. of Medical Ethics, 1974–89 (Amulree Fellow, 1991–; Vice Pres., 1999–); Chaplain to Univ. of London, 1969–89; Prebendary of St Paul's Cathedral, 1977–89. Leverhulme Sen. Educnl Fellowship, 1976–79. Chairman: Cttee on Welfare of Czechoslovak Med. Students in Britain, 1968–69; Educn Sub-Cttee, Faculty of History and Phil. of Medicine, Apothecaries Soc., 1976–81; Church, Commerce and Industry Project, 1991–95: N Kent NHS Chaplaincy Service, 1993–96; Jt Chm., Kent Police Ecumenical Chaplaincy Cttee, 1993–2001; Force Chaplain, Kent Co. Constab., 1996–2001. Member: SCM Trust Assoc. Exec., 1965–79; Univ. Chaplains' Cttee, C of E Bd of Educn, 1968–70; Archbishop of Canterbury's Counsellors on Foreign Relations, 1971–82; BCC East/West Relations Adv. Cttee, 1971–81; Liberal Party Foreign Affairs Panel (Chm. East Europe Sub-Cttee), 1974–81; St Christopher's Hospice Educn Cttee, 1982–89; Wkg Party on ethics of med. involvement in torture, 1989–91; Chm., IME working party on ethics of prolonging life and assisting death, 1991–98; Chm., Univ. of Greenwich Res. Ethics Cttee, 1995–2003. Chairman: Medway Enterprise Agency, 1993–98; Medway Business Support Partnership, 1994–96; Medway Business Point Ltd, 1996–98. Dir, Firmstart Medway Ltd, 1991–2000. C of E rep. on Churches Council of Health and Healing, 1975–76. Mem., Gen. Synod of C of E, 1994–2002; Sec., Assoc. of English Cathedrals, 1994–2002; Mem., Church Heritage Forum, 1999–2002. Chm., HMS Cavalier Meml Steering Gp, 2000–07. Chm., Governing Body, King's School, Rochester, 1989–2003; Pres., St Bartholomew's Hosp., Rochester, 1989–2003. Founder, Jl of Medical Ethics, 1975. FRSocMed 1976. Hon. FRCP 2007. Patriarchal Cross (Oeconomos Stavrophor), Romanian Orthodox Church, 1975. *Publications:* (ed) Matters of Life and Death, 1970; (with K. M. Boyd and B. Callaghan, SJ) Life Before Birth, 1986; The Saints of Rochester, 2003; (with L. A. Reynolds and E. M. Tansey) Medical Ethics Education in Britain 1963–93, 2007; A Benefice of Saints, 2013. *Recreations:* East European affairs, gardening, domestic architecture. *Address:* Hill House, Westhall, Halesworth, Suffolk IP19 8QZ. *T:* (01502) 575364. *Club:* Reform.

SHOTTON, Dr Keith Crawford, CEng, FIET; CPhys, FInstP; Head of Management and Technology Services Division, Department of Trade and Industry, 1994–96; *b* 11 Sept. 1943; *s* of William Crawford Shotton and Mary Margaret Shotton (*née* Smith); *m* 1969, Maria Elizabeth Gonszor; two *d. Educ:* Newcastle upon Tyne Royal Grammar Sch.; Trinity Coll., Cambridge (Schol.; MA, PhD). CPhys, FInstP 1982; CEng, FIET (FIEE 1988). Post-doctoral Fellow (laser physics and spectroscopy), NRCC, 1969–71; National Physical Laboratory: mem. team measuring speed of light, 1971–77; Head, Ultrasonics Metrology Unit, 1977–80; Head, Marketing and Inf. Services, 1980–84; DCSO, Supt, Div. of Radiation Sci. and Acoustics, 1984–87; Department of Trade and Industry: Dir, Radio Technology, Radio Communications Div., 1987–90; Hd, IT Div., 1990–92; Hd, Inf. and Manufg Technols Div., 1992–93; Hd, Technol. Progs and Services Div., 1993–94. *Publications:* papers in sci. jls, principally in spectroscopy, laser physics, ultrasonics and instrumentation. *Recreations:* family, walking, gardens, books, food.

SHOVELTON, Dame Helena, DBE 1999; Chair, 2020health, since 2012; *b* 28 May 1945; *d* of late Denis George Richards, OBE and Barbara Smethurst; *m* 1968, Walter Patrick Shovelton, CB, CMG (*d* 2012). *Educ:* North London Collegiate Sch.; Regent St Poly. (HND Business Studies); Strathclyde Univ. (MBA 1998). Manager, Tunbridge Wells and Dist CAB, 1987–94; National Association of Citizens Advice Bureaux: Council Mem., 1989–90; Vice-Chm., 1990–94; Chm., 1994–99. Mem., 1995–98, Chair, 1998–2001, Audit Commn; Chief Exec., British Lung Foundn, 2002–12; Member: Local Govt Commn, 1995–98 (Dep. Chm., 1996–98); Banking Code Standards Bd (formerly Ind. Review Body for Banking and Mortgage Lending Codes), 1997–2000; Competition (formerly Monopolies and Mergers) Commn, 1997–2004; Better Regulation Task Force, 1997–99; Nat. Lottery Commn, 1999–2000; NHBC, 2009– (non-exec. Dir, 2012–; Chair, Consumer Cttee, 2012–). Chm., Independent Review Panel on Continuing Care, E Sussex, Brighton and Hove HA, 1996–97. Non-exec. Dir, Energy Saving Trust, 1998–2009. Trustee: RAF Benevolent Fund, 1997–2005; Independent Age, 2013–. Volunteer, Islington Foodbank. FRSA 1995; CCMI 2001. Hon. FRCP 2006. British Thoracic Soc. Medal, 2011. *Recreations:* films, theatre, friends.

SHOWALTER, Prof. Elaine, PhD; FRSL; Professor of English and Avalon Foundation Professor of Humanities, Princeton University, 1984–2003, now Emerita; *b* 21 Jan. 1941; *d* of Paul Cottler and Violet Rottenberg; *m* 1963, English Showalter; one *s* one *d. Educ:* Bryn Mawr Coll. (BA 1962); Univ. of California, Davis (PhD 1970). Departments of English: Douglass Coll., 1966–78; Rutgers Univ., 1966–84. Pres., Modern Language Assoc. of America, 1998. FRSL 2012. *Publications:* A Literature of Their Own, 1977; The Female Malady, 1985; Sexual Anarchy, 1990; Sister's Choice: tradition and change in American women's writing, 1991; (jtly) Hysteria Beyond Freud, 1993; Hystories: hysterical epidemics and modern culture, 1997; Inventing Herself: claiming a feminist intellectual heritage, 2001; Teaching Literature, 2002; Faculty Towers, 2005; A Jury of Her Peers: American women writers from Anne Bradstreet to Annie Proulx, 2009. *Address:* 4620 North Park Avenue #405E, Chevy Chase, MD 20815–4579, USA. *T:* (301) 6563248. *Club:* Princeton (New York).

SHREEVE, Ven. David Herbert; Archdeacon of Bradford, 1984–99, now Emeritus; *b* 18 Jan. 1934; *s* of Hubert Ernest and Ivy Eleanor Shreeve; *m* 1957, Barbara (*née* Fogden); one *s* one *d. Educ:* Southfield School, Oxford; St Peter's Coll., Oxford (MA); Ridley Hall, Cambridge. Asst Curate, St Andrew's Church, Plymouth, 1959–64; Vicar: St Anne's, Bermondsey, 1964–71; St Luke's, Eccleshill, 1971–84; RD of Calverley, 1978–84. Mem., Gen. Synod and Proctor in Convocation, 1977–90, 1993–98; Mem., Dioceses Commn, 1988–98. Hon. Canon of Bradford Cathedral, 1983–84. *Recreations:* choral singing, travel, photography. *Address:* 26 Kingsley Drive, Harrogate, N Yorks HG1 4TJ. *T:* (01423) 886479.

SHRESTHA, Surya Prasad; Ambassador of Nepal to the Court of St James's, 1992–97; *b* 1 March 1937; *s* of late L. P. Shrestha and Mrs G. K. Shrestha; *m* 1958, Ginni Baba Shrestha; two *s* two *d. Educ:* Tribhuvan Univ. (MA Pol Sci.); LSE (Dip. Econs and Social Admin). Joined HM Govt service, Nepal, 1958; Section Officer, Parlt Secretariat and Min. of Develt, 1958–63; Under Secretary: Min. of Home and Panchayat, 1963–65; Election Commn, 1965–66; Jt Zonal Comr, 1970–74, Zonal Comr, 1974–78, Bagmati Zone; Actg Sec., Home and Panchayat Min., 1978–79; Sec. of Industry and Commerce, 1979–83; Jt Mem., Nat. Planning Commn, 1983–85; Chief Election Comr, 1985–92. Prabal Gorkha Dakshin Bahu, III Cl. (Nepal), 1966, Prasiddha, II Cl., 1976; Trishakti Patta, Vikhyat, III Cl. (Nepal), 1973, Suvikhyat, II Cl., 1991. FRGS 1996. *Publications:* Democracy Prevails: general election in Nepal, 1991. *Recreations:* reading, gardening. *Address:* PO Box 2482, Jagaran Marg-130, Maharajgung (Chakrapath), Kathmandu, Nepal. *T:* (1) 4720708, 4721135.

SHREWSBURY, Bishop Suffragan of, since 2009; **Rt Rev. Mark James Rylands;** *b* 11 July 1961; *m* 1986, Amanda Byrom (Preb. Amanda Rylands); one *s* one *d. Educ:* Shrewsbury Sch.; St Hild and St Bede Coll., Durham Univ. (BA 1983); Trinity Coll., Bristol (BA 1987); Sheffield Univ. (MA 2006). Ordained deacon, 1987, priest, 1988; Asst Curate, St George's, Stockport, 1987–91; Vicar, Acton and Worleston, Church Minshull and Wettenhall, 1991–97; Team Rector, Langport Area Team Ministry, 1997–2002; Diocesan Missioner, Dio. of Exeter, 2002–09; Canon Residentiary, Exeter Cathedral, 2002–09. *Recreations:* cricket, fishing, butterflies. *Address:* Athlone House, 68 London Road, Shrewsbury SY2 6PG. *T:* (01743) 235867, *Fax:* (01743) 243296. *E:* bishop.shrewsbury@lichfield.anglican.org.

See also P. C. Byrom.

SHREWSBURY, Bishop of, (RC), since 2010; **Rt Rev. Mark Davies;** *b* Manchester, 12 May 1959. *Educ:* St Richard's Infant Sch., St Robert's Primary Sch., Manchester; Broadstone Hall Co. Primary Sch., St Anne's High Sch., Stockport; Ushaw Coll., Univ. of Durham. Ordained priest, 1984; Assistant Priest: Our Lady of Grace, Prestwich, 1984; St Mary's, Swinton, 1984–88; Private Sec. to RC Bishop of Salford, 1988–92; Parish Priest, St John Bosco, Blackley, 1992–2003; Vicar Gen., Diocese of Salford, 2003–09; Parish Priest: St Teresa's, Little Lever, 2003–05; St Joseph's, Longsight, 2005–07; Holy Family, Wigan, 2008–09. *Address:* Diocese of Shrewsbury, 2 Park Road South, Prenton, Wirral CH43 4UX.

SHREWSBURY AND WATERFORD, 22nd Earl of, *cr* 1442 and 1446; **Charles Henry John Benedict Crofton Chetwynd Chetwynd-Talbot;** DL; Baron Talbot, 1733; 7th Earl Talbot, Viscount Ingestre, 1784; Premier Earl on the Rolls of England and Ireland, Hereditary Great Seneschal or Lord High Steward of Ireland; Lord Dungarvan; *b* 18 Dec. 1952; *s* of 21st Earl of Shrewsbury and Waterford, and Nadine (*d* 2003), *yr d* of late Brig.-Gen. C. R. Crofton, CBE; *S* father, 1980; *m* 1974, Deborah, *o d* of late Noel Hutchinson; two *s* one *d. Educ:* Harrow. Director: Britannia Building Soc., 1984–92 (Dep. Chm., 1987–89; Jt Dep. Chm., 1989–92); Richmount Enterprise Zone Managers, 1988–94. Mem. Exec. Cttee, 1988–, Chm., 2000–, Staffs Br., Game Conservancy Trust. Pres., Staffordshire Soc., 1989–91; Vice-Pres., Midland & West Assoc. of Building Socs, 1984–92; Pres., BSA, 1993–97. Chairman: Firearms Consultative Cttee, 1994–99; British Shooting Sports Council, 2000–08 (Pres., 2008–14). Chancellor, Univ. of Wolverhampton, 1993–99. Elected Mem., H of L, 1999. President: British Inst. of Innkeeping, 1996–97; Staffs & Birmingham Agricl Soc., 2000–01; Vice-Pres., Staffs Assoc. of Clubs for Young People, 2000–. Patron, Staffs Br., BRCS, 1989–92. Hon. President: Lord Roberts Wkshops and SSAFA (Wolverhampton Br.), 1987–; Staffs Small Bore Rifle Assoc., 1988–; Gun Trade Assoc., 2000–; Hon. Vice-Pres., Rugeley Rugby FC. Hon. Pres., Shropshire Hospice, 1983–88. Patron of 10 livings. Hon. Col, A Sqdn Royal Mercian and Lancastrian (formerly Staffs) Yeomanry, 2004–07. DL Stafford, 1994. Hon. LLD Wolverhampton, 1994. *Recreations:* shooting, fishing. *Heir: s* Viscount Ingestre, *qv. Address:* Throstles House, Birdsgrove Lane, Ashbourne, Derbys DE6 2BP.

SHRIBMAN, Sheila Joan, CBE 2011; FRCP, FRCPCH, FRCGP; Consultant Paediatrician, Northampton General Hospital, 1985–2011; National Clinical Director for Children, Young People and Maternity Services (formerly for Children), Department of Health, 2005–13; *b* 8 March 1951; *d* of Wilfred and Margaret Norval; *m* 1981, Dr Jonathan Shribman; two *s* one *d. Educ:* Girton Coll., Cambridge (BA 1972; MB BChir 1976); St George's Hosp., London. FRCP 1993; FRCPCH 1996; FRCGP 2010. Paediatric trng posts at St George's, Brompton, Queen Charlotte's and Gt Ormond St Hosps; Med. Dir, Northampton Gen. Hosp., 1995–2005. Registrar, RCPCH, 2003–05. *Recreations:* travel, books, cookery, family. *Address:* 25A Ridge Hill, Dartmouth, Devon TQ6 9PE. *T:* (01803) 834651. *E:* sheila@shribman.co.uk. *Club:* Royal Society of Medicine.

SHRIMPLIN, John Steven; consultant, 1994–2011; UK Member, European Space Agency Appeals Board, 2000–10; *b* 9 May 1934; *s* of late John Reginald Shrimplin and Kathleen Mary (*née* Stevens); *m* 1957, Hazel Baughen; two *s*. *Educ:* Royal Grammar Sch., Colchester; King's Coll., London (BSc Maths). Joined RAE, Farnborough, 1956; Defence Operational Analysis Estabt, 1966; JSSC, 1970; Weapons Dept, RAE, 1971; Defence R&D Staff, British Embassy, Washington, 1972; Asst Dir, Future Systems, Air Systems Controllerate, MoD PE, 1974; Asst Chief Scientist, RAF, 1978; Head of Weapons Dept, RAE, 1983; Dep. Hd, British Defence Staff, and Minister/Counsellor, Defence Equipment, British Embassy, Washington, DC, 1985–88; Dir, Defence Science (Studies), MoD, 1988–91; Dep. Dir Gen. and Dir, Space Technol., BNSC, 1991–94. UK Rep., Eur. Space Policy Cttee, 1994–99. Pres., Old Colcerian Soc., 2010–11. FRAeS 1993. *Recreations:* travel, camping, walking. *Address:* c/o National Westminster Bank, 2 Alexandra Road, Farnborough, Hants GU14 6BZ.

SHRIMSLEY, Bernard; journalist and novelist; *b* 13 Jan. 1931; *er s* of John and Alice Shrimsley, London; *m* 1952, Norma Jessie Alexandra, *d* of Albert and Maude Porter, Southport; one *d*. *Educ:* Kilburn Grammar School, Northampton. Press Association, 1947–48; Southport Guardian, 1948–49 and 1951–53; RAF, 1949–51; Daily Mirror, 1953–58 and 1961–68; Sunday Express, 1958–61; Editor, Daily Post, Liverpool, 1968–69; Dep. Editor, 1969–72, Editor, 1972–75, The Sun; Editor, News of the World, and Dir, News Group Newspapers Ltd, 1975–80; Editor-designate (subseq. Editor), The Mail on Sunday, and Dir (subseq. Vice-Chm.), The Mail on Sunday Ltd, 1980–82; Asst Editor, 1983–86, Associate Editor, 1986–96, Daily Express; media consultant, Referendum Party, 1996–97; leader writer, Press Gazette, 1999–2002. Member: Press Council, 1989–90 (Jt Vice-Chm., 1990); Defence, Press and Broadcasting Cttee, 1989–93. Mem. judging acad., British Press Awards, 1988–2007. *Publications:* The Candidates, 1968; Lion Rampant, 1984 (US Book of the Month Choice); The Silly Season, 2003. *Club:* Garrick.

SHRIMSLEY, Robert Gideon; Managing Editor, F.T.com, and Assistant Editor, Financial Times, since 2009; *b* 21 Sept. 1964; *s* of late Anthony Shrimsley and of Yvonne Shrimsley; *m* 1997, Reeve Lewis; one *s* one *d*. *Educ:* St Nicholas Preparatory Sch.; University College Sch.; London Sch. of Economics (BSc Econs 1985). Reporter: Darlington Evening Despatch, 1986; Kentish Times, 1986–88; Sunday Telegraph, 1988–89; Reporter, 1989–92, political staff, 1992–95, Daily Telegraph; Lobby Corresp., Financial Times, 1995–96; Chief Pol Corresp., Daily Telegraph, 1996–2000; Financial Times: Chief Pol Corresp., 2000–02; UK News Ed., 2002–04; columnist, 2004–05; News Ed., 2005–09. *Recreations:* cinema, reading, walking on Dartmoor, trying to persuade my son to watch QPR rather than Arsenal, spending time with my family. *Address:* Financial Times, 1 Southwark Bridge, SE1 9HL. *T:* (020) 7873 3000.

SHTAUBER, Dr Zvi; Director, Institute for National Security Studies, Israel, 2006–08 (Head, Jaffee Center for Strategic Studies, Tel Aviv University, 2005–08); company director; *b* 15 July 1947; *m* Nitza Rousso; two *s* one *d*. *Educ:* Fletcher Sch. of Law and Diplomacy; Harvard Business Sch.; Hebrew Univ. of Jerusalem. Brig. Gen., Israel Defence Force, 1970–95; Vice-Pres., Ben Gurion Univ. of Negev, 1996–99; Foreign Policy Advr to Prime Minister of Israel, 1999–2000; Ambassador of Israel to the Court of St James's, 2001–04.

SHUCKBURGH, Sir James Rupert Charles, 14th Bt *cr* 1660, of Shuckburgh, Warwickshire; *b* 4 Jan. 1978; *er s* of Sir Rupert Charles Gerald Shuckburgh, 13th Bt and of Judith (*née* Mackaness); *S* father, 2012. *Heir:* *b* Peter Gerald William Shuckburgh, *b* 1982. *Address:* c/o Shuckburgh Hall, Daventry, Northants NN11 6DT.

SHUCKSMITH, Prof. (David) Mark, OBE 2009; PhD; FAcSS; Professor of Planning, since 2005, and Director, Newcastle Institute for Social Renewal, since 2012, University of Newcastle upon Tyne; *b* 25 Aug. 1953; *s* of Thomas David Shucksmith and Gwladys Inga Shucksmith; *m* 1979, Janet Susan Raper; two *d*. *Educ:* Sidney Sussex Coll., Cambridge (BA 1976); Univ. of Newcastle upon Tyne (MSc; PhD Agricl Econs 1987). University of Aberdeen: Lectr, 1981–87; Sen. Lectr, 1987–89; Reader, Dept of Land Econ., 1989–93; Prof. of Land Economy, 1993–2004; Dir, Arkleton Centre for Rural Develt Res., 1995–2004. Vis. Prof., Univ. of Trondheim, 2006–08. Co-Dir, Scottish Centre for Res. on Social Justice, 2001–04. Joseph Rowntree Foundation: Advr, Action in Rural Areas prog., 1995–; Sec., Rural Housing Policy Forum, 2005–06. Member: Bd, Countryside Agency, 2005–06; Affordable Rural Housing Commn, 2005–06; Bd, Commn for Rural Communities, 2006–13. Chm., Cttee of Enquiry on Crofting, 2007–08. Programme Chairman: World Rural Sociol. Congress, 2004; European Soc. Rural Sociol. Congress, 2015; First Vice-Pres., Internat. Rural Sociol. Assoc., 2004–08 (Mem. Council, 2012–Aug. 2016); Mem., Exec. Cttee, Eur. Soc. of Rural Sociol., 2009–. Trustee: Arkleton Trust, 2011–; ACRE 2014–. Carnegie Fellow, Carnegie UK Trust, 2015. FAcSS (AcSS 2010). *Publications:* No Homes for Locals?, 1981; Rural Housing in Scotland: recent research and policy, 1987; Housebuilding in Britain's Countryside, 1990; (jtly) Rural Scotland Today: the best of both worlds, 1996; Exclusive Countryside?: social inclusion and regeneration in rural Britain, 2000; (jtly) Housing in the European Countryside, 2003; (jtly) Young People in Rural Europe, 2004; (jtly) CAP and the Regions: the territorial impact of the Common Agricultural Policy, 2005; (jtly) Comparing Rural Development: continuity and change in the countryside of Western Europe, 2009; (jtly) From Community to Consumption: new and classical themes in rural sociological research, 2010; (jtly) Rural Transformations and Rural Policies in the US and UK, 2012; Future Directions in Rural Development, 2012; (jtly) International Handbook of Rural Studies, 2016; contrib. numerous articles to learned jls. *Recreations:* music, reading novels, hill-walking, finding coffee shops. *Address:* School of Architecture, Planning and Landscape, University of Newcastle upon Tyne, Claremont Tower, Newcastle upon Tyne NE1 7RU. *T:* (0191) 208 6942. *E:* m.shucksmith@ncl.ac.uk.

SHUE, Prof. Vivienne B., PhD; FBA 2008; Leverhulme Professor of Contemporary China, and Director, Contemporary China Studies Programme, University of Oxford, 2002, now Emeritus; Fellow of St Antony's College, Oxford, 2002, now Emeritus. *Educ:* Vassar Coll., NY (BA 1967); St Antony's Coll., Oxford (BLitt 1969); Harvard Univ. (PhD 1975). Asst Prof., 1976–81, Associate Prof., 1981–82, Dept of Pol Sci., Yale Univ.; Associate Prof., 1982–87, Prof. of Govt, 1987–95, Frank and Rosa Rhodes Prof. of Chinese Govt, 1995–2004, Cornell Univ. *Publications:* Peasant China in Transition, 1980; The Reach of the State, 1988; (ed jtly) State Power and Social Forces, 1994; (with Marc Blecher) Tethered Deer: government and economy in a Chinese county, 1996; (ed with C. Wong) Paying for Progress in China, 2007; contrib. learned jls. *Address:* c/o St Antony's College, Oxford OX2 6JF.

SHUFFREY, Ralph Frederick Dendy, CB 1983; CVO 1981; Deputy Under-Secretary of State and Principal Establishment Officer, Home Office, 1980–84; *b* 9 Dec. 1925; *s* of late Frederick Arthur Shuffrey, MC and Mary Shuffrey (*née* Dendy); *m* 1953, Sheila, *d* of late Brig. John Lingham, CB, DSO, MC, and Juliet Judd; one *s* one *d*. *Educ:* Shrewsbury; Balliol Coll., Oxford. Served Army, 1944–47 (Captain). Entered Home Office, 1951; Private Sec. to Parly Under-Sec. of State, 1956–57; Private Sec. to Home Sec., 1965–66; Asst Sec., 1966–72; Asst Under-Sec. of State, 1972–80. Chairman: The Cranstoun Projects Ltd, 1988–97; Fire Service Res. and Trng Trust, 1989–2004. Hon. Sec., Soc. for Individual Freedom, 1985–89. *Address:* Flat D, Campden House, 29 Sheffield Terrace, W8 7ND. *Club:* Reform.

SHUKER, Gavin; MP (Lab and Co-op) Luton South, since 2010; *b* 10 Oct. 1981; *m* 2007, Lucie Moore; one *d*. *Educ:* Icknield High Sch.; Luton Sixth Form Coll.; Girton Coll., Cambridge (BA Soc. and Pol Sci. 2003). Associate Pastor, Cambridge, 2003–06, Church Leader, Luton, 2006–, City Life Church; charity worker, Fusion UK, 2003–08; Endis Ltd, 2008–10. Shadow Minister for Water and Waste, 2011–13, for Internat. Develt, 2013–15. *Address:* House of Commons, SW1A 0AA.

SHUKLA, Rashmita, CBE 2007; Regional Director, Midlands and East, Public Health England, since 2013; *b* 4 July 1960; *d* of Himatlal Shukla and Mrudula Shukla; *m* 1992, Dr Vinod Patel. *Educ:* Univ. of Southampton Med. Sch. (BM 1984). MRCP 1988, FRCP 2007; FFPH 2001. Leicestershire Health Authority: Consultant in Communicable Disease/Public Health Medicine, 1994–2001; Actg Dir of Public Health, 2000–01; Director of Public Health: Eastern Leicester PCT, 2001–04; Leicester City West PCT, 2004; Regl Dir of Public Health, W Midlands DoH, 2004–13. Hon. Sen. Lectr, Univ. of Leicester, 2003–. *Publications:* articles in Communicable Disease Review, Sexually Transmitted Infections, Jl of Public Health Medicine and Postgraduate Med. Jl. *Recreations:* cycling, ski-ing, reading, supporting local Rugby team (Leicester Tigers). *Address:* Public Health England, 1st Floor, 5 St Philip's Place, Birmingham B3 2PW. *T:* (0121) 232 9267. *E:* Rashmi.Shukla@phe.gov.uk.

SHUKMAN, David Roderick, FRGS; Science Editor, BBC News, since 2012; *b* 30 May 1958; *s* of late Dr Harold Shukman and of Rev. Dr Ann Shukman; *m* 1988, Jessica Therese Pryce-Jones; two *s* one *d*. *Educ:* Eton Coll.; Durham Univ. (BA Hons Geog.). Reporter, Coventry Evening Telegraph, 1980–83; joined BBC, 1983: trainee, News, 1983–85; reporter, NI, 1985–87; Defence Corresp., TV News, 1987–95; Europe Corresp., Brussels, 1995–99; World Affairs Corresp., News, 1999–2003; Envmt and Sci. Corresp., News, 2003–12. FRGS 2007. *Publications:* (with B. Brown) All Necessary Means, 1991; The Sorcerer's Challenge: fears and hopes for the weapons of the next millennium, 1995, US edn as Tomorrow's War, 1996; Reporting Live from the End of the World, 2010; An Iceberg as Big as Manhattan, 2011; contribs to RUSI Jl, Brassey's Defence Yearbook. *Recreations:* cooking, diving, surfing. *Address:* BBC News Centre, Broadcasting House, Portland Place, W1A 1AA. *E:* david.shukman@bbc.co.uk. *Club:* Frontline.

SHULMAN, Alexandra, OBE 2005; Editor, British Vogue, since 1992; *b* 13 Nov. 1957; *d* of late Milton Shulman and of Drusilla Beyfus, *qv*; *m* 1994, Paul (marr. diss. 2005), *s* of late Rev. Dr Robert W. Spike, NY; one *s*. *Educ:* St Paul's Girls' Sch.; Sussex Univ. (BA Social Anthropology). Tatler: Commissioning Editor, 1982–84; Features Editor, 1984–87; Sunday Telegraph: Editor, Women's Page, 1987; Dep. Editor, 7 Days Mag., 1987–88; Features Editor, Vogue, 1988–90; Editor, GQ, 1990–92. Dir, Condé Nast Pubns, 1997–2002. Vis. Prof., Univ. of the Arts, London, 2003–. Trustee: Nat. Portrait Gall., 1999–2008; Arts Foundn, 2001–10; Royal Marsden Cancer Charity, 2009–. Hon. MA Univ. for Creative Arts, 2010. *Publications:* Can We Still Be Friends, 2012; The Parrots, 2015. *Address:* Condé Nast Publications, Vogue House, Hanover Square, W1S 1JU. *T:* (020) 7152 3471.

See also Marchioness of Normanby.

SHULMAN, Drusilla Norman; *see* Beyfus, D. N.

SHULMAN, Neville, CBE 2005 (OBE 1995); Director, British Centre, International Theatre Institute, 1992; *m* 1970, Emma Broide; two *s* one *d*. ACA 1961, FCA 1971. Chartered Accountant, in private practice, 1961–. Vice Pres., NCH Action for Children, 1989; Vice Chm., UK UNESCO Culture Cttee, 2005. Director: Theatre Forum, 2002; Shepperton Studios Ltd, 2003–. Freeman, City of London, 1992; Liveryman, Co. of Blacksmiths, 1992. FRGS 1990. *Publications:* Exit of a Dragonfly, 1985; Zen in the Art of Climbing Mountains, 1992; On Top of Africa, 1995; Zen Explorations in Remotest New Guinea, 1997; Some Like it Cold, 2001; Climbing the Equator, 2003. *Recreations:* mountaineering, exploring, theatre, film, writing. *Address:* 35A Huntsworth Mews, Gloucester Place, NW1 6DB. *Clubs:* Travellers, Explorers (Fellow, 2002), Rotary.

SHULTZ, George Pratt; Secretary of State, United States of America, 1982–89; Distinguished Fellow, Hoover Institution, since 1989; *b* New York City, 13 Dec. 1920; *s* of Birl E. Shultz and Margaret Pratt; *m* 1946, Helena Maria O'Brien (*d* 1995); two *s* three *d*; *m* 1997, Charlotte Mailliard Swig (Hon. CVO 2007). *Educ:* Princeton Univ., 1942 (BA Econ); Massachusetts Inst. of Technology, 1949 (PhD Industrial Econ). Served War, US Marine Corps, Pacific, 1942; Major, 1945. Faculty, MIT, 1949–57; Sen. staff economist, President's Council of Economic Advisers, 1955–56 (on leave, MIT); Univ. of Chicago, Graduate Sch. of Business: Prof. of Industrial Relations, 1957–68; Dean, 1962–69; Prof. of Management and Public Policy, Stanford Univ., Graduate Sch. of Business, 1974. Secretary of Labor, 1969–July 1, 1970; Dir, Office of Management and Budget, 1970–72; Secretary of the Treasury, 1972–74; Exec. Vice-Pres., Bechtel Corp., 1974–75, Pres. 1975–77; Vice-Chm., Bechtel Corp., 1977–81 (Dir); Pres., Bechtel Group Inc., San Francisco, 1981–82. Chairman: President's Economic Policy Adv. Bd, 1981–82; Internat. Council, J. P. Morgan, 1989–2009; Adv. Council, Inst. of Internat. Studies, 1989–; Adv. Bd, Accenture Energy, 2002–07; Theranos Inc., 2011–. Director: General Motors Corp., 1981–82, 1989–91; Boeing Corp., 1989–93; Bechtel Gp Inc., 1989–2009; Tandem Computers Inc., 1989–92; Chevron Corp., 1989–93; Gulfstream Aerospace Corp., 1992–99; AirTouch Communications, 1994–98; Gilead Scis, 1996–2006; Charles Schwab & Co. Inc., 1997–2004; Unext, 2000–03; Infrastructure World, 2000–03; Accretive Health Associates, 2004–11; Mem., GM Corporate Adv. Council. Chm., State of California Gov's Econ. Policy Adv. Bd, 1995–98, Council of Econ. Advrs, 2004–09. US Chm., N American Forum, 2005–09; Chairman: Adv. Council, Precourt Inst. for Energy Efficiency, Stanford Univ., 2007–; Ext. Adv. Bd, MIT Energy Initiative, 2007–; Energy Taskforce, Hoover Inst., 2007–; Adv. Council, Precourt Inst. for Energy, Stanford Univ., 2011–. Hon. Dr of Laws: Notre Dame Univ., 1969; Loyola Univ., 1972; Pennsylvania, 1973; Rochester, 1973; Princeton, 1973; Carnegie-Mellon Univ., 1975; Columbia, 2001; Williams Coll., 2008; Peking, 2009. *Publications:* Pressures on Wage Decisions, 1950; The Dynamics of a Labor Market (with C. A. Myers), 1951; Labor Problems: cases and readings (with J. R. Coleman), 1953; Management Organization and the Computer (with T. L. Whisler), 1960; Strategies for the Displaced Worker (with Arnold R. Weber), 1966; Guidelines, Informal Controls, and the Marketplace (with Robert Z. Aliber), 1966; Workers and Wages in the Urban Labor Market (with Albert Rees), 1970; Leaders and Followers in an Age of Ambiguity, 1975; Economic Policy Beyond the Headlines (with Kenneth W. Dam), 1977, 2nd edn 1998; Turmoil and Triumph: my years as Secretary of State, 1993; (with John Shoven) Putting Our House in Order: a guide to social security and healthcare reform, 2008; Ideas & Action, Featuring 10 Commandments for Negotiations, 2010; (ed jtly) Ending Government Bailouts as We Know Them, 2010; Issues on My Mind: strategies for the future, 2013; (ed jtly) Game Changers: energy on the move, 2014; (jtly) Nuclear Security: the problems and the road ahead, 2014. *Recreation:* golf. *Address:* Hoover Institution, Stanford University, Stanford, CA 94305–6010, USA.

SHUTER, Jo; Headteacher, Quintin Kynaston School, Marlborough Hill, 2002–13; education consultant. *Educ:* Univ. of Bristol (BA Psychol. and Social Sci.); Univ. of Birmingham (PGCE Social Scis/Physical Educn). Asst Headteacher, Phoenix High Sch., Shepherds Bush, 1993–99; Dep. Headteacher, Broomfield Sch., N London, 1999–2000; Sen. Dep. Headteacher, Hertswood Sch., Borehamwood, 2000–01. Nat. Headteacher of Year (Secondary Sch.), Teaching Awards Trust, 2007.

SHUTLER, (Ronald) Rex (Barry), CB 1992; FRICS; FAAV; Chairman, Leasehold Valuation Tribunal and Rent Assessment Panel, 1994–2001 (Vice President, 1994–99); *b* 27 June 1933; *s* of Ronald Edgar Coggin Shutler and Helena Emily Shutler (*née* Lawes); *m* 1958, Patricia Elizabeth Longman; two *s*. *Educ:* Hardye's, Dorchester. Articled pupil and assistant, chartered surveyors, Dorchester, 1952–59; joined Valuation Office (Inland Revenue), 1959; District Valuer, Hereford and Worcester, 1970; Superintending Valuer, Wales, 1976; Dep.

Chief Valuer, 1984–88; Chief Valuer, then Chief Exec., Valuation Office Agency, 1988–94. FRICS 1972; FAAV 1962; Hon. FSVA 1994. *Recreations:* golf, country pursuits, gardening, bridge. *Club:* Bank House Golf & Country.

SHUTT, family name of **Baron Shutt of Greetland**.

SHUTT OF GREETLAND, Baron *cr* 2000 (Life Peer), of Greetland and Stainland in the county of West Yorkshire; **David Trevor Shutt,** OBE 1993; PC 2009; FCA; *b* 16 March 1942; *s* of Edward Angus Shutt and Ruth Satterthwaite Shutt (*née* Berry); *m* 1965, Margaret Edith Pemberton; two *s* one *d*. *Educ:* Pudsey Grammar Sch. FCA 1969. Smithson Blackburn & Co., Leeds: Articled Clerk, 1959–64; Audit Clerk, 1964–66; Bousfield Waite & Co., Halifax: Taxation Asst, 1967–70; Partner, 1970–94; Consultant, 1994–2001. Mem. (L then Lib Dem) Calderdale MBC, 1973–90 and 1995–2003 (Mayor, 1982–83). Dir, Joseph Rowntree Reform Trust Ltd, 1975–2010 (Vice Chm., 1987–2005; Chm., 2007–10); Trustee, Joseph Rowntree Charitable Trust, 1985–2010. Treas., Inst. for Citizenship, 1995–2002. Contested: (L): Sowerby, 1970, Feb. and Oct. 1974, 1979; (L/Alliance): Calder Valley, 1983, 1987; (Lib Dem): Pudsey, 1992. House of Lords: Lib Dem Asst Whip, 2001–02, Dep. Chief Whip, 2002–05, Chief Whip, 2005–12; Coalition Dep. Chief Whip, 2010–12; Lib Dem spokesman on internat. develt, 2001–02, on NI, 2001–05; govt spokesman on culture, media and sport, on NI and on transport, 2010–12; Captain of the Yeomen of the Guard (Dep. Chief Whip, H of L), 2010–12. Freeman of Calderdale, 2000. Paul Harris Fellow, Rotary Club, 1999. Citoyen d'honneur, Commune de Riorges (France), 1983. *Recreations:* transport, travel. *Address:* Woodfield, 197 Saddleworth Road, Greetland, Halifax, West Yorkshire HX4 8LZ. *T:* (01422) 375276.

SHUTTLE, Penelope (Diane); writer and poet; *b* 12 May 1947; *d* of Jack Frederick Shuttle and Joan Shepherdess Lipscombe; *m* Peter Redgrove, FRSL (*d* 2003); one *d*. *Educ:* Staines Grammar Sch.; Matthew Arnold County Secondary Sch., Middx. Radio plays: The Girl who Lost her Glove, 1975 (Jt 3rd Prize Winner, Radio Times Drama Bursaries Comp., 1974); The Dauntless Girl, 1978. Poetry recorded for Poetry Room, Harvard Univ. Arts Council Awards, 1969, 1972 and 1985; Greenwood Poetry Prize, 1972; E. C. Gregory Award for Poetry, 1974. *Publications: novels:* An Excusable Vengeance, 1967; All the Usual Hours of Sleeping, 1969; Wailing Monkey Embracing a Tree, 1974; Rainsplitter in the Zodiac Garden, 1976; Mirror of the Giant, 1979; *poetry:* Nostalgia Neurosis, 1968; Midwinter Mandala, 1973; Photographs of Persephone, 1973; Autumn Piano, 1973; Songbook of the Snow, 1973; Webs on Fire, 1977; The Orchard Upstairs, 1980; The Child-Stealer, 1983; The Lion from Rio, 1986; Adventures with my Horse, 1988; Taxing the Rain, 1992; Building a City for Jamie, 1996; Selected Poems, 1998; A Leaf out of his Book, 1999; Redgrove's Wife, 2006; Sandgrain and Hourglass (new poems), 2010; Unsent: new and selected poems, 2012; In the Snowy Air (pamphlet), 2014; *with Peter Redgrove:* The Hermaphrodite Album (poems), 1973; The Terrors of Dr Treviles (novel), 1974; The Wise Wound (psychology), 1978, 5th edn 1999; Alchemy for Women, 1995. *Recreations:* listening to music, Hatha Yoga, walking, reading, contemplation. *Address:* c/o David Higham Associates Ltd, 7th Floor, Waverley House, 7–12 Noel Street, W1F 8GQ.

SHUTTLEWORTH, 5th Baron *cr* 1902, of Gawthorpe; **Charles Geoffrey Nicholas Kay-Shuttleworth,** KCVO 2011; JP; Bt 1850; Lord-Lieutenant and Custos Rotulorum of Lancashire, since 1997; *b* 2 Aug. 1948; *s* of 4th Baron Shuttleworth, MC, and Anne Elizabeth (*d* 1991), *er d* of late Col Geoffrey Phillips, CBE, DSO; *S* father, 1975; *m* 1975, Mrs Ann Mary Barclay, *d* of James Whatman, MC; three *s*. *Educ:* Eton. Trainee Surveyor, Raby Estates, Co. Durham, 1966–70; Vigers, Chartered Surveyors, 1970–77; Partner, Burton, Barnes & Vigers, Chartered Surveyors, 1977–96; National & Provincial Building Society: Dir, 1983–96; Chm., 1994–96; Director: Burnley Bldg Soc., 1978–82 (Vice-Chm., 1982); Rank Foundn, 1993–2015; Abbey National plc, 1996–2004 (Dep. Chm., 1996–99); Rural Solutions Ltd, 1999–2007 (Chm., 2005–07); Chairman: Abbey National Gp Pension Funds Trustee Co., 2002–12; Santander UK Gp Pension Scheme Trustees Ltd, 2012–. Chairman: Rural Develt Commn, 1990–97; Lancs Small Industries Cttee, COSIRA, 1978–83; Lancs Youth Clubs Assoc., 1980–86, Pres., 1986–2012; Member: Skelmersdale Develt Corp., 1982–85; NW Regional Cttee, National Trust, 1980–89; Council, CBI, 1993–96; Council, Duchy of Lancaster, 1998–2014 (Chm., 2006–14). Chm., Assoc. of Lord-Lieutenants, 2008–. President: Royal Lancashire Agricl Soc., 1985–86, 2000–01; Assoc. of Lancastrians in London, 1986–87 and 1997. Pres., RFCA, NW, 2011–15 (Vice-Pres., 1997–2011, 2015–). Chm. of Trustees, Yorkshire Dales Millennium Trust, 2000–05. Mem. Council, Lancaster Univ., 1990–93; Governor, Giggleswick Sch., 1981–2006 (Chm., 1984–97). Hon. Fellow: Univ. of Central Lancs, 1996; Myerscough Coll., 2002. Hon. Colonel: 4th (V) Bn, Queen's Lancs Regt, 1996–99; Lancastrian and Cumbrian Vol., 1999–2005. FRICS, 1983–2002. JP 1997, DL Lancs, 1986. KStJ 1997 (Pres., Council for Lancs, 1997–2012). *Heir: s* Hon. Thomas Edward Kay-Shuttleworth [*b* 29 Sept. 1976; *m* 2002, Clare Barbara Tozer; one *s* two *d*]. *Address:* Heber House, Leck, Carnforth, Lancs LA6 2JG. *Clubs:* Brooks's, MCC.

SHUTTLEWORTH, Kenneth Owen; Chief Executive, Make Ltd, since 2004; *b* 10 Sept. 1952; *s* of Owen William Shuttleworth and late Ilene Doris; *m* 1987, Seana Ann Brennan (marr. diss. 2006); one *s* one *d*; *m* 2008, Claire Nicola Dexter; one *s*. *Educ:* Leicester Poly. (DipArch Dist. 1977). RIBA 1978. Registered architect, 1978; Dir, Foster and Partners, 1984–2003. Projects include: 30 St Mary Axe; City Hall, London; Nottingham Univ. Campus; St Paul's inf. kiosk; Grosvenor Waterside; 55 Baker Street; Cube Birmingham. Mem., CABE, 2003–11. Hon. DDes De Montfort 1994; Hon. DSc Westminster, 2007; Hon. DLit Nottingham, 2009; Hon. Dr UEL. FRSA. *Recreations:* painting, landscape drawing. *Address:* Make Ltd, 32 Cleveland Street, W1T 4JY. *T:* (020) 7636 5151, *Fax:* (020) 7636 5252. *E:* kenshuttleworth@makearchitects.com.

SHUTTLEWORTH, Prof. Sally Ann, PhD; FBA 2015; Professor of English Literature, University of Oxford, since 2005; Fellow, St Anne's College, Oxford, since 2005; *b* Sheffield, 5 Sept. 1952; *d* of Kenneth and Barbara Shuttleworth; *m* 1988, John Christie; two *d*. *Educ:* Univ. of York (BA 1st Cl. Hons English Lit. and Sociol. 1974); Darwin Coll., Cambridge (PhD English Lit. 1980). Asst Prof., English Dept, Princeton Univ., 1980–83; Lectr, 1983–91, Sen. Lectr, 1991–94, Sch. of English, Univ. of Leeds; University of Sheffield: Prof. of English Lit., 1994–2005; Hd of Dept, 1996–99; Dean of Arts, 1999–2003; Hd, Humanities Div., Univ. of Oxford, 2005–11. Frank Knox Fellow, Harvard Univ., 1978–79; Soc. for Humanities Fellow, Cornell Univ., 1986–87; Leverhulme Res. Fellow, 1994–95; British Acad. Readership, 2003–05. Member: Peer Rev. Coll., AHRC, 2004– (Strategic Reviewer, 2009–); Res. Awards Adv. Cttee, Leverhulme Trust, 2010–. AHRC Science in Culture prog. award, 2013–; Eur. Res. Council Advanced Investigator Award, 2014–. *Publications:* George Eliot and Nineteenth-Century Science: the make-believe of a beginning, 1984; (ed with John Christie) Nature Transfigured: science and literature, 1700–1900, 1989; (ed jtly) Body/Politics: women and the discourses of science, 1990; Charlotte Brontë and Victorian Psychology, 1996; (ed with J. Bourne Taylor) Embodied Selves: an anthology of psychological texts, 1830–1890, 1998; (ed jtly) Memory and Memorials, 1789–1914: literary and cultural perspectives, 2000; (jtly) Science in the Nineteenth-Century Periodical: reading the magazine of nature, 2004; (ed jtly) Science Serialised: representations of the sciences in nineteenth-century periodicals, 2004; (ed jtly) Culture and Science in the Nineteenth-Century Media, 2004; The Mind of the Child: child development in literature, science and medicine, 1840–1900, 2010 (British Soc. for Lit. and Sci. Prize). *Recreations:* family, walking on moors and mountains, wild swimming, citizen science. *Address:* St Anne's College, Woodstock Road, Oxford OX2 6HS. *T:* (01865) 274800. *E:* sally.shuttleworth@st-annes.ox.ac.uk.

SIBBETT, Prof. Wilson, CBE 2001; PhD; FRS 1997; FInstP; FRSE; Wardlaw Professor of Natural Philosophy, School of Physics and Astronomy, University of St Andrews, 1997–2014, now Emeritus; *b* 15 March 1948; *s* of John Sibbett and Margaret (*née* McLeister); *m* 1979, Barbara Anne Brown; three *d*. *Educ:* Ballymena Tech. Coll.; Queen's Univ., Belfast (BSc 1st Cl. Hons Physics); Imperial Coll., London (PhD Laser Physics 1973). FInstP 1986. Blackett Laboratory, Imperial College, London: Postdoctoral Res. Asst, 1973–77; Lectr in Physics, 1977–84; Reader, 1984–85; University of St Andrews: Prof., 1985–2014; Head, Physics Dept, 1985–88; Chm., 1988–94, Dir of Research, 1994–2005, Sch. of Physics and Astronomy. Mem., EPSRC, 1998–2001; Chm., Scottish Science Adv. Cttee, 2002–06. Mem. Council, Royal Soc., 2011–; Vice Pres., Physical Scis, RSE, 2011–. Mem., St Andrews Rotary Club. FRSE 1988; Fellow: Optical Soc. of America, 1998; Eur. Optical Soc., 2008. Hon. LLD Dundee, 2002; Hon. DSc: Dublin, 2005; Glasgow, 2012; DUniv Strathclyde, 2012. Hubert Schardin Gold Medal for Res. in Ultrafast Lasers and Diagnostics, 1978; C. V. Boys Prize and Medal for Exptl Physics, Inst. of Physics, 1993; Rank Prize for Optoelectronics, 1997; Rumford Medal, Royal Soc., 2000; Quantum Electronics Prize, European Physical Soc., 2002; Royal Medal, RSE, 2009; Charles Hard Townes Award, Optical Soc. of America, 2011. *Publications:* numerous on laser physics and related diagnostic techniques in internat. scientific jls. *Recreations:* golf, gardening, DIY. *Address:* School of Physics and Astronomy, University of St Andrews, North Haugh, St Andrews, Fife KY16 9SS. *T:* (01334) 463100. *Clubs:* Rotary (St Andrews); Royal and Ancient Golf, New Golf (St Andrews).

SIBERRY, (William) Richard; QC 1989; a Deputy High Court Judge, since 2002; *b* 11 Dec. 1950; *s* of late John William Morgan Siberry; *m* 1976, Julia Christine Lancaster. *Educ:* King's Coll., Taunton; Pembroke Coll., Cambridge (MA, LLB). Fellow, Pembroke Coll., Cambridge, 1973–75. Called to the Bar, Middle Temple, 1974, Bencher, 2002. Asst Recorder, 1997–2000; Recorder, 2000–10. *Recreations:* music, gardening, walking, photography, North West Highlands of Scotland. *Address:* Essex Court Chambers, 24 Lincoln's Inn Fields, WC2A 3EG. *T:* (020) 7813 8000. *Club:* Royal Automobile.

SIBLEY, Dame Antoinette, (Dame Antoinette Corbett), DBE 1996 (CBE 1973); Prima Ballerina, The Royal Ballet, Covent Garden; President, Royal Academy of Dance (formerly of Dancing), 1991–2012 (Vice-President, 1989–91); guest coach, Royal Ballet, since 1991; Governor, Royal Ballet Board, since 2000; *b* 27 Feb. 1939; *d* of late Edward G. Sibley and Winifred M. Sibley (*née* Smith); *m* 1964, Michael Somes, CBE (marr. diss. 1973; he *d* 1994); *m* 1974, Panton Corbett; one *s* one *d*. *Educ:* Arts Educational Sch. and Royal Ballet Sch. 1st performance on stage as Student with Royal Ballet at Covent Garden, a swan, Jan. 1956; joined company, July 1956; appeared with the company or as guest artist in most opera houses worldwide; iconic dancing partnership with Sir Anthony Dowell spanned three decades. Leading rôle in: Swan Lake, Sleeping Beauty, Giselle, Coppelia, Cinderella, The Nutcracker, La Fille Mal Gardée, Romeo and Juliet, Harlequin in April, Les Rendezvous, Jabez and the Devil (created the rôle of Mary), La Fête Etrange, The Rake's Progress, Hamlet, Ballet Imperial, Two Pigeons, La Bayadère, Symphonic Variations, Scènes de Ballet, Lilac Garden, Daphnis and Chloe, Pas de Quatre (Dolin's), Konservatoriet, A Month in the Country, Raymonda Act III, The Dream (created Titania), Laurentia, Good Humoured Ladies, Aristocrat in Mam'zelle Angot, Façade, Song of the Earth, Monotones (created rôle), Jazz Calendar (created Friday's Child), Enigma Variations (created Dorabella), Thais (created pas de deux), Anastasia (created Kshessinska), Afternoon of a Faun, Triad (created the Girl), Pavanne (created pas de deux), Manon (created title rôle), Soupirs (created pas de deux), L'invitation au voyage (created), Impromptu (created pas de deux), Varii Capricci (created La Capricciosa), Fleeting Figures (created rôle); retired from dancing, 1989. *Film:* The Turning Point (with Baryshnikov), 1978. *Relevant publications:* Classical Ballet—the Flow of Movement, by Tamara Karsavina, 1962; Sibley and Dowell, by Nicholas Dromgoole and Leslie Spatt, 1976; Antoinette Sibley, 1981, photographs with text by Mary Clarke; Reflections of a Ballerina, by Barbara Newman, 1986. *Recreations:* watching sport, opera, reading. *Address:* 24 Chapel Street, SW1X 7BY.

SIBSON, Angela Margaret, OBE 2010; Diocesan Secretary, Diocese of Lincoln, since 2014; *b* 1 May 1949; *d* of Robert Sibson, Maryport, Cumbria and Joan Sibson (*née* Stafford); *m* 1971, Tom Ridler (*d* 2001); one *s* one *d*. *Educ:* Univ. of Birmingham (BA 1970); Queen Mary and Westfield Coll., London (MSc 2000). Chief Exec. Officer, Mothers' Union, 1993–99; Chief Executive: Relate, 2000–06; Commn for the Compact, 2007; Nat. Acad. for Parenting Practitioners, 2007–10; Diocesan Sec., Dio. of Chichester, 2011–14. *Recreations:* history, gardening, inter-generational studies and support.

SIBSON, Prof. Richard Hugh, PhD; FRS 2003; FRSNZ; Professor of Geology, University of Otago, New Zealand, 1990–2009, now Emeritus (Head, Department of Geology, 1990–96); *b* 28 Nov. 1945; *s* of Richard Broadley Sibson and Joan Winifred Sibson (*née* Fleming); *m* 1999, Prof. Francesca Cancarini Ghisetti, Catania, Italy. *Educ:* King's Coll., Otahuhu, Auckland; Univ. of Auckland (BSc 1st Cl. Hons Geol. 1968; Dist. Alumnus 2010); Imperial Coll., London (MSc, DIC Structural Geol. 1970; PhD 1977). Jun. Scientific Officer, Geophysics Div., DSIR, NZ, 1969; Lectr in Structural Geol., Imperial Coll., London, 1973–81; Vis. Scientist, Office of Earthquake Studies, US Geol Survey, Menlo Park, Calif, 1981; Asst Prof., 1982–83, Associate Prof., 1984–87, Prof., 1988–90, Dept of Geol Scis, UCSB. Francis Birch Lectr, Amer. Geophysical Union, 2012; Umbgrove Lectr, Univ. of Utrecht, 2015. FGS 1973; FRSNZ 1993; FAAAS 2006; Fellow: Geol Soc. of America, 1991; American Geophysical Union, 1999; Soc. of Econ. Geologists, 2010. Dist. Res. Medal, Univ. of Otago, 2003; Wollaston Medal, Geol Soc. of London, 2010; Structural Geol. and Tectonics Career Contribn Award, Geol. Soc. of America, 2011. *Publications:* contrib. numerous scientific res. papers to geol and geophysical jls on earthquake source mechanics in relation to structure, mechanics and mineralisation of crustal fault zones. *Recreations:* recorded music, hill and coastal walking, sea-kayaking, fly-fishing. *Address:* 60 Brabant Drive, Ruby Bay, Mapua 7005, New Zealand. *T:* (3) 5403713. *E:* rick.sibson@otago.ac.nz.

SIBSON, Prof. Robin, PhD; Chief Executive, Higher Education Statistics Agency, 2001–09 (Board Member, 1996–2000); *b* 4 May 1944; *o s* of late Robert and Florence Elizabeth Sibson; *m* 1975, Heather Gail Gulliver; two *s*. *Educ:* Sutton County Grammar Sch.; King's Coll., Cambridge (Schol.; Wrangler, Maths Tripos Pt II, 1965; BA 1966; Smith's Prize, 1968; MA, PhD 1970). CStat 1993. Fellow, King's Coll., 1968–76, Lectr in Math. Stats, 1971–76, Univ. of Cambridge; University of Bath: Prof. of Stats, 1976–94; Head, Sch. of Maths, 1979–82; Pro-Vice-Chancellor, 1989–94; Vice-Chancellor, Univ. of Kent at Canterbury, 1994–2001. Member: various SSRC/ESRC and SERC cttees, 1980–85; Science Bd, SERC, 1986–89; Wildfowl Trust Sci. Adv. Cttee, 1979–83; UK Acad. Mem., Higher Educn and Res. Cttee, Council of Europe, 1997–2002 (Mem. Bureau, 2000–02). Mem. Corp., Canterbury Coll., 1995–2001. Hon. DCL Kent, 2002. *Publications:* (with N. Jardine) Mathematical Taxonomy, 1971; papers in learned jls.

SIDDALL, Jonathan Charles; Chief Executive, Civil Mediation Council, since 2013; Protector, Spirit of 2012, since 2014; *b* 6 July 1954; *s* of John Siddall and Joan Siddall; *m* 1988, Nicola Ann Glover; two *d*. *Educ:* Rugby Sch.; Univ. of Birmingham (LLB Hons 1976). Called to the Bar, Middle Temple, 1978; Accredited Mediator, CEDR, 1999. Pupillage, 1979–80; in-house Lawyer, Internat. Mgt Gp, 1980–83; Gen. Sec., British Univs Sports Fedn, 1984–86; Sec., Cumberland Lawn Tennis Club, 1987–90; Sec. and Campaign Co-ordinator, Law Aid Trust, 1990–91; Dep. Sec., LTA, 1992–98; Dir, Sports Dispute Resolution Panel Ltd, 1999–2006; Chief Exec., LandAid Charitable Trust Ltd, 2007–12; Dir, Commercial Educn Trust, 2012–15. *Recreations:* golf, tennis, ski-ing, amateur dramatics. *Clubs:* Cumberland Lawn Tennis; Jesters; Highgate Golf.

SIDDALL, Victoria May; Director, Frieze Art Fairs (Frieze London, Frieze New York and Frieze Masters), since 2014; *b* Belfast, 8 Dec. 1977; *d* of Stephen and Jill Siddall. *Educ:* Uppingham Sch.; Bristol Univ. (BA Hons). Christie's, London, 2000–04; Hd of Devel, Frieze, 2004–11; Dir, Frieze Masters, 2011–14. *Address:* Frieze, 1 Montclare Street, E2 7EU. *T:* (020) 3372 6111.

SIDDELEY, family name of **Baron Kenilworth**.

SIDDELEY, Randle; *see* Kenilworth, 4th Baron.

SIDDIQ, Irfan, OBE 2005; HM Diplomatic Service; Ambassador to Azerbaijan, since 2013; *b* London, 27 Jan. 1977; *s* of late Mohammed Siddiq Noor and of Nusrat Siddiq. *Educ:* University Coll., Oxford (BA Hons PPE 1998). Entered FCO, 1998; Second Sec. (Econ.), New Delhi, 1999–2000; Arabic Lang. Trng, 2000–02; Second Sec. (Pol), Cairo, 2002–03; First Sec. (Pol), Coalition Provisional Authy, Baghdad, 2003–04; on secondment to US State Dept, Washington, 2004–05; Private Sec. to Sec. of State for Foreign and Commonwealth Affairs, 2005–07; Dep. Hd of Mission, Syria, 2007–10, Iraq, 2010–11; Hd, Arab Partnership Dept, FCO, 2011–13. *Recreations:* football, literature, current affairs, trekking. *Address:* British Embassy Baku, Landmark 2, 45A Khagani, AZ 1010, Azerbaijan. *T:* 12 437 7855. *E:* irfan.siddiq@fco.gov.uk.

SIDDIQ, Tulip, (Mrs C. W. St J. Percy); MP (Lab) Hampstead and Kilburn, since 2015; *b* London, 16 Sept. 1982; *d* of Dr Shafiq Siddiq and Sheikh Rehana; *m* 2013, Christian William St John Percy. *Educ:* University Coll. London (BA); King's Coll. London (MA); Birkbeck, Univ. of London (MSc). Work for Amnesty Internat.; researcher: Philip Gould Associates; GLA; Brunswick Gp LLP. Mem. (Lab) Camden LBC, 2010–14 (Cabinet Mem. for Culture and Communities, 2010–14). *Address:* House of Commons, SW1A 0AA. *T:* (020) 7219 3000.

SIDDIQUI, Prof. Mona, OBE 2011; PhD; FRSE; Professor of Islamic and Interreligious Studies, Edinburgh Divinity School, University of Edinburgh, since 2011; *b* 3 May 1963; *d* of Abdul Ali and Hasina Khatoon; *m* 1991, Farhaj Ahmed Siddiqui; three *s*. *Educ:* Leeds Univ. (BA Hons Arabic and French); Manchester Univ. (MA; PhD 1992). Lectr in Islamic Law, Glasgow Caledonian Univ., 1993–95; University of Glasgow: Sen. Lectr in Arabic and Islamic Studies, 1995–2006; Hd, Dept of Theol. and Religious Studies, 2002–05; Prof. of Islamic Studies, 2006–11; Mem. Court, 2004. Member: Central Religious Adv. Council, BBC, 1998–2005; Global Agenda Council on Faith, World Economic Forum, 2008–09; Chair, Scottish Religious Adv. Council, BBC, 2005–; Comr, Calman Commn on Scottish Devolution, 2008–09. FRSE 2005. FRSA 2005. Hon. DCL Huddersfield, 2009; Hon. DLitt: Leicester, 2009; Roehampton, 2014. *Publications:* How to Read the Qur'an, 2007; Islam (4 vols), 2010; The Good Muslim: reflections on classical Islamic law and theology, 2012; (ed) The Routledge Reader on Christian-Muslim Relations, 2012; Christians, Muslims and Jesus, 2013; My Way: a Muslim woman's journey, 2014; contrib. articles on inter-religious dialogue and Islamic law to various internat. jls. *Recreations:* cooking, interior design. *Address:* Edinburgh Divinity School, Mound Place, Edinburgh EH1 2LX. *T:* (0131) 650 7912. *E:* mona.siddiqui@ed.ac.uk.

SIDDLE, Anne Elizabeth; *see* Willis, A. E.

SIDDLE, Prof. Kenneth, PhD; Professor of Molecular Endocrinology, University of Cambridge, since 1990; Fellow, since 1982 and Vice-Master, since 2012, Churchill College, Cambridge; *b* 30 March 1947; *s* of Fred and Vera Siddle; *m* 1st, 1971, Yvonne Marie Kennedy (marr. diss. 1994); one *s*; 2nd, 1996, Anne Elizabeth Willis, *qv*; one *s*. *Educ:* Morecambe Grammar Sch.; Downing Coll., Cambridge (BA 1969). MA, PhD 1973. Lectr, Dept Medical Biochemistry, Welsh Nat. Sch. Med., Cardiff, 1971–78; Meres Sen. Student for Med. Research, St John's Coll., Cambridge, 1978–81; Wellcome Lectr, Dept Clinical Biochem., Univ. of Cambridge, 1981–90. Vis. Scientist, Joslin Diabetes Center and Harvard Med. Sch., 1989–90. Hon. Treas., Cambridge Univ. CC, 1990–. Chm. Editl Bd, Biochemical Jl, 1995–99. *Publications:* articles in biochem. jls. *Recreations:* mountaineering (especially Munro bagging), cricket, bird watching, gardening. *Address:* 6 Church Street, Wing, Oakham, Rutland LE15 8RS. *T:* (01572) 737675. *Clubs:* MCC; Hawks (Cambridge); Lancashire County Cricket.

SIDDLE, Oliver Richard, CB 1995; OBE 1983; General Manager, Enterprises Group, and Assistant Director-General, British Council, 1992–96; retired; *b* 11 March 1936; *s* of George Siddle and Grace (*née* Hatfield); *m* 1964 (marr. diss. 1995); one *s* one *d*. *Educ:* Hymers Coll., Hull; Queen's Coll., Oxford (BA 2nd Cl. Hons Mod. Hist. 1959). Joined British Council, 1961: Budget Dept, 1961–63; Poland, 1963–65; Argentina, 1965–68; Nigeria, 1968–70; Mgt Trng, Heriot-Watt Univ., 1970–71; Staff Trng Dept, 1971–74; Dir, Budget Dept, 1974–76; Representative: Peru, 1976–80; Hong Kong, 1980–85; Malaysia, 1985–87; Gen. Manager, Direct Teaching, 1987–92. *Recreations:* hill-walking, gardening, drawing. *Address:* 24320 La Tour Blanche, France.

SIDDONS, Michael Powell; Wales Herald of Arms Extraordinary (Herodr Arbennig Cymru), 1994–2010; *b* 4 June 1928; *s* of Bertram Siddons and Enid Mary Powell; *m* 1951, Denise Maria Jacqueline Dambre; three *s* (and one *d* decd). *Educ:* Shrewsbury Sch.; Trinity Coll., Cambridge (MA, MB BCh); St Thomas' Hosp. MFOM 1983; Licence en médecine du Travail, Univ. Catholique de Louvain, 1980. Casualty and anaesthetics officer, then house physician, St Thomas' Hosp., London, 1952–53; Nat. Service, RAMC, Malaya, 1953–55; general medical practitioner, Pontypool, 1955–74; Commission of European Communities: MO, Med. Service, Brussels, 1974–78; Head, Medical Service, Brussels Staff, 1978–87. Mem., Académie Internat. d'Héraldique, 2000; FSA 1987; FHS 1996; FSG 1998. Hon. DLitt Wales, 1997. *Publications:* The Development of Welsh Heraldry, vol. I, 1991, vols II and III, 1993, vol. IV, 2006; Welsh Pedigree Rolls, 1996; Visitations by the Heralds in Wales, 1996; Visitation of Herefordshire 1634, 2002; Heraldic Badges in England and Wales, 2009; The Heraldry of Foreigners in England 1400–1700, 2010; A Dictionary of Mottoes in England and Wales, 2014; contribs to books on heraldic and genealogical subjects and articles in jls. *Recreations:* gardening especially magnolias, medieval Welsh heraldry, genealogy. *Address:* Castagnon, 32800 Eauze, France.

SIDELL, Ron Daniel; architect; Sidell Gibson Architects (formerly Sidell Gibson Partnership LLP) (private practice), since 1970; *b* 20 April 1941; *s* of Daniel Sidell and Dorothy Eady; *m* Sally Hodgson; one *d*. *Educ:* Canterbury Coll. of Architecture; York Univ. Projects in London and Germany include: Unilever, Lloyds, Cazenove, Prudential, Rothschilds, European Bank and Civic Bldgs; Crown Jewel House and Windsor Castle reconstruction; One New Change, St Paul's; masterplans: Paddington Central; Birmingham Snow Hill redevelt. Winner: Grand Buildings Trafalgar Square Internat. Competition, 1986; City of Winchester Central Redevelt Proposal Comp., 1989. *Recreation:* just about most things. *Address:* (office) 35 Soho Square, W1D 3QX. *T:* (020) 3179 9000.

SIDHU, Navjot, (Jo); QC 2012; *b* Perivale, 4 Nov. 1965; *s* of Pritam Singh Sidhu and Surjit Kaur Sidhu; *m* 1996, Luna Tiwana; two *d*. *Educ:* Villiers High Sch.; Wadham Coll., Oxford (BA Hons PPE 1987); London Sch. of Econs and Pol Sci. (MSc Politics of the World Economy 1989); Coll. of Law (CPE 1992); Inns of Court Sch. of Law (BVC 1993). Policy and Res. Officer, London Bor. of Ealing, 1988; Sen. Researcher, BBC, 1989; Tutor in Econs (pt-time), 1989–91; called to the Bar, Lincoln's Inn, 1993, Bencher, 2014; in practice as a barrister, 1993–. Pres., Soc. of Asian Lawyers, 2014–. Mem., Ealing LBC, 1994–98. Chm. of Govs, Beaconsfield Primary Sch., 1997–. *Publications:* (contrib.) Cases that Changed our Lives, 2010; articles in Criminal Law and Justice Weekly, Criminal Bar Qly and The Guardian. *Recreations:* sport and fitness, travel, motoring, comedy, mentoring. *Address:* 25 Bedford Row, WC1R 4HD. *T:* (020) 7067 1500. *E:* jo.sidhu@sky.com.

SIDI, Marianne; *see* Elliott, Marianne.

SIDMOUTH, 8th Viscount *cr* 1805; **Jeremy Francis Addington;** *b* 29 July 1947; *s* of 7th Viscount and Barbara Mary Addington (*née* Rochford); *S* father, 2005; *m* 1st, 1970, Grete Henningsen (marr. diss.); one *s* one *d*; 2nd, 1986, Una Coogan (*d* 2009); one *s* two *d*. *Educ:* Ampleforth. *Heir:* *s* Hon. John Addington, *b* 29 Nov. 1990.

SIDNEY, family name of **Viscount De L'Isle**.

SIDWELL, Dr Elizabeth Mary, CBE 2009; FRGS; Schools Commissioner for England, 2011–13; *b* Johannesburg, 29 Sept. 1949; *d* of Richard Archibald Freeman and Mary Willmott Freeman (*née* Alderton); *m* (marr. diss. 1978); two *s*. *Educ:* Ursuline High Sch., Brentwood, Essex; Queen Mary Coll., Univ. of London (BSc Hons 1972; PhD 1976); Hughes Hall, Cambridge (PGCE 1978). FRGS 1998. TEFL Teacher: Anglo World Lang. Sch., Cambridge, 1978–80; Forest Sch., E17, 1980–91, Dep. Hd, 1985–91; Principal: Haberdashers' Aske's Hatcham Girls' Sch., 1991–95; Haberdashers' Aske's Hatcham Coll., 1995–2005; CEO, Haberdashers' Aske's Fedn, 2005–11; Lead Educnl Consultant, Aske's Consultancy Services, 2005–11. OFSTED Inspector, 1995–. Exec. Coach, Specialist Schs and Acads Trust, 1995–2011 (Trustee, 2007–11); Sen. Educn Advr, Baker Dearing Trust, 2013–. Mem., HMC, 1996–2011. Founder, Aske's Annual Educn Lecture series, 1995–. Governor: Wellington Coll., 2008–15; Forest Sch., E17, 2012–. MRI 2000; FRSA. Freeman, City of London, 2007; Liveryman, Haberdashers' Co., 2009–. *Recreations:* family, walking, theatre, travel, Hearing Dogs for the Deaf, Riding for the Disabled. *Address:* 12 Forest Court, E11 1PL. *T:* (020) 8530 4773, 07798 791738. *E:* lizsidwell29@googlemail.com.

SIEFF, Hon. Sir David (Daniel), Kt 1999; Chairman, Newbury Racecourse plc, 1998–2010 (Member of Board, 1988–2010); non-executive Director, Benesco Charity Ltd, since 2005; *b* 22 March 1939; *s* of Baron Sieff of Brimpton, OBE, and late Rosalie Cottage; *m* 1962, Jennifer Walton; two *s*. *Educ:* Repton. Joined Marks & Spencer, 1957: Dir, 1972–97; non-exec. Dir, 1997–2001. Pt-time Mem., NFC, 1972–78; non-exec. Chm., FIBI Bank (UK) Plc (formerly First Internat. Bank of Israel (UK) Ltd), 1994–2004; Chm., ukbetting, 2001–04; non-exec. Dir, GET plc, 2003–06. Chm., British Retail Consortium, 1998–2002. Chairman, North Metropolitan Conciliation Cttee of Race Relations Board, 1969–71; Vice-Chm., Inst. of Race Relations, 1971–72; Member: Policy Studies Inst. (formerly PEP), 1976–84; Bd, Business in the Community; Council, Industrial Soc., 1975–90. Governor: Weizmann Inst. of Science, Rehovot, Israel, 1978– (Chm. Exec. Cttee, UK Foundn, 1984–2000); Shenkar Coll. of Textile Technology (Israel), 1980–; Hon. Pres., British ORT, 1983–. Trustee, Glyndebourne Arts Trust, 1971–2000. Pres., Racehorse Owners Assoc., 1975–78; Chairman: Racing Welfare Charities, 1988–2000; Nat. Lottery Charities Bd, 1994–99; Member: Jockey Club, 1977–; Horserace Totalisator Bd, 1991–98; British Horseracing Bd, 1998–2001. Trustee, Mentor Foundn; Vice Pres., St Andrew's Youth Club. FRSA 1989. *E:* david@d-d-s.biz. *Clubs:* White's, Jockey.

SIEGERT, Prof. Martin John, PhD; FRSE; Co-Director, Grantham Institute, Imperial College London, since 2014; *b* Walthamstow, London, 19 Nov. 1967; *s* of David Alan Siegert and Kathleen May Siegert; *m* 2001, Maggie Robertson; one *s*. *Educ:* Sudbury Upper Sch.; Univ. of Reading (BSc Geol Geophysics 1989); Pembroke Coll., Cambridge (PhD 1993). Lectr in Phys. Geog., Univ. of Wales, Aberystwyth, 1994–98; University of Bristol: Lectr, 1999–2002, Reader, 2002–03, in Phys. Geog.; Prof. of Phys. Geog., 2003–06; Prof. of Geoscis, 2006–12, Hd, Sch. of GeoScis, 2006–11, Univ. of Edinburgh; Prof. of Geoscis, Univ. of Bristol, 2012–14. Chief Scientist, UK prog. investigating Lake Ellsworth, W Antarctica, 2009–14. FRSE 2007. Martha T. Muse Prize, Tinker Foundn, 2013. *Publications:* Ice Sheets and Late Quaternary Environmental Change, 2001; over 150 papers in scientific jls, incl. Nature and Science, on Antarctic glaciol. and subglacial lake exploration. *Recreations:* running around Bristol Downs, walking in countryside, watching football (especially Leyton Orient), playing golf. *Address:* Grantham Institute, Imperial College London, South Kensington, SW7 2AZ. *T:* (020) 7594 9667, *Fax:* (020) 7594 9668. *E:* m.siegert@imperial.ac.uk.

SIEGHART, Mary Ann Corinna Howard; writer and broadcaster; *b* 6 Aug. 1961; *d* of Paul Sieghart and Felicity Ann Sieghart (*née* Baer); *m* 1989, David Prichard; two *d*. *Educ:* Cobham Hall; Bedales Sch.; Wadham Coll., Oxford (MA). Occasional feature and leader writer (part-time), Daily Telegraph, 1980–82; Eurobond Correspondent and Lex Columnist, Financial Times, 1982–86; City Editor, Today, 1986; Political Correspondent, Economist, 1986–88; The Times: Asst Editor, 1988–2007; Opinion Page Editor, 1988–91; Arts Editor, 1989–90; Political Leader Writer, 1990–2007; acting Editor on Sundays, 1997–99; columnist, 1998–2007; Equity Partner, The Browser, 2008–12; columnist, The Independent, 2010–12. Television: presenter: The World This Week; The Brains Trust; The Big Picture Show; Powerhouse; radio: presenter, Newshour, Profile, The Week in Westminster, Beyond Westminster, One to One; guest interviewer, Start the Week. Founding Cttee Mem., Women in Journalism, 1995–98; Member: Adv. Council and Steering Cttee, New Europe, 1999–2006; Steering Gp, "No" Campaign, 2000–04; Council, Tate Modern, 2008–. Member: Social Studies Adv. Bd, Oxford Univ., 1999–2003; Adv. Panel, IntoUniversity, 2007–. Non-executive Director: Henderson Smaller Cos Investment Trust, 2008–; DLN Digital Ltd, 2011–; The Merchants Trust plc, 2014–; Content Bd, Ofcom, 2014–. Chm., Social Market Foundn, 2010–. Trustee: Nat. Heritage Meml Fund, 1997–2002; The Radcliffe Trust, 2006–; Inst. of Art and Ideas, 2012–. Vice Pres., Nat. Assoc. for Gifted Children, 1996–. Vice-Chair, New Deal for Communities, N Fulham, 2001–06. Laurence Stern Fellow, Washington Post, 1984. Harold Wincott Young Financial Journalist of the Year, 1983; Commended, Young Journalist of the Year, British Press Awards, 1983. *Recreations:* travel to remote places, singing in choirs, art, architecture, music, theatre, geometric doodling, reading fiction. *E:* sieghart@journalist.com. *W:* www.maryannsieghart.com. *Clubs:* Groucho, Chelsea Arts, Ivy.

See also W. M. T. S. Sieghart.

SIEGHART, William Matthew Timothy Stephen; Chairman: Forward Thinking, since 2004; Somerset House Trust, since 2015; *b* 14 April 1960; *s* of Paul Sieghart and Felicity Ann Sieghart (*née* Baer); *m* 1996, Molly Dineen; one *s* two *d*. *Educ:* Eton Coll.; St Anne's Coll., Oxford (MA Hons PPE). Founder and Chm., Forward Publishing, 1986–2001. Director: Groucho Club plc, 1995–2001; Hammer Films, 1998–2007; Vrumi, 2014–. Vice-Pres., Arts and Business, 2001–; Dir, Index on Censorship, 1999–2000. Dir, Forward Gp, 1998–2006. Founder and Chm., Forward Arts Foundn, 1993–; Chm., Arts Foundn, 2002–. Mem. Council, Arts Council England (formerly Arts Council of England), 2000–06 (Chm., Lottery Panel, 2000–05). Author, ind. review for DCMS, E-Lending in Public Libraries in England, 2013; Chm., Govt Adv. Panel on public library service in England, 2014 (report publd 2014). Trustee: Citizenship Foundn, 1994–2011; and Mem. Council, RSA, 1995–99; Esmée Fairbairn Foundn, 1998–; YCTV, 1998–2001; Writer's and Scholar's Educnl Trust, 1999–2000; The Poetry Archive, 2001–05; Internat. Prize for Arab Fiction, 2007–14; Free Word, 2008–; Reprieve, 2008–; Brit Docs, 2013–. Sen. Adv. Fellow, UK Defence Acad., 2004–10. Founder and Chm., Streetsmart (Action for the Homeless), 1998–. Gov., British Inst. of Human Rights, 1998–2013. Founder: Nat. Poetry Day, 1995–; Bedtime Reading Week, 2000–05; Big Arts Week, 2001–08. *Publications:* (ed) The Forward Book of Poetry, annually 1993–; (ed) Poems of the Decade, 2001, 2nd edn 2011; The Swing Factory, 2004; Winning Words, 2012. *Recreations:* travelling, playing and watching sport, poetry. *Address:* 50

Albemarle Street, W1S 4BD. *T:* (020) 7493 4361. *E:* sieghart1@mac.com. *Clubs:* Brooks's, Groucho, MCC; Queenwood Golf, Aldeburgh Golf.
See also M. A. C. H. Sieghart.

SIGMON, Robert Leland; lawyer; *b* Roanoke, Va, 3 April 1929; *s* of Ottis Leland Sigmon and Aubrey Virginia (*née* Bishop); *m* 1st, 1963, Marianne Rita Gellner (marr. diss.; she *d* 2005); 2nd, 1992, Jean Mary Anderson. *Educ:* Univ. of Virginia; Sorbonne; London Sch. of Economics. BA, DJur. Member of the Bar: US Supreme Court; Court of Appeals, Second and District of Columbia Circuits; Virginia; District of Columbia. Vice-Pres., Pilgrims Soc. of GB, 1993– (Chm., Exec. Cttee, 1977–93); Founder Member: Associates of the Victoria and Albert Museum, 1976 (Dir, 1976–87); Amer. and Internat. Friends of V&A Mus. (Trustee, 1985–2000). Mem., Council of Management, British Inst. of Internat. and Comparative Law, 1982–2006. Trustee: American Sch. in London, 1977–91; Magna Carta Trust, 1984–94; Vice-Chm., Mid-Atlantic Club of London, 1977–96; Vice-Pres., European-Atlantic Gp, 1978–94; Member: Exec. Cttee, Amer. Soc. in London, 1969– (Chm. 1974); Amer. Soc. of Internat. Law; Selden Soc.; Guild of St Bride's Church, Fleet Street; Ends of the Earth; Gov., E-SU, 1984–90. Chevalier du Tastevin. *Publications:* contribs to legal periodicals. *Recreations:* collecting antiquarian books, oenology. *Address:* Flat 46, Queen Alexandra Mansions, Judd Street, WC1H 9DQ. *Club:* Reform.

SIGURDSSON, Niels P.; Ministry of Foreign Affairs, Iceland, 1990–96; *b* Reykjavik, 10 Feb. 1926; *s* of Sigurdur B. Sigurdsson and Karitas Einarsdóttir; *m* 1953, Olafia Rafnsdóttir; two *s* one *d*. *Educ:* Univ. of Iceland (Law). Joined Diplomatic Service 1952; First Sec., Paris Embassy, 1956–60; Dep. Permanent Rep. to NATO and OECD, 1957–60; Dir, Internat. Policy Div., Min. of Foreign Affairs, Reykjavik, 1961–67; Delegate to UN Gen. Assembly, 1965; Ambassador and Permanent Rep. of Iceland to N Atlantic Council, 1967–71; Ambassador: to Belgium and EEC, 1968–71; to UK, 1971–76; to Fed. Republic of Germany, 1976–78; Ministry of Foreign Affairs, Reykjavik, 1979–84; Ambassador to Norway, 1985–89. *Recreations:* swimming, riding. *Address:* Naustabryggja 55, 110 Reykjavík, Iceland.

SIKORA, Prof. Karol, FRCP, FRCR, FFPM; Dean, Buckingham Medical School, since 2007; Chief Medical Officer (formerly Medical Director), Cancer Partners UK, since 2006; *b* 17 June 1948; *s* of Witold Karol Sikora and Thomasina Sikora; *m* 1974, Alison Mary Rice; one *s* two *d*. *Educ:* Dulwich Coll.; Corpus Christi Coll., Cambridge (MA, MB, BChir, PhD); Middlesex Hospital. FRCR 1980; FRCP 1988; FFPM 2002. Middlesex Hosp., 1972; Hammersmith Hosp., 1973; MRC Clinical Fellow, Lab. for Molecular Biol., Cambridge, 1974–77; Clinical Fellow, Stanford Univ., 1978–79; Dir, Ludwig Inst. for Cancer Research, Cambridge, 1980–86; Prof. of Clin. Oncol., RPMS, then ICSM, Hammersmith Hosp., 1986–2007; Dep. Dir (Clinical Res.), ICRF, 1995–97; Chief, WHO Cancer Prog., Lyon, France, 1997–99. Vis. Prof. of Cancer Medicine, Hammersmith Hosp., 1999–. Vice Pres., Global Clinical Res. (Oncology), Pharmacia Corp., 1999–2002; Special Advr on cancer services, HCA Internat., 2002–06. *Publications:* Monoclonal Antibodies, 1984; Interferon, 1985; Cancer: a student guide, 1988; (ed jtly) Treatment of Cancer, 1990, 6th edn 2015; Fight Cancer, 1990; Genes and Cancer, 1990; (with N. Bosanquet) The Economics of Cancer Care, 2006; contrib. Gene Therapy. *Recreations:* boating, travelling, rock climbing. *Address:* 21 Dorset Square, NW1 6QG. *T:* (020) 7724 8086. *Clubs:* Athenæum, Polish Hearth.

SILBER, Dr Evelyn Ann, FMA; Hon. Professorial Research Fellow, University of Glasgow, since 2006; *b* 22 May 1949; *d* of late Martin Helmut Silber and Mavis Evelyn (*née* Giles). *Educ:* Hatfield Girls' Grammar Sch.; New Hall, Cambridge (MA); Univ. of Pennsylvania (MA); Clare Hall, Cambridge (PhD). Guide, Hatfield House, 1965–70; Thouron Fellow, Univ. of Penn., 1972–73; copy-writer and media controller, Associated Book Publishers, 1973–74; publicity manager, Addison Wesley Publishers, 1974–75; Leverhulme Res. Fellow in Hist. of Art, 1975–76; Lectr, Hist. of Art, Glasgow Univ., 1978; Birmingham Museum and Art Gallery: Asst Keeper (Fine Art), 1979–82; Dep. Keeper (Painting and Sculpture), 1982–85; Birmingham Museums and Art Gallery: Asst Dir, Public Services, 1985–94; Head of Central Museums, 1994–95; Director: Leeds Mus and Galls, 1995–2001; Hunterian Mus. and Art Gall., Univ. of Glasgow, 2001–06. Mem. Council, Ikon Gall., 1981–88. Member: Bd, Cultural Heritage NTO (formerly Museums Trng Inst.), 1996–2003; Historic Envmt Adv. Council for Scotland, 2006–09. Chm., Scottish Archaeol Finds Allocation Panel, 2012–. Chm., Charles Rennie Mackintosh Soc., 2006–12. Chm., Queen's Park Arena Ltd, 2011–. FMA 1996; FRSA 2000. *Publications:* The Sculpture of Epstein, 1986; (with T. Friedman) Jacob Epstein Sculpture and Drawings, 1987; Gaudier-Brzeska: Life and Art, 1996. *Recreations:* travel, music, walking, gardening. *Address:* School of Culture and Creative Arts, University of Glasgow, 8 University Gardens, Glasgow G12 8QQ. *Club:* Royal Over-Seas League.

SILBER, Hon. Sir Stephen (Robert), Kt 1999; a Judge of the High Court of Justice, Queen's Bench Division, 1999–2014; *b* 26 March 1944; *s* of late J. J. Silber and Marguerite Silber; *m* 1982, Lucinda, *d* of late Lt-Col David St John Edwards; one *s* one *d*. *Educ:* William Ellis Sch.; University Coll. London; Trinity Coll., Cambridge. Called to Bar, Gray's Inn, 1968, Bencher, 1994 (Vice-Treas., 2013; Treas., 2014). QC 1987; a Recorder, 1987–99; a Dep. High Court Judge, 1995–99. A Judge, Employment Appeal Tribunal, 2004–14; Dep. Chm., Security Vetting Appeals Panel, 2009–. Law Comr for England and Wales, 1994–99. Mem., Criminal Law Cttee, Judicial Studies Bd, 1994–99. Mem. Adv. Council, Inst. of Eur. and Comparative Law, Univ. of Oxford, 2004–; Distinguished Judicial Visitor, UCL, 2011–. Pres., Travel and Tourism Law Assoc., 2002–. *Recreations:* walking, music, watching sport, theatre. *Address:* c/o Royal Courts of Justice, Strand, WC2A 2LL.

SILBERT, Roxana Alba; Artistic Director, Birmingham Repertory Theatre, since 2012; *b* La Plata, Argentina, 12 May 1964; *d* of Moises Silbert and Yolanda Silbert; *m* Chahine Yavroyan. *Educ:* Eaton (City of Norwich) Comp. Sch.; New Hall, Cambridge (BA Hons Eng. Lit. 1986). Associate Dir, Royal Court Th., 1996–98; Literary Dir, Traverse Th., 2001–04; Artistic Dir, Paines Plough Theatre Co., 2005–09; Associate Dir, RSC, 2009–12. *E:* roxana.silbert@birmingham-rep.co.uk.

SILCOCK, David Thomas; road safety consultant; Chief Executive, Global Road Safety Partnership, 2002–08; *b* 2 March 1945; *s* of John and Marjorie Silcock; *m* 1st, 1967, Lesley Maureen Reeves (marr. diss. 1994); three *d*; 2nd, 1996, Annette de Villiers Herholdt. *Educ:* Churchill Coll., Cambridge (BA 1966, MA 1970); Imperial Coll., London (MSc 1970). CEng, MICE, 1971. Engr, Canadian Pacific Railway Co. and Consultant, N. D. Lea and Assocs, Vancouver, 1967–69; various transport consultancy assignments, Halcrow Fox and Assocs, UK, 1969–74; Sen. Associate, Halcrow Fox and Assocs (London), and Man. Dir, Halcrow Fox and Assocs (Hong Kong), 1974–79; Dep. Dir, Transport Ops Res. Gp, Univ. of Newcastle upon Tyne, 1979–92; Ross Silcock, subseq. Babtie Group: Partner, Ross Silcock Partnership, 1986–96; Man. Dir, Ross Silcock Ltd, transportation and road safety consultants, 1996–2001; Divl Dir, Babtie Gp Ltd, 2001–02. Mem. Council, 1995–96, Dir, 1996–2001, British Consultants Bureau. Mem. Editl Bd, Transport Reviews (internat. jl), 1989–92. *Publications:* over 90 tech. articles in fields of transport and road safety. *Recreations:* walking, music.

SILJA, Anja; German opera singer; *b* Berlin, 17 April 1940; parents both actors; *m* 1980, Christoph von Dohnányi, *qv* (marr. diss.); one *s* two *d*. Started career at age 10; first opera engagement, Staatstheater Braunschweig, 1956; débuts: Stuttgart State Opera, Frankfurt Opera, 1958; Bayreuth Fest. (Senta in The Flying Dutchman), 1960; has appeared widely in USA, Japan and Europe, in all major opera houses, incl. Salzburg, and Glyndebourne Fest. (début, 1989); repertoire includes: all major Wagner rôles, Salome, Lulu, Fidelio, Elektra, Jenůfa, The Makropulos Case, Erwartung, Pierrot Lunaire, Dialogues des Carmélites, etc. Has made recordings and videos. *Address:* c/o Artists Management Zürich/Rita Schütz, Rütistrasse 52, 8044 Zürich-Gockhausen, Switzerland.

SILK, Rev. Mgr David; *see* Silk, Rev. Mgr R. D.

SILK, Dennis Raoul Whitehall, CBE 1995; MA; Warden of Radley College, 1968–91; Chairman, Test and County Cricket Board, 1994–96; *b* 8 Oct. 1931; 2nd *s* of late Rev. Dr Claude Whitehall Silk and Mrs Louise Silk; *m* 1963, Diana Merilyn, 2nd *d* of W. F. Milton, Pitminster, Somerset; two *s* two *d*. *Educ:* Christ's Hosp.; Sidney Sussex Coll., Cambridge (Exhibr). MA (History) Cantab. Asst Master, Marlborough Coll., 1955–68 (Housemaster, 1957–68). JP Abingdon, 1972–89. *Publications:* Cricket for Schools, 1964; Attacking Cricket, 1965; Siegfried Sassoon and the Great War, 1975. *Recreations:* antiquarian, literary, sporting (Blues in cricket (Capt. Cambridge Univ. CC, 1955) and Rugby football). *Address:* Sturts Barn, Huntham Lane, Stoke St Gregory, Taunton, Somerset TA3 6EG. *T:* (01823) 490348. *Clubs:* East India, Devonshire, Sports and Public Schools, MCC (Pres., 1992–94); Hawks (Cambridge).

SILK, Sir (Evan) Paul, KCB 2015; Associate, Global Partners Governance, since 2013; *b* 8 Feb. 1952; *s* of late Evan Silk and Joan Silk (*née* King); *m* 1986, Kathryn Barnes; three *s*. *Educ:* Christ Coll., Brecon; Brasenose Coll., Oxford (John Watson Scholar; MA 1st Cl. Hons Lit.Hum.); Princeton Univ.; Open Univ. (Dip. French 2013). A Clerk in H of C, 1975–77 and 1979–2001: Energy Cttee, 1984–89; Home Affairs Cttee, 1989–93; Foreign Affairs Cttee, 1998–2001; NI Office, 1977–79; occasional work with Council of Europe Parly Assembly, 1976–99; Clerk to Nat. Assembly for Wales, 2001–07; Dir of Strategic Projects, H of C, 2007–10; Chair, Commn on Devolution to Wales, 2011–14. Member, Board of Visitors: HM Prison Ashford, 1981–90; HM Prison Belmarsh, 1991–93. Occasional work with Westminster Foundn for Democracy, 2010–. Pres., Study of Parlt Gp, 2015–. Hon. Prof., Wales Governance Centre, Sch. of Law and Politics (formerly Eur. Studies), Cardiff Univ., 2011–. Trustee, Oxford Univ. Student Union, 2011–15. Patron, Tools for Self-Reliance Cymru, 2013–. Dir, RWCMD, 2014–; Gov., Univ. of S Wales, 2014–; Chm. of Govs, Christ Coll., Brecon, 2014–. *Publications:* (with R. Walters) How Parliament Works, 1987, 4th edn 1998; (with P. Evans) Parliamentary Assembly of the Council of Europe: practice and procedure, 10th edn 2008, 11th edn 2013; contribs to other works on Parliament. *Recreation:* living in countryside. *Address:* Mill Cottage, Crickhowell NP8 1SA. *E:* paulsilk@aol.com. *Clubs:* Chelsea Arts; Ebbw Vale Rugby Football; Gwernyfed Rugby Football.

SILK, Prof. Joseph Ivor, PhD; FRS 1999; Savilian Professor of Astronomy, Oxford University, 1999–2011, now Emeritus; Fellow, New College, Oxford, 1999–2011, now Emeritus; *b* 3 Dec. 1942; *s* of Philip and Sylvie Silk; *m* 1st, 1968, Margaret Wendy Kuhn (marr. diss. 1998); two *s*; 2nd, 2001, Jacqueline Riffault. *Educ:* Clare Coll., Cambridge (MA 1963); Harvard Univ. (PhD 1968). Research Fellow: Inst. of Astronomy, Cambridge Univ., 1968–69; Princeton Univ. Observatory, 1969–70; University of California at Berkeley: Prof. of Astronomy, 1970; Miller Res. Prof., 1980–81; Prof. of Physics, 1988. Alfred P. Sloan Foundn Fellow, 1972–74; Guggenheim Fellow, 1975–76; Leon Lectr, Univ. of Penn, 1984; Hooker Dist. Vis. Prof., McMaster Univ., 1987; Bearden Vis. Prof., Johns Hopkins Univ., 1994; Sackler Fellow, Inst. Astronomy, Cambridge, 1997; Tercentenary Fellow, Emmanuel Coll., Cambridge, 1997; Blaise-Pascal Prof., Inst. d'Astrophysique, Paris, 1997–98; Biermann Lectr, Max-Planck Inst. für Astrophys., Garching, 1997. FAAAS 1987; Fellow, APS, 1996. Hon. Mem., French Physical Soc., 1997. *Publications:* The Big Bang, 1980, 3rd edn 2001; (jtly) Star Formation, 1980; The Left Hand of Creation, 1983, rev. edn 1994; Cosmic Enigmas, 1994; A Short History of the Universe, 1994; Horizons of Cosmology: exploring worlds seen and unseen, 2009; contrib. numerous articles to refereed jls. *Recreation:* ski-ing. *Address:* Physics Department (Astrophysics), Denys Wilkinson Building, Keble Road, Oxford OX1 3RH. *T:* (01865) 273300; New College, Oxford OX1 3BN.

SILK, Prof. Michael Stephen, FBA 2009; Professor of Classical and Comparative Literature, King's College London, since 2006; *b* 11 June 1941; *s* of Norman and Ada Silk; *m* 1964, Laurel Evans; one *s* two *d*. *Educ:* King Edward's Sch., Birmingham; St John's Coll., Cambridge (BA 1964; MA 1967; PhD 1969). Res. Fellow, St John's Coll., Cambridge, 1967–70; King's College London: Lectr in Classics, 1970–85; Reader in Classics, 1985–91; Head, Dept of Classics, 1993–97; Prof. of Greek Lang. and Lit., 1991–2006. Leverhulme Major Res. Fellowship, 2000–03. Vis. Prof., Greek and Comparative Lit., Boston Univ., 2003, 2005, 2007; Adjunct Prof., Univ. of North Carolina, Chapel Hill, 2012–. Co-founder and co-editor, Dialogos, 1994–99. FKC 2010. *Publications:* Interaction in Poetic Imagery, 1974; (with J. P. Stern) Nietzsche on Tragedy, 1981, rev. edn 1983; Homer: the Iliad, 1987, 2nd edn 2004 (trans. Greek 2009); (ed) Tragedy and the Tragic: Greek theatre and beyond, 1996; Aristophanes and the Definition of Comedy, 2000; (ed with A. Hirst) Alexandria, Real and Imagined, 2004; (ed with A. Georgakopoulou) Standard Languages and Language Standards: Greek, past and present, 2009; (with I. Gildenhard and R. Barrow) The Classical Tradition: art, literature, thought, 2013; articles and reviews in classical and literary jls and collections. *Recreations:* poetry, jazz, standard popular songs, cricket. *Address:* Department of Classics, King's College London, Strand, WC2R 2LS. *T:* (020) 7848 2627.

SILK, Sir Paul; *see* Silk, Sir E. P.

SILK, Rev. Mgr (Robert) David; Bishop of Ballarat, 1994–2003; Hon. Assistant Bishop, Diocese of Exeter, 2004–10; *b* 23 Aug. 1936; *s* of Robert Reeve Silk and Winifred Patience Silk; *m* 1957, Joyce Irene Bracey; one *s* one *d*. *Educ:* Gillingham Grammar School; Univ. of Exeter (BA Hons Theology 1958); St Stephen's House, Oxford. Deacon 1959, priest 1960, Rochester; Curate: St Barnabas, Gillingham, 1959–63; Holy Redeemer, Lamorbey, 1963–69; Priest-in-Charge of the Good Shepherd, Blackfen, 1967–69; Rector of Swanscombe, 1969–75; Rector of Beckenham, St George, 1975–80; Team Rector, Holy Spirit, Leicester, 1982–88; Archdeacon of Leicester, 1980–94; Priest i/c of Amberley with N Stoke, Parham, Greatham and Wiggonholt, and Hon. Asst Bishop, Dio. of Chichester, 2003–04; received into RC Church and ordained deacon and priest, 2011. Proctor in Convocation, 1970–94; Prolocutor of Lower House of Convocation of Canterbury, 1980–94; Member of Liturgical Commn, 1976–91; Chm., Leicester Council of Faiths, 1986–93; Moderator, Churches Commn for Inter-Faith Relations (formerly Cttee for Relations with Peoples of Other Faiths), 1990–93; Pres., Victorian Council of Churches, 1995–97; Member: Anglican-Lutheran Commn, 1995–2003 (Chm., 2001–03); Liturgy Commn, 1996–2003; Chairman: Leaders of Faith Communities Forum, Victoria, 1996–2003; Glastonbury Pilgrimage Assoc., 2003–09. Appointed Chaplain by His Holiness Pope Benedict XVI, 2012. *Publications:* Prayers for Use at the Alternative Services, 1980; Compline—an Alternative Order, 1980; In Penitence and Faith, 1988. *Recreations:* Richard III Society, Leicester FC, theatre. *Address:* 1 Centenary Way, Torquay TQ2 7SB. *E:* david.silk3@btopenworld.com.

SILK, Robert K.; *see* Kilroy-Silk.

SILKIN, Barony of (*cr* 1950); title disclaimed by 3rd Baron; *see under* Silkin, Christopher Lewis.

SILKIN, Christopher Lewis; *b* 12 Sept. 1947; *s* of Baron Silkin of Dulwich (Life Peer), PC, QC and his 1st wife, Elaine Violet (*née* Stamp); *S* uncle, 2001, as 3rd Baron Silkin, but disclaimed his peerage for life; one *s* one *d* by Carolyn Theobald. *Educ:* Dulwich; LLB London 1974. Admitted solicitor, 1977.

SILLARS, James; management consultant; Assistant to Secretary-General, Arab-British Chamber of Commerce, 1993–2002; *b* Ayr, 4 Oct. 1937; *s* of Matthew Sillars; *m* 1st, 1957; one *s* one *d*; 2nd, 1981, Mrs Margo MacDonald, MSP (*d* 2014). *Educ:* Newton Park Sch., Ayr; Ayr Academy. Former official, Fire Brigades Union; Past Member Ayr Town Council and Ayr County Council Educn Cttee. Head of Organization and Social Services Dept, Scottish TUC, 1968–70. Full-time Labour Party agent, 1964 and 1966 elections. Contested (SNP): Linlithgow, 1987; Glasgow, Govan, 1992. MP: (Lab) South Ayrshire, March 1970–1976, (SLP) 1976–79; (SNP) Glasgow, Govan, Nov. 1988–1992. Among the founders of the Scottish Labour Party, Jan. 1976. Man. Dir, Scoted Ltd, 1980–83. Especially interested in education, social services, industrial relations, development policies. *Publications:* Scotland—the Case for Optimism, 1986; Labour Party pamphlets on Scottish Nationalism; Tribune Gp pamphlet on Democracy within the Labour Party. *Recreations:* reading, golf. *Address:* 97 Grange Loan, Edinburgh EH9 2ED.

SILLEM, Jeremy William; Managing Partner, Spencer House Partners LLP, since 2005; *b* London, 4 July 1950; *s* of Arthur and Patricia Sillem; divorced; two *d*. *Educ:* Downside Sch.; Brasenose Coll., Oxford (MA). Lazard Brothers, London, 1971–85, latterly Exec. Dir; Lazard Frères and Co., NY, 1985–95, latterly Gen. Partner and Hd of Corp. Finance; Chief Exec., Lazard Capital Mkts, London, 1995–2000; Chm., Bear Stearns Internat., 2000–04. Director: Martin Currie Hldgs, 2007–14; CDC Gp, 2011–14. Mem., Adv. Bd and Hon. Treas., Reform, 2004–. *Recreations:* fishing, shooting. *Address:* Spencer House Partners LLP, 15 St James's Place, SW1A 1NP. *T:* (020) 7647 8529. *E:* j.sillem@spencerhousepartners.com. *Club:* Brooks's.

SILLERY, William Moore, OBE 2002; DL; Headmaster, Belfast Royal Academy, 1980–2000; *b* 14 March 1941; *s* of William and Adeline Sillery; *m* 1963, Elizabeth Margaret Dunwoody; two *d*. *Educ:* Methodist Coll., Belfast; St Catharine's Coll., Cambridge. Head of Modern Languages, Belfast Royal Academy, 1968, Vice-Principal 1974, Deputy Headmaster 1976. Educnl Advr, Ulster Television, 1985–94. Chm., Ministerial Working Party on Modern Langs in NI Curriculum, 1991; Member: NI Cttee, UFC, 1989–93; Belfast Educn and Liby Bd, 1994–97; Cttee, HMC, 1998–99; Chm., Irish Div., HMC, 1998–99. Lay Mem., Solicitors' Disciplinary Tribunal, NI, 1999–2012. Chm., Arion Selection Panel, British Council, 2003–06. Gov., Methodist Coll., Belfast, 2007–14. DL Belfast, 1997. *Recreations:* golf, bridge. *Address:* Ardmore, 15 Saintfield Road, Belfast BT8 7AE. *T:* (028) 9064 5260. *Club:* Belvoir Park (Belfast).

SILLITO, Prof. Adam Murdin, PhD; FMedSci; Professor of Visual Science, 1987–2014, now Emeritus, and Director, 1991–2006, Institute of Ophthalmology, University College London; *b* 31 March 1944; *s* of Adam Cheswardine Sillito and Jean Mary Sillito, Amington, Tamworth; *m* Sharon Pascoe; one *s* one *d*. *Educ:* Univ. of Birmingham (MRC Schol.; BSc, PhD). Res. Fellow, Dept of Physiol., Univ. of Birmingham, 1968–70; Sir Henry Wellcome Travelling Fellow, Dept of Physiol., Johns Hopkins Med. Sch., Baltimore, 1970–71; Lectr, 1971–79, Wellcome Trust Sen. Lectr, 1979–82, Med. Sch., Birmingham; Prof. and Hd of Dept of Physiol., UC, Cardiff, 1982–87. Mem. Editl Bd, Jl Physiol., 1979–86; Co-Ed., Exptl Brain Res., 1989–; Mem., Adv. Cttee, Plenum Press Cerebral Cortex series, 1991–. Non-exec. Dir, Moorfields NHS Trust, 1994–2006 (Mem. Bd, Moorfields Eye Hosp., 1992–94). Medical Research Council: Member: Neurosci. Grants Cttee, 1982–86; Neurosci. Bd, 1991–95; Non-clinical Trng and Career Develt Panel, 1993–95. Chairman: Res. Cttee, BPMF, 1990–94; Electrophysiol. Panel, Prog. Cttee, ARVO, 1996–99; Member: Surgery Task Force—Technol. Transfer of Minimal Access Surgery, ACOST Med. Res. and Health Cttee, 1992; Human Frontiers Fellowship Panel, 1994–98. Chm., Brain Res. Assoc., 1980–83; Member: Physiol Soc. (Mem. Cttee, 1982–86); IBRO; British Neurosci. Assoc.; Soc. for Neurosci.; Assoc. for Res. in Vision and Ophthalmology (Mem., Prog. Cttee, 1996–99); Eur. Neurosci. Assoc. Founder FMedSci, 1998. Hon. Fellow, UCL. *Publications:* (ed jtly) Progress in Brain Research, 1990; Mechanisms of the GABA Action in the Visual System, 1992; (ed with G. Burnstock) Nervous Control of the Eye, 2000; numerous contribs to learned jls on mechanisms of vision. *Recreations:* dreaming of better things, learning and speculating. *Address:* Department of Visual Neuroscience, Institute of Ophthalmology, University College London, Bath Street, EC1V 9EL. *T:* (020) 7608 6801. *E:* a.sillito@ucl.ac.uk.

SILLITOE, Prof. Paul, PhD, ScD; FBA 2006; Professor of Anthropology, Durham University, since 1997; *s* of Frank Arthur George Sillitoe and Doris Mary Sillitoe (*née* Graves); *m* 1972, Jacqueline Ann Bryan; two *s*. *Educ:* Durham Univ. (BA, MA Anthropol.); Trinity Coll., Cambridge (PhD 1976, ScD Social Anthropol. 2001); Open Univ. (BA Nat. Scis); Newcastle Univ. (MSc Soil Sci.); Wye Coll., London Univ. (MSc Agricl Scis). Field work in New Guinea and projects in S Asia and Gulf region. Work with internat. develt agencies. *Publications:* Give and Take, 1979; Roots of the Earth, 1983; Made in Niugini, 1988; The Bogaia of the Muller Ranges, 1994; A Place Against Time, 1996; An Introduction to the Anthropology of Melanesia, 1998; Social Change in Melanesia, 2000; (jtly) Horticulture in Papua New Guinea, 2002; Managing Animals in New Guinea, 2003; (jtly) Indigenous Knowledge Inquiries, 2005; (jtly) Grass-Clearing Man, 2009; From Land to Mouth, 2010 (ed) Sustainable Development, 2014; (ed) Indigenous Studies and Engaged Anthropology, 2015. *Recreation:* urban peasant occupations. *Address:* Anthropology Department, Durham University, Dawson Building, South Road, Durham DH1 3LE. *T:* (0191) 334 6190, *Fax:* (0191) 334 6101. *E:* paul.sillitoe@durham.ac.uk.

SILLS, Dame Eileen, DBE 2015 (CBE 2004); Chief Nurse and Director of Patient Experience, Guy's and St Thomas' NHS Foundation Trust, since 2005; *b* Stockport, 21 June 1962; *d* of William Henry McQuinn and Eileen Jenifer Ann McQuinn; *m* 1988, Michael David Sills; two *d*. *Educ:* Tottenham Technol. Coll. (Dip. Nursing); London Sch. of Hygiene and Tropical Medicine (MSc Health Services Mgt). RN 1983. Jun. and sen. nursing posts, Stepping Hill Hosp., Withington Hosp., N Middx Hosp., 1983–95; Sen. Nurse, then Dep. Gen. Manager, Royal Free NHS Trust, 1995–99; Dir of Nursing, Royal Nat. Orthopaedic Hosp., 1999–2001; Dir of Nursing and Dep. Chief Exec., Whipps Cross Hosp., 2001–05. Visiting Professor: KCL, 2005–; London South Bank Univ., 2005–. *Recreation:* keeping fit. *Address:* Guy's and St Thomas' NHS Foundation Trust, St Thomas' Hospital, Westminster Bridge Road, SE1 7EH.

SILMAN, Prof. Alan Jonathan, FRCP, FMedSci; Consultant, Arthritis Research UK (formerly Campaign), since 2015 (Medical Director, 2007–14); part-time Professor: of Medicine, Keele University, since 2015; of Musculoskeletal Health, University of Oxford, since 2015; *b* 4 Dec. 1951; *m* 1979, Ruth Abrams; two *s* one *d*. *Educ:* Leeds Univ. (MB ChB); LSHTM (MScSocMed 1979); MD London 1985. MRCP 1977, FRCP 1992; MFCM 1980, FFCM 1988; FMedSci 2001. House Surgeon, then House Physician, St James Univ. Teaching Hosp., Leeds, 1974–75; SHO, Professorial Dept of Paediatrics, Royal Liverpool Children's Hosp., 1975–76; SHO/Registrar, N Manchester Gen. Hosp., 1976–77; DHSS Bursary and Hon. Registrar, SE Thames RHA, 1977–79; Lectr, 1979–82, Sen. Lectr, 1982–88, in Clinical Epidemiology, London Hosp. Med. Coll.; Hon. Sen. Registrar, 1979–82, Hon. Consultant, 1982–88, Tower Hamlets Health Dist; ARC Prof. of Rheumatic Disease Epidemiology and Dir, ARC Epidemiology Res. Unit, Univ. of Manchester, 1989–2007. Hon. Consultant in Rheumatology, Manchester Royal Infirmary, 1989–. Chair, NICE Technol. Appraisals Appeal Panel, 2014–. Hon. DSc: E Anglia, 2009; Keele, 2012. *Publications:* (with M. Hochberg) Epidemiology of the Rheumatic Diseases, 2001; (ed jtly) Rheumatology, 3rd edn 2004 to 6th edn 2010; over 500 res. articles on rheumatic diseases. *Address:* Arthritis Research UK, 41 Portland Place, W1B 1QH. *T:* (020) 7307 2254. *E:* a.silman@arthritisresearchuk.org.

SILSOE, 3rd Baron *cr* 1963, of Silsoe, co. Bedford; **Simon Rupert Trustram Eve;** Bt 1943; *b* 17 April 1966; *o s* of 2nd Baron Silsoe, QC and of Bridget Min (*née* Hart-Davis); *S* father, 2005; *m* Julie C. Legge. *Heir: uncle* Hon. Peter Nanton Trustram Eve, OBE [*b* 2 May 1930; *m* 1961, Petronilla Letiere Sheldon (*née* Elliott); two *s*].

SILUNGWE, Hon. Annel Musenga; Hon. Mr Justice Silungwe; Judge of the High Court and acting Judge of the Supreme Court, Namibia, 1999–2009; Judge, Court of Appeal, Seychelles, 1992; *b* 10 Jan. 1936; *s* of late Solo Musenga Silungwe and Janet Nakafunda Silungwe; *m* 1960, Abigail Nanyangwe; one *s* four *d*. *Educ:* Council of Legal Educn; Univ. of Zambia (LLM 1977). Called to the Bar, Inner Temple, 1966; State Counsel, Zambia, 1974; Judge of the High Court, Zambia, 1971–73; Minister of Legal Affairs and Attorney-General, 1973–75; Chief Justice of Zambia, 1975–92; Dir, Justice Trng Centre, Ministry of Justice, Namibia, 1994–99. Chairman: Judicial Services Commn, 1975–92; Council of Legal Educn, 1975–92; Council of Law Reporting, 1975–92; Technical Cttee on Drafting the Zambian Constitution, 2011–14. Award of Merit, Rotary Internat. Dist 9210, 1989. *Publications:* contrib. learned jls. *Recreations:* music, photography, reading, golf. *T:* and *Fax:* (home) (61) 242705.

SILVER, Caroline Louise; Partner and Managing Director, Moelis & Co., since 2009; *b* Wokingham, Berks, 30 Dec. 1962; *d* of Henry and Louise Nery; *m* 1986, Mark Silver; one *s* one *d*. *Educ:* Ranelagh Grammar Sch., Bracknell; Durham Univ. (BA Hons English with Spanish). ACA 1987. Price Waterhouse, 1984–88; Corporate Finance Exec., Morgan Grenfell & Co. Ltd, 1988–90; Dir, Internat., Deutsche Morgan Grenfell, 1990–94; Vice Chairman: Global Investment Banking, Morgan Stanley Inc., 1994–2007; Investment Banking, Merrill Lynch Inc./Bank of America, 2007–09. Non-executive Director: London Ambulance Service, 2005–14; PZ Cussons plc, 2014–. Trustee V&A Mus., 2014–. *Recreations:* opera, safaris, scuba diving, racehorse ownership, family, Africa, arts and design. *Address:* Moelis & Co., First Floor, Condor House, 10 St Paul Churchyard, EC4M 8AL. *T:* (020) 7634 3578. *E:* caroline.silver@moelis.com.

SILVER, Clinton Vita, CBE 1993; Chairman, British Fashion Council, 1994–97; Deputy Chairman, 1991–94, and Managing Director, 1990–94, Marks & Spencer plc; *b* 26 Sept. 1929; *s* of Sidney (Mick) Silver and Mina Silver (*née* Gabriel); *m* 1973, Patricia Ann (Jill) Vernon; one *s* one *d*. *Educ:* Upton House Sch.; Southampton Univ. (BSc Econ). Nat. Service, 1950–52. Joined Marks & Spencer, 1952; Alternate Dir, 1974; Dir, 1978. Director: Hillsdown Hldgs, 1994–98; Pentland Group plc, 1994–99; Tommy Hilfiger Corp., 1994–2006. Member: Bd, Youth and Music, 1987–99 (Patron, 1999–2000); Southampton Univ. Develt Trust, 1992–2002 (Patron, 2002–); Chm., Israel/Diaspora Trust, 1989–2003; Trustee, Jewish Assoc. for Business Ethics, 1995–2006 (Chm. Trustees, 1995–97). CCMI (CBIM 1991); CompTI 1994. Hon. DLitt Southampton, 1997. *Recreations:* gardening, music. *Clubs:* Athenæum; Phyllis Court (Henley-on-Thames).

SILVER, Prof. Ian Adair; Professor of Comparative Pathology, University of Bristol, 1970–93, Emeritus Professor of Pathology, since 1993; Adjunct Professor of Neurology, University of Pennsylvania, 1977–2006; *b* 28 Dec. 1927; *s* of Captain George James Silver and Nora Adair Silver; *m* 1st, 1950, Dr Marian Scrase (*d* 1994), *d* of Dr F. J. Scrase; two *s* two *d*; 2nd, 1996, Prof. Maria Erecińska, *d* of Prof. K Ereciński. *Educ:* Rugby School; Corpus Christi Coll., Cambridge (BA, MA); Royal Veterinary Coll. MRCVS 1952, FRCVS 1990. University of Cambridge: Univ. Demonstrator, Zoology, 1952–57; Univ. Lectr, Anatomy, 1957–70; Official Fellow and Coll. Lectr, Churchill Coll., 1965–70; Sen. Tutor for Advanced Students, Churchill Coll., 1966–70; University of Bristol: Hd, Dept of Path., later Path. and Microbiol., 1981–93; Dean, Faculty of Medicine, 1987–90; Sen. Res. Fellow, 1994–2015; Chm., Inst. of Clinical Neuroscience, 2000–; Chm., Burden Neurological Inst., 2006–. Chm., Southmead Health Services NHS Trust, Bristol, 1992–99. Vis. Fellow, Weitzmann Inst., Rehovot, 1963; Vis. Prof., Louisiana Tech. Univ., 1973; Royal Soc. Vis. Prof., Fed. Univ. of Rio de Janeiro, 1977. Mem., SERC Biol. Scis Cttee, 1975–80; President: Internat. Soc. for O_2 Transport to Tissue, 1976 and 1986; RCVS, 1985–86 and 1987 (Sen. Vice-Pres., 1986–87 and 1987–88). Fellow, Anatomical Soc., 2012. Hon. BVetStuds, RVC. RAgS Silver Medal, 1952; Sir Frederick Hobday Meml Medal, British Equine Vet. Assoc., 1982; Dalrymple-Champneys Medal, BVA, 1984. *Publications:* Editor of scientific books, 1971–; numerous articles in scientific jls. *Recreations:* farming, exploring, fishing, DIY. *Address:* Centre for Comparative and Clinical Anatomy, School of Veterinary Sciences, University of Bristol, Southwell Street, Bristol BS2 8EJ. *T:* (0117) 928 8362.

SILVER, Dame Ruth (Muldoon), DBE 2006 (CBE 1998); Principal and Chief Executive Officer, Lewisham College, London, 1991–2009; *b* 23 Jan. 1945; *d* of Francis Faughnan and Catherine Muldoon; *m* 1970, Anthony Silver (marr. diss. 1985); partner, Andrew Mingay; one *d*. *Educ:* Hamilton Acad.; Univ. of Glasgow (NUM schol.; MA Lit. and Psychol. 1966); Univ. of Southampton (Dip. Educn Psychol. 1968); Tavistock Inst. of Human Relations (clinical trng); Univ. of London (Dip. Educn Mgt 1978); Polytech. of Central London (MA 1983). Teaching in schs, Hackney, and Trng Psychologist, Woodberry Down Child Guidance Clinic, 1968–70; in training and work (pt-time), ILEA, 1970–75; BBC broadcaster and author in community youth develts, 1975–77; ILEA inspectorate, DES, 1977–80; Policy Principal in Youth Develt Team, MSC, 1980–82; academic consultant to MSC, 1982–83; Hd of Faculty, Southwark Coll., 1983–86; Vice Principal and actg Principal, Newham Community Coll., 1986–91. Vis. Scholar, Lucy Cavendish Coll. Centre for Women Leaders, Cambridge, 1988–. Broadcaster, lectr and author on equal opportunities and leading orgnl change. Member: Bd, British Trng Internat., 1997–99; Bd, Council for Ind. and Higher Educn, 1999– (Trustee, 1999–); Post 16 e-Learning Task Force, 2002–04; Standing Conf. of E London Principals, 2003–; Women and Work Commn, 2004–; Strategic Skills Commn, 2004–; Review Gp, students with learning difficulties and disabilities, LSC, 2004–; Nat. Skills Forum, 2005–; London Skills and Employment Bd, 2006–08; Chair, Bd, Learning and Skills Improvement Service (formerly Further Educn Improvement Agency), 2008–; Co Chair, Skills Commn. Founder Member: Further Educn NTO, 1999–2001; Higher Educn Policy Inst., 1999–; Centre for Excellence in Leadership, 2001–05; Adv. Forum, Learning and Skills Res. Centre, 2002–; Acad. Adv. Bd, NHSU, 2004–05; EDGE, 2004–10; acted as Scrutineer to Cabinet Office's ministerial network on social exclusion, 2000–02; Chm., Wkg Gp on Faiths and Further Educn, LSC/Nat. Ecumenical Agency in Further Educn, 2005–. Chief Assessor, Trng of Principals' Qualifications in England, 2006–08. Trustee: Working Men's Coll., 1995– (Chm. Govs, 1995–2008); Laban Coll., 2000; Lottie Betts-Priddy Educn Trust, 2004–; Baker Dearing Educnl Trust, 2009; Jamie Oliver Foundn, 2010. Bd Mem., London Internat. Fest. of Theatre, 1999–2004. FRSA 1994; FCGI 2003. Hon. DSocSc Southampton, 2001; Hon. DEd London Southbank, 2005. *Publications:* Making a Living, 1977; Personal Effectiveness and Young People, 1983; Guidance of Young People, 1984; Changing College Culture, 1984; (with Julian Gravatt) Further Education Re-formed, 2000; regular contribs to TES on further educn. *Recreations:* Martha, cinema, talking, reading, wondering. *Address:* 52 Fortess Road, NW5 2HG.

SILVERMAN, Prof. Bernard Walter, FRS 1997; FAcSS; Chief Scientific Adviser to the Home Office, since 2010; Professor of Statistics, since 2003, and Senior Research Fellow, Smith School for Enterprise and the Environment, since 2010, University of Oxford; *b* 22 Feb. 1952; *s* of Elias Silverman and Chana Szajna Silverman (*née* Korn); *m* 1985, Dr Rowena Fowler; one *s*. *Educ:* City of London Sch.; Jesus Coll., Cambridge (BA 1973; PhD 1978; ScD 1989; Hon. Fellow, 2003; MMath 2011); Southern Theol Educn and Trng Scheme (BTh). CStat. Research Fellow, Jesus Coll., Cambridge, 1975–77; Calculator Develt Manager, Sinclair Radionics, 1976–77; Weir Fellow, University Coll., Oxford, and Jun. Lectr, Oxford

Univ., 1977–78; University of Bath: Lectr, Reader, and Prof. of Statistics, 1978–93; Head, Sch. of Math. Scis, 1988–91; University of Bristol: Prof. of Stats, 1993–2003; Henry Overton Wills Prof. of Maths, 1999–2003, now Emeritus; Provost, Inst. for Advanced Studies, 2000–03; Master of St Peter's Coll., Oxford, 2003–09. Professorial Res. Associate, Wellcome Trust Centre for Human Genetics, Univ. of Oxford, 2010–15; Vis. Prof., LSE, 2010–13; various vis. appts at foreign univs, 1978–; Fellow, Center for Advanced Study in Behavioral Scis, Stanford, 1997–98. Ed., Annals of Stats, 2007–09. Non-exec. Dir, Defence Analytical Services Agency, MoD, 2003–09. Mem., GM Sci. Rev. Panel, 2002–04; Chm., Peer Rev. Panel, Project for Sustainable Develt of Heathrow, 2005–06. Mem., AHRC, 2012–. President: Inst. of Mathematical Stats, 2000–01; Royal Statistical Soc., 2010; Chairman: Jt Mathematical Council of UK, 2003–06; UK Maths Trust, 2004–10; Mem. Council, Royal Soc., 2009–10. MAE 2001; FAcSS (AcSS 2014). Ordained deacon, 1999, priest, 2000; Hon. Curate, 1999–2003, Associate Parish Priest, 2003–05, St Paul's Clifton, and St Mary's, Cotham, Bristol; Proctor in Convocation, Gen. Synod of C of E, 2000–03; Associate Priest, St Giles and St Margaret's, Oxford, 2009–15. Hon. Fellow, St Chad's Coll., Durham, 2010. Guy Medals in Bronze, 1984, and Silver, 1995, Royal Statistical Soc.; (N American) Cttee of Presidents of Statistical Socs' Award, 1991. Hon. DSc St Andrews, 2014. *Publications:* Density Estimation for Statistics and Data Analysis, 1986; (with P. J. Green) Nonparametric Regression and Generalized Linear Models, 1994; (with J. O. Ramsay) Functional Data Analysis, 1997, 2nd edn 2005; (with J. O. Ramsay) Applied Functional Data Analysis, 2002; numerous papers in learned jls.

SILVERMAN, Prof. (Hugh) Richard, OBE 2000; Professor of Architecture, University of Wales, Cardiff (formerly University of Wales College of Cardiff), 1986–99, now Emeritus (Head of Welsh School of Architecture, 1986–97); *b* 23 Sept. 1940; *m* 1963, Kay Sønderskov-Madsen; two *d. Educ:* Edinburgh Univ. (MSc Soc. Sci). Lectr, then Sen. Lectr, Univ. of Bristol, 1971–82. Partner, Alec French Partnership, Architects, Bristol, 1984–86. Built project, 1 Bridewell St, Bristol, 1985 (RIBA Regl Award). Mem. Board, Cardiff Bay Develt Corp., 1990–2000; Director: Edward Ware Homes, Bristol, 2002–03; Under the Sky Urban Renewal, 2004–13. FRSA 1989–2010.

SILVERS, Robert B.; Editor, New York Review of Books, since 2006 (Co-Founder and Co-Editor, 1963–2006); *b* New York, 31 Dec. 1929; *s* of James J. Silvers and Rose (Roden) Silvers. *Educ:* Univ. of Chicago (AB 1947); École des Sciences Politiques, Paris (Cert. 1956). Press Sec. to Gov. Chester Bowles, 1950. Served with US Army, SHAPE, 1952. Joined Editl Bd, Paris Review, 1954, Paris Editor, 1956–59; Associate Editor, Harper's mag., NYC, 1959–63. Trustee: Ditchley Foundn, 1996–; NY Public Liby, 1997–; Paris Review Foundn, 2002–. Member: Amer. Acad. of Arts and Scis; Century Assoc.; Council on Foreign Relns. Hon. FBA 2013. Hon. LittD: Harvard, 2007; Columbia, 2014; Oxford, 2014. Literarian Award for Outstanding Service to Amer. Lit. Community (jtly), Amer. Book Foundn, 2006; Ivan Sandrof Lifetime Achievement Award, Nat. Book Critics Circle Awards, 2012; Hadada Award, Paris Rev., 2012; Nat. Humanities Medal, Nat. Endowment for the Humanities, 2012. Légion d'Honneur (France); Ordre Nat. du Merité (France). *Publications:* (ed) Writing in America, 1962; (ed) Hidden Histories of Science, 1995; (ed) Doing It: five performing arts, 2001; (ed jtly) The Legacy of Isaiah Berlin, 2001; (ed jtly) Striking Terror: America's new war, 2002; (ed jtly) The Company They Kept: writers on unforgettable friendships, 2006, vol. 2, 2011; (ed) Consequences to Come, 2008; (ed jtly) The New York Review Abroad: fifty years of international reportage, 2013; (trans), La Gangrène. *Address:* New York Review of Books, 435 Hudson Street, 3rd Floor, New York, NY 10014, USA. *T:* (212) 7578070. *E:* rsilvers@nybooks.com. *Club:* Knickerbocker (NY).

SILVERSTONE, Daniel William; Chair, René Cassin, since 2014; *b* 29 Sept. 1951; *s* of Jack and Liesl Silverstone; *m* 1988, Judith Anne Hunt, *qv*; two step *d. Educ:* Univ. of Sussex (BA Hons Politics); Univ. of Manchester (MA Govt). Greater London Council: Prin. Race Relns Advr, 1982–84; Dep. Dir, Personnel, 1984–86; Dep. Dir, Personnel, ILEA, 1986–89; Dep. Dir, Educn, London Bor. of Hackney, 1989–95; Dir, London Boroughs Grants, 1995–2001; Chief Exec., CRE, 2001–04; Principal Associate, Global Diversity Practice, Norman Broadbent, 2004; CEO, London Remade, 2004–09; Exec. Dir, Interights, 2010–12. Mem., Commn for a Sustainable London 2012, 2008–10; Chair, Leadership Gp, Refugee Council, 2008–. Special Advr, England Cttee, Big Lottery Fund, 2014– (Mem., 2010–14). Gov., Parliament Hill Sch. FRSA 1998. *Publications:* (jtly) The System, 1981. *Recreations:* modern jazz, books, film, tennis, Tottenham Hotspur. *E:* daniel@dsilverstone.co.uk.

SILVERSTONE, Judith Anne; *see* Hunt, J. A.

SILVERTON, Kate; broadcaster and journalist with BBC, since 2003; *b* Waltham Abbey, Essex, 4 Aug. 1970; *d* of Terence George and Patricia Ann Silverton; *m* 2010, Mike Heron; one *s* one *d. Educ:* West Hatch High Sch., Chigwell; Univ. of Durham (BSc Psychol., and Arabic and Middle Eastern Studies). Volunteer, Operation Raleigh, 1990; Corporate Finance, Barclays de Zoete Wedd, 1994–96; with BBC, 1996–98: travel and traffic reporter, Breakfast Show, Radio Newcastle, 1997–98; reporter and presenter: Look North, 1997–98; Evening News, Tyne Tees Television, 1998–2000; The Wright Stuff, Channel 5, 2000–02; presenter: World Travel, Travel Channel, 2003; Third Degree, BBC 3, 2003; 3D, Sky News, 2003; BBC: co-presenter: Five Live Breakfast Show, Radio 5 Live, 2004; Weekend with Rod Liddle and Kate Silverton, 2004; reporter and presenter, News Channel, 2004–; reporter, Panorama, 2006–; News Foreign Corresp., Iraq, 2006, Afghanistan, 2009; reporter and presenter: Breakfast News, 2006–; One O'Clock News, 2008–; Six O'Clock News, 2008–; presenter: Ultimate Wild Water, 2007; Big Cat Live, 2008; Propertywatch, 2009; Ten O'Clock News, 2009; Kate Silverton Show, Radio 5 Live, 2009–11. Patron, Tusk Trust, 2014–; Ambassador, The Journalists' Charity. *Recreations:* outdoor pursuits, adventure sports, swimming, triathlon, travelling. *E:* enquiries@katesilverton.com. *W:* www.katesilverton.com.

SILVESTER, Frederick John; author; Chairman and Managing Director, Advocacy (formerly Advocacy Partnership) Ltd, 1986–2000; *b* 20 Sept. 1933; *s* of William Thomas Silvester and Kathleen Gertrude (*née* Jones); *m* 1971, Victoria Ann, *d* of James Harold and Mary Lloyd Davies; two *d. Educ:* Sir George Monoux Grammar Sch.; Sidney Sussex Coll., Cambridge. Called to the Bar, Gray's Inn, 1957. Teacher, Wolstanton Grammar School, 1955–57; Political Education Officer, Conservative Political Centre, 1957–60. Member, Walthamstow Borough Council, 1961–64; Chairman, Walthamstow West Conservative Association, 1961–64. MP (C): Walthamstow West, Sept. 1967–70; Manchester, Withington, Feb. 1974–1987; contested (C) same seat, 1987. An Opposition Whip, 1974–76; PPS to Sec. of State for Employment, 1979–81, to Sec. of State for NI, 1981–83. Member: Public Accounts Cttee, 1983–87; Procedure Cttee, 1983–87; Exec., 1922 Cttee, 1985–87; Vice-Chm., Cons. Employment Cttee, 1976–79. Sen. Associate Dir, J. Walter Thompson, 1970–88. *Publications:* The Northern Briton, 1984; Global Speak: the five untruths, 2005; Rape of democracy, 2008; Facing Up to Human Rights, 2012, 2nd edn as Facing Up to Human Rights: why Britain should leave the Strasbourg Court, 2013. *Address:* 27 King Edward Walk, SE1 7PR.

SIM, Andrew Fraser; Consultant, Kennedys, solicitors, 1999–2005; *b* 27 Nov. 1948; *s* of Donald Fraser Sim and Pamela Jean Sim; *m* 1975, Antonia Rolfe Tweedie Aitken; two *s* one *d. Educ:* Haileybury Coll., Herts; City of London Poly. (BA Business Law). Admitted Solicitor. British Railways Board: Asst Solicitor, 1975; Head of Litigation, 1982; Dep. Solicitor, 1986–93; Solicitor, 1993–99. *Recreations:* cricket, golf, fishing.

SIMEON, Sir Stephen George Barrington, 9th Bt *cr* 1815, of Grazeley, Berkshire; *b* 29 Oct. 1970; *s* of Sir Richard Edmund Barrington Simeon, 8th Bt and of Agnes Joan Simeon (*née* Weld); *S* father, 2013, but his name does not appear on the Official Roll of the Baronetage; *m* 1996, Michelle Owens; one *s* one d. *Heir: s* Ewan Barrington Harold Simeon, *b* 4 June 1998.

SIMEONE, Reginald Nicola, CBE 1985; FRMetS; Adviser to the Chairman, Nuclear Electric plc, 1990–96; *b* 12 July 1927; *s* of late Nicola Francisco Simeone, FCIS, and Phyllis Simeone (*née* Iles); *m* 1954, Josephine Frances Hope; two *s. Educ:* Raynes Park Grammar Sch.; St John's Coll., Cambridge (Schol.; MA). FRMetS 1993. Instructor Lieut (Meteorol), Royal Navy, 1947–50; Admiralty: Asst Principal, 1950–55; Principal, 1955–59; UKAEA: Finance Br., 1959–61; Economics and Programmes Br., 1961–65; Chief Personnel Officer, AWRE, 1965–69; Principal Estabts Officer, 1970–76; Authority Personnel Officer, 1976–84; Comptroller and Bd Mem. for Finance and Administration, 1984–88; Advr to the Chm., 1988–90. Chm., Atomic Energy Constabulary Police Cttee, 1985–90; Exec. Vice Pres., European Atomic Energy Soc., 1987–91. *Recreations:* European travel, theatre, opera, ballet, music, meteorology. *Address:* 31 Portsmouth Avenue, Thames Ditton, Surrey KT7 0RU.

SIMINOVITCH, Dr Louis, CC 1989 (OC 1980); PhD, FRS 1980; FRSC 1965; Director, Samuel Lunenfeld Research Institute of Mount Sinai Hospital (formerly Mount Sinai Hospital Research Institute), 1983–94, now Director Emeritus (University Professor Emeritus, 1985), and Senior Fellow, Massey College, since 2009, University of Toronto; *b* Montreal, PQ, 1 May 1920; *s* of Nathan Siminovitch and Goldie Watchman; *m* 1944, Elinore, *d* of late Harry Faierman; three *d. Educ:* McGill Univ. (BSc 1941, PhD 1944; Arts and Sci. schol. 1939, Sir William McDonald schol. 1940, Anne Molson prize in Chem. 1941). With NRC at Ottawa and Chalk River, Ont., 1944–47; NRC Studentship and Fellowship, 1942–44; Canadian Royal Soc. Fellowship, 1947–49; with Centre Nat. de la Recherche Scientifique, Paris, 1949–53; Nat. Cancer Inst. Canadian Fellowships, 1953–55; Connaught Med. Res. Labs, Univ. of Toronto, 1953–56. Sen. Scientist, 1956–69 and Head, Div. of Biolog. Research, 1958–69, Ontario Cancer Inst., Univ. of Toronto; Chm., Dept of Med. Cell Biology, Univ. of Toronto, 1969–72; Chm., Dept of Med. Genetics, 1972–79, Univ. Prof., 1976–85, Special Advr to Dean on Res., 1994–, Toronto Univ.; Geneticist-in-Chief, Hosp. for Sick Children, Toronto, 1976–85. Founding Mem. and Pres., Editorial Bd, Science Forum, 1966–79; Pres., Canadian Cell Biology Soc., 1967. Member: Bd of Dirs, Nat. Cancer Inst. of Canada, 1975–85 (Pres., 1982–84); Nat. Bd of Dirs, Canadian Cancer Soc., 1981–84; Bd, Ontario Cancer Treatment and Res. Foundn, 1979–94; Scientific Adv. Cttee, Connaught Res. Inst., 1980–84; Alfred P. Sloan, Jr, Selection Cttee, General Motors Cancer Res. Foundn, 1980–81, 1983–84; Health Res. and Develt Council of Ont, 1983–86. Chairman: Scientific Advisory Committee: Ontario Cancer Treatment and Res. Foundn, 1985–99; Loeb Inst. for Med. Res., Ottawa, 1988–99; Rotman Res. Inst., Toronto, 1988–; Phagetech, 1998–2005; Scientific Advisory Board: Bioniche Inc., 1996–98; Cytochroma Inc., 1999–2001; Member, Scientific Advisory Committee: Montreal Neurol Inst., 1992– (Mem., Neuro. Adv. Council, 1997–2001); Glycodesign, 1996–2001; Member, Scientific Advisory Board: Apoptogen Inc., 1995–2000; Univ. Medical Discoveries Inc., 1996–2006; GeminX, 1997–2000; Lorus (formerly Genesense) Technologies Inc., 1998–; Ottawa Gen. Hosp. Res. Inst., 1998–2000; Genetic Diagnostics, 2003–. Member: Hybrisens Ltd, 1995–98; Program Adv. and Sci. Adv. Cttee, Tanenbaum Chairs, Univ. of Toronto, 1995–2000; Scientific Adv. Bd, Canadian Med. Discoveries Fund, 1998–2002; Bd, Premier's Res. Excellence Awards Prog., 1998–2005; Bd, Viventia Biotech, 2000–06. Member: Bd of Dirs, Ottawa Civic Hosp. & Loeb Res. Inst. Corp., 1996–2000; Bd, Baycrest Centre for Geriatric Care, Toronto, 1998– (Consultant to Vice-Pres. Res. and Co-Chm. Res. Adv. Cttee, 1994–; Chm., Sci. Adv. Cttee, KLARU, 1997–). Founding Editor: Virology, 1960–80; Cell, 1973–81; Ed., Jl of Molecular and Cellular Biology, 1980–90; Member Editorial Board: Jl Cancer Surveys (London), 1980–89; Somatic Cell and Molecular Genetics, 1984–2005. Foreign Associate, NAS, 1999. Hon. DSc: Meml Univ., Newfoundland, 1978; McMaster Univ., 1978; Hon. Dr: Univ. of Montreal, 1990; McGill Univ., Montreal, 1990; Univ. of Western Ont, London, 1990; Univ. of Toronto, 1995; Univ. of Guelph, 2001. Flavelle Gold Medal, RSC, 1978; Univ. of Toronto Alumni Assoc. Award, 1978; Izaak Walton Killam Meml Prize, 1981; Gairdner Foundn Wightman Award, 1981; Medal of Achievement Award, Institut de Recherches Cliniques de Montreal, 1985; Environmental Mutagen Society Award, Baltimore, Maryland, 1986; R. P. Taylor Award, Canadian Cancer Soc., Nat. Cancer Inst., 1986; Distinguished Service Award, Canadian Soc. for Clinical Investigation, 1990; Toronto Biotechnol. Initiative Community Service Award, 1991; Canadian Medical Hall of Fame, 1997; Canadian Sci. and Engrg Hall of Fame, 2008. Silver Jubilee Medal, 1977; Gov.-Gen.'s Commemorative Medal for 125th Anniversary of Canadian Confedn, 1992; Lifetime Achievement Award, Toronto Biotechnol. Initiative, 2006. Has specialised in the study of bacterial and somatic cell genetics. *Publications:* many contribs to scientific and learned journals. *Address:* c/o Samuel Lunenfeld Research Institute of Mount Sinai Hospital, 600 University Avenue, Room 778D, Toronto, ON M5G 1X5, Canada; Apt 805, 130 Carlton Street, Toronto, ON M5A 4K3, Canada.

SIMITIS, Konstantinos, DJur; MP (PASOK) Piraeus, 1985–2009; Prime Minister of Greece, 1996–2004; Leader, Panhellenic Socialist Movement, 1996–2004; *b* Athens, 23 June 1936; *s* of George Simitis and Fani Cristopoulou; *m* Daphne Arkadiou; two *d. Educ:* Univ. of Marburg (DJur 1959); LSE. Lawyer of the Supreme Court, 1961; Reader in Law, Univ. of Konstanz, Germany, 1971; Prof. of Commercial Law and Civil Law, Justus Liebig Univ., Germany, 1971–75; Prof. of Commercial Law, Panteion Univ. of Political and Social Scis, Athens, 1977. Member: Nat. Council, Panhellenic Liberation Movt, 1970; PASOK, 1974–. Minister: of Agriculture, 1981–85; of Nat. Econ., 1985–87; of Educn and Religious Affairs, 1989–90; of Industry and Commerce, 1993–95. *Publications:* The Structural Opposition, 1979; Policy for Economic Stabilisation, 1989; Nationalistic Populism or National Strategy?, 1992; Towards a Vigorous Society, Towards a Vigorous Greece, 1995; Politics for a Creative Greece, 2005; Strategy and Perspectives, 2006; books and articles on legal and econ. matters. *Address:* Akademias 35, 10672 Athens, Greece.

SIMLER, Hon. Dame Ingrid (Ann), DBE 2013; **Hon. Mrs Justice Simler;** a Judge of the High Court of Justice, Queen's Bench Division, since 2013; *b* 17 Sept. 1963; *d* of Derek and Judy Simler; *m* 1991, John Bernstein; two *s* two *d. Educ:* Henrietta Barnett Sch.; Sidney Sussex Coll., Cambridge (BA 1985; MA); Europa Inst., Univ. of Amsterdam (Dip. EC Law 1986). Called to the Bar, Inner Temple, 1987, Bencher, 2008; a Recorder, 2002–13; Jun. Counsel to IR, 2002–06; QC 2006; a Dep. High Ct Judge, 2010–13. Chm., Equality and Diversity Cttee, Bar Council, 2003–11; Mem., Equal Treatment Adv. Cttee, Judicial Studies Bd, 2007–11. Gen. Editor, Jordans Employment Law Service, 2007–. *Publications:* (contrib.) Tottel Discrimination Law. *Recreations:* theatre, travel, being with my children. *Address:* Royal Courts of Justice, Strand, WC2A 2LL.

SIMM, Ian Richard; Chief Executive, Impax Asset Management Group plc, since 2005; *b* Ilkley, Yorks; *s* of John and Marjorie Simm; *m* 1999, Helen Dell; one *s* one *d. Educ:* St John's Coll., Cambridge (BA Natural Scis 1988); Harvard Univ. (MPA 1993). Consultant: EC, 1988–89; Envmtl Resources Ltd, 1990–91; McKinsey & Co., 1993–96; Dir, Impax Capital, 1996–98; Founder and Man. Dir, Impax Asset Mgt Ltd, 1998–2005. Non-exec. Dir, NERC, 2013–. *Recreations:* sailing, tennis, family. *Address:* c/o Impax Asset Management, Norfolk House, 31 St James's Square, SW1Y 4JR. *T:* (020) 7434 1122. *E:* i.simm@impaxam.com.

SIMMERS, Graeme Maxwell, CBE 1998 (OBE 1982); DL; Chairman, Scottish Sports Council, 1992–99; *b* 2 May 1935; *s* of W. Maxwell Simmers and Gwen Simmers; *m* 1965, Jennifer Roxburgh; two *s* two *d. Educ:* Glasgow Acad.; Loretto Sch. CA 1959. National

Service, commnd Royal Marines, 1959–61. Sen. Partner, S. Easton Simmers & Co., 1960–86; Dir, Scottish Highland Hotels Gp, 1962–92 (Chm., 1972–92). Mem., Scottish Tourist Bd, 1979–86; British Hospitality Association (formerly British Hotels & Restaurants Association): Chm., Bd of Management, 1987–88; Mem. Nat. Exec., 1991–97. Chm., Forth Valley Acute Hosps NHS Trust, 2002–04; non-exec. Mem., Forth Valley Health Bd, 2002–10. Governor: Loretto Sch., 1968–2000 (Chm., 1992–99); Queen's Coll., Glasgow, 1989–93; Mem. Court, Stirling Univ., 2000–10. DL Stirling and Falkirk, 2004. Hon. Col, RM Reserve, Scotland, 2000–06. Elder, Killearn Kirk. DUniv Stirling, 2012. *Address:* 11 Crawford Gardens, St Andrews, Fife KY16 8XG. *Clubs:* All England Lawn Tennis; Royal & Ancient Golf (Chm., Championship Cttee, 1988–91; Captain, 2001–02); Prestwick Golf, Loch Lomond Golf, Pine Valley Golf.

SIMMONDS, Andrew John; QC 1999; a Deputy High Court Judge, since 2006; *b* 9 May 1957; *s* of late Ernest Simmonds and of Sybil Simmonds; *m* 1981, Kathleen Moyse; one *d.* *Educ:* Sevenoaks Sch., Kent; St John's Coll., Cambridge (MA). Called to the Bar, Middle Temple, 1980, Bencher, 2012. *Recreations:* alpine ski-ing, running. *Address:* 5 Stone Buildings, Lincoln's Inn, WC2A 3XT. *T:* (020) 7242 6201.

SIMMONDS, Brigid Mary, OBE 2006; Chief Executive, British Beer and Pub Association, since 2009; *b* 17 April 1958; *d* of Rev. Dermot Quinlan and Edna Quinlan; *m* 1984, Gavin Simmonds; two *s* one *d.* *Educ:* St Margaret's Sch., Bushey; WRAC Coll., Camberley. Short Service Commn, WRAC, 1978–86: Hong Kong, 1982–84; MoD, 1984–86. Dir, Mktg and PR, S & P Architects, 1986–91; Chief Exec., Business In Sport and Leisure, 1992–2009. Mem., then Chm., Lottery Panel, 1994–2000, Mem. Bd, 1998–2004, Sport England; Chm., Sport and Recreation Alliance (formerly CCPR), 2005–11 (Mem. Bd, 2000–12; Vice Pres., 2012–); Dir, Tourism Alliance, 2005– (Chm., 2005–06, 2011–12). Non-exec. Dir, Quintus PA, 2006–08. Shine Industry Expert of the Year Award, 2007; Leisure Report Industry Individual Award, 2007. *Publications:* Developing Partnerships in Sport and Leisure, 1996. *Recreations:* sport (running and tennis), reading, music. *Address:* British Beer and Pub Association, Ground Floor, Brewers Hall, Aldermanbury Square, EC2V 7HR. *T:* (020) 7627 9162, *Fax:* (020) 7627 9179. *E:* bsimmonds@beerandpub.com.

SIMMONDS, Christopher Albert; a District Judge, Principal Registry of the Family Division, since 2010; *b* Chatham, Kent, 24 May 1973; *s* of late Albert Simmonds and of Ruth Simmonds; *m* 1999, Louise Hudson. *Educ:* Hertfordshire Univ. (LLB Hons); London Guildhall Univ. (Law Soc. Annual Prize for Outstanding Perf. 1997). Admitted as solicitor, 1999; with Stantons, Solicitors, Strood; Solicitor, later Partner, Stephens & Son, Chatham; Founder, Davis Simmonds & Donaghey Solicitors, Sen. Partner, 2004–10. Comr, Judicial Appointments Commn, 2014–. *Recreations:* walking with my dogs, gardening, reading, caring for our chickens, sailing. *Address:* Principal Registry of the Family Division, First Avenue House, 42–49 High Holborn, WC1V 6NP.

SIMMONDS, John Andrew; Registrar in Bankruptcy, High Court of Justice, 1993–2011; *b* 8 March 1939; *s* of Frank Andrew Simmonds and Eugenie Marie Alexandra (*née* Longyear); *m*; one *s.* *Educ:* Holloway Grammar Sch. Admitted solicitor, 1968; Partner, Stafford Clark & Co., 1971–93. Mem., Insolvency Practitioners Tribunal, 1987–2011. Conducted first electronic winding-up court, 2011. *Publications:* Statutory Demands: use and abuse, 1992; contributions to: Report by Lord Justice Otton, Litigants in Person in the High Court, 1995–96; Report by Mr Justice Ferris, Insolvency Practitioner Remuneration, 1999–2000. *Address:* Dulwich and Herts.

SIMMONDS, Rt Hon. Sir Kennedy (Alphonse), KCMG 2004; PC 1984; Prime Minister, Federation of St Christopher (St Kitts) and Nevis, 1983–95; *b* 12 April 1936; *s* of Bronte Clarke and Arthur Simmonds; *m* 1976, Mary Camella (*née* Matthew); three *s* two *d.* *Educ:* St Kitts and Nevis Grammar School; Leeward Islands Scholar, 1954; Univ. of West Indies (studies in Medicine), 1955–62. Senior Bench Chemist, Sugar Assoc. Res. Lab., St Kitts, 1955; Internship, Kingston Public Hosp., 1963; medical practice, St Kitts, Anguilla and Nevis, 1964–66; postgrad. studies, Princess Margaret Hosp., Bahamas, 1966; Resident in Anaesthesiology, Pittsburgh, 1968–69; medical practice, St Kitts, 1969–80; Premier of St Christopher (St Kitts) and Nevis, 1980–83. Foundn Mem., People's Action Movement Opposition Party, 1965, Pres., People's Action Movement, 1976. Fellow, Amer. Coll. of Anaesthesiology, 1970. Medal of Honour, Anguilla, 2005. *Recreations:* tennis, cricket, football, video taping. *Address:* PO Box 167, Earle Morne Development, Basseterre, St Kitts, West Indies.

SIMMONDS, Rt Hon. Mark (Jonathan Mortlock); PC 2014; Managing Director, Kroll, since 2015; *b* 12 April 1964; *s* of Neil Mortlock Simmonds and Mary Griffith Simmonds; *m* 1994, Lizbeth Josefina Hanomancin; one *s* two *d.* *Educ:* Trent Poly. (BSc Hons). MRICS 1987. With Savills, 1986–88; Partner, Strutt & Parker, 1988–96; Dir, C. B. Hillier Parker, 1996–98; Man. Dir, 1998–2001, Chm., 2001–12, CEO, 2014–, Mortlock Simmonds Brown (formerly Mortlock Simmonds). MP (C) Boston and Skegness, 2001–15. Shadow Minister: for Public Services, Health and Educn, subseq. Educn, 2003–04; for Foreign Affairs, 2004–05; for Internat. Develt, 2005–07; for Health, 2007–10; PPS to Sec. of State, DEFRA, 2010–12; Parly Under-Sec. of State, FCO, 2012–14. *Recreations:* family, Rugby, tennis, history, reading.

SIMMONDS, Posy, MBE 2002; FRSL; freelance illustrator/cartoonist, since 1969; *b* 9 Aug. 1945; *d* of late Reginald A. C. Simmonds and Betty Cahusac; *m* 1974, Richard Graham Hollis, *qv.* *Educ:* Queen Anne's Sch., Caversham; L'Ecole des Beaux Arts, Paris; Central Sch. of Art and Design, London (BA Art and Design). Cartoonist: The Guardian, 1977–87, 1988–90, 1992–; The Spectator, 1988–90. Exhibitions: The Cartoon Gall. (formerly the Workshop), 1974, 1976, 1979, 1981, 1982, 1984; Mus. of Modern Art, Oxford, 1981; Manor House Mus. & Art Gall., Ilkley, 1985; Belgian Comic Strip Centre, Brussels, 2012. TV documentary, Tresoddit for Easter, 1991. FRSL 2005. Hon. DArt Plymouth, 1993; Hon. DLitt Exeter, 2007. Cartoonist of the Year: Granada TV/What The Papers Say, 1980; British Press Awards, 1981; Nat. Art Liby Illustrations Award, 1998. *Publications:* Bear Book, 1969; Mrs Weber's Diary, 1979; True Love, 1981; Pick of Posy, 1982; (illustrator) Daisy Ashford, The Young Visiters, 1984; Very Posy, 1985; Fred, 1987 (filmed as Famous Fred, 1997); Pure Posy, 1987; Lulu and the Flying Babies, 1988; The Chocolate Wedding, 1990; (illustrator) Hilaire Belloc, Matilda, who told such Dreadful Lies, 1991; Mustn't Grumble, 1993; Bouncing Buffalo, 1994; F-Freezing ABC, 1995; (illustrator) Hilaire Belloc, Cautionary Tales, 1998; Gemma Bovery, 1999 (filmed, 2014); (illustrator) Folio Book of Humorous Verse, 2002; Lavender, 2003; Literary Life, 2003; Baker Cat, 2004; Tamara Drewe, 2007 (Grand Prix 2009 de la critique bande dessinée) (filmed, 2010); Mrs Weber's Omnibus, 2012. *Address:* c/o United Agents, 12–26 Lexington Street, W1F 0LE. *T:* (020) 3214 0800.

See also R. J. Simmonds.

SIMMONDS, Richard James, CBE 1996; farmer and forester; Chairman, London and Economic Properties, 2002–13; *b* 2 Aug. 1944; *s* of late Reginald A. C. Simmonds and Betty Cahusac; *m* 1967, Mary (*née* Stewart); one *s* two *d.* *Educ:* Trinity Coll., Glenalmond. Councillor, Berkshire CC (Chm. of Environment, Property, Transport, and Development Cttees), 1973–79. National Vice-Chm. of Young Conservatives, 1973–75; Founding Vice-Chm. of Young European Democrats, 1974; Personal Asst to Rt Hon. Edward Heath, 1973–75; MEP (C) Midlands W, 1979–84, Wight and Hampshire E, 1984–94; PPS to Sir James Scott-Hopkins, Leader of European Democratic Gp, European Parlt, 1979–82; Cons. spokesman on youth and educn, European Parlt, 1982–84, on budget control, 1984–87; Whip, 1987–89; Chief Whip, 1992–94. Mem., Agric., Fisheries, Food and Rural Develt Cttee, 1992–94; Expert Advr, Eur. Commn, 1997–. Fellow of Parly & Industry Trust. Chairman: Countryside Commn, 1995–99; Ind. Transport Commn, 1999–2001. Pres., A>B Global Inc., 2005–. Mem. Council, PDSA, 1995–2001. Founding Pres., Mounted Games Assoc. of GB, 1984–; President: Royal E Berks Agricl Assoc., 1995; Jersey Cattle Soc., 1997. Fellow, Waitangi Foundn, NZ, 1996. Chm. of Governors, Berkshire Coll. of Agriculture, 1979–92; Mem. Adv. Cttee, Centre for Agric. Strategy, Reading Univ., 1998–2001. ARAgS 1997. Hon. Pres., Fair Weather Golfing Soc., 2011–. *Publications:* The Common Agricultural Policy—a sad misnomer, 1979; An A to Z of Myths and Misunderstandings of the European Community, 1981, 3rd edn 1993; (jtly) Cork Declaration on Rural Development, 1996; European Parliamentary report on farm animal welfare, 1985, 1987, 1990; report on prodn, processing, politics and potential of NZ meat (P4 report), 1996. *Recreations:* resisting bureaucracy, getting things done. *Address:* Dyars, Cookham Dean, Berkshire SL6 9PJ. *Clubs:* Royal Ascot Racing; Ancient Britons, Tamworth; OPB Sailing (Hon. Cdre, 1999–).

See also Posy Simmonds.

SIMMONS, His Honour Alan Gerald; a Circuit Judge, 1990–2006; *b* 7 Sept. 1936; *s* of late Maurice Simmons and Sophie Simmons (*née* Lasserson); *m* 1961, Mia, *d* of late Emanuel and Lisa Rosenstein; one *s* one *d.* *Educ:* Bedford Modern Sch.; Quintin Sch.; Inns of Court Sch. of Law. RAF, 1956–58. Director: Aslon Labs; Record Productions (Surrey); Ashcourt. Called to the Bar, Gray's Inn, 1968 (Lee Essay Prize; Holker Sen Exhibn); SE Circuit; Assistant Recorder, 1985; Recorder, 1989. Mem., Mental Health Rev. Tribunal, 1993–2000. Member: Board of Deputies of British Jews, 1982–88; Council, United Synagogue, 1979–93. *Recreations:* music, reading, (formerly) fencing.

SIMMONS, Alick George; Deputy Chief Veterinary Officer, Department for Environment, Food and Rural Affairs, since 2007; *b* Birmingham, 18 May 1956; *s* of Douglas George Simmons and Mary Alexina Simmons; *m* 1985, Elizabeth Ann Crabbe; one *s* one *d.* *Educ:* Paisley Grammar Sch.; Glasgow Univ. (BVMS 1978); Univ. of Edinburgh (MSc Tropical Vet. Medicine 1984; Dip. Applied Animal Behaviour and Animal Welfare 1991). MRCVS 1978. Private practice, 1978–81; Vet. Officer, Govt of Belize, 1981–83; Vet. Officer, MAFF, Aberdeen, 1985–91; Sen. Vet. Officer, MAFF, London, 1991–95; Divl Vet. Manager, MAFF, 1996–2001; Hd, Endemic Diseases and Zoonoses, DEFRA, 2001–04; Vet. Dir, Food Standards Agency, 2004–07. Mem., Somerset Ornithological Soc. *Recreations:* keen amateur naturalist, mostly reformed twitcher, frustrated photographer and deluded outdoorsman. *Address:* Department for Environment, Food and Rural Affairs, Nobel House, 17 Smith Square, SW1P 3JR. *T:* (020) 7238 6385, *Fax:* (020) 7238 5875. *E:* alick.simmons@defra.gsi.gov.uk.

SIMMONS, Sir David (Anthony Cathcart), KA 2001; BCH 2001; QC 1984; Chief Justice of Barbados, 2002–10; Chairman, Integrity Commission of Turks and Caicos Islands, since 2010; *b* 28 April 1940; *s* of late Kenneth G. Simmons and of Sybil Louise Simmons; *m* 1966, Marie MacCormack, QC; one *s* one *d.* *Educ:* London Sch. of Econs and Pol Sci. (LLB Hons 1963; LLM 1965). Called to the Bar, Lincoln's Inn, 1968, Hon. Bencher, 2006; joined law chambers of Henry Forde, QC, Barbados, 1970; private law practice, 1970–85 and 1986–94; Lectr in Law (pt-time), Univ. of WI, 1970–75; Chairman: Nat. Housing Corp., 1976–79; Caribbean Broadcasting Corp., 1979–81; Nat. Sports Council, 1982–85. MP, Barbados, 1976–81, 1985–2001; Mem., Barbados House of Assembly, 1981–85; Attorney General, 1985–86 and 1994–2001. Caribbean Court of Justice: Chairman: Prep. Cttee for establishment, 1999–2001; Regl Judicial Legal Services Cttee, 2003–04; High Level Task Force for inauguration, 2004–05. Mem., Barbados Cricket Assoc. Hon. Fellow, Univ. of WI, 2003. Hon. LLD LSE, 2003. *Recreations:* reading, sports, collecting calypso music, playing trumpet. *Club:* Barbados Turf (Appellate Steward).

SIMMONS, Fr Eric, CR; Prior of St Michael's Priory, Burleigh Street, London, 1993–98; *b* 3 Aug. 1930. *Educ:* Univ. of Leeds (BA Phil 1951). Coll. of the Resurrection, Mirfield, 1951; deacon, 1953, priest, 1954; Curate of St Luke, Chesterton, 1953–57; Chaplain, University Coll. of N Staffordshire, 1957–61; licensed to officiate: Dio. Wakefield, 1963–65 and 1967–; Dio. Ripon, 1965–67; Warden and Prior of Hostel of the Resurrection, Leeds, 1966–67; subseq. Novice Guardian, CR, looking after young Community members; Superior, Community of the Resurrection, Mirfield, Yorks, 1974–87; permission to officiate, Dio. London, 1989–98; the Community is an Anglican monastic foundation engaged in evangelism and teaching work, based in Yorkshire. *Address:* House of the Resurrection, Mirfield, W Yorks WF14 0BN.

SIMMONS, Guy Lintorn, LVO 1961; HM Diplomatic Service, retired; *b* 27 Feb. 1925; *s* of late Captain Geoffrey Larpent Simmons, RN and Frances Gladys Simmons (*née* Wright); *m* 1951, Sheila Jacob; three *d.* *Educ:* Bradfield Coll.; Oriel Coll., Oxford. RAF, 1943–46; CRO, 1949; 2nd Sec., British High Commn: Lahore, 1950; Dacca, 1952; CRO, 1954–58 and 1964–66; 1st Sec.: Bombay, 1958; New Delhi, 1961; Commercial Counsellor: New Delhi, 1966–68; Cairo, 1968–71; Head of Trade Policy Dept, FCO, 1971–73; Diplomatic Service Inspectorate, 1973–76; Commercial Counsellor, Copenhagen, 1976–79; Consul-General: Karachi, 1979–82; Montreal, 1982–84; FCO, 1984–90. Chm., Crouch End Open Space, 1992–94. *Recreation:* the arts. *Address:* 29 Wood Vale, N10 3DJ.

SIMMONS, Prof. Ian Gordon, PhD, DLitt; FSA; FBA 1997; Professor of Geography, University of Durham, 1981–2001, now Emeritus; *b* 22 Jan. 1937; *s* of Charles Frederick Simmons and Christina Mary Simmons (*née* Merrills); *m* 1962, Carol Mary Saunders; one *s* one *d.* *Educ:* UCL (BSc 1959; PhD 1962); Durham Univ. (DLitt 1990). CGeog 2002. Lectr, 1962–70, Sen. Lectr, 1970–76, Reader, 1976–77, in Geography, Univ. of Durham; Prof. of Geography, Univ. of Bristol, 1977–81. ACLS Postdoctoral Fellow, Univ. of Calif at Berkeley, 1964–65; Churchill Meml Travelling Fellow, 1970–71. Chm., Benchmarking Panel for Geography, QAA, 1999–2001; Mem. Geog. Panel, RAE, 1996–2001. FSA 1980; MAE 1994. Hon. DSc Aberdeen, 2005. Victoria Medal, RGS, 1998. Writer on medieval and early modern landscape history of E Lincs at www.durham.ac.uk/east-lincs-history. *Publications:* Ecology of Natural Resources, 1974 (trans. Polish 1979, Spanish 1982); Biogeography, 1979 (trans. Spanish 1982); Changing the Face of the Earth, 1989, 2nd edn 1996; Earth, Air and Water, 1993 (trans. German 1983); Interpreting Nature, 1993; Environmental History, 1993 (trans. Swedish 1994); The Environmental Impact of Later Mesolithic Cultures, 1996; Humanity and Environment: a cultural ecology, 1997 (trans. Portuguese 2001, Japanese 2003); An Environmental History of Great Britain, 2001; An Environmental History of the Moorlands of England and Wales, 2003; A Global Environmental History, 2008 (trans. Croatian 2010); (with K. J. Gregory) Environmental Sciences: a student's companion, 2009; 44 chapters in edited collections and about 115 papers in learned jls. *Recreations:* music, poetry, channel zapping. *Address:* Department of Geography, Lower Mountjoy, South Road, Durham DH1 3LE. *T:* (0191) 386 1570. *E:* i.g.simmons@durham.ac.uk.

SIMMONS, John Barry Eves, OBE 1987; VMH 1986; Curator: Castle Howard Arboretum Trust, 1997–2006; Royal Botanic Gardens, Kew, 1972–95; *b* 30 May 1937; *s* of Alfred John and Gladys Enid Simmons; *m* 1958, Valerie Lilian Dugan; two *s* one *d.* *Educ:* Harrow County Grammar Sch.; Herts Coll. of Agric. and Hort.; Regent Street Polytechnic; Sch. of Horticulture, Kew. MHort 1962, FIHort 1984; FIBiol 1988–2004; FLS 2004. Royal Botanic Gardens, Kew: Supervisor, Tropical Propagation Unit, 1961–64; Asst Curator, Temperate Section, 1964–68; Deputy Curator, 1968–72. Chm., Nat. Council for Conservation of Plants and Gardens, 1994–97 (Mem. Council, 1985–97; Vice-Chm., 1991–94; Pres., Norfolk Gp, 1993–2002); Member: RHS Award and Judging Cttees, 1969–2007; Longwood Gardens (Pennsylvania) Visiting Cttee, 1984–91; Westonbirt Arboretum Consultative Cttee, 1986–2004; Chm., Bedgebury Pinetum Consultative Cttee, 1992–2003; Dir, Flora for Fauna,

1997–2000; Trustee, Stanley Smith (UK) Horticultural Trust, 1994–. Pres., Inst. of Horticulture, 1987–88. Chm., N Norfolk Voluntary Gp, Diabetes UK, 2011–. Gov., Writtle Agricl Coll., 1990–93. *Publications:* The Life of Plants, 1974, 2nd edn 1990; (series editor) Kew Gardening Guides, 1987–; (gen. editor) Kew Gardens Book of Indoor Plants, 1988; (jtly) The Gardens of William Morris, 1998; (jtly) English Plants for your Garden, 2000; Managing the Wet Garden, 2008; ed and contrib. to learned jls. *Recreations:* photography, walking, gardening (own garden!).

SIMMONS, Air Marshal Sir Michael (George), KCB 1989 (CB 1988); AFC 1976; Member, Air Force Board, Defence Council, 1989–92; *b* 8 May 1937; *s* of George and Thelma Simmons; *m* 1964, Jean Aliwell; two *d. Educ:* Shrewsbury Sch.; RAF Coll., Cranwell. Commissioned 1958; No 6 Squadron, Cyprus, 1959–61; ADC to AOC-in-C FTC, 1961–64; No 39 Sqdn, Malta, 1964–66; No 13 Sqdn, Malta, 1966–67; No 51 Sqdn, Wyton, 1967–69; RN Staff Coll., 1970; MoD, 1971–72; OC No XV Sqdn, Germany, 1973–76; MoD, 1976–79; OC RAF Cottesmore, 1980–82; MoD, 1982–84; SASO, HQ Strike Comd, 1984–85; AOC No 1 Gp, RAF, 1985–87; ACAS, 1987–89; Dep. Controller Aircraft, MoD, 1989–92. ADC to the Queen, 1980–81. Mem. Council, RAF Benevolent Fund, 1994–2006. Chm. Bd of Govs, Duke of Kent Sch., 1994–96. *Recreations:* clock repairing, gardening, golf. *Club:* Royal Air Force.

SIMMONS, Richard John, CBE 1995; FCA; Chairman: BPP University of Professional Studies, since 2010; Inclusive Learning, since 2010; Skill Boosters, since 2010; Senior Partner, Andersen (formerly Arthur Andersen), 1996–2001, Senior Adviser, 2002; *b* 2 June 1947; *s* of John Eric Simmons and Joy Mary Simmons (*née* Foat); *m* 1983, Veronica Sinkins; one *s* one *d. Educ:* Moseley GS, Birmingham; London School of Economics (BSc Econs); Haas Business Sch., Univ. of California, Berkeley. FCA 1971. Joined Arthur Andersen, subseq. Andersen, 1968; Partner, 1979–2001. Asst Sec., Internat. Accounting Standards Cttee, 1973–75. Non-executive Director: Cranfield Information Technology Inst., 1987–89; Westminster Forum Ltd, 1999–2013; Chairman: Atticmedia Ltd, 2007–10; Shimmer Productions Ltd, 2008–10; Rewind Creative Media Ltd, 2008–10; CET Primary Schools Ltd, 2011–14; Risk Mosaic; Dir, GreenAcre Films Ltd, 2010–14. Chairman: Bow Gp, 1980–81; CBlu Adv. Council, 2000–02; Member: Shadow Nat. Accounts Commn, 2000–01; Bd of Treasurers, Cons. Party, 2002–03. Mem., Develt Bd, Royal Acad. of Arts, 1995–2002. Dir, Constable Trust, 2003–14; Trustee, Foundn for Social and Econ. Thinking, 2003– (Chm., Governing Council, 2005–14). Gov., Moat Sch., 2003–14. FRSA 2004. *Recreations:* horse racing, tennis, gardening. *Clubs:* Carlton (Hon. Treas., 1995–2001, Hon. Mem., 2006–, Political Cttee), United and Cecil.

SIMMONS, Richard Thomas, PhD; FRGS; Chief Executive, Commission for Architecture and the Built Environment, 2004–11; *b* 17 Feb. 1953; *s* of Laurence and Audrey Simmons; *m* 1976, Elizabeth Mary; two *s* two *d. Educ:* Univ. of Sheffield (BA Hons 1974); South Bank Polytech. (BTP (Postgrad.) 1982); Univ. of Leicester (PhD 1995). MRTPI 1984; FRGS 2010. Town Planner, London Bor. of Hackney, 1978–85; Sen. Planning Officer, Inner Cities Directorate, DoE, 1985–87; Develt Manager, LDDC, 1987–93; Chief Exec., Dalston City Challenge, 1993–97; Dir of Develt and Envmt, Medway Council, 1997–2004. Vis. Prof. of City Design and Regeneration, Univ. of Greenwich, 2011–14; Vis. Lectr, Bartlett Sch. of Planning, UCL, 2015–. Mem., SE Design Review Panel, Design South East, 2015–. Mem., Acad. of Urbanism, 2006. FRSA. Hon. FRIBA 2011. DUniv Oxford Brookes, 2010. *Recreations:* climbing, scouting, DJing, reading science fiction and detective novels.

SIMMONS, Prof. Robert Malcolm, FRS 1995; Professor of Biophysics, King's College London, 1983–2001, now Emeritus; *b* 23 Jan. 1938; *s* of Stanley Laurence Simmons and Marjorie Amys; *m* 1967, Mary Ann (Anna) Ross; one *s* one *d. Educ:* King's College London (BSc Physics 1960; FKC 1996); Royal Institution (PhD London 1965); University College London (MSc Physiol. 1967). CBiol, FRSB (FIBiol 2000). Department of Physiology, University College London: Sharpey Scholar, 1967–70; Lectr, 1970–79; MRC Res. Fellow, 1979–81; King's College London: MRC Cell Biophysics Unit, 1981–83; Associate Dir, 1983–91; Head of Dept of Biophysics, 1983–88; Head of Div. of Biomolecular Scis, 1988–91; Hon. Dir, MRC Muscle and Cell Motility Unit, 1991–2001; Dir, Randall Centre (formerly Randall Inst.), 1995–2001. *Publications:* contribs on physiol. and biophys to learned jls. *Recreations:* music, fishing. *Address:* 1 Woodborough Road, Pewsey, Wilts SN9 5NH.

SIMMONS, Rosemary Ann; freelance artist, writer and curator, since 1975; *b* 19 Oct. 1932; *d* of Donald and Alys Simmons; *m* 1974, Anthony H. Christie (*d* 1994); two step *s* three step *d. Educ:* Chelsea Sch. of Art (NDD and Chelsea Dip. 1955). Graphic Designer, Curwen Press, 1955–58; Dir, Curwen Gall., 1965–71; Man. Dir, Curwen Prints Ltd, 1971–75. Chm., Combe Down Heritage Soc., 2004–14. President: Bath Artist Printmakers, 2006–; Combe Down Stone Legacy Trust, 2015–. Founder Ed., 1990–98, Consultant Ed., 1998–, Printmaking Today. Hon. RE 1990. *Publications:* Printmaking in Easy Steps, 1977; Collecting Original Prints, 1980; (with Katie Clemson) The Complete Manual of Relief Printmaking, 1988; A Dictionary of Printmaking Terms, 2002; Collecting Original Prints, 2005; Mr & Mrs Ralph Allen at home, 2015. *Recreations:* supporting Printmaking Today, art and science, gardens, the company of friends. *Address:* 12 Greendown Place, Combe Down, Bath BA2 5DD. *T:* (01225) 833301. *E:* rosyprint@care4free.net.

SIMMONS, Sir Stanley (Clifford), Kt 1993; FRCS, FRCOG; Consultant Obstetrician and Gynaecologist, Windsor, 1965–92; *b* 28 July 1927; *s* of Lewis Alfred and Ann Simmons; *m* 1956, Ann Wine; one *s* three *d. Educ:* Hurstpierpoint Coll.; St Mary's Hosp., London Univ. (MB BS 1951). FRCS 1957, FRCOG 1971. National Service, Royal West African Frontier Force, 1953–55. Resident MO, Queen Charlotte's Hosp. and Chelsea Hosp. for Women, 1955–56; Registrar, St Mary's Hosp. Paddington, 1957–59; Sen. Registrar, St Thomas' Hosp., 1960–64. Member: GMC, 1975–84; Council, RCOG, 1971–72, 1973–78, 1982– (Vice-Pres., 1986; Sen. Vice-Pres., 1987; Pres., 1990–93); Council, RCS (co-opted), 1984–86; President: Hosp. Consultants and Specialists Assoc., 1972; Windsor Med. Soc., 1983; Section of Obst. and Gyn., RSocMed, 1985. Hon. FRCSE 1994; Hon. FRACOG 1992; Hon. FACOG 1993; Hon. Fellow, Inst. of Gynaecologists, RCPI, 1993. *Publications:* (jtly) General Surgery in Gynaecological Practice, 1974; contribs to med. jls. *Recreations:* flying, sailing, golf, ski-ing, painting. *Address:* 23 Chapel Square, Virginia Park, Virginia Water, Surrey GU25 4SZ. *T:* (01344) 844029. *Clubs:* Royal Society of Medicine, Royal Ocean Racing; Wentworth.

SIMMONS, Timothy Michael John, CVO 2008; Assistant Director, Human Resources Strategy, Talent and Performance Management, Foreign and Commonwealth Office, 2009–10; *b* 8 April 1960; *m* 1989, Caroline Mary Radcliffe; two *s. Educ:* Univ. of East Anglia (BA Jt Hons 1981). Entered FCO, 1982; Nuclear Energy Dept, FCO, 1982–85; Third, later Second Sec., Warsaw, 1985–87; First Secretary: FCO, 1987–93; UK Mission to UN, Geneva, 1993–97; Price Waterhouse, subseq. PricewaterhouseCoopers, 1997–99 (on secondment); Asst Dir, Personnel Comd, FCO, 1999–2001; Dep. Hd of Mission, Warsaw, 2001–04; Ambassador to Slovenia, 2005–09. *Recreations:* reading, music, miniature wargames.

SIMMONS, Tom Christopher; Town Clerk, Corporation of London, 1998–2003; *b* 29 Oct. 1942; *s* of Tom Francis Simmons and Mary Simmons; *m* 1971, Barbara Loxley (*d* 2009); one *s. Educ:* Nottingham Univ. (BA Law 1963). Admitted Solicitor, 1968. Borough Sec., Chelmsford BC, 1973–83; Dep. Town Clerk, 1983–95, City Sec., 1996–98, Corp. of London. Sec., Mus. of London, 1990–2003; Clerk: Nat. Crime Squad Authy, 1998–2003; Nat. Criminal Intelligence Service Authy, 1998–2003. Board Member: and Hon. Treas., Mosaic Housing Assoc. (formerly New Islington and Hackney Housing Assoc.), 2003–06; Family Mosaic Housing Assoc., 2006–08. *Recreations:* water colour painting, gardening, walking. *Address:* 20 Great Oaks, Hutton, Brentwood, Essex CM13 1AZ.

SIMMS, Andrew Mark; author; campaigner; Fellow, New Economics Foundation, since 2011; Co-Founder, New Weather Institute, 2013; *b* Chelmsford, 23 April 1965; *s* of David Simms and June Simms; *m* 1995, Rachel Maybank; one *d. Educ:* Poly. of Central London (BA Hons Film and Photography); London Sch. of Econs (MSc Develt (Internat. Pol Econ.)). Campaigns officer, British Trust for Conservation Volunteers, 1987–88; freelance envmt writer and Green Party Nat. Youth Spokesperson, 1988–90; Co-ordinator, The Other Economic Summit, New Econs Foundn, 1991; Campaign and Press Officer, Oxfam, 1992–93; freelance researcher for Internat. Inst. for Envmt and Develt, Shadow Minister for Overseas Develt and World Develt Movement, 1993–95; Campaign Communications Manager, Christian Aid, 1995–99; New Economics Foundation: Hd, Global Econ. Prog., 1999–2001; Policy Dir, 2002–11; Hd, Climate Change Prog., 2002–10. Advr on develt alternatives, Global Witness, 2015– (Hd of Envmtl Investigations, 2013). Trustee: Energy and Resource Inst., Europe, 2003–; Greenpeace UK, 2004–12; 10:10 UK, 2010–12; 10:10 Internat., 2010–12; Transition Network, 2014–. Associate Ed., Resurgence mag., 2002–. *Publications:* Ecological Debt: global warming and the wealth of nations, 2005, 2nd edn 2009; Tescopoly: how one shop came out on top and why it matters, 2007; (with Joe Smith) Do Good Lives have to Cost the Earth?, 2008; (with David Boyle) The New Economics: a bigger picture, 2009; (with David Boyle) Eminent Corporations, 2010; Cancel the Apocalypse, 2013. *Recreations:* coffee and conversation, trees (appreciating them), bicycles, film, photography, writing and drawing, paradigm shifting, running. *Address:* c/o New Economics Foundation, 10 Salamanca Place, SE1 7HB. *T:* (020) 7820 6300, *Fax:* (020) 7820 6301. *E:* andrewsimms.uk@gmail.com.

SIMMS, Sir Neville (Ian), Kt 1998; FREng, FICE, FCIOB; Chairman, Thames Tideway Tunnel Ltd, since 2013; *b* 11 Sept. 1944; *s* of late Arthur Neville Simms and Anne Davidson Simms (*née* McCulloch). *Educ:* Queen Elizabeth's GS, Crediton; Univ. of Newcastle upon Tyne (BSc 1st cl. Hons 1966); Univ. of Glasgow (MEng 1971). CEng 1970; FICE 1995; FCIOB 1995; FREng (FEng 1996). Structural Engr, Ove Arup and Partners, 1966–69; joined Tarmac plc as Sect. Engr, Roads Div., Tarmac Civil Engrg, 1970; Chief Exec., Tarmac Construction Ltd, 1988–92; Gp Chief Exec., 1992–99, Dep. Chm., 1994–99, Tarmac plc; Chief Exec., 1999–2000, Chm., 1999–2005, Carillion plc. Dir, Bank of England, 1995–2002; non-executive Director: Courtaulds, 1994–98; Private Finance Panel Ltd, 1994–99; National Power, 1998–2000; Operating Partner, Duke St Capital, 2006–08; Chm., 2000–11, Dep. Chm., 2011–15, Internat. Power plc, later GDF SUEZ Energy Internat.; Chairman: Equiniti Gp Ltd, 2009–11; OasisIP LLC (Abu Dhabi), 2009–14. Chairman: BITC (W Midlands), 1998–2001; BITC Solent Regl Leadership Team, 2006–07; Govt Sustainable Procurement Task Force, 2005–06; Member: Pres.'s Cttee, CBI, 1997–2010, 2012–; New Deal Task Force, 1999–2001; Trade Partners UK-Business Adv. Panel, 2001–03. Trustee, BRE Trust (formerly Foundn for Built Envmt), 2002– (Chm., 2006–15). Gov., Ashridge Mgt Coll., 2000–11 (Dep. Chm., 2006–11). MInstD 1995; CCMI (CIMgt 1992); FRSA 1992. Hon. DTech Wolverhampton Univ., 1997; Dr *hc* Edinburgh, 2000; Dr Eng Glasgow, 2001. *Address:* Thames Tideway Tunnel Ltd, The Point, 37 North Wharf Road, W2 1AF.

SIMON, family name of **Viscount Simon,** and of **Barons Simon of Highbury** and **Simon of Wythenshawe**.

SIMON, 3rd Viscount *cr* 1940; **Jan David Simon;** a Deputy Speaker, House of Lords, since 1999; *b* 20 July 1940; *o s* of 2nd Viscount Simon, CMG; *S* father, 1993; *m* 1969, Mary Elizabeth, *d* of late John J. Burns, Sydney, NSW; one *d. Educ:* Westminster; Sch. of Navigation, Univ. of Southampton; Sydney Tech. Coll. Dep. Chm. of Cttees, H of L, 1998–; Member, Select Committee: on Procedure of H of L, 1999–2002; on Personal Bills, 2004–; on Standing Orders (Private Bills), 2004–; elected Mem., H of L, 1999. Fellow, Univ. of Hertfordshire, 2013. Younger Brother, Trinity House, 2007. *Heir:* none. *Address:* House of Lords, SW1A 0PW.

SIMON OF HIGHBURY, Baron *cr* 1997 (Life Peer), of Canonbury in the London Borough of Islington; **David Alec Gwyn Simon,** Kt 1995; CBE 1991; *b* 24 July 1939; *s* of late Roger Albert Damas Jules Simon and Barbara (*née* Hudd); *m* 1st, 1964, Hanne (*née* Mohn) (marr. diss. 1987); two *s*; 2nd, 1992, Sarah (*née* Roderick Smith). *Educ:* Christ's Hospital; Gonville and Caius College, Cambridge (MA Hons; Hon. Fellow 2001); MBA INSEAD. Joined BP 1961; a Man. Dir, 1985–97, CEO, 1992–95 and Chm., 1995–97, BP. A Dir, Bank of England, 1995–97. Minister of State, HM Treasury and DTI, 1997–99; Advr, Cabinet Office, 1999–2003. Mem., Prodi Gp advising on Enlargement Implications, EU, 1999. Sen. Advr (formerly Dir), Morgan Stanley Internat., 2000–; Director: Unilever, 2000–09 (Dep. Chm., 2006–09); Suez Group, 2001–; Sen. Advr, MWM, 2010–. Member: International Council and UK Adv. Bd, INSEAD, 1985–2008; Internat. Adv. Bd, Dana Gas, 2006–; Chm., Adv. Bd, Montrose Associates, 2009–; Vice Chm., European Round Table, 1993–97. Mem., Cambridge Univ. Council, 2005–10 (Dep. Chm., 2007–10). Gov., Inst. for Govt, 2009–. Cadman Medal, Inst. of Petroleum, 1997. Grand Officer, Order of Leopold (Belgium), 2005 (Comdr, 2001). *Recreations:* golf, books, music. *Address:* 1 St James's Square, SW1Y 4PD. *Clubs:* Athenæum, Brooks's.

SIMON OF WYTHENSHAWE, 3rd Baron *cr* 1947, of Didsbury, City of Manchester; **Matthew Simon;** artisan; Principal Lecturer, Sheffield Hallam University, 1998–2011; *b* 10 April 1955; *o s* of 2nd Baron Simon of Wythenshawe and of (Anthea) Daphne (*née* May); *S* father, 2002, but does not use the title; *m* 1987, Sally Mitchell (*d* 2014); two *d. Educ:* St Paul's Sch.; Balliol Coll., Oxford (BA 1978); Manchester Poly. (PhD 1983). CEng; MIMechE 1991. Sen. Lectr, Dept Mech. Engrg, Manchester Metropolitan Univ. (formerly Manchester Poly.), 1983–98; Lectr, Univ. of Zimbabwe, Harare, 1988–90. *Heir: cousin* Michael Ben Simon, *b* 3 March 1970.

SIMON, (Dominic) Crispin (Adam), CBE 2015; Chief Executive Officer, Rex Bionics plc, since 2014; *b* London, 25 March 1958; *s* of Baron Simon of Glaisdale, PC and of Fay Elizabeth Leicester (*née* Pearson); *m* 1983, Georgina Brown; one *s* one *d* (and one *s* decd). *Educ:* Westminster Sch.; Lincoln Coll., Oxford (BA PPE 1979; MA). NM Rothschild and Sons, 1979–85; McKinsey & Co., 1985–87; Division Dir, Bowater plc, 1987–95; Division Pres., Smith & Nephew plc, 1995–98; Chief Exec., Biocompatibles International plc, 1998–2011; Man. Dir, Trade Gp, UK Trade and Investment, 2012–14. Non-exec. Dir, NHS Trust Develt Authy, 2013–; Mem., Governance Bd, UK Healthcare. *Recreations:* Bath Rugby, theatre, Jack Russell terriers. *Address:* Rex Bionics plc, Thame Park, Thame Park Road, Thame, Oxon OX9 3PU. *E:* crispin.simon@rexbionics.com. *Club:* Reform.

See also Rt Hon. Sir P. C. H. Simon.

SIMON, Jacob Michael Henry, FSA; Editor, Walpole Society, 1981–89 and since 2013; Research Fellow, National Portrait Gallery, since 2011 (Chief Curator, 2001–11); *b* 29 Sept. 1946; *s* of John Eric Henry Simon and Josephine (*née* Sammone); partner, Jenny Bescoby; two *s. Educ:* Christ's Coll., Cambridge (BA 1969; MA 1972). FMA 1988; FSA 1992. Trainee Asst, Temple Newsam House, Leeds, 1971–73; Asst Curator, Iveagh Bequest, Kenwood, 1973–83; Curator, 18th century portraits, NPG, 1983–2001. Mem. Council and Cttee, NT, 1969–2000; Trustee, Grimsthorpe and Drummond Castle Trust, 1989–2005. *Publications:* (ed) Handel: a celebration of his life and times 1685–1759, 1985; The Art of the Picture Frame:

artists, patrons and the framing of portraits in Britain, 1996; Thomas Johnson's The Life of the Author, 2003. *Recreations:* walking, book collecting. *Address:* National Portrait Gallery, WC2H 0HE. *T:* (020) 7306 0055, *Fax:* (020) 7306 0056. *E:* jsimon@npg.org.uk.

SIMON, Prof. Leon Melvyn, PhD; FRS 2003; FAA; Robert Grimmett Professor of Mathematics, Stanford University, now Emeritus Professor; *b* 6 July 1945. *Educ:* Univ. of Adelaide (BSc 1967; PhD 1971). FAA 1983. Lectr in Math., Flinders Univ., 1972–73; Asst Prof., Stanford Univ., 1973–76; Vis. Prof., Univ. of Adelaide, 1976–77; Associate Prof., Univ. of Minnesota, 1977–78; Professor of Mathematics: Univ. of Melbourne, 1978–81; ANU, 1981. *Address:* Department of Mathematics, Stanford University, 450 Serra Mall, Building 380, Stanford, CA 94305–2125, USA.

SIMON, Neil; playwright; *b* NYC, 4 July 1927; *s* of Irving and Mamie Simon; *m* 1st, 1953, Joan Baim (*d* 1973); 2nd, 1973, Marsha Mason; 3rd, 1987, Diane Lander; 4th, Elaine Joyce. *Educ:* De Witt Clinton High Sch.; entered Army Air Force Reserve training programme as an engineering student at New York University; discharged with rank of corporal, 1946. Went to New York Offices of Warner Brothers Pictures to work in mail room. Hon. LHD Hofstra Univ., 1981; Dr *hc* Williams Coll., 1984. *Screenplays include:* After The Fox (produced 1966); Barefoot in the Park, 1967; The Odd Couple, 1968; The Out-of-Towners, 1970; Plaza Suite, 1971; The Last of the Red Hot Lovers, 1972; The Heartbreak Kid, 1973; The Prisoner of 2nd Avenue, 1975; The Sunshine Boys, 1975; Murder by Death, 1976; The Goodbye Girl, 1977 (and TV film, 2004); The Cheap Detective, 1978; California Suite, 1978; Chapter Two, 1979; Seems Like Old Times, 1980; Only When I Laugh, 1981; I Ought To Be In Pictures, 1982; Max Dugan Returns, 1983; adapt. Lonely Guy, 1984; The Slugger's Wife, 1984; Brighton Beach Memoirs, 1986; Biloxi Blues, 1988; The Marrying Man, 1991; Broadway Bound (TV film), 1992; Lost in Yonkers, 1993; Jake's Women (TV film), 1996; London Suite (TV film), 1996; The Odd Couple II, 1998; Laughter on the 23rd Floor (TV film), 2001; other films based on his stage plays: Come Blow Your Horn, 1963; Sweet Charity, 1969; The Star-Spangled Girl, 1971. *Plays produced:* Come Blow Your Horn, 1961 (publ. 1961); (jtly) Little Me, 1962 (publ. 1979), rev. version 1982, West End 1984; Barefoot in the Park, 1963 (publ. 1964); The Odd Couple, 1965 (publ. 1966), West End 1996, NY revival 2005; (jtly) Sweet Charity, 1966 (publ. 1966), NY revivals 1986 and 2005, West End revival, 2010; The Star-Spangled Girl, 1966 (publ. 1967); Plaza Suite, 1968 (publ. 1969); (jtly) Promises, Promises, 1968 (publ. 1970), NY revival, 2010; Last of the Red Hot Lovers, 1969 (publ. 1970), Criterion, 1979; The Gingerbread Lady, 1970 (publ. 1971); The Prisoner of Second Avenue, 1971 (publ. 1972), West End revival, 2010; The Sunshine Boys, 1972 (publ. 1973), West End revival, 2012; The Good Doctor, 1973 (publ. 1974); God's Favorite, 1974 (publ. 1975); California Suite, 1976 (publ. 1977); Chapter Two, 1977 (publ. 1979), West End 1996; (jtly) They're Playing Our Song, 1979 (publ. 1980); I Ought To Be In Pictures, 1980 (publ. 1981); Fools, 1981 (publ. 1982); Brighton Beach Memoirs, 1983 (publ. 1984), NT, 1986, West End, 1987; Biloxi Blues, 1985 (Tony Award for Best Play, 1985) (publ. 1986); The Odd Couple (female version), 1985 (publ. 1992); Broadway Bound, 1986 (publ. 1988); Rumors, 1988 (publ. 1990), Chichester, 1990; Lost in Yonkers, 1991 (Pulitzer Prize, Tony Award for Best Play, 1991) (publ. 1992), West End, 1992; Jake's Women, 1992 (publ. 1994); (jtly) The Goodbye Girl, 1993; Laughter on the 23rd Floor, 1993 (publ. 1995), West End 1996; London Suite, 1995; Proposals, 1997; The Dinner Party, 2000; Hotel Suite, 2000; 45 Seconds from Broadway, 2001; Oscar and Felix, LA, 2002 (publ. 2004); Rose's Dilemma, 2004 (publ. 2004, also publ. as Rose and Walsh, 2013). *Publications:* Rewrites: a memoir, 1996; The Play Goes On, 1999. *Address:* c/o Gary DaSilva, 111 N Sepulveda Boulevard #250, Manhattan Beach, CA 90266, USA. *T:* (310) 3185665, *Fax:* (310) 3182114. *E:* mail@garydasilva.com.

SIMON, Paul; American singer and songwriter; *b* 13 Oct. 1941; *s* of Louis and Belle Simon; *m* 1st, Peggy Harper (marr. diss.); one *s*; 2nd, 1983, Carrie Fisher (marr. diss.); 3rd, 1992, Edie Brickell; two *s* one *d*. *Educ:* Queens Coll. (BA Eng. Lit.). Mem., Simon and Garfunkel, 1964–71; solo performer, 1971–. *Songs* include: *with Art Garfunkel:* The Sounds of Silence; Homeward Bound; I Am a Rock; 59th Street Bridge Song (Feelin' Groovy); Scarborough Fair/Canticle; Mrs Robinson; The Boxer; Bridge Over Troubled Water; Cecilia; *solo:* American Tune; Loves Me Like a Rock; Still Crazy After All These Years; 50 Ways to Leave Your Lover; Slip Slidin' Away; Something So Right; Hearts and Bones; Graceland; You Can Call Me Al; Diamonds on the Soles of her Shoes; Under African Skies; The Rhythm of the Saints; albums include: (with Derek Walcott) Songs from The Capeman, 1997; You're the One, 2000; So Beautiful or So What, 2011; *films:* performer (with Art Garfunkel) and composer of soundtrack, The Graduate, 1967; actor, Annie Hall, 1977; writer of screenplay and score, One-Trick Pony, 1980; musical, The Capeman (lyrics with Derek Walcott), 1998. Numerous Grammy Awards. *Publications:* At the Zoo, 1991.

SIMON, Rt Hon. Sir Peregrine (Charles Hugo), Kt 2002; PC 2015; FLS; **Rt Hon. Lord Justice Simon;** a Lord Justice of Appeal, since 2015; *b* 20 June 1950; *s* of Baron Simon of Glaisdale, PC and of Fay Elizabeth Leicester (*née* Pearson); *m* 1980, Francesca Fortescue Hitchins; two *s* two *d*. *Educ:* Westminster School; Trinity Hall, Cambridge (MA). Called to the Bar, Middle Temple, 1973, Bencher, 1999; QC 1991; a Recorder, 1998–2002; a Dep. High Court Judge, 1999–2002; a Judge of the High Court, QBD, 2002–15; Presiding Judge, North Eastern Circuit, 2006–08. Mem. Council, Zool Soc., 1992–96 (Vice-Pres., 1995–96). *Address:* Royal Courts of Justice, Strand, WC2A 2LL.

SIMON, Robin John Hughes, FSA; art historian; Founder and Editor, The British Art Journal, since 1999; *b* 23 July 1947; *s* of Most Rev. (William) Glyn (Hughes) Simon, sometime Archbishop of Wales, and Sarah Sheila Ellen (*née* Roberts); *m* 1st, 1971, Jette Margaret Brooke (*see* J. M. Guillebaud) (marr. diss.); one *s* one *d*; 2nd, 1979, Joanna Christine Ross; one *d*. *Educ:* Cardiff High Sch.; Univ. of Exeter (BA Hons English; DLitt 2008); Courtauld Inst. of Art (MA Hist. European Art). FSA 1998. Lectr in Hist. of Art and English, Univ. of Nottingham, 1972–78; Historic Bldgs Rep., NT, 1979–80; Dir, Inst. European Studies, London, 1980–90; Editor, Apollo, 1990–97; Hd of Publications, NACF, and Ed., Art Qly, Annual Review, 1997–98. Vis. Lectr in Hist. of Art, Univ. of Warwick, 1978; Vis. Prof. in Hist. of Art and Architecture, Westminster Coll., Fulton, Mo, 1989; Vis. Prof. in English, 2007–13, Hon. Prof. of English, 2013–, UCL. Arts Corresp., 1987–90, Art Critic, 1990–, Daily Mail; columnist, Tatler, 1994–98. Delmas Foundn Fellow, Venice, 1978. Co-Curator, Richard Wilson and the Transformation of European Landscape Painting exhibn, Yale Center for British Art, Nat. Mus. of Wales, Cardiff, 2014. Paul Mellon Lectr in British Art, Nat. Gall., London and Yale Center for British Art, New Haven, 2013. Member: Council, 1991–96, Exec. and Editl Cttee, 1993–96, 2005–10, Walpole Soc.; Adv. Council, Paul Mellon Centre for Studies in British Art, 1993–98; Exec. Cttee, Assoc. of Art Historians, 1993–96; Cttee, Courtauld Assoc. (formerly Courtauld Assoc. of Former Students), 1992– (Chm., 1998–2010); Johnson Club, 1995–; Member, Advisory Committee: Battle of Britain Meml, 2001–02; Thomas Jones (1742–1803) Exhibn, 2001–03; Mem. Centenary Cttee, Nat. Mus. of Wales, 2006–07; Trustee, Foundling Mus., 2008–09. Editor-in-Chief, The Royal Academy: its history and collections, 2009–. Writer of commissioned entertainments including: Hogarth versus Handel, perf. Middle Temple, 2000; Music and Monarchs, perf. Villa Decius, Cracow, 2002; From Pencerrig to Pozzuoli, perf. Swansea Arts Fest., 2003. Patron, Lord Leighton Centenary Trust, 1994–96. *Publications:* (with Alastair Smart) The Art of Cricket, 1983; The Portrait in Britain and America, 1987; Hogarth, France and British Art, 2007; *edited:* Buckingham Palace: a complete guide, 1993; The King's Apartments, Hampton Court Palace, 1994; (with Gervase Jackson-Stops) The National Trust 1895–1995: 100 great treasures, 1995; Lord Leighton 1830–1896 and Leighton House, 1996; (with Christopher Woodward) A Rake's Progress: from Hogarth to Hockney, 1997; (with Rhian Harris) Enlightened Self-interest: the Foundling Hospital and Hogarth, 1997; Oxford: art and architecture, 1997; Somerset House: the building and collections, 2001; Public Artist, Private Passions: the world of Edward Linley Sambourne, 2001; (with Natasha McEnroe) The Tyranny of Treatment: Samuel Johnson, his friends, and Georgian medicine, 2003; Hogarth's Children, 2007; contrib. Oxford DNB; articles in British Art Jl, Apollo, Burlington Mag., TLS, Papers of Brit. Sch. at Rome, Spectator, Tatler, Opera Now, Country Life, Sunday Times, Mail on Sunday, etc. *Recreations:* cricket (Captain, Poor Fred's XI), music. *Address:* The British Art Journal, 46 Grove Lane, SE5 8ST. *T:* (020) 7787 6944. *Clubs:* Garrick, MCC.

SIMON, Siôn Llewelyn; Member (Lab) West Midlands Region, European Parliament, since 2014; *b* 23 Dec. 1968; *s* of Jeffrey Simon and Anne Loverini Simon (*née* Jones; now Owen); *m* 1992, Elizabeth Jane Middleton (marr. diss. 2003); one *s* two *d*. *Educ:* Handsworth Grammar Sch., Birmingham; Magdalen Coll., Oxford (BA PPE 1990). Res. Asst to George Robertson, MP, 1990–93; Sen. Manager, Guinness plc, 1993–95; freelance writer, 1995–97; columnist: Daily Telegraph, 1997–2001; News of the World, 2000–01; Associate Ed., The Spectator, 1997–2002. MP (Lab) Birmingham, Erdington, 2001–10. Parly Under-Sec. of State, DIUS, 2008–09, DCMS, 2009–10. *Address:* European Parliament, Rue Wiertz, 1047 Brussels, Belgium.

SIMON, Susannah Kate; HM Diplomatic Service; Director, European Reform, Department for Business, Innovation and Skills, since 2013; *b* 7 June 1964; *d* of Peter and Sheila Simon; *m* 1994, Mikhail Kubekov; one *s*. *Educ:* Lady Eleanor Holles Sch., Hampton; St Hilda's Coll., Oxford (BA Hons Modern Langs). Entered FCO, 1988; Third, later Second Sec., Bonn, 1989–92; Second Sec., Almaty, 1992–93; FCO, 1994–99; First Sec. (EU), Berlin, 1999–2003; Dir, Eur. Policy, Immigration and Nationality Directorate, Home Office (on secondment), 2003–06; Hd, Climate Change and Energy Gp, FCO, 2006–09; Dir, Jt Internat. Unit for Educn, Employment and Social Affairs, DWP, BIS and DfE (on secondment), 2010–11; Dir, Migration Directorate, FCO, 2011–13. *Recreation:* gardening. *Address:* c/o Foreign and Commonwealth Office, King Charles Street, SW1A 2AH. *E:* susannah.simon@fco.gov.uk.

SIMON, Tobias Robert Mark, (Toby); JP; Secretary to London Probation Board, 2002–05; *b* 31 May 1948; *s* of A. P. W., (Tim), Simon and B. M. Simon; *m* 2001, Mrs Margaret Anne McAlpine; two step *s* one step *d*. *Educ:* Bryanston Sch., Dorset; Trinity Hall, Cambridge (MA); BA Open Univ. 1976. Department of Health and Social Security, 1969–87; Sen. Lectr, Civil Service Coll., 1984–87; Sec., Chartered Soc. of Physiotherapy, 1987–96. Gen. Manager, Assoc. of Anaesthetists of GB and Ireland, Jan.–Aug. 2000; Interim Chief Exec., 2001–02, Gov., 2004–10, Inst. of Optimum Nutrition. Chm. Scrutiny Commn, London Fire and Civil Defence Authy, 1999–2000; Mem., London Fire and Emergency Planning Authy, 2000–02; Member: Regl Legal Services Cttee for London, 2000–04; Professional Conduct Panel (formerly Investigating Cttee), Inst. of Legal Executives, 2002–11. A Gen. Comr of Income Tax, 2001–09; Mem., First-tier Tribunal (Tax), 2009–. Mem. (Lab) Enfield LBC, 1998–2002 and 2006– (Chairman: Social Inclusion Scrutiny Panel, 2000–02; Overview and Scrutiny Cttee, 2010–14; Pension Cttee, 2010–; Planning Cttee, 2014–). Governor: Enfield County Sch., 1996–2004; Edmonton County Sch., 1999–2009; Gladys Aylward Sch., 2006–10; Chm. Govs, Brettenham Prim. Sch., 2010–. JP North London and Family Courts, 1998. *Address:* 39 Raleigh Road, Enfield EN2 6UD. *T:* (020) 8363 3684. *E:* cllr.Toby.Simon@enfield.gov.uk.

SIMONDS, Gavin Napier; Chairman, Snell Group, 2009–14; *b* 1 Jan. 1955; *s* of Duncan and Monica Simonds; *m* 1980, Venetia Steele; one *s* three *d*. *Educ:* Eton Coll. FCA 1980. Trainee, Peat Marwick Mitchell, 1975–81; Corporate Finance Exec., Rowe & Pitman, 1982–85; Corporate Finance Dir, UBS, 1985–88; Dir, Kleinwort Benson Ltd, 1988–93; Jt Man. Dir, Intercontinental Hotels Gp, 1993–96; Founding Dir, ResidenSea, 1997–2000; Consultant/Dir, various cos, 2000–04; Chairman: Peacock Gp plc, 2004–06; Jessops plc, 2004–07; Club Co., 2004–06; Red Funnel Gp, 2004–07; Craegmoor Healthcare, 2006–08; Classic Hospitals, 2006–08; Apollo Gp, 2006–09; Ez Revenue Mgt Systems, 2011–12; non-executive Director: Sunseeker Internat. Hldgs, 2010; A-Gas Internat., 2011–15. *Recreations:* family, sailing, tennis. *Club:* Seaview Yacht.

SIMONDS-GOODING, Anthony James Joseph, CBE 2010; company director; *b* 10 Sept. 1937; *s* of Major and Mrs Hamilton Simonds-Gooding; *m* 1st, 1961, Fiona (*née* Menzies) (marr. diss. 1982); three *s* two *d* (and one *s* decd); 2nd, 1982, Marjorie Anne, *d* of late William and Wendy Pennock; one step *s*. *Educ:* Ampleforth Coll.; BRNC, Dartmouth. Served RN, 1953–59; Unilever, 1960–73; Marketing Dir, subseq. Man. Dir (UK), finally Gp Man. Dir, Whitbread & Co. plc, 1973–85; Saatchi plc, 1985–87 (Chm. and Chief Exec. of all communication and advertising cos worldwide); Chief Exec., British Satellite Broadcasting, 1987–90. Chairman: Aqueduct Enterprises, 1992–94; Ammirati Puris Lintas, 1994–96; Clark & Taylor (Dir, 1996–99); OMG plc, 2001–; Pimco Properties, 2002–; Director: Robinson and Sons, Chesterfield, 1993–99; Lilliput Group, 1993–94; Community Hosps Gp plc, 1995–2001; Newell & Sorrell, 1996–99; Kunick plc, 1997–2004; Blick plc, 1997–2002; CLK.MPL, 1999–2006; Corporate Edge, 1999–2006. Chairman: D&AD, 1992–2010; Design Business Assoc., 2003–08; Rose Theatre, Kingston, 2008–15. Director: ICA, 1992–94; Macmillan Cancer Relief (formerly Cancer Relief Macmillan Fund), 1992–2001; Brixton Prison Bd, 1994–97. Trustee: Rainbow Trust, 2001–04; Sea Cadets Assoc., 2001–03; Chm., Haven Breast Cancer Trust, 2013–. *Recreations:* family, opera, sport, travel, oil painting. *Clubs:* Garrick, Chelsea Arts, Hurlingham.

SIMONS, Joanna Lesley, CBE 2011; Chief Executive, Oxfordshire County Council, and Clerk to the Lieutenancy, since 2005; *b* 16 Aug. 1959; *d* of late Frank Simons and Philippa Simons; *m* 1987, Richard John Robinson, *qv* (marr. diss. 2010). *Educ:* Lady Margaret Sch., Fulham; Open Univ. Business Sch. (MBA 2002). FCIH 1987. Estates Officer, Hammersmith and Fulham LBC, 1980–83; Neighbourhood Manager, Newcastle CC, 1983–87; Dist Housing Officer, Barnet LBC, 1987–89; Asst Dir of Housing, Hounslow LBC, 1989–95; Dir of Housing, Greenwich LBC, 1995–2001; Chief Exec., Sutton LBC, 2001–05. Non-executive Director: South London Business, 2003–05; Government Office for the South East, 2009–11. Chair, ACCE, 2013–15. Board Member: London Wildlife Trust, 1981–83, 1988–93; Notting Hill Housing Trust, 1996–2005; Trustee: Leadership Centre for Local Govt, 2010–13; Shelter, 2012–. Mem. Ct, Oxford Brookes Univ., 2007– (Chm. of Govs, 2008–12; Pro-Chancellor, 2011–12). FRSA 2006. DUniv Oxford Brookes, 2014. *Recreations:* travel, cooking, entertaining, walking. *Address:* Oxfordshire County Council, County Hall, New Road, Oxford OX1 1ND. *T:* (01865) 815330. *E:* joanna.simons@oxfordshire.gov.uk.

SIMONS, Prof. John Philip, PhD, ScD; FRS 1989; CChem, FRSC; Dr Lee's Professor of Chemistry, Oxford University, 1993–99, now Emeritus; Fellow of Exeter College, Oxford, 1993–99, now Emeritus; *b* 20 April 1934; *s* of Mark Isaac Simons and Rose (*née* Pepper); *m* 1st, 1956, Althea Mary (*née* Screaton) (*d* 1989); three *s*; 2nd, 1992, Elizabeth Ann Corps. *Educ:* Haberdashers' Aske's Hampstead Sch.; Sidney Sussex Coll., Cambridge (BA; PhD 1958; ScD 1975). CChem, FRSC 1975. Chemistry Department, University of Birmingham: ICI Fellow, 1959; Lectr, 1961; Reader in Photochemistry, 1977; Prof. of Photochem., 1979; Prof. of Physical Chemistry, Univ. of Nottingham, 1981–93. JSPS Fellow, Univ. of Kyoto, 1992; Erskine Fellow, Univ. of Canterbury, NZ, 1996; Dist. Vis. Prof., Texas A&M Univ., 1995; Visiting Professor: Univ. of Pittsburgh, 1998; Univ. Paul Sabatier, Toulouse, 1998; Vis. Miller Prof., Univ. of Calif, Berkeley, 2000. Lectures: Tilden, RSC, 1983; Tri-Jt, Univ. of Southern Calif, UCLA, CIT, 1988; Pimentel, UC Berkeley, 1998; Spiers, RSC, 1999; Burton, KCL, 2001; Humphry Davy, Royal Soc., 2001; Liversidge, RSC, 2007. Vice Pres., and Hon. Sec., 1981–93, Pres., 1993–95, Faraday Div., RSC. Member: Chemistry Cttee, 1983–85, Laser Facility Cttee, 1983–87, SERC; Comité de Direction, CNRS Lab. de Photophysique

Moléculaire, Orsay, 1985–90, 2004–05; specially promoted scientific programme panel, NATO, 1985–88; Council, Royal Soc., 1999–2000; Scientific Adv. Cttee, FOM Inst., The Netherlands, 2004–06. Adv. Councillor, Ramsay Meml Fellowship Trust, 1991–2006. Ed., PhysChemComm, 1998–2002. Member Editorial Boards: Molecular Physics, 1980–96; Chemical Physics Letters, 1982–99; Jl Chem. Soc. Faraday Trans, 1990–98; Chemical Physics, 1994–2006; Phys Chem Chem Phys, 1998–2013. Leverhulme Emeritus Fellow, 2009–10. Hon. DSc Birmingham, 2002. Chemical Dynamics Award, 1994, Polanyi Medal, 1996, RSC; Davy Medal, Royal Soc., 2007. Citoyen d'Honneur de la Ville de Toulouse, 1997. *Publications:* Photochemistry and Spectroscopy, 1970; research papers in learned jls of molecular/chemical/biophysics. *Recreations:* (writing), reading, walking, talking. *Address:* Physical and Theoretical Chemistry Laboratory, South Parks Road, Oxford OX1 3QZ. *T:* (01865) 275400.

SIMONS, Jonathan Michael; Master of Senior (formerly Supreme) Court Costs Office (Taxing Master), since 2001; *b* 15 June 1947; *s* of Eric Louis Simons and Eta Simons; *m* 1972, Judith Priscilla Cohen; one *s* one *d. Educ:* Priestmead Primary Sch., Harrow; Hasmonean Grammar Sch., Hendon. Admitted solicitor, 1971; Partner: Hart Fortgang, Solicitors, 1973–92; Simons Platman-Rechnic, Solicitors, 1993–98; Dep. Taxing Master, Supreme Court, 1996–2001. *Recreations:* history, travel, golf, supporting Brentford Football Club. *Address:* Senior Court Costs Office, Royal Courts of Justice, Thomas More Building, Strand, WC2A 2LL. *T:* (020) 7947 6459. *E:* Master.Simons@judiciary.gsi.gov.uk. *Club:* MCC.

SIMONS, Prof. Peter Murray, PhD; FBA 2004; Professor of Philosophy, Trinity College Dublin, since 2009; *b* 23 March 1950; *s* of Jack Simons and Marjorie Nita Simons (*née* Brown); *m* 1973, Susan Jane Walker; one *s* one *d. Educ:* Univ. of Manchester (BSc (Maths) 1971; MA 1973, PhD 1975 (Philos.)); Univ. of Salzburg (Habilitation Philos. 1986); Trinity Coll. Dublin (MA 2009). Asst Librarian, Univ. of Manchester, 1975–77; Lectr in Philos., Bolton Inst., 1977–80; Lectr, 1980–95, Hon. Prof., 1996–, in Philos., Univ. of Salzburg; Prof. of Philosophy, Univ. of Leeds, 1995–2009. British Acad. Reader, 2004–06. Consultant, Ontek Corp., 1989–2001. MAE 2006; MRIA 2013. FTCD 2010. Hon. PhD Bolton, 2012. *Publications:* Parts, 1987; Philosophy and Logic in Central Europe from Bolzano to Tarski, 1992; about 240 articles in learned jls. *Recreations:* walking, choral singing, reading history, classical music. *Address:* Department of Philosophy, Trinity College Dublin, Dublin 2, Ireland. *T:* (1) 8961671, *Fax:* (1) 6715760. *E:* psimons@tcd.ie.

SIMONS, Richard Brian; Lecturer in Broadcasting and Journalism, University of West Scotland, since 2013; Managing Director, Norbury Media Ltd, 2008–14; *b* 5 Nov. 1952; *s* of Harry Simons and Ann Lily Simons (*née* Gold); one *s* one *d*; *m* 2001, Lisa, *d* of late Ronald Hazlehurst and of Kathleen Hazlehurst; one *s* one *d. Educ:* Royal Grammar Sch., High Wycombe; Exeter Coll., Oxford (BA Hons PPE). Independent Television News Ltd: Trainee TV Journalist, 1974–75; Writer, News at Ten, and Reporter, News at One, 1976–78; Prog. Editor and News Editor, News At One, 1979; Special Progs Producer, Foreign News Editor and Home News Editor, 1980–84; Head of Investigative Unit, and Associate Producer, D-Day: 40 Years On, 1984; Associate Prod., VE Day: 40 Years On, 1985; Sports Editor, and Mem., ITV Sport Network Cttee, 1985; Editor, World Cup Mexico, 1986; News Editor, 'Vote '87', General Election Results Special, 1986; Special Productions Editor, 1988–90; Commissioning Editor, Factual Progs, 1992–94, Head of Features, 1995–96, Carlton TV; Dir of Progs, Meridian Broadcasting, 1994–2000; Develt Dir, New Media Productions, United Broadcasting & Entertainment, 2000; Dir of TV, CSS-Stellar plc, 2001; Hd of Develt, GMTV, 2002–04; Man. Dir, Banana Split Prodns, 2006–08. Dir, 2entertain Ltd, 2006–08. *Recreations:* my children, piano, papers and TV for pleasure, tennis. *E:* Richardsimons@norburymedia.co.uk.

SIMOR, Jessica Margaret Poppaea; QC 2013; *b* London, 1968; *d* of Peter Simor and Anne Simor; *m* 2000, Philippe Haag; one *s* one *d. Educ:* St Paul's Girls' Sch.; Bryanston Sch.; St Catherine's Coll., Oxford (MA 1986); City Univ., London (CPE 1992); King's Coll. London (Dip. EU Law 1993). Called to the Bar, Middle Temple, 1992; in practice as barrister, Monckton Chambers, 1992–2000; Founder Mem., Matrix Chambers, 2000–. Lawyer, Eur. Commn of Human Rights, 1995–96; Legal Advr, Human Rights Ombudsman, Bosnia, 1996–97. *Publications:* Human Rights Practice, 2000 (Gen. Editor, 2000–). *Recreations:* reading, music, dance, theatre. *Address:* 2 The Old Orchard, NW3 2TR; Matrix Chambers, Griffin Building, Gray's Inn, WC1R 5LN. *E:* jessicasimor@matrixlaw.co.uk.

SIMPKINS, Christopher John; Director General, Royal British Legion, since 2007; *b* Hornchurch, 28 Jan. 1952; *s* of Walter and Constance Simpkins; *m* 1974, Denise Dickens; one *s* one *d. Educ:* John Taylor High Sch.; Dovecliff Grammar Sch.; Birmingham Poly.; Stafford Coll. of Further Educn; Local Govt Trng Bd (Dip. Municipal Admin). Dep. Town Clerk, Tamworth BC, 1984–88; Chief Executive: South Holland DC, 1988–2003; Falkland Is Govt, 2003–07. Executive Vice Chairman: Falkland Is Develt Corp., 2003–07; Falkland Hldgs, 2003–07; Director: S Lincs Enterprise Agency and Venture Capital Ltd, 1993–99; Lincs Trng and Enterprise Council, 1996–98; Lincs and Rutland Connexions, 2001–03; Stanley Services, 2003–07; Member: Trent Reg. NHS Modernisation Bd, 2000–02 (Chm., Inequalities Task Force, 2000–02); Nat. Rural Affairs Forum, 2002–03. Chm., Corp., Stamford Coll. of Further Educn, 2000–03. Trustee: Officers' Assoc., 2007–12; Nat. Meml Arboretum, 2007–11 and 2014–; Poppy Scotland, 2011–. FInstD 2014. DL Lincs, 2011–15. DUniv Loughborough, 2011. *Recreations:* good company, good food, good wine, motoring, gardening, cycling, commuting. *Address:* Royal British Legion, 199 Borough High Street, SE1 1AA. *Club:* Royal Over-Seas League.

SIMPKINS, Peter B.; *see* Bowen-Simpkins.

SIMPKISS, (Richard) Jonathan; His Honour Judge Simpkiss; a Circuit Judge, since 2004; a Deputy High Court Judge and Designated Civil Judge for Kent, Surrey and Sussex, since 2005; a Senior Circuit Judge, since 2010; *b* 21 Oct. 1951; *s* of Dr Michael Simpkiss and late Eileen Simpkiss; *m* 1985, Elizabeth Anne Weaver; two *d. Educ:* Magdalene Coll., Cambridge (BA 1974). Called to the Bar, Middle Temple, 1975, Bencher of Lincoln's Inn, 2003; a Recorder, 2000–04. *Recreations:* salmon fishing, shooting, gardening, wine. *Club:* Flyfishers'.

SIMPSON, family name of **Baron Simpson of Dunkeld**.

SIMPSON OF DUNKELD, Baron *cr* 1997 (Life Peer), of Dunkeld in Perth and Kinross; **George Simpson,** FCCA; FIMI; FCIT; Chief Executive, Marconi (formerly General Electric Co.) plc, 1996–2001; *b* 2 July 1942; *s* of William Simpson and Elizabeth Simpson; *m* 1964, Eva Chalmers; one *s* one *d. Educ:* Morgan Acad., Dundee; Dundee Inst. of Technology. ACIS. Sen. Accountant, Gas Industry, Scotland, 1962–69; Central Audit Man., BLMC, 1969–73; Financial Controller, Leyland Truck and Bus Div., 1973–76; Dir of Accounting, Leyland Cars, 1976–78; Finance and Systems Dir, Leyland Trucks, 1978–80; Managing Director: Coventry Climax Ltd, 1980–83; Freight Rover Ltd, 1983–86; Chief Exec. Officer, Leyland DAF, 1986–88; Man. Dir, 1989–91, Chm., 1991–94, and Chief Exec., 1991–92, Rover Gp; Dep. Chief Exec., BAe, 1992–94 (Dir, 1990–94); Chairman: Ballast Nedam Construction Ltd, 1992–94; Arlington Securities, 1993–94; Chief Exec., Lucas Industries plc, 1994–96. Mem., H of L, 1997–2015. Non-executive Director: Pilkington plc, 1992–99; ICI plc, 1995–2001; Nestlé SA, 1999–2004; Alstom SA, 1998–2005; Triumph Gp Inc., 2000; HBOS, 2001–02; Member, Supervisory Board: Northern Venture Capital, 1992; Pro Share, 1992–94. Member: Exec. Cttee, SMMT, 1986 (Vice Pres., 1986–95, Pres., 1995–96, Council); Senate, Engrg Council, 1996–2002. Industrial Prof., Warwick Univ., 1991. *Recreations:* golf, squash and Rugby (now spectating). *Clubs:* Royal Automobile; Royal Birkdale Golf, New Zealand Golf (Weybridge), Gleneagles Golf, Rosemount Golf (Blairgowrie), Pine Valley Golf (NJ); Kenilworth RFC.

SIMPSON, His Honour Alan; a Circuit Judge, 1985–2000; *b* 17 April 1937; *s* of William Henry Simpson and Gladys Simpson; *m* 1965, Maureen O'Shea; one *s* one *d. Educ:* Leeds Grammar Sch.; Corpus Christi Coll., Oxford (MA). Called to the Bar, Inner Temple, 1962; a Recorder, 1975–85. Prosecuting Counsel to DHSS, North Eastern Circuit, 1977–85. Admin. Steward, 1994–, Vice-Chm., 2000–04, Chm., 2004, BBB of C. *Recreations:* music, books, sport. *Address:* Leeds Combined Court Centre, Oxford Row, Leeds LS1 3BG.

SIMPSON, Alan Francis, OBE 2000; author and scriptwriter since 1951 (in collaboration with Ray Galton, *qv*); *b* 27 Nov. 1929; *s* of Francis and Lilian Simpson; *m* 1958, Kathleen Phillips (*d* 1978). *Educ:* Mitcham Grammar Sch. *Television:* Hancock's Half Hour, 1954–61 (adaptation and trans., Fleksnes, Scandinavian TV, film and stage); Comedy Playhouse, 1962–63; Steptoe and Son, 1962–74 (US TV version, Sanford and Son; Dutch TV, Stiefbeen And Zoon; Scandinavian TV, Albert Och Herbert; Portuguese TV, Camilo & Filho); Galton-Simpson Comedy, 1969; Clochemerle, 1971; Casanova '74, 1974; Dawson's Weekly, 1975; The Galton and Simpson Playhouse, 1976–77; Paul Merton in Galton & Simpson's..., 1996, 1997; Fleksnes Fataliteter (specially written last episode of Hancock), Scandinavian TV, 2002; *films:* The Rebel, 1960; The Bargee, 1963; The Wrong Arm of the Law, 1963; The Spy with a Cold Nose, 1966; Loot, 1969; Steptoe and Son, 1971; Steptoe and Son Ride Again, 1973; Den Siste Fleksnes (Scandinavia), 1974; Skraphandlerne (Scandinavia), 1975; *theatre:* Way Out in Piccadilly, 1966; The Wind in the Sassafras Trees, 1968; Albert och Herbert (Sweden), 1981; Fleksnes (Norway), 1983; Mordet på Skolgatan 15 (Sweden), 1984; Steptoe and Son, UK tour, 2012–13; *radio:* The Galton & Simpson Radio Playhouse, 1998–99; Galton and Simpson's Half Hour, 2009; The Missing Hancocks, 2014. Awards: Scriptwriters of the Year, 1959 (Guild of TV Producers and Directors); Best TV Comedy Series (Steptoe and Son, 1962, 1963, 1964, 1965 (Screenwriters Guild)); John Logie Baird Award (for outstanding contribution to Television), 1964; Best Comedy Series (Stiefbeen And Zoon, Dutch TV), 1966; Best Comedy Screenplay (Steptoe and Son, Screenwriters Guild), 1972; Best TV Series, Portugal Golden Globe (Camilo & Filho), 1995. *Publications:* (jointly with Ray Galton, *qv*): Hancock, 1961; Steptoe and Son, 1963; The Reunion and Other Plays, 1966; Hancock Scripts, 1974; The Best of Hancock, 1986; Masters of Sitcom: from Hancock to Steptoe, 2011. *Recreations:* Hampton & Richmond Borough FC (Pres.), gourmet travelling, guest speaking. *Address:* c/o Tessa Le Bars Management, 54 Birchwood Road, Petts Wood, Kent BR5 1NZ. *T:* (01689) 837084. *W:* www.galtonandsimpson.com.

SIMPSON, Alan John; independent writer, thinker and campaigner on energy and climate policies; Advisor, Friends of the Earth, since 2010; *b* 20 Sept. 1948; *s* of Reginald James and Marjorie Simpson; *m* (marr. diss.); one *d* two *s*; *m* 2005, Pascale Quiviger; one *d. Educ:* Bootle Grammar Sch.; Nottingham Poly. (BSc Econ). Asst Gen. Sec., Nottingham Council of Voluntary Service, 1970–72; Develt Officer, Home Office Pilot Programme (Non Custodial Treatment of Offenders), 1972–74; Community Worker, Nottingham Areas Project, 1974–78; Res. and Inf. Officer, Nottingham Racial Equality Council, 1979–92. Cllr, Notts CC, 1985–93. MP (Lab) Nottingham S, 1992–2010. Govt Special Advr on renewable energy to DECC, 2009–10. Member: CND; Action Aid. *Publications:* (contrib.) Issues in Community Education, 1980; Stacking the Decks: race, inequality and council housing, 1981; I'll Never Forget What's His Name: one year on from the Scarman Report, 1982; (contrib.) The Right to a Home, 1984; Cuckoos in the Nest—Task Forces and urban policy, 1988; (with M. Read, MEP) Against a Rising Tide—racism, Europe and 1992, 1991; Beyond the Famished Road—defence and common security, 1994; (contrib.) Football and Commons People, 1994; (contrib.) What the Three Main Parties Are Not Telling You, 2015. *Recreations:* tennis, football (lifelong supporter, Everton FC), vegetarian cooking, eclectic interest in music and reading.

SIMPSON, Very Rev. Alison Jane; Rector, St Columba's Episcopal Church, Nairn, since 2009; Dean of Moray, Ross and Caithness, since 2014; *b* Dumfries, 15 Sept. 1960; *d* of George Fazakerley and Daisy Clark; *m* 1992, Stephen William Simpson. *Educ:* Dumfries Acad.; St Andrews Univ. (BSc Marine Biol. 1983; BD 1986); Princeton Theol Seminary (MTh 1987). Associate Minister, Ellon, Aberdeenshire, 1988–90; Minister, Maud with Savoch Parish, Aberdeenshire, 1990–97; sabbatical study, 1997–99; ordained deacon and priest, 1999; Curate, St Mary-on-the-Rock, Ellon, 1999–2002; Rector, Holy Trinity, Keith, 2002–09. Synod Clerk, Dio. of Moray, Ross and Caithness, 2012–13. *Recreations:* hill-walking, climbing, canoeing, travel, theatre, playing bagpipes. *Address:* St Columba's Rectory, 3 Queen Street, Nairn IV12 4AA. *T:* (01667) 452458. *E:* revalison433@btinternet.com. *Club:* Scottish Midweek Mountaineering (Pres., 2010–12).

SIMPSON, Anthony Maurice Herbert, TD 1973; Manager, DAPHNE Programme, Justice and Home Affairs Task Force, later Directorate General, Justice and Home Affairs, European Commission, 1996–2000; *b* 28 Oct. 1935; *y s* of late Lt-Col Maurice Rowton Simpson, OBE, TD, DL and Mrs Renée Claire Simpson; *m* 1961, Penelope Gillian, *d* of late Howard Dixon Spackman; one *s* two *d. Educ:* Rugby; Magdalene College, Cambridge. BA 1959, LLM (LLB 1961), MA 1963. Leics and Derbys (PAO) Yeomanry, 1956–59; 21st and 23rd SAS Regts (TA), 1959–74, Major 1968. Called to Bar, Inner Temple, 1961; practised Midland and Oxford Circuit, 1961–75; Mem., Legal Service of European Commn, Brussels, 1975–79; MEP (C) Northamptonshire, later Northamptonshire and S Leics, 1979–94; contested (C) Northamptonshire and Blaby, Eur. Parly elecns, 1994; Quaestor of the European Parlt, 1979–87, and 1989–94; EDG spokesman on develt and co-operation, 1987–89; Mem., Inspectorate-Gen. of Services, Eur. Commn, 1994–96. Contested (C) West Leicester, Feb. and Oct. 1974. Treas., Eur. Foundn for Street Children Worldwide, 2003–11; Chm., UK Sect., AIACE, 2005–09. Mem., Bd of Govs, De Montfort Univ., 2004–08. Common Market Law Editor, Current Law, 1965–72. *Recreations:* walking, travelling. *Address:* 17 Alderney Street, SW1V 4ES. *T:* (020) 7233 9344. *Club:* Travellers.

SIMPSON, Brian, OBE 2015; Member (Lab) North West England, European Parliament, 2006–14; *b* Leigh, Lancs, 6 Feb. 1953; *s* of late John Hartley Simpson and Freda Simpson; *m* 1975, Linda Jane Gwynn; one *s* two *d. Educ:* Golborne Comprehensive Sch., Wigan; W Midlands Coll. of Educn, Walsall (Cert Ed). Teacher, City of Liverpool, 1974–89. Member: Merseyside CC, 1981–85; Warrington BC, 1987–91. MEP (Lab) Cheshire E, 1989–99, NW Reg., England, 1999–2004. Chm., Transport and Tourism Cttee, EP, 2010–14. Campaign Dir, NW Rail Campaign, 1994–96; Chm., Heritage Railway Assoc., 2014– (Vice Pres., 2000–14); Vice Pres., Warrington RSPCA, 1996–; Pres., Warrington Rugby League Referees Soc., 1997–. *Recreations:* Rugby League, cricket, military history, heritage and modern railways. *Clubs:* Golborne Sports and Social (Wigan), Golborne Cricket (Pres., 1992–).

SIMPSON, Air Vice-Marshal Charles Ednam; Director (Scotland), Royal Air Force Benevolent Fund, 1989–94; *b* 24 Sept. 1929; *s* of Charles and Margaret Simpson; *m* 1955, Margaret Riddell; two *s* one *d. Educ:* Stirling and Falkirk High Schools; Univ. of Glasgow (MB ChB); University of London (MSc). FFOM 1986; MFCM. British Defence Staff, Washington DC, 1975; Dep. Dir, Aviation Medicine, RAF, 1978; CO, RAF Hosp., Wegberg, 1981; CO, Princess Alexandra Hosp., Wroughton, 1982; Dir of Health and Research, RAF, 1984; Asst Surgeon General (Envmtl Medicine and Res.), 1985; PMO HQ

RAF Strike Comd, 1986–89; QHS 1985–89. HM Comr, Queen Victoria Sch., Dunblane, 1990–2000 (Chm. Bd, 1997–2000). *Recreation:* birdwatching. *Address:* 12 Balmyle Grove, Dunblane, Perthshire FK15 0QB. *T:* (01786) 822191. *Club:* Royal Air Force.

SIMPSON, Claire Margaret; *see* Ward, C. M.

SIMPSON, David; District Judge (Magistrates' Courts) (formerly Metropolitan Stipendiary Magistrate), 1993–2012; *b* 29 July 1947; *s* of Albert Edward Simpson and Lily Simpson; *m* 1975, Jane Richards; one *s*. *Educ:* N Cestrian GS, Altrincham; Worthing High Sch. for Boys; King's Coll., London (LLM 1987). Admitted a solicitor, 1974. British Bank of ME, 1966–67; Court Clerk, Magistrates' Court: Worthing, 1967–74; Mansfield, 1975–76; Dep. Clerk, 1976–82, Clerk, 1982–93, to the Justices, Uxbridge. Part-time Immigration Special Adjudicator, 1996–2000. Vice-Pres., Assoc. of Magisterial Officers, 1981–82; Member: Council, Justices' Clerks' Soc., 1987–93; Magisterial Cttee, Judicial Studies Bd, 1990–93, 2003–12; Inner London Magistrates' Courts' Cttee, 1998–2001; Youth Justice Bd, 2003–13; Local Safeguarding Children's Bd, Royal Borough of Windsor and Maidenhead, 2013–; Safeguarding Cttee, C of E Dio. in Europe, 2013–. Member: Adv. Panel on Children's Viewing, BBFC, 1999–2010; Windsor Learning Partnership, 2015–; Lay Mem., Sec. of State for Transport's Medical Adv. Bd, 2012–. Gov., Windsor Boys' Sch., 2002–15.

SIMPSON, David; MP (DemU) Upper Bann, since 2005; *b* 16 Feb. 1959; *m* Elaine Elizabeth; one adopted *s* two adopted *d*. *Educ:* Killicomaine High Sch.; Coll. of Business Studies, Belfast. Businessman. Mem. (DemU), Craigavon BC, 2001–10; Mayor of Craigavon, 2004–05. Mem. (DemU) Upper Bann, NI Assembly, 2003–10. *Address:* (office) 13 Thomas Street, Portadown, Craigavon, Co. Armagh BT62 3NP; House of Commons, SW1A 0AA.

SIMPSON, David Rae Fisher; Economic Adviser, Standard Life Assurance Co., 1988–2001; Deputy Chairman, Water Industry Commission for Scotland, 2005–12; *b* 29 Nov. 1936; *s* of late David Ebenezer Simpson and Roberta Muriel Wilson; *m* 1st, 1980, Barbara Dianne Goalen (marr. diss. 2008), *d* of late N. and Mrs G. Inglis, Edinburgh; one *s* (and one step *s* one step *d*); 2nd, 2009, Judith Mary Riley, widow of Prof. E. C. Riley. *Educ:* Skerry's Coll.; Edinburgh and Harvard Univs. MA 1st cl. hons Econs Edinburgh; PhD Econs Harvard. Instr in Econs, Harvard Univ., 1963–64; Assoc. Statistician, UN HQ, NY, 1964–65; Res. Officer, Econ. Res. Inst., Dublin, 1965–67; Lectr in Pol Economy, UCL, 1967–69; Sen. Lectr in Econs, Univ. of Stirling, 1969–74; University of Strathclyde: Prof. and Dir, Fraser of Allander Inst., 1975–80, Res. Prof., 1980–85; Prof., Dept of Economics, 1985–88. Contested (SNP) Berwick and E Lothian Division, 1970 and Feb. 1974. *Publications:* Problems of Input-Output Tables and Analysis, 1966; General Equilibrium Analysis, 1975; The Political Economy of Growth, 1983; The Challenge of New Technology, 1987; The End of Macro Economics?, 1994; Regulating Pensions, 1996; Re-Thinking Economic Behaviour, 2000; The Rediscovery of Classical Economics, 2013; articles in Econometrica, Financial Times, Scientific American, Spectator. *Recreation:* tilting at windmills. *Address:* The Old Kitchen, Tyninghame House, East Lothian EH42 1XW.

SIMPSON, David Richard Salisbury, OBE 1989; Founder and Director, International Agency on Tobacco and Health, since 1991; *b* 1 Oct. 1945; *s* of late Richard Salisbury Simpson and Joan Margaret Simpson (*née* Braund). *Educ:* Merchiston Castle School, Edinburgh. ACA 1969; FCA 1979 (but resigned from Institute, 1981). Teacher at Cadet College, Hasan Abdal, West Pakistan, 1963–64 (VSO). Peat, Marwick, Mitchell & Co., Chartered Accountants, 1964–72; Scottish Director, Shelter, Campaign for the Homeless, 1972–74; Director: Amnesty International (British Section), 1974–79; ASH, 1979–90. Sundry journalism, broadcasting and public lectures. Hon. Consultant, Clin. Trial Service Unit and Epidemiol Studies Unit, Oxford Univ., 1991–. Vis. Prof., LSHTM, 2000–. News Ed., Tobacco Control, 1993–2012. Trustee, Pier Arts Centre, Stromness, 1994–2012. *Publications:* Doctors and Tobacco: medicine's big challenge, 2000; (with J. Crofton) Tobacco: a global threat, 2002. *Recreations:* friends, reading, music, hill-walking, Orkney. *Address:* Clinical Trial Service Unit, Richard Doll Building, Old Road Campus, Roosevelt Drive, Headington, Oxford OX3 7LF.

SIMPSON, Lt-Col (Retd) David Sackville Bruce, CBE 1990; Chief Executive, Civil Service Catering Organisation, 1981–91, retired; *b* 18 March 1930; *s* of Henry and Violet Simpson; *m* 1956, Margaret Elizabeth Goslin; two *s* three *d*. *Educ:* Brockley Grammar Sch.; Westminster Technical Coll. FIH. Regular Officer, Army Catering Corps (retd in rank of Lt-Col), 1950–75; Principal Education Catering Organiser, Inner London Education Authority, 1975–81. *Recreations:* golf, squash. *Address:* 1 Tavistock Road, Fleet, Hants GU51 4EH. *T:* (01252) 625795.

SIMPSON, Dennis Charles; business consultant and lecturer; Managing Director, Axtel (UK) Ltd, 1986–88; *b* 24 Oct. 1931; *s* of late Arthur and Helen Simpson; *m* 1st, 1964, Margery Bruce Anderson (marr. diss.); three *s* one *d*; 2nd, 1983, Susan Gaynor Conway-Williams. *Educ:* Manchester Univ. (BA). FInstPS. 2nd Lieut Royal Signals, 1952–54; commercial appts, Philips Electrical Industries, 1956–63; Group Purchasing Manager, STC Ltd, 1963–66; Gp Purchasing Controller, Rank Organisation, 1966–69; Gen. Man., Cam Gears (S Wales) Ltd, 1969–72; Industrial Dir for Wales, Dept of Industry, 1972–75; Industrial Dir for Wales, Welsh Office, 1975–76; Business Agent, Welsh Develt Agency, 1983–85. Chairman: Spencer Harris Ltd, 1976–81; Grainger Hydraulics Ltd, 1976–81; Wellfield Engineering, 1976–81; Director: Beechwood Holdings, 1976–81; Gower Technology Ltd, 1983–87; Video Interactive Systems Ltd, 1983–87; Gower Alarms Ltd, 1985–87; Video Interactive Teaching Aids Ltd, 1985–87. *Recreations:* golf, bridge, reading war histories.

SIMPSON, Derek; Joint General Secretary, Unite, 2007–10 (General Secretary, Amicus, 2004–07, on merger with Transport and General Workers' Union); *b* 23 Dec. 1944; *m* Freda; three *c*. *Educ:* Sheffield Central Tech. Sch.; Open Univ. (BA 1987). Engrg apprentice, Firth Brown Tools, 1960–66; with Balfour Darwin, 1966–81; full-time official, AEU, 1981–2002; elected Gen. Sec., Amicus-AEEU, 2002; Jt Gen. Sec., Amicus, 2002–04. *Address:* Unite, 128 Theobalds Road, Holborn, WC1X 8TN.

SIMPSON, Edward Alexander, CB 1993; Director, Northern Ireland Court Service, 1987–95; *b* 25 Dec. 1935; *s* of late Robert Simpson and Eva (*née* Graham); *m* 1960, Audrey Gordon; two *s*. *Educ:* Regent House Sch., Newtownards; Queen's Univ., Belfast (BSc Econ). Joined Ministry of Finance, 1953; various posts in Mins of Health and Local Govt and DoE, 1956–77; Asst Sec., Transportation and the Fire Service, 1977–81; Belfast Develt Officer, 1981–87. *Recreations:* golf, walking, gardening, wine, school governor. *Address:* 28 Londonderry Avenue, Comber, Newtownards BT23 5ES.

SIMPSON, Edward Hugh, CB 1976; FSS 1946; Deputy Secretary, Department of Education and Science, 1973–82; *b* 10 Dec. 1922; *o s* of Hugh and Mary Simpson, of Brookfield, Ballymena, Co. Antrim; *m* 1947, Rebecca (*d* 2012), *er d* of Sam and Elizabeth Gibson, Ernevale, Kesh, Co. Fermanagh; one *s* one *d*. *Educ:* Coleraine Academical Institution; Queen's Univ., Belfast (BSc (1st cl. Hons Mathematics), 1942); Mathematical Statistics res., Christ's Coll., Cambridge (Scholar), 1945–47. Foreign Office, Bletchley Park, 1942–45; Min. of Education, 1947–50 and 1952–56; HM Treasury, 1950–52; Commonwealth Fund Fellow, USA, 1956–57; Private Sec. to Lord President of Council and Lord Privy Seal, 1957–60; Dep. Dir, Commonwealth Educn Liaison Unit, 1960–62; Sec., Commonwealth Educn Conf., New Delhi, 1962; Asst Sec., DES, 1962–68; Under-Sec., Civil Service Dept, 1968–71, DES, 1971–73. Sen. Hon. Res. Fellow, Birmingham Univ., 1983–88; Vis. Res. Fellow, Univ. of Warwick, 1993–95. Chairman: Nat. Assessment Panel, Schools Curriculum Award, 1983–95; Educn Grants Adv. Service, 1987–93; Gov. and Chm., Professional Cttee, Bishop Grosseteste Coll., Lincoln, 1984–99; Trustee, Educn 2000, 1987–93. Consultant, Educn Management Information Exchange, 1986–89; Chm. Govs, Dixons City Technol. Coll., 1989–99. FRSA 1991. Hon. LLD Hull, 1992. *Publications:* articles in statistical and educn journals, and on history of Bletchley Park. *Address:* Flat 36, Dove Court, Swan Lane, Faringdon, Oxon SN7 7AB. *E:* edw.reb@gmail.com. *Club:* Athenæum.

SIMPSON, Prof. Elizabeth, OBE 2004; FRS 2010; FMedSci; Professor of Immunogenetics, Imperial College London (formerly Royal Postgraduate Medical School, subsequently Imperial College School, then Faculty, of Medicine, London University), 1994–2004, now Emeritus Professor of Transplantation Biology; Head of Transplantation Biology Group, 1984–2004, and Deputy Director, 1994–2004, MRC Clinical Sciences Centre, Hammersmith Hospital (formerly Clinical Research Centre, Harrow); *b* 29 April 1939; *d* of J. H. G. Browne and O. R. Browne (*née* Wood); *m* 1963 (marr. diss. 1973); one *d* with Prof. Peter Charles Leonard Beverley, *qv*. *Educ:* Old Palace Sch. for Girls, Croydon; Girton Coll., Cambridge (BA Nat. Sci. 1960; VetMB 1963; MA 1964). Vet. Surg., private practice, Canada, 1963–65; Res. Virologist, Ottawa, 1965–66; Univ. Demonstrator in Animal Pathology, Cambridge Univ., 1966–69; Research Scientist: NIMR, 1969–71; Clin. Res. Centre, Harrow, 1971–84. Visiting Scientist: All India Inst. Med. Res., Delhi, 1971; Nat. Inst. Health, Bethesda, 1972–73; Jackson Lab., Maine, 1976–. Mem., peer review research funding cttees, MRC, AFRC, CRUK, Wellcome Trust, Royal Soc., ERC, 1983–. FMedSci 1999. Hon. FRCVS 2010. Hon. DSc Imperial Coll. London, 2015. *Publications:* (ed) T Cell Receptors, 1995; A Thousand Natural Shocks, 2011; reviews and scientific papers on transplantation, immunology and genetics in jls. *Recreations:* writing, reading, music, swimming. *Address:* Transplantation Biology Group, Imperial College London, Hammersmith Hospital, Du Cane Road, W12 0NN.

SIMPSON, Frances Clare; *see* Nash, F. C.

SIMPSON, Sir Gilbert, (Sir Gil), KNZM 2000; QSM 1986; Founder and Chief Executive, Jolly Good Software Pty Ltd, since 2006; *b* 5 April 1948; *m* 1998, Joy Reilly. *Educ:* Christchurch Boys' High Sch. Clerk, Nat. Bank of NZ, 1967–71; Sen. Programmer, NZ Aluminium Shelters, 1971–74; Data Processing Manager, Whitcoulls NZ, 1974–78; formed own co., 1978; CEO, Aoraki Corp. Ltd, 1982–2003; Dir, Jade Software Corp., 2003–06. Dir, Reserve Bank of NZ, 1997. Pres., Royal Soc. of NZ, 2000. Fellow: NZ Computer Soc., 1998; NZ Inst. Mgt, 1999; NZ Inst. Dirs, 2000. *Recreations:* tramping, flying, railway enthusiast, following cricket and Rugby.

SIMPSON, Ian Christopher; QC (Scot.) 2005; Sheriff of Lothian and Borders at Edinburgh, 2006; Temporary High Court Judge, 2004–07; *b* 5 July 1949; *s* of David F. Simpson and J. O. S. Simpson (*née* Dickie); *m* 1973, Anne Strang; two *s*. *Educ:* Glenalmond; Edinburgh Univ. (LLB). Admitted Faculty of Advocates, 1974; Floating Sheriff, 1988–91; Sheriff: at Airdrie, 1991–2003; of Tayside, Central and Fife at Dunfermline, 2003–06. *Publications: novels:* Murder on Page One, 2012; Murder on the Second Tee, 2014; Murder in Court Three, 2015. *Recreations:* golf, travel, reading. *Address:* 30 Cluny Drive, Edinburgh EH10 6DP. *T:* (0131) 447 3363. *W:* www.iansimpsonauthor.co.uk. *Clubs:* Royal and Ancient (St Andrews); Luffness Golf.

SIMPSON, James; *see* Simpson, William J.

SIMPSON, Very Rev. James Alexander; an Extra Chaplain to the Queen in Scotland, since 2004 (Chaplain, 1992–2004); Moderator of the General Assembly of the Church of Scotland, 1994–95; *b* 9 March 1934; *s* of Robert and Marion Simpson; *m* 1960, Helen Gray McCorquodale; three *s* two *d*. *Educ:* Glasgow Univ. (BSc Hons 1955; BD 1958); Union Seminary, New York (STM 1959). Minister: Grahamston Church, Falkirk, 1960–66; St John's Renfield Church, Glasgow, 1966–76; Dornoch Cathedral, 1976–97; Interim Minister: Almondbank Tibbermore, Perth, 1997–98; Brechin Cathedral, 1998–99. Hon. DD Aberdeen, 1995. *Publications:* There is a Time To, 1971; Marriage Questions Today, 1975; Doubts Are Not Enough, 1982; Holy Wit, 1986, 4th edn 2002; Laughter Lines, 1988, 2nd edn 1991; The Master Mind, 1989; History of Dornoch Cathedral, 1989; More Holy Wit, 1990; Keywords of Faith, 1992; Royal Dornoch Golf Club (a pictorial history), 1992; All about Christmas, 1994; The Laugh shall be First, 1998; Life, Love and Laughter, 2002, 2nd edn 2003; A Funny Way of Being Serious, 2005; At Our Age, 2010; The Magic of Words, 2013. *Address:* Dornoch, Perth Road, Bankfoot, Perth PH1 4ED. *Club:* Royal Dornoch Golf (Captain, 1993).

SIMPSON, James Walter Thorburn, OBE 2007; RIBA; FRIAS; Partner, Simpson & Brown, Architects, 1977–2010, Consultant, since 2010; *b* 27 July 1944; *s* of Robert Alison Crighton Simpson, TD, FRIBA, and Rosemary Euphemia (*née* Morrison); *m* 1968, Ann Mary Bunney; two *d*. *Educ:* Belhaven Hill Sch.; Trinity Coll., Glenalmond; Edinburgh Coll. of Art (BArch Hons). RIBA 1970; FRIAS 1985. Trained as architect with Ian G. Lindsay and with Sir Bernard Feilden, 1972–77 (work on St Paul's, Norwich and St Giles' Cathedral, Edinburgh); estabd Simpson & Brown, with Stewart Brown, 1977. Building projects in Scotland and NE England, including: St Giles' Cathedral; Alderman Fenwick's House, Newcastle-upon-Tyne; Auchinleck House, Ayrshire; Kinlochmoidart House, Inverness-shire; Rosslyn Castle and Chapel, Midlothian; 26–31 Charlotte Square, Edinburgh. Curator, William Adam Exhibn, Scottish Nat. Portrait Gall., 1989. Surveyor of the Fabric, York Minster, 1994–95. Mem., Ancient Monuments Bd for Scotland, 1984–96. Comr, Royal Commn on Ancient and Historical Monuments of Scotland, 1997–2006. *Publications:* Vitruvius Scoticus, 1980, repr. 2011; The Care of Historic Buildings and Ancient Monuments by Government Departments in Scotland, 1995; The British Standard Guide to the Principles of the Conservation of Historic Buildings, 1998. *Recreations:* playing Scottish small pipes, Norfolk Terriers, thinking about architecture, learning Gaelic, India. *Address:* (office) St Ninian's Manse, Quayside Street, Edinburgh EH6 6EJ. *T:* (0131) 555 4678; 40 Raeburn Place, Edinburgh EH4 1HL. *T:* (0131) 332 7294.

SIMPSON, Jane Ann; *see* Plant, J. A.

SIMPSON, Dr Jennifer Linda, OBE 2000; FRCPE; Founder, European Association of Medical Managers (Acting Chairman, 2010); Associate Director, Revalidation Support Team, Department of Health, 2011; *b* 18 April 1953; *d* of Dr I. M. Simpson and Janette Simpson; *m* 1981, Dr Gavin M. M. Thoms (marr. diss. 2010); one *s* two *d*; *m* 2011, Tim Scott. *Educ:* Univ. of Manchester Med. Sch. (MB ChB, DCH); Sheffield Business Sch. (MBA, DBA). Clinical posts in Manchester and Sheffield, 1976–80; clinical and managerial posts, Sheffield Children's Hosp., 1983–90; Dir, Resource Mgt, Mersey RHA, 1990–94. Clinical Advr, Resource Mgt Team, DoH, 1991–93. Founder and Chief Exec., British Assoc. of Med. Managers, 1991–2010; Pres., Inst. of Healthcare Mgt, 2011–12. Vis. Prof., Centre for Leadership, York Univ.; Vis. Fellow, Cranfield Sch. of Mgt. *Publications:* Clinicians as Managers, 1994; Clinical Governance in the New NHS, 1997; Appraisal in Action, 1998; The Duties of the Medical Director, 2001; Consultant Careers: times of change, 2001; Making Sense: a career framework for medical management, 2003. *Recreations:* music, working with a talented group of musicians running an independent recording label, physical fitness, and sheer enjoyment of my three children. *E:* jenny@jennysimpson.com.

SIMPSON, John Andrew, OBE 2014; lexicographer, writer and researcher; Chief Editor, Oxford English Dictionary, 1993–2013; Fellow, 1991–2013, now Emeritus, and Dean of Degrees, since 2014, Kellogg College (formerly Rewley House), Oxford; *b* 13 Oct. 1953; *s* of Robert Morris Simpson and Joan Margaret (*née* Sersale); *m* 1976, Hilary Croxford; two *d*. *Educ:* Dean Close Sch., Cheltenham; Univ. of York (BA Hons English Literature); Univ. of Reading (MA Medieval Studies). Editorial Asst, Supplement to OED, 1976–79; Editor, Concise Oxford Dictionary of Proverbs, 1979–81; Sen. Editor, Supplement to OED, 1981–84; Editor (New Words), OED, 1984–86; Co-editor, OED, 1986–93. Mem., Faculty of English, Univ. of Oxford, 1993–. Editl Consultant, Australian National Dictionary, 1986–88. Mem. Adv. Cttee, Opera del Vocabolario Italiano, Florence, 2003–05. Vis. Asst Prof., Dept of English, Univ. of Waterloo, Ont, Canada, 1985. Mem., Philolog. Soc., 1994–; Founding Mem. and Mem. Exec. Cttee, European Fedn of Nat. Instns for Lang., 2003–. BBC TV series, Balderdash & Piffle, 2006, 2007. FRSA 2007. Hon. LittD: ANU, 1999; Leicester, 2015. Editor (with Harald Beck), James Joyce Online Notes, 2011–; Project Leader, Pittville History Works. *Publications:* (ed) Concise Oxford Dictionary of Proverbs, 1982, 3rd edn 1998; (contrib.) Oxford English, 1986; (contrib.) Words, 1989; (ed) Oxford English Dictionary, 2nd edn (with Edmund Weiner) 1989, 3rd edn (online) 2000–; (contrib.) Wörterbücher: ein internationales Handbuch zur Lexikographie, 1990; (ed with John Ayto) Oxford Dictionary of Modern Slang, 1992, 2nd edn 2008 as Stone the Crows: Oxford Dictionary of Modern Slang; (ed with Edmund Weiner) OED Additions series, vols 1 and 2, 1993, (Gen. Ed.) vol. 3, 1997; The First English Dictionary 1604, 2007; The First Dictionary of Slang 1699, 2010; Superstitions: omens, charms, cures 1787, 2011; Ware's Victorian Dictionary of Slang and Phrase, 2013; articles in Medium Aevum, English Today, Dublin James Joyce Qly, and other lexicographical and linguistic publications. *Address:* 67 Prestbury Road, Cheltenham, Glos GL52 2BY. *E:* john.simpson@kellogg.ox.ac.uk.

SIMPSON, John Anthony, CVO 2002; RIBA; architect; Principal, John Simpson & Partners, since 1980; *b* 9 Nov. 1954; *s* of late John Simpson and of Lydia Simpson; *m* 1990, Erica; two *s* one *d*. *Educ:* Marlborough Coll.; UCL (BSc Hons; DipArch). RIBA 1981. Main commissions: Paternoster Square Develt, City of London, 1990–96 (AIA Honor Award for Urban Design); W Range of Gonville Court, Gonville and Caius Coll., Cambridge, 1993–98 (RICS Conservation Award); Brownsword Market Bldg, Poundbury, 1996–2000; Queen's Gallery, Buckingham Palace, 1998–2002 (RIBA and Royal Fine Art Commn Trust awards, 2003); St Mary's Ch Hall and Vicarage, Old Church St, Chelsea, 1998–2002 (RBKC Envmt Award); masterplan for 4500 new houses, Swindon Southern Develt Area, 2001–05; Carhart Mansion, 5th Avenue, NY, 2002–05 (Palladio Award, 2007; Stanford White Award, Inst. of Classical Architecture, 2012); redevelt of Rochester Row Police Stn site at 68 Vincent Square, Westminster, 2003–08; redevelt of Royal Worcester Porcelain Wks, Worcester, 2004; Stanhope redevelt, 5th Ave, NY, 2005–07; Pipe Partridge Bldg, Lady Margaret Hall, Oxford, 2005–10 (Classical Bldg of Yr Award, Georgian Gp, 2010); Gisborne Ct, Peterhouse, Cambridge; New Birley Schs, Elliott Schs, Lyttleton Schs, Jafar Debating Chamber, Museum of Antiquities and McCrum Yard, Eton Coll., 2015; representation of Kensington Palace for Queen's Diamond Jubilee; current commissions: Forthergill Bldg and Duffield Graduate Centre, Lady Margaret Hall, Oxford; Sch. of Architecture, Univ. of Notre Dame, USA; Defence and Nat. Rehabilitation Centre, Stanford Hall; two music halls and museum, Royal Coll. of Music. Arthur Ross Award for Excellence in Classical Tradition, Inst. of Classical Architecture, 2008; Philippe Rotthier European Prize for the reconstruction of the City, 2008. *Recreations:* music, opera, swimming, vintage motor cars. *Address:* (office) 29 Great James Street, WC1N 3ES. *T:* (020) 7405 1285, *Fax:* (020) 7831 1781.

SIMPSON, Very Rev. John Arthur, OBE 2001; Dean of Canterbury, 1986–2000, now Emeritus; *b* 7 June 1933; *s* of Arthur Simpson and Mary Esther Simpson; *m* 1968, Ruth Marian (*née* Dibbens); one *s* two *d*. *Educ:* Cathays High School, Cardiff; Keble Coll., Oxford (BA, 2nd cl. Mod. History 1956, MA 1960); Clifton Theological Coll. Deacon 1958, priest 1959; Curate: Leyton, 1958–59; Christ Church, Orpington, 1959–62; Tutor, Oak Hill Theol Coll., 1962–72; Vicar of Ridge, Herts, 1972–79; Director of Ordinands and Post-Ordination Training, Diocese of St Albans, 1975–81; Hon. Canon of St Albans Cathedral, 1977–79; Residentiary Canon, St Albans, and Priest-in-charge of Ridge, 1979–81; Archdeacon of Canterbury and Canon Res. of Canterbury Cathedral, 1981–86. Dir, Ecclesiastical Insurance Group (formerly Ecclesiastical Insurance Office), 1983–2000. Chm. Govs, King's Sch., Canterbury, 1986–2000. Hon. DD Kent, 1994. *Recreations:* travel, theatre, opera. *Address:* Flat D, 9 Earls Avenue, Folkestone, Kent CT20 2HW.

SIMPSON, John (Cody Fidler-), CBE 1991; World (formerly Foreign) Affairs Editor, BBC, since 1988; *b* 9 Aug. 1944; *s* of Roy Simpson Fidler-Simpson and Joyce Leila Vivienne Cody; *m* 1965, Diane Jean Petteys (marr. diss. 1995), El Cajon, California; two *d*; *m* 1996, Adèle Krüger; one *s*. *Educ:* St Paul's School; Magdalene Coll., Cambridge (MA; Hon. Fellow, 1999). FRGS 1990. Reporter, BBC Radio News, 1970; BBC correspondent, Dublin, 1972; Common Market correspondent (based in Brussels), 1975; Southern Africa correspondent (based in Johannesburg), 1977; Diplomatic correspondent, BBC Television News, 1978; BBC Political Editor, 1980; Presenter and Correspondent, BBC-TV News, 1981; Diplomatic Editor, BBC-TV, 1982–88. Associate Editor, The Spectator, 1991–96. Pres., Chelsea Soc., 2013–. Chancellor, Roehampton Univ., 2005–14. Freeman, City of London, 2011. Hon. DLitt: De Montfort, 1995; Nottingham, 2000; Dundee, Southampton, 2003; St Andrews, Roehampton, 2005. RTS Journalist of the Year, 1990, 2000; BAFTA Award, 1992, 2000; Peabody Award, USA, 1998; Internat. Emmy Award for reporting in Afghanistan, 2002; Bayeux War Correspondent's Award, 2002; RTS award for reporting in Afghanistan and Iraq, 2002; Mungo Park Medal, RSGS, 2004; Internat. Ischia Prize for journalism, Italy, 2010; Churchillian Award, 2012. *Publications:* (ed jtly) The Best of Granta, 1966; The Disappeared: voices from a secret war, 1985; Behind Iranian Lines, 1988; Despatches from the Barricades, 1990; From the House of War: Baghdad and the Gulf, 1991; The Darkness Crumbles: the death of Communism, 1992; In the Forests of the Night: drug-running and terrorism in Peru, 1993; (ed) The Oxford Book of Exile, 1995; (jtly) Lifting the Veil: life in revolutionary Iran, 1995; Wars Against Saddam, 2003; Unreliable Sources, 2010; *autobiography:* Strange Places, Questionable People, 1998; A Mad World, My Masters: tales from a traveller's life, 2000; News from No Man's Land, 2002; Days from a Different World, 2005; Not Quite World's End, 2007; *novels:* Moscow Requiem, 1981; A Fine And Private Place, 1983. *Recreations:* collecting obscure books, travelling to obscure places, and returning to Suffolk. *Address:* c/o Kruger Cowne Ltd, Unit 7C, Chelsea Wharf, 15 Lots Road, SW10 0QJ. *Clubs:* Garrick, Travellers, Chelsea Arts.

SIMPSON, (John Ernest) Peter, FRCS; Director, Health Management Systems, 1996–99; *b* 30 Jan. 1942; *s* of John and Alice Bewick Simpson; *m* 1st, 1964, Valerie Joan Lamb (marr. diss. 1987); one *s* one *d*; 2nd, 1996, Elizabeth Anne Lang. *Educ:* Jesus Coll., Oxford (MA, BM BCh); St Thomas's Hosp. Med. Sch. (Schol.). MFPHM. Surgical training, St Thomas' and Northwich Park Hosps, 1966–78; Lectr, Community Medicine, St Thomas' Hosp., 1974–75; Tutor, King's Fund Coll., 1975–78; Management, Planning Policy and Internat. Divs, DHSS, 1978–88; Regl MO, Mersey RHA, 1988–93; Med. Advr, London Implementation Gp, 1993–96. Pres., British Assoc. of Day Surgery, 1998–2001. Pres., Osler Club of London, 2011–13. *Publications:* Going Home (from hospital) (ed jtly), 1981; articles on day case surgery and organisation of surgical and other clinical services. *Recreations:* golf, music. *Address:* Flat 13, Rosemary Gate, 14 Esher Park Avenue, Esher, Surrey KT10 9NZ. *T:* (01372) 463319. *Clubs:* Royal Society of Medicine; Royal Mid Surrey Golf.

SIMPSON, Julia Elizabeth; Chief of Staff, International Airlines Group, since 2011; *b* 15 May 1958; *d* of Jack Victor Simpson and Ellen Kathleen Simpson (*née* Powell); *m* 2002, Graham Hassell (*d* 2009); two *d*. *Educ:* Lady Margaret Sch., Fulham; Royal Acad. of Dancing; Univ. of Warwick (BA Spanish and European Studies); Salamanca Univ. (1978). News reporter, Iberia Daily Sun and Majorca Daily Bulletin, 1982–84; News Ed., Nat. Union of Civil and Public Servants, 1985–93; Hd of Communications, CWU, 1993–96; Asst Chief Exec., London Bor. of Camden, 1996–98; Head of News: DfEE, 1998–2001; Home Office, 2001–02; Dir of Communications, Home Office, 2002–06; Strategic Communications Advr to Prime Minister, 2006–07; Dir of Corporate Communications, British Airways, 2007–11. Mem. Bd, Iberia and British Airways, 2012–. Freelance subed. and reviewer, Egon Ronay's Guide: And Baby Comes Too, 1988–89. Gov., Robinsfield Infants Sch. and Barrow Hill Junior Sch., London, 1992–2001. *Recreations:* tennis, hispanophile, birds, dance, London, my lovely daughters. *Address:* International Airlines Group, 2 World Business Centre Heathrow, Newall Road, London Heathrow Airport, Hounslow TW6 2SF.

SIMPSON, Rt Hon. Keith (Robert); PC 2015; MP (C) Broadland, since 2010 (Mid Norfolk, 1997–2010); *b* 29 March 1949; *s* of Harry Simpson and Jean Simpson (*née* Day); *m* 1984, Pepita Hollingsworth; one *s*. *Educ:* Thorpe Grammar Sch.; Univ. of Hull (BA Hons 1970). Postgrad. res., KCL, 1970–72; Sen. Lectr in War Studies, RMA Sandhurst, 1973–86; Hd of Oversea and Defence Section, Cons. Res. Dept, 1986–88; Special Advr to Sec. of State for Defence, 1988–90; Dir, Cranfield Security Studies Inst., Cranfield Univ., 1991–97. Opposition front bench spokesman on defence, 1998–99 and 2002–05, on agriculture, 2001–02, on foreign affairs, 2005–10; an Opposition Whip, 1999–2001; PPS to Foreign Sec., 2010–. Member: DEFRA Select Cttee, 2001–02; Parly Intelligence and Security Cttee, 2015–. Sec., Cons. backbench Defence Cttee, 1997–98; Mem., H of C Catering Cttee, 1997–98; Chm., Cons. History Gp, 2003–. Member: Lord Chancellor's Adv. Council on Nat. Records and Archives, 2006–08; Prime Minister's First World War Centenary Adv. Gp, 2013–. Member: RUSI, 1970–; IISS, 1975–; British Commn for Mil. History, 1980–; Comr, Commonwealth War Graves Commn, 2008–. Trustee, Hist. of Parlt Trust, 2005–10. *Publications:* The Old Contemptibles, 1981; (ed) A Nation in Arms, 1985; History of the German Army, 1985; (ed) The War the Infantry Knew 1914–1919, 1987; Waffen SS, 1990. *Recreations:* collecting books, cinema, visiting restaurants, walking battlefields, observing ambitious people. *Address:* House of Commons, SW1A 0AA. *T:* (020) 7219 4053.

SIMPSON, Mark Taylor; QC 2008; barrister; *b* Maidstone, 5 Jan. 1963; *s* of His Honour Keith Taylor Simpson and of Dorothy May Simpson; *m* 1987, Janet McDowell; two *s* one *d*. *Educ:* King's Sch., Canterbury; Oriel Coll., Oxford (BA Hons Classics 1986); Hughes Hall, Cambridge (PGCE 1987); City Univ., London (Dip. Law 1991); King's Coll. London (Dip. Eur. Law 1995). Teacher of Classics, St Paul's Sch., Barnes, 1987–90; called to the Bar, Middle Temple, 1992. *Publications:* (Gen. Ed.) Professional Negligence and Liability, 2000–; (Associate Ed.) Clerk & Lindsell on Torts, 19th edn, 2006, 20th edn, 2010. *Recreations:* golf, tennis, travel, reading. *Address:* Fountain Court Chambers, Temple, EC4Y 9DH. *T:* (020) 7583 3335, *Fax:* (020) 7353 0329. *E:* ms@fountaincourt.co.uk. *Club:* Rye Golf.

SIMPSON, Meg; *see* Hillier, M.

SIMPSON, Rear-Adm. Michael Frank, CB 1985; CEng, FIMechE; FRAeS; Chairman, Aircraft Engineering Division, Hunting Aviation Ltd, 1994–98; *b* 27 Sept. 1928; *s* of Robert Michael Simpson and Florence Mabel Simpson; *m* 1973, Sandra MacDonald (*née* Clift); two *s* one *d*. *Educ:* King Edward VI Sch., Bath; RN Engrg Coll., Manadon; RAF Tech. Coll., Henlow. CEng, FIMechE 1983; FRAeS 1983. Joined RN, 1944; qual. as Air Engr Officer, 1956; served in FAA Sqdns, cruisers and carriers; served with US Navy on exchange, 1964–66; Air Engr Officer, HMS Ark Royal, 1970–72; MoD appts, 1972–78; Supt, RN Aircraft Yard, Fleetlands, 1978–80; Cdre, RN Barracks, Portsmouth, 1981–83; Dir Gen. Aircraft (Naval), 1983–85; Dir and Gen. Man., 1985–88, Man. Dir, Field, later Hunting, Airmotive Ltd, 1988–94; Chm., Somet Ltd, 1988. Mem. Council and Dir, SBAC, 1994–98. Chairman: RN/RM Children's Home Management Cttee, 1980–83; RN Athletics Assoc., 1981–83. Mem. Court, Cranfield Inst. of Technology, 1983–86. *Publications:* The View From Below: memoir of an Aircraft Artificer 1949/51, 2013; articles on helicopter engrg in Jl of RN Engrg; article on helicopter environmental design, 1974. *Recreations:* sailing, ski-ing, shooting, making things, military history, swimming. *Address:* Keppel, Blackhills, Esher, Surrey KT10 9JW. *Clubs:* Army and Navy; Royal Naval Sailing Association (Captain, Portsmouth Br., 1981–83); Royal Navy Ski.

SIMPSON, Morag; *see* Macdonald, M.

SIMPSON, Prof. Patricia Ann, DèsSc; FRS 2000; Wellcome Trust Principal Fellow, 2000–10, and Professor of Comparative Embryology, 2003–11, now Emeritus, Department of Zoology, University of Cambridge; Fellow of Newnham College, Cambridge, since 2000; *b* 9 Dec. 1945; *d* of James Alfred Simpson and Peggy Anderson Simpson. *Educ:* Univ. of Southampton (BSc Hons); Univ. Pierre et Marie Curie, Paris (DèsSc). Scientific research at: Inst. d'Embryologie et Tératologie Experimentale, Nogent sur Marne, Paris, 1968–72; Center for Pathobiol., Univ. of Calif, Irvine, 1972–74; Centre de Génétique Moléculaire, Gif sur Yvette, France, 1975–80; Inst. de Génétique et de Biologie Moléculaire et Cellulaire, Univ. Louis Pasteur, Strasbourg (Res. Dir, 1981–2000). Silver Medal, CNRS, France, 1993; Waddington Medal, British Soc. for Develtl Biol., 2008. *Publications:* The Notch Receptors, 1994. *Recreations:* hiking in remote corners of the world, woodwork, boating. *Address:* Department of Zoology, Downing Street, Cambridge CB2 3EJ. *T:* (01223) 336669.

SIMPSON, Peter; *see* Simpson, J. E. P.

SIMPSON, Sir Peter (Austin), Kt 2011; OBE 2006; education consultant, since 2013; Chief Executive Officer, Brooke Weston Trust, 2007–13; *b* North Shields, 27 April 1950; *s* of Henry and Dorothy Simpson; *m* 1972 (marr. diss. 1995); two *s*. *Educ:* Open Univ. (BA 1975); Univ. of Leicester (MA 1996). Science teacher: Waltham Forest, 1971; Northants, 1972–75; Sharnbrook Upper Sch., 1975–83; Dir of Electronics, Abergele High Sch., 1983–85; Inspector of Sci. and Technol., Walsall Local Authy, 1985–92; Vice Principal, 1992–99, Principal, 1999–2007, Brooke Weston. *Recreations:* amateur radio (callsign G3XQZ), sailing, walking. *Address:* Orchard House, 8 Church Road, Egleton, Oakham, Rutland LE15 8AD. *T:* (01572) 722300. *E:* psimpson@brookeweston.org.

SIMPSON, Sir Peter (Jeffery), Kt 2006; MD; FRCA, FRCP; President, Royal College of Anaesthetists, 2003–06; Consultant Anaesthetist, Frenchay Hospital, Bristol, 1982–2007; *b* 17 Dec. 1946; *s* of Thomas Simpson and Barbara Josephine (*née* Greenwood); *m* 1969, Jane Carpenter-Jacobs; one *s* three *d*. *Educ:* Bryanston Sch., Blandford; St Bartholomew's Hosp. Med. Sch., London (MB BS 1970; MD 1978). MRCS 1970; LRCP 1970; FRCA (FFARCS 1975); FRCP 2005. Registrar and Lectr in Anaesthetics, St Bartholomew's Hosp., 1972–76; Sen. Registrar in Anaesthetics, Oxford, 1976–78; Consultant Sen. Lectr in Anaesthetics, Univ. of Bristol, 1978–82. Chairman: Nat. Confidential Enquiry into Patient Outcome and Death (formerly Nat. Confidential Enquiry into Perioperative Deaths), 2002–05; UK Donation Ethics Cttee, 2010–13; Mem. and Dep. Chm., Postgrad. Medical Educn and Trng Bd, 2004–06. Mem. Council, Royal Coll. of Anaesthetists, 1997–2007 (Vice Pres., 2001–03). Chm. Examination Cttee, European Acad. of Anaesthesiology, 1999–2005; Pres., European Soc. of Anaesthesiology, 2006–07. MRSocMed 1994. Hon. Mem., German Soc. of Anaesthesiology, 2007–. Hon. FCARCSI 2006; Hon. FRCS 2007. *Publications:* Understanding Anaesthesia, 1982, 4th edn 2001; 600 MCQ's in Anaesthesia: basic science, 1985; 600 MCQ's in Anaesthesia: clinical practice, 1986. *Recreations:* golf, walking, choral singing, bird-watching, classical music, opera. *Address:* 2 St Hilary Close, Stoke Bishop, Bristol BS9 1DA. *T:* (0117) 968 1537, *Fax:* (0117) 904 8725. *E:* pjsimpson@blueyonder.co.uk. *Club:* Bristol and Clifton Golf.

SIMPSON, Richard John, FRCPsych; Member (Lab) Mid Scotland and Fife, Scottish Parliament, since 2007; *b* 22 Oct. 1942; *s* of John and Norah Simpson; *m* 1967, Christine McGregor; two *s*. *Educ:* Edinburgh Univ. (MB ChB; DPM). FRCPsych 1994; MRCGP 1996, FRCGP 2013. Pres., Scottish Union of Students, 1967–69. GP, Stirling, 1970–99; psychiatrist, 1970–99; consultant addiction psychiatrist, 2003–07. MSP (Lab) Ochil, 1999–2003; Scottish Executive: Dep. Minister for Justice, 2001–02; Shadow Minister for Public Health, 2007–. Hon. Prof., Stirling Univ., 1997. *Publications:* numerous papers and articles in medical research. *Recreations:* watching Rugby, golf. *Address:* Scottish Parliament, Edinburgh EH99 1SP.

SIMPSON, Robert Brian; Chairman, Antenna Audio Ltd, 2001–03; *b* 12 Sept. 1944; *s* of Harold and Clara Simpson; *m* 1966, Vivienne Jones; three *s*. *Educ:* Liverpool Inst.; University Coll. London (BA 1966). Asst to Marketing Dir, Holt, Rinehart & Winston (Publishers) Ltd, 1966–68; Asst Develt Manager, later Develt Manager, and Dep. Hd of Inf. Services, Consumers' Assoc., 1968–73; Marketing Manager, Universal News Services Ltd, 1973–74; Marketing Dir, later Man. Dir, University Microfilms Internat. Ltd, 1974–79; Marketing and Develt Manager, later Commercial Manager, Press Assoc., 1979–86; Chief Exec., Universal News Services Ltd, 1986–90; Chm. and Chief Exec., PNA Ltd, 1989–90; Chief Exec., The Press Assoc. Ltd, 1990–2000 (Dir, 1989–2000). Chairman: Two-Ten Communications Ltd, 1990–99; Tellex Monitors Ltd, 1990–99; PA News Ltd, 1994–2000; PA Listings Ltd, 1996–2000; PA WeatherCentre Ltd, 1997–2000; Director: Canada NewsWire, 1986–2000; PA Sporting Life Ltd, 1996–2000; World Assoc. of Newspapers, 1997–2000. Pres., Eur. Alliance of Press Agencies, 1998–99 (Mem., 1990–2000); Mem. Council, CPU, 1995–2000. *Recreations:* music, walking, reading, gardening.

SIMPSON, Robert Watson, (Robin); Director, Brewers and Licensed Retailers Association (formerly Brewers' Society), 1993–98; *b* 14 June 1940; *s* of Robert Simpson and Susan Simpson (*née* Rolland). *Educ:* Perth Academy; University of St Andrews (BSc Hons). Board of Trade (Patent Office), 1962; Dept of Trade (Aviation), 1973; Dept of Industry (Indust. Develt Unit), 1976; Dept of Trade (Shipping), 1979; Department of Trade and Industry: (Management Services and Manpower), 1982; Under Sec., and NE Regl Dir, 1986; Head, Business Task Force Div. (incl. Envmt Unit), 1990–92; Head, Steel, Metals and Minerals Div., 1992. JP W London, 2001–07. *Recreations:* history, commemorative pottery.

SIMPSON, Robin Muschamp Garry; QC 1971; *b* 19 June 1927; *s* of Ronald Maitland Simpson, actor and Lila Maravan Simpson (*née* Muschamp); *m* 1st, 1956, Avril Carolyn Harrisson; one *s* one *d*; 2nd, 1968, Mary Faith Laughton-Scott; one *s* one *d*. *Educ:* Charterhouse; Peterhouse, Cambridge (MA). Called to Bar, Middle Temple, 1951, Bencher, 1979; SE Circuit; former Mem., Surrey and S London Sessions; a Recorder of the Crown Court, 1976–86. Mem., CCC Bar Mess. Appeal Steward, British Boxing Bd of Control. Mem., Friends of Hardwick. *Recreation:* Real tennis (Mem., Dedanists Club). *Address:* 116 Station Road, Barnes, SW13 0NB. *T:* (020) 8878 9898. *Clubs:* Pratt's, MCC.

SIMPSON, Sir Roderick Alexander C.; *see* Cordy-Simpson.

SIMPSON, Sally Anne; *see* Hatfield, S. A.

SIMPSON, Prof. Stephen James, AC 2015; PhD; FRS 2013; FAA; Professor, School of Biological Sciences, since 2005, and Academic Director, Charles Perkins Centre, since 2012, University of Sydney; Executive Director, Obesity Australia, since 2014; *b* 26 June 1957; *s* of Arthur Leonard and Patricia Simpson; *m* 1984, Lesley Kathryn Dowie; two *s*. *Educ:* C of E Grammar Sch., Brisbane; Univ. of Queensland (BSc Hons 1978); King's Coll., London (PhD 1982); MA Oxon 1986. FAA 2007. Univ. of Qld Travelling Schol., 1979–82; University of Oxford: MRC post-doctoral res. asst, Dept of Exptl Psychol., 1982–83; Demonstrator, Dept of Zool., 1983–86; Lectr in Entomol., 1986–98 and Curator, 1986–2005, Hope Entomol Collections; Reader in Zool., 1996–98; Prof., 1998–2004; Vis. Prof., 2005–08; Associate Hd, Dept of Zool., 2000–04; Principal Curator, Univ. Mus. of Natural Hist., 1989–92; Fellow, Linacre Coll., 1986–88, Jesus Coll., 1988–2004, Oxford; Federation Fellow, 2005–10, Aust. Res. Council Laureate Fellow, 2010–14, Sch. of Biol Scis, Univ. of Sydney. Guest Prof. in Animal Behaviour, Univ. of Basel, 1990; Dist. Vis. Prof., Univ. of Arizona, 1999. Fellow, Wissenschaftskolleg (Inst. for Advanced Study), Berlin, 2002–03. NSW Scientist of Year, NSW State Govt, 2009; Wigglesworth Medal, Royal Entomological Soc. of London, 2011. *Publications:* The Right Fly, 1996 (US edn as Angler's Fly Identifier, 1996); Anglers' Flies, 1997; The Nature of Nutrition: a unifying framework from animal adaptation to human obesity, 2012; ed books and scientific papers. *Recreations:* fishing, cookery. *Address:* School of Biological Sciences, University of Sydney, NSW 2006, Australia.

SIMPSON, Susan Margaret; *see* Haird, S. M.

SIMPSON, Prof. Thomas James, PhD, DSc; FRS 2001; CChem, FRSC; FRSE; Professor of Organic Chemistry, since 1990, Alfred Capper Pass Professor of Chemistry, since 2005, University of Bristol; *b* 23 Feb. 1947; *s* of Thomas Simpson and Hughina Ross Hay; *m* 1st, 1972, Elizabeth Crosthwaite Nattrass; one *s* one *d*; 2nd, 1987, Prof. Mary Norval. *Educ:* Univ. of Edinburgh (BSc 1st Cl. Hons 1969; Macfarlan-Smith Prize; DSc 1986); Univ. of Bristol (PhD 1973). Sen. Univ. Demonstrator, Dept of Organic Chem., Univ. of Liverpool, 1973–74; Research Fellow: Res. Sch. of Chem., ANU, 1974–76; Dept of Organic Chem., Univ. of Liverpool, 1977–78; Lectr, Dept of Chem., Univ. of Edinburgh, 1978–88; Prof. of Organic Chem., Univ. of Leicester, 1988–89. Royal Society of Chemistry: Tilden Lectr, 2001; Simonsen Lectr, 2002; Hugo Müller Lectr, 2004; Mem., Perkin Council, 1989–96 (Vice-Pres., 1993–95); Mem., 1989–93, Chm., 1993–96, Perkin Div. Standing Cttee on Meetings; Chm., Internat. Adv. Bd, Natural Product Reports; Mem., Editl Bd, Chem. in Britain, 1994–2000. FRSE 2006. Corday-Morgan Medal and Prize, 1984, Natural Products Chemistry Medal, 2007, Rita and John Cornforth Award, 2013, RSC. *Publications:* contrib. numerous original papers and review articles. *Recreations:* mountain walking, food and wine. *Address:* School of Chemistry, University of Bristol, Bristol BS8 1TS. *T:* (0117) 928 7656.

SIMPSON, William George; international library and heritage consultant, since 2008; Director of the John Rylands Library and University Librarian, University of Manchester, 2002–07; *b* 27 June 1945; *s* of William Anion Simpson and Sarah Jane Simpson; *m* 1968, Margaret Lilian Pollard; two *d*. *Educ:* Liverpool Inst.; Univ. of Liverpool (BA); MA Dublin 1995. MCLIP. Gilroy Scholar in Semitic Languages, Univ. of Aberdeen, 1968; Asst Librarian, Univ. of Durham, 1969–73; Asst Librarian, Sub-Librarian and Senior Sub-Librarian, John Rylands Univ. Library of Manchester, 1973–85; University Librarian: Surrey, 1985–90; London, 1990–94; Librarian and Coll. Archivist, TCD, 1994–2002. Chairman: Guildford Inst., 1987–90; Amer. Studies Library Gp, 1992–94; Mem., Humanities and Social Scis Adv. Cttee, 1991–92, London Adv. Cttee, 1992–94, British Library; Dir, Consortium of University Res. Libraries, 1992–97 and 2003–05; Curator, Oxford Univ. Libraries, 2002–07. UK Advr to British Univ. in Egypt, 2008–11. Dir, IRIS, 1994–2003; Member: An Chomhairle Leabharlanna (Liby Council of Ireland), 1995–2002; Council for Library Co-operation, 1995–2002 (Chm., 1998–2000); Nat. Preservation Adv. Cttee, 1994–96; Nat. Preservation Office Mgt Cttee, 1996–2002 (Chm., 1999–2002); Working Gp on UK Literary Heritage, 2005–08; Chairman: CONUL, 1997–99; Standing Cttee on Legal Deposit, 1999–2001; Sec., Div. of Library Mgt and Admin, LIBER, 2002–07. Fellow, Salzburg Foundn, 2004–. Trustee: Worth Library, 1997–; The People's History Mus., 2003–05; Working Class Movement Library, 2007–; Frome Heritage Mus., 2014–. Mem., Internat. Editl Bd, Jl of Library Administration, 2004–12. FRSA 1988. Jubilee Medal, Charles Univ., Prague, 1998. *Publications:* Libraries, Languages and the Interpretation of the Past, 1988; articles in learned and professional jls and press. *Recreations:* astronomy, genealogy, languages, travel, Everton FC. *Address:* 1 Woolmer Villas, Petersfield Road, Greatham, Liss, Hants GU33 6AY.

SIMPSON, Prof. (William) James, PhD; Donald P. and Katherine B. Loker Professor of English and American Literature and Language, Harvard University, since 2006 (Professor of English and American Literature and Language, 2004–06); *b* 16 March 1954; *s* of R. C. Simpson and M. A. Simpson (*née* MacDougall); *m* 1982, Luisella Maria Brunetti; two *s* one *d*. *Educ:* Scotch Coll., Melbourne; Univ. of Melbourne (BA Hons); St Edmund Hall, Oxford (MPhil); Girton Coll., Cambridge (PhD 1996). Lectr in English Lit., Westfield Coll., Univ. of London, 1981–89; University of Cambridge: Fellow, Girton Coll., 1989–2003; Lectr in English, and Lectr, Girton Coll., 1989–99; Prof. of Medieval and Renaissance English, 1999–2003. *Publications:* Piers Plowman: an introduction to the B-text, 1990; Sciences and the Self in Medieval Poetry, 1995; Reform and Cultural Revolution 1350–1547, 2002; Burning to Read: English fundamentalism and its Reformation opponents, 2007; Under the Hammer: iconoclasm in the Anglo-American tradition, 2010; contrib. articles to Medium Aevum, Rev. English Studies, Speculum, Traditio, Jl Medieval & Early Modern Studies, etc. *Recreation:* conversation. *Address:* Department of English and American Literature and Language, Harvard University, Barker Center, 12 Quincy Street, Cambridge, MA 02138, USA. *E:* jsimpson@fas.harvard.edu.

SIMS, Prof. Andrew Charles Petter, MD; FRCP, FRCPsych, FRCPE; Professor of Psychiatry, 1979–2000, Chairman, Division of Psychiatry and Behavioural Sciences in Relation to Medicine, 1994–97, University of Leeds; Consultant Psychiatrist, St James's University Hospital, 1979–2000; *b* 5 Nov. 1938; *s* of late Dr Charles Henry Sims and Dr Norah Winifred Kennan Sims (*née* Petter); *m* 1964, Ruth Marie Harvey; two *s* two *d*. *Educ:* Monkton Combe Sch.; Emmanuel Coll., Cambridge (MA; MD 1973); Westminster Hosp. DObstRCOG; FRCPsych 1979; FRCPE 1993; FRCP 1997. House Surgeon, Westminster Hosp., 1963–64; Registrar in Psychiatry, Manchester Royal Infirmary, 1966–69; Consultant Psychiatrist, All Saints Hosp., Birmingham, 1971–76; Sen. Lectr, Univ. of Birmingham, 1976–79; Head of Dept of Psychiatry, Univ. of Leeds, 1980–83, 1986–89, 1994–97. Royal College of Psychiatrists: Sub-Dean, 1984–87; Dean, 1987–90; Pres., 1990–93; Dir, Continuing Professional Develt, 1993–97; Chm., Spirituality and Psychiatry Special Interest Gp, 2003–05. Chairman: Confidential Inquiry into Homicides and Suicides by Mentally Ill People, 1993–96; Schizophrenia Cttee, Clinical Standards Adv. Gp, DoH, 1994–95; Health Adv. Service 2000, 1997–98. Mem., GMC, 1994–99. Patron: John Young Foundation, 1991–; Assoc. for Pastoral Care in Mental Health, 1994–; Interhealth, 1998–; Leeds Faith in Schs, 2011–. Hon. FCPS (Pak) 1994; Hon. FCMSA 1997. MD Lambeth, 1995. Editor: Advances in Psychiatric Treatment, 1994–2003; Developing Mental Health, 2002–05. *Publications:* Neurosis in Society, 1983; Psychiatry (Concise Medical Textbooks), 5th edn (with Sir William Trethowan), 1983, 6th edn (with D. Owens), 1993; (with W. I. Hume) Lecture Notes in Behavioural Sciences, 1984; Symptoms in the Mind: introduction to descriptive psychopathology, 1988 (Italian edn 1993, Portuguese edn 2000, Korean edn 2008, Japanese edn 2009), 3rd edn 2002; (with R. P. Snaith) Anxiety in Clinical Practice, 1988 (German edn 1993); Speech and Language Disorders in Psychiatry, 1995; (with C. Williams) Disorders of Volition, 1999; Is Faith Delusion?, 2009 (Dutch edn 2010); (with C. C. H. Cook and A. Powell) Spirituality and Psychiatry, 2009. *Recreations:* gardening, music, theatre, walking. *Address:* Church Farm House, Alveley, Bridgnorth, Shropshire WV15 6ND. *Clubs:* Christian Medical Fellowship, Royal Society of Medicine.

SIMS, Prof. Christopher A., PhD; Professor of Economics, since 1999, and John F. Sherrerd '52 University Professor of Economics, since 2012, Princeton University; *b* Washington, DC, 21 Oct. 1942; *s* of Albert Sims and Ruth Sims (*née* Leiserson); *m* 1967, Catherine Sears; two *s* one *d*. *Educ:* Harvard Coll. (BA Maths 1963); Univ. of Calif, Berkeley; Harvard Univ. (PhD Econs 1968). Instructor in econs, 1967–68, Asst Prof. of Econs, 1968–70, Harvard Univ.; Associate Prof. of Econs, 1970–74, Prof. of Econs, 1974–90, Univ. of Minnesota; Henry Ford II Prof. of Econs, Yale Univ., 1990–99; Harold H. Helm '20 Prof. of Econs, Princeton Univ., 2004–12. Visiting Professor: Yale Univ., 1974; MIT, 1979–80; Visiting Scholar: Fed. Reserve Bank of Atlanta, 1995–; Fed. Reserve Bank of NY, 1994–97, 2004– (Resident Schol., 2012–13); Fed. Reserve Bank of Philadelphia, 2000–03; IMF, 2003–. Consultant: Fed. Reserve Bank of Minneapolis, 1983 and 1986–87; Fed. Nat. Mortgage Assoc., 1999–2002. President: Econometric Soc., 1995 (Fellow 1975); Amer. Econ. Assoc., 2012. Member: Amer. Acad. Arts and Scis, 1988; NAS, 1989. (Jtly) Nobel Prize in Econ. Scis, 2011. *Publications:* contribs to learned jls incl. Rev. Econs and Stats, Econometrica, Annals Math. Stats, Amer. Econ. Rev., Jl Amer. Statistical Assoc. *Address:* Department of Economics, Princeton University, 104 Fisher Hall, Princeton, NJ 08544–1021, USA.

SIMS, Ven. Christopher Sidney; Archdeacon of Walsall, 2009–14; *b* Shipley, W Yorks, 9 Sept. 1949; *s* of Rev. Sidney Sims and Dorothy Sims; *m* 1972, Catherine Virginia Thomson; three *s*. *Educ:* Wycliffe Hall, Oxford (Cert. Theol.). Ordained deacon, 1977, priest, 1978; Asst Curate, St John the Evangelist, Walmley, Sutton Coldfield, 1977–80; Vicar: St Cyprian with St Chad, Hay Mill, Birmingham, 1980–88; St Michael, Stanwix, with St Mark, Belah, Carlisle, 1988–96; Rural Dean, Carlisle, 1990–95; Priest-in-charge, Allhallows and Torpenhow, Boltongate with Ireby and Uldale, Bassenthwaite with Isel and Setmurthy, 1996–2001; Team Rector, Binsey Team Ministry, Cumbria, 2001–03; Vicar, Shrewsbury Abbey and St Peter, Monkmoor, 2003–09; Rural Dean, Shrewsbury, 2008–09. Hon. Canon, Carlisle Cathedral, 1991–96. *Recreations:* cricket, football.

SIMS, Prof. Geoffrey Donald, OBE 1971; FREng; Vice-Chancellor, University of Sheffield, 1974–90; *b* 13 Dec. 1926; *s* of Albert Edward Hope Sims and Jessie Elizabeth Sims; *m* 1949, Pamela Audrey Richings; one *s* two *d*. *Educ:* Wembley County Grammar School; Imperial College of Science and Technology, London. Research physicist, GEC, 1948–54; Sen. Scientific Officer, UKAEA, 1954–56; Lecturer/Senior Lecturer, University College, London, 1956–63; University of Southampton: Prof. and Head of Dept of Electronics, 1963–74; Dean, Faculty of Engrg, 1967–70; Senior Dep. Vice-Chancellor, 1970–72. Member: Council, British Association for the Advancement of Science, 1965–69 (Chm., Sheffield Area Council, 1974–); EDC for Electronics Industry, 1966–75; Adv. Cttee for Scientific and Technical Information, 1969–74; CNAA Electrical Engineering Bd, 1970–73; Planning Cttee for British Library, 1971–73 (Chm., British Library R&D Adv. Cttee, 1975–81); Adv. Council, Science Museum, 1972–84; British Nat. Cttee for Physics, 1972–78; Royal Soc. Cttee on Sci. Information, 1972–81; Electronics Res. Council, 1973–74; Annan Cttee on Future of Broadcasting, 1974–77; Naval Educn Adv. Cttee, 1974–79; Trent RHA, 1975–84; British Council Engrg and Tech. Adv. Cttee, 1976–84 (Chm.); Interim Action Cttee on British Film Industry, 1977–81; EEC Adv. Cttee on Scientific and Technical Trng, 1977–81; Univs Council for Adult and Continuing Educn, 1978–84 (Chm., 1980–84); CNAA, 1979–83; Liaison Cttee on Highly Qualified Technol Manpower, 1979–82; Council, Nat. Inst. of Adult Educn, 1980–84; SRC, later SERC Engrg Bd, 1980–84; Inter Univ. and Polytechnic Council, 1981–91 (IUC and Exec. Cttee, 1974–81; Vice-Chm., IUPC, 1985–91); Cttee for Internat. Co-operation in Higher Educn, 1981–94 (Vice-Chm., 1985–91); EEC Adv. Cttee on Programme Management, 1981–84; BBC Engrg Adv. Cttee, 1981–90 (Chm.); Council, Fellowship of Engrg, 1986–88; Museums and Galleries Commn, 1983–88; Hong Kong City Polytechnic Sub-cttee, 1984–86, Hong Kong Univ. of Sci. and Technol. Sub-cttee, 1987–91, UPGC, Hong Kong; Mem. of Council and Hon. Dep. Treas., ACU, 1984–90; Chm., Council for Commonwealth Educn, 1991–96. UK rep. on Perm. Cttee of Conf. of European Rectors, 1981–84; *ad personam* rep. on Perm. Cttee and Bureau of Conf. of European Rectors, 1984–94; rep. on Liaison Cttee, Rectors' Confs of EEC Mem. States, 1985–90 (Pres., 1987–89). Chairman of Governors: Southampton College of Technology, 1967–69; Southampton Sch. of Navigation, 1972–74; Sheffield High Sch., 1978–85; Fellow, Midland Chapter, Woodard Schools, 1977–97 (Hon. Fellow, 1997); Custos, Worksop Coll., 1984–92. Trustee, Church Burgesses Trust, Sheffield, 1984–2015 (Capital, 1988–89, 1999–2000; Chm., Educnl Foundn, 1992–2013). FIET (FIEE 1963); FCGI 1980; FREng (FEng 1980); FRSocMed 2002. Hon. Fellow, Sheffield City Polytechnic, 1990. Hon. DSc: Southampton, 1979; Huddersfield, 2001; Hon. ScD Allegheny Coll., Penn, USA, 1989; Hon. DSc (Eng) QUB, 1990; Hon. LLD: Dundee, 1987; Sheffield, 1991. Symons Medal, ACU, 1991. Co-founder Mem., 1966, Reviews Editor, 1969–91, Chm., 1982–98, Jl of Materials Science Bd. *Publications:* Microwave Tubes and Semiconductor Devices (with I. M. Stephenson), 1963; Variational Techniques in Electromagnetism (trans.), 1965; numerous papers on microwaves, electronics and education in learned jls. *Recreations:* travel, music. *Address:* Ingleside, 70 Whirlow Lane, Sheffield S11 9QF. *T:* (0114) 236 6196, *Fax:* (0114) 236 6196. *E:* gdsims@blueyonder.co.uk.

SIMS, Prof. Mark Rayner, PhD; Professor of Astrobiology and Space Instrumentation, University of Leicester, since 2008; *b* Bristol, 10 Feb. 1956; *s* of Norman and Sheila Sims. *Educ:* Wellsway Sch., Keynsham, Bristol; Univ. of Leicester (BSc Physics with Astrophysics 1977; PhD 1982). Res. Fellow, ESA, 1981–84; Res. Associate, 1984–91, Res. Fellow, 1991–2008, Univ. of Leicester. *Publications:* contribs to scientific and technical jls. *Recreations:* birdwatching, photography, walking, golf, dancing, badminton. *Address:* Space Research Centre, Department of Physics and Astronomy, University of Leicester, Leicester LE1 7RH. *T:* (0116) 252 3513. *E:* mrs@le.ac.uk.

SIMS, Monica Louie, OBE 1971; MA, LRAM, LGSM; Vice President, British Board of Film Classification, 1985–98; *d* of late Albert Charles Sims and Eva Elizabeth Preen, both of Gloucester. *Educ:* Girls' High School, Gloucester; St Hugh's College, Oxford. Tutor in Literature and Drama, Dept of Adult Educn, Hull Univ., 1947–50; Educn Tutor, Nat. Fedn of Women's Institutes, 1950–53; BBC Sound Talks Producer, 1953–55; BBC Television Producer, 1955–64; Editor of Woman's Hour, BBC, 1964–67; Head of Children's Programmes, BBC TV, 1967–78; Controller, BBC Radio 4, 1978–83; Dir of Programmes, BBC Radio, 1983–84; Dir of Prodn, Children's Film and TV Foundn, 1985–97. Chm., Careers Adv. Bd, Univ. of Bristol, 1991–99. Hon. DLitt Bristol, 2000.

SIMS, Sir Roger (Edward), Kt 1996; JP; *b* 27 Jan. 1930; *s* of late Herbert William Sims and Annie Amy Savidge; *m* 1957, Angela Mathews (*d* 2015); two *s* one *d*. *Educ:* City Boys' Grammar Sch., Leicester; St Olave's Grammar Sch., London. MCInstM. National Service, 1948–50. Coutts & Co., 1950–51; Campbell Booker Carter Ltd, 1953–62; Dodwell & Co. Ltd, 1962–90; Dir, Inchcape International Ltd, 1981–90. Contested (C) Shoreditch and Finsbury, 1966 and 1970. MP (C) Chislehurst, Feb. 1974–1997. PPS to Home Sec., 1979–83. Mem., Nat. Commn of Inquiry into the Prevention of Child Abuse, 1995–96. Mem., GMC, 1989–99. Mem., Central Exec. Cttee, NSPCC, 1980–93. Chm., Bromley Voluntary Sector Trust, 1997–2001. Mem. Chislehurst and Sidcup UDC, 1956–62. JP Bromley, 1960–72 (Dep. Chm. 1970–72); Chm., Juvenile Panel, 1971–72. *Recreations:* swimming; music, especially singing (Mem. Royal Choral Soc., 1950–2008). *Address:* 68 Towncourt Crescent, Petts Wood, Orpington, Kent BR5 1PJ. *Club:* Bromley Conservative (Bromley).

SIMS, Sonia Lisa; a District Judge (Magistrates' Courts), since 2002; Designated District Judge for Stratford, since 2011, and for East London, since 2012; *b* 8 Jan. 1957; *d* of Beryl Leonora Sims (*née* Lang). *Educ:* St John of Jerusalem Primary Sch.; Dalston Co. Grammar Sch.; Kingsway Princeton Coll.; City of London Poly. Trainee legal executive: Richard Sandler & Co., 1975–77; Rance & Co., 1978–81; Legal Exec., then Asst Solicitor, 1981–88, Partner, 1988–98, Whitelock & Storr; Consultant, Traymans, 1998–2002. Dep. Dist Judge, 1998–2002. Member: London Criminal Courts Cttee, 1999–2003; Criminal Justice Council, 2011–. Mem., Legal Aid Rev. Cttee (formerly Legal Aid Bd), Legal Services Commn, 1989– (Chm., 1995–2002). Mem., Local Cttee, Highbury and City, 1989–2002, Regl Mem., City of London, 1999–2000, Duty Solicitor Schemes. Associate, 1978, and Fellow, 1984, Inst. Legal Execs. *Recreations:* dance, music, travelling, good food, good wine and song, humour, all things of a Latin flavour, friends, children, animals, a challenge. *Address:* c/o Stratford Magistrates' Court, 389–397 High Street, Stratford, E15 4SB. *T:* (020) 8437 6051.

SIMS-WILLIAMS, Prof. Nicholas John, PhD; FBA 1988; Research Professor of Iranian and Central Asian Studies, School of Oriental and African Studies, University of London, 2004–07 and 2012–15, now Emeritus (Professorial Research Associate, 2008–12); *b* 11 April 1949; twin *s* of late Rev. M. V. S. Sims-Williams; *m* 1972, Ursula Mary Judith, *d* of late Prof. Hugh Seton-Watson, CBE, FBA; two *d*. *Educ:* Trinity Hall, Cambridge (BA, MA; PhD 1978). Res. Fellow, Gonville and Caius Coll., Cambridge, 1975–76; SOAS, University of London: Lectr in Iranian Langs, 1976–89; Reader in Iranian Studies, 1989–94; Prof. of Iranian and Central Asian Studies, 1994–2004. Visiting Professor: Collège de France, 1998–99; Macquarie Univ., 1998–2000; Univ. of Rome 'La Sapienza', 2001. British Acad. Res. Reader, 1992–94; Leverhulme Major Res. Fellow, 2002–04. MAE 2012. Corresp. Mem., Austrian Acad. of Scis, 1990; Associé Etranger, Acad. des Inscriptions et Belles Lettres, Inst de France, 2002; Mem., Amer. Philosophical Soc., 2014. Hon. Mem., Amer. Oriental Soc., 2011. Hirayama Prize for Silk Road Studies, 1996; Denis Sinor Medal for Inner Asian Studies, RAS, 2015. *Publications:* The Christian Sogdian manuscript C2, 1985 (Prix Ghirshman, Inst. de France, 1988); Sogdian and other Iranian Inscriptions of the Upper Indus, vol. I, 1989, vol. II, 1992; (with James Hamilton) Documents turco-sogdiens du IXe–Xe siècle de Touen-houang, 1990; Partita, 1993; Serenade, 1997; New Light on Ancient Afghanistan: the decipherment of Bactrian, 1997; Bactrian Documents from Northern Afghanistan, vol. I, 2001, rev. edn 2012, vol. II, 2007 (World Prize for Book of the Year, Iran, 2009), vol. III, 2012; In Memoriam (string trio), 2002; Bactrian Personal Names, 2010; (with Judith A. Lerner) Seals, Sealings and Tokens from Bactria to Gandhara, 2011; (with D. Durkin-Meisterernst) Dictionary of Manichaean Sogdian and Bactrian, 2012; Iranian manuscripts in Syriac script in the Berlin Turfan collection, 2012; Biblical and Other Christian Sogdian Texts from the Turfan Collection, 2014; The Life of Serapion and other Christian Sogdian texts from the manuscripts E25 and E26, 2015; *festschrift:* Exegisti Monumenta, ed W. Sundermann, A. Hintze and F. de Blois, 2009; contrib. on Iranian and Central Asian langs and culture to learned jls. *Recreation:* music. *Address:* 11 Park Parade, Cambridge CB5 8AL. *E:* ns5@soas.ac.uk.

See also P. P. Sims-Williams.

SIMS-WILLIAMS, Prof. Patrick Philip, PhD; FBA 1996; Professor of Celtic Studies, Aberystwyth University (formerly University College of Wales, Aberystwyth, then University of Wales, Aberystwyth), 1994–2014, now Emeritus; *b* 11 April 1949; twin *s* of late Rev. Michael Sims-Williams and Kathleen (*née* Wenborn); *m* 1986, Prof. Marged Haycock; one *s* one *d*. *Educ:* Borden GS, Sittingbourne; Trinity Hall, Cambridge (BA 1972; MA 1975); PhD Birmingham 1980. Cambridge University: Lectr, Dept of Anglo-Saxon, Norse and Celtic, 1977–93; British Acad. Res. Reader, 1988–90; Reader in Celtic and Anglo-Saxon, 1993; Fellow, St John's Coll., 1977–93. O'Donnell Lectr, Oxford Univ., 1981–82, Edinburgh Univ., 1986, Univ. of Wales, 2000–01; Bergin Lectr, UCD, 2015. Leverhulme Major Res. Fellow, 2003–06. Dir, British Acad. proj., The Development of the Welsh Language, 2007–. Mem., Royal Commn on Ancient and Historical Monuments of Wales, 1998–2008. Council Member: Irish Texts Soc., 1991–97; Philological Soc., 1997–2000; British Acad., 2012–15; Pres., Internat. Congress of Celtic Studies, 2011–. Editor, Cambrian Medieval Celtic Studies, 1981–. Gollancz Prize, British Acad., 1992; Antiquity Prize, 1998; G. T. Clark Award, Cambrian Archaeol Assoc., 2007; Vernam Hull Prize, Univ. of Wales, 2011. *Publications:* Religion and Literature in Western England 600–800, 1990; Britain and Early Christian Europe, 1995; Ptolemy: towards a linguistic atlas of the earliest Celtic place-names of Europe, 2000; The Celtic Inscriptions of Britain, 2003; New Approaches to Celtic Place-names in Ptolemy's Geography, 2005; Ancient Celtic Place-names in Europe and Asia Minor, 2006; The Iron House in Ireland, 2006; (with Georges Cousin) Additions to Alfred Holder's Celtic Thesaurus, 2006; Studies on Celtic Languages Before the Year 1000, 2007; (with M. E. Raybould) The Geography of Celtic Personal Names in the Latin Inscriptions of the Roman Empire, 2007; (with M. E. Raybould) A Corpus of Latin Inscriptions of the Roman Empire Containing Celtic Personal Names, 2007, Introduction and Supplement, 2009; Irish Influence on Medieval Welsh Literature, 2010; Rhai Addasiadau Cymraeg Canol o Sieffre o Fynwy, 2011. *Recreations:* music, sailing, carpentry. *Address:* Department of Welsh, Aberystwyth University, Aberystwyth SY23 2AX. *T:* (01970) 622137.

See also N. J. Sims-Williams.

SINCLAIR, family name of **Earl of Caithness, Viscount Thurso** and **Baron Sinclair of Cleeve**.

SINCLAIR, 18th Lord *cr* 1449 (Scot.); **Matthew Murray Kennedy St Clair;** Director, Saint Property Ltd, since 2001; *b* 9 Dec. 1968; *s* of 17th Lord Sinclair, CVO and of Anne Lettice, *yr d* of Sir Richard Cotterell, 5th Bt, CBE; *S* father, 2004; *m* 2005, Laura Cicely, *y d* of Jonathan Coode, DL; two *s*. *Educ:* Glenalmond; RAC Cirencester. MRICS. *Heir: s* Harry Murray Kennedy St Clair, Master of Sinclair, *b* 6 Oct. 2007. *Address:* Knocknalling, St Johns Town of Dalry, Castle Douglas DG7 3ST. *E:* mstc@saintproperty.com. *Club:* New (Edinburgh).

SINCLAIR OF CLEEVE, 3rd Baron *cr* 1957, of Cleeve, Somerset; **John Lawrence Robert Sinclair;** *b* 6 Jan. 1953; *s* of 2nd Baron Sinclair of Cleeve, OBE, and Patricia, *d* of late Major Lawrence Hellyer; *S* father, 1985; *m* 1997, Shereen Khan; one *d*. *Educ:* Winchester College; Manchester Univ. Technical support and Gov., an Inner London comprehensive sch., 1984–94. Founding Mem. and Sec., Hackney Local Economic Trading System, 1992. Interest in archaeology and campaigning. *Recreations:* motor cycling, mime, music, construction, design, marathons.

SINCLAIR, Andrew Annandale; author; Managing Director, Timon Films, since 1967; *b* 21 Jan. 1935; *m* 1960, Marianne, *d* of Mr and Mrs Arsène Alexandre; *m* 1972, Miranda, *o d* of Mr and Hon. Mrs George Seymour; one *s*; *m* 1984, Sonia Lady Melchett (*see* S. E. Sinclair), *d* of Dr and Mrs Roland Graham. *Educ:* Eton Coll.; Trinity Coll., Cambridge (BA, PhD); Harvard. Ensign, Coldstream Guards, 1953–55. Harkness Fellow of the Commonwealth Fund, 1959–61; Dir of Historical Studies, Churchill Coll., Cambridge, 1961–63; Fellow of American Council of Learned Societies, 1963–64; Lectr in American History, University Coll., London, 1965–67. FRSL 1973; Fellow Soc. of American Historians, 1974; FRSA 2007. Somerset Maugham Literary Prize, 1966. *Directed films:* Under Milk Wood, 1971; Dylan on Dylan, 2003. *Publications:* The Breaking of Bumbo, 1958; My Friend Judas, 1959; The Project, 1960; Prohibition, 1962; The Hallelujah Bum, 1963; The Available Man: Warren E. Harding, 1964; The Better Half, 1964; The Raker, 1965; Concise History of the United States, 1966; Albion Triptych: Gog, 1967, Magog, 1972, King Ludd, 1988; The Greek Anthology, 1967; Adventures in the Skin Trade, 1968; The Last of the Best, 1969; Guevara, 1970; Dylan Thomas: poet of his people, 1975; The Surrey Cat, 1976; The Savage, 1977; Jack: the biography of Jack London, 1977; A Patriot for Hire, 1978; John Ford, 1979; The Facts in the Case of E. A. Poe, 1979; Corsair, 1981; The Other Victoria, 1981; Sir Walter Raleigh and the Age of Discovery, 1984; Beau Bumbo, 1985; The Red and the Blue, 1986; Spiegel, 1987; War Like a Wasp, 1989; (ed) The War Decade, an anthology of the 1940s, 1989; The Need to Give, 1990; The Far Corners of the Earth, 1991; The Naked Savage, 1991; The Strength of the Hills, 1992; The Sword and the Grail, 1993; Francis Bacon: his life and violent times, 1993; In Love and Anger, 1994; Arts and Cultures: the history of the fifty years of the Arts Council of Great Britain, 1995; Jerusalem: the endless crusade, 1996; Death by Fame: a life of Elisabeth Empress of Austria, 1998; The Discovery of the Grail, 1998; Dylan the Bard: a life of Dylan Thomas, 1999; The Secret Scroll, 2001; Blood & Kin, 2002; An Anatomy of Terror, 2003; Rosslyn, 2005; Viva Che!, 2006; The Grail, 2007; Man and Horse, 2008; Down Under Milk Wood, 2014. *Recreations:* old cities, old movies. *Address:* Flat 20, Millennium House, 132 Grosvenor Road, SW1V 3JY. *Clubs:* Garrick, Chelsea Arts.

SINCLAIR, Angus Hugh; Secretary to the Speaker, House of Commons, 2005–10; *b* 4 Nov. 1952; *s* of late Dr Hugh Melville Sinclair and Diana Grieve; *m* 1981 (marr. diss. 2002); one *s* one *d*. *Educ:* Merchiston Castle Sch.; Durham Univ. (BA Hons Geog. 1974). Asst Master, Wellingborough Sch., 1975; joined RN, 1975; served submarines and surface ships; Comdr (Trng) Britannia RNC, 1993–95; Sec. C-in-C Fleet, 1995–99; Naval Attaché, Rome, 1999–2002; Defence Attaché, Malta, 2001–02; Dir, RN Logistics, 2002–05. Editor: Encyclopaedia Britannia, 1993–95; Norsworthy's Epitome, 1996–97. *Recreations:* endeavouring to persevere, striving for parsimony. *Clubs:* Royal Navy of 1919, Naval; Moffat Cricket.

SINCLAIR, Prof. Anthony Ronald Entrican, DPhil; FRS 2002; FRSC; Professor of Zoology, University of British Columbia, 1987–2009, now Emeritus; *b* 25 March 1944; *s* of Sir Ronald Ormiston Sinclair, KBE and Ellen Isobelle Sinclair; *m* 1966, Anne Catherine Begbie; two *d*. *Educ:* Pembroke Coll., Oxford (BA 1966, MA 1970; DPhil 1970). Res. Officer, Animal Behaviour Res. Gp, Oxford Univ., 1970; Staff Ecologist, Serengeti Res. Inst., Tanzania, 1970–73; Res. Scientist, Div. of Ecol. and Wildlife, CSIRO, Australia, 1973–75; University of British Columbia: Asst Prof., 1975–81, Associate Prof., 1981–87, Dept of Zool.; Dir, Centre for Biodiversity Res., 1996–2002. FRSC 1996. Aldo Leopold Medal, Wildlife Soc., 2013. *Publications:* The African Buffalo, 1977; (ed with M. Norton-Griffiths) Serengeti, 1979, 2nd edn 1995; (with G. Caughley) Wildlife Ecology, 1994; (ed with P. Arcese) Serengeti II, 1995; (ed jtly) Conserving Nature's Diversity, 2000; (with J. Fryxell and G. Caughley) Wildlife Ecology, Conservation and Management, 2006, 3rd edn 2014; (ed with C. Packer, S. Mduma and J. Fryxell) Serengeti III, 2008; Serengeti Story, 2012; (ed jtly) Serengeti IV, 2015; contrib. scientific papers concerning ecology and conservation to leading jls, incl. Jl Animal Ecol., Ecol., Nature, Science. *Address:* Department of Zoology, University of British Columbia, 6270 University Boulevard, Vancouver, BC V6T 1Z4, Canada. *T:* (604) 2751563, *Fax:* (604) 8222416. *E:* sinclair@zoology.ubc.ca.

SINCLAIR, Carolyn Elizabeth Cunningham, (Mrs S. J. Bowen); Director, Constitutional and Community Policy Directorate, and Registrar of the Baronetage, Home Office, 1996–2001; *b* 13 July 1944; *d* of John Archibald Sinclair and Grace Margaret Stuart Sinclair (*née* Cunningham); *m* 1979, Stephen John Bowen. *Educ:* Laurel Bank Sch., Glasgow; Brown Univ., RI; Edinburgh Univ. (MA Hist.); Univ. of E Africa (Leverhulme Schol.; MA Pol Sci.). Joined FCO, 1968; Vienna, 1970–73; Private Sec. to Minister of State, 1977–78; transferred to HM Treasury, 1979; Prime Minister's Policy Unit, 1988–92; transf. to Home Office, as Asst Under-Sec. of State, 1992. *Recreations:* gardening, listening to music, reading, seeing friends.

SINCLAIR, Charles James Francis, CBE 2009; FCA; Chairman, Associated British Foods plc, since 2009 (non-executive Director, since 2008); *b* 4 April 1948; *s* of Sir George (Evelyn) Sinclair, CMG, OBE and Katharine Jane Sinclair (*née* Burdekin); *m* 1974, Nicola Bayliss; two *s*. *Educ:* Winchester Coll.; Magdalen Coll., Oxford (BA). ACA 1974, FCA 1980. VSO, Zambia, 1966–67. Dearden Farrow, CA, 1970–75; joined Associated Newspapers Holdings, 1975; Asst Man. Dir and Mem. Main Bd, 1986; Man. Dir, 1988 (Associated Newspapers

Holdings became the wholly-owned operating subsid. of Daily Mail and General Trust, 1988); Gp Chief Exec., Daily Mail and General Trust plc, 1988–2008. Non-executive Director: Euromoney Institutional Investor PLC, 1985–2008; Schroders plc, 1990–2004; Reuters Group plc, 1994–2005; SVG Capital plc, 2005–13; Mem., UK Adv. Bd, Spencer Stuart, 2006–12 (Chm., 2009–12). Chm. of Trustees, Minack Theatre Trust, Porthcurno, Cornwall, 1985–; Mem., UK Cttee, VSO, 2006–11. Mem., Adv. Bd, Reuters Inst. for Study of Journalism, Univ. of Oxford, 2007–10. Gov., Courtauld Inst. of Art, 2011–14; Warden, Winchester Coll., 2014– (Fellow, 2010). *Recreations:* theatre, opera, fishing, ski-ing. *Address:* Associated British Foods plc, Weston Centre, 10 Grosvenor Street, W1K 4QY. *Clubs:* Athenæum, Flyfishers'; Vincent's (Oxford).

SINCLAIR, Sir Clive (Marles), Kt 1983; Chairman, Sinclair Research Ltd, since 1979; *b* 30 July 1940; *s* of late George William Carter Sinclair and Thora Edith Ella (*née* Marles); *m* 1st, 1962, Ann (*née* Trevor Briscoe) (marr. diss. 1985; she *d* 2004); two *s* one *d*; 2nd, 2010, Angie Bowness. *Educ:* Boxgrove Prep. Sch., Guildford; Highgate; Reading; St George's Coll., Weybridge. Editor, Bernards Publishers Ltd, 1958–61; Chairman: Sinclair Radionics Ltd, 1962–79; Sinclair Browne Ltd, 1981–85; Cambridge Computer Ltd, 1986–90; Dir, Shaye Communications Ltd, 1986–91. Vis. Fellow, Robinson Coll., Cambridge, 1982–85; Vis. Prof., Dept of Elec. Engrg, Imperial Coll. of Science, Technol. and Medicine, London, 1984–92 (Hon. Fellow, 1984). Chm., British Mensa, 1980–97 (Hon. Pres., 2001–). Hon. Fellow UMIST, 1984. Hon. DSc: Bath, 1983; Warwick, 1983; Heriot-Watt, 1983. Mullard Award, Royal Soc., 1984. *Publications:* Practical Transistor Receivers, 1959; British Semiconductor Survey, 1963. *Recreations:* music, poetry, mathematics, science, poker. *Address:* 1A Spring Gardens, Trafalgar Square, SW1A 2BB. *T:* (office) (020) 7839 6868, *Fax:* (020) 7839 6622, *T:* (home) (020) 7839 7744. *Clubs:* National Liberal, Royal Automobile.

SINCLAIR, Douglas, CBE 2001; Member, since 2007 and Chairman, since 2014, Accounts Commission for Scotland (Deputy Chairman, 2009–14); *b* 28 Jan. 1946; *s* of Douglas Matheson Sinclair and Agnes Jack Sinclair; *m* 1969, Mairi MacPhee; two *d*. *Educ:* Edinburgh Univ. (MA Hons Politics). Admin. Asst, Midlothian, E Lothian and Peebles Social Work Dept, 1969–72; Admin. Officer, Barnardo's, Scotland, 1972–75; Depute Dir of Admin, 1975–78, Dir of Admin, 1978–85, Western Isles Is Council; Chief Executive: Ross and Cromarty DC, 1985–90; Central Regl Council, 1990–95; COSLA, 1995–99; Fife Council, 1999–2006. Chair, Scottish Consumer Council, later Consumer Focus Scotland, 2006–13; Chm., Scotland Cttee, Consumer Futures, 2013–14; Mem., Audit and Adv. Cttee, Scottish Public Services Ombudsman. Dir, St Andrews Botanic Garden Trust. *Recreations:* Scottish literature, music, gardening, walking. *Address:* Accounts Commission for Scotland, 110 George Street, Edinburgh EH2 4LH.

SINCLAIR, Fiona Mary; QC 2013; *b* Chester; *d* of John Mark Sinclair and Emily Georgina Sinclair; partner, Paul Maung-Maung; one *s*. *Educ:* Jesus Coll., Cambridge (BA 1987; LLM 1998). Called to the Bar, Inner Temple, 1989; Mem., Lincoln's Inn, 2000–; in practice as a barrister, specialising in internat. and domestic construction, professional liability and insurance dispute resolution. *Publications:* (ed) Jackson and Powell on Professional Negligence, 3rd edn 1992 to 7th edn 2012. *Recreations:* ski-ing, mountaineering, Italy, reading. *Address:* Four New Square, Lincoln's Inn, WC2A 3RJ. *T:* (020) 7822 2000. *E:* f.sinclair@4newsquare.com.

SINCLAIR, Maj.-Gen. George Brian, CB 1983; CBE 1975; Engineer-in-Chief (Army), 1980–83; *b* 21 July 1928; *s* of Thomas S. Sinclair and Blanche Sinclair; *m* 1953, Edna Margaret Richardson (*d* 2011); two *s* one *d*. *Educ:* Christ's College, Finchley; RMA Sandhurst. Commissioned, Royal Engineers, 1948; served UK, BAOR, Korea, and Christmas Island, 1948–66; Directing Staff, Staff College, Camberley, 1967–69; CRE, Near East, 1970–71; Col GS, HQ 1st British Corps, 1972–74; Nat. Defence Coll., India, 1975; Commandant Royal School of Military Engineering, 1976–77; BGS, Military Operations, MoD, 1978–80. Col Comdt, RE, 1983–91; Hon. Col, Engineer and Transport Staff Corps, 1988–93. Vice Pres., Red R (formerly Register of Engrs for Disaster Relief), 1985–98; Trustee: Imperial War Mus., 1990–2000; RE Museum Foundn, 1993–2001. Mem., Smeatonian Soc. of Civil Engrs, 1985–. Governor, King's Sch., Rochester, 1984–97. Freeman, City of London, 1981. DL Kent, 1996–97. *Publications:* The Staff Corps: the history of the Engineer and Logistic Staff Corps RE, 2001. *Recreations:* hill walking, bird watching and discussion. *Address:* Brockie's Hole, The Croft, St Boswells, Roxburghshire TD6 0AE. *Club:* Army and Navy (Chm., 1995–97; Trustee, 1999–2006).

SINCLAIR, Rt Rev. (Gordon) Keith; *see* Birkenhead, Bishop Suffragan of.

SINCLAIR, Rt Hon. Ian (McCahon), AC 2001; PC 1977; Chairman, Foundation for Rural and Regional Renewal, since 1999; *b* 10 June 1929; *s* of George McCahon Sinclair and Gertrude Hazel Sinclair; *m* 1st, 1956, Margaret Tarrant (*d* 1967); one *s* two *d*; 2nd, 1970, Rosemary Fenton; one *s*. *Educ:* Knox Grammar Sch., Wahroonga, NSW; Sydney Univ. BA, LLB. Barrister; grazier. Mem. Legislative Council, NSW, 1961–63; MP (Nat.) New England, NSW, 1963–98; Minister for: Social Services, 1965–68; Trade and Industry (Minister Assisting Minister), 1966–71; Shipping and Transport, 1968–71; Primary Industry, 1971–72; Leader of House for Opposition, 1974–75; Country Party spokesman for Defence, Foreign Affairs, Law and Agriculture, 1973; Opposition spokesman on primary industry, 1974–75; Leader of House, 1975–79; Minister for: Agriculture and N Territory, Nov.–Dec. 1975; Primary Industry, 1975–79; Special Trade Representations, 1980; Communications, 1980–82; Defence, 1982–83; Leader of the House for the Opposition, 1983–89; Shadow Minister: Defence, 1983–87; Trade and Resources, 1987–89; of State, Jan.–May 1994; Speaker, House of Reps, Australia, 1998. Member Committee: House of Reps Standing Orders, 1974–79, 1980–82, 1983–84; Privileges, 1980–82; Legal and Constitutional Affairs, 1990–98; Jt Foreign Affairs, Defence and Trade, 1990–98 (Chm., 1996–98); Nat. Crime Authority, 1990–98; Member: Jt Standing Cttee on Migration Regulations, 1990–98; Jt Cttee on Corps and Securities, 1990–98; Parly Code of Conduct Working Gp, 1994–96. Perm. Rep., Exec., IPU, 1996–98; Chm., Aust. Parly Gps for UK, PNG, Uruguay and Vietnam, 1996–98. Dep. Leader, 1971–84, Leader, 1984–89, Nat. Party of Australia. Dir, Farmers and Graziers Cooperative Ltd, 1962–65. Chairman: Australian Constitutional Convention, 1998; Australian Rural Summit, 1999; Australian Sheep Cooperative Res. Centre, 2002–07; Co-Chairman: NSW Drugs Summit, 1999; NSW Salinity Summit, 2000; SA Economic Summit, 2003; NSW Health Care Adv. Council, 2005–11. Chairman: Good Beginnings (Australia), 2000–10; Australia Taiwan Business Council, 2000–08; Dir, Regl Australia Inst., 2011–. President: Austcare, 2000–09; Murray Darling Basin Commn, 2003–08; Scouts Australia (NSW), 2003–. Adjunct Prof. of Social Scis (Pol Sci.), Univ. of New England, 2000–. DUniv New England, 1999; Hon. DLitt Southern Cross, 2005. *Address:* Mulberry Farm, Dumaresq Island, NSW 2430, Australia. *T:* (2) 65538276, *Fax:* (2) 65538358. *E:* iansinclair@ozemail.com.au. *Clubs:* Australian, University and Schools (Sydney).

SINCLAIR, James Boyd A.; *see* Alexander-Sinclair.

SINCLAIR, Rev. Jane Elizabeth Margaret; Canon Steward, Westminster Abbey, since 2014; *b* 1956. *Educ:* St Hugh's Coll., Oxford (BA 1978; MA 1980); St John's Coll., Nottingham (BA Nottingham Univ. 1982). Ordained deaconess, 1983, deacon, 1987, priest, 1994; Deaconess, St Paul's, Herne Hill, London, 1983–86; Chaplain, and Lectr in Liturgy and Pastoral Studies, St John's Coll., Nottingham, 1986–93; Canon Residentiary and Precentor, 1993–2003, Hon. Canon, 2003–07, Sheffield Cathedral; Vicar, Rotherham, 2003–07; Sec., Convocation of York, 2005–07; Archdeacon of Stow and Lindsey, 2007–14. Member: Liturgical Commn of C of E, 1986–2001; Archbishop's Commn on Church Music, 1989–92; Gen. Synod of C of E, 1995–2007; Clergy Discipline Commn, 2013–; Comr, Cathedrals Fabric Commn for England, 2001–10. *Address:* 2 Little Cloister, SW1P 3PL. *E:* jane.sinclair@westminister-abbey.org.

SINCLAIR, Jeremy Theodorson; Chairman, M & C Saatchi plc, since 2004 (Founder and Partner, since 1995); *b* 4 Nov. 1946; *s* of Lilian Theodora Sinclair and Donald Alan Forrester Sinclair; *m* 1976, Jacqueline Margaret Metcalfe; two *s* one *d*. *Educ:* Rannoch Sch., Perthshire; Watford Art Sch. Saatchi & Saatchi and Co.: Jt Founder, 1970; Dir, 1973–95; Head of Creative Dept, 1973–86; Chairman: UK Agency, 1982–86; Saatchi & Saatchi International, 1986–95. Pres., D&AD, 1987. Chm., Art Acad., 1999–2007; Mem., Exec. Cttee, Sch. of Econ. Sci., London, 1987–2007; Chm., Ind. Educnl Assoc. Ltd, 2007– (Gov., 1999–). Organiser, Art in Action, 2004–14. Trustee: Jyotirnidhi Nyasa Trust, 2000–; Tony Blair Faith Foundn, 2008– (Chm., 2015–). *Publications:* Brutal Simplicity of Thought, 2011; Faces, Faces, Faces, 2015. *Recreations:* philosophy, economics, Italy. *Address:* M & C Saatchi plc, 36 Golden Square, W1F 9EE. *T:* (020) 7543 4500.

SINCLAIR, Karen; Member (Lab) Clwyd South, National Assembly for Wales, 1999–2011; *b* 20 Nov. 1952; *m* 1973, Mike Sinclair; one *s* one *d*. *Educ:* Grove Park Girls' Sch., Wrexham; Cartrefle Coll., Wrexham. Contracted Care Manager of home for learning disabled adults, Wrexham Social Services, 1990–99. CAB Advr, 1995–97. Member (Lab): Glyndwr DC, 1988–95; Denbighshire CC, 1997–99. Minister for Assembly Business, Nat. Assembly for Wales, 2003–05. Mem., N Wales Cancer Forum, 2010–. *Recreations:* reading, gentle walking, family.

SINCLAIR, Rt Rev. Keith; *see* Sinclair, Rt Rev. G. K.

SINCLAIR, Lindsay Neil; Group Chief Executive, NFU Mutual Insurance Society, since 2008; *b* Palmerston North, NZ, 19 Aug. 1956; *s* of Graeme Sinclair and Ann Sinclair (*née* O'Keeffe); *m* 1984, Janet Scholma; two *d*. *Educ:* Poole Grammar Sch. ACIB 1990. Bank Officer: Midland Bank, UK, 1974–76; Barclays Internat., UK, France and Netherlands Antilles, 1976–85; Standard Chartered Bank, Bahrain, San Francisco, Hong Kong, Sri Lanka, 1985–95; Sen. Manager, Commercial Banking, Amsterdam, 1996–98, Hd, Intermediary Banking, 1998–99, ING Gp; Hd, Business Develt, 1999–2002, CEO UK, 2002–07, ING Direct. Mem. Bd, Internat. Cooperative and Mutual Insce Fedn, 2008–. Trustee, NFU Mutual Charitable Trust, 2008–. *Recreations:* researching the Pratt family of Castlemartyr 1647–, reading (history and travel), listening to music, walking, the arts. *Address:* NFU Mutual, Tiddington Road, Stratford upon Avon CV37 7BJ. *T:* (01789) 265388.

SINCLAIR, Martin John; Executive Leader (formerly Assistant Auditor General), National Audit Office, since 1999; *b* 24 April 1957; *s* of late Malcolm Sinclair and of Susan Sinclair; *m* 1996, Joke Pouw; one *s* one *d*. *Educ:* Glasgow Univ. (MPhil Town and Regl Planning). CPFA 1985. Joined Nat. Audit Office, 1981 (Mem., Mgt Bd, 1999–). *Recreations:* hill-walking, swimming, reading. *Address:* National Audit Office, 157–197 Buckingham Palace Road, SW1W 9SP. *T:* (020) 7798 7180.

SINCLAIR, Matthew John Hayes; Senior Consultant, Europe Economics, since 2014; *b* Reading, 10 Dec. 1983; *s* of Michael Paul and Michelle Anne Sinclair; *m* 2013, Arianna Capuani. *Educ:* London Sch. of Econs and Pol Sci. (BSc Econs and Econ. Hist.; MSc Econ. Hist.). Taxpayers' Alliance: Policy Analyst, 2007–08; Res. Dir, 2008–12; Chief Exec., 2012–14. *Publications:* (ed) How to Cut Public Spending and Still Win an Election, 2010; Let Them Eat Carbon: the price of failing climate change policies, and how governments and big business profit from them, 2011. *Address:* Europe Economics, Chancery House, 53–64 Chancery Lane, WC2A 1QU. *E:* Matthew.Sinclair@europe-economics.com.

SINCLAIR, Rt Rev. Maurice Walter; an Hon. Assistant Bishop, Diocese of Birmingham, since 2002; *b* 20 Jan. 1937; *s* of Maurice and Dorothea Sinclair; *m* 1962, Gillian (*née* Spooner); four *s*. *Educ:* Chigwell Sch.; Nottingham Univ. (BSc 1959); Leicester Univ. (PGCE 1960); Tyndale Hall, Bristol. Asst Master, Brays Grove County Secondary Sch., Harlow, Essex, 1960–62. Ordained, 1964; Asst Curate, St John's Church, Boscombe, 1964–67; Missionary, South American Missionary Soc., serving in Argentina, 1967–78; Personnel Sec., 1979–83, Asst Gen. Sec., 1983–84, South American Missionary Soc.; Principal, Crowther Hall, Selly Oak Colls, 1984–90; Bp of Northern Argentina, 1990–2001 and Presiding Bp (Primate), Province of Southern Cone of America, 1995–2001. Dean, All Saints Cathedral, Cairo, 2004–05; Hon. Asst Bp, Dio. Egypt, 2009–. Faculty Mem., Alexandria Sch. of Theol., 2006–. Hon. DD Nashotah House Seminary, 2001. Ibo chief, Nigeria, 1987. *Publications:* Green Finger of God, 1980; Ripening Harvest Gathering Storm, 1988; Way of Faithfulness, 1999; To Mend the Net, 2001; Pathways of Wisdom, 2010. *Recreations:* gardening, hill walking, running. *Address:* 55 Selly Wick Drive, Selly Park, Birmingham B29 7JQ. *T:* (0121) 471 2617.

SINCLAIR, Murray Alexander; Solicitor to Scottish Government and Head, Government Legal Service for Scotland, since 2007; *b* Falkirk, 29 May 1961; *s* of late Peter Sinclair and of Kathleen Sinclair; one *s* one *d*. *Educ:* Dollar Acad.; Christ Church, Oxford (MA Hons Juris.); Univ. of Edinburgh (LLB with Dist.; DipLP). Trained, qualified and practised as solicitor with Dundas and Wilson CS, 1985–89; joined Scottish Office, 1989; legal advr to depts incl. Justice Dept, 1989–97; Mem. and legal advr, Constitution Gp, 1997–99; Sen. Civil Service, 1999; Head: Legal Div., 1999–2004; Constitution and Parly Secretariat, 2004–07. *Recreations:* walking, football, reading, staring at the night sky. *Address:* Scottish Government, Victoria Quay, Edinburgh EH6 6QQ. *T:* (0131) 244 0531. *E:* murray.sinclair@scotland.gsi.gov.uk.

SINCLAIR, Rear-Adm. the Hon. Peter Ross, AC 1992 (AO (mil.) 1986); Governor of New South Wales, 1990–96; farmer, Flagship Poll Hereford Stud; *b* 16 Nov. 1934; *s* of late G. P. Sinclair; *m* 1957, Shirley, *d* of J. A. McLellan; one *s* two *d*. *Educ:* North Sydney Boys' High Sch.; Royal Aust. Naval Coll.; Royal Coll. of Defence Studies. jssc. Joined RAN 1948; served HM Australian ships Australia, Tobruk, Vengeance, Arunta, Swan, Sydney, Vendetta, Vampire, Penguin, HMS Maidstone, HMS Jutland; CO HMAS Duchess, 1970–72; CO HMAS Hobart, 1974–77; Dir, Naval Plans, 1979–80; Dir-Gen., Mil. Staff Branch, Strategic and Internat. Policy Div., Defence Dept, 1980–82; Chief of Staff, 1983–84; First Comdt, Aust. Defence Force Acad., 1984–86; Maritime Comdr Australia, 1986–90 and Dep. Chief of Naval Staff, 1989. Chm. Council, Order of Australia, 1996–2002. Hon. FIEAust 1994; CPEng 1994. DUniv Sydney, 1992. KStJ 1991. *Recreations:* painting, sketching, whittling, reading, cricket, golf, tennis. *Address:* Post Office, Tea Gardens, NSW 2324, Australia.

SINCLAIR, Sir Robert (John), Kt 2001; Chairman: Lae Builders & Contractors Ltd, since 1974; Lae International Hotel Ltd, since 1977; *b* 21 Nov. 1943; *s* of William Arthur Sinclair; *m* 1985, Phuong Lan; three *s* two *d*. *Educ:* St Mary's Primary High Sch., PNG. Chm., PNG Post Ltd, 2000–. Chm., PNG Apprenticeship Bd, 1996–. *Recreation:* breeding thoroughbred horses. *Address:* PO Box 1730, Lae, Papua New Guinea. *T:* (675) 4724109, *Fax:* (675) 4725494. *Clubs:* Papua (Port Moresby); Royal Yacht (Lae).

SINCLAIR, Sonia Elizabeth, (Mrs A. A. Sinclair); Board Member, Royal Court Theatre, 1974–84; *b* 6 Sept. 1925; *d* of Col R. H. Graham; *m* 1st, 1947, Hon. Julian Mond, later 3rd Baron Melchett (*d* 1973); one *s* two *d*; 2nd, 1984, Dr Andrew Annandale Sinclair, *qv*. *Educ:* Royal School, Bath. Board Member: NSPCC, 1960–70; Nat. Theatre, then RNT, 1984–94. JP Marylebone, 1962–72. *Publications:* Tell Me, Honestly, 1964; Someone is Missing, 1987; Passionate Quests, 1991. *Recreations:* reading, walking, swimming, foreign travel. *Address:* Flat 20, Millennium House, 132 Grosvenor Road, SW1V 3JY. *T:* (020) 7976 6958.

See also Baron Melchett.

SINCLAIR, Susan Myraid; Sheriff of North Strathclyde at Paisley, since 2002; *b* 16 Sept. 1958; *d* of William Stevenson Sinclair and Myraid Elizabeth Sinclair; *m* 1983, David Robert Adie. *Educ:* Glasgow Univ. (MA Hons; LLB; DLP). Solicitor, 1983; Advocate, 1988; Pt-time Chm., Appeals Service, 1996–2001; Temp. Sheriff, 1998–99; Pt-time Sheriff, 2000–01; All Scotland Floating Sheriff, 2001–02. Pt-time tutor, Univ. of Glasgow, 1995–97. *Recreations:* sailing, scuba diving, walking, reading, theatre.

SINCLAIR, Sir William (Robert Francis), 11th Bt *cr* 1704 (NS), of Dunbeath, Caithness-shire; entrepreneur, since 2011; *b* London, 27 March 1979; *s* of Sir Patrick Robert Richard Sinclair, 10th Bt and of Susan Catherine Beresford Davies, *e d* of Geoffrey Clive Davies, OBE; *S* father, 2011; *m* 2011, Piriyah Sivagnanam, MB BS, BSc, MRCS; one *s*. *Educ:* Winchester Coll.; Imperial Coll., London; South Bank Univ. (BEng Civil Engrg). Engrg Surveyor, MAL Ltd, 2006–11; Man. Dir, H2I Ltd, 2011–. *Recreations:* cycling, field sports, kite surfing. *Heir: s* Robert (John Pulavan) Sinclair, *b* 6 March 2013. *Address:* 209 Greenkeepers Road, Great Denham, Bedford MK40 4RQ.

SINCLAIR-LOCKHART, Sir Simon (John Edward Francis), 15th Bt *cr* 1636 (NS); *b* 22 July 1941; *s* of Sir Muir Edward Sinclair-Lockhart, 14th Bt, and of Olga Ann, *d* of late Claude Victor White-Parsons, Hawkes Bay, NZ; *S* father, 1985; *m* 1973, Felicity Edith, *d* of late I. L. C. Stewart, NZ; one *s* one *d* (and one *s* decd). *Heir: yr* twin *s* James Lachlan Sinclair-Lockhart, *b* 12 Sept. 1973. *Address:* 62 Muritai Crescent, Havelock North, Hawke's Bay, New Zealand.

SINCLAIR-STEVENSON, Christopher Terence; literary agent, since 1995; *b* 27 June 1939; *s* of late George Sinclair-Stevenson, MBE and Gloria Sinclair-Stevenson; *m* 1965, Deborah Susan (*née* Walker-Smith). *Educ:* Eton Coll.; St John's Coll., Cambridge (MA). Joined Hamish Hamilton Ltd, 1961, Dir, 1970, Man. Dir, 1974–89; Man. Dir, Sinclair-Stevenson Ltd, 1989–92; Publisher, Sinclair-Stevenson, and Editor-in-Chief, Reed Consumer Books, 1992–95; Consultant, Sinclair-Stevenson, 1995–96. *Publications:* The Gordon Highlanders, 1968; Inglorious Rebellion, 1971; The Life of a Regiment, 1974; Blood Royal, 1979; That Sweet Enemy, 1987; (ed) Enjoy!, 2000. *Recreations:* music, travel, food, the written word. *Address:* 3 South Terrace, SW7 2TB. *T:* (020) 7584 8087.

SINCLAIRE, Nicole; Member, West Midlands Region, European Parliament, 2009–14 (UK Ind, 2009–10, Ind, 2010–12, We Demand a Referendum, 2012–14); *b* London, 26 July 1968. *Educ:* Univ. of Kent. New Business Liaison Officer, Lloyds Blackhorse Life; Store Manager, Gateway Food Mkts; hospitality, Cyprus; Hd Office Manager, UKIP; Political Advr to Michael Nattrass, MEP. Contested (We Demand a Referendum) W Midlands, EP, 2014. *Publications:* Never Give Up: standing tall through adversity (autobiog.), 2013. *Recreations:* foreign travel, playing football, avid supporter of Liverpool FC.

SINDALL, Adrian John, CMG 1993; HM Diplomatic Service, retired; Chairman, Council for British Research in the Levant, 1997–2005; *b* 5 Oct. 1937; *s* of Stephen Sindall and Clare Mallet; *m* 1st, 1958; one *s* one *d*; 2nd, 1978, Jill Margaret Cowley. *Educ:* Battersea Grammar Sch. FO, 1956–58; ME Centre for Arab Studies, 1958–60; Third Sec. (Commercial), Baghdad, 1960–62; Second Sec., British Embassy, Rabat, 1962–67; First Secretary: FCO, 1967–70; Beirut, 1970–72; First Sec. and Head of Chancery, British Embassy, Lima, 1972–76; FCO, 1976–79; Counsellor, Head of Chancery and Consul-Gen., Amman, 1979–82; Hd of S America Dept, FCO, 1982–85; Consul-Gen., Sydney, 1985–88; ME Marketing Dir, Defence Export Services Orgn, MoD, on secondment, 1988–91; High Comr, Brunei, 1991–94; Ambassador to Syria, 1994–96. Sen. Diplomatic Consultant, Landair Internat. Chairman: Gtr London Fund for the Blind, 1997–99; Internat. Adv. Panel, Nat. Lottery Charities Bd, 1997–2003; Arab-British Centre, 1997–2001; Vice-Chm., Medical Aid for Palestinians, 1997–99; Mem. Adv. Council, London Middle East Inst., SOAS (formerly Mem. Adv. Bd, Centre for Near and Middle Eastern Studies), 1997–2010. Mem., RIIA. SPMB (Negara Brunei Darussalam), 1992. *Address:* 11 The Woodlands, Kings Worthy, Hants SO23 7QQ. *Club:* English-Speaking Union.

SINDALL, Barry John; Chief Executive, Grammar Schools Headteachers Association, since 2008; Headmaster, Colyton Grammar School, Devon, 1990–2008; *b* 20 Oct. 1945; *s* of Reginald and Kathleen Sindall; *m* 1975, Margaret Eleanor Barker; one *s* one *d*. *Educ:* Univ. of Exeter (MEd). Teacher of Hist., Duncan Bowen Secondary Mod. Sch., Ashford, Kent, 1967–68; Hd of Humanities, R. M. Bailey High Sch., Nassau, Bahamas, 1968–76; Dir of Studies, Colyton GS, 1976–88; Dep. Headteacher, Torquay Boys' GS, 1988–90. Consultant Hd to Nat. Leading Edge prog., 2006–13. Trustee, W of England Sch. for Young People with Little or No Sight, 2010–. FRSA 1994. *Recreations:* amateur dramatics, cricket, fell-walking, ski-ing, lifelong supporter of Tranmere Rovers. *Club:* Somerset County Cricket.

SINES, Prof. David Thomas, CBE 2010; PhD; FRCN; Pro Vice Chancellor and Executive Dean, Faculty of Society and Health, Buckinghamshire New University, 2009–14, now Emeritus Professor and Associate; *b* Woking, 7 April 1954; *s* of Thomas Sines and Anne Patricia Sines; *m* (marr. diss.); one *s*. *Educ:* Brunel Univ. (BSc Hons Sociol./Psychol. with Nursing 1977); Univ. of Southampton (PhD 1990); Univ. of Ulster (PGCHE 1993). FRCN 1989. Community Charge Nurse, NW Surrey Dist Health Authy, 1977–79; Community Nursing Officer, Richmond, Twickenham and Roehampton Health Authy, 1979–85; Dir, Nursing and Gen. Manager, Winchester HA, 1985–90; Prof. of Community Health Nursing, and Hd, Sch. of Health Scis, Univ. of Ulster, 1990–99; Prof. of Community Health Care Nursing, and Exec. Dean, Health and Social Care, London South Bank Univ., 1999–2009. Associate non-exec. Dir, Bucks Hosps NHS Trust, 2012–; non-exec. Dir, Central London Community Healthcare NHS Trust, 2012–. Dir, British Sch. of Osteopathy, 2007–13. Trustee, Burdett Nursing Trust, 2014–. *Publications:* Community Health Care Nursing, 1995, 5th edn 2013. *Recreations:* walking, reading, theatre, cinema. *Address:* Buckinghamshire New University, 106 Oxford Road, Uxbridge, Middx UB8 1NA. *T:* 07787 002297. *E:* david.sines@icloud.com.

SINGARES ROBINSON, Ariadne Elizabeth; Ambassador of Panama to the Court of St James's, 2000–04; *b* Panama, 24 Sept. 1961; *m* Andrew Ian Robinson; one *d*. *Educ:* Knox Sch., Long Island, NY; Le Château Mont-Choisi, Geneva; Stony Brook Univ., NY; Parson Sch. of Design, Manhattan; New York Univ. A designer and personal asst to Gerald Franklin, Canadian designer of haute couture, NY, 1985–88. Member: Breast Cancer Assoc., Race for Life; City Harvest; Meals on Wheels; volunteer, St Lucas Hosp., Manhattan.

SINGER, His Honour Harold Samuel; a Circuit Judge, 1984–2003; *b* 17 July 1935; *s* of Ellis and Minnie Singer; *m* 1966, Adèle Berenice Emanuel; one *s* two *d*. *Educ:* Salford Grammar School; Fitzwilliam House, Cambridge (MA). Called to the Bar, Gray's Inn, 1957; a Recorder, 1981–84. *Recreations:* music, painting, books, photography.

SINGER, Sir (Jan) Peter, Kt 1993; family dispute resolution facilitator, mediator and arbitrator, since 2010; *b* 10 Sept. 1944; *s* of late Dr Hanus Kurt Singer and Anita Singer; *m* 1st, 1970, Julia Mary Caney (marr. diss. 2006; she *d* 2011); one *s* one *d*; 2nd, 2010, Maria Healy. *Educ:* King Edward's School, Birmingham; Selwyn College, Cambridge. MCIArb 2012. Called to the Bar, Inner Temple, 1967, Bencher, 1993; QC 1987; a Recorder, 1987–93; Judge of the High Court of Justice, Family Div., 1993–2010; NE Circuit Liaison Judge, 1993–2001. A Chm., Family Law Bar Assoc., 1990–92 (Sec., 1980–83, Treasurer, 1983–90); Member: Matrimonial Causes Rule Cttee, 1981–85; Senate of Inns of Court and Bar, 1983–86; Law Soc. Legal Aid Cttee, 1984–89; Gen. Council of the Bar, 1990–92. Vice-Pres., European Chapter, Internat. Acad. of Matrimonial Lawyers, 1992–93. Joint Editor: Capitalise (software), 1998–; @eGlance (software), 2001–; Care (software), 2003–07; www.FamilyArbitrator.com, 2012–. *Publications:* (ed jtly) Rayden on Divorce, 14th edn, 1983; (ed jtly) At A Glance, annually 1992–; (Consulting Ed.) Essential Family Practice, 2000–02; (ed jtly) Financial Remedies Practice, annually, 2012–. *Recreations:* travel, avoiding vegetating. *Address:* 1 Hare Court, Temple, EC4Y 7BE. *E:* SirPeterSinger.ADR@dsl.pipex.com.

SINGER, Norbert, CBE 1990; PhD; FRSC; Vice Chancellor, University of Greenwich (formerly Director, Thames Polytechnic), 1978–93; *b* 3 May 1931; *s* of late Salomon Singer and Mina Korn; *m* Brenda Margaret Walter, *e d* of late Richard and Gladys Walter, Tunbridge Wells, Kent. *Educ:* Highbury County School; Queen Mary Coll., London (BSc, PhD). CChem, FRSC. Research Chemist and Project Leader, Morgan Crucible Co. Ltd, 1954–57; Lecturer, Senior Lectr, Principal Lectr and Dep. Head of Department, Dept of Chemistry, Northern Polytechnic, 1958–70; Head of Dept of Life Sciences 1971–74, Professor of Life Sciences 1972–74, Polytechnic of Central London; Asst Dir, then Dep. Dir, Polytechnic of N London, 1974–78. Vis. Prof., Univ. of Westminster, 1996–99. Council for National Academic Awards: Mem., 1982–88; Chm., Reviews Co-ordination Sub-Cttee, 1984–87; Vice Chm., Cttee for Academic and Institutional Policy, 1985–87; Mem., Accreditation Cttee, 1987–89; Chm., Cttee for CATs, 1990–93. Mem., MSC Nat. Steering Gp, TVEI, 1984–88 (Mem., Quality and Standards Gp, 1987–89). Chairman: Bexley HA, 1993–94; Oxleas (formerly Bexley Community Health) NHS Trust, 1994–2001. Chm., Governing Body, Rose Bruford Coll., 1994–99; Governor: London Inst., 1993–99; Nene Coll., Northants, 1993–97; St Peter's C of E Primary Sch., Tunbridge Wells, 1995–2004 (Chm., 2004–10). Fellow: QMW, 1993; Nene Coll., 1998. Hon. DSc Greenwich, 1993. *Publications:* research papers in electrochemistry, theoretical chemistry and surface chemistry in scientific jls. *Recreation:* reading. *Address:* Croft Lodge, Bayhall Road, Tunbridge Wells, Kent TN2 4TP. *T:* (01892) 523821.

SINGER, Hon. Sir Peter; *see* Singer, Hon. Sir J. P.

SINGER, Philip Francis; QC 1994; a Recorder, 1989–2013; *b* 1 Dec. 1940; *s* of late Abraham Singer and Sylvia Singer (*née* Hyman); *m* 1978, Heather Angela Cutt. *Educ:* Bedford Modern Sch.; Bishop's Stortford Coll.; St John's Coll., Cambridge (MA, LLM). Called to the Bar, Inner Temple, 1964.

SINGER, Sara Catherine; *see* Nathan, S. C.

SINGER, Susan Honor; educational consultant, since 2003; Headmistress, Guildford High School, 1991–2002; *b* 23 Feb. 1942; *d* of late Brig. John James McCully, DSO and Honor Goad McCully (*née* Ward, later Mrs E. B. Elliott); *m* 1964, Christopher Ronald Morgan Singer; one *s* two *d*. *Educ:* St Mary's, Calne; Open Univ. (BA); Garnett Coll. (PGCE). Set up and ran pre-school playgroup, E Sheen, 1968–74; St Paul's Girls' School: maths teacher, 1980–91; Head of Middle School, 1988–91; Head of Maths, 1990–91. President: GSA, 2001; Mathematical Assoc., 2005–06. *Recreation:* transatlantic sailing 1907 gaff cutter. *Address:* 39 East Sheen Avenue, SW14 8AR. *T:* (020) 8876 4031.

SINGH, family name of **Baron Singh of Wimbledon**.

SINGH OF WIMBLEDON, Baron *cr* 2011 (Life Peer), of Wimbledon in the London Borough of Merton; **Indarjit Singh,** CBE 2009 (OBE 1996); JP; CEng; Director, Network of Sikh Organisations (UK), since 1995; *b* 17 Sept. 1932; *s* of Dr Diwan Singh and Kundan K. Singh; *m* 1962, Dr Kanwaljit Kaur; two *d*. *Educ:* Birmingham Univ. (MCom, MBA). CEng 1967; MIMinE 1967. Worked in sen. positions in mining and civil engrg, 1955–75: NCB, 1955–59, 1965–67; manager of mines, India, 1959–65; with Costain, 1967–75; mgt consultant in various areas of local govt, Gtr London, 1975–. Founder Mem., 1987–, Vice Chair, 2010–, Interfaith-Network UK (Co-Chair, 1989–92); hon. work for Sikh community and in promotion of inter-faith understanding, 1993–. Mem., All Party Parly Gp for Religious Educn, 2012; Vice Chair, All Party Parly Gp for Freedom of Religion and Belief, 2013–. Editor, Sikh Messenger (qly mag.), 1984–. Has made broadcasts on religious and current affairs, incl. Any Questions, Thought for the Day. JP Wimbledon, 1984. UK Templeton Prize for the promotion of inter-faith understanding, 1989; Inter-faith Medallion for services to religious broadcasting, BBC and CCJ, 1991. Hon. DLitt Coventry, 2002; Hon. DLaws Leicester, 2004. *Recreations:* writing, broadcasting, debating, grandchildren. *Address:* 43 Dorset Road, Merton Park, SW19 3EZ. *T:* (020) 8540 4148. *E:* sikhmessenger@aol.com.

SINGH, Darra, OBE 2004; Partner, Government and Public Sector team, Ernst & Young, since 2013 (Executive Director, 2012–13); *b* 26 July 1959; *s* of Lachsman Singh and Gurmit Kaur; *m* 1995, Monika Singh; one *d*. *Educ:* Fairfax Secondary Sch., Bradford; Newcastle upon Tyne Poly. (BA Hons Law 1981). Housing caseworker, Tyneside Housing Aid Centre, 1983; Housing Advr, London Housing Aid Centre, 1983–85; housing campaign worker, Housing Campaign for Single People, 1985–88; Sen. Policy and Res. Officer, London Housing Unit, 1988–90; Regl Dir, North British Housing Assoc., 1990–92; Chief Executive: Asra Greater London Housing Assoc., 1992–95; Hexagon Housing Assoc., 1995–2000; Regl Dir, Audit Commn, 2000–01; Chief Executive: Luton BC, 2001–05; Ealing LBC, 2005–09; Jobcentre Plus, DWP, 2009–11; Chair, Communities and Victims Panel, 2011–12. Mem., Balance of Funding Review Gp, ODPM, 2004. Chm., Commn of Integration and Cohesion, 2006–07. *Recreations:* motor bikes, guitar-based bands, films. *Address:* (office) 1 More London Place, SE1 2AF.

SINGH, Deepak; Senior Vice President, RR Donnelley & Sons, since 2011; *b* Ethiopia, 1964; *s* of Surjan Singh and Suman L. Singh; *m* 1986, Sally Ruth Westwood; one *s* two *d*. *Educ:* Univ. of York (BA Hons Pols). Team Leader, Jaguar Cars Ltd, 1988–91; Application Services Manager, Facilities Technology Ltd, 1992–95; Sen. Proj. Manager, AstraZeneca plc, 1997–2000; Exec. Vice Pres., T-Mobile, 2001–06; Dir Gen. and Chief Inf. Officer, HMRC, 2006–09; Man. Dir, Cable & Wireless plc, 2009–10. *Recreations:* investing in the stock market, golf, football, politics and current affairs.

SINGH, Gurbux; Strategic Account Director, Department for Work and Pensions, 2012–14; *b* Punjab, India, 4 Dec. 1950; *s* of Parkesh Singh and Shaminder Kaur; *m* 2001, Siobhan Maguire; three *s*. *Educ:* Univ. of Sussex (BA Hons Pol Sci.). Housing Specialist, CRC, 1972–77; housing and local govt, CRE, 1977–83; Housing Services, GLC, 1983–85; Dep. Dir of Housing, Brent BC, 1985–87; Dir of Housing, 1987–89, Chief Exec., 1989–2000, Haringey BC; Chair, CRE, 2000–02; Man. Dir, Diverse Solutions, Mgt Consultancy, 2005–10; Contract Dir, SERCO Civil Govt, 2008–11. Mem., Home Sec.'s Race Relns Forum, 1998; Dir, N London TEC, 1990–2000; Mem. Bd, Food Standards Agency, 2000–02; Nat. Dir, Civic Educn and Democracy, Research Triangle Inst., Iraq, 2003–04. *Recreation:* supporting Wolverhampton Wanderers and the Indian cricket team. *Address:* 6 Hollycroft Gardens, Tettenhall, Wolverhampton WV6 8FB. *T:* (01902) 755366, 07810 874189.

SINGH, Kanwar N.; *see* Natwar-Singh.

SINGH, Karamjit Sukhminder, CBE 2000; Northern Ireland Judicial Appointments Ombudsman, 2006–April 2016; Chairman, University Hospitals of Leicester NHS Trust, since 2014; *b* 11 March 1950; *s* of Tara Singh and Chanan Kaur; *m* 1972, Jaswir Kaur (*d* 2014); two *s*. *Educ:* Univ. of Warwick (MA). Res. Associate, Industrial Relns Res. Unit, Univ. of Warwick, 1971–75; Caseworker, Leicester CRC, 1975–78; Sen. Exec. Officer, CRE, 1978–82; Principal Officer, W Midlands CC, 1982–84; Asst Co. Clerk, Leics CC, 1984–87; Member: Police Complaints Authy for England and Wales, 1987–90 and 1991–94; Parole Bd for England and Wales, 1994–97. Harkness Fellow, US, 1990–91. Member: Data Protection Tribunal, 1997–2003; Criminal Cases Review Commn, 1997–2006; Regulatory Decisions Cttee, FSA, 2002–06; QC Selection Panel for England and Wales, 2005–11; Social Fund Commissioner: for GB, 2009–13; for NI, 2009–15. Chm., Coventry and Warwicks NHS Partnership Trust, 2006–09. Member: Area Manpower Bd for Coventry and Warwicks, 1984–87; Industrial Tribunals Panel for England and Wales, 1986–96; Complaints Audit Cttee, Immigration and Nationality Dept, Home Office, 1994–97; Judicial Studies Bd, 1994–99; Ind. Mem., W Midlands Police Authy, 1994–96; Member: CS Commn, 1996–2000; UK Electoral Commn, 2001–10. FRSA 1995; CCMI 2002. Trustee: Citizenship Foundn, 1993–2000; Lloyds TSB Foundn for England and Wales, 2001–06; British Lung Foundn, 2007–09; Joseph Rowntree Foundn, 2014–. *Recreations:* family, reading, charity work in India.

SINGH, Laleshwar Kumar Narayan, CCH 1996; High Commissioner for Guyana in London, 1993–2015; also non-resident Ambassador to The Netherlands, 1993–2015, the Republic of France, 1995–2015, the Russian Federation, 1995–2015, the Czech Republic, 1997–2015 and the Holy See, 1998–2015; *b* 2 April 1941; *s* of late Mr and Mrs Narayan, Windsor Forest, Guyana; *m* 1971, Latchmin Ramrattan; one *s* one *d*. *Educ:* Windsor Forest Govt Sch., Guyana; Indian Educn Trust Coll., Guyana. Left Guyana, 1961; Mem., Lincoln's Inn; Clerk to the Justices, Inner London Magistrates' Courts Service, 1971–93: Bow St, Marlborough St, Highbury Corner, Clerkenwell; Old St; Principal Chief Clerk's Office, Horseferry Rd; Personnel Officer, 1988–89.

SINGH, Manmohan, DPhil; Member, Rajya Sabha, since 1991; Prime Minister of India, 2004–14, and Finance Minister, 2012–14; *b* 26 Sept. 1932; *m* Gursharan Kaur; three *d*. *Educ:* Punjab Univ.; St John's Coll., Cambridge (BA 1957); Nuffield Coll., Oxford (DPhil 1962). Lectr, Punjab Univ., 1957–69; Prof., Delhi Sch. of Econs, 1969–71; Secretariat, UNCTAD; Econ. Advr, Min. of Foreign Trade, India, 1971–72; Chief Econ. Advr, 1972–76, Sec., 1976–80, Min. of Finance; Dir, 1976–80, Gov., 1982–85, Reserve Bank of India; Mem.-Sec., 1980–82, Dep. Chm., 1985–87, Planning Commn; Sec.-Gen. and Comr, South Commn, Geneva, 1987–90; Advr to Prime Minister, 1990–91; Union Finance Minister, 1991–96; Leader of the Opposition, 1998–2004. Chm., Univ. Grants Commn. Hon. DCL Oxon, 2005; Hon. LLD Cantab, 2006. Padma Vibhushan, 1987. *Publications:* India's Export Trends and Prospects for Self-Sustained Growth, 1964. *Address:* 3 Motilal Nehru Place, New Delhi 110011, India. *E:* manmohan@gov.in.

SINGH, Margaret Stella, (Mrs Christopher Cook), CBE 1996; Chair, Association of District Councils, 1993–95; *b* 10 Aug. 1945; *d* of Edward Richard Jones and Stella Jones; *m* 1st (marr. diss.); one *s* one *d*; 2nd, 2001, Christopher Cook; one step *d*. Working in and for local govt, 1962–; Mem. (Lab) Reading BC, 1976–95. Lay Mem., W Norfolk Primary Care Trust, 2000–06; Vice Chair, Norwich and W Norfolk CAB, 2009–. Bd Mem., Broadlands Housing Assoc., 2004–10. Trustee, Meridian East, 2008–. *Recreations:* reading, walking the dogs, listening to people. *Address:* Chiswick House, Creake Road, Burnham Market, Norfolk PE31 8EN.

SINGH, His Honour Sir Mota, Kt 2010; QC 1978; a Circuit Judge, 1982–2002; *b* 26 July 1930; *s* of Dalip Singh and Harnam Kaur; *m* 1950, Swaran Kaur; two *s* one *d*. *Educ:* Duke of Gloucester Sch., Nairobi, Kenya; Hon. Soc. of Lincoln's Inn. Called to the Bar, 1956. Left school, 1947; Solicitor's Clerk, Nairobi, 1948–54; Lincoln's Inn, London, 1954–56; Advocate, High Court of Kenya, 1957–65; Alderman, City of Nairobi, 1958–63; Vice-Chm., Kenya Justice; Sec., Law Soc. of Kenya, 1963–64. A Deputy Circuit Judge, 1976–82; a Recorder of the Crown Court, 1979–82; Bencher, Lincoln's Inn, 2002. Member: London Rent Assessment Panel, 1965–67; Race Relations Bd, 1968–77; Parole Bd, 2009–12; Chm., Immigration Adv. Service, 2000–10. Chm., Statutory Cttee, RPSGB, 2007–09. Vice-Pres., Barnardo's. Chairman: Eur. Sect., World Sikh Council, 1998–; Guru Nanak Internat. Educn Fund, Punjab, India, 2006–; Vice-Chm., Bharatiya Vidya Bhavan, Inst. of Indian Art and Culture, 2010–. Patron: World Council of Faiths; Swami Narayan Temple, Neasden; Ben Samuel Trust. Lifetime Achievement Award, Asian Jewels Awards, 2003. Hon. LLD Guru Nanak Dev Univ., Amritsar, 1981. *Recreations:* reading; formerly cricket (represented Kenya). *Club:* MCC.

SINGH, Sir Pritpal, Kt 2005; Head, Drayton Manor High School, since 1994; *b* 22 June 1953; *s* of Dr Gurbuxsh Singh and Vidya Vati; *m* 1983, Elizabeth Szulc; two *s*. *Educ:* Chelsea Coll., Univ. of London (BSc (Hons) Chemistry 1975; PGCE 1979; MA 1986). Head of Chemistry, Feltham Sch., 1982–86; Head of Science, Vyne Sch., 1986–89; Dep. Head, Cranford Community Sch., 1989–94. Non-exec. Dir, E Berks NHS Trust, 1999–2001. Mem., Educn Cttee, Royal Soc., 2003–04; Jt Dir, London Leadership Strategy, 2005–06; Chm., Nat. Awards Panel, PTA-UK (formerly Nat. Confedn of PTAs), 2010–. Mem. Council, Imperial Soc. of Knights Bachelor, 2011–. Mem., Educators' Co., 2013–. Promethean Award for Head Teacher of the Year, London, Teaching Awards Trust, 2004. *Recreations:* history, Rugby, sport, travel, music. *Address:* Drayton Manor High School, Drayton Bridge Road, W7 1EU. *T:* (020) 8357 1900, *Fax:* (020) 8357 1901.

SINGH, Hon. Sir Rabinder, Kt 2011; a Judge of the High Court, Queen's Bench Division, since 2011; a Presiding Judge, South Eastern Circuit, since 2013; *b* 6 March 1964; *s* of late Lakhinder Singh and Swarn Kaur; *m* 1989, Alison Joy Baigent; two *s*. *Educ:* Bristol Grammar Sch.; Trinity Coll., Cambridge (BA Hons 1985; MA Hons 2013); Univ. of Calif, Berkeley (Harkness Fellow; LLM 1986). Lectr in Law, Univ. of Nottingham, 1986–88; called to the Bar, Lincoln's Inn, 1989, Bencher, 2009; QC 2002; in practice as barrister, 1989–2011; a Dep. High Court Judge, 2003–11; a Recorder, 2004–11. Visitor, Brunel Univ., 2006–14. Hon. LLD: London Metropolitan, 2004; Nottingham, 2011. *Publications:* The Future of Human Rights in the United Kingdom, 1997; (jtly) Human Rights: judicial enforcement in the United Kingdom, 2008; contrib. articles to Public Law, Judicial Rev. and Eur. Human Rights Law Rev. *Recreations:* walking, drama, film, opera, saxophone. *Address:* Royal Courts of Justice, Strand, WC2A 2LL.

SINGH, Rameshwar, (Ray), CBE 2001; a District Judge, 1997–2010; *s* of late Brijmohan Singh and Ram Kumari; *m* Gwynneth, BSc; three *s*. *Educ:* Deenbandhu High Sch., Fiji; Council of Legal Educn. Called to the Bar, Middle Temple, 1969. In practice as barrister, Wales and Chester Circuit, 1969–97; Dep. Dist Judge, 1992–97. Chm. (pt-time), Child Support Appeals Tribunal, 1993–97; Ind. Chm. (pt-time), Complaints against Nat. Assembly for Wales, 2000. Mem., CRE for England and Wales, 1996–2002. Member: Adv. Cttee on Drugs and Alcohol Abuse to Sec. of State for Wales, 1996–2000; Nat. Assembly for Wales Adv. Cttee, 1999–2000. Mem., S Wales Criminal Justice Cttee, 1996. Chairman: Challenges for the Future, Birmingham, 2000–01; Formal Investigation into the Prison Service, 2000; Stephen Lawrence Inquiry Commn, 2002; Mem., Rees Commn: student support system and tuition fee regime to Wales, 2004–05. Non-exec. Dir, Gwalia Housing, 1999. Mem., Family Mediators Assoc., 2011–. FLBA. Mem., Hon. Soc. of Middle Temple. Mem., Age Concern, Wales, 1999. Governor: Swansea Inst. for Higher Educn, 2000–09; Swansea Coll., 2002–09; Gower Coll., 2010–. *Recreations:* mountain walking, cooking, watching cricket, Rugby. *Address:* Maranatha, Main Road, Cilfrew, Neath, West Glamorgan SA10 8LU. *Clubs:* Neath Cricket; Bonymaen Rugby Football.

SINGH, Reuben; Chairman and Chief Executive Officer, alldayPA, 2002; Chairman, Reuben Singh Group of Companies, 2000; *b* 20 Sept. 1976. *Educ:* William Hulme's Grammar Sch., Manchester. Founded first company, Miss Attitude, 1994; launched IT Golden Fund, 2001. Member: Competitiveness Council, DTI, 1999–2001; Small Business Council, DTI, 2000–02. British Ambassador for Entrepreneurship, 1999; Chm., Genesis Initiative, 2000–02. British Entrepreneur of the Year, 2002; Asian Entrepreneur of the Year, 2002; World Sikh Personality of the Year, 2003; listed as Youngest Self-made Millionaire, Guinness Book of World Records, 1998. *Recreation:* inspiring future entrepreneurs younger than myself.

SINGH, Simon Lehna, MBE 2003; PhD; writer, journalist and television producer; *b* 19 Sept. 1964; *s* of Mengha and Sawarn Singh; *m* 2007, Anita Anand, broadcaster; one *s*. *Educ:* Imperial Coll., London (BSc Physics 1987); Emmanuel Coll., Cambridge (PhD Physics 1990). Joined Science Dept, BBC, 1991, producer, director and broadcaster, radio and TV; Dir, Fermat's Last Theorem (documentary), 1996 (BAFTA Award for best documentary); presenter, Science of Secrecy (series), Channel 4, 2001. Trustee, Science Mus., 2002–06. *Publications:* Fermat's Last Theorem, 1997; The Code Book, 1999; Big Bang, 2004; (with E. Ernst) Trick or Treatment?, 2008; The Simpsons and their Mathematical Secrets, 2013. *Recreations:* games of chance, observing solar eclipses. *Address:* Morley House, 36 Acreman Street, Sherborne, Dorset DT9 3NX. *E:* simon@simonsingh.net.

SINGH, Vijay; golfer; *b* Fiji, 22 Feb. 1963; *m* Ardena Seth; one *s*. *Educ:* Univ. of N Carolina. Professional golfer, 1982–; joined PGA Tour, 1983; wins include: Malaysian Championship, 1984; Malaysian Open, 1992, 2001; Buick Classic, 1993, 1995, 2004, 2005; Toyota World Match Play Championship, 1997; Buick Open, 1997, 2004; US PGA Championship, 1998, 2004; US Masters, 2000; Singapore Masters, 2001; Tour Championship, 2002; Pebble Beach Nat. Pro-Am, 2004; Canadian Open, 2004; Sony Open, 2005; Chrysler Championship, 2005. Member: President's Cup Team, 1994, 1996, 1998, 2000, 2003; World Cup Team, 2002.

SINGLETON, Barry Neill; QC 1989; *b* 12 April 1946; *s* of late Clifford and Moyna Singleton; *m* 1971, Anne Mary Potter; one *s* two *d*. *Educ:* Downside Sch.; Gonville and Caius Coll., Cambridge (MA). Called to the Bar, Gray's Inn, 1968.

SINGLETON, Sir Roger, Kt 2006; CBE 1997; Chief Executive, Barnardo's, 1984–2006; consultant, government advisor and interim manager, since 2006; *b* 6 Nov. 1942; *s* of late Malcolm and Ethel Singleton, Nether Edge, Sheffield; *m* 1966, Ann Hasler; two *d*. *Educ:* City Grammar Sch., Sheffield; Durham Univ. (MA); Bath Univ. (MSc; Hon. LLD 2011); London Univ. (DipSocStud); Leeds (Cert. Ed.). Accredited Mediator. Appts in care and educn of vulnerable young people, 1961–71; professional adviser to Children's Regional Planning Cttee, 1971–74; Dep. Dir, Dr Barnardo's, 1974–84. Non-exec. Dir, Capacitybuilders, 2006–11. Chairman: Ind. Safeguarding Authy (formerly Ind. Barring Bd), 2007–12; Panel on Independence of Voluntary Sector, 2012–15; Govt Chief Advr on Safety of Children, 2009–10. Dir, SafeguardingFirst Ltd, 2013– (Consultant, 2012–13). Trustee, Nat. Council of Voluntary Child Care Organisations, 1984–2002 (Chm., 1990–92). Chair, Princess of Wales Meml Fund, 2006–13 (Trustee, 2001–13). Trustee, Lumos (formerly Children's High Level Gp), 2006–14. Pres., Friends of St Andrew's Ch, Shalford, 2006–; Vice-Pres., Perennial (Gardeners' Royal Benevolent Soc.), 2014– (Chm., 2006–14); Patron, Ann Craft Trust, 2012–. CCMI (FBIM 1982); FRSA 1991. *Publications:* contribs to professional jls. *Recreation:* timber framed buildings. *E:* rogersingleton42@gmail.com. *Club:* Reform.

SINGLETON, Sarah Louise; QC 2006; **Her Honour Judge Singleton;** a Circuit Judge, since 2012; *b* 9 March 1962; *d* of James and Beryl Singleton. *Educ:* Goff's Oak Primary Sch., Herts; Roedean; Lancaster Girls' Grammar Sch.; Hertford Coll., Oxford (BA Juris. 1982). Called to the Bar, Middle Temple, 1983, Bencher, 2010; barrister, 1983–2012; Recorder, 2000–12; a Deputy High Court Judge, 2011. Chancellor, Diocese of Sheffield, 2014– (Dep. Chancellor, 2013–14). *Recreations:* running, cycling, book clubs. *Address:* Sessions House, Lancaster Road, Preston, Lancs PR1 2PD.

SINGLETON, Valerie, OBE 1994; television broadcaster, travel writer for newspapers and magazines; with BBC, 1962–93; *b* 9 April 1937; *d* of late Wing Comdr Denis G. Singleton, OBE and Eileen Singleton, LRAM. *Educ:* Arts Educational Sch. (3 times Drama Cup); RADA (schol.). Bromley Rep.; commercial voice-overs; TV advertising magazines; joined BBC as announcer, 1962; presenter: Blue Peter, 1962–71; Blue Peter Special Assignments, covering capital cities, islands, famous houses, 1972–75, and Rivers Niagara and Yukon, 1980; Val Meets the VIPs, 1972–75; Nationwide, 1972–78; Tonight, and Tonight in Town, 1978–79; Echoes of Holocaust, documentary, BBC 2, Midweek, Radio 4, 1980; The Money Programme, BBC 2, 1980–88; Radio 4 PM, 1981–93; (jtly) Travel UK, Central TV, 1992; Backdate, Channel 4, 1996; Playback, History Channel, 2 series, 1998, 1999; numerous other radio and TV progs; corporate videos, business confs. Dir, simplicity Computers with Envelope software, 2008–. *Recreations:* sailing, ski-ing, water ski-ing, photography, exploring London, travelling… especially cities, riding, pottering in museums and antique shops. *Address:* c/o Panmedia, 18 Montrose Crescent, N12 0ED. *Clubs:* Hurlingham, Chelsea Arts.

SINGLETON, William Brian, CBE 1974; FRCVS; retired; Director, Animal Health Trust, 1977–88; *b* 23 Feb. 1923; *s* of William Max Singleton and Blanche May Singleton; *m* 1947, Hilda Stott; two *s* one *d* (and one *s* decd). *Educ:* Queen Elizabeth Grammar Sch., Darlington; Royal (Dick) Sch. of Vet. Studies, Edinburgh. Vis. Prof. Surgery, Ontario Vet. Coll., Guelph, Canada, 1973–74; Hon. Vet. Advr to Jockey Club, 1977–88. Member: Govt Cttee of Inquiry into Future Role of Veterinary Profession in GB (Chm., Sir Michael Swann), 1971–75; UGC Wkg Pty on Vet. Educn into the 21st Century (Chm., Sir Ralph Riley, FRS), 1987–89. President: British Small Animal Vet. Assoc., 1960–61; RCVS, 1969–70; World Small Animal Vet. Assoc., 1975–77; BEVA, 1988–89. Hon. Diplomate, Amer. Coll. of Vet. Surgeons, 1973; Hon. DVM & S Edinburgh, 1993. ARPS 2001. Dalrymple-Champneys Award, 1987. *Publications:* (contrib.) Canine Medicine and Therapeutics, 1979; numerous papers on veterinary orthopaedics and comparative medicine. *Recreations:* gardening, photography, bird watching. *Address:* Martlets, Back Lane, Blakeney, Holt, Norfolk NR25 7NP. *T:* (01263) 740246. *Club:* Farmers.

SINHA, 6th Baron *cr* 1919, of Raipur; **Arup Kumar Sinha;** *b* 23 April 1966; *er s* of 5th Baron Sinha and of Lolita, *d* of Deb Kumar Das; *S* father, 1999; *m* 1st, 1993, Deborah Jane Tidswell (marr. diss. 1995); 2nd, 2002, Penny Askins. *Heir:* *b* Hon. Dilip Kumar Sinha, *b* 28 May 1967.

SINKER, Isabel Margaret; *see* Dedring, I. M.

SINKINSON, Philip Andrew, OBE 2006; HM Diplomatic Service, retired; High Commissioner to The Gambia, 2006–11; *b* 7 Oct. 1950; *m* 1971, Clare Maria Catherine Jarvis; one *s*. Bd of Inland Revenue, 1967–70; entered FCO, 1970; Warsaw, 1973–74; FCO, 1974; E Berlin, 1974–75; Rome, 1975–76; FCO, 1976–78; Rio de Janeiro, 1978; Quito, 1978–79; Prague, 1979–81; FCO, 1981–82; Blantyre, 1982–85; Lilongwe, 1985–86; FCO, 1986–92; Second Sec. (Commercial), São Paulo, 1992–95; on secondment to British Olympic Assoc., Atlanta, 1995–96; First Sec. (Commercial), Lisbon, 1996–2001; Dep. High Comr, Jamaica, 2001–05. Chm., Bournemouth RFC, 2014–. Patron, Bansang Hosp. Appeal, 2012–.

SINNATT, Maj.-Gen. Martin Henry, CB 1984; *b* 28 Jan. 1928; *s* of Dr O. S. Sinnatt and Mrs M. H. Sinnatt (*née* Randall); *m* 1957, Susan Rosemary Clarke; four *d*. *Educ:* Hitchin Grammar School; Hertford College, Oxford (1 Year Army Short Course); RMA Sandhurst. Commissioned RTR, 1948; served Germany, Korea, UK, Hong Kong, 1948–58; psc 1959; Aden, 1959–62; Germany and UK, 1962–64; MA to C-in-C AFNE, Norway, 1964–66; jssc 1967; Germany and UK, 1967–69; CO 4 RTR, BAOR, 1969–71; Nat. Defence Coll., 1971–72; Comdr RAC, 1 (BR) Corps, BAOR, 1972–74; Dir Operational Requirements MoD, 1974–77; rcds 1978; Dir, Combat Development (Army), 1979–81; Chief of Staff to

Live Oak, SHAPE, 1982–84; completed service, 1984. Sen. Exec. and Sec., Kennel Club, 1984–93. *Address:* Meadowside Farmhouse, Tulls Lane, Standford, Bordon, Hants GU35 8RB.

SINNOTT, John Brian, CBE 2010; Chief Executive, Leicestershire County Council and Clerk of Lieutenancy, since 1994; *s* of William John Sinnott and Mary Josephine Sinnott (*née* Foley); *m* 1970, Helen Mary Turner; two *s* two *d*. *Educ:* St Mary's Coll., Crosby; Univ. of Liverpool (MA, Dip. Public Admin). Liverpool CC, 1970–74; PA to Chm. and Leader of Council, Head of Leader's office, Merseyside CC, 1974–86; Management Consultant, Coopers and Lybrand Associates, 1986–87; Leicestershire County Council: Asst, then Sen. Asst, County Clerk, 1987–90; Asst Chief Exec., 1990–92; Dir, Corporate Management, 1992–94. Director: Leics TEC, 1994–2001; Leics Business Point (Business Link), 1995–2001; Leics Develt Agency, 1998–2003; Heart of the Nat. Forest Foundn, 1998–2004; Leics and Rutland Sport, 2005–; Leics Econ. Partnership, 2007–09; Prospect Leics, 2009–11. Chm., ACCE, 2001–02. Chairman: Leics Cricket Bd, 2001–06; Everton FC Shareholders' Assoc., 2003–04. *Publications:* papers in local govt jls. *Recreations:* sport, cricket literature, history of rock music. *Address:* County Hall, Glenfield, Leicester LE3 8RA. *T:* (0116) 305 6000. *Club:* Everton Football.

SINOUSSI, Françoise Claire; *see* Barré-Sinoussi, F. C.

SINTON, William Baldie, OBE 1999; HM Diplomatic Service, retired; *b* 17 June 1946; *s* of late John William Sinton and Isabella McCrae Sinton (*née* Baldie); *m* 1995, Jane S. B. Aryee. *Educ:* Bristol Cathedral Sch.; Kirkcaldy High Sch.; Edinburgh Univ. (MA 1968). Third Sec., FCO, 1968; Third later Second Sec., Prague, 1970; Second later First Sec., UK Delegn to NATO, Brussels, 1973; FCO, 1977–81; First Sec. (Commercial), Algiers, 1981; FCO, 1985–96; Ambassador to Panama, 1996–99; Ambassador to Algeria, 1999–2001; Ambassador to Bolivia, 2001–05. Clerk, Cttee Office, H of L, 2006–14. *Address:* 22 Fairburn Court, St John's Avenue, SW15 2AU. *Clubs:* Reform; Lundin Golf.

SINYOR, Joseph, (Joe); Chairman, Global Garden Products, since 2014; *b* 16 Aug. 1957; *s* of Samuel Joseph Sinyor and Claire Sinyor; *m* 1987, Pamela Caroline Neild Collis; two *s* one *d*. *Educ:* Jesus Coll., Cambridge; London Business Sch. (MBA). Corporate Finance Exec., J. Henry Schroder Wagg, 1983–85; Sen. Engagement Manager, McKinsey & Co. Inc., 1985–90; Gp Chief Exec., Pepe Gp plc, 1990–93; Man. Dir, Dillon's Bookstores Ltd, 1994–98; Man. Dir, Sony UK Ltd, 1998–2000; Chief Exec., Newspapers, Trinity Mirror plc, 2000–03; Man. Dir, Terra Firma Capital Partners, 2003–06; Operating Partner (formerly Man. Dir), Strategic Value Partners LLP, 2007–11; Hd, Value Creation Gp, Actis, 2011–14. Non-executive Director: Channel 4 TV Corp., 1998–2004; Ideal Standard Internat., 2014–. *Recreations:* opera, ski-ing, walking. *Address:* 70 Sheldon Avenue, N6 4ND.

SIONE, Hon. Sir Tomu (Malaefone), GCMG 2001; OBE 1989; MP Niutao and Niulakifa Islands, Tuvalu, 1970–2002 and 2006–10; Chairman of the Caucus, 2006–10; *b* 17 Nov. 1941; *m* 1979, Segali Lusia; four *s* two *d*. Journalist, 1962–68. Gov.-Gen., Tuvalu, 1993–94. Speaker, Parlt of Tuvalu, 1998–2006. *Recreation:* fishing. *Address:* Niutao Island, Tuvalu.

SIPPINGS, Gwenda Margaret; Head, Knowledge and Information Management, Medical Defence Union, since 2011; *b* London, 20 April 1957; *d* of David Hughes and Dr Joan Hughes (*née* Isaac); *m* 1984, Andrew John Sippings. *Educ:* Dame Alice Harpur Sch., Bedford; Univ. of Wales, Aberystwyth (BLib 1978; MLib 1986). FCLIP 2002. Reference Librarian Reader Services Team, Bedford Central Liby, 1978–84; Asst Database Adminr, BT Prestel, 1984–86; Inf. Specialist, 1987–88, Trng Manager, 1989, ASLIB; Hd, Accommodation Information Unit, BTA, 1989–94; Hd, Information, Clifford Chance, 1994–2002; Dir, Information Resources, Bd of Inland Revenue, subseq. Dir, Knowledge Resources, HMRC, 2002–06; Ind. Records Consultant, London Bor. of Southwark, 2007–09; Hd, Information and Res., Linklaters LLP, 2009–11. Hon. Deptl Fellow of Information Studies, Univ. of Aberystwyth, 2010–. Trustee and Chm., Council, Cymmrodorion Soc., 2003–. Trustee and Archivist, Old Students Assoc., Aberystwyth, 2012–. FRSA 2002–14. Editor, Business Information Review, 2008–10. *Publications:* articles in professional information jls. *Address:* 69 Friern Watch Avenue, N12 9NY. *T:* 07877 803252; Cysgod y Llyfrgell, 5 Bryn Ardwyn, Aberystwyth SY23 1ED. *E:* gwenda@gwendasippings.com.

SIRKS, Prof. (Adriaan Johan) Boudewijn; Regius Professor of Civil Law, University of Oxford, and Fellow of All Souls College, Oxford, 2006–14, now Emeritus. *Educ:* Leyden Univ. (LLM 1972); Univ. of Amsterdam (PhD 1984). Formerly: Lectr, Hist. of Roman Law, Utrecht State Univ.; Associate Prof. of Legal Techniques, Univ. of Amsterdam; Prof. of Legal Hist. and Private Law, Johann Wolfgang Goethe Univ., Frankfurt am Main, 1998–2006. Corresp. Mem., Koninklijke Nederlandse Akademie van Wetenschappen, 2002. Kt, Order of the Lion (Netherlands). *Publications:* Food for Rome, 1991; (jtly) Ein früh-byzantinisches Szenario für die Amtswechslung in der Sitonie, 1996; The Theodosian Code: a study, 2007; (ed jtly) Papyri in Memory of P. J. Sijpesteijn, 2007. *Address:* All Souls College, Oxford OX1 4AL. *E:* boudewijn.sirks@law.ox.ac.uk.

SIRLEAF, Ellen Eugenia J.; *see* Johnson Sirleaf.

SIRRINGHAUS, Prof. Henning, PhD; FRS 2009; Hitachi Professor of Electron Device Physics, University of Cambridge, since 2004; Fellow, Churchill College, Cambridge, since 1999. *Educ:* Eidgenössische Technische Hochschule Zürich (BSc; PhD). Postdoctoral Res. Fellow, Princeton Univ., 1995–96; Univ. of Cambridge, 1997–. Co-founder and Chief Scientist, Plastic Logic Ltd, 2000–. Mullard Award, Royal Soc., 2003. *Publications:* contribs to jls incl. Nature Nanotechnol., Nature Materials, Nature. *Address:* Microelectronics Research Centre, Cavendish Laboratory, Department of Physics, University of Cambridge, J J Thomson Avenue, Cambridge CB3 0HE.

SISSLING, David Anthony; Chief Executive, Kettering General Hospital NHS Foundation Trust, since 2014; *b* St Albans, 5 Nov. 1957; *s* of Brian Sissling and late Moira Sissling; *m* 2007, Caroline Angelina Godfrey; two *s*. *Educ:* Thornbury Grammar Sch., subseq. Marlwood Comp. Sch.; Univ. of Birmingham (BA Geog. 1978). Merchant seaman, Blue Star Ship Mgt, 1978–80; Personnel Manager, Northern Foods, 1980–85; Personnel Manager, 1985–89, Gen. Manager, 1989–93, Robinson & Sons Ltd; Leicester Royal Infirmary NHS Trust: Business Manager, 1993–96; Dir, Contracts, 1996–98; Chief Exec., 1998–2000; Chief Executive: Northampton HA, 2000–02; Leicestershire, Northamptonshire and Rutland Strategic HA, 2002–06; NI Health and Social Care Authy, 2006–08; Prog. Dir, Healthcare for London, 2008–09; Chief Exec., Abertawe Bro Morgannwg Univ. Health Bd, 2009–11; Chief Exec., NHS Wales and Dir Gen., Dept of Health, Social Services and Children, Welsh Govt, 2011–14. *Recreations:* golf, running, ski-ing, football (Leicester City), Rugby (Leicester Tigers), dining out, cookery. *Address:* Kettering General Hospital NHS Foundation Trust, Kettering General Hospital, Rothwell Road, Kettering, Northants NN16 8UZ.

SISSON, Rosemary Anne; writer since 1929; *b* 13 Oct. 1923; *d* of Prof. C. J. Sisson, MA, DèsL and Vera Kathleen (*née* Ginn). *Educ:* Cheltenham Ladies' Coll.; University Coll., London (BA Hons English); Newnham Coll., Cambridge (MLit). Served War, Royal Observer Corps, 1943–45. Instr in English, Univ. of Wisconsin, 1949; Lecturer in English: UCL, 1950–53; Univ. of Birmingham, 1953–54; Dramatic Critic, Stratford-upon-Avon Herald, 1954–57; after prodn of first play, The Queen and the Welshman, became full-time writer, 1957. Co-Chm., Writers Guild of GB, 1979 and 1980 (Pres., 1995–98); Hon. Sec., Dramatists' Club, 1984–2008; Mem., BAFTA (Mem. Council, 1995–98). Laurel Award, for service to writers, 1985; Prince Michael of Kent Award, for services to SSAFA, 1987. *Plays:* The Queen and the Welshman, 1957; Fear Came to Supper, 1958; The Splendid Outcasts, 1959; The Royal Captivity, 1960; Bitter Sanctuary, 1963; I Married a Clever Girl, 1967; Ghost on Tiptoe (with Robert Morley), 1974; The Dark Horse, 1978. Contributed to *TV series:* Shadow of the Tower; Catherine of Aragon, in The Six Wives of Henry VIII; The Marriage Game, in Elizabeth R; Upstairs, Downstairs; The Duchess of Duke Street; A Town Like Alice; The Young Indiana Jones Chronicles; *TV scripts:* Irish RM; Seal Morning; The Manions of America; The Bretts (creator of series). *Film scripts* include: Ride a Wild Pony; Escape from the Dark; Candleshoe; Watcher in the Woods; The Black Cauldron (full-length animation film) (all for Walt Disney); The Wind in the Willows (animation film), 1983 (also TV series, 1984). *Other scripts:* Heart of a Nation (Son-et-Lumière), Horse Guards Parade, 1983; Dawn to Dusk, Royal Tournament, 1984; Joy to the World, Royal Albert Hall, 1988–97; Royal Military Tattoo, 2000; All the Queen's Horses, 2002; Debt of Honour, Greenwich, 2007; Not Forgotten Association, 90th Birthday, Buckingham Palace, 2010. *Publications: children's books:* The Adventures of Ambrose, 1951; The Young Shakespeare, 1959; The Young Jane Austen, 1962; The Young Shaftesbury, 1964; *novels:* The Exciseman, 1972; The Killer of Horseman's Flats, 1973; The Stratford Story, 1975; Escape from the Dark, 1976; The Queen and the Welshman, 1979; The Manions of America, 1982; Bury Love Deep, 1985; Beneath the Visiting Moon, 1986; The Bretts, 1987; Footstep on the Stair, 1999; First Love, Last Love, 2002; *poetry:* Rosemary for Remembrance, 1995. *Recreations:* travel, walking, riding, writing poetry, being a great-aunt. *Address:* 167 New King's Road, Parson's Green, SW6 4SN.

SISSONS, Sir (John Gerald) Patrick, Kt 2012; MD; FRCP, FRCPath; Professor of Medicine, 1988–2005, Regius Professor of Physic, 2005–12, University of Cambridge; Fellow of Darwin College, Cambridge, since 1988; *b* 28 June 1945; *s* of Gerald William Sissons and Georgina Margaret Cockin; *m* 1971, Jennifer Ann Scovell (marr. diss. 1987); two *d*. *Educ:* Felsted Sch.; St Mary's Hosp. Med. Sch. (MB, MD). FRCP 1983; FRCPath 1995. Hosp. appts, St Mary's, St George's and Hammersmith Hosps, 1968–71; Registrar and Lectr, Dept of Medicine, RPMS, 1972–77; NIH Research Fellow and Asst Mem., Res. Inst. of Scripps Clinic, California, 1977–80; Wellcome Sen. Lectr, Depts of Medicine and Virology, RPMS, 1980–86; Prof. of Infectious Diseases, RPMS, 1987. Hon. Consultant Physician, Cambridge Univ. Hosps (formerly Addenbrooke's) NHS Trust, 1988–2012. Founder FMedSci 1998 (Vice Pres., 2010–). *Publications:* papers on immunology and pathogenesis of virus infections. *Recreation:* travel.

SISSONS, Michael; *see* Sissons, T. M. B.

SISSONS, Sir Patrick; *see* Sissons, Sir J. G. P.

SISSONS, Peter George; journalist, broadcaster and writer; *b* 17 July 1942; *s* of late George Robert Percival Sissons and Elsie Emma Evans; *m* 1965, Sylvia Bennett; two *s* one *d*. *Educ:* Liverpool Inst. High Sch. for Boys; University College Oxford (MA PPE). Independent Television News: graduate trainee, 1964; general reporter, 1967; industrial corresp., 1970; indust. editor, 1972–78; presenter, News at One, 1978–82; presenter: Channel Four News, 1982–89; BBC TV 6 o'clock news, 1989–93; BBC TV 9 o'clock news, 1993–2000; BBC TV 10 o'clock news, 2000–03; presenter, BBC News 24, 2003–09; Chm., BBC TV Question Time, 1989–93; occasional presenter, Breakfast with Frost, 2002–05. Mem., Hillsborough Ind. Panel, 2010–12. Vice Pres., Liverpool Sch. of Tropical Medicine, 2013–. Hon. Fellow, Liverpool John Moores Univ., 1997. Hon. LLD Liverpool, 2002. Broadcasting Press Guild Award, 1984; RTS Judges' Award, 1988; Newscaster of the Year, TRIC, 2001. *Publications:* When One Door Closes (memoir), 2011. *Recreations:* relaxing, supporting Liverpool FC.

SISSONS, (Thomas) Michael (Beswick); Senior Consultant, The Peters Fraser and Dunlop Group Ltd, since 1999 (Managing Director, 1988–94; Chairman, 1988–99); *b* 13 Oct. 1934; *s* of Captain T. E. B. Sissons (killed in action, 1940) and late Marjorie (*née* Shepherd); *m* 1st, 1960, Nicola Ann Fowler (marr. diss. 1974); one *s* one *d*; 2nd, 1974, Ilze Kadegis (marr. diss. 1992); two *d*; 3rd, 1992, Serena Palmer. *Educ:* Winchester Coll.; Exeter Coll., Oxford (BA 1958, MA 1964). National Service, 2nd Lieut 13/18 Royal Hussars, 1953–55. Lectr in History, Tulane Univ., New Orleans, USA, 1958–59; joined A. D. Peters, Literary Agent, 1959; Dir, 1965, Chm. and Man. Dir, 1973–88, A. D. Peters & Co. Ltd. Chm., Cardinall's Musick Ltd, 2006–11. Pres., Assoc. of Authors' Agents, 1978–81; Director: London Broadcasting Co., 1973–75; Groucho Club plc, 1985–2001; Mem. Council, Consumers Assoc., 1974–77. Board Member: BFSS, 1994–95; Countryside Movt, 1995–97. Patron, Saïd Business Sch., Univ. of Oxford, 2009– (Mem., Business Adv. Forum, 2006–09). *Publications:* (ed with Philip French) Age of Austerity, 1963, repr. 1986; (ed) A Countryside for All, 2001. *Recreations:* football, gardening, cricket, music. *Address:* Raceyard House, Fawler Road, Kingston Lisle, Wantage, Oxon OX12 9QH. *T:* (01367) 820724. *Clubs:* Boodle's, Groucho, MCC (Mem. Cttee, 1984–87, 1993–2000; Chairman: Arts and Liby Sub-Cttee, 1985–93; Marketing and Public Affairs Sub-Cttee, 1995–2000).

SITWELL, Sir George (Reresby Sacheverell), 8th Bt *cr* 1808, of Renishaw, Derbyshire; *b* London, 22 April 1967; *er s* of late Francis Trajan Sacheverell Sitwell, *yr s* of 6th Bt, and of Susanna Carolyn, *d* of Rt Hon. Sir Ronald Hibbert Cross, 1st Bt, KCMG, KCVO; *S* uncle, 2009, but his name does not appear on the Official Roll of the Baronetage; *m* 2008, Martha Louise, 2nd *d* of late Justin Robert de Blank. *Educ:* Eton Coll.; Edinburgh Univ. (MA Hons). Merchant banker, 1990–98; J & M Entertainment, 1998–2000; Co-founder and Director: Interquest Gp plc, 2000–06; Crossover Capital Ltd, 2001–. *Recreations:* travel, reading, dogs. *Heir: b* William Ronald Sacheverell Sitwell [*b* 2 Oct. 1969; *m* 1999, Laura Barbara, *d* of Euan Norman Jersey McCorquodale; one *s* one *d*]. *Clubs:* Brooks's, Pratt's.

SITWELL, Peter Sacheverell W.; *see* Wilmot-Sitwell.

SIU, Gordon Kwing-Chue, GBS 2002; CBE 1997; JP; Secretary for Planning and Lands, Hong Kong, 1999–2002; *b* 29 Nov. 1945; *s* of Siu Wood-chuen and Chan Shuk-ming; *m* 1999, Cynthia Wong Lok-yee; two *s* by a previous marriage. *Educ:* Birmingham Univ. (MSocSci). Joined Hong Kong Civil Service, 1966; Sec.-Gen., Office of Members of Exec. and Legislative Councils, 1985; Postmaster Gen., 1988; Comr for Transport, 1989; Dir, New Airport Projects Co-ordination Office, 1992; Secretary for: Economic Services, 1993; Transport, 1996; Hd, Central Policy Unit, 1997. Founder and Chm., Music For Our Young Foundn, 2009–. *Recreations:* reading, swimming, golf. *Clubs:* Hong Kong Golf, Hong Kong Jockey.

SIZELAND, Paul Raymond, CMG 2006; HM Diplomatic Service, retired; Director, Economic Development, City of London Corporation, since 2008 (Assistant Director, City, European and International Affairs, 2006–08); *b* 19 Feb. 1952; *s* of Raymond Sizeland and Patricia Sizeland (*née* Dudley); *m* 1976, Vasantha, *d* of late James Kanaka and Nancy Jesudasan; two *d*. *Educ:* Dulwich Coll.; Bradford Univ. (BTech Hons Applied Biol. 1975). MIPD 1995. VSO teacher, St Stephen's Coll., Trinidad, 1970–71; Res. Student, Rowett Res. Inst., Aberdeen, 1973–74; CMS volunteer teacher, Ida Scudder Sch., Vellore, S India, 1976–78; Med. Rep. for Essex and Suffolk, Merrell Pharmaceuticals, 1978–80; joined HM Diplomatic Service, 1980; Third Sec., UK Delegn to NATO, Brussels, 1981–84; Commercial Attaché, Doha, 1985–86; Second Sec., FCO, 1986–88; First Sec., Political/Develt, Lagos, 1988–91; Private Sec. to Lord Carrington, Chm., EU Conf. on former Yugoslavia, 1991–92; Head, Career Develt Unit, FCO, 1992–95; Dep. Head, Personnel Mgt Dept, FCO, 1995–96; Dep. Hd of Mission, Bangkok, 1996–2000; Consul Gen., Shanghai, 2000–03; Dir, Consular Services, FCO, 2003–06. Trustee, Prisoners Abroad, 2006. *Recreations:* family, Millwall FC supporter, travel, books, music, Kipling Society. *Address:* PO Box 270, Guildhall, EC2P 2EJ.

SKAISGIRYTĖ LIAUŠKIENĖ, Asta; Ambassador of the Republic of Lithuania to the Court of St James's, since 2012; *b* 20 March 1966; *m*; one *c*. *Educ:* Vilnius Univ. (MA Romanic-Germanic Philology 1989); Internat. Inst. of Public Admin, France (Internat. Relns). Correspondent, Atgimimas, weekly newspaper, 1989–90; Hd, Inter-Parliamentary Relns Dept, Supreme Council, Rep. of Lithuania, 1990–92; First Sec., 1993–94, Hd, 1994–95, W Eur. Div., Political Dept, Min. of Foreign Affairs; Advr for Internat. Relns, Govt of Lithuania, 1995–98; Ambassador to France, 1998–2003; non-resident Ambassador to Tunisian Republic, 2002–03; Ambassador-at-Large, Eur. Affairs Dept, 2003, Hd, Personnel Dept, 2003–06, Min. of Foreign Affairs; Ambassador to Israel, 2006–09; non-resident Ambassador to S Africa, 2007–09; Vice Minister of Foreign Affairs, 2009–12. Comdr, Légion d'Honneur (France), 2001; Commemorative Medal for 13th Jan. (Lithuania), 2003; Comdr Cross, Order of Merit (Lithuania), 2003; Grand Officer, Order of Merit (France), 2004. *Address:* Embassy of the Republic of Lithuania, Lithuania House, 2 Bessborough Gardens, SW1V 2JE.

SKARBEK, Marjorie Shiona, (Countess Skarbek); *see* Wallace, M. S.

SKEA, Prof. James Ferguson, CBE 2013 (OBE 2004); Professor of Sustainable Energy, Centre for Environmental Policy, since 2009, and Research Councils UK Energy Programme Strategy Fellow, since 2012, Imperial College London; *b* 1 Sept. 1953; *s* of Colin Hill Skea and Margaret Ferguson Skea; *m* 1976, Jane Howley (marr. diss. 2001); one *s* one *d*. *Educ:* Grove Acad., Broughty Ferry; Univ. of Edinburgh (BSc 1st cl. Hons); Clare Coll., Cambridge (PhD 1979). Res. Asst, Cavendish Lab., 1978–81; Vis. Res. Associate, Carnegie-Mellon Univ., 1981–83; Res. Fellow, 1983–94, Professorial Fellow, 1994–98, Science Policy Res. Unit; Director: Global Envmtl Change Prog., ESRC, 1995–98; PSI, 1998–2004; UK Energy Res. Centre, 2004–12. Member: UK Climate Change Cttee, 2008–; Bureau of the Intergovernmental Panel on Climate Change, 2008–15. Pres., Energy Inst., 2015–. FRSA 2000; FEI 2005. Hon. FSE 2011. Melchett Award, Energy Inst., 2010. *Publications:* Acid Politics, 1991; Standards, Innovation, Competitiveness and Policy, 1995; Clean and Competitive, 1997; Pollution for Sale, 1998; Energy 2050, 2011. *Recreations:* walking the South Downs, mountain biking, losing keys. *Address:* Flat 13, 17–19 Nevern Place, SW5 9NR. *T:* (020) 3581 7688. *E:* j.skea@ic.ac.uk.

SKEAPING, Lucie; musician, writer and broadcaster; Presenter, The Early Music Show, BBC Radio 3, since 1995; Co-Founder, 1973, and Director, since 1978, The City Waites; Founder and Director, The Burning Bush, since 1992; *d* of Dr Bernard Finch, GP and Patricia Finch, sculptor; *m* 1974, Roderick Skeaping; one *s*. *Educ:* King Alfred Sch., London; Henrietta Barnett Sch., London; Arts Educnl Sch., London; RCM. Performances of early and trad. English and Jewish music with ensembles, The City Waites and The Burning Bush, 1973–; presenter: music and children's programmes, BBC TV, 1980–85; performances with Michael Nyman Band, Sadista Sisters, Martin Best Consort, 1980–90; music documentaries and features for radio. Artistic Dir, Windsor Fest., 1995–99. Producer, historical recordings for Soundalive Music, 1994–96; collaborations include: projects and performances for RNT, Rambert Dance Co., RSC, Cultural Co-operation, Shakespeare's Globe; vocal soundtracks include: History of Britain, BBC TV; The Pianist (film), 2002. Mem. Judging Panel, Live Music Now, 2006– (Ambassador, 2009–); contrib. to govt singing in schools initiative 'Sing Up', 2008. Patron, Finchley Children's Music Gp, 1995–. Mem., Samuel Pepys Club, 2006–. *Publications:* Let's Make Tudor Music, 1999; Broadside Ballads, 2005 (Best Classical Music Pubn, Music Industry Awards, 2006); (ed jtly) Singing Simpkin and other Bawdy Jigs: musical comedy on the Shakespearean stage, 2014; contribs to BBC Music Magazine, BBC History Magazine, Early Music Today. *Address:* 19 Patshull Road, NW5 2JX. *T:* 07931 373133. *E:* lucieskeaping@hotmail.com. *W:* www.lucieskeaping.co.uk.

SKEFFINGTON, family name of **Viscount Massereene and Ferrard**.

SKEGG, Sir David (Christopher Graham), KNZM (DCNZM 2009); OBE 1990; DPhil; FRSNZ; Vice-Chancellor, University of Otago, 2004–11, now Emeritus Professor; President, Royal Society of New Zealand, since 2012; *b* 16 Dec. 1947; *s* of Donald and Margaret Skegg; *m* 1973, Dr Keren Mary Cargo; two *d*. *Educ:* King's Coll., Auckland; Univ. of Auckland; Univ. of Otago (BMedSc 1970; MB ChB 1972); Univ. of Oxford (DPhil 1979). FAFPHM 1994; FFPHM 1999. Rhodes Scholar, Balliol Coll., Oxford, 1973, 1975–76. House Physician, Waikato Hosp., NZ, 1974; Lectr in Epidemiology, Univ. of Oxford, 1976–79; University of Otago: Prof. of Preventive and Social Medicine, 1980–2004; Fellow, Knox Coll., 1980–. Vis. Fellow, Wolfson Coll., Oxford, 1986. Consultant to WHO, Geneva, 1984–2004 and 2009– (Chm., Scientific and Tech. Adv. Gp, WHO Dept of Reproductive Health and Res., 2011–); Chairman: Health Res. Council of NZ, 1991–94; Public Health Commn, 1992–95; BSE Expert Sci. Panel, 1996–2011; Res. Cttee, Universities NZ, 2004–10; Matariki Network of Univs, 2010–11; NZ Sci. Bd, 2011–12. Sec., Rhodes Scholarships in NZ, 2004–13. Trustee: NZ Antarctic Res. Inst., 2012–; Antarctic Heritage Trust, 2012–. FRSNZ 1992. Hon. Life Mem., Otago Inst., 2010. Hon LLD Otago, 2011. NZ Commem. Medal, 1990; Sir Charles Hercus Medal, Royal Soc. of NZ, 1999; Dist. Res. Medal, Univ. of Otago, 2003. *Publications:* scientific articles on cancer causes and control, contraceptive and drug safety and epidemiology of multiple sclerosis and AIDS. *Recreations:* books, art history, walking. *Address:* PO Box 6023, Dunedin 9059, New Zealand. *T:* (3) 4795774.

SKEGGS, Sir Clifford (George), Kt 1987; JP; FNZIM; Founder, 1952, and former Chairman and Chief Executive, Skeggs Group; Director of various public and private companies; Mayor, Dunedin City, 1978–89; *b* 19 March 1931; *s* of George Henry Skeggs and Beatrice Hannah (*née* Heathcote); *m* 1952, Marie Eleanor Ledgerwood; three *s*. *Educ:* Southland Technical Coll., New Zealand. Mem., 1968–80, Chm., 1973–77, Otago Harbour Bd. City Councillor, Dunedin, 1972–77. Mem. Council, Univ. of Otago, 1981–89. FNZIM 1985; Mem., Inst. of Dirs, 1984. JP Dunedin, 1978. OStJ 1987. *Publications:* contrib. fishing and general business publications. *Recreations:* yachting, golf, flying, power boating, squash, keen follower of Rugby. *Address:* Skeggs Group, PO Box 2615, Frankton, Queenstown 9349, New Zealand. *Club:* Dunedin (Dunedin).

SKEHEL, Sir John (James), Kt 1996; PhD; FRS 1984; Director, MRC National Institute for Medical Research, 1987–2006, now Visiting Scientist; *b* 27 Feb. 1941; *s* of Joseph and Annie Josephine Skehel; *m* 1962, Anita Varley; two *s*. *Educ:* St Mary's Coll., Blackburn; University College of Wales, Aberystwyth (BSc); UMIST (PhD). Post-doctoral Fellow, Marischal Coll., Aberdeen, 1965–68; Fellow, Helen Hay Whitney Foundn, 1968–71; MRC National Institute for Medical Research: Mem., Scientific Staff, 1971–2006; Head of Div. of Virology, 1984–87. Dir, World Influenza Centre, 1975–93. Leeuwenhoek Lecture, Royal Soc., 1990. Hon. Professor: Liverpool John Moores Univ. (formerly Liverpool Poly. Sch. of Nat. Sci.), 1990–; Div. of Virology, UCL, 2003–; Vis. Prof. of Virology, Glasgow Univ., 1997–. Biol Sec. and Vice-Pres., Royal Soc., 2013–. Mem., EMBO, 1983; MAE, 1992. Founder FMedSci 1998 (Vice-Pres., 2001–07). Hon. Mem., Soc. for Gen. Microbiol., 2004. Foreign Associate, NAS, 2014–. Hon. Fellow, Univ. of Wales, 2004. Hon. DSc: CNAA, 1990; London, 2004; Liverpool John Moores, 2007; La Laurea *hc* Medicina E Chirurgia, Univ. of Padua, 2010. Wilhelm Feldberg prize, Feldberg Foundn, 1986; Robert Koch prize, Robert Koch Foundn, 1987; Prix Louis Jeantet de Médecine, Jeantet Foundn, 1988; Internat. Prize in Virology, ICN Pharmaceuticals, 1992; Royal Medal, Royal Soc., 2003; Ernst Chain Prize, Imperial Coll., London, 2004; Grand Prix, Louis D Foundn, Institut de France, 2007. *Publications:* numerous scientific articles in various jls. *Address:* MRC National Institute for Medical Research, The Ridgeway, Mill Hill, NW7 1AA. *T:* (020) 8816 2256.

SKELLETT, Colin Frank, OBE 2012; CChem, FRSC; FCIWEM; Chief Executive, Wessex Water, since 1988; *b* 13 June 1945; *s* of Harry and Ivy Skellett; *m* 1st, 1963, Jennifer Trout (marr. diss.); two *s* one *d*; 2nd, 2010, Theresa McDermott. *Educ:* City Univ. (MSc). CChem 1971, FRSC 1990. Chemist, Nottingham CC, 1961–69; Sen. Chemist, Bath CC, 1970–74; operational and mgt posts, Wessex Water, 1974–88. Non-executive Chairman: Jarvis plc, 2000–02; Regen South West Ltd, 2002–07; European Connoisseurs Travel, 2006–; Bath Hotel & Spa Ltd, 2013–; Vice-Chm., Azurix Services, 1999–2001; Director: YTL Utilities UK Ltd, 2002–; GWE/Business West, 2008– (Jt Chm., 2008–13); Chairman: Future Bath Plus, 2008–12; Bd, West of England Local Enterprise Partnership, 2011–. Bd Mem., SW RDA, 2001–07. Trustee: WaterAid, 1995–2003; Money Advice Trust, 2000–02. Churchill Fellow, 1983. Master, Soc. of Merchant Venturers, 2009–10. Hon. DEng West of England, 2014. *Publications:* various technical papers on water and waste water treatment. *Recreations:* walking, theatre, music, charity fundraising. *Address:* (office) Wessex Water, Claverton Down, Bath BA2 7WW. *T:* (01225) 526000.

SKELLORN, Kathryn Mair; QC 2014; *b* Cardiff, 4 June 1971; *m* 2004; three *d*. *Educ:* Heaton Grammar Sch., Newcastle upon Tyne; Clifton High Sch., Bristol; Magdalen Coll., Oxford (MA Juris. 1992); Inns of Court Sch. of Law. Gray's Inn Jun. Schol., 1992–93; called to the Bar, Gray's Inn, 1993; in practice as a barrister, 1993–; Children Act specialist. Trustee, Nonita Glenday Fund, 2013–. *Recreations:* running, cookery, writing. *Address:* St John's Chambers, 101 Victoria Street, Bristol BS1 6PU. *E:* Kathryn.skellornqc@stjohnschambers.co.uk.

SKELLY, Michael Anthony; Headmaster, Westcliff High School for Boys, since 2012 (Deputy Headmaster, 2010–12); *b* Dublin, 1 Nov. 1971; *s* of Michael and Mary Skelly; *m* Maria Morris. *Educ:* Patrician Coll.; St Patrick's Coll., Maynooth (BA Econs and Music 1992); Open Univ. (MA Open and Distance Educn). Asst Choir Dir, Palestrina Choir, Dublin Pro-Cathedral, 1992–93; Teacher of Econs, 1994–2000, Dir, Sixth Form Studies, 2000–03, Westcliff High Sch. for Boys; Dep. Headmaster, 2003–09, Actg Headmaster, 2009–10, Calday Grange GS. *Recreations:* theatre, concerts, opera, school governor (infant), economic literature. *Address:* Westcliff High School for Boys, Kenilworth Gardens, Westcliff on Sea, Essex SS0 0BP. *T:* (01702) 475443. *E:* skellym@whsb.essex.sch.uk.

SKELLY, William Alan; Deputy Chief Constable, Devon and Cornwall Police, since 2013; *b* Dundee, 29 Nov. 1966; *s* of William Skelly and Gladys Emily Skelly (*née* Wood); *m* Alison Margaret Dobbie; two *d*; partner, Jane Wilkin. *Educ:* Auchterhouse Primary Sch., Angus; Newtyle Secondary Sch., Angus; Harris Acad., Dundee; Edinburgh Univ. (BSc Maths 1988; MBA 1997); Cambridge Univ. (Dip. Criminol. 2004). Joined Lothian and Borders Police, 1990; plain clothed and uniformed roles, 1990–99; Project Officer, Local Govt Section, Audit Scotland (on secondment), 1999–2000; Inspector, 1999–2001; Chief Inspector, 2001–02; Temp. Supt, then Supt, later Chief Supt, 2002–07; Strategic Comd Course, Bramshill, 2004; on secondment to Metropolitan Police, 2005, as Leader, Immigration Crime Team, then i/c UK Campaign targeting criminals involved in trafficking women for sexual exploitation; Asst Chief Constable (Crime and Operational Support), 2007–08; Temp. Dep. Chief Constable, 2008–09; HM Inspector of Constabulary for Scotland (on secondment), 2009–10; Asst Chief Constable, Lothian and Borders Police, 2011–13. Internat. Visitor Leadership Prog., US State Dept, 2007. Mem. Bd, Scottish Inst. of Policing Res., 2009. Mem., Adv. Gp, Place2Be (children's charity), 2010–. Chm., volleyball section, Police Sport UK. Hon. Col, Kentucky, 2007. Queen's Golden Jubilee Medal, 2002. *Publications:* Public Servant Scotland, 2010. *Recreations:* volleyball (played European match as mem., GB Police team competing against Finland, 2009), learning the guitar (consistently guilty of terrible crimes against many respected songs).

SKELMERSDALE, 7th Baron *cr* 1828; **Roger Bootle-Wilbraham;** Director, Broadleigh Nurseries Ltd, 1991–2013 (Managing Director, 1973–81); *b* 2 April 1945; *o s* of 6th Baron Skelmersdale, DSO, MC, and Ann (*d* 1974), *d* of late Percy Cuthbert Quilter; *S* father, 1973; *m* 1972, Christine Joan, *o d* of Roy Morgan; one *s* one *d*. *Educ:* Eton; Lord Wandsworth Coll., Basingstoke; Somerset Farm Institute; Hadlow Coll. VSO (Zambia), 1969–71; Proprietor, Broadleigh Gardens, 1972; Vice-Chm., Co En Co, 1979–81. A Lord in Waiting (Govt Whip), 1981–86; Parly Under-Sec. of State, DoE, 1986–87; Parly Under-Sec. of State, DHSS, 1987–88, Dept of Social Security, 1988–89, NI Office, 1989–90; House of Lords: Dep. Chm. of cttees, 1991–96; Dep. Speaker, 1996–2003; elected Mem., 1999; an Opposition Whip, 2003–05; Opposition spokesman on work and pensions, 2005–09, Home Office, 2009–10. Dep. Speaker, Cttees, 2010–; Mem., Select Cttee on Communications, 2010–. President: Somerset Trust for Nature Conservation, 1980–; British Naturalists Assoc., 1980–85. Chm., Stroke Assoc., 1993–2004. Gov., Castle Sch., Taunton, 1993–97. *Recreations:* gardening, reading, bridge playing. *Heir:* *s* Hon. Andrew Bootle-Wilbraham [*b* 9 Aug. 1977; *m* 2005, Fenella Jane, *yr d* of Jonathan Richmond Edwards; two *s*]. *Address:* c/o House of Lords, SW1A 0PW.

SKELTON, Nicholas David, (Nick), OBE 2012; show jumper; *b* 30 Dec. 1957; *s* of David Frank Skelton and Norma Skelton (*née* Brindley); *m* 1982, Sarah Poile; two *s*. Jun. European Champion, 1975; British Champion, 1981, on St James; European Championships: team gold medal, 1985, 1987, 1989, team silver medal, 1991, 1993, 1995, team bronze medal, 2011, individual bronze medal, on Apollo, 1987, on Carlo, 2011; World Championships: team bronze medals, 1982, 1990, 1998, team silver medal, and individual bronze medal, on Apollo, 1986; winner: King George V Gold Cup, on St James, 1984, on Limited Edition, 1993, 1996, on Hopes Are High, 1999; Hickstead Derby, on J Nick, 1987, on Apollo, 1988, 1989; Grand Prix in Britain, Canada, France, Germany, Ireland, USA; Member: Nations Cup team, 1978–; British Team, 1978–; Olympic team, 1988, 1992, 1996, 2004, 2008, 2012 (Gold Medal, team jumping). Chef d'équipe, British team, Nations Cup, Lisbon, 2001. *Publications:* Only Falls and Horses (autobiog.), 2001.

SKELTON, Peter John, OBE 1997; Director, Tunisia, 2005–09, and Director, Business Support Services, Near East and North Africa Region, 2008–09, British Council; Volunteer, Refugee Support Devon (Ltd), since 2013; *b* 24 Sept. 1949; *s* of John Frederick and Gwendoline Mabel Skelton; *m* 1st, 1971, Heather Morrison (marr. diss. 2009); one *s* one *d*; 2nd, 2009, Trupti Desai; one *s*. *Educ:* Queen Elizabeth's Grammar Sch., Barnet; Durham Univ. (BA Hons Modern Arabic Studies 1971); UCNW, Bangor (PGCE (TEFL) 1973). Desk Officer, FCO, 1971; British Council: Asst Rep., Jordan, 1977–81, Peru, 1982–84; Dep. Rep., Wales, 1984–86, Zambia, 1986–88; Dir, Hamburg, 1989–93, E Jerusalem (West Bank and Gaza), 1993–98; Regl Dir, Eastern and Central Africa, and Dir, Kenya, 1998–2000; Dir, Cyprus, 2000–05. CSV Volunteer Co-ordinator, BBC Radio Devon, 2010–13. Parent Gov., Clyst St Mary Primary Sch., Devon, 2014–. *Recreations:* family, Tottenham Hotspur, all sport, cycling, playing guitar, Hospital Radio Exeter, editing the Clyst Valley News. *Address:* c/o British Council Association, 10 Spring Gardens, SW1A 2BN. *T:* (020) 7930 8466.

SKELTON, Robert William, OBE 1989; Keeper, Indian Department, Victoria and Albert Museum, 1978–88; *b* 11 June 1929; *s* of John William Skelton and Victoria (*née* Wright); *m* 1954, Frances Aird; three *s*. *Educ:* Tiffin Boys' Sch., Kingston-upon-Thames. Joined Indian Section of Victoria and Albert Museum, 1950; Asst Keeper, 1960; Dep. Keeper, 1972; Nuffield Travelling Fellow in India, 1962. Mem. Council: Royal Asiatic Soc., 1970–73, 1975–78, 1988–92; Soc. for S Asian Studies, 1984–94; Trustee: Asia House Trust (London), 1977–2008; Indian Nat. Trust for Art and Cultural Heritage, UK, 1991–2008. *Publications:* Indian Miniatures from the XVth to XIXth Centuries, 1961; Rajasthani Temple Hangings of the Krishna Cult, 1973; (jtly) Islamic Painting and Arts of the Book, 1976; (jtly) the Indian Painting, 1978; (jtly) Arts of Bengal, 1979; (jtly) The Indian Heritage, 1982; (jtly) Islamic Art in the Keir Collection, 1988; (jtly) The Indian Portrait 1560–1860, 2010; (jtly) Ragamala Paintings from India, 2011; (jtly) Beyond Extravagance: a Royal collection of gems and jewels, 2013; various contribs to art periodicals and conf. proc., 1956–. *Recreations:* chamber music, walking. *Address:* 10 Spencer Road, South Croydon CR2 7EH. *E:* robertskelton@blueyonder.co.uk.

SKEMPTON, Howard While; composer; *b* Chester, 31 Oct. 1947; *s* of late Ivor Skempton and Leslie Skempton; *m* 1984, Susan Lordon (*d* 2008); one *s*. *Educ:* Birkenhead Sch.; Ealing Technical Coll. Composition Tutor, Birmingham Conservatoire, 2005–. *Compositions include:* Lento, 1991; Six Figures, for solo cello, 1998; Five Preludes, for guitar, 1999; Chamber Concerto, for 15 players; Concerto for Hurdy-Gurdy and Percussion; Tendrils, for string quartet; The Moon is Flashing, song cycle for tenor and orch.; Only the Sound Remains, for viola and ensemble; Song's Eternity, choral; Five Rings Triples, for eight church bells, 2012; Piano Concerto, 2015. Hon. RAM 2012. *Recreations:* art, theatre, friendship. *Address:* 4 Pleasant Way, Leamington Spa CV32 5XA. *T:* (01926) 338739. *E:* howardskempton@aol.com.

See also Maj. Gen. K. Skempton.

SKEMPTON, Maj. Gen. Keith, CBE 1997; DL; Defence Sector Lead (formerly defence consultant), Capita Property and Infrastructure Ltd (formerly Capita Symonds), since 2010; *b* 22 Feb. 1949; *s* of late Dr Ivor Skempton and Leslie Skempton; *m* 1971, Susan Lawrence; one *d*. *Educ:* Birkenhead Sch.; Liverpool Coll. of Building; Mons OCS; Army Staff Coll., Camberley. Commnd Cheshire Regt, 1969; served UK, ME and FE; COS, 33 Armd Bde, 1982–83; MA to GOC NI, 1986–88; CO, 1st Bn, Cheshire Regt, 1988–91 (mentioned in despatches, 1988, 1990, NI); DCS, 1st Armd Div., 1991–93; DACOS, G4 Ops and Plans, HQ Land Comd, 1993–96; COS, HQ British Forces Cyprus, 1996–98; DCS, Support, HQ ARRC, 1998–2001 (QCVS 1999, Kosovo op.); ACOS, HQ AFSOUTH, 2001–03; Col, 22nd (Cheshire) Regt, 1999–2006. Business Develt Dir, Denis Ferranti Gp, 2006–07; Operations Dir, Chester Cathedral, 2007–08. Pres., SSAFA (Cheshire Br.), 2011–. Trustee, Cheshire Military Mus., 1998–. FCMI 2003; MInstD 2003. DL Cheshire, 2006. *Recreations:* sailing, game shooting, ski-ing, motor vehicles. *Address:* Regimental Headquarters, Mercian Regiment (Cheshire), The Castle, Chester CH1 2DN. *T:* (01244) 327617, (mobile) 07788 415366. *E:* keithskempton@hotmail.com, keith.skempton@capita.co.uk. *Clubs:* Army and Navy; Chester City, Cheshire Pitt.

See also H. W. Skempton.

SKENE, Alison Jean Katherine, MBE 2015; Director, Skene Group, since 1972; Vice Lord-Lieutenant of Aberdeen City, 2007–14; *b* 26 May 1939; *d* of Alexander Lamont and Alexa Lee Lamont (*née* Will); *m* 1964, Charles Pirie Skene; one *s* two *d*. *Educ:* High Sch. for Girls, Aberdeen; Univ. of Aberdeen (MA); Aberdeen Trng Coll. Teacher of French, 1961–65. Pres., Jun. Chamber Wives Gp, 1970–71; Committee Member: St John Assoc., 1984–90; Queens Cross/Harlaw Community Council, 1987–94; Grampian/Houston Assoc., 1989–2002. Mem., Gen. Council, Business Cttee, 1980–2007, Court, 1990–2002, Aberdeen Univ. Mem. Cttee, Elphinstone Inst. Friends' Assoc., 1996–2005. Burgess of Guild, City of Aberdeen, 1998. DL Aberdeen, 1999. Pres., St Nicholas Probus Club, 2006–07. OStJ 2000 (SSStJ 1987). *Recreations:* spending time with grandsons, Hamish, Cameron, Charlie and Oscar, walking, travelling, golfing, reading, crosswords. *Address:* 21 Rubislaw Den North, Aberdeen AB15 4AL. *T:* (01224) 317517. *E:* alison.skene@theskenegroup.com. *Club:* Aberdeen Ladies' Golf.

SKENE, Prudence Patricia, CBE 2000; Governance Associate, Clore Leadership Programme, since 2009; *b* 9 Jan. 1944; *d* of Robert Worboys Skene and Phyllis Monica Skene (*née* Langley); *m* 1986, Brian Henry Wray (*d* 2002); one step *s* one step *d*. *Educ:* Francis Holland Sch., London; Open Univ. (BA Hons. 1st Cl. 2009). Dep. Administrator, The Round House, Chalk Farm, 1973–75; Ballet Rambert: Administrator, 1975–78; Admin. Dir, 1978–84; Exec. Dir, 1984–86; Exec. Producer, English Shakespeare Co., 1987–90 and 1992; Dir, The Arts Foundn, 1993–98. Non-executive Director: Theatre Royal, Bath, 1998–2003; Royal United Hosp. Bath NHS Trust, 1999–2003; Chairman: Arvon Foundn, 2000–05; Rambert Dance Co., 2000–09; Free Word, 2010–14. Mem., Arts Council of England (formerly Arts Council of GB), 1992–2000 (Chairman: Dance Panel, 1992–96; Lottery Panel, 1996–2000). Vice-Pres., 1985–89, Pres., 1991–92, Theatrical Management Assoc.; Chm., Dancers Resettlement Trust and Vice-Chm., Dancers Resettlement Fund, 1988–92. Trustee: Cardiff Old Liby Trust, 1996–2000; Stephen Spender Trust (formerly Meml Fund), 2000– (Chm., 2013–); Friends of the V&A, 2004–10; NESTA, 2006–07; Nureyev Foundn, 2007–. FRSA 1992. *Recreations:* travel, food, the performing arts. *Address:* 19a Eccleston Street, SW1W 9LX.

SKEOCH, (Norman) Keith; Chief Executive: Standard Life Investments, since 2004 (Executive Director and Chief Investment Officer, 1999–2004); Standard Life plc, since 2015 (Executive Director, 2006); *b* Ouston, 5 Nov. 1956; *s* of Norman and Audrey Skeoch; *m* 1981, Andrea Ball; two *s*. *Educ:* Prior Pursglove Coll.; Univ. of Sussex (BA Hons); Univ. of Warwick (MA). Govt Econ. Service, 1979–80; James Capel: Internat. Economist, 1980–99; Chief Economist and Associate Partner, 1984–99; Sen. Exec. (Partner), 1986–99; Dir, Econs and Strategy and Mem., James Capel & Co. Bd, 1993–99; Man. Dir, Internat. Equities, 1998–99; Standard Life Assurance Co.: Mem., Gp Exec., 2003–; Exec. Dir, 2006–. Chm., SLCP (Private Equity), 2004–15. Non-executive Director: HDFC Asset Mgt, India, 2006–; HDFC Life, India, 2006–. Mem., Chancellor's Wkg Gp on Rights Issues, 2007. Mem., Sen. Practitioner Panel, FSA, 2006; Mem., Adv. Panel on impact of financial crisis, 2010, Dir, and Mem., Codes and Standards Cttee and Audit Cttee, 2012, Financial Reporting Council. Dir, ABI, 2007 (Chm., Investment Cttee); Dir, Investment Mgt Assoc., 2007 (Chm., Asset Mgt Cttee). Chm., Instnl Shareholders Cttee, 2009. Mem., Adv. Council, Instnl Investor Cttee, 2011–14. FCSI 2005; Fellow, Soc. of Business Economists, 2012. Hon. DBA Teesside, 2011; DUniv Sussex, 2015. *Recreations:* fly fishing, music, watching Rugby. *Address:* Standard Life Investments Ltd, 1 George Street, Edinburgh EH2 2LL. *T:* (0131) 245 5046. *Club:* Reform.

SKERRIT, Hon. Roosevelt; MHA (Lab) Vieille Case, Dominica, since 2000; Prime Minister of Dominica, since 2004; Minister for Finance, since 2004, and for Foreign Affairs and Information Technology, since 2010; *b* 8 June 1972; one *s*; *m* 2013, Melissa Poponne; one *s*. *Educ:* New Mexico State Univ. (Dip. Secondary Educn 1995); Univ. of Mississippi (BA Hons Psychol. and English 1997). Quality Assce Officer, JUC Factory, Dominica; teacher, Portsmouth Secondary Sch.; Supervisor, Student Activity Center, Univ. of Mississippi; Database Manager/Advr, Offshore Firm; Lectr, Dominica State Coll., 1997–99. Minister: for Sports and Youth Affairs, 2000; for Educn, Sports and Youth Affairs, 2000–04. Mem., Exec. Bd, UNESCO. Mem. Council, Univ. of WI (Member: F and GP Cttee; Strategy Cttee). Leader, Dominica Labour Party, 2004–.

SKEWIS, (William) Iain, PhD; Principal Consultant, Maldwyn Development Consultancy and Action with Impact (formerly Maldwyn Development Consultancy and Rural Development Solutions), since 2009; Coordinator, Soccer Destinations, since 2006; Marketing Advisor, Euroworld Sports, since 2009; *s* of John Jamieson and Margaret Middlemass Skewis; *m* 1963, Jessie Frame Weir; two *s* one *d*. *Educ:* Hamilton Academy; Univ. of Glasgow (BSc, PhD). FTS 1987. British Rail, 1961–63; Transport Holding Co., 1963–66; Highlands and Islands Develt Bd, 1966–72; Yorkshire and Humberside Develt, 1973–77; Chief Executive: Develt Bd for Rural Wales, 1977–90; Enterprise SW Shropshire, 1998–2009. Dir, Develt Consultancy, 1995–2009. Chm., Regl Studies Assoc., 1990–93. Chairman: British Isles Soccer Tournaments Assoc., 1996–2010; Football Assoc. of Wales Premier Cup, 1998–2008. *Recreation:* soccer. *Address:* Rock House, The Square, Montgomery, Powys SY15 6PA. *T:* (01686) 668276. *E:* wiskewis@online.rednet.co.uk.

SKIDELSKY, family name of **Baron Skidelsky**.

SKIDELSKY, Baron *cr* 1991 (Life Peer), of Tilton in the County of East Sussex; **Robert Jacob Alexander Skidelsky,** DPhil; FRSL; FRHistS; FBA 1994; Professor of Political Economy, Warwick University, 1990–2007, now Emeritus; *b* 25 April 1939; *s* of late Boris Skidelsky and Galia Sapelkin; *m* 1970, Augusta Mary Clarissa Hope; two *s* one *d*. *Educ:* Brighton Coll.; Jesus Coll., Oxford (BA and MA Mod. Hist.; DPhil; Hon. Fellow, 1997). FRHistS 1973; FRSL 1978. Res. Fellow: Nuffield Coll., Oxford, 1965–68; British Acad., 1968–70; Associate Prof. of History, Sch. of Advanced Internat. Studies, Johns Hopkins Univ., Washington, DC, 1970–76; Head, Dept of History, Philosophy and Eur. Studies, Polytechnic of N London, 1976–78; Prof. of Internat. Studies, Warwick Univ., 1978–90. Director: Stilwell Financial Inc., 2001–03; Janus Capital, 2003–11; Gtr Europe Fund, 2005–09; Sistema, 2008–10; Rusnano Capital, 2010–. Dir, 1989–91, Chm., 1991–2001, Social Market Foundn; Mem., Policy Cttee, SDP, 1988–90. Opposition Spokesman on: Culture, Media and Sport, H of L, 1997–98; Treasury affairs, 1998–99. Chairman: Charleston Trust, 1987–92; Hands Off Reading Campaign, 1994–98. Member: Adv. Council on Public Records, 1988–93; Schools Examinations and Assessment Council, 1992–93; Council, Royal Economic Soc., 2007–; Adv. Council, Inst. for New Economic Thinking, 2010–. Mem., Bd of Dirs, Moscow Sch. of Pol Studies, 1999–; Exec. Sec., UK/Russia Roundtable, 2005–07. Governor: Portsmouth Univ., 1994–97; Brighton Coll., 1998–2004 (Chm. of Govs, 2004–); Wilton Park Academic Council, 2003–09. Hon. DLit: Buckingham, 1997; Rome, 2010; Warwick, 2011. *Publications:* Politicians and the Slump, 1967, 2nd edn 1994; English Progressive Schools, 1969; Oswald Mosley, 1975; (ed) The End of the Keynesian Era, 1977; (ed, with Michael Holroyd) William Gerhardie's God's Fifth Column, 1981; John Maynard Keynes, vol. 1 1883–1920, Hopes Betrayed, 1983, vol. 2 1921–1937, The Economist as Saviour (Wolfson History Prize), 1992, vol. 3 1937–1946, Fighting for Britain (Duff Cooper, Lionel Gelber, James Tait Black Meml and Council on Foreign Relations Prizes), 2000, abridged edn in one vol. 2003; (ed) Thatcherism, 1988; Interests and Obsessions, 1993; The World After Communism, 1995; Keynes, 1996; Keynes: return of the master, 2009; (with Edward Skidelsky) How Much is Enough?: the love of money, and the case for the good life, 2012. *Recreations:* music, travelling, sport, conversation. *Address:* Saxon Lodge, Saxon Lane, Seaford, East Sussex BN25 1QL. *T:* (01323) 890941.

SKIDMORE, Christopher James, FRHistS; MP (C) Kingswood, since 2010; author, since 2004; *b* Bristol, 17 May 1981; *s* of Robert and Elaine Skidmore. *Educ:* Bristol Grammar Sch.; Christ Church, Oxford (BA Hons Double First; MSt). FRHistS 2010. Advr, Cons. Party, 2006–09; Tutor, 2009–10, Hon. Res. Fellow, 2012–, Bristol Univ. Member: Health Select Cttee, 2010–13; Educn Select Cttee, 2012–14; Policy Bd, No 10 Downing St, 2013–. FRSA. *Publications:* Edward VI: the lost king, 2007; Death and the Virgin, 2010; After the Coalition, 2011; Britannia Unchained, 2012; Bosworth: the birth of the Tudors, 2013. *Address:* House of Commons, SW1A 0AA. *T:* (020) 7219 7094. *E:* chris.skidmore.mp@parliament.uk.

SKIDMORE, Jeffrey, OBE 2015; Artistic Director and Conductor, Ex Cathedra, since 1969; *b* 27 Feb. 1951; *s* of Ernest and Lily Mary Skidmore; *m* 1974, Janet Mary Moore; two *s* one *d*. *Educ:* Magdalen Coll., Oxford (BA). Head of Music: Hagley Park Sch., Rugeley, 1978–80; John Wilmott Sch., Birmingham, 1980–92. Hon. Res. Fellow, Univ. of Birmingham, 1998–; Hon. Fellow, Birmingham Conservatoire, 2001. Has made recordings. *Address:* Ex Cathedra, CBSO Centre, Berkley Street, Birmingham B1 2LF. *T:* (0121) 616 3411. *E:* info@excathedra.co.uk.

SKILBECK, Diana Margaret, MBE 2012; Headmistress, The Queen's School, Chester, 1989–2001; *b* 14 Nov. 1942; *d* of late William Allen Skilbeck and Elsie Almond Skilbeck. *Educ:* Wirral County Grammar School for Girls, Cheshire; Furzedown Coll., London (Teacher's Cert.); BA Hons London (External). Assistant Teacher: Mendell Primary Sch., 1964–67; Gayton Primary Sch., 1967–69; Wirral County Grammar Sch., 1969–74; Head of Geography, Wirral County Grammar Sch., 1974–78; Dep. Headmistress, West Kirby Grammar Sch., 1978–83; Headmistress, Sheffield High School, GPDST, 1983–89. Hon. MA Chester, 2015. *Recreations:* inland waterways, walking, singing, reading, industrial archaeology.

SKILBECK, Prof. Malcolm, AO 2014; education consultant and writer; Emeritus Professor, Deakin University, Australia, 1986; *b* 22 Sept. 1932; *s* of Charles Harrison Skilbeck and Elsie Muriel Nash Skilbeck; *m* Helen Connell. *Educ:* Univ. of Sydney (BA); Acad. DipEd London, PhD London; MA Illinois. Secondary school teacher and adult educn teacher, 1958–63; Lectr, Univ. of Bristol, 1963–71; Prof., New Univ. of Ulster, 1971–75; Dir, Australian Curriculum Develt Centre, 1975–81; Dir of Studies, Schs Council for Curriculum and Exams for England and Wales, 1981–83; Prof. of Education, Univ. of London, 1981–85; Vice-Chancellor and Pres., Deakin Univ., Australia, 1986–91; Dep. Dir (Educn), Directorate of Educn, Employment, Labour and Social Affairs, OECD, 1991–97. Active in voluntary organizations concerned with educn for internat. understanding, e.g. Chm., World Educn Fellowship, 1981–85. Currently researching history of nature ideas in art, religion, science and educn. Hon. DLitt NUI, 2000. *Publications:* John Dewey, 1970; (jtly) Classroom and Culture, 1976; (jtly) Inservice Education and Training, 1977; A Core Curriculum for the Common School 1982; (ed) Evaluating the Curriculum in the Eighties, 1984; School Based Curriculum Development, 1984; Readings in School-Based Curriculum Development, 1984; Curriculum Reform, 1990; The Vocational Quest, 1994; (jtly) Redefining Tertiary Education, 1998; Access and Equity in Higher Education, 2000; Education for All: 2000 assessment, 2000; numerous contribs to jls, project reports, etc. *Recreations:* landcare, winemaking, reading.

SKILTON, Ven. Christopher John; Archdeacon of Croydon, since 2013; *b* 19 March 1955; *s* of John Hampsheir Skilton and Kathleen Ada Skilton; *m* 1980, Barbara Kilgour; one *s* two *d*. *Educ:* Magdalene Coll., Cambridge (BA 1976, MA 1980); Wycliffe Hall, Oxford; St John's Coll., Nottingham (MA in Mission/Ministry 1996). Ordained deacon, 1980, priest, 1981; Curate: St Mary, Ealing, 1980–84; Newborough and Leigh St John, Wimborne, 1984–88; Team Vicar, St Paul, Great Baddow, 1988–95; Team Rector, Sanderstead, 1995–2003; RD, Croydon S, 2000–03; Archdeacon of Lambeth, 2004–13; Priest-in-charge, St Mark's, Kennington, 2008–09. *Recreations:* gardening, cricket, recent British politics, The Archers, classical music, classic and contemporary fiction. *Address:* 2a Sefton Road, Croydon CR0 7HR. *T:* (020) 8656 4017; (office) St Matthew's House, 100 George Street, Croydon CR0 1PE. *T:* (020) 8256 9633. *E:* chris.skilton@southwark.anglican.org.

SKILTON, Prof. David John; Professor of English, 1988–2009, now Emeritus, and Research Professor, 2002–11, Cardiff University (formerly University of Wales College of Cardiff); *b* 10 July 1942; *s* of Henry C. S. Skilton and Iris F. M. Skilton; *m* 1st, 1976, Marvid E. G. Kennedy-Finlayson (marr. diss.); 2nd, 1984, Joanne V. Papworth; one *s* one *d*. *Educ:* Tollington Grammar Sch., London; King's Coll., Cambridge (MA, MLitt); Univ. of Copenhagen. Lectr, Glasgow Univ., 1970–80; Professor of English: St David's University Coll., Lampeter, 1980–86; UWIST, 1986–88; Head of School of English, Communication and Philosophy, UWCC, then Cardiff Univ., 1988–2002; Pro Vice-Chancellor, UWCC, 1992–96; Dean, Faculty of Humanities, Cardiff Univ., 1997–99. Mem., Nat. Curriculum English Working Group, 1988–89; Trustee, Brainwave Project Trust (formerly Roald Dahl Arts Project), 1996– (Chair, 2011–). Literary Adviser to Trollope Soc., 1988–; Editor, Trollope Soc. edn of novels of Anthony Trollope, 1988–99; Founding Ed., Jl of Illustration

Studies, 2007–; co-author, Database of Mid-Victorian Illustration, 2007–. FRSA 2001; FEA 2002. *Publications:* Anthony Trollope and his Contemporaries, 1972, 2nd edn 1996; Defoe to the Victorians, 1977, 2nd edn 1985; The Early and Mid-Victorian Novel, 1993. *Recreations:* music, Scandinavian culture. *Address:* School of English, Communication and Philosophy, Cardiff University, Cardiff CF10 3EU. *T:* (029) 2087 4000.

SKINGLE, Diana; HM Diplomatic Service, retired; High Commissioner to Seychelles, 2004–07; *b* 3 May 1947; *d* of Eric Barry Skingle and Joyce Ada Skingle; *m* 2011, Christopher John Marshall Carrington. *Educ:* Chatham Grammar Sch. for Girls; Open Univ. (BSc Hons; Dip Env and Dev); Birkbeck Coll., London (MSc Merit Pols and Sociol.). Joined Commonwealth Office, subseq. FCO, 1966; Kampala, 1970; FCO, 1972; Abidjan, 1974; Vila, 1975; Prague, 1977; Casablanca, 1979; Second Secretary: FCO, 1982; (Aid/Commercial) Georgetown, 1985; (Develt) Bridgetown, 1986; First Secretary: (Information) UK Delegn to NATO, Brussels, 1988; FCO, 1993; Dep. Hd of Mission, Addis Ababa, 2001–04. *Recreations:* cats, walking.

SKINGSLEY, Air Chief Marshal Sir Anthony (Gerald), GBE 1992 KCB 1986 (CB 1983); Deputy Commander-in-Chief, Allied Forces Central Europe, 1989–92, retired; *b* 19 Oct. 1933; *s* of Edward Roberts Skingsley; *m* 1957, Lilwen; two *s* one *d. Educ:* Cambridge Univ. (BA, MA). Commissioned RAFVR 1954, RAF 1955; several flying appointments, then Flt Comdr 13 Sqdn, 1961–62; OC Ops Sqdn, RAF Akrotiri, 1962–63; RAF Staff Coll., Bracknell, 1964; OC 45 Sqdn, RAF Tengah, Singapore, 1965–67; jssc Latimer, 1968; RAF Project Officer for Tornado in MoD, 1968–71; OC 214 Sqdn, RAF Marham, 1972–74; Station Comdr, RAF Laarbruch, Germany, 1974–76; Hon. ADC to the Queen, 1976–78; Asst Chief of Staff, Offensive Ops, HQ 2nd ATAF, 1977; RCDS 1978; Director of Air Staff Plans, MoD, 1978–80; Asst Chief of Staff, Plans and Policy, SHAPE, 1980–83; Comdt, RAF Staff Coll., Bracknell, 1983–84; ACAS, 1985–86; Air Mem. for Personnel, 1986–87; C-in-C RAF Germany, and Comdr, Second ATAF, 1987–89. Mem., Allgemeine Rheinlaendische Industrie Gesellschaft, 1975. Pres., RAFA, Luxembourg, 1992–2010; Mem. Adv. Council, Atlantic Council, 1993–. *Recreations:* travel, off-shore sailing, music, golf. *Address:* c/o National Westminster Bank, 43 Swan Street, West Malling, Kent ME19 6HF. *Club:* Royal Air Force.

SKINNER, Angus Mackinnon Cumming; writer; *b* 4 Jan. 1950; *s* of Dr Theodore Skinner, OBE and Morag Mackinnon Skinner; *m* (marr. diss. 2001); one *s* two *d. Educ:* Univ. of Edinburgh (BSc 1971); London Univ. (CQSW 1973); Strathclyde Univ. (MBA 1988); Pennsylvania Univ. (Master of Applied Positive Psychol., 2006); Univ. of Oxford (Dip. Local History, 2002); Open Univ. (MA Art History, 2015). Social Worker, Cheshire and Kent, 1971–75; Social Work Manager, Lothian, 1975–87; Depute Dir, Borders, 1987–91; Chief Social Work Advr, Scottish Office, 1991–92; Chief Insp. of Social Work Services for Scotland, Scottish Office, subseq. Scottish Exec. Educn Dept, 1992–2005. Mem., Charter for Compassion. Founding Fellow: Inst. of Contemp. Scotland, 2000; Internat. Positive Psychol Assoc., 2006; FRSA. *Publications:* Another Kind of Home, 1992; Leadership in Social Care, 1999, 2009. *Recreations:* family, friends, learning.

SKINNER, Charles Edward; Founder and Director, Your Reputation Matters Ltd, since 2014; *b* 27 July 1951; *s* of late Charles John Henry Skinner and Nell Skinner (*née* Seward); *m* 1973, Caroline Mary Gregory; one *d. Educ:* Nightingale Sch., Wanstead, London. Editorial Trainee, Industrial Daily News, 1968; Editorial Asst, Maclean-Hunter News Publishing, 1969–71; Asst Ed., IPC Business Press, 1971–75; Central Office of Information: Information Officer, N Amer. Desk, Overseas Press and Radio, 1975; Sen. Press Officer, ME Desk, and Defence Correspondent, 1981; Hd, UK and Overseas Radio, 1985; Dir, Films, Television and Radio, 1988–90; Hd, Mktg and Corporate Communication, Home Office, 1990–97; Dir, Govt Information and Communication Service Develt Centre, Cabinet Office, 1997–99; Hd of Mktg, DETR, 1999–2002; Dir of Communication, DfT, 2002–04; Head: of Communication, Tower Hamlets Council, 2007–09; of Communications and Consultation, Haringey Council, 2005–07 and 2009–12. Chm., Whitehall Hds of Marketing, 2000–04. FRSA 1993; FCIPR (FIPR 2004). *Publications:* (ed) MI5 - The Security Service, 1993. *Recreations:* opera, political biography, horology, naval history, cycling, motorcycling, old friends. *Club:* Royal Automobile.

SKINNER, Prof. Christopher John, CBE 2010; PhD; FBA 2004; Professor of Statistics, London School of Economics and Political Science, since 2011; *b* 12 March 1953; *s* of Richard Skinner and Daphne Skinner; *m* 1998, Sheila (*née* Hinchliffe) (*d* 2010); two *s. Educ:* Trinity Coll., Cambridge (BA 1975); LSE (MSc 1976); Univ. of Southampton (PhD 1982). Lectr, 1982–89, Sen. Lectr, 1989–94, Prof., 1994–2011, Univ. of Southampton. *Publications:* (ed jtly) Analysis of Complex Surveys, 1989; (ed with R. Chambers) Analysis of Survey Data, 2003. *Recreations:* cinema, music. *Address:* Department of Statistics, London School of Economics and Political Science, Houghton Street, WC2A 2AE. *T:* (020) 7405 7686.

SKINNER, David; Chief Executive, Co-operative Wholesale Society Ltd, 1992–96; *b* 27 Oct. 1931; *s* of late David Skinner and Mary (*née* Davidson); *m* 1st, 1956, Elizabeth Vera Harben (marr. diss. 1976); one *s* one *d*; 2nd, 1996, Morag J. L. Mar (*née* Busby). *Educ:* Gateshead Grammar Sch.; Nottingham Univ. (BSc). Nat. Service, RNVR, 1953–55. Mgt Trainee, Yorkshire Imperial Metals, 1955–57; Productivity Services Manager, Distillers' Co., 1957–60; Mgt Consultant, 1960–68; Food Divl Manager, Scottish CWS, 1969–73; Co-operative Wholesale Society Ltd: Non Food Controller, 1974–83; Retail Controller and Dep. Chief Exec. (Retail & Services), 1983–92. *Recreations:* comfortable travelling, easy gardening. *Address:* Rowan Tree Cottage, Pannal Road, Follifoot, Harrogate HG3 1DR.

SKINNER, David Victor, FRCS, FRCSE, FRCSGlas, FRCEM, FIMCRCSE; Consultant, Emergency Department, John Radcliffe Hospital, Oxford, 1993–2011, now Emeritus; Dean, Faculty of Accident and Emergency Medicine, 2000–04; *b* 6 May 1948; *s* of Victor and Joan Skinner; *m* 1975, Alison Rosemary (*née* Earley); one *s* one *d. Educ:* Haberdashers' Aske's Sch.; Royal Free Hosp., London (MB BS 1975). FRCSE 1981; FRCS 1990; FRCSGlas 1993; FIMCRCSE 2004. Consultant, Emergency Dept, St Bartholomew's Hosp., London, 1986–93; Med. Dir, Bart's City Lifesaver; Hon. Sen. Lectr, Oxford Med. Sch. Chair, project exec. team, trauma guidelines, NICE, 2013–. Gov., RNLI. Trustee, Maternal and Childhealth Advocacy Internat., 2013–. Service Medal, OStJ, 2003. *Publications:* (ed jtly) Cambridge Textbook of Accident and Emergency Medicine, 1997; (ed jtly) Trauma Care, 1998; (ed jtly) Trauma (A Companion to Bailey and Love's Short Practice of Surgery), 1999; (ed jtly) ABC of Major Trauma, 4th edn 2013. *Recreations:* family, home, Portugal, Scottish Highlands, the Swan yacht Red Beauty, the Scuderia, British motorcycles (old) and cars (new). *Address:* Northcott, Chiltern Road, Chesham Bois, Amersham, Bucks HP6 5PH. *E:* mvf4312r@googlemail.com.

SKINNER, Dennis Edward; MP (Lab) Bolsover, since 1970; *b* 11 Feb. 1932; good working-class mining stock; *m* 1960; one *s* two *d. Educ:* Tupton Hall Grammar Sch.; Ruskin Coll., Oxford. Miner, Parkhouse Colliery and Glapwell Colliery, 1949–70. Mem., Nat. Exec. Cttee of Labour Party, 1978–92, 1994–98, 1999–; Vice-Chm., Labour Party, 1987–88, Chm., 1988–89; Pres., Derbyshire Miners (NUM), 1966–70; Pres., NE Derbys Constituency Labour Party, 1968–71; Derbyshire CC, 1964–70; Clay Cross UDC, 1960–70. *Publications:* Sailing Close to the Wind: reminiscences, 2014. *Recreations:* tennis, cycling, walking. *Address:* House of Commons, SW1A 0AA. *T:* (01773) 581027. *Clubs:* Miners' Welfares in Derbyshire; Bestwood Working Men's.

SKINNER, Frank; entertainer, since 1987; *b* 28 Jan. 1957; *s* of John and Doris Collins; *né* Chris Collins, changed name to Frank Skinner, 1987. *Educ:* Birmingham Polytech. (BA Hons English 1981); Univ. of Warwick (MA English 1982). Numerous stand-up performances incl. London Palladium, 1996, and Battersea Power Station, 1997; UK tour, 2007; appearances in West End include: Art, 1999; Cooking with Elvis, 2000; Baddiel & Skinner Unplanned, 2001; Credit Crunch Cabaret (host), Lyric, 2009; Frank Skinner & Friends, Noel Coward Th., 2012; Frank Skinner: Man In A Suit, Soho Th., 2013, Leicester Sq. Th. and UK tour, 2014; *television:* Fantasy Football League (with David Baddiel), 5 series, 1994–2005 (VHE Award of Excellence for Top Comedy Prog., 1994); The Frank Skinner Show, 8 series, 1995–2005; Baddiel & Skinner Unplanned (with David Baddiel), 5 series, 2000–05; (writer and star) Shane, 2 series, 2004–05; Frank Skinner's Opinionated, 3 series, 2010–11; Frank Skinner on George Formby, 2011; Room 101, 5 series; I Love My Country, 2013; Sky Arts Portrait Artist of the Year, 2 series, 2013–14; Sky Arts Landscape Artist of the Year, 2015; Taskmaster, 2015; *radio:* Saturday morning show for Absolute Radio, 2009– (Sony Award for Best Entertainment Prog., 2011); Don't Start, 2011, 2012, 2015; The Rest is History, Radio 4, 2014–15. Number one single (with David Baddiel and The Lightning Seeds), Three Lions, 1996 and 1998. Columnist, The Times, 2009–11. Pres., Dr Johnson Soc., 2010–11. In Conversation with Archbishop of Canterbury, Dr Rowan Williams, Canterbury Cath., 2011. DUniv: UCE, 2006; Wolverhampton, 2009. Perrier Comedy Award, 1991; Best Comedy Entertainment Personality, British Comedy Awards, 2001; Variety Club Award for Comedy, 2001; London's Favourite Comedy Act, Capital Awards, 2005; Radio Academy Award, 2014. *Publications:* Frank Skinner on Frank Skinner, 2001; Frank Skinner on the Road, 2008; Dispatches from the Sofa: the collected wisdom of Frank Skinner, 2011. *Recreations:* watching football, playing ukulele, visiting art galleries. *Address:* Avalon Management Group Ltd, 4A Exmoor Street, W10 6BD.

SKINNER, Air Vice-Marshal Graham, CBE 1999 (MBE 1982); CEng, FIMechE, FRAeS; non-executive Director, Short Brothers plc, Belfast, Bombardier Aerostructures and Engineering Services (formerly Bombardier Aerospace), since 2000; *b* 16 Sept. 1945; s of late Frederick and Phyllis Skinner; *m* 1969, Margaret Christine Hacon; one *s* one *d. Educ:* Hampton Sch.; RAF Tech. Coll., Henlow; Bristol Univ. (BSc); Loughborough Univ. (MSc). CEng 1972; MRAeS 1980, FRAeS 2003; FIMechE 1990; FCILT (FILT 1997). Commnd Engr Br., RAF, 1964; served at Odiham, Sharjah, Coltishall, Leconfield, Kemble, 1967–78; RAF Staff Coll., Bracknell, 1978; air weapons staff, MoD, London, 1979–83; OC Engrg Wing, RAF Valley, 1983–85; various engrg posts and SO Engrg and Supply, HQ 38 Gp, Strike Comd, 1986–95; Air Cdre, Policy and Plans, HQ Logistics Comd, 1996–97; Dir, Support Mgt (RAF), 1997–99; COS, 1999–2000; last AOC-in-C Logistics Comd, 1999; Mem. Mgt Bd, Defence Logistics Orgn, 1999–2000; retd RAF, 2000. Vis. Prof., Acquisition and Logistics Unit, RMCS, Shrivenham, at Cranfield Univ., 2000–05. Mil. Advr, Marshall Aerospace, Cambridge, 2000–09; Defence Advr, Symbia, 2002–09 (non-exec. Dir, 2003–09); Dir, Insider Publishing Ltd, 2003–13. Freeman, City of London, 2000–; Liveryman, Engineers' Co., 2000– (Clerk, 2003–09; Master, 2013–14). Gov., Hampton Sch., Middx, 2001–. *Publications:* contrib. various articles to professional jls on aerospace engrg and defence logistics. *Recreations:* golf, watercolour painting. *Address:* Rokesly, 63 Sandelswood End, Beaconsfield, Bucks HP9 2AA. *T:* (01494) 672350. *Club:* Royal Air Force.

SKINNER, Sir Keith; *see* Skinner, Sir T. K. H.

SKINNER, Paul David, CBE 2014; Chairman, Defence Equipment and Support, Ministry of Defence, since 2014; *b* 24 Dec. 1944; *s* of William Stanley Skinner and Elizabeth Ann Skinner; *m* 1971, Rita Jacqueline Oldak; two *s. Educ:* Pembroke Coll., Cambridge (BA Law; Fellow Commoner); Manchester Business Sch. (Univ. of Manchester Dist. Alumnus, 2009). Royal Dutch/Shell Group of Companies, 1963–2003: sen. appts in UK and Greece, 1974–76, Nigeria, 1976–78, NZ, 1984–87, Norway, 1987–91; Gp Man. Dir and Man. Dir, Shell Transport and Trading Co. plc, 2000–03; Chm., Shell Canada, 2001–03. Chairman: Rio Tinto plc, 2003–09 (non-exec. Dir, 2001–09); Rio Tinto Ltd, 2003–09 (non-exec. Dir, 2001–09); non-executive Director: Standard Chartered plc, 2003–15; Tetra Laval Gp, 2005–15; Air Liquide SA, 2006–; PricewaterhouseCoopers LLP, 2010–; Mem., Adv. Bd, Norton Rose Fulbright LLP, 2014–. Chm., Infrastructure UK, HM Treasury, 2009–13. Pres., UK Chamber of Shipping, 1997–98; Chairman: ICC UK, 2005–08; Commonwealth Business Council, 2007–09. UK Business Ambassador, 2008–12. Member: Bd, Eur./Asian Business Sch., INSEAD, 1999–2011; Eur. Round Table of Industrialists, 2005–09; Defence Bd (formerly Mgt Bd), MoD, 2006–09, 2014–; Defence Adv. Forum, 2009–10. Liveryman, Co. of Shipwrights, 2000–. *Recreations:* opera, ski-ing, fly-fishing, boating. *Address:* PO Box 65129, SW1P 9LY. *T:* (020) 7885 7104. *E:* paul@skinnerlondon.com. *Clubs:* Royal Automobile; Hawks (Cambridge).

SKINNER, Peter William; Member (Lab) South East Region, England, European Parliament, 1999–2014 (Kent West, 1994–99); Director of Political Affairs, Allianz Group, Munich, since 2014; *b* 1 June 1959; *s* of William James Skinner and Jean Theresa Skinner; *m* 1st, 1990, Julie Doreen (marr. diss. 2006); one *d*, and one step *s* one step *d*; 2nd, 2006, Kimberly Strycharz; two *s. Educ:* Bradford Univ. (BSc); Warwick Univ. (Post Grad. Cert. in Industl Relns); Greenwich Univ. (PGCE 1992). Industrial Relations Officer, 1982; Course Dir for HNC in Business and Finance, North West Kent Coll. of Technol., 1989–94. European Parliament: Member: Employment and Social Affairs Cttee, 1994–99; Educn, Culture, Media and Youth Cttee, 1997–99; Economic and Monetary Affairs Cttee, 2000–04; Internat. Trade Cttee, 2011–14; Rapporteur on: Health and Safety Rapporteur, 1995–2014; Solvency II and Reinsurance Directive; liaison with HM Treasury EP Delegn, 2002–10; Lab. spokesman on employment and social affairs, 1996–2000, on economic and monetary affairs, 2002–14. Mem., Transatlantic Economic Council, 2005–09. Mem., Educn and Employment Policy Commn, Lab Party, 1995–. Fellow, Univ. of Sunderland, 2003.

SKINNER, Prof. Quentin Robert Duthie, FRHistS; FBA 1981; Barber Beaumont Professor of the Humanities, Queen Mary University of London, since 2008; *b* 26 Nov. 1940; 2nd *s* of late Alexander Skinner, CBE, and Winifred Skinner (*née* Duthie), MA; *m* 2nd, 1979, Susan Deborah Thorpe James, MA, PhD; one *s* one *d. Educ:* Bedford Sch.; Gonville and Caius Coll., Cambridge (BA 1962, MA 1965; Hon. Fellow, 1997). FRHistS 1971. Cambridge University: Lectr in History, 1967–78; Prof. of Political Sci., 1978–96; Chm., Faculty of Hist., 1993–95; Regius Prof. of History, 1996–2008; Pro-Vice-Chancellor, 1999; Fellow, 1962–2008, now Hon. Fellow, Vice Master, 1997–99, Christ's Coll., Cambridge. Visiting Fellow: Research Sch. of Social Science, ANU, 1970, 1994; Humanities Res. Centre, ANU, 1989, 1994, 2006; Institute for Advanced Study, Princeton: Mem., School of Historical Studies, 1974–75; longer-term Mem., School of Social Science, 1976–79; Professeur invité, Collège de France, 1997; Vis. Schol., Center for Eur. Studies, Harvard Univ., 2008; Dist. Vis. Prof., Northwestern Univ., 2011; Rockefeller Vis. Prof., Princeton Univ., 2013–14; Spinoza Prof., Univ. of Amsterdam, 2014. Member: Council, British Acad., 1987–90; Res. Council, Eur. Univ. Inst., Florence, 2003–08; Prize Cttee, Balzan Foundn, 2009–. Lecture series: Gauss Seminars, Princeton Univ., 1980; Carlyle, Oxford Univ., 1980; Messenger, Cornell Univ., 1983; Tanner, Harvard Univ., 1984; T. S. Eliot Meml, Univ. of Kent, 1995; Ford, Oxford Univ., 2003; Adorno, Univ. of Frankfurt, 2005; Clarendon, Oxford Univ., 2011; Clark, Trinity Coll., Cambridge, 2012; Academia Sinica, Taiwan, 2013. Fellow, Wissenschaftskolleg zu Berlin, 2003–04; Corresp. Fellow, Österreichische Akademie der Wissenschaften, 2009. Foreign Hon. Mem., Amer. Acad. of Arts and Sciences, 1986; Foreign Member: Amer. Phil Soc., 1997; Accademia Nazionale dei Lincei, 2007; Hon. Mem., Univ. Adolfo Ibáñez, Santiago, 2009. MAE 1989. FRSA 1996. Hon. MRIA 1999. Hon. Fellow, QMW, 1999.

Hon. LittD: Chicago, East Anglia, 1992; Helsinki, 1997; Leuven, 2004; Harvard, St Andrews, 2005; Aberdeen, Athens, 2007; Oslo, 2011; Copenhagen, 2014; Hon. DLitt Oxford, 2000. Benjamin Lippincott Award, Amer. Pol Sci. Assoc., 2001; Sir Isaiah Berlin Prize, British Pol Studies Assoc., 2006; Balzan Foundn Prize, 2006; David Easton Award, Amer. Pol Sci. Assoc., 2007; Bielefelder Wissenschaftspreis, 2008. *Publications:* (ed jtly and contrib.) Philosophy, Politics and Society, Series 4, 1972; The Foundations of Modern Political Thought, Vol. 1, The Renaissance, 1978; Vol. 2, The Age of Reformation, 1978 (Wolfson History Prize, 1979); Machiavelli, 1981; (ed jtly and contrib.) Philosophy in History, 1984; (ed and contrib.) The Return of Grand Theory in the Human Sciences, 1985; (ed jtly and contrib.) The Cambridge History of Renaissance Philosophy, 1988; Meaning and Context: Quentin Skinner and his critics, ed J. H. Tully, 1988; (ed and introd) Machiavelli: The Prince, 1988; (ed jtly and contrib.) Machiavelli and Republicanism, 1990; (ed jtly and contrib.) Political Discourse in Early-modern Britain, 1992; (ed jtly) Milton and Republicanism, 1995; Reason and Rhetoric in the Philosophy of Hobbes, 1996; Liberty Before Liberalism, 1998; Visions of Politics, Vol. 1, Regarding Method, 2002, Vol. 2, Renaissance Virtues, 2002, Vol. 3, Hobbes and Civil Science, 2002; (ed jtly and contrib.) Republicanism: a shared European heritage, 2 vols, 2002; (ed jtly and contrib.) States and Citizens, 2003; (ed jtly) Thomas Hobbes: writings on common law and hereditary right, 2005; Hobbes and Republican Liberty, 2008; (ed jtly and contrib.) Sovereignty in Fragments, 2010; (ed) Families and States in Western Europe, 2011; (ed jtly and contrib.) Freedom and the Construction of Europe, 2 vols, 2013; Forensic Shakespeare, 2014. *Address:* School of History, Queen Mary University of London, Mile End Road, E1 4NS.

SKINNER, Robert George; Chief Executive, Lending Standards Board, since 2009; *b* 8 Aug. 1955; *s* of George and Mary Patricia Skinner; *m* 1974, Sheila White; one *s* one *d* (and one *d* decd). *Educ:* St Peter's Coll., Oxford (MA Physics). ACIB 1979. Barclays Bank Plc, 1976–2003: Mgt Develt Prog., 1976–80; Assistant Manager: Sunbury Br., 1981–82; Hounslow Br., 1982–84; Manager, Energy Dept, 1984–87; PA to Gp Chm., 1987–89; Man. Dir, Swaziland, 1989–92; Corporate Dir, Energy Finance Team, 1992–93; UK Personal Sector Network Dir, 1993–98; Mktg Dir, Private Banking Div., 1998–2003; Dir Gen., Money Advice Trust, 2003–06; Chief Exec., Banking Code Standards Bd, 2006–09. Non-exec. Dir, Money Advice Service, 2012–. Fellow, Inst. Financial Services, 1998. *Recreations:* triathlons, photography, travel. *Address:* Lending Standards Board, Level 17, City Tower, 40 Basinghall Street, EC2V 5DE. *T:* (020) 7012 0085, *Fax:* (020) 7374 4414. *E:* robertskinner@lstdb.org.uk.

SKINNER, Sir (Thomas) Keith (Hewitt), 4th Bt *cr* 1912; Director, Reed International, 1980–90; Chairman and Chief Executive, Reed Publishing and Reed Regional Publishing, 1982–90, and other companies; *b* 6 Dec. 1927; *s* of Sir (Thomas) Gordon Skinner, 3rd Bt, and Mollie Barbara (*d* 1965), *d* of Herbert William Girling; *S* father, 1972; *m* 1959, Jill, *d* of Cedric Ivor Tuckett; two *s*. *Educ:* Charterhouse. Managing Director, Thomas Skinner & Co. (Publishers) Ltd, 1952–60; also Director, Iliffe & Co. Ltd, 1958–65; Director, Iliffe-NTP Ltd; Chairman: Industrial Trade Fairs Holdings Ltd, 1977–92; Business Press Internat., 1970–84. *Recreations:* publishing, shooting, fishing, gardening, golf. *Heir: s* Thomas James Hewitt Skinner, *b* 11 Sept. 1962. *Address:* Wood Farm, Reydon, near Southwold, Suffolk IP18 6SL.

SKINNER, Zoe Ann; *see* Billingham, Z. A.

SKIPPER, Mark David; DL; Chief Executive, Northern Ballet, since 1996; *b* Brighton, 23 July 1961; *s* of David and Diane Skipper; civil partnership 2006, Neil Jarman. *Educ:* Kings Manor Sch., Shoreham. Barclays Bank, 1979–84; freelance stage manager, 1984–87; Northern Ballet: Dep. Stage Manager, 1987; Co. Manager, 1988–95; Hd of Planning, 1995–96. DL W Yorks, 2010. *Recreations:* all types of theatre, fine dining, travel. *Address:* c/o Northern Ballet, Quarry Hill, Leeds LS2 7PA. *T:* (0113) 220 8000. *E:* mark.skipper@northernballet.com.

SKIPWITH, Sir Patrick Alexander d'Estoteville, 12th Bt *cr* 1622; consultant editor and translator (trading as Traduscience), since 2003; *b* 1 Sept. 1938; *o s* of Grey d'Estoteville Townsend Skipwith (killed in action, 1942), Flying Officer, RAFVR, and Sofka (*d* 1994), *d* of late Prince Peter Dolgorouky; *S* grandfather, 1950; *m* 1st, 1964, Gillian Patricia (marr. diss. 1970; she *d* 2012), *d* of late Charles F. Harwood; one *s* one *d*; 2nd, 1972, Ashkhain (marr. diss. 1997; she *d* 2006), *d* of late Bedros Atikian, Calgary, Alta; 3rd, 1997, Martine Sophie (marr. diss 2011), *d* of late Joseph de Wilde, Theillay, France; twin *s*; 4th, 2012, Katherine Jane, *d* of Derek Mahon, Kinsale, Eire; one *s*. *Educ:* Harrow; Dublin (MA); London (DIC, PhD). With Ocean Mining Inc., in Tasmania, 1966–67, Malaysia, 1967–69, W Africa, 1969–70; with Min. of Petroleum and Mineral Resources, Saudi Arabia, 1970–71 and 1972–73. Editor, Bureau de Recherches Géologiques et Minières, Jiddah, 1973–86; consultant editor/translator (trading as GeoEdit), 1986–96; Hd of Translation, BRGM, Orléans, 1996–2003; Man. Dir, Immel Publishing Ltd, 1988–89. *Heir: s* Alexander Sebastian Grey d'Estoteville Skipwith [*b* 9 April 1969; *m* 2006, Anne, *d* of late Paul Tolstoy-Miloslavsky; one *s* one *d*]. *Address:* 14 Wilton Rise, York YO24 4BW. *Club:* Chelsea Arts.

SKIPWORTH, Kevin Leslie, CVO 2011 (LVO 2000); JP; Agent General for Western Australia, London, 2012–15; *b* Kalgoorlie, WA, 27 July 1947; *s* of late Donald John Skipworth and Sheila Edith Skipworth (*née* McAlister); *m* 1970, Edith Ann True; one *s* three *d*. *Educ:* CBC Leederville; Perth Technical Coll. (Dip. Public Admin; Cert. Personnel Mgt). Private Sec. to Ministers of the Crown, Govt of WA, 1977–83; Exec. Officer to Premier of WA, 1983–85; Dir, Office of Agent Gen. for WA, London, 1986–88; Chief of Protocol, Min. of the Premier and Cabinet, WA, 1988–90; Official Sec. and CEO, Governor's Establishment, WA, 1991–2011. Chm., Govt Domain Reserve Bd, 1991–2011; Mem. Council, Govt House Foundn of WA, 1991–2011. Mem., Royal Assoc. of Justices of WA, 1986–. Patron, UK tour, Youth Theatre Perth, Australia, 2012–. Member: Britain-Australia Soc., 2012–15; Cook Soc., 2012–. JP W Australia, 1986. *Recreations:* tennis, golf, family and grandchildren, theatre arts, fishing. *Address:* 35 Marbella Drive, Hillarys, WA 6025, Australia. *T:* (4) 06672105. *E:* skipwest38@gmail.com. *Club:* Royal Over-Seas League.

SKIPWORTH, Mark; Deputy Editor, The Telegraph, since 2014; *b* Kingston upon Hull, 27 Jan. 1959; *s* of late George and Jean Marjorie Skipworth; *m* 1981, Julie Alison Patricia Deegan; two *s* one *d*. *Educ:* Sydney Smith Sch., Hull; St John's Coll., Oxford (BA Modern Hist.). Reporter, Sheffield Star, 1980–84; writer, Which? mag., 1984–89; reporter, Daily Telegraph, 1989; Sunday Times: consumer affairs corresp., 1990–93; Dep. Insight Ed., 1994–95; News Ed., 1995–97; Man. Ed. (News), 1998–2008; Exec. Ed. (Sport), 2008, Exec. Ed., 2009–14, Telegraph Media Gp. *Publications:* (with A. Billen) Oxford Type: the best of Isis, 1984; The Scotch Whisky Book, 1987; (with G. Hadfield) Class, 1994. *Recreations:* piano and piano accordion. *Address:* Daily Telegraph, 111 Buckingham Palace Road, SW1W 0DT. *T:* (020) 7931 2414. *E:* mark.skipworth@telegraph.co.uk.

SKITT, Baden Henry, CBE 1997; BEM 1969; QPM 1990; Lay Member, Office for Judicial Complaints Review Body, 2006–12; *b* 5 Dec. 1941; *s* of late Frederick Albert Skitt and Laura Kathleen (*née* Oakley). *Educ:* Rugeley Grammar Sch., Staffs; St Paul's Coll., Cheltenham (Dip of PE; CertEd). Schoolmaster, Sir Wilfrid Martineau Sch., Birmingham, 1963–67; Constable to Supt, Birmingham City, later W Midlands, Police, 1967–82; Chief Supt, 1982–84, Comdr, 1984–86, Metropolitan Police; Dep. Chief Constable, Northants, 1986–90; Chief Constable, Herts, 1990–94; Asst Comr, Metropolitan Police, 1994–97. Mem., Criminal Cases Review Commn, 1997–2006. Chm., Personnel and Training Cttee, 1993–96, Chm., Internat. Affairs Adv. Cttee, 1996–97, ACPO. Dir, Police Extended Interviews, 1995–97. Member: Police Adv. Bd, 1993–97; Police Trng Council, 1993–97; Police Advr, Police Negotiating Bd, 1994–96. Dir, Educnl Broadcasting Services Trust, 1992–2008; Advr, Council of Europe Cttee for prevention of torture and inhuman and degrading treatment or punishment, 2001–. Trustee: Police Convalescent Home, 1995–97; Youth Sport Trust, 1995–97. Advr, N London Common Purpose, 1995–97. Patron, Revolving Doors Agency, 1995–97. CCMI 2002. *Publications:* (jtly) In Service Training: a new approach, 1974; (jtly) Education 2000, 1984; contrib. to learned jls. *Recreations:* the history and travelling of inland waterways, Rugby football, music.

SKLYANIN, Prof. Evgeny Konstantinovich, PhD; FRS 2008; Professor of Mathematics, University of York; *b* Leningrad. *Educ:* Steklov Inst., St Petersburg (MSc, PhD). Formerly Reader in Maths, Univ. of York. *Publications:* contribs to jls incl. Contemporary Maths, Phil Trans Royal Soc., Sigma, Indagationes Mathematicae. *Address:* Department of Mathematics, University of York, Heslington, York YO10 5DD.

SKOLL, Lindsay Samantha; HM Diplomatic Service; Minister-Counsellor, Foreign and Commonwealth Office, since 2015; *b* 26 Sept. 1970; *d* of Gordon Stent and Linda Stent; *m* 2005, Richard Skoll; one *s*, and one step *s* one step *d*. *Educ:* Queen's Sch., Chester; Univ. of Nottingham (BA Hons 1st Cl. Hist. with Russian); Edinburgh (TEFL Dip). Counsellor, Internat. Relns, JET Prog., Japan, 1992–95; Lewis Communications, Internat. PR, 1996; joined FCO, 1996; Information Dept, 1996–97; Media Services Officer, G8 and EU Presidency, 1997–98; Hd, VIP Visits Section, Conf. and Visits Gp, 1999–2001; Hd, Korea and Mongolia Section, NE Asia Pacific Dept, 2001–02; Japanese lang. trng, 2002; on secondment to Cabinet Office, 2002–04; Dep. Hd of Mission, Pyongyang, 2004–06; Whitehall Liaison Dept, FCO, 2006–07; Middle East Dept, FCO, 2010; Dep. Hd (Climate), Climate Change and Energy Dept, FCO, 2010–12; High Comr to the Seychelles, 2012–15. *Recreations:* food and wine, travel and languages, country pursuits, singing, piano, beachcombing. *Address:* c/o Foreign and Commonwealth Office, King Charles Street, SW1A 2AH. *E:* lindsay.skoll@fco.gov.uk.

SKOLNICK, Prof. Maurice, PhD; FRS 2009; Professor of Condensed Matter Physics, since 1991, and Co-Director, EPSRC National Centre for III-V Technologies, University of Sheffield. *Educ:* Univ. of Oxford (PhD 1975). Postdoctoral res., Max-Planck Inst., Grenoble, 1976–77; RSRE, Malvern, 1978–91 (SPSO, 1988–91). EPSRC Sen. Res. Fellow, 2001–06. Chm., Semiconductor Gp, Inst. of Physics, 2006–09. Chm., Semiconductor Commn, and a Vice Pres., IUPAP, 2002–05. Mott Medal and Prize, Inst. of Physics, 2002. *Publications:* contribs to jls incl. Physics Rev. Letters, Physics Rev., Applied Physics Letters. *Address:* Department of Physics and Astronomy, Hicks Building, Hounsfield Road, Sheffield S3 7RH.

SKOTT, Maria; *see* Nikolajeva, M.

SKOU, Prof. Jens Christian, MD; Professor, Institute of Biophysics, Aarhus University, 1978–88, now Emeritus; *b* Lemvig, Denmark, 8 Oct. 1918; *s* of Magnus Martinus Skou and Ane Margrethe (*née* Knak); *m* 1947, Ellen-Margrethe Nielsen; two *d*. *Educ:* Univ. of Copenhagen (MD 1944); Univ. of Aarhus (DMedSci 1954). Intern, 1944–45, Resident, 1945–46, Hjørring Hosp.; Resident, Orthopaedic Hosp., Aarhus, 1946–47; Institute of Physiology, Aarhus University: Asst Prof., 1947–54; Associate Prof., 1954–63; Prof. and Chm., Inst. Physiol., 1963–78. Member: Danish Royal Acad. Scis, 1965; Deutsche Acad. der Naturforscher Leopoldina, 1977; EMBO, 1978; For. Associate, US Nat. Acad. of Scis, 1988; For. Hon. Mem., Amer. Acad. of Arts and Scis, 1999; Hon. Member: Japanese Biochem. Soc., 1988; American Physiol. Soc., 1990; Academia Europaea, 1993; Internat. Acad. of Humanism, 2002. Hon. DMedSci Copenhagen, 1986. Leo Prize, 1954; Novo Prize, 1965; Consul Carlsen Prize, 1973; A. Retzius Gold Medal, Swedish Med. Assoc., 1977; Fernström Foundn Prize, 1985; Prakash Datta Medal, Fedn European Biochem. Socs, 1985; (jtly) Nobel Prize for Chemistry, 1997. *Recreations:* classical music, yachting, ski-ing, fishing. *Address:* Rislundvej 9, 8240 Risskov, Denmark. *T:* 86177918; (office) Institute of Biophysics, Ole Worms Allé 185, 8000C Aarhus, Denmark. *T:* 89422929, *Fax:* 86129599. *E:* jcs@biophys.au.dk.

SKOURIS, Prof. Vassilios; Judge, 1999–2015, President, 2003–15, Court of Justice of the European Union (formerly Communities); *b* 6 March 1948; *s* of Panagiotis and Katerina Skouris; *m* Vassiliki Papaïoannou; one *s* one *d*. *Educ:* Free Univ. of Berlin; Univ. of Hamburg (Dr jur 1973). Asst Prof. of Constitutional and Admin. Law, Univ. of Hamburg, 1978; Professor of Public Law: Dimokriteio Univ. of Thrace, 1977–80; Bielefeld Univ., Germany, 1980–82; Prof., Aristoteleio Univ. of Thessaloniki, 1982–; Dir of Res., 1985–90, Sec., 1990–97, Centre for Internat. and Eur. Econ. Law, Thessaloniki. Minister for Internal Affairs, Greece, 1989 and 1996. Mem., Higher Selection Bd for Greek Civil Servants, 1994–96. Mem., Acad. Council, Acad. Eur. Law, Trier, 1995–. Pres., Greek Assoc. for Eur. Law, 1992–94. Hon. LLD: Thrace, 2004; Vilnius, 2005; Münster, 2007; Bucharest, 2009; Paris II Panthéon-Assas, 2010; Deutsche Hochschule für Verwaltungswissenschaften, 2005. Grand Officier, Ordre of Merit (Italy), 2005; Ehrenkreuz für Wissenschaft und Kunst, 1st Cl. (Austria), 2005; Grand Cross, Order of Makarios III (Cyprus), 2006; Commandeur de la Légion d'Honneur (France), 2008. *Publications:* (contrib.) Constitutional Review and Legislation: an international comparison, ed C. Landfried, 1988; (contrib.) Advertising and Constitutional Rights in Europe: a study in comparative constitutional law, 1994; (contrib.) Verfassung im Diskurs der Welt, 2004; (contrib.) The Future of the European Judicial System: the constitutional role of European courts, 2005; contribs to Eur. Business Law Rev. *Address:* c/o Court of Justice of the European Union, Boulevard Konrad Adenauer, 2925 Luxembourg.

SKUDDER, Taryn Jane; *see* Lee, T. J.

SKUSE, Prof. David Henry, MD; FRCP, FRCPsych, FRCPCH; Professor of Behavioural and Brain Sciences, Institute of Child Health, University College London, since 1994; Hon. Consultant in Child and Adolescent Psychiatry, Great Ormond Street Hospital for Children, since 1985; *b* Bristol, 25 Jan. 1949; *s* of Henry Lawrence Skuse and Kathleen Mary Skuse (*née* Holten); *m* 1993, Linda Rose Dowdney; one step *s* one step *d*. *Educ:* Manchester Univ. (MB, ChB 1973; MD 1985). FRCP 1991; FRCPsych 1993; FRCPCH 1997. SHO, Oxford United Hosps (Gen. Medicine), 1974–76; Registrar, 1976–78, Sen. Registrar, 1979–85, Maudsley Hosp.; Lectr, Inst. of Psychiatry, KCL, 1979–85; Wellcome Trust Sen. Lectr, Inst. of Child Health, 1985–90, Sen. Lectr, 1990–94, UCL. Vis. Prof., Mayo Clinic, 2001–. Ed., Jl Child Psychol. and Psychiatry, 1992–2001; Ed., Internat. Psychiatry, 2013– (Co-Ed., 2009–13). Treas., British Neuropsychiatry Assoc., 1998–. *Publications:* (ed jtly) Motherhood in Human and Nonhuman Primates: biosocial determinants, 1994; (jtly) Schedule for Oral-Motor Assessment, 2000; (ed jtly) Child Psychology and Psychiatry: frameworks for practice, 2011; contrib. papers to scientific jls on child neuropsychiatry, theory and practice. *Recreations:* cycling, walking, running, travel. *Address:* Behavioural and Brain Sciences Unit, Institute of Child Health, 30 Guilford Street, WC1N 1EH. *T:* (020) 7905 2168. *E:* d.skuse@ucl.ac.uk.

SKWEYIYA, Zola Sidney Themba, LLD; High Commissioner of the Republic of South Africa to the United Kingdom, 2009–13; Special Envoy of South Africa to the Middle East, 2014–15; *b* Simons Town, South Africa, 14 April 1942; *m* Thuthukile. *Educ:* Primary schs, New Brighton and Retreat, Cape Town; Lovedale High Sch., Fort Hare (scholarship); Univ. of Leipzig (LLD 1978). African National Congress: joined at age 14, 1956; forced into exile, 1963, and moved to Lusaka, then to Germany; Chief Rep. to OAU, 1981–83; Hd, Legal and Constitutional Dept, 1984; Chm., Constitution Cttee, 1985–2000, involved in drawing up South Africa's new democratic constitution; Mem., Nat. Exec. Cttee, 1985–; returned from exile, 1990. MP, S Africa, 1994–2009; Minister: of Public Service and Admin, 1994–99; of Social Develt, 1999–2009. Founder and first Pres., Nat. Commn for the Rights of Children,

1990–95; President: Commonwealth Assoc. of Public Admin and Mgt, 1995–2000; Mgt of Social Transformations Prog., UNESCO, 2005–09. *Recreations:* reading, general interest in sports.

SLABAS, Prof. Antoni Ryszard, DPhil; Professor of Plant Sciences, 1990–2013, now Emeritus, Director of Research, Department of Biological Sciences, 1995–2000, and Director, Durham Centre for Crop Improvement Technology, 2010–12, University of Durham; *b* 30 July 1948; *s* of Franciszek Slabas and Wiera Ruban. *Educ:* Bishop Thomas Grant Sch.; QMC, Univ. of London (BSc); St Edmund Hall, Oxford (DPhil). Postdoctoral Fellow: Univ. of Sheffield, 1974–75; UCL, 1975–77; Unilever Research Laboratory, Sharnbrook, Bedford: Mem., Basic Studies Unit, 1977–80; Gp Leader, Lipid Enzymology, 1980–85; Section Manager, Protein Chem., 1985–86; Plant Molecular Biol. Prog. Leader, 1986–87; Sen. Molecular Biologist, 1988; Section Manager, Cell Scis, 1989–90. Mem., EC Seeds of Tomorrow Scientific Steering Cttee, 1990–; Agricultural and Food Research Council: Member: Engrg Bd, 1992–94; Plants and Envmt Res. Cttee, 1992–94; Wkg Gp, Protein Sci., 1992; Bd of Metabolic Regulation, 1992–94. Member: Cttee, Biochem. Soc. Lipid Gp, 1984–88; Health and Life Scis Panel, 1994–99, Food Chain and Crops for Industry Panel, 1999–2001, Technol. Foresight Prog., OST; Management Cttee, Agricl Systems Directorate, BBSRC, 1994–98; Governing Body, Scottish Crops Res. Inst., 1995–2004; Sci. Strategy Adv. Cttee, Nat. Inst. of Agricl Botany, 2010–. Founder, 2000, and Co-Dir, 2000–, Creative Gene Technology. Member, Editorial Board: Biochem. Jl, 1989–2001; Plant Molecular Biol., 1991–2002; Proteomics, 2005–. *Publications:* various in area of plant and microbial lipid biochem., enzymology and gene cloning; contrib. Science, Jl Biol Chem., Eur. Jl Biochem., Biochim. Biophys. Acta, Biochem. Jl, Nature, Plant Jl, Plant Cell. *Recreations:* book collecting, classical music, walking, feeding swans by hand. *Address:* Department of Biological Sciences, University of Durham, South Road, Durham DH1 3LE. *T:* (0191) 334 1354.

SLACK, Dr (Charles) Roger, FRS 1989; FRSNZ 1983; Senior Scientist, New Zealand Institute for Crop and Food Research Ltd, 1989–2000, retired; *b* 22 April 1937; *s* of Albert Oram Slack and Eva (*née* Simister); *m* 1963, Pamela Mary Shaw; one *s* one *d*. *Educ:* Audenshaw Grammar Sch., Lancs; Sch. of Agriculture, Univ. of Nottingham (BSc; PhD 1962). Biochemist, David North Plant Res. Centre, CSR Co. Ltd, Brisbane, Australia, 1962–70; Leader, Biochemistry Group, 1970–84, Leader, Crop Physiology Group and Dep. Dir, Plant Physiol. Div., 1984–89, DSIR, NZ; Sen. Scientist, Crop Res. Div., DSIR, NZ, subseq. NZ Inst. for Crop and Food Res. Ltd, 1989. Charles F. Kettering Award for Photosynthesis Res., Amer. Soc. of Plant Physiologists, 1980; Rank Prize for Nutrition, 1981. *Publications:* scientific pubns, mainly on aspects of photosynthesis and plant lipid synthesis. *Recreations:* bird watching, hiking, trout fishing, gardening. *Address:* 30 Ihaka Street, Palmerston North, New Zealand 4410. *T:* (6) 3572966.

SLACK, Prof. Jonathan Michael Wyndham, PhD; FMedSci; Tulloch Professor of Stem Cell Biology, Genetics and Genomics, University of Minnesota, 2007–13, now Emeritus (Director, Stem Cell Institute, 2007–12); Emeritus Professor, University of Bath, 2009; *b* 10 Sept. 1949; *s* of Ronald Slack and Pamela Zoe Slack (*née* Gregory); *m* 1980, Janet Elizabeth Blaker; two *d*. *Educ:* Balliol Coll., Oxford (BA 1st. cl. Hons (Biochem.) 1971); Edinburgh Univ. (PhD 1974). Res. Fellow, Middlesex Hosp. Med. Sch., 1974–76; Res. Scientist, later Sen. and Principal Scientist, ICRF, 1976–95; Prof. of Develtl Biology, 1995–2007, Hd, Dept of Biol. and Biochem., 2000–06, Univ. of Bath. Mem., EMBO, 1993. FMedSci 2004. Waddington Medal, British Soc. Develtl Biol., 2002; Rank Prize, Biochem. Soc., 2009. *Publications:* From Egg to Embryo, 1983, 2nd edn 1991; Egg and Ego, 1999; Essential Developmental Biology, 2001, 3rd edn 2013; Stem Cells: a very short introduction, 2012; Genes: a very short introduction, 2014; numerous scientific papers. *Recreations:* walking, learning Turkish, playing the melodeon, Morris dancing. *Address:* Department of Biology and Biochemistry, University of Bath, Bath BA2 7AY.

SLACK, Michael Dennis; Founder and Chairman, Temporary Cover Ltd, since 2002; *b* Sudbury, 20 Oct. 1942; *s* of Dennis Slack and Stella Fyfe; one *s*. *Educ:* Kent Coll., Canterbury. Various posts, insce industry, 1960–80; Founder, Stuart Fyfe & Partners Ltd, 1980; Founder and Chm., Road Runner Gp, subseq. Fyfe Gp, 1989–2008. Mem., Insce Brokers' Registration Council, 1989–2002; Founder Dir, Gen. Insce Standards Council, 1999–2003; non-exec. Dir, FSA, 2004–09. Dir, Inst. of Insce Brokers, 1992–97; Founder Chm., Assoc. of Insce Intermediaries and Brokers, 1997; Mem. Main Bd, Brit. Insce Brokers' Assoc., 2002–. FCMI. Mem., Co. of Insurers. Mem., RYA. *Recreations:* sailing, boating. *Clubs:* Royal London Yacht; Royal Thames Yacht; City Livery Yacht.

SLACK, Prof. Paul Alexander, DPhil, DLitt; FBA 1990; FRHistS; Principal of Linacre College, Oxford, 1996–2010; Titular Professor of Early Modern Social History, University of Oxford, 1999–2010, now Emeritus; *b* 23 Jan. 1943; *s* of Isaac Slack and Helen (*née* Firth); *m* 1965, Diana Gillian Manby (*d* 2003); two *d*. *Educ:* Bradford Grammar Sch.; St John's Coll., Oxford (Casberd Exhibnr and Schol.; 1st cl. Hons Mod. Hist. 1964; MA; DPhil 1972; DLitt 2010; Hon. Fellow, 1998). FRHistS 1972. A. M. P. Read Schol., Oxford Univ., and Harmsworth Sen. Schol., Merton Coll., Oxford, 1965–66; Jun. Res. Fellow, Balliol Coll., Oxford, 1966–69; Lectr in Hist., York Univ., 1969–72; Oxford University: Fellow and Tutor, 1973–96 (Emeritus Fellow, 1996–), Sub-Rector, 1983, Sen. Tutor, 1984–86 and 1991–92, Exeter Coll.; Reader in Modern Hist., 1990–96; Jun. Proctor, 1986–87; Mem., Hebdomadal Council, 1987–2008; Chm., Gen. Bd of Faculties, 1995–96; Pro-Vice-Chancellor, 1997–2000; Pro-Vice-Chancellor (Acad. Services and Univ. Collections), 2000–05; Delegate, OUP, 2000–13. Vis. Prof., Univ. of S Carolina, 1980; Vis. Res. Associate, Rikkyo Univ., Tokyo, 1988. Ford's Lectr in British History, Oxford, 1994–95; Aylmer Memorial Lectr, York, 2003; Stenton Lectr, Reading, 2010. Member: Internat. Commn for Hist. of Towns, 1976–; Humanities Res. Bd, 1994–95. Pres., Soc. for Social Hist. of Medicine, 1991; Member, Council: RHistS, 1984–87; British Acad., 1994–95. Editor, Past and Present, 1985–94. Hon. Fellow: Balliol Coll., Oxford, 2009; Linacre Coll., Oxford, 2010. DUniv York, 2005. *Publications:* (ed with Peter Clark) Crisis and Order in English Towns 1500–1700, 1972; (ed) Poverty in Early Stuart Salisbury, 1975; (with P. Clark) English Towns in Transition 1500–1700, 1976 (Japanese edn 1989); (ed) Rebellion, Popular Protest and the Social Order in Early Modern England, 1984; The Impact of Plague in Tudor and Stuart England, 1985; Poverty and Policy in Tudor and Stuart England, 1988; The English Poor Law 1531–1782, 1990; (ed with T. Ranger) Epidemics and Ideas, 1992; (ed jtly) Public Duty and Private Conscience in Seventeenth-Century England, 1993; From Reformation to Improvement: public welfare in early modern England, 1999; (ed) Environments and Historical Change, 1999; (ed jtly) Civil Histories: essays presented to Sir Keith Thomas, 2000; (ed jtly) The Peopling of Britain, 2002; Plague: a very short introduction, 2012; The Invention of Improvement: information and material progress in seventeenth-century England, 2015; contribs to learned jls. *Recreations:* opera, fell-walking. *Address:* Linacre College, Oxford OX1 3JA. *T:* (01865) 271650.

SLACK, Roger; *see* Slack, C. R.

SLACK, Stephen; Head, Legal Office of the Church of England and Chief Legal Adviser to the Archbishops' Council, since 2001; Chief Legal Adviser and Registrar, General Synod of the Church of England, since 2001; Joint Registrar of the Provinces of Canterbury and York, since 2001; Official Solicitor to the Church Commissioners, since 2009; *b* 29 Dec. 1954; *s* of Thomas and Ada Genary Slack; *m* 1982, Georgiana Sophia (*née* Shaw); one *s* two *d*. *Educ:* Aylesbury Grammar Sch.; Christ Church, Oxford (MA). Solicitor in private practice, 1979–84; Charity Commission: Sen. Lawyer, Liverpool, 1984–89; Hd, Legal Sect., Taunton, 1989–2001. *Recreations:* gardening, music, historic buildings. *Address:* Church House, Great Smith Street, SW1P 3AZ. *Clubs:* Athenæum; Devon and Exeter Instn (Exeter).

SLACK, Sir William (Willatt), KCVO 1990; MA, MCh, BM, FRCS; Consultant Surgeon, Middlesex Hospital, 1962–91, now Emeritus Surgeon; Senior Lecturer in Surgery, 1962–91, and Dean, 1983–87, Middlesex Hospital Medical School; Dean, Faculty of Clinical Sciences, University College and Middlesex School of Medicine, University College London, 1987–91; also Surgeon: Hospital of St John and St Elizabeth, 1970–88; King Edward VII Hospital for Officers, 1975–91; *b* 22 Feb. 1925; *s* of late Cecil Moorhouse Slack, MC, and Dora Slack (*née* Willatt); *m* 1951, Joan, 4th *d* of late Lt-Col Talbot H. Wheelwright, OBE; two *s* two *d*. *Educ:* Winchester Coll.; New Coll., Oxford; Middlesex Hosp. Med. Sch. Ho. Surg., Surgical Registrar and Sen. Surgical Registrar, Middx Hosp., 1950–59; Jun. Registrar, St Bartholomew's Hosp., 1953; Fulbright Scholar, R. & E. Hosp., Univ. of Illinois, Chicago, 1959. Surgeon to the Queen, 1975–83; Serjeant Surgeon to the Queen, 1983–90. Hon. Consultant, RBL, 1984–2007. Hon. Fellow, UCL, 1987. Master, Barbers' Co., 1991–92. *Publications:* various surgical articles in med. jls and textbooks. *Recreations:* ski-ing, gardening; Oxford blue for Association football, 1946. *Address:* Hillside Cottage, Tower Road, Stawell, near Bridgwater, Somerset TA7 9AJ. *T:* (01278) 722719.

SLADE, Adrian Carnegie, CBE 1988; PR and TV training consultant, 1991–2002; political journalist, 2002–12; *b* 25 May 1936; *y s* of late George Penkivil Slade, KC and Mary Albinia Alice Slade; *m* 1960, Susan Elizabeth Forsyth; one *s* one *d*. *Educ:* Eton Coll.; Trinity Coll., Cambridge (BA Law). Pres., Cambridge Footlights, 1959. Writer, J. Walter Thompson, 1959–64; S. H. Benson, 1964–71, Dir, 1970–71; Co-Founder and Managing Director: Slade Monico Bluff Ltd, 1971–75; Slade Bluff & Bigg Ltd, 1975–86; Slade Hamilton Fenech Ltd, 1986–91. Director: Orange Tree Th., Richmond, 1986–98 (Chm., 1991–98); Adzido, 1998–2004 (Chm., 2001–04). Trustee, One plus One, 1987–97 (Chm., 1990–97). Mem. (L) Richmond, GLC, 1981–86 (Leader, L/SDP Alliance Gp, 1982–86). Contested: (L) Putney, 1966, Feb. and Oct. 1974; (L/SDP Alliance) Wimbledon, 1987. Pres., Liberal Party, 1987–88; Jt Pres., 1988, Vice-Pres., 1988–89, Liberal Democrats. *Recreations:* music, theatre, films, piano playing, song writing, golf, photography, political interviewing. *Address:* 28 St Leonard's Road, SW14 7LX. *T:* (020) 8876 8712.

See also Rt Hon. Sir C. J. Slade.

SLADE, Sir Benjamin Julian Alfred, 7th Bt *cr* 1831; Chairman: Shirlstar Holdings Ltd; Pyman Bell (Holdings) Ltd; *b* 22 May 1946; *s* of Sir Michael Slade, 6th Bt and Angela (*d* 1959), *d* of Captain Orlando Chichester; *S* father, 1962; *m* 1977, Pauline Carol (marr. diss. 1991), *er d* of Major Claude Myburgh. *Educ:* Millfield Sch. Chm., Shirlstar Container Transport Ltd, 1973–95. Chm., Wilshaw Plc, 2005–09. Mem., Worshipful Co. of Ironmongers. Freeman, City of London, 1979. *Recreations:* racing, polo, bridge. *Heir:* none. *Address:* Maunsel House, North Newton, North Petherton, Bridgwater, Somerset TA7 0BU. *T:* (01278) 661076, (Sec.) (01278) 663107, *Fax:* (01278) 661124. *E:* info@maunselhouse.co.uk; (office) Woodlands Castle, Ruishton, Taunton, Somerset TA3 5LU. *T:* (01823) 444955. *E:* info@woodlandscastle.co.uk. *Club:* White's.

SLADE, Prof. Christina Mary, (Mrs Robert Hamilton), PhD; Vice-Chancellor, Bath Spa University, since 2012; *b* Adelaide, SA, 29 June 1953; *d* of John Slade and Gwenyth Slade; *m* 1976, Robert Hamilton; one *s* one *d*. *Educ:* Presbyterian Girls' Coll., Adelaide; Australian National Univ. (BA 1st Cl. 1974; PhD 1982); Univ. of New England (DipEd 1986). Lectr, then Sen. Lectr, Univ. of Canberra, 1990–96; Harkness Fellow, New York Univ., 1996–97; Vis. Prof., Univ. Iberoamericana, Mexico and Instituto Tecnológico de Monterrey, Mexico City, 1997–2001; Hd, Sch. of Creative Communications, Univ. of Canberra, 2001–03; Dean, Humanities, Macquarie Univ., Sydney, 2003–08; Prof. of Media Theory, 2004–10, Vis. Prof., 2010–11, Univ. of Utrecht; Dean, Arts and Soc. Scis, City Univ., London, 2009–12. *Publications:* The Real Thing: doing philosophy with media, 2002; A Tale of Two Women, 2008; (ed with M. Möllering) From Migrant to Citizen, 2010. *Address:* Bath Spa University, Newton Park, Newton St Loe, Bath BA2 9BN. *T:* (01225) 875510. *E:* c.slade@bathspa.ac.uk. *Clubs:* Athenæum; Queen Adelaide (Adelaide).

SLADE, Rt Hon. Sir Christopher John, Kt 1975; PC 1982; a Lord Justice of Appeal, 1982–91; *b* 2 June 1927; *e s* of late George Penkivil Slade, KC, and Mary Albinia Alice Slade; *m* 1958, Jane Gwenllian Armstrong Buckley, *d* of Rt Hon. Sir Denys Buckley, PC, MBE; one *s* three *d*. *Educ:* Eton (Scholar); New Coll., Oxford (Scholar). Eldon Law Scholar, 1950. Called to Bar, Inner Temple, 1951; joined Lincoln's Inn *ad eundem*, 1954, Bencher, 1973 (Treas., 1994). In practice at Chancery Bar, 1951–75; QC 1965; Attorney General, Duchy of Lancaster and Attorney and Serjeant Within the County Palatine of Lancaster, 1972–75; a Judge of the High Ct, Chancery Division, 1975–82; a Judge of Restrictive Practices Ct, 1980–82, Pres., 1981–82. Member: Gen. Council of the Bar, 1958–62, 1965–69; Senate of Four Inns of Court, 1966–69; Lord Chancellor's Legal Educn Cttee, 1969–71. Master, Ironmongers' Co., 1973. *Address:* 40 Rivermead Court, Ranelagh Gardens, SW6 3RX. *Club:* Garrick.

See also A. C. Slade.

SLADE, Hon. Dame Elizabeth Ann, DBE 2008; **Hon. Mrs Justice Slade;** a Judge of the High Court of Justice, Queen's Bench Division, since 2008; *b* 12 May 1949; *d* of late Dr Charles and Henriette Slade; *m* 1975; two *d*. *Educ:* Wycombe Abbey Sch.; Lady Margaret Hall, Oxford (Exhibnr, MA; Hon. Fellow, 2009). Called to the Bar, Inner Temple, 1972, Bencher, 1990. QC 1992; Asst Recorder, 1995–98; Recorder, 1998–2008; Dep. High Court Judge, 1998–2008; additional pt-time Judge, Employment Appeal Tribunal, 2000–03. Member, Administrative Tribunal: BIS, 1999–2008 (Vice Pres., 2008); EBRD, 2008. Chm., Sex Discrimination Cttee, Bar Council, 2000–02. Hon. Vice Pres., Employment Law Bar Assoc., 1998– (Chm., 1995–97). Trustee, Free Representation Unit, 1998–2002. *Publications:* Tolley's Employment Handbook, 1978, to 7th edn (ed jtly) 1991. *Recreations:* theatre, art, music. *Address:* Royal Courts of Justice, Strand, WC2A 2LL.

SLADE, Laurie George; Insurance Ombudsman, 1994–96 and 1999–2000; *b* Nairobi, 12 Feb. 1944; *yr s* of Humphrey Slade and Constance Laing Gordon. *Educ:* Duke of York Sch., Nairobi; Magdalen Coll., Oxford (MA); London Univ. Inst. of Educn (PGCE). Called to the Bar, Lincoln's Inn, 1966. Stage management and acting in professional theatre and TV, Kenya and UK, 1967–70; teaching, 1972–75; Advocate, Kenya High Court, 1975–81; Legal Advr, CIArb and Dep. Registrar, London Court of Internat. Arbitration, 1982–88; Dep. Insurance Ombudsman, 1988–94; Independent Investigator, SIB, then FSA, 1996–99. Mem., Insurance Brokers' Registration Council, 1997–98. Mem., British and Irish Ombudsman Assoc., 1993–2008; Chm., FSA Ombudsman Steering Gp, 1998. Voluntary counsellor, Hounslow Social Services, 1988–94; counselling and psychotherapy practice and consultancy, 1991–; UKCP Registered Psychoanalytic Psychotherapist, 1999; Hon. Psychotherapist, Charing Cross Hosp., 2000–05; social dreaming practitioner, 2002–. Mem., Guild of Psychotherapists, 1999–; Founder Mem., Internat. Neuro-Psychoanalysis Soc., 2000–; Mem., Confedn for Analytical Psychology (formerly Confedn of Analytical Psychologists), 2002–; Founder Associate, Gordon Lawrence Foundn for Promotion of Social Dreaming, 2013–. Wrote plays: Out of Africa, 1988 and Karen's Tale, 1996 (both after Karen Blixen); Joe & I, 2005; The Father, 2012 (after August Strindberg), BBC Radio 3, 2013; Marriage, 2013 (after Nikolai Gogol). *Publications:* professional papers and contribs to learned jls. *Recreations:* theatre, painting (2 solo exhibns in Kenya, 1974, 1979).

SLADE, Patrick Buxton M.; *see* Mitford-Slade.

SLADE, William Charles; Vice-Principal, 1998–2000, Consultant, 2000–02, King's College London; *b* 20 June 1939; *s* of late Charles Slade and Phyllis (*née* Littlejohns); *m* 1961, Elizabeth Lyn Roberts; two *d*. *Educ:* St Julian's High Sch., Newport, Gwent; UC of Swansea (BSc; Pres., Students' Union, 1960–61). ACMA 1966. Guest Keen Iron and Steel Ltd, 1961–66; Management Accountant: Tunnel Cement Ltd, 1966–71; Pye TMC Ltd, 1971–75; Finance Officer, 1975–77, Sec., 1977–85, Chelsea Coll., Univ. of London; Sec., 1986–98, Mem. Council, 1998–2000, KCL (FKC 1989). Chm., Univ. of London Purchasing Consortium, 1991–94. Mem. Council, Greenacre Sch. for Girls, 1980–95. Member: NADFAS (Epsom branch), 2002–, (Ashtead branch), 2014–; Epsom Literary Soc., 2003–13 (Cttee Mem., 2005–12; Chm., 2009–12). *Recreations:* theatre, golf, Rugby football. *Address:* 1b The Murreys, Ashtead, Surrey KT21 2LU. *T:* (01372) 273847. *Club:* Royal Automobile.

SLADEK, Nancy; Editor, since 1999, and Proprietor, since 2005, Literary Review; *b* London, 7 Dec. 1960; *d* of Milan Sladek and Hana Sladek (*née* Kozeluhova); one *s* by Andrea Chiari-Gaggia. *Educ:* Heathfield Sch., Ascot; Univ. of Geneva (LèsL). Dep. Ed., Literary Rev., 1989–99. *Address:* Literary Review, 44 Lexington Street, W1F 0LW. *T:* (020) 7437 9392, *Fax:* (020) 7734 1844. *E:* nancy@literaryreview.co.uk. *Club:* Academy.

SLADEN, Teresa; Secretary of the Victorian Society, 1987–93; *b* 16 Sept. 1939; *d* of Robert John Fawcett and Anne (*née* Fairlie Clarke); *m* 1961, David Sladen; one *s* two *d*. *Educ:* Birkbeck Coll., London Univ. (BA Hons Hist. of Art/Italian); Courtauld Inst. (MA Medieval Art and Architecture, 1978). Royal Commn on Historical Monuments, 1978–79; part-time lectr and freelance researcher, 1980–82; Architectural Advr, Victorian Soc., 1983–87. Trustee and Cttee Mem., Mausolea & Monuments Trust, 1997–2008 (Chm., 1998–2000); Vice-Chm., Victorian Soc., 1998–2001; Member: Southwark DAC, 1993–2002; Adv. Bd for Redundant Churches, 1999–2008. *Publications:* (contrib.) The Albert Memorial, 2000; (contrib.) St Paul's Cathedral, 2004; contrib. to Jl of Garden History. *Recreations:* drawing, 19th century stained glass and painted decoration, 19th century novels.

SLANE, Viscount; Rory Nicholas Burton Conyngham; *b* 28 Feb. 2010; *s* and *heir* of Earl of Mount Charles, *qv*.

SLANEY, Prof. Sir Geoffrey, KBE 1984; FRCS; Barling Professor, Head of Department of Surgery, Queen Elizabeth Hospital, Birmingham University, 1971–86, now Emeritus; Hon. Consultant Surgeon: United Birmingham Hospitals and Regional Hospital Board, 1959–2002; Royal Prince Alfred Hospital, Sydney, since 1981; President, Royal College of Surgeons of England, 1982–86; Hon. Consulting Surgeon Emeritus, City of London and Hackney Health Authority, 1983; *b* 19 Sept. 1922; *er s* of Richard and Gladys Lois Slaney; *m* 1956, Josephine Mary Davy; one *s* two *d*. *Educ:* Brewood Grammar Sch.; Univs of Birmingham, London and Illinois, USA. MB, ChB (Birmingham) 1947, FRCS 1953, MS (Ill) 1956, ChM (Birmingham) 1961; Hon. FRCSI 1983; Hon. FRACS 1983; Hon. FCSSL 1984; Hon. FACS 1985; Hon. FCSSA 1986; Hon. FRCSCan 1986; Hon. FRCA (Hon. FFARCS 1987). Ho. Surg. and Surgical Registrar, Gen. Hosp. Birmingham, 1947–48. Captain RAMC, 1948–50. Surgical Registrar, Coventry, London and Hackney Hosps, 1950–53; Surgical Registrar, Lectr in Surgery and Surgical Research Fellow, Queen Elizabeth Hosp., Birmingham, 1953–59; Hunterian Prof., RCS, 1961–62; Prof. of Surgery, Univ. of Birmingham, 1966–87. Non-exec. Dir, St Martins Hosps, 1987–2001. Member: London Adv. Group to Sec. of State, DHSS, 1980–81; Ministerial Adv. Gp on Med. Manpower, 1985–86; Res. Liaison Gp, DHSS, 1979–85; Midlands Med. Appeals Tribunal, 1964–94; Med. Adv. Bd, Internat. Hosp. Gp, 1986–94. Former External Examr in Surgery to Univs of: Newcastle upon Tyne, London, Cambridge, Oxford, Liverpool, Nat. Univ. of Ireland, Lagos, Zimbabwe, and Licentiate Cttee, Hong Kong; Advisor in Surgery, Univs of Bristol and London. Lectures: Richardson Meml, Massachusetts Gen. Hosp., Boston, USA, 1975; Pybus Meml, Newcastle, 1978; Simpson Smith Meml, London, 1979; Legg Meml, KCH, London, 1982; Chesledon, St Thomas' Hosp., London, 1983; Miles Meml, London, 1983; Berrill Meml, Coventry, 1984; Sandblom, Lund, Sweden, 1984; Sir John Frazer Meml, Edinburgh, 1984; Tung Wah Inaugural, Tung Wah Hosp., Hong Kong, 1986; Sir Ernest Finch Meml, Sheffield, 1986; Hunterian Oration, RCS, 1987; Budd Meml, Bristol, 1987; Annual Guest Lecture, Chicago Surgical Soc., 1987; Barney Brooks Meml, Vanderbilt Univ., Tennessee, 1987; Rutherford-Morison, Newcastle, 1987; Walter C. Mackenzie, Edmonton, 1988; Francis C. Moore, Boston, 1988; Joseph C. Finneran, Indianapolis, 1988; Annual Oration, Osler Club, 1988; Qvist Meml, Royal Free Hosp., 1988; Duke Sesquicentennial, NC, 1988; Telford Meml, Manchester, 1989; (first) Bryan Brooke, Ileostomy Assoc., 1990. Visiting Professor: Durban, Cape Town, Witwatersrand, 1970; Sir Logan Campbell and RACS, NZ, 1977; Univ. of Calif and Cedars-Sinai Hosp., LA, 1978; Pearce Gould, Middlesex Hosp., 1980; McIlrath Guest, Sydney, 1981; G. B. Ong, Univ. of Hong Kong, 1983 (Ong Inaugural Lecture); Foundn Culpepper Prof., Univ. of California, 1984; Madras Med. Coll., and Univ. of Istanbul, 1986; Univ. of Alberta, Edmonton, 1988; Harvard, 1988; Uniformed Services Univ., Bethesda, 1988; Duke Univ., 1988; Wernicke-Marks-Elk, Univ. of Zimbabwe, 1989. Mem. Council, RCS, 1975–87; Member: Moynihan Chirurgical Club (Pres., 1986–87); James IV Assoc. of Surgeons (Pres., 1985–86); Internat. Surgical Gp (Pres., 1985–86); Surgical Research Soc.; Internat. Soc. of Cardio-Vascular Surgeons; Vascular Surgical Soc., GB (Pres., 1974–75); Chm., Assoc. of Profs of Surgery of GB and Ireland, 1979–82. Mem. Council, Univ. of Zimbabwe, 1973–82. Fellow: RSM; Assoc. of Surgeons GB and Ire. (Mem. Council, 1966–76, Treasurer, 1970–76); Assoc. Clinical Anatomists; Amer. Surgical Assoc. Hon. Life Member: Los Angeles Surgical Soc.; Chicago Surgical Soc.; Warren H. Cole Surgical Soc.; William H. Scott Surgical Soc.; Hon. Member: Grey Turner Surgical Club; Assoc. of Surgeons of India. Hon. Freeman, Barbers' Co. Jacksonian Prize and Medal, RCS, 1959; Pybus Meml Medal, NE Surgical Soc., 1978; Miles Medal, Royal Marsden Hosp., 1983; Vanderbilt Univ. Medal, 1987; Brooke Medal, Ileostomy Assoc. of GB and Ireland, 1990. Mem. Editl Bd, British Jl of Surgery, 1970–84; Co-Chief Editor, Jl of Cardio-Vascular Surgery, 1988–92. *Publications:* Metabolic Derangements in Gastrointestinal Surgery (with B. N. Brooke), 1967 (USA); (jtly) Cancer of the Large Bowel, 1991; numerous contribs to med. and surg. jls. *Recreations:* fishing, family, sculpture and carving. *Address:* 3 Mason View, Laugherne Park, Martley, Worcester WR6 6RQ. *T:* (01886) 887890.

SLANEY, (William) Simon (Rodolph) K.; *see* Kenyon-Slaney.

SLATER, Bill; *see* Slater, W. J.

SLATER, Dr David Homfray, CB 1996; Director, Cambrensis Ltd, since 2001; Chief Scientist, Willworth Enterprises Ltd, since 2008; *b* 16 Oct. 1940; *m* 1964, Edith Mildred Price; four *d*. *Educ:* University College of Wales Aberystwyth (BSc, PhD). CChem, FRIC, FIChemE, CEng, FInstE. Research Associate, Ohio State Univ., 1966–69; Sen. Res. Fellow, Dept of Chemistry, Univ. of Southampton, 1969–70; Lectr in Combustion, Dept of Chem. Engineering and Chem. Technology, Imperial College London, 1970–75; Cremer and Warner: Sen. Scientist, 1975; Partner, 1979–81; Founding Dir, Technica, 1981–91; Chief Inspector, HM Inspectorate of Pollution, 1991–96; Dir, Pollution Prevention and Control, Envmt Agency, 1996–98; Dir, Oxera Envmtl, 1998–2001; Principal Partner, Acona Gp, 2001–05; Chairman: RLtec, 2003–09; NIREX CLG Ltd, 2005–07; non-executive Director: Alsitek Ltd, 2010–; Tidal Lagoon (Swansea Bay) plc, 2012–. Specialist Advr to Envmt, Transport and Regl Affairs Select Cttee, H of C, 1999–2000; Envmtl Advr, Better Regulation Task Force, Cabinet Office, 2000. Chm., Envmtl Gp, Regulatory Policy Inst., Oxford, 2001–03. Associate, Envmtl Change Unit, Oxford Univ., 1999–2001; Royal Acad. of Engrg Vis. Prof., UMIST, 2002–06; Adjunct Prof., Industrial Adv. Panel, KCL, 2002. Hon. Professor: of Life Sciences, Univ. of Wales, Aberystwyth, 1991; Sch. of Engrg, Cardiff Univ., 2009–. Chm. and Trustee, SEE – It Working. Mem. Court, Cranfield Univ., 1997–2001. *Publications:* numerous contribs to sci. jls and conference procs. *Recreations:* music, horses. *Club:* Athenæum.

SLATER, Prof. Edward Charles, ScD; FRS 1975; FAA; Professor of Physiological Chemistry, University of Amsterdam, The Netherlands, 1955–85; *b* 16 Jan. 1917; *s* of Edward Brunton Slater and Violet Podmore; *m* 1940, Marion Winifred Hutley; one *d*. *Educ:* Melbourne Univ. (BSc, MSc); Cambridge Univ. (PhD, ScD). Biochemist, Australian Inst. of Anatomy, Canberra, Aust., 1939–46; Research Fellow, Molteno Inst., Univ. of Cambridge, UK, 1946–55. Pres., Internat. Union of Biochem., 1988–91. Member: Royal Netherlands Acad. of Science and Letters, 1964; Hollandsche Maatschappij van Wetenschappen, 1970; Hon. Member: Amer. Soc. of Biological Chemists, 1971; Japanese Biochemical Soc., 1973; The Biochemical Soc., 1987; Nederlandse Vereniging voor Biochemie, 1989; For. Mem., Royal Swedish Acad. of Sciences, 1975; Hon. For. Mem., Académie Royal de Méd., Belgium, 1982; Corresp. Mem., Acad. Nacional de Ciencias Exactas, Físicas y Naturales, Argentina, 1973; FAA (Corresp. Mem., Australian Acad. of Sci., 1985). Hon. DSc Southampton, 1993; Hon. DBiolSci Bari, 1998. Kt, Order of the Netherlands Lion, 1984. *Publications:* Biochimica et Biophysica Acta: story of a biochemical journal, 1986; 475 contribs to learned jls. *Recreation:* yachting. *Address:* Suite 3/1, Richmond Painswick, Stroud Road, Painswick, Glos GL6 6UL. *T:* (01452) 810787.

SLATER, Francesca; *see* Wiley, F.

SLATER, Prof. Gillian Lesley, (Mrs Ian Huntley); DL; DPhil; Vice-Chancellor, Bournemouth University, 1994–2005; *b* 13 Jan. 1949; *d* of Leonard William Henry Filtness and Adeline Mary Filtness; *m* 1st, 1970, John Bruce Slater (marr. diss. 1983); two *d*; 2nd, 1988, Ian David Huntley. *Educ:* Sutton High Sch. for Girls; St Hugh's Coll., Oxford (BA 1970; MSc 1971; MA, DPhil 1973). FIMA 1982; CMath 1991. Lectr, Poly. of South Bank, 1973–79; Sen. Lectr, 1979–84, Prin. Lectr, 1984–86, Sheffield City Poly., 1979–86; Head of Dept of Math. and Physics, 1986–89, Asst Dir and Dean of Science and Engrg, 1989–92, Manchester Poly.; Pro-Vice-Chancellor, Manchester Metropolitan Univ., 1992–94. Governor: UEL, 2006–08; Talbot Heath Sch. (Dep. Chm.), 2006–09; Sherborne Sch., 2009–13. DL Dorset, 2006. *Publications:* Essential Mathematics for Software Engineers, 1987; (with A. Norcliffe) Mathematics for Software Construction, 1991; numerous articles in learned jls. *Recreations:* listening to classical orchestral music, handweaving. *Address:* 2 Strata, 150 Canford Cliffs Road, Poole BH13 7ER.

SLATER, James Derrick, FCA; Chairman, Salar Properties Ltd, since 1983; Deputy Chairman, Agrifirma Services Ltd, since 2008; *b* 13 March 1929; *o s* of Hubert and Jessica Slater; *m* 1965, Helen Wyndham Goodwyn; two *s* two *d*. *Educ:* Preston Manor County Sch. Accountant and then Gen. Man. to a gp of metal finishing cos, 1953–55; Sec., Park Royal Vehicles Ltd, 1955–58; Dep. Sales Dir, Leyland Motor Corp. Ltd, 1963; Chm., Slater Walker Securities Ltd, 1964–75; Dir, BLMC, 1969–75. Dep. Chm., Galahad Gold, 2003–08. FCA 1963 (ACA 1953). *Publications:* Return to Go, 1977; The Zulu Principle, 1992; Investment Made Easy, 1994; Pep Up Your Wealth, 1994; Beyond the Zulu Principle, 1996; How to Become a Millionaire, 2000; *for children:* Goldenrod, 1978; A. Mazing Monsters, 1979; Grasshopper and the Unwise Owl, 1979; The Boy Who Saved Earth, 1979. *Recreations:* bridge, salmon fishing.

SLATER, Adm. Sir John Cunningham Kirkwood, (Sir Jock), GCB 1992 (KCB 1988); LVO 1971; DL; First Sea Lord and Chief of Naval Staff, and First and Principal Naval Aide-de-Camp to the Queen, 1995–98; *b* 27 March 1938; *s* of late Dr James K. Slater, OBE, MD, FRCPE and M. C. B. Slater (*née* Bramwell); *m* 1972, Ann Frances, *d* of late Mr and Mrs W. P. Scott of Orkney; two *s*. *Educ:* Edinburgh Academy; Sedbergh. BRNC Dartmouth, 1956–58; served HM Ships Troubridge, Yaxham, HM Yacht Britannia, Cassandra, 1959–64; Comd HMS Soberton, 1965; specialised in navigation, HMS Dryad, 1965–66; HM Ships Victorious and Scarborough (Dartmouth Training Sqdn), 1966–68; Equerry to HM the Queen, 1968–71; Comdr 1971; Comd, HMS Jupiter, 1972–73; Directorate of Naval Ops, MoD, 1973–75; Captain 1976; Comd, HMS Kent, 1976–77; RCDS 1978; Asst Dir of Naval Warfare, MoD, 1979–81; Comd, HMS Illustrious, 1982–83; Captain, Sch. of Maritime Ops and Comd, HMS Dryad, 1983–85; Rear Adm. 1985; ACDS (Policy and Nuclear), 1985–87; Vice-Adm., 1987; Flag Officer, Scotland and NI, and NATO Comdr Northern sub area Eastern Atlantic, Comdr Nore sub area Channel and Naval Base Comdr, Rosyth, 1987–89; Chief of Fleet Support (Mem., Admiralty Bd), 1989–91; Adm. 1991; C-in-C, Fleet, Allied C-in-C, Channel, and Eastern Atlantic, 1991–92; VCDS, 1993–95. Non-executive Director: VTGp (formerly Vosper Thornycroft Hldgs) plc, 1999–2004; Lockheed Martin UK Ltd, 2000–08; Consultant, Bristow Helicopters, 2001–04. Vice Pres., RUSI, 1995–98 (Vice Chm., 1993–95); Chm., RNLI, 2004–08 (Council, 1999–2008; Chm., Ops Cttee, 2001–02; Dep. Chm., 2002–04; Chm. Emeritus, 2008); Mem., Bd of Mgt, BNSC, 1986–87. Chm., Royal Navy Club of 1765 and 1785, 2001–04; Chm., White Ensign Assoc., 2002–05 (Mem. Council, 1999–2008; Vice Pres., 2008–); Vice-Pres., British Forces Foundn, 2002– (Vice-Chm., 1999–2002); Pres., Royal Navy and Royal Marines Charity, 2008–11. Chm., Imperial War Mus., 2001–06 (Trustee, 1999–2006); Pres., Amer. Air Mus. in Britain, 2001–06. Mem., Nat. Youth Orchestra of GB, 1955. Gov., Sedbergh Sch., 1997–2002. Elder Brother, Trinity Hse, 1995 (Younger Brother, 1978–95). Freeman, City of London, 1989; Liveryman, Shipwrights' Co., 1991– (Mem. Ct of Assts, 2005–; Prime Warden, 2011, 2012). DL Hants, 1999. Hon. DSc: Cranfield, 1998; Southampton, 2008. Comdr Legion of Merit (US), 1997. *Recreation:* outdoor. *Address:* c/o Naval Secretary, Fleet Headquarters, Whale Island, Portsmouth PO2 8BY. *Clubs:* Army and Navy; Liphook Golf.

See also P. J. B. Slater.

SLATER, Dr John Morton; agricultural economic consultant, since 1998; *b* 21 Aug. 1938; *s* of Rev. Percy William Slater and Evelyn Maude Morton Slater; *m* 1972, Susan Mary Black, *d* of Rev. Dr John Ferguson Park and Mary Davis McCaughey Park; two *s* one *d*. *Educ:* Durham Sch.; Univ. of Nottingham (BSc Agric. Sc 1961); Univ. of Toronto (MS Agric. Econ. 1963); Univ. of Illinois (L. J. Norton Meml Fellow; PhD 1965). Lectr, Univ. of Manchester, 1965–70; Consultant, FAO, 1966–67; Ministry of Agriculture, Fisheries and Food: Economic Advr, 1970–84; Head of Econs and Stats (Food) Div., 1984–92; Head of Econs (Internat.) Div., 1992–96; Head of Econs and Stats Gp, 1996–98. Special Advr, H of L Select Cttee on Science and Technol., 1999–2000. Master, Worshipful Co. of Turners, 1999–2000; Chm., Millennium Masters Assoc., 2003–06. MRI. *Publications:* (ed) Fifty Years of the National Food Survey 1940–1990, 1991. *Recreations:* cricket, golf, bridge. *Address:* 28 Swains Lane, N6 6QR. *T:* (020) 7485 1238. *E:* slaterconsult@gmail.com. *Clubs:* City Livery (Hon. Sec., 2002–03), United Wards, MCC.

SLATER, Jonathan; Director General, Head Office and Commissioning Services, Ministry of Defence; *b* London, 29 Nov. 1961; *s* of Christopher and Julia Slater; *m* 2001, Jane Ramsey; two *s* one *d*. *Educ:* Univ. of York (BSc Maths); Univ. of Sussex (MSc Operational Res.). Operational Res. Analyst, British Rlys Bd, 1985–88; Sen. Policy Analyst, Newnham BC, 1988–90; Islington Borough Council: Prin. Policy Develt Officer, 1990–93; Contract Services Manager, 1993–95; Asst Chief Exec., 1995–98; Exec. Dir, 1998–2000; Dep. Chief Exec. and Dir of Educn, 2000–01; Director: Cabinet Office, 2001–05; Prime Minister's Delivery Unit, 2005–06; Performance and Improvement, Nat. Offender Mgt Service, 2006–08; Chief Exec., Office for Criminal Justice Reform, 2008–09; Director General:

Transforming Justice, MoJ, 2009–11; Transformation and Corporate Strategy, MoD, 2011. *Recreations:* piano playing, tennis, musical theatre. *Address:* Ministry of Defence, Main Building, Whitehall, SW1A 2HB.

SLATER, Judith Mary; HM Diplomatic Service; Deputy High Commissioner and Director, UK Trade and Investment, Singapore, since 2011; *b* 26 June 1964; *d* of George Norris Stewart Slater and Valerie Mary Slater (*née* Pratt); *m* 1998, Philip Frederick de Waal; one *s* one *d*. *Educ:* Howell's Sch., Denbigh; St John's Coll., Cambridge (BA 1987). Joined HM Diplomatic Service, 1988; Third, then Second Sec. (Political), Canberra, 1989–93; First Sec., FCO, 1993; Private Sec. to Minister of State, 1994; First Sec. (Press and Public Affairs), New Delhi, 1997–2001; Asst Dir, Personnel Policy, FCO, 2001–04; Consul-Gen., Houston, 2004–07; Dep. High Comr, Pretoria, 2007–11. *Recreations:* golf, tennis, cinema. *Address:* c/o Foreign and Commonwealth Office, King Charles Street, SW1A 2AH.

SLATER, Rt Rev. Keith Francis; Bishop of Grafton, NSW, 2003–13; *b* 13 Dec. 1949; *s* of George Richard Slater and Edna May Slater (*née* Eriksen); *m* 1969, Lorraine Margaret Halvorson; two *s*. *Educ:* Univ. of Qld (BA); St Francis Theol Coll., Brisbane (ThL); Kelvin Grove Teachers' Coll., Brisbane (Dip. Teaching); Brisbane Coll. of Theology (MMin 2007). Ordained deacon and priest, 1975; Asst Curate, St Saviour's, Gladstone, 1975–78; Priest i/c, 1978–80, Rector, 1980–82, St Peter's, Springsure; Rector: St Luke's, Ekibin, Brisbane, 1982–87; St Saviour's, Gladstone, 1987–94; St Clement's-on-the-Hill, Stafford, Brisbane, 1994–2003; Archdeacon of Lilley, Brisbane, 1996–2003. Provincial Minister (Aust. Province), 1993–99, Minister Gen., 1999–2005, Third Order of Soc. of St Francis; Episcopal Advr, Nat. Secretariat Anglican Cursillo Movt of Australia, 2009–13. Mem. Bd, Foundn of St George's Coll., Jerusalem, 2008–. *Address:* 470 Main Western Road, Tamborine Mountain, Qld 4272, Australia. *E:* keithfslater@gmail.com.

SLATER, Kenneth Frederick, FREng, FIET; engineering and defence consultant, retired; *b* 31 July 1925; *s* of Charles Frederick and Emily Gertrude Slater; *m* 1965, Marjorie Gladys Beadsworth (*d* 2007), Northampton; *m* 2011, Mary Maiden, widow. *Educ:* Hull Grammar Sch.; Manchester Univ. (BSc Tech (Hons)). Admiralty Signal Estab. Extension, 1943–46; RRE, 1949–63; UK Mem., NATO Air Defence Planning Team, 1964; Supt, Radar Div., RRE, 1965–68; Asst Dir of Electronics R&D, Min. of Technology, 1968–70, Dir, 1970–71; Head of various groups, RRE, 1971–76; Dep. Dir, RSRE, 1976–78; Dir, Admiralty Surface Weapons Estabt, Portsmouth, 1978–84; Dir of Engrg, Marconi Underwater Systems Ltd, 1984–88. Vis. Prof., UCL, 1995–. Liveryman, Engineers' Co., 1992. FREng (FEng 1985). *Publications:* specialist contribs on Radar to Encyclopaedia Britannica and Encyclopaedic Dictionary of Physics; technical articles. *Recreations:* photography, music. *Address:* Flat 22 Silverdale, Racefield Road, Altrincham WA14 4AP. *T:* (0161) 941 1828.

SLATER, Prof. Michael Derek, MBE 2014; DPhil; Professor of Victorian Literature, Birkbeck College, University of London, 1991–2001, now Emeritus; *b* 29 Dec. 1936; *s* of Jesse Slater and Valentine Blanche (*née* Clément). *Educ:* Reading Sch.; Balliol Coll., Oxford (Goldsmith Schol., Charles Oldham Schol., MA, DPhil 1965). Birkbeck College, University of London: Res. Asst, 1962–65; Asst Lectr in English, 1965–67; Lectr in English, 1967–79; Sen. Lectr, 1979–83; Reader, 1983–91. Dist. Vis. Prof., Ohio State Univ., 1975–76; Visiting Professor: Univ. of Debrecen, Hungary, 1992; Univ. of Kyoto, Japan, 1995, 2005; Evelyn Wrench Lectr, English-Speaking Union of USA, 2011. Tennyson Soc. annual Lect., 1997; Lee Seng Tee Dist. Lect., Wolfson Coll., Cambridge, 2012. President: Dickens Soc. of America, 1973; Internat. Dickens Fellowship, 1988–90. Chm. Trustees, Dickens House Mus., 1996–99, 2000–02, now Hon. Academic Advr. Hon. Fellow, Birkbeck Coll., 2001; Sen. Res. Fellow, Inst. of English Studies, Univ. of London, 2002–. Editor, The Dickensian, 1968–77. *Publications:* The Catalogue of the Suzannet Charles Dickens Collection, 1975; (ed) Dickens 1970, 1970; Dickens on America and the Americans, 1978; Dickens and Women, 1983, 2nd edn 1986; (with N. Bentley and N. Burgis) The Dickens Index, 1988; (ed) The Dent Uniform Edition of Dickens's Journalism, Vol. 1 1994, Vol. 2 1996, Vol. 3 1998, (with J. Drew) Vol. 4 2000; The Intelligent Person's Guide to Dickens, 2000, reissued as The Genius of Dickens, 2011; Douglas Jerrold 1803–1857, 2002; Biographical Memoir of Kathleen Tillotson, 2006; Very Interesting People: Charles Dickens, 2007; Charles Dickens, 2009; The Great Charles Dickens Scandal, 2012; contrib. Oxford DNB. *Recreations:* theatre, visiting literary museums. *Address:* 8 Ridgmount Gardens, WC1E 7AP. *T:* (020) 7580 3252.

SLATER, Prof. Nigel Kenneth Harry, PhD; FREng, CEng, FIChemE; Professor of Chemical Engineering, since 2000, and Pro-Vice-Chancellor, from Jan. 2016, Cambridge University (Head, Department of Chemical Engineering and Biotechnology, 2010–15); Fellow, 1978–85 and since 2000, and President, 2009–13, Fitzwilliam College, Cambridge; *b* 22 March 1953; *s* of Arthur Geoffrey Slater; *m* 1976, Kay Bendle; one *s* two *d*. *Educ:* Bolton Sch.; Sidney Sussex Coll., Cambridge (MA; PhD). CEng 1990; FREng 2004; FIChemE 1997. Asst Lectr, 1979–82, Lectr, 1982–85, in Chemical Engrg, Cambridge Univ.; Bioprocessing Section Manager, Unilever Research NL, 1985–90; Head of Bioprocess Dept, Wellcome Foundation Ltd, 1990–95; Prof. and Head of Dept of Chem. Engrg and Applied Chemistry, Aston Univ., 1995–2000. Hon. Prof., Tianjin Univ. of Sci. and Technol., 2013–. Director: Birmingham Technology Ltd, 1995–2000; Cobra Bio-Manufacturing plc, 2002–10; Founder, Cobra Biosciences Ltd, 1997. Chm., Chemical and Pharmaceuticals Directorate, BBSRC, 1993–96; Mem. Governing Body, Silsoe Res. Inst., 1996–2000. Governor, King Edward VI Foundn, 1997–2000. *Publications:* numerous articles in learned science and engrg jls. *Recreation:* golf. *Address:* Shenstone House, 3 St Bernard's Road, Sutton Coldfield, W Midlands B72 1LE. *T:* (0121) 321 2349.

SLATER, Rt Rev. Paul John; *see* Richmond, Bishop Suffragan of.

SLATER, Prof. Peter James Bramwell, FRSE; Kennedy Professor of Natural History, University of St Andrews, 1984–2008, now Professor Emeritus; *b* 26 Dec. 1942; *s* of Dr James Kirkwood Slater, OBE and Margaret Claire Byrom Slater (*née* Bramwell); *m* 1968, Elisabeth Priscilla Vernon Smith; two *s*. *Educ:* Edinburgh Academy; Glenalmond; Univ. of Edinburgh (BSc 1964; PhD 1968; DSc 1983). FRSB (FIBiol 1986); FRSE 1991. Shaw Macfie Lang Fellow, 1964–66, Demonstrator in Zoology, 1966–68, Univ. of Edinburgh; Lectr in Biology, Univ. of Sussex, 1968–84; University of St Andrews: Head, Sch. of Biol and Med. Scis, 1992–97; Dean, Faculty of Sci., 1998–2002. Chm., Heads of Univ. Biol Scis, 1994–96. Association for Study of Animal Behaviour: Hon. Sec., 1973–78; Hon. Pres., 1986–89; Medallist, 1999. European Editor, Animal Behaviour, 1979–82; Editor: Advances in the Study of Behavior, 1989–2005 (Associate Editor, 1982–88); Science Progress, 1983–89. *Publications:* Sex Hormones and Behaviour, 1978; (ed with T. R. Halliday) Animal Behaviour, 1983; An Introduction to Ethology, 1985; (ed) Collins Encyclopaedia of Animal Behaviour, 1986; (ed with T. R. Halliday) Evolution and Behaviour, 1994; (with C. K. Catchpole) Bird Song: biological themes and variations, 1995, 2nd edn 2008; Essentials of Animal Behaviour, 1999; numerous articles in learned jls. *Recreations:* ornithology, writing, listening to music. *Address:* Vagaland, Stromness, Orkney KW16 3AW. *T:* (01856) 850148.

See also Sir J. C. K. Slater.

SLATER, William Bell, CBE 1982; VRD 1959; FCILT; Chairman, The Mersey Docks & Harbour Co., 1987–93; Managing Director, The Cunard Steam-Ship Co. plc, 1974–85 (Director, 1971–85 and 1986–88); Director, Trafalgar House plc, 1975–88; *b* 7 Jan. 1925; *s* of William Bell and Mamie Slater; *m* 1950, Jean Mary Kiernan (*d* 2010); two *s*. *Educ:* Lancaster Royal Grammar Sch. FCILT (FCIT 1970). National Service, RM, 1943–47 (Captain, 3rd Commando Bde); RM Reserve, 1949–63 (Lt-Col and CO Merseyside Unit, 1959–63; Hon. Col, 1986–91). Trainee, Thos & Jno Brocklebank Ltd, 1947, Dir 1966–85, also Chm.; Ops Dir, 1968, Dep. Man. Dir, 1969, Man. Dir, 1971–72, Chm. 1972–85, Cunard Brocklebank Ltd. Director: Atlantic Container Line Ltd, 1968–85 (Chm., 1977–78 and 1982–83); Associated Container Transportation (Australia) Ltd, 1974–85 (Chm., 1982–85); Associated Container Transportation Ltd, 1974–85 (Chm., 1982–85); The Mersey Docks & Harbour Co., 1980–93 (Dep. Chm., 1985–87; Chm., 1987–93). External Dir, British Internat. Freight Assoc., 1989–94. Vice-Pres., CIT, 1984–87; Pres., Inst. of Freight Forwarders Ltd, 1987–88. Gen. Comr of Income Tax, 1987–99. Order of El Istiqlal (2nd Cl.), Jordan, 1972. *Recreations:* Rugby and cricket (formerly Senior Club player). *Club:* Naval.

SLATER, William John, CBE 1998 (OBE 1982); President, British Amateur Gymnastics Association, 1989–2000; Director of National Services, Sports Council, 1984–89; *b* 29 April 1927; *s* of John Rothwell Slater and Ethel May Slater; *m* 1952, Marion Warr; two *s* two *d*. *Educ:* Clitheroe Royal Grammar Sch.; Carnegie Coll. of Physical Educn; Univ. of Birmingham (BSc 1960). Dir of Phys. Educn, Univ. of Liverpool, 1964–70; Dir of Phys. Educn, Univ. of Birmingham, 1970–83. Member: Central Adv. Council for Educn (Newsom Cttee), 1961–63; Cttee of Enquiry into Association Football (Chester Cttee), 1966–68; Sports Council, 1974–83; Nat. Olympic Cttee, 1990–2000. Chm., Grants Cttee, Sports Aid Foundn, 1978–97. Wolverhampton Wanderers Football Club, 1952–62: Football League Championship medal, 1954–55, 1957–58, 1958–59; FA Cup winner's medal, 1960; rep. England in Association Football, 1951–60; Olympic Games, Helsinki, 1952; World Cup (Assoc. Football), Sweden, 1958. Hon. MSc Birmingham, 1990; Hon. DEd Wolverhampton, 2003. Footballer of the Year, 1960.

SLATKIN, Leonard; conductor; music director; Music Director: Detroit Symphony Orchestra, since 2008; Orchestre National de Lyon, since 2010; National Symphony Orchestra, Washington, 1995–2008; Chief Conductor, BBC Symphony Orchestra, 2000–04; *b* Los Angeles, 1 Sept. 1944; *s* of Felix Slatkin and Eleanor Slatkin (*née* Aller); *m* 1986, Linda Hohenfeld; one *s*; *m* 2011, Cindy McTee. *Educ:* Indiana Univ.; LA City Coll.; Juilliard Sch. of Music. Conducting début as Asst Conductor, Youth Symphony Orch. of NY, Carnegie Hall, 1966; Asst Conductor, Juilliard Opera Theater and Dance Dept, 1967; St Louis Symphony Youth Orchestra: Founder, Music Dir and Conductor, 1969–75; Musical Advr, 1984–96; St Louis Symphony Orchestra: Asst Conductor, 1968–71; Associate Conductor, 1971–74; Music Dir and Conductor, 1979–95; Music Dir, New Orleans Philharmonic Symphony, 1977–78; débuts: with Chicago Symphony, NY Philharmonic, Philadelphia Orch., RPO, 1974; with USSR orchs, 1976–77; Tokyo, 1986; Metropolitan Opera, 1991. Guest conductor with orchs throughout world incl. Concertgebouw, English Chamber Orch., LPO, LSO, Vienna State Opera, Stuttgart Opera; Principal Guest Conductor: Minnesota Orch., 1974–79; Philharmonia, 1997–2000; RPO, 2005–; Los Angeles Philharmonic, 2005–07; Pittsburgh SO, 2008–; Music Advr, Nashville SO, 2006–09. Has made numerous recordings. Mem., Nat. Acad. Recording Arts and Scis, 1985. Holds hon. doctorates. Grammy Awards, 1984, 1991 and 1994. Declaration of Honor (Silver) (Austria), 1986; Nat. Medal of Arts, USA, 2003. *Compositions:* The Raven, 1971; Rhymes and Sonnets, 1974; Dialogue for Two Cellos and Orchestra, 1975; Absurd Alphabed-time Stories, 1976; Extensions, 1, 2, 3 and 4, 1973–75.

SLATTERY, Dr David Antony Douglas, MBE (mil.) 1958; Chief Medical Officer, Rolls-Royce plc, 1973–92; Dean, Faculty of Occupational Medicine, Royal College of Physicians, 1988–91 (Vice-Dean, 1986–88); *b* 28 Jan. 1930; *s* of Rear-Adm. Sir Matthew Slattery, KBE, CB and Mica Mary Slattery (*née* Swain); *m* 1st, 1954, Mary Winifred Miller; two *s* two *d*; 2nd, 1974, Claire Louise McGuinness; one *s*. *Educ:* Ampleforth Coll.; St Thomas' Hosp., London. MB BS; FFOM RCPI 1977; FFOM RCP 1981; FRCP 1986. Capt., RAMC, 1954–58. MO, E Midlands Gas Bd, 1959–69; Manager, Health and Safety, BSC, Rotherham, 1969–73. Special Lectr, Dept of Community Health, Nottingham Univ., 1978–93; Vis. Prof., Dept of Occupational Health, Univ. of Liverpool, 1992–97. Consultant Advr in occupational medicine, RAF, 1987–96; Advr on occupational health policy, Mersey RHA, 1992–94. Dir, Occupational Health Service, Aintree Hosps NHS Trust, 1993–94. Member: Standing Med. Adv. Cttee, DHSS, 1988–91; Adv. Bd, CS Occupational Health Service, 1988–91. Industrial Health Advr, Derbys Br., BRCS, 1976–93. *Publications:* The Pattens: the story of an Ulster-Scots family in Ireland, 2008; papers on occupational medicine and the employment of the disabled. *Recreations:* history, fishing, people. *Address:* 99 South Quay, Wapping Dock, Liverpool L3 4BW. *T:* (0151) 707 2022.

SLAUGHTER, Andrew Francis; MP (Lab) Hammersmith, since 2010 (Ealing, Acton and Shepherd's Bush, 2005–10); *b* 29 Sept. 1960; *s* of late Alfred Frederick Slaughter and Marie Frances Slaughter. *Educ:* Univ. of Exeter; Coll. of Law; Inns of Court Sch. of Law. Called to the Bar, Middle Temple, 1993; barrister, Bridewell Chambers, 1993–2006, Lamb Chambers, 2006–. Mem., Hammersmith and Fulham LBC, 1986–2006 (Dep. Leader, 1991–96; Leader, 1996–2005). *Address:* House of Commons, SW1A 0AA. *T:* (020) 7219 4990.

SLAUGHTER, Audrey Cecelia, (Mrs Denis Lanigan); writer and freelance journalist; *d* of Frederick George Smith and Ethel Louise Smith; *m* 1st, 1949, W. A. Slaughter (marr. diss.); one *s* one *d*; 2nd, 1979, Charles Vere Wintour, CBE (*d* 1999); 3rd, 2002, Denis Lanigan, CBE (*d* 2009). *Educ:* Chislehurst High Sch.; Stand Grammar Sch., Manchester. Editor, Honey magazine, 1960; founded Petticoat magazine, 1964; columnist, Evening News, 1968; joined National Magazine Co., to edit Vanity Fair, 1969; founded and funded own magazine, Over 21, 1970; after sale to Morgan Grampian, 1972, remained as Dir and Editor until 1979; Associate Editor, Sunday Times, 1979; with husband founded Sunday Express colour magazine, 1981; Founder Editor, Working Woman magazine, 1984–86; Lifestyle Editor, The Independent, 1986–87; Editorial Consultant, Burda Publications, Germany, 1987–88. *Publications:* Every Man Should Have One (with Margaret Goodman), 1969; Getting Through…, 1981; Working Woman's Handbook, 1986; Your Brilliant Career, 1987; Private View (novel), 1990; Blooming (novel), 1992; Unknown Country (novel), 1994. *Recreations:* classical music, theatre, painting.

SLAUGHTER, Giles David, MA; Headmaster, University College School, 1983–96; *b* 11 July 1937; *s* of Gerald Slaughter and Enid Lillian Slaughter (*née* Crane); *m* 1965, Gillian Rothwell Shepherd; three *d*. *Educ:* Royal Masonic School; King's College, Cambridge. MA. Pierrepont School, Frensham, 1961–65; Campbell College, Belfast, 1965–68; Stockport Grammar School, 1968–70; Housemaster, Ormiston House, Campbell Coll., 1970–73; Headmaster, Solihull School, 1973–82. Non-exec. Dir, Heckett MultiServ plc, 1999–2002. Chm., London and SE, ISIS, 1995–98. Governor: Godolphin and Latymer Sch., 1988–99; Cobham Hall, 1989–2000; Aldwickbury Sch., 1974–2003; King's Coll. Sch., Wimbledon, 1995–2008; Woodbridge Sch., 1997–2007. JP Solihull, 1977–82. Church Warden, St Mary's, Ufford, 2007–12. *Recreations:* gardening, cricket, golf, theatre. *Address:* 6 Church Lane, Lower Ufford, Woodbridge, Suffolk IP13 6DS.

SLAYMAKER, Christine Ann, CBE 2014; Principal and Chief Executive, Farnborough College of Technology, since 2001; *b* Emsworth, Hants, 7 May 1958; *d* of Mervyn Ronald and Lillian Ann Johnson; *m* 2010, James Henry Slaymaker; one *s* by a previous marriage. *Educ:* Purbrook Park Co. Grammar Sch.; Portsmouth Poly. (BA Hons Business Studies 1980; Cert Ed 1983). Dir of Mktg, Croydon Coll., 1985–87; Vice Principal, Salisbury Coll., 1987–98; Principal, Brinsbury Coll., 1998–2001. Mem., SE England Regl Assembly, 2007–09. Proto-Council Mem., Inst. of FE, 2014–. Board Member: Farnborough Aerospace Consortium, 2007–; Enterprise M3 LEP, 2014–. Advr, RE Educn Trust, 2007–. Governor: Frimley Park Hosp. NHS Trust, 2005–06; Talavera Infants Sch., Aldershot, 2012–; Treloar Sch. and Coll.,

2014–. MCIM 1985. *Recreations:* friends and family, holidays and travelling, swimming to keep fit. *Address:* Farnborough College of Technology, Boundary Road, Farnborough, Hants GU14 6SB. *T:* (01252) 407001, *Fax:* (01252) 407002. *E:* c.slaymaker@farn-ct.ac.uk.

SLEDGE, Ven. Richard Kitson; Archdeacon of Huntingdon, 1978–96; *b* 13 April 1930; *s* of Sydney Kitson and Mary Sylvia Sledge; *m* 1958, Patricia Henley (*née* Sear); one *s* two *d* (and one *s* decd). *Educ:* Epsom College; Peterhouse, Cambridge (MA). Curate of Emmanuel, Plymouth, 1954–57; Curate-in-charge of St Stephen's, Exeter, 1957–63; Rector: Dronfield, 1963–78; Hemingford Abbots, 1978–89. *Address:* 7 Budge Close, Brampton, Huntingdon, Cambs PE28 4PL. *T:* (01480) 437789.

SLEE, Prof. Richard; artist; Professor, University of the Arts London (formerly The London Institute), 1992–2012, now Emeritus (Principal Lecturer, Camberwell College of Arts, 1998–2011); *b* 8 May 1946; *s* of Richard and Margaret Slee; *m* 1977, Diana Gill (marr. diss. 1987); one *d*. *Educ:* Carlisle Coll. of Art and Design; Central Sch. of Art and Design (BA 1st cl. Hons Ceramics 1970); Royal Coll. of Art (MA Design degree by project 1988). Full-time Lectr, Hastings Coll. of Further Educn, 1973–75; Vis. Lectr, Central Saint Martin's Coll. of Art and Design and Brighton Poly., and pt-time Sen. Lectr, Harrow Sch. of Art, 1975–90; Sen. Lectr, Camberwell Coll. of Arts, 1990–98. Theodore Randall Internat. Chair in Ceramic Art, Sch. of Art and Design, Alfred Univ., USA, 2011. External Examiner: Department of Ceramics: Camberwell Coll. of Arts, 1985–87; Loughborough Coll. of Art, 1987–90; Glasgow Sch. of Art, 1998–2002; Dept of Goldsmithing, Silversmithing, Metalwork and Jewellery (MA), RCA, 2007–10. Mem., Setting-up Grants Cttee, Crafts Council, 2000–04. Jerwood Prize, 2001. *Recreation:* pottery. *Address:* c/o Hales Gallery, Tea Building, 7 Bethnal Green Road, E1 6LA. *T:* (020) 7033 1938, *Fax:* (020) 7033 1939. *E:* info@halesgallery.com.

SLEEMAN, His Honour Stuart Philip; a Circuit Judge, 1993–2012; a Deputy Circuit Judge, since 2012; *b* 9 May 1947; *s* of His Honour (Stuart) Colin Sleeman; *m* 1973, Elisabeth Nina Brann; one *s* two *d*. *Educ:* Cranleigh Sch.; Merton Coll., Oxford (BA Jurisprudence 1969; MA 1972). Called to the Bar, Gray's Inn, 1970; a Recorder, 1986–93. Tutor Judge, Civil and Family, Judicial Studies Bd, 2003–12; Designated Family Judge, Guildford Care Centre, 2003–11. Chm., Bar Disciplinary Tribunal, 2014–. Chm., Old Cranleighan Soc., 1984–97; Gov., Cranleigh Sch., 1989–2005. Liveryman, Fruiterers' Co., 2009–. *Recreations:* music, history (in particular the Reformation), formerly hockey (Oxford Occasionals).

SLEEP, Wayne Philip Colin, OBE 1998; dancer, actor, choreographer; *b* Plymouth, 17 July 1948. *Educ:* Hartlepool; Royal Ballet Sch. (Leverhulme Scholar). Graduated into Royal Ballet, 1966; Soloist, 1970; Principal, 1973; roles in: Giselle; Dancers at a Gathering; The Nutcracker; Romeo and Juliet; The Grand Tour; Elite Syncopations; Swan Lake; The Four Seasons; Les Patineurs; Petroushka (title role); Cinderella; The Dream; Pineapple Poll; Mam'zelle Angot; 4th Symphony; La Fille mal gardée; A Month in the Country; A Good Night's Sleep (gala); Coppelia, English Nat. Ballet, 1994; chor., with Robert North, David & Goliath; also roles in operas, A Midsummer Night's Dream and Aida; roles created for him by Sir Frederick Ashton, Dame Ninette de Valois, Sir Kenneth MacMillan, Rudolf Nureyev, John Neumeier, Joe Layton and many others. *Theatre:* Ariel in The Tempest, New Shakespeare Co.; title role in Pinocchio, Birmingham Rep.; genie in Aladdin, Palladium; soldier in The Soldier's Tale, QEH, 1980 and 1981; Truffaldino in The Servant of Two Masters; chor. and played lead in The Point, Mermaid; Mr Mistoffelees in Cats, New London, 1981; co-starred in Song and Dance, Palace, 1982, Shaftesbury, 1990 (video, 1984); Cabaret, Strand, 1986; chor. Savoy Suite, 1993; The History of Dance, tour, 1995; Chitty Chitty Bang Bang, London Palladium, 2003; Into Thin Air!, New Players, 2005; High Society, tour, 2007; Cabaret, tour, 2008. Formed own company, DASH, 1980: Chichester Fest., 1980, national tour and Sadler's Wells, 1982, Apollo Victoria and national tour, Christmas season, Dominion, 1983; danced in and jtly choreographed Bits and Pieces, Dominion, 1989; Hollywood and Broadway tour, 1996–97; World of Classical Ballet tour, 1998; Precious Little Sleep tour, 2011; has directed several charity galas including 90 Years of Dance, 1995 and Stars of the Night, 1997. Teaches workshops around the world. *Films:* The Virgin Soldiers; The First Great Train Robbery; The Tales of Beatrix Potter, 1971. Chor. films and television, inc. Adam's Rib, Death on the Nile, and appeared in many television progs inc. Dizzy Feet and series, The Hot Shoe Show, 1983, 1984; Big Ballet, 2014; Tony Lumpkin in She Stoops to Conquer, radio. Patron: Wheelchair Dance Assoc.; Dance Teachers Benevolent Fund; Benesh Dance Inst. Hon. DLitt Exeter. Show Business Personality of the Year, 1983. *Publications:* Variations on Wayne Sleep, 1983; Precious Little Sleep (autobiog.), 1996. *Recreation:* entertaining.

SLEIGH, Andrew Crofton, FInstP; Director, Pinoak Innovation Consulting, since 2010; *b* 4 Nov. 1950; *s* of Arthur Ffennell Crofton Sleigh and Margaret Sleigh; *m* 1986, Christine Mattick; one *s* one *d*. *Educ:* Portsmouth Grammar Sch.; Maret Sch., Washington; Havant Grammar Sch.; St Catherine's Coll., Oxford (MA Physics). FInstP 2000. Superintendent, Pattern Processing and Machine Intelligence Div., RSRE, 1985–90; Director: of Science, Central Staff, MoD, 1990–93; Operation Studies Sector, DRA, 1993–94; Chief Exec., Defence Operational Analysis Centre, MoD, 1994–95; Man. Dir, Centre for Defence Analysis, DERA, 1995–98; Dir Gen. for Inf. and Communications Services, MoD, 1999–2001; UK Principal, NATO C4I Bd, 1998–2001; Capability Manager for Information Superiority, MoD Defence Equipment Capability Customer, 1999–2001; QinetiQ plc: Man. Dir, Defence Solutions, 2001–03; Man. Dir, Knowledge and Information Systems Div., 2003–05; Gp Man. Dir, Defence and Technol. Sector, 2005–07; Gp Chief Technol. Officer, 2007–09; Sen. Sci. Advr, 2009. Member: DTI Spectrum Mgt Adv. Gp, 1998–2002; OFCOM Spectrum Mgt Adv. Bd, 2003–; Res. and Develt Gp, NDIC, 2007–08; Hartwell Gp on Climate Change, 2011–14; Bd, Birmingham Science City, 2012–; Vice-Chm., Security Adv. Gp, Framework Prog. 7, EC, 2008–12. Council Mem., RUSI, 2002–06. Adjunct Prof., Imperial Coll. Business Sch. (formerly Tanaka Business Sch.), Imperial Coll. London, 2008–12. Chm., GeoLang Hldgs Ltd, 2013–; Vice Chm., EU Horizon 2020 Secure Societies Adv. Gp, 2014–; non-executive Director: Worcester Acute Hosps Trust, 2011–; Alta Innovations Ltd, 2011–; Vislink plc, 2011–14. Hon. Fellow, Worcester Univ., 2008. W Midlands Ambassador, 2005–07. Chairman: Malvern Fest. Fringe, 1977–82; Wyvern Trust Ltd, 1984–90. *Publications:* (with O. J. Braddick) The Physical and Biological Processing of Images, 1983. *Recreations:* ski-ing, windsurfing, helping my wife run the farm. *Club:* Savile.

SLEIGHT, Prof. Peter, MD (Cantab), DM (Oxon), FRCP; FACC; Field-Marshal Alexander Professor of Cardiovascular Medicine in the University of Oxford, and Fellow of Exeter College, Oxford, 1973–94, now Emeritus Professor and Fellow; Hon. Consultant Physician, Oxford Radcliffe Hospitals NHS Trust (formerly Oxford Health Authority), 1964–2011, Observer status, since 2012; *b* 27 June 1929; *s* of William and Mary Sleight, Boston Spa, Yorks; *m* 1953, Gillian France; two *s*. *Educ:* Leeds Grammar Sch.; Gonville and Caius Coll., Cambridge; St Bartholomew's Hosp., London. Ho. Phys. and Ho. Surg., Med. and Surg. Professorial Units, Bart's, 1953; Sen. Registrar, St George's Hosp., London, 1959–64; Bissinger Fellow, Cardiovascular Research Inst., Univ. of California, San Francisco, 1961–63; MRC Scientific Officer, Depts of Physiology and Medicine, Univ. of Oxford, 1964–66; Consultant Physician, Radcliffe Infirmary, Oxford, 1966–73. Visiting Prof., Univ. of Sydney (Warren McDonald Sen. Overseas Fellow of Aust. Heart Foundn), 1972–73; Hon. Prof. of Medicine, Federal Univ. of Pernambuco, 1975. Civil Consultant in Medicine, RAF, 1985–94. Co-Chairman: Heart Outcomes Prevention Evaluation Study Gp, 1995–2000; ON TARGET Study Gp, 2000–08; SEARCH, Heart Protection Study. Vice Pres., ASH, 1994– (Chm., 1982–93); President: British Hypertension Soc., 1993–95; World Hypertension League, 1995–2001; Member Council: Internat. Soc. of Hypertension, 1978–86; Eur. Soc. of Cardiology, 1983–88; Hon. Mem., Eur. Soc. of Hypertension, 2001. Mem. Editl Bd, British Heart Jl, 1976–83; Editor: Jl of Cardiovascular Res., 1983–92; Jl of Cardiovascular Risk, 1994–2001. Hon. MD Gdansk, 2000. Young Investigators Award, 1963, Bishop Lectr, 2004, Internat. Lecture, 2008, Amer. Coll. of Cardiology; Evian Prize, 1988; Merck Sharp and Dohme Award, Internat. Soc. of Hypertension, 1990; Galen Medal for Therapeutics, Soc. of Apothecaries, 2000; Sen. Internat. Award, Aspirin Foundn, 2000; MacKenzie Medal, British Cardiac Soc., 2003; Lifetime Achievement Award, Eur. Soc. Hypertension, 2005; Award for Lifetime Res., Russian Fedn Soc. of Cardiology, 2005; Gold Medal, Eur. Soc. of Cardiology, 2010; Jl of Physiol. Medal, 2011; Paton Lectr, Physiol Soc., 2014. *Films:* Control of Circulation; History of Hypertension (Medal, BMA Scientific Film Competition, 1981). *Publications:* Modern Trends in Cardiology, 1976; (ed) Arterial Baroreceptors and Hypertension, 1981; Hypertension, 1982; (ed) Scientific Foundations of Cardiology, 1983; (with D. Eckberg) Human arterial baroreflexes in Health and Disease, 1992; contribs on nervous control of the circulation, hypertension, treatment of myocardial infarction and Lipid res. in: Circulation Research; Jl Physiol; Lancet; clinical trials in: Lancet; New England Jl of Medicine; Circulation Research; Heart; Eur. Heart Jl; BMJ; Clinical Sci. *Recreation:* travel. *Address:* Wayside, 32 Crown Road, Wheatley, Oxon OX33 1UL. *Club:* Royal Air Force.

SLEIGHT, Sir Richard, 4th Bt *cr* 1920, of Weelsby Hall, Clee; *b* 27 May 1946; *s* of Sir John Frederick Sleight, 3rd Bt and of Jacqueline Margaret, *o d* of late Maj. H. R. Carter, Brisbane, Queensland; *S* father, 1990; *m* 1978, Marie-Thérèse, *o d* of O. M. Stepan; two *s*. *Heir:* *s* James Alexander Sleight, *b* 5 Jan. 1981. *Address:* c/o National Westminster Bank, 6 High Street, Teddington, Middlesex TW11 8EP.

SLEIMAN, Gen. Michel; President of Lebanon, 2008–14; *b* Amchit-Jbeil, 21 Nov. 1948; *m* Wafaa; one *s* two *d*. *Educ:* Lebanese Univ. (BA Pol and Admin. Scis 1980). Graduated Mil. Acad., 2nd Lieut, 1970; Inf. Platoon Comdr; Co. Comdr; Bn Comdr; Trainer, Mil. Acad. and NCO Sch.; Chief, Mount Lebanon Intelligence Section, 1990–91; Staff Sec., 1991–93; Commander: 11th Inf. Bde, 1993–96; 6th Inf. Bde, 1996–98; C-in-C, Lebanese Army, 1998–2008. Dr *hc:* Moscow State Inst. for Internat. Relns, 2010; Nat. Univ. of Third of February, Buenos Aires, 2012. Holds numerous decorations and medals, including: OM, 1st Grade, 1998, Extraordinary Grade, 2008 (Lebanon); Military Medal (Lebanon), 2003; Medal of Honour (Arab Fedn), 2004; OM, Grade of Excellence (Syria), 2005; Grand Cross, Order of Merit (Italy), 2008; Grand Croix, Légion d'Honneur (France), 2009; Mil. Order (Oman), 2009; Collar: Order of Isabella la Catholique (Spain), 2009; Moubarak the Great (Kuwait), 2009; Order Pro Merito Melitensi (Malta), 2009; Grand Collar: Order of Makarios III (Cyprus), 2010; Nat. Order of Southern Cross (Brazil), 2010; Nat. Order of the Cedar, 2010; Necklace of Independence, Qatar, 2010; Kt Grand Cross, Order of St Charles (Monaco), 2011.

SLESSOR, Catherine Helen; Editor, The Architectural Review, 2010–15; *b* Aberdeen, 15 Nov. 1960; *d* of Donald Munro Slessor and Christina Catherine Slessor (*née* MacDonald). *Educ:* St Margaret's Sch. for Girls, Aberdeen; Univ. of Edinburgh (MA Architecture 1983; DipArch 1984). RIBA Pt 3 1986. Architectl Asst in private practice, 1984–87; Tech. Editor, The Architects' Jl, 1987–91; Asst Editor, 1992–93, Dep. Editor, 1993–2009, The Architectural Review. *Publications:* Eco-Tech, 1997; Concrete Regionalism, 1998. *Recreations:* art, architecture, gardening, opera, cinema, ice skating.

SLEVIN, Maurice Louis, MD; FRCP; Consultant Physician, Medical Oncology Department, St Bartholomew's and Homerton Hospitals, 1982–2008; Hon. Consultant, Barts Health NHS Trust (formerly Barts and the London NHS Trust); Founding Partner and Consultant Medical Oncologist, Leaders in Oncology Care (formerly London Oncology Clinic), since 2005; *b* 2 July 1949; *s* of David Slevin and Nita (*née* Rosenbaum); *m* 1st, 1975, Cherry Jacobsohn (marr. diss. 1987); two *d*; 2nd, 1993, Nicola Jane Harris; one *s* one *d*. *Educ:* Univ. of Cape Town (MB ChB 1973; MD 1984). MRCP 1978, FRCP 1989. Registrar in General Medicine, Groote Schuur Hosp., Cape Town, 1977–78; Registrar in Med. Oncology, St Bartholomew's Hosp., 1978–80, Sen. Registrar, 1980–82. Chm. and Trustee, Cancerbackup (formerly BACUP), 1987–2008; Trustee, Macmillan Cancer Support, 2008–09. *Publications:* Randomised Trials in Cancer, 1986; Metastases, 1988; Challenging Cancer: from chaos to control, 1991; Cancer: the facts, 1996; Cancer: how worthwhile is non-curative treatment?, 1998; numerous pubns on clinical oncology, clinical pharmacology and psychosocial oncology. *Address:* 95 Harley Street, W1G 6AF. *T:* (020) 7317 2525.

SLIGO, 12th Marquess of, *cr* 1800; **Sebastian Ulick Browne;** Baron Mount Eagle 1760; Viscount Westport 1768; Earl of Altamont 1771; Earl of Clanricarde 1543 and 1800; Baron Monteagle (UK) 1806; *b* 27 May 1964; *s* of Captain Lord Ulicke Browne, RA and his 2nd wife, Fiona Browne (*née* Glenn); *S* cousin 2014; *m* 1984, Christina Maria Suaznabar (marr. diss. 1992); one *s* one *d*. *Educ:* Rugby. Residential property consultant. *Heir:* *s* Lord Christopher Ulick Browne, Earl of Altamont, *b* 14 Nov. 1988.

SLIM, family name of **Viscount Slim**.

SLIM, 2nd Viscount *cr* 1960, of Yarralumla and Bishopston; **John Douglas Slim,** OBE 1973; DL; Chairman, 1976–91, and non-executive Deputy Chairman, 1991–98, Peek plc (formerly Peek Holdings); Director, Trailfinders Ltd, 1984–2007, and a number of other companies; *b* 20 July 1927; *s* of Field Marshal the 1st Viscount Slim, KG, GCB, GCMG, GCVO, GBE, DSO, MC, and Aileen (*d* 1993), *d* of Rev. J. A. Robertson, MA, Edinburgh; *S* father, 1970; *m* 1958, Elisabeth, *d* of Arthur Rawdon Spinney, CBE; two *s* one *d*. *Educ:* Prince of Wales Royal Indian Military College, Dehra Dun. Indian Army, 6 Gurkha Rifles, 1945–48; Argyll and Sutherland Highlanders, 1948; SAS, 1952; Staff Coll., Camberley, 1961; Brigade Major, HQ Highland Infantry Bde (TA), 1962–64; JSSC 1964; Lt-Col 1967; Comdr, 22 Special Air Service Regt, 1967–70; GSO1 (Special Forces) HQ UK Land Forces, 1970–72; retired 1972. Elected Mem., H of L, 1999. Vice-Pres., Britain-Australia Soc., 1988– (Chm., 1978–84); Vice-Chm., Arab-British Chamber of Commerce and Industry, 1977–96. President: Burma Star Assoc., 1971–; SAS Assoc., 2000–11 (Patron, 2011–); Trustee, Royal Commonwealth Ex-Services League, 1996–. Patron, Prospect Burma, 1985–. Master, Clothworkers' Co., 1995–96. DL Greater London, 1988. FRGS 1983. *Heir:* *s* Hon. Mark William Rawdon Slim [*b* 13 Feb. 1960; *m* 1992, Harriet Laura, *yr d* of Jonathan Harrison; three *s*]. *Address:* House of Lords, Westminster, SW1A 0PW. *Clubs:* White's, Special Forces.

SLINGER, His Honour Edward; a Circuit Judge, 1995–2010; *b* 2 Feb. 1938; *s* of Thomas Slinger and Rhoda (*née* Bradshaw); *m* 1965, Rosalind Margaret Jewitt; two *s* two *d*. *Educ:* Accrington Grammar Sch.; Balliol Coll., Oxford (Dist. Law Mods 1956; BA 1958). Admitted solicitor (with Hons), 1961; Partner, Ramsbottom & Co., Solicitors, Blackburn, 1964–95; Dep. Registrar, 1982–88; Asst Recorder, 1988–92; Recorder, 1992–95. Pres., Blackburn Incorporated Law Assoc., 1986; Member: Immigration Law Sub-cttee, Law Soc., 1990–95; Immigration Appeal Tribunal, 1997–2005; Chairperson List, Panel of Arbitrators, Sport Resolution Panel, 2007–14; Parole Bd, 2009–. Lancashire County Cricket Club: Captain, 2nd XI, 1967–75; Mem. Cttee, 1969–99; Trustee, 1978–96; Vice-Chm., 1985–98; Vice-Pres., 2000–. Mem., Discipline Cttee, TCCB (now ECB), 1990–; Mem., Jury of Appeal, Horse of the Year Show, 2000–14. Governor: Samlesbury C of E Sch., Lancs, 1986–; Westholme Sch., Blackburn, 1985– (Vice-Chm., 2002–12). *Recreations:* cricket, gardening. *Clubs:* MCC, Lansdowne.

SLINGO, Dame Julia (Mary), DBE 2014 (OBE 2008); FRS 2015; PhD; Chief Scientist, Meteorological Office, since 2009; *b* 13 Dec. 1950; *d* of late Herbert Walker and Lucy Mary Walker (*née* Hirons); *m* 1978, Anthony Slingo (*d* 2008); two *d*. *Educ:* King's High Sch. for Girls, Warwick; Univ. of Bristol (BSc Physics; PhD Atmospheric Physics). Scientist, Meteorol

Office, 1972–80; Consultant, European Centre for Medium Range Weather Forecasts, 1981–85; Scientist, Nat. Center for Atmospheric Res., Boulder, Colo, 1986–90; University of Reading: Sen. Scientist, then Dep. Dir, NERC Centre for Global Atmospheric Modelling, 1990–2002; Dir, NERC Centre for Global Atmospheric Modelling, then Dir of Climate Res., Nat. Centre for Atmospheric Sci., 2002–08; Prof. of Meteorology, 2000–; Founding Dir, Walker Inst. for Climate System Res., 2006–07. Mem., NERC, 2009–. Vice-Pres., 2003–05, 2007–08, Pres., 2008–10, RMetS. Member, Scientific Committees: of Met Office; of Eur. Centre for Medium-Range Weather Forecasts; of Centre for Ocean-Land-Atmosphere Studies; of Internat. Centre for Theoretical Physics; Mem., Jt Sci. Cttee, World Climate Res. Prog., 2006–. Hon. FRSC 2015. Hon. DSc: Bristol, 2010; Reading, 2011; Exeter, 2014; Edinburgh, 2014. *Publications:* over 100 papers in leading jls. *Recreations:* music, walking, gardening. *Address:* Meteorological Office, Fitzroy Road, Exeter EX1 3PB.

SLINN, David Arthur, CMG 2008; OBE 2000; HM Diplomatic Service, retired; Ambassador to Croatia, 2012–15; *b* 16 April 1959; *s* of Ronald Geoffrey Slinn and Christine Mary Slinn; *m* 2012, Heidi Alberta Hulan; one *d. Educ:* Univ. of Salford (BA Hons Mod Langs 1981). Joined FCO, 1981; Third Sec., UK Delegn to Conf. on Disarmament, Geneva, 1983–86; Second Secretary: Ulaanbaatar, 1987–89; Pretoria/Cape Town, 1990–93; FCO, 1993–95; Chargé d'Affaires, Tirana, 1995–96; First Sec. (Commercial), 1996–98, (Political), 1998–99, Belgrade; Head, British Liaison Office, Pristina, Kosovo, 1999–2000; HCSC 2001; seconded to EU/NATO, former Yugoslav Rep. of Macedonia, 2001–02; Ambassador, Democratic People's Republic of Korea, 2002–05; UK Regl Co-ordinator, Southern Afghanistan, 2007–08; Hd of Office Mitrovica, Internat. Civilian Office, Kosovo, 2008–09 (on secondment); Hd, Afghanistan Drugs and Justice Unit, FCO, 2009–11. FRSA 2005. *Recreations:* sport (watching and participating), military history, malt whiskey. *E:* davidslinn@gmail.com.

SLIPMAN, Sue, OBE 1994; Director, Foundation Trust Network, NHS Confederation, 2004–12; *b* 3 Aug. 1949; *d* of Marks Slipman and Doris Barham; one *s. Educ:* Stockwell Manor Comprehensive School; Univ. of Wales (BA Hons 1st Class English; Post Graduate Cert Ed); Univs of Leeds and London. Sec. and Nat. Pres., Nat. Union of Students, 1975–78; Mem., Adv. Council for Adult and Continuing Educn, 1978–79; Area Officer, Nat. Union of Public Employees, 1979–85; Director: Nat. Council for One Parent Families, 1985–95; London TEC Council, 1995–96; Gas Consumers' Council, 1996–98; Dir for Social Responsibility, 1998–2001, for External Relns and Compliance, 2001–02, Camelot Gp plc; Chm., Financial Ombudsman Service Ltd, 2003–05. Mem. Exec., NCCL, 1974–75; Vice-Chair, British Youth Council, 1977–78; Chair: Women for Social Democracy, 1983–86; Advice Guidance and Counselling Lead Body, 1992–; Member: Exec. and Chair of Training, 300 Group, 1985–86; Exec., London Voluntary Service Council, 1986; Women's Issues Wkg Gp, Dept of Employment, 1990–94; Better Regulation Task Force, 1997–2001. Director: London East TEC, 1990; Social Market Foundn, 1992–93. Non-exec. Dir, King's Coll. Hosp. NHS Foundn Trust, 2012–. Trustee, NEST Corporation, 2010–15. *Publications:* chapter in The Re-Birth of Britain, 1983; Helping Ourselves to Power: a handbook for women on the skills of public life, 1986.

SLOAN, Paul Kay; QC 2001; **His Honour Judge Sloan;** a Circuit Judge, since 2011; a Senior Circuit Judge, since 2014; Honorary Recorder of Newcastle; *b* Essex; *s* of late Stanley Buchanan Sloan and of Susan Ann Sloan (*née* Usherwood). *Educ:* City of London Sch.; Queen Mary Coll., Univ. of London (LLB). Called to the Bar, Inner Temple, 1981; Asst Recorder, 1998–2000; Recorder, 2000–11. Chm., Barmark, 2004–07; tutor judge, Judicial Coll., 2007–. *Address:* Newcastle upon Tyne Combined Court Centre, The Quayside, Newcastle Upon Tyne NE1 3LA.

SLOANE, Ian Christopher; HM Diplomatic Service, retired; *b* 28 Jan. 1938; *s* of Albert Henry Sloane and Ivy Rose (*née* Dennis); *m* 1968, June Barton; two *s. Educ:* Lewes Co. Grammar Sch. for Boys; DMS Poly. of Central London 1971. Joined FO, 1956; RAF, 1957–59; FO, 1959–60; MECAS, 1960–61; Vice-Consul: Khartoum, 1961–64; Algiers, 1964–66; Saigon, 1967; 2nd Secretary: Dacca, 1967; Lahore, 1967–70; FCO, 1970–73; UK Disarmament Delegn, Geneva, 1973–74; 1st Sec., Hd of Chancery and Consul, Seoul, 1974–77; 1st Sec. (Econ.), Bonn, 1978–82; W European Dept, FCO, 1983–85; Cultural Attaché, Moscow, 1985; 1st Sec. (Commercial), Ankara, 1986–88; Overseas Estate Dept, FCO, 1989–90; Counsellor and Dep. Consul-Gen., New York, 1990–93; Ambassador to Mongolia, 1994–96. Chm. Bd of Trustees, Electronic Aids for the Blind, 1997–2002; Exec. Dir, Prospect Burma, 1998–2007; Administrator, British-Egyptian Foundn for Children with Special Needs, 2000–08. *Recreations:* tennis, bridge, collecting antique maps, travelling. *Address:* 2/242 Lawrence Road, Mount Waverley, Vic 3149, Australia.

SLOANE, Prof. Peter James, PhD; FRSE; Director, Welsh Economy Labour Market Evaluation and Research Centre, Swansea University (formerly University of Wales, Swansea), 2002–08, now Professor Emeritus; Research Fellow, Institute for the Study of Labour, Bonn, since 2001; *b* 6 Aug. 1942; *s* of John Joseph Sloane and Elizabeth (*née* Clarke); *m* 1969, Avril Mary Urquhart; one *s. Educ:* Cheadle Hulme Sch.; Univ. of Sheffield (BAEcon Hons 1964); Univ. of Strathclyde (PhD 1966). FRSE 1997. Asst Lectr in Pol Econ., Univ. of Aberdeen, 1966–67, Lectr in Pol Econ., 1967–69; Lectr in Indust. Econs, Univ. of Nottingham, 1969–75; Economic Adviser, Unit for Manpower Studies, Dept of Employment (on secondment), 1973–74; Prof. of Econs and Management, Paisley Coll., 1975–84; Jaffrey Prof. of Political Econ., 1984–2002, now Emeritus, Vice Principal and Dean of Social Scis and Law, 1996–2002, Univ. of Aberdeen. Vis. Prof. (Commonwealth Fellow), Faculty of Business, McMaster Univ., Canada, 1978; Vis. Prof., Indiana Univ., 1996; Hon. Professorial Fellow, Univ. of Melbourne, 2007–10; Adjunct Prof., Nat. Inst. of Labour Studies, Flinders Univ., 2010–. Member: ESRC (formerly SSRC), 1979–85 (Mem., Peer Review Coll., 2010–); Mergers Cttee, SHEFC, 1994–97; Council, Scottish Economic Soc., 1983–2001. Sec., REconS Conf. of Heads of Univ. Depts of Econs, 1990–97. Vice-Pres., Internat. Assoc. of Sports Economists, 2000–10. FRSA 1997. *Publications:* (with B. Chiplin) Sex Discrimination in the Labour Market, 1976; (ed) Women and Low Pay, 1980; (with H. C. Jain) Equal Employment Issues, 1981; (with B. Chiplin) Tackling Discrimination, 1982; (with D. Carline *et al*) Labour Economics, 1985; (ed jtly) Low Pay and Earnings Mobility in Europe, 1998; (jtly) Employment Equity and Affirmative Action, 2003; (jtly) The Economics of Sport, 2004; (jtly) Modern Labour Economics, 2013; (ed jtly) Handbook on the Economics of Professional Football, 2014; monographs on changing patterns of working hours, discrimination and on sport in the market; articles in learned jls, incl. Econ. Jl, Economica, Econs Letters, Applied Econs, Bull. Econ. Res., Oxford Bull. of Econ. Stats, Scottish Jl of Pol Econ., British Jl of Indust. Relations, Managerial and Decision Econs, Lab., Lab. Econs, Ind. and Lab. Relns Review, Educn Econs, Nat. Inst. Econ. Review, Jl of Health Econs, Manchester School, Oxford Econs Papers, Regl Studies, Econ. Record, Econs of Educn Rev., Cambridge Jl Econs. *Recreation:* sport. *Address:* 5 Willowbrook Gardens, Mayals, Swansea SA3 5EB. *T:* (01792) 517511. *Club:* Pennard Golf.

SLOBODA, Prof. John Anthony, PhD; FBA 2004; Professor of Psychology, Keele University, 1991–2008 (part-time, 2004–08), now Emeritus; Research Professor, Guildhall School of Music and Drama, since 2009; Co-Director, Every Casualty (formerly Every Casualty Programme, Oxford Research Group), since 2007 (Executive Director (part-time), Oxford Research Group, 2004–10); *b* 6 June 1950; *s* of late Mieczyslaw Herman Sloboda and of Mary Edna Sloboda; *m* 1980, Judith Nussbaum (marr. diss. 1991); one *d. Educ:* St Benedict's Sch., Ealing; Queen's Coll., Oxford (MA 1st cl. (Psychol. and Philos.) 1971); UCL (PhD (Experimental Psychol.) 1974). Lectr, 1974–87, Sen. Lectr, 1987–91, in Psychol., Keele Univ. Mem. Exec. Council, European Soc. for the Cognitive Scis of Music, 1994–2009. Associate Researcher and Co-Founder, Iraq Body Count, 2003–. *Publications:* The Musical Mind: the cognitive psychology of music, 1985; Music and Emotion: theory and research, 2001; Exploring the Musical Mind, 2005; Psychology for Musicians, 2007; Beyond Terror, 2007; Handbook of Music and Emotion, 2010. *Recreation:* choral singing. *Address:* Every Casualty, Development House, 56–64 Leonard Street, EC2Y 4LT. *T:* (020) 7549 0298, *Fax:* (020) 7681 1668. *E:* john.sloboda@everycasualty.org.

SLOCOCK, Caroline Ann, (Mrs C. A. Nightingale); Director, Civil Exchange, since 2011; *b* 30 Dec. 1956; *d* of Horace Slocock and Florence (Joyce) Slocock (*née* Wheelton); *m* 1990, John Nightingale; two *d. Educ:* Talbot Heath Sch., Bournemouth; University Coll. London (BA Hons English Lang. and Lit. 1978). Joined Dept of Employment, 1982; Private Sec. to Sec. of State for Employment, 1985–87; Mem., Next Steps Project Team, Cabinet Office, 1988–89; Private Sec. (Home Affairs) to Prime Minister, 1989–91; HM Treasury: Head: Spending Team Br. on Employment, 1991–92; Treasury Personnel, 1993–96; Sen. Policy Advr on Expenditure, 1997–2000; Jt Hd, Early Years and Childcare Unit, DfES, 2000–02; Chief Executive: Equal Opportunities Commn, 2002–07; Refugee and Migrant Justice (formerly Refugee Legal Centre), 2007–10. *Recreations:* gardening, photography, reading, swimming, walking, tweeting. *E:* carolineslocock@civilexchange.org.uk.

SLOCOMBE, Gillian Mary, CBE 2015; Chief Guide, Girlguiding UK, since 2011; *b* Exmouth, 25 Dec. 1955; *d* of Frederick and Beryl Bolt; *m* 1977, Nicholas Slocombe; two *s. Educ:* Bishop Blackall Grammar Sch., Exeter; Exeter Coll., Exeter (Inst. of Legal Execs 1976). Legal exec., 1975–84; youth justice worker (pt-time), 2000–10; Manager, The Buddy (formerly Teenage Parents' Buddy) Project, Som, 2010–. Chair, Nat. Appropriate Adult Network, 2010–11. Parish Councillor, North Curry, 2002–08. *Recreations:* sport, gym, swimming, travelling, theatre, walking, family guiding. *Address:* Girlguiding UK, 17–19 Buckingham Palace Road, SW1W 0PT. *T:* (020) 7834 6242, *Fax:* (020) 7828 8317. *E:* Gill.Slocombe@girlguiding.org.uk. *Club:* Camping and Caravanning (Hon. Vice-Pres., 2011–).

SLOGGETT, Jolyon Edward, OBE 1995; CEng, Hon. FIMarEST, FRINA, FICS; Secretary, Institute of Marine Engineers, 1986–98; *b* 30 May 1933; *s* of Edward Cornelius Sloggett and Lena May (*née* Norton); *m* 1970, Patricia Marjorie Iverson Ward; two *d. Educ:* John Lyon Sch.; Univ. of Glasgow (BSc). CDipAF. William Denny & Brothers Ltd, Leven Shipyard, Dumbarton, 1951–57 and 1959–60. Served, Royal Navy, TA Sub Lieut (E), RNVR, 1957–58; Houlder Brothers & Co. Ltd, 1960–78, Director, 1972–78; Man. Dir, Offshore, British Shipbuilders Corp., 1978–81; Dir, Vickers Shipbuilding Group, 1979–80; Chm., Vickers Offshore (Projects & Development) Ltd, 1979–81; Consultant to Marine and Offshore Industries, 1981–86. *Publications:* Shipping Finance, 1984, 2nd edn 1998. *Recreations:* sailing, gardening, woodwork. *Address:* Corstone Farm, Broadwoodkelly, Winkleigh, Devon EX19 8EF. *T:* (01837) 851441. *E:* jsloggett5@gmail.com.

SLOMAN, Anne, OBE 2004; Chair, Church Buildings Council, 2009–14; Member, Archbishops' Council, 2003–09; *b* 24 April 1944; *d* of John Bibby and Kay Bibby (*née* Harvey); *m* 1st, 1966, Andrew Duncan-Jones (marr. diss. 1971); 2nd, 1972, Martyn George Morgan Sloman; two *s. Educ:* Farlington; St Hilda's Coll., Oxford (BA (Hons) PPE 1966). BBC journalist, programme maker and policy adviser, 1967–2003: Ed., Gen. Election Results Progs, 1974–92; Dep. Ed., Today Prog., 1981–82; Ed., Special Current Affairs (Radio), 1983–93; Dep. Hd, Weekly Progs (TV and Radio), 1993–96; Chief Political Advr, 1996–2003. Mem. Council, RIIA, 1992–2002. Guest Lectr, Berkeley, Southern Illinois and S Dakota Univs; Faculty, Salzburg Seminar, 2004. Vice Patron, Norfolk Community Foundn, 2011– (Trustee, 2005–10; Vice-Chm., 2006–10). Press Guild Award for Outstanding Prog., 1986 (The Thatcher Phenomenon), 1988 (My Country Right or Wrong). *Publications:* (with David Butler) British Political Facts, 2nd edn (1900–1968), 1968 to 5th edn (1900–1980), 1980; (with Hugo Young): No Minister, 1982; But Chancellor, 1984; The Thatcher Phenomenon, 1986; (with Simon Jenkins) With Respect Ambassador, 1985. *Recreations:* my garden, travel, looking at pictures, theatre, ballet. *Address:* All Saints Cottage, Bale Road, Sharrington, Norfolk NR24 2PF. *Club:* Fakenham Cricket.

SLOMAN, Prof. Morris Samuel, PhD; FREng, FIEEE, FIET, FBCS; Professor of Distributed Systems Management, Imperial College London, since 1996; *b* Kwe Kwe, Southern Rhodesia, 5 Dec. 1947; *s* of Reuben Sloman and Hannah Sloman (*née* Rest); *m* 1975, Ruth Cass; two *d. Educ:* Univ. of Cape Town (BSc 1st Cl. Electrical Engrg 1970); Univ. of Essex (PhD 1974). CEng 1990; FBCS 2003; FIET 2004; FREng 2006; FIEEE 2011. Systems programmer, GEC Computers Ltd, 1974–75; Department of Computing, Imperial College London: Lectr, 1976–88; Sen. Lectr, 1988–92; Reader, 1992–96; Dep. Hd, 2004–14; Dean, 2010–13. Co-Ed., IEE/IOP/BCS Distributed Systems Engrg, 1993–99; Ed.-in-Chief, 2011–13, Adv. Bd, 2014–, IEEE Trans on Network and Service Mgt; Member: Adv. Bd, Jl Network and Systems Mgt, 1994–; Editl Adv. Bd, Internat. Jl Network Mgt, 2009–. Mem., Defence Security Adv. Cttee, Information Security Bd, MoD, 2006–08. Mem., Computing Panel, RAE 2001, 1998–2001; Deputy Chairman: Computing Panel, RAE 2008, 2005–08; Computing Sci. and Informatics Sub-panel, REF 2014, 2011–14. Member: Information and Communication Technologies Strategic Adv. Team, EPSRC, 2002–04; Exec. Cttee, UK Cttee for Res. on Computing, 2005–14. Member: Assessment Panel for Ireland Univs ICT Res., Forfás Ireland, 2002; Internat. Adv. Council, INESC ID-Lisboa, Portugal Res. Inst., 2005–. Dan Stokesberry Meml Award for dist. contribn to growth in field of network mgt, IEEE/IFIP. *Publications:* (with J. Kramer) Distributed Systems and Computer Networks, 1987; (ed) Network and Distributed Systems Management, 1994; contrib. jl and conf. papers on distributed computing systems, network security and mgt and policy based mgt. *Recreations:* theatre, classical music, going to the gym. *Address:* Department of Computing, Imperial College London, 180 Queen's Gate, SW7 2RH. *T:* (020) 7594 8279, *Fax:* (020) 7594 8282. *E:* m.sloman@imperial.ac.uk.

SLOSS; *see* Butler-Sloss.

SLOT, His Honour Peter Maurice Joseph; a Circuit Judge, 1980–97; *b* 3 Dec. 1932; *s* of Joseph and Marie Slot; *m* 1962, Mary Eiluned Lewis; two *s* three *d. Educ:* Bradfield Coll.; St John's Coll., Oxford (MA). Called to Bar, Inner Temple, 1957. A Recorder of the Crown Court, 1974–80. *Recreations:* golf, creating harmony. *Address:* The Red House, Betchworth, Surrey RH3 7DR. *T:* (01737) 842010. *Club:* Walton Heath Golf.

SLUMBERS, Martin Richard; Secretary, Royal and Ancient Golf Club of St Andrews, since 2015; *b* Brighton, 19 March 1960; *s* of George Denzil and Maureen Slumbers; *m* 1985, Jill Elizabeth Norman; two *s. Educ:* Lancing Coll.; Birmingham Univ. (BSc). ACA 1981. Chartered Accountant, Price Waterhouse, 1982–86; Salomon Brothers: financial mgt and control roles, 1986–94; Chief Financial Officer, Asia, 1994–97, Europe, 1997–98; Deutsche Bank: Global Business Area Controller, Sales and Trading, 1998–2001; Dep. Chief Operating Officer, Corporate and Investment Bank, 2001–03; Global Head and Chief Operating Officer, Orgn, 2004–13; CEO, Deutsche Bank Operation Internat. Global Services, 2005–13; Global Head, Investment Banking Ops, 2006–13, Global Business Services, 2007–13. *Address:* Royal and Ancient Golf Club, St Andrews, Fife KY16 9JD. *T:* (01334) 400000, *Fax:* (01334) 460001. *E:* TheSecretary@RandAgc.org. *Club:* Worplesdon Golf.

SMALL, Gareth, FRAM; Principal Trumpet, Hallé Orchestra, since 2008; *b* Swansea, 14 Nov. 1970; *s* of Tony and Gillian Small; *m* 2005, Katherine Brown; two *s. Educ:* Gowerton Comprehensive Sch., Swansea; Royal Acad. of Music (GRSM Hons 1992). LTCL 1988;

LRAM 1993, ARAM 1997, FRAM 2014. Co-Principal Trumpet: Hallé Orch., 1993–2008; London Brass, 2002–. *Recreations:* golf, Welsh Rugby, wine, family. *Address:* 80 Grove Park, Knutsford, Cheshire WA16 8QB. *T:* 07973 197148. *E:* garethsmall@yahoo.co.uk.

SMALL, Prof. John Rankin, CBE 1991; Professor of Accountancy and Finance, Heriot-Watt University, 1967–98, now Emeritus; *b* 28 Feb. 1933; *s* of David and Annie Small; *m* 1957, Catherine Wood; one *s* two *d. Educ:* Harris Academy, Dundee; Dundee Sch. of Econs. BScEcon London; FCCA, FCMA, JDipMA. Dunlop Rubber Co., 1956–60; Lectr, Univ. of Edinburgh, 1960–64; Sen. Lectr, Univ. of Glasgow, 1964–67; Heriot-Watt University: Head, Dept of Accountancy and Finance, 1967–90; Dean of Faculty of Econ. and Social Studies, 1972–74; Vice-Principal, 1974–78, 1987–90; Dep. Principal, 1990–94. Director: Edinburgh Instruments Ltd, 1976–2003; Orkney Water Test Centre, Ltd, 1987–96; Environment and Resource Technology Ltd, 1991–99; Petroleum Science and Technology Ltd, 1992–97; Computer Application Services, 1997–2007; Mem. Bd, Scottish Homes, 1993–2002. Chm., Nat. Appeal Panel for Entry to Pharmaceutical Lists (Scotland), 1987–95. Trustee, Nat. Library of Scotland, 1991–99. Pres., Assoc. of Certified Accountants, 1982 (Mem. Council, 1971–99); Member: Educn Cttee, Internat. Fedn of Accountants, 1978–85 (Chm., 1978–82); Commn for Local Authority Accounts in Scotland, 1982–92 (Chm., 1983–92); Chm., Inst. of Offshore Engrg, 1988–90. Hon. DLitt Heriot-Watt, 1996. *Publications:* (jtly) Introduction to Managerial Economics, 1966; (contrib.) Business and Accounting in Europe, 1973; (jtly) Accounting, 1991; articles in accounting and financial jls on accounting and financial management. *Recreation:* golf. *Address:* 39 Caiystane Terrace, Edinburgh EH10 6ST. *T:* (0131) 445 2638. *Club:* New (Edinburgh).

SMALL, Jonathan Edwin; QC 2006; *b* 6 Aug. 1967; *s* of late Lensworth Small, E Grinstead, formerly Kingston, Jamaica, and of Marion Small (*née* Hickson). *Educ:* Greenfields Sch., E Sussex; Nottingham Univ. (BA Hist.); City Univ. (Dip. Law). Called to the Bar, Lincoln's Inn, 1990; joined Falcon Chambers, 1992; in practice, specialising in law of real property. Mem., Bar Council, 1994–97 and 2005–08. *Recreations:* polo, hunting, music. *Address:* Falcon Chambers, Falcon Court, Fleet Street, EC4Y 1AA. *T:* (020) 7353 2484.

SMALL, Peter John, CB 1999; Permanent Secretary, Department of Agriculture and Rural Development, Northern Ireland, 1996–2003; *b* 21 July 1946; *s* of John and Kathleen Small; *m* 1971, Pamela Hanna; two *s. Educ:* Univ. of London (LLB ext.). Northern Ireland Civil Service: Dept of Finance and Personnel, 1966–94: Treasury Officer of Accounts, 1986–88; Dir of Personnel, 1988–94; Finance Dir, Dept of Health and Social Services, 1994–96. *Recreations:* golf, gardening, reading, music, soccer.

SMALLBONE, Graham, MBE 2011; Headmaster, Oakham School, 1985–96; *b* 5 April 1934; *s* of Dr E. G. Smallbone and Jane Mann; *m* 1959, Dorothea Ruth Löw; two *s* two *d. Educ:* Uppingham School (music scholar); Worcester College, Oxford (Hadow Scholar; MA; Pres., Oxford Univ. Music Club, 1957). ARCO, ARCM. 2nd Lieut, RA, 1952–54. Asst Master, Oundle Sch., 1958–61; Director of Music: Dean Close Sch., 1961–66; Marlborough Coll., 1967–71; Precentor and Director of Music, Eton, 1971–85. Pres., Music Masters' Assoc., 1975; Warden, Music in Educn Section, ISM, 1977; Pres., International Cello Centre, 1985–2000. Conductor: Cheltenham Chamber Orch., 1963–66; N Wilts Orch., 1966–71; Windsor and Eton Choral Soc., 1971–85. Chm., Peterborough Cathedral Fabric Adv. Cttee, 1990–. Chm. of Govs, Purcell Sch., 1998–2010; Governor: Yehudi Menuhin Sch., 1989–2011; NYO, 1992–2012. FRSA. *Recreations:* music, golf, photography, reading. *Address:* The Old Manse, 56 High Street, Chinnor, Oxon OX39 4DH. *T:* (01844) 354572.

SMALLDON, Ven. Keith; Archdeacon of St Davids, 2011–13; *b* Newport, Monmouthshire, 14 Aug. 1948; *s* of Herbert and Edith Smalldon; *m* 1969, (Patricia) Anne McDonough; one *s* one *d. Educ:* Hartridge High Sch.; St John's Coll., Ystrad Meurig; St Michael and All Angels Theol Coll., Llandaff (DipTh Univ. of Wales 1971); Open Univ. (BA 1976); Univ. of Newcastle upon Tyne (MA Applied Theol. 1994). Midland Bank Ltd, 1966–67; ordained deacon, 1971, priest, 1972; Curate: Cwmbran, 1971–73; Chepstow, 1973–75; Youth Advr, Dio. of Bradford, 1975–79; Sen. Youth and Community Officer (Trng), Bradford Metropolitan Council, 1979–82; Youth and Community Officer, Dio. of Manchester, 1982–90; Advr for Clergy Trng, Dio. of Carlisle, 1990–94; Team Rector, Daventry, 1994–98; Rector, Llantwit Major, 1998–2003; Dir of Ministry and Res. Canon, Dio. of Swansea and Brecon, 2003–11. Chaplain: Danetre Hosp., 1994–98; Daventry, 1995–98, Llantwit Major, 1998–2003, Milford Haven, 2011–13, RBL. *Recreations:* photography, railways, film soundtracks, reading, Belgian ale, watching sport esp. speedway, soccer and Rugby League. *Address:* 41 Horsham Close, Banbury OX16 1XP. *T:* (01295) 269281. *E:* keithsmalldon@btinternet.com.

SMALLEY, Very Rev. Stephen Stewart; Dean of Chester, 1987–2001; *b* 11 May 1931; *s* of Arthur Thomas Smalley and May Elizabeth Selina Smalley; *m* 1974, Susan Jane Paterson (*d* 1995); one *s* one *d. Educ:* Jesus Coll., Cambridge (MA, PhD); Eden Theological Seminary, USA (BD). Assistant Curate, St Paul's, Portman Square, London, 1958–60; Chaplain of Peterhouse, Cambridge, 1960–63; Lectr and Sen. Lectr in Religious Studies, Univ. of Ibadan, Nigeria, 1963–69; Lectr in New Testament, Univ. of Manchester, 1970–77, Sen. Lectr, 1977 (also Warden of St Anselm Hall, 1972–77); Canon Residentiary and Precentor of Coventry Cathedral, 1977–86, Vice-Provost, 1986. Vis. Prof., Univ. of Chester (formerly Chester Coll., then UC, Chester), 2001–. Mem., C of E Doctrine Commn, 1981–86. Mem., Studiorum Novi Testamenti Soc., 1965–. Manson Meml Lectr, Univ. of Manchester, 1986. Hon. LLD Liverpool, 2001. *Publications:* Building for Worship, 1967; Heaven and Hell (Ibadan), 1968; The Spirit's Power (Achimota), 1972; ed, Christ and Spirit in the New Testament, 1973; John: Evangelist and Interpreter, 1978, USA 1984, 2nd edn 1998; 1, 2, 3 John, 1984, 2nd edn 2007; Thunder and Love, 1994; The Revelation to John, 2005; Hope for Ever, 2005; numerous articles in learned jls, incl. New Testament Studies, Novum Testamentum, Jl of Biblical Lit. *Recreations:* literature, music, drama, travel. *Address:* The Old Hall, The Folly, Longborough, Glos GL56 0QS. *T:* (01451) 830238. *Clubs:* City, Business (Chester), Pitt (Cheshire).

SMALLMAN, Barry Granger, CMG 1976; CVO 1972; HM Diplomatic Service, retired; Founder, Granger Consultancies, 1984; *b* 22 Feb. 1924; *s* of late C. Stanley Smallman, CBE, ARCM, and Ruby Marian Granger; *m* 1952, Sheila Knight (*d* 2009); two *s* one *d. Educ:* St Paul's School; Trinity College, Cambridge (Major Scholar, MA). Served War of 1939–45, Intelligence Corps, Australia 1944–46. Joined Colonial Office, 1947; Assistant Private Secretary to Secretary of State, 1951–52; Principal, 1953; attached to United Kingdom Delegation to United Nations, New York, 1956–57, 1958, 1961, 1962; seconded to Government of Western Nigeria, Senior Assistant Secretary, Governor's Office, Ibadan, 1959–60; transferred to CRO, 1961; British Deputy High Comr in Sierra Leone, 1963–64; British Dep. High Comr in NZ, 1964–67; Imp. Defence Coll., 1968; FCO, 1969–71; Counsellor and Consul-Gen., British Embassy, Bangkok, 1971–74; British High Comr to Bangladesh, 1975–78; Resident Diplomatic Service Chm., Civil Service Selection Bd, 1978–81; High Comr to Jamaica and non-resident Ambassador to Haiti, 1982–84. Mem. Governing Council: SPCK, 1984–99 (Vice Chm., 1993–99); Leprosy Mission, 1985–97; St Lawrence Coll., Ramsgate, 1984–97 (Vice-Pres., 1997–2005); Benenden Sch., 1985–92 (Chm., 1986–92). Reader, C of E, 1996–. *Recreations:* reading, crosswords, making and listening to music, light verse, bird watching. *Address:* Beacon Lodge, Benenden, Kent TN17 4BU. *T:* (01580) 240625.

SMALLMAN, David Leslie, LVO 1990; HM Diplomatic Service, retired; Historical Records Adviser, Foreign and Commonwealth Office, 2000–05; *b* 29 April 1940; *s* of late Leslie Alfred Smallman and Millicent Jean (*née* Burton); *m* 1st, 1967 (marr. diss.); one *s*; 2nd, 1979, Sandra Jill (*née* Browne); one step *s* one step *d. Educ:* St Clement Danes; Kingston upon Hull Univ.; London Business Sch. RAFVR/RAF, 1958–60. Nat. Assistance Bd, 1961–66; Colonial, later Foreign and Commonwealth, Office, 1966–67; served Rawalpindi, Islamabad, Nicosia, 1967–72; attached DTI, 1973; Singapore, 1973–77; FCO, 1977; Consul, Aden, 1981–83; Head of Chancery, Rangoon, 1983–87; Head of Royal Matters, FCO, 1987–90; Dep. High Comr, Port of Spain, 1990–94; Gov. and C-in-C, St Helena and Dependencies, 1995–99 (first Gov. to visit Nightingale Is, Inaccessible Is and Gough Is.). Pres., 1995–98, Patron, 1998–99, St Helena Cricket Assoc. (played for Governor's XI, 1996–98); Founder, Governor's Cup internat. yacht race. Promoter, internat. sporting links, Louis Glanville Associates, 1999–. Trustee, Charles Wallace Burma Trust, 2005–10 (Chm., 2006–10). Mem., Towcester PROBUS, 2006–. MIEx; MCIM. *Publications:* (as Louis Glanville) The BEAM (short stories), 1976; Quincentenary, 2003; One of The Queen's Men, 2012; articles, incl. on travel (some as Louis Glanville). *Recreations:* novels, history and security, walking, attending match days at Lord's Cricket Ground. *Address:* The Old School, Blakesley, Northamptonshire NN12 8RS. *Clubs:* MCC (Life Mem.); Royal Cornwall Yacht; Queen's Park Cricket (Trinidad); St Helena Yacht (Hon. Life Mem.).

SMALLMAN, Ven. Wilhelmina T.; Archdeacon of Southend, since 2013; *b* Edgware, 29 Oct. 1956; *d* of Hector Abiodan Agbe and Catherine Watson Inglis Agbe; *m* 1992, Christopher Duncan Smallman; three *d. Educ:* Central Sch. of Speech and Drama (BEd Hons Drama, English and Voice 1988); Middlesex Univ. (BA Hons Contextual Theol. 2006); N Thames Ministerial Trng Course. Asst Principal, John Kelly Girls Tech. Coll., 2005; ordained deacon, 2006, priest, 2008; Assistant Curate: St Paul's, Harrow, 2006–07; St John the Evangelist, Stanmore, 2007–10; Team Vicar, St Margaret's, Barking, 2010–13. Chair of Govs, George Carey Sch., Barking, 2011. *Recreations:* theatre, travel, National Trust, family, film, singing. *Address:* The Archdeacon's Lodge, 459 Rayleigh Road, Benfleet, Essex SS7 3TH. *E:* msmallman@chelmsford.anglican.org.

SMALLRIDGE, Peter William, CBE 1995; Chair, Avante Care and Support (formerly Partnership), since 2012; *b* 8 Aug. 1943; *s* of William Smallridge and Eileen (*née* Wilson); *m* 1965, Margaret Collis; two *s* one *d. Educ:* Sutton High Sch.; Chichester High Sch.; North-Western Polytechnic (CSW 1965); LSE (Dip. Mental Health 1970). Sen. Mental Health Social Worker, W Sussex CC, 1965–71; Area Officer, W Sussex Social Services, 1971–73; Sen. Lectr, Croydon Coll., 1973–75; Divl Manager, Social Services, Norfolk CC, 1975–82; Dep. Dir, 1982–83, Dir, 1983–91, Social Services, Warwicks CC; Dir of Social Services, Kent CC, 1991–98; Chairman: W Kent HA, 1998–2002; Ashford PCT, 2002–06; Kent and Medway NHS and Socialcare Partnership Trust, 2006–11. Dir, Initiatives in Care Ltd, 2002–12. Pres., Assoc. of Dirs of Social Services, 1992–93. Nat. Trustee, BRCS, 1997–2004; Trustee, Smith's Charity, 1999–2014. *Recreations:* reading, walking, golf, travel. *Address:* Maltmans Hill Barn, Maltmans Hill, Smarden, Kent TN27 8RD.

SMALLWOOD, Christopher Rafton; Chairman, St George's University Hospitals NHS Foundation Trust (formerly Healthcare NHS Trust), since 2011; *b* 13 Aug. 1947; *s* of James Rafton Smallwood and Josephine Smallwood (*née* Mortimer); *m* 1979, Ingeborg Hedwig Eva Wiesler; one *s* one *d. Educ:* Lancaster Royal Grammar Sch.; Exeter Coll., Oxford (MA 1st Cl. Hons PPE); Nuffield Coll., Oxford (MPhil Econs). Lecturer in Economics: Exeter Coll., Oxford, 1971–72; Edinburgh Univ., 1972–76; Special Advr, Constitution Unit, Cabinet Office, 1974–75; Econ. Advr, HM Treasury, 1976–81; Dir of Policy, SDP, 1981–83; Chief Economist, British Petroleum plc, 1983–86; Econs Ed., Sunday Times, 1986–89; Strategic Develt Dir, TSB Gp and Dir, TSB Bank, 1989–94; Partner: Makinson Cowell Ltd, 1994–98; Brunswick Gp Ltd, 1998–2001; Chief Economic Advr, Barclays plc, 2002–05. Member: Competition Commn, 2001–09; Sec. of State's Econ. Adv. Panel, BIS, 2013–. Chairman: Hounslow PCT, 2007–09; Kingston Hosp. NHS Trust, 2009–11. Dir, Lombard Street Associates, 2005–. *Recreations:* golf, opera, theatre. *Address:* St George's University Hospitals NHS Foundation Trust, St George's Hospital, Blackshaw Road, SW17 0QT. *Club:* Reform.

See also J. D. M. Smallwood.

SMALLWOOD, (James) Douglas (Mortimer); Chair, Princess Alexandra Hospital NHS Trust, since 2013; *b* 10 June 1955; *s* of James Rafton Smallwood and Josephine Smallwood (*née* Mortimer); *m* 1983, Sally Rayner; one *s* one *d. Educ:* Lancaster Royal Grammar Sch.; Exeter Coll., Oxford (MA). FCIH. CEO, Worcestershire Housing Assoc., 1983–87; Dir, Halifax Building Soc., 1987–2001; Man. Dir, HBOS plc, 2001–04; Chief Exec., Diabetes UK, 2004–10. Non-exec. Co-Chair, Long Term Conditions Prog. Bd, 2008–10, Consultant, 2010–13, E of England Strategic HA, later NHS Midlands and East; Mem., NHS Equality and Diversity Council, 2009–12. Non-exec. Dir, E and N Herts NHS Trust, 2011–13. Mem. Bd (non-exec.), Centrepoint, 2002–08. Chm., Headway Herts, 2013–. Trustee, Herts and Middx Wildlife Trust, 2011–13. *Recreations:* running, gardening, birdwatching. *Club:* Reform.

See also C. R. Smallwood.

SMALLWOOD, Stuart David, PhD; Headmaster, Bishop Wordsworth's School, Salisbury, since 2002 (Deputy Headmaster, 1998–2002); *b* 21 Feb. 1962; *s* of James Smallwood and Pamela Smallwood; *m* 1988, Charlotte Burlend; two *s* one *d. Educ:* Leeds Univ. (BSc Earth Scis 1982); Darwin Coll., Cambridge (PhD Geol 1986); Bristol Univ. (PGCE Geog 1989); NPQH 2002. Head of Geography, then of Humanities, Sir Thomas Rich's Sch., Gloucester, 1989–98. *Recreations:* ornithology, middle distance running. *Address:* Bishop Wordsworth's School, 11 The Close, Salisbury SP1 2ED. *T:* (01722) 333851, *Fax:* (01722) 325899. *E:* sds@bws.wilts.sch.uk.

SMALLWOOD, Trevor, OBE 1995; DL; Chairman: Advanced Transport Systems, 2000–12; LDJ Design & Display Ltd, 2003–09; UKRD Group, since 2006 (Director, 2001–06); Stage Electrics, since 2012; *b* 4 Nov. 1947; *s* of late Eric Smallwood and of Vera Smallwood; *m* 1986, Caroline Mary Ball; two *s* two *d. Educ:* Mexborough Grammar Sch. MILT. Mgt Trainee, Yorkshire Traction, 1966; National Bus Co., 1970–80; Traffic Manager, Potteries Motor Traction, 1980–82; Man. Dir, Bristol Country Bus, 1983; purchased Badgerline from Dept of Transport, 1986; developed and floated Badgerline, 1993; merged with GRT to become FirstBus, 1995, renamed FirstGroup, 1997, Exec. Chm., 1995–99; Chm., WestCom Media Ltd, 1999–2001. Director: Bristol Water plc, 1999–2008; Brandon Hire plc, 2004–06; Chairman: Catalist Ltd, 2002–06; Coull Ltd, 2005–06. Chm., Quartet Community Foundn (formerly Gtr Bristol Foundn), 2000–06. Pres., Confedn of Public Transport, 1994. Pres., St Monica Trust, 2009–. Chm., Colston's Girls' School Trust, Bristol, 2001–. DL Somerset, 2003. Master, Soc. of Merchant Venturers, 2009. *Recreations:* football, cricket, running.

SMART; *see* de Bernière-Smart.

SMART, David Eynon; Managing Director, and Head, Investment Solutions Europe, Middle East and Africa Region, Franklin Templeton Solutions, since 2014; *b* Hampton Court, 4 July 1961; *s* of Donald Smart and Malvyn Smart; *m* 1989, Rona Shiach; two *s* two *d. Educ:* St Paul's Sch.; St John's Coll., Cambridge (BA Classics 1982). Fund Manager, Barings, 1982–85; Asst Dir, County Natwest Investment Mgt Ltd, 1985–88; Sen. Vice Pres., 1988–90, Man. Dir, 1990–2002, Fiduciary Trust Internat. Ltd; Co-CEO, Franklin Templeton Investment Mgt Ltd, 2006–12. National Trust: Chm., Investment Cttee, 2008–; Mem. Council, 2012–; Trustee, 2015–. *Publications:* contrib. article in Central Banking Qly Jl. *Recreations:* tennis, croquet, antiquarian books, piano, wine. *E:* d.smart421@btinternet.com. *Clubs:* Brooks's, Royal Automobile, MCC, Pilgrims.

SMART, Ian Stewart; Sole Principal, Ian S. Smart & Co., since 1991; President, Law Society of Scotland, 2009–10; *b* Paisley. *Educ:* Univ. of Glasgow (LLB). Admitted Solicitor, 1980; with Pattison & Sim; Partner, Ross, Harper & Murray, 1988–91. Law Society of Scotland: Mem. Council, 1997–2008; Dep. Pres., 2007–09. *Address:* Ian S. Smart & Co., 3 Annan House, Town Centre, Cumbernauld G67 1DP.

SMART, John Dalziel Beveridge, CVO 2008; Lord-Lieutenant of Kincardineshire, 1999–2007; *b* Edinburgh, 12 Aug. 1932; *s* of George Beveridge Smart and Christina Mary Ann Smart (*née* MacDonald); *m* 1960, Valerie Bigelow Blaber (*d* 2014); two *s*. *Educ:* Harrow; Admin. Staff Coll. Nat. Service, 2nd Lieut, Black Watch, RHR, Korea, 1952; PA to COS, 1953. With J. & J. Smart (Brechin) Ltd, 1953–64 (Dir, 1954–64); Dir, Don Brothers Buist & Co., 1964–87 (Man. Dir, 1985–87), retd. Chm., British Polyolefin Textile Assoc., 1986–97. Chm., Scottish-American Community Relns Cttee, 1990–93. Mem., Queen's Bodyguard for Scotland (Royal Co. of Archers), 1974–. Mem., St Andrews Mgt Inst., 1989. DL Kincardineshire, 1993–99. Dean, Guildry of Brechin, 1991–93. *Recreation:* looking for the things that I have lost. *Address:* Kincardine, 9a The Glebe, Edzell, Brechin DD9 7SZ. *T:* (01356) 648416. *E:* smart@kincardine9.plus.com.

SMART, Kenneth Peter Ross, CBE 1996; Chief Inspector of Air Accidents, Department for Transport (formerly Department of Transport, then Department of Transport, Local Government and the Regions), 1990–2005; *b* 28 April 1946; *s* of Peter Smart and Evelyn Smart (*née* Ross); *m* 1st, 1969, Kathleen Rouse (marr. diss.); one *s* one *d*; 2nd, 1993, Christine Palmer. *Educ:* Coll. of Electronics, Malvern (FTC); Worcester Tech. Coll. (HNC Aero Engrg); Open Univ. (BA). Aircraft Engrg apprentice, Min. of Aviation, 1962–67; Technical Officer, RRE, 1967–75; Inspector of Accidents, Dept of Trade, 1975–82; Principal Inspector of Accidents, 1982–86, Dep. Chief Inspector of Accidents, 1986–90, Dept of Transport. Non-exec. Dir, British Airways, 2005–. Mem. Council, The Air League. Trustee, Vulcan to the Sky Trust. *Recreations:* mountaineering, tennis, sailing, classic motorcycle restoration, walking, golf, Southampton FC. *Address:* 4 Clandon Drive, Boyatt Wood, Eastleigh, Hants SO50 4QQ.

SMART, Air Vice-Marshal Michael David; DL; Director, Meer Consultants Ltd, 2000–10; *b* 18 March 1942; *s* of Gerald Sidney Smart and Keziah Smart (*née* Edwards); *m* 1964, Sheelagh Ann Gent; one *d* (and one *d* decd). *Educ:* Trinity Sch. of John Whitgift, Croydon; BA Open Univ. Joined RAF Secretarial Branch, 1960; Air Sec.'s Branch, 1973–76 and 1983–85; ndc 1979; Comd, Admin Wing, RAF Coltishall, 1982–83; CO RAF Hereford, 1985–88; Sen. Personnel Staff Officer, HQ Strike Command, 1988–89; RCDS, 1990; Dir, Ground Training, 1991–92; Air Cdre, Training Support, 1993; Dir of Personnel, 1994–95; C of S to Air Mem. for Personnel, 1995–98. Dir, Govt Services, Arthur Andersen Business Consulting, 1998–2000. Chm., Herefordshire, SSAFA, 2003–; Vice Chm. (Air), Council of Reserve Forces, 2004–; Council Mem., Forces Pension Soc., 1998–2010; Chm., Forces Pension Soc. Charitable Fund, 2010–. Mem., Herefordshire Armed Forces Community Covenant Gp, 2012–. Trustee, Regular Forces Employment Assoc., 1999–2009. Hon. Pres., W Mercian Wing, ATC, 2011–. DL Herefordshire, 2006. *Recreations:* track and field athletics and cross country, travelling, cooking, gardening. *Address:* c/o Drummonds Bank, 49 Charing Cross, SW1A 2DX. *Club:* Royal Air Force.

SMART, Peter Geoffrey; Headmaster, Wallington County Grammar School, 2010–13; *b* Streatham, London, 29 Jan. 1953; *s* of Geoffrey Reginald Ernest Smart and Doreen Ivy Smart (*née* Kipling); *m* 1st, 1984 (marr. diss. 2010); two *d*; 2nd, 2011, Chiquita Louise Hunt. *Educ:* Spencer Park Sch., Wandsworth; Chelsea Coll., Univ. of London (BSc Hons Maths 1975; PGCE Maths Educn 1976). NPQH 2003; Chartered London Teacher, 2007. Wallington County Grammar School: Teacher of Maths, 1976–2013; Hd of Maths, 1988–99; Asst Hd, 1993–2005; Dep. Hd, 2005–09; Actg Hd, 2009–10. Member: RHS; Nat. Trust; Hardy Plant Soc. *Recreations:* cricket, tennis, opera, classical music, gardening, walking, nature. *E:* peter135smart@googlemail.com.

SMART, Rosamund H.; *see* Horwood-Smart.

SMART, Timothy Spencer; HM Diplomatic Service; Ambassador to the Republic of Madagascar, since 2012; *b* Wimbledon, 17 Sept. 1974; *s* of Simon and Elizabeth Smart. *Educ:* Taunton Sch., Som; Bristol Univ. (BA Hons Ancient Hist.); Peterhouse, Cambridge (MPhil Classics 1995). Business analyst, JP Morgan, 1997–98; entered FCO, 1999; OSCE Dept, FCO, 1999–2000; Second Sec., Tel Aviv, 2001–04; Hd of Chancery, Basra, 2004–05; Hd, EU, Middle E and N Africa Team, FCO, 2005–06; Press Sec. to Perm. Under Sec. of State, FCO, 2006–07; Hd, Strategic Communications Unit and Dep. Hd, Public Diplomacy Gp, FCO, 2007–08; High Comr to the Solomon Islands, 2008–11; Chargé d'Affaires, Fiji, 2011–12. *Publications:* (ed) Engagement: public diplomacy in a globalised world, 2008. *Recreations:* kite surfing, ski-ing, scuba diving, learning the guitar, reading history, archaeology and the New Scientist. *Address:* British Embassy, Tour Zital Ankorondrano, Ravoninahitriniarivo Street, Antananarivo 101, Madagascar. *E:* Timothy.Smart@fco.gov.uk.

SMEATON, John Joseph; Chief Executive (formerly National Director), Society for the Protection of Unborn Children, since 1996; *b* 20 Feb. 1951; *s* of John Henry Smeaton and Marguerite Amy Smeaton; *m* 1984, Josephine Ann Toner (*née* Clarke); one *s* one *d*, and two step *s*. *Educ:* Salesian Coll., Battersea; Greyfriars Hall, Oxford (MA Eng. Lang. and Lit.); London Univ. (Cert Ed). English Teacher, 1973–75 (full-time), 1975–78 (part-time), Salesian Coll., Battersea; Head of English, Whitefriars, Cheltenham, 1975–76; part-time volunteer worker, 1976–78, Gen. Sec., 1978–96, SPUC. Mem., Nat. Assoc. of Catholic Families, 2006. KSC 1984. *Recreations:* reading, enjoying company of my family. *Address:* Society for the Protection of Unborn Children, 3 Whitacre Mews, Stannary Street, SE11 4AB. *T:* (020) 7091 7091. *Club:* New Cavendish.

SMEDLEY, George; *see* Smedley, R. R. G. B.

SMEDLEY, Nicholas John; educational consultant and film historian; *b* 23 Nov. 1959; *s* of Albert Glyn Smedley and Barbara Mary (*née* Sansom); partner, 1983, Kate Jennings. *Educ:* UCL (BA 1st cl. Hons (Hist.) 1981); Birkbeck Coll., London (PhD (Hist.) 1992). Lord Chancellor's Department: Admin. trainee, 1981–84; HEO, 1984–86; Grade 7, 1986–88; freelance advr to Dir, BFI, 1988–92; Dir, HR, PRO, 1992–94; Grade 7, Ct Service HQ, 1994–96; Grade 5, Dir Crown Ct Ops, 1996–99; Grade 3, Chief Exec., Public Trust Office, 1999–2001; Dir, Criminal Justice, LCD, then DCA, 2001–04; Dir, Asylum and Diversity, 2004–05, Diversity, 2005–06, DCA; on secondment as Res. Dir, Prince of Wales's Charities Office, 2006–08. Dir, Rosemary Works Sch., 2012–. *Publications:* The Dead Locust (novella), 2008; A Divided World: Hollywood cinema and émigré directors in the era of Roosevelt and Hitler, 1933–1948, 2011; The Roots of Modern Hollywood: the persistence of values in American cinema from the New Deal to the present day, 2014; articles on Hollywood film hist.; booklets on British film and TV. *Recreations:* opera, ballet, theatre, cinema, travel. *E:* nickandkate@yahoo.com. *Clubs:* Athenæum; Kennels (Goodwood).

SMEDLEY, (Roscoe Relph) George (Boleyne); Barrister; Counsellor, HM Diplomatic Service, retired; *b* 3 Sept. 1919; *o s* of late Charles Boleyne Smedley and Aimie Blaine Smedley (*née* Relph); *m* 1st, 1947, Muriel Hallaway Murray (*d* 1975), *o d* of late Arthur Stanley Murray; one *s*; 2nd, 1979, Margaret Gerrard Gourlay (*d* 1991), *oc* of late Augustus Thorburn Hallaway and *widow* of Dr John Stewart Gourlay; 3rd, 1993, Marjorie Drummond (*d* 1994), *d* of late John Leonard Haslam and *widow* of David Drummond; 4th, 2004, Margaret Mavis Linton (*d* 2006), *d* of late Alfred Kenneth Loxley Hamilton, and *widow* of William Riddell Linton. *Educ:* King's Sch., Ely; King's Coll., London (LLB). Called to Bar: Inner Temple; (*ad eundem*) Lincoln's Inn. Artists Rifles TA; commnd S Lancs Regt, 1940; Indian Army, 1942–46 (Captain); Foreign Office, 1937 and 1946; Foreign Service (subseq. Diplomatic Service): Rangoon, 1947; Maymyo, 1950; Brussels, 1952; Baghdad, 1954; FO, 1958; Beirut, 1963; Kuwait, 1965; FCO, 1969; Consul-Gen., Lubumbashi, 1972–74; British Mil. Govt, Berlin, 1974–76; FCO 1976; Head of Nationality and Treaty Dept, 1977–79. Part-time appointments (since retirement): Adjudicator under Immigration Act 1971; Inspector, Planning Inspectorate, Depts of the Environment and Transport; Dep. Traffic Comr for N Eastern Traffic Area; Legal Mem., Mental Health Review Tribunal; Chm., Rent Assessment Cttee; Mem., No 2 Dip. Service Appeal Bd. Churchwarden; Mem., diocesan and deanery synods. *Recreations:* forestry, reading. *Address:* Garden House, Whorlton, Barnard Castle, Co. Durham DL12 8XQ. *T:* (01833) 627381. *Club:* Royal Over-Seas League.

SMEDLEY, Susan M.; *see* Marsden, S.

SMEE, Clive Harrod, CB 1997; Visiting Professor of Economics, University of Surrey, since 1995; *b* 29 April 1942; *s* of Victor Woolley Smee and Leila Olive Smee (*née* Harrod); *m* 1975, Denise Eileen Sell; one *s* two *d*. *Educ:* Royal Grammar Sch., Guildford; LSE (BSc Econ); Indiana Univ. (MBA); Inst. of Commonwealth Studies, Oxford. British Council, Nigeria, 1966–68; Economic Advr, ODM, 1969–75; Sen. Economic Advr, DHSS, 1975–82; Nuffield and Leverhulme Travelling Fellow, USA and Canada, 1978–79; Advr, Central Policy Review Staff, 1982–83; Sen. Economic Advr, HM Treasury, 1983–84; Chief Economic Adviser: DHSS, 1984–88; DSS, 1988–89; DoH, 1988–2002; Sen. Policy Advr, NZ Treasury, 2002–04. Consultant: NZ Treasury, 1988; NZ Dept of Health, 1991. Chm., OECD Social Policy Working Party, 1987–90; Member: Internat. Co-ordinating Cttee, Commonwealth Fund, 1998–2004; Economics Adv. Panel, Home Office, 2006–08; Ind. Adv. Cttee on Develt Impact, DFID, 2007–10. Trustee, Medicines and People, 2006–12. Queen Mother Meml Fellow, Nuffield Trust, 2003–04. *Publications:* Speaking Truth to Power, 2005; articles on economics in learned jls. *Recreations:* painting, walking, gardening, cycling; Anna, David and Elizabeth. *Address:* Appletree House, Ockham Road North, East Horsley, Surrey KT24 6PU.

SMEE, John Charles O.; *see* Odling-Smee.

SMEE, Paul; Director General, Council of Mortgage Lenders, since 2011; *b* Liverpool, 27 Dec. 1956; *s* of Mirek and Rene Smee; *m* 1983, Penny Fulbeck; one *s* one *d*. *Educ:* Liverpool Coll.; Wadham Coll., Oxford (MA). DTI, 1978–88; Hd of Public Policy and Internat. Affairs, Stock Exchange, 1988–94; Hd, Life Insce, ABI, 1994–96; Dir, Public Affairs, ITC, 1996–99; Dir Gen., Assoc. of Ind. Financial Advrs, 1999–2004; Chief Exec., Payment Council/APACS, 2005–11. *Recreations:* reading, theatre, opera, family. *Address:* Council of Mortgage Lenders, North West Wing, Bush House, Aldwych, WC2B 4PJ. *E:* paul.smee@cml.org.uk. *Club:* Surrey County Cricket.

SMEETH, Ruth Lauren; MP (Lab) Stoke-on-Trent North, since 2015; *b* Edinburgh, 29 June 1979; *d* of Lucille Kelly; *m* 2004, Michael Smeeth. *Educ:* Downend Comprehensive Sch.; Alton Sixth Form Coll.; Birmingham Univ. (BSocSc Hons; Postgrad. Dip. PR). Sen. researcher, Amicus/AEEU, 2000–04; Hd of Govt Relns, Sodexo, 2004–05; Dir, Public Affairs, Bicom, 2005–07; Public Affairs Manager, Nestlé UK, 2007; Campaign Co-ordinator, CST, 2008–10; Dep. Dir, Hope Not Hate, 2010–15. *Recreations:* cinema, reading, travel. *Address:* House of Commons, SW1A 0AA. *T:* (020) 7219 4844. *E:* ruth.smeeth.mp@parliament.uk. *Club:* Naval and Military.

SMELLIE, David Craig Shaw; Partner, Farrer & Co. LLP, since 1996; *b* Glasgow, 20 Oct. 1964; *s* of Prof. Martin Smellie and Dr Florence Smellie; *m* 1991, Lady Emma Caroline de Vere Beauclerk, *d* of Duke of St Albans, *qv*; one *s* two *d*. *Educ:* Glenalmond Coll.; St John's Coll., Cambridge (BA 1986); Coll. of Law, Guildford. Admitted solicitor, 1989; Solicitor, Farrer & Co., 1989–91 and 1993–96; served HM Diplomatic Service, FCO, 1992–93; Mem., Mgt Bd, Farrer & Co. LLP, 2007–13. Vis. Fellow, Eton Coll., 2013. Mem. Council, Radley Coll., 2003–. Governor: James Allen's Girls' Sch., 2002–12; Dulwich Prep. Sch., London and Cranbrook, 2011– (Chm., 2014–). *Publications:* Common Employment Problems, 2000. *Recreations:* running, walking, opera, travel. *Address:* Farrer & Co. LLP, 66 Lincoln's Inn Fields, WC2A 3LH. *T:* (020) 7242 2022, *Fax:* (020) 7404 5127. *E:* dcs@farrer.co.uk. *Club:* New (Edinburgh).

SMETHAM, Andrew James, MA; Headmaster, The Purbeck School, Wareham, Dorset, 1985–2002; *b* 22 Feb. 1937; *s* of Arthur James Smetham and Eunice (*née* Jones); *m* 1964, Sandra Mary Owen; two *s*. *Educ:* Vaynor and Penderyn Grammar Sch., Cefn Coed, Breconshire; King's Coll., Univ. of London (BA (Hons German) 1959, DipEd 1964, MA (Educn) 1968). Assistant Master: Wandsworth Sch., 1960–66; Sedgehill Sch., 1966–70; Dep. Headmaster, Holloway Sch., 1970–74; Headmaster, Wandsworth Sch., 1974–84. *Recreation:* music. *Address:* Hethfelton Farmhouse, Hethfelton, Wareham, Dorset BH20 6HJ. *T:* (01929) 761637.

SMETHURST, Richard Good, MA; Provost, Worcester College, Oxford, 1991–2011; Pro Vice-Chancellor, University of Oxford, 1997–2011; *b* 17 Jan. 1941; *s* of Thomas Good Smethurst and Madeleine Nora Foulkes; *m* 1964, Dorothy Joan (*née* Mitchenall); two *s* two *d*; *m* 2000, Prof. Susan Edith Gillingham (*née* Mull); two step *d*. *Educ:* Liverpool Coll.; Worcester Coll., Oxford (Webb Medley Jun. Schol. 1962; BA 1st Cl. 1963; MA; Hon. Fellow, 2011); Nuffield Coll., Oxford. Research Fellow: St Edmund Hall, Oxford, 1964–65; Inst. for Commonwealth Studies, Oxford, 1965–66 (Consultant, UN/FAO World Food Program); University of Oxford: Fellow and Tutor in Economics, St Edmund Hall, 1966–67; Fellow and Tutor in Economics, Worcester Coll., and Univ. Lectr in Economics, 1967–76; Dir, Dept for External Studies, and Professorial Fellow, Worcester Coll., 1976–89; Supernumerary Fellow, Worcester Coll., and Chm., Gen. Bd of Faculties, 1989–91; non-exec. Dir, Nuffield Orthopaedic Centre, Oxford, 1992–2000. Economic Adviser, HM Treasury, 1969–71; Policy Adviser, Prime Minister's Policy Unit, 1975–76. Dir, IMRO, 1987–99. Member: Adv. Council for Adult and Continuing Educn, DES, 1977–83; Monopolies and Mergers Commn, 1978–89 (Dep. Chm., 1986–89); UGC/NAB Continuing Educn Standing Cttee, 1984–88; Acad. Consultative Cttee, Open Univ., 1986–92; Adv. Bd, Music at Oxford, 1988–94; Consumer Panel, FSA, 1998–2004. Chm., Unit for Develt of Adult Continuing Educn, 1991–92. Trustee: Eur. Community Baroque Orch., 1986–93; Oxford Philomusica, 2003–. Mem. Council, Templeton Coll., Oxford (formerly Oxford Management Centre), 1982–95; Life Governor, Liverpool Coll., 1968. Foundn Hon. Fellow, Kellogg Coll., Oxford, 1990; Hon. Fellow: St Edmund Hall, Oxford, 1991; St Catharine's Coll., Cambridge, 2002. *Publications:* Impact of Food Aid on Donor Countries (with G. R. Allen), 1967; contribs to New Thinking About Welfare, 1969; Economic System in the UK, 1977, 2nd edn 1979; New Directions in Adult and Continuing Education, 1979; Continuing Education in Universities and Polytechnics, 1982; contrib. Jl of Development Studies, Oxford Rev. of Educn, Studies in Adult Education. *Recreations:* good food, travel. *Address:* 43 Cranham Street, Oxford OX2 6DD. *T:* (01865) 552837. *E:* richard.smethurst@worc.ox.ac.uk.

SMILEY, Lt-Col Sir John (Philip), 4th Bt *cr* 1903, of Drumalis, Larne, Co. Antrim and Gallowhill, Paisley, Co. Renfrew; *b* 24 Feb. 1934; *s* of Sir Hugh Houston Smiley, 3rd Bt and Nancy Elizabeth Louise Hardy (*née* Beaton) (*d* 1999); *S* father, 1990; *m* 1963, Davina Elizabeth, *e d* of late Denis Charles Griffiths; two *s* one *d*. *Educ:* Eton Coll.; RMA Sandhurst. Commnd Grenadier Guards, 1954; ADC to Governor of Bermuda, 1961–62; served in Cyprus, BAOR, Hong Kong; Lt-Col, 1981; retired 1986. Russell Reynolds Associates,

1986–89. Governor, Oundle Sch., 1987–99. Mem., Ct of Assts, Worshipful Co. of Grocers, 1987– (Master, 1992–93). *Recreations:* gardening, travel. *Heir: s* Christopher Hugh Charles Smiley [*b* 7 Feb. 1968; *m* 1998, Clare Annabel, *y d* of Maj. Henry Blosse-Lynch; three *s*]. *Address:* Cornerway House, Chobham, Woking, Surrey GU24 8SW. *T:* (01276) 858992. *Club:* Army and Navy.

SMILEY, Miranda Caroline; *see* Sawyer, M. C.

SMILEY, Prof. Timothy John, PhD; FBA 1984; Knightbridge Professor of Philosophy, University of Cambridge, 1980–98; Fellow of Clare College, Cambridge, since 1955; *b* 13 Nov. 1930; *s* of Prof. M. T. Smiley and Mrs T. M. Smiley (*née* Browne); *m* 1955, Benita Mary Bentley; four *d. Educ:* Ardwyn Grammar Sch., Aberystwyth; Ampleforth Coll.; Fribourg Univ.; Clare Coll., Cambridge (BA 1952, Math. Tripos; MA, PhD 1956). Holt Scholarship, Gray's Inn, 1954; called to the Bar, 1956. Pilot Officer, RAFVR, 1954. Scientific Officer, Air Min., 1955–56; Clare Coll., Cambridge: Res. Fellow, 1955–59; Asst Tutor, 1959–65; Sen. Tutor, 1966–69; Asst Lectr in Phil., Cambridge Univ., 1957–62, Lectr, 1962–79. Vis. Professor: Cornell Univ., 1964; Univ. of Virginia, 1972; Yale Univ., 1975; Univ. of Notre Dame, 1986; Yale Univ., 1990. Sec. for Postgrad. Studies, 1992–94, Mem., Humanities Res. Bd, 1994–96, British Acad. *Publications:* (with D. J. Shoesmith) Multiple-conclusion Logic, 1978; (with Alex Oliver) Plural Logic, 2013; articles in phil and math. jls. *Recreation:* orienteering. *Address:* Clare College, Cambridge CB2 1TL. *T:* (01223) 352152.

SMILEY, Xan de Crespigny; journalist; Editor at Large, The Economist, since 2014; *b* Hanover, 1 May 1949; *s* of Col David de Crespigny Smiley, LVO, OBE, MC and Bar and Moyra Eileen Smiley (*née* Montagu-Douglas-Scott); *m* 1983, Hon. Jane Acton; two *s* and two step *d. Educ:* Eton Coll.; New Coll., Oxford (MA Russian and Modern Hist.). Commentator, BBC Radio Ext. Service, 1974–75; corresp., Spectator and Observer, in Africa, 1975–77; Ed., 1977–81, co-owner, 1981–92, Africa Confidential; leader writer, The Times, 1981–83; foreign affairs writer, The Economist, 1983–86; Moscow corresp., Daily Telegraph, 1986–89; Washington corresp., Sunday Telegraph, 1989–92; Political Ed. and Bagehot columnist, 1992–94, Europe Ed., 1995–2003, Middle East and Africa Ed., 2003–14, The Economist. Mem. Council, Chatham House, 2010–. *Recreations:* genealogy, shooting, food, sport (Mem., British Ski Team, 1969; winner, Oxford and Cambridge downhill race, 1969). *Address:* Lower Farm, Taston, Chipping Norton, Oxon OX7 3JL. *E:* xansmiley@economist.com. *Clubs:* Beefsteak, Pratt's, Grillions.

SMIT, Sir Timothy (Bartel), KBE 2012 (Hon. KBE 2011; Hon. CBE 2002); Executive Vice Chairman, Eden Project, since 2014 (Chief Executive, 1999–2013); Executive Chairman, Eden Regeneration Ltd, since 2013; Director, Lost Gardens of Heligan, since 1990; *b* Scheveningen, The Hague, Holland, 25 Sept. 1954; *s* of Jan Adrianus Bartel Smit and Anthea Margaret Smit (*née* Fairclough); adopted British citizenship, 2012; *m* 1978, Laura Candace Pinsent (marr. diss. 2013); three *s* one *d. Educ:* Cranbrook Sch.; Univ. of Durham (BA Hons Archaeol. and Anthropology). Archaeologist, 1977–78; record producer and composer, 1978–90; with John Nelson discovered, 1990, and restored Heligan estate, Cornwall, now open to visitors and known internationally as Lost Gardens of Heligan (Gardener of Year, Country Life, 1995; Garden of Year, Good Guide to Britain, 1999); Co-Founder, Eden Project, 1994 (scientific instn featuring conservatories inside a 34 acre, 200ft deep clay pit near St Austell). Mem. Bd, Prince's Trust Business Div., 1999–2005. Dir, Hurst Lodge Sch. Ltd Co. Vice-Pres., Garden History Soc.; Patron: Green Space; Nat. Council for Sch. Leadership; Cornwall Garden Soc. Hon. Fellow, St Catherine's Coll., Oxford, 2003. Hon. MSc Gen. Sci. Plymouth, 1998; Hon. LLD Exeter, 2001; Warwick, 2002; Wolverhampton, 2003; Bradford, 2003; Reading, 2003; DUniv: UCE, 2005; Open, 2005; West of England, 2006; Oxford Brookes, 2006. Outstanding Contribution to Tourism, English Tourism Council, 2000; Alchemist Award, 2001; Social Entrepreneur of the Year, Southern Region, 2001; Lord Lloyd of Kilgerran Award, Foundn for Sci. & Tech., 2003; Albert Medal, Royal Soc. of Arts, 2003. *Publications:* The Lost Gardens of Heligan, 1997 (Illustrated Book of Year, BCA, 1998); The Complete Works: secrets locked in silence, 1999; (with Philip McMillan Browse) The Heligan Vegetable Bible, 2000; Eden, 2001, 10th Anniv. edn 2011. *Recreations:* music, reading, film, art, theatre. *Address:* Eden Project, Bodelva, Cornwall PL24 2SG.

SMITH; *see* Carleton-Smith.

SMITH; *see* Darwall Smith.

SMITH; *see* Dixon-Smith, family name of Baron Dixon-Smith.

SMITH; *see* Ferguson-Smith.

SMITH; *see* Gordon-Smith.

SMITH; *see* Hamilton-Smith, family name of Baron Colwyn.

SMITH; *see* Hastie-Smith.

SMITH; *see* Llewellyn Smith and Llewellyn-Smith.

SMITH; *see* Mackenzie Smith and McKenzie Smith.

SMITH; *see* Stewart-Smith.

SMITH; *see* Stuart-Smith.

SMITH; *see* Warnock-Smith.

SMITH, family name of **Viscount Hambleden, Barons Bicester, Kirkhill, Smith of Clifton, Smith of Kelvin** and **Smith of Leigh,** and **Baroness Smith of Gilmorehill**.

SMITH OF BASILDON, Baroness *cr* 2010 (Life Peer), of Basildon in the County of Essex; **Angela Evans Smith;** PC 2009; Vice President, Local Government Association, since 2010; *b* 7 Jan. 1959; *d* of Patrick Joseph Evans and Emily Meikle Evans (*née* Russell); *m* 1978, Nigel J. M. Smith. *Educ:* Chalvedon Comprehensive Sch., Basildon; Leicester Poly. (BA Hons Public Admin). Part-time shop asst, J Sainsbury, 1975–77; Trainee Accountant, Newham LBC, 1981–83; Head of Pol and Public Relations, League Against Cruel Sports, 1983–95; Researcher, Alun Michael, MP, 1995–97. Mem. (Lab) Essex CC, 1989–97. Contested (Lab) Southend W, 1987. MP (Lab and Co-op) Basildon, 1997–2010; contested (Lab and Co-op) S Basildon and E Thurrock, 2010. PPS to Minister of State, Home Office, 1999–2001; an Asst Govt Whip, 2001–02; Parliamentary Under-Secretary of State: NI Office, 2002–06; DCLG, 2006–07; PPS to Prime Minister, 2007–09; Minister of State (Minister for the Third Sector), Cabinet Office, 2009–10. Shadow Leader of H of L, 2015–. Chair: Resolving Chaos, 2012–; Prodn Exchange, 2014–. Hon. Pres., St Clere's Co-operative Acad. Trust, 2012–; Patron: Basildon Women's Aid, 1998–; Sugarloaf Riding for the Disabled, 2012–; Stanford and Corringham Sch. Trust, 2014–. *Address:* House of Lords, SW1A 0PW.

SMITH OF CLIFTON, Baron *cr* 1997 (Life Peer), of Mountsandel, in the co. of Londonderry; **Trevor Arthur Smith,** Kt 1996; FRHistS, FAcSS; Vice-Chancellor, University of Ulster, 1991–99; *b* 14 June 1937; *e s* of late Arthur James Smith and Vera Gladys Smith (*née* Cross); *m* 1st, 1960, Brenda Susan (*née* Eustace) (marr. diss. 1973); two *s*; 2nd, 1979, Julia Donnithorne (*née* Bullock); one *d. Educ:* LSE (BSc Econ 1958). Schoolteacher, LCC, 1958–59; temp. Asst Lectr, Exeter Univ., 1959–60; Research Officer, Acton Soc. Trust, 1960–62; Lectr in Politics, Hull Univ., 1962–67; Queen Mary College, later Queen Mary & Westfield College, London: Lectr, then Sen. Lectr, in Political Studies, 1967–83; Prof., Political Studies, 1983–91; Head of Dept, 1972–85; Dean of Social Studies, 1979–82; Pro-Principal, 1985–87; Sen. Pro-Principal, 1987–89; Sen. Vice-Prin., 1989–91; Hon. Fellow, 2003. Vis. Associate Prof., California State Univ., LA, 1969. Director: Job Ownership Ltd, 1978–85; New Society Ltd, 1986–88; Statesman & Nation Publishing Co. Ltd, 1988–90; G. Duckworth & Co., 1990–95. Mem., Tower Hamlets DHA, 1987–91 (Vice Chm., 1989–91); non-exec. Mem., N Yorks HA, 2000–02. Vice Pres., Patients' Assoc. of UK, 1988–97. Chm., Conf. of Rectors in Ireland, 1997. Vice-Pres., Political Studies Assoc. of UK, 1989– (Chm., 1988–89; Pres., 1991–93); Dep. Pres., Inst. of Citizenship Studies, 1991–2001; Member: Admin. Bd, Internat. Assoc. of Univs, 1995–96; Editl Bd, Government and Opposition, 1995–2013; UK Socrates Council, 1993–99 (Chm., 1996–99). Contested (L) Lewisham W, 1959. House of Lords: Lib Dem Spokesman on NI, 2000–11; Chm., Select Cttee on Animals in Scientific Procedures, 2001–02; Member: Select Cttee on Communications, 2004–06; Select Cttee on Constitution, 2005–08; Select Sub-Cttee on Lords' Interests, 2006–08; Ad Hoc Select Cttee on Barnett Formula, 2008–09; Select Cttee on Works of Art, 2010, on Econ. Affairs, 2010–15; Sci. and Technol. Sub-Cttee on Complementary and Alternative Medicine, 1999–2000; EU Sub-Cttee E (Law and Instns), 2000–01. Trustee: Joseph Rowntree Reform (formerly Social Service) Trust, 1975–2006 (Chm., 1987–99); Stroke Assoc., 2002–05. Pres., Belfast Civic Trust, 1995–99; Member Board: Taste of Ulster, 1996–99; Opera NI, 1997–99. Governor: Sir John Cass and Redcoats Sch., 1979–84; Univ. of Haifa, 1985–92; Bell Educnl Trust, 1988–93. Hon. Mem. Senate, Fachhochschule Augsburg, 1994. FRHistS 1986; FICPD 1998. CCMI (CBIM 1992); FRSA 1994. FAcSS (AcSS 2000). Hon. LLD: Dublin, 1992; Hull, 1993; Belfast, 1995; NUI, 1996; Hon. DHL Alabama, 1998; Hon. DLitt Ulster, 2002. *Publications:* (with M. Argyle) Training Managers, 1962; (with A. M. Rees) Town Councillors, 1964; Town and County Hall, 1966; Anti-Politics, 1972; (jtly) Direct Action and Democratic Politics, 1972; The Politics of the Corporate Economy, 1979; (with A. Young) The Fixers, 1996; numerous articles. *Address:* House of Lords, SW1A 0PW. *Club:* Reform.

SMITH OF FINSBURY, Baron *cr* 2005 (Life Peer), of Finsbury in the London Borough of Islington; **Christopher Robert Smith;** PC 1997; PhD; Chairman, Advertising Standards Authority, since 2007; Master, Pembroke College, Cambridge, since 2015; *b* 24 July 1951; *s* of Colin Smith and Gladys (*née* Luscombe). *Educ:* Cassiobury Primary Sch., Watford; George Watson's Coll., Edinburgh; Pembroke Coll., Cambridge Univ. (BA 1st Cl. Hons 1972, PhD 1979; Hon. Fellow, 2005–15); Harvard Univ., Mass (Kennedy Scholar, 1975–76). Develt Sec., Shaftesbury Soc. Housing Assoc., 1977–80; Develt Co-ordinator, Soc. for Co-operative Dwellings, 1980–83. Dir, Clore Leadership Prog., 2003–08. Chm., London Cultural Consortium, 2005–08. Sen. Advr, Walt Disney Co., 2001–07; non-exec. Dir, PPL, 2006–. Councillor, London Bor. of Islington, 1978–83 (Chief Whip, 1978–79; Chm., Housing Cttee, 1981–83). MP (Lab) Islington South and Finsbury, 1983–2005. Opposition spokesman on treasury and economic affairs, 1987–92; principal opposition spokesman on environmental protection, 1992–94, on Nat. Heritage, 1994–95, on social security, 1995–96, on health, 1996–97; Sec. of State for Culture, Media and Sport, and Chm., Millennium Commn, 1997–2001. Chairman: Environment Agency, 2008–14; Task Force on Shale Gas, 2015–. Non-exec. Dir, Spencer Ogden, 2014–. Chairman: Tribune Gp of MPs, 1988–89 (Sec., 1985–88); Labour Campaign for Criminal Justice, 1985–88; Bd, Tribune Newspaper, 1990–93; Bd, New Century Magazine, 1993–96. Pres., Socialist Envmt and Resources Assoc., 1992–2007; Mem. Exec., Fabian Soc., 1990–97 (Chm., 1996–97). Mem., Cttee on Standards in Public Life, 2001–05. Pres., Cambridge Union, 1972; Vice-Chm., Young Fabian Gp, 1974–75; Chm., Charing Cross Br., ASTMS, 1980–83; Member: Exec., NCCL, 1986–88; Bd, Shelter, 1986–92; Exec. Cttee, Nat. Trust, 1995–97; Bd, RNT, 2001–09; Bd, Donmar Warehouse, 2001–03 (Chm., 2003–15); Film Policy Rev., DCMS, 2011–12. Chairman: Classic FM Consumer Panel, 2001–07; Man Booker Prize Judges, 2004; Art Fund, 2014– (Chm. Judges, ArtFund Prize for Museums, 2012). Vis. Prof. in Culture and the Creative Industries, Univ. of the Arts, London (formerly London Inst.), 2002–; Vis. Fellow, Ashridge Business Sch., 2007–. Founding Dir, Clore Leadership Prog., 2003–08. Governor: Sadler's Wells Theatre, 1987–97; Univ. of the Arts, 2005–08; Trustee: John Muir Trust, 1991–97; The Sixteen, 2013–; Chm., Wordsworth Trust, 2002–. Pres., Ramblers' Assoc., 2004–08. Hon. FRIBA 2000; Hon. Sen. Fellow, RCA, 2007; Hon. FKC 2008; Hon. Fellow, Cumbria Univ., 2010. Hon. DArts City, 2003; DUniv Lancaster, 2011. *Publications:* Creative Britain, 1998; (jtly) Suicide of the West, 2006. *Recreations:* mountaineering, literature, theatre, music. *Address:* House of Lords, SW1A 0PW.

SMITH OF GILMOREHILL, Baroness *cr* 1995 (Life Peer), of Gilmorehill in the City of Glasgow; **Elizabeth Margaret Smith;** DL; *b* 4 June 1940; *d* of Frederick William Moncrieff Bennett and Elizabeth Waters Irvine Shanks; *m* 1967, Rt Hon. John Smith, PC, QC (Scot.), MP (*d* 1994); three *d. Educ:* Hutchesons' Girls' Grammar Sch.; Univ. of Glasgow (MA, DipEd). Admin. Asst, 1962–64, Scottish Sec., 1982–88, Great Britain-USSR Assoc.; teacher of French, 1964–68. Mem., Press Complaints Commn, 1995–2001. Chm., Edinburgh Festival Fringe, 1995–2012; non-executive Director: Scottish Media Group plc (formerly Scottish Television), 1995–97; Deutsche Bank (formerly Deutsche Morgan Grenfell) (Scotland), 1996–2003; City Inn Ltd, 2001–10; Member: BP Adv. Bd, Scotland, 1996–2004; Adv. Bd, Know How Fund, 1998–99. Mem. Adv. Council, Russo-British Chamber of Commerce, 1996–; Mem. Bd, Covent Garden Fest., 1997–2001. Pres., Scottish Opera, 1997–2012. Trustee: John Smith Meml Trust, 1995–; BHF, 1995–98; ESU, 1995–2001; Centre for European Reform, 1996–2003; World Monument Fund, 1996–2000; Hakluyt Foundn, 1998–2001; Mariinsky Theatre Trust, 2001–. Pres., Birkbeck Coll., London, 1998–2003. DL Edinburgh, 1996. Hon. LLD Glasgow, 1998. *Recreations:* family, cinema, music, theatre, travel. *Address:* House of Lords, SW1A 0PW.

SMITH OF HINDHEAD, Baron *cr* 2015 (Life Peer), of Hindhead in the County of Surrey; **Philip Roland Smith,** CBE 2013; Chief Executive (formerly National Secretary), Association of Conservative Clubs. *Address:* Association of Conservative Clubs, 24 Old Queen Street, SW1H 9HP.

SMITH OF KELVIN, Baron *cr* 2008 (Life Peer), of Kelvin in the City of Glasgow; **Robert Haldane Smith,** KT 2013; Kt 1999; CA; FCIBS; Chairman: Commonwealth Games Organising Committee, Glasgow 2014 Ltd, 2008–15; Green Investment Bank, since 2012; Forth Ports, since 2015; IMI plc, since 2015; Clyde Gateway, since 2015; *b* 8 Aug. 1944; *s* of Robert Haldane Smith and Jean Smith (*née* Adams); *m* 1969, Alison Marjorie Bell; two *d. Educ:* Allan Glen's Sch., Glasgow. CA 1968; FCIBS 1993. With ICFC, 1968–82; Royal Bank of Scotland plc, 1983–85; Man. Dir, Charterhouse Develt Capital Ltd, 1985–89; Chm., Morgan Grenfell Develt Capital Ltd, 1989–2001 (Chief Exec., 1989–96); Chief Exec., Morgan Grenfell Asset Mgt Ltd, 1996–2000; Vice Chm., Deutsche Asset Mgt, 2000–02. Chairman: The Weir Gp plc, 2002–13; SSE plc (formerly Scottish and Southern Energy plc), 2005–15. Director: MFI Furniture Gp plc, 1987–2000; Stakis plc, 1997–99 (Chm., 1998–99); Bank of Scotland, 1998–2000; Aegon UK, 2002–09; Standard Bank Gp Ltd, 2003–; 3i plc, 2004–09. Vice-Pres., China-Britain Business Council, 2003–08. Dir, FSA, 1997–2000. Scottish Gov., BBC, 1999–2004; Bd Mem., British Council, 2002–05. Member: Financial Reporting Council, 2001–04 (Chm., FRC Gp on Guidance to Audit Cttees, 2003); Judicial Appts Bd, 2002–07; Scottish Council of Econ. Advrs, 2007–10. Chm. Smith Gp Adv. Gp to Scottish Govt (formerly Scottish Exec.) on young people not in educn, employment or trng, 2006–12. Pres., RHASS, 2010–11. Pres., ICA of Scotland, 1996–97. Chm., Bd of Trustees, Nat. Museums of Scotland, 1993–2002 (Trustee, 1985–2002); Mem., Museums and Galls Commn, 1988–98 (Vice Chm., 1996–98). Pres., British Assoc. of Friends of Museums, 1995–2005. Patron: Foundn Scotland (formerly Scottish Community Foundn), 2008–15;

Capital Appeal, Prince and Princess of Wales Hospice, 2013–. Chm., BBC Children in Need, 2003–04. Chancellor: UWS (formerly Paisley Univ.), 2003–13; Strathclyde Univ., 2013–. Dr *hc* Edinburgh, 1999; DUniv: Glasgow, 2001; Paisley, 2003. *Publications:* (jtly) Managing Your Company's Finances, 1981. *Recreation:* Inchmarnock Island. *Address:* Inchmarnock, Porthouse, Straad, Rothesay, Bute PA2 0QF. *T:* (01700) 500132.

SMITH OF LEIGH, Baron *cr* 1999 (Life Peer), of Wigan in the county of Greater Manchester; **Peter Richard Charles Smith;** Lecturer, Manchester College of Art and Technology, 1974–2001; Chairman, Greater Manchester Combined Authority, since 2011; *b* 24 July 1945; *s* of Ronald Ernest Smith and Kathleen (*née* Hocken); *m* 1968, Joy Lesley (*née* Booth); one *d*. *Educ:* Bolton Sch.; LSE (BScEcon); Garnett Coll. of Educn (CertEd FE); Salford Univ. (MSc Urban Studies). Lectr, Walbrook Coll., 1969–74. Mem. (Lab) Wigan MBC, 1978– (Chm. Finance, 1982–91; Leader, 1991–). North West Regional Assembly: Vice Chm., 1998–99; Chm., 1999–2000; Chm. Exec. Bd, 2005–09. Board Member: Manchester Airport plc, 1986–2001 (Chm., 1989–90); Manchester Airports Gp plc, 2001–. Chm., Assoc. of Gtr Manchester Authorities, 2000–. Hon. Freeman, Wigan, 2011. Hon DLaws Manchester Metropolitan, 2012. *Recreations:* gardening, reading political biographies, jazz. *Address:* Mysevin, Old Hall Mill Lane, Atherton, Manchester M46 0RG. *T:* (01942) 676127.

SMITH OF NEWNHAM, Baroness *cr* 2014 (Life Peer), of Crosby in the County of Merseyside; **Julie Elizabeth Smith,** DPhil; Fellow in Politics, Robinson College, since 1997, Senior Lecturer, since 2004, and Director, European Centre, Department of Politics and International Studies, since 2013, University of Cambridge; *b* Liverpool, 1 June 1969; *d* of Hugh Francis Smith and Eileen Elizabeth Smith (*née* Murphy). *Educ:* Merchant Taylors' Sch. for Girls, Crosby; Brasenose Coll., Oxford (MA PPE); St Antony's Coll., Oxford (MPhil, DPhil Politics). Hd, 1999–2003, Assoc. Fellow, 2003–07, European Prog., RIIA (Chatham House). Hanseatic Scholar, Univ. of Hamburg, 1995–97; Vis. Prof., Internat. Relns and European Studies Prog., Central European Univ., Budapest, 1997. Mem. (Lib Dem) Cambridge CC, 2003–15 (Exec. Cllr for Arts and Recreation, 2006–10, for Customer Services and Resources, 2012–14; Hon. Councillor, 2015). Mem., Lib Dem Federal Policy Cttee, 2005– (Vice Chm., 2012–). Mem. Council and Trustee, Cambridge Univ. Catholic Assoc., 2009–; Trustee, Gladstone Library, 2014–. *Publications:* Voice of the People: the European Parliament in the 1990s, 1995; (ed jtly) Eminent Europeans: personalities who shaped contemporary Europe, 1996 (trans. Czech, 1998); A Sense of Liberty: a short history of the Liberal International 1947–97, 1997; (ed jtly) Democracy in the New Europe, 1999; Europe's Elected Parliament, 1999; (jtly) The New Bilateralism: the UK's bilateral relations within the EU, 2002; (ed jtly) Through the Paper Curtain: insiders and outsiders in the New Europe, 2003; Reinvigorating European Elections: the implications of electing the European Commission, 2005; (Series Ed.) New Horizons in European Politics, 2011–; (ed jtly and contrib.) Palgrave Handbook on National Parliaments and the European Union, 2015. *Recreations:* theatre, ballet (watching), yoga (practice), travel, spending time with family and friends. *Address:* Robinson College, Cambridge CB3 9AN. *T:* (01223) 766259, (020) 7219 3214. *E:* jes42@parliament.uk.

SMITH, Rt Hon. Lady; Anne Smith; PC 2013; a Senator of the College of Justice in Scotland, since 2001; *b* 16 March 1955; *d* of John Mather and Jessica Douglas; *m* 1979, David Alexander Smith, WS; one *s* one *d*. *Educ:* Cheadle Girls' Grammar Sch.; Edinburgh Univ. (LLB Hons). Apprenticeship with Shepherd & Wedderburn WS, 1977–79; pupil of James McGhie, 1979–80; admitted Faculty of Advocates, 1980; QC (Scot.) 1993; Advocate Depute, 2000–01. Hon. Bencher, Gray's Inn, 2008. Chm., Royal Scottish Nat. Orch. Foundn, 2008–. *Recreations:* music, walking, gardening, cooking for friends and family. *Address:* Parliament House, Edinburgh EH1 1RF. *T:* (0131) 225 2595.

SMITH, Adam de la Falaise Brett B.; *see* Brett-Smith.

SMITH, His Honour Adrian Charles; a Circuit Judge, 1996–2014; First-tier Tribunal Judge (formerly Legal Member), Mental Health Review Tribunal (Restricted), 2002–14; *b* 25 Nov. 1950; *s* of late Fred Smith and Jenny Smith; *m* 1973, Sallie Ann Palmer (*d* 1994); two *d*. *Educ:* Blackpool Grammar Sch.; Queen Mary Coll., Univ. of London (LLB (Hons)). Called to the Bar, Lincoln's Inn, 1973; in practice on Northern Circuit, 1974–96; a Recorder, 1994–96. Mem., Liverpool Witness Support Mgt Cttee, 1990–93; Legal Mem., NW Mental Health Review Tribunal, 1994–96. *Recreations:* world travel, theatre, fell walking. *Club:* Waterloo Rugby Union.

SMITH, Sir Adrian (Frederick Melhuish), Kt 2011; PhD; FRS 2001; Vice-Chancellor, University of London, since 2012; *b* 9 Sept. 1946; *s* of late Claude Herbert Melhuish Smith and Jean Margaret Eileen Smith (*née* Hunt); one *s*; partner, Lucy Lauris Heller, *qv*. *Educ:* Teignmouth Grammar Sch.; Selwyn Coll., Cambridge (MA 1968; Hon. Fellow, 2013); University Coll. London (MSc 1969; PhD 1971). Jun. Lectr, 1971–72, Univ. Lectr, 1972–74, in Maths, Univ. of Oxford; Tutorial Fellow in Maths, Keble Coll., Oxford, 1971–74; Lectr in Stats, UCL, 1974–77; Prof. of Mathematical Stats, Univ. of Nottingham, 1977–90; Prof. of Stats, Imperial Coll. of Sci., Technology and Medicine, 1990–98 (Vis. Prof., 1998–2008); Principal, QMW, subseq. Queen Mary, Univ. of London, 1998–2008; Dir Gen., Sci. and Res., DIUS, then BIS, 2008–10; Dir Gen., Knowledge and Innovation, BIS, 2010–12. Dir, Imperial College Consultants, 1992–98 (Chm. of Bd, 1996–98). Member: Math. Cttee, SERC, 1985–91 (Chm., 1988–91); Sci. Bd, SERC, 1988–91; Technical Opportunities Panel, EPSRC, 1997–2000; Stats Adv. Cttee, ONS, 1997–99; Chair: UK Inquiry into Post-14 Maths Educn, 2002–03; London Higher, 2004–06; Council for Mathematical Scis, 2013–; Dep. Chair, UK Statistics Authy, 2008, 2012–. Chm. Bd, Diamond Synchrotron Ltd, Harwell, 2014–. Pres., Royal Statistical Soc., 1995–97 (Guy Medal in Bronze, 1977, in Silver, 1993). Member: Governing Body, London Business Sch., 1998–2008; Council, St George's Medical Sch., 2002–04; Dep. Vice-Chancellor, Univ. of London, 2006–08. FIS 1980. Hon. Fellow, Keble Coll., Oxford, 2014. Hon. DSc: City, 2003; Loughborough, 2006; Plymouth, 2011; Imperial Coll. London, 2013; Hon. DLit QMUL, 2009. *Publications:* (jtly) The Statistical Analysis of Finite Mixture Models, 1985; (jtly) Bayesian Theory, 1994; (jtly) Bayesian Methods for Nonlinear Classification and Regression, 2002; (trans. jtly) Bruno de Finetti, Theory of Probability, vol. I, 1974, vol. II, 1975; papers in statistical jls. *Recreations:* jazz, opera, cooking, internet chess. *Address:* University of London, Senate House, Malet Street, WC1E 7HU. *Club:* Reform.

SMITH, Prof. Alan, DPhil; UNESCO Professor of Education, University of Ulster, since 2000; *b* Belfast, 18 Jan. 1954; *s* of Walter Smith and Barbara Smith (*née* Stanex); *m* 1981, Elaine Steele; two *d*. *Educ:* Univ. of Ulster (BSc Hons; DPhil 1985). Teacher, NI and Zimbabwe, 1978–84; Research Fellow, Centre for Study of Conflict, Univ. of Ulster, 1985–96; Nuffield Foundn nominee to Integrated Educn Fund, 1992–99. Consultant to Dept of Education, NI, DFID, Council of Europe, UNICEF and World Bank, 1997–. Founding Chm., NI Council for Integrated Educn, 1987–89. Member: UNESCO Adv. Cttee on Peace, Human Rights and Democracy, Paris, 2000–04; Internat. Assessment Bd, Postgrad. Scholarship Scheme, Irish Res. Council, 2002–06 (Mem., Sen. Fellowships Bd, 2006–08); Civic Engagement Empowerment and Respect for Diversity External Adv. Cttee, World Bank, 2003–05; Global Monitoring Report Adv. Gp, Education for All, 2010–11. Vis. Prof., Hong Kong Inst. of Educn, 2006–07. Trustee, Speedwell Envmtl Centre, 1990–96. *Publications:* contribs to acad. jls on educn and conflict in NI, peace, human rights and democracy. *Address:* School of Education, University of Ulster, Coleraine, Northern Ireland BT52 1SA. *T:* (028) 7032 4137.

SMITH, Alan Christopher, CBE 1996; Chief Executive, Test and County Cricket Board, 1987–96; *b* 25 Oct. 1936; *s* of Herbert Sidney and Elsie Smith; *m* 1963, Anne Elizabeth Boddy; one *s* one *d*. *Educ:* King Edward's Sch., Birmingham; Brasenose Coll., Oxford (BA). Played cricket: Oxford Univ. CC, 1958–60 (Captain, 1959 and 1960); Warwicks CCC, 1958–74 (Captain, 1968–74); rep. England in six Test Matches, Australia and NZ, 1962–63. Gen. Sec., Warwicks CCC, 1976–86; England overseas cricket tours: Asst Manager, Australia, 1974–75; Manager: West Indies, 1981; Fiji, NZ and Pakistan, 1984. Mem., England Cricket Selection Cttee, 1969–73, 1982–86; ICC Referee, 1998–2002. Director: Royds Advertising and Marketing, 1971–86; Aston Villa Football Club plc, 1972–78. President: Brasenose Soc., 1999–2000; OUCC, 2000–09. *Recreations:* both football codes, golf, bridge, motoring. *Address:* The Old Farmhouse, Wyck Rissington, Gloucestershire GL54 2PN. *T:* (01451) 820509. *Clubs:* MCC, I Zingari; Vincent's (Oxford); Warwickshire CC.

SMITH, Alan Edward, CBE 2005; PhD; FRS 2010; Senior Vice President, Research, 1989–2011 and Chief Scientific Officer, 1996–2011, Genzyme Corporation, Cambridge, Mass; Lady Margaret Beaufort Fellow, Christ's College, Cambridge, since 2012; *b* Fareham, Hants, 9 Oct. 1945; *s* of late William George Smith and Hilda Annie Smith; *m* 1st, 1979, Eva Paucha (*d* 1988); one *s* one *d*; 2nd, 1991, Mary Loeken (marr. diss. 2004); three *s*. *Educ:* Price's Sch., Fareham; Christ's Coll., Cambridge (BA Nat. Scis Tripos Biochem. 1967); MRC Lab. of Molecular Biol., Cambridge (PhD 1984). Scientific Staff, ICRF, 1972–80; Hd, Biochem. Div., NIMR, 1980–84; Scientific Dir and Vice Pres., Integrated Genetics, Inc., Framingham, Mass, 1984–89. Member, Board of Directors: Genzyme Transgenics Corp., 1993–2000; Cambridge in America, 2001–10, 2012–; Genzyme Therapeutics Ltd, 2006–11; Arecor Ltd, 2008–. Member, Scientific Advisory Board: Health Care Ventures, Princeton, NJ, 1999–2011; Massachusetts Life Scis Center, 2008–; Pharnext, Paris, 2009–; ImmuneXcite, Lexington, Mass, 2014–. Mem., Bd of Dirs, 1999–2000, Adv. Bd, 2002–07, Amer. Soc. of Gene Therapy. Chm., Cambridge in America, 2014–. *Publications:* over 140 articles in learned jls incl. Cell, Nature, PNAS, Science; 38 reviews and chapters; 11 US patents. *Recreations:* Early English watercolours, mowing stripes, travelling hopefully. *Address:* 111 Plain Road, Wayland, MA 01778, USA. *T:* (617) 2304572. *E:* alanesmith@me.com.

SMITH, Alan Frederick; Chairman, Acambis (formerly Peptide Therapeutics) plc, 1999–2006 (non-executive Director, 1995–2006); *b* 21 July 1944; *s* of Frederick Herbert Smith and Winifred Alice Bella (*née* Farthing); *m* 1966, Judith Mary Forshaw (marr. diss. 1991); one *s* one *d*. *Educ:* Gosfield Sch., Essex. CIPFA. Trainee, Colchester BC, 1961–66; Ipswich County Borough Council: Sen. Accountant, 1966–72; Asst Treas., 1972–74; Principal Accountant, Anglian Water Authy, 1974–75; Asst Dir of Finance, Southern Water Authy, 1975–80; Dir of Finance, Anglian Water Authy, 1980–89; Dep. Man. Dir and Dir of Finance, 1989–90, Gp Man. Dir, 1990–97, Anglian Water PLC. *Recreations:* walking, photography.

SMITH, Rt Rev. Alan Gregory Clayton; *see* St Albans, Bishop of.

SMITH, Alan Keith Patrick; non-executive Chairman, Space NK Ltd, since 1997; *b* 17 March 1941; *s* of Ernest and Mary Smith; *m* 1st, 1968, Veronica Soskin (marr. diss.); one *s* one *d*; 2nd, 1983, Joan Peregrine; two *s*. *Educ:* St Michael's Coll., Leeds; Edinburgh Univ. (MA). Marks & Spencer, 1964–93, Dir, 1978–93; Chief Exec., Kingfisher, 1993–95; Dir, Smith Peregrine Ltd, 1996–. Non-executive: Chm., Storehouse, then Mothercare, plc, 2000–02; Director: Colefax Gp, 1994–; Whitehead Mann Gp, 1997–2006; Planet Organic Ltd, 2000–; Tangent Communications, 2010–13. Governor: South Bank Bd, 1995–2008; Arts & Business, 1999–2007. *Recreations:* family, wine collecting, walking, cooking. *Clubs:* Brooks's, MCC.

SMITH, Alasdair; *see* Smith, M. A. M.

SMITH, Alexander; *b* Kilwinning, 2 Dec. 1943. *Educ:* Irvine Royal Acad. Former gardener. Chm., 1983–87, Trade Union Liaison Officer, 1986–88, Cunninghame S CLP; former Chm., Irvine and District Trades Council. MEP (Lab) Scotland S, 1989–99. Member: TGWU (Mem., Regl, Public Service and Political Cttees); Scottish CND; Anti-Apartheid Movement; Amnesty Internat.; Latin American Solidarity Campaign.

SMITH, Rt Hon. Sir (Alexander) Lockwood, KNZM 2013; High Commissioner for New Zealand in the United Kingdom, since 2013; Speaker, House of Representatives, New Zealand, 2008–13; *b* Paparoa, NZ, 13 Nov. 1948; *s* of David and Heather Smith; *m* 2009, Alexandra Lang (*née* Morrison). *Educ:* Matakohe Primary Sch.; Ruawai Dist High Sch.; Auckland Grammar Sch.; Massey Univ. (BAgrSc; MAgrSc Hons); Univ. of Adelaide (PhD Animal Sci. 1980). Jun. Lectr, Massey Univ., 1971–72; Commonwealth Schol., 1973–76; Mktg Manager, NZ Dairy Bd, Central and SE Asia Area, 1981–83. MP (Nat.) Kaipara, 1984–96, Rodney, 1996–2011, NZ, 2011–13. Minister: responsible for Nat. Liby, and for Educn Rev. Office, 1990–95; of Educn, 1990–95; of Agric. and of Forestry, 1996; Dep. Minister of Finance, 1996; Minister: responsible for Contact Energy, 1996–99; for Internat. Trade, 1997–99; Associate Minister of Finance, 1998–99; Minister of Tourism, 1999. Dist. Alumni Award, Massey Univ., 2010. *Publications:* Maize Silage: a study of the nutritive value of ensiled zea mays, 1973; Ruminant Protein Metabolism: a study of the nitrogenous transactions of the small intestinal muscosa, 1979. *Recreations:* beef cattle farming, singing, weight training, rowing, surf lifesaving. *Address:* New Zealand High Commission, New Zealand House, 80 Haymarket, SW1Y 4TQ. *Club:* Lyall Bay Surf Lifesaving.

SMITH, Alexander M.; *see* McCall Smith.

SMITH, Alfred Nicholas Hardstaff L.; *see* Leigh-Smith.

SMITH, Alwyn; *see* Smith, Ernest A.

SMITH, Alyn; Member (SNP) Scotland, European Parliament, since 2004; *b* 15 Sept. 1973; *s* of Edward and Jane Smith. *Educ:* Univ. of Leeds (LLB Hons 1994); Univ. of Heidelberg; Coll. of Europe, Warsaw (MA European Studies 1995); Nottingham Law Sch. (Dip. Legal Practice 1996). Clifford Chance, Solicitors, 1997–99; Anderson Strathern, Solicitors, 2000–02; Gp Advr, Justice, Business and Europe, SNP Gp, Scottish Parlt, 2002–04. Dir, Turning Point Scotland. Trustee, LGBT Youth Scotland. Hon. Vice Pres., Scottish SPCA. *Address:* TechCube, 1 Summerhall, Edinburgh EH9 1PL. *E:* alyn.smith@europarl.europa.eu.

SMITH, Andrea Catherine; *see* Catherwood, A. C.

SMITH, Sir Andreas W.; *see* Whittam Smith.

SMITH, Andrew; QC (Scot.) 2002; advocate and barrister; *b* 22 Jan. 1963; *s* of David Abercrombie Smith and Margaret Smith; *m* 1st, Jane Russell (marr. diss. 2009); one *s* two *d*; 2nd, 2014, Jane Munro. *Educ:* Eastwood High Sch.; Dundee Univ. (LLB Hons 1985; DipLP 1986); Edinburgh Univ. (Dip. Advanced Legal Studies 1987). Admitted advocate, 1988; called to the Bar, Gray's Inn, 2006; Member: Compass Chambers, Edinburgh (Hd, 2006–09); Crown Office Chambers, London. Former Assessor, Gen. Teaching Council of Scotland; apptd under Proceeds of Crime Act 2002 as Statutory Appointed Person. *Recreations:* travel, motorcycling, cycling, running, vicarious round the world yachting. *T:* (0131) 226 5071.

SMITH, Dr Andrew Benjamin, FRS 2002; FRSE; Senior Research Scientist, Natural History Museum, since 1991; *b* 6 Feb. 1954; *s* of Benjamin Butler Smith and Elsie Marjory (*née* Fleming); *m* 1976, Mary Patricia Cumming Simpson; two *d*. *Educ:* Univ. of Edinburgh (BSc 1st Cl. Hons Geol. 1976; DSc 1993); Univ. of Exeter (PhD Biol Sci. 1979). Lectr, Dept of Geol., Univ. of Liverpool, 1981–82; Dept of Palaeontol., Natural History Mus., 1982– (Res. Scientist, 1982–91). FRSE 1996. *Publications:* Echinoid Palaeobiology, 1984;

Systematics and the Fossil Record, 1994; edited jointly: Echinoderm Phylogeny and Evolutionary Biology, 1988; Fossils of the Chalk, 1988, revd edn 2002; Echinoderm Research 1995, 1996; contrib. numerous scientific papers and monographs. *Address:* Department of Palaeontology, Natural History Museum, Cromwell Road, SW7 5BD. *T:* (020) 7942 5217, *Fax:* (020) 7942 5546. *E:* a.smith@nhm.ac.uk.

SMITH, Hon. Sir Andrew (Charles), Kt 2000; **Hon. Mr Justice Andrew Smith;** a Judge of the High Court of Justice, Queen's Bench Division, since 2000; Judge in charge, Commercial Court, 2008–09; *b* 31 Dec. 1947; *s* of Charles George Smith and Winifrid Smith; *m* 1986, Indu Nathoo; one *s* two *d.* *Educ:* Wyggeston Grammar Sch. for Boys, Leicester; Wadham Coll., Oxford (BA). Called to Bar, Middle Temple, 1974, Bencher, 1999. QC 1990; a Recorder, 1996–2000; Presiding Judge, NE Circuit, 2003–06. *Address:* Royal Courts of Justice, Strand, WC2A 2LL. *Club:* Reform.

SMITH, Rt Hon. Andrew (David); PC 1997; MP (Lab) Oxford East, since 1987; *b* 1 Feb. 1951; *m*; one step *s.* *Educ:* Reading Grammar Sch.; St John's Coll., Oxford. Joined Labour Party, 1973. Mem., Oxford City Council, 1976–87 (Chairman: Recreation Cttee, 1980–83; Planning Cttee, 1984–87). Opposition spokesman on higher and continuing educn, 1988–92, on Treasury and Economic Affairs, 1992–94, on transport, 1996–97; Shadow Chief Sec. to HM Treasury, 1994–96; Minister of State, DFEE, 1997–99; Chief Sec. to HM Treasury, 1999–2002; Sec. of State for Work and Pensions, 2002–04. Contested (Lab) Oxford E, 1983. Chm., Bd, Oxford Brookes Univ. (formerly Oxford Poly.), 1987–93. *Address:* Unit A, Bishops Mews, Transport Way, Oxford OX4 6HD; House of Commons, SW1A 0AA.

SMITH, Andrew Duncan; QC 2012; a Recorder, since 2009; *b* Grantham, Lincs, 14 Oct. 1974; *s* of Dr Duncan Smith and Patricia Smith; *m* 2006, Kate Hollingsworth; one *s* one *d.* *Educ:* St Hugh's Coll., Oxford (BA Juris. 1996; MA). Called to the Bar, Middle Temple, 1997; in practice as a barrister, specialising in criminal law, 1997–. *Address:* St Philips Chambers, 55 Temple Row, Birmingham B2 5LS. *T:* (0121) 246 0200. *Club:* Nottinghamshire County Cricket.

SMITH, Andrew Paul H.; *see* Hudson-Smith.

SMITH, Sir Andrew (Thomas), 5th Bt *cr* 1897, of Stratford Place, St Marylebone, London; Account Director, New Zealand Media and Entertainment (formerly The Radio Network), Wellington, since 2012; *b* 17 Oct. 1965; *er s* of Sir Gilbert Smith, 4th Bt and of Patricia Christine Smith (*née* Cooper); *S* father, 2003; one *s* one *d*; *m* 2007, Erin Katrina, *d* of Perry Aspros; one *s.* Account Dir, Mail Marketing Service, New Zealand Post, 2008–10. *Heir: s* Samuel James Thomas Smith, *b* 29 Aug. 2009.

SMITH, Angela Christine; MP (Lab) Penistone and Stocksbridge, since 2010 (Sheffield Hillsborough, 2005–10); *b* 16 Aug. 1961; *d* of Thomas Edward Smith and Patricia Ann Smith; *m* 2005, Steven Wilson; one step *s* one step *d.* *Educ:* Univ. of Nottingham (BA 1st cl. Hons (English studies) 1990); Newnham Coll., Cambridge. Lectr, Dearne Valley Coll., Wath on Dearne, 1994–2003. Mem., Sheffield CC, 1996–2005 (Chm., Finance, 1998–99; Cabinet Mem. for Educn and Trng, 2002–05). Opposition Whip, 2010–11; Shadow Dep. Leader of the House, 2011–14; Shadow Minister, DEFRA, 2014–15. *Recreations:* hill-walking, bird watching, cooking. *Address:* Area Regeneration Centre, Town Hall, Manchester Road, Stocksbridge S36 2DT. *T:* (0114) 283 1855, *Fax:* (0114) 283 1850; House of Commons, SW1A 0AA. *T:* (020) 7219 6713. *E:* smithac@parliament.uk.

SMITH, Anne; *see* Smith, Rt Hon. Lady.

SMITH, Anne; Chief Executive, Primary Care Respiratory Society UK (formerly General Practice Airways Group), since 2004; *b* 6 May 1961; *d* of John and Gerry Bradley; *m* 2000, Amahl Smith. *Educ:* Christ's Coll., Cambridge (MA; tennis blue). Product Manager, then Gp Product Manager, Merck Sharp and Dohme Ltd, 1982–89; Allen & Hanburys: Mktg Manager, 1989–94; Business Zone Manager, 1994–96; Glaxo Wellcome UK Ltd, 1989–98: Regl Business Dir, 1994–96; Dir, Respiratory Mktg, 1996–98; Chief Exec., Nat. Asthma Campaign, 1998–2001; management consultant, 2001–04. Mem., Technol. Appraisal Cttee, NICE, 2002–04; Trustee, Long Term Med. Conditions Alliance, 2000–05. *Recreations:* travelling, hill walking, gardening, cycling, tennis. *E:* anne_smith@btconnect.com.

SMITH, Anne Margaret Brearley; *see* Luther, A. M.

SMITH, Annette Dionne K.; *see* Karmiloff-Smith.

SMITH, Lt-Gen. Sir Anthony Arthur D.; *see* Denison-Smith.

SMITH, Anthony David, CBE 1987; President, 1988–2005, and Hon. Fellow, 2005, Magdalen College, Oxford; *b* 14 March 1938; *s* of Henry and Esther Smith. *Educ:* Brasenose Coll., Oxford (BA; Hon. Fellow, 1999). BBC TV Current Affairs Producer, 1960–71; Fellow, St Antony's Coll., Oxford, 1971–76; Director, BFI, 1979–88 (Fellow 1988). Bd Mem., Channel Four Television Co., 1980–84. Member: Arts Council, 1990–94; Bd of Dirs, The Sixteen, 2006–; Council, RADA, 2007–. Member: Internat. Bd, Russia Mus., St Petersburg, 2009–; Internat. Adv. Bd, Tomsk State Univ., 2014–. Chairman: Writers and Scholars Educnl Trust, 1989–99 (Mem., 1982–); Jan Hus Educnl Foundn, 1989–2002; Chair: Hill Foundn, 1998–; Oxford-Russia Fund, 2004–; Trustee: Cambodia Trust, 1990–99; Med. Res. Foundn, 2005–14; Kidu Foundn of Bhutan, 2011–; Indian Nat. Trust for Art and Cultural Heritage UK, 2012–14. *Publications:* The Shadow in the Cave: the broadcaster, the audience and the state, 1973, 2nd edn 1976; British Broadcasting, 1974; The British Press since the War, 1976; Subsidies and the Press in Europe, 1977; The Politics of Information, 1978; Television and Political Life, 1979; The Newspaper: an international history, 1979; Newspapers and Democracy, 1980; Goodbye Gutenberg—the newspaper revolution of the 1980s, 1980; The Geopolitics of Information, 1980; The Age of the Behemoths, 1991; From Books to Bytes, 1993; The Oxford Illustrated History of Television, 1995; Software for the Self: culture and technology, 1996; (with F. Webster) The Postmodern University?, 1997. *Address:* Albany, Piccadilly, W1J 0AX. *Clubs:* Garrick, Grillions, Beefsteak.

SMITH, Prof. (Anthony) David, DPhil; FMedSci; Professor of Pharmacology, 1984–2005, now Emeritus, and Deputy Head, Division of Medical Sciences, 2000–05, University of Oxford; Director, Oxford Project to Investigate Memory and Ageing, 1988–2008, now Founding Director; Fellow, Lady Margaret Hall, Oxford, 1984–2005, now Emeritus Fellow; *b* 16 Sept. 1938; *s* of Rev. William Beddard Smith and Evelyn Smith; *m* 1st, 1962, Wendy Diana Lee (marr. diss. 1974); one *s* one *d*; 2nd, 1975, Dr Ingegerd Östman; one *s.* *Educ:* Kingswood Sch., Bath; Christ Church, Oxford (Bostock Exhibnr; BA 1963, MA 1966, DPhil 1966). Royal Soc. Stothert Res. Fellow, Oxford, 1966–70; Res. Lectr, Christ Church, Oxford, 1966–71; Wellcome Res. Fellow, Oxford, 1970–71; Univ. Lectr in Pharmacology and Student of Christ Church, 1971–84; Hd, Dept of Pharmacol., Univ. of Oxford, 1984–2000. Hon. Dir, MRC Anatomical Neuropharmacology Unit, Oxford, 1985–98, Hon. Assoc. Dir, 1998. Member: Gen. Bd of the Faculties, Oxford, 1980–84; Neurosciences Bd, MRC, 1983–88; Physiol Soc.; Pharmacol Soc.; Chm., Scientific Adv. Bd, Alzheimer's Res. Trust, 1998–2003. Dir of Pubns, IBRO, 1977–95; Editor: Methods in the Neurosciences (IBRO Handbook Series), 1981–; Neuroscience, 1976–2002; Mem., editorial bds of various scientific jls. FMedSci 2000. Hon. Res. Fellow, Alzheimer's Res. Trust, 2007. Mem., Norwegian Acad. of Sci. and Letters, 1996; Hon. Mem., Hungarian Acad. of Sci., 1998. Dr *hc* Szeged Univ., 1993; MD *hc* Lund Univ., 1998. (Seventh) Gaddum Meml Prize, British Pharmacol Soc., 1979. *Publications:* (ed) Handbook of Physiology, Section 7 Vol. 6, 1974; (ed) Commentaries in the Neurosciences, 1980; articles on neuropharmacology and Alzheimer's disease in jls. *Recreations:* art, music, travel. *Address:* University Department of Pharmacology, Mansfield Road, Oxford OX1 3QT. *E:* david.smith@pharm.ox.ac.uk.

SMITH, Anthony Donald Raymond, CMG 2008; Chief Executive Officer, Westminster Foundation for Democracy, since 2014; *b* 8 Nov. 1958; *s* of Raymond and Flora Smith; *m* 1986, Kerry Rankine; one *s* one *d.* *Educ:* Univ. of Chicago High Sch.; Amherst Coll. (BA); Warwick Univ. (LLB). Joined FCO, 1986; Second, later First Sec., Madrid, 1988–91; First Sec., FCO, 1991–96; Head, EU Dept, then S Africa Dept, DFID, 1996–2006; Dir, Eur. Pol Affairs, FCO, 2006–08; Dir, Europe and Donor Relations, then Internat. Relations Div., DFID, 2008–14. *Recreations:* tennis, canoeing, pruning. *Address:* Westminster Foundation for Democracy, Artillery House, 11–19 Artillery Row, SW1P 1RT.

SMITH, Anthony Glen; Managing Consultant, Cambridge Education, since 2014; Lead for Local Authorities, Mott MacDonald Group (formerly Manager, Local Authority Division, then Director, Children's Services, then Director, Health and Education UK, Cambridge Education), 2005–14; *b* 29 July 1955; *s* of Bernard Neil Smith and Jean Margaret Smith; *m* 1978, Anne McLaren; one *s* one *d.* *Educ:* Price's Sch., Fareham; Christ's Coll., Cambridge (BA 1977; MA 1980); Open Univ. (MA 2015). Asst Teacher of Geog., Weston Favell Upper Sch., Northampton, 1977–81; Head of Geog., Sir Frank Markham Sch., Milton Keynes, 1981–84; Asst, later Sen. Educn Officer, Wilts CC, 1984–89; Devon County Council: Area Educn Officer, 1989–91; Sen. Educn Officer, 1991–94; Asst Chief Educn Officer, 1994–96; Dep. Chief Educn Officer, 1996–98; Dir of Educn, Arts and Libraries, 1998–2003; Dir of Learning and Culture, 2003, Dir for Children's Services, 2004–05, Torbay Council. Director: Carillion Academies Trust; Sandwell Futures; Leeds Local Educn Partnership; Chm., Diocese of Salisbury Academies Trust, 2013–. *Recreations:* cricket, antique maps, watercolour painting, furniture restoration, gardening, family. *Address:* Trafalgar House, Dawlish Road, Teignmouth, Devon TQ14 8TQ. *T:* (01626) 774289. *Club:* Hawks (Cambridge).

SMITH, Cdre Anthony Philip M.; *see* Masterton-Smith.

SMITH, Prof. Anthony Terry Hanmer, LLD; Professor, Faculty of Law, Victoria University of Wellington, since 2015 (Pro Vice-Chancellor and Dean, 2007–15); Fellow, Gonville and Caius College, Cambridge, since 1973; *b* 12 Jan. 1947; *s* of William Duncan Hanmer Smith and Rima Patricia Smith (*née* Donnelly); *m* 1968, Gillian Innes (marr. diss. 1981); one *s.* *Educ:* St Bede's Coll., Christchurch, NZ; Univ. of Canterbury (LLB; LLM); PhD 1985, LLD 1999, Cantab. Barrister and solicitor, High Court of NZ, 1979; called to the Bar, Middle Temple, 1992 (Hon. Bencher, 2001). Asst Lectr, Univ. of Canterbury, 1970–72; Lectr in Law, 1973–81, and Tutor, 1974–81, Gonville and Caius Coll., Cambridge; Reader in Law, 1981–85, and Dean of Faculty, 1984, Univ. of Durham; Prof. of Law, 1986–90, and Head of Dept, 1988–90, Univ. of Reading; Prof. of Criminal and Public Laws, 1996–2006, and Chm., Faculty of Law, 1999–2001, Univ. of Cambridge. Arthur Goodhart Vis. Prof., Univ. of Cambridge, 2015–Sept. 2016. *Publications:* Offences Against Public Order, 1987; Property Offences, 1994; (ed jtly) Harm and Culpability, 1996; (with Sir David Eady) The Law of Contempt, 1998, 4th edn 2011; (ed) Glanville Williams: Learning the Law, 15th edn, 2013. *Recreations:* cookery, travelling, architecture, wine. *Address:* 86 Bolton Street, Wellington, New Zealand. *Clubs:* Athenæum; Wellington (Wellington, NZ).

SMITH, Anthony Thomas; QC 1977; *b* 21 June 1935; *s* of Sydney Ernest Smith and Winston Victoria Smith; *m* 1959, Letitia Ann Wheldon Griffith; one *s* two *d.* *Educ:* Northampton, Stafford, and Hinckley Grammar Schs; King's Coll., Cambridge (Exhibnr; MA). Called to the Bar, Inner Temple, 1958, Bencher, 1985; a Recorder, 1977. Flying Officer, RAF, 1958–60. Founder and Chm., Birmingham Free Representation Scheme. *Recreations:* music, reading, the countryside. *Address:* No5 Chambers, Fountain Court, Steelhouse Lane, Birmingham B4 6DR.

SMITH, Arnold Terence, MBE 1963; HM Diplomatic Service, retired; *b* 7 Oct. 1922; *s* of Thomas Smith and Minnie Louisa (*née* Mole); *m* 1st, 1944, Mary James (*d* 1983), Preston, Yorks; one *s* one *d*; 2nd, 1985, Brenda Day (*née* Edwards), Edmonton (*d* 2012); one step *s.* *Educ:* Christ Church, Dover; Coll. of Technol., Dover. Enlisted HM Forces, Army, 1939; served War, 1939–45; released, 1947. Joined CRO, 1948; Attaché, Karachi, 1952–56; Second Sec., Madras, 1956–60; CRO, 1960–61; First Sec., Kuala Lumpur, 1961–65; Consul, Oslo, 1965–69; FCO, 1969–73; Head of Chancery, Mbabane, 1973–77; Head of Admin, Nairobi, 1977–78; Counsellor and Consul-Gen., Lagos, Nigeria, 1978–80. *Recreations:* hiking, gardening, golf, swimming. *Address:* Grunters, Cavendish Road, Clare, Suffolk CO10 8PJ. *T:* (01787) 277918.

SMITH, (Arthur) Jeffrey, CEng, FREng; FIMMM; Senior Consultant, Wardell Armstrong (Mining, Minerals Engineering and Environmental Consultants), since 2009 (Partner, 1983–2009, Managing Partner, 1994–2006; Chairman, 2006–09); *b* 1 Feb. 1947; *s* of Alfred and Doris Smith; *m* 1st (marr. diss. 2008); one *s* one *d*; 2nd, 2009, Fiona Mary Bazley. *Educ:* Univ. of Newcastle upon Tyne (BSc Engrg (Mech. and Mining) 1968; BSc Hons (Mining Engrg) 1969). CEng 1971; FIMMM 1988. Tech. asst to colliery manager, Golborne, NCB, 1971–73; Sen. Mining Engr, 1973–75, Associate, 1975–82, K. Wardell & Partners, subseq. Wardell Armstrong. Mem. Bd, British Geol Survey, 2000–08. Pres., IMMM, 2004–05. Mem. Council, Keele Univ., 2000–08. FREng 2001. Freeman, City of London, 1996; Mem., Co. of Engrs, 1999. *Recreations:* golf, boating, classic cars, music (playing guitar (in private!)); opposing: the nanny state; political spin; Federalist Europe; social engineering; red tape. *Address:* Wardell Armstrong, Sir Henry Doulton House, Forge Lane, Etruria, Stoke on Trent ST1 5BD. *T:* 0845 111 7777, *Fax:* 0845 111 8888. *E:* arthurjeffsmith@gmail.com.

SMITH, Prof. Austin Gerard, PhD; FRS 2006; FRSE; MRC Professor of Stem Cell Biology, and Director, Wellcome Trust Centre for Stem Cell Research, University of Cambridge, since 2006. *Educ:* Univ. of Oxford (BA). FRSE 2003. University of Edinburgh: Prof. of Stem Cell Biol.; Dir, BBSRC Centre for Genome Res., 1998; Dir, MRC Centre of Develt in Stem Cell Biol.; Chm., Inst. for Stem Cell Res., 2005–06. Louis-Jeantet Prize for Medicine, 2010. *Publications:* articles in learned jls. *Address:* Wellcome Trust Centre for Stem Cell Research, University of Cambridge, Tennis Court Road, Cambridge CB2 1QR.

SMITH, Barney; *see* Smith, L. B.

SMITH, Prof. Barry Edward, PhD; Head of Nitrogen Fixation Laboratory, 1987–2000, Associate Research Director, 1994–2000, Leverhulme Fellow, 2001–03, John Innes Centre (formerly AFRC Institute of Plant Science Research); *b* 15 Nov. 1939; *s* of late Ernest Smith and Agnes Mary Smith (*née* DeFraine); *m* 1963, Pamela Heather Pullen; one *s* one *d.* *Educ:* Dr Challoner's Grammar Sch., Amersham; Royal Melbourne Tech. Coll., Australia; Hatfield Tech. Coll.; Univ. of Exeter (BSc); Univ. of East Anglia (PhD). Lab. technician, ICIANZ, 1956–59; ICI, 1959–60; res. appts, Univ. of Washington, Seattle, 1966–68, Univ. of Oxford, 1968–69; ARC, subseq. AFRC, Unit of Nitrogen Fixation, 1969–87; Asst Dir, 1986–87. Vis. Prof., Univ. of Essex, 1988–98; Hon. Professorial Fellow, Univ. of Sussex, 1989–95; Hon. Prof., UEA, 1995–. *Publications:* numerous articles in sci. jls and chapters in books on excited state chem., nitrogen fixation and on denitrification. *Address:* 61 Church Lane, Eaton, Norwich NR4 6NY.

SMITH, Bartholomew Evan Eric; Chairman, Amber Foundation, since 1994; *b* 1 Feb. 1955; *s* of Sir John (Lindsay Eric) Smith, CH, CBE and of Christian Margaret Smith, OBE; *m* 1987, Catherine, *d* of Gavin and Mary Rowan Hamilton; three *s* one *d.* *Educ:* Eton Coll.; New Coll., Oxford. Littlemore Scientific Engrg Co., 1976–84; Dir, Lundy Co. Ltd, 1984–;

Chairman: Smith Hamilton Ltd, 1989–; Coexis Ltd, 1990–2005 (Dir, 1985–2008); White Waltham Airfield Ltd, 1992–. Chm., Landmark Trust, 1995–2001. *Recreations:* flying, farming. *Address:* Garden House, Cornwall Gardens, SW7 4BQ; Shottesbrooke Farm, White Waltham, Berks SL6 3SD. *E:* b@rtysmith.com. *Clubs:* Pratt's, MCC; West London Aero (White Waltham).

SMITH, Prof. Bernard Geoffrey Norman, PhD; FDSRCS, FDSRCSE; Professor Emeritus, Guy's, King's and St Thomas' Dental Institute (formerly United Medical and Dental Schools), London University, at Guy's Hospital (Professor, and Head, Division of Conservative Dentistry, 1991–2003); *b* 23 Sept. 1938; *s* of Roland and Dora Smith; *m* 1962, Susan Greenwood; one *s* one *d. Educ:* University Coll. London (BDS 1963); Univ. of Michigan (MSc 1968); PhD London Hosp. Dental Sch. 1974. FDSRCS 1970; MRD RCS 1994; FDSRCSE 1995. Lectr, London Hosp. Dental Sch., 1968–75; Senior Lecturer and Hon. Consultant: Royal Dental Hosp., London, 1975–83; UMDS, Guy's Hosp., 1983–91. Hon. Consultant to the Army, 1982–. *Publications:* Planning and Making Crowns and Bridges, 1986, 4th edn 2006; (jtly) Clinical Handling of Dental Materials, 1986, 2nd edn 1995; (jtly) Pickard's Manual of Operative Dentistry, 6th edn 1990 to 8th edn 2003; contrib. papers to restorative and conservative dentistry jls. *Recreations:* rebuilding and restoring old houses, making furniture. *Address:* 175 Clapham Road, SW9 0QE. *T:* (020) 7274 8464, *Fax:* (020) 7924 9447. *E:* bernard.g.smith@talk21.com.

SMITH, Beverley; *see* Smith, Jenkyn B.

SMITH, Bob and Roberta; *see* Brill, P.

SMITH, Sir Brian; *see* Smith, Sir E. B.

SMITH, Sir Brian; *see* Smith, Sir N. B.

SMITH, Brian, CPFA; Chief Executive, Stoke on Trent City Council, 1992–2002; *b* 16 May 1947; *s* of Albert Frederick and Gladys Smith; *m* 1972, Susan Jane Lund; two *s. Educ:* Bristol Univ. (BA Hons). Graduate trainee accountant, Derbyshire CC, 1968; Accountancy Asst, Berkshire CC, 1972; Group Technical Officer, South Yorkshire CC, 1974; Asst County Treasurer, Dorset CC, 1976; Sen. Asst County Treasurer, Avon CC, 1979; Dep. County Treasurer, 1981, County Treasurer, 1983, Staffordshire CC. Chm., Surrey Ambulance NHS Trust, 2004–06 (non-exec. Dir, 2003–04); non-exec. Dir, Surrey PCT, 2006–11. Chm., Inst. of Public Finance Ltd, 2004–11. Public Mem., Network Rail, 2011–14. Hon. Sec., Soc. of County Treasurers, 1990–92; Hon. Treasurer: CIPFA, 2001–04 (Vice-Pres., 1998–99; Pres., 1999–2000); UNICEF UK, 2002–11. *Publications:* various articles in local govt finance jls. *Recreations:* music, gardening, travel.
See also T. J. Smith.

SMITH, Ven. Brian; Archdeacon of the Isle of Man, 2005–11, now Emeritus; *b* 15 July 1944; *s* of William Charles Freeman Smith and Frances Smith; *m* 1967, Christine Ann Masterman; one *s* one *d. Educ:* Preston Grammar Sch., Lancs; Barton Peveril Grammar Sch., Eastleigh, Hants; Salisbury and Wells Theol Coll.; Westminster Coll., Oxford (MTh 1995). In commerce and industry, 1960–71. Ordained deacon, 1974, priest, 1975; Curate, St Thomas, Pennywell with St Oswald, Grindon, Sunderland, 1974–77; Chaplain, RAF, 1977–95; Vicar, St John, Keswick, 1995–2005; RD, Derwent, 1998–2005; Priest-in-charge, St Bridget, Bridekirk, 2002–04; Vicar, St George, Douglas, 2005–11. Mem., Gen. Synod, C of E, 2005–11. Hon. Canon, Carlisle Cathedral, 1999–2005. *Recreations:* walking, golf, DIY. *Address:* The Coach House, The Street, Westward, Wigton, Cumbria CA7 8AF.

SMITH, Rt Rev. Brian Arthur; Bishop of Edinburgh, 2001–11; *b* 15 Aug. 1943; *s* of late Arthur and Doris Marion Smith; *m* 1970, Elizabeth Berring (*née* Hutchinson); two *d. Educ:* George Heriot's School, Edinburgh; Edinburgh Univ. (MA Mental Philosophy 1966); Fitzwilliam Coll., Cambridge (BA Theology 1968; MA 1972); Westcott House, Cambridge; Jesus Coll., Cambridge (MLitt 1973). Curate of Cuddesdon, 1972–79; Tutor in Doctrine, Cuddesdon Coll., Oxford, 1972–75; Dir of Studies, Ripon Coll., Cuddesdon, 1975–78, Senior Tutor 1978–79; Diocese of Wakefield: Priest-in-charge of Cragg Vale, 1979–85; Dir of In-Service Training, 1979–81; Dir of Ministerial Trng, 1981–87; Warden of Readers, 1981–87; Sec. of Dio. Board of Ministry, 1979–87; Hon. Canon of Wakefield, 1981–87; Proctor in Convocation, 1985–87; Archdeacon of Craven, 1987–93; Bp Suffragan of Tonbridge, 1993–2001. Hon. Lectr, St Augustine's Theol Sch., Botswana, 2013, 2015. Vice-Chairman, Northern Ordination Course, 1985–93. Chm., Churches Together in Kent, 1999–2001; Vice-Pres., Modern Church (formerly Modern Churchpeople's Union), 2009–. Mem., Scotland Cttee, UNESCO, 2008–. Dir, Waverley Care, 2002–11. Gov., Loretto Sch., 2012–; Trustee, St Mary's Music Sch., 2010–. A Director, Scottish Jl of Theology, 1977–81. *Recreations:* browsing in junk shops, walking, reading, music, short-wave radio listening. *Address:* Flat E, 2A Dean Path, Edinburgh EH4 3BA. *T:* (0131) 220 6097. *E:* bishopsmith@btinternet.com. *Club:* New (Edinburgh).

SMITH, Brian Stanley, FSA, FRHistS; Secretary, Royal Commission on Historical Manuscripts, 1982–92; *b* 15 May 1932; *s* of late Ernest Stanley Smith and Dorothy (*née* Palmer); *m* 1963, Alison Margaret Hemming; two *d. Educ:* Bloxham; Keble College, Oxford (Holroyd Scholar). MA 1957. FSA 1972, FRHistS 1980. Archivist, Worcestershire, 1956–58, Essex, 1958–60, Gloucestershire, 1961–68; County Archivist, Gloucestershire, 1968–79; Asst Sec., Royal Commn on Historical Manuscripts, 1980–81. Part-time Editor, Victoria County History of Gloucestershire, 1968–70; Editor, Bristol and Gloucestershire Archaeological Soc., 1971–79 (Pres., 1986–87). Chm., Soc. of Archivists, 1979–80; Vice Pres., British Records Assoc., 1993–2005; Chm., Herefords Victoria County History Trust, 1997–2007; Pres., Woolhope Club, Herefords, 2001–02. Lay Mem., Gloucester Diocesan Synod, 1972–76. *Publications:* History of Malvern, 1964, 2nd edn 1978; (with Elizabeth Ralph) History of Bristol and Gloucestershire, 1972, 3rd edn 1996; The Cotswolds, 1976, 2nd edn 1992; History of Bloxham School, 1978; Manuscript Sources for the History of St Helena, 1996; Herefordshire Maps 1577–1800, 2004, supplement 2012; Turnastone, 2010; articles in learned jls on local history and archives. *Recreation:* hill-walking. *Address:* Bryn Farm, Vowchurch Common, Hereford HR2 0RL.

SMITH, Brian William, AO 1988; PhD, FIEAust; Vice-Chancellor and Professor, University of Western Sydney, 1989–94; *b* 24 June 1938; *s* of William Lyle Smith and Grace Ellen Smith; *m* 1961, Josephine Peden; two *d* (one *s* decd). *Educ:* Univ. of Melbourne (BEng); Univ. of Cambridge (PhD). Australian Paper Manufacturers Ltd, 1964–70; Consolidated Electronic Industries Ltd, 1971–73; Head, School of Electrical Engineering, 1973–77, Dean, Faculty of Engineering, 1977–79, Dir, 1979–89, Royal Melbourne Inst. of Technology. Chairman of Board: UniSuper Ltd, 1994–2006; Cooperative Res. Centre for Intelligent Manufg Systems and Technologies, 1995–2006. Hon. LLD Hong Kong Baptist Univ., 1999. *Recreations:* music, golf, writing. *Address:* 60 Faraday Street, Carlton, Vic 3053, Australia. *Clubs:* Greenacres Golf, Melbourne Cricket.

SMITH, Dr Bruce Gordon, CBE 1999 (OBE 1992); FREng, FIET; Chairman, Smith Institute for Industrial Mathematics and System Engineering, since 1993; *b* 4 Oct. 1939; *s* of William Francis Smith and Georgina Lucy May Smith (*née* Tompkins); *m* 1964, Rosemary Jane Martineau (*d* 2007); two *s* two *d. Educ:* Dulwich Coll.; Christ Church, Oxford (BA 1st cl. Hons Physics 1961; DPhil 1964; MA 1968). FIET (FIEE 1978; MIEE 1971); FREng (FEng 1998). Res. Associate, Univ. of Chicago, 1964–65; mem., tech. staff, Bellcomm Inc., 1965–68; Prin. Engr, Decca Radar Ltd, 1968–71; Man. Dir, 1971–87, Chm., 1987–97, Smith System Engineering Ltd; Chairman: Industrial Technology Securities Ltd, 1995– (Dir, 1985–95); Univ. of Southampton Hldgs Ltd, 2001–06; Imagineer Systems Ltd, 2002–14; Director: Gordon and Co., 1996–; British Maritime Technology Ltd, 1996–99; Southampton Innovations Ltd, 1998–2003; Esys Ltd, 1999–2001; Innovision Res. and Technol. plc, 2001–04; Southampton Asset Mgt Ltd, 2002–03; IPGroup (formerly IP2IPO Gp) plc, 2002–15 (Chm., 2007–15); Orbital Optics Ltd, 2006–09; Mirriad Ltd, 2010–14; Oregan Networks Ltd, 2011–. Domus Fellow, St Catherine's Coll., Oxford, 1991–. Chm., ESRC, 1994–2001; Member: Plenary Bd, RAE, 1987–91; BNSC Earth Observation Prog. Bd, 1986–2001 (Chm., 1998–2001); Exec. Cttee, Parly Space Cttee, 1989–97; Industrial R&D Adv. Cttee, EC, 1996–99; Chm., UK Industrial Space Cttee, 1992–94. Chm., Eur. Assoc. of Remote Sensing Cos, 1987–91 (Treas., British Assoc., 1985–95); Pres., Assoc. of Ind. Res. and Technol. Orgns, 1991–93; UK Deleg. and Pres., Eur. Assoc. of Contract Res. Orgns, 1995–97; Member: Council, SBAC, 1992–94; Bd, British Antarctic Survey, 2001–07. Chm., Nat. Space Sci. Centre, 1997–2005. Vice-Chm., Surrey Br., Business Div., Prince's Trust, 1991–2002; Chm., Rainbow Seed Fund, 2002–13; Trustee: Gordon Foundn, 1997–; Radio Communications Foundn, 2003–08. Vice-Chm. of Council, Southampton Univ., 2001–05 (Mem. Council, 2000–06); Gov., ICSTM, 1999–2005. Pres., Alleyn Club, 2011–12. Hon. Fellow, Inst. of Mathematics and its Applications, 2010. Hon. DSc Leicester, 2001. *Recreations:* mountain walking, dinghy sailing, cycling, music. *Address:* 11 Oxdowne Close, Cobham, Surrey KT11 2SZ. *T:* (01372) 843526. *Club:* Athenæum.

SMITH, Catherine; MP (Lab) Lancaster and Fleetwood, since 2015; *b* Barrow-in-Furness, 16 July 1985; *d* of Alan and Joyce Smith. *Educ:* Lancaster Univ. (BA Hons Gender and Sociol. 2006). Campaigns and Policy Officer, British Assoc. of Social Workers, 2011–15. Contested (Lab) Wyre and Preston N, 2010. *Address:* House of Commons, SW1A 0AA. *T:* (020) 7219 6001. *E:* cat.smith.mp@parliament.uk.

SMITH, Cecil Raymond Julian H.; *see* Humphery-Smith.

SMITH, Ceri Ivor Daniel; Director, Shareholder Executive, Department for Business, Innovation and Skills, since 2013; *b* Greenwich, 23 April 1973; *s* of Lawrence F. T. Smith, OBE and Judith M. Smith; *m* 2002, Jessica Mary Lovell; two *s* one *d. Educ:* Emmanuel Coll., Cambridge (BA Soc. and Pol Scis 1995). Academic Affairs Officer, Students' Union, Univ. of Cambridge, 1995–96; HM Treasury, 1996–2003; DTI, 2003–04; HM Treasury, 2004–07; Dir, Business Envmt Unit, BERR, 2007–09; Department for Business, Innovation and Skills: Dir, New Industry, New Jobs, 2009–10; Dir, Business Envmt and Growth and Dir, Office of Life Scis, 2010–11; Dir, Labour Mkt, 2011–13. Gov., Acland Burghley Sch., London, 2005–. *Recreation:* my family. *E:* ceri.smith@bis.gsi.gov.uk.

SMITH, Sir Charles B.; *see* Bracewell-Smith.

SMITH, Charles M.; *see* Miller Smith.

SMITH, (Charles) Philip, MBE 2000; ARCA; book-art maker; Proprietor, Philip Smith Book Arts, since 1961; *b* 10 June 1928; *s* of Henry Mason Smith and Emily Mary Mildon Smith (*née* Pennington); *m* 1957, Dorothy Mary Weighill; three *s. Educ:* Ackworth Sch. (Soc. of Friends), Yorks; Southport Sch. of Art and Crafts; Royal Coll. of Art (ARCA 1st Cl. Hons 1954). Nat. Service, RAF, 1946–49. Teacher of drawing, modelling and bookbinding, Malvern Sch. of Art, 1955–57; Asst to Sydney Cockerell (rare-book conservator), 1957–61. Ed., The New Bookbinder (internat. jl), 1980–95. Dir of Studies in Graphic Design (pt-time), NE London Poly., 1961–71. Inventor: maril (use of leather waste), UK patent, 1969; Lap-Back book structure, US and UK patents, 1992. Mem., BM Team Florence Flood Disaster, 1966–67. Fellow, Designer Bookbinders, 1957 (Pres., 1977–79; Hon. Fellow, 2012); Mem., Soc. of Bookbinders, 1991–; MCSD (MSIAD 1972). Mem., Soc. for Study of Normal Psychol., 1955–. Hon. Member: Meister der Einbandkunst, 1971; Center for Book Arts, NY, 1984; Canadian Bookbinders and Book Artists Guild, 1987. Work in exhibns internationally; solo exhibn of works in London and Switzerland, 1971, and US/Canadian collections, Portland, Oregon, Bloomington, Indiana; *work in collections:* Royal Collection; BL; V&A Mus.; Royal Coll., Holland; NY Public Liby, Spencer Coll.; Harry Ransome Humanities Res. Center, Univ. of Texas; Marriott Liby, Salt Lake City; Lilly Liby, Indiana, and other public and private collections worldwide. 1st Open Prize, Thomas Harrison Meml Comp., 1957; Gold Medals: 2nd Internat. Bienal, São Paulo, 1972; EEC Bookbinding Comp., 1993; Silver Medal: Paris Internat. Comp., 1992; 1st and 2nd Internat. Comps for Book as Art, Italy, 1998 and 2002; 1st Prize, Czech Republic Bookbinding Art, 2004. *Publications:* The Lord of the Rings and Other Bookbindings of Philip Smith, 1970; New Directions in Bookbinding, 1974; The Book: art and object, 1982; contrib. articles and introdns to many books, exhibn catalogues, etc. *Recreations:* non-duality philosophy (Oneness of All), creation of visual metaphors, writing, inventing, painting, table-tennis. *Address:* The Book House, The Street, Yatton Keynell, Chippenham, Wilts SN14 7BH. *T:* and *Fax:* (01249) 782597. *E:* philipsmithbookart@gmail.com.

SMITH, Charles Robert S.; *see* Saumarez Smith.

SMITH, Chloe; MP (C) Norwich North, since July 2009; *b* May 1982; *d* of David and Claire Smith; *m* 2013, Sandy McFadzean. *Educ:* Univ. of York (BA Hons 1st Class Eng. Lit.). Mgt Consultant, Deloitte, until 2009. An Asst Govt Whip, 2010–11; Economic Sec., HM Treasury, 2011–12; Parly Under-Sec. of State, Cabinet Office, 2012–13. *Address:* House of Commons, SW1A 0AA.

SMITH, Dr Christopher, FRCPath; science broadcaster and writer; Consultant Clinical Virologist, University of Cambridge, since 2011; Fellow, Queens' College, Cambridge, since 2006; *b* Chelmsford, 16 Jan. 1975; *s* of Geoffrey Smith and Jacqueline Smith; *m* 2003, Dr Sarah Urquhart; one *s* one *d. Educ:* Felsted Sch.; King Edward VI Grammar Sch., Chelmsford; London Hosp. Med. Coll.; University Coll. London (BSc Neurosci. 1996); Trinity Coll., Cambridge (MB BChir 2001; PhD 2001). FRCPath 2010. Surgical House Officer, Broomfield Hosp., 2001–02; Med. House Officer, Addenbrooke's Hosp., Cambridge, 2002; Med. SHO, Hammersmith Hosp., 2003; Registrar and Clinical Lectr in Virol., Univ. of Cambridge, 2003–11. Founder and Man. Editor, The Naked Scientist, 2001–; Man. Dir, Naked Science Ltd, 2008–. Weekly broadcasts on BBC Radio 5 Live and on Australian and S African radio. Vice Pres., Public Understanding of Sci., Genetics Soc., 2011–. *Publications:* Naked Science, 2006; The Naked Scientist, 2006; Return of the Naked Scientists, 2008; (with Dave Ansell) Crisp Packet Fireworks, 2008; Stripping Down Science, 2010; Everyday Life Under the Microscope, 2012; The Naked Scientist, 2013. *Recreations:* walking, four-wheel drive excursions, reading. *Address:* The Naked Scientists, Institute of Continuing Education, University of Cambridge, Madingley Hall, Cambridge CB23 8AQ. *T:* (01223) 761756, *Fax:* 07092 019697. *E:* chris@thenakedscientists.com.

SMITH, Christopher Brian P.; *see* Powell-Smith.

SMITH, Christopher Frank; QC 2009; *b* Leicester, 3 Dec. 1964; *s* of John Christopher Smith and Isabel Mary Smith; *m* 1995, Natalie Louise McGowan; one *d. Educ:* Oundle Sch.; Southampton Univ. (LLB 1st class Hons). Called to the Bar, Inner Temple, 1989; CEDR Accredited Mediator, 2007. *Publications:* (contrib.) Seafarer's Rights, 2005; (ed jtly) Scrutton on Charterparties and Bills of Lading, 21st edn 2008 to 22nd edn 2011. *Recreations:* carriage driving, riding, sailing. *Address:* Essex Court Chambers, 24 Lincoln's Inn Fields, WC2A 3EG. *T:* (020) 7813 8000, *Fax:* (020) 7813 8080. *E:* csmith@essexcourt.net. *Club:* Royal London Yacht.

SMITH, Rev. Christopher Hughes; Supernumerary Methodist Minister; President of the Methodist Conference, 1985–86; *b* 30 Nov. 1929; *s* of Rev. Bernard Hughes Smith and Dorothy Lucy Smith; *m* 1956, Margaret Jean Smith (*d* 2011); three *s* and one foster *s*. *Educ:* Bolton School; Emmanuel College and Wesley House, Cambridge. MA Cantab. Intercollegiate Sec., SCM, 1955–58; ordained at Methodist Conf., Newcastle upon Tyne, 1958; Leicester South Methodist Circuit, 1958–65; Birmingham South-West Methodist Circuit, 1965–74; Chm., Birmingham Methodist Dist, 1974–87; Lancaster Methodist Circuit, 1987–88; Gen. Sec., Div. of Educn and Youth, Methodist Ch, 1988–95. Pres., Nat. Christian Educn Council, 1995–99. Mem. Court, Univ. of Surrey, Roehampton, 2000–04. Hon. Fellow: Selly Oak Colls, 1992; Roehampton Inst., 1997; Southlands Coll., Roehampton Univ., 2004. Hon. MA Birmingham, 1985. *Publications:* (contrib.) Queen's Sermons, 1973; Music of the Heart—Methodist Spirituality, 1991; (contrib.) A Dictionary of Methodism, 2000; (contrib.) Reflections on Ministry, 2004; contribs to Methodist Recorder, Epworth Review, Ichthus. *Recreations:* gardening, music, books, walking. *Address:* 12 Spean Court, Wollaton Road, Nottingham NG8 1GL.

SMITH, Christopher John Addison, CBE 2013; FCA; Chief of Staff to Archbishop of Canterbury, 2003–13; *b* 30 March 1949; *s* of Rev. Canon Anthony Cecil Addison Smith and Muriel Patricia Addison Smith; *m* 1973, Nina Jane Perry; two *d*. *Educ:* Univ. of East Anglia (BA Hons). FCA 1980. With Price Waterhouse, London, 1970–93, Human Resources Partner, 1989–93; Gen. Sec., Diocese of London, 1993–99; Gen. Manager, C. Hoare & Co. Bankers, 1999–2003. Mem., Gen. Synod, Church of England, 1995–2000. Vice Chm. Govs, Southwark Coll. of Further Educn, 1987–94; Dep. Chm. Govs, James Allen's Girls' Sch., 1994–2004. Hon. Treas., Holy Trinity Brompton, 1974–91. Chm. Council, St John's Coll., Nottingham, 2014–; Member: Council, Corp. of Church Hse, 2014–; Bd, Send A Cow UK, 2014–; Bd, Abbeyfield Homes, 2015– (Chm., Audit Cttee, 2015–); Treas., Gordon Russell Design Museum, 2014–. Trustee, St Martin-in-the-Fields Charity, 2014–. *Recreations:* theatre, music, reading, railways. *Club:* Reform.

SMITH, Rev. Canon Christopher Milne; Vicar of the Minster Church of St George, Doncaster, 2002–10; Chaplain to the Queen, 2004–14; *b* 7 Sept. 1944; *s* of Alastair Gordon Smith and Marjorie Boulton Smith; *m* 1971, Christine Wright; three *s* one *d*. *Educ:* Selwyn Coll., Cambridge (BA (Theol.) 1966, MA 1970); Cuddesdon Theol Coll. Ordained deacon, 1969, priest, 1970; Curate, Our Lady and St Nicholas, Liverpool, 1969–74; Team Vicar, St Andrew's, Tower Hill, Kirkby, 1974–81; Rector, St Mary's, Walton-on-the-Hill, Liverpool, 1981–91; Canon Residentiary, Sheffield Cathedral, 1991–2002 (Hon. Canon, 2003–). Advr on the Paranormal to Bishop of Sheffield, 1997–2004. *Recreations:* contract bridge, gardening, philately. *Address:* 14 Ravensdowne, Berwick-upon-Tweed, Northumberland TD15 1HX. *T:* (01289) 330735. *E:* smith@revcm.fsnet.co.uk.

SMITH, Christopher Shaw G.; *see* Gibson-Smith.

SMITH, Claire Helen; HM Diplomatic Service, retired; Director, CH Smith Consulting Ltd, since 2014; *b* 23 Dec. 1956; *d* of late Norman Eric Stubbs and Helen Evelyn Stubbs; *m* 1986, Michael Forbes Smith, *qv*; one *s* one *d*. *Educ:* Queen Mary Coll., London (BA Hons 1979); Open Univ. (Postgrad. Cert. Business Admin 2008). FCO 1979; Second Sec., Peking, 1983; First Sec., FCO, 1985; Credit Suisse, Zurich, 1990–94; seconded to Auswärtiges Amt, Bonn, 1994–97; First Sec., Bonn, 1997–99; Counsellor, Islamabad, 1999–2001; on loan to Assessments Staff, Cabinet Office, 2001–04; Hd, Whitehall Liaison Dept, FCO, 2004–07. Non-exec. Dir, Mott Macdonald Gp Ltd, 2008–12. Vis. Prof., UEA London, 2011–13. Mem., Security Vetting Appeals Panel, 2009–. Mem., St Laurence Educnl Trust (formerly Abbot's Adv. Cttee), Ampleforth Coll., 2010–. Gov., Curwen Primary Sch., Plaistow, London E13, 2008–13 (Chair of Govs, 2009–11). *Recreations:* reading detective novels, travel. *Club:* Royal Over-Seas League.

SMITH, Clive Adrian S.; *see* Stafford Smith.

SMITH, Colin Deverell, OBE 2011; Chairman, Poundland Group Holdings (formerly Poundland Holdings), 2002–12 (non-executive Director, 2012–14); *b* 21 May 1947; *m* 1971, Kathy Morgan; two *s*. *Educ:* All Saints Sch., Bloxham, Banbury; Liverpool Univ. (BCom 1969). FCA 1973. Qualified with Arthur Andersen, Manchester; Argyll Foods: Gp Financial Controller and Co. Sec., 1979–83; Argyll Gp, subseq. Safeway plc: Gp Financial Controller and Co. Sec., 1983–84; Dir, 1984–99; Finance Dir, 1989–93; Gp Chief Exec., 1993–99. Chairman: Blueheath Hldgs (formerly Blue Heath Direct), 2000–06; Masstock Gp Hldgs, 2007–08; Assured Food Standards, 2003–09; non-executive Director: McBride plc, 2002–11; Hilton Food Gp plc, 2010–. Trustee, SCF, 2001–05; Chair of Trustees, Challenge Network, 2012–. *Recreations:* Rugby, travel, walking, military history, interesting vehicles.

SMITH, Prof. Colin John, CBE 1997; Professor of Oral Pathology, Sheffield University, 1973–2003, now Emeritus (Dean of Dental Studies, School of Clinical Dentistry, 1978–84 and 1988–2000; Deputy Dean, Faculty of Medicine, 2000–02); *b* 7 June 1938; *s* of Rowland William John Smith and Doris Emily Smith (*née* Lover); *m* 1st, 1962, Mary Margaret Kathrine MacMahon (marr. diss. 1995); three *d*; 2nd, 1995, Eunice Turner (*née* Acaster). *Educ:* Purley County Grammar Sch. for Boys; Royal Dental Hosp. Sch. of Dental Surgery, Univ. of London (BDS Hons, PhD). FDSRCS, FRCPath. House Surgeon, Royal Dental Hosp., 1961–62; MRC Scientific Asst, 1962–63, Prophit Cancer Res. Student, 1964–68, Dept of Dental Sci., RCS; Wellcome Travelling Res. Fellow, Dept of Oral Path., Royal Dental Coll., Copenhagen, 1968–69; Nuffield Dental Res. Fellow, Dept of Morbid Anatomy, RPMS, 1969–71; Sen. Lectr and Res. Fellow, Dept of Oral Medicine and Path., Guy's Hosp. Dental Sch., 1971–72; Dir, Charles Clifford Dental Hosp., Central Sheffield Univ. Hosps NHS Trust, 1998–2001. Charles Tomes Lectr, RCS, 1987. Member: GDC, 1979–84, 1994–2003 (Chm., Dental Auxiliaries Cttee, 1999–2003; Mem., Fitness to Practise Cttee, 2003–11; Co-Chair, Panel of Visitors to Dental Schs, 2003–05); Nuffield Foundn Cttee of Inquiry into Dental Educn, 1978–80; Nuffield Foundn Cttee of Inquiry into Educn and Trng of Personnel Auxiliary to Dentistry, 1992–93; MRC Dental Cttee, 1973–84 (Scientific Sec., 1975–84) and Physiological Systems and Disorders Bd, 1988–92; MRC/DHSS/SERC Joint Dental Cttee, 1988–93 (Vice-Chm.); Council, Odontological Sect., RSocMed, 1973–76 and 1989–92 (Pres., 1990–91); Dental Educn Adv. Council, 1978–2000 (Hon. Sec., 1985–90; Chm., 1990–92); British Soc. for Oral Pathology, 1975– (Pres., 1980–81; Life Mem., 2007); Internat. Assoc. of Oral Pathologists, 1983– (Mem. Council, 1988–2004; Pres., 2000–02; Hon. Life Mem., 2006–); Assoc. for Dental Educn in Europe, 1982–2004 (Sec. Gen., 1984–87; Editor, 1989–92); Internat. Assoc. for Dental Res., 1963–2004 (Internat. Relns Cttee, 1982–84; Ethics Cttee, 1992–95); UGC Dental Sub-Cttee, 1985–89; UGC Dental Review Working Party, 1986–88; UFC Medical Cttee, 1989–92; British Council Medical Adv. Cttee, 1985–91; Standing Dental Adv. Cttee, 1992–96; Clinical Standards Adv. Gp, 1995–99; CVCP Task Force on Clin. Acad. Careers, 1996–98; WHO Expert Adv. Panel on Oral Health, 1989–98. Ed.-in-chief, Jl of Oral Pathology and Medicine, 1993–99. Hon. Treasurer, Alpine Garden Soc., 2003–11 (Ferrier Charlton Award, 2011). Hon. Mem., Hungarian Dental Assoc., 1991. Founder FMedSci 1998. Hon. DSc Sheffield, 2004. Colgate Prize, British Div., Internat. Assoc. for Dental Res., 1964. *Publications:* (jtly) Oral Cancer: epidemiology, etiology and pathology, 1990; (jtly) Histological typing of cancer and precancer of the oral mucosa, 1997; chapters in books and contribs to professional jls. *Recreations:* lawn tennis, walking, gardening, listening to classical music, theatre. *Address:* Hooper House, Playing Fields Lane, Elmley Road, Ashton-under-Hill, Evesham WR11 7RF. *T:* (01386) 881281. *Club:* Royal Society of Medicine.

SMITH, His Honour Colin Milner; QC 1985; a Circuit Judge, 1991–2009; *b* 2 Nov. 1936; *s* of late Alan Milner Smith and Vera Ivy Smith; *m* 1979, Moira Soraya, *d* of late Reginald Braybrooke; one *s* one *d*. *Educ:* Tonbridge; Brasenose College, Oxford (MA); Univ. of Chicago (JD). Called to the Bar, Gray's Inn, 1962; a Recorder, 1987–91. *Publications:* (jtly) The Law of Betting, Gaming and Lotteries, 1987. *Recreations:* cricket, ski-ing, reading. *Clubs:* MCC, Roehampton.

SMITH, Colin Roderick, CVO 1984; CBE 1995; QPM 1987; an appeals commissioner, 2001–11; HM Inspector of Constabulary, 1991–2000; *s* of Humphrey and Marie Smith; *m* 1961, Patricia Joan Coppin. *Educ:* Dorking County and Bexhill Grammar Schools; Univ. of Birmingham (BSocSc, Hons Social Admin.); rcds 1981. Royal Army Service Corps (Lieut), 18 Co. (Amph), 1959–62; East Sussex Constabulary, later Sussex Police, from Constable to Chief Supt, 1962–77; Asst Chief Constable, Thames Valley Police, 1977–82; Dep. Asst Comr, Metropolitan Police, 1982–85 (incl. founder, Royalty and Diplomatic Protection Dept); Chief Constable, Thames Valley Police, 1985–91. Mem., Police Authority, UKAEA Constabulary, 2000–05. With Sir John Chilcot, review of N Ireland nat. security, 2002–03. Advr to Chm. Council, SSAFA, 2012– (Caseworker, 2001–11; Dorset Chm., 2005–11; Trustee, 2006–11; W of England Regl Rep., 2006–11; Chm., Nat. Br. Support Cttee, 2006–09; Hon. Life Mem., 2011; Dorset Vice-Pres., 2012). *Recreation:* walking.

SMITH, Cyril Stanley, CBE 1985; MSc, PhD; Secretary to Economic and Social Research Council (formerly Social Science Research Council), 1975–85; *b* 21 July 1925; *s* of Walter and Beatrice May Smith; *m* 1968, Eileen Cameron; two *d* (by first marr.). *Educ:* Plaistow Municipal Secondary Sch.; London Sch. of Economics. HM Forces, Dorset Regt, 1943–47. Univ. of Birmingham, 1950–51; Univ. of Sheffield, 1951–52; Dulwich Coll. Mission, 1952–56; Nat. Coal Board, 1956–61; Univ. of Manchester, 1961–71; Civil Service Coll., 1971–75. Man. Dir, ReStrat, 1985–90. Visiting Prof., Univ. of Virginia, 1965; Academic Visitor, Nuffield Coll., Oxford, 1980–81, 1985–86; Senior Res. Fellow, Wissenschaftszentrum Berlin für Sozialforschung, 1987. British Nat. Expert, European Poverty Prog., 1977–82. Mem., Sec. of State's Cttee on Inequalities in Health, DHSS, 1977–80. Chm., British Sociological Assoc., 1972–74; Pres., Sociol. Sect., British Assoc., 1979. *Publications:* Adolescence, 1968; (sen. author) The Wincroft Youth Project, 1972; (ed jtly) Society and Leisure in Britain, 1973; numerous articles on youth, leisure and developments in social science.

SMITH, Prof. David; *see* Smith, Anthony D.

SMITH, Prof. David, FRS 1988; CPhys, FInstP; Professor, Institute of Science and Technology in Medicine (formerly Department of Biomedical Engineering and Medical Physics), University of Keele, since 1999 (Visiting Professor, 1995–99); Director and Company Secretary, Trans Spectra Ltd, since 2001; *b* 26 Nov. 1935; *s* of J. and F. L. Smith. *Educ:* Keele Univ. (BA 1959); DSc 1975, PhD 1962, Birmingham Univ. FInstP 1973. Res. Fellow, 1962, Prof. of Chemical Physics, 1984–90, Birmingham Univ.; Prof. of Physics, Institut für Ionenphysik der Universität Innsbruck, Austria, 1991–95. Hon. DSc Keele, 1990. *Publications:* numerous res. pubns and review articles in physics, chemistry and astrophysics, for learned jls incl. British Inst. of Physics jls, Amer. Inst. of Physics jls, Breath Research, Analytical Chemistry. *Recreations:* classical music, sport. *Address:* 9 The Elms, Porthill, Newcastle-under-Lyme, Staffs ST5 8RP; Institute of Science and Technology in Medicine, University of Keele, Thornburrow Drive, Hartshill, Stoke-on-Trent, Staffs ST4 7QB.

SMITH, David Andrew; Director, SonVida Wine, since 2014; Manager, SonVida Vineyard, since 2014; *b* 5 March 1952; *s* of John and Patricia Smith; *m* 1996, Sonia Ruseler; one *s* one *d*, and two *s* from former marriage. *Educ:* Lincoln Coll., Oxford (BA Hons, MA Hons). Reuters Correspondent, Spain and Italy, 1975–78; Africa Correspondent, 1979–81, Middle East Correspondent, 1982–86, ITN; Channel 4 News: Diplomatic Correspondent, 1987–89; Moscow Correspondent, 1989–90; Washington Correspondent, 1991–2003. Dir, UN Office, Washington, 2004–06; Special Advr, UN, 2006–10; Dir, UN Office, Argentina, 2010–14. Vis. Prof., Univ. of Michigan, 1986–87. Member: Adv. Bd, OMFIF UK, 2014–; Bd, British Hospital, Argentina, 2014–; Bd, Conciencia NGO, Latin America, 2014–. Hon. Patron, VacProject, Lincoln Coll., Oxford, 2008–. RTS Award, 1983; NY TV Fest. Award, 2000. *Publications:* Mugabe: a biography, 1981; Prisoners of God: conflict of Arab and Israeli, 1987; Dream On: a memoir, 2010. *Recreations:* fatherhood, golf, study of wine. *Address:* 2670 Austria, 11A, 1425 Buenos Aires, Argentina. *E:* davidsmith.un@gmail.com. *Club:* Reform.

SMITH, David Arthur George, OBE 1996; Headmaster of Bradford Grammar School, 1974–96; *b* 17 Dec. 1934; *o s* of Stanley George and Winifred Smith, Bath, Somerset; *m* 1957, Jennifer, *o d* of John and Rhoda Anning, Launceston, Cornwall; one *s* two *d*. *Educ:* City of Bath Boys' Sch.; Balliol Coll., Oxford. MA, Dip. Ed (Oxon). Assistant Master, Manchester Grammar Sch., 1957–62; Head of History, Rossall School, 1963–70; Headmaster, The King's School, Peterborough, 1970–74. Chm., HMC, 1988. Mem., Parole Bd, 1995–2001. JP West Yorks, 1975–2003, Thames Valley, 2003–04. Chm., Woburn Parish Council, 2006–. *Publications:* (with John Thorn and Roger Lockyer) A History of England, 1961; Left and Right in Twentieth Century Europe, 1970; Russia of the Tsars, 1971. *Recreations:* writing, walking. *Club:* East India.

SMITH, David Buchanan, FSAScot; Sheriff of North Strathclyde at Kilmarnock, 1975–2001; *b* 31 Oct. 1936; *s* of William Adam Smith and Irene Mary Calderwood Hogarth; *m* 1961, Hazel Mary Sinclair; one *s* one *d* (and one *s* decd). *Educ:* Paisley Grammar Sch.; Glasgow Univ. (MA); Edinburgh Univ. (LLB). Harry Dalgety Scholarship, 1961, 1962. Advocate, 1961; Standing Junior Counsel to Scottish Educn Dept, 1968–75. Tutor, Faculty of Law, Univ. of Edinburgh, 1964–72. Res. Associate, Nat. Mus of Scotland, 2002–. Member Council: Stair Soc., 1994– (Vice Chm. Council, 1998–); Scottish Nat. Dictionary Assoc., 1994–2002; Sheriffs' Assoc., 1998–2001 (Treas., 1979–89; archivist, 1989–); Scottish Language Dictionaries, 2002–; Mem., Scottish Records Adv. Council, 2001–08. Trustee: The Scottish Curling Museum Trust, 1980–; Scottish Curling Trust (formerly Royal Caledonian Curling Club Charitable Trust); President: Ayr Curling Club, 1995–96; Eglinton County Curling Game, 2000–04. Lifetime Achievement Award, Royal Caledonian Curling Club, 2005. *Publications:* Curling: an illustrated history, 1981; The Roaring Game: memories of Scottish curling, 1985; (contrib.) The Laws of Scotland: Stair Memorial Encyclopedia, vol. 6, 1988; George Washington Wilson in Ayrshire, 1991; (contrib.) Atlas of Scottish History to 1707, 1996; (contrib.) Macphail, Sheriff Court Practice, 2nd edn 1999; (contrib.) Sport, Scotland and the Scots, 2000; (contrib.) Oxford Companion to Scottish History, 2001; (contrib.) Encyclopaedia of Traditional British Rural Sports, 2005; articles in Scots Law Times, Juridical Rev., Jl of Law Soc. of Scotland, Scottish Book Collector, The Medal, Rev. of Scottish Culture, Scottish Curler, Procs of Soc. of Antiquaries of Scotland, Book of the Old Edinburgh Club, and newspapers. *Recreations:* history of the law and institutions of Scotland, curling, collecting curliana, music, architecture, grandchildren. *Address:* 72 South Beach, Troon, Ayrshire KA10 6EG. *T:* (01292) 312130. *E:* dvdsmith1936@gmail.com.

SMITH, Prof. David Burton, PhD; Raymond Williams Research Professor in Cultural History of Wales, Swansea University, since 2005; Chair, Arts Council Wales, 2006–April 2016; *b* Tonypandy, Rhondda, 11 Feb. 1945; *s* of Burton Smith and Enid Wyn Smith (*née* Owen); *m* 1969, Norette Ann Wyson; three *s*. *Educ:* Porth Co. Sch.; Barry Grammar Sch.; Balliol Coll., Oxford (BA 1st Cl. Hons Hist. 1966); Columbia Univ., NYC (MA Comparative Lit. 1967); University Coll. of Swansea; PhD Wales 1976. Lecturer in History: Univ. of Lancaster, 1969–71; Univ. Coll. of Swansea, 1971–76; Lectr in Hist. of Wales, Univ. Coll., Cardiff, 1976–85; Personal Chair, Univ. of Wales, 1986–93; Simon Senior Fellow,

Manchester Univ., 1992–93; Ed., BBC Radio Wales, 1993; Hd of Progs, BBC Wales, 1994–2000; Pro-Vice-Chancellor, Univ. of Glamorgan, 2000–05. Presenter and writer, Wales! Wales?, BBC TV, 1984. Series Ed., Library of Wales, 2006–. *Publications:* (jtly) The Fed: history of South Wales miners in the 20th century, 1980; (jtly) Fields of Praise: official history of Welsh Rugby Union, 1980; Lewis Jones: writers of Wales, 1982; Wales! Wales?, 1984; Aneurin Bevan and the World of South Wales, 1993; Wales: a question for history, 1999; Raymond Williams: a warrior's tale, 2008; In the Frame: memory and society 1910–2010, 2010; Dream On, 2013. *Recreations:* watching Welsh club Rugby, collecting contemporary Welsh art, sea swimming, dog walking, drinking Languedoc wines. *Address:* Rockcliffe, 66 Redbrink Crescent, Barry Island, Vale of Glamorgan CF62 5TU. *T:* (01446) 721064. *E:* daibsmith@btinternet.com. *Club:* Pontypridd Rugby Football.
See also O. Smith.

SMITH, Sir David C.; *see* Calvert-Smith.

SMITH, Sir David (Cecil), Kt 1986; FRS 1975; FRSE; Principal and Vice-Chancellor, University of Edinburgh, 1987–93; President, Wolfson College, Oxford, 1994–2000; *b* 21 May 1930; *s* of William John Smith and Elva Emily Smith; *m* 1965, Lesley Margaret Mollison Mutch; two *s* one *d*. *Educ:* Colston's Sch., Bristol; St Paul's Sch., London; Queen's Coll., Oxford (Browne Schol., MA, DPhil; Hon. Fellow 2000). Christopher Welch Res. Schol., Oxford, 1951–54; Swedish Inst. Schol., Uppsala Univ., 1951–52; Browne Res. Fellow, Queen's Coll., Oxford, 1956–59; Harkness Fellow, Univ. Calif, Berkeley, 1959–60; Oxford University: Univ. Lectr, Dept Agric., 1960–74; Mem., Linacre Coll., 1962–64, Hon. Fellow, 1988; Royal Soc. Res. Fellow, 1964–71, Tutorial Fellow and Tutor for Admissions, 1971–74, Hon. Fellow, 1987, Wadham Coll.; Melville Wills Prof. of Botany, Bristol Univ., 1974–80; Sibthorpian Prof. of Rural Economy, and Fellow of St John's Coll., Oxford Univ., 1980–87. Vis. Prof., UCLA, 1968. Chairman: NERC Aquatic Life Scis Cttee, 1978–81; Member: AFRC (formerly ARC), 1982–88; Consultative Bd, JCO for Res. in Agric. and Food, 1981–83; SERC Science Board, 1983–85; Co-ordinating Cttee on Marine Sci. and Technology, 1987–91; ABRC, 1989–90; Commn on Scottish Educn, 1994–96. President: British Lichen Soc., 1972–74; British Mycological Soc., 1980; Soc. for Experimental Biol., 1983–85 (Vice-Pres., 1981–83); Internat. Soc. Endocytobiology, 1981–89; Scottish Assoc. for Marine Sci., 1994–2000; Linnean Soc., 2000–03. Royal Society: a Vice-Pres., 1978–80, 1983–87; Biological Sec., 1983–87. Bidder Lecture, Soc. for Experimental Biology, 1985; Sir Joseph Banks Lectures, Australian bicentennial, 1988; L. F. Power Meml Lecture, James Cook Univ., 1988. Editor and Trustee, New Phytologist, 1965–85. FRSE 1988. Hon. FRCPEd 1993; Hon. FRCSEd 1994. Hon. DSc: Liverpool, Exeter, 1986; Hull, 1987; Aberdeen, 1990; Napier, Heriot-Watt, 1993; Oxford Brookes, 1996; Hon. LLD: Pennsylvania, 1990; Queen's Univ., Ontario, 1991; Dr *hc* Edinburgh, 1994. Linnean Medal, Linnean Soc., 1989. Commendatore dell'Ordine al Merito della Repubblica Italiana, 1991; Comdr, Order of Merit, Republic of Poland, 1994. *Publications:* (with A. Douglas) The Biology of Symbiosis, 1987; various articles on symbiosis, in New Phytol., Proc. Royal Soc., Biol. Rev., etc. *Address:* 13 Abbotsford Park, Edinburgh EH10 5DZ.

SMITH, Air Marshal Sir David H.; *see* Harcourt-Smith.

SMITH, David Henry; Economics Editor, since 1989, Policy Adviser, since 1995, Assistant Editor, since 1998, The Sunday Times; *b* 3 April 1954; *s* of Charles Henry Smith and Elizabeth Mary Smith (*née* Williams), Walsall; *m* 1980, Jane Howells, Tenby; two *s* two *d*. *Educ:* West Bromwich Grammar Sch.; UC Cardiff (BSc Econ 1st cl. hons; Tassie Medallion, 1975); Worcester Coll., Oxford; Birkbeck Coll., London (MSc Econ). Economic report writer, Lloyds Bank, 1976–77; economist, Henley Centre for Forecasting, 1977–79; economics and business writer, Now! magazine, 1979–81; Asst Editor, Financial Weekly, 1981–84; Economics Corresp., The Times, 1984–89. Visiting Professor: Cardiff Univ., 2007–; Nottingham Univ., 2011–. Dir, UK Economics Ltd, 2011–. FRSA 1999. Wincott Sen. Financial Journalist of the Year, 2003; Econ. Commentator of Year, Editl Intelligence Comment Awards, 2013; Business Journalist of the Year, London Press Award, 2014. *Publications:* The Rise and Fall of Monetarism, 1987; Mrs Thatcher's Economics, 1988; North and South, 1989, 2nd edn 1994; From Boom to Bust, 1992, 2nd edn 1993; Mrs Thatcher's Economics: her legacy, 1992; UK Current Economic Policy, 1994, 2nd edn 1999; Job Insecurity *vs* Labour Market Flexibility, 1996; Eurofutures, 1997; Will Europe Work?, 1999; (ed) Welfare, Work and Poverty, 2000; Free Lunch, 2003, 2nd edn 2012; The Dragon and the Elephant: China, India and the new world order, 2007; The Age of Instability, 2010; Something Will Turn Up, 2015. *Recreations:* squash, golf, music, racketball, tennis. *Address:* 1 London Bridge Street, SE1 9GF. *T:* (020) 7782 5750. *E:* david@economicsuk.com. *Club:* Bexley Lawn Tennis and Squash.

SMITH, Sir David (Iser), KCVO 1990 (CVO 1977); AO 1986; BA; Director, Winston Churchill Memorial Trust, 1999–2013; Official Secretary to the Governor-General of Australia, 1973–90; Secretary of the Order of Australia, 1975–90; *b* 9 Aug. 1933; *s* of late W. M. Smith; *m* 1955, June F., *d* of late M. A. W. Forestier; three *s*. *Educ:* Scotch Coll., Melbourne; Melbourne Univ.; Australian National Univ., Canberra (BA). Commnd CMF, Melb. Univ. Regt, 1956. Entered Aust. Public Service, 1954; Dept of Customs and Excise, Melb., 1954–57; Trng Officer, Dept of the Interior, Canberra, 1957–58; Private Sec. to Minister for the Interior and Minister for Works, 1958–63; Exec. Asst to Sec., Dept of the Interior, 1963–66; Exec. Officer (Govt), Dept of the Interior, 1966–69; Sen. Adviser, Govt Br., Prime Minister's Dept, 1969–71; Sec., Federal Exec. Council, 1971–73; Asst Sec., Govt Br., Dept of the Prime Minister and Cabinet, 1972–73. Attached to The Queen's Household, Buckingham Palace, June–July 1975. Director: FAI Life Insurance Soc. Ltd, 1991–96; FAI Life Ltd, 1991–96. Australian National University: Vis. Fellow in Pol Sci., Res. Sch. of Social Scis, 1991–92; Vis. Fellow, 1998–99, Vis. Scholar, 2000–07, Faculty of Law. Dir, Canberra Symphony Orch., 1976–96 (Chm., 1991–93). Dir, Nat. Heart Foundn of Aust., 1991–97. Mem., Adv. Council, Old Parliament Hse, 2014–. Pres., Samuel Griffith Soc., 2006–10. Vice-Pres., Scout Assoc. of Australia, 1991–99 (Dist Comr, Capital Hill Dist, 1971–74). KStJ 1991 (CStJ 1974). *Publications:* Head of State: the Governor-General, the monarchy, the republic and the dismissal, 2005. *Recreations:* music, reading. *Address:* 1/36 Shackleton Circuit, Mawson, ACT 2607, Australia. *T:* (2) 62865094. *Club:* Commonwealth (Canberra).

SMITH, Rt Rev. David James; an Hon. Assistant Bishop, Diocese in Europe, and Diocese of York, since 2002; *b* 14 July 1935; *s* of Stanley James and Gwendolen Emie Smith; *m* 1961, Mary Hunter Moult; one *s* one *d*. *Educ:* Hertford Grammar School; King's College, London (AKC; FKC 1999). Assistant Curate: All Saints, Gosforth, 1959–62; St Francis, High Heaton, 1962–64; Long Benton, 1964–68; Vicar: Longhirst with Hebron, 1968–75; St Mary, Monkseaton, 1975–81; Felton, 1982–83; Archdeacon of Lindisfarne, 1981–87; Bishop Suffragan of Maidstone, 1987–92; Bishop to the Forces, 1990–92; Bishop of Bradford, 1992–2002. DUniv Bradford, 2001. *Recreations:* fell walking, reading novels. *Address:* 34 Cedar Glade, Dunnington, York YO19 5QZ. *T:* (01904) 481225. *E:* david@djmhs.force9.co.uk.

SMITH, David James, CB 2009; FCIPS; Managing Director, Procurement Direction Ltd, since 2014; *b* Leyton, 2 Oct. 1954; *s* of James William Smith and Marjorie Dorothy Jesse Smith; partner, Jane Nicolson; three *s*. *Educ:* Downsell Sch., Leyton; Leyton Co. High Sch. for Boys. Home Office, 1973–88; Sen. Procurement Advr, HM Treasury, 1988–91; Dep. Hd of Procurement, 1991–96, Hd of Procurement, 1996–2002, Inland Revenue; Commercial Dir, DWP, 2002–13; Govt Dep. Chief Procurement Officer and Crown Rep., 2011–13. Mem., Falkland Is Rev. Cttee, Cabinet Office, 1982–83. Gov., Saxon Sch., Shepperton, 2000–03. MCIPS 1998 (Mem., Bd of Mgt, 2005–08, 2010–; Vice Pres., 2010–11; Pres., 2011–12), FCIPS 2009. *Recreations:* music (popular), listening and playing guitar/keyboard/vocal (with 'The Front Covers'), sport (Mem., Essex CCC; season ticket holder, West Ham United FC), football referee (FA qualified). *Address:* Procurement Direction Ltd, 11 Whitehall Crescent, Chessington, Surrey KT9 1NF. *T:* 07771 591409. *E:* davidjamessmith@blueyonder.co.uk.

SMITH, David James Benwell T.; *see* Taylor-Smith.

SMITH, David John; Deputy non-executive Chairman, Vitesse Media plc, since 2012; *b* 4 Oct. 1949; *s* of Frederick and Olive Smith; *m* 2006, Julia Stanton; one *s*. *Educ:* Durham Univ. (Teaching Cert.). Wolters Kluwer, NV: Chief Executive Officer: Wayland Publishers, 1995–2001; Stanley Thornes, 1992–2001; Educn/Learning, 1999–2001; Legal, Tax and Business Europe, 2001–02; CEO, Taylor & Francis Gp plc, 2002–04; Chairman: T&F Informa plc, 2004–05; Sherston Publishing, 2006–09; Executive Chairman: Granada Learning, 2006–09; Critical Information Group plc, 2009–12. *Recreations:* horse-racing, gardening, tennis, golf.

SMITH, David John Leslie, PhD; CEng, FRAeS; Director of Group Services, Defence Research Agency, 1991–94; *b* 8 Oct. 1938; *s* of late Arthur George Smith and Gertrude Mary Smith; *m* 1962, Wendy Lavinia (*née* Smith); two *d*. *Educ:* Cinderford Tech. Coll.; N Glos Tech. Coll.; Coll. of Aeronautics (MSc); Univ. of London (PhD); rcds. Mech. Engrg Apprentice, Rotol Ltd, 1954–59; Nat. Gas Turbine Estabt, Min. of Aviation, 1961, Head of Turbomachinery Dept, 1973; RCDS 1979; Ministry of Defence (PE): Dir, Aircraft Mech. and Elect. Equipment, Controllerate of Aircraft, 1980–81; Head of Aero. Dept, RAE, 1981–84; Dep. Dir (Marine Technology), 1984–85, Dep. Dir (Planning), 1986–87, ARE; Hd, Defence Res. Study Team, MoD, 1988; Asst Under-Sec. of State (Civilian Management) (Specialists), MoD, 1988–91. *Publications:* contribs to learned jls on gas turbine technology and fluid mechanics. *Recreations:* garden (including exhibiting flowers), oil and watercolour painting. *Address:* Kyrle Grange, Peterstow, Ross-on-Wye, Herefordshire HR9 6JZ.

SMITH, David Mark; Chief Executive, Energy Networks Association, since 2007 (Deputy Chief Executive, 2003–07); *b* Middlesbrough, 17 April 1964; *s* of Derek and Beryl Smith. *Educ:* Teesside Poly. (BA Hons). PR Officer, Cleveland CC, 1983–89; Press and PR Officer, Assoc. of County Councils, 1989–91; Press and Public Affairs Manager, London Ambulance Service, 1991–94; Hd, Membership and Mktg, Finance and Leasing Assoc., 1994–2000; Dir, Corporate Affairs, British Retail Consortium, 2000–03. *Recreations:* cooking, reading, collecting vinyl records, local history. *Address:* Energy Networks Association, 6th Floor, Dean Bradley House, 52 Horseferry Road, SW1P 2AF. *T:* (020) 7706 5100. *E:* david.smith@energynetworks.org.

SMITH, Prof. David Marshall, PhD; FBA 2009; Professor of Geography, Queen Mary College, later Queen Mary, University of London, 1973–2001, now Emeritus; *b* Birmingham, 1936; *s* of James Marshall Smith and Elizabeth Winifred Smith; *m* 1961, Margaret Harrup (*d* 2002); one *s* one *d*. *Educ:* Solihull Sch.; Univ. of Nottingham (BA 1958; PhD 1961). Lectr in Geog., Univ. of Manchester, 1963–66; Prof., Southern Illinois Univ., 1966–70; short-term posts at Univs of Florida, Natal, Witwatersrand and New England, 1970–73. *Publications:* The Industrial Archaeology of the East Midlands, 1965; Industrial Britain: the North West, 1969; Industrial Location: an economic geographical analysis, 1971; (with Margaret Smith) The United States: how they live and work, 1973; The Geography of Social Well-being in the United States: an introduction to territorial social indicators, 1973; Patterns in Human Geography: an introduction to numerical methods, 1975; Human Geography: a welfare approach, 1977; Where the Grass is Greener: living in an unequal world, 1979; (ed) Living under Apartheid: aspects of urbanization and social change in South Africa, 1982; Geography, Inequality and Society, 1987; (ed) The Apartheid City and Beyond: urbanization and social change in South Africa, 1992; Geography and Social Justice, 1994; Moral Geographies: ethics in a world of difference, 2000; *edited jointly:* Social Problems and the City: geographical perspectives, 1979; Qualitative Methods in Human Geography, 1988; Social Problems and the City: new perspectives, 1989; Shared Space, Divided Space: essays on conflict and territorial organization, 1990; Geography and Ethics: journeys in a moral terrain, 1999; Geographies and Moralities: international perspectives on development, justice and place, 2004; Society, Economy, Environment: towards the sustainable city, 2005. *Recreations:* reading, music. *Address:* 41 Traps Hill, Loughton, Essex IG10 1SZ.

SMITH, David S.; *see* Sands Smith.

SMITH, Dame Dela, DBE 2001; DL; Executive Director, Darlington Education Village, 2006–10 (Chief Executive, 2004–06); *b* 10 Oct. 1952; *d* of John Henthorne Wood and Norah Wood (*née* Read); *m* 1976, Colin Smith. *Educ:* schs in York, Bristol and Cambridge; Durham Univ. (AdvDip); Middleton St George Coll. (Cert Ed). Teacher, Dinsdale Park Residential Sch., nr Darlington, 1975–84; Dep. Head Teacher, 1984–85, Headteacher, 1985–92, Mayfair Special Sch. (Severe Learning Difficulties); Headteacher, Beaumont Hill Special Educnl Needs Centre, subseq. Beaumont Hill Technol. Coll., Primary Sch. and Information, Communication and Technol. Centre, 1992–2004. Mem., Adv. Panel, Nat. Forum for Neurosci. in Special Educn, 2011–. Dir, Ski Peisey, 2004–. Patron and Vice-Chair, Educn Centre for Children with Downs Syndrome, 2007– (Chair of Trustees, 2010–); Chm. Bd, Ascent Acad. Trust (formerly Ascent Trust), 2012– (Gov., Barbara Priestman Special Sch., 2012–); Mem., Horizons (formerly Abbey Hill, then Horizons Multi) Acad. Trust, 2012–; Mem., Hurworth Acad. Trust (formerly Hurworth Primary Acad. Sch.), 2013–; Dir, North East Schools Trust, 2014–. DL Durham, 2001. *Recreations:* walking, travelling, reading, jewellery making, charity and voluntary work. *Address:* 20 West Green, Heighington, Co. Durham DL5 6RA. *T:* (01325) 314905.

SMITH, Delia, CBE 2009 (OBE 1995); cookery writer and broadcaster; *m* Michael Wynn Jones. Several BBC TV series; cookery writer, Evening Standard, later the Standard, 1972–85; columnist, Radio Times; launched Delia Online Cookery Sch., 2013. Director: Norwich City FC, 1996–; Delia's Canary Catering, 1999–2011. FRTS 1996. Hon. Fellow, Liverpool John Moores, 2000; Hon. DLitt: Nottingham, 1996; UEA, 1999. BAFTA Special Award, 2013. Is a Roman Catholic. *Publications:* How to Cheat at Cooking, 1971; Country Fare, 1973; Recipes from Country Inns and Restaurants, 1973; Family Fare, book 1, 1973, book 2, 1974; Evening Standard Cook Book, 1974; Country recipes from "Look East", 1975; More Country Recipes from "Look East", 1976; Frugal Food, 1976; Book of Cakes, 1977; Recipes from "Look East", 1977; Food for our Times, 1978; Cookery Course, part 1, 1978, part 2, 1979, part 3, 1981, The Complete Cookery Course, 1982; A Feast for Lent, 1983; A Feast for Advent, 1983; One is Fun, 1985; (ed) Food Aid Cookery Book, 1986; A Journey into God, 1988; Delia Smith's Christmas, 1990; Delia Smith's Summer Collection, 1993; Delia Smith's Winter Collection, 1995; Delia's Red Nose Collection (Comic Relief), 1997; Delia's How to Cook, Book One, 1998, Book Two, 1999, Book Three, 2001; Delia's Chocolate Collection (Comic Relief), 2001; Delia's Vegetarian Collection, 2002; The Delia Collection: Soup, Chicken, Chocolate, Fish, 2003; Italian, Pork, 2004; Delia's Kitchen Garden, 2004; Baking, 2005; Puddings, 2006; How to Cheat at Cooking, 2008; Delia's Frugal Food, 2008; Delia's Complete How to Cook, 2009; Delia's Happy Christmas, 2009; Delia's Cakes, 2013.

SMITH, Denis M.; *see* Mack Smith.

SMITH, Derek; management consultant; *b* 26 Sept. 1948; *s* of Arthur Edmund Smith and Hazel Smith (*née* Proudlove); *m* 1st, 1970, Carol Anne Susan Cunio (marr. diss. 2003); one *s* one *d*; 2nd, 2003, Ruth Patricia Harrison; one *s*. *Educ:* Univ. of Wales (BSc Hons Econs); Univ. of Strathclyde (Postgrad. Dip. in Russian Lang.). Gen. Manager, Frenchay Hosp., 1982–87; Dist Gen. Manager, S Beds HA, 1987–90; Chief Exec., King's Healthcare NHS Trust, 1990–99; Man. Dir, 1999–2001, Chm., 2000–01, London Underground Ltd; Chief Exec., Hammersmith Hosps NHS Trust, 2001–07. Chm., NHS Elect, 2004–06. *Recreations:* tennis, music, sailing, golf.

SMITH, Derek Cyril; Under-Secretary, Export Credits Guarantee Department, 1974–87, retired; *b* 29 Jan. 1927; *s* of Albert Cyril and Edith Mary Elizabeth Smith; *m* 1st, 1949, Ursula Kulich (marr. diss. 1967); two *d*; 2nd, 1967, Nina Munday; one *s*. *Educ:* Pinner Grammar Sch.; St Catherine's Soc., Oxford. BA Mod. History 1951. Asst Principal, Min. of Materials, 1952–55; BoT, 1955–57: Asst Private Sec., Minister of State; Private Sec., Parly Sec.; Principal, ECGD, 1958–67; Asst Sec., BoT and DTI, 1967–72: Sec. to Lord Cromer's Survey of Capital Projects Contracting Overseas; Asst Sec., ECGD, 1972–74. *Recreation:* reading. *Address:* Somerleigh Court Nursing Home, Somerleigh Road, Dorchester DT1 1AQ.

SMITH, Derek Frank; Alternate Executive Director of the World Bank, and Counsellor (Overseas Develt), Washington, 1979–84; *b* 11 Feb. 1929; *s* of late Frank H. and Rose V. Smith; *m* 1954, Anne Carpenter (*d* 2007); one *s* one *d*. *Educ:* Chatham House Sch., Ramsgate. Served RAF, 1947–49. Colonial Office, 1949–66: Sec., Develt and Welfare Org. in WI, 1956–58; transf. to Min. of Overseas Develt, 1966; First Financial Adviser, British Develt Div. in the Caribbean, 1966–68; Principal, India Sect., ODA, 1968–72; Asst Sec., 1972; Founder Head of Southern African Develt Div., 1972–75; Establishment Officer, 1976–78, Head of UN Dept B, 1978–79, ODA. Consultant: ODA, 1985; World Bank, 1986–87. Chairman: Sevenoaks Area NT Association, 1992–96; Probus Club, Sevenoaks, 1997–98. *Address:* 3 The Close, Montreal Park, Sevenoaks, Kent TN13 2HE. *T:* (01732) 452534.

SMITH, Prof. Derek James, PhD; Professor of Infectious Disease Informatics, University of Cambridge, since 2007; *b* 27 Sept. 1959; *s* of Dorothy Mabel Smith. *Educ:* Pensby High Sch.; Univ. of Bradford (BSc); Univ. of New Mexico (MSc; PhD 1997). Software Engr, Texas Instruments, UK, 1982–83; Res. Scientist, Texas Instruments Res. Labs, USA, 1983–92; Graduate Fellow, Santa Fe Inst., 1992–97; Postdoctoral Fellow, Univ. of New Mexico, 1998–99; Res. Scientist, Dept of Virol., Erasmus Med. Centre, Rotterdam, 1999–; Chief Scientist, Popular Power Inc., San Francisco, 2000–01; Scientist, Eatoni Ergonomics, NY, 2001; Res. Associate, Dept of Zool., Univ. of Cambridge, 2003–07; Sen. Res. Fellow, Fogarty Internat. Center, NIH, 2008–. Dir and Mem., Eur. Scientific Wkg Gp on Influenza, 2002–10 (Vice Pres., 2007–10; Mem., Exec. Cttee, 2007–10); Temp. Advr, WHO, 2005–; Mem., Sci. Bd, Santa Fe Inst., 2011–; Dir, WHO Collaborating Centre on Modeling, Evolution and Control of Emerging Infectious Diseases, Cambridge Univ.; Dir, Centre for Pathogen Evolution, Cambridge Univ. Dir's Pioneer Award, NIH, 2005. *Publications:* scientific papers in learned jls on evolution, immunol., virol., vaccination, computational biol., bioinformatics, epidemiology, public health, computer sci., computer design, integrated circuit design; patents on computer design and information encoding. *Address:* Department of Zoology, University of Cambridge, Downing Street, Cambridge CB2 3EJ.

SMITH, Desmond; *see* Smith, S. D.

SMITH, Douglas Armitage, CB 2005; Chief Executive, Child Support Agency, 2000–05; *b* 8 April 1947; *s* of James and Joan Smith; *m* 1968, Maureen Buckroyd; one *s* one *d*. *Educ:* Leeds Central High Sch.; Open Univ. (BA Hons). Board of Inland Revenue: Asst Dir, IT, 1989–93; Director: Change, 1993–95; Self Assessment, 1995–98; Business Ops, 1998–2000. Pres., Assoc. of Inspectors of Taxes, 1986–88. *Recreations:* smallholding/brewery in France, travelling, horse-racing, sport, reading. *Club:* Boxmoor Social.

SMITH, Drew; *see* Smith, F. D.

SMITH, Drew; Member (Lab) Glasgow, Scottish Parliament, since 2011; *b* Broxburn, 1982; *s* of Andrew and Mary Valentine Smith. *Educ:* St Kentigern's Acad., Blackburn; Aberdeen Univ. (MA Hons Politics and Internat. Relns 2004); Glasgow Univ. (Postgrad. Dip. Human Rights and Internat. Politics). Parly Asst to Pauline McNeill, MSP, 2005–08; PR and Social Mktg Manager, Paths for All Partnership, 2008–10; Officer Manager/Sen. Parly Asst to Ann McKechin, MP, 2010–11. *Recreations:* music, reading, walking, theatre, cinema. *Address:* Scottish Parliament, Holyrood, Edinburgh EH1 1SP. *T:* (0131) 348 6208. *E:* drew.smith.msp@scottish.parliament.uk.

SMITH, Sir Dudley (Gordon), Kt 1983; DL; retired politician and management consultant; *b* 14 Nov. 1926; *o s* of late Hugh William and Florence Elizabeth Smith, Cambridge; *m* 1st, 1958 (marr. diss. 1975); one *s* two *d*; 2nd, 1976 (marr. diss. 2011). *Educ:* Chichester High Sch., Sussex. Worked for various provincial and national newspapers, as journalist and senior executive, 1943–66; Asst News Editor, Sunday Express, 1953–59. Vice-Chm. Southgate Conservative Assoc., 1958–59; CC Middlesex, 1958–65; Chief Whip of Majority Group, 1961–63. A Divl Dir, Beecham Group, 1966–70. Contested (C) Camberwell-Peckham, 1955. MP (C) Brentford and Chiswick, 1959–66; Warwick and Leamington, 1968–97; contested (C) Warwick and Leamington, 1997. PPS to Sec. for Tech. Co-operation, 1963–64; an Opposition Whip, 1964–66; an Opposition Spokesman on Employment and Productivity, 1969–70; Parliamentary Under-Secretary of State: Dept of Employment, 1970–74; (Army) MoD, 1974. Vice Chm., Parly Select Cttee on Race Relations and Immigration, 1974–79. UK delegate to Council of Europe and WEU, 1979–97 (Sec.-Gen., European Democratic Gp, 1983–96; Chm., WEU Defence Cttee, 1989–93; Pres., WEU Assembly, 1993–97; Hon. Associate, WEU, 1997; Hon. Associate, Council of Europe, 1998); a Founder Mem., CSCE Assembly, 1992. Sen. official observer, elecns in Turkey, Russia, Chile, Bulgaria, Slovenia and Azerbaijan for, variously, Council of Europe, CSCE, then OSCE, and EDG, 1983–2008. Promoted Town and Country Planning (Amendment) Act, 1977, as a private member. Governor: Mill Hill Sch., 1958–89; N London Collegiate Sch., 1962–80; Chm., United & Cecil Club, 1975–80. Freeman, City of London. DL Warwickshire, 1988. Order of the Horseman of Madara, 1st cl. (Bulgaria), 1994; Comdr, Order of Isabella la Católica (Spain), 1994. *Publications:* Harold Wilson: A Critical Biography, 1964; etc. *Recreations:* books, travel, music, wild life and wilderness preservation. *Address:* Church Farm, Weston-under-Wetherley, near Leamington Spa, Warwicks CV33 9BY. *T:* (01926) 632352.

SMITH, Dugal N.; *see* Nisbet-Smith.

SMITH, Edward; *see* Smith, J. E. K.

SMITH, Elaine Agnes; Member (Lab) Coatbridge and Chryston, Scottish Parliament, since 1999; Deputy Presiding Officer, Scottish Parliament, since 2011; *b* 7 May 1963; *m* 1996, James Vann Smith; one *s*. *Educ:* St Patrick's High Sch., Coatbridge; Glasgow Coll. (BA Hons Social Sci. (Econs and Politics)); St Andrews Teacher Trng Coll. (PGCE); DPSM 1995. Teacher, 1986; work in retail industry, Women's Aid Advice Worker and supply teacher, 1987; Local Authy Homeless Officer and Urban Prog. Asst Co-ordinator, 1988–90; posts in local authy depts, Monklands DC and W Highland Regl Council, 1990–97; Volunteers Manager, 1997–98; Supply Teacher, 1999. *Recreations:* family life, reading, swimming, cinema, cooking, supporting local youth Rugby. *Address:* Scottish Parliament, Holyrood, Edinburgh EH99 1SP. *T:* (0131) 348 5824. *E:* elaine.smith.msp@scottish.parliament.uk.

SMITH, Elizabeth H.; *see* Hallam Smith.

SMITH, Elizabeth Jane; Member (C) Scotland Mid and Fife, Scottish Parliament, since 2007; *b* 27 Feb. 1960; *d* of James Smith and (Margaret) Thelma Smith (*née* Moncrieff). *Educ:* George Watson's Coll., Edinburgh; Univ. of Edinburgh (MA Hons Econs and Politics 1982; DipEd 1983). Teacher, George Watson's Coll., 1983–98; Schoolteacher Fellow Commoner, Corpus Christi Coll., Cambridge, 1992; Political Advr to Sir Malcolm Rifkind, 1998–2001; Hd, Chairman's Office, Scottish Cons. and Unionist Party, 2001–03; self-employed political consultant, 2003–05; pt-time teacher, George Watson's Coll., 2005–06. *Publications:* Outdoor Adventures, 2003; An Illustrated History of George Watson's Ladies' College, 2006. *Recreations:* cricket, hill-walking, photography, travel. *Address:* Stables Cottage, Woodend, Madderty PH7 3PA. *E:* elizabeth.smith.msp@scottish.parliament.uk. *Club:* New (Edinburgh).

SMITH, Elizabeth Jean, OBE 2004; Consultant, Transforming Broadcasting, since 2010; *b* 15 Aug. 1936; *d* of Lt-Gen. Sir Robert Hay, KCIE; *m* 1960, Geoffrey Smith; one *s* one *d*. *Educ:* St George's Sch., Edinburgh; Univ. of Edinburgh (MA Hons Hist. 1958). BBC Radio: Studio Manager, 1958–61; News Producer, 1961–70; Current Affairs Producer, 1970–78; Producer for BBC Current Affairs TV, 1978–79; Sen. Asst, BBC Secretariat, 1979–81; BBC World Service: Asst Head, Central Talks and Features, 1981–84; Head, Current Affairs, 1984–87; Controller, English Services, 1987–94; Sec.-Gen., Commonwealth Broadcasting Assoc., 1994–2010. Member: Council, RIIA, 1992–97; Bd, Population Communications Internat., 1994–2002; Bd, Internat. Trng and Res. Consultancies, 1994–98; Bd, Westminster Foundn for Democracy, 1998–2001; Communications and Inf. Cttee, UK Nat. Commn for UNESCO, 2006–11. Chair: Voice of the Listener and Viewer Trust, 2006–08; Commonwealth Media Gp, 2011–. Trustee: Oneworld Broadcasting Trust, 1994–2000; Commonwealth Human Rights Initiative, 1998–2010; Television Trust for the Envmt, 2000–04. Consumer columnist, The Listener, 1978–80. Fellow, Radio Acad., 1996 (Mem. Bd, 1990–94). Trustee, Royal Commonwealth Soc., 2010–14. Hon. DLit Westminster, 2014. *Publications:* (as Elizabeth Hay) Sambo Sahib: the story of Helen Bannerman, 1981; Sayonara Sanbo, 1993; A Road Map to Public Service Broadcasting, 2012. *Recreations:* gardening, walking, travelling in the developing world. *T:* (020) 7226 3519, *Fax:* (020) 7354 0188. *E:* elizabeth.smith226@gmail.com. *Clubs:* Reform, Royal Over-Seas League.

SMITH, Emilie; *see* Savage-Smith, E.

SMITH, Emma; author; *b* 21 Aug. 1923; *m* 1951, Richard Stewart-Jones (*d* 1957); one *s* one *d*. *Publications:* Maidens' Trip, 1948 (John Llewellyn Rhys Meml Prize, 1948), reissued 2009; The Far Cry, 1949 (James Tait Black Meml Prize, 1949); Emily, 1959; Out of Hand, 1963; Emily's Voyage, 1966; No Way of Telling, 1972; The Opportunity of a Lifetime, 1978; The Great Western Beach (memoir), 2008; As Green as Grass: growing up before, during and after the Second World War (memoir), 2013. *Address:* c/o Curtis Brown, 28–29 Haymarket, SW1Y 4SP.

SMITH, Sir (Eric) Brian, Kt 1999; PhD, DSc; FRSC; Vice-Chancellor, Cardiff University (formerly Principal, University of Wales College of Cardiff), 1993–2001; *b* 10 Oct. 1933; *s* of Eric Smith and Dilys Olwen (*née* Hughes); *m* 1st, 1957, Margaret Barr (marr. diss. 1978); two *s* one *d*; 2nd, 1983, Regina Arvidson Ball; two step *d*. *Educ:* Alun Grammar Sch., Mold; Wirral Grammar Sch.; Univ. of Liverpool (BSc; PhD 1957); MA Oxon 1960, DSc Oxon 1988. FRSC 1981. Res. Associate, Univ. of Calif, Berkeley, 1957–59; Oxford University: ICI Fellow, 1959–60; Lectr in Physical Chemistry, 1960–88; Member: Gen. Bd of Faculties, 1980–87 (Chm., 1985–87); Hebdomadal Council, 1985–93; St Catherine's College: Fellow, 1960–88; Master, 1988–93; Hon. Fellow, 1993; Dir, Isis Innovation, 1988–97. Vis. Prof., Univ. of Calif, Riverside, 1967; Vis. Lectr, Stanford Univ., 1983, 1984 and 1985; Priestley Lectr, RSC, 1986. Chm., Thermodynamics and Statistical Mechanics Section, RSC, 1979–83; Member Board: WDA, 1998–2002; HEFCW, 2003–11; Dir, Higher Aims Ltd, 2002–. Vice-Chm., Oxford Soc. Cttee, 1988–2005; Trustee: Oxford Univ. Soc., 2005–06; Liverpool Sch. of Tropical Medicine, 2004–13. Dir, Cardiff Internat. Fest. of Musical Theatre, 2001–07. Mem. Bd, Univ. of Glamorgan, 2002–06. Mem., Magic Circle, 2015–. FLSW 2012. Hon. Fellow, UWCM, 2003. Hon. DSc Glamorgan, 2000; Hon. LLD Wales, 2001. Pott's Medal, Univ. of Liverpool, 1969. *Publications:* (jtly) Virial Coefficients of Pure Gases and Mixtures, 1969, 2nd edn 1980; Basic Chemical Thermodynamics, 1973, 6th edn 2013; (jtly) Intermolecular Forces: origin and determination, 1981; (jtly) Forces between Molecules, 1986; Basic Physical Chemistry, 2012; papers in scientific jls. *Recreation:* mountaineering. *Address:* Appletree House, 2 Boults Lane, Old Marston, Oxford OX3 0PW. *Clubs:* Alpine; Gorphwysfa.

SMITH, Prof. (Ernest) Alwyn, CBE 1986; PhD; Professor of Epidemiology and Social Oncology, University of Manchester, 1979–90; Chairman, Lancaster Health Authority, 1991–94; *b* 9 Nov. 1925; *s* of Ernest Smith and Constance Barbara Smith; *m* 1950, Doreen Preston (*d* 2012); one *s* one *d*. *Educ:* Queen Mary's Sch., Walsall; Birmingham Univ. MB, PhD; FRCP 1970; FRCGP 1973; FFCM 1974. Served War, RM, 1943–46. Res. Fellow in Social Medicine, Birmingham Univ., 1952–55; WHO Vis. Lectr, Univ. of Malaya, 1956–58; Lectr, Univ. of St Andrews, 1959–61; Sen. Lectr, Univ. of Edinburgh, 1961–66; First Dir, Social Paediatric Res. Gp, Glasgow, 1966–67; Prof. of Community Medicine, Univ. of Manchester, 1967–79. Pres., FCM, 1981–86. *Publications:* Genetics in Medicine, 1966; The Science of Social Medicine, 1968; (ed) Cancer Control, 1979; (ed) Recent Advances in Community Medicine, 1982; papers on epidemiological subjects in Lancet, British Jl of Epidemiol., etc. *Recreations:* music, bird watching, sailing. *Address:* Plum Tree Cottage, 17 Silverdale Road, Arnside, Cumbria, via Carnforth LA5 0AH. *T:* (01524) 761976.

SMITH, Ewen Dale, FSAScot; Director, Hunterian Museum and Art Gallery, University of Glasgow, 2006–09; *b* 14 Sept. 1946; *s* of Norman Smith and Greta Smith (*née* Holton); *m* 1976, Kathleen Ann Kane; two *d*. *Educ:* George Heriot's Sch., Edinburgh; Univ. Nacional Autónoma de México; Univ. of Glasgow (MA, MLitt). MCIPD 1992. Cost clerk, Scottish & Newcastle Breweries Ltd, 1964–69; Investment Analyst, Ivory & Sime, 1969–74; fund-raiser, UNA, 1980–82; Adminr, Open Univ., 1982–85; University of Glasgow: Adminr, CPD Unit, 1985–89, Univ. Staff Develt Service, 1989–94; Planning Unit Adminr, Academic Services, 1994–99; Dep. Dir, Hunterian Mus. and Art Gall., 1999–2006. Member: Bd, Scottish Museums Council, 2007; Recognition Cttee, Mus and Galls Scotland, 2012–. Mem. Council, Soc. of Antiquaries of Scotland, 2013–. Trustee and Hon. Treas., Assoc. Certificated Field Archaeologists, 2010–. FSAScot 1988. *Publications:* general articles. *Recreations:* archaeological field surveying, hill-walking, listing things alphabetically, reading, waiting for Aberdeen FC's next European Final.

SMITH, Fiona Mary; *see* Watt, F. M.

SMITH, Sir Francis Graham-, Kt 1986; FRS 1970; Langworthy Professor of Physics, Manchester University, 1987–90, now Emeritus (Professor of Radio Astronomy, 1964–74 and 1981–87); Director, Nuffield Radio Astronomy Laboratories, 1981–88; Astronomer Royal, 1982–90; *b* 25 April 1923; *s* of Claud Henry and Cicely Winifred Smith; *m* 1945, Dorothy Elizabeth (*née* Palmer); three *s* one *d*. *Educ:* Epsom Coll.; Rossall Sch.; Downing Coll., Cambridge. Nat. Sci. Tripos, Downing Coll., 1941–43 and 1946–47; PhD Cantab 1952. Telecommunications Research Estab., Malvern, 1943–46; Cavendish Lab., 1947–64; 1851 Exhibnr 1951–52; Warren Research Fellow of Royal Soc., 1959–64; Fellow of Downing Coll., 1953–64, Hon. Fellow 1970; Dir-Designate, 1974–75, Dir, 1976–81, Royal Greenwich Observatory. Vis. Prof. of Astronomy, Univ. of Sussex, 1975. Sec., Royal

Astronomical Soc., 1964–71, Pres., 1975–77. Mem. Council and Physical Sec., 1988–94, Vice-Pres., 1990–94, Royal Soc.; For. Associate, RSSAf, 1988. Hon. DSc: QUB, 1986; Keele, 1987; Birmingham, 1989; TCD, 1990; Nottingham, 1990; Manchester, 1993; Liverpool, 2003; Salford, 2003. Royal Medal, Royal Soc., 1987; Glazebrook Medal, Inst. of Physics, 1991. *Publications:* Radio Astronomy, 1960; (with J. H. Thomson) Optics, 1971; Pulsars, 1977; (with Sir Bernard Lovell) Pathways to the Universe, 1988; (with A. G. Lyne) Pulsar Astronomy, 1990, 4th edn 2012; (with B. F. Burke) Introduction to Radio Astronomy, 1997, 3rd edn 2010; (with T. A. King) Optics and Photonics, 2000, 2nd edn (with T. A. King and Dan Wilkins) 2007; Unseen Cosmos, 2013; papers in Monthly Notices of RAS, Nature and other scientific jls. *Recreations:* beekeeping, walking. *Address:* Jodrell Bank Observatory, Macclesfield, Cheshire SK11 9DL; Old School House, Henbury, Macclesfield, Cheshire SK11 9PH.

SMITH, Prof. Frank Thomas, FRS 1984; Goldsmid Professor of Applied Mathematics in the University of London, at University College London, since 1984; *b* 24 Feb. 1948; *s* of Leslie Maxwell Smith and Catherine Matilda Smith; *m* 1972, Valerie Sheila (*née* Hearn); three *d. Educ:* Bournemouth Grammar Sch.; Jesus Coll., Oxford (BA; DPhil); University College London. Research Fellow in Theoretical Aerodynamics Unit, Southampton, 1972–73; Lectr in Maths Dept, Imperial Coll., London, 1973–78; Vis. Scientist, Applied Mathematics Dept, Univ. of Western Ontario, Canada, 1978–79; Reader in Maths Dept, 1979–83, Prof. in Maths, 1983–84, Imperial Coll., London. Director: Lighthill Inst., 2006–; London Taught Course Centre, 2007–. *Publications:* on applied mathematics, fluid mechanics, industrial modelling, biomedical modelling, societal models, computing and natural sciences, in jls. *Recreations:* the family, reading, music, sport. *Address:* Mathematics Department, University College London, Gower Street, WC1E 6BT. *T:* (020) 7679 2837.

SMITH, Frank William G.; *see* Glaves-Smith.

SMITH, (Fraser) Drew; Director, Food By Design (formerly Food Factory), since 1991; senior adviser on food strategy, London Docklands Development Corporation, 1995–98; *b* 30 March 1950; *s* of Frank and Beatrice Smith; *m* 1988, Susan Maloney; one *s* one *d. Educ:* Westminster School. Worked on Student magazine, 1967; IPC magazines, 1969–72; Westminster Press Newspapers, 1972–81. Editor, Good Food Guide, 1982–89; launched: Good Food Directory, 1985; Budget Good Food Guide, 1986–88; Head of Media Develt, Dir's Office, Consumers' Assoc., 1988–90; Publishing Dir, Alfresco Leisure Publications, 1990–92. Director: Taste Publishing; West India Co. Columnist, Guardian, 1982–; creator, TV Food File, Channel 4. Chm., Guild of Food Writers, 1990. Trustee, Jane Grigson Liby. Chief Judge, British Cheese Awards, 1995, 1996. Restaurant Writer of the Year, 1981, 1988. *Publications:* Modern Cooking, 1990; Food Watch, 1994; Baby Food Watch, 1995; Good Food, 1995; The Circus (novel), 1997; Food Industry and the Internet, 2001; Oyster: a world history, 2010. *Recreations:* walking, music, cooking, people.

SMITH, Geoffrey John; writer and broadcaster; *b* Mich, USA, 23 Aug. 1943; *s* of Earl Willard Smith and Marian Kay Smith (*née* Eisele); *m* 1968, Lenore Ketola (marr. diss. 1985; she *d* 2003); *m* 1995, Janette Grant; one *s. Educ:* Central High Sch., Bay City, Mich; Univ. of Michigan (BA English 1966); Univ. of Wisconsin (Woodrow Wilson Fellow; MA English 1967). Musician, 1959–69; Instr in English, Eastern Michigan Univ., 1967–68; NDEA Title IV Fellow, Univ. of Virginia, 1970–73; freelance writer and lectr, 1973–93; Lectr in English and American Lit., City Univ., 1979–91, City Lit., 1986–92. Music Critic and Consultant, Country Life, 1977–; Arts Corresp., The Economist, 1988–; columnist, BBC Music Mag., 2001–; Presenter, BBC Radio 3, 1988–: documentaries, interviews and concerts; series on Gilbert and Sullivan; CD Review; Jazz Record Requests, 1991–2012; Geoffrey Smith's Jazz, 2012–. *Publications:* The Savoy Operas, 1983; Stéphane Grappelli, 1987; 100 Jazz Legends, 2011; contrib. poetry to Encounter, Mandeville Press, The Tablet. *Recreations:* tennis, jogging, family outings, 'gaping and dawdling' (Henry James). *Address:* BBC Radio 3, Broadcasting House, W1A 1AA. *T:* (020) 7580 4468, *Fax:* (020) 7765 5052.

SMITH, Prof. Geoffrey Lilley, PhD; FRS 2003; Wellcome Trust Principal Research Fellow, since 2000; Professor of Pathology, University of Cambridge, since 2011; Fellow, Emmanuel College, Cambridge, since 2011; *b* 23 July 1955; *s* of Irvine Battinson Smith and Kathleen Lilley Smith; *m* 1979, Tessa Marie Trico; two *s* two *d. Educ:* Bootham Sch., York; Univ. of Leeds (BSc Hons Microbiol./Biochem. 1977); Nat. Inst. for Med. Res., London (PhD 1981). Wellcome Trust Fellow, Div. of Virology, NIMR, London, 1980–81; Vis. Fellow, Lab. of Viral Diseases, Nat. Inst. of Allergy and Infectious Diseases, NIH, Bethesda, 1981–84; Lectr in Virology, Dept of Pathology, Univ. of Cambridge, 1985–89; Jenner Fellow, Lister Inst. of Preventive Medicine, 1988–92; Reader in Bacteriology, 1989–96, Prof. of Virology, 1996–2000, Sir William Dunn Sch. of Pathology, Univ. of Oxford; EPA Sen. Res. Fellow, Wadham Coll., Oxford, 1989–2000; Prof. of Virology, Imperial Coll. London, 2000–11. Chm., WHO Adv. Cttee for Variola Virus Res., 2004–07, 2009–; International Union of Microbiological Societies: Vice-Chm., 2002–05, Chm., 2005–08, Virology Div.; Pres., 2011–14; Member: MRC Infection and Immunity Bd, 2004–09; Royal Soc. Cttee on Scientific Aspects of Internat. Security, 2005–08 (Chm., 2009–12); New Agents Cttee, CRUK, 2008–10; Royal Soc. Adv. Gp to Sci. Policy Centre, 2009–12; Wellcome Trust Expert Review Gp, 2010–; Scientific Adv. Bd, Bernard Nocht Inst., Hamburg, 2011–; Biomedical Panel, Univ. Res. Grant Cttee, Hong Kong, 2012–; Chm., Scientific Adv. Bd, Friedrich-Loeffler Inst., Germany, 2015– (Vice-Chm., 2011–15). Gov., Lister Inst. of Preventive Medicine, 2003–13. FRSB (FIBiol 2000); FMedSci 2000. Mem., German National Acad. of Scis Leopoldina, 2011. GlaxoSmithKline Internat. Mem. of the Year Award, American Soc. for Microbiol., 2012. Ed.-in-Chief, Jl of Gen. Virology, 2003–07. *Publications:* editor of several books and author of over 50 book chapters and over 248 scientific papers, and several patents. *Recreations:* hockey, cricket, chess, bridge, gardening, carpentry, hill-walking. *Address:* Department of Pathology, University of Cambridge, Tennis Court Road, Cambridge CB2 1QP. *T:* (01223) 333692. *E:* gls37@cam.ac.uk.

SMITH, George D.; *see* Davey Smith.

SMITH, Prof. George David William, DPhil; FRS 1996; FRSC; CEng, FIMMM; CPhys, FInstP; Professor of Materials Science, University of Oxford, 1996–2010, now Emeritus (Head of Department of Materials, 2000–05); Professorial Fellow, Trinity College, Oxford, 1992–2010, now Emeritus (Tutorial Fellow, 1991–92); *b* 28 March 1943; *s* of George Alfred William Smith and Grace Violet Hannah Dayton Smith; *m* 1968, Josephine Ann Halford (*d* 2014); two *s. Educ:* St Benedict's Sch., Aldershot; Salesian Coll., Farnborough; Corpus Christi Coll., Oxford (Scholar; BA Hons Metallurgy 1965; MA, DPhil 1968; Hon. Fellow, 2008). CEng 1978; CPhys, FInstP 1996; FIMMM (FIM 1996); FRSC 2003. SRC Res. Fellow, 1968–70; Jun. Res. Fellow, 1968–72, Res. Fellow, 1972–77, Wolfson Coll., Oxford; Oxford University: Res. Fellow, Dept of Metallurgy, 1970–75; Sen. Res. Fellow, 1975–77; Lectr in Metallurgy, 1977–92; George Kelley Reader in Metallurgy, 1992–96; Fellow, St Cross Coll., Oxford, 1977–91, Emeritus Fellow, 1991–. Adv. Prof., Chongqing Univ., China, 2005–; Hon. Prof., Univ. of Sci. and Technol., Beijing, 2005–. Man. Dir, Oxford Nanoscience Ltd (formerly Kindbrisk Ltd), 1987–2002 (Chm., 2002–04); Chm., Polaron plc, 2004–06; Scientific Advr, Tokamak Energy Ltd (formerly Tokamak Solutions UK Ltd), 2010–. Councillor (L), W Oxon DC, 1973–76. Co-Chm., UK Materials Congress, 1998. Mem., OST Foresight Panel for Materials, 1999–2003. Hatfield Meml Lect., Univ. of Sheffield, 2011; Hume Rothery Meml Lect., Univ. of Oxford, 2014. Pres., Internat. Field Emission Soc., 1990–93; Member: Council, Inst. of Materials, Minerals and Mining (formerly of Materials), 1997–2004 (Vice-Pres., 2002–03); Council, Royal Soc., 2002–04. Freeman, Armourers' and Brasiers' Co., 1998 (Liveryman, 2003). FRSA 1997. Sir George Beilby Medal and Prize, SCI, RSC, Inst. Metals, 1985; (jtly) Vanadium Award, 1985, Rosenhain Medal and Prize, 1991, Inst. of Metals; Nat. Innovative Measurement Award, DTI, 2004; Gold Medal, Acta Materialia Inc., 2005; Platinum Medal, 2006, Material World Publication Prize, 2013, IMMM. *Publications:* (with M. K. Miller) Atom Probe Microanalysis: principles and applications to materials problems, 1989 (trans. Russian 1993, Chinese 1994); (jtly) Atom Probe Field Ion Microscopy, 1996; numerous contribs to scientific jls. *Recreations:* walking, fishing, bird watching, travel. *Address:* Trinity College, Oxford OX1 3BH. *T:* (01865) 273700.

SMITH, Dr George Elwood; Head, Device Concepts Department, Bell Laboratories, Murray Hill, New Jersey, 1964–86; *b* White Plains, NY, 10 May 1930; *s* of George F. and Lillian Smith; partner, Janet Lee Murphy; one *s* two *d. Educ:* Univ. of Pennsylvania (BA Physics 1955); Univ. of Chicago (MS 1956; PhD Physics 1959). Mem., Tech. Staff, Res. Area, Bell Labs, Murray Hill, NJ, 1959–64. Founding Ed., IEEE pubn, Electron Device Letters, 1980–86. Member: US NAE, 1983–; Pi Mu Epsilon, 1985–; Phi Beta Kappa, 1985–; Sigma Xi, 1985–. Fellow, APS, 1963; FIEEE 1966. Ballantine Medal, Franklin Inst., 1973; Morris N. Liebmann Award, 1974, Electron Devices Soc. Dist. Service Award, 1997, Device Res. Conf. Breakthrough Award, 1999, IEEE; Progress Medal, Photographic Soc. of America, 1986; Prize for invention of Charge Coupled Device, Foundn for Computer and Communications Promotion, 1999; Edwin Land Medal, Optical Soc. of Amer., 2001; Charles Stark Draper Prize, NAE, 2006; (jtly) Nobel Prize in Physics, 2009. *Publications:* contrib. over 40 papers; 31 US patents. *Recreation:* sailing (started world cruise with Janet Murphy aboard 9.5 meter sailing vessel, Apogee, 1986; completed in 2003 after 55,000 miles of ocean sailing). *Address:* 221 Teaneck Road, PO Box 787, Barnegat, NJ 08005, USA. *T:* (609) 6983738. *E:* apogee2@comcast.net.

SMITH, Rt Hon. (George) Iain D.; *see* Duncan Smith.

SMITH, (George) Neil, CMG 1987; HM Diplomatic Service, retired; *b* 12 July 1936; *s* of George Smith and Ena (*née* Hill); *m* 1956, Elvi Vappu Hämäläinen (*d* 2013); one *s* one *d. Educ:* King Edward VII Sch., Sheffield. Joined HM Foreign (subseq. Diplomatic) Service, 1953; served RAF, 1954–56; Foreign Office, 1957; Rangoon, 1958–61; 2nd Sec., Berne, 1961–65; Diplomatic Service Administration, 1965–66; 1st Sec., CO, 1966–68; British Mil. Govt, Berlin, 1969–73; FCO, 1973–77; Counsellor (Commercial), Helsinki, 1977–80; Consul-Gen., Zürich and Principality of Liechtenstein, 1980–85; Head of Trade Relations and Exports Dept, FCO, 1985–87; RCDS, 1988; Ambassador to Finland, 1989–95. Sec. Gen., Soc. of London Art Dealers, 1996–2001; Sec., British Art Market Fedn, 1996–2001. *Recreations:* music, golf. *Address:* 5 Linton Falls, Linton in Craven, N Yorks BD23 6BQ.

SMITH, Prof. Gerald Stanton, FBA 2001; Professor of Russian, 1986–2003, and Fellow of New College, 1986–2003, now Emeritus, University of Oxford; *b* 17 April 1938; *s* of Thomas Arthur Smith and Ruth Annie Stanton; *m* 1st, 1961, Frances Wetherill (marr. diss. 1981); one *s* one *d*; 2nd, 1982, Barbara Heldt; one step *s* (and one step *d* decd). *Educ:* Stretford Grammar Sch.; Sch. of Slavonic and E European Studies, Univ. of London (BA 1964 PhD 1977); DLitt Oxon 1996. Lectr in Russian, Univ. of Nottingham, 1964–71, Univ. of Birmingham, 1971–79; Univ. Research Fellow, Univ. of Liverpool, 1980–82. Visiting Professor: Indiana Univ., 1984; Univ. of California, Berkeley, 1984; Private Scholar, Social Scis and Humanities Res. Council, Canada, 1985; John Simon Guggenheim Meml Fellow, 1986. Pres., MHRA, 2000. *Publications:* (ed) Alexander Galich, Songs and Poems, 1983; Songs to Seven Strings, 1984; Russian Inside and Out, 1989; (ed) D. S. Mirsky, Uncollected Writings on Russian Literature, 1989; Contemporary Russian Poetry: a bilingual anthology, 1993; D. S. Mirsky: Letters to P. P. Suvchinskii, 1995; (co-ed and trans.) M. L. Gasparov, A History of European Versification, 1996; (ed and trans.) Boris Slutsky, Things That Happened, 1999; D. S. Mirsky: a Russian-English life, 2000; Vzglyad izvne: Izbrannye stat´i o russkoi poezii i poetike, 2002; (ed and trans.) Lev Loseff, As I Said, 2012; papers in learned jls. *Recreation:* jazz music. *Address:* 15 Dale Close, Oxford OX1 1TU.

SMITH, Geraldine; *see* Smith, Maria G.

SMITH, Gilbert, PhD; Member of Board, National Patient Safety Agency, 2001–05 (Acting Chairman, 2005); Vice Chairman, Northern Stage, 2004 (Board Member, 2002). *Educ:* Brentwood Sch., Essex; Univ. of Leeds (BA Hons 1966); Univ. of Essex (MA 1967); Univ. of Aberdeen (PhD 1973). Research Fellow and Attached Worker, MRC Medical Sociology Unit, Univ. of Aberdeen, 1969–73; Res. Advr, Central Research Unit, Scottish Office, Edinburgh, 1973–75; Sen. Lectr, then Reader, Dept of Social Admin and Social Work, Univ. of Glasgow, 1975–81; University of Hull: Prof. of Social Admin, 1981–96; Head, Dept of Social Admin, 1982–84; Foundn Head, Dept of Social Policy and Professional Studies, 1984–85; Dean, Faculty of Social Scis, 1985–87; Vice-Chancellor and Chief Exec., Univ. of Northumbria at Newcastle, 1996–2001. Sen. Travelling Scholar in Australia, ACU, 1988. Chm., E Yorks HA, then E Riding Health, 1990–93. Dep. Dir, R&D, DoH and NHS Exec., 1993–96. Foundn Trustee, Social Care Inst. for Excellence, 2001–02. Numerous board appts, directorships, commns and adv. posts with univs, res. councils, res. funding agencies, publishers, foundns, arts bodies, Govt depts, ACU, UUK and British Council. Mem., Corbridge with Halton and Newton Hall PCC, 2002. Elder, Church of Scotland. Mem., Amnesty Internat. Editor, Jl of Social Policy, 1991–93. DUniv Moscow State Univ. of Mgt, 1998. *Publications:* Social Work and the Sociology of Organisations, 1970, 2nd rev. edn 1979 (trans. Japanese and Korean); Social Need: policy practice and research, 1980 (trans. Japanese); (with C. Cantley) Assessing Health Care: a study in organisational evaluation, 1985; numerous book chapters; contrib. articles in professional and academic jls of social policy, sociology, social work and healthcare.

SMITH, Godfrey, FRSL; writer; *b* 12 May 1926; *s* of Reginald Montague Smith and Ada May Smith (*née* Damen); *m* 1951, Mary (*d* 1997), *d* of Jakub Schoenfeld, formerly of Vienna; three *d. Educ:* Surbiton County Sch.; Eggars Grammar Sch.; Worcester Coll., Oxford (MA; Pres. of Oxford Union Soc. 1950). RAF, 1944–47. Joined Sunday Times as PA to Lord Kemsley, 1951; News Editor, 1956; Asst Editor, 1959; Special Projects Editor, 1964–65; Editor, Magazine, 1965–72, Associate Editor, 1972–91; fiction critic, 1974; Editor, Weekly Review, 1972–79; columnist, 1979–2004; Director, 1968–81. Regent's Lectr, Univ. of California, 1970. Pres., Charlton Cricket Club, 1981–2006. FRSL 1995. *Publications: novels:* The Flaw in the Crystal, 1954; The Friends, 1957; The Business of Loving, 1961 (Book Society Choice); The Network, 1965; Caviare, 1976; *non-fiction:* The English Companion, 1984; The English Season, 1987; The English Reader, 1988; *anthologies:* The Best of Nat Gubbins, 1978; A World of Love, 1982; Beyond the Tingle Quotient, 1982; How it Was in the War, 1989; Take the Ball and Run, 1991. *Recreation:* chums. *Address:* Village Farmhouse, Charlton, Malmesbury, Wilts SN16 9DL. *T:* (01666) 822479; 10 Kensington Park Mews, W11 2EY. *T:* (020) 7727 4155. *Clubs:* Garrick, Savile.

SMITH, Godric William Naylor, CBE 2004; Co-Founder, Inc. (Incorporated London Ltd), since 2013; *b* 29 March 1965; *s* of Eric and Phyl Smith; *m* 1991, Julia Barnes; two *s. Educ:* Perse Sch., Cambridge; Worcester Coll., Oxford (MA Lit Hum 1987). Appeals Manager, SANE, 1988–91; Sen. Inf. Officer, 1991–94, Chief Press Officer, 1995, DoH; Prime Minister's Office, 1996–2006: Dep. Press Sec., 1998–2001; Prime Minister's Official Spokesman, 2001–03; Hd of Strategic Communications, 2004–06; Dir of Communications, ODA, 2006–11; Dir of Govt Communications for London 2012 (on secondment from ODA), 2011–12; Interim Exec. Dir of Govt Communications, 2012. *Recreations:* watching Cambridge United, cycling, family. *Address:* Inc., Two John Street, WC1N 2ES.

SMITH, Prof. Gordon Campbell Sinclair, MD, PhD, DSc; FRCOG; FMedSci; Professor of Obstetrics and Gynaecology, since 2001, and Head of Department of Obstetrics and Gynaecology, since 2004, University of Cambridge; Honorary Consultant in Maternal Fetal Medicine, Addenbrooke's Hospital, Cambridge, since 2001; Fellow, Hughes Hall, Cambridge, since 2014; *b* 11 May 1965; *s* of Robert (Roy) Smith and Peggy Smith; *m* 1986, Nicola Wilkinson; two *d*. *Educ:* Bankhead Primary Sch., Glasgow; Stonelaw High Sch., Glasgow; Univ. of Glasgow (BSc 1st Cl. Hons Physiol. 1986; MB ChB 1990; MD 1995; PhD 2001; DSc 2012). MRCOG 1996, FRCOG 2008. House officer and registrar appts, Glasgow, 1990–92 and 1993–96; Wellcome Trust Research Fellow: Dept of Physiol., Univ. of Glasgow, 1992–93; Dept of Physiol., Cornell Univ., Ithaca, NY, 1996–99; sub specialist trainee in Maternal-Fetal Medicine, Glasgow, 1999–2001. FMedSci 2010. *Publications:* contrib. numerous res. papers on physiol., pharmacol. and obstetrics to learned jls, incl. Lancet, BMJ, New England Jl of Medicine, Jl of Amer. Med. Assoc., Nature. *Recreations:* fly fishing, walking, reading. *Address:* Department of Obstetrics and Gynaecology, University of Cambridge, Box 223, The Rosie Hospital, Robinson Way, Cambridge CB2 0SW. *T:* (01223) 336871, *Fax:* (01223) 215327. *E:* paoandghod@medschl.cam.ac.uk.

SMITH, Gordon James, CBE 2004; Resident Director for Scotland, IBM, 1997–2007; *b* 17 Dec. 1947; *s* of Stanley and Agnes Smith; *m* 2001, Margaret McKenzie; two *s* two *d*. *Educ:* Univ. of Stirling (BA 2003). IBM: joined 1970; various appts, 1970–97. Chairman: Business Enterprise Trusts, 1996–99; CBI Scotland, 2003–05; Regl Chms Cttee, CBI, 2005–06. Dir, Dunfermline Bldg Soc., 2006–09. Board Member: Scottish Qualifications Authy, 2000–04; Young Enterprise Scotland, 2000–04; Trust Bd, Scottish Chamber Orch., 2000–04. *Recreations:* golf, travel, cooking.

SMITH, Graeme David; His Honour Judge Graeme Smith; a Circuit Judge, since 2015; *b* London, 16 Nov. 1963; *s* of David and Patricia Smith; *m* 1986, Helen; two *s* one *d*. *Educ:* Archbishop Tenison's Grammar Sch.; Emmanuel Coll., Cambridge (BA 1985; MA); Coll. of Law, London. Admitted as solicitor, 1988; Partner, Pannone & Partners, Manchester, 1991–2003; Dep. Dist Judge, 1999–2003; Dist Judge, 2003–15; Recorder, 2008–15. Gen. Ed., Jordan's Civil Court Service, 2014–. *Publications:* Was the Tomb Empty?, 2014. *Recreations:* reading, model making, spending time with family and friends. *Address:* Bolton Combined Court, Blackhorse Street, Bolton BL1 1SU. *T:* (01204) 392881.

SMITH, Very Rev. Graham Charles Morell; Dean of Norwich, 2004–13, now Dean Emeritus; *b* 7 Nov. 1947; *s* of Philip and Helen Smith; *m* 1975, Carys Evans; one *s* two *d*. *Educ:* Whitgift Sch., Croydon; Univ. of Durham (BA Hons Theology 1974); Westcott House, Cambridge. Ordained deacon, 1976, priest, 1977; Asst Curate, All Saints, Tooting Graveney, 1976–80; Team Vicar, St Paul's, Thamesmead, 1980–87; Team Rector, Kidlington with Hampton Poyle, 1987–97; Rural Dean of Oxford, 1988–94; Rector of Leeds, 1997–2004; Hon. Canon, Ripon Cathedral, 1997–2004. *Recreations:* classic cars, theatre and cinema, biography, music, novels, hill walking. *Address:* Blacksmith's Cottage, Church Street, Ashreigney, nr Chulmleigh, Devon EX18 7LP.

SMITH, Grahame; General Secretary, Scottish Trades Union Congress, since 2006; *b* 8 Jan. 1959; *s* of Thomas Smith and Joyce Smith; partner, Liz Campbell; two *s*. *Educ:* Strathclyde Univ. (BA Hons). Asst Sec., 1986–96, Dep. Gen. Sec., 1996–2006, Scottish TUC. *Address:* Scottish Trades Union Congress, 333 Woodlands Road, Glasgow G3 6NG. *T:* (0141) 337 8100, *Fax:* (0141) 337 8101. *E:* gsmith@stuc.org.uk.

SMITH, Maj. Gen. Gregory Stephen, CB 2013; TD 1994; QVRM 2009; Chief Executive, Royal Norfolk Agricultural Association, since 2012; *b* Norwich, 18 May 1956; *s* of James Lee and Geraldine Mary Smith; *m* 1982, Rebecca Elizabeth Read; two *s* one *d*. *Educ:* Norwich Sch.; Univ. of Newcastle upon Tyne (BSc Hons Agricl and Food Mktg). Director: Taylor Nelson Sofres plc, 1992–2000; Ipsos MORI (formerly Market and Opinion Res. Internat. (MORI) Ltd, 2001–09; Founder, Read Smith Consulting, 2010. Chair, Internat. Adv. Bd, Newcastle Univ. Business Sch., 2009–14; Mem. Court, Newcastle Univ., 2011–. CO 5 (V) RGJ, 1996–99; Dir, Army Reserves, 2006–09; ACDS (Reserves and Cadets), MoD, 2010–13. Chair, East Anglia Reserves' and Cadets' Assoc., 2014–; Pres., UK Reserve Forces Assoc., 2014–. Director: Norfolk Showground Ltd, 2012–; Innovation for Agriculture, 2013–14; Norfolk Showground Develts Ltd, 2014–. DL Bucks, 1998–2011. MInstD 2001. FRSA. Trustee, The Rifles, 2009–14. *Recreations:* sailing, walking, the Norfolk Broads. *Address:* Norfolk Showground, Dereham Road, Costessey, Norwich, Norfolk NR5 0TT. *T:* (01603) 748931. *Clubs:* Army and Navy; Norfolk (Norwich); Horning Sailing.

SMITH, Prof. Hamilton Othanel; Scientific Director, Synthetic Biology and Bioenergy Groups, J. Craig Venter Institute, San Diego, since 2006 (Scientific Director, Institute for Biological Energy Alternatives, 2002–06); *b* 23 Aug. 1931; *s* of Bunnie Othanel Smith and Tommie Harkey Smith; *m* 1957, Elizabeth Anne Bolton; four *s* one *d*. *Educ:* Univ. of Illinois; Univ. of California (AB); Johns Hopkins Univ. Sch. of Medicine (MD). Research Associate, Dept of Human Genetics, Univ. of Michigan, 1964–67; Johns Hopkins University School of Medicine: Asst Prof. of Microbiology, 1967–69; Associate Prof. of Microbiology, 1969–73; Prof. of Microbiology, 1973–81; Prof. of Molecular Biology and Genetics, 1981–2002; Celera Genomics Corp., 1998–2002. During sabbatical leave in Zürich, worked in collaboration with Prof. Dr M. L. Birnstiel, Inst. für Molekularbiologie II der Univ. Zürich, 1975–76; Vis. Prof., Inst. of Molecular Pathol., Vienna, 1990–91. Nobel Prize in Medicine (jtly), 1978. *Publications:* A restriction enzyme from *Hemophilus influenzae:* I. Purification and general properties (with K. W. Wilcox), in Jl Mol. Biol. *51*, 379, 1970; A restriction enzyme from *Hemophilus influenzae:* II. Base sequence of the recognition site (with T. J. Kelly), in Jl Mol. Biol. *51*, 393, 1970. *Recreations:* piano, classical music. *Address:* J. Craig Venter Institute, 4120 Capricorn Lane, La Jolla, CA 92037, USA.

SMITH, Harvey; *see* Smith, Robert H.

SMITH, Helen Sylvester, MA; Headmistress, Perse School for Girls, Cambridge, 1989–2001; *b* 7 Jan. 1942; *d* of late S. J. Smith and K. R. Smith. *Educ:* King Edward VI High Sch. for Girls, Birmingham; St Hilda's College, Oxford (BA 1963, MA 1967 Maths); Hughes Hall, Cambridge (PGCE 1964). Cheltenham Ladies' College, 1964–69; International School of Brussels, 1969–71; Perse Sch. for Girls, 1971–2001 (Dep. Head, 1979–82, 1988–89). *Recreations:* music, gardening. *Address:* 6A Cavendish Avenue, Cambridge CB1 7US. *T:* (01223) 249200.

SMITH, Henry Edward Millar; MP (C) Crawley, since 2010; *b* Epsom, 14 May 1969; *s* of John Edwin Smith and Josephine Anne Smith (*née* Millar); *m* 1994, Jennifer Lois Ricks; one *s* one *d* (and one *s* decd). *Educ:* University Coll. London (BA Hons Philosophy 1991). Mem. (C) W Sussex CC, 1997–2010 (Leader, 2003–10). Contested (C) Crawley, 2001, 2005. *Publications:* (jtly) Direct Democracy, 2005. *Recreations:* family, ski-ing, vexillology. *Address:* House of Commons, SW1A 0AA. *T:* (020) 7219 7043. *E:* henry.smith.mp@parliament.uk.

SMITH, Col Henry Owen H.; *see* Hugh Smith.

SMITH, Prof. Henry Sidney, FBA 1985; Edwards Professor of Egyptology, 1970–86, Head of Department of Egyptology, 1970–88, University College London, now Professor Emeritus; *b* 14 June 1928; *s* of Prof. Sidney Smith, FBA, and Mary, *d* of H. W. Parker; *m* 1961, Hazel Flory Leeper (*d* 1991). *Educ:* Merchant Taylors' Sch., Northwood; Christ's Coll., Cambridge (MA); DLit London, 1987. Lectr in Egyptology, Univ. of Cambridge, 1954–63; Budge Fellow in Egyptology, Christ's Coll., Cambridge, 1955–63; Reader in Egyptian Archaeology, University Coll. London, 1963–70. Field Dir for Egypt Exploration Soc. in Nubia, 1961, 1964–65, and at Saqqara and Memphis, Egypt, 1970–88. *Publications:* Preliminary Reports of the Egypt Exploration Society's Nubian Survey, 1962; A Visit to Ancient Egypt, 1974; The Fortress of Buhen: the inscriptions, 1976; The Fortress of Buhen: the archaeological report, 1979; (with W. J. Tait) Saqqara Demotic Papyri I, 1983; The Anubieion at Saqqara, Vol. I (with D. G. Jeffreys), 1988, Vol. II (with L. L. Giddy), 1992; (with Sue Davies): The Sacred Animal Necropolis at North Saqqara: the falcon complex and catacomb, the archaeological report, 2005; The Sacred Animal Necropolis at North Saqqara: the main temple complex, 2006; (with C. A. R. Andrews and Sue Davies) The Sacred Animal Necropolis at North Saqqara: the mother of Apis inscriptions, 2011; articles in Kush, Jl of Egyptian Arch., Orientalia, Rev. d'Egyptologie, Bull. Inst. Français d'Arch. Or., Z für Äg. Sprache und Altertumskunde, etc.

SMITH, Iain-Mór L.; *see* Lindsay-Smith.

SMITH, Iain William; senior consultant on Scottish public policy, since 2012; Policy and Engagement Officer, Inclusion Scotland, since 2013; *b* 1 May 1960; *s* of William Smith and Jane Allison Smith (*née* Farmer). *Educ:* Bell Baxter High Sch., Cupar; Newcastle upon Tyne Univ. (BA Hons Politics and Econs). Fife Regional Council: Mem. (Lib Dem), 1982–96; Sec., Alliance Gp, 1982–86; Leader of Opposition, 1986–96; Mem. (Lib Dem), and Leader of Opposition, Fife Council, 1995–99. MSP (Lib Dem) NE Fife, 1999–2011. Dep. Minister for Parlt, Scottish Exec., 1999–2000; spokesman on local govt and transport, 2003–05, on education, 2005–07, for Europe, external relns and culture, 2007–11. Scottish Parliament: Convener: Procedures Cttee, 2003–05; Educn Cttee, 2005–07; Economy, Energy and Tourism Cttee, 2008–11; Mem., Eur. and External Affairs Cttee, 2007–08. Convener, Lib Dems Scottish Parly Party, 2007–11; Policy and Information Officer, CHILDREN 1ST, 2012. Contested (Lib Dem) North East Fife, Scottish Parlt, 2011. *Recreations:* sport (mainly football and cricket), cinema, travel, reading, theatre. *Address:* Ambler Cottage, 14 Melville Road, Ladybank, Cupar, Fife KY15 7LU. *T:* (01337) 831115.

SMITH, Prof. Ian Edward, MD; FRCP, FRCPE; Professor of Cancer Medicine, Institute of Cancer Research, University of London, since 2000; Consultant Cancer Physician, since 1978, and Head of Breast Unit, since 2003, Royal Marsden Hospital, London; *b* 16 May 1946; *s* of late David Nicol Smith and Nettie, (Bunty), Thompson Smith (*née* Millar); *m* 1978, Suzanne Dorothy Mackey; three *d*. *Educ:* High Sch. of Dundee; Edinburgh Univ. (BSc Hons 1968; MB ChB 1971; MD 1978). FRCPE 1984; FRCP 1988. House Physician, SHO, then Registrar, Royal Infirmary, Edinburgh, 1971–73; Med. Registrar, Royal Marsden Hosp., London, 1973–75; Res. Fellow, Inst. of Cancer Res., London, 1975–76; UICC Travelling Fellow, Harvard Med. Sch., Boston, 1976–77; Lectr, Royal Marsden Hosp., 1977–78; Head of Section of Medicine, Inst. of Cancer Res., 1994–; Head of Lung Unit, 1994–2001, Med. Dir, 2000–03, Royal Marsden Hosp. Lectures worldwide on breast cancer and new cancer therapies. Chairman: Assoc. of Cancer Physicians, 1995–98; UKCCCR Lung Gp, 1999–; NCRI Lung Clinical Trials Gp, 2000–03; British Breast Gp, 2007–; UK Breast Intergroup, 2007–. Member: Amer. Soc. of Clin. Oncology, 1978; British Assoc. for Cancer Res., 1978; Eur. Soc. of Med. Oncology, 1991. *Publications:* (jtly) Autologous Bone Marrow Transplantation, 1984; (jtly) Medical Management of Breast Cancer, 1991; multiple papers, articles and contribs to books on breast cancer. *Recreations:* ski-ing, supporting Chelsea, reading. *Address:* Royal Marsden Hospital, Fulham Road, SW3 6JJ. *T:* (020) 7808 2751; Royal Marsden Hospital, Downs Road, Sutton, Surrey SM2 5PT.

SMITH, Ian Knight; HM Diplomatic Service, retired; Counsellor and Deputy Head of Mission, Berne, 1993–97; *b* 18 June 1938; *m* 1st, 1964, Glenys Audrey Hayter (*d* 1981); one *s*; 2nd, 1989, Ellen Ragnhild Sweet-Escott; one *s* one *d*. FCO, 1962; Mexico City, 1964; Second Secretary: Calcutta, 1967; Caracas, 1969; First Secretary: FCO, 1972; UKREP Brussels, 1982; FCO, 1987; on secondment as Counsellor to EEC, 1989, to DSS, 1991.

SMITH, Ian Richard; Chairman, Four Seasons Health Care, since 2012; *b* 22 Jan. 1954; *s* of Albert and Drusilla Smith; *m* 1989, Caroline Firstbrook; three *c*. *Educ:* St Edmund Hall, Oxford (MA Hons); Univ. of Harvard (MBA high dist.). Gen. Manager, Jordan, Royal Dutch Shell, 1978–86; Chief Exec., Europe, Monitor (strategy consulting), 1986–98; Chief Exec., Europe, Exel (Transportation), 1998–2004; CEO, General Healthcare, 2004–06; Chief Exec., Taylor Woodrow plc, 2007; Mem., Govt Rev. of Royal Mail and UK Postal Sector (Hooper Rev.), 2008; Chm., Parly Rev. on Civil Service Reform (Smith Rev.), 2009; CEO, Reed Elsevier, 2009; Partner, Governance for Owners, 2011–12. Advr to Quartet Rep., 2009–12. *Publications:* Mosquito Pathfinder, 2002; Building a World Class NHS, 2007. *Recreations:* sports, politics, history. *Club:* Royal Automobile.

See also Prof. S. K. Smith.

SMITH, Prof. Ian William Murison, PhD; FRS 1995; CChem, FRSC; Senior Research Fellow, Department of Chemistry, University of Cambridge, since 2002; Mason Professor of Chemistry, University of Birmingham, 1991–2002, now Emeritus; *b* 15 June 1937; *s* of William Murison Smith and Margaret Moir Smith; *m* 1961, Susan Morrish; two *s* two *d*. *Educ:* Giggleswick Sch.; Christ's Coll., Cambridge (BA, MA, PhD). Cambridge University: ICI Res. Fellow, 1965–66; Demonstrator, 1966–71, Lectr, 1971–85, in Physical Chem.; Christ's College: Res. Fellow, 1963–66, Fellow, 1966–85; Tutor, 1968–77; Dir of Studies, 1972–85; Fellow Commoner, 2003–; University of Birmingham: Prof. of Chemistry, 1985–2002; Head, Sch. of Chem., 1989–93, 2001. Visiting Professor: Univ. of California, Berkeley, 1980, 1996; Univ. of Rennes I, 1999; Jt Inst. in Lab. Astrophysics Fellow, Univ. of Colorado, 2000. Stauffer Dist. Lectr, USC, 2000; Wilhelm Jost Meml Lectr, Germany, 2003. Royal Society of Chemistry: Liversidge Lectr, 2001–02; Pres., Faraday Div., 2001–03; Special Award for reaction kinetics, 1982; Tilden Medal, 1983; Polanyi Medal, 1990. Hon. Dr rer. nat. Duisburg-Essen, 2007. EU Descartes Prize, 2000. *Publications:* Kinetics and Dynamics of Elementary Gas Reactions, 1980; (ed) Physical Chemistry of Fast Reactions: reaction dynamics, 1980; (ed) Modern Gas Kinetics, 1987; (ed) Low Temperatures and Cold Molecules, 2008; (ed) Astrochemistry and Astrobiology, 2013; numerous contribs to learned jls. *Recreations:* Guardian crosswords, reading, theatre, grandchildren. *Address:* University Chemical Laboratories, Lensfield Road, Cambridge CB2 1EW; 36 Grantchester Road, Cambridge CB3 9ED.

SMITH, Prof. Ivor Ramsay, FREng; Professor of Electrical Power Engineering, Loughborough University (formerly Loughborough University of Technology), since 1974; *b* 8 Oct. 1929; *s* of Howard Smith and Elsie Emily Smith; *m* 1962, Pamela Mary Voake; three *s*. *Educ:* Univ. of Bristol (BSc, PhD, DSc), CEng, FIET (FIEE 1974); FREng (FEng 1988); Sen. MIEEE 2011 (MIEEE 2010). Design and Develt Engr, GEC, Birmingham, 1956–59; Lectr, Sen. Lectr, Reader, Univ. of Birmingham, 1959–74; Loughborough University of Technology: Hd, Dept of Electronic and Electrical Engrg, 1980–90; Dean of Engrg, 1983–86; Pro-Vice-Chancellor, 1987–91. Director: Loughborough Consultants Ltd, 1980–; E Midlands Regl Technology Network, 1989–. Ind. Mem., Defence Scientific Adv. Council, 2003–. *Publications:* (jtly) Magnetocumulative Generators, 2000; Explosively Driven Pulsed Power, 2005; over 450 technical papers and articles on range of power engrg topics, incl. the efficient computation of power supply systems and the prodn, processing and application of very large pulses of electrical energy for various pulsed power applications. *Recreations:* gardening, walking, reading. *Address:* School of Electronic, Electrical and Systems Engineering, Loughborough University, Loughborough, Leics LE11 3TU. *T:* (01509) 227005.

SMITH, Rt Hon. Jacqueline Jill, (Jacqui); PC 2003; consultant, trainer, coach and commentator; Chair, University Hospitals Birmingham NHS Foundation Trust, since 2013; *b* 3 Nov. 1962; *d* of Michael and Jill Smith; *m* 1987, Richard James Timney; two *s. Educ:* Hertford Coll., Oxford (BA Hons PPE); Worcester Coll. of Higher Education (PGCE). Res. Asst, Terry Davis, MP, 1984–85; Teacher: Arrow Vale High Sch., Redditch, 1986–88; Worcester Sixth Form Coll., 1988–90; Head of Econs, and GNVQ Co-ordinator, Haybridge High Sch., 1990–97. Mem. (Lab) Redditch BC, 1991–97. Contested (Lab) Mid Worcestershire, 1992. MP (Lab) Redditch, 1997–2010; contested (Lab) same seat, 2010. Parly Under-Sec. of State, DfEE, 1999–2001; Minister of State: DoH, 2001–03; DTI, 2003–05; Minister of State (Minister for Schs), DfES, 2005–06; Parly Sec. to HM Treasury (Govt Chief Whip), 2006–07; Sec. of State for the Home Dept, 2007–09. Chair, Public Affairs Practice, Westbourne Communications, 2015–; Associate, Global Partners Governance, 2012–. Chair, Precious Trust, 2011–. *Recreations:* family, friends, football, theatre. *E:* smithjacqui@live.co.uk.

SMITH, James Cadzow, CBE 1989; DRC, FREng; FRSE; Chairman, Natural Environment Research Council, 1997–2000; *b* 28 Nov. 1927; *s* of James Smith and Margaret Ann Cadzow; *m* 1954, Moira Barrie Hogg; one *s* one *d. Educ:* Bellvue Secondary Sch.; Heriot-Watt Coll.; Strathclyde Univ. FIMechE 1960; FIET (FIEE 1960); FIMarEST (FIMarE 1960); FREng (FEng 1988); FRSE 1981. Engineer Officer, Mercantile Marine, 1948–53; engineering and managerial appts in fossil and nuclear power generation with SSEB and CEGB, 1953–73; Dir of Engineering, N Ireland Electricity Service, 1973–74; Dep. Chm. and Chief Exec., 1975–77; Chm., E Midlands Electricity Bd, 1977–82; Chm. and Chief Exec., Eastern Electricity Bd, 1982–90; Chief Exec., 1990–93, and Chm., 1990–95, Eastern Electricity plc, later Eastern Gp. Pres., IEE, 1989–90. Dir, N. M. Rothschild & Sons Ltd, 1991–97. Freeman, City of London, 1984; Liveryman, 1984, Master, 1997–98, Engineers' Co. Hon. LLD Strathclyde, 1988. *Recreations:* music, drama, mountaineering. *Address:* 20 Hartley Court, 84 Woodstock Road, Oxford OX2 7PF.

SMITH, Dr James Cuthbert, FRS 1993; FMedSci; Deputy Chief Executive Officer and Chief of Strategy, Medical Research Council, since 2014; Director of Research, Francis Crick Institute, since 2015; *b* 31 Dec. 1954; *s* of late Leslie Cuthbert Smith and Freda Sarah (*née* Wragg); *m* 1979, Fiona Mary Watt, *qv*; two *s* one *d. Educ:* Latymer Upper Sch.; Christ's Coll., Cambridge (BA 1976; MA 1979; Hon. Fellow, 2009); London Univ. (PhD 1979). NATO Postdoctoral Fellow, Sidney Farber Cancer Inst. and Harvard Med. Sch., 1979–81; ICRF Postdoctoral Fellow, 1981–84; National Institute for Medical Research: Mem., Scientific Staff, 1984–2000; Head, Div. of Develtl Biol., 1991–2000; Head, Genes and Cellular Controls Gp, 1996–2000; John Humphrey Plummer Prof. of Develtl Biol., Univ. of Cambridge, 2001–08; Fellow of Christ's Coll., Cambridge, 2001–08; Chm., Wellcome Trust/CRUK Gurdon Inst. (formerly Wellcome Trust and CRUK Inst. of Cancer and Develtl Biol.), 2001–08; Dir, MRC Nat. Inst. for Med. Res., 2009–15. Chm., British Soc. for Developmental Biol., 1994–99; Mem., EMBO, 1992. Howard Hughes Internat. Res. Scholar, 1993–97. Fellow, European Acad. of Cancer Scis, 2009. Founder FMedSci 1998. FRSA 2009. Scientific Medal, Zool Soc. of London, 1989; Otto Mangold Prize, Ges. für Entwicklungsbiologie, 1991; EMBO Medal, 1993; Feldberg Foundn Award, 2000; (jtly) William Bate Hardy Prize, Cambridge Phil Soc., 2001; Waddington Medal, British Soc. for Develtl Biology, 2013. *Publications:* (ed jtly) The Molecular Basis of Positional Signalling, 1989; (with L. Wolpert and others) Principles of Development, 2nd edn 2001, 3rd edn 2007; scientific articles in various jls. *Recreations:* cycling, running, music, reading. *Address:* Francis Crick Institute, Mill Hill Laboratory, The Ridgeway, NW7 1AA. *T:* (020) 8816 2048, 07802 745798, *Fax:* (020) 8816 2041. *E:* jim.smith@crick.ac.uk.

SMITH, Jane Caroline Rebecca P.; *see* Parker-Smith.

SMITH, Jane L.; *see* Lewin Smith.

SMITH, Rt Hon. Dame Janet (Hilary), (Dame Janet Mathieson), DBE 1992; PC 2002; a Lord Justice of Appeal, 2002–11; *b* 29 Nov. 1940; *d* of Alexander Roe and Margaret Holt; *m* 1st, 1959, Edward Stuart Smith; two *s* one *d*; 2nd, 1984, Robin Edward Alexander Mathieson. *Educ:* Bolton School. Called to the Bar, Lincoln's Inn, 1972, Bencher, 1992 (Treas., 2012); QC 1986; a Recorder, 1988–92; a Judge of the High Ct of Justice, QBD, 1992–2002; a Judge of the Employment Appeal Tribunal, 1994–2002; Presiding Judge, N Eastern Circuit, 1995–98. Pres., Council, Inns of Court, 2006–09. Chairman: Shipman Inquiry, 2001–05; BBC review into allegations of sexual abuse by Jimmy Savile, 2012–15. Mem., Criminal Injuries Compensation Bd, 1988–92; Chm., Security Vetting Appeals Panel, 2000–09; Ind. Assessor of Compensation for Miscarriages of Justice, 2011–15. Chm., Civil Cttee, Judicial Studies Bd, 2000–04. Chancellor, Manchester Metropolitan Univ., 2003–09. Pres., Personal Injuries Bar Assoc., 2009–11. Chm., Buxton Arts Festival, 2007–14. Hon. LLD: Manchester Metropolitan, 2002; Lancaster, 2005. *Recreations:* gardening, music.

SMITH, Jeff; Head of Music, BBC Radio 2 and BBC Radio 6 Music, since 2007; *b* Fleetwood, Lancs, 24 Dec. 1960; *s* of William Henry Smith and Joyce Smith; *m* 2013, Deborah Stanley; one *s* one *d. Educ:* Baines' Sch., Poulton-le-Fylde; North Cheshire Coll., Warrington; Univ. of Manchester (BA Communication Studies). Producer, BBC World Service, 1984–87; Programme Manager, TFM Radio, 1987–90; BBC Radio 1: Producer and Creator, Evening Session, 1990–93; Editor, Mainstream Progs and Music Manager, 1993–95; Dir, Progs, Wise Buddah Independent Prodn, 1995–97; Hd, Music Policy, BBC Radio 1, 1997–2000; Prog. Controller, 95.8 Capital FM, 2000–03; Programming Dir, Napster UK and Internat., 2004–07. Commnd music drama for BBC Radio 2, Darkside, 2013; creator, music drama for BBC Radio, Queens of Noise: Shout to the Top, 2014. *Address:* BBC Radio 2, 99 Great Portland Street, W1A 1AA. *E:* jeff.smith@bbc.co.uk.

SMITH, Jeffrey; *see* Smith, A. J.

SMITH, Jeffrey; MP (Lab) Manchester Withington, since 2015; *b* Withington, 26 Jan. 1963; *s* of Allan Smith and Deidre Smith. *Educ:* Old Moat Primary Sch.; Univ. of Manchester (BA(Econ) Hons 1984). Event manager, 1985–2010; DJ, 1992–2011. Mem. (Lab) Manchester CC, 1997–2015 (Executive Member: for Educn and Children's Services; for Finance; for Housing and Regeneration). Mem., Envmtl Audit Select Cttee, 2015–. Mem. Bd, Southway. Governor: Old Moat Primary Sch.; Parrs Wood High Sch. *Address:* House of Commons, SW1A 0AA.

SMITH, Prof. (Jenkyn) Beverley, FRHistS; FLSW; Research Professor of Welsh History, University of Wales, Aberystwyth, 1995–98, now Emeritus Professor; Commissioner, 1984–99, Chairman, 1991–99, Royal Commission on Ancient and Historical Monuments for Wales; *b* 27 Sept. 1931; *s* of Cecil Nelson Smith and Hannah Jane (*née* Jenkins); *m* 1966, Llinos Olwen Wyn Vaughan, PhD, FRHistS, medieval historian; two *s. Educ:* Gowerton Grammar Sch.; UCW, Aberystwyth (BA, MA). FRHistS 1967. National Service, 1954–56. Researcher, Bd of Celtic Studies, Univ. of Wales, 1956–58; Asst Keeper, Dept of MSS and Records, Nat. Library of Wales, 1958–60; Lectr 1960–67, Sen. Lectr 1967–78, Reader 1978–86, Sir John Williams Prof. of Welsh History, 1986–95, Dept of Welsh History, UCW, Aberystwyth. Sir John Rhys Vis. Fellow, Univ. of Oxford, 1978–79. Member: Court and Council, Nat. Library of Wales, 1974–84; Bd of Celtic Studies, Univ. of Wales, 1965–2007 (Sec., History and Law Cttee, 1979–85, Chm. 1985–91); Ancient Monuments Bd for Wales, 1992–98. FLSW 2013. Jt Editor, Bulletin of Bd of Celtic Studies, 1972–93; Editor, 1994–96, Chief Editor, 1996–2010, Studia Celtica. *Publications:* Llywelyn ap Gruffudd, Tywysog Cymru, 1986; Llywelyn ap Gruffudd, Prince of Wales, 1998, 2nd edn 2014; (ed) Medieval Welsh Society, Selected Essays by T. Jones Pierce, 1972; (ed with G. H. Jenkins) Politics and Society in Wales 1840–1922, 1988; (ed with Llinos Beverley Smith) History of Merioneth, vol. II, The Middle Ages, 2001; Princes and Castles: the thirteenth-century legacy, 2010; articles in English Hist. Review, Welsh Hist. Review, Bulletin Bd of Celtic Studies, Studio Celtica and other jls. *Address:* Erw'r Llan, Llanbadarn Road, Aberystwyth, Ceredigion SY23 1EY.

SMITH, Hon. Dame Jennifer, DBE 2005; JP; MP (Progressive Lab) St George's North, Bermuda, 1989–2012; Minister of Education, 2010–12; *d* of late Eugene Wilberforce Smith and Lillian Smith (*née* De Shields). *Educ:* Bermuda; Art Inst., Pittsburgh. Formerly newspaper and magazine editor, radio and TV promotions manager and choreographer. Mem., Senate of Bermuda, 1980–89; Premier of Bermuda, 1998–2003; Minister of Educn, 1998–99; Dep. Speaker, House of Assembly, 2003–10. Dep. Leader, 1994–96, Leader, 1996–2003, Progressive Labour Party. Exec. Mem., 2005–07, Vice-Chm., 2006–07, Commonwealth Parly Assoc. Election Observer, Bangladesh, Commonwealth Secretariat, 2008. Member: Bermuda Inst. of Ocean Scis; Bd of Trustees, Bermuda Nat. Gall.; Bermuda Heritage Assoc.; Bermuda Musical and Dramatic Soc.; Bermuda Dance Foundn; Masterworks of Bermuda. Hon. DHumLit: Mount St Vincent, Halifax, Canada, 2000; Morris Brown Coll., Atlanta, USA, 2000; Hon. DHum Art Inst. of Pittsburgh, 2003. *Publications:* Voice of Change, 2003.

SMITH, Jennifer A.; Principal, Harrogate Ladies' College, 1993–95; *b* 11 March 1950; *d* of Geoffrey and Elsie Bird; *m* 1974, Michael Smith; one *d. Educ:* Leeds Univ. (BSc Hons Physics, PGCE); Open Univ. (BA); Liverpool Univ. (MEd). Asst teacher, Physics, 1973–83, Head of Physics, 1983–85, St Richard Gwyn High Sch., Clwyd; Sen. Project Tutor, Science and Electronics, Bodelwyddan TVEI Centre, 1985–88; Dep. Head Teacher, West Kirby Grammar Sch. for Girls, 1988–93. Mem., Treuddyn Community Council, 2008 (Chair, 2010–). Chair, Trueddyn Community Assoc., 2009–. *Recreations:* ski-ing, climbing, music, theatre, computing.

SMITH, Jeremy Fox Eric; DL; Chairman, Smith St Aubyn (Holdings) plc, 1973–86, retired; *b* 17 Nov. 1928; *s* of late Captain E. C. E. Smith, MC, and B. H. Smith (*née* Williams); *m* 1st, 1953, Julia Mary Rona, DL (*d* 2004), *d* of Sir Walter Burrell, 8th Bt, CBE, TD; two *s* two *d*; 2nd, 2008, Lady Gillian Moyra Katherine Kertesz, *d* of 6th Marquess of Exeter, KCMG, DL. *Educ:* Eton; New College, Oxford. Chairman, Transparent Paper Ltd, 1965–76. Chairman, London Discount Market Assoc., 1978–80. Trustee, Henry Smith's Charity, 1971–97. DL 1988, High Sheriff, 1992–93, West Sussex. *Address:* The Old Rectory, Slaugham, Haywards Heath, W Sussex RH17 6AG. *T:* (01444) 400341. *Clubs:* Beefsteak; Pitt; Leander (Henley on Thames); Cavalry and Guards.

See also Fortune, Duchess of Grafton, Earl of Verulam, Countess of Verulam.

SMITH, Jeremy James Russell; Director, Advocacy International Ltd, since 2010; *b* 12 June 1947; *s* of Horace James Smith and Joan Alistair Russell. *Educ:* Peterhouse, Cambridge (BA Law 1968). Called to the Bar, Lincoln's Inn, 1969; Barrister, 1971–78; Sen. Legal Adviser, Brent Community Law Centre, 1978–83; Legal Services Liaison Officer, GLC, 1983–86; Clerk and Legal Advr, ILEA, 1986–89; Dir of Law and Admin, 1989–90, Chief Exec., 1990–95, London Borough of Camden; Dir, Local Govt Internat. Bureau, 1996–2002; Secretary General: IULA, 2002–04; CEMR, 2002–09. *Recreations:* history, current affairs, music, rambling. *Address:* Advocacy International Ltd, 51 Clarence Gate Gardens, Glentworth Street, NW1 6QS. *E:* jeremy.smith@advocacyinternational.co.uk.

SMITH, Joan Alison; journalist and novelist; *b* London, 27 Aug. 1953; *d* of Alan Smith and Ann Anita Smith (*née* Coltman); *m* 1985, Francis James Baird Wheen, *qv* (marr. diss. 1993); partner, 2003–10, Denis MacShane, *qv. Educ:* Girls' Grammar Sch., Stevenage; Basingstoke High Sch. for Girls; Univ. of Reading (BA Hons Latin). Reporter: Evening Gazette, Blackpool, 1976–78; Piccadilly Radio, Manchester, 1978–79; Sunday Times, 1979–84; freelance journalist, 1984–. Exec. Dir, Hacked Off, 2014–15. Non-exec. Dir, ALCS, 2010–. Chair, Writers in Prison Cttee, English PEN, 2000–04; Co-Chair, Mayor of London's Violence Against Women and Girls Panel, 2013–. Adjunct Associate Prof., Edith Cowan Univ., WA, 2002–05. Pres., Creators' Rights Alliance, 2011–13. Hon. Associate, Nat. Secular Soc., 2001; Dist. Supporter, British Humanist Assoc., 2013. FRSA. *Publications: non-fiction:* Clouds of Deceit, 1985; Misogynies, 1989; (ed) Femmes de Siècle, 1992; Hungry for You, 1996; Different for Girls, 1998; Moralities, 2001; The Public Woman, 2013; *novels:* A Masculine Ending, 1987; Why Aren't They Screaming?, 1988; Don't Leave Me This Way, 1990; What Men Say, 1993; Full Stop, 1995; What Will Survive, 2007; Down with the Royals, 2015. *Address:* c/o Peters Fraser & Dunlop, Drury House, 34–43 Russell Street, WC2B 5HA. *T:* (020) 7344 1000. *E:* info@pfd.co.uk.

SMITH, Joanna Angela; QC 2009; *b* London, 27 April 1968; *d* of Dr W. H. Smith and Pamela Smith (now Dickson); *m* 1994, Mark James Vanhegan, *qv*; two *d. Educ:* King's Sch., Ely; Christ Church, Oxford (MA 1st Cl. Juris.). Called to the Bar, Lincoln's Inn, 1990; in practice as barrister specialising in commercial litigation, professional negligence, construction and regulation. *Recreations:* wandering at a leisurely pace across Europe, laughing with my children, running. *Address:* Wilberforce Chambers, 8 New Square, Lincoln's Inn, WC2A 3QP. *T:* (020) 7306 0102, *Fax:* (020) 7306 0095. *E:* jsmith@wilberforce.co.uk.

SMITH, Jock; *see* Smith, John M. M.

SMITH, Sir John (Alfred), Kt 1994; QPM 1986; Deputy Commissioner of the Metropolitan Police, 1991–95; *b* 21 Sept. 1938; *s* of Ruth Alice and Alfred Joseph Smith; *m* 1960, Joan Maria Smith; one *s* one *d. Educ:* St Olave's and St Saviour's Grammar School. Irish Guards, 1959–62. Metropolitan Police, 1962; Head, Scotland Yard drugs squad, 1979; Commander 'P' (Bromley-Lewisham) Dist, 1980; Dep. Chief Constable, Surrey Constabulary, 1981; Metropolitan Police: Dep. Asst Comr, 1984; Inspectorate and Force Reorganisation Team, 1985; Asst Comr, 1987–90; Management Support Dept, 1987–89; Specialist Ops Dept, 1989–90; Inspector of Constabulary for SE England, 1990–91. Dir, Sabrewatch Ltd, 1995–2000. Mem., Ind. Commn on Policing for NI, 1998–99. Pres., ACPO, 1993–94. Consultant, Football Assoc., 1995–98; non-exec. Dir, Brighton and Hove Albion FC, 1997–2000, 2002–07; Member: Cttee, AA, 1996–99; Govt Football Task Force Wkg Gp, 1997–99; Trustee: Drinking Fountain Assoc., 1995–2013; English Nat. Stadium Trust, 1997–98. *Recreations:* gardening, sport spectating, walking. *Address:* 23 Winterbourne, Horsham, West Sussex RH12 5JW. *T:* (01403) 211076.

SMITH, John Allan Raymond, CBE 2008; PhD; FRCS, FRCSE; Consultant General Surgeon, Northern General Hospital NHS Trust (formerly Northern General Hospital, Sheffield), 1985–2007; President, Royal College of Surgeons of Edinburgh, 2003–06 (a Vice-President, 1997–2000); *b* 24 Nov. 1942; *s* of Alexander Macintyre Smith and Evelyn Joyce Smith; *m* 1979, Valerie Fullalove; two *s* three *d. Educ:* Boroughmuir Sch., Edinburgh; Edinburgh Univ. (MB ChB 1966); Aberdeen Univ. (PhD 1979). FRCS 1972; FRCSE 1972. House Officer, Royal Infirmary of Edinburgh, 1966–67; SSC, RAMC, 1967–72; Registrar, Dumfries and Galloway Royal Infirmary, and Royal Infirmary, Aberdeen, 1972–73; Res. Fellow, Lectr in Surgery and Sen. Surgical Registrar, Grampian Health Bd, 1972–78; Sen. Lectr in Surgery and Cons. Surgeon, Royal Hallamshire Hosp., Sheffield, 1978–85. Chm., Jt Cttee for Higher Surgical Trng, 2000–03; Med. Mem., 2006–10, Chair, Assessment Cttee, 2009–10, PMETB; Mem., Postgrad. Bd, GMC, 2010–11. Non-exec. Dir, Portsmouth Hosps NHS Trust, 2015–. Editor, Complications in Surgery series, 1985. Trustee, Diverse Abilities Plus, Dorset, 2013–. *Publications:* (jtly) Wounds and Wound Management, 1992; (ed jtly and contrib.) Pye's Surgical Handicraft. *Recreations:* family, sport, cooking, wine. *Address:* Hadley Wood, 2 Castlewood, Ringwood, Hants BH24 2AX. *T:* (01425) 291196.

SMITH, John Barry, FCCA; Chief Operating Officer, Burberry Group plc, since 2013 (non-executive Director, 2009–13); *b* 16 Aug. 1957; *s* of Kenneth William Smith and Elsie Smith (*née* Jackson); *m* 1993, Catherine Esther Heywood Hewetson (marr. diss. 2010); two *s* one *d*. *Educ:* South London Coll. (FCCA 1980); Harvard Business Sch. (AMP 1997). Chartered Certified Accountant: Bocock, Bew & Co., Chartered Accountants, 1973–75; BR Gp subsidiaries, 1975–83; BRB, 1983–90; BBC, 1990–2012: Dir of Finance, 1996–2004; Mem. Exec. Bd, 1996–2009; Chief Operating Officer, 2004–05; CEO, BBC Worldwide, 2004–12. Director: Vickers PLC, 1999–2000; UK Enterprise Adv. Bd, Zurich Financial Services, 2000–01; Severn Trent PLC, 2003–08. Member: 100 Gp of Finance Dirs, 2000–05; Public Services Productivity Panel, 2000–06; Accounting Standards Bd, 2001–04. Dir, Henley Festival, 2004–. Vice Pres., RTS. FRTS 2001; FRSA 2005. Hon. FRIBA 2004. *Address:* Burberry Group plc, Horseferry House, Horseferry Road, SW1P 2AW.

SMITH, (John) Edward (Kitson), CBE 2014; FCA; Deputy Chairman, WWF-UK, since 2014 (Chairman, 2008–14); *b* Calcutta, 24 Oct. 1954; *s* of late Jack Smith and Edith Smith; *m* 1981, Jennifer Linton; one *s* two *d*. *Educ:* St Dunstan's Coll., Catford; London Metropolitan Univ. (BA Hons). FCA 2000. CPFA 2013. Coopers & Lybrand, then PricewaterhouseCoopers, 1977–2007: Hd, Educn Practice, 1989–93; Exec. Partner, UK Audit, 1994–97; Global Leader, Learning and Develt, 1998–99; Mem., UK Bd, 2000–03; Sen. Partner and Global Assurance Chief Operating Officer and Strategy Chm., 2004–07. Financial Advr, DES, 1987–89; Mem. Bd, DfT, 2008–; Chm., Crown Commercial Services, Cabinet Office, 2014–. Member: Competition Commn, 2009–14; NHS England (formerly NHS Commissioning Bd), 2011–15; Competition and Markets Authy, 2014–; Chairman: NHS Monitor, 2015–; NHS Trust Develt Authy, 2015–. Member: Adv. Bd, Opportunity Now, 2001–13; Bd, Demos, 2008–10. Mem. Bd, HEFCE, 2004–11; Chm., Student Loans Co., 2010–13. Mem., Commn on Future of Women's Sport, 2008–13. Chm., British Univs and Colls Sport, 2008–14. Mem. Bd, WWF Internat., 2008–14. Trustee and Treas., Work Foundn, 2007–10; Mem. Council and Treas., Chatham House, 2008–. Pro-Chancellor and Chm. Council, Univ. of Birmingham, 2010–; Gov., Univ. (formerly Poly.) of N London, 1991–95. FRSA 2001. Hon. LLD: Bath, 2009; Roehampton, 2013; Aberdeen, 2014. *Publications:* Breakpoint/Breakthrough Strategies for Worklife Balance in the 21st Century, 1999; Accounting for People, 2003; Diversity Dimensions, 2004; (jtly) Papering Over the Cracks, 2006. *Recreations:* golf, cooking, wine collecting, travel, opera. *Address:* Old Mill Leat, Vicarage Hill, Westerham, Kent TN16 1TJ. *T:* 07711 793312. *E:* ed.smith@jeks.co.uk. *Clubs:* Athenaeum, Lansdowne; Wildernesse Golf.

SMITH, (John) Edward (McKenzie) L.; *see* Lucie-Smith.

SMITH, John Frederick; Lord Mayor of Cardiff, 1990–91 (Deputy Lord Mayor, 1988–89; Consort to Deputy Lord Mayor, 2005–06); *b* 28 Sept. 1934; *s* of Charles Frederick Smith and Teresa Smith (*née* O'Brian); *m* 1962, Irene Rice (*d* 1982); one *s*. *Educ:* St Cuthbert's Jun. Sch.; St Illtyd's Grammar Sch.; Gwent Inst. of Higher Educn, 1981–82 (Dip. Trade Union Studies); University Coll., Cardiff, 1982–85 (BScEcon). Engrg apprenticeship, Edward Curran Engrg, 1951–56; Merchant Navy Engr, Blue Funnel and Andrew Weir, 1956–62; Steel Industry, GKN S Wales, 1964–81; Housing Officer, Adamsdown Housing Assoc. Ltd, 1985–96. Member (Lab), Cardiff City Council, 1972–96, Cardiff County Council, 1995–2004: Chairman: Housing and Public Works Cttee, 1973–75; Land Cttee, 1987–90; Chief Whip, 1995–99; Chair, Economic Develt, 1996–99; Presiding Officer, 1999–2000; Mem., S Glamorgan CC, 1973–81. Chm., S Wales Film Commn, 1996–99. Chm., Cardiff Older Persons' Forum, 2007–09. JP Cardiff, 1977–87; DL S Glam, 1999. *Recreations:* music, spectator of Cardiff RFC and Wales RU, Shakespeare, cooking. *Address:* 128 Corporation Road, Grangetown, Cardiff CF11 7AX. *T:* (029) 2033 3193.

SMITH, Sir John Hamilton S.; *see* Spencer-Smith.

SMITH, John Hilary, CBE 1970 (OBE 1964); Secretary, Imperial College, London, and Clerk to the Governors, 1979–89 (Fellow, 1992); *b* 20 March 1928; 2nd *s* of late P. R. Smith, OBE and Edith Prince; *m* 1964, Mary Sylvester Head; two *s* one *d*. *Educ:* Cardinal Vaughan Sch., London; University Coll. London (Fellow, 1987); University Coll., Oxford. BA Hons London 1948; MA Oxon 1991. Mil. service, 1948–50, commnd Queen's Own Royal W Kent Regt. Cadet, Northern Nigerian Administration, 1951; Supervisor, Admin. Service Trng, 1960; Dep. Sec. to Premier, 1963; Dir Staff, Develt Centre, 1964; Perm. Sec., Min. of Finance, Benue Plateau State, 1968; Vis. Lectr, Duke Univ., 1970; Financial Sec., British Solomon Is, 1970; Governor of Gilbert and Ellice Islands, 1973–76, of Gilbert Islands, 1976–78. Procurator, 1990–94, and Fellow, 1991–94, University Coll., Oxford. Public Orator, Univ. of London, 1991–94. Director: Fleming Ventures, 1985–98; Empire Mus. Ltd, 2001–14. Mem. Council, Scout Assoc., 1980–98 (Chm., Cttee of Council, 1984–88); Pres., Pacific Is Soc. of UK and Ireland, 1981–85. Governor: St Mary's Coll., Strawberry Hill, 1980–88; Cardinal Vaughan School, 1982–88; Heythrop Coll., 1986–93 (Fellow, 2002); Member, Board of Management: LSHTM, 1989–98 (Treas., 1993–98; Fellow, 1999); St Mary's Sch., Shaftesbury, 1993–2001 (Chm. Govs, 1994–2001). Sir Arthur Keith Medal, RCS, 2008; Ana Tokabeti Kiribati (Kiribati), 2009. *Publications:* How to Write Letters that get Results, 1965; Colonial Cadet in Nigeria, 1968; (ed) Administering Empire, 1999; An Island in the Autumn, 2010; articles in S Atlantic Quarterly, Administration, Jl of Overseas Administration, Nigeria. *Recreations:* walking, writing, music. *Address:* 282 Old Bath Road, Cheltenham, Glos GL53 9AP. *Club:* Athenæum.

SMITH, Sir John Jonah W.; *see* Walker-Smith.

SMITH, John Mitchell Melvin, (Jock), WS; Partner, Masson & Glennie, Solicitors, Peterhead, 1957–94, retired; *b* 5 July 1930; *s* of John Mitchell Smith and Barbara Edda Smith or Glennie; *m* 1958, Elisabeth Marion Slight; two *s* one *d*. *Educ:* Fettes College; Edinburgh Univ. (BL). Pres., Law Soc. of Scotland, 1987–88. *Recreations:* golf, theatre. *Address:* 1 Winton Terrace, Edinburgh EH10 7AP.

SMITH, Sir John Rathborne V.; *see* Vassar-Smith.

SMITH, (John) Stephen; QC 2000; a Recorder, since 2004; a Deputy High Court Judge, since 2006; *b* 30 June 1960; *s* of John Slater Smith and Nancy Smith (*née* Clayton); *m* 1982, Lorraine Dunn; four *s* one *d*. *Educ:* Walton High Sch., Nelson; University Coll., Oxford (BA 1st Cl. Jurisprudence). Called to the Bar: Middle Temple, 1983; Eastern Caribbean (BVI), 1994; Bahamas, 2004; Isle of Man, 2007; Cayman Islands, 2010. *Recreations:* family, alpaca farming, deer. *Address:* Erskine Chambers, 33 Chancery Lane, WC2A 1EN. *T:* (020) 7242 5532. *E:* ssmith@erskinechambers.com.

SMITH, John William Patrick; *b* 17 March 1951; *s* of John Henry Smith and Margaret Mary (*née* Collins); *m* 1971, Kathleen Mulvaney; two *s* one *d*. *Educ:* Penarth County Sch.; Gwent Coll. of Higher Educn (Dip. in Indust. Relations and Trade Union Studies); UCW Cardiff (BSc (Econ) Hons). Building worker, 1966–68; RAF, 1967–71; joiner, 1971–76; mature student, 1976–83; University Tutor, 1983–85; Sen. Lectr in Business Studies, 1985–89; Chief Exec., Gwent Image Partnership, 1992–97. MP (Lab) Vale of Glamorgan, May 1989–1992 and 1997–2010; contested (Lab) same seat, 1992. PPS to Dep. Leader of the Opposition, 1989–92, to Minister of State for the Armed Forces, 1997–98, to Minister of State (Minister of Transport), DETR, 1998–99. Mem., Select Cttee on Welsh Affairs, 1990–92; formerly Parly spokesperson for Vale of Glam. *Recreations:* reading, boating, walking. *Clubs:* West End Labour; Sea View Labour (Barry).

SMITH, Jon; Chief Executive Officer, First Artist Company Ltd, since 2011; *b* London, 20 Sept. 1952; *s* of Mick and Rosemary Smith; *m* 1st, 1976, Lee M. (*d* 1981); 2nd, 1986, Janine; two *s*. *Educ:* Orange Hill Grammar Sch.; Kingsway Coll. of Further Educn. Chief Exec., London Monarchs, 1991; CEO, 2001–10, Exec. Vice Chm., 2011, First Artist Corp. plc. Mem., Govt Cttee on Replacement of Tobacco Sponsorship in Sport, 1998. Non-exec. Dir, British Taekwondo, 2013–. Mem. Bd, Inst. of Child Health, 1987. Trustee, Lee Smith Foundn, 1982–. Patron, British Stammering Assoc., 2004. FInstD. *Recreations:* charity work, extreme challenges, family management. *Address:* First Artist Company Ltd, First Artist House, 85a Wembley Hill Road, Wembley, Middx HA9 8BU. *T:* (020) 8900 1818. *E:* jons@firstartist.com.

SMITH, Jonathan A.; *see* Ashley-Smith.

SMITH, Ven. Jonathan Peter; Archdeacon of St Albans, since 2008; *b* Guildford, 10 Nov. 1955; *s* of John Smith and Dorothea Smith. *Educ:* Ipswich Sch.; King's Coll., London (BD, AKC 1977); Queens' Coll., Cambridge (PGCE 1978); Westcott House, Cambridge. Ordained deacon, 1980, priest, 1981; Assistant Curate: All Saints', Gosforth, 1980–82; Waltham Abbey, 1982–85; Chaplain, City Univ., 1985–88; Rector, Harrold and Carlton with Chellington, 1988–97; Vicar, St John's, Harpenden, 1997–2008. Rural Dean, Wheathampstead, 1999–2004. Chaplain, Bedfordshire Police, 1990–97. *Recreations:* Association Football, travel, opera, proroguing committees, the company of friends. *T:* (01727) 818121. *Clubs:* Farmers; Bridgman Bowls (Bedfordshire).

SMITH, Jonathan Simon Christopher R.; *see* Riley-Smith.

SMITH, Dr Joseph, FRHistS; Editor, History: Journal of the Historical Association, 2000–10; Reader in American Diplomatic History, University of Exeter, 1995–2010; *b* 2 May 1945; *m* 1971, Marjorie Rachael Eaves. *Educ:* Grey Coll., Univ. of Durham (BA 1966); UCL (PhD 1970). FRHistS 1979. Research Assistant: UCL, 1969–70; Inst. of Latin American Studies, Univ. of London, 1970–71; Lectr in History, Univ. of Exeter, 1971–95. Visiting Professor of History: Coll. of William and Mary, Va, 1976–77; Univ. of Colorado at Denver, 1990–91. Fulbright Schol., 1990–91. Historical Association: Mem. Council, 1985–2003; Chm. of Pubns, 1995–2000; Vice-Pres., 2002–03. FHA 2007. Ed., The Annual Bull. of Histl Literature, 1990–99. Rio Branco Prize, Casa do Brasil, London, 1971. *Publications:* Illusions of Conflict, 1979; The Cold War, 1989, 2nd edn 1998; Origins of NATO, 1990; Unequal Giants, 1991; The Spanish-American War, 1994; Historical Dictionary of the Cold War, 2000; History of Brazil, 2002; The United States and Latin America, 2005; Historical Dictionary of United States-Latin American Relations, 2007; Brazil and the United States, 2010. *Recreations:* travel, tennis. *Address:* 1 California Close, Exeter, Devon EX4 5ET.

SMITH, Sir Joseph (William Grenville), Kt 1991; MD; FRCP; FRCPath; FFPH; Director, Public Health Laboratory Service, 1985–92; *b* 14 Nov. 1930; *s* of Douglas Ralph and Hannah Letitia Margaret Smith; *m* 1954, Nira Jean (*née* Davies); one *s*. *Educ:* Cathays High School, Cardiff; Welsh Nat. Sch. of Medicine (MD 1966); Dip. Bact., London Univ., 1960; FRCPath 1975; FFPH (FFCM 1976); FRCP 1987. FRSB (FIBiol 1978). Lectr, 1960–63, Sen. Lectr, 1963–65, Dept of Bacteriology and Immunology, LSHTM; Consultant Clinical Bacteriologist, Radcliffe Infirmary, Oxford, 1965–69; Gen. Practitioner, Islington, 1970–71; Consultant Epidemiologist, Dep. Dir, Epidemiological Res. Lab., PHLS, 1971–76; Dir, Nat. Inst. for Biological Standards and Control, 1976–85. Consultant on immunisation to British Army, 1985–96. Special Prof., Nottingham Univ., 1989–94. Member: Cttee on Safety of Medicines, 1978–86 (Chm., Biol Sub-Cttee, 1981–86); Jt Cttee on Vaccination and Immunisation, 1976–93 (Chm., Influenza, Measles and Rubella Sub-Cttees, 1979–93); British Pharmacopoeia Commn, 1976–85 (Chm., Immunization Cttee, 1977–85); MRC, 1989–92; Council, RCPath, 1988–90; Adv. Gp on Rabies Quarantine, MAFF, 1997–98; Chairman: Cttee on Vaccination and Immunization Procedures, MRC, 1976–93; Simian Virus Cttee, MRC, 1982–93; Tropical Medicine Res. Bd, MRC, 1989–90; World Health Organisation: Chm., Expert Adv. Gp on Immunization, 1993–95, Chm., Poliomyelitis Commn, 1995–2006, Eur. Reg.; Chm., Global Polio Commn, 2001–03 (Co-Chm., 1998–2001). Mem., Ct of Govs and Bd of Management, LSHTM, 1994–97 (Chm. Bd of Mgt, 1995–97). Hon. DipHIC, LSHTM, 1999. *Publications:* (with E. B. Adams and D. R. Laurence) Tetanus, 1969; papers on tetanus, immunization, and epidemiology of infections in scientific and med. jls. *Recreation:* the arts.

SMITH, Julia Clare; *see* Buckingham, J. C.

SMITH, Julian; MP (C) Skipton and Ripon, since 2010; an Assistant Government Whip, since 2015; *b* Stirling, 30 Aug. 1971; *m* 2003, Amanda. *Educ:* Balfron Sch.; Millfield Sch.; Univ. of Birmingham (BA Hons English and Hist.). Founder and Man. Dir, Arq Internat., recruitment co., 1999–2010, non-exec. Dir, 2010–12. *Address:* House of Commons, SW1A 0AA.

SMITH, Sir Julian (Stanley), KNZM 2013; OBE 1994; Chairman and Managing Director, Allied Press Ltd, since 1986; *b* Dunedin, NZ, 29 Oct. 1943; *s* of Stanley David Smith and Mary Smith; *m* 1972, Beverley Anne Scott; two *s* one *d*. *Educ:* John McGlashan Coll.; Univ. of Otago. Co. Sec., Lovell Reilly Ltd, 1967–70; Gen. Manager and Dir, John M. Fraser and Co. Ltd, 1970–79; Man. Dir, Otago Press and Produce Ltd, 1979–86. Dir, NZ Press Assoc., 1983– (Chm., 1983–90, 2002–06); Mem., Newspaper Publishers' Assoc., 1983– (Pres., 2002–06). Pres., Otago Chamber of Commerce, 1993–94. Chm., Bd of Trustees, John McGlashan Coll., 1996–98. Hon. Col, 4th Otago Southland Bn Gp, 1998–2008. Patron, Otago Aero Club Inc., 2005–. FInstD 2009. *Recreations:* vintage cars, golf, boating. *Address:* Windover, 22 Belmont Lane, Dunedin 9013, New Zealand. *T:* (office) (3) 4793561, *Fax:* (3) 4747420. *E:* jcs@alliedpress.co.nz. *Clubs:* Dunedin, Commerce of Otago (Pres., 1992; Patron, 2010–) (Dunedin); Rolls-Royce Enthusiasts', Bentley Drivers (UK); Vintage Car of NZ; Waikouaiti Golf.

SMITH, Julian William; His Honour Judge Julian Smith; a Circuit Judge, since 2015; *b* Darlington, Co. Durham, 22 May 1968; *s* of Sir Graham William Smith, CBE and Jeanne Lilian Ann Smith; *m* 1995, Louise; two *s* two *d*. *Educ:* Dartford Grammar Sch. LLB. Called to the Bar, Inner Temple, 1991; in practice as barrister, 1991–2015; a Recorder, 2009–15. Hd of Chambers, New Park Court Chambers, Newcastle upon Tyne, 2010–15. *Recreations:* family, music, travel, early morning walks. *Address:* c/o The Law Courts, Barker Road, Maidstone, Kent ME16 8EQ. *T:* (01622) 202000.

SMITH, Justin D.; *see* Davis Smith.

SMITH, Karen Denise; Managing Director, Tuesday's Child Television, since 2012; *b* 16 June 1970; *d* of Peter A. Smith and Janet E. Smith; partner, Paul R. Jacobs; one *s* one *d* (twins). *Educ:* Univ. of Liverpool (BA Hons English 1991). Producer, presenter, reporter, BBC Radio York, 1992–95; Producer, NMTV, 1996–97; Producer, 1998, Dep. Editor, 1999, Editor, 2000–01, This Morning, Granada Television; Series Producer, Endemol UK, 2002–04; Exec. Producer, Strictly Come Dancing, BBC, 2003–04 (Rose d'Or Award, 2005); Sen. Editor, BBC Entertainment, 2004–06; Creative Hd, BBC Format Entertainment, 2006; Creative Dir, BBC Entertainment, 2007; Jt Man. Dir, Shine TV, 2008–12.

SMITH, Karen Jane; *see* Holt, K. J.

SMITH, Karen Jane W.; *see* Walden-Smith.

SMITH, Katherine Emma, (Kassie); QC 2013; *b* Reading, 25 Nov. 1969; *d* of Keith Edward Smith and Marjorie Patricia, (Paddy), Smith; *m* 2007, Dominic Geer; one *s* one *d*. *Educ:* Sir William Perkins's Sch., Chertsey; Lincoln Coll., Oxford (MA 1991); Corpus Christi Coll., Oxford (BCL 1994). Called to the Bar, Inner Temple, 1995; in practice as a barrister, specialising in EU, public and competition law, Monckton Chambers, 1995–. *Publications:* (ed jtly) Competition Litigation in the UK, 2005. *Recreations:* family, good food and good wine. *Address:* Monckton Chambers, 1–2 Raymond Buildings, Gray's Inn, WC1R 5NR. *T:* (020) 7405 7211, *Fax:* (020) 7405 2084. *E:* ksmith@monckton.com.

SMITH, Prof. Kenneth George Campbell, PhD; FRCP, FRACP, FRCPA, FMedSci; Professor of Medicine and Head of Department of Medicine, University of Cambridge, since 2010 (Genzyme Professor of Experimental Medicine, 2006–10); Fellow, Pembroke College, Cambridge, since 1998 (Director of Studies in Clinical Medicine, 1998–2013); Senior Clinical Fellow, National Institute of Health Research, since 2015; *b* 18 April 1963; *s* of Trevor James Sylvester Smith and Margery Leonie Smith (*née* Campbell); two *s*; one *d*. *Educ:* Bell Post Hill Primary Sch.; Geelong Coll.; Univ. of Melbourne (BMedSc 1985; MB BS 1987; PhD 1996); Pembroke Coll., Cambridge (MA 2000). FRACP 1994; FRCPA 1999; FRCP 2002. Intern, RMO and Med. and Nephrology Registrar, 1988–94, Asst Nephrologist, 1995–96, Royal Melbourne Hosp.; Dir, Studies in Clinical Medicine, and J. Alexander Scott Fellow in Anatomy, Ormond Coll., Univ. of Melbourne, 1992–96; Univ. Lectr, 1996–2004, Reader, 2004–06, in Renal Medicine, Univ. of Cambridge. Hon. Consultant Physician, Addenbrooke's Hosp., Cambridge, 1996–. Khoo Oon Teik Prof. of Nephrology, Univ. of Singapore, 2007–. FHEA (ILTM 2003); FMedSci 2006. Lister Inst. Res. Prize, 2007. *Publications:* articles on immunology and medicine. *Recreations:* Real tennis, reading, natural history. *Address:* Cambridge Institute for Medical Research, Box 139, Addenbrooke's Hospital, Cambridge CB2 0XY. *T:* (01223) 762645, *Fax:* (01223) 762640. *E:* kgcs2@cam.ac.uk. *Clubs:* Melbourne Cricket; Cambridge Real Tennis.

SMITH, Sir Kevin, Kt 2007; CBE 1997; FRAeS; Partner, Unitas Capital Pte Ltd, Hong Kong, since 2012; *b* 22 May 1954. *Educ:* Burnley Coll.; Lancashire Poly. (BA Hons). British Aerospace: Contract Officer, 1980–90; Commercial Dir, 1990–91; Dep. Man. Dir, 1991–93, Man. Dir, 1993–95, Mil. Aircraft Div.; British Aerospace plc: Man. Dir, Business Ops, 1995–98; Dep. Gp Man. Dir, New Business, 1998–99; Man. Dir, GKN Aerospace, 1999–2003; Chief Exec., GKN plc, 2003–11. Non-exec. Dir, Scottish and Southern Energy plc, 2004–08. Dir, SBAC, 2003–07 (Pres., 2004–05; Dep. Pres., 2005–07). CCMI. FRAeS 1993.

SMITH, Kingsley Ward, OBE 2007; DL; non-executive Chairman, Newcastle Hospitals NHS Foundation Trust (formerly Newcastle Hospitals Foundation Trust), since 2007; Adviser, NSK (Europe), since 2004; Clerk to the Lieutenancy, since 1990; *b* 24 Oct. 1946; *s* of Peter and Doris Evelyn Smith; *m* 1st, 1968, Kathy Rutherford (marr. diss. 1999); two *s*; 2nd, 2004, Sayoko Barbour. *Educ:* Blue Coat Secondary Sch., Walsall, Staffs; Dame Allan's Boys' Sch., Newcastle upon Tyne. CPFA (IPFA 1970). Trainee Accountant, Gateshead CBC, 1964–67; Durham County Council: Accountant, subseq. Sen. Accountant, 1967–76; Chief Internal Auditor, 1976–79; Sen. Asst County Treasurer, 1979–81; Dep. County Treasurer, 1981–84; County Treasurer, 1984–88; Chief Exec., 1988–2005; Exec. Chm., Co. Durham Develt Co., 2005–07; Interim Chief Exec., Teesdale DC, 2005–06. Non-exec. Dir, Durham Co. Waste Mgt Co., 2005–07; Chm., Time for Success, 2007–09. Mem., LSC, Co. Durham, 2001–05; Chm., Prince's Trust Regl Council, 1999–2005; formerly: founder Mem., Durham TEC; Chairman: ACCE; Fujtsu Response Gp; E Durham Task Force; Co. Durham Connexions Partnership; Co. Durham Youth Offending Service; Mem., Nat. Coalfields Task Force. DL Durham, 2011. *Recreations:* golfing, fishing, walking his labrador (Sam).

SMITH, Kirstie Louise Stewart-; *see* Hamilton, K. L.

SMITH, Laura; *see* Duncan, A. L. A.

SMITH, Lawrence Edward; yachting consultant, since 1971; *b* 19 Feb. 1956; *s* of Harold and Jean Smith; *m* 1991, Penny Jane Smith (*née* Haydock); two *s* two *d* (of whom one *s* one *d* are twins). *Educ:* Bury Grammar Sch. America's Cup: Skipper, British challenger, Lionheart, 1980, Victory, 1983. Winning skipper: Fastnet Race, 1985; Admiral's Cup, 1989. Whitbread Round the World Race: Skipper, Rothmans, 1990 (4th), Intrum Justitia, 1994 (2nd), Silk Cut, 1997–98 (5th). Skipper, UK crew, Soling class, Olympic Games, 1988, 1992 (Bronze medal). Dragon Class World Champion, 2011. *Publications:* Dinghy Helming, 1985; Dinghy Tuning, 1986; Yacht Tuning, 1987; Science of Speed, 1994. *Recreations:* golf, tennis.

SMITH, Lawrence Roger Hines, FSA; Keeper of Japanese Antiquities, 1987–97, and Senior Keeper, 1995–97, British Museum, now Keeper Emeritus; *b* 19 Feb. 1941; *s* of Frank Ernest Smith and Eva Lilian Smith (*née* Hines); *m* 1st, 1965, Louise Geraldine Gallini (marr. diss. 1986); one *s* five *d*; 2nd, 1993, Louise Elaine Woodroff; one *d*. *Educ:* Collyer's Grammar Sch., Horsham; Queens' Coll., Cambridge (Foundn Schol.; BA). British Museum: Asst Keeper, Dept of Manuscripts, 1962; Dept of Oriental Antiquities, 1965; Dep. Keeper, 1976; Keeper, 1977. British Acad. Exchange Fellow, Nihon Gakujutsu Shinkōkai, Kyoto, 1974–75. Academic adviser, Great Japan Exhibn, RA, 1981–82, and contrib. to catalogue. Mem. (Lib Dem), Broadland DC, 2003–07. Uchiyama Prize, Ukiyoe Soc. of Japan, 1986. *Publications:* Netsuke: the miniature sculpture of Japan (with R. Barker), 1976; Flowers in Art from East and West (with P. Hulton), 1979; Japanese Prints: 300 years of albums and books (with J. Hillier), 1980; Japanese Decorative Arts 1600–1900 (with V. Harris), 1982; The Japanese Print since 1900, 1983; Contemporary Japanese Prints, 1985; (ed) Ukiyoe: images of unknown Japan, 1988; (ed) Japanese Art: masterpieces in the British Museum, 1990; Nihonga: traditional Japanese painting, 1991; Japanese Prints 1912–1989: woodblocks and stencils, 1994; Japanese Prints during the Allied Occupation 1945–52, 2002; contribs to BM multi-cultural catalogues; articles and reviews in learned jls; conference and symposium papers. *Recreations:* walking, running, bellringing, music, wine. *Address:* 15 Repton Close, Aylsham, Norfolk NR11 6JE. *T:* (01263) 734499. *E:* lrhsumisu@paston.co.uk.

SMITH, Leonard Wayne; QC 2008; *b* Sydney, Australia, 21 July 1959; *s* of Leonard Bryan Smith and Beatrice Wendy Smith (*née* Bawden); *m* 1984, Anne Terese Walker; two *s* one *d*. *Educ:* Univ. of Sydney (BA, LLM). Called to the Bar: NSW, 1986; Australia, 1987; Gray's Inn, 1991; in practice as barrister specialising in corporate and regulatory crime, serious fraud and general criminal law. *Recreations:* golf, cricket, reading, travelling on Swiss railways. *Address:* Carmelite Chambers, 9 Carmelite Street, EC4Y 0DR. *Clubs:* Kibworth Golf (Kibworth Beauchamp); Luffenham Heath Golf.

SMITH, Prof. Lewis Lauchlan, PhD; FRCPath; FBTS; Interim Director, Centre for Translational Therapeutics, University of Leicester, 2009–12; *b* 21 Aug. 1947; *s* of Lewis Smith and Margaret (*née* Wilson); *m* 1972, Susan Lisbeth Baynes; one *s* two *d*. *Educ:* Hatfield Poly. (BSc, PhD). MRCPath 1990, FRCPath 1997. ICI Central Toxicology Laboratory: Res. Scientist, 1971–80; Sen. Scientist, 1980–85; Hd, Biochem. Toxicology Sect., 1985–91; Dir, Toxicology Unit, 1991–98, and Inst. for Envmt and Health, 1993–98, MRC; Dir, Syngenta (formerly Zeneca) Central Toxicology Lab., 1998–2002; Hd of Develt, Syngenta Crop Protection AG, Basel, Switzerland, 2002–09. *Publications:* numerous in res. jls on mechanisms of toxicity and cellular biochem. *Recreations:* golf, eating, dieting. *E:* lls10@leicester.ac.uk.

SMITH, Llewellyn Thomas; *b* 16 April 1944; *m* 1969, Pamela Williams (*d* 2008); two *s* one *d*. *Educ:* Cardiff University. Formerly with Pilkington Glass, George Wimpey and Workers' Educational Assoc. MEP (Lab) SE Wales, 1984–94; MP (Lab) Blaenau Gwent, 1992–2005. Mem., CND. *Address:* The Mount, Uplands, Tynewydd, Newbridge NP11 3RH.

SMITH, Lloyd Barnaby, (Barney), CMG 2002; HM Diplomatic Service, retired; Editor, Asian Affairs, since 2005; *b* 21 July 1945; *s* of Arthur and Zena Smith; *m* 1st, 1972, Nicola Mary Whitehead (marr. diss.); 2nd, 1983, Elizabeth Mary Sumner; one *s* one *d*. *Educ:* Merchant Taylors' Sch., Moor Park; Brasenose Coll., Oxford (MA). Joined Diplomatic Service, 1968; Third, later Second Sec., Bangkok, 1970–74; First Secretary: FCO, 1974–77; Paris, 1977–78; Head of Chancery, Dublin, 1978–81; Ecole Nat. d'Admin, Paris, 1981–82; First Sec., then Counsellor, UK Repn to EEC, Brussels, 1982–86; Counsellor, Bangkok, 1987–90; Dir, Know How Fund for Eastern Europe, 1990–92; Head, S Asia Dept, FCO, 1993–95; Ambassador: to Nepal, 1995–99; to Thailand, also accredited to Laos, 2000–03. Non-exec. Dir, 2006–14, Chm., 2011–14, Coastal Energy Co. Ltd. *Recreation:* sailing.

SMITH, Rt Hon. Sir Lockwood; *see* Smith, Rt Hon. Sir A. L.

SMITH, Prof. Lorraine Nancy, PhD; Professor of Nursing, University of Glasgow, 1990–2012, now Emeritus (Head, Nursing and Midwifery School, 1999–2001; Head of Department, 1990–99); *b* 29 June 1949; *d* of Geoffrey Leonard Millington and Ida May (*née* Attfield); *m* 1975, Christopher Murray Smith; one *s* one *d*. *Educ:* Univ. of Ottawa (BScN); Univ. of Manchester (MEd, PhD). Staff Nurse, Ottawa, 1971–73; Team Leader, Montreal, 1973–76; Sister, Withington Hosp., Manchester, 1976–77; Lectr, Dept of Nursing Studies, Univ. of Manchester, 1977–90. Member: Clin. Standards Adv. Gp (UK); Standards Cttee, Nat. Bd for Scotland, 1997–2000; RCN UK Rep., Work Gp, Eur. Nurse Researchers, 1999–2008 (Chm., 2005–08); Mem. Bd, RCN Scotland, 2009–10. Chair: RCN Res. Soc. Scotland, 1999–2005; Sign Guideline 120, 2008–10. *Publications:* articles in Advanced Jl of Nursing, Clinical Rehabilitation, BMJ, Cerebrovascular Diseases. *Recreations:* ski-ing, sailing, reading, bridge. *Address:* Nursing & Health Care, University of Glasgow, 59 Oakfield Avenue, Glasgow G12 8LL. *T:* (0141) 330 5498. *Clubs:* S Caernarvonshire Yacht, Abersoch Golf (Abersoch, N Wales).

SMITH, Dame Maggie, (Dame Margaret Natalie Cross), CH 2014; DBE 1990 (CBE 1970); actress; Director, United British Artists, since 1982; *b* 28 Dec. 1934; *d* of Nathaniel Smith and Margaret Little (*née* Hutton); *m* 1st, 1967, Robert Graham Stephens (later Sir Robert Stephens) (marr. diss. 1975; he *d* 1995); two *s*; 2nd, 1975, Beverley Cross (*d* 1998). *Educ:* Oxford High School for Girls. Studied at Oxford Playhouse School under Isabel van Beers. First appearance, June 1952, as Viola in OUDS Twelfth Night; 1st New York appearance, Ethel Barrymore Theatre, June 1956, as comedienne in New Faces. Played in Share My Lettuce, Lyric, Hammersmith, 1957; The Stepmother, St Martin's, 1958. Old Vic Co., 1959–60 season: The Double Dealer; As You Like It; Richard II; The Merry Wives of Windsor; What Every Woman Knows; Rhinoceros, Strand, 1960; Strip the Willow, Cambridge, 1960; The Rehearsal, Globe, 1961; The Private Ear and The Public Eye (Evening Standard Drama Award, best actress of 1962), Globe, 1962; Mary, Mary, Queen's, 1963 (Variety Club of Gt Britain, best actress of the year); The Country Wife, Chichester, 1969; Design for Living, LA, 1971; Private Lives, Queen's, 1972, Globe, 1973, NY, 1975 (Variety Club of GB Stage Actress Award, 1972); Peter Pan, Coliseum, 1973; Snap, Vaudeville, 1974; Night and Day, Phoenix, 1979; Virginia, Haymarket, 1981 (Standard Best Actress Award, 1982); The Way of the World, Chichester and Haymarket, 1984 (Standard Best Actress Award, 1985); Interpreters, Queen's, 1985; Lettice and Lovage, Globe, 1987, NY, 1990 (Tony Award, best leading actress, 1990); The Importance of Being Earnest, Aldwych, 1993; Three Tall Women, Wyndham's, 1994, 1995; Talking Heads, Chichester, 1996, Comedy Theatre, 1997, Australian tour, 2004; A Delicate Balance, Haymarket, 1997; Lady in the Van, Queen's, 1999; The Breath of Life, Haymarket, 2002; The Lady from Dubuque, Haymarket, 2007; *at National Theatre:* The Recruiting Officer, 1963; Othello, The Master Builder, Hay Fever, 1964; Much Ado About Nothing, Miss Julie, 1965; A Bond Honoured, 1966; The Beaux' Stratagem, 1970 (also USA); Hedda Gabler, 1970 (Evening Standard Best Actress award); War Plays, 1985; Coming in to Land, 1986; *at Festival Theatre, Stratford, Ontario:* 1976: Antony and Cleopatra, The Way of the World, Measure for Measure, The Three Sisters; 1977: Midsummer Night's Dream, Richard III, The Guardsman, As You Like It, Hay Fever; 1978: As You Like It, Macbeth, Private Lives; 1980: Virginia; Much Ado About Nothing. *Films:* The VIP's, 1963; The Pumpkin Eater, 1964; Young Cassidy, 1965; Othello, 1966; The Honey Pot, 1967; Hot Millions, 1968 (Variety Club of GB Award); The Prime of Miss Jean Brodie, 1968 (Oscar; SFTA award); Oh! What a Lovely War, 1968; Love and Pain (and the Whole Damned Thing), 1973; Travels with my Aunt, 1973; Murder by Death, 1976; California Suite, 1977 (Oscar); Death on the Nile, 1978; Quartet, 1981; Clash of the Titans, 1981; Evil Under the Sun, 1982; The Missionary, 1982; A Private Function, 1984 (BAFTA award, Best Actress, 1985); The Loves of Lily, 1985; A Room with a View, 1986 (Variety Club of GB Award; BAFTA award, Best Actress, 1986); The Lonely Passion of Judith Hearn, 1989 (Evening Standard British Films Award, 1988, and Best Film Actress BAFTA Award, 1988); Hook, 1992; Sister Act, 1992; The Secret Garden, 1993; Sister Act II, 1994; Richard III, 1996; The First Wives Club, 1996; Washington Square, 1998; Tea with Mussolini, 1999 (Best Supporting Actress, BAFTA, 2000); The Last September, 2000; Harry Potter and the Philosopher's Stone, 2001; Gosford Park, 2002; Divine Secrets of the Ya-Ya Sisterhood, 2002; Harry Potter and the Chamber of Secrets, 2002; Harry Potter and the Prisoner of Azkaban, 2004; Ladies in Lavender, 2004; Harry Potter and the Goblet of Fire, 2005; Keeping Mum, 2005; Becoming Jane, Harry Potter and the Order of the Phoenix, 2007; Harry Potter and the Half-Blood Prince, 2009; Nanny McPhee and the Big Bang, From Time to Time, Harry Potter and the Deathly Hallows, Part 1, 2010, Part 2, 2011; The Best Exotic Marigold Hotel, Quartet, 2012; My Old Lady, 2014; The Second Best Exotic Marigold Hotel, The Lady in the Van, 2015; *television:* Talking Heads: Bed Among the Lentils, 1989 (RTS Award); Memento Mori, 1992; Suddenly Last Summer, 1993; All The King's Men, 1999; David Copperfield, 1999; My House in Umbria, 2003 (Emmy Award for Best Actress); Capturing Mary, 2007; Downton Abbey, 2010, 2011, 2012, 2013, 2014, 2015 (Best Supporting Actress, Emmy Award, 2011 and 2012, Golden Globe Awards, 2012, Best Actress in a Drama Series, Screen Actors Guild Awards, 2014). Fellow: BFI; BAFTA. Hon. DLitt: St Andrews, 1971; Cambridge, 1995. Hanbury Shakespeare Prize, 1991. *Recreation:* reading. *Address:* c/o Independent Talent Agency Ltd, 40 Whitfield Street, W1T 2RH.

See also T. Stephens.

SMITH, Marcus Alexander; QC 2010; *b* 1 July 1967; *s* of Ronald Smith and Hannelore Smith; *m* 1998, Louise Merrett; one *s* one *d*. *Educ:* Balliol Coll., Oxford (BA 1988; BCL 1990; MA 1992); Univ. of Munich. Called to the Bar, Lincoln's Inn, 1991; in practice as barrister, specialising in commercial and regulatory law, 1991–; pt-time Chm., Competition Appeal Tribunal, 2009. Lectr in Law, Balliol Coll., 1991–94. *Publications:* Private International Law of Reinsurance and Insurance, 2006; The Law of Assignment, 2007, 2nd edn 2013. *Recreations:* Norfolk, writing. *Address:* Fountain Court Chambers, Temple, EC4Y 9DH. *T:* (020) 7583 3335. *E:* mas@fountaincourt.co.uk.

SMITH, Margaret Elizabeth; Lord Provost and Lord-Lieutenant of Aberdeen City, 1999–2003; *b* 10 Aug. 1931. *Educ:* Twickenham Grammar Sch.; Southport High Sch. for Girls; Lady Mabel Coll., Rotherham (DipPE 1953). Physical Education Teacher: Fleetwood Grammar Sch., 1953–58; Blairgowrie High Sch., 1958–67; Youth Officer, Chichester CC, 1967–73; Neighbourhood Worker, Easterhouse, Glasgow, 1973–78; Housing Worker, Scottish Special Housing Assoc., Glasgow, 1978–81; Community Educn Area Officer,

Grampian Regl Council, 1981–91. Aberdeen District, now City, Council: Mem. (Lab), 1988–2003; Leader of Council, 1996–99; Mem., Drug Strategy Task Gp, 1996–99; Chair, Community Planning Core Gp; COSLA Rep., 1997–99; Convenor, Women's and Equal Opportunities Cttee, 1992–96. Lord High Adm., Northern Seas, 1999–2003; Vice Adm., Coast of GB and Ireland, 1999–2003. President: World Energy Cities Partnership, 2000–02; Voluntary Service, Aberdeen, 1999–2003; Aberdeen Br., RNLI, 1999–2003; Comr, Northern Lighthouse Bd, 1999–2003; Chair: Froghall Community Project, 1995–99; Aberdeen Alternative Fest. Trust, 1999–2001; Member: Sunnybank Community Educn Mgt Cttee, 1988–2003; NE Scotland Econ. Develt Partnership, 1997–99; Aberdeen Gomel Trust, 1999–2003; Aberdeen Safer Communities Trust, 1999–2003; Aberdeen Bulawayo Trust, 1999–2003; Patron: Mental Health, Aberdeen, 1999; Aberdeen Internat. Youth Fest., 1999. Hon. DL: Robert Gordon, Aberdeen, 1999; Aberdeen, 2004. *Recreations:* walking, theatre and concerts, family and friends, learning Russian, Aberdeen FC. *Address:* 49 Froghall Terrace, Aberdeen AB24 3JP.

SMITH, Margaret Joy; Member (Lib Dem) Edinburgh West, Scottish Parliament, 1999–2011; *b* 18 Feb. 1961; *d* of late John Murray and of Anna Murray; *m* 1983, Douglas Robert Smith (marr. diss. 2004); one *s* one *d*; civil partnership 2006, Suzanne Main; three step *s. Educ:* Edinburgh Univ. (MA Gen. Arts). Pensions Administrator, Guardian Royal Exchange Assurance, 1982–83; Civil Servant (EO), Registers of Scotland, 1983–88; tour guide and freelance journalist, 1988–90; Scottish Officer, UNA, 1990–96; Political Organiser, Edinburgh W Liberal Democrats, 1996–97. Mem. (Lib Dem) Edinburgh CC, 1995–99. Scottish Parliament: Convenor, Health and Community Care Cttee, 1999–2003; Lib Dem spokesperson on justice, 2003–05, on transport and local govt, 2005; Chief Whip (Lib Dem), 2005–07; Lib Dem Shadow Cabinet Sec. for Justice, 2007–11. Contested (Lib Dem) Edinburgh W, Scottish Parlt, 2011. *Recreations:* golf, reading. *Club:* Ravelston Golf (Edinburgh).

SMITH, Margaret Osborne B.; *see* Bickford Smith.

SMITH, (Maria) Geraldine; *b* 29 Aug. 1961; *d* of John and Ann Smith. *Educ:* Morecambe Bay Primary Sch.; Morecambe High Sch. Postal Administrator, Royal Mail, 1980–97. MP (Lab) Morecambe and Lunesdale, 1997–2010; contested (Lab) same seat, 2010. *Recreations:* chess, walking.

SMITH, Marion Helen; QC 2015; *b* Isleworth, 24 Dec. 1956; *d* of Arthur Owen Smith and Isabel Mary Smith (*née* Wiseman); *m* 1980, Alex Macgregor Mason; two *d. Educ:* Howell's Sch., Llandaff, Cardiff; Queen Mary Coll., Univ. of London (LLB); London Sch. of Econs and Pol Sci. (LLM). Called to the Bar, Gray's Inn, 1981; in practice as barrister, 1981–. *Recreations:* theatre, travel, reading. *Address:* 39 Essex Street, WC2R 3AT. *T:* (020) 7832 1111. *E:* marion.smithqc@39essex.com.

SMITH, Marion Wallace, RSA 2005; sculptor; Secretary, Royal Scottish Academy, since 2012; *b* St Andrews, 14 Feb. 1969; *d* of Alistair Wallace Smith and Patricia Christian Hall Smith (*née* Bodie). *Educ:* Gray's Sch. of Art, Aberdeen (BA Hons Fine Art 1991). ARSA 1998. Artist/technician, Scottish Sculpture Workshop, Aberdeenshire, 1994–96; Workshop Manager, Glasgow Sculpture Studios, 1996–98; Gall. Manager, Crawford Arts Centre, St Andrews, 1998; fine art technician, Glasgow Sch. of Art, 1999–2004. Has exhibited in UK, Scandinavia, France and Japan; *solo exhibitions* include: Crawford Arts Centre, St Andrews, 1997; Bonhoga Gall., Shetland, 2004; Patriothall Gall., Edinburgh, 2005; Park Gall., Falkirk, 2009; *group exhibitions* include: Sculptors' Prints, 2013, Scottish Drawings, 2015, RSA; first granite commn, Brittany, 2002; *commissions* throughout UK, including: Fire Ball, Linlithgow, 2007; The Plough and the Reaper, Anstruther, 2009; Panmure Passage, Dundee, 2009; HMT Lancastria Meml, Clydebank, 2011; Loch Leven, Kinross-shire, 2014. *Recreations:* exploring landscapes, social history, cooking, gardening. *Address:* Royal Scottish Academy, The Mound, Edinburgh EH2 2EL. *T:* (0131) 225 6671. *E:* info@royalscottishacademy.org.

SMITH, Prof. Mark Edmund, PhD; FInstP; Vice-Chancellor, Lancaster University, since 2012. *Educ:* Churchill Coll., Cambridge (BA Natural Scis 1984); Univ. of Warwick (PhD). Application scientist, Bruker Analytische Messtechnik, Germany; Res. Scientist, CSIRO, Australia; Lectr, then Reader, Univ. of Kent, 1992–98; University of Warwick: Reader, 1998; Prof. of Physics; Chair, Faculty of Sci., 2005; Pro-Vice-Chancellor for Res., 2007; Dep. Vice-Chancellor, until 2012. Member: EPSRC Coll.; HEFCW, 2003–15. Member, Board: UK Research Reserve; JISC. Mem., Ampère Prize Cttee, French Acad. Scis. *Publications:* contribs to jls incl. Jl Amer. Chem. Soc., Applied Magnetic Resonance, Jl Magnetic Resonance, Jl Materials Chem., Chem. Materials, Jl Materials Res. *Address:* University House, Lancaster University, Bailrigg, Lancaster LA1 4YW.

SMITH, Mark Gordon M.; *see* Milliken-Smith.

SMITH, Sir Martin (Gregory), Kt 2013; Founding Partner, Beaumont Partners LLP, since 2009; *b* 2 Feb. 1943; *s* of late Archibald Gregory Smith, OBE, and Mary Eleanor Smith (*née* Malone); *m* 1971, Elise Barr Becket (OBE 2015); one *s* one *d. Educ:* St Albans Sch.; St Edmund Hall, Oxford (BA, MA); Stanford Univ., Calif (MBA, AM Econ). Brewer, A. Guinness Son & Co. (Dublin) Ltd, 1964–69; McKinsey & Co. Inc., 1971–73; Dir, Citicorp Internat. Bank Ltd, 1974–80; Chm., Bankers Trust Internat., 1980–83; Co-founder, Phoenix Securities, 1983–97; Chairman: Phoenix Partnership, 1990–97; Phoenix Fund Managers, 1990–97; Eur. Investment Banking, Donaldson, Lufkin & Jenrette, 1997–2000; Amerindo Internet Fund PLC, 2000–06; GP Bullhound, 2005–; Worldwide Healthcare Trust PLC (formerly Finsbury Worldwide Pharmaceutical Ltd), 2008–; Director: New Star Asset Management, 2000–09; Phoenix Equity Partners, 2000–06; Odgers, Ray & Berndtson, 2001–09; Oxford Capital Partners, 2010–; Energy Works plc, 2014–; Sen. Advr, Bain Capital, 2001–09; Mem., Adv. Bd, IDDAS Ltd, 2005–08; Chm., Adv. Bd, Episode 1 LLP, 2013–. Chairman: Bath Mozartfest, 2000–09; ENO, 2001–05; Orchestra of Age of Enlightenment, 2011– (Mem. Bd, 1985–). Deputy Chairman: South Bank Centre, 1992–97; Science Mus., 1999–2009; Trustee: IMS Prussia Cove, 1999–; Becket Collection, 1999–2014; Wigmore Hall, 2000–14; Tetbury Music Fest., 2006–; Dir, Glyndebourne Arts Trust, 2007–. Mem., Science Mus. Foundn, 2012–. Visitor, Ashmolean Museum, 2006–14. Governor: RAM, 2006–; Ditchley Foundn, 2013–. Mem., Prince's Council of Charities, 2009–10. Founder, Smith Sch. of Enterprise and the Envmt, Oxford Univ., 2007; Mem., Chancellor's Ct of Benefactors, Oxford Univ., 2009–. Liveryman, Co. of Musicians, 2000–. St Edmund Fellow, St Edmund Hall, Oxford, 2001. FRGS 2015. Hon. FRAM 2003; Hon. Fellow, Science Mus., 2009. *Recreations:* music, conducting, riding, ski-ing, golf, sailing, Real tennis. *Address:* Beaumont Partners, 29 Beaumont Street, Oxford OX1 2NP. *T:* (01865) 594370. *E:* martin.smith@beaumontpartners.com. *Clubs:* Brooks's, Garrick, MCC; Eastward Ho! (USA); Huntercombe Golf.

SMITH, Maj. Gen. Martin Linn, MBE 1998; Commandant General Royal Marines and Commander United Kingdom Amphibious Forces, since 2014; *b* Pembury, Kent, 30 July 1962; *s* of Edward Linn Smith and Joanne Smith (*née* Liddell); *m* 1997, Susan Jane Robinson. *Educ:* Sevenoaks Sch., Univ. of Bristol (BSc Zoology). Joined Royal Marines, 1984; CO, 30 Cdo Information Exploitation Gp, 2003–05; Dep. Comdr, 2008–10, Comdr, 2011–13, 3 Cdo Bde; HCSC 2010; rcds 2013–14. *Recreations:* mountaineering, sea kayaking, sailing. *Address:* Fieldhouse Building, PP301, HMS Excellent, Whale Island, Portsmouth PO2 8ER. *T:* (023) 9254 8044, *Fax:* (023) 9254 8374. *E:* NAVYCAF-ADC@mod.uk.

SMITH, Canon Maurice John, CB 2007; Diocesan Director of Education, Church of England Manchester Diocese, since 2007; *b* 16 March 1955; *s* of George and Edna Smith; *m* 1980, Alison Mary Jones; two *s. Educ:* Quarry Bank Comp. Sch.; Univ. of Wales (BA Hons 1976); Univ. of Manchester (MA Econ 1983); Univ. of Central Lancashire (MBA Dist. 1991); Manchester Metropolitan Univ. (MRes (Educn and Soc.) 2007). Office for Standards in Education: HMI, 1996–2002; Dir, Early Years, 2002–06; HM Chief Inspector, 2006. Hon. Lay Canon, Manchester Cathedral, 2012. Pres., Bangor Old Stars on Merseyside, 1982–. *Recreations:* wandering around my garden in the evening, saying my prayers and contemplating the meaning of life. *Address:* Church of England Manchester Diocese, Church House, 90 Deansgate, Manchester M3 2GH.

SMITH, Most Rev. Michael; *see* Meath, Bishop of, (RC).

SMITH, Michael A.; *see* Acton Smith.

SMITH, Michael Anthony; Comment Editor, The Times, since 2014; *b* Bristol, 9 March 1968; *s* of Patrick and Frances Smith; *m* 2004, Charlotte Smith; one *s* one *d. Educ:* King Edward's Sch., Bath; Univ. of York (BA Hons). Reporter: Western Gazette, 1992–93; The People, 1993–95; Asst News Ed., 1995–97, Associate News Ed., 1997–99, Daily Mail; Asst Ed., 1999–2001, Dep. Ed., 2001–02, Metro; Exec. News Ed., Evening Standard, 2002–04; News Ed., 2005–06, Foreign Ed., 2006–08, Internat. Comment Ed., 2008, Daily Telegraph; Dep. Home Ed., 2009–11, Home Ed., 2011–12, Hd of News, 2012–14, The Times. *Recreation:* bagging Betty's in North Yorkshire. *Address:* The Times, 1 London Bridge Street, SE1 9GF. *T:* (020) 7782 5999. *E:* mike.smith@thetimes.co.uk. *Clubs:* Lyke Wake Walk; Godfrey Evans Cricket.

SMITH, Michael Forbes; Director General, Chartered Institute of Arbitrators, 2006–12; Founding Director, The Tempered and True Consultancy (diplomacy skills, international briefing), 2004–06; *b* 4 June 1948; *s* of Forbes Weir Smith and Elizabeth Smith (*née* Mackie); *m* 1st, 1974, Christian Joanna Kersley (marr. diss. 1983, annulled 1986); one *d*; 2nd, 1986, Claire Helen Stubbs (*see* C. H. Smith); one *s* one *d. Educ:* Aberdeen Grammar Sch.; Southampton Univ. (BSc Hons Geog.); Heythrop Coll., London Univ. (MA Christianity and Interreligious Relns 2013). BoT, 1966–68; commnd Gordon Highlanders, 1971, retd as Captain, 1978. HM Diplomatic Service, 1978–2004: Second Sec., FCO, 1978–79; Second, later First, Sec. and Hd of Chancery, Addis Ababa, 1979–83; Pol Advr to Civil Comr, later Gov., Falkland Is, Port Stanley, 1983–85; First Sec., FCO (SE Asia Dept, later FO Spokesman), 1985–89; Consul (Commercial), Zürich, 1990–94; Hd, Press and Public Affairs, Bonn, 1994–99; Dep. High Comr, Islamabad, 1999–2002; Ambassador to Republic of Tajikistan, 2002–04. Advr, Gulf Internat. Minerals Ltd, 2004–06. Non-exec. Dir, IDRS Ltd, 2007–11; Chm., City Disputes Panel Ltd, 2011–12 (non-exec. Dir, 2007–11). FRGS 1971; FRSA 1991; FSAScot 1995; MCIArb 2007; Accredited Mediator 2007; Dip. IoD, 2010. Mem., Appeal Cttee and Church Council, Farm St Ch, Mayfair, 1986–90; Vice-Pres., St Thomas More Parish Council, Bonn, 1996–99. Chm., Bonn Caledonian Soc., 1995–99; Mem., Northern Meeting, 2008–. Pres., St Francis Leprosy Guild, 2015– (Vice Pres., 2014–15). Mem., Highland Soc. of London, 2010–. *Publications:* contributor: Diplomacy in the 21st Century series, 2006, Diplomatic Acad. of London; Piping Times; Arbitration. *Recreations:* music, Scotland, Yachtmaster offshore, field and winter sports, entertaining and conviviality. *Clubs:* Army and Navy, Little Ship (Cdre, 2015–); Royal Findhorn Yacht.

SMITH, Michael Gerard A.; *see* Austin-Smith.

SMITH, Michael John W.; *see* Winkworth-Smith.

SMITH, Michael Lynas, OBE; Chief Executive, Livability, 2010–12; *b* Bolton, 22 April 1946; *s* of Alfred Smith and Ruby Smith; *m* 1970, Lynda Veronica; one *s* one *d. Educ:* Bedford Modern Sch.; Open Univ. (BA 1980); Camberley Staff Coll.; Royal Mil. Coll. of Sci. (MSc 1995); Exeter (Mktg 1996). MCIPD 1980. Served RAF; Chief Executive: St Loye's Foundn, 1994–96; Enham, 1996–2010. Non-executive Member of Board: Royal Devon and Exeter, 1995–96; North and Mid Hampshire HA, 1996–99; Hampshire and IoW Strategic HA, 1999–2006; Hampshire Partnership NHS Foundn Trust, 2007–10; R2M Ltd, 2006–10. *Recreations:* running, rugger, antique clocks. *Club:* Royal Air Force.

SMITH, Prof. (Murdo) Alasdair (Macdonald); DL; DPhil; Inquiry Chair (formerly a Panel Deputy Chairman), Competition and Markets Authority, since 2014; Professor of Economics, 1981–2007, and Vice-Chancellor, 1998–2007, University of Sussex, Research Professor of Economics, since 2007; *b* 9 Feb. 1949; *s* of late John Smith and Isabella Smith (*née* Mackenzie); *m* Sherry Ferdman; two *d. Educ:* Nicolson Inst., Stornoway; Univ. of Glasgow (MA 1969); London Sch. of Econs (MSc 1970); DPhil Oxford 1973. Lecturer: University Coll., Oxford, 1970–72; LSE, 1972–81. Vis. Prof. of Econs, Coll. of Europe, 1991–98. Chm., Armed Forces Pay Review Body, 2010–13; Dep. Chm., Competition Commn, 2012–14. DL E Sussex, 2001. Hon. DSc(Econ) Warsaw, 2004; Hon. LLD Sussex, 2008. *Publications:* A Mathematical Introduction to Economics, 1982; (ed with P. Krugman) Empirical Studies of Strategic Trade Policy, 1994; articles on international economics in learned jls. *Recreations:* walking, gardening, cooking, twittering @AlasdairMSmith. *Address:* 11 Gundreda Road, Lewes BN7 1PT. *T:* (01273) 472940. *E:* alasdair@sussex.ac.uk.

SMITH, Neil; *see* Smith, G. N.

SMITH, Prof. Neilson Voyne, FBA 1999; Professor of Linguistics, University College London, 1982–2006, now Emeritus; *b* 21 June 1939; *s* of Voyne Smith and Lilian Freda Smith (*née* Rose); *m* 1966, Saraswati Keskar; two *s. Educ:* Trinity College, Cambridge (BA 1961, MA 1964); UCL (PhD 1964). Lectr in W African Languages, SOAS, 1964–70; Harkness Fellow, MIT and UCLA, 1966–68; Lectr in Linguistics and W African Languages, SOAS, 1970–72; University College London: Reader in Linguistics, 1972–81; Hd, Dept of Phonetics and Linguistics, 1983–90; Vice-Dean, 1992–94. Pres., Assoc. of Heads and Profs of Linguistics, 1993–94. Chm., Linguistics Assoc., 1980–86. Hon. Mem., Linguistic Soc. of America, 1999. *Publications:* An Outline Grammar of Nupe, 1967; The Acquisition of Phonology, 1973; (with Deirdre Wilson) Modern Linguistics, 1979; (ed) Mutual Knowledge, 1982; Speculative Linguistics, 1983; The Twitter Machine, 1989; (with Ianthi Tsimpli) The Mind of a Savant, 1995; Chomsky: ideas and ideals, 1999, 3rd edn (with N. Allott) 2015; Language, Bananas and Bonobos, 2002; Language, Frogs and Savants, 2005; Acquiring Phonology: a cross-generational case-study, 2010; (jtly) The Signs of a Savant: language against the odds, 2011; articles in learned jls. *Recreations:* music, walking, travel, playing with children. *Address:* 32 Long Buftlers, Harpenden, Herts AL5 1JE; Department of Linguistics, University College London, Chandler House, Wakefield Street, WC1N 1PF. *T:* (020) 7580 5928. *E:* smithnv@gmail.com.

SMITH, Nicholas Desmond John; MP (Lab) Blaenau Gwent, since 2010; *b* Cardiff, 14 Jan. 1960; *s* of William Thomas Smith and Alma Anne Smith; *m* (marr. diss.); two *d. Educ:* Coventry Univ. (BA Hist., Pols and Internat. Relns 1981); Birkbeck Coll., London (MSc Econ. and Social Change 1991). Constituency Organiser to Frank Dobson, MP, 1989–91; Organiser, Wales Labour Party, 1991–93; Hd, Membership Develt, Labour Party, 1993–98; consultant on internat. campaigning, 1998–2000; Campaign Manager, Public Policy, NSPCC, 2000–04; Sec. Gen., Eur. Parly Labour Party, 2005–06; Dir, Policy and Partnerships, Royal Coll. of Speech and Lang. Therapists, 2006–10. PPS to Shadow Work and Pensions Sec., 2010–11, to Shadow Foreign Sec., 2011–15. Mem., Public

Accounts Cttee, 2010–. Member: Aneurin Bevan Soc.; Fabian Soc. FRGS. *Recreations:* hiking, singing, reading, chess. *Address:* House of Commons, SW1A 0AA. *T:* (020) 7219 7018. *E:* nick.smith.mp@parliament.uk.

SMITH, Nicholas George Edward L.; *see* Loraine-Smith.

SMITH, Nicholas Paul; Headteacher, Torquay Girls' Grammar School, since 2007; *b* Brighton, 9 Sept. 1964; *s* of C. and R. Smith; *m* 1993, Caroline Inglethorpe; one *s* one *d*. *Educ:* Cardinal Newman Sch., Hove; Royal Free Hosp. Sch. of Medicine, Univ. of London (MB BS 1987); Inst. of Educn, Univ. of London (PGCE Sci. 1993); Nat. Coll. of Sch. Leadership (NPQH 2005). Jun. Hse Officer, Royal E Sussex Hosp., Hastings and Fazakerley Hosp., Liverpool, 1988–89; Penguin Keeper, London Zoo, 1991; teaching in Cornwall, 1993–2002; Dir, Sixth Form, Liskeard Community Coll., 2002–04; Dep. Hd, Devonport High Sch. for Girls, 2004–07. *Recreations:* running, walking, fitness, annoying my family by being pedantic. *Address:* Torquay Girls' Grammar School, 30 Shiphay Lane, Torquay, Devon TQ2 7DY. *T:* (01803) 613215, *Fax:* (01803) 616724. *E:* admin@tggsacademy.org.

SMITH, Nigel Christopher S.; *see* Starmer-Smith.

SMITH, Nigel Watkin Roberts, CB 2011; Chairman, Spikes Cavell, since 2011; *b* Newcastle upon Tyne, 9 June 1954; *s* of Captain Peter Watkin Roberts Smith and Brenda Smith; *m* 1982, Heather Scott; two *d*. *Educ:* Skinners' Grammar Sch., Tunbridge Wells; Bristol Poly. (BA Hons Business Studies 1976); Henley Mgt Coll. (GMC 1987). Dowty Group plc: grad. commercial apprentice, 1972–76; Personnel Exec./Manager, Dowty Rotol, 1976–86; Dir of Projects, Dowty Fuel Systems, 1986–88; Man. Dir, Dowty Aerospace Aviation Services, 1988–92; Commercial Dir, Dowty Landing Gear, 1993; Managing Director: GEC Marconi Ltd, 1993–95; Pandrol Internat., 1995; Charter plc: Chief Operating Officer, 1995–98; CEO, 1998–2001; on sabbatical and consulting, 2001–03; Pres., Invensys Rail Systems, 2003–06; Second Perm. Sec. and Chief Exec., Office of Govt Commerce, HM Treasury, 2007–10. Non-executive Director: Sellafield Ltd, 2012–; Sepura plc, 2013–. Mem. Bd, BT Major Projects Centre, Saïd Business Sch., Oxford Univ., 2010–. FCIPS 2007. *Recreations:* family, France, golf, walking, opera, Newcastle United FC. *E:* nigel@charleswood.me.uk.

SMITH, Niove Rachel J., (Nia); *see* Janis Smith.

SMITH, Sir (Norman) Brian, Kt 1998; CBE 1980; Chairman, Cable and Wireless HKT (formerly Hong Kong Telecommunications) Ltd, 1995–97 and 1998–2000 (non-executive Director, 1997–98); *b* 10 Sept. 1928; *s* of late Vincent and Louise Smith; *m* 1955, Phyllis Crossley; one *s* one *d* (and one *s* decd). *Educ:* Sir John Deane's Grammar Sch., Northwich; Manchester Univ. (PhD Phys. Chemistry, 1954). FTI 1981. Joined ICI Ltd, Terylene Council, 1954; Fibres Division: Textile Develt Dir, 1969; Dep. Chm., 1972; Chm., 1975–78; ICI Main Bd, 1978–85; Director: Fiber Industries Inc., 1972–83; Canadian Industries Ltd, 1981–85; Territorial Dir for the Americas, and Chm., ICI Americas Inc., 1981–85 (Dir, 1980–85); Non-exec. Dir, Carrington Viyella Ltd, 1979–81. Chairman: Metal Box plc, subseq. MB Group, 1986–89 (Dep. Chm., 1985–86); Lister & Co., 1991–94 (Dir, 1985–94; Dep. Chm., 1990–91); BAA plc, 1991–98; Cable and Wireless, 1995–98 (Dir, 1988–95); Hydron Ltd, 1994–2000; Director: Davy Corp., 1986–91; Yorkshire Chemicals, 1990–91; Mercury Communications, 1990–93; Berisford plc, 1990–96. Pres., British Textile Confedn, 1977–79; Chairman: Man-Made Fibres Producers Cttee, 1976–78; EDC for Wool Textile Industry, 1979–81; Priorities Bd for R&D in Agric. and Food, 1987–92; Heatherwood and Wexham Park Hosps Trust, 1991–97; Dir, John Cabot CTC Bristol Trust, 1997–98; Mem., BOTB, 1980–81, 1983–87 (Chm., N American Adv. Group, 1983–87). Chm., Standing Conf. on Schools' Sci. and Technology, 1992–96. Dir, Oxford Dio. Bd of Finance, 1990–2006. Freeman, City of London, 1986; Liveryman, Glovers' Co., 1986. Hon. DBA Buckingham, 1990. *Recreations:* sailing, tennis, gardening.

SMITH, Norman Jack, MA, MPhil, PhD; FEI; consultant and author; Chairman, Petroleum Venture Management Ltd, 2001–05; *b* 14 April 1936; *s* of late Maurice Leslie and Ellen Dorothy Smith; *m* 1967, Valerie Ann, *o d* of late Capt. A. E. Frost and Mrs M. Frost; one *s* one *d*. *Educ:* Grammar Sch., Henley-on-Thames; Oriel Coll., Oxford (MA); City Univ. (MPhil); Aberdeen Univ. (PhD); Harvard Univ. (Mgt Develt Prog.); CEDEP, France. Dexion Ltd, 1957; Vickers Ltd, 1960; Baring Brothers & Co. Ltd, 1969; seconded as Industrial Director, 1977, Dir-Gen., 1978–80, Offshore Supplies Office, Dept of Energy; Chairman: British Underwater Engineering Ltd, 1980–83; Mentor Engineering Consultants, 1987–92; Man. Dir, Smith Rea Energy Associates Ltd, 1981–2000; Director: Smith Rea Energy Analysts, 1985–2000; Smith Rea Energy Aberdeen, 1990–2000; Gas Transmission, 1989–95; Capcis, 1999–2000. Mem., Offshore Energy Technology Bd, 1978–80. Council Mem., Canterbury Archaeol Trust, 2003–07; Chm., Friends of Canterbury Archaeol Trust, 2003–07. Patron, Oriel Coll. Develt Trust, 2003–11. Fellow, Soc. of Business Economists; FEI (FInstPet 1978). *Publications:* The Sea of Lost Opportunity: North Sea oil and gas, British industry and the Offshore Supplies Office, 2011; sundry articles in economic and oil industry jls and think-tank papers. *Recreations:* walking, swimming, history, writing, reading. *Club:* Oxford and Cambridge.

SMITH, Owen; MP (Lab) Pontypridd, since 2010; *b* Morecambe, Lancs, 2 May 1970; *s* of Prof. David Burton Smith, *qv*; *m* 1995, Liz; two *s* one *d*. *Educ:* Sussex Univ. (BA Hist. and French). Producer, BBC Radio and TV, 1992–2002; Govt Special Advr to Wales Office, 2002, to NI Office, 2003–05; Hd, Govt Affairs, Pfizer Ltd, 2005–07; Dir, Corporate Affairs and Health Econs, Amgen Ltd, 2008–09. Shadow Minister, Wales Office, 2010–11; Mem., Shadow Health Team, 2010–11; Shadow Exchequer Sec. 2011–12; Shadow Sec. of State for Wales, 2012–15, for Work and Pensions, 2015–. Contested (Lab) Blaenau Gwent, June 2006. *Recreations:* family, fishing, reading, Rugby. *Address:* House of Commons, SW1A 0AA. *T:* (020) 7219 7128, (constituency office) (01443) 401122. *E:* owen.smith.mp@parliament.uk. *Club:* Pontypridd Rugby Football.

SMITH, Patrick J.; *see* Janson-Smith.

SMITH, Paul; Chairman, Eversheds LLP, since 2014; *b* Burnley, Lancs, 14 Nov. 1956; *s* of Fred Smith and Eileen Bartlett; *m* 1981, Carole; two *s* one *d*. *Educ:* Burnley Grammar Sch.; Univ. of Warwick (LLB). Articled clerk, then solicitor, Freshfields, 1980–84; Eversheds, 1984–. *Recreations:* puppetry, cooking, theatre, gardening. *Address:* Eversheds LLP, 1 Wood Street, EC2V 7WS.

SMITH, Paul Adrian, CBE 2012; Chairman: Celador Entertainment Ltd (formerly Complete Communications Corporation Ltd), since 1986; Celador Films Ltd, since 1999 (Joint Managing Director, 1999–2008); Celador Radio Broadcasting Ltd, since 2004; Celador Theatrical Productions Ltd, since 2009; *b* 16 Jan. 1947; *s* of Clifford Bryce Smith and Marjorie Doreen Smith (*née* Walker); *m* 1980, Sarah Anne King; one *s* one *d*. *Educ:* Royal Belfast Academical Instn. Joined BBC TV as trainee projectionist, 1966, various posts, incl. prodn manager and director, 1966–73; freelance television producer/dir, 1973–82; created It'll Be All Right on the Night, 1977; established: Complete Video Facilities, 1981; Celador Prodns, 1983 (Chm., 1983–2006); Complete Communications Corp., 1986; Celador Films, 1999; launched Who Wants to be a Millionaire? on UK TV, 1998, on US TV, 1999, sold worldwide rights, 2006. Estabd UK radio stations: The Coast, 2008; The Breeze, 2010; Jack FM, 2011; Sam FM; Palm FM; Fire Radio. Executive Producer (films): Dirty Pretty Things, 2002 (12 industry awards, inc. Best Film, British Ind. Film Awards, 2003, and Evening Standard Film Awards, 2003); The Descent, Separate Lies, 2005; Slumdog Millionaire, 2008 (awards incl. 8 Acad. Awards, 7 BAFTA Awards, 4 Golden Globe Awards); The Descent: Part 2, 2009; The Scouting Book for Boys, Centurion, 2010. BAFTA Award, 1999; Emmy Award, USA, 2000 and 2001. Hon. DSc Ulster, 2012; Hon. Dr Media Southhampton Solent, 2014. *Recreations:* travelling, motor yachting, photography, cinema, collecting original sixties records, family and home. *Address:* Celador Entertainment Ltd, 39 Long Acre, WC2E 9LG. *T:* (020) 7845 6802. *E:* psmith@celador.co.uk.

SMITH, Sir Paul (Brierley), Kt 2000; CBE 1994; RDI 1991; fashion designer; Chairman, Paul Smith Ltd; *b* 5 July 1946; *s* of late Harold and Marjorie Smith; *m* 2000, Pauline Denyer. *Educ:* Beeston Fields Grammar Sch. Opened own shop, 1970 (part-time), 1974 (full time); has shops in London, Nottingham, NY, LA, Paris, Milan, Moscow, Hong Kong, Singapore, San Francisco, Antwerp, Melbourne, Hamburg, Amsterdam and over 250 in Japan; exporter to numerous other countries; Nottingham and London-based design studios. Paul Smith True Brit exhibn, Design Mus., 1995; Hello, My Name is Paul Smith, Design Mus., 2013. Freeman, City of Nottingham, 1997. Hon. FRIBA 2007. Hon. MDes Nottingham Trent, 1991. Queen's Award for Export, 1995; Queen's Award for Enterprise, Internat. Trade, 2009; Outstanding Achievement in Fashion Award, British Fashion Awards, 2011. *Address:* Paul Smith Ltd, 20 Kean Street, WC2B 4AS. *T:* (020) 7836 7828.

SMITH, Paul James; Chief Executive, City and County of Swansea, 2006–11; *b* Colchester, 11 Nov. 1955; *s* of late Henry Joseph Smith and Jessie Elizabeth Mackenzie; *m* 1980, Keri Ann Jones; one *s*. *Educ:* Colchester Royal Grammar Sch.; Univ. of Wales Inst. of Science and Technol. (BSc Hons Town Planning; Postgrad. Dip. Town Planning). Asst Dir (Housing), Cardiff CC, 1988–91; Gloucester City Council: City Housing Officer, 1991–96; Dir, Community Services, 1996–2001; Chief Exec., 2001–06. Non-exec. Dir, Severnside Housing, 2013– (Chm., 2013–). Trustee, Citizens Advice Shropshire, 2012–15. Mem., Munslow Parish Council, 2012– (Chm., 2014–). *Recreations:* Colchester United FC, night sky, real ale and malt whisky. *E:* paulsmith.pjs@gmail.com.

SMITH, Paul Jonathan, OBE 1999; Director, USA, British Council, and Cultural Counsellor, British Embassy, Washington, since 2012; *b* 30 May 1956; *s* of late Arthur Godfrey Smith and Constance Mildred Smith (*née* Phelps); *m* 1999, Viveka Kumari; two *s* one *d*. *Educ:* King Edward's Sch., Birmingham; Queens' Coll., Cambridge (BA Hons double 1st 1978, MA 1982). Lectr in Lit., St Stephen's Coll., Univ. of Delhi, 1978–80; British Council: Asst Dir, Kano, 1983–85, Lagos, 1985–87; Dep. Dir, Drama and Dance Dept, 1987–89; Acting Director, Burma, Chile and Berlin, 1989–90; Dep. Dir, Dhaka, 1990–95; Director: NZ, 1995–99; Arts, 1999–2000; W India, 2000–05; Egypt, and Cultural Counsellor, British Embassy, Cairo, 2005–10; Afghanistan, and Cultural Counsellor, British Embassy, Kabul, 2010–12. Pres., EU Nat. Insts of Culture (Washington DC Cluster), 2013–14. Mem., Adv. Bd, Caravan, 2013–. Member, Board of Trustees: American Sch. of Bombay, 2003–05; Modern Sci. and Arts Univ., Cairo; Turquoise Mt Foundn, Afghanistan, 2010–12 (Mem., Bd of US Trustees, 2012–); US Friends of British Council, 2012–; Founder Mem., Bd of Trustees, British Univ. of Egypt, 2008–10. *Publications:* (contrib. sections on Shakespeare and Wordsworth) Reference Guide to English Literature, 2nd edn 1991; (contrib.) Colonial and Postcolonial Shakespeares, 2001; (contrib.) British-Egyptian Relations from Suez to the Present, 2007; Full Fathom Five: Shakespeare's old seas and new oceans, 2009; (contrib.) Vintage Shakespeare: new perspectives from India and Abroad, 2010. *Recreations:* directing Shakespeare, all arts, particularly literature, drama and film. *Address:* c/o Foreign and Commonwealth Office, King Charles Street, SW1A 2AH. *T:* (USA) (202) 6317368. *E:* paul.smith@britishcouncil.org.

SMITH, Prof. Paul Julian, PhD; FBA 2008; Distinguished Professor of Hispanic and Luso-Brazilian Literatures and Languages, Graduate Center, City University of New York, since 2010; *b* 11 Nov. 1956; *s* of Albert Charles Smith and Margaret (*née* Tovey). *Educ:* Cambridge Univ. (BA 1980; MA 1982; PhD 1984). Res. Fellow, Trinity Hall, Cambridge, 1983–84; Lectr, QMC, London Univ., 1984–88; Reader, QMW, 1989–91; Prof. of Spanish, 1991–2010, Hd, Dept of Spanish and Portuguese, 1991–2001 and 2006–07, Cambridge Univ.; Fellow, Trinity Hall, Cambridge, 1991–2010. *Publications:* Quevedo on Parnassus, 1987; Writing in the Margin: Spanish literature of the Golden Age, 1988; The Body Hispanic: gender and sexuality in Spanish and Spanish American literature, 1989; A Critical Guide to El Buscón, 1991; Representing the Other: race, text and gender in Spanish and Spanish American narrative, 1992; Laws of Desire: questions of homosexuality in Spanish writing and film, 1992; Desire Unlimited: the cinema of Pedro Almodóvar, 1994; Vision Machines: cinema, literature and sexuality in Spain and Cuba, 1996; The Theatre of García Lorca: text, performance and psychoanalysis, 1998; The Moderns: time, space and subjectivity in contemporary Spanish culture, 2000; Contemporary Spanish Culture: television, fashion, art and film, 2003; Spanish Visual Culture: cinema, television, internet, 2007; Spanish Practices: literature, cinema, television, 2012. *Address:* Hispanic and Luso-Brazilian Literatures, Graduate Center, City University of New York, 365 Fifth Avenue, New York, NY 10016, USA.

SMITH, Dr Paul Philip; Secretary General, Botanic Gardens Conservation International, since 2015; *b* Bexley, 8 Jan. 1964; *s* of Robert Langley Smith and Sheila Margaret Smith; *m* 1994, Deborah Ann Shah; one *d*. *Educ:* Univ. of Kent (BSc Hons Microbiol. 1986; PhD Ecol. 1991). Plant ecologist: N Luangwa Nat. Park, Zambia, 1993–96; Royal Botanic Gdns, Kew, 1997–2000; Internat. Co-ordinator, Millennium Seed Bank, 2000–05; Hd, Millennium Seed Bank, Royal Botanic Gds, Kew, 2005–14. FRGS 2012; FLS 2012. *Publications:* Common Trees, Shrubs and Grasses of the Luangwa Valley, 1995; The Ecological Survey of Zambia, 2001; Field Guide to the Trees and Shrubs of the Miombo Woodland, 2004; Vegetation Atlas of Madagascar, 2007; contrib. papers to jls. *Recreations:* painting, walking, travel. *Address:* Botanic Gardens Conservation International, Descanso House, 199 Kew Road, Richmond, Surrey TW9 3BW. *T:* (020) 8332 5953. *E:* paul.smith@bgci.org.

SMITH, Penelope R.; *see* Russell-Smith.

SMITH, Peter Alan, FCA; Director, NM Rothschild & Sons Ltd, since 2001; *b* 5 Aug. 1946; *s* of Dudley Vaughan Smith and Beatrice Ellen (*née* Sketcher); *m* 1971, Cherry Blandford; two *s*. *Educ:* Mill Hill Sch.; Univ. of Southampton (BSc); Wharton Sch., Univ. of Pennsylvania (AMP). FCA 1970. PricewaterhouseCoopers (formerly Coopers & Lybrand), 1967–2000: Partner, 1975–2000 (Senior Partner, 1998–2000); Chm., 1994–98; Mem., Global Leadership Team, 1998–2000. Dir and Dep. Chm., Equitable Life Assce Soc., 2001–10; Director: Safeway plc, 2002–04; Savills plc, 2004– (Chm., 2004–); Templeton Emerging Markets Investment Trust plc, 2004– (Chm., 2007–); Associated British Foods plc, 2007–; Land Restoration Trust, 2009– (Chm., 2009–); Chm., RAC plc, 2003–05. Hon. Treas., UK Housing Trust, 1979–83. Member: Finance Cttee, Nat. Trust, 1991–98, 2001–05; Cttee on Corporate Governance, 1996–97; Council, ICAEW, 1997–2003 (Treas., 2001–03); POW Business Leaders Forum, 1994–2000; President's Cttee, 1994–98, F and GP Cttee, 1999–2008, CBI. Liveryman, Chartered Accountants' Co., 1993–. FRSA 1993; CCMI 1994. *Publications:* Housing Association Accounts and Their Audit, 1980. *Recreations:* golf, gardens. *Address:* (office) New Court, St Swithin's Lane, EC4N 8AL. *Clubs:* Carlton, Walbrook; Beaconsfield Golf.

SMITH, Peter Bruce, MA; Head Master, Bradfield College, 1985–2003; *b* 18 March 1944; *s* of Alexander D. Smith and Grace Smith; *m* 1968, Diana Margaret Morgan; two *d*. *Educ:* Magdalen College School, Oxford; Lincoln College, Oxford (Old Members Scholar; MA). Asst Master, Rugby Sch., 1967–85 (Head of Hist. Dept, 1973–77, Housemaster of School Field, 1977–85). Mem. Governing Body, Downe House Sch., 1985–89; Gov., Abbey Sch.,

2005 (Chm., 2007–13). Captain Oxfordshire County Cricket Club, 1971–77 (Minor Counties Champions, 1974). *Recreations:* antiquarian, sporting, literary. *Club:* Vincent's (Oxford).

SMITH, Prof. Peter Charles; Professor of Health Policy, 2009–13, now Emeritus, and Co-Director, Centre for Health Policy, 2010–13, Imperial College London; *b* 29 July 1952; *s* of Dennis John Smith and Evelyn Mary Smith (*née* Rush); *m* 1986, Sally Jane Stone; one *d*. *Educ:* Birkenhead Sch.; Oriel Coll., Oxford (MA Maths 1974). Res. Fellow, Univ. of Cambridge, 1977–82; University of York: Lectr, 1984–94; Reader, 1994–96; Prof. of Economics, 1996–2009; Dir, Centre for Health Economics, 2005–09. Sen. Res. Associate, WHO Eur. Observatory on Health Systems and Policy, 2007–; Sen. Associate, Nuffield Trust, 2008–. Member: DoH Adv. Cttee on Resource Allocation, 1997–2002; Audit Commn, 2003–09; Co-operation and Competition Panel, NHS, 2009–14; Health England, DoH Adv. Gp to Minister for Public Health, 2007–10; Ind. Inquiry into Modernising Med. Careers, 2007–08; Wkg Party on Future Doctor and Patient, RCP, 2008–10. Chm., UK Centre for Measurement of Govt Activity, 2005–08. Member: Scientific Peer Rev. Gp, WHO, 2001–02; Global Agenda Council on Healthcare Systems, WEF, 2008–10. Council Mem., Royal Statistical Soc., 2002–06. Vis. Prof., LSE, 2005–; Hon. Professor: Univ. of St Andrews, 1997–2007; Monash Univ., 2006–11; Univ. of York, 2011–. Hon. FRCP, 2010. Founding Editor-in-Chief, Health Care Mgt Science, 1997–2005; Ed., Health Policy, 2011–. *Publications:* (ed) Outcome Measurement in the Public Sector, 1996; (ed) Reforming Markets in Health Care, 2000; (ed) Measuring Up: improving health system performance in OECD countries, 2002; Formula Funding of Public Services, 2006; (jtly) Measuring Efficiency in Health Care, 2006; (ed jtly) Performance Measurement for Health System Improvement: experiences, challenges and prospects, 2009; (ed) Health Care Systems in Developing and Transition Economies: the role of research evidence, 2009; (ed with S. Glied) Oxford Handbook of Health Economics, 2011; (ed with I. Papanicolas) Health System Performance Comparison: an agenda for policy, information and research, 2013; (ed jtly) Paying for Performance in Healthcare: implications for health system performance and accountability, 2014; over 150 papers in acad. jls. *Recreations:* bridge, allotment gardening, jazz, finding safe cycling routes. *Address:* Imperial College Business School, SW7 2AZ. *E:* peter.smith@imperial.ac.uk.

SMITH, Peter Claudius G.; *see* Gautier-Smith.

SMITH, Most Rev. Peter David; *see* Southwark, Archbishop of, (RC).

SMITH, Peter David V.; *see* Vicary-Smith.

SMITH, Sir Peter Frank Graham N.; *see* Newson-Smith.

SMITH, Prof. Peter George, CBE 2001; Professor of Tropical Epidemiology, London School of Hygiene and Tropical Medicine, since 1989; *b* 3 May 1942; *s* of George Henry Smith and Lily Smith (*née* Phillips); *m* 1999, Jill Margaret Routledge; one *s*, and one step *s* one step *d*. *Educ:* City Univ. (BSc Applied Maths 1st Class 1963; DSc Med. Stats 1983). Statistical Res. Unit, MRC, 1965–67; Clinical and Population Cytogenetics Unit, MRC, 1967–69; Makerere Univ. Med. Sch., Uganda, 1970–71; WHO Internat. Agency for Res. on Cancer, Uganda, 1971–72; Cancer Epidemiology and Clinical Trials Unit, ICRF, Oxford, 1972–79; Dept of Epidemiology, Harvard Sch. of Public Health, 1975; Sen. Lectr, 1979–86, Reader, 1986–89, Hd, Dept of Epidemiol. and Population Scis, 1990–97, Hd, Dept of Infectious and Tropical Diseases, 1997–2002, LSHTM. WHO Tropical Diseases Res. Prog., Geneva, 1987–88. Chairman: Global Adv. Cttee on Vaccine Safety, WHO, 2009–11 (Mem., 2005–11; Dep. Chm., 2006–09); Prog. Bd for Global Health and Vaccination Res., Res. Council of Norway, 2011–; Member: WHO, MRC, and DoH Cttees, incl. Spongiform Encephalopathy Adv. Cttee, 1996–2004 (Chair, 2001–04); Nuffield Council on Bioethics, 2003–09 (Dep. Chm., 2006–09); Bd of Mgt, Medicines for Malaria Venture, 2009–12. Gov., Wellcome Trust, 2004–14. FMedSci 1999. Hon. MFPHM, then Hon. MFPH, 1991–2013. Donald Reid Medal, LSHTM, 2003. *Publications:* (ed with R. H. Morrow) Field Trials of health interventions in developing countries, 1996; (ed with R. H. Morrow and D. A. Ross) Field Trials of Health Interventions: a toolbox, 2015; numerous contribs to med. res. literature. *Recreations:* gardening, walking, cycling, swimming. *Address:* MRC Tropical Epidemiology Group, Department of Infectious Disease Epidemiology, London School of Hygiene and Tropical Medicine, Keppel Street, WC1E 7HT. *T:* (020) 7927 2246.

SMITH, Peter J.; *see* Jefferson Smith.

SMITH, Peter John, CPFA; Chairman, Gateshead Health NHS Foundation Trust (formerly NHS Trust), 1998–2012; *b* 31 Dec. 1936; *s* of Frank and Sarah Ann Smith; *m* 1st, Marie Louise Smith (marr. diss. 2001); one *s* one *d*; 2nd, 2001, Judith Anne Brown. *Educ:* Rastrick Grammar Sch., Brighouse, W Yorkshire. Trainee Accountant, Huddersfield CBC, 1953–59; Accountancy Asst, Bradford CBC, 1959–61; Asst Chief Accountant, Chester CBC, 1961–63; Computer Manager, Keighley BC, 1963–66; Asst City Treasurer, Gloucester CBC, 1966–69; Dep. Borough Treasurer, Gateshead CBC, 1969–73; Asst County Treasurer, Tyne and Wear CC, 1973–74, Dep. County Treasurer, 1974–80, County Treasurer, 1980–86. Gen. Manager, Tyne and Wear Residuary Body, 1985–88. Treasurer: NE Regional Airport Jt Cttee, 1980–86; Northumbria Police Authority, 1980–86; Northumbria Probation and After Care Cttee, 1980–86; Mem., Tyne and Wear Passenger Transport Exec. Bd, 1981–86. Director: N American Property Unit Trust, 1982–93; Northern Investors Co., 1983–86; Westgate Trust, 1990–92; Chairman: Gateshead Healthcare and Community NHS Trusts, 1992–98; Northern Clinical Waste Consortium, 1994–2012. Mem. Bd, NHS Foundn Trust Network, 2006–10. *Recreations:* fell walking, bridge. *Address:* Wheatsheaf House, 19 Station Road, Beamish, Co. Durham DH9 0QU. *T:* (0191) 370 0481.

SMITH, Peter John, CBE 1995; HM Diplomatic Service, retired; Governor, Cayman Islands, 1999–2002; *b* 15 May 1942; *s* of late John S. Smith and Irene (*née* Waple); *m* 1964, Suzanne Pauline Duffin; one *s* one *d*. *Educ:* St Dunstan's Coll., London. Joined FO, 1962; Vietnamese lang. student, then 3rd Sec., Saigon, 1964–67; Commercial Attaché, Paris, 1968–69; Commercial Publicity Officer, British Information Services, NY, 1970–73; FCO, 1973–76; 1st Sec., Commercial, Mexico City, 1976–80; Dep. High Comr, Port Louis, Mauritius, 1981–84; FCO, 1984–86; Deputy Consul General: Montreal, 1987–88; Toronto (also Dir, Trade and Investment), 1988–92; RCDS 1992; Ambassador to Madagascar and concurrently Ambassador (non-resident) to The Comoros, 1993–96; High Comr to Lesotho, 1996–99. *Recreations:* golf, cricket, chess, bridge. *Address:* Abbey Gardens, Abbey Street, Cerne Abbas, Dorset DT2 7JQ. *Club:* MCC.

SMITH, Peter Lincoln Chivers, FRCS, FRCP; cardiothoracic surgeon; Consultant Cardiothoracic Surgeon, Imperial College Healthcare NHS Trust (formerly Hammersmith Hospital, then Hammersmith Hospitals NHS Trust), 1987–2012; *b* 20 Sept. 1948; *s* of Alfred Stanley Chivers Smith and Cynthia Enid (*née* Anstee); *m* 1976, Susan Margaret Evans; one *s* two *d*. *Educ:* St Bartholomew's Hosp., Univ. of London (MB, BS 1975). MRCP 1978, FRCP 1997; FRCS 1980. General surgical trng, St Bartholomew's Hosp., 1976–79; cardiothoracic surgical trng, St Bartholomew's, Royal Brompton, Middlesex, Harefield and Hammersmith Hosps, 1979–86. Hunterian Prof., 1986–87, and Mem. Ct of Examiners, 1995–2003, RCS. FESC 2001; FETCS 2001. *Publications:* (jtly) The Brain and Cardiac Surgery, 1993; numerous scientific pubns on cardiac and thoracic surgical topics. *Recreations:* music, travelling. *Address:* Field House, Ferry Road, Orford, Woodbridge, Suffolk IP12 2NR. *Clubs:* Royal Automobile, Royal Society of Medicine.

SMITH, (Peter) Patrick J.; *see* Janson-Smith.

SMITH, His Honour Peter William; a Circuit Judge, 1994–2009; *b* 31 Dec. 1945; *s* of late William and Bessie Smith; *m* 1970, Vanessa Mary (*née* Wildash); one *s*. *Educ:* Arnold Sch., Blackpool; Downing Coll., Cambridge (MA). Called to the Bar, Middle Temple, 1969. Practised (as William Smith) on Northern Circuit; a Dep. Judge Advocate, 1983–84; a Recorder, 1991–94. Mem., Mental Health Review Tribunal, 1993–2012. *Recreation:* weekends in the Lake District.

SMITH, Peter William G.; *see* Greig-Smith.

SMITH, Hon. Sir Peter (Winston), Kt 2002; **Hon. Mr Justice Peter Smith;** a Judge of the High Court of Justice, Chancery Division, since 2002; *b* 1 May 1952; *s* of George Arthur Smith and Iris Muriel Smith; *m* 1980, Diane Dalgleish; one *s* two *d*. *Educ:* Selwyn Coll., Cambridge (BA 1974; MA 1976); Coll. of Law. Called to the Bar, Lincoln's Inn, 1975, Bencher, 2000. Lectr, Manchester Univ., 1977–83; practice on Northern Circuit, 1979–2002; QC 1992; Asst Recorder, 1994–97; Actg Deemster, IOM, 1994–2002; a Deputy High Court Judge, 1996–2002; a Recorder, 1997–2002. *Recreations:* Titanic Historical Society, Friend of Royal Naval Museum and HMS Victory, Jackie Fisher fan, reading military history, football. *Address:* Royal Courts of Justice, 7 Rolls Building, Chancery Division, Fetter Lane, EC4A 1NL.

SMITH, Philip; *see* Smith, C. P.

SMITH, Philip Andrew B.; *see* Brook Smith.

SMITH, Ralph Andrew; QC (Scot.) 1999; a Deputy Judge of the Upper Tribunal, since 2012; Legal Member, Lands Tribunal for Scotland, since 2014; *b* 22 March 1961; *s* of Rev. Ralph Colley Philip Smith and Florence Howat Smith; *m* 1989, Lucy Moore Inglis; one *s* one *d*. *Educ:* Edinburgh Acad.; Kelvinside Acad.; Aberdeen Univ. (LLB 1981; DLP 1982). Admitted to Faculty of Advocates, 1985; formerly in practice, specialising in commercial law and planning; Jun. Counsel to Lord Pres. of Court of Session, 1989–90; Standing Jun. Counsel to DoE (Scotland), 1992–99. *Publications:* contribs to Scots Law Times. *Recreations:* field sports, Scottish Jun. Foil Fencing Champion, 1982. *Address:* Castlemains, Gifford, E Lothian EH41 4PL. *Club:* New (Edinburgh).

SMITH, Rt Rev. Raymond George; Senior Associate Minister, Church Hull Anglican Parish, Sydney, since 2014; *b* 7 March 1936; *s* of Gordon William Smith and Alice Mary (*née* Brett); *m* 1960, Shirley Jeanette Gilmore; three *s*. *Educ:* Australian Coll. of Theology (ThSchol); Univ. of New England (BA, Dip Cont. Ed, MEd). Parish priest, dio. of Armidale, 1959–76; Dir of Christian Educn and Archdeacon, Armidale, 1977–86; Dir of Extension Ministries, Trinity Episcopal Sch. for Ministry, Ambridge, Pa, USA, 1986–90; Rector of Wanniassa, 1990–93, and Archdeacon of S Canberra, 1991–93, dio. of Canberra and Goulburn; Bp of Liverpool, NSW, and an Asst Bp of Sydney, 1993–2001; Senior Associate Minister: St Clement, Mosman, NSW, 2002–04; St Philip's, York Street, Sydney, 2005–13. Chair, Next Phase Ministry Cttee, Anglican Deaconess Inst., dio. of Sydney, 2012–. *Publications:* People Caring for People, 1990. *Recreations:* swimming, cycling, photography, stamp collecting, Australian history. *Address:* 20/3A Blackwall Point Road, Abbotsford, NSW 2046, Australia.

SMITH, Richard James Crosbie W.; *see* Wilmot-Smith.

SMITH, Prof. Richard John, ScD; FBA 2007; Professor of Econometric Theory and Economic Statistics, and Director, Centre for Research in Microeconomics, University of Cambridge, since 2006; Lecturer in Economics and Fellow of Gonville and Caius College, Cambridge, since 2005; *b* Redhill, 14 May 1949; *s* of John Hayden Smith and Irene Smith (*née* Barlow); *m* 1975, Margaret Veronica Assumpta Breen. *Educ:* Bromley Grammar Sch.; Bournemouth Sch.; Churchill Coll., Cambridge (BA 1972); Univ. of Essex (MA 1976); PhD 1989, ScD 2010, Cantab. Res. Asst, SSRC Inflation Workshop, 1975–76, Lectr in Econometrics, 1976–89, Univ. of Manchester; Lectr in Econometrics, 1989–95, Reader in Theoretical Econometrics, 1995, Univ. of Cambridge; Coll. Lectr in Econs and Fellow, 1989–95, Dir of Studies in Econs, 1992–94, Gonville and Caius Coll., Cambridge; Professor: of Econs, Univ. of Bristol, 1995–2002; of Econometrics, Univ. of Warwick, 2002–05; Reader in Theoretical Econometrics, Univ. of Cambridge, 2005–06. Visiting Professor: Queen's Univ., Canada, 1983–84; Univ. of Montreal, 1994, 2001, 2006; CREST-INSEE, Paris, 1993, 1996, 2004; Univ. of Calif, Berkeley, 2006; Vis. Fellow, NIESR, 1997–; Centre Fellow, Centre for Microdata Methods and Practice, UCL and IFS, 2001–; 2002 Leverhulme Maj. Res. Fellow, 2003–06. Mem., Academic Econometric Panel, ONS, 1997–2003. Mem., Eur. Standing Cttee, 2002–04, GB and Ireland Regl Consultant, 2003–08, Fellow, 2007, Econometric Soc. Mem., Exec. Cttee, 2007–, Mem. Council, 2007–, REconS. Gov., NIESR, 2004–. Mem., Editl Bd, Rev. of Econ. Studies, 1986–94; Associate Ed., Econometrica, 1995–2007; Co-Ed., Econometric Theory, 2000–08 (Mem., Adv. Bd, 2010–); Man. Ed., Econometrics Jl, 2007– (Founding Ed., 1997–2001). *Publications:* contribs to Biometrika, Econometrica, Econometric Theory, Jl Econometrics, Jl Amer. Statistical Assoc., Rev. Econ. Studies, Jl Business and Econ. Stats. *Recreations:* fell walking, Manchester United FC, FC United of Manchester, Manchester United Supporters Trust, modernist architecture, theatre, film, reading. *Address:* Faculty of Economics, University of Cambridge, Austin Robinson Building, Sidgwick Avenue, Cambridge CB3 9DD. *T:* (01223) 335230, *Fax:* (01223) 335475. *E:* rjs27@econ.cam.ac.uk.

SMITH, Richard Lloyd; QC 2001; a Recorder, since 2000; *b* 28 Jan. 1963; *s* of Lloyd and Dorothy Smith; *m* 1990, Anna Sara Webb; one *s* one *d*. *Educ:* King's Coll. London (LLB). Called to the Bar, Middle Temple, 1986. *Recreations:* Rugby, Leeds United Football Club. *Address:* Guildhall Chambers, 23 Broad Street, Bristol BS1 2HG. *T:* (0117) 927 3366.

SMITH, Prof. Richard Lyttleton, PhD; Mark L. Reed III Distinguished Professor of Statistics, since 2004, and Professor of Biostatistics, School of Public Health, since 2008, University of North Carolina (Professor of Statistics, 1991–2004 (on leave, 1994–96)); Director, Statistical and Applied Mathematical Sciences Institute, North Carolina, since 2010; *b* 31 March 1953; *s* of Stanley Lyttleton Smith and Hilary Margaret (*née* James); *m* 2002, Amy Grady; two *s*. *Educ:* Jesus Coll., Univ. of Oxford (BA Maths 1975; MA 1985); Cornell Univ., USA (PhD Ops Res. 1979). Lectr in Stats, Imperial Coll., London, 1979–85; Prof. of Statistics, Univ. of Surrey, 1985–90; Prof. of Statistical Sci., Univ. of Cambridge, 1994–96. Guy Medal in Silver, Royal Statistical Soc., 1991. *Publications:* (jtly) Statistical Analysis of Reliability Data, 1991; (with G. Alastair Young) Essentials of Statistical Inference, 2005; contrib. to Jl Roy. Statistical Soc., Proc. Royal Soc., Biometrika, Annals of Stats, etc. *Recreations:* cross-country and road running, chess, bridge, music. *Address:* 4314 Oak Hill Road, Chapel Hill, NC 27514–9731, USA.

SMITH, Prof. Richard Michael, PhD; FRHistS; FBA 1991; Professor of Historical Geography and Demography, 2003–11, now Emeritus, and Head, Department of Geography, 2007–10, University of Cambridge; Director, Cambridge Group for the History of Population and Social Structure, 1994–2012; Fellow, Downing College, Cambridge, 1994–2010, now Emeritus (Vice-Master, 2004–10); *b* 3 Jan. 1946; *s* of Louis Gordon Smith and Elsie Fanny (*née* Ward); *m* 1971, Margaret Anne McFadden. *Educ:* Earls Colne Grammar Sch.; University Coll. London (BA Hons); St Catharine's Coll., Cambridge (MA 1977; PhD 1974). Lectr in Population Studies, Plymouth Poly., 1973–74; Cambridge University: Asst Lectr in Histl Geography, 1974–76; Sen. Res. Officer, 1976–81, Asst Dir, 1981–83,

Cambridge Gp for the Hist. of Population and Social Structure; Fellow, 1977–83, Tutor, 1979–83, Fitzwilliam Coll.; Oxford University: Univ. Lectr in Histl Demography, 1983–89; Fellow, All Souls Coll., 1983–94; Reader in Hist. of Medicine and Dir, Wellcome Unit for Hist. of Medicine, 1990–94; Reader in Historical Demography, Cambridge Univ., 1996–2003. Mem. Council, British Soc. for Population Studies, 1987–91; Pres., Economic History Soc., 2007–10. Sir John Neale Lectr, 1996. Editor: Social Hist. of Medicine, 1986–92; Economic History Review, 2001–07. *Publications:* (ed jtly) Bastardy and its Comparative History, 1980; (ed) Land, Kinship and Lifecycle, 1984; (ed jtly) The World We Have Gained: histories of population and social structure, 1986; (ed jtly) Life, Death and the Elderly: historical perspectives, 1991; (ed jtly) Medieval Society and the Manor Court, 1996; contribs to Annales ESC, Jl of Family Hist., Trans RHistS, Ageing and Society, Law and Hist. Rev., Population and Develt Rev. *Recreations:* listening to music, especially jazz and classical. *Address:* Cambridge Group for the History of Population and Social Structure, Sir William Hardy Building, Department of Geography, Downing Place, Cambridge CB2 3EN. *T:* (01223) 333182.

SMITH, Richard Philip Morley R.; *see* Reay-Smith.

SMITH, Richard Sydney William, CBE 2000; Chief Executive, UnitedHealth Europe, 2004; Visiting Professor, London School of Hygiene and Tropical Medicine, since 1996; *b* 11 March 1952; *s* of Sydney Smith and Hazel Smith (*née* Kirk); *m* 1977, Linda Jean Arnott; two *s* one *d*. *Educ:* Roan Grammar Sch., London; Edinburgh Univ. (BSc 1973; MB ChB 1976); Stanford Univ. (MSc in Management 1990). MFPHM 1992, FFPH (FFPHM 1997); FRCPE 1992; MRCP 1993, FRCP 1995; FRCGP 1997; FRCSE 2000. Hosp. jobs in Scotland and New Zealand, 1976–79; British Medical Journal: Asst Editor, 1979; Sen. Asst Editor, 1984; Editor, and Chief Exec., BMJ Publishing Gp, 1991–2004. BBC Breakfast Time doctor, 1983–87. Founder, 1998, and Vice-Chm., 2001–04, Cttee on Publication Ethics; Member: Internat. Cttee of Med. Jl Editors, 1991–2004; Bd, World Assoc. of Med. Editors, 1994–2000; Editorial Boards: Nat. Med. Jl of India, 1992–2002; Ceylon Med. Jl, 1996–2002; Canadian Med. Assoc. Jl, 1997–2002; Hong Kong Jl of Family Practice, 1998–2002. Prof. of Med. Journalism, Univ. of Nottingham, 1993–2001. Chm., Foresight Wkg Pty on Inf. and Health, 2000; Member: UK Panel for Health and Biomed. Res. Integrity, 2006–; Medicines Partnership Taskforce, Nat. Prescribing Centre, 2006–. Member: Bd, Public Liby of Sci., 2004–; Adv. Bd, Global Trial Bank, 2005–. Mem. Gov. Council, St George's Hosp. Med. Sch., 2004–. Patron: Contact a Family, 1985–; Project Hope UK, 2004– (Mem. Bd, 1996–2002). Founder FMedSci 1998; Fellow, Acad. of Gen. Educn, Karnataka, India, 1993. HealthWatch Award, 2004. *Publications:* Alcohol Problems, 1982; Prison Health Care, 1984; The Good Health Kit, 1987; Unemployment and Health, 1987; (ed) Health of the Nation, 1991; (ed) Rationing in Action, 1993; (ed jtly) Management for Doctors, 1995; (ed jtly) Scientific Basis of Health Services, 1996; The Trouble with Medical Journals, 2006; articles in learned jls; contrib. Guardian. *Recreations:* jazz, cycling, running, wine, talking first and thinking second.

SMITH, Robert B.; *see* Bettley-Smith.

SMITH, Robert Carr, CBE 1989; PhD; Vice-Chancellor, Kingston University, 1992–97 (Director, Kingston Polytechnic, 1982–92); *b* 19 Nov. 1935; *s* of late Edward Albert Smith and Olive Winifred Smith; *m* 1960, Rosalie Mary (*née* Spencer) (*d* 2004); one *s* one *d*. *Educ:* Queen Elizabeth's School, Barnet; Southampton Univ. (BSc); London Univ. (PhD). Research Asst, Guy's Hosp. Med. Sch., 1957–61; Lectr, Senior Lectr, Reader, Prof. of Electronics, Southampton Univ., 1961–82. Seconded to DoE, 1973–74. Chairman: Engineering Profs' Conf., 1980–82; Polytechnics and Colls Employers' Forum, 1988–90; Vice-Chm., Cttee of Dirs of Polytechnics, 1988–89; Member: Design Council, 1983–88; Council for Industry and Higher Educn, 1985–97; Council, Inst. for Manpower Studies, 1987–95; PCFC, 1988–93; TEC for Kingston, Merton and Wandsworth, 1989–97; Higher Educn Statistics Agency, 1993–97; Univs and Colls Employers' Assoc., 1994–97. Pt-time Chief Exec., SEARCH (careers service for Kingston, Merton and Wandsworth), 1998; Chm. Bd, Prospects Services Ltd, 2003–08. Chm., Bd of Govs, IoW Further Educn Coll., 1999–2003 and 2007–10; Governor: Treloars Sch. and Coll., 2008–13; Wolf Fields Primary Sch. Trustee, Prospects Acads Trust, 2013–15. Hon. Fellow, St George's Hosp. Med. Sch., 1998. Freeman, Royal Borough of Kingston upon Thames, 1997. *Publications:* research papers on radiation physics, laser physics, new technology. *Recreations:* visual arts, classical music, local history, research on stained glass artist Keith New. *Address:* 40 Oakbark House, High Street, Brentford, Middx TW8 8LF.

SMITH, Sir Robert (Courtney), Kt 1987; CBE 1980; FRSE; MA, CA; Chairman, Alliance and Second Alliance Trust, 1984–96; *b* 10 Sept. 1927; 4th *s* of late John Smith, DL, JP, and Agnes Smith, Glasgow and Symington; *m* 1954, Moira Rose, *d* of late Wilfred H. Macdougall, CA, Glasgow; one *s* two *d* (and one *s* decd). *Educ:* Kelvinside Academy, Glasgow; Sedbergh Sch.; Trinity Coll., Cambridge. BA 1950, MA 1957. Served, Royal Marines, 1945–47, and RMFVR, 1951–57; Hon. Col, RM Reserves Scotland, 1992–96. Partner, Arthur Young McClelland Moores & Co., Chartered Accountants, 1957–78. Director: Standard Life Assurance, 1975–94 (Chm., 1982–88); Sidlaw Gp, 1977–97 (Chm., 1980–88); Wm Collins, 1978–89 (Vice-Chm., 1979–89); Volvo Trucks (GB), later Volvo Truck and Bus, 1979–98; Edinburgh Investment Trust, 1983–98; British Alcan Aluminium, 1983–99; Bank of Scotland, 1985–97. Mem., Scottish Industrial Develt Adv. Bd, 1972–88 (Chm., 1981–88); Pres., Business Archives Council of Scotland, 1986–97; Chancellor's Assessor, Glasgow Univ., 1984–96. Mem., Horserace Betting Levy Bd, 1977–82; Deacon Convener, Trades House of Glasgow, 1976–78; Dir, Merchants House of Glasgow, 1991–96. Mem. Council, Inst. of Chartered Accountants of Scotland, 1974–79. Trustee, Carnegie Trust for Univs of Scotland, 1982–2002. FRSE 1988. Hon. LLD: Glasgow, 1978; Aberdeen, 1991. CStJ 2004. *Address:* The Old Rectory, Cathedral Street, Dunkeld, Perthshire PH8 0AW. *T:* (01350) 727574. *Clubs:* East India; Western (Glasgow); Hawks (Cambridge).

SMITH, Robert Daglish, CMG 1998; Executive Director, UK Committee for UNICEF, 1980–99; *b* 2 July 1934; *s* of Robert Ramsay Smith and Jessie Smith (*née* Daglish); *m* 1984, Ursula Schmidt-Brümmer (*née* Stollenwerk) (*d* 2010). *Educ:* Dulwich Coll.; Queens' Coll., Cambridge (MA). Nat. Service, Royal Signals, 1953–55. Master, King's Sch., Canterbury, 1960–65; Lectr, Newland Park Coll. of Education, 1965–67; Consultant, Wells Management Consultants, 1968–70; freelance mgt consultant in fundraising and arts admin, 1970–74; Dir, East Midlands Arts Assoc., 1974–80. Sec., 1976–78, Chair, 1979–80, Standing Cttee of Regl Arts Assocs; Treas., Council, Children's Rights Alliance for England (formerly Children's Rights Office), 1992–2004. Trustee, NSPCC, 1999–2008; Mem. Council, Shakespeare's Globe, 2005–09 (Mem. Internat. Cttee, 2000–05); Bd Mem., UNA, 2002–07. FRSA 1990. *Recreations:* music, opera, theatre, travel. *Address:* Lynde House Care Home, 28 Cambridge Park, Twickenham TW1 2JB.

SMITH, (Robert) Harvey; show jumper, farmer; *b* 29 Dec. 1938; *m* 1st, Irene Shuttleworth (marr. diss. 1986); two *s*; 2nd, 1987, Susan Dye. First major win with Farmer's Boy. Leading Show Jumper of the Year; other major wins include: King George V Cup, Royal Internat. Horse Show, 1958; has won the John Player Trophy 7 times, King George V Gold Cup once, and the British Jumping Derby 4 times; Grand Prix and Prix des Nations wins in UK, Ireland, Europe and USA; took part in Olympic Games, 1968 and 1972; best-known mounts: Farmer's Boy, Mattie Brown, Olympic Star, O'Malley, Salvador, Harvester. BBC TV Commentator, Los Angeles Olympics, 1984. Assists wife in training of racehorses. *Publications:* Show Jumping with Harvey Smith, 1979; Bedside Jumping, 1985.

See also R. W. Smith.

SMITH, Prof. Robert Henry Tufrey, AM 1998; PhD; Chancellor, University of Ballarat, Australia, 2005–12, now Emeritus Chancellor; *b* 22 May 1935; *s* of late Robert Davidson Smith and Gladys Smith (*née* Tufrey); *m* 1959, Elisabeth Jones; one *s* one *d*. *Educ:* Farrer Memorial Agricultural High Sch., Tamworth, NSW; Univ. of New England, NSW (BA, 1st Cl. Hons Geography); Northwestern Univ. (MA); ANU (PhD). Lectr in Geography, Univ. of Melbourne, 1961–62; University of Wisconsin: Asst Prof. of Geography, 1962–64; Associate Prof., 1964–67; Prof., 1967–70; Chm., African Studies Programme, 1968–69 (on leave, 1964–66: Associate Res. Fellow, Nigerian Inst. for Social and Econ. Res., and Hon. Vis. Lectr in Geography, Univ. of Ibadan, 1964–65; Vis. Fellow, Dept of Geography, Univ. of Sydney, 1965–66); Prof. of Geography and Head of Dept, Queen's Univ., Kingston, Ontario, 1970–72; Prof. of Geography, Monash Univ., 1972–75 (Chm. of Dept, 1973–75; Associate Dean, Faculty of Arts, 1974–75); University of British Columbia: Prof. of Geography, 1975–85; Head of Dept, 1975–80; Associate Vice-Pres., Academic, 1979–83; Vice-Pres., Academic, 1983–85; Pres. *pro tem*, March–Nov. 1985; Vice-Chancellor, Univ. of WA, 1985–89; Chm., Nat. Bd of Employment, Educn and Trng, Aust., 1989–90; Vice-Chancellor, Univ. of New England, Australia, 1990–93; Exec. Dir and Pres., 1994–97, Sen. Consultant, 1997–99, Australian Educn Office, Washington; Dep. Chancellor, Southern Cross Univ., 1998–2002. *Address:* PO Box 5046, Victoria Point, Qld 4165, Australia.

SMITH, Sir Robert Hill, 3rd Bt *cr* 1945, of Crowmallie, Co. Aberdeen; *b* 15 April 1958; *s* of Sir (William) Gordon Smith, 2nd Bt, VRD, and of Diana (*née* Goodchild); *S* father, 1983; *m* 1993, Fiona Anne Cormack; three *d*. *Educ:* Merchant Taylors' School; King's Coll., Aberdeen Univ. Contested (SDP/Lib Alliance), Aberdeen North, 1987. MP (Lib Dem) W Aberdeenshire and Kincardine, 1997–2015; contested (Lib Dem) same seat, 2015. Mem. (Lib Dem) Aberdeenshire Unitary Council, 1995–97. Vice Chm., Grampian Jt Police Bd, 1995–97. Gen. Council Assessor, Aberdeen Univ. Court, 1994–98. *Heir: b* Charles Gordon Smith [*b* 21 April 1959; *m* 1990, Dr Ann Maria Kennedy; two *s* one *d*]. *Address:* Crowmallie House, Pitcaple, Inverurie, Aberdeenshire AB51 5HR. *T:* (01330) 820330. *E:* bobsmith@cix.co.uk.

SMITH, Robert Lee, CB 2004; Director General, Regional Development Group, Office of the Deputy Prime Minister, 2004–05. *Educ:* St Dunstan's Coll., Catford; Magdalene Coll., Cambridge (MA Eng. Lit.). Entered Civil Service as Administrative Trainee, 1974; DES, later DFE, then DFEE, subseq. DfES, 1981–2000: Principal Private Sec. to Sec. of State for Educn and Science, 1985–87; Under Sec., Pupils and Parents Br., 1994; Dir, Pupil Support and Inclusion Gp (formerly Pupils, Parents and Youth), 1995–2000; Dir Gen., Regional Co-ordination Unit, DETR, subseq. Cabinet Office, then ODPM, 2000–04. Public Sector Chm., Inst. of Mgt/CS Network, 1995–2000. Mem., Young People and Families Cttee, Joseph Rowntree Foundn, 1997–2000; Co-Chm., Social Policy Forum, 2003. *Recreation:* folk dancing and music.

SMITH, Robert Walter; show jumper; *b* 12 June 1961; *e s* of (Robert) Harvey Smith, *qv*, and Irene Smith; one *s* three *d*. Member: GB junior and senior European events teams, 1977–; British Nations Cup Team, 1979–; World Class Performance Squad, 1999–2005; Gold team medal and Bronze individual medal, Jun. European Championships, 1977; Bronze team medal, European Championships, 1997; King George V Gold Cup winner, 1979, 1988, 1998. British Open Champion, 2005 and 2006; British Masters Champion, 2009. Top ranking rider and owner, BSJA, 2002. *Address:* Brookfurlong Farm, High Cross, Shrewley, Warwickshire CV35 7BD. *T:* (01926) 843886.

SMITH, Robin Anthony, TD 1978; DL; Consultant, DLA Piper (formerly Dibb Lupton Alsop, then DLA), solicitors, 1999–2008; Chairman, Leeds Building Society, 2007–13; *b* 15 Feb. 1943; *s* of late Tom Sumerfield Smith and Mary Smith; *m* 1967, Jennifer Elizabeth Roslington; one *s* one *d*. *Educ:* St Michael's Coll.; Manchester Univ. (LLB). Solicitor, admitted 1966; joined Dibb Lupton & Co., 1966; Partner, 1966–99; Man. Partner, 1988–93; Sen. Partner, Dibb Lupton & Co., later Dibb Lupton Broomhead, then Dibb Lupton Alsop, 1993–98. Mem. Council, Law Society, 1982–91; Pres., Leeds Law Soc., 1993–94. Non-executive Director: Leeds (formerly Leeds & Holbeck) Bldg Soc., 1998–2013; Coutts & Co., 1999–2006; Town Centre Securities plc, 1999–2009; Bartlett Gp Hldgs Ltd, 2000–. Gov., Stonyhurst Coll., 1989–98. Commnd 5th Bn LI, TA, 1966; retired 1985, Lt-Col. DL W Yorks, 1991. KSG 2002. *Recreations:* golf, cricket. *Clubs:* Army and Navy, MCC; Alwoodley Golf; Yorkshire CC (Mem. Bd, 2000–; Pres., 2000–04; Chm., 2002–05; Vice Chm., 2005–); Scarborough CC; Western Province Cricket (S Africa).

SMITH, Robin F.; *see* Field-Smith.

SMITH, Robin Jeremy O.; *see* Ord-Smith.

SMITH, Rt Rev. Robin Jonathan Norman; Suffragan Bishop of Hertford, 1990–2001; Hon. Assistant Bishop, diocese of St Albans, since 2001; *b* 14 Aug. 1936; *s* of Richard Norman and Blanche Spurling Smith; *m* 1961, Hon. Lois Jean, *d* of Baron Pearson, CBE, PC; three *s* one *d*. *Educ:* Bedford Sch.; Worcester Coll., Oxford (MA); Ridley Hall, Cambridge. RAF Regiment Commission, 1955–57. Curate, St Margaret's, Barking, 1962–67; Chaplain, Lee Abbey, 1967–72; Vicar, Chesham St Mary, 1972–80; Rector, Great Chesham, 1980–90. Hon. Canon, Christ Church, Oxford, 1988–90. *Recreations:* gardening, walking. *Address:* 7 Aysgarth Road, Redbourn, Herts AL3 7PJ.

SMITH, Prof. Roderick Arthur, PhD, ScD; FREng, FIMechE, FIMMM; Research Professor, Imperial College London, since 2011 (Professor and Head of Department of Mechanical Engineering, 2000–05; Royal Academy of Engineering Research Professor, 2006–11); Chief Scientific Adviser, Department for Transport, 2011–14; *b* 26 Dec. 1947; *s* of Eric and Gladys Mary Smith; *m* 1975, Yayoi Yamanoi. *Educ:* Hulme Grammar Sch., Oldham; St John's Coll., Oxford (BA, MA); Queens' Coll., Cambridge (MA; PhD 1975; ScD 1998; Hon. Fellow 2015). CEng 1976; FIMechE 1991; FIMMM (FIM 1992); FREng 1999. Queens' College, Cambridge: Godfrey Mitchell Res. Fellow, 1975–78; Official Fellow, College Lectr and Dir of Studies, 1978–88; Asst Lectr, Engrg Dept, Cambridge Univ., 1977–80, Lectr, 1980–88; Sheffield University: Prof. of Mech. and Process Engrg, 1988–2000; Hd, Dept of Mech. and Process Engrg, 1992–95; Royal Acad. of Engrg/BR Res. Prof., 1995–2000; Chm., Advanced Rly Res. Centre, 1993–2000; Warden, Stephenson Hall, 1992–2000. Sen. Vis. Res. Fellow, St John's Coll., Oxford, 2005–06; Vis. Prof., Oxford Univ., 2012–. Chm., Coll. of Rly Technol., Derby, 1996–97. Consultant to: British Steel plc, 1986–89; BR, 1992–96 (Mem. Bd, Res. and Tech. Cttee, 1992–96). Mem., Res. and Tech. Cttee, AEA Technology, 1997–2006. Chm., Heathrow Airport Consultative Cttee, 2015–. Institution of Mechanical Engineers: Mem. Council, 1999–; Trustee, 2006–; Dep. Pres., 2010–11; Pres., 2011–12. Trustee, Nat. Mus. of Science and Industry, 2002–10. FCGI 2000. Hon. DEng: Lincoln, 2012; Sheffield, 2015. *Publications:* Thirty Years of Fatigue Crack Growth, 1986; Innovative Teaching in Engineering, 1991; Engineering for Crowd Safety, 1993; ed books; papers and articles on mech. engrg, design, manufacture, engrg educn and crowd engrg. *Recreations:* mountaineering, reading, history, Japan: its people and technology; conversation, wine. *Address:* Department of Mechanical Engineering, Imperial College London, Exhibition Road, SW7 2AZ. *T:* (020) 7594 7007. *Clubs:* Oxford and Cambridge, Alpine; Fell and Rock (Lake District).

SMITH, Rodger H.; *see* Hayward Smith.

SMITH, Roger Huntington, FRCP, FRCPE; Joint Vice President, Royal College of Physicians of Edinburgh, 2005–06 (Vice President, 2003–05); *b* 9 April 1945; *s* of John Smith and Evelyn Smith; *m* 1971, Judith Elizabeth Martin; two *s*. *Educ:* Wallasey Grammar Sch.; Univ. of Edinburgh (BSc Hons (Physiol.) 1966; MB ChB 1969). FRCPE 1983; FRCP 1987. Consultant Physician and Cardiologist, Univ. Hosp. of N Tees, 1979–2007; Hon. Clinical Lectr, Univ. of Newcastle, 2000–. Associate Mem., 2001–08, Mem., Fitness to Practise Panel, 2001–13, GMC; Mem., Med. Panel, Nat. Patient Safety Authy, 2003–06; Public Interest Mem., Public Practice Cttee, ICAS, 2008–13. Royal College of Physicians of Edinburgh: Chm., Collegiate Mems Cttee, 1979; Mem. Council, 1992–93, 1996–2002; Sec., 2001–03. *Publications:* articles on early work in infective endocarditis, pioneering res. in acute thrombolysis (with H. A. Dewar), substantial trialling of thrombolytics in acute infarction. *Recreations:* serious singer (formerly Mem., Edinburgh Festival Chorus, and for 25 years of chamber choir, Michelmas Singers), village politics, gardening, classical music, art, walking in the Lake District, newly initiated golfer. *Address:* The Sheiling, High Street, Wolviston, Stockton on Tees TS22 5JS.

SMITH, Roger John; Chairman, Cotton Spring Farm Ltd (family holding company), since 1975; *b* 20 April 1939; *s* of Horace W. Smith and Marjorie E. Pummery; *m* 1962, Margaret R. Campbell; one *s* two *d*. *Educ:* Bedford School. Nat. Service, Subaltern, RCT, 1958–60. Dir, Family Group business, incl. Lea Heating Merchants (later part of Tricentrol), 1960–70; Man. Dir, Commercial Div., 1971–75, Dir, Special Projects, 1976–78, Tricentrol International; Dir, Group Co-ordination, Tricentrol, 1978–81; Man. Dir, Commercial Div., 1981–83; Dep. Chm., Tricentrol plc, 1983–88; Chm. and Chief Exec., Trimoco plc, 1987–92. Dir, Close Brothers AIM (VCT) plc, and other cos. Chairman: European Motor Hlgs plc, 1994–2007; Harpenden Building Society, 1999–2009. President: Retail Motor Industry Fedn, 1991–93; Internat. Orgn for Motor Trade and Repair, 1998–2000. Sloan Fellow, Stanford Univ., 1976. Chm., Lord's Taverners, 2000–02. Board Mem., Univ. of Herts. Chm., Central Finance Bd, Methodist Church, 2000–. Master, Coachmakers' and Coach Harnessmakers' Co., 2006. *Recreations:* sailing, shooting, tennis, reading. *Address:* Cotton Spring, Flamstead, Herts AL3 8AF. *Clubs:* Royal Automobile, Royal Thames Yacht.

SMITH, Roger John Gladstone, OBE 2008; legal researcher, consultant and journalist, since 2012; *b* 20 June 1948; *s* of late Kenneth Smith and Alice Smith; partner, Sue Berger; one *s* one *d*. *Educ:* York Univ. (BA 1970). Admitted solicitor, 1973; Solicitor, Camden Community Law Centre, 1973–75; Dir, W Hampstead Community Law Centre, 1975–79; Solicitor, Child Poverty Action Gp, 1980–86; Director: Legal Action Gp, 1986–98; Legal Educn and Training, Law Soc., 1998–2001; Justice, 2001–12. Hon. Prof., Kent Law Sch., 1998–; Vis. Prof., London South Bank Univ., 2008–. Hon. LLD Westminster, 2007. *Publications:* Children and the Courts, 1981; A Strategy for Justice, 1992; Shaping the Future: new directions in legal services, 1995; Achieving Civil Justice, 1996; Justice: redressing the balance, 1997; Legal Aid Contracting: lessons from North America, 1998; (jtly) Effective Criminal Defence Rights in Europe, 2010; (jtly) Face to Face Legal Services and their Alternatives: global lessons from the digital revolution, 2013; Digital Delivery of Legal Services to People on Low Incomes, 2015. *Recreations:* sailing, reading, managing an allotment, struggling with classical guitar. *E:* rogerjgsmith@gmail.com.

SMITH, Roger L.; *see* Lane-Smith.

SMITH, Roland Hedley, CMG 1994; HM Diplomatic Service, retired; Clerk, Wakefield and Tetley Trust (formerly Wakefield Trust), since 2004; *b* 11 April 1943; *s* of late Alan Hedley Smith and of Elizabeth Louise Smith; *m* 1971, Katherine Jane Lawrence; two *d*. *Educ:* King Edward VII School, Sheffield; Keble College, Oxford (BA 1st cl. hons 1965, MA 1981). Third Sec., Foreign Office, 1967; Second Sec., Moscow, 1969; Second, later First Sec., UK Delegn to NATO, Brussels, 1971; First Sec., FCO, 1974; First Sec. and Cultural Attaché, Moscow, 1978; FCO, 1980; attached to Internat. Inst. for Strategic Studies, 1983; Political Advr and Hd of Chancery, British Mil. Govt, Berlin, 1984–88; Dep. Hd, Sci., Energy and Nuclear Dept, FCO, 1988–90; Hd of Non-Proliferation and Defence Dept, FCO, 1990–92; Minister and Dep. Perm. Rep., UK Delegn to NATO, Brussels, 1992–95; Asst Under-Sec. of State, then Dir, (Internat. Security), FCO, 1995–98; Ambassador to Ukraine, 1999–2002. Dir, St Ethelburga's Centre for Reconciliation and Peace, 2002–04. *Publications:* Soviet Policy Towards West Germany, 1985. *Recreations:* music, esp. choral singing, football (Sheffield United), trams. *Address:* Wakefield and Tetley Trust, Oxford House, Derbyshire Street, E2 6HG.

SMITH, Prof. Roland Ralph Redfern, DPhil; FBA 2010; Lincoln Professor of Classical Archaeology and Art, University of Oxford, since 1995; *b* 30 Jan. 1954; *s* of Rupert and Elinor Smith; *m* 1988, Ingrid Gaitet. *Educ:* Fettes Coll., Edinburgh; Pembroke Coll., Oxford (BA 1977; MPhil 1979); Magdalen Coll., Oxford (DPhil 1983). Fellow, Magdalen Coll., Oxford, 1981–86; Asst Prof. of Classical Archaeology, 1986–90, Associate Prof., 1990–95, Inst. of Fine Arts, NY Univ. Harkness Fellow, Princeton, 1983–85; Alexander von Humboldt Fellow, Munich, 1991–92. Dir, Excavations at Aphrodisias, Caria, 1991–. *Publications:* Hellenistic Royal Portraits, 1988; Hellenistic Sculpture, 1991; The Monument of C. Julius Zoilos, 1993; Roman Portrait Statuary from Aphrodisias, 2006; (with B. Dignas) Historical and Religious Memory in the Ancient World, 2012; The Marble Reliefs from the Julio-Claudian Sebasteion at Aphrodisias, 2013; contrib. learned jls. *Address:* Ashmolean Museum, Oxford OX1 2PH.

SMITH, Ronald Angus, OBE 2009; General Secretary, Educational Institute of Scotland, 1995–2012; *b* 9 June 1951; *s* of William Angus and Daisy Smith; *m* 1976, Mary A. Lambie; one *s* one *d*. *Educ:* Anderson Educnl Inst., Lerwick; Univ. of Aberdeen (MA 1972); Aberdeen Coll. of Educn (PGCE 1973). Teacher, later Principal Teacher, Latin and Modern Studies, Broxburn Acad., W Lothian, 1973–88; Asst Sec., Educnl Inst. of Scotland, 1988–95. Hon. FEIS 2003. *Recreation:* Livingston FC.

SMITH, Ronald George B.; *see* Barclay-Smith, R. G.

SMITH, Ronald Good; Sheriff of North Strathclyde, 1984–99; *b* 24 July 1933; *s* of Adam Smith and Selina Spence Smith; *m* 1962, Joan Robertson Beharrie; two *s*. *Educ:* Glasgow University (BL 1962). Private practice to 1984. *Recreations:* philately, photography, gardening, reading. *Address:* 8 Lomond View, Symington, Ayrshire KA1 5QS. *T:* (01563) 830763.

SMITH, Rosemary Ann; Headmistress, Wimbledon High School, GPDST, 1982–92; *b* 10 Feb. 1932; *d* of late Harold Edward Wincott, CBE, editor of the Investors Chronicle, and Joyce Mary Wincott; *m* 1954, Rev. Canon Graham Francis Smith (*d* 2008); two *s* two *d*. *Educ:* Brighton and Hove High School, GPDST; Westfield College, Univ. of London (BA Hons); London Univ. Inst. of Education (post grad. Cert. in Education). Assistant Teacher: Central Foundation Girls' School, 1964–69; Rosa Bassett Girls' School, 1970–77; Furzedown Secondary School, 1977–80; Deputy Head, Rowan High School, 1980–82. Mem. Council, GDST (formerly GPDST), 1993–2005. *Recreations:* theatre, gardening, reading. *Address:* 1 Bentley Road, Chorlton-cum-Hardy, Manchester M21 9WD. *T:* (01608) 605594.

SMITH, Air Marshal Sir Roy David A.; *see* Austen-Smith.

SMITH, Royston Matthew, GM 2012; MP (C) Southampton, Itchen, since 2015; *b* Harefield, Southampton, 13 May 1964; *s* of Frank Wilmot Smith and Marie Cecilia Smith (*née* Page). RAF Kinloss (Nimrod), 1980–83; RAF St Mawgan (Nimrod), 1983–86; RAF Lyneham (Hercules C130), 1986–88; RAF Laarbruch, Germany (Tornado GR4), 1988–90; maintenance engr, BA, Heathrow, 1990–2006. Mem. (C), Southampton CC, 2000– (Leader of Council, 2010–12). Mem., Hants Fire and Rescue Authy, 2000–15 (Chm., 2009–15). Gov., Southampton Solent Univ. Contested (C) Southampton, Itchen, 2010. *Address:* House of Commons, SW1A 0AA.

SMITH, Ruby McGregor; *see* McGregor-Smith, R.

SMITH, Gen. Sir Rupert (Anthony), KCB 1996; DSO 1991 (and Bar 1996); OBE 1982; QGM 1978; Deputy Supreme Allied Commander, Europe, 1998–2001; Aide-de-Camp General to the Queen, 2000–01; *b* 13 Dec. 1943; *s* of late Gp Captain Irving Smith, CBE, DFC (and Bar) and Joan Smith (*née* Debenham). Parachute Regt, 1964; Dep. Comdt, Staff Coll., Camberley, 1989–90; Comdr, 1st Armoured Div., BAOR, Gulf, 1990–92; ACDS (Ops), 1992–94; Comdr, UN Protection Force Bosnia-Herzegovina, 1995; GOC and Dir of Military Ops, NI, 1996–98. Lt Col, 1980; Col, 1985; Brig., 1986; Maj.-Gen., 1990; Lt-Gen., 1995. *Publications:* The Utility of Force: the art of war in the modern world, 2005. *Address:* c/o RHQ The Parachute Regiment, Merville Barracks, Colchester CO2 7UT.

SMITH, Sandra Mary; *see* Thomas, Sandra M.

SMITH, Sandra Melanie, (Mrs K. M. Whittaker); Head of Conservation, Victoria and Albert Museum, since 2002; *b* 28 Oct. 1962; *d* of Anthony Smith and Margaret Smith; *m* 1985, Kenneth Martin Whittaker; one *s* two *d*. *Educ:* Institute of Archaeology, London (BSc Hons Archaeol Conservation and Material Sci.). Accredited Mem. UKIC 2000; FIIC 2002. British Museum: Hd of Ceramics and Glass Conservation, Dept of Conservation, 1992–97; Hd, Inorganic Materials Gp, 1997–2002; Actg Keeper, Conservation, 2002. Treas., Internat. Inst. for Conservation of Historic and Artistic Works, 2006–10. Trustee: Gabo Trust, 2011–; Inst. of Conservation, 2011–14. Advr on Conservation, Queen Elizabeth Scholarship Trust, 2010–. Chief Ed., V&A Conservation Jl, 2002–. *Publications:* (contrib.) The Art of the Conservator, 1992; (ed jtly) Past Practice, Future Prospects, 2001. *Recreations:* walking, gardening, cycling. *Address:* Department of Conservation, Victoria and Albert Museum, South Kensington, SW7 2RL. *T:* (020) 7942 2132. *E:* sm.smith@vam.ac.uk.

SMITH, Sarah Jane; University Secretary, University of Edinburgh, since 2013; *b* Babraham, Cambs, 29 July 1962; *d* of Michael Waddington Smith and Frances Sheila Smith; *m* 2008, Norman McBeath. *Educ:* St Hugh's Coll., Oxford (BA Hons PPE 1984); Imperial Coll., London (MBA 1996); Harvard Business Sch. (AMP 2005). Department for Transport: Private Sec. to Minister for Aviation and Shipping, 1987–89; Hd, Internat. Shipping Br., 1989–93; Hd, Internat. Aviation Br., 1993–95; Department for International Development: Hd of Section, Latin Amer. and Caribbean Dept, 1996–98; Dep. Hd, Aid Policy and Resource Dept, 1998–99; Hd, Eastern Asia and Pacific Dept, 1999–2001; Scottish Executive, later Scottish Government: Hd, Children and Families Div., 2001–04; Hd, Strategy and Delivery Unit, 2004–06; Director: Strategy, 2006–07; Children, Young People and Social Care, 2008–11; Children and Families, 2011; Learning, 2011–12; Associate Vice-Principal, Univ. of Edinburgh, 2007–08 (on secondment). Non-exec. Dir, Bd, Archangels Informal Investment, 2004–07. Vis. Prof., Univ. of Edinburgh, 2008–13. *Recreations:* reading, theatre, art, fencing, creative writing. *Address:* University of Edinburgh, Old College, South Bridge, Edinburgh EH8 9YL.

SMITH, Shaun Malden; QC 2008; a Recorder, since 2001; *b* Sheffield, 3 March 1959; *s* of Jack and Jean Smith; *m* 1991, Janet Wilson. *Educ:* Grenoside Jun. Sch.; Ecclesfield Comp. Sch.; Sheffield Univ. (LLB Law 1980); Inns of Court Sch. of Law. Called to the Bar, Gray's Inn, 1981, Bencher, 2013; in practice as barrister specialising in crime; Figtree Chambers, Sheffield, 1982–90, King Street Chambers, Leicester, 1990–92, 1 High Pavement Chambers, Nottingham, 1992– (Jt Hd of Chambers, 2011–). Sen. Barrister Mem., QC Appointments Panel, 2014–. Bar Vocational Course Examiner: Nottingham, 2003–06; College of Law, 2006–10; External Examiner, Nottingham Trent LLM, 2012–. Vis. Prof of Law, Univ. of Law, 2015–. *Recreations:* music (particularly Indie bands), reading, running, walking, golf, supporting Sheffield Wednesday. *Address:* 1 High Pavement Chambers, Nottingham NG1 1HF. *T:* (0115) 941 8218, *Fax:* (0115) 941 8240. *E:* shaunsmithqc@highpavement.co.uk.

SMITH, Simon John Meredith, CMG 2015; HM Diplomatic Service; Ambassador to Ukraine, 2012–15; *b* 14 Jan. 1958; *s* of Philip and Mary Smith (*née* Williams); *m* 1984, Sian Rosemary Stickings, MBE; two *d*. *Educ:* Triple C Sch., Grand Cayman; Clifton Coll.; Wadham Coll., Oxford (BA Modern Langs 1980; MA 1984); SOAS, London (Japanese). Dept of Employment, 1981–86, Manager, Unemployment Benefit Office, Tottenham, 1983–84; joined FCO, 1986; Second, then First Sec. (Econ.), Tokyo, 1989–92; Dep. Hd, S European Dept, FCO, 1995–97; Counsellor (Econ./Commercial), Moscow, 1998–2002; Hd, NE Asia and Pacific Dept, 2002–04, Hd, Eastern Dept, 2004–05, Dir, Russia, South Caucasus and Central Asia, 2005–07, FCO; Ambassador to Austria, and UK Perm. Rep. to internat. orgns in Vienna, 2007–12; UK Gov., IAEA, 2007–12. Mem., Adv. Bd, UCL Sch. of Slavonic and E European Studies, 2006–07. Vice Chm., UN Commn on Crime Prevention and Criminal Justice, 2009. *Recreations:* vicarious sport, tromboning, seeking the key to all Slavologies. *Address:* c/o Foreign and Commonwealth Office, King Charles Street, SW1A 2AH.

SMITH, Prof. (Stanley) Desmond, OBE 1998; FRS 1976; FRSE 1972; Professor of Physics and Head of Department of Physics, Heriot-Watt University, Edinburgh, 1970–96, now Professor Emeritus (Dean of the Faculty of Science, 1981–84); Chairman and Founder, Edinburgh Instruments Ltd, 1971–2012; Founder, Director and Chairman, Edinburgh Biosciences Ltd, since 2003; *b* 3 March 1931; *s* of Henry George Stanley Smith and Sarah Emily Ruth Smith; *m* 1956, Gillian Anne Parish; one *s* one *d*. *Educ:* Cotham Grammar Sch., Bristol; Bristol Univ. (BSc, DSc); Reading Univ. (PhD). SSO, RAE, Farnborough, 1956–58; Research Asst, Dept of Meteorology, Imperial Coll., London, 1958–59; Lectr, then Reader, Univ. of Reading, 1960–70. Member: ACARD, 1985–87; Defence Scientific Adv. Council, 1985–91; Astronomy, Space & Radio Bd, Engrg Bd, SERC, 1985–88; ACOST, Cabinet Office, 1987–88. Principal Investigator, Scottish Collaborative Initiative in Optoelectronics, 1991–97. Mem. Council, Inst. of Physics, 1984–87; Chm., Scottish Optoelectronics Assoc., 1996–98. Hon. DSc Heriot-Watt, 2003. C. V. Boys Prizeman, Inst. of Physics, 1976; Educn in Partnership with Industry or Commerce Prize, DTI, 1982; Technical or Business Innovation in Electronics Prize, Electronics Weekly, 1986; James Scott Prize, RSE, 1987; Royal Medal, RSE, 2011. *Publications:* (with J. T. Houghton) Infra-red Physics, 1966; Optoelectronic Devices, 1995; 226 papers on interference filters, semi-conductors, lasers, satellite meteorology, nonlinear optics, optical computing, application of fluorescence to cataract detection, lasers and LEDs to non-invasive treatment and instrumentation. *Recreations:* ski-ing, mountaineering, golf. *Address:* Tree Tops, 29D Gillespie Road, Colinton, Edinburgh EH13 0NW. *T:* (0131) 441 7225, (office) (01506) 429274. *E:* des@edinbio.com, desgillsmith@gmail.com; 106 Corniche du Pinateau, Chaillol 1600, 05260 St Michel de Chaillol, France. *T:* (4) 92500881. *E:* stanley-desmond.smith@orange.fr.

SMITH, Stephen; *see* Smith, J. S.

SMITH, Stephen, MA; educational consultant, since 2010; Headmaster, Bedford Modern School, 1996–2009; Secretary, Forum of Independent Day Schools Ltd, since 2011; *b* 8 Aug. 1948; *s* of late Joseph Leslie Smith and Audrey May Smith; *m* 1970, Janice Susan Allen; one *s* one *d*. *Educ:* Loughborough Grammar Sch.; Regent's Park Coll., Oxford (BA Modern History 1969; Cert. Ed. 1970; MA 1974). Loughborough Grammar School: Asst History Master, 1970–87; Junior Housemaster, 1976–79; Head of General Studies, 1983–87; Head of

History, 1987–93; Dep. Headmaster, Birkenhead Sch., 1993–96. Chm., HMC/GSA Sports Subcttee, 2001–09; Chm., Teaching and Learning Cttee, and Gov., Haberdashers' Aske's Boys Sch., 2007–14. Chm., Colmworth History Soc., 2000–. *Recreations:* piano, organ, singing, oenology, Church and youth work, local history. *Address:* Bramble Cottage, Chapel Lane, Colmworth, Beds MK44 2JY.

SMITH, Prof. Stephen Kevin, DSc, MD; FRCOG; FMedSci; Dean of Medicine, Dentistry and Health Sciences, University of Melbourne, since 2013; *b* 8 March 1951; *s* of Albert and Drusilla Smith; *m* 1978, Catriona Maclean Hobkirk Smith; one *s* two *d*. *Educ:* Birkenhead Sch.; Westminster Med. Sch., Univ. of London (MB BS 1974; MD 1982); DSc London 2002. FRCOG 1998 (MRCOG 1979); FRSB (FIBiol 1997). Lecturer: Univ. of Edinburgh, 1979–82; Univ. of Sheffield, 1982–85; Cons. Gynaecologist, MRC Reproductive Biology Unit, Edinburgh, 1985–88; Prof. of Obstetrics and Gynaecol., Univ. of Cambridge Clin. Sch., Rosie Maternity, subseq. Addenbrooke's, Hosp., Cambridge, 1988–2004; Fellow, Fitzwilliam Coll., Cambridge, 1991–2004; Principal, Faculty of Medicine, 2004–11, Pro-Rector, 2010–11, Imperial Coll. London; CEO, Imperial Coll. Healthcare NHS Trust, 2007–11; Founding Dean, Lee Kong Chian Sch. of Medicine, and Vice Pres. (Res.), Nanyang Technological Univ., Singapore, 2010–13. Founder FMedSci 1998. FRSA. *Publications:* numerous contribs to sci. and med. pubns on the subject of Reproductive Medicine. *Recreations:* flying, football, music, natural history, politics. *Address:* Office of the Dean, Medicine, Dentistry and Health Sciences, University of Melbourne, Victoria 3010, Australia.

See also I. R. Smith.

SMITH, Stephen Philip M.; *see* Moverley Smith.

SMITH, Prof. Stephen Robert, PhD; Professor of Economics, University College London, since 1997 (Dean, Faculty of Social and Historical Sciences, 2008–13); *b* Durham, 25 Nov. 1955; *s* of Dr Russell Smith and Katherine Smith (*née* Truman); *m* 1987, Beverley Stanford. *Educ:* Durham Johnston Secondary Sch.; Wadham Coll., Oxford (BA Hons PPE); Manchester Univ. (MA (Econ)); University Coll. London (PhD Econs 1997). Econ. Asst, Dept of Industry, 1977–82; Econ. Advr, Dept of Trade, 1982–85; Institute for Fiscal Studies: Sen. Res. Officer, 1985–87; Programme Dir, 1987–90; Dep. Dir, 1990–97. Vis. Prof., Sciences Po, Paris, 2013–14. *Publications:* Britain's Shadow Economy, 1986; (jtly) Fiscal Harmonisation, 1988; Green Taxes and Charges: policy and practice in Britain and Germany, 1995; Environmental Economics: a very short introduction, 2011; Taxation: a very short introduction, 2015; monographs and acad. papers. *Recreations:* modern German literature, railway journeys (real and imagined). *Address:* Department of Economics, University College London, WC1E 6BT. *T:* (020) 7679 5882. *E:* stephen.smith@ucl.ac.uk.

SMITH, Maj.-Gen. Stephen Robert C.; *see* Carr-Smith.

SMITH, Stephen Wynn B.; *see* Boys Smith.

SMITH, Sir Steven Murray, (Sir Steve), Kt 2011; PhD; FAcSS; Vice-Chancellor and Chief Executive, University of Exeter, since 2002; *b* 4 Feb. 1952; *s* of late William Smith and of Doris Smith; *m* 2013, Dr Jeannie Forbes. *Educ:* Univ. of Southampton (BSc Soc. Scis 1973; MSc 1974; PhD 1978). Lectr in Politics, Huddersfield Poly., 1976–78; Lectr, 1979–85, Sen. Lectr, 1985–90, Prof., 1990–92, of Internat. Relns, UEA; Prof. of Internat. Politics, 1992–2002, Pro Vice Chancellor, 1999–2002, UCW, Aberystwyth, subseq. Univ. of Wales, Aberystwyth. Hon. Prof., Jilin Univ., China, 2007–. President: Internat. Studies Assoc., 2003–04; UUK, 2009–11; Chm., Bd of Trustees, UCAS, 2012–. Hon. Fellow: Aberystwyth Univ., 2010; UWIC, 2011. FAcSS (AcSS 2000). Hon. DSc Southampton, 2004; Hon. DEd W of England, 2010. President's Global Leadership Award, Univ. of S Florida, 2012. *Publications:* Foreign Policy Adaptation, 1981; (ed with I. Forbes) Politics and Human Nature, 1983; (ed with M. Clarke) Foreign Policy Implementation, 1985; (ed) International Relations, 1985; (ed with R. Crockatt) The Cold War Past and Present, 1987; (ed jtly) British Foreign Policy, 1988; (ed with R. Little) Belief Systems and International Relations, 1988; (with M. Hollis) Explaining and Understanding International Relations, 1990; (jtly) Deciding Factors in British Politics, 1991; (ed with W. Carlsnaes) European Foreign Policy, 1994; (ed with K. Booth) International Relations Theory Today, 1995; (ed jtly) International Theory, 1995; (ed with J. Baylis) The Globalization of World Politics, 1997, 6th edn 2014; (ed jtly) International Relations Theory, 2007, 3rd edn 2013; (ed jtly) Foreign Policy, 2008, 2nd edn 2012; (jtly) Introduction to Global Politics, 2011, 2nd edn 2013. *Recreations:* Norwich City FC, theatre, music, firework displays, arctophile. *Address:* Vice-Chancellor's Office, University of Exeter, Northcote House, Queen's Drive, Exeter EX4 4QJ. *T:* (01392) 723000. *E:* vice-chancellor@exeter.ac.uk.

SMITH, Stuart Graham, OBE 2009; FRICS; Director: All England Lawn Tennis Ground plc, 1997–2013; International Tennis Federation, 2009–15; *b* Paddington, 18 Feb. 1946; *s* of James Pettigrew and Ethel Mary Smith; *m* 1968, Marilyn Lesley; three *s*. *Educ:* John Ruskin Grammar Sch., Croydon; St Catharine's Coll., Cambridge (BA 1967; MA 1971). FRICS 1982. Partner, Collier & Madge, Chartered Surveyors, 1969–85; Dir, Lambert Smith Hampton, Chartered Surveyors, 1985–2002. Pres., LTA, 2006–09. *Recreations:* Association Football, gardening, family, tennis. *Address:* Upper Pryors, Cowden, Kent TN8 7HB. *T:* (01342) 850384. *E:* sgscowden@tiscali.co.uk. *Club:* All England Lawn Tennis.

SMITH, Rt Rev. Stuart Meldrum; Assistant Bishop, Diocese of Adelaide, 1992–98; *b* 8 June 1928; *s* of late F. R. and O. E. Smith; *m* 1st, 1957, Margaret (*d* 2006), *d* of J. L. F. and D. M. Sando; three *s* two *d*; 2nd, 2008, Judith Kay Nurton. *Educ:* Univ. of Adelaide (BA Hons English); St Michael's House, SSM (Scholar in Theol. (Hons), ACT). Ordained 1953; Asst Curate, Glenelg, 1954–56; Mission Chaplain, Meadows, 1956–57; Domestic Chaplain, Bishop of Adelaide, and Precentor, St Peter's Cathedral, 1957–58; Priest-in-charge, Kilburn, 1958–61; Editor, Adelaide Church Guardian, 1959–61 and 1965–76; Rector: Clare, 1961–65; Coromandel Valley (with Blackwood, Eden Hills and Belair), 1965–69; Belair, 1969–72; Unley, 1972–84; Canon of Adelaide, 1974–84; Archdeacon: of Sturt, 1976–84; of Adelaide, 1984–92; Dir of Home Mission and Evangelism, 1984–92. Acting Dean, St Peter's Cathedral, Adelaide, 1998–99; Associate in Ministry, St John's, Adelaide, 2000. Visiting Lecturer: St Barnabas Coll., 1966–81; St Michael's House, 1975–77. Hon. Chaplain, Walford C of E Girls' Grammar Sch., 1973–75. Mem., Gen. Synod and Gen. Synod Standing Cttee, 1979–98. Chm., Council of Govs, Pulteney Grammar Sch., 1973–97. *Recreations:* walking, reading, gardening. *Address:* 8 Fairway Avenue, Glenelg North, SA 5045, Australia. *T:* (8) 82952210.

SMITH, Susan Gwynneth, OBE 2009; Chair, Local Government Boundary Commission for Wales, 2001–08 (Member, 1996–2001); *b* 18 Dec. 1946; *d* of George Henry David Abbott and Victoria Gwynneth May Abbott; *m* 1969, David Charles Smith. *Educ:* Tiffin Sch. for Girls, Kingston-upon-Thames; University Coll. London (LLB ext. 1970). Admitted as solicitor, 1970; Asst Solicitor, Hammersmith and Fulham LBC, 1970–73; Sen. Solicitor, then Asst Borough Solicitor, 1973–78, Borough Solicitor, 1978–92, Wandsworth LBC; Dir, Admin. and Legal Services, Cardiff CC, 1992–96. Mem., Parly Boundary Commn for Wales, 1998–2008. Mem., Standing Orders Commn, Nat. Assembly for Wales, 1998–99. Chair, Standards Cttee, Pembrokeshire CC, 2001–10. Non-exec. Dir, Cardiff and Vale NHS Trust, 2000–02. Ind. Adjudicator for Local Authorities in Wales, 2003–08. *Recreations:* reading, music, choral singing, visiting Venice. *E:* smith.sycamores@btinternet.com.

SMITH, Prof. Susan Jane, DPhil; FBA 2008; FRSE; FAcSS; Mistress of Girton College, Cambridge, since 2009. *Educ:* St Anne's Coll., Oxford (BA Geog. 1977; Hon. Fellow); Nuffield Coll., Oxford (DPhil 1982). Research Fellow: St Peter's Coll., Oxford, 1981–82; Dept of Govt, Brunel Univ., 1984–85; Dept of Social and Economic Res., Univ. of Glasgow, 1985–90; Ogilvie Prof. of Geog., Univ. of Edinburgh, 1990–2004; Prof. of Geog. and Dir, Inst. of Advanced Study, Durham Univ., 2004–09. Adjunct Prof., Sch. of Global Studies, RMIT Univ., Melbourne, 2008–; Hon. Prof. of Social and Econ. Geog., Univ. of Cambridge, 2011–. FAcSS (Founding AcSS 1999). FRSE 2000. *Publications:* (ed with P. Jackson) Social Interaction and Ethnic Segregation, 1981; (ed jtly) Ethnic Segregation in Cities, 1981; (with P. Jackson) Exploring Social Geography, 1984; Crime, Space and Society, 1986; (ed with J. Mercer) New Perspectives on 'Race' and Housing in Britain, 1987; The Politics of 'Race' and Residence, 1989; (jtly) Housing and Social Policy, 1990; (ed jtly) Housing for Health, 1991; (jtly) Children at Risk?, 1995; (jtly) A Review of Flexible Mortgages, 2002; (ed with R. Pain) Critical GeoPolitics of Fear, 2008; (ed with M. Munro) The Microstructures of Housing Markets, 2009; (ed jtly) Handbook of Social Geographies, 2010; (ed with B. A. Searle) The Blackwell Companion to the Economics of Housing: the housing wealth of nations, 2010; (Ed. in Chief) International Encyclopaedia of Housing and Home, 2012; contribs to books and academic jls. *Recreation:* brass band and early music enthusiast. *Address:* Girton College, Cambridge CB3 0JG.

SMITH, Terence Charles; Chief Executive, Fundsmith LLP, since 2010; *b* 15 May 1953; *s* of Ernest George and Eva Ada Smith; *m* 1974, Barbara Mary George; two *d*. *Educ:* Stratford Grammar Sch.; University Coll., Cardiff (BA); Management Coll., Henley (MBA). Mgt trainee, then Gp Finance Manager, Barclays Bank, 1974–83; Bank Analyst, W. Greenwell & Co., 1984–86; Hd, Financial Desk, BZW, 1986–88; Bank Analyst, James Capel, 1988–89; Hd of Res., UBS Phillips & Drew, 1990–92; Bank Analyst, 1992–96, Dir, 1996–2000, Chief Exec., 2000, Collins Stewart; Collins Stewart acquired Tullett, 2003 and Prebon, 2004; Collins Stewart Tullett Prebon demerged, 2006; Chm., 2006–10, Dep. Chm., 2010, Collins Stewart; Chief Exec., Tullett Prebon, 2006–14. ACIB 1976; Series 24, Nat. Assoc. of Securities Dealers. *Publications:* Accounting for Growth, 1992, 2nd edn 1996. *Recreations:* boxing, shooting. *Address:* Fundsmith LLP, 33 Cavendish Square, W1G 0PW. *T:* (020) 3551 6337.

SMITH, Thomas C.; *see* Cavalier-Smith.

SMITH, Thomas Jonathan; QC 2014; *b* Wakefield, 27 Jan. 1976; *s* of Brian Smith, *qv*; *m* 2008, Janice Wong; one *s* one *d* (and one *d* decd). *Educ:* Walton High Sch., Stafford; Clare Coll., Cambridge (BA 1997; LLM 1998). Called to the Bar, Middle Temple, 1999; in practice as barrister, specialising in commercial and financial law, 1999–. *Recreations:* ski-ing, travel, family, Rugby League. *Address:* 3–4 South Square, Gray's Inn, WC1R 5HP. *T:* (020) 7696 9900, *Fax:* (020) 7696 9911. *E:* tomsmith@southsquare.com.

SMITH, Timothy; *see* Smith, W. T. C.

SMITH, Rt Rev. Timothy D.; *see* Dudley-Smith.

SMITH, Timothy John; Director, Nevill Hovey & Co. Ltd Chartered Accountants, since 2002; *b* 5 Oct. 1947; *s* of late Captain Norman Wesley Smith, CBE and Nancy Phyllis Smith; *m* 1980, Jennifer Jane Scott-Hopkins, *d* of Sir James Scott-Hopkins; two *s*. *Educ:* Harrow Sch.; St Peter's Coll., Oxford (MA). FCA; CTA. Articled with Gibson, Harris & Turnbull, 1969; Audit Sen., Peat, Marwick, Mitchell & Co., 1971; Company Sec., Coubro & Scrutton (Hldgs) Ltd, 1973. Sec., Parly and Law Cttee, ICA, 1979–82. Pres., Oxford Univ. Conservative Assoc., 1968; Chm., Coningsby Club, 1977–78. MP (C): Ashfield, April 1977–1979; Beaconsfield, May 1982–1997. PPS to Chief Sec. HM Treasury, 1983, to Sec. of State for Home Dept, 1983–85; a Vice Chm. and Treas., Conservative Party, 1992–94; Parly Under-Sec. of State, NI Office, 1994. Member: Public Accts Cttee, 1987–92, 1995–97; Select Cttee on NI, 1994–97; Vice-Chm., Cons. Finance Cttee, 1987–92. Partner, 2001–13, Consultant, 2013–15, H. M. Williams Chartered Accountants. Mem., Truro Diocesan Synod, 2012–. Vice-Chm., Cornwall Area Conservatives, 2009–12. Director: Quality South West Ltd, 2003–07; Harbour Centre (Plymouth), 2004–08; W Country Renewables Ltd, 2011–13. Mem. Council, ICA, 1992–94. Chm., Launceston Abbeyfield Soc., 2003–10; Treasurer: St Petroc's Soc., 2005–14; Cornwall Community Foundn, 2009–; Cornwall and Devon Countryman's Fair, 2011–; N Cornwall Cons. Assoc., 2014–. *Recreations:* theatre, gardening, tennis. *Address:* Queen's Acre, Boyton, Launceston, Cornwall PL15 9RJ.

SMITH, Timothy John; Technical Director, Tesco plc, since 2012; *b* Sheffield, 15 Nov. 1955; *s* of John and Patricia Smith; *m* 1982, Sheila Truman; one *s* two *d*. *Educ:* Withernsea High Sch.; Leeds Univ. (BSc Microbiol. and Zool.). Unigate plc, 1978–80; gen. mgt, 1981–90, Divl Dir, 1990–94, Northern Foods; Pres. and CEO, Sara Lee UK, 1994–99; Dir, Express Dairies plc, 1999–2005; Chief Executive: Arla Foods UK plc, 2005–08; Food Standards Agency, 2008–12. Mem., Musicians' Union. *Recreations:* getting wet, guitar, cycling a long way. *Address:* Tesco plc, New Tesco House, Delamare Road, Cheshunt, Herts EN8 9SL. *Club:* Farmers.

SMITH, Timothy Peter P.; *see* Pigott-Smith.

SMITH, Vanessa Frances H.; *see* Hall-Smith.

SMITH, Prof. Vernon Lomax, PhD; Professor of Economics and Law, Chapman University, Orange, California, since 2008; Professor of Economics and Law, George Mason University, 2001–08, now Emeritus; *b* 1 Jan. 1927; *s* of Vernon Chessman Smith and Lulu Belle Smith (*née* Lomax, then Bougher); *m* Candace C. Smith. *Educ:* North High Sch., Kansas; CIT (BS 1949); Univ. of Kansas (MA 1952); Harvard Univ. (PhD 1955). Purdue University, Indiana: Mem., Mgt Scis Res. Gp, 1955–56; Asst Prof., 1956–58, Associate Prof., 1958–61, Prof. of Econs, 1961–64, Krannert Prof., 1964–67; Professor of Economics: Brown Univ., Rhode Island, 1967–68; Univ. of Mass, Amherst, 1968–75; Prof. of Econs, 1975–88, Regents Prof., 1988–2001, Univ. of Arizona, Tucson. Vis. Associate Prof., Stanford Univ., 1961–62; Fellow, Center for Advanced Study in Behavioral Scis, Calif, 1972–73; Sherman Fairchild Dist. Scholar, CIT, 1973–74; Vis. Prof., USC and CIT, 1974–75; Adjunct Scholar, Cato Inst., Washington, 1983–. (Jtly) Nobel Prize for Econs, 2002. *Publications:* include: (jtly) Economics: an analytical approach, 1958; Investment and Production, 1961; Economics of Natural and Environmental Resources, 1977; (ed) Research in Experimental Economics, vol. 1, 1979, vol. 2, 1982, vol. 3, 1985; (ed) Schools of Economic Thought, 1990; Papers in Experimental Economics, 1991; Experiments in Decision, Organization and Exchange, 1993; Bargaining and Market Behavior: essays in experimental economics, 2000; Rationality in Economics, 2008; Discovery - A Memoir, 2008; articles in jls. *Address:* Dale E. Fowler School of Law, Chapman University, One University Drive, Orange, CA 92866, USA.

SMITH, Vincent Neil; solicitor; Visiting Fellow, British Institute of International and Comparative Law, since 2010; Affiliate Professor in Law, ESCP Europe Business School, since 2014; *b* 11 Dec. 1962; *m* 1997, Barbara Cross; one *s*. *Educ:* Univ. of Surrey (BSc Hons); Univ. of Liège (licence spéciale en droit européen). Admitted solicitor, 1990; Simmons & Simmons, 1988–98; Partner, Pinsent Curtis, 1999–2000; Sen. Legal Advr, Office of Telecommunications, 2000–02; Office of Fair Trading: Dir, Competition Policy Co-ordination, and Dep. Divisional Dir, 2002–03; Dir, Competition Enforcement Div., 2003–06; Sen. Dir for Competition, 2006–07; Partner: Cohen, Milstein, Hausfeld & Toll, later Hausfeld & Co. LLP, 2007–10; Sheppard & Smith, 2011–13. *Address:* British Institute of International and Comparative Law, Charles Clore House, 17 Russell Square, WC1B 5JP. *E:* v.smith@biicl.org.

SMITH, Walter Purvis, CB 1982 OBE 1960 (MBE 1945); Director General, Ordnance Survey, 1977–85, retired; *b* 8 March 1920; *s* of John William Smith and Margaret Jane (*née* Purvis); *m* 1946, Bettie Cox (*d* 2011); one *s* one *d*. *Educ:* Wellfield Grammar Sch., Co. Durham; St Edmund Hall, Oxford (MA). FRICS 1951. Commnd RE (Survey), 1940; served War, UK and Europe, 1940–46; CO 135 Survey Engr Regt (TA), 1957–60. Directorate of Colonial (later Overseas) Surveys: served in Ghana, Tanzania, Malaŵi, 1946–50; Gen. Man., Air Survey Co. of Rhodesia Ltd, 1950–54; Fairey Surveys Ltd, 1954–75 (Man. Dir, 1969–75); Adviser: Surveying and Mapping, UN, NY, 1975–77; Ordnance Survey Review Cttee, 1978–79. Mem., Field Mission, Argentine-Chile Frontier Case, 1965. 15th British Commonwealth Lectr, RAeS, 1968. Dir, Sys Scan (UK) Ltd, 1985–90. President: Photogrammetric Soc., 1972–73; European Council of Heads of National Mapping Agencies, 1982–84; Eur. Orgn for Photogrammetric Res., 1984–85; Guild of Surveyors, 1985–88; Chm., National Cttee for Photogrammetry and Remote Sensing, 1985–88; Dep. Chm., Govt Cttee of Enquiry into Handling of Geographical Information, 1985–87; Mem., Gen. Council, RICS, 1967–70 (Chm., Land Survey Cttee, 1963–64). Patron's Medal, RGS, 1985. *Publications:* papers and technical jls. *Recreations:* music, woodworking. *Address:* 15 Forest Gardens, Lyndhurst, Hants SO43 7AF. *T:* (023) 8028 2566.

SMITH, Warren James; Lord-Lieutenant of Greater Manchester, since 2007; *b* Manchester, 1 July 1948; *s* of William James Smith and Rowena Smith (*née* Gore). Various appts in banking and property development cos, 1965–2008. JP Manchester 1983–2003; DL 1995–2007, High Sheriff, 1997–98, Custos Rotulorum, 2007–, Gtr Manchester. High Steward, Manchester Cathedral, 2009–. President: Gtr Manchester W Co. Scout Council, 2007–; County Priory Gp, St John Gtr Manchester, 2007–. Hon. Col, Gtr Manchester ACF, 2007–; Pres., ATC, 2008–. Chairman: Turning Point, 1995–98; Manchester Concert Hall Trust (Bridgewater Hall), 1995–2015; Trustee, Hallé Orch., 1989–2001; Mem., Hallé Concert Soc. Hon. DLitt Salford 2011; Hon. LLD Bolton, 2011. KStJ 2011 (CStJ 2008). Medal of Honour, Manchester Univ., 2011. *Recreations:* gardening, the arts, fine wines. *Address:* Greater Manchester Lieutenancy Office, Gaddum House, 6 Great Jackson Street, Manchester M15 4AX. *T:* (0161) 834 0490, *Fax:* (0161) 835 1539. *E:* deputy@gmlo.org. *Club:* Salford Lads and Girls.

SMITH, (Warwick) Timothy (Cresswell); His Honour Judge Timothy Smith; a Circuit Judge, since 2014; *b* Liverpool, 16 June 1959; *s* of Peter and Prudence Smith; *m* 1986, Siân Layzell; two *s* one *d*. *Educ:* Birkenhead Sch.; Trinity Coll., Cambridge (BA 1981). FCIArb 1997. Called to the Bar, Middle Temple, 1982; in practice as barrister, 1982–2014; Asst Recorder, 2000, Recorder, 2000–14. *Recreations:* theatre, cinema, fair weather sailing.

SMITH, Wendy Alison K.; *see* Kenway-Smith.

SMITH, Wilbur Addison; author; *b* 9 Jan. 1933; *m* 1971, Danielle Antoinette Thomas (*d* 1999); *m* 2000, Mokhiniso Rakhimova; two *s* one *d* by former marriages. *Educ:* Michaelhouse, Natal; Rhodes Univ. (BCom). Business executive, 1954–58; factory owner, 1958–64; full-time author, 1964–. *Publications:* When the Lion Feeds, 1964; Dark of the Sun, 1965; Sound of Thunder, 1966; Shout at the Devil, 1968; Gold Mine, 1970; Diamond Hunters, 1971; The Sunbird, 1972; Eagle in the Sky, 1974; Eye of the Tiger, 1975; Cry Wolf, 1976; Sparrow Falls, 1977; Hungry as the Sea, 1978; Wild Justice, 1979; A Falcon Flies, 1980; Men of Men, 1981; The Angels Weep, 1982; The Leopard hunts in Darkness, 1984; The Burning Shore, 1985; Power of the Sword, 1986; Rage, 1987; A Time to Die, 1989; Golden Fox, 1990; Elephant Song, 1991; River God, 1993; The Seventh Scroll, 1995; Birds of Prey, 1997; Monsoon, 1999; Warlock, 2001; Blue Horizon, 2003; A Triumph of the Sun, 2005; The Quest, 2007; Assegai, 2009; Those in Peril, 2011; Vicious Circle, 2013; Desert God, 2014; Golden Lion, 2015. *Recreations:* fly fishing, big game angling, wing shooting, ski-ing, scuba diving.

SMITH, Sir William Antony John R.; *see* Reardon Smith.

SMITH, William Austin N.; *see* Nimmo Smith, Rt Hon. Lord.

SMITH, (William) Nigel W.; *see* Wenban-Smith.

SMITH, William Peter; *see* Smith, His Honour P. W.

SMITH, Zoë Philippa; Her Honour Judge Zoë Smith; DL; a Circuit Judge, since 1999; *b* 16 May 1949; *d* of late Basil Gerrard Smith and of Marjorie Elizabeth Smith (*née* Artz). *Educ:* Queenswood, Hatfield. Called to the Bar, Gray's Inn, 1970, Bencher, 2012; in practice at the Bar, 1970–99; a Recorder, 1991–99. Hon. Recorder, Reading. 2010. DL Berks, 2011. *Recreation:* dining out. *Address:* Oxford Crown Court, St Aldates OX1 1TL.

SMITH-BINGHAM, Col Jeremy David; Director General, British Equestrian Federation, 1994–97; *b* 29 July 1939; *s* of Col Oswald Cyril Smith-Bingham and Vera Mabel Smith-Bingham (*née* Johnson); *m* 1969, Priscilla Mary Incledon-Webber; three *s*. *Educ:* Cheam; Eton; RMA, Sandhurst. Commnd Royal Horse Guards (The Blues), 1959; Lt Col, 1981; jssc, 1982; CO, The Blues and Royals, 1982–85; CO, Tactical Sch., RAC, 1985–87; Col, 1987; Chief Exercise Planner, HQ N Army Gp, 1987–90; Comdr, Household Cavalry, and Silver Stick to the Queen, 1990–93; COS, HQ London Dist, 1993–94. Hon. Col, Royal Devon Yeomanry, 2013–. Pres., N Devon Cons. Assoc., 2010–. *Recreations:* horses, tennis, rackets, ski-ing, water sports, fishing, shooting, golf, gardening. *Address:* St Brannocks House, Braunton, Devon EX33 1HN. *T:* (01271) 812270. *E:* mail@stbrannocks.com. *Clubs:* White's, Cavalry and Guards, Queen's.

SMITH-CAMERON, Rev. Canon Ivor Gill; Chaplain to the Queen, 1995–99; *b* 12 Nov. 1929; *s* of James Smith-Cameron and Cynthia Smith-Cameron (*née* Fitzgerald). *Educ:* Madras Christian Coll., India (MA Eng. Lang. and Lit.); Coll. of the Resurrection, Mirfield, Yorks. Ordained deacon, 1954; priest, 1955; Curate, St George's, Rumboldswyke, Chichester, 1954–58; Chaplain, London Univ., 1958–72; Canon Residentiary and Diocesan Missioner, Dio. Southwark, 1972–92; Asst Curate, All Saints, Battersea, 1992–94; retd 1994; Canon Residentiary Emeritus, 1994. Hon. DD Serampore Coll., India, 2004. *Publications:* Pilgrimage: an exploration into God, 1982; The Church of Many Colours, 1998; New Lamps, 2000. *Recreations:* cooking, jam making, reading, walking. *Address:* 24 Holmewood Gardens, SW2 3RS. *T:* (020) 8678 8977. *E:* ivorsmithcameron@yahoo.co.uk.

SMITH-DODSWORTH, Sir David (John), 9th Bt *cr* 1784, of Newland Park and Thornton Watlass, Yorkshire; company director, since 1992; *b* Rotorua, NZ, 23 Oct. 1963; *s* of Sir John Christopher Smith-Dodsworth, 8th Bt and his 1st wife, Margaret Anne (*née* Jones); *S* father, 2012; *m* 1996, Elizabeth Anne Brady; one *s* one *d*. *Educ:* Ampleforth. Farming career. *Heir: s* Matthew David Smith-Dodsworth, *b* 26 May 2002. *Address:* Thornton Watlass Hall, Ripon, N Yorks HG4 4AS. *T:* (01677) 422803. *E:* sirdavid@twhall.co.uk.

SMITH-GORDON, Sir (Lionel) Eldred (Peter), 5th Bt *cr* 1838; engaged in book publishing, since 1960; *b* 7 May 1935; *s* of Sir Lionel Eldred Pottinger Smith-Gordon, 4th Bt, and Eileen Laura (*d* 1979), *d* of late Captain H. G. Adams-Connor, CVO; *S* father, 1976; *m* 1962, Sandra Rosamund Ann, *d* of late Wing Commander Walter Farley, DFC and Mrs Dennis Poore; one *s* one *d*. *Educ:* Eton College; Trinity College, Oxford. *Heir: s* Lionel George Eldred Smith-Gordon [*b* 1 July 1964; *m* 1993, Kumi, *d* of Masashi Suzuki, Japan; two *s* one *d*]. *Address:* 13 Shalcomb Street, SW10 0HZ. *T:* (020) 7352 8506. *E:* publisher@smithgordon.com.

SMITH-LAITTAN, James, CMG 1995; HM Diplomatic Service, retired; *b* 13 May 1939; *s* of James Alexander and Etta Smith; *m* 1969, Mary Susan Messer; three *d*. *Educ:* Buckie High Sch.; North West London Poly. Nat. Service, 1st Queen's Dragoon Guards, 1958–60; Admiralty, 1961–62; joined CRO, 1963; Dacca, 1964–66; FCO, 1966–68; Brussels, 1968; Rabat, 1969–72; Accra, 1972–75; Rome, 1975–79; Asst Overseas Insp., FCO, 1979–82; Trade Comr, Hong Kong and concurrently Consul, Macao, 1982–86; Asst Head, Migration and Visa Dept, FCO, 1987–90; Commercial Mgt and Exports Dept, FCO, 1990–91; Trade Counsellor and Head of China Trade Unit, Hong Kong, 1991–95; Consul-Gen., Auckland, 1996–99. *Recreations:* hill-walking, family, travel. *Club:* Hong Kong (Hong Kong).

SMITH-MARRIOTT, Sir Peter Francis, 12th Bt *cr* 1774, of Sydling St Nicholas, Dorset; *b* 14 Feb. 1927; *yr s* of Sir Ralph George Cavendish Smith-Marriott, 10th Bt and Phyllis Elizabeth (*née* Kemp); *S* brother, 2013; *m* 1961, Jean Graham Martin (*née* Ritchie); five *s* (incl. twins). *Educ:* Bristol Cathedral Sch. *Heir: s* Martin Ralph Smith-Marriott, *b* 30 Dec. 1962.

SMITHERS, Prof. Alan George, PhD; CPsychol; author and broadcaster; Professor of Education and Director, Centre for Education and Employment Research, University of Buckingham, since 2004; *b* 20 May 1938; *s* of late Alfred Edward Smithers and Queenie Lilian Smithers; *m* 1962, Angela Grace Wykes (marr. diss. 2003); two *d*. *Educ:* King's Coll., Univ. of London (BSc, PhD 1966); Bradford Univ. (MSc, PhD 1974); Univ. of Manchester (MEd 1981). CPsychol 1988. Lecturer in: Biol., Coll. of St Mark and St John, Chelsea, 1962–64; Botany, Birkbeck Coll., Univ. of London, 1964–67; Research Fellow, then Sen. Lectr in Educn, Bradford Univ., 1967–76; Prof. of Educn, Univ. of Manchester, 1977–96; seconded to British Petroleum, 1991–92; Prof. of Educn (Policy Res.), Brunel Univ., 1996–98; Sydney Jones Prof. of Educn, Liverpool Univ., 1998–2004. Member: Nat. Curriculum Council, 1992–93; Beaumont Cttee on Vocational Qualifications, 1995–96; Special Advr, H of C Educn and Employment Cttee, 1997–2001, Educn and Skills Cttee, 2001–07, Children, Schs and Families Cttee, 2007–10, Educn Cttee, 2010–15. Fellow, Soc. for Res. into Higher Educn, 1986. *Publications:* Sandwich Courses: an integrated education?, 1976; The Progress of Mature Students, 1986; What Employers Want of Higher Education, 1988; Graduates in the Police Service, 1990; Gender, Primary Schools and the National Curriculum, 1991; The Vocational Route into Higher Education, 1991; Every Child in Britain, 1991; Assessing the Value, 1992; All Our Futures: Britain's education revolution, 1993; The New Zealand Qualifications Framework, 1997; Assessment in Primary Schools, 1998; Teacher Qualifications, 2003; England's Education, 2004; Blair's Education: an international perspective, 2007; A-Level Trends, annually, 2011–; GCSE Trends, annually, 2011–; Educating the Highly Able, 2012; Confusion in the Ranks, 2013; book chapters; contrib. papers to jls of biology, psychol. and educn; *with Dr Pamela Robinson:* The Shortage of Maths and Physics Teachers, 1988; The Growth of Mixed A-Levels, 1988; Increasing Participation in Higher Education, 1989; Teacher Loss, 1990; Trends in Science and Technology Manpower Demands and Mobilities, 1990; Teacher Provision in the Sciences, 1991; Teacher Provision: trends and perceptions, 1991; Staffing Secondary Schools in the Nineties, 1991; Beyond Compulsory Schooling, 1991; Teacher Turnover, 1991; Technology in the National Curriculum, 1992; Technology at A-Level, 1992; General Studies: breadth at A-Level?, 1993; Changing Colleges: further education in the market place, 1993; Technology Teachers, 1994; The Impact of Double Science, 1994; Post-18 Education: growth, change, prospect, 1995; Affording Teachers, 1995; Co-educational and Single-Sex Schooling, 1995; Trends in Higher Education, 1996; Technology in Secondary Schools, 1997; Staffing Our Schools, 1997; Co-educational and Single-Sex Schooling Revisited, 1997; Degrees of Choice, 1998; Teacher Supply: passing problem or impending crisis?, 1998; The Good Teacher Training Guide, annually, 1998–; Teacher Supply: old story or new chapter?, 1999; Further Education Re-formed, 2000; Coping with Teacher Shortages, 2000; Talking Heads, 2000; Attracting Teachers, 2000; Teachers Leaving, 2001; Factors in Teachers' Decisions to Leave the Profession, 2003; The Reality of School Staffing, 2003; Teacher Turnover, Wastage and Movements between Schools, 2005; Physics in Schools and Colleges, 2005; Five Years On, 2006; Patterns and Policies in Physics Education, 2006; The Paradox of Single Sex and Coeducation, 2006; Bucking the Trend, 2007; School Headships: present and future, 2007; The Diploma: a disaster waiting to happen, 2008; Physics in Schools IV: the teachers, 2008; HMC Schools, 2008; Specialist Science Schools, 2009; Physics Participation and Policies, 2009; Worlds Apart, 2010; Choice and Selection in Education, 2010; The Science and Mathematics Teaching Workforce, 2014. *Recreations:* walking, theatre. *Address:* Centre for Education and Employment Research, University of Buckingham, Buckingham MK18 1EG. *T:* (01280) 820270, *Fax:* (01280) 820343. *E:* alan.smithers@buckingham.ac.uk.

SMITHERS, Jonathan Robert Saville; Senior Partner, CooperBurnett, Solicitors, since 2015 (Partner, since 1989); President, Law Society of England and Wales, 2015–July 2016 (Vice President, 2014–15); *b* Pembury, Kent, 3 May 1962; *s* of David and Margaret Smithers; *m* 1987, Mathea Blankers; two *d*. *Educ:* Beacon Sch., Crowborough, Sussex; Nottingham Trent Univ. (LLB). Admitted Solicitor, 1986; joined CooperBurnett, Solicitors, 1984. Mem. Council, Law Soc. of England and Wales, 2007–. Mem., Rules Cttee, Land Registry, 2012–. President: Tunbridge Wells, Tonbridge and Dist Law Soc., 2002; Kent Law Soc., 2007–08. *Recreation:* Oriana Singers. *Address:* CooperBurnett, Napier House, 14–16 Mount Ephraim Road, Tunbridge Wells, Kent TN1 1EE. *T:* (01892) 515022. *E:* jrs@cooperburnett.com.

SMITHIES, Frederick Albert; General Secretary, National Association of Schoolmasters and Union of Women Teachers, 1983–90; *b* 12 May 1929; *s* of Frederick Albert and Lilian Smithies; *m* 1960, Olga Margaret Yates. *Educ:* St Mary's Coll., Blackburn, Lancs; St Mary's Coll., Twickenham, Middx. Schoolteacher: Accrington, Lancs, 1948–60; Northampton, 1960–76. NAS/UWT (before 1975, NAS): Nat. Executive Member, 1966–76; Chm. of Education Cttee, 1972–76; Vice-President, 1976; Asst Gen. Secretary, 1976–81; Dep. Gen. Secretary, 1981–82; Gen. Sec. Designate, 1982–83. Member: Exec. Bd, European Trade Union Cttee for Educn, 1982–93; TUC Gen. Council, 1983–89; Exec. Bd, Internat. Fedn of Free Teachers' Unions, 1985–93 (Hon. Treas., 1989–93). *Recreations:* reading, music, theatre. *Address:* High Street, Guilsborough, Northampton NN6 8PY.

SMITHIES, Prof. Oliver, DPhil; Excellence Professor in Pathology, then Weatherspoon Eminent Distinguished Professor, University of North Carolina at Chapel Hill, since 1988; *b* Halifax, W Yorks, 23 June 1925; *s* of William Smithies and Doris Smithies (*née* Sykes); *m* 1st, Lois Kitze (marr. diss. 1978); 2nd, Dr Nobuyo Maeda. *Educ:* Heath Grammar Sch., Halifax; Balliol Coll., Oxford (Brackenbury Schol.; BA 1st Cl. Physiol.; MA 1951; DPhil Biochem. 1951; Hon. Fellow). Postdoctoral Fellow, Dept of Chem., Univ. of Wisconsin, 1951–53; Associate Res. Mem., Connaught Med. Res. Labs, Univ. of Toronto, 1953–60; Asst, Associate, then Leon J. Cole and Hilldale Prof. of Genetics and Med. Genetics, Univ. of Wisconsin, Madison, 1960–88. FAAAS 1986. Foreign Mem., Royal Soc., 1998. Hon. DSc Oxford, 2011. (Jtly) Nobel Prize in Medicine, 2007. *Publications:* contribs to Physiol. Rev., Biochem. Jl, Science, Proc. NAS, Nature. *Address:* Department of Pathology and Laboratory Medicine, University of North Carolina at Chapel Hill, Room 701 Brinkhaus-Bullitt Building, Chapel Hill, NC 27599–7525, USA.

SMITHSON, Michael; polling analyst, writer and blogger; Editor, politicalbetting.com, since 2004; *b* 11 May 1946; *s* of late Arthur Smithson and Doris Smithson (*née* Simpson); *m* 1969, Jacqueline Anne Cowan; one *s* two *d*. *Educ:* Burnage GS, Manchester; London Sch. of Econs (LLB). Thomson Orgn Grad. Trng Scheme, with Newcastle Jl and Evening Chronicle, 1968–71; BBC Radio News: Mem., Editl Staff, 1971–78; Duty Ed., 1978–80; Dep. Hd, BBC TV Licence Campaign, 1980–81; i/c Corporate Publicity Unit, BBC, 1982–84; Dir, Public Relns, RSPCA, 1984–88; Mgt Consultant, 1988–91, Dir, 1990–91, Finite Gp plc; Man. Dir, Pemberley Associates, 1991–94; Dir of Fundraising, LSE, 1994–96; Develt Dir, Univ. of Cambridge, and Fellow of Queens' Coll., Cambridge, 1996–99; Dir of Develt, Univ. of Oxford, 1999–2005; Fellow, Magdalen Coll., Oxford, 2000–05; Dir of Develt and Alumni

Relns, Univ. of York, 2005–07. Councillor (Lib Dem): Beds CC, 1990–96; Bedford BC, 1996–2000. Contested (Lib Dem) N Beds, 1992. *Recreations:* talking politics, cycling, enjoying fine teas, my family. *Address:* 5 Devon Road, Bedford, Beds MK40 3DJ.

SMOLIRA, Rev. David Richard, SJ; Parish Priest, St Ignatius Catholic Parish, Stamford Hill, since 2014; *b* 9 Sept. 1955; *s* of late Mieczyslaw Smolira and Eileen Smolira (*née* Taylor). *Educ:* Manchester Univ. (BSc); Heythrop Coll., London Univ. (BD); Liverpool Univ. (Advanced DipSocSc with CQSW); St Louis Univ., USA (MSocWork); Loyola Chicago Univ., USA (MSc). UKCP Registered Psychotherapist, until 2006; organisational develt consultant. Entered Society of Jesus, 1978; ordained priest, 1988; Dir, Home & Away Project, Catholic Children's Soc., 1989–94; Provincial Asst for Formation, SJ, 1997–99; Provincial Superior of the British Province, SJ, 1999–2005; Founding Dir, 2006–10, Pres., 2010–14, Jesuit Inst. SA; Regl Superior, Jesuits, SA, 2008–14. *Recreations:* gardening, natural history, photography. *Address:* St Ignatius Jesuit Community, 27 High Road, Stamford Hill, N15 6ND.

SMOOT, Prof. George F., PhD; Professor, Physics Department, 1994, now Emeritus, and Founding Director, Berkeley Center for Cosmological Physics, since 2007, University of California, Berkeley; *b* 1945; *s* of George and Talicia Smoot; *m* Maxine. *Educ:* Massachusetts Inst. of Technol. (BS 1966; PhD 1970). Research Physicist: Space Sciences Lab., Univ. of California, Berkeley, 1971–; Lawrence Berkeley National Lab., 1974–. (Jtly) Nobel Prize in Physics, 2006. *Publications:* (with K. Davidson) Wrinkles in Time, 1993; articles in jls. *Address:* Department of Physics, University of California, Berkeley, 366 LeConte Hall, Berkeley, CA 94720, USA.

SMOUHA, Joseph; QC 2003; *b* 20 Jan. 1963; *s* of Brian and Hana Smouha; *m* 1994, Lucy Howard; two *s*. *Educ:* Harrow Sch.; Magdalene Coll., Cambridge (MA); New York Univ. Sch. of Law (Kenneson Fellow; Fulbright Schol.). Called to the Bar, Middle Temple, 1986, Bencher, 2010; specializes in internat. commercial law. Chm., Commercial Bar Assoc., 2013–15. Dir, English Concert, 2003–. *Recreations:* opera, ski-ing, walking, tennis, clarinet player. *Address:* Essex Court Chambers, 24 Lincoln's Inn Fields, WC2A 3EG. *T:* (020) 7813 8000, *Fax:* (020) 7813 8080.

SMOUT, Prof. (Thomas) Christopher, CBE 1994; PhD; FBA 1988; FRSE; FSAScot; Director, Institute for Environmental History, University of St Andrews, 1992–2001; Historiographer to the Queen in Scotland, since 1993; *b* 19 Dec. 1933; *s* of Sir Arthur and Lady (Hilda) Smout; *m* 1959, Anne-Marie Schøning; one *s* one *d*. *Educ:* The Leys Sch., Cambridge; Clare Coll., Cambridge (MA; PhD 1960). FRSE 1975; FSAScot 1991. Dept of Economic History, Edinburgh University: Asst Lectr, 1959; Lectr, 1962; Reader, 1964; Prof. of Econ. History, 1970; University of St Andrews: Prof. of Scottish History, 1980–91; Dir, St John's House Centre for Advanced Histl Studies, 1992–97. Visiting Professor: Strathclyde Univ., 1991–97; Dundee Univ., 1993–2005; York Univ., 1998–99; Hon. Prof., Stirling Univ., 2000–06. Member: Cttee for Scotland, Nature Conservancy Council, 1986–91; Bd, NCC (Scotland), 1991–92; Bd, Scottish Natural Heritage, 1992–98 (Dep. Chm., 1992–97); Royal Commn on Ancient and Historic Monuments of Scotland, 1987–2000 (Vice-Chm., 2000); Bd of Trustees, Nat. Museums of Scotland, 1991–95; Royal Commn on Historical Manuscripts, 1999–2003; Adv. Council on Public and Private Records, 2003–04. Chm., Scottish Coastal Archaeol. and the Problem of Erosion Trust, 2002–12; Chm., Strathmartine Trust, 2013–; Trustee, Woodland Trust, 1998–2004. Patron, Scottish Native Woods, 2004–. Hon. Fellow, TCD, 1995. Hon. DSSc QUB, 1995; Hon. DSc (SocSci) Edinburgh, 1996; Hon. DLitt: St Andrews, 1999; Glasgow, 2001; DUniv Stirling, 2002. Patrick Geddes Medal, RSGS, 2014. *Publications:* Scottish Trade on the Eve of Union, 1963; A History of the Scottish People, 1969; (with I. Levitt) The State of the Scottish Working Class in 1843, 1979; A Century of the Scottish People, 1986; (with S. Wood) Scottish Voices, 1990; (with A. Gibson) Prices, Food and Wages in Scotland, 1995; Nature Contested, 2000; (jtly) A History of the Native Woodlands of Scotland 1500–1920, 2005; Exploring Environmental History: selected essays, 2009; (with M. Stewart) The Firth of Forth: an environmental history, 2012. *Recreations:* birdwatching, butterflies, bees. *Address:* Upper Flat, Chesterhill, Shore Road, Anstruther, Fife KY10 3DZ. *T:* (01333) 310330. *E:* christopher@smout.org.

SMURFIT, Sir Michael (William Joseph), KBE 2005; Chairman, Smurfit Kappa Group, 2005–07; *b* 7 Aug. 1936; *s* of late Jefferson Smurfit; *m* 1st, Norma Treisman (marr. diss.); two *s* two *d*; 2nd, Birgitta Beimark; two *s*. Joined Jefferson Smurfit & Sons Ltd, Dublin, 1955; founded Jefferson Smurfit Packaging Ltd, Lancs, 1961; Jefferson Smurfit & Sons Ltd, subseq. Jefferson Smurfit Group: Dir, 1964; Jt Man. Dir, 1966–69; Dep. Chm., 1969–77; Chief Exec., 1977–2002; Chm., 1977–2005. Owner of K Club, host to Ryder Cup 2006. *Publications:* A Life Worth Living (autobiog.), 2014.

SMYTH, Clare, MBE 2013; Chef Patron, Restaurant Gordon Ramsay, since 2012 (Head Chef, 2007–13); *b* Ballymoney, NI, 6 Sept. 1978; *d* of William Boyce Smyth and Doreen Brenda Margret Smyth. *Educ:* Dunluce High Sch.; Highbury Coll., Portsmouth. Commis chef, Bibendum, Chelsea; head chef, St Enodoc Hotel, Rock; chef de partie, later sen. sous chef, Restaurant Gordon Ramsay, 2002–05; worked as private chef, France, then at Louis XV, Monaco, 2005–07. *Address:* Restaurant Gordon Ramsay, 68 Royal Hospital Road, SW3 4HP.

SMYTH, David William; QC (NI) 1989; **His Honour Judge Smyth;** a County Court Judge, Ards Division, Northern Ireland, 2011; *b* 12 Nov. 1948; *s* of late William McKeag Smyth and Eva Maud Smyth (*née* Moran); *m* 1977, Anthea Linda Hall-Thompson, DL; one *s* two *d* (and one *d* decd). *Educ:* Methodist Coll., Belfast; Queen's Univ., Belfast (Porter Scholar, 1967; LLB 1971). Called to the NI Bar, 1972, Bencher, 1997, Treas., 2009–10; political res., London, 1972–74; called to the Bar, Gray's Inn, 1978, Ireland, 1989; a County Court Judge, Fermanagh and Tyrone Div., 1990–97, Antrim Div., 1997–2011, NI. Chairman: Legal Aid Adv. Bd, NI, 1994–2005; NI Council on Alcohol, 1996–98; Council of County Court Judges, 2005–; Member: Franco-British-Irish Judicial Co-operation Cttee, 1997–; Criminal Justice Wkg Gp on Drugs, 2002; Cttee, Anglo-French Judicial Gp, 2002; Youth Conferencing Adv. Gp, 2003; Lands Tribunal, 2014–; President: Addiction NI (formerly NI Community Addiction Service), 1998–; Methodist Coll. Belfast Former Pupils Assoc., 2012–14. Chm. Bd of Advrs, Inst. of Criminology, QUB, 2002–. Trustee, N Belfast Wkg Men's Club, 1974–. Winston Churchill Scholar, 2002. FRSA 2009. *Publications:* contrib. to NI Legal Qly and Jl of Judicial Studies Bd (Ire.). *Recreations:* cycling, opera, history. *Address:* Royal Courts of Justice, Chichester Street, Belfast BT1 3JE. *E:* davidsmyth80@icloud.com.

SMYTH, Desmond; *see* Smyth, J. D.

SMYTH, Joan Rutherford, CBE 1998; Chairman, Progressive Building Society, 2005–12 (Director, 2001–12); Director, Eirgrid, since 2009; *b* 29 Dec. 1946; *d* of David James Hunter and Kathleen McRoberts (*née* Carson); *m* 1983, John Vernon Smyth. *Educ:* Glenlola Collegiate Sch., Bangor; Dalriada Sch., Ballymoney; Queen's Univ., Belfast (BSc Econ.). Employee Relns Manager, Gallaher Ltd, 1969–89; Partner, Allen & Smyth, 1989–92; Chair and Chief Exec., EOC for NI, 1992–99. Chm., NI Transport Hldg Co., 1999–2005; Dir, Trinity Housing (formerly Choice Housing, then Sanctuary Housing Assoc.), 2002–12. Member: Bd, British Council, 1999–2002 (Chm., NI Cttee, 1999–2003); Steering Gp, Women's Nat. Commn, 1999–2002; NI QC Appts Panel, 2005–07; Ind. Assessor of Public Appts, 2005–12. Chm., Chief Executives Forum, NI, 2001–08; Chair, Women's Fund for NI, 2012–. President: GB and Ireland Fedn, Soroptimist Internat., 2002–03; British Red Cross, NI, 2005–12; Confedn of Ulster Socs, 2005–12; North Down Guides, 2007–12. Vice-Pres., Railway Preservation Soc. of Ireland, 2012–. Trustee, 2009–10, Mem., Adv. Bd, 2010–, Gender Action for Peace and Security, UK. CIPD 1998. Trustee, Bangor Drama Club, 2013–. Hon. LLD Ulster, 2000. *Recreations:* golf, drama. *Address:* 12 Shandon Park East, Bangor, Co. Down, Northern Ireland BT20 5HN. *T:* and *Fax:* (028) 9146 9889. *E:* joanrsmyth@btinternet.com.

SMYTH, Prof. John Fletcher, MD; FRCPE, FRCP, FRCSE, FRCR; FRSE; Professor of Medical Oncology, 1979–2008, Assistant Principal, since 2009, University of Edinburgh (Director of Cancer Research Centre, 2002–05); Hon. Director, Cancer Research UK (formerly Imperial Cancer Research Fund) Medical Oncology Unit, Edinburgh, 1980–2005; *b* 26 Oct. 1945; *s* of Henry James Robert Smyth and Doreen Stanger (*née* Fletcher); *m* 1st, 1973, Catherine Ellis; two *d* (marr. diss. 1992); 2nd, 1995, Ann Cull; two step *d*. *Educ:* Bryanston Sch.; Trinity Coll., Cambridge (choral exhibnr; BA 1967; MA 1971); St Bartholomew's Hosp. (MB BChir 1970); MD Cantab 1976; MSc London 1975. FRCPE 1981; MRCP 1973, FRCP 1983; FRCSE 1994; FRCR 1995; FRSE 1996. House Officer posts: St Bartholomew's Hosp. and RPMS, London, 1970–72; Asst Lectr, Dept of Med. Oncology, St Bartholomew's Hosp., 1972–73; CRC Res. Fellowship, Inst. Cancer Res., 1973–75; MRC Travelling Fellowship, Nat. Cancer Inst., USA, 1975–76; Sen. Lectr, Inst. Cancer Res., 1976–79. Honorary Consultant Physician: Royal Marsden Hosp. and Brompton Hosp., 1977–79; Lothian Health Bd, 1979–2008; Vis. Prof. of Medicine and Associate Dir for Med. Res., Univ. of Chicago, 1979. Chm., Expert Adv. Gp for Haematol. and Oncology for Commn on Human Medicines, 2006–13; Member: Cttee on Safety of Medicines, 1999–2005; Scientific Adv. Gp for Oncology, EMEA, 2005–07. Member: Council, 1990–94, Bd, 2001–10, EORTC; EORTC Charitable Trust, 1990– (Vice Chm., 2014–); Council, UICC, 1990–94; President: European Soc. of Med. Oncology, 1991–93; Fedn of European Cancer Socs, 2005–07 (Treas., 1992–97). Ed.-in-Chief, European Jl of Cancer, 2001–10. Founder Mem., Monteverdi Choir, 1967– (Trustee, 2014–). Gov., Bryanston Sch., 1979–2014. *Publications:* Basic Principles of Cancer Chemotherapy, 1980; The Management of Lung Cancer, 1984; Communicating with Cancer Patients, 2013; more than 300 contribs to various med. and scientific jls on cancer medicine, pharmacology, clinical and exptl cancer therapeutics. *Recreations:* flying and singing (sometimes simultaneously). *Address:* 18 Inverleith Avenue South, Edinburgh EH3 5QA. *T:* (0131) 552 3775. *Club:* Athenæum.

SMYTH, John Jackson; QC 1979; barrister-at-law; Executive Director, Justice Alliance of South Africa, since 2007; *b* 27 June 1941; *e s* of late Col Edward Hugh Jackson Smyth, FRCSEd, and Ursula Helen Lucie (*née* Ross); *m* 1968, Josephine Anne, *er d* of late Walter Leggott and Miriam Moss Leggott, Manor Farm, Burtoft, Lincs; one *s* three *d*. *Educ:* Strathcona Sch., Calgary, Alberta; St Lawrence Coll.; Trinity Hall, Cambridge. MA, LLB (Cantab); Trinity Coll., Bristol; Regent Coll., Vancouver. Called to Bar, Inner Temple (Major Schol.), 1965. A Recorder, 1978–84. Dir, Zambesi Ministries, Zimbabwe, 1986–2002; Nat. Dir, Christian Lawyers' Assoc. of SA, 2002–03; legal advr and media spokesperson, Doctors for Life Internat., 2004–09. *Publications:* Discovering Christianity Today, 1985, 2nd edn 2003; Following Christ Today, 1987; Jabulani Bible Reading Notes, 1990–2002; Forgiven, 2009, 2nd rev. edn 2013; Tremendous Teens, 2011. *Recreations:* ski-ing, sailing, trout fishing, tennis, mountain walking; nine grandchildren, squash. *Address:* 1 Ruskin Road, Bergvliet, Cape Town 7945, South Africa. *T:* (21) 7133259, *Fax:* 865452833, *T:* and *Fax:* (21) 7133259. *E:* john@justicealliance.co.za. *W:* www.jjs.za.net. *Club:* Kelvin Grove (Cape Town).

SMYTH, (Joseph) Desmond, CBE 2000; FCA; Managing Director, Ulster Television, 1983–99; *b* 20 April 1950; *s* of Andrew and Annie Elizabeth Smyth; *m* 1975, Irene Janette (*née* Dale); one *s* one *d*. *Educ:* Limavady Grammar School; Queen's University, Belfast. BSc (Jt Hons Pure Maths and Statistics). Accountancy articles, Coopers and Lybrand, 1971–75; Ulster Television: Chief Accountant, 1975–76; Financial Controller and Company Secretary, 1976–83. Dir, Viridian (formerly NIE) plc, 1996–2005. Pres., NI Chamber of Commerce and Industry, 1991–92. FRTS 1993. *Recreations:* fishing, gardening. *E:* desmondsmyth@yahoo.co.uk.

SMYTH, Karin; MP (Lab) Bristol South, since 2015; *b* London, 8 Sept. 1964; *m*; three *s*. *Educ:* Bishopshalt Sch.; Uxbridge Tech. Coll.; Univ. of E Anglia (BA Econ. and Social Studies 1988); Univ. of Bath (MBA 1995). Joined NHS as Manager, 1988; Pol Asst to Valerie Davey, MP, 1997–2001; non-exec. Dir, Bristol N PCT, 2002–06; Ind. Project and Interim Manager, 2008–10; Locality Manager, South Bristol Consortium, 2010–. Mem., Public Accounts Select Cttee, 2015–. Trustee, Bristol Deaf Centre, 2007–08. Governor: St Werburgh's Park Nursery Sch. and Children's Centre; St Thomas More Secondary Sch., 1996–2000. *Address:* House of Commons, SW1A 0AA.

SMYTH, Liam Cledwyn L.; *see* Laurence Smyth.

SMYTH, Rev. Martin; *see* Smyth, Rev. W. M.

SMYTH, Michael Thomas, CBE 2009; lawyer, consultant; *b* 3 March 1957; 2nd *s* of Rev. Kenneth Smyth and Freda Smyth; *m* 1983, Joyce Anne Young; one *s* one *d*. *Educ:* Royal Belfast Academical Instn; Clare Coll., Cambridge (MA). Admitted solicitor, 1982; Partner, 1990–2010, Head of Public Policy, 2003–10, Clifford Chance. Chairman: Public Concern at Work, 2001–11; Social Welfare Law Coalition, 2006–11. Mem., Press Complaints Commn, 2011–14. Visiting Professor: QMUL, 2011–; Univ. of Essex, 2011–. Associate Fellow, Centre for Public Law, Univ. of Cambridge, 2010–. Chairman: Internat. Senior Lawyers' Project (UK), 2011–; Law for Life: Foundn for Public Legal Educn, 2011–; Community Links, 2012–; Member: Lawyers Adv. Bd, Wesleyan Assurance Soc., 2011–; Adv. Bd, Project Associates, 2012; Lord Chancellor's Adv. Council on Nat. Records and Archives, 2014–. FRSA. Hon. QC 2014. *Publications:* Business and the Human Rights Act, 2000; (jtly) The Law of Political Donations, 2012. *Club:* Reform.

SMYTH, Richard Ian; Principal, Fulwood Academy, 2010–14; *b* 19 Nov. 1951; *s* of Ronald and Elsa Smyth; *m* 1983, Nicole Adrienne Ryser; one *s* two *d*. *Educ:* Sedbergh Sch.; Emmanuel Coll., Cambridge (BA 1974; PGCE). Asst Master, Christ's Hosp., 1975–77; worked in family baking and confectionery business, 1977–81; Lay Asst to Anglican Vicar of Berne, Switzerland, 1981–82; Asst Master, Gresham's Sch., 1982–85; Housemaster, Wellington Coll., 1985–92; Headmaster: King's Sch., Bruton, 1993–2004; St Peter's Sch., York, 2004–09. *Recreations:* cricket, golf, Rugby, ski-ing, alpine flowers, roses. *Club:* MCC.

SMYTH, Prof. Rosalind Louise, CBE 2015; MD; FRCPCH, FMedSci; Professor of Child Health and Director, Institute of Child Health, University College London, since 2012; *b* 28 Sept. 1958; *d* of Robert Smyth and Louisa Smyth (*née* Noble); *m* 1986, Andrew Richard Bowhay; one *s* one *d*. *Educ:* Down High Sch., Downpatrick; Clare Coll., Cambridge (BA 1980; MA 1984); Westminster Med. Sch. (MB BS 1985; MD 1993). DCH 1985; MRCP 1986; FRCPCH 1997. Jun. posts, Westminster and St Stephen's Hosps, Westminster Children's Hosp. and KCH, 1983–86; Registrar, Ipswich Hosp., 1987–88; Res. Registrar, Papworth Hosp., 1988–90; Sen. Registrar, 1990–93, Consultant Paediatrician, 1994–96, Alder Hey Children's Hosp.; University of Liverpool: Sen. Lectr, Dept of Child Health, 1996–99; Brough Prof. of Paediatric Medicine, 1999–2012; Hd, Div. of Child Health, 2001–12. Sen. Investigator, NIHR, 2008–. Dir, UK Medicines for Children Res. Network, 2005–12; Chm., Paediatric Expert Adv. Gp to Commn on Human Medicines, 2006–13. Non-exec. Dir, Gt Ormond St Hosp. NHS Foundn Trust, 2013–. FMedSci 2006. *Publications:* (ed with J. V. Craig) The Evidence-based Manual for Nurses, 2002; (ed jtly) Forfar and Arneil's Textbook of Paediatrics, 6th edn 2003; numerous contribs to med. jls and books. *Recreations:* reading, ski-ing, running, gardening. *Address:* Institute of Child Health, University College London, 30 Guilford Street, WC1N 1EH. *T:* (020) 7905 2189, *Fax:* (020) 7905 2820.

SMYTH, Thomas Weyland B.; *see* Bowyer, T. W.

SMYTH, Dr Sir Timothy (John), 2nd Bt *cr* 1956, of Teignmouth, Co. Devon; consultant, since 2011; *b* 16 April 1953; *s* of Julian Smyth (*d* 1974) and late Phyllis, *d* of John Francis Cannon; *S* grandfather, Brig. Rt Hon. Sir John Smyth, 1st Bt, VC, MC, 1983; *m* 1981, Bernadette Mary, *d* of Leo Askew (marr. diss. 2005); two *s* two *d*. *Educ:* Univ. of New South Wales. MB, BS 1977; LLB 1987; MBA (AGSM) 1985; FRACMA 1985. Resident Medical Officer, 1977–79; Medical Administrator, Prince Henry Hosp., Prince of Wales Hosp. Gp, Sydney, 1980–86; Chief Exec. Officer, Sydney Health Service, 1986–88; Gen. Man., St George Hosp., Sydney, 1988–91; CEO, Hunter Area Health Service, 1992–97; Dep. Dir-Gen., Policy, DoH, NSW, 1997–2000; Health Partner, DLA Phillips Fox (formerly Phillips Fox) Lawyers, 2000–08; Dep. Dir-Gen., Health System Performance Div., DoH, NSW, 2008–11. *Heir: s* Brendan Julian Smyth, *b* 4 Oct. 1981. *Address:* PO Box 264, Enmore, NSW 2042, Australia.

SMYTH, Rev. (William) Martin; *b* 15 June 1931; *s* of James Smyth, JP, and Minnie Kane; *m* 1957, Kathleen Jean Johnston, BA; two *d* (and one *d* decd). *Educ:* Methodist Coll., Belfast; Magee University Coll., Londonderry; Trinity Coll., Dublin (BA 1953, BD 1961); Assembly's Coll., Belfast. Assistant Minister, Lowe Memorial, Finaghy, 1953–57; Raffrey Presbyterian Church, Crossgar, 1957–63; Alexandra Presbyterian Church, Belfast, 1963–82. Member, Northern Ireland Convention, 1975; Mem. (UU) Belfast S, NI Assembly, 1982–86 (Chm., Health and Social Services Cttee, 1983–84; Chm., Finance and Personnel Cttee, 1984–86). MP (UU) Belfast South, March 1982–2005 (resigned seat Dec. 1985 in protest against Anglo-Irish Agreement; re-elected Jan. 1986). Chief UU Whip, 1995–2000; Member, Select Committee: for Social Services, 1983–90; on Health, 1990–97; on NI Affairs, 2001–05. Member Executive: UK Branch, IPU, 1985–92, 1995–2005; CPA, 1986–2005. Ulster Unionist Council: Chm. Exec., 1974–76; Vice-Pres. 1974–2000; Hon. Sec., 2000–01; Pres., 2001–03. Dir, Ormeau Business Park, 1988–. Member, Council: Belfast Bible Coll., 1974–2013; Christian Witness to Israel, 1990–. Governor, Belfast City Mission. Grand Master, Grand Orange Lodge of Ireland, 1972–96; Grand Master of World Orange Council, 1974–82, Pres., 1985–88; Hon. Past Grand Master, Canada, and Hon. Deputy Grand Master, USA, NZ, NSW, of Orange Order. *Publications:* (ed) Faith for Today, 1961; pamphlets: Why Presbyterian?, 1963; Till Death Us Do Part, 1965; In Defence of Ulster, 1970; The Battle for Northern Ireland, 1972; A Federated People, 1988; (contrib.) Forbidden Faith, 2010; occasional papers, and articles in Christian Irishman, Evangelical Quarterly, Biblical Theology. *Recreations:* reading, photography; former Rugby player (capped for Magee University College). *Address:* 6 Mornington, Annadale Avenue, Belfast BT7 3JS. *T:* and *Fax:* (028) 90643816. *E:* wms1690@btinternet.com.

SMYTH-OSBOURNE, Maj. Gen. Edward Alexander, CBE 2012; General Officer Commanding London District and Major General Household Division, since 2013; *b* Plymouth, 18 May 1964; *s* of late George William Smyth-Osbourne and Ann Katherine Louisa Smyth-Osbourne; *m* 1996, Lucy Helen Turner; one *s* one *d*. *Educ:* Eton; Univ. of St Andrews (MA). Joined Army, 1983; CO, Household Cavalry Regt, 2005–08; Comdr, 38 (Irish) Bde, 2010–11; Dir, Force Reintegration, HQ ISAF, Afghanistan, 2012–13. *Recreations:* shooting, fishing, walking, ski-ing, sailing, gardening, rural life, collecting books. *Address:* 29 The Close, Salisbury, Wilts SP1 2EJ. *Club:* Buck's.

SMYTHE, Brig. Michael, OBE 1989; Clerk to the Vintners' Company, 1997–2012; *b* 30 April 1948; *s* of Peter and Kay Smythe; *m* 1st, 1976, Sally Paget-Cooke (marr. diss. 2001); one *s* one *d*; 2nd, 2004, Carole James. *Educ:* Ratcliffe Coll. Commnd RA, 1968: Adjt, King's Troop, RHA, 1975–78; psc 1980; CO 94th Regt, RA, 1986–88; MA to C-in-C UKLF, 1988–90; HCSC 1990; COS 2nd Inf. Div., 1990–91; Comdr, RA 1st Armd Div., 1991–93; rcds 1994; Brig., HQ Land, 1995–96. *Recreations:* ski-ing, walking, wine.

SNAPE, Baron *cr* 2004 (Life Peer), of Wednesbury in the County of West Midlands; **Peter Charles Snape;** transport consultant; *b* 12 Feb. 1942; *s* of late Thomas and Kathleen Snape; *m* 1st, 1963 (marr. diss. 1980); two *d*; 2nd, 2004, Janet Manley. *Educ:* St Joseph's RC Sch., Stockport; St Winifred's Sch., Stockport; Dialstone Secondary Modern, Stockport. Railway signalman, 1957–61; regular soldier, RE and RCT, 1961–67; goods guard, 1967–70; clerical officer BR, 1970–74. Non-exec. Dir, W Midlands Travel, 1992–97; Chm., Travel W Midlands, 1997–2000. MP (Lab) West Bromwich East, Feb. 1974–2001. An Asst Govt Whip, 1975–77; a Lord Comr, HM Treasury, 1977–79; opposition spokesman for Defence, 1979–82, for Home Affairs, 1982–83, for Transport, 1983–92. Member: Council of Europe and WEU, May–Nov. 1975; N Atlantic Assembly, 1980–83. Consultant: National Express Gp, 2001–07; First Gp plc, 2007–09. Chm., Bus Appeals Body, 2009–13; Nat. Patron, Community Transport, 2008–13. Fellow, Inst. of Travel and Tourism, 2008–. Mem., Bredbury and Romiley UDC, 1971–74 (Chm., Finance Cttee). Chm., Stockport County AFC, 2011–13 (Dir, 2010–13). Hon. Freeman, Borough of Sandwell, 2010. *Address:* Hildercroft, 281 Highfield Road, Hall Green, Birmingham B28 0BU.

SNAPE, Edward George Crighton; theatre producer and impresario; Chief Executive, Fiery Angel Ltd, since 2001; *b* London, 7 Feb. 1966; *s* of John and Alison Snape; *m* 1999, Marilyn Eardley; one *s* one *d*. *Educ:* Taverham High Sch., Norwich; Norwich City Coll. Co-founder: The Ticketmachine Group, 1993; Fiery Dragons, 2011. Dir, Arts Th., London, 2000–05. Producer: The Complete Works of William Shakespeare: Abridged, Criterion, and UK tour, 1992; Salad Days, Vaudeville, 1996; Kindertransport, Vaudeville, 1997; Bugsy Malone, Queen's Th., 1998; Fascinating Aida, Vaudeville and Theatre Royal, Haymarket, 2003; Oleanna, Garrick, 2004; The 39 Steps, Criterion, 2006 (Olivier Award, 2007), UK tour and NY, 2008; Swallows and Amazons, Vaudeville, 2011; Goodnight Mr Tom, nat. tour, 2011, Phoenix, 2013; The Ladykillers, Gielgud Th., 2012; Another Country, Trafalgar Studios, 2014; Ghost Stories, Arts, 2014; To Kill A Mockingbird, Barbican, 2015; Kenneth Branagh Th. Co. prodns, Garrick, 2015. Mem. Exec. Bd, Soc. of London Theatre, 2011–. *Recreation:* anything apart from theatre. *Address:* Fiery Angel Partners LLP, 2nd Floor, National House, 60-66 Wardour Street, W1F 0TA. *T:* (020) 7292 8888. *E:* esnape@fiery-angel.com. *Clubs:* Garrick, Ivy.

SNAPE, Royden Eric; a Recorder of the Crown Court, 1979–92; *b* 20 April 1922; *s* of John Robert and Gwladys Constance Snape; *m* 1949, Unity Frances Money; one *s* one *d*. *Educ:* Bromsgrove Sch. Served War, Royal Regt of Artillery (Field), 1940–46; Adjt, 80th Field Regt, 1945. Admitted Solicitor, 1949; a Deputy Circuit Judge, 1975. Chairman: Med. Appeal Tribunal, 1985–94; Disability Appeal Tribunal, 1992–94. Governor, St John's Sch., Porthcawl, 1971–88 (Chm., 1971–72). *Recreations:* golf, Rugby Union football, cricket, swimming. *Address:* 7 Cae Rex, Llanblethian, Vale of Glamorgan CF71 7JS. *T:* (01446) 772362. *Club:* Royal Porthcawl Golf.

SNASHALL, Prof. David Charles, FRCP; Professor of Occupational Medicine, King's College School of Medicine, University of London, since 2011 (Senior Lecturer, 1982–2011); Honorary Consultant and Clinical Director (formerly Head of Service), Occupational Health and Safety Services, Guy's and St Thomas' NHS Foundation Trust (formerly Guy's and St Thomas' Hospitals), since 1982; *b* 3 Feb. 1943; *s* of Cyril Francis Snashall and Phyllis Mary Snashall; partner, Carolyn Graham; three *d*. *Educ:* Haberdashers' Aske's Sch., Hatcham; Edinburgh Univ. (MB ChB 1968); Univ. of Wales Coll. of Cardiff (LLM 1996); London Sch. of Hygiene and Tropical Medicine (MSc 1979). FFOM 1987; FRCP 1993; FFOMI 2004; FFTM (Glas) 2006. Jun. med. posts, Warwick, Edinburgh, Paris and Vancouver, 1968–73; Chief Medical Officer: Majes Project, Peru, 1975–77; Mufindi Project, Tanzania, 1981–82. Chief Medical Adviser: FCO, 1989–98; HSE, 1998–2003. Pres., Faculty of Occupational Medicine, RCP, 2005–08. Member: GMC, 1989–2003; Council, BMA, 2009–12. *Publications:* ABC of Work Related Disorders, 1997; (with D. Patel) ABC of Occupational and Environmental Medicine, 2003, 2nd edn 2012. *Recreations:* climbing, gardening, European languages, cycling, cooking, jazz. *Address:* 2 Charity Cottages, Petsoe End, Emberton, Bucks MK46 5JL. *E:* david.snashall1@btinternet.com.

SNEATH, David Rupert, TD 1991, and Bar 2000; DL; Fee-Paid Employment Judge, Nottingham, 2010–12 and 2014–15 (Sheffield, 2012–14); *b* 7 June 1948; *s* of John and Stella Doreen Sneath; *m* 1st, 1971, Anna Minding (marr. diss. 1984); two *d*; 2nd, 1986, Carol Parsons. *Educ:* Pembroke Coll., Cambridge (MA). Called to the Bar, Inner Temple, 1970; in practice at the Bar, Nottingham, 1971–92; pt-time Chm., 1983–92, full-time Chm., 1992–98, Industrial Tribunals; Regl Chm., Employment Tribunals, later Regl Employment Judge, Leeds, 1998–2010. Commnd TA, 1969; TA Comd and Staff Course, Camberley, 1989; Comd, 3rd Bn Worcestershire and Sherwood Foresters Regt (V), 1991; Col (TA) 1994; Dep. Hon. Col D (WFR) Co., E of England Regt, 1999–2007; Chief Mil. Ops, Office of Staff Judge Advocate, Multinat. Corps, Iraq, 2006. Pres., Territorial Commns Bd, 1997–99. Asst Sec. Gen., Interallied Confedn of Reserve Officers, 1996–98. County Vice-Pres., Notts, RBL, 2004–. Trustee: Worcs and Sherwood Foresters Regt, 1996–2007; Sherwood Foresters Mus., 1996–; Mercian Regt, 2009–. Speaker at seminars for judiciary on discrimination, European Law Acad., 2008–15. DL Notts 1998. Bronze Star Medal (USA), 2006. *Publications:* Employment Tribunals, 2005; (jtly) booklet on pensions loss in employment tribunals. *Recreations:* flute playing, choral singing, opera, theatre, ski-ing, cycling for charity (coast to coast, 2014, 2015). *Address:* 7 Kirkby Road, Ravenshead, Nottingham NG15 9HD. *T:* (01623) 456310. *Club:* Army and Navy.

SNEDDEN, David King, CA; Chairman, Trinity International Holdings, 1994–98 (Chief Executive and Managing Director, 1982–93; Deputy Chairman, 1993–94); Chairman, Liverpool Daily Post and Echo, 1985–96; *b* 23 Feb. 1933; *s* of David King Snedden and Isabella (*née* Martin); *m* 1st, 1958 (marr. diss. 1995); two *s* one *d*; 2nd, 2012, Jane Foye. *Educ:* Daniel Stewart's College, Edinburgh. CA 1956. Flying Officer, RAF, 1956–57. Investment Adviser, Guinness Mahon, 1958–59; Chief Accountant, Scotsman Publications Ltd, Thomson British Publications Ltd, Thomson Scottish Associates Ltd, 1959–64; Commercial Controller, The Scotsman Publications Ltd, 1964–66; Managing Director: Belfast Telegraph Newspapers Ltd, 1967–70 (Director, 1979–82); The Scotsman Publications Ltd, 1970–78 (Director, 1970–82). Thomson Regional Newspapers Ltd: Dir, 1974–82; Gp Asst Man. Dir, 1979–80; Jt Man. Dir, 1980–82. Chm., Norcor Holdings PLC, 1994–99; Director: Radio Forth Ltd, 1973–77; BSkyB, 1994–97; Scottish Council Research Inst. Ltd, 1975–77; The Press Association Ltd, 1984–94 (Vice-Chm., 1988; Chm., 1989–94); Reuters Holdings PLC, 1988–94. Pres., Scottish Daily Newspaper Soc., 1975–78; Mem., Press Council, 1976–80. *Recreations:* golf, hill walking, fishing. *Address:* Upper Ouchnoire, Boat of Garten PH24 3BX. *Clubs:* Bruntsfield Links Golfing Society; Scarista Golf (Isle of Harris).

SNELGROVE, Anne Christine; *b* 7 Aug. 1957; *d* of Eric and Chris Stamper; *m* 1978, Michael H. Snelgrove. *Educ:* Ranelagh Sch., Bracknell; King Alfred's Coll., Winchester (BEd (Hons) 1979); City Univ. (MA 1986). Teacher of English and Drama, 1979–86; vocational educn curriculum advr, 1986–95, consultant, 1995–97; political office mgr, 1997–99; community relns mgr, 2001–04. MP (Lab) Swindon S, 2005–10; contested (Lab) same seat, 2010, 2015. PPS to the Prime Minister, 2009–10.

SNELGROVE, Rt Rev. Donald George, TD 1972; an Hon. Assistant Bishop, Diocese of Lincoln, since 1995; Bishop Suffragan of Hull, 1981–94; *b* 21 April 1925; *s* of William Henry Snelgrove and Beatrice Snelgrove (*née* Upshell); *m* 1949, Sylvia May Lowe (*d* 1998); one *s* one *d*. *Educ:* Queens' Coll. and Ridley Hall, Cambridge (MA). Served War, commn (Exec. Br.) RNVR, 1943–46. Cambridge, 1946–50; ordained, 1950; Curate: St Thomas, Oakwood, 1950–53; St Anselm's, Hatch End, Dio. London, 1953–56; Vicar of: Dronfield with Unstone, Dio. Derby, 1956–62; Hessle, Dio. York, 1963–70; Archdeacon of the East Riding, 1970–81. Rural Dean of Hull, 1966–70; Canon of York, 1969–81. Chm., Central Church Fund, 1985–2001; Director: Central Bd of Finance, 1975–99; Ecclesiastical Insurance Gp, 1978–94; Church Schools Co., 1981–97; Clergy Stipend Trust, 1985–; Allchurches, 1992–. Chaplain T&AVR, 1960–73. Chm., Linnaeus Centre, 1994–2002. Director: Cornwall Independent Trust Fund, 1998–2003; Cornwall Develt Foundn, 2003–06; Mem. Council, Univ. of Hull, 1988–95. Hon. DD Hull, 1997.

SNELL, Arthur Gordon; Director, Aegis Defence Services Ltd, 2014–; *b* Brighton, 30 Oct. 1975; *s* of Roderick Saxon Snell and Cecilia Mary Snell (*née* Gordon Clark); *m* 2006, Charlotte Bigland; one *s* one *d*. *Educ:* Bedales; Magdalen Coll., Oxford (BA 1st Cl. Hons Modern Hist.; MA 2003); Birkbeck Coll., Univ. of London (MSc (Dist.) Internat. Security and Global Governance). Entered FCO, 1998; Second Secretary: Harare, 2000–01; Abuja, 2001–03; First Secretary: Sana'a, 2003–05; Baghdad, 2005–06; Dep. Hd, Counter-Terrorism Dept, FCO, 2008–10; Dep. Hd of Mission, Helmand Provincial Reconstruction Team, Lashkar Gah, 2010; High Comr, Trinidad and Tobago, 2011–14. *Publications:* contribs to Asian Affairs, Alpine Jl, Caribbean Jl Internat. Relns and Diplomacy. *Recreations:* mountaineering, ski-touring, rock-climbing, sailing. *Clubs:* Alpine, Savile, Travellers.

SNELL, John Nicholas B.; *see* Blashford-Snell.

SNELL, Paul Stephen, CBE 2009; independent consultant and executive coach, since 2009; Chief Inspector, Commission for Social Care Inspection, 2006–09; *b* 29 June 1955; *s* of Bernard Lionel Snell and Gabrielle Irene Snell (*née* Allman). *Educ:* Warwick Univ. (BA Hons Sociology 1976; MA, CQSW 1979). Social Worker, 1977–84, District Manager, 1984–88, Coventry CC; Area Manager, 1988–89, Asst Dir, Social Services, 1989–95, Birmingham CC; Chief Social Services Officer, Bexley LBC, 1995–97; Dir of Social Services, Nottingham CC, 1997–2004; Dir of Inspection, Regulation and Review, Commn for Social Care Inspection, 2004–06. Member, Board: Action for Children, 2009–; Ofsted, 2011–. *Recreations:* reading, theatre, French cinema, good food. *Address:* 3 Lindsay Square, SW1V 3SB.

SNELLGROVE, David Llewellyn, LittD, PhD; FBA 1969; Professor of Tibetan in the University of London, 1974–82, now Emeritus Professor (Reader, 1960–74, Lecturer, 1950–60); Founder Director of Institute of Tibetan Studies, Tring, 1966–82; *b* Portsmouth, 29 June 1920; *s* of Lt-Comdr Clifford Snellgrove, RN, and Eleanor Maud Snellgrove. *Educ:* Christ's Hospital, Horsham; Southampton Univ.; Queens' Coll., Cambridge. Served War of 1939–45: commissioned in Infantry, 1942; Intell. Officer in India until 1946. Then started seriously on oriental studies at Cambridge, 1946, cont. Rome, 1949–50. BA Cantab 1949, MA Cantab 1953; PhD London 1954; LittD Cantab 1969. Made expedns to India and the Himalayas, 1953–54, 1956, 1960, 1964, 1967, 1974–75, 1978–80, 1982, continued with regular travel in Indonesia, 1987–94, to Cambodia, 1995–; founded with Mr Hugh E. Richardson an Inst. of Tibetan Studies, 1966. Apptd Consultant to Vatican in new Secretariat for non-Christian Religions, 1967. Many professional visits abroad, mainly to W Europe and USA. Burton Medal, RAS, 2004. *Publications:* Buddhist Himalaya, 1957; The Hevajra Tantra, 1959; Himalayan Pilgrimage, 1961, 2nd edn 1981; Four Lamas of Dolpo, 1967; The Nine Ways of Bon, 1967, repr. 1980; (with H. E. Richardson) A Cultural History of Tibet, 1968, 4th edn 2003; (with T. Skorupski) The Cultural Heritage of Ladakh, vol. I, 1977, vol. II, 1980; (ed) The Image of the Buddha, 1978; Indo-Tibetan Buddhism, 1987, 2nd edn 2003;

Asian Commitment, 2000; Khmer Civilization and Angkor, 2001; Angkor Before and After: a cultural history of the Khmers, 2004; Religion as History—Religion as Myth, 2005; articles in Arts Asiatiques (Paris), Bulletin of the Secretariat for non-Christian Religions (Rome), etc. *Address:* Via Vista 7, 10060 Lusernetta, Italy. *W:* www.dlsnellgrove.com.

SNELSON, Rear Adm. David George, CB 2004; RN retired; Chief Harbour Master, Port of London Authority, 2007–11; *b* 27 May 1951; *s* of W. M. Snelson; *m* 1973, Ruth Mary Clayton; two *s*. *Educ:* Alleyne's Grammar Sch., Uttoxeter, Staffs; BRNC, Dartmouth. Comdr, HMS Liverpool, 1987–88; Naval Asst to Controller of Navy, 1989–92; Staff Ops Officer, Comdr UK Task Gp, 1993–95; Comdr, HMS Liverpool, and Captain 3rd Destroyer Sqdn, 1996–98; Dir, Naval Ops, 1998–99, Naval Staff, 1999–2000, MoD; Captain, HMS Ark Royal, 2001–02; Comdr UK Maritime Force, 2002–04; COS (Warfare) to C-in-C Fleet, 2004–06. Chm., Thames Trng Alliance, 2011–13. Non-executive Director: Maritime and Coastguard Agency, 2012–; Port of Milford Haven, 2012–. Mem., Hon. Co. of Master Mariners, 2007. Elder Brother, Trinity House, 2013. FNI 2004. Officer, Operation Telic Legion of Merit (USA), 2003. *Recreations:* sailing, reading. *Address:* Trinity House, Tower Hill, EC3N 4DH.

SNELSON, Rev. William Thomas; Communications Officer, Anglican Centre in Rome, since 2015 (Development Officer, 2008–14); General Secretary, Churches Together in England, 1997–2008; *b* 10 March 1945; *s* of Samuel and Dorothy Snelson; *m* 1968, Beryl Griffiths; one *s* one *d*. *Educ:* Exeter Coll., Oxford (BA 1967); Fitzwilliam Coll., Cambridge (BA 1969; MA 1975); Westcott House, Cambridge. Ordained deacon, 1969, priest, 1970; Curate: Godalming, 1969–72; Leeds Parish Church, 1972–75; Vicar: Chapel Allerton, Leeds, 1975–81; Bardsey, Leeds, 1981–93; W Yorks County Ecumenical Officer, 1993–97. *Publications:* Enriching Communion, 2006. *Recreations:* bridge, opera, continental holidays, choral singing. *E:* bill.snelson@btopenworld.com.

SNODDY, (Matthew) Raymond, OBE 2000; freelance journalist; Presenter, Newswatch, BBC Television, 2005–12; *b* 31 Jan. 1946; *s* of Matthew and Mary Snoddy; *m* 1970, Diana Elizabeth Jaroszek; one *s* one *d*. *Educ:* Larne Grammar Sch., NI; Queen's Univ., Belfast; BA Hons Open Univ. Reporter: Middx Advertiser, 1966–68; Oxford Mail, 1968–71; Parly staff, The Times, 1971–72; Visnews, 1972–74; Dep. Eur. Editor, LA Times and Washington Post News Service, 1974–78; Financial Times, 1978–97; Media Ed., The Times, 1997–2004. Presenter, Hard News series, Channel 4, 1988–90. FRSA 2004. Chairman's Award, British Press Awards, 1992. *Publications:* The Good, the Bad and the Unacceptable, 1992; Green Finger: the rise of Michael Green and Carlton Communications, 1996; (with J. Ashworth) It Could be You: the untold story of the UK National Lottery, 2000. *Recreations:* opera, tennis, chess, drinking and eating, supporting Queens Park Rangers. *Address:* 30 Bushey Road, Ickenham, Middx UB10 8JP. *T:* (01895) 639377. *E:* Raymond.Snoddy@gmail.com. *Club:* Uxbridge Tennis.

SNODGRASS, Prof. Anthony McElrea, FSA; FBA 1979; Laurence Professor of Classical Archaeology, University of Cambridge, 1976–2001; Fellow of Clare College, Cambridge, since 1977; *b* 7 July 1934; *s* of William McElrea Snodgrass, MC (Major, RAMC), and Kathleen Mabel (*née* Owen); *m* 1st, 1959, Ann Elizabeth Vaughan (marr. diss.); three *d*; 2nd, 1983, Annemarie Künzl; one *s*. *Educ:* Marlborough Coll.; Worcester Coll., Oxford (BA 1959; MA, DPhil 1963; Hon. Fellow, 1999). FSA 1978. Served with RAF in Iraq, 1953–55 (National Service). Student of the British School, Athens, 1959–60; University of Edinburgh: Lectr in Classical Archaeology, 1961; Reader, 1969; Prof., 1975. Sather Classical Vis. Prof., Univ. of California, Berkeley, 1984–85; Geddes-Harrower Vis. Prof., Aberdeen, 1995–96. Sen. Fellow, Harvard Univ. Center for Hellenic Studies, 2001–. Myres Meml Lectr, Oxford, 1981; Context and Human Society Lectr, Boston Univ., 2002. Chm., British Cttee for the Reunification of Parthenon Marbles, 2002–10. British Academy: Vice-Pres., 1990–92; Mem., Humanities Res. Bd, 1994–95. Corresponding Member: German Archaeol. Inst., 1977; Archaeol Inst. of America, 2009; Overseas Fellow, Russian Acad. of Scis, 2003. FRSA 2005. Hon. DLitt Edinburgh, 2008; DLitt Hum. Chicago, 2009. *Publications:* Early Greek Armour and Weapons, 1964; Arms and Armour of the Greeks, 1967; The Dark Age of Greece, 1971; Archaic Greece, 1980; Narration and Allusion in Early Greek Art, 1982; An Archaeology of Greece, 1987; Homer and the Artists, 1998; Archaeology and the Emergence of Greece (collected papers), 2006; contrib. Jl of Hellenic Studies, Proc. of Prehistoric Soc., Gnomon, etc. *Recreations:* mountaineering, ski-ing. *Address:* Clare College, Cambridge CB2 1TL. *Clubs:* Alpine, Alpine Ski.

SNOW, Adrian John, MA, MEd; construction consultant; *b* 20 March 1939; *e s* of Edward Percy John Snow and Marjory Ellen Nicholls; *m* 1963 (marr. diss. 1994); one *s* one *d*. *Educ:* Hurstpierpoint Coll.; Trinity Coll., Dublin (BA, MA, HDipEd; Kt of the Campanile; Hon. Sec., Trinity Week); Reading Univ. (MEd). Asst Master, The New Beacon, Sevenoaks, 1958–59; RAF Pilot Officer, 1963; Assistant Master: King's Sch., Sherborne, 1964; High Sch., Dublin, 1964–65 (part-time); Brighton Coll., 1965–66; The Oratory School: Head of Econ. and Pol Studies, 1966–73; Head of Hist., 1967–73; Housemaster, 1967–73; acting Headmaster, Sept. 1972–Mar. 1973; Headmaster, 1973–88; farmer (part-time), Gellifelen, Gwyddgrug, 1975–94. Warden, Oratory Sch. Assoc., 1989–93; Director: Oratory Construction Ltd, 1988–93; Oratory Trading Ltd, 1990–93. Governor: Prior Park Coll., 1981–87 (Mem., Action Cttee, 1980–81); Moreton Hall Prep. Sch., 1984–93; St Mary's Sch., Ascot, 1986–94; St Edward's Sch. and Highlands Sch., Reading, 1987–2001 (Chm., 1990–2001); Rendcomb Coll., 2004–11; St Edward's Sch., Cheltenham, 2004–06. Member: Berks Cttee, Prince's Trust, 1989–93 (Vice-Chm., 1990–91); Tennis Cttee, Tennis and Rackets Assoc., 1990–94 (Chm., Court Develt Cttee, 1992–2006; Develt Officer, 1994–2006); Hon. Court Develt Officer, Internat. Real Tennis Professionals Assoc., 2007–11. Pres., Old Oratorian CC, 1994–; Vice-Pres., Friends of Hardwick Tennis Court, 2009– (Hon. Treas., 1990–97; Chm., 1996–2009). Hon. Treas., Churches Together In Cirencester, 2011–. Mem., F and GP Cttee, St Peter's Catholic Ch, Cirencester, 2012– (Chm., 2013–). *Recreations:* athletics (univ. colour), cricket, hockey (Jun. Internat. triallist), Real Tennis, Rugby (Combined Univs), bridge, croquet. *Address:* The Dormer House, Clarks Hay, South Cerney, Glos GL7 5UA.

SNOW, Alexander Charles Wallace; Chief Executive Officer, Lansdowne Partners Ltd, since 2013; *b* London, 29 April 1969; *s* of late Peter Wallace Snow and of Sally Snow (*née* Hambro, now Sally, Viscountess Hampden); *m* 2009, Elizabeth; two *s* one *d*. *Educ:* Harrow Sch.; Univ. of St Andrews (MA Hons). Director: BZW; Credit Suisse First Boston; Chief Executive Officer: Evolution Gp plc; Williams de Broë Ltd; Evolution Securities Ltd, 2003–12; Dir, Investec Bank plc, 2012–13. Chm., IP2IPO plc, 2002–05. *Recreations:* walking, cricket. *T:* (020) 7290 5500. *E:* asnow@lansdownepartners.com. *Club:* White's.

SNOW, Antony Edmund; Chairman, Hill and Knowlton, Europe, Middle East and Africa, Ltd, 1990–98; *b* 5 Dec. 1932; 2nd *s* of Thomas Maitland Snow, CMG; *m* 1961, Caroline Wilson; one *s* two *d*. *Educ:* Sherborne Sch.; New College, Oxford. National Service, commnd in 10th Royal Hussars, 1952–53; Royal Wiltshire Yeomanry, TA, 1953–63. W. S. Crawford, 1958; joined Charles Barker & Sons, 1961, Dep. Chm., 1975, Chm. and Chief Exec., Charles Barker plc, 1983–88; Chm., 1992–98, non-exec. Dir, 1999–2008, Hill and Knowlton (UK). Non-exec. Dir, Hogg Gp plc (formerly Hogg Robinson & Gardner Mountain), 1989–94; Chm., Fraseer Trust, 1996–2002. Vice-Pres., Market Planning, Steuben Glass, 1976; Dep. Dir, Corning Museum of Glass, 1976 (Trustee, 1983–2012, now Trustee Emeritus); Director: Rockwell Museum, 1979; Heatherley Sch. of Fine Art, 2012–15. Member: Cttee of Management, Courtauld Institute of Art, 1984–89; Exec. Cttee, Nat. Art-Collections Fund, 1985–2008; Ancient Monuments Cttee, English Heritage, 1988–91; Design Council, 1989–94. Trustee: Monteverdi Choir, 1988–2001; V&A Mus., 1996–2002. Mem. Council, RCA, 1994–2002. *Recreations:* English watercolours, fishing. *Address:* 1 Tedworth House, Tedworth Square, SW3 4DU. *Club:* Cavalry and Guards.

See also T. Snow.

SNOW, Rear Adm. Christopher Allen, CBE 2002; DL; Flag Officer Sea Training, 2009–11; Rear Admiral Surface Ships, 2009–11; director, mentor and advisor; *b* 16 April 1958; *s* of Rear Adm. Kenneth Arthur Snow, CB and of Pamela Elizabeth Snow; *m* 1983, Helen Maria Young; one *s* one *d*. *Educ:* Jun. King's Sch., Canterbury; Churcher's Coll., Petersfield; Durham Univ. (BA Hons Archaeol.). Joined RN, 1976; 2nd Navigator, HM Yacht Britannia, 1982; i/c HM Prize Tiger Bay (ex-ARA Islas Malvinas), 1983; Navigator, HMS Birmingham, 1983–85; PWO(U), HMS Hermione and HMS Jupiter, 1985–87; Torpedo Officer, HMS Tireless, 1987–89; SWO(U) to FOST, 1990–92; i/c HMS Atherstone, 1993, Iron Duke, 1994–96; Mil. Asst to VCDS, 1996–98; i/c HMS Coventry, 1998–99; Asst Dir, Partnerships and Internat. Relns, Navy, MoD, 2002–01; Ops Team Leader, PJHQ Northwood, for UK Response Post 9/11 and for ops in Afghanistan, 2001–02; ACOS, Progs and Resources, Fleet HQ, 2002–04; Dir, Navy Resources and Plans, MoD, 2004–05; i/c HMS Ocean, 2005–06; Sen. Directing Staff (Navy), RCDS, 2007; Dep. Comdr, Naval Striking Forces NATO, and Comdr, Striking Forces NATO Maritime Force, 2008–09. Martitime Advr, H of C Defence Cttee, 2011–; Senior Jt Maritime Mentor to NATO and UK JSCSC, 2012–. Strategic Leadership Consultation, Windsor Leadership Trust, 2007. Non-exec. Dir, Northern Devon Healthcare Trust, 2011–15; non-exec. Advr, Real Visual, 2012–; Man. Dir, Chris Snow Consulting Ltd, 2014–. MInstD 2011. Gov., Kelly Coll. Sch., Tavistock, 2009–14 (Chair of Govs, 2013–14); Chair of Govs, Mount Kelly Foundn, 2014–. DL Devon 2011. *Recreations:* sailing, walking Dartmoor and the coastal footpath, follows the Lamerton Hunt on foot.

SNOW, John William, PhD; Chairman, Cerberus Capital Management, LP, since 2006; Secretary of the Treasury, United States of America, 2003–06; *b* 2 Aug. 1939; *s* of William Dean Snow and Catharine Snow (*née* Howard); *m* 1st, 1964, Frederica Wheeler (marr. diss. 1973); two *s*; 2nd, 1973, Carolyn Kalk; one *s*. *Educ:* Univ. of Toledo (BA 1962); Univ. of Virginia (PhD 1965); George Washington Univ. (LLB 1967). Asst Prof. of Econs, Univ. of Maryland, 1965–67; Associate, Wheeler & Wheeler, law firm, 1967–72; US Department of Transportation: Asst Gen. Counsel, 1972–73; Dep. Asst Sec. for Policy, Plans and Internat. Affairs, 1973–74; Asst Sec. for Govtl Affairs, 1974–75; Dep. Under-Sec., 1975–76; Administrator, Nat. Highway Traffic Safety Admin, 1976–77; Vice-Pres., of Govt Affairs, Chessie Systems Inc., 1977–80; CSX Corporation: Sen. Vice-Pres., Corp. Services, 1980–84; Exec. Vice-Pres., 1984–85; Pres. and CEO, Chessie System Railroads, 1985–86, CSX Rail Transport, 1986–87, CSX Transport, 1987–88; Chief Operating Officer, 1988–89; Pres., 1988–2001; CEO, 1989–2003; Chm., 1991–2003. Co-Chm., Nat. Commn on Financial Instn Reform, Recovery and Enforcement, 1992–93; Chm., Business Roundtable, 1994–96. Adjunct Prof. of Law, George Washington Univ., 1972–75; Vis. Prof. of Econs, Univ. of Virginia, 1977. *Publications:* Perspectives in Economics, 1969. *Address:* Cerberus Capital Management, LP, 875 Third Avenue, New York, NY 10022, USA.

SNOW, Jonathan George, (Jon); television journalist; Presenter, Channel Four News, since 1989; *b* 28 Sept. 1947; *s* of late Rt Rev. George Snow and Joan Snow; two *d* with former partner, Madeleine Colvin; *m* 2010, Dr Precious Lunga. *Educ:* St Edward's School, Oxford; Liverpool Univ. (no degree; sent down following political disturbances, 1970). VSO, Uganda, 1967–68; Co-ordinator, New Horizon Youth Centre, Covent Garden, 1970–73 (Chm., 1986–); Journalist, Independent Radio News, LBC, 1973–76; Independent Television News: Reporter, 1976–83; Washington Correspondent, 1983–86; Diplomatic Editor, 1986–89; main presenter, Election '92, ITV. Visiting Professor: Broadcast Journalism, Nottingham Trent Univ., 1992–2001; Media Studies, Univ. of Stirling, 2001–07; Univ. of Coventry, 2009–13. Chairman: Prison Reform Trust, 1992–97; On The Line Steering Gp, 1999–2003. Chm., Heart of England Forest Trust, 2014–; Dep. Chm., Media Trust, 1995–; Trustee: Noel Buxton Trust, 1992–; Chelsea Physic Garden, 1993–2003; Nat. Gallery, 1999–2008; Stephen Lawrence Trust, 1999–2003; Tate Gall., 2000–08; Ashmolean Mus., Oxford, 2010–; Mem. Council, Tate Modern, 2002–07; Chm., Tate Friends, 2010–. Chancellor, Oxford Brookes Univ., 2001–08. Member: UK-India Round Table, 2002–; Pontignano UK/India Cttee, 2008–. Pres., Cycle Touring Club GB, 2007–. Hon. FRIBA, 2005. Hon. DLitt: Nottingham Trent, 1994; Sussex, 2015; DPhil Open, 2001; Hon. LittD Liverpool, 2011; Hon. Dr Edinburgh, 2012. Monte Carlo Golden Nymph Award, for Eritrea Air Attack reporting, 1979; TV Reporter of the Year, for Afghanistan, Iran and Iraq reporting, RTS, 1980; Valiant for Truth Award, for El Salvador reporting, 1982; Internat. Award, for El Salvador reporting, RTS, 1982; Home News Award, for Kegworth Air Crash reporting, RTS, 1989; RTS Presenter of the Year, 1994, 2002, 2006, 2008, 2010, 2012; Richard Dimbleby Award, BAFTA, 2005; RTS Journalist of the Year, 2005; BAFTA Fellowship, 2015. *Publications:* Atlas of Today, 1987; (contrib.) Sons and Mothers, 1996; Shooting History, 2004. *Address:* Channel Four News, ITN, 200 Gray's Inn Road, WC1X 8HB. *T:* (020) 7430 4237. *E:* jon.snow@itn.co.uk. *W:* www.twitter.com/jonsnowc4. *Club:* Chelsea Arts.

SNOW, Rt Rev. Martyn James; *see* Tewkesbury, Bishop Suffragan of.

SNOW, Peter John, CBE 2006; television presenter, reporter and author; *b* Dublin, 20 April 1938; *s* of Brig. John F. Snow, CBE and Peggy Mary Pringle; *m* 1st, 1964, Alison Carter (marr. diss. 1975); one *s* one *d*; 2nd, 1976, Ann MacMillan; one *s* two *d*. *Educ:* Wellington College; Balliol College, Oxford (BA Hons Greats 1962). 2nd Lieut, Somerset Light Infantry, 1956–58, served Plymouth and Warminster. Independent Television News: newscaster and reporter, 1962–66; diplomatic and defence corresp., 1966–79; events covered include: Cyprus, 1964; Vietnam, Laos, Malaysia, 1968–70; China, 1972; Mideast war, 1973; Nigerian civil war, 1969; Oman, 1975; Rhodesia, 1965–79; Britain and EEC, 1970–73; co-presenter, Gen. Elections, Feb. and Oct. 1974, 1979; BBC: television: presenter, Newsnight, 1979–97; events covered or reported include: Zimbabwe independence, 1980; Falklands war, 1982; S Africa, 1986; co-presenter, Gen. Elections, 1983, 1987, 1992, 1997, 2001 and 2005, and US elections; presenter: Tomorrow's World, 1997–2001; (with Dan Snow): Battlefield Britain, 2004; Peter and Dan Snow: 20th Century Battlefields, 2007; radio: Random Edition, 1997–; Mastermind, 1998–2000; Masterteam, 2001–05. Vice-Patron, Jubilee Sailing Trust. Judges Award, RTS, 1998. *Publications:* (jtly) Leila's Hijack War, 1970; Hussein: a biography, 1972; (with Dan Snow) Battlefield Britain, 2004; (with Dan Snow) The World's Greatest Twentieth Century Battlefields, 2007; To War with Wellington, 2010; When Britain Burned the White House: the 1814 invasion of Washington, 2013; (with Dan Snow) The Waterloo Experience, 2015. *Recreations:* sailing (skipper Cerulean, Atlantic Rally crossing, 2001), ski-ing, model railways, photography. *E:* p.snow@athenaeumclub.co.uk. *Clubs:* Athenæum; Royal Cruising.

SNOW, Thomas; Director, Oxford University Careers Service (formerly Secretary, Oxford University Appointments Committee), 1970–96; Fellow, New College, Oxford, 1973–96, then Emeritus; *b* 16 June 1929; *e s* of Thomas Maitland Snow, CMG; *m* 1961, Elena Tidmarsh; two *s* one *d*. *Educ:* Winchester Coll.; New Coll., Oxford. Joined Crittall Manufacturing Co. Ltd as Management Trainee, 1952; Dir 1966; Director: Crittall Hope Ltd, Darlington Simpson Rolling Mills, Minex Metals Ltd, 1968. Marriage Counsellor, 1964–70; Chm., Oxfordshire Relate (formerly Oxford Marriage Guidance Council), 1974–90; Member: Cttee of Management, Oxford Univ. Counselling Service, 1992–94 (Chm., 1994–96); Standing Cttee, Assoc. of Graduate Careers Adv. Services, 1973–77, 1985–89. Chm., Central and N Oxford Branch, Oxford Preservation Trust, 2008–10; Dir and Co-Sec.,

Murray Ct, Oxford, 2007–. Trustee: Thomas Wall Trust, 1980–99; Secure Retirement Assoc., 1996–2007 (Dep. Chm., 2002–07); Ethox, 1998–2002; Governor: Harpur Trust, 1996–2001; Bedford Sch., 1996–2001. Fellow, Winchester Coll., 1985–98. Mem. (Lab.), Witham UDC, Essex, 1957–61 (Mem., 1957–61, Chm., 1959–61, Finance Cttee); Mem. (Lib Dem), Oxfordshire CC, 1997–2001. JP Braintree, Essex, 1964–69. *Address:* Flat 9, Murray Court, 80 Banbury Road, Oxford OX2 6LQ.

See also A. E. Snow.

SNOWBALL, Priscilla Deborah, (Cilla), CBE 2009; Group Chairman and Group Chief Executive, Abbott Mead Vickers BBDO, since 2006; *b* 1 Oct. 1958; *d* of late Rev. Frank Chadwick and Gwen Chadwick; *m* 1987, Geoff Snowball (marr. diss. 2007); two *s* one *d*. *Educ:* Sch. of St Mary and St Anne, Abbots Bromley; Birmingham Univ. (BA Hons French). Allen Brady and Marsh, 1981–83; Ogilvy and Mather, 1983–92; Abbott Mead Vickers.BBDO Ltd, 1992–: New Business Dir, 1992–94; Hd, Client Service, 1994–99; Man. Dir, 2000–02; Chief Exec., 2002–04; Chm., 2004–10. Non-executive Director: Fishburn Hedges, 1996–; Arcadia plc, 1999–2001. Chm., Advertising Assoc., 2012–; Mem., Women's Business Council, 2012–. Non-exec. Dir, Macmillan Cancer Support, 2004–08. Trustee, BITC, 2005–11. Trustee, Comic Relief, 2011–. Lay Mem. Council, Univ. of Birmingham, 2010–13. *Recreations:* travel, music, family. *Address:* Abbott Mead Vickers BBDO, 151 Marylebone Road, NW1 5QE. *T:* (020) 7616 3652, *Fax:* (020) 7616 3700. *Clubs:* Thirty, Women in Advertising and Communications London (Past Pres.), Marketing Gp of GB (Past Chm.).

SNOWDEN, Prof. Sir Christopher (Maxwell), Kt 2012; PhD; FRS 2005; FREng, FIEEE, FIET; Vice Chancellor and Professor, University of Southampton, since 2015; *b* 5 March 1956; *s* of William and Barbara Snowden; *m* 1993, Irena Lewandowska; two *s*. *Educ:* Univ. of Leeds (BSc Hons, MSc; PhD 1982). FIET (FIEE 1993); FIEEE 1996. Applications Engr, Mullard Applications Lab., Surrey, 1977–78; Lectr, Dept of Electronics, Univ. of York, 1982–83; University of Leeds, 1983–2005: Lectr, then Sen. Lectr, Dept of Electronic and Electrical Engrg, 1983–92; on secondment as Sen. Staff Scientist, M/A-COM Inc., Corporate R&D, Mass, 1990–91; Prof. of Microwave Engrg, 1992–2005; Hd, Sch. of Electronic and Electrical Engrg, 1995–98; Dir, Inst. of Microwaves and Photonics, 1997–98; Pres. (formerly Chief Exec.) and Vice Chancellor, and Univ. Prof., Univ. of Surrey, 2005–15. Filtronic plc: Exec. Dir of Technol., 1998–99; Jt CEO, 1999–2001; CEO, Compound Semiconductors, 2001–03; Chief Exec., Filtronic ICS, 2003–05. UK Govt Rep., Governance Bd, Jt Res. Centre, EC, 2011–. Non-executive Director: Intense Ltd, 2004–09; Cenamps Ltd, 2003–06; SSTL Ltd, 2005–06; Res. Parks Develts Ltd, 2005–15; Univ. of Surrey Seed Fund Ltd, 2005–09; Engineering Technol. Bd Ltd, 2007–09; InnovateUK (formerly Technol. Strategy Bd), 2009–15; non-exec. Chm., HERO Ltd, 2006–08. Mem. Bd, UUK, 2007– (Chm., Employment, Industry and Business Policy Cttee, 2007–11; Chm., England and NI Council, 2011–; Vice-Pres., 2011–13; Pres., 2013–15). Distinguished Lectr, IEEE (Electron Devices Soc.), 1996–2006. Member: Electromagnetics Acad., MIT, 1990–; SE England Sci., Engrg and Technol. Adv. Council, 2005–11; Council, EPSRC, 2006–12; Nat. Centre for Univs and Business (formerly Council for Industry and Higher Educn), 2006–; PM's Adv. Council for Sci. and Technol., 2011–; UK Govt Foresight Adv. Bd, 2011–. UK Rep., Governance Bd, Jt Res. Centre, EU Commn, 2011–12; Council, Royal Soc., 2011–12. Vice-Pres., Eur. Microwave Assoc., 2003–06 (Chm., Eur. Microwave Week, 2006); Vice-Pres., 2006–07, Dep. Pres., 2007–09, Pres., 2009–10, IET; Vice-Pres., RAEng, 2008–13 (Chair, Engrg Policy Cttee, 2008–13). FREng 2000; FRSA 2000; FCGI 2005. Mem., Council of Govs, Royal Surrey Co. Hosp. NHS Trust, 2009–10. Dir, ERA Foundn, 2010–. Patron: Surrey Community Develt Trust, 2005–09; Surrey Youth Focus, 2009–; Daphne Jackson Trust, 2009– (Chm., 2005–09). Microwave Prize, 1999, Dist. Educator Award, 2009, IEEE; Eur. Microwave Assoc. Outstanding Career Award, 2012; Silver Medal, Royal Acad. of Engrg, 2004. *Publications:* Introduction to Semiconductor Device Modelling, 1986 (trans. Japanese 1988); (ed jtly and contrib.) Semiconductor Device Modelling, 1987; INCA Interactive Circuit Analysis, 1988; Semiconductor Device Modelling, 1988; (ed and contrib.) Semiconductor Device Modelling, 1989; (ed jtly and contrib.) Compound Semiconductor Device Modelling, 1993; (jtly) International Conference on Computational Electronics, 1993; contrib. numerous papers in IEEE, IEE and other learned jls. *Recreations:* photography, painting. *Address:* Vice-Chancellor's Office, Highfield Campus, University of Southampton, University Road, Southampton SO17 1BJ. *Club:* Athenæum.

SNOWDEN, Hon. Sir Richard Andrew, Kt 2015; **Hon. Mr Justice Snowden;** a Judge of the High Court, Chancery Division, since 2015; *b* 22 March 1962; *s* of late Dr Paul Snowden and of Patricia Snowden; *m* 1988, Kirsti Niinisalo; two *s*. *Educ:* Downing Coll., Cambridge (MA); Harvard Law Sch. (LLM). Called to the Bar, Lincoln's Inn, 1986, Bencher, 2010; Jun. Counsel to the Crown (A Panel), 1999–2003; QC 2003; a Recorder, 2006–15; a Dep. High Court Judge, Chancery Div., 2008–15. Mem., Insolvency Rules Cttee, 2002–12. *Publications:* (ed jtly) Company Directors: law and liability, 1997; (ed jtly) Lightman and Moss, The Law of Receivers and Administrators of Companies, 3rd edn 2000, 5th edn as The Law of Administrators and Receivers of Companies, 2011. *Recreations:* Rugby refereeing, cricket, golf, rowing, music. *Address:* Royal Courts of Justice, Rolls Building, Fetter Lane, EC4A 1NL.

SNOWDON, 1st Earl of, *cr* 1961; **Antony Charles Robert Armstrong-Jones,** GCVO 1969; RDI 1978; FCSD; Viscount Linley, 1961; Baron Armstrong-Jones (Life Peer), 1999; Constable of Caernarfon Castle since 1963; Provost, Royal College of Art, 1995–2003; *b* 7 March 1930; *s* of Ronald Owen Lloyd Armstrong-Jones, MBE, QC, DL (*d* 1966), and Anne (*d* 1992), *o d* of Lt-Col Leonard Messel, OBE (later Countess of Rosse); *m* 1st, 1960, HRH The Princess Margaret (marr. diss. 1978; she *d* 2002); one *s* one *d*; 2nd, 1978, Lucy Lindsay-Hogg, *d* of Donald Davies; one *d*. *Educ:* Eton; Jesus Coll., Cambridge (coxed winning Univ. crew, 1950). Joined Staff of Council of Industrial Design, 1961, continued on a consultative basis, 1962–87, also an Editorial Adviser of Design Magazine, 1961–87; an Artistic Adviser to the Sunday Times and Sunday Times Publications Ltd, 1962–90; photographer, Telegraph Magazine, 1990–94. Designed: Snowdon Aviary, London Zoo, 1965; Chairmobile, 1972. A Vice President: National Fund for Research for Crippling Diseases; Prince of Wales Adv. Cttee on Disability; Patron, Circle of Guide Dog Owners; Chm., Working Party on Integrating the Disabled (Report 1976); Pres. for England, Cttee, International Year for Disabled People, 1981. Vice Pres., Kensington Soc. Founder, Snowdon Award Scheme, 1980. Hon. Fellow: Institute of British Photographers; Royal Photographic Soc.; Manchester College of Art and Design; Hon. Member: North Wales Society of Architects; South Wales Institute of Architects; Royal Welsh Yacht Club; Patron: Welsh Nat. Rowing Club; Metropolitan Union of YMCAs; British Water Ski Federation. President: Contemp. Art Society for Wales; Welsh Theatre Company; Mem. Council, English Stage Co., 1978–82. Senior Fellow, RCA, 1986. FRSA. Dr *hc* Bradford, 1989; Hon. LLD Bath, 1989; Hon. DLitt Portsmouth, 1994. Silver Progress Medal, RPS, 1985. *Television films:* Don't Count the Candles, 1968 (2 Hollywood Emmy Awards; St George Prize, Venice; awards at Prague and Barcelona film festivals); Love of a Kind, 1969; Born to be Small, 1971 (Chicago Hugo Award); Happy being Happy, 1973; Mary Kingsley, 1975; Burke and Wills, 1975; Peter, Tina and Steve, 1977; Snowdon on Camera, BBC (presenter), 1981. *Exhibitions include:* Photocall, London, 1958; Assignments, Cologne, London, Brussels, USA, 1972, Japan, Canada, Denmark, Holland, 1975, Australia, 1976, France, 1977; Serendipity, Brighton, Bradford, 1989, Bath, 1990; Snowdon on Stage, RNT and Prague, 1997; Photographs by Snowdon: a retrospective, NPG, 2000; Snowdon, Chris Beetles Gall., 2006; Snowdon: a life in view, NPG, 2014. *Publications:* London, 1958; Malta (in collaboration), 1958; Private View (in collaboration), 1965; A View of Venice, 1972; Assignments, 1972; Inchcape Review, 1977; (jtly) Pride of the Shires, 1979; Personal View, 1979; Sittings, 1983; Israel: a first view, 1986; (with Viscount Tonypandy) My Wales, 1986; Stills 1983–1987, 1987; Public Appearances 1987–1991, 1991; Wild Flowers, 1995; (jtly) Hong Kong: portraits of power, 1995; Snowdon on Stage, 1996; Wild Fruit, 1997; London, Sight Unseen, 1999; Photographs by Snowdon 1952–2000, 2000; Snowdon on Russia, 2003; India by Snowdon, 2008. *Heir: s* Viscount Linley, *qv*. *Address:* 22 Launceston Place, W8 5RL. *Clubs:* Buck's, Oxford and Cambridge; Leander (Henley-on-Thames); Hawks (Cambridge).

See also under Royal Family, and Earl of Rosse.

SNOWDON, Leslie Colin; Scotland Editor, The Times, since 2015; *b* RAF Cosford, 23 June 1961; *s* of Alex and Jackie Snowdon; *m* 1984, Fiona Allison MacGregor; two *s* one *d*. *Educ:* Annan Acad.; Univ. of Edinburgh (MA Hons). Photographer, Dumfriesshire Newspapers, 1984–89; Photographer and Sub-editor, Dumfries and Galloway Standard, 1989–94; The Scotsman: Sub-ed., 1994–96; Chief Pol Sub-ed., 1996–97; Chief Sports Sub-ed., 1997–98; Dep. Sports Ed., 1998–99; Sports Ed., Sunday Times Scotland, 1999–2000; Dep. Sports Ed., The Sunday Times, 2000–03; Editor: Sunday Times Scotland, 2003–06; Scotland on Sunday, 2006–09; Sports Ed., Daily Mail, 2009–15. *Recreations:* hill-walking accompanied by two terriers: Woody and Max, sport, exercise, music, cooking, wine. *Address:* The Times, 1 London Bridge Street, SE1 9GF.

SNOWLING, (George) Christopher (Edward); Legal Member, Mental Health Review Tribunal, 1992–2007; *b* 12 Aug. 1934; *s* of George Edward Snowling and Winifred Beryl (*née* Cave); *m* 1961, Flora Skells; one *s* one *d*. *Educ:* The Mercers' Sch.; Fitzwilliam House, Cambridge (MA). Served RAF, 1953–55 (commnd in Fighter Control Br.). Admitted Solicitor, 1961; various local govt posts, Grantham Bor., Margate Bor., Eastbourne Co. Bor. and Assoc. of Municipal Corpns, 1958–71; Law Society: Legal Aid Admin, 1971–78; Secretary: Educn and Trng, 1978–85, Professional Purposes, 1985–86; Dir, Legal Aid, 1986–89; private practice, 1989–92. Mem., Cuckfield UDC, 1971–74; Mid Sussex District Council: Mem. (C), 1973–2015; Chm., 1981–82, 1986–87, 1987–88; Chm., Policy and Resources Cttee, 1988–91; Leader majority gp, 1991–95; Leader largest minority gp, 1995–99; Leader majority gp, Leader of Council, and Chm. Policy and Resources Cttee, 1999–2001; Chairman: Central Area Planning Cttee, 2001–03; Service Review and Performance Panel, 2001–03; Dep. Leader, 2003–06; Cabinet Mem. for Resources, subseq. Corporate Services, 2003–06, for Health and Community, 2006–; Chm., Planning and Traffic Cttee, 2003–11. Vice Chm., Brighton and Mid Sussex Res. Ethics Cttee, 2004–07; Alternate Vice Chm., Brighton and Sussex (formerly Brighton E) Res. Ethics Cttee, 2008–11; Mem., Crawley & Horsham Local Res. Ethics Cttee, 1994–2003 (Chm., 2003). Member: Council, Assoc. of Dist Councils, 1990–97; cttees, LGA, 1996–98; W Sussex (formerly Shadow W Sussex) Health and Wellbeing Bd, 2011–15; Affinity Sutton S and SW Regl Scrutiny Bd, 2012–; Sussex (formerly Shadow Sussex) Police and Crime Panel, 2012–15. Member: Mid Downs CHC, 1988–96; Lindfield Parish Council, 1995– (Vice Chm., 1999–2003; Chm., Planning and Traffic Cttee, 2003–11); Lindfield Rural Parish Council, 2003–15. Pres., Lindfield Br., Mid Sussex Cons Assoc., 2010–. Pres., Old Mercers' Club, 1998–99 (Trustee, Old Mercers' Benevolent Fund, 2008–). *Recreations:* painting, gardening, enjoying retirement. *Address:* Eldon Lodge, Pondcroft Road, Lindfield, West Sussex RH16 2HQ. *T:* (01444) 482172.

SNOWLING, Prof. Margaret Jean, PhD; FBA 2009; FMedSci; President, St John's College, Oxford, since 2012; *b* 15 July 1955; *d* of Walter and Jean Snowling; *m* 1st, 1986, Christopher Parker (marr. diss. 1992); one *s*; 2nd, 1995, Charles Hulme, *qv*; three step *d*. *Educ:* Univ. of Bristol (BSc Psychol. 1976); University Coll. London (PhD Psychol. 1979). Dip. Clin. Psychol., BPsS, 1988. National Hospital College of Speech Sciences, London: Lectr in Psychology, 1979–88; Sen. Lectr, 1988–89; Principal, 1989–92; Professor of Psychology: Univ. of Newcastle upon Tyne, 1992–94; Univ. of York, 1994–2012. Vice-Pres., British Dyslexia Assoc., 1997. FMedSci 2008. Hon. DSc: Goldsmiths, Univ. of London, 2007; UCL, 2014. *Publications:* (ed) Children's Written Language Difficulties, 1985; Dyslexia: a cognitive developmental perspective, 1987, 2nd edn 2000; (ed jtly) Dyslexia: integrating theory and practice, 1991; (ed jtly) Reading Development and Dyslexia, 1994; (ed jtly) Dyslexia, Speech and Language: a practitioner's handbook, 1996; (ed jtly) Dyslexia, Biology and Cognition, 1997; (ed jtly) The Science of Reading: a handbook, 2005; (ed jtly) Neurocognitive Approaches to Developmental Disorders, 2008; (jtly) Developmental Disorders of Language, Learning and Cognition, 2009; (jtly) Developing Language and Literacy, 2011; (jtly) Developing Reading Comprehension, 2013. *Recreations:* walking, entertaining, music. *Address:* St John's College, St Giles, Oxford OX1 3JP. *T:* (01865) 277419.

SNOWMAN, (Michael) Nicholas, OBE 2014; General Director, Opéra National du Rhin, 2002–09; Chairman, Wartski, since 2002 (Co-Chairman, 1997–2002); Chargé de Mission, Maire de Strasbourg, 2009–12; *b* 18 March 1944; *s* of late Kenneth Snowman and Sallie Snowman (*née* Moghi-Levkine); *m* 1983, Margo Michelle Rouard; one *s*. *Educ:* Hall Sch., London; Highgate Sch., London; Magdalene Coll., Cambridge (BA Hons Eng. Lit.). Asst to Hd of Music Staff, Glyndebourne Fest., 1967–69; Co-Founder and Gen. Man., London Sinfonietta, 1968–72; Administrator, Music Th. Ensemble, 1968–71; Artistic Dir, IRCAM, Centre d'Art et de Culture Georges Pompidou, 1972–86; Gen. Dir (Arts), 1986–92, Chief Exec., 1992–98, South Bank Centre, London; Gen. Dir, Glyndebourne, 1998–2000. Co-Founder, 1975, Artistic Advr, 1975–92, Bd Mem., 1992–, Vice-Chm., 1998–, Ensemble InterContemporain, Paris; Mem. Music Cttee, Venice Biennale, 1979–86; Artistic Dir, Projects in 1980 (Stravinsky), 1981 (Webern), 1983 (Boulez), Fest. d'Automne de Paris; Programme Consultant, Cité de la Musique, La Villette, Paris, 1991. Mem. Bd, Cultural Olympiad, 2012–13. Mem. British Sect., 1995–2000, French Sect., 2009–, Franco-British Council. Trustee, New Berlioz Edition, 1996–; Board Member: Music Restored, 2010–; Monteverdi Choir and Orchestra, 2012–; Chm., L'Association Monteverdi, 2013–. Gov., RAM, 1998–2006 (Hon. RAM 1999; Patron, 2011–). Hon. Fellow, Bangor Univ., 2015. Officier de l'Ordre des Arts et des Lettres (France), 1990 (Chevalier, 1985); Order of Cultural Merit (Poland), 1990; Chevalier: l'Ordre National du Mérite (France), 1995; Légion d'Honneur (France), 2008. *Publications:* (co-ed) The Best of Granta, 1967; (series ed.) The Contemporary Composers; papers and articles on music, architecture, cultural policy. *Recreations:* films, eating, spy novels, France. *Address:* Wartski, 14 Grafton Street, W1S 4DE.

SNOXELL, David Raymond; HM Diplomatic Service, retired; High Commissioner, Mauritius, 2000–04; *b* 18 Nov. 1944; *s* of late Gordon William Snoxell and of Norah Snoxell; *m* 1971, Anne Carter; two *s* one *d*. *Educ:* Bishop Vesey's Grammar Sch., Sutton Coldfield; Bristol Univ. (BA Hons Hist. 1966); Aston Univ. (Dip. Personnel Mgt 1967). MIPD. UNA Volunteer, Senegal, 1967–68; joined FCO, 1969; Islamabad, 1973–76; UK Mission to Geneva, 1976–81; FCO, 1981–86; Dir, British Information Services, NY, 1986–91; Dep. Head of Drugs and Internat. Crime Dept, FCO, 1991–94; Dep. Head of Southern Africa Dept, FCO, 1994–96; Ambassador to Senegal and concurrently to Mali, Guinea, Guinea Bissau and Cape Verde, 1997–2000. Co-ordinator, Chagos Islands All-Party Parly Gp, 2008–. Chm., Marine Educn Trust, 2009–. *Recreations:* choral singing, local history. *Address:* Old Mill Cottage, Bassetsbury Lane, High Wycombe, Bucks HP11 1QZ. *T:* (01494) 529318.

SNYDER, Prof. Allan Whitenack, FRS 1990; FAA; FTSE; 150th Anniversary Chair of Science and the Mind and University Professor, University of Sydney, 1999–2013, now Professor Emeritus; *s* of Edward H. Snyder, philanthropist, and Zelda (*née* Cotton), Broadway actress and psychodramatherapist; one *s* one *d*. *Educ:* Central High Sch., Phil. (AB); Pennsylvania State Univ. (BS); MIT (SM); Harvard Univ. (MS); University Coll. London

(PhD); DSc London. Greenland Ice Cap Communications Project, 1961; Gen. Telecom. and Elec. Res. Lab., 1963–67; Cons. to Brit. PO and Standard Telecom. Lab., 1968–70; Nat. Sci. Foundn Fellow, Yale Univ., 1970–71; Professorial Fellow, IAS, ANU, 1971–77; John Simon Guggenheim Fellow, Yale Univ. Med. Sch., 1977–78; Institute for Advanced Studies, Australian National University: Prof. of Optical Physics and Visual Scis, 1978–98; Hd, Dept of Applied Maths, 1980–83; Hd, Optical Scis Centre, 1987–2003; Peter Karmel Chair and Dist. Prof., 1999–2006, now Prof. Emeritus; Dir, Centre for the Mind, ANU, 1997–2005, Univ. of Sydney, 1999–2012; Royal Soc. Guest Res. Fellow, Cambridge Univ., 1987. Foundn Dir, Aust. Photonics Cooperative Res. Centre, 1992–95. Associate Editor, Jl of Optical Soc. of America, 1981–83. Fellow, Optical Soc. of Amer., 1980; Foundn Fellow, Nat. Vision Res. Inst. of Aust., 1983. A. E. Mills Meml Orator, RACP, 1996; Harrie Massey Prize and Lect., Inst. of Phys, 1996; Inaug. Edwin Flack Lect., Australian Olympic Cttee, 1998; Clifford Paterson Prize and Lect., Royal Soc., 2001. Edgeworth David Medal, Royal Soc. NSW, 1974; Research Medal, Royal Soc. Vic, 1974; Thomas Rankin Lyle Medal, Aust. Acad. of Sci., 1985; Stuart Sutherland Meml Medal, Aust. Acad. of Technological Sci. and Engrg, 1991; CSIRO External Medal for Research, 1995; Australia Prize, 1997; Tall Poppy Prize, Australian Inst. of Political Sci., 2000; Marconi Internat. Prize, 2001; Australian Centenary Medal, 2003. *Publications:* Photoreceptor Optics, 1975; Optical Waveguide Theory, 1983; Optical Waveguide Sciences, 1983; What Makes a Champion, 2002; articles on the mind, the visual system of animals and on the physics of light propagation in internat. sci. jls. *Recreations:* art, culture, swimming, snorkelling. *Address:* Department of Physiology, University of Sydney Medical School, NSW 2006, Australia. *T:* (418) 633247, *Fax:* (2) 93518534. *E:* allan@centreforthemind.com.

SNYDER, Sir Michael (John), Kt 2008; Senior Partner: Kingston Smith LLP, Chartered Accountants, since 1990; Kingston Smith Consulting LLP, since 2009; *b* 30 July 1950; *s* of Elsworth and Pauline Snyder; *m* 1974, Mary Dickinson; two *d. Educ:* Brentwood Sch.; City of London Coll. FCA 1973. Chairman: Cheviot Capital Ltd, 1983–2006; Kingston Sorel Internat. (KS Internat.), 1990–; Kingston Smith Services Ltd (formerly Kingston Smith Consultants Ltd), 1997–; Kingston Smith Financial Advisers Ltd, 1997–; Devonshire Corporate Finance Ltd, 2001–; HR Insight Ltd, 2005–. Mem., Lee Valley Regl Park Authy, 1993–2008. Member: Bd, Thames Gateway London Partnership, 2000–11; Gateway to London, 2001–11 (Chm., 2008–11). Chm., Assoc. of Practising Accountants, 1992–. Chm., London Business Loans, 2007–; Dir, GLE Loan Finance Ltd, 2014–. Mem., Leaders Cttee, 2003–08, Vice Chm., London Councils (formerly Assoc. of London Govt), 2003–08. Chm., Nat. Business Angels Network, 1998–2004. Mem. Bd, Film London, 2004–08. Trustee, Academy Sponsor Trust, 2005–10. MCSI. FInstD 1986. Corporation of London: Dep., Ward of Cordwainer, 1993–; Member: Policy and Resources Cttee, 1994– (Chm., 2003–08); Chancellor's High Level Gp on Financial Services, 2008; Chairman: Professional Services Global Competitiveness Gp, 2008–09; Professional and Business Services Gp, 2010–12; Co-Chm., Professional and Business Services Council, 2012–; Member: Ct of Common Council, 1986–; Finance Cttee, 1992– (Chm., 1998–2003); City Lands and Bridge House Estates Cttee, 1998–2003. Mem., Securities Inst., 1997–. Liveryman and Member of Court: Co. of Needlemakers, 1980– (Master, 2005–06); Tallow Chandlers' Co., 1990– (Master, 2012–13). Hon. Treas., Bow Bells Assoc. Governor: London Metropolitan Univ., 1999–2010; City of London Sch. for Girls, 1989– (Chm., 2013–); Brentwood Sch., 1992– (Hon. Treas., 1992–2010; Vice Chm., 2005–). FInstD 1986. FRSA 2008. Hon. DSc City, 2001. Grand Cross, Order of Merit (FRG), 1998. *Recreations:* music, gardening, narrow boating. *Address:* Kingston Smith LLP, Devonshire House, 60 Goswell Road, EC1M 7AD. *T:* (020) 7566 4000, *Fax:* (020) 7689 6300. *E:* mjs@kingstonsmith.co.uk. *Clubs:* Ward of Cordwainer (Vice Pres.); City Pickwick.

SOAME, Sir Richard (John) Buckworth-Herne-, 13th Bt *cr* 1697, of Sheen, Surrey; *b* 17 Aug. 1970; *o s* of Sir Charles John Buckworth-Herne-Soame, 12th Bt and Eileen Margaret Mary Buckworth-Herne-Soame (*née* Minton); *S* father 2013, but his name does not yet appear on the Official Roll of the Baronetage. *Heir:* none.

SOAMES, Rt Hon. Sir (Arthur) Nicholas (Winston), Kt 2014; PC 2011; MP (C) Mid Sussex, since 1997 (Crawley, 1983–97); *b* 12 Feb. 1948; *s* of Baron Soames, GCMG, GCVO, CH, CBE, PC and Lady Soames, LG, DBE; *m* 1st, 1981, Catherine Weatherall (marr. diss. 1990); one *s*; 2nd, 1993, Serena, *d* of Sir John L. E. Smith, CH, CBE; one *s* one *d. Educ:* Eton. Served 11th Hussars (PAO), 1967–70 (2nd Lieut); Equerry to the Prince of Wales, 1970–72; Asst Dir, Sedgwick Group, 1976–82. PPS to Minister of State for Employment, 1984–85, to Sec. of State, DoE, 1987–89, to Sec. of State, DTI, 1989–90; Parly Sec., MAFF, 1992–94; Minister of State for the Armed Forces, MoD, 1994–97; Shadow Defence Sec., 2003–05. Pres., Conservative Middle East Council, 2010–. Mem., Commonwealth War Graves Commn, 2003–08. *Recreation:* country pursuits. *Address:* House of Commons, SW1A 0AA. *T:* (020) 7219 3000. *Clubs:* White's, Turf, Pratt's, Beefsteak.

See also Hon. E. M. Soames, Hon. R. C. Soames.

SOAMES, Hon. Emma (Mary); Editor-at-Large, Saga magazine, and Director, Saga Media, since 2008; *b* 6 Sept. 1949; *d* of Baron Soames, GCMG, GCVO, CH, CBE, PC and Lady Soames, LG, DBE; *m* 1981, James MacManus (marr. diss. 1989); one *d. Educ:* Hamilton House Sch. for Girls; Queen's Coll., London; Sorbonne, Univ. of Paris; Ecole des Sciences Politiques. Journalist, Evening Standard, 1974–81; Editor, Literary Review, 1984–86; Features Editor, Vogue, 1986–88; Editor: Tatler, 1988–90; Evening Standard mag., 1992–94; Telegraph mag., 1994–2002; Ed., Saga mag. and Editl Dir, Saga Publishing Ltd, 2002–08. Trustee: Turner Contemporary Art Trust, 2005–13; Fine Cell Work, 2012–; Swarovski Foundn, 2014–. Editor of Year Award for Gen. Interest and Current Affairs, BSME, 2003. *Recreations:* travel, gardening, self education.

See also Rt Hon. Sir A. N. W. Soames, Hon. R. C. Soames.

SOAMES, Rt Hon. Sir Nicholas; *see* Soames, Rt Hon. Sir A. N. W.

SOAMES, Hon. Rupert Christopher, OBE 2010; Chief Executive, Serco Group plc, since 2014; *b* 18 May 1959; *s* of Baron Soames, GCMG, GCVO, CH, CBE, PC and Lady Soames, LG, DBE; *m* 1988, Camilla Dunne; two *s* one *d. Educ:* Eton; Worcester Coll., Oxford (BA). Pres., Oxford Union, 1981. With GEC plc, 1982–96 (Man. Dir, Avery Berkel UK); Misys plc, 1996–2002 (Chief Exec., Banking and Securities Div., 2000–02); Chief Exec., Aggreko plc, 2003–14. *Recreations:* country sports, food and wine. *Address:* Serco Group plc, Serco House, 16 Bartley Wood Business Park, Bartley Way, Hook, Hants RG27 9UY. *Clubs:* White's, Turf, Pratt's.

See also Rt Hon. Sir A. N. W. Soames, Hon. E. M. Soames.

SOANE, Tim; Managing Partner, Persuasion Associates (formerly The Soanes) Ltd, since 2010; *b* London, 9 May 1953; *s* of Morris Soane and Lore Soane (*née* Garratt); *m* 1975, Giorgina Perugini; one *s. Educ:* Dulwich Coll., London. BoT and Dept of Industry, 1974–92, incl. Private Sec. to Parly Under Sec. of State, DTI, 1985–86; Department of Trade and Industry: Director: Electrical Manufg, 1993–96; Competitiveness, 1996–99; Change and Knowledge Mgt, 2000–04; HR, 2001–03; Dir, Partnership, Employment Relns, DTI, later BERR, 2004–08; Dir, Regulatory Innovation, Better Regulation Exec., BIS, 2009–10. *Recreations:* Italy, web 2.0, genealogy, bridge. *Address:* Fulham, SW6 3RU. *T:* (020) 7736 2396; Barga, Lucca 55051, Italy. *T:* (0583) 1801382. *E:* mail@soane.net. *Club:* Hurlingham.

SOANES, Zebedee; broadcaster, BBC Radio and Television, since 1998; *b* Great Yarmouth, 24 June 1976; *s* of Rev. Robert Soanes and Jeanette Soanes. *Educ:* Univ. of E Anglia (BA Hons English and American Studies 1997). Actor, 1995–; teacher of speech and drama, Langley Sch., Norfolk, 1997–98; freelance broadcaster, BBC Radio Norfolk, 1997–98; Continuity Announcer, BBC Network TV, 1998–2002; newsreader, BBC Radio 4, 2001–; launched BBC Four, 2002; presenter, BBC Proms, BBC TV, 2006–; reporter, From Our Own Correspondent, BBC Radio, 2008–; presenter, Saturday Classics, BBC Radio 3, 2012. Voice of God, Noye's Fludde by Benjamin Britten, Aldeburgh Music, 2013. Patron: Awards for Young Musicians, 2013–; British Assoc. for Performing Arts Medicine, 2014–. *Recreations:* theatre, classical music, travel, The Highgate Society, Suffolk. *Address:* c/o BBC Radio 4, Broadcasting House, W1A 1AA. *W:* www.zebsoanes.com. *Club:* Two Brydges.

SOAR, Adm. Sir Trevor (Alan), KCB 2009; OBE 1994; Commander-in-Chief Fleet and Commander Allied Maritime Command Northwood, 2009–12; Vice-Admiral of the United Kingdom, 2009–12; Director, Trevor Soar Strategic Consulting Ltd, since 2012; *b* 21 March 1957; *s* of Colin and Hazel Soar; *m* 1978, Anne Matlock; two *s. Educ:* Loughborough Grammar Sch.; BRNC Dartmouth. Joined RN, 1975; qualified submariner, 1978; Captain: HMS Ocelot, 1987–90; HMS Talent, 1991–94; Navy Plans and Prog., MoD, 1996; Captain, HMS Chatham, 1997–98; Asst Dir Warfare, Navy Plans and Prog., then Captain Navy Plans, Navy Resources and Plans, MoD, 1998–2000; Dir Naval Staff responsible for pan-Navy policy across Defence, 2000–02; Captain, HMS Invincible, 2002–04; Rear Adm. 2004; Capability Manager (Precision Attack), 2004–06; Chief of Materiel (Fleet), Defence Equipment and Support, MoD, 2007–09. Younger Brother, Trinity House, 2002–. Freeman: City of London, 2004; Lightmongers' Co. Hon. DEng Heriot-Watt, 2005. President: Training Ship Wizard, 1990–; Training Ship Modwena, 2012–; Adm., City Livery Yacht Club, 2014–. Chm., The Leaders Club, 2013–. *Recreations:* Royal Navy Rugby Football Union (Past Pres.), supporter of Leicester Tigers. *Address:* c/o Naval Secretary, Leach Building, Whale Island, Portsmouth, Hants PO2 8BY. *E:* trevor.soar@me.com. *Clubs:* Army and Navy, Royal Navy of 1765 and 1785.

SOARES, Dr Mário Alberto Nobre Lopes; President of Portugal, 1986–96; Member, Council of State, Portugal; *b* 7 Dec. 1924; *s* of João Lopes Soares and Elisa Nobre Soares; *m* 1949, Maria Barroso Soares; one *s* one *d. Educ:* Univ. of Lisbon (BA 1951; JD 1957); Faculty of Law, Faculty of History and Philosophy, Sorbonne. LèsL, LenD. Leader, United Democratic Youth Movement and Mem., Central Cttee, 1946–48; Mem. Exec., Social Democratic Action, 1952–60; Democratic Opposition candidate, Lisbon, legis. elections, 1965, 1969; deported to São Tomé, March–Nov. 1968; Rep., Internat. League of Human Rights; imprisoned 12 times; exile, Paris, 1970–74; Founder, Portuguese Socialist Party, 1973, Sec. Gen., 1973–86; elected to Legis. Assembly as Mem. (Socialist Party) for Lisbon, 1974; Minister of Foreign Affairs, 1974–75; Minister without Portfolio, 1975; Deputy, Constituent Assembly, 1975, Legis. Assembly, 1976; Prime Minister of Portugal, 1976–77, 1978, 1983–85; Leader of Opposition, 1978–83. Mem., European Parlt, 1999–2004. Pres., Mário Soares Foundn, 1996–. Pres., Jury, Félix Houphouët-Boigny Peace Prize, UNESCO, 2010–. Joseph Lemaire Prize, 1975; Internat. Prize of Human Rights, NY, 1977; Robert Schuman Prize, Strasbourg, 1987, etc; numerous hon. degrees, decorations and orders. *Publications:* A Juventude Não Está com o Estado Novo, 1946; As idéias político-sociais de Teófilo Braga, 1950; A Justificação Jurídica da Restauração e a Teoria da Origem Popular do Poder Político, 1954; Escritos Políticos, 1969; Le Portugal Baillonné, 1972 (Portuguese edn, Portugal Amordaçado, 1947; also trans. English, Italian, German and Spanish); Destruir o Sistema, Construir uma Vida Nova, 1973; Caminho Difícil, do Salazarismo ao Caetanismo, 1973; Escritos do Exílio, 1975; (with Willy Brandt and Bruno Kreisky) Liberdade para Portugal, 1975; Democratização e Descolonização, 1975; Portugal, que Revolução? (interviews with Dominique Pouchin), 1976 (also French, German, Italian and Spanish edns); Relatório as II Congresso do Partido Socialista, 1976; A Europa Connosco, 1976; Na Posse do I Governo Constitucional, 1976; Na Hora da Verdade, 1976; Na Reestruturação do I Governo Constitucional, 1977; Medidas Económicas de Emergência, 1978; Na Posse do II Governo Constitucional, 1978; Em Defesa do Estado Democrático, 1978; Encarar o Futuro com Esperança, 1978; Existe o Eurocomunismo?, 1978; O Futuro será o Socialismo Democrático, 1979; Partido Socialista, Fronteira da Liberdade, 1979; Confiar no Partido Socialista, Apostar em Portugal, 1979; Soares Responde a Artur Portela, 1980; Apelo Irrecusável, 1981; Resposta Socialista para o Mundo em Crise, 1983; Persistir, 1984; A Árvore e a Floresta, 1985; Intervenções (collected speeches): Vol. I, 1987; Vol. II, 1988; Vol. III, 1989; Vol. IV, 1990; Vol. V, 1991; Vol. VI, 1992; Vol. VII, 1993; Vol. VIII, 1994; Vol. IX, 1995; Vol. X, 1996; Moderador e Árbitro, 1995; (with F. H. Cardoso) O Mundo em Português - um diálogo, 1998; Português e Europeu, 2000; Porto Alegre e Nova Iorque: um mundo dividido, 2002; Incursões Literárias, 2003; Um Mundo Inquietante, 2003; Mário Soares e Sérgio Sousa Pinto - Diálogo de Gerações, 2003; (jtly) Mémoire Vivante, 2003; (jtly) A Incerteza dos Tempos, 2003; Um diálogo ibérico no contexto europeu e mundial, 2004; Poemas da Minha Vida, 2004; A Minha Experiência prisional, 2004; A Crise. E agora?, 2005; O Que Falta Dizer, 2005; Um Mundo em Mudança, 2009, O Elogio da Política, 2009; Em luta por um Mundo melhor, 2010. *Recreations:* bibliophile; collector of contemporary Portuguese paintings. *Address:* Fundação Mário Soares, Rua de S Bento No. 176, 1200–821 Lisbon, Portugal.

SOBER, Phillip, FCA; consultant; non-executive Director: Liberty International (formerly Transatlantic Holdings, then Liberty International Holdings), 1983–2002; Capital and Counties, 1993–2002; Capital Shopping Centres, 1994–2002; *b* 1 April 1931; *s* of Abraham and Sandra Sober; *m* 1957, Vivien Louise Oppenheimer; two *d* (and one *d* decd). *Educ:* Haberdashers' Aske's. Qual. as Chartered Accountant, 1953; FCA 1963. Stoy Hayward, Chartered Accountants: Partner, 1958; Internat. Partner, 1975–90; Sen. Partner, 1985–90. Eur. Regl Dir, Horwath Internat., 1990–94. Crown Estate Comr, 1983–94. Mem. Council, UK Central Council for Nursing, Midwifery and Health Visiting, 1980–83. Pres., Norwood Child Care, 1990–94. Trustee, Royal Opera House Trust, 1985–91. Gov., London Inst. Higher Educn Corp., 1994–2003; Mem. Council, London Univ., 1999–2008. *Publications:* articles in prof. press on various subjects but primarily on property co. accounting. *Recreations:* interested in all the arts, partic. music; golf main sporting activity. *Address:* Flat 1, 5 Sheffield Terrace, W8 7NG. *T:* (020) 3220 0165. *Clubs:* Savile, Royal Automobile, Hurlingham.

SOBERS, Sir Garfield St Auburn, (Sir Garry), Kt 1975; AO 2003; OCC; former cricketer; Consultant, Barbados Tourism Authority, since 1980; *b* Bridgetown, Barbados, 28 July 1936; *m* 1969, Prudence Kirby (marr. diss.); two *s* one *d. Educ:* Bay Street Sch., Barbados. First major match, 1953, for Barbados; played in 93 Test Matches for West Indies, 39 as Captain, 1953–74 (made world record Test Match score, Kingston, 1958); captained West Indies and Barbados teams, 1965–74; Captain of Nottinghamshire CCC, 1968–74. On retirement from Test cricket held the following world records in Test Matches: 365 not out; 26 centuries; 235 wickets; 110 catches. *Publications:* Cricket Advance, 1965; Cricket Crusader, 1966; King Cricket, 1967; (with J. S. Barker) Cricket in the Sun, 1967; Bonaventure and the Flashing Blade, 1967; (with Brian Scovell) Sobers: Twenty Years At The Top (autobiog.), 1988; (jtly) The Changing Face of Cricket, 1995; (with Bob Harris) Garry Sobers: my autobiography, 2002. *Address:* Barbados Tourism Authority, PO Box 242, Harbour Road, Bridgetown, Barbados, West Indies. *Fax:* 4264080.

SODANO, His Eminence Cardinal Angelo, STD, JCD; Secretary of State to His Holiness the Pope, 1990–2006, now Emeritus; Dean, Sacred College of Cardinals, since 2005; *b* Asti, Italy, 23 Nov. 1927; *s* of Giovanni Sodano and Delfina (*née* Brignolo). *Educ:* Seminario di Asti; Pontifical Università Gregoriana (STD); Pontifical Università Lateranense (JCD). Ordained priest, 1950; Titular Archbishop, 1978; Apostolic Nuncio, Chile, 1978–88; Sec., Council for Public Affairs of Church, later Section for Relns of Holy See with States, 1988–90. Several hon. distinctions. *Address:* c/o Secretariat of State, 00120 Vatican City State.

SODIWALA, Vijay; Chief Operating Officer, TheBlogTV and Userfarm, since 2011; *b* Kenya, 28 Aug. 1967; *s* of Tansukh and Anuradha Sodiwala; *m* 1995, Minakshi; two *d. Educ:* City Univ. (BSc Hons Electrical and Electronic Engrg); London Business Sch. (MBA). Analyst, NatWest Bank, 1989–92; Consultant: Seer Technologies, 1993–97; Compass Gp, 1997–99; Consultant, Man. Dir and CEO, Sky+ News Corp., 1999–2004; Man. Dir, Video Networks, 2004–07; Consultant, Wireless Infrastructure Gp, 2007–08; Man. Dir, Chime Communications, 2008–10. Chm., Bilbary, 2011. Non-executive Director: Ofsted, 2008–; One Housing Gp, 2010–. *Recreation:* travel.

SODOR AND MAN, Bishop of, since 2008; **Rt Rev. Robert Mar Erskine Paterson;** *b* Cardiff, 27 Feb. 1949; *s* of David Donaldson Paterson and Letitia Paterson; *m* 1971, Pauline Anne Laing; one *s* two *d. Educ:* St John's Coll., Univ. of Durham (BA 1971; Van Mildert Scholar 1971; DipTh 1972); MA Dunelm 1982. Ordained deacon, 1972, priest, 1973; Assistant Curate: Harpurhey, Manchester, 1972–73; Sketty, Swansea, 1973–78; Rector, Llangattock and Llangynidr, 1978–83; Vicar, Gabalfa, Cardiff, 1983–94; Team Rector, Cowbridge, 1994–2000; Principal Officer, Council for Mission and Ministry, Church in Wales, 2000–06; Chaplain to Archbishop of York, 2006–08; Dean, Cathedral Church of St German, Peel, 2008–11. Chm., Central Readers' Council, 2009–; Vice-Chairman: Theol Educn for the Anglican Communion, 2002–09; Liturgical Commn, 2008–; Vice-Chair and Mem. Bd, Fresh Expressions, 2009–13. *Publications:* Short, Sharp and Off the Point: a guide to good and bad preaching, 1987; The Monarch Book of Christian Wisdom, 1997; (contrib.) Common Worship Today, 2000; (contrib.) The Book of Common Prayer Worldwide, 2006. *Recreations:* early music, walking, cycling, theatre, reading. *Address:* Thie yn Aspick, 4 The Falls, Douglas, Isle of Man IM4 4PZ. *T:* (01624) 622108. *E:* bishop@sodorandman.im.

SODOR AND MAN, Dean of; *see* Godfrey, Very Rev. N. P.

SOFAT, Janardan, FCA; Director, Addidi Wealth (formerly AJS Wealth Management) Ltd, since 2006; Chairman, Dartford and Gravesham NHS Trust, since 2014; *b* 11 May 1958; *s* of Didar Chand Sofat and Ved Kumari Sofat; *m* 1981, Anna Mathur; two *d. Educ:* Univ. of Hull (BSc Econ). FCA 1992. Finance Dir, J. S. Hamilton Ltd, 1983–90; Chief Exec., AJS Financial Consultants Ltd, 1990–97; Ops Dir, Business Link London E, 1997–2000; Regional Dir, Small Business Service, 2000–04; Regl Comr for SE, NHS Appts Commn, subseq. Appts Commn, 2004–07; Chm., Kent Probation Area, Nat. Probation Services, 2007–14. Non-exec. Dir, W Kent HA, 1994–2000; Chm., Medway NHS Trust, 2000–04. Chm., Medway Racial Equality Council, 2001–11; Chief Operating Officer, Business Link for London, 2004–05. Trustee, Mencap, 2005–09. *Recreations:* family, good food, travel. *Address:* 47 Pilgrims Road, Halling, Kent ME2 1HN. *E:* sofat@mail.com.

SOFER, Mrs Anne Hallowell; Chief Education Officer, London Borough of Tower Hamlets, 1989–97; *b* 19 April 1937; *d* of Geoffrey Crowther (later Baron Crowther) and Margaret Worth; *m* 1958, Jonathan Sofer (*d* 2003); two *s* one *d. Educ:* St Paul's Sch.; Swarthmore Coll., USA; Somerville Coll., Oxford (MA); DipEd London. Secretary, National Assoc. of Governors and Managers, 1972–75; Additional Member, ILEA Education Cttee, 1974–77; Chairman, ILEA Schools Sub-Cttee, 1978–81; Mem. (SDP), GLC/ILEA for St Pancras N, Oct. 1981–86 (by-election) (Labour, 1977–81). Dir, Channel Four Television Co. Ltd, 1981–83; Columnist, The Times, 1983–87. Mem., SDP Nat. Cttee, 1982–87. Contested Hampstead and Highgate (SDP) 1983, (SDP/Alliance) 1987. Trustee, Nuffield Foundn, 1990–2005. Chm., Nat. Children's Bureau, 2000–06. *Publications:* (with Tyrrell Burgess) The School Governors and Managers Handbook and Training Guide, 1978; The London Left Takeover, 1987. *Address:* 46 Regent's Park Road, NW1 7SX. *T:* (020) 7722 8970.

SOGA, Prof. Kenichi, PhD; FREng, FICE; Professor of Civil Engineering, University of Cambridge, since 2007; Fellow, Churchill College, Cambridge, since 1995; *b* New York, 5 Nov. 1964; *s* of Naohiro and Kuniko Soga; *m* 1999, Mikiko Ashikari; one *d. Educ:* Kyoto Univ. (BSc 1987; MEng 1989); Univ. of Calif, Berkeley (PhD 1994). FICE 2007; FREng 2013. Res. Asst, Univ. of Calif, Berkeley, 1991–94; University of Cambridge: Lectr, 1994–2000, Sen. Lectr, 2000–03, Geotechnic Gp; Reader, 2003–07. George Stephenson Medal, 2006, Crampton Prize, 2007, Telford Gold Medal, 2010, ICE. *Publications:* (with J. K. Mitchell) Fundamentals of Soil Behavior, 3rd edn 2005. *Address:* Department of Engineering, University of Cambridge, Trumpington Street, Cambridge CB2 1PZ. *T:* (01223) 332713, *Fax:* (01223) 339713. *E:* ks207@cam.ac.uk.

SOHLMAN, (Per) Michael (Sverre Rolfsson); Executive Director, Nobel Foundation, 1992–2011; *b* 24 May 1944; *s* of Rolf Rolfsson Sohlman and Zinaida Sohlman (*née* Yarotskaya); *m* 1965, Margareta Borg-Sohlman (marr. diss. 1980); one *s* two *d. Educ:* Univ. of Uppsala (BA 1964). Asst Sec., Commn on Environmental Problems, 1969–70; Min. of Industry, 1972–74; Internat. Div., 1974–76, Budget Dept, 1976, Min. of Finance; Financial Counsellor, Permt Swedish Delegn to OECD, Paris, 1977–80; Res. Dept, Social-Democratic Parly Gp, 1981–82; Head of Planning, Econ. Dept, 1982–84, Dir of Budget, 1985–87, Min. of Finance; Under-Sec. of State, Min. of Agriculture, 1987–89; Under-Sec. of State for Foreign Trade, Min. for Foreign Affairs, 1989–91. Chm. Bd, Swedish Inst. of Internat. Affairs. Member: Stockholm Inst. of Transition Econs, 1990–; Swedish Internat. Develt Agency, 1995–98; Chm., Bd of Dirs, Royal Dramatic Theatre, Stockholm, 1993–96. Member: Royal Swedish Acad. of Scis, 1996; Acad. of Engineering Scis, 1995. Hon. DHL Gustavus Adolphus Coll., 1992. *Address:* c/o Nobel Foundation, PO Box 5232, 102 45 Stockholm, Sweden. *T:* (8) 6630920.

SOKOL, Christopher John Francis; QC 2006; *b* 22 April 1953; *s* of Emil Sokol and Madge Sokol (*née* Woolley); four *d. Educ:* Brighton Coll.; Trinity Coll., Cambridge (BA 1974, MA 1977). Called to the Bar, Lincoln's Inn, 1976, Bencher, 2002; in practice, specialising in tax law. *Publications:* contribs to professional jls. *Recreations:* travel, country sports, old books, fencing, wine. *Address:* Temple Tax Chambers, 3 Temple Gardens, Temple, EC4Y 9AU. *T:* (020) 7353 7884, *Fax:* (020) 7583 2044. *E:* clerks@templetax.com. *Clubs:* Lansdowne, Buck's.

SOKOLOV, Dr Avril, FBA 1996; Reader in Russian, University of Durham, 1989–96, Emeritus since 1996; *b* 4 May 1930; *d* of Frederick Cresswell Pyman and Frances Gwenneth Pyman (*née* Holman), MBE; *m* 1963, Kirill Konstantinovich Sokolov (*d* 2004); one *d. Educ:* Newnham Coll., Cambridge (BA Mod. Langs 1951; PhD 1958). FCIL (FIL 1949). British Council post-grad. scholarship to Leningrad, 1959–61; freelance writer on and translator of Russian lit., 1962–75; lived in Moscow, 1963–74; University of Durham: part-time Lectr in Russian Lit., 1975–77; Lectr, 1977–86; Sen. Lectr, 1986–89. Mem., Soc. of Authors (Translators' Section), 1974–. Hon. Mem., Blok Gp, Russian Acad. of Scis, 2002–; Mem. Hon. Cttee, Fondn Centre d'Etudes Vjatcheslav Ivanov, Rome, 2005. Cert. of Merit, Moscow Patriarchate, 1973. *Publications:* as Avril Pyman: The Distant Thunder: a life of Aleksandr Blok, Vol. I, 1979 (trans. Russian 2005); The Release of Harmony: a life of Aleksandr Blok, Vol. II, 1980 (trans. Russian 2006); Aleksandr Blok's The Twelve, 1989; A History of Russian Symbolism, 1994 (trans. Russian 1998); (contrib.) Mapping Lives: the uses of biography, 2002; (trans.) Requiem, by Anna Akhmatova, 2002; Pavel Florensky: a quiet genius, 2010 (trans. Italian 2010); ed and trans. works by Blok, Bulgakov, Shvarts; trans. poetry, prose, art books; numerous articles on Russian Symbolism and later 20th century literature. *Recreations:* travelling, art, theatre, cinema. *Address:* 213 Gilesgate, Durham DH1 1QN. *T:* (0191) 384 2482.

SOLA, Maggie; *see* Koumi, M.

SOLANA MADARIAGA, Javier, Hon. KCMG 1999; Secretary-General, and High Representative for Common Foreign and Security Policy, European Union, 1999–2009; Secretary-General, Western European Union, 1999–2009; Head, European Defence Agency, 2004–09; *b* 14 July 1942; *s* of Luis Solana and Obulia Madariaga; *m* 1972, Concepción Giménez; two *c. Educ:* Colegio del Pilar; Univ. Complutense de Madrid (PhD Physics). Fulbright Schol., USA, 1968. Asst to Prof., Univ. of Valencia, 1968–71, then Univ. Autónoma de Madrid; Mem. Exec., Federación Socialista Madrileña and Federación de Trabajadores de la Enseñanza, Unión General de Trabajadores; Prof. of Physical Scis, Univ. Complutense de Madrid. Mem., Congress of Deputies for Madrid; Mem., Fed. Exec. Cttee, PSOE (Press Sec. and Sec. for Res. and Programmes); Minister of: Culture, and Govt Spokesman, 1982–88; Educn and Sci., 1988–92; Foreign Affairs, 1992–95; Sec.-Gen., NATO, 1995–99. Pres., Madariaga - College of Europe Foundn. *Publications:* several on physics and solid state physics. *Recreations:* swimming, jogging, tennis, paddle tennis.

SOLANDT, Jean Bernard; Chairman: Schroder France SA, 1992–97; J. Henry Schroder & Co. Ltd, 1994–97; Director, Woolwich Building Society, 1993–98; *b* 23 Dec. 1936; *s* of Alfred Solandt and Mathilde Braun Solandt; *m* 1966, Sheila Hammill; one *s* one *d. Educ:* Lycée Pasteur, Strasbourg; Collège Technique Commercial, Strasbourg. Société Générale, Strasbourg, Paris, London, 1954–68; Schroder Gp, 1968–97: Director: J. Henry Schroder & Co., 1973; Schroders plc, 1982; IBJ Schroder Bank & Trust Co. Inc., 1984–86; Schroders Japan Ltd, 1984–95; Schroder & Co. Inc., 1986–96; Schroder Wertheim Hldgs Inc., 1986–97; Schroder Wertheim & Co. Inc., 1986–97; Schroders Asia, 1991; Schroders AG, 1992; Chairman: Schroder Securities Ltd, 1985–89; Schroder Structured Investments Inc., 1995–97. Director: Royal Trust Co. of Canada (London) Ltd, 1978–82; Banca Woolwich SpA, 1996–98; Banque Woolwich SA, 1996–98. Mem. Exec. Cttee, BBA, 1990–94. Advr, Royal Trustees Investment Cttee, 1991–96. Hon. FCIB. *Recreations:* walking, driving, music. *Address:* 27 Heathgate, NW11 7AP. *T:* (020) 8458 2950; La Clapière, 84190 Vacqueyras, France.

SOLANKI, Ramniklal Chhaganlal, CBE 2007 (OBE 1999); author; Editor-in-Chief: Garavi Gujarat, newsweekly, since 1968 (US edition, since 1992); Asian Trader, business journal, with controlled circulation in English, Gujarati and Urdu, since 1985; GG2, since 1990; Pharmacy Business, since 1998; Asian Hospitality, since 2002; Eastern Eye Newspaper, since 2009; Asian Rich List, since 2010; GG2 Power 101, since 2011; AAHOA Lodging Business, since 2011; Asian Rich List Midlands, since 2013; Correspondent, Janmabhoomi Group, Bombay, since 1968; *b* 12 July 1931; *s* of Chhaganlal Kalidas and Mrs Ichchhaben Solanki, Surat, Gujarat, India; *m* 1955, Mrs Parvatiben, *d* of Makanji Dullabhji Chavda, Nani Pethan, India; two *s* two *d. Educ:* Irish Presbyterian Mission Sch., Surat (Matriculation Gold Medal, 1949); MTB Coll., Gujarat Univ. (BA(Econ)); Sarvajanik Law Coll., Surat, Gujarat (LLB). Pres., Rander Student Union, 1950–54; Sec., Surat Dist Students' Assoc., 1954–55. Sub-Editor, Nutan Bharat and Lok Vani, Surat, 1954–56; freelance columnist for several newspapers, while serving State Govt in India, 1956–63; London correspondent, Gujarat Mitra Surat, 1964–68; European Correspondent, Janmabhoomi Gp of Newspapers, 1968–; Managing Director: Garavi Gujarat Publications Ltd, Garavi Gujarat Property Ltd and Asian Media Marketing Gp (USA) Inc.; Asian Trade Publications Ltd (columnist of thought of the week on Indian philosophy, Garavi Gujarat, newsweekly). Member: Soc. of Editors (formerly Guild of British Newspaper Editors), 1976–; Asian Adv. Cttee, BBC, 1976–80; Nat. Centre for Ind. Language Trng Steering Gp, 1976–; Exec. Cttee, Gujarati Arya Kshtriya Maha Sabha UK, 1979–84; Exec. Cttee, Gujarati Arya Assoc., 1974–84 (Vice-Pres., 1980–81, 1982–83); CPU, 1964–; Foreign Press Assoc., 1984–; Parly Press Gallery, House of Commons; Sec., Indian Journalists Assoc. of Europe, 1978–79. Founder: Asian Trader Awards for Retail Excellence, 1989; (and Mem. Judging Panel), annual GG2 Leadership and Diversity Awards, 1999; Pharmacy Business Awards, 2001; (and Mem., Judging Panel) Asian Business Awards, 2010. Trustee, Gandhi Bapu Meml Trust, 1993–. Best Reporter of the Year in Gujarati, 1970. *Publications:* contrib. many articles. *Recreations:* reading, writing. *Address:* (office) Garavi Gujarat House, 1/2 Silex Street, SE1 0DW. *T:* (020) 7928 1234, *Fax:* (020) 7261 0055. *E:* ram@gujarat.co.uk; (office) 2020 Beaver Ruin Road, Norcross, Atlanta, GA 30071, USA. *T:* (770) 2637728, *Fax:* (770) 2638617; (office) AMG Business Solutions Pvt Ltd, Commerce House II, Satya Marg, Bodakdev, Ahmedabad, 380054, Gujarat, India. *T:* (79) 40005000.

SOLARI TUDELA, Luis; Ambassador of Peru to the Court of St James's, and concurrently to Ireland, 2004–06; *b* 5 Dec. 1935; *s* of Luis Solari Saco and Rosa Tudela Salmón; *m* 1961, Martha Reinoso Castañeda; one *s* one *d. Educ:* Catholic Univ., Lima (graduate in law); Diplomatic Acad., Peru (postgrad. dip.); Institut des Hautes Etudes Internationales, Geneva (postgrad. dip.). Third Sec., 1961; Second Sec., 1966; Ambassador to Panama, 1977–82; Prof. of Internat. Law, Central Univ., Panama, 1978–82; Ambassador to Italy, 1986–88; Vice Minister of Foreign Affairs and Sec. Gen. *ad interim*, 1990; Ambassador to the Holy See, and concurrently to Croatia, Cyprus and Malta, 1992–95; Juridical Advr to Min. of Foreign Affairs, 2002; Sec. of Foreign Policy, 2002–03; Vice Minister and Sec. Gen. of Foreign Affairs, 2003–04. Prof. in Public Internat. Law, Univ. of Lima, Villarreal Univ., San Martin de Porres Univ. and Diplomatic Acad. of Peru, 1986–2004. Mem., Internat. Law Commn, 1987–91. Grand Cross: Order of Peruvian Sun, 1985; Order of Merit for Dist. Services (Peru), 2000. Knight, Order of Condor of Andes (Bolivia), 1955; Grand Cross: Order of Vasco Núñez de Balboa (Panama), 1982; Ordo Pianus (Holy See), 1995; SMO Malta, 1995; Order of Rio Branco (Brazil), 2003; Order of Bernardo O'Higgins (Chile), 2004. *Publications:* Derecho Internacional Público, 1982, 10th edn 2011. *E:* solaritudela@hotmail.com. *Clubs:* Nacional, Regatas (Lima); Jockey Club del Perú.

SOLBES MIRA, Pedro; Second Deputy Vice President and Minister of Economy and Finance, Spain, 2004–09; Chairman, Supervisory Board, European Financial Reporting Advisory Group, 2009; *b* 31 Aug. 1942; *m* 1973, Pilar Castro; one *s* two *d. Educ:* Univ. of Madrid (BL, Dr Pol Scis); Univ. Libre de Bruxelles (Dip. in European Econs). Entered Min. of Foreign Trade, Spain, 1968; Commercial Counsellor, Spanish Mission to EC, 1973–78; Special Advr to Minister for Relns with EC, 1978–79; Dir Gen. of Commercial Policy, Min. of Econs and Trade, 1979–82; Gen. Sec., Min. of Econs and Finance, 1982–85; Sec. of State for Relns with EC, 1985–91; Minister of Agriculture, Food and Fisheries, 1991–93; Minister of Econs and Finance, 1993–96; Deputy (Socialist Party), Cortes, 1996–99; European Comr for Econs and Monetary Affairs, 1999–2004. Chm., EBRD, 1994.

SOLCAN, Natalia; Ambassador of Moldova to the Court of St James's, 2008–10; *b* Floresti, Moldova. Lectr, Acad. of Econ. Studies of Moldova, 1995–97; Sen. Consultant, Foreign Relns Service and Protocol, Presidency of Moldova, 1997–2001; linguistic studies, Princes Coll., London, 2001–03; Counsellor: Directorate for Europe and N America, Min. of Foreign Affairs, 2003–04; Mission to EC, 2004–06; Control and Internal Audit Div., Cabinet of Dep. Prime Minister and Minister, Min. of Foreign Affairs and Eur. Integration, 2006–07; Hd, Political Cooperation with EU Div., Dept of Eur. Integration, Min. of Foreign Affairs and Eur. Integration, 2007–08. *Address:* c/o Embassy of the Republic of Moldova, 5 Dolphin Square, Edensor Road, W4 2ST.

SOLESBURY, William Booth; researcher and writer, since 2010; Senior Visiting Research Fellow, King's College London, since 2005; *b* 10 April 1940; *s* of William and Hannah Solesbury; *m* 1966, Felicity Andrew; one *s* two *d. Educ:* Hertford Grammar Sch.; Univ. of Cambridge (BA Hons Geography); Univ. of Liverpool (MCD Town Planning). London County Council, 1961–65; London Borough of Camden, 1965–66; City of Munich, 1966–67; Min. of Housing, 1967–72; NATO Res. Fellow, Univ. of California, Berkeley, 1973; Dept of Environment, 1974–89; Gwilym Gibbon Res. Fellow, Nuffield Coll., Oxford,

1989–90; Sec., ESRC, 1990–95; res. mgt consultant, 1995–2010. Sen. Vis. Res. Fellow, Queen Mary, Univ. of London, 2005–. *Publications:* Policy in Urban Planning, 1974; World Cities, City Worlds, 2013; articles in Public Administration, Policy and Politics, Public Money and Management, Research Fortnight. *Recreations:* home life, films, reading, travel. *Address:* 1 Dolby Road, SW6 3NE. *T:* (020) 7736 2155.

SOLESBY, Tessa Audrey Hilda, CMG 1986; HM Diplomatic Service, retired; Leader, UK Delegation to Conference on Disarmament, Geneva (with personal rank of Ambassador), 1987–92; *b* 5 April 1932; *d* of Charles Solesby and Hilda Solesby (*née* Willis). *Educ:* Clifton High School; St Hugh's College, Oxford. MA; Hon. Fellow, 1988. Min. of Labour and Nat. Service, 1954–55; joined Diplomatic Service, 1956; FO, 1956; Manila, 1957–59; Lisbon, 1959–62; FO, 1962–64; First Sec., UK Mission to UN, Geneva, 1964–68; FO, 1968–70; First Sec., UK Mission to UN, NY, 1970–72; FCO, 1972–75, Counsellor, 1975; on secondment to NATO Internat. Staff, Brussels, 1975–78; Counsellor, East Berlin, 1978–81; temp. Minister, UK Mission to UN, NY, 1981–82; Head of Central African Dept, FCO, 1982–86; Minister, Pretoria, 1986–87. *Recreations:* hill-walking, music. *Address:* c/o Foreign and Commonwealth Office, SW1A 2AH.

SOLEY, Baron *cr* 2005 (Life Peer), of Hammersmith in the London Borough of Hammersmith and Fulham; **Clive Stafford Soley;** Campaign Director, Future Heathrow, 2005–11; *b* 7 May 1939. *Educ:* Downshall Sec. Modern School; Newbattle Abbey Coll.; Strathclyde Univ. (BA Hons); Southampton Univ. (Dip. in Applied Social Studies). Various appointments; Probation Officer, 1970–75; Senior Probation Officer, 1975–79. Chairman: Alcohol Educn Centre, 1977–83; Mary Seacole Meml Statue Appeal, 2003–; Arab-Jewish Forum, 2003–. MP (Lab): Hammersmith N, 1979–83; Hammersmith, 1983–97; Ealing, Acton and Shepherd's Bush, 1997–2005. Opposition front bench spokesman on N Ireland, 1981–84, on Home Affairs, 1984–87, on Housing, 1987–92. Chairman: Select Cttee on NI, 1995–97; All Party Parly Gp on Parenting, 1994–96; Intergovtl Orgns Select Cttee, H of L, 2007–. Chm., PLP, 1997–2001; Mem., NEC, Lab. Pty, 1998–2001. *Publications:* (jtly) Regulating the Press, 2000. *Address:* House of Lords, SW1A 0PW.

SOLKIN, Prof. David Hersh, PhD; FBA 2012; Walter H. Annenberg Professor of the History of Art, since 2010, and Dean and Deputy Director, since 2007, Courtauld Institute of Art (Professor of the Social History of Art, 2002–10); *b* Montreal, 16 March 1951; *s* of Wolf William Solkin and Elaine Waddington (*née* Robinson); *m* 1st, 1979, Sally Marie Kolker (*d* 1999); one *s* one *d*; 2nd, 2010, Gillian Archer; one step *d*. *Educ:* Harvard Coll. (AB *magna cum laude* Fine Arts); Courtauld Inst. of Art (MA with Dist.); Yale Univ. (PhD Hist. of Art 1978). Asst Prof., Dept of Fine Arts, Univ. of BC, 1978–85; Courtauld Institute of Art: Lectr in Hist. of Art, 1986–93; Reader, 1993–2002; Dep. Dir, 1994–96. Paul Mellon Lectr, 2004–05. Guest Curator, Turner and the Masters exhibn, Tate Britain, London, Grand Palais, Paris and Museo del Prado, Madrid, 2009–10; Sen. Res. Fellow, Paul Mellon Centre, 2010–11. *Publications:* Richard Wilson: the landscape of reaction, 1982; Painting for Money: the visual arts and the public sphere in eighteenth-century England, 1993; (ed and jt author) Art on the Line: the Royal Academy exhibitions at Somerset House 1780–1836, 2001; Painting out of the Ordinary: modernity and the art of everyday life in early nineteenth-century Britain, 2008; (ed and jt author) Turner and the Masters, 2009. *Recreations:* collecting art, swimming, supporting Tottenham Hotspur. *Address:* Courtauld Institute of Art, Somerset House, Strand, WC2R 0RN. *T:* (020) 7848 2806, *Fax:* (020) 7848 2412. *E:* david.solkin@courtauld.ac.uk.

SOLLEY, Stephen Malcolm; QC 1989; a Recorder, since 1989; *b* 5 Nov. 1946; *s* of late Leslie Solley, sometime MP, and José Solley; *m* 1971, Helen Olivia Cox; four *s*. *Educ:* University College London (LLB 1968). Called to the Bar, Inner Temple, 1969, Bencher, 1998 (Master of the Cellar, 2000–). The Recorder, South Eastern Circuit, 1984–87. Chm., Bar Human Rights Cttee, 1999–2003. Trustee, Reprieve, 2008–. Dir, Hackney Empire Theatre, 1994–2013. *Recreations:* jazz, opera, wine, football. *Address:* Charter Chambers, 33 John Street, WC1N 2AT. *T:* (020) 7618 4400. *Club:* Les Six.

SOLLOWAY, Amanda Jane; MP (C) Derby North, since 2015; *b* 6 June 1961. *Educ:* Bramcote Hills Grammar Sch. Tennis player; Hd of Trng and Devlt, Baird Clothing, 1998–2009; mgt consultant, 2009–. Mem., Business, Innovation and Skills Select Cttee, 2015–. Chair, Cons. Friends of Internat. Devlt. Mem., Ockbrook and Borrowash Parish Council, 2011. FCIPD. *Publications:* (with A. Cartwright) Emotional Intelligence: activities for developing you and your business, 2009. *Address:* House of Commons, SW1A 0AA.

SOLOMON, Ashley Darren; musician; Professor, since 1994 and Head, Historical Performance, since 2006, Royal College of Music; Director, Florilegium, since 1991; *b* Hove, 15 March 1968; *s* of Henry Solomon and Meta Solomon; *m* 1998, Dr Sarah Tunkel; four *d*. *Educ:* Haberdashers' Aske's Sch. for Boys; Royal Acad. of Music (BMus; LRAM; ARAM). Dir, Arakaendar Bolivia Choir, 2005–. Hon. RCM 2000. *Recreations:* family, sport. *Address:* 21 Village Road, N3 1TL. *T:* (020) 8346 2896. *E:* asolomon@rcm.ac.uk, ashleysolomon@florilegium.org.uk.

SOLOMON, Prof. David Henry, AM 1990; PhD, DSc; FRS 2004; FAA, FRACI, FTSE, FIChemE; Professorial Fellow, Department of Chemical and Biomolecular Engineering, University of Melbourne, since 1996; *b* 19 Nov. 1929; *s* of H. J. Solomon and Mary Solomon; *m* 1954, Harriet Valerie Dawn Newport; three *d*. *Educ:* Sydney Technical Coll.; NSW Univ. of Technol. (BSc Hons 1952; MSc 1954; PhD 1959); Univ. of NSW (DSc 1968). ASTC; FRACI 1966; FTSE 1975; FIChemE 2007. Joined, 1946, Leader, 1955–63, Resin and Polymer Resin BALM Paints Ltd; Demonstrator and Teaching Fellow, Univ. of NSW, 1953–55; Commonwealth Scientific and Industrial Research Organization (Australia): Div. of Applied Mineralogy, 1963–70; Chief Res. Scientist, Div. of Applied Chemistry, 1970–74; Chief, Div. of Chemicals and Polymers, 1974–89; Dep. Dir, Inst. of Industrial Technol., 1989–90; Hd of Sch. and ICI Aust.–Masson Prof. of Chemistry, Sch. of Chemistry, Univ. of Melbourne, 1990–94. Pres., RACI, 1979–80. FAA 1975. Victoria Prize, Govt of Vic, Australia, 2006; (jtly) Australian Prime Minister's Sci. Prize, 2011. *Publications:* Chemistry of Organic Film Formers, 1967, 2nd edn 1977; (ed) Step-Growth Polymerizations: kinetics and mechanisms, 1972; The Catalytic Properties of Pigments, 1977; Chemistry of Pigments and Fillers, 1983; The Chemistry of Free Radical Polymerization, 1995. *Recreation:* fishing. *Address:* Department of Chemical and Biomolecular Engineering, University of Melbourne, Vic 3010, Australia. *T:* (3) 8344 8200, *Fax:* (3) 8344 4153. *E:* davids@unimelb.edu.au.

SOLOMON, David Joseph; Senior Partner, D. J. Freeman, solicitors, 1992–96; *b* 31 Dec. 1930; *s* of Sydney and Rosie Harriet Solomon; *m* 1959, Hazel Boam; one *s* two *d*. *Educ:* Torquay Grammar Sch.; Univ. of Manchester (LLB). Admitted as solicitor, 1955. Partner, Nabarro Nathanson, 1961–68; Head of Property Dept, 1976–90, Chief Exec., 1990–93, D. J. Freeman. Chm., Oriental Art Fund plc (formerly Carter Asian Arts PLC), 1996–2009. Trustee: Highgate Literary and Scientific Instn, 1999–2006 (Pres., 1993–98); Public Art Develt Trust, 1996–2002 (Chm., Public Art Develt Trust, 1998–2001). Mem. Council, Oriental Ceramic Soc., 1988–91, 1994–97, 1998–2001, 2003–06. *Recreations:* Chinese ceramics, music, poetry, architecture, art, wine, the championing of unjustly neglected writers. *Address:* Russell House, 9 South Grove, N6 6BS. *T:* (020) 8341 6454; 6 Rue de Cussy, Longecourt les Culetre, 21230 Arnay le Duc, France. *T:* 380900555. *Club:* Athenæum.

SOLOMON, Sir Harry, Kt 1991; Deputy Chairman, Portland Trust, since 2003; Director, Q Tec Analytics Ltd (formerly Monitor/Quest Ltd), since 2008; *b* 20 March 1937; *s* of Jacob and Belle Solomon; *m* 1962, Judith Diana Manuel; one *s* two *d*. *Educ:* St Albans School; Law Society School of Law. Qualified solicitor, 1960; in private practice, 1960–75; Hillsdown Holdings: Man. Dir, 1975–84; Jt Chm., 1984–87; Chm., 1987–93; Dir, 1993–97; Chm., Harvey Hldgs, 1994–2000; Director: West City (QEC) Ltd, 2003–06; Falkland Islands Hldgs plc, 1999–2009. Pres., Help Medicine, RCP, 1990–97. Trustee, Nat. Life Story Collection, 2005–14. Hon. FRCP 1992. *Recreations:* jogging, tennis, theatre, collector of historical autographed letters. *Address:* Hillsdown House, 32 Hampstead High Street, NW3 1QD.

SOLOMON, Kate Victoria; *see* Branigan, K. V.

SOLOMON, Nicola; Chief Executive (formerly General Secretary), Society of Authors, since 2011; *b* Pembury, 1 May 1960; *d* of Aaron Kenneth Solomon and Rosalie Ursula Solomon; *m* 1991, Rabbi Jonathan Wittenberg; one *s* two *d*. *Educ:* Paddock Wood County Primary Sch.; Tonbridge Grammar Sch. for Girls; Univ. of Warwick (LLB Hons 1981). Admitted solicitor, 1984; trainee solicitor, Taylor, Tyrell, Lewis and Craig, 1982–84; solicitor, Norton Rose, 1985; Stephen Innocent, later Finers Stephens Innocent: solicitor, 1985–88; Partner, 1988–2007; Hd, IP and Media Dept, 2002–07; Consultant, 2007–11. A Dep. District Judge, 1998–. Freeman, City of London, 2008; Freeman, Stationers' and Newspaper Makers' Co., 2008. *Publications:* (jtly) Personal Injury Litigation, 7th edn 1992 to 10th edn 2002; articles on IP law, publishing, fashion. *Recreations:* family, reading, gardening, people, laughter, nature. *Address:* Society of Authors, 84 Drayton Gardens, SW10 9SB. *T:* (020) 7373 6642. *E:* nsolomon@societyofauthors.org.

SOLOMON, Rabbi Dr Norman; Fellow, Oxford Centre for Hebrew and Jewish Studies, 1995–2000; Lecturer, Faculty of Theology, University of Oxford, 1995–2001; *b* Cardiff, 31 May 1933; *s* of late Phillip Solomon and Esther Solomon (*née* Lewis); *m* 1st, 1955, Devora, (Doris), Strauss (*d* 1998); three *s* one *d*; 2nd, 2000, Dr Hilary Nissenbaum. *Educ:* Cardiff High Sch.; St John's Coll., Cambridge (BA 1954); Univ. of Manchester (PhD 1966). London Univ. (BMus 1958); ARCM 1956. Rabbi: Whitefield Synagogue, Manchester, 1961–66; Greenbank Drive Synagogue, Liverpool, 1966–74; Hampstead Synagogue, 1974–83; Central Synagogue, Birmingham, 1994; Lectr in Judaism, 1983–89, Dir, Centre for Study of Judaism and Jewish/Christian Relations, 1989–94, Selly Oak Colls, Birmingham. Vis. Lectr, Oxford Centre for Postgraduate Hebrew Studies, 1985–94; Koerner Vis. Fellow, Oxford Centre for Hebrew and Jewish Studies, 1994–95; Scholar-in-Residence, Mandelbaum House, Univ. of Sydney, 2004. Mem., Commn on Religion and Belief in British Public Life, 2013–15. Editor, Jewish Christian Relations, 1985–91. Adviser, Internat. CCJ, 1988–; Specialist Adviser, CNAA, 1989–92. Vice-Pres., World Congress of Faiths, 1998– (Vice-Chm., 1992–98); President: Birmingham Inter-Faiths Council, 1984–85; British Assoc. for Jewish Studies, 1994; Soc. for Jewish Studies, 2006–. FBIS 1986. 15th Annual Sir Sigmund Sternberg Award, CCJ, 1993; Distinguished Service Medal, Univ. of San Francisco, 2001. *Publications:* Judaism and World Religion, 1991; The Analytic Movement, 1993; Judaism: a very short introduction, 1996; Historical Dictionary of the Jewish Religion, 1998; (ed) Abraham's Children, 2006; The Talmud: selections, 2009; Torah from Heaven, 2012; (ed) Ernest Bloch Studies, 2015; articles in learned jls. *Recreation:* playing chamber music. *Address:* Oxford Centre for Hebrew and Jewish Studies, Clarendon Institute, Walton Street, Oxford OX1 4QG. *T:* (01865) 377946. *W:* www.normansolomon.info.

SOLOMONS, Anthony Nathan, FCA; Chairman: Singer & Friedlander Ltd, 1976–99 (Chief Executive, 1973–90); Singer & Friedlander Group plc, 1987–99; *b* 26 Jan. 1930; *s* of Leslie Emanuel Solomons and Susie Schneiders; *m* 1957, Jean Golding; two *d*. Qual. as chartered accountant, 1953; FCA 1963. National Service, 1953–54: commnd Dorset Regt. Articled 1952; Accountant, Kennedy, Fox & Oldfield, 1955; Asst Accountant, then Chief Accountant, Lobitos Oilfields Ltd, 1955–58; Singer & Friedlander, 1958–99: successively Exec. Dir, Man. Dir, and Jt Chief Exec.

SOLOW, Prof. Robert Merton; Professor of Economics, Massachusetts Institute of Technology, 1949–95, now Emeritus; *b* 23 Aug. 1924; *s* of Milton H. Solow and Hannah Solow (*née* Sarney); *m* 1945, Barbara Lewis; two *s* one *d*. *Educ:* New York City schools; Harvard College (BA 1947); Harvard University (MA 1949, PhD 1951). Served US forces, 1942–45 (Bronze Star, 1944). Joined MIT Faculty as Asst Prof. of Statistics, 1949, Inst. Prof. of Economics, 1974–95. Senior Economist, Council of Economic Advisers, 1961–62. Eastman Prof. and Fellow of Balliol Coll., Oxford, 1968–69; Overseas Fellow, Churchill Coll., Cambridge, 1984, 1991; Robert K. Merton Foundn Fellow, Russell Sage Foundn, 2007–. President: Econometric Soc., 1965; Amer. Econ. Assoc., 1976; Member: Amer. Acad. of Arts and Scis, 1963; Nat. Acad. of Sciences, USA, 1972; Accademia dei Lincei, 1984; Corresp. Mem., British Acad., 1975; Mem., Amer. Philosophical Soc., 1974–. Hon. degrees: Chicago, 1967; Brown, 1972; Williams, 1974; Paris I, 1975; Warwick, 1976; Lehigh, 1977; Geneva, Wesleyan, 1982; Tulane, 1983; Yale, 1986; Bryant, 1987; Massachusetts at Boston, Boston Coll., 1989; Colgate, Dartmouth, Helsinki, 1990; New York at Albany, 1991; Harvard, Glasgow, Chile, 1992; Conservatoire Nat. des Arts et Métiers, Paris, 1995; Colorado Sch. of Mines, 1996; New York, 2000; Rensselaer Poly. Inst., 2003; New Sch. Univ., NY, 2006; Rochester, 2007; Iowa, 2008. Nobel Prize for Economics, 1987; Nat. Medal of Sci., USA, 1996. Order of Merit (Germany), 1995. *Publications:* Linear Programming and Economic Analysis (with P. Samuelson and R. Dorfman), 1958; Capital Theory and the Rate of Return, 1964; The Sources of Unemployment in the US, 1964; Growth Theory: an exposition, 1970, 2nd edn 1999; The Labor Market as a Social Institution, 1990; (with F. Hahn) A Critical Essay on Modern Macroeconomic Theory, 1995; Learning from Learning by Doing, 1996; (with J. Taylor) Inflation, Unemployment and Monetary Policy, 1998; Monopolistic Competition and Macroeconomic Theory, 1998; Work and Welfare, 1998; articles in learned jls. *Address:* 1010 Waltham Street, Apt 328, Lexington, MA 02421–8057, USA. *T:* (781) 5385412.

SOLTI, (Anne) Valerie, (Lady Solti); Chairman, Solti Foundation to assist young musicians, since 1998; President, Sadler's Wells Theatre, since 2002 (Trustee and Governor, since 1995); Hungarian Government Global Ambassador for Culture, since 2007; *b* Leeds, 19 Aug. 1937; *d* of William Pitts and Nancy Pitts; *m* 1st, 1960, James Sargant; 2nd, 1967, Sir Georg Solti, KBE; two *d*. *Educ:* Leeds Girls High Sch.; Royal Acad. of Dramatic Art (Licentiate). (As Valerie Pitts) TV and radio announcer, 1960–70, interviewer, 1960–67, BBC; freelance writer and broadcaster, 1967–97; programmes include: Face the Music, 1971–81, Town and Around, South at Six, BBC; North East Roundabout, Tyne Tees TV; for children: Playschool, BBC, 1967–70; Extraordinary, Gammon and Spinach, Yorkshire TV, 1978–81; contrib. to radio progs in UK and US. Appeared in play, Roseland's Variation on a Theme, W End, 1958–59. Dir, 1998, Trustee, 1999–, Chm., 1999–2006, Mariinsky Th. Trust; Chm., Devlt Campaign for rebuilding Sadler's Wells Th., 1990–98. Mem., BBC Adv. Bd (SE), 1975–80. Adviser: Hungarian Cultural Centre; Liszt Acad., Budapest. Jt Pres., Jewish Music Inst., 2000. Trustee: Hampstead Old People's Housing Trust, 1975–83; LPO, 1980–86 (Chm., Friends); Voice of the Listener; Eur. Orgn for Res. Treatment of Cancer. Hon. Trustee, Chicago SO, 1997–. Gov., Brit Sch. for Performing Arts and Technol., 1997–2006. Patron: Longborough Fest. Opera, 2007. Patron, Frankfurt Internat. Conducting Comp., 2000–; Geneva Internat. Comp.; Jeunesse Musicale Suisse; Mem. Jury, Whittaker Prize for Trios. Comdr, Hungarian Cross with Star, 2002; Pro Cultura Hungarica, 2006; Hungarian Order of Merit, 2012. *Recreations:* swimming, sailing, walking, travelling by steam train, music and theatre. *Address:* c/o Solti Foundation, PO Box 67, 1410 Waterloo, Belgium. *E:* Soltioffice51@googlemail.com. *Club:* Athenæum.

See also G. T. Solti-Dupas.

SOLTI-DUPAS, Gabrielle Teresa; Head, Junior School, South Hampstead High School, since 2013; *b* London, 25 April 1970; *d* of Sir Georg Solti, KBE and Anne Valerie Solti, *qv*; *m* 1998, Frederic Dupas; one *s* one *d*. *Educ:* Francis Holland Sch.; King's Sch., Canterbury; Jesus Coll., Oxford (BA Hons Mod. Hist. 1991); Inst. of Educn, London (PGCE 1997). Intern, EC, 1991–92; Mktg Exec., Nestlé, 1992–94; Teacher, Trevor Roberts Prep. Sch., 1994–96; Teacher, then Dep. Headteacher, Primrose Hill Prim. Sch., 1997–2003; Head, Jun. Sch., Notting Hill and Ealing High Sch., 2003–13. Trustee, Solti Foundn for Young Musicians, 1999–. *Recreations:* classical music, travel, playing with my son, cooking and eating. *Address:* Junior School, South Hampstead High School, 5 Netherhall Gardens, NW3 5RN.

SOLYMAR, Prof. Laszlo, FRS 1995; PhD; Senior Research Fellow, Department of Electrical and Electronic Engineering, Imperial College London, since 2004; Professor of Applied Electromagnetism, University of Oxford, 1992–97, now Emeritus Professor; Professorial Fellow of Hertford College, Oxford, 1986–97, now Emeritus Fellow; *b* 24 Jan. 1930; *s* of Pál and Aranka Solymar; *m* 1955, Marianne Klopfer; two *d*. *Educ:* Technical University, Budapest (Hungarian equivalents of BSc and PhD in Engineering). Lectr, Technical Univ., Budapest, 1952–53; Research Engineer, Res. Inst. for Telecommunications, Budapest, 1953–56; Res. Engineer, Standard Telecom Labs, Harlow, 1956–65; Fellow in Engineering, Brasenose Coll., Oxford, 1966–86 (Emeritus Fellow, 2011); Lectr, 1971–86, Donald Pollock Reader in Engrg Sci., 1986–92, Univ. of Oxford. Visiting Professor: Ecole Normale Supérieure, Paris, 1965–66; Tech. Univ. of Denmark, 1972–73; Univ. Osnabrück, 1987; Tech. Univ., Berlin, 1990; Univ. Autónoma, Madrid, 1993, 1995; Tech. Univ., Budapest, 1994; ICSTM, 2000–. Consultant: Tech. Univ. of Denmark, 1973–76; Thomson-CSF, Orsay, 1984; British Telecom, 1986–88; GEC Wembley, 1986–88; Pilkington Technol. Centre, 1989–90. Faraday Medal, IEE, 1992. Anaxagoras, Archimedes, Hypatia (radio plays with John Wain), 1991. *Publications:* Lectures on the Electrical Properties of Materials (with D. Walsh), 1970, 9th edn 2014; Superconductive Tunnelling and Applications, 1972; (ed) A Review of the Principles of Electrical and Electronic Engineering, 1974; Lectures on Electromagnetic Theory, 1976, 2nd edn 1984; (with D. J. Cooke) Volume Holography and Volume Gratings, 1981; Lectures on Fourier Series, 1988; (jtly) The Physics and Applications of Photorefractive Materials, 1996; Getting the Message: a history of communications, 1999; (with E. Shamonina) Waves in Metamaterials, 2008; The Rhineland War: 1936, 2012; The Portrait of a Genius, 2013; (with J. Wain) Three Scientists of the Ancient World, 2013; Anatomy of Assassinations, 2013; Past, Present and Future, 2014; articles. *Recreations:* history, languages, chess, swimming. *Address:* Department of Electrical and Electronic Engineering, Imperial College London, Exhibition Road, SW7 2AZ. *T:* (020) 7594 6301.

SÓLYOM, László; Professor, Faculty of Law, Péter Pázmány Catholic University, Budapest, 1995–2012; President, Republic of Hungary, 2005–10; *b* Pécs, 3 Jan. 1942; *m* Erzsébet Nagy; one *s* one *d*. *Educ:* Univ. of Pécs (grad 1965); Univ. of Jena (Dr 1969); Dr Pol and Legal Scis, Hungarian Acad. Scis, 1981. Asst Lectr, Inst. Civil Law, Friedrich Schiller Univ. of Jena, 1966–69; Fellow, Inst. Political and Legal Scis, Hungarian Acad. Scis, 1969–78; Librarian, Liby of Parlt, 1975; Associate Prof., 1978–83, Prof., 1983–98, Dept of Civil Law, Eötvös Loránd Univ., Budapest. Justice, 1989, Dep. Pres., 1990, Pres., three times, 1990–98, Constitutional Court, Hungary. Vis. Prof., Univ. of Cologne, 1999–2000. Mem., Hungarian Acad. Scis, 2013 (Corresp. Mem., 2001). Hon. Dr: Cologne, 1999; Johann Wolfgang Goethe, 2006; Yonsei, 2009. Humboldt Prize to foreign social scientists, 1998. *Publications:* A polgári jogi felelősség hanyatlása (The Decline of Civil Law Liability), 1977, 1980; Környezetvédelem és polgári jog (Environmental Protection and Civil Law), 1980; A személyiségi jogok elmélete (The Theory of Personality Rights), 1983; Die Persönlichkeitsrechte, 1984; (ed with M. Szabó) A Zöld Hullám: Olvasókönyv a környezetvédelmi társadalmi mozgalmakról (The Green Wave: a reader on environmental social movements), 1988; (with Georg Brunner) Versassungsgerichtsbarkeit in Ungarn, 1995; (with Georg Brunner) Constitutional Judiciary in a New Democracy: the Hungarian Constitutional Court, 2000; Az alkotmánybíráskodás kezdetei Magyarországon (The Beginnings of Constitutional Jurisdiction in Hungary), 2001; Pártok és érdekszervezetek az Alkotmányban (Parties and Interest Organisations in the Constitution), 2004; Egy elnökség lenyomata (Imprints of a Presidency), 2010. *Address:* Kelenhegyi ut 32, 1118 Budapest, Hungary.

SOMARE, Rt Hon. Sir Michael (Thomas), GCMG 1990; CH 1978; PC 1977; MP; Prime Minister of Papua New Guinea, 1975–80, 1982–85 and 2002–11; *b* 9 April 1936; *m* 1965, Veronica Bula Kaiap; three *s* two *d*. *Educ:* Sogeri Secondary Sch. Admin. Coll. Teaching, 1956–62; Asst Area Educn Officer, Madang, 1962–63; Broadcasts Officer, Dept of Information and Extension Services, Wewack, 1963–66; Journalism, 1966–68. Member for E Sepik Region (Nat. Parlt), PNG House of Assembly, 1968–; Parly Leader, Pangu Pati, 1968–93; First Chief Minister, 1972–75; first Prime Minister, 1975; Leader of Opposition in House of Assembly, 1980–82; Minister for Foreign Affairs, 1988–94; National Alliance Leader. Gov., E Sepik Province, PNG, 1995–2002. Dep. Chm., Exec. Council, 1972–73, Chm., 1973–75. Mem., Second Select Cttee on Constitutional Develt, 1968–72; Mem. Adv. Cttee, Australian Broadcasting Commission. *Publications:* Sana: an autobiography. *Recreations:* golf, fishing, reading. *Address:* Karan, Murik Lakes, East Sepik, Papua New Guinea.

SOMAVIA, Juan O.; Special Adviser on Inter-regional Policy Cooperation, United Nations, since 2013; *m*; two *c*. *Educ:* Catholic Univ. of Chile; Univ. of Paris. Joined Min. of Foreign Relations, Chile; Mem. Bd of Dirs and Vice Pres. for Latin America, Inter-Press Service, 1976–87; Sec. Gen., S American Peace Commn, 1987; Perm. Rep. of Chile to UN, NY, 1990–99; Dir Gen., Internat. Labour Orgn, 1999–2012; former consultant to GATT and UNDP. Founder and Dir, Latin American Inst. for Transnational Studies. Dr *hc* Univ. Central, Chile, 2012. Leonidas Proaño Prize, Latin American Human Rights Assoc. *Address:* c/o Economic Commission for Latin America and the Caribbean, Casilla 179–D, Santiago 7630412, Chile.

SOMERLEYTON, 4th Baron *cr* 1916; **Hugh Francis Savile Crossley;** Bt 1863; *b* Norwich, 27 Sept. 1971; *s* of 3rd Baron Somerleyton, GCVO, and of Belinda Maris, OBE (*née* Loyd); *S* father, 2012; *m* 2009, Lara Kate Bailey; one *s* two *d*. *Educ:* Eton; Anglia Polytechnic Univ. (BA Hist. 1st cl.). Entrepreneur: developed Dish Dash Middle-Eastern restaurant chain, 2000–04, Hot Chip kiosks chain, 2012. Estate manager, Somerleyton Estate, 2005– (Duke's Head pub, 2005–; Fritton Hse Hotel, 2006–). Chm., Waveney Tourism, 2008–11. *Recreations:* Middle East and Islam, tennis, running, forestry, history. *Heir: s* Hon. John de Bathe Savile Turner Crossley, *b* 9 Feb. 2010. *Address:* Somerleyton Hall, Lovingland, Suffolk NR32 5QQ. *T:* (01502) 734901. *Club:* Soho House.

SOMERS, 9th Baron *cr* 1784; **Philip Sebastian Somers Cocks;** Bt 1772; *b* 4 Jan. 1948; *o s* of John Sebastian Somers Cocks, CVO, CBE (*d* 1964), and late Marjorie Olive (*née* Weller); *S* cousin, 1995. *Educ:* abroad; Elston Hall, Newark; Craig-y-Parc, Cardiff. *Recreations:* opera, music generally, foreign travel. *Heir: cousin* Alan Bromley Cocks [*b* 28 May 1930; *m* 1955, Pamela Fay, *d* of A. H. Gourlay, Christchurch, NZ; three *d* (one *s* decd)].

See also Hon. A. G. Somers Cocks.

SOMERS, Shaw Stefano, MD; FRCS; Specialist Upper Gastrointestinal and Bariatric Surgeon; Consultant Surgeon: Portsmouth Hospitals NHS Trust, since 1998; The London Clinic, since 2007; Director, Streamline Surgical Group, since 2008; *b* London, 7 Aug. 1962; *s* of Derek and Edelweiss Somers; *m* 1991, Joanne Ward; two *s*. *Educ:* Latymer Sch., Edmonton; Univ. of Leeds (BSc Hons Pathol. 1983; MB ChB Medicine 1986; MD Surgery 1992). FRCS 1992. Lectr in Surgery, Univ. of Leeds, 1994–95; Associate Prof. of Surgery, Prince of Wales Hosp., Hong Kong, 1995–97; Sen. Lectr in Surgery, Univ. of Leeds, 1997–98. Presenter, TV series: Fat Doctor, 2006–; Food Hospital, 2011–12. *Recreations:* off-road cycling, ski-ing, travel, wild mushrooms, Italian wine, collecting fountain pens. *Address:* The Sudbury Clinic, Harrow, Middx HA1 3RX; Department of Upper Gastrointestinal Surgery, Portsmouth Hospitals NHS Trust, Portsmouth PO6 3LY. *T:* 0845 643 1400. *E:* info@shawsomers.com.

SOMERS COCKS, Hon. Anna Gwenllian, (Hon. Mrs Allemandi), OBE 2011; FSA; Group Editorial Director, Giornale dell' Arte and The Art Newspaper, since 2003; Chief Executive Officer, Umberto Allemandi and Co. Publishing Ltd, since 2012; *b* 18 April 1950; *d* of late John Sebastian Somers Cocks, CVO, CBE and Marjorie Olive Weller; *m* 1st, 1971, Martin Walker (marr. diss.); 2nd, 1978, John Hardy (marr. diss.); one *s* one *d*; 3rd, 1991, Umberto Allemandi. *Educ:* abroad; Convent of the Sacred Heart, Woldingham; St Anne's College, Oxford (MA); Courtauld Inst., Univ. of London (MA). Asst Keeper, Dept of Metalwork, 1973–85, Dept of Ceramics, 1985–87, Victoria and Albert Museum; Editor: Apollo Magazine, 1987–90; The Art Newspaper, 1990–94, 1996–2003. Chm., Umberto Allemandi Publishing, 1995–96. Member: Mus., New Buildings and Refurbishment Panel, Heritage Lottery Fund, 1996–97; Adv. Council, Sotheby's Inst. of Art, 2002–; Trustee: Gilbert Collection, 1998–; Cass Sculpture Foundn, 2004–13. Gov., Courtauld Inst., 2010–. Chm., Venice in Peril, 1999–2012. Mem., Ateneo Veneto, 2007. Annual Prize, Nat. Art Collections Fund, 1992; European Women of Achievement Award (Arts and Media), 2006; Advocate Award, Internat. Inst. of Conservation, 2011; Istituto Veneto Prize for journalism about Venice, 2013. Commendatore, Ordine della Stella della Solidarietà Italiana (Italy), 2004. *Publications:* The Victoria and Albert Museum: the making of the collection, 1980; (ed and jt author) Princely Magnificence: court jewels of the Renaissance, 1980; (with C. Truman) Renaissance Jewels, Gold Boxes and Objets de Vertu in the Thyssen Collection, 1985; journalism in The Daily Telegraph etc, articles in magazines, incl. NY Rev. of Books. *Recreations:* learning Arabic, travelling in the Middle and Far East. *Address:* via Giulio 6, Turin 10122, Italy.

See also Baron Somers.

SOMERSET, family name of **Duke of Beaufort** and **Baron Raglan**.

SOMERSET, 19th Duke of, *cr* 1547; **John Michael Edward Seymour;** DL; FRICS; Baron Seymour 1547; Bt 1611; *b* 30 Dec. 1952; *s* of 18th Duke of Somerset and Gwendoline Collette (Jane) (*d* 2005), 2nd *d* of Major J. C. C. Thomas; *S* father, 1984; *m* 1978, Judith-Rose, *d* of J. F. C. Hull, *qv*; two *s* two *d*. *Educ:* Eton. Elected Mem., H of L, 2014. DL: Wilts, 1993, Devon, 2003. *Heir: s* Lord Seymour, *qv*. *Address:* Berry Pomeroy, Totnes, Devon TQ9 6NJ.

SOMERTON, Viscount; James Shaun Christian Welbore Ellis Agar; *b* 7 Sept. 1982; *s* and *heir* of 6th Earl of Normanton, *qv*; *m* 2012, Lady Lucy Caroline Alexander, *yr d* of Earl Alexander of Tunis, *qv*; one *d*. *Educ:* Harrow Sch.; Santa Clara Univ., Calif; RAC Cirencester. *Address:* Somerley, Ringwood, Hants BH24 3PL.

SOMERVILLE, Prof. Christopher Roland, PhD; FRS 1991; Director, Energy Biosciences Institute, and Professor of Plant and Microbial Biology, University of California, Berkeley, since 2007; *b* 11 Oct. 1947; *s* of Hubert Roland Somerville and Teresa Marie (*née* Bond); *m* 1976, Shauna Christine Phimester. *Educ:* Univ. of Alberta, Canada (PhD, BS). Asst Prof. of Genetics, Univ. of Alberta, Canada, 1980–82; Associate Prof. of Botany and Genetics, Michigan State Univ., Mich, 1982–86; Prof. of Botany and Genetics, Michigan State Univ., 1982–93; Dir, Carnegie Instn for Science and Prof. of Biology, Stanford Univ., 1994–2007. (Jtly) Balzan Prize in Plant Molecular Genetics, Internat. Balzan Foundn, Italy, 2006. *Publications:* numerous research articles on genetics, physiology and biochemistry of plants. *Recreation:* sailing. *Address:* Energy Biosciences Institute, Melvin Calvin Laboratory MC5230, Berkeley, CA 94720–5230, USA.

SOMERVILLE, Sir James Lockett Charles A.; *see* Agnew-Somerville.

SOMERVILLE, Prof. Jane, MD; FRCP; Consultant Cardiologist, Grown-Up Congenital Heart Disease Clinic: Middlesex Hospital, University College London, 1997–2003; Mater Die Hospital, Malta, since 2006; Emeritus Professor of Cardiology, Imperial College School of Medicine, 1999; *b* 24 Jan. 1933; *d* of Joseph Bertram Platnauer and Pearl Ashton; *m* 1957, Dr Walter Somerville, CBE, FRCP (*d* 2005); three *s* one *d*. *Educ:* Queen's Coll., London; Guy's Hosp., London Univ. MB, BS (Treasurer's Gold Medal for Clin. Surg.) 1955; MD 1966. MRCS 1955; FRCP 1973 (LRCP 1955, MRCP 1957). FACC 1972. Med. Registrar, Guy's Hosp., 1956–58; Registrar, Nat. Heart Hosp., 1958–59; First Asst to Dr Paul Wood, 1959–63, Sen. Lectr 1964–74, Inst. of Cardiol.; Hon. Cons. Phys., Nat. Heart Hosp., 1967–74, Hosp. for Sick Children, Gt Ormond St, 1968–88; Consultant Physician: Nat. Heart Hosp., then Royal Brompton & Nat. Heart Hosp., 1974–99; Cardiac Dept, Grown-Up Congenital Heart Disease Clinic, St Bartholomew's Hosp., 1988–92. Lectr in Cardiovascular Disease, Turin Univ., 1973. Vis. Prof. and Guest Lectr, Europe, ME, USA, Mexico, S America, USSR, China; Lectures: St Cyres, Imperial Coll., London, 1976; 6th Mahboubian, NY, 1981; World Congress Gold Medal, Bombay, 1982; Edgar Mannheimer, Hamburg, 1987; John Keith, Montreal, 1988; Tudor Edwards, RCP, 1991; Paul Wood, British Cardiac Soc., 1995; McCue, Washington, 1997; Henry Neufeld, Israel, 1999; Dan G. McNamara, American Coll. of Cardiol., Chicago, 2012. Chm., Staff Cttee, 1988–89, Jt Adv. Cttee, 1989–90, Nat. Heart Hosp.; Chm., Cardiol. Cttee, Royal Brompton & Nat. Heart Hosp., 1990–99. Sci. Sec., World Congress, Paed. Cardiol., 1980; Advr on congenital heart disease, Sec. of State's Hon. Med. Adv. Panel on driving and disorders of cardiovascular system, 1986–96; Advr to Florence, Trieste and Baltic States on setting up Grown-up Congenital Heart Disease Services. Founder, 1993, Pres., 2004–, Grown-Up Congenital Heart Patient Assoc. (Chm., 1993–2003); Member: Assoc. Eur. Pæd. Cardiol.; British Cardiac Soc. (Mem., Paediatric Cardiol. Services Sub-cttee, 1987–; Chm., Wkg Pty on Grown-up Congenital Heart Disease, 2002); RSocMed; Harveian Soc.; 300 Gp; Sci. Council, Monaco Cardiothoracic Centre. Hon. Member: Argentine Pæd. Soc.; Chilean Cardiac Soc.; Argentine Soc. of Cardiol.; Brazilian Cardiac Soc.; Argentine Cardiac Soc.; French Cardiac Soc.; Italian Cardiac Soc.; Spanish Cardiac Soc. Founding Fellow, Eur. Soc. of Cardiol. Member: Council, Stonham Housing Assoc.; Governing Council, Beaconhouse Educn Gp, 2009–. Gov., Nat. Heart and Chest Hosps, 1977–82, 1988–90; Chm. Council, Queen's Coll., London, 2000–07. Woman of the Year, 1968. Gold Medal, Eur. Soc. of Cardiol., 2008; Dist. Service Award, Amer. Coll. of Cardiol., 2009. *Publications:* numerous contribs to med. lit. on heart disease in children, adolescents and adults, congenital heart disease and results of cardiac surgery; chapters in Paul Wood's Diseases of Heart and Circulation (3rd edn), Oxford Textbook of Medicine, and Perspectives in Pediatric Cardiology, Vols I and II. *Recreations:* collecting, roof gardening, travel, opera, 7 grandchildren. *Address:* 30 York House, 39 Upper Montagu Street, W1H 1FR. *T:* (020) 7262 2144, *Fax:* (020) 7724 2238; 81 Harley Street, W1G 8PP.

SOMERVILLE, Brig. Sir (John) Nicholas, Kt 1985; CBE 1975; self-employed consultant, personnel selection, 1984–2003; *b* 16 Jan. 1924; *s* of Brig. Desmond Henry Sykes Somerville and Moira Burke Somerville; *m* 1951, Jenifer Dorothea Nash; one *s* two *d*. *Educ:* Winchester College. Commissioned, The South Wales Borderers, 24th Regt, 1943; served: France and Germany, D-day—VE day, 1944–45 (despatches 1945); BAOR, War Office, FARELF, Aden, 1967–68 (despatches 1968); Directing Staff, JSSC, 1967–69; Comdt, Junior Div., Staff Coll., 1969–72; Dir of Army Recruiting, 1973–75; retired, 1978. Managing Director, Saladin Security Ltd, 1981–84; voluntary consultant responsible for designing Cons. Party Parly selection board procedure, 1980–92. *Recreations:* sailing, gardening, house designing. *Address:* Deptford Cottage, Deptford Lane, Greywell, Hook, Hants RG29 1BS. *T:* (01256) 702796.

SOMERVILLE, Julia Mary Fownes, OBE 2013; broadcaster and journalist; *b* 14 July 1947; *d* of late John Arthur Fownes Somerville, CB, CBE, and of Julia Elizabeth (*née* Payne); *m* 1st, 1970, Stephen Band (marr. diss. 1975); 2nd, 1984, Ray Gowdridge (separated, 1992); one *s* one *d*; partner, Sir Jeremy Dixon, *qv*. *Educ:* Headington Sch., Oxford; Sussex Univ. (BA Hons English 1969). IPC Magazines, 1969–70; ed., company newspaper, ITT Creed, 1970–72; BBC Radio News: journalist, 1972–79; news reporter, 1979–81; labour/industrial correspondent, 1981–84; Newscaster: Nine o'clock News, BBC TV, 1984–87; ITN, 1987–2001; presenter, Rip Off Britain, BBC TV, 2011–. Mem., Marshall Aid Commn, 1998–2000. Chm., Adv. Cttee, Govt Art Collection, 2003–13. Supporter, Advance Housing & Support Ltd, 1995–; Patron: British Brain and Spine Foundn, 1993; Children of Chernobyl Fund, 1993; Friends United Network, 1993; Samantha Dickson Res. Trust, 1997; Barnet Cancer Care, 1998; Vice Patron, Apex Trust, 1995; Companion, Headway. *Recreations:* music, reading, wining, dining, walking. *Club:* Peg's.

SOMERVILLE, Sir Lockett; *see* Agnew-Somerville.

SOMERVILLE, Brig. Sir Nicholas; *see* Somerville, Sir J. N.

SOMERVILLE, Shirley-Anne; Campaign Strategist, Scottish National Party, since 2012; *b* 2 Sept. 1974. *Educ:* Kirkcaldy High Sch.; Univ. of Strathclyde (BA Hons Econs and Pol. 1996); Univ. of Stirling (Dip. Housing Studies 1999); Queen Margaret Univ. Coll. (Dip. Public Relns). Policy and Public Affairs Officer, Chartered Inst. of Housing, 2001–04; Media and Campaigns Officer, Royal Coll. of Nursing, 2004–07; public affairs consultant, 2011. MSP (SNP) Lothians, Sept. 2007–2011; contested (SNP) Edinburgh Northern and Leith, Scottish Parlt, 2011. Trustee, Shelter UK, 2011–. *Recreations:* hill-walking, golf.

SOMMARUGA, Cornelio; Chairman, Foundation for the Future, Amman, 2008–11, now Honorary Chairman; *b* 29 Dec. 1932; *s* of Carlo Sommaruga and Anna-Maria Valagussa; *m* 1957, Ornella Marzorati; two *s* four *d*. *Educ:* schs in Rome and Lugano; Univs of Zürich (LLD 1957), Paris and Rome. Bank trainee, Zürich, 1957–59; joined Swiss Diplomatic Service, 1960: Attaché, Swiss Embassy, The Hague, 1961; Sec., Bonn, 1962–64; Rome, 1965–68; Dep. Hd of Delegn to EFTA, GATT, UNCTAD and ECE/UN, Geneva, 1969–73; Dep. Sec. Gen., EFTA, 1973–75; Minister plenipotentiary, Div. of Commerce, Fed. Dept of Public Economy, Berne, 1976; Amb., 1977; Delegate, Fed. Council for Trade Agreements, 1980–83; State Sec. for External Econ. Affairs, 1984–86. President: Internat. Cttee of the Red Cross, 1987–99 (Hon. Mem., 2000); Initiatives of Change Internat. (formerly Moral Rearmament) Assoc., 2002–06, now Hon.; Chm., Geneva Internat. Centre for Humanitarian De-mining, 2000–08, now Hon. Chm; Chm., Internat. Cancer Foundn, Geneva, 2006–09. Member: Panel on UN Peace Operations, 2000; Internat. Commn on Intervention and State Sovereignty, 2001. Hon. Dr: (Political Affairs) Fribourg, 1985; (Internat. Relns) Minho, Braga, 1990; (Medicine) Bologna, 1991; (Internat. Law) Nice-Sophia Antipolis, 1992; (Law) Seoul Nat. Univ., 1992; (Law) Geneva, 1997; (Internat. Relns) Webster Univ., 1998; (Law) Insubria, Como, 2008. Presidential Award, Tel Aviv Univ., 1995; Dr Jean Mayer Global Citizens Award, Tufts Univ., 2003; Presidential Award, Peace Univ., 2009. *Publications:* La posizione costituzionale del Capo dello Stato nelle Costituzioni francese ed italiana del dopoguerra, 1957; numerous articles in jls and periodicals; *relevant publication:* Cornelio Sommaruga: diplomatie im Dienste der Menschlichkeit, by Jürg Bischoff, 2004. *Address:* 16 chemin des Crêts-de-Champel, 1206 Geneva, Switzerland. *T:* (22) 3474552. *E:* cornelio.sommaruga@bluewin.ch.

SOMMER, Peter Michael; Managing Director, Virtual City Associates, since 1981; expert witness and author, since 1985; *b* 21 April 1943; *s* of Fritz and Beate Sommer. *Educ:* King Edward VI Five Ways Sch., Birmingham; St Catherine's Coll., Oxford (BA 1965, MA Hons Juris. 1967). Editor: Harrap Books, 1966–73; Paladin Books, 1973–77; Dep. Editl Dir, Granada Paperbacks, 1977–81; Tech. Dir, Data Integrity, 1987–98; Sen. Res. Fellow, Inf. Systems and Innovation (formerly Inf. Systems Integrity) Gp, Dept of Mgt (formerly Inf. Systems Dept), LSE, 1994–2008; Vis. Prof., Inf. Systems and Innovation Gp, Dept of Mgt, LSE, 2008–11. Specialist Advr, H of C Trade and Industry Select Cttee, 1998–2001. Vis. Sen. Res. Fellow, Faculty of Maths, Computing and Technology (formerly Maths and Computing), 2006–08, Vis. Reader, 2008–13, Open Univ.; Vis. Prof., De Montfort Univ., 2011–. Jt Lead Assessor, Computing, Council for Registration of Forensic Practitioners, 2005–09. Ext. Examr, Defence Acad. of UK (Cranfield Univ.), 2002–06. Member: Adv. Council, Foundn for Information Policy Res., 2001–; Scientific Adv. Panel for Emergency Response, 2003–09; Digital Evidence Specialist Gp, Forensic Sci. Regulator, 2008–; Digital Forensics Adv. Cttee for Standards, Nederlands Register Gerechtelijk Desindien, 2014–. Self-employed expert in digital forensics: major instructions include: Rome Labs hack, 1997; Wonderland Club of internet paedophiles (Op. Cathedral), 2001; DrinkorDie software piracy conspiracy (Op. Blossom), 2005; State of SA *v* Zuma and Thales, 2005–09; Op. Crevice terrorism, 2006–07; Sorrell *v* FullSix defamation, 2007; PharmaCare Labs Pty *v* Commonwealth of Australia, 2010; Operation Alpine (Child Exploitation and Online Protection Centre), 2010–11; Special Tribunal on Lebanon, 2011–13; Al-Sweady Public Inquiry, 2012–14; Internat. Criminal Court (Uhuru Kenyatta), 2012–14; R *v* Moazzem Begg, 2014–15. FBCS 2014. FRSA 2013. *Publications:* Guide to Electronic Publishing, 1982; The PC Security Guide, 1993, 2nd edn 1994; (contrib.) Fraud: law, procedure and practice, 2004; Digital Evidence: a guide for directors and corporate advisors, 2005, 2nd edn 2009; Digital Evidence, Digital Investigations and E-Disclosure, 2005, 4th edn 2013; (jtly) Reducing Systematic Cybersecurity Risk, 2011; *as Hugo Cornwall:* The Hacker's Handbook, 1985; Data Theft, 1987; The Industrial Espionage Handbook, 1991; articles in learned jls incl. Criminal Law Rev., Telecommunications Law Rev., IEEE Security and Privacy. *Recreations:* reading, book collecting, gardening, jazz, amateur radio, the ethical abuse of technology. *Address:* PO Box 6447, N4 4RX. *E:* peter@pmsommer.com.

SOMMERLAD, Brian Clive, FRCS, FRCPCH; Consultant Plastic Surgeon: St Andrew's Centre, Broomfield Hospital, Chelmsford (formerly St Andrew's Hospital, Billericay), 1978–2010, now Hon. Consultant; The London Hospital, 1978–2010; Great Ormond Street Hospital for Children, 1995–2010, now Hon. Consultant; Ospedale Pediatrico Bambino Gesu, Rome; *b* 1 Feb. 1942; *s* of Verdun and Winsome Sommerlad; *m* 1971, Gwyneth Watkins; four *s* one *d*. *Educ:* Newington Coll., Sydney; Sydney Univ. (MB BS 1966). FRCS 1971. Jun. and Sen. MO, Sydney Hosp., 1966–67; Surgical Registrar, UCH, 1969–73; Surgeon, Australian Surgical Team, Bien Hoa, Vietnam, 1971; Sen. Registrar in Plastic Surgery, London, Billericay and Glasgow, 1974–78. Hunterian Prof., RCS, 1999. President: Plastic Surgery Section, RSocMed, 1985–86; Craniofacial Soc. of GB, 1997–98; British Assoc. of Plastic Surgeons, 1998. Hon. FRCSLT 1998; Hon. FRCSE 2001. Active Service Medal (Australia), 1994; Vietnam Logistic and Support Medal (Australia), 1994. *Publications:* co-editor: Recent Advances in Plastic Surgery 3, 1985; Recent Advances in Plastic Surgery 4, 1992; Recent Advances in Plastic Surgery 5, 1996; book chapters; contrib. papers to several jls on many subjects, but especially cleft lip and palate. *Recreations:* sailing, running (including occasional marathons), ski-ing, theatre, supporting cleft lip and palate services in the developing world. *Address:* The Old Vicarage, 17 Lodge Road, Writtle, Chelmsford, Essex CM1 3HY. *T:* (01245) 422477, *Fax:* (01245) 421901. *E:* brian@sommerlad.co.uk.

SOMOGYI, Prof. Peter, PhD, DSc; FRS 2000; Professor of Neurobiology, University of Oxford, since 1996; Director, MRC Anatomical Neuropharmacology Unit, Oxford, since 1998; Nicholas Kurti Senior Research Fellow, Brasenose College, Oxford, since 2004. *Educ:* Loránd Eötvös Univ., Budapest (PhD); Semmelweis Med. Sch., Budapest; Univ. of Oxford; Flinders Med. Centre, SA, Australia. Associate, later Co-Dir, MRC Anatomical Neuropharmacology Unit, Oxford, 1985–98. FMedSci 2006; Fellow, Hungarian Acad. Scis, 2013. Dr and Prof. *hc*: Eötvös Loránd Univ., Budapest, 2013; Zurich, 2014. Brain Prize, Lundbeck Foundn, 2011; Semmelweis Budapest Award, 2012. Commander's Cross, Order of Merit (Hungary), 2012. *Address:* MRC Anatomical Neuropharmacology Unit, Mansfield Road, Oxford OX1 3TH; 129 Staunton Road, Oxford OX3 7TN.

SØNDERGÅRD, Thomas; Principal Conductor, BBC National Orchestra of Wales, since 2012; *b* Holstebro, Denmark, 4 Oct. 1969. *Educ:* Royal Danish Acad. of Music. Mem., EU Youth Orch., 1989–92; teacher, Royal Danish Acad. of Music, Copenhagen, 2001–02; Principal Conductor, Norwegian Radio Orch., 2009–12. Guest conductor appearances worldwide; Principal Guest Conductor, Royal Scottish Nat. Orch., 2012–. Queen Ingrid Prize for services to music (Denmark), 2011. *Address:* c/o Askonas Holt Ltd, Lincoln House, 300 High Holborn, WC1V 7JH. *T:* (020) 7400 1700. *E:* info@askonasholt.co.uk.

SONDHEIM, Stephen Joshua; composer-lyricist; *b* 22 March 1930; *s* of Herbert Sondheim and Janet (*née* Fox). *Educ:* Williams Coll. (BA 1950). Lyrics: West Side Story, 1957; Gypsy, 1959; Do I Hear a Waltz?, 1965; (additional lyrics) Candide, 1973; music and lyrics: A Funny Thing Happened on the Way to the Forum, 1962; Anyone Can Whistle, 1964; Company, 1970; Follies, 1971; A Little Night Music, 1973 (filmed, 1976); The Frogs, 1974; Pacific Overtures, 1976; Sweeney Todd, 1979; Merrily We Roll Along, 1981; Sunday in the Park with George, 1984 (Pulitzer Prize, 1985); Into The Woods, 1987 (filmed, 2015); Assassins, 1991; Passion, 1994; Bounce, 2003; Road Show, 2011; incidental music: The Girls of Summer, 1956; Invitation to a March, 1961; Twigs, 1971; film scores: Stavisky, 1974; Reds, 1981; Dick Tracy, 1990; Sweeney Todd: The Demon Barber of Fleet Street, 2008; co-author, The Last of Sheila (film), 1973; songs for Evening Primrose (TV), 1966; *play:* co-author, Getting Away with Murder, 1996; anthologies: Side By Side By Sondheim, 1976; Marry Me A Little, 1981; You're Gonna Love Tomorrow, 1983; Putting It Together, 1992. Vis. Prof. of Drama, and Fellow of St Catherine's Coll., Oxford, Jan.–June 1990. Mem. Council, Dramatists Guild, 1963 (Pres., 1973–81); Mem., AAIL, 1983. Hon. Doctorate, Williams Coll., 1971. Tony Awards and New York Drama Critics' Circle Award for Company, Follies, A Little Night Music, Sweeney Todd, Into the Woods, and Passion; London Evening Standard Best Musical Award for Into the Woods; New York Drama Critics' Circle Award for Pacific Overtures and Sunday in the Park with George; London Evening Standard Best Musical Award, 1987, and SWET Laurence Olivier Award, 1988, for Follies; Ivor Novello Internat. Award, 2011; Critics' Circle Award for Services to the Arts, 2011. *Publications:* (book and vocal score): West Side Story, 1958; Gypsy, 1960; A Funny Thing Happened on the Way to the Forum, 1963; Anyone Can Whistle, 1965; Do I Hear a Waltz?, 1966; Company, 1971; Follies, 1972; A Little Night Music, 1974; Pacific Overtures, 1977; Sweeney Todd, 1979; Sunday in the Park with George, 1986; Into the Woods, 1989; Assassins, 1991; Passion, 1996; Finishing the Hat: collected lyrics 1954–1981, 2010; Look, I Made a Hat, 2011. *Address:* c/o John Breglio, Paul, Weiss, Rifkind, Wharton & Garrison, 1285 Avenue of the Americas, New York, NY 10019–6064, USA.

SONDHEIMER, Prof. Ernst Helmut, MA, ScD; Professor Emeritus of Mathematics, University of London; *b* Stuttgart, 8 Sept. 1923; *er s* of late Max and Ida Sondheimer; *m* 1950, Janet Harrington Matthews, PhD (*d* 2007); one *s* one *d*. *Educ:* Reformrealgymnasium Stuttgart; University College School; Trinity Coll., Cambridge. Smith's Prize, 1947; Fellow of Trinity Coll., 1948–52; Research Fellow, H. H. Wills Physical Lab., University of Bristol, 1948–49; Research Associate, Massachusetts Inst. of Technology, 1949–50; London University: Lecturer in Mathematics, Imperial College of Science and Technology, 1951–54; Reader in Applied Mathematics, Queen Mary Coll., 1954–60; Prof. of Mathematics, Westfield Coll., 1960–82. Vis. Research Asst Prof. of Physics, Univ. of Illinois, USA, 1958–59; Vis. Prof. of Theoretical Physics, University of Cologne, 1967. FKC 1985; Fellow, Queen Mary and Westfield Coll., London, 1989. Editor, Alpine Journal, 1986–91. *Publications:* (with S. Doniach) Green's Functions for Solid State Physicists, 1974, repr. 1998; (with A. Rogerson) Numbers and Infinity, 1981, repr. 2006; papers on the electron theory of metals. *Recreations:* German history, German expressionist painting, mountains, alpine and Himalayan plants, contract bridge. *Address:* 51 Cholmeley Crescent, Highgate, N6 5EX. *T:* (020) 8340 6607. *Club:* Alpine.

SONDHI, Ranjit, CBE 1999; a Civil Service Commissioner, 2007–12; *b* 22 Oct. 1950; *s* of Prem Lal Sondhi and Kanta Sondhi; *m* 1979, Anita Bhalla; one *s* one *d*. *Educ:* Bedford Sch.; Univ. of Birmingham (BSc Hons Physics). Handsworth Action Centre, Birmingham, 1972–76; Dir, Asian Resource Centre, Birmingham, 1976–85; Sen. Lectr, Westhill Coll., Birmingham, 1985–2007. Freelance lectr and researcher, 1975–2003. A Gov., BBC, 1998–2006; Member: IBA, 1987–90; Radio Authority, 1991–94; Chairman: Jt Council of Welfare for Immigrants, West Midlands, 1987–90; Refugee Employment, Trng and Educn Forum, 1990–93; Home Sec.'s Race Equality Adv. Panel, 2003–; Dep. Chm., CRE, 1993–95 (Mem., 1991–93); Member: Digbeth Trust, 1986–90; Prince's Youth Business Trust, Birmingham, 1986–91; Royal Jubilee and Prince's Trust, Birmingham, 1986–88; Admin. Council, Prince's Trust, 1986–88; Council for Educn and Trng in Youth and Community Work, 1987–90; Ethnic Minorities Adv. Cttee, Judicial Studies Bd, 1991–95; John Feeney Charitable Trust, 1991–2003; Glidewell Panel of Enquiry into Immigration and Asylum Bill, 1996; Lord Chancellor's Adv. Cttee on Legal Educn and Conduct, 1997–99; DFEE Task Force on Disability Rights, 1997–99; Tenant Services Authy, 2009–12; Judicial Appts Commn, 2012–14; Criminal Cases Rev. Commn, 2012–. Trustee: Nat. Primary Centre, 1993–2007 (Chm., 2003–07); Nat. Gall., 2000–08. Director: Birmingham TEC, 1990–93; Birmingham HA, 1998–2002; Chm., Heart of Birmingham Primary Care Trust, 2002–11; Vice-Chm., Sandwell and W Birmingham CCG, 2011–. Vis. Prof., Diversity Cohesion and Intercultural Relns, Coventry Univ., 2010. FRSA 1988. DUniv: UCE, 2003; Birmingham, 2010; Hon. DLitt Wolverhampton. *Publications:* (jtly) Race in the Provincial Press, 1977; Divided Families, 1987; contribs to: Ethnicity and Social Work, 1982; Community Work and Racism, 1982; Minorities: community and identity, 1983; Analysing Inter-cultural Communication, 1987; Community Work in the Nineties, 1994; (ed jtly) 20 Years After the RRA76, 1999. (contrib.) Intercultural Europe, 2000; Equality and Diversity in Birmingham, 2005; Navigating Difference, 2006. *Recreations:* Indian classical music, yoga, travel, antiquarian books. *Address:* 89 Hamstead Hall Avenue, Handsworth Wood, Birmingham B20 1JU.

SONENBERG, Prof. Nahum, OC 2010; PhD; FRS 2006; FRSC; James McGill Professor, Department of Biochemistry, McGill University; *b* Wetzlar, Germany, 29 Dec. 1946; *s* of Meyer Sonenberg and Fradl Sonenberg (*née* Kutchinsky); *m* 1972, Yocheved Shrot; two *d*. *Educ:* Tel-Aviv Univ. (BSc, MSc); Weizmann Inst. of Sci. (PhD 1976). Chaim Weizmann Fellow, Roche Inst. of Molecular Biol., NJ, 1976–79; Asst Prof., 1979–82, Associate Prof., 1983–86, Prof., 1987–, Dept of Biochem., McGill Univ. Internat. Res. Scholar, Howard Hughes Med. Inst.; Dist. Scientist, CIHR. FRSC 1992. Robert L. Noble Prize, Nat. Cancer Inst. of Canada, 2002; Killam Prize for Health Scis, 2005; Gairdner Award, 2008; Rosenstiel Award, Brandeis Univ., 2012; Wolf Prize, Wolf Foundn, 2014. *Publications:* articles in jls. *Address:* Department of Biochemistry, McGill University, McIntyre Medical Building, 3655 Promenade Sir William Osler, Montreal, QC H3G 1Y6, Canada.

SONNABEND, Yolanda; painter, portraitist and theatre designer; *b* 26 March 1935; *d* of Dr Henry Sonnabend and Dr Fira Sonnabend (*née* Sandler). *Educ:* Eveline High Sch., Bulawayo; Slade Sch. of Fine Art (Dip.). Lectr in Theatre Design, Slade Sch. of Fine Art, 1989–2001. Fellow, UCL, 2002. *Painting: exhibitions* include: Whitechapel Art Gall. (solo), 1975; Serpentine Gall. (solo), 1986; Amphitheatre, ROH, 2000; portraits of Stephen Hawking and others, Nat. Portrait Gall.; portrait for Pembroke Coll., Cambridge; portrait of Lord Rees for

Royal Soc.; *theatre design: installations:* Japan, Denmark, Poland; *ballet* productions: for Royal Ballet, incl. Swan Lake and works for Kenneth Macmillan (Requiem, My Brother My Sister); for La Scala, Milan; for K Ballet Co., Tokyo: Swan Lake, 2003; The Nutcracker, 2005; Le Corsaire, 2007; The Beethoven, with symphony and symphonic ballet, 2008; Romeo and Juliet, 2010; Strasbourg; Lisbon; Stuttgart; Hong Kong; Nice; Chicago; Boston; *opera* productions: Aldeburgh; Sadler's Wells; Italy; *theatre* includes: Oxford Playhouse; RSC; Old Vic; *film:* The Tempest, 1980. Garrick Milne Prize for Theatrical Portraiture, 2000. *Recreation:* usual diversions. *Address:* 30 Hamilton Terrace, NW8 9UG. *T:* (020) 7286 9616.

SOOD, Prof. Ajay Kumar, Padma Shri, 2013; PhD; FRS 2015; Professor, Department of Physics, Indian Institute of Science, Bangalore, India, since 1994; *b* Gwalior, India, 26 June 1951; *s* of Ishwar Singh and Bimla Devi; *m* 1980, Anita Sood; one *s* one *d.* *Educ:* Punjab Univ., Chandigarh (BSc Physics 1971; MS Physics 1972); Indian Inst. of Sci., Bangalore (PhD Physics 1982). Scientist, Indira Gandhi Centre for Atomic Res., Kalpakkam, India, 1973–88; postdoctoral res., Max Planck Inst. für Festkörperforschung, Stuttgart, 1983–85; Associate Prof., Dept of Physics, 1988–94, Divl Chm., Div. of Physical and Math. Scis, 1998–2008, Indian Inst. of Sci., Bangalore. Hon. Prof., Jawaharlal Nehru Centre for Advanced Scientific Res., Bangalore, 1993–. Exec. Ed., Solid State Communications; Co-Ed., Europhysics Letters, 2012–; Member: Internat. Editl Adv. Bd, Particle, 2012–; Editl Bd, Scientific Reports, 2013–. Mem., Scientific Adv. Council to Prime Minister of India, 2009–14. Chm., Res. Council, Nat. Physical Lab., New Delhi. Sec. Gen., World Acad. of Scis, 2013–15. Vice Pres., Indian Nat. Sci. Acad., 2008–10; Pres., Indian Acad. of Scis, 2010–12. FASc 1991; Fellow, Nat. Acad. of Scis, India 1995; FNA 1996; Fellow, World Acad. of Sci., 2002. Mem., Asia-Pacific Acad. of Materials, 2008. Awards include: Award in Physics, Third World Acad. of Scis, 2000; Homi Jehangir Bhabha Medal, Indian Nat. Sci. Acad., 2002; Millennium Gold Medal, 2000, M. N. Saha Birth Centenary Award, 2003–04, Award for outstanding contribs to Sci., 2014, Indian Sci. Congress; Goyal Prize in Physics, Kurukshatra Univ., 2003; Nat. Award in Nanosci. and Nanotechnol., Dept of Sci. and Technol., Govt of India, 2006; Lifetime Achievement Award, 2006, Vigyan Ratan Award, 2010, Punjab Univ.; Bangalore Nano Award, Govt of Karnataka, 2010; G. M. Modi Award for Sci., 2012; R. D. Birla Award for Excellence in Physics, Indian Physics Assoc., 2014. *Publications:* contribs to scientific jls incl. Nature Physics, Procs NAS, Nature Communications, Physical Rev. Letters, Soft Matter, Science, Nature Nanotechnol., Clin. Chem. *Recreations:* classical music, sports. *Address:* Department of Physics, Indian Institute of Science, Bangalore 560012, India. *T:* 8023602238, *Fax:* 823602602. *E:* asood@physics.iisc.ernet.in.

SOOLE, Michael Alexander; QC 2002; a Recorder, since 2000; *b* 18 July 1954; *yr s* of late Brian Alfred Seymour Soole and Rosemary Una Soole (*née* Salt); *m* 2002, Catherine Gavine Marshall (*née* Gardiner); three step *s* two step *d.* *Educ:* Berkhamsted Sch. (schol.); University Coll., Oxford (schol.; MA). Pres., Oxford Union, 1974. Called to the Bar, Inner Temple, 1977, Bencher, 2008; practising barrister, 1978–. Chm., Technol. and Construction Bar Assoc., 2013–15. Contested (SDP), Aylesbury, 1983, 1987. Mem. Bd, Christian Aid, 1991–2002. Trustee, Oxford Literary and Debating Union Trust, 2005– (Chm., 2013–). *Recreation:* conversation. *Address:* 4 New Square, Lincoln's Inn, WC2A 3RJ. *T:* (020) 7822 2000, *Fax:* (020) 7822 2001. *Clubs:* Beefsteak, Buck's.

SOPEL, Jon(athan); North America Editor, BBC, since 2014; *b* 22 May 1959; *s* of late Myer Sopel and Miriam Sopel; *m* 1988, Linda Twissell; one *s* one *d.* *Educ:* Christ's Coll. Finchley; Univ. of Southampton (BA Politics 1981). BBC: Radio Solent, 1983–87; reporter, World at One, Radio 4, 1987–89; Political Correspondent, 1989–98; Chief Political Correspondent, 1998–99; Paris Correspondent, 1999–2003; Presenter: News Channel (formerly BBC News 24), 2003; reported on war in Afghanistan, 2001, on war in Iraq, 2003, on tsunami, from Sri Lanka, 2004–05; Presenter, The Politics Show, BBC One, 2005–11; Global with Sopel, World News, 2013–14; has presented PM and Today progs, Radio 4. Political Journalist of the Year, 2007. *Publications:* Tony Blair: the moderniser, 1994; contrib. widely to newspapers and mags. *Recreations:* travel, tennis, golf, running, cinema, watching football. *Address:* BBC News Centre, Broadcasting House, Portland Place, W1A 1AA. *E:* jon.sopel@bbc.co.uk.

SOPER, Dr Alan Kenneth, FRS 2014; STFC Senior Fellow, STFC Rutherford Appleton Laboratory, since 2009; *b* Romford, Essex, 16 June 1951; *s* of Stanley John Soper and Joan Jessamine Soper (*née* Ayling); *m* 1981, Krista Ann McAuley; two *d.* *Educ:* Campion Sch., Hornchurch, Essex; Univ. of Leicester (BSc Hons; PhD 1977). Post-doctoral Fellow, Physics Dept, Univ. of Guelph, Canada, 1977–79; staff mem., Los Alamos Nat. Lab., USA, 1979–82; Asst Prof., Dept of Physics, Univ. of Guelph, 1982–86; Instrument Scientist, 1986–97, Gp Leader, 1997–2009, STFC Rutherford Appleton Lab. *Publications:* contribs to jls incl. Jl Chem. Physics, Jl Physical Chem., Physical Rev. Letters, Chem. Physics. *Recreations:* cycling, gardening, classical music. *Address:* ISIS Facility, STFC Rutherford Appleton Laboratory, Harwell Oxford, Didcot, Oxon OX11 0QX.

SOPER, Andrew Keith; HM Diplomatic Service; Minister Counsellor (Political and Press), New Delhi, since 2013; *b* 6 July 1960; *s* of late Rev. Brian Soper and of Doreen Soper; *m* 1987, Kathryn Garrett Stevens; one *s* one *d.* *Educ:* Cranbrook Sch., Kent; Sidney Sussex Coll., Cambridge (MA, PGCE). Student helper, Flying Angel Club, Fremantle, Australia, 1978–79; Teacher, Woodstock Sch., Uttar Pradesh, India, 1983–84; Admin. Trainee, DES, 1984–85; entered FCO, 1985; Second, later First, Sec. (Chancery), Mexico City, 1987–90; First Secretary: FCO, 1990–95; Washington, 1995–99; FCO, 1999–2001; Counsellor and Dep. Hd of Mission, Brasilia, 2001–04; Hd, Sustainable Develt and Commonwealth Gp, FCO, 2004–07; High Comr, Republic of Mozambique, 2007–10; Ambassador to Latvia, 2010–13. *Recreations:* tennis, bridge, music, reading, travelling. *Address:* c/o Foreign and Commonwealth Office, King Charles Street, SW1A 2AH. *Club:* Royal Over-Seas League.

SOPER, Rt Rev. (Andrew) Laurence, OSB; STD; General Treasurer, Benedictine Confederation, 2002–11; Titular Abbot of St Alban's, 2000–11; *b* 17 Sept. 1943; *s* of late Alan and Anne Soper. *Educ:* St Benedict's Sch., Ealing; Blackfriars, Oxford; Sant Anselmo, Rome (STD); Strawberry Hill (PGCE; Hon. Fellow, 1996). Banking until 1964; entered Novitiate at Ealing, 1964; St Benedict's School: Master, 1973–83; Bursar, 1975–91; Prior, 1984–91; Asst Chaplain, Harrow Sch., 1981–91; Abbot of Ealing, 1991–2000. Mem. Council, Union of Monastic Superiors, 1994–99 (Chm., 1995–99). Episcopal Vicar for Religious for Westminster (Western Area), 1995–2001. FRSA. *Publications:* (ed with Rev. Peter Elliott) Thoughts of Jesus Christ, 1970; articles and thesis on T. H. Green and 19th century English theology. *Recreations:* reading, hill walking.

SOPER, Tony; freelance writer; *b* Southampton, 10 Jan. 1929; *s* of Albert Ernest Soper and Ellaline May Soper; *m* 1971, Hilary Claire Brooke; two *s.* *Educ:* Devonport High Sch. Joined BBC as youth-in-training, 1947; Technical Asst, 1947–49; Studio Manager, 1949–55; Features Producer, BBC Bristol, 1955–57; Film Producer, BBC Natural Hist. Unit, 1957–63; writer and presenter, BBC wildlife series incl. Wildtrack, Beside the Sea, Animal Design, Discovering Birds, Soper at Large, Nature, Birdwatch, 1963–90; expedition leader for Noble Caledonia, Lindblad Expeditions and Quark Expeditions, 1990–2010; lecturer for P&O, Holland America and Crystal Cruises. *Publications:* The Bird Table Book, 1965, 7th edn 2006; Penguins, 1967, 2nd edn 1987; Owls, 1970, 2nd edn 1989; Oceans of Birds, 1989; The Shell Book of the Shore, 1991; Antarctica, 1995, 6th edn 2013; The Arctic, 2001, 3rd edn 2012; Wildlife of the North Atlantic, 2008; The Northwest Passage, 2012. *Recreations:* beachcombing, seagoing. *E:* tonysoper@btinternet.com.

SORABJI, Sir Richard Rustom Kharsedji, Kt 2014; CBE 1999; FBA 1989; Professor of Ancient Philosophy, King's College London, 1981–2000, now Emeritus; Supernumerary Fellow, Wolfson College, Oxford, 1996–2002, now Hon. Fellow; *b* 8 Nov. 1934; *s* of Richard Kaikushru Sorabji and late Mary Katherine (*née* Monkhouse); *m* 1958, Margaret Anne Catherine Taster; one *s* two *d.* *Educ:* Dragon Sch.; Charterhouse; Pembroke Coll., Oxford (BA Greats; MA; BPhil). CS Commn in Russian Lang. Cornell University: joined Sage Sch. of Philosophy, 1962; Associate Prof., 1968; Sen. Res. Fellow, Soc. of Humanities, 1979; King's College, London, 1970–: Designer and Dir, King's Coll. Centre for Philosophical Studies, 1989–91; FKC 1990; British Acad./Wolfson Res. Prof., 1996–99; Chm., Bd of Philosophical Studies, London Univ., 1979–82; Dir, Inst. of Classical Studies, London, 1991–96. Sen. Fellow, Council of Humanities, Princeton Univ., 1985; Vis. Prof., Indian Council of Philos. Res., 1989 and 2004; Adjunct Prof., Philosophy Dept, Univ. of Texas at Austin, 2000–; Ranieri Vis. Scholar, New York Univ., 2000–03; Vis. Prof., CUNY Graduate Center, 2004–07 and 2010; Cyprus Global Distinguished Prof., New York Univ., 2007–09. Member: Common Room, Wolfson Coll., Oxford, 1991–96; Sen. Common Room, Pembroke Coll., Oxford, 1992–. Gresham Prof. of Rhetoric, 2000–03. Lectures: Read-Tuckwell, Bristol, 1985; Simon, Toronto, 1990; Gray, Cambridge, 1991; Townsend, Cornell, 1991–92; Gaisford, Oxford, 1993; Webster, Stanford, 1994; Donnellan, Dublin, 1995; Radhakrishnan Meml, Indian Inst. of Advanced Study, Simla, 1996; Gifford, St Andrews, 1997, Edinburgh, 1997; Prentice, Princeton, 1998. Pres., Aristotelian Soc., 1985–86. Founder and dir of internat. project for translating the Ancient Commentators on Aristotle (100 vols of trans., 5 vols of exposition), 1985–. Foreign Honorary Member: Amer. Acad. of Arts and Scis, 1997; Royal Flemish Acad. of Arts and Scis, Belgium, 2008. Hon. DLitt: Union Coll., Schenectady, 2007; McGill Univ., 2009. *Publications:* Aristotle on Memory, 1973, 2nd edn 2004; (ed jtly) Articles on Aristotle, 4 vols, 1975–79; Necessity, Cause and Blame, 1980; Time, Creation and the Continuum, 1983; (ed) Philoponus and the Rejection of Aristotelian Science, 1987, 2nd edn 2010; (ed) The Ancient Commentators on Aristotle, 100 vols, 1987–; Matter, Space and Motion, 1988 (Choice Award for Outstanding Academic Book, 1989–90); (ed) Aristotle Transformed, 1990; Animal Minds and Human Morals: the origins of the western debate, 1993; (ed) Aristotle and After, Supplement 68 to the Bulletin of Inst. of Classical Studies, 1997; Emotion and Peace of Mind: from Stoic agitation to Christian temptation, 2000; Philosophy of the Commentators 200–600 AD, 3 vols, 2004; (contrib.) Metaphysics, Soul and Ethics in Ancient Thought: themes from the work of Richard Sorabji, 2005; (ed jtly) The Ethics of War: shared problems in different traditions, 2005; Self: ancient and modern insights about individuality, life and death, 2006; (ed jtly) Greek and Roman Philosophy 100 BC–200 AD, 2 vols, 2007; Opening Doors: the untold story of Cornelia Sorabji, reformer, lawyer and champion of women's rights in India, 2010; Gandhi and the Stoics: modern experiments on ancient values, 2012; Perception, Conscience and Will, 2013; Electrifying New Zealand, Russia and India: the three lives of Engineer Allan Monkhouse, 2014; Moral Conscience through the Ages, 2015. *Recreations:* architecture, archaeology, occasional verses. *Address:* Wolfson College, Oxford OX2 6UD.

SORBIE, Prof. Kenneth Stuart, DPhil; FRSE; Professor of Petroleum Engineering, Heriot-Watt University, since 1992; *b* Prestwick, 15 Jan. 1950; *s* of late Kenneth Sorbie and of Lucy (*née* Ferguson); *m* 1976, Prof. Sheila Riddell; two *d.* *Educ:* Strathclyde Univ. (BSc 1st cl. Hons, 1972); Sussex Univ. (DPhil 1975). Res. Fellow, Cambridge Univ., 1975–76; teaching and lecturing, 1976–80; Group leader, oil res. and enhanced oil recovery, AEE Winfrith, 1980–88; Lectr, 1988–90, Reader, 1990–92, Heriot-Watt Univ. Vis. Prof., China Univ. of Petroleum, Qingdao, 2010. Mem., Soc. of Petroleum Engrs, 1985. FRSE 2001. Tech. Achievement Award, Soc. of Core Analysts, 2004; Improved Oil Recovery Pioneer Award, Soc. Petroleum Engrs, 2008; Lifetime Achievement Award, RSC, 2013. *Publications:* Polymer Improved Oil Recovery, 1991; over 400 technical papers on petroleum-related research. *Recreations:* listening to and collecting classical music, particularly Renaissance masses and lute music, guitar and chamber music; hill walking, running, weight training—but also fond of good food and wine, alas! *Address:* Institute of Petroleum Engineering, Heriot-Watt University, Edinburgh EH14 4AS. *T:* (0131) 451 3139, *Fax:* (0131) 451 3127. *E:* ken.sorbie@pet.hw.ac.uk.

SORENSEN, (Kenneth) Eric (Correll); Chief Executive, Thames Gateway London Partnership, 2003–08; *b* 15 Oct. 1942; *m* Susan; two *s* one *d.* *Educ:* Bedford Sch.; Keele Univ. (BA(Hons) Econs and History). Voluntary work, India; joined DoE, 1967; Private Sec. to Sec. of State for Envmt, 1977; NW Regl Dir, Depts of the Envmt and Transport, 1980–81; Dir, Merseyside Task Force, DoE, 1981–84; Dir, Inner Cities Directorate, DoE, 1984–87; Head of Urban Policy Unit, Cabinet Office, 1987–88; Dir of Personnel Management and Trng, Depts of Envmt and Transport, 1988–90; Dep. Sec., Housing and Construction Comd, DoE, 1990–91; Chief Executive: LDDC, 1991–97; Millennium Commn, 1997–98; London Develt Partnership, 1998. Civil Service Comr (part-time), 1992–95. Chm., Royal Docks Trust (London); Dep. Chm., St Katharine and Shadwell Trust. Non-exec. Dir, Homerton Univ. Hosp. NHS Foundn Trust, 2005. Gov., Museum of London, 2008–.

SORIANO, Kathleen; Director of Exhibitions, Royal Academy of Arts, 2009–14; Director, Kathleen Soriano Ltd, since 2014; *b* London, 18 July 1963; *d* of Salvador Soriano and Kathleen Soriano; *m* 1995, Peter Greenhough; one *d.* *Educ:* Putney High Sch.; Univ. of Louisville; Univ. of Leicester (BA Hons Combined Arts). RA, 1986–89; Hd, Exhibns and Collections, NPG, 1989–2006; Dir, Compton Verney, Warwicks, 2006–09. Member: Bd, Tourism W Midlands, 2006–09; Women Leaders in Mus Steering Gp, 2008–11; Bd, Sainsbury Centre, UEA, 2008–10; Contemp. Art Panel, Nat. Trust, 2009–12; Contemp. Art Panel, English Heritage, 2011–12; Comité d'orientation stratégique, Réunion des Musées Nationaux, Grand Palais, Paris, 2014–; Chair: Arts Adv. Cttee, Churches Conservation Trust, 2015–; Exhibns and Collections Cttee, House of Illustration, 2014–. Judge: Sky Arts Portrait Artist of Year, 2013–14; Sky Arts Landscape Artist of the Year, 2015. Trustee: MLA W Midlands, 2007–09; Student Hubs Oxford, 2012–14; House of Illustration, 2012–; Patron: Crisis Charity Art Commn, 2011–14; Stroke Assoc., 2014–; volunteer, Oxford Foodbank, 2014–. Clore Leadership Fellow, 2004; Grad., Salzburg Global Seminar, 2007. Hon. Kentucky Col, 1982. *Publications:* Compton Verney, 2009; Australia, 2013, Anselm Kiefer, 2014, Eileen Cooper, RA, 2015. *E:* kathleen.soriano@outlook.com. *Clubs:* Arts, Quo Vadis.

SORKIN, (Alexander) Michael; Vice-Chairman, N M Rothschild & Sons, since 2001; *b* 2 March 1943; *s* of Jose Sorkin and Hildegard Ruth Sorkin; *m* 1977, Angela Lucille Berman; one *s* two *d.* *Educ:* St Paul's Sch.; Manchester Univ. (BA (Hons) Econs). Chartered accountant. Joined Hambros, 1968; Dir, 1973–2001, Vice Chm., 1987–2001, SG Hambros (formerly Hambros Bank Ltd); Dep. Chm., Hambros Bank Ltd, 1995–98; Dir, Hambros plc, 1986–98; Man. Dir, SG Hambros, 1998–2001. *Recreations:* golf, tennis, football, opera. *Address:* N M Rothschild & Sons Ltd, New Court, St Swithin's Lane, EC4N 8AL.

SOROS, Flora; *see* Fraser, F.

SOROS, George; President, Soros Fund Management, since 1973; Founder and Chairman, Open Society Foundations; *b* Budapest, 12 Aug. 1930; *s* of Tivadar Soros and Elisabeth Soros (*née* Szucs); *m* 1960, Annaliese Witschak (marr. diss. 1983); two *s* one *d*; *m* 1983, Susan Weber (marr. diss. 2005); two *s*; *m* 2013, Tamiko Bolton. *Educ:* LSE, London Univ. (BS 1952). Arbitrage trader, F. M. Mayer, NYC, 1956–59; Economic Analyst, Wertheim & Co., NYC, 1959–63; Vice Pres., Arnhold and S. Bleichroeder, NYC, 1963–73. Member: Exec. Cttee, Helsinki Watch, 1982–; Cttee, Americas Watch, 1982–; Council on Foreign Relations, 1988–. Chm. and Founding Pres., Central European Univ., Prague, Budapest, 1991. Mem., RIIA, 1990. Hon. DCL Oxford, 1990; Hon. DHL Yale, 1991. *Publications:* The Alchemy of

Finance, 1987, 2nd edn 1994; Opening the Soviet System, 1990; Underwriting Democracy, 1991; (jtly) Soros on Soros: staying ahead of the curve, 1995; The Crisis of Global Capitalism (Open Society Endangered), 1998; Open Society: reforming global capitalism, 2000; George Soros on Globalisation, 2002; The Bubble of American Supremacy, 2004; The Age of Fallibility: consequences of the war on terror, 2006; The New Paradigm for Financial Markets: the credit crisis of 2008 and what it means, 2008; (with G. P. Schmitz) The Tragedy of the European Union: disintegration or revival?, 2014. *Address:* Soros Fund Management, 888 7th Avenue, Suite 3300, New York, NY 10106–0001, USA. *Clubs:* Brooks's; Queen's; NY Athletic, Town Tennis.

SORRELL, Sir John (William), Kt 2008; CBE 1996; Chairman: Sorrell Foundation, since 1999; London Design Festival, since 2002; *b* 28 Feb. 1945; *s* of late John William Sorrell and Elizabeth Jane Sorrell (*née* Taylor); *m* 1974, Frances Mary Newell; two *s* one *d*. *Educ:* Hornsey Coll. of Art (NDD 1964). Designer, Main Wolff & Partners, 1964; Partner, Goodwin Sorrell, 1964–71; Design Manager, Wolff Olins, 1971–76; Newell & Sorrell, subseq. Interbrand Newell & Sorrell: Founder, 1976; Partner, 1976–83; Chm., 1983–2000. Chairman: Design Council, 1994–2000; CABE, 2004–09; Creative Industries Fedn, 2014–. A Vice-Pres., CSD, 1989–92; Chm., Design Business Assoc., 1990–92. Chairman: NHS London Design Adv. Gp, 2001–03; UK Trade & Investment Creative Industries Adv. Bd, 2007–12; Member: BR Architecture and Design Panel, 1991–93; RSA Design Adv. Gp, 1991–93; Panel 2000, FCO, 1998–2000; Culture and Creativity Adv. Gp, DCMS, 2002–03; Adv. Gp on Sch. Bldgs Design, 2002–04, London Challenge Ministerial Adv. Gp, 2002–06, DfES; Public Diplomacy Strategy Bd, FCO, 2002–06; Design and Technol. Alliance, Home Office, 2007–12; Creative Economy Prog. Ministerial Steering Bd, DCMS, 2008–09. UK Business Ambassador, 2009–. Chm., Univ. of the Arts London, 2013–. Gov., Design Dimension, 1991–93. Chm., Victory Ceremonies Medal Panel, 2012 Olympics, 2010–12. Trustee, RIBA Trust, 2004–05. Hon. Mem., Romanian Design Foundn, 1996. Hon. FRIBA 2002; Hon. FREng 2009; Hon. Fellow, UC Falmouth, 2006. CCMI 2006. Hon. DDes: De Montfort, 1997; Greenwich, 2007; Hon. Dr: London Inst., 1999; Middlesex, 2006; Huddersfield, 2014; Hon. PhD London Metropolitan, 2006. Bicentenary Medal, RSA, 1998. *Publications:* Creative Island, 2002; Joined up Design for Schools, 2005; Creative Island II, 2009; The Virtuous Circle, 2014. *Recreations:* architecture, Arsenal, art, film. *Clubs:* Chelsea Arts, Groucho.

SORRELL, Sir Martin (Stuart), Kt 2000; Group Chief Executive, WPP Group, since 1986; *b* 14 Feb. 1945; *s* of late Jack and Sally Sorrell; *m* 1971, Sandra Carol Ann Finestone (marr. diss. 2005); three *s*; *m* 2008, Cristiana Falcone. *Educ:* Haberdashers' Aske's School; Christ's College, Cambridge (MA); Harvard Graduate School of Business (MBA 1968). Consultant, Glendinning Associates, Conn, 1968–69; Vice-Pres., Mark McCormack Orgn, London, 1970–74; Dir, James Gulliver Associates, 1975–77; Gp Financial Dir, Saatchi & Saatchi, 1977–86. Non-executive Director: Colefax & Fowler Gp plc, 1997–2003; Alpha Topco Ltd; Alcoa; Bloomberg Family Foundn. Mem. Bd, NASDAQ, 2001–04. Chm., Adv. Gp, KPMG, 2002–07; Member, Advisory Board: Bowmark Capital Gp, 2009–; Stanhope Capital, 2011–; Mem., ATP Mktg Adv. Bd, 2001–; Internat. Adv. Bd, CBI, 2002–. Modern Apprenticeship Taskforce, DfES, 2003–. Mem., Engrg and Technol. Bd, 2002. Mem., Business Council, US, 2009–. Chairman: Mayor of London Internat. Business Adv. Council, 2008–; Internat. Business Council, WEF, 2010–; Mayor of Rome Internat. Business Adv. Council, 2010–; Internat. Business Adv. Council, Jerusalem, 2012–; Vice-Chm., Shanghai Internat. Business Leaders Adv. Council, 2010–. Member: Adv. Bd, Internat. Graduate Sch. of Mgt, Univ. of Navarra, Spain, 1989–; Deans Adv. Council, Boston Univ. Sch. of Mgt, 1998–; Bd of Dirs of Associates, Harvard Business Sch., 1998–2005 (Mem., Adv. Bd, 1998–); Bd, Indian Sch. of Business, 1998–; Internat. Adv. Bd, Russian Mus., St Petersburg, 2009–; Internat. Adv. Bd, China Europe Internat. Business Sch., 2012–. Mem., Council for Excellence in Mgt and Leadership, 1999–. Ambassador for British Business, 1997–2010. Member: Bd and Cttee, Special Olympics, 2000–05; Corporate Adv. Gp, Tate Gall., 2000–; Bd, Paley Center for Media, NY, 2002–; Adv. Gp, England 2018 FIFA World Cup Bid, 2009–. Gov., London Business Sch., 1990–2012 (Dep. Chm., 1998–). Trustee, Cambridge Foundn, 1990–; Patron: Christ's Coll., Cambridge; British Mus., 2011–; Hon. Patron, Cambridge. *Recreations:* ski-ing, cricket. *Address:* WPP, 27 Farm Street, W1J 5RJ. *T:* (020) 7408 2204. *Clubs:* Reform, MCC; Harvard (New York).

SORRELL, Robert Michael, PhD; Vice President, Public Partnerships, BP, since 2008; *b* London, 3 Oct. 1959; *s* of Robert Arthur Sorrell and Shirley Peggy Sorrell; *m* 1988, Karen Chapman; three *d*. *Educ:* Queen Elizabeth Coll., Univ. of London (BSc Chem. 1st Cl. Hons 1982); St John's Coll., Cambridge (PhD 1985). Royal Soc. Fellow, Univ. of Wurzburg, 1985; Sen. Demonstrator, St Aidan's Coll., Univ. of Durham, 1986; BP: joined, 1987; Res. and Develt Team Leader, 1987–91; Mkt Develt Manager, 1991–93; Customer Service Gp Manager, 1993–98; Mktg Manager, 1998–2001; Mktg Dir, Europe and Asia, 2001–03; Technol. Strategy Manager, Downstream, 2003–05; Technol. Vice Pres., Business Mktg, 2005–06; Vice Pres., Technol. Strategy, Downstream, 2006–08. Non-exec. Dir, Breathing Buildings Ltd, 2010–. Member: Strategic Adv. Cttee (Energy), EPSRC, 2010– (Chm., 2014–); UK Technol. Strategy Bd, 2011–; Main Panel B, UK REF, 2011–14; UK Energy Res. Partnership, 2014–; Energy Catalyst Adv. Bd, 2014–; Sci. and Technol. Adv. Council, Nat. Physical Lab., 2015–. Chair, Audit and Risk Cttee, Innovate UK, 2014–. Fellow, Centre for Sci. and Policy, Univ. of Cambridge, 2010–13. Mem., Governing and Prog. Mgt Bd, BP Internat. Centre for Advanced Materials, 2013–. FRSC 2012; FInstD 2014. *Recreations:* family, gardening, music, theatre, cycling. *Address:* BP International Ltd, Chertsey Road, Sunbury-on-Thames, Middx TW16 7LN. *T:* 07769 881350. *E:* robert.sorrell@uk.bp.com.

SOSA, Hon. Sir Manuel, Kt 2014; OB 2012; CBE 1998; **Hon. Mr Justice Sosa;** a Judge, since 1999, and President, since 2011, Court of Appeal of Belize; *b* Corozal Town, British Honduras, 24 Dec. 1950; *s* of Marcelino and Augustina Sosa; *m* 1981, Elba Rosado; one *s* two *d*. *Educ:* Univ. of W Indies (LLB Hons 1974); Norman Manley Law Sch., Jamaica (Cert. Legal Ed. 1976). Admitted as Attorney-at-Law, Belize, 1976; licensed to practice as NP, 1981; Sen. Counsel, Belize, 1986; Temp. Justice, 1993–98, Justice, 1998–99, Supreme Court of Belize. Mem., Bd of Dirs, Central Bank of Belize, 1993–97. Mem., Belize Adv. Council, 1987–97. Pres., Bar Assoc. of Belize, 1988–89. *Publications:* contrib. W Indian Law Jl. *Recreations:* walking, jogging, reading, listening to music. *Address:* Court of Appeal, 1 Treasury Lane, Belize City, Belize.

SOSKICE, Prof. David William, FBA 2013; School Professor of Political Science and Economics, London School of Economics and Political Science, since 2012; *b* London, 6 July 1942; *s* of Rt Hon. Baron Stow Hill, QC; *m* 1st, 1966, Alison Black (marr. diss.); one *s* one *d*; 2nd, 1991, Nicola Mary Lacey, *qv*. *Educ:* Winchester Coll.; Trinity Coll., Oxford; Nuffield Coll., Oxford (MA; Hon. Fellow, 2015). Economics Fellow, University Coll., Oxford, 1967–90; Res. Dir, Wissenschaft Zentrum, Berlin, 1990–2005; Res. Prof., Pol Sci. Dept, Duke Univ., 2005–12; Res. Prof. of Comparative Pol Economy, Univ. of Oxford, 2007–12. Vis. Prof., Scuola Superiore St Anna, Pisa, 2000–02; Semans Distinguished Vis. Prof., Dept of Pol Sci., Duke Univ., 2001; Mars Vis. Prof., Dept of Pol Sci., Yale Univ., 2004; Vis. Prof., Dept of Govt, Harvard Univ., 2007. Pres., Eur. Pol Sci. Assoc., 2011–13. *Publications:* (with R. Flanagan and L. Ulman) Unionism, Economic Stabilization, and Incomes Policies: European experiences, 1983; (with W. Carlin) Macroeconomics and the Wage Bargain, 1992; (ed with P. A. Hall) Varieties of Capitalism, 2001; (with W. Carlin) Macroeconomics: institutions, instability and financial institutions, 2015. *Address:* 19 Church Row, Hampstead, NW3 6UP. *E:* d.w.soskice@lse.ac.uk.

SOSKICE, Prof. Janet Martin, DPhil; Professor of Philosophical Theology, University of Cambridge, since 2009; Fellow, since 1988, and President, since 2014, Jesus College, Cambridge; *b* 16 May 1951; *d* of Alison M. Martin and F. Claire Jamieson; *m* 1982, Oliver C. H. Soskice; two *d*. *Educ:* Cornell Univ. (BA); Sheffield Univ. (MA); Oxford Univ. (DPhil 1982); Heythrop Coll., Univ. of London (DD). Gordon Milburn Jun. Res. Fellow, Oxford Univ. and Somerville Coll., 1980–83; Lectr, Ripon Coll., Cuddesdon, 1983–88; University of Cambridge: Lectr, 1988–2001; Reader in Philos. Theol., 2001–09; Chm. Bd, Faculty of Divinity, 2014–. Canada Commonwealth Fellow, 1996; British Acad. Sen. Res. Fellow, 2000–01. Visiting Professor: Univ. of Uppsala, 1992; Univ. of Calgary, 1996; Univ. of Virginia, 2006; Eugene McCarthy Vis. Prof., Gregorian Univ., 1997. Lectures: Stanton, Univ. of Cambridge, 1997–99; Richards, Univ. of Virginia, 2006. Ecumenical Advr to Archbp of Canterbury, 1990–96. Chm. Bd, Margaret Beaufort Inst. of Theol., 1998–2005. Mem., Bd of Dirs, Concilium, 1998–2006 (Ed., some issues of Concilium). President: Catholic Theol Assoc. of GB, 1992–94; Soc. for Study of Theol., 2008–11. Trustee, The Tablet, 2013–. *Publications:* Metaphor and Religious Language, 1985, Japanese edn 1992; (ed) After Eve, 1990; (ed jtly) Medicine and Moral Reasoning, 1994; (ed with Diana Lipton) Feminism and Theology, 2003; (ed jtly) Fields of Faith, 2005; The Kindness of God, 2007; Sisters of Sinai: how two lady adventurers found the hidden Gospels, 2009. *Recreations:* ski-ing, travel. *Address:* Jesus College, Cambridge CB5 8BL. *T:* (01223) 339606, *Fax:* (01223) 339313.

SOSKICE, Nicola Mary; *see* Lacey, N. M.

SOUBRY, Rt Hon. Anna (Mary); PC 2015; MP (C) Broxtowe, since 2010; Minister of State (Minister for Business and Enterprise), Department for Business, Innovation and Skills, since 2015; *b* Lincoln, 7 Dec. 1956; *d* of David and Frances Soubry; two *d*; partner, Neil Davidson, CBE. *Educ:* Hartland Comprehensive Sch., Worksop; Univ. of Birmingham (LLB). Presenter and reporter, Central Television, 1984–92; called to the Bar, Inner Temple, 1995; in practice as barrister, 1995–2010. Parly Under-Sec. of State, DoH, 2012–13; Parly Under-Sec. of State, 2013–14, Minister of State, 2014–15, MoD. Contested (C) Gedling, 2005. *Recreations:* gardening, cooking, ski-ing, watching football, cricket and Rugby. *Address:* House of Commons, SW1A 0AA. *T:* (020) 7219 7211. *E:* anna.soubry.mp@parliament.uk.

SOUEIF, Ahdaf; writer; *b* 23 March 1950; *d* of Mustapha Soueif and Fatma Moussa; *m* 1st, 1972, Sherif Hosni (marr. diss. 1977); 2nd, 1981, Ian Hamilton (*d* 2001); two *s*. *Educ:* schs in Cairo and London; Cairo Univ. (BA English Lit. 1971); American Univ. in Cairo (MA English Lit. 1973); Univ. of Lancaster (PhD Linguistics 1978). Cairo University: Associate Lectr, 1971–79; Lectr, 1979–84; Project Leader and Arabic Ed., Cassel Ltd (Macmillan Inc.), London and Cairo, 1978–84; Associate Prof. of Linguistics, King Saud Univ., Riyadh, 1987–89; Exec. Officer, Al-Furqan Islamic Heritage Foundn, London, 1989–2008. Columnist, al-Shorouk News, Cairo, 2011–. Member: Amnesty Internat., 1990–; Cttee for Advancement of Arab-British Understanding, 1995–. Member: Egyptian-British Soc., 1990–; Egyptian Writers' Union, Egypt, 1999–; PEN, Egypt, 1999–; PEN, UK, 1999–. Patron, Caine Prize for African Lit., 2010– (Mem. Bd, 2002–10); Trustee: Internat. Prize for Arab Fiction, 2011–; BM, 2012–. Founding Chm., Engaged Events (charity), 2007–. Editor, Reflections on Islamic Art, 2012. Fellow: Lannan Foundn, USA, 2002; Bogliasco Foundn, Italy, 2002; FRSL 2003. Hon. DLitt: Lancaster, 2004; London Metropolitan, 2004; Exeter, 2008. Mahmoud Darwish Award, 2010. *Publications: fiction:* Aisha: a collection of short stories, 1983; In the Eye of the Sun, 1992; Sandpiper and Other Stories, 1996; Zīnat al-Ḥayāh wa Qiṣas Ukhrā (collection of stories in Arabic), 1996 (Best Short Stories of the Year Award, Cairo Book Fair); Ahdāf Suwayf: Mukhtārāt min A'mālihā (collection of Arabic writings), 1998; The Map of Love, 1999; I Think of You (short stories), 2007; *non-fiction:* Mezzaterra: fragments from the common ground (essays), 2004; Cairo: my city, our revolution, 2012, new edn as Cairo: a city transformed, 2013; *translation:* In Deepest Night (play), 1998; I Saw Ramallah, memoir by Mourid al-Barghouti, 2000. *Recreations:* friends, film, music, cooking. *Address:* c/o Wylie Agency, 17 Bedford Square, WC1B 3JA. *T:* (020) 7908 5900, *Fax:* (020) 7908 5901. *E:* cbuchan@wylieagency.co.uk. *W:* www.ahdafsoueif.com. *Clubs:* Frontline; Gezira (Cairo).

SOUHAMI, Prof. Robert Leon, CBE 2004; MD, DSc; FRCP, FRCR, FMedSci; Professor of Medicine, University College London, 1997–2001, now Emeritus; Executive Director of Policy and Communications, 2003–05, Director of Clinical Research and Training, 2001–03, Cancer Research UK; *b* 26 April 1938; *s* of John Souhami and Freda Harris; *m* 1966. *Educ:* St Marylebone Grammar Sch.; University Coll. Hosp. Med. Sch. (BSc, MB BS). MD 1975; FRCP 1979; FRCR 1992. Hon. Lectr, St Mary's Hosp. Med. Sch., 1969–71; Sen. Registrar, UCH, 1971–73; Consultant Physician, Poole Gen. Hosp., 1973–75; Consultant Physician and Sen. Lectr, UCH, 1975–87; Kathleen Ferrier Prof. of Clinical Oncology, UCMSM, subseq. UCL Med. Sch., 1987–97; Dean, Faculty of Clinical Scis, 1997–99, Principal, 1999–2001, UCL Med. Sch., subseq. Royal Free and UC Med. Sch., UCL; Hon. Consultant Physician, Whittington Hosp. and Royal Nat. Orthopaedic Hosp., 1976–2001. Chairman: Cancer Therapy Cttee, MRC, 1987–93; Protocol Review Cttee, EORTC, 1994–97; Sci. Adv. Bd, London Res. Inst., 2006–12; Mem., Sci. Adv. Bd, MRC Clinical Scis Centre, 2008–; Member, Science Council: Institut Curie, 1999–2010; Centre Leon Bérard, 2001–08; Institut Bergonié, 2003–08. Fellow: UCL, 1990; Faculty of Medicine, Imperial Coll. London, 2012. FMedSci 1998. Foreign Sec., Acad. of Med. Scis, 2008–13. Hon. DSc Inst. Cancer Res., 2009. *Publications:* Tutorials in Differential Diagnosis, 1974, 4th edn 2003; Cancer and its Management, 1986, 5th edn 2005; Textbook of Medicine, 1990, 4th edn 2002; (ed) Oxford Textbook of Oncology, 2001; clinical and scientific articles on aspects of cancer.

SOULBURY, 4th Viscount *cr* 1954; **Prof. Oliver Peter Ramsbotham,** PhD; Honorary Visiting Professor of Conflict Resolution, Department of Peace Studies, University of Bradford, since 2002 (Professor of Peace Studies and Head of Department, 1999–2002); *b* 27 Oct. 1943; *er s* of Hon. Sir Peter Ramsbotham, GCMG, GCVO, (3rd Viscount Soulbury, but did not use the title) and Frances Marie Massie (*née* Blomfield); *S* father, 2010; *m* 1965, Meredith Anne, *o d* of Brian Jones; three *s*. *Educ:* Eton; University Coll., Oxford (BA 1965); Univ. of Bradford (PhD). Consultant and writer, Oxford Res. Gp (Chm. Bd, 2007–13); Dept of Peace Studies, Univ. of Bradford, 1991–. Mem., Adv. Panel, Conflict Analysis Res. Centre, Univ. of Kent. Pres., Conflict Res. Soc. *Publications:* (jtly) Humanitarian Intervention in Contemporary Conflict, 1996; (jtly) The Crescent and the Cross: Muslim and Christian approaches to war and peace, 1997; Islam, Christianity and Humanitarian Intervention, 1997; (jtly) Contemporary Conflict Resolution: the prevention, management and resolution of deadly conflict, 1999, 3rd edn 2011; (ed jtly) Peacekeeping and Conflict Resolution, 2000; Transforming Violent Conflict: radical disagreement, dialogue and survival, 2010; over 60 articles and papers. *Heir: s* Hon. Edward Herwald Ramsbotham, *b* 8 July 1966. *Address:* Department of Peace Studies, Pemberton Building, University of Bradford, Bradford, W Yorks BD7 1DP.

SOULSBY, family name of **Baron Soulsby of Swaffham Prior**.

SOULSBY OF SWAFFHAM PRIOR, Baron *cr* 1990 (Life Peer), of Swaffham Prior in the County of Cambridgeshire; **Ernest Jackson Lawson Soulsby;** Professor of Animal Pathology and Dean, Faculty of Veterinary Medicine, University of Cambridge, 1978–93, now Emeritus Professor; Fellow, Wolfson College, Cambridge, 1978–93, Hon. Fellow, 2004; *b* 23 June 1926; *s* of William George Lawson Soulsby and Agnes Soulsby; *m* 1st, 1950, Margaret Macdonald; one *s* one *d*; 2nd, 1962, Georgina Elizabeth Annette Williams (*d* 2014). *Educ:* Queen Elizabeth Grammar Sch., Penrith; Univ. of Edinburgh. MRCVS; DVSM; PhD; MA (Cantab). CBiol; FIBiol 1998, Hon. FRSB (Hon. FIBiol 2002). Veterinary Officer, City of Edinburgh, 1949–52; Lectr in Clinical Parasitology, Univ. of Bristol, 1952–54; Univ. Lectr in Animal Pathology, Univ. of Cambridge, 1954–63; Prof. of Parasitology, Univ. of Pennsylvania, 1964–78. Ian McMaster Fellow, CSIRO, 1958; Sen. Vis. Fellow, EEC, Poland, 1961; WHO Vis. Worker, USSR, 1962; UN Special Fund Expert, IAEA, Vienna and Zemun, Yugoslavia, 1964; Ford Foundn Visiting Prof., Univ. of Ibadan, 1964; Richard Merton Guest Prof., Justus Liebig Univ., 1974–75; Vis. Prof. Univ. of Qld, 1992. Lectures: Hume Meml, Univ. Fedn Animal Welfare, 1985; Wooldridge Meml, BVA, 1986; Sir Frederick Hobday Meml, British Equine Vet. Assoc., 1986; Richard Turk Meml, Texas A & M Univ., 1991; Harben, RIPH&H, 1991; Stoll Meml, NJ, 1995; Clive Behrens, Leeds Univ., 1996; Stoll-Stunkard, Amer. Soc. Parasitol., 1997; Bourne, St George's Univ., Grenada, 2001; Boyd Orr, Nutrition Soc., 2002; Windref, St George's Univ., Grenada, 2004; Steele Meml, Univ. of Texas, 2005; Garrod, British Soc. Antimicrobial Therapy, 2008. Member: AFRC, 1984–89 (Chm., Animal Res. Grants Bd, 1986–89); Vet. Adv. Cttee, Horserace Betting Levy Bd, 1984–97 (Chm., 1985–97); EEC Adv. Cttee on Vet. Trng, 1981–86; Animal Procedure Cttee, Home Office, 1986–95. Royal College of Veterinary Surgeons: Mem. Council, 1978–93; Jun. Vice-Pres., 1983; Pres., 1984; Sen. Vice-Pres., 1985; Hon. Fellow, 1997. President: World Assoc. Adv. Vet. Parasit., 1963–67 (Hon. Mem., 1985); Helminthol. Soc., Washington, 1970–71 (Hon. Mem., 1990); Cambridge Soc. for Comp. Medicine, 1984–85; Vet. Res. Club, 1985–86; Pet Adv. Cttee, 1997–; RSocMed, 1998–2000 (Pres., Comp. Medicine Section, 1993–95; Hon. Fellow, 1996); RIPH, then RSPH, 2004–; Parly and Sci. Cttee, 2004–08; Windward Islands Res. and Educn Foundn, 2008–. Council Mem., Amer. Soc. Parasitologists, 1974–78. Corresponding Member: German Parasitology Soc.; Acad. Royale de Médecine de Belgique; Hon. Member: Mexican Parasitology Soc.; Argentinian Parasitological Soc.; BVA; British Soc. for Parasitology; World Innovation Foundn; Hon. Life Member: British Small Animal Vet. Assoc.; British Soc. Antimicrobial Therapy; Expert Advisor and Consultant, and Member, Scientific Groups: various internat. agencies and govts. Chm., Companion Animal Welfare Council, 1999–; Member: Council, Internat. League for Protection of Horses, 1997–2002; Soc. for Protection of Animals Abroad, 1997–2004. Patron: Vet. Benevolent Fund, 1996; Fund for Replacement of Animals in Med. Experiments, 1997–. Founder FMedSci 1998. Hon. FRCPath 2005. Hon. AM 1972, Hon. DSc 1984, Univ. of Pennsylvania; Hon. DVMS: Edinburgh, 1991; Glasgow, 2001; Hon. DVM: León, 1993; Liverpool, 2004; Hon. DSc: Univ. of Peradeniya, Sri Lanka, 1994; St George's Univ., Grenada, 2005; Lincoln, 2007. R. N. Chaudhury Gold Medal, Calcutta Sch. of Tropical Med., Calcutta, 1976; Behring-Bilharz Prize, Cairo, 1977; Ludwig-Schunk Prize, Justus-Liebig Universität, Giessen, 1979; Diploma and Medal, XXI World Vet. Congress, Moscow, 1979; Distinguished Parasitologist Award, Amer. Assoc. of Vet. Parasitologists, 1987; Friedrich Mussenmeier Medal, Humboldt Univ., 1990; World Assoc. for Advancement of Vet. Parasitology/Pfizer Excellence in Teaching Award, 1993; Chiron Award, BVA, 1998; Equestrian Vet. Achievement Award, Animal Health Trust, 2005; Dist. Service Award and Mike Fisher Meml Award, St George's Univ., Grenada, 2006; Wight Award, British Small Animals Veterinary Assoc., 2009. *Publications:* Textbook of Veterinary Clinical Parasitology, 1965; Biology of Parasites, 1966; Reaction of the Host to Parasitism, 1968; Helminths, Arthropods and Protozoa of Domesticated Animals, 6th edn 1968, 7th edn 1982; Immunity to Animal Parasites, 1972; Parasitic Zoonoses, 1974; Pathophysiology of Parasitic Infections, 1976; Epidemiology and Control of Nematodiasis in Cattle, 1981; Immunology, Immunopathology and Immunoprophylaxis of Parasitic Infections, Vols I, II, III & IV, 1986; Zoonoses, 1998; articles in jls of parasitology, immunology and pathology. *Recreations:* travel, gardening, photography. *Address:* House of Lords, SW1A 0PW. *Club:* Farmers.

SOULSBY, Sir Peter (Alfred), Kt 1999; Mayor of Leicester (Lab), since 2011; *b* 27 Dec. 1948; *s* of late Robert and of Mary Soulsby; *m* 1969, Alison Prime (*d* 2011); three *d*. *Educ:* Minchenden Sch., Southgate; City of Leicester Coll. (BEd Leicester Univ.). Teacher of children with special educational needs, 1973–90. Mem. (Lab), Leicester City Council, 1973–2003 (Leader, 1981–94 and 1995–99). MP (Lab) Leicester S, 2005–April 2011. Mem., Audit Commission, 1994–2000. Vice-Chairman: Waterways Trust, 1999–2003; British Waterways Bd, 2000–04 (Mem., 1998–2004). *Address:* City Mayor's Office, 7th Floor, Block B, New Walk Centre, Welford Place, Leicester LE1 6ZG.

SOUNDY, Andrew John; Senior Partner, Ashurst Morris Crisp (Solicitors), 1992–98; *b* 29 March 1940; *s* of Harold Cecil Soundy and Adele Monica Templeton (*née* Westley); *m* 1963, Jill Marion Steiner; one *s* two *d*. *Educ:* Boxgrove Sch.; Shrewsbury Sch.; Trinity Coll., Cambridge (BA, MA). Ashurst Morris Crisp: articled clerk, 1963–66; qualified as solicitor, 1966; Partner, 1969. Non-exec. Dir, EWFact plc, 1994–98 (Chm., 1997–98). Vice Pres., 1998–2009, Trustee (Dir), 2003–10, The Lord Slynn of Hadley Eur. Law Foundn. Director: St Michael's Hospice, Basingstoke, 1996– (Chm., 2007–11; Pres., 2011–); Anglo-Russian Opera and Ballet Trust, 2001–. Mem. Bd Govs, De Montfort Univ., 2001–05. Churchwarden, Parish of Mattingley, 2002–10, now Emeritus. FRSA 1993. *Recreations:* countryside, shooting, opera, maintenance of historic buildings. *Address:* Gainsborough House, 69 High Street, Odiham, Hants RG29 1LB. *T:* (01256) 704290. *Clubs:* Cavalry and Guards, City Law, Bishopsgate Ward.

SOUNESS, Graeme James; Manager, Newcastle United Football Club, 2004–06; Commentator, Sky TV, since 2006; *b* 6 May 1953; *s* of James and Elizabeth Souness; *m* 1994, Karen; one *s*, and two *s* one *d* from previous marriage. *Educ:* Carrickvale Sch., Edinburgh. Professional football player: Tottenham Hotspur, 1969–73; Middlesbrough FC, 1973–78; Liverpool FC, 1978–84 (3 European Cups, 1978, 1981 and 1984; 5 League Championships, 1979–84 and 4 League Cups, 1981–84); Sampdoria, Italy, 1984–86; played for Scotland, 1975–86 (54 full caps); Manager: Glasgow Rangers, 1986–91 (also player, 1986–90; 4 Scottish League Championships, 1987, 1989, 1990, 1991; 4 Scottish League Cups, 1987–90); Liverpool FC, 1991–94 (FA Cup, 1992); Galatasaray, Turkey, 1995–96 (Turkish Cup, 1996); Southampton FC, 1996–97; Torino, Italy, 1997–98; Benfica, Portugal, 1998–99; Blackburn Rovers, 2000–04 (Worthington Cup, 2002). *Publications:* (with B. Harris) No Half Measures, 1984; A Manager's Diary, 1990. *Recreations:* golf, gardening, walking.

SOUROZH, Archbishop of, (Russian Orthodox), since 2010; **Rt Rev. Elisey Ilia Ganaba;** Bishop of Bogorodsk, since 2006; *b* St Petersburg, 1 Aug. 1962. Head, Russian Ecclesiastical Mission in Jerusalem, 2002–06. *Address:* 67 Ennismore Gardens, SW7 1NH. *T:* (020) 7584 0086, *Fax:* (020) 7584 9864. *E:* sourozhdiocese@me.com.

SOUTAR, Air Marshal Sir Charles (John Williamson), KBE 1978 (MBE 1958); Director-General, Medical Services (RAF), 1978–81; *b* 12 June 1920; *s* of Charles Alexander Soutar and Mary Helen (*née* Watson); *m* 1944, Joy Dorée Upton (*d* 2004); one *s* two *d*. *Educ:* Brentwood Sch.; London Hosp. MB, BS, LMSSA, FFCM, DPH, DIH. Commissioned RAF, 1946. Various appts, then PMO, Middle East Command, 1967–68; Dep. Dir, Med. Organisation, RAF, 1968–70; OC, PMRAF Hosp., Halton, 1970–73; Comdt, RAF Inst. of Aviation Medicine, 1973–75; PMO, Strike Command, 1975–78. QHS 1974–81. CStJ 1972. *Recreations:* sport, gardening, ornithology, music. *Club:* Royal Air Force.

SOUTAR, David Strang; Consultant Plastic Surgeon, Nuffield Health Glasgow Hospital, since 2008; *b* 19 Dec. 1947; *s* of Alexander Anderson Soutar and Lizbeth Agnes Bailey Soutar; *m* 1972, Myra (*née* Banks); two *s* one *d*. *Educ:* Univ. of Aberdeen (MB ChB 1972; ChM 1987). Registrar, Gen. Surgery, Grampian Health Bd, 1975–78; Registrar, then Sen. Registrar, Plastic Surgery, 1978–81, Consultant Plastic Surgeon, 1981–2008, W of Scotland Regional Plastic Surgery Unit, Canniesburn Hosp., Bearsden, Glasgow. Hon. Clinical Sen. Lectr, Univ. of Glasgow, 1981–2009. Chm., Div. of Trauma and Related Services, N Glasgow Univ. Hosps NHS Div., 2002–06. *Publications:* Practical Guide to Free Tissue Transfer, 1986; Microvascular Surgery and Free Tissue Transfer, 1993; Excision and Reconstruction in Head and Neck Cancer, 1994; contrib. 30 chapters in books and over 80 papers in peer-reviewed jls. *Recreations:* music, travel, golf. *Address:* Nuffield Health Glasgow Hospital, 25 Beaconsfield Road, Glasgow G12 0PJ. *T:* (0141) 334 9441, *Fax:* (0141) 339 1352.

SOUTAR, Ian; *see* Soutar, S. I.

SOUTAR, Michael James; Chief Executive, ShortList Media Ltd, since 2007; *b* Dundee, 8 Nov. 1966; *s* of David Bruce Soutar and Patricia Grace Anne Buik; *m* 1994, Beverly; one *s* and one step *s*. *Educ:* Glenrothes High Sch., Fife; Univ. of Michigan (Exec. MBA 2004). Editor: Smash Hits, 1990–94; FHM, 1994–97; Man. Dir, Kiss FM, 1997–99; Ed. in Chief, Maxim USA, 1999–2000; Man. Dir, IPC Ignite, 2000–03; Editl Dir, IPC Media, 2003–06; Founder, Crash Test Media Ltd, 2006–. Chm., Wallpaper Media, 2001–03. Trustee, Comic Relief, 2003–10. *Recreations:* running, cooking, reading, travelling, Arsenal FC. *Address:* ShortList Media Ltd, 26–34 Emerald Street, WC1N 3QA. *T:* (020) 7611 9702. *E:* mike.soutar@shortlist.com. *Clubs:* Soho House, Ivy, Hospital, Paramount.

SOUTAR, (Samuel) Ian; HM Diplomatic Service, retired; Ambassador to Bulgaria, 2001–03; *b* 2 June 1945; *s* of James Soutar and Maud Soutar (*née* McNinch); *m* 1968, Mary Isabella Boyle; one *s* one *d*. *Educ:* Ballymena Acad.; Trinity Coll. Dublin (BA Mod. Langs and Lit.). FCO, 1968–70; UK Delegn to EC, 1970–72; Saigon, 1972–74; First Sec., FCO, 1974–76; Private Sec. to Parly Under-Sec. of State, 1976–77; Washington, 1977–81; FCO, 1981–86; Dep. High Comr, Wellington, 1986–91; RCDS 1991; Head, Inf. Systems Div. (Ops), FCO, 1991–95; Head, Library and Records Dept, FCO, 1995–97; UK Perm. Rep. to Conf. on Disarmament, Geneva, 1997–2001. Mem., Lord Chancellor's Adv. Council on Nat. Records and Archives, 2008–14. *Recreations:* walking, listening to music. *Address:* Flat 10, 2 Graystone Road, Whitstable, Kent CT5 2NB.

SOUTER, Sir Brian, Kt 2011; Chairman, Stagecoach Group plc, 1980–2002 and since 2013 (Chief Executive, 2002–13); *b* 1954; *s* of late Iain and Catherine Souter; *m* 1988, Elizabeth McGoldrick; three *s* one *d*. *Educ:* Dundee Univ.; Univ. of Strathclyde (BA Accountancy). CA; MCIT. *Address:* Stagecoach Group plc, 10 Dunkeld Road, Perth PH1 5TW.
See also A. H. Gloag.

SOUTER, Carole Lesley, CBE 2011; FSA; Chief Executive (formerly Director), Heritage Lottery Fund, since 2003; *b* 2 May 1957; *d* of late Richard Teague and June Teague; *m* 1979, David Norman Souter; one *s* one *d*. *Educ:* Truro High Sch. for Girls; St Austell 6th Form Coll.; Jesus Coll., Oxford (BA Hons PPE); Birkbeck Coll., London (MA Victorian Studies). Various posts, DHSS, later DSS, 1978–2000; Dir, Planning and Develt, English Heritage, 2000–03. Dir, Nat. Communities Resource Centre, 2013–. Trustee: London (formerly SE London, then Capital) Community Foundn, 1996–2013 (Chm., 2004–07); London Bombings Relief Charitable Fund, 2005–08; Creativity, Culture and Education, 2008–; Kent Wildlife Trust, 2012–. FRSA 2003; FSA 2014. *Recreations:* gardening, visiting historic sites, museums and galleries, theatre. *Address:* Heritage Lottery Fund, 7 Holbein Place, SW1W 8NR. *T:* (020) 7591 6011, *Fax:* (020) 7591 6013. *E:* caroles@hlf.org.uk.

SOUTER, David Hackett; Associate Justice of the Supreme Court of the United States, 1990–2009; *b* 17 Sept. 1939. *Educ:* Harvard Univ. (LLB); Oxford Univ. (Rhodes Scholar; MA). Admitted to NH Bar; Associate, Orr & Reno, Concord, NH, 1966–68; Asst Attorney-Gen., 1968–71, Dep. Attorney-Gen., 1976, Attorney-Gen., 1976–78, New Hampshire; Associate Justice: NH Superior Court, 1978–83; NH Supreme Court, 1983–90. *Address:* c/o Supreme Court Building, 1 First Street NE, Washington, DC 20543, USA.

SOUTH, Martin Christopher; Chief Executive Officer: Marsh Ltd, since 2007; Marsh Asia-Pacific, since 2013; *b* Kenya, 4 Jan. 1965; *s* of Anthony and Adelheid South; *m* 2010, Traci Alford; one *s* three *d* by a previous marriage. *Educ:* Charterhouse Sch. Minet Gp, 1983–85; C T Bowring, later Marsh Ltd, 1985–96; Zurich Re, 1996–2000; Chief Executive Officer: Zurich London, 2000–04; Zurich Specialities, 2003; Internat. Business Div., Zurich Financial Services, 2003–07; Marsh Europe, 2012. Dep. Pres., Insce Inst. of London, 2010–11. *Recreations:* ski-ing, tennis, family, epicurean activities. *Address:* 8 Marina View #09–02, Asia Square Tower 1, Singapore 018960. *T:* 69228333. *E:* martin.south@marsh.com.

SOUTH, William Lawrence, CBE 1988; FIET; Director, Philips Electronics, 1982–94; management consultant, 1991–2002; *b* 3 May 1933; *s* of Laurence and Anne South; *m* 1960, Lesley (*née* Donaldson); one *s* two *d*. *Educ:* Purley County Grammar Sch. FIET (FIEE 1992). RAF, 1951–55 (Pilot, 511 and 220 Sqdns). Director: Pye of Cambridge, 1977–81; Origin Holdings, 1990–92; Greenwich Healthcare NHS Trust, 1995–2003. Member: NPL Supervisory Bd, 1988–96; ITAB, 1988–93; SERC Engrg Bd, 1992–94. Freeman, City of London, 1991; Liveryman, Co. of Information Technologists, 1992–. Hon. DTech Greenwich, 2004. *Recreations:* sailing, music. *Address:* 14 Harbour Way, Emsworth, Hants PO10 7BE. *Club:* Chichester Yacht.

SOUTH AUSTRALIA, Metropolitan of; *see* Adelaide, Archbishop of.

SOUTHALL, Anna Catherine, OBE 2013; Vice Chairman: Big Lottery Fund, 2006–14 (Member Board, 2004–06); Wales Millennium Centre, since 2011; *b* 9 June 1948; *d* of Stephen Readhead Southall and Philippa (Cadbury) Southall; *m* 1st, 1975, Neil Burton (marr. diss. 1978); 2nd, 1983, Christopher Serle (marr. diss. 2003); two *s*. *Educ:* Univ. of E Anglia (BA Hons 1970); Gateshead Tech. Coll. (Post Grad. Dip. 1974). Ecclesiastical Insce Office, 1970; Adv. Bd for Redundant Churches, Church Comrs, 1970–71; teacher, Shoreditch Secondary Sch., ILEA (full and part-time), 1971–74; Conservator, Polychrome Monuments (freelance), 1974–75; Senior Conservator: S Eastern Museums' Service, 1975–81; Tate Gall., London, 1981–96; Asst Dir, 1996–98, Dir, 1998–2002, Nat. Museums and Galls of Wales; Chief Exec., Resource: The Council for Museums, Archives and Libraries, 2002–03. Chm., Barrow Cadbury Trust, 1996–2006. Member: Govt's Spoliation Adv. Panel, 2000–10; Adv. Panel on Futurebuilders, 2005–08. *Publications:* numerous contribs on 18th and 19th century British artists' materials and techniques in conf. papers, exhibn catalogues and professional jls. *Recreations:* my small-holding in Wales, family and friends, and sharing their sporting and cultural interests.

SOUTHAMPTON, 7th Baron *cr* 1780; **Edward Charles FitzRoy;** *b* Norwich, 8 July 1955; *s* of 6th Baron Southampton and Pamela Anne FitzRoy (*née* Henniker); *S* father, 2015; *m* 1978, Rachel Caroline Vincent Millett; one *s* three *d*. *Educ:* Gresham's Sch., Holt; Royal Agricl Coll., Cirencester. *Recreations:* painting, current affairs, reading, shooting. *Heir:* *s* Hon. Charles Edward Millett FitzRoy, *b* 18 Jan. 1983. *Address:* Venn Farm, Morchard Bishop, Crediton, Devon EX17 6SQ. *E:* ecfitz57@yahoo.co.uk.

SOUTHAMPTON, Bishop Suffragan of, since 2010; **Rt Rev. Jonathan Hugh Frost;** *b* 26 Sept. 1964; *s* of late Peter Clifford Frost and of Jean Lucelle Frost; *m* 1988, Christine Cuckow; three *c*. *Educ:* Univ. of Aberdeen (BD 1988); Nottingham Univ. (MTh 1999); Ridley Hall, Cambridge. Ordained deacon, 1993, priest, 1994; Asst Curate, St Giles, Bridgford, 1993–97; Rector, St Peter's, Ash, 1997–2002; Chaplain, Univ. of Surrey, 2002–10; Canon Res., Guildford Cathedral, 2002–10. Tutor, Local Ministry Prog., Dio. of Guildford, 1999–2010; Bishop of Guildford's Advr for Inter-Faith Relns, 2007–10. DUniv Surrey, 2012. *Recreation:* lifelong supporter of Fulham Football Club. *Address:* Bishop's House, St Mary's Church Close, Wessex Lane, Southampton SO18 2ST.

SOUTHAN, Elizabeth Andreas; *see* Evatt, Hon. E. A.

SOUTHAN, His Honour Robert Joseph; a Circuit Judge, 1986–2001; *b* 13 July 1928; *s* of late Thomas Southan and of Kathleen Southan; *m* 1960, Elizabeth Andreas Evatt, *qv*; one *d* (one *s* decd). *Educ:* Rugby; St Edmund Hall, Oxford (MA); University Coll., London (LLM); Open Univ. (BA Hons 2008). Called to the Bar, Inner Temple, 1953; called to the Bar of NSW, 1976; a Recorder, 1983–86. *Recreations:* theatre, opera, sailing, tennis. *Clubs:* Royal Corinthian Yacht, Bar Yacht; Cumberland Lawn Tennis.

SOUTHBY, Sir John (Richard Bilbe), 3rd Bt *cr* 1937, of Burford, Co. Oxford; *b* 2 April 1948; *s* of Sir Archibald Richard Charles Southby, 2nd Bt, OBE and Olive Marion (*d* 1991), *d* of late Sir Thomas Bilbe-Robinson; *S* father, 1988; *m* 1971, Victoria Jane, *d* of John Wilfred Sturrock; two *s* one *d*. *Educ:* Peterhouse, Marandellas, Rhodesia; Loughborough Univ. of Technology (BSc Elec. Eng). CEng, MIET. East Midlands Electricity: Graduate Trainee, 1971; Asst Engineer 1973, O & M Engineer 1976, Shepshed, Leics; Senior Asst Engineer 1979, O & M Engineer 1981, Boston, Lincs; District Engineer, Grantham, 1986; Dist Manager, then Gen. Manager, Milton Keynes, 1991; Network Gen. Manager Northampton, 1996–99. Pres., Milton Keynes Business Leaders (formerly Milton Keynes Large Employers Assoc.), 1998– (Chm., 1994–98); Chm., Milton Keynes Police Area Adv. Cttee, 1995–99; Mem. Bd, Milton Keynes Economic Partnership, 1994–99; Dir, Milton Keynes Theatre and Gallery Mgt Co., 1996–2000; non-exec. Dir, Milton Keynes Gen. NHS Trust, 2001–08. Pres., Milton Keynes Rotary Club, 1997–98 (Sen. Vice Pres., 1996–97; Sec., 1999–2004, 2006–12); Asst Sec., 1998–99, 2012–14, Sec., 1999–2004, 2014–, Asst Gov., 2006–09, Rotary Dist 1260. FCMI. *Recreations:* ski-ing, gardening, music, DIY, photography. *Heir: s* Peter John Southby [*b* 20 Aug. 1973; *m* 1995, Katherine Margaret, *d* of Dr R. N. Priestland; three *s*]. *Address:* Lomagundi, High Street, Nash, Bucks MK17 0EP.

SOUTHEND, Archdeacon of; *see* Smallman, Ven. W. T.

SOUTHERN, Dr David Boardman; QC 2014; barrister; Director and Visiting Professor, School of Tax Law, Queen Mary, University of London, since 1998; *b* Bexhill-on-Sea, 12 May 1946; *s* of Leslie Southern and Emily Southern (*née* Boardman); *m* 1975, Jane Heslop; one *s* one *d*. *Educ:* Christ Church, Oxford (Open, Dixon and Sen. Scholar; BA, MPhil; DPhil 1976); Bonn Univ. CTA (Fellow) 1998 (FIIT 2009). Lectr, Univ. of Kent at Canterbury, 1973–82; called to the Bar, Lincoln's Inn, 1982, Bencher, 2010; Legal Advr, Bd of Inland Revenue, 1983–90; Tax Advr, Lloyds Bank, 1990–97; in practice as a barrister, 1997–. Treas., Bar Council, 2004–07. *Publications:* Governing Germany, 1990; Taxation of Corporate Debt and Financial Instruments, 1997, 10th edn as Taxation of Loan Relationships and Derivative Contracts, 2015; articles in legal and tax jls. *Recreations:* Germany, opera, theatre. *Address:* Temple Tax Chambers, 3 Temple Gardens, Temple, EC4Y 9AU. *T:* (020) 7353 7884. *E:* David.SouthernQC@templetax.com. *Club:* Athenæum.

SOUTHERN, Graham; Director, Blain|Southern Gallery, since 2010; *b* Cornwall, 21 Sept. 1960; *s* of John and Barbara Southern; *m* 1995, Antje Schmitt; two *d*. Christie's London: Specialist, Modern and Impressionist Dept, 1985–88, Modern British Dept, 1988–94; Founding Dir, Post War and Contemporary British Art Dept, 1994–97; Dir, Contemporary Art Dept, 1997–2001; Director: Christie Manson & Wood, 1990–2001; Anthony d'Offay Gall., London, 2001; Founding Dir, Haunch of Venison Gall., 2002–10. Trustee, Public Catalogue Foundn, 2008–. Adjudicator, Prince's Drawing Sch., 2011–. *Club:* Chelsea Arts.

SOUTHERN, Rt Rev. Humphrey Ivo John; Principal, Ripon College, Cuddesdon, since 2015; an Honorary Assistant Bishop, Diocese of Oxford, since 2015; Suffragan Bishop of Repton, 2007–15; *b* 17 Sept. 1960; *s* of late Guy Hugo Southern and of Rosamund Antonia Southern; *m* 1996, Emma Jane, *o d* of Robin and Brenda Lush; two *d*. *Educ:* Harrow Sch.; Westminster Tutors; Christ Church, Oxford (MA 1986); Ripon Coll., Cuddesdon. Ordained deacon, 1986, priest, 1987; Assistant Curate: St Margaret's, Rainham, Kent, 1986–89; Walton-on-the-Hill, Liverpool, 1989–92; Vicar and Team Rector, Hale with Badshot Lea, Farnham, Surrey, 1992–99; Ecumenical Officer, Dio. of Guildford, 1992–99; Team Rector, Tisbury and Nadder Valley, Wilts, 1999–2007. Chm., House of Clergy, Dio. of Salisbury, 2004–07; Non-res. Canon and Prebendary, Salisbury Cathedral, 2006–07; Warden of Readers, Dio. of Derby, 2009–10; Chair: Derbyshire Churches and Church of N India Partnership, 2009–15; Derby Diocesan Bd of Educn, 2013–15. Occasional contrib., Pause for Thought, BBC Radio 2, 2009–11. *Publications:* contrib. to Theology. *Recreations:* conversation, cooking, horse racing, English Bull Terriers, bonfires, reading widely and walking gently. *Address:* Ripon College, Cuddesdon, Oxford OX44 9EX. *T:* (01865) 877400. *E:* Principal@rcc.ac.uk. *Club:* Brooks's.

SOUTHERN, Paul David; a Judge of the Upper Tribunal (Immigration and Asylum Chamber) (formerly a Senior Immigration Judge, Asylum and Immigration Tribunal), since 2006; Principal Resident Judge of the Upper Tribunal (Immigration and Asylum Chamber), since 2011; *b* 3 Feb. 1954; *m* 1987, Anne Prosser; three *s* one *d*. *Educ:* Tetherdown Primary Sch.; William Ellis Grammar Sch.; Lanchester Poly. (BA Hons Business Law 1976). Admitted as solicitor, 1979; Dep. Dist Judge, 2000–; Immigration Adjudicator, 2002–05; Immigration Judge, 2005–06. *Recreation:* motorcycling. *Address:* Upper Tribunal (Immigration and Asylum Tribunal), Field House, 15/25 Bream's Buildings, EC4A 1DZ.

SOUTHERN, Dr Peter Campbell David; Director, International College Spain, 2009–13; *b* 28 Feb. 1947; *s* of Sir Richard Southern, FBA; *m* 1972, Dinah Mitchell; two *s*. *Educ:* Dragon Sch., Oxford; Magdalen College Sch., Oxford; Merton Coll., Oxford (MA); Edinburgh Univ. (PhD). Malosa Secondary Sch., Malawi, 1964–65; Tutorial Asst, Edinburgh Univ., 1970–71; Asst Master, Dulwich Coll., 1973–78; Head of History Dept, Westminster Sch., 1978–85; Head Master: Bancroft's Sch., 1985–96; Christ's Hospital, 1996–2007. Governor: Dulwich Coll., 2007–12; Bancroft's Sch., 2008–. History Awarder and Reviser, Oxford and Cambridge Examn Bd, 1980–90; Sec., Nat. Centre for Cued Speech, 1990–92. Vice-Chm., Redbridge and Waltham Forest Dist HA, 1993–96. Trustee, Lumos, 2007–12. *Publications:* articles on P. G. Wodehouse. *Recreations:* sailing, golf.

SOUTHERN, Richard Michael; QC 2006; *b* Yorks, 1964; *s* of Michael and Merle Southern; *m* 2001, Yvette Austin; two *d*. *Educ:* St Catharine's Coll., Cambridge (BA 1986). Called to the Bar, Middle Temple, 1987; in practice as barrister specialising in commercial litigation. Mem., Oxford & Cambridge Sailing Soc. *Recreation:* sailing. *Address:* 7 King's Bench Walk, Temple, EC4Y 7DS. *T:* (020) 7910 8300. *E:* rsouthern@7kbw.co.uk. *Clubs:* Bar Yacht, Royal Corinthian Yacht (Cowes).

SOUTHESK, Earl of; Charles Duff Carnegie; *b* 1 July 1989; *s* and *heir* of Duke of Fife, *qv*.

SOUTHEY, (David) Hugh; QC 2010; a Recorder of the Crown Court, since 2009; *b* Redhill, 29 Feb. 1964; *s* of David Southey and Mary Southey; *m* 1989, Jacqueline Margaret Peirce. *Educ:* Salvatorian Coll.; Harrow Weald 6th Form Coll.; Imperial Coll., London (MEng); City of London Poly. Trainee solicitor, Lewis Silkin, 1989–91; admitted solicitor, 1991; solicitor, Glazer Delmar, 1991–96; called to the Bar, Inner Temple, 1996; barrister, Tooks Chambers, 1997–2013, Matrix Chambers, 2013–. *Publications:* (jtly) A Criminal Practitioner's Guide to Judicial Review and Case Stated, 1999; (jtly) United Kingdom Human Rights Reports, 2000–; (jtly) Judicial Review: a practical guide, 2004, 2nd edn 2012. *Recreations:* cricket, running, ski-ing, theatre, contemporary music, Marco and Maggie. *Address:* Matrix Chambers, Griffin Building, Gray's Inn, WC1R 5LN. *E:* hughsouthey@matrixlaw.co.uk.

SOUTHGATE, Sir Colin (Grieve), Kt 1992; Chairman, Whitehead Mann Group plc, 2003–06 (non-executive Director, 1997–2006); *b* 24 July 1938; *s* of Cyril Alfred and Edith Isabelle Southgate; *m* 1962, Sally Patricia Mead; two *s* two *d*. *Educ:* City of London Sch. ICT, later ICL, 1960–70; formed Software Sciences, 1970; apptd Chief Exec., BOC Computer Services Div. on sale of Software Sciences to BOC, 1980–82; Chief Executive: THORN EMI Information Technology, 1983; THORN EMI, subseq. EMI Gp plc, 1989–99 (Dir, 1984–99); Dir, 1990–96, Chm., 1993–96, PowerGen; Dir, Bank of England, 1991–99; Chm., Terence Chapman Gp plc, 1999–2003 (non-exec. Dir, 1997–99). Chm., Royal Opera House, Covent Gdn, 1998–2003; Trustee: Nat. Gall., 1998–2005; Music Sound Foundn, 1998–2002. Vice Patron, Home Farm Develt Trust, 1991– (Trustee, 1988–91). *Recreation:* gardening.

SOUTHGATE, Joanna Mary; *see* Donaldson, J. M.

SOUTHGATE, Dame Lesley (Jill), DBE 1999; DSc; FRCP, FRCGP; Professor of Medical Education, St George's, University of London, since 2004; *b* 25 Sept. 1943; *m* Richard Boyd Bennet, GP; three *c*. *Educ:* Liverpool Univ. (MB ChB 1967); Univ. of Western Ontario (MClinSci 1980). MRCGP 1974, FRCGP 1985; FRCP 1997. House surgeon and phys., St Helen's Hosp.; W. K. Kellogg Fellow, Univ. of Western Ontario; former GP, Hoddesdon; Sen. Lectr, then Prof. of Gen. Practice, 1992–95, St Bartholomew's Hosp. Med. Coll.; Prof. of Primary Care and Medical Educn, Royal Free and University College Med. Sch. (formerly at UCL), 1995–2004; founder Mem., Centre for Health Informatics and Multiprofessional Educn, UCL. Convenor, Panel of MRCGP Examnrs, 1994–99; Chm., Perf. Assessment Implementation Gp, GMC, 1994–2004; Mem., Postgrad. Med. Educn and Trng Bd, 2003–06. President: RCGP, 2000–03; ASME, 2006–09. Mem. Bd, Royal Vet. Sch. Mem. at Large, Nat. Bd Med. Examnrs, Philadelphia. Trustee, Thalidomide Trust, 2010–15. Founder FMedSci 1998. Hon. FAcadMed. *Publications:* (contrib.) The Certification and Recertification of Doctors, 1993; (jtly) Infection, 1997; (contrib.) Teaching Medicine in the Community, 1997; contrib. to learned jls. *Address:* Department of Medical Education, St George's, University of London, Cranmer Terrace, SW17 0RE. *T:* (020) 7288 5209. *E:* lesley.southgate@sgul.ac.uk.

SOUTHGATE, Robert; Chairman, Birmingham Royal Ballet, 2000–04 (Vice-Chairman, 1994–99); *b* 20 Jan. 1934; *s* of Robert Bevis Southgate and Ann Southgate (*née* Boyes); *m* 1st, 1957, Elizabeth Benson; four *s*; 2nd, 2002, Ann Yeandle (*d* 2015), *d* of Edward Yeandle and Kate (*née* Walker). *Educ:* Morecambe Grammar Sch. Work on national newspapers, 1954–64; Dep. Northern Editor, The Sun, 1964–68; Reporter and Presenter, ITN, 1969–78; Presenter, Thames TV, 1978–80; Controller, News and Current Affairs: TVS, 1980–84; Central TV, 1984–92; non-executive Director: Meridian TV, 1995–97; Central Broadcasting, 1994–97 (former Dep. Man. Dir and Man. Dir). Mem., Arts Council, 1993–97; Chairman: W Midlands Regl Arts Bd, 1992–97; City of Birmingham Touring Opera, 1992–97; Dir, Birmingham Rep. Th., 1996–2002. *Recreations:* Lyric Theatre, travel, food, wine.

SOUTHGATE, Dr Vaughan Robert; DL; FZS, FRSB; President, Linnean Society of London, 2009–12; *b* Kempston, 13 May 1944; *s* of Stanley Robert Double and Hilda Louisa Peggy Southgate (*née* Dean); *m* 1966, Marilyn Kuhn; one *s* one *d*. *Educ:* Bedford Modern Sch.; University Coll. of Wales, Aberystwyth (BSc); Christ's Coll., Cambridge (PhD 1969). FZS 1970; MInstBiol 1980, FRSB (FInstBiol 1988). Natural History Museum: Jun. Res. Fellow, 1968–71; SSO, 1971–76; PSO, 1976–92; SPSO (Individual Merit), 1992–2004. Hd, Biomed. Parasitol. Div. and Dir, WHO Collaborating Centre for Identification of schistosomes and their snail intermediate hosts, 1983–2004; Mem., Expert Cttee on parasitic diseases (schistosomiasis), WHO, 1986–2011. Ed., Jl Natural Hist., 1972–83. Royal Society of Tropical Medicine and Hygiene: Fellow, 1970; Mem. Council, 1979–82; Hon. Sec., 1986–91; Vice Pres., 1993–95. FRSocMed 2006. Linnean Society of London: Fellow, 1988; Zool Sec., 1997–2009; Vice Pres., 1998–2008; Pres. Elect, 2008–09. Hon. Fellow, Dept of Biol., UCL, 2002–12. British Society for Parasitology: Mem., 1965–; Mem. Council, 1975–77; Chm., Autumn Symposium Cttee, 1984–88. Mem., Beds and Luton Crimebeat, 2006–. Trustee: John Spedan Lewis Foundn, 2001–; Bedford Hosps Charity, 2008–; Chm., Trustees, Friends of Cople Ch, 2003–15. Patron, The Higgins, Bedford (formerly Cecil Higgins Art Gall. and Bedford Mus.), 2009–. Mem., Bedford Camera Club (Pres., 2008–10); President: London Soc. of Old Aberystwythians, 2012–14; Old Bedford Modernians, 2013–14 (Vice-Pres., 2012–13); Bedford Millennium Probus Club, 2014–15 (Vice-Pres., 2013–14); Mem., Biggleswade Ivel Rotary Club, 2000–11 (Paul Harris Fellow, 2009; Hon. Mem., 2014). Mem., Beds High Sheriff's Panel, 2008–12. High Sheriff, 2007–08, DL 2009–, Beds. C. A. Wright Meml Medal, British Soc. of Parasitol., 1990. *Publications:* contrib. chapters in books; contrib. articles to learned jls specialising in parasitol. and tropical medicine. *Recreations:* fly fishing, shooting, photography, natural history, family. *Address:* The Coach House, Woodlands Close, Cople, Bedford MK44 3UE. *T:* (01234) 838714. *E:* V.Southgate714@btinternet.com. *Clubs:* Royal Society of Medicine; Sheerhatch Shoot; Roxton Park Trout Fishery.

SOUTHGATE, Sir William (David), Kt 1995; conductor and composer; *b* Waipukurau, NZ, 4 Aug. 1941; *s* of Alfred John Southgate and Phyllis (*née* Maden); *m* 1967, (Alison) Rosemary Martin, *d* of (Alexander James) Lloyd Martin and (Gwendolene) Noel (*née* McGeorge). *Educ:* Otago Boys' High Sch.; Otago Univ. (MA Hons First Cl.; BMus Hons First Cl.); Guildhall Sch. of Music and Drama (Ricordi Conducting Prize). Worked in UK with variety of musical orgns incl. Phoenix Opera Co., RSC and BBC TV, 1969–74; worked in NZ, 1974–; Musical Dir, then Principal Guest Conductor, Christchurch Symphony Orch., 1986–97, Conductor Laureate, 1997–; Guest Conductor, NZ Symphony Orch., 1975–, and all main NZ orchs and opera cos; Musical Director: Royal NZ Ballet, 1976–93; Wellington Youth Orch., 1978–90; Wellington Regional Orch.; Conductor, Wellington City Opera Co. Has conducted orchs in Europe, NZ and Australia, incl. Hallé, Royal Philharmonic, Berlin Radio Symphony, and Sydney Symphony. Own arts and music progs on TV and radio in NZ. Patron: Wellington Audio Club; Performing Arts Comp. Assoc. of NZ; New Plymouth Orch. Hon. DMus Otago, 1994. Queen's Sesquicentennial Medal, NZ, 1990; Kirk-Burnand and Brown Citation, Composers' Assoc. of NZ, 1993; NZ Music Award, 2003. Internationally accredited as major interpreter of classic/romantic symphonic repertoire in Wand to Furtwangler/German tradition. *Compositions include:* Capital Variations, 1983; Symphony No 1, 1984; Symphony No 2, 1988; Erewhon (for wind quintet), 1989; Cello Concerto, 1991; Psalmody, 1992; Hamlet (ballet), 1992, Hamlet Suite, 1993; Overture: Réjouissance, 1994; Symphony No 3, 1997; In Emmanuel's Land (piano quartet), 2003. *Recreations:* golf, billiards, snooker, sports of all kinds (Otago Univ. soccer blue), dining with friends, gardening. *Address:* PO Box 25 261, Featherston Street, Wellington 6146, New Zealand.

SOUTHWARD, Eileen; *see* Cooper, Eileen.

SOUTHWARD, Sir Nigel (Ralph), KCVO 2003 (CVO 1995; LVO 1985); Apothecary to the Queen, Apothecary to the Household and to the Households of Princess Alice Duchess of Gloucester and the Duke and Duchess of Gloucester, 1975–2003; *b* 8 Feb. 1941; *s* of Sir Ralph Southward, KCVO; *m* 1965, Annette, *d* of J. H. Hoffmann; one *s* two *d*. *Educ:* Rugby Sch.; Trinity Hall, Cambridge; Middlesex Hosp. Med. Sch. MA, MB, BChir, 1965; MRCP 1969. Ho. Surg., Middx Hosp., 1965; Ho. Phys., Royal Berkshire Hosp., Reading, 1966; Ho. Phys., Central Middx Hosp., 1966; Casualty MO, Middx Hosp., 1967; Vis. MO, King Edward VII Hosp. for Officers, 1972–2003. Apothecary to the Households of Princess

Margaret Countess of Snowdon, 1975–2002, and of Queen Elizabeth the Queen Mother, 1986–2002. *Recreations:* sailing, golf, ski-ing. *Address:* Drokesfield, Bucklers Hard, Beaulieu, Hants SO42 7XE. *T:* (01590) 616252. *Clubs:* Royal Yacht Squadron, Royal Cruising.

SOUTHWARK, Archbishop of, (RC), since 2010; **Most Rev. Peter David Smith;** *b* 21 Oct. 1943. *Educ:* Clapham Coll.; Univ. of Exeter (LLB 1966); St John's Seminary, Wonersh; Angelicum Univ., Rome (JCD *summa cum laude* 1977). Coutts Bank, London, 1962–63; ordained priest, 1972; Asst Priest, St Francis de Sales and St Gertrude, Stockwell, 1972–74; Prof. of Canon Law, St John's Seminary, Wonersh, 1977–84; Parish Priest, St Andrew's, Thornton Heath, 1984–85; Rector, St John's Seminary, Wonersh, 1985–95; Bishop of E Anglia, 1995–2001; Archbishop of Cardiff, (RC), 2001–10. Vice-Officialis and Judge, Diocesan Marriage Tribunal, 1977; Officialis, Metropolitan Tribunal, 1980–85. Bishops' Conference: Mem., Cttee for Ministerial Formation, 1989–95; Chairman: Cttee for Marriage and Family Life, 1995–2001; Dept for Christian Responsibility and Citizenship, 1998–; Central Religious Adv. Cttee, 2001–04; Vice Pres., 2009–. Chairman: Catholic Truth Soc., 1993–2007; Catholic Assoc. Pilgrimage Trust, 1998–2001; Vice-Chm., Catholic Agency for Social Concern, 1996–2001. Mem. Mgt Cttee, Catholic Educn Service, 1998–2001. Hon. Fellow: Univ. of Wales, Lampeter, 2004; Cardiff Univ., 2006. Sub-Prelate and Chaplain, Order of St John of Jerusalem, 2002. KC*HS 2010. *Address:* Archbishop's House, 150 St George's Road, Southwark, SE1 6HX.

SOUTHWARK, Bishop of, since 2011; **Rt Rev. Christopher Thomas James Chessun;** *b* 5 Aug. 1956; twin *s* of late Thomas Frederick Chessun and Joyce Rosemary Chessun. *Educ:* Hampton Grammar Sch.; University Coll., Oxford (BA Hons Modern Hist. 1978; MA 1982); Trinity Hall, Cambridge (BA Hons Pt II Theol. Tripos 1982); Westcott House Theol Coll., Cambridge. Ordained deacon, 1983, priest, 1984; Asst Curate, St Michael and All Angels, Sandhurst, 1983–87; Sen. Curate, St Mary, Portsea, 1987–89; Chaplain and Minor Canon, St Paul's Cathedral, 1989–93; Vocations Advr, Dio. London, 1991–93; Rector of St Dunstan and All Saints', Stepney, 1993–2001; Area Dean, Tower Hamlets, 1997–2001; Archdeacon of Northolt, 2001–05; Area Bishop of Woolwich, 2005–11. Bishop for Urban Life and Faith, 2010–13. Took seat, H of L, 2014. Freeman, City of London, 1993; Hon. Chaplain, 1992–, Freeman and Hon. Liveryman, 2001, Needlemakers' Co. *Recreations:* music, history, travel, overseas church links. *Address:* Bishop's House, 38 Tooting Bec Gardens, SW16 1QZ. *T:* (020) 8769 3256, *Fax:* 0843 290 6894; Trinity House, 4 Chapel Court, Borough High Street, SE1 1HW. *T:* (020) 7939 9420. *E:* bishop.christopher@southwark.anglican.org.

SOUTHWARK, Auxiliary Bishops in, (RC); *see* Hendricks, Rt Rev. P. J.

SOUTHWARK, Dean of; *see* Nunn, Very Rev. A. P.

SOUTHWARK, Archdeacon of; *see* Steen, Ven. J. E.

SOUTHWELL, family name of **Viscount Southwell.**

SOUTHWELL, 7th Viscount *cr* 1776; **Pyers Anthony Joseph Southwell;** Bt 1662; Baron Southwell, 1717; International Management and Marketing Consultant, now retired; *b* 14 Sept. 1930; *s* of Hon. Francis Joseph Southwell (2nd *s* of 5th Viscount) and Agnes Mary Annette Southwell (*née* Clifford); *S* uncle, 1960; *m* 1955, Barbara Jacqueline Raynes; two *s.* *Educ:* Beaumont Coll., Old Windsor, Berks; Royal Military Academy, Sandhurst. Commissioned into 8th King's Royal Irish Hussars, 1951; resigned commission, 1955. *Recreation:* golf. *Heir: s* Hon. Richard Andrew Pyers Southwell [*b* 15 June 1956; *m* 1985, Alison Margaret Huntington; one *d* (one *s* decd)]. *Address:* PO Box 62211, 8062 Paphos, Cyprus. *T:* 26950227. *Clubs:* Army and Navy, MCC.

SOUTHWELL AND NOTTINGHAM, Bishop of, since 2015; **Rt Rev. Paul Gavin Williams;** *b* Weston-Super-Mare, 16 Jan. 1968; *s* of Bryan Williams and Heather Williams; *m* 1997, Sarah Cossham; three *s.* *Educ:* Court Fields Comp. Sch., Wellington, Som; Richard Huish Coll., Taunton; Grey Coll., Univ. of Durham (BA Hons Theology 1989); Wycliffe Hall, Oxford. Youth Pastor, St Andrew's Church, Oxford, 1989–90; ordained deacon, 1992, priest, 1993; Curate, St James's Church, Muswell Hill, 1992–95; Associate Vicar, Christ Church, Clifton, Bristol, 1995–99; Rector, St James, Gerrards Cross with Fulmer, 1999–2009; Area Bishop of Kensington, 2009–15. Hon. Canon, Christ Church, Oxford, 2007–09. *Recreations:* fell-walking, football, choral music, family. *Address:* Jubilee House, 8 Westgate, Southwell, Notts NG25 0JH.

SOUTHWELL, Dean of; *no new appointment at time of going to press.*

SOUTHWELL, His Honour Edward; *see* Southwell, His Honour R. C. E.

SOUTHWELL, Richard Charles; QC 1977; *s* of late Sir Philip Southwell, CBE, MC and Mary Burnett (*née* Scarratt); *m* Belinda Mary, *d* of late Col F. H. Pownall, MC; two *s* one *d.* Former Judge of the Courts of Appeal of Jersey and Guernsey. Commercial Arbitrator. Treasurer, Inner Temple, 2002. Pres., Lloyd's Appeal Tribunal, 1997–2010. Lt Bailiff, Guernsey Royal Ct, 2005–14. Lay Canon, Salisbury Cathedral, 2007–12, now Lay Canon Emeritus; Chm., House of Laity, Salisbury Diocesan Synod, 2006–10; former Lay Co-Chm., Heytesbury Deanery Synod. Chm. Trustees, Wessex MS Therapy Centre; Vice Chm. Trustees, Hosp. of St John and St Katherine, Heytesbury; Former Founding Trustee, Tropical Health and Educn Trust. Former Chm. of Govs: St Mary's Sch., Calne (now Patron); Warminster Sch. (now Patron). *Address:* Serle Court, 6 New Square, Lincoln's Inn, WC2A 3QS. *T:* (020) 7242 6105, *Fax:* (020) 7405 4004. *E:* clerks@serlecourt.co.uk.

SOUTHWELL, His Honour (Richard Charles) Edward; a Circuit Judge, 2000–13; *b* 31 March 1946; *s* of Dr Neville Southwell and Elizabeth Southwell; *m* 1974, Judith Mary Bowdage; one *s* two *d* (and one *s* decd). *Educ:* Charterhouse Sch. Called to the Bar, Inner Temple, 1970. *Recreations:* golf, sailing, ski-ing, motoring. *Clubs:* MCC; West Surrey Golf; Royal London Yacht; Bar Yacht.

SOUTHWELL, Robin, OBE 1999; FRAeS; Chief Executive Officer, Airbus Group UK (formerly EADS UK) Ltd, 2005–14; *b* 10 April 1960; *s* of Peter and Susan Southwell; *m* 1988, Sally Deakin (*d* 2010); one *s* one *d.* *Educ:* Univ. of Hull (BA Hons). FRAeS 1998. With British Aerospace, then BAE Systems, 1981–2000 (Gp Man. Dir, Customer Solutions and Support, 1998–2000); Chief Executive Officer: W. S. Atkins plc, 2001–02; AirTanker Ltd, 2002–05. Non-exec. Dir, Chloride Gp Plc, 2002–08; Dir, David Linley Hldgs, 2014–. Pres., UK Aerospace, Defence and Security Orgn, 2012–14. *Recreations:* family, football.

SOUTHWOOD, Prof. David John, PhD; Professor of Physics, 1986–2008, Senior Research Investigator, since 2011, Imperial College London; *b* 30 June 1945; *s* of H. H. J. Southwood and H. M. Southwood; *m* 1967, Susan Elizabeth Fricker; two *s* one *d.* *Educ:* Torquay Boys' Grammar Sch.; Queen Mary Coll., London (BA; Hon. Fellow 2003); Imperial Coll., London (PhD, DIC). UCLA 1970; Lectr, 1971–86, Head of Physics Dept, 1994–97, Imperial Coll., London; on leave of absence as Hd, Earth Observation Strategy, ESA, Paris, 1997–2000; Dir of Sci., 2001–08, Dir of Sci. and Robotic Exploration, 2008–11, ESA. Vis. Prof., 1976, Regents' Prof., 2000, UCLA; Vis. Prof., Plymouth Univ., 2011–; Dist. Vis. Scholar, Jet Propulsion Lab., Calif Inst. of Technol., Pasadena, 2011– (Mem. Adv. Council, 2011–); Hon. Prof., Univ. of Lancaster, 2013–. Mem., SERC Boards, 1989–94; Chairman: Commn D, COSPAR, 1986–92; Space Sci. Adv. Cttee, ESA, 1990–93; Sci. Prog. Cttee, ESA, 1993–96; Sci. Adv. Cttee, Internat. Space Sci. Inst., 1995–2001; Trustees, Inst. for Space Policy and Law, Univ. of London, 2013–; Mem. Steering Bd, UK Space Agency, 2011–. Pres., RAS, 2012–14 (Vice-Pres., 1989–91; Trustee, 2010–11). Fellow, Amer. Geophys. Union (James B. Macelwane Award, 1981); Mem., Internat. Acad. of Astronautics, 1999; For. Mem., Nat. Acad. of Air and Space, France, 2005. FRAeS 2011. Hon. DSc Plymouth, 2011; Hon. Dr Bern, 2012. Silver Medal, Royal Aerospace Soc., 2005; Gold Medal, Eur. Aerospace Socs, 2007; Sir Arthur Clarke Award for exceptional space achievement, Space Educnl Trust, 2011; Public Service Award, NASA, 2011. *Publications:* numerous contribs in solar terrestrial physics and planetary science to learned jls. *Recreations:* reading, theatre, cinema. *Address:* Space and Atmospheric Physics Group, Physics Department, Imperial College London, South Kensington Campus, SW7 2BZ. *T:* (020) 7594 7679. *E:* d.southwood@imperial.ac.uk.

SOUTHWOOD, Sara Michel; *see* Selwood, S. M.

SOUTHWORTH, Benedict; Chief Executive, Ramblers, since 2012; *b* Preston, Lancs, 28 Aug. 1965; *s* of Edmund Campion Southworth and Kathleen Southworth; *m* 1997, Michaela Claire O'Brien; two *d.* *Educ:* Preston Catholic Coll.; Newman Coll., Preston; Univ. of Liverpool (BA Hons Pol Theory and Instns 1987); Univ. of East London (MSc Architecture: Advanced Envmtl and Energy Studies (distance learning) 2011). Campaigner, Friends of the Earth, England, Wales and NI, 1990–95; Campaign Manager, Newbury Bypass Campaign, 1995–96; Coordinator, Mgt Support Proj., NSW Community Legal Centres Secretariat, 1996–98; Campaigns Manager, Greenpeace Australia-Pacific, 1998–2001; Dir, Internat. Climate Campaign, Greenpeace Internat., 2001–03; Campaigns Prog. Dir, Internat. Secretariat, Amnesty Internat., 2003–05; Dir, World Develt Movement, 2005–09; charity consultant, 2009–12. Member, Board: 38 Degrees Ltd, 2009–; 38 Degrees Trust, 2010–; Mem., Mgt Cttee, People and Planet Student Activities Ltd, 2009–. Gov., Oxted Sch., 2013–14. *Recreations:* walking, archery, democracy, family history, British post-apocalyptic TV, growing fruit and herbs. *Address:* Ramblers, 2nd Floor Camelford House, 87–90 Albert Embankment, SE1 7TW. *T:* (020) 7339 8500. *E:* benedict.southworth@ntlworld.com.

SOUTHWORTH, Helen Mary; Chief Executive, Age Isle of Man, since 2014; *b* 13 Nov. 1956; *m* Edmund Southworth; one *s.* *Educ:* Larkhill Convent Sch., Preston; Univ. of Lancaster (BA Hons). Director: Age Concern, St Helens; Grosvenor Housing Assoc.; St Helens and Knowsley HA. Mem. (Lab) St Helens MBC, 1994–98 (Chm., Leisure Cttee, 1994–96). Contested (Lab) Wirral S, 1992. MP (Lab) Warrington S, 1997–2010.

SOWARD, Prof. Andrew Michael, FRS 1991; Professor of Applied Mathematics, University of Exeter, 1996–2009, now Emeritus; Strategic Research Adviser, School of Mathematics and Statistics, Newcastle University, since 2011; *b* 20 Oct. 1943; *s* of Arthur Layton Soward and Sybil Jessica Lilian Soward (*née* Greathurst); *m* 1968, Elaine Celia McCaully; one *s* one *d.* *Educ:* St Edward's Sch., Oxford; Queen's College, Cambridge (BA 1st cl. Hons Maths 1965; PhD 1969; ScD 1984). University of Newcastle upon Tyne: Lectr, 1971, Reader, 1981–86, Dept of Maths and Stats; Head, Div. of Applied Maths, 1985–95; Prof. of Fluid Dynamics, 1986–95. Visiting appointments: Courant Inst. of Mathematical Scis, NY, 1969–70; CIRES, Boulder, Colorado, 1970–71; IGPP, UCLA, 1977–78. Editor, Jl of Geophysical and Astrophysical Fluid Dynamics, 1991–. *Publications:* contribs to learned jls. *Address:* 1 Stephenson Terrace, Wylam, Northumberland NE41 8LA. *Club:* Fell and Rock Climbing.

SOWDEN, Susan, (Mrs Philip Sowden); Registrar, Headington School, Oxford, 2007–15; *b* 10 June 1951; *d* of Albert Henry Letley and Ethel May Letley; *m* 1st, 1973, Michael Geoffrey Bodinham (marr. diss. 1990); one *s* two *d*; 2nd, 2000, Philip Sowden. *Educ:* Clarendon House Grammar Sch. for Girls, Ramsgate; King's Coll., London (BSc 2nd Cl. Hons; AKC; PGCE); Open Univ. (Adv. Dip Ed Man). Geography teacher, Peers Upper Comprehensive, Oxford, 1973–77 and 1984–85; Headington School, Oxford: Geog. teacher, 1985–87; Head of Dept, 1987; Housemistress, 1988; Head of Lower Sixth, 1991–93; Dep. Head, 1993–94; Headmistress, St Mary's Sch., Wantage, 1994–2006. Sen. examng posts with EMREB, Southern Examng Gp and Northern Exams and Assessment Bd. Gov., Twyford Sch., 2003–10. Lay Minister (formerly Reader), Church of England, 1993–. *Publications:* articles in Britain and the British (pubd in Poland). *Recreations:* walking, reading, theatre, canoeing, camping, music.

SOWDEN, Terence Cubitt; QC 1989; HM's Solicitor General for Jersey, 1986–93; *b* 30 July 1929; *s* of George Henry Sowden, RNR, Master Mariner and Margaret Duncan Cubitt; *m* 1955, Doreen Mary Lucas (*d* 1983); two *d* (one *s* decd); *m* 1999, Jacqueline Carol Ince. *Educ:* Victoria Coll. Prep. Sch.; Victoria Coll.; Hendon Tech. Coll., London. Called to the Bar, Middle Temple, 1951; Advocate, Royal Court of Jersey, 1951; in private practice in Jersey, 1951–85; Deputy for St Helier, States of Jersey, 1960–63; Sen. Partner, Crill Cubitt Sowden & Tomes, Advocates and Solicitors, 1962–83. Juge d'Instruction, 1994–99. Relief Stipendiary Magistrate for Jersey, 2000–04. Ind. Mem., Temporary Release Assessment Panel, HM Prison, La Moye, Jersey, 2006–09. *Publications:* (with Paul Matthews) The Jersey Law of Trusts, 1988, 3rd edn 1994. *Recreations:* writing, walking the low tide. *Address:* La Rousse, Le Bourg, La Grande Route de la Côte, St Clement, Jersey, Channel Islands JE2 6FY.

SOWERBY, Rt Rev. Mark Crispin Rake; *see* Horsham, Area Bishop of.

SOWREY, Air Marshal Sir Frederick (Beresford), KCB 1978 (CB 1968); CBE 1965; AFC 1954; *b* 14 Sept. 1922; *s* of late Group Captain Frederick Sowrey, DSO, MC, AFC; *m* 1946, Anne Margaret (*d* 2014), *d* of late Captain C. T. A. Bunbury, OBE, RN; one *s* one *d.* *Educ:* Charterhouse. Joined RAF 1940; flying training in Canada, 1941; Fighter-reconnaissance Squadron, European theatre, 1942–44; Flying Instructors Sch., 1944; trng Airborne Forces (despatches), 1945; No 615 (Co. of Surrey) Squadron, RAuxAF ('Winston Churchill's Own'), 1946–48; Fighter Gunnery Sch., 1949–50, comdg 615 Sqdn, 1951–54; RAF Staff Coll., Bracknell, 1954; Chiefs of Staff Secretariat, 1955–58; comdg No 46 Sqdn, 1958–60; Personal Staff Officer to CAS, 1960–62; comdg RAF Abingdon, 1962–64; IDC 1965; SASO, Middle East Comd (Aden), 1966–67; Comdr, RAF Aden, Nov. 1967; Dir Defence Policy, MoD, 1968–70; SASO, RAF Trng Comd, 1970–72; Comdt, Nat. Defence Coll., 1972–75; Dir-Gen. RAF Training, 1975–77; UK Representative, Permanent Military Deputies Group CENTO, 1977–79. Research Fellow, IISS, 1980–81. Pres., Sussex Indust. Archaeology Soc., 1993– (Chm., 1981–93); Mem., Bd of Conservators, Ashdown Forest, 1984–99; Vice-Pres., Victory Services Assoc., 1994– (Pres., 1989–93; Chm., 1985–89); Life Vice-Pres., RAF Historical Soc., 1996 (Founder Chm., 1986–96); Trustee, Guild of Aviation Artists, 1990–2007 (Vice-Pres., 2007–). *Publications:* contributed to: D-Day Encyclopaedia, 1994; Oxford Dictionary of National Biography, 2004; articles and book reviews in defence jls. *Recreations:* watching motor-racing (world class records in a supercharged Cooper, 1956), veteran cars (London/Brighton run), mechanical devices of any kind and age, working in the Sussex High Weald Area of Outstanding Natural Beauty. *Club:* Royal Air Force.

SOYINKA, Wole; Nigerian writer; *b* 13 July 1934; *s* of Ayo and Eniola Soyinka; *m*; *c.* *Educ:* Univ. of Ibadan, Nigeria; Univ. of Leeds. Res. Fellow in Drama, Univ. of Ibadan, 1960–61; Lectr in English, Univ. of Ife, 1962–63; Sen. Lectr in English, Univ. of Lagos, 1965–67; political prisoner, 1967–69; Artistic Dir and Head of Dept of Theatre Arts, Univ. of Ibadan, 1969–72; Res. Prof. in Dramatic Literature, 1972, Prof. of Comparative Literature, 1976–85, Emeritus Prof., 2004–, Univ. of Ife (later Obafemi Awolowo Univ., Iwe-Ife); Goldwin Smith Prof. of Africana Studies and Theatre, Cornell Univ., 1988–92; Elias Ghanen Chair of Creative Writing, Univ. of Nevada, until 2005; President's Marymount Inst. Prof. in Residence, Loyola Marymount Univ., 2007–. Fellow: Churchill Coll., Cambridge, 1973–74; Dubois Inst., Harvard Univ., 2004–. Reith Lectr, BBC Radio 4, 2004. Hon. DLitt: Leeds, 1973; Yale, 1981; Paul Valéry, 1984; Morehouse Coll., 1988. Nobel Prize for Literature, 1986; AGIP/Enrico Mattei Award for the Humanities, 1986. *Publications: plays:* The Lion and the Jewel, 1959; The Swamp Dwellers, 1959; A Dance of the Forests, 1960; The Trials of Brother Jero, 1961; The Strong Breed, 1962; The Road, 1964; Kongi's Harvest, 1965; Madmen and Specialists, 1971; Before the Blackout, 1971; Jero's Metamorphosis, 1973; Camwood on the Leaves, 1973; The Bacchae of Euripides, 1974; Death and the King's Horsemen, 1975; Opera Wonyosi, 1978; A Play of Giants, 1984; From Zia with Love, 1992; A Scourge of Hyacinths, 1992; The Beatification of Area Boy, 1995; *novels:* The Interpreters, 1964; The Forest of a Thousand Daemons (trans.), Season of Anomy, 1973; *poetry:* Idanre and other poems, 1967; A Shuttle in the Crypt, 1972; (ed) Poems of Black Africa, 1975; Ogun Abibman, 1977; Mandela's Earth and other Poems, 1989; Selected Poems, 2002; Samarkand And Other Markets I Have Known, 2002; *non-fiction:* The Man Died (prison memoirs), 1972; Myth, Literature and the African World (lectures), 1972; Ake, the Years of Childhood (autobiog.), 1982; Art, Dialogue and Outrage (essays), 1988; Isara: a voyage around "Essay" (biog.), 1989; Ibadan (memoir), 1995; The Open Sore of a Continent, 1996; The Burden of Memory, the Muse of Forgiveness (essays), 1999; Climate of Fear: the quest for dignity in a dehumanized world (essays), 2005; You Must Set Forth At Dawn (memoirs), 2006.

SPACEY, Kevin, Hon. KBE 2015 (Hon. CBE 2010); actor, director and producer; Artistic Director, Old Vic, 2004–15 (Trustee, 2000–04); *b* 26 July 1959; *né* Kevin Spacey Fowler; *s* of Thomas and Kathleen Fowler. *Educ:* Chatsworth High Sch., LA; Juilliard Drama Sch., NY. Cameron Mackintosh Vis. Prof. of Contemporary Th., St Catherine's Coll., Oxford, 2008–09. MacTaggart Lectr, Edinburgh Internat. TV Fest., 2013. *Theatre includes:* Ghosts, NY, 1982; Hurlyburly, 1985; Long Day's Journey into Night, 1986; National Anthems, Long Wharf Th., New Haven, CT, 1988, Old Vic, 2005; Lost in Yonkers, NY (Tony Award), 1991; The Iceman Cometh, Almeida, 1998, NY 1999; The Philadelphia Story, Richard II (Critics' Circle Award), Old Vic, 2005; A Moon for the Misbegotten, Old Vic, 2006, NY 2007; Speed-the-Plow, Old Vic, 2008; Inherit the Wind, Old Vic, 2009; Richard III, Old Vic, 2011; Clarence Darrow, Old Vic, 2014. *Television includes:* Wiseguy (series), 1988; The Murder of Mary Phagan, 1988; Fall from Grace, 1990; When You Remember Me, 1990; Darrow, 1991; House of Cards, 2013, 2014 (Golden Globe Award, 2015), 2015. *Films include:* Working Girl, 1988; See No Evil, Hear No Evil, Dad, 1989; A Show of Force, Henry and June, 1990; Glengarry Glen Ross, Consenting Adults, 1992; The Ref, Swimming with Sharks (also co-prod.), 1994; Outbreak, The Usual Suspects (Acad. Award for Best Supporting Actor), Seven, 1995; Looking for Richard, A Time to Kill, 1996; L. A. Confidential, Midnight in the Garden of Good and Evil, 1997; The Negotiator, 1998; The Big Kahuna (also prod.), 1999; American Beauty (Academy, BAFTA and London Film Critics' Circle Awards for Best Actor), Hurlyburly, Ordinary Decent Criminal, 2000; Pay it Forward, 2001; K-PAX, The Shipping News, 2002; The Life of David Gale, 2003; Beyond the Sea (also dir and prod.), 2004; The United States of Leland (also prod.), 2005; Superman, 2006; Fred Claus, 2007; 21, 2008; The Men Who Stare At Goats, 2009; Shrink, 2010; Horrible Bosses, 2011; Margin Call, 2012; Dir, Albino Alligator, 1996; Producer: Interstate 84, 2000; Uncle Frank, 2002; Triggerstreet.com, 2004. *Address:* c/o William Morris Endeavor Entertainment, 9601 Wilshire Boulevard, Beverly Hills, CA 90210, USA.

SPACIE, Maj.-Gen. Keith, CB 1987; OBE 1974; Chairman, Sudbury Consultants Ltd, 1989–2000; *b* 21 June 1935; *s* of Frederick and Kathleen Spacie; *m* 1961, Valerie Rich (*d* 2008); one *s*. Commnd Royal Lincolns, 1955; transf. Parachute Regt, 1959; Staff Coll., Camberley, 1966; DAA&QMG 16 Parachute Bde, 1968–70; Staff, RMA, Sandhurst, 1970–72; Comd, 3rd Bn Parachute Regt, 1973–75; SHAPE, 1976–78; Comdr 7 Field Force, 1979–81; RCDS, 1982; Mil. Comr and Comdr, British Forces Falkland Is, 1983–84; Dir of Army Training, 1984–87. Pres., Arnhem 1944 Fellowship, 2013–. Pres., Milocarian Athletic Club, 2012–. *Recreations:* cross-country running, athletics, walking, battlefield touring. *Clubs:* Army and Navy; Thames Hare and Hounds.

SPACKMAN, Brig. John William Charles, PhD; Director, KC3 NET Ltd, 2007–09; *b* 12 May 1932; *s* of Lt-Col Robert Thomas Spackman, MBE and Ann (*née* Rees); *m* 1955, Jeanette Vera; two *s* one *d*. *Educ:* Cyfarthfa Castle Grammar School, Merthyr Tydfil; Wellington Grammar School; RMCS. BSc 1st cl. Hons London (external) 1960, PhD 1964; MSc (Management Sci.) UMIST, 1968; Open Univ. (BA Humanities with Eng. Lit. 2015). Nat. Service, 1950–52; Regular Commission, RAOC, 1952; Regtl appts, 1952–72; Project Wavell, 1969–72; RARDE, 1972–75; Senior Mil. Officer, Chem. Defence and Microbiological Defence Estab., Porton Down, 1975–78; Branch Chief, Inf. Systems Div., SHAPE, 1978–80; Dir, Supply Computer Services, 1980–83; retired from Army, 1983 (Brig.); Under Sec., and Dir, Social Security Operational Strategy, DHSS, 1983–87; Director: Computing and Information Services, BT, 1987–90; Eur. Telecommunications Informatics Services, 1991–93; Management Systems Unit, Govt of Malta, 1993–96; KFKI (CSC), Hungary, 1993–2004; Logan Orviss Internat., 1993–2009; Intelligent Networks Ltd, 1997–98. FBCS 1987 (MBCS 1970); CITP 2007; CEng 1990; MCMI (MBIM 1970); MInstD 1983. Liveryman, Information Technologists' Co., 1989 (Mem., 1987). Freeman, City of London, 1987. *Recreations:* gardening, hill walking, opera. *Address:* The Hermitage, Snow Street, Roydon, Diss, Norfolk IP22 5RZ. *T:* (01379) 651650.

SPACKMAN, Michael John; special consultant, NERA Economic Consulting (formerly National Economic Research Associates), since 2007 (affiliated consultant, 1996–2007); Visiting Senior Fellow, Grantham Institute for Climate Change and the Environment, London School of Economics and Political Science, since 2010 (Visiting Fellow, Centre for Analysis of Risk and Regulation, 2001–10); *b* 8 Oct. 1936; *s* of late Geoffrey Spackman and Audrey (*née* Morecombe); *m* 1965, Judith Ann Leathem; two *s* two *d*. *Educ:* Malvern Coll.; Clare Coll., Cambridge (MA); Queen Mary Coll., London (MScEcon). Served RA (2nd Lieut), 1955–57; Physicist, UKAEA, Capenhurst, 1960–69; Sen. Physicist/Engr, Nuclear Power Gp Ltd, 1969–71; PSO, then Economic Advr, Dept of Energy, 1971–77; Economic Advr, HM Treasury, 1977–79; Dir of Econs and Accountancy, CS Coll., 1979–80; Hd of Public Services Econs Div., HM Treasury, 1980–85; Under Sec., 1985; Hd of Public Expenditure Econs Gp, HM Treasury, 1985–91 and 1993–95; Chief Economic Advr, Dept of Transport, 1991–93. Gwilym Gibbon Res. Fellow, Nuffield Coll., Oxford, 1995–96. *Recreations:* walking, climbing. *Address:* 44 Gibson Square, Islington, N1 0RA. *T:* (020) 7359 1053.

SPALDING, Alistair William, CBE 2012; Chief Executive and Artistic Director, Sadler's Wells, since 2004 (Director of Programming, 2000–04); *b* 25 Aug. 1957; *s* of Robert and Pauline Spalding; *m* 2000, Katy McPhee; one *s*. *Educ:* Hatfield Poly. (BA Hons Combined Studies in Humanities); Edge Hill Coll. (PGCE). Arts Programmer, Hawth Th., Crawley, 1988–94; Hd of Dance and Performance, South Bank Centre, London, 1994–2000. Chm., Dance UK, 2004–09. Mem. Council, Arts Council England, 2009–. Chevalier des Arts et des Lettres (France), 2005. *Recreations:* swimming, hill walking. *E:* artisticdirector@sadlerswells.com. *Club:* 2 Brydges.

SPALDING, Prof. (Dudley) Brian, MA, ScD; FRS 1983; FREng, FIMechE, FInstF; Professor of Heat Transfer, London University, 1958–88, now Emeritus, and Head, Computational Fluid Dynamics Unit, Imperial College of Science, Technology and Medicine, 1981–88; Managing Director, Concentration, Heat & Momentum Ltd, since 1975; *b* New Malden, Surrey, 9 Jan. 1923; *s* of H. A. Spalding; *m* 1st, Eda Ilse-Lotte (*née* Goericke); two *s* two *d*; 2nd, Colleen (*née* King); two *s*. *Educ:* King's College Sch., Wimbledon; The Queen's Coll., Oxford (BA 1944; MA 1948); Pembroke Coll., Cambridge (PhD 1952; ScD 1966). Bataafsche Petroleum Matschapij, 1944–45; Ministry of Supply, 1945–47; National Physical Laboratory, 1947–48; ICI Research Fellow at Cambridge Univ., 1948–50; Cambridge University Demonstrator in Engineering, 1950–54; Reader in Applied Heat, Imperial College of Science and Technology, 1954–58. Man. Dir, Combustion, Heat and Mass Transfer Ltd, 1970–75; Chm., CHAM of N America Inc., 1977–91. FREng (FEng 1989). Member: Russian Acad. of Scis, 1994; Ukrainian Nat. Acad. of Scis, 1994. Hon. Dr Moscow Energy Inst., 2013; Hon. DSc Imperial Coll. London, 2014. Internat. Energy Prize, Global Energy, 2009; Benjamin Franklin Medal in Mechanical Engineering, Franklin Inst., 2010; A. V. Luikov Prize, Acad. of Scis of Belarus, 2010; Huw Edwards Award, Inst. of Physics, 2011; 75th Anniversary Medal, Heat Transfer Div., ASME, 2013. *Publications:* Some Fundamentals of Combustion, 1955; (with E. H. Cole) Engineering Thermodynamics, 1958; Convective Mass Transfer, 1963; (with S. V. Patankar) Heat and Mass Transfer in Boundary Layers, 1967, rev. edn 1970; (co-author) Heat and Mass Transfer in Recirculating Flows, 1969; (with B. E. Launder) Mathematical Models of Turbulence, 1972; GENMIX: a general computer program for two-dimensional parabolic phenomena, 1978; Combustion and Mass Transfer, 1979; (jtly) Heat Exchanger Design Handbook, 1982; Numerical Prediction of Flow, Heat Transfer, Turbulence and Combustion (selected works), 1983; numerous scientific papers. *Recreations:* music, poetry. *Address:* Concentration Heat & Momentum Ltd, Bakery House, 40 High Street, Wimbledon Village, SW19 5AU.

SPALDING, Prof. Frances, CBE 2005; PhD; art historian, biographer and critic; Editor, The Burlington Magazine, since 2015; *b* 16 July 1950; *d* of Hedley Stinston Crabtree and Margaret (*née* Holiday); *m* 1974, Julian Spalding, *qv* (marr. diss. 1991); one *s*. *Educ:* Farringtons Sch.; Univ. of Nottingham (BA Hons 1972); PhD CNAA 1988. Lectr in Art Hist., Sheffield City Poly., 1978–88; ind. scholar, 1989–99; Lectr in Art Hist., 2000–02, Reader in 20th Century British Art, 2002–07, Prof. of Art History, 2007–15, Univ. of Newcastle upon Tyne. Res. co-ordinator, Writers-in-Prison Cttee, 1991–93, Mem. Exec. Cttee, English Centre of Internat. PEN, 1997–2004 (Vice-Chm., 2000). Member, Council: Charleston Trust, 1990–2011 (Emeritus Trustee, 2011); RSL, 2005–09; Editor, Charleston Mag., 1992–2000. Ashby Lectr, 1997, Vis. Fellow, 1998, Clare Hall, Cambridge; Assoc. Vis. Mem., Darwin Coll., Cambridge, 2002; Paul Mellon Sen. Res. Fellow and Vis. Res. Fellow, Newnham Coll. Cambridge, 2005–06. Trustee: Hampstead Church Music Trust, 1999–; NW Essex Art Collection, 2014–. FRSL 1984; Hon. FRCA 1998. *Publications:* Magnificent Dreams: Burne-Jones and the late Victorians, 1978; Whistler, 1979, rev. edn 1994; Roger Fry: art and life, 1980, rev. edn 1999; Vanessa Bell, 1983; British Art since 1900, 1986; Stevie Smith: a critical biography, 1988, rev. edn 2002; A Dictionary of 20th Century British Painters and Sculptors, 1990; Paper Darts: selected letters of Virginia Woolf, 1991; Dance Till the Stars Come Down: a biography of John Minton, 1991, rev. edn 2005; Duncan Grant, 1997; The Tate: a history, 1998; The Bloomsbury Group, 1998, rev. edn 2005; Gwen Raverat: friends, family and affections, 2001; Ravilious in Public, 2003; (with David Fraser Jenkins) John Piper in the 1930s: abstraction on the beach, 2003; John Piper, Myfanwy Piper: lives in art, 2009; Prunella Clough: regions unmapped, 2012; Virginia Woolf: art, life and vision, 2014; contrib. TLS, Guardian, Burlington Mag., etc. *Recreation:* music. *Address:* c/o Coleridge & Rogers, 20 Powis Mews, W11 1JN. *T:* (020) 7221 3717; The Flat, 70 Gloucester Crescent, NW1 7EG. *Club:* PEN.

SPALDING, Julian, FMA; writer and broadcaster; Master, Guild of St George (John Ruskin's Guild), 1996–2005 (Director, 1983–2005; Companion, 1978); *b* 15 June 1947; *s* of Eric Peter Spalding and Margaret Grace Savager; *m* 1st, 1974, Frances (*née* Crabtree) (*see* F. Spalding) (marr. diss. 1991); one *s*; 2nd, 1991, Gillian (*née* Tait), conservation advisor. *Educ:* Chislehurst and Sidcup Grammar Sch. for Boys; Univ. of Nottingham (BA Hons Fine Art). Dip. Museums Assoc., 1973; FMA 1983. Art Assistant: Leicester Museum and Art Gall., 1970; Durham Light Infantry Mus. and Arts Centre, 1971; Sheffield City Art Galleries: Keeper, Mappin Art Gall., 1972–76; Dep. Dir, 1976–82; Dir of Arts, Sheffield City Council, 1982–85; Dir, Manchester City Art Galls, 1985–89; Acting Dir, Nat. Mus. of Labour History, 1987–88; Dir, Glasgow Museums and Art Galls, 1989–98. Res. Fellow, Nat. Mus. of Denmark, Copenhagen, 1999–2000. Art Panel Mem., Arts Council of GB, 1978–82 (Chm., Exhibns Sub-Cttee, 1981–82 and 1986–); Founder: Art Galleries Assoc., 1976 (Mem. Cttee, 1976–89, Chm., 1987–89); Campaign for Drawing, 2000. Member: Crafts Council, 1986–90 (Member: Projects and Orgn Cttee, 1985–87; Purchasing Cttee, 1986–90; Exhibns Cttee, 1986–90); British Council, 1987–96 (Mem., Fine Arts Adv. Cttee, 1987–96). Dir, Niki de Saint Phalle Foundn, 1994. BBC broadcaster (talks and reviews); Third Ear, BBC Radio Three, 1988. *Publications:* L. S. Lowry, 1979; Three Little Books on Painting, 1984; Is There Life in Museums?, 1990; Glasgow Gallery of Modern Art, 1996; The Poetic Museum: reviving historic collections, 2002; The Eclipse of Art: tackling the crisis in art today, 2003; The Art of Wonder: a history of seeing, 2005 (Sir Banister Fletcher Award, Authors' Club, 2006); Peter Angermann: art and life, 2009; The Best Art You've Never Seen: 101 hidden treasures from around the world, 2010; Con Art: why you should sell your Damien Hirsts while you can, 2012; Nothing On: a satirical novel about contemporary art, 2012; The Art of Peter Angermann, 2012; (contrib.) Summers of Discontent: the purpose of the arts today, 2014; pamphlets and exhibition catalogues, including: Modern British Painting 1900–1960, 1975; Fragments against Ruin, 1981; Francis Davison, 1983; George Fullard Drawings, 1984; The Forgotten Fifties, 1984; Modern Art in Manchester, 1986; The Art of Watercolour, 1987; L. S. Lowry, 1987; Ken Currie, 1988; Funfair or Church?, RSA, 1989; Glasgow's Great British Art Exhibition, 1990; Clouds and Tigers: the art of Hock Aun Teh, 1996; Elisabeth Frink Catalogue Raisonné, 2012; contrib. Art Newspaper, Museums Jl, Jackdaw. *Recreations:* drawing, gardening. *Address:* 90 Grassmarket, Edinburgh EH1 2JR. *E:* julian.spalding@ukgateway.net.

SPALL, Timothy Leonard, OBE 2000; actor, since 1978; *b* 27 Feb. 1957; *s* of Joseph and Sylvia Spall; *m* 1981, Shane Baker; one *s* two *d*. *Educ:* Battersea Co. Comprehensive Sch.; Kingsway and Princeton Coll.; RADA. Birmingham Rep., 1978–79; *theatre* includes: Royal Shakespeare Co., 1978–80: Merry Wives of Windsor; Nicholas Nickleby; The Three Sisters; National Theatre: Saint Joan, 1985; Mandragola, 1985; Le Bourgeois Gentilhomme, 1993; A Midsummer Night's Dream, 1994; This is a Chair, Royal Court, 1996; *television* includes: The Brylcreem Boys, 1978; Auf Wiedersehen Pet, 4 series, 1983–84, 2002–04, Christmas Special, 2004; Roots, 1993; Frank Stubbs Promotes, 1994–95; Outside Edge, 1994–96; Neville's Island, 1997; Our Mutual Friend, 1997; Shooting the Past, 1999; The Thing About Vince, 2000; Vacuuming Completely Nude in Paradise, 2001; Perfect Strangers, 2001; Bodily Harm, 2002; Cherished, 2005; Mr Harvey Lights a Candle, 2005; The Street, 2006, 2007; Mysterious Creatures, 2006; A Room with a View, 2007; Oliver Twist, 2007; The Street, 2008–09; Gunrush, 2009; The Fattest Man in Britain, 2009; The Syndicate, 2012; Blandings, 2013–14; The Enfield Haunting, 2015; documentaries: Timothy Spall: Somewhere at Sea, 2010; Timothy Spall: Back at Sea, 2011; Timothy Spall: All at Sea, 2013; *films* include: Quadrophenia, 1978; Gothic, 1986; The Sheltering Sky, 1989; Life is Sweet, 1990; Secrets and Lies, Hamlet, 1996; The Wisdom of Crocodiles, Still Crazy, 1998; Topsy Turvy, Clandestine Marriage, 1999; Love's Labours Lost, Vatel, 2000; Lucky Break, Intimacy, 2001; Rock Star, Vanilla Sky, All or Nothing, 2002; Nicholas Nickleby, My House in Umbria, Gettin' Square, The Last Samurai, 2003; Harry Potter and the Prisoner of Azkaban, Lemony Snicket's A Series of Unfortunate Events, 2004; Harry Potter and the Goblet of Fire, 2005; Pierrepoint, 2006; Enchanted, Death Defying Acts, 2007; Sweeney Todd: The Demon Barber of Fleet Street, Appaloosa, 2008; The Damned United, Harry Potter and the Half-Blood Prince, From Time to Time, Desert Flower, 2009; Heartless, Harry Potter and the Deathly Hallows, Pt 1, 2010; The King's Speech, Wake Wood, Harry Potter and the Deathly Hallows, Pt 2, Reuniting the Rubins, 2011; Comes a Bright Day, Ginger & Rosa, Love Bite, 2012; Love Punch, Mr Turner, 2014. Patron: Horniman Mus., 1999–; ChildHope, 2002–.

Fellow, Goldsmiths, Univ. of London, 2011; FRSA 2000. *Recreations:* boating, strolling. *Address:* c/o Markham, Froggatt & Irwin, 4 Windmill Street, W1T 2HZ. *T:* (020) 7636 4412. *Club:* Colony.

SPALTON, Prof. David John, FRCS, FRCP, FRCOphth; Consultant Ophthalmic Surgeon, St Thomas' Hospital, London, 1983–2012, now Emeritus; Professor of Ophthalmology, King's College, London, since 2010; *s* of John and Babs Spalton; *m* 1979, Catherine Bompas; three *s*. *Educ:* Buxton Coll., Buxton, Derbys; Westminster Med. Sch., London (MB BS 1970). FRCS 1976; FRCOphth 1989; FRCP 1992. RSO, Moorfields Eye Hosp., 1973–77; Consultant Ophthalmic Surgeon, Charing Cross Hosp., 1980–83. Hon. Consultant Ophthalmic Surgeon: Royal Hosp., Chelsea, 1989–2012; King Edward VII's Hosp. (Sister Agnes), London, 1998–; Hon. Civilian Advr in Ophthalmology, Metropolitan Police, 1999–. Ridley Medal Lectr, Eur. Soc. of Cataract and Refractive Surgeons, 2011. Pres., UK and Ireland Soc. of Cataract and Refractive Surgeons, 2007–09. Member: Amer. Soc. of Cataract and Refractive Surgeons, 1992–; Board, Eur. Soc. of Cataract and Refractive Surgeons, 2006–13 (Pres., Jan. 2016–). *Publications:* (ed jtly) Atlas of Clinical Ophthalmology, 1985 (Best Med. Textbook of Year, Abbott Prize for Med. Writing), 3rd edn 2004 (BMA prize for Best Med. Textbook of Year); over 170 peer-reviewed scientific papers. *Recreations:* my family and other animals, fly fishing, gardening, ophthalmology. *Address:* The London Clinic Eye Centre, 119 Harley Street, W1G 6AU. *T:* (020) 7935 6174. *E:* profspalton@gmail.com. *W:* www.davidspalton.com. *Club:* Garrick.

SPALVINS, Janis Gunars, (John); Chairman: Galufo Pty Ltd, since 1991; Westall Pty Ltd, since 1981; *b* 26 May 1936; *s* of Peter Spalvins and Hilda Blumentals; *m* 1961, Cecily Westall Rymill (*d* 1991); two *s*. *Educ:* Concordia College, Adelaide; Univ. of Adelaide (BEc). FCIS 1961; FASA 1967. Camelec Group of Cos, 1955–73 (Group Sec./Dir, subsidiary cos); Adelaide Steamship Co.: Asst Gen. Manager, 1973; Gen. Manager, 1977; Chief Gen. Manager and Dir, 1979; Man. Dir, 1981–91. Dir and Chief Exec., David Jones Ltd, 1980–91. Mem., Business Council of Australia, 1986–91. FAIM; MInstD Australia, 1981. *Recreations:* snow ski-ing, water ski-ing, tennis, sailing. *Address:* Galufo Pty, 2 Brookside Road, Springfield, SA 5062, Australia. *T:* (8) 83792965. *Club:* Cruising Yacht Club of SA (Adelaide).

SPANIER, Suzy Peta, (Mrs D. G. Spanier); *see* Menkes, S. P.

SPARKE, Andrew Philip; Director, Andrew Sparke Consulting, since 2009; Owner, APS Publications, since 2013; *b* 22 July 1956; *s* of Philip Aubrey Sparke and Sheila Myrtle Sparke; *m* 1980, Laura Emma Simmons; one *s* one *d*; partner, Elizabeth Mary Bennett; one *s* (and one *s* decd). *Educ:* Manchester Univ. (LLB Hons 1977). Technician and Surveying Asst, S Hams DC, 1974; admitted Solicitor, 1980. Articled Clerk, Derby CC, 1978–80; Printing Asst, BP, 1981; Solicitor, Kingston upon Hull CC, 1981–85; Asst Town Clerk, 1985–90, Dep. Dir of Corporate Services, 1990–94, Enfield LBC; Chief Exec., Lincoln CC, 1994–99; Clerk to W Midlands Police Authy, 1999–2005; Chief Exec., Dudley MBC, 1999–2008. Adviser: Public Sector plc, 2008–; Leaps & Bounds (Inspiring Change) Trust Ltd, 2008–. *Publications:* The Compulsory Competitive Tendering Guide, 1993, rev. edn 1995; The Practical Guide to Externalising Local Authority Services, 1994; The Butterworths Best Value Manual, 1999; Broken English, 2013; Indie Publishing: the journey made easy, 2013; Abuse Cocaine & Soft Furnishings (novel), 2013; Copper Trance & Motorways (novel), 2014; In Search Of…, 2014. *Recreations:* writing fiction, travel, ski-ing, badminton, Chelsea FC. *Address:* 4 Oakleigh Road, Old Swinford, Stourbridge DY8 2JX. *T:* (01384) 390401.

SPARKE, Prof. Penelope Anne, PhD; Professor of Design History, Kingston University, since 1999; *b* London, 6 Nov. 1948; *d* of Kenneth Stanley Sparke and Jacqueline Anne Sparke; *m* 1987, John William Small (marr. diss. 2014); three *d*. *Educ:* Green Sch. for Girls, Isleworth; Sussex Univ. (BA 1971; PGCE 1972); Brighton Poly. (PhD 1975). Lectr in Design History, Brighton Poly., 1972–82; Lectr in Design History, RCA, 1982–99; Dean, Faculty of Art, Design and Music, 1999–2005, Pro-Vice Chancellor, Res. and Enterprise, 2005–14, Kingston Univ. *Publications:* (ed) Design by Choice, 1981; Ettore Sottsass Jnr, 1982; Consultant Design: the history and practice of the designer in industry, 1983; Modern Furniture, 1986; Electrical Appliances, 1986; Japanese Design, 1986; (ed) Did Britain Make It?, 1986; An Introduction to Design and Culture, 1900 to the present, 1986, 3rd edn 2012; Design in Context, 1987; Italian Design, 1988; (ed) The Plastics Age: from modernity to postmodernity, 1990; As Long as It's Pink, 1995, rev. edn 2010; A Century of Design: design pioneers of the twentieth-century, 1998; Design Directory: Great Britain, 2001; A Century of Car Design, 2002; (ed jtly) Women's Places: architecture and design 1860–1960, 2003; (ed jtly) Interior Design and Identity, 2004; Elsie de Wolfe: the birth of modern decoration, 2005; (ed jtly) The Modern Period Room: the construction of the exhibited interior 1870–1950, 2005; The Modern Interior, 2008; The Genius of Design, 2009; Japanese Design, 2009; (ed jtly) European Design Since 1985: shaping the new century, 2009; (ed jtly) Designing the Modern Interior: from the Victorians to today, 2009; (ed jtly) Biography and the Interior, 2013. *Recreations:* swimming, historic houses. *Address:* Galveston Lodge, Galveston Road, Putney, SW15 2SA. *T:* (020) 8870 9115, 07799 348650. *E:* penny.sparke@btinternet.com.

SPARKES, Andrew James, CMG 2007; HM Diplomatic Service, retired; Ambassador to Nepal, 2013–15; *b* 4 July 1959; *s* of Rev. James Reginald Sparkes and Brenda Mary Sparkes (*née* Brown); *m* 1985, Jean Mary Meakin (marr. diss. 2003); one *s* one *d*. *Educ:* King Edward's Sch., Edgbaston; Manchester Grammar Sch.; Trinity Hall, Cambridge (MA Hons). MCIPD 1999. English teacher, Japan, 1981–82; joined HM Diplomatic Service, 1983; Second Sec., Political, Ankara, 1985–88; Hd, Political Section, Bangkok, 1992–95; Asst Dir, Personnel Mgt, FCO, 1996–97; on secondment as Dir, Service Exports, DTI, 1997–99; Dep. Hd of Mission, Jakarta, 1999–2001; Dep. High Comr, S Africa, 2001–04; Ambassador: Congo, 2004–07; Kosovo, 2008–10; Dep. Hd, EU Rule of Law Mission, Kosovo, 2010–12 (Acting Hd, 2012). *Recreations:* music, writing poetry, sailing, golf. *Address:* c/o Foreign and Commonwealth Office, King Charles Street, SW1A 2AH. *Clubs:* Oakland Park Golf (Chalfont St Giles); Tanjung Lesung Sailing (W Java, Indonesia).

SPARKES, Jonathan Winston; Chief Executive, Crisis, since 2014; *b* Elston, Notts, 3 March 1968; *s* of late Donald and Mary Sparkes. *Educ:* Loughborough Univ. (BSc Hons Mgt Sci. 1990). FCIPD 2008. Gp HR Dir, Generics Gp, 1995–2002; Hd of HR, Cambridgeshire CC, 2002–04; HR Dir, 2004–06, Chief Exec., 2006–09, Scope; Director: Workforce Develt, Cornwall and Isles of Scilly PCT, 2010; HR and Orgnl Develt, Royal Cornwall Hosps NHS Trust, 2010–11; Chief Operating Officer, UNICEF UK, 2012–14. *Publications:* (jtly) Leading HR, 2001. *Recreations:* reading, films, travel. *Address:* Crisis, 66 Commercial Street, E1 6LT.

SPARKS, Leslie Thomas, OBE 1997; RIBA; consultant architect/planner, specialising in conservation and urban design, since 1999; *b* 3 March 1943; *s* of Eric and Dorothy Leonie Sparks; *m* 1967, Yvonne Ann Sawyer; one *s* one *d*. *Educ:* Kingston Coll. of Art (DipArch); Central London Poly. (DipTP). RIBA 1971; MRTPI 1973. Severn Gorge Projects Manager, Telford Develt Corp., 1977–80; Dir, Envmtl Services, Bath CC, 1980–90; Dir, Planning and Architecture, Birmingham CC, 1991–99; Planning Inspector (pt-time), 1999–2002. Vis. Prof., UWE, 1998–2007. Chm., Expert Panel on Historic Buildings and Land, Heritage Lottery Fund, 1999–2001. Commissioner: CABE, 1999–2006; English Heritage, 2001–08 (Chm., Adv. Cttee, Historic Built Envmt, 2002–03); Chairman: English Heritage/CABE Urban Panel, 2003–10; West Midlands Design Rev. Panel, 2007–; CABE/Crossrail Design Rev. Panel, 2009–; West Midlands Cttee, Heritage Lottery Fund, 2010–April 2016; Steering Gp, Ironbridge World Heritage Site, 2011–. Hon. Life Mem., English Historic Towns Forum, 1992. Patron, Urban Design Gp, 1997–2010; Trustee, Birmingham Conservation Trust, 1999–2012. FRSA 1981. Hon. DDes UWE, 2000. *Recreations:* painting, music, Rugby, cricket, architecture, historic towns.

SPARKS, Prof. (Robert) Stephen (John), CBE 2010; FRS 1988; Chaning Wills Professor of Geology, Bristol University, since 1990 (Professor of Geology, since 1989); Natural Environment Research Council Professor of Earth Sciences, 1998–2003; *b* 15 May 1949; *s* of Kenneth Grenfell Sparks and Ruth Joan Rugman; *m* 1971, Ann Elizabeth Talbot; two *s*. *Educ:* Imperial College London (BSc Hons 1971, PhD 1974). Postdoctoral fellowships, Lancaster Univ., 1974–76, Univ. of Rhode Island, 1976–78, studying physics of volcanic eruptions; Cambridge University: Demonstrator, 1978–82; Lectr in Geology, 1982–89; Fellow, Trinity Hall, 1981–89; Chief Scientist, Montserrat Volcano Observatory, 1997–99. Sherman Fairchild Dist. Scholar, Calif Inst. of Technology, 1987; Hon. Res. Fellow, Nat. History Mus., 2002–05. Studies of volcanic eruptions: Heimaey, Iceland, 1973; Etna, 1975; Soufrière, St Vincent, WI, 1979; Mount St Helens, 1980; Soufrière Hills, Montserrat, WI, 1996–. Chm., Adv. Cttee for Maths Educn, 2012–15; Mem. Council, Royal Soc., 2015–. Trustee, Natural Hist. Mus., 2015–. President: Geol Soc. of London, 1994–96; Internat. Assoc. of Volcanology and Chemistry of Earth's Interior, 1999–2003. Bakerian Lectr, Royal Soc., 2000. Fellow, Amer. Geophys. Union, 1999. Hon. DSc: Université Blaise Pascal, Clermont-Ferrand, 1999; Lancaster Univ., 2000; Inst. de Physique du Globe, Paris, 2005. Wager Prize for Volcanology, Internat. Assoc. of Volcanology and Chemistry of Earth's Interior, 1983; Bigsby Medal, 1985, Murchison Medal, 1998, Geol Soc.; Arthur L. Day Medal, Geol Soc. of America, 2000; Arthur Holmes Medal, European Geosciences Union, 2004; Thorarinsson Medal, IAVCEI, 2008; Vetlesen Prize, 2015. *Publications:* Volcanic Plumes, 1997; over 400 papers on physics of volcanic eruptions, geology of young volcanoes and origins of volcanism. *Recreations:* music, cricket, travel, cooking. *Address:* Walnut Cottage, 19 Brinsea Road, Congresbury, Bristol BS49 5JF.

SPARROW, Bryan, CMG 1992; HM Diplomatic Service, retired; Ambassador to Croatia, 1992–94; *b* 8 June 1933; *m* 1958, Fiona Mary Mylechreest; one *s* one *d*. *Educ:* Hemel Hempstead Grammar Sch.; Pembroke Coll., Oxford (BA Hons; MA). Served Army, 1951–53. Belgrade, 1958–61; FO, 1961–64; Moscow, 1964–66; Tunis, 1967–68; Casablanca, 1968–70; FO, 1970–72; Kinshasa, 1972–76; Prague, 1976–78; Counsellor (Commercial), Belgrade, 1978–81; Ambassador, United Republic of Cameroon, 1981–84, and concurrently to Republic of Equatorial Guinea and Central African Republic, 1982–84; Canadian Nat. Defence Coll., 1984–85; Consul-General: Toronto, 1985–89; Lyon, 1989–92. *Recreations:* gardening, travel. *Address:* The Haven, The Green Avenue, Ambleside, Cumbria LA22 9AU.

SPARROW, Sir John, Kt 1984; Chairman, Horserace Betting Levy Board, 1991–98; *b* 4 June 1933; *s* of Richard A. and Winifred R. Sparrow; *m* 1967, Cynthia Whitehouse. *Educ:* Coldfall Primary Sch.; Stationers' Company's School; London School of Economics (BSc Econ 1954; Hon. Fellow, 1994). FCA 1957–97. With Rawlinson & Hunter, Chartered Accountants, 1954–59; Ford Motor Co. Ltd, 1960; AEI-Hotpoint Ltd, 1960–63; United Leasing Corporation, 1963–64; Morgan Grenfell Group (formerly Morgan Grenfell & Co.), 1964–88; Dir, Morgan Grenfell Gp (formerly Morgan Grenfell Hldgs), 1971–88; Chairman: Morgan Grenfell Asset Management, 1985–88; Morgan Grenfell Laurie Hldgs, 1985–88. National & Provincial Building Society: Mem., London Adv. Bd, 1986–89; Dir, 1989–96; Dep. Chm., 1994–96; Chm., Universities Superannuation Scheme Ltd, 1988–96. Chm., Mather & Platt, 1979–81; Director: Federated Chemicals, 1969–78 (Chm., 1974–78); Harris Lebus, 1973–79; United Gas Industries, 1974–82 (Dep. Chm., 1981–82); Coalite Group plc, 1974–82, 1984–89; Gas and Oil Acreage, 1975–78; Tioxide Gp, 1977–78; Peterborough Develt Corp., 1981–88; Short Brothers plc, 1984–89 (Dep. Chm., 1985–89); ASW Holdings Plc, 1987–93; Regalian Properties PLC, 1990–93. Seconded as Head of Central Policy Review Staff, Cabinet Office, 1982–83. Chm., EDC for Process Plant Industry, 1984–85; Chairman: National Stud, 1988–91; Horseracing Forensic Lab., 1991–98. Gov., LSE, 1984–2003 (Vice-Chm. Govs, 1984–93; Actg Chm., 1987–88); Pres., Old Stationers' Assoc., 1995–96. Hon. Fellow, Wolfson Coll., Cambridge, 1987. *Recreations:* cricket, crosswords, horse-racing, reading, lunching. *Address:* Padbury Lodge, Padbury, Buckingham MK18 2AJ. *Club:* MCC.

SPAWFORTH, David Meredith, MA; Headmaster, Merchiston Castle School, Edinburgh, 1981–98; *b* 2 Jan. 1938; *s* of Lawrence and Gwen Spawforth, Wakefield, Yorks; *m* 1963, Yvonne Mary Gude; one *s* one *d*. *Educ:* Silcoates School; Hertford Coll., Oxford (Heath Harrison Travelling Schol.; MA Mod. Langs). Assistant Master: Winchester Coll., 1961–64; Wellington Coll., 1964–80; Housemaster, Wellington Coll., 1968–80. British Petroleum Education Fellow, Keble Coll., Oxford, 1977. FRSA 1994. *Recreations:* gardening, France, history, theatre, walking, sailing, model railways. *Address:* Kimberley, Netherbarns, Galashiels, Selkirkshire TD1 3NW.

SPEAIGHT, Anthony Hugh; QC 1995; *b* 31 July 1948; *s* of late George Victor Speaight and Mary Olive Speaight (*née* Mudd); *m* 1991, Gabrielle Anne Kooy-Lister; two *s* one *d*. *Educ:* St Benedict's Sch., Ealing; Lincoln Coll., Oxford (MA; Sec., Oxford Union Soc., 1970). Called to the Bar, Middle Temple, 1973 (Bencher, 2004). Member: Bar Council, 1986–92, 1998–2000; Bar Working Party on Televising Courts, 1990; Chm., Bar Council Access to the Bar Cttee, 2004–06. Mem., Govt Commn on UK Bill of Rights, 2011–12. Chm., Editl Bd, Counsel, jl of Bar of England and Wales, 1990–94. Schuman Silver Medal, FVS Foundn, Germany, 1976. *Publications:* (with G. Stone) The Law of Defective Premises, 1982; Architects Legal Handbook, (ed jtly) 3rd edn 1982 to (ed) 9th edn 2010; (ed jtly) Butterworths Professional Negligence Service, 2 vols, 2000. *Recreations:* theatre, cricket. *Address:* 4 Pump Court, Temple, EC4Y 7AN. *T:* (020) 7842 5555. *Clubs:* Carlton (Chm., Political Cttee, 2009–13), Hurlingham.

SPEAKMAN, William, VC 1951; *b* 21 Sept. 1927; *m* 1st, 1956, Rachel Snitch; one *s*; 2nd, Jill; one *d*. *Educ:* Wellington Road Senior Boys' Sch., Altrincham. Entered Army as Private. Served Korean War, 1950–53 (VC), King's Own Scottish Borderers. *Recreations:* swimming, ski-ing.

SPEARING, Prof. Anthony Colin, LittD; William R. Kenan Professor of English, University of Virginia, since 1989 (Professor of English, since 1987); *b* 31 Jan. 1936; *s* of Frederick Spearing and Gertrude Spearing (*née* Calnin); *m* 1961, Elizabeth; one *s* one *d*. *Educ:* Alleyn's Sch., Dulwich; Jesus Coll., Cambridge (BA 1957; MA 1960); Cambridge Univ. (LittD 2014). University of Cambridge: W. M. Tapp Res. Fellow, Gonville and Caius Coll., 1959–60; Univ. Asst Lectr in English, 1960–64; Supernumerary Fellow, Gonville and Caius Coll., 1960; Official Fellow, Queens' Coll., 1960–87; Univ. Lectr in English, 1964–85; Dir of Studies in English, Queens' Coll., 1967–85; Reader in Medieval English Literature, 1985–87; Life Fellow, Queens' Coll., 1987. Vis. Prof. of English, Univ. of Virginia, 1979–80, 1984. Hon. PhD Lund, 2011. *Publications:* Criticism and Medieval Poetry, 1964, 2nd edn 1972; The Gawain-Poet: a critical study, 1970; Chaucer: Troilus and Criseyde, 1976; Medieval Dream-Poetry, 1976; Medieval to Renaissance in English Poetry, 1985; Readings in Medieval Poetry, 1987; The Medieval Poet as Voyeur, 1993; (trans.) The Cloud of Unknowing, 2001; Textual Subjectivity, 2005; Medieval Autographies, 2012; texts, articles in learned jls. *Address:* Department of English, 219 Bryan Hall, University of Virginia, PO Box 400121, Charlottesville, VA 22904–4121, USA.

SPEARING, Nigel John; *b* 8 Oct. 1930; *s* of late Austen and of May Spearing; *m* 1956, Wendy, *d* of Percy and Molly Newman, Newport, Mon; one *s* two *d*. *Educ:* Latymer Upper School, Hammersmith. Ranks and commission, Royal Signals, 1950–52; St Catharine's Coll., Cambridge, 1953–56. Mem., NUT, 1955–. Tutor, Wandsworth School, 1956–68 (Sen.

Geography Master, 1967–68); Director, Thameside Research and Development Group, Inst. of Community Studies, 1968–69; Housemaster, Elliott School, Putney, 1969–70. Chairman: Barons Court Labour Party, 1961–63; Hammersmith Local Govt Cttee of the Labour Party, 1966–68. Co-opted Mem. GLC Planning and Transport Cttees, 1966–73. Contested (Lab) Warwick and Leamington, 1964. MP (Lab): Acton, 1970–74; Newham S, May 1974–1997. Introd Private Members Bill, which became Industrial Diseases (Notification) Act 1981. Secretary: Parly Lab. Party Educn Gp, 1971–74; Parly Inland Waterways Gp, 1970–74; Member Select Cttee: Overseas Develt, 1973–74, 1977–79; Members' Interests, 1974–75; Procedure, 1975–79; Sound Broadcasting, 1978–83; European (formerly EEC) Legislation, 1979–97 (Chm., 1983–92); Foreign and Commonwealth Affairs, 1980–87; Chair, Parly Affairs Cttee, PLP, 1989–97. Jt Pres., London Dockland Forum, 1998–; Vice-Pres., River Thames Soc., 1975–2008; Pres., Socialist Envmt and Resources Assoc., 1977–86; Chm., British Anti-Common Market Campaign, 1977–83; a Vice-Pres., Campaign for Ind. Britain, 1997–. Mem. Bd, Christian Aid, 1987–91. Mem., Congregational Church and URC, 1947–. *Publications:* The Thames Barrier-Barrage Controversy (Inst. of Community Studies), 1969. *Recreations:* rowing, cycling, reading. *Address:* 92 Boileau Road, SW13 9BP. *T:* (020) 8748 9266.

SPEARMAN, Sir Alexander Young Richard Mainwaring, 5th Bt *cr* 1840; *b* 3 Feb. 1969; *s* of Sir Alexander Bowyer Spearman, 4th Bt, and Martha, *d* of John Green, Naauwpoort, S Africa; *S* father, 1977; *m* 1st, 1994, Anne Stine (marr. diss. 1997), *d* of K. Munch; 2nd, 1997, Theresa Jean, *d* of Dr Thomas Sutcliffe; one *s*. *Heir: s* Alexander Axel Spearman, *b* 9 March 1999.

SPEARMAN, John; Chairman: Playback Ltd, 1987–2011; Scholz & Friends, 2002–10; FrameStore Group, since 2001; *b* 25 Nov. 1941; *s* of Thomas Spearman and Elizabeth Alexandra Spearman (*née* Leadbeater); *m* 1st, 1966, Susan Elizabeth Henderson Elms (marr. diss. 1986); one *s* one *d*; 2nd, 1988, Angela Josephine van Praag; one *d*. *Educ:* Trinity Coll., Dublin (MA). Unilever Grad. Trng Scheme; Lintas Ltd; London Press Exchange; Collett Dickenson Pearce, 1972–89: Man. Dir, 1982–83; Chm. and Chief Exec., 1983–89; Chief Exec., 1992–97, Dep. Chm., 1996–97, Classic FM; Operating Partner, Cognetas LLP, 1995–2008. Chm., Laser Sales (LWT), 1990–93. Member: Government Lead Body for Design, 1991–94; Arts Council of England, 1996–98. Patron Dir, RIBA. Trustee, World Monuments Fund. FRSA 1996. *Recreations:* music, sailing, ski-ing, walking, gardening. *Address:* c/o FrameStore Ltd, 19–23 Wells Street, W1T 3PQ. *Clubs:* Athenæum, Hurlingham; Royal Irish Yacht (Dublin).

See also T. D. Spearman.

SPEARMAN, Richard; QC 1996; a Recorder, since 2000; a Deputy High Court Judge, Chancery Division, since 2013; *b* 19 Jan. 1953; *s* of late Clement Spearman, CBE and Olwen Regina Spearman (*née* Morgan); *m* 1983, Sandra Elizabeth Harris; three *d*. *Educ:* Bedales; King's Coll., Cambridge. Called to the Bar, Middle Temple, 1977, Bencher, 2006. An Asst Recorder, 1998–2000; Hd of Chambers, 4–5 Gray's Inn Square, 2012. *Publications:* (with F. A. Philpott) Sale of Goods Litigation, 1983, 2nd edn 1994; (contrib.) Information Rights, Coppel, 2004, 3rd edn 2010. *Recreations:* racquet sports, ski-ing, family. *Address:* 39 Essex Street, Essex Street, WC2R 3AT. *T:* (020) 7832 1111. *Clubs:* Brooks's, Hurlingham, MCC.

SPEARMAN, Prof. Thomas David, PhD; President, Royal Irish Academy, 1999–2002; Pro-Chancellor, University of Dublin, 2009–12; *b* 25 March 1937; *s* of Thomas Spearman and Elizabeth Alexandra Spearman (*née* Leadbeater); *m* 1961, Juanita Smale; one *s* two *d*. *Educ:* Greenlanes Sch., Dublin; Mountjoy Sch., Dublin; Trinity Coll., Dublin (BA, MA); St John's Coll., Cambridge (PhD 1961). Res. Fellow, UCL and CERN, Geneva, 1961–62; Res. Associate, Univ. of Ill, 1962–64; Lectr in Theoretical Physics, Univ. of Durham, 1964–66; Univ. Prof. of Natural Philosophy, Univ. of Dublin, 1966–97; Trinity College, Dublin: Fellow, 1969, Sen. Fellow, 1994–97, Fellow Emeritus, 1997; Vice-Provost, 1991–97. Chm., Trustee Savings Bank, Dublin, 1989–92. Mem. Council, Dublin Inst. for Advanced Studies, 1999–2002. MAE 1988 (Treas., 1989–2000); Chm., Eur. Acads' Sci. Adv. Council, 2004–08; Vice-Pres., 1983–89, Mem., Governing Council, 1999–2002, ESF; Mem., ESTA, 1994–98. Mem., Rep. Body, C of I, 1968–2001. Gov. and Guardian, Nat. Gall. of Ireland, 1999–2002. *Publications:* (with A. D. Martin) Elementary Particle Theory, 1970; contrib. papers in elementary particle theory, inverse problems and history of science. *Recreations:* walking, reading, gardening, looking at pictures, listening to music. *Address:* St Elmo, Marlborough Road, Glenageary, Co. Dublin, Ireland; Trinity College, Dublin 2, Ireland. *Clubs:* Kildare Street and University, Royal Dublin Soc. (Dublin).

See also J. Spearman.

SPECK, Adrian; QC 2012; *b* Brighton, 15 Jan. 1969; *s* of Neil Speck and Doreen Hobden; *m* 1995, Kathryn Anne Wilson; one *s* one *d*. *Educ:* Seaford Head Comprehensive Sch.; King's Coll., Cambridge (BA 1991). Called to the Bar, Gray's Inn, 1993; in practice as a barrister, specialising in intellectual property law, 1994–. *Publications:* (jtly) The Modern Law of Copyright and Designs, 3rd edn 2000, 4th edn 2011. *Recreations:* long distance gardening, especially vegetables and soft fruit. *Address:* 8 New Square, Lincoln's Inn, WC2A 3QP. *T:* (020) 7405 4321.

SPECTOR, Prof. Roy Geoffrey, MD, PhD; FRCP, FRCPath; Professor of Applied Pharmacology, Guy's Hospital Medical School, 1972–89, now Emeritus; Hon. Physician, Guy's Hospital, since 1967; *b* 27 Aug. 1931; *s* of Paul Spector and Esther Cohen; *m* 1st, 1960, Evie Joan Freeman (marr. diss. 1979); two *s* one *d*; 2nd, 1986, Dr Annette Skinner, botanist. *Educ:* Roundhay Sch., Leeds; Sch. of Medicine, Leeds Univ. (MB, ChB, MD); Guy's Hosp. Med. Sch., Univ. of London (PhD 1964; Dip. in Biochem. 1966). FRCP 1971; FRCPath 1976. Lectr in Paediatric Res. Unit, Guy's Hosp., 1961–67; Guy's Hosp. Medical School, subseq. United Medical and Dental Schools of Guy's and St Thomas's Hosps: Reader in Pharmacology, 1968–71; Sub Dean for Admissions, 1975–89; Chm., Div. of Pharmacology, 1985–88. Vis. Prof. in Clin. Pharmacology, West China Med. Univ., Chengdu, 1986–87. External Examiner, Hong Kong Univ., 1994–95 and 1996–97. Vice Chm., British Univs' Film Council, 1976–87. FRSocMed. *Publications:* (jtly) The Nerve Cell, 1964, 2nd edn 1986; (jtly) Clinical Pharmacology in Dentistry, 1975, 6th edn 1995; (jtly) Mechanisms in Pharmacology and Therapeutics, 1976; (jtly) Aids to Pharmacology, 1980, 3rd edn 1993; (jtly) Textbook of Clinical Pharmacology, 1981, 2nd edn 1986, (contrib.) 3rd edn, 1994; (jtly) Aids to Clinical Pharmacology and Therapeutics, 1984, 3rd edn 1993; (jtly) Common Drug Treatments in Psychiatry, 1984; Catechism in Clinical Pharmacology Therapeutics, 1986; (jtly) Drugs and Medicines, 1989; (contrib.) Handbook of Clinical Research, 1994; contribs to jls on pathology, medicine, gen. science, and applied pharmacology. *Recreations:* cookery, music. *Address:* 3 St Kilda Road, Orpington, Kent BR6 0ES. *T:* (01689) 810069. *E:* r.spector@ntlworld.com.

SPECTOR, Prof. Timothy David, MD; FRCP; Professor of Genetic Epidemiology, and Director, Department of Twin Research and Genetic Epidemiology (formerly Twin Research Unit), King's College London, since 1993; Consultant Rheumatologist, St Thomas' Hospital, since 1993; *b* 14 July 1958; *s* of Walter and June Spector; *m* 1988, Veronique Bataille; one *s* one *d*. *Educ:* St Bartholomew's Hosp. Med. Sch. (MB BS 1982); London Sch. of Hygiene and Tropical Medicine (MSc 1986); MD London 1989. FRCP 1995. SHO in Medicine, 2-year Eur. rotation, St Bartholomew's Hosp., UCL and Brussels, 1983–85; Wellcome Res. Fellow in Clin. Epidemiol., London Hosp. Med. Coll., 1985–88; Sen. Registrar in Rheumatol., St Bartholomew's Hosp., 1988–93. *Publications:* An Introduction to General Pathology, 1999; Your Genes Unzipped, 2003; The Diet Myth, 2015; medical articles. *Recreations:* ski-ing, sailing, wine. *Address:* Department of Twin Research and Genetic Epidemiology, King's College London, St Thomas' Campus, Lambeth Palace Road, SE1 7EH. *E:* tim.spector@kcl.ac.uk.

SPEDDING, John Henry Fryer F.; *see* Fryer-Spedding.

SPEED, Anthony James, CBE 1999; QPM 1991; Police Adviser on public order: City of London Police Committee, 1999; Metropolitan Police, 2004; Singapore Police, 2006; *b* 23 Feb. 1941; *m* 1961, Patricia Elizabeth Boyle; one *s* three *d*. *Educ:* Thomas Calton Technical Sch., Dulwich. Metropolitan Police, 1957–99: Personal Protection Officer to the Prince of Wales, 1969; Scarman Inquiries into Red Lion Square Disorders, 1974, Brixton Disorders, 1981; Divl Comdr, Brixton, 1981–83; posts in Westminster, 1983–99, Asst Comr, Central Area, 1994–99. Chm., Football Licensing Authy, 2003–09. DL Greater London, 1999; Representative DL London Borough of Hounslow, 2000–05, Lambeth, 2005–09. *Recreation:* golf.

SPEED, Sir (Herbert) Keith, Kt 1992; RD 1967; DL; Director, Folkestone & Dover Water Services (formerly Folkestone and District Water Co.), 1986–2007; *b* 11 March 1934; *s* of late Herbert Victor Speed and Dorothy Barbara (*née* Mumford); *m* 1961, Peggy Voss Clarke; two *s* one *d* (and one *s* decd). *Educ:* Greenhill Sch., Evesham; Bedford Modern Sch.; RNC, Dartmouth and Greenwich. Officer, RN, 1947–56; Lt-Comdr RNR, 1964–79. Sales Man., Amos (Electronics) Ltd, 1957–60; Marketing Man., Plysu Products Ltd, 1960–65; Officer, Conservative Res. Dept, 1965–68. MP (C): Meriden, March 1968–Feb. 1974; Ashford, Oct. 1974–1997. An Asst Govt Whip, 1970–71; a Lord Comr of HM Treasury, 1971–72; Parly Under-Sec. of State, DoE, 1972–74; Opposition spokesman on local govt, 1976–77, on home affairs, 1977–79; Parly Under Sec. of State for Defence for RN, 1979–81; Mem., Parly Select Cttee on Defence, 1983–87; UK Rep. to Parly Assembly of Council of Europe and WEU, 1987–97. Parliamentary Consultant: Professional Assoc. of Teachers, 1982–97; Assoc. for Instrumentation, Control and Automation Industry in UK, 1983–87. DL Kent, 1996. *Publications:* Blue Print for Britain, 1965; Sea Change, 1982; contribs to various political and defence jls. *Recreations:* classical music, reading. *Address:* Strood House, Rolvenden, Cranbrook, Kent TN17 4JJ. *Club:* Garrick.

See also J. J. Speed.

SPEED, Jeffery John, CBE 1991; Director of Fundraising and Treasurer's Department, Conservative Central Office, 1995–96; *b* 3 Oct. 1936; *s* of late Herbert Victor Speed and Dorothy Barbara Speed (*née* Mumford); *m* 1985, Hilary Anne Busfield, *d* of late Haley Busfield, Mayfield, Sussex. *Educ:* Bedford Modern Sch. General Motors (Vauxhall), 1955–58; Sales Manager, later Sales Dir, Tompkins Moss Gp, 1959–65; Conservative Party Agent, 1965–78; Dep. Central Office Agent, S Eastern Area, 1978–82; Central Office Agent: E Midlands Area, 1982–88; Greater London Area, 1988–93; Dir, Constituency Services, Cons. Central Office, 1993–95. Election Agent for: Rt Hon. Iain MacLeod, 1970; Cecil Parkinson, Nov. 1970; Rt Hon. Edward Heath, Feb. and Oct. 1974. FInstLM (FISM 1995; MISM 1993). FRSA 1993; FRGS 2003. *Publications:* Tudor Townscapes, 2000; articles in Internat. Map Collectors' Jl. *Recreations:* antique maps (especially those by John Speed, 1552–1629), oenology, travel (particularly in Spain), musical theatre and film.

See also Sir H. K. Speed.

SPEED, Sir Keith; *see* Speed, Sir H. K.

SPEED, Malcolm Walter; Chairman, Brian Ward & Partners, since 2009; *b* 14 Sept. 1948; *s* of Walter and Audrey Speed; *m* 1971, Allison Cutter; three *d*. *Educ:* Melbourne Univ. (LLB). Admitted barrister and solicitor, Melbourne, 1971; called to Victorian Bar, 1981; Solicitor, 1971–81, Barrister, 1981–94, Melbourne; sports consultant, and Exec. Chm., Basketball Australia, 1994–97; Chief Executive: Australian Cricket Bd, 1997–2001; ICC, 2001–08. Sen. Fellow, Melbourne Law Sch., Univ. of Melbourne. *Recreations:* golf, cricket, walking, reading, Australian history. *Address:* Brian Ward & Partners Pty Ltd, Level 1, 555 Lonsdale Street, Melbourne, Vic 3000, Australia. *Clubs:* Wentworth Golf; Australian, Melbourne Cricket.

SPEED, Stephen John Charles; Director, Energy Development, Department for Energy and Climate Change, since 2012; *b* Liverpool, 28 May 1962; *s* of John Raymond Speed and Sheila Veronica Speed (*née* Kelly); *m* 1992, Louise Elizabeth Nash; one *d*. *Educ:* St Edward's Coll., Liverpool; Univ. of Sheffield (BSc Hons Physics 1983); Imperial Coll. London (MBA 1998). Researcher, nano-metrology and X-ray optics, Nat. Physical Lab., 1983–89; Department of Trade and Industry: Eur. Policy, 1989–90; Post Office Sponsorship, 1990–91; Private Secretary: to Sec. of State for Trade and Industry, 1991–92; to Parly Under Sec. of State, 1992; Service Mgt Directorate, 1992–94; Prog. Finance Coordinator, 1994–97; Dep. Dir, Sci. Res. Policy and Funding, OST, 1999–2003; Dep. Dir, Broadband and Telecoms, DTI, 2003–05; Dir, Regl Econ. Develt, DTI, subseq. BERR, 2005–07; Inspector Gen. and Chief Exec., Insolvency Service, 2007–12; Acting Dir Gen., Internat. Climate Change and Energy Efficiency, DECC, 2013–14. Chm., ACE (formerly Assoc. of Chief Execs of Govt Bodies), 2011–12; Vice-Chm., Internat. Assoc. of Insolvency Regulators, 2011–12. *Recreations:* cycling, ski-ing, walking, music. *Address:* Department of Energy and Climate Change, 3 Whitehall Place, SW1A 2AW.

SPEED, Prof. Terence Paul, PhD; FRS 2013; Honorary Research Associate and Laboratory Head, Walter and Eliza Hall Institute of Medical Research, since 2015 (Senior Principal Research Scientist, 1997–2015); *b* Victor Harbor, SA, 14 March 1943; *s* of Harold Hector Speed and Jeanette Elizabeth Speed (*née* Hacklin); *m* 1964, Freda Elizabeth Pollard. *Educ:* University High Sch., Melbourne; Univ. of Melbourne (BSc Hons 1965); Monash Univ. (PhD 1969; DipEd 1969). Tutor, 1965–66, Sen. Tutor, 1966–67, Lectr, 1967–69, Dept of Maths, Monash Univ.; Lectr, Dept of Probability and Stats, Univ. of Sheffield, 1969–73; Associate Prof., 1974–75, Prof., 1975–82, Dept of Maths, Univ. of WA; Chief, Div. of Maths and Stats, CSIRO, 1983–87; Prof. of Statistics, 1987–2009, now Prof. Emeritus, Univ. of Calif, Berkeley. Walter and Eliza Hall Institute of Medical Research: Hd, Genetics and Bioinformatics Div., 1997–2005; Hd, Bioinformatics Div., 2005–14. Hon. DSc: WA, 2005; Chicago, 2014. *Publications:* (trans.) J. Neveu, Discrete Parameter Martingales, 1974; (trans. with T. Hida) T. Hida, Brownian Motion, 1980; (ed with L. Rade) Teaching Statistics in the Computer Age: proceedings of the Round Table Conference on the impact of calculators and computers on teaching statistics, 1985; (ed with M. S. Waterman) Genetic Mapping and DNA Sequencing, 1996; (with D. Nolan) Stat Labs: mathematical statistics through applications, 2000; (ed) Statistical Analysis of Gene Expression Microarray Data, 2003; (ed jtly) Research in Computational Molecular Biology: proceedings of the 11th Annual International Conference RECOMB, 2007; (with Deborah Nolan) Probability and Statistics: essays in honor of David A. Freedman, 2008; approx. 300 articles on maths, statistics, genetics and genomics in jls. *Recreations:* running, reading, opera, movies. *Address:* Walter and Eliza Hall Institute of Medical Research, 1G Royal Parade, Parkville, Vic 3052, Australia. *T:* (3) 93452697, *Fax:* (3) 93470852. *E:* terry@wehi.edu.au; Department of Statistics, 367 Evans Hall #3860, University of California, Berkeley, CA 94720–3860, USA. *T:* (510) 6422781, *Fax:* (510) 6427892. *E:* terrys@berkeley.edu.

SPEIGHT, Prof. Paul Michael, PhD; FDSRCPSGlas, FRCPath; Professor of Oral Pathology and Consultant Histopathologist, University of Sheffield, since 2003 (Dean, School of Clinical Dentistry, 2007–15); *b* Harrogate, Yorks, 25 Oct. 1954; *s* of John Maurice Speight and Beryl Estelle Speight (*née* Somerwell); *m* 1989, Prof. Paula Farthing; two *s* two *d*. *Educ:* Harrogate Grammar Sch.; Univ. of Manchester (BDS 1978); Univ. of Dundee (PhD 1984). FDSRCPSGlas 1982; FRCPath 1989; FDSRCS *ad eundem* 1998; FDSRCSEd *ad hominem*

2003. Sen. Lectr in Oral Pathol., London Hosp. Med. Coll., 1985–89; University College London: Hd, Oral Pathol., Eastman Dental Inst., 1990–2003; Prof. of Oral Pathol., 1997–2003; Hd, Cellular Pathol., UCL Hosps NHS Trust, 2002–03. President: British Soc. for Oral and Maxillofacial Pathol., 2000–03; Internat. Assoc. of Oral Pathologists, 2006–09; British Soc. for Oral and Dental Res., 2009–11. Chairman: Dental Schs Council, 2011–14; Scottish Bd for Academic Dentistry, 2014–. Member: Bd, Faculty of Dental Surgery, RCS, 2011– (Chm., Res. Cttee, 2011–, Awards Cttee, 2015–); Panel A3, REF 2014, 2011–14; Dental Prog. Bd, Health Educn England, 2012–14. *Publications:* Cysts of the Oral and Maxillofacial Regions (with M. Shear), 4th edn 2007; 250 papers in learned jls; 12 book chapters; over 180 research presentations. *Recreations:* ski-ing, hill walking, travel, family, cafés, vintage cameras, photography, reading (novels and biographies). *Address:* School of Clinical Dentistry, University of Sheffield, Claremont Crescent, Sheffield S10 2TA. *T:* (0114) 271 7802, *Fax:* (0114) 279 7050. *E:* p.speight@sheffield.ac.uk.

SPEIGHT, Rebecca; Chief Executive Officer, Woodland Trust, since 2014; *b* Dorchester, 20 June 1967; *d* of Richard and Elizabeth Speight. *Educ:* St Genevieve's Convent, Dorchester; Canford Sch., Wimborne; Durham Univ. (BA English Lang. and Lit.); Heriot-Watt Univ. (MBA). Local Govt Officer, Lothian Regl Council, 1990–95; Sen. Consultant, 1995–99, Dir, 1999–2000, Smythe Dorward Lambert; Gen. Manager, 2000–05, Midlands Dir, 2005–14, National Trust. *Recreations:* walking, cinema, singing, arts. *Address:* Woodland Trust, Kempton Way, Grantham, Lincs NG31 6LL. *T:* 0343 770 5598. *E:* beccyspeight@woodlandtrust.org.uk.

SPEIRS, Robert; Chairman, Stagecoach Group plc, 2002–10 (Director, 1996–2010); *b* 23 Oct. 1936; *s* of John and Isabella Speirs; *m* 1958, Patricia Holt; two *s*. *Educ:* Alleyne's Grammar Sch., Uttoxeter. Cooper Bros, London, 1964–68; Tax Administrator, Texaco Ltd, 1968–77; Tax/Finance Dir, BNOC, subseq. Britoil plc, 1977–88; Finance Director: Olympia and York Canary Wharf Ltd, 1988–93; Royal Bank of Scotland Gp plc, 1993–98; Chairman: Miller Gp Ltd, 1999–2008; Bell Gp plc, 1999–2004; Dir, Canary Wharf Gp plc, 1999–2004. *Recreations:* hill-walking, gardening, military history. *Address:* Arden, Pitts Lane, Pitts Haven, Binstead, Isle of Wight PO33 3AX. *T:* (01983) 568708. *E:* bob.speirs@btopenworld.com.

SPELLAR, Rt Hon. John (Francis); PC 2001; MP (Lab) Warley, since 1997 (Warley West, 1992–97); *b* 5 Aug. 1947; *s* of William David and Phyllis Kathleen Spellar; *m* 1981, Anne Rosalind Wilmot (*d* 2003); one *d*. *Educ:* Bromley Parish Primary Sch.; Dulwich Coll.; St Edmund Hall, Oxford (BA PPE). Electrical, Electronic, Telecommunication and Plumbing Union: Res. Officer, 1969–76; Nat. Officer, 1976–92. Contested (Lab) Bromley, 1970. MP (Lab) Birmingham Northfield, 1982–83; contested (Lab) same seat, 1983, 1987. Parly Under-Sec. of State, 1997–99, Minister of State, 1999–2001, MoD; Minister of State (Minister for Transport), DTLR, then DFT, 2001–03; Minister of State, NI Office, 2003–05; Comptroller of HM Household, 2008–10; Opposition Dep. Chief Whip, 2010; Opposition Dep. Spokesman on Foreign Affairs, 2010–15. *Recreation:* gardening. *Address:* House of Commons, SW1A 0AA. *T:* (020) 7219 0674. *Clubs:* Bromley Labour; Brandhall Labour.

SPELLER, John Christopher, MA (Ed); JP; Headteacher, Norton Knatchbull School, 1997–2010; *b* 10 May 1949; *s* of Sydney and Doris Speller, Woodford Green, Essex; *m* 1981, Jennifer Edgar; twin *s* one *d*. *Educ:* Forest Sch., London; Hatfield Coll., Univ. of Durham (BA Hons French; PGCE); Open Univ. (MA Educn). Asst Teacher, Davenant Foundn Sch., Essex, 1972–76; Head of Languages, Grahame Park Comp. Sch., Barnet, 1977–80; Head of Upper Sch., Nicholas Comp. Sch., Basildon, 1981–83; Dep. Head, Ilford County High Sch. for Boys, 1983–89; Headteacher, Liverpool Blue Coat Sch., 1989–97. PGCE Tutor, Open Univ., 2011–. JP E Kent, 2011. *Recreations:* cricket, walking, travel (UK and abroad), voluntary education advisory and regulatory work, incl. school governor, independent appeals panel membership. *Address:* 45 Joyce Close, Cranbrook, Kent TN17 3LZ. *E:* johncspeller@hotmail.co.uk.

SPELLER, Marcelle Elizabeth, OBE 2011; Founder, 2008, and Chairman, since 2014, Localgiving.com (Chief Executive Officer, 2008–14); *b* Manchester, 6 March 1950; *d* of Vernor Speller and Antonia Speller-Kuijpers. *Educ:* Gumley House Grammar Sch.; Univ. of East Anglia (BSc); INSEAD (MBA 1982). Grad. Trainee, British Railways Bd, 1971–74; Account Manager, Lintas, then Benton & Bowles, London, 1974–77; Account Dir, Young & Rubicam, then Doyle Dane Bernbach, Amsterdam, 1977–81; Sen. Manager, European Projects, Heineken BV, Amsterdam, 1982–84; Sen. Mktg Manager, Europe, Avis Car Rental, 1985–86; Vice-Pres., Mktg, EMEA, Inter-Continental Hotels, 1987–88; Vice-Pres., UK Strategic Planning and Irish Ops, American Express, 1988–89; ind. mktg consultant, 1989–92; Bd Dir, Mktg and Sales, Air UK Ltd, 1992–93; Speller Coundley Associates, 1993–96; Co-Founder and Jt Man. Dir, Holiday-Rentals.com, 1996–2005. *Recreations:* hill-walking, horse riding, classical music. *Address:* Localgiving.com, 6th Floor, 233 High Holborn, WC1V 7DN. *E:* marcelle.speller@localgiving.com.

SPELLER, Paul Anthony; HM Diplomatic Service, retired; Director, International Office, Liberal Democrat Party, 2008–12; Secretary General, Liberal Democrats Abroad, 2010–12; *b* 21 Jan. 1954; *s* of Cecil Edmund Kirby Speller and Shelagh Maureen Clifford Speller; *m* 1998, Jane Hennessy. *Educ:* Wellington Coll.; University Coll. London (BSc Econ 1976). Joined FCO, 1979; Soviet Dept, 1979–83; Nuclear Energy Dept, 1983–86; Second, later First, Sec., Bonn, 1986–89; EU Dept, 1989–91; Private Sec. to Parly Under-Sec. of State, 1991–93; First Sec., UK Repn to EU, Brussels, 1993–96; Southern Eur. Dept, 1996–98; Dep. Governor, Gibraltar, 1998–2002; Dep. Hd of Mission, Jakarta, 2002–05; Hd, SE Asia and Pacific Dept (formerly Gp), FCO, 2005–08. *Recreations:* cricket, tennis, theatre, guitars.

SPELLMAN, (Irene) Ruth, OBE 2007; Chief Executive, Workers' Educational Association, since 2012; *b* 14 Aug. 1951; *d* of Vernon A. Hewlett and Jean Hewlett (*née* Weir); *m* 1979, Dr William Spellman (*d* 2009); one *s* two *d*; *m* 2014, Timothy David Melville-Ross, *qv*. *Educ:* Girton Coll., Cambridge (BA Hons Econs and Pol Sci. 1972). FCIPD 1992. National Coal Board: Investment Analyst, Pension Fund, 1972–73; Industrial Relns Asst, Manpower and Industrial Res., 1973–76; Educn and Trng Advr, NEDO, 1976–86 (pt-time, 1978–86); Consultant in HR and Managing Change, then Managing Consultant, Coopers & Lybrand, 1986–91; Dir, HR, NSPCC, 1991–98; Chief Exec., Investors in People UK, 1998–2006; CEO, IMechE, 2007–08; Chief Exec., Chartered Mgt Inst., 2008–12. Member: Council, Open Univ., 2010–; Bd, NIACE, 2012–. FRSA 2003. Hon. DSc Cranfield, 2010. *Publications:* Economic Consequences of New Technology, 1981; Perspectives in Managing Change, 1990; Management and Leaders Who Can, 2011. *Recreations:* music (violin, singing), literature, politics. *Address:* 9 Maybury Mews, Highgate, N6 5YT. *T:* 07824 865389.

SPELMAN, Rt Hon. Caroline (Alice); PC 2010; MP (C) Meriden, since 1997; Second Church Estates Commissioner, since 2015; *b* 4 May 1958; *d* of Marshall Cormack and Helen Margaret Greenfield; *m* 1987, Mark Gerald Spelman; two *s* one *d*. *Educ:* Herts and Essex Grammar Sch. for Girls; Queen Mary Coll., London (BA 1st cl. Hons European Studies). Sugar Beet Advr, NFU, 1981–84; Dep. Dir, European Confedn of Sugar Beet Growers, Paris, 1984–89; Dir, Spelman, Cormack and Associates (food and biotechnology consultancy), 1989–2009. Contested (C) Bassetlaw, 1992. Shadow Secretary of State: for internat. develt, 2001–03; for envmt, 2003–04; for local and devolved govt affairs, 2004–05; DCLG, 2006–07; Shadow Minister: for women, 2001–04; ODPM, 2005–06; Chm., Cons. Party, 2007–09; Shadow Sec. of State for Communities and Local Govt, 2009–10; Sec. of State for Envmt, Food and Rural Affairs, 2010–12. Member: Envmtl Audit Cttee, 2013–15; Jt Cttee on Modern Slavery Bill, 2014. Chm., Parliament Choir, 2013–15. Vice-Pres., Tearfund, 2013–. *Publications:* The Non-Food Uses of Agricultural Raw Materials, 1994. *Recreations:* tennis, hockey, singing. *Address:* House of Commons, SW1A 0AA. *T:* (020) 7219 4189.

SPENCE, Prof. Alastair Andrew, CBE 1993; MD; FRCA, FRCSE, FRCPG, FRCPE, FRCS; Professor of Anaesthetics, University of Edinburgh, 1984–98, now Emeritus; *b* 18 Sept. 1936; *s* of James Glendinning Spence and Margaret Macdonald; *m* 1963, Maureen Isobel Aitchison; two *s*. *Educ:* Ayr Acad.; Glasgow Univ. FRCA (FFARCS 1964); FRCPG 1980; FRCSE 1991; FRCPE 1994; FRCS 1994. Western Infirmary, Glasgow, 1961–65; MRC Res. Fellow, Univ. of Glasgow Dept of Surgery, 1965–66; Steinberg Res. Fellow and Clinical Asst to Prof. of Anaesthesia, Univ. of Leeds, 1966–69; Sen. Lectr and Head of Dept of Anaesthesia, later Reader and Prof., Western Infirmary, Glasgow, 1969–84. Hon. Consultant Anaesthetist, Lothian Health Bd, then Royal Infirmary of Edinburgh Trust, 1984–98. Lewis H. Wright Meml Lect., Amer. Soc. of Anesthesiologists, 2006. Member: Clinical Standards Adv. Gp, 1994–99; Adv. Cttee on Distinction Awards, 1992–2000 (Dir and Med. Vice-Chm., Scottish Sub-Cttee, 1995–98); Scottish Adv. Cttee on Distinction Awards, 1998–2000. Pres., Royal Coll. of Anaesthetists, 1991–94 (Vice-Pres., 1988–91). Hon. FDS 1994; Hon. FRCEM (Hon. FFAEM 1997). Editor, British Jl of Anaesthesia, 1973–83 (Chm. Bd, 1983–91). *Publications:* books, chapters and papers on anaesthesia and respiratory care. *Recreations:* golf, gardening. *Address:* Harewood, Kilmacolm, Renfrewshire PA13 4HX. *T:* (01505) 872962.

SPENCE, Prof. (Andrew) Michael, PhD; Philip H. Knight Professor of Management, and Dean, Graduate School of Business, Stanford University, 1990–99, now Professor Emeritus; William R. Berkley Professor in Economics and Business, Stern Business School, New York University, since 2010; *b* 7 Nov. 1943; *s* of Ernest John Hamilton Spence and Mary Jane Spence (*née* Gotschal); *m* 1st, Ann Bennett (marr. diss.); one *s* two *d*; 2nd, 1997, Monica Cappuccini (marr. diss.); 3rd, 2006, Giuliana Ferraino; one *s*. *Educ:* Princeton Univ. (BA Philosophy 1966); Oxford Univ. (Rhodes Schol.; MA Maths 1968); Harvard Univ. (PhD Econs 1972). Asst Prof. of Pol Econ., Kennedy Sch. of Govt, Harvard Univ., 1971–75; Associate Prof. of Econs, Stanford Univ., 1973–75; Harvard University: Hon. Res. Fellow, 1975–76, Vis. Prof., 1976–77, Econs Dept; Prof. of Econs, 1977–83, and Prof. of Business Admin, 1979–83; George Gund Prof. of Econs and Business Admin, 1983–86; Chm., Econs Dept, 1983–84; Dean, Faculty of Arts and Scis, 1984–90. Mem., Econs Adv. Cttee, Sloan Foundn, 1979–. Chm., Commn on Growth and Develt, 2006–09. Affiliate, 1999–2009, Sen. Advr, 2009–, Oak Hill Investment Mgt (formerly Oak Hill Venture Partners). Mem. Bd, Stanford Mgt Co., 2008–. Consulting Advr, PIMCO, 2009–. Mem., editl bds of jls incl. Amer. Econs Rev., Bell Jl Econs, Jl of Econ. Theory and Public Policy, at various times. Fellow: Econometric Soc., 1975; Amer. Acad. Arts and Scis, 1983. John Bates Clark Medal, Amer. Econ. Assoc., 1981; (jtly) Nobel Prize for Econs, 2001. *Publications:* Market Signaling: informational transfer in hiring and related processes, 1974; (jtly) Industrial Organization in an Open Economy, 1980; (jtly) Competitive Structure in Investment Banking, 1983; contrib. numerous articles to professional jls incl. Bell Jl Econs, Qly Jl Econs, Econometrica. *Recreations:* windsurfing, motorcycle riding, golf. *Address:* Ohana Investors, 899 Northgate Drive, Suite 301, San Rafael, CA 94903, USA. *E:* mspence98@gmail.com.

SPENCE, Bill; *see* Spence, J. W.

SPENCE, Prof. Charles Jason, PhD; Professor of Experimental Psychology, University of Oxford, since 1997; Fellow, Somerville College, Oxford, since 1997; *b* Leeds, 18 June 1969; *s* of Allan Wright Spence and Norah Spence; *m* 2008, Barbara Maria Vargas-Escobar. *Educ:* Balliol Coll., Oxford (BA 1991); Corpus Christi Coll., Cambridge (PhD 1995). Jun. Res. Fellow, St John's Coll., Cambridge, 1994–97. Presidential Vis. Prof., Temple Univ., Philadelphia, 2015. Eur. Psychologist of Year, European Soc. for Cognitive Psychol., 2003; 10th Exptl Psychol. Prize, EPsS, 2003; Friedrich Wilhelm Bessel Res. Award, Alexander von Humboldt Foundn, Germany, 2005; IG Nobel Prize for Nutrition, Annals of Improbable Res. mag., 2008. *Publications:* The Secrets of the Senses, 2002; (with J. Driver) Crossmodal Space and Crossmodal Attention, 2004; (jtly) The Handbook of Multisensory Processing, 2004; (with C. Ho) The Multisensory Driver, 2008; (with A. Gallace) In Touch with the Future: the sense of touch from cognitive neuroscience to virtual reality, 2014; (with B. Piqueras-Fiszman) The Perfect Meal: the multisensory science of food and dining, 2014 (Prose Prize for Popular Science, 2015). *Recreation:* neurogastronomy. *Address:* Department of Experimental Psychology, University of Oxford, South Parks Road, Oxford OX1 3UD. *T:* (01865) 271364, *Fax:* (01865) 310447. *E:* charles.spence@psy.ox.ac.uk.

SPENCE, Christopher Alexander, CBE 2006 (MBE 1992); Chief Executive: National Centre for Volunteering, since 1998; Volunteering England, 2004–07; Hon. President, London Lighthouse, 1996–2000; *b* 24 April 1944; *s* of late Robert Donald Spence and Margaret Summerford Spence; *m* 1990, Nancy Corbin Meadors Kline. *Educ:* Bromsgrove Sch.; South West London Coll. (Dip. in Counselling Skills). Dir, Task Force, 1968–70; Private Sec. to Speaker of House of Commons, 1970–76; freelance organisational devel consultant, 1976–86; Founder and Dir, London Lighthouse, 1986–96. Dir, Oxfordshire Learning Disability NHS Trust, 1996–2002 (Vice-Chm., 1998–2002). Founding Chair, Pan London HIV/AIDS Providers Consortium, 1992–96; Chair, HIV Project, 1997– (Dir, 1995–97). Chm., Diana, Princess of Wales Meml Fund, 1999–2006 (Trustee, 1998–2006; Chair, Grants Cttee, 1998–2006). Pres., Eur. Volunteer Centre, 2002–07. FRSA 1998. Hon. Fellow, Univ. of Wales, Lampeter, 1999. *Publications:* (with Nancy Kline) At Least a Hundred Principles of Love, 1985, revd edn 1994; AIDS: time to reclaim our power, 1986; On Watch: views from the Lighthouse, 1996. *Recreations:* gardening, reading, writing, walking, vegetarian cooking, cats with challenging behaviour. *Address:* Lower Farm Orchard, Preston Crowmarsh, Wallingford, Oxon OX10 6SL. *T:* (01491) 835266.

SPENCE, Christopher John; Chairman, English Trust Co. Ltd, 1991–2002 (Managing Director, 1978–91); *b* 4 June 1937; *s* of late Brig. Ian Fleming Morris Spence, OBE, MC, TD, ADC and Ruth Spence (*née* Peacock); *m* 1st, 1960, Merle Aurelia (marr. diss. 1968), *er d* of Sir Leonard Ropner, Bt; one *d* (one *s* decd); 2nd, 1970, Susan, *d* of late Brig. Michael Morley, MBE; one *s* one *d*. *Educ:* Marlborough. 2nd Lieut, 10 Royal Hussars (PWO), 1955–57; Royal Wilts Yeomanry, 1957–66. Mem., London Stock Exchange, 1959–78. Sen. Steward, Jockey Club, 1998–2003. Chairman: Nat. Stud Ltd, 2007–11; Newbury Racecourse plc, 2010–11 (Dir, 2003–15). High Sheriff, Berks, 1996–97. *Recreations:* racing, shooting, golf. *Address:* Chieveley Manor, Newbury, Berks RG20 8UT. *T:* (01635) 248208. *Club:* Jockey.

SPENCE, David Lane, CA; London Senior Partner, Grant Thornton, 1998–2006; *b* 5 Oct. 1943; *s* of Dr Alex S. Spence and Edith F. Spence; *m* 1966, Beverley Esther Cardale; one *s* two *d*. *Educ:* Fettes Coll., Edinburgh; Univ. of Surrey (BA 2012). CA 1967. C. F. Middleton & Co., 1962–67; Grant Thornton (formerly Thornton Baker), 1967–2006: Partner, 1970; Eur. Practice Partner, 1974–80; Exec. Partner, 1983–89. DTI Inspector, 1989 and 1992. Chm., Chartered Accountants Jt Ethics Cttee, 1995–97. Pres., Inst. Chartered Accountants of Scotland, 1998–99 (Vice-Pres., 1996–98). Mem. Council, Royal Holloway, Univ. of London, 2010–. Trustee, Debra, 2009–. *Recreations:* golf, occasional cycling, tinkering with old MGs. *Address:* Hendred, Hatton Hill, Windlesham, Surrey GU20 6AB. *Clubs:* Caledonian; Sunningdale, Royal and Ancient Golf.

SPENCE, Rt Rev. (David) Ralph; Bishop of Niagara, 1997–2008; *b* 10 March 1942; *m* Carol Anne Spence; one *s* two *d*. *Educ:* Univ. of Guelph (BA 1964); Wycliffe Coll. (LTh 1968). Ordained priest, 1968; Asst Curate, St George's, Guelph, 1968–70; Rector: St Bartholomew, Hamilton, 1970–74; St John, Thorold, 1974–82; St Luke's, Burlington,

1982–97; Archdeacon of Trafalgar, 1992–97. Chancellor, Renison University Coll., Univ. of Waterloo, 2008–. Hon. DD: Wycliffe Coll., 1999; Trinity Coll., Toronto, 2000; Huron Coll., 2004. Albion Herald Extraordinary, 2006.

SPENCE, James William, (Bill); Lord-Lieutenant, Orkney, since 2014 (Vice Lord-Lieutenant, 2011–14); *b* St Ola, Orkney, 19 Jan. 1945; *s* of late James William Spence and Margaret Duncan Spence (*née* Peace); *m* 1st, 1971, Margaret Paplay Stevenson (*d* 2000); two *s* (and one *s* decd); 2nd, 2003, Susan Mary Price. *Educ:* Stenness Public Sch.; Firth Jun. Secondary Sch.; Leith Nautical Coll.; Robert Gordon's Inst. of Technol., Aberdeen (Master Mariner 1971); Univ. of Wales, Cardiff (BSc Maritime Law and Maritime Econs 1974). Served Merchant Navy, 1961–74: apprentice deck officer, Watts Watts & Co. Ltd, 1961–65; certificated deck officer, NZ Shipping Co. (P&O Steam Navigation Co. Ltd), 1965–74. Temp. asst site co-ordinator, Scapa Flow Project, Micoperi SpA, 1974–75; John Jolly, Shipbrokers and Stevedores, Kirkwall: Manager, 1975; Jun. Partner, 1976–77; Sen. Partner, 1978–; Man. Dir and Proprietor, 1978–; Chm. Bd, 2003–. MRIN 1971; MNI 1972; MICS 1979. Mem., Kirkwall Community Council, 1978–82. Member: Kirkwall Port Employers' Assoc., 1975– (Chm., 1979–87); Orkney Pilotage Cttee, 1979–88. Kirkwall Station, RNLI: Dep. Launching Authy, 1976–87; Stn Hon. Sec., 1987–96; Chm., Br. Cttee, 1997–2004. Vice Consul for Norway, 1976–77, Actg Consul, 1977–78, Consul, 1978–2015; Vice Consul for Netherlands, 1978–94. Chm., Assoc. of Hon. Norwegian Consuls in UK and Ireland, 1993–95 (Vice Chm., 1991–93). Chm., Orkney Riding Club, BHS, 1985–92 (Mem., 1984–). Trustee, Pier Arts Centre Trust, Orkney, 1980–91 (Chm., 1989–91). DL Orkney, 1988. Hon. Sheriff, Grampian, Highland and Islands in Kirkwall, 2000–. Comdr, Royal Norwegian Order of Merit, 1987; Chevalier, Order of Orange-Nassau (Netherlands), 1994. *Recreations:* oenophilist, equestrian matters, Orcadian history, vintage motoring. *Address:* Alton House, Kirkwall, Orkney KW15 1NA. *T:* (01856) 872268. *E:* bs3920@yahoo.com, ll@johnjolly.co.uk.

SPENCE, Canon John Andrew, CBE 2013 (OBE 2006; MBE 1999); DL; Governor, Church Commissioners, 2005–13; *b* Edinburgh, 30 Jan. 1951; *s* of Henry John Spence and Thelma Spence; *m* 1974, Yvonne May Cameron; one *s* two *d*. *Educ:* George Watson's Coll., Edinburgh; Trinity Coll., Dublin (BA Hons Econs); Harvard Business Sch. (PMD Exec. Educn). Lloyds Banking Group, 1973–2005: posts include: Man. Dir, Business Banking, 1994–98; Chief Exec., Lloyds TSB Scotland, 1998–2000; Managing Director: Branch Networks, 2000–01; Retail Distribn, 2001–03; Dir, Policy and Risk, 2003–05. Non-executive Director: HMRC, 2005–12; Capital for Enterprise Ltd, 2005–13; Callcredit Information Gp Ltd, 2006–09; Skipton Gp Hldgs Ltd, 2009–10; Chm., Spicer Haart Gp, 2010–. Dep. Chm., BITC, 2000–. President: Enable, 1999–2010; Royal Zool Soc. of Scotland, 2007–; Chairman: Vitalise, 2005–10; Action for Blind People, 2007–10; Essex Community Foundn, 2009–14; SE Local Enterprise Partnership, 2011–13; Finance Cttee, Archbishops' Council, 2013–; Treas., Queen Elizabeth Diamond Jubilee Trust, 2013–. Lay Canon, Chelmsford Cathedral, 2006–. Member, Board: Anglia Ruskin Univ., 2010–; Money Advice Service, 2012–14. Mem. (C), Essex CC, 2013– (Mem. Cabinet for Finance, 2014–). DL Essex, 2008. Hon. DEd Anglia Ruskin, 2009. *Recreations:* cooking, eating, drinking, listening to sport and arts, motorcycling, swimmimg. *Address:* Cuton Hall, Chelmer Village Way, Chelmsford, Essex CM2 6TD. *T:* (01245) 465108. *E:* john.spence@hotmail.co.uk.

SPENCE, Prof. Jonathan Dermot, CMG 2001; PhD; Sterling Professor of History, Yale University, 1993, now Emeritus; *b* 11 Aug. 1936; *s* of Dermot Gordon Chesson Spence and Muriel Evelyn Crailsham; *m* 1st, 1962, Helen Alexander (marr. diss. 1993); two *s*; 2nd, 1993, Annping Chin; one step *s* one step *d*. *Educ:* Winchester Coll.; Clare Coll., Cambridge (BA 1959; Hon. Fellow, 2006); Yale Univ. (MA 1961; PhD 1965). Yale University: Asst Prof., then Prof., 1966–, Chm., 1984–86, History Dept; George Burton Prof., 1976; Dir, Div. of Humanities, 1981–83; Mem. Bd of Govs, Yale Univ. Press, 1994–. Hon. Prof., Univ. of Nanjing, 1994–2008; Guggenheim Fellow, 1979–80; MacArthur Fellow, 1988–92. Council of Scholars, Library of Congress, 1988–96. Fellow: Amer. Acad. of Arts and Scis, 1985; Amer. Philosophical Soc., 1993; Corresp. FBA 1997. Hon. degrees from 8 American colls, and Chinese Univ. of Hong Kong, 1996; Hon. DLitt: Oxon, 2003; Cambridge, 2013. *Publications:* Ts'ao Yin and the K'ang-hsi Emperor: bondservant and master, 1966, 2nd edn 1988; To Change China: Western advisers in China 1620–1960, 1969, 2nd edn 1980; Emperor of China: self-portrait of K'ang-hsi, 1974; The Death of Woman Wang, 1978; (ed with John E. Wills) From Ming to Ch'ing: conquest, region and continuity in seventeenth-century China, 1979; The Gate of Heavenly Peace: the Chinese and their revolution 1895–1980, 1981; The Memory Palace of Matteo Ricci, 1984; The Question of Hu, 1988; The Search for Modern China, 1990, 2nd edn 1999; Chinese Roundabout: essays in history and culture, 1992; God's Chinese Son: the Taiping heavenly kingdom of Hong Xiuquan, 1996; (with Annping Chin) The Chinese Century: a photographic history of the last hundred years, 1996; The Chan's Great Continent: China in Western minds, 1998; Mao Zedong, 1999; Treason by the Book, 2001; Return to Dragon Mountain: memories of a late Ming man, 2007. *Recreation:* gardening. *Address:* 691 Forest Road, West Haven, CT 06516, USA. *Clubs:* Athenæum; Yale (New York City).

SPENCE, Dr Joseph Arthur Francis; Master, Dulwich College, since 2009; *b* 18 Dec. 1959; *s* of Joseph Arthur Spence and Lenice Mary Spence (*nee* Woolley); *m* 1985, Angela Margaret Alexander Fiddes; two *s* one *d*. *Educ:* St Philip's Grammar Sch., Edgbaston; Salesian Coll., Battersea; Univ. of Reading (BA Hons Modern History and Politics); Birkbeck Coll., London (PhD 1991). Master in College, Eton Coll., 1992–2002; Headmaster, Oakham Sch., 2002–09. Governor: St John's Sch., Cambridge, 2005–; Dragon Sch., Oxford, 2007–; Isle of Sheppey Acad., 2009–; Windlesham House, 2011–. Trustee: Demarco Archive Trust, 2007–; Dulwich Picture Gall., 2011–; Inspiring Futures Foundn, 2011–. *Publications:* (ed) The Sayings of W. B. Yeats, 1993; (ed) The Sayings of G. B. Shaw, 1993; (ed) The Sayings of Jonathan Swift, 1994; contrib. to Oxford DNB, TLS, Irish Historical Studies. *Address:* Dulwich College, Dulwich, SE21 7LD. *T:* (020) 8693 3601. *E:* spencejaf@dulwich.org.uk. *Club:* Athenæum.

SPENCE, Malcolm Hugh; QC 1979; a Recorder, 1985–99; a Deputy High Court Judge, 1988–99; barrister-at-law, 1958–2012; *b* 23 March 1934; *s* of late Dr Allan William and Martha Lena Spence; *m* 1967, Jennifer Jane, *d* of Lt-Gen. Sir George Cole, KCB, CBE; one *s* one *d*. *Educ:* Summer Fields, Oxford; Stowe Sch.; Gonville and Caius Coll., Cambridge (MA, LLM). Gray's Inn: James Mould Schol., Holker Sen. Exhibnr, Lee Prizeman; called to the Bar, 1958; Bencher, 1988. Worcester Regt, First Lieut, 1954. Marshal to Mr Justice McNair, 1957; Pupil to Mr Nigel Bridge (later Lord Bridge of Harwich), 1958; entered chambers of Mr John Widgery, QC, 1958; practised mainly in Town and Country Planning and Compensation for Compulsory Purchase; Asst Recorder, 1982–85. Chm., Planning and Envmt (formerly Local Govt Planning and Envmtl) Bar Assoc., 1994–98. Chartered Arbitrator, 2003; Accredited Mediator, 2006; FCIArb 1999. Freeman, City of London, 2001; Liveryman, Arbitrators' Co., 2001. Chm., Wagner Soc., 2002–08. *Publications:* (jtly) Rating Law and Valuation, 1961; The Chambers of Marshall Hall: 125 years, 2005. *Recreations:* trout and salmon fishing, forestry, golf (Captain: Cambridge University Stymies, 1957; Old Stoic Golfing Soc., 1972; Semi-finalist, Scandinavian Amateur Championship, 1964), opera. *Address:* 1 Gray's Inn Square, WC1R 5AA. *T:* (020) 7405 4379; Scamadale, Arisaig, Inverness-shire PH39 4NS. *T:* (01687) 450698. *Club:* Hawks (Cambridge).

SPENCE, Michael; *see* Spence, A. M.

SPENCE, Michael James, DPhil; Vice-Chancellor and Principal, University of Sydney, since 2008; *b* Sydney, 10 Jan. 1962; *s* of James Spence and Judith Fay Spence; *m* 1990, Beth Ann Peterson (*d* 2012); two *s* three *d*; *m* 2015, Jenny Seon-Young Ihn. *Educ:* Univ. of Sydney (BA Hons 1985; LLB Hons 1987); St Catherine's Coll., Oxford (DPhil 1996); St Stephen's House, Oxford (Post Grad. Dip. Theol. 2005). Fellow and Tutor in Law, 1992–2008, Dean, 1993 and 1995–2000, St Catherine's Coll., Oxford; University of Oxford: Chairman: Law Faculty, 2001–02; Law Bd, 2002–04; Hd, Social Scis Div., 2005–08. Consultant, Olswang Solicitors, 1997–2008. Curate, Cowley Parish, Oxford, 2006–08. Member: Bd, NSW Bd of Studies, Teaching and Educnl Standards, 2014–; Hong Kong Quality Assurance Council, 2015–. *Publications:* Protecting Reliance: the emergent doctrine of equitable estoppel, 1999; (with A. Ohly) The Law of Comparative Advertising, 1999; (ed jtly) The Modern Law of Patents, 2005; Intellectual Property, 2007; contribs to jls incl. Current Legal Problems, Law Qly Rev. *Recreations:* oboe, piano, Chinese, Korean, walking, cycling. *Address:* Office of the Vice-Chancellor and Principal, Main Quadrangle–A14, University of Sydney, NSW 2006, Australia. *T:* (2) 93515051, *Fax:* (2) 93514596. *E:* vice.chancellor@sydney.edu.au. *Clubs:* Oxford and Cambridge; Australian (Melbourne).

SPENCE, Prof. Nicola Jane, PhD; Chief Plant Health Officer, Department for Environment, Food and Rural Affairs, since 2014; *b* W Runton, Norfolk, 22 Feb. 1961; *d* of Sqdn Leader John Spence and Leoné Spence; *m* 1993, Julian Horsley; one *s* one *d*. *Educ:* Mount Sch., York; Bridlington High Sch.; Univ. of Durham (BSc Botany 1982); Birkbeck Coll., Univ. of London (MSc Microbiol. 1986); Univ. of Birmingham (PhD Plant Virology 1992). Res. Scientist, Horticulture Res. Internat., Wellesbourne, 1987–2003; Team Leader, Internat. Plant Health, 2003–06, Hd of Plant Health, 2006–09, Central Sci. Lab., York; Chief Scientist, Food and Envmt Res. Agency, York, 2009–10; Chief Exec., Science City York, 2010–14. Special Prof. in Plant Pathol., Univ. of Nottingham, 2007–. Trustee, Royal Botanic Gdns, Kew, 2009–. *Publications:* The Distribution, Identification, Ecology and Control of Bean Common Mosaic Virus in Africa, 1992; (contrib.) The Gene-for-Gene Relationship in Host-Parasite Interactions, 1997; (contrib.) Biotic Interactions in Plant-Pathogen Associations, 2001; (contrib. with A. J. Murant) Compendium of Umbelliferous Crop Diseases, 2002; (contrib. with S. L. Hughes) Handbook of Plant Virology, 2005; contrib. papers to learned jls, incl. Plant Pathol., Outlook in Agriculture, Plant Disease, Jl Virological Methods, Annals Applied Biol., Jl Phytopathol., Eur. Jl Plant Pathol., Bulgarian Jl Agricl Sci., Archives of Virol., Jl Applied Econs. *Recreations:* walking, cycling, surfing, ski-ing. *Address:* Department for Environment, Food and Rural Affairs, Nobel House, 17 Smith Square, SW1P 3JR. *Club:* Farmers.

SPENCE, Rt Rev. Ralph; *see* Spence, Rt Rev. D. R.

SPENCE, Prof. Robert, FREng; Professor of Information Engineering, Imperial College of Science, Technology and Medicine, 1984–2000, now Emeritus; *b* 11 July 1933; *s* of Robert Whitehair Spence and Minnie Grace Spence (*née* Wood); *m* 1960, Kathleen Potts (*d* 2003); one *s* one *d*. *Educ:* Hymers Coll., Hull; Hull Coll. of Technology (BScEng Hons London External 1954); Imperial College, London (DIC 1955; PhDEng 1959; DScEng 1983); Dr RCA 1997. FCGI; FREng (FEng 1990). Hull Corp. Telephones, 1950–51; General Dynamics/Electronics, Rochester, NY, 1959–62; Department of Electrical Engineering, Imperial College: Lectr, 1962–68; Reader, 1968–84. Vis. Erskine Fellow, Univ. of Canterbury, NZ, 2002; Vis. Fellow, Manchester Business Sch., 2009–. Hon. Prof., Univ. of Waikato, 2007–. Chm. and Founding Dir, Interactive Solutions Ltd, 1985–90. Officier de l'Ordre des Palmes Académiques (France), 1995 (Chevalier, 1985). *Publications:* Linear Active Networks, 1970; Tellegen's Theorem and Electrical Networks, 1970 (trans. Russian and Chinese); Resistive Circuit Theory, 1974; Modern Network Theory, 1978; Sensitivity and Optimization, 1980; Circuit Analysis by Computer, 1986; Tolerance Design of Electronic Circuits, 1988 (trans. Japanese); Information Visualization, 2001; Information Visualization: design for interaction, 2007 (trans. Chinese); Introductory Circuits, 2008; Rapid Serial Visual Presentation, 2013; Information Visualization: an introduction, 2014; numerous papers in learned jls. *Recreation:* mosaic sculpture. *Address:* 1 Regent's Close, Whyteleafe, Surrey CR3 0AH. *T:* (020) 8668 3649.

SPENCE, Ronald Blackwood, CB 1997; Chairman: Probation Board for Northern Ireland, 2004–12; Northern Ireland Legal Services Commission, 2010–15 (Member, 2003–15); Deputy Chairman, National Heritage Memorial Fund and Heritage Lottery Fund, 2006–13; *b* 13 July 1941; *s* of Harold Spence and Margaret Spence (*née* McClure); *m* 1st, 1964, Julia Fitton (marr. diss. 1989); one *s* one *d*; 2nd, 1989, Sarah McKnight. *Educ:* Methodist Coll., Belfast; Queen's Univ., Belfast (BA Hons). Entered NICS as Asst Principal, 1963; Principal, Min. of Devel t, 1967–74; Asst Sec., DoE, 1974–80; Head, Econ. and Social Div., NI Office, 1980–82; Under Sec., Dept of Finance and Personnel, 1982–85; Head, Central Secretariat, 1985–90; Under Sec., Dept of Econ. Develt, 1990–94; Permanent Secretary: DoE (NI), 1994–99; Dept for Regl Develt (NI), 1999–2001. Chairman: NI Partnership Bd, 1996–2001; NI Events Co., 1997–2002; The Change Alliance, 2001–09; Blackwood Enterprises Ltd, 2001–09; Ulster Sports Mus. Assoc., 2008–. Mem. Council, Univ. of Ulster, 2007–08. Hon. Sen. Res. Fellow, Inst. of Governance, QUB, 2001–07. *Recreation:* golf.

SPENCE, Simon Peter; QC 2009; barrister, since 1985; a Recorder, since 2007; *b* York, 29 June 1963; *s* of Arthur John Spence and Nora Emily Spence (*née* Mills); *m* 1990, Diane Mavis Horsey (marr. diss. 2008); two *s* two *d*. *Educ:* Pocklington Sch.; De Montfort Univ. (LLB Hons 1984); Inns of Court Sch. of Law. Called to the Bar, Inner Temple, 1985; in practice as barrister specialising in criminal law. Mem., Bd of Dirs, Th. Royal, Bury St Edmunds, 2000–07; Chm., Bd of Trustees, Co-Opera Co., 2012–. FRSA 2006. *Recreations:* walking, reading, opera, theatre, classical music (listening and singing), jazz, cooking, history. *Address:* 18 Red Lion Court, EC4A 3EB. *T:* (020) 7520 6000, *Fax:* (020) 7520 6248. *E:* Simon.Spence@18rlc.co.uk; Dere Street Chambers, 14 Toft Green, York YO1 6JT. *Club:* Farmers (Bury St Edmunds).

SPENCE, His Honour Stanley Brian; a Circuit Judge, 1991–2006; Resident Judge, Reading Crown Court, 1999–2006; *b* 3 May 1937; *s* of George Henry Spence and Sarah Spence (*née* Hoad); *m* 1961, Victoria Rosaleen Tapper; one *s* one *d*. *Educ:* Portsmouth Grammar Sch.; Britannia Royal Naval College, Dartmouth. Commissioned Supply and Secretariat Specialisation, RN, 1958; served: HMS Eagle; Staff of FO2 FEF; Portsmouth; 3rd Frigate Sqdn; HMS St Vincent; legal training, 1966–68; called to the Bar, Middle Temple, 1968; served: HMS Terror, Singapore; Staff of Commander FEF; 8th Frigate Sqdn; Legal Advr to C-in-C Naval Home Command and Flag Officer Spithead; retired from RN, 1975; Office of Judge Advocate General of the Forces (Army and RAF), 1975–90; Recorder of the Crown Court, 1987–91. *Recreations:* maintaining a cottage in France, wine.

SPENCER, family name of **Earl Spencer,** and **Viscount Churchill**.

SPENCER, 9th Earl *cr* 1765; **Charles Edward Maurice Spencer;** DL; Baron and Viscount Spencer 1761; Viscount Althorp 1765; Viscount Althorp (UK) 1905; writer; *b* 20 May 1964; *s* of 8th Earl Spencer, LVO and Hon. Frances Ruth Burke Roche, *yr d* of 4th Baron Fermoy; *S* father, 1992; *m* 1st, 1989, Victoria (marr. diss. 1997), *d* of John Lockwood; one *s* three *d* (incl. twin *d*); 2nd, 2001, Caroline Victoria Freud (*née* Hutton) (marr. diss. 2009); one *s* one *d*; 3rd, 2011, Mrs Karen Gordon (*née* Villeneuve); one *d*. *Educ:* Maidwell Hall; Eton College; Magdalen Coll., Oxford. Page of Honour to HM the Queen, 1977–79; contributing correspondent, NBC News, 1987–91 and 1993–95; reporter, Granada Television, 1991–93; presenter, NBC Super Channel, 1995–96; writer, Planet Wild, 1998–2000; freelance writer, 2001–. DL Northants, 2005. *Publications:* Althorp: the story of an English home, 1998; The

Spencer Family, 1999; Blenheim: battle for Europe, 2004; Prince Rupert: the last cavalier, 2007; Killers of the King, 2014. *Heir:* *s* Viscount Althorp, *qv.* *Address:* Althorp, Northampton NN7 4HG.

SPENCER, Raine, Countess; *b* 9 Sept. 1929; *d* of late Alexander George McCorquodale and Dame Barbara Cartland, DBE; *m* 1st, 1948, 9th Earl of Dartmouth (marr. diss. 1976); three *s* one *d*; 2nd, 1976, 8th Earl Spencer, LVO; 3rd, 1993, Comte Jean-François de Chambrun (marr. diss. 1996). Westminster City Councillor, 1954–65 (served on various cttees); Member: for Lewisham West, LCC, 1958–65 (served on Town Planning, Parks, Staff Appeals Cttees); for Richmond upon Thames, GLC, 1967–73; GLC Gen. Purposes Cttee, 1971–73; Chm., GLC Historic Buildings Bd, 1968–71; Mem., Environmental Planning Cttee, 1967–71; Chm., Covent Garden Develt Cttee, 1971–72; Chm., Govt working party on Human Habitat in connection with UN Conf. on Environment, Stockholm (June 1972), 1971–72 (report: How Do You Want to Live?); Chm., UK Exec., European Architectural Heritage Year, 1975. British Tourist Authority: Member: Infrastructure Cttee, 1972–86; Board, 1982–93; Chairman: Spas Cttee, 1982–83; Accommodation Cttee (formerly Hotels and Restaurants Cttee), 1983–93; Develt Cttee, 1986–93; Commended Hotels Panel, 1986–90; Cttee, Britain Welcomes Japan, 1990–92; Come to Britain Awards, 1990–93; Member: English Tourist Bd, 1971–75; Adv. Council, V&A Museum, 1980–83; Cttee of Honour, Business Sponsorship of the Arts, 1980; Tourism Deptl Adv. Council, Surrey Univ.; Commn de Tourisme Prestige, Nice, 1993–95. Mem. Jury, improvement of Promenade des Anglais, Nice, 1993–95. Formerly LCC Voluntary Care Cttee Worker, Wandsworth and Vauxhall. Director: Harrods International Ltd, 1996–; Harrods (Management) Ltd, 2001–; Harrods Estates, 2006–. Hon. Dr Laws, Dartmouth Coll., USA. *Publications:* What Is Our Heritage?, 1975; The Spencers on Spas (with photographs by Earl Spencer), 1983; Japan and the East (with photographs by Earl Spencer), 1986. *Address:* Sprimont Lodge, 2A Sprimont Place, SW3 3HU. *T:* 07917 000941, *Fax:* (office) (020) 7225 2021; Whiteway House, Chudleigh, Newton Abbot, Devon TQ13 0DY.

See also Earl of Dartmouth, Hon. H. Legge.

SPENCER, Charles Easdale; theatre critic, Daily Telegraph, 1991–2014; *b* 4 March 1955; *s* of Graham Easdale Spencer and Dorothy Aileen Spencer (*née* Brundan); *m* 1983, Nicola Katrak; one *s.* *Educ:* Charterhouse; Balliol Coll., Oxford (BA Hons Eng. Lang. and Lit.). Surrey Daily Advertiser, 1976–79; Arts Reporter, Evening Standard, 1979–84; Chief Sub-editor, The Stage, 1984–86; Dep. Theatre Critic, London Daily News, 1986–87; Asst Arts Editor and Dep. Theatre Critic, Daily Telegraph, 1987–91. Pres., Critics' Circle, 2008–10. Critic of the Year, British Press Awards, 1999, 2008. *Publications:* I Nearly Died, 1994; Full Personal Service, 1996; Under the Influence, 2000. *Recreations:* food, music, staring into space. *Address:* 16 Derwent Close, Claygate, Esher, Surrey KT10 0RF. *T:* (01372) 465591.

SPENCER, Sir Derek (Harold), Kt 1992; QC 1980; QC (NI) 1992; a Recorder, 1979–92 and 1998–2001; *b* 31 March 1936; *s* of Thomas Harold Spencer and Gladys Spencer (*née* Heslop); *m* 1st, 1960, Joan (*née* Nutter) (marr. diss.; she *d* 2012); two *s* one *d*; 2nd, 1988, Caroline Alexandra (*d* 2003), *yr d* of Dr Franziskus Pärn, Hamburg; one *s.* *Educ:* Clitheroe Royal Grammar Sch.; Keble Coll., Oxford (MA, BCL). 2nd Lieut, King's Own Royal Regt, 1954–56; served in Nigeria. Part-time Law Tutor, Keble Coll., Oxford, 1960–64; called to the Bar, Gray's Inn, 1961 (Holt Scholar; Arden Scholar; Bencher, 1991–2012); in practice SE Circuit. Councillor, London Borough of Camden, 1978–83; Dep. Leader, Conservative Gp, London Borough of Camden, 1979–81. Contested (C) Leicester South, 1987. MP (C): Leicester South, 1983–87; Brighton Pavilion, 1992–97; contested (C) same seat, 1997. PPS: to Home Office Ministers, 1986; to the Attorney General, 1986–87; Solicitor-Gen., 1992–97. Joint Sec. Cons. Parly Legal Affairs Cttee, 1985–87. Vice-Chm., St Pancras North Cons. Assoc., 1977–78; Treas., City of London and Westminster Cons. Assoc., 1990–91. *Recreations:* reading, swimming, walking.

SPENCER, Prof. Harrison Clark, MD; President and Chief Executive Officer, Association of Schools of Public Health, Washington, since 2000; *b* 22 Sept. 1944; *s* of Harrison C. and Dorothy M. Spencer; *m* 1977, Christine Michel; two *s.* *Educ:* Haverford Coll. (BA 1965); Johns Hopkins Univ. (MD 1969); Univ. of Calif at Berkeley (MPH 1972); DTM&H London 1972. FACP 1986; FACPM. Intern in Medicine, Vanderbilt Univ., 1969–70; Med. Resident, USPHS Hosp., San Francisco, 1970–71; Epidemic Intelligence Service Officer, CDC Atlanta, 1972–74; Sen. Med. Resident, Univ. of Calif at San Francisco, 1974–75; Med. Res. Officer, Central American Res. Station, El Salvador, 1975–77; MO, Bureau of Tropical Diseases, CDC, 1977–79; SMO and Malaria Res. Co-ordinator, Clin. Res. Center, Kenya Med. Res. Inst., Nairobi, 1979–84; MO, Malaria Action Prog., WHO, Geneva, 1984–87; Chief, Parasitic Diseases Br., CDC, Atlanta, 1987–91; Dean: Sch. of Public Health and Tropical Medicine, Tulane Univ., 1991–95; LSHTM, London Univ., 1996–2000. *Publications:* over 100 articles on epidemiology, malaria, community-based health, internat. health and tropical medicine. *Recreations:* music, ballet, tennis. *Address:* Association of Schools of Public Health, 1900 M Street NW, Suite 710, Washington, DC 20036, USA.

SPENCER, Isobel; *see* Johnstone, I. T.

SPENCER, James; QC 1991; **His Honour Judge Spencer;** a Circuit Judge, since 2001; *b* 27 May 1947; *s* of James Henry Spencer and Irene Dulcie (*née* Wilson). *Educ:* The King's Sch., Pontefract; Univ. of Newcastle upon Tyne (LLB). Admitted solicitor, 1971; called to the Bar, Gray's Inn, 1975. A Recorder, 1990–2001. A Pres., Mental Health Review Tribunal, 1999–. Mem., Parole Bd, 2002–09. *Recreations:* reading history, cooking and the occasional light exercise. *Address:* Combined Court Centre, 1 Oxford Row, Leeds LS1 3BG.

SPENCER, Janet; *see* Carsten, J.

SPENCER, Prof. John Rason; Professor of Law, University of Cambridge, 1995–2013, now Emeritus; Fellow, Selwyn College, Cambridge, 1970–2013, now Emeritus; Bye Fellow, Murray Edwards College, since 2014; *b* 19 March 1946; *s* of Donald Edward Spencer and Catherine Mary Spencer (*née* Cozens); *m* 1972, Rosemary Stewartson; one *s* two *d.* *Educ:* Blandford Grammar Sch.; Selwyn Coll., Cambridge (MA; LLB; LLD 2007). Cambridge University: Asst Lectr, Law Faculty, 1973–76; Lectr, 1976–91; Reader, 1991–95; Chm., Law Faculty, 1995–97; Dep. Vice Chancellor, 2014–15. Ganshof van der Meersch Vis. Prof., Université Libre de Bruxelles, 2015. Mem., Calcutt Cttee on Privacy and Related Matters, 1990; Consultant, Criminal Courts Review, 2000. Hon. QC 2003; Academic Bencher, Inner Temple, 2003; Hon. Member of Chambers: Hardwicke Bldg, 2003; 15 New Bridge St, 2014. DenD *hc* Poitiers, 2004. Chevalier, Ordre des Palmes Académiques (France), 2000. *Publications:* Jackson's Machinery of Justice, 8th edn 1989; (with Rhona Flin) The Evidence of Children: the law and the psychology, 1990, 2nd edn 1993; La procédure pénale anglaise (Que sais-je?), 1998; (jtly) European Criminal Procedures, 2002; Evidence of Bad Character, 2006, 2nd edn 2009; Hearsay Evidence in Criminal Proceedings, 2008, 2nd edn 2014; (jtly) Children and Cross-examination: time to change the rules?, 2012. *Address:* Murray Edwards College, Cambridge CB3 0DF.

SPENCER, Dr Jonathan Page, CB 2002; Chairman, Church of England Pensions Board, since 2009; company director and public policy consultant, since 2006; *b* 24 April 1949; *s* of John Spencer and Doreen (*née* Page); *m* 1976, Caroline Sarah Armitage; one *s* two *d.* *Educ:* Bournemouth Sch.; Downing Coll., Cambridge (BA); Oxford Univ. (DPhil). ICI Res. Fellow, Oxford, 1973–74; joined Department of Trade and Industry, 1974: Principal, 1977; Principal Private Sec. to successive Secs of State, 1982–83; Asst Sec., 1983; Cabinet Office, 1987–89; Under Sec., 1991; Dir, Insurance Div., then Directorate, 1991–97; Director General: Resources and Services, 1997–2000; Business Competitiveness, 2000–02; Dir Gen., Policy, then Clients and Policy, LCD, later DCA, 2002–05. Member: Admin. Justice & Tribunals Council (formerly Council on Tribunals), 2005–13; SRA (formerly Law Soc. Regulation Bd), 2006–09; Gibraltar Financial Services Commn, 2011–. Non-exec. Dir, East Kent Hosps Univ. NHS Foundn Trust, 2007– (Dep. Chair, 2010–). *Recreations:* music, keeping the house up and the garden down. *Address:* Little Eggarton, Godmersham, Canterbury, Kent CT4 7DY.

SPENCER, Prof. Jonathan Robert, DPhil; FRSE; Regius Professor of South Asian Language, Culture and Society, University of Edinburgh, since 2014 (Professor of Anthropology of South Asia, 1999–2014); *b* Dorking, 23 Dec. 1954; *s* of George Spencer and Maisie Spencer; *m* 1st, 1987, Julia Swannell (*d* 1992); 2nd, 1994, Prof. Janet Carsten, *qv*; one *d.* *Educ:* Univ. of Edinburgh (MA Hons Social Anthropol. 1977); Univ. of Chicago (AM 1981); Univ. of Oxford (DPhil 1986). Lecturer: Univ. of Sussex, 1987; LSE, 1989–90; Univ. of Edinburgh, 1990–99. FRSE 2011. *Publications:* A Sinhala Village in a Time of Trouble, 1990, 2nd edn 2000; Anthropology, Politics and the State, 2007; Checkpoint, Temple, Church and Mosque, 2014. *Recreations:* books, jazz, family. *Address:* School of Social and Political Science, University of Edinburgh, Edinburgh EH8 9LL. *T:* (0131) 650 3944. *E:* jonathan.spencer@ed.ac.uk.

SPENCER, Mark Steven; MP (C) Sherwood, since 2010; *b* 20 Jan. 1970; *s* of Cyril and Dorothy Spencer; *m* Claire; one *s* one *d.* *Educ:* Colonel Frank Seely Sch., Calverton; Shuttleworth Agricl Coll. (Nat. Cert. Agric.). Farmer, Spring Lane Farm, Nottingham; Proprietor, Floralands Garden Village, Lambley. Member (C): Gedling BC, 2003–; Notts CC, 2005–. *Address:* House of Commons, SW1A 0AA.

SPENCER, Martin Benedict; QC 2003; *b* 19 June 1956; *s* of late Dr Seymour Spencer and Margaret Spencer; *m* 1977, Lisbet Steengaard Jensen; two *s* one *d.* *Educ:* Hertford Coll., Oxford (MA, BCL). Called to the Bar, Inner Temple, 1979, Bencher, 2011; in practice, Hailsham Chambers, 1981– (Hd of Chambers, 2009–). *Publications:* (jtly) The Danish Criminal Code, 1999; (jtly) The Civil Procedure Rules in Action, 2000; (contrib.) Risk Management and Litigation in Obstetrics and Gynaecology, ed by R. V. Clements, 2001; (contrib.) McGregor on Damages, 19th edn 2014. *Recreation:* music (Member: St Albans Bach Choir; Carillon Chamber Choir). *Address:* Hailsham Chambers, 4 Paper Buildings, Temple, EC4Y 7EX. *Club:* Danish.

See also M. G. Spencer.

SPENCER, Matthew Dominic; Director, Green Alliance, since 2010; *b* London, 1964; *s* of Brian Spencer and Ann Spencer; *m* 1999, Eleanor Knight; two *d.* *Educ:* Whitehaven Grammar Sch.; Heaton Comp.; Univ. of Liverpool (BSc Hons Envmtl Biol. 1987). Internat. Coordinator, Rio Mazan Project, Ecuador, 1989–92; Campaigner, then Campaign Manager, subseq. Campaign Dir, Greenpeace UK, 1994–2003; Founder Chief Exec., Regen SW, 2003–08; Hd, Govt Affairs, Carbon Trust, 2008–10. Mem., Renewables Adv. Bd, 2005–10, CCS Develt Forum, 2010–12, DECC. *Recreations:* mountains, family, cycling, wildlife. *Address:* Green Alliance, 36 Buckingham Palace Road, SW1W 0RE. *T:* (020) 7233 7433.

SPENCER, Michael Alan; Group Chief Executive, ICAP plc, since 1999; Treasurer, Conservative Party, 2007–10; *b* 30 May 1955; *s* of Oscar and Diana Spencer; *m* 1983, Lorraine Geraldine Murphy (marr. diss. 2011); two *s* one *d.* *Educ:* Worth Abbey; Corpus Christi Coll., Oxford (MA). Analyst, Simon & Coates, 1976–80; Vice Pres., Drexel Burnham Lambert, 1981–83; Dir, Charles Fulton, 1983–86; Chairman: Intercapital, 1986–99; Numis plc, 2003–09. *Recreations:* running, riding, shooting, wine, art, politics. *Address:* ICAP plc, 1–2 Broadgate, EC2M 7UR. *T:* (020) 7050 7400, *Fax:* (020) 7050 7116. *Clubs:* Turf, White's, 5 Hertford Street.

SPENCER, Michael Gerald; QC 1989; a Recorder, 1987–2005; *b* 1 Dec. 1947; *s* of Dr Seymour J. G. Spencer and late Margaret (*née* Behn); *m* 1969, Catherine Helen (*née* Dickinson); three *s.* *Educ:* Ampleforth Coll.; Hertford Coll., Oxford (MA Hons). Called to the Bar, Inner Temple, 1970, Bencher, 1996; Mem., Oxford Circuit, 1971, Midland and Oxford, then Midland, Circuit, 1972–. Dir, Yattendon Gp (formerly Yattendon Investment Trust), 1992–. Member: Hertford Coll. Boat Club Soc.; Ampleforth Soc. Chm. and Trustee, Ampleforth Beagles, 1995–. *Publications:* (contrib.) Medical Negligence, 1990; (contrib.) Doctors, Patients and the Law, 1992. *Recreations:* golf, reading, classical music, beagling, paragliding, ski-ing. *Address:* Crown Office Chambers, 2 Crown Office Row, Temple, EC4Y 7HJ. *T:* (020) 7797 8100. *Clubs:* Pegasus, Bar Yacht, Chiltern Rugby Football; Beaconsfield Golf, Inner Temple Golf, Bar Golf.

See also M. B. Spencer.

SPENCER, Dr Neal Andrew; Keeper, Department of Ancient Egypt and Sudan, British Museum, since 2012; *b* Brussels, 18 Dec. 1974; *s* of Edward John Spencer and Catherine Spencer (*née* Hunt). *Educ:* Downing Coll., Cambridge (BA Egyptol. 1996; PhD 2001). British Museum: Asst Keeper, Dept of Ancient Egypt and Sudan, 2000–11; Manager, Internat. Trng Prog., 2006–11. *Publications:* A Naos of Nekhthorheb from Bubastis, 2006; The Gayer Anderson Cat, 2007; Kom Firin I: the Ramesside Temple and the site survey, 2008; (jtly) The International Training Programme: towards a global network, 2011; Kom Firin II: the urban fabric and landscape, 2014. *Recreations:* music, food and wine, history of London. *Address:* British Museum, Great Russell Street, WC1B 3DG. *T:* (020) 7323 8311. *E:* nspencer@britishmuseum.org.

SPENCER, Hon. Sir Robin (Godfrey), Kt 2010; **Hon. Mr Justice Spencer;** a Judge of the High Court, Queen's Bench Division, since 2010; a Presiding Judge, South Eastern Circuit, since 2013; *b* 8 July 1955; *s* of late Eric Spencer and of Audrey Elaine Spencer (*née* Brown); *m* 1978, Julia Margaret Eileen Burley; three *d.* *Educ:* King's Sch., Chester; Emmanuel Coll., Cambridge (MA). Called to the Bar, Gray's Inn, 1978 (Holker Sen. Award; Colyer Prize), Bencher, 2005; in practice, Wales and Chester Circuit, 1978–2010, Leader, 2004–06; an Asst Recorder, 1993–98; a Recorder, 1998–2010; QC 1999; a Dep. High Ct Judge, 2001–10. *Recreations:* music, cricket, football, Methodist history. *Address:* Royal Courts of Justice, WC2A 2LL.

SPENCER, Dame Rosemary (Jane), DCMG 1999 (CMG 1991); HM Diplomatic Service, retired; Ambassador to the Netherlands, 1996–2001; *b* 1 April 1941; *d* of Air Vice-Marshal Geoffrey Roger Cole Spencer, CB, CBE, and Juliet Mary Spencer (*née* Warwick). *Educ:* Upper Chine Sch., Shanklin, IoW; St Hilda's Coll., Oxford (BA Hons Modern Langs). Joined Foreign Office, 1962; FO, 1962–65; Third Secretary, Nairobi, 1965–67; Second Sec., FCO, 1967–70; Second Sec., UK Delegn to EEC, and Private Sec. to Hon. Sir Con O'Neill, Official Leader of UK negotiating team, 1970–71; First Sec., Office of UK Permanent Representative to EEC, Brussels, 1972–73; First Sec. (Economic), Lagos, 1974–77; First Sec., Asst Head of Rhodesia Dept, FCO, 1977–80; RCDS 1980; Counsellor (Agric. and Economic Affairs), Paris, 1980–84; Counsellor (External Relations), Office of UK Perm. Rep. to EEC, 1984–87; Hd of European Community Dept (External), FCO, 1987–89; Asst Under-Sec. of State, FCO, 1989–92; Minister and Hd of British Embassy Berlin Office, 1993–96. Member: Salisbury Cathedral Chapter, 2001–07; Salisbury Cathedral Council, 2002–; Bd, Salisbury Festival, 2003–12; Council, Wyndham Place Charlemagne Trust, 2009– (Trustee, 2013–); Pres., Salisbury Civic Soc., 2007–. Lay Canon, Salisbury Cathedral, 2006–. Trustee: Heinz Koeppler Trust, 2001–09 (Chm., 2005–09); Magna Carta Trust, 2002–; World Faiths Develt Dialogue, 2002–05. Chm., Nikaean Club, 2002–12. Member: Council and Court, Imperial Coll., London Univ., 2001–05; Council, St Swithun's Sch., 2001–04; Gov., Internat. Coll.,

Sherborne Sch., 2001–11; Hon. Pres., Berlin British Sch., 2002–. *Recreations:* country walking, travel, the arts. *Address:* c/o FCO Association, Room K G/117 King Charles Street, SW1A 2AH. *Clubs:* Oxford and Cambridge; International (Berlin).

SPENCER, Sarah Ann, CBE 2007; PhD; Director, Global Exchange on Migration and Diversity, Centre on Migration, Policy and Society, University of Oxford, since 2014 (Open Society Fellow (formerly Director of Policy Research, then Associate Director, later Deputy Director), 2003–14); Chair, Equality and Diversity Forum, 2002–12; *b* 11 Dec. 1952; *d* of late Dr I. O. B. Spencer and of Dr Elspeth Wilkinson; *m* 1978, Brian Anthony Hackland, *qv*; two *s*. *Educ:* Nottingham Univ. (BA Hons); University Coll. London (MPhil); Erasmus Univ. (PhD 2012). Researcher, Law Faculty, UCL, 1977–79; Res. Officer, Cobden Trust (Civil Liberties Charity), 1979–84, Dir 1984–85; Gen. Sec., NCCL, 1985–89; Res. Fellow, 1990–2003, Dir, Citizenship and Governance (formerly Human Rights) Prog., 1994–2003, IPPR. Member: Home Office Task Force on Implementation of the Human Rights Act, 1998–2001; Commn on Future of Multi-Ethnic Britain, 1999–2000; CRE, 2002–06 (Dep. Chm., 2003–05; Chm., Inquiry into site provision for Gypsies and Travellers, 2004–06); DTI Task Force Commn on Equality and Human Rights, 2003–05; Task Gp on Gypsies and Travellers, DCLG, 2006–07; Sen. Stakeholder Gp, Govt Equality Office, 2008–. Advr, Cabinet Office, 2000 and 2002–03. Vis. Prof., Human Rights Centre, Univ. of Essex, 2002–. Associate Mem., Nuffield Coll., Oxford, 2004–08. Trustee, National Flood Forum, 2011–14. Gov., British Inst. of Human Rights, 2002–. Advr, Atlantic Philanthropies (Ireland), 2006–. Editor, Rights Jl, 1979–84. FRSA. *Publications:* Called to Account: police accountability in England and Wales, 1985; (jtly) The New Prevention of Terrorism Act, 1985; The Role of Police Authorities during the Miners' Strike, 1985; (jtly) A British Bill of Rights, 1990; (jtly) Accountable Policing: effectiveness, empowerment and equity, 1993; (ed) Strangers and Citizens: a positive approach to migrants and refugees, 1994; (ed) Immigration as an Economic Asset: the German experience, 1994; Migrants, Refugees and the Boundaries of Citizenship, 1995; (jtly) A UK Human Rights Commission, 1998; (jtly) Mainstreaming Human Rights in Whitehall and Westminster, 1999; (jtly) Migration: an economic and social analysis, 2001; (jtly) Reluctant Witness, 2001; (jtly) Them and Us? The Public, Offenders and the Criminal Justice System, 2002; (ed) The Politics of Migration: managing opportunity, conflict and change, 2003; (jtly) Age as an Equality Issue: legal and policy perspectives, 2003; (jtly) Age Equality Comes of Age, 2003; (jtly) Fair Enough: Central and East European migrants in low wage employment in the UK, 2006; (contrib.) Blair's Britain, 1997–2007, 2007; (jtly) Migrant Care Workers in Ageing Societies, 2009; The Migration Debate, 2011. *Address:* (office) 58 Banbury Road, Oxford OX2 6QS.

SPENCER, His Honour Shaun Michael; QC 1988; a Circuit Judge, 2002–14; a Deputy High Court Judge, 1999–2014; Designated Civil Judge, Bradford Group of County Courts, 2008–12; *b* 4 Feb. 1944; *s* of late Edward Michael Spencer, Leeds and Barbara Spencer (*née* Williams); *m* 1971, Nicola, *e d* of F. G. Greenwood, Tockwith, York; three *s* two *d*. *Educ:* Middleton Boys' Sch., Leeds; Cockburn High Sch., Leeds; King's Coll., Newcastle (Univ. of Durham); Open Univ. (Dip. Classical Studies 2010). LLB 1st cl. Hons 1965. Asst Lectr and Lectr in Law, Univ. of Sheffield, 1965–68; called to the Bar, Lincoln's Inn, 1968, Bencher, 1997; a Recorder, 1985–2002. *Recreations:* singing, cookery, books. *Address:* 34A Rutland Drive, Harrogate, N Yorks HG1 2NX.

SPENCER, Thomas Newnham Bayley, (Tom); Executive Director, European Centre for Public Affairs, Templeton College, Oxford, 1987–89, then at University of Surrey, then at Brunel University, 1999–2011; Vice-Chairman, Institute for Environmental Security, The Hague, since 2002 (Vice Chairman, Global Military Advisory Council, since 2012); Visiting Professor of Public Affairs: Brunel University, since 2003; University of Chester, since 2010; *b* 10 April 1948; *s* of Thomas Henry Newnham Spencer and Anne Hester (*née* Readett-Bayley); *m* 1979, Elizabeth Nan Maltby, *er d* of late Captain Ronald Edgar Bath and of Doreen Lester (*née* Bush); two *d* and one step *d*. *Educ:* Nautical Coll., Pangbourne; Southampton Univ. (BSc Social Sciences). Peat, Marwick, Mitchell & Co., 1972–75; Asst to Dir, Britain-in-Europe Campaign, 1975; J. Walter Thompson & Co., 1975–79. Associate Dean, Templeton Coll., Oxford, 1984–89. MEP (C) Derbyshire, 1979–84, contested same seat, 1984; MEP (C) Surrey West, 1989–94, Surrey, 1994–99. European Democratic Group: Dep. Chief Whip, 1989–91; spokesman on: Social Affairs and Employment, 1979–81; External Econ. Relations, 1982–84; Social Affairs, 1993–94; Chm., British Section, EPP Gp, 1994–95; European Parliament: Member: Envmt, Public Health and Consumer Affairs Cttee, 1991–99; Institutional Affairs Cttee, 1991–94; Foreign Affairs Cttee, 1993–99; Chairman: Cttee on Foreign Affairs, Security and Defence Policy, 1997–99; delegn to Czech, Slovene and Slovak Republics, 1993–99; Jt Parly Cttee with Czech Republic, 1995–97. Chm., European Union Cons. and Christian-Democratic Students, 1971–73; Mem. Council, Cons. Gp for Europe, 1999–. Member: Global Legislators for a Balanced Environment, 1989–99; Commn on Globalisation, 2000–03; Professional Practice Panel, European Public Affairs Consultants' Assoc. Convenor, Global Public Affairs Network, 2011–. Chm., Counterpart Europe, 2000–02. Vis. Prof., Global Governance, Univ. of Surrey, 2000–04. Sen. Advr, Inst. for Global Envmtl Strategies, Japan, 1997–2001. Pres., Globe Internat., 1995–99; Patron, Global Commons Inst. Trust, 1997–. Member: Bd of Trustees, Friends of Europe, 2000; Council, Federal Trust, 2003–. Mem. Court, Univ. of Surrey, 1992–; Member, Advisory Board: Centre for Corporate and Public Affairs, Manchester Metropolitan Univ., 2000–; Centre for Res. on the European Matrix, Univ. of Surrey, 2012–. Member Editorial Board: Eur. Business Jl, 1991–2003; Jl of Public Affairs, 2000–. Robert Schuman Silver Medal, 1974; Green Ribbon Award for most envmtl MEP, Forum for the Future, 1999. Great Golden Medal for Merit (Republic of Austria), 1995. *Publications:* Public Affairs and Power: essays in a time of fear, 2003; Everything Flows: essays on public affairs and change, 2005; Challenge and Response: essays on public affairs and transparency, 2006; The Future of Public Trust: public affairs in a time of crisis, 2009. *Recreations:* gardening, opera, Conservative Party. *Address:* Barford Court, Lampard Lane, Churt, Surrey GU10 2HJ. *Clubs:* Carlton, Brass Monkey.

SPENCER, Timothy John; QC 2001; a Recorder, since 2000; *b* 6 Nov. 1958; *s* of John Spencer and Muriel Spencer (*née* Rowe); *m* 1983, Ann Fiona Rigg; two *s* one *d* (of whom one *s* one *d* are twins). *Educ:* Baines Grammar Sch.; Downing Coll., Cambridge (MA Hons Law). 1st Lieut, 1st RTR, 1978. Called to the Bar, Middle Temple, 1982; Asst Recorder, 1998–2000. *Recreations:* Preston North End, Lancashire County Cricket Club, gardening. *Address:* 7 Bedford Row, WC1R 4BS. *T:* (020) 7242 3555. *Club:* MCC.

SPENCER-CHURCHILL, family name of **Duke of Marlborough**.

SPENCER-NAIRN, Sir Robert (Arnold), 3rd Bt *cr* 1933; Vice Lord-Lieutenant of Fife, 1996–2008; *b* 11 Oct. 1933; *s* of Sir Douglas Spencer-Nairn, 2nd Bt, TD, and Elizabeth Livingston (*d* 1985), *d* of late Arnold J. Henderson; *S* father, 1970; *m* 1963, Joanna Elizabeth, *d* of late Lt-Comdr G. S. Salt, RN; two *s* one *d*. *Educ:* Eton College; Trinity Hall, Cambridge (MA). Fellow, Game Conservancy, 1993. Mem. Council, Macmillan Cancer Support (formerly Macmillan Cancer Relief), 1997–2008. DL Fife, 1995. *Heir: s* James Robert Spencer-Nairn [*b* 7 Dec. 1966; *m* 1994, Dominique Jane, *o d* of Michael Williamson and Mrs Charles Newman; two *s*]. *Address:* Barham, Cupar, Fife KY15 5RG. *Clubs:* Royal and Ancient Golf (St Andrews); Falkland Palace Royal Tennis.

SPENCER-SMITH, Sir John Hamilton, 7th Bt *cr* 1804; *b* 18 March 1947; *s* of Sir Thomas Cospatric Hamilton-Spencer-Smith, 6th Bt, and Lucy Ashton, *o d* of late Thomas Ashton Ingram, Hopes, Norton-sub-Hamdon, Somerset; *S* father, 1959; *m* 1980, Christine (marr. diss. 1990), *d* of late John Theodore Charles Osborne, Durrington, Worthing, Sussex; one *d*. *Educ:* Milton Abbey; Lackham College of Agriculture, Wilts. *Heir: cousin* Michael Philip Spencer-Smith, *b* 2 April 1952.

SPENCER WILLS; *see* Wills.

SPENS, family name of **Baron Spens**.

SPENS, 4th Baron *cr* 1959, of Blairsanquar, Fife; **Patrick Nathaniel George Spens;** Head, Market Monitoring, Financial Conduct Authority, since 2013; *b* 14 Oct. 1968; *s* of 3rd Baron Spens and of Barbara Janet Lindsay Spens; *S* father, 2001; *m* 1998, Hon. Philippa Patricia Lennox-Boyd, *yr d* of Viscount Boyd of Merton, *qv*; one *s* two *d*. *Educ:* Rugby. Strauss Turnbull, 1987–93; Merrill Lynch International, 1993–99; Dir, 1999–2005, Man. Dir, 2001–05, Schroder Salomon Smith Barney, subseq. Citigroup; Partner, Copenhagen Capital LLP, 2005–09; Hd, Mkt Monitoring, FSA, 2009–13. *Recreations:* racing, claret. *Heir: s* Hon. Peter Lathallan Spens, *b* 3 March 2000. *Address:* Top Floor, 23 Earls Court Square, SW5 9BY. *Clubs:* Bluebird; Cercle de Deauville.

SPENS, David Patrick; QC 1995; a Recorder of the Crown Court, since 1994; *b* 2 May 1950; *s* of late Hugh Stuart Spens and Mary Jean Drake (*née* Reinhold); *m* 1st, 1979, Danièle Irving (marr. diss. 2003); two *d*; 2nd, 2010, Robbin Leak-Piccioni. *Educ:* Rugby Sch.; Univ. of Kent at Canterbury (BA). Called to the Bar, Inner Temple, 1973, Bencher, 2005; Junior Treasury Counsel, CCC, 1988–95; Leader, S Eastern Circuit, 2007–08. Chm., Criminal Bar Assoc., 2004–05. *Address:* QEB Hollis Whiteman, 1–2 Laurence Pountney Hill, EC4R 0EU. *T:* (020) 7933 8855.

SPENS, John Alexander, RD 1970; WS; Partner, Maclay, Murray & Spens, Solicitors, Glasgow and Edinburgh, 1960–91, later Consultant; *b* 7 June 1933; *s* of Thomas Patrick Spens and Nancy F. Spens (*née* Anderson); *m* 1961, Finella Jane, *d* of Donald Duff Gilroy; two *s* one *d* (and one *s* decd). *Educ:* Cargilfield; Rugby School; Corpus Christi College, Cambridge (BA); Glasgow Univ. (LLB). WS 1977. Director: Scottish Amicable Life Assurance Soc., 1963–97 (Chairman, 1978–81); Standard Property Investment PLC, 1977–87. Carrick Pursuivant, 1974–85; Albany Herald, 1985–2011. *Recreations:* sailing, countryside and opera. *Address:* The Old Manse, Gartocharn, Dunbartonshire G83 8RX. *T:* (01389) 830456. *Clubs:* Naval; Western (Glasgow).

SPENS, Michael Colin Barkley, MA; Headmaster, Fettes College, since 1998; *b* 22 Sept. 1950; *s* of Richard Vernon Spens and (Theodora) Margaret Yuille Spens (*née* Barkley); *m* 1989, Deborah Susan Lane; one *s* two *d*. *Educ:* Marlborough Coll.; Selwyn Coll., Cambridge (BA 1972; MA Natural Scis 1976). Asst Master, Rathkeale Coll., NZ, 1968–69; Mktg Dept, United Biscuits plc, 1973–74; Asst Master, 1974–93, Housemaster, 1984–93, Radley Coll.; Headmaster, Caldicott Sch., 1993–98. Liveryman, Grocers' Co., 1981–. *Recreations:* mountaineering, golf, bridge, crosswords, geology, electronics, wood turning, gardening. *Address:* Headmaster's Lodge, Fettes College, Edinburgh EH4 1QX. *T:* (0131) 311 6701. *Clubs:* Hawks (Cambridge); New (Edinburgh); Denham Golf; Royal and Ancient Golf (St Andrews); Hon. Company of Edinburgh Golfers (Muirfield).

SPERRYN, Simon George; consultant, since 2010; Chief Executive, Chartered Institute of Purchasing and Supply, 2008–09; *b* 7 April 1946; *s* of George Roland Neville Sperryn and Wendy Sperryn (*née* King); *m* 1993, Jessica Alice Hayes (marr. diss. 2008); two *s* one *d*. *Educ:* Rydal School; Pembroke College, Cambridge (MA); Cranfield School of Management (MBA). Birmingham Chamber of Commerce and Industry, 1967–77; Chief Executive: Northants Chamber of Commerce and Industry, 1979–85; Manchester Chamber of Commerce and Industry, 1986–92; London Chamber of Commerce and Industry, 1992–2000; Chief Exec., Lloyd's Market Assoc., 2001–06. Director: Manchester TEC, 1989–92; Manchester Camerata, 1989–92 (Chm.); Business Link London, 1995–2000; Stylites Ltd, 2010–. Non-exec. Dir, Professional Assocs Res. Network, 2011–. British Chambers of Commerce: Mem. Nat. Council, 1986–97; Dir, 1998–2000; Pres., British Chambers of Commerce Executives, 1994, 1995; Administrator, London Chamber of Commerce and Industry Commercial Educn Trust, 1992–2000; Mem. UK Council, ICC, 2000–06; Accreditation Assessor, 2013–. Vice Pres., World Chambers Fedn, 2000; Dir, Internat. Fedn of Purchasing and Supply Mgt, 2008–09. Mem. Council, Chartered Insurance Inst., 2003–06. Chm., City of London Early Years Develt and Childcare Partnership, 1998–2000. Mem., London Regl Cttee, FEFC, 1996–2000. Trustee, UNIAID, 2002–10 (Dep. Chm., 2006–10). Gov., UC Salford, 1988–92. Freeman, City of London, 1998. CCMI; FRSA; MIEx. *Address:* 33 Halifax Road, Cambridge CB4 3QB.

SPICELEY, Peter Joseph, MBE 1976; HM Diplomatic Service, retired; Ambassador to Costa Rica, 1999–2002; *b* 5 March 1942; *s* of late Robert Joseph Spiceley and Lucy Violet Spiceley; *m* 1965, Cecilia Orozco-Lemus; two *d*. *Educ:* Trinity Sch. of John Whitgift, Croydon. Entered Diplomatic Service, 1961; FCO, 1961–64; Bogotá, 1964–66; DSAO, 1966–69; Lima, 1969–72; Second Sec., Yaoundé, 1972–74; Consul, Douala, 1974–76; Second, later First, Sec., Quito, 1976–81; FCO, 1982–86; Consul, Miami, 1986–90; Asst Head of Aviation Dept, FCO, 1991–94; Dep. Consul-Gen. and Dir of Trade Promotion, Sydney, 1994–98. *Recreations:* travel, reading. *Address:* Flat 41, 2 Tavistock Road, Croydon, Surrey CR0 2AS.

SPICER, family name of **Baron Spicer**.

SPICER, Baron *cr* 2010 (Life Peer), of Cropthorne in the County of Worcestershire; **William Michael Hardy Spicer,** Kt 1996; PC 2013; *b* 22 Jan. 1943; *s* of late Brig. L. H. Spicer; *m* 1967, Patricia Ann Hunter; one *s* two *d*. *Educ:* Wellington Coll. (Head Boy); Emmanuel Coll., Cambridge (MA Econs). Asst to Editor, The Statist, 1964–66; Conservative Research Dept, 1966–68; Dir, Conservative Systems Research Centre, 1968–70; Man. Dir, Economic Models Ltd, 1970–80. MP (C) S Worcestershire, Feb. 1974–1997, W Worcestershire, 1997–2010. PPS, Dept of Trade, 1979–81; Parly Under Sec. of State, 1984–87, and Minister for Aviation, 1985–87, Dept of Transport; Parly Under Sec. of State (Minister for Coal and Power), Dept of Energy, 1987–90; Minister of State (Minister for Housing and Planning), DoE, 1990. Mem., Treasury Select Cttee, 1997–2001; Chm., Treasury Sub-Cttee, 1991–2001. Chm., 1922 Cttee, 2001–10 (Mem. Exec., 1997–99). Conservative Party: a Vice-Chm., 1981–83; Dep. Chm., 1983–84; Mem. Bd, 2001–10; Chm., Finance & Audit Cttee, 2007–10. Chairman: Parly OST, 1990; Parly and Scientific Cttee, 1996–99; European Res. Gp, 1994–2001; Political and Parly Honours Cttee, 2012–. Pres., Assoc. of Electricity (formerly Ind. Power) Producers, 1996–2012; Chm., Energy UK, 2012–15. Gov., Wellington Coll., 1992–2005. Chm. and Captain, Lords and Commons Tennis Club, 1997–2006. *Publications:* A Treaty Too Far, 1992; The Challenge from the East, 1996; *novels:* Final Act, 1981; Prime Minister Spy, 1986; Cotswold Manners, 1989; Cotswold Murders, 1990; Cotswold Mistress, 1992; Cotswold Moles, 1993; The Spicer Diaries, 2012; contrib. Jl Royal Inst. Public Admin. *Recreations:* painting, tennis, writing, bridge. *Address:* House of Lords, SW1A 0PW. *Clubs:* Garrick, Pratt's.

SPICER, Harriet Greville; coach and mentor, since 2008; Partner, Working Edge Coaching and Mentoring, since 2007; Governor, since 2008, Member of Council, since 2011, and Member, Audit Committee, since 2014, London School of Economics and Political Science; *b* 24 April 1950; *d* of James Spicer and Patricia Spicer (*née* Palmer); one *s* one *d*. *Educ:* St Anne's Coll., Oxford (BA Hons English Lit.). Virago Press Ltd, 1973–96, Man. Dir, 1990–96. Mem., 1999–2005, Chair, 2001–02, Nat. Lottery Commn. Chm., The Friendly Almshouses, 2002–05. Mentor and Trainer, UpRising Foundn and Young Foundn Accelerator Prog.,

2010–. Adviser: Talk for Health, 2014–; Carers Trust Advance Prog., 2015–. Mem., Judicial Appts Commn, 2006–12. Govt Equalities Office, 2009–11; Croydon Social Work Acad., 2011–13. Advr, Piccadilly Dance Orch., 2007–12. *Recreations:* friends, reading, music, theatre.

SPICER, Sir Nicholas (Adrian Albert), 5th Bt *cr* 1906, of Lancaster Gate, Paddington; General Medical Practitioner, 1982–2007; *b* 28 Oct. 1953; *o s* of (Sir) Peter James Spicer (4th Bt, but did not use the title) and Margaret (*née* Wilson); *S* father, 1993; *m* 1st, 1992, Patricia Carol Dye (marr. diss. 2008); two *s*; 2nd, 2012, Priscilla Anne Davey (*née* Kennedy). *Educ:* Eton; Birmingham Univ. (MB ChB 1977). *Recreations:* amateur singing, mowing. *Heir: s* James Peter Warwick Spicer, *b* 12 June 1993. *Address:* Tower House, Burley, Craven Arms, Shropshire SY7 9LN.

ŠPIDLA, Dr Vladimír; Member, European Commission, 2004–10; *b* Prague, 22 April 1951; *s* of Václav and Dagmar Špidla; *m* 1st; two *s*; 2nd, Viktorie; one *s* one *d*. *Educ:* Charles Univ., Prague (PhD Hist. and Prehist.). Formerly archaeologist, worker at historical monuments, sawmill worker and worker in dairy and livestock industry. Jindřichův Hradec: Vice-Pres. for Educn, Health Service, Social Affairs and Culture, Dist Cttee, 1990–91; Dir, Labour Office, 1991–96; Mem. (CSSD) Chamber of Deps, Czech Republic, 1996–2004; Dep. Prime Minister and Minister of Labour and Social Affairs, 1998–2002; Prime Minister, 2002–04. Czech Social Democratic Party: Founding Mem., S Bohemian Br., 1989; joined party leadership, 1992; Vice-Chm., 1997–2001; Chm., 2001–04. *Recreations:* care of historical monuments, books, cross-country running, other outdoor sports.

SPIEGELHALTER, Sir David (John), Kt 2014; OBE 2006; FRS 2005; Winton Professor for the Public Understanding of Risk, University of Cambridge, since 2007; *b* 16 Aug. 1953; *s* of Edmund Spiegelhalter and late Faith Spiegelhalter (*née* Baker); *m* 1978, Eva Sommerschield (marr. diss. 1987); one *d*; partner, 1988, Kate Bull; one *d* (and one *s* decd). *Educ:* Barnstaple Grammar Sch.; Keble Coll., Oxford (BA); University Coll. London (PhD 1978). Lectr, Univ. of Calif, Berkeley, 1977–78; Res. Asst, Univ. of Nottingham, 1978–81; MRC Biostatistics Unit, Cambridge, 1981–2012 (Sen. Scientist, 1986–2012; Hon. Prof., 2006–). Hon. FIRM, 2011; Hon. FRCP 2013. Hon. DSc: Aalborg, Denmark, 1994; Plymouth, 2010; Heriot-Watt, 2013; Bath, 2013. Weldon Meml Prize, Univ. of Oxford, 2010; Science Communication Award, Soc. of Biol., 2011. *Publications:* (jtly) Leucocyte Typing III: White Cell Differentiation Antigens, 1987; (jtly) Machine Learning, Neural and Statistical Classification, 1994; (jtly) Markov Chain Monte Carlo Methods in Practice, 1996; (jtly) Bayesian Analysis in Probabilistic Networks, 1999; (jtly) Bayesian Approaches to Clinical Trials and Health Care Evaluation, 2004; (jtly) The Norm Chronicles: stories and numbers about danger, 2013; Sex By Numbers: what statistics can tell us about sexual behaviour, 2015; papers in Jl Royal Statistical Soc., etc. *Recreations:* trekking, samba drumming, making stained-glass panels, watching old films with family, talking to Michael Traynor. *Address:* Department of Pure Mathematics and Mathematical Statistics, Centre for Mathematical Sciences, University of Cambridge, Wilberforce Road, Cambridge CB3 0WB.

SPIELBERG, Steven, Hon. KBE 2001; American film director and producer; *b* 18 Dec. 1947; *s* of Arnold Spielberg and Leah (*née* Posner); *m* 1985, Amy Irving (marr. diss. 1989); one *s*; *m* Kate Capshaw; one *s* two *d*, and one adopted *s* one adopted *d*. *Educ:* Calif State Coll. TV Director, Universal Pictures, 1968. Founder: Amblin Entertainment; DreamWorks SKG. Fellow, BAFTA, 1986. *Films include: directed:* Sugarland Express, 1974; Jaws, 1975; Close Encounters of the Third Kind, 1977; 1941, 1979; Raiders of the Lost Ark, 1981; (also produced) E.T., 1982; (also produced) Twilight Zone—the movie, 1983; Indiana Jones and the Temple of Doom, 1984; The Color Purple, 1985; Empire of the Sun, 1988; Indiana Jones and the Last Crusade, 1989; Hook, 1991; Jurassic Park, 1992; Schindler's List, 1994; The Lost World: Jurassic Park, 1997; Amistad, 1998; Saving Private Ryan, 1998; A. I. Artificial Intelligence, 2001; Minority Report, 2002; Catch Me If You Can, 2003; The Terminal, 2004; War of the Worlds, 2005; Munich, 2006; Indiana Jones and the Kingdom of the Crystal Skull, 2008; The Adventures of Tintin: The Secret of the Unicorn, 2011; War Horse, 2012; Lincoln, 2013; *produced:* I Wanna Hold Your Hand, 1978; (also co-wrote) Poltergeist, 1982; Gremlins, 1984; The Goonies, 1985; Young Sherlock Holmes, 1985; Back to the Future, 1986; Who Framed Roger Rabbit, 1988; Always, 1990; The Flintstones, 1994; Casper, 1995; Men in Black, 1997; The Last Days, 1999; Flags of Our Fathers, 2006; Transformers, 2007; Eagle Eye, 2008; Transformers: Revenge of the Fallen, 2009; The Lovely Bones, 2010; Super 8, 2011. *Television series:* co-prod., Band of Brothers, 2001; executive producer: Into the West, 2006; United States of Tara, 2009–11; The Pacific, 2010; Falling Skies, 2011–14; Terra Nova, 2011; Smash, 2012–13; Extant, 2014–15. *Publications:* (jtly) Close Encounters of the Third Kind. *Address:* Amblin Entertainment, 100 Universal City Plaza, Universal City, CA 91608, USA.

SPIELMAN, Amanda Mary Victoria; Chairman, Office of Qualifications and Examinations Regulation, since 2011; Education Adviser, ARK, since 2013; *b* London, 22 May 1961; *d* of Sebastian Robinson and Prof. Olivia Robinson; *m* 1996, Adam Spielman; two *d*. *Educ:* Clare Coll., Cambridge (BA Hons Maths and Law 1982); Inst. of Educn, Univ. of London (MA Comparative Educn 2002). ACA 1985. KMG Thomson McLintock, 1982–86; Kleinwort Benson, 1986–92; Director: Newstead Capital, 1992–94; Bridgewater Business Analysis, 1994–95; Principal, Mercer Mgt Consulting, Boston, 1995–97; Nomura Principal Finance, USA and UK, 1997–2001; educn consultancy, 2002–04; Res. and Devlt Dir, ARK Schools, 2005–13. Mem. Council, Inst. of Educn, Univ. of London, 2011–. Trustee: Pilotlight, 2001–04; New Schools Network, 2009–11; Mem. Bd, Wales Millennium Centre, 2004–11; Governor: Evelyn Grace Acad., 2008–; Bolingbroke Acad., 2012–. *Recreations:* Alpine walking, cooking. *Address:* Office of Qualifications and Examinations Regulation, Spring Place, Herald Avenue, Coventry CV5 6UB; ARK, 65 Kingsway, WC2B 6TD. *E:* amanda@spielman.co.uk.

SPIELMANN, Dean Frank; Judge, since 2004, and President, since 2012, European Court of Human Rights; *b* Luxembourg, 26 Oct. 1962; *s* of Alphonse Spielmann and Catherine Spielmann (*née* Hildgen); partner, Veerle Willems. *Educ:* Univ. Catholique de Louvain (Licence en droit 1988); Fitzwilliam Coll., Cambridge (Foreign and Commonwealth Schol.; LLM Internat. Law 1990; Hon. Fellow 2013). Asst Lectr and Res. Asst, Univ. of Louvain, 1991–97; Lecturer: Univ. of Luxembourg, 1996–2006; Univ. of Nancy, 1997–2009; barrister, Luxembourg Bar: Avocat, 1989–92; Avocat à la Cour, 1992–2004; Section Pres., 2011–12, Vice-Pres., 2012, Eur. Court of Human Rights. Hon. Prof., UCL, 2014–. Mem., Inst. Grand-Ducal, Luxembourg, 2005–. Co-founder and Co-dir, Annales du droit luxembourgeois, 22 vols, 1990–. Member: Adv. Commn of Human Rights, Luxembourg, 2000–04; EU Network of Ind. Experts in Fundamental Rights, 2002–04. Hon. Bencher, Gray's Inn, 2013–. Dr *hc* Yerevan, 2013; Cluj-Napoca, 2015; Bucharest, 2015. Kt Grand Cross, Equestrian Order of St Agatha (San Marino), 2014. *Publications:* (jtly) La Convention européenne des droits de l'homme et le droit luxembourgeois, 1991; L'effet potentiel de la Convention européenne des droits de l'homme entre personnes privées, 1995; (with Nathalie Hustin-Denies) L'infraction inachevée en droit pénal comparé, 1997; Le Luxembourg devant la Cour européenne des droits de l'homme (Recueil de jurisprudence 1995–2003), 2003; (with Alphonse Spielmann) Droit pénal général luxembourgeois, 2002, 2nd edn 2004; (jtly) La Convention européenne des droits de l'homme, un instrument vivant, Mélanges offerts à Christos Rozakis, 2011; contrib. articles to legal periodicals. *Recreations:* music, organ playing, history. *Address:* European Court of Human Rights, 67075 Strasbourg, France. *T:* 388412018, *Fax:* 388412730. *E:* dean.spielmann@echr.coe.int. *Club:* Oxford and Cambridge.

SPIERS, Sir Donald (Maurice), Kt 1993; CB 1987; TD 1966; FREng; Chairman, Farnborough Aerospace Consortium, since 2003; *b* 27 Jan. 1934; *s* of Harold Herbert Spiers and Emma (*née* Foster); *m* 1958, Sylvia Mary Lowman (*d* 2014); two *s*. *Educ:* Raynes Park County Grammar Sch.; Trinity Coll., Cambridge (MA). CEng. Commnd RE, 1952–54. de Havilland Engine Co., Hatfield, 1957–60; joined Air Min. as SSO, 1960; operational res. on deterrence, 1960–63; trials and analysis, Aden and Radfan, 1964; Kestrel evaluation trial, 1965; Scientific Adviser to FEAF, Singapore, 1967–70; Asst Chief Scientist (RAF), MoD, 1972–77; Asst Dir, Mil. Aircraft Projs, MoD (PE), 1978; Dir of Aircraft Post Design Services, MoD (PE), 1979–81; Dir Gen. Aircraft 1, MoD (PE), 1981–84; Dep. Controller Aircraft, MoD (PE), 1984–86; Controller of R&D Estabts, later of Estabts, Res. and Nuclear Programmes, and Hd of Profession Defence Engrg Service, MoD, 1986–89; Controller Aircraft, and Head of Profession Defence Sci. and Engrg, MoD, 1989–94. Chairman: European Helicopter Industries Ltd, 1998–2004; Farnborough Enterprise Hub, 2004–08; AgustaWestland International, 2004–09. Director: Computing Devices Co. Ltd, 1994–2001 (Chm., 1997–2001); Meggitt plc, 1995–2003 (Chm., 1998–2001); Messier-Dowty Internat. Ltd, 1998–2004; TAG Aviation (UK) Ltd, 1999–2005; General Dynamics UK Ltd, 2001–10. Hon. FRAeS (Vice Pres., 1993–95; Pres., 1995–96). Pres., Popular Flying Assoc., 1997–2000. Gold Medal, RAeS, 1989. *Recreations:* mending cars, mowing lawns. *Address:* 20 Paddock Close, Camberley, Surrey GU15 2BN. *Club:* Royal Air Force.

SPIERS, Prof. Edward Michael, PhD; FRHistS; Professor of Strategic Studies, University of Leeds, since 1993; *b* 18 Oct. 1947; *s* of Ronald Arthur Spiers, DSC and Margaret Carlisle Laing Spiers (*née* Manson); *m* 1971, Fiona Elizabeth McLeod; one *s* one *d*. *Educ:* Royal High Sch., Edinburgh; Edinburgh Univ. (MA, PhD). FRHistS 1980. University of Leeds: Defence Lectr, 1975–85; Lectr in History, 1985–87; Reader in Strategic Studies, 1987–93; Chm., School of History, 1994–97; Dean, 1999–2002, Pro-Dean, 2006–11, of Res. (Arts), of Res. and Evaluation, 2011–; Actg Pro-Vice Chancellor for Res. and Innovation, 2011. Vis. Lectr, Univ. of Alberta, 1987; Leverhulme Res. Fellow, 1991–92. Chief Examiner, Army, 1992–2002; Peer Reviewer, AHRC, 2004–. Mem. (C), Edinburgh DC, 1974. *Publications:* Haldane: an army reformer, 1980; The Army and Society 1815–1914, 1980; Radical General: Sir George de Lacy Evans 1787–1870, 1983; Chemical Warfare, 1986; Chemical Weaponry: a continuing challenge, 1989; The Late Victorian Army 1868–1902, 1992; Chemical and Biological Weapons: a study of proliferation, 1994; (ed) Sudan: the reconquest reappraised, 1998; Weapons of Mass Destruction, 2000; The Victorian Soldier in Africa, 2004; The Scottish Soldier and Empire 1854–1902, 2006; A History of Chemical and Biological Weapons, 2010; (ed) Letters from Ladysmith: eyewitness accounts from the South African War, 2010; (co-ed) A Military History of Scotland, 2012 (Scottish History Book of the Year, Saltire Soc., 2012; Templer Medal, Soc. for Army Histl Res., 2012); (ed) Letters from Kimberley: eyewitness accounts from the South African war, 2013; Engines for Empire: the Victorian military and its use of railways, 2015. *Recreation:* supporting the Green Bay Packers. *Address:* 170 Alwoodley Lane, Leeds LS17 7PF. *T:* (0113) 268 5493. *Club:* Army and Navy.

SPIERS, John Raymond; Chairman, John Spiers Publishing Ltd, since 1988; Senior Research Fellow, Institute of English Studies, School of Advanced Study, University of London, since 2003; Professorial Research Fellow, Global Policy Institute, London Metropolitan University, since 2013; *b* 30 Sept. 1941; *s* of Horace Henry Spiers and Kate Dawson (*née* Root); *m* 1967, Prof. Margaret Ann Boden, *qv* (marr. diss. 1981); one *s* one *d*; *m* 2003, Leigh Richardson (*née* Radford); one step *s* one step *d*. *Educ:* Redhill Sch., E Sutton, Kent; Catford Coll. of Commerce; Univ. of Sussex (BA 1st Cl. Hons Hist. 1968). Writer and publisher, 1960–; Founder: Harvester Press Ltd (Chm., 1969–88); Harvester Press Microform Pubns Ltd (Chm., 1973–87) (Queen's Award for Export Achievement, 1986); Wheatsheaf Books Ltd (Chm., 1980–88). Special Advr to Dep. Chm., Cons. Party, 1989–90; Consultant Dir, Special Services Dept, Cons. Central Office, 1990–94; Mem., Citizens' Charter Adv. Panel to PM, 1994; Dep. Treas., Cons. Party SE England Area, 1990–92 (Mem., SE Area Council, 1990–92); Pres., Brighton Kemp Town Cons. Assoc., 1991–95. Founder and Chm., Brighton Business Gp, 1989–95. Health Policy Advr, Social Market Foundn, 1994–99; Chairman: Brighton HA, 1991–92; Brighton Health Care NHS Trust, 1992–94; National Association of Health Authorities and Trusts: Mem., Nat. Council and Exec. Cttee, 1993–94; Chm., Nat. Conf. Cttee, 1993–94; Co-Chm., S Thames Network, 1994; Vice-Chm., Provider Cttee, 1993–94; Member: NHS Mgt Exec. Adv. Gps, 1991–98; Bd, Nat. Care Standards Commn, 2001–04. Chairman: Patients Assoc., 1995–97 (Actg Chief Exec., 1995–96); Health Policy Cttee, Centre for Policy Studies, 1997–99; Founding Chm., Civitas: Inst. for Study of Civil Soc., 1999–2000; Member: Exec. Bd, Internat. Health Policy and Management Inst., 1994–98; Adv. Council, Health and Welfare Unit, IEA, 1989–92, 1997–99; (co-opted), Nat. Exec., Voluntary Euthanasia Soc., 1997–99. Co-Chm., The Radical Soc., 1991–2001; Mem., Adv. Council, Reform, 2001–10. Vice-Chm., Grant Maintained Schools Foundn, 1992–98 (Trustee, 1992–98). Trustee: Choice in Educn, 1990–92; Trident Trust, 1992–99 (Vice Chm., 1993–94; Chm., 1994–97); Brighton Internat. Arts Fest., 1989–96; English Nat. Schs Orch., 1998–2004; League of Mercy, 1999–2004 (Companion, 2002); Shakespeare Authorship Trust, 2002–05 (Associate, 2005–); Ruskin Foundn, 2002–08; Pres., Gissing Foundn, 2005–. Chm., Alumni Soc., 1983–2004 (Hon. Fellow, 1998; Vice-Pres., 2002), and Mem. Court, 1989–, Univ. of Sussex. Visiting Fellow: NHS Staff Coll., Wales, 1995–2010; King's Fund Mgt Coll., 1996–2010; IEA, 2003–10; Ruskin Prog., Univ. of Lancaster, 2005–; Res. Fellow, 1997–2011, Sen. Res. Fellow, Health and Welfare Unit, 1998–99, Head of Health Care Studies, 1999–2000, IEA; Ext. Prof., Business Sch., 1998–2001, Ext. Prof., then Vis. Prof., Sch. of Humanities and Social Studies, 2001–12, Univ. of Glamorgan; Adjunct Schol., Cascade Policy Inst., Portland, Oregon, 1999. Librarian and Mem. Nat. Council, Francis Bacon Soc., 1998–2005 (Vice-Chm., 2003–05). Pres., Hoxton Hawks Vintage Cycling Club, 2006–. Fellow, Progressive Vision, 2007–10. Companion, Guild of St George, 1971 (Founding Editor, The Companion, 2000–04; Dir, 2001–04). Freeman, City of London, 2000. FRSA 1994. DUniv Sussex, 1994. JP E Sussex, 1988–90. Companion's Cross, League of Mercy, 2002. Kt Grand Cross, Order of St Stanislaus (Poland), 1998. *Publications:* (with P. Coustillas) The Re-discovery of George Gissing, Novelist, 1971; The Invisible Hospital and the Secret Garden: an insider's commentary on the NHS reforms, 1995; Who Owns Our Bodies?: making moral choices in health care, 1997; (ed) Dilemmas in Modern Health Care, 1997; The Realities of Rationing: priority setting in the National Health Service, 1999; Coming, Ready or Not: the present, future and politics of the NHS, 2003; Patients, Power and Responsibility in British Health Care, 2003; (ed) George Gissing and the City: cultural crisis and the making of books in late-Victorian England, 2005; Serious About Series, 2007; Who Decides Who Decides?, 2008; (ed) The Culture of the Publisher's Series (2 vols), 2011; Just the Ticket!: railway library fiction of the 19th century, 2015; contrib. Health Service Jl, British Jl of Health Management, Health Summary, Healthcare Today, Health Director, Sunday Telegraph, Guardian, Daily Express, Independent, English Literature in Transition, Jl of Printing Historical Soc., Sunday Times, Gissing Jl, Publishing History. *Recreations:* collecting 19th century novels (and reading them), writing, walking, supporting The Arsenal, exploring inland waterways. *E:* jr.spiers@btinternet.com.

SPIERS, Air Cdre Reginald James, OBE 1972; FRAeS; *b* 8 Nov. 1928; *s* of Alfred James Oscar and Rose Emma Alice Spiers; *m* 1956, Cynthia Jeanette Williams; two *d*. *Educ:* Haberdashers' Aske's Sch.; RAF Coll., Cranwell. FRAeS 1975. Commissioned 1949; 247 and 64 Fighter Sqdns, 1950–54; Graduate, Empire Test Pilots' Sch., 1955; Fighter Test Sqdn, A&AEE, 1955–58; CO 4 Fighter Sqdn, 1958–61; PSO to C-in-C RAF Germany, 1961–63; RAF Staff Coll., 1964; FCO, 1965–67; CO RAF Masirah, 1967–68; Chief Test Flying

Instructor, ETPS, 1968–71; Air Warfare Course, 1972; Air Secretary's Dept, MoD, 1972–73; MA to Governor of Gibraltar, 1973–75; CO Experimental Flying Dept, RAE Farnborough, 1975–78; Director, Defence Operational Requirements Staff, MoD, 1978–79; Comdt, A&AEE, Boscombe Down, 1979–83, retd. Marketing Exec., Marconi, later GEC, Avionics, 1984–91. *Recreations:* aviation, painting. *Address:* Barnside, Penton Mewsey, near Andover, Hants SP11 0RQ. *T:* (01264) 772376. *Club:* Royal Air Force.

SPIERS, Ronald Ian; consultant on international affairs, since 1992; Under-Secretary-General, Department of Political and General Assembly Affairs and Secretariat Services, United Nations, 1989–92; *b* 9 July 1925; *s* of Tomas H. and Blanca De P. Spiers; *m* 1949, Patience Baker; one *s* three *d*. *Educ:* Dartmouth Coll., New Hampshire (BA); Princeton Univ. (Master in Public Affairs, PhD). Mem., US Delegn to UN, 1956–60; US Department of State: Dir, Office of Disarmament and Arms Control, 1960–62; Dir, Office of NATO Affairs, 1962–66; Political Counsellor, London, 1966–69; Asst Sec. of State, Politico-Military Affairs, 1969–73; Ambassador to the Bahamas, 1973–74; Minister, London, 1974–77; Ambassador to Turkey, 1977–80; Asst Sec. of State, Bureau of Intelligence and Research, Dept of State, 1980–81; Ambassador to Pakistan, 1981–83; Under Sec. of State for Management, 1983–89. *Recreations:* swimming, music, theatre-going, gardening, adult education. *Address:* 5 Timber Lane, Apt K312, Exeter, NH 03833, USA.

SPIERS, Shaun Mark; Chief Executive, Campaign to Protect Rural England, since 2004; *b* 23 April 1962; *s* of Charles Gordon Spiers and Ann Kathleen Spiers (*née* Hutton); *m* 2006, Louise Humphrey; one *s* two *d*. *Educ:* St John's Coll., Oxford (BA Hons PPE); King's Coll. London (MA War Studies). Political Officer, SE Co-op., 1987–94. MEP (Lab Co-op) London SE, 1994–99; contested (Lab) London Region, 1999. Chief Exec., Assoc. of British Credit Unions, 1999–2004. *Recreation:* cooking. *Address:* (office) 5–11 Lavington Street, SE1 0NZ. *E:* shauns@cpre.org.uk.

SPIGELMAN, James Jacob, AC 2000; Chairman, Australian Broadcasting Corporation, since 2012; *b* 1 Jan. 1946; *s* of Majloch and Gucia Spigelman; *m* 1979, Alice Kalmar; one *s* two *d*. *Educ:* Maroubra Bay Public Sch.; Sydney Boys' High Sch.; Univ. of Sydney (BA, LLB). Sen. Advr and Principal Private Sec. to Prime Minister, 1972–75; Sec., Dept of Media, 1975; called to the Bar, NSW, 1976; in practice at NSW Bar, 1980–98; QC (NSW) 1986; Actg Solicitor Gen., NSW, 1997; Lieut-Gov. and Chief Justice, NSW, 1998–2011. Arbitrator, One Essex Ct, London, 2011–; Non-Permanent Judge, HK Ct of Final Appeal, 2013–. Chm., Nat. Liby of Australia, 2010–12. *Publications:* Secrecy: political censorship in Australia, 1972; (jtly) The Nuclear Barons, 1981; Becket and Henry, 2004; Statutory Interpretation and Human Rights, 2008; Speeches of a Chief Justice, 2008; Opening Law Term, 2010; Transitions in the Court: ceremonial speeches of Chief Justice Spigelman, 1998–2011, 2012. *Recreations:* swimming, recumbency, walking.

SPIKINGS, Barry Peter; Partner, Spikings Entertainment (formerly Pleskow/Spikings Partnership), international production and distribution of feature films, since 1992; *b* Boston, Lincs, 23 Nov. 1939; *m* 1st, 1962, Judith Anne; one *s* one *d*; 2nd, 1978, Dorothy; two step *d*. *Educ:* Boston Grammar School. Joint Managing Director: British Lion Films Ltd, 1973–75; EMI Films Ltd, 1975–78; Director, EMI Films Inc., 1975–78; Chm. and Chief Exec. Officer, EMI Film and Theatre Corp., 1978–80; Chm., Elstree Studios, 1978–82; Chm. and Chief Exec., Thorn EMI Films Worldwide, 1980–82; Pres. and Chief Operating Officer, Nelson Entertainment Inc., 1986–91. Member: Acad. of Motion Picture Arts and Scis; BAFTA. Oscar award as Producer of Best Picture of the Year, for The Deer Hunter, 1979; elected one of America's Greatest Hundred Movies by Amer. Film Inst., 1999; other films include: as producer: Conduct Unbecoming; The Man Who Fell to Earth; Convoy; Texasville; Beyond Rangoon; Lone Survivor; as distributor: Close Encounters of the Third Kind; The Deep; City Slickers; When Harry Met Sally; The Last Emperor. Hon. DArts Lincoln, 2006. *Recreation:* making films.

SPILLANTINI, Prof. Maria Grazia, PhD; FRS 2013; FMedSci; William Scholl Professor of Molecular Neurology, Department of Clinical Neurosciences, University of Cambridge, since 2007; Fellow of Clare Hall, Cambridge, since 1994; *b* Arezzo, Italy, 10 Nov. 1957; *d* of late Otello Spillantini and Leonide Spillantini (*née* Mazzoni); partner, Michel Goedert, *qv*; one *s*. *Educ:* Liceo Scientifico Piero della Francesca, Sansepolcro; Univ. of Florence (Laurea Biol Scis 1981); Peterhouse, Cambridge and MRC Lab. of Molecular Biol. (PhD Molecular Biol. 1993). Mem., Scientific Staff, Nat. Res. Council Inst. of Cell Biol., Rome, 1992–93, 1995–96; Res. Scientist, MRC Lab. of Molecular Biol., 1993–95; Cambridge Centre for Brain Repair, University of Cambridge: Sen. Res. Associate, 1996–97; William Scholl Lectr in Neurol. (non clinical), 1997–2002; William Scholl Reader in Molecular Neurol., 2002–07. FMedSci 2010. Citizen, Caprese Michelangelo, 2002. Potamkin Prize, Amer. Acad. of Neurol., 2000; Alessandro Agnoli Prize, Italian League Against Movement Disorders and Dementia, 2003; Fair Play Prize for Scientific Res., Semplicemente Donna, 2013; Cotzias Prize, Spanish Soc. of Neurol., 2014. *Publications:* contrib. res. papers and reviews in scientific jls. *Recreations:* walking, travelling, watching old movies. *Address:* John Van Geest Centre for Brain Repair, University of Cambridge, Forvie Site, Robinson Way, Cambridge CB2 0PY. *T:* (01223) 331160, *Fax:* (01223) 331174. *E:* mgs11@cam.ac.uk.

SPILLER, John Anthony Walsh, MBE 1979; Technical Adviser to Organisation for Security and Co-operation in Europe/Office for Democratic Institutions and Human Rights Mission, Montenegro, on secondment to Foreign and Commonwealth Office, 1998; *b* 29 Dec. 1942; *s* of C. H. Spiller and Sarah (*née* Walsh), Moycullen, Co. Galway, Eire; *m* 1972, Angela, *d* of Surtees Gleghorn; one *s* one *d*. *Educ:* County Secondary Sch., Bideford; North Devon College. Member Executive, Nat. League of Young Liberals, 1960–61; Organiser, Torrington Constituency Liberal Assoc., 1962–64; Divl Liberal Agent, Cornwall (Northern) Parly Constituency, 1965–71; Northern Regional Organiser (Election Agent, Rochdale By-elecn 1972 and Berwick-upon-Tweed By-elecn 1973), 1972–74; Nat. Agent, Liberal Central Assoc., 1974–76; Mem., Liberal Party Gen. Elecn Campaign Cttee, and Press Officer, Gen. Elections Feb. and Oct. 1974; Western Area Agent, 1977–80; Advisor, African Peoples Union, Independence Elections, Zimbabwe, 1980; By-elecn and Marginal Seats Agent, Liberal Party Org. Headquarters, 1981–82; Sec. Gen., Liberal Party, 1983–85; Co. Liaison Officer, Devonshire PHAB Organisation UK, 1990–92; Sen. Consultant, Western Approaches PR Ltd, 1993–96. Chm., Lib Dem Campaign, Cornwall (Northern), Gen. Elecn 1992; Advr, Electoral Reform Soc., Democracy Conf., Lithuania, 1992, Estonia, 1995, Croatia, 1997. Conf. Deleg., Moscow, 1995, Armenia, 1995; Observer, Elections: Republic of Georgia, 1995; Bosnia Herzegovina, 1996, Estonia, 1999, on behalf of OSCE. Mem. Bd of Management, Gladstone Benevolent Fund, 1980–98 (Sec. 1980, Hon. Sec., 1993). *Recreations:* golf, walking in Connemara. *Address:* 34 Fore Street, Northam, Bideford, Devon EX39 1AW.

SPILLER, Prof. Robin Charles, MD; FRCP; Professor of Gastroenterology, Nottingham University, since 2000; *b* Limpsfield, 3 April 1950; *s* of Reginald Harvey Spiller and Margaret Spiller; *m* 1978, Susan Angela Smith; one *s* two *d*. *Educ:* Whitgift Sch., Croydon; Magdalene Coll., Cambridge (BA 1971; BChir 1975; MB 1976; MD 1986); London Sch. of Econs and Pol Sci. (MSc). MRCP 1977, FRCP 1993. Trng in London, incl. Registrar posts at Charing Cross, W Middx and Central Middx Hosps, 1975–84; MRC Travelling Fellow, Mayo Clinic, Minn, 1984–85; Sen. Registrar, Central Middx Hosp., 1985–88; Consultant Physician, Nottingham Univ. Hosps, 1988–2000. *Publications:* (ed jtly) Irritable Bowel Syndrome: a clinician's guide, 2002; (ed with D. Grundy) Pathophysiology of the enteric nervous system: a basis for understanding functional diseases, 2004. *Recreations:* hill walking, sailing, gardening, stone carving. *Address:* Nottingham Digestive Diseases Centre, Nottingham University Hospitals NHS Trust, Queen's Medical Centre Campus, Clifton Boulevard, Nottingham NG7 2UH. *T:* (0115) 823 1090, *Fax:* (0115) 823 1409. *E:* robin.spiller@nottingham.ac.uk.

SPINDLER, Susan Mary; consultant and writer, since 2008; Deputy Director, Drama, Entertainment and Children's, BBC, 2005–07; *b* 1 March 1955; *d* of Kenneth Spindler and Elsie Spindler (*née* Knapper); *m* 1980, Peter Guy Brown, two *s* one *d*. *Educ:* Wycombe High Sch.; Newnham Coll., Cambridge (BA Hons English 1977). Grad. trainee, Thomson Newspapers, 1978–80; BBC, 1980–2007: prodn trainee, 1980–82; Asst Producer and Producer, 1983–88; Producer, Doctors to Be, 1988–92; Ed., QED, 1992–94; Dep. Hd, Sci. Dept, 1994–96; Chief Advr, Editl Policy, 1997; Hd of Strategy, Drama, 1998–99; Controller, Drama Production, 1999–2000; Controller, Factual Drama and New Media, 2000–01; Project Dir, Making It Happen, 2002–04. *Publications:* The Tomorrow's World Book of Food, 1984; Doctors to Be, 1992. *E:* susanspindler@gmail.com.

SPINK, Andrew John Murray; QC 2003; a Recorder, since 2005; a Deputy High Court Judge, since 2008; *b* 21 April 1962; *s* of Nigel Spink and Penny Spink; *m* 1994, Susan Katherine Vivien Taylor; one *s* two *d*. *Educ:* Sherborne Sch.; Queens' Coll., Cambridge (MA). Called to the Bar, Middle Temple, 1985, Bencher, 2010. *Address:* Outer Temple Chambers, Outer Temple, 222 Strand, WC2R 1BA. *T:* (020) 7353 6381, *Fax:* (020) 7583 1786.

SPINK, Air Marshal Clifford Rodney, CB 2002; CBE 1992 (OBE 1989); FRAeS; Managing Director, Clifford Spink Associates Ltd, since 2003; Chairman, Spitfire Ltd, since 2005; Director, Contingency Planning Associates Ltd, since 2004; *b* 17 May 1946; *s* of Ronald Charles Spink and Beryl Spink (*née* Phillips); *m* 1977, Caroline Anne Smith; one *s* one *d*. *Educ:* Sheerness Sch.; Halton Apprentice, RAF Coll., Cranwell. FRAeS 1997. Commissioned RAF 1968; Sqn Pilot, 111/56 Sqn, 1970–76; Instructor, RMA Sandhurst, 1976–78; Flight Comdr, 111 Sqn, 1979–82; NDC, 1982–83; HQ RAF Germany, 1983–86; OC No 74 (Fighter) Sqn, 1986–89; Stn Comdr and Dep. Comdr British Forces, Falkland Islands, 1989–90; Detachment Comdr, Dhahran, Gulf conflict, 1990–91; Stn Comdr, RAF Coningsby, 1990–93; rcds, 1993; SASO, No 11 Group, 1993–95; COS No 18 Group, 1995–96; AOC No 11/18 Gp, 1996–98; DG, Saudi Armed Forces Project, 1998–2002; retired RAF, 2003. Chairman: Atlantic Reconnaissance, 2003–06; London Ashford Airport Ltd, 2004–10. President: ROC Assoc., 1996–; Battle of Britain Meml Flight Assoc., 2007. FCMI (FIMgt 1992). Liveryman, Hon. Co. of Air Pilots, (formerly GAPAN), 2004– (Master, 2012–13). *Recreations:* vintage aircraft flying, winter sports, golf. *Club:* Royal Air Force.

SPINK, Dr Robert Michael; *b* 1 Aug. 1948; *s* of George and Brenda Spink; *m* 1968, Janet Mary Barham (marr. diss. 2002); three *s* one *d*. *Educ:* Manchester Univ. (research and academic prizes; BSc 1st Cl. Hons Eng 1971); Cranfield Inst. of Technology (MSc Indust Eng 1974; PhD, Sch. of Management, 1989). CEng, MIProdE, MIIM, MIMC, CDipAF. Mill labourer, 1962–64; RAF, 1964–66; EMI Electronics, 1966–77 (Engrg Apprentice; EMI Graduate Apprentice of the Year, 1971); Management consultant, 1977–; Dir and Co-Owner, Seafarer Navigation International, 1980–84; industrial engr, 1984–; Dir, Bournemouth Internat. Airport, 1989–93. Dorset County Councillor, 1985–93 (Chm., Educn Policy Cttee, 1989–91); Mem., Dorset Police Authy, 1985–93. Contested (C) Castle Point, 1997. MP Castle Point, 1992–97 and 2001–10 (C, 1992–97 and 2001–08, UK Ind, 2008, Ind 2008–10); contested (Ind) same seat, 2010. PPS to Minister of State, Dept of Employment, then Home Office, 1994–97. Mem., Educn Select Cttee, 1992–97; Vice Chm., Backbench Employment Cttee, 1993–94; Chm., All Party Parly Gp for Prisoners Abroad, 1995–97. Dep. Chm., Poole Cons. Assoc., 1984–92; Mem. Nat. Exec., Baby Life Support Systems Charity, 1985–92. MCMI. *Recreations:* occasional marathons, gardening, potter.

SPINKS, Mary Cecilia, CBE 2010; RGN; health services consultant, specialising in risk management, audit and expert opinion on malpractice, 1993–2010; *b* 20 Sept. 1940; *d* of Francis and Mary Clark; *m* 1st, 1961, Robert Donn (marr. diss. 1975); 2nd, 1992, Leslie Oswald Spinks (*d* 2014). *Educ:* St Vincent's Convent, Cork; Student Nurse, Whipps Cross Hosp. (RGN 1962); DipN London; William Rathbone Coll.; Thames Polytechnic (DMS). Post-graduate Staff Nurse, Charing Cross Hosp., 1962; Theatre Sister, St Mary's Hosp., Paddington, 1963–64; Theatre Sister, Nursing Officer, Sen. Nursing Officer, Bromley AHA, 1964–83; Dir, Nursing Services, Lewisham and N Southwark HA, 1983–84; Chief Nursing Officer and Dir, Consumer Affairs, Brighton HA, 1984–90; Regl Nursing Officer, NE Thames RHA, 1990–93. Former chm. and mem., nursing, health, editorial and advisory cttees; Chm., Nat. Assoc. of Theatre Nurses, 1975–78; Member: Maidstone HA, 1985–90; NHS Training Authy, 1988–91. Chm., E Berks Community Trust, 1998–2002 (Life Vice Pres., Windsor League of Friends). Dir, Florence Nightingale Foundn, 1996–2010 (Vice Pres., 2010–). Vis. Prof., Univ. of Ulster, 2007–11. MRSM 1992. *Publications:* From SRN to CBE: celebrating 50 remarkable years in nursing, 2014; numerous contribs to professional jls. *Recreations:* horse-racing, cricket, gardening. *Address:* 2 Somerford Close, Maidenhead, Berks SL6 8EJ. *T:* (01628) 675526.

SPIRA, Catherine Ruth, (Kate); *see* Pakenham, C. R.

SPIRO, Prof. Stephen George, MD; FRCP; Professor of Respiratory Medicine, University College London, 1997–2009; Consultant Physician, University College London Hospitals NHS Trust, 1997–2009, now Hon. Consultant, Royal Brompton Hospital and University College London Hospitals; *b* 24 Aug. 1942; *s* of late Ludwig Spiro and Anna Spiro (*née* Freidmann); *m* 1971, Alison Mary Brown; three *s*. *Educ:* Manchester Univ. (BSc Anatomy 1964; MB ChB 1967; MD 1975). FRCP 1981. Consultant Physician, Royal Brompton Hosp., 1977–93. Res. Fellow, Hammersmith Hosp., 1971–73; Sen. Registrar, Royal Brompton Hosp., 1973–77; Clin. Dir of Med. Services, 1994–2000, Med. Dir, 2001–03, UCL Hosps NHS Trust. Fulbright-Hayes Travelling Scholarship, Seattle, 1975–76. Visiting Professor: South African Respiratory Soc., 1993; Univ. of Queensland, Australia, 1994. Chairman: London Lung Cancer Clinical Trials Gp, 1997–2008; N London Cancer Network for Lung Cancer, 1997–2008; Rennie Grove Hospice Care, 2013–; Vice-Chairman: NE London Adv. Cttee for Clinical Excellence, 2003–08; British Lung Foundn, 2008–. President: European Respiratory Soc., 1996–97; British Thoracic Soc., 2004. Trustee, Chai Cancer Care, 1994–. Chief Investigator, CRUK nat. trial of screening for lung cancer in high risk populations, 2006–. British Thoracic Soc. Medal, 2013. Exec. Ed., Thorax, 1991–95. *Publications:* Drug Treatment of Respiratory Disease, 1994; (jtly) New Perspectives on Lung Cancer, 1994; Carcinoma of the Lung, 1995, 2nd edn 2001; (ed) Self-Assessment Colour Review of Respiratory Medicine, 1997, 3rd edn 2012; The Lung in Auto-Immune Disease, 1997; (ed) Comprehensive Respiratory Medicine, 1999, 4th edn as Clinical Respiratory Medicine, 2012; Sarcoidosis, 2012; over 300 articles and chapters in textbooks. *Recreations:* tennis, flyfishing, worrying about Arsenal, home handyman. *Address:* 66 Grange Gardens, Pinner, Middx HA5 5QF. *Clubs:* Croxley Hall Fly Fishery; Eastcote Tennis.

SPITTLE, Graham Nigel, CBE 2008; Chief Technology Officer, Europe, and Vice-President, Software Group, IBM, since 2010; *b* Lewisham, 2 Nov. 1955; *s* of Richard and Ruby Spittle; *m* 1983, Julie Ann Wooldridge; two *s*. *Educ:* Edinburgh Univ. (MA Hons). FBCS 2001. Ford Motor Co., 1978–85; joined IBM, 1985: Internat. Assignment, IBM NY, 1995–97; Dir, MQSeries Develt, 2000–01; Vice-Pres., Develt, IBM UK and Dir, IBM Hursley Lab., 2001–07; Vice-Pres., Software, IBM UK and Ireland, 2007–10. Chm., Technol. Strategy Bd, 2002–11. Visiting Professor: Edinburgh Univ., 2002–; Southampton

Univ., 2002–; Bristol Univ., 2007–. Member: Ct of Benefactors, Oxford Univ., 2001–; Council, Southampton Univ., 2008–. FRSA 2008. Hon. DSc Southampton, 2005. *Recreations:* music, sailing, motor racing, astronomy.

SPITTLE, His Honour Leslie; a Circuit Judge, 1996–2010; a Deputy Circuit Judge, since 2010; *b* 14 Nov. 1940; *s* of Samuel and Irene Spittle; *m* 1963, Brenda Clayton; three *s*. *Educ:* Teesside Poly. (ACIS); Hull Univ. (LLB). Mgt trainee, Head Wrightson & Co., 1956–62; Lectr in Law, Econs and Accountancy, Bradford Tech. Coll., 1965–66; Sen. Lectr in Law, Teesside Poly., 1966–70. Called to the Bar, Gray's Inn, 1970; in private practice, 1970–96. Mem., Parole Bd, 2010–. Paul Harris Fellow, Teesside West Rotary Club. Visitor, Teesside Univ. *Recreations:* family, friends, National Trust volunteer.

SPITTLE, Dr Margaret Flora, (Mrs David Hare), OBE 2004; FRCP, FRCR; Consultant Clinical Oncologist: University College Hospital (formerly at Middlesex Hospital), since 1971; St John's Centre for Diseases of the Skin, St Thomas' Hospital, since 1971; *b* 10 Nov. 1939; *d* of Edwin William Spittle and Ada Florence Spittle (*née* Axam); *m* 1st, 1965, Dr Clive Lucas Harmer (marr. diss. 1977); two *d*; 2nd, 1986, David John Hare. *Educ:* King's Coll., London (AKC 1963; MSc 1969); Westminster Hosp. Med. Sch. (MB BS 1963). MRCS 1963; LRCP 1963, MRCP 1993, FRCP 1995; DMRT 1966; FRCR (Rohan Williams Gold Medal) 1968. Sen. Registrar, Radiotherapy Dept, Westminster Hosp., 1969; Instr, Radiation Div., Stanford Univ. Med. Centre, 1970; Hon. Consultant Clinical Oncologist: W Middx Univ. Hosp., 1971–2002; Royal Nat. Throat, Nose and Ear Hosp., 1986–; St Luke's Hosp. for the Clergy, 1993–. Civilian Consultant Advr in Radiation Medicine, RN, 2000–. Member: Nat. Radiation Protection Bd, 1991–98; Govt Adv. Cttee on Breast Screening, 1986–; Govt Cttee on Medicine and Radiation in the Envmt, 1993–; Govt Adv. Gp on Ionizing Radiation, 1995–; DoH Commng Gp for Health of the Nation Projects, 1996; Defence Nuclear Safety Cttee, 2002–; Depleted Uranium Oversight Bd, 2002–. Chairman: Multicentre Cancer Chemotherapy Gp, 1985–; UK AIDS Oncology Gp, 1988–. Vice-President: RSocMed, 1994–96 (Sen. Hon. Treas., 1988–94; Pres., Oncology Sect., 1987, Radiology Sect., 1989); Royal Coll. of Radiologists, 1995–96 (Dean, Faculty of Clin. Oncology, 1994–96); Pres., Assoc. of Head and Neck Oncologists of GB, 1990–92. *Publications:* chapters and articles on cancer of breast, head and neck, skin, and AIDS-related malignancy. *Recreations:* family, flying, golf, ski-ing, gardening. *Address:* The Manor House, 20 Beaconsfield Road, Claygate, Surrey KT10 0PW. *T:* (01372) 465540. *Clubs:* Royal Automobile, Royal Society of Medicine.

SPITZ, Prof. Lewis, PhD; FRCS, FRCSE, FRCPCH; Nuffield Professor of Paediatric Surgery, and Head of Surgical Unit, Institute of Child Health, London, 1979–2004, now Emeritus Nuffield Professor; Consultant Surgeon, Great Ormond Street Hospital for Children Trust (formerly Hospital for Sick Children, Great Ormond Street), 1979–2006, now Hon. Consultant Surgeon; *b* 25 Aug. 1939; *s* of Woolf and Selma Spitz; *m* 1972, Louise Ruth Dyzenhaus; one *s* one *d*. *Educ:* Univ. of Pretoria (MB, ChB); Univ. of the Witwatersrand (PhD). FRCS (*ad eundem*) 1980; FRCSE 1969; FRCPCH 1997, Hon. FRCPCH 2004; FACS 2012. Smith and Nephew Fellow, Liverpool and London, 1971; Paediatric Surgeon, Johannesburg, 1971–74; Consultant Paediatric Surgeon, Sheffield Children's Hosp., 1974–79. Hon. Consultant in Paediatric Surgery to the Army, 1983–2006. Windermere Vis. Prof., Univ. of Melbourne, 1988; Chafin-Snyder Vis. Prof., Children's Hosp., UCLA, 1992; Santuli Vis. Prof., Babies Hosp., Columbia Univ., NY, 1992; Penman Vis. Prof., Red Cross Meml Hosp. and Univ. of Cape Town, 2000; Guttman Vis. Prof., Montreal, 2000; Jewitt Vis. Prof., Children's Hosp. of Buffalo, 2001–; Visiting Professor: Toronto, 1991; Seattle, 1992; Univ. of Hong Kong, 1993; Indianapolis, Pittsburgh, Washington, 1995; Royal Coll. of Surgeons, Thailand, 1995; Ann Arbor, 1997; Royal Coll. of Surgeons, Korea, 1997; Japanese Surgical Soc., 1998; Albert Einstein Coll. of Medicine, NY, 1999; Univ. of Alabama, 2003; Kansas, 2005; Adelaide, 2005; Chile, 2005. Hunterian Prof., RCS, 2001–02; Lectures: Sulamaa, Children's Hosp., Univ. of Helsinki, 1993 (Sulamaa Medal, 1990); Amer. Pediatric Surgical Assoc., 1995; P. Rickham Meml, Liverpool, 2004; J. Grosfeld, Indianapolis, 2005; Jl of Pediatric Surgery, Amer. Pediatric Surgical Assoc., 2011; Stephen Gans Meml, Amer. Acad. of Pediatrics, 2013. Member: British Assoc. of Paediatric Surgeons (Pres., 1996–98); Assoc. of Surgeons of GB and Ireland; BPA (Mem. Acad. Bd, 1991–93); British Soc. of Gastroenterology; Med. Bd, Tracheo-oesophageal Support Soc., 1982–; Invited Mem., RCS, 1997–2000; Chm., Specialist Adv. Cttee in Paediatric Surgery, 1994–2004 (RCS Rep., 1991–96); RCS Rep on Intercollegiate Bd of Paediatric Surgery, 1994–97. Television: Your Life in their Hands, BBC TV: The baby who could not swallow, 1984; Siamese Twins, 1986; Separating Twins, BBC TV, 2005. Exec. Editor, Progress in Paediatric Surgery, 1982; Member, Editorial Board: Jl of Paediatric Surgery, 1980–; Archives of Diseases in Childhood, 1984–89; Turkish Jl of Paediatric Surgery, 1987–; Jl of RCSE, 1992–97; Associate Editor, Pediatric Surgery International, 1986–2004; Editorial Consultant: Surgery in Childhood International, 1996–; Annals of College of Surgery of Hong Kong, 1996–. Patron, Children's Wish, 1998. MRSocMed. Hon. FAAP 1987; Hon. FRCPH 2004; Hon. FRCSI 2005; Hon. Fellow, Inst. of Child Health, UCL, 2011; Hon. FACS 2012; Hon. FCSSA; Hon. FCMSA. Hon. Mem., Paediatric Surgical Assocs of Switzerland, Austria, Greece, Germany, Asia, America and S Africa. Hon. MD: Sheffield, 2002; Witwatersrand, 2008. Bronze Medal, Nordik Soc. of Paediatric Surgeons, 1990; James Spence Medal, RCPCH, 2004; Denis Browne Gold Medal, Brit. Assoc. of Paediatric Surgeons, 2004; Clement-Price Thomas Award, RCS, 2004; Rehbein Medal, German Assoc. of Paediatric Surgeons, 2008; Rehbein Medal, Eur. Pediatric Surgical Assoc., 2010; Ladd Medal, Amer. Assoc. of Pediatrics (Surgical Section), 2012. *Publications:* A Colour Atlas of Paediatric Surgical Diagnosis, 1981; A Colour Atlas of Surgery for Undescended Testes, 1984; Paediatric Surgery, 4th edn (with H. H. Nixon) 1988 (Rob and Smith Operative Surgery series), 7th edn as Operative Paediatric Surgery (with A. G. Coran) 2013; (ed jtly) The Great Ormond Street Colour Handbook of Paediatrics & Child Health, 2007; Visual Handbook of Paediatrics and Child Health: the core, 2008; chapters in books on paediatrics and surgery; articles on oesophageal atresia, oesophageal replacement, gastro-oesophageal reflux, neonatal surgical conditions, paediatric oncology, and conjoined twins. *Recreations:* sport, reading, food and wine. *Address:* 78 Wood Vale, N10 3DN.

SPOFFORTH, (David) Mark, OBE 2014; FCA; Partner, Spofforths, Chartered Accountants, since 1982 (Managing Partner, 1997–2000, 2010–12); President, Institute of Chartered Accountants in England and Wales, 2012–13 (Deputy President, 2011–12); *b* Worthing, Sussex, 26 July 1956; *s* of Michael Gordon Spofforth and Joan Mary Spofforth (*née* Marsh); *m* 1983, Dorothy Lesley (*d* 2007); one *s* one *d*; *m* 2015, Veronica Anne. *Educ:* Durham Univ. (BSc). FCA 1982; CTA 2005. Coopers and Lybrand, 1979–82. Institute of Chartered Accountants in England and Wales: Member: Council, 1993– (Chm., 2003–05); Main Bd (formerly Exec.), 1998–2007, 2009–; Tech. Adv. Cttee, 1985–94; Gen. Practitioner Bd, 1993–99 (Chm., 1995–98); Remuneration Cttee, 2010–13; Chm., Educn and Trng Bd, 2000–03, 2005–07. Mem., Internat. Accounting Educn Standards Bd, 2005–10 (Dep. Chm., 2009–10). Bd Observer, IFAC, 2014–. Broadcaster, BBC Southern Counties Radio, 1996–2006. Gov., Sion Sch., Worthing, 1987–. Trustee, Thalidomide Trust 2013–. Liveryman: Horners' Co., 1979– (Master, 2009); Chartered Accountants' Co., 2005– (Jun. Warden, 2013–14; Sen. Warden, 2014–15). *Recreations:* watching Rugby, watching international swimming (daughter, Gemma, is a 2008 and 2012 Olympian and world record holder in 100m backstroke event), scuba diving. *Address:* Spofforths, 9 Donnington Park, 85 Birdham Road, Chichester, Sussex PO20 7AJ. *T:* (01243) 787627. *E:* markspofforth@spofforths.co.uk. *Clubs:* City Livery, Carlton.

SPOKES, Ann; *see* Spokes Symonds, A. H.

SPOKES, John Arthur Clayton; QC 1973; *b* 6 Feb. 1931; 2nd *s* of late Peter Spencer Spokes and Lilla Jane Spokes (*née* Clayton), Oxford; *m* 1961, Jean, *yr d* of late Dr Robert McLean and Jean Symington McLean (*née* Barr), Carluke; one *s* one *d*. *Educ:* Westminster Sch.; Brasenose Coll., Oxford (BA 1954; MA 1959); Univ. of Southampton (MA 2000). Nat. Service, Royal Artillery, 1949–51 (commnd 1950). Called to Bar, Gray's Inn, 1955, Bencher, 1985; a Recorder, 1972–93. Chm., Data Protection, subseq. Inf., Tribunal, 1985–2001. Chancellor, Dio. of Winchester, 1985–93. *Recreation:* local history. *Address:* 31 Southgate Street, Winchester, Hants SO23 9EB. *Club:* Leander (Henley-on-Thames).

See also A. H. Spokes Symonds.

SPOKES SYMONDS, Ann (Hazel); Chairman, Age Concern England, 1983–86 (Vice-President, 1987–94; Patron, 1994–2010); *b* 10 Nov. 1925; *d* of Peter Spencer Spokes and Lilla Jane Spokes (*née* Clayton); *m* 1980, (John) Richard (Charters) Symonds (*d* 2006). *Educ:* Wychwood Sch., Oxford; Masters Sch., Dobbs Ferry, NY, USA; St Anne's Coll., Oxford (BA 1947; MA). Organising Secretary: Oxford Council of Social Service, 1959–74; Age Concern Oxford, 1958–80. Dir, ATV, 1978–81; Mem. W Midlands Bd, Central Ind. Television plc, 1981–92. Mem., Thames Valley Police Authy, 1973–85; Chm., No 5 Police Dist Authy Cttee, 1982–85; Vice-Chm., Personal Social Services Council, 1978–80; Chm., Social Services Cttee, ACC, 1978–82; Mem. Bd, Anchor Housing Assoc., 1976–83, 1985–94; Member: Prince of Wales' Adv. Gp on Disability, 1983–90; Oftel Adv. Cttee for Disabled and Elderly People, 1985–91; Hearing Aid Council, 1986–89; Trustee, CERT, 1986–89. Member: Oxford City Council, 1957–95 (Lord Mayor, 1976–77; Hon. Alderman, 1995–); Oxfordshire CC, 1974–85 (Chm., 1981–83). Contested (C) NE Leicester, 1959, Brigg, 1966 and 1970. Mem., Soc. of Authors, 1992–. FRSA 1991. *Publications:* Celebrating Age: an anthology, 1987; Havens Across the Sea, 1990; The Great Grosvenor Hotel Scandal, 1993; Storks, Black Bags and Gooseberry Bushes, 1993; The Changing Faces of Wolvercote, Wytham and Godstow, 1997, 2nd edn 2011; The Changing Faces of North Oxford, Books One and Two, 1998; The Changing Faces of Iffley, 1999; The Changing Faces of Rose Hill, 2000; Oxfordshire People and the Forgotten War: the Anglo-Boer conflict 1899–1902, 2002; (with Richard Symonds) Follow Me: a dog's view of the gospel story, 2006; (with Chris Nichols) The Changing Faces of Summertown and Cutteslowe, Book Two, 2009; (with Nigel Morgan) The Origins of Oxford Street Names, 2010, 2nd edn 2011; Also-Rans: the injustice of history, 2014. *Recreations:* lawn tennis, golf, photography, enjoying cats. *Address:* 43 Davenant Road, Oxford OX2 8BU. *T:* (01865) 515661.

See also J. A. C. Spokes.

SPOONER, Sir James (Douglas), Kt 1981; Director, John Swire & Sons, 1970–2003; *b* 11 July 1932; *s* of late Vice-Adm. E. J. Spooner, DSO, and Megan Spooner (*née* Megan Foster, the singer); *m* 1958, Jane Alyson, *d* of late Sir Gerald Glover; two *s* one *d*. *Educ:* Eton Coll. (Fellow, 1990); Christ Church, Oxford. Chartered Accountant 1962; Partner, Dixon Wilson & Co., Chartered Accountants, 1963–72; Chm., Vantona Viyella, subseq. Coats Viyella, 1969–89. Chm., NAAFI, 1973–86 (Dir, 1968–86); Director: Abingworth, 1973–91; Morgan Crucible, 1978–97 (Chm., 1983–97); J. Sainsbury, 1981–94; Barclays Bank, 1983–94; Hogg Robinson Gp, 1971–85 (Dep. Chm., 1971–85); Dep. Chm., Royal Opera House, Covent Garden, 1992–97 (Dir, 1987–97); Chm. of Trustees, British Telecom Pension Scheme, 1992–98. Chm. Council, King's College London, 1986–98; Gov., RAM, 1997–2006. *Recreations:* music, history. *Address:* Pytchley House, Pytchley, Kettering, Northants NN14 1EH. *Clubs:* Beefsteak, Brooks's.

SPOTTISWOODE, Clare Mary Joan, CBE 1999; Chairman, Gas Strategies Ltd, since 2000; Member, Future of Banking Commission, 2009–10; *b* 20 March 1953; *d* of late Charlotte and of Tony Spottiswoode; *m* 1977, Oliver Richards; one *s* three *d*. *Educ:* Cheltenham Ladies' Coll.; Clare Coll., Cambridge (MA Maths Pt 1, Economics Pt 2); Yale Univ. (MPhil). HM Treasury, 1977–80; Spottiswoode Trading, 1980–84 (wholesale importing business); Chm. and Chief Exec., Spottiswoode and Spottiswoode (micro computer software), 1984–90; Dir Gen. of Gas Supply, 1993–98; Sen. Vice Pres. of Regulatory Affairs, Europe, Azurix, Enron, 1998–99; Mem., Mgt Gp, PA Consulting Gp, 1999–2000; Dep. Chm., British Energy, 2001–07; Policyholder Advocate, Aviva, 2006–09. Dir, BioFuels, 2003–07; Chairman: Flow Energy, 2011–; Magnox, 2011–14; non-executive Director: Tullow Oil plc, 2002–11; Energy Solutions, 2009–13; Ilika, 2010–; G4S, 2010–; EnQuest plc, 2011–; RBC Europe Ltd, 2012–14; Ind. Dir, Payments Council, 2012–. Hon. DSc Brunel, 1997. *Publications:* Quill, 1984; Abacus, 1984. *Recreations:* children, gardening, theatre.

SPRACKLING, David Martin; Parliamentary Counsel, since 2009; *b* Nottingham, 3 April 1963; *s* of Dr Peter Sprackling and Dr Margaret Sprackling (*née* Hughes). *Educ:* Nottingham High Sch.; Jesus Coll., Cambridge (BA Hons 1985); Worcester Coll., Oxford (MLitt Theol. 1995). Admitted as solicitor, 1988; Solicitor, Martineau Johnson, 1988–90; joined Parly Counsel Office, 1995; Asst Parly Counsel, 1995–99; Sen. Asst Parly Counsel, 1999–2003; on secondment to Law Commn, 1999–2001; Dep. Parly Counsel, 2003–09. *Recreations:* travel, books, languages, singing. *Address:* Office of the Parliamentary Counsel, 1 Horse Guards Road, SW1A 2HQ. *T:* (020) 7276 6561. *E:* david.sprackling@cabinet-office.x.gsi.gov.uk.

SPRAGGS, Rear-Adm. Trevor Owen Keith, CB 1983; CEng, FIET; Chief of Staff to Commander-in-Chief, Naval Home Command, 1981–83; *b* 17 June 1926; *s* of Cecil James Spraggs and Gladys Maude (*née* Morey); *m* 1st, 1955, Mary Patricia Light (*d* 1983); two *s*; 2nd, 1986, Gwynedd Kate (*née* Adams) (*d* 2011), *widow* of Reginald A. W. Green, CEng, MIMechE. *Educ:* Portsmouth Grammar Sch.; St John's Coll., Southsea; Imperial College of Science and Technology, London (BScEng, ACGI). Joined Royal Navy, 1945; courses: HM Ships: King Alfred, Leander, Harrier, 1945–47; Admiralty Compass Obs., Slough, 1948; BRNC, Dartmouth, 1948–50; HM Ships: Dryad, Vanguard, Vernon, Collingwood, Ariel, Falcon, 1950–61; AEI, Manchester, 1962; RNEC, 1962–66; HMS Collingwood, 1966–69 and 1972–75; RNEC, 1969–72, and, as Dean, 1979–80; Dean, RNC, Greenwich, 1975–77; Dir of Naval Trng Support, Dir of Naval Educn and Trng Support, 1977–79; Chief Naval Instr Officer, 1981–83. ADC to the Queen, 1979. Member: Nautical Studies Bd of CNAA, 1975–80; Maritime Studies Adv. Cttee of Plymouth Polytech., 1979–80; Cttee of Management, Royal Hosp. Sch., Holbrook, 1981–83; Governor: Fareham Technical Coll., 1972–75; RN Sch. for Officers' Daughters, Haslemere, 1975–77. Pres., Combined Services and RN Amateur Athletic Assocs, 1981–83. *Recreation:* gardening. *Address:* 46 Sinah Lane, Hayling Island, Hants PO11 0HH. *Club:* Royal Naval Sailing Association.

SPRAGUE, David Keith, MVO 1972; HM Diplomatic Service, retired; High Commissioner, Sierra Leone, 1991–93; *b* 20 Feb. 1935; *m* 1958, Audrey Mellon; two *s* one *d*. *Educ:* King Edward VI Grammar Sch., Camp Hill, Birmingham. Foreign Office, 1953; Nat. Service, 1953–55; FO, 1955, served Addis Ababa, Paris, Belgrade, Budapest, Kuala Lumpur, Abidjan, Sofia, and FCO; Dep. High Comr, Madras, 1986–89; Ambassador to Mongolia, 1989–91. *Recreations:* playing with words, bridge, heathers. *Address:* 18 Springfield Road, Exmouth EX8 3JX.

SPRAKE, Anthony Douglas; HM Diplomatic Service, retired; Consul-General, Melbourne, 2001–03; *b* 16 July 1944; *s* of Douglas Alfred Sprake and Doris Elizabeth Sprake (*née* Grindley); *m* 1977, Jane Bonner McNeill; one *s* (and one *s* decd). *Educ:* City of Bath Boys' Sch.; Univ. of Keele (BA Hons Maths and Physics). Asst Principal, Min. of Labour, 1968–72; Private Sec. to Parly Under-Sec. of State for Employment, 1972–73; Principal, Dept of Employment, 1973–77; Labour Attaché, British Embassy, Brussels, 1977–79; joined

Diplomatic Service, 1980: FCO, 1980–82; Dep. High Comr, Freetown, Sierra Leone, 1982–85; Defence Dept, FCO, 1986–88; MoD (on secondment), 1989; Counsellor (Commercial), The Hague, 1990–94; Head, Cultural Relns Dept, FCO, 1994–96; Minister and Consul Gen., Peking, 1996–2000; Hd, China and Hong Kong Dept, FCO, 2000. *Recreations:* sailing, theatre, bridge. *Address:* 1 Chapel Street, Woodbridge, Suffolk IP12 4NF. *T:* (01394) 380006.

SPRANGE, Thomas Kimpton; QC 2015; Partner, King & Spalding International LLP, since 2011; *b* Sydney, Australia, 21 Feb. 1972; *s* of Michael Sprange and Rosemary Sprange; two *s* one *d*. *Educ:* Cranbrook Sch.; Univ. of Sydney (DipLaw); Univ. of New South Wales (LLM). Admitted Solicitor, 2001; Associate, Vandervords, 1998–2000; Barlow Lyde & Gilbert, 2000–02; Steptoe & Johnson, 2002–11 (Partner, 2004–11). *Recreations:* swimming (Red Top Swim), martial arts (KO Muay Thai), reading, cinema, travel. *Address:* c/o King & Spalding International LLP, 125 Old Broad Street, EC2N 1AR. *T:* (020) 7551 7529. *E:* tsprange@kslaw.com.

SPRATT, Prof. Brian Geoffrey, CBE 2008; PhD; FMedSci; FRS 1993; Professor of Molecular Microbiology, Imperial College Faculty of Medicine, since 2001 (Head of Department of Infectious Disease Epidemiology, 2004–12); *b* 21 March 1947; *s* of Clarence Albert Spratt and Marjory Alice (*née* Jeffreys); *m* 1st, 1986, Dr Jennifer Broome-Smith (marr. diss. 1995); one *s*; 2nd, 1995, Dr Jiaji Zhou; one *s*. *Educ:* Tonbridge Sch.; University Coll. London (BSc, PhD). Research Fellow: Princeton Univ., 1973–75; Leicester Univ., 1975–80; Sussex University: Lectr in Biochem., 1980–87; Reader in Molecular Genetics, 1987–89; Prof., 1989–98; Prof. of Biology, Oxford Univ., 1998–2001; Wellcome Trust Principal Res. Fellow, 1989–2014. Founder FMedSci 1998. Fellow, Amer. Acad. of Microbiol., 2003. Fleming Award, Soc. for Gen. Microbiol., 1982; Pfizer Award, 1983; Hoechst-Roussel Award, Amer. Soc. for Microbiol., 1993; Kitasato Medal for Microbial Chemistry, Kitasato Inst., Japan, 1995; Leeuwenhoek Lect. and Medal, Royal Soc., 2003; Garrod Medal, British Soc. for Antimicrobial Chemotherapy, 2011; GlaxoSmithKline Internat. Award, Amer. Soc. for Microbiol., 2011. *Publications:* numerous pubns on microbiol. and genetics in learned jls. *Address:* Department of Infectious Disease Epidemiology, Imperial College Faculty of Medicine, St Mary's Hospital, W2 1PG. *T:* (020) 7594 3625.

SPRAY, Martin Coulson, CBE 2013; Chief Executive, Wildfowl and Wetlands Trust, since 2004; *b* London, 16 June 1951; *s* of Lionel Spray and Constance Spray; *m* 1977, Marian Madden; one *s* one *d*. *Educ:* Tiffin Boys' Sch., Kingston upon Thames; University Coll. of Swansea (BSc Hons). Mgt positions, SRC, subseq. SERC, 1974–88; Area Manager, WWF, 1988–91; Chief Exec., Berks, Bucks and Oxfordshire Wildlife Trust, 1991–2004; Actg Chief Exec., RSNC, 2003–04. Chm., North Wessex Downs Area of Outstanding Natural Beauty, 2001–03. Chm., Marine Conservation Soc., 2010–. MInstD 2006. Hon. DSc Roehampton, 2013. *Recreations:* countryside, travel, family, friends. *Address:* Wildfowl and Wetlands Trust, Slimbridge, Glos GL2 7BT. *T:* (01453) 891131, *Fax:* (01453) 890827. *E:* Martin.Spray@wwt.org.uk. *Clubs:* Athenæum, Farmers.

SPRENT, Prof. Janet Irene, OBE 1996; DSc; FRSE; Professor of Plant Biology, University of Dundee, 1989–98, now Emeritus (Deputy Principal, 1995–98); *b* 10 Jan. 1934; *d* of James William and Dorothy May Findlater; *m* 1955, Peter Sprent. *Educ:* Slough High Sch. for Girls; Imperial Coll. of Science and Technol., London (BSc; ARCS 1954); Univ. of Tasmania (PhD 1958); Univ. of London (DSc 1988). FRSE 1990. Scientific Officer, Rothamsted Exptl Stn, 1954–55; ICIANZ Res. Fellow, Univ. of Tasmania, 1955–58; Botany Mistress, Rochester Girls' Grammar Sch., 1959–61; Lectr, subseq. Sen. Lectr, Goldsmiths' Coll., London, 1960–67; University of Dundee: successively Res. Fellow, Lectr, Sen. Lectr and Reader, 1967–89; Dean, Faculty of Science and Engrg, 1987–89; Hd, Dept of Biol Scis, 1992–95. Hon. Res. Fellow, James Hutton (formerly Scottish Crop Res.) Inst., 1991–. Extensive overseas collaboration, e.g. Australia, Brazil, Kenya, in nitrogen fixing crop and tree research. Member: Council, NERC, 1991–95; SHEFC, 1992–96; (ind.) JNCC, 1994–2000; Bd, Scottish Natural Heritage, 2001–07; Royal Commn on Envmtl Pollution, 2002–08. Trustee, 2007–15, Res. Associate, 2015–, Royal Botanic Gardens, Edinburgh. Mem. Governing Body and Trustee, MacAulay Land Use Res. Inst., 1990–2001 (Chm., 1995–2001). Hon. DAgrSc Uppsala, 2010. *Publications:* The Biology of Nitrogen Fixing Organisms, 1979; The Ecology of the Nitrogen Cycle, 1987; (with P. Sprent) Nitrogen Fixing Organisms: pure and applied aspects, 1990; (with P. Sprent) Suilven's World, 1995; Nodulation in Legumes, 2001; Legume Nodulation: a global perspective, 2009; papers in scientific jls and chapters in books and symposium vols. *Recreations:* walking, gardening, music. *Address:* 32 Birkhill Avenue, Wormit, Newport on Tay, Fife DD6 8PW. *T:* (01382) 541706. *Club:* Farmers.

SPRIDDELL, Peter Henry; Director: Capital & Counties plc, 1988–94; Capital Shopping Centres plc, 1994–2000; Royal Artillery Museums Ltd, 1990–94; *b* 18 Aug. 1928; *s* of Thomas Henry Spriddell and Eva Florence Spriddell; *m* 1952, Joyce Patricia (*née* Haycock); two *s* one *d*. *Educ:* Plymouth Coll.; Exeter Coll., Oxford (MA); Harvard Business Sch. Marks & Spencer: store management, 1951–68; Sen. Exec. Store Operations, 1968–70; Dir, 1970–88; Alternate Exec. Dir, 1970–72; Exec. Dir Personnel, 1972–75; Exec. Dir Store Operations, Transport, Building and Store Develt, Real Estate, 1975–88; Dir, NFC, 1978–82; non-exec. Mem., British Rail Property Bd, 1986–2001. Mem. Bd, British Council of Shopping Centres, 1983–95 (Pres., 1988–89; Hon. Life Mem., 1998). Mem. Council, 1978–94, Barclay Fellow, 1994–2003, Hon. Life Fellow, 2003, Templeton Coll., Oxford (formerly Oxford Centre for Management Studies). Mem. Cttee, Wine Soc., 1998–2000. FRSA. Freeman, City of London; Liveryman, Worshipful Co. of Paviors, 1984. *Recreations:* music, golf. *Club:* Moor Park Golf.

SPRING, family name of **Baron Risby**.

SPRING, Sir Dryden (Thomas), Kt 1994; dairy farmer; Director, 1983–98, Chairman, 1989–98, New Zealand Dairy Board; *b* 6 Oct. 1939; *s* of Maurice Spring and Violet Grace Spring; *m* 1st, 1960, Christine Margaret McCarthy (marr. diss. 2002); three *s* three *d*; 2nd, 2003, Margaret Skews. *Educ:* Walton Primary Sch.; Matamata Coll. NZ Co-operative Dairy Co. Ltd: Dir, 1973–98; Dep. Chm., 1979–82; Chm., 1982–89. Director: Rural Banking and Finance Corp., 1974–88; Maramarua Coalfields Ltd, 1978–84; Nufarm (formerly Fernz Corp.) Ltd, 1982–2004; Goodman Fielder Ltd, 1989–2003 (Dep. Chm., 2000–03); Nat. Bank of NZ, 1994–2003; Maersk New Zealand Ltd, 1999–2004; Fletcher Building Ltd, 2001–11; Sky City Entertainment Group Ltd, 2003–11; Port of Tauranga Ltd, 2004–14, and other cos; Chairman: WEL Networks Ltd, 1999–2005; Ericsson Communications NZ Ltd, 1999–2003; Tenon (formerly Fletcher Challenge Forests) Ltd, 2001–04; ANZ Nat. Bank, 2006–12 (Dir, 2003–12); Dep. Chm., Ports of Auckland Ltd, 1988–94. Member: Prime Minister's Enterprise Council, 1991–94; Asian Pacific Econ. Co-operation Eminent Persons Gp, 1994–96; Internat. Adv. Bd, Chile Pacific Foundn, 2005–; Chm., Asia 2000 Foundn of NZ, 2001–06. Hon. Chm., NZ/Philippines Business Council, 1992–98. Chm., ASEAN/NZ Combined Business Council, 1998–99; NZ Chm., Business Adv. Council, Asia Pacific Econ. Co-operation, 2000–06; Patron, NZ/Thailand Business Council, 1995–98. Fellow, 1993, Dist. Fellow, 2000, Inst. of Dirs in NZ; Paul Harris Fellow, 2010. Life Mem., Federated Farmers of NZ (Waikato), 1987. Dist. Fellow, Massey Univ. of Agric., 1999. Hon. DSc Massey, 2000; Hon. Dr Waikato, 2014. NZ Commemoration Medal, 1990; NZ Bus. Hall of Fame, 2013. *Recreations:* sport, reading. *Address:* 15 Awanui Place, Matamata 3400, New Zealand. *Clubs:* Wellington; Matamata.

SPRING, Richard, (Dick); non-executive Deputy Chairman, Financial Exchange Co. of Ireland, since 2008 (Executive Vice Chairman, 1997–2008); Chairman, Industrial Development Ireland, since 1998; *b* 29 Aug. 1950; *s* of late Daniel and Anne Spring; *m* 1977, Kristi Lee Hutcheson; two *s* one *d*. *Educ:* Mt St Joseph Coll., Roscrea; Trinity Coll., Dublin (BA 1972). Called to the Bar, King's Inns, Dublin, 1975; in practice on Munster Circuit, 1977–81. Mem. Dáil (TD) (Lab), N Kerry, 1981–2002. Minister of State, Dept of Justice, 1981–82; Dep. Prime Minister of Ireland, 1982–87 and 1993–97; Minister for the Environment, 1982–83; Minister for Energy, 1983–87; Minister for Foreign Affairs, 1993–97. Leader of Irish Labour Party, 1982–97. Director: Repak Ltd, 2006–13; Allied Irish Banks, 2009–; Goodbody Stockbroking Ltd, 2012–; Chairman: Fexco Stockbroking Ltd, 2002–12; Alder Capital, 2004– (Dir, 2000–); Altobridge Ltd, 2006– (Dir, 2002–). Chm., Réalta HIV Global Foundn, 2005–. Associate Fellow, Kennedy Sch. of Govt, Harvard, 1998–; Fellow, Salzburg Seminar, 1998–. *Recreations:* swimming, reading, golf, walking. *Address:* Ridge Lodge, The Spa, Tralee, Co. Kerry, Ireland. *T:* (87) 2391200. *E:* dspring@fexco.com.

SPRING, Stephanie, (Stevie), FIPA, FMS; Chairman, BBC Children in Need, since 2008; *b* 10 June 1957; *d* of William Harold Spring and Marlene Maud Spring (*née* Coleman, now Green). *Educ:* Eggars Grammar Sch., Alton; Univ. of Kent, Canterbury (LLB Hons 1978). FIPA 1996; FMS 2004. Mktg Manager, Alpine Hldgs, 1978–82; Business Develt, TV-am, 1982–84; Business Dir, Grey Advertising, 1984–88; Dep. Man. Dir, Gold Greenlees Trott, 1988–92; Managing Director: Woollams Moira Gaskin O'Malley, 1992–94; Young & Rubicam, 1994–2000; Chief Executive: Clear Channel UK, 2000–06; Future plc, 2006–12; Luxup, 2013. Sen. Ind. Dir, Engine Gp, 2012–14; Chm., ITG Gp, 2014–. Non-exec. Dir, Co-operative Gp, 2015– (Chm., Remuneration Cttee, 2015–). Chm., Fedn of Groundwork Trusts, 2001–08. Trustee, Arts & Business, 2006–09. Hon. PhD Kent, 2011. *Recreations:* travel, socialising, swimming, running. *Address:* 34 Courtnell Street, W2 5BX. *E:* stevie@steviespring.com. *Clubs:* Soho House, Thirty, WACL.

SPRING RICE, family name of **Baron Monteagle of Brandon**.

SPRINGALL, Diana; artist; *b* 16 Sept. 1938; *d* of William Gordon Alexander and Stella Alice Fuller; *m* 1960, Ernest Thomas Springall (marr. diss. 1975); two *s*. *Educ:* Goldsmiths' Coll. Sch. of Art (NDD Painting 1960; ATC 1961); City and Guilds of London Inst. (Embroidery 1963); Univ. of London (Dip. Hist. of Art 1968). Hd, Art Dept, West Heath Sch., Sevenoaks, 1961–63; Lectr, Fashion Dept, Maidstone Coll. of Art, 1963–68; Principal Lectr and Hd, Dept of Fashion and Textiles, Stockwell Coll. of Educn, Bromley, 1968–80; Panel Lectr, V&A Mus., 1980–. Chm. and Emeritus Mem., Embroiderers' Guild, 1978–85; Chm. and Fellow, Soc. of Designer-Craftsmen, 1987–90. Design consultant, Embroidery (TV series), BBC TV, 1980; Twelve British Embroiderers (exhibn), Tokyo, 1985; retrospective exhibn, Knitting and Stitching Show, London, Dublin and Harrogate, 2011. FRSA. Broderers' Prize, Broderers' Co., 2011. *Publications:* Canvas Embroidery, 1969; Embroidery, 1980; Twelve British Embroiderers, 1985; Design for Embroidery, 1988; Inspired to Stitch, 2005; An Embroiderer's Eye, 2009; *relevant publication*: Diana Springall A Brave Eye, by June Hill, 2011. *Recreations:* gardening, cooking, travel. *Address:* Oast Cottage, 2 Park Lane, Kemsing, Sevenoaks, Kent TN15 6NU. *T:* and *Fax:* (01732) 761501. *E:* dianaspringall@btinternet.com.

SPRINGETT, Ven. Robert Wilfred; Archdeacon of Cheltenham, since 2010; *b* Chelmsford, 15 Sept. 1962; *s* of Jack and Patricia Springett; *m* 1991, Helen Bates; two *d*. *Educ:* Brentwood Sch.; Chelmsford Coll.; Lincoln Theological Coll.; Nottingham Univ.; King's Coll., London. Ordained deacon, 1989, priest, 1990; Curate: St James', Colchester, 1989; St Martin's, Basildon, 1992; Priest in Charge, South Ockendon and Belhus Park, 1994–2001; Area Dean, Thurrock, 1998–2001; Rector, Wanstead, 2001–10; Area Dean, Redbridge, 2008–10. Hon. Canon, Chelmsford, 2008–10. *Recreations:* travel, dog walking, ski-ing. *Address:* 1 Gloucester Road, Tewkesbury GL20 5SS. *T:* (01452) 410022. *E:* archdchelt@glosdioc.org.uk.

SPRINGFORD, Prof. Michael, PhD; FInstP; H. O. Wills Professor of Physics, 1996–2001, and Director, Physics Laboratory, 1994–2001, University of Bristol, now Emeritus Professor of Physics; *b* 10 Jan. 1936; *s* of Stanley Walter Springford and Lilian Springford (*née* Tyler); *m* 1st, 1958, Kathleen Elizabeth Wyatt (marr. diss. 1983); two *s* one *d*; 2nd, 1991, Maria Sergeyevna (*née* Morosova). *Educ:* Durham Univ. (BSc); Hull Univ. (PhD). Nat. Res. Council of Canada, 1962–64; Univ. of Sussex, 1964–89; Prof. of Experimental Physics, Univ. of Bristol, 1989–2001. Mott Prize Lectr, and Charles Vernon Boys Medal and Prize, 1995, Guthrie Medal and Prize, 2003, Inst. of Physics. *Publications:* (ed) Electrons at the Fermi Surface, 1980; (ed) Electron: a centenary volume, 1997; papers on the quantum properties of condensed matter in learned jls. *Recreations:* piano, writing, hill walking, cooking, pursuit of quietness. *Address:* 12A Royal York Crescent, Bristol BS8 4JY. *E:* m.springford@bristol.ac.uk.

SPRINGMAN, Prof. Sarah Marcella, CBE 2012 (OBE 1997); PhD; CEng, FREng, FICE; Professor of Geotechnical Engineering, Department of Civil, Environmental and Geomatic Engineering, since 1997, and Rector, since 2015, Eidgenössische Technische Hochschule (Swiss Federal Institute of Technology), Zurich (Deputy Head of Department, 2013–14); *b* 26 Dec. 1956; *d* of late (Paul) Michael Eyre Springman and Dame Ann Marcella Springman, DBE. *Educ:* Wycombe Abbey Sch.; Girton Coll., Cambridge (MA; Roscoe Meml Prize 1978; Hon. Fellow, 2015); St Catharine's Coll., Cambridge (MPhil); Magdalene Coll., Cambridge (PhD 1989; Hon. Fellow, 2014). 11 blues/half blues in lacrosse, tennis, squash, cross country, swimming, athletics. CEng 1993; FICE 2005; FREng 2009. Engr, Sir Alexander Gibb & Partners, UK, Australia and Fiji, 1979–83; Cambridge University: Soil Mechanics Group, Engineering Department: Res. Asst, 1984–88; Res. Associate, 1989–90; Asst Lectr, 1990–93; Lectr, 1993–96; Res. Fellow, 1988–90, Lectr and Fellow, 1991–96, Magdalene Coll.; Chm. and Initiator, Lang. Prog. for Engrs, 1992–96. Lectures: Cross Canada, Canadian Geotech. Soc., 2010; Suklje, Slovenian Geotech. Soc., 2011. Member: Swisscode Commn Geodesign, 1998–2003; Swiss Natural Hazards Competence Centre, 1998–; Swiss Council for Sci. and Technol., 2000–07; Peer Review Coll., EPSRC, 2005–09, 2013–14; Swiss Platform for Natural Hazards, PLANAT, 2008–15; Bd, Implenia AG, 2013–14. MInstRE 1990; Member: Women's Engrg Soc., 1983– (Fellow, 2015); Swiss Soc. of Engrs and Architects, 1999–; Swiss Acad. of Engrg Scis, 2015–; Res. Cttee, RAEng, 2011–; Search Cttee, Queen Elizabeth Prize for Engrg, 2012; Swiss Geotech. Soc., 2013–14; Chm., Tech. Cttee on Physical Modelling in Geotechnics, Internat. Soc. for Soil Mechanics and Geotech. Engrg, 2005–10. Regl Ed., Internat. Jl of Physical Modelling in Geotechnics, 2007–14; Associate Ed., Permafrost and Periglacial Processes, 2013–14. Mem., British Triathlon Team, 1984–93 (Nat. Champion 11 times, European Champion 3 times, European Team Champion 5 times); Mem., GB World Cup Rowing team, 1997; Vice Pres., Internat. Triathlon Union, 1992–96, 2008– (Hon. Mem., 2001); Gov., World Masters Games, 1993–2002; Member: UK (formerly GB) Sports Council, 1993–2001; Exec. Bd, British Triathlon, 2005–12 (Pres., 2007–12); Nat. Olympic Cttee, British Olympic Assoc., 2008–12; Bd, UK Sport, 2013–; Bd, English Inst. of Sport, 2014. Governor: Marlborough Coll., 1991–94; Wycombe Abbey Sch., 1993–96. FRSA 1993 (Life Fellow 2005). Hon. DSc Bath, 2013. Lifetime Achievement Award, Sunday Times and Sky Sportswoman of Year Awards, 2013. *Publications:* (ed) Constitutive and Centrifuge Modelling: two extremes, 2002; (ed jtly) Permafrost, 2003; Physical Modelling in Geotechnics (2 vols), 2010; contrib. geotechnical jls. *Recreations:* sculling/rowing, triathlon, cross-country ski-ing, opera. *Address:* ETH Zürich, Rectorate, HG F61, Rämistrasse 101, 8092 Zürich,

Switzerland; Institute for Geotechnical Engineering, 8093 Zürich, Switzerland. *T:* (44) 6333805, *Fax:* (44) 6331079. *Clubs:* Cambridge Triathlon (Cambridge) (Pres., 1996–); Leander (Henley); Belvoir (Zurich).

SPROT, Lt-Col Aidan Mark, MC 1944; JP; landed proprietor and farmer (Haystoun Estate); Lord-Lieutenant of Tweeddale, 1980–94; *b* 17 June 1919; *s* of Major Mark Sprot of Riddell. *Educ:* Stowe. Commissioned Royal Scots Greys, 1940; served: Middle East, 1941–43; Italy, 1943–44; NW Europe, 1944–45, and after the war in Germany, Libya, Egypt, Jordan and UK; Adjt 1945–46; CO, 1959–62, retired. Councillor, Peeblesshire CC, 1963–75; JP 1966, DL 1966–80, Peeblesshire. Member, Royal Company of Archers (Queen's Body Guard for Scotland), 1950–; Pres., Lowlands of Scotland, TAVRA, 1986–89. Vice-Pres., RHASS, 1986; Trustee, Royal Scottish Agricl Benevolent Instn, 1989–98. British Red Cross Society: County Dir, 1966–74, Patron, 1983–98, Tweeddale Br.; Patron, Borders Br., 1998–; County Comr, 1968–73, Chm., 1975–80, Pres., 1980–94, Tweeddale Scout Assoc.; President: Borders Area Scout Assoc., 1994–99; Lothian Fedn of Boys' Clubs, 1988–96. Hon. President: Tweeddale Soc., 1995–; Peebles Br., RBL, Scotland, 1990–; Hon. Mem., Rotary Club, Peebles, 1986–. Hon. Sec., Royal Caledonian Hunt, 1964–74 (Hon. Mem., 2007). Mem., Service Chaplains Cttee, Church of Scotland, 1974–82 and 1985–92. Freeman, Tweeddale Dist, 1994. Scout Medal of Merit, 1994; Badge of Honour, BRCS, 1998. *Publications:* Swifter than Eagles—War Memoirs 1939–1945, 1998. *Recreations:* country pursuits, motor cycle touring. *Address:* Crookston, Peebles EH45 9JQ. *T:* (01721) 740209. *Club:* New (Edinburgh).

SPRÜTH, Monika Ilse Gabriele; Co-owner, Sprüth Magers, contemporary art gallery, since 1998; *b* Memmingen, Germany, 18 May 1949; *d* of Gerhard Merfort and Hannelore Sprüth; one *s* one *d*. *Educ:* Rheinisch-Westfälische Technische Hochschule, Aachen (Dip Ing Architecture 1975). Diplom Ingenieur, Stadtplanungsamt Oberhausen, 1975–79; Teacher of construction, maths and art, Fachhochschule für Bauwesen, Cologne, 1981–83; Founder, Monika Sprüth Gallery, 1983; merged with Galerie Philomene Magers as Sprüth Magers, Cologne, 1998; Sprüth Magers, Munich, opened 2001; addnl project space for young and emerging art in Munich, opened 2002; Sprüth Magers, London, opened 2003, Berlin, 2008, LA, 2016. *Recreation:* soccer. *Address:* Sprüth Magers, Oranienburger Strasse 18, 10178 Berlin, Germany. *E:* info@spruethmagers.com.

SPRY, Christopher John, CBE 2002; self-employed healthcare management consultant, since 2006; Director, OD Partnerships Network, 2001–11; *b* 29 Aug. 1946; *s* of late Reginald Charles Spry and Kathleen Edith Spry (*née* Hobart); *m* 1st, Jean Banks (marr. diss. 1989); two *s*; 2nd, 1989, Judith Christina (*née* Ryder). *Educ:* Sir Roger Manwood's Sch., Sandwich; Exeter Univ. (BA 1967). AHSM. Dep. Hosp. Sec., Lewisham Hosp., 1970; Hosp. Sec., Nottingham Gen. Hosp., 1973; Asst Dist Administrator, S Nottingham, 1975, Dist Administrator, 1978; Dist Administrator, 1981, Dist Gen. Manager, 1984, Newcastle HA; Regl Gen. Manager, SW Thames RHA, 1989–94; Regl Dir, NHS Exec., S Thames, 1994–96; Chief Exec., Gtr Glasgow Health Bd, 1996–2001. Non-exec. Dir, Dorset County Hosp. NHS Federation Trust (formerly W Dorset Gen. Hosps NHS Trust), 2005–10. Dir, Redwood House Mgt Co., 2010–14. Vis. Prof., Glasgow Univ., 2001. *Recreations:* the Arts, enjoying townscapes, travel, biographies, history, modern novels, keeping fit. *Address:* 31 Redwood House, Charlton Down, Dorchester, Dorset DT2 9UH.

SPUFFORD, Prof. Peter, PhD, LittD; FSA; FRHistS; FBA 1994; Professor of European History, University of Cambridge, 2000–01, now Emeritus; Fellow, Queens' College, Cambridge, since 1979; *b* 18 Aug. 1934; *s* of late Douglas Henry Spufford and Nancy Gwendoline Spufford (*née* Battagel); *m* 1962, Honor Margaret Clark (Prof. Margaret Spufford, OBE, FBA) (*d* 2014); one *s* (one *d* decd). *Educ:* Kingswood Sch.; Jesus Coll., Cambridge (BA 1956; MA 1960; PhD 1963; LittD 1990). FRNS 1955; FRHistS 1968; FSG 1969; FSA 1990. Res. Fellow, Jesus Coll., Cambridge, 1958–60; Asst Lectr, Lectr, Sen. Lectr and Reader, Univ. of Keele, 1960–79; University of Cambridge: Lectr, 1979–90; Reader in Econ. History, 1990–2000. Visiting Fellow: Clare Hall, Cambridge, 1969–70; Netherlands Inst. for Advanced Study, 1992–93; Vis. Prof. of Burgundian Studies, 1972–73, Vis. Prof., Econ. Studies, 1993, Leuven; Guest, Japan Acad., 2003; Guest of the Rector, Netherlands Inst. for Advanced Study, 2005 (Ortelius Lecture, 2005). Vice-Pres., Soc. of Genealogists, 1997–; Chm., British Records Soc., 1985–2010; Mem. Council, Soc. of Antiquaries, 1996–99. Hon. Member: Koninklijk Genootschap voor Munt-en Penningkunde, 1992–; Société Royale de Numismatique de Belgique, 2011; British Numismatic Soc., 2012. Medallist, Royal Numismatic Soc., 2005; Van Gelder Medal, Univ. of Leiden, 2006. *Publications:* Origins of the English Parliament, 1967; Monetary Problems and Policies in the Burgundian Netherlands 1433–1496, 1970; Handbook of Medieval Exchange, 1986; (ed with N. J. Mayhew) Later Medieval Mints, 1988; Money and Its Use in Medieval Europe, 1988; (ed with G. H. Martin) Records of the Nation, 1990; (ed) Index to the Probate Accounts of England and Wales, 2 vols, 1999; Power and Profit: the merchant in medieval Europe, 2002; From Antwerp to London: the decline of financial centres in Europe, 2005; How Rarely Did Medieval Merchants Use Coin?, 2008; chapters in: Cambridge Economic History of Europe, vol. 3, 1965, vol. 2, 2nd edn, 1987; New Cambridge Medieval History, vi, 1999. *Address:* Queens' College, Cambridge CB3 9ET. *T:* (01223) 335511.

SPUNNER, Lt Gen. Sir Barnabas William Benjamin W.; *see* White-Spunner.

SPURGEON, Prof. Sarah Katherine, OBE 2015; DPhil; CEng, FREng; CMath; FIET; Professor of Control Engineering, and Head of School, University of Kent, since 2008; *b* Wolverhampton, 4 Dec. 1963; *d* of Michael and Sheila Mudge; *m* 1986, Dr Christopher Thomas Spurgeon; two *s* one *d*. *Educ:* Ounsdale High Sch., Wombourne; Univ. of York (BSc Hons Maths; DPhil Electronics 1988). CEng 1996; CMath 1996; FIET 2006; FREng 2008. Department of Engineering, University of Leicester: Lectr, 1991–95; Sen. Lectr, 1995–2000; Reader, 2000–02; Prof. of Engrg, 2002–08; Hd, Dept of Engrg, 2005–08. Chm., UK Automatic Control Council, 2008–11. FInstMC 2004; FIMA; SMIEE 2004. *Publications:* Sliding Mode Control, Theory and Applications, 1998; (ed) Variable Structure Systems: from principles to implementation, 2004. *Recreation:* gardening. *Address:* School of Engineering and Digital Arts, University of Kent, Canterbury, Kent CT2 7NT. *T:* (01227) 823258, *Fax:* (01227) 456084. *E:* s.k.spurgeon@kent.ac.uk.

SPURLING, Hilary; *see* Spurling, S. H.

SPURLING, Sir John (Damian), KCVO 2012; OBE 1999; Chairman, PetPartners Inc., USA, since 2004; *b* Ilford, 11 July 1939; *s* of William Edgar Spurling and Winnefred Spurling; *m* 1989, Gwyneth Wycherley. *Educ:* St David's Coll., Johannesburg; St Ignatius Coll., London. Dir, Kenya Advertising Corp., 1963–70; Chairman and Chief Executive Officer: Advertising Associates, Kenya, 1970–82; Pet Protect Ltd, 1984–2001; PetPartners Ltd, 2002–09. Trustee, Hon. Treas. and Fellow, Animal Health Trust, 1999–; Chm., London Marathon, 2008– (Trustee, London Marathon Charitable Trust, 2008–); Vice-Pres., Kennel Club, 2011– (Trustee, Kennel Club Charitable Trust, 2009–15); Trustee, Foundn of Coll. of St George, Windsor Castle, 2011–. Mem., Lord's Taverners. *Recreations:* golf playing, watching all sport except football, travelling. *T:* 07974 735819. *E:* john@spurls.co.uk. *Clubs:* Oriental, Caledonian; Sunningdale Golf; Muthaiga Country (Nairobi).

SPURLING, (Susan) Hilary, CBE 2007; biographer; *b* 25 Dec. 1940; *d* of Gilbert Alexander Forrest and Emily Maureen Forrest; *m* 1961, John Spurling; two *s* one *d*. *Educ:* Somerville Coll., Oxford (BA; Hon. Fellow, 2006). FRSL 2005. Theatre Critic of the Spectator, 1964–70, Literary Editor, 1966–70. Founding Chair, Fellowship Scheme, 1999, Hon. Mem., 2008, Royal Literary Fund. Hon. Dr Anglia Ruskin, 2007. (Jtly) Heywood Hill Lit. Prize, 2003. *Publications:* Ivy When Young: the early life of I. Compton-Burnett 1884–1919, 1974; Handbook to Anthony Powell's Music of Time, 1977; Secrets of a Woman's Heart: the later life of I. Compton-Burnett 1920–1969, 1984 (Duff Cooper Meml Prize, 1984; Heinemann Literary Award (jtly), 1985); Elinor Fettiplace's Receipt Book, 1986; Paul Scott, A Life, 1990; Paper Spirits, 1992; The Unknown Matisse 1869–1908, vol. i, 1998; La Grande Thérèse, 1999; The Girl from the Fiction Department: a portrait of Sonia Orwell, 2002; Matisse the Master, A Life of Henry Matisse: the conquest of colour 1909–1954 (Whitbread Book of the Year, Los Angeles Times Biography Prize), 2005; Burying the Bones: Pearl Buck in China, 2010 (James Tait Black Prize). *Recreations:* reading, ratting, country walks. *Address:* c/o David Higham Associates, 7th Floor, Waverley House, 7–12 Noel Street, W1F 8GQ.

SPURR, Margaret Anne, OBE 1994; DL; Headmistress, Bolton School, Girls' Division, 1979–94; Governor, BBC, 1993–98; *b* 7 Oct. 1933; *m* 1st, 1953, John Spurr (*d* 2003); one *s* one *d*; 2nd, 2009, Prof. Peter Young (*d* 2011). *Educ:* Abbeydale Girls' Grammar Sch., Sheffield; Univ. of Keele. BA (Hons); PGCE. Tutor: Eng. Lit., Univ. of Glasgow, 1971; Eng. Lit. Dept, Adult Educn, Univ. of Keele, 1972–73. Chm., Scholaservices, 1990–94. Sen. Examiner, Univ. of London, 1971–80. Pres., GSA, 1985–86. Chairman: Nat. ISIS Cttee, 1987–90; BBC English Nat. Forum, 1994–98; Member: Adv. Cttee, American Studies Resources Centre, Polytechnic of Central London, 1977–90; Scholarship Selection Cttee, ESU, 1983–94; CBI Schools Panel, 1985–89; Exec. Cttee, GBGSA, 1994–99. Vice-Provost, Woodard Corp., 1994–98. Governor: Kent Coll., Tunbridge Wells, 1993–99; John Moores Univ., Liverpool, 1994–98; Colfe's Sch., 1995–2009; Stafford Coll. of Further Educn, 1996–2000; Newton Prep. Sch., Battersea, 1999–2006; Univ. of Lincoln, 2008–; Life Gov., Liverpool Coll., 2001; Mem. Governing Council, Keele Univ., 1996–2007. Trustee: School Fees Trust Fund, 1994–2000; Raven Mason Collection, Univ. of Keele, 2001–07; Westminster Abbey Article 26 Fund, 2009–14. Dir, SFS Gp, 1999–2005; Mid-Atlantic Club, 2000–05. Pres., Staffs Soc., 1999–2001. Chm., Croxden Parochial Charities Trusts, 2001. Mem., Exec. Cttee, Lichfield Br., Prayer Book Soc., 2002–04. Dir, Helena Kennedy Scholarship Fund, 2008–14. FRSA 1991. Freeman, City of London, 2006. DL Staffs, 1998. Hon. DLitt Keele, 1995. *Publications:* (ed) A Curriculum for Capability, 1986; (ed) Girls First, 1987. *Recreations:* gardening, poetry, music. *Address:* New Cottage, Parwich, Ashbourne, Derbys DE6 1QJ. *Club:* Reform.

SPURR, Dr (Michael) Stephen, DPhil; Head Master, Westminster School, 2005–14; *b* 9 Oct. 1953; *s* of late (Arthur) Michael (Marshall) Spurr and of Patricia (Ann) Spurr (*née* Newall); *m* 1982, Susanna Armani; one *s* one *d*. *Educ:* King's Sch., Canterbury; Sydney Grammar Sch.; Univ. of Sydney (BA 1st cl. Hons Classics 1975); Corpus Christi Coll., Univ. of Oxford (Oxford Ancient History Prize, 1981; DPhil 1984). Rome Scholar, British Sch. at Rome, 1981–82; Lectr in Classics and Ancient History, ANU, 1982–83; Eton College, 1984–2000: Curator, Myers Mus. of Egyptian Art, 1989–2000; Hd of Classics, 1992–96; House Master, 1996–2000; Hd of College and Headmaster, Upper Sch., Clifton Coll., Bristol, 2000–05. *Publications:* Arable Cultivation in Roman Italy, 1986; Egyptian Art at Eton College, 1995; (trans.) Another Sea by Claudio Magris, 1993; (contrib.) The Oxford Classical Dictionary, 1996; various articles and reviews. *Recreations:* Roman archaeology, Egyptology, mountaineering, Mediterranean agriculture.

SPY, James; Sheriff of North Strathclyde at Paisley, since 1988; *b* 1 Dec. 1952; *s* of James Spy and Jean Learmond; *m* 1980, Jennifer Margaret Malcolm; three *d*. *Educ:* Hermitage Acad., Helensburgh; Glasgow Univ. (LLB Hons). Admitted Solicitor, 1976; passed Advocate, 1979. *Recreations:* music, clocks, model ships, model trains. *Address:* St Ann's, 171 Nithsdale Road, Glasgow G41 5QS.

SPYER, Prof. (Kenneth) Michael, PhD, DSc; FMedSci; Sophia Jex-Blake Professor of Physiology, UCL Medical School (formerly Royal Free and University College Medical School), University College London, 1980–2010, now Emeritus; Chairman, St George's, University of London, since 2013; *b* 15 Sept. 1943; *s* of late Harris Spyer and Rebecca Spyer (*née* Jacobs); *m* 1971, Christine Spalton; two *s*. *Educ:* Coopers' Co. Sch.; Univ. of Sheffield (BSc); Univ. of Birmingham (PhD 1969; DSc 1979). Res. Fellow, Univ. of Birmingham Med. Sch., 1969–72; Royal Soc. European Prog. Fellow, Instituto de Fisologia, Pisa, 1972–73; Res. Fellow, 1973–78, Sen. Res. Fellow, 1978–80, Dept of Physiology, Univ. of Birmingham; joined Royal Free Hosp. Sch. of Medicine, 1980; Dir, Neural Control Gp, BHF, 1985–2000; Head, Jt Depts of Physiology, UCL and Royal Free Hosp. Sch. of Medicine, 1994–99; Dir, Autonomic Neurosci. Inst., 1997–2010; Dean, Royal Free and UC Med. Sch., UCL, 2001–06 (Dean, Royal Free Campus, 1998–2001); Vice-Provost (Biomedicine), 2002–06, (Enterprise), 2006–10, UCL. Chm., NHS London, 2010–13. Pres., Physiological Soc., 2010–12. Founder FMedSci 1998. Hon. FRCP 2002. Hon. MD Lisbon, 1991. *Publications:* (ed jtly) Central Regulation of Autonomic Functions, 1990; papers in Jl of Physiology, Neurosci., Brain Res., Amer. Jl of Physiology, Jl of Autonomic Nervous System, Exptl Physiology, Science, Nature. *Recreations:* fly fishing, travelling (particularly in Italy), gardening, books, fine arts, bookbinding. *Address:* University College London, Gower Street, WC1E 6BT.

SPYROPOULOS, Andrea; Project Manager, Alder Hey Children's NHS Foundation Trust, since 2012; President, Royal College of Nursing, 2010–14; *b* Liverpool, 1954; *d* of Albert and Margaret Styles; *m* 1985, Sotiris Spyropoulos; one *s*. *Educ:* John Moores Univ. (BA Hons Health Studies 1995; LLB Hons 2000); Univ. of Wales, Cardiff (Cert Ed 1992; LLM 2004). RGN 1976; SCM 1979; DPSN; RNT 1992; English Nat. Bd No 7 1995. Staff nurse, sister, stomacare specialist, Sefton Gen. Hosp., 1976–78; pupil, then staff midwife, Countess of Chester Hosp., 1978–79; Nursing Officer, Chandris Cruise Line, 1979–80; Sister, Occupational Health, Darjerba, Evia, Greece, 1980–81; various posts, incl. mgt, sister, tutor, Royal Liverpool and Broadgreen Univ. Hosps, 1981–90; Sen. Lectr in law professional issues, John Moores Univ., 1991–2000. Bid Manager, Health Care Projects, 2001–06; Clin. Strategist, UK and Canada, Health Care Projects Social Infrastructure, 2006–12. Non-exec. Dir, Clatterbridge Centre for Oncol., 1998–2007. Mem., Honour Soc. of Nursing, Sigma Theta Tau Internat., 2011. Hon. DSc Lincoln, 2014. *Recreations:* family, community activity, Life President of Riverside Residents' Association. *Address:* Alder Hey Children's NHS Foundation Trust, Eaton Road, Liverpool L12 1AP. *T:* (0151) 282 4783, 07780 977111. *E:* andrea.spyropoulos@alderhey.nhs.uk.

SQUAIR, George Alexander; non-executive Chairman, British Approvals Service for Cables, 1993–2002; *b* 26 July 1929; *s* of Alexander Squair and Elizabeth (*née* Macdonald); *m* 1953, Joy Honeybone (*d* 2013); two *s* one *d*. *Educ:* Woolwich Polytechnic; Oxford Technical Coll.; Southampton Univ. CEng, FIET (FIEE 1986); CIMgt (CBIM 1984). Gen. distribution engrg posts, 1950–68; Southern, later South Eastern, Electricity Board, subseq. SEEBOARD: 1st Asst Dist Engr, 1968–69; Dist Engr, Swindon, 1969–70; Area Engr, Newbury, 1970–73; Dist Manager, Oxford, 1973–74; Area Manager, Newbury, 1974–78; Mem., Exec. Bd, 1976–78; Dep. Chm., 1978–83; Chm. and Chief Exec., 1983–92. *Recreations:* reading, golf. *Address:* Mews Cottage, Swallow Grove Farmhouse, Mangrove Lane, Hertford SG13 8QG.

SQUIRE, Dr (Clifford) William, CMG 1978; LVO 1972; HM Diplomatic Service, retired; Chairman, Grenzebach Glier Europe, 1996–2008; *b* 7 Oct. 1928; *s* of Clifford John Squire and Eleanor Eliza Harpley; *m* 1st, 1959, Marie José Carlier (*d* 1973); one *s* two *d* (and one *s* decd); 2nd, 1976, Sarah Laetitia Hutchison (*see* S. L. Squire); one *s* one *d*. *Educ:* Royal Masonic Sch., Bushey; St John's Coll., Oxford; Coll. of Europe, Bruges. PhD London 1979. British Army, 1947–49. Nigerian Admin. Service, 1953–59; FO, 1959–60; British Legation, Bucharest, 1961–63; FO, 1963–65; UK Mission to UN, New York, 1965–69; Head of

Chancery, Bangkok, 1969–72; Head of SE Asian Dept, FCO, 1972–75; Extramural Fellow, Sch. of Oriental and African Studies, London Univ., 1975–76; Counsellor, later Head of Chancery, Washington, 1976–79; Ambassador to Senegal, 1979–82, concurrently to Cape Verde Is, Guinea (Bissau), Guinea (Conakry), Mali and Mauritania; Asst Under-Sec. of State, FCO, 1982–84; Ambassador to Israel, 1984–88. Develt Dir, Univ. of Cambridge, 1988–96; Fellow of Wolfson Coll., Cambridge, 1988–96. *Publications:* University Fundraising in Britain, 2014. *Address:* 11A Chaucer Road, Cambridge CB2 7EB. *Club:* Travellers.

SQUIRE, Peter John; Headmaster, Bedford Modern School, 1977–96; *b* 15 Feb. 1937; *s* of Leslie Ernest Squire and Doris Eileen Squire; *m* 1965, Susan Elizabeth (*née* Edwards); one *s* one *d*. *Educ:* King Edward's Sch., Birmingham; Jesus Coll., Oxford (BA 1960, MA 1964); Pembroke Coll. and Dept of Educn, Cambridge (Cert. in Educn 1961). Asst Master, Monkton Combe Sch., Bath, 1961–65; Haberdashers' Aske's Sch., Elstree, 1965–77: Sen. Boarding Housemaster, 1968–77; Sen. History Master, 1970–77. Reporting Inspector, HMC/ISI Inspections, 1994–2004. Chm., Bedfordshire Victim Support, 1997–2001. Mem., Whitgift Council, 1997–2014. *Recreations:* foreign travel, gardening, antique collecting. *Address:* 98A Bromham Road, Biddenham, Bedford MK40 4AH. *T:* (01234) 342373.

SQUIRE, Air Chief Marshal Sir Peter (Ted), GCB 2001 (KCB 1997); DFC 1982; AFC 1979; DL; Chief of the Air Staff, 2000–03; Air Aide-de-Camp to the Queen, 1999–2003; *b* 7 Oct. 1945; *s* of late Wing Comdr Frank Squire, DSO, DFC and Margaret Pascoe Squire (*née* Trump); *m* 1970, Carolyn Joynson; three *s*. *Educ:* King's Sch., Bruton. psc(n). Flying and Staff appts include: commnd 1966; 20 Sqn, Singapore, 1968–70; 4 FTS, Anglesey, 1970–73; 3 (F) Sqn, Germany, 1975–78; OC1 (F) Sqn, 1981–83; Personal Staff Officer to AOC-in-C Strike Comd, 1984–86; Station Comdr, RAF Cottesmore, 1986–88; Dir Air Offensive, 1989–91; SASO, RAF Strike Comd, 1991–93; AOC No 1 Gp, 1993–94; ACAS, 1994–96; DCDS (Progs and Personnel), MoD, 1996–99; AOC-in-C, Strike Comd and Comdr Allied Air Forces NW Europe, 1999–2000. Mem., CWGC, 2003–08 (Vice-Chm., 2005–08). Trustee, Imperial War Mus., 2003–11 (Chm., 2006–11); Pres., American Air Mus. in Britain, 2006–15. Pres., Devon and Somerset Wing ATC, 2012–. Liveryman: Hon. Co. of Air Pilots (formerly GAPAN); Coachmakers' Co.; Hon. Freeman, Barbers' Co. FRAeS 1995. Gov., King's Sch., Bruton, 1990–2011 (Chm., 2004–11). DL Devon, 2008. Hon. DSc Cranfield, 2001. *Recreation:* golf. *Address:* c/o National Westminster Bank, 5 South Street, Wincanton BA9 9DJ. *Club:* Royal Air Force (Pres., 2013–).

SQUIRE, Robin Clifford; Trust Secretary: Veolia Havering Riverside (formerly ES Cleanaway Havering Riverside) Trust and Veolia Pitsea Marshes (formerly ES Cleanaway Pitsea Marshes) Trust, 2002–13; Veolia North Thames Trust, since 2013; *b* 12 July 1944; *s* of late Sidney John Squire and Mabel Alice Squire (*née* Gilmore); *m* 1981, Susan Margaret Fey, OBE (marr. diss. 2007), *d* of late Arthur Frederick Branch and Mahala Branch (*née* Parker); one step *s* one step *d*. *Educ:* Tiffin School, Kingston-upon-Thames. FCA. Qualified as Chartered Accountant, 1966; joined Lombard Banking Ltd (subsequently Lombard North Central Ltd) as Accountant, 1968, becoming Dep. Chief Accountant, 1972–79. Dir Advocacy Ltd, 1997–2000. Councillor, London Borough of Sutton, 1968–82; Chm., Finance Cttee, 1972–76; Leader of Council, 1976–79. Chm., Greater London Young Conservatives, 1973; Vice-Chm., Nat. Young Conservatives, 1974–75. Personal Asst to Rt Hon. Robert Carr, Gen. Election, Feb. 1974; contested (C) Havering, Hornchurch, Oct. 1974. MP (C) Hornchurch, 1979–97; contested (C) same seat, 1997, 2001. PPS to Minister of State for Transport, 1983–85, to Rt Hon. Chris Patten, Chm. of Cons. Party, 1991–92; Parliamentary Under-Secretary of State: DoE, 1992–93; DFE, later DFEE, 1993–97. Mem., Commons Select Cttee on Environment, 1979–83 and 1987–91, on European Legislation, 1985–88; Sec., Cons. Parly European Affairs Cttee, 1979–80; Vice-Chm., Cons. Parly Trade Cttee, 1980–83; Chm., Cons. Parly Environment Cttee, 1990–91 (Jt Vice-Chm., 1985–89); Originator of Local Govt (Access to Information) Act, 1985. Chm., Cons. Action for Electoral Reform, 1983–86 (Vice-Chm., 1982–83); Dep. Chm., Anglo-Asian Cons. Soc., 1982–83. Comr, Nat. Lottery Commn, 1999; Adjudicator for Schs Orgns and Admissions, 1999. Mem. Bd, Shelter, 1982–91; Dir, Link Assured Homes series of cos, 1988–92. Chm., Assoc. of Distributive Envmtl Bodies, 2005–07. Freeman, City of London, 2003; Liveryman, Co. of Makers of Playing Cards, 2003–. *Publications:* (jtly) Set the Party Free, 1969. *Recreations:* films, ballroom dancing, duplicate bridge, classical music, meditation, gnosticism, reiki healing. *Address:* Flat 3, 63 Millbank, SW1P 4RW.

SQUIRE, Rosemary Anne, (Lady Panter), OBE 2008; Joint Chief Executive (formerly Executive Director), Ambassador Theatre Group Ltd, since 1997; *b* 27 May 1956; *d* of late Donald Squire and of Mary Squire (*née* Sykes); *m* 1st, 1982, Alan Brodie (marr. diss. 1994); one *s* one *d*; 2nd, 1994, Howard Hugh Panter (*see* Sir Howard Panter); one *d*. *Educ:* Nottingham High Sch. for Girls; Southampton Univ. (BA 1st Cl. Hons Spanish with Catalan and French 1979); Brown Univ. (Postgrad. Schol. 1979). Gen. Manager, Maybox Gp plc, 1984–88; Gen. Manager, 1988–90, Exec. Dir, 1990–97, Turnstyle Gp Ltd. Mem., Arts Council England, 2009–. Pres., SOLT, 2005–08. Hon. DLitt Southampton, 2009. EY UK Entrepreneur of the Year, 2014. *Recreations:* gardens, walking, reading. *Address:* Ambassador Theatre Group, 2nd Floor, Alexander House, Church Path, Woking, Surrey GU21 6EJ. *T:* (01483) 545804, *Fax:* (01483) 770477. *E:* rosemarysquire@theambassadors.com. *Club:* Ivy.

SQUIRE, Sara Laetitia, (Sarah); HM Diplomatic Service, retired; President, Hughes Hall, Cambridge, 2006–14; *b* 18 July 1949; *d* of Michael Duncan Hutchison and Margery Betty Hutchison (*née* Martin); *m* 1976, (Clifford) William Squire, *qv*; one *s* one *d*. *Educ:* St Paul's Girls' Sch.; Newnham Coll., Cambridge (BA Hons Hist., MA). Entered HM Diplomatic Service, 1971: FCO, 1971–72; Tel Aviv, 1972–75; SE Asian Dept, FCO, 1975–76; Washington, 1977–79; Falkland Is Dept, FCO, 1982–84; Tel Aviv, 1986–88; Policy Officer, Cambridge CC, 1989–90; Sen. Inf. Officer, COI, 1990–95; Dep. Dir, Know How Fund, FCO, 1995–96; Dep. Hd, Central Eur. Dept, FCO, 1996–99; Ambassador to Estonia, 2000–03; Gp Dir, FCO Services, FCO, 2004–06. Adv. Bd, SSEES, UCL, 2006–12. Dep. Vice Chancellor, Cambridge Univ., 2008–14; Syndic, Fitzwilliam Mus., 2007–12. Deputy Chairman: Cambridge Commonwealth and Overseas Trusts, 2009–15; Cambridge Alumni Adv. Bd, 2010–14. Trustee, PHG Foundn, 2008–10; Trustee, United Learning, and Mem. Gp Bd, United Church Schs Trust, 2013–. Canon and Mem. Lay Chapter, Ely Cath., 2013–. *Address:* 11a Chaucer Road, Cambridge CB2 7EB. *T:* (01223) 329547. *Club:* Oxford and Cambridge.

SQUIRE, William; *see* Squire, C. W.

SQUIRES, (Charles) Ian; Controller, ITV News Operations and Current Affairs, 2011–15; *b* 22 April 1951; *s* of Charles Ian Squires and Mary Squires; *m* 1993, Vanessa Marie Sweet; two *d*. *Educ:* Bede Grammar Sch., Sunderland; University Coll. London (BA Hons English). Westminster Press, 1973–75; Current Affairs and Editor, Omnibus, BBC TV, 1975–86; freelance producer, 1986–88; Head of Network TV, North West, BBC, 1988–90; Managing Director: Zenith North, 1990–94; Carlton Studios, 1994–2004; ITV Central (formerly Central Broadcasting), 1996–2008; Director of Regional Production: ITV News Gp, 2004–08; ITV plc, 2008–09; Controller, ITV Regions and Current Affairs, 2009–11. Chm., EMMedia, 2001–05; Director: West Midlands Life, 1999–2003; NEC, 2005–10; Birmingham City Univ. (formerly Univ. of Central England), 2005–09; Fair Cities (Birmingham), 2005–07; Midland Heart Housing Assoc., 2007–09. Chairman: Birmingham City Pride, 2001–04; Marketing Birmingham, 2004–09; Birmingham Repertory Theatre, 2005–13; Dir, Birmingham Hippodrome Theatre, 2005–09; Mem. Bd and Gov., RSC, 2014–. Pres., Birmingham Chamber of Commerce and Industry, 2004–05 (Vice-Pres., 2002–04). BAFTA Award, Best Arts Prog., for A Simple Man (TV ballet on life of L. S. Lowry), 1987. *Recreations:* theatre, history, cycling, writing. *Address:* Manor Cottage, Bottom Lane, Bisbrooke, Rutland LE15 9EJ. *T:* (01572) 821340. *Club:* Royal Automobile.

SRINIVASAN, Krishnan; Deputy Secretary-General, Commonwealth Secretariat, 1995–2002; *b* 15 Feb. 1937; *s* of late Captain C. Srinivasan, Indian Navy, and Rukmani Chari; *m* 1975, Brinda Mukerjea; one *s*. *Educ:* Bedford Sch.; Christ Church, Oxford (MA; Boxing Blue, 1956; Hon. Mem., SCR). Joined Indian Foreign Service, 1959; Chargé d'Affaires, Tripoli, 1968–71; High Comr to Zambia and Botswana, 1974–77; Consul-Gen., NY, 1977–80; High Comr to Nigeria, and Ambassador to Benin and Cameroon, 1980–83; Ambassador, Netherlands, 1986–89; High Comr, Bangladesh, 1989–92; Perm. Sec., Min. of External Affairs, 1992–94; Foreign Secretary, 1994–95. Visiting Fellow: Wolfson Coll., Cambridge, 2002–05; Centre of Internat. Studies, Cambridge, 2002–05; Sen. Res. Fellow, Inst. of Commonwealth Studies, Univ. of London, 2002–08; Fellow: Azad Inst. of Asian Studies, Calcutta, 2006–; Swedish Collegium, 2008, 2012–13. Dist. Vis. Schol., Netherlands Inst. for Advanced Study, 2003–04; Vis. Prof., Indian Admin. Staff Coll., 2004–. Ramsden Sermon, Oxford, 2002. Hind Ratna, 2001; Chevalier de l'Ordre de la Valeur (Cameroon), 2007. *Publications:* Selections in Two Keys, 1974; The Water's Edge, 1975; The Eccentricity Factor, 1980; The Fourth Profile, 1991; A Fizzle Yield, 1992; Tricks of the Trade, 2000; The Eccentric Effect, 2001; The Ugly Ambassador, 2003; Guesswork, 2005; The Rise, Decline and Future of the British Commonwealth, 2005; The Jamdani Revolution, 2008; (with Prof. J. B. L. Mayall) Towards the New Horizon: world order in the 21st century, 2009; The Invisible African, 2012; Diplomatic Channels, 2012; Europe in Emerging Asia, 2015; book reviews and articles on internat. relns in Indian and foreign newspapers and jls. *Recreations:* music, watching sports. *Address:* Flat 8, Courtleigh, 126 Earls Court Road, W8 6QL. *Clubs:* Royal Over-Seas League; Vincent's (Oxford); Bengal (Calcutta); International Centre (New Delhi); Habitat Centre (New Delhi).

SRINIVASAN, Prof. Mandyam Veerambudi, AM 2012; PhD; FRS 2001; FAA; Professor of Visual Neuroscience, Queensland Brain Institute, University of Queensland, since 2007; *b* 15 Sept. 1948; *s* of Mandyam Veerambudi Sundararajan and Mandyam Veerambudi Vedavalli Ammal; *m* Jaishree Srinivasan. *Educ:* Bangalore Univ. (BE 1st Cl. Electrical Engrg 1968); Indian Inst. of Sci., Bangalore (Masters in Applied Electronics and Servomechanisms 1970); Yale Univ. (MPhil 1973, PhD 1976, Engrg and Applied Sci.). Res. Scientist, Dept of Ophthalmol. and Visual Sci., Yale Univ. Sch. of Medicine, 1977–78; Res. Fellow, Depts of Neurobiol. and Applied Maths, ANU, 1978–82; Asst Prof. of Biophysics, Dept of Neurobiol., Univ. of Zurich, 1982–85; Australian National University: Fellow, Visual Sciences, 1985–91, Sen. Fellow, 1992–93, Prof. of Visual Sci., 1994–2006, Res. Sch. of Biol Scis; Dir, Centre for Visual Sci., 1994–96 and 2000–06. Daimler-Benz Fellow, Inst. Advanced Studies, Berlin, 1996–97. FAA 1995; Fellow, Acad. of Scis of Developing World, 2006. Hon. DSc Neuroethol., ANU, 1994; Dr *hc* Zurich, 2002. Australian Prime Minister's Sci. Prize, 2006; UK Rank Prize in Optoelectronics, 2008; Dist. Alumni Award, Indian Inst. Sci., 2009. *Publications:* (ed with S. Venkatesh) From Living Eyes to Seeing Machines, 1997; (jtly) Flying Insects and Robots, 2009; contrib. numerous res. articles and rev. chapters, one internat. patent. *Address:* Queensland Brain Institute, University of Queensland, St Lucia, Qld 4072, Australia; (home) 42 Rosecliffe Street, Highgate Hill, Brisbane, Qld 4101, Australia.

SRISKANDARAJAH, Dr Dhananjayan; Secretary General, CIVICUS, since 2013; *b* Jaffna, Sri Lanka, 31 Dec. 1975; *s* of Prof. N. Sriskandarajah and Dr Sridevy Sriskandarajah; *m* 2003, Suzanne Lambert; two *s* one *d*. *Educ:* James Ruse Agricl High Sch., Sydney, NSW; Univ. of Sydney (BEc (Social Scis) Hons 1997); Magdalen Coll., Oxford (MPhil Develt Studies 2000; DPhil 2005). Institute for Public Policy Research: researcher, 2004–06; Associate Dir, 2006–08; Dep. Dir, 2008; Dir, Royal Commonwealth Soc., 2009–12; Interim Dir, Commonwealth Foundn, 2011–12 (on secondment). Non-exec. Dir, Equality Works Ltd, 2007–08. Trustee: Ockenden Internat., 2004–; Praxis Community Projects, 2006–12; Baring Foundn, 2009–; Internat. Alert, 2012–. Vice Pres. and Dir, Univ. of Sydney Union, 1995–97; Fellow, Univ. of Sydney Senate, 1996–97. Young Global Leader, WEF, 2012. *Publications:* (jtly) Brits Abroad: mapping the scale and nature of British emigration, 2006; (jtly) Development on the Move: measuring and optimising migration's social and economic impacts, 2010; (ed and contrib.) Queen and the Commonwealth, 2012; contrib. articles to learned jls incl. Contemp. S Asia, Geog., Health, Internat. Migration, Oxford Develt Studies, Social Policy Rev., Studies in Christian Ethics, Third World Qly and World Econs. *Recreations:* travel, family, planespotting. *Address:* CIVICUS House, 24 Gwigwi Mrwebi Street, Newtown 2001, Johannesburg, South Africa.

STABLE, His Honour (Rondle) Owen (Charles); QC 1963; a Circuit Judge, 1979–95; Senior Circuit Judge, Snaresbrook Crown Court, 1982–95; *b* 28 Jan. 1923; *yr s* of late Rt Hon. Sir Wintringham Norton Stable, MC, and Lucie Haden (*née* Freeman); *m* 1949, Yvonne Brook (*d* 2010), *y d* of late Maj. L. B. Holliday, OBE; two *d*. *Educ:* Winchester. Served with Rifle Bde, 1940–46 (Captain). Barrister, Middle Temple, 1948; Bencher, 1969. Dep. Chm., QS, Herts, 1963–71; a Recorder of the Crown Court, 1972–79. Board of Trade Inspector: Cadco Group of Cos, 1963–64; H. S. Whiteside & Co. Ltd, 1965–67; International Learning Systems Corp. Ltd, 1969–71; Pergamon Press, 1969–73. Sec. National Reference Tribunal for the Coal Mining Industry, 1953–64; Chancellor of Diocese of Bangor, 1959–88; Member, Governing Body of the Church in Wales, 1960–88; Licensed Parochial Lay Reader, Diocese of St Albans, 1961–2003; Member: General Council of the Bar, 1962–66; Senate of 4 Inns of Court, 1971–74; Senate of the Inns of Court and the Bar, 1974–75. Chm., Horserace Betting Levy Appeal Tribunal, 1969–74. Mem. Council, Benslow Music Trust, 1995–2001; Chm., Benslow Develt Appeal, 1995–2000. JP Hertfordshire, 1963–71. *Publications:* (with R. M. Stuttard) A Review of Coursing, 1971. *Recreations:* listening to music, playing the flute. *Address:* Buckler's Hall, Much Hadham, Herts SG10 6EB. *T:* (01279) 842604. *Club:* Boodle's.

STACE, Prof. Anthony John, PhD; FRS 2002; FRSC; Professor of Physical Chemistry, University of Nottingham, since 2004. *Educ:* Univ. of Essex (BA, PhD). Univ. of Sussex, 1974–77; Advanced Res. Fellow, SERC, Univ. of Southampton, 1977–83; Lectr, 1984–93, Prof. of Chemistry, 1993–2004, Univ. of Sussex. Tilden Medal and Lectr, RSC, 1995; Aston Medal, British Mass Spectrometry Soc., 2013. *Address:* School of Chemistry, University of Nottingham, University Park, Nottingham NG7 2RD.

STACEY, Hon. Lady; Valerie Elizabeth Stacey; a Senator of the College of Justice in Scotland, since 2009; a Judge of the Employment Appeal Tribunal, since 2013; *b* 25 May 1954; *d* of James and Helen Thom; *m* 1981, Andrew Stacey; two *s*. *Educ:* Elgin Acad.; Edinburgh Univ. (LLB Hons). Solicitor, 1978–86; admitted to Faculty of Advocates, 1987 (Vice Dean, 2004–07); Advocate Depute, 1993–96; Standing Jun. Counsel to Home Office in Scotland, 1996–99; Temp. Sheriff, 1997–99; QC (Scot.) 1999. Member: Sentencing Commn for Scotland, 2003–06; Judicial Appts Bd for Scotland, 2005–07. *Recreation:* listening to music. *Address:* Parliament House, Parliament Square, Edinburgh EH1 1RQ.

STACEY, Air Marshal Graham Edward, CB 2011; MBE 1988; Deputy Commander Joint Force Command Brunssum, since 2013; *b* London, 1 Sept. 1959; *s* of Kenneth and Kay Stacey; *m* 2007, Maria Stuttaford; one *s* one *d*. *Educ:* Epsom Coll.; Leeds Univ. (BSc Hons); King's Coll. London (MA). Joined RAF, 1980; in comd RAF Honington, 2001–03; Dep. Sen. British Mil. Advr, Iraq, 2003; rcds 2004; Asst COS J7 UK PJHQ, 2005–07; Dir, J3 Ops, NATO Jt Forces Comd Brunssum, 2007–09; Sen. British Mil. Advr, US Central Comd, 2009–10; Comdr British Forces Cyprus and Adminr Sovereign Base Areas, 2010–12. Chm., RAF Rugby Union, 2001–06. *Recreations:* travel, cycling, squash, amateur chef.

STACEY, Mary Elizabeth; Her Honour Judge Stacey; a Circuit Judge, since 2014; *b* 15 May 1961; *d* of Rev. Nicolas David Stacey, *qv*; *m* 2004, Stuart Bell; two *s*. *Educ:* Keble Coll., Oxford (BA Hons English 1982; MA). Admitted solicitor, 1987; solicitor in private practice, 1987–98; Partner and Hd of Equality, 1993–98, Consultant, 1999–2003, Thompsons, Solicitors; Chm., Industrial Tribunal, then Employment Tribunals, later Employment Judge, 2003–14 (part-time Chm., 1997–2003); a Recorder, 2007–14. Ind. Chair, Jt Negotiating Cttee for Higher Educn Staff, 2001–07. Dep. Chm., Central Arbitration Cttee, 2000–. Mem., Gtr London Magistrates' Courts Authy, 1999–2003 (Chm., Audit Cttee). Mem., CIPD (Law Faculty), 1995–2014. Chm., Industrial Law Soc., 2006–10 (Hon. Vice-Pres., 2011–). Chm., Visitatorial Bd, Oxford Univ., 2009–14; Ind. Mem. Council, Goldsmiths, Univ. of London, 2008–14; Mem., Equal Treatment Adv. Cttee, Judicial Coll., 2011–14. Trustee, Midlands Legal Support Trust, 2014–. *Publications:* Part-time Workers and the Law, 1995; Challenging Disability Discrimination at Work, 2001; Discrimination Law Handbook, 2002, 2nd edn 2006. *Address:* Birmingham Crown Court, Queen Elizabeth II Law Courts, 1 Newton Street, Birmingham B4 7NA.

STACEY, Michael Albert; Chairman: Meggitt plc, 2001–04 (Chief Executive Officer, 1995–2001); McKechnie Group, 2001–05; Dynacast International, 2002–05; *b* 25 Jan. 1939; *s* of William Robert Stacey and Ivy May Stacey; *m* 1st, 1962, Anne Jenkins (marr. diss. 1970); two *s*; 2nd, 1970, Jean Brymer (marr. diss. 1997); 3rd, 1997, Elizabeth Jane Collins. *Educ:* City of Bath Sch. for Boys; Univ. of Hull (BSc Hons Physics). Res. Officer, Joseph Lucas Res. Centre, 1960–70; prodn engr, mktg, and factory manager, 1970–82; Managing Director: Lucas Automotive Electronics, 1982–87; Lucas Aerospace UK, 1987–90; Meggitt Aerospace, 1990–94. Dir and Chm., Rubicon plc, 1994–99; Dep. Chm., Avio SpA, Italy, 2007–10; Director: Sidlaw plc, 1997–98; Vitec plc, 1999–2003; Marshalls plc, 2000–03. Director: Dorset Chamber of Commerce and Industry, 1995–2000; Dorset TEC, 1996–2001. *Recreations:* golf, Rugby, gardening. *Address:* 8 Highland Road, Wimborne, Dorset BH21 2QN. *Clubs:* Royal Air Force; Rushmore Golf.

STACEY, Morna Dorothy, (Mrs W. D. Stacey); *see* Hooker, M. D.

STACEY, Rev. Nicolas David; Chairman, East Thames Housing Group (formerly East London Housing Association), 1993–98; *b* 27 Nov. 1927; *s* of late David and Gwen Stacey; *m* 1955, Hon. Anne Bridgeman, *er d* of 2nd Viscount Bridgeman, KBE, CB, DSO, MC; one *s* two *d*. *Educ:* RNC, Dartmouth; St Edmund Hall, Oxford (hons degree Mod. Hist.); Cuddesdon Theol Coll., Oxford. Midshipman, HMS Anson, 1945–46; Sub-Lt, 1946–48. Asst Curate, St Mark's, Portsea, 1953–58; Domestic Chap. to Bp of Birmingham, 1958–60; Rector of Woolwich, 1960–68; Dean of London Borough of Greenwich, 1965–68; Dep. Dir of Oxfam, 1968–70; Director of Social Services: London Borough of Ealing, 1971–74; Kent County Council, 1974–85; Dir, AIDS Policy Unit, sponsored by Citizen Action, 1988–89. Vice-Chm., TV South Charitable Trust, 1988–92. Six Preacher, Canterbury Cathedral, 1984–89. Sporting career: internat. sprinter, 1948–52, incl. British Empire Games, 1949, and Olympic Games, 1952 (semi-finalist 200 metres and finalist 4×400 metres relay); Pres., OUAC, 1951; winner, Oxf. v Camb. 220 yds, 1948–51; Captain, Combined Oxf. and Camb. Athletic Team, 1951. Cross of St Augustine, 2005. *Publications:* Who Cares (autobiog.), 1971. *Address:* 9 City Gardens, Iron Bar Lane, Canterbury CT1 2HR. *T:* (01227) 785499. *E:* nicolasstacey@btinternet.com.
See also M. E. Stacey.

STACEY, Valerie Elizabeth; *see* Stacey, Hon. Lady.

STACEY, Very Rev. Victor George; Dean, St Patrick's Cathedral, Dublin, since 2012; *b* Newtownbarry, Co. Wexford, 19 March 1944; *s* of George William Stacey and Norah Eleanor Stacey (*née* Young). *Educ:* Kilkenny Coll.; Mountjoy Sch.; University Coll., Dublin (BA Hons; Dip. Applied Psychol.); Trinity Coll., Dublin; Queen's Univ., Belfast (MTh). Yorks Insurance Co. Ltd, 1960–66. Ordained deacon, 1972, priest, 1973; Assistant Curate: Derriaghy, 1972–76; Knock, 1976–79; Hd, Southern Church Mission, Down, 1979–86; Rector: Santry and Glasnevin, Dublin, 1986–95; Dun Laoghaire, Dublin, 1995–2012. *Recreations:* music, travel, theatre, walking, dining. *Address:* St Patrick's Cathedral, St Patrick's Close, Dublin 8, Ireland. *T:* (1) 4539472, *Fax:* (1) 4755449. *E:* dean@stpatrickscathedral.ie. *Clubs:* University (Dublin); Royal Irish Yacht; National Yacht.

STACK, Most Rev. George; *see* Cardiff, Archbishop of, (RC).

STACY, Graham Henry, CBE 1993; FCA; Chairman, Sanctuary Housing Association, 2004–09 (Treasurer, 1995–2004); *b* 23 May 1933; *s* of Norman Winny Stacy and Winifred Frances Stacy (*née* Wood); *m* 1958, Mary Fereday; one *s* three *d*. *Educ:* Stationers' Co.'s Sch. FCA 1955. Articled to Walter Smee Will & Co., 1950–55; Nat. Service, RN (Sub-Lieut), 1955–57; joined Price Waterhouse, 1957: Partner, 1968–93; Dir of Technical Services, 1976–88; Dir of Professional Standards (UK and Europe), 1988–93; Mem., Policy Cttee, 1987–93. Member: Auditing Practices Cttee, 1976–84; Accounting Standards Cttee, 1986–90; Accounting Standards Bd, 1990–94. Mem., Monopolies and Mergers, subseq. Competition, Commn, 1995–2001. Hon. Treas., URC in UK, 1995–2002. *Recreations:* bridge, reading, painting watercolours, DIY.

STADLEN, Hon. Sir Nicholas Felix, Kt 2007; a Judge of the High Court of Justice, Queen's Bench Division, 2007–13; *b* 3 May 1950; *s* of late Peter Stadlen and Hedi (*née* Simon); *m* 1972, Frances Edith Howarth, *d* of T. E. B. and Margaret Howarth; three *s*. *Educ:* St Paul's School (Scholar); Trinity Coll., Cambridge (Open Scholarship and McGill Exhibition; BA Hons Classics Part 1, History Part 2). Pres., Cambridge Union Soc., 1970. First in order of merit, Part 1 Bar Exams, 1975; called to the Bar, Inner Temple, 1976. QC 1991; Asst Recorder, 1997–2000; Recorder, 2000–07. Mem., Bar Council Public Affairs Cttee, 1987; Chm., Bar Caribbean pro bono Cttee, 1999–2007. Chm. of Trustees, Volunteer Reading Help, 2005–08. First Sec., British-Irish Assoc., 1972–74. *Publications:* (with Michael Barnes) Gulbenkian Foundation Reports on National Music and Drama Education, 1974–75; (contrib.) Convention: an account of the 1976 US Democratic Party Presidential Nominating Convention, 1976. *Recreation:* listening to classical music.

STAFFORD, 15th Baron *cr* 1640; **Francis Melfort William Fitzherbert;** DL; Chancellor, Staffordshire University, since 2014; *b* 13 March 1954; *s* of 14th Baron Stafford and of Morag Nada, *yr d* of late Lt-Col Alastair Campbell; *S* father, 1986; *m* 1980, Katharine Mary Codrington; two *s* two *d*. *Educ:* Ampleforth College; Reading Univ.; RAC, Cirencester. Director (non-executive): Tarmac Industrial Products Div., 1987–93; Mid Staffs Mental Health Foundn, 1990–99; Hanley Economic BS, 1992–2014 (Vice Chm., 2005–14). Pro-Chancellor, Keele Univ., 1993–2004. Pres., Staffs CCC, 1999–2008; Pres. and Patron various orgns in North Staffs. Chm., Countryside Learning, 2010–. Governor, Harper Adams University (formerly Agricl) Coll., 1990–2007 (Chm. Govs, 2004–07). DL Stafford, 1994; High Sheriff, Staffs, 2005. DUniv: Keele, 2005; Staffs, 2006; Hon. DLitt Harper Adams, 2009; Hon. DSc Aston, 2011. *Recreations:* shooting, cricket, golf. *Heir:* *s* Hon. Benjamin John Basil Fitzherbert [*b* 8 Nov. 1983; *m* 2011, Georgina, *d* of Hon. Thomas Anthony Hewlett]. *Address:* Swynnerton Park, Stone, Staffordshire ST15 0QE. *T:* (01782) 796228. *Club:* Lord's Taverners.

STAFFORD, Marquis of; James Granville Egerton; *b* 12 Aug. 1975; *s* and *heir* of Duke of Sutherland, *qv*; *m* 2007, Barbara Ruth, *d* of Dr Graham Schneider, Vienna; four *d*. *Educ:* Eton Coll., Windsor; Univ. of Edinburgh. *Address:* Ley Farm, Stetchworth, Newmarket, Suffolk CB8 9TX.

STAFFORD, Bishop Suffragan of, since 2010; **Rt Rev. Geoffrey Peter Annas;** *b* London, 29 Nov. 1953; *s* of Derek and Betty Annas; *m* 1987, Ann Clover; one *s* one *d*. *Educ:* Therfield County Secondary Sch., Leatherhead; Univ. of Leicester (BA Hons Sociol. 1975; DipSW, CQSW 1977); Salisbury and Wells Theol Coll. (BTh Hons Southampton 1983). Sen. Social Worker, Surrey CC, 1975–80; ordained deacon, 1983, priest, 1984; Curate, Holy Trinity with St Matthew, Elephant and Castle, Dio. of Southwark, 1983–87; Team Vicar, St Christopher's, Walworth, and Coll. Missioner, Pembroke Coll., Cambridge, 1987–94; Vicar, St Christopher's, Thornhill, Southampton, 1994–2010; Theatre Chaplaincy UK (formerly Actors' Church Union)): Chaplain, Mayflower Th., Southampton, 1996–2010, Regent Th., Stoke on Trent, 2011–; Mem. Council, 2009–. Asst Area Dean, Southampton, 2007–10; Canon, Winchester Cathedral, 2007–10. *Recreations:* theatre (Actors' Church Union Chaplain of Regent Theatre, Stoke on Trent), holidays in Greece. *Address:* Ash Garth, 6a Broughton Crescent, Barlaston, Stoke on Trent ST12 9DD. *T:* (01782) 373308, *Fax:* (01782) 373705. *E:* bishop.stafford@lichfield.anglican.org.

STAFFORD, Andrew Bruce; QC 2000; *b* 30 March 1957; *s* of Cyril Henry Stafford and Audrey Estelle Stafford; *m* 1982, Catherine Anne, *d* of Derek and Kathleen Johnson; one *s* four *d*. *Educ:* Royal Grammar Sch., Newcastle upon Tyne; Trinity Hall, Cambridge (BA Law, MA). Called to the Bar, Middle Temple, 1980, Bencher 2008. Part-time Chm., Employment Tribunals, 2000–08. Jt Editor, Transfer of Undertakings, 2006–; Mem., Adv. Bd, Gore-Browne on Companies, 2007–. *Publications:* (with Stuart Ritchie) Fiduciary Duties: directors and employees, 2008, 2nd edn 2015. *Recreations:* art, theatre, Newcastle United, Apostrophe Chambers. *Address:* Kobre & Kim LLP, Tower 42, 25 Old Broad Street, EC2N 1HQ. *Club:* Athenæum.

STAFFORD, David Valentine; Secretary, Economic and Social Research Council, 1988–90; *b* 14 Feb. 1930; *s* of Augustus Everard and Emily Blanche Stafford; *m* 1953, Aileen Patricia Wood; one *s* one *d*. *Educ:* Rutlish School, Merton. Dept of Educn and Science, 1951–88; Sec., Open Univ. Planning Cttee, 1967–69. Acting Chm., ESRC, Feb.–Sept. 1988. *Recreations:* reading, gardening. *Address:* 10 Duke Street, Bath, Somerset BA2 4AG. *T:* (01225) 938479.
See also N. D. Stafford.

STAFFORD, Prof. Nicholas David, FRCS; Professor of Head and Neck Surgery and Otolaryngology, University of Hull, 1995–2015 (Director, Postgraduate Medical Institute (formerly Head, Postgraduate School of Medicine), 1997–2012); Director, Research and Development, Hull and East Yorkshire Hospitals NHS Trust, since 2013; *b* 13 Aug. 1954; *s* of David Valentine Stafford, *qv*; *m* 1977, Heather Gay Sims; four *d*. *Educ:* Farnborough Grammar Sch.; Univ. of Leeds (MB ChB 1977). FRCS 1983. Various SHO posts, 1978–82; Registrar in ENT Surgery, RNTNEH, 1982–84; Sen. Registrar in ENT/Head and Neck Surgery, Royal Marsden Hosp. and St Mary's Hosp., London, 1985–89; Consultant Head and Neck/ENT Surgeon, St Mary's, Ealing and Charing Cross Hosps, 1989–95. Résident Etranger, Inst. Gustave-Roussy, Paris, 1987–88. Chm. Trustees, Hull and E Yorks Med. Res. Centre Appeal, 2002–; Trustee, Hull and E Yorks Cardiac Trust Fund, 2006–. *Publications:* (with R. Youngs) Colour Aids: ENT, 1988, 3rd edn 2006; (ed with J. Waldron) Management of Oral Cancer, 1989; contribs mainly in field of head and neck oncology. *Recreation:* classic cars. *Address:* 29 Eastgate, Beverley HU17 0DR. *T:* (01482) 871541. *Clubs:* Alvis Owners; Abarth Owners.

STAFFORD, Peter Moore, FCA; Director and Trustee, Rathbone Training Ltd, 2002–11; Member, Board of Partners, Deloitte & Touche (formerly Touche Ross & Co.), 1990–2000 (Chairman, 1992–95); *b* 24 April 1942; *s* of late Harry Shaw Stafford and May Alexandra (*née* Moore); *m* 1973, Elspeth Anne, *d* of James Steel Harvey; one *s* one *d*. *Educ:* Charterhouse. FCA 1976 (ACA 1965). Articled Clerk, Garnett Crewdson & Co., Manchester, 1960–64; Arthur Andersen, 1966–68; Partner, 1968–71, Garnett Crewdson & Co., merged with Spicer & Oppenheim: Partner, 1971–90; Managing Partner, 1990; merged with Touche Ross & Co. Member: Council for Industry and Higher Educn, 1993–97; Professional Standards Dept, ICAEW, 1998–2002. Governor, Terra Nova Sch., 1976–2004. *Recreations:* travel, gardening. *Address:* Goostrey, Cheshire. *T:* (01477) 533339. *Clubs:* Royal Over-Seas League; St James's (Manchester) (Hon. Treas., 2002–04).

STAFFORD-CLARK, Maxwell Robert Guthrie Stewart, (Max); artistic director and founder, Out of Joint Theatre Company, since 1993; *b* 17 March 1941; *s* of late Dr David Stafford-Clark, FRCP, FRCPsych and Dorothy Stewart (*née* Oldfield); *m* 1st, 1971, Carole Hayman; 2nd, 1981, Ann Pennington; one *d*; 3rd, 2010, Stella Feehily. *Educ:* Felsted School; Riverdale Country Day School, NY; Trinity College, Dublin. Associate dir, Traverse, 1966, artistic dir, 1968–70; dir, Traverse Workshop Co., 1970–74; founder, Joint Stock Theatre Group, 1974; Artistic Dir, English Stage Company at Royal Court Theatre, 1979–93. Productions include: Cloud 9, 1980; Top Girls, 1982; Falkland Sound, 1983; Tom and Viv, Rat in the Skull, 1984; Serious Money, 1987; Our Country's Good, 1988; King Lear, 1993; The Steward of Christendom, 1995; Shopping and Fucking, 1996; Blue Heart, 1997; Feelgood, 2001; Duck, The Permanent Way, 2003, Macbeth, Talking to Terrorists, 2004; O Go My Man, The Overwhelming, 2006; The Convict's Opera, 2008; Dreams of Violence, Mixed Up North, 2009; Andersen's English, The Big Fellah, 2010; A Dish of Tea with Dr Johnson, Bang Bang Bang, 2011; This May Hurt a Bit, Pitcairn, 2014; Crouch, Touch, Pause, Engage, All That Fall, 2015. *Publications:* Letters to George, 1989; Taking Stock, 2006; Our Country's Good: page to stage, 2010; Journal of the Plague Year, 2014. *Address:* 7 Thane Works, Thane Villas, N7 7NU.

STAFFORD SMITH, Clive Adrian, OBE 2000; Founder and Counsel, Reprieve; *b* 9 July 1959; *s* of Richard Stafford Smith and Jean Stafford Smith; *m* 1998, Emily MacSween Bolton; one *s*. *Educ:* Radley Coll., Abingdon; Univ. of North Carolina, Chapel Hill (John Motley Morehead Scholar; BA Pol Sci. 1981); Columbia Law Sch., NY (Harlan Fiske Stone Merit Scholar 1982, 1983, 1984; JD 1984). Staff attorney, Southern Prisoners' Defense Cttee, subseq. Southern Center for Human Rights, Atlanta, Ga, 1984–93; Dir, Louisiana Capital Assistance Center, New Orleans, 1993–2004. Patron, Lifelines. Documentaries: Fourteen Days in May, 1987; The Journey, 1988; Murder in Room 1215, 1997; The Death Belt, 2003; Torture (presenter), 2005. Hon. LLM Wolverhampton, 2001; Hon. DCL City, 2006; Hon. DLaws: Staffs, 2006; Oxford Brookes, 2008; Exeter, 2009; Bath, 2011; Bournemouth, 2011. Lifetime Achievement Award, Law Soc., 2003; Benjamin Smith Award, ACLU, La, 2004; Gandhi Peace Award, 2005; Contrarian Prize, 2014. *Publications:* (contrib.) A Punishment in Search of a Crime, 1989; Bad Men: Guantanamo and the secret prisons, 2007; Injustice, 2012. *Address:* Reprieve, PO Box 72054, London, EC3P 3BZ. *T:* (020) 7553 8140, *Fax:* (020) 7553 8189. *E:* clive@reprieve.org.uk. *Club:* Chelsea Arts.

STAGG, Sir (Charles) Richard (Vernon), KCMG 2008 (CMG 2001); HM Diplomatic Service, retired; Chairman, Rothschild (India), since 2015; *b* 27 Sept. 1955; *s* of Walter and Elise Patricia Stagg; *m* 1982, Arabella Clare Faber; three *s* two *d*. *Educ:* Winchester; Oriel Coll., Oxford. Joined Diplomatic Service, 1977; FCO, 1977–79; Sofia, 1979–82; The Hague, 1982–85; FCO, 1985–86; UK Repn to EC, Brussels, 1987–88; FCO, 1988–91; UK Repn to EC, Brussels, 1991–93; Private Sec. to Foreign Sec., 1993–96; Head, EU (Ext.) Dept, FCO, 1996–98; Ambassador to Bulgaria, 1998–2001; Dir of Information, 2001–03, Dir Gen. (Corporate Affairs), 2003–07, FCO; High Comr to India, 2007–11; Ambassador to Afghanistan, 2012–15. *Recreations:* racing, gardening. *Clubs:* Turf, Beefsteak; Millennium.

STAHEL, Rolf; Chairman, Chesyl Pharma Ltd, since 2003; non-executive Chairman: Connexios Lifesciences Pvt Ltd, Bangalore, since 2009; Midatech Ltd, since 2014; Ergomed Clinical Research Ltd, since 2014; *b* 21 April 1944; *s* of Hermann Stahel and Bluette Maillard; *m* 1970, Ewa Stachurska; two *s*. *Educ:* Kantonsschule, Lucerne (Dip. Kfm (CH) Business Studies, 1962; Handels Matura, 1963); 97th AMP, Harvard. Sales Administration, Rhône Poulenc, Switzerland, 1963–67; Wellcome: Rep., UK, 1967; Asst Manager, Switzerland, 1968; Gen. Manager, Italy, 1969–74; Man. Dir, Wellcome Thailand, 1974–79; Regl Dir, Wellcome Singapore, 1979–90; Dir of Marketing, Wellcome plc, UK, 1990–94; Chief Exec., Shire Pharmaceuticals Gp plc, 1994–2003. Non-executive Chairman: Newron Pharmaceuticals SPA, 2004–14; PowderMed Ltd, 2005–06; Cosmo SPA, 2006–12 (Dep. Chm., 2004–06); EUSA Pharma Inc., 2007–12. Mem., Adv. Bd, Imperial Coll. Business Sch., 2007–. FRSA 1996; MInstD 1997. CEO of Year, Global Pharmaceutical Award, Informa, 2001; Techmark award, 2003; UK Lifetime Achievement Award, Bioindustry Assoc., 2009. *Recreations:* golf, opera, musicals. *Address:* Neatham, Sleepers Hill, Winchester, Hants SO22 4NB. *T:* (01962) 868224. *E:* rstahel@chesyl.com. *Clubs:* Royal Automobile, Harvard Business School; South Winchester Golf.

STAINES, Paul DeLaire; Director and Chief Investment Officer, Global & General Nominees Ltd (Hong Kong), since 2009; Founder and Editor, Guido Fawkes, since 2004; *b* London, 11 Feb. 1967; *s* of Terril DeLaire Staines and Mary DeLaire Staines; *m* 2003, Orla Murphy; two *d*. *Educ:* Salvatorian Coll., Harrow. Broker, Capital Mkts, Yamaichi Europe, London, 1996–97; Fund Manager, Mondial Global Investors LLC, 1997–2001; Trader, Westminster Investors (Bahamas) Ltd, 2002–03; Investment Advisor: United Growth Opportunities LLC, 2004–05; Global & Gen. Nominees Ltd, St Kitts and Nevis, 2007–11; Co-Founder and Man. Dir, MessageSpace Ltd, 2011–13. *Publications:* In the Grip of the Sandinistas: human rights in Nicaragua, 1979–89, 1989; The Big Red Book of New Labour Sleaze, 2007. *T:* 07092 840531, *Fax:* 07092 012337. *E:* paul.staines@order-order.com. *Club:* St Anne's Waterford Tennis.

STAIR, 14th Earl of, *cr* 1703; **John David James Dalrymple;** Bt 1664 and 1698 (Scot); Viscount Stair, Lord Glenluce and Stranraer, 1690; Viscount Dalrymple, Lord Newliston, 1703; Baron Oxenfoord (UK), 1841; *b* 4 Sept. 1961; *s* of 13th Earl of Stair, KCVO, MBE and of Davina Katharine, *d* of late Hon. Sir David Bowes-Lyon, KCVO; *S* father, 1996; *m* 2006, Hon. Emily Mary Julia Stonor, 2nd *d* of Baron Camoys, *qv*; one *s* one *d*. Commnd Scots Guards, 1982. Elected Mem., H of L, 2008. *Heir: s* Viscount Dalrymple, *qv*.

STAIR, Claire; *see* Wilcox, C.

STAIR, Julian Francis, PhD; potter, since 1981; *b* 9 March 1955; *s* of Derek Anthony Guthrie (*né* Plank) and Christine Marie Stair (*née* Kelly); *m* 1992, Claire Wilcox, *qv*; two *d* (one *s* decd). *Educ:* Camberwell Sch. of Art (BA Hons 1978); Royal Coll. of Art (MA 1981; PhD 2003). Sen. Lectr, Univ. of Surrey, 1983–98. Fellow in Craft and Criticism, Univ. of Newcastle, 1997–99; Vis. Lectr, Brighton Univ., Westminster Univ. and Cardiff Univ., 1998–2006; Vis. Prof. of Ceramics and Theory, Camberwell Coll. of Art, Univ. of London, 2003–; Res. Fellow, RCA, 2004. Crafts Council: Trustee, 2000–06; Interim Chm., 2005–06; Dep. Chm., 2006–08. Trustee, Contemporary Applied Arts, 1997–2003. FRSA. *Publications:* (ed) The Body Politic: the role of the body and contemporary craft, 2000; (contrib.) The Persistence of Craft, ed by Paul Greenhalgh, 2002; contribs to The Times, Art in America, Crafts, Ceramic Review and New Art Examiner. *Recreations:* croquet, bird watching, walking, cinema. *Address:* 127 Court Lane, Dulwich, SE21 7EE. *T:* (020) 8693 8012. *E:* studio@julianstair.com.

STAITE, Sara Elizabeth, (Mrs John Peet); Her Honour Judge Staite; a Circuit Judge, since 2010; *b* Sussex, 17 Aug. 1957; *d* of Anthony Staite; *m* 1990, John Peet; two *s* one *d*. *Educ:* Cheltenham Ladies' Coll.; Leeds Univ. (LLB). Called to the Bar, Inner Temple, 1979; in practice as a barrister specialising in ancillary relief, 1980–2010. *Recreations:* walking, gardening, theatre. *Address:* Chelmsford County Court, Priory Place, New London Road, Chelmsford CM2 0PP.

STAMER, Sir Peter (Tomlinson), 6th Bt *cr* 1809, of Beauchamp, Dublin; *b* 19 Nov. 1951; *o s* of Sir (Lovelace) Anthony Stamer, 5th Bt and Stella Huguette (*née* Binnie); *S* father, 2012; *m* 1st, 1979, Dinah Louise Berry (marr. diss. 1989); one *s* one *d*; 2nd, 1999, Vera Řeháková (marr. diss. 2002). *Educ:* Malvern; Southampton Univ. RAF 1972–89 (Sqdn Ldr 1988). *Heir: s* William Peter Alexander Stamer, *b* 20 Sept. 1983.

STAMP, family name of **Baron Stamp**.

STAMP, 4th Baron *cr* 1938, of Shortlands; **Trevor Charles Bosworth Stamp,** MD; FRCP; Hon. Consultant Physician, Royal National Orthopaedic Hospital, since 1999; Consultant Physician and Director, Department of Bone and Mineral Metabolism, Institute of Orthopaedics, Royal National Orthopaedic Hospital, 1974–99; *b* 18 Sept. 1935; *s* of 3rd Baron Stamp, MD, FRCPath and Frances Hammond (*d* 1998), *d* of late Charles Henry Bosworth, Evanston, Illinois, USA; *S* father, 1987; *m* 1st, 1963, Anne Carolynn Churchill (marr. diss. 1971); two *d*; 2nd, 1975, Carol Anne (marr. diss. 1997), *d* of late Robert Keith Russell; one *s* one *d*. *Educ:* The Leys School; Gonville and Caius Coll., Cambridge; Yale Univ.; St Mary's Hosp. Medical School. MSc (Yale) 1957; MD (Cantab) 1972; FRCP 1978. Qualified in medicine, 1960; Med. Registrar, Professorial Medical Unit, St Mary's Hosp., 1964–66; Hon. Senior Registrar 1968–73, and Hon. Sen. Lecturer 1972–73, Dept of Human Metabolism, University College Hosp. and Medical School; Hon. Consultant Physician and Sen. Lectr, Middlesex Hosp. and UCL School of Medicine, 1974–99, now Emeritus Consultant, UCL Hosps. Mem., Scientific Adv. Bd, Nat. Osteoporosis Soc. Patron, Nat. Assoc. for Relief of Paget's Disease; Vice-Patron, British Sch. of Osteopathy. Hon. Life Member: Bone and Tooth Soc.; Internat. Skeletal Soc. Prix André Lichtwitz, France, 1973. *Publications:* numerous papers on disorders of mineral metabolism. *Recreations:* music, golf, contract bridge. *Heir: s* Hon. Nicholas Charles Trevor Stamp, *b* 27 Feb. 1978.

STAMP, Gavin Mark, MA, PhD; FSA; architectural historian and writer; *b* 15 March 1948; *s* of Barry Hartnell Stamp and Norah Clare (*née* Rich); *m* 1st, 1982, Alexandra Frances Artley (marr. diss. 2007); two *d*; 2nd, 2014, Rosemary Hill. *Educ:* Dulwich Coll.; Gonville and Caius Coll., Cambridge (MA, PhD). Lectr, 1990–99, Sen. Lectr, 1999–2003, Mackintosh Sch. of Architecture, Glasgow Sch. of Art; Mellon Sen. Fellow and Bye-Fellow, Gonville and Caius Coll., Cambridge, 2003–04. Hon. Prof., Univ. of Cambridge, 2010–. Contributor to The Spectator, The Independent, Daily Telegraph, Private Eye, Architects' Jl, etc. Chm., Twentieth Century (formerly Thirties) Soc., 1983–2007; Founder and Chm., Alexander Thomson Soc., 1991–2003. Hon. Prof., Glasgow Univ., 2003. FSA 1998. Hon. FRIAS 1994; Hon. FRIBA 1998. *Publications:* The Architect's Calendar, 1973; Silent Cities, 1977; (text only) Temples of Power, 1979; (jtly) The Victorian Buildings of London 1837–1887, 1980; Robert Weir Schultz and his work for the Marquesses of Bute, 1981; The Great Perspectivists, 1982; The Changing Metropolis, 1984; The English House 1860–1914, 1986; (jtly) The Church in Crisis, 1986; The Telephone Boxes, 1989; (ed jtly) Greek Thomson, 1994; (ed) Recollections of Sir Gilbert Scott, 1995; Alexander 'Greek' Thomson, 1999; Edwin Lutyens Country Houses, 2001; (ed jtly) Lutyens Abroad, 2002; An Architect of Promise: George Gilbert Scott junior and the late Gothic revival, 2002; The Memorial to the Missing of the Somme, 2006; Britain's Lost Cities, 2007; Lost Victorian Britain, 2010; Anti-Ugly: excursions in English architecture and design, 2013; articles in Arch. History, Arch. Design, Jl of RSA, etc. *Address:* 15 Belle Vue Court, Devonshire Road, SE23 3SY. *E:* gavin.stamp@btopenworld.com.

STAMP, Malcolm Frederick, CBE 2002; Chief Executive, Metro North Hospital and Health Service, Brisbane, Queensland, 2013–14; *b* 29 Dec. 1952; *s* of Frederick and Elizabeth Stamp; *m* Linda (marr. diss.); two *d*. *Educ:* Stand Grammar Sch. Unit Gen. Manager, N Manchester HA, 1982–86; District General Manager: Crewe HA, 1986–88; Liverpool HA, 1988–90; Chief Executive: Royal Liverpool Univ. Hosps NHS Trust, 1990–94; Norfolk and Norwich Univ. Hosp. NHS Trust, 1994–2002; Addenbrooke's NHS Trust, then Cambridge Univ. Hosps NHS Foundn Trust, 2002–06; Waikato Dist Health Bd, 2006–07; Provider Agency, NHS London, 2007–09; University Hosps Coventry and Warwickshire NHS Trust, 2009–11; Mid Essex Hosp. Service NHS Trust, 2011–13. Mem., IMS, 1975; MIHM 1978. Hon. DCL UEA, 2000. *Publications:* Appraisal for Consultants in the NHS, 2000. *Recreations:* football, gardening, family.

STAMP, Terence Henry; actor and author; *b* 22 July 1938; *s* of Thomas Stamp and Ethel Esther Perrott. *Educ:* Plaistow County Grammar School; Webber-Douglas Dramatic Acad. (Amhurst Webber Meml Schol., 1958). *Films include:* Billy Budd, 1962; The Collector, 1964; Far from the Madding Crowd, 1966; Blue, 1967; Spirits of the Dead (Fellini sect.), 1967; Theorem, 1968; Superman, 1977; Meetings with Remarkable Men, 1977; Superman 2, 1978; The Hit, 1984; Legal Eagles, 1985; Wall Street, 1987; Young Guns, 1988; The Sicilian, 1988; Prince of Shadows, or Beltenebros, 1993; The Real McCoy, 1994; The Adventures of Priscilla the Queen of the Desert, 1994; Bliss, 1995; Limited Edition, 1995; Kiss the Sky, 1998; Love Walked In, 1998; The Limey, 1999; Red Planet, 2000; My Wife is an Actress, 2002; My Boss's Daughter, 2003; The Haunted Mansion, 2003; These Foolish Things, 2006; Valkyrie, 2009; Song for Marion, 2013; *stage:* Alfie, Morosco, NY, 1965; Dracula, Shaftesbury, 1978; Lady from the Sea, Roundhouse, 1979. Launched, with Elizabeth Buxton, Stamp Collection range of organic food, 1994. Hon. DArts East London, 1993. *Publications:* autobiography: Stamp Album, 1987; Coming Attractions, 1988; Double Feature, 1989; The Night (novel), 1992; (with Elizabeth Buxton) The Stamp Collection Cookbook, 1997; Rare Stamps: reflections on living, breathing, and acting, 2012. *Club:* New York Athletic (New York).

STANAGE, Rt Rev. Thomas Shaun; Bishop of Bloemfontein, 1982–97; *b* 6 April 1932; *s* of late Robert and Edith Clarice Stanage. *Educ:* King James I Grammar Sch., Bishop Auckland; Univ. of Oxford (MA, Hons Theology, 1956). Curate, St Faith, Great Crosby, 1958–61; Minister of Conventional District of St Andrews, Orford, 1961–63; Vicar, St Andrew, Orford, 1963–70; Rector, All Saints, Somerset West, 1970–75; Dean of Kimberley, 1975–78; Bishop Suffragan of Johannesburg, 1978–82. Liaison Bishop to Missions to Seafarers, Southern Africa. Lectr in Systematic Theol., Biblical Studies and Religious Educn, Univ. of Orange Free State, 1998–2001. Hon. DD Nashotah Theol Sem., Wisconsin, 1986. *Recreation:* music (organ, violin and piano). *Address:* Walden, 42a Union Avenue, Waverley, Bloemfontein 9301, S Africa. *Clubs:* Bloemfontein; Good Hope Flying, Cape Aero (Cape Town).

STANBRIDGE, Roger Andrew; Headteacher, Stratford-upon-Avon Grammar School for Girls, 1991–2005; *b* 22 June 1948; *s* of Bert and Kit Stanbridge; *m* 1972, Sandy Black; three *d*. *Educ:* Varndean Boys' Grammar Sch., Brighton; Hull Univ. (BSc 1969); Univ. of Newcastle upon Tyne. Hd of Sci., Moulton Sch., Northampton, 1980–87; Dep. Headteacher, Stratford-upon-Avon Grammar Sch. for Girls, 1987–91. Principal Examiner: for Cambridge Assessment (formerly Univ. of Cambridge Local Exams Syndicate), 1988–; for Edexcel, 2005–09. *Recreations:* overseas travel, supporter of Brighton and Hove Albion FC. *E:* zen79983@zen.co.uk.

STANBROOK, Clive St George Clement, OBE 1987; QC 1989; Senior Counsel, McDermott Will & Emery Belgium LLP (formerly Stanbrook & Hooper, then McDermott, Will & Emery/Stanbrook), since 2013 (Partner, 1980–2013); *b* 10 April 1948; *s* of late Ivor Robert Stanbrook and Joan Stanbrook (*née* Clement); *m* 1971, Julia Suzanne Hillary; one *s* three *d*. *Educ:* Dragon Sch.; Westminster; University Coll. London. Called to the Bar, Inner Temple, 1972; called to Turks and Caicos Bar, 1986, New York Bar, 1988. Founded Stanbrook & Hooper, 1980. President: British Chamber of Commerce for Belgium and Luxembourg, 1985–87; Exec. Cttee, Overseas Countries and Territories Assoc., EU, 2004–08. *Publications:* Extradition: the law and practice, 1979, 2nd edn 2000; Dumping: manual of EEC rules, 1980; Dumping and Subsidies, 1982, 3rd edn (with A. P. Bentley) 1996. *Recreations:* tennis, travel. *Address:* McDermott Will & Emery Belgium LLP, Avenue des Nerviens 9–31, Brussels 1040, Belgium.

STANCIOFF, Ivan; Ambassador-at-Large for Bulgaria, since 1994; *b* 1 April 1929; *s* of late Ivan Robert Stancioff and Marion (*née* Mitchell); *m* 1st, 1957, Deirdre O'Donnell (marr. diss.); two *s* two *d*; 2nd, Alexandra Lawrence. *Educ:* Georgetown Univ., Washington (BA); New York Univ. Sch. of Business. Economist, Amer. and Foreign Power Corp., 1957–60; Dir Marketing, IBM World Trade Corp., São Paulo, 1961–63; Rio, 1963–65; Paris, 1965–70; Manager, ITT, Athens, 1970; Vice-Pres., ITEL Corp., London, 1971–74; Dir, Safestore Ltd, London, 1975–77; Vice-Pres., Storage Technol. Corp., London, 1977–81; Dir, Cresta Marketing SA, Geneva, 1981–90; Advr to UDF, Sofia, 1990–91; Ambassador to UK, 1991–94; Minister of Foreign Affairs, Bulgaria, 1994–95. Dir, Inst. for Intercultural Relations, Sofia, 1992; Chm., Karin Dom Foundn, 1995–. FLS. Good Conduct Medal, US Army, 1956; Commander, Legion of Honour (France), 1994; Grand Cross, Rio Branco (Brazil), 2002; Star of Solidarity, Italy, 2006; Stara Planina 1st cl., Bulgaria, 2010. *Recreations:* history, gardening, travel, painting. *Address:* 28 Cresswell Place, SW10 9RB.

STANCLIFFE, Rt Rev. David Staffurth, FRSCM; Bishop of Salisbury, 1993–2010; an Honorary Assistant Bishop: Diocese of Europe, since 2011; Diocese of Durham, since 2013; *b* 1 Oct. 1942; *s* of late Very Rev. Michael Staffurth Stancliffe; *m* 1965, Sarah Loveday Smith; one *s* two *d*. *Educ:* Westminster School; Trinity College, Oxford (MA; Hon. Fellow 2003); Cuddesdon Theological College. Assistant Curate, St Bartholomew's, Armley, Leeds, 1967–70; Chaplain to Clifton Coll., Bristol, 1970–77; Canon Residentiary of Portsmouth Cathedral, Diocesan Director of Ordinands and Lay Ministry Adviser, 1977–82; Provost of Portsmouth, 1982–93. Hon. Fellow, 1999–2010, Fellow, 2010–, St Chad's Coll., Durham. Member: Gen. Synod, 1985–2010; Liturgical Commn, 1986–2005 (Chm., 1993–2005); Cathedrals' Fabric Commn, 1991–2001. Pres., Council, Marlborough Coll., 1994–2010. Vice-Pres., RSCM, 2005–. FRSCM 2001; Hon. FGCM 2005. Hon. DLitt Portsmouth, 1993; DD Lambeth, 2004. *Publications:* God's Pattern: shaping our worship, ministry and life, 2003; The Pilgrim Prayer Book, 2003; Celebrating Daily Prayer, 2005; The Lion Companion to Church Architecture, 2008; The Gospels in Art, Music and Literature: the story of salvation in three media, 2014. *Recreations:* old music, Italy. *Address:* Butts House, 15 The Butts, Stanhope, Bishop Auckland, Co. Durham DL13 2UQ. *T:* (01388) 526912. *E:* d.s.stancliffe@durham.ac.uk.

See also M. J. Stancliffe.

STANCLIFFE, Martin John, FSA; RIBA; Surveyor to the Fabric, St Paul's Cathedral, 1990–2011, Surveyor Emeritus, 2013; *b* 28 Dec. 1944; *s* of Very Rev. Michael Staffurth Stancliffe and Barbara Elizabeth Tatlow; *m* 1979, Sara Judith Sanders; two *d*. *Educ:* Westminster Sch.; Magdalene Coll., Cambridge (MA, DipArch). AABC. Dir, Martin Stancliffe Architects, 1975–2004; Partner (formerly Strategy Partner, then Sen. Principal), Purcell (formerly Purcell Miller Tritton), 2004–15, now Consultant. Architect to: Lichfield Cath., 1983–2003; Southwell Minster, 1989–2009; Christ Church Cath., Oxford, 1990–95; Consultant Architect to Canterbury Cath., 2014–. Member: Exec. Cttee, Council for the Care of Churches, 1980–91; Cathedrals' Fabric Commn for England, 1991–2001;

Archbishops' Commn on Cathedrals, 1992–94; Historic Bldgs and Areas Adv. Cttee, English Heritage, 1995–2001; Expert Adv. Panel on Bldgs and Land, Heritage Lottery Fund, 1997–99; Cultural Tourism Cttee, ICOMOS UK, 1997–; Fabric Adv. Cttee, York Minster, 2007–. Chairman: Cathedral Architects Assoc., 1999–2005; York Consortium for Conservation and Craftsmanship, 2005–. Trustee: York Civic Trust, 2008–; Landmark Trust, 2011–. Marvin Breckinridge Patterson Lectr, Univ. of Maryland, 2000. Hon. Vis. Fellow, Dept of Archaeol., Univ. of York, 2002–. FSA 1995. *Publications:* (contrib.) St Paul's: the Cathedral Church of London 604–2004, 2004. *Recreations:* the baroque oboe, old buildings, sailing. *Address:* 16 Bootham Terrace, York YO30 7DH. *T:* (01904) 630105.

See also Rt Rev. D. S. Stancliffe.

STANDAGE, Simon Andrew Thomas; violinist; *b* 8 Nov. 1941; *s* of Thomas Ralph Standage and Henrietta Florence Sugg; *m* 1964, Jennifer Ward; three *s*. *Educ:* Bryanston Sch.; King's Coll., Cambridge (MA). Harkness Fellow, 1967–69; Sub-leader, English Chamber Orch., 1974–78; leader and soloist, English Concert, 1973–91; Founder and Leader, Salomon String Quartet, 1981–; founded Collegium Musicum 90, 1990; Associate Dir, Acad. of Ancient Music, 1991–95. Professor of Baroque Violin: Royal Acad. of Music, 1983–; Dresdner Akademie für Alte Musik, 1993–2004; Franz Liszt Acad. of Music, 2010–. Has made numerous recordings. Hon. RAM 2009. Georg Philipp Telemann Prize, City of Magdeburg, 2010; Medal of Honour, Polish Min. of Culture and Nat. Heritage, 2008. *Recreation:* crosswords. *Address:* 106 Hervey Road, Blackheath, SE3 8BX. *T:* (020) 8319 3372.

See also T. W. Standage.

STANDAGE, Thomas William; Deputy Editor and Head of Digital Strategy, The Economist, since 2015; *b* London, 1969; *s* of Simon Andrew Thomas Standage, *qv*; *m* 1996, Kirstin McKee; one *s* one *d*. *Educ:* Dulwich Coll.; Worcester Coll., Oxford (BEng Engrg and Computer Sci.). Freelance journalist and photographer, 1992–96; Dep. Ed., Technol., Daily Telegraph, 1996–98; The Economist: Sci. and Technol. Corresp., 1998–2003; Technol. Ed., 2003–06; Business Ed., 2006–09; Business Affairs Ed., 2009–10; Digital Ed., 2010–15. *Publications:* The Victorian Internet, 1998, 3rd edn 2014; The Neptune File, 2000; The Mechanical Turk, 2002; A History of the World in Six Glasses, 2005; An Edible History of Humanity, 2009; Writing on the Wall, 2013. *Recreations:* playing the drums, food and wine, video games. *Address:* The Economist, 25 St James's Street, SW1A 1HG. *T:* (020) 7830 7131. *E:* tws@economist.com.

STANDEN, Iain Gordon; Chief Executive Officer, Bletchley Park Trust, since 2012; *b* Lincoln, 2 April 1963; *s* of Kenneth Standen and Janet Standen; *m* 1989, Anna Robertson; two *s* one *d*. *Educ:* Christ's Hospital; King's Coll. London (BA Geog. 1985); Royal Mil. Acad. Sandhurst; Cranfield Univ. (MA Mil. Studies 1996). Royal Corps of Signals, British Army: Univ. Cadet, 1982–85; Regtl Duty, GB, Cyprus, NI and Germany, 1986–95; psc 1996; D Army Plans, MoD, 1996–99; OC 20 Armoured Bde HQ and Signal Sqdn, 1999–2001; COS 1 Signal Bde, 2001–02; SO1 Orgn & Deployment HQ Signal Officer in Chief (Army), 2002–03; CO Jt Service Signal Unit, Cyprus, 2003–05; COS HQ Signal Officer in Chief (Army), 2005–08; Chief Campaign Plans HQ Multinat. Force-Iraq, Baghdad, 2008; Dep. Hd NEC Prog. Office, MoD, 2009–10; Comd Jt Service Signals Orgn, 2010–11. Pt-time battlefield tour guide, 2000–. *Recreations:* studying history, travel, listening to live music, long-distance running. *Address:* Bletchley Park Trust, The Mansion, Bletchley Park, Milton Keynes, Bucks MK3 6EB. *T:* (01908) 272682. *Club:* Army and Navy.

STANDING, John; *see* Leon, Sir J. R.

STANDING, Rev. Dr Roger; Principal, Spurgeon's College, since 2013; *b* Downham Market, Norfolk, 19 April 1959; *s* of John and Margaret Standing; *m* 1978, Marion Neale; one *s* two *d*. *Educ:* Downham Market Secondary Modern Sch.; Norfolk Coll. of Arts and Technol.; Univ. of Manchester (BA 1984; MPhil 1992); Denver Seminary, Colo (DMin. 2000). Evangelist, Liverpool Central Hall, 1978–81; Methodist Minister, Horsforth, 1984–90; Baptist Minister, W Croydon, 1990–2001; Regl Minister, Southern Counties Baptist Assoc., 2001–07; Spurgeon's College, London: Tutor, 2007–09; Dir of Trng, 2009–11; Dep. Principal, 2011–13. FRSA. *Publications:* Preaching for the Unchurched, 2002; Finding the Plot, 2004, 2nd edn 2012; Re-emerging Church, 2008; As a Fire by Burning, 2013; Mosaic Evangelism, 2013; The Forward Movement, 2015. *Recreations:* Norwich City Football Club, writing, music, sport. *Address:* Spurgeon's College, South Norwood Hill, SE25 6DJ. *T:* (020) 8653 0850. *E:* r.standing@spurgeons.ac.uk.

STANDRING, Prof. Susan Margaret, MBE 2015; PhD, DSc; FRSB; Professor of Anatomy, 2007–09, now Emeritus, and Head, Department of Anatomy and Human Sciences (formerly Division of Anatomy, Cell and Human Biology), 2000–09, School of Biomedical and Health Sciences (formerly Guy's, King's and St Thomas' School of Biomedical Sciences), King's College London; *b* 22 Feb. 1947; *d* of William and Margaret Hall; *m* 1970, Guy Lewis Standring (*d* 2014); two *d*. *Educ:* Sch. of St Clare, Penzance; Guy's Hosp. Medical Sch., Univ. of London (BSc, PhD; DSc); King's Coll. London (Postgrad. Dip. in Teacher Educn Medicine and Dentistry). FRSB (FSB 2010). Reader in Experimental Neurobiology, UMDS of Guy's and St Thomas' Hosps, 1989–98; Admissions Dean for Medicine, UMDS, subseq. GKT, KCL, 1996–2002; Prof. of Experimental Neurobiol., Sch. of Biomed. and Health Scis (formerly GKT Sch. of Biomed. Scis), KCL, 1998–2007. President: Peripheral Nerve Soc., 2001–03; Anatomical Soc. (formerly Anatomical Soc. of GB and Ireland), 2008–10; Mem., Court of Examiners, 2002–, Anatomy Develt Tutor, 2008–13, RCS. Trustee: Damilola Taylor Trust, 2005–07; Changing Faces, 2008–10; Hunterian Collection, RCS, 2012–. FKC 2008. Hon. FRCS 2009. *Publications:* Gray's Anatomy, (section ed.) 37th edn 1989, 38th edn 1995, (ed.-in-chief) 39th edn 2005, 40th edn 2008; (as Susan Hall) over 150 papers in peer-reviewed scientific jls. *Recreations:* walking, reading, gardening. *Address:* School of Biomedical and Health Sciences, King's College London, Hodgkin Building, Guy's Campus, SE1 1UL. *T:* (020) 7848 6083. *E:* susan.standring@kcl.ac.uk.

STANES, Ven. Ian Thomas; Archdeacon of Loughborough, 1992–2005, now Archdeacon Emeritus; *b* 29 Jan. 1939; *s* of Sydney Stanes and Iris Stanes (*née* Hulme); *m* 1962, Sylvia Alice (*née* Drew); one *d* (one *s* decd). *Educ:* Sheffield Univ. (BSc 1962); Linacre Coll., Oxford (BA 1965; MA 1969); Wycliffe Hall, Oxford. Ordained: deacon, 1965; priest, 1966; Curate, Holy Apostles, Leicester, 1965–69; Vicar, Broom Leys, Coalville, Leicester, 1969–76; Priest Warden, Marrick Priory, Ripon, 1976–82; Willesden Area Officer for Mission, Ministry and Evangelism, London, 1982–92. Prebendary, St Paul's Cathedral, 1989–92. *Recreations:* walking, photography, theatre, singing, music, art appreciation, model and stamp collecting, reading. *Address:* 192 Bath Road, Bradford on Avon, Wilts BA15 1SP. *T:* (01225) 309036. *E:* istanes@btinternet.com.

STANESBY, Rev. Canon Derek Malcolm, PhD; Canon of St George's Chapel, Windsor, 1985–97 (Steward, 1987–94; Treasurer, 1994–97); *b* 28 March 1931; *s* of Laurence J. C. Stanesby and late Elsie L. Stanesby (*née* Stean); *m* 1958, Christine A. Payne; three *s* one *d*. *Educ:* Orange Hill Central School, London; Northampton Polytechnic, London; Leeds Univ. (BA Hons); Manchester Univ. (MEd, PhD); College of the Resurrection, Mirfield. GPO Radio Research Station, Dollis Hill, 1947–51; RAF (Navigator), 1951–53. Ordained, 1958; Curate: Old Lakenham, Norwich, 1958–61; St Mary, Welling, Dio. Southwark, 1961–63; Vicar, St Mark, Bury, Dio. Manchester, 1963–67; Rector, St Chad, Ladybarn, Manchester, 1967–85. Mem., Archbishop's Commn on Christian Doctrine, 1986–91. *Publications:* Science, Reason and Religion, 1985; (contrib.) Theology, Evolution and the Mind, 2009; various articles and papers. *Recreations:* hill walking, sailing, woodwork, idling. *Address:* 32 Elizabeth Way, Uppingham, Rutland LE15 9PQ. *T:* (01572) 821298. *Club:* Royal Air Force.

STANFORD, Rear Adm. Christopher David, CB 2002; Partner, Odgers Berndtson (formerly Odgers Ray and Berndtson), Executive Search, since 2002 (Head of Global Healthcare Practice (formerly Head of Practice (Healthcare and Life Sciences), 2002–15); *b* 15 Feb. 1950; *s* of late Joseph Gerald Stanford and Dr Elspeth Stanford (*née* Harrison); *m* 1972, Angela Mary, (Annie), *d* of late Commander Derek G. M. Gardner, VRD, RSMA; one *s* three *d*. *Educ:* St Paul's Sch.; Britannia RN Coll., Dartmouth; Merton Coll., Oxford (MA History and French). Joined RN 1967; served HM Ships Puma, Jupiter, Hubberston, Exmouth, Newcastle, Antrim, Brilliant, Fife; commanded: HMS Boxer, 1988–89; HMS Coventry and First Frigate Sqdn, 1993–94; Asst Dir (Ships), Directorate of Operational Requirements, 1990–93; rcds 1995; Dir, Naval Staff Duties, 1995–97; Dir, Operational Capability, 1997–98; COS to Surgeon Gen., MoD, 1999–2002. FNI (Vice Pres., 1999–2007). Gov., King Edward VII's Hosp., 2008–. Lay Chm., St Lawrence, Cucklington PCC, 2002–. Freeman: City of London, 2000; Master Mariners' Co., 2000; Younger Brother, Trinity House, 2006. Chm., Combined Services Rugby Union, 2001–02; Vice President: RN Rugby Union, 1996–2002; N Dorset RFC, 1999–; Chairman: Royal Naval Lay Readers Soc., 1999–2002; Somerset and Dorset Sea Cadet Assoc., 2002–12. Mem. Council, White Ensign Assoc., 2009–. DUniv UCE, 2002. OStJ 2001. *Publications:* contribs to learned and professional jls on maritime, health and leadership issues. *Recreations:* art, maritime affairs, industrial archaeology (especially railways), healthcare. *Address:* Odgers Berndtson, 20 Cannon Street, EC4M 6XD. *Clubs:* Naval and Military, Royal Naval of 1765 and 1785, Hon. Society of Anchorites (Pres., 2003), Chelsea Arts.

STANFORD, James Keith Edward, OBE 1999; Director General, Leonard Cheshire Foundation, 1991–98; a Vice President, Leonard Cheshire, 2000–12; *b* 12 April 1937; *s* of late Lt-Col J. K. Stanford, OBE, MC, author and naturalist, and Eleanor Stanford; *m* 1964, Carol Susan Harbord; one *s* one *d*. *Educ:* Rugby Sch.; RMA Sandhurst. 17th/21st Lancers, 1955–64; IBM Corp., 1965–72; Industry and City, 1973–90; Chm., David Brown Corp., 1987–90; Dir, Aerospace Engrg, 1990–94. Chm., Edward Stanford Gp Ltd, 2009–11. Vice-Chm., Holiday Care Service, 1991–99. March Dir, Countryside Alliance, 1999–2004. Dir, Dorset NHS Ambulance Trust, 2001–05. Chm., Cranborne Chase and W Wilts Area of Outstanding Natural Beauty, 2009–15. Chm. of Govs, Milton Abbey Sch., 2004–08. *Recreation:* countryside activities. *Address:* Nippards Farmhouse, Whitsbury, nr Fordingbridge SP6 3QB.

See also Earl of Radnor.

STANFORD, Martin; Presenter, Sky News, since 1991; *b* Didcot, 2 May 1958; *s* of Rev. P. Guy Stanford and Barbara Alice Stanford; *m* Sarah Strike; three *s*. BBC Transcription Recording Unit, 1977–79; BBC Radio Oxford, 1979–81; BBC Trng Dept, 1981; BBC Radio Northampton, 1982–86; BBC TV South, 1986–89; British Satellite Broadcasting TV, 1989–90; freelance producer and reporter, 1991. Lay Steward, St George's Chapel, Windsor Castle. *Recreations:* technology, theatre, family, boating. *Address:* Sky News, Grant Way, Isleworth, Middx TW7 5QD. *T:* (020) 7705 3000. *E:* martin.stanford@bskyb.com.

STANFORD, Peter James; writer, journalist and broadcaster; *b* 23 Nov. 1961; *s* of late Reginald James Hughes Stanford and Mary Catherine (*née* Fleming); *m* 1995, Siobhan, *d* of James Cross and late Celine Cross; one *s* one *d*. *Educ:* St Anselm's Coll., Birkenhead; Merton Coll., Oxford (BA Hons 1983). Reporter, The Tablet, 1983–84; News Editor, 1984–88, Editor, 1988–92, The Catholic Herald. Feature writer: for various titles incl. Guardian, Independent; for Daily Telegraph, 2007–; Columnist, The Tablet, 2003–. Chm., ASPIRE (Assoc. for Spinal Res., Reintegration and Rehabilitation), 1992–2001 and 2005–11. Dir, Candoco Dance Co., 1994–98 (Patron, 1998–). Dir, Frank Longford Charitable Trust, 2002–. Panellist: FutureWatch, TV, 1996; radio: The Moral Maze, 1996; Vice or Virtue, 1997; Presenter: The Mission, TV, 1997; various Radio 2, Radio 4 and BBC World Service documentaries, 1999–. *Publications:* (ed) Hidden Hands: child workers around the world, 1988; (with Simon Lee) Believing Bishops, 1990; (ed) The Seven Deadly Sins, 1990; (with Kate Saunders) Catholics and Sex, 1992 (televised, 1992; Bronze Medal, NY TV Fest., 1993); Cardinal Hume and the changing face of English Catholicism, 1993; Lord Longford: an authorised life, 1994; revd edn as The Outcasts' Outcast, 2003; (with Gerard Noel) The Anatomy of the Catholic Church, 1994; (with Leanda de Lisle) The Catholics and their Houses, 1995; The Devil: a biography, 1996 (televised 1998); The She-Pope: a quest for the truth behind the mystery of Pope Joan, 1998 (televised 1998); Bronwen Astor: her life and times, 2000; Heaven: a travellers' guide, 2002; Being a Dad, 2004; (ed) Why I'm Still a Catholic, 2005; (ed with Julian Filochowski) Opening Up, 2005; C. Day-Lewis: a biography, 2007; Teach Yourself Catholicism, 2008; A Life of Christ, 2009; The Extra Mile: a 21st century pilgrimage, 2010; (ed) The Death of a Child, 2011; How to Read a Graveyard: journeys in the company of the dead, 2013; Judas Iscariot: the troubling history of the renegade apostle, 2015. *Recreations:* old cars, my children, north Norfolk. *Address:* c/o Sheil Land Associates, 52 Doughty Street, WC1N 2LS. *W:* www.peterstanford.co.uk.

STANGER, David Harry, OBE 1987; FCQI; CQP; Partner, Al Hoty-Stanger Ltd, Saudi Arabia/United Arab Emirates, since 1975; Chairman and Managing Director, David H. Stanger sprl, 1997–2000; *b* 14 Feb. 1939; *s* of Charles Harry Stanger, CBE and Florence Bessie Hepworth Stanger; *m* 1963, Jill Patricia (*née* Barnes); one *s* two *d*. *Educ:* Oundle Sch.; Millfield Sch. FCQI (FIQA 1982); MSocIS 1982; CQP 2007; MInstRE. Served Corps of RE, 1960–66; joined R. H. Harry Stanger, 1966; Chm. and Man. Dir, Harry Stanger Ltd, 1975–90 (Sen. Partner, 1972–90); non-exec. Chm., Stanger Consultants Ltd, 1990–93. Chm., Adv. Cttee, NAMAS, 1985–87. Secretary General: Union Internationale des Laboratoires Indépendants, 1983–93 and 2001–03 (Mem. Governing Bd, 1997–2010; Hon. Mem., 1993–); Eur. Orgn for Testing and Certification, 1993–97. Member: Steering Cttee, NATLAS, 1981–87; Adv. Council for Calibration and Measurement, 1982–87; Council, EUROLAB, 1990–93; Adv. and Technical Cttee, Dubai Accreditation Centre, 2008–10; CQI Adv. Council, 2007–10; Chairman: Standards, Quality and Measurement Adv. Cttee, 1988–92; British Measurement and Testing Assoc., 1990–93 (Associate Mem., 2009–); Inst. of Quality Assurance, 1990–93 (a Vice-Pres., 1986–2010); Adv. Bd, Brunel Centre for Manufacturing Metrology, 1991–93; ILAC Lab. Cttee, 1998–2002 (Mem., 1998–). FInstD 1982; FRSA 1989. Pingat Peringatan, Malaysia, 1966; Pingat Jasa Malaysia, 2009. *Recreation:* collecting vintage wines. *Address:* 7C Forth Mansions, Ta'Xbiex Seafront, Ta'Xbiex, XBX 1027, Malta. *E:* dhstanger1@gmail.com.

STANHOPE, family name of **Earl of Harrington**.

STANHOPE, Janet Anne, (Lady Stanhope); Special Adviser to Devon and Cornwall Police and Crime Commissioner, since 2012; *b* 3 Oct. 1952; *d* of late Thomas Flynn and Anne Flynn (*née* Atkinson); *m* 1975, Adm. Sir Mark Stanhope, *qv*; one *d*. *Educ:* Nottingham High Sch. for Girls; Somerville Coll., Oxford (MA Hons Physics). CIPFA 1978. Trainee stockbroker, Montagu, Loebl, Stanley & Co., 1974–75; trainee accountant, W Sussex CC, 1975–77; Devon County Council: various accountancy posts, 1977–93; Dep. Co. Treas., 1993–98; Dep. Dir of Resources, 1998–2000; Dir of Resources, 2000–04. Ind. Mem., Devon and Cornwall Police Authy, 2009–12. Mem., Exeter Southernhay Rotary Club, 1994– (Pres., 2011–12). Lady Sponsor, RFA Cardigan Bay, 2005–; Pres., Central London Cttee, RNLI, 2009–13; Trustee, RN and RM Charity, 2008–14. Chm. Govs, Maynard Sch., 2013– (Gov., 2008–13). *Recreations:* reading, spending time with the family, playing bridge, golf. *Address:* Following Seas, 6 Barton Close, Exton, Exeter, Devon EX3 0PE.

STANHOPE, Adm. Sir Mark, GCB 2010 (KCB 2004); OBE 1988; FNI; DL; First Sea Lord and Chief of the Naval Staff, 2009–13; First and Principal Naval Aide-de-Camp to the Queen, 2009–13; *b* 26 March 1952; *s* of late Frederick William Stanhope and Sheila Mary Hattemore (*née* Cutler); *m* 1975, Janet Anne Flynn (*see* J. A. Stanhope); one *d*. *Educ:* London Nautical Sch.; Worthing High Sch.; St Peter's Coll., Oxford (MA Hons Physics; Hon. Fellow 2009). FNI 2008. Joined Royal Navy, 1970: Commanding Officer: HMS Orpheus, 1982–84; HMS Splendid, 1987–88; Submarine Comd Course (Teacher), 1989–90; HMS London, 1991–92; Capt., Submarine Sea Trng, 1993–94; Dep. Principal Staff Officer to CDS, MoD, 1994–96; rcds 1997; CO and ADC, HMS Illustrious, 1998–2000; Dir, Operational Mgt, NATO Regl Comd N, 2000–01; on secondment to Cabinet Office, 2002; Dep. C-in-C Fleet, 2002–04; Dep. Supreme Allied Comdr (Transformation), 2004–07; C-in-C Fleet and Comdr Allied Maritime Component Comd Northwood, 2007–09; Vice-Adm. of the UK, 2007–09. Dir, White Ensign Assoc., 2013– (Life Mem., 2007). President: Marine Soc. and Sea Cadets, 2014–; Britannia Assoc., 2014–; Assoc. of RN Officers, 2015–; Chm., Naval Review, 2014–. Trustee, Royal Museums Greenwich, 2015–. Member: RNSA; RUSI, 2003–. Life Mem., Guild of Freemen of London, 1993. Freeman, City of London, 1993; Liveryman, Upholders' Co., 1996; Hon. Member: Co. of Master Mariners, 2009–13; Co. of Shipwrights, 2010–. Younger Brother, Trinity House, 2003. DL Devon, 2013. Hon. DSc Plymouth, 2012. Meritorious Service Medal, NATO, 2007; Prince Hendrik Medal, Netherlands Navy, 2010. Legion of Merit (USA), 2007; Commemorative Medal (Slovak Republic), 2007; Order of Adm. Padilla (Colombia), 2008; Tong-il Medal, Order of Nat. Security Merit (S Korea), 2011; Norwegian Defence Medal with Laurel, 2011. *Publications:* contribs to Naval Rev., RUSI, military pubns. *Recreations:* family life, reading, sailing, golf. *E:* stanhopemark@hotmail.com. *Clubs:* Army and Navy, Royal Navy of 1765 and 1785.

STANIER, Sir Beville (Douglas), 3rd Bt *cr* 1917, of Peplow Hall, Market Drayton, Shropshire; Chairman of Trustees, Shotover Estate, Oxon, since 2006 (Trustee, since 1973); Member (C), Aylesbury Vale District Council, since 1999 (Cabinet Member, Environment and Health, since 2003); *b* 20 April 1934; *o s* of Brig. Sir Alexander Stanier, 2nd Bt, DSO, MC and Dorothy Gladys Miller (*d* 1973); *S* father, 1995; *m* 1st, 1963, Shelagh Sinnott (*d* 2007); one *s* two *d*; 2nd, 2010, Nerena Stephenson (*née* Villiers) (*d* 2015). *Educ:* Eton Coll. Joined Welsh Guards, 1952; commnd 2nd Lieut, 1953; Lieut, 1955; Captain, 1958; ADC to Governor-General of Australia, 1959–60. Stockbroker with Kitcat & Aitken, 1960–76 (Partner, 1968–76). Chairman: Buckingham Constituency Cons. Assoc., 1999–2003; Oxon and Bucks Area Cons. Party, 2003–04. *Recreations:* shooting, cricket. *Heir: s* Alexander James Sinnott Stanier, *b* 10 April 1970. *Address:* Kings Close House, Whaddon, Buckinghamshire MK17 0NG. *T:* (01908) 501738, 07778 305419. *Club:* MCC.

STANIFORTH, Martin John; non-executive Director, Local Care Direct, 2005–13; *b* 11 Feb. 1953; *s* of late Trevor Staniforth and Doris Nellie Staniforth (*née* Quaife). *Educ:* Kingston Grammar Sch., Kingston upon Thames; Univ. of Newcastle upon Tyne (BA Hons Eng. Lang. and Lit.); Open Univ. (MA 2008). Joined DHSS as Admin. Trainee, 1975, Principal, 1985–91; Department of Health: Asst Sec., 1991–96; Hd of Corp. Affairs, NHS Exec., 1996–99; Dep. Dir of Human Resources, subseq. Workforce, 1999–2005. Mem., Registration and Conduct Cttees, Gen. Social Care Council, 2007–12. Mem. Council, Leeds Civic Trust, 2006–14. Chm., Leeds Mencap, 2010–. Trustee, Leeds Library, 2013–. *Recreations:* hill walking, opera going, cricket watching. *Address:* 2 Ashwood Terrace, Leeds LS6 2EH. *Club:* New Headingley (Leeds).

STANIFORTH, Sarah Elizabeth, (Hon. Lady Porritt), CBE 2015; President, International Institute for Conservation of Historic and Artistic Works, since 2013 (Vice-President, 1998–2005); *b* 14 Jan. 1953; *d* of Malcolm Arthur Staniforth and Bridget Christian Salkeld Hall; *m* 1986, Hon. Sir Jonathon Porritt, *qv*; two *d*. *Educ:* St Hilda's Coll., Oxford (BA Hons); Courtauld Inst. of Art, London Univ. (Dip Conservation of Paintings). Higher Scientific Officer, Scientific Dept, Nat. Gall., 1980–85; National Trust: Advr on Paintings Conservation and Envmtl Control, 1985–2004; Head Conservator, 2002–04; Historic Properties Dir, 2005–11; Museums and Collections Dir, 2011–14. Trustee, Hunterian Collection, RCS, 1997–2008; Westminster Abbey Fabric Comr, 1998–. Chair, Nat. Heritage Sci. Forum, 2013–14. Chm., Accreditation Cttee, UKIC, 2002–05; Ind. Museums Councillor, Museums Assoc., 2005–; Mem. Council, Assoc. of Ind. Museums, 2011–14. Mem. SW Cttee, HLF, 2015–. Trustee: Hunterian Collection, RCS, 2011–; Pilgrim Trust, 2011–; Landmark Trust, 2014–; English Heritage, 2015–. FSA 2010; FRSA 2010. *Publications:* (ed jtly) Durability and Change, 1994; (ed with C. Sitwell) Studies in the History of Painting Restoration, 1998; (ed jtly) National Trust Manual of Housekeeping, 2005; (ed) Historical Perspectives on Preventive Conservation, 2013; papers in mus. and conservation jls and conf. procs. *Recreation:* swimming. *Address:* 9 Lypiatt Terrace, Lypiatt Road, Cheltenham, Glos GL50 2SX.

STANLEY, family name of **Earl of Derby** and **Baron Stanley of Alderley**.

STANLEY, Lord; Edward John Robin Stanley; *b* 21 April 1998; *s* and *heir* of Earl of Derby, *qv*. *Educ:* Ludgrove; Eton Coll. A Page of Honour to the Queen, 2008–12.

STANLEY OF ALDERLEY, 9th Baron *cr* 1839; **Richard Oliver Stanley;** Bt 1660; Baron Sheffield (Ire.) 1783; Baron Eddisbury 1848; *b* 24 April 1956; *e s* of 8th Baron Stanley of Alderley and Jane Barrett Stanley (*née* Hartley); *S* father, 2013; *m* 1983, Carla Mary Angela McKenzie; three *d* (one *s* decd). *Educ:* St Edward's Sch., Oxford; University Coll., London (BSc). *Heir: b* Hon. Charles Ernest Stanley [*b* 30 June1960; *m* 1989, Beverley Ann Emmitt; three *d*].

STANLEY, Alison; Partner, Bindmans LLP, since 1995; *b* Kent, UK. *Educ:* Univ. of Sussex (BA Hons English 1979); Coll. of Law. Admitted solicitor, 1984; Winstanley-Burgess, 1983–86; Evans Butler Smith, 1986–87; Jt Council for the Welfare of Immigrants, 1988–92; Racial Discrimination Legal Defence Fund, 1992–93; Deighton Guedalla, 1993–94; Bindmans LLP, 1994–. *Publications:* The Rights of Third Country Nationals in the New European Order, 1994; (jtly) Putting Children First: a guide for immigration practitioners, 2002; Asylum Seekers: a guide to current legislation, 2001; (jtly) Asylum: a guide to recent legislation, 2004; The Asylum and Immigration Tribunal: practice and procedure, 2005; (jtly) Representation at Immigration Appeals, 2006. *Address:* Bindmanns LLP, 236 Grays Inn Road, WC1X 8HB. *T:* (020) 7833 4433, *Fax:* (020) 7837 9792. *E:* a.stanley@bindmans.com.

STANLEY, Barbara Elizabeth; Independent Schools Specialist, Association of School and College Leaders, since 2015; *b* Belfast, 2 July 1950; *d* of John Morrison Hunter, CBE and I. Elizabeth Hunter; *m* 1978, Graham Stanley; two *d*. *Educ:* Glenlola Collegiate Sch., Bangor, Co. Down; Queen's Univ., Belfast (BA Hons 1972); Leicester Univ. (PGCE 1973). Teacher: Devizes Sch., 1973–75; Glenlola Collegiate Sch., 1975–86; Hd of House, Forest Sch., Snaresbrook, 1986–90; Hd of Geog., St Bernard's Convent, 1990–92; Dep. Headmistress, Channing Sch., 1992–95; Headmistress, Bedford High Sch., 1995–2000; Principal, Alexandra Coll., Dublin, 2000–02; Headmistress, The Abbey School, Reading, 2002–14. FRGS 2001. Mem. and speaker, Corrymeela Community (NI reconciliation community), 1970–. *Recreations:* church and community involvement, geographical interests, amateur dramatics, travel, hill walking. *Address:* Northcote, Swallowfield Street, Swallowfield, Reading RG7 1QX. *T:* 07793 249385. *E:* Barbara.Stanley@ascl.org.uk.

STANLEY, Clare Fiona Louise; QC 2015; *b* Adelaide, Australia, 25 Jan. 1967; *d* of Dr Philip Edward Stanley and Prof. Margaret Anne Stanley, *qv*; *m* 1998, Geoffrey Charles Chapman; one *s* one *d*. *Educ:* King's Sch., Ely; Univ. of Adelaide (BEc); Downing Coll., Cambridge (BA Law 1993). Called to the Bar, 1994; in practice as barrister, 1994–. *Recreations:* swimming, music, cooking, travelling. *Address:* Wilberforce Chambers, 8 New Square, Lincoln's Inn, WC2A 3QP. *T:* (020) 7306 0102, *Fax:* (020) 7306 0095. *E:* cstanley@wilberforce.co.uk.

STANLEY, David Raymond; sustainability and environmental management adviser, since 1998; Director: E3 Ltd, environmental consultancy, since 1998; Institute of Environmental Management Assessment, since 2013; Pasture-Fed Livestock Association, since 2013; *b* Bristol, 18 April 1946; *s* of Raymond Frank Stanley and Gwyneth Kate Stanley; *m* 1973, Patricia Jane Cross; one *s* one *d*. *Educ:* Cotham Grammar Sch.; RAF Coll.; Open Univ. (BA Envmtl Studies and Econs 1983). Dip. Internat. Envmtl Mgt 2003; CEnv 2004. Dock worker, Avonmouth Docks, 1964–65. Served RAF, 1965–84: Air Liaison Officer, 16 Parachute Bde, 1973–75; Flt Comdr, Hunters, Tactical Weapons Unit, 1976–78; 1 (F) Sqdn Harriers, 1979–81; Lectr in Defence Strategy, Dept of Air Warfare, 1982–84; retired in rank of Sqdn Leader, 1984. Regl Trng Manager, Anglian Water, 1984–89; Regl Admin Manager, NRA, 1989–92; Hd, Envmtl Mgt, Envmt Agency, 1993–97. Envmtl Auditor, 1998. Vis. Lectr and envmtl advr, Nat. Sch. of Govt, 1998–2012; Visiting Lecturer: in Sustainable Estate Mgt, Reading Univ., 2002–10; in Sustainable Agric., Centre for Alternative Technol., 2007–10. Mem., UK Wkg Party, ISO14000 Internat. Envmtl Mgt Standard, 1994–96. Farmer; zero carbon Pedigree Lincoln Red Beef producer, 1998–. MIEMA (MIEMgt 1998), FIEMA 2005. Lincolnshire Envmtl Award for Farming, Lincolnshire Wildlife Trust, 2012. *Publications:* Achieving the UK GHG Reduction Commitments Through Food, 2001. *Recreations:* sequestrating carbon through grassland, shooting and stalking, gardening, producing sustainability videos. *Address:* Holly House, Camp Lane, Grimley, Worcs WR2 6LX. *T:* (01905) 641529. *E:* dave@sustainability.works.

STANLEY, Prof. Eric Gerald, MA (Oxford); AM (Yale); PhD (Birmingham); FBA 1985; Rawlinson and Bosworth Professor of Anglo-Saxon in the University of Oxford, and Fellow of Pembroke College, Oxford, 1977–91; Emeritus Professor and Fellow, since 1991; *b* 19 Oct. 1923; *m* 1959, Mary Bateman, MD, FRCP; one *d*. *Educ:* Queen Elizabeth's Grammar Sch., Blackburn; University Coll., Oxford. Lectr in Eng. Lang. and Lit., Birmingham Univ., 1951–62; Reader in Eng. Lang. and Lit., 1962–64, Prof. of English, 1964–75, Univ. of London at QMC; Prof. of English, Yale Univ., 1975–76. Mem., Mediaeval Acad. of America, 1975– (Corresp. Fellow, 2008–); Corresponding Member: Fryske Akad., Netherlands, 1991–; Bavarian Acad. of Scis, 1994–. Sir Israel Gollancz Meml Lectr, British Acad., 1984. Co-Editor, 1963–2002, Adv. Ed., 2003–, Notes and Queries. Hon. DSL Univ. of Trinity Coll., Toronto; Hon. DLaws Toronto. *Publications:* (ed) The Owl and the Nightingale, 1960, 2nd edn 1972; The Search for Anglo-Saxon Paganism, 1975; A Collection of Papers with Emphasis on Old English Literature, 1987; In the Foreground: Beowulf, 1994; Die altenglische Rechtspflege, 1999; Imagining the Anglo-Saxon Past, 2000; academic articles. *Address:* 18 Walton Street, Oxford OX1 2HQ. *E:* eric.stanley@pmb.ox.ac.uk. *Club:* Athenæum.

STANLEY, Prof. Fiona Juliet, AC 1996; MD; Patron, Telethon Kids Institute (formerly Telethon Institute for Child Health Research), since 2012 (Director, 1990–2012); Professor, 1990–2012, Distinguished Research Professor, since 2012, School of Paediatrics and Child Health, University of Western Australia; Chair, Australian Research Alliance for Children and Youth, 2007–11 (Chief Executive Officer, 2001–04; Executive Director, 2004–07); *b* 1 Aug. 1946; *d* of Prof. Neville Stanley and Muriel MacDonald Stanley; *m* 1973, Prof. Geoffrey Shellam; two *d*. *Educ:* Univ. of Western Australia (MB BS 1970; MD 1986); LSHTM, Univ. of London (MSc 1976). FFPH (FFPHM 1989); FAFPHM 1991; FRACP 1994; FRANZCOG 1995; FASSA 1996; FAA 2002. Doctor, Princess Margaret Hosp. Aboriginal Clinic, Perth, 1972; Scientific Staff, MRC Social Medicine Unit, 1972–73, NH & MRC Fellow in Clin. Scis, 1974–75, LSHTM; vis. appt, Nat. Inst. Child Health and Human Develt, NIH, 1976; University of Western Australia: NH & MRC Clin. Scis Res. Fellow, Unit of Clin. Epidemiology, Dept of Medicine, 1977; SMO (Child Health), Community and Child Health Services, Public Health Dept, 1978–79; Dep. Dir, 1980–88, Dir, 1988–90, NH & MRC Res. Unit in Epidemiology and Preventive Medicine. Dir, 2013 Fest. of Ideas, Univ. of Melbourne, 2012–. Vice Chancellor's Fellow, Univ. of Melbourne, 2012–. Hon. FRACGP 2004; Hon. FRCPCH 2006. Hon. DSc Murdoch, 1998; DUniv Queensland Univ. of Tech., 2001; Hon. MD: Sydney, 2005; Melbourne, 2008. Australian of the Year, Nat. Australia Day Council, 2003. *Publications:* (ed jtly) The Epidemiology of Prematurity, 1977; (ed jtly) The Epidemiology of the Cerebral Palsies, 1984; (ed) The Role of Epidemiology and Perinatal Databases for both Research and Care, 1997; (jtly) The Cerebral Palsies: epidemiology and causal pathways, 2000; (jtly) Children of the Lucky Country?: how Australian society has turned its back on children and why children matter, 2005; papers in learned jls, reports, and chapters in books. *Recreations:* bushwalking, swimming. *Address:* Telethon Kids Institute, PO Box 855, West Perth, WA 6872, Australia. *T:* (8) 9489 7968.

STANLEY, Rev. Canon John Alexander, OBE 1999; Vicar of Huyton, since 1974; Chaplain to the Queen, 1993–2001; *b* 20 May 1931; *s* of Edward Alexander Stanley and Lucy Vida Stanley; *m* 1956, (Flora) Elaine Wilkes; three *s* two *d*. *Educ:* Birkenhead Sch.; Tyndale Hall Theol Coll., Bristol. Assistant Curate: All Saints', Preston, 1956; St Mark's, St Helens, 1960; Vicar, St Cuthbert's, Everton, Liverpool, 1963; Priest in Charge, St Saviour, Everton, 1969; Vicar, St Saviour with St Cuthbert, Everton, 1970; Area Dean of Huyton, 1989–2003; Hon. Canon of Liverpool Cathedral, 1987–. Mem., Gen. Synod, and Proctor in Convocation, 1973–2000; Chm., Diocesan House of Clergy, 1979–85; Prolocutor, York Convocation, 1990–2000. A Church Comr, 1983–99 (Mem., Bd of Govs, 1989–99); Member: Crown Appointments Commn, 1992–2000; Archbishops' Council, 1999–2000. Mem., BCC, 1984–87; Trustee, Church Urban Fund, 1987–2003. *Recreations:* golf, bees, photography. *Address:* The Vicarage, Huyton, Merseyside L36 7SA. *T:* (0151) 449 3900, *Fax:* (0151) 480 6002. *E:* John.Stanley@btinternet.com.

STANLEY, Prof. John Knowles, FRCSE, FRCS; Professor of Hand Surgery, Manchester University, 1996–2009, now Emeritus; Consultant Hand Surgeon, Wrightington Hospital, Wigan, 1979–2011; Vice President, Royal College of Surgeons, 2010–12; *b* Cardiff, 30 March 1944; *s* of Frederick John and Mary Thelma Stanley; *m* 1964, Gail Simpson; one *s* one *d*. *Educ:* Oswestry Boys' High Sch.; Liverpool Univ. (MB ChB 1968; MChOrth 1975). FRCSE 1973; FRCS 1974. Senior Registrar in Orthopaedics: Broadgreen Hosp., 1974; Royal Southern Hosp., 1974; Royal Liverpool Hosp., 1975; Wrightington Hosp., 1975; Broadgreen Hosp., 1976; rotation, Royal Southern Hosp. and Broadgreen Hosp., 1977–79. Robert Jones' Lect., British Orthopaedic Assoc., 2004; Hunterian Prof., RCS, 2010; Visiting Professor: Yoshiba Univ., NY, 1988; Dept of Orthopaedics and Plastic and Reconstructive Surgery, Univ. of Marseille, 1989; Pellenburg Hosp. Leuven Univ., Belgium, 1991; St Joseph's Hosp., Univ. of London, Ontario, 1991; Univ. of Otago Med. Sch., NZ, 1997; Royal Coll. of Surgeons, Australasia, 1998; Mayo Clinic, Rochester, USA, 2001; Univ. of Cape Town, 2001; Univ. of Bloemfontein, 2001; Univ. of Durban, 2001; Univ. of Pretoria, 2001; Univ. of Stellenbosch, 2001; NZ Soc. of Surgery of the Hand, Napier NZ Orthopaedic Soc., 2002; Aust. Orthopaedic and Hand Soc., 2003; Asia/Pacific Orthopaedic Soc., 2004; Mgt of Complex Elbow Problems, Hand Rehabilitation Foundn, Philadelphia, 2005. *Publications:* Wrist Arthroscopy, 1994; contrib. articles to learned jls. *Recreations:* golf, military aircraft, gliding, travelling, volunteer and friend, Manchester Mus. of Sci. and Industry. *Address:* 20 Derby Street West, Ormskirk, Lancs L39 3NH. *T:* and *Fax:* (01695) 575210. *E:* profstanley@btinternet.com. *Club:* Ormskirk Golf.

STANLEY, John Mallalieu; Director of Legal Services A, Department of Trade and Industry, 1996–2001; *b* 30 Sept. 1941; *s* of William and Rose Margaret Stanley; *m* 1968, Christine Mary Cunningham; two *s* one *d*. *Educ:* Welwyn Garden City Grammar Sch.; Clare College, Cambridge (MA). Solicitor. Church, Adams, Tatham & Co., 1965–68; Jaques & Co.,

1968–75; Department of Industry, later of Trade and Industry, 1975–2001: Under Sec. (Legal), 1989–96. Chairman: Meridian Money Advice, 2002–; Greenwich Charities, 2008–. *Address:* 12 Westcombe Park Road, SE3 7RB.

STANLEY, Rt Hon. Sir John (Paul), Kt 1988; PC 1984; *b* 19 Jan. 1942; *s* of late Mr and Mrs H. Stanley; *m* 1968, Susan Elizabeth Giles; one *s* one *d* (and one *s* decd). *Educ:* Repton Sch.; Lincoln Coll., Oxford (MA). Conservative Research Dept with responsibility for Housing, 1967–68; Research Associate, Internat. Inst. for Strategic Studies, 1968–69; Rio Tinto-Zinc Corp. Ltd, 1969–79. MP (C) Tonbridge and Malling, Feb. 1974–2015. PPS to Rt Hon. Margaret Thatcher, 1976–79; Minister of State (Minister for Housing and Construction), DoE, 1979–83; Minister of State: for the Armed Forces, MoD, 1983–87; Northern Ireland Office, 1987–88. Mem., Parly Select Cttee on Nationalised Industries, 1974, on Foreign Affairs, 1992–2015. Mem., NATO Parly Assembly, 2001–15. Director: Fidelity Japanese Values plc, 1994–2005; Henderson High Income Trust plc, 1997–2007. Trustee, ActionAid, 1989–99. *Publications:* (jtly) The International Trade in Arms, 1972. *Recreations:* music, sailing.

STANLEY, Khatun; *see* Sapnara, K.

STANLEY, Prof. Margaret Anne, OBE 2004; PhD; Professor of Epithelial Biology, University of Cambridge, 2001–09, now Emeritus; Fellow, Christ's College, Cambridge, since 1990; *b* 19 July 1939; *d* of Colin Campbell Coutts and Clara Coutts; *m* 1964, Philip Edward Stanley; one *s* one *d*. *Educ:* Bedford Coll., London (BSc); Univ. of Bristol (PhD 1964). Sen. Lectr in Pathol., Univ. of Adelaide, S Australia, 1974–80; Lectr in Pathol., 1980–96, Reader in Epithelial Biol., 1996–2001, Univ. of Cambridge. FMedSci 2004; Hon. FRCOG 2008. *Publications:* numerous articles in peer-reviewed jls. *Recreation:* cooking. *Address:* Department of Pathology, University of Cambridge, Tennis Court Road, Cambridge CB2 1QP. *T:* (01223) 333690, *Fax:* (01223) 333346. *E:* mas1001@cam.ac.uk.
See also C. F. L. Stanley.

STANLEY, Martin Edward; author and adviser on effective government, since 2010; Chief Executive, Turks and Caicos Islands Government, 2009, 2011; *b* 1 Nov. 1948; *s* of Edward Alan and Dorothy Stanley; *m* 1971, Marilyn Joan Lewis (marr. diss. 1992); one *s*; *m* 1996, Janice Margaret Munday, *qv*; one *s* (and one *s* decd). *Educ:* Royal GS, Newcastle upon Tyne; Magdalen Coll., Oxford (BA Hons). Inland Revenue, 1971–80; Department of Trade and Industry, 1980–98: various posts, 1980–87; Head, Industry/Educn Unit, 1987–90; Principal Private Sec., 1990–92; Hd of Vehicles, Metals and Minerals Div., later Engrg Automotive and Metals Div., 1992–96; Chief Exec., Oil and Gas Projects and Supplies Office, then Infrastructure and Energy Projects Directorate, 1996–98; Dir, Better Regulation, then Regulatory Impact, Unit, Cabinet Office, 1998–2000; Chief Executive: Postal Services Commn, 2000–04; Competition Commn, 2004–09. Hon. Fellow, Manchester Univ., 2013. Editor: www.civilservant.org.uk, 2000–; www.regulation.org.uk, 2010–. *Publications:* How to be a Civil Servant, 2000, 2nd edn 2004. *Recreations:* walking, sailing. *Address:* 68 Richborne Terrace, SW8 1AX. *E:* 68rtsw8@gmail.com.

STANLEY, Oliver Duncan; Chairman, 1972–97 and Director, 1972–2000, Rathbone Brothers (formerly Comprehensive Financial Services) PLC; *b* 5 June 1925; *s* of Bernard Stanley and Mabel Best; *m* 1954, Ruth Brenner, JP, BA (*d* 2002); one *s* three *d*. *Educ:* Christ Church, Oxford (MA); Harvard Univ., USA. Called to the Bar, Middle Temple, 1963. Served War, 8 Hussars, 1943–47. HM Inspector of Taxes, 1952–65; Dir, Gray Dawes Bank, 1966–72; founded Comprehensive Financial Services Gp of Cos, 1971. Chief Taxation Adviser, CLA, 1975–83 (Mem., Tax Cttee, 1983–2002). Chairman: Profile Books Ltd, 1996–2005; Esterel Ltd, 2003–; Dir, Axa Equity and Law, 1992–97. Member: Soc. of Authors, 1967–; Council of Legal Educn, 1992–96. Gov., Inns of Court Sch. of Law, 1996–99. Trustee: Age Concern Barnet, 2003–12; Barnet Carers, 2015– (Trustee and Chm., 2007–13). Hon. Fellow, Liverpool John Moores Univ., 2011. *Publications:* A Guide to Taxation, 1967; Taxology, 1971; Creation and Protection of Capital, 1974; Taxation of Farmers and Landowners, 1981, 31st edn 2012; Offshore Tax Planning, 1986; Hotel Victoire (novel), 2007; 1941 (novel), 2008; contrib. The Times and The Sunday Times, 1966–83; numerous articles in legal and agricultural periodicals. *Recreations:* music, French language and literature. *Club:* Travellers.

STANLEY, Hon. Peter Hugh Charles; Manager: New England Stud, since 1990; Stanley House Stud, since 1993; *b* London, 4 March 1964; *s* of late Hon. Hugh Henry Montagu Stanley and of Mary Rose Stanley (*née* Birch, now Spiegelberg); *m* 1990, Hon. Frances Caroline Burke Roche, *d* of 5th Baron Fermoy; two *s* one *d*. *Educ:* Ludgrove; Eton Coll. Chairman: New Astley Club, 2009–; Jockey Club Rooms, 2012–; non-exec. Dir, Jockey Club Estates, 2010–; Steward, Jockey Club, 2014–. *Recreations:* shooting, horseracing. *Address:* New England Stud, Newmarket, Suffolk CB8 0XA. *T:* (01223) 811249, *Fax:* (01223) 812723. *E:* stanley@newenglandstud.com.
See also Earl of Derby, Baron Fermoy.

STANNARD, Ven. Colin Percy, TD 1966; Archdeacon of Carlisle and Residentiary Canon of Carlisle Cathedral, 1984–93, now Archdeacon and Canon Emeritus; *b* 8 Feb. 1924; *s* of Percy and Grace Adelaide Stannard; *m* 1950, Joan Callow; one *s* two *d*. *Educ:* Woodbridge School; Selwyn Coll., Cambridge (BA 1947, MA 1949); Lincoln Theological Coll. Deacon 1949, priest 1950; Curate, St James Cathedral, Bury St Edmunds, 1949–52; Priest-in-charge, St Martin's, Grimsby, 1952–55; CF (TA), 1953–67; Vicar: St James's, Barrow-in-Furness, 1955–64; St John the Baptist's, Upperby, 1964–70; Rector of Gosforth, 1970–75; RD of Calder, 1970–75; Hon. Canon of Carlisle, 1975–84; Priest-in-charge of Natland, 1975–76, Vicar, 1976–84; RD of Kendal, 1975–84. *Recreations:* walking, bringing order out of chaos—especially in gardens. *Address:* Flat 4, Manormead Supported Housing, Tilford Road, Hindhead, Surrey GU26 6RA. *T:* (01428) 601504.

STANNARD, Prof. (Frank) Russell, OBE 1998; PhD; Professor of Physics, Open University, 1971–98, now Emeritus; *b* 24 Dec. 1931; *s* of Frank and Lillie Stannard; *m* 1984, Glenys Margaret Hawkins; two *s* two *d*, and two step *s* (and one step *s* decd). *Educ:* University Coll. London (BSc 1953; PhD 1956; Fellow, 2000). FInstP 1973. Res. Asst, UCL, 1956–59; Res. Physicist, Radiation Lab., Berkeley, 1959–60; Lectr, UCL, 1960–69; Open University: Reader, 1969–71; Hd, Physics Dept, 1971–75 and 1977–92; Pro Vice Chancellor, 1975–77. Mem., Center of Theological Inquiry, Princeton, 1988–89. Trustee, John Templeton Foundn, 1993–99 and 2000–06. Bragg Medal, Inst. of Physics, 2000. *Publications: for adults:* Science and the Renewal of Belief, 1982; Grounds for Reasonable Belief, 1989; Doing Away with God?, 1993; Science and Wonders, 1996; The God Experiment, 1999; The New World of Mr Tompkins, 1999; God for the 21st Century, 2000; Why?, 2003; Relativity, 2008; The End of Discovery, 2010; Science and Belief, 2012; *for children:* The Time and Space of Uncle Albert, 1989; Black Holes and Uncle Albert, 1991; Here I Am!, 1992; World of 1001 Mysteries, 1993; Uncle Albert and the Quantum Quest, 1994; Our Universe, 1995; A Short History of God, Me and the Universe, 1995; Letters to Uncle Albert, 1996; More Letters to Uncle Albert, 1997; Ask Uncle Albert: 100½ tricky science questions answered, 1998; The Curious History of God, 1998; Space, Time, Rhythm and Rhyme, 1999; Lab Cats on the Move, Lab Cats Get up Steam, Lab Cats Switch On, and Lab Cats See the Light, 2001; Dr Dyer's Academy, 2002; Virtutopia, 2003; over 60 articles in jls incl. Physical Rev., Physical Rev. Letters, Nature, Physics Letters, Procs of Physical Soc., etc. *Recreations:* sculpture, attending opera, ballet and concerts, enjoying 16 grandchildren and three great grandchildren. *Address:* 21 Alwins Field, Leighton Buzzard, Beds LU7 2UF. *T:* (01525) 371106. *E:* russell.stannard@tesco.net.

STANNARD, Jill; Chief Executive, Cumbria County Council, 2009–13; *b* Romford, Essex, 5 Dec. 1957; *d* of Jack and Marie Stannard; *m* 1997, Chris Taylor. *Educ:* Southampton Univ. (BSc, CQSW). Asst Dir, Hants CC, 2001–05; Corporate Dir, Adults and Cultural Services, Cumbria CC, 2005–09. Non-exec. Dir, Cumbria Partnership NHS Trust, 2014–. *Recreation:* walking in Cumbria.

STANNARD, Russell; *see* Stannard, F. R.

STANSBY, John; Chairman, UIE (UK) Ltd, 1974–2000 (UK parent company of UIE Scotland Ltd and subsidiary of Bouygues Group); Director, Bouygues UK, 1998–2000; *b* 2 July 1930; *s* of late Dumon Stansby and Vera Margaret Main; *m* 1966, Anna Maria Kruschewsky; one *d* and one step *s* one step *d*. *Educ:* Oundle; Jesus Coll., Cambridge (Schol., MA). FInstPet. Commissioned, Queen's Royal Regt, 1949; Service, 1949–50, Somaliland Scouts. Domestic Fuels Manager, Shell Mex & BP Ltd, 1955–62; Sen. Mktg Consultant, AIC Ltd, 1962–66; Dir, Rank Leisure Services, Rank Organisation, 1966–70; Dir, P&O Energy, P&OSN Co., 1970–74; Chm., Dumon Stansby & Co. Ltd, 1974–2000; Dep. Chm., London Transport Exec., 1978–80; Chairman: SAUR (UK) Ltd, 1986–89; Cementation-SAUR Water Services Ltd, 1986–88; Bouygues (UK) Ltd, 1987–2005; SAUR UK Development PLC, 1989–91; Dep. Chm., Energy Resources Ltd, 1990–92. Mem. Develt Bd, Almeida Th., 1990–2000. European Bobsleigh Champion, 1952. Chevalier de l'Ordre Nat. du Mérite (France), 1997. *Recreations:* theatre, church music, history. *Address:* Apt 5, 17 Cranley Gardens, SW7 3BD. *T:* (020) 7835 1913, *Fax:* (020) 7373 1455. *Club:* Travellers.

STANSFIELD, George Norman, CBE 1985 (OBE 1980); HM Diplomatic Service, retired; *b* 28 Feb. 1926; *s* of George Stansfield and Martha Alice (*née* Leadbetter); *m* 1947, Elizabeth Margaret Williams. *Educ:* Liscard High Sch. Served War, RAF, 1944–47. Ministries of Food and Supply, 1948–58; Private Sec. to Dir-Gen. of Armament Prodn, 1958–61; CRO, 1961; Second Secretary: Calcutta, 1962–66; Port of Spain, 1966–68; First Secretary: FCO, 1968–71; Singapore, 1971–74; Consul, Durban, 1974–78; FCO, 1978; Counsellor, and Head of Overseas Estate Dept, 1980–82; High Comr, Solomon Islands, 1982–86. Training consultant and instructor, FCO, 1986–2002. *Recreations:* sailing, wildlife. *Address:* Deryn's Wood, 80 Westfield Road, Woking, Surrey GU22 9QA. *Clubs:* Civil Service; Clandon Regis Golf.

STANSFIELD, Jill Veronica; Executive Director for Communities, London Borough of Barnet, 2006–09 (Director of Children's Services, 2002–06); *b* 18 Sept. 1951; *d* of Richard and Ivy Stansfield; *m* 1977, Paul Temple. *Educ:* Royal Holloway Coll., London (BA Hons Hist. 1973); Warwick Business Sch. (MPA 2005). Administrative officer, GLC and ILEA, 1973–89; Asst Dir, 1989–95, Actg Dir, 1995–96, of Educn, Lambeth BC; Strategic Dir of Learning and Develt, Milton Keynes Council, 1996–2002. Member: Barnet Coll. Corp., 2003–11; Bd, Milton Keynes Gall., 2003– (Vice Chair, 2013–); Barnet and Southgate Coll. Corp., 2011– (Chair, 2012–13). *Recreations:* gardening, playing the piano, art.

STANSFIELD, Piers Alistair; QC 2012; *b* Welwyn Garden City, 16 Aug. 1970; *s* of Jeffrey Stansfield and Alison Buchanan; *m* 2000, Rachel Claire Murdoch; two *s* one *d*. *Educ:* Loretto Sch., E Lothian; Bristol Univ. (LLB 1992); Inns of Court Sch. of Law. Called to the Bar, Inner Temple, 1993; in practice as barrister, specialising in construction, professional negligence and energy, 1993–. *Publications:* (contrib.) Keating on Construction Contracts, 9th edn 2012; (contrib.) Keating on NEC 3, 2012. *Recreations:* cycling, art, family. *Address:* Keating Chambers, 15 Essex Street, WC2R 3AA. *T:* (020) 7544 2600. *E:* pstansfield@keatingchambers.com.

STANSGATE, 3rd Viscount *cr* 1942, of Stansgate, co. Essex; **Stephen Michael Wedgwood Benn;** Director of Parliamentary Affairs, Society of Biology; *b* 21 Aug. 1951; *e s* of Rt Hon. Tony Benn, PC (who disclaimed his peerage for life, 1963); *S* father, 2014; *m* 1988, Ishika Nita, *d* of Stuart Ashley Bowes; one *s* one *d*. *Educ:* Holland Park Sch.; Keele Univ. *Heir: s* Hon. Daniel John Wedgwood Benn, *b* 10 Dec. 1991.
See also Rt Hon. H. J. W. Benn.

STANSTED, Archdeacon of; *see* King, Ven. R. L. C.

STANTON, Alan William, OBE 2014; RA 2009; RDI 2005; RIBA; Director, Stanton Williams Architects, since 1985; *b* 19 April 1944; *s* of William and Irene Stanton; *m* 1st, 1967, Marilyn Tindall (marr. diss. 1983); one *d*; *m* 2nd, 1985, Wendy Robin; one *d*. *Educ:* Architectural Assoc., London (AA Dip. Hons); Univ. of California, Los Angeles (MArch). RIBA 1979. Architect: with Norman Foster, 1967–68; Centre Pompidou, Paris (Piano & Rogers), 1970–77; in private practice, 1978–85 (projects in Paris, Italy and London); in partnership with Paul Williams, 1985–: award-winning projects in UK, Switzerland and Italy include: Casa Fontana, Lugano, 2000; Wellcome Trust Millennium Seed Bank, Sussex, 2000; Whitby Abbey Mus. and Visitor Centre, 2002; Tower Hill Environs, London, 2004; Compton Verney Art Gall., 2004; Belgrade Theatre extension, Coventry, 2007; House of Fraser, Bristol, 2008; Bourne Hill Offices, Salisbury, 2010; Sainsbury Lab., Cambridge, 2011. Lectr, AA, 1978–81. Mem., Design Rev. Panel, CABE, 2001–05. Mem. Council and Vice Pres., AA, 2000–04. Trustee, Open-City, 2013–. Has lectured in Europe and USA. FRSA 1993. SADG Medal 1967. *Publications:* numerous contribs to architectural books and jls. *Address:* Stanton Williams, 36 Graham Street, N1 8GJ. *T:* (020) 7880 6400, *Fax:* (020) 7880 6401. *E:* info@stantonwilliams.com.

STANTON, David, CB 2000; Director (Grade 3), Analytical Services Division, Department for Work and Pensions (formerly Department of Social Security), 1992–2002; *b* 5 Nov. 1942; *s* of Frederick Charles Patrick Stanton and Ethel (*née* Cout); *m* 1967, Isobel Joan Blair; one *s* one *d*. *Educ:* Bishop's Stortford Coll.; Worcester Coll., Oxford (BA PPE 1965); LSE (MSc(Econ) 1970). ODI/Nuffield Fellow, Govt of Uganda, 1965–67; Lectr, Brunel Univ., 1967–70; Economic Adviser: Min. of Transport, 1970; Min. of Housing, then DoE, 1971–74; HM Treasury, 1974–75; Senior Economic Adviser: seconded to Hong Kong Govt, 1975–77; also Head of Unit for Manpower Studies, Dept of Employment, 1977–81; Econs Br., Dept of Employment, 1981–83; also Dir, Employment Market Res. Unit, 1983–87; Chief Economist (Grade 3), Dept of Employment, 1988–92. Econ. Advr, Turner Pensions Commn, 2003–04. Chm., Indicators Sub Gp, Social Protection Cttee, EC, 2001–09. *Recreations:* people, dogs and other animals, singing.

STANTON, Rev. Canon David John; Canon Treasurer and Almoner, Westminster Abbey, since 2013; *b* London, 10 Oct. 1960; *s* of Peter Frederick Stanton and Frances Margaret Stanton (*née* Grumitt); *m* 1990, Sarah Jane Norris; two *d*. *Educ:* Exeter Cathedral Sch.; Blundell's Sch.; St Andrews Univ. (MTh); Exeter Univ. (MA); Cuddesdon Theol Coll., Oxford. Ordained deacon, 1985, priest, 1986; Curate, Beckenham Parish Ch, 1985–88; Asst Chaplain and Tutor, Shrewsbury Sch., 1988–90; Priest in Charge: St Mary Abbotskerswell, 1990–94; St John Bovey Tracey, 1994–2005; Chaplain, Plymouth Univ., 1992–97; Rural Dean, Moreton, 1998–2005; Diocese of Exeter: Vocations Chaplain, 1995–2005; Warden of Readers, 1996–2005; Mem., Bishop's Council and Bd of Educn, 2000–03; Diocesan Moderator and Chair, SW Dioceses, 2002–05; Diocesan Dir of Ordinands, 2003–05; Residentiary Canon (Precentor and Pastor), Worcester, 2005–13; Diocese of Worcester: Member: Diocesan Adv. Cttee for Care of Churches, 2005–13; Bishops' Selection Advr for Ordained Ministry, 2006–13; Ind. Mem., Worcester Cathedral Council, 2005–13. A Church Comr, 2010–14 (Mem., Assets Cttee, 2011–14). Ind. Mem., Standards Cttee, Worcester CC, 2008–13; Mem., Lord Chancellor's Adv. Cttee (W Mercia) on Justices of the Peace, 2010–13; non-exec. Mem., Wales Audit Office, 2011–14. Sec. of State Mem., Dartmoor Nat. Park Authy, 2002–05. Vice Chair, Inter-Divl Res. Ethics Cttee, Oxford Univ., 2010–. Governor:

Heathfield C of E Sch., 1994–2005; Stover Sch., 2003–07; Westminster Sch., 2013–; Westminster Abbey Choir Sch., 2013–. FSA(Scot) 1989. FRSA 1998. Distinguished Friend, Oxford Univ., 2015. *Publications:* contribs to theol jls. *Recreations:* sport, the arts, the countryside. *Address:* 1 Little Cloister, Westminster Abbey, SW1P 3PL. *T:* (020) 7654 4804. *E:* david.stanton@westminster-abbey.org. *Club:* Travellers.

STANTON, David Leslie, CMG 2014; Chairman of Trustees, UNICEF UK, 2004–13; Director, Friends Trusts Ltd, 2009–15; *b* 29 April 1943; *s* of Leslie Stanton and C. Mary Stanton (*née* Staynes); *m* 1989, Rosemary Jane Brown; one *d*. *Educ:* Bootham Sch., York; Balliol Coll., Oxford (BA Hons). Asst Principal, ODM, 1965–69; SSRC Sen. Scholarship, Oxford Univ., 1969–71; Principal, ODA, 1971–75; First Sec., Office of UK Permanent Rep. to EC, 1975–77; Mem., Bd of Dirs, Asian Develt Bank, 1979–82; Head of Dept, ODA, 1982–92; Advr, Finance and Admin, EBRD, 1990–91 (on secondment); Mem. Bd of Dirs, World Bank Gp, 1992–97; UK Ambassador and Perm. Delegate to UNESCO, 1997–2003. Mem., Exec. Bd, 1997–2003, Chm., Finance and Admin. Commn, 2000–01, UNESCO. Chm., Campaign for Nubia and Cairo Museums, 2002–03. Mem., Quaker Peace and Social Witness Central Cttee, 2014–. Vice Chair of Govs, Canonbury Sch., 2003–06. *Recreations:* mountaineering, ski-ing, painting, gardening. *Address:* 11 Canonbury Park South, N1 2JR. *E:* davidstanton@canonburypark.plus.com.

STANTON, Louise Jane, OBE 2012; HM Diplomatic Service; Deputy Head, Counter Proliferation Department, Foreign and Commonwealth Office, since 2013; *b* Bedfordshire, 14 Aug. 1968; *d* of Robert Charles Stanton and Jane Rosannah Sinclair (*née* Baker). *Educ:* Dominican Convent Benoni, S Africa; Dame Alice Harpur Sch., Bedford; Queen Mary and Westfield Coll., Univ. of London (BA Hons German and Linguistics 1990); Univ. of Sussex (Dip. Human Resource Mgt 2003); King's Coll. London (MA Internat. Security and Strategic Studies, 2013). Entered FCO, 1990; Desk Officer for Brunei, SE Asia Dept, FCO, 1990–91; Japanese lang. trng, 1991–93; Third Sec. (Commercial), Tokyo, 1993–96; Worldwide Floater, 1997–98 (incl. British Liaison Officer, Nagano Winter Olympics, Japan, 1998); Dep. Hd of Peacekeeping, UN Dept, FCO, 1999–2001; Hd, Personnel Unit, HR Gp, FCO Services, 2001–03; HR Manager for Consular Directorate, UK Visas and Protocol Div., FCO, 2004; HR Manager and Team Leader for Directorate Gen., Economic, FCO, 2004–06; Dep. Hd of Mission, Slovenia, 2006–08; High Comr, Malta, 2009–12; rcds, 2012. MCIPD 2004. *Recreations:* slow food, wine, cooking, dancing, travel, my iPhone. *Address:* c/o Foreign and Commonwealth Office, King Charles Street, SW1A 2AH.

STANTON, Lyndon, PhD; non-executive Director: Environment Agency, 2002–09; Nuclear Decommissioning Authority, 2004–08; *b* 22 Dec. 1942; *s* of late Joseph Reginald Stanton and of Violet Hazel Stanton (*née* Sears); *m* 1964, Carol Ann Smith; two *d*. *Educ:* Newport High Sch. for Boys; Univ. of Wales (BSc 1st cl. Hons; PhD); Emmanuel Coll., Cambridge (Salters' Res. Fellowship). Various tech. and commercial appts, ICI Ltd, UK and Brussels, 1969–79; Arco Chemical Europe: Gen. Manager, Sales and Mktg, 1979–81; Manager, Mergers and Acquisitions, 1981–83; Business Manager, Urethanes, 1983–88; Dir of Business Develt, 1988–91; Vice Pres., Business Mgt, 1991–94; Pres. and Chief Exec., Arco Chemical Europe, 1994–98, subseq. Lyondell Chemical Europe, 1998–2000. Chm., Industry Cttee, and Southern Reg. Adv. Panel, EA, 2002–09. Trustee: Prince of Wales's Phoenix Trust, 1996–2004 (Chm., 2003–04); Earthwatch Europe, 1997–2002; Churches Conservation Trust, 1999–2005 (Dep. Chm., 2001–05); Norden Farm Centre for Arts, 2002–12. Liveryman, Horners' Co., 2000– (Mem., Ct of Assts, 2004–). *Publications:* scientific papers on nonlinear optics, scattering and atomic and molecular physics in learned jls, various business pubns and speeches in conf. procs. *Recreations:* water sports (esp. scuba diving), collecting antique furniture and antiquarian scientific books, photography, music. *Address:* Broadley, 11 Woodlands Ride, Ascot, Berks SL5 9HP. *T:* (01344) 626904, *Fax:* (01344) 627045. *E:* lyndon.stanton@btinternet.com. *Club:* Athenæum.

STANTON, Prof. Stuart Lawrence Richard, FRCS, FRCSE, FRCOG; Professor of Pelvic Surgery and Urogynaecology, St George's Hospital Medical School, 1997–2003, now Emeritus Professor; Consultant Gynaecologist and Director of Urogynaecology Unit, St George's Hospital, 1984–2003; in practice as private gynaecologist, urogynaecologist and medico-legal consultant, 1974–2012; *b* 24 Oct. 1938; *s* of Michael Arthur Stanton and Sarah (*née* Joseph); *m* 1965, Anne Frances Goldsmith (marr. diss. 1991); three *d*; *m* 1991, Julia Heller; one *s* one *d*. *Educ:* City of London Sch.; London Hosp. Med. Sch. (MB BS 1961). FRCS 1966; FRCSE 1966; FRCOG 1987. Surgical Registrar, Royal Masonic Hosp., 1964–65; SHO, Queen Charlotte's Hosp., 1967; Res. Registrar, Inst. of Urology, London, 1971–72; Sen. Registrar, Dept of Obstetrics and Gynaecology, St George's Hosp., London, 1972–74; Consultant Obstetrician and Gynaecologist, St Helier Hosp., 1974–84. Lectures: William Blair Bell Meml, 1974, William Meredith Fletcher Shaw, 1996, RCOG; Victor Bonney, RCS, 1984; J. Marion Sims, Amer. Urogynecologic Soc., 1995. Pres., British Soc. of Urogynaecology, 2003–. Vice Chm., Hadassah UK, 2011– (Chm., 2010–11). FRSocMed 1975. Hon. FRANZCOG 2000. *Publications:* (ed jtly) Surgery of Female Incontinence, 1980, 2nd edn 1986; Clinical Gynaecologic Urology, 1984; (ed) The Principles of Gynaecological Surgery, 1987; Gynaecology in the Elderly, 1988; (ed jtly) Gynaecology, 1992, 3rd edn 2003; (ed jtly) Pelvic Floor Re-education, 1994, 2nd edn 2008; (ed jtly) Clinical Urogynaecology, 1999; (ed jtly) Urinary Tract Infections in the Female, 2000. *Recreations:* family, photography, modern ceramics, biographies, music. *Address:* 1 Church Hill, SW19 7BN. *E:* stuartstanton@hotmail.co.uk.

STAPELY, Sue; solicitor; independent reputation management consultant with Sue Stapely Consulting Ltd, since 2001; *b* 11 July 1946; *d* of Stanley Sly and Kathleen MacIvor; two *s*; *m* 2012, David Fitt. *Educ:* Kingston Univ. (LLB Hons); Coll. of Law (Solicitors Final Exam.). Production posts, BBC TV, 1966–73; Manager, various CABx, 1973–83; Partner, Heald Nickinson (solicitors), 1985–89; Hd of PR, Law Soc., 1989–96 (Mem., 1989–); Dir, Fishburn Hedges, 1996–2001. Contested (SDP) Chertsey and Walton, 1987. Mem., Nat. Exec. Cttee, SDP, 1986–88; Chm., Women for Social Democracy, 1987–88; Founding Nat. Chm., 300 Group, 1986–88. Member Board: SW Thames RHA, 1993–94; London Ambulance Service, 1993–94; Countryside Agency, 2000–03; LAMDA, 1998–; Spare Tyre Theatre Co., 1999–2012; Brighton Fest., 2006–; Media Standards Trust, 2007–; Mem. Develt Council, Royal Court Theatre, 1998–2006. Mem. Bd, Dignity in Dying (formerly Voluntary Euthanasia Soc.), 2004–06. Trustee, Solicitors' Pro Bono Gp. FRSA 1994; FCIPR (FIPR 2002). *Publications:* Media Relations for Lawyers, 1994, 2nd edn 2003. *Recreations:* conversation, travel, theatre, fast cars. *Address:* Wood Lane House, Cherington, Warwicks CV36 5HY; Star Cottage, Little Compton, Glos GL56 0RY.

STAPLE, George Warren, CB 1996; Partner, Clifford Chance, 1987–92 and 1997–2001, Consultant, 2001–12; Director, Serious Fraud Office, 1992–97; *b* 13 Sept. 1940; *s* of late Kenneth Harry Staple and Betty Mary Staple; *m* 1968, Olivia Deirdre Lowry; two *s* two *d*. *Educ:* Haileybury. Articled to Walker Charlesworth and Jefferson, Westminster, and Coll. of Law, 1958–62; Associate with Condon and Forsyth, NY, 1963; admitted Solicitor, 1964; Asst Solicitor, 1964–67, Partner, 1967–87, Clifford-Turner & Co. Legal Assessor, Disciplinary Cttee, Stock Exchange, 1978–92; DTI Inspector, Consolidated Gold Fields, 1986, Aldermanbury Trust, 1988; a Chairman, Authorisation and Disciplinary Tribunals: of The Securities Assoc., 1987–91; of Securities and Futures Authy, 1991–92; Member: Commercial Court Cttee, 1977–92; Law Adv. Cttee, British Council, 1998–2001; Sen. Salaries Review Body, 2000–04; Tribunal Panel, Accountancy and Actuarial Discipline Bd, 2005–13; Chairman: Fraud Adv. Panel, 1998–2003; Review Bd for Govt Contracts, 2002–09. Mem. Council, Law Soc., 1986–2000 (Treas., 1989–92). Trustee: Romney Marsh Historic Churches Trust, 2002–; Royal Humane Soc., 2007–. Gov., City of London Polytechnic, subseq. London Guildhall Univ., 1982–94; Chm. Govs, Haileybury, 2001–08. Hon. QC 1997; Hon. Bencher, Inner Temple, 2000. *Recreations:* cricket, walking, gardening. *Address:* Clifford Chance, 10 Upper Bank Street, E14 5JJ. *Clubs:* Brooks's, City of London, MCC.

See also W. P. Staple.

STAPLE, William Philip; non-executive Deputy Chairman, Westhouse Holdings plc, 2011–14 (Managing Partner, Westhouse Securities LLP, then Chief Executive, Hanson Westhouse Ltd, later Chief Executive, Westhouse Holdings plc, 2005–11); *b* 28 Sept. 1947; *s* of late Kenneth Harry Staple and Betty Mary Staple (*née* Lemon); *m* 1977, Jennifer Frances Walker (marr. diss. 1986); one *s* one *d*. *Educ:* Haileybury; Coll. of Law. Called to the Bar, Inner Temple, 1971; Executive at Cazenove, 1972–81; N. M. Rothschild and Sons Ltd: Asst Dir, 1981–86; Dir, 1986–94 and 1996–99; Dir Gen., Takeover Panel, 1994–96; Man. Dir, Benfield Advisory, 1999–2001; Dir, Corporate Finance, Brown, Shipley & Co. Ltd, 2001–04. *Recreations:* golf, theatre, reading. *Address:* 18 Calico House, SW11 3TN. *E:* billstaple@hotmail.co.uk. *Clubs:* White's, City of London.

See also G. W. Staple.

STAPLEFORD, Sally Anne, OBE 1999; President, National Ice Skating Association of UK Ltd, 1995–2006; *b* 7 July 1945; *d* of Richard Harvey Stapleford and Alice Elizabeth Stapleford. *Educ:* Streatham Hill High Sch.; Clapham High Sch.; private tutor. British Jun. Ice Skating Champion, 1961; Southern Regl Sen. Ice Skating Champion, 1961–63; Gold Medal: Britain, and Canada, 1961; America, 1962; British Sen. Ice Skating Champion, 1963–68; competed in: European Championships, 1963–68 (Silver Medal, 1965); World Championships, 1964–68; Winter Olympics, 1964, 1968; won Edinburgh Internat. Trophy, 1968. Nat. judge and referee, 1968–2006; internat. judge and referee, 1972–2003; National Ice Skating Association (formerly National Skating Association): Mem., Governing Body, 1970–; Chm., Ice Figure Cttee, 1989–94; Vice-Chm., Fedn of Ice Skating, 1990; Technical Orgnr, internat. figure skating events in UK; Mem., 1988–92, Chm., 1992–2002, Figure Skating Technical Cttee, Internat. Skating Union; Mem., Nat. Olympic Cttee, 1994–99. *Address:* Flat 3, St Valery, 54 Beulah Hill, Upper Norwood, SE19 3ER. *T:* (020) 8771 0778.

STAPLES, Brian Lynn; Chairman: Pendle (UK) Ltd, since 2003; Effective Waste Solutions Ltd, 2003–09; European Scanning Centre, since 2008; St Joseph's Hospital Ltd, since 2014; *b* 6 April 1945; *s* of Stanley Holt Staples and Catherine Emma Annie Staples (*née* Walding); *m* 1st, 1965; one *d*; 2nd, 1973; one *s* two *d*; 3rd, 1999, Anne-Marie Smith; two *s*. *Educ:* Sweyne Grammar Sch., Rayleigh. Joined Tarmac Group, 1964; Chief Executive: Tarmac Construction, 1991–94; United Utilities Plc (formerly North West Water Gp), 1994–97; Amey PLC, 1997–2003; Dir and Chief Exec., Scottish BioPower Ltd, 2003–07. Chm., Scottish Resources Gp, 2005–11 (non-exec. Dir, Mining Scotland Gp, 2004; Dep. Chm., Mining (Scotland) Ltd, 2006). *Recreations:* Rugby, music, theatre, outdoor pursuits. *Address:* Pendle House, Castle Hill, Prestbury, Cheshire SK10 4AR.

STAPLES, (Hubert Anthony) Justin, CMG 1981; HM Diplomatic Service, retired; Ambassador to Finland, 1986–89; *b* 14 Nov. 1929; *s* of late Francis Hammond Staples, formerly ICS, and Catherine Margaret Mary Pownall; *m* 1962, Susan Angela Collingwood Carter; one *s* one *d*. *Educ:* Downside; Oriel Coll., Oxford. Served in RAF 1952–54 (Pilot Officer). Entered Foreign (later Diplomatic) Service, 1954; 3rd Sec., Bangkok, 1955; Foreign Office, 1959; 1st Sec., Berlin (Dep. Political Adviser), 1962; Vientiane, 1965 (acted as Chargé d'Affaires in 1966 and 1967); transf. to FO and seconded to Cabinet Office, 1968; Counsellor, UK Delegn to NATO, Brussels, 1971; Counsellor and Consul-General, Bangkok, 1974 (acted as Chargé d'affaires, 1975 and 1977); Counsellor, Dublin, 1978–81; Ambassador to Thailand, 1981–86 and concurrently to Laos, 1985–86. Pres., Anglo-Finnish Soc., 1993–2014. Order of the Lion (Finland), 2003. *Recreation:* golf. *Address:* 48 Crescent Road, Kingston, Surrey KT2 7RF. *Clubs:* Travellers (Chm., 2003–06); Roehampton; Royal Bangkok Sports (Bangkok).

STAPLETON, Annamarie; *see* Phelps, A.

STAPLETON, Air Vice-Marshal Deryck Cameron, CB 1960; CBE 1948; DFC; AFC; psa; *b* 15 Jan. 1918; *s* of John Rouse Stapleton, OBE, Sarnia, Natal; *m* 1942, Ethleen Joan Clifford, *d* of late Sir Cuthbert William Whiteside. *Educ:* King Edward VI Sch., Totnes. Joined RAF, 1936; served Transjordan and Palestine (AFC), 1937–39; War of 1939–45 (DFC). Middle East, N Africa, Italy. Asst Sec. (Air), War Cabinet Offices, 1945–46; Secretary, Chiefs of Staff Cttee, Ministry of Defence, 1947–49; OC RAF, Odiham, 1949–51; subsequently, Plans, Fighter Comd HQ and Ops at AFCENT Fontainebleau; then OC, RAF, Oldenburg (Germany); Plans, Bomber Comd HQ, 1957–60; Air Ministry, 1960–62; Dir, Defence Plans, Min. of Defence, 1963–64; AOC No 1 Group, RAF Bomber Command, 1964–66; Comdt, RAF Staff Coll., Bracknell, 1966–68. BAC Area Manager, Libya, 1969–70; BAC Rep. CENTO Area, Tehran, later BAe Chief Exec. Iran, and Man. Dir, Irano-British Dynamics Co. Iran, 1970–79; Rep. BAe, Beijing, China, and Chm., British Cos Assoc., Beijing, 1979–83. *Publications:* (jtly) Winged Promises, 1996. *Recreation:* most sports.

STAPLETON, Very Rev. Henry Edward Champneys, MBE 2009; Dean of Carlisle, 1988–98; *b* 17 June 1932; *s* of Edward Parker Stapleton and Frances Mary Champneys; *m* 1964, Mary Deborah Sapwell; two *d*. *Educ:* Lancing College; Pembroke Coll., Cambridge (BA 1954, MA 1958); Ely Theological Coll. Deacon 1956, priest 1957, York; Assistant Curate: St Olave with St Giles, 1956–59; Pocklington, 1959–61; Vicar of Seaton Ross with Everingham, Harswell and Bielby, 1961–67; RD of Weighton, 1966–67; Rector of Skelton, 1967–75; Vicar of Wroxham with Hoveton, 1975–81; Priest in Charge of Belaugh, 1976–81, with Hoveton St Peter, 1979–81; Canon Residentiary and Precentor of Rochester Cathedral, 1981–88; Warden of Readers, 1981–88. Sec., York Diocesan Adv. Cttee, 1959–75; Church Comr, 1993–98; Member: Council for the Care of Churches, 1965–91; Churches Conservation Trust (formerly Redundant Churches Fund), 1976–98; Royal Commn on Historical Manuscripts, 1992–2002. Chm., Incorp. Church Building Soc., 2002–13. Trustee, Nat. Churches Trust (formerly Historic Churches Preservation Trust), 1983–2008. Chm., Cathedral Libraries and Archives Assoc., 1988–97; Member: Liby Cttee, Lambeth Palace, 1999–2006; Archbishops' Adv. Panel for Archives and Libraries, 2006–12. Fellow, Woodard Corp., 1990–2002. FSA 1974. Editor, Cathedral, 1976–82. Hon. Fellow, Univ. of Northumbria, Newcastle, 1995. *Publications:* Skelton Village, 1971; Heirs without Title, 1974; The Skilful Master Builder, 1975; The Model Working Parson, 1976; (ed and contrib.) Churchyards Handbook, 2nd edn 1976, 3rd edn 1988; articles in Churchscape and other ecclesiastical jls. *Recreations:* the writings of R. H. Benson, genealogy, visiting churches, second-hand bookshops. *Address:* Rockland House, 20 Marsh Gardens, Honley, Holmfirth, W Yorks HD9 6AF. *T:* (01484) 666629. *E:* hec.stapleton@talktalk.net.

STAPLETON, Nigel John; Chairman, Postal Services Commission, 2004–10; Chairman of Trustees, Mineworkers Pension Scheme, since 2009; *b* 1 Nov. 1946; *s* of Frederick Ernest John Stapleton and Katie Margaret Stapleton (*née* Tyson); *m* 1982, Johanna Augusta Molhoek; one *s* one *d*. *Educ:* City of London Sch.; Fitzwilliam Coll., Cambridge (MA; Hon. Fellow 1998). Planning, finance and gen. mgt positions, incl. Vice Pres., Finance, Unilever United States Inc., Unilever plc, 1968–86; Reed International plc: Dir, 1986–99; Finance Dir, 1986–96; Dep. Chm., 1994–97; Chm., 1997–99; Co-Chm., 1996–98, Co-Chief Exec., 1998–99, Reed Elsevier plc; Chairman: Veronis, Suhler Internat. Ltd, 1999–2002; Uniq plc, 2001–06. Dir, London Stock Exchange, 2001–10. Non-executive Director: Allied Domecq plc, 1992–99; Marconi plc (formerly GEC), 1997–2002; Axa UK (formerly Sun Life and Provincial Hldgs) plc, 1999–2002; Reliance Security Gp Ltd, 2002–11; Independent Director:

Kazpost, 2008–13; Real Estate Fund Samruk Kazyna, 2011–13; Sovereign Wealth Fund Samruk Kazyna, 2013–. Ind. Trustee, Nat. Grid UK Pension Scheme, 2012–. Trustee, Royal Opera House Trust, 1999–2001. *Recreations:* theatre, opera, travel, tennis. *Club:* Oxford and Cambridge.

STAPLETON, Prof. Richard Christopher, PhD; Professor of Finance (part-time), University of Manchester, 2003–14; *b* 11 Oct. 1942; *s* of Leonard Stapleton and Rosamund Kathleen May Stapleton; *m* 1968, Linda Cairns; one *s* one *d*. *Educ:* Univ. of Sheffield (BAEcon, PhD Business Studies); Open Univ. (BA Maths). Lectr in Business Finance, Sheffield Univ., 1965–73; Asst Prof. of Finance, New York Univ., 1973–76; Sen. Res. Fellow, 1976–77, Nat. West. Bank Prof. of Business Finance, 1977–86, Manchester Business Sch., Univ. of Manchester; Fellow, Churchill Coll., Cambridge, 1986–89; Wolfson Prof. of Finance, Lancaster Univ., 1989–98; Prof. of Finance, Strathclyde Univ., 1998–2003. Hon. MBA Manchester, 1980. *Publications:* The Theory of Corporate Finance, 1970; International Tax Systems and Financing Policy, 1978; Capital Markets and Corporate Financial Decisions, 1980; contrib. Econ. Jl, Jl of Finance, Jl of Financial Econs, Qly Jl of Econs. *Recreations:* running, golf, reading, travel.

STAPLETON, Victoria Lucy Annabel, (Mrs Jonathan Pilkington); Founder and Creative Director, Brora Ltd, since 1993; *b* Chelmsford, 5 April 1967; *d* of David Stapleton and Annabel Stapleton; *m* 1999, Jonathan Pilkington; three *d*. *Educ:* St Mary's Sch., Ascot; Univ. of East Anglia (BA). Film prodn asst, 1988–89; Founder, Pyjamarama, 1989–91; Account Manager, Lindsay Hiscox Designs, 1991–92; Retail Manager, Hunters of Brora, 1992–93. *Recreations:* art exhibitions, theatre, adventures, fishing, ski-ing, golf. *Address:* Brora Ltd, 5–6 The Orbital Centre, Gunnels Wood Road, Stevenage, Herts SG1 2NB. *T:* (01438) 744300.

STAPLETON-COTTON, family name of **Viscount Combermere**.

STARGARDT, Lyndal Anne; *see* Roper, L. A.

STARK, David; *see* Stark, J. D. S.

STARK, George Robert, PhD; FRS 1990; Distinguished Scientist, Lerner Research Institute, Cleveland Clinic Foundation, since 2002 (Chairman, 1992–2002); *b* 4 July 1933; *s* of Jack and Florence Stark; *m* 1956, Mary Beck; one *s* one *d*. *Educ:* Columbia College, NY (BA 1955); Columbia Univ., NY (Chemistry; PhD 1959). Asst Prof., Rockefeller Univ., 1961; Stanford University: Asst Prof., 1963; Associate Prof., 1966; Prof. of Biochemistry, 1971; ICRF, 1983–92 (Associate Dir of Res., 1989–92). Member: European Molecular Biol. Orgn, 1985; NAS, USA, 1987; Inst. of Medicine, USA, 2002. *Publications:* contribs to scientific jls. *Recreations:* sports, stamps, books, records. *Address:* Cleveland Clinic Foundation, 9500 Euclid Avenue, Cleveland, OH 44195, USA. *T:* (216) 4443900, *Fax:* (216) 4443279.

STARK, (John) David (Sinclair), CEng; Chairman, Norcros Group (Trustee) Ltd, 2005–09 (Director, 1999–2009); *b* 16 April 1939; *s* of John and Bertha Stark; *m* 1964, Pamela Margaret Reed; one *s* one *d*. *Educ:* St Bees Sch., Cumberland; Leeds Univ. (BSc). CEng, MIET (MIEE 1966). GEC plc, 1960–62; Morgan Crucible plc, 1962–76; Bestobell plc, 1976–81; Man. Dir, Bestobell Australia Ltd, 1981–84; Divl Chief Exec., Unitech plc, 1984–85; Divl Dir, 1985–86, Dir, 1986–97, Tomkins plc; Chm., Glentay, subseq. Brauer Technologies, Ltd, 1997–2004; Dir, Norcros plc, 1997–99. Non-exec. Dir, Royal Mint, 2000–04 (Chm., 2002–04). Mem., Monopolies and Mergers, subseq. Competition, Commn, 1998–2005. Gov., Esher Church Sch., 1998–2006. *Recreations:* inland waterways, opera, amateur dramatics. *Address:* Tara, 15 Copsem Drive, Esher, Surrey KT10 9HD. *T:* (01372) 466781.

STARK, Jürgen; independent economist, since 2012; Member, Executive Board, European Central Bank, 2006–11; *b* 31 May 1948. *Educ:* Univ. of Hohenheim (first degree in econs 1973; DEc 1975); Eberhard Karls Univ., Tübingen. Res. Asst, Univ. of Hohenheim, 1973–78; Official, Econ. Policy Dept, Min. of Econs, Germany, 1978–88; First Sec., Perm. Repn of Fed. Rep. of Germany to GATT, Geneva, 1982–83; Hd of Div., For. Trade and Payments, Money and For. Currency, Financial Mkts, Federal Chancellery, 1988–92; Ministry of Finance: Dep. Hd of Dept, Nat. Monetary Policy, Capital Mkt Policy, Germany as Financial Centre, Borrowing, 1992; Hd of Dept, Internat. Monetary and Financial Relns, Financial Relns in EC, 1993–94; State Sec. and Personal Rep. of Federal Chancellor in preps for G7/G8 Econ. Summits, 1995–98; Vice Pres., Deutsche Bundesbank, 1998–2006. Hon. Prof., Faculty of Econs, Eberhard Karls Univ., Tübingen, 2005–. Alternate Gov. and Delegate for Germany to IMF, 1995–2006; Member: Monetary Cttee, 1995–98, Econ. and Financial Cttee, 1999–2011, EU; G7 and G10 Deputies, 1995–2006, G20 Deputies, 1999–2006; Internat. Relns Cttee, ESCB, 1998–2006; Cttee on Global Financial System (G10, BIS), 1998–2006; Financial Stability Forum, 1999–2006. Member Supervisory Board: Deutsche Telekom AG, 1995–98; Deutsche Bahn AG, 1995–98; German Investment and Develt Corp., 1997–98; Dep. Mem., Bd of Dirs, BIS, 1998–2006. Dep. Chm., Ifo Inst., Munich, 1999–; Chm., Univ. of Hildesheim Foundn, 2003–. Trustee, Bertelsmann Foundn, 2012–.

STARKEY, Amy; Regional Director, East, Jockey Club Racecourses, since 2012; *b* York, 27 April 1981; *d* of Steven and Deborah Starkey. *Educ:* All Saints RC Sch., York; Trinity and All Saints Coll., Leeds Univ. (BA Business Mgt). Commercial Exec., Northern Racing, Sedgefield and Newcastle Racecourses, 2002–05; Jockey Club: Managing Director: Huntingdon Racecourse, 2005–08; Kempton Park Racecourse, 2008–12. *Recreations:* horseracing, reading, snowboarding. *Address:* 4 The Gallops, Old Station Road, Newmarket CB8 8LA. *E:* amy.starkey@thejockeyclub.co.uk.

STARKEY, Dr David Robert, CBE 2007; FSA; FRHistS; historian and broadcaster; *b* 3 Jan. 1945; *s* of Robert Starkey and Elsie Starkey (*née* Lyon). *Educ:* Kendal GS; Fitzwilliam Coll., Cambridge (Open Schol.; Hon. Fellow, 2006). FRHistS 1984; FSA 1994. Fitzwilliam College, Cambridge: Res. Fellow, 1970–72; Vis. Fellow, 1998–2001; Bye-Fellow, 2001–06; Pres., Fitzwilliam Soc., 2003–04. Lectr in History, Dept of Internat. History, LSE, 1972–98. Vis. Vernon Prof. of Biography, Dartmouth Coll., New Hampshire, 1987, 1989; British Council Specialist Visitor, Australia, 1989; Hon. Vis. Prof. of History, Univ. of Kent, 2007–. Guest Curator: Henry VIII: a European court in England, Nat. Maritime Mus., 1991; Elizabeth, Nat. Maritime Mus., 2003; Making History, RA, 2007; Lost Faces, Philip Mould Ltd, 2007; Henry VIII: man and monarch, British Library, 2009; Royal River: power, pageantry and the Thames, Nat. Maritime Mus., 2012. Presenter and writer of television series: This Land of England, 1985; Henry VIII, 1998 (Indie Award, 2002); Elizabeth I, 2000; Six Wives of Henry VIII, 2001 (Silver Medal, NY Festivals World, 2004; Cine Golden Eagle, Thirteen/WNET, NY, 2006); The Unknown Tudors, 2002; Monarchy, 2004–07; Starkey's Last Word, 2006; Henry VIII: Mind of a Tyrant, 2009; The Churchills, 2012; Music and Monarchy, 2013; David Starkey's Magna Carta, 2015; presenter and writer: TV prog., Kate and William: Romance and the Royals, 2011; (with Lucy Worsley), A Night at Hampton Court Palace, 2015; contributor, TV series: The Genius of British Art, 2010; Jamie's Dream School, 2011; panellist, Moral Maze, BBC Radio 4, 1992–2001; Presenter, Starkey on Saturday, then Starkey on Sunday, Talk Radio, 1995–98. Mem., Commemorative Plaques Wkg Gp, English Heritage, 1993–2006; Pres., Soc. for Court Studies, 1996–2005. Vice-Pres., Tory Campaign for Homosexual Equality, 1994–. Liveryman, Co. of Barbers, 1999– (Freeman, 1992). Mem. Editl Bd, History Today, 1980–; Hon. Associate: Rationalist Press Assoc., 1995–; Nat. Secular Soc., 1999–. Hon. Commodore, Nat. Maritime Mus., 2005; Trustee and Hon. Commodore, Mary Rose Trust. Hon. DLitt: Lancaster, 2004; Kent, 2006. Norton Medlicott Medal, for services to history, Historical Assoc., 2001. *Publications:* (jtly) This Land of England, 1985; The Reign of Henry VIII: personalities and politics, 1985, 3rd edn 2002; (ed jtly) Revolution Reassessed: revisions in the history of Tudor government and administration, 1986; (ed) The English Court from the Wars of the Roses to the Civil War, 1987; (ed) Rivals in Power: the lives and letters of the great Tudor dynasties, 1990; Henry VIII: a European court in England, 1991; (ed jtly) The Inventory of Henry VIII, vol. I, 1998; Elizabeth: apprenticeship, 2000 (W H Smith Award for Biog./Autobiog., 2001); Six Wives: the Queens of Henry VIII, 2003; The Monarchy of England, vol. 1: the beginnings, 2004; Monarchy: from the Middle Ages to Modernity, 2006; Henry: virtuous prince, 2008; Crown and Country: a history of England through the monarchy, 2010; (with K. Greening) Music and Monarchy, 2013; Magna Carta: the true story behind the charter, 2015; contribs to newspapers, numerous articles in learned jls. *Recreations:* decorating, gardening, treading on toes. *Address:* Fitzwilliam College, Cambridge CB3 0DG.

STARKEY, Sir John (Philip), 3rd Bt *cr* 1935; DL; *b* 8 May 1938; *s* of Sir William Randle Starkey, 2nd Bt, and Irene Myrtle Starkey (*née* Francklin) (*d* 1965); *S* father, 1977; *m* 1966, Victoria Henrietta Fleetwood (marr. diss. 2014), *y d* of Lt-Col Christopher Fuller, TD; one *s* three *d*. *Educ:* Eton College; Christ Church, Oxford. Sloan Fellow, London Business School. Notts: DL, 1981; High Sheriff, 1987–88. *Recreations:* cricket, painting, golf. *Heir: s* Henry John Starkey [*b* 13 Oct. 1973; *m* 2002, Georgina Gemma, *y d* of Richard Whittington; two *s*]. *Address:* Norwood Park, Southwell, Notts NG25 0PF. *Club:* MCC.

STARKEY, Dr Phyllis Margaret; *b* 4 Jan. 1947; *d* of Dr John Williams and Catherine Hooson Williams (*née* Owen); *m* 1969, Hugh Walton Starkey; two *d*. *Educ:* Perse Sch. for Girls, Cambridge; Lady Margaret Hall, Oxford (BA Biochem.); Clare Hall, Cambridge (PhD). Research posts: Strangeways Lab., Cambridge, 1970–81; Sir Wm Dunn Sch. of Pathology, Oxford, 1981–84; Lectr in Obstetrics and Gynaecology, 1984–93, and Fellow of Somerville Coll., 1987–93, Univ. of Oxford; Head of Assessment, BBSRC, 1993–97. Sen. Associate Mem., St Antony's Coll., Oxford, 2011–. Mem. (Lab) Oxford City Council, 1983–97 (Leader, 1990–93); Chm., Local Govt Inf. Unit, 1992–97. MP (Lab) Milton Keynes SW, 1997–2010; contested (Lab) Milton Keynes S, 2010. PPS to FCO Ministers, 2001–02, to Minister of State (Minister for Europe), FCO, 2002–05. Mem., Foreign Affairs Select Cttee, 1999–2001; Chm., Select Cttee for DCLG (formerly ODPM), 2005–10. Chm., POST, 2002–05. Mem. Bd, St Martin of Tours Housing Assoc., 2011–; Ind. Mem. Bd, Landscape Inst., 2013–; Mem., Community Bd, Greensquare Housing Assoc., 2014–; Chm., Jericho Wharf Trust, 2012–. Trustee, Med. Aid for Palestinians, 2011–. *Publications:* numerous scientific articles in learned jls. *Recreations:* gardening, cinema, walking. *Address:* 8 Walton Crescent, Oxford OX1 2JG.

STARLING, Keith Andrew; Headmaster, The Judd School, 1986–2004; *b* 12 June 1944; *s* of Stanley Ernest Starling and Gladys Joyce Starling; *m* 1968, Jacqueline Eagers; two *s*. *Educ:* The Perse Sch.; Fitzwilliam Coll., Cambridge (MA, CertEd). Asst Master, Lancaster Royal Grammar Sch., 1968–71; Head of Geography, Sedbergh Sch., 1971–80; Dep. Headmaster, Portsmouth Grammar Sch., 1980–86. Gov., Stamford Endowed Schs, 2005–15. Treas., Percy Whitlock Trust, 2012–; Trustee, Hosp. of St John and St Anne, Oakham, 2014–. Liveryman, Skinners' Co., 2004–. *Recreations:* music, walking. *Address:* Elderberry Cottage, Orchard Close, Egleton, Rutland LE15 8AG.

STARLING, Nicholas James; Director, Nick Starling Consultancy, since 2014; Director of General Insurance (formerly Director of General Insurance and Health), Association of British Insurers, 2005–13; *b* 16 March 1956; *s* of Richard James Starling and late Helen Mary Starling; *m* 1984, Catherine Susannah Thompson; two *d*. *Educ:* George Watson's Coll., Edinburgh; St John's Coll., Cambridge (BA Archaeol. and Anthropology 1977); St John's Coll., Oxford (DPhil 1983). Theodor Heuss Fellow, Univ. of Cologne, 1981–82; Randall Maciver Student in Archaeol., Queen's Coll., Oxford, 1982–83; Department of Transport: joined, 1984; Pvte Sec. to Minister for Roads and Traffic, 1986–88; Principal, 1988–94; Asst Sec., 1994–98; Dep. Dir, Internat. Aviation, 1994–98; Hd, Nuclear and Hazardous Installations Policy, 1998–2000, Dir, Safety Policy, 2000–03, Policy Dir, 2003–05, HSE. *Publications:* various articles in archaeol. jls. *Recreations:* family, music, especially Schubert, singing, cooking, Guardian crossword. *E:* nick_starling@hotmail.com.

STARMER, Sir Keir, KCB 2014; QC 2002; MP (Lab) Holborn and St Pancras, since 2015; *b* 2 Sept. 1962; *s* of Rod and late Jo Starmer; *m* 2007, Victoria Alexander; one *s* one *d*. *Educ:* Reigate Grammar Sch.; Leeds Univ. (LLB 1st Cl. Hons 1985); St Edmund Hall, Oxford (BCL 1986; Hon. Fellow, 2012). Called to the Bar: Middle Temple, 1987, Bencher, 2009; St Lucia, 1997; St Vincent, 1997; Belize, 2002. Dir of Public Prosecutions, 2008–13. Fellow, Human Rights Centre, Essex Univ., 1998–. Human Rights Advr to NI Policing Bd, 2003–08. Mem., Foreign Sec.'s Adv. Panel on the Death Penalty, 2002–08. Mem., Governance Adv. Bd, British Council, 2002–07. Mem. Council, Justice, 1999–2008. DUniv Essex, 2011; Hon. DLaws Leeds, 2012. Human Rights Lawyer of the Year Award, Justice/Liberty, 2001. *Publications:* (ed) Justice in Error, 1995; Three Pillars of Liberty: political rights and freedom in the UK, 1996; Signing up for Human Rights: the UK and international standards, 1998; (ed) Miscarriages of Justice, 1999; European Human Rights Law, 1999; Blackstone's Human Rights Digest, 2001; Criminal Justice, Police Powers and Human Rights, 2001; (contrib.) Human Rights Principles, 2001; (contrib.) Mithani's Directors' Disqualification, 2001; (contrib.) Human Rights and Civil Practice, 2001; contribs to Public Law. *Recreations:* football, classical music. *Address:* House of Commons, SW1A 0AA.

STARMER-SMITH, Nigel Christopher; International Rugby Board consultant and TV commentator, since 2002; *b* 25 Dec. 1944; *s* of late Harry Starmer-Smith and Joan Mary Starmer-Smith (*née* Keep); *m* 1973, Rosamund Mary Bartlett; one *s* (and one *s* one *d* decd). *Educ:* Magdalen Coll. Sch., Oxford; University Coll., Oxford (MA). Schoolmaster, Epsom Coll., 1967; Producer and Reporter, BBC Radio Outside Broadcasts, 1971; Sports Commentator, BBC TV, 1973–2002; Commentator, ITV Rugby World Cup, 2003; Presenter and Commentator, Rugby Special; commentator, hockey and other sports. Publisher and Editor, Rugby World and Post magazine, 1984–93. Former Rugby Union international: Harlequins, Oxford Univ., Barbarians, England. Gov., Shiplake Coll., 2003–. Trustee, Reading and Dist Hospitals Charity, 1991–. *Publications:* include: The Barbarians, 1977; Rugby: a way of life, 1986. *Recreations:* family, tennis, piano playing, horse racing, gardening. *Address:* Cobblers Cottage, Skirmett, Henley-on-Thames RG9 6TD. *T:* (01491) 639422. *Clubs:* Vincent's (Oxford); Leander (Henley); Harlequins FC.

STARR, Lesley Ann; *see* Page, L. A.

STARR, Nicholas Frederick, CBE 2013; Executive Director, National Theatre, 2002–14; *b* Swanley, Kent, 23 Oct. 1957; *s* of Anthony and Marian Starr. *Educ:* Chislehurst and Sidcup Grammar Sch.; Merton Coll., Oxford (BA Hons English Lang. and Lit.). Lectr, Oxford Coll. of Further Educn, 1980–83; Mktg Officer, Cambridge Th. Co., 1983–84; Mktg Manager, Half Moon Th., 1984–86; Mktg Manager, Paton Walker Associates, 1986–87; Press Officer, 1987–91, Hd of Planning, 1991–96, RNT; Dir, Warwick Arts Centre, 1996–97; Exec. Dir, Almeida Th., 1997–2001; Dir, US Prodns, 2001–02. Chm., Battersea Arts Centre, 2001–09; Bd Dir, Soc. of London Theatre, 2003–12. Chm. Trustees, Bush Th., 2009–; Trustee: NESTA, 2007–13; Young Vic Th., 2007–12. *Recreations:* piano-playing, gardening. *Address:* Abbey Farmhouse, Abbey Road, Faversham ME13 7BL.

STATMAN, Philip Richard; His Honour Judge Statman; a Circuit Judge, since 2002; *b* 28 March 1953; *s* of Martin and Evelyn Statman; *m* 1997, Mary Louise Cameron (*d* 2006); two *s*. *Educ:* Mid Essex Tech. Coll. (LLB Hons London (ext.)); Inns of Court Sch. of Law.

Called to the Bar, Middle Temple, 1975; specialised in criminal law; Asst Recorder, 1997–2000; a Recorder, 2000–02. *Recreations:* travel, Association Football, cinema, literature, antiques. *Address:* Maidstone Combined Court Centre, Barker Road, Maidstone ME16 8EQ. *T:* (01622) 202000.

STAUNTON, Imelda Mary Philomena Bernadette, OBE 2006; actress, since 1976; *b* 9 Jan. 1956; *d* of Joseph Staunton and Bridie McNicholas; *m* 1983, Jim Carter, actor; one *d*. *Educ:* La Sainte Union Convent, Highgate; RADA. *Theatre* includes: rep., 1976–81; The Corn is Green, Old Vic, 1985; Calico, Duke of York's, 2004; There Came a Gypsy Riding, Almeida, 2007; Entertaining Mr Sloane, Trafalgar Studios, 2009; A Delicate Balance, Almeida, 2011; Sweeney Todd, Chichester, 2011 (Olivier Award for Best Actress in a Musical, 2013), Adelphi, 2012; Circle Mirror Transformation, Rose Lipman Building, 2013; Good People, Hampstead, transf. Noël Coward Th., 2014; Gypsy, Chichester, 2014, Savoy, 2015; *National Theatre:* Guys and Dolls, 1982, 1996; Beggar's Opera, Chorus of Disapproval (Olivier Award, best supporting actress), 1985; Life × 3, 2000, transf. Old Vic; *Royal Shakespeare Company:* Fair Maid of the West, Wizard of Oz, 1986; Uncle Vanya, Vaudeville, 1988; Into the Woods, Phoenix, 1990 (Olivier Award, best actress in a musical, 1991); *television* includes: The Singing Detective, 1986; Yellowbacks, 1990; Sleeping Life; Roots; Up the Garden Path, 1990; Antonia & Jane; Is it Legal?; Murder, 2002; Cambridge Spies, 2003; Fingersmith, 2005; Cranford, 2007, 2009; Psychoville, 2010–11; The Girl, 2012; That Day We Sang, 2014; *films* include: Peter's Friends, 1992; Much Ado About Nothing, 1993; Deadly Advice, 1994; Sense and Sensibility, Twelfth Night, Remember Me, 1996; Shakespeare in Love, 1999; Rat, 2001; Crush, 2002; Blackball, Virgin of Liverpool, Bright Young Things, 2003; Vera Drake, 2004 (BAFTA Award, best actress, 2005); Nanny McPhee, 2005; Freedom Writers, 2006; Harry Potter and the Order of the Phoenix, 2007; Three and Out, A Bunch of Amateurs, 2008; Another Year, Harry Potter and the Deathly Hallows, Pt 1, 2010; The Awakening, 2011; Pride, 2014; Maleficent, 2014. *Address:* c/o ARG, 4A Exmoor Street, W10 6BD.

STAUNTON, Prof. James, PhD; FRS 1998; Professor of Chemical Biology, 1999–2002, and Fellow of St John's College, since 1969, University of Cambridge; *b* 18 March 1935; *s* of James and Elizabeth Staunton; *m* 1961, Dr Ruth Mary Berry, MB, ChB. *Educ:* St Edward's Coll., Liverpool; Univ. of Liverpool (BSc 1956; PhD 1959); MA Cantab 1969. Postdoctoral Fellow, Stanford Univ., 1959–60; Fellow, 1960–62, Lectr in Organic Chemistry, 1962–69, Liverpool Univ.; Lectr in Organic Chemistry, 1969–78, Reader, 1978–99, Cambridge Univ. Natural Products Award, 1987, Tilden Medal, 1989, Robert Robinson Award, 2001, RSC. *Publications:* Primary Metabolism: a mechanistic approach, 1978; articles in chemical and biochemical jls. *Recreations:* walking, cycling, gardening, travel, DIY. *Address:* St John's College, Cambridge CB2 1TP.

STAUNTON, Marie, CBE 2013; Chief Executive: Plan International UK, 2000–12; Interact Worldwide, 2009–12; *b* 28 May 1952; *d* of Ann and Austin Staunton; *m* 1986, James Albert Provan; two *d*. *Educ:* Lancaster Univ.; College of Law (BA). Solicitor. Head of casework for Simon Community Hostels for Addicts, Alcoholics and Homeless Families (England, NI and Eire), 1970–72; Articled Clerk and Solicitor in private practice and Law Centres, 1976–83; Legal Officer, NCCL, 1983–87; Dir, British Section, Amnesty Internat., 1987–90 (Vice-Chm., Internat. Exec. Cttee, 1993–95); Publishing Dir, Longman Law Tax & Finance, then Financial Times Law & Tax, 1990–96; Ed., Solicitors' Jl, 1990–95; Dep. Dir, UK Cttee for UNICEF, 1997–2000. Non-exec. Dir, Crown Agents, 2013–. UK Ind. Mem., Mgt Bd, EU Fundamental Rights Agency, 2007–12. Trustee, Disasters Emergency Cttee, 2011–12; Chairman, Trustees: Equality and Diversity Forum, 2012–; Raleigh Internat., 2013–. *Publications:* Data Protection: putting the record straight, 1987; Because I am a Girl, 2010; contribs to NCCL works; chapters in books on allied subjects.

STAVERT, Most Rev. Alexander Bruce; Metropolitan of the Ecclesiastical Province of Canada, and Archbishop of Quebec, 2004–09; *b* 1 April 1940; *s* of Ewart and Kathleen Stavert; *m* 1982, Diana Greig; one *s* two *d*. *Educ:* Lower Canada Coll., Montreal; Bishop's Univ., Lennoxville, PQ (BA 1961): Trinity Coll., Univ. of Toronto (STB 1964; MTh, 1976). Incumbent of Schefferville, Quebec, 1964–69; Fellow, 1969–70, Chaplain, 1970–76, Trinity Coll., Univ. of Toronto; Incumbent, St Clement's Mission East, St Paul's River, PQ, 1976–81; Chaplain, Bishop's Univ., Lennoxville, 1981–84; Dean and Rector, St Alban's Cathedral, Prince Albert, Sask., 1984–91; Bishop of Quebec, 1991–2009. Hon. DD Toronto, 1986. *Recreations:* swimming, ski-ing. *Address:* c/o Church House, 31 rue des Jardins, Québec, QC G1R 4L6, Canada. *T:* (418) 6923858. *Club:* Garrison (Québec).

STAVORDALE, Lord; Simon James Fox-Strangways; *b* 25 Aug. 1972; *s* and *heir* of Earl of Ilchester, *qv*.

STEAD, Prof. Christian Karlson, ONZ 2007; CBE 1985; PhD, DLitt; FRSL; FEA; writer; Professor of English, University of Auckland, 1968–86, now Emeritus; *b* 17 Oct. 1932; *s* of James Walter Ambrose Stead and Olive Ethel Stead; *m* 1955, Kathleen Elizabeth Roberts; one *s* two *d*. *Educ:* Mt Albert Grammar Sch.; Univ. of NZ (MA 1955); Univ. of Bristol (PhD 1962); Univ. of Auckland (DLitt 1981). Lectr in English, Univ. of New England, NSW, 1956–57; Michael Hiatt Baker Schol., Univ. of Bristol, 1957–59; Lectr, then Sen. Lectr in English, 1960–64, Associate Prof., 1964–68, Univ. of Auckland. Nuffield Fellow, London, 1965; Hon. Vis. Fellow, UCL, 1977; Fulbright Travelling Fellow, UCLA, 1987; Sen. Vis. Fellow, St John's Coll., Oxford, 1996–97. Katherine Mansfield Menton Fellow, 1972; Arts Laureate, Waitakere City, 2006; Bogliasco Foundn Fellow in Arts, 2007, 2011. FRSL 1995; FEA 2003. Hon. DLitt Bristol, 2001. Jessie McKay Award for Poetry, PEN NZ, 1972; NZ Book Award, for Poetry, 1976, for Fiction, 1985, 1995; Distinguished Citizen Award, Auckland, 2007; Distinguished Alumni Award, Univ. of Auckland, 2008; Prime Minister's Award for Fiction, NZ, 2009; Sunday Times EFG Private Bank Short Story Award, 2010; Open Internat. Award, Hippocrates Prize for Poetry and Medicine, 2010; Honoured NZ Writer, Auckland Writers Fest., 2015. *Publications:* South-West of Eden: a memoir, 1932–56, 2010; *poetry:* Whether the Will is Free, 1964; Crossing the Bar, 1972; Quesada, 1975; Walking Westward, 1978; Geographies, 1981; Paris, 1984; Poems of a Decade, 1985; Between, 1987; Voices, 1990; Straw into Gold: poems new and selected, 1997; The Right Thing, 2000; Dog, 2002; The Red Tram, 2004; The Black River, 2007; Collected Poems, 1951–2006, 2008 (Montana Book Award, Creative NZ, 2009); The Yellow Buoy, 2013; *fiction:* Smith's Dream, 1971; Five for the Symbol (stories), 1981; All Visitors Ashore, 1984; The Death of the Body, 1986; Sister Hollywood, 1988; The End of the Century at the End of the World, 1991; The Singing Whakapapa, 1994; Villa Vittoria, 1996; The Blind Blonde with Candles in her Hair (stories), 1998; Talking about O'Dwyer, 1999; The Secret History of Modernism, 2002; Mansfield: a novel, 2004; My Name Was Judas, 2006; Risk, 2012; *literary criticism:* The New Poetic, 1964; In the Glass Case: essays on New Zealand literature, 1981; Pound, Yeats, Eliot and the Modernist Movement, 1986; Answering to the Language, 1989; The Writer at Work, 2000; Kin of Place: essays on twenty New Zealand writers, 2002; Book Self: the reader as writer and the writer as critic, 2008; *edited:* New Zealand Short Stories, 2nd series, 1966; Measure for Measure: a casebook, 1971; Letters and Journals of Katherine Mansfield, 1977; Collected Stories of Maurice Duggan, 1981; Faber Book of Contemporary South Pacific Stories, 1993; Werner Forman's New Zealand (photographs with commentary), 1995. *Recreations:* swimming, music, walking. *Address:* 37 Tohunga Crescent, Auckland 1052, New Zealand.

STEAD, Ian Mathieson, PhD; FSA; FBA 1991; Deputy Keeper, Department of Prehistoric and Romano-British Antiquities, British Museum, 1977–96 (Assistant Keeper, 1974–77); *b* 9 Jan. 1936; *er s* of Sidney William Stead and Edith Johann (*née* Mathieson); *m* 1962, Sheelagh Mary Johnson; one *s* one *d*. *Educ:* Nunthorpe Grammar Sch., York; Fitzwilliam House, Cambridge Univ. (MA; PhD 1965). FSA 1966. Asst Inspector of Ancient Monuments, 1962, Inspector, 1964–74, Min. of Works. Chairman: Herts Archaeol Council, 1970–75; Humberside Jt Archaeol Cttee, 1974–81; Sec., Prehistoric Soc., 1974–76. Hon. Life Mem., Yorks Philosophical Soc., 1982; Corresp. Mem., Deutsches Archäologisches Institut, 1976. Silver Medal, Yorks Archaeol Soc. 2005. *Publications:* La Tène Cultures of Eastern Yorkshire, 1965; Winterton Roman Villa, 1976; Arras Culture, 1979; (with J.-L. Flouest) Iron Age Cemeteries in Champagne, 1979; Rudston Roman Villa, 1980; The Gauls, 1981; Celtic Art in Britain, 1985, 2nd edn 1996; Battersea Shield, 1985; (with J. B. Bourke and D. Brothwell) Lindow Man, the Body in the Bog, 1986; (with V. Rigby) Baldock, 1986; (with V. Rigby) Verulamium, the King Harry Lane Site, 1989; Iron Age Cemeteries in East Yorkshire, 1991; (with Karen Hughes) Early Celtic Designs, 1997; The Salisbury Hoard, 1998 (British Archaeol Awards Book Award, 2000); (with V. Rigby) The Morel Collection, 1999; British Iron Age Swords and Scabbards, 2006; (with J.-L. Flouest and V. Rigby) Iron Age and Roman Burials in Champagne, 2006; papers in learned jls. *Address:* Adam House, 11 Ogleforth, York YO1 7JG.

STEAD, Rt Rev. John; *see* Willochra, Bishop of.

STEADMAN, Alison, OBE 2000; actress; *b* Liverpool, 26 Aug. 1946; *d* of late George Percival Steadman and Marjorie Steadman; *m* 1973, Mike Leigh, *qv* (marr. diss. 2001); two *s*. *Theatre includes:* Abigail's Party, Hampstead (Best Actress, Evening Standard Awards), 1977; Joking Apart, Globe, 1979; Uncle Vanya, Hampstead, 1979; Cinderella and her Naughty Sisters, Lyric, Hammersmith, 1980; A Handful of Dust, Lyric, Hammersmith, 1982; Tartuffe, Maydays, RSC, 1985; Kafka's Dick, Royal Court, 1986; Cat on a Hot Tin Roof, NT, 1988; The Rise and Fall of Little Voice, Aldwych (Olivier Best Actress Award), 1992; Marvin's Room, Hampstead, transf. Comedy, 1993; When We Are Married, Chichester, transf. Savoy, 1996; The Provok'd Wife, Old Vic, 1997; The Memory of Water, Vaudeville, 1999; Entertaining Mr Sloane, Arts, 2001; The Woman Who Cooked Her Husband, New Ambassadors, 2002; Losing Louis, Hampstead, transf. Trafalgar Studios, Whitehall, 2005, nat. tour, 2006; Enjoy, Th. Royal, Bath, 2008, transf. Gielgud, 2009; Blithe Spirit, Th Royal, Bath, transf. Apollo, 2011; Here, Rose Th., Kingston, 2012; Thérèse Raquin, Th. Royal, Bath, 2014; *television includes:* Nuts in May, 1976; Through the Night, 1976; Abigail's Party, 1977; Our Flesh and Blood, 1978; Pasmore, 1980; P'tang Yang Kipperbang, 1982; The Singing Detective, 1986; Virtuoso, 1989; A Small Mourning, 1989; News Hounds, Gone to the Dogs, 1990; Gone to Seed, 1991; Selling Hitler, 1992; Pride and Prejudice, 1995; Wimbledon Poisoner, 1995; Karaoke, 1996; No Bananas, 1996; The Missing Postman, 1997; Let Them Eat Cake, 1999; Fat Friends, 2000, 2002, 2004, 2005; Adrian Mole: The Cappuccino Years, 2001; The Worst Week of my Life, 2004; The Worst Christmas of My Life, 2006; The Last Detective, 2006; The Dinner Party, 2007; Fanny Hill, 2007; Gavin and Stacey, 2007–09; King of the Teds, 2012; Civil Arrangement, 2012; The Syndicate, 2013; Love and Marriage, 2013; Alison Steadman's Shetland, 2014; Boomers, 2014–15; The Secrets, 2014; *radio includes:* Beyond Black, 2010; Clarissa, 2010; A Tale of Two Cities, 2012; Bird Island, 2012; Gloomsbury, 2012, 2014; *films include:* Champions, 1983; A Private Function, 1984; Number One, 1985; Clockwise, 1986; The Adventures of Baron Münchhausen, Shirley Valentine, Wilt, 1989; Life is Sweet, Blame it on the Bellboy, 1991; Topsy-Turvy, 1999; DIY Hard, 2002; Chunky Monkey, The Life and Death of Peter Sellers, 2004; Peterman, 2014. Hon. MA Univ. of East London, 1996; DU Essex, 2003. *Address:* c/o ARG, 4A Exmoor Street, W10 6BD.

STEADMAN, Dr John Hubert; consultant in regulatory and environmental toxicology and environmental health, 1996–2013; *b* 10 Aug. 1938; *s* of late Dr Harry Hubert Steadman and Janet Gilchrist Steadman (*née* MacDonald); *m* 1972, Dr Anthea Howell; one *s* one *d*. *Educ:* Wimbledon Coll.; Guy's Hosp. (MB, BS); University Coll. London (MSc). University College Hospital, London: Beit Meml Fellowship, 1968–72; Sen. Registrar, Dept of Haematology, 1972–78, with secondments to Ahmadu Bello Univ. Hosp., Nigeria, 1973, and Royal Perth Hosp., WA, 1974; Cons. Haematologist, King George Hosp., Ilford, 1978–81; MO 1981, SMO 1982, PMO 1984, DHSS; SPMO, Head of Div. of Toxicology and Envmtl Health, subseq. Health Aspects of Envmt and Food, DoH, 1988–93; Hd of Consumer and Envmtl Safety, Unilever, 1993–96. Expert Advr on food safety, WHO, 1988–93. *Publications:* articles in learned jls on regulatory toxicology, haematology and biochemistry. *Recreations:* cooking, languages, cosmology. *Address:* 38 Kingswood Avenue, NW6 6LS.

See also J. M. M. Curtis-Raleigh.

STEADMAN, Ven. Mark John; Archdeacon of Stow and Lindsey, since 2015; *b* 20 May 1974; *s* of John Edward Steadman and Gloria Ann Steadman (*née* Williams). *Educ:* Southampton Univ. (LLB 1995); Westcott House, Cambridge; Christ's Coll., Cambridge (MA 2005). Called to the Bar, Inner Temple, 1996; ordained deacon, 2002, priest, 2003; Curate, St Mary's, Portsea, 2002–05; Priest-in-charge, St Philip's, Camberwell, 2005–12; Area Dean, Bermondsey, 2008–11; Chaplain to the Bishop of Southwark, 2011–15. *Recreations:* opera, travel, cooking. *Address:* Edward King House, Minster Yard, Lincoln LN2 1PU. *T:* (01522) 504050.

STEADMAN, Ralph Idris; freelance cartoonist, artist and writer; *b* 15 May 1936; *s* of Lionel Raphael Steadman (English), and Gwendoline (Welsh); *m* 1st, 1959, Sheila Thwaite (marr. diss. 1971); two *s* two *d*; 2nd, 1972, Anna Deverson; one *d*. *Educ:* Abergele Grammar Sch.; London Coll. of Printing and Graphic Arts. Apprentice, de Havilland Aircraft Co., 1952; Cartoonist, Kemsley (Thomson) Newspapers, 1956–59; freelance for Punch, Private Eye, Telegraph, during 1960s; Political Cartoonist, New Statesman, 1978–80; retired to work on book about Leonardo da Vinci; as a positive political statement, refuses to draw another politician; 15 Save the Children originals auctioned in aid of Ethiopia Fund, 1990. Retrospective exhibitions: Nat. Theatre, 1977; Royal Festival Hall, 1984; Cartoon Mus., 2013; exhibitions: Wilhelm Busch Mus., Hannover, 1988; October Gall. (sculptures and silk screen prints), 1990, Gulf war collages, 1991; Peacock Gall., Aberdeen, 1993; Aberdeen City Art Gall., 1994; The Lord is an Animal, One on One Gall., Denver, USA, 1997; Contemporary Satirists, RA, 1997; Les Sixties, Les Invalides, Paris, transf. Brighton, 1997; centenary Lewis Carroll exhibn, Warrington Mus., 1998; Making a Mark, William Havu Gall., Denver, 2000; Who? Me! No!! Why?? (pictures and artefacts from book Doodaaa), NY, 2003. Designed set of stamps of Halley's Comet, 1986; opera libretto and concept, Plague and the Moonflower, Exeter Cathedral and Festival, 1989 (artist-in-residence), St Paul's Cathedral, 1989, Canterbury Cathedral and Festival, 1990, performed as Hearts Betrayed, St Martin-in-the-Fields, 1993, televised 1995, recorded 1999; libretto and concept, Love Underground, Norwich Fest., 1997; artist-in-residence, Cheltenham Fest., 1994; designer, Gulliver's Travels, Theatr Clwyd, 1995; artist-in-residence, Leviathan series of films, BBC2, 1999; designer of set and costumes, The Crucible, Royal Ballet, 2000. Writer, dir and performer, TV film, Hanging Garden Centres of Kent, 1992; artist, film, For No Good Reason, 2014. Hon. Fellow, Kent Inst. of Art and Design, 1993. Hon. DLitt Kent, 1995. D & AD Gold Award (for outstanding contribution to illustration), 1977, and Silver Award (for outstanding editorial illustration), 1977; Black Humour Award, France, 1986; W. H. Smith Illustration Award for best illustrated book for last five years, 1987; BBC Design Award for postage stamps, 1987; Empire Award (for involvement with film Withnail and I), Empire Magazine, 1996; Milton Caniff Award, Nat. Cartoonists Soc. of America, 2005; Star of Saatchi and Saatchi Clio Creative Hero Show, 2008. *Publications:* Jelly Book, 1968; Still Life with Raspberry: collected drawings, 1969; The Little Red Computer, 1970; Dogs Bodies, 1971; Bumper to Bumper Book, 1973; Two Donkeys and the Bridge, 1974; Flowers for the Moon, 1974; America: drawings, 1975; America: collected drawings, 1977 (rev. edn, Scar Strangled Banger, 1987); Between the Eyes, 1984; Paranoids, 1986; The Grapes of Ralph, 1992; Teddy! Where are you?, 1994; Untrodden Grapes, 2005; The Joke's Over: memories of Hunter S. Thompson, 2006; *written and illustrated:* Sigmund Freud, 1979 (as The Penguin Sigmund Freud, 1982); A Leg in the Wind and other Canine Curses, 1982; I, Leonardo, 1983; That's My Dad, 1986 (Critici in Erba Prize, 1987); The Big I Am, 1988; No Room to Swing a Cat, 1989; Near the Bone, 1990; Tales of the Weirrd, 1990; Still Life with Bottle, Whisky According to Ralph Steadman, 1994; Jones of Colorado, 1995; Gonzo: the art, 1998; little.com, 2000; Garibaldi's Biscuits, 2008; designed and printed, Steam Press Broadsheets; Proud Too Be Weirrd, 2013; *illustrated:* Frank Dickens, Fly Away Peter, 1961, 2008; Mischa Damjan: The Big Squirrel and the Little Rhinoceros, 1962; The False Flamingoes, 1963; The Little Prince and the Tiger Cat, 1964; Two Cats in America, 1968; Richard Ingrams, The Tale of Driver Grope, 1964; Love and Marriage, 1964; Daisy Ashford, Where Love Lies Deepest, 1964; Fiona Saint, The Yellow Flowers, 1965; Alice in Wonderland, 1967; Midnight, 1967; Tariq Ali, The Thoughts of Chairman Harold, 1968; Dr Hunter S. Thompson: Fear and Loathing in Las Vegas, 1972, 25th anniv. edn, 1997; The Curse of Lono, 1984, 2nd (limited) edn 2004; Kurt Baumann, The Watchdog and the Lazy Dog, 1974; Contemporary Poets set to Music series, 1972; Through the Looking Glass, 1972; Night Edge: poems, 1973; The Poor Mouth, 1973; John Letts Limericks, 1974; The Hunting of the Snark, 1975; Dmitri Sidjanski, Cherrywood Cannon, 1978; Bernard Stone: Emergency Mouse, 1978; Inspector Mouse, 1980; Quasimodo Mouse, 1984; Ted Hughes, The Threshold (limited edn), 1979; Adrian Mitchell, For Beauty Douglas, 1982; Flann O'Brien, More of Myles, 1982; Wolf Mankowitz, The Devil in Texas, 1984; Treasure Island, 1985; The Complete Alice and The Hunting of the Snark, 1986; Friendship (short stories), 1990 (in aid of John McCarthy); Animal Farm, 50th anniv. edn, 1995; Adrian Mitchell, Heart on the Left, Poems 1953–1984, 1997; Roald Dahl, The Mildenhall Treasure, 1999; Doodaaa: the balletic art of Gavin Twinge (novel), 2002; Ambrose Bierce, The Devil's Dictionary, 2003; Fahrenheit 451, 50th anniv. limited edn, 2003; Hunter S. Thompson, Fire in the Nuts, 2004; Will Self, PsychoGeography, 2007; Will Self, Psycho Too, 2009; Ralph Steadman's Extinct Boids, 2012. *Recreations:* gardening (planted vineyard), collecting, writing, sheep husbandry, fishing, guitar, trumpet. *W:* www.ralphsteadman.com. *Club:* Chelsea Arts.

STEAR, Air Chief Marshal Sir Michael (James Douglas), KCB 1990; CBE 1982; QCVSA 1969; DL; Deputy Commander-in-Chief, Allied Forces Central Europe, 1992–96; *b* 11 Oct. 1938; *s* of late Melbourne Douglas Stear and Barbara Jane Stear (*née* Fletcher); *m* 1966, Elizabeth Jane (*d* 2015), *d* of late Donald Edward Macrae, FRCS and Janet Wallace Macpherson Macrae (*née* Simpson); two *s* one *d*. *Educ:* Monkton Combe Sch.; Emmanuel Coll., Cambridge (MA; CU Air Sqn (RAFVR), 1959–62). Nat. Service, RAF, 1957–59. Joined RAF, 1962; served on 1 Sqn, Hunters, 1964–67, on 208 Sqn, Hunters, Persian Gulf, 1967–69; exchange tour with USAF, F4 Phantom, 1969–71; RAF Staff Coll., 1972; Air Sec.'s Br., MoD, 1972–74; OC 17 Sqn, Phantom, Germany, 1974–76; OC 56 Sqn, Phantom, RAF Wattisham, 1976; PSO to CAS, MoD, 1976–79; OC RAF Gutersloh and Harrier Force Comdr, RAF Germany, 1980–82; Asst C of S (Ops), HQ 2 ATAF, 1982; Air Cdre Plans, HQ Strike Command, 1982–85; AOC No 11 Gp, UK Air Defence, 1985–87; ACDS (Nato/UK), MoD, 1987–89; AOC No 18 Gp, Maritime, and Comdr Maritime Air Eastern Atlantic and Channel, 1989–92. Mem., Commonwealth War Graves Commn, 1998–2003. Member: RUSI, 1989–99; Council, Malcolm Clubs, 1988–2003; RFU Cttee, 1987–98 (Mgt Bd Jt Vice-Chm. (admin), 1997–98); Air League, 1999–; Pres., RAF RU, 1992–97 (Chm., 1983–86). Nat. Pres., RAFA, 1998–2002 (Vice-Pres., 1997–98; Life Vice-Pres., 2002–; Service Vice-Pres., Europe Area, 1992–96); Pres., RAF and Allied Air Forces Monument Service Cttee, 2010–; Hon. Pres., Devon & Som Wing, ATC, 2000–11. Pres., Exeter and District Br. Cttee, ESU, 2013– (Mem., 2009–; Progs Sec., 2009–12; Vice Chm., 2010–12; Chm., 2012–13). FRAeS 1997–2011. DL Devon, 2000. *Recreations:* Rugby football, gardening, fishing, shooting, music – jazz to grand opera, history – ancient and modern. *Club:* Royal Air Force (Vice-Pres., 1990–98).

STEAR, Roderick Morton, (Rory); Executive Chairman, Flambard Holdings Ltd, since 2007; non-executive Chairman, Lifeline Energy Ltd, since 2011; *b* 17 March 1959; *s* of Robert and Natalie Stear; *m* 1995, Kristine Joy Pearson. *Educ:* Grey High Sch., Port Elizabeth, SA; Rhodes Univ., SA. Founder and Man. Dir, Seeff Corporate Finance, 1990–94; Founder and Exec. Chm., Freeplay Energy Gp, 1994–2008; Exec. Chm., MobileWave Gp (formerly Fieldbury) plc, 1995–2013. Chm., Minlam Asset Mgt LLP, 2009–11. Member, President Nelson Mandela's business delegation: to UK, 1996; to USA, 1998. Student, Birthing of Grants prog., MIT, 2000. Member: Dean's Council, John F. Kennedy Sch. of Govt, Harvard Univ., 2005–14; Adv. Bd, Business Sch., Nelson Mandela Univ., Port Elizabeth, SA, 2005– (Chm., 2005–); Adv. Bd, Melton Foundn, 2014–. Mem., African Business Roundtable, 1995. Member: Global Agenda Council on Renewable Energies, World Economic Forum, 2008–11; Pres. of S Africa's Business Delegn to UK and to India, 2010. Founder, Lifeline Energy (formerly Freeplay Foundn), 1998. CNN Principal Voice, 2007; Hero of the Envmt, Time, 2007. *Recreations:* golf, gym, music, reading. *Address:* Flambard Holdings Ltd, 2 Stone Buildings, Lincoln's Inn, WC2A 3TH. *E:* rstear@flambardholdings.com. *Clubs:* Royal Automobile; Jockey (S Africa); Steenberg Golf.

STEARNS, Elizabeth Jane Elford, FFFLM; HM Coroner, Eastern District, Greater London, 1998–2011; *b* 20 Nov. 1946; *d* of Cecil Smith and Audrey Quelch; *m* 1972, Michael Patrick Stearns; three *s*. *Educ:* Wycombe Abbey Sch.; Guy's Hosp. Dental and Med. Schs, London (BDS Hons, LDS RCS 1970; MB BS 1974). FFFLM 2006. Assistant Deputy Coroner: City of London, 1993; N London, 1994–95; Dep. Coroner, N London, 1995–98. Called to the Bar, 1997. Examr for Dips in Forensic Med. Scis. Pres., SE Coroners' Soc., 2005–06; Vice-Pres., Faculty of Forensic and Legal Medicine, RCP, 2006–10.

STEBBING, Nowell, PhD; Chairman, Pharmagene plc (formerly Pharmagene Laboratories Ltd), 1996–2003; *b* 5 Sept. 1941; *s* of Lionel Charles Stebbing and Margarita (*née* Behrenz); *m* 1st, 1963, Nancy Lynah (marr. diss.); two *d* (one *s* decd); 2nd, 1973, Birgit Griffiths (*née* Evjen); one *s*. *Educ:* Michael Hall Sch., Sussex; Univ. of Edinburgh (BSc Hons 1964; PhD 1968). Demonstrator, Univ. of Edinburgh, 1967–69; Director of Biology: G. D. Searle & Co., 1969–79; Genentech Inc., San Francisco, 1979–82; Vice-Pres., Scientific Affairs, Amgen Inc., Thousand Oaks, Calif, 1982–86; Gen. Manager, Res., ICI Pharmaceuticals, UK, 1986–93; Chief Exec. and Dep. Chm., Chiroscience Gp PLC, 1993–95. Chm., Axis Genetics, 1995–99. *Publications:* numerous papers and articles in scientific and med. jls and books. *Recreations:* theatre, old cars, gardens, wine making in Italy.

STEDMAN JONES, Prof. Gareth, DPhil; FBA 2013; Professor of the History of Ideas, Queen Mary University of London, since 2010; Co-Director, Centre for History and Economics, Cambridge, since 1991; Fellow of King's College, Cambridge, since 1974; *b* 17 Dec. 1942; *s* of Lewis and Joan Olive Stedman Jones; one *s* by Prof. Sally Alexander; one *s* by Prof. Miri Rubin. *Educ:* St Paul's Sch.; Lincoln Coll., Oxford (BA 1964); Nuffield Coll., Oxford (DPhil 1970). Res. Fellow, Nuffield Coll., Oxford, 1967–70; Sen. Associate Mem., St Antony's Coll., Oxford, 1971–72; Humboldt Stiftung Fellow, Dept of Philosophy, Goethe Univ., Frankfurt, 1973–74; University of Cambridge: Lectr in History, 1979–86; Reader in History of Social Thought, 1986–97; Prof. of Political Thought (formerly Political Sci.), 1997–2010. Mem., CNRS, 2005–10. Mem., Editl Bd, New Left Review, 1964–81; Jt Founder and Jt Ed., History Workshop Jl, 1976–. *Publications:* Outcast London, 1971, 3rd edn 2013; Languages of Class, 1983; Klassen, Politik, Sprache, 1988; (ed) Charles Fourier, The Theory of the Four Movements, trans. I. Patterson, 1994; (ed) Karl Marx and Friedrich Engels, The Communist Manifesto, 2002 (trans. German 2013); An End to Poverty?, 2004 (trans. French 2007); Columbia, 2005; (ed) Religion and the Political Imagination, 2010; (ed jtly) Cambridge History of Nineteenth-Century Political Thought, 2011. *Recreations:* country walks, collecting old books, cricket. *Address:* King's College, Cambridge CB2 1ST. *T:* (01223) 331120.

STEDMAN-SCOTT, Baroness *cr* 2010 (Life Peer), of Rolvenden in the County of Kent; **Deborah Stedman-Scott,** OBE 2008; DL; Chief Executive, Tomorrow's People, since 2005; *b* Paddington, London, 23 Nov. 1955; *d* of Jack and Doreen Margaret Scott; civil partnership 2006, Gabrielle Joy Stedman-Scott. *Educ:* Ensham Secondary Sch. for Girls; Southwark Tech. Coll.; Salvation Army Trng Coll. Nat. Westminster Bank, 1972–76; The Salvation Army, 1978–83; Royal Tunbridge Wells Chamber of Commerce, 1983–84; Tomorrow's People Trust: Devel Manager, Hastings, 1984–86; Manager, Kent and Sussex Area, 1986–88, SE Region, 1988–93; Nat. Ops Dir, 1993–95; Trust Dir, 1995–2005. DL E Sussex, 2007. Charity Principal of the Year, UK Charity Awards, 2005. *Recreations:* reading, art - particularly Lowry, travelling, opera. *Address:* House of Lords, SW1A 0PW. *T:* (020) 7219 8919. *E:* stedmanscottd@parliament.uk.

STEEDEN, Dr Michael Frank, FRAeS; Corporate Adviser, Defence Science and Technology Laboratory, 2012–14; *b* London, 23 March 1952; *s* of Frank and late Joyce Steeden; *m* 1975, Hilary Bridget Alison Ambrose; one *s* one *d*. *Educ:* Judd Sch., Tonbridge, Kent; King's Coll. London (BSc Hons Physics; PhD Nuclear Structure Physics 1981); Open Univ. (MBA). CDipAF 1996. FInstP 1995–2012; FRAeS 1995. PSO, AWRE, 1983–87; Hd, Atomic Co-ordinating Office, UK Embassy, Washington, 1987–89; Asst Dir, Guided Weapons Air, 1989–91, Dir, Mil. Aircraft Procurement, 1991–94, MoD Procurement Exec.; rcds 1995; Dir, Air Systems Sector, 1996–98, Aircraft Test and Evaluation, 1998–2000, DERA; Pres. and Man. Dir, Computing Devices Co. Ltd, 2000–02; Dir, Civil Air Transport, Soc. of British Aerospace Cos, 2002–06; Tech. Dir, 2006–09, Dir, Strategic Relns, 2009–12, Defence Sci. and Technol. Lab. Non-executive Director: Ploughshare Innovations Ltd, 2007–; Tetricus Ltd, 2007–10. Pres., RAeS, 2009–10 (Chm., Medals and Awards Cttee). FInstD 2008–13. Liveryman, Engrs' Co., 2005–12. *Publications:* contribs to Jl Physics G, World Defence Systems. *Recreations:* guitar, modern jive, family history, archery, current affairs.

STEEDMAN, Prof. Carolyn Kay, PhD; FBA 2011; Professor of History, University of Warwick, 1999–2013, now Emeritus; *b* 20 March 1947. *Educ:* Rosa Bassett Grammar Sch. for Girls, London; Univ. of Sussex (BA Hons English and Amer. Studies 1968); Newnham Coll., Cambridge (MLitt 1974; PhD 1989). Teacher, E Sussex and Warwicks, 1974–81; Institute of Education, University of London: project asst to Lang. in the Multicultural Primary Classroom Project, 1982–83; Fellow, Sociol. Dept, 1983–84; University of Warwick: Lectr, 1984–88, Sen. Lectr, 1988–91, Reader, 1991–93, Dept of Arts Educn; Reader, 1993–95, Prof. of Social Hist., 1995–98, Dir, 1998–99, Centre for Study of Social Hist. ESRC Res. Prof., 2004–07. Vis. Prof., Univ. of Michigan, Ann Arbor, 1992. Sen. Simon Res. Fellow, Univ. of Manchester, 1990–91. *Publications:* The Tidy House, 1982 (Fawcett Soc. Book Prize, 1983); Policing the Victorian Community, 1984; (ed jtly) Language, Gender and Childhood, 1984; Landscape for a Good Woman, 1986; The Radical Soldier's Tale: John Pearman, 1819–1908, 1988; Childhood, Culture and Class in Britain: Margaret McMillan, 1860–1931, 1990; Past Tenses: essays on writing, history and autobiography, 1980–1990, 1992; Strange Dislocations: childhood and the idea of human interiority, 1780–1930, 1995; Dust, 2001; Master and Servant: love and labour in the English industrial age, 2007; Labours Lost: domestic service and the making of modern England, 2009; An Everyday Life of the English Working Class: work self, and sociability in the early nineteenth century, 2013. *Address:* Department of History, University of Warwick, Humanities Building, University Road, Coventry CV4 7AL.

STEEDMAN, Prof. Mark, PhD; FRSE; FBA 2002; Professor of Cognitive Science, University of Edinburgh, since 1998; *b* 18 Sept. 1946; *s* of George and Nan Steedman; *m* 1987, Prof. Bonnie Lynn Webber. *Educ:* Univ. of Sussex (BSc); Univ. of Edinburgh (PhD 1973). Res. Fellow, Univ. of Sussex, 1973–76; Lectr in Psychology, Univ. of Warwick, 1976–83; Lectr, 1983–86, Reader, 1986–88, in Computational Linguistics, Univ. of Edinburgh; Associate Prof. of Computer and Inf. Sci., 1988–92, Prof., 1992–98, Adjunct Prof., 1998–, Univ. of Pennsylvania. FAAAI 1993; FRSE 2002; MAE 2006; Fellow, Assoc. of Computational Linguistics, 2012. *Publications:* Surface Structure and Interpretation, 1996; The Syntactic Process, 2000; Taking Scope, 2012; articles in Linguistics & Philosophy, Cognition, Cognitive Science, Linguistic Inquiry, Computational Linguistics, etc. *Recreations:* jazz, hill-climbing. *Address:* School of Informatics, University of Edinburgh, 10 Crichton Street, Edinburgh EH8 9AB. *T:* (0131) 650 4631, *Fax:* (0131) 650 6626.

STEEDMAN, Dr Robert Russell, OBE 1997; RSA 1979 (ARSA 1973); RIBA; FRIAS; MLI; Partner, Morris and Steedman, Architects and Landscape Architects, Edinburgh, 1959–2002; *b* 3 Jan. 1929; *s* of late Robert Smith Steedman and Helen Hope Brazier; *m* 1st, 1956, Susan Elizabeth (marr. diss. 1974), *d* of Sir Robert Scott, GCMG, CBE; one *s* two *d*; 2nd, 1977, Martha Hamilton, OBE (*d* 2015). *Educ:* Loretto Sch.; School of Architecture, Edinburgh College of Art (DA); Univ. of Pennsylvania (MLA). RIBA 1955; ALI 1979. Lieut, RWAFF, 1947–48. Worked in office, Alfred Roth, Zürich, 1953. Architectural works include: Principal's House, Univ. of Stirling; Head Offices for Christian Salvesen, Edinburgh; Administration Building for Shell UK Exploration and Production; Moss Morran Fife; Restoration of Old Waterworks, Perth, to form Tourist Information Centre and Offices; Nat. Lighthouse Mus., Fraserburgh. Ten Civic Trust Awards, 1963–88; British Steel Award, 1971; Saltire Award, 1971, 1999; RIBA Award for Scotland, 1974 and 1989; European Architectural Heritage Medal, 1975; Assoc. for Preservation of Rural Scotland Award, 1977 and 1989. Chm., Central Scotland Woodlands Project, 1984–87; Member: Countryside Commn for Scotland, 1980–88; Adv. Panel on Management of Popular Mountain Areas in Scotland, 1989; Royal Fine Art Commn for Scotland, 1984–96 (Dep. Chm., 1994–96); Council, Nat. Trust for Scotland, 1999–2005; Sec., Royal Scottish Acad., 1983–90 (Mem. Council 1981–, Dep. Pres. 1982–83, 2000–01); Mem. Bd, Friends of Royal Scottish Acad., 1984–92; Governor, Edinburgh College of Art, 1974–88; Mem., Edinburgh Festival Soc., 1978–; past Mem. Council, RIAS and Soc. of Scottish Artists. Trustee: House of Falkland, 1999–; St Andrews Preservation Trust, 2002–10 (Hon. Pres., 2014–); Royal Scottish Acad. Foundn, 2012–. Member Panel: Saltire Patrick Geddes Award, 1995–; Assoc. for Protection of Rural Scotland Annual Awards, 1995–99. Hon. Senior, St Leonards Sch., 1987–. FRSA 1995. Hon. DLitt St Andrews, 2006; DUniv Stirling, 2011. Gold Medal for Lifetime Achievement in Architecture, RIAS, 2009; Architecture Lifetime Achievement Award, Scottish Design Awards, 2009. *Recreations:* hill-walking, photography, redesigning other people's houses. *Address:* Muir of Blebo, Blebocraigs, by Cupar, Fife KY15 5UG. *T:* (01334) 850781. *Clubs:* New (Edinburgh); Royal & Ancient Golf (St Andrews).

See also R. S. Steedman.

STEEDMAN, (Robert) Scott, CBE 2010; PhD; FREng; Director of Standards, British Standards Institution, since 2012; *b* Edinburgh, 10 Sept. 1958; *s* of Dr Robert Russell Steedman, *qv*; *m* 1st, 1981, Zoreh Kazemzadeh (marr. diss. 2002); one *s* one *d*; 2nd, 2005, Hon. Dr Deborah Jane, *d* of Baron Keith of Kinkel, GBE, PC. *Educ:* Edinburgh Acad.; Univ. of Manchester Inst. of Sci. and Technol. (BSc 1980); Queens' Coll., Cambridge (MPhil 1983); St Catharine's College, Cambridge (PhD 1985). CEng 1989; FICE 1994; FREng 2001;

FInstRE 2009. University of Cambridge: Fellow, St Catharine's Coll., 1983–93; Lectr, Dept of Engrg, 1983–90; Director: Gibb Ltd, 1993–2000; Whitbybird & Partners Ltd, 2000–03; ind. consultant, 2003–06; Director: Strategy, High-Point Rendel Ltd, 2006–09; Engrg, Foster Wheeler Energy, 2009–10; BRE Global Ltd, 2010–11. Non-exec. Dir, Port of London Authy, 2009–15. Ind. Mem., Defence Scientific Adv. Council, 2005–11. Vice President: Royal Acad. of Engrg, 2003–09; ICE, 2005–09. *Recreations:* family, Bhutan, ski-ing, sailing. *Address:* 42 Hillgate Place, W8 7ST. *T:* (020) 7727 9663. *Club:* New (Edinburgh).
See also Hon. H. G. Keith.

STEEDS, Prof. John Wickham, FRS 1988; FInstP; Professor of Physics, since 1985, Henry Overton Wills Professor, 2002–06, and Leverhulme Emeritus Research Fellow, 2008–11, Bristol University; *b* 9 Feb. 1940; *s* of John Henry William Steeds and Ethel Amelia Tyler; *m* 1969, Diana Mary Kettlewell; two *d. Educ:* University College London (BSc 1961); PhD Cantab 1965. FInstP 1991. Research Fellow, Selwyn Coll., Cambridge, 1964–67; IBM Res. Fellow, 1966–67; Fellow, Selwyn Coll., Cambridge, 1967; Bristol University: Lectr in Physics, 1967–77; Reader, 1977–85; Hd of Microstructural Gp, 1985–2001; Dir, Interface Analysis Centre, 1990–2001; Hd of Physics Dept, 2001–05. Visiting Professor: Univ. of Santiago, Chile, 1971; Univ. of California, Berkeley, 1981. Chairman: Science Res. Foundn, Emersons Green, 1989–99; Commn on Electron Diffraction, Internat. Union of Crystallography, 1993–99; Emersons Innovations Ltd, 1999–2006; Mem., Council, European Pole Univ., Lille, 1993–97. Pres., W of England Metals and Materials Assoc., 2003–04. Patient Gov., Univ. Hosps Bristol Foundn Trust, 2010–May 2016 (Lead Gov., 2010–11). Holweck Medal and Prize, French Physical Soc., 1996; Gjønnes Medal, Internat. Union of Crystallography, 2014. *Publications:* Introduction to Anisotropic Elasticity Theory of Dislocations, 1973; (with J. F. Mansfield) Electron Diffraction of Phases in Alloys, 1984; (ed jtly) Thin Film Diamond, 1994; papers on electron diffraction, materials science and solid state physics. *Recreations:* tennis, overseas travel. *Address:* Hall Floor Flat 4, Codrington Place, Clifton, Bristol BS8 3DE. *T:* (0117) 973 2183.

STEEL, family name of **Baron Steel of Aikwood**.

STEEL OF AIKWOOD, Baron *cr* 1997 (Life Peer), of Ettrick Forest in the Scottish Borders; **David Martin Scott Steel,** KT 2004; KBE 1990; PC 1977; DL; journalist and broadcaster; Member (Lib Dem) Lothians, and Presiding Officer, Scottish Parliament, 1999–2003; Lord High Commissioner, General Assembly, Church of Scotland, 2003 and 2004; *b* Scotland, 31 March 1938; *s* of late Very Rev. Dr David Steel; *m* 1962, Judith Mary, *d* of W. D. MacGregor, CBE, Dunblane; two *s* one *d. Educ:* Prince of Wales School, Nairobi, Kenya; George Watson's Coll.; Edinburgh Univ. (MA 1960; LLB 1962). President: Edinburgh University Liberals, 1959; Students' Representative Council, 1960. Asst Secretary, Scottish Liberal Party, 1962–64. MP (L 1965–88, Lib Dem 1988–97) Roxburgh, Selkirk and Peebles, 1965–83, Tweeddale, Ettrick and Lauderdale, 1983–97; youngest member of 1964–66 Parliament. Liberal Chief Whip, 1970–75; Mem. Parly Delegn to UN Gen. Assembly, 1967; Sponsor, Private Member's Bill to reform law on abortion, 1966–67. Pres., Africa All Party Parly Gp, 2011–. Leader of Liberal Party, 1976–88; Co-Founder, Social and Liberal Democrats, 1988. Pres., Liberal International, 1994–96. President: Anti-Apartheid Movement of GB, 1966–70; Med. Aid for Palestinians, 1996–2004; Scottish Castles Assoc., 2002–10; Chairman: Shelter, Scotland, 1969–73; Countryside Movement, 1995–96; Patron, Prostate Cancer Scotland (formerly Scottish Assoc. of Prostate Cancer Support Gps), 2002–. Mem., British Council of Churches, 1971–75. Chubb Fellow, Yale Univ., 1987; Vis. Fellow, St Antony's Coll., Oxford, 2013. BBC television interviewer in Scotland, 1964–65; Presenter of STV weekly religious programme, 1966–67, and for Granada, 1969, and BBC, 1971–76. Pres., Jaguar Drivers' Club, 2007–. Rector, Edinburgh Univ., 1982–85. DL Roxburgh, Ettrick and Lauderdale, 1990–2013. Awarded Freedom of Tweeddale, 1988, of Ettrick and Lauderdale, 1990. Hon. FRCOG, 2013. DUniv: Stirling, 1991; Heriot-Watt, 1996; Open, 2001; Hon. DLitt Buckingham; Hon. LLD: Edinburgh, 1997; Strathclyde, 2000; Aberdeen, 2001; St Andrews, 2003; Glasgow Caledonian, 2004; Brunel, 2010. Commander's Cross, Order of Merit (Germany), 1992; Chevalier, Légion d'Honneur (France), 2003; Order of Brilliant Star (Taiwan), 2004. *Publications:* Boost for the Borders, 1964; Out of Control, 1968; No Entry, 1969; The Liberal Way Forward, 1975; A New Political Agenda, 1976; Militant for the Reasonable Man, 1977; New Majority for a New Parliament, 1978; High Ground of Politics, 1979; A House Divided, 1980; (with Judy Steel) Border Country, 1985; (presenter) Partners in One Nation: a new vision of Britain 2000, 1985; (with Judy Steel) Mary Stuart's Scotland, 1987; Against Goliath: David Steel's autobiography, 1989; contrib. to The Times, The Guardian, The Scotsman, other newspapers and political weeklies. *Recreations:* angling, classic car rallying (bronze medallion in London - Cape Town, 1998). *Address:* House of Lords, SW1A 0PW; Ettrick Lodge, Selkirk TD7 4LE. *Clubs:* National Liberal, Royal Over-Seas League.
See also C. M. Steel.

STEEL, Dame (Anne) Heather, (Dame Heather Beattie), DBE 1993; a Judge of the High Court of Justice, Queen's Bench Division, 1993–2001; Judge of the Courts of Appeal of Jersey and Guernsey, 2004–12; *b* 3 July 1940; *d* of late His Honour Edward Steel and Mary Evelyn Griffith Steel; *m* 1967, David Kerr-Muir Beattie; one *s* one *d. Educ:* Howell's School, Denbigh; Liverpool University (LLB). Called to the Bar, Gray's Inn, 1963, Bencher, 1993; practice on N Circuit; Prosecuting Counsel to DHSS on N Circuit, 1984–86; a Recorder, 1984–86; a Circuit Judge, 1986–93. Mem., Criminal Cttee, Judicial Studies Bd, 1992–95. President: Merseyside Medico Legal Soc., 1992–94; Law Faculty Assoc., Liverpool Univ., 1994–. Member: Council, Rossall Sch., 1990–2002; Adv. Council, Soc. for Advanced Legal Studies, 2001–. Mem., Guild of Freeman, City of London, 1996–. Freeman, City of London, 1993; Liveryman: Pattenmakers' Co., 1993 (Master, 2003–04); Fan Makers' Co., 2005. *Recreations:* theatre, gardening, art, antiques.
See also E. M. Steel.

STEEL, Prof. (Christopher) Michael, PhD, DSc; Professor in Medical Science, University of St Andrews, 1994–2005, now Emeritus; *b* 25 Jan. 1940; *s* of late Very Rev. David Steel; *m* 1962, Dr Judith Margaret Spratt, MBE; two *s* one *d. Educ:* Prince of Wales Sch., Nairobi; George Watson's Coll., Edinburgh; Univ. of Edinburgh (BSc Hons, MB, ChB Hons, PhD, DSc). FRCPE; FRCSE (*ad hominem*) 1994; FRCPath; FRSE. Jun. hosp. posts in Edinburgh teaching hosps, 1965–68; Graduate Res. Fellow, Univ. of Edinburgh Faculty of Medicine, 1968–71; Mem. of Clin. Sci. Staff, MRC Human Genetics Unit, Edinburgh, 1971–93 (Asst Dir, 1979–93); MRC Travelling Res. Fellow, Univ. of Nairobi Med. Sch., 1972–73. Hon. Cons., Lothian Health Bd, 1976–. Member: Adv. Cttee, UK Gene Therapy, 1995–2000; MRC Adv. Bd, 2000–05; Bd, Worldwide Cancer Res. (formerly Assoc. for Internat. Cancer Res.), 2003–; Bd, Med. Res. Scotland, 2005–10. Founder FMedSci 1998. *Publications:* (with D. K. Apps and B. B. Cohen) Biochemistry: a concise text for medical students, 1992; papers on molecular biology of cancer in learned jls. *Recreations:* golf, theatre, DIY. *Address:* Breakers, 3a The Scores, St Andrews, Fife KY16 9AR. *T:* (01334) 472877.
See also Baron Steel of Aikwood.

STEEL, Danielle; *see* Schüelein-Steel, D. F.

STEEL, Vice Adm. Sir David (George), KBE 2015 (CBE 2009); DL; Second Sea Lord and Chief of Naval Personnel and Training, 2012–15; *b* Walthamstow, 6 April 1961; *s* of George Malcolm Steel and Doreen Steel. *Educ:* Rossall Sch., Fleetwood; Britannia Royal Naval Coll.; Durham Univ. (BA Hons Law 1983); Inns of Court Sch. of Law. Joined Royal Navy, 1979. Called to the Bar, Middle Temple, 1987, Bencher, 2014; in practice as barrister, 1987–. Comdr (Supply) HMS Invincible, 1998–2000; CSO (Personnel and Logistics) C-in-C Fleet, 2000–02; Sec. to First Sea Lord and Chief of Naval Staff, 2002–05; Naval Base Comdr, Portsmouth, 2005–09; Chief Naval Logistics Officer, 2008–15; Naval Sec. and COS (Personnel), 2010–12. QCVS 1999. Freeman, City of London, 2010. Yr Brother, Trinity House, 2014. DL Hants, 2014. *Recreations:* gardening, cycling, international relations, Windsor Leadership Trust.

STEEL, Sir David (William), Kt 1998; commercial arbitrator and mediator, since 2011; a Judge of the High Court of Justice, Queen's Bench Division, 1998–2011; a Judge of the Commercial Court, 1998–2011 (Judge in charge, 2006–07); *b* 7 May 1943; *s* of Sir Lincoln Steel and late Barbara (*née* Goldschmidt); *m* 1970, Charlotte Elizabeth Ramsay; two *s. Educ:* Eton Coll.; Keble Coll., Oxford (MA Hons Jurisprudence). Called to the Bar, Inner Temple, 1966, Bencher, 1991; with Coudert Bros (Attorneys), New York, 1967–68; commenced practice in England, 1969; Junior Counsel to the Treasury (Common Law) 1978–81; Junior Counsel to the Treasury (Admiralty), 1978–81; QC 1981; a Recorder, 1991–98; a Dep. High Court Judge, 1993–98, 2011–; Judge, Admiralty Ct, 1998–2011; Presiding Judge, Western Circuit, 2002–06; Judge, Ct of Dubai Internat. Financial Centre, 2011–. Wreck Commissioner for England and Wales, 1982–98; Mem., panel of Lloyd's Salvage Arbitrators, 1982–98. Chm., Commercial Bar Assoc., 1990–91; Mem., Lord Chancellor's Adv. Cttee on Legal Educn and Conduct, 1994–98. Chm., OUBC Trust Fund Cttee, 1990–93. Mem., Dubai World Tribunal, 2012–. Younger Brother, Trinity House, 2012–. *Publications:* Editor: Temperley: Merchant Shipping Acts, 1976–98; Forms and Precedents: British Shipping Laws, 1977–98; Kennedy: Salvage, 1981–98. *Recreations:* golf, reading, fishing, sailing. *Address:* 10 Fleet Street, EC4Y 1AU. *Club:* Garrick.

STEEL, Donald MacLennan Arklay; golf correspondent and golf course architect; *b* 23 Aug. 1937; *s* of William Arklay Steel and Catherine Fanny (*née* Jacobs), internat. golfer; *m* 1988, Rachel Ellen. *Educ:* Fettes Coll.; Christ's Coll., Cambridge (MA). Golf correspondent: Sunday Telegraph, 1961–90; Country Life, 1983–93; golf course architect, 1965–: with C. K. Cotton, Pennink, Lawrie and Partners; with C. K. Cotton, Pennink, Steel & Co.; with Donald Steel & Co. President: British Inst. of Golf Course Architects, 1989–91 (Hon. Sec., 1971–83; Chm., 1983–86); Assoc. of Golf Writers, 1993–98 (Treas., 1977–90); English Golf Union, 2006. *Publications:* (ed jtly) Shell World Encyclopaedia of Golf, 1975; (ed) Guinness Book of Golf Facts and Feats, 1980; Bedside Books of Golf, 1965, 1971; The Classic Links, 1992; (ed) 14 edns, The Golf Course Guide of the British Isles (Sunday Telegraph), 1968–96; (jtly) Traditions and Change: the Royal and Ancient Golf Club 1939–2004, 2004; The Open: golf's oldest Major, 2010. *Recreations:* cricket, wine. *Address:* 1 March Square, Chichester, West Sussex PO19 5AN. *T:* (01243) 528506. *Clubs:* MCC; Hawks (Cambridge); Royal and Ancient Golf.

STEEL, Her Honour Elizabeth Mary, (Mrs Stuart Christie); DL; a Circuit Judge, 1991–2007; *b* 28 Nov. 1936; *d* of His Honour Edward Steel and Mary Evelyn Griffith Steel (*née* Roberts); *m* 1972, Stuart Christie (*d* 2011); one *s* one *d. Educ:* Howell's Sch., Denbigh; Liverpool Univ. (LLB). Admitted solicitor, 1960; Partner, John A. Behn Twyford & Co., 1968–80; Partner, Cuff Roberts, 1980–91; a Recorder, 1989. Member: Cripps Cttee, 1967–69; Race Relations Bd, 1970–78; Council, Radio Merseyside, 1974–78; Gen. Adv. Council, BBC, 1979–82 (Chm., NW Adv. Council). Member: Law Soc., 1960; Liverpool Law Soc., 1960 (Pres., 1989–90); Chm., Steering Cttee, Hillsborough Solicitors' Gp, 1989–91. Member: Royal Liverpool Univ. Hosp. NHS Trust, 1991; Liverpool Playhouse Bd, 1968–95 (Vice-Pres., 1995–99). Nat. Vice-Chm., YCs, 1965–67. Pres., Merseyside Br., ESU, 2006–. Chm., Royal Court Liverpool Trust Ltd, 2008–13; Trustee, Liverpool Cathedral Centenary Trust, 2003–10. Gov., Liverpool John Moores Univ., 2001–12 (Hon. Fellow, 2013). DL Merseyside, 1991. Hon. LLD Liverpool, 2007. *Recreations:* theatre (amateur and professional), music, needlework, cooking, entertaining, being entertained. *Address:* 70 Knowsley Road, Cressington Park, Liverpool L19 0PG. *E:* elizabeth_christie@hotmail.com. *Club:* Athenæum (Pres., 2002–03) (Liverpool).
See also Dame A. H. Steel.

STEEL, Dame Heather; *see* Steel, Dame A. H.

STEEL, Henry, CMG 1976; OBE 1965; Principal Legal Adviser: Government of British Antarctic Territory, 1989–2005; Government of British Indian Ocean Territory, 1991–2005; consultant on international and commonwealth law; *b* 13 Jan. 1926; *yr s* of late Raphael Steel; *m* 1960, Jennifer Isobel Margaret, *d* of late Brig. M. M. Simpson, MBE; two *s* two *d. Educ:* Christ's Coll., Finchley; New Coll., Oxford. BA Oxon 1950. Military Service, RASC and Intell. Corps, 1944–47. Called to Bar, Lincoln's Inn, 1951; Legal Asst, Colonial Office, 1955; Senior Legal Asst, CO, 1960; Asst Legal Adviser, CRO, 1965; Legal Counsellor, FCO, 1967–73; Legal Adviser, UK Mission to UN, NY, 1973–76; Legal Counsellor, FCO, 1976–79; Asst Under-Sec. of State (on loan to Law Officers' Dept), 1979; Legal Adviser to Governor of Southern Rhodesia, 1979–80; Asst Legal Secretary (Under-Secretary), Law Officers' Dept, 1980–83, Legal Sec. (Dep. Sec.), 1983–86; Dir, Commonwealth Legal Adv. Service, British Inst. of Internat. and Comparative Law, 1986–87; Leader, UK Delegn to UN Human Rights Commn, 1987–92 and 1994–97; special consultant to FCO on human rights reporting, 1992–2003. *Address:* College Place, Chapel Lane, Bledington, Oxon OX7 6UZ.

STEEL, John Brychan; QC 1993; a Recorder, Midland Circuit, since 2000; *b* 4 June 1954; *s* of late John Exton Steel and Valentine Brychan-Rees; *m* 1981, Susan Rebecca Fraser; two *s* one *d. Educ:* Harrow Sch.; Durham Univ. (BSc Hons Chem.; Hon. Fellow, Durham Law Sch., 2010). Pres., Durham Univ. Athletic Union, 1975–76; Capt., Durham Univ. Ski Club, 1975. Lieut, Inns of Court and City Yeomanry, 1977–81; called to the Bar, Gray's Inn, 1978 (Gray's Inn Moots Prize, 1979), Bencher, 2006 (Mem., Mgt Cttee, 2011–13 (Chm., 2012–13); Master of Estate, 2011–12); Attorney-General's Suppl. Panel (Common Law), 1989–93; an Asst Recorder, 1998–2000. Mem. Cttee, Planning and Envmtl Bar Assoc., 2008–12. Hon. Legal Advr, Air League, 2002–; Mem., Air Squadron, 2002–; Hon. Legal Advr and Trustee, Bentley Priory Battle of Britain Trust, 2006–; Trustee: Mission Aviation Fellowship, 2008–12; Blenheim Palace, 2009–. Chm., Strategic Develt Bd, 2009–11, Mem. Bd, Durham Global Securities Inst., 2011–, Durham Univ.; Chm., Oxford Airport Gen. Aviation Gp, 2009–. Jt Founder, Busoga Trust, 1982–. Dep. Chm., Ski Club of GB, 1980–82; Chm., Kandahar Racing, 1998–2000. FRGS 2002; FRAeS 2003; FRSA 2006; FCIArb 2014. *Recreations:* ski-ing, flying, walking. *Address:* 39 Essex Street, WC2R 3AT. *T:* (020) 7832 1111. *Clubs:* Boodle's; Kandahar (Chm., 1992–97).

STEEL, Prof. Karen, PhD; FRS 2009; Professor of Sensory Function, Wolfson Centre for Age-Related Diseases, King's College London, since 2012. *Educ:* Univ. of Leeds (BSc Genetics and Zool. 1974); University Coll. London (PhD 1978). Postdoctoral Fellow, MRC Inst. of Hearing Res., Nottingham, then postdoctoral role at Inst. für Zoologie, Munich, 1978–83; res. role, MRC Inst. of Hearing Res., Nottingham, 1983–2003; Principal Investigator for the Genetics of Deafness and Founder, Mouse Genetics Prog., Wellcome Trust Sanger Inst., 2003–12. Hon. Prof. of Genetics, Univ. of Nottingham, 1995. Mem., Scientific Adv. Bd, Mouse Genome Database. Scientific Adviser: Deafness Res. UK; SENSE. FMedSci 2004. Brain Prize, Grete Lundbeck Eur. Brain Res. Foundn, 2012. *Publications:* contribs to jls incl. Nature Genetics, Neurosci., Human Molecular Genetics, Molecular and Cell. Biol. *Address:* Wolfson Centre for Age-Related Diseases, King's College London, Wolfson Wing, Hodgkin Building, Guy's Campus, SE1 1UL.

STEEL, Michael; *see* Steel, C. M.

STEEL, Patricia Ann, OBE 1990; Secretary, Institution of Highways and Transportation, 1973–90; *b* 30 Oct. 1941; *d* of Thomas Norman Steel and Winifred Steel. *Educ:* Hunmanby Hall, near Filey, Yorks; Exeter Univ. (BA). Parly Liaison, Chamber of Shipping of UK and British Shipping Fedn, 1968–71; Sec., Highway and Traffic Technicians Assoc., 1972–73. Director: LRT, 1984–91; Docklands Light Railway, 1984–91 (Chm., 1988–89); Victoria Coach Station Ltd, 1988–91. Non-executive Director: TRL, 1992–96; Richmond, Twickenham and Roehampton Healthcare NHS Trust, 1992–99; NHS Litigation Authy, 2002–08. Mem., Occupational Pensions Bd, 1979–84; Non-legal (formerly Lay) Mem., Transport Tribunal, 1999–2012. *Recreations:* music, travel, politics.

STEEL, Robert, CBE 1979; Secretary-General, Royal Institution of Chartered Surveyors, 1968–85 (Fellow, 1961; Hon. Member, 1985); *b* 7 April 1920; *e s* of late John Thomas Steel and Jane (*née* Gordon), Wooler, Northumberland; *m* 1943, Averal Frances (*d* 2007), *d* of Arthur Pettitt; one *s* one *d*. *Educ:* Duke's Sch., Alnwick, Northumb.; Univ. of London (BSc 1945); Gray's Inn (Barrister, 1956). Surveyor, 1937–46; Asst Sec., Under Sec., RICS, 1946–61; Dir of Town Development, Basingstoke, 1962–67. Hon. Sec.-Gen., Internat. Fedn of Surveyors, 1967–69, Vice-Pres., 1970–72, Hon. Mem., 1983; Hon. Sec., Commonwealth Assoc. of Surveying and Land Economy, 1969–90; Sec., Aubrey Barker Trust, 1970–96; Member: South East Economic Planning Council, 1974–76; Council, British Consultants Bureau, 1977–85. Chm., Geometers Liaison Cttee, EEC, 1972–86. Hon. Editor, Commonwealth Surveying and Land Economy, 1975–90. Founder Mem., 1977, Mem. Ct of Assts, 1977–94, Master, 1988–89, Worshipful Co. of Chartered Surveyors. Organised national networks of beacons for Queen's Silver Jubilee celebrations, 1977, and for the Wedding of Prince Charles and Lady Diana Spencer, 1981. Raised: £71,210 for RICS Benev. Fund by sponsored walk of 1000 miles, John O'Groats to Land's End, 1979; £66,333 for RICS Benev. Fund and The Prince's Trust by walk of 1100 miles, Cape Wrath to Dover and London, 1985; £113,739 for Lord Mayor of London's Charity Appeal for Children, 1988, by walk of 1,200 miles from Strathy Point, Sutherland, to Portland Bill, Dorset, and London; £133,500 for National Trust Enterprise Neptune, 1990, by walk of 2,000 miles around the perimeter of England; £116,820 for Nat. Trust Centenary 1995 by walk of 4,444 miles around the perimeter of mainland Britain; £80,015 for RICS Benev. Fund and Marie Curie Cancer Care, by walk of 2,000 kms, Iona to Canterbury, 2000; £75,000 for RICS Benev. Fund, Macmillan Cancer Support and Treloar Trust, by walk of 650 miles, Balmoral to Snowdon, 2007. Hon. Member: Bulgarian Mountain Rescue Service, 1964; Union Belge des Géomètres Experts, 1976; Hon. Fellow, Inst. of Surveyors, Malaysia, 1983. Hon. LLD Aberdeen, 1985. Distinguished Service Award, Surveyors Inst. of Sri Lanka, 1986; Help the Aged Tunstall Golden Award for Outstanding Achievement, 1995. Silver Jubilee Medal, 1977. *Publications:* The Housing Repairs and Rent Act, 1954; The Rent Act, 1957; Steel Nuggets: a personal chronicle, 2002; Walking Wonderlands: an account of eight long walks, 2009; contrib. professional jls and internat. conferences. *Recreations:* mountain walking, travel, music, family genealogy.

STEELE, Prof. Fiona Alison, OBE 2011; PhD; FBA 2009; Professor of Social Statistics, University of Bristol, since 2008; Professor of Statistics, London School of Economics and Political Science, since 2013. *Educ:* Univ. of Edinburgh (BSc 1st Cl. Hons Maths and Stats 1992); Univ. of Southampton (MSc Social Stats with Dist. 1993; PhD Stats 1996). Lectr in Stats and Res. Methodology, LSE, 1996–2001; Res. Lectr in Stats, Inst. of Educn, Univ. of London, 2001–05; Reader in Social Stats, 2005–08, Dir, Centre for Multilevel Modelling, 2010–13, Univ. of Bristol. Vis. Fellow, Centre for Advanced Study, Norwegian Acad. Sci. and Letters, 2007. *Publications:* (jtly) A User's Guide to MLwiN, Version 2.10, 2009; contribs to Public Opinion Qly, Jl Royal Statistical Soc., Demography. *Address:* Centre for Multilevel Modelling, Graduate School of Education, University of Bristol, 2 Priory Road, Bristol BS8 1TX; Department of Statistics, London School of Economics and Political Science, Houghton Street, WC2A 2AE.

STEELE, Ven. Gordon John; Archdeacon of Oakham, since 2012; *b* Stoke Newington, 6 April 1955; *s* of Henry John Steele and Jean MacKechnie Steele; *m* 1991, Helen Beverley Maria Rixon; one *s* one *d*. *Educ:* Owen's Grammar Sch., London; Univ. of Kent (BA 1976); Worcester Coll., Oxford (BA 1982; MA 1987). Diocesan Treas., Tanzania, 1977–80; ordained deacon, 1984, priest, 1985; Curate, St John the Baptist, Greenhill, Harrow, 1984–88; pt-time Chaplain to the Bishop of Willesden, 1987–92; Team Vicar, St Andrew's, Uxbridge, 1988–94; Vicar: St Alban's, Northampton, 1994–2001; St John the Baptist, Peterborough, 2001–12; Rural Dean of Peterborough, 2004–10. Hon. Canon, Peterborough Cath., 2004–. *Recreations:* travel, music, family. *Address:* The Diocesan Office, The Palace, Peterborough PE1 1YB. *T:* (01733) 887017, *Fax:* (01733) 555271. *E:* archdeacon.oakham@peterborough-diocese.org.uk.

STEELE, John Charles; Chair, Armed Forces Pay Review Body, since 2013 (Member, since 2009); *b* Essex, 10 Aug. 1942; *s* of Charles and Florence Steele; *m* 1965, Jennifer Knopp; two *s*. *Educ:* Royal Liberty Grammar Sch.; SE Essex Tech. Coll. (HND Business Studies 1963; Dip. Personnel Mgt 1968). Ford Motor Company: Mgt trainee, 1961–63; Personnel Officer, 1963–67; IBM UK Ltd: Job Evaluation Officer, 1967–69; Personnel Manager, 1969–74; assignment, IBM Europe as Personnel Ops Manager, 1974–76; Personnel and Communications Dir, Gen. Business Gp, 1976–81; Personnel Dir, Data Processing Gp, 1981–83; assignment, IBM Corp. as Internat. Compensation Dir, 1983–84; Internat. Employee Relns Dir, 1984–85; UK Personnel Dir, 1985–89; British Telecommunications plc: Personnel Dir, BT UK, 1989–90; Gp Personnel Dir and Mem., Exec. Cttee, 1990–2002; Chm., Adv. Council, Accenture HR Services, 2002–03. Mem. Bd, Orgn Resources Counsellors Inc. (NY), 2005–12. Member: Teacher Trng Authy, 1998–2001; Council, ACAS, 2001–07. Mem., Court of Govs, Henley Mgt Coll., 1996–2007 (Hon. Fellow 2008). Trustee, Industrial Relns Counsellors Inc. (NY), 2013–. FIPD (FIPM 1981); FCIPD 2003; FRSA. *Recreations:* opera, ballet, golf, theatre, family. *Address:* Armed Forces Pay Review Body, Office of Manpower Economics, Fleetbank House, 2–6 Salisbury Square, EC4Y 8JX. *T:* (020) 7211 8203. *E:* john.c.steele@btopenworld.com. *Clubs:* Athenæum, Royal Air Force.

STEELE, John Ernest, FCIPS; consultant to shipbuilding and allied industries, 1989–94; Director, Morganite Special Carbons Ltd, 1990–97; *b* 4 June 1935; *s* of William Steele and Amelia Steele (*née* Graham); *m* 1958, Lucy Wilkinson; one *s* three *d*. *Educ:* Rutherford College of Technology, Newcastle upon Tyne. MNECInst. Swan Hunter and Wigham Richardson Ltd: apprentice shipbuilder, 1951–56; Management Progression, 1956–68; Swan Hunter Shipbuilders Ltd: Local Dir, 1968–71; Purchasing Dir, 1971–74; Dep. Chm. and Dep. Chief Exec., 1974–78; Chief Exec., 1977–82; Chm. and Chief Exec., 1978–82; British Shipbuilders: Div. Man. Dir, Composite Yards, 1981–83; part time Bd Mem., 1979–82; Exec. Bd Mem., Offshore, 1982–84; a Corp. Man. Dir, Offshore, 1982–84; Exec. Bd Mem., Procurement, 1984–85; Corporate Man. Dir, Procurement and Special Projects, 1985–89; North East Shipbuilders Ltd: Commercial Dir, 1986–88; Man. Dir, 1988–89. Chairman: Cammell Laird Shipbuilders Ltd, 1981–84; V. O. Offshore Ltd, 1982–84; Scott Lithgow Ltd, 1983–84; Lyon Street Railway Ltd, 1977–84; Vosper Thorneycroft (UK) Ltd, 1984–86; Sunderland Forge Services, 1987–89; Exec. Cttee, Rigby Metal Components Ltd, 1990–91. British Cttee Mem., Det Norske Veritas, 1981–91. Director: Euroroute Construction Ltd, 1985–89; Sunderland Shipbuilders Ltd, 1988–89; non-exec. Dir, Gibraltar Shiprepair Ltd, 1987–90. Freeman, Shipwrights' Co. *Recreations:* Rugby football, golf, reading.

STEELE, John Martin, CB 1995; OBE 1986 (MBE 1979); TD 1970; DL; a Civil Service Commissioner for Northern Ireland, 1999–2006; *b* 20 May 1938; *s* of John and Margaret Steele; *m* 1st, 1961, Molly Fulton (*d* 1988); one *s* two *d*; 2nd, 1992, Margaret Norma Armstrong, ISO. *Educ:* Belfast High Sch.; Queen's Univ., Belfast. Various posts, NI Civil Service, 1962–66; staff of NI Parlt, 1966–72; Dept of Community Relations, 1972–73; Second Clerk Asst, NI Assembly, 1973–74; Co-Sec., Gardiner Cttee on measures to deal with terrorism in NI, 1974; Second Clerk Asst, NI Constitutional Convention, 1975–76; DoE, NI, 1976–78; DHSS, NI, 1978–82; Dir, NI Court Service, 1982–87; Northern Ireland Office: Controller of Prisons, 1987–92; Dir, Security, 1992–96; Sen. Dir (Belfast), and Dir, Policing and Security, 1996–98. Mem., TA, 1958–85; formerly Dep. Comd 23 Artillery Bde and CO 102 Air Defence Regt, RA(V); Hon. Colonel: 102 AD Regt, 1987–93; 105 AD Regt, 1998–2004; Pres., NI Area, RAA; Vice-Chm., Council of NI War Meml Bldg, 2008–. Director: Multi-Cultural Resource Centre, Belfast, 2008–12; North City Training, Belfast, 2008–13. Chm., Bryson Charitable Gp (formerly Bryson House), Belfast, 2001–08. DL Belfast, 1992. FRSA 2009. *Recreations:* gardening, fly-fishing, reading, cooking. *Clubs:* Army and Navy; Ulster Reform (Belfast).

STEELE, Jonathan Peter; journalist and author; Chief Reporter, Middle East Eye, since 2014; Senior Foreign Correspondent and Assistant Editor, The Guardian, 1994–2009; *b* Oxford, 15 Feb. 1941; *s* of Paul Herbert Steele and Gabriele Steele (*née* Wiegand); *m* 1967, Ruth Gordin; two *s*. *Educ:* Eton Coll.; King's Coll., Cambridge (BA 1963); Yale Univ. (MA 1965). The Guardian: reporter, 1965–67; leader-writer, 1967–71; E Eur. corresp., 1971–75; Washington corresp., 1975–79; Foreign News Ed., 1979–82; Chief Foreign Corresp., 1982–88; Moscow corresp., 1988–94. Member: Exec. Cttee of Council, Chatham Hse, 2005–10; Adv. Bd, SSEES, 2006–. Hon. DLitt Herts, 2009. Internat. Reporter of Year, British Press Awards, 1981, 1991; James Cameron Award, 1998; Media Award, Amnesty Internat., 1999; Martha Gellhorn Special Award, 2006; Press Award, One World Media, 2011. *Publications:* (with Ruth First and Christabel Gurney) The South African Connection, 1972; Eastern Europe since Stalin, 1974; Socialism with a German Face, 1977; (with Noam Chomsky and John Gittings) Superpowers in Collision, 1982; (with Eric Abraham) Andropov in Power, 1984; The Limits of Soviet Power, 1985; Eternal Russia, 1994; Defeat: why they lost Iraq, 2008; Ghosts of Afghanistan, 2011. *Recreations:* tennis, yoga, reading, walking. *Address:* 8 Wren Street, WC1X 0HA. *T:* (020) 7837 9743. *Club:* Athenæum.

STEELE, Maj.-Gen. Michael Chandos Merrett, MBE 1972; DL; Chief of Joint Services Liaison Organization, Bonn, 1983–86; Regimental Comptroller, Royal Artillery, 1989–2001; *b* 1 Dec. 1931; *s* of late William Chandos Steele and Daisy Rhoda Steele (*née* Merrett); *m* 1961, Judith Ann Huxford; two *s* one *d*. *Educ:* Westminster School; RMA Sandhurst. Commissioned RA, 1952; Staff Coll., Camberley, 1962; BM RA, 53rd Welsh Div., 1965–67; BM, 8th Inf. Brigade, 1970–72; CO 22nd Light Air Defence Regt, RA, 1972–74; GSO1, HQ DRA, 1974–76; Comdr, 7th Artillery Brigade, 1976–78; Nat. Defence Coll., Canada, 1978–79; BGS, Defence Sales Organization, 1979–82. Col Comdt, RA, 1988–94. Hon. Col 104 Air Defence Regt, RA(V), 1987–96. Chm., Tree Council, 1994–96. Trustee, Haig Homes, 1998–2003. DL Surrey, 1996. *Recreations:* lawn tennis, gardening. *Address:* Elders, Masons Bridge Road, Redhill, Surrey RH1 5LE. *T:* (01737) 763982.

STEELE, Richard Charles, FRSB, FICFor; Director General, Nature Conservancy Council, 1980–88; *b* 26 May 1928; *s* of Richard Orson Steele and Helen Curtis Steele (*née* Robertson); *m* 1956, Anne Freda Nelson; two *s* one *d*. *Educ:* Univ. of Wales (BSc Forestry and Botany); Univ. of Oxford. National Service, 1946–48. Assistant Conservator of Forests, Colonial Forest Service (later HMOCS), Tanganyika (later Tanzania), 1951–63; Head: Woodland Management Section, Nature Conservancy, Monks Wood, 1963–73; Terrestrial Life Sciences Section, Natural Environment Research Council, London, 1973–78; Division of Scientific Services, NERC Inst. of Terrestrial Ecology, Cambridge, 1978–80. Past Pres., Inst. of Foresters of Gt Britain. *Publications:* Wildlife Conservation in Woodlands, 1972; ed, Monks Wood: a nature reserve record, 1974; numerous papers on nature conservation, ecology and forestry in professional and scientific jls. *Recreations:* hill-walking, gardening, collecting books on natural history and E African travel. *Address:* 11 Hallgarth Close, Corbridge, Northumberland NE45 5BS. *T:* (01434) 633041.

STEELE, Prof. Robert James Campbell, MD; FRCSE, FRCS, FCSHK, FRCPE; Professor of Surgery (formerly of Surgical Oncology), University of Dundee, since 1996; Director, Scottish Bowel Cancer Screening Programme, since 2009; *b* 5 March 1952; *s* of Robert Steele and Elizabeth (*née* Sheridan); *m* 1st, 1981, Susan Cachia (marr. diss. 2007); one *s* two *d*; 2nd, 2008, Prof. Annie Anderson. *Educ:* Univ. of Edinburgh (BSc; MB ChB; MD). FRCSE 1984; FRCS 1995; FCSHK 1995; FRCPE 2012. Lecturer in Surgery: Univ. of Edinburgh, 1980–85; Chinese Univ. of Hong Kong, 1985–86; Univ. of Aberdeen, 1986–90; Sen. Lectr and Reader in Surgery, Univ. of Nottingham, 1990–95. Chm., Scottish Cancer Foundn, 2010–. Mem. Council, RCSE, 2005–. *Publications:* Practical Management of Acute Gastrointestinal Bleeding, 1993; Gastrin Receptors in Gastrointestinal Tumours, 1993; Essential Surgical Practice, 2002; many articles in learned jls. *Recreations:* music, Scottish country dancing, country sports. *Address:* Medical Research Institute, Mailbox 4, Ninewells Hospital and Medical School, Dundee DD1 9SY. *T:* (01382) 383452, *Fax:* (01382) 383615. *E:* r.j.c.steele@dundee.ac.uk.

STEELE, Tommy, (Thomas Hicks), OBE 1979; actor; *b* Bermondsey, London, 17 Dec. 1936; *s* of late Thomas Walter Hicks and Elizabeth Ellen (*née* Bennett); *m* 1960, Ann Donoghue; one *d*. *Educ:* Bacon's Sch. for Boys, Bermondsey. First appearance on stage in variety, Empire Theatre, Sunderland, Nov. 1956; first London appearance, variety, Dominion Theatre, 1957; Buttons in Rodgers and Hammerstein's Cinderella, Coliseum, 1958; Tony Lumpkin in She Stoops to Conquer, Old Vic, 1960; Arthur Kipps in Half a Sixpence, Cambridge Theatre, London, 1963–64 and Broadhurst Theatre (first NY appearance), 1965; Truffaldino in The Servant of Two Masters, Queen's, 1969; Dick Whittington, London Palladium, 1969; Meet Me In London, Adelphi, 1971; Jack Point, in The Yeomen of the Guard, City of London Fest., 1978; London Palladium: The Tommy Steele Show, 1973; Hans Andersen, 1974 and 1977; one-man show, Prince of Wales, 1979; Singin' in the Rain (also dir.), 1983; Some Like It Hot, Prince Edward, (also dir.), 1992; What a Show!, Prince of Wales, 1995; Scrooge (title rôle), UK tour, 2003, London Palladium, 2005, 2012, UK and Dublin tour, 2010; Dr Doolittle, UK tour, 2008; The Glenn Miller Story, UK tour, 2015; *films:* Kill Me Tomorrow, 1956; The Tommy Steele Story; The Duke Wore Jeans; Tommy the Toreador; Touch It Light; It's All Happening; The Happiest Millionaire; Half a Sixpence; Finian's Rainbow; Where's Jack?; *television:* wrote and acted in Quincy's Quest, 1979. Composed and recorded, My Life, My Song, 1974; composed: A Portrait of Pablo, 1985; Rock Suite—an Elderly Person's Guide to Rock, 1987. Hon. DLitt South Bank, 1998. *Publications:* Quincy, 1981; The Final Run, 1983; Bermondsey Boy, 2007. *Recreations:* tennis, squash, sculpture, painting.

STEELE-BODGER, Michael Roland, CBE 1990; veterinary surgeon in private practice, retired; *b* 4 Sept. 1925; *s* of late Henry William Steele-Bodger and Kathrine Macdonald; *m* 1955, Violet Mary St Clair Murray; two *s* one *d*. *Educ:* Rugby Sch.; Gonville and Caius Coll., Cambridge. MRCVS. Mem., Sports Council, 1976–82. England Rugby Selector, 1954–70; Pres., RFU, 1973–74; Mem., Internat. Rugby Football Bd, 1974–84; Chm., Four Home Rugby Unions' Tours Cttee, 1976–88; Pres., Barbarians FC, 1987–. Cambridge Univ. Rugby Blue, Captain 1946; England Rugby Internat., 1947–48. Founder and organiser, Steele-Bodger's XV v Cambridge Univ., 1948–. *Recreation:* interest in all sport. *Address:* Laxford Lodge, Bonehill, Tamworth, Staffs B78 3HY. *T:* (01827) 251001. *Clubs:* East India, Devonshire, Sports and Public Schools (Life Pres.); Hawks (Cambridge).

STEELE-PERKINS, Crispian G.; trumpet soloist; *b* 18 Dec. 1944; *s* of Dr Guy Steele-Perkins and Sylvia de Courcey Steele-Perkins; *m* 1st, 1967, Angela Helen Hall (*d* 1991); one *s* two *d*; 2nd, 1995, Jane Elizabeth Mary (*née* Steele-Perkins). *Educ:* Marlborough Coll.; Guildhall Sch. of Music (LGSM, AGSM; Alumni 1995). Has performed with: Sadler's Wells (later ENO), 1966–73; London Gabrieli Brass Ensemble, 1974–84; RPO, 1976–80; English Baroque Soloists, 1980–91; The King's Consort, 1985–. *Address:* Dormy Cottage, 204 Cooden Sea Road, Bexhill-on-Sea, E Sussex TN39 4TR. *T:* (01424) 842401, (01306) 885339. *E:* crispiansp@trumpet1.co.uk. *W:* www.crispiansteeleperkins.com.

STEEMERS, Prof. Koen Alexander, PhD; RIBA; Professor of Sustainable Design, University of Cambridge, since 2005 (Head of Department of Architecture, 2008–14); Fellow, Jesus College, Cambridge, since 2014; *b* 21 Nov. 1961; *s* of Theo and Greetje Steemers; *m* 1992, Jeanette Peasey; two *s*. *Educ:* European Sch., Karlsruhe; Springdale First Sch., Dorset; Queen Elizabeth's Sch., Dorset; European Sch., Brussels; Univ. of Bath (BSc, BArch); Darwin Coll., Cambridge (MPhil 1988; PhD 1992). RIBA 1991; ARB. Architect: ECD, London, 1984 and 1988–91; Borchers Metzner Kramar, Darmstadt, 1986–87; Cambridge University: Res. Associate, then Sen. Res. Associate, 1992–95; Lectr, 1995–2000; Sen. Lectr, 2000–03; Reader in Envmtl Design, 2003–05; Dir, Martin Centre for Architectural and Urban Studies, 2002–08; Fellow, Wolfson Coll., Cambridge, 1998–2014. Dir, Cambridge Architectural Res. Ltd, 1991–. Guest Prof., Chongqing Univ., China, 2002–; Vis. Prof., Kyung Hee Univ., Republic of Korea, 2010–12. Pres., Passive and Low Energy Architecture Internat., 2005–11. *Publications:* (jtly) Daylighting in Architecture, 1993; (with N. V. Baker) Energy and Environment in Architecture, 2000; (with N. V. Baker) Daylight Design in Architecture, 2002; (jtly) The Selective Environment, 2002; (with M. A. Steane) Environmental Diversity in Architecture, 2004. *Recreation:* red wine and Roquefort. *Address:* Department of Architecture, University of Cambridge, 1 Scroope Terrace, Cambridge CB2 1PX.

STEEN, Anthony David, CBE 2015; barrister; youth leader; social worker; underwriter; *b* 22 July 1939; *s* of late Stephen Nicholas Steen; *m* 1965, Carolyn Padfield, educational psychologist; one *s* one *d*. *Educ:* Westminster Sch.; occasional student University Coll., London. Called to Bar, Gray's Inn, 1962; practising Barrister, 1962–74; Defence Counsel, MoD (Court Martials), 1964–68. Lectr in Law, Council of Legal Educn, 1964–67; Adv. Tutor, Sch. of Environment, Central London Poly., 1982–83. Youth Club Leader, E London Settlement, 1959–64; Founder, 1964, and First Director, 1964–68, Task Force recruiting young people to help London's old and lonely, with Govt support; Govt Foundn YVFF, tackling urban deprivation, 1968–74; Consultant to Canadian Govt on student and employment matters, 1970–71; Special Envoy to Home Sec. on tackling human trafficking, 2013–14. MP (C) Liverpool Wavertree, Feb. 1974–1983, S Hams, 1983–97, Totnes, 1997–2010. PPS to Sec. of State for Nat. Heritage, 1992–94. Member, Select Committee: on Race Relations, 1975–79; on the Envmt, 1991–94; on European Scrutiny, 1997–2010. Chairman: Backbench gps on Youth and Young Children, 1976–79; Cons. Cttee on Cities, Urban and New Town Affairs, 1979–83; Parly Urban and Inner City Cttee, 1987–90; Parly Cttee on Deregulation, 1993–97; All-Party Gp on Trafficking of Women and Children, 2006–10; Vice-Chairman: Health and Social Services Cttee, 1979–80; All-Party Fisheries Cttee, 1997–2010; Secretary: Parly Caribbean Gp, 1979–2010 (Vice-Chm.); Cons. back bench Trade and Industry Cttee, 1997–99; 1922 Cttee, 2001–10; Founder Mem., All Party Friends of Cycling, 1975–88. Chm., Chm.'s Unit Marginal Seats, 1982–84, Minority Parties Unit, 1999–2000, Cons. Central Office. Vice-Chm., Envmt Cttee, 1983–85; Chairman: Prime Minister's Cons. Deregulation Cttee, 1993–97; Sane Planning Gp, 1989–96; West Country Mems, 1992–94; Member: Parly Population and Develt Gp; Commons and Lord's Cycle Gp; Services Cttee; Chm., Cons. Friends of English Wine; Jt Nat. Chm., Impact 80's Campaign. Chm., Human Trafficking Foundn, 2010–; Special Advr, All-Party Gp on Human Trafficking, 2010–. Member: Exec. Council, NPFA; Board, Community Transport; Council of Reference, Internat. Christian Relief; Council Mem., Anglo-Jewish Assoc.; Founder Mem., CSA Monitoring Gp; Chm., Outlandos Charitable Trust, 1980–97; Vice-Chm., Task Force Trust, 1964–; Vice-President: Ecology Bldg Soc.; Internat. Centre for Child Studies; Bentley Operatic Soc.; S Hams Young Farmers; Assoc. of District Councils; Marlborough with S Huish Horticultural Soc.; Devon CPRE; Dartmoor Preservation Assoc.; Trustee: Educn Extra; Dartington Summer Arts Foundn; Patron: Liverpool's Open Circle for Detached Youth Work; St Luke's Hospice, Plymouth; Kidscape; Sustrans. Pres., Devon Youth Assoc. *Publications:* New Life for Old Cities, 1981; Tested Ideas for Political Success, 1983, 7th edn 1991; Public Land Utilisation Management Schemes (Plums), 1988. *Recreations:* Dartmouth, piano playing, chess. *Clubs:* Royal Automobile; Churchill (Liverpool); Totnes Conservative (South Hams).

STEEN, Ven. Dr Jane Elizabeth; Archdeacon of Southwark, since 2013; *b* Thornton Heath, 1964; *m* 1990, Pip Steen. *Educ:* Newnham Coll., Cambridge (BA 1987; PhD 1992); Trinity Coll., Cambridge; Westcott House, Cambridge. Ordained deacon, 1996, priest, 1997; Curate, Chipping Barnet with Arkley, 1996–99; Chaplain to Bishop of Southwark, 1999–2005; Canon Chancellor, Southwark Cath., 2005–13; Dir of Ministerial Educn, Dio. of Southwark, 2005–13. *Publications:* (contrib.) Samuel Johnson's Pendulum, 2012; contribs to jls incl. New Rambler, Theology. *Recreations:* walking, reading, gardening, cooking. *Address:* Trinity House, 4 Chapel Court, Borough High Street, SE1 1HW. *T:* (020) 7939 9409. *E:* jane.steen@southwark.anglican.org.

STEER, Sir Alan (William), Kt 2004; Headmaster, Seven Kings High School, Redbridge, 1985–2008; *b* 30 Jan. 1948; *s* of Jack and Esther Steer; *m* 1970, Julie Hodgkin. *Educ:* Magdalen Coll. Sch., Oxford; Univ. of Warwick (BA Hons 1970). Teacher: West Leeds Boys' High Sch., Leeds, 1971–76; Weavers Sch., Wellingborough, 1976–82; Dep. Hd, then Actg Hd, Grange Park Sch., Herts, 1982–85. FRSA. *Recreations:* political cartoons, Fulham Football Club, ancient history, gardening.

STEER, David; QC 1993; a Recorder, 1991–2005; *b* 15 June 1951; *s* of Alcombe Steer and Nancy Steer; *m* 1974, Elizabeth May Hide; one *s*. *Educ:* Rainford High Sch.; Manchester Poly. (BA Hons Law). Called to the Bar, Middle Temple, 1974, Bencher, 2001; Hd of Chambers, 1992–2012; in practice as barrister, 1974–2012. Mem., Bar Council, 1995–97, 2002–04. Leader, Northern Circuit, 2002–04. *Recreations:* Rugby League, gardening, horse-riding.

STEER, Deirdre V.; *see* Clancy, D. V.

STEER, James Kelly, CEng, FCILT; transport consultant; Founder, 1978, and Director, since 2005, Steer Davies Gleave (Managing Director, 1978–2002); Director and Founder, Greengauge 21, since 2005; *b* 7 Dec. 1948; *s* of Desmond and Josephine Steer; *m* 1973, Adrianne Jenifer Harris (*d* 1979); two *s*; partner, Mary Anderson Wright; one *d*. *Educ:* Somers Park Primary Sch., Malvern; Worcester Royal Grammar Sch.; University of Wales Swansea (BSc Hons Civil Engrg); Imperial Coll., London (MSc Transport; DIC). CEng 1975; MICE 1975; MCIHT (MIHT 1975); FCILT (MCIT 1976, FCIT 1999). Asst Engr, Freeman Fox Wilbur Smith Associates, 1969–71; Consultant, Alan M. Voorhees Associates, then Associate, MVA, 1972–78; on secondment to Strategic Rail Authy as Mem., Exec. and Man. Dir, Strategic Planning, 2002–05. Mem., West End Commn, 2012–13. Non-exec. Dir, GCR Develt Ltd, 2011–14. Dir, High Speed Rail Industry Leaders Gp, 2015–. Pres., CILT, 2013–14 (Vice-Pres., 2009–13). Columnist, Transport Times, 2005–. Pres., Railway Study Assoc., 2008–09. Ambassador, Transport Systems Catapult, 2014–. *Publications:* contrib. jl articles on rail, LRT, economic appraisal, research, finance and planning. *Recreations:* boating, admiring grand-children, overlong hikes. *Address:* Steer Davies Gleave, 28–32 Upper Ground, SE1 9PD.

STEER, Dr Peter Anthony; Chief Executive, Great Ormond Street Hospital for Children NHS Foundation Trust, since 2015; *b* Australia, 15 Feb. 1959; *m* 1983, Glenys. *Educ:* Univ. of Queensland (MB BS 1981). FRACP (Paediatrics) 1989; FRCPC (Paediatrics) 2003; FAAP 2005. Mater Adult Hospital, Brisbane: Intern, 1982; Jun. Resident MO, 1983; Sen. MO/Med. Registrar, 1984; Sen. Registrar/Neonatology, 1988, Actg Staff Neonatologist, 1988–89, Nat. Women's Hosp., Auckland; Neonatal Fellowship, McMaster Univ., Hamilton, 1989–91; Staff Neonatologist and Dir, Post-Grad. Educn, Mater Mother's Hosp. and Mater Children's Hosp., Brisbane, 1991–94; Actg Med. Superintendent, Mater Children's Hosp., Brisbane, 1995; Neonatolotist, Mater Mother's Hosp., Brisbane, 1995–2000; Exec. Dir, Mater Children's Public and Private Hosps, Brisbane, 1995–2000; Neonatologist and Dir, Centre for Clin. Studies - Women's and Children's Health (formerly Mater Perinatal Epidemiol. Unit), Mater Hosp., Brisbane, 2001; Div. Chief, Clin. Dir and Academic Hd, Div. of Neonatol., McMaster Univ., Hamilton, 2001; Neonatologist and Dir, Centre for Clin. Studies - Women's and Children's Health, Mater Hosp., Brisbane, 2002–03; Chief of Paediatrics, St Joseph's Healthcare, Hamilton, 2003–08; Chief, Dept of Paediatrics, Pres., McMaster Children's Hosp., Hamilton, 2003–08; Prof. and Chair, Dept for Paediatrics, McMaster Univ., Hamilton, 2003–08; Exec. Lead, McMaster Univ. Med. Centre, Hamilton Health Services, Hamilton, 2005–08. Chief Exec., Children's Health Queensland Hosp. and Health Services, Queensland Health, Brisbane, 2009–14. University of Queensland: Adjunct Associate Prof., Dept for Paediatrics and Child Health, 1995–2000; Associate Prof., Central Clin. Sch., Fac. of Health Scis, 2002–03; Adjunct Prof., Sch. of Public Health, Queensland Univ. of Technol., Brisbane, 2003–08. GAICD 2011. *Address:* Great Ormond Street Hospital for Children NHS Foundation Trust, Executive Office, Level 2, Paul O'Gorman Building, Great Ormond Street, WC1N 3JH. *T:* (020) 7813 8330.

STEERE, Gordon Ernest L.; *see* Lee-Steere.

STEFF-LANGSTON, Group Captain John Antony, MBE 1959; Executive Secretary, Royal Astronomical Society, 1980–91; *b* 5 Nov. 1926; *s* of William Austen Paul Steff-Langston, organist and composer, and Ethel Maude (*née* Fletcher); *m* 1959, Joyce Marian Brown. *Educ:* Cathedral Choir Sch., Canterbury; King's Sch., Canterbury; Pembroke Coll., Cambridge. RAF Coll., 1945–46; 45 Sqn, Ceylon, 1948; 61 Gp, Kenley, 1949; 34 Sqn, 1950–51; 80 Sqn, Hong Kong, 1951–54; 540, 58 and 82 Sqns, Wyton and Singapore, 1955–57; HQ 3 Gp, 1957–59; 80 Sqn, Germany, 1959–62; Staff Coll., Andover, 1962–63; Air Sec.'s Dept, 1963–65; OC 114 Sqn, Benson, 1966–68; aws 1968; CO Northolt, 1969–71; Defence Advr to High Comrs to NZ and Fiji, 1971–74; sowc Greenwich, 1974–75; AMPs Dept, 1975–78; retd 1978. FCMI (FBIM 1978); FRAS 1992. Affiliate, RAeS 1987. Freeman, City of London, 1994; Liveryman, Fletchers' Co., 1994–. *Recreations:* ornithology, photography, travel, music, cricket. *Address:* 6 Beech Wood, Church Hill, Caterham, Surrey CR3 6SB. *T:* (01883) 344348. *Club:* Royal Air Force.

STEFFENSEN, Anne Hedensted; Director General, Danish Shipowners' Association, since 2013; *b* Aalborg, 14 Nov. 1963; *d* of Palle H. Steffensen and Tove Steffensen; *m* 1989, Lars Lundorf Nielsen; three *d*. *Educ:* Univ. of Aarhus (Cant. Scient. Pol.); London Sch. of Econs and Pol Sci. (MSc); Univ. of Oslo (Exam. Philasoficum). Ministry of Foreign Affairs, Denmark: Hd of Section, 1990–92, 1996–98; Dep. Hd, Commercial Dept, London, 1992–95; Dep. Consul Gen., New York, 1998–2000; Chief Consultant, Financial Dept, 2000–01; Hd of Dept, Bilateral Relns, 2001–03, Hd of Dept, Secretariat, 2003–04, Trade Council; Under Sec. of State for Trade, 2004–06; State Sec. for Trade and Corporate Resources, 2006–11; Ambassador of Denmark to the Court of St James's, 2011–13. Knight, Order of Dannebrog, 1 Degree (Denmark), 2008. *Recreations:* contemporary literature, walking and running, good food (fish). *Address:* Danish Shipowners' Association, Amaliegade 33, 1256 Copenhagen K, Denmark. *Club:* Danish.

STEGGLE, Terence Harry, CMG 1990; HM Diplomatic Service, retired; Ambassador to Paraguay, 1989–91; *b* 4 March 1932; *s* of Henry Richard Steggle and Jane Steggle; *m* 1st, 1954, Odette Marie (*née* Audisio) (*d* 1988); two *d*; 2nd, 1989, Annemarie Klara Johanne (*née* Wohle). *Educ:* Chislehurst and Sidcup County Grammar School. Crown Agents, 1950–57; Lieut RA (TA), 1951–53; seconded to Govt of E Nigeria, 1957–58, 1960–62; FO 1963; served Laos, 1963, France, 1964, Zaire, 1970, Bolivia, 1978–82; Ambassador to Panama, 1983–86; Consul-Gen., São Paulo, 1986–87; Counsellor, FCO, 1987–89. *Recreations:* reading, internet. *Address:* c/o Foreign and Commonwealth Office, SW1A 2AH.

STEGMANN, Graham Murray, CBE 2006; independent development consultant, since 2011; Special Adviser to President of African Development Bank, 2006–11; *b* 1 Nov. 1948; *s* of Andrew Murray Stegmann and Mary Isobel Stegmann; *m* 1979, Carol Anne Mayle; one *s* two *d*. *Educ:* University Coll., Rhodesia (BA Hons London); Fitzwilliam Coll., Cambridge (Commonwealth Schol.; MLitt 1979). Posts with DFID and FCO in London and abroad, 1975–96: Hd of Div., N, Central and Southern Africa, Malaŵi, 1986–89; Hd of Estabts, 1989–93; Hd, Develt Div., Southern Africa, Pretoria, 1993–95; Department for International Development: Hd, Aid Policy Resources, then Principal Finance Officer, 1996–2000; Africa Dir, 2000–04; Strategic Advr, 2004–06 and Dir, 2005. Chm., SciDev.Net. Internat. Trustee, British Red Cross, 2007–12. *Recreations:* tennis, cricket, squash, travel. *Address:* London. *T:* 07742 103136. *E:* graham.stegmann@btinternet.com.

STEICHEN, René; Chairman of Board, Société Européene des Satellites, since 1996; *b* Luxembourg, 27 Nov. 1942; *s* of Félix Steichen and Hélène Rausch; *m* 1975, Marianne Belche; two *s* one *d*. *Educ:* Lycée Classique, Diekirch; Cours Supérieurs, Luxembourg; Univ. of Aix-en-Provence; Univ. of Paris (LLD); Institut d'Etudes Politiques, Paris (Dip. Econs and Finance 1966). Qualified as notary, then solicitor, 1969; practised in Diekirch, 1969–84. Mem., Diekirch DC, 1969–84, Mayor, 1974–84. MP (Social Christian) North constituency, Luxembourg, 1979–93; Sec. of State for Agric. and Viticulture, 1984–89; Minister for Agric., Viticulture and Rural Develt and Minister for Cultural Affairs and Scientific Res., 1989–93; Mem., Commn of the European Communities, 1993–95; Sen. Partner, Arendt & Medernach, Luxembourg and Brussels, 1995–2010. *Address:* 36 rue Clairefontaine, 9201 Diekirch, Luxembourg.

STEIN, Christopher Richard, (Rick), OBE 2003; broadcaster; Chef, The Seafood Restaurant, Padstow, since 1975; *b* 4 Jan. 1947; *s* of late Eric and Dorothy Stein; *m* 1st, 1975, Jill Newstead (OBE 2013) (marr. diss. 2007); three *s*; 2nd, 2011, Sarah Burns. *Educ:* Uppingham; New Coll., Oxford (BA English Lit. 1971). Proprietor: St Petroc's Hotel, Rick Stein's Café, Stein's Gift Shop, Stein's Patisserie, Stein's Deli, Stein's Fish & Chips, Padstow Seafood School, Stein's Fisheries (all in Padstow); Rick Stein's Fish & Chips, Falmouth; Rick Stein at Bannisters, Mollymook, Australia; Rick Stein Winchester; Rick Stein Porthleven; Rick Stein Fistral; Tenant, Cornish Arms, St Merryn. Presenter, BBC TV series: Rick Stein's Taste of the Sea, 1995; Rick Stein's Fruits of the Sea, 1997; Rick Stein's Seafood Odyssey, 1999; Fresh Food, 1999; Rick Stein's Seafood Lovers' Guide, 2000 (Glenfiddich Food and Drink Award, for best TV prog., 2001; Glenfiddich Trophy, 2001); Rick Stein's Food Heroes, 2002; Rick Stein's Food Heroes: another helping, 2004; Rick Stein's French Odyssey, 2005; Rick Stein in Du Maurier Country, 2006; Rick Stein and the Japanese Ambassador, 2006; Rick Stein's Mediterranean Escapes, 2007; Rick Stein's Far Eastern Odyssey, 2009; Rick Stein's Spain, 2011; Rick Stein Tastes the Blues, 2011; Rick Stein's Indian Odyssey, 2013; Rick Stein: From Venice to Istanbul, 2015. *Publications:* English

Seafood Cookery, 1988 (Glenfiddich Cook Book of the Year, 1989); Taste of the Sea, 1995 (André Simon Cook Book of the Year, 1996); Fish, 1996; Fruits of the Sea, 1997; Rick Stein's Seafood Odyssey, 1999; Rick Stein's Seafood Lovers' Guide, 2000; Rick Stein's Seafood, 2001 (James Beard Award, 2005); Rick Stein's Food Heroes, 2002; Rick Stein's Guide to the Food Heroes of Britain, 2003; Rick Stein's Food Heroes: another helping, 2004; Rick Stein's French Odyssey, 2005; Rick Stein's Mediterranean Escapes, 2007; Coast to Coast, 2008: Rick Stein's Far Eastern Odyssey, 2009; Rick Stein's Spain, 2011; Rick Stein's India, 2013; Under a Mackerel Sky: a memoir, 2013; Fish and Shellfish, 2014; Rick Stein: From Venice to Istanbul, 2015. *Address:* The Seafood Restaurant, Riverside, Padstow, Cornwall PL28 8BY. *T:* (01841) 532700. *Clubs:* Groucho, Chelsea Arts, Ivy.

STEIN, Colin Norman Ralph; Sheriff of Tayside Central and Fife at Arbroath, 1991–2011; *b* 14 June 1948; *s* of late Colin Hunter Stein and of Margaret Lindsay Stein; *m* 1979, Dr Linda McNaught; one *s*. *Educ:* Glenalmond Coll.; Durham Univ. (BA Hons Modern History); Edinburgh Univ. (LLB). Admitted Member of Faculty of Advocates, 1975. Standing Jun. Counsel to MoD (RAF), Scotland, 1983–91; Temp. Sheriff, 1987–91. *Recreations:* angling, gardening.

STEIN, Paul Jonathan, CEng, FREng, FIET, FRAeS; Chief Scientific Officer, Rolls-Royce plc, since 2010; *b* London, 26 July 1957; *s* of late Philip Stein and of Greta Stein (now Bennett); *m* 2007, Juliet Esther Goodden; two step *s*; two *d* from a previous marriage. *Educ:* Beverley Boys' Sch., New Malden; King's Coll., London (BScEng Electronic Engrg). CEng 1995; FIET 2003; FREng 2006; FRAeS 2009. Electronic Engr, Philips Research Labs, 1978–84; Advanced Develt Manager, MEL, 1984–91; Business Sector Manager, Thomson UK, 1991–93; Roke Manor Research: Business Unit Dir, Radio Communications Dept, 1993–96; Man. Dir, 1996–2006; Sci. and Technol. Dir, MoD, 2006–09. Mem., Siemens UK Exec. Mgt Bd, 2000–06. *Recreations:* electronics, computing, guitar, motorcycling. *Address:* Rolls-Royce plc, 65 Buckingham Gate, SW1E 6AT. *T:* (01332) 249575, *Fax:* (01332) 249408.

STEIN, Prof. Peter Gonville, FBA 1974; JP; Regius Professor of Civil Law in the University of Cambridge, 1968–93, now Emeritus; Fellow of Queens' College, Cambridge, since 1968; *b* 29 May 1926; *o s* of late Walter Stein, MA, Solicitor, and Effie Drummond Stein (*née* Walker); *m* 1st, 1953, Janet Chamberlain (marr. diss. 1978); three *d*; 2nd, 1978, Anne M. Howard (*née* Sayer); one step *s*. *Educ:* Liverpool Coll. (Life Gov., 1976); Gonville and Caius Coll., Camb. (Hon. Fellow, 1999); University of Pavia. Served in RN, Sub-lieut (Sp) RNVR, 1944–47. Admitted a Solicitor, 1951; Asst Lecturer in Law, Nottingham Univ., 1952–53; Lecturer in Jurisprudence, 1953–56, Prof. of Jurisprudence, 1956–68, Dean of Faculty of Law, 1961–64, Aberdeen Univ.; Chm., Faculty Bd of Law, Cambridge, 1973–76; Vice Pres., Queens' Coll., 1974–81 (Acting Pres., 1976 and 1980–81). Visiting Prof. of Law: Univ. of Virginia, 1965–66, 1978–79; Colorado, 1966; Witwatersrand, 1970; Louisiana State, 1974, 1977, 1983, 1985; Chicago, 1985, 1988, 1990, 1992, 1995; Padua and Palermo, 1991; Tulane, New Orleans, 1992, 1996 and 1998; Salerno, 1994; Lateran, Rome, 1997; Lectures: R. M. Jones, QUB, 1978; Irvine, Cornell, 1979; Sherman, Boston, 1979; Tucker, Louisiana State, 1985; David Murray, Glasgow, 1987; Maccabaean, British Acad., 1995. Fellow, Winchester Coll., 1976–91. Member: Council, Max Planck Inst. for European Legal History, Frankfurt, 1966–88; Council, Internat. Assoc. of Legal History, 1970– (Vice-Pres., 1985–); Internat. Acad. of Comparative Law, 1987–; Sec. of State for Scotland's Working Party on Hospital Endowments, 1966–69; Bd of Management, Royal Cornhill and Assoc. (Mental) Hospitals, Aberdeen, 1963–68 (Chm. 1967–68); UGC, 1971–75; US-UK Educnl (Fulbright) Commn, 1985–91; Council, British Acad., 1988–90; Acad. of European Lawyers, 1992– (Pres., 2008–). Chm., Ely Diocesan Trust Cttee, 1987–94. Pres., Soc. of Public Teachers of Law, 1980–81; Vice-Pres., Selden Soc., 1984–87. Foreign Fellow: Accad. di Scienze morali e politiche, Naples, 1982; Accademia Nazionale dei Lincei, Rome, 1987; Corresp. Fellow, Accademia degli Intronati, Siena, 1988; Fellow, Academia Europaea, 1989; Foreign Fellow, Koninklijke Academie voor Wetenschappen, Belgium, 1991. JP Cambridge, 1970 (Supplementary List, 1988). Hon. QC 1993. Hon. Dr jur Göttingen, 1980; Hon. Dott. Giur. Ferrara, 1991; Hon. LLD Aberdeen, 2000; Hon. Dr: Perugia, 2001; Paris II, 2001. *Publications:* Fault in the formation of Contract in Roman Law and Scots Law, 1958; editor, Buckland's Textbook of Roman Law, 3rd edn, 1963; Regulae Iuris: from juristic rules to legal maxims, 1966; Roman Law in Scotland in Ius Romanum Medii Aevi, 1968; Roman Law and English Jurisprudence (inaugural lect.), 1969; (with J. Shand) Legal Values in Western Society, 1974, Italian edn 1981; (ed jtly) Adam Smith's Lectures on Jurisprudence, 1978; Legal Evolution, 1980, Japanese edn 1987; (ed jtly) Studies in Justinian's Institutes, 1983; Legal Institutions: the development of dispute settlement, 1984, Italian edn 1987; The Character and Influence of the Roman Civil Law: historical essays, 1988; (with F. de Zulueta) The Teaching of Roman Law in England around 1200, 1990; (ed and contrib.) Notaries Public in England since the Reformation (English and Italian edns), 1991; Roman Law in European History, 1999 (German trans., 1996, Spanish and Italian trans., 2001, Japanese trans., 2003, French trans., 2004, Hungarian trans., 2005; Basque trans., 2014); articles in legal periodicals mainly on Roman Law and legal history. *Address:* 36 Wimpole Road, Great Eversden, Cambridge CB23 1HR. *T:* (01223) 262349.

See also Lord Howard of Effingham.

STEIN, Richard Stenton; Partner, Solicitor, Leigh Day, since 1993; *b* Geneva, Switzerland, 15 Dec. 1954; *s* of late Gunther Stein and of Zabelle Stein (*née* Yardumian, now Stenton); *m* 1993, Maria Duggan (marr. diss. 2011); one *s* one *d*; partner, Sally Lovell. *Educ:* William Ellis Sch., Highgate; Leeds Univ. (BA Hons Pol Studies); Manchester Univ. (PGCE); Poly. of Central London (DipLaw); Inns of Court Sch. of Law; University Coll. London (LLM). Lecturer: Trowbridge Coll., 1978–79; Hackney Coll., 1979–81; called to the Bar, Inner Temple, 1982; Campaigns Co-ordinator, Camden Tribunal and Rights Unit, 1982–88; Solicitor, 1988–90, Principal Solicitor, 1990–93, London Bor. of Lewisham; admitted Solicitor, 1994. Mem. (Lab) Camden LBC, 1983–86. Trustee, Public Law Project, 2000–. *Publications:* (with W. Birtles) Planning and Environmental Law, 1994. *Recreations:* fell walking, gardening, DIY, Green Party, Chelsea FC, badminton, running (slowly). *Address:* 32 Silverdale Court, 142–148 Goswell Road, EC1V 7DU. *T:* 07976 780305; Brook Cottage, Llanveynoe, Longtown, Herefordshire HR2 0NE. *E:* rstein@leighday.co.uk, richardstein1@icloud.com.

STEIN, Rick; *see* Stein, C. R.

STEIN, Samuel; QC 2009; *b* Canterbury, 5 March 1964; *s* of Maurice and Gillian Stein; *m* 1997, Karen Stubbs. *Educ:* South Bank Poly. (LLB). Called to the Bar, Inner Temple, 1988, Bencher, 2011; in practice as barrister, specialising in crime, 1988–. Mem., Bar Standards Bd, 2010– (Chm., Pupillage Cttee, 2009–; Chm., Quality Assce Cttee, 2010–). *Recreation:* trying to sail. *Address:* Mansfield Chambers, 5 Chancery Lane, WC2A 1LG. *Club:* Herne Bay Sailing.

STEIN, Thea Suzanna Ruth; Chief Executive, Carers Trust, since 2012; *b* London, 1964; *d* of Clive and June Stein. *Educ:* Haberdashers' Aske's Sch. for Girls; St Anne's Coll., Oxford (BA Psychol. and Physiol.; MA); Univ. of London (MBA). Clinical Psychol. trng, London Regl Health Service; clinical psychologist and family therapist, Barnet, Camden and Islington, 1986–93; Public Health Lead on Mental Health, then Dep. Dir, Commissioning, Hillingdon HA, 1993–97; Dep. Chief Exec., Dumfries and Galloway Health Bd; on secondment, working on Health Plan, Scottish Parliament; Chief Exec., Leeds NE PCT, 2002–06; Yorkshire and Humber Regional Development Agency: Exec. Dir, 2006–10; Chief Exec., 2010–12. Non-exec. Dir, St Annes Housing Assoc., 2005–09. Gov., Leeds Beckett (formerly Leeds Metropolitan) Univ., 2011–. *Recreations:* astanga yoga, collecting cookery books, enthusiastic novice beekeeper, reading (anything from the cereal box onwards). *Address:* Stockport, Manchester. *E:* theasrstein@gmail.com. *W:* www.twitter.com/thea_stein.

STEINBERG, Prof. Hannah; Professor Emerita of Psychopharmacology, University of London, since 1989; Hon. Research Professor in Psychology, School of Social Science, Middlesex University, 1992–2001; *b* 16 March; *d* of late Michael Steinberg, doctor of law, and Marie (*née* Wein). *Educ:* Schwarzwaldschule, Vienna; Putney High School; Queen Anne's School, Caversham; Univ. of Reading (Cert. Comm.); Denton Secretarial Coll., London; University College London (BA 1st cl. Hons Psychology, PhD; Troughton Schol., 1948–50); DSc Psychopharmacol., London, 2002. FBPsS 1959 (Hon. Fellow, 2007), CPsychol 1990. Pres., Univ. of London Union, 1947–48; Univ. of London Postgrad. Studentship in Psychol., 1948–50. Sec. to Man. Dir, Omes Ltd, 1943–44. Part-time Lectr, LSE, 1951; University College London: Asst Lectr in Pharmacology, 1954–55; Lectr, 1955–62; Reader in Psychopharmacology, 1962–70; Prof. of Psychopharmacology (first in W Europe and USA), 1970–92; Head of Psychopharmacology Gp, Dept of Psychology, 1979–92; Hon. Res. Fellow, Dept of Psychol., 1992–. Hon. Consulting Clinical Psychologist, Dept of Psychological Medicine, Royal Free Hosp., 1970. Member MRC working parties on: Biochemistry and Pharmacology of Drug Dependence, 1968–73; Biological Aspects of Drug Dependence, 1971–75. Vice-President: Collegium Internationale Neuro-Psychopharmacologicum (CINP), 1968–74 (Emeritus Fellow, 1996; Pioneer Award, 2008); Brit. Assoc. for Psychopharmacology, 1974–76 (Mem., 1st Council, 1974; Hon. Mem., 1989; launched Hannah Steinberg-Wolfson Foundn annual bursary, 2011); Mem., Biological Council, 1977–80. Distinguished Affiliate of Amer. Psychol Assoc., Psychopharmacology Div., 1978–; Founder Member: European Coll. of Neuropsychopharmacology; European Behavioural Pharmacol Soc.; British Psychological Society: Mem., 1954; Ed., Bulletin, 1955–62; First Hon. Sec., Psychology of Sport and Exercise Section, 1995–2000. Member: British Pharmacol Soc. (Mem., Editl Bd, 1965–72); Experimental Psychol. Soc.; Soc. for Study of Addiction; European Health Psychol Soc.; Soc. for Medicines Res. Convener, Academic Women's Achievement Gp, 1979–92. Accredited Sport Psychologist, British Assoc. of Sport and Exercise Scis, 1992. Special Trustee, Middx Hosp., 1989–92. Discovered (with E. A. Sykes) mutual potentiation of amphetamine and barbiturate drugs ('purple hearts'), 1963; Initiator (with E. A. Sykes), Steinberg Principle on new develts in conservation areas, Steinberg v Sec. of State for the Envmt, Planning Law Reports, vol. 2, 1989. British Assoc. for Psychopharmacology/AstraZeneca Lifetime Achievement Award, 2001. Past ed. of scientific jls. *Publications:* (trans. and ed jtly) Animals and Men, 1951; organiser of symposia, workshops and editor: (jtly) Animal Behaviour and Drug Action, 1963; Scientific Basis of Drug Dependence, 1968; (jtly) Psychopharmacology, Sexual Disorders and Drug Abuse, 1972; Joint Editor, Occasional Publications of British Psychological Society: Exercise Addiction, 1995; Quality and Quantity, 1996; Teams and Teamwork, 1996; Cognitive Enhancement, 1997; What Sport Psychologists Do, 1998; Sport Psychology in Practice: the early stages, 2000; chapters and reviews on psychopharmacology, drug addiction, drug combinations, psychological benefits and hazards of physical exercise, exercise addiction, creativity and writer's block. *Address:* c/o Pharmacology Department, University College London, WC1E 6BT. *T:* (020) 7267 4783, *Fax:* (020) 7267 4780.

STEINBERG, Max Laurence, CBE 2013 (OBE 1998); Chief Executive, Liverpool Vision, since 2010; *b* Liverpool, 22 Jan. 1952; *s* of Ronald Steinberg and Golda Steinberg; *m* 1975, Sharon Abisgold; one *s* one *d*. *Educ:* King David High Sch., Liverpool. Regl Dir, Merseyside Housing Corp., 1987–95; Housing Corporation, Liverpool: Dir, NW and Merseyside, 1995–2001; Dir, Investment and Regeneration - North, 2001–03; Chief Executive: Elevate East Lancashire, 2003–08; Regenerate Pennine Lancashire Ltd, 2009–10. Mem., Social Exclusion Unit's Policy Action Team 7, 1997; Mem. Bd, Nat. Housing and Planning Advice Unit, 2006–10. Chairman: Riverside Housing Gp, 2014–; Internat. Fest. for Business, 2014, 2016. Trust Mem., Royal Court Theatre, Liverpool. Chm., European Inst. for Urban Affairs, Liverpool John Moores Univ., 2001–. Chm. Govs, King David High Sch., 1999–2013. FRSA. *Recreations:* theatre, cinema, family, reading, travel. *Address:* Liverpool Vision, 10th Floor, Cunard Building, Water Street, Liverpool L3 9PP. *T:* (0151) 600 2998. *E:* msteinberg@liverpoolvision.co.uk.

STEINBERGER, Prof. Jack; Physicist, European Center for Particle Physics, CERN, Geneva, 1968–86; *b* 25 May 1921; *s* of Ludwig and Bertha Steinberger; *m* 1st, 1943, Joan Beauregard; two *s*; 2nd, 1962, Cynthia Eve Alff; one *s* one *d*. *Educ:* New Trier Township High Sch.; Armour Inst. of Technology; Univ. of Chicago (BS Chem. 1942; PhD Phys 1948). Mem., Inst. of Advanced Study, Princeton, 1948–49; Asst, Univ. of California, Berkeley, 1949–50; Prof., Columbia Univ., 1950–68 (Higgins Prof., 1965–68). Vis. Prof. of Physics, Scuola Normale Superiore, Pisa, 1986. Member: Nat. Acad. of Sciences; Amer. Acad. of Arts and Sciences; Heidelberg Acad. of Science; Accad. Nationale dei Lincei. Hon. Dr: Autònoma, Barcelona; Dortmund; Würzburg; Glasgow; Clermont-Ferrand. (Jtly) President's Science Award, USA, 1988; (jtly) Nobel Prize for Physics, 1988; Mateuzzi Medal, Soc. Italiana della Scienze, 1991. *Publications:* papers in learned jls on discoveries leading to better understanding of elementary particles. *Recreations:* flute; formerly mountaineering, tennis, yachting. *Address:* CERN, 1211 Geneva 23, Switzerland; 25 Ch. des Merles, 1213 Onex, Switzerland.

STEINBRÜCK, Peer; Member (SPD), Bundestag, Germany, since 2009; Minister of Finance, Germany, 2005–09; *b* Hamburg, 10 Jan. 1947; *m* 1976, Gertrud Isbary; one *s* two *d*. *Educ:* Christian-Albrechts Univ., Kiel (degree in econs 1974). Military service, 1968–70; Federal Government of Germany: Construction Ministry (Regl Planning), 1974–76; Planning Gp, Min. of Res. and Technol., 1976–77; Personal Sec. to Ministers Matthöfer and Hauff, 1977–78; div. responsible for Ministry of Res. and Technol., Federal Chancellery, 1978–81; Econs Directorate, Perm. Mission of Federal Rep. of Germany, E Berlin, 1981; Personal Sec. to Minister of Res. and Technol., 1981–82; Co-ordinating Desk Officer, envmtl protection, SPD Parly Gp, Bundestag, 1983–85; North Rhine-Westphalia: Desk Officer for nat. econ. policy, Planning Gp, Min. of Envmt and Agric., 1985–86; Hd, Office of the Premier, 1986–90; Schleswig-Holstein: State Secretary: Min. of Nature, Envmt and Land Develt, 1990–92; Min. of Econs, Technol. and Transportation, 1992–93; Minister of Econs, Technol. and Transportation, 1993–98; North Rhine-Westphalia: Minister of Econs and Small Business, Technol. and Transportation, 1998–2000; Finance Minister, 2000–02; Mem., State Assembly, 2002; Premier, 2002–05. Joined SPD, 1969 (a Dep. Chm., 2005–). *Address:* Deutscher Bundestag, Platz der Republik, 11011 Berlin, Germany.

STEINBY, Prof. Eva Margareta, FSA; Professor of Archaeology of the Roman Empire, and Fellow of All Souls College, University of Oxford, 1994–2004; *b* 21 Nov. 1938; *d* of Kaarlo Erkki Wilén and Doris Margareta Steinby. *Educ:* Univ. of Helsinki (Hum. Kand. 1963; Fil. Kand. 1964; Fil. Lic. 1970; Fil. Dr 1976); MA Oxon 1995. FSA 1997. Institutum Romanum Finlandiae, Rome: Asst, 1973–77; Dir, 1979–82 and 1992–94; Sen. Res. Fellow, Finnish Acad., Helsinki, 1985–92. Docent in History, Univ. of Helsinki, 1977–; Vis. Fellow, All Souls Coll., Oxford, 1990–91. Fellow, Suomen Historiallinen Seura, 1978; Corresp. Fellow, Pontificia Accademia Romana di Archeologia, 1982, Fellow, 1993; Fellow: Societas Scientiarum Fennica, 1983; Academia Scientiarum Fennica, 2000; Corresp. Fellow, Deutsches Archäologisches Institut, 1984; For. Hon. Mem., Archaeol Inst. of America, 1998. Medaglia d'Oro per Benemeriti Culturali (Italy), 1983; Finnish Cultural Foundn Prize, 2003. Officer, 1st Cl., Order of White Rose (Finland), 1991. *Publications:* La cronologia delle figlinae doliari urbane, 1976; Lateres signati Ostienses, Vol. I 1977, Vol. II 1978; Indici complementari ai bolli doliari urbani (CIL, XV, 1), 1987; (ed) Lacus Iuturnae I, 1989; (ed) Lexicon

Topographicum Urbis Romae, 6 vols, 1993–2000; (ed) Ianiculum-Gianicolo, 1997; La necropoli della Via Triumphalis: il tratto sotto l'Autoparco vaticano, 2003; Edilizia pubblica e potere politico nella Roma repubblicana, 2012; Lacus Iuturnae II, Saggi degli anni 1982–85, (ed and contrib.) 1. Saggi e conclusioni, (ed) 2. Materiali, 2012; articles in Italian, German and Finnish learned jls. *Address:* Kalevank 61 A 13, 00180 Helsinki, Finland. *T:* (9) 6852829.

STEINER, Achim; Executive Director, United Nations Environment Programme, since 2006; Director-General, United Nations Office, Nairobi, 2009–11; *b* Carazinho, Brazil, 17 May 1961; *s* of Roland Steiner and Helga Steiner; *m* 2001, Elizabeth Clare Rihoy; two *s*. *Educ:* Worcester Coll., Oxford (BA 1983); Sch. of Oriental and African Studies, Univ. of London (MA 1985); German Development Inst.; Harvard Business Sch. Tech. Advr, Masaara Shams Omania, Sultanate of Oman, 1979–80; community develt worker, Anthyodhaya Sangh, 1983–84; GTZ: Tech. Advr, 1986–88; Desk Officer, Asia/Middle East, 1988–89; Policy Advr, 1989–91; International Union for Conservation of Nature: Prog. Coordinator, Regl Office for S Africa, 1991–94; Sen. Policy Advr, Global Policy Unit, 1994–97; Chief Tech. Advr, Mekong River Commn, 1997–98; Sec. Gen., World Commn on Dams, 1998–2001; Dir Gen., IUCN, 2001–05. *Address:* (office) PO Box 47074, 00100 Nairobi, Kenya. *T:* (20) 7624001, (20) 7624002, *Fax:* (20) 7624275, (20) 7624006. *E:* executiveoffice@unep.org.

STEINER, Prof. (Francis) George, MA, DPhil; FBA 1998; FRSL; Fellow, Churchill College, Cambridge, since 1961; Weidenfeld Professor of Comparative Literature, and Fellow of St Anne's College, Oxford, 1994–95; *b* 23 April 1929; *s* of Dr F. G. and Mrs E. Steiner; *m* 1955, Zara Shakow (*see* Z. Steiner); one *s* one *d*. *Educ:* Paris (BèsL); Univ. of Chicago (BA); Harvard (MA); Oxford (DPhil). Member, staff of the Economist, in London, 1952–56; Inst. for Advanced Study, Princeton, 1956–58; Gauss Lectr, Princeton Univ., 1959–60; Prof. of English and Comparative Literature, Univ. of Geneva, 1974–94, Prof. Emeritus, 1994–. Lectures: Massey, 1974; Leslie Stephen, Cambridge, 1986; W. P. Ker, 1986, Gifford, 1990, Univ. of Glasgow; Page-Barbour, Univ. of Virginia, 1987; Paul Tillich, Harvard, 1999. Fulbright Professorship, 1958–69; Vis. Prof., Collège de France, 1992; Charles Eliot Norton Prof., Harvard, 2001–02. Pres., English Assoc., 1975; Corresp. Mem., (Federal) German Acad. of Literature, 1981; Hon. Mem., Amer. Acad. of Arts and Scis, 1989; Hon. RA 2000. FRSL 1964. Hon. Fellow: Balliol Coll., Oxford, 1995; St Anne's Coll., Oxford, 1998. Hon. DLitt: East Anglia, 1976; Louvain, 1980; Mount Holyoke Coll., USA, 1983; Bristol, 1989; Glasgow, 1990; Liège, 1990; Ulster, 1993; Durham, 1995; Kenyan Coll., USA, 1996; Trinity Coll., Dublin, 1996; Rome, 1998; Sorbonne, 1998; Salamanca, 2002; Athens, 2004; Bologna, 2006; London, 2006; Lisbon, 2009; Dr *hc* École Normale Supérieure, Paris, 2014. O. Henry Short Story Award, 1958; Guggenheim Fellowship, 1971–72; Zabel Award of Nat. Inst. of Arts and Letters of the US, 1970; Faulkner Stipend for Fiction, PEN, 1983; PEN Macmillan Fiction Prize, 1993; Truman Capote Lifetime Award for Lit., 1999; Prince of Asturias Prize, Spain, 2001; Ludwig Börne Prize, Germany, 2003; Mondello Prize, Italy, 2004; Redonda Prize, Spain, 2007. Chevalier de la Légion d'Honneur (France), 1984; Comdr, Ordre des Arts et des Lettres (France), 2001. *Publications:* Tolstoy or Dostoevsky, 1958; The Death of Tragedy, 1960; Anno Domini, 1964; Language and Silence, 1967; Extraterritorial, 1971; In Bluebeard's Castle, 1971; The Sporting Scene: White Knights in Reykjavik, 1973; After Babel, 1975 (adapted for TV as The Tongues of Men, 1977); Heidegger, 1978; On Difficulty and Other Essays, 1978; The Portage to San Cristobal of A. H., 1981; Antigones, 1984; George Steiner: a reader, 1984; Real Presences: is there anything in what we say?, 1989; Proofs and Three Parables, 1992; The Deeps of the Sea (fiction), 1996; No Passion Spent, 1996; Errata: an examined life, 1997; Grammars of Creation, 2001; Lessons of the Masters, 2003; My Unwritten Books, 2008; George Steiner at the 'New Yorker', 2009; The Poetry of Thought, 2012; Un long samedi, 2014. *Recreations:* music, chess, mountain walking. *Address:* 32 Barrow Road, Cambridge CB2 2AS. *Clubs:* Athenæum; Harvard (New York).

STEINER, Prof. Hillel Isaac, PhD; FBA 1999; Professor of Political Philosophy, University of Manchester, 1995–2009, now Emeritus; *b* 1942; *m* 1966. *Educ:* Univ. of Toronto (BA); Carleton Univ. (MA); Univ. of Manchester (PhD). Lectr in Politics and Public Admin, Univ. of Saskatchewan, 1966–67; Res. Associate, 1967–71, Lectr, then Sen. Lectr, 1971–95, Reader, 1995, in Pol Philosophy, Univ. of Manchester. *Publications:* Essay on Rights, 1994; A Debate Over Rights, 1998; Left-Libertarianism and its Critics, 2000; Freedom: a philosophical anthology, 2007; contrib. to learned jls.

STEINER, Prof. Ullrich; Professor of Soft Matter Physics, Adolphe Merkle Institute, University of Fribourg; *b* 27 March 1963; *s* of Richard Steiner and Elisabeth Steiner (*née* Konrad); *m* 1995, Barbara Gorodecki; one *d*. *Educ:* Dip. Physics; Dr rer. nat.; Habilitation. Prof. of Polymer Science, Univ. of Groningen, 1999–2004; John Humphrey Plummer Prof. of Physics of Materials, Univ. of Cambridge, 2004. (Jtly) Raymond and Beverley Sackler Prize for Physical Scis, Tel Aviv Univ., 2002. *Publications:* 60 articles in scientific jls; 3 patents. *Recreations:* ski-ing, sailing, cycling. *Address:* Adolphe Merkle Institute, Chemin des Verdiers, 1700 Fribourg, Switzerland.

STEINER, Dr Zara, FBA 2007; Fellow, New Hall, Cambridge, 1965–96, Fellow Emeritus, 1997; *b* 6 Nov. 1928; *d* of Joseph and Frances Shakow; *m* 1955, Prof. (Francis) George Steiner, *qv*; one *s* one *d*. *Educ:* Swarthmore Coll. (BA 1948); St Anne's Coll., Oxford (BA 1950); Radcliffe Coll., Harvard Univ. (PhD 1962). Lectr, Center of Internat. Studies, Princeton Univ., 1957–58 and 1960–61. Visiting Professor: Stanford Univ., Calif, 1979–80; Inst. Univ. des Hautes Etudes Internationales, Geneva, 1980–81; Univ. of N Carolina, 1985. Hon. DLitt: S, Sewanee, Tennessee, 1997; E Anglia, 2011. *Publications:* The State Department and the Foreign Service, 1958; Present Problems of the Foreign Service, 1961; The Foreign Office and Foreign Policy 1898–1914, 1969, rev. edn 1986; Britain and the Origins of the First World War, 1977, 2nd edn (with K. Neilson), 2005; (ed) The Times Survey of Foreign Ministries of the World, 1982; The Lights that Failed: European international history 1919–1933, 2005; (ed jtly) History and Neorealism, 2010; The Triumph of the Dark: European international history, 1933–39, 2011; articles in jls incl. Jl Modern Hist., Historical Jl, Relns Internationales, Diplomacy and Statecraft. *Recreation:* dog walking. *Address:* 32 Barrow Road, Cambridge CB2 8AS. *T:* (01223) 461043. *E:* zs202@hermes.cam.ac.uk. *Club:* Lansdowne.

STEINFELD, Alan Geoffrey; QC 1987; *b* 13 July 1946; *s* of Henry Chaim Steinfeld and Deborah Steinfeld; *m* 1976, Josephine Nicole (*née* Gros); two *s*. *Educ:* City of London Sch.; Downing Coll., Cambridge (BA Hons, LLB). Arnold McNair Schol. in Internat. Law, 1967; Whewell Schol. in Internat. Law, 1968. Called to the Bar, Lincoln's Inn, 1968, Bencher, 1996; commenced pupillage at the Bar, 1968, practice at the Bar, 1969; a Dep. High Court Judge, 1995–. *Recreations:* tennis, sailing, opera. *Address:* (chambers) 24 Old Buildings, Lincoln's Inn, WC2A 3UP. *T:* (020) 7691 2424. *Club:* Royal Automobile.

STEINMEIER, Frank-Walter; Member (SPD), Bundestag, Germany, since 2009; Minister for Foreign Affairs, since 2013; *b* 5 Jan. 1956; *s* of Walter Steinmeier and Ursula Steinmeier (*née* Broy); *m* 1995, Elke Büdenbender; one *d*. *Educ:* Blomberg Grammar Sch.; Justus Liebig Univ., Giessen (1st State Law Exam 1982, 2nd State Law Exam 1986; Doctorate 1991). State Chancellery of Lower Saxony: Hd, Dept, 1994–96, responsible for policy guidelines and interministerial co-ordination and planning; State Sec. and Head, 1996–98; State Sec., Federal Chancellery and Comr for Federal Intelligence Services, 1998–99; Hd, Federal Chancellery, 1999–2005; Minister for Foreign Affairs, 2005–09, Vice-Chancellor, 2007–09, Germany; Leader of the Opposition, 2009–13. Cavaliere di Gran Croce, 2006. *Publications:* Made in Germany; Sicherheit im Wandel (The Changing Face of Security); Bürger ohne Obdach (Citizens without Shelter). *Address:* Deutscher Bundestag, Platz der Republik, 11011 Berlin, Germany.

STEITZ, Prof. Thomas Arthur, PhD; Professor of Molecular Biophysics and Biochemistry, since 1979, and Sterling Professor, since 2001, Yale University; Investigator, Howard Hughes Medical Institute, since 1986; *b* Milwaukee, 23 Aug. 1940; *s* of Arthur R. and Catherine Steitz; *m* 1966, Joan Argetsinger; one *s*. *Educ:* Lawrence Coll., Appleton, Wisconsin (BA 1962); Harvard Univ. (PhD Biochem. and Molecular Biol. 1966). Postdoctoral res., MRC Lab. of Molecular Biol., Cambridge, 1967–70; Yale University: Asst Prof. of Molecular Biophysics and Biochem., 1970–74; Associate Prof., 1974–79; Actg Dir, Div. of Biol Scis, 1981; Eugene Higgins Prof. of Molecular Biophysics and Biochem., 1994–2001; Chm., Dept of Molecular Biophysics and Biochem., 2000–03. Macy Fellow, Max-Planck Inst. for Biophysical Chem., Göttingen, Germany and MRC Lab. of Molecular Biol., Cambridge, 1976–77; Fairchild Schol., CIT, 1984–85. Lectures include: Paul Doty, 2000, Frank H. Westheimer Medal Symposium, 2004, Harvard Univ.; Bateson Meml, 15th John Innes Symposium, Norwich, 2003; Norden, Univ. of Mass, 2006; Francis Crick Nobel, Salk Inst., 2008; George E. Palade Dist., Wayne State Univ., 2008; EMBL Dist. Vis. Lectr, Heidelberg, 2008; A* Star Biomed. Res. Council Dist. Vis. Lectr, Singapore, 2008; Arthur Birch Vis. Lectr, ANU, 2008. Member, Editorial Board: Qly Rev. Biophysics, 1986–91; Structure, 1991–; Proteins, 1991–96; Annual Rev. Biochem., 1997–2002; Current Opinion in Structural Biol., 1998–. Co-founder and Chm., Scientific Adv. Bd, Rib-X Pharmaceuticals, Inc., New Haven, Conn, 2001–. Mem., Cttee on Microgravity Res., Space Studies Bd, Nat. Res. Council, Washington, 1987–92. Member: Bd of Scientific Advrs, Jane Coffin Childs Meml Fund for Med. Res., New Haven, 1998–2006; Scientific Adv. Council, Walter and Eliza Hall Inst. Med. Res., Vic, Australia, 2001–. Member: NAS, 1990; Amer. Acad. Arts and Scis, 1990; Conn Acad. Sci. and Engrg, 1991. Foreign Mem., Royal Soc., 2011. Fellow, Amer. Acad. Microbiol., 2003. Hon. DSc Lawrence, 1981. Awards include: Pfizer Award in Enzyme Chem., Amer. Chem. Soc., 1980; Rosenstiel Award for Dist. Work in Basic Med. Scis, Brandeis Univ., 2001; Newcomb Cleveland Prize, AAAS, 2001; Lucia R. Briggs Dist. Achievement Award, Lawrence Univ., 2002; Frank H. Westheimer Medal, Harvard Univ., 2004; Keio Med. Sci. Prize, Keio Univ., 2006; Gairdner Internat. Award, Gairdner Foundn, 2007; George E. Palade Gold Medal, Wayne State Univ., 2008; (jtly) Nobel Prize in Chem., 2009; Connecticut Medal of Sci., 2013. *Publications:* contribs to jls incl. Nature, Science, Cell, EMBO Jl, Procs of NAS, Molecular Cell. *Recreations:* gardening, sailing, hiking, ski-ing. *Address:* Department of Molecular Biophysics and Biochemistry, Howard Hughes Medical Institute, Yale University, Bass Center, Room 418, PO Box 208114, 266 Whitney Avenue, New Haven, CT 06520–8114, USA. *T:* (203) 4325617. *E:* thomas.steitz@yale.edu.

STELL, Edward Jedidiah; Parliamentary Counsel, since 2005; *b* 8 June 1962; *s* of late Christopher Fyson Stell, OBE and of Dorothy Jean Stell (*née* Mackay); *m* 1991, Jocelyn Helen Whyte; two *s* one *d*. *Educ:* Merchant Taylors' Sch., Northwood; Corpus Christi Coll., Oxford (BA 1985, MA 1988). Articled clerk, 1988–90, asst solicitor, 1990–93, Ashurst Morris Crisp; Office of the Parly Counsel, 1993–. *Recreations:* cycling, books. *Address:* Office of the Parliamentary Counsel, 1 Horse Guards Road, SW1A 2HQ.

STELMACH, Hon. Edward Michael; MLA (Progressive C) Fort Saskatchewan-Vegreville, Canada, 2004–12 (Vegreville-Viking, 1993–2004); Premier of Alberta and Minister for Public Affairs Bureau, 2006–11; Leader, Progressive Conservative Party, 2006–11; *b* 11 May 1951; *s* of Michael Stelmach and Nancy Stelmach; *m* Marie Warshawski; four *c*. *Educ:* Univ. of Alberta. Mixed farm business, 1973–. Minister: of Agriculture, Food and Rural Devel, 1997–99; of Infrastructure, 1999–2001; of Transportation, 2001–04; of Internat. and Intergovtl Relns, 2004–06. Vice Chm., Genalta Power, 2012–. Chm. Bd, Vegreville Health Unit; Member Board: Archer Meml Hosp.; Lamont Auxiliary Hosp. and Nursing Home; Covenant Health, 2012–. Member: Andrew Co-op. Assoc.; Lamont 4-H Dist Council; Andrew 4-H Beef Club. Hon. LLD Alberta, 2013. *Recreations:* golf, reading.

STELZER, Irwin Mark, PhD; Director, Economic Policy Studies, and Senior Fellow, Hudson Institute, since 1998; President, Irwin M. Stelzer Associates, since 1981; Columnist, Sunday Times, since 1985; *b* 22 May 1932; *s* of Abraham Stelzer and Fanny Dolgins Stelzer; *m* 1981, Marian Faris Stuntz; one *s*. *Educ:* New York Univ. (BA 1951; MA 1952); Cornell Univ. (PhD 1954). Researcher and consultant, 1951–61; Lectr, New York Univ., and City Coll., NY, 1951–61; Teaching Asst, Cornell Univ., 1953–54; Instr, Univ. of Connecticut, 1954–55; Pres., Nat. Economic Res. Associates, 1961–81; Dir, Energy and Envmtl Policy Center, Harvard Univ., 1985–88; Resident Schol., American Enterprise Inst., 1990–98. Vis. Fellow, Nuffield Coll., Oxford, 2004–; Sen. Res. Fellow, Smith Inst., 2005–10. Mem., Pres., Adv. Cttee to US Trade Rep. Mem. Bd of Dirs, Regulatory Policy Inst., Oxford, 2000–08; Dir, Centre for Policy Studies, 2010–. Mem., Vis. Cttee, Harris Sch., Univ. of Chicago, 2007–13. Mem., Editl Bd, Public Interest. *Publications:* Selected Antitrust Cases: landmark decisions, 1955; The Antitrust Laws: a primer, 1996, 4th edn 2001; Neoconservatism, 2004; contrib. to Public Interest, Commentary and other jls. *Recreation:* photography. *Clubs:* Reform, Royal Automobile; Cosmos, Metropolitan (Washington).

STEMBRIDGE, David Harry; QC 1990; a Recorder of the Crown Court, 1977–97; *b* 23 Dec. 1932; *s* of Percy G. Stembridge and Emily W. Stembridge; *m* 1956, Therese C. Furer; three *s* one *d*. *Educ:* St Chad's Cathedral Choir Sch., Lichfield; Bromsgrove Sch.; Birmingham Univ. (LLB Hons). Called to the Bar, Gray's Inn, 1955; practising barrister, 1956–2003. *Recreations:* music, sailing. *Address:* Omega, 101 Court Road, Newton Ferrers, Plymouth PL8 1DE. *Club:* Bar Yacht.

STEMPLOWSKI, Prof. Ryszard; Professor of Human Sciences, Akademia Ignatianum, Cracow, since 2010; *b* 25 March 1939; *s* of Kazimierz Stemplowski and Eugenia Białecka; *m* 1975, Irena Zasłona; two *d*. *Educ:* Tech. Lycée (Civil Build.), Bydgoszcz; Tech. Univ., Wrocław; Univ. of Wrocław (LLM 1968); Inst. of History, Polish Acad. of Scis (PhD 1973); Dr Habilitatus (Hist.) Warsaw Univ., 1999. Res. Fellow, Inst. of History, Polish Acad. of Scis, 1973–90; Chief of Chancellery of Sejm (Chamber of Deputies), Poland, 1990–93; Polish Ambassador to UK, 1994–99; Dir, Polish Inst. of Internat. Affairs, Warsaw, 1999–2004; Prof. of Political Theory, Warsaw Sch. of Econs, 2001–05; Prof. of History and Internat. Relns, Jagiellonian Univ., Cracow, 2005–10. Ed., Polish Diplomatic Rev., 2000–04. Vis. Fellow, St Antony's Coll., Oxford, 1974; Vis. Scholar and Alexander von Humboldt Fellow, Univ. of Cologne, 1981–82. Interfaith Golden Medallion, Peace Through Dialogue, UK, 1999. Kt Cross, Order of Polonia Restituta (Poland), 2000; Grand Cross of Merit, Constantinian Order of St George (House of Bourbon Two Sicilies), 1996. *Publications:* Dependence and Defiance: Argentina and rivalries among USA, UK and Germany 1930–46, 1975, 2nd edn 2014; (jtly) History of Latin America 1850–1980, 3 vols, 1978–80; (jtly) Economic Nationalism in East Central Europe and South America 1918–39, 1990; (jtly) The Slavic Settlers in Misiones 1897–1947, 1992; State-Socialism in the Actually Existing Capitalism: Chile 1932, 1996, 2nd edn 2013; Development of Polish Foreign Policy, 2004; An Introduction to Polish Foreign Policy Analysis, 2006, 2nd edn 2007; Government Projects and Theoretical Concepts of European Integration, 2007, 2nd edn 2012; (ed) On the State of Latin American States: approaching the bicentenary, 2009; Political Philosophy of the Integration of States in Europe (20th-21st centuries), 2010, 2nd edn 2012; (ed) Europe—Latin America: looking at each other?, 2010; (ed) The Poles, Ruthenians and Ukrainians, Argentines: the agricultural colonization of Misiones, 1892–2009, 2011, 2nd edn 2013; On Policy-Making and Policy-

Analysing, 2013; other works and translations in Polish, German, Spanish, English, Russian. *Recreations:* music, cosmology, reading bilingual editions of poems. *E:* ryszard@stemplowski.pl. *W:* www.stemplowski.pl.

STEPAN, Prof. Alfred, PhD; FBA 1997; Wallace S. Sayre Professor of Government, Columbia University, New York, 1999, now Emeritus; Director, Center for the Study of Democracy, Toleration, and Religion, 2006; *b* 22 July 1936; *s* of Alfred C. Stepan, Jr and Mary Louise Quinn; *m* 1964, Nancy Leys; one *s* one *d.* *Educ:* Univ. of Notre Dame (BA 1958); Balliol Coll., Oxford (BA PPE 1960; MA 1963); Columbia Univ. (PhD Comparative Politics 1969). Special Corresp., Economist, 1964; Staff Mem., Social Sci. Dept, Rand Corp., 1966–69; Yale University: Asst Prof., Associate Prof., and Prof. of Political Science, 1970–83; Dir, Concilium on Internat. and Area Studies, 1982–83; Columbia University: Dean, Sch. of Internat. and Public Affairs, 1983–91; Prof. of Political Sci., 1983–87; Burgess Prof. of Political Sci., 1987–93; first Rector and Pres., Central European Univ., Budapest, Prague and Warsaw, 1993–96; Gladstone Prof. of Govt, and Fellow of All Souls Coll., Oxford Univ., 1996–99. Guggenheim Fellow, 1974–75; Vis. Prof. and Lectr to numerous acad. bodies and confs, USA, Europe, S America and Asia. Former Member: Bd of Govs, Foreign Policy Assoc.; NEC, Americas Watch. Former Chm., Richard Tucker Music Foundn. Fellow, Amer. Acad. of Arts and Scis. Member, Editorial Board: Jl of Democracy, 1989–; Government and Opposition, 1996–; Jl of Civil Soc. Hon. Fellow, St Antony's Coll., Oxford, 2006. Karl Deutsch Award, Internat. Political Sci. Assoc., 2012. Mem., Order of Rio Branco (Brazil), 2002. *Publications:* The Military in Politics: changing patterns in Brazil, 1971; The State and Society: Peru in comparative perspective, 1978; Rethinking Military Politics: Brazil and the southern cone, 1988; (with Juan J. Linz) Problems of Democratic Transition and Consolidation: Southern Europe, South America and post-Communist Europe, 1996; Arguing Comparative Politics, 2001; (with Juan J. Linz and Yogendra Yadav) Crafting State-Nations: India and other multinational democracies, 2011; editor, jt editor and contrib. to numerous other works and learned jls. *Recreations:* opera, gardening, walking. *Address:* 210 Riverside Drive, New York, NY 10025, USA; 8 Frognal Gardens, NW3 6UX.

STEPHANOPOULOS, Konstantinos; President of Greece, 1995–2005; *b* Patras, 1926; *s* of Demetrius and Vrisiis Stephanopoulos; *m* 1959, Eugenia El Stounopoulou; two *s* one *d.* *Educ:* Univ. of Athens. Private law practice, 1954–74. MP for Achaia: (Nat. Radical Union), 1964; (New Democracy Party), 1974–89; (Party of Democratic Renewal), 1989–93; Under-Sec. of Commerce, 1974; Minister of the Interior, 1974–76; Minister of Social Services, 1976–77; Prime Minister's Office, 1977–81; Parly Rep., New Democracy Party, 1981–85; Leader, Party of Democratic Renewal, 1985–94.

STEPHEN, family name of **Baron Stephen**.

STEPHEN, Baron *cr* 2011 (Life Peer), of Lower Deeside in the City of Aberdeen; **Nicol Ross Stephen;** *b* 23 March 1960; *s* of R. A. Nicol Stephen and Sheila G. Stephen; *m* Caris Doig; two *s* two *d.* *Educ:* Robert Gordon's Coll., Aberdeen; Aberdeen Univ. (LLB 1980); Edinburgh Univ. (DipLP 1981). Admitted Solicitor, 1983; C&PH Chalmers, 1981–83; Milne & Mackinnon, 1983–88; Sen. Corporate Finance Manager, Touche Ross & Co., 1988–90. Dir, Glassbox Ltd, 1992–99. Mem. (Lib Dem) Grampian Regl Council, 1982–92 (Chm., Econ. Develt and Planning Cttee, 1986–91). MP (Lib Dem) Kincardine and Deeside, Nov. 1991–1992. MSP (Lib Dem) Aberdeen S, 1999–2011. Scottish Executive: Dep. Minister for Enterprise and Lifelong Learning, 1999–2000, for Educn, Europe and Ext. Affairs, 2000–01, for Educn and Young People, 2001–03; Minister for Transport, 2003–05; Dep. First Minister, and Minister for Enterprise and Lifelong Learning, 2005–07. Leader, Scottish Lib Dems, 2005–08. Contested: Kincardine and Deeside, (L/All) 1987, (Lib Dem) 1992; (Lib Dem) Aberdeen S, 1997. *Recreations:* golf, swimming. *Address:* House of Lords, SW1A 0PW.

STEPHEN, Alexander, OBE 2009; FCCA; Chief Executive, Dundee City Council, 1995–2009; *b* 17 Sept. 1948; *m* Joyce Robertson; one *s* one *d.* FCCA 1977. Local govt posts, 1970–2009; Chief Exec., Dundee City DC, 1991–95. Treas., Revival, 1991–. *Address:* 1 Golspie Terrace, Dundee DD5 2PW. *T:* (01382) 776895.

STEPHEN, Barrie Michael Lace; *see* Stephen, Michael.

STEPHEN, David; *see* Stephen, J. D.

STEPHEN, Dr (George) Martin; Director of Education, GEMS (UK), 2012–14; *b* 18 July 1949; *s* of Sir Andrew Stephen, MB, ChB and late Lady Stephen (*née* Frances Barker); *m* 1971, Jennifer Elaine Fisher, JP; three *s.* *Educ:* Uppingham Sch.; Univ. of Leeds (BA); Univ. of Sheffield (Dip Ed, Dist., PhD; Hallam Prize for Educn, 1971). Child supervisor, Leeds and Oxford Remand Homes, 1966–67; Teacher of English, Uppingham, 1971–72, Haileybury, 1972–83 (and Housemaster); Second Master, Sedbergh, 1983–87; Headmaster, Perse Sch. for Boys, Cambridge, 1987–94; High Master: Manchester Grammar Sch., 1994–2004; St Paul's Sch., 2004–11. Vis. Lectr, Manchester Univ., 2001–04. Member: ESRC, 1990–2000; Naval Review, 1992–2000; Community Service Volunteers' Educnl Adv. Council, 1994–; HMC/GSA Univ. Admissions Working Gp, 1994–2004; British Assoc. for Sport and Law, 1995–98; Chm., HMC, 2004 (Chm., Community Service Cttee, 1992–95); non-exec. Chm., Clarendon Academies, 2011–. Associate Mem., Combination Room, GCCC, 1988–94. Member: Portico Library, Manchester, 1995–2000; Bd, Royal Exchange Theatre, Manchester, 1999–2004; Bd, LAMDA, 2004–10. Trustee: Project Trust, 1994–; Nat. Youth Advocacy Service, 2010–; Member, Board: Never Such Innocence, 2013–; Educate a Child, 2015–. Mem. Court, Univ. of Salford, 2000–04; Governor: Withington Sch., Manchester, 1994–2002; Pownall Hall Sch., Wilmslow, 1994–2004; Ducie High Sch., Moss Side, 1995–2004; Orley Farm Sch., 2004–11; Manchester City Acad., 1998–2004; The Hall Sch., Hampstead, 2004–11; Durston House Sch., 2005–11; London Acad. of Excellence, 2012; Sidra School, 2014–; Mem. Council, United World Schools, 2014–. FRSA 1996. Hon. DEd De Montfort, 1997. *Publications:* An Introductory Guide to English Literature, 1984; Studying Shakespeare, 1984; British Warship Designs since 1906, 1985; English Literature, 1986, 4th edn 1999; (ed) Never Such Innocence, 1988, 3rd edn 1993; Sea Battles in Close Up, 1988, 2nd edn 1996; The Fighting Admirals, 1991; (ed) The Best of Saki, 1993, 2nd edn 1996; The Price of Pity: poetry, history and myth in the Great War, 1996; (contrib.) Machiavelli, Marketing and Management, 2000; The Desperate Remedy, 2002; The Conscience of the King, 2004; The Galleons' Grave, 2005; The Rebel Heart, 2007; (contrib.) Sea Stories, 2007; The Diary of a Stroke, 2008; (contrib.) The School of Freedom: a liberal education reader from Plato to the present day, 2009; The Coming of the King, 2011; Scapegoat: the death of 'Prince of Wales' and 'Repulse', 2014; Poetry and Myths of the Great War: how poets altered our perception of history, 2014; Never Such Innocence (play), 2014; Educating the More Able Student: what works and why, 2015; contrib. York Notes series; articles and reviews for various jls. *Recreations:* writing, drama, pen and ink drawing, field and water sports, music. *Address:* 23 Merthyr Terrace, SW13 8DL; Thornage Watermill, Holt Road, Thornage, Norfolk NR25 7QN. *Clubs:* Athenæum, East India (Hon. Mem.), Garrick.

STEPHEN, Henrietta Hamilton, (Rita), MBE 1973; National Officer, GMB, 1989–91; *b* 9 Dec. 1925; *d* of late James Pithie Stephen, engine driver, Montrose and late Mary Hamilton Morton, South Queensferry. *Educ:* Wolseley Street and King's Park Elem. Schs, Glasgow; Queen's Park Sen. Secondary, Glasgow; Glasgow Univ. (extra-mural); LSE (TUC Schol.). McGill Univ. and Canada/US Travel, 1958–59. Law office junior, 1941; Clerk, Labour Exchange (Mem. MLSA), 1941–42; Post Office Telephonist, 1942–60; Officer, Union of Post Office Workers, Glasgow Br., 1942–60; Member: UPW Parly Panel, 1957; London and Home Counties Area Organiser, CAWU, 1960–65; Nat. Sec., CAWU, subseq. APEX, 1965–89. Editor, The Clerk, 1965–71; Union Educn Officer, 1965–72; Delegate: TUC; Labour Party Annual Confs; Member: EDC for Food and Drink Manufacturing, 1976–90; Food Standards Cttee, 1968–80; Mary Macarthur Educnl Trust, 1965–2010; Distributive Industry Trng Bd, 1968–73; Monopolies and Mergers Commn, 1973–83; British Wool Marketing Bd, 1973–88; Trustee: Duke of Edinburgh's Commonwealth Study Conferences, 1968–91; Mary Macarthur Holiday Trust, 1993– (Vice Chair, 2009–). Mem., TUC Women's Adv. Cttee, 1983; Chair, Nat. Jt Cttee of Working Women's Organisations, 1983–84. Mem., Adv. Council, Canadian Caribbean Emerging Leaders Conference, 2011. Life Mem., Work Foundn (formerly Industrial Soc.), 1992–. Member: Gen. Cttee, Greenwich and Woolwich Labour Party, 1995–; Exec. Cttee, Greenwich Link, 2008–. Mem., Court of Govs, LSE, 1976–2005 (Gov. Emeritus, 2005). *Publications:* (jtly) Training Shop Stewards, 1968; (with Roy Moore) Statistics for Negotiators, 1973; contrib. Clerk, Industrial Soc. Jl, Target, etc. *Recreations:* food, walking, conversation, travel, theatre, reading. *Address:* 3 Pond Road, SE3 9JL. *T:* and *Fax:* (020) 8852 7797. *E:* hstephen25@o2.co.uk.

STEPHEN, (John) David; Director, European Movement, 2004–06; *b* 3 April 1942; *s* of late John Stephen and Anne Eileen Stephen; *m* 1968, Susan Dorothy (*née* Harris); three *s* one *d.* *Educ:* Denbigh Road Primary Sch., Luton; Luton Grammar Sch.; King's Coll., Cambridge (BA Mod. Langs, 1964); Univ. of San Marcos, Lima, Peru; Univ. of Essex (MA Govt, 1968). Educn Officer, CRC, 1969–70; with Runnymede Trust, 1970–75 (Dir, 1973–75); Latin American Regional Rep., Internat. Univ. Exchange Fund, 1975–77; Special Adviser to Sec. of State for Foreign and Commonwealth Affairs, 1977–79; Editor, International Affairs, 1979–83; Dir, UK Immigrants Advisory Service, 1983–84; Commonwealth Development Corporation: Mem., Management Bd, 1984–92; Head of External Relations, 1985–89; Dir of Corporate Relns, 1989–92; Principal Officer, Exec. Office of Sec.-Gen., UN, 1992–96 and March–Sept. 1997; Dir, UN Verification Mission, Guatemala, June 1996–Feb. 1997; Rep. of UN Sec.-Gen., and Dir, UN Office for Somalia, 1997–2001; Rep. of UN Sec.-Gen., and Hd, UN Peace-building Support Office for Guinea-Bissau, 2002–04. Chm., Action for a Global Climate Community, 2009–13; Bd Mem., Internat. Action Network on Small Arms, 2009–13. EU Election Observer, Madagascar, 2013; Advr and Election Observer, All-Party Parly Gp on Guinea-Bissau, 2014. Trustee, Action Aid, 1981–92. Contested: (SDP-Liberal Alliance) N Luton, 1983, 1987; (Lib Dem) Norwich N, 2010. *Address:* Raggot Hill Cottage, North Tamerton, Cornwall EX22 6RJ. *Club:* Royal Automobile.

STEPHEN, Martin; *see* Stephen, George M.

STEPHEN, Mhairi Margaret, QC (Scot.) 2015; Sheriff Principal of Lothian and Borders, since 2011; *b* 22 Jan. 1954; *d* of William Strachan Stephen and Alexandrina Wood Stephen (*née* Grassam). *Educ:* George Watson's Ladies' Coll.; Univ. of Edinburgh (BA 1974; LLB 1976). With Allan McDougall & Co., SSC, Edinburgh, 1976–97, Partner, 1981–97; Sheriff of Lothian and Borders at Edinburgh, 1997–2011. Gov., Dean Orphanage and Cauvin's Trust, 2004–14. *Recreations:* curling, hill-walking, golf, music. *Address:* Sheriff Principal's Chambers, Edinburgh Sheriff Court, 27 Chambers Street, Edinburgh EH1 1LB. *T:* (0131) 225 2525. *Clubs:* New (Edinburgh); Murrayfield Golf, Murrayfield Curling.

STEPHEN, Michael; Group Deputy Chairman, Symphony Environmental Technologies plc, since 2007; *b* 25 Sept. 1942; *s* of late Harry Lace Stephen and Edna Florence Stephen; *m* 1989, Virginia Mary (*née* de Trensé). *Educ:* Stanford Univ. (LLM 1971); Harvard Univ. Admitted Solicitor, 1964 (DistCompany Law); called to the Bar, Inner Temple, 1966 (Hons); commissioned, The Life Guards, 1966–70; Harkness Fellowship in Internat. Law, 1970–72; Asst Legal Adviser, UK Delegn to UN, 1971; London Bar practice, 1972–87; Internat. Trade and Public Affairs Consultant, 1988–92. Chm., Severnside Internat. Airport Consortium, 2000–05. County Councillor, Essex, 1985–91; Mem., Nat. Exec., ACC, 1989–91; contested (C) Doncaster North, 1983. MP (C) Shoreham, 1992–97. Member: Select Cttee on the Environment, 1994–97; Trade and Industry Select Cttee, 1996–97; European Standing Cttee, 1994–97. Vice Chm., Cons. Parly Home Affairs and Legal Cttees, 1994–97. Chm., Planning Cttee, Chelsea Soc., 2015–. Author: S. 36 Criminal Justice Act, 1988; Bail (Amendment) Act, 1993. *Publications:* numerous political pamphlets. *Recreations:* tennis, sailing, history, theatre. *E:* kkrkyz@gmail.com.

STEPHEN, Rt Hon. Sir Ninian (Martin), KG 1994; AK 1982; GCMG 1982; GCVO 1982; KBE 1972; PC 1979; Governor-General of Australia, 1982–89; *b* 15 June 1923; *o s* of late Frederick Stephen and Barbara Stephen (*née* Cruickshank); *m* 1949, Valery Mary, *d* of late A. Q. Sinclair and of Mrs G. M. Sinclair; five *d.* *Educ:* George Watson's Sch., Edinburgh; Edinburgh Acad.; St Paul's Sch., London; Chillon Coll., Switzerland; Scotch Coll., Melbourne; Melbourne Univ. (LLB). Served War, HM Forces (Australian Army), 1941–46. Admitted as Barrister and Solicitor, in State of Victoria, 1949; signed Roll of Victorian Bar, 1951; QC 1966. Appointed Judge of Supreme Court of Victoria, 1970; Justice of High Court of Australia, 1972–82; Australian Ambassador for the Envmt, 1989–92; Chm., Anglo-Irish Talks (2nd strand), 1992; Judge, Internat. War Crimes Tribunal for Yugoslavia, 1993–97; Chm., UN Expert Gp on Cambodia, 1998–99. Mem., Ethics Commn, IOC, 2000–. Hon. Bencher, Gray's Inn, 1981. Chm., Nat. Liby of Aust., 1989–94. Hon. Liveryman, Clothworkers' Co., 1991. Hon. LLD: Sydney, 1984; Melbourne, 1985; Griffith, 1988; Hon. DLitt WA, 1993. KStJ 1982. Comdr, Legion of Honour (France), 1993. *Address:* Flat 13/1, 193 Domain Road, South Yarra, Vic 3141, Australia.

STEPHEN, Peter James; Lord Lieutenant and Lord Provost, City of Aberdeen, 2007–12; *b* 24 April 1937; *m* 1960, Sandra McDonald; one *s* one *d.* *Educ:* Robert Gordon's Coll., Aberdeen. Nat. Service, RAF, 1955–57. Union Bank of Scotland Ltd, subseq. Bank of Scotland: mgt apprentice, 1953; Accountant, 1969, Asst Manager, 1973, Stirling Br.; Manager, Strathaven, Lanarkshire, 1977; Senior Manager: Fraserburgh, 1982; Kirkcaldy, 1989–91; self-employed business consultant, 1992–96; Inland Revenue Tax Comr, 1999–2007. Mem. (Scottish Lib Dem), Aberdeen CC, 2002–12. Mem., Chartered Inst. of Banking in Scotland, 1961. Dhc Aberdeen, 2012. OStJ 2009. *Recreation:* outdoor mostly. *Clubs:* Rotary, Probus (Aberdeen).

STEPHEN, Rita; *see* Stephen, H. H.

STEPHENS, Anthony William, CB 1989; CMG 1976; Deputy Under Secretary of State, Northern Ireland Office, 1985–90; *b* 9 Jan. 1930; *s* of late Donald Martyn Stephens and Norah Stephens (*née* Smith-Cleburne); *m* 1954, Mytyl Joy, *d* of late William Gay Burdett; four *d.* *Educ:* Bradfield Coll.; Bristol Univ. (LLB); Corpus Christi Coll., Cambridge. RM (commnd), 1948–50. Colonial Administrative Service, 1953; District Officer, Kenya, 1954–63; Home Civil Service, 1964; Principal, MoD, 1964–70; Asst Private Sec. to successive Secretaries of State for Defence, 1970–71; Asst Sec., 1971; Chief Officer, Sovereign Base Areas, Cyprus, 1974–76; Under Sec., NI Office, 1976–79; Asst Under Sec. of State, General Staff, 1979–83, Ordnance, 1983–84, MoD. Trustee, Sherborne House Trust, 1995–2004. *Recreations:* travel and the outdoor life, music, theatre. *Address:* Virginia Cottage, Bradford Abbas, Sherborne, Dorset DT9 6SA. *Club:* Royal Over-Seas League.

STEPHENS, Barbara Marion, (Mrs T. J. Stephens), OBE 2002; Director, Student Casework, Open University, since 2014; *b* 25 Aug. 1951; *d* of late Sydney and of Edna Webb; *m* 1970, Trevor James Stephens. *Educ:* Mid-Essex Technical Coll. (HNC Engrg); NE London Poly. (DMS); City Univ. (MBA Engrg Mgt). IEng; MIET (MIProdE 1976); MIIE (MIET 1992). Mechanical technician apprentice, Marconi Co., 1969–73; various technical and managerial posts, Marconi Communication Systems Ltd, 1973–88; Industrial Advr, Electronic Applications, NEDO, 1988–92; Dir of Ops, then Chief Exec., W Cumbria Develt Agency,

1993–98; Chief Exec., Local Govt Commn for England, 1998–2002; Hd of Public Sector, subseq. Higher Educn, Practice, kmc internat., 2002–07; Principal, Carbon Leadership, 2007–09; Regl Dir, Open Univ. in London, 2009–11; Dir, Student Coursework and Special Projects, Open Univ., 2011–14. Co. Sec., Carbon-NfP Ltd, 2008–14. Member: Engineering Council, 1990–96; HEFCE, 1995–2002; Adv. Forum (formerly Council) for Develt of RN Personnel, 1995–2002 (Chm., 2001–02); a Dir, Assoc. of MBAs, 2001–06 (Chm., 2005–06). Chm., NHSU, 2003–05. Non-executive Director: Cumbria Ambulance Service NHS Trust, 1996–98; EBS Trust, 2001–08. Board Member: New Opportunities Fund, 2001–04; Univ. of Cumbria, 2007–12; Equality Challenge Unit, 2008–; London Higher, 2009–14. Lay Mem., Professional Conduct and Complaints Cttee, Gen. Council of Bar, 2000–09 (Lay Vice Chm., 2006–09). FCMI (FIMgt 1994; MBIM 1978); FRSA 1992. DUniv Bradford, 2005. *Address:* Edgefield, 120A Stainburn Road, Workington, Cumbria CA14 1ST. *T:* (01900) 871095.

STEPHENS, Sir Barrie; *see* Stephens, Sir E. B.

STEPHENS, Sir Benjamin; *see* Stephens, Sir W. B. S.

STEPHENS, Catherine Anne, (Mrs C. P. G. Qadir), OBE 1996; Acting Director, Education and Society, until 2011, and Member of Executive Board, 2007–11, British Council (Director, Innovation, 2007); *b* 24 Feb. 1951; *d* of Geoffrey Francis Stephens and Jeannine Christianne Langer Stephens; *m* 1998, Cecil Parvaiz Ghulam Qadir; one *d*, and one step *s*. *Educ:* Univ. of Hull (BA 1st Cl. American Studies 1978). Sec., George G. Harrap, 1970; Personal Asst, Penguin Books, 1970–71; Sec., UNESCO, Paris, 1972–73; Admin. Asst, US Peace Corps, Kabul, 1973–74; joined British Council, 1978: Asst, Educnl Contracts Dept, 1978–81; Zimbabwe, 1981–82; Asst Rep., Cameroon, 1982–85; Regl Officer, Central and E Africa S of Sahara Dept, 1985–88; First Sec., Develt, New Delhi, 1988–93; Deputy Director: Indonesia, 1993–96; India, 1996–2000; Regl Dir, W Africa, 2001–03; Dir, Africa and Asia, 2003–07. *Recreations:* travel, reading.

STEPHENS, Christopher; MP (SNP) Glasgow South West, since 2015; *b* Glasgow, 20 March 1973; *m*. *Educ:* Trinity High Sch., Renfrew. With Glasgow CC. Lead negotiator, UNISON, Glasgow. Mem., Nat. Exec. Cttee, SNP. Contested (SNP) Glasgow Pollock, Scottish Parlt, 2007, 2011. *Address:* House of Commons, SW1A 0AA.

STEPHENS, Christopher Berkeley; Chairman, Judicial Appointments Commission, since 2011; *b* London, 28 April 1948; *s* of Sir David Stephens, KCB, CVO and (Mary) Clemency Stephens (*née* Gore Browne); *m* 1976, Anne Justine Margaret Lloyd Morgan; two *s* one *d*. *Educ:* Christ Church, Oxford (MA PPE 1970); St John's Coll., Nottingham (BA Theol. 1973). Prodn Trainee, United Biscuits, 1973–75; Human Resources Manager: Unilever plc, 1975–76; Nestlé SA, 1976–84; Unisys, 1984–88; Human Resources Director: Bet plc (Rentokil), 1988–93; Gen. Utilities (Vivendi), 1994–96; Gp HR Dir, Exel plc (DHL), 1996–2004. Member: CS Commn, 2005–09; Sen. Salaries Rev. Bd, 2009–11. Sen. Ind. Dir, WSP plc, 2003–12; Chm., Traidcraft plc, 2006–11; non-exec. Dir, Holidaybreak plc, 2008–11. Gov., Gordonstoun Sch., 2012–. *Recreations:* allotment gardening, walking. *Address:* Judicial Appointments Commission, 1st Floor, 102 Petty France, SW1H 9AJ. *E:* christopher.stephens@jac.gsi.gov.uk.

STEPHENS, Prof. Christopher David, OBE 1999; FDSRCS, FDSRCSE; Professor of Child Dental Health, University of Bristol, 1984–2002, now Emeritus; *b* 29 May 1942; *s* of late Wilfred Ernest Donnington Stephens, OBE, PhD, and of Phyllis Margaret Stephens (*née* Lecroissette); *m* 1966, Marion Kay Prest; two *s*. *Educ:* Dulwich Coll.; Guy's Hosp. Dental Sch. (BDS); MDS Bristol. DOrthRCS 1968, MOrthRCS 1988; FDSRCSE 1970; FDSRCS 1986. Hse Surgeon, 1965, Registrar in Children's Dentistry, 1966–69, Guy's Hosp. Dental Sch.; Registrar in Orthodontics, Royal Dental Hosp., 1969–71; Lectr in Orthodontics, 1971–76, Consultant Sen. Lectr in Orthodontics, 1976–84, Univ. of Bristol. Civil Consultant in Orthodontics to RAF, 1988–2005. Mem., Standing Dental Adv. Cttee, 1992–98. Pres., British Orthodontic Soc., 2001–02. Hon. Life Mem., European Orthodontic Soc., 2003. Fellow, BDA, 2004. Ballard Medal, Consultant Orthodontists Gp, 2003. *Publications:* (jtly) Functional Orthodontic Appliances, 1990; (with K. G. Isaacson) Practical Orthodontic Assessment, 1990; (jtly) A Textbook of Orthodontics, 2nd edn 1992; A History of the University of Bristol Dental School, 2012; The Rev. Dr Thomas Sedgwick Whalley and the Queen of Bath, 2014; contrib. numerous papers to refereed jls. *Recreations:* amateur radio, dry stone-walling, woodland management, walking. *Address:* 12 Berkshire Road, Bristol BS7 8EX. *T:* (0117) 942 9944.

STEPHENS, Sir (Edwin) Barrie, Kt 1998; CEng; Chairman, 1990–98, Hon. President, since 1998, Siebe plc. *Educ:* Christ Coll., Brecon; Manchester Univ. CEng 1962. Industrial Engr, General Dynamics, USA, 1954; Production Manager, Barden Corp., Conn, USA, 1962; Dir of Manufg, Barden Corp. Ltd, UK, 1962–63; Man. Dir, Siebe Gorman and Co. Ltd, 1963–75; Gp Man. Dir and CEO, Siebe Gorman Hldgs Ltd, 1975–86; Vice-Chm., 1987–90, CEO, 1987–93, Siebe plc. Hon. DSc Plymouth, 1993. *Club:* Carlton.

STEPHENS, Prof. Elan Closs, CBE 2001; Professor of Communications and Creative Industries, Aberystwyth University (formerly University of Wales, Aberystwyth), 2001–11, now Emeritus; Trustee (for Wales), BBC Trust, since 2010; *b* 16 June 1948; *d* of William Jones and Mair Closs Roberts (*née* Williams); *m* 1972, Roy Stephens (*d* 1989); one *s* one *d*. *Educ:* Ysgol Dyffryn Nantlle, Penygroes; Somerville Coll., Oxford (Open Schol.; BA 1969). University of Wales, Aberystwyth: Lectr, 1976–84; Hd of Dept, 1984–91; Sen. Lectr, 1994–2001. Member: Broadcasting Council for Wales, 1984–89; S4C Authy, 1990–95; Council, Nat. Liby of Wales, 1995–2005; Wales Adv. Cttee, CRE, 2003–; Vice-Chm., Welsh Language Bd, 1994–99; Chairman: Welsh Fourth Channel Authy, 1998–2006; Chwarae Teg, 2002–04; Wales Adv. Cttee, British Council, 2005–. Governor: BFI, 2001–07; Univ. of Glamorgan, 2002. FRSA 2002. Hon. Fellow, Trinity Coll., Carmarthen, 2004. High Sheriff, Dyfed, 2012–13. *Publications:* chapters and articles on Welsh theatre and media policy. *Recreations:* reading, theatre, television, film, cookery and eating out with friends. *Address:* Fronhyfryd, Ffordd Llanbadarn, Aberystwyth SY23 1EY. *T:* (01970) 625653.

STEPHENS, Eldridge, OBE 2009; High Commissioner for St Lucia in the United Kingdom, 2008–12; *b* St Lucia, 19 Oct. 1946; *s* of Emmanuel Octave and Mary Anna Stephens; *m* 1972, Peternise Peter; one *s*. *Educ:* Vieux Fort Boys Primary Sch.; St Mary's Coll.; Sir Arthur Lewis Community Coll. Primary sch. teacher, 1962–71; St Lucia Civil Service, 1971; Traffic Superintendent, LIAT (1974) Ltd, 1971–94; Man. Dir, Phoenix Services Ltd and Hewanorra Air Cargo Services, 1994–2008. Mem., Vieux Fort Town Council, 1974–79 (Chm., 1989–91). MP and Dep. Speaker, House of Assembly, 1982–87. Dep. Chm., Nat. Develt Corp., 1987–95; Dir, Windward & Leeward Brewery, 1987–95; Dir, Housing and Urban Develt Corp., 1996–97; Dep. Chm., Develt Control Authy, 2007–08; Dir, St Lucia Bureau of Standards, 2007–08. Founder and Pres., Sports and Cultural Orgn, 1969; Manager/Sec., Goodwill Fishermen Co-op., 1972–74; Chm., Develt Cttee, Southern Carnival, 1980–81; Pres., Parents and Teachers Assoc. Vieux Fort Comp. Sec. Sch., 1989–91; Dist Gov. and Chm. Council of Govs, Lions Club Internat., 1999–2001; Chm. Council, St John's, St Lucia, 2002–08. JP 1987. OStJ 2004. *Recreations:* sports (football, cricket and athletics), travelling, volunteering. *Address:* Moule a Chique, Vieux Fort, St Lucia. *T:* 4546268. *E:* eldridges@candw.lc. *Club:* Lions Club International (Vieux Fort).

STEPHENS, Jean Marie; Chief Executive Officer, RSM International Ltd, since 2006; *b* Calif, USA, 1959. *Educ:* Univ. of Redlands, Calif (BSc Accounting 1981); California State Univ., San Bernardino (MS Finance 1990). Partner and Hd, Audit Practice, Fleming Reiss & Co., 1990–94; Sen. Manager, 1994–2001, Partner, 2001–11, RSM McGladrey; Chief Operating Officer, RSM Internat. Ltd, 2003–06. Pres., Inland Empire Chapter, YWCA, 1992–96; Vice Pres., Finance, Inland Empire Symphony, 1995; Treas., United Way, 1995. MInstD. Hon. Dr Humane Letters Redlands, 2009. Athena Award for Outstanding Business Woman of the Year, San Bernardino Chamber of Commerce, 1993. *Address:* RSM International Ltd, 11 Old Jewry, 2nd Floor, EC2R 8DU. *T:* (020) 7601 1080, *Fax:* (020) 7601 1090. *E:* jean.stephens@rsmi.com.

STEPHENS, Sir Jonathan (Andrew de Sievrac), KCB 2013; Permanent Under-Secretary, Northern Ireland Office, since 2014; *b* 8 Feb. 1960; *s* of Prescot and Peggy Stephens; *m* 1983, Rev. Penny; one *s* one *d*. *Educ:* Sevenoaks Sch.; Christ Church, Oxford (MA). NI Office, 1983–89; HM Treasury, 1989–92; Northern Ireland Office, 1992–2000: Principal Private Sec., 1993–94; Associate Pol Dir, 1996–2000; Dir, Modernising Public Services, Cabinet Office, 2000–01; Dir, Public Services, 2001–03, Public Spending, 2003–04, Man. Dir, Public Services, 2004–06, HM Treasury; Permanent Secretary: DCMS, 2006–13; HM Treasury, 2013–14. *Address:* Northern Ireland Office, 1 Horseguards Road, SW1A 2HQ.

STEPHENS, Malcolm George, CB 1991; Group Chairman, International Financial Consulting, since 1998; Chairman, IFC Training, 2001–11; *b* 14 July 1937; *s* of Frank Ernest Stephens and Janet (*née* McQueen); *m* 1975, Lynette Marie Caffery, Brisbane, Australia. *Educ:* St Michael's and All Angels; Shooters Hill Grammar Sch.; St John's Coll., Oxford (Casberd Scholar; BA 1st Cl. Hons PPE; MA 1995). National Service, RAOC, 1956–58. CRO, 1953; British High Commission: Ghana, 1959–62; Kenya, 1963–65; Export Credits Guarantee Dept, 1965–82: Principal, 1970; seconded to Civil Service Coll., 1971–72; Asst Sec., 1974; Estab. Officer, 1977; Under Sec., 1978; Head of Proj. Gp B, 1978–79; Principal Finance Officer, 1979–82; Internat. Finance Dir, Barclays Bank Internat. Ltd, 1982–84; Dir, Barclays Export Services, 1984–87; Export Finance Dir, Barclays Bank PLC, 1985–87; Chief Executive: ECGD, 1987–91; London Chamber of Commerce and Industry, 1991–92; Pres., 1989–91, Sec.-Gen., 1992–98, Internat. Union of Credit and Investment Insurers (Berne Union); Man. Dir and Dep. Chm., Commonwealth Investment Guarantee Agency, 1998–99; Exec. Dir, IPCIS, 1999–2001. Chm., Del Credere Insurance Services Ltd, 1999–2001; Director: European Capital, 1992–2000; Arab-British Chamber of Commerce, 1992–95; Major Projects Assoc., 1995–99; Berry, Palmer & Lyle, 1997–2001; EULER Internat., 1998–2000. Mem. Adv. Council, Zurich Emerging Markets, 2001–14; Advr to Sinosure, China, 2000–; Consultant: to EU PHARE Prog., 1997–99; to World Bank, 1997–2001; Eur. Commn, 1999–2000, 2011; OECD (Russia), 2001; APEC, 2002, 2003; Asian Develt Bank, 2005; Govt of Chile, 1999, of Bangladesh, 1999, of Iran, 2000, of Sri Lanka, 2000, of S Africa, 2000, 2002, of Australia, 2000, 2001, 2002, 2003, of NZ, 2001, of Turkey, 2001, of Canada, 2001, 2003, 2007, 2008, 2009, of Fiji, 2003, of Romania, 2007, of Singapore, 2011–12. Advr, CDR Internat., 1998–2000; Exec. Vice-Pres., SGA Internat., Florida, 1998–2000. Member: Overseas Projects Bd, 1985–87; BOTB, 1987–91. Vis. Schol., IMF, 1998–99. Member: Cook Soc., 2002–; Australia Britain Soc., 2002–; Order of Australia Assoc., 2004– (Treas., Southern Highlands Gp, 2005–). Nat. Hon. Sec., Assoc. of Australian Decorative and Fine Arts Socs, 2012–14 (Nat. Vice Chm., 2010–11); Chm., Southern Highlands Australia Britain Soc., 2012– (Treas., 2006–12); Pres., Southern Highlands Opera Appreciation Gp, 2013 (Dep. Pres., 2012). FCIB (FIB 1984); FIEx 1987; MICM 1990. *Publications:* The Changing Role of Export Credit Agencies, 1999. *Recreations:* gardening, reading, tapestry, watching cricket and football (Charlton Athletic). *Address:* 38 Argyle Street, Bong Bong Hill, Moss Vale, NSW 2577, Australia. *Clubs:* Union, University and Schools (Sydney).

STEPHENS, Mark Howard, CBE 2011; lawyer; broadcaster; writer; lecturer; Senior Member, Howard Kennedy (formerly Finers Stephens Innocent, later HowardKennedyFSI) LLP, since 1999; Mediator, since 2007; *b* Old Windsor, Berks, 7 April 1957; *s* of Howard Stephens and Evelyn Phyllis Stephens (*née* Banks); *m* 1982, Donna Michelle Coote; three *d*. *Educ:* St Paul's Secondary Modern Sch.; Cambridge Manor Acad. for Dramatic Arts; Strode's Grammar Sch.; North East London Poly. (BA Hons Law); Coll. of Law. Legal Dir, Art Law, 1982–84; Founder and Sen. Partner, Stephens Innocent, solicitors, 1983–99. Member: British Copyright Council, 1986–98; Bd, ICSTIS, 1990–96; Founder Chm., Policy Bd, 1996–99, Vice Chm., 1999–2003, Internet Watch Foundn. Chm., Mgt Cttee, Prog. in Comparative Media Law and Policy, Wolfson Coll., Centre for Socio-Legal Studies, Univ. of Oxford, 1997–. Trustee: Index on Censorship, 2002–12 (Hon. Solicitor, 2012–); Bianca Jagger Human Rights Foundn, 2007–; Bd, Internat. Law Book Trust; Founding Trustee, Solicitors' Pro Bono Gp, 1997–2004; Chairman: Solicitors' Law Fest., 1998–2001; Greenwich and Docklands Internat. Fests, 1999–2004; Contemp. Art Soc., 2010–14 (Trustee, 1987–2009; Hon. Solicitor, 2002–09); Design Artists Copyright Soc., 2011–; Media Law Defence Initiative, 2011–; Global Network Initiative, 2014–. Mem., FCO Free Expression Adv. Bd, 2002–. Mem. Exec. Cttee and Dir, Commonwealth Lawyers Assoc., 2007– (Vice Pres., 2011–13; Pres., 2013–); Mem. Human Rights Council, IBA, 2009– (Trial Observer, 2005). Patron, Internat. Alert, 2011–. Ind. Dir, ISI, 2011–. Chm. Govs, Univ. of E London, 2009–; Gov., Rose Bruford Coll. of Theatre and Performance, 2003–07. Gov., Wanstead C of E Primary Sch., 1996–2002. Freeman, City of London, 1989; Liveryman, Stationers' Co., 2004; Freeman, Solicitors' Co., 2005. Hon. DLaws East London, 2001. *Publications:* (contrib.) Miscarriages of Justice: a review of justice in error, 1999; (contrib.) International Libel and Privacy Handbook, 2005; (contrib.) This is Not a Book about Gavin Turk, 2012; (contrib) La Presunción de Inocencia Y Los Juicios Paralelos, 2013; (contrib.) Media Law and Ethics in the 21st Century, 2014. *Recreations:* bees, badinage and dandyism. *Address:* Howard Kennedy LLP, No 1, London Bridge, SE1 9BG. *T:* (020) 3755 5725, *Fax:* (020) 3650 7075. *E:* mark.stephens@howardkennedy.com. *Clubs:* Chelsea Football; Aston Martin Owners.

STEPHENS, His Honour Martin; *see* Stephens, His Honour S. M.

STEPHENS, Rt Rev. Peter; *see* Stephens, Rt Rev. W. P.

STEPHENS, Peter Norman Stuart; Director, News Group Newspapers, 1978–87, Editorial Director, 1981–87; *b* 19 Dec. 1927; *s* of J. G. Stephens; *m* 1950, Constance Mary Ratheram; two *s* one *d*. *Educ:* Mundella Grammar Sch., Nottingham. Newark Advertiser, 1945–48; Northern Echo, 1948–50; Daily Dispatch, 1950–55; Daily Mirror, Manchester, 1955–57; Asst Editor, Newcastle Journal, 1957–60; Asst Editor, Evening Chronicle, Newcastle, 1960–62, Editor 1962–66; Editor, Newcastle Journal, 1966–70; Asst Editor, The Sun, 1970–72, Dep. Editor 1972; Associate Editor, News of the World, 1973, Editor, 1974–75; Associate Editor, The Sun, 1975–81. *Publications:* (ed) Newark: the magic of malt, 1993; Grey Sanctuary: the story of the Newark Friary, 1996; P. S. on a life in newspapers, 2003. *Recreations:* the printed word, Derby County FC. *Address:* 6 Homefield Road, Sevenoaks, Kent TN13 2DU.

STEPHENS, Philip Francis Christopher; Associate Editor and Columnist, Financial Times, since 2003; *b* 2 June 1953; *s* of Haydn Stephens and Theresa (*née* Martin); partner, Patty Hemingway; one *s* one *d*. *Educ:* Wimbledon Coll.; Worcester Coll., Oxford (BA Hons Mod. Hist.). Correspondent London and Brussels, Reuters, 1979–83; Financial Times: Econs Correspondent, 1983–88; Political Ed., 1988–94; Political Commentator, 1994–99; Ed., UK Edn, 1999–2003. Fulbright Fellow, LA Times, 1988. Gov., 2006–, Mem. Council, 2008–, Vice-Chm., 2013–, The Ditchley Foundn; Member: Adv. Council, IPPR, 2010–; Steering Gp, Anglo-French Colloque. David Wait Meml Prize for Outstanding Political Journalism, RTZ, 2002; Political Journalist of the Year, Political Studies Assoc., 2004; Political Journalist of the Year, British Press Awards, 2008. *Publications:* Politics and the Pound, 1996; Tony Blair:

the price of leadership, 2004. *Recreations:* trying to understand history, chauffeuring Jess and Ben. *Address:* c/o Financial Times, 1 Southwark Bridge, SE1 9HL. *E:* stephenspfc@hotmail.com. *Club:* Chelsea Football.

STEPHENS, Simon William; playwright; Artistic Associate, Lyric Theatre, Hammersmith, since 2009; *b* Manchester, 6 Feb. 1971; *s* of Graham Stephens and Carole Stephens; *m* 2005, Polly Heath; two *s* one *d*. *Educ:* Stockport Sch.; Univ. of York (BA Hons Hist. 1992); London Inst. of Educn (PGCE 1998). Resident Dramatist: Royal Court Th., 2000; Royal Exchange, 2000; NT, 2007. *Plays include:* Bluebird, 1998; Herons, 2001; Port, 2002; Christmas, 2003; One Minute, 2003; Country Music, 2004; On the Shore of the Wide World, 2005; Motortown, 2006; Pornography, 2007; Harper Regan, 2008; Punk Rock, 2009; Sea Wall, 2009; Marine Parade, 2010; The Trial of Ubu, 2010; (jtly) A Thousand Stars Explode in the Sky, 2010; T5, 2010; Wastwater, 2011; Three Kingdoms, 2011–12; (adaptation) The Curious Incident of the Dog in the Night-Time, 2012; (adaptation) A Doll's House, 2012; Morning, 2012; Blindsided, 2014; Birdland, 2014; (trans.) The Cherry Orchard, 2014; Carmen Disruption, 2015; The Funfair, 2015; Song from Far Away, 2015. *Publications: plays:* Bluebird, 1998; Herons, 2001; Port, 2002; Christmas, 2003; One Minute, 2003; Country Music, 2004; On the Shore of the Wide World, 2005; Motortown, 2006; Pornography, 2007; Harper Regan, 2008; Punk Rock, 2009; (jtly) Marine Parade, 2010; The Trial of Ubu, 2010; (jtly) A Thousand Stars Explode in the Sky, 2010; Wastwater and T5, 2011; Three Kingdoms, 2012. *Recreations:* drinking wine, listening to dissonant music, playing with my children, irresponsible evils of Tweeting. *Address:* Lyric Theatre, Lyric Square, Hammersmith, W6 0QL. *E:* s_stephensuk@yahoo.co.uk. *W:* www.twitter.com/StephensSimon.

STEPHENS, His Honour (Stephen) Martin; QC 1982; a Circuit Judge 1986–2012; a Judge of the Central Criminal Court, 1999–2012; *b* 26 June 1939; *s* of late Abraham Stephens and Freda Stephens, Swansea; *m* 1965, Patricia Alison, *d* of late Joseph and Anne Morris, Mapperley, Nottingham; one *s* one *d* (and one *s* decd). *Educ:* Swansea Grammar Sch.; Wadham Coll., Oxford (MA). Called to the Bar, Middle Temple, 1963, Bencher, 2004; Wales and Chester Circuit; a Recorder, 1979–86. Mem., Parole Bd, 1995–2001, 2010–. Mem., Criminal Cttee, 1995–2000, Main Bd, 1997–2000, Judicial Studies Bd. *Recreations:* cricket, theatre.

STEPHENS, Toby; actor; *b* 21 April 1969; *s* of Sir Robert Graham Stephens and of Dame Maggie Smith, *qv*; *m* 2001, Anna-Louise Plowman; one *s* one *d*. *Educ:* Aldro Sch.; Seaford Coll.; LAMDA. Crewed, Chichester Festival Th., 1986 and 1987; *theatre* includes: Tartuffe, Playhouse, 1991; Royal Shakespeare Company: All's Well That Ends Well, Antony and Cleopatra, Tamburlaine, Unfinished Business, Wallenstein, 1992; Coriolanus, A Midsummer Night's Dream, Measure for Measure, 1994; Hamlet, The Pilate Workshop, 2004; A Streetcar Named Desire, Haymarket, 1996; Phèdre, Britannicus, Almeida, 1998, transf. NY, 1999; Ring Round the Moon, NY, 1999; Japes, The Royal Family, Haymarket, 2001; Betrayal, Donmar Warehouse, The Country Wife, Haymarket, 2007; A Doll's House, Donmar Warehouse, 2009; The Real Thing, Old Vic, 2010; Danton's Death, NT, 2010; Private Lives, Chichester Festival Th., 2012, Gielgud, 2013; *films* include: Photographing Fairies, 1997; Cousin Bette, 1998; Onegin, 1999; Space Cowboys, 2000; Possession, Die Another Day, 2002; Severance, 2006; All Things to All Men, 2013; *television* includes: The Camomile Lawn, 1992; The Tenant of Wildfell Hall, 1996; The Great Gatsby, 2000; Perfect Strangers, 2001; Cambridge Spies, Poirot - Five Little Pigs, 2003; The Queen's Sister, 2005; The Best Man, Sharpe's Challenge, Jane Eyre, 2006; Wired, 2008; Vexed, 2010, 2012; Black Sails, 2015. *Address:* c/o United Agents, 12–26 Lexington Street, W1F 0LE.

STEPHENS, Sir (William) Ben(jamin Synge), Kt 2007; **Hon. Mr Justice Stephens;** a Judge of the High Court of Justice, Northern Ireland, since 2007; *b* 28 Dec. 1954; *s* of Denis Synge Stephens and Gladys Joyce Stephens (*née* Clarke); *m* 1982, Nicola Gladys Skrine; one *s* one *d*. *Educ:* Swanbourne House Sch., Swanbourne, Bucks; Campbell Coll., Belfast; Manchester Univ. (LLB 1st cl. Hons). Called to the Bar: NI, 1977; Lincoln's Inn, 1978; Ireland, 1996; QC (NI) 1996. Vice-Chm., Gen. Council of the Bar of NI, 2006–07. *Address:* Royal Courts of Justice, Belfast BT1 3JF.

STEPHENS, Rt Rev. Prof. (William) Peter; Bishop of The Gambia and Presiding Bishop of Methodist Church in The Gambia, 2010–12, now Presiding Bishop Emeritus; Minister, West Penwith Circuit, since 2014; *b* 16 May 1934; *s* of Alfred Cyril William Joseph Stephens and Jennie Eudora Stephens (*née* Trewavas). *Educ:* Lescudjack Sch., Penzance; Truro Sch.; Clare Coll., Cambridge (MA, BD); Wesley House, Cambridge; Univs of Lund, Strasbourg (Docteur ès Sciences Religieuses) and Münster. Asst Tutor, Hartley Victoria Coll., Manchester, 1958–61; ordained, Methodist Ministry, 1960; Minister in Nottingham and Methodist Chaplain to Univ. of Nottingham, 1961–65; Minister, Shirley, Croydon, 1967–71; Ranmoor Prof. of Church History, Hartley Victoria Coll., Manchester, 1971–73; Randles Prof. of Historical and Systematic Theology, Wesley Coll., Bristol, 1973–80; Res. Fellow, 1980–81, Lectr in Church History, 1981–86, Queen's Coll., Birmingham; University of Aberdeen: Prof. of Church History, 1986–99; Dean, 1987–89, Provost 1989–90, Faculty of Divinity. Vis. Prof., 2001–04, Hon. Univ. Fellow, 2004–07, Exeter Univ. Pres., Methodist Conf., 1998–99; Superintendent Minister, Plymouth Methodist Mission, 1999–2000; Minister, Mint Church, Exeter, and Methodist Chaplain, Exeter Univ., 2000–02; Superintendent Minister, Liskeard and Looe Circuit, 2002–03; Chm. and Gen. Superintendent, Methodist Church in The Gambia, 2003–04; Minister, Uckfield and Lewes, 2004–06; Minister, Camborne Circuit, 2006–09 (Superintendent Minister, 2007–08); Dep. Superintendent, Redruth Circuit, 2008–09; Minister, Camborne-Redruth Circuit, 2009–10; Superintendent Minister, Saltash Circuit, 2012–14. Mem., Bristol City Council, 1976–83. Member: Central Cttee, Conf. of European Churches, 1974–92; Conservative and Churches Standing Cttee, 1998–2006. Sec., Soc. for the Study of Theology, 1963–77; Pres., Soc. for Reformation Studies, 1995–98. Max Geilinger Prize, Switzerland, 1997. *Publications:* (trans. jtly) Luther's Works, Vol. 41, 1966; The Holy Spirit in the Theology of Martin Bucer, 1970; Faith and Love, 1971; The Theology of Huldrych Zwingli, 1986 (French edn 1999); Zwingli: An Introduction to His Thought, 1992 (German edn 1997; Korean edn 2007); Methodism in Europe, 1993; (ed) The Bible, the Reformation and the Church, 1995; contributions to religious works; articles and reviews in learned jls and other pubns. *Recreations:* squash, swimming, gardening, cliff-walking, theatre, opera. *Address:* Trewavas House, 8 Polwithen Road, Penzance, Cornwall TR18 4JS. *E:* williampeter.stephens@yahoo.com.

STEPHENSON, Andrew; MP (C) Pendle, since 2010; *b* 17 Feb. 1981; *s* of Malcolm and Ann Stephenson. *Educ:* Poynton Co. High Sch.; Royal Holloway, Univ. of London (BSc Business Mgt 2002). Partner, Stephenson and Threader, 2002–10. Mem. (C), Macclesfield BC, 2003–07. Vice Chm., (Youth) Conservative Party, 2010–13. *Address:* House of Commons, SW1A 0AA.

STEPHENSON, Ashley; *see* Stephenson, R. A. S.

STEPHENSON, Charles Lyon, TD 1972; Vice Lord-Lieutenant of Derbyshire, 2004–10; *b* 15 Aug. 1935; *s* of Col C. E. K. Stephenson and Nancy Stephenson; *m* 1st, 1960, Jane Tinker (marr. diss. 1972); two *s* one *d*; 2nd, 1974, Hon. Sarah Norrie. *Educ:* Eton Coll. Employed in family engrg business Stephenson Blake (Holdings) Ltd, 1956–2000, Gp Man. Dir, 1985–2000. Non-executive Director: Bramber Engrg Co. Ltd, 1980–87; Lyon and Lyon plc, 1982–90; Director: Carlton Main Brickworks Ltd, 1977–; Kestrel Travel Consultancy Ltd, 1998–; Hotel and Catering Staff Supplies Ltd, 1998–. Chairman: Derbys Br., Rural Develt Commn, 1987–93; Wynkin de Worde Soc., 1990; Derbys Br., SSAFA Forces Help, 2001–13. High Sheriff, 1984–85, DL, 2004, Derbys. *Recreations:* gardening, shooting, fishing, theatre, travel. *Address:* The Cottage, Great Longstone, Bakewell, Derbyshire DE45 1UA. *T:* (01629) 640213, *Fax:* (01629) 640135. *E:* Charles@kestreltravel.com. *Club:* Cavalry and Guards.

STEPHENSON, Darryl Leslie; DL; Managing Director, Hardmoor Associates Ltd, since 2005; Chief Executive, Hull City Council, since 2012; *b* 4 Sept. 1950; *s* of late Lawrence Stephenson and of Olga Mary Stephenson; *m* 1984, Susan Marialuisa Lockwood; one *s* one *d*. *Educ:* Warwick Sch.; Trent Poly. (BA Hons); Coll. of Law, Chester; Univ. of Birmingham (Advanced Mgt Develt Prog., 1986). Admitted Solicitor, 1980. Articled Clerk, W Bromwich CBC, 1972–74; Solicitor, Warwick DC, 1974–80; Principal Asst Chief Exec., Leicester CC, 1980–89; Dep. Town Clerk, subseq. Town Clerk and Chief Exec., Hull CC, 1989–95; Chief Exec., ER of Yorks Unitary Council, 1995–2005; Interim Chief Exec., NE Lincs Council, March–Nov. 2004; Strategic Advr, Deloitte, 2005–12. Vis. Prof., Univ. of Hull, 2005–. Co. Sec., Humber Forum Ltd, 1992–2005. Clerk to: Humber Bridge Bd, 1993–96, 2010–; Humberside Police Authy, 1996–97; Lord Lieut, E Riding of Yorks, 1996–2005; Sec., N Eastern Sea Fisheries Cttee, 1996–2005; Humberside Police Appts Cttee, 2004–. Chm., E Riding Drug Action Team, 1995–2002; Mem. Council, Hull and E Riding Chamber of Commerce, Industry and Shipping, 1995–. Member: Adjudication Panel for England, 2002–; Bd, Hull Pathfinders, 2004–; First-tier Tribunal (Local Govt Standards), 2010–. Mem. of Court, Univ. of Hull, 1993–; Gov., Beverley Coll., 1998–. Chm., AgeUK E Riding, 2007–; Trustee: Age Concern E Yorks, 2005–; Beverley Meml Hall, 2006–. DL ER of Yorks, 2005. Hon. LLD Hull, 2006. *Recreations:* motor boating, music, painting, food and wine. *Address:* Hardmoor Grange, Hardmoor Lane, Hotham, ER Yorks YO43 4UJ. *Club:* Portcullis (Warwick).

STEPHENSON, David Arnold; QC (Scot.) 2009; *b* Dumfries, 6 June 1959; *s* of Arnold Stephenson and Sylvia Walker Stephenson; *m* Catherine Johan Paterson; three *d*. *Educ:* Royal High Sch. of Edinburgh; Univ. of Aberdeen (LLB Hons, DipLP). Admitted as solicitor, 1983; solicitor in private practice, 1982–90; Advocate at Scottish Bar, specialising in professional negligence, personal injury, insce and medical law, 1991–; Westwater Advocates, 1991–2013; Ampersand Advocates, 2013–. Mem., Mason Inst. for Medicine, Life Scis and the Law, Univ. of Edinburgh, 2013–. Chm., Scottish Govt panel to consider and determine disputes regarding General Medical Services contracts, 2014–. *Recreations:* cycling, walking, arts, music and literature, travel, family. *Address:* Advocates' Library, Parliament House, Edinburgh EH1 1RF.

STEPHENSON, Rev. Canon Eric George; Vicar, St George's Church, East Boldon, 1985–2008; Chaplain to the Queen, 2002–11; *b* 26 April 1941; *s* of Albert and Nora Stephenson. *Educ:* Bede Coll., Durham (Teaching Cert., 1963); Birmingham Univ. (DipTh 1965; Dip. Liturgy and Architecture 1966). Ordained deacon, 1966, priest, 1967; Curate: St John the Baptist, Wakefield, 1966–69; Seaham with Seaham Harbour, Durham, 1969–73; Cockerton, Darlington, 1973–75; Licence to officiate, 1975–85; Teacher, Haughton Comp. Sch., Darlington, 1975–85. Area Dean of Jarrow, 1992–2001; Non-residentiary Canon, 1993–2008, Canon Emeritus, 2008, Durham Cathedral. *Recreations:* current affairs, history, archaeology, music appreciation.

STEPHENSON, George Anthony C.; *see* Carter-Stephenson.

STEPHENSON, Sir Henry Upton, 3rd Bt *cr* 1936; TD; Director: Stephenson Blake & Co. Ltd, 1952–75; Stephenson, Blake (Holdings) Ltd, 1972–99; *b* 26 Nov. 1926; *s* of Lt-Col Sir Henry Francis Blake Stephenson, 2nd Bt, OBE, TD, and Joan, *d* of Major John Herbert Upton (formerly Upton Cottrell-Dormer); *S* father, 1982, but his name does not appear on the Official Roll of the Baronetage; *m* 1962, Susan, *o d* of Major J. E. Clowes, Ashbourne, Derbyshire; four *d*. *Educ:* Eton. Formerly Major, QO Yorkshire Dragoons. High Sheriff of Derbyshire, 1975. *Heir: cousin* Matthew Francis Timothy Stephenson [*b* 24 Aug. 1960; *m* 1984, Philippa Delphine Lincoln; one *s* two *d*]. *Address:* Tissington Cottage, Rowland, Bakewell, Derbyshire DE45 1NR.

STEPHENSON, Prof. Hugh; writer and journalist; Professor of Journalism, City University, 1986–2003, now Emeritus; *b* 18 July 1938; *s* of late Sir Hugh Stephenson; *m* 1st, 1962, Auriol Stevens, *qv* (marr. diss. 1987); two *s* one *d*; 2nd, 1990, Diana Eden. *Educ:* Winchester Coll.; New Coll., Oxford (BA); Univ. of Calif, Berkeley. Pres., Oxford Union, 1962. HM Diplomatic Service, 1964–68; joined The Times, 1968; Editor, The Times Business News, 1972–81; Editor, The New Statesman, 1982–86. Dir, Eur. Journalism Centre, Maastricht, 1993–2008 (Chm., 1995–2002). Mem., Cttee to Review Functioning of Financial Instns, 1977–80. Councillor, London Bor. of Wandsworth, 1971–78. Dir, History Today Ltd, 1981–2014 (Chm., 2011–14). FRSA 1987. *Publications:* The Coming Clash, 1972; Mrs Thatcher's First Year, 1980; Claret and Chips, 1982; (jtly) Libel and the Media, 1997; Secrets of the Setters, 2005. *Address:* 7 Clifton Terrace, Brighton, E Sussex BN1 3HA.

STEPHENSON, Lynne, (Mrs Chaim Stephenson); *see* Banks, L. R.

STEPHENSON, Paul, OBE 2009; Regional Director, Wales and the West, Focus Consultancy Ltd, 1992–2000; *b* 6 May 1937; *s* of Olive Stephenson; *m* 1965, Joyce Annikie; one *s* one *d*. *Educ:* Westhill Coll. of Educn, Selly Oak, Birmingham. MCIPR (MIPR 1978). Youth Tutor, St Paul's, Bristol, 1962–68; Sen. Community Relations Officer, Coventry, 1968–72; National Youth Trng Officer, Community Relations Commn, 1972–77; Sen. Liaison Officer, CRE, 1980–92. Chm., Muhammad Ali Sports Develt Assoc., Brixton and Lambeth, 1974–; Member: British Sports Council, 1976–82; Press Council, 1984–90. Chm., Bristol Legacy Commn, 2008–. Freeman, City of Bristol, 2007. *Recreations:* travel, cinema, reading, international politics. *Address:* 12 Downs Park East, Westbury Park, Bristol BS6 7QD. *T:* (0117) 962 3638.

STEPHENSON, Sir Paul (Robert), Kt 2008; QPM 2000; Commissioner, Metropolitan Police, 2009–11 (Deputy Commissioner, 2005–09); *b* 26 Sept. 1953; *s* of late Jack Stephenson and of Rose Cathryne (*née* Sullivan); *m* 1974, Lynda, *d* of late James Alexander Parker; three *d*. *Educ:* Bacup and Rawtenstall Grammar Sch. Mgt trainee, E. Sutton & Son, 1973–75; with Lancashire Constabulary, 1975–94: Chief Inspector, 1986; Supt, 1988; Asst Chief Constable, Merseyside, 1994–99; Dep. Chief Constable, 1999–2001, Chief Constable, 2002–05, Lancs Constabulary. Company dir, 2012–. Ind. Regulatory Dir, British Horse Racing Authy, 2015–. Trustee, Crimestoppers, 2012–. Hon. Fellow, Univ. of Central Lancs, 2007. CCMI 2008. *Recreations:* country sports, reading.

STEPHENSON, (Robert) Ashley (Shute), LVO 1990 (MVO 1979); FCIHort; Bailiff of the Royal Parks, 1980–90; *b* 1 Sept. 1927; *s* of late James Stephenson and Agnes Maud Stephenson; *m* 1955, Isabel Dunn; one *s* one *d*. *Educ:* Walbottle Secondary Sch. Diploma in Horticulture, RHS, Wisley, 1954; MIHort 1987, FCIHort (FIHort 1998). Apprenticeship, Newcastle upon Tyne Parks Dept, 1942; served RASC, Palestine and Cyprus, 1946; Landscape Gardener, Donald Ireland Ltd, 1949; Student, RHS's gardens, Wisley, 1952; Royal Parks, 1954–90: Supt, Regent's Park, 1969; Supt, Central Royal Parks, 1972. Gardening Correspondent, The Times, 1982–87. President: British Pelargonium and Geranium Soc., 1983–95; South East in Bloom, 2001 (Chm., 1990–2001); Member: Cttee, RHS, 1981–; London in Bloom Cttee, English Tourism Council (formerly English Tourist Bd), 1980–91 (Vice-Chm., 1983); Chm., Floral Jersey, 1990–2001; Nat. Chm., Britain in Bloom, 1991–2001; Mem., The Queen's Anniversary Cttee 1952–92, 1992– (Chm., Horticl Cttee, 1992–). Contributor to television and radio programmes; regularly on BBC Radio Sussex gardening programmes; gardening correspondent to professional and amateur papers.

Publications: The Garden Planner, 1981; contribs to nat. press. *Recreations:* sport, judging horticultural shows, natural history, walking, golf. *Address:* 17 Sandore Road, Seaford, E Sussex BN25 3PZ.

STEPHENSON, Prof. Terence John, DM; FRCP, FRCPCH, FRCSE, FRCOG; Nuffield Professor of Child Health, University College London, since 2009; Honorary Consultant Paediatrician, University College Hospital and Great Ormond Street Hospital, since 2009; *b* 6 Dec. 1957; *s* of late James Ewing Stephenson and Cora Bell Stephenson (*née* Elliott); *m* 1987, Amanda Jane Lilley (marr. diss. 2011); one *s* one *d*; partner, Alison Johns. *Educ:* Larne Grammar Sch.; Bristol Univ. (BSc 1st Cl. Hons); Imperial Coll. London; New Coll., Oxford (BM BCh); DM Nottingham 1992. MRCP 1986, FRCP 1995; FRCPCH 1997; FRCSE 2015; FRCOG 2015. Jun. hosp. appts at John Radcliffe Hosp., Oxford, Royal United Hosp., Bath, St Thomas' Hosp., London, Nat. Hosp. for Nervous Diseases, Queen Sq. and UCH, London, 1983–86; University of Nottingham: Lectr in Child Health, 1986–90; Sen. Lectr, 1990–96; Prof. of Child Health, 1996–2009; Dean, Faculty of Medicine and Health Scis, 2003–09, Nottingham Univ. Sometime advisor: Official Solicitor to Supreme Court, 1997; DoH, 1999–2006; Eur. Agency for Evaluation of Med. Products, 2001–05. External Examiner: UCL; TCD; UC, Galway; Univs of Hong Kong, Leicester, Birmingham and Putra. Vice Chm., Adv. Gp for Nat. Specialised Services, 2011–13; Chm., Ext. Review Panel, Expert Clinical Advice - Medicines and Healthcare products Regulatory Agency Medical Devices, 2014; Mem., Ind. Panel Inquiry into Child Sexual Abuse, 2014–15. Treas., Council of Heads of Med. Schs, 2005–09. Vice-Pres. for Res. and Sci., 2007–09, Pres., 2009–12, RCPCH; Chairman: Acad. of Medical Royal Colls, 2012–15; GMC, 2015–. Pres., Trent Paediatric Soc., 1999–2005; Sec., Neonatal Soc., 2001–03; Treas., Paediatric Res. Soc., 2001–03. Trustee, NSPCC, 2011–14. Hon. Sec., Assoc. of Clinical Profs of Paediatrics, 2003–05. Hon. FRACP 2010; Hon. FRCPI 2013; Hon. Fellow, HK Acad. of Pharmacy 2013; Hon. FRCS 2014; Hon. FRCGP 2014; Hon. FRCA 2015; Hon. FCAI 2015. *Publications:* (with H. Wallace) Clinical Paediatrics for Post Graduate Examinations, 1991, 2nd edn 1995; (with C. O'Callaghan) Pocket Paediatrics, 1992, 2nd edn 2003; (with C. O'Callaghan) Data Interpretation for the MRCP, 1994; (jtly) Pocket Neonatology, 2000; (jtly) Short Cases for the MRCPCH, 2004; (jtly) How to Write a Guideline, 2008; Swine Flu: the facts, 2009; contrib. numerous peer-reviewed papers in various fields of child health and disease. *Recreations:* golf (badly), football and Rugby (former competitor, now spectator), skiing, ecclesiastical architecture, piano, guitar. *Address:* Institute of Child Health, University College London, 30 Guilford Street, WC1N 1EH. *T:* (020) 7092 6000. *Clubs:* Lansdowne, 1942; Paediatric Visiting, Medical Pilgrims.

STEPHENSON, Prof. Thomas, PhD; CEng, FREng; FIChemE; Professor, since 1994, and Pro-Vice-Chancellor Research, since 2014, Cranfield University; *b* Cambridge, 26 Nov. 1957; *s* of Andrew and Viiu Stephenson; *m* 1985, Gillian Horrell; two *d*. *Educ:* Newport Grammar Sch., Essex; York Univ. (BSc Biochem. 1979); Imperial Coll. London (PhD Civil Engrg 1983). FCIWEM 1994; CEng 1999; FIChemE 2001; FREng 2010. Sen. Lectr in Biochem. Engrg, Teesside Poly., 1986–90; Cranfield Institute of Technology, subseq. Cranfield University: Dep. Dir of Water Scis, 1990–92; Dir of Water Scis, 1992–2004; Hd, Sch. of Applied Scis, 2004–14. Managing Director: Cranfield Innovative Manufg Ltd, 2004–; Cranfield Impact Centre Ltd, 2004–; Tech. Dir, 2005–10, Chm., 2010–, Water Innovate Ltd; Chm., British Water, 2010–12. FHEA 2007. *Recreations:* cycling, pubs, reading, collecting sewage treatment textbooks. *Address:* Cranfield University, Cranfield MK43 0BD. *T:* (01234) 754054. *E:* t.stephenson@cranfield.ac.uk.

STEPHENSON, Air Vice-Marshal Tom Birkett, CB 1982; Assistant Chief of Defence Staff (Signals), 1980–82, retired; *b* 18 Aug. 1926; *s* of Richard and Isabel Stephenson; *m* 1951, Rosemary Patricia (*née* Kaye) (*d* 1984); one *s* three *d*. *Educ:* Workington Secondary Sch.; Manchester Univ.; Southampton Univ. (DipEl). Commissioned in RAF Engrg Branch, 1945; Staff Coll., 1962; Wing Comdr, Station and Staff appointments, until 1967; Command Electrical Engr, HQASC, 1967–69; Dep. Director Op. Requirements, 1969–72; AOEng, HQ NEAF, 1972–74; RCDS 1975; Director of Signals (Air), 1976–79. *Recreations:* sport, walking, reading. *Address:* c/o National Westminster Bank, High Street, Maidenhead SL6 1PY. *Club:* Royal Air Force.

STEPNEY, Area Bishop of, since 2011; **Rt Rev. Adrian Newman;** *b* 21 Dec. 1958; *s* of John Henry Newman and Ruth Doreen Newman; *m* 1981, Gillian Ann Hayes; three *s*. *Educ:* Univ. of Bristol (BSc (Econ.) 1980); Trinity Theol Coll., Bristol (DipHE (Theol.) 1985; MPhil (Theol.) 1989). Ordained deacon, 1985, priest, 1986; Curate, St Mark's, Forest Gate, 1985–89; Vicar, Hillsborough and Wadsley Bridge, Sheffield, 1989–96; Rector, St Martin in the Bull Ring, Birmingham, 1996–2004; Dean of Rochester, 2005–11. *Recreations:* sport, music, reading. *Address:* 63 Coborn Road, E3 2DB. *T:* (020) 7932 1140, *Fax:* (020) 8981 8015. *E:* bishop.stepney@london.anglican.org.

STEPTOE, Prof. Andrew Patrick Arthur, DPhil; FMedSci, FBPsS, FAcSS; British Heart Foundation Professor of Psychology, since 2000 and Director, Institute of Epidemiology and Health Care, since 2011, University College London; *b* 24 April 1951; *s* of Patrick Christopher Steptoe, CBE, FRS, and Sheena Macleod Steptoe; *m* 1st, 1980, Jane Horncastle (marr. diss. 1984); one *s*; 2nd, 1991, (Frances) Jane Wardle, *qv*; one *s*. *Educ:* Gonville and Caius Coll., Cambridge (BA 1972; MA 1976); Magdalen Coll., Oxford (DPhil 1976); DSc London, 1995. FBPsS 1988. Res. Lectr, Christ Church Coll., Oxford, 1975–77; St George's Hospital Medical School: Lectr in Psychology, 1977–81; Sen. Lectr, 1981–87; Reader, 1987–88; Prof. of Psychology, 1988–2000; Chm. Acad. Bd, 1997–99; Dep. Hd, 2005–11, Hd, 2011, Dept of Epidemiol. and Public Health, UCL. President: Soc. of Psychosomatic Res., 1983–85; Internat. Soc. of Behavioral Medicine, 1994–96. Editor, British Jl of Health Psychology, 1995–2001; Associate Editor: Psychophysiology, 1982–86; Jl of Psychosomatic Res., 1989–97; British Jl of Clinical Psychology, 1992–95; Annals of Behavioral Medicine, 1992–97. FAcSS (AcSS 2001); MAE 2003. FMedSci 2008. *Publications:* Psychological Factors in Cardiovascular Disorders, 1981; Problems of Pain and Stress, 1982; Health Care and Human Behaviour, 1984; Clinical and Methodological Issues in Cardiovascular Psychophysiology, 1985; The Mozart-Da Ponte Operas, 1988; Behavioural Medicine in Cardiovascular Disorders, 1988; Stress, Personal Control and Health, 1989; Psychosocial Processes and Health, 1994; Mozart, 1996; Genius and the Mind: studies of creativity and temperament, 1998; Depression and Physical Illness, 2006; Handbook of Behavioral Medicine, 2010; Stress and Cardiovascular Disease, 2012. *Recreations:* music, theatre, reading, family, running. *Address:* Department of Epidemiology and Public Health, University College London, 1–19 Torrington Place, WC1E 6BT. *T:* (020) 7679 1804, *Fax:* (020) 7916 8542. *E:* a.steptoe@ucl.ac.uk.

STEPTOE, (Frances) Jane; *see* Wardle, F. J.

STERCKX, Prof. Roel, PhD; FBA 2013; Joseph Needham Professor of Chinese History, Science and Civilisation, since 2008, and Head, Department of East Asian Studies, since 2014, University of Cambridge (Professor of Chinese, 2007–08); Fellow of Clare College, Cambridge, since 2006; *b* 13 May 1969; *s* of Herman Sterckx and Angèle Sterckx (*née* Vos); *m* 2003, Dr Ang Cheng Eng; one *s*. *Educ:* Gemeentelijke Basisschool Retie, Belgium; St Jan Berchmans Coll., Mol; Katholieke Universiteit Leuven (BA, MA Sinology and Hist. 1991; PGCE 1991); National Taiwan Univ., Taipei (studied philosophy 1992); Univ. of Cambridge (MPhil 1993; PhD Oriental Studies 1997); DPhil Oxon 1998. Jun. Res. Fellow, Wolfson Coll., Oxford, 1997–2000; Asst Prof. of E Asian Studies, Univ. of Arizona, 2000–02; University of Cambridge: Univ. Lectr, then Sen. Lectr, in Chinese Studies, 2002–07; Chairman: Dept of E Asian Studies, 2007–10; Faculty of Asian and Middle Eastern Studies, 2013; Race and Equality Champion, 2013–. Vis. Fellow, Academia Sinica, Taipei, Republic of China, 2011–12. Sec.-Gen., Eur. Assoc. for Chinese Studies, 2006–12; Member: Conseil d'Admin, Ecole Française d'Extrême-Orient, Paris, 2009–11; Eur. Fellowship Panel, Chiang Ching-kuo Foundn, 2011–. Trustee: Needham Res. Inst., 2007–; Percival David Foundn of Chinese Art, 2011–15. FRAS 2006; FRHistS 2006. *Publications:* The Animal and the Daemon in Early China, 2002; Of Tripod and Palate: food, politics and religion in traditional China, 2005; Of Self and Spirits: exploring 'shen' in China, 2007; Food, Sacrifice and Sagehood in Early China, 2011; Energia Vitale: il cosmo nel pensiero cinese antico, 2012; various scholarly articles. *Recreations:* music, gardening, fishing. *Address:* Clare College, Trinity Lane, Cambridge CB2 1TL.

STERLING, family name of **Baron Sterling of Plaistow**.

STERLING OF PLAISTOW, Baron *cr* 1991 (Life Peer), of Pall Mall in the City of Westminster; **Jeffrey Maurice Sterling,** GCVO 2002; Kt 1985; CBE 1977; Executive Chairman, The Peninsular and Oriental Steam Navigation Company, 1983–2005; Chairman: Sterling Guarantee Trust, since 2005; P&O Princess Cruises, 2000–03; Swan Hellenic, 2007–15, now Hon. President; Hebridean Island Cruises, 2009–15, now Hon. President; Chairman and Joint Founder, Motability, since 1994 (Chairman of Executive, since 1977); Chairman of Trustees, National Maritime Museum, 2005–13; *b* 27 Dec. 1934; *s* of late Harry and of Alice Sterling; *m* 1985, Dorothy Ann Smith; one *d*. *Educ:* Reigate Grammar Sch.; Preston Manor County Sch.; Guildhall School of Music. Paul Schweder & Co. (Stock Exchange), 1955–57; G. Eberstadt & Co., 1957–62; Fin. Dir, General Guarantee Corp., 1962–64; Man. Dir, Gula Investments Ltd, 1964–69; Chm., Sterling Guarantee Trust plc, 1969–85, when it merged with P&O Steam Navigation Co. Mem., British Airways Bd, 1979–82. Special Advr to Sec. of State for Industry, later for Trade and Industry, 1982–90. Mem. Exec., 1966–, Chm. Organisation Cttee, 1969–73, World ORT Union; Chm., ORT Technical Services, 1974–; Vice-Pres., British ORT, 1978–; President: Gen. Council of British Shipping, 1990–91; EC Shipowners' Assocs, 1992–94. Dep. Chm. and Hon. Treasurer, London Celebrations Cttee, Queen's Silver Jubilee, 1975–83; Chm., Queen's Golden Jubilee Weekend Trust, 2002. Chm., Young Vic Co., 1975–83; Chm., of the Governors, Royal Ballet Sch., 1983–99; Gov., Royal Ballet, 1986–99. Pres., AJEX, 2012–. Freeman, City of London. Hon. Captain, 1991, Hon. Cdre, 2005, Hon. Rear Adm., 2010, Hon. Vice Adm., 2015, RNR. Elder Brother, Trinity House, 1991. Hon. FIMarEST (Hon. FIMarE 1991); Hon. FICS 1992; Hon. MRICS 1993; FSVA 1995; Hon. FRINA 1997. Hon. DBA Nottingham Trent, 1995; Hon. DCL Durham, 1996; Hon. DSc City, 2006. Interfaith Medallion, Internat. CCJ, 2003. KStJ 1998. Grand Officer, Order of May (Argentina), 2002; Officer's Cross, Order of Merit (Germany), 2004; Officier, Légion d'Honneur (France), 2005. *Recreations:* music, the arts. *Clubs:* Garrick, Hurlingham.

STERLING, David Robert; Permanent Secretary, Department of Finance and Personnel, Northern Ireland, since 2014; *b* 7 March 1958; *s* of Ronald and Kathleen Sterling; *m* 1987, Lynda Elaine Robinson; one *s* one *d*. *Educ:* Royal Belfast Academical Instn; Univ. of Ulster (MSc). Northern Ireland Civil Service, 1978–: Police Authority; NI Office; Dept of Finance and Personnel; Dep. Sec., Dept for Regl Develt, 2003–08; Dep. Sec., 2008–09, Perm. Sec., 2009–14, Dept of Enterprise, Trade and Investment. *Recreations:* golf, cycling, walking. *E:* david.sterling@dfpni.gov.uk.

STERLING, Dr (Isobel Jane) Nuala, CBE 1993; FRCP; Consultant Physician in Geriatric Medicine, Southampton University Hospitals NHS Trust (formerly Royal South Hants Hospital), 1979–2002, now Emeritus; *b* 12 Feb. 1937; *d* of Prof. F. Bradbury and Mrs J. Bradbury; *m* 1961, Dr G. M. Sterling; five *s* (one *d* decd). *Educ:* Friends' Sch., Saffron Walden; King's Coll. and St George's Hosp., London (MB BS 1960). MRCS LRCP 1960; MRCP 1971, FRCP 1982. House Officer and Registrar posts, St George's Hosp., 1960–67; in general practice: London, 1963–64; Oxford, 1968; Lectr in Medicine, Univ. of Calif., San Francisco, 1969–70; Sen. House Officer then Registrar, Oxford, 1970–71; Sen. Registrar and Lectr in Geriatric Medicine, Southampton Univ. Hosps, 1972–79. Member: Standing Med. Adv. Cttee to Sec. of State for Health, 1986–96 (Chm., 1990–94); Clinical Standards Adv. Gp, 1990–94; Ind. Review Panel on Advertising of Medicines, 2000–; Vice-Chairman: Wessex Regl Adv. Cttee on Distinction Awards, 1998–99; Southern Regl Adv. Cttee on Distinction Awards, 2000–03. Royal College of Physicians: Chm., Standing Cttee of Mems, 1978–79; Mem., Jt Consultants Cttee, 1986–92; Pres., Medical Women's Fedn, 1989–90. Trustee: Wessex Medical Trust, 1999–2004; King Edward VII Hosp., Midhurst, 2000–06. *Publications:* research publications on immunology and cancer, endocrine and respiratory disorders in the elderly, provision of medical services and training. *Recreations:* music, modern art, growing orchids and lilies (Mem. Cttee, 2006–, Chm., 2012–, RHS Lily Gp), gardening (Mem., RHS Bulb Cttee, 2013–), watching cricket. *Address:* Vermont House, East Boldre, Hants SO42 7WX.

STERLING, Prof. Sir Michael (John Howard), Kt 2012; FREng, FIET; FInstMC; Chairman: Science and Technology Facilities Council, since 2009; OCEPS Ltd, since 1990; *b* 9 Feb. 1946; *s* of Richard Howard Sterling and Joan Valeria Sterling (*née* Skinner); *m* 1969, Wendy Karla Anstead; two *s*. *Educ:* Hampton Grammar Sch., Middx; Univ. of Sheffield (BEng 1968; PhD 1971; DEng 1988). CEng 1975. Student apprentice, AEI, 1964–68; research engineer, GEC-Elliott Process Automation, 1968–71; Sheffield University: Lectr in Control Engineering, 1971–78; Industrial Liaison Officer, 1976–80; Sen. Lectr in Control Engineering, 1978–80; Prof. of Engineering, Univ. of Durham, 1980–90 (Dir, Microprocessor Centre, 1980–85); Vice-Chancellor and Principal: Brunel Univ., 1990–2001 (Emeritus Prof., 2001); Birmingham Univ., 2001–09 (Emeritus Prof., 2009). Chairman: WASMACS Ltd, 1994–2002; MidMAN, 2001. Director: UCAS, 2001–06; COBUILD Ltd, 2001–09; Universitas 21, 2001–09. Member: UUK (formerly CVCP), 1990–2009 (Mem. Council, 1994–95); Cttee for Internat. Co-op. in Higher Educn, British Council, 1991–96. Chairman: Univs Statistical Record, 1992–95; Higher Educn Stats Agency, 1992–2003; Jt Performance Indicators Wkg Gp, Higher Educn Councils for England, Scotland and Wales, 1992–95; Russell Gp, 2003–06; STEMNET, 2006–11; Member: Quality Assessment Cttee, 1992–95, Additional Student Numbers and Funds Adv. Gp, 1997–99, HEFCE; Mech. Aeronautical and Prodn Engrg Assessment Panel, RAE, 1992, 1996; Bd, W Midlands Higher Educn Assoc., 2001–09; Bd, AWM, 2003–09; Science Review Gp, DECC, 2011–12; Lead Expert Gp on Manufg, BIS, 2012–14; Chairman: AWM ITC Steering Gp, 2002–09; IET/DECC Transmission Costing Gp, 2011–12. Member: Electricity Supply Res. Council, 1987–89; Engrg Bd, SERC, 1989–92; Engrg Council, 1994–96; Prime Minister's Council for Sci. and Technol., 2004–14. Academic Grand Master, Energy Systems, Chinese Govt, 2014–. Guest Prof., South Eastern Univ., China, 2014–. FREng (FEng 1991; Member: Standing Cttee for Educn, Trng and Competence to Practise, 1993–97; Membership Panel, 2000–02 (Chm., 2002–05); Membership Cttee, 2002–05 (Chm., 2005–08)); FInstMC 1983 (Mem. Cttee, 1975–80, Chm., 1979–80, S Yorks Sect.; Mem. Council, 1983–91; Vice Pres., 1985–88; Nat. Pres., 1988); FIEE 1985 (Mem. Council, 1991–93 and 1997–2002; Chm., Qualifications Bd, 1997–2002; Vice-Pres., 1997–2000; Dep. Pres., 2000–02; Pres., 2002–03). FRSA 1984. CCMI 2002. Dir, W London TEC, 1999–2001 (Dir, Charitable Trust, 1999–2001). Governor: Hampton Sch., 1991–2001 (Chm., 1997–2001); Burnham Grammar Sch., 1991–2001; Pres., Elmhurst Sch. for Dance, 2002–09. Trustee: Hillingdon Partnership Trust, 1993–98; Barber Inst. of Fine Art, 2001–09. Freeman, City of London, 1996; Liveryman, Engineers' Co., 1998–. Fellow, Engrg Acad. of the Czech Republic, 2008. Hon. Fellow, Inst. of Measurement and Control, 2003; Hon. FIET, 2006. Hon. DEng: Sheffield,

1995; Brunel, 2008; Hon. Dr: Tashkent, Uzbekistan, 1999; West Bohemia, Czech Republic, 2001; Medal of Honour, Univ. of Bohemia, Czech Republic, 2000. *Publications:* Power Systems Control, 1978; contribs to: Large Scale Systems Engineering Applications, 1980; Computer Control of Industrial Processes, 1982; Real Time Computer Control, 1984; Comparative Models for Electrical Load Forecasting, 1985; over 120 papers in learned jls. *Recreations:* gardening, DIY, computers, model engineering.

STERLING, Nuala; *see* Sterling, I. J. N.

STERN, family name of **Baron Stern of Brentford**.

STERN, Baroness *cr* 1999 (Life Peer), of Vauxhall, in the London Borough of Lambeth; **Vivien Helen Stern,** CBE 1992; Secretary-General, Penal Reform International, 1989–2006; Senior Research Fellow, International Centre for Prison Studies, King's College, London, 1997–2010; *b* 25 Sept. 1941; *d* of Frederick Stern and Renate Mills; *m* Andrew Gerard Coyle, *qv*. *Educ:* Kent Coll., Pembury, Kent; Bristol Univ. (BA, MLitt, CertEd). Lectr in Further Educn until 1970; Community Relations Commn, 1970–77; Dir, NACRO, 1977–96. Vis. Fellow, Nuffield Coll., Oxford, 1984–91; Vis. Prof., Essex Univ., 2011–14. Member: Special Programmes Bd, Manpower Services Commn, 1980–82; Youth Training Bd, 1982–88; Gen. Adv. Council, IBA, 1982–87; Cttee on the Prison Disciplinary System, 1984–85; Adv. Council, PSI, 1993–96; Bd, Assoc. for Prevention of Torture, Geneva, 1993–99; Bd, Eisenhower Foundn, Washington, 1993–2007; Law Adv. Council, 1995–2001, Governance Adv. Cttee, 2002–06, British Council; Adv. Council, ILANUD (UN Latin Amer. Inst. for Prevention of Crime and Treatment of Offenders), 2001–; Council, Français Incarcérés au Loin, 2001–07; Co-Chm., Know Violence in Childhood, 2014–; Bd, Internat. Legal Foundn, NY, 2014–. Convener, Scottish Consortium on Crime and Criminal Justice, 2003–09. Member: Select Cttee on EU, H of L, 1999–2003; Jt Cttee on Human Rights, 2004–08; Jt Cttee on Statutory Instruments, H of L, 2010–15; Select Cttee on Inquiries Act 2005, H of L, 2013–14; Secondary Legislation Cttee, H of L, 2014–. Chm., Govt Rev. on how rape complaints are handled by public authorities, 2009–10 (report pub. 2010). Pres., New Bridge, 2001–05. Pres., Assoc. of Members of Ind. Monitoring Bds, 2004–. Trustee, Civil Liberties Trust, 2009–. Hon. Fellow, LSE, 1997. Hon. LLD: Bristol, 1990; Oxford Brookes, 1996; Glasgow, 2012; DUniv Stirling, 2008; Hon. DLaws Edinburgh, 2010; Hon. DCL Kent, 2014. Margaret Mead Award for contribution to social justice, Internat. Assoc. for Residential & Community Alternatives, 1995. *Publications:* Bricks of Shame, 1987; Imprisoned by Our Prisons, 1989; Deprived of their Liberty, a report for Caribbean Rights, 1990; A Sin Against the Future: imprisonment in the world, 1998; Alternatives to Prison in Developing Countries, 1999; (ed) Sentenced to Die?: the problem of TB in prisons in Eastern Europe and Central Asia, 1999; Developing Alternatives to Prison in East and Central Europe and Central Asia: a guidance handbook, 2002; Creating Criminals: prisons and people in a market society, 2006. *Address:* House of Lords, SW1A 0PW.

STERN OF BRENTFORD, Baron *cr* 2007 (Life Peer), of Elsted in the County of West Sussex and of Wimbledon in the London Borough of Merton; **Nicholas Herbert Stern,** Kt 2004; FBA 1993; FRS 2014; I. G. Patel Professor of Economics and Government, Chairman, Grantham Institute on Climate Change and the Environment, and Director, India Observatory, London School of Economics, since 2007; President, British Academy, since 2013; *b* 22 April 1946; *s* of Adalbert Stern and Marion Fatima Stern; *m* 1968, Susan Ruth (*née* Chesterton); two *s* one *d*. *Educ:* Peterhouse, Cambridge (BA Mathematics; Hon. Fellow, 2006); Nuffield Coll., Oxford (DPhilEcon). Jun. Res. Fellow, The Queen's Coll., Oxford, 1969–70; Fellow/Tutor in Econs, St Catherine's Coll., and Univ. Lectr, Oxford, 1970–77; Prof. of Econs, Univ. of Warwick, 1978–85; Sir John Hicks Prof. of Econs, LSE, 1986–97; Chief Economist, 1994–99, and Special Counsellor to Pres., 1997–99, EBRD; School Prof. of Econs, LSE, 1999–2003 (on leave of absence); Chief Economist and Sen. Vice-Pres., World Bank, 2000–03; HM Treasury: Second Perm. Sec., Hd of Govt Econ. Service and Hd Review on Econs of Climate Change, 2003–05 (report published 2006); Man. Dir, Budget and Public Finance, 2003–04. Dir of Policy and Res., Prime Minister's Commn for Africa, 2004–05. Trustee, BM, 2008– (Vice-Chm., 2012–). Research Associate/Visiting Professor: MIT, 1972; Ecole Polytech., 1977; Indian Statistical Inst. (Overseas Vis. Fellow of British Acad., 1974–75, and Ford Foundn Vis. Prof., 1981–82); People's Univ. of China, Beijing, 1988, Hon. Prof., 2001; Prof., Collège de France, 2009–10. Mem., American Philosophical Soc., 2015. For. Hon. Mem., Amer. Acad. of Arts and Scis, 1998. Fellow, Econometric Soc., 1978. Hon. Fellow: St Catherine's Coll., Oxford, 2003; Queen's Coll., Oxford, 2007. Hon. DSc Warwick, 2006; Hon. Dr: Cambridge, Nottingham, Exeter, Sussex, Roehampton, Geneva Sch. of Diplomacy and Internat. Relns, 2007; Sheffield, York, E Anglia, 2008; Brighton, Paris-Dauphine, Technische Berlin, 2009. Prizes include: Blue Planet, 2009; Leontief, 2010; BBVA Foundn Frontiers of Knowledge Award, 2011; Schumpeter Award, 2015. Editor, Journal of Public Economics, 1980–98. *Publications:* An Appraisal of Tea Production on Smallholdings in Kenya, 1972; (ed jtly) Theories of Economic Growth, 1973; (jtly) Crime, the Police and Criminal Statistics, 1979; (jtly) Palanpur: the economy of an Indian village, 1982; (jtly) The Theory of Taxation for Developing Countries, 1987; (jtly) Economic Development in Palanpur over Five Decades, 1998; (jtly) Growth and Empowerment: making development happen, 2005; Economics of Climate Change, 2007; A Blueprint for a Safer Planet: how to manage climate change and create a new era of progress and prosperity, 2009; Why Are We Waiting? The logic, urgency, and promise of tackling climate change, 2015; articles in American Econ. Rev., Econ. Jl, Rev. of Econ. Studies, Jl of Public Econs, Jl of Develt Econs, Jl of Econ. Theory, Econs and Phil., and others. *Recreations:* reading novels, walking, watching sport, food. *Address:* London School of Economics, Houghton Street, WC2A 2AE.

STERN, Prof. Claudio Daniel, DPhil, DSc; FRS 2008; J. Z. Young Professor, since 2001, and Head, 2001–11, Department of Cell and Developmental Biology (formerly Department of Anatomy and Developmental Biology), University College London; *b* 9 Feb. 1954; *s* of Erico and Trude Stern; *m* 2000, Andrea Streit. *Educ:* Univ. of Sussex (BSc Hons Biol Scis 1975; DPhil Develtl Biol. 1978); Univ. of Oxford (DSc Physiol Scis 1994). FRSB (FIBiol 2008). Res. Fellow, UCL, 1978–84; Univ. Demonstrator, Univ. of Cambridge, 1984–85; Univ. Lectr, Univ. of Oxford, and Fellow, Christ Church, Oxford, 1985–94; Prof. and Chm. of Genetics and Develt, Columbia Univ., NY, 1994–2001. Pres., Internat. Soc. for Develtl Biol., 2010–14. Member: Ibero-Amer. Molecular Biol. Orgn, 1998; EMBO, 2002; MAE 2013. Foreign Hon. Mem., Amer. Acad. of Arts and Scis, 2014. FMedSci 2001. Foreign Fellow, Latin-Amer. Acad. of Scis, 2001. Waddington Medal, British Soc. for Develtl Biol., 2006. *Publications:* (jtly) The Making of the Nervous System, 1988; (with P. W. Ingham) Gastrulation (Development 1992 supplement), 1992; (with P. W. H. Holland) Essential Developmental Biology: a practical approach, 1993 (trans. Japanese); (jtly) Cellular and Molecular Procedures in Developmental Biology, 1998; Gastrulation: from cells to embryo, 2004; more than 200 articles in internat. learned jls inc. Nature, Science, Cell, Neuron, Developmental Cell, Development and others. *Recreations:* playing Baroque and Renaissance woodwind musical instruments, gastronomy. *Address:* Department of Cell and Developmental Biology, Anatomy Building, University College London, Gower Street, WC1E 6BT.

STERN, Ian Michael; QC 2006; a Recorder, since 2000; *b* 26 Jan. 1957; *s* of Harold and Laura Stern; *m* 1987, Helen Appleton; three *d*. *Educ:* Queen Elizabeth's Grammar Sch. for Boys, Barnet; Univ. of Warwick (BA Hons Pol Sci 1979); City Univ., London (Dip. Law 1982). Called to the Bar, Inner Temple, 1983, Bencher, 2011; in practice as a barrister; Asst Recorder, 1998–2000. *Recreations:* running, travel, family. *Address:* 2 Bedford Row, WC1R 4BU. *T:* (020) 7440 8888, *Fax:* (020) 7242 1738. *E:* istern@2bedfordrow.co.uk.

STERN, John Andrew; freelance writer; Editor at Large, All Out Cricket, since 2012; *b* 12 March 1970; *s* of Peter and Gill Stern; *m* 2004, Clare Alison Henderson; two step *d*. *Educ:* Arnold House; King's Sch., Canterbury; Univ. of Manchester (BA Hons Classics). Hayters Sports Agency, 1992–97; freelance sports writer, 1997–2001 (mostly cricket reporting for The Times and Sunday Times); cricket columnist, Sunday Times, 1998–; Dep. Ed., Wisden Cricket Monthly, 2001–03; Ed., The Wisden Cricketer, 2003–11. *Publications:* Cricket: the definitive guide to the international game, 2012; (with Marcus Williams) The Essential Wisden: an anthology of 150 years of Wisden Cricketers' Almanack, 2013; (with Rob Maier) Youth Cricket Coaching, 2013; (contrib.) Wisden Cricketers' Almanack, annually 1999–. *Recreations:* cricket, golf, travel, wine.

STERN, Michael Charles, FCA; Proprietor and Partner, Michael Stern & Co., 1998–2012, now consultant; Company Secretary, since 2005, and Director, since 2014, Lafferty Ltd; Director, Shalimar Accountancy Ltd, since 2012; Company Secretary, Gandlake Ltd, since 2012; *b* 3 Aug. 1942; *s* of late Maurice Leonard Stern and Rose Stern; *m* 1976, Dr Jillian Denise Aldridge; one *d*. *Educ:* Christ's College Grammar School, Finchley. Mem. ICA 1964; FCA 1969. Partner, Percy Phillips & Co., Accountants, 1964–80; Partner, Halpern & Woolf, Chartered Accountants, 1980–92; Consultant, Cohen Arnold & Co., 1992–98. Chm., The Bow Group, 1977–78; co-opted Mem., Educn Cttee, Borough of Ealing, 1980–83. Contested (C) Derby S, 1979. MP (C) Bristol NW, 1983–97; contested (C) same seat, 1997. PPS to Minister of State, HM Treasury, 1986–87, to Paymaster General, 1987–89, to Minister for Corporate Affairs, DTI, 1991. Chief Finance Officer, 1988–91, Vice-Chm., 1991–92, Cons. party. *Publications:* papers for The Bow Group. *Recreation:* chess. *Address:* 61 Shalimar Gardens, Acton, W3 9JG. *Clubs:* Royal Automobile, United and Cecil.

STERNBERG, Prof. Michael Joseph Ezra, DPhil; FRSB; Professor of Structural Bioinformatics, since 2001, and Director, Centre for Integrative Systems Biology and Bioinformatics, since 2011, Imperial College London; *b* London, 24 June 1951; *s* of Charles Sternberg and Klara Sternberg; *m* 1984, Michelle Bernice Wolfson; one *s* one *d*. *Educ:* Hendon Co. Grammar Sch.; Gonville and Caius Coll., Cambridge (BA 1st Cl. Nat. Scis Theoretical Physics 1972); Imperial Coll. London (MSc Computing); Wolfson Coll., Oxford (DPhil Molecular Biophysics 1978). Postdoctoral Res., Lab. of Molecular Biophysics, Oxford, 1977–83; Royal Soc. Univ. Res. Fellow and Lectr, Crystallography Dept, Birkbeck Coll., Univ. of London, 1983–88; Hd, Biomolecular Modelling Lab., Imperial Cancer Res. Fund, 1988–2001. Founder and Dir, Equinox Pharma Ltd, 2001–. Member: Strategy Bd, BBSRC, 2003–04; Scientific Adv. Bd, Inst. of Food Res., 2007–. Co-developer, Phyre2 protein structure prediction web server. FRSB (FIBiol 2001). Lectures to schs and teachers. Mem. Editl Bd, Jl of Molecular Biol., 2005–. *Publications:* (with A. R. Rees) From Cells to Atoms: an illustrated introduction to molecular biology, 1984; (jtly) Protein Engineering: a practical approach, 1992; Protein Structure Prediction: a practical approach, 1996; contrib. articles to jls incl. Nature, Proc. NAS, Jl of Molecular Biol., Proteins, Human Mutation, Bioinformatics. *Recreations:* swimming, family. *Address:* Sir Ernst Chain Building, Imperial College London, SW7 2AZ.

STERNBERG, Michael Vivian; QC 2008; barrister; *b* Belsize Park, London, 12 Sept. 1951; *s* of Sir Sigmund Sternberg, *qv* and late Ruth Sternberg; *m* 1975, Dr Janine Levinson; one *s* two *d*. *Educ:* Carmel Coll., Wallingford; Queens' Coll., Cambridge (BA 1973, LLB 1975). Called to the Bar, Gray's Inn, 1975, Bencher, 2014; Mem., Inner Temple, 2006; in practice as barrister, 1975–, specialising in all aspects of family law, esp. allocation of resources on divorce; 4 Paper Buildings, 1994–. Asst Sec., Family Law Bar Assoc., 1986–88. Qualified collaborative lawyer, 2010; qualified mediator, 2011. Trustee, Sternberg Charitable Foundn, 1983–; Jt Convenor, Legal Gp, 2005–, Chm., Trustees, 2009–, Three Faiths Forum. Gov., NLCS, 1974–2009. Freeman, City of London, 1983; Liveryman, Horners' Co., 1986–. MCIArb 2012. FRSA 2007. Silver Benemerenza Medal, Sacred Mil. Constantinian Order of St George, 1990; Knight, Royal Order of Francis I, 2011. *Publications:* (contrib.) Pension and Marriage Breakdown, 2005, 2nd edn as Pensions and Family Breakdown, 2008. *Recreations:* walking, Mozart, family law. *Address:* 4 Paper Buildings, EC4Y 7EX. *T:* (020) 7583 0816, *Fax:* (020) 7353 4979. *E:* clerks@4pb.com. *Club:* Reform.

STERNBERG, Sir Sigmund, Kt 1976; JP; Chairman, Sternberg Charitable Foundation, since 1968; *b* Budapest, 2 June 1921; *s* of late Abraham and Elizabeth Sternberg; *m* 1970, Hazel (*née* Everett Jones) (*d* 2014); one *s* one *d*, and one *s* one *d* from a previous marriage. Chairman: Martin Slowe Estates Ltd, 1971–; St Charles Gp, HMC, 1974; Inst. for Archaeo-Metallurgical Studies, 2010 (Hon. Pres., 2010–). Hon. Life Pres., Labour Finance and Industry Gp, 2002– (Dep. Chm., 1972–93); Life Vice Pres., Royal Coll. of Speech and Lang. Therapists, 2002– (Sen. Vice-Pres., 1995–2002). Life Pres., Movt for Reform Judaism (formerly Reform Synagogues of GB), 2011– (Pres., 1998–2011); Patron: Internat. Council of Christians and Jews; Board of Deputies of British Jews Charitable Trust, 2005–; Hon. Gov., Hebrew Univ. of Jerusalem, 2012– (Gov., 1970–2012; Hon. Fellow, 2011); Life Pres., Sternberg Centre for Judaism, 1996; Co-Founder, Three Faiths Forum (Christians, Muslims & Jews Dialogue Gp), 1997; Sen. Religious Advr, World Econ. Forum, 2002–. Life Mem., Magistrates' Assoc., 1965. Mem., John Templeton Foundn, 1998– (Templeton Prize for Progress in Religion, 1998). Founding Patron, Anne Frank Trust, 1991–. Vice Pres., London Jewish Cultural Centre, 2006–. Hon. Vice Pres., Inst. for Business Ethics, 2010. Mem., Court, Essex Univ., 1976–2009. Vice-Pres., Keston Inst., 2003–15. Freeman, City of London, 1970; Liveryman, Co. of Horners. JP Middlesex, 1965. Hon. Life Fellow, Inst. of Dirs, 2007; Hon. Mem., Rotary Club of London, 2012–. FRSA 1979. Life FRSocMed 2002; Hon. FCST 1989; Hon. Fellow, UCL, 2001. DU: Essex, 1996; Hebrew Union Coll., Cincinnati, 2000; DUniv Open, 1998; Hon. LLD Leicester, 2007; Hon. DHLitt Richmond American Internat., 2008. Paul Harris Fellow, Rotary Foundn of Rotary Internat., 1989 (Rotary Internat. Award of Honour, 1998); Medal of Merit, Warsaw Univ., 1995; Wilhelm Leuschner Medal, Wiesbaden, 1998; (jtly) St Robert Bellarmine Medal, Gregorian Univ., 2002; (jtly) Dist. Service Award, Internat. CCJ, 2005; Lifetime Achievement Award, First, 2008. OStJ 1988. KC★SG 1985; Order of Orthodox Hospitallers (1st Class with Star and Badge of Religion), 1986; Order of Merit (Poland), 1989, Comdr's Cross, 1992, Comdr's Cross with Star, 1999; Order of the Gold Star (Hungary), 1990; Commander's Cross, 1st cl. (Austria), 1992; Comdr of the Order of Civil Merit (Spain), 1993; Comdr, Order of Honour (Greece), 1996; Comdr, Royal Order of Polar Star (Sweden), 1997; Order of Commendatore (Italy), 1999; Gran Oficial, Orden de Mayo al Merito (Argentina), 1999; Grand Cross, Order of Bernardo O'Higgins (Chile), 2000; Order of Ukraine, 2001; Order of Merit with star (Portugal), 2002; Officier, Légion d'Honneur (France), 2003; Order of Madara Horseman (Bulgaria), 2003; Order of White Two-Armed Cross (Slovakia), 2003; Order of Francisco de Miranda (Venezuela), 2004; Comdr's Cross, Order of Merit (Hungary), 2004; Knight Grand Cross, Royal Order of Francis I, 2005; Knight Comdr's Cross, Order of Merit (Germany), 2006 (Comdr's Cross, 1993); Comdr, Order Pentru Merit (Romania), 2007; St Mellitus Medal, 2008; Officer, Order of Wissam Alouite (Morocco), 2009. *Relevant publication:* The Knight with many Hats by Emma Klein, 2012. *Recreations:* reading the religious press, swimming. *Address:* Star House, 104 Grafton Road, NW5 4BA. *Club:* City Livery.

See also M. V. Sternberg.

STEVELY, Prof. William Stewart, CBE 2004; DPhil; FRSB; Principal and Vice-Chancellor, Robert Gordon University, 1997–2005; Chairman, NHS Ayrshire and Arran, 2006–11; *b* 6 April 1943; *s* of Robert Reid Stevely and Catherine Callow Stevely; *m* 1968, Sheila Anne Stalker; three *s* two *d*. *Educ:* Ardrossan Acad.; Glasgow Univ. (BSc 1965; DipEd 1973); St Catherine's Coll., Oxford (DPhil 1968). FRSB (FIBiol 1988). Asst Lectr, 1968–70,

Lectr, 1970–83, Sen. Lectr, 1983–88, in Biochemistry, Univ. of Glasgow; Prof. and Head of Dept of Biology, 1988–92, Vice Principal, 1992–97, Paisley Coll. of Tech., then Univ. of Paisley. Chm., Scottish Council, Inst. of Biology, 1993–95. Chm., UCAS, 2001–05; Member: Nat. Bd for Nursing, Midwifery and Health Visiting for Scotland, 1992–2002; SHEFC, 1993–96; Bd, QAA, 1998–2002; Bd, Scottish Enterprise Grampian (formerly Grampian Enterprise) Ltd, 1998–2006; Bd, Scottish Univs for Industry, 2004–08; Bd, Skills Development Scotland, 2008–11. Member: Council, Inst. for Learning and Teaching in Higher Educn, 1998–2000; Bd, SRUC (formerly Scottish Agricl Coll.), 2005–13 (Vice Chm., 2007–13); Council, Open Univ., 2009– (Vice Chm., 2011–). Convener, Universities Scotland, 2002–04. Fellow, SCDI, 2006. Hon. LLD Aberdeen, 2004; Hon. DEd Robert Gordon, 2005; DUniv Paisley, 2007. *Publications:* papers on herpes viruses. *Address:* 10 Evergreen Estate, Coalhall, Ayr KA6 6PQ.

STEVEN, Dr Andrew John Maclean; Member, Scottish Law Commission, since 2011; *b* Banff, 8 Nov. 1972; *s* of Rev. Harold Andrew Maclean Steven and Mary Allison Steven (*née* Little). *Educ:* Banff Acad.; Univ. of Edinburgh (LLB Hons 1994; PhD 1998; DipLP 1998). Admitted solicitor, 1999; NP 1999; WS 2009. University of Edinburgh: Lectr in Law, 2000–10; Sen. Lectr in Law, 2010–. *Publications:* Pledge and Lien, 2008; (with G. L. Gretton) Property, Trusts and Succession, 2009, 2nd edn 2013; papers in learned jls. *Address:* Scottish Law Commission, 140 Causewayside, Edinburgh EH9 1PR. *T:* (0131) 668 2131.

STEVEN, Rosemary Margaret; Chief Executive, Warrington Hospital NHS Trust, 1993–98; *b* 2 Nov. 1945; *d* of Donald and Margaret Robson; *m* 1983, Michael A. Knights (*d* 2005); *m* 2008, Angus C. Steven. *Educ:* Houghton-le-Spring Grammar School; Coll. of Nursing, Sunderland AHA. RGN, OND. Clinical nursing career, 1962–75 (Ward Sister posts, Sunderland and Harrogate); Nursing Officer, Harrogate, 1975–78; Sen. Nursing Officer, North Tees, Stockton, 1978–80; Dir of Nursing, Central Manchester HA, 1981–85; Unit Gen. Manager and Dist Nursing Officer, Manchester Royal Eye Hosp., 1985–88; Regl Nursing Officer, 1988–90, Dep. Chief Exec., 1989–91, Mersey RHA; Exec. Dir, NHS Mgt Exec. Trust Monitoring Unit (NW), 1991–93. Mem., S Manchester HA, 1983–88; Sec. and Chief Exec., Ophthalmic Nursing Bd, 1983–88. Gov., Salford Royal NHS Foundn Trust (Lead Gov., 2007–). *Publications:* articles in nursing and health service papers. *Recreations:* music (piano; Friends of Hallé), fashion. *Address:* 21 Crossfield Drive, Worsley, Manchester M28 1GP. *Club:* Soroptomist International (Manchester).

STEVENS, family name of **Barons Stevens of Kirkwhelpington** and **Stevens of Ludgate**.

STEVENS OF KIRKWHELPINGTON, Baron *cr* 2005 (Life Peer), of Kirkwhelpington in the county of Northumberland; **John Arthur Stevens,** Kt 2000; QPM 1992; DL; Commissioner, Metropolitan Police, 2000–05; Senior Adviser to the Prime Minister on International Security Issues, since 2007; *b* 21 Oct. 1942; *s* of C. J. and S. Stevens; *m*; two *s* one *d*. *Educ:* St Lawrence Coll., Ramsgate; Leicester Univ. (LLB Hons; LLD 2000); Southampton Univ. (MPhil). Joined Metropolitan Police, 1963; DS, Police Staff Coll., 1983–84; Asst Chief Constable, Hampshire Constabulary, 1986–89; Dep. Chief Constable, Cambridgeshire Constabulary, 1989–91; Chief Constable, Northumbria, 1991–96; HM Inspector of Constabulary, 1996–98; Dep. Comr, Metropolitan Police, 1998–99. Chairman: Jt Cttee on Offender Profiling, 1991; ACPO Crime Prevention Sub-Cttee, 1994. Chm., NI Enquiry into alleged collusion between paramil. and security forces (Stevens Enquiry), 1989–92; headed Enquiry into alleged malpractice at Nat. Criminal Intelligence Service, 1994–96; 'Stevens 3' NI Enquiry into Collusion, 1999–2003; inquiry into the deaths of Diana, Princess of Wales and Dodi Al-Fayed, 2003–06. Advr, Forensic Sci. Service; Advr to Govts of S Africa, Jamaica and Romania on police matters and anti corruption, 2002–; Chairman: Strategic Adv. Panel, Interpol, 2005–; Monitor Quest (formerly Quest) Ltd, 2005–; Skills for Security, 2005–. Vis. Prof., City Univ., NY, 1984–85; Vis. Lectr, Internat. Crime Prevention Centre, Canada, 1998–; Sen. Mem., 1996–, Hon. Fellow, 2000, Wolfson Coll., Cambridge. Chancellor, Northumbria Univ., 2005–. Pres., Aircraft Owners and Pilots Assoc., 2005–. Patron, Northumbria Youth Action, 2000–; Patron of charities, Brixton and Romania. Hon. Col, Northumbria Cadet Force, 2006–. Freeman, City of London, 2002. DL: Greater London, 2001; Northumberland, 2007. FRSA 2002. Hon. DCL Northumbria, 2001; Hon. LLD Newcastle, 2006; Hon. PhD London Metropolitan, 2008; Hon. DLitt Newcastle, 2008. KStJ 2002. Hon. Air Cdre, RAAF, 2008–. *Publications:* Not for the Faint-hearted (autobiog.), 2005. *Recreations:* walking, cricket, squash, Rugby, flying (qualified pilot). *Address:* House of Lords, SW1A 0PW. *Clubs:* East India, Royal Air Force; Northern Counties, Durham County Cricket (Pres., 2004–06; Dir, 2006–).

STEVENS OF LUDGATE, Baron *cr* 1987 (Life Peer), of Ludgate in the City of London; **David Robert Stevens;** Chairman: United News & Media (formerly United Newspapers plc), 1981–99 (Director, 1974–99); Express Newspapers, 1985–99 (Deputy Chairman, since 2014); *b* 26 May 1936; *s* of late (Arthur) Edwin Stevens, CBE; *m* 1st Patricia Rose (marr. diss. 1971); one *s* one *d*; 2nd, 1977, Melissa Milicevich (*d* 1989); 3rd, 1990, Meriza Giori. *Educ:* Stowe Sch.; Sidney Sussex Coll., Cambridge (MA Hons Econ; Hon. Fellow, 1991). 2nd Lieut, Royal Artillery, 1955–56. Management Trainee, Elliott Automation, 1959; Director: Hill Samuel Securities, 1959–68; Drayton Group, 1968–74; Man. Dir, 1974–80, Chm., 1985–86, Drayton Montagu Investment Mgt. Chairman: Alexander Proudfoot Hldgs (formerly City & Foreign), 1976–95; Drayton Far East, 1976–93; English & International, 1976–79; Consolidated Venture (formerly Montagu Boston), 1979–93; Drayton Consolidated, 1980–92; Drayton Japan, 1980–88; Oak Industries, 1989–96; Mid States, 1989–95; Premier Asset Mgt plc, 1997–2001; PNC Tele.Com (formerly Personal Number Co.), 1998–2002; Chief Exec., 1980–87, Chm., 1980–93, Montagu Investment Management, subseq. INVESCO MIM Management; Dep. Chm., 1987–89, Chm., 1989–93, Britannia Arrow Hldgs, subseq. INVESCO MIM. Chm., EDC for Civil Engrg, 1984–86. Dir, ENO, 1980–87. Founder Dir, Helicopter Emergency Rescue Service, London Hosp., 1988. Patron, RCS, 1998. Grand Order of Southern Cross (Brazil), 1993. *Recreations:* golf, gardening. *Address:* House of Lords, SW1A 0PW. *Clubs:* White's; Sunningdale Golf, Swinley Golf.

STEVENS, Andrew John; Chief Executive Officer, Cobham plc, 2010–12; *b* Sedgley, W Midlands, 30 Aug. 1956; *s* of Alfred Stevens and Margaret Stevens; *m* 1980, Elizabeth Crabb; two *d*. *Educ:* Aston Univ. (BSc Hons 1st cl. 1978). CEng 1982; FIET 2001; FRAeS 2001. Provident Gp Trng Scheme, 1972–76; Dowty Group plc, subseq. TI Group plc, 1976–94: student apprentice, 1976–78; Dowty Rotol Ltd: machinist, 1978; Proj. Engr, Propellers and Gearboxes, 1978–80; Landing Gear Controller, 1980–82; Dep. Prodn Engrg Manager, 1982–86; Exec. Dir, Works, 1986–89; Prodn Dir and Mem. Bd, 1989–90; Mem. Bd, Dowty Aerospace IOM, 1989–92; Designate Dir and Gen. Manager, 1990–92, Dir and Gen. Manager, 1992–94, Landing Gear UK; Sector Exec., Cable Mgt, Bowthorpe plc, 1994–96; Messier Dowty International: Man. Dir UK, 1996–97; Man. Dir Europe, 1997–99; Man. Dir, Defence Aerospace, Bristol, Rolls-Royce plc, 2001–03; Cobham plc: Gp Pres., Aerospace Systems, 2003–05; Chief Operating Officer, 2005–09. Non-executive Director: De La Rue plc, 2013–; CAE Inc., 2013–; Héroux-Devtek Inc., 2014–. Ext. Examr, Brunel Univ., 1992–94. *Recreations:* walking, gardening, cars and driving.

STEVENS, Prof. Anne Frances, PhD; Professor of European Studies, Aston University, 1998–2008, now Emeritus (Head, School of Languages and European Studies, 1998–2003); *b* 28 Dec. 1942; *d* of late Robert Ross, FLS and Margaret Helen Ross (*née* Steadman); *m* 1966, Handley Michael Gambrell Stevens, *qv*; two *d* (and one *d* decd). *Educ:* Blackheath High Sch. for Girls; Newnham Coll., Cambridge (BA 1964; MA 1975); LSE, Univ. of London (MSc Econ (with distinction) 1975; PhD 1980). Asst Principal, Dept of Technical Co-operation, ODM, 1964–66; part-time Lectr, Univ. of Malaya, 1966–68; HEO, British High Commn, Kuala Lumpur, 1968–69; School of European Studies, University of Sussex: Lectr in Politics, 1978–90; Dean, 1988–90; Prof. of European Studies, Univ. of Kent at Canterbury, 1991–98. *Publications:* (jtly) Hostile Brothers: competition and closure in the European electronics industry, 1990; The Government and Politics of France, 1992, 3rd edn 2003; Brussels Bureaucrats: the administration of the European Union, 2000; Women, Power and Politics, 2007; articles on comparative admin. *Recreations:* walking, watching opera, needlework. *Address:* Flat 1, 20 Netherhall Gardens, NW3 5TH. *T:* (020) 7794 0874.

STEVENS, Annette; *see* King, Annette.

STEVENS, Anthony John; Post Graduate Veterinary Dean for London and South East England, Royal College of Veterinary Surgeons/British Veterinary Association, 1986–97; engaged in consultancy and literary work; *b* 29 July 1926; *s* of John Walker Stevens and Hilda Stevens; *m* 1954, Patricia Frances, *d* of Robert Gill, Ponteland; one *s* two *d*. *Educ:* Liverpool and Manchester Univs; Magdalene Coll., Cambridge. MA, BVSc, MRCVS, DipBact. Veterinary Investigation Officer, Cambridge, 1956–65; Animal Health Expert for UNO, 1959–63; Suptg Veterinary Investigation Officer, Leeds, 1965–68; Ministry of Agriculture, Fisheries and Food: Dep. Dir, Central Vet. Lab., 1968–71; Asst Chief Vet. Officer, 1971–73; Dep. Chief Vet. Officer, 1973–78; Dir, Vet. Labs, MAFF, 1979–86. External Examr, Dublin, Liverpool and Edinburgh Univs, 1964–70. Past Pres., Veterinary Research Club. Vice Pres., Zoological Soc., 1989–90 and 1995–98 (Mem. Council, 1987–91, 1994–98). Vice Chm., Surrey Industrial History Gp, 1990–2002. FRSA. *Publications:* UN/FAO Manual of Diagnostic Techniques; regular contributor to Veterinary Record, etc. *Recreations:* industrial archaeology particularly canals, all forms of livestock. *Address:* Marigold Cottage, Great Halfpenny Farm, Guildford, Surrey GU4 8PY. *T:* (01483) 565375.

STEVENS, Auriol, (Lady Ashworth); freelance journalist, retired; Editor, Times Higher Education Supplement, 1992–2002; *d* of Capt. E. B. K. Stevens and Ruth M. Stevens Howard; *m* 1st, 1962, Prof. Hugh Stephenson, *qv* (marr. diss. 1987); 2nd, 1988, Dr J. M. Ashworth (*see* Sir J. M. Ashworth). *Educ:* Somerville Coll., Oxford (BA Hons); London Univ. (Dip. (Ext.)). Freelance journalist, 1962–72; TES, 1972–78; educn corresp., Observer, 1978–83; reporter, A Week in Politics, TV, 1983–86; Dir, Univs Inf. Unit, Cttee of Vice-Chancellors, 1986–92. Chm. Govs, Elliot Sch., Putney, 1981–85; Council Member: PSI, 1985–91; RCA, 1998–2006 (Vice-Chm., 2004–06); Essex Univ., 2002–12 (Pro-Chancellor, 2005–12; Hon. Fellow, 2013); Educn Review Gp, 2008–; Governor: UEL, 2002–05; St Helena Sch., Colchester, 2009–. Member: Exec. Cttee, Forum UK, 1999–2003; Inst. of Cancer Res., 2000–; Exec. Cttee, Wivenhoe Soc., 2003–06. Hon. FRCA 2007. Hon. DLitt Nottingham Trent, 2003. *Publications:* Clever Children in Comprehensive Schools, 1978; The State of the Universities, 1991; Women in the Media, 1998. *Recreations:* history, textiles, sailing, gardening, grandchildren. *Address:* Garden House, Wivenhoe, Essex CO7 9BD. *Clubs:* Royal Over-Seas League; Wivenhoe Sailing.

STEVENS, Christopher Paul C.; *see* Claxton Stevens, C. P.

STEVENS, Rt Rev. Dr Douglas; Bishop of Riverina, 2005–12; Rector, Parish of Mt Gravatt, since 2012; *b* 19 May 1952; *s* of Robert Henry Stevens and Dorothy Phyllis Cooper; *m* 1979, Denise Karen; two *d*. *Educ:* Newcastle Univ., NSW (BA); Aust. Coll. of Theol. (BTh Hons); Univ. of Dublin (MPhil); Melbourne Coll. of Divinity (Dr of Ministry Studies). Rector: Merriwa, 1981–84; Botton Point, 1986–90; Wingham, 1990–94; Nambucca Heads, 1994–99; Tweed Heads, 1999–2005. *Address:* St Bartholomew's Anglican Church, PO Box 275, Mt Gravatt, Qld 4122, Australia.

STEVENS, Glenn Robert; Chairman and Governor, Reserve Bank of Australia, since 2006; *b* 23 Jan. 1958; *s* of Robert Frank Hollis Stevens and Audrey Grace Stevens; *m* 1983, Susan Elizabeth Dunbar; two *d*. *Educ:* Univ. of Sydney (BEc Hons 1979); Univ. of Western Ontario (MA Econ 1985). Reserve Bank of Australia: joined, 1980; Head: Econ. Analysis Dept, 1992–95; Internat. Dept, 1995–96; Asst Gov. (Econ.), 1996–2001; Dep. Gov., 2001–06. Vis. Scholar, Fed. Reserve Bank of San Francisco, 1990. *Recreation:* flying. *Address:* Reserve Bank of Australia, 65 Martin Place, Sydney, NSW 2000, Australia. *T:* (2) 95518111, *Fax:* (2) 95518030. *E:* governor@rba.gov.au.

STEVENS, Handley Michael Gambrell, PhD; Under Secretary, Department of Transport, 1983–94; *b* 29 June 1941; *s* of Ernest Norman Stevens and Kathleen Emily Gambrell; *m* 1966, Anne Frances Ross (*see* A. F. Stevens); two *d* (and one *d* decd). *Educ:* The Leys Sch., Cambridge; Phillips Acad., Andover, Mass (E-SU schol.); King's Coll., Cambridge (BA 1963; MA 1971; PhD 2007). Joined Foreign Office, 1964; Third, later Second, Sec., Kuala Lumpur, 1966; Asst Private Sec. to the Lord Privy Seal, 1970; Principal: CSD, 1971; DTI, 1973; Asst Sec., Dept of Trade, 1976. Vis. Res. Associate, Eur. Inst., LSE, 1994–2007. *Publications:* Transport Policy in Britain, 1998; Brussels Bureaucrats?, 2000; Transport Policy in the European Union, 2003; Air Transport and the European Union, 2010. *Recreations:* music, hill walking, travel. *Address:* 20 Netherhall Gardens, NW3 5TH.

STEVENS, Howard Linton; QC 2012; *b* Kent, 6 March 1965; *s* of Donald John Stevens and Shirley Marion Stevens; *m* 1995, Anthea Lucy Michaelson-Yeates; two *d*. *Educ:* Tonbridge Sch.; Univ. of Durham (BA Jt Hons); City Univ. (DipLaw). Called to the Bar, Middle Temple, 1990; barrister in independent practice, 1990–. *Recreations:* family, travel, ski-ing, restoring Grade II listed home. *Address:* 3 Hare Court, Temple, EC4Y 7BJ. *T:* (020) 7415 7800. *E:* howardstevens@3harecourt.com.

STEVENS, Jo; MP (Lab) Cardiff Central, since 2015; *b* Swansea, 6 Sept. 1966. *Educ:* Ysgol Uwchradd Argoed; Elfed High Sch.; Univ. of Manchester (LLB Hons 1988); Manchester Poly. (CPE 1989). Admitted Solicitor, 1991; Solicitor and Dir, Thompsons Solicitors, 1989–2015. *Recreations:* football, cricket, Rugby, darts. *Address:* House of Commons, SW1A 0AA. *E:* jo.stevens.mp@parliament.uk. *Clubs:* Cardiff City Football, Glamorgan County Cricket.

STEVENS, John Christopher Courtenay; Adviser, THS Partners LLP (formerly THS Capital Fund), since 1999; *b* 23 May 1955; *s* of Sir John Melior Stevens, KCMG, DSO, OBE. *Educ:* Winchester Coll.; Magdalen Coll., Oxford (BA Jurisprudence). Foreign exchange and Bond trader, Banque Indosuez, Paris, 1976–77; Bayerische Hypotheken und Wechselbank, Munich, 1977–78; Morgan Grenfell, London, 1979–89, Internat. Dir, 1986–89; Advr, St James's Place Capital plc, 1989. MEP (C) Thames Valley, 1989–99. Contested (Ind) Buckingham, 2010. Vis. Sen. Hon. Fellow, LSE IDEAS, 2011–. *Recreations:* riding, ski-ing. *Address:* 40 Smith Square, SW1P 3HL.

STEVENS, Hon. John Paul; Associate Justice, Supreme Court of the United States, 1975–2010; *b* 20 April 1920; *s* of Ernest James Stevens and Elizabeth Stevens (*née* Street); *m* 1st, 1942, Elizabeth Jane Sheeren; one *s* three *d*; 2nd, 1979, Maryan Mulholland. *Educ:* Univ. of Chicago (AB 1941); Northwestern Univ. (JD 1947). Served War, USNR, 1942–45 (Bronze Star). Law Clerk to US Supreme Ct Justice Wiley Rutledge, 1947–48; Associate, Poppenhusen, Johnston, Thompson & Raymond, 1948–50; Associate Counsel, sub-cttee on Study Monopoly Power, Cttee on Judiciary, US House of Reps, 1951; Partner, Rothschild, Hart, Stevens & Barry, 1952–70; US Circuit Judge, 1970–75. Lectr, anti-trust law, Northwestern Univ. Sch. of Law, 1953; Univ. of Chicago Law Sch., 1954–55; Mem., Attorney-Gen.'s Nat. Cttee to study Anti-Trust Laws, 1953–55. Mem., Chicago Bar Assoc. (2nd Vice-Pres. 1970). Order of Coif, Phi Beta Kappa, Psi Upsilon, Phi Delta Phi. Presidential

Medal of Freedom (USA), 2012. *Publications:* chap. in book, Mr Justice (ed Dunham and Kurland); contrib. to Antitrust Developments: a supp. to Report of Attorney-Gen.'s Nat. Cttee to Study the Anti-trust Laws, 1955–58; various articles etc, in Ill. Law Rev., Proc. confs, and reports. *Recreations:* flying, tennis, bridge, reading, travel. *Address:* c/o Supreme Court of the United States, Washington, DC 20543, USA.

STEVENS, John Williams, CB 1988; Member, 1989–90, Deputy Chairman, 1991–94, Civil Service Appeal Board; *b* 27 Feb. 1929; *s* of John Williams and Kathleen Stevens; *m* 1949, Grace Stevens; one *s* one *d*. *Educ:* St Ives School. Min. of Supply, 1952; UK Defence Res. and Supply Staff, Australia, 1958–61; HM Treasury, 1966; Civil Service Dept, 1969–73; Price Commn, 1973–74; Head of Personnel, Stock Exchange, 1975–76; Principal Private Sec. to Lord Pres. of the Council and Leader of the House of Commons, 1977–79, to Chancellor of Duchy of Lancaster and Leader of the House, 1979–80; Principal Estabts and Finance Officer, Cabinet Office, 1980–89; Under Sec. 1984. *Recreations:* Cornwall, reading, theatre. *Address:* 14 Highbury Crescent, Portsmouth Road, Camberley, Surrey GU15 1JZ.

STEVENS, Sir Kenneth (Allen), KNZM 2009 (DCNZM 2007); Owner and Manager, Glidepath Ltd, 1972–2008; Chairman, Glidepath Group, since 1997; *b* Christchurch, NZ, 1 Feb. 1944; *s* of Arthur Edward Stevens and Marion Glover Cotter; *m* Glenice Jean McKenzie; one *s* one *d*. *Educ:* Seddon Memorial Tech. Coll., Auckland. Chm., NZ Aviation Jt Action Gp, 1994–97. Chairman: Export New Zealand, 2008– (Mem. Bd, NZ Export Inst., 1980–83); Howick Ltd, 2008–; Member: Bd of Trustees, Asia NZ Foundn, 2007–; Bd, Icehouse, 2008–. Business Champion, Export Year 2007, 2006–07. Mem., Experimental Aircraft Assoc., Milwaukee, 2003–12. Trustee: Vex Robotics, NZ, 2010–; NZ Business Mentors, 2010–. *Recreations:* Rugby, boating, cricket, mentoring exporters. *Address:* Glidepath Group, 30 Cartwright Road, Glen Eden, Auckland 0602, New Zealand. *T:* (9) 8183354, *Fax:* (9) 8189994. *E:* ken.stevens@glidepathgroup.com. *Club:* Royal New Zealand Yacht Squadron.

STEVENS, Lewis David, MBE 1982; management and industrial engineering consultant (self-employed), since 1979; *b* 13 April 1936; *s* of Richard and Winnifred Stevens; *m* 1959, Margaret Eileen Gibson; two *s* one *d*. *Educ:* Oldbury Grammar Sch.; Liverpool Univ.; Lanchester Coll. RAF 1956–58. Various engrg cos, mainly in industrial engrg and production management positions, 1958–79. Mem., Nuneaton Borough Council, 1966–72. MP (C) Nuneaton, 1983–92; contested (C) Nuneaton, 1992. *Address:* 151 Sherbourne Avenue, Nuneaton, Warwicks CV10 9JN. *T:* (024) 7674 4541.

STEVENS, Marie Adelaide Grizella; regulatory consultant to gaming industry, since 2004; Director, Prometheus Bound Ltd, since 2010; *b* London, 5 July 1950; *d* of David Henry John Griffiths Powell and Judith Amy Powell (*née* Lennard); *m* 1st, 1973, David John Stevens (marr. diss. 1988); one *s* two *d*; 2nd, 1988, David Cooper; one *s* one *d*, and one step *s* one step *d*. *Educ:* Wadhurst Coll.; London Sch. of Econs and Pol Sci. (LLB Hons); Coll. of Law. Admitted solicitor, 1974; Slaughter and May, 1972–77; Gp Solicitor, Ladbrokes, 1987–97. Chm., 888 Hldgs plc, 2005–06. Mem., Gaming Bd for GB, 1999–2004; Chm., Adv. Bd, Global Leaders in Law, 2010–. Trustee, Royal Armouries, 2008–12. *Recreations:* children and grandchildren, dollhouses, vintage fairs, 20th century English women literature, making lists. *Address:* 3 Wilton Crescent, SW1X 8RN. *T:* (020) 7245 0005. *E:* mariestevens@btconnect.com. *Clubs:* Annabel's, Union.

STEVENS, Philip Simeon St J.; *see* St John-Stevens.

STEVENS, Dr Robert Bocking; Of Counsel, Covington & Burling, Washington and London, since 1992; Senior Research Fellow, Constitution Unit, University College London, since 2001; *b* 8 June 1933; *s* of John Skevington Stevens and Enid Dorothy Stevens; *m* 1st, 1961, Rosemary Anne Wallace (marr. diss. 1982); one *s* one *d*; 2nd, 1985, Katherine Booth; one *d*. *Educ:* Oakham Sch.; Keble Coll., Oxford (BA 1956; BCL 1956; MA 1959; DCL 1984; Hon. Fellow, 1983); Yale Univ. (LLM 1958). Called to the Bar, Gray's Inn, 1956, Bencher, 1999. Yale University: Asst Prof. of Law, 1959–61; Associate Prof., 1961–65; Prof., 1965–76; Provost, Tulane Univ., 1976–78; Pres., Haverford Coll., 1978–87; Chancellor, Univ. of Calif., Santa Cruz, 1987–91; Master, Pembroke Coll., Oxford, 1993–2001 (Hon. Fellow, 2001). Mem., Nat. Council of the Humanities, 1982–88. Chairman: Marshall Aid Commemoration Commn, 1995–2000; Sulgrave Manor Trust, 2002–06. Gov., Abingdon Sch., 1993–2000. Hon. LLD: NY Law Sch., 1984; Villanova, 1985; Pennsylvania, 1987; Hon. DLitt Haverford Coll., 1991. *Publications:* (with B. S. Yamey) The Restrictive Practices Court, 1965; (with B. Abel-Smith) Lawyers and the Courts, 1967; (with B. Abel-Smith) In Search of Justice, 1968; Income Security, 1970; (with R. A. Stevens) Welfare Medicine in America, 1974; Law and Politics, 1978; The American Law School, 1983; The Independence of the Judiciary, 1993; The English Judges, 2002, 2nd edn 2005; From University to Uni, 2004, rev. edn 2005. *Recreations:* history, politics, scepticism. *Address:* 19 Burgess Mead, Oxford OX2 6XP. *T:* (01865) 558420; Covington & Burling, 265 Strand, WC2R 1BH. *T:* (020) 7067 2000. *Clubs:* Reform; Elizabethan (New Haven, Conn).

STEVENS, Rear Adm. Robert Patrick, CB 2000; Managing Director, Stevens Marine Ltd, since 2013; *b* 14 March 1948; *s* of late Major Philip Joseph Stevens, RMP and Peggy Stevens (*née* Marshall); *m* 1973, Vivien Roberts; one *s* one *d*. *Educ:* Prince Rupert Sch., Wilhelmshaven; BRNC, Dartmouth. Commanding Officer: HMS Odin, 1979–81; comdg officers qualifying course, HMS Dolphin, 1983–85; HMS Torbay, 1985–88; USN War Coll., 1988–89; Asst Dir, Strategic Systems, MoD, 1989–91; Captain: 7th Frigate Sqdn and CO, HMS Argonaut, 1992–93; Navy Presentation team, 1993–94; Dir, Jt Warfare, MoD, 1994–98; FO, Submarines, Comdr Submarines (NATO), Eastern Atlantic and NW, and COS (Ops) to C-in-C Fleet, 1998–2001; COS to Comdr Allied Naval Forces Southern Europe, and Sen. British Officer Southern Reg., 2002–05. CEO, British Marine Fedn, 2006–12. Chm., Solent Marine Forum, 2013–14. Pres., RN Football Assoc., 1998–2005; Trustee, 1851 Trust (Americas Cup), 2014–. Mem., RNSA. Liveryman, Shipwrights' Co., 2006–. *Recreations:* tennis, ski-ing, sailing. *Address:* Long Reach, Hensting Lane, Fishers Pond, Hants SO50 7HH. *Clubs:* Royal Navy of 1765 and 1785; South West Shingles Yacht; Meon Valley Golf.

STEVENS, Simon Laurence; Chief Executive, NHS England, since 2014; *b* Birmingham, 4 Aug. 1966; *s* of Laurence and Vivien Stevens; *m* 1998, Maggie Thurer; one *s* one *d*. *Educ:* St Bartholomew's Comprehensive Sch., Newbury; Balliol Coll., Oxford (BA Hons PPE 1987; MA); Strathclyde Univ. (MBA 1996). Econ. develt analyst, Guyana, 1987–88; NHS Mgt Trng Scheme, Newcastle upon Tyne and Asst Gen. Manager, NW Durham Hosps, 1988–90; Gen. Manager, Psychiatric Hosps, Northumberland and N Tyneside, 1990–92; Gp Manager, Guy's and St Thomas' Hosps, 1992–94; Harkness Fellow, Columbia Univ./NYC Health Dept, 1994–95; Exec. Dir, E Sussex, Brighton and Hove HA, 1995–97; Policy Advr to Sec. of State for Health, DoH, 1997–2001; Prime Minister's Health Advr, 10 Downing St Policy Unit, 2001–04; Pres., United Health Europe, 2004–06; CEO, United Healthcare Medicare, USA, 2006–09; Pres., Global Health and Exec. Vice Pres., United Health Gp, USA, 2009–14. Vis. Prof., LSE, 2004–08. Mem. (Lab), Lambeth LBC, 1998–2002. Director: Medicare Rights Center, NY, 2009–13; Amil, Brazil, 2012–13; Commonwealth Fund, NY, 2013–. Director: Minnesota Histl Soc., 2008–13; Minnesota Opera, 2008–13. Trustee: King's Fund, 2007–11; Nuffield Trust, 2012–14. DUniv Birmingham, 2015. *Recreations:* family, books, cooking without recipes. *Address:* c/o NHS England, 80 London Road, SE1 6LH. *E:* england.ce@nhs.net.

STEVENS, Timothy John, OBE 2000; FSA; Director, Gilbert Collection, Somerset House, 2002–08 (Executive Director, Hermitage Rooms, 2001–03); *b* 17 Jan. 1940; *s* of Seymour Stevens and Joan Rudgard; *m* 1969, Caroline Sankey; twin *s*. *Educ:* King's Sch., Canterbury; Hertford Coll., Oxford (MA); Courtauld Inst., Univ. of London (Academic Diploma, History of Art). Walker Art Gallery: Asst Keeper of British Art, 1964–65; Keeper of Foreign Art, 1965–67; Dep. Dir, 1967–70; Dir, 1971–74; Dir, Merseyside CC Art Galls, 1974–86; Dep. Dir, Nat. Museums and Galleries on Merseyside, 1986–87; Keeper of Art, Nat. Mus. of Wales, 1987–94; Asst Dir (Collections), V&A Mus., 1994–2000. Trustee: NACF, 2000–11; Leeds Castle Foundn, 2008–. Hon. LittD Liverpool, 1985. Chevalier de l'Ordre des Arts et des Lettres (France), 1988. *Recreation:* gardening. *Address:* Luddenham Court, Faversham, Kent ME13 0TH.

STEVENS, Rt Rev. Timothy John; Bishop of Leicester, 1999–2015; *b* 31 Dec. 1946; *s* of late Ralph and Jean Ursula Stevens; *m* 1973, Wendi Kathleen; one *s* one *d*. *Educ:* Chigwell Sch.; Selwyn Coll., Cambridge (BA 1968; MA 1972); Ripon Hall, Oxford (Dip Th). BOAC, 1968–72; FCO, 1972–73. Ordained priest, 1976; Curate, East Ham, 1976–79; Team Vicar, Upton Park, 1979–80; Team Rector, Canvey Island, 1980–88; Bp of Chelmsford's Urban Officer, 1988–91; Archdeacon of West Ham, 1991–95; Bishop Suffragan of Dunwich, 1995–99. Hon. Canon of Chelmsford, 1987–95. Chm., Urban Bishops' Panel, Gen. Synod of C of E, 2001–06; Member: Archbps' Council, 2006–15; Standing Cttee, House of Bishops, 2006–10; Convenor of the Lords Spiritual, H of L, 2009–15. Chm., Council, Children's Soc., 2004–10. Mem. Bd of Govs, De Montfort Univ., 2006–13; Chm. Bd of Govs, Westcott House Theol Coll., 2006–12. Took seat in H of L, 2004. Hon. DCL De Montfort, 2002; Hon. DLitt Leicester, 2003. *Recreations:* golf, cricket. *Address:* 62 Horringer Road, Bury St Edmunds, Suffolk IP33 2DR.

STEVENS-HOARE, Michelle, (Brie); QC 2013; *b* Wokingham, 21 Oct. 1963; *d* of Edward John Stevens-Hoare and Jacqueline Stevens-Hoare; civil partnership 2006, Paula Louise Ives. *Educ:* Kendrick Girls' Grammar Sch., Reading; London Sch. of Econs and Pol Sci. (LLB, LLM); Inns of Court Sch. of Law. Called to the Bar, Middle Temple, 1986; in practice as a barrister specialising in property law, 1986–. First-tier Tribunal Judge, Property Chamber (Land Registration) (pt-time), 2005–. Ambassador, Stonewall, 2013–; Mem. Bd, Freehold, 2012–. *Publications:* (contrib.) The Law and Practice of Compromise, 5th edn 2002 to 7th edn 2010; (contrib.) Cousins: the law of mortgages, 2nd edn 2001 to 3rd edn 2010. *Recreations:* roller coasters, motorbikes, international travel, good food. *Address:* Hardwicke, New Square, Lincoln's Inn, WC2A 3SB. *T:* (020) 7242 2523, *Fax:* (020) 7691 1234. *E:* brie@hardwicke.co.uk.

STEVENSON, family name of **Barons Stevenson of Balmacara** and **Stevenson of Coddenham**.

STEVENSON OF BALMACARA, Baron *cr* 2010 (Life Peer), of Little Missenden in the County of Buckinghamshire; **Robert Wilfrid, (Wilf), Stevenson;** Senior Policy Adviser, Prime Minister's Office, 2008–10; *b* 19 April 1947; *s* of James Alexander Stevenson and Elizabeth Anne Stevenson (*née* Macrae); *m* 1st, 1972, Jennifer Grace Antonio (marr. diss. 1979); 2nd, 1991, (Elizabeth) Ann Minogue, *qv*; one *s* two *d*. *Educ:* Edinburgh Academy; University College, Oxford (MA Natural Sciences, Chemistry); Napier Polytechnic (ACCA). Research Officer, Edinburgh Univ. Students' Assoc., 1970–74; Sec., Napier Coll., Edinburgh, 1974–87; Dep. Dir, 1987–88, Dir, 1988–97, BFI; Dir, Smith Inst., 1997–2008. Chm., Foundn for Credit Counselling, 2010–15. Governor: Prestwood Lodge Sch., 2008–10; Chiltern Way Fedn Sch., 2010–14. Hon. DArts Napier, 2008. *Publications:* (ed) Gordon Brown Speeches, 2006; (ed) Moving Britain Forward, 2006; (ed) The Change We Choose: speeches 2007–2009, 2010. *Recreations:* cinema, bee keeping, bridge. *Address:* Missenden House, Little Missenden, Amersham, Bucks HP7 0RD. *T:* (01494) 890689. *E:* wilf@wilfstevenson.co.uk.

STEVENSON OF BALMACARA, Lady; *see* Minogue, E. A.

STEVENSON OF CODDENHAM, Baron *cr* 1999 (Life Peer), of Coddenham, in the county of Suffolk; **Henry Dennistoun Stevenson, (Dennis),** Kt 1998; CBE 1981; DL; *b* 19 July 1945; *s* of Alexander James Stevenson and Sylvia Florence Stevenson (*née* Ingleby); *m* 1972, Charlotte Susan, *d* of Hon. Sir Peter Vanneck, GBE, CB, AFC, AE; four *s*. *Educ:* Glenalmond; King's Coll., Cambridge (MA). Chairman: SRU Gp of cos, 1972–96; GPA, then AerFi, Gp, 1993–2000; Pearson plc, 1997–2005 (Dir, 1986–97); Dir, Halifax plc, 1999–2009; Chm., HBOS plc, 2001–09; Gov., Bank of Scotland, 2006–09; Director: British Technology Gp, 1979–89; Tyne Tees Television, 1982–87; Manpower Inc. (formerly Blue Arrow), 1988–2006; Thames Television plc, 1991–93; J. Rothschild Assurance plc, 1991–97; J. Rothschild Assurance Hldgs plc, 1991–99; English Partnerships, 1993–99; Bd, BSkyB Gp plc, 1994–2000; Lazard Bros, 1997–2000; Whitehall Trust Ltd, 1997–2004; St James's Place Capital, 1997–2002 (Hon. Pres., 2002–04); Economist Newspapers, 1998–2011; Western Union Co., 2006–12; Loudwater Investment Partners Ltd, 2007–12; Culture and Sport Glasgow, 2007–09; Cloaca Maxima Ltd, 2010–13; Waterstones Hldgs Ltd, 2011–; Inter Mediate, 2011–. Chm., Trustees, Tate Gall., 1989–98. Chairman: Newton Aycliffe and Peterlee New Town Develt Corp., 1971–80; Intermediate Technology Develt Gp, 1983–90; Director: Nat. Building Agency, 1977–81; LDDC, 1981–88. Chairman: govt working party on role of voluntary movements and youth in the envmt, 1971, '50 Million Volunteers' (HMSO); Ind. Adv. Cttee on Pop Fests, 1972–76, 'Pop Festivals, Report and Code of Practice' (HMSO); Advr on Agricl Marketing to Minister of Agric., 1979–83; Special Advr to PM and Sec. of State for Educn on use of IT in Educn, 1997–2000; Chairman: H of L Appts Commn, 2000–09; Arts and Media Honours Cttee, 2008–12; Member: Panel on Takeovers and Mergers, 1992–2000; Bd, British Council, 1996–2003; Standards Cttee, Westminster CC, 2008–12; H of L Works of Art Cttee, 2009–14. Chairman: NAYC, 1973–81; Sinfonia 21 (formerly Docklands Sinfonietta), 1989–99; Aldeburgh Music (formerly Aldeburgh Prodns), 2000–12; MQ: Transforming Mental Health, 2013–; Director: Glyndebourne Prodns, 1998–; London Music Masters, 2011–; Inst. for Govt, 2008–13. Pres., Aldeburgh Music, 2012–. Trustee: Tate Gall. Foundn, 1998–; Horse's Mouth, 2006–. Mem. Admin. Council, Royal Jubilee Trusts, 1978–80. Chancellor, Univ. of the Arts London (formerly London Institute), 2000–10. Governor: LSE, 1995–99; London Business Sch., 1999–2002. DL Suffolk, 2008. *Recreation:* home. *Clubs:* Brooks's, Garrick, MCC.

STEVENSON, (Andrew) John; MP (C) Carlisle, since 2010; *b* Aberdeen, 4 July 1963; *s* of Andrew Lochart Stevenson and Jane Wilson Stevenson. *Educ:* Aberdeen Grammar Sch.; Dundee Univ. (MA Hons Hist. and Pols); Chester Law Coll. Admitted solicitor, 1990; Partner, Bendles Solicitors, Carlisle, 1994–. Mem. (C) Carlisle CC, 1999–2010. *Recreation:* sport. *Address:* Wood Villa, Great Corby, Carlisle CA4 8LL. *E:* john.stevenson.mp@parliament.uk.

STEVENSON, Anne Katharine, (Mrs Peter Lucas); poet; *b* Cambridge, England, 3 Jan. 1933; *d* of Charles Leslie Stevenson, philosopher, and Louise Destler Stevenson; *m* 1987, Peter David Lucas; two *s* one *d* by previous marriages. *Educ:* Univ. of Michigan, Ann Arbor (BA 1954, Major Hopwood Award 1954; MA 1961; Athena Award for dist. alumni 1990). School teacher, 1955–61; Advertising Manager (as Mrs A. Hitchcock), A&C Black Publishers Ltd, 1956–57; Fellow: Radcliff Inst., Harvard, 1970–71; in Writing, Univ. of Dundee, 1973–75; Lady Margaret Hall, Oxford, 1975–77; Bulmershe Coll., Reading, 1977–78; Northern Arts Fellow, Newcastle and Durham, 1982–86; Fellow in Writing, Edinburgh Univ., 1987–89. FEA 2002. Hon. Fellow, St Chad's Coll., Durham Univ., 2010. Hon. DLitt: Loughborough, 1997; Durham, 2005; Hull, 2006; Michigan, 2008; Newcastle, 2010; London, 2010. Poetry

Award, Scottish Arts Council, 1974; Cholmondeley Award, Soc. of Authors, 1997; Writer's Award, Northern Rock Foundn, 2002; Neglected Masters Award, Poetry Foundn, USA, 2007; Lannan Literary Award for Lifetime Achievement for Poetry, 2007; Aiken-Taylor Award, Sewanee Rev., 2007. *Publications: poetry:* Living in America, 1965; Reversals, 1967; Correspondences, 1974; Travelling Behind Glass, 1974; Enough of Green, 1977; Minute by Glass Minute, 1982; The Fiction Makers, 1985; Winter Time (pamphlet), 1986; Selected Poems, 1987; The Other House, 1990; Four and a Half Dancing Men, 1993; Collected Poems, 1996; Granny Scarecrow, 2000; Hearing with my Fingers (pamphlet), 2001; A Report from the Border, 2003; Poems 1955–2005, 2006; A Lament for the Makers, 2006; Stone Milk, 2007; Selected Poems, 2008; Astonishment, 2012; *criticism and biography:* Elizabeth Bishop, 1966; Bitter Fame: a life of Sylvia Plath, 1989; Five Looks at Elizabeth Bishop, 1998, 2nd edn 2006; Between the Iceberg and the Ship (essays in criticism), 1998; trans., Eugene Dubnov, The Thousand-Year Minutes, 2013; contrib. articles and revs to TLS, Poetry Nation Rev., Poetry Rev., Hudson Rev., Michigan Qly Rev., and to many other poetry pubns in UK and USA; *festschrift:* The Way You Say the World, 2003; (ed Angela Leighton) Voyages over Voices: critical essays on Anne Stevenson, 2010. *Recreations:* good music, good company, laughter. *Address:* 38 Western Hill, Durham DH1 4RJ. *T:* (0191) 386 2115; Pwllymarch, Llanbedr, Gwynedd, N Wales LL45 2PL. *T:* (01341) 241208.

STEVENSON, Christopher Terence S.; *see* Sinclair-Stevenson.

STEVENSON, Prof. David John, PhD; FRS 1993; Marvin L. Goldberger (formerly George Van Osdol) Professor of Planetary Science, California Institute of Technology, since 1995; *b* 2 Sept. 1948; *s* of Ian McIvor Stevenson and Gwenyth (*née* Carroll). *Educ:* Rongotai Coll.; Victoria Univ., Wellington, NZ (BSc, BSc Hons, MSc); Cornell Univ., NY (PhD). Res. Fellow, ANU, 1976–78; Asst Prof., UCLA, 1978–80; California Institute of Technology: Associate Prof., 1980–84; Prof. of Planetary Science, 1984–95; Chm., Div. of Geol and Planetary Scis, 1989–94. Fellow, Amer. Geophysical Union, 1986 (Whipple Award, 1994; Hess Medal, 1998). Hon. DSc Victoria Univ. of Wellington, 2002. Urey Prize, Amer. Astronomical Soc., 1984. *Publications:* numerous papers in learned jls, principally in earth and planetary scis. *Recreations:* hiking, biking. *Address:* Division of Geological and Planetary Sciences, California Institute of Technology, Pasadena, CA 91125, USA. *T:* (626) 3956534.

STEVENSON, Prof. Freda Kathryn, DPhil; FRCPath, FMedSci; Professor of Immunology, and Consultant (non-clinical) Immunologist, University of Southampton, since 1997; *b* 27 April 1939; *d* of Richard Pollard Hartley and Joyce Elizabeth Hartley; *m* 1963, George Telford Stevenson, *qv*; three *s*. *Educ:* Univ. of Manchester (BSc 1960, MSc 1961); St Hugh's Coll., Oxford (DPhil 1964). FRCPath 1995. Lectr in Biochem., Univ. of Sydney, 1965–67; Post-doctoral Fellow, Univ. of Oxford, and Lectr in Biochem., Oriel Coll., Oxford, 1967–70; Southampton General Hospital: MRC Staff (external), 1970–73, Tenovus Post-doctoral Fellow, 1973–81, Tenovus Lab.; PSO, Regl Immunology Service, 1981–86; Top Grade SO, 1986–97; Reader in Immunology, Southampton Univ., 1986–97. Mem., Assoc. of Sen. Mems, St Hugh's Coll., Oxford. FMedSci 2000. *Publications:* over 200 peer-reviewed articles, mainly in internat. jls, in field of immunology with focus on strategies to vaccinate against cancer using genetic technology and on the nature and behaviour of human B-cell malignancies. *Recreations:* music, literature, walking. *Address:* University of Southampton, Cancer Sciences Division, Somers Cancer Research Building, Mailpoint 891, Southampton General Hospital, Tremona Road, Southampton SO16 6YD. *T:* (023) 8079 6923, *Fax:* (023) 8070 1385. *E:* fs@soton.ac.uk; Sudbury House, Sudbury Lane, Longworth, Abingdon OX13 5EL. *T:* (01865) 820646.

STEVENSON, Prof. George Telford; Professor of Immunochemistry, Faculty of Medicine, University of Southampton, 1974–97, now Emeritus; *b* 18 April 1932; *s* of Ernest George Stevenson and Mary Josephine Madden; *m* 1963, Freda Kathryn Hartley (*see* F. K. Stevenson); three *s*. *Educ:* North Sydney High Sch.; Univ. of Sydney (MB, BS; MD); Univ. of Oxford (DPhil). Resident MO, 1955–56, Resident Pathologist, 1957, Sydney Hosp.; Research Fellow, Dept of Medicine, Univ. of Sydney, 1958–61; Nuffield Dominions Demonstrator, Dept of Biochemistry, Univ. of Oxford, 1962–64; Sen. Research Fellow, Dept of Biochemistry, Univ. of Sydney, 1965–66; Scientific Staff, MRC Immunochemistry Unit, Univ. of Oxford, 1967–70; Dir, Tenovus Research Lab., Southampton Gen. Hosp., 1970–97; Consultant Immunologist, Southampton Univ. Hosps, 1976–97, now Hon. Consultant Immunologist. Hammer Prize for Cancer Research (jtly) (Armand Hammer Foundn, LA), 1982. *Publications:* Immunological Investigation of Lymphoid Neoplasms (with J. L. Smith and T. J. Hamblin), 1983; research papers on immunology and cancer, considered mainly at molecular level. *Address:* Sudbury House, Sudbury Lane, Longworth, Abingdon OX13 5EL. *T:* (01865) 820646.

STEVENSON, George William; *b* 30 Aug. 1938; *s* of Harold and Elsie May Stevenson; *m* 1st, 1958, Doreen June (decd); two *s* one *d*; 2nd, 1991, Pauline Brookes. *Educ:* Uttoxeter Road Primary School; Queensberry Road Secondary School, Stoke-on-Trent. Pottery caster, 1953–57; coal miner, 1957–66; transport driver, 1966–84; shop steward, TGWU 5/24 Branch, 1968–84 (Mem., 1964–; Chm., 1975–81). Deputy Leader: Stoke-on-Trent City Council, 1972–83; Staffs County Council, 1981–85. MEP (Lab) Staffs East, 1984–94; Pres., Eur. Parlt Delegn for Relations with S Asia, 1989–92 (Vice-Pres., 1984–89). MP (Lab) Stoke on Trent South, 1992–2005. Member, Select Committee: on European Legislation, 1995–2005; on Environment, Transport and the Regions, 1997–2005; Mem., Speaker's Panel of Chairmen. Chairman: All-Party Tibet Gp, 1995–2005; PLP Agric. Cttee, 1993–2001. *Recreations:* walking, cinema, travel, reading.

STEVENSON, Sir Hugh (Alexander), Kt 2010; Chairman, Equitas Ltd, 1998–2009; *b* 7 Sept. 1942; *s* of William Hugh Stevenson and Elizabeth Margaret (*née* Wallace); *m* 1965, Catherine May Peacock; two *s* two *d*. *Educ:* Harrow Sch.; University Coll., Oxford (BA 1964; Hon. Fellow 1999); Harvard Business School (AMP 103). Admitted as solicitor, 1967; with Linklaters & Paines, 1964–70; with S. G. Warburg & Co., 1970–92; Dir, S. G. Warburg Gp plc, 1986–95; Chairman: Mercury Asset Management Gp plc, 1992–98 (Dir, 1986–98); The Merchants Trust plc, 2000–10 (Dir, 1999–2010); Standard Life Investments, 2004–08 (Dir, 2000–04); Dir, Standard Life plc (formerly Standard Life Assurance), 1999–2008. Director: British Museum Co., 1984–2006; Securities Inst., 1994–98 (Hon. FSI 1998); IMRO, 1995–2000; FSA, 2004–10 (Dep. Chm., 2009–10). Mem., Adv. Cttee on Business Appts, 2010–15 (Interim Chm., 2014). Chm., Instnl Fund Managers Assoc., 1998–99. Hon. Treas., Inst. of Child Health, 1991–96 (Hon. Fellow 1996); Chairman: The Sick Children's Trust, 1982–99; Gt Ormond St Hosp. Redevelt Adv. Bd (formerly Gt Ormond St Hosp. Develt Trust), 1999–2006; Special Trustee, Gt Ormond St Hosp., 1996–2007. Hon. Treas., Millennium Bridge Trust, 1998–2002. Chm., Swinley Forest Golf Club, 2007–. Hon. Fellow, UCL, 2000.

See also R. W. Ellis, Dame E. A. Griffiths.

STEVENSON, (James Alexander) Stewart; Member (SNP) Banffshire and Buchan Coast, Scottish Parliament, since 2011 (Banff and Buchan, June 2001–2011); *b* 15 Oct. 1946; *s* of late James Thomas Middleton Stevenson, MB ChB and Helen Mary Berry MacGregor, MA; *m* 1969, Sandra Isabel Pirie, MA. *Educ:* Bell Baxter Sch., Cupar; Univ. of Aberdeen (MA 1969). Various technology posts, later Dir of Technology Innovation, Bank of Scotland, 1969–99; pt-time Lectr, Sch. of Mgt, Heriot-Watt Univ., 2001–. Scottish Parliament: contested (SNP) Linlithgow, 1999; Shadow Dep. Minister for Health and Social Justice, 2003–07; Minister for Transport, Infrastructure and Climate Change, 2007–10, for Envmt and Climate Change, 2011–12. Member: Rural Develt Cttee, 2001–03; Justice Cttee, 2001–03. Mem., SNP, 1961–. *Recreations:* computing, travel, public speaking. *Address:* Scottish Parliament, Edinburgh EH99 1SP; (constituency) Unit 8, Burnside Business Centre, Burnside Road, Peterhead, Aberdeenshire AB42 3AW. *Clubs:* Edinburgh Flying; Moray Flying.

STEVENSON, Prof. Jane Barbara, (Mrs P. R. K. A. Davidson), PhD; Regius Professor of Humanity, University of Aberdeen, since 2007; *b* 12 Feb. 1959; *d* of John Lynn Stevenson and Winifred Mary Stevenson (*née* Temple); *m* 1989, Prof. Peter Robert Keith Andrew Davidson, *qv*. *Educ:* Haberdashers' Aske's Sch. for Girls, Elstree; Newnham Coll., Cambridge (BA 1981; PhD 1986). Drapers' Res. Fellow, Pembroke Coll., Cambridge, 1985–88; Lectr in Late Antique and Early Medieval Hist., Univ. of Sheffield, 1988–95; Sen. Res. Fellow, Univ. of Warwick, 1995–2000; University of Aberdeen: Reader in English, 2000–02; Reader in Postclassical Latin and Renaissance Studies, Sch. of Divinity, Hist. and Philosophy, 2002–05; Prof. of Latin, 2005–07. *Publications:* Women Writers in English Literature, 1992; The Laterculus Malalianus and the School of Archbishop Theodore, 1995; Several Deceptions, 1999; London Bridges, 2000; Astraea, 2001; The Pretender, 2002; The Empress of the Last Days, 2003; Good Women, 2005; Women Latin Poets: language, gender and authority from antiquity to the Eighteenth Century, 2005; Edward Burra: Twentieth Century eye, 2007; edited with Peter Davidson: Walter Scott, Old Mortality, 1993; The Closet of Sir Kenelm Digby, Kt, Opened, 1997; Early Modern Women Poets, 2001. *Recreations:* sleeping, being nice to cats. *Address:* Burnside House, Turriff, Aberdeenshire AB53 5PP. *T:* (01888) 562244. *E:* janebstevenson@yahoo.com.

STEVENSON, Dr John, FRHistS; Reader in History, University of Oxford, 1994–2006; President, William Cobbett Society, since 2013; *b* 26 Sept. 1946; *s* of John Stevenson and Bridget Stevenson; *m* 1971, Jacqueline Patricia Johns. *Educ:* Boteler GS, Warrington; Worcester Coll., Oxford (MA 1968; DPhil 1975). Lectr in Hist., Oriel Coll., Oxford, 1971–76; Lectr, 1976, Sen. Lectr, 1979, Reader in History, 1986–90, Univ. of Sheffield; Fellow and Tutor, Worcester Coll., Oxford, 1990–2006; Fellow, Greyfriars Hall, Oxford, 2006–08; Vis. Fellow, Oriel Coll., Oxford, 2007–09. Editor, English Historical Rev., 1996–2000. *Publications:* (with R. E. Quinault) Popular Protest and Public Order, 1974; Social Conditions in Britain between the Wars, 1977; London in the Age of Reform, 1977; (jtly) Crime and Law in Nineteenth Century Britain, 1978; Popular Disturbances in England, 1700–1870, 1979, 2nd edn 1992; (with M. Bentley) High and Low Politics in Modern Britain, 1983; British Society 1914–45, 1984; (with A. J. Fletcher) Order and Disorder in early modern England, 1985; (with S. Salter), The Working Class and Politics in Europe and America 1929–1945, 1990; The Macmillan Dictionary of British and European History since 1914, 1991; (with A. O'Day) Irish Historical Documents since 1800, 1992; Third Party Politics since 1945, 1993; (with J. C. Binfield) Sport, Culture and Politics, 1993; (with J. Gregory) The Longman Companion to the Eighteenth Century, 1999; (jtly) Advancing with the Army 1790–1850, 2006; with C. P. Cook: The Slump: society and politics during the Depression, 1977, new edn 2009; The Longman Atlas of Modern British History, 1978; British Historical Facts 1760–1830, 1980; The Longman Handbook of Modern British History 1714–1980, 1983, 4th edn 2001; The Longman Handbook to Modern European History 1760–1985, 1987, 2nd edn 1998; British Historical Facts 1688–1760, 1988; The Longman Handbook of World History since 1914, 1991; The Longman Companion to Britain since 1945, 1996, 2nd edn 2000; The Longman Handbook of the Modern World, 1998; The History of Europe, 2002; The Longman Handbook of Twentieth Century Europe, 2003; The Routledge Companion to European History since 1763, 2005; The Routledge Companion to World History since 1914, 2005; (jtly) Advancing with the Army, 2006; (with J. Grande and R. Thomas) The Opinions of William Cobbett, 2013; (with C. P. Cook) The History of British Elections since 1689, 2014; (ed with J. Grande) William Cobbett, Romanticism and the Enlightenment: contexts and legacy, 2015. *Recreations:* book-collecting, gardening. *Address:* Merrifield, Down St Mary, Crediton, Devon EX17 6ED.

STEVENSON, John; *see* Stevenson, A. J.

STEVENSON, Joseph Aidan; non-executive Director, Johnson Matthey plc, 1991–95; Chairman, Young Group plc, 1992–95; *b* 19 April 1931; *s* of Robert and Bridget Stevenson; *m* 1956, Marjorie Skinner; one *s* two *d*. *Educ:* Birmingham Univ. (BSc Hons Metallurgy). Instr Lieut, RN, 1955–58. Joined Johnson Matthey, 1958, as development metallurgist; held a number of sen. management, operating and div. dirships within the Johnson Matthey Gp; Gp Exec. Dir, 1982–91; Chief Exec. Officer, 1989–91. Chm. of Govs, Combe Bank Ind. Girls' Sch., Kent, 1985–91. Royal London Society for the Blind: Mem. Council, 1990–98 (Vice-Chm., 1995–98); Special Advr, Workbridge Scheme for employment of blind people, 1998–2005; Chm. Govs, RLSB Coll. of Further Educn (Dorton House), 1995–98. FIMMM (FIM 1990; Mem. Council, 1991–93). Liveryman: Goldsmiths' Co.; Clockmakers' Co. Distinguished Achievement Award, Inst. of Precious Metals, 1989.

STEVENSON, Julia Charlotte; *see* Palca, J. C.

STEVENSON, Juliet Anne Virginia, CBE 1999; actress; Associate Artist, Royal Shakespeare Company; *b* 30 Oct. 1956; partner, Hugh Brody; one *s* one *d*. *Educ:* RADA (Bancroft Gold Medal). With Royal Shakespeare Company, 1978–86: Les Liaisons Dangereuses; As You Like It; Troilus and Cressida; Measure for Measure; A Midsummer Night's Dream; The Witch of Edmonton; Money; Henry IV parts I and II; Once in a Lifetime; The White Guard; Hippolytus; Antony and Cleopatra; The Churchill Play; Breaking the Silence; *other plays* include: Yerma, NT, 1987; Hedda Gabler, NT, 1989; Burn This, Hampstead, transf. Lyric, 1990; Death and the Maiden, Royal Court, transf. Duke of York's, 1991; The Duchess of Malfi, Greenwich, transf. Wyndhams, 1995; Caucasian Chalk Circle, RNT, 1997; Not I, and Footfalls, RSC and European tour, 1998; Private Lives, RNT, 1999; The Country, 2000, Alice Trilogy, 2005, Royal Court; The Seagull, NT, 2006; Duet for One, Almeida, transf. Gielgud, 2009; The Heretic, Royal Court, 2011; Happy Days, Young Vic, 2014, 2015; *films* include: Drowning by Numbers, 1988; Ladder of Swords, 1990; Truly, Madly, Deeply, 1991; The Trial, 1993; The Secret Rapture, 1994; Emma, 1996; Bend It Like Beckham, 2002; Food of Love, 2002; Nicholas Nickleby, 2003; Mona Lisa Smile, 2004; Being Julia, 2004; Pierrepoint, 2006; Breaking and Entering, 2006; Infamous, 2007; And When Did You Last See Your Father?, 2007; The Secret of Moonacre, 2008; Desert Flower, 2009; The Letters, 2013; Diana, 2013; several television rôles. *Publications:* (jtly) Clamorous Voices, 1988; (jtly) Fifty Shades of Feminism, 2013.

STEVENSON, Katharine Jane; *see* Marshall, K. J.

STEVENSON, Michael Charles; global education consultant, since 2013; Vice President of Global Public Sector: Strategy, Education and Healthcare, Cisco Systems, 2012–13 (Vice President of Global Education, 2007–12); *b* 14 Aug. 1960; *s* of Michael Anthony and Ena Elizabeth Stevenson; *m* 1987, Deborah Frances Taylor; one *s* two *d*. *Educ:* Doncaster Grammar Sch.; Christ Church, Oxford (LitHum). British Broadcasting Corporation, 1983–2003: trainee, 1983; Producer, Talks and Documentaries, Radio, 1984; Producer, News and Current Affairs, TV, 1988; Chief Assistant, Policy and Planning Unit, 1990; Dep. Editor, On The Record, 1991; Secretary, 1992–96; Dep. Dir, Regl Broadcasting, 1996–99; Dir of Educn, 1999–2000; Jt Dir, Factual and Learning, 2000–03; Department for Education and Skills: Dir of Strategy and Communications, 2003–05; Dir of Technology and Chief Information Officer, 2005–06. Non-executive Director: Granada Learning, 2007–10; Surrey and Borders Partnership NHS Foundn Trust, 2011–. Sen. Associate, NESTA, 2014–. Expert Advr, OECD, 2014–. Mem. Bd, Re:source, then MLA, 2000–06. Mem. Council, Nat. Coll.

for Sch. Leadership, 2000–03. Sir Huw Wheldon Fellow, Univ. of Wales, 1989; Sen. Res. Fellow, Nat. Centre for Univs and Businesses, 2013–. Hon. Prof., Glasgow Caledonian Univ., 2013–. *Recreation:* sport. *Address:* 49 Thurleigh Road, SW12 8TZ.

STEVENSON, Maj.-Gen. Paul Timothy, OBE 1985 (MBE 1975); Clerk to Carpenters' Co., 1992–2007; *b* 9 March 1940; *s* of Ernest Stevenson and Dorothy Stevenson (*née* Trehearn); *m* 1965, Ann Douglas Drysdale; one *s* one *d*. *Educ:* Bloxham Sch. Commissioned Royal Marines 1958; 41 Commando, 1960; 45 Commando, Aden, 1962; HMS Mohawk, Gulf and W Indies, 1965–68; Army Staff Coll., 1972; 45 Commando, 1973–75; HMS Bulwark, 1975; Instructor, RN Staff Coll., 1978; SO Plans, HQ Land Forces, Falklands Campaign, 1982; CO 42 Commando, 1983; NATO Defence Coll., 1986; Dir, RM Personnel, 1987–88; RCDS 1989; Comdr, British Forces, Falkland Is, 1989–90. Pres., RMA, 1997–2002. Pres., Glos Co., RBL, 2011–14. Modern Pentathlon British Team, 1962–69 (Olympic Team Manager, 1964); Biathlon British Team, 1965. *Recreations:* field sports, golf, gardening, ski-ing. *Address:* Lacys, Wortley, Wotton-under-Edge, Glos GL12 7QP.

STEVENSON, Robert Lindsay, (Robert Lindsay); actor; *b* 13 Dec. 1949; *s* of late Norman Stevenson and Joyce Stevenson; one *d* by Diana Weston; *m* 2006, Rosemarie Ford; two *s*. *Educ:* Gladstone Boys' Sch., Ilkeston; Clarendon Coll.; RADA. *Theatre:* The Roses of Eyam, 1970, Guys and Dolls, 1972, Northcott, Exeter; Godspell, Wyndhams, 1973; The Changeling, Riverside Studios, 1978; Trelawny of the Wells, Old Vic, 1980; How I Got That Story, Hampstead, 1981; Me and My Girl, Adelphi, 1985, NY, 1986 (Laurence Olivier Award, 1985; Tony Award, 1987); Becket, 1991, Cyrano de Bergerac, 1992, Th. Royal, Haymarket; Oliver!, Palladium, 1996 (Laurence Olivier Award, 1997); Richard III, RSC, 1998, Savoy, 1999; Power, RNT, 2003; The Entertainer, Old Vic, 2007; Aristo, Chichester, 2008; Onassis, Novello Th., 2010; The Lion in Winter, Th. Royal, Haymarket, 2011; Dirty Rotten Scoundrels, Savoy, 2014; Royal Exchange, Manchester: The Cherry Orchard; Lower Depths; Hamlet, 1983 (and UK tour); Beaux Stratagem; Philoctetes; Julius Caesar; Leaping Ginger; Three Musketeers. *Films:* That'll Be the Day, 1973; Three for All, 1974; Strike It Rich, 1990; Fierce Creatures, 1997; Remember Me?, 1997; Divorcing Jack, 1998; Wimbledon, 2004; Grace of Monaco, 2014. *Television:* Get Some In, 1975–77; Citizen Smith, 1977; Twelfth Night, 1980; Seconds Out, 1981; All's Well That Ends Well, 1981; A Midsummer Night's Dream, 1981; Cymbeline, 1982; Give Us a Break, 1983; King Lear, 1984; Much Ado About Nothing, 1984; Confessional, 1989; Bert Rigby, You're a Fool, 1989; Nightingales, 1990; GBH, 1991 (BAFTA Award, RTS Award, 1992); Genghis Cohn, 1993; The Wimbledon Poisoner, 1994; Jake's Progress, 1995; The Office, 1996; Brazen Hussies, 1996; Goodbye My Love, 1997; Hornblower, 1998, 1999, 2001, 2003; Oliver Twist, 1999; My Family (11 series), 2000–11; Hawk, 2001; Don't Eat the Neighbours, 2001; Friends and Crocodiles, 2005, 2006; A Very Social Secretary, 2005; Jericho, 2005; Gideon's Daughter, 2006; The Trial of Tony Blair, 2007; Spy, 2011. *Publications:* Letting Go (autobiog.), 2009. *Address:* c/o Hamilton Hodell Ltd, 20 Golden Square, W1F 9JL.

STEVENSON, Stewart; *see* Stevenson, J. A. S.

STEVENSON, Struan John Stirton; author and political consultant; Member (C) Scotland, European Parliament, 1999–2014; *b* 4 April 1948; *s* of late Robert Harvey Ure Stevenson and Elizabeth Robertson (*née* Stirton); *m* 1974, Patricia Anne Taylor; two *s*. *Educ:* Strathallan Sch.; West of Scotland Agricl Coll. (DipAgr 1970). Member (C): Girvan DC, 1970–74; Kyle and Carrick DC, 1974–92 (Leader, 1986–88); Conservative Gp Leader, COSLA, 1986–88; Scottish agriculture spokesman, 1992–97, Scottish spokesman on envmt, transport, media, arts, heritage and tourism, 1997–98, Conservative Party. European Parliament: UK spokesman on fisheries, and dep. UK spokesman on agric., 1999–2002, 2004–14; Chm., 2002–04, Sen. Vice Pres., 2009–14, Fisheries Cttee; Vice-Pres., EPP-ED Gp, 2005–09; President: Climate Change, Biodiversity and Sustainable Develt Intergroup, 2009–14; Delegn for Relations with Iraq, 2009–14. Personal Rep. of Chm.-in-Office Responsible for Envmt, OSCE, 2010. Contested (C): Carrick, Cumnock and Doon Valley, 1987; Edinburgh S, 1992; Dumfries, 1997; NE Scotland, EP elecn, Nov. 1998. Chm., Tuesday Club, 1998–2001 (Hon. Pres., 2001–). Pres., European Iraqi Freedom Assoc., 2014–. Hon. Prof., Semey State Shakarim Univ., Kazakhstan, 2007. Hon. DSc State Med. Acad. of Semipalatinsk, Kazakhstan, 2000. Hon. Citizen, Semipalatinsk, Kazakhstan, 2003. Shapagat Medal, Kazakhstan, 2007. *Publications:* Crying Forever, 2006; The Refugee Crisis in Iraq, 2009; Green Biotechnology: sowing the seeds for a better future, 2010; Stalin's Legacy: the Soviet war on nature, 2012; So Much Wind: the myth of green energy, 2013; Self Sacrifice: life with the Iranian Mojahedin, 2015. *Recreations:* contemporary art, music, opera, poetry, theatre, cinema, photography. *Club:* New (Edinburgh).

STEVENSON, Timothy Edwin Paul, OBE 2004; Lord-Lieutenant of Oxfordshire, since 2008; Chairman, Johnson Matthey plc, since 2011; *b* 14 May 1948; *s* of late Derek Paul Stevenson, CBE; *m* 1973, Marion Emma Lander Johnston; three *d*. *Educ:* Canford Sch., Dorset; Worcester Coll., Oxford (BA Jurisp.). Called to the Bar, Inner Temple, 1971. Burmah Castrol: Asst Gp Legal Advr, 1975–77; Gp Planning Manager, 1977–81; Chief Exec., Castrol España, 1981–85; Marketing Manager, Develt, 1985–86; Manager, Corporate Develt, 1986–88; Chief Exec., Expandite Gp, 1988–90; Chief Exec., Fuels Gp, 1990–93; Dir, Lubricants, 1993–98; Chief Exec., 1998–2000; Chairman: Travis Perkins plc, 2001–10; Morgan Crucible Co. plc, 2006–12. Non-executive Director: DfES, 1997–2004; Partnerships UK Ltd, 2000–04; Tribal Gp plc, 2004–08; Sen. Ind. Dir, and Chm. Audit Cttee, National Express, 2001–05. Mem. Council, Modern Art Oxford (formerly MOMA, Oxford), 1998–2004. Chm. Govs, Oxford Brookes Univ., 2004–08 (Gov., 2002–). Sloan Fellow, London Business Sch., 1988. DL Oxon, 2006. DUniv Oxford Brookes, 2009. *Recreations:* hill walking, reading, music. *Address:* 263 Woodstock Road, Oxford OX2 7AE. *T:* (01865) 515477; Johnson Matthey plc, 25 Farringdon Street, EC4A 4AB.

STEW, Timothy David, MBE 1996; HM Diplomatic Service; High Commissioner, Trinidad and Tobago, since 2015; *b* Oxford, 8 Oct. 1966; *s* of David John Stew and Gillian Primrose Stew; partner, Amanda Parsons; one *s* one *d*. *Educ:* Magdalen Coll. Sch., Oxford; Liverpool Univ. (BA Jt Hons English and Latin 1988). Entered FCO, 1988; Arabic lang. trng, Cairo, 1990; Press Officer, Riyadh, 1991–95; Political Officer, Sarajevo, 1995–96; Dep. High Comr, Belize, 1996–99; Head: Iraq Humanitarian and Sanctions Gp, FCO, 2000–03; Pol/Econ. Teams, Cairo, 2003–06; Dep. Ambassador, Kuwait, 2007–10; Sen. Finance Strategist, 2010; Hd, Arab Partnership Dept, FCO, 2010–15. *Recreations:* family, music, dog walking. *Address:* BFPO 5565, FCO, West End Road, Ruislip HA4 6EP. *T:* (Trinidad and Tobago) 3746194. *E:* tim.stew@fco.gov.uk.

STEWARD, Rear Adm. Cedric John, CB 1984; Chief of Naval Staff, New Zealand, 1983–86, retired; *b* 31 Jan. 1931; *s* of Ethelbert Harold Steward and Anne Isabelle Steward; *m* 1952, Marie Antoinette Gurr; three *s*. *Educ:* Northcote College, Auckland, NZ; RNC Dartmouth; RNC Greenwich. Served: HMS Devonshire, 1950; HMS Illustrious, 1950; HMS Glory, 1951 (Korean Campaign and UN Medals, 1951); HMAS Australia, HMAS Barcoo, 1952; HM NZ Ships Hawea, 1953, Kaniere, 1954 (NZ GSM Korea 2002), Tamaki, 1955–58, Stawell, 1958–59; HMAS Creswell (RAN College), 1959–62; HM NZ Ships Rotoiti, 1962–63 (Antarctic support, Operation Deep Freeze), Tamaki, 1963–64, Royalist, 1965–66 (Confrontation; Naval GSM Malaya 2002), Philomel, 1966, Inverell (in Command), 1966–67; JSSC Latimer, 1968; RNZN Liaison Officer Australia and Dep. Head, NZ Defence Liaison Staff, Canberra, 1969–73; in Command, HMNZS Otago, NZ Force SE Asia, 1973–74; in Command and Captain F11, HMNZS Canterbury, 1974–75; Defence HQ, 1976–77; RCDS, 1978; Dep. Chief of Naval Staff, NZ, 1979–81; Commodore, Auckland, and NZ Maritime Comdr, 1981–83. Life Mem., US Naval Inst., 1983; Mem., Australian Naval Inst., 1993. NZ Armed Forces Medal and Clasp, 1984; NZ Operational Service Medal, 2002; NZ Defence Service Medal, 2011. Pingat Jasa Malaysia, 2006. *Recreation:* philately. *Club:* Auckland Racing (Ellerslie).

STEWARD, Dr Katherine Mary; Director, Board Leadership Programme, and Assistant Director, Leadership, King's Fund, since 2006; *b* Malaysia, 18 April 1964; *d* of Robert Edward Alan Steward and Rosemary Steward (*née* Mather); *m* 1994, (Achilles) James Daunt, *s* of Sir Timothy Lewis Achilles Daunt, *qv*; two *d*. *Educ:* Presdales Sch.; Haileybury; Girton Coll., Cambridge (BA Hons 1986); Imperial Coll. of Sci., Technol. and Medicine, London (MBA 1990; PhD 1994). Overseas Develt Consultant, Cambridge Educn Consultants, 1986–89; Co-owner, Daunt Books, 1989–; Orgn Develt Consultant, OASiS, 1994–97; Sen. Consultant, KPMG, 1997; Vice Pres., Emerging Local Corporates, Citigroup, 1997–2000; freelance, 2001; business transformation at H of C Liby, 2002; Associate, Judge Business Sch., 2002; Hd, Governance Policy, Monitor, 2005–06. Trustee: Kaloko Trust, 2010–15; Amref Health Africa, 2012–15; Oxfam, 2013– (Chair, Recruitment and Develt Gp, 2013–; Mem., Remuneration Cttee, 2013–). *Recreations:* travelling, books, living well. *Address:* 39 Downshire Hill, NW3 1NU; King's Fund, 11–13 Cavendish Square, W1G 0AN. *T:* 07774 221780. *E:* k.steward@kingsfund.org.uk.

STEWART; *see* Vane-Tempest-Stewart, family name of Marquess of Londonderry.

STEWART, family name of **Earl of Galloway** and **Baron Stewartby**.

STEWART, Hon. Lord; Angus Stewart; a Senator of the College of Justice in Scotland, since 2010; *b* 14 Dec. 1946; *s* of late Archibald Ian Balfour Stewart, CBE, BL, FSAScot and of Ailsa Rosamund Mary Massey; *m* 1975, Jennifer Margaret Stewart; one *d*. *Educ:* Edinburgh Acad.; Balliol Coll., Oxford (BA); Edinburgh Univ. (LLB). Called to the Scottish Bar, 1975; QC (Scot.) 1988. Keeper, Advocates' Liby, 1994–2002. Sen. Advocate Depute, 2005–08; Leading Counsel, Billy Wright Inquiry, NI, 2008–10. Chm., Scottish Council of Law Reporting, 1997–2001. Trustee: Nat. Liby of Scotland, 1994–2005; Stewart Heritage Trust, 1994–2001; Internat. E Boat Class Assoc., 1993–. Chm., Abbotsford Liby Project, 1996–2002. President: Stewart Soc., 2001–04; Stair Soc., 2013–. *Address:* Court of Session, Parliament House, Edinburgh EH1 1RQ. *T:* (0131) 225 2595.

See also P. L. McI. Stewart.

STEWART, Dame Adrienne; *see* Stewart, Dame E. A.

STEWART, Sir Alan (d'Arcy), 13th Bt *cr* 1623; yachtbuilder; *b* 29 Nov. 1932; *s* of Sir Jocelyn Harry Stewart, 12th Bt, and Constance Mary (*d* 1940), *d* of D'Arcy Shillaber; *S* father, 1982; *m* 1952, Patricia, *d* of Lawrence Turner; two *s* two *d*. *Educ:* All Saints College, Bathurst, NSW. *Heir: s* Nicholas Courtney d'Arcy Stewart, BSc, HDipEd, *b* 4 Aug. 1953. *Address:* One Acre, Ramelton, Co. Donegal, Ireland.

STEWART, Alastair James, OBE 2006; ITV News presenter; *b* 22 June 1952; *s* of late Group Captain James F. Stewart and Joan Mary Stewart (*née* Lord); *m* 1978, Sally Ann Jung; three *s* one *d*. *Educ:* St Augustine's Abbey Sch., Ramsgate; Univ. of Bristol. Dep. Pres., Nat. Union of Students, 1974–76. Reporter and presenter, Southern ITV, 1976–80; industrial corresp., ITN, 1980; presenter, ITN: News at Ten, 1981; Channel 4 News, 1983; News at One, 1985; News at 5.45, 1986; Parliament Programme, 1988; News at Ten, 1989, 1991–92; Washington corresp., 1990–91; London Tonight, 1993–2009; Live with Alastair Stewart, ITV News Channel, 2003–05; ITV News at 10.30, 2006–09; ITV Lunchtime News, 2007–; ITV News at 10, 2009–; ITV News at 6.30, 2009–; presenter: BBC Radio, 1994; Missing, LWT, 1992–96; The Carlton Debates, 1993–2006; The Sunday Prog. with Alastair Stewart, GMTV, 1994–2001; Police, Camera, Action, Carlton TV, 1994–2003, ITV, 2007–09; Ask Ken, 2001–08; Moral of the Story, ITV, 2006–07. Commentator and presenter, numerous parly programmes and State occasions, UK and overseas, incl. first live transmission from House of Lords, 1985, House of Commons, 1989; ITV General Election, 1987, 1992, 1997, 2005, 2010, 2015; Gulf War and liberation of Kuwait, 1991; Who Wants to be a London Mayor?, 2000; King of the Castle, 2001; Funeral of Pope John Paul II, 2005; London's Mayor - You Decide, 2008; moderator, Party Leader's Debate, ITV, 2010. Trustee, Just a Drop, 2004–08. Vice President: Homestart UK, 1997–; Action for Children (formerly NCH Action for Children), 1998–. Patron: Lord Mayor Treloar Coll.; Hope Medical; Kids 4 Kids, 2003–; Samantha Dixon Trust, 2003–; Loomba Trust, 2005–12; Scope, 2006–; Naomi House Hospice, 2014–; Vice Patron: Missing Person's Helpline, 1993–; Zito Trust, 1995–; SANE, 1999–. Ambassador: Investors in People, 2002–; Crisis, 2007–; CARE Internat. UK, 2006–. Governor, Ravensbourne Coll., 2006–14. Hon. LLD Bristol, 2007; Hon. DLitt: Plymouth, 2010; Winchester, 2011; Hon. DArt Sunderland, 2012. Annual Award, RBL, 1996; Face of London, RTS, 2002; Presenter of the Year, RTS, 2004. *Recreations:* travel, cartography, a catholic taste in music. *Address:* ITN, 200 Gray's Inn Road, WC1X 8XZ. *T:* (020) 7833 3000.

STEWART, Alastair Lindsay; QC (Scot.) 1995; Sheriff of Tayside, Central and Fife at Dundee, 1990–2004; Temporary Judge in Supreme Courts, Scotland, 1996–2013; *b* 28 Nov. 1938; *s* of Alexander Lindsay Stewart and Anna Stewart; *m* 1st, 1968, Annabel Claire Stewart (marr. diss. 1991), *yr d* of late Prof. W. McC. Stewart; two *s*; 2nd, 1991, Sheila Anne Mackinnon (*née* Flockhart), *o d* of late David H. Flockhart. *Educ:* Edinburgh Academy; St Edmund Hall, Oxford (BA); Univ. of Edinburgh (LLB). Admitted to Faculty of Advocates, 1963; Tutor, Faculty of Law, Univ. of Edinburgh, 1963–73; Standing Junior Counsel to Registrar of Restrictive Trading Agreements, 1968–70; Advocate Depute, 1970–73; Sheriff of South Strathclyde, Dumfries and Galloway, at Airdrie, 1973–79, of Grampian, Highland and Islands, at Aberdeen and Stonehaven, 1979–90; Interim Sheriff Principal, Lothian and Borders, Glasgow and Strathkelvin, 2005. Chairman: Grampian Family Conciliation Service, 1984–87 (Hon. Pres., 1987–90); Scottish Assoc. of Family Conciliation Services, 1986–89. Mem., Judicial Studies Cttee, 2000–04. Governor, Robert Gordon's Inst. of Technology, 1982–90 (Vice-Chm. of Governors, 1985–90). Hon. Prof., Sch. of Law (formerly Faculty of Law and Accountancy), Univ. of Dundee, 2001–13. Editor, Scottish Civil Law Reports, 1992–95. *Publications:* (contrib.) Sheriff Court Practice, by I. D. Macphail, 1988, jt gen. editor, 2nd edn, vol. 1 1998, vol. 2 2002; The Scottish Criminal Courts in Action, 1990, 2nd edn 1997; Evidence reissue, Stair Memorial Encyclopædia of the Laws of Scotland, 2006; various articles in legal jls. *Recreations:* reading, music, walking. *Address:* 86 Albany Road, Broughty Ferry, Dundee DD5 1JQ. *T:* (01382) 477580. *Club:* Western (Glasgow).

STEWART, Sir Alastair (Robin), 3rd Bt *cr* 1960, of Strathgarry, Perth; *b* 26 Sept. 1925; 2nd *s* of Sir Kenneth Dugald Stewart, 1st Bt, GBE and Noel (*d* 1946), *yr d* of Kenric Brodribb, Melbourne; *S* brother, 1992; *m* 1953, Patricia Helen, MBE, ARIBA, *d* of late J. A. Merrett; three *d* (one *s* decd). *Educ:* Marlborough Coll. Lieut, 1st Royal Gloucestershire Hussars, 1945–47. Dir, Neale & Wilkinson Ltd, 1947–71; Man. Dir, Stewart & Harvey Ltd, 1971–90. *Recreation:* gardening. *Heir:* none. *Address:* Walters Cottage, North Hill, Little Baddow, Chelmsford, Essex CM3 4TQ. *T:* (01245) 222445.

STEWART, Alec James, OBE 2003 (MBE 1998); cricketer; *b* 8 April 1963; *s* of Michael James, (Micky), Stewart and Sheila Marie Macdonald Stewart; *m* 1991, Lynn Blades; one *s* one *d*. *Educ:* Tiffin Boys' Sch. Joined Surrey County Cricket Club, 1981, capped 1985, Captain, 1992–97, retired from County team, 2003; Test début, 1989; Mem., 1989–2003, Captain, 1998–99, England Test team; played 133 Test Matches, scored 15 centuries, took 263 catches, 14 stumpings; overseas tours with England team: W Indies, 1989–90, 1993–94 (Vice Capt.), 1997–98; Australia and NZ, 1990–91; India and Sri Lanka, 1992–93; Australia, 1994–95,

1998–99, 2002–03; S Africa, 1995–96, 1999–2000; Zimbabwe and NZ, 1996–97. *Publications:* (with Brian Murgatroyd) Alec Stewart: a Captain's Diary, 1999; Playing for Keeps (autobiog.), 2003. *Address:* c/o Surrey County Cricket Club, The Oval, SE11 5SS.

STEWART, Alexandra Joy; Recruitment Consultant, since 2003, Head of Global Higher Education Practice, since 2004, and Equity Partner, Saxton Bampfylde Ltd (formerly Saxton Bampfylde Hever Ltd), since 2010; *b* 11 April 1953; *d* of Charles Stewart and Myrtle Stewart (*née* Sheppard); *m* 1st, 1976, Andrew Smyth (marr. diss. 1990); one *d*; 2nd, 1991, Michael McBride (*d* 2014). *Educ:* Bexhill Grammar Sch. for Girls; Durham Univ. (BA Hons). Joined DES, 1975; admin trainee, 1975–79; Private Sec. to Minister for Educn, 1979–81; Principal, 1981–88; Assistant Secretary: Hd of City Technol. Unit, 1988–92; with DNH, subseq. DCMS, 1992–2003; Hd of Sports Div., then Finance Dir, 1992–99; Dir, Museums, Galleries, Libraries and Heritage, subseq. Art and Culture, 1999–2003. *Recreations:* my family, gardening, the South Downs, poultry. *Address:* Saxton Bampfylde Ltd, 35 Old Queen Street, SW1H 9JA.

STEWART, Allan; *see* Stewart, J. A.

STEWART, Andrew Fleming; QC (Scot.) 2009; *b* Dundee, 12 Sept. 1963; *s* of Rev. Gordon Grant Stewart and late Elspeth Margaret Stewart (*née* Farquharson); *m* 1992, Dr Lesley Katherine Dawson; two *d*. *Educ:* Perth High Sch.; Edinburgh Univ. (LLB Hons 1985). Admitted Faculty of Advocates, 1996; Standing Jun. Counsel to DTI, 2000–09; Advocate Depute, 2009–13; Mem., Scottish Civil Justice Council, 2014–. Clerk of the Faculty of Advocates, 2003–09; Pres., Scottish Tax Tribunals, 2015–. Vis. Lectr, Univ. de Lorraine (formerly Univ. de Nancy 2), 1993–. Chm., Scottish Churches Cttee, 2007–. Ed., Session Cases, 2001–. *Publications:* articles in legal jls, etc. *Recreations:* family, Scottish dance music, golf. *Address:* Advocates Library, Parliament House, Edinburgh EH1 1RF. *Clubs:* New (Edinburgh); Blairgowrie Golf, Bruntsfield Links Golfing Society.

STEWART, Brian Edward; HM Diplomatic Service, retired; Ambassador to Algeria, 2004–05; *b* 4 Feb. 1950; *s* of late Edward Stewart and of Carrol Stewart (*née* Medcalf); *m* 1975, Anne Cockerill. *Educ:* Melsetter Sch., Southern Rhodesia; Keith Grammar Sch., Scotland; Keele Univ. (BA Hons). Entered FCO, 1972; MECAS, Lebanon, 1973–75; 3rd, later 2nd Sec., Amman, 1975–78; on loan to Cabinet Office, 1978–80; First Sec., FCO, 1980–82; First Secretary and Head of Chancery: Singapore, 1982–85; Tunis, 1986–89; First Sec., FCO, 1989–93; Dep. Hd of Mission, Damascus, 1993–96; Counsellor, FCO, 1996–98; Dep. Hd of Mission and Counsellor, Kuwait, 1998–2001; FCO, 2002; rcds 2003. *Publications:* (contrib.) The Arabists of Shemlan, 2006. *Recreations:* restoring and maintaining potential classic cars, tackling essential household DIY, playing tennis and cricket with more enthusiasm than skill. *Address:* c/o Foreign and Commonwealth Office, King Charles Street, SW1A 2AH.

STEWART, Sir Brian (John), Kt 2002; CBE 1996; Chairman: Miller Group Ltd, 2009–12; C&C, since 2010; *b* 9 April 1945; *m* 1971, Seonaid Duncan; two *s* one *d*. *Educ:* Edinburgh Univ. (MSc). Mem., Scottish Inst. of Chartered Accountants. Scottish and Newcastle Breweries, subseq. Scottish and Newcastle plc: joined 1976; Finance Dir, 1988–91; Gp Chief Exec., 1991–2000; Dep. Chm., 1997–2000; Chm., 2000–03; non-exec. Chm., 2003–08. Dir, Booker, 1993–99; Chm., Standard Life Assurance Co., 2003–07 (Dir, 1993–2007). *Recreations:* golf, ski-ing.

STEWART, Rev. Dr Charles Edward; Chaplain, Royal Hospital School, 2000–10; *b* 10 June 1946; *s* of Charles Stewart and Mary Stewart (*née* McDougall); *m* 1970, Margaret Marion Smith; two *s* one *d*. *Educ:* Strathclyde Univ. (BSc; PhD); Glasgow Univ. (BD); Edinburgh Univ. (MTh). Ordained, C of S, 1976; Chaplain: HMS Sea Hawk, RNAS Culdrose, 1976–78; Clyde Submarine Base, 1978–80; Staff of Flag Officer 3rd Flotilla, 1980; Chaplain: HMS Hermes, Falklands Conflict, 1981; HMS Neptune, 1982–85; HMS Drake and Staff of Flag Officer Plymouth, 1985–87; HMS Raleigh, 1987–90; BRNC, Dartmouth, 1990–93; Asst Dir Naval Chaplaincy Service, 1992–94; HMS Invincible, Bosnia, 1994–96; Dir Naval Chaplaincy Service, 1996–97; Dir Gen. Naval Chaplaincy Service, 1997–2000; Chaplain of the Fleet, 1998–2000. QHC 1996–2000. South Atlantic Medal, 1982; NATO Medal, 1995. *Recreations:* gardening, water colours (painting), music, hill walking, photography.

STEWART, Colin MacDonald, CB 1983; FIA; Directing Actuary, Government Actuary's Department, 1974–84; *b* 26 Dec. 1922; *s* of John Stewart and Lillias Cecilia MacDonald Fraser; *m* 1948, Gladys Edith Thwaites (*d* 2003); three *d*. *Educ:* Queen's Park Secondary Sch., Glasgow. Clerical Officer, Rosyth Dockyard, 1939–42. Served War: Fleet Air Arm (Lieut (A) RNVR), 1942–46. Govt Actuary's Dept, London, 1946–84. Head of Actuarial Res., Godwins Ltd, 1985–88. FIA 1953. *Publications:* The Students' Society Log 1960–85, 1985; (contrib.) Life, Death and Money, 1998; numerous articles on actuarial and demographic subjects in British and internat. jls. *Recreations:* genealogical research, foreign travel, grandchilding. *Address:* 8 The Chase, Coulsdon, Surrey CR5 2EG. *T:* (020) 8660 3966.

STEWART, Sir David James H.; *see* Henderson-Stewart.

STEWART, David John; Member (Lab) Highlands and Islands, Scottish Parliament, since 2007; *b* 5 May 1956; *s* of John and Alice Stewart; *m* 1982, Linda MacDonald; one *s* one *d*. *Educ:* Paisley Coll. (BA Hons); Stirling Univ. (Dip. Social Wk, CQSW); Open Univ. (Professional Dip. Mgt). Social work manager, 1980–97; Asst Dir for Rural Affairs, SCVO, 2005–07. Member (Lab): Nithsdale DC, 1984–86; Inverness DC, 1988–96 (Dep. Leader, Labour Gp). Contested (Lab): Inverness, Nairn and Lochaber, 1987 and 1992; Inverness, Nairn, Badenoch and Strathspey, 2005. MP (Lab) Inverness E, Nairn and Lochaber, 1997–2005. Scottish Parliament: a Labour Whip, 2007–11 (Chief Whip, 2008–11); Shadow Envmt Minister, 2007–08; Shadow Minister for Transport and Islands, 2015–; Convener, Petitions Cttee, 2011–15; Mem., Scottish Parly Corporate Body, 2011–15. *Address:* Scottish Parliament, Edinburgh EH99 1SP.

STEWART, Captain Sir David (John Christopher), 7th Bt *cr* 1803, of Athenree, Tyrone; *b* 19 June 1935; *s* of Sir Hugh Charlie Godfray Stewart, 6th Bt and his 1st wife, Rosemary Elinor Dorothy, *d* of Maj. George Peacocke; *S* father, 1994; *m* 1959, Bridget Anne, *er d* of late Patrick W. Sim; three *d*. *Educ:* Bradfield Coll.; RMA Sandhurst. Commnd Royal Inniskilling Fusiliers, 1956; seconded to Trucial Oman Scouts, 1957–58 (Jebel Akhdar Campaign, 1957); Adjt 1958; served in Trucial States, Oman and Muscat, 1957–58, Germany, 1958–59, Kenya, 1960–62 (Kuwait Operation, 1961), UN Peacekeeping Force, Cyprus, 1964; retd as Captain, 1965. Representative for E. S. & A. Robinson, Bristol, 1965–69; Director: Maurice James Holdings, Coventry, 1969–77; Papropak UK, 1977–79; self-employed, 1979–; owner, George Inn, Middlezoy, Somerset, 1982–85. Hon. Organiser, RBL Poppy Appeal, Wiveliscombe, 1996–2002; Hon. Treas., Friends of Somerset SSAFA-Forces Help, 1998–2006; Hon. Pres., Trucial Oman Scouts Assoc., 2014–. Medal, Order of Tower of Al Qassimi (UAE), 2003. *Recreations:* golf, cricket. *Heir:* half *b* Hugh Nicholas Stewart [*b* 20 April 1955; *m* 1976, Anna Leeke; one *s* three *d*]. *Address:* 16 Blackdown View, Curry Rivel, Langport, Somerset TA10 0ER. *Clubs:* MCC; XL.

STEWART, Dawn Jacquelyn; *see* Austwick, D. J.

STEWART, Dame (Ellen) Adrienne, (Lady Stewart), DNZM 2015 (ONZM 2006); Director, PDL Holdings Ltd, 1982–2001; *b* Melbourne, 6 Feb. 1936; *d* of Joseph Peake and Ellen Mabel Peake (*née* Parker); *m* 1970, Sir Robertson Huntly Stewart, CBE (*d* 2007); two *s*. *Educ:* Presbyterian Ladies' Coll., Melbourne. Dir, Trustbank Canterbury, 1980–85. Chair, Christchurch Symphony Orch. Foundn, 2002–; Governing Patron, Art and Industry Biennial Trust, 1998–; Mem., Coll. of Arts Adv. Panel, Univ. of Canterbury; Trustee, Christchurch Cathedral Foundn, and Canon Almoner; Patron: Univ. of Canterbury Foundn; Court Theatre Supporters; Woolston Brass Band; Fedn of Australasian Brass Bands; National Australia Brass. FNZIM; Dist. Fellow, NZ Inst. of Dirs. Hon. LLD Canterbury, 2011. QSM 1995; Patron of the Year, Arts Foundn of NZ, 2009. *Recreations:* arts, music. *Address:* PO Box 2043, Christchurch, New Zealand. *T:* (3) 3485040. *E:* adrienne.stewart@masthead.co.nz. *Clubs:* Zonta (Past Pres.), Christchurch (Christchurch).

STEWART, George Girdwood, CB 1979; MC 1945; TD 1954; Cairngorm Estate Adviser, Highlands and Islands Enterprise, 1988–98; *b* 12 Dec. 1919; *o s* of late Herbert A. Stewart, BSc, and of Janetta Dunlop Girdwood; *m* 1950, Shelagh Jean Morven Murray (*d* 2004); one *s* one *d*. *Educ:* Kelvinside Academy, Glasgow; Glasgow Univ.; Edinburgh Univ. (BSc). Served RA, 1940–46 (MC, despatches); CO 278 (Lowland) Field Regt RA (TA), 1957–60. Dist Officer, Forestry Commn, 1949–61; Asst Conservator, 1961–67; Conservator, West Scotland, 1967–69; Comr for Forest and Estate Management, 1969–79; National Trust for Scotland: Mem., Council, 1975–79; Rep., Branklyn Garden, Perth, 1980–84; Regional Rep., Central and Tayside, 1984–88; Forestry Consultant, 1989–93. Specialist advr, Select Cttee on EEC Forestry Policy, 1986; Associate Dir, Oakwood Envmtl, 1990–2003. Member: BR Bd Envmt Panel, 1980–90; Countryside Commn for Scotland, 1981–88; Chm., Scottish Wildlife Trust, 1981–87; Cairngorm Mountain Trust (formerly Cairngorm Recreation Trust), 1986–. Pres., Scottish Nat. Ski Council, 1988–94 (Hon. Vice-Pres., 1998–2014). Pres., Scottish Ski Club, 1971–75; Vice-Pres., Nat. Ski Fedn of GB; Chm., Alpine Racing Cttee, 1975–78. Mem., British Team, ITF Veterans World Team Tennis Championships, 1999, 2001, 2002; Winner of Doubles, ITF Super-Seniors World Individual Championships, 2006, 2007. FRSA; FICFor; Hon. FLI. Nat. Service to Sport Award, Scottish Sports Council, 1995. Olympic torch bearer, Newburgh, Fife, 2012. *Recreations:* ski-ing, tennis, studying Scottish painting. *Address:* 11 Mansfield Road, Scone, Perth PH2 6SA. *T:* (01738) 551815. *Club:* Ski Club of Great Britain.

STEWART, Prof. George Russell, PhD, DSc; Dean, Faculty of Life and Physical Sciences, University of Western Australia, 2002–10 (Executive Dean, Faculty of Science, 1998–2001); *b* 25 Feb. 1944; *s* of George and Isobella Stewart; *m* 1978, Janice Anne Grimes; three *d*. *Educ:* Pinner County Grammar Sch.; Univ. of Bristol (BSc 1965; PhD 1968); DSc London 1991. Lectr in Botany, Univ. of Manchester, 1968–81; London University: Prof. of Botany and Head of Dept, Birkbeck Coll., 1981–85; Quain Prof. of Botany, 1985–91 and Head of Dept of Biology, 1987–91, UCL; Dean of Faculty of Sci., 1990–91; Prof. of Botany, Univ. of Queensland, 1992–98. Vis. Lectr, Dept of Biology, Univ. of Lagos, Nigeria; Visiting Professor: Dept of Botany, Univ. of Queensland, Aust.; Dept of Biology, Univ. of Campinas, Brazil; Dept of Biology, Univ. of WA. Member: Plants and Envmt Cttee, AFRC, 1989–91; Plants and Envmt Res. Bd, AFRC (Chm., 1989–91); Agriculture Cttee, Long Ashton Res. Station, 1990–91; Inter-Agency Cttee on Res. into Global Envmtl Change (Working Gp 2), 1990–91; Zool Parks Authy, WA, 2006–08. Mem., Bd of Dirs, SciTech Discovery Centre, 1999–2008. Dep. Pres., WA Br., Australia-China Business Council, 2005–07. Foreign expert consultant, Beijing Assoc. for Sci., 2008–. Hon. Mem., Shanghai Assoc. for Sci. and Tech., 2006. *Publications:* (ed jtly) The Genetic Manipulation of Plants and its Application to Agriculture, 1984; numerous scientific papers on plant physiology and metabolism and chapters in books and conf. proc. *Recreations:* cycling, cooking. *Address:* c/o Faculty of Life and Physical Sciences, M011, University of Western Australia, Crawley, WA 6009, Australia.

STEWART, Gillian Mary, CB 2003; Head of Children and Young People's Group, Scottish Executive Education Department, 1999–2002; *b* 2 June 1945; *d* of John Knott and Nora Elizabeth Knott; marr. diss.; two *s*. *Educ:* Blyth Grammar Sch.; Univ. of Durham (BA Hons Class 1 German). Joined Scottish Office, 1970; posts in educn and social work; Asst Sec., 1984; posts in historic buildings and local govt; Under-Sec., 1992; Hd of Criminal Justice Gp, 1992–97; Hd of Social Work Services Gp, Home Dept, 1997–99. Mem., Council and Scottish Cttee, Barnardo's, 2003–14. *Recreations:* swimming, walking, music, theatre, travel.

STEWART, Prof. Gordon Thallon, MD; FFPH; Mechan Professor of Public Health, University of Glasgow, 1972–84, now Emeritus Professor; Hon. Consultant in Epidemiology and Preventive Medicine, Glasgow Area Health Board; *b* 5 Feb. 1919; *s* of John Stewart and Mary L. Thallon; *m* 1946, Joan Kego; two *s* two *d*; *m* 1975, Neena Walker. *Educ:* Paisley Grammar Sch.; Univs of Glasgow and Liverpool. BSc 1939; MB, ChB 1942; DTM&H 1947; MD (High Commendation) 1949; FRCPath 1964; FFPH (FFCM 1972); MRCPGlas 1972; FRCPGlas 1975. House Phys. and House Surg., 1942–43; Surg. Lieut RNVR, 1943–46; Res. Fellow (MRC), Univ. of Liverpool, 1946–48; Sen. Registrar and Tutor, Wright-Fleming Inst., St Mary's Hosp., London, 1948–52; Cons. Pathologist, SW Metrop. Regional Hosp. Bd, 1954–63; Res. Worker at MRC Labs Carshalton, 1955–63; Prof. of Epidem. and Path., Univ. of N Carolina, 1964–68; Watkins Prof. of Epidem., Tulane Univ. Med. Center, New Orleans, 1968–72. Vis. Prof., Dow Med. Coll., Karachi, 1952–53 and Cornell Univ. Med. Coll., 1970–71; Cons. to WHO Blue Nile Health Plan, Sudan, and to NYC Dept of Health; Mem., Presidential Commn on AIDS, S Africa; Founding Mem., Rethinking AIDS, USA, 1986; dir of progs on urban deprivation and control of disease; Vis. Lectr and Examr, various univs in UK and overseas. Sen. Fellow, Nat. Science Foundn, Washington, 1964; Delta omega, 1969. Ed., C. C. Thomas American Lect. Series. *Publications:* (ed) Trends in Epidemiology, 1972; (ed jtly) Penicillin Allergy, 1970; Penicillin Group of Drugs, 1965; papers on chemotherapy of infectious diseases, drug allergy, epidemiology and etiology of HIV/AIDS in various med. and sci. jls. *Recreations:* gardening, drawing, music. *Address:* 29/8 Inverleith Place, Edinburgh EH3 5QD.

STEWART, Iain Aitken; MP (C) Milton Keynes South, since 2010; *b* 18 Sept. 1972; *s* of James Stewart and Leila Stewart. *Educ:* Hutchesons' Grammar Sch., Glasgow; Univ. of Exeter (BA Pols 1993); Chartered Mgt Inst. (Dip. Mgt 2006). Trainee chartered accountant, Coopers & Lybrand, 1993–94; Hd, Research, Scottish Cons Party, 1994–98; Dep. Dir, 1998–2001, Dir, 2001–06, Parly Resources Unit, H of C; Associate, Odgers Berndtson (formerly Odgers, Ray & Berndtson), 2006–10. Contested (C) Glasgow Rutherglen, Scottish Parlt, 1999; contested (C) Milton Keynes SW, 2001, 2005. PPS to Sec. of State for Transport, 2013–15, to Sec. of State for Scotland, 2015–. Mem., Transport Select Cttee, 2010–13. Mem. (C), Shenley Brook End and Tattenhoe Parish Council, 2005–11. *Address:* House of Commons, SW1A 0AA.

STEWART, Prof. Iain Alastair, PhD; FBCS; Professor of Computer Science, Durham University, since 2002; *b* Durham, 16 March 1961; *s* of Allan and Dorothy Stewart; *m* 1988, Sheila; two *s* one *d*. *Educ:* Royal Grammar Sch., Newcastle upon Tyne; Christ Church, Oxford (MA Maths); Queen Mary Coll., London (PhD Maths 1986). FBCS 1997. Lectr, Computer Lab., Univ. of Newcastle upon Tyne, 1986–92; Lectr, 1992–94, Sen. Lectr, 1994–95, Reader, 1995–96, University Coll. of Swansea; Prof. of Computer Sci., Leicester Univ., 1996–2002. *Publications:* contribs to learned jls on maths and computer sci. *Recreations:* supporting Newcastle United, cinema, fly fishing, rambling. *Address:* School of Engineering and Computing Sciences, Durham University, South Road, Durham DH1 3LE. *T:* (0191) 334 1720. *E:* i.a.stewart@durham.ac.uk.

STEWART, Ian; City Mayor of Salford, since 2012; *b* 28 Aug. 1950; *s* of John and Helen Stewart; *m* 1968, Merilyn Holding; two *s* one *d*. *Educ:* David Livingstone Primary Meml Sch., Blantyre; Calder Street Secondary, Blantyre; Alfred Turner Secondary Modern Sch., Salford; Stretford Technical Coll.; Manchester Metropolitan Univ. Regl Officer, TGWU, 1978–97. MP (Lab) Eccles, 1997–2010. PPS to Minister of State for Industry and Energy, subseq. for Energy and Construction, 2001–03, to Minister of State (Minister for Energy, the Post Office,

E-Govt and Corporate Social Responsibility), 2003–04, DTI; PPS to Financial Sec. to HM Treasury, 2004–05; PPS to Sec. of State, DTI, 2005–06. Member: Deregulation Select Cttee, 1997–2001; Information Select Cttee, 1998–2001; Innovation, Sci. and Skills Select Cttee, 2007–10; PLP Employment and Trng Cttee, 1997–2010; PLP Trade and Industry Cttee, 1997–2010; PLP Foreign Affairs Cttee, 1997–2010; Exec., PITCOM, 1998–2010; Chm., All Party Community Media Gp, 2002–10; Founder and Vice Chm., All Party China Gp, 1997–2010 (Mem., GB China Centre Exec., 1997–2010); Chm., Parly Gp for Vaccine Damaged Children, 1998–2001. Defence Sports Advr to Minister of State (Minister for Sport), DCMS, 2002–10; former Govt Rep. for Defence Sports. Founder, Eur. Foundn for Social Partnership and Continuing Trng Initiatives, 1993. Member: Unite (formerly TGWU), 1965–; UK Soc. of Industrial Tutors, 1980–; Manchester Industrial Relations Soc., 1994–; Member: Internat. Soc. of Industrial Relations, 1996–; Council, Eur. Informatics Market, 1998–2010; Council, Eur. Information Soc. Fellow, Industry and Parlt Trust, 1997; Vis. Fellow, Salford Univ., 1998.

STEWART, Prof. Ian George; Professor of Economics, University of Edinburgh, 1967–84; *b* 24 June 1923; *s* of David Tweedie Stewart, MA and Ada Doris Montgomery Haldane; *m* 1949, Mary Katharine Oddie; one *s* two *d. Educ:* Fettes Coll.; Univ. of St Andrews (MA 1st Class Hons); MA Cantab 1954. Pilot, RAF, 1942–46. Commonwealth Fund Fellow, 1948–50. Research Officer, Dept of Applied Economics, Univ. of Cambridge, 1950–57; University of Edinburgh: Lectr in Economics, 1957–58; Sen. Lectr, 1958–61; Reader, 1961–67; Curator of Patronage, 1979–84. Vis. Associate Prof., Univ. of Michigan, 1962; Vis. Prof., Univ. of S Carolina, 1975. Dir, Scottish Provident Instn, 1980–90, Dep. Chm., 1983–85. Mem., British Library Bd, 1980–87. Governor, Fettes Coll., 1976–89. *Publications:* National Income of Nigeria (with A. R. Prest), 1953; (ed) Economic Development and Structural Change, 1969; articles in jls and bank reviews. *Recreations:* golf, fishing, gardening. *Club:* New (Edinburgh).

STEWART, Rev. Canon Ian Guild; Priest-in-charge, St David, Inverbervie, 1992–2008; Rector, St Mary and St Peter, Montrose, 1992–2008; Dean of Brechin, 2007–08; *b* 1943. *Educ:* Edinburgh Theol Coll. Ordained deacon, 1984, priest, 1985; Non-Stipendiary Minister, St Mary Magdalene, Dundee, 1984–87; Non-Stipendiary Minister, 1987–90, Asst Curate, 1990–92, St Martin, Dundee; Non-Stipendiary Minister, 1987–90, Asst Curate, 1990–92, St John the Baptist, Dundee. Canon, St Paul's Cathedral, Dundee, 2001–12, now Canon Emeritus. *Address:* 36 Forbes Road, Edinburgh EH10 4ED.

STEWART, Ian James, CB 1997; Director, Cambridge Concepts Ltd, since 2007; *b* 30 Aug. 1946; *m* 1967, Morag Gardiner Duncan; two *d. Educ:* Perth Acad. Area Dir, Newcastle Benefits Directorate, 1990–92; Mem. Bd of Mgt and Dir, Benefits Agency, DSS, 1993–95; Project Dir, Jobseeker's Allowance, DfEE, 1995–97; Dir Gen., Benefit Fraud Inspectorate, DSS, 1997–99; Chief Executive: Bradford CC, 1999–2003; Cambs CC, 2003–07.

STEWART, Ian James; Editor, Scotland on Sunday, since 2009, and The Scotsman, since 2012; *b* Kingston-upon-Thames, 4 Aug. 1960; *s* of William Stewart and Colina Stewart; *m* 1988, Lesley Innes; one *s* one *d. Educ:* Royal High Sch., Edinburgh; Napier Coll. (HND Journalism Studies 1986). Royal Marines, 1979–82; reporter, Nottingham Evening Post, 1986–91; News Editor, The Scotsman, 1991–98; Assistant Editor: Daily Mail, 1998–99; Scotland on Sunday, 1999–2001; Editor, Edinburgh Evening News, 2001–04; Dep. Editor, The Scotsman, 2004–12. *Recreation:* mainly worrying. *Address:* The Scotsman, 108 Holyrood Road, Edinburgh EH8 8AS. *T:* (0131) 620 8626, *Fax:* (0131) 620 8617.

STEWART, Prof. Ian Nicholas, PhD; FRS 2001; CMath, FIMA; Professor of Mathematics, University of Warwick, 1990–2009, now Emeritus Professor; *b* 24 Sept. 1945; *s* of Arthur Reginald Stewart and Marjorie Kathleen Stewart (*née* Diwell); *m* 1970, Avril Bernice Montgomery; two *s. Educ:* Cambridge Univ. (MA); Univ. of Warwick (PhD). FIMA 1993; CMath 1993; CBiol 2003–07, FIBiol 2003–07. University of Warwick: Lectr, 1969–84; Reader, 1984–90. Humboldt Fellow, Tübingen, 1974; Vis. Fellow, Auckland, 1976; Associate Prof., Storrs, Conn, 1977–78; Professor: Carbondale, Ill, 1978; Houston, Texas, 1983–84; Gresham Prof. of Geometry, 1994; Adjunct Prof., Houston Univ., 2001–. Author, Incredible Numbers iPad app, 2014. Hon. DSc: Westminster, 1999; Louvain, 2000; Kingston, 2003. Michael Faraday Medal, Royal Soc., 1995; IMA Gold Medal, 2000; Ferran Sunyer i Balaguer Prize, 2001; Public Understanding of Sci. and Tech. Award, AAAS, 2002; Zeeman Medal, London Math. Soc., 2009; (jtly) Lewis Thomas Prize, Rockefeller Univ., 2015. *Publications* include: Galois Theory, 1973; Concepts of Modern Mathematics, 1975; Catastrophe Theory and its Applications, 1978; The Problems of Mathematics, 1987; Does God Play Dice?, 1989; Game Set & Math, 1991; Another Fine Math You've Got Me Into, 1992; Fearful Symmetry, 1992; The Collapse of Chaos, 1994; Nature's Numbers, 1995; From Here to Infinity, 1996; Figments of Reality, 1997; The Magical Maze, 1997; Life's Other Secret, 1998; (jtly) The Science of Discworld, 1999; (jtly) Wheelers, 2000; Flatterland, 2001; What Shape is a Snowflake?, 2001; The Annotated Flatland, 2001; (jtly) The Science of Discworld II: the globe, 2002; (jtly) Evolving the Alien, 2002; (jtly) What Does a Martian Look Like?, 2004; Math Hysteria, 2004; (jtly) Heaven, 2004; (jtly) The Science of Discworld III: Darwin's watch, 2005; The Mayor of Uglyville's Dilemma, 2005; Letters to a Young Mathematician, 2006; How to Cut a Cake, 2006; Why Beauty is Truth: the history of symmetry, 2007; Professor Stewart's Cabinet of Mathematical Curiosities, 2008; Professor Stewart's Hoard of Mathematical Treasures, 2009; Cows in the Maze, 2010; Mathematics of Life, 2011; Seventeen Equations that Changed the World, 2012; Great Mathematical Problems, 2013; (jtly) The Science of Discworld IV: Judgement Day, 2013; Symmetry: a very short introduction, 2013; Professor Stewart's Casebook of Mathematical Mysteries, 2014; Professor Stewart's Incredible Numbers, 2015. *Recreations:* science fiction, painting, guitar, keeping fish, geology, Egyptology, snorkelling. *Address:* Mathematics Institute, University of Warwick, Coventry CV4 7AL.

STEWART, Sir Jackie; *see* Stewart, Sir John Young.

STEWART, James Alexander Gustave Harold, OBE 2007; FICE; Chairman, Global Infrastructure, KPMG, since 2011; *b* London, 29 April 1962; *s* of H. Ivan Stewart; *m* 1988, Gill; two *s* two *d. Educ:* Harrow Sch.; Univ. of Oxford (BA Chem.). Dir, Hambros Bank, 1984–98; Chief Executive: Partnerships UK, 2000–09; Infrastructure UK, 2009–11. Non-exec. Dir, Sport England, 2006–13. *Recreations:* golf, photography, walking. *Address:* Goddards Green House, Goddards Green Road, Benenden, Kent TN17 4AR. *Club:* Rye Golf.

STEWART, James Harvey; former consultant in healthcare management; Chief Executive (formerly District General Manager), Barking and Havering (formerly Barking, Havering and Brentwood) Health Authority, 1985–95; *b* 15 Aug. 1939; *s* of Harvey Stewart and Annie (*née* Gray); *m* 1965, Fiona Maria Maclay Reid (*d* 2004); three *s* one *d*; *m* 2015, Sally Ann Marsh (*nee* Childerley). *Educ:* Peterhead Acad.; Aberdeen Univ. (MA 1962); Manchester Univ. (DSA 1964). Hosp. Sec., Princess Margaret Rose Orthopaedic Hosp., Edinburgh, 1965–67; Principal Admin. Asst, 1967–68, and Dep. Gp Sec. and sometime Acting Gp Sec., 1968–73, York A HMC; Area Administrator, 1973–82, and Dist Administrator, 1982–83, Northumberland AHA; Regional Administrator, East Anglian RHA, 1983–85. Mem., Cambridge CHC, 1999–2002; Bd Mem., S Cambs PCT, 2002–05. Hon. Treasurer, Assoc. of Chief Administrators of Health Authorities in England and Wales, 1982–85 (Mem. Council, 1975–82). Member: (Lib Dem) S Cambs DC, 1998– (Chm., 2007–09); Hardwick Parish Council, 1999–. Mem., Cambridge Rotary Club, 1983– (Pres., 1998–99). Hon. Pres., Cambs Rehab. Club for Visually Handicapped, 1999–2010; Trustee, Cambridgeshire Soc. for Blind (Camsight), 2005–. Chm., Cambridge Friends of Nat. Trust for Scotland, 2014–. *Recreations:* music, reading, walking, sport. *Club:* National Liberal.

STEWART, Sir (James) Moray, KCB 1995 (CB 1990); Chairman, Board of Management, North Glasgow College, 2005–08 (Member, since 1996); President, SSAFA (formerly SSAFA-Forces Help), Fife, 2003–15; *b* 21 June 1938; third *s* of James and Evelyn Stewart; *m* 1963, Dorothy May Batey, *o d* of Alan and Maud Batey; three *s. Educ:* Marlborough Coll.; Univ. of Keele (BA First Cl. Hons History and Econs). Sec., Univ. of Keele Union, 1960–61. Breakdown and Information Service Operator, AA, 1956–57; Asst Master, Northcliffe Sch., Bognor Regis, 1957–58; Asst Principal, Air Min., 1962–65; Private Sec. to 2nd Permanent Under Sec. of State (RAF), MoD, 1965–66; Principal, MoD, 1966–70; First Sec. (Defence), UK Delegn to NATO, 1970–73; Asst Sec., MoD, 1974–75; Private Sec. to successive Secs of State for NI, 1975–77; Dir, Naval Manpower Requirements, MoD, 1977; Dir, Defence Policy Staff, MoD, 1978–80; Asst Under Sec. of State, MoD, 1980–84; Asst Sec. Gen. for Defence Planning and Policy, NATO, 1984–86; Dep. Under Sec. of State, Personnel and Logistics, 1986–88, Defence Procurement, 1988–90, MoD; Second Permanent Under Sec. of State, MoD, 1990–96. Chm., CS Healthcare, 1993–2000. Commissioner: Royal Hosp. Chelsea, 1986–88; Queen Victoria Sch., Dunblane, 1996–2006; Trustee, Imperial War Museum, 1986–88; Mem. Council, RUSI, 1988–92. Vice Pres., Eurodefense UK, 2002–09. Vice Pres., Civil Service RFU, 1993–. Chairman: Arvon Foundn in Scotland, 1998–2003; Elie Harbour Trust, 1999–2007; Member: Bd, Assoc. of Scotland's Colls, 2005–08; Cttee, Elie and Earlsferry Hist. Soc., 2009–. Trustee, Pegasus Trust, 1993–. Hon. DLitt Keele, 1995. *Recreations:* reading, listening to music. *Address:* c/o Drummonds, Royal Bank of Scotland, 49 Charing Cross, SW1A 2DX. *Clubs:* Farmers; New, Royal Scots (Edinburgh); Golf House (Elie).

STEWART, His Honour James Simeon Hamilton; QC 1982; a Circuit Judge, 2002–12; Resident Judge, Bradford Crown Court, 2009–12; *b* 2 May 1943; *s* of late Henry Hamilton Stewart, MD, FRCS and Edna Mary Hamilton Stewart, JP; *m* 1st, 1972, Helen Margaret Whiteley (*d* 1998); one *d* (and one *d* decd); 2nd, 2006, Deborah Marion Rakusen (*née* Rose). *Educ:* Cheltenham Coll.; Univ. of Leeds (LLB Hons). Called to the Bar, Inner Temple, 1966, Bencher, 1992. A Recorder, 1982–2002; a Dep. High Court Judge, 1993–2002. Hon. Recorder of Bradford, 2009–12. *Recreations:* cricket, golf, British Heart Foundation. *Club:* Yorkshire Taverners (Leeds).

STEWART, (John) Allan; *b* 1 June 1942; *s* of Edward MacPherson Stewart and Eadie Barrie Stewart; *m* 1973, Marjorie Sally, (Susie), Gourlay (*see* M. S. Stewart); one *s* one *d. Educ:* Bell Baxter High Sch., Cupar; St Andrews Univ. (1st Cl. Hons MA 1964); Harvard Univ. (Rotary Internat. Foundn Fellow, 1964–65). Lectr in Pol Economy, St Andrews Univ., 1965–70 (Warden, John Burnet Hall, 1968–70); Confederation of British Industry: Head of Regional Develt Dept, 1971–73; Dep. Dir (Econs), 1973–76; Scottish Sec., 1976–78; Scottish Dir, 1978–79. Councillor, London Bor. of Bromley, 1975–76. Contested (C) Dundee E, 1970. MP (C): E Renfrewshire, 1979–83; Eastwood, 1983–97. PPS to Minister of State for Energy, 1981; Parly Under-Sec. of State, Scottish Office, 1981–86 and 1990–95. Mem., Select Cttee on Scottish Affairs, 1979–81 and 1995–97. Mem., Chairman's Panel, H of C, 1996–97. *Publications:* (with Harry Conroy) The Long March of the Market Men, 1996; articles in academic and gen. pubns on econ. and pol affairs. *Recreations:* sport, travel to Menorca. *Address:* Broadlie View, 8 Holehouse Brae, Neilston, E Renfrewshire G78 3LU. *E:* jallanstewart@hotmail.com.

STEWART, Lt Col John Cochrane; farmer, since 1999; Lord-Lieutenant of Clackmannanshire, since 2014; *b* Edinburgh, 21 Aug. 1957; *s* of Lt-Col Sir Robert (Christie) Stewart, *qv*; *m* 1999, Katie Dook; one *s* two *d. Educ:* Aysgarth Sch.; Eton Coll. Served Scots Guards, 1977–99: Platoon Comdr, 1977–81; Adjt, Cyprus, 1984–86; Co. Comd, 1986–90, 1992–94; MoD, 1990–92, 1996–97; 2 i/c, 1994–96, CO, 1997–99, 1st Bn. Equerry, 1981–84, Extra Equerry, 1999–, to the Duke of Kent. Golf tour operator, JCS Golf, 2002–. Adjt, Royal Co. of Archers, 2010–. Chm., Scots Guards Assoc., 2004–15. *Recreations:* golf, shooting, ski-ing, tennis. *Address:* Arndean, Dollar, Clackmannanshire FK14 7NH. *T:* (01259) 743525, 07940 530499. *E:* johnny@arndean.co.uk. *Clubs:* Muirfield Golf; Royal & Ancient Golf (St Andrews).

STEWART, Rt Rev. John Craig; Episcopal Chaplain, Diocese of Ballarat, Victoria, since 2010; *b* 10 Aug. 1940; *s* of J. J. Stewart; *m* 1967, Janine (*née* Schahinger); two *s. Educ:* Newington Coll., Sydney; Wesley Coll., Melbourne; Ridley Theol Coll., Melbourne. Ordained: deacon, 1965; priest, 1966; Curate, S Australia, 1965–68; Associate Priest, St John's, Crawley, 1968–70; Vicar: St Aidan's, Parkdale, 1970–74; St Luke's, Frankston, 1974–79; Gen. Sec., Church Missionary Soc., Victoria, 1979–84; Asst Bishop, Dio. Melbourne, 1984–2001; Rector, Parish of Woodend, Vic, 2001–04; Associate Priest, Parish of Holy Trinity, Bacchus Marsh, Vic, 2005–10. *Publications:* From London to Dartmoor, 1996; From Bolton to Ballarat, 1996; From Peebles to Port Phillip, 2006; From Penicuik to Penola, 2009. *Recreations:* family history, geology, music. *Address:* PO Box 928, Bacchus Marsh, Vic 3340, Australia.

STEWART, Prof. John David, DPhil; Professor of Local Government and Administration, Birmingham University, 1971–96, Hon. Professor, 1996–99, Emeritus Professor, since 1999; *b* 19 March 1929; *s* of Dr David Stewart and Phyllis Stewart (*née* Crossley); *m* 1953, Theresa Stewart, *qv*; two *s* two *d. Educ:* Stockport Grammar Sch.; Balliol Coll., Oxford (MA 1966); Nuffield Coll., Oxford (DPhil 1966). Industrial Relns Dept, NCB, 1954–66; Birmingham University: Sen. Lectr, 1966–71, Dir, 1976–83, Inst. of Local Govt Studies; Hd of Sch. of Public Policy, 1990–93. Member: Layfield Cttee on Local Govt Finance, 1974–76; Acad. Adv. Panel on local govt, DETR, 1997–98. President's Award for Outstanding Contribn to Local Govt, SOLACE, 2007; Local Govt Chronicle Lifetime Achievement Award, 2013. *Publications:* British Pressure Groups, 1958; Management in Local Government, 1971; The Responsive Local Authority, 1974; (jtly) Corporate Management in English Local Government, 1974; Local Government: the conditions of local choice, 1983; (jtly) The Case for Local Government, 1983; Understanding the Management of Local Government, 1988; (jtly) The Politics of Hung Authorities, 1992; Management for the Public Domain, 1994; (jtly) The Changing Organisation and Management of Local Government, 1994; (ed jtly) Local Government in the 1990s, 1995; The Nature of British Local Government, 2000; Modernising British Local Government, 2003. *Recreations:* gardening, walking. *Address:* 15 Selly Wick Road, Birmingham B29 7JJ. *T:* (0121) 472 1512. *E:* johnstewart@tinyonline.co.uk.

STEWART, John Duncan Maclean; Chairman, Heathrow Association for the Control of Air Noise, since 1998; *b* Bulawayo, 17 June 1949; *s* of James and Mary Stewart. *Educ:* Bristol Poly. (Dip. Social Policy). Co-ordinator, Lambeth Public Transport Gp, 1981–90; Hon. Chm., 1987–90, Chm., 1990–97, Alarm UK. Hon. Chair: Road Peace, 1994–2000; Slower Speeds Initiative, 1996–2005; UK Noise Assoc., 2000–; Transport 2000, 2001–08. *Publications:* Roadblock, 1995; Rough Crossing, 1998; Roads for People: policies for liveable streets, 2001; The Night Flight Question, 2005; Location, Location, Location, 2006; Victory Against All the Odds: the story of how the campaign to stop a third runway was won, 2010; Why Noise Matters, 2011. *Address:* 13 Stockwell Road, SW9 9AU. *E:* johnstewart2@btconnect.com.

STEWART, John Hall; Sheriff of South Strathclyde, Dumfries and Galloway at Hamilton (formerly at Airdrie), 1985–2010; *b* 15 March 1944; *s* of Cecil Francis Wilson Stewart and Mary Fyfe Hall or Stewart; *m* 1968, Marion MacCalman; one *s* two *d*. *Educ:* Airdrie Acad.; St Andrews Univ. (LLB). Advocate. Enrolled solicitor, 1970–77; Mem. Faculty of Advocates, 1978–. *Recreations:* scuba diving, spectator sports, his grandchildren. *Address:* 43 Grieve Croft, Bothwell, Glasgow G71 8LU. *T:* (01698) 853854. *Clubs:* Uddingston Rugby (Past Pres.), Uddingston Cricket and Sports (Past Pres.).

STEWART, John Morrison, FCIB; Chairman, Legal & General Group plc, since 2010; Group Chief Executive, National Australia Bank, 2004–08 (Executive Director, Principal Board, and Chief Executive of European Operations, 2003–04); Chairman, Guide Dogs for the Blind Association, since 2012; *b* 31 May 1949; *s* of Peter and Jane Stewart; *m* 1971, Sylvia Jameson; one *s* one *d*. *Educ:* Boroughmuir Sch., Edinburgh; Open Univ. (BA 1975). ACII 1979; FCIB 1989. Posts with Legal & General; Woolwich Building Society: joined 1977, as Br. Manager; Asst Gen. Manager, Insurance Services, 1988–91; General Manager: Financial Services, 1991–92; Retail Ops, 1992–95; Group Ops Dir, 1995–96; Gp Chief Exec., Woolwich Bldg Soc., subseq. Woolwich plc, 1996–2000; Dep. Gp Chief Exec., Barclays Bank, 2000–03. Chm., Woolwich Ind. Financial Adv. Services (Dir, 1989–95); Director: Banca Woolwich, Italy, 1996–2000; Banque Woolwich, France, 1996–2000. Non-executive Director: Business Council, Australia, 2006–08; Telstra Corp. Ltd, 2008–11; Bank of England, 2009–; Financial Reporting Council, 2014–. Pres., CIB, 2002–03 (Dep. Pres., 2001–02); Chm., Australian Bankers' Assoc., 2007–08. Member: Business-Govt Adv. Gp on nat. security, 2004–08; Prime Minister's task gp on emissions trading, 2007. Chm., Southern Cross Stud, 2009–. CCMI (CIMgt 1996). Hon. DLitt Heriot-Watt, 1997. *Recreation:* sailing.

STEWART, Sir (John) Simon (Watson), 6th Bt *cr* 1920, of Balgownie; MD, FRCP, FRCR; Consultant in Clinical Oncology at St Mary's Hospital and Imperial College School of Medicine (formerly Royal Postgraduate Medical School), since 1989; *b* 5 July 1955; *s* of Sir John Keith Watson Stewart, 5th Bt and of Mary Elizabeth, *d* of John Francis Moxon; *S* father, 1990; *m* 1978, Dr Catherine Stewart, *d* of H. Gordon Bond; one *s* one *d*. *Educ:* Uppingham Sch.; Charing Cross Hosp. Med. Sch. BSc (1st cl. Hons) 1977; MB BS Lond. 1980; MRCP 1983, FRCP 1994; FRCR 1986; MD 1989. *Heir: s* John Hamish Watson Stewart, *b* 12 Dec. 1983. *Address:* 8 Chiswick Wharf, Chiswick, W4 2SR. *T:* (020) 8995 2213. *Club:* Oriental.

STEWART, Sir John Young, (Sir Jackie), Kt 2001; OBE 1972; racing driver, retired 1973; developed Gleneagles Jackie Stewart Shooting School; Chairman, Stewart Grand Prix Ltd, 1996–2000; *b* 11 June 1939; *s* of late Robert Paul Stewart and of Jean Clark Young; *m* 1962, Helen McGregor; two *s*. *Educ:* Dumbarton Academy. First raced, 1961; competed in 4 meetings, 1961–62, driving for Barry Filer, Glasgow; drove for Ecurie Ecosse and other private entrants, winning 14 out of 23 starts, 1963; 28 wins out of 53 starts, 1964; drove Formula 1 for BRM, 1965–67 and for Ken Tyrrell, 1968–73; has won Australian, New Zealand, Swedish, Mediterranean, Japanese and many other non-championship major internat. Grands Prix; set up new world record by winning his 26th World Championship Grand Prix (Zandvoort), July 1973, and 27th (Nurburgring), Aug. 1973; 3rd in World Championship, 1965; 2nd in 1968 and 1972; World Champion, 1969, 1971, 1973. Global Ambassador, Royal Bank of Scotland, 2004–12; Strategic Advr, Genii Business Exchange, 2011–13. Chm., Motorsport Steering Cttee, Cranfield Univ., 2000–07. President: Dyslexia Scotland, 2004–; Springfield Club, 1976–; Vice President: British Dyslexia Assoc., 1998–; Vice-Chm. and Founding Trustee, Scottish Internat. Educn Trust, 1970– (Mem., Internat. Adv. Bd to the Scottish Parlt, 2002–10). Founder, Trustee and Chm., Grand Prix Mechanics Charitable Trust, 1987–. Hon. Prof., Stirling, 2001–. Hon. Dr Automotive Engrg, Lawrence Inst. of Technology, Mich, USA, 1973; Hon. DEng: Glasgow Caledonian, 1986; Heriot-Watt, 1996; Glasgow, 2001; Hon. Dr: Cranfield, 1998; Stirling, 1998; Edinburgh, 2006; Edinburgh Napier, 2013; Hon. DSc St Andrews, 2008. BARC Gold Medal, 1971, 1973. Daily Express Sportsman of the Year, 1971, 1973; World Sportsman of the Year, 1973; BBC Sports Personality of the Year, 1973; Scottish Sportsman of the Year, 1973; Sports Illustrated American Sportsman of the Year, 1973; ABC Sports Personality of the Year, 1973; Seagrove Trophy, 1973, 1999. *Film:* Weekend of a Champion, 1972. *Publications:* World Champion, 1970 (with Eric Dymock); Faster!, 1972 (with Peter Manso); On the Road, 1983; (with Alan Henry) Jackie Stewart's Principles of Performance Driving, 1986; The Jackie Stewart Book of Shooting, 1991; Winning is Not Enough: the autobiography, 2007; Collage: Jackie Stewart's Grand Prix album, 2010. *Recreations:* golf, fishing, tennis, shooting (Mem. Scottish and British Teams for Clay Pigeon shooting; former Scottish, English, Irish, Welsh and British Champion; won Coupe des Nations, 1959 and 1960; reserve for two-man team, 1960 Olympics). *Clubs:* (Hon.) Royal Automobile, British Racing Drivers' (Pres., 2000–06; Vice Pres., 2006–); Royal and Ancient (St Andrews); (Hon.) Gleneagles; Sunningdale; Loch Lomond Golf; Geneva Golf; Domaine Imperial, Club De Bonmont (Switzerland).

STEWART, Joseph Martin, OBE 1994; JP; Director of Human Resources, Police Service of Northern Ireland, since 2001; *b* 5 Nov. 1955; *s* of late Joseph Aloysius Stewart and of Annie Margaret Mary Stewart (*née* Friel); *m* 1978, Deirdre Ann Ritchie. *Educ:* Queen's Univ., Belfast (LLB Hons 1978); Univ. of Ulster (Post Grad. Dip. in Mgt Studies 1980). Engineering Employers Federation (NI) Association: Asst Indust. Relns Officer, 1978–80; Indust. Relns Officer, 1980–85; Dir, 1985–90; Personnel Dir, Harland & Wolff Shipbuilding and Heavy Industries Ltd, 1990–95; Sec. and Chief Exec., Police Authy for NI, 1995–2001. JP Ards Circuit, 1990. *Recreations:* game shooting, pedigree sheep breeding, motorcycle touring. *Address:* Police Service of Northern Ireland Lisnasharragh, 42 Montgomery Road, Belfast BT6 9LD. *Club:* Ulster Reform (Belfast).

STEWART, Kevin Morrice; Member (SNP) Aberdeen Central, Scottish Parliament, since 2011; *b* Aberdeen, 3 June 1968; *s* of Michael Stewart and Sandra Stewart. *Educ:* Summerhill Acad., Aberdeen; Univ. of Aberdeen (degree unfinished due to lack of finances). Worked at ASDA, then in family retail business. Mem. (SNP), Aberdeen CC, 1999– (Leader, SNP Gp, 1999–2011; Dep. Leader of Council, 2007–11). Mem., ACC, 1999–2012. Convener, Local Govt and Regeneration Cttee, Scottish Parlt, 2012–. Chm., Nestrans, 2007–11. Burgess, Guild of Burgh of Aberdeen, 2008–. *Recreation:* reading. *Address:* Scottish Parliament, Edinburgh EH99 1SP. *T:* (0131) 348 6382; (office) Third Floor, 27 John Street, Aberdeen AB25 1BT. *T:* (01224) 624719. *E:* kevin.stewart.msp@scottish.parliament.uk. *W:* www.twitter.com/KevinStewartMSP.

STEWART, Sir Ludovic Houston S.; *see* Shaw Stewart.

STEWART, Marjorie Sally, (Susie); Vice Lord-Lieutenant of Renfrewshire, since 2007; *b* Glasgow, 13 Aug. 1941; *d* of Colin W. H. Gourlay and Aileen M. Gourlay (*née* Millen); *m* 1973, (John) Allan Stewart, *qv*; one *s* one *d*. *Educ:* St Leonards Sch., St Andrews; St Andrews Univ. (MA Spanish and French 1962); Edinburgh Univ. (Postgrad. Dip. Social Studies 1963). FFPH 2001. Ed., Dept of Community Medicine, St Thomas' Hosp. Med. Sch., 1966–76; Technical Editor: BMA Special Jls, 1977–84; Panel of Social Medicine and Epidemiol., Eur. Communities, 1984–90; Exec. Sec., Scottish Forum for Public Health Medicine, 1990–95; Res. Manager, Dept of Public Health, Univ. of Glasgow, 1995–98. DL Renfrewshire, 1996. *Publications:* (with Walter W. Holland): Screening in Health Care, 1990; Public Health: the vision and the challenge, 1997; Screening in Disease Prevention: what works?, 2005. *Recreations:* creative writing, reading, gardening, dogs and cats, wildlife, tapestry, Menorca, beekeeping. *Address:* Broadlie View, 8 Holehouse Brae, Neilston, E Renfrewshire G78 3LU. *T:* (0141) 881 2698. *E:* susiestewart113@btopenworld.com. *Club:* Western (Glasgow).

STEWART, Michael James; Reader in Political Economy, University College, London University, 1969–94, now Emeritus; *b* 6 Feb. 1933; *s* of late John Innes Mackintosh Stewart; *m* 1962, Frances Kaldor, *d* of Baron Kaldor, FBA; one *s* two *d* (and one *d* decd). *Educ:* Campbell Coll., Belfast; St Edward's Sch., Oxford; Magdalen Coll., Oxford (1st cl. PPE 1955). Asst Res. Officer, Oxford Univ. Inst. of Statistics, 1955–56; Barnett Fellow, Cornell Univ., 1956–57; Econ. Asst, HM Treasury, 1957–60; Sec. to Council on Prices, Productivity and Incomes, 1960–61; Econ. Adviser, HM Treasury, 1961–62, Cabinet Office, 1964–67 (Senior Econ. Advr, 1967), Kenya Treasury, 1967–69; Special Adviser to Sec. of State for Trade, Apr.–Oct. 1974; Economic Adviser to Malta Labour Party, 1970–73; Special Econ. Advr to Foreign Sec., 1977–78. Guest Scholar, Brookings Instn, Washington, DC, 1978–79. Mem., Acad. Adv. Panel, Bank of England, 1977–83. Contested (Lab): Folkestone and Hythe, 1964; Croydon North-West, 1966. Asst Editor, Nat. Inst. Econ. Review, 1962–64. Consultant to various UN agencies, 1971–. *Publications:* Keynes and After, 1967; The Jekyll and Hyde Years: politics and economic policy since 1964, 1977; Controlling the Economic Future: policy dilemmas in a shrinking world, 1983; (with Peter Jay) Apocalypse 2000: economic breakdown and the suicide of democracy 1989–2000, 1987; Keynes in the 1990s: a return to economic sanity, 1993. *Recreations:* looking at paintings, eating at restaurants in France. *Address:* 79 South Hill Park, NW3 2SS. *T:* (020) 7435 3686. *Club:* Oxford and Cambridge.

STEWART, Sir Moray; *see* Stewart, Sir J. M.

STEWART, Neill Alastair; His Honour Judge Stewart; a Circuit Judge, since 1999; *b* 8 June 1947; *yr s* of James Robertson Stewart, CBE; *m* 2000, Tiffany, *d* of His Honour William Llewellyn Monro Davies, *qv*; one *s* one *d*. *Educ:* Whitgift Sch.; Clare Coll., Cambridge (BA Mech. Scis Tripos). Engr, Sir Alexander Gibb & Partners, 1968–70; called to the Bar, Middle Temple, 1973; in practice at the Bar, 1975–99. *Address:* c/o Guildford Crown Court, Bedford Road, Guildford GU1 4ST.

STEWART, Nicholas John Cameron; QC 1987; *b* 16 April 1947; *s* of John Cameron Stewart and Margaret Mary (*née* Botsford); *m* 1974, Pamela Jean Windham (marr. diss. 2000); one *s* two *d*, one *d* by Dr Tabea Lauktien. *Educ:* Bedford Modern Sch.; Worcester Coll., Oxford (BA). CDipAF. Called to the Bar, Inner Temple, 1971, Bencher, 1999; Dep. High Ct Judge, Chancery Div., 1991–. Chm., Bar Human Rights Cttee, 1994–98. Pres., Union Internationale des Avocats, 2001–02. Narrator, No Further Questions, BBC Radio series, 1993 and 1995. *Recreations:* walking, Spain, photography. *Address:* Ely Place Chambers, 30 Ely Place, EC1N 6TD.

STEWART, Nikola Caroline, (Mrs A. R. Milne); Sheriff of South Strathclyde, Dumfries and Galloway at Lanark, since 2000; *b* 29 July 1956; *d* of James Lumsden Stewart and Joyce Elizabeth Stewart (*née* Urquhart); *m* 1989, Alastair Robert Milne; two *d*. *Educ:* Harris Acad., Dundee; Dundee Univ. (MA, LLB, DipLP). Admitted Advocate, 1987; called to the Scottish Bar, 1987; in practice as advocate, 1987–2000; Temp. Sheriff, 1997–99. Chm., Child Support Appeal Tribunals, 1990–97. *Address:* Medwynbrae, Carlops Road, West Linton EH46 7DS.

STEWART, Norman MacLeod; Senior Partner, 1984–97, Consultant, 1997–99, Allan, Black & McCaskie; President, The Law Society of Scotland, 1985–86; *b* 2 Dec. 1934; *s* of George and Elspeth Stewart; *m* 1959, Mary Slater Campbell; four *d*. *Educ:* Elgin Acad.; Univ. of Edinburgh (BL); SSC. Alex. Morison & Co., WS, Edinburgh, 1954–58; Allan, Black & McCaskie, Solicitors, Elgin, 1959–99, Partner, 1961–97. Law Society of Scotland: Mem. Council, 1976–87; Convener: Public Relations Cttee, 1979–81; Professional Practice Cttee, 1981–84; Vice-Pres., 1984–85. Chm., Elgin and Lossiemouth Harbour Bd, 1993–2009. Hon. Mem., American Bar Assoc., 1985–. *Recreations:* walking, golf, music, Spanish culture. *Address:* 25 Saltcoats Gardens, Bellsquarry South, Livingston, W Lothian EH54 9JD. *T:* (01506) 419439. *E:* norman666@btinternet.com.

STEWART, Patricia Ann; Deputy Chief Executive, Food Standards Agency, 2003–07; *b* 22 March 1949; *d* of late Walter William Stewart and Freda Dorothy Stewart (*née* Rolfe); *m* 1st, 1978, Jeremy Gye Colman, *qv* (marr. diss.); 2nd, 1996, Lt Comdr Nicholas Austen Bates, RN. *Educ:* Palmer's Grammar Sch. for Girls, Grays; Univ. of Sussex (BSc (Maths with Electronic Engrg) 1970). FSS 1975. Statistician: Civil Service Dept, 1970–79; Local Govt Finance, DoE, 1979–83, seconded to EC, Luxembourg, 1983; Department of Health: Chief Statistician, 1984–86; Assistant Secretary: NHS Finance, 1986–89; NHS Liaison, 1989–91; Facilities and Corporate Mgt, 1991–95; Public Health Div., 1996–97; Food Standards Agency: Implementation Div., 1997–2000; Dir, Corporate Resources and Strategy, 2000–07. *Recreations:* music (singing, playing the viol; Chair, Southern Early Music Forum, 2010–), contributing to village life, computers and gadgets, reading, boating. *E:* pas_ww@btinternet.com.

STEWART, Sir Patrick, Kt 2010; OBE 2001; actor; *b* 13 July 1940; *s* of late Alfred Stewart and Gladys Stewart (*née* Barrowclough); *m* 1st, 1966, Sheila Falconer (marr. diss. 1990); one *s* one *d*; 2nd, 2002, Wendy Neuss (marr. diss.); 3rd, 2013, Sunny Ozell. *Educ:* Mirfield Secondary Modern Sch.; Bristol Old Vic Theatre Sch. Joined RSC, 1966, Associate Artist, 1967–87; CEO, Flying Freehold Prodns, 1998–. *Theatre includes:* Antony and Cleopatra, 1979; Henry IV, RSC, 1984; Yonadab, NT, 1986; Who's Afraid of Virginia Woolf?, Young Vic, 1987; A Christmas Carol (one-man show), NY, 1991, 1992, Albery, 2005; The Tempest, NY, 1995; Othello, Washington, 1997; The Ride Down Mount Morgan, NY, 1998, 2000; The Master Builder, Albery, 2003; A Life in the Theatre, Apollo, 2005; Antony and Cleopatra, RSC, 2006; The Tempest, RSC, 2006, transf. Novello, 2007; Twelfth Night, Chichester, 2007; Macbeth, Chichester, transf. Gielgud, 2007; Hamlet, RSC, 2008; Waiting for Godot, UK tour then Th. Royal, Haymarket, 2009, NY 2013; Bingo, Chichester, 2010, transf. Young Vic, 2012; The Merchant of Venice, RSC, 2011; No Man's Land, NY, 2013; *television includes:* Hedda, 1975; I Claudius, 1976; Oedipus Rex, 1976; Tinker Tailor Soldier Spy, 1979; Hamlet, Prince of Denmark, 1980; Smiley's People, 1982; Maybury, 1980; The Mozart Inquest, 1985; The Devil's Disciple, 1987; Star Trek: The Next Generation (series), 1987–94; Death Train, 1993; The Canterville Ghost (also co-prod), 1996; Moby Dick, 1998; A Christmas Carol (also prod), 1999; King of Texas (also prod), 2002; The Lion in Winter (also prod), 2003; Eleventh Hour, 2006; Hamlet, 2009; Richard II, 2012; Blunt Talk (US), 2015; *films include:* Excalibur, 1981; Dune, 1984; Lady Jane, 1986; LA Story, 1991; Robin Hood: Men in Tights, 1993; Gunmen, 1994; Star Trek: Generations, 1994; Jeffrey, 1996; Star Trek: First Contact, 1996; Conspiracy Theory, 1997; Masterminds, 1997; Dad Savage, 1998; Star Trek: Insurrection, 1998; X Men, 2000; Star Trek: Nemesis, 2002; X2, 2003; Steamboy, 2005; X-Men: The Last Stand, 2006; X Men: Days of Future Past, 2014; Green Room, 2015. Cameron Mackintosh Vis. Prof. of Contemporary Th., Univ. of Oxford, 2007. Chancellor, 2004–, Prof. of Performing Arts, 2008, Univ. of Huddersfield. Emeritus Fellow, St Catherine's Coll., Oxford, 2010–. *Address:* c/o Independent Talent Group Ltd, 40 Whitfield Street, W1T 2RH.

STEWART, Patrick Loudon McIain, MBE 2000; Consultant, Messrs Stewart Balfour & Sutherland, Solicitors, Campbeltown, Argyll, 2000–13; Lord-Lieutenant, Argyll and Bute, since 2011 (Vice Lord-Lieutenant, 2003–11); *b* 25 July 1945; *s* of late Archibald Ian Balfour Stewart, CBE and of Ailsa Rosamund Mary Stewart (*née* Massey); *m* 1969, Mary Anne McLellan; one *s* one *d*. *Educ:* Dalintober Primary Sch.; Edinburgh Acad.; Edinburgh Univ. (LLB). WS 1968; NP 1968. Partner, 1970–82, Sen. Partner, 1982–2000, Stewart Balfour & Sutherland, Solicitors. Asst Sec., 1970–74, Sec., 1974–2009, Adminr, 2009–14, Clyde Fishermen's Assoc.; Marine Envmt, then Marine Legislation Consultant, Scottish Fishermen's Fedn, 2009–12. Clerk to Comrs of Income Tax, Argyll-Islay, 1972–2009. DL Argyll and

Bute, 1987. Hon. Sheriff at Campbeltown, 1997–. CO, Campbeltown Unit, Sea Cadet Corps, 1972–88; Mem., Sea Cadet Council, 1983–93; Trustee, Sea Cadet Assoc., 2000–04; Life Vice Pres., Marine Soc. and Sea Cadets, 2005. Cadet Forces Medal, 1984. *Recreations:* sailing, field sports. *Address:* PO Box 9261, Campbeltown, Argyll PA28 6YE. *T:* (01586) 551717. *E:* plms@talktalk.net.

See also Hon. Lord Stewart.

STEWART, Dame Pieter (Ane), DNZM 2012; Founder and Managing Director, New Zealand Fashion Week, 1999–2015, now Consulting Director; *b* Christchurch, NZ; *d* of Reginald George McKenzie and Joan McKenzie; *m* 1968, Peter Maxwell Stewart; one *s* three *d*. *Educ:* St Margaret's Coll., Christchurch. Anaesthetic and Operating Theatre Sec., North Canterbury Hosp. Bd, 1965–68; Founder, Pieters Model Agency and Sch., 1981; Associate Editor, Fashion Quarterly mag., 1985–87; Founder, Pieter Stewart Promotions, public relns and promotions co., 1988; coordinated Corbans Fashion Collections, annual TV special, 1990–95; produced and coordinated Wella Fashion Collections and Wella Fashion Report, TV specials, 1996–99; launched NZ Fashion Festival, 2010. Member: Bd, St Margaret's Coll. Trust, 1992–2003 (Chm., 1994–2003); Bd, Ind. Schs Assoc., 1996–2003 (Dep. Chm., 1999–2003); Trust Bd, Sir George Seymour Coll. of Travel and Tourism, 1997–2004. Former Mem., Exec. Cttee, Child Cancer Soc.; former Coordinator, Child Cancer Foundn House. MInstD. *Recreations:* family activities, sailing, reading, cooking. *Address:* Heatherlea Homestead, Darfield 7572, New Zealand. *T:* (9) 3778033, *Fax:* (3) 3180891. *E:* pieter@pieterstewart.com. *Clubs:* Global Women; Windwhistle Winter Sports.

STEWART, Col Robert Alexander, (Bob), DSO 1993; MP (C) Beckenham, since 2010; *b* 7 July 1949; *s* of late A. A. Stewart, MC and Marguerita Joan Stewart; *m* 1st (marr. diss. 1993); one *s* one *d*; 2nd, 1994, Claire Podbielski; one *s* three *d*. *Educ:* Chigwell Sch.; RMA Sandhurst; Univ. of Wales, Aberystwyth (BSc 1st Cl. Hons Internat. Politics). Commnd, Cheshire Regt, 1969; Instructor, RMA, 1979–80; Army Staff Coll., Camberley, 1981; Company Comdr, N Ireland, 1982–83; Staff Officer, MoD, 1984–85; 2 i/c 1st Bn Cheshire Regt, 1986–87; JSSC 1988; MA to Chm., NATO Mil. Cttee, HQ NATO, Brussels, 1989–91; CO, 1st Bn Cheshire Regt, 1991–93; Chief of Policy, SHAPE, 1994–95; resigned Regular Army, 1996; JSDC, 1997–98. Sen. Consultant, Public Affairs, Hill & Knowlton (UK) Ltd, 1996–98; Sen. Vice Pres., WorldSpace UK, 1998–2001; Dir, Action Leadership, 2001–10. Mem., Defence Select Cttee, 2010–; Chm., All-Party Parly Gp for Army, 2010–. Non-exec. Chm., Premier Gold Resources, 2012–15. Chm., Ind. Defence Media Assoc., 2003–10. Patron: Elifar Foundn, 2007–; Bede Griffiths Charitable Trust (UK), 2014–. Companion, RAF Regt Officers' Dinner Club. *Publications:* Broken Lives, 1993; Thoughts on Leadership, 2004; Leadership under Pressure, 2009. *Recreations:* writing, history. *Address:* House of Commons, SW1A 0AA. *T:* 07771 863894. *Clubs:* Army and Navy, Royal Air Force.

STEWART, Lt-Col Sir Robert (Christie), KCVO 2002; CBE 1983; TD 1962; Lord-Lieutenant of Clackmannan, 1994–2001; *b* 3 Aug. 1926; *m* 1953, Ann Grizel Cochrane; three *s* two *d*. *Educ:* Eton; University College, Oxford. Lt Scots Guards, 1945–49. Oxford Univ., 1949–51 (BA Agric.). TA, 7 Argyll and Sutherland Highlanders, 1948–66; Lt-Col Comdg 7 A & SH, 1963–66. Hon. Col, 1/51 Highland Volunteers, 1972–75. Chm. and Pres., Bd of Governors, E of Scotland Coll. of Agric., 1970–83. Chm., Kinross CC, 1963–73. DL Kinross, 1956, Vice Lieut, 1958; Lord-Lieutenant, Kinross-shire, 1966–74. Mem., Queen's Bodyguard for Scotland, 1961–. *Address:* Mains of Arndean, by Dollar, Clackmannanshire FK14 7NT. *T:* (01259) 742527. *Club:* Royal Perth Golfing Society.

See also Countess of Romney, Lt-Col J. C. Stewart.

STEWART, Roderick David, CBE 2007; singer and songwriter; *b* 10 Jan. 1945; *s* of Robert Joseph Stewart and Elsie Stewart; *m* 1st, 1979, Alana Collins (marr. diss. 1984); one *s* one *d*; 2nd, 1990, Rachel Hunter (marr. diss.); one *s* one *d*; one *d* by Kelly Emberg; 3rd, 2007, Penny Lancaster; two *s*. *Educ:* William Grimshaw Secondary Modern Sch., Hornsey. Singer with Jeff Beck Group, 1968–69, with The Faces, 1969–75. Albums include: with Jeff Beck Group: Truth, 1968; Cosa Nostra Beck Ola, 1969; with The Faces: First Step, 1970; Long Player, 1971; A Nod's as Good as a Wink…To a Blind Horse, 1971; Ooh La La, 1973; Coast to Coast, 1974; solo: An Old Raincoat Won't Ever Let You Down, 1969; Gasoline Alley, 1970; Every Picture Tells a Story, 1971; Never a Dull Moment, 1972; Smiler, 1974; Atlantic Crossing, 1975; A Night on the Town, 1976; Foot Loose and Fancy Free, 1977; Blondes Have More Fun, 1978; Foolish Behaviour, 1980; Tonight I'm Yours, 1981; Body Wishes, 1983; Camouflage, 1984; Every Beat of My Heart, 1986; Out of Order, 1988; Vagabond Heart, 1991; A Spanner in the Works, 1995; When We Were the New Boys, 1998; Human, 2001; It Had To Be You—The Great American Songbook, 2002; Sweet Little Rock N Roller, 2002; As Time Goes By—The Great American Songbook, Vol. II, 2003; Stardust—The Great American Songbook, Vol. III, 2004; Thanks For The Memory—The Great American Songbook, Vol. IV, 2005; Still the Same, 2006; Soulbook, 2009; Fly Me To The Moon—The Great American Songbook, Vol. V, 2010; Merry Christmas, Baby, 2012; Time 2013. *Publications:* Rod: the autobiography, 2012. *Address:* c/o Sony Music Entertainment UK, 9 Derry Street, W8 5HY.

STEWART, Roderick James Nugent, (Rory), OBE 2004; MP (C) Penrith and The Border, since 2010; Parliamentary Under-Secretary of State, Department for Environment, Food and Rural Affairs, since 2015; *b* 3 Jan. 1973; *s* of Brian Thomas Webster Stewart, CMG; *m* 2012, Shoshana Clark; one *s*. *Educ:* Eton; Balliol Coll., Oxford (MA). Served Black Watch (RHR), 1991–92. Entered FCO, 1995; Second Secretary: Jakarta, 1997–99; Montenegro, 1999–2000; crossed Iran, Afghanistan, Pakistan, India and Nepal on foot, 2000–02; Dep. Governorate Co-ordinator, Al Amarah, Coalition Provisional Authy, 2003–04; Sen. Advr, Nasiriyah, 2004; Fellow, Carr Center, Harvard Univ., 2004–05; Chief Exec., Turquoise Mt Foundn, Afghanistan, 2005–08; Ryan Family Prof. of Human Rights and Dir, Carr Center for Human Rights Policy, Harvard Univ., 2008–10. Member: Foreign Affairs Select Cttee, 2010–15; Defence Select Cttee, 2014–15 (Chm., 2014–15). Gov., Internat. Res. Develt Council, 2008–10. Presenter, The Legacy of Lawrence of Arabia, 2010, Afghanistan: the Great Game, 2012, BBC TV. FRSL 2008. DUniv Stirling, 2009; Hon. Dr American Univ. Paris, 2011. Livingston Medal, RSGS, 2010. *Publications:* The Places in Between, 2004 (Ondaatje Prize, RSL, 2005); Occupational Hazards, 2006; (jtly) Can Intervention Work?, 2011; The Marches, 2014. *Recreations:* walking, history, trees. *Address:* House of Commons, SW1A 0AA. *Clubs:* Athenæum, Travellers, Beefsteak.

STEWART, Roger Paul Davidson; QC 2001; a Recorder, since 2002; *b* 17 Aug. 1963; *s* of late Martin Neil Davidson Stewart and of Elizabeth Janet Stewart (*née* Porter); *m* 1st, 1988, Georgina Louise Smith (marr. diss. 2011); two *s* one *d*; 2nd, 2011, Elizabeth Jane Wiseman; one *d* and two step *s* two step *d*. *Educ:* Oundle Sch.; Jesus Coll., Cambridge (MA, LLM). Called to the Bar, Inner Temple, 1986, Bencher, 2002; Barrister, Lincoln's Inn, 2000–; Hd of Chambers, 2006–10. *Publications:* (ed) Jackson and Powell on Professional Negligence, 3rd edn 1992, 4th edn 1997, (gen. ed.) 5th edn 2002, 7th edn 2012. *Recreations:* sailing, ski-ing, reading military history. *Address:* 4 New Square, Lincoln's Inn, WC2A 3RJ. *Clubs:* National Liberal; Lost Valley Mountaineering (Glencoe).

STEWART, Rory; *see* Stewart, R. J. N.

STEWART, Rosemary Gordon, (Mrs I. M. James), PhD; author of management books; *d* of William George Stewart and Sylvia Gordon Stewart (*née* Sulley); *m* 1961, Ioan Mackenzie James, *qv*. *Educ:* Univ. of British Columbia (BSc); London School of Economics, Univ. of London (MSc, PhD). Dir, Acton Soc. Trust, 1956–61; Res. Fellow, London Sch. of Economics, 1964–66; Fellow in Organizational Behaviour, Templeton Coll. (formerly Oxford Centre for Mgt Studies), 1967–93; Co-Dir, Oxford Health Care Mgt Inst., Templeton Coll., Oxford, 1993–2000. Organiser, NHS Chairs Workshop, 1993–. Mem. Bd, Centre for Develt and Population Activities, Washington, 1988–2004. Mem., Oxfordshire Res. Ethics Cttee, 2001–09. Gov., Headington Sch., Oxford, 1991–2003. FRSocMed 2008; Hon. Fellow, Green Templeton (formerly Templeton) Coll., Oxford, 2000. Hon. DPhil Uppsala, 1998. *Publications:* (jtly) The Boss: the life and times of the British businessman, 1958; The Reality of Management, 1963, 3rd edn 1997; Managers and their Jobs, 1967, 2nd edn 1988; The Reality of Organizations, 1970, 3rd edn 1993; How Computers Affect Management, 1971; Contrasts in Management, 1976 (John Player Award for best British mgt book); (contrib.) The District Administrator in the NHS, 1982; Leading in the NHS, 1989, 2nd edn 1995; Managing Today and Tomorrow, 1994; (jtly) The Diversity of Management, 1994; (contrib.) Managing in Britain and Germany, 1994; (ed) Managerial Work, 1998; (ed) Management of Health Care, 1998; Evidence-based Management, 2001; The Struggle for Artistic Success, 2014. *Recreations:* travel, painting, art history, golf, gardening. *Address:* Saïd Business School, Egrove Park, Oxford OX1 5NY.

STEWART, Sir Simon; *see* Stewart, Sir J. S. W.

STEWART, Hon. Sir Stephen (Paul), Kt 2013; **Hon. Mr Justice Stewart;** a Judge of the High Court of Justice, Queen's Bench Division, since 2013; *b* 9 Oct. 1953; *s* of Cyril Stewart and Phyllis Mary Stewart; *m* 1980, Prof. (Mary) Felicity Dyer; one *s* one *d*. *Educ:* Stand GS, Whitefield, Manchester; St Peter's Coll., Oxford (MA; half blue for badminton); Open Univ. (BA 1st cl. Hons Mod. Langs (French and Spanish), 2012). Called to the Bar, Middle Temple, 1975 (Harmsworth Major Exhibnr, 1973; Harmsworth Schol., 1975), Bencher, 2013; in practice on Northern Circuit; QC 1996; Asst Recorder, 1995–99; a Recorder, 1999–2003; Dep. Judge, Technol. and Construction Court, 2000–03; a Circuit Judge, 2003–13; Senior Circuit Judge and Designated Civil Judge: Liverpool, 2003–11; Gtr Manchester, 2011–13; Queen's Bench Admin. Court Judge, N and NE Circuits, 2014–. *Recreations:* running, music, foreign languages, writing poetry. *Address:* Royal Courts of Justice, Strand, WC2A 2LL. *Club:* East India.

STEWART, Susie; *see* Stewart, M. S.

STEWART, Suzanne Freda; *see* Norwood, Her Honour S. F.

STEWART, Theresa; Member (Lab), Birmingham City Council, 1970–2002 (Leader, 1993–99); Lord Mayor of Birmingham, 2000–01; *b* 24 Aug. 1930; *d* of John Raisman and Ray Raisman (*née* Baker); *m* 1953, John David Stewart, *qv*; two *s* two *d*. *Educ:* Cowper Street Sch., Leeds; Allerton High Sch., Leeds; Somerville Coll., Oxford (MA; Hon. Fellow, 2001). Member: Birmingham Regl Hosp. Bd, 1968–71; W Midland CC, 1974–77; Birmingham City Council: Chair: Birmingham Community Develt Project, 1973–76; Social Services Cttee, 1981–82 and 1984–87; Direct Labour Contract Services Cttee, 1989–93; Policy and Resources Cttee, 1997–99; W Midlands Jt Cttee, 1998–2001. Vice-Chm., AMA Social Services Cttee, 1985–87; Chair, W Midlands LGA, 1999–2000 (Sen. Vice Chair, 1998–99). Chm., Assoc. of Direct Labour Orgns, 1994–95. Hon. LLD Birmingham, 2000. *Recreations:* relaxing in a hot bath with a good book, walking, cooking. *Address:* 15 Selly Wick Road, Birmingham B29 7JJ. *T:* (0121) 472 1512.

STEWART, Sir William (Duncan Paterson), Kt 1994; PhD, DSc; FRS 1977; FRSE; Chief Scientific Adviser, Cabinet Office, 1990–95; President, Royal Society of Edinburgh, 1999–2002; *b* 7 June 1935; *s* of John and Margaret Stewart; *m* 1st, 1958, Catherine MacLeod (*d* 1998); one *s* decd; 2nd, 2000, Elizabeth Smales. *Educ:* Bowmore Junior Secondary Sch., Isle-of-Islay; Dunoon Grammar Sch.; Glasgow Univ. (BSc, PhD, DSc). FRSE 1973. Asst Lectr, Univ. of Nottingham, 1961–63; Lectr, Westfield Coll., Univ. of London, 1963–68; Boyd Baxter Prof. of Biology, 1968–95, Vice-Principal, 1985–87, Univ. of Dundee; Sec. and Chief Exec., AFRC, 1988–90. Head, UK Office of Sci. and Technol., 1992–95. Chairman: Microbiol Res. Authy, Porton Down, 1999–2002; HPA, 2003–09. Chairman: Internat. Cttee on Microbial Ecology, 1983–86; Royal Soc. Biotechnology and Educn Wkg Gp, 1980–81; Independent Adv. Gp on Gruinard Is., 1985–87; President: British Phycological Soc., 1975–77; Council, Scottish Marine Biol. Assoc., 1985–87; Bioindustry Assoc., 1995–99; BAAS, 2000–01; Member: Council, Marine Biol. Assoc., 1973–76, 1977–80, 1981–84; British Nat. Cttee for problems of environment, 1979–85; UNESCO Panel on Microbiology, 1975–81; Council, NERC, 1979–85; Internat. Cell Res. Org., 1979–84; Royal Soc. Study Gp on Science Educn, 1981–82; Council, Royal Soc., 1984–86 (Vice-Pres., 1995–97); Royal Commn on Environmental Pollution, 1986–88; DSAC, 1990–95. Chairman: Govt Technol. Foresight Steering Gp, 1993–95; Govt Sci. and Engrg Base Co-ordinating Cttee, 1993–95; Ind. Expert Gp on Mobile Phones and Health, 1999–2000; Nat. Radiological Protection Bd, 2003–05; Mem., DTI Link Steering Gp, 1990–94. Dir (non-exec.), Water Research Centre plc, 1995–2002; Chm., Cyclacel Ltd, 1998–2002. Member, Governing Body: Scottish Hort. Res. Inst., 1971–80; Scottish Crop Res. Inst., 1980–88; Macaulay Land Use Res. Inst., 1987–88; Trustee, Royal Botanic Gardens, Kew, 2006–11. Chairman: Dundee Teaching Hosps NHS Trust, 1997–99; Tayside Univ. Hosps NHS Trust, 1999–2000. 25 hon. degrees and fellowships. President's Medal, Royal Acad. Engrg, 1995. *Publications:* Nitrogen Fixation in Plants, 1966; (jtly) The Blue-Green Algae, 1973; Algal Physiology and Biochemistry, 1974; (ed) Nitrogen Fixation by Free-living Organisms, 1975; (ed jtly) Nitrogen Fixation, 1980; (ed jtly) The Nitrogen Cycle of the United Kingdom, 1984; Mobile Phones and Health, 2000; over 250 papers in learned jls of repute. *Recreations:* watching soccer, watching people, DIY, playing the bagpipes (occasionally). *Address:* 1 Clarendon Drive, Perth Road, Dundee DD2 1JU. *Club:* Dundee United.

STEWART-CLARK, Sir John, (Sir Jack), 3rd Bt *cr* 1918; Chairman, Dundas Castle Ltd, since 1999; Member (C) European Parliament, East Sussex and Kent South, 1994–99 (Sussex East, 1979–94); a Vice-President, 1992–97; *b* 17 Sept. 1929; *e s* of Sir Stewart Stewart-Clark, 2nd Bt, and Jane Pamela (*d* 1993), *d* of late Major Arundell Clarke; *S* father, 1971; *m* 1958, Lydia Frederike, *d* of J. W. Loudon, Holland; one *s* four *d*. *Educ:* Eton; Balliol College, Oxford; Harvard Business School. Commissioned with HM Coldstream Guards, 1948–49. Oxford, 1949–52. With J. & P. Coats Ltd, 1952–69; Managing Director: J. & P. Coats, Pakistan, Ltd, 1961–67; J. A. Carp's Garenfabrieken, Holland, 1967–69; Philips Industries, 1971–79: Managing Director: Philips Electrical Ltd, London, 1971–75; Pye of Cambridge Ltd, 1975–79. Director: A. T. Kearney Ltd, 1979–92; Low and Bonar plc, 1980–95; Pioneer Concrete plc, 1986–99; TSB Scotland, 1986–89. Pres. Supervisory Bd, Eur. Inst. for Security, 1984–86; Mem. Council, RUSI, 1979–83. Dir and Trustee, Eur. Centre for Work and Society, 1982–2005; Mem., Bd of Govs, Eur. Inst. for Media, 1995–2000; Chairman: Conf. of Regions of North Western Europe, 1986–92; Eur. Parliamentarians and Industrialists Council, 1990–99. European Drugs Monitoring Centre: Mem., Mgt Bd, 1999–2006; Mem., Policy Bureau, 2001–06; Trustee, Mentor UK Foundn, 1999–2014. Chm., EP delegn to Canada, 1979–84; Mem., EP delegn to Japan, 1984–94. Treas., Eur. Democratic Group, 1979–92. Member Royal Company of Archers, Queen's Body Guard for Scotland. Contested (U) North Aberdeen, Gen. Election, 1959. *Publications:* Competition Law in the European Community, 1990; It's My Problem As Well: drugs prevention and education, 1993. *Recreations:* golf, tennis, photography, vintage cars. *Heir: s* Alexander Dudley Stewart-Clark, *b* 21 Nov. 1960. *Address:* Dundas Castle, South Queensferry, near Edinburgh EH30 9SP. *T:* (0131) 331 1114. *Club:* White's.

STEWART-JONES, Mrs Richard; *see* Smith, Emma.

STEWART-RICHARDSON, Sir Simon (Alaisdair), 17th Bt *cr* 1630; *b* 9 June 1947; *er s* of Sir Ian Rorie Hay Stewart-Richardson, 16th Bt, and of Audrey Meryl (who *m* 1975, Patrick Allan Pearson Robertson, CMG), *e d* of late Claude Odlum; *S* father, 1969; *m* 1990, Marilene Cabal do Nascimento (marr. diss.); one *s* one *d*. *Educ:* Trinity College, Glenalmond. *Heir: s* Jason Rorie Stewart-Richardson, *b* 5 Oct. 1990. *Address:* Lynedale, Longcross, near Chertsey, Surrey KT16 0DP. *T:* (01932) 872329.

STEWART-ROBERTS, Phyllida Katharine, CVO 2009; OBE 1995; Lord-Lieutenant, East Sussex, 2000–08 (Vice Lord-Lieutenant, 1996–2000); Superintendent-in-Chief, St John Ambulance Brigade, 1990–93; *b* 19 Aug. 1933; *d* of Lt-Col Walter Harold Bamfield, Royal Welch Fusiliers and Veronica Grissell; *m* 1955, Andrew Kerr Stewart-Roberts; one *s* one *d*. *Educ:* Tormead Sch.; Royal Acad. of Music (DipEd). Primary sch. teacher, LCC, 1954–57; Love Walk Hostel for Disabled Workers: Mem., Management Cttee, 1972–94; Vice Chm., 1980–83; Chm., 1983–89; Pres., 1994–2000. Trustee: Community Service Volunteers, 1984–2012; Orders of St John Care Trust, 1994–2005; Defence Medical Welfare Service, 2000–12; Member: Management Cttee, Habinteg Housing Assoc., 1988–96 (Chm., Southern Cttee, 1994–96); St John Ambulance Brigade, Sussex, 1962–89, 1994–2000; Jt Pres., Council of Order of St John, Sussex, 2000–08 (County Pres., 1984–89; Chm., 1995–2000); Chm., Jt Cttee, Order of St John of Jerusalem and BRCS, 1991–2001 (Mem., 1990–2001); Mem., Florence Nightingale Foundn, 1990–2000; Vice-Pres., VAD Assoc., 1989–95. Mem. Council, Sussex Univ., 1995–2001 (Vice-Chm., 1999–2001). Pres., Friends of Lewes Victoria Hosp., 2009–; Vice-Pres., Sussex Housing and Care, 2009–. JP Inner London, 1980–95. DL E Sussex, 1991. DUniv Sussex, 2009. DStJ 1993. *Recreations:* needlework, the gentler country pursuits. *Address:* Mount Harry Lodge, Offham, Lewes, E Sussex BN7 3QW.

STEWART-SMITH, Christopher Dudley, CBE 1995; DL; Chairman, Cautley Ltd, since 1997; Producer, Stanley Hall Opera, since 2001; *b* 21 Jan. 1941; *s* of late Ean Stewart-Smith and Edmee von Wallerstain und Marnegg; *m* 1964, Olivia Barstow (marr. diss. 1989); one *s* two *d*. *Educ:* Winchester; King's Coll., Cambridge (MA Mod Langs); MIT (SM Management). Courtaulds, 1962–65; McKinsey & Co. Management Consultants, 1966–71; joined Sterling Guarantee Trust, 1971, Dir, 1973; served on main bd after merger with Town & City Properties and later with P&OSNCo., until 1986; Chairman: Earls Court and Olympia Exhibns Gp, 1974–85; Sutcliffe Catering Gp, 1975–85; Butlers Warehousing & Distribution, 1971–85; Sterling Guards, 1974–85; P&O Cruises, Swan Hellenic, and Princess Cruises, 1985–86; Conder Group plc, 1987–92; Collett Dickenson Pearce Internat., 1990–91; Producer Responsibility Gp and V-Wrag, 1994–96; London & Henley Ltd, 1995–98; Healthcall Gp plc, 1991–98; Leighton & Henley PLC, 2007–14. Director: Outer London Reg. Bd, 1984–88, Southern Adv. Bd, 1988–92, Nat. Westminster Bank; Williamson Tea Holdings, 1986–94; Life Sciences Internat., 1987–97; Erith plc, 1992–95; Strategic Partnership, 1997–2000; Gartmore SNT plc, 1998–2005; Brompton Bicycle Ltd, 2000–. Chm., London Chamber of Commerce and Industry, 1988–90; Pres., British Chambers of Commerce, 1992–94; Vice-Pres. and Hd of UK Delegn, Eurochambres SA, Brussels, 1994–2002. Member: Council, Worldaware, 1988–2000 (Trustee, 2000–02); Council of Management, Acad. of St Martin-in-the-Fields, 1990–93; Cttee, Royal Tournament, 1976–85; Vice-Pres., Olympia Internat. Showjumping, 1977–85; Hon. Mem., Royal Smithfield Club, 1985–. Trustee, Personal Support Unit, Royal Courts of Justice, 2001–12. Chm. of Govs, Oundle Sch., 2001–04. Mem. Ct of Assts, Grocers' Co., 1990– (Master, 1996). Pres., Essex Club, 2010–11. High Sheriff, Essex, 2006–07; DL Essex, 2008. *Recreations:* organic farming, design of gardens and buildings, tennis, shooting, ski-ing. *Address:* 52 Westbourne Terrace, W2 3UJ. *T:* (020) 7262 0514. *Club:* Travellers.

STEWART-SMITH, Kirstie Louise; *see* Hamilton, K. L.

STEWARTBY, Baron *cr* 1992 (Life Peer), of Portmoak in the District of Perth and Kinross; **Bernard Harold Ian Halley Stewart of Stewartby,** Kt 1991; PC 1989; RD 1972; FBA 1981; FRSE 1986; *b* 10 Aug. 1935; *s* of late Prof. H. C. Stewart of Stewartby, CBE and Dorothy Irene (*née* Lowen); *m* 1966, Hon. Deborah Charlotte Buchan, JP, *d* of 3rd Baron Tweedsmuir; one *s* two *d*. *Educ:* Haileybury; Jesus Coll., Cambridge (1st cl. hons Class. Tripos; MA; LittD 1978; Hon. Fellow, 1994). Nat. Service, RNVR, 1954–56; subseq. Lt-Comdr RNR. Seccombe, Marshall & Campion Ltd, bill brokers, 1959–60; joined Brown, Shipley & Co. Ltd, 1960, Dir 1971–83; Director: Diploma plc, 1990–2007; Standard Chartered plc, 1990–2004 (Dep. Chm., 1993–2004); Chm., Throgmorton Trust, 1990–2005; Dep. Chm., Amlin, 1995–2006. Mem., SIB, later FSA, 1993–97. MP (C) Hitchin, Feb. 1974–1983, N Herts, 1983–92. PPS to Chancellor of the Exchequer, 1979–83; Parly Under-Sec. of State for Defence Procurement, MoD, Jan.–Oct. 1983; Economic Sec. to HM Treasury, 1983–87; Minister of State: for the Armed Forces, MoD, 1987–88; NI Office, 1988–89. Jt Sec., Cons. Parly Finance Cttee, 1975–76, 1977–79; Member: Public Expenditure Cttee, 1977–79; Public Accounts Cttee, 1991–92. UK rep., Eur. Budget Council, 1983–85; responsible for: Trustee Savings Banks Act, 1985; Building Socs Act, 1986; Banking Act, 1987. Trustee, Parly Contributory Pension Fund, 2000–05. Mem. British Academy Cttee for Sylloge of Coins of British Isles, 1967– (Chm., 1993–2003); Numismatic advr, NACF, 1988–; Chm., Treasure Valuation Cttee, 1996–2001. Hon. Treas., Westminster Cttee for Protection of Children, 1960–70, Vice-Chm., 1975–92. FSA (Mem. Council 1974–76); FSAScot; Dir, British Numismatic Soc., 1965–75 (Sanford Saltus Gold Medal 1971); FRNS (medallist 1996). Mem. Council, British Museum Soc., 1975–76. Life Governor, 1977, Mem. Council, 1980–95, Haileybury; Trustee, Sir Halley Stewart Trust, 1978– (Pres., 2002–). Hon. Vice-Pres., 1989, Pres., 2007–10, Stewart Soc. Pres., St John Ambulance for Herts, 2007– (County Vice-Pres., 1978–2007); KStJ 1992. *Publications:* The Scottish Coinage, 1955, 2nd edn 1967; Scottish Mints, 1971; (ed with C. N. L. Brooke and others) Studies in Numismatic Method, 1983; (with C. E. Blunt and C. S. S. Lyon) Coinage in Tenth-Century England, 1989; (with C. E. Challis and others) New History of the Royal Mint, 1992; English Coins 1180–1551, 2009; many papers in Proc. Soc. Antiquaries of Scotland, Numismatic Chronicle, British Numismatic Jl, etc. *Recreations:* history; tennis (Captain CU Tennis Club, 1958–59; 1st string v Oxford, 1958 and 1959; winner Coupe de Bordeaux 1959; led 1st Oxford and Cambridge Tennis and Rackets team to USA, 1958); Homer. *Address:* House of Lords, SW1A 0PW. *Clubs:* Beefsteak, MCC; New (Edinburgh); Hawks, Pitt (Cambridge).

STEYN, family name of **Baron Steyn**.

STEYN, Baron *cr* 1995 (Life Peer), of Swafield in the county of Norfolk; **Johan Steyn,** Kt 1985; PC 1992; a Lord of Appeal in Ordinary, 1995–2005; *b* 15 Aug. 1932; *m* Susan Leonore (*née* Lewis); two *s* two *d* by previous marriage, and one step *s* one step *d*. *Educ:* Jan van Riebeeck Sch., Cape Town, S Africa; Univ. of Stellenbosch, S Africa (BA, LLB); University Coll., Oxford (MA; Hon. Fellow, 1995). Cape Province Rhodes Scholar, 1955; commenced practice at S African Bar, 1958; Sen. Counsel of Supreme Court of SA, 1970; settled in UK; commenced practice at English Bar, 1973 (Bencher, Lincoln's Inn, 1985); QC 1979; a Presiding Judge, Northern Circuit, 1989–91; Judge of the High Court, QBD, 1985–91; a Lord Justice of Appeal, 1992–95. Member: Supreme Court Rule Cttee, 1985–89; Deptl Adv. Cttee on Arbitration Law, 1986–89 (Chm., 1990–94); Chairman: Race Relations Cttee of the Bar, 1987–88; Lord Chancellor's Adv. Cttee on Legal Educn and Conduct, 1994–96; Takeover Appeal Bd, 2006–. Chm., Adv. Council, Centre for Commercial Law Studies, QMW, 1993–94. Pres., British Insce Law Assoc., 1992–94. Hon. Member: Amer. Law Inst., 1999; Soc. of Legal Scholars, 2002; Hon. Fellow, UCL, 2005. Hon. LLD: QMW, 1997; UEA, 1998; Cape Town, 2007. *Address:* House of Lords, SW1A 0PW.
See also K. M. Steyn.

STEYN, Karen Margaret; QC 2014; *b* Cape Town, 20 Oct. 1970; *d* of Baron Steyn, *qv* and Jean Steyn; *m* 1997, Alexander Glassbrook; two *s*. *Educ:* Tonbridge Grammar Sch.; Univ. of Liverpool (BA Hons Hist.); City Univ. (CPE). Called to the Bar, Middle Temple, 1995; in practice as a barrister, specialising in public law, human rights, information law and public internat. law, 4–5 Gray's Inn Square, 1996–2000, 11 King's Bench Walk, 2000–. *Recreations:* family, friends, forests and oceans. *Address:* 11 King's Bench Walk, Temple, EC4Y 7EQ. *T:* (020) 7632 8500. *E:* karen.steyn@11kbw.com.

STHEEMAN, Robert Alexander Talma, CB 2008; Chief Executive, United Kingdom Debt Management Office, since 2003; *b* 7 June 1959; *s* of Sape Talma Stheeman and Cécile Talma Stheeman (*née* Mendelssohn Bartholdy); *m* 1989, Elisabeth Haas; four *s*. *Educ:* Stowe Sch.; Chamber of Commerce, Hamburg (Bank Business Degree 1982). Vereins-und Westbank AG, Hamburg, 1979–85; Deutsche Bank AG, Frankfurt and London, 1986–2002 (Dir, 1991–2002). *Recreations:* family, music, walking. *Address:* United Kingdom Debt Management Office, Eastcheap Court, 11 Philpot Lane, EC3M 8UD. *T:* (020) 7862 6500, *Fax:* (020) 7862 6509. *E:* robert.stheeman@dmo.gsi.gov.uk.

STIBBARD, Peter Jack, CStat; Head, Labour Market Statistics Group, Central Statistical Office, 1995–96; international consultancies, 1996–99; *b* 15 May 1936; *s* of late Frederick Stibbard and Gladys Stibbard (*née* Daines); *m* 1964, Christine Fuller; two *d*. *Educ:* City of Norwich Grammar School; Hull Univ. (BSc Econ). Served RAF, 1954–56. Kodak Ltd, 1959–64; Thos Potterton Ltd, 1964–66; Greater London Council, 1966–68; Central Statistical Office, 1968–82; HM Treasury, 1982–85; Under Sec., Statistics Div. 2, DTI, 1985–89; Dir of Statistics, Dept of Employment, 1989–95. *Publications:* articles in official and trade jls. *Address:* 62 Allington Drive, Tonbridge, Kent TN10 4HH.

STIBBON, Emma Louise, RA 2013; artist; *b* Münster, Germany, 1 March 1962; *d* of Gen. Sir John James Stibbon, KCB, OBE and of Jean Ferguson Stibbon. *Educ:* Goldsmiths, Univ. of London (BA Fine Art 1984); Univ. of West of England (MA Res. Fine Art 2005). Sen. Lectr in Fine Art (pt-time), Univ. of Brighton, 2008–. Artist residencies include: Derek Hill Schol., British Sch. at Rome, 2010; Arctic Circle Expedn to Svalbard, 2013; Friends of Scott Polar Res. Inst./HMS Protector Artist Placement in Antarctica, 2013. *Solo exhibitions* include: Glacial Shift, Scott Polar Res. Inst., 2008; Stadtlandschaften, Stadtmuseum, Berlin, 2009; Now's the Time, upstairs berlin, 2010; Falls the Shadow, ROOM, London, 2011; Terra Infirma, Rabley Contemporary Drawing Centre, 2013; Ice Mirage, Galerie Bastian, Berlin, 2015; Ice Limit, Polar Mus., Cambridge, 2015. *Recreations:* walking, mountains, ruins.

STIGLITZ, Prof. Joseph Eugene, PhD; Professor of Economics, Columbia Business School, Columbia University, since 2001; *b* 9 Feb. 1943; *m*; two *s* two *d*. *Educ:* Amherst Coll. (BA 1964); MIT (PhD 1967); Fitzwilliam Coll., Cambridge Univ. (MA 1970; Hon. Fellow, 2006). Professor of Economics: Yale Univ. 1970–74; Stanford Univ., 1974–76; Drummond Prof. of Political Economy, Oxford Univ. and All Souls Coll., 1976–79; Prof. of Economics, Princeton Univ., 1979–88; Prof. of Econs, Stanford Univ., 1992–2001. Mem., 1993–97, Chm., 1995–97, Council of Econ. Advrs to Pres. of USA; Chief Economist, World Bank, 1997–2000. Fellowships: Nat. Sci. Foundn, 1964–65; Fulbright, 1965–66; SSRC Faculty, 1969–70; Guggenheim, 1969–70; Oskar Morgenstern Distinguished Fellowship, Mathematica and Inst. for Advanced Study, Princeton, 1978–79. Consultant: Nat. Sci. Foundn, 1972–75; Ford Foundn Energy Policy Study, 1973; Dept of Labor (Pensions and Labor Turnover), 1974; Dept of Interior (Offshore Oil Leasing Programs), 1975; Federal Energy Admin (Intertemporal Biases in Market Allocation of Natural Resources), 1975–79; World Bank (Cost Benefit Analysis; Urban Rural Migration; Natural Resources), 1975–; Electric Power Res. Inst., 1976–; OECD; Office of Fair Trading; Treasury (Office of Tax Analysis), 1980; US AID (commodity price stabilization), 1977; Inter-American Development Bank; Bell Laboratories; Bell Communications Research; State of Alaska; Seneca Indian Nation. Chm., Brooks World Poverty Inst., Univ. of Manchester, 2006. Internat. Prize, Academia Lincei, 1988; Union des Assurances de Paris Scientific Prize, 1989; Rechtenwald Prize, 1999. Gen. Editor, Econometric Soc. Reprint Series; Associate Editor: Jl of Economic Theory, 1968–73; American Economic Rev., 1972–75; Jl of Economic Perspectives, 1988–93; Co-editor, Jl of Public Economics, 1968–83; American Editor, Rev. of Economic Studies, 1968–76; Editorial Bd, World Bank Economic Review, The Geneva Papers, Revista de Econometrica, Assicurazioni. Vice-Pres., American Econ. Assoc., 1985. Fellow: Econometric Soc., 1972 (Sec./Treasurer, 1972–75); Amer. Acad. of Arts and Scis; Inst. for Policy Reform, 1990–; American Philosophical Assoc.; NAS; Senior Fellow: Hoover Instn, 1988–93; Brookings Instn, Washington, 2000–01. Corresp. FBA 1993; Foreign Mem., Royal Soc., 2009. Hon. MA Yale, 1970; Hon. DHL Amherst, 1974; Hon. Dr: Pomona Coll.; New Sch.; Northwestern; Bard Coll.; Toronto; Naumur; Leuven; Ben Gurion; Barcelona; Bucharest; Lisbon Tech.; Charles Univ., Prague. John Bates Clark Medal, Amer. Econ. Assoc.; (jtly) Nobel Prize for Economics, 2001. *Publications:* (ed) Collected Scientific Papers of P. A. Samuelson, 1965; (ed with H. Uzawa) Readings in Modern Theory of Economic Growth, 1969; (with A. B. Atkinson) Lectures in Public Finance, 1980; (with D. Newbery) The Economic Impact of Price Stabilization, 1980; Economics of the Public Sector, 1986; Globalization and its Discontents, 2002; Making Globalization Work, 2006; (with L. Bilmes) The Three Trillion Dollar War: the true cost of the Iraq conflict, 2008; Freefall: free markets and the sinking of the global economy, 2010; Creating a Learning Society: a new approach to growth, development and social progress, 2014; The Great Divide: unequal societies and what we can do about them, 2015; contribs on economics of growth, development, natural resources, information, uncertainty, imperfect competition, corporate finance and public finance in Amer. Econ. Rev., Qly Jl of Econs, Jl of Pol Econ., Econometrica, Internat. Econ. Rev., Econ. Jl, Rev. of Econ. Studies, Jl of Public Econs, Jl of Econ. Theory, Oxford Econ. Papers. *Address:* Room 814, Uris Hall, Columbia Business School, New York, NY 10027, USA. *T:* (212) 8540671.

STIHLER, Catherine Dalling; Member (Lab) Scotland, European Parliament, since 1999; *b* 30 July 1973; *d* of Gordon McLeish Taylor and Catherine Doreen Taylor; *m* 2000, David Stihler; one *s*. *Educ:* Coltness High Sch., Wishaw; Univ. of St Andrews (MA Hons Geography and Internat. Relns 1996; MLitt Internat. Security Studies 1998). Pres., Univ. of St Andrews Students' Assoc., 1994–95. Young Labour Representative: Exec. Cttee, SLP, 1993–95; Lab Party NEC, 1995–97; Women's Rep. and Local Orgns Rep., SLP Exec., 1997–99. Researcher and facilitator to Anne Begg, MP, 1997–99. Contested (Lab) Angus, 1997. European Parliament Parliamentary Labour Group: health spokesperson, 1999–2004; spokesperson on fisheries and regl develt; Dep. Leader, 2004–06; Whip, 2014–. European Parliament: Pres., Health Intergroup, 2000–02; Mem., Internal Market and Consumer Protection Cttee, 2009– (Vice-Chm., 2014–); Substitute, Econ. and Monetary Affairs Cttee, 2009–; MEP Ed., Parliament mag., 2002–11. Rector, Univ. of St Andrews, 2015–. *Publications:* (contrib.) Women and the Military, 2000. *Recreations:* running marathons, yoga, swimming, music, film, studying languages. *Address:* European Parliament, Rue Wiertz, 1047 Brussels, Belgium.

STILGOE, Sir Richard (Henry Simpson), Kt 2012; OBE 1998; DL; songwriter, lyricist, entertainer and broadcaster, since 1962; *b* 28 March 1943; *s* of late John Henry Tweedie Stilgoe and Joan Lucy Strutt Stilgoe; *m* 1st, 1964, Elizabeth Caroline Gross; one *s* one *d*; 2nd, 1975, Annabel Margaret Hunt; two *s* one *d*. *Educ:* Liverpool Coll.; Monkton Combe Sch.; Clare Coll., Cambridge (choral exhibnr). One-man show worldwide, incl. Windsor Castle, 1982 and British Embassy, Washington, 1986; Two-man show with Peter Skellern, 1985–2002. Author and composer: Bodywork, 1987; Brilliant the Dinosaur, 1991; Orpheus the Mythical, 2010; librettist: Road Rage, Garsington Opera, 2013; The Freedom Game,

2015. Word-processor for Andrew Lloyd Webber on Cats, Starlight Express and Phantom of the Opera. Stilgoe Saturday Concerts, RFH, 1999–2005. Founder and Trustee, Orpheus Centre (music and disabled people), 1985–; Founder and Chm., Alchemy Foundn, 1985–; Pres., Surrey Care Trust, 1986–2000; Trustee, Nat. Foundn for Youth Music, 1999–2012 (Chm., 2007–12). FRSA 1992. Hon. ARAM 2003; Hon. RCM 2012. Hon. Fellow, Liverpool John Moores Univ., 2008. Hon. DLitt: Greenwich, 1999; Southampton, 2005; DUniv Surrey, 2014. Monaco Radio Prize, 1984, 1991, 1996; NY Radio Fest. Gold Award, 1989; Prix Italia, 1991. DL, 1996, High Sheriff, 1998, Surrey. *Publications:* The Richard Stilgoe Letters, 1981; Brilliant The Dinosaur, 1994. *Recreations:* sailing, cricket, architecture, building, music, demolition, children. *Address:* c/o The Orpheus Centre, Trevereux Manor, Limpsfield Chart, Oxted, Surrey RH8 0TL. *Clubs:* MCC, Lord's Taverners (Pres., 2003); Surrey CC (Pres., 2005).

STILITZ, Daniel Malachi; QC 2010; barrister; *b* London, 1 Aug. 1968; *s* of Ivor Bernard Stilitz and Linda Stilitz; *m* 1996, Ruth Walker; two *s* one *d*. *Educ:* William Ellis Sch.; New Coll., Oxford (BA Hons PPE 1990); City Univ. (DipLaw 1991; MA 1992). Called to the Bar, Lincoln's Inn, 1992; in practice as barrister, specialising in employment, commercial and public law. Mediator, CEDR, 1997. *Recreations:* photography, music, reading. *Address:* 11KBW, 11 King's Bench Walk, Temple, EC4Y 7EQ. *T:* (020) 7632 8500, *Fax:* (020) 7583 9123. *E:* daniel.stilitz@11kbw.com.

STILLMAN, Dr Bruce William, AO 1999; FRS 1993; Chief Executive Officer, since 2000, President, since 2003, Cold Spring Harbor Laboratory, New York (Director, 1994–2003); *b* Melbourne, Australia, 16 Oct. 1953; *s* of Graham Leslie Stillman and Jessie May (*née* England); *m* 1981, Grace Angela Begley; one *s* one *d*. *Educ:* Glen Waverley High Sch.; Sydney Boys' High Sch.; Univ. of Sydney (BSc Hons); ANU (PhD). Cold Spring Harbor Laboratory, New York: Damon Runyon-Walter Winchell Postdoctoral Res. Fellow, 1979–80; Staff Investigator, 1981–82; Sen. Staff Investigator, 1983–85; Sen. Scientist, 1985–90; Asst Dir, 1990–93; Adjunct Prof. of Microbiology, SUNY, 1982–. Damon Runyon-Walter Winchell Cancer Fund Fellow, 1979–80; Rita Allen Foundn Scholar, 1982–87; Charter Fellow, Molecular Medicine Soc., 1995. Lectures: Harvey Soc., 1993; Nieuwland, Univ. of Notre Dame, 1993; Doty, Harvard Univ., 1998. For. Associate, NAS, USA, 2000; Fellow, Amer. Acad. of Microbiol., 2000. Hon. DHL Hofstra, 2001; Hon. DSc NY Inst. Tech. Commonwealth Postgrad. Award, 1976–80; Merit Award, NIH, 1986. *Publications:* numerous scientific pubns. *Address:* Cold Spring Harbor Laboratory, One Bungtown Road, Cold Spring Harbor, NY 11724, USA. *T:* (516) 3678383.

STIMSON, Prof. Gerald Vivian, PhD; Director, Knowledge-Action-Change, since 2010; *b* 10 April 1945; *s* of late Geoffrey Edward Vivian Stimson and Maud Ellen Stimson; *m* 1st, 1971, Carol Anne Fowler (marr. diss. 1992, she *d* 1997); two *s*; 2nd, 1993, Elizabeth Louise Vivian Tacey; one *s*. *Educ:* City of London Sch.; London Sch. of Econs (BSc 1966; MSc 1967); Inst. of Psychiatry, Univ. of London (PhD 1971). Res. worker, Addiction Res. Unit, Inst. of Psychiatry, Univ. of London, 1967–71; Res. Fellow, Med. Sociology Res. Centre, UC of Swansea, 1971–75; London University: Lectr, then Sen. Lectr, Addiction Res. Unit, Inst. Psychiatry, 1975–78; Goldsmiths' College: Sen. Lectr in Sociology, 1978–89; Head, Sociology Dept, 1980–83; Dir, Monitoring Res. Gp, Sociology Dept, 1987–89; Imperial College: Dir, Centre for Res. on Drugs and Health Behaviour, 1990–2004; Prof. of Sociology of Health Behaviour, 1991–2004, now Emeritus; Hd, Dept of Social Science and Medicine, 1997–2004. Exec. Dir, Internat. Harm Reduction Assoc., 2004–10. Fulbright Schol., NY Univ., 1983; Vis. Prof., Univ. of W London (formerly Thames Valley Univ.), 1995–2000; Hon. Prof., LSHTM, 2006–. Advisory Council on Misuse of Drugs: Mem., 1984–99; Mem., Wkg Gp on AIDS and Drug Misuse, 1987–92; Chm., Stats Inf. and Res. Cttee, 1990–99; Member: Council, Inst. for Study of Drug Dependence, 1985–90 (Vice-Chm., 1987); Scientific Cttee, Eur. Monitoring Centre for Drugs and Drug Addiction, 1994–97; Founder Member: UK Harm Reduction Alliance, 2001 (Chm., 2001–02); Nicotine Policy Network, 2013. Pres., Action on Hepatitis C, 2000–04. Member, Editorial Board: Addiction, 1982–2006; Addiction Res., 1991–2000; AIDS, 1993–96; Ed., Internat. Jl Drug Policy, 2000–; Founder, Sociology of Health and Illness. Trustee, AIDS Educnl and Res. Trust, 1995–2003. Internat. Rolleston Award, Harm Reduction Internat., 2010. *Publications:* Heroin and Behaviour: diversity among addicts attending London clinics, 1973; (with B. Webb) Going to See the Doctor: the consultation process in general practice, 1975; (with E. Oppenheimer) Heroin Addiction: treatment and control in Britain, 1982; (ed jtly) AIDS and Drug Misuse: the challenge for policy and practice in the 1990s, 1990; (ed jtly) Drug Injecting and HIV Infection: global issues and local responses, 1998; (ed jtly) Drug Use in London, 1998; (ed jtly) Drugs and the Future: brain science, addiction and society, 2006; (ed) Drinking in Context: patterns, interventions and partnerships, 2006. *Recreations:* walking, the countryside, travel. *Club:* Athenæum.

STIMSON, Robert Frederick, CBE 1992; Governor and Commander-in-Chief of St Helena and its Dependencies, 1988–91; *b* 16 May 1939; *s* of Frederick Henry Stimson and Gladys Alma Stimson (*née* Joel); *m* 1st, 1961, Margaret Faith Kerry (*d* 2004); two *s* one *d*; 2nd, 2012, Penn Pusao; one *s*. *Educ:* Rendcomb Coll.; Queen Mary Coll., London (BSc First Cl. Hons; MSc (by thesis) mathematical physics). HM Diplomatic Service: FO, 1966–67; Saigon, 1967–68; Singapore, 1968–70; Cabinet Office, 1970–73; Mexico City, 1973–75; FCO, 1975–80; Counsellor, East Berlin, 1980–81; Head of Home Inspectorate, 1982–83; Counsellor and Hd of Chancery, Dublin, 1984–87. Order of Aztec Eagle, Mexico, 1975. *Publications:* contrib. Jl Physics and Chemistry of Solids.

STINCHCOMBE, Paul David; QC 2011; barrister; *b* 25 April 1962; *s* of Lionel Walter Stinchcombe and Pauline Sylvia Ann (*née* Hawkins); *m* 1990, Suzanne Jean Gardiner; two *s* one *d*. *Educ:* Royal Grammar Sch., High Wycombe; Trinity Coll., Cambridge (Sen. Schol.; BA Law double 1st cl. Hons 1983); Harvard Law Sch. (Frank Knox Fellow; LLM 1984). Called to the Bar, Lincoln's Inn, 1985; in practice at the Bar, 1985–. Vis. Fellow, Centre of Public Law, Cambridge Univ., 2005–06. Mem. (Lab), Camden Council, 1990–94 (Chm., Labour Gp, 1992–94). MP (Lab) Wellingborough, 1997–2005; contested (Lab) same seat, 2005. *Recreations:* football, cricket, golf. *Address:* 39 Essex Street, WC2R 3AT.

STING; *see* Sumner, G. M.

STIPRAIS, Eduards; Under-Secretary of State - Political Director, Ministry of Foreign Affairs, Latvia, since 2013; *b* Riga, 19 Feb. 1969; *s* of Andreas Stiprais and Ludmila Stipra; *m* 2004, Zanda Grauze. *Educ:* Univ. of Latvia (Dip. Econs 1993). Desk Officer, Min. of Foreign Trade, Latvia, 1992–93; Ministry of Foreign Affairs: Sen. Desk Officer, 1993; Hd, EC/EFTA Relns Div., 1993–94; Dep. Dir, Dept of Internat. Econ. Relns, 1994–95; Second Sec., 1995, First Sec., 1995–98, Mission of Latvia to EU, Brussels; Hd, Task Force for preparations of EU accession negotiations, 1998–99, Secretariat of Delegn for EU accession negotiations, 1999–2003; Ambassador: and Dep. Hd of Mission of Latvia to EU, Brussels, 2003–04; and Dep. Perm. Rep. of Latvia to EU, 2004; and Perm. Rep. of Latvia to EU, 2004–07; Hd, State President's Chancellery, 2007–08; Ambassador and Hd of Directorate for Bilateral Relns, 2009; Ambassador to Court of St James's, 2009–13. Officer, Order of Three Stars (Latvia), 2004; Chevalier, Order of Merit (Ukraine), 2009. *Recreations:* travelling, walking, basketball, reading. *Address:* Ministry of Foreign Affairs, K.Valdemara Street 3, Riga 1395, Latvia. *T:* 67016209, *Fax:* 67288121. *E:* eduards.stiprais@mfa.gov.lv. *Clubs:* Travellers; Circle Royal Gaulois (Brussels).

STIRLING, Alison Nancy; Sheriff of Grampian, Highland and Islands at Aberdeen, since 2014; *b* Stirling, 14 May 1965; *d* of Robert Louis Stirling and Dorothy Jean Stirling; *m* (marr. diss.); one *s*. *Educ:* Dollar Acad.; Univ. of Edinburgh (MA Hons 1987; LLB 1992). Admitted to Faculty of Advocates, 1997; Sheriff (pt-time), 2011–14. Dep. Ed., Session Cases, 2001–15. *Publications:* (contrib.) Green's Litigation Styles, 2001–; (contrib.) Litigation Styles: family actions and adoption, 2010. *Recreations:* foreign travel, Turkish speaker, swimming, cycling. *Address:* Sheriff Court House, Castle Street, Aberdeen AB10 1WP.

STIRLING, Prof. Andrew Charles, DPhil; Professor of Science and Technology Policy, since 2006, and Co-Director, ESRC Centre on Social, Technological and Environmental Pathways to Sustainability, since 2006, University of Sussex; *b* Portsmouth, 3 March 1961; *s* of Charles and Diana Stirling; partner, Vanessa Topsy Jewell; two *s* one *d*. *Educ:* Westfield Comprehensive Sch., Yeovil; Yeovil Tertiary Coll.; Univ. of Edinburgh (MA Hons Archaeol. and Social Anthropol. 1984); Univ. of Sussex (DPhil Sci. and Technol. Policy 1995). Field archaeologist, Univ. of Edinburgh, 1984; Greenpeace International: campaigner, 1985–87; Campaign Dir, 1987–90; Mem. Bd, 1994–98; University of Sussex: Res. Fellow, 1993–2000; Sen. Lectr and Sen. Fellow, 2000–06; Res. Dir, SPRU - sci. and technol. policy res., 2007–13. Mem., Energy Policy Consultative Cttee, 1998–2001, Expert Gp on Sci. and Governance, 2005–08, EU Commn; Member: UK Adv. Cttee on Toxic Substances, 1999–2004; UK Genetic Modification Sci. Rev. Panel, 2002–04; Sci. Adv. Council, DEFRA, 2004–11; Sciencewise Steering Cttee, DIUS, later BIS, 2008–; Steering Gp on Neurosci. and Policy, Royal Soc., 2010–; Working Gp on Emerging Biotechnologies, Nuffield Council on Bioethics, 2010–; Res. Cttee, ESRC, 2010–. Mem. Bd, Greenpeace UK Ltd, 2010–. Member, Editorial Board: Jl Risk Res., 1999–; Technol. Analysis and Strategic Mgt, 2007–; Minerva, 2007–; Nature EMBO Reports, 2009–; Jl Envmtl and Societal Transitions, 2010–. *Publications:* On Science and Precaution in the Management of Technological Risk, 1999; (ed jtly) The Precautionary Principle in the Twentieth Century: late lessons from early warnings, 2002; (ed jtly) Precautionary Risk Appraisal and Management: an orientation for meeting the precautionary principle in the European Union, 2009; (jtly) Dynamic Sustainabilities: technology, environment, social justice, 2010; contribs to jls incl. Energy Policy, Envmt and Planning C, Nature EMBO Reports, Futures, Ecol. and Society, Global Envmtl Change, Annals of NY Acad. Scis, Res. Policy, Royal Soc. Interface, Sci., Technol. and Human Values, Sustainable Develt, Yearbook of Eur. Envmtl Law. *Recreations:* backpacking/cycling, field archaeology, history, mythology, music, politics. *Address:* SPRU - science and technology policy research, Jubilee Building, University of Sussex, Brighton, E Sussex BN1 9SL. *T:* (01273) 877118, *Fax:* (01273) 685865. *E:* a.c.stirling@sussex.ac.uk.

STIRLING, Sir Angus (Duncan Æneas), Kt 1994; Director-General, National Trust, 1983–95 (Deputy Director-General, 1979–83); *b* 10 Dec. 1933; *s* of late Duncan Alexander Stirling and Lady Marjorie Murray, *e d* of 8th Earl of Dunmore, VC, DSO, MVO; *m* 1959, Armyne Morar Helen Schofield, *e d* of late W. G. B. Schofield and Hon. Armyne Astley, *d* of 21st Baron Hastings; one *s* two *d*. *Educ:* Eton Coll.; Trinity Coll., Cambridge; London Univ. (Extra Mural) (Dip. History of Art). Christie, Manson and Woods Ltd, 1954–57; Lazard Bros and Co. Ltd, 1957–66; Asst Dir, Paul Mellon Foundn for British Art, 1966–69 (Jt Dir, 1969–70); Dep. Sec.-General, Arts Council of GB, 1971–79. Sen. Policy Advr, Nat. Heritage Meml Fund, 1996–97; Chairman: Greenwich Foundn for RNC, 1996–2003; JNCC, 1997–2002. Mem., Govt Task Force on Tourism and the Envmt, 1991. Mem. Bd, Royal Opera House, Covent Garden, 1979–96 (Chm., 1991–96); Mem., Council, Friends of Covent Garden, 1981–2011 (Chm., 1981–91); Dep. Chm., Royal Ballet Bd, 1988–91; a Gov., Royal Ballet, 1988–96; Member: Crafts Council, 1980–85; Council of Management, Byam Shaw Sch. of Art, 1965–89; Bd of Trustees, Courtauld Inst. of Art, 1981–83, 2002–14; Adv. Council, London Symphony Orchestra, 1979–; Bd of Governors, Live Music Now, 1982–89; Bd of Trustees, The Theatres Trust, 1983–91; Bd of Trustees, Heritage of London Trust, 1983–95; Tourism Cttee, ICOMOS UK, 1993–2003; Council, RSCM, 1996–98; Fabric Adv. Cttee, Wells Cathedral, 2001–. Chm., Adv. Panel for Local Heritage Initiative, Countryside Commn, 1998–99; Chm., Policy Cttee, 1996–2001, Pres., Som Br., 2002–07, CPRE; Mem. Adv. Cttee, Stowe Landscape Gardens, 1996–; Trustee: Stowe House Preservation Trust, 1998–2012; Samuel Courtauld Trust (formerly Home House (Courtauld Collection)), 1983–2012; World Monuments Fund in Britain, 1996–2008. President: Friends of Holland Park, 2003–; NADFAS Kensington and Chelsea, 2008–. Vice Patron, Almshouses Assoc., 2000–09 (Chm., Adv. Panel, Patron's Award, 2001–03). Member, Board of Governors: Gresham Sch., 1999–2007; City and Guilds Art Sch., 2003–11. CCMI. Hon. FTCL 2004. Mem., Court, Fishmongers' Co., 1991– (Prime Warden, 2004–05; Chm., Fisheries Cttee, 2007–14). Hon. Fellow, Courtauld Inst. of Art, 2015. Hon. DLitt: Leicester, 1995; Greenwich, 2002. *Recreations:* painting, music, travel, walking. *Address:* 30 Upper Addison Gardens, W14 8AJ. *Clubs:* Garrick, Brooks's, Beefsteak, Grillions.

STIRLING, Prof. Charles James Matthew, FRS 1986; CChem, FRSC; Professor of Organic Chemistry, University of Sheffield, 1990–98, now Emeritus; *b* 8 Dec. 1930; *s* of Brig. Alexander Dickson Stirling, DSO, MB, ChB, DPH, RAMC, and Isobel Millicent Stirling, MA, DipPsych; *m* 1956, Eileen Gibson Powell, BA, MEd (*d* 2012), *yr d* of William Leslie and Elsie May Powell; two *d* (and one *d* decd). *Educ:* Edinburgh Acad.; Univ. of St Andrews (Harkness Exhibn; BSc; Biochem. Medal 1951); Univ. of London (PhD, DSc). FRSC, CChem 1967. Civil Service Jun. Res. Fellowship, Porton, 1955, Sen. Fellowship, 1956; ICI Fellowship, Univ. of Edinburgh, 1957; Lectr, QUB, 1959; Reader in Org. Chem., KCL, 1965; University of Wales, Bangor: Prof. of Organic Chemistry, 1969–81; Dean of Faculty of Science, 1977–79; Hd of Dept of Chemistry, 1981–90; Sheffield University: Hd, Dept of Chemistry, 1991–94; Dir, Engrg and Physical Scis Div., Grad. Sch., 1994–97; Public Orator, 1995–. Visiting Professor: Hebrew Univ. of Jerusalem, 1981; ANU, Canberra, 1999; Akademia Jan Dlugosz, Czestochowa, 2013. Royal Instn Christmas Lects, BBC TV, 1992. Mem., IUPAC Commn on Physical Organic Chemistry, 1992–95. Mem., Perkin Council, RSC, 1971–93 (Vice-Pres., 1985–88 and 1991–93, Pres., 1989–91); Pres., Section B (Chemistry), BAAS, 1990; Pres., Yorks and Humberside Sect., ASE, 1993–95. Founding FLSW 2010. Hon. Mem., Società Chimica Italiana, 2002. Hon. Fellow, Univ. of Wales, Bangor, 2004. Hon. DSc: St Andrews, 1994; Aix-Marseille, 1999; Sheffield, 2007. Award for Organic Reaction Mechanisms, RSC, 1988; Millennium Commn Award, 1999. *Publications:* Radicals in Organic Chemistry, 1965; (ed) Organic Sulphur Chemistry, 1975; (ed) The Chemistry of the Sulphonium Group, 1981; (ed) The Chemistry of Sulphones and Sulphoxides, 1988; numerous res. papers mainly in Jls of RSC. *Recreations:* choral music, the collection of chiral objects, furniture restoration. *Address:* Department of Chemistry, University of Sheffield, Sheffield S3 7HF. *T:* (0114) 222 9453; 114 Westbourne Road, Sheffield S10 2QT.

STIRLING, James; *see* Stirling, W. J.

STIRLING of Garden, Col Sir James, KCVO 2006; CBE 1987; TD; FRICS; Lord-Lieutenant of Stirling and Falkirk, 1983–2005; *b* 8 Sept. 1930; *s* of Col Archibald Stirling of Garden, OBE; *m* 1958, Fiona Janetta Sophia Wood Parker; two *s* two *d*. *Educ:* Rugby; Trinity Coll., Cambridge (BA; Dip. Estate Mgt). FRICS 1966. Commnd Argyll and Sutherland Highlanders, 1950; served in Korea, wounded; transf. 7th Bn TA, comd 1965–67, 3rd Bn, 1967–68. Chartered Surveyor in private practice. Partner, K. Ryden and Partners, Chartered Surveyors, 1962–89. Director: Local Bd, Scotland and N Ireland, Woolwich Building Soc., 1973–97; Scottish Widows and Life Insurance Fund, 1975–96. Hon. Sheriff, Stirling, 1998. DL 1970, Vice-Lieutenant 1979–83, Stirling. Hon. Guild Brother, Stirling Guildry, 1996. Chm., Highland TAVR Assoc., 1982–87 (Pres., 1992–97). Hon. Col, 3/51st Highland

Volunteers, TA, 1979–86. DUniv Stirling, 2004. GCStJ 2005 (KStJ 1987; Prior, Order of St John, Scotland, 1995–2009). *Address:* Dambrae, Buchlyvie, Stirlingshire FK8 3NR. *T:* (01360) 850225. *Club:* New (Edinburgh).

STIRLING, John Fullarton; JP; Librarian, University of Exeter, 1972–94; *b* 12 April 1931; *s* of Reginald Stirling and Jeanette Sybil (*née* Fullarton); *m* 1960, Sheila Mary Fane; two *d.* *Educ:* Waterloo Grammar Sch.; Univ. of Liverpool (BA 1st Cl. Hons 1953; MA 1962). Asst, Liverpool Public Libraries, 1953–56; Asst Librarian, UCL, 1956–62; Sub-librarian, 1962–64, Dep. Librarian, 1964–66, Univ. of York; Librarian, Univ. of Stirling, 1966–71; Librarian designate, Univ. of Exeter, 1971–72. Member: various cttees, SCONUL, 1977–; UGC Working Gp on Liby Automation, 1986; British Liby Cttee for Bibliographic Services, 1987. JP Exeter, 1976. *Publications:* (ed) University Librarianship, 1981; contrib. various professional jls. *Recreations:* woodcarving, puppetry. *Address:* c/o Devon and Exeter Institution, 7 Cathedral Close EX1 1EZ. *T:* (01392) 274727. *Club:* Devon and Exeter Institution (Chm., 2001–04) (Exeter).

STIRLING, Prof. (William) James, CBE 2006; PhD; FRS 1999; Provost, Imperial College London, since 2013; *b* 4 Feb. 1953; *s* of late John Easton Stirling and Margaret Eleanor Stirling (*née* Norris); *m* 1975, Paula Helene Close; one *s* one *d.* *Educ:* Belfast Royal Acad.; Peterhouse, Cambridge (MA, PhD 1979; Hon. Fellow 2013). CPhys, FInstP 1992. Res. Associate, Univ. of Washington, 1979–81; Res. Fellow, Peterhouse, 1981–83; Fellow and Staff Mem., CERN, Geneva, 1983–86; University of Durham: Lectr, 1986–89, Sen. Lectr, 1989–90, Reader, 1990–92, Prof., 1992–2008, Depts of Math. Scis and Physics; Dir, Inst. for Particle Physics Phenomenology, 2000–05; Pro-Vice-Chancellor (Res.), 2005–08; University of Cambridge: Jacksonian Prof. of Natural Philosophy, 2008–13; Hd of Dept, Cavendish Lab., 2011–13; Fellow, Peterhouse, Cambridge, 2008–13. SERC and PPARC Sen. Fellow, 1993–98. Chm., Sci. Cttee, PPARC, 2001–03. Member, Council: Royal Soc., 2007–08; STFC, 2009–15. Gov., Royal Grammar Sch., Newcastle, 1996–2005. FCGI 2015. Humboldt Res. Award, 1997. *Publications:* (jtly) QCD and Collider Physics, 1996; numerous articles on elementary particle theory in learned jls. *Recreations:* playing and listening to Irish music, supporting Irish Rugby, various outdoor activities. *Address:* Provost's Office, Level 4 Faculty Building, Imperial College London, Exhibition Road, SW7 2AZ. *E:* provost@imperial.ac.uk.

STIRLING-HAMILTON, Sir Malcolm William Bruce, 14th Bt *cr* 1673 (NS), of Preston, Haddingtonshire; *b* 6 Aug. 1979; *s* of Sir Bruce Stirling-Hamilton, 13th Bt and of Stephanie (who *m* 1990, Anthony Tinsley), *d* of Dr William Campbell, LRCP, LRCS; *S* father, 1989. *Educ:* Stowe. *Heir: cousin* Rev. Andrew Robert Hamilton [*b* 5 Sept. 1937; *m* 1972, Josephine Mary, *d* of Reginald Sargant].

STIRRAT, Canon Prof. Gordon Macmillan, MA, MD; FRCOG; Research Fellow, Centre for Ethics in Medicine, 2011–14 (Senior Research Fellow, 2000–10); Professor of Obstetrics and Gynaecology, University of Bristol, 1982–2000, now Emeritus; *b* 12 March 1940; *s* of Alexander and Caroline Mary Stirrat; *m* 1965, Janeen Mary (*née* Brown); three *d.* *Educ:* Hutchesons' Boys' Grammar Sch., Glasgow; Glasgow Univ. (MB, ChB); MA Oxon, MD London. FRCOG 1981. Jun. hosp. doctor appts, Glasgow and environs, and London, 1964–71; Lectr, St Mary's Hosp. Med. Sch., London, 1971–75; Clinical Reader, Univ. of Oxford, 1975–81; Dean, Faculty of Medicine, 1990–93, Pro-Vice-Chancellor, 1993–97, Univ. of Bristol. Dep. Chm., Bristol and Dist HA, 1991–96. Member: Acad. of Experts, 1996–2004 (Fellow, 2004–09); Expert Witness Inst., 1997–2006. Chm., House of Laity, Bristol Dio., 2003–12. Lay Canon, Bristol Cathedral, 2008–10, now Emeritus. Hon. Vice-Pres., IME, 2012–. *Publications:* Legalised Abortion: the continuing dilemma, 1979; Obstetrics Pocket Consultant, 1981, 2nd edn 1986; Aids to Reproductive Biology, 1982; (jtly) You and Your Baby—a Mother's Guide to Health, 1982; Aids to Obstetrics and Gynaecology, 1983, 4th edn 1996; (jtly) The Immune System in Disease, 1992; (jtly) Handbook of Obstetric Management, 1996; (jtly) Notes on Obstetrics and Gynaecology, 2002; (jtly) Medical Ethics and Law for Doctors of Tomorrow, 2010. *Recreations:* fly-fishing, walking, photography. *Address:* Malpas Lodge, 24 Henbury Road, Westbury-on-Trym, Bristol BS9 3HJ. *T:* (0117) 950 5310.

STIRRUP, family name of **Baron Stirrup**.

STIRRUP, Baron *cr* 2011 (Life Peer), of Marylebone in the City of Westminster; **Marshal of the Royal Air Force Graham Eric, (Jock), Stirrup,** KG 2013; GCB 2005 (KCB 2002; CB 2000); AFC 1983; FRAeS; Chief of the Defence Staff, 2006–10; Air Aide-de-Camp to the Queen, since 2003; *b* 4 Dec. 1949; *s* of William Hamilton Stirrup and Jacqueline Brenda Stirrup (*née* Coulson); *m* 1976, Mary Alexandra Elliott; one *s.* *Educ:* Merchant Taylors' Sch., Northwood; Royal Air Force Coll., Cranwell. Qualified Flying Instr, 1971–73; Loan Service, Sultan of Oman's Air Force, 1973–75; Fighter Reconnaissance Pilot, 1976–78; Exchange Pilot, USAF, 1978–81; Flt Comdr, 1982–84; OC No II (Army Co-operation) Sqn, 1985–87; PSO to CAS, 1987–90; OC RAF Marham, 1990–92; rcds, 1993; Dir, Air Force Plans and Progs, MoD, 1994–97; AOC No 1 Gp, 1997–98; ACAS, 1998–2000; Dep. C-in-C, Strike Comd, Comdr NATO Combined Air Ops Centre 9, and Dir European Air Gp, 2000–02; Dep. Chief of Defence Staff (Equipment Capability), MoD, 2002–03; Chief of Air Staff, MoD, 2003–06. FCMI (FIMgt 1983); FRAeS 1991. Hon. DSc Cranfield, 2005. *Recreations:* golf, music, theatre, history. *Address:* House of Lords, SW1A 0PW. *Clubs:* Royal Air Force, Beefsteak.

STIRTON, Prof. Charles Howard, PhD; FLS; botanist, mentor, writer; *b* 25 Nov. 1946; *s* of late Charles Aubrey and Elizabeth Maud Stirton; *m* 1979, Jana Žantovská; one *d.* *Educ:* Univ. of Natal (BSc, BSc Hons, MSc); Univ. of Cape Town (PhD 1989). Botanist, Botanical Res. Inst., Pretoria, 1975–82; S African Liaison Botanist, 1979–82, B. A. Krukoff Botanist for Neotropical Legumes, 1982–87, Royal Botanic Gardens, Kew; Associate Prof., Univ. of Natal, Pietermaritzburg, 1988–90; self-employed, 1990; economic botanist, 1990–92, Dep. Dir, and Dir, Sci. and Horticulture, 1992–96, Royal Botanic Gardens, Kew; Founding Dir, Nat. Botanic Gdn of Wales, 1996–2002. Chm., Contextua, 2002–05. Dir, St Vincent Capital Ltd, 2010–; Founding Dir, Matara Gdns of Wellbeing, 2012–. Vis. Prof., Univ. of Reading, 1993–96; Hon. Prof., Univ. of Wales, 1997–2002; Hon. Res. Associate, Univ. of Cape Town, 2008–. Trustee, Gateway Gardens Trust, 2003–10. Mentor, Mellon Foundn, 2007–09. Founding Trustee, Ourobos Res. and Educn Trust; Scientific Advr, Overberg Lowlands Conservation Trust, 2013– (Founding Trustee, 2012–13). FLS 1975. Hon. DSc Glamorgan, 2001. *Publications:* (ed) Plant Invaders: beautiful but dangerous, 1978; (ed with J. Zarucchi) Advances in Legume Biology, 1990; (ed) Advances in Legume Systematics 3, 1987; (ed) The Changing World of Weeds, 1995; contrib. numerous scientific papers. *Recreations:* gardening, postcards, photography, philately, postal history, writing, books, travelling, cinema. *E:* chstirton@gmail.com. *W:* http://chstirton.wordpress.com.

STOATE, Dr Howard Geoffrey Alvan, FRCGP; general practitioner; Chairman, NHS Bexley Clinical Commissioning Group (formerly Clinical Cabinet, Bexley Primary Care Trust), since 2011; *b* 14 April 1954; *s* of Alvan Stoate and Maisie Stoate (*née* Russell); *m* 1979, Deborah Jane Dunkerley; two *s.* *Educ:* Kingston Grammar Sch.; King's Coll., London (MB BS 1977; MSc 1989). DRCOG 1981; FRCGP 1994. GP training, Joyce Green Hosp., Dartford, 1978–81; gen. med. practice, Albion Surgery, Bexleyheath, 1982–; GP Tutor, Queen Mary's Hosp., Sidcup, 1989–2006; Chm., Local Res. Ethics Cttee, Bexley HA, 1995–97; Vice-Chm., Regl Graduate Educn Bd, South Thames, 1997–99. Mem. (Lab) Dartford BC, 1990–99 (Chm., Finance and Corporate Business Cttee, 1996–99); Vice Pres., Dartford Racial Equality Council. MP (Lab) Dartford, 1997–2010. PPS to Minister of State for Crime Reduction, Policy and Community Safety, Home Office, 2001–03; PPS to Minister for the Arts, 2003–05. Mem., Health Select Cttee, 1997–2001 and 2005–10; Co-Chairman: All Party Parly Gp on Primary Care and Public Health, 1998–2010; All Party Parly Gp on Obesity, 2002–10; Chairman: All Party Pharmacy Gp, 2000–10; All Party Gp on Men's Health, 2001–10. Mem. Assembly, Univ. of Greenwich, 1997–. *Recreations:* running, sailing, travelling, reading, car building.

STOATE, Jane Elizabeth; *see* Davidson, J. E.

STOBART, John; a District Judge (Magistrates' Courts), 2004–15; *b* 6 May 1948; *s* of Joe and Jean Stobart; *m* 2001, Tracey Kirwin. *Educ:* Birmingham Univ. (LLB Hons 1971); Inns of Court Sch. of Law. Called to the Bar, Gray's Inn, 1974; in practice as barrister, specialising in crime, 1974–2004; a Dep. Dist Judge, 1999–2004. *Recreations:* golf, ski-ing, sailing, drinking and eating.

STOCK, Francine Elizabeth; writer and broadcaster; *b* 14 March 1958; *d* of John Hubert Stock and Jean Anne Stock (*née* Mallet); *m* 1987, Robert Lance Hughes; two *d.* *Educ:* St Catherine's, Bramley; Jesus Coll., Oxford (MA Hons Modern Langs; Hon. Fellow, 2007). Journalist, Petroleum Economist, 1980–82; joined BBC, 1983: Producer, The World at One, 1983–85; reporter: Money Prog., 1986–87; and Presenter, Newsnight, 1988–93; Presenter: Europe on the Brink series, 1993; Money Prog., 1995–96; Antiques Show, 1997–98; Front Row, 1998–2004; The Film Programme, 2004–. Film Critic, The Tablet, 2008–. Chair, Tate Members' Council, 2005–10; a Judge, Man Booker Prize, 2003; Mem. Cttee, Kim Scott Walwyn Prize 2003–; Chair of Judges, Gulbenkian Prize for Mus and Galls, 2007; Vice Pres., Hay Fest., 2009–. Guest Curator, From Page to Screen Fest., 2012. Patron, Borderlines Film Fest., 2012–. Trustee, Sidney Nolan Trust, 2011–. Hon. MA Worcester, 2006. *Publications:* A Foreign Country, 1999; Man-Made Fibre, 2002; In Glorious Technicolor: a century of film and how it has shaped us, 2011. *Address:* c/o Aitken Alexander Associates, 291 Gray's Inn Road, WC1X 8EB.

STOCK, Rt Rev. Marcus Nigel Ralph Peter; *see* Leeds, Bishop of, (RC).

STOCK, Very Rev. Victor Andrew, OAM 2002; Dean of Guildford, 2002–12, now Dean Emeritus; Priest Vicar, Westminster Abbey, since 2012; *b* 24 Dec. 1944; *s* of Arthur and Violet Stock. *Educ:* Christopher Wren Sch.; King's Coll., London (AKC 1968); St Boniface Coll., Warminster. Ordained deacon, 1969, priest, 1970; Curate, Pinner, 1969–73; Resident Chaplain, London Univ. Church of Christ the King, Gordon Sq., 1973–79; Rector: Friern Barnet, 1979–86; St Mary le Bow, City of London, 1986–2002. Mem., Gen. Synod, 1980–86. Chaplain, UK/Europe Gp, Order of Australia Assoc., 1988–. Pres., Sion Coll., 1994–95. Gov., Emmanuel Sch., 2013–. FRSA 1995. DUniv Surrey, 2012. *Publications:* Taking Stock: confessions of a city priest (autobiog.), 2001. *Recreations:* gardening, London, travel, politics, broadcasting. *Address:* 62 Bramwell House, Churchill Gardens, SW1V 3DS. *Clubs:* Reform; Guildford County.

STOCK, Rt Rev. (William) Nigel; Bishop at Lambeth, since 2013; Bishop for the Falkland Islands, since 2014; Bishop to the Forces, since 2014; an Honorary Assistant Bishop, Diocese of London, since 2013; an Honorary Assistant Bishop, Diocese of Southwark, since 2013; *b* 29 Jan. 1950; *s* of Ian Heath Stock, MC, and Elizabeth Mary Stock; *m* 1973, Carolyne Grace (*née* Greswell); three *s.* *Educ:* Durham Sch.; Durham Univ. (BA Hons Law and Politics); Ripon Coll., Cuddesdon (Oxford Univ. DipTh). Ordained deacon, 1976, priest, 1977; Asst Curate, Stockton St Peter, Durham, 1976–79; Priest-in-charge, Taraka St Peter, Aipo Rongo, PNG, 1979–84; Vicar, St Mark, Shiremoor, Newcastle, 1985–91; Team Rector, North Shields Team Ministry, 1991–98; RD, Tynemouth, 1992–98; Hon. Canon, Newcastle Cathedral, 1997–98; Residentiary Canon, Durham Cathedral, 1998–2000; Bishop Suffragan of Stockport, 2000–07; Bishop of St Edmundsbury and Ipswich, 2007–13. Commissary for Archbp of PNG, 1986–2015. Entered House of Lords, 2011. *Recreations:* walking, photography, travel. *Address:* Lambeth Palace, SE1 7JU. *T:* (020) 7898 1211. *E:* nigel.stock@lambethpalace.org.

STOCKDALE, David Andrew; QC 1995; **His Honour Judge Stockdale;** a Circuit Judge, since 2010; Senior Circuit Judge and Honorary Recorder of Manchester, since 2013; a Deputy High Court Judge, Queen's Bench Division, since 2008; *b* 9 May 1951; 2nd *s* of late John Ramsden Stockdale and Jean Stewart Stockdale (*née* Shelley); *m* 1985, Melanie Jane, *e d* of late Anthony Benson and Barbara Benson; one *s* three *d.* *Educ:* Giggleswick Sch.; Pembroke Coll., Oxford (MA Lit.Hum.). Called to the Bar, Middle Temple, 1975, Bencher, 2003; in practice on Northern Circuit, 1976–2010 (Jun., 1978; Treas., 2008–10); Asst Recorder, 1990–93; Recorder, 1993–2010. Governor: Giggleswick Sch., 1982– (Chm. of Govs, 1997–2007); Terra Nova Sch., 2000–08. *Recreations:* the outdoors, motorcycling, remote Scotland. *Address:* Courts of Justice, Crown Square, Manchester M3 3FL. *T:* (0161) 954 1800. *Club:* Sloane.

STOCKDALE, His Honour Eric; a Circuit Judge, 1972–94; *b* 8 Feb. 1929; *m* 1952, Joan (*née* Berry); two *s.* *Educ:* Collyer's Sch., Horsham; London Sch. of Economics; LLB, BScEcon, LLM, PhD (Lond.); MSc (Cranfield). 2nd Lieut, RA, 1947–49; Lieut, RARO, 1952–84. Called to the Bar, Middle Temple, 1950, Bencher, 2004; practised in London and on Midland Circuit until 1972; admitted to State Bar, Calif, 1983. Mem., Supreme Court Procedure Cttee, 1982–94. Tech. Advr, Central Council of Probation Cttees, 1979–84; Vice-Pres., NACRO, 1980–94 (Mem. Council, 1970–80); President: British Soc. of Criminology, 1978–81; Soc. of English and Amer. Lawyers, 1986–89 (Chm., 1984–86). Member: Central Council for Educn and Trng in Social Work, 1984–89; Parole Board, 1985–89; Criminal Injuries Compensation Bd, 1995–2000; Criminal Injuries Compensation Appeals Panel, 1997–2005. Vis. Prof., Queen Mary and Westfield Coll., London Univ., 1989–93. Governor, 1977–89, Vis. Fellow, 1986–94, Vis. Prof., 1994–2009, Univ. of Hertfordshire (formerly Hatfield Poly.). Consultant Ed., Blackstone's Criminal Practice, first 16 edns, 1991–2006. Hon. LLD Hertfordshire, 1995. *Publications:* The Court and the Offender, 1967; A Study of Bedford Prison 1660–1877, 1977; Law and Order in Georgian Bedfordshire, 1982; The Probation Volunteer, 1985; (with Keith Devlin) Sentencing, 1987; (ed with Silvia Casale) Criminal Justice Under Stress, 1992; 'Tis Treason, My Good Man!, 2005; (with Randy J. Holland) Middle Temple Lawyers and the American Revolution, 2007; From Wig and Pen to Computer, 2008; The Man Who Shot the President - and other lawyers, 2008; Further and Worse Particulars, 2009; (contrib.) History of the Middle Temple, 2011; Send for Benson!, 2015. *Address:* 20 Lyonsdown Road, New Barnet, Herts EN5 1JE. *T:* (020) 8449 7181. *Club:* Athenæum.

STOCKDALE, Sir Thomas (Minshull), 2nd Bt *cr* 1960, of Hoddington, Co. Southampton; *b* 7 Jan. 1940; *s* of Sir Edmund Villiers Minshull Stockdale, 1st Bt and Hon. Louise Fermor-Hesketh (*d* 1994), *er d* of 1st Lord Hesketh; *S* father, 1989; *m* 1965, Jacqueline Ha-Van-Vuong (*d* 2010); one *s* one *d.* *Educ:* Eton; Worcester Coll., Oxford (MA). Called to Bar, Inner Temple, 1966; Bencher, Lincoln's Inn, 1994. *Recreations:* shooting, travel. *Heir:* *s* John Minshull Stockdale, *b* 13 Dec. 1967. *Address:* Manor Farm, Weston Patrick, Basingstoke, Hants RG25 2NT. *Clubs:* Turf, MCC.

STOCKEN, Oliver Henry James, CBE 2013; Chairman, Stanhope plc, since 2000; *b* 22 Dec. 1941; *s* of late Henry Edmund West Stocken and Sheila Guiscard Stocken (*née* Steele); *m* 1967, Sally Forbes Dishon; two *s* one *d.* *Educ:* Felsted Sch.; University Coll., Oxford (BA). FCA 1978. Director: N M Rothschild & Sons Limited, 1968–77; Esperanza Trade & Transport, 1977–79; Barclays Merchant Bank, 1979–81; Man. Dir, Barclays Australia, 1982–84; Finance Director: BZW, 1985–93; Barclays plc, 1993–99. Non-executive Director:

Steel Burrill Jones Group plc, 1992–96; MEPC plc, 1995–2000; Pilkington plc, 1998–2006; Rank plc, 1998–2006; Bunzl plc, 1998–2000; 3i Group plc, 1999–2009 (Dep. Chm., 2002–09); Novar plc, 2000–05; GUS plc, 2000–06; Standard Chartered Bank plc, 2004–14. Chairman: Rutland Trust, 1999–2007; Lupus Capital plc, 1999–2002; Oval Insurance Gp, 2006–11; Home Retail Gp, 2006–12. Trustee: Natural Hist. Mus., 1999–2013 (Chm., 2006–13); Henley River and Rowing Mus., 2002–09; Chichester Fest. Th., 2010–; Care (UK), 2012– (Chm., 2012–). Mem. Council, RCA, 1998–2007 (Treas., 2002–07). Chairman, Trustees: Children's Leukaemia Trust, 1993–2002; Devas Club, 1997–2004. Gov., Felsted Sch., 2008–. *Recreations:* golf, running, Rugby, cricket. *Address:* 25c Marryat Road, Wimbledon, SW19 5BB. *Clubs:* Brooks's, Garrick, MCC (Mem. Cttee, 1998–, Treas., 2000–06, Trustee, 2007–09, Chm., 2009–15); Royal Wimbledon Golf, West Sussex Golf.

STOCKER, Diane Louise; *see* Corner, D. L.

STOCKER, John Wilcox, AO 1999; PhD; FRACP; Principal, Foursight Associates Pty Ltd, since 1996; *b* 23 April 1945; *s* of W. R. Stocker and Gladys Noelle Davies; *m* 1973, Joanne Elizabeth Gross; two *d. Educ:* Wesley Coll., Univ. of Melbourne (MB BS BMedSc). FTS. RMO, Royal Melbourne Hosp., 1970–72; Res. Scientist, Walter & Eliza Hall Inst. of Med. Res., 1974–76; Mem., Basel Inst. of Immunology, 1976–78; Central Res. Unit, 1979–84; Dir, Pharm. Res., Hoffman-La Roche & Co., Basel, 1986–87; Dir, Vic. Govt Strategic Res. Foundn, 1988–93; Chief Exec., CSIRO, 1990–95; Govt Chief Scientist, Australia, 1996–99. Founding Man. Dir, AMRAD, 1987–90; Director: Gene Shears Pty, 1992–96; Cambridge Antibody Technology Ltd, 1995–2006; Telstra Corp., 1996–; Circadian Technologies Pty Ltd, 1996–2009; Rothschild Bioscience Managers Ltd, 1996–98; Nufarm Ltd, 1998–; Chairman: Sigma Co. Ltd, 1999–2005; Sigma Pharmaceuticals Ltd, 2005–09. Chairman: Australian Sci. Technol. and Engrg Council, 1997–98; Grape and Wine R&D Corp., 1997–2004; CSIRO, 2007–10; Mem., numerous Industry and Govt sci. orgns. Centenary Medal, Australia, 2003. *Publications:* scientific papers, contribs to learned jls. *Recreations:* tennis, tiling, viticulture, reading. *Address:* Foursight Associates Pty Ltd, Level 15, 1 Nicholson Street, Melbourne, Vic 3000, Australia. *Club:* Winzergenossenschaft zur Landskron (Switzerland).

STOCKING, Dame Barbara (Mary), (Dame Barbara MacInnes), DBE 2008 (CBE 2000); President, Murray Edwards College, Cambridge, since 2013; *b* 28 July 1951; *d* of Percy Frederick Stocking and Mary Stocking; *m* 1981, Dr R. John MacInnes; two *s. Educ:* New Hall, Cambridge (BA); Univ. of Wisconsin (MS). Teaching Asst, Dept of Physiology and Biophysics, Univ. of Illinois, 1972–73; Staff Associate, Nat. Acad. of Scis, Washington, 1974–76; Jt Research Fellow, Nuffield Provincial Hosps Trust and Centre for Med. Res., Univ. of Sussex, 1977–79; Sec., WHO Independent Commn on Long Term Prospects of Onchocerciasis Control Programme, LSHTM, 1979–91; Fellow in Health Policy, Innovation and Evaluation, King's Fund Coll., 1983–86; Dir, King's Fund Centre for Health Services Develt, 1987–93; Chief Executive: Oxford RHA, 1993–94; Anglia and Oxford RHA, 1994–96; Regl Dir, Anglia and Oxford, 1994–98, South East, 1999–2000, NHS Exec., DoH; Dir, NHS Modernisation Agency, 2000–01 (on secondment); Chief Exec., Oxfam GB, 2001–13. Chair: NHS Patient Partnership Steering Gp, 1993–98; NHS Resource Allocation Gp, 1995–97. Member: UK Harkness Fellowships Adv. and Selection Cttee, 1989–95; NHS Central R&D Cttee, 1992–96. Member: UN Inter Agency Standing Cttee for Humanitarian Response, 2006–; High Level Panel on delivering Millennium Develt Goals, FAO, 2006–; Founder Bd Mem., Global Humanitarian Forum, 2007–; Mem. Bd, Cabinet Office, 2010–15. Hon. DSc: Luton, 1998; Oxford Brookes, 1999; Loughborough, 2003. *Publications:* (jtly) The Image and the Reality: a case study of the impacts of medical technology, 1978; Initiative and Inertia: case studies in the health services, 1985; (ed) Expensive Medical Technologies, 1988; (Series Editor) A Study of the Diffusion of Medical Technology in Europe, 3 vols, 1991; (jtly) Criteria for Change, 1991; Medical Advances: the future shape of acute services, 1991. *Recreations:* music, family.

STOCKMANN, Caroline Anne; Chief Financial Officer, British Council, since 2014; *b* Leeds, 26 Oct. 1961; *d* of John Anthony Stockmann and Anita Edith Elizabeth Stockmann; *m* 1996, Michael John Thurlow Stuttard; two *c. Educ:* Durham Univ. (BA Hons); Guildhall Sch. of Music and Drama (LGSM). FCA; DChA. Freelance musician and teacher, 1986–88; course leader, Lancaster Dio., 1988–90; trainee accountant, KPMG, 1990–94; Sen. Internal Auditor, Cadbury Schweppes, 1994–95; Financial Controller, Granada plc, 1995–96; Financial Accountant/Controller, 1996–99, Finance Dir, Benelux, 2000–01, Bestfoods; Vice Pres. Finance, Unilever Foods Europe, 2001–04; Chief Financial Officer/Chief Inf. Officer, Unilever Thailand, 2004–06; Hd, Business Planning, Novartis, 2006–07; Finance and Commercial Dir, Southbank Centre, 2007–09; Dir, Internat. Progs, Sue Ryder Care, 2010; Chief Financial Officer, Save the Children Internat., 2010–14. Trustee: Sue Ryder Care, 2008–10; The Brooke, 2011–14. Mem., Adv. Bd, Rehearsal Orch., 2008–12; Treas., Epsom Symphony Orch., 2010–14. Member: Adv. Bd, Faculty of Arts and Humanities, Durham Univ., 2012–; Audit Cttee, Univ. of Cambridge, 2014–15. Foundn Gov., St Gregory's Comp. Sch., 2013–. *Recreations:* bell ringing, musician, reading, DJ, fell walking, family, school governor, cooking, travel, languages. *Address:* British Council, 10 Spring Gardens, SW1A 2BN. *T:* (020) 7389 4955. *E:* caroline.stockmann@britishcouncil.org.

STOCKPORT, Bishop Suffragan of, since 2015; **Rt Rev. Elizabeth Jane Holden Lane;** *b* High Wycombe, 8 Dec. 1966; *d* of Dennis and Helen Holden; *m* 1990, Rev. George Lane; one *s* one *d. Educ:* Manchester High Sch. for Girls; St Peter's Coll., Oxford (MA); St John's Coll., Cranmer Hall, Durham (DipMin). Ordained deacon, 1993, priest, 1994; Curate, St James, Blackburn, 1993–96; Permission to officiate, Dio. of York, 1996–99; Hosp. Chaplain, Hull, 1998–99; Social Responsibility Officer, Dio. of Chester, 2000–02; Team Vicar, St George's Stockport, 2002–07; Asst Dir of Ordinands, Dio. of Chester, 2005–07; Vicar, St Peter's, Hale and St Elizabeth's, Ashley, 2007–14; Dean of Women in Ministry, Dio. of Chester, 2010–14. Participant Observer, House of Bishops, 2013. Hon. DD Univ. of Wales Trinity St David. *Recreations:* reading, performing arts, sport, music, cryptic crosswords. *Address:* Bishop's Lodge, Back Lane, Dunham Town, Altrincham, Cheshire WA14 4SG. *T:* (0161) 928 5611. *E:* bpstockport@chester.anglican.org.

STOCKTON, 2nd Earl of, *cr* 1984; **Alexander Daniel Alan Macmillan;** Viscount Macmillan of Ovenden, 1984; *b* Oswestry, Shropshire, 10 Oct. 1943; *s* of Viscount Macmillan of Ovenden, PC, MP (*d* 1984) and of Katharine Viscountess Macmillan of Ovenden, DBE; *S* grandfather, 1986; *m* 1st, 1970, Hélène Birgitte Hamilton (marr. diss. 1991); one *s* two *d*; 2nd, 1995, Miranda Elizabeth Louise, Lady Nuttall (marr. diss. 2010), *d* of Richard Quarry and Diana, Lady Mancroft; 3rd, 2012, Linda Shirley Rimington. *Educ:* Eton; Université de Paris; Strathclyde Univ. FRICS 1999. Sub Ed., Glasgow Herald, 1964–66; Reporter, Daily Telegraph, 1966–68; Foreign Corresp., Daily Telegraph and Sunday Telegraph, 1968–74; Corresp., BBC TV and Radio, Toronto Star, San Francisco Examiner, 1969–74; Macmillan Publishers: Dir, 1974–80; Man. Dir, 1980–86; Chm., 1986–2000; Pres., Internat. Gp, 2000–06. Mem. Council, Publishers Assoc., 1980–88. Contested (C) Bristol, EP elecns, 1994; MEP (C) SW Region, England, 1999–2004. Mem. (C), S Bucks DC, 2011–. FRSA 1987. Liveryman: Worshipful Co. of Merchant Taylors, 1972 (Mem., Ct of Assts, 1987–; Master, 1992–93); Worshipful Co. of Stationers and Newspaper Makers, 1973 (Mem., Ct of Assts, 1996–2008). DUniv Strathclyde, 1993; Hon. DLitt: De Montfort, 1993; Westminster, 1995; London Inst., 2003. *Heir: s* Viscount Macmillan of Ovenden, *qv. Address:* Flat M, 9 Warwick Square, SW1V 2AA. *T:* (020) 7834 6004; The Priory, Old Mill Road, Denham Village, Bucks UB9 5AS. *T:* (01895) 834181, 07860 461497. *E:* thepriory@dbac.co.uk. *Clubs:* Beefsteak, Pratt's.

STOCKWIN, Prof. (James) Arthur (Ainscow), OBE 2009; Nissan Professor of Modern Japanese Studies, and Director of Nissan Institute of Japanese Studies, University of Oxford, 1982–2003; Fellow, St Antony's College, Oxford, 1982–2003, now Emeritus (Sub-Warden, 1999–2001); *b* 28 Nov. 1935; *s* of Wilfred Arthur Stockwin and Edith Mary Stockwin; *m* 1960, Audrey Lucretia Hobson Stockwin (*née* Wood); one *s* two *d* (and one *s* decd). *Educ:* Exeter Coll., Oxford Univ. (MA); Australian Nat. Univ. (PhD). Australian National University: Lectr, Dept of Political Science, 1964–66; Sen. Lectr, 1966–72; Reader, 1972–81. Pres., British Assoc. of Japanese Studies, 1994–95. Gen. Ed., Nissan Inst.—Routledge Japanese Studies Series, 1984–. Japan Foundn Prize, 2009. Order of the Rising Sun (Japan), 2004. *Publications:* The Japanese Socialist Party and Neutralism, 1968; (ed) Japan and Australia in the Seventies, 1972; Japan, Divided Politics in a Growth Economy, 1975, 2nd edn 1982; Why Japan Matters, 1983; (jtly, also ed) Dynamic and Immobilist Politics in Japan, 1988; (trans.) Junji Banno, The Establishment of the Japanese Constitutional System, 1992; The Story of Tim, 1993; (ed jtly) The Vitality of Japan: sources of national strength and weakness, 1997; Governing Japan, 1999, new edn 2008; Dictionary of the Modern Politics of Japan, 2003; Collected Writings of J. A. A. Stockwin, Part I, 2004; Thirty-Odd Feet Below Belgium: an affair of letters in the Great War 1915–1916, 2005; (trans.) Michael Lucken et al., Japan's Postwar, 2011; The Writings of J. A. A. Stockwin: Japanese foreign policy and understanding Japanese politics, 2 vols, 2012; (trans.) Sébastien Lechevalier, The Great Transformation of Japanese Capitalism, 2014; (trans.) Junji Banno, Japan's Modern History, 1857–1937: a new political narrative, 2014; articles, largely on Japanese politics and foreign policy, in Pacific Affairs, Japanese Studies, Asia-Pacific Review, Japan Forum, etc. *Recreations:* languages, running. *Address:* Glym Cottage, Glympton Road, Wootton, Woodstock, Oxon OX20 1EL. *T:* (01993) 811449. *W:* www.arthurstockwin.co.uk.

STODDART, family name of **Baron Stoddart of Swindon**.

STODDART OF SWINDON, Baron *cr* 1983 (Life Peer), of Reading in the Royal County of Berkshire; **David Leonard Stoddart;** *b* 4 May 1926; *s* of Arthur Leonard Stoddart, coal miner, and Queenie Victoria Stoddart (*née* Price); *m* 1961, Jennifer Percival-Alwyn; two *s* (one *d* by previous marr.). *Educ:* elementary; St Clement Danes and Henley Grammar Schools. Youth in training, PO Telephones, 1942–44; business on own account, 1944–46; Railway Clerk, 1947–49; Hospital Clerk, 1949–51; Power Station Clerical Worker, 1951–70. Joined Labour Party, 1947; Reading County Borough Council: Member, 1954–72; served at various times as Chairman of Housing, Transport and Finance Cttees; Leader, Labour Group of Councillors, 1962–72; Leader of Council, 1967–72. Contested (Lab) Newbury, 1959 and 1964, Swindon, 1969, 1983. MP (Lab) Swindon, 1970–83; PPS to Minister for Housing and Construction, 1974–75; an Asst Govt Whip, 1975; a Lord Comr, HM Treasury, 1976–77; an opposition whip, and opposition spokesman on energy, House of Lords, 1983–88. Chairman: Alliance Against the European Constitution (formerly Anti-Maastricht Alliance), 1992–2007; Global Britain, 1998–; Jt Pres., Campaign for an Ind. Britain, 2007–11 (Chm., 1985–2007); Mem. Council, Freedom Assoc., 2006–. *Recreations:* gardening, music. *Address:* Sintra, 37A Bath Road, Reading, Berks RG1 6HL. *T:* (0118) 957 6726.

STODDART, Anne Elizabeth, CMG 1996; HM Diplomatic Service, retired; Deputy Permanent Representative (Economic Affairs), UK Mission to the United Nations, Geneva, 1991–96; *b* 29 March 1937; *d* of late James Stoddart and Ann Jack Stoddart (*née* Inglis). *Educ:* Kirby Grammar School, Middlesbrough; Somerville College, Oxford. MA. Entered Foreign Office, 1960; British Military Govt, Berlin, 1963–67; FCO, 1967–70; First Secretary (Economic), Ankara, 1970–73; Head of Chancery, Colombo, 1974–76; FCO, 1977–81; Dep. Permanent UK Rep. to Council of Europe, Strasbourg, 1981–87; seconded to External Eur. Policy Div., DTI, 1987–91. *Address:* Flat 1, 63 The Avenue, Richmond, Surrey TW9 2AH.

STODDART, Caroline Ann Tuke; *see* Malone, C. A. T.

STODDART, Charles Norman, PhD; Sheriff of Lothian and Borders at Edinburgh, 1995–2009; *b* 4 April 1948; *s* of Robert Stoddart and Margaret (*née* Allenby); *m* 1981, Anne Lees; one *d. Educ:* Edinburgh Univ. (LLB, PhD); McGill Univ. (LLM). Admitted Solicitor, 1972, practised, 1972–73, 1980–88; Lectr in Scots Law, Edinburgh Univ., 1973–80; Sheriff of N Strathclyde at Paisley, 1988–95. Dir, Judicial Studies in Scotland, 1997–2000. Member: Maclean Cttee on Serious, Violent and Sexual Offenders, 1999–2000; Sentencing Commn for Scotland, 2003–06; Civil Courts Rev. Policy Gp, 2007–09; Post-corroboration Safeguards Rev., 2014–15. Mem., Parole Bd for Scotland, 2011–14. Editor, Green's Criminal Law Bulletin, 1992–2008. *Publications:* (with H. Neilson) The Law and Practice of Legal Aid in Scotland, 1979, 4th edn 1994; (with C. H. W. Gane and J. Chalmers) A Casebook on Scottish Criminal Law, 1980, 4th edn 2009; Bible John (crime documentary), 1980; (with C. H. W. Gane) Cases and Materials on Scottish Criminal Procedure, 1983, 2nd edn 1994; Criminal Warrants, 1991, 2nd edn 1999; contribs to professional jls. *Recreations:* music, foreign travel.

STODDART, Christopher West; Chief Executive Officer, ATR plc (formerly Go Racing), 2001–03; *b* 10 April 1950; *s* of Dr Ian West Stoddart and Bridget Stoddart (*née* Pilditch); *m* 1st, 1972, Deborah Ounsted (marr. diss. 1984); 2nd, 1985, Dr Hazel Grasmere, *d* of Hon. Robert and Evelyn Grasmere, USA. *Educ:* Winchester Coll.; Churchill Coll., Cambridge (BA Hons 1971). Joined CS, 1971; DoE, 1971–75; Research Sec., Centre for Envmtl Studies, 1976–80; Regl Companies Sec., 1980–81, Sec. 1981–82, ITCA; Tyne Tees Television: Gen. Manager, 1982–83; Dir of Resources, 1983–88; Man. Dir and Chief Exec., Satellite Information Services Ltd, 1988–92; Man. Dir, GMTV, 1992–2001. Non-exec. Dir, Sterling Publishing Gp, 1999–2001. Chm., Trustees, Changing Faces, 1999–2002. *Publications:* The Inner City as Testing Ground for Government-funded Research, 1980. *Recreations:* mountaineering, photography, travel.

STODDART, Sir (James) Fraser, Kt 2007; FRS 1994; CChem, FRSC; FRSE; Board of Trustees Professor of Chemistry, and Director, Center for Chemistry of Integrated Systems, Northwestern University, since 2008; Kavli Professor of NanoSystems Science, University of California at Los Angeles, 2003–07, Emeritus Professor of Chemistry, 2008; *b* 24 May 1942; *s* of Thomas Fraser Stoddart and Jane Spalding Hislop Stoddart; *m* 1968, Norma Agnes Scholan (*d* 2004); two *d. Educ:* Melville Coll., Edinburgh; Univ. of Edinburgh (BSc 1964; PhD 1966; DSc 1980). CChem, FRSC 1978. Nat. Res. Council of Canada Post-doctoral Fellow, Queen's Univ., Canada, 1967–69; University of Sheffield: ICI Res. Fellow, subseq. Lectr in Chemistry, 1970–82; seconded to Catalysis Gp, ICI Corporate Lab., Runcorn, 1978–81; Reader in Chemistry, 1982–91; Prof. of Organic Chem., 1990–97, Hd, Sch. of Chem., 1993–97, Univ. of Birmingham; Winstein Prof. of Organic Chemistry, 1997–2003, Dir, California NanoSystems Inst., 2003–07, UCLA. Vis. Lectr, Univ. of Parana, Brazil, 1972; SRC Sen. Vis. Fellow, UCLA, 1978; Visiting Professor: Texas A&M Univ., 1980; Univ. of Messina, Italy, 1986–88; Mulhouse, France, 1987. FRSE 2008; Fellow, American Acad. of Arts and Scis, 2012. Mem., NAS, 2014. Hon. DSc: Birmingham, 2005; Twente, 2006; Sheffield, 2008; Trinity Coll. Dublin, 2009; St Andrews, 2010. Awards include: Internat. Izatt-Christensen in macrocyclic chem., 1993; Arthur C. Cope Schol. Award, 1999, Arthur C. Cope Award, 2008, ACS; Nagoya Gold Medal in Organic Chemistry, Nagoya Univ., Japan, 2004; Alumnus of the Year Award, Univ. of Edinburgh, 2005; Fusion Award, Univ. of Nevada, 2006; King Faisal Internat. Award in Sci. (Chemistry), King Faisal Foundn, 2007; Davy Medal, Royal Soc., 2008; Royal Medal, RSE, 2010. Mem., various editl bds in Europe and USA. *Publications:* over 1000 papers, reviews and monographs in Angewandte Chemie, Chemistry—A Europ. Jl, Jl of the American Chemical Soc. on nanoscale science and self-assembly processes. *Address:* Department of Chemistry, Northwestern University, 2145 Sheridan Road, Evanston, IL 60208–3113, USA.

STODDART, Prof. John Little, CBE 1994; PhD, DSc; FRSB; FRAgS; Director of Research, Institute of Grassland and Environmental Research, Agricultural and Food Research Council, 1988–93; *b* 1 Oct. 1933; *s* of John Little Stoddart and Margaret Pickering Dye; *m* 1957, Wendy Dalton Leardie; one *d* (one *s* decd). *Educ:* South Shields High Sch. for Boys; University Coll., Durham (BSc Botany 1954); University of Wales, Aberystwyth (PhD 1961); Durham Univ. (DSc 1973). FRSB (FIBiol 1984); ARPS 1985; FRAgS 1993. Nat. Service, RA, UK, Hong Kong and Malaya, 1954–56. Fulbright-Hays Sen. Fellow, 1966–67; Res. Associate, Mich. State Univ./Atomic Energy Commn Plant Res. Lab., 1966–67; Welsh Plant Breeding Station: Dep. Dir, 1985–87; Dir, 1987–88; Head of Plants and Soils Div., 1985–88. Hon. Prof., Sch. of Agric. and Biol Scis, Univ. of Wales, 1988–95. Chm., Plant Sci. Prog. Adv. Cttee, ODA, 1995–98. Mem. Council, NIAB, 1988–93. Non-executive Director: Derwen NHS Trust (W Wales), 1994–97; Pembrokeshire & Derwen NHS Trust, 1997–2008; IGER Technologies, 2000–03. Trustee, Stapledon Meml Trust, 1996–2007 (Mem., 1988–). *Publications:* scientific articles, reviews and contribs to scientific books. *Recreations:* photography (pictorial), golf. *Club:* St David's (Aberystwyth).

STODDART, John Maurice, CBE 1995; Principal and Vice-Chancellor, Sheffield Hallam University, 1992–98 (Principal, Sheffield City Polytechnic, 1983–92); *b* 18 Sept. 1938; *s* of Gordon Stoddart and May (*née* Ledder). *Educ:* Wallasey Grammar Sch.; Univ. of Reading (BA Pol Econ.). Teacher, Wallasey GS, 1960–62; Lectr, Mid Cheshire Coll. of Further Educn, 1962–64; Lectr, Enfield Coll., 1964–70; Head, Dept of Econs and Business Studies, Sheffield Polytechnic, 1970–72; Asst Dir, NE London Polytechnic, 1972–76; Dir, Hull Coll. of Higher Educn (now Univ. of Humberside), 1976–83. Dir, Sheffield Science Park Co. Ltd, 1988–96; Deputy Chairman: Northern Gen. Hosp. NHS Trust, 1999–2001; Sheffield Teaching Hosps NHS Trust, 2001–06. Chm., CNAA Cttee for Business and Management, 1985–88 (Chm., Undergrad. Courses Bd, 1976–83); Mem., CNAA, 1982–88, 1991–93; Chm., Cttee of Dirs of Polys, 1990–93 (Vice-Chm., 1988–90). Member: Sea Fisheries Trng Council, 1976–80; Architects Registration Council, UK, 1979–85; Council for Industry and Educn, 1989–94; Council for Educn and Trng in Social Work, 1989–94; BTEC, 1991–95; Chm., Higher Educn Quality Council, 1992–97. Member: Court, Univ. of Hull, 1976–83; Council, Univ. of Sheffield, 1983–92. Companion, British Business Graduates Soc., 1983; Hon. Fellow: Humberside Coll., 1983; Univ. of Bolton, 2005. FRSA 1977. CCMI (FBIM 1977; CBIM 1990). Hon. DEd CNAA, 1992; Hon. DLitt Coventry, 1993; DUniv: Middlesex, 1993; Sheffield Hallam, 1998; Hon. LLD Sheffield, 1998. *Publications:* articles on business and management educn. *Address:* 6 Tapton Park Gardens, Sheffield S10 3FP. *T:* (0114) 230 5467. *Clubs:* Reform; Leander (Henley-on-Thames).

STODDART, Michael Craig, FCA; Chairman, Electra Investment Trust, 1986–2000; Senior Business Advisor, Stonehage Fleming Family and Partners (formerly Fleming Family and Partners), since 2001; *b* 27 March 1932; *s* of late Frank Ogle Boyd Stoddart and Barbara (*née* Craig); *m* 1961, (Susan) Brigid (*née* O'Halloran); two *s* two *d*. *Educ:* Abberley Hall, Worcs; Marlborough Coll. Chartered Accountant 1955; joined Singer & Friedlander, 1955: resp. for opening provincial network; retired as Jt Chief Exec., 1973; Dep. Chm. and Chief Exec., Electra Investment Trust, 1974–86; pioneered into substantial unlisted investments, incl. developing venture capital arm; Chm., Electra Kingsway Gp, 1989–95. Non-executive Chairman: Britax (formerly BSC) plc, 1994–2000; Elderstreet Millennium (formerly Gartmore) Venture Capital Trust plc, 1996–2007; non-executive Director: Bullough, 1968–2002; Chesterfield Properties plc, 1997–99; Private Investors Capital Ltd, 1997–2004, and other UK cos. Underwriting Mem. of Lloyd's, 1972–96. Chm., Foundn for Entrepreneurial Mgt, London Business Sch., 1997–2004. (Mem., Develt Bd); Mem. Bd, Britech Foundn Ltd, 1999–2002. *Recreations:* country pursuits, shooting, golf, theatre. *Address:* Stonehage Fleming Family and Partners, 15 Suffolk Street, SW1Y 4HG; Compton House, Kinver, Worcs DY7 5LY; 27 Crown Reach, 145 Grosvenor Road, SW1V 3JU. *Clubs:* Boodle's, Pratt's.

STODDART, Dr Simon Kenneth Fladgate, FSA; Fellow, Magdalene College, Cambridge, since 1998; Reader in Prehistory, University of Cambridge, since 2013; *b* 8 Nov. 1958; *s* of Kenneth Bowring Stoddart and Daphne Elizabeth Fladgate (*née* Hughes); *m* 1983, Dr Caroline Ann Tuke Malone, *qv*; two *d*. *Educ:* Winchester Coll.; Magdalene Coll., Cambridge (BA 1980; PhD 1987); Univ. of Michigan (MA 1983). FSA 1994. Rome Schol. in Archaeol., British Sch. at Rome, 1980–81; Power Schol., Univ. of Michigan, 1981–83; Res. Fellow, Magdalene Coll., Cambridge, 1986–89; Lecturer: Univ. of York, 1988–90; Univ. of Bristol, 1990–94 (Sen. Lectr, 1994–96); University of Cambridge: Lectr, 1996–2000; Sen. Lectr, 2000–14. Ed., Antiquity, 2001–02. Charter Fellow, Wolfson Coll., Oxford, 1992–93; Balsdon Fellow, British Sch. at Rome, 2004; Res. Associate Prof., State Univ. of NY, 2004–06. MCIfA (MIFA 1987). *Publications:* (ed with C. Malone) Papers in Italian Archaeology, Vols 1–4, 1985; (with N. Spivey) Etruscan Italy, 1990; (ed with C. Mathers) Development and Decline in the Mediterranean Bronze Age, 1994; (ed with C. Malone) Territory, Time and State: the archaeological development of the Gubbio Basin, 1994; (ed) Landscapes from Antiquity, 2000; (ed with G. Carr) Celts from Antiquity, 2002; (ed with C. Malone) Mortuary Ritual in Prehistoric Malta, 2009; Historical Dictionary of the Etruscans, 2009; (ed with G. Cifani and S. Neil) Landscape, Ethnicity and Identity in the Archaic Mediterranean, 2012; (ed with C. Popa) Fingerprinting the Iron Age, 2014; contrib. acad. articles. *Recreations:* walking, travel, cycling, recycling. *Address:* Magdalene College, Cambridge CB3 0AG. *T:* (01223) 332168.

STODDART, Thomas; photo-journalist; *b* 28 Nov. 1953; *s* of Tommy and Kathleen Stoddart. *Educ:* Seahouses Secondary Sch., Northumberland. Freelance photographer working on humanitarian issues, such as the siege of Sarajevo, 1992–97, Sudan famine, and AIDS catastrophe in Sub-Saharan Africa, for internat. magazines, incl. Time, Newsweek, Stern, and Sunday Times Mag. Member: RPS; RGS. *Publications:* Sarajevo, 1998; A Day in the Life of Africa, 2002. *Recreations:* lifelong fan of Newcastle United, watching sport, photography, enjoying good food, friends and wine. *Address:* 13 Tradewinds Court, Asher Way, E1W 2JB. *E:* tom@tomstoddart.com.

STOER, John Edmund; Head Master, St Aloysius' College, Glasgow, 2004–13; *b* Point Fortin, Trinidad, 7 May 1954; *s* of Edmund Stoer and Lilly Stoer; *m* 1983, Janet Lewis; one *s* one *d*. *Educ:* Douai Sch.; Bristol Univ. (BA Theol. and Sociol.); Inst. of Educn, Univ. of London (PGCE). Teacher, St Thomas More Sch., Chelsea, 1978–81; Hd of Religious Educn, St Philip Howard Sch., 1981–84; Dir, Sixth Form, Gunnersbury Catholic Sch., 1984–89; Dep. Hd, Campion Sch., 1989–94; Headmaster, St Joseph's Coll., Stoke-on-Trent, 1994–2004. *Recreation:* researching inter-religious dialogue.

STOKE-UPON-TRENT, Archdeacon of; *see* Parker, Ven. M. J.

STOKER, Dr Dennis James, FRCP, FRCS, FRCR; Consultant Radiologist: Royal National Orthopaedic Hospital, 1972–93, and 1997–2002, now Emeritus; St George's Hospital, 1972–87; London Clinic, 1976–93; King Edward VII Hospital for Officers, 1985–98; part-time consultant, Frimley Park Hospital, 1994–2008; *b* 22 March 1928; *yr s* of Dr George Morris Stoker and Elsie Margaret Stoker (*née* Macqueen); *m* 1st, 1951, Anne Sylvia Nelson Forster (*d* 1997); two *s* two *d*; 2nd, 1999, Sheila Mary Mercer. *Educ:* Oundle Sch.; Guy's Hosp. Med. Sch. MB BS; DMRD; FRCR (FFR RCS 1972); FRCP 1976; FRCS 1992. Guy's Hosp. appts, 1951–52; RAF Med. Branch, 1951–68; served Cyprus and Aden; Wing Comdr (retd). Consultant Physician, RAF, 1964–68; Registrar and Sen. Registrar, Diagnostic Radiology, St George's Hosp., London, 1968–72; Sen. Lectr and Dir of Radiological Studies, 1977–93, Dean, 1987–91, Inst. of Orthopaedics. Royal Society of Medicine: Fellow, 1958; Mem. Council, Section of Radiol., 1975–77; Vice-Pres., 1978–80; Royal College of Radiologists: Fellow, 1976; Examr, 1981–84 and 1985–88; George Simon Lectr, 1988; Dean and Vice-Pres., 1989–91; Robert Knox Lectr, 1992. Fellow, British Orth. Assoc.; Founder Mem., Internat. Skeletal Soc., 1974– (Medal, 1993). Special Trustee, Royal Nat. Orthopaedic Hosp., 1984–2000 (Chm., 1992–98). Editor, Skeletal Radiology, 1984–96; Mem., Editl Bd, Clinical Radiology, 1974–84. *Publications:* Knee Arthrography, 1980; (jtly) Self Assessment in Orthopaedic Radiology, 1988; The Radiology of Skeletal Disorders, 1990; chapters in textbooks; papers on metabolic medicine, tropical disease and skeletal radiology. *Recreations:* philology, medical history, genealogy. *Address:* 3 Pearce's Orchard, Henley-on-Thames, Oxon RG9 2LF. *T:* (01491) 575756. *Clubs:* Royal Air Force; Phyllis Court (Henley).

STOKER, John Francis; charity adviser; *b* 11 Sept. 1950; *s* of Francis Charles Stoker and Joyce Stoker (*née* Barnwell); *m* 1982, Julie Puddicombe. *Educ:* King Edward's Sch., Birmingham; Brasenose Coll., Oxford (BA Lit.Hum.). Department of the Environment: Admin. Trainee, 1973–78; Principal, 1978; Tenant's Right to Buy, 1979–81; Alternatives to Rates, 1981–83; Cabinet Office, 1983–85; Grade 5, 1985; Envmt White Paper Div., 1990–92; Grade 3, 1992; Regl Dir, Govt Office for Merseyside, 1992–96; Dep. Dir Gen., 1997–98, Dir Gen., 1998–99, Nat. Lottery; Chief Charity Comr, 1999–2004. Chief Exec., London Bombings Relief Charitable Fund, 2005. Comr for the Compact (between Govt and voluntary/community sector), 2006–07. Mem., SRA (formerly Law Soc. Regulation Bd), 2006–09. Mem. Ct, Univ. of Greenwich, 2010– (Mem., Audit Cttee; Chair, Staffing Cttee). FRSA. *Recreations:* books, music, ski-ing. *Club:* Travellers.

STOKES, Dr Adrian Victor, OBE 1983; CChem; CEng; FBCS; Chief Executive, CAT Ltd, since 2000; *b* 25 June 1945; *s* of Alfred Samuel and Edna Stokes; *m* (marr. diss.). *Educ:* Orange Hill Grammar School, Edgware; University College London (BSc (1st cl. Hons) 1966; PhD 1970); Univ. of Hertfordshire (LLB 1st cl. Hons 2014); Postgrad. Cert. Commercial Mediation 2014. CChem 1976; MRSC 1976; FBCS 1978; CEng 1990; CSci 2004; CITP 2004. Research Programmer, GEC-Computers Ltd, 1969–71; Research Asst, Inst. of Computer Science, 1971–73; Research Fellow, UCL, 1973–77; Sen. Research Fellow and Sen. Lectr, Hatfield Polytechnic, 1977–81; Dir of Computing, St Thomas' Hosp., 1981–88 (King's Fund Fellow, 1981–84); Consultant, 1986–88 (on secondment), Principal Consultant, 1989–97, NHS Centre for IT, then Inf. Mgt Centre; Asst Dir, NHS Inf. Mgt Centre, 1997–99; Jt Dir, NHS Inf. Authy (Standards), 1999–2000. Man. Dir, Elvis Memories (UK) Ltd, 2001–15. Chairman: European Workshop for Open Systems Expert Gp on Healthcare, 1991–97; BSI Inf. Communications and Technol. Sector (formerly Systems Assembly) and Exec. Cttee, 2000–. Vis. Prof., Nene Coll., 1994–96 (Hon. Vis. Prof., 1996–99); Hon. Research Fellow, King Alfred's Coll., Winchester, 2001–04. Non-executive Director: NHS Barnet (formerly Barnet Primary Care Trust), 2001–11; Nat. Clinical Assessment Authy, 2001–05; Special Trustee, RNOH Charity (formerly Royal Nat. Orthopaedic Hosp. NHS Trust), 2003–13. Mem., Administrative Justice & Tribunals Council (formerly Council on Tribunals), 2003–11. Member: Silver Jubilee Cttee on Improving Access for Disabled People, 1977–78; Cttee on Restrictions Against Disabled People, 1979–81; Social Security Adv. Cttee, 1980–2001; Dept of Transport Panel of Advisers on Disability, 1983–85; Disabled Persons' Transport Adv. Cttee, 1986–89; First-tier Tribunal (Social Entitlement Chamber) (formerly Disability Appeal Tribunal), 1992–. Chm., Disabled Drivers' Motor Club, 1972–82, 1991–94, 1997–2000, Vice-Pres., 1982–2005; Chm., Exec. Cttee, RADAR, 1985–92 (Vice-Pres., 1999–). Governor, Motability, 1978–; Trustee: PHAB, 1982–90; Independent Living (1993) Fund, 1993–2002; Independent Living (Extension) Fund, 1993–2002; Mobility Choice, 1998–2013; Disabled Motoring UK (formerly Mobilise Orgn), 2005– (Life Vice-Pres., 2005, Vice-Chm., 2007–09 and 2012–13, Chm., 2009–12, Treas., 2013–). Freeman, City of London, 1988; Freeman, Co. of Information Technologists, 1988. Gov., Univ. of Hertfordshire, 2005–11. MCMI (MBIM 1986); FInstD 1986; FRSA 1997. Hon. DSc Hertfordshire, 1994. Mem., Editl Bd, Tribunals jl, 2015–. *Publications:* An Introduction to Data Processing Networks, 1978; Viewdata: a public information utility, 1979, 2nd edn 1980; The Concise Encyclopaedia of Computer Terminology, 1981; Networks, 1981; (with C. Saiady) What to Read in Microcomputing, 1982; Concise Encyclopaedia of Information Technology, 1982, 3rd edn 1986, USA edn 1983; Integrated Office Systems, 1982; (with M. D. Bacon and J. M. Bacon) Computer Networks: fundamentals and practice, 1984; Overview of Data Communications, 1985; The A to Z of Business Computing, 1986; Communications Standards, 1986; OSI Standards and Acronyms, 1987, 3rd edn 1991; (with H. de Glanville) The BJHC Abbreviary, 1995; numerous papers and articles, mainly concerned with computer technology. *Recreations:* philately, science fiction, collecting Elvis Presley records, computer programming. *Address:* 97 Millway, Mill Hill, NW7 3JL. *T:* (020) 8959 6665, 07785 502766.

STOKES, Dr Alistair Michael; Chairman, Solent NHS Trust (formerly Solent Healthcare), since 2010; *b* 22 July 1948; *s* of Alan Philip and Janet Ross Stokes; *m* 1970, Stephanie Mary Garland; two *d*. *Educ:* University College, Cardiff (BSc, PhD). With Pharmacia AB (Sweden), 1974–76; Monsanto Co., St Louis, USA, 1976–82; Glaxo Pharmaceuticals, 1982–85; Regional Gen. Manager, Yorkshire RHA, 1985–87; Dir, Glaxo Pharmaceuticals, 1987–90; Dir and Chief Operating Officer, Porton Internat., 1990–95; CEO, Speywood Pharmaceuticals, then Ipsen Ltd, 1995–2007. Chairman: Stowic PLC, 1998–99; Quadrant Healthcare PLC, 1999–2000; Ipsen Ltd, 2007–10; Ipsen Biopharm Ltd, 2007–10. Director: Octagen Corp., 1999–2008; Spirogen Ltd, 2003–10. Chm., E Berks Community Health NHS Trust, 1993–98. Gov., Univ. of W London (formerly Thames Valley Univ.), 2007–. FInstD 2009. *Publications:* Plasma Proteins, 1977; biochemical and scientific papers. *Recreations:* music, cricket, travel. *Address:* Solent NHS Trust, Adelaide Health Centre, William MacLeod Way, Southampton SO16 4XE. *Clubs:* Naval and Military, Royal Society of Medicine.

STOKES, Antony; *see* Stokes, N. A. D.

STOKES, Prof. Martin, DPhil; FBA 2012; King Edward Professor of Music, King's College London, since 2012. *Educ:* Univ. of Oxford (BA 1984; DPhil Social Anthropol. 1989). Lectr, Dept of Social Anthropol., QUB, 1989–97; Associate Prof. of Music, Univ. of Chicago, 1997–2007; Lectr in Ethnomusicol., then Prof. of Music, Univ. of Oxford, 2007–12; Fellow, St John's Coll., Oxford, 2007–12. Vis. Prof., Bogazici Univ., Istanbul; Hon. Prof., Univ. of Copenhagen; Vis. Bloch Prof., Univ. of Calif, Berkeley, 2013. Dent Medal, Royal Musical Assoc., 2010. *Publications:* The Arabesk Debate: music and musicians in modern Turkey, 1992, 2nd edn 2012; (ed) Ethnicity, Identity and Music: the musical construction of place, 1994, 2nd edn 1997; (ed jtly) Nationalism, Minorities and Diasporas: identities and rights in the Middle East, 1996; (ed jtly) Celtic Modern: music on the global fringe, 2004; The Republic of Love: cultural intimacy in Turkish popular music, 2010. *Address:* Music Department, King's College London, Strand Campus, WC2R 2LS.

STOKES, Michael George Thomas; QC 1994; **His Honour Judge Michael Stokes;** a Senior Circuit Judge, since 2006 (a Circuit Judge, since 2001); Resident Judge, Nottingham Crown Court, since 2006; Hon. Recorder of Nottingham, since 2007; a Deputy High Court Judge, since 2010; a Judge of the First-tier Tribunal (Health Education and Social Care Chamber), since 2013; *b* 30 May 1948; *e s* of late M. P. Stokes and E. Stokes, Leyland, Lancs; *m* 1994, Alison Hamilton Pollock; one *s* one *d*. *Educ:* Preston Catholic Coll.; Univ. of Leeds (LLB Hons 1970). Asst Lectr, Univ. of Nottingham, 1970–72; called to the Bar, Gray's Inn, 1971, Bencher, 2013; in practice on Midland and Oxford Circuit, 1973–2001; Asst Recorder, 1986–90, Recorder, 1990–2001; Res. Judge, Leicester Crown Ct, 2002–06. Pres., Mental Health Review Tribunals, 1999–2007. Circuit Rep., Remuneration and Terms of Work (formerly Fees & Legal Aid) Cttee, Bar Council, 1996–2000; Mem., Northants Criminal

Justice Strategy Cttee, 2000–01. Vis. Prof. of Law, Nottingham Trent Univ., 2013–. Governor: Haddon Park High Sch., Nottingham, 2007–09; Sycamore Primary Sch., Nottingham, 2010–13; Ratcliffe Coll., Leics, 2012–. *Recreations:* racing, France, gardening, writing. *Address:* c/o Nottingham Crown Court, 60 Canal Street, Nottingham NG1 7EL.

STOKES, Dr (Nigel) Antony (David), LVO 1996; HM Diplomatic Service; Ambassador to Socialist Republic of Vietnam, 2010–14; *b* 21 Jan. 1965. *Educ:* Queens' Coll., Cambridge (BA 1986); University Coll., London (PhD 1990). With Schlumberger Ltd, 1989–90; Mars GB, 1990–94; Centre for Exploitation of Sci. and Technol., 1994; entered FCO, 1994; Security Policy Dept, FCO, 1994–96; First Sec. (Pol), Bangkok, 1996–99; Pol Counsellor, Seoul, 2000–04; Hd, Tsunami Response Team, Bangkok, 2005; Hd, S Asia, FCO, 2005–08; Hd of Mission, Riga, 2009–10. *Address:* c/o Foreign and Commonwealth Office, King Charles Street, SW1A 2AH.

STOKES, Rear Adm. Richard; Assistant Chief of Naval Staff (Support), since 2015; *b* Cannock, Staffs, 9 May 1963; *s* of Maurice Richard Stokes and Denise Stokes; *m* 2011, Claire Hall; two *s*. *Educ:* Royal Naval Engrg Coll. (BScEng); Royal Mil. Coll. of Sci. (MDA). Tactical Weapons Engr Officer, HMS Resolution, 1987–89; Weapon Engr Officer, HMS Ocelot, 1989–90; Mgt Planner, Flag Officer Submarines, 1992–95; Weapon Engr Officer, HMS Torbay, 1995–97; Weapon Engrg Instructor, Submarine Sea Trng, 1998; Sqdn Weapon Engrg Officer, First Submarine Sqdn, 1999–2001; Logistics, Infrastructure and Engrg Support SO, Directorate of Naval Resources and Plans, MoD, 2001–03; Engr Officers Appointer, Directorate of Naval Officer Appts, 2003–05; Asst Dir, Capability Strategy, Directorate of Equipt Planning, MoD, 2005–08; Asst Dir, Career Mgt (Engrs), 2008–10; rcds 2011; Dir, RN Defence Reform Implementation Prog., 2011–12; Hd, Nuclear Capabilities, MoD, 2012–15. *Recreations:* ski-ing, sailing, mountain walking, music. *Address:* c/o Naval Secretary, Navy Command Headquarters, Leach Building, Whale Island, Portsmouth PO2 8BY.

STOKES, Simon George Garbutt; Artistic Director, Theatre Royal Plymouth, since 1998; *b* Llansantffraid, Wales, 22 Oct. 1950; *s* of Rev. George Smithson Garbutt Stokes and Betty Stokes; *m* (marr. diss.). *Educ:* Barnard Castle Sch., Co. Durham; Bristol Old Vic Th. Sch. Artistic Dir, Bush Th., London, 1976–87; Artistic Associate and Dir of Develt, Turnstyle Gp, 1988–95; freelance directing internationally, 1988–98. Director: Sputnik Th. Co., 2009–; Dance Consortium, 2011–. Gov., British American Drama Acad., 2000–. DArts Plymouth, 2014. *Recreation:* glass of wine with convivial company speaking wise words or chatting the breeze…. *Address:* Theatre Royal Plymouth, Royal Parade, Plymouth PL1 2TR. *T:* (01752) 230340. *E:* simon.stokes@theatreroyal.com.

STOKOE, Maj. Gen. John Douglas, CB 1999; CBE 1991 (MBE 1981); Chairman, Debut Services Ltd, since 2006; *b* 30 Dec. 1947; *s* of late Major John Alexander Gordon Stokoe and Elsie Mary Stokoe; *m* 1972, Jenny (*née* Beach); one *s* two *d*. *Educ:* Richmond Grammar Sch.; Army Apprentices Coll., Harrogate; RMA, Sandhurst. Commnd Royal Signals, 1968; served Far East, UK and BAOR; Comdr Communications, Germany, 1991–93; Higher Comd and Staff Course, 1992; DCS, Germany, 1993–94; rcds 1994; Dir, Army Staff Duties, 1994–97; DCS, HQ Land Comd, 1997–98; Dep. C-in-C, HQ Land Comd and Insp. Gen., TA, 1998–99. Defence Business Develt Dir, Amey Gp, 1999–2001; Man. Dir, Amey Defence, 2001–03; Director: Defence, Lend Lease, 2003–04; Corporate Affairs, Lend Lease Europe, 2004–06; Dir, Central Govt, Defence and Nat. Security (formerly Defence), 2006–09, Man. Dir, UK Nat. Govt Div., 2009–11, BT; Dir, Strategy, Dassault Systèmes UK, 2015–. Non-exec. Dir, Salisbury NHS Foundn Trust, 2008–12. Chairman: Regular Forces Employment Assoc., 2008–13; Defence Med. Welfare Service, 2013–. Col Comdt, RCS, 1998–2004; Hon. Col, 31 (City of London) Signal Regt (Vols), 2002–07; Hon. Col, FANY, 2006–08. *Recreations:* fell walking, sailing, water colour artist.

STOLLER, Dr Anthony David, CBE 2004; Chair: Joseph Rowntree Foundation, since 2011 (Deputy Chair, 2005–11); Joseph Rowntree Housing Trust, since 2011 (Deputy Chair, 2009–11); *b* 14 May 1947; *s* of Louis and Pearl Stoller; *m* 1969, Andrea Lewisohn; one *s* one *d*. *Educ:* Hendon County Grammar Sch.; Gonville and Caius Coll., Cambridge (MA, LLB); Bournemouth Univ. (PhD 2015). Head of Radio Programming, IBA, 1974–79; Dir, Assoc. of Ind. Radio Contractors, 1979–81; Man. Dir, Thames Valley Broadcasting, 1981–85; John Lewis Partnership, 1985–95: Man. Dir, Tyrrell and Green, 1987–95; Chief Exec., Radio Authy, 1995–2003; External Relations Dir, Ofcom, 2003–06. Member: Administrative Appeals Chamber, Upper Tribunal; Gen. Regulatory Chamber, First-tier Tribunal, 2010–11. Mem., Competition Commn, 2009–14. Chm., Winchester Action on Climate Change, 2014–. Ed., The Friends Quarterly, 2008–. *Publications:* Wrestling with The Angel, 2001; Sounds of Your Life: the history of independent radio in the UK, 2010. *Recreations:* cricket, sailing, music. *Address:* 16 Denham Close, Hyde, Winchester SO23 7BL.

STOLLIDAY, Deborah Mary; *see* Jenkins, D. M.

STOLTENBERG, Jens; Secretary General, NATO, since 2014; *b* Oslo, 16 March 1959; *m* Ingrid Schulerud; two *c*. *Educ:* Univ. of Oslo (postgrad. degree Econs 1987). Statistics Norway; State Sec., Min. of Envmt, 1990–91. MP Norway, 1991–2014; Minister of Industry and Energy, 1993–96, of Finance, 1996–97; Prime Minister of Norway, 2000–01 and 2005–13. Leader, Norwegian Labour Party, 2002–14. *Address:* NATO, Boulevard Leopold III, 1110 Brussels, Belgium.

STOMBERG, Dr Rolf Wilhelm Heinrich; non-executive Chairman, Management Consulting Group (formerly Proudfoot Consulting), 2000–08; *b* Emden, Germany, 10 April 1940; *s* of Friedrich Stomberg and Johanna (*née* Meiners). *Educ:* Univ. of Hamburg (Dipl. Kfm. 1966; Dr rer. pol. 1969). Apprenticeship in shipping; Asst Prof., Univ. of Hamburg, 1966–69; joined BP Group, 1970; Finance Dir and Mem., Bd of Mgt, Deutsche BP, 1981–83; Oilstream Dir, 1983–86; Dep. Chm., Deutsche BP, 1986–89; Chm., Europe-Continental Div., BP Oil Internat., 1988; Chm., Bd of Mgt, Deutsche BP, 1989–91; CEO, BP Oil Europe, 1990; Chm., BP Europe, 1994; Man. Dir, BP plc and CEO, BP Oil Internat., 1995–97. Non-executive Chairman: John Mowlem & Co. PLC, 1999–2001; Unipoly SA, Luxembourg, 1999–2002; non-executive Director: Smith & Nephew, 1998–2009; Cordiant Communications plc, 1998–2003; Scania AB, 1998–2004; Stinnes AG, 1998–2003; TPG Gp, 1998–2008; Reed Elsevier plc, 1999–2007. Mem. Adv. Bd, Dresdner Bank AG, 1991–2003; Chm., Supervisory Bd, Lanxess AG, 2005–. Vis. Prof., Imperial Coll., London, 1997–2004.

STONE, family name of **Baron Stone of Blackheath**.

STONE OF BLACKHEATH, Baron *cr* 1997 (Life Peer), of Blackheath in the London Borough of Greenwich; **Andrew Zelig Stone;** *b* 7 Sept. 1942; *s* of Sydney Stone and Louise Sophia Stone (*née* Gould); *m* 1973, Vivienne Wendy Lee; one *s* two *d*. *Educ:* Cardiff High School. Joined Marks & Spencer, 1966: Dir, 1990–99; Jt Man. Dir, 1994–99. Chairman, Falcon Power, 2012–14; Deputy Chairman: Deal Gp Media plc, 2005–08; Sindicatum Carbon Capital Hldgs Ltd, 2007–09; non-executive Director: Thorn plc, 1996–98; Design Ville Ltd, 2001–03; N. Brown Gp, 2002–14; Ted Baker plc, 2002–05; Moon Valley Enterprises, 2009–14; Mem., Adv. Bd, McDonald's Restaurants, 2005–07. Chm., Dipex, 2004–. Mem., Nat. Adv. Cttee on Culture and Creativity in Educn, 1998–2001. Non-executive Director: Science Media Centre, 2001–07; ODI, 2002–05. Governor: Weizmann Inst. of Sci., 1996–07 (Life Mem., 2009); Tel Aviv Univ., 2000–05; British Univ. of Egypt, 2006–; Mem., European Council, Ben Gurion Univ., 2002–08. Trustee, The Olive Tree Project, 2003–09; Dir, Sindicatum Climate Change Foundn, 2009–12. Hon. Vice Pres., Reform Synagogues of GB, 2000–. Patron, The Forgiveness Project, 2004–. Risk Comr, RCA, 2007–09. Hon. Dr Law Oxford Brookes, 1998; Hon. DDes Kingston, 1999. *Recreations:* reading, walking, thinking. *Address:* House of Lords, SW1A 0PW.

STONE, Maj.-Gen. Anthony Charles Peter, CB 1994; independent defence policy and security analyst, writer and commentator, since 2009; *b* 25 March 1939; *s* of late Major Charles C. Stone and Kathleen M. Stone (*née* Grogan); *m* 1967, (Elizabeth) Mary, *d* of Rev. Canon Gideon Davies; two *s*. *Educ:* St Joseph's Coll.; RMA, Sandhurst; Staff Coll., Camberley. Commnd RA, 1960; served in light, field, medium, heavy, locating and air defence artillery in BAOR, FE and ME and in various general and weapons staff appts in MoD; commanded 5th Regt, RA, 1980–83; founded Special OP Troop, 1982; Col, Defence Progs Staff, MoD, 1983–84; Mil. Dir of Studies, RMCS, 1985–86; Ministry of Defence: Dir of Operational Requirements (Land), 1986–89; Dir of Light Weapons Projects, 1989–90; Dir Gen. Policy and Special Projects (VMGO), 1990–92; Dir Gen. Land Fighting Systems, MoD (PE), 1992–95. Chm. and Man. Dir, The Nash Partnership Ltd, internat. defence advrs, 1996–2005; Defence Advr, Gracemoor Consultants (UK) Ltd, 1997–2006; Military Advr, PricewaterhouseCoopers, 2006–08; Military Advr to Bd, Simrad Optronics, Norway, 2007–10. Internat. Conference Chm., IQPC Defence, 2004–10. Hon. Col, 5th Regt, RA, 1990–2008; Col Comdt, 1993–2001, Rep. Col Comdt, 1998, Royal Regt of Artillery. Vis. Res. Fellow, Dept of Defence Studies, Univ. of York, 1996. Army Mem., Steering Cttee, UK Defence Forum, 1997–2007; Member: European-Atlantic Gp, 1999–2007; Military Commentators' Circle, 2013–. FRUSI 1997. *Publications:* papers on defence, security, policy and acquisition. *Recreations:* family, sudoku, writing, tennis. *Club:* Army and Navy.

STONE, Sir Christopher, Kt 2013; Chief Executive, Arthur Terry Learning Partnership, since 2012 (Executive Headteacher, 2008–12); *b* Liverpool, 7 April 1958; *m* 1981, Kathryn Turvey; two *s*. *Educ:* Caereinion High Sch.; St Katharine's Coll. (BEd 1980 (Hons 1981)); Univ. of Leicester (MA 1989). Teacher of Physical Educn, Hist. and Life Skills, John Hanson Sch., Andover, Hants, 1981–86; Hd of Performing and Creative Arts and Sixth Form, Ousedale Sch., Newport Pagnell, Bucks, 1986–92; Dep. Headteacher, Byng Kenrick Central Sch., Birmingham, 1992–95; Headteacher: Perry Beeches Sch., Birmingham, 1995–2000; Arthur Terry Sch., Birmingham, 2000–08. Nat. Leader in Educn, 2008–. Chm., Birmingham Sch. Improvement Gp, 2010–12. *Recreations:* all sport, walking, travelling, family. *Address:* Arthur Terry Learning Partnership, Kittoe Road, Four Oaks, Sutton Coldfield B74 4RZ. *T:* (0121) 323 2221, (direct) (0121) 323 1134, *Fax:* (0121) 308 8033. *E:* cstone@arthurterry.bham.sch.uk.

STONE, David Lewis, MD; FRCP; Consultant Cardiologist, 1988–2010, and Medical Director, 2002–09, Papworth Hospital; *b* 31 May 1948; *s* of Sidney David Stone and Dorothy Stone; *m* 1972, Helen Sharman; one *s* one *d*. *Educ:* Bancroft's Sch.; Charing Cross Hosp. Med. Sch., London (BSc 1968; BBS 1971; MD 1985); MA Cantab 2001; King's Coll. London (MA 2010). MRCP 1974, FRCP 1992. Associate Lectr, Faculty of Clinical Medicine, Univ. of Cambridge, 1997–2009. Consultant Cardiologist, W Suffolk Hosps, 1988–2007. *Publications:* (contrib.) The Future of the NHS, 2006; articles in field of cardiac imaging. *Recreations:* music, travel, literature. *Address:* 18 Bigwood Road, NW11 7BD. *T:* (020) 8728 0438. *E:* stonedavid1@mac.com.

STONE, David Radcliffe, CBE 2010 (OBE 1997); CEng, FIMMM; Chairman, Sheffield Teaching Hospitals NHS Foundation Trust (formerly Sheffield Teaching Hospitals NHS Trust), 2001–11; Interim Chairman, Mid Yorkshire NHS Trust, 2012; *b* 19 Sept. 1935; *s* of Arthur Thomas Stone and Esther Stone; *m* 1st, 1959, Janet Clarke (*d* 1996); two *d*; 2nd, 2010, Jean Amy Day (*née* Broddley). *Educ:* Barking Abbey Sch., Essex; Univ. of Manchester (BSc Hons 1957). CEng 1983; FIMMM (FIM 1994). Manager, United Steel Cos Ltd, 1957–68; Consultant, PA Mgt Consultants, 1968–73; Works Dir, Firth Brown Ltd, 1973–78; Managing Director: Doncaster Sheffield Ltd, 1978–85; Stocksbridge Engrg Steels Ltd, 1985–89; UES Steels 1989–94; United Engrg Steels Ltd, 1994–96. Pres., British Iron and Steel Producers Assoc., 1993–94. Chairman: Weston Park Hosp. NHS Trust, 1997–99; Central Sheffield Univ. Hosps NHS Trust, 1999–2001; S Yorks Forum, 1997–2001; Convenor, UK Univ. Hosps Chairs Gp, 2004–08; Interim Chm., Mid Staffs NHS Foundn Trust, 2009. Trustee: Weston Park Cancer Care Appeal, 1996–2010; Freshgate Foundn, 1996–; Sheffield Botanical Gardens, 1997–2011. Pres., Longshaw Sheepdog Trials Assoc., 2012–13. Guardian, Sheffield Assay Office, 1998–2010. Freeman, City of London, 1995; Liveryman, Co. of Blacksmiths, 1997–; Master Cutler, Co. of Cutlers in Hallamshire, 1995–96 (Freeman, 1979–). Hon. LittD Sheffield, 2010. Hon. Consul, Finland, 1996–2014. Knight (1st Class), Order of the Lion of Finland. *Recreations:* golf, gardening, fishing, music. *Address:* Broadlea, North Green, East Drayton, near Retford, Notts DN22 0LF. *T:* (01777) 248315. *E:* davidr.stone@btinternet.com. *Club:* Hallamshire and Lindrick Golf.

STONE, Prof. Diane Lesley, PhD; Professor of Politics and International Studies, University of Warwick, since 2007; Professor of Governance, Murdoch University, since 2013; *b* Collie, WA, 22 April 1964; *d* of Roy John and Pauline Hilda Stone; *m* 1990, Richard Higgott. *Educ:* Murdoch Univ. (BA Hons Asian Studies and Pol and Social Theory); Australian Nat. Univ. (MA; PhD Pol Sci. and Internat. Relns 1993). Tutor, Murdoch Univ., 1990; Fulbright Schol., Public Policy Prog., Georgetown Univ., 1991; Lectr, Manchester Metropolitan Univ., 1993–95; Lectr, then Reader, Univ. of Warwick, 1996–2006; Marie Curie Chair and Foundn Prof. of Public Policy, Central Eur. Univ., 2004–08; Winthrop Prof. in Politics and Internat. Relations, Univ. of Western Australia, 2010–13. Mem., Steering Cttee, 2004–, Chm., 2006–08, Researchers Alliance for Develt. Mem., Governing Body, Global Develt Network, 2001–04. Trustee and Mem. Council, ODI, 2000–08. *Publications:* Capturing the Political Imagination: think tanks and the policy process, 1996; (ed with S. Maxwell) Global Knowledge Networks and Development, 2005; (ed with C. Wright) The World Bank and Governance, 2006; contrib. articles to jls. *Recreations:* swimming, travel. *Address:* Politics and International Studies, University of Warwick, Coventry CV4 7AL. *T:* 07968 19177. *E:* diane.stone@warwick.ac.uk.

STONE, Emma Ace; *see* Gladstone, E. A.

STONE, Evan David Robert; QC 1979; a Recorder of the Crown Court, 1979–98; a Deputy High Court Judge, 1979–98; *b* 26 Aug. 1928; *s* of Laurence George and Lillian Stone; *m* 1959, Gisela Bridget Mann; one *s*. *Educ:* Berkhamsted; Worcester Coll., Oxford (MA). National Service (commnd, Army), 1947–49; served Middle East and UK. Called to Bar, Inner Temple, 1954, Bencher, 1985; sometime HM Deputy Coroner: Inner West London; West Middlesex; City of London. Mem. Senate of Inns of Court and the Bar, 1985–86. Formerly Associate Editor, Medico-Legal Journal. Councillor, later Alderman, London Borough of Islington, 1969–74 (Dep. Leader, later Leader of Opposition). Chm., City and Hackney HA, 1984–92. Mem., Criminal Injuries Compensation Bd, 1989–2002. Governor: Moorfields Eye Hosp., 1970–79; Highbury Grove Sch., 1971–86 (Chm. of Governors, 1978–83). Hon. Sec., 2008, Pres. elect, 2009, Pres., 2010, Vice-Pres., 2011–12, Harveian Soc. of London; Mem. Council, Osler Club of London, 2006–14. Liveryman, Barbers' Co., 1999. *Publications:* Forensic Medicine, 1987 (with Prof. H. Johnson); contrib. Social Welfare and the Citizen (paperback), 1957; contribs to Medico-Legal Jl and other professional jls. *Recreations:* reading, writing, sport, listening to music. *Address:* 60 Canonbury Park South, N1 2JG. *T:* (020) 7226 6820; The Mill House, Ridgewell, Halstead, Essex CO9 4SR. *T:* (01440) 785338. *Clubs:* Garrick, MCC.

STONE, Gerald Charles, PhD; FBA 1992; University Lecturer in non-Russian Slavonic Languages, Oxford University, and Fellow of Hertford College, Oxford, 1972–99; *b* 22 Aug. 1932; *s* of Albert Leslie Stone and Grace Madeline Stone (*née* Varndell); *m* 1st, 1953, Charlotte Johanna Steinbach (marr. diss. 1973); two *s* one *d*; 2nd, 1974, Vera Fedorovna Konnova; one *d*. *Educ:* Windsor Grammar Sch.; School of Slavonic Studies, London Univ. (BA 1964; PhD 1969). Nat. service, Army, Trieste, 1951–53. Metropolitan Police, 1953–64; Asst Master, Bexhill Grammar Sch., 1964–65; Asst Lectr, 1966–67, Lectr, 1967–71, Nottingham Univ.; Asst Dir of Res., Cambridge Univ., 1971–72. General Editor, Oxford Slavonic Papers, 1983–94. *Publications:* The Smallest Slavonic Nation: the Sorbs of Lusatia, 1972; (with B. Comrie) The Russian Language since the Revolution, 1978; An Introduction to Polish, 1980, 2nd edn 1992; (ed with D. Worth) The Formation of the Slavonic Literary Languages, 1985; (ed) Kěrluše, 1995; (with B. Comrie and M. Polinsky) The Russian Language in the Twentieth Century, 1996; (ed) Kjarliže, 1996; (ed) A Dictionarie of the Vulgar Russe Tongue Attributed to Mark Ridley, 1996; Upper Sorbian-English Dictionary, 2002; Der erste Beitrag zur sorbischen Sprachgeographie, 2003; The Göda Manuscript 1701, 2009; Slav Outposts in Central European History: the Wends, Sorbs and Kashubs, 2015. *Recreations:* gardening, walking, visiting pubs. *Address:* 6 Lathbury Road, Oxford OX2 7AU. *T:* (01865) 558227.

STONE, Ven. Godfrey Owen; Archdeacon of Stoke-upon-Trent, 2002–13; *b* 15 Dec. 1949; *s* of Guy and Shirley Stone; *m* 1977, Dot Caswell; one *s* one *d*. *Educ:* Exeter Coll., Oxford (BA Geog. 1971, Theol. 1978); W Midlands Coll. of Educn (PGCE 1972); Sheffield Univ. (Dip. Leadership, Renewal and Mission Studies, 1997). Ordained deacon, 1981, priest, 1982; Asst Curate, Rushden-with-Newton Bromswold, 1981–87; Dir, Pastoral Studies, Wycliffe Hall, Oxford, 1987–92; Team Rector, Bucknall Team Ministry, 1992–2002; RD, Stoke-upon-Trent, 1998–2002. Associate, Church Mission Soc., 2014–. FRGS 2009. *Recreations:* walking, gardening, travel, meteorology, music. *Address:* 12 William Lucy Way, Jericho, Oxford OX2 6EQ.

STONE, His Honour Gregory; QC 1994; a Circuit Judge, 2001–12; a Deputy High Court Judge, 2008–12; *b* 12 Dec. 1946; *s* of Frederick Albert Leslie Stone and Marion Gerda Stone (*née* Heller); *m* (separated); three *d*. *Educ:* Chislehurst and Sidcup Grammar Sch.; St Joseph's Coll., London; Université de Rennes; Queen's Coll., Oxford (MA); Univ. of Manchester (Dip. Econ. Develt (distinction) 1971; MA (Econ.) 1972). Sen. Economist, Morgan Grenfell, 1974–76; called to the Bar, Inner Temple, 1976, Bencher, 2008; Standing Counsel to DTI for Criminal Matters on South Eastern Circuit, 1989–90; a Recorder, 2000–01. *Publications:* The Law of Defective Premises, 1982; The Architect's Legal Handbook, 2nd edn 1978, to 8th edn 2009. *Recreations:* travel, walking, cinema, theatre, opera, architecture, landscape. *Club:* Athenæum.

STONE, James Hume Walter Miéville; Member (Lib Dem) Caithness, Sutherland and Easter Ross, Scottish Parliament, 1999–2011; *b* 16 June 1954; *s* of Edward Reginald Stone and Susannah Gladys Hume (*née* Waddell-Dudley); *m* 1981, Flora Kathleen Margaret Armstrong; one *s* two *d*. *Educ:* Tain Royal Acad.; Gordonstoun Sch.; St Andrews Univ. (MA 1977). Cleaner, Loch Kishorn, fish-gutter, Faroe Is, English teacher, Sicily, 1977–79; stores clerk, Wimpey Internat., 1979–81; Asst Site Administrator, then Site Administrator, subseq. Project Co-ordinator, Bechtel GB Ltd, 1981–84; Admin. Manager, Odfjell Drilling and Consulting Co. Ltd, 1984–86; Dir, Highland Fine Cheeses Ltd, 1986–94; Mem., Cromarty Firth Port Authy, 1998–2000; freelance newspaper columnist and broadcaster, 1990–. Chm., Tain Community Council, 1984; Member: (Ind, 1986–88, Lib Dem, 1988–96) Ross and Cromarty DC, 1986–96 (Vice Chm., Policy and Resources); (Lib Dem) Highland Council, 1995–99 (Vice-Chm., Finance); Scottish Constitutional Convention, 1988–96; Scottish Lib Dem agriculture spokesman, 1998–99; Scottish Parliament: Lib Dem spokesman on educn and children, 1999–2000, on Highlands and Fisheries, 2000–01, on equal opportunities, 2001–03, on finance, 2002–03, on enterprise, lifelong learning and tourism, 2003–07; on housing, 2008; dep. spokesman on health, 2008; Mem., Holyrood Progress Gp, 2000–04; Co-Convener: Cross Pty Gp on tackling debt, 2004; Cross Pty Gp on Scottish economy, 2005; Cross Pty Gp on oil and gas, 2007 (Vice-Convener, 2003–07); Convener: Subordinate Legislation Cttee, 2007; Cross Pty Gp on Russia, 2008; Dep. Convener, Communities Cttee, 2006–07; Chm., Scottish Parlt Business Exchange, 2004–06 (Dir, 2003). Mem., Exec. Cttee (Scotland), CPA, 2005. Chm., Dornoch Firth Fest., 1990–92; Director: Highland Fest., 1994–2000; Grey Coast Theatre, 2000–. Trustee: Tain Guildry Trust, 1987–; Tain Mus. Trust, 1992–; Highland Building Preservation Trust, 1995–2002. Gov., Eden Court Th., Inverness, 1995–99. FRSA. *Recreations:* shooting, reading, music, gardening, funghi, steam engines, the identification of butterflies. *Address:* Knockbreck, Tain IV19 1LZ. *T:* (01862) 894829. *Clubs:* New (Edinburgh); Armagh (N Ireland).

STONE, Prof. James McLellan, PhD; Professor, since 2003, and Director, Graduate Studies, Department of Astrophysical Sciences, Princeton University; *b* 29 Nov. 1962; *s* of William and Helen Stone; *m* 1984, Penelope Janet (*née* Rose); two *d*. *Educ:* Queen's Univ., Kingston, Ont. (BS Hons, MS); Univ. of Illinois, Champaign-Urbana (PhD 1990). Postdoctoral Fellow, Univ. of Illinois, 1990–92; Prof., Dept of Astronomy, Univ. of Maryland, College Park, 1992–2002; Prof. of Mathematical Physics, Cambridge Univ., 2002–03. *Publications:* contrib. numerous papers to refereed jls. *Recreations:* hiking, ski-ing. *Address:* Department of Astrophysical Sciences, Princeton University, Peyton Hall, Ivy Lane, Princeton, NJ 08544–1001, USA.

STONE, Joseph; QC 2013; *b* 28 Jan. 1964; *s* of Nicholas Stone and Lorraine Stone; *m* 2001, Keir Posner; one *d*. *Educ:* Brighton Coll.; Hammersmith and West London Coll.; Manchester Univ. (BA 1st Cl. Hons Pols and Phil. 1985). Called to the Bar, Inner Temple, 1989; in practice specialising in criminal defence, homicide. *Recreations:* swimming, sailing, windsurfing. *Address:* 53–54 Doughty Street, WC1N 2LS. *T:* (020) 7404 1313.

STONE, Lucy Madeline, (Mrs C. Coleman); QC 2001; *b* 16 Oct. 1959; *d* of late Alexander Stone and of Rene Stone; *m* 1994, Charles Coleman; one *s*. *Educ:* Newnham Coll., Cambridge (MA 1984); Inns of Court Sch. of Law. Called to the Bar, Middle Temple, 1983, Bencher, 2010; specialist in divorce law. *Recreations:* family, entertaining, reading. *Address:* Queen Elizabeth Building, Temple, EC4Y 9BS. *T:* (020) 7797 7837.

STONE, Prof. Norman; Professor of International Relations, Bilkent University, Ankara, since 1997 (on leave at Koç University, Istanbul, 2005–07); *b* 8 March 1941; *s* of late Norman Stone and Mary Stone (*née* Pettigrew); *m* 1st, 1966, Nicole Aubry (marr. diss. 1977); two *s*; 2nd, 1982, Christine Margaret Booker (*née* Verity); one *s*. *Educ:* Glasgow Acad.; Gonville and Caius Coll., Cambridge (MA). Research student in Austria and Hungary, 1962–65; University of Cambridge: Research Fellow, Gonville and Caius Coll., 1965–67; Univ. Lectr in Russian History, 1967–84; Fellow and Dir of Studies in History, Jesus Coll., 1971–79; Fellow of Trinity Coll., 1979–84; Prof. of Modern History, and Fellow, Worcester Coll., Univ. of Oxford, 1984–97. Vis. Lectr, Sydney Univ., 1978. Trustee, Margaret Thatcher Foundn, 1991–. Order of Merit (Polish Republic), 1993. *Publications:* The Eastern Front 1914–1917, 1975, 3rd edn 1978 (Wolfson History Prize, 1976); Hitler, 1980; Europe Transformed 1878–1919 (Fontana History of Europe), 1983; (ed jtly) Czechoslovakia, 1989; (jtly) The Other Russia, 1990; The Russian Chronicles, 1990; World War One: a short history, 2007; The Atlantic and its Enemies: a personal history of the Cold War, 2010; Turkey: a short history, 2011; WWII: a short history, 2013; thirteen translations. *Recreations:* bridge, music, languages, Turkey. *Address:* 22 St Margaret's Road, Oxford OX2 6RX. *T:* (Turkey) (312) 2901088. *E:* norman@bilkent.edu.tr.

STONE, Oliver William; actor, screenwriter and director; *b* NYC, 15 Sept. 1946; *s* of Louis Stone and Jacqueline Stone (*née* Goddet). *Educ:* Yale Univ.; NY Univ. (BFA). Film Sch. Teacher, Cholon, Vietnam, 1965–66; wiper, US Merchant Marine, 1966; served US Army, Vietnam, 1967–68 (Purple Heart with oak leaf cluster, Bronze Star); taxi driver, NYC, 1971. *Screenwriter:* Seizure, 1974; Midnight Express, 1978 (Acad. Award, Writers' Guild of Amer. Award); The Hand, 1981; (with J. Milius) Conan the Barbarian, 1982; Scarface, 1983; (with M. Cimino) Year of the Dragon, 1985; (with D. L. Henry) 8 Million Ways to Die, 1986; (with R. Boyle) Salvador, 1986; (also Dir) Platoon, 1986 (Acad. Award, Dirs Guild of Amer. Award, BAFTA Award); *co-writer:* Evita, 1996; *co-writer and director:* Wall Street, 1987; Talk Radio, 1988; The Doors, 1991; *screenwriter, producer and director:* Born on the Fourth of July, 1989 (Acad. Award, 1990); JFK, 1991; Heaven & Earth, 1993; Natural Born Killers, 1994; Nixon, 1995; Any Given Sunday, 1999; Commandante, 2003; Persona Non Grata, 2003, Looking for Fidel, 2004; Alexander, 2005; Wall Street: Money Never Sleeps, 2010; Savages, 2012; *co-writer, producer and director:* Oliver Stone's Untold History of the United States (TV series), 2013; *producer and director:* World Trade Center, 2006; *director:* U-Turn, 1997; W., 2008; South of the Border, 2010; *producer:* Reversal of Fortune, 1990; Blue Steel, 1990; South Central, 1992; Zebrahead, 1992; The Joy Luck Club, 1993; New Age, 1994; Wild Palms (TV mini-series), 1993; Freeway, 1996; The People vs Larry Flynt, 1996; Saviour, 1998; *executive producer:* Iron Maze, 1991; Killer: A Journal of Murder, 1996; (HBO) Indictment: The McMartin Preschool, 1995; The Last Day of Kennedy and King, 1998; The Corrupter, 1999; The Day Reagan Was Shot, 2001. Member: Writers' Guild of America; Directors' Guild of America; Acad. of Motion Picture Arts and Scis. *Publications:* A Child's Night Dream, 1997; The Untold History of the United States, 2013.

STONE, Maj.-Gen. Patrick Philip Dennant, CB 1992; CBE 1984 (OBE 1981 MBE 1975); Director General, Personal Services (Army), 1988–91; *b* 7 Feb. 1939; *s* of Philip Hartley Stone and Elsie Maude Stone (*née* Dennant); *m* 1967, Christine Iredale Trent; two *s* one *d*. *Educ:* Christ's Hospital; psc 1972. Nat. Service, 1959; commissioned East Anglian Regt, 1959; seconded 6 KAR, 1960–62 (Tanganyika); served British Guyana and Aden, 1962–65; ADC to Governor of W Australia, 1965–67; RAF Staff Coll., 1972; Comd 2nd Bn, Royal Anglian Regt, 1977–80 (UK and Berlin); Chief of Staff, 1st Armoured Div., 1981–84; Comdr, Berlin Inf. Bde, 1985–86; Dep. Mil. Sec. (B), 1987. Dep. Col, Royal Anglian Regt, 1986–91, Col, 1991–97; Col Comdt, Mil. Provost Staff Corps, 1988–92; Dep. Col Comdt, AGC, 1992–93. *Recreations:* country interests, travel, conservation, veteran and classic cars. *Address:* c/o Lloyds Bank, 90A Mill Road, Cambridge. *Club:* Army and Navy.

STONE, Prof. Richard Thomas Horner; Professor of Law, University of Lincoln, 2003–14, now Emeritus; *b* 7 March 1951; *s* of late Rev. Ross Stone and Bettine Stone (*née* Horner); *m* 1973, Margaret Peerman; one *s* three *d*. *Educ:* Reading Sch.; Southampton Univ. (LLB); Hull Univ. (LLM 1978). Called to the Bar, Gray's Inn, 1998. Leicester University: Lectr in Law, 1975–89; Sen. Lectr in Law, 1989–93; Dean, Faculty of Law, 1987–90; Resident Dir, Sunway Coll., Malaysia, 1989; Prof., 1993–97, Dean, 1996–97, Nottingham Law Sch., Nottingham Trent Univ.; Principal, Inns of Court Sch. of Law, 1997–2001. Vis. Lectr, Loughborough Univ., 1978–91; Visiting Professor: City Univ., 1997–2002; UC, Northampton, 2002–04. FRSA 1998. *Publications:* Entry, Search and Seizure, 1985, 5th edn 2013; Textbook on Civil Liberties, 1994, 10th edn 2014; Principles of Contract Law, 1994, 11th edn, as Modern Law of Contract (with James Devenney), 2015; Law of Agency, 1996; Offences Against the Person, 1999; (with Ralph Cunnington) Text, Cases and Materials on Contract Law, 2007, 3rd edn (with James Devenney), 2014; articles in legal jls. *Recreations:* books, music. *Address:* Lincoln Law School, University of Lincoln, Brayford Pool, Lincoln LN6 7TS. *E:* rstone@lincoln.ac.uk.

STONE, Rt Rev. Ronald Francis, AM 2008; Ministry Development Officer, 2004–08, Vicar General, 2008, and Archdeacon, since 2009, Diocese of Bendigo; Executive Assistant to Bishop of Bendigo, since 2007; *b* Armadale, Vic, 10 Sept. 1938; *s* of late Allan Francis Stone and Beatrice Rose Stone (*née* Hubber); *m* 1964, Lisbeth Joan Williams; two *s* one *d*. *Educ:* Caulfield South High Sch.; Caulfield Tech. Coll.; Taylors' Coll., Melbourne; St John's Coll., Morpeth, NSW (ThL 1963). Rector of Kerang, 1969–83; Canon, All Saints Cathedral, Bendigo, 1979–82; Archdeacon of Bendigo, 1983–92; VG, Diocese of Bendigo, 1983–92; Provincial Officer, Province of Victoria, 1988–92; Asst Bishop of Tasmania, 1992–96; Bishop of Rockhampton, 1996–2003. Convener, Gen. Synod Rural Ministry Task Gp, 1991–98; Member: Gen. Synod Ministry and Trng Commn, 1991–98; Episcopal Standards Commn, 2004–11. Chairman: Bd of Dirs, Anglican Superannuation Australia, 1999–2003; Nat. Home Mission Fund—Anglican Outback Fund, 2007–11. Editor, The Anglican Gazette, 1997–2003. *Publications:* A Kangaroo is Designed to Move Forward…But Which Direction for the Rural and Remote Area Church?, 1998 (Felix Arnott Meml Lect.); paper on rural ministry in Bush Telegraph. *Recreations:* gardening, philately, furniture restoration, golf, music, radio broadcasting. *Address:* 18 Hewitt Avenue, Bendigo, Vic 3550, Australia. *T:* (3) 54436099. *E:* stonebgo@bigpond.net.au. *Club:* Barham.

STONE, Dr Timothy John, CBE 2010; CEng, FICE; Expert of the Board, European Investment Bank, since 2003; *b* Rotherham, 11 May 1951; *s* of Jack and Kathleen Elsa Stone; *m* 1977, Joanne Mary Egan Lee; one *s* one *d*. *Educ:* Maltby Grammar Sch.; St Catherine's Coll., Oxford (MA; DPhil 1976). MBCS 1982; CEng 1985; FICE 2010. Sen. Manager, Arthur Andersen, 1976–83; Man. Dir, Chase Manhattan Bank, NY, 1983–89; Dir, S. G. Warburg & Co., 1989–95; Partner, and Chm., Global Infrastructure and Projects, KPMG, 1995–2011. Sen. Advr to Sec. of State for Energy and Climate Change, 2007–13; Expert Chair, Office for Nuclear Develt, DECC, 2008–13. Non-executive Director: Anglian Water Gp, 2011–; Horizon Nuclear Power, 2014–. Hon. FNucI 2012. *Recreations:* double bass playing (classical), classical music, computing. *Club:* Reform.

STONE, Prof. Trevor William, PhD, DSc; FBPhS; Professor of Pharmacology, University of Glasgow, since 1989; *b* 7 Oct. 1947; *s* of late Thomas William Stone and Alice Stone (*née* Reynolds); *m* 1st, 1971, Anne Corina (marr. diss. 2003); 2nd, 2005, Dr Lynda Gail Ramsey (*née* Darlington). *Educ:* Sch. of Pharmacy, London Univ. (BPharm 1969; DSc 1983); Aberdeen Univ. (PhD 1972). Lectr in Physiology, Univ. of Aberdeen, 1970–77; Sen. Lectr, 1977–83, Reader, 1983–86, Prof., 1986–88, in Neurosci., St George's Hosp. Sch. of Medicine, Univ. of London. Res. Fellow, Nat. Inst. of Mental Health, Washington, 1974, 1977; Vis. Prof. of Pharmacology, Univ. of Auckland, 1988. Man. Dir, Imagery, 1984–89; Dir of Res., Shinkanco, 2001–; Dir, PharmaLinks, 2002–10. Mem., Inst. of Neuroscis and Psychol., 2010–. FRSocMed; FBPhS (FBPharmacolS 2005). Hon. FRCP 2011. Hon. Mem., Portuguese Pharmacol Soc., 1989. *Publications:* Microiontophoresis and Pressure Ejection, 1985; Purines: basic and clinical aspects, 1989; Quinolinic Acid and Kynurenines, 1989; Adenosine in the Nervous System, 1991; CNS Transmitters and Neuromodulators, I 1994, II and III 1995, IV 1996; Neuropharmacology, 1995; Pills, Potions & Poisons, 2000; over 400 sci. papers. *Recreations:* piano, photography, snooker, music, work. *Address:* West Medical Building, University of Glasgow, Glasgow G12 8QQ. *T:* (0141) 330 4481.

STONE-FEWINGS, Nancy; *see* Carroll, N.

STONEHAM, family name of **Baron Stoneham of Droxford**.

STONEHAM OF DROXFORD, Baron *cr* 2011 (Life Peer), of the Meon Valley in the County of Hampshire; **Benjamin Russell Mackintosh Stoneham;** Chairman and Director, Housing and Care 21, since 2011; *b* Tunbridge Wells, 24 Aug. 1948; *m* 1975, Anne Kristine MacKintosh (MBE 2012); two *s* one *d*. *Educ:* Harrow Sch.; Christ's Coll., Cambridge (BA Econs 1970); Warwick Univ. (MA Industrial Relns 1971); London Business Sch.

(Advanced Sen. Mgt Prog. 1990). Res. Officer, Dept of Social and Admin. Studies, Univ. of Oxford, 1971–74; trainee, 1974–76, staff officer to Chm., 1976–78, Hd, Wages Planning Unit 1978–79, NCB; Nat. Officer, NUR, 1979–82; Portsmouth and Sunderland Newspapers plc, 1982–99; Man. Dir, Portsmouth Publishing and Printing Ltd, 1989–99; Gp Prodn Dir and Personnel Dir, News Internat., 2000–03; Ops Dir, Liberal Democrat HQ, 2003–10. Mem. (SDP) Herts CC, 1985–89. Contested: (Lab) Saffron Walden, 1977, 1979; (SDP/Alliance) Stevenage, 1983, 1987. Founder Member: SDP, 1981 (Mem., Federal Exec., 1986–88); Lib Dem, 1988. Chairman and Director: Portsmouth Harbour Renaissance Ltd, 1996–2005; First Wessex Housing Gp, 2007–12; Dir, Thames Gateway-Thurrock Urban Develt Corp., 2004–11. *Address:* House of Lords, SW1A 0PW.

STONER, Christopher Paul; QC 2010; *b* Shoreham by Sea, W Sussex, 29 April 1967; *s* of Gordon and Marie Stoner; *m* 2005, Lydia Simpson. *Educ:* Shoreham Coll.; Univ. of East Anglia (LLB 1st Cl.). Called to the Bar, Lincoln's Inn, 1991; in practice as barrister, specialising in property litigation, sports, regulatory and disciplinary law. *Recreations:* Bath Rugby, motor racing. *Address:* Serle Court, 6 New Square, Lincoln's Inn, WC2A 3QS. *T:* (020) 7242 6105. *E:* cstoner@serlecourt.co.uk.

STONES, (Elsie) Margaret, AM 1988; MBE 1977; botanical artist; *b* 28 Aug. 1920; *d* of Frederick Stones and Agnes Kirkwood (*née* Fleming). *Educ:* Swinburne Technical Coll., Melbourne; Melbourne National Gall. Art Sch. Came to England, 1951; working independently as botanical artist, 1951–: at Royal Botanic Gardens, Kew; Nat. Hist. Museum; Royal Horticultural Soc., and at other botanical instns; Contrib. Artist to Curtis's Botanical Magazine, 1957–82. Drawings (water-colour): 20, Aust. plants, National Library, Canberra, 1962–63; 250, Tasmanian endemic plants, 1962–77; Basalt Plains flora, Melbourne Univ., 1975–76; Vis. Botanical Artist, Louisiana State Univ., 1977–86 (200 drawings of Louisiana flora, exhibited: Fitzwilliam, Cambridge, Royal Botanic Garden, Edinburgh, Ashmolean Mus., Oxford, 1991). Tapestries commissioned for Govt House, Victoria (Victorian Tapestry Workshop), 2004. Exhibitions: Colnaghi's, London, 1967–; retrospective, Melbourne Univ., 1976; Louisiana Drawings, Smithsonian, USA, 1980, Louisiana State Mus., 1985, Univ. of Virginia, 1993; Baskett & Day, 1984, 1989; Boston Athenæum, 1993; 50 year retrospective, Nat. Gall. of Victoria, Melbourne, 1996; group exhibn, Arte Botanica, Botanical Art into the Third Millennium, Museo Della Grafica, Pisa, 2013. Workshop, Cornell Univ., USA, 1990. Hon. DSc: Louisiana State Univ. Baton Rouge, 1986; Melbourne Univ., 1989; DUniv Swinburne, 2003; Hon. DLitt Tasmania, 2008. Eloise Payne Luquer Medal, Garden Club of Amer., 1987; Gold Veitch Meml Medal, RHS, 1989. *Publications:* The Endemic Flora of Tasmania (text by W. M. Curtis), 6 Parts, 1967–78; Flora of Louisiana: water-colour drawings, 1991; Beauty in Truth: the botanical art of Margaret Stones (text by Irena Zdanowicz), 1996; illus. various books. *Recreations:* gardening, reading. *Address:* 26 Hunter Street, Hawthorn, Vic 3122, Australia. *T:* (3) 98183320.

STONHAM, Rt Rev. Dom Paul, OSB; Abbot of Belmont, since 2000; *b* 22 Feb. 1947; *s* of Robert Stonham and Anna Maria (*née* Frezzini). *Educ:* Univ. of Birmingham (BA (Hons) Mod. Langs 1969); Coll. Sant'Anselmo, Rome (STB 1975). Housemaster, Belmont Abbey Sch., 1975–81; Parish Priest, Tambogrande, Peru, 1981–86; Superior, Monasterio de la Encarnación, Peru, 1986–2000; Prof., Seminario Arquidiocesano, Piura, Peru, 1988–2000; Parish Priest, San Lorenzo, Peru, 1994–98. Dean, Herefordshire, 2001–11. Mem., Equipe Internat. Alliance Inter Monastères, 2001–. *Recreations:* reading, walking, music, travel, animal life. *Address:* Belmont Abbey, Hereford HR2 9RZ. *T:* (01432) 374718. *E:* abbot@belmontabbey.org.uk.

STONHOUSE, Rev. Canon Sir Michael Philip, 19th Bt *cr* 1628 and 15th Bt *cr* 1670, of Radley, Berkshire; Rector and Incumbent, St John's Minster and Associated Churches, Lloydminster, Saskatchewan, since 2007; *b* 4 Sept. 1948; *er s* of Sir Philip Allan Stonhouse, 18th Bt and 14th Bt, and Winnifred Emily (*d* 1989), *e d* of J. M. Shield; *S* father, 1993; *m* 1977, Colleen Coucill; three *s*. *Educ:* Medicine Hat Coll., Univ. of Alberta (BA); Wycliffe Coll. (MDiv). Ordained deacon, 1977, priest, 1978, dio. Calgary, Canada. Asst Curate, St Peter's, Calgary, 1977–80; Rector and Incumbent: Parkland Parish, Alberta, 1980–87; St Mark's Innisfail and St Matthew's Bowden, Alberta, 1987–92; St James, Saskatoon, Saskatchewan, 1992–2007; Canon, Dio. of Saskatoon, 2006. Prolocutor, Provincial Synod of Rupert's Land, 2009–. *Heir: s* Allan James Stonhouse, *b* 20 March 1981. *Address:* 202–4827–46 Street, Lloydminster, Saskatchewan, SK S9V 0J6, Canada.

STONIER, Prof. Peter David, PhD; consultant in pharmaceutical medicine, since 2000; Director of Education and Training, Faculty of Pharmaceutical Medicine, Royal Colleges of Physicians of the UK, since 2003; *b* 29 April 1945; *s* of Frederick Stonier and Phyllis Maud Stonier; *m* 1989, Elizabeth Margaret Thomas; one *s* one *d*. *Educ:* Cheadle Hulme Sch.; Univ. of Birmingham (BSc 1st cl. Hons 1966); Univ. of Sheffield (PhD 1969); Univ. of Manchester (MB ChB Hons 1974); Open Univ. (BA 1990). FFPM 1989; FRCPE 1993; MRCPsych 1994; FRCP 1998. House Officer, Manchester Royal Infirmary, 1974–75; Senior House Officer: Univ. Hosp. S Manchester, 1975–76; Leicester Royal Infirmary, 1976–77; Med. Advr, 1977–80, Head of Med. Services, 1980–81, Med. Dir, 1982–2000, and Bd Mem., 1994–2000, Hoechst UK Ltd, later Hoechst Roussel Ltd, then Hoechst Marion Roussel Ltd. Gp Med. Dir, Amdipharm plc, 2004–13; Med. Dir, Axess Ltd, 2005–. Visiting Professor: Univ. of Surrey, 1992–2010 (Course Dir, MSc in Pharmaceutical Medicine, 1993–2001); KCL, 1998–. Member: Pharm. Industry Trng Council, 1998–2002; Appeal Panel, NICE, 2000–; Bd, PharmaTrain, 2009–14; Bd, PharmaTrain Fedn, 2014–. Chm., British Assoc. of Pharmaceut. Physicians, 1988–90; Mem. Council, British Assoc. of Psychopharmacology, 1993–97; Council, RCP, 1997–2001; Faculty of Pharmaceutical Medicine, Royal Colleges of Physicians of UK: Vice Pres., 1992–96, Pres., 1997–2001; Mem., Bd of Examrs, 1994–97; Chm., Fellowship Cttee, 1997–2001; Convenor and Chair, Task Force for Specialist Trng in Pharmaceut. Medicine, 1995–99. Pres., Internat. Fedn of Assocs of Pharmaceut. Physicians, 1996–98. FRSocMed 1982 (Pres., Sect. of Pharmaceut. Medicine and Res., 1994–96); FMS 1999; FRSA 2000. Founder Ed., Pharmaceutical Physician, 1989–98; Associate Editor, Human Psychopharmacology, 1990–2007; Internat. Jl of Pharmaceut. Medicine, 1997–. Lifetime Achievement Award, Acad. of Pharmaceutical Physicians & Investigators, 2006. *Publications:* (ed jtly) Perspectives in Psychiatry, 1988; (ed with I. Hindmarch) Human Psychopharmacology: methods and measures, vol. 1 1988, vol. 2 1989, vol. 3 1991, vol. 4 1993, vol. 5 1996, vol. 6 1997; (ed) Discovering New Medicines: careers in pharmaceutical research and development, 1994, 2nd edn as Careers with the Pharmaceutical Industry, 2003; (ed jtly) Clinical Research Manual, 1994–; (ed jtly) Medical Marketing Manual, 2001; (ed jtly) Principles and Practice of Pharmaceutical Medicine, 2002, 3rd edn 2010; (ed jtly) Paediatric Clinical Research Manual, 2005; articles on psychopharmacology and pharmaceut. medicine. *Recreations:* opera, gardening, travel. *Address:* 5 Branstone Road, Kew, Richmond-on-Thames, Surrey TW9 3LB. *T:* (020) 8948 5069.

STONOR, family name of **Baron Camoys**.

STONOR, Sara Jane; Vice Lord-Lieutenant of East Sussex, since 2008; professional embroiderer and cushion maker; *b* Portsmouth, 22 June 1948; *d* of Rt Rev. Gerald Alexander Ellison, KCVO and of Jane Elizabeth Ellison; *m* 1969, Desmond Michael Stonor; one *s* one *d*. *Educ:* Moreton Hall; Château Brilliantmont, Lausanne. Chm., Chichester Cathedral Restoration Trust, 2003–08; Member: Chichester Cathedral Council, 2001–; Chichester Cathedral Chapter, 2002–; Provincial Panel, Clergy Discipline Measure, 2003–; Exec., Assoc. of English Cathedrals, 2010–15; Council, St John, Sussex, 2011–12; Centenary Appeals Cttee, Charleston Manor Farmhouse, 2014–. Trustee, Sussex Historic Churches Trust, 2011–. Vice-Chm., Trustees, De La Warr Pavilion, Bexhill-on-Sea, 2008–14. Patron, Friends of Crowborough Meml Hosp., 2013–. Vice Pres., E Sussex Magistrates Assoc., 2014–. DL E Sussex, 2001–08. Churchwarden, St Bartholomew's, Burwash, 1996–2003. *Recreations:* walking, needlework, art, music, theatre, cooking. *Address:* Pound Platt, Northbridge Street, Robertsbridge, E Sussex TN32 5NY. *T:* (01580) 880569. *E:* sara@stonor.org.uk.

STONOR, Air Marshal Sir Thomas (Henry), KCB 1989; Group Director and Controller, National Air Traffic Services, 1988–91; *b* 5 March 1936; *s* of Alphonsus and Ann Stonor; *m* 1964, Robin Antoinette, *er d* of Wilfrid and Rita Budd; two *s* one *d*. *Educ:* St Cuthbert's High Sch., Newcastle upon Tyne; King's Coll., Univ. of Durham (BSc (Mech Eng) 1957). Commissioned, RAF, 1959; served No 3 Sqn, 2ATAF, 1961–64; CFS, 6 FTS and RAF Coll., Cranwell, 1964–67; No 231 Operational Conversion Unit, 1967–69; RAF Staff Coll., Bracknell, 1970; HQ, RAF Germany, 1971–73; OC 31 Sqn, 1974–76; Mil. Asst to VCDS, MoD, 1976–78; OC RAF Coltishall, 1978–80; RCDS, 1981; Inspector of Flight Safety, RAF, 1982–84; Dir of Control (Airspace Policy), NATS, 1985–86; Dep. Controller, NATS, 1986–88. Sen. Consultant, Siemens Plessey Systems, 1991–98; Defence Advr, BT Defence Sales Sector, 1991–2003; non-exec. Dir, Parity PLC (formerly COMAC Gp), 1994–2001. *Recreations:* gardening, music. *Address:* 213 Woodstock Road, Oxford OX2 7AD. *Club:* Royal Air Force.

STOPFORD, family name of **Earl of Courtown**.

STOPFORD, Viscount; James Richard Ian Montagu Stopford; *b* 30 March 1988; *s* and *heir* of Earl of Courtown, *qv*. *Educ:* Eton; Univ. of Durham; BPP Law Sch. (Grad. Dip. Law; Legal Practice Course). *Recreations:* ski-ing, Rugby.

STOPFORD, Maj.-Gen. Stephen Robert Anthony, CB 1988; MBE 1971; Director General Fighting Vehicles and Engineer Equipment, Ministry of Defence (Procurement Executive), 1985–89; *b* 1 April 1934; *s* of Comdr Robert Stopford, RN, and Elsie Stopford; *m* 1963, Vanessa (*née* Baron). *Educ:* Downside; Millfield. MIET. Commissioned Royal Scots Greys, 1954; regimental service and various staff appts until 1977; Project Manager, MBT80, 1977–80; Military Attaché, Washington, 1983–85. Dir, David Brown Vehicle Transmissions Ltd, 1990–99. *Recreations:* sailing, scuba diving, shooting. *Address:* 18 Thornton Avenue, SW2 4HG. *T:* (020) 8674 1416.

STOPPARD, Miriam, (Lady Hogg), OBE 2010; MD; FRCP; writer and broadcaster; Founder and Executive Chairman, Miriam Stoppard Lifetime Ltd, since 2001; *b* 12 May 1937; *d* of Sydney and Jenny Stern; *m* 1st, 1972, Sir Tom Stoppard, *qv* (marr. diss. 1992); two *s* and two step *s*; 2nd, 1997, Sir Christopher Hogg, *qv*. *Educ:* Newcastle upon Tyne Central High Sch. (State Scholar, 1955); Royal Free Hosp. Sch. of Medicine, Univ. of London (Prize for Experimental Physiol., 1958); King's Coll. Med. Sch. (Univ. of Durham), Newcastle upon Tyne (MB, BS Durham, 1961; MD Newcastle, 1966). FRCP 1998 (MRCP 1964). Royal Victoria Infirmary, King's Coll. Hosp., Newcastle upon Tyne: House Surg., 1961; House Phys., 1962; Sen. House Officer in Medicine, 1962–63; Univ. of Bristol: Res. Fellow, Dept of Chem. Pathol., 1963–65 (MRC Scholar in Chem. Pathol.); Registrar in Dermatol., 1965–66 (MRC Scholar in Dermatol.); Sen. Registrar in Dermatol., 1966–68; Syntex Pharmaceuticals Ltd: Associate Med. Dir, 1968; Dep. Med. Dir, 1971; Med. Dir, 1974; Dep. Man. Dir, 1976; Man. Dir, 1977–81. TV series: Where There's Life (5 series), 1981; Baby & Co. (2 series), 1984; Woman to Woman, 1985; Miriam Stoppard's Health and Beauty Show, 1988; Dear Miriam, 1989. MRSocMed (Mem. Dermatol. Sect., Endocrinol. Sect.); Member: Heberden Soc.; Brit. Assoc. of Rheumatology and Rehabilitation. Hon. DSc Durham, 2000; Hon. DCL Newcastle, 2004. *Publications:* Miriam Stoppard's Book of Baby Care, 1977; (contrib.) My Medical School, 1978; Miriam Stoppard's Book of Health Care, 1979; The Face and Body Book, 1980; Everywoman's Lifeguide, 1982; Your Baby, 1982; Fifty Plus Lifeguide, 1982; Your Growing Child, 1983; Baby Care Book, 1983; Pregnancy and Birth Book, 1984; Baby and Child Medical Handbook, 1986; Everygirl's Lifeguide, 1987; Feeding Your Family, 1987; Miriam Stoppard's Health and Beauty Book, 1988; Every Woman's Medical Handbook, 1988; Lose 7 lb in 7 Days, 1990; Test Your Child, 1991; The Magic of Sex, 1991; Conception, Pregnancy and Birth, 1993; The Menopause, 1994; Questions Children Ask and How to Answer Them, 1997; Sex Ed—Growing up, Relationships and Sex, 1997; The New Parent, 1998; Healthcare series (15 titles), 1998–2002; Drugs Info File, 1999; Baby's Play and Learn Pack, 2000; Women's Health Handbook, 2001; Teach Your Child, 2001; Family Health Guide, 2002; Baby First Aid, 2003; Defying Age, 2003; The Grandparent's Book: making the most of a very special relationship, 2006; My Pregnancy Planner, 2007; Bonding with Your Bump, 2008; Grandparents: enjoying and caring for your grandchild, 2011; Trusted Advice series (6 titles), 2011–12; over 40 pubns in med. jls. *Recreations:* my family, gardening. *Address:* Miriam Stoppard Lifetime Ltd, 131–151 Great Titchfield Street, W1W 5BB.

STOPPARD, Sir Tom, OM 2000; Kt 1997; CBE 1978; FRSL; playwright and novelist; *b* 3 July 1937; *yr s* of late Eugene Straussler and of Mrs Martha Stoppard; *m* 1st, 1965, Jose (marr. diss. 1972), *yr d* of John and Alice Ingle; two *s*; 2nd, 1972, Dr Miriam Moore-Robinson (*see* Miriam Stoppard) (marr. diss. 1992); two *s*; 3rd, 2014, Sabrina Guinness. *Educ:* abroad; Dolphin Sch., Notts; Pocklington, Yorks. Journalist: Western Daily Press, Bristol, 1954–58; Bristol Evening World, 1958–60; freelance, 1960–63. *Plays:* Enter a Free Man, London, 1968 (TV play, A Walk on the Water, 1963); Rosencrantz and Guildenstern are Dead, Nat. Theatre, 1967, subseq. NY, etc (Tony Award, NY, 1968; NY Drama Critics Circle Award, 1968); The Real Inspector Hound, London, 1968; After Magritte, Ambiance Theatre, 1970; Dogg's Our Pet, Ambiance Theatre, 1972; Jumpers, National Theatre, 1972 (Evening Standard Award); Travesties, Aldwych, 1974 (Evening Standard Award; Tony Award, NY, 1976); Dirty Linen, Newfoundland, Ambiance Theatre, 1976; Every Good Boy Deserves Favour (music-theatre), 1977; Night and Day, Phoenix, 1978 (Evening Standard Award); Dogg's Hamlet and Cahoot's Macbeth, Collegiate, 1979; Undiscovered Country (adaptation), NT, 1979; On the Razzle, NT, 1981; The Real Thing, Strand, 1982 (Standard Award), subseq. NY (Tony Award, 1984); Rough Crossing (adaptation), NT, 1984; Dalliance (adaptation), NT, 1986; Hapgood, Aldwych, 1988; Arcadia, NT, 1993 (Evening Standard Award; Olivier Award); Indian Ink, Aldwych, 1995; The Seagull (trans.), Old Vic, 1997; The Invention of Love, NT, 1997 (Evening Standard Award); The Coast of Utopia (trilogy), NT, 2002, NY (Tony Award), 2007; Henry IV (adaptation), Donmar Warehouse, 2004; Heroes (trans.), Wyndham's, 2005; Rock 'n' Roll, Royal Court, transf. Duke of York's (Best Play, London Evening Standard Theatre Awards, and Critics' Circle Theatre Awards), 2006; Ivanov (adaptation), Wyndham's, 2008; The Cherry Orchard (adaptation), Harvey Th., NY, 2009; The Hard Problem, NT, 2015; *radio:* The Dissolution of Dominic Boot, 1964; M is for Moon Among Other Things, 1964; If You're Glad I'll Be Frank, 1965; Albert's Bridge, 1967 (Prix Italia); Where Are They Now?, 1970; Artist Descending a Staircase, 1972; The Dog it was That Died, 1982 (Giles Cooper Award; televised 1988); In the Native State, 1991; Dark Side, 2013; *television:* A Separate Peace, 1966; Teeth, 1967; Another Moon Called Earth, 1967; Neutral Ground, 1968; (with Clive Exton) Boundaries, 1975; (adapted) Three Men in a Boat, 1976; Professional Foul, 1977; Squaring the Circle, 1984; (adapted) Parade's End, 2012; *screenplays:* (with T. Wiseman) The Romantic Englishwoman, 1975; Despair, 1978; The Human Factor, 1979; (with Terry Gilliam and Charles McKeown) Brazil, 1985; Empire of the Sun, 1987; Rosencrantz and Guildenstern are Dead, 1990 (also dir); The Russian House, 1991; Billy Bathgate, 1991; (with Marc Norman) Shakespeare in Love (Oscar Award for Best Screenplay), 1999; Enigma, 2001; Anna Karenina, 2012. Mem. Bd, RNT, 1982–2003. Pres., London Library, 2004–. Hon. degrees: Bristol, 1976; Brunel, 1979; Leeds, 1980; Sussex, 1980; London, 1982; Kenyon Coll., 1984; York, 1984. John Whiting Award, Arts Council, 1967;

Evening Standard Award for Most Promising Playwright, 1968; Shakespeare Prize, 1979; Praemium Imperiale, Japan Art Soc., 2009; (jtly) PEN Pinter Prize, 2013. *Publications:* (short stories) Introduction 2, 1964; (novel) Lord Malquist and Mr Moon, 1965; *plays:* Rosencrantz and Guildenstern are Dead, 1967; The Real Inspector Hound, 1968; Albert's Bridge, 1968; Enter a Free Man, 1968; After Magritte, 1971; Jumpers, 1972; Artists Descending a Staircase, and, Where Are They Now?, 1973; Travesties, 1975; Dirty Linen, and New-Found-Land, 1976; Every Good Boy Deserves Favour, 1978; Professional Foul, 1978; Night and Day, 1978; Undiscovered Country, 1980; Dogg's Hamlet, Cahoot's Macbeth, 1980; On the Razzle, 1982; The Real Thing, 1983; The Dog it was that Died, 1983; Squaring the Circle, 1984; Four plays for radio, 1984; Rough Crossing, 1985; Dalliance and Undiscovered Country, 1986; (trans.) Largo Desolato, by Vaclav Havel, 1987; Hapgood, 1988; In the Native State, 1991; Arcadia, 1993; The Television Plays 1965–1984, 1993; The Invention of Love, 1997; The Coast of Utopia, 2002; Henry IV, 2004; Heroes, 2005; Rock 'n' Roll, 2006. *Address:* c/o United Agents, 12–26 Lexington Street, W1F 0LE.

STOPPS, Ian Robert, CBE 2003; FRAeS; Chairman and Founder, McLean Partnership, since 2007; Chairman, McLean Advisory, since 2007; Chairman, Raytheon UK, since 2012; *b* 7 Oct. 1946; *s* of late Rowland Arthur Stopps and Megan Maynard Stopps; *m* 1969, Alexandra Margaret Gebbie; two *d. Educ:* Loughborough Univ. of Technol. (BSc 1st cl. Hons (Mech. Engrg) 1969). MIMechE 1969; MASME 1970; FRAeS 2005. Various posts with GE Co. (USA), 1971–87; General Manager: Dynamic Products, BF Goodrich, 1987–90; GE-Aerospace-Europe, 1990–93; Pres., European Region, Martin Marietta, London, 1993–95; merged with Lockheed, 1995 to form Lockheed Martin; Pres., Western Europe Region, Lockheed Martin Corp., 1995–99. Chief Exec., Lockheed Martin UK Ltd, 1999–2009; Chm., Arundel Aerospace and Defence Systems Ltd, 2010–12; Chm., 2003–05, Mem. Adv. Bd, 2005–, British American Business Inc. (BABi). Chm. Adv. Bd, Sch. of Business and Econs, Loughborough Univ., 2011–; Mem. Adv. Bd, Centre for Blast Injury Studies, Imperial Coll. London, 2011–; Member Council: SBAC, 1996–2009; RUSI, 2002–04; UK Council for Electronic Business, 2006–09; Mem. of Ct, Cranfield Univ., 2002–09. Hon. DTech Loughborough, 2014. *Publications:* contribs to ASME, IMechE and RUSI jls. *Recreations:* county and national squash and lawn tennis, Real tennis, golf, travel. *Clubs:* Foxhills; Queen's.

STOPS, Timothy William Ashcroft J.; *see* Jackson-Stops.

STORER, David George; Under Secretary, Department of Social Security (formerly of Health and Social Security), 1984–89; *b* 27 June 1929; *s* of Herbert Edwards Storer; *m* 1960, Jean Mary Isobel Jenkin; one *s* two *d. Educ:* Monmouth School; St John's Coll., Cambridge (MA). Assistant Principal, Min. of Labour, 1952; Principal, 1957; Cabinet Office, 1963–66; Asst Secretary, Dept of Employment, 1966–73; Director, Training Opportunities Scheme, 1973–77; Dir of Corporate Services, MSC, 1977–84. *Recreations:* reading history, still walking. *Address:* 5a Carlton Road, Redhill, Surrey RH1 2BY.

STORER, James Donald, CEng, MRAeS; author and museum consultant; Keeper, Department of Science, Technology and Working Life, Royal Museum of Scotland, Edinburgh, 1985–88; *b* 11 Jan. 1928; *s* of James Arthur Storer and Elizabeth May Gartshore (*née* Pirie); *m* 1955, Shirley Anne (*née* Kent); one *s* one *d. Educ:* Hemsworth Grammar Sch., Yorks; Imperial Coll., London (BSc Hons, ACGI). MRAeS (AFRAeS 1958). Design Office, Vickers Armstrongs (Aircraft) Ltd, and British Aircraft Corporation, Weybridge, 1948–66; Dept of Technology, Royal Scottish Museum, 1966–85. Hon. Sec., British Aviation Preservation Council, 1990–95 (Vice-Pres., 1996); Chm., Friends of Ironbridge Gorge Museum, 1994–98. *Publications:* Steel and Engineering, 1959; Behind the Scenes in an Aircraft Factory, 1965; It's Made Like This: Cars, 1967; The World We Are Making: Aviation, 1968; A Simple History of the Steam Engine, 1969; How to Run An Airport, 1971; How We Find Out About Flight, 1973; Flying Feats, 1977; Book of the Air, 1979; Great Inventions, 1980; (jtly) Encyclopedia of Transport, 1983; (jtly) East Fortune: Museum of Flight and history of the airfield, 1983; The Silver Burdett Encyclopedia of Transport: Air, 1984; Ship Models in the Royal Scottish Museum, 1986; The Conservation of Industrial Collections, 1989; (jtly) Fly Past, Fly Present, 1995; (contrib.) Biographical Dictionary of the History of Technology, 1996; (jtly) Industry and Transport in Scottish Museums, 1997; Liverpool on Wheels, 1998. *Recreations:* aircraft preservation, industrial archaeology, gardening. *Address:* 41 Campion Way, Sheringham, Norfolk NR26 8UN. *T:* (01263) 825086.

STORER, Robert Andrew; Consultant: Harbottle & Lewis LLP, since 2007; Film Finances Ltd, since 2007; *b* Burton-on-Trent, 29 April 1947; *s* of Horace and Nancy Storer; *m* 1982, Linda Pritchard; one *s* two *d. Educ:* Buxton Coll., Derbys; London Sch. of Econs and Pol Sci. (LLB 1968). Admitted as solicitor, 1971; joined Harbottle & Lewis, 1969; Partner, 1975–2007; Hd, Film and TV Dept, 1980–2007; Sen. Partner, 2000–09. Mem., BAFTA, 1998–. *Recreations:* golf, tennis, watching Fulham FC and Middlesex Cricket, film, theatre, bridge. *Address:* 35 Gerard Road, Barnes, SW13 9QH. *T:* (020) 8748 1898. *E:* robert.storer@harbottle.com. *Club:* Roehampton (Dir).

STORER, Prof. Roy; Professor of Prosthodontics, 1968–92 and Dean of Dentistry, 1977–92 (Clinical Sub-Dean, 1970–77), The Dental School, University of Newcastle upon Tyne, Professor Emeritus, since 1992; *b* 21 Feb. 1928; *s* of late Harry and Jessie Storer; *m* 1953, Kathleen Mary Frances Pitman; one *s* two *d. Educ:* Wallasey Grammar Sch.; Univ. of Liverpool. LDS (Liverpool) 1950; FDSRCS 1954; MSc (Liverpool) 1960; DRD RCS Ed, 1978. House Surg., 1950, and Registrar, 1952–54, United Liverpool Hosps; Lieut (later Captain) Royal Army Dental Corps, 1950–52; Lectr in Dental Prosthetics, Univ. of Liverpool, 1954–61; Visiting Associate Prof., Northwestern Univ., Chicago, 1961–62; Sen. Lectr in Dental Prosthetics, Univ. of Liverpool, 1962–67; Hon. Cons. Dental Surgeon: United Liverpool Hosps, 1962–67; United Newcastle Hosps (later Newcastle Health Authority), 1968–92. Chm., Div. of Dentistry, Newcastle Univ. Hosps, 1972–75. Mem. Council and Sec., British Soc. for the Study of Prosthetic Dentistry, 1960–69 (Pres., 1968–69); Member: GDC, 1977–92 (Chm. Educn Cttee, 1986–91); Bd of Faculty, RCS, 1982–90; Dental Sub-Cttee, UGC, 1982–89; EC Dental Cttee for trng of dental practitioners, 1986–93; Med. Cttee, UFC, 1989–92. Pres., Med. Rugby Football Club (Newcastle), 1968–82; Mem. Bd of Dirs, Durham CCC, 1994–98. Mem., Northern Sports Council, 1973–88; External Examiner in Dental Subjects: Univs of Belfast, Birmingham, Bristol, Dublin, Dundee, Leeds, London, Newcastle upon Tyne, RCS, and RCPSGlas. Church Warden, St Mary the Virgin, Ponteland, 2000–04. *Publications:* A Laboratory Course in Dental Materials for Dental Hygienists (with D. C. Smith), 1963; Immediate and Replacement Dentures (with J. N. Anderson), 3rd edn, 1981; papers on sci. and clin. subjects in dental and med. jls. *Recreations:* cricket, Rugby football, gardening, vexillology. *Address:* 164 Eastern Way, Darras Hall, Ponteland, Newcastle upon Tyne NE20 9RH. *T:* (01661) 823286. *Clubs:* MCC, East India.

STOREY, Baron *cr* 2011 (Life Peer), of Childwall in the City of Liverpool; **Michael John Storey,** CBE 2002 (OBE 1994); Headteacher, Plantation County Primary School, Halewood, Knowsley, 1986–2012; Member (Lib Dem), Liverpool City Council, 1973–2011 (Leader, 1998–2005); Lord Mayor, City of Liverpool, 2009–10; *b* 25 May 1949; *m* Carole; one *d. Educ:* Liverpool Univ. (BEd). Teacher: Prescot C of E Primary Sch.; New Hutte Primary Sch., Halewood; Deputy Headteacher, Halsnead Primary Sch., Whiston; Headteacher, St Gabriel's C of E Primary Sch., Huyton. Liverpool City Council: Chm., Educn Cttee, and Dep. Leader, 1980–83; Leader, Lib Dem Opposition, 1991–98. Member, Board: Mersey Partnership, 1993–2008; Liverpool Vision (Dep. Chm.); North West Develt Agency: Speke Garston Develt Co. *Address:* 36 Countisbury Drive, Liverpool L16 0JJ; House of Lords, SW1A 0PW. *W:* www.twitter.com/LordStorey.

STOREY, Alastair Dunbar; Founder Chairman and Chief Executive Officer, WSH Ltd (owner of hospitality businesses BaxterStorey, benugo, Searcys, Holroyd Howe, Caterlink and Portico), since 2000; *b* Fyvie, Aberdeenshire, 22 Jan. 1953; *s* of Robert Storey and May Storey; *m* 1977, Elizabeth Linden; one *s* four *d. Educ:* Robert Gordon's Coll., Aberdeen; Strathclyde Univ. (BA); Harvard Business Sch. (PMD). Mgt trainee, later Man. Dir, Sutcliffe Catering, 1975–96; Gp Man. Dir, Granada Food Services, 1996–99. Vice Pres., Food Service Europe, 2012–; Dir, British Hospitality Assoc., 2013–. Chm., Trustees, Gold Service Scholarship, 2012–. Gov., Royal Acad. of Culinary Arts, 2012–. Trustee, Nicholli Spinal Injury Foundn, 2014–. Hon. DLitt West London, 2013. *Recreations:* food and wine, art, reading, family, cycling, ski-ing and other sports, guitar. *Address:* WSH Ltd, TVP 2, 300 Thames Valley Park Drive, Reading, Berks RG6 1PT. *T:* (0118) 935 6700, *Fax:* (0118) 935 6701. *E:* astorey@baxterstorey.com.

STOREY, Christopher Thomas; QC 1995; a Recorder, 2000–15; *b* 13 Feb. 1945; *s* of Leslie Hall Storey and Joan Storey; *m* 1968, Hilary Johnston; two *s. Educ:* Rugby Sch. Chartered Accountant, 1967; Glass & Edwards, Liverpool, 1964–68; Price Waterhouse & Co., 1968–70; A. E. Smith Coggins Group, 1970–72; Stacey's, 1972–74; private practice as Chartered Accountant, 1974–82; called to the Bar, Lincoln's Inn, 1979; practising Barrister, NE Circuit, 1982–2007; an Asst Recorder, 1996–2000. *Recreations:* music, cricket, classic cars, flying light aircraft (instructor), undergardening. *Address:* Park Lane Plowden, 19 Westgate, Leeds LS1 2RD. *T:* (0113) 228 5000.

STOREY, David Malcolm; writer and dramatist; *b* 13 July 1933; *s* of Frank Richmond Storey and Lily (*née* Cartwright); *m* 1956, Barbara Rudd Hamilton; two *s* two *d. Educ:* Queen Elizabeth Grammar Sch., Wakefield, Yorks; Slade School of Fine Art, London. Fellow, UCL, 1974. *Plays:* The Restoration of Arnold Middleton, 1967 (Evening Standard Award); In Celebration, 1969 (Los Angeles Critics' Award); The Contractor, 1969 (Writer of the Year Award, Variety Club of GB, NY Critics' Award) (televised, 1989); Home, 1970 (Evening Standard Award, Critics' Award, NY); The Changing Room, 1971 (Critics' Award, NY); Cromwell, 1973; The Farm, 1973; Life Class, 1974; Mother's Day, 1976; Sisters, 1978; Early Days, 1980; The March on Russia, 1989; Stages, 1992. *Publications:* This Sporting Life, 1960 (Macmillan Fiction Award, US); Flight into Camden, 1960 (John Llewellyn Rhys Meml Prize); Radcliffe, 1963 (Somerset Maugham Award); Pasmore, 1972 (Geoffrey Faber Meml Prize, 1973); A Temporary Life, 1973; Edward, 1973; Saville, 1976 (Booker Prize, 1976); A Prodigal Child, 1982; Present Times, 1984; Storey's Lives: poems 1951–1991, 1992; A Serious Man, 1998; as it happened, 2002; Thin-Ice Skater, 2004. *Address:* c/o Jonathan Cape, Random House, 20 Vauxhall Bridge Road, SW1V 2SA.

STOREY, Dr Hugo Henry; a Judge of the Upper Tribunal (Immigration and Asylum Chamber) (formerly a Vice President, Immigration Appeal Tribunal, later a Senior Immigration Judge, Asylum and Immigration Tribunal), 2000–15; *b* 30 Sept. 1945; *s* of Harry MacIntosh Storey and Barbara Storey; *m* 1983, Sehba Haroon; three *s. Educ:* N Sydney Boys' High Sch.; Univ. of Sydney (BA Hons 1967; Medal in Govt); Balliol Coll., Oxford (BPhil Politics); Nuffield Coll., Oxford; Univ. of Leeds (PhD 1988). Adult educn teaching, legal res., and journalism, 1971–76; Organiser, Tribunal Assistance Unit, Chapeltown CAB, 1976–78; Sen. Legal Worker, Chapeltown and Harehills Law Centre, 1978–88; Human Rights Fellow, Council of Europe, 1983–88; legal worker, John Howell & Co., 1989–90; Sen. Lectr, Law Dept, Leeds Poly., 1990–91; Lectr and Dep. Dir for Study of Law in Europe, Law Dept, 1991–95, Hon. Res. Fellow, 1995–98, Univ. of Leeds. Adjudicator, Immigration Appellate Authy, 1995–2000. Mem. Council, Internat. Assoc. Refugee Law Judges, 1998–. *Publications:* (jtly) I Want to Appeal: a guide to Supplementary Benefit Appeal Tribunals, 1978; (jtly) Social Security Appeals: a guide to National Insurance Local Tribunals and Medical Appeal Tribunals, 1980; (with G. Crawford) Sacked? Made Redundant? Your Rights if You Lose Your Job: a guide to Industrial Tribunals and the Employment Appeal Tribunal, 1981; (with W. Collins) Immigrants and the Welfare State, 1985; (ed jtly) Asylum Law, 1995; (ed jtly) Butterworth's Immigration Law Handbook, 2001; contribs to various legal jls in UK, Europe and internat. *Recreations:* family, travel, golf, writing poetry (esp. haiku), music, chess.

STOREY, Jeremy Brian; QC 1994; a Recorder, since 1995; Deputy Judge of the Technology and Construction Court (formerly Official Referee), since 1996; a Deputy High Court Judge, since 2008; Deemster, Isle of Man Courts, since 2009 (Acting Deemster, 1999–2009); *b* 21 Oct. 1952; *s* of late Captain James Mackie Storey and Veronica Walmsley; *m* 1981, Carolyn Margaret Ansell; two *d. Educ:* Uppingham Sch.; Downing Coll., Cambridge (Scholar; BA Law 1st Class, MA). MCIArb 1999 (ACIArb 1997). Called to the Bar, Inner Temple, 1974, Bencher, 2006; Asst Recorder, 1991–95; Head of Chambers, 2008–. Asst Boundary Comr for Eng. and Wales, 2000–. Member: ADR Chambers (UK) Ltd; Western Circuit; Technology and Construction Bar Assoc.; Commercial Bar Assoc.; Soc. of Construction Law; Professional Negligence Bar Assoc.; Soc. for Computers and Law; Panel, WIPO Arbitration and Mediation Center, Geneva; ACI Panel of Arbitrators; ACI Panel of Mediators; Civil Mediation Council. *Recreations:* travel, cricket, theatre. *Address:* 4 Pump Court, Temple, EC4Y 7AN. *T:* (020) 7842 5555. *Clubs:* MCC; Glamorgan CC.

STOREY, Maurice, CB 2003; CEng, FIMarEST; FRINA; Chief Executive, Maritime and Coastguard Agency, 1998–2003; Hon. Chairman, Evergreen-Marine UK Ltd (formerly Hatsu Marine Ltd), since 2007 (Chairman, 2003–06, Hon. Chairman, 2006–07, Hatsu Marine Ltd); *b* 14 June 1943; *s* of Albert Henry Storey and Violet Esther Storey; *m* 1987, Linda Mears; two *s* one *d. Educ:* HNC Naval Architecture 1963. CEng 1969; FRINA 1969; FIMarEST 1972. Apprentice, Swan Hunter Shipbuilders, 1958–62; Ship Repair Manager, Swan Hunter Ship Repairers, 1962–67; Asst to Marine Superintendent, then Tech. Superintendent, Shaw Savill Line, 1967–72; Hd, Tech. Dept, Kuwait Oil Tanker Co., 1972–76; Director: Sea Containers Ltd, 1976–90; Hoverspeed Ltd, 1986–90; Ship and Port Mgt, Stena Line Ltd, 1990–98; non-exec. Dir, James Fisher plc, 2003–13. Chm. and Dir, Fishguard and Rosslare Rlys and Harbours Co., 1992–98; Dir, Soc. du Terminal Transmanche de Dieppe, 1992–98. Chamber of Shipping UK: Vice-Chm., Cruise Ship and Ferry Section, 1991–96; Chm., Marine Policy Cttee, 1996–98; Vice-Pres., 2005–06; Pres., 2006–07. Pres., Inst. of Marine Engrg, Sci. and Tech., 2005–06. RNLI: Mem. Council, 2002–14; Mem. Technical Cttee, 2003–14; Vice Pres., 2014–. Trustee, Historic Dockyard Chatham, 2007–. Hon. MBA Nottingham Trent, 2000. *Recreations:* walking, golf. *Address:* 69 Greenhill, Staplehurst, Tonbridge, Kent TN12 0SU. *T:* and *Fax:* (01580) 890530.

STOREY, Most Rev. Patricia; *see* Meath and Kildare, Bishop of.

STOREY, Paul Mark; QC 2001; a Recorder, since 2000; a Deputy High Court Judge, since 2004; *b* 12 March 1957; *s* of late George Daniel Storey and Denise Edna Storey (*née* Baker); *m* 1st, 1977, Margaret Jane Aucott (marr. diss. 1994); two *d*; 2nd, 1994, Alexa Roseann Rea; three *s* one *d. Educ:* Notre Dame Sch., Lingfield; John Fisher Sch., Purley; N London Poly.; Newcastle Poly.; UCL; Inns of Court Law Sch.; BA Hons; CPE. Called to the Bar, Lincoln's Inn, 1982; in practice as barrister, 1983–; Asst Recorder, 1999–2000. *Publications:* contrib. various articles to Family Law. *Recreations:* football (Fulham FC), cycling, Rugby (Harlequins RFC), cricket, my family. *Address:* (chambers) 29 Bedford Row, WC1R 4HE.

STOREY, Hon. Sir Richard, 2nd Bt *cr* 1960; CBE 1996; DL; Chairman of Portsmouth and Sunderland Newspapers plc, 1973–98 (Director, 1962–99); *b* 23 Jan. 1937; *s* of Baron Buckton (Life Peer) and Elisabeth (*d* 1951), *d* of late Brig.-Gen. W. J. Woodcock, DSO; *S* to baronetcy of father, 1978; *m* 1961, Virginia Anne, 3rd *d* of Sir Kenelm Cayley, 10th Bt; one *s* two *d*. *Educ:* Winchester; Trinity Coll., Cambridge (BA, LLB). National service commission, RNVR, 1956. Called to the Bar, Inner Temple, 1962. Administers agricultural land and woodland in Yorkshire. Director: One Stop Community Stores Ltd, 1971–98; Croydon Cable, 1983–89; Reuters Hldgs PLC, 1986–92; Press Association Ltd, 1986–95 (Chm., 1991–95); Fleming Enterprise Investment Trust PLC, 1989–2002 (Chm., 1996–2002); Foreign & Colonial Smaller Cos PLC, 1993–2002; Sunderland PLC, 1996–2004; eFinancialNews Ltd, 2000–06. Chm., York Health Services Trust, 1991–97. Member: Nat. Council and Exec., CLA, 1980–84, Yorks Exec., CLA (Chm., 1974–76); Employment Policy Cttee, CBI, 1984–88, CBI Regl Council, Yorks and Humberside, 1974–76; Press Council, 1980–86; Pres., Newspaper Soc., 1990–91 (Mem. Council, 1980–98). Chairman: Sir Harold Hillier Arboretum Management Cttee, 1989–2005; Internat. Dendrology Soc., 2007–12; Trustee: Royal Botanic Gardens Kew Foundn, 1990–2004; Castle Howard Arboretum Trust, 1997–2013. Mem. Council: INCA-FIEJ Res. Assoc., 1983–88; European Newspaper Publishers' Assoc., 1991–96. Contested (C): Don Valley, 1966; Huddersfield W, 1970. High Sheriff, 1992–93, DL 1998, N Yorks. Trustee, Hope and Homes for Children, 2002–09. Hon. Fellow, Univ. of Portsmouth, 1989. Hon. DLitt Sunderland Poly., 1992. Veitch Meml Medal, RHS, 2005. *Recreations:* architecture, silviculture, dendrology. *Heir: s* Kenelm Storey [*b* 4 Jan. 1963; *m* 2001, Karen, *d* of Keith Prothero; one *s* two *d*]. *Address:* Settrington Grange, Malton, Yorks YO17 8NU. *T:* (01944) 768200; 11 Zetland House, Marloes Road, W8 5LB. *T:* (020) 7937 8823. *E:* storey.london@btinternet.com.

STOREY, Dame Sarah (Joanne), DBE 2013 (OBE 2009; MBE 1998); athlete, since 1992; *b* Manchester, Oct. 1977; *née* Bailey; *m* 2007, Barney Storey, MBE; one *d*. *Educ:* Leeds Metropolitan Univ. (BSc (Hons) Sport and Exercise Sci. 1999). GB internat. swimmer, 1992–2005; GB internat. cyclist, 2005–; Paralympic Games Barcelona 1992, Atlanta 1996, Sydney 2000, Athens 2004, Beijing 2008, London 2012 (11 Gold Medals (5 swimming, 6 cycling), 8 Silver Medals (swimming), 3 Bronze Medals (swimming)); Team England, Commonwealth Games, Delhi, 2010; GB Team Pursuit Squad, Track World Cup, Manchester, 2011 (Gold Medal), Cali, Colombia, 2011 (Gold Medal); winner: 27 World Championship titles (6 swimming, 21 cycling); 21 Europ. titles (18 swimming, 3 cycling); 7 World Cup titles (5 paracycling, 2 able-bodied cycling). Dir, Team Storey Sport Ltd, 2009–. Member: VioRed Racing Team, subseq. Breast Cancer Care Cycling Team, 2012–14; Pearl Izumi Sports Tours Internat. Women's Cycling Team, 2014–. *Address:* Team Storey Sport Ltd, PO Box 80, Disley, Cheshire SK12 2WF.

STOREY, Susannah Jemima; Director, Corporate Strategy and Change, Department of Energy and Climate Change, since 2013; *b* London, 7 March 1973; *d* of Tom Storey and Victoria Storey; *m* 2003, Robin Hooper; two *d*. *Educ:* Benenden Sch.; St John's Coll., Cambridge (BA Hist. 1995). SFA Rep. 1996. UK Corporate Finance, Schroders, 1996–2000; UK M&A, Citigroup Global Markets, 2000–07; Shareholder Executive, BIS (formerly BERR), 2007–13, incl. Dir, Royal Mail and Postal Services, 2010–12. Non-exec. Dir, Post Office Ltd, 2012–. *Recreations:* family, art. *Address:* Department of Energy and Climate Change, 3 Whitehall Place, SW1A 2AW.

STORKEY, Elaine; President, Tear Fund, 1997–2013; *b* 1 Oct. 1943; *d* of James and Anne Lively; *m* 1968, Alan James Storkey; three *s*. *Educ:* UCW, Aberystwyth (BA); McMaster Univ., Ontario (MA); York Univ. Tutor, Manchester Coll., Oxford, 1967–68; Res. Fellow, Univ. of Stirling, 1968–69; Tutor, then Lectr, Open Univ., 1976–90; Exec. Dir, Inst. for Contemporary Christianity, 1990–98. Dir of Training, Church Army, 2009–12. Visiting Professor: Calvin Coll., USA, 1980–81; Covenant Coll., Chattanooga, USA, 1981–82; Vis. Scholar, KCL, 1996–; New Coll. Schol., Univ. of NSW, 1997; Sen. Res. Fellow, Wycliffe Hall, Univ. of Oxford, 2003–07; Micah Lectr, Port au Prince, Haiti, 2008; Templeton-Cambridge Journalism Fellow, 2009; Frumentius Vis. Scholar, Graduate Sch. of Theology, Addis Ababa, Ethiopia, 2010. Associate Ed., Third Way, 1988–. Member: Cathedrals Commn, 1992–96; Crown Nominations (formerly Crown Appts) Commn, 2002–08; Gen. Synod of C of E, 1987–; Gen. Assembly of C of S, 2014; Forum for the Future, 1994–2001; Emerging Mkts Symposium, 2013–; founding Mem., Restored, 2010–. Pres., Fulcrum, 2011–. Reviewer, Free Thinking, BBC Radio 3, 2013–. Vice-Pres., Gloucestershire Univ. (formerly Cheltenham & Gloucester Coll.), 1995–. Mem., High Table, Newnham Coll., Cambridge, 2008–. Mem., RSA, 2012. Hon. Fellow, Aberystwyth Univ., 2013. DD Lambeth 1998; Hon. PhD Gloucester, 2000. Kuyper Prize, Princeton Theol Seminary, 2016. *Publications:* What's Right with Feminism, 1986, 2nd edn 2013; Mary's Story, Mary's Song, 1993; The Search for Intimacy, 1995; Magnify the Lord, 1998; (with Margaret Hebblethwaite) Conversations on Christian Feminism, 1999; Men and Women: created or constructed, 2000; Origins of Difference, 2002; Word on the Street, 2003; Scars Across Humanity, 2015; contrib. to Scottish Jl Theol., Gospel and Culture, The Independent, Church Times, Dagen (Sweden). *Recreations:* broadcasting, making film documentaries. *Address:* (home) The Old School, Coton, Cambs CB23 7PL. *T:* (01954) 212381.

STORMER, Prof. Horst Ludwig, PhD; physicist; Professor of Physics and Applied Physics, Columbia University, 1998, now Emeritus; Adjunct Physics Director, Lucent Technologies (formerly AT&T Bell Laboratories), 1997–2006; *b* Frankfurt am Main, 6 April 1949; *s* of Karl Ludwig Stormer and Marie Stormer (*née* Ihrig); *m* 1982, Dominique A. Parchet. *Educ:* Univ. of Stuttgart (PhD 1977). AT&T Bell Laboratories: Mem., Technical Staff, 1978–83; Dept Head, 1983–92; Dir, Physical Res. Lab., 1992–97. Bell Labs Fellow, 1983. Mem., US Nat. Acad. of Scis, 1999. Buckley Prize, 1984; Otto Klung Prize, Free Univ., Berlin, 1985; Benjamin Franklin Medal, 1998; (jtly) Nobel Prize for Physics, 1998; NYC Mayor's Award for Excellence in Sci. and Technol., 2000. Officier de la Légion d'Honneur (France), 1999; Grosse Verdienstkreuz mit Stern (Germany), 1999. *Address:* Department of Physics, Columbia University, 704 Pupin Hall, New York, NY 10027, USA.

STORMONT, Viscount; Alexander David Mungo Murray; *b* 17 Oct. 1956; *s* and *heir* of 8th Earl of Mansfield and Mansfield, *qv*; *m* 1985, Sophia Mary Veronica, *o d* of Biden Ashbrooke, St John, Jersey; one *s* three *d*. *Educ:* Eton. Member: Scottish Council, HHA, 1993–2007; Tay and District Salmon Fisheries Bd, 2000–11. *Heir: s* Master of Stormont, *qv*. *Address:* Scone Palace, Perthshire PH2 6BD.

STORMONT, Master of; Hon. William Philip David Mungo Murray; *b* 1 Nov. 1988; *s* and *heir* of Viscount Stormont, *qv*. ADC to Grand Master of Order of Malta, 2011–.

STORMONTH DARLING, Peter; Director, Soditic Limited, since 2007; *b* 29 Sept. 1932; *s* of Patrick Stormonth Darling and Edith Mary Ormston Lamb; *m* 1st, 1958, Candis Hitzig; three *d*; 2nd, 1971, Maureen O'Leary (*d* 2015). *Educ:* Winchester; New Coll., Oxford (MA). 2nd Lieut, Black Watch, 1950–53, served Korean War; RAFVR, 1953–56. Dir, 1967–2001, Chm., 1995–2001, Deltec Panamerica, then Deltec Internat., SA. Chairman: Mercury Asset Mgt Gp, 1979–92 (Dir, 1969–98); Mercury International Investment Trust, 1990–98; Mercury European Investment (formerly Mercury Europe Privatisation) Trust, 1994–2004; Atlas Capital Gp (incorporating Deltec Internat. Gp), 2001–06; Alta Advisers Ltd, 2004–07. Director: S. G. Warburg & Co. Ltd, 1967–85 (Vice-Chm., 1977–85); S. G. Warburg Group plc, 1974–94; Europe Fund, 1990–2000; Scottish Equitable plc, 1992–99; Merrill Lynch UK (formerly Mercury Keystone) Investment Co., 1992–2002; Greenwich Associates, 1993–2006; Scottish and Southern Energy (formerly Scottish Hydro-Electric) plc, 1994–2000; Sagitta Asset Mgt Ltd, 1996–2003; Guardian Capital Gp Ltd (Canada), 1998–2013; Aegon (UK) plc, 1999–2003; Invesco Perpetual Select Trust plc, 2001–08; Howard de Walden Estates Ltd, 2001–14; Galahad Gold plc, 2005–08. Director: The UK Fund Inc., 1994–2000; Advent Capital Hldgs, 2006–09; Genagro Services Ltd, 2008–14. Member: UN Pension Fund Investments Cttee, 1990–2005; Exec. (formerly Finance and Investments) Cttee, IISS, 1994–2007; Finance Cttee, World Monuments Fund, 2002–11. Chm. Council, Winchester Coll. Soc., 2007–09. *Publications:* City Cinderella, 1999. *Address:* Soditic Limited, 12 Charles II Street, SW1Y 4QU.

STOTHARD, Sir Peter (Michael), Kt 2003; Editor, The Times Literary Supplement, since 2002; *b* 28 Feb. 1951; *s* of late Wilfred Max Stothard and of Patricia J. Stothard (*née* Savage); *m* 1980, Sally Ceris Emerson; one *s* one *d*. *Educ:* Brentwood Sch., Essex; Trinity Coll., Oxford (BA Lit Hum.; MA; Hon. Fellow, 2000). BBC journalist, 1974–77; with Shell Internat. Petroleum, 1977–79; business and political writer, Sunday Times, 1979–80; The Times: Features Ed. and Leader writer, 1980–86; Dep. Ed., 1986–92; US Ed., 1989–92; Editor, 1992–2002. Chairman of Judges: Forward Poetry Prize, 2003; Hessell Tiltman Prize for History, 2004; Man Booker Prize, 2012. Pres., Classical Assoc., 2011–12. Dir, Roundhouse Trust, 2004–10. President's Medal, British Acad., 2013; Criticos Prize, 2013. *Publications:* Thirty Days: a month at the heart of Blair's war, 2003; On the Spartacus Road: a spectacular journey through ancient Italy, 2010; Alexandria: the last nights of Cleopatra, 2013. *Recreation:* ancient and modern literature. *Address:* The Times Literary Supplement, 1 London Bridge Street, SE1 9GF. *Club:* Garrick.

STOTT, Sir Adrian, 4th Bt *cr* 1920; management consultant, since 1989; *b* 7 Oct. 1948; *s* of Sir Philip Sidney Stott, 3rd Bt, and Cicely Florence (*d* 1996), *o d* of Bertram Ellingham; *S* father, 1979. *Educ:* Univ. of British Columbia (BSc (Maths) 1968, MSc (Town Planning) 1974); Univ. of Waterloo, Ont (MMaths (Computer Science) 1971). Dir of Planning for a rural region of BC, 1974; formed own consulting practice, 1977; property develt, gen. management and town planning consultant, 1977–85; Manager: BC Govt Real Estate Portfolio, 1980; Islands Trust (coastal conservation and property develt control agency), 1985; Man. Dir, direct sales marketing company, 1986–88. Mem., Assoc. for Computing Machinery. *Recreations:* music, inland waterways, politics. *Heir: b* Vyvyan Philip Stott, *b* 5 Aug. 1952.

STOTT, Andrew Charles, CBE 2011; Director of Digital Engagement, Government Communications, Cabinet Office, 2009–10; *b* 11 Sept. 1955; *s* of Prof. Peter Frank Stott and Vera Stott (*née* Watkins). *Educ:* Westminster Sch.; Clare Coll., Cambridge (BA 1976). Civil Service Dept, 1976; Prime Minister's Efficiency Unit, 1983–85; HM Prison Service, 1985–87; DSS, 1987–2001; Dir, Digital Infrastructure and e-Champion, DWP, 2001–03; Modernisation Dir, DfT, 2003–04; Hd, Service Transformation, e-Govt Unit, later Dep. Govt Chief Information Officer and Dir, Service Transformation, Cabinet Office, 2004–08. Mem., Public Sector Transparency Bd, Cabinet Office, 2011–. Sen. Consultant, World Bank, 2012–. *Recreation:* walking. *Address:* PO Box 191, Sevenoaks, Kent TN13 2AW. *E:* andrew.stott@dirdigeng.com.

STOTT, Kathryn Linda; pianist; *b* 10 Dec. 1958; *d* of Desmond Stott and Elsie Stott (*née* Cheetham); *m* 1st, 1979, Michael Ardron (marr. diss. 1983); 2nd, 1983, John Elliott (marr. diss. 1997); one *d*. *Educ:* Yehudi Menuhin Sch.; Royal Coll. of Music, London (ARCM). Regular duo partner of Yo-Yo Ma, Truls Mork, Natalie Clein, Christian Poltera, Noriko Ogawa; has worked with all major British orchs; recitals throughout UK; tours of Europe, USA and Far East; world premières of concertos by Graham Fitkin, George Lloyd, Michael Nyman and Sir Peter Maxwell Davies. Artistic Director: Fauré and the French Connection, 1995; Piano 2000, Piano 2003; Incontri in terra de Siena. Visiting Professor: RAM, 2004–; Chetham's Sch. of Music, 2004–. Member: Bd, Halle Orchs; Nordoff Robbins Music Therapy. Numerous recordings. Chevalier de l'Ordre des Arts et des Lettres (France), 1996. *Recreations:* food, travel, Italian language. *Address:* c/o Jane Ward, 60 Shrewsbury Road, Oxton, Wirral CH43 2HY.

STOTT, Kenneth Campbell; actor; *b* Edinburgh, 19 Oct. 1954; *s* of David and Antonia Stott; one *s*; partner, Nina Gehl. *Educ:* George Heriot's Sch., Edinburgh; Mountview Th. Sch., London. *Theatre* includes: appearances with RSC; The Sea, RNT, 1992; Art, Wyndham's, 1996; Faith Healer, Almeida, 2001; God of Carnage, Gielgud, 2008, NY 2009; A View From the Bridge, Duke of York's, 2009; Uncle Vanya, Vaudeville Th., 2012; *films* include: Shallow Grave, 1994; Franz Kafka's It's a Wonderful Life, 1995; Fever Pitch, 1997; The Debt Collectors, 1999; Charlie Wilson's War, 2007; One Day, 2011; The Hobbit: An Unexpected Journey, 2012; The Hobbit: The Desolation of Smaug, 2013; The Hobbit: The Battle of the Five Armies, 2014; *television* includes: The Singing Detective, 1986; Your Cheatin' Heart, 1990; Takin' Over the Asylum, 1994; Silent Witness, 1996; The Vice, 1999–2003; Messiah, 2001–05; The Key, 2003; Rebus, 2006–07; Hancock and Joan, 2008; Toast, 2010; The Runaway (series), 2011; The Missing, 2014; An Inspector Calls, 2015. *Recreations:* watching Heart of Midlothian FC, dining out, visiting galleries. *Club:* Chelsea Arts.

STOUGHTON-HARRIS, Anthony Geoffrey, CBE 1989; DL; FCA; Deputy Chairman, Nationwide Building Society, 1990–95; *b* 5 June 1932; *s* of Geoffrey Stoughton-Harris and Kathleen Mary (*née* Baker Brown); *m* 1959, Elizabeth Thackery (*née* White); one *s* two *d*. *Educ:* Sherborne Sch., Dorset. FCA 1956. Partner, Norton Keen & Co., chartered accountants, 1958–74; Maidenhead & Berkshire Building Society, subseq. South of England, London & South of England, Anglia, Nationwide Anglia, then Nationwide Building Society: Dir, 1967–95; Man. Dir, 1975; Chief Gen. Manager, 1983–87; Vice-Chm., 1987–90. Chm., Electronic Funds Transfer Ltd, 1984–89; Director: Southern Electric, 1981–98 (Dep. Chm., 1993–98); Guardian Royal Exchange, 1990–95. Gen. Comr, Inland Revenue, 1982–2000. Part-time Treasurer, W Herts Main Drainage Authority, 1964–70. Chairman: BSA, 1987–89; Northants TEC, 1990–95; Northants Chamber of Commerce, Trng and Enterprise, 1995–96. FCBSI. DL 1994, High Sheriff, 2000, Northants. *Recreations:* sport, gardening, DIY. *Address:* The Beeches, 26 Granville Road, Limpsfield, Oxted, Surrey RH8 0DA. *T:* (01883) 717026.

STOURTON, family name of **Baron Mowbray, Segrave and Stourton**.

STOURTON, Edward John Ivo; Presenter, BBC News and Current Affairs programmes, since 1993; *b* 24 Nov. 1957; *s* of Nigel John Ivo Stourton, CBE, and Rosemary Jennifer Rushworth Stourton (*née* Abbott), JP; *m* 1st, 1980, Margaret (marr. diss. 2001), *e d* of Sir James Napier Finnie McEwen, 2nd Bt; two *s* one *d*; 2nd, 2002, Fiona Murch, *d* of late John Edward King. *Educ:* Ampleforth; Trinity Coll., Cambridge (MA; Pres., Cambridge Union, Lent, 1979). Joined ITN, 1979; founder mem., Channel 4 News, 1982, Washington Corresp., 1986–88; Paris Corresp., BBC TV, 1988–90; Diplomatic Ed., ITN, 1990–93; BBC Television: Presenter: One O'Clock News, 1993–99; Call Ed Stourton, 1997–98; Reporter: Correspondent, 1996–2001; Panorama, 1998; Presenter, Today, 1999–2009, Sunday, 2001– (Main Presenter, 2010–), Radio 4; has written and presented series for BBC2 and Radio 4, incl. Asia Gold (Sony Gold Award for Current Affairs, 1997), and Israel Accused (Amnesty Award for best television current affairs prog., 2001). *Publications:* Absolute Truth: the Catholic Church in the world today, 1998; In the Footsteps of St Paul, 2004; Paul of Tarsus: a visionary life, 2005; John Paul II: man of history, 2006; It's a PC World: what it means to live in a land gone politically correct, 2008; Diary of a Dog Walker, 2011; (ed) Trinity: a portrait, 2011; Cruel Crossing: escaping Hitler across the Pyrenees, 2013. *Recreations:*

conversation, buying books, croquet, racing demon. *Address:* c/o Curtis Brown, 5th Floor Haymarket House, 28–29 Haymarket, SW1Y 4SP. *T:* (020) 7393 4400. *Clubs:* Hurlingham, Travellers.

STOUT, Andrea Mary; *see* Sutcliffe, A. M.

STOUT, Prof. Robert William, MD, DSc; FRCP, FMedSci; Professor of Geriatric Medicine, Queen's University, Belfast, 1976–2007, now Emeritus; Director of Research and Development, Northern Ireland Health and Personal Social Services, 2001–08; *b* 6 March 1942; *s* of William Ferguson Stout, CB and Muriel Stout (*née* Kilner); *m* 1969, Helena Patricia Willis (*d* 2015); two *s* one *d*. *Educ:* Campbell Coll., Belfast (schol.); Queen's Univ., Belfast (MD, DSc). FRCP 1979; FRCPE 1979–2014; FRCPI 1989–2014; FRCPGlas 1994. MRC Eli Lilly Foreign Educnl Fellow, Univ. of Washington Sch. of Medicine, Seattle, 1971–73; Queen's University, Belfast: BHF Sen. Res. Fellow, 1974; Sen. Lectr in Medicine, 1975; Dean, Faculty of Medicine, 1991–96; Provost for Medicine and Health Scis, 1993–98; Dean, Faculty of Medicine and Health Scis, 1998–2001. Mem., GMC, 1991–2003 (Member: Standards Cttee, 1993–94; Educn Cttee, 1992–93, 1995–98, 1999–2002). Chairman: Specialty Adv. Cttee on Geriatric Medicine, Jt Cttee on Higher Med. Trng, 1986–92; Benchmark Cttee for Medicine, QAA, 2000–02; Main Panel B (Clinical Medicine), 2008 RAE; Member, Health & Social Services Boards: Southern, 1982–91; Eastern, 1993–2002; Member: Royal Commn on Long-Term Care for the Elderly, 1997–99; Distinction and Meritorious Awards Cttee for NI, 2001–04; Health Res. Bd, Dublin, 2002–07; Public Inquiry into C.diff outbreak, Northern HSC Trust, NI, 2009–10; Dep. Chm. and Med. Dir, NI Clinical Excellence Awards Cttee, 2005–14. Vice-Pres., Age Concern Northern Ireland, 1988–2001 (Chm., 1985–88). NI Regl Advr, RCP, 1984–90; British Geriatrics Society: Mem., Council, 1984–90; Chm., NI Reg., 1984–90; Mem., Exec., 1987–90; Chm., Editl Bd, Age and Ageing, 1999–2002; Pres.-elect, 2000–02; Pres., 2002–04. Jt Chm., Centre for Ageing Res. and Develt in Ireland, 2005–; Mem., NI Cttee, 2007–15 (Chm., 2009–15), Mem. Council, 2009–15, Stroke Assoc.; Mem., Bd of Dirs, Extra Care NI, 2008–13. Mem., Bd of Govs, Methodist Coll., Belfast, 1983–2002 (Chm., 1994–97); Chm. Bd of Govs, Edgehill Theol Coll., Belfast, 2005–11; Governor, Research in Ageing, 1989–2001 (Mem., Med. Adv. Cttee, 1982–89). Visiting Professor: Univ. of Auckland, NZ, 1990; Hong Kong Geriatric Soc., 1993. Founder FMedSci 1998. *Publications:* Hormones and Atherosclerosis, 1982; Arterial Disease in the Elderly, 1984; Diabetes and Atherosclerosis, 1992; articles in scientific jls on geriatric medicine and related topics. *Recreations:* golf, gardening, reading. *Address:* 3 Larch Hill Drive, Craigavad, Co. Down BT18 0JS. *T:* (028) 9042 2253. *Club:* Royal Belfast Golf.

STOUTE, Sir Michael (Ronald), Kt 1998; race horse trainer, since 1972; *b* 22 Oct. 1945; *m*; one *s* one *d*. *Educ:* Harrison College, Barbados. Leading flat racing trainer, 1981, 1986, 1989, 1994, 1997, 2000, 2003, 2005, 2006 and 2009; trained: Derby winners, Shergar, 1981, Shahrastani, 1986, Kris Kin, 2003, North Light, 2004; Workforce, 2010; Irish Derby winners, Shergar, 1981, Shareef Dancer, 1983, Shahrastani, 1986; 1000 Guineas winners, Musical Bliss, 1989, Russian Rhythm, 2003; Irish 1000 Guineas winner, Sonic Lady, 1986; 2000 Guineas Winners, Shadeed, 1985, Doyoun, 1988, Entrepreneur, 1997, King's Best, 2000, Golan, 2001; Irish 2000 Guineas winner, Shaadi, 1989; Oaks winners, Fair Salinia, 1978, Unite, 1987; Irish Oaks winners, Fair Salinia, 1978, Colorspin, 1986, Unite, 1987, Melodist, 1988, Pure Grain, 1995, Petrushka, 2000; St Leger winner, Conduit, 2008; Breeders Cup Turf winners, Pilsudski, 1996, Kalanisi, 2000, Conduit, 2008, 2009; Breeders' Cup Filly and Mare Turf winner: Islington, 2003; Dank, 2013; Japan Cup winner, Singspiel, 1996, Pilsudski, 1997; Dubai World Cup winner, Singspiel, 1997; Gold Cup, Royal Ascot winner, Estimate, 2013; Beverley D. Stakes winner, Dank, 2013. *Recreations:* golf, deep sea fishing. *Address:* Freemason Lodge, Bury Road, Newmarket, Suffolk CB8 7BY. *T:* (01638) 663801.

STOW AND LINDSEY, Archdeacon of; *see* Steadman, Ven. M. J.

STOW, Graham Harold, CBE 2004; DL; Executive Vice Chairman, Britannia Building Society, 2002–03 (Group Chief Executive, 1999–2002); Chairman, Home and Legacy Insurance Services, 2003–06; *b* 29 April 1944; *s* of Joseph Stow and Carrie Stow (*née* Meakin); *m* 1st, 1966, Susan Goldingay (marr. diss. 1983); two *s* (and one *s* decd); 2nd, 1984, Christine Probert. *Educ:* Liverpool Collegiate Sch. Captain, Royal Signals (TA), 1976–82. Retail Ops, then Divl Dir, Personnel, Littlewoods Orgn, 1962–82; Dir, Marlar Internat., 1982–84; ASDA Group plc: Personnel Dir, ASDA Stores, 1984–87; Gp Human Resources Dir, 1987–88; Man. Dir, 1988–89, Chief Exec., 1989–91, ASDA Stores; Director: George Davies Corp., 1991–92; Sandpiper Consultants, 1992; Exec. Vice Pres., Minet Gp, 1992–96; Retail Ops Dir, 1996–98, Dep. Gp Chief Exec., 1998–99, Britannia Building Soc. Non-executive Director: Northern Racing, 2001–07 (Chm., 2004–07); Uttoxeter Leisure & Develt Co., 2003–04; Co-op. Financial Services, 2003–09; Co-op. Bank, 2003–09; CIS, 2003–09; Co-op. Gen. Insce, 2006–09; Co-op. Food Div., 2007–09; non-exec. Chm., Iprism Underwriting Agency Ltd, 2006–; Mem., Adv. Bd, Kiddy & Partners, 2004–11. Chm., Building Socs Assoc., 2002–03 (Dep. Chm., 2001–02). Chm., Staffordshire Moorlands Local Agenda 21 Cttee, 1999–2001; Ind. Bd Mem., DSS, 2000–01; non-executive Director: DWP, 2001–05; Jobcentre Plus, 2003–05. Chm., InStaffs, 2007–09. Trustee: Second World War Experience Centre, 2003–07 (Chm. of Trustees, 1998–2002); Staffordshire Yeomanry Mus., 2007–12 (Chm. of Trustees, 2008–11); Lichfield Cathedral, 2007–11 (Dep. Chm. of Trustees, 2009–11). Chm. of Trustees, Staffs Community Foundn, 2008–11. Member: Regl Council, Nat. Meml Arboretum, 2008– (Trustee, 2010–11); Council, St John Ambulance, Staffs, 2009–11. Pres., Inst. of Home Econs, 1990–91; Mem., Council and Court, Leeds Univ., 1991–94; Vice Chm. of Govs, Harrogate GS, 1989–91; Governor: Leeds GS, 1989–94; Staffordshire Univ., 1999–2009 (Dep. Chm., 2002–04, Chm., 2004–09); Denstone Coll., 1999–2001. Mem., HAC. Hon. Col, Staffs and W Midland Army Cadet Force, 2008–15; Chm., 2008–13, Trustee, 2015–, Friends of Staffs and W Midlands (N) Army Cadet Force Trust. FCIPD (FIPD 1986); FRSA 1990; FCIB 2002. Freeman, City of London, 1994; Liveryman, Co. of Curriers, 1994– (Master, 2013–14). High Sheriff, 2007–08, DL 2009, Staffs. DUniv Staffordshire, 2009. *Recreations:* military history, collecting Irish stamps 1922 to 1939. *Clubs:* Special Forces, City Livery; Potters' (Stoke-on-Trent); Burton (Burton upon Trent).

STOW, Sir Matthew P.; *see* Philipson-Stow.

STOW, His Honour Timothy Montague Fenwick; QC 1989; a Circuit Judge, 2000–13; *b* 31 Jan. 1943; *s* of late Geoffrey Montague Fenwick Stow and Joan Fortescue Stow (*née* Flannery); *m* 1965, Alisoun Mary Francis Homberger; one *s* one *d*. *Educ:* Eton Coll. Called to the Bar, Gray's Inn, 1965, Bencher, 1998; became a tenant in common law chambers of David Croom-Johnson, QC (later Lord Justice Croom-Johnson), 1966; Hd of Chambers, 1998; a Recorder, 1989–2000. *Recreations:* swimming, chain sawing, tennis, foreign travel, music, looking after their country property. *E:* tmfstow@gmail.com.

STOW, William Llewelyn, CMG 2002; Director General and Head of Policy and Support Career Home, Department for Environment, Food and Rural Affairs, 2009–12; *b* 11 Jan. 1948; *s* of Alfred Frank and Elizabeth Mary Stow; *m* 1976, Rosemary Ellen Burrows; two *s*. *Educ:* Eastbourne Grammar Sch.; Churchill Coll., Cambridge (MA). Joined DTI, 1971; seconded to FCO, 1980–83 (UK Delegn to OECD) and 1985–88 (UK Perm. Repn to EC, Brussels); Internal European Policy, 1988–91; Financial and Resource Management, 1991–94; Hd, EC and Trade Policy Div., 1994–96; Dep. Dir-Gen., Trade Policy and Europe, 1996–98; Dir, Employment Relns, 1998; UK Dep. Perm. Rep. to EU, 1999–2003; Dir Gen., Envmt, 2003–07, Strategy and Evidence Gp, 2007–09, DEFRA. Mem. Bd, Sustrans Ltd, 2011– (Chm., 2015–). Chairman: Radnorshire Wildlife Trust, 2012–; Wildlife Trusts Wales, 2013–; Bd Mem., Council, Wildlife Trusts UK, 2012–. *Recreations:* hill and coastal walking, bird-watching, cricket, reading, cycling.

STOWELL OF BEESTON, Baroness *cr* 2011 (Life Peer), of Beeston in the County of Nottinghamshire; **Tina Wendy Stowell,** MBE 1996; PC 2014; Leader of the House of Lords and Lord Privy Seal, since 2014; *b* Nottingham, 2 July 1967; *d* of David and Margaret Stowell. *Educ:* Chilwell Comprehensive; Broxtowe Coll. of Further Educn. PA to Dir, RAF Regt, MoD, 1986–88; PA to Counsellor (Defence Supply), Defence Section, British Embassy, Washington, 1988–91; PA to Chief Press Sec., Press Office, Prime Minister's Office, 1991–96; various posts, private sector cos, 1996–98; Dep. Chief of Staff to Leader of Cons. Party and Leader of the Opposition, 1998–2001; BBC: Dep. Sec., 2001–03; Hd of Communications to Chm. and Governing Body, 2003–08; Hd of Corporate Affairs, 2008–10; independent strategic communications consultant, 2010–11; Dir, Tina Stowell Associates, 2010–11. A Baroness in Waiting (Govt Whip), 2011–13; Parly Under-Sec. of State, DCLG, 2013–14. *Address:* House of Lords, SW1A 0PW. *T:* (020) 7219 5353. *E:* stowellt@parliament.uk. *W:* www.tinastowell.co.uk, www.twitter.com/tinastowell.

STOWELL, Dr Michael James, FRS 1984; Research Director, Alcan International Ltd, 1990–94; *b* 10 July 1935; *s* of Albert James Stowell and Kathleen Maud (*née* Poole); *m* 1st, 1962, Rosemary Allen (marr. diss. 1990; she *d* 2007); one *s* one *d*; 2nd, 1995, Kerry June Brice (*née* Kern) (*d* 1998). *Educ:* St Julian's High Sch., Newport; Bristol Univ. (BSc 1957, PhD 1961). Res. Scientist and Gp Leader, Tube Investments Research Labs, 1960–78; Research Manager, Materials Dept, TI Research, 1978–88; Prin. Consulting Scientist, Alcan Internat. Ltd, 1989–90. Post-doctoral Res. Fellow, Ohio State Univ., 1962–63; Res. Fellow, Univ. of Minnesota, 1970; Dist. Res. Fellow, Dept of Materials Sci. and Metallurgy, Univ. of Cambridge, 1999–2013. L. B. Pfeil Medal, Metals Soc., 1976; Sir Robert Hadfield Medal, Metals Soc., 1981. *Publications:* papers on electron microscopy, epitaxy, nucleation theory, superplasticity and physical metallurgy, in various jls. *Recreation:* music. *Address:* 7 Marking's Field, Saffron Walden, Essex CB10 2BB. *T:* (01799) 500112. *E:* stowell290@virginmedia.com.

STRABANE, Viscount; James Alfred Nicholas Hamilton; *b* 30 Oct. 2005; *s* and *heir* of Marquess of Hamilton, *qv*.

STRABOLGI, 12th Baron *cr* 1318, of England; **Andrew David Whitley Kenworthy;** Software Architect/Big Data Engineer, inovex GmbH, Pforzheim, Germany, since 2008; *b* London, 25 Jan. 1967; *s* of late Rev. Hon. Jonathan Malcolm Atholl Kenworthy and of Victoria Kenworthy (*née* Hewitt); *S* uncle, 2010; *m* 1998; one *s* one *d*. *Educ:* Pembroke Coll., Cambridge (BA Engrg Tripos 1989; MA 1993). *Heir: s* Hon. Joel Brendan Kenworthy, *b* 3 Sept. 2004.

STRACEY, Sir John (Simon), 9th Bt *cr* 1818; *b* 30 Nov. 1938; *s* of Captain Algernon Augustus Henry Stracey (2nd *s* of 6th Bt) (*d* 1940) and Olive Beryl (*d* 1972), *d* of late Major Charles Robert Eustace Radclyffe; *S* cousin, 1971; *m* 1968, Martha Maria, *d* of late Johann Egger; two *d*. *Heir: cousin* Henry Mounteney Stracey [*b* 24 April 1920; *m* 1st, 1943, Susanna, *d* of Adair Tracey; one *d*; 2nd, 1950, Lysbeth, *o d* of Charles Ashford, NZ; one *s* one *d*; 3rd, 1961, Jeltje, *y d* of Scholte de Boer]. *Address:* Holbeam Wood Cottage, Wallcrouch, Wadhurst, East Sussex TN5 7JT. *T:* and *Fax:* (01580) 201061.

STRACHAN, Alan Lockhart Thomson; theatre director, writer and broadcaster; *b* 3 Sept. 1946; *s* of Roualeyn Robert Scott Strachan and Ellen Strachan (*née* Graham); *m* 1977, Jennifer Piercey-Thompson. *Educ:* Morgan Acad., Dundee; St Andrews Univ. (MA); Merton Coll., Oxford (BLitt). Associate Dir, Mermaid Theatre, 1970–75; Artistic Director: Greenwich Th., 1978–88; Theatre of Comedy Co., 1991–97; Churchill Theatre, Bromley, 1995–97. *Productions directed include: Mermaid:* The Watched Pot, 1970; John Bull's Other Island, The Old Boys, 1971; (co-deviser) Cowardy Custard, 1972; Misalliance, 1973; Children, (co-deviser and dir) Cole, 1974; *Greenwich:* An Audience Called Edouard, 1978; The Play's the Thing, I Sent a Letter to my Love, 1979; Private Lives (transf. Duchess), Time and the Conways, 1980; Present Laughter (transf. Vaudeville), The Golden Age, The Doctor's Dilemma, 1981; Design for Living (transf. Globe), The Paranormalist, French Without Tears, 1982; The Dining Room, An Inspector Calls, A Streetcar Named Desire, 1983 (transf. Mermaid, 1984); The Glass Menagerie, Biography, 1985; One of Us, Relatively Speaking, For King and Country, 1986; The Viewing, The Perfect Party, 1987; How the Other Half Loves (transf. Duke of York's), 1988; *freelance:* Family and a Fortune, Apollo, 1975; (deviser and dir) Shakespeare's People, world tours, 1975–78; Confusions, Apollo, 1976; (also jt author) Yahoo, Queen's, 1976; Just Between Ourselves, Queen's, 1977; The Immortal Haydon, Mermaid, 1977 (transf. Greenwich, 1978); Bedroom Farce, Amsterdam, 1978; Noël and Gertie, King's Head, 1983, Comedy, 1989; (replacement cast) Woman in Mind, Vaudeville, 1987; The Deep Blue Sea, Haymarket, 1988; Re: Joyce!, Fortune, 1988 (transf. Vaudeville, 1989; USA, 1990), Vaudeville, 1991; (replacement cast) Henceforward…, Vaudeville, 1989; June Moon, Scarborough, 1989, Hampstead, transf. Vaudeville, 1992; Toekomstmuziek, Amsterdam, 1989; Alphabetical Order, Scarborough, 1990; (replacement cast) Man of the Moment, Globe, 1990; Other People's Money, Lyric, 1990; Taking Steps, NY, 1991; London Assurance, Dublin, 1993; Make Way for Lucia, Bromley and tour, 1995; Switchback, Bromley and tour, 1996; Høfeber, Copenhagen, 1996; All Things Considered, Scarborough, 1996, Hampstead, 1997; Loot, W Yorks Playhouse, 1996; Live and Kidding, Duchess, 1997; Mrs Warren's Profession, Guildford and tour, 1997; Hooikoorts, Amsterdam, 1997; New Edna—The Spectacle!, Haymarket, 1998; Troilus and Cressida, Regent's Park, 1998; How the Other Half Loves, Oxford Playhouse and tour, 1998; The Merry Wives of Windsor, Regent's Park, 1999; Private Lives, Far East tour, 1999; Hobson's Choice, Scarborough, 1999; Larkin with Women, Scarborough, 1999, Orange Tree Th., Richmond, 2006; A Midsummer Night's Dream, Regent's Park, 2000, 2001; Harvey, Singapore, 2000; The Real Thing, Bristol Old Vic and tour, 2001, Plymouth and tour, 2002; Henry IV, Pt One, Regent's Park, 2004; Going Straight, Windsor and tour, 2004; Glorious!, Birmingham Rep., transf. Duchess, 2005; Entertaining Angels, Chichester, 2006, revised version, Bath and tour, 2009; The Letter, Wyndham's, 2007; How the Other Half Loves, Bath and tour, 2007; Absurd Person Singular, Garrick, 2007, tour, 2009; Year of the Rat, W Yorks Playhouse, 2008; Relatively Speaking, Bath and tour, 2008; Balmoral, Bath and tour, 2009; The Promise, Orange Tree Th., Richmond, 2010; (revised) Cowardy Custard, Guildford and tour, 2011; Three Days in May, Trafalgar Studios, 2011; Storm in a Flower Vase, Arts Th., 2013; Mrs P.C., Chichester, 2015. *Producer/co-Producer:* Out of Order, tour, 1991; The Pocket Dream, Albery, 1992; Six Degrees of Separation, Royal Court, transf. Comedy, 1992; Hay Fever (also dir), Albery, 1992; Happy Families, tour, 1993; Hysteria, Royal Court, 1993; Under Their Hats (also devised), King's Head, 1994; The Prime of Miss Jean Brodie (also dir.), Strand, 1994; (exec. prod.) Love on a Branch Line, BBC1, 1994. *Publications:* Secret Dreams: a biography of Michael Redgrave, 2004; Putting It On: the West End Theatre of Michael Codron, 2010; contribs to periodicals and newspapers. *Recreations:* music, tennis, travelling. *Address:* Kirklands, St Martins, Perthshire PH2 6AL. *T:* (01821) 640580.

STRACHAN, Major Benjamin Leckie, CMG 1978; HM Diplomatic Service, retired; Special Adviser (Middle East), Foreign and Commonwealth Office, 1990–91; *b* 4 Jan. 1924; *e s* of late Dr C. G. Strachan, MC FRCPE and Annie Primrose (*née* Leckie); *m* 1958, Lize Lund; three *s*, and one step *s* one step *d*. *Educ:* Rossall Sch. (Scholar); RMCS; Univ. of Aberdeen (MA 2005). Royal Dragoons, 1944; France and Germany Campaign, 1944–45 (despatches); 4th QO Hussars, Malayan Campaign, 1948–51; Middle East Centre for Arab Studies,

1952–53; GSO2, HQ British Troops Egypt, 1954–55; Technical Staff Course, RMCS, 1956–58; 10th Royal Hussars, 1959–61; GSO2, WO, 1961; retd from Army and joined Foreign (subseq. Diplomatic) Service, 1961; 1st Sec., FO, 1961–62; Information Adviser to Governor of Aden, 1962–63; FO, 1964–66; Commercial Sec., Kuwait, 1966–69; Counsellor, Amman, 1969–71; Trade Comr, Toronto, 1971–74; Consul General, Vancouver, 1974–76; Ambassador to Yemen Arab Republic, 1977–78, and to Republic of Jibuti (non-resident), 1978, to the Lebanon, 1978–81, to Algeria, 1981–84. Principal, Mill of Strachan Language Inst., 1984–89. Vice Chm., Kincardine and Deeside Lib Dems, 1993–95; Chm., W Aberdeenshire and Kincardine Lib Dems, 1995–2000 (Pres., 2000–14); Mem. Policy Cttee, Scottish Lib Dems, 1998–. *Publications:* The Skirts of Alpha: an alternative to the Materialist Philosophy. *Recreations:* crofting, writing. *Address:* Mill of Strachan, Strachan, Kincardineshire AB31 6NS. *T:* (01330) 850663. *Club:* Lansdowne.

STRACHAN, Crispian; *see* Strachan, J. C.

STRACHAN, (Douglas) Mark (Arthur); QC 1987; SC (Hong Kong) 2013; a Recorder, 1990–2002; a Deputy High Court Judge, Queen's Bench Division, 1993–2002; *b* 25 Sept. 1946; *s* of late William Arthur Watkin Strachan and Joyce Olive Strachan; *m* 1995, Elizabeth Vickery; one *s*. *Educ:* Orange Hill Grammar Sch., Edgware, Middx; St Catherine's Coll., Oxford (Open Exhibnr in Eng. Lit.; BCL, MA); Nancy Univ. (French Govt Schol.). Called to the Bar, Inner Temple, 1969 (Major Schol. 1969–71), Hong Kong, 2002; Asst Recorder, 1987–90. *Publications:* contributor to Modern Law Rev. *Recreations:* son Charlie, France, Far East, antiques, paintings, food.

STRACHAN, Sir Hew (Francis Anthony), Kt 2013; PhD; FRSE; Professor of International Relations, University of St Andrews, since 2015; Chichele Professor of The History of War, University of Oxford, 2002–15; Fellow of All Souls College, Oxford, 2002–15, now Emeritus; Lord Lieutenant of Tweeddale, since 2014; *b* 1 Sept. 1949; *s* of late Michael Francis Strachan, CBE and Iris Strachan; *m* 1st, 1971, Catherine Margaret Blackburn (marr. diss. 1980); two *d*; 2nd, 1982, Pamela Dorothy Tennant (*née* Symes); one *s*, and one step *s* one step *d*. *Educ:* Rugby; Corpus Christi Coll., Cambridge (MA, PhD 1977). FRSE 2003. Res. Fellow, Corpus Christi Coll., Cambridge, 1975–78; Sen. Lectr in War Studies, RMA, Sandhurst, 1978–79; Corpus Christi College, Cambridge: Fellow, 1979–92, Life Fellow, 1992; Admissions Tutor, 1981–88, Sen. Tutor, 1989–92; Dean of Coll., 1981–86; Prof. of Modern Hist., 1992–2001, and Dir, Scottish Centre for War Studies, 1996–2001, Glasgow Univ.; Dir, Oxford Prog. (formerly Leverhulme Prog.) on the Changing Character of War, Univ. of Oxford, 2004–12. Vis. Prof., Royal Norwegian Air Force Acad., 2000–; Sir Howard Kippenberger Vis. Prof., Victoria Univ. of Wellington, NZ, 2009; Major Res. Fellow, Leverhulme Trust, 2008–11; Inaugural Humanitas Vis. Prof. in War Studies, Univ. of Cambridge, 2011. Lees Knowles Lectr, Cambridge, 1995; Thank Offering to Britain Fellow, British Acad., 1998–99. Comr, Commonwealth War Graves Commn, 2006–; Mem., Chief of the Defence Staff's Strategic Adv. Panel, 2010–; Advr, Jt Parly Cttee, Nat. Security Strategy, 2011–; Chm., Prime Minister's Taskforce on the Military Covenant, 2010. Member: First World War Centenary Adv. Gp, 2012–; Scottish Cttee for Centenary of First World War, 2013–; Comité Scientifique du Mission du Centenaire, France, 2013–. Trustee, Imperial War Mus., 2010–. Member of Council: Lancing Coll., 1982–90; Nat. Army Mus., 1994–2003; IISS, 2012–; Governor: Rugby Sch., 1985–2007; Stowe Sch., 1990–2002. Mem., Royal Co. of Archers, Queen's Bodyguard for Scotland, 1996– (Mem., Council, 2003–12; Brigadier, 2008–). DUniv Paisley, 2005. DL Tweeddale, 2006. *Publications:* British Military Uniforms 1768–1796, 1975; History of Cambridge University Officers' Training Corps, 1976; European Armies and the Conduct of War, 1983; Wellington's Legacy: the reform of the British Army, 1984; From Waterloo to Balaclava: tactics, technology and the British Army 1815–1854, 1985 (Templer Medal, Soc. for Army Histl Res.); The Politics of the British Army, 1997 (Westminster Medal, RUSI); (ed) Oxford Illustrated History of the First World War, 1998, 2nd edn 2014; (ed) The British Army, Manpower and Society, 2000; The First World War: vol. 1, To Arms, 2001; The First World War: a new illustrated history, 2003; (ed) Big Wars and Small Wars, 2006; Clausewitz's On War: a biography, 2007; (ed jtly) Clausewitz in the 21st Century, 2007; (ed jtly) The Changing Character of War, 2011; (ed jtly) La guerre irrégulière, 2011; (ed jtly) How Fighting Ends, 2012; (ed jtly) British Generals in Blair's Wars, 2013; The Direction of War: contemporary strategy in historical perspective, 2013. *Recreations:* shooting, Rugby football (now spectating). *Address:* Glenhighton, Broughton, by Biggar ML12 6JF. *Clubs:* Hawks (Cambridge); New (Edinburgh).

STRACHAN, James Murray; photographer; *b* 10 Nov. 1953; *s* of Eric Alexander Howison Strachan and Jacqueline Georgina Strachan. *Educ:* King's Sch., Canterbury; Christ's Coll., Cambridge (exhibnr, BA); London Coll. of Printing. Chase Manhattan Bank, 1976–77; joined Merrill Lynch, 1977, Exec. Dir, 1982–86, Man. Dir, 1986–89; writer and photographer, 1989–97; Associate Photographer, Getty Images (formerly Tony Stone), 1990–; Chief Exec., 1997–2002, Chm., 2002–07, Vice Pres., 2008–, RNID (Mem., Finance Cttee and Trustee, 1994–96); Chm., Audit Commn, 2002–06. Mem. Court, Bank of England, 2006–09 (Mem., Audit Cttee, 2006–09). Vis. Fellow, 2005–11, Sen. Vis. Fellow, 2011–13, LSE. Rotating Chair, Disability Charities Consortium, 1997–2002; Co-Chair: Task Force on Social Services Provision for Deaf and Hard of Hearing People, 1998–2002; NHS Modernising Hearing Aid Services Gp, 1999–2002; Chm., Task Force on Audiology Services, 2000–02; Member: Ministerial Disability Rights Task Force, 1997–99; Ministerial Disability Benefits Forum, 1998–99; Bd and Audit Cttee, Ofgem, 2000–04; Bd, Community Fund, 2001–03; Comr for Communications, Disability Rights Commn, 1999–2002. Non-executive Director: Legal and General Gp plc, 2003–11 (Mem., Remuneration Cttee, 2003–10, Risk Cttee, 2010–11); Welsh Water Ltd, 2007– (Mem., Audit Cttee; Chm., Remuneration Cttee, 2010–); JP Morgan Asian Investment Trust plc, 2009– (Mem., Audit Cttee); Sarasin and Partners LLP, 2008– (Chm., Remuneration Cttee, 2008–); Care UK plc, 2006–10 (Chm. Remuneration Cttee); Social Finance Ltd, 2008–; FSA, 2009–13 (Mem., Audit and Remuneration Cttees, 2009–13); Towergate Insurance, 2011–14 (Chm., Risk Cttee, 2012–14). Ext. Mem., DTI Transition Gp (Energy), 2001–02; Ind. Mem., DTI Business Bd, 2002–04. Mem., Adv. Gp on Diversity, NCVO, 2001–03; Pres., Midland Regl Assoc. for Deaf, 2001–. Trustee: Save the Children, 1999–2002; Somerset House Trust, 2003–08 (Chm., Audit and Finance Cttee, 2006–08). Leadership Patron, Nat. Coll. of School Leadership, 2003–10. Hon. Fellow, Univ. of the Arts, London (formerly London Inst.), 2002. *Publications:* Madrid, 1991; numerous illustrated travel books as photographer; contrib. The Times, Financial Times and Sunday Times. *Recreations:* film, reading, swimming, tennis. *Address:* 10B Wedderburn Road, NW3 5QG. *E:* james.strachan@mac.com.

STRACHAN, James Oliver John; QC 2013; *b* London, 17 May 1971; *s* of John Strachan and Caroline Strachan; *m* 2000, Imogen; two *s* one *d*. *Educ:* Winchester Coll.; St Peter's Coll., Oxford (BA Hons). Called to the Bar, Middle Temple, 1996; Attorney Gen.'s Counsel to Crown 'A' Panel, 2008–13. *Recreations:* theatre, opera, tennis, Real tennis, sailing, fishing. *Address:* 39 Essex Street, WC2R 3AT. *T:* (020) 7832 1111, *Fax:* (020) 7353 3978. *E:* james.strachan@39essex.com. *Club:* Garrick.

STRACHAN, Jeremy Alan Watkin; Secretary, British Medical Association, 2001–04; *b* 14 Dec. 1944; *s* of William Arthur Watkin Strachan and Joyce Olive Strachan; *m* 1976, Margaret Elizabeth McVay; two step *d*. *Educ:* Haberdashers' Aske's Sch., Elstree; St Catharine's Coll., Cambridge (MA, LLM). Called to the Bar, Inner Temple, 1969 (Paul Methven Entrance Schol.); Legal Asst, Law Commn, 1967–72; Legal Advr, BSC, 1972–78; Principal Legal Advr and Hd, Legal and Patent Services, ICL, 1978–84; Gp Legal Advr, Standard Telephones and Cables, 1984–85; Dir, Gp Legal Services, and Corporate Affairs, Glaxo Hldgs, 1986–91; Exec. Dir, responsible for legal services, corporate policy and public affairs, and business develt, Glaxo Wellcome, 1992–2000. Co. Sec., Forensic Science Service Ltd, 2005–12. Non-exec. Dir, NHS Business Services Authy, 2005–13. Vice-Chm., Disciplinary Appeals Cttee, CIMA, 2005–12. *Recreations:* France, Victoria & Albert Museum, controversy.

STRACHAN, (John) Crispian, CBE 2003; QPM 1996; DL; Director, Holyoake CIR Ltd, since 2011; *b* 5 July 1949; *s* of late Dr (Mark) Noel Strachan and Barbara Joan Strachan; *m* 1974, Denise Anne Farmer; one *s* three *d*. *Educ:* Jesus Coll., Oxford (BA Jurisp 1971; MA 1989); Sheffield Univ. (MA Criminology 1972). Joined Metropolitan Police, 1972; Inspector, 1977–83; Chief Inspector, 1983–87; Superintendent, 1987–90; Chief Superintendent, 1990–93; Asst Chief Constable, Strathclyde Police, 1993–98; Chief Constable, Northumbria Police, 1998–2005. Vis. Schol. in Applied Criminol. and Police Mgt, Cambridge Inst. of Criminology, 2011–. Dep. County Pres., St John Ambulance Northumbria, 2006–14. Trustee: Royal Grammar Sch. (Newcastle upon Tyne) Educnl Trust, 2006–; St Mary the Virgin Estate Mgt Charity, 2010–. DL Tyne and Wear, 2002. OStJ 2005. *Publications:* (with A. Comben) A Short Guide to Policing in the UK, 1992; (contrib.) Clinical Forensic Medicine, 3rd edn 2009. *Recreations:* woodworking, photography, the countryside, family above all. *Address:* Clifton House, Clifton, Morpeth, Northumberland NE61 6DQ. *E:* crispianstrachan@gmail.com.

STRACHAN, Mark; *see* Strachan, D. M. A.

STRACHAN, Peter; Managing Director, Serco Caledonian Sleeper, since 2014; *b* Aberdeen, 29 Aug. 1959; *s* of Alexander Strachan and Ina Strachan (*née* Mitchell); *m* 1981, Fiona Jill Colgate; two *s*. *Educ:* Kirkcudbright Acad.; Univ. of Durham (BA Hons). MIRO 2005. British Rail: graduate trainee, 1980–82; local and line mgt posts, 1982–90; Intercity Manager, Birmingham, 1990–93; Dir, Midlands, Railtrack, 1993–97; Man. Dir, North Western Trains, 1997–98; Chief Exec. (Rail), National Express Australia, 1999–2003; Man. Dir, Arriva Trains Wales, 2003–05; Route Dir, London North Western, Network Rail, 2005–09; Chief Exec., TransLink Transit Authy, Brisbane, 2009–11; Dir Gen., Major Projects and London, DfT, 2011–13; Bid Dir, Serco Gp Pty Ltd, Sydney, 2013–14. *Recreations:* football, golf, opera.

STRACHAN, Dame Valerie (Patricia Marie), DCB 1998 (CB 1991); Chairman, HM Customs and Excise, 1993–2000; *b* 10 Jan. 1940; *d* of John Jonas Nicholls and Louise Nicholls; *m* 1965, John Strachan; one *s* one *d*. *Educ:* Newland High Sch., Hull; Manchester Univ. (BA). Joined HM Customs and Excise, 1961; Dept of Economic Affairs, 1964; Home Office, 1966; Principal, HM Customs and Excise, 1966; Treasury, 1972; Asst Secretary, HM Customs and Excise, 1974, Comr, 1980; Head, Joint Management Unit, HM Treasury/Cabinet Office, 1985–87; a Dep. Chm., Bd of Customs and Excise, 1987–93. External Mem., H of L Audit Cttee, 2002–08. Mem. Panel, Rosemary Nelson Inquiry, 2005–11; Mem., Judicial Appts Commn, 2012–. Chm., Communications and Public Service (formerly CS, PO and BT) Lifeboat Fund, 1998–2004; Dep. Chair, Community Fund (formerly Nat. Lottery Charities Bd), 2000–04; Vice Chm., Big Lottery Fund, 2004–06. Pres., British Internat. Freight Assoc., 2002–04. Chairman: Govs, James Allen's Girls' Sch., 2004–09; Council, Univ. of Southampton, 2006–12. CCMI. Hon. LLD: Manchester, 1995; Southampton, 2013.

STRACHEY, family name of **Baron O'Hagan**.

STRACHEY, Sir Henry Leofric Benvenuto, 7th Bt *cr* 1801, of Sutton Court, Somerset; *b* 17 April 1947; *o s* of John Ralph Severs Strachey and Rosemary Strachey (*née* Mavor); *S* kinsman (Charles Strachey, who did not use the title) 2014, but his name does not yet appear on the Official Roll of the Baronetage; *m* 1st, 1971, Julie Margaret Hutchens (marr. diss. 1982); 2nd, 1983, Susan Christine Skinner. *Heir:* none.

STRADBROKE, 6th Earl of, *cr* 1821; **Robert Keith Rous;** Bt 1660; Baron Rous 1796; Viscount Dunwich 1821; grazier, Mount Fyans Station, Darlington, Victoria; *b* 25 March 1937; *s* of 5th Earl of Stradbroke and Pamela Catherine Mabell (*d* 1972), *d* of Captain Hon. Edward James Kay-Shuttleworth; *S* father, 1983, but does not use the title; *m* 1960, Dawn Antoinette (marr. diss. 1977), *d* of Thomas Edward Beverley, Brisbane; two *s* five *d*; 2nd, 1977, Roseanna Mary Blanche, *d* of late Francis Reitman, MD; six *s* two *d*. *Educ:* Harrow. *Recreation:* making babies. *Heir:* *s* Viscount Dunwich, *qv*. *Address:* Box 383, Richmond, Vic 3121, Australia. *T:* (4) 27901294, *Fax:* (3) 98152668.

STRADLING, Donald George; Group Personnel Director, John Laing & Son Ltd, then John Laing plc, 1969–89; Director, Quantum Care, 2000–04; *b* 7 Sept. 1929; *s* of George Frederic and Olive Emily Stradling; *m* 1st, 1955, Mary Anne Hartridge (*d* 2000); two *d*; 2nd, 2004, Elizabeth Lilian Jane Dennis (*née* Hewitt). *Educ:* Clifton Coll.; Magdalen Coll., Oxford (Open Exhibnr; MA). CIPM. School Master, St Albans Sch., 1954–55; Group Trng and Educn Officer, John Laing & Son Ltd, Building and Civil Engrg Contractors, 1955. Vis. Prof., Univ. of Salford, 1989–94. Comr, Manpower Services Commn, 1980–82; Mem. Council, Inst. of Manpower Studies, 1975–81; Member: Employment Policy Cttee, CBI, 1978–84, 1986–91; Council, CBI, 1982–86; FCEC Wages and Industrial Cttee, 1978–95; Council, FCEC, 1985–95; National Steering Gp, New Technical and Vocational Educn Initiative, 1983–88; NHS Trng Authy, 1985–89. Director: Building and Civil Engrg Benefits Scheme (Trustee, 1984–2004); Building and Civil Engrg Holidays Scheme Management, 1984–2004; Construction ITB, 1985–90. Vice-Pres., Inst. of Personnel Management, 1974–76. Vice-Chm. of Governors, St Albans High Sch., 1977–95; Mem. Council, Tyndale House, 1977–96. Liveryman, Glaziers' and Painters of Glass Co., 1983–95, 2003–. Hon. PhD Internat. Management Centre, Buckingham, 1987; Hon. DSc Salford, 1995. *Publications:* contribs on music and musical instruments, et al. to New Bible Dictionary, 1962. *Recreations:* listening to music (espec. opera), walking. *Address:* Courts Edge, 12 The Warren, Harpenden, Herts AL5 2NH.

STRAFFORD, 8th Earl of, *cr* 1847; **Thomas Edmund Byng;** Baron Strafford, 1835; Viscount Enfield, 1847; nurseryman, riverkeeper and artist's companion; *b* 26 Sept. 1936; *s* of 7th Earl of Strafford, and Maria Magdalena Elizabeth, *d* of late Henry Cloete, CMG, Alphen, S Africa; *S* father, 1984; *m* 1963, Jennifer Mary (marr. diss. 1981), *er d* of late Rt Hon. W. M. May, FCA, PC, MP, and of Mrs May, Mertoun Hall, Holywood, Co. Down; two *s* two *d*; 2nd, 1981, Mrs Julia Mary Howard, (Judy), *d* of Sir Dennis Pilcher, CBE. *Educ:* Eton; Clare Coll., Cambridge. Lieut, Royal Sussex Regt (National Service). Councillor, Winchester and District, 1983–87. *Recreations:* gardening, travelling. *Heir:* *s* Viscount Enfield, *qv*. *Address:* Apple Tree Cottage, Easton, Winchester, Hants SO21 1EF. *T:* (01962) 779467.

See also Hon. J. E. Byng.

STRAKER, Anita, CB 2001; OBE 1990; *b* 22 June 1938; *d* of David William Barham and Laura Barham; *m* 1961, Patrick Vincent Straker; four *s*. *Educ:* Weston-super-Mare Grammar Sch. for Girls; University Coll. London (BSc Hons); Royal Holloway Coll., Univ. of London (MSc); Univ. of Cambridge Inst. of Educn (PGCE). Teacher, 1961–62 and 1968–74; Inspector for maths, Surrey LEA, 1974–78; Gen. Advr, Wilts LEA, 1978–83; Dir, Microelectronics Educn Prog. Primary Project, DES, 1983–86; Dist Inspector, ILEA, 1986–89; Principal Advr, Berks LEA, 1989–93; Dep. Dir of Educn, Camden LEA, 1993–96; Dir, Nat. Numeracy Strategy, DFE, then DfEE, 1996–2000; Dir, Key Stage 3 Nat. Strategy, DfEE, then DfES, 2000–02. Hon. LLD UEA, 2002. *Publications:* Mathematics for Gifted Pupils, 1980; Children Using Computers, 1988; Mathematics from China, 1990; Primary Maths Extension Activities, 1991; Talking Points in Mathematics, 1993; Mental Maths (series), 1994; Home Maths (series), 1998; Exploring Maths (series), 2008. *Recreations:* holidays abroad, cooking, reading, swimming. *Address:* Mundays, St Mary Bourne, Andover, Hants SP11 6AY. *T:* (01264) 738474.

STRAKER, Timothy Derrick; QC 1996; a Recorder, since 2000; a Deputy High Court Judge, since 2010; acting Justice of Appeal, Court of Appeal of the Falklands, since 2011; *b* 25 May 1955; *s* of late Derrick Straker, solicitor, and Dorothy Elizabeth, *o d* of late Brig. T. L. Rogers, CBE; *m* 1982, Ann Horton Baylis (marr. diss. 2007); two *d*. *Educ:* Malvern Coll.; Downing Coll., Cambridge (BA 1st Cl. Hons Law, MA). Called to the Bar: Gray's Inn, 1977 (Holt Schol.), Bencher, 2004; Lincoln's Inn, *ad eundem*, 1979; NI, 2001; Trinidad and Tobago, 2001; in practice at the Bar, 1977–; an Asst Recorder, 1998–2000. Jt Hd of Chambers, 2002–12, 2013–. Election Comr for various petitions, 2007–; Advr to Home Sec. under Animals (Scientific Procedures) Act, 2011–. Member: Admin. Law Bar Assoc., 1986–; Local Govt, Planning and Envmtl Bar Assoc., 1986–; Crown Office Users' Cttee, 1993–2000; Administrative Court Users' Assoc., 2000–; Parly Bar Mess, 2011–. Gov. and Mem. Council, Malvern Coll., 2011–. Contrib. Ed., Civil Court Practice, 1999–2008. *Publications:* Annotated Current Law Statutes, 1994; (Consultant Ed.) Registration of Political Parties: a guide to Returning Officers, 1999; (with Iain Goldrein) Human Rights and Judicial Review: case studies in context, 2000; Information Rights, 2004; Electoral Administration Act, 2006; contrib. Halsbury's Laws of England (Public Health and Environmental Protection, 2000; Local Government, 2001; Markets, 2002); contrib. Rights of Way Law Review, Judicial Review. *Recreations:* theatre, history, rackets (with Steve Tulley, finalists, Winchester Invitation Doubles, 2011 and 2013, winners, Tonbridge Tournament, 2013, finalists, 2014). *Address:* 4–5 Gray's Inn Square, Gray's Inn, WC1R 5AH. *T:* (020) 7404 5252. *Clubs:* Lansdowne, Oxford and Cambridge; Manchester Tennis and Racquet; St Paul's Rackets.

STRAND, Prof. Kenneth T.; Professor, Department of Economics, Simon Fraser University, 1968–86, now Emeritus; *b* Yakima, Wash, 30 June 1931; Canadian citizen since 1974; *m* 1960, Elna K. Tomaske; no *c*. *Educ:* Washington State Coll. (BA); Univ. of Wisconsin (PhD, MS). Woodrow Wilson Fellow, 1955–56; Ford Foundn Fellow, 1957–58; Herfurth Award, Univ. of Wisconsin, 1961 (for PhD thesis). Asst Exec. Sec., Hanford Contractors Negotiation Cttee, Richland, Wash, 1953–55; Asst Prof., Washington State Univ., 1959–60; Asst Prof., Oberlin Coll., 1960–65 (on leave, 1963–65); Economist, Manpower and Social Affairs Div., OECD, Paris, 1964–66; Assoc. Prof., Dept of Econs, Simon Fraser Univ., 1966–68; Pres., Simon Fraser Univ., 1969–74 (Acting Pres., 1968–69). Mem., Canadian Industrial Relations Assoc. (Pres., 1983). Hon. LLD Simon Fraser Univ., 1983. FRSA 1972. *Publications:* Jurisdictional Disputes in Construction: The Causes, The Joint Board and the NLRB, 1961; contribs to Review of Econs and Statistics, Amer. Econ. Review, Industrial Relations, Sociaal Mannblad Arbeid. *Recreations:* fishing, ski-ing. *Address:* PO Box 5009, Lac Le Jeune, BC V1S 1Y8, Canada.

STRANG, David James Reid, QPM 2002; Chief Inspector of Prisons for Scotland, since 2013; *b* Glasgow, 9 April 1958; *s* of William Guthrie Strang and Morag Langlands Strang; *m* 1981, Alison; one *s* two *d*. *Educ:* Glasgow Acad.; Loretto Sch.; Univ. of Durham (BSc 1980); Birkbeck Coll., London (MSc 1989). Metropolitan Police, 1980–98; Asst Chief Constable, Lothian and Borders Police, 1998–2001; Chief Constable: Dumfries and Galloway Constabulary, 2001–07; Lothian and Borders Police, 2007–13. *Address:* HM Prisons Inspectorate, Saughton House, Broomhouse Drive, Edinburgh EH11 3XD.

STRANG, Rt Hon. Gavin (Steel); PC 1997; *b* 10 July 1943; *s* of James Steel Strang and Marie Strang (*née* Finkle); *m*. *Educ:* Univs of Edinburgh and Cambridge. BSc Hons Edinburgh, 1964; DipAgricSci Cambridge, 1965; PhD Edinburgh, 1968. Mem., Tayside Econ. Planning Consultative Group, 1966–68; Scientist with ARC, 1968–70. MP (Lab) Edinburgh E, 1970–97 and 2005–10, Edinburgh E and Musselburgh, 1997–2005. Opposition front bench spokesman on Scottish affairs, 1972–73, on energy, 1973–74; Parly Under-Sec. of State, Dept of Energy, March–Oct. 1974; Parly Sec., MAFF, 1974–79; Opposition front bench spokesman on agriculture, 1979–82, on employment, 1987–89, on food, agriculture and rural affairs, 1992–97; Mem., Shadow Cabinet, 1994–97; Minister for Transport, 1997–98. Chm., PLP Defence Group, 1984–87. *Publications:* articles in Animal Production. *Recreations:* golf, swimming, watching football. *E:* gavin.s.strang@gmail.com.

STRANG, Prof. John Stanley, MD; FRCPsych; FRCP; Professor of the Addictions, Institute of Psychiatry and Director, National Addiction Centre, since 1995, and Head, Addictions Department, since 2009, King's College, London; Director, Addictions Clinical Academic Group, King's Health Partners, since 2010; *b* 12 May 1950; *s* of late William John Strang, CBE, FRS, and of Margaret Nicholas Strang (*née* Howells); *m* 1984, Jennifer Abbey; two *s* (one *d* decd). *Educ:* Bryanston Sch., Dorset; Guy's Hosp. Med. Sch. (MB BS 1973; MD 1995). FRCPsych 1994; FRCP 2006. Consultant psychiatrist in drug dependence: Manchester, 1982–86; Maudsley Hosp., London, 1986–; Getty Sen. Lectr in the Addictions, Nat. Addiction Centre, Inst. of Psychiatry, 1991–95. Consultant Advr (drugs), DoH, 1986–2003. Mem., Adv. Council on Misuse of Drugs, 1989–2001. Hon. FAChAM 2005. *Publications:* (with G. Stimson) AIDS and Drug Misuse: the challenge for policy and practice in the 1990s, 1990; (jtly) Drugs, Alcohol and Tobacco: making the science and policy connections, 1993; (with M. Gossop) Heroin Addiction and Drug Policy: the British system, 1994; (with J. Sheridan) Drug Misuse and Community Pharmacy, 2002; (with G. Tober) Methadone Matters, 2003; (with M. Gossop) Heroin Addiction and the British System, 2 vols, 2005; (with T. Babor *et al*) Drug Policy and the Public Good, 2010; (with P. Miller *et al*) Addiction Research Methods, 2010; (jtly) New Heroin-Assisted Treatment: recent evidence and current practices of supervised injectable heroin treatment in Europe and beyond, 2012. *Address:* National Addiction Centre, Addiction Sciences Building, 4 Windsor Walk, SE5 8AF. *T:* (020) 7848 0438. *Club:* Athenæum.

STRANG STEEL, Major Sir (Fiennes) Michael, 3rd Bt *cr* 1938, of Philiphaugh, Selkirk; CBE 1999; Vice Lord-Lieutenant, Borders Region (Roxburgh, Ettrick and Lauderdale), since 2008; *b* 22 Feb. 1943; *s* of Sir (Fiennes) William Strang Steel, 2nd Bt and Joan Strang Steel (*d* 1982), *d* of Brig.-Gen. Sir Brodie Haldane Henderson, KCMG, CB; *S* father, 1992; *m* 1977, Sarah Jane Russell; two *s* one *d*. *Educ:* Eton. Major, 17/21 Lancers, 1962–80, retd. Forestry Comr, 1988–99. Lieut, Royal Co. of Archers, Queen's Body Guard for Scotland, 2010– (Ensign, 2007–10). DL Borders Region (Districts of Roxburgh, Ettrick & Lauderdale), 1990. *Heir:* *s* (Fiennes) Edward Strang Steel, *b* 8 Nov. 1978. *Address:* Philiphaugh, Selkirk TD7 5LX. *Club:* Cavalry and Guards.

STRANGE, 17th Baron *cr* 1628; **Adam Humphrey Drummond;** *b* 20 April 1953; *s* of Captain Humphrey ap Evans, MC, who assumed name of Drummond of Megginch by decree of Lord Lyon, 1965, and Baroness Strange (16th in line); *S* mother, 2005; *m* 1988, Hon. Mary Emma Jeronima Dewar, *d* of Baron Forteviot, *qv*; one *s* one *d*. *Educ:* Eton; RMA Sandhurst; Heriot-Watt Univ. (MSc (Housing)). MCIH 2007. Major, Grenadier Guards, retd. Farmer. Mem., Queen's Body Guard for Scotland (Royal Co. of Archers). *Heir:* *s* Hon. John Adam Humphrey Drummond, *b* 3 Nov. 1992. *Club:* Perth.

STRANGE, Rt Rev. Mark Jeremy; *see* Moray, Ross and Caithness, Bishop of.

STRANGWAYS; *see* Fox-Strangways, family name of Earl of Ilchester.

STRANRAER-MULL, Very Rev. Gerald; Dean of Aberdeen and Orkney, 1988–2008, now Emeritus; Rector of Ellon and Cruden Bay, 1972–2008; *b* 24 Nov. 1942; *s* of Gerald and Lena Stranraer-Mull; *m* 1967, Glynis Mary Kempe (*d* 2015); one *s* one *d* (and one *s* decd). *Educ:* Woodhouse Grove School, Apperley Bridge; King's College, London (AKC 1969); Saint Augustine's College, Canterbury. Journalist, 1960–66. Curate: Hexham Abbey, 1970–72; Corbridge, 1972; Priest-in-Charge of St Peter's, Peterhead, 2001–04. Editor of Aberdeen and Buchan Churchman, 1976–84, 1991–94; Director of Training for Ministry, Diocese of Aberdeen and Orkney, 1982–90; Canon of Saint Andrew's Cathedral, Aberdeen, 1981–2008. Dir of Ordinands, Dio. of Moray, Ross and Caithness, 2014–. Director: Oil Chaplaincy Trust, 1993–2008; Duncraig, Iona (formerly Iona Cornerstone Foundn), 1995–2009. Warden, Soc. of Our Lady of the Isles, Isle of Fetlar, Shetland, 2006–. Hon. Priest-in-Charge, St Paul's, Strathnairn, 2009–12; Hon. Priest, St Michael and All Angels, Inverness, 2011–14. FSAScot 2011. *Publications:* A Turbulent House: the Augustinians at Hexham, 1970; View of the Diocese, 1977; A Church for Scotland: the story of the Scottish Episcopal Church, 2000, 3rd edn 2012; Steps on the Way: the history of the Scottish Episcopal Church 1513–2013, 2013. *Address:* 75 The Cairns, Muir of Ord, Ross-shire IV6 7AT. *T:* (01463) 870986.

STRASBURGER, Baron *cr* 2011 (Life Peer), of Langridge in the County of Somerset; **Paul Cline Strasburger;** businessman and philanthropist; *b* 31 July 1946. *Address:* House of Lords, SW1A 0PW.

STRATFORD, Ian Dodd; Managing Director, Bodis Associates, since 2009; *b* 26 June 1954; *s* of John and Elsie Stratford; *m* 1994, Debra Jean Wolstenholme; one *s* one *d*. *Educ:* Univ. of Salford (BSc Hons Geog. 1977); Newcastle Business Sch., Northumbria Univ. (Postgrad. Cert. in Coaching 2010). MCIH 1982. Area Housing Manager, Middlesbrough, 1983–88; Dep. Dir, 1987–90, Dir, 1990–97, of Housing, Enfield LBC; Exec. Dir, Personal Services, 1997–2000, Dep. Chief Exec., 2000–02, Thurrock Council; Chief Exec., Newcastle CC, 2002–08. Chm., London Business Innovation Centre, 1995–97; Clerk, Tyne and Wear PTA, 2002–08; non-exec. Dir, Nexus Transport Exec., 2002–08; Director: NewcastleGateshead Initiative, 2002–08; Tyne and Wear Develt Co., 2002–08; My Life Plus CIC, 2013–. Company Sec., Newcastle Th. Royal, 2002–08; Member of Board: Newcastle Science City, 2005–08; NewcastleGateshead City Develt Co., 2008; Lay Mem., Court, Univ. of Newcastle upon Tyne, 2005–10. *Recreations:* live music, sailing, walking in Northumberland, Tyne Rowing Club, volunteer fundraiser. *E:* ianstratford@talktalk.net.

STRATFORD, Jemima Lucy; QC 2010; *b* London, 23 July 1968. *Educ:* S Hampstead High Sch.; New Coll., Oxford (BA Modern Hist.); City Univ. (Dip. Law). Called to the Bar, Middle Temple, 1993; tenant at Brick Court Chambers, specialising in EU, public law and human rights, 1995–. *Address:* Brick Court Chambers, 7–8 Essex Street, WC2R 3LD.

STRATFORD, Neil Martin; Keeper of Medieval and Later Antiquities, 1975–98, Keeper Emeritus, 1998–2001, British Museum; *b* 26 April 1938; *s* of late Dr Martin Gould Stratford and Dr Mavis Stratford (*née* Beddall); *m* 1966, Anita Jennifer Lewis; two *d*. *Educ:* Marlborough Coll.; Magdalene Coll., Cambridge (BA Hons English 1961, MA); Courtauld Inst., London Univ. (BA Hons History of Art 1966). 2nd Lieut Coldstream Guards, 1956–58; Trainee Kleinwort, Benson, Lonsdale Ltd, 1961–63; Lecturer, Westfield Coll., London Univ., 1969–75; Prof. of Hist. of Medieval Art, Ecole Nationale des Chartes, Paris, 2000–03. British Academy/Leverhulme Sen. Res. Fellow, 1991; Mem., Inst. for Advanced Study, Princeton, 1998–99; Appleton Vis. Prof., Florida State Univ., 2000; Vis. Sen. Lecturing Fellow, Duke Univ., 2006. Chm., St Albans Cathedral Fabric Cttee, 1995–; Member: Conseil Scientifique, Société Française d'Archéologie, 1994– (Gold Medal, 2011); Comité d'orientation scientifique et culturelle, Centre des monuments nationaux, 2011–; Pres., Comité scientifique pour la restauration et mise en valeur de l'ancienne abbaye de Cluny, 2005–. Liveryman, Haberdashers' Co., 1959–. Hon. Mem., Académie de Dijon, 1975; For. Mem., Société Nationale des Antiquaires de France, 1985; Associate Mem., Acad. des Inscriptions et Belles-Lettres, 2012 (For. Corresp. Mem., 2002). FSA 1976. Comdr, Ordre des Arts et des Lettres (France), 2013 (Officier, 2006). *Publications:* La Sculpture Oubliée de Vézelay, 1984; Catalogue of Medieval Enamels in the British Museum, vol. II, Northern Romanesque Enamel, 1993; Westminster Kings and the medieval Palace of Westminster, 1995; The Lewis Chessmen and the enigma of the hoard, 1997; Studies in Burgundian Romanesque Sculpture, 1998; La Frise romane monumental de Souvigny, 2002; Chronos et Cosmos: le pilier roman de Souvigny, 2005; (ed and principal contrib.) Cluny 910–2010: onze siècles de rayonnement, 2010; (ed and principal contrib.) Corpus de la sculpture de Cluny: les parties orientales de la Grande Eglise Cluny III, 2011; articles in French and English periodicals. *Recreations:* opera, food and wine, cricket and football. *Address:* 17 Church Row, NW3 6UP. *T:* (020) 7794 5688. *Clubs:* Beefsteak, Garrick, MCC, I Zingari; University Pitt, Hawks (Cambridge).

STRATFORD, Ven. Dr Timothy Richard; Archdeacon of Leicester, since 2012; *b* Liverpool, 26 Feb. 1961; *s* of George Alexander Stratford and Vera June Stratford; *m* 1986, Jennifer Anne Stanley; three *s*. *Educ:* Knowsley Hey Comprehensive; Univ. of York (BSc Hons 1982); Wycliffe Hall, Oxford (CTh); Sheffield Univ. (PhD 2008). Ordained deacon, 1986, priest, 1987; Assistant Curate: Mossley Hill Parish Church, 1986–89; St Helens Parish Church, 1989–91; Chaplain to Bishop of Liverpool, 1991–94; Vicar, Good Shepherd, W Derby, 1994–2003; Team Rector, Kirkby, 2003–12. *Publications:* Interactive Preaching, 1998; Liturgy and Technology, 1999; Liturgy and Urban Mission, 2002; Using Common Worship: a service of the word, 2002; Worship Window of the Urban Church, 2006. *Recreations:* photography, mountain biking, music. *Address:* St Martin's House, 7 Peacock Lane, Leicester LE1 5PZ. *T:* (0116) 261 5309. *E:* tim.stratford@leccofe.org.

STRATHALLAN, Viscount; James David Drummond; Director, End of the Road Festival Ltd, since 2014; *b* 24 Oct. 1965; *s* and *heir* of Earl of Perth, *qv*.

STRATHALMOND, 3rd Baron *cr* 1955; **William Roberton Fraser,** CA; Finance Director, Gerling at Lloyd's (formerly Owen & Wilby Underwriting Agency) Ltd, 1995–2000; *b* 22 July 1947; *s* of 2nd Baron Strathalmond, CMG, OBE, TD, and of Letitia, *d* of late Walter Krementz, New Jersey, USA; *S* father, 1976; *m* 1973, Amanda Rose, *yr d* of Rev. Gordon Clifford Taylor; two *s* one *d*. *Educ:* Loretto. Man. Dir, London Wall Members Agency Ltd, 1986–91 (Dir, 1985–91); Dir, London Wall Hldgs plc, 1986–91; Chm., R. W. Sturge Ltd, 1991–94. Dir, N Atlantic Salmon Fund (UK), 2003–08. Pres., RSAS AgeCare, 2008– (Chm. Trustees, 1984–2001; Vice-Pres., 2001–08); Trustee, Medusa Trust, 2013–. Liveryman, Girdlers' Co., 1979– (Master, 2010–11). *Heir:* *s* Hon. William Gordon Fraser [*b* 24 Sept. 1976; *m* 2011, Charlotte, *d* of Dr Ralph Stephenson; one *s* one *d*]. *Address:* Holt House, Elstead, Surrey GU8 6LF.

STRATHAVON, Lord; Cosmo Alistair Gordon; *b* 27 July 2009; *s* and *heir* of Earl of Aboyne, *qv*.

STRATHCARRON, 3rd Baron *cr* 1936; **Ian David Patrick Macpherson;** Bt 1933; Senior Partner, Unicorn Publishing Group LLP, since 2010; Partner, Art Resolve LLP, since 2012; *b* 31 March 1949; *er s* of 2nd Baron Strathcarron and Diana Hawtrey Curle (*née* Deane); *S* father, 2006; *m* 1974, Gillian Rosamund Allison; one *s* one *d*. *Educ:* Hill House Sch.; Horris Hill; Eton; Hollingbourne Manor; Grenoble Univ. Proprietor and Ed., Japan Europa Press Agency, 1970–2005; Partner, Strathcarron & Co., 1974. Trustee, Nat. Motor Museum, Beaulieu. *Publications:* Invisibilty, 2004; Black Beach, 2007; Joy Unconfined! Lord Byron's Grand Tour Re-toured, 2010; Innocence & War, Mark Twain's Holy Land Tour Re-toured, 2011; Living with Life, 2012; The Indian Equator: Mark Twain's India revisited, 2013. *Heir:* *s* Hon. Rory David Alasdair Macpherson, *b* 15 April 1982. *W:* www.istrath.com.

STRATHCLYDE, 2nd Baron *cr* 1955, of Barskimming; **Thomas Galloway Dunlop du Roy de Blicquy Galbraith,** CH 2013; PC 1995; Leader of the House of Lords and Chancellor of the Duchy of Lancaster, 2010–13; *b* 22 Feb. 1960; *s* of Hon. Sir Thomas Galloway Dunlop Galbraith, KBE, MP (*d* 1982) (*e s* of 1st Baron) and Simone Clothilde Fernande Marie Ghislaine (*d* 1991), *e d* of late Jean du Roy de Blicquy; *S* grandfather, 1985; *m* 1992, Jane, *er d* of John Skinner; three *d*. *Educ:* Wellington College; Univ. of East Anglia (BA 1982); Université d'Aix-en-Provence. Insurance Broker, Bain Dawes, subseq. Bain Clarkson Ltd, 1982–88. Contested (C) Merseyside East, European Parly Election, 1984. Spokesman for DTI, Treasury and Scotland, H of L, 1988–89; Govt Whip, 1988–89; Parly Under-Sec. of State, Dept of Employment, 1989–90, DoE, 1990, 1992–93, Scottish Office (Minister for Agric. and Fisheries), 1990–92, DTI, 1993–94; Minister of State, DTI, 1994; Captain of the Hon. Corps of Gentlemen at Arms (Govt Chief Whip in H of L), 1994–97; Opposition Chief Whip, House of Lords, 1997–98; elected Mem., H of L, 1999; Leader of the Opposition, H of L, 1998–2010. Director: Trafalgar Capital Management Ltd, 2001–10 (Chm., 2001–10); Scottish Mortgage Investment Trust plc, 2004–10; Galena Asset Management Ltd, 2004–10; Marketform Group Ltd, 2004–10; Hampden Agencies Ltd, 2008–10; non-exec. Dir, Trafigura, 2013–. Gov., Wellington Coll., 2010–. *Heir: b* Hon. Charles William du Roy de Blicquy Galbraith [*b* 20 May 1962; *m* 1992, Bridget, *d* of Brian Reeve; three *s* one *d*]. *Address:* House of Lords, SW1A 0PW. *T:* (020) 7219 5353.

STRATHCONA AND MOUNT ROYAL, 4th Baron *cr* 1900; **Donald Euan Palmer Howard;** *b* 26 Nov. 1923; *s* of 3rd Baron Strathcona and Mount Royal and Diana Evelyn (*d* 1985), twin *d* of 1st Baron Wakehurst; *S* father, 1959; *m* 1st, 1954, Lady Jane Mary Waldegrave (marr. diss. 1977), 2nd *d* of 12th Earl Waldegrave, KG, GCVO; two *s* four *d* (incl. twin *s* and *d*); 2nd, 1978, Patricia (*née* Thomas), *widow* of John Middleton. *Educ:* King's Mead, Seaford; Eton; Trinity Coll., Cambridge; McGill University, Montreal (1947–50). Served War of 1939–45: RN, 1942–47: Midshipman, RNVR, 1943; Lieutenant, 1945. With Urwick, Orr and Partners (Industrial Consultants), 1950–56. Lord in Waiting (Govt Whip), 1973–74; Parly Under-Sec. of State for Defence (RAF), MoD, 1974; Jt Dep. Leader of the Opposition, House of Lords, 1976–79; Minister of State, MoD, 1979–81. Dir, Computing Devices, Hastings, 1981–92. Chm., Maritime Foundn, 1950–2012. Chairman, Bath Festival Society, 1966–70. Dep. Chm., SS Great Britain Project, 1970–73; Founder Chm., Coastal Forces Heritage Trust, 1995–; President: Falkland Is Trust, 1982; Steamboat Assoc. of GB, 1972–; Pilots' Assoc., 1959–80; Mem. Council, RN Mus., 1982–95. Prime Warden, Fishermen's Co., 1965. *Recreations:* gardening, sailing. *Heir: s* Hon. Donald Alexander Smith Howard [*b* 24 June 1961; *m* 1992, Jane Maree, *d* of Shaun Gibb; one *s* one *d*]. *Address:* Millers Cottage, Isle of Colonsay, Argyll PA61 7YR. *T:* (01951) 200301. *Clubs:* Brooks's, Pratt's.

STRATHEDEN, 7th Baron *cr* 1836, **AND CAMPBELL,** 7th Baron *cr* 1841; **David Anthony Campbell;** *b* 13 Feb. 1963; *o s* of 6th Baron Stratheden and Campbell and Hilary Ann Holland (*née* Turner); *S* father, 2011; *m* 1993, Jennifer Margaret Owens; two *d*. *Educ:* Qld, Australia. *Heir:* none. *Address:* 71 Magpie Lane, Cooroy, Qld 4563, Australia.

STRATHERN, Prof. Andrew Jamieson, PhD; Andrew Mellon Professor of Anthropology, University of Pittsburgh, since 1987; Emeritus Professor of Anthropology, University of London; Hon. Research Fellow, Institute of Papua New Guinea Studies, Port Moresby, since 1977 (Director, 1981–86); *b* 19 Jan. 1939; *s* of Robert Strathern and Mary Strathern (*née* Sharp); *m* 1963, Ann Marilyn Evans (marr. diss. 1986); two *s* one *d*; *m* 1997, Pamela J. Stewart. *Educ:* Colchester Royal Grammar Sch.; Trinity Coll., Cambridge (BA, PhD). Research Fellow, Trinity Coll., Cambridge, 1965–68; Research Fellow, then Fellow, Australian National Univ., 1969–72; Professor, later Vis. Professor, Dept of Anthropology and Sociology, Univ. of Papua New Guinea, 1973–77; Prof. of Anthropology and Hd of Dept of Anthropology, UCL, 1976–83. Hon. Mem., Phi Beta Kappa, 1993. Rivers Memorial Medal, RAI, 1976. 10th Independence Anniv. Medal (PNG), 1987. *Publications:* The Rope of Moka, 1971; One Father, One Blood, 1972; (with M. Strathern) Self-decoration in Mount Hagen, 1972; Melpa Amb Kenan, 1974; Myths and Legends from Mt Hagen, 1977; Beneath the Andaiya Tree, 1977; Ongka, 1979; (with Malcolm Kirk) Man as Art, 1981; Inequality in New Guinea Highlands Societies, 1982; Wiru Laa, 1983; A line of power, 1984; (ed jtly) Strauss, The Mi Culture of the Mount Hagen People, 1990; (with P. Birnbaum) Faces of Papua New Guinea, 1991; Landmarks: reflections on anthropology, 1993; Voices of Conflict, 1993; Ru, 1993; Body Thoughts, 1996; (ed jtly) Millennial Markers, 1997; (ed jtly) Bodies and Persons, 1998; (ed jtly) Identity Work, 2000; (jtly) Oceania: an introduction to the cultures and identities of Pacific Islanders, 2002; with P. J. Stewart: A Death to Pay For: individual voices, 1998; Curing and Healing, 1999; Collaborations and Conflicts: a leader through time, 1999; Arrow Talk, 2000; The Python's Back: pathways of comparison between Indonesia and Melanesia, 2000; Minorities and Memories: survivals and extinctions in Scotland and western Europe, 2001; Humors and Substances: ideas of the body in New Guinea, 2001; Gender, Song and Sensibility: folktales and folksongs in the Highlands New Guinea, 2002; Remaking the World: myth, mining and ritual change among the Duna of Papua New Guinea, 2002; Violence: theory and ethnography, 2002; (ed) Landscape, Memory and History, 2003; Witchcraft, Sorcery, Rumors and Gossip, 2004; Empowering the Past, Confronting the Future, 2004; (ed) Terror and Violence: imagination and the unimaginable, 2006; (ed) Asian Ritual Systems: syncretisms and ruptures, 2007; (ed) Exchange and Sacrifice, 2008; (ed) Religious and Ritual Change, 2009 (Chinese edn 2010); (ed) Ritual, 2010; Kinship in Action: self and group, 2011; Peace-making and the Imagination: Papua New Guinea perspectives, 2011; articles in Man, Oceania, Ethnology, Jl Polyn Soc., Amer. Anthropology, Amer. Ethnology, Mankind, Bijdragen, Jl de la Soc. des Océanistes, Oral History, Bikmaus, Pacific Studies, Ethos, Jl of Ethnomusicology, Canberra Anthropology, Historische Anthropologie, Aust. Jl of Anthropology, Ethnohistory. *Address:* Department of Anthropology, University of Pittsburgh, Pittsburgh, PA 15260, USA. *T:* (office) (412) 6487519.

STRATHERN, Dame (Ann) Marilyn, DBE 2001; FBA 1987; Mistress of Girton College, Cambridge, 1998–2009; William Wyse Professor of Social Anthropology, University of Cambridge, 1993–2008; *b* 6 March 1941; *d* of Eric Charles Evans and Joyce Florence Evans; *m* 1963, Andrew Jamieson Strathern, *qv* (marr. diss. 1986); twin *s* one *d*. *Educ:* Bromley High Sch. (GPDST); Girton Coll., Cambridge (MA, PhD). Asst Curator, Mus. of Ethnology, Cambridge, 1966–68; Res. Fellow, ANU, 1970–72 and 1974–75; Bye-Fellow, Sen. Res. Fellow, then Official Fellow, Girton Coll., 1976–83; Fellow and Lectr, Trinity Coll., Cambridge, 1984–85 (Hon. Fellow, 1999); Prof. and Hd of Dept of Social Anthropology, Manchester Univ., 1985–93; Professorial Fellow, Girton Coll., Cambridge, 1993–98 (Life Fellow, 2009). Sen. Res. Fellow, ANU, 1983–84; Vis. Prof., Univ. of California, Berkeley, 1984. Hon. Foreign Mem., Amer. Acad. Arts and Scis, 1996; Hon. Life Pres., Assoc. of Social Anthropologists, 2008. Hon. DSc (Soc Sci): Edinburgh, 1993; Copenhagen, 1994; Hon. DLitt: Oxford, 2004; St Andrews, 2013; Hon. DSc: Helsinki, 2006; Panteion, Athens, 2006; Durham, 2007; Hon. PhD Papua New Guinea, 2009; Hon. DSocSc: QUB 2009; Yale, 2010; Universidad del País Vasco, 2011; KCL, 2011. Rivers Meml Medal, 1976, Huxley Meml Medal, 2004, RAI; Viking Fund Medal, Wenner-Gren Foundn for Anthropol Res., NY, 2003; Leverhulme Medal, British Acad., 2012. *Publications:* Self-Decoration in Mt Hagen (jtly), 1971; Women In Between, 1972; (co-ed) Nature, Culture and Gender, 1980; Kinship at the Core: an anthropology of Elmdon, Essex, 1981; (ed) Dealing with Inequality, 1987; The Gender of the Gift, 1988; Partial Connections, 1991; (ed) Big Men and Great Men in Melanesia, 1991; After Nature, 1992; Reproducing the Future, 1992; (jtly) Technologies of Procreation, 1993; (ed) Shifting Contexts, 1995; Property, Substance and Effect, 1999; (ed) Audit Cultures, 2000; (ed) Transactions and Creations, 2004; Kinship, Law and the Unexpected, 2005. *Address:* c/o Girton College, Cambridge CB3 0JG.

STRATHMORE AND KINGHORNE, 18th Earl of, *cr* 1677 (Scot.); Earl (UK) *cr* 1937; **Michael Fergus Bowes Lyon;** DL; Lord Glamis, 1445; Earl of Kinghorne, Lord Lyon and Glamis, 1606; Viscount Lyon, Lord Glamis, Tannadyce, Sidlaw and Strathdichtie, 1677; Baron Bowes (UK), 1887; Captain, Scots Guards; *b* 7 June 1957; *s* of 17th Earl of Strathmore and Kinghorne and of Mary Pamela, DL, *d* of Brig. Norman Duncan McCorquodale, MC; *S* father, 1987; *m* 1984, Isobel (marr. diss. 2004), *yr d* of Capt. A. E. Weatherall, Cowhill, Dumfries; three *s*; *m* 2005, Dr Damaris Stuart-William (marr. diss. 2008); one *s*; *m* 2012, Karen Rose Baxter. *Educ:* Univ. of Aberdeen (BLE 1979). Page of Honour to HM Queen Elizabeth The Queen Mother, 1971–73; commissioned, Scots Guards, 1980. A Lord in Waiting (Govt Whip), 1989–91; Captain of the Yeomen of the Guard (Dep. Govt Chief Whip), 1991–94. Director: Polypipe PLC, 1994–99; Lancaster PLC, 1994–99. Pres., Boys' Brigade, 1994–99. DL Angus, 1993. *Heir: s* Lord Glamis, *qv*. *Address:* Glamis Castle, Forfar, Angus DD8 1QJ. *Clubs:* Turf, Pratt's, Mark's; Third Guards'; Perth (Perth).

STRATHNAVER, Lord; Alistair Charles St Clair Sutherland; Master of Sutherland; with Sutherland Estates, since 1978; Vice Lord-Lieutenant of Sutherland, since 1993; *b* 7 Jan. 1947; *e s* of Charles Noel Janson, and the Countess of Sutherland, *qv*; *heir* to mother's titles; *m* 1st, 1968, Eileen Elizabeth, *o d* of Richard Wheeler Baker, Jr, Princeton, NJ; two *d*; 2nd, 1980, Gillian, *er d* of Robert Murray, Gourock, Renfrewshire; one *s* one *d*. *Educ:* Eton; Christ Church, Oxford. BA. Metropolitan Police, 1969–74; with IBM UK Ltd, 1975–78. DL Sutherland, 1991. *Heir: s* Hon. Alexander Charles Robert Sutherland, *b* 1 Oct. 1981. *Address:* Sutherland Estates Office, Golspie, Sutherland KW10 6RP. *T:* (01408) 633268.

STRATHSPEY, 6th Baron *cr* 1884; **James Patrick Trevor Grant of Grant;** Bt (NS) 1625; Chief of Clan Grant; *b* 9 Sept. 1943; *s* of 5th Baron and his 1st wife, Alice, *oc* of late Francis Bowe; *S* father, 1992; *m* 1st, 1966, Linda (marr. diss. 1984), *d* of David Piggott; three *d*; 2nd, 1985, Margaret (marr. diss. 1993), *d* of Robert Drummond. *Heir:* half *b* Hon. Michael Patrick Francis Grant of Grant, *b* 22 April 1953.

STRATTON, Frances; Headteacher, and geology teacher, South Wilts Grammar School, 2003–11; *b* 21 Jan. 1952; *d* of Thomas and Mary Clift; *m* 1973, Brian Stratton (marr. diss. 2003); one *s*. *Educ:* St Catherine's Primary Sch.; Hollies Convent Grammar Sch.; University Coll. of Wales, Aberystwyth (BSc Hons Geol.; PGCE). Luton Sixth Form College: Teacher of Geol., 1974–98; Hd of Sci., 1990–92; Dir, then Asst Principal, 1992–98; Dep. Hd, 1998–2002, Actg Hd, 2002–03, Corfe Hills Sch., Dorset. Chief Examr for Geol. A Level, 2000–. FGS. *Publications:* Action Science, 1994; OCR AS and A2 Geology, 2008. *Recreations:* gardening, walking the Dorset Jurassic coast, geological holidays.

STRATTON, Sir Michael (Rudolf), Kt 2013; PhD; FRCPath, FMedSci; FRS 2008; Director, since 2010, and Head, Cancer Genome Project, since 2000, Wellcome Trust Sanger Institute (formerly Sanger Centre) (Deputy Director, 2006–10); Professor of Cancer Genetics, Institute of Cancer Research, since 1997; *b* 22 June 1957; *s* of Henry Stratton and Nita Stratton; *m* 1981, Dr Judith Breuer; one *s* one *d*. *Educ:* Brasenose Coll., Oxford (BA Physiol Scis); Guy's Hosp. Med. Sch., London (MB BS 1982); Inst. Cancer Res., London (PhD 1989). MRCPath 1991, FRCPath 2008. House and res. posts at Guy's Hosp., Beckenham Hosp., Inst. Psychiatry and Westminster Hosp., 1982–84; Registrar in Histopathol., RPMS, Hammersmith Hosp., 1984–86; MRC Trng Fellow, Inst. Cancer Res., 1986–89; Sen. Registrar, Dept Neuropathol., Inst. Psychiatry, 1989–91; Institute of Cancer Research: Team Leader, 1991–; Reader in Molecular Genetics of Cancer, 1996–97. Hon. Consultant, Royal Marsden Hosp., 1992–. FMedSci 1999. *Publications:* contrib. papers on genetic basis of cancer. *Address:* Wellcome Trust Sanger Institute, Genome Campus, Hinxton, Cambridge CB10 1SA.

STRAUSFELD, Prof. Nicholas James, PhD; FRS 2002; Regents Professor of Neurobiology, since 1987, MacArthur Fellow, since 1995, and Director, Center for Insect Science, since 2005, University of Arizona, Tucson (Guggenheim Fellow, 1994); *b* 22 Oct. 1942. *Educ:* University Coll. London (BSc 1965; PhD 1968). Scientist, Max Planck Inst. for Biol Cybernetics, Tübingen, Germany, 1970–75; Gp Leader, Neurobiol., EMBL, 1975–86. *Publications:* Atlas of an Insect Brain, 1976; (jtly) Neuroanatomical Techniques: insect nervous system, 1981; Functional Neuroanatomy, 1984; contrib. learned jls. *Address:* Division of Neurobiology, University of Arizona, Arizona Research Laboratories, 611 Gould-Simpson Building, Tucson, AZ 85721, USA.

STRAUSS, Nicholas Albert; QC 1984; a Recorder, since 2000; *b* 29 July 1942; *s* of late Walter Strauss and Ilse Strauss (*née* Leon); *m* 1972, Christine M. MacColl; two *d*. *Educ:* Highgate School; Jesus College, Cambridge (BA 1964; LLB 1965). Called to the Bar, Middle Temple, 1965 (Harmsworth Scholar); a Dep. High Court Judge, 1995–. *Address:* 1 Essex Court, Temple, EC4Y 9AR. *T:* (020) 7583 2000.

STRAUSS, Toby; Group Director, Insurance, Lloyds Banking Group, and Chief Executive, Scottish Widows, 2011–15; *b* London, 4 Oct. 1959; *m* 1995, Cressida; one *s* one *d*. *Educ:* St Paul's Sch., London; Loughborough Univ. (BTech Mech. Engrg). Account Manager, IBM, 1984–88; Founder, Psiax, 1988–92; Associate Partner, McKinsey & Co., 1993–99; Man. Dir, Charcol, 1999–2003; Chief Exec., John Scott & Partners, 2003–05; Chm., OrderWork, 2005–08; Chief Exec., Chief Operating Officer and Man. Dir, Aviva Life UK, 2008–11. Trustee, Macmillan Cancer Support, 2013–. *Recreations:* sailing, cycling.

STRAUSS-KAHN, Dominique Gaston André; Managing Director, International Monetary Fund, 2007–11; *b* 25 April 1949; *s* of Gilbert Strauss-Kahn and Jacqueline (*née* Fellus); *m* 1991, Anne Sinclair; four *c* from previous marriages. *Educ:* Lycée de Monaco; Lycée Carnot à Paris; Univ. de Paris X-Nanterre (DEconSc). Lectr, Univ. de Nancy II, 1977–80; Scientific Advr, l'Institut national de la statistique et des études économiques, 1978–80; Dir, Cerepi, CNRS, 1980–; Prof., Univ. de Paris X-Nanterre, 1981; Hd, Dept of Finance, Gen. Commn of the Nat. Plan, 1982–84, Asst Comr, 1984–86. Mem., Exec. Cttee, Socialist Party, 1983– (Nat. Sec., 1984–89). National Assembly, France: Deputy (Soc.) from Haute-Savoie, 1986–88, from Val-d'Oise, 1988–91, 2001–07; Pres., Commn of Finance, 1988–91; Minister: in Dept of Finance, 1991–92; for Industry and Foreign Trade, 1992–93; of the Econ. and of Finance, 1997–99. Mayor, 1995–97, Dep. Mayor, 1997–2001, Sarcelles. *Publications:* Economie de la famille et Accumulation patrimoniale, 1977; (jtly) La Richesse des Français, 1977; (jtly) L'Epargne et la Retraite, 1982. *Address:* BP26, 95203 Sarcelles, France.

STRAW, Alice Elizabeth, (Mrs J. W. Straw); *see* Perkins, A. E.

STRAW, Edward; writer; Chairman of Trustees, Demos, 2007–08; *b* Buckhurst Hill, Essex, 16 Jan. 1949; *s* of Walter Arthur Whitaker Straw and Joan Sylvia Straw; *m* 2008, Lindsey Colbourne; three *s* two *d* from previous marriages. *Educ:* Staples Rd Prim. Sch., Loughton; Brentwood Sch.; Univ. of Manchester (BSc Engrg 1971); Manchester Business Sch. (MBA 1973). Coopers & Lybrand, subseq. PricewaterhouseCoopers: Local Govt Consultant, 1982–88; Partner, Govt Services, and Dir of Quality, 1988–94; Hd, Entertainment and Media Consulting, EMEA, 1994–2002; Partner, Central Govt, 2002–08; Bd Dir, 1996–98; Global Bd Dir, 1997–2002. Chm., 1994–2000, Vice-Pres., 2000–, Relate. Founder Trustee, Family and Parenting Inst., 1999–2007; Trustee, Stroud Valley Arts, 2003–. Orgnl Architect, New Labour, 1992–95. FCMI. *Publications:* Relative Values, 1998; The Dead Generalist, 2004; Stand and Deliver: a design for successful government, 2014; numerous articles on relationships, public engagement, and media industries. *Recreations:* thinking, camping, entertaining with words, electronic music composition. *Address:* 17 Blue Lion Place, SE1 4PU. *W:* www.edstraw.com.

STRAW, Rt Hon. John Whitaker, (Rt Hon. Jack); PC 1997; *b* 3 Aug. 1946; *s* of Walter Arthur Whitaker Straw and Joan Sylvia Straw; *m* 1st, 1968, Anthea Lilian Weston (marr. diss. 1978); (one *d* decd); 2nd, 1978, Alice Elizabeth Perkins, *qv*; one *s* one *d*. *Educ:* Brentwood Sch., Essex; Univ. of Leeds (LLB 1967); Inns of Court Sch. of Law. Called to Bar, Inner Temple, 1972, Bencher, 1997. Political Advr to Sec. of State for Social Services, 1974–76; Special Advr to Sec. of State for Environment, 1976–77; on staff of Granada TV (World in Action), 1977–79. Pres., Leeds Univ. Union, 1967–68; Pres., Nat. Union of Students, 1969–71; Mem., Islington Borough Council, 1971–78; Dep. Leader, Inner London Educn Authority, 1973–74; Mem., Labour Party's Nat. Exec. Sub-Cttee on Educn and Science, 1970–82; Chm., Jt Adv. Cttee on Polytechnic of N London, 1973–75. Vice-Pres., Assoc. of District Councils, 1984–. Contested (Lab) Tonbridge and Malling, Feb. 1974. MP (Lab) Blackburn, 1979–2015. Opposition spokesman on the Treasury, 1980–83, on the environment, 1983–87; Principal Opposition Spokesman on educn, 1987–92, on the envmt (local govt), 1992–94, on home affairs, 1994–97; Sec. of State for the Home Office, 1997–2001; Sec. of State for Foreign and Commonwealth Affairs, 2001–06; Lord Privy Seal and Leader of H of C, 2006–07; Lord Chancellor and Sec. of State for Justice, 2007–10; Shadow Lord Chancellor and Sec. of State for Justice, 2010. Mem., Shadow Cabinet, 1987–97 and 2010. Mem., NEC, Labour Pty, 1994–95. Mem., Commn on Freedom of Information, 2015–. Vis. Fellow, Nuffield Coll., Oxford, 1990–98; Vis. Prof., UCL, 2011–. Member Council: Inst. for Fiscal Studies, 1983–96; Lancaster Univ., 1988–91; Governor: Blackburn Coll., 1990–; Pimlico Sch., 1994–2000 (Chm., 1995–98); Mem., Adv. Council, Oxford Centre for Islamic Studies, 2007–. Hon. Vice-Pres., Blackburn Rovers FC, 1998–. Fellow, Royal Statistical Soc., 1995. Hon. LLD: Leeds, 1999; Brunel, 2007. Order of the Republic Medal (Turkey), 2012. *Publications:* Granada Guildhall Lecture, 1969; University of Leeds Convocation Lecture, 1978; Policy and Ideology, 1993; Last Man Standing, 2012; Hamlyn Lectures, 2013; contrib. pamphlets, articles. *Recreations:* walking, cycling, cooking puddings, music.

See also E. Straw.

STREAMS, Peter John, CMG 1986; HM Diplomatic Service, retired; Ambassador to Sudan, 1991–94; *b* 8 March 1935; *s* of Horace Stanley Streams and Isabel Esther (*née* Ellaway); *m* 1956, Margareta Decker (*d* 2012); two *s* one *d*. *Educ:* Wallington County Grammar Sch. BoT, 1953; Bombay, 1960, Calcutta, 1962, Oslo, 1966; FCO, 1970; Mexico, 1973; FCO, 1977, Counsellor, 1979; Consul-Gen., Karachi, 1982; Counsellor, Stockholm, 1985; Ambassador to Honduras and concurrently to El Salvador, 1989. Head, EU Monitoring Mission to former Yugoslavia, 1998. *Address:* c/o Foreign and Commonwealth Office, SW1A 2AH.

STREATFEILD-JAMES, David Stewart; QC 2001; a Recorder, since 2010; *b* 22 Oct. 1963; *e s* of Capt. John Jocelyn Streatfeild-James, *qv*; *m* 1991, Alison; two *s* two *d*. *Educ:* Charterhouse; University Coll., Oxford. Called to the Bar, Inner Temple, 1986. *Recreations:* family, sport, gardening, cookery. *Address:* The Manor, Queen Charlton, Bristol BS31 2SH. *T:* (0117) 986 2025.

STREATFEILD-JAMES, Captain John Jocelyn; RN retired; *b* 14 April 1929; *s* of late Comdr Rev. Eric Cardew Streatfeild-James, OBE, and Elizabeth Ann (*née* Kirby); *m* 1962, Sally Madeline (*née* Stewart); three *s* (one *d* decd). *Educ:* RNC, Dartmouth. Specialist in Undersea Warfare. Naval Cadet, 1943–47; Midshipman, 1947–49; Sub-Lt, 1949–51; Lieutenant: Minesweeping, Diving and Anti-Bandit Ops, Far East Stn, 1951; Officer and Rating Trng, Home Stn, 1952–53; specialised in Undersea Warfare, 1954–55; Ship and Staff Duties, Far East Stn, 1955–57; Exchange Service, RAN, 1957–59; Lieutenant-Commander: instructed Officers specialising in Undersea Warfare, 1960–61; Sea Duty, Staff of Flag Officer Flotillas, Home Stn, 1962–63; Sen. Instr, Jt Anti-Submarine Sch., HMS Sea Eagle, 1964–65; Commander: Staff of C-in-C Western Fleet and C-in-C Eastern Atlantic Area, 1965–67; Jt Services Staff Coll., 1968; Staff of Comdr Allied Naval Forces, Southern Europe, Malta, 1968–71; HMS Dryad, 1971–73; Captain: Sen. Officers' War Course, RNC, Greenwich, 1974; Dir, OPCON Proj., 1974–77; HMS Howard (i/c), Head of British Defence Liaison Staff, Ottawa, and Defence Advr to British High Comr in Canada, 1978–80 (as Cdre); HMS Excellent (i/c), 1981–82; ADC to the Queen, 1982–83. *Recreations:* sailing, carpentry, painting. *Address:* South Lodge, Tower Road, Hindhead, Surrey GU26 6SP. *T:* (01428) 606064.

See also D. S. Streatfeild-James.

STREATOR, Edward (James); consultant; *b* 12 Dec. 1930; *s* of Edward J. and Ella S. Streator; *m* 1957, Priscilla Craig Kenney; one *s* two *d*. *Educ:* Princeton Univ. (AB). US Naval Reserve, served to Lieut (jg), 1952–56; entered Foreign Service, 1956; Third Sec., US Embassy, Addis Ababa, 1958–60; Second Sec., Lomé, 1960–62; Office of Intelligence and Research, Dept of State, 1962–64; Staff Asst to Sec. of State, 1964–66; First Sec., US Mission to NATO, 1966–69; Dep. Director, then Director, Office of NATO Affairs, Dept of State, 1969–75; Dep. US Permanent Representative to NATO, Brussels, 1975–77; Minister, US Embassy, London, 1977–84; US Ambassador to OECD, 1984–87. Mem., South Bank Bd, 1990–99. Member: Council, RUSI, 1988–92; Exec. Cttee, IISS, 1988–99; Bd, British Amer. Arts Assoc., 1989–99; Develt Cttee, Nat. Gallery, 1991–95; Adv. Bd, Fulbright Commn, 1995–2001; Chm., New Atlantic Initiative, 1996–98. President: American Chamber of Commerce (UK), 1989–94; European Council, American Chambers of Commerce, 1992–95. Mem., Bd of Overseers, Whitehead Sch. of Diplomacy and Internat. Relations, Seton Hall Univ., 2009–13. Mem. Exec. Cttee, The Pilgrims, 1984–2000; Governor: Ditchley Foundn, 1984–; ESU, 1989–95; President: Northcote Parkinson Fund, 2007–08 (Trustee, 2004–08); Train Foundation, 2008– (Trustee, 2008–). Hon. FRSA 1992. Benjamin Franklin Medal, RSA, 1992. *Recreation:* swimming. *Address:* 535 Park Avenue, New York, NY 10065–8198, USA. *T:* (212) 4866688. *E:* estreator@nyc.rr.com. *Clubs:* White's, Beefsteak; Metropolitan (Washington); Mill Reef (Antigua); Century Association, Knickerbocker (New York).

STREEP, Mary Louise, (Meryl); American actress; *b* 22 June 1949; *d* of Harry and Mary Streep; *m* 1978, Donald Gummer; one *s* three *d*. *Educ:* Vassar Coll. (BA 1971); Yale (MA 1975). *Stage appearances include:* New York Shakespeare Fest., 1976; Alice in Concert, NY Public Theater, 1981; The Seagull, NY, 2001; Mother Courage and Her Children, NY, 2006; *television appearances include:* The Deadliest Season (film), 1977; Holocaust, 1978; Angels in America (film), 2004; *films include:* The Deer Hunter, 1978; Manhattan, 1979; The Seduction of Joe Tynan, 1979; Kramer versus Kramer, 1979 (Academy Award, 1980); The French Lieutenant's Woman (BAFTA Award), 1981; Sophie's Choice (Academy Award), Still of the Night, 1982; Silkwood, 1983; Falling in Love, 1984; Plenty, Out of Africa, 1985; Heartburn, 1986; Ironweed, 1987; A Cry in the Dark, 1989; She-Devil, 1990; Postcards from the Edge, Defending your Life, 1991; Death Becomes Her, 1992; The House of the Spirits, 1994; The River Wild, The Bridges of Madison County, 1995; Before and After, 1996; Marvin's Room, 1997; Dancing at Lughnasa, 1998; One True Thing, 1999; Music of the Heart, 2000; The Hours, Adaptation, 2003; Stuck on You, The Manchurian Candidate, Lemony Snicket's A Series of Unfortunate Events, 2004; Prime, The Devil Wears Prada, 2006; A Prairie Home Companion, Evening, Rendition, Lions for Lambs, 2007; Mamma Mia!, 2008; Doubt, Julie and Julia, 2009; It's Complicated, 2010; The Iron Lady (Best Actress, BAFTA and Academy Awards), 2012; Hope Springs, 2012; August: Osage County, The Giver, 2014; Into The Woods, 2015; Ricki and the Flash, 2015. Hon. DFA: Dartmouth Coll., 1981; Yale, 1983. *Address:* c/o Creative Artists Agency, 2000 Avenue of the Stars, Los Angeles, CA 90067, USA.

STREET, Hon. Anthony Austin; manager and company director; *b* 8 Feb. 1926; *s* of late Brig. the Hon. G. A. Street, MC, MHR; *m* 1951, Valerie Erica, *d* of J. A. Rickard; three *s*. *Educ:* Melbourne C of E Grammar Sch. RAN, 1945–46. MP (L) Corangamite, Vic, 1966–84 (resigned); Mem., various Govt Mems Cttees, 1967–71; Mem., Fed. Exec. Council, 1971–; Asst Minister for Labour and Nat. Service, 1971–72; Mem., Opposition Exec., 1973–75 (Special Asst to Leader of Opposition and Shadow Minister for Labour and Immigration, March–Nov. 1975); Minister for Labour and Immigration, Caretaker Ministry after dissolution of Parliament, Nov. 1975; Minister for Employment and Industrial Relations and Minister Assisting Prime Minister in Public Service Matters, 1975–78; Minister for: Industrial Relations, 1978–80; Foreign Affairs, 1980–83. Chm., Fed. Rural Cttee, Liberal Party, 1970–74. *Recreations:* cricket, golf, tennis, flying. *Address:* 153 The Terrace, Ocean Grove, Vic 3226, Australia. *Clubs:* MCC; Melbourne; Barwon Heads Golf.

STREET, Hon. Sir Laurence (Whistler), AC 1989; KCMG 1976; QC (NSW) 1963; commercial mediator; Lieutenant-Governor of New South Wales, 1974–89; Chief Justice of New South Wales, 1974–88; *b* Sydney, 3 July 1926; *s* of Hon. Sir Kenneth Street, KCMG; *m* 1st, 1952, Susan Gai, AM, *d* of E. A. S. Watt; two *s* two *d*; 2nd, Penelope Patricia, *d* of G. Ferguson; one *d*. *Educ:* Cranbrook Sch., Sydney; Univ. of Sydney (LLB Hons). RANVR, incl. war service in Pacific, 1943–47; Comdr, Sen. Officer RANR Legal Br., 1964–65. Admitted to NSW Bar, 1951; Judge, Supreme Court of NSW, 1965–74; Judge of Appeal, 1972–74; Chief Judge in Equity, 1972–74. Director: John Fairfax Holdings Ltd, 1991–97 (Chm., 1994–97); Monte Paschi Aust. Ltd, 1992–97. Lectr in Procedure, Univ. of Sydney, 1962–63, Lectr in Bankruptcy, 1964–65; Member: Public Accountants Regn Bd, 1962–65; Companies Auditors Bd, 1962–65; Pres., Courts-Martial Appeal Tribunal, 1971–74; Chairman: Aust. Commercial Disputes Centre Planning Cttee, 1985–86; Aust. Govt Internat. Legal Services Adv. Council, 1990; Aust. Mem., WIPO Arbitration Consultative Commn, Geneva, 1994–2003; Aust. Govt Designated Conciliator, ICSID, Washington, 1995–. Mem. Court, London Court of Internat. Arbitration, 1988–2003 (Pres., Asia-Pacific Council, 1989–2006). Pres., Aust. Br., 1990–94, World Pres., 1990–92, Life Vice-Pres., 1992, Internat. Law Assoc.; Chm., Judiciary Appeals Bd and Drug Tribunal, NSW Rugby League, 1989–. President: Sydney Univ. Law Grads Assoc., 1963–65; Cranbrook Sch. Council, 1966–74; St John Amb. Aust. (NSW), 1974–2006. Hon. Col, 1st/15th Royal NSW Lancers, 1986–96. FCIArb 1992. Hon. FIArbA 1989; Hon. Fellow, Aust. Inst. of Bldg, 2004. Hon. LLD: Sydney, 1984; Macquarie, 1989; Univ. of Technol., Sydney, 1998 (Fellow, 1990); Hon. DEc New England, 1996. KStJ 1976. Grand Officer of Merit, SMO Malta, 1977. *Clubs:* Union, University & Schools (Sydney); Royal Sydney Golf.

STREET, Prof. Peter Ronald, PhD; Development Director, Genus International Consultancy, 1999; Director, Produce Studies Ltd, 1992; *b* 4 May 1944; *s* of Leslie Arthur John and Winifred Marjorie Street; *m* 1969, Christine Hill; two *d*. *Educ:* Univ. of Reading (BScAgr, PhD Management and Econs). Lectr in Management and Econs, Faculty of Agricl Sci., Univ. of Nottingham, 1971–74; Tropical Products Institute: Principal Res. Officer, 1974–82; Sen. Principal Res. Officer and Head, Mkting and Industrial Econs Dept, 1982–85; Mem., Directorate Bd, 1982–85; Dir and Chief Economist, Produce Studies Ltd, 1985–89; Prof. of Agricl Systems and Head, Dept of Agriculture, Univ. of Reading, 1989–92. Visiting Professor: Imperial Coll., London, 1998–; RAU (formerly RAC), 2000–. Chm., Selskya Zhign Consultants, Moscow, 1994–; Mem. Bd, British Consultants Bureau, 1999; Man. Dir, GFA-RACE Partners Ltd, 2000; Vice Pres., Online Global Commodities Exchange, 2000–. Numerous internat. consultancy assignments. MCMI (MBIM 1972). *Publications:* (ed with J. G. W. Jones) Systems Theory Applied to Agriculture and the Food Chain, 1990. *Recreations:* gardening, fly fishing. *Address:* Brooklyn, Crow, Ringwood, Hants BH24 3EA. *T:* (01425) 475222.

STREET, Sarah Elizabeth; *see* Brown, Sarah Elizabeth.

STREET, Dame Susan (Ruth), DCB 2005; strategic advisor, Deloitte LLP, 2006–12; *b* 11 Aug. 1949; *d* of late Dr Stefan Galeski and of Anna Galeski; *m* 1972, Richard Street; one *s* one *d*. *Educ:* St Andrews Univ. (MA Philosophy). Home Office, 1974–2001: Course Dir, Top Mgt Prog., Cabinet Office, 1989–91 (on secondment); Supervising Consultant, Price Waterhouse, 1991–94; Director: Central Drugs Co-ordination Unit, Cabinet Office, 1994–96 (on secondment); Fire and Emergency Planning, 1996–99; Sentencing and Correctional Policy, 1999–2000; Criminal Policy, 2000–01; Permanent Sec., DCMS, 2001–06. Non-executive Director: MoJ, 2009–15; Adlens, 2014–. Exec. Coach, Praesta, 2015–. Associate Mem., BUPA, 2007–; Associate Fellow, Inst. for Govt, 2010–. Trustee, Royal Opera House, 2007–15; Gov., Royal Ballet, 2007–. FRSA 1992; CCMI 2007. Mem., Firefighters' Co., 2014–. *Recreations:* family, ballet, theatre, remedial tennis. *Address:* 85 South Lodge, Circus Road, NW8 9EU.

STREET-PORTER, Janet; journalist and broadcaster, since 1967; Editor-at-large, The Independent on Sunday, since 2001 (Editor, 1999–2001); *b* 27 Dec. 1946; *m* 1st, 1967, Tim Street-Porter (marr. diss. 1975); 2nd, 1976, A. M. M. Elliott, *qv* (marr. diss. 1978); 3rd, 1978, Frank Cvitanovich (marr. diss. 1988; he *d* 1995). *Educ:* Lady Margaret Grammar Sch., Fulham; Architectural Assoc. TV presenter, 1975–; TV producer, 1981–; Exec., BBC TV, 1988–94; Man. Dir, Live TV, 1994–95. Pres., Ramblers Assoc., 1994–97. Trustee, Sci. Mus. Gp (formerly NMSI), 2008–14. FRTS 1994. Hon. FRIBA 2001. Award for originality, BAFTA, 1988; Prix Italia, 1993. *Publications:* The British Teapot, 1977; Scandal, 1981; Coast to Coast, 1998; As the Crow Flies, 1999; Baggage: my childhood, 2004; Fallout, 2006; Life's Too F***ing Short, 2008; Don't Let the B*****ds Get You Down, 2009. *Recreations:* walking, talking, modern art. *Address:* c/o Sophie Lauriemore, Factual Management, 105 Tanners Hill, SE8 4QD. *T:* (020) 8694 1626. *E:* sl@factualmanagement.com.

STREETEN, Paul Patrick, DLitt; Professor, Boston University, 1980–93, now Emeritus (Director: Center for Asian Development Studies, 1980–84; World Development Institute, 1984–90); *b* 18 July 1917; *e s* of Wilhelm Hornig, Vienna; changed name to Streeten under Army Council Instruction, 1943; *m* 1951, Ann Hilary Palmer, *d* of Edgar Higgins, Woodstock, Vermont; two *d*, and one step *s*. *Educ:* Vienna; Aberdeen Univ.; Balliol Coll., Oxford (Hon. Schol.); 1st cl. PPE, 1947; Student, Nuffield Coll., Oxford, 1947–48. DLitt Oxon, 1976. Mil. service in Commandos, 1941–43; wounded in Sicily, 1943. Fellow, Balliol Coll., Oxford, 1948–66 (Hon. Fellow, 1986); Associate, Oxford Univ. Inst. of Econs and Statistics, 1960–64; Dep. Dir-Gen., Econ. Planning Staff, Min. of Overseas Develt, 1964–66; Prof. of Econs, Fellow, Acting and Dep. Dir of Inst. of Develt Studies, Sussex Univ., 1966–68; Warden of Queen Elizabeth House, Dir, Inst. of Commonwealth Studies, Univ. of Oxford, and Fellow of Balliol Coll., 1968–78; Special Adviser, World Bank, 1976–79; Dir of Studies, Overseas Develt Council, 1979–80. Rockefeller Fellow, USA, 1950–51; Fellow, Johns Hopkins Univ., Baltimore, 1955–56; Fellow, Center for Advanced Studies, Wesleyan Univ., Conn.; Vis. Prof., Econ. Develt Inst. of World Bank, 1984–86; Jean Monnet Prof., European Univ. Inst., Florence, 1991. Sec., Oxford Econ. Papers, until 1961, Mem. Edit. Bd, 1971–78; Editor, Bulletin of Oxford Univ. Inst. of Econs and Statistics, 1961–64; Chm. Editorial Bd, World Develt, 1972–2003. Member: UK Nat. Commn of Unesco, 1966; Provisional Council of Univ. of Mauritius, 1966–72; Commonwealth Develt Corp., 1967–72; Statutory Commn, Royal Univ. of Malta, 1972–; Royal Commn on Environmental Pollution, 1974–76. Mem., Internat. Adv. Panel, Canadian Univ. Service Overseas. Vice-Chm., Social Sciences Adv. Cttee, 1971; Member, Governing Body: Queen Elizabeth House, Oxford, 1966–68; Inst. of Develt Studies, Univ. of Sussex, 1968–80 (Vice-Chm.); Dominion Students' Hall Trust, London House; Mem. Council, Overseas Develt Institute, until 1979. Pres., UK Chapter, Soc. for Internat. Develt until 1976. Mem., Phi Beta Delta. Hon. Fellow, Inst. of Develt

Studies, Sussex, 1980. Raffaele Mattioli Lectr, Milan, 1991. Hon. LLD Aberdeen, 1980; Hon. DLitt Malta, 1992. Development Prize, Justus Liebig Univ., Giessen, 1987; Leontief Prize, Global Develt and Envmt Inst., Tufts Univ., 2001. Silver Sign of Honour (Vienna), 2002. *Publications:* (ed) Value in Social Theory, 1958; Economic Integration, 1961, 2nd edn 1964; (contrib.) Economic Growth in Britain, 1966; The Teaching of Development Economics, 1967; (ed with M. Lipton) Crisis in Indian Planning, 1968; (contrib. to) Gunnar Myrdal, Asian Drama, 1968; (ed) Unfashionable Economics, 1970; (ed, with Hugh Corbet) Commonwealth Policy in a Global Context, 1971; Frontiers of Development Studies, 1972; (ed) Trade Strategies for Development, 1973; The Limits of Development Research, 1975; (with S. Lall) Foreign Investment, Transnationals and Developing Countries, 1977; Development Perspectives, 1981; First Things First, 1981; (ed with Richard Jolly) Recent Issues in World Development, 1981; (ed with H. Maier) Human Resources, Employment and Development, 1983; What Price Food?, 1987; (ed) Beyond Adjustment, 1988; Mobilizing Human Potential, 1989; Paul Streeten in South Africa, 1992; Strategics for Human Development, 1994; (co-ed) The UN and the Bretton Woods Institutions, 1995; Thinking About Development, 1995; Globalisation: threat or opportunity, 2001; Essays in Social and Economic Development, 2010; contribs to learned journals; *festschrift:* (ed S. Lall and F. Stewart) Theory and Reality in Development, 1986. *Address:* 65 Moores MI Mt Rose Road, Hopewell, NJ 08525–2401, USA.

STREETER, Gary Nicholas; MP (C) South West Devon, since 1997 (Plymouth Sutton, 1992–97); *b* 2 Oct. 1955; *s* of Kenneth Victor Streeter and Shirley Nellie (*née* Keable); *m* 1978, Janet Stevens; one *s* one *d. Educ:* Tiverton Grammar Sch.; King's Coll., London (LLB 1st cl. Hons). Articled at Coward Chance, London, 1978–80; admitted solicitor, 1980; joined Foot & Bowden, solicitors, Plymouth, 1980, Partner, 1984–99. Plymouth City Council: Mem., 1986–92; Chm., Housing Cttee, 1989–91. PPS to Solicitor-General, 1993–95, and to Attorney-General, 1994–95; an Asst Govt Whip, 1995–96; Parly Sec., Lord Chancellor's Dept, 1996–97; Opposition front bench spokesman on European affairs, 1997–98; Shadow Sec. of State for Internat. Develt, 1998–2001; Shadow Minister of State for Foreign Affairs, 2003–04. Member: Panel of Chairs (formerly Chairmen's Panel), 2008–15; Speaker's Cttee overseeing Electoral Commn, 2008–; Ecclesiastical Cttee, 2010–15; Chairman: Christians in Parliament, 2010–; Westminster Foundn for Democracy, 2010–. A Vice Chm., Cons. Party, 2001–02; Chm., Cons. Party Internat. Office, 2005–08. *Publications:* (ed) There is Such a Thing as Society, 2002. *Recreation:* lover of cricket and Rugby. *Address:* House of Commons, SW1A 0AA. *T:* (020) 7219 4070.

STREETING, Wesley Paul William; MP (Lab) Ilford North, since 2015; *b* London, 21 Jan. 1983. *Educ:* Westminster City Sch.; Selwyn Coll., Cambridge (BA Hist.). Pres., Cambridge Univ. Students' Union, 2004–05; Vice Pres. (Educn), 2006–10, Pres., 2008–10, NUS; Chief Exec., Helena Kennedy Foundn, 2010–12; Hd of Educn, Stonewall, 2012–13; Associate, Magic Breakfast, 2015. Mem. (Lab) Redbridge LBC, 2010– (Dep. Leader, 2014–15). *Recreations:* theatre, cinema, walking, travelling. *Address:* House of Commons, SW1A 0AA. *T:* (020) 7219 6132. *E:* wes.streeting.mp@parliament.uk.

STREETON, Sir Terence (George), KBE 1989 (MBE 1969); CMG 1981; HM Diplomatic Service, retired; Chairman: Healthco Pvt Ltd, Harare, 1994–2008; Director, Contact International Ltd, Harare, 1992–2007; *b* 12 Jan. 1930; *er s* of late Alfred Victor Streeton and Edith Streeton (*née* Deiton); *m* 1962, Molly Horsburgh; two *s* two *d. Educ:* Wellingborough Grammar School. Inland Revenue, 1946; Prison Commission, 1947; Government Communications Headquarters, 1952; Foreign Office (Diplomatic Wireless Service), 1953; Diplomatic Service, 1965–89: First Secretary, Bonn, 1966; FCO, 1970; First Secretary and Head of Chancery, Bombay, 1972; Counsellor and Head of Joint Admin Office, Brussels, 1975; Head of Finance Dept, FCO, 1979; Asst Under-Sec. of State and Prin. Finance Officer, FCO, 1982–83; High Comr to Bangladesh, 1983–89. Pres., Bangladesh-British Chamber of Commerce, 1993–97. *Recreation:* collecting fountain pens. *Address:* 189 Billing Road, Northampton NN1 5RS. *T:* (01604) 473510. *Club:* Northampton and County (Northampton).

STREISAND, Barbra Joan; singer, actress, director, producer, writer, composer, philanthropist; *b* Brooklyn, NY, 24 April 1942; *d* of Emanuel and Diana Streisand; *m* 1963, Elliott Gould (marr. diss. 1971); one *s*; *m* 1998, James Brolin. *Educ:* Erasmus Hall High Sch. Nightclub début, Bon Soir, Greenwich Village, 1961; NY theatre début, Another Evening with Harry Stoones, 1961; musical comedy, I Can Get It For You Wholesale, 1962 (NY Critics' Best Supporting Actress Award, 1962); musical, Funny Girl, NY, 1964, London, 1966 (Best Foreign Actress, Variety Poll Award, 1966). Special Tony Award, 1970. *Films:* Funny Girl, 1968 (Golden Globe Award, Acad. Award, 1968); Hello Dolly, 1969; On a Clear Day You Can See Forever, 1970; The Owl and the Pussycat, 1971; What's Up Doc?, 1972; Up the Sandbox, 1972; The Way We Were, 1973; For Pete's Sake, 1974; Funny Lady, 1975; A Star is Born (also prod), 1976; The Main Event (also prod), 1979; All Night Long, 1981; Yentl (also co-wrote, dir. and prod), 1984 (Golden Globe Award for Best Picture and Best Dir); Nuts (also prod), 1987; The Prince of Tides (also dir. and prod), 1990; The Mirror Has Two Faces (also dir. and co-prod), 1997; Meet the Fockers, 2005; Little Fockers, 2010. *Television specials:* My Name is Barbra, 1965 (5 Emmy Awards, Peabody Award); Color Me Barbra, 1966; Belle of 14th Street, 1967; A Happening in Central Park, 1968; Musical Instrument, 1973; One Voice, 1986; Barbra Streisand, the Concert (also prod and co-dir.), 1994 (Peabody Award, 3 Cable Ace Awards, 5 Emmy Awards); Serving in Silence: the Margarethe Cammermeyer story (exec. prod.), 1995. Began recording career, 1962; Grammy Awards for best female pop vocalist, 1963, 1964, 1965, 1977, 1986, for best songwriter (with Paul Williams), 1977; (jtly) Acad. Award for composing best song (Evergreen), 1976; awarded: 50 Gold Albums (exceeded only by Elvis Presley and The Beatles); 30 Platinum Albums; 13 Multi-Platinum Albums (most for any female artist). *Albums include:* People, 1965; My Name is Barbra, 1965; The Way We Were, 1974; Guilty, 1980; The Broadway Album, 1986; Just for the Record (retrospective album), 1991; Back to Broadway, 1993; Barbra Streisand, the Concert (double album and video), 1994; The Mirror Has Two Faces (soundtrack), 1996; Higher Ground, 1997; A Love Like Ours, 1999; Christmas Memories, 2001; Guilty Pleasures, 2005; Love Is The Answer, 2009; What Matters Most, 2011; Release Me, 2012; Partners, 2014. *Address:* Barwood Films, 330 West 58th Street, Suite 301, New York, NY 10019, USA.

STRETTON, James; Chairman, Trustees, Lloyd's Pension Scheme, 2010–14; *b* 16 Dec. 1943; *s* of Donald and Muriel Stretton; *m* 1968, Isobel Robertson; two *d. Educ:* Laxton Grammar Sch., Oundle; Worcester Coll., Oxford (BA Maths). FFA 1970–2008. Standard Life Assurance Company, 1965–2001: Asst Pensions Manager, 1974–77; Asst Investment Manager, 1977–84; General Manager (Ops), 1984–88; Dep. Man. Dir, 1988–94; Chief Exec., UK Ops, 1994–2001. Chm., Wise Gp, 2002–09. Dir, Bank of England, 1998–2003; Chm., Bank of England Pension Fund Trustee Co., 2001–05; Member: Franchise Bd, Lloyd's of London, 2003–09; Disciplinary Bd of Actuarial profession, 2004–06. Member: Scottish New Deal Adv. Task Force, 1997–99; Scottish Business Forum, 1998–99. Pres., YouthLink Scotland, 1994–2000. Director: PIA, 1992–94; Scottish Community Educn Council, 1996–99. Chm., Foresight Ageing Population Panel, 1999–2000. Dir, Edinburgh Internat. Fest. Ltd, 1997–2008; Chm., Lammermuir Fest., 2010–. Mem. Court, 1996–2002, Rector's Assessor, 2003–06, Univ. of Edinburgh. *Recreations:* music, reading, gardening. *Address:* 15 Letham Mains, Haddington EH41 4NW.

STRETTON, His Honour Peter John; a Circuit Judge, 1986–2002; *b* 14 June 1938; *s* of Frank and Ella Stretton; *m* 1973, Eleanor Anne Wait; three *s* one *d. Educ:* Bedford Modern Sch. Called to the Bar, Middle Temple, 1962; Head of Chambers, 1985. A Recorder, 1982–86. *Recreations:* squash, gardening, golf.

STREVENS, Bonnie Jean Holford; *see* Blackburn, B. J.

STRICK, Robert Charles Gordon; Clerk to the Drapers' Company, 1980–93 (Liveryman, Court of Assistants, 1994); *b* 23 March 1931; *m* 1960, Jennifer Mary Hathway (*d* 2013); one *s* one *d. Educ:* Royal Grammar Sch., Guildford; Sidney Sussex Coll., Cambridge (MA). Served RA, 1949–51; TA, 1951–55. Spicers Ltd, 1954–55; joined HMOCS, 1955; Dist Officer, Fiji, 1955–59; Sec., Burns Commn into Natural Resources and Population Trends, 1959–60; Asst Sec., Suva, 1960–61; Sec. to Govt, Tonga, 1961–63; Develt Officer and Divl Comr, 1963–67, Sec. for Natural Resources, 1967–71, Fiji; retired 1971; Under Sec., ICA, 1971–72; Asst Sec.-Gen., RICS, 1972–80; Clerk, Chartered Surveyors' Co., 1977–80. Hon. Member: CGLI, 1991; Shrewsbury Co. of Drapers, 1992. Hon. Old Student, Aberystwyth, 1993. Hon. Fellow, Queen Mary, London Univ. (formerly QMW), 1993. Hon. DLitt Coll. of William and Mary, Virginia, USA, 1993. Grand Cross, Order of Crown (Tonga), 2010. *Recreations:* the countryside, walking, golf, gardening. *Address:* Lane End, Sheep Lane, Midhurst GU29 9NT. *T:* (01730) 813151.

STRICKLAND, Benjamin Vincent Michael, FCA; Group Managing Director (Group Strategy, Finances and Operations), and Director, Schroders PLC, 1983–91; *b* 20 Sept. 1939; *s* of Maj.-Gen. Eugene Vincent Michael Strickland, CMG, DSO, OBE, MM, and of Barbara Mary Farquharson Meares Lamb, *d* of Major Benjamin Lamb, RFA; *m* 1965, Tessa Mary Edwina, *d* of Rear-Adm. John Grant, CB, DSO; one *s* one *d. Educ:* Mayfield Coll.; University Coll., Oxford, 1960–63 (MA PPE); Harvard Business Sch. (AMPDip 1978). FCA 1967. Lieutenant: 17/21 Lancers, BAOR, 1959–60; Inns of Court and City Yeomanry, 1963–67. Joined Price Waterhouse & Co., 1963, Manager, 1967–68; joined J. Henry Schroder Wagg & Co. in Corp. Finance, 1968: Director: Schroder Wagg, 1974–91; Schroders Internat., 1975–85; Chm., G. D. Peters Engineering, 1972–74; Dir, Property Hldgs Internat. (USA), 1974–75; Chm. and Chief Exec., Schroders Australia, 1978–82. Adviser: *inter alia,* on strategy to City law firm, to media gp, on mission and finances to Westminster Cathedral; mentor to chief execs, 2005–12. Mem. steering gp, Vision for London, 1991–2000. Chm., Chester Street Insce Assoc. (formerly Iron Trades Insce Gp), 1996–. Voluntary reading help and leader of hist. club and book club in Falconbrook Primary Sch., 2004–. Mem. Council, St George's Med. Sch., 1984–87. FRSA. *Publications:* Bow Group pamphlet on Resources of the Sea (with Laurance Reed), 1965. *Recreations:* travel, reading, family, military and general history, theatre, film. *Address:* 23 Juer Street, SW11 4RE. *T:* (020) 7585 2970. *Clubs:* Boodle's, Hurlingham.

STRICKLAND-CONSTABLE, Sir Frederic, 12th Bt *cr* 1641, of Boynton, Yorkshire; *b* 21 Oct. 1944; *er s* of Sir Robert Frederick Strickland-Constable, 11th Bt and Lettice, *yr d* of Major Frederick Strickland; *S* father, 1994; *m* 1981, Pauline Margaret Harding (*d* 2009), one *s* one *d. Educ:* Westminster; Corpus Christi Coll., Cambridge (BA); London Business Sch. (MSc). *Heir: s* Charles Strickland-Constable, *b* 10 Oct. 1985. *Address:* c/o Estate Office, Castle Howard, York YO60 7DA.

STRIDE, Melvyn John; MP (C) Central Devon, since 2010; a Lord Commissioner of HM Treasury (Government Whip), since 2015; *b* 30 Sept. 1961; *m* 2005, Michelle King Hughes; three *d. Educ:* Portsmouth Grammar Sch.; St Edmund Hall, Oxford (BA PPE 1984). President: Oxford Univ. Cons. Assoc., 1981; Oxford Union, 1984. Founder and Owner, Venture Mktg Gp, 1987–. An Asst Govt Whip, 2014–15. *Address:* House of Commons, SW1A 0AA.

STRIKE, Prof. Peter, PhD; Professor of Genetics, and Vice Chancellor and Chief Executive, University of Cumbria, since 2011; *b* Barrow in Furness, 26 Nov. 1948; *s* of Fred and Kathleen Rose Strike; *m* 1970, Christine M. (marr. diss. 2001); *m* 2004, Jill Hughes (*d* 2004); *m* 2011, Victoria Geraldine Bruce (*see* Dame V. G. Bruce); one *s* one *d* and one step *s* three step *d. Educ:* Barrow in Furness Grammar Sch. for Boys; Univ. of Sussex (BSc Hons Biochem. 1970); Univ. of Newcastle upon Tyne (PhD Biochem. 1974). University of Liverpool: Lectr, 1974–84; Sen. Lectr, 1984–88; Reader, 1988–93; Prof. of Genetics and Microbiol., 1993–2002; Dir of Teaching (Life Scis), 1999–2002; Prof. of Genetics and Vice Principal, Res. and Knowledge Transfer, Napier Univ., Edinburgh, 2002–07; Prof. of Genetics and Dep. Vice Chancellor, Res. and Innovation, Northumbria Univ., 2007–10; Prof. of Genetics and Dep. Vice Chancellor (Res., Knowledge Transfer and Business Engagement), Univ. of Sunderland, 2010–11. Vis. Res. Fellow, Yale Univ., 1983. Sen. Trng Officer, RNR (Liverpool Univs RN Unit), 1984–2002 (Lt Comdr, RNR). *Publications:* articles on molecular biol. and genetics. *Recreations:* sailing, hill-walking. *Address:* 15 Cade Hill Road, Stocksfield, Northumberland NE43 7PB. *T:* (01661) 842325, 07747 760915, (01228) 888882. *E:* peter.strike@cumbria.ac.uk.

STRIKER, Prof. Gisela, DPhil; Walter C. Klein Professor of Philosophy and of the Classics, Harvard University, 2002–11, now Emerita (Professor of Classical Philosophy, 2000–02); *b* 26 Nov. 1943. *Educ:* Univ. of Göttingen (DPhil 1969). Asst Prof., 1970–83, Prof., 1983–86, Univ. of Göttingen; Prof., Dept of Philosophy, Columbia Univ., NY, 1986–89; Prof. of Classical Philosophy, 1989–90, George Martin Lane Prof. of Philosophy and Classics, 1990–97, Harvard Univ.; Laurence Prof. of Ancient Philosophy, Univ. of Cambridge, and Fellow, Trinity Coll., Cambridge, 1997–2000. *Publications:* Essays on Hellenistic Epistemology and Ethics, 1996; (trans. and commentary) Aristotle, Prior Analytics book I, 2009; articles in learned jls. *Address:* Langenfelder Strasse 71, 22769 Hamburg, Germany.

STRINGER, Prof. Christopher Brian, PhD, DSc; FRS 2004; Research Leader in Human Origins, Natural History Museum, London, since 2006 (Head, Human Origins Programme, 1990–93 and 1999–2006); *b* 31 Dec. 1947; *s* of late George Albert Stringer and Evelyn Beatrice Stringer, and foster *s* of late Harry Kennett and Lilian Kennett; *m* 1977, Rosemary Susan Margaret (marr. diss. 2004); two *s* one *d. Educ:* UCL (BSc Hons (Anthropol.) 1969); Univ. of Bristol (PhD 1974; DSc 1990). Natural History Museum, London, 1973–: Sen. Res. Fellow, 1973–77; SSO, 1977–87; PSO, 1987–94; Hd, Anthropology, 1989–90; Individual Merit Promotion Band 2, 1994. Vis. Prof., Royal Holloway, London, 1998–; Res. Associate, Centre for Ecology and Evolution, UCL, 1999–; Dir, Ancient Human Occupation of Britain project, 2001–. Vis. Lectr, Dept of Anthropol., Harvard Univ., 1979. Lectures: Lyell, BAAS, 1988; Radcliffe, Green Coll., Oxford, 1996; Dalrymple, Univ. of Glasgow, 2001; Mulvaney, ANU, 2001; Darwin, Centre for Ecology and Evolution, London, 2003; Annual Science, Natural History Mus., London, 2011; Galton, Galton Inst., 2011; Millennium Distinguished Lectr, Amer. Anthropol Assoc., 2000. FAAAS 2012. Hon. FSA 2010. Hon. Dr of Laws Bristol, 2000; Hon. DSc Kent, 2009. Osman Hill Medal, Primate Soc. of GB, 1998; Henry Stopes Medal, Geologists' Assoc., 2000; Rivers Meml Medal, RAI, 2004; Frink Medal, Zool Soc. of London, 2009; Coke Medal, Geol Soc., 2011; James Croll Medal, Quaternary Res. Assoc., 2012. *Publications:* (ed) Aspects of Human Evolution, 1981; (with A. Gray) Our Fossil Relatives, 1983; (ed with P. Mellars) The Human Revolution: behavioural and biological perspectives in the origins of modern humans, 1989; (with P. Andrews) Human Evolution: an illustrated guide, 1989; (ed jtly) The Origin of Modern Humans and the Impact of Chronometric Dating, 1993; (with C. Gamble) In Search of the Neanderthals: solving the puzzle of human origins, 1993 (Archaeol. Bk of the Year, 1994); (with R. McKie) African Exodus, 1996, 2nd edn 1997; (jtly) Westbury Cave: the Natural History Museum excavations 1976–1984, 1999; (ed jtly) Neanderthals on the Edge: 150th anniversary conference of the Forbes' Quarry discovery, Gibraltar, 2000; (with J. Weiner) The Piltdown Forgery, 2003;

(with P. Andrews) The Complete World of Human Evolution, 2005, 2nd edn 2011; *Homo britannicus*, 2006 (Kistler Book Award, 2008; British Archaeological Book Award, 2008); The Origin of Our Species, 2011; (ed jtly) The Ancient Human Occupation of Britain, 2011; Lone Survivors, 2012; (jtly) Neanderthals in Context: a report of the 1995–1998 excavations at Gorham's and Vanguard Caves, Gibraltar, 2012; (ed jtly) Culture Evolves, 2012; (with R. Dinnis) Britain: one million years of the human story, 2014; articles in learned jls. *Recreations:* music, current affairs, travel, watching soccer, astronomy. *Address:* Department of Earth Sciences, Natural History Museum, Cromwell Road, SW7 5BD. *Clubs:* Tetrapods; West Ham United Football.

STRINGER, Sir Donald (Edgar), Kt 1993; CBE 1987; *b* 21 Aug. 1930; *o s* of late Donald Bertram Frederick and Marjorie Stringer, Croydon; *m* 1957, Pamela Irene Totty; three *s*. *Educ:* Whitgift Sch., Croydon. Served Army, RMP, 1951–53. Conservative Party Agent, Fulham, Harrow and Honiton, 1954–65; Conservative Central Office: Dep. Area Agent, W Midlands, 1965–71; Central Office Agent: Northern Area, 1971–73; Greater London Area, 1973–88; Wessex Area, 1988–93. Member: Cons. Agents Exam. Bd, 1987–93; Agents Employment Adv. Cttee, 1988–93. Chm., Salisbury Abbeyfield Soc., 1996–2006. Treas.-Trustee, Fovant Badges Soc., 2001–07. Mem., Guild of Freemen, City of London, 1988. *Recreations:* walking, military history, philately.

STRINGER, Graham Eric; MP (Lab) Blackley and Broughton, since 2010 (Manchester Blackley, 1997–2010); *b* 17 Feb. 1950; *s* of late Albert Stringer and Brenda Stringer; *m* 1999, Kathryn Carr; one *s*, and one step *s* one step *d*. *Educ:* Moston Brook High Sch.; Sheffield Univ. (BSc Hons Chemistry). Analytical chemist. Mem. (Lab), Manchester City Council, 1979–98 (Leader, 1984–96; Chm., Policy and Resources Cttee); Chm., Manchester Airport, 1996–97. Parly Sec., Cabinet Office, 1999–2001; a Lord Comr of HM Treasury (Govt Whip), 2001–02. *Address:* House of Commons, SW1A 0AA.

STRINGER, Sir Howard, Kt 2000; Chairman, Sony Corporation, 2005–13 (Board Member, 1999–2013; Vice Chairman, 2003–05; Group Chief Executive Officer and Representative Corporate Executive Officer, 2005–12; President, 2009–12); Chairman, Sony Corporation of America, 1998–2013 (Chief Executive Officer, 1998–2012); *b* Cardiff, 19 Feb. 1942; naturalised US citizen, 1985 (dual nationality); *s* of late Harry Stringer, MBE and Marjorie Mary Stringer; *m* 1978, Jennifer Kinmond Patterson; one *s* one *d*. *Educ:* Oundle Sch.; Merton Coll., Oxford (BA Modern History 1964; MA; Hon. Fellow, 2000). Served US Army, Vietnam, 1965–67 (Commendation Medal). Joined CBS Inc., 1965; Executive Producer: CBS Reports, 1976–81; CBS Evening News, 1981–84; Exec. Vice Pres., 1984–86, Pres., 1986–88, CBS News; Pres., CBS Broadcast Gp, 1988–95; Chm. and CEO, Tele-TV, 1995–97. Joined Sony Corp. of America, 1997; Corp. Hd, Sony Corp. Entertainment Business Gp, 2003–13; Board Member: Sony BMG, 2004–13; Sony Ericsson, 2006–13. Non-executive Director: TalkTalk, 2012–; BBC, 2013–. Board Member: Amer. Theater Wing; Amer. Friends of BM; NY Presbyterian Hosp.; Carnegie Hall. Chm., Bd of Trustees, Amer. Film Inst., 1999– (Mem., 1989–); Trustee, Paley Center for Media (Visionary award, 2007). Chm. Bd, Saïd Business Sch., Oxford Univ., 2013–. Hon. FRWCMD 2001. Hon. PhD London Inst., 2003; Hon. Dr Glamorgan, 2005; Hon. DLitt: Oxford, 2012; Swansea, 2013. Foundn Award, Internat. Radio and TV Soc., 1994; Steven J. Ross Humanitarian Award, UJA-Fedn of NY, 1999; Internat. Emmy (Founders) Award, 2002; Phoenix House Award for Public Service, 2002; Medal of Honor, St George Soc., 2004; Dist. Service Award, Lincoln Center for the Performing Arts, 2006.

STRINGER, Prof. Dame Joan (Kathleen), DBE 2009 (CBE 2001); PhD; FRSE; Principal and Vice-Chancellor, Edinburgh Napier (formerly Napier) University, 2003–13; *b* 12 May 1948; *d* of Francis James and Doris Joan Bourne; *m* 1993, Roelof Marinus Mali. *Educ:* Portland House High Sch., Stoke-on-Trent; Stoke-on-Trent Coll. of Art; Keele Univ. (BA, CertEd, PhD Politics 1986). Graphic designer, ICL, 1966–70; Local Govt Officer, Staffs, 1970–74; teacher, Sudbury Open Prison, Derbys, 1978–80; Robert Gordon University: Lectr, 1980–88; Head, Sch. of Public Admin and Law, 1988–91; Asst Principal, 1991–96; Queen Margaret College, subseq. Queen Margaret University College, Edinburgh: Principal and Vice Patron, 1996–2002. Comr (Scotland), EOC, 1995–2001; Chm. Wkg Gp, NI Equality Commn, 1999. Mem., Scottish Parlt Consultative Steering Gp and Financial Issues Adv. Gp, 1998–99; Comr, Scottish Election Commn, 1999–2000; Chm., Scottish Exec. Strategic Gp on Women, 2003. Mem., HFEA, 1996–99. Vice-Convener, Univs Scotland (formerly Cttee of Scottish Higher Educn Prins), 1998–2002; Chair, Education UK Scotland, 2006–12. Member: CVCP Commn on Univ. Career Opportunities, 1996–2001; Scottish Cttee, Cttee of Inquiry into Higher Educn (Dearing Cttee), 1996–97; Scottish Council for Postgrad. Med. and Dental Educn, 1999–2002; Scottish Health Minister's Learning Together Strategy Implementation Gp, 2000–01; Exec. Cttee, Scottish Council Develt and Industry, 1998–2013; Scottish Cttee, British Council, 2000–12; Bd, Higher Educn Careers Services Unit, 2000–05; DoH Wkg Gp on modernisation of SHO, 2001–02; Adv. Gp, Scottish Nursing and Midwifery Educn Council, 2001–02; UUK Equality Challenge Steering Gp, 2001–03; Bd, UCEA, 2001–10; Judicial Appts Bd for Scotland, 2002–08; Bd, QAA, 2002–06; Bd, Higher Educn Statistics Agency, 2003–13; Bd, Leadership Foundn for Higher Educn, 2005–10; Bd, UCAS, 2009–13. Sen. HE Advr, British Council, 2013–15. Convener, SCVO, 2001–07. Non-exec. Dir, Grampian Health Bd, 1994–96. Convenor, Product Standards Cttee, Scottish Quality Salmon, 2001–03. Non-executive Director: City Refrigeration Holdings Ltd, 2013–; Grant Property Investment, 2013–. Member: Develt Adv. Bd, Scottish Opera and Ballet, 2000–02; Bd, National Theatre of Scotland, 2009–; Bd, Scottish Improvement Sci. Collaborating Centre, 2014–. Mem., Bd of Mgt, Aberdeen Coll., 1992–96. Member Council: World Assoc. for Co-op. Educn, 1998–2003; Edinburgh Internat. Festival Soc., 1999–2005; IoD, 2013–; RSE, 2014–; Chair: Edinburgh City Theatres Trust, 2013–; Scotch Whisky Action Fund, 2014–. Trustee, David Hume Inst., 2004–; Community Integrated Care, 2013– (Chm., 2014–); Fellow, 48 Group Club, 2006. CCMI (CIMgt 1999; MIMgt 1990); FRSA 1994; FRSE 2001. Hon. DLitt Keele; Hon. Dr: Edinburgh, 2011; Open Univ., 2014. *Publications:* contrib. articles in field of politics with particular ref. to British Public Admin and employment and trng policy. *Recreations:* music (especially opera), gardening, cats.

STROHM, Prof. Paul Holzworth, PhD; Anna S. Garbedian Professor of the Humanities and Professor of Medieval Literature, Columbia University, 2003–11, now Emeritus; Emeritus Fellow, St Anne's College, University of Oxford, since 2003; *b* 30 July 1938; *s* of Paul H. Strohm and Catherine Poole Strohm; *m* 1st, 1960, Jean Sprowl (marr. diss. 1977); two *s*; 2nd, 2008, Claire P. Harman. *Educ:* Amherst Coll. (BA 1960); Univ. of California, Berkeley (PhD 1965); Univ. of Oxford (MPhil 1998). Indiana University: Asst Prof., 1965–68; Associate Prof., 1968–73; Full Prof. of English, 1973–98; J. R. R. Tolkien Prof. of Medieval Lang. and Lit., and Fellow, St Anne's Coll., Oxford Univ., 1998–2003. Guggenheim Fellow, 1994–95; Vis. Fellow, Clare Hall, Cambridge, 1994–95; Henry R. Luce Fellow, Nat. Humanities Center, 1996–97; Leverhulme Vis. Prof., 2012–13, Hon. Professorial Fellow, 2013–, QMUL. First Vice Pres., Amer. Assoc. of Univ. Profs, 1985–86, Ed., Academe: Bull. of AAUP, 1986–92; Pres., New Chaucer Soc., 1998–2000. *Publications:* Social Chaucer, 1989; Hochon's Arrow: the social imagination of medieval texts, 1992; England's Empty Throne: usurpation and the language of legitimation, 1998; Theory and the Premodern Text, 2000; Politique, 2005; Middle English, 2008; Conscience: a very short introduction, 2011; The Poet's Tale: Chaucer and the year that made The Canterbury Tales, 2015. *Address:* 560 Carroll Street, Apt 12A, Brooklyn, New York, NY 11215, USA; 76 Southfield Road, Oxford OX4 1PA.

STROHM, Prof. Reinhard, PhD; FBA 1993; Professor of Music, Oxford University, 2007–10, now Emeritus; Fellow, Wadham College, Oxford, 1996–2007, now Emeritus; *b* 4 Aug. 1942. *Educ:* Tech. Univ., Berlin (PhD 1971). Lectr, then Reader, in Music, KCL, 1975–83; Prof. of Music Hist., Yale Univ., 1983–89; Reader, 1990–91, Prof. of Histl Musicology, 1991–96, KCL; Heather Prof. of Music, Univ. of Oxford, 1996–2007. Edward J. Dent Medal, Royal Musical Assoc., 1977. *Publications:* Italienische Opernarien des frühen Settecento, 1976; Die italienische Oper im 18 Jahrhundert, 1979, 2nd edn 1991; Music in Late Medieval Bruges, 1985, 2nd edn 1990; Essays on Handel and Italian Opera, 1985; The Rise of European Music 1380–1500, 1993; Dramma per Musica: Italian opera seria of the 18th century, 1997; (ed) The Eighteenth-century Diaspora of Italian Music and Musicians, 2001; (ed with B. J. Blackburn) Music as Concept and Practice in the Late Middle Ages, 2001; The Operas of Antonio Vivaldi, 2008; many contribs to books and learned jls. *Recreations:* travel, mountaineering. *Address:* Faculty of Music, St Aldate's, Oxford OX1 1DB; 19 Hunt Close, Bicester, Oxon OX26 6HX.

STRONACH, David Brian, OBE 1975; FSA; Professor of Near Eastern Studies, University of California, Berkeley, 1981–2004, now Emeritus (Chair of Department, 1994–97); *b* 10 June 1931; *s* of Ian David Stronach, MB, FRCSE, and Marjorie Jessie Duncan (*née* Minto); *m* 1966, Ruth Vaadia; two *d*. *Educ:* Gordonstoun; St John's Coll., Cambridge (MA). Pres., Cambridge Univ. Archaeological Field Club, 1954. British Inst. of Archaeology at Ankara: Scholar, 1955–56; Fellow, 1957–58; Fellow, British Sch. of Archaeology in Iraq, 1957–60; Brit. Acad. Archaeological Attaché in Iran, 1960–61; Dir, British Inst. of Persian Studies, 1961–80, Hon. Vice Pres., 1981–; Curator of Near Eastern Archaeol., Hearst (formerly Lowie) Mus. of Anthropol., Berkeley, 1982–2001. Asst on excavations at: Istanbul, 1954; Tell Rifa'at, 1956; Beycesultan, 1956–57; Hacilar, 1957–59; Nimrud, 1957–60; Charsada, 1958. Director, excavations at: Ras al'Amiya, 1960; Yarim Tepe, 1960–62; Pasargadae, 1961–63; Tepe Nush-i Jan, 1967–77; Nineveh, 1987–90; Co-director, excavations at: Shahr-i Qumis, 1967–78; Horom, 1992–93; Velikent, 1994–97; Erebuni, 2007–10. Mem., Internat. Cttee of Internat. Congresses of Iranian Art and Archaeology, 1968–80. Hagop Kevorkian Visiting Lectr in Iranian Art and Archaeology, Univ. of Pennsylvania, 1967; Lectures: Rhind, Edin., 1973; Norton, Amer. Inst. of Archaeology, 1980; Columbia in Iranian Studies, Columbia Univ., 1986; Leventritt, Harvard Univ., 1991; Cohodas, Hebrew Union Coll., Jerusalem, 1992; McNicoll, Univ. of Sydney, 1994. Vis. Prof. of Archaeology, Hebrew Univ., Jerusalem, 1977; Vis. Prof. of Archaeology and Iranian Studies, Univ. of Arizona, Tucson, 1980–81; Vis. Prof., Collège de France, Paris, 1999; Walker Ames Prof., Univ. of Washington, 2002. Mem., German Archaeological Inst., 1973 (Corresp. Mem., 1966); Associate Mem., Royal Belgian Acad., 1988–. Ghirshman Prize, Académie des Inscriptions et Belles-Lettres, Paris, 1979; Sir Percy Sykes Meml Medal, Royal Soc. for Asian Affairs, 1980; Gold Medal, Archaeol Inst. of America, 2004. Adv. Editor: Jl of Mithraic Studies, 1976–79; Iran, 1981–96; Iranica Antiqua, 1984–; Bulletin of Asia Inst., 1986–; Amer. Jl of Archaeol., 1989–96; Ancient West and East, 2002–. *Publications:* Pasargadae, a Report on the Excavations conducted by the British Institute of Persian Studies, 1978; (with M. Roaf) Nush-i Jan I, The Major Buildings of the Median Settlement, 2007; (ed with A. Mousavi) Irans Erbe in Flugbildern von Georg Gerster, 2009; (ed with A. Mousavi) Ancient Iran from the Air, 2012; archaeological articles in: Jl of Near Eastern Studies; Iran; Iraq; Anatolian Studies, etc. *Recreations:* fly fishing, mediaeval architecture, tribal carpets; repr. Cambridge in athletics, 1953. *Address:* Department of Near Eastern Studies, University of California, Berkeley, CA 94720–1940, USA. *Clubs:* Achilles; Hawks (Cambridge); Explorers (New York).

STRONG, Benjamin James Quentin; QC 2014; *b* 6 Aug. 1968; *s* of Harry and Mary Strong; *m* 2002, Anita Drew; one *s*. *Educ:* Nottingham High Sch.; Jesus Coll., Cambridge (BA 1991). Admitted as solicitor, 1994; Solicitor, Slaughter and May, 1994–2001; called to the Bar, Middle Temple, 2001; in practice as a barrister, specialising in commercial litigation, 2002–. *Address:* One Essex Court, Temple, EC4Y 9AR. *T:* (020) 7583 2000. *E:* bstrong@oeclaw.co.uk.

STRONG, Hilary Jane Veronica; Director: Strong Ideas Ltd, since 2011; Making Theatre Gaining Skills CIC, since 2014; *b* 3 June 1957; *d* of Robert Hedley Strong and Estelle Flora Strong (*née* Morris). *Educ:* Chichester High Sch. for Girls; Lombard Sch. of Dancing. Freelance stage-manager and actress, 1979–83; Administrator: Merlin Theatre, Frome, 1986–88; Natural Theatre Co., Bath, 1989–94; Dir, Edinburgh Festival Fringe, 1994–99; Exec. Dir, Greenwich Theatre, 1999–2007; estabd Greenwich Musical Theatre Acad., 2003; Dir, Nat. Council for Drama Trng, 2007–10. Member Board: Nat. Campaign for Arts, 1990–92; Dance Base, Edinburgh, 1995–99; Mem., Arts Council of England, 1998–2002. *Recreation:* travelling on buses abroad. *E:* hilary@strong-ideas.co.uk.

STRONG, Jaqueline Ann Mary; education consultant, 2004–10; *b* 2 Oct. 1944; *d* of Donald Cameron McKeand and Gwendoline Mary Ann McKeand (*née* Graham); *m* 1966, Roger Francis Strong (*d* 2014). *Educ:* Sexey's Grammar Sch.; Chipping Sodbury Grammar Sch.; Univ. of Wales (BSc, DipEd 1st cl.); Univ. of Bristol (MEd). Teacher, St Julian's Jun. High Sch., Newport, 1966–69; Lectr, Rhydyfelin Coll. of FE, 1967–70; teacher: Belfast, 1970–73; St Peter's Comp. Sch., Huntingdon, 1974, Dep. Head Teacher, 1974–81; Warden, The Village Coll., Bassingbourn, 1981–88; Asst Dir of Educn, Cambs CC, 1988–93; Director of Education: Leeds MDC, 1993–95; Leics CC, 1995–2004. Mem., Exec. Bd, Encounter, 1984–2008. Mem. Council, Univ. of Loughborough, 1995–2012. Voluntary worker for animal charities, Blue Cross and Pets as Therapy, 2000–. *Publications:* articles in educational magazines. *Recreations:* singing, exotic foreign travel, photography, walking, reading, concert and theatre going, taking in unwanted Great Danes.

STRONG, Liam; Partner, since 2007, and Chief Executive Officer, since 2009, Cerberus European Capital Advisers LLP; Chairman, Virtual IT, since 2002; *b* 6 Jan. 1945; *s* of Gerald Strong and Geraldine Strong (*née* Crozier); *m* 1970, Jacqueline Gray; one *s* one *d*. *Educ:* Trinity Coll., Dublin. Procter & Gamble, 1967–71; Reckitt & Colman, 1971–88; Dir of Mktg and Ops, British Airways, 1988–91; Chief Executive: Sears plc, 1991–97; MCI (formerly WorldCom) Internat., 1997–2001; Teleglobe Inc., 2003–06. Chairman: Torex, 2009–12; Greenstar, 2014–; Director: Aercap Holdings NV, 2006– (Vice-Chm., 2011–13); Admiral, 2013–. Chm., UK Govt Telecoms Adv. Bd, 2002–05. Gov., Ashridge Management Coll., 1996–. *Recreations:* sailing, history, charity.

STRONG, Liza; *see* Marshall, L.

STRONG, Hon. Maurice Frederick; PC (Can.) 1993; OC 1976; FRSC 1987; Senior Advisor to the President, World Bank, since 1995; Special Advisor to Secretary-General of the United Nations, 1998–2005; *b* 29 April 1929; *s* of Frederick Milton Strong and late Mary Fyfe Strong; *m* 1st, 1950 (marr. diss. 1980); two *s* two *d*; 2nd, 1981, Hanne Marstrand; one foster *d*. *Educ:* Public and High Sch., Oak Lake, Manitoba, Canada. Served in UN Secretariat, 1947; worked in industry and Pres. or Dir, various Canadian and internat. corporations, 1948–66; Dir-Gen., External Aid Office (later Canadian Internat. Develt Agency), Canadian Govt, 1966–71; Under-Sec.-Gen. with responsibility for envmtl affairs, and Sec.-Gen. of 1972 Conf. on the Human Environment, Stockholm, 1971–72; Exec. Dir, UN Envmtl Programme, 1972–75; Pres., Chm. of Bd and Chm. of Exec. Cttee, Petro-Canada, 1976–78; Chm. of Bd, AZL Resources Inc., USA, 1978–83; Under-Sec.-Gen., UN, 1985–87 and 1989–92; Exec. Co-ordinator, UN Office for Emergency Ops in Africa, NY, 1985–87; Sec.-Gen., UN 1992 Conf. on Envmt and Develt, 1990–92; Under-Sec. Gen. and Exec. Co-ordinator for UN Reform, 1997. Chm. and CEO, Ontario Hydro, 1992–95; Chairman: Quantum Energy Technols Corp., subseq. Super Critical Combustion; Technology

Development Corp.; Strovest Hldgs Inc.; formerly: Dir, Massey Ferguson, Canada; Dir, Mem. Exec. Cttee and Vice Chm., Canada Develt Corp., Toronto; Chm., Canada Develt Investment Corp., Vancouver. Chairman: Centre for Internat. Management Studies, Geneva, 1971–78; American Water Development, Denver, 1986; Internat. Energy Develt Corp., Geneva (also Special Advr); Bd of Govs, Internat. Develt Res. Centre, 1977–78; Co-Chm., Interaction Policy Bd, Vienna; Vice-Chm. and Dir, Soc. Gén. pour l'Energie et les Ressources, Geneva, 1980–86; Foundn Dir, World Economic Forum. Chm., Internat. Adv. Gp, CH2M Hill Cos Ltd; Member: Internat. Adv. Bd, Toyota Motor Corp.; Adv. Bd, Lamont-Doherty Observatory; Bd, Bretton Woods Cttee, Washington; World Commn on Envmt and Develt; Alt. Gov., IBRD, ADB, Caribbean Develt Bank. President: World Fedn of UN Assocs, 1987; Better World Soc., 1988; Chairman: North South Energy Roundtable, Washington; North South Energy Roundtable, Rome; World Resources Inst.; Earth Council; Stockholm Envmt Inst.; Adv. Cttee, UN Univ., Tokyo, Japan; Pres. Council and Rector, UN Univ. for Peace; Mem., and Chm. Exec. Cttee, UN Foundn. Director: Leadership for Envmt and Develt; Lindisfarne Assoc.; Mem., Internat. Asia Soc., NY. Trustee: Rockefeller Foundn, 1971–78; Aspen Inst., 1971; Internat. Foundn for Develt Alternatives. Hon. Prof., Peking Univ., 2004. FRSA. Holds numerous hon. degrees from univs and colls in Canada, USA and UK. First UN Internat. Envmt Prize. Order of the Star of the North (Sweden); Comdr, Order of the Golden Ark (Netherlands). *Publications:* Where on Earth are We Going?, 2000; articles in various jls, including Foreign Affairs Magazine, Natural History Magazine. *Recreations:* swimming, skin-diving, farming, reading. *Clubs:* Yale (New York); University (Toronto).

STRONG, Sir Roy (Colin), Kt 1982; PhD; FSA; FRSL; writer and historian, diarist, lecturer, critic, columnist, contributor to radio and television and organiser of exhibitions, gardener; Director, Oman Productions Ltd; *b* 23 Aug. 1935; *s* of G. E. C. Strong; *m* 1971, Julia Trevelyan Oman, CBE, RDI (*d* 2003). *Educ:* Edmonton Co. Grammar Sch.; Queen Mary Coll., London (Fellow, 1976); Warburg Inst., London. Asst Keeper, 1959, Director, Keeper and Secretary 1967–73, Nat. Portrait Gallery; Dir, Victoria and Albert Museum, 1974–87. Ferens Prof. of Fine Art, Univ. of Hull, 1972. Walls Lectures, Pierpont Morgan Library, 1974; Andrew Carnduff Ritchie Lectr, Yale Univ., 1999. Member: Fine Arts Adv. Cttee, British Council, 1974–87; Westminster Abbey Architectl Panel, 1975–89; Council, RCA, 1979–87; Arts Council of GB, 1983–87 (Chm., Arts Panel, 1983–87); Vice-Chm., South Bank Centre (formerly South Bank Bd), 1985–90. High Bailiff and Searcher of the Sanctuary, Westminster Abbey, 2000–. Pres., 2001–02, 2004–, Vice-Pres., 2002–04, Garden History Soc.; Vice-Pres., RSPCA, 2000–05. Trustee: Arundel Castle, 1974–86; Chevening, 1974–87; Sutton Place, 1982–84; Patron, Pallant House, Chichester, 1986– (Trustee, 1980–86). Writer and presenter, TV series incl. Royal Gardens 1992; The Diets That Time Forgot, 2008; (contrib.) The Genius of British Art, 2010. Sen. Fellow, RCA, 1983; FRSL. Hon. DLitt: Leeds, 1983; Keele, 1984; Hon. MA Worcester, 2005. Shakespeare Prize, FVS Foundn, Hamburg, 1980. *Publications:* Portraits of Queen Elizabeth I, 1963; (with J. A. van Dorsten) Leicester's Triumph, 1964; Holbein and Henry VIII, 1967; Tudor and Jacobean Portraits, 1969; The English Icon: Elizabethan and Jacobean Portraiture, 1969; (with Julia Trevelyan Oman) Elizabeth R, 1971; Van Dyck: Charles I on Horseback, 1972; (with Julia Trevelyan Oman) Mary Queen of Scots, 1972; (with Stephen Orgel) Inigo Jones: the theatre of the Stuart court, 1973; contrib. Burke's Guide to the Royal Family, 1973; Splendour at Court: Renaissance Spectacle and the Theatre of Power, 1973; (with Colin Ford) An Early Victorian Album: the Hill-Adamson collection, 1974; Nicholas Hilliard, 1975; (contrib.) Spirit of the Age, 1975; The Cult of Elizabeth: Elizabethan Portraiture and Pageantry, 1977; And When Did You Last See Your Father?, 1978; The Renaissance Garden in England, 1979; (contrib.) The Garden, 1979; Britannia Triumphans: Inigo Jones, Rubens and Whitehall Palace, 1980; (introd.) Holbein, 1980; (contrib.) Designing for the Dancer, 1981; (jtly) The English Miniature, 1981; (with Julia Trevelyan Oman) The English Year, 1982; (contrib.) Pelican Guide to English Literature vol. 3, 1982; (with J. Murrell) Artists of the Tudor Court, 1983; The English Renaissance Miniature, 1983; (contrib.) Glyndebourne: a celebration, 1984; Art & Power, 1984; Strong Points, 1985; Henry, Prince of Wales and England's Lost Renaissance, 1986; (contrib.) For Veronica Wedgwood These, 1986; Creating Small Gardens, 1986; Gloriana, Portraits of Queen Elizabeth I, 1987; A Small Garden Designer's Handbook, 1987; Cecil Beaton: the Royal Portraits, 1988; Creating Small Formal Gardens, 1989; (contrib.) British Theatre Design, 1989; Lost Treasures of Britain, 1990; (contrib.) Sir Philip Sidney's Achievements, 1990; (contrib.) England and the Continental Renaissance, 1990; (ed) A Celebration of Gardens, 1991; The Garden Trellis, 1991; Small Period Gardens, 1992; Royal Gardens, 1992; A Country Life, 1994; Successful Small Gardens, 1994; William Larkin, 1995; The Tudor and Stuart Monarchy, vol. I, Tudor, 1995, vol. II, Elizabethan, 1996, vol. III, Jacobean and Caroline, 1998; The Story of Britain, 1996; Country Life 1897–1997: the English Arcadia, 1996; The Roy Strong Diaries 1967–1987, 1997; (with Julia Trevelyan Oman) On Happiness, 1998; The Spirit of Britain, 1999, 2nd edn as The Arts in Britain: a history, 2004; Garden Party, 2000; The Artist and the Garden, 2000; Ornament in the Small Garden, 2001; Feast: a history of grand eating, 2002; The Laskett: the story of a garden, 2003; Passions Past and Present, 2005; Coronation: a history of kingship and the British monarchy, 2005; A Little History of the English Country Church, 2007; Visions of England, 2011; Self-Portrait as a Young Man, 2013; Remaking a Garden: the Laskett transformed, 2014; (with John Swannell) Sir Portrait, 2015. *Recreations:* gardening, keeping fit, cycling. *Address:* The Laskett, Much Birch, Herefords HR2 8HZ. *Club:* Garrick.

STRONG, Prof. Russell Walker, AC 2001; CMG 1987; RFD 1995; FRCS, FRACS, FACS; FRACDS; Professor of Surgery, University of Queensland, 1992–2004, now Emeritus; Director of Surgery, Princess Alexandra Hospital, Brisbane, 1981–2004; *b* 4 April 1938; *s* of Aubrey and Anne Strong; *m* 1960, Judith Bardsley; two *d*. *Educ:* Lismore High Sch.; Univ. of Sydney (BDS); Charing Cross Hosp. Med. Sch., Univ. of London (MB BS). LRCP 1965; MRCS 1965, FRCS 1970; FRACDS 1966; FRACS 1974; FACS 1984, Hon. FACS 2008. Intern, Bromley Hosp., Kent, 1965–66; Tutor in Anatomy, Charing Cross Hosp. Med. Sch., 1966–67; SHO, Birmingham Accident Hosp., 1968; Surgical Registrar: Charing Cross Hosp., 1969; St Helier Hosp., 1970–71; Sen. Surgical Registrar, Whittington Hosp., 1972–73; Surgical Supervisor, Princess Alexandra Hosp., Brisbane, 1973–80. Vis. Prof. and Guest Lectr on numerous occasions worldwide. James IV Surgical Traveller, 1987; Vis. Schol., Pembroke Coll., Cambridge, 2001. Hon. Fellow: Assoc. of Surgeons of GB and Ireland, 1996; Surgical Res. Soc. of SA, 1996; Hon. FRCSE 2001; Distinguished Academician, Acad. of Medicine, Singapore, 1998; Hon. Mem., Internat. Coll. of Surgeons, 1989; Hon. Fellow, American Surgical Assoc., 2003. Inaugural Award for Excellence in Surgery, RACS, 1993; Prize, Internat. Soc. of Surgeons, 2001; Brand Laureate Award, Malaysia, 2012. Knight Comdr, Distinguished Order of Malaysia, 2010. *Publications:* contrib. book chapters and numerous articles in scientific jls. *Recreations:* golf, tennis. *Address:* U5313 Farringford, 197 King Arthur TCE, Tennyson, Brisbane, Qld 4105, Australia. *T:* (7) 38481130.

STRONGE, Christopher James; Partner, Coopers & Lybrand Deloitte, 1967–92; *b* 16 Aug. 1933; *s* of Reginald Herbert James Stronge and Doreen Marjorie Stronge; *m* 1964, Gabrielle; one *s* one *d*. *Educ:* Chigwell Sch.; Magdalene Coll., Cambridge (MA Math.). FCA. Deloitte Haskins & Sells: joined 1957; Partner 1967; Dep. Sen. Partner, 1985. Member: Accounting Standards Cttee, 1980–83; Internat. Accounting Standards Cttee, 1985–90; Treasurer, RIIA, 1981–91. *Recreations:* opera, golf, sailing.

STRONGE, Sir James Anselan Maxwell, 10th Bt *cr* 1803; *b* 17 July 1946; *s* of Maxwell Du Pré James Stronge (*d* 1973) (*ggs* of 2nd Bt) and Eileen Mary (*d* 1976), *d* of Rt Hon. Maurice Marcus McCausland, PC, Drenagh, Limavady, Co. Londonderry; *S* cousin, 1981, but his name does not appear on the Official Roll of the Baronetage. *Heir:* none. *Address:* Camphill Community Clanabogan, 15 Drudgeon Road, Clanabogan, Omagh, Co. Tyrone BT78 1TJ.

STRONGMAN, Ian Melville, TD 1993; a District Judge (Magistrates' Courts), since 2011; *b* St Dennis, Cornwall, 1958; *s* of Ronald Strongman and Lilian Strongman; *m* 1984, Carol Gray; two *s*. *Educ:* Univ. of Leeds (LLB 1980). Called to the Bar, Lincoln's Inn, 1981; in practice as a barrister, 8 Fountain Court, Birmingham, 1986–2011, Hd of Chambers, 1997–2011; a Dep. Dist Judge, 1999–2011. Served TA, Staffs Regt (rank of Major). *Recreations:* walking, water colour painting. *Address:* Victoria Law Courts, Corporation Street, Birmingham B4 6QA.

STROUD, family name of **Baroness Stroud**.

STROUD, Baroness *cr* 2015 (Life Peer), of Fulham in the London Borough of Hammersmith and Fulham; **Philippa Claire Stroud;** Special Adviser, Department for Work and Pensions, 2010–15; *b* Whitestone, Devon, 2 April 1965; *d* of Peter and Wendy Duffy; *m* 1989, David Stroud; three *c*. *Educ:* St Catherine's Sch., Bramley; Univ. of Birmingham (BA Hons). Work in Hong Kong and Macau amongst addict community, 1987–89; Founder, King's Arms Project (night shelter and hostel), Bedford, 1989–98; Exec. Dir, Bridge Project, Birmingham, 1998; Centre for Social Justice: Co-founder, 2004; Exec. Dir, 2004–10; Chm., Implementation Strategy Bd, 2008–10; Dir, Policy, 2008–10. Contested (C): Birmingham Ladywood, 2005; Sutton and Cheam, 2010. *Publications:* God's Heart for the Poor, 1999.

STROUD, Dr Michael Adrian, OBE 1993; FRCP, FRCPE; Senior Lecturer and Consultant in Medicine, Gastroenterology and Nutrition, Southampton General Hospital, since 1998 (Research Fellow in Nutrition and Gastroenterology, 1995–98); *b* 17 April 1955; *s* of Victor and Vivienne Stroud; *m* 1987, Thea de Moel; one *s* one *d*. *Educ:* University Coll. London (BSc; Fellow 2005); St George's Hosp. Med. Sch. (MB, BS, MD); FRCP 1994; FRCPE 1994. Med. trng, St George's Hosp., London, 1973–79; postgrad. trng and work in various NHS hosps, 1979–89; govt res. in survival and endurance physiology, 1989–95. Has taken part in many expeditions to Polar regions, incl. the first unassisted crossing of Antarctica on foot, with Sir Ranulph Fiennes, 1992–93; Land Rover 7x7x7 Challenge (7 marathons in 7 days on 7 continents), with Sir Ranulph, 2003. Hon. DSc Robert Gordon, 2006. Polar Medal, 1995. *Publications:* Shadows on the Wasteland: crossing Antarctica with Ranulph Fiennes, 1993; Survival of the Fittest, 1998; articles on thermal and survival physiology, endurance exercise, and nutrition in med. jls. *Recreations:* climbing, multi-sport endurance events. *Address:* Institute of Human Nutrition, Southampton General Hospital, Tremona Road, Southampton SO16 6YD. *T:* (023) 8079 6317.

STROWGER, (Gaston) Jack, CBE 1976; Managing Director, Thorn Electrical Industries, 1970–79; *b* 8 Feb. 1916; *s* of Alfred Henry Strowger, Lowestoft boat-owner, and Lily Ellen Tripp; *m* 1939, Katherine Ellen Gilbert; two *s* one *d*. *Educ:* Lowestoft Grammar School. Joined London Electrical Supply Co., 1934; HM Forces, 1939–43. Joined TEI, as an Accountant, 1943; Group Chief Accountant, 1952; joined Tricity Finance Corp. as Dir, 1959; Exec. Dir, TEI, 1961; full Dir 1966; Financial Dir 1967; Dep. Chm., Tricity Finance Corp., 1968; Chm., Thorn-Ericsson, 1974–81. Dir (non-exec.), Hornby Hobbies (Chm., 1981–93). FCMI. *Recreations:* gardening, bowling. *Address:* 43 Blake Court, 1 Newsholme Drive, Winchmore Hill, N21 1SQ.

STROYAN, Rt Rev. John Ronald Angus; *see* Warwick, Bishop Suffragan of.

STROYAN, His Honour Ronald Angus Ropner; QC 1972; a Circuit Judge, 1975–96; a Senior Circuit Judge, 1993–96; Hon. Recorder of Newcastle upon Tyne, 1993–96; *b* 27 Nov. 1924; *e s* of Ronald S. Stroyan of Boreland, Killin; *m* 1st, 1952, Elisabeth Anna Grant (marr. diss. 1965), *y d* of Col J. P. Grant of Rothiemurchus; one *s* two *d*; 2nd, 1967, Jill Annette Johnston, *d* of late Sir Douglas Marshall; one *s*, and two step *s* two step *d*. *Educ:* Harrow School; Trinity College, Cambridge; BA(Hons). Served 1943–45 with The Black Watch (NW Europe); attd Argyll and Sutherland Highlanders, Palestine, 1945–47 (despatches); Captain; later with Black Watch TA. Barrister-at-Law, 1950, Inner Temple. Dep. Chm., North Riding QS, 1962–70, Chm., 1970–71; a Recorder of the Crown Court, 1972–75. Member: Gen. Council of the Bar, 1963–67, 1969–73 and 1975; Parole Bd, 1996–2002. Chm., West Rannoch Deer Management Gp, 1989–2003. *Recreation:* country sports. *Address:* Boreland, Killin, Perthshire FK21 8TT. *T:* (01567) 820252. *Club:* Caledonian.

See also Bishop Suffragan of Warwick.

STRUDWICK, Maj. Gen. Mark Jeremy, CBE 1990; Chief Executive, The Prince's Scottish Youth Business Trust, 2000–12; Chairman, Scottish Veterans' Residences, since 2001; *b* 19 April 1945; *s* of late Ronald Strudwick and Mary Strudwick (*née* Beresford); *m* 1st, 1970, Janet Elizabeth Coleridge Vivers (*d* 2013); one *s* one *d*; 2nd, 2015, Sue Garrett-Cox (*née* Guest); two step *s* one step *d*. *Educ:* St Edmund's Sch., Canterbury; RMA Sandhurst. Commnd Royal Scots (The Royal Regt), 1966; served UK, BAOR, Cyprus, Canada, India, NI (despatches twice); Comd, 1st Bn Royal Scots, 1984–87; Instr, Staff Coll., 1987–88; ACOS HQ NI, 1988–90; Higher Comd and Staff Course, 1989; Comd 3 Inf. Bde, 1990–91; NDC New Delhi, 1992; Dep. Mil. Sec., MoD, 1993–95; Dir of Infantry, 1996–97; ADC to the Queen, 1996–97; GOC Scotland and Gov. of Edinburgh Castle, 1997–2000. Col, Royal Scots, 1995–2005; Col Comdt, Scottish Div., 1997–2000. Mem., Queen's Body Guard for Scotland, Royal Company of Archers, 1994 (Brig. 2006). Dir, Royal Edinburgh Military Tattoo, 2007–15; Chm., Scottish Nat. War Meml, 2009–. Trustee, Historic Scotland Foundn, 2001–15; President: Highland and Lowland Brigades Club, 2007–; Soc. of Friends of St Andrew's, Jerusalem, 2011–15. Cdre, Infantry Sailing Assoc., 1997–2000. Governor: Royal Sch., Bath, 1993–2000; Gordonstoun Sch., 1999–2007; Excelsior Acad., Newcastle, 2009–15. KStJ 2015; Prior, Order of St John, Scotland, 2015–. *Recreations:* fishing, golf, shooting, sailing. *Club:* Royal Scots (Trustee, 1995–; Chm., 2014–) (Edinburgh).

STRUNIN, Prof. Leo, MD; FRCA; BOC Professor of Anaesthesia, Bart's and The London School of Medicine and Dentistry, Queen Mary (formerly London Hospital Medical College, then St Bartholomew's and Royal London School of Medicine and Dentistry, Queen Mary and Westfield College), University of London, 1990–2003, now Emeritus Professor; *b* 19 Nov. 1937; *m* 1968, Jane Smith. *Educ:* Univ. of Durham (MB BS 1960); Univ. of Newcastle upon Tyne (MD 1974). FRCA (FFARCS 1964); FRCP(C) 1980. Training posts, Newcastle upon Tyne, Sunderland, Manchester and London, 1960–67; Lectr, 1967–69, Sen. Lectr, 1969–72, Anaesthetics Unit, London Hosp. Med. Coll.; Sen. Lectr, 1972–74, Prof., 1975–79, Anaesthetic Dept, King's Coll. Hosp. and Med. Sch.; Prof. and Head, Dept of Anaesthesia, Univ. of Calgary, Canada, 1980–90. President: RCAnaes, 1997–2000; Assoc. of Anaesthetists of GB and Ire., 2000–02. *Publications:* Anaesthesia and the Liver, 1977; (with S. Thomson) Anaesthesia and the Liver, 1992; (with J. A. Stamford) Neuroprotection, 1996. *Recreation:* whippet and greyhound racing. *Address:* The Grange, Firsby, Spilsby, Lincs PE23 5QL. *T:* (01754) 830585. *Club:* Athenæum.

STRUTHERS, Alastair James, OBE 1995; *b* 25 July 1929; *s* of Alexander Struthers and Elizabeth Struthers (*née* Hutchison); *m* 1967, Elizabeth Henderson (*d* 2014); three *d*. *Educ:* Stowe; Trinity Coll., Cambridge (MA). Chairman: J. & A. Gardner & Co. Ltd, 1962–; Scottish National Trust plc, 1983–98; Caledonian MacBrayne Ltd, 1990–94. Chairman: Steamship Mutual Underwriting Assoc., 1988–95; Steamship Mutual Trustees (Bermuda) Ltd,

2000–. Dir, Hamilton Park Racecourse, 1973–. Chm., Racing and Thoroughbred Breeding Trng Bd, 1992–98. Comr, Northern Lighthouse Bd, 1980–99. Dep. Sen. Steward, Jockey Club, 1990–94. *Recreations:* racing, shooting, golf. *Address:* Garden Cottage, Craigmaddie, Milngavie, by Glasgow G62 8LB. *T:* (0141) 956 1262. *Club:* Western (Glasgow).

STRUTHERS, Prof. Allan David, MD; FRCP, FESC; FRSE; FMedSci; Professor of Cardiovascular Medicine, since 1992, and Head, Division of Medicine and Therapeutics, since 2002, University of Dundee; *b* Glasgow, 14 Aug. 1952; *s* of Dr David Struthers and Margaret Struthers; *m* 1979, Julia Elizabeth Anne Diggens; one *s* one *d.* *Educ:* Hutchesons' Boys' Grammar Sch., Glasgow; Univ. of Glasgow (BSc Hons Biochem. 1973; MB ChB Hons 1977; MD 1984); FRCPE 1990; FRCPG 1990; FRCP 1992; FESC 1994; FRSE 2010; FMedSci 2011. Sen. Med. Registrar, RPMS and Hammersmith Hosp., London, 1982–85; Wellcome Sen. Lectr, Univ. of Dundee, 1985–89. Chairman: SIGN Guidelines on Heart Failure, 2003–07; Nat. Scientific Adv. Cttee, TENOVUS charity, 2004–; Heart Failure Clinical Standards, NHS Quality Improvement Scotland, 2008–; SIGN/RCPSG CPD Cttee, 2009–. SmithKline Beecham Prize, Brit. Pharmacol Soc., 1990. *Publications:* Atrial Natriuretic Peptide, 1993; papers on B-type natriuretic peptide (BNP), aldosterone antagonists and xanthine oxidase inhibitors in cardiovascular jls. *Recreations:* cycling, walking, travel, opera. *Address:* Division of Medicine and Therapeutics, Ninewells Hospital and Medical School, Dundee DD1 9SY. *T:* (01382) 383013, *Fax:* (01382) 644972. *E:* a.d.struthers@dundee.ac.uk.

STRUTT, family name of **Barons Belper** and **Rayleigh**.

STUART; *see* Crichton-Stuart, family name of Marquess of Bute.

STUART, family name of **Earl Castle Stewart, Earl of Moray** and **Viscount Stuart of Findhorn**.

STUART, Viscount; Andrew Richard Charles Stuart; lecturer, now retired; *b* 7 Oct. 1953; *s* and *heir* of 8th Earl Castle Stewart, *qv*; *m* 1st, 1973, Annie Le Poulain (marr. diss. 2003), St Malo, France; one *d*; 2nd, 2009, Carol Ann Reid. *Educ:* Wynstones, Glos; Millfield, Som.; Univ. of Exeter. *Recreations:* running, hiking, bellringing, cycling, sailing. *Address:* The Old Barn, Stone Lane, E Pennard, Shepton Mallet, Somerset BA4 6RZ.

STUART OF FINDHORN, 3rd Viscount *cr* 1959, of Findhorn co. Moray; **Dominic Stuart;** *b* 25 March 1948; *s* of 2nd Viscount Stuart of Findhorn and his 1st wife, Grizel Mary Wilfreda, *d* of D. T. Fyfe and *widow* of Michael Gillilan; *S* father, 1999, but does not use the title; *m* 1979, Yvonne Lucienne (marr. diss. 2002), *d* of Edgar Després. *Educ:* Eton. *Heir: half-b* Hon. Andrew Moray Stuart, *b* 20 Oct. 1957.

STUART, Hon. Sir Antony James Cobham E.; *see* Edwards-Stuart.

STUART, (Charles) Murray, CBE 1995; Chairman, Scottish Power, 1992–2000 (Director, 1990–2000); *b* 28 July 1933; *s* of Charles Maitland Stuart and Grace Forrester Stuart (*née* Kerr); *m* 1963, Netta Caroline; one *s* one *d.* *Educ:* Glasgow Acad.; Glasgow Univ. (MA, LLB). Scottish Chartered Accountant; CA. With P. & W. McLellan, Ford Motor Co., Sheffield Twist Drill & Steel Co., and Unicorn Industries, 1961–73; Finance Dir, Hepworths, 1973–74; Finance Dir and Dep. Man. Dir, ICL, 1974–81; Metal Box, subseq. MB Group: Finance Dir, Dir—Finance, Planning and Admin, 1981–86; Man. Dir, Dec. 1986–Dec. 1987; Gp Chief Exec., 1988–89; Chm., 1989–90; Finance Dir, 1990–91, Chief Exec., 1991, Berisford International. Vice Chm., CMB Packaging SA, 1989–90; Vice-Chm. and Dir, Hill Samuel, 1992–93; Chairman: Hill Samuel Scotland, 1993–94; Intermediate Capital Group PLC, 1993–2001; Hammersmith Hospitals NHS Trust, 1996–2000; non-executive Director: Save & Prosper Insurance, 1987–91; Save & Prosper Securities, 1988–91; Hunter Saphir, 1991–92; Clerical Medical & General Life Assurance Soc., 1993–96; Royal Bank of Scotland Gp, 1996–2002; Royal Bank of Scotland, 1996–2002; Willis Corroon Gp plc, 1996–97; CMG plc, 1998–2002; Old Mutual PLC, 1999–2003; Nat. Westminster Bank, 2000–02; Administrateur, 2000–09, and Prés., Comité des comptes et de l'audit, 2004–09, Veolia Environnement SA; Mem., European Adv. Bd, Credit Lyonnais, 2000–04. Dep. Chm., Audit Commn, 1991–95 (Mem., 1986–95); Mem., Private Finance Initiative Panel, 1995–97. Mem., W Surrey and NE Hants HA, 1990–93. Mem., Meteorological Office, 1994–98. Non-exec. Dir, Royal Scottish Nat. Orch., 1998–2000. DUniv: Paisley, 1999; Glasgow, 2001. *Recreations:* theatre, gardening, travel. *Address:* Longacre, Guildford Road, Chobham, Woking, Surrey GU24 8EA. *T:* (01276) 857144. *Club:* Caledonian.

STUART, Christopher Charles; HM Diplomatic Service, retired; Ambassador to Mongolia, 2012–15; *m* 1986, Isabelle Julie Louise Brown; one *s.* Develt chemist, 1982–86; Inspector of Health and Safety, HSE, 1986–96; Lectr (pt-time), Basford Hall Coll., 1993–97; entered FCO, 1997; First Sec., Sci. and Technol., Tokyo, 1997–2001; Hd, Near East and N Africa Unit, UK Trade and Investment, 2001–02; Japanese lang. trng, 2003–04; Hd, Investment and Dep. Consul Gen., W Japan, 2004–07; Consul Gen., and Hd, UK Trade and Investment, Osaka, 2007–09; Dir, Corporate Develt, Energy Technologies Inst. (on secondment), 2009–12.

STUART, Prof. David Ian, PhD; FMedSci; FRS 1996; MRC Professor of Structural Biology, since 1996, and Joint Head of Division of Structural Biology, Wellcome Trust Centre for Human Genetics, University of Oxford; Fellow of Hertford College, Oxford, since 1985. *Educ:* London Univ. (BSc); PhD Bristol; MA Oxon. Lectr in Structural Molecular Biology, Univ. of Oxford, 1985–96. Life Sci. Dir, Diamond Light Source, 2008–. FMedSci 2006. Hon. DSc Leeds, 2011; Hon. Dr Helsinki. *Address:* Wellcome Trust Centre for Human Genetics, Roosevelt Drive, Headington, Oxford OX3 7BN.

STUART, Duncan, CMG 1989; HM Diplomatic Service, retired; *b* 1 July 1934; *s* of late Ian Cameron Stuart and Patricia Forbes; *m* 1961, Leonore Luise Liederwald; one *s* one *d.* *Educ:* Rugby Sch.; Brasenose Coll., Oxford (MA). Served 1st Bn Oxfordshire and Bucks LI, 1955–57 (2nd Lieut). Joined Foreign, later Diplomatic, Service, 1959; Office of Political Advr, Berlin, 1960–61; FO, 1961–64; Helsinki, 1964–66; Head of Chancery, Dar-es-Salaam, 1966–69; FCO, 1969–70; Helsinki, 1970–74; FCO, 1974–80; Counsellor, Bonn, 1980–83; FCO, 1983–86; Counsellor, Washington, 1986–88; FCO, 1988–92; Advr, MoD, 1992–94; Special Ops Exec. Advr, FCO, 1996–2002. Chm. and Chief Exec., Cyrus Internat., 1994–95. Gov., St Clare's, Oxford, 1991–2008. *Address:* c/o C. Hoare & Co., 37 Fleet Street, EC4P 4DQ. *Clubs:* Oxford and Cambridge, Special Forces.

STUART, Rt Hon. Gisela (Gschaider); PC 2015; MP (Lab) Birmingham Edgbaston, since 1997; *b* 26 Nov. 1955; *d* of late Martin and of Liane Gschaider; *m* 1st, 1980, Robert Scott Stuart (marr. diss. 2000); two *s*; 2nd, 2010, Derek John Scott (*d* 2012). *Educ:* Staatliche Realschule, Vilsbiburg; Manchester Poly.; London Univ. (LLB 1991). Dep. Dir, London Book Fair, 1982; Law Lectr, Worcester Coll. of Technol., 1992–97; res. in pension law, Birmingham Univ., 1995–97. PPS to Minister of State, Home Office, 1998–99; Parly Under-Sec. of State, DoH, 1999–2001. Member: Social Security Select Cttee, 1997–98; Foreign Affairs Select Cttee, 2001–10; Defence Select Cttee, 2010–15; Intelligence and Security Cttee, 2015–; Chair, All Party Parly Gp on Kazakhstan, 2015–. Mem. Presidium, Convention on Future of Europe. Associate Ed., 2001–05, Ed., 2006–, The House mag. Member: Ext. Bd, Birmingham Business Sch., 2007–; London Univ. Ext. Prog., 2008–. Trustee: Henry Jackson Soc., 2006–; Reading Force, 2014–; Armed Forces Parly Scheme, 2014–. Hon. Dr Aston, 2008; DUniv Birmingham City, 2015. Bundesverdienstkreuz (Germany), 2008. *Publications:* The Making of Europe's Constitution, 2003. *Address:* House of Commons, SW1A 0AA. *T:* (020) 7219 3000. *E:* stuartg@parliament.uk.

STUART, Graham Charles; MP (C) Beverley and Holderness, since 2005; *b* 12 March 1962; *s* of late Dr Peter Stuart and of Joan Stuart; *m* 1989, Anne Crawshaw; two *d.* *Educ:* Glenalmond Coll.; Selwyn Coll., Cambridge. Dir, CSL Publishing Ltd, 1987–. Mem. (C) Cambridge CC, 1998–2004 (Leader, Cons. Gp, 2000–04). Chairman: Educn Select Cttee, 2010–15; All Party Parly Gp on Rural Services. Vice-Pres., Globe Internat., 2007–. Chm., Cambridge Univ. Cons. Assoc., 1985. *Recreations:* cricket, cycling, motorcycling. *Address:* House of Commons, SW1A 0AA. *T:* (020) 7219 4340. *E:* graham@grahamstuart.com.

STUART, Ven. Canon Herbert James, CB 1983; Canon Emeritus of Lincoln Cathedral, since 1983 (Canon, 1980–83); *b* 16 Nov. 1926; *s* of Joseph and Jane Stuart; *m* 1955, Adrienne Le Fanu; two *s* one *d.* *Educ:* Mountjoy School, Dublin; Trinity Coll., Dublin (BA Hons, MA). Priest, 1950; served in Church of Ireland, 1950–55; Chaplain, RAF, 1955; Asst Chaplain-in-Chief, RAF, 1973; Chaplain-in-Chief and Archdeacon, RAF, 1980–83; QHC, 1978–83; Rector of Cherbury, 1983–87. *Recreations:* gardening, travel, books. *Club:* Royal Air Force.

STUART, Rt Rev. Ian Campbell; an Hon. Assistant Bishop, Diocese of Liverpool, 1999–2011; Pro Vice-Chancellor (formerly Assistant Vice-Chancellor), Liverpool Hope University, 2005–11, now Pro Vice-Chancellor Emeritus; *b* 17 Nov. 1942; *s* of Campbell Stuart and Ruth Estelle Stuart (*née* Butcher); *m* 1976, Megan Helen Williams; one *s* two *d.* *Educ:* Univ. of New England (BA, Cert Ed); Univ. of Melbourne (MA, DipEdAdmin). Headmaster, Christchurch Grammar Sch., Melbourne, 1977–84; ordained deacon and priest, 1985; Principal, Trinity Anglican Sch., Queensland, 1984–93; Warden, St Mark's Coll., James Cook Univ., 1993–96; Principal, All Souls' and St Gabriel's Sch., 1993–98; Diocese of North Queensland: Archdeacon, 1989–92; Asst Bishop, and Bishop Administrator, 1992–98; Chaplain, 1999–2001, Provost and Dir, Student Services, 2001–05, Liverpool Hope Univ. *Recreations:* reading, travel. *Address:* Pro Vice-Chancellor's Office, Liverpool Hope University, Hope Park, Liverpool L16 9JD. *T:* (0151) 291 3547.

STUART, Sir (James) Keith, Kt 1986; Chairman, Associated British Ports Holdings PLC, 1983–2002; *b* 4 March 1940; *s* of James and Marjorie Stuart; *m* 1966, Kathleen Anne Pinder (*née* Woodman); three *s* one *d.* *Educ:* King George V School, Southport; Gonville and Caius College, Cambridge (MA). FCILT. District Manager, South Western Electricity Bd, 1970–72; British Transport Docks Board: Sec., 1972–75; Gen. Manager, 1976–77; Man. Dir, 1977–82; Dep. Chm., 1980–82; Chm., 1982–83. Dir, Internat. Assoc. of Ports and Harbors, 1983–2000 (Vice-Pres., 1985–87); Pres., Inst. of Freight Forwarders, 1983–84. Director: Royal Ordnance Factories, 1983–85; BAA Plc, 1986–92; Seeboard plc, 1989–96 (Chm., 1992–96); City of London Investment Trust plc, 1999–2011; RMC Group plc, 1999–2005; Mallett plc, 2005–06. Consultant, Gas and Electricity Markets Authy, 2007– (Mem., 2000–06). Chm., UK-S Africa Trade Assoc., 1988–93; Vice-Chairman: UK-Southern Africa Business Assoc., 1994–95; Southern Africa Business Assoc., 1995–2002. Chartered Inst. of Transport: Mem. Council, 1979–88; Vice-Pres., 1982–83; Pres., 1985–86. Pres. and Chm. Bd, British Quality Foundn, 1997–2001. Freeman, City of London, 1985; Liveryman, Clockmakers' Co., 1987 (Mem. Ct of Assts, 1998–). Vice-Chm., Mgt Bd, London Mozart Players, 2002–09. Gov., NYO of GB, 1997–2004; Chm., Trinity Coll. London, 2009–15, now Pres. Emeritus (Dir, 1992–2009); Trustee: Trinity Coll. of Music, 2001– (Gov., 1991–2003; Chm., 2008–); Cambridge Univ. Musical Soc., 2012– (Chm., 2012–15). FRSA. Hon. FTCL 1998. *Recreation:* music. *Clubs:* Brooks's, Oxford and Cambridge (Trustee, 1989–94).

STUART, Prof. (John) Trevor, FRS 1974; Professor of Theoretical Fluid Mechanics, Imperial College of Science, Technology and Medicine, University of London, 1966–94, now Emeritus; Dean, Royal College of Science, 1990–93; *b* 28 Jan. 1929; *s* of Horace Stuart and Phyllis Emily Stuart (*née* Potter); *m* 1957, Christine Mary (*née* Tracy); two *s* one *d.* *Educ:* Gateway Sch., Leicester; Imperial Coll., London. BSc 1949, PhD 1951; FIC 1998. Aerodynamics Div., Nat. Physical Lab., Teddington, 1951–66; Sen. Principal Scientific Officer (Special Merit), 1961; Hd, Maths Dept, Imperial Coll., London, 1974–79, 1983–86. Vis. Lectr, Dept of Maths, MIT, 1956–57; Vis. Prof. of Maths, MIT, 1965–66; Vis. Prof. of Theoretical Fluid Mechanics, Brown Univ., 1978–; Hon. Prof., Tianjin Univ., China, 1983–. Member: Council, Royal Soc., 1982–84; SERC, 1989–94 (Chm., Mathematics Cttee, 1985–88). Pres., London Mathematical Soc., 2000–02 (Vice-Pres., 1999–2000). Editor, Biographical Memoirs of the Royal Soc., 2012–15. 1st Stewartson Meml Lectr, Long Beach, Calif., 1985; 1st DiPrima Meml Lectr, Troy, NY, 1985; Ludwig Prandtl Meml Lectr, Dortmund, 1986. Hon. ScD: Brown Univ., 1986; East Anglia, 1987. Senior Whitehead Prize, London Mathematical Soc., 1984; Otto Laporte Award, Amer. Physical Soc., 1987. *Publications:* (contrib.) Laminar Boundary Layers, ed L. Rosenhead, 1963; articles in Proc. Royal Soc., Phil. Trans Royal Soc., Jl Fluid Mech., Proc. 10th Internat. Cong. Appl. Mech., Jl Lub. Tech. (ASME). *Recreations:* theatre, music, gardening, reading, ornithology. *Address:* Mathematics Department, Imperial College, SW7 2AZ. *T:* (020) 7594 8535; 3 Steeple Close, Wimbledon, SW19 5AD. *T:* (020) 8946 7019. *E:* t.stuart@imperial.ac.uk.

STUART, Sir Keith; *see* Stuart, Sir J. K.

STUART, Prof. Sir Kenneth (Lamonte), Kt 1977; MD, FRCP, FRCPE, FACP, FFPM, FFPH, DTM&H; Hon. Medical and Scientific Adviser, Barbados High Commission, since 1991; *b* 16 June 1920; *s* of Egbert and Louise Stuart; *m* 1958, Barbara Cecille Ashby; one *s* two *d.* *Educ:* Harrison Coll., Barbados; Queen's Univ., Belfast (MB, BCh, BAO 1948). Consultant Physician, University Coll. Hospital of the West Indies, 1954–76; University of the West Indies: Prof. of Medicine, 1966–76; Dean, Medical Faculty, 1969–71; Head, Dept of Medicine, 1972–76; Mem. Council, 1971–76; Medical Adviser, Commonwealth Secretariat, 1976–84. Rockefeller Foundation Fellow in Cardiology, Massachusetts Gen. Hosp., Boston, 1956–57; Wellcome Foundation Research Fellow, Harvard Univ., Boston, 1960–61; Gresham Prof. of Physic, 1988–92. Consultant to WHO on Cardiovascular Disorders, 1969–89. Chairman: Commonwealth Caribbean MRC, 1989–96; Adv. Council, Centre for Caribbean Medicine, UK, 1998; Commonwealth Health Res. Inter-regional Consultation, 1998–. Chm., Scientific Adv. Bd, BeeVital, 2005–. Chm., Court of Governors, LSHTM, 1982–86; Member: Council, Liverpool Sch. of Tropical Medicine, 1980–97; Council, UMDS Guy's and St Thomas's Hosps, 1994–98; Council, KCL, 1998–2001; Court of Governors, Internat. Develt Res. Centre of Canada, 1985–90; Council, London Lighthouse, 1994–2000; Central Council, Royal Over-Seas League, 1994–2001. Trustee, Schools, subseq. Students, Partnership Worldwide, 1986–; Chm., Errol Barrow Meml Trust, 1989–2000; Dir, Internat. Medical Educn Trust 2000, 2000–. Freeman, City of London, 1994. Hon. DSc QUB, 1986. *Publications:* articles on hepatic and cardiovascular disorders in medical journals. *Recreations:* tennis, music. *Address:* 3 The Garth, Cobham, Surrey KT11 2DZ. *Club:* Athenæum.

STUART, Marian Elizabeth; consultant on social issues, particularly child care projects, Department of Health, 1993–99; *b* 17 July 1944; *d* of William and Greta Stuart; one *s* one *d.* *Educ:* Eye Grammar School, Suffolk; Mount Grace Comprehensive School, Potters Bar; Leicester Univ. (MA). Joined Min. of Health as Asst Principal, 1967; Principal, DHSS, 1971; Asst Sec., 1979; Dep. Chief Inspector of Social Services, 1988; Under Sec., Finance Div., DoH, 1989–93; Resident Chm., CSSB, 1993–99 (on secondment). *Publications:* (jtly) Progress on Safeguards for Children Living Away from Home: a review of action since the People Like Us report, 2004; (jtly) Safeguards for Vulnerable Children, 2004. *Recreations:* golf, reading, bridge. *Address:* 18 Tower Rise, Richmond, Surrey TW9 2TS. *T:* (020) 8404 9709.

STUART, Sir Mark M.; *see* Moody-Stuart.

STUART, Prof. Mary, DPhil; Vice Chancellor, University of Lincoln, since 2009; *b* Cape Town, SA, 4 March 1957; *d* of Thomas Cleary and Isobel Cleary (now Thompson); *m* 1978, Douglas Ian Stuart; two *d*. *Educ:* Chisipite Sen. Sch., Salisbury, Rhodesia; Univ. of Cape Town (BA Hist. and Drama 1979); Open Univ. (BA Hons Social Scis 1990; DPhil Social Policy 1998). Community Th. Coordinator and People's Educn Worker, People's Space Th., Cape Town, 1979–81; drama teacher, Westminster Play Assoc., 1981–82; Dir, Cast Underground Community Th., London, 1984–87; Lectr in Women's Educn, Streatham and Tooting Adult Educn Inst., 1987–89; Sen. Lectr in Special Educn, Lambeth Community Coll., 1990–91; University of Sussex: Lectr in Continuing Educn, 1991–95; Asst Dir, Centre for Continuing Educn, 1995–2000; Dir, Inst. of Educn, 2000–01; Pro Vice Chancellor, 2000–05; Dep. Vice Chancellor, Kingston Univ., 2006–09. Associate Res. Dir, Nat. Co-ordinating Team for HEFCE, DfES and LSC, 2001–05; Mem. Bd, HEFCE, 2015–. *Publications:* Engaging with Difference: the 'other' in adult education (with A. Thomson), 1995; Collaborating for Change: managing widening participation in further and higher education, 2002; Not Quite Sisters: women with learning difficulties and social policy, 2002; Social Mobility and Higher Education: the life experiences of first generation entrants in higher education, 2012; contrib. chapters in books; contribs to Oral Hist., Jl Access Studies, Jl Access and Credit Studies, Adults Learning, Jl Access Policy and Practice, Internat. Jl of Lifelong Educn and Active Learning. *Recreations:* modern art, travel, jazz, theatre, film. *Address:* Vice Chancellor's Office, University of Lincoln, Brayford Pool, Lincoln LN6 7TS. *T:* (01522) 886100, *Fax:* (01522) 886200. *E:* mstuart@lincoln.ac.uk.

STUART, Moira, OBE 2001; Presenter, Radio 2 Breakfast News, since 2010; *b* 2 Sept. 1949; *d* of Harold and Marjorie Stuart. Joined BBC Radio as prodn asst, Talks and Documentaries Dept, 1981; newsreader, Radio 4; presenter of news progs incl. News After Noon, 5.40 News, Nine O'Clock News, Six O'Clock News; Presenter, Breakfast News, 2000–06. Presenter of radio and TV progs incl.: The Quincy Jones Story, Best of Jazz, Open Forum, Holiday Programme, Cashing In, Moira Stuart in Search of Wilberforce; Strong and Sassy: inspiring women of jazz, Radio 4, 2011; Kings of Cool, Radio 2, 2012; Moira Stuart Show, Radio 2, 2014–. Mem., Human Genetics Adv. Commn, 1996–99. Dr hc Edinburgh, 2006. *Address:* c/o Knight Ayton Management, 35 Great James Street, WC1N 3HB.

STUART, Murray; *see* Stuart, C. M.

STUART, Nicholas Willoughby, CB 1990; Director General for Lifelong Learning, Department for Education and Skills (formerly Department for Education and Employment), 2000–01; *b* 2 Oct. 1942; *s* of late Douglas Willoughby Stuart and Margaret Eileen Stuart; *m* 1st, 1963, Sarah Mustard (marr. diss. 1974); one *d* (one *s* decd); 2nd, 1975, Susan Jane Fletcher; one *s* one *d*. *Educ:* Harrow Sch.; Christ Church Coll., Oxford (MA). Asst Principal, DES, 1964–68; Private Sec. to Minister for the Arts, 1968–69; Principal, DES, 1969–73; Private Secretary to: Head of the Civil Service, 1973; Prime Minister, 1973–76; Asst Sec., DES, 1976–78; Advr, Cabinet of Pres. of EEC, 1978–80; Under Sec., 1981–87, Dep. Sec., 1987–92, DES; Dir of Resources and Strategy, Dept of Employment, 1992–95; Dir Gen. for Employment and Lifelong Learning, later for Employment, Lifelong Learning and Internat. Directorate, DFEE, 1995–2000. Bd Mem., Investors in People (UK), 1995–2001; Dir, UFI Ltd, 2001–07. Pres., Nat. Inst. of Adult Contg Educn, 2012– (Vice-Pres., 2001–03; Chm., 2003–12); Council Member: Univ. of London Inst. of Educn, 2001–10; C&G, 2001–02; GDST, 2002–13; Member: QCA, 2002–10; Bd, CAFCASS, 2003–12. Trustee: Harrow Mission, 2001–; PSI, 2002–09; Specialist Schs and Acads Trust, 2003–12 (Chm., 2009–12); Primary Shakespeare Co., 2014–; Mem., Grants Cttee, John Lyon's Charity, 1996– (Chm., 2002–10); Hon. Treas., British Assoc. for Adoption and Fostering, 2015–. Governor: John Lyon's Sch., 1996–2005; Harrow Sch., 1996–09; South Hampstead High Sch., 1997–2002; Edward Wilson Sch., 2001–12 (Chm.). *Recreations:* collecting Tunbridgeware, cruising the canals.

STUART, Sir Phillip (Luttrell), 9th Bt *cr* 1660; late F/O RCAF; former President, Agassiz Industries Ltd; *b* 7 Sept. 1937; *s* of late Luttrell Hamilton Stuart and Irene Ethel Jackman; *S* uncle, Sir Houlton John Stuart, 8th Bt, 1959, but his name does not appear on the Official Roll of the Baronetage; *m* 1st, 1962, Marlene Rose Muth (marr. diss. 1968); one *d*; 2nd, 1969, Beverley Clare Pieri; one *s* one *d*. *Educ:* Vancouver. Enlisted RCAF, Nov. 1955; commnd FO (1957–62). *Heir: s* Geoffrey Phillip Stuart [*b* 5 July 1973; *m* 1999, Ashley Glen; one *s* one *d*]. *Address:* #50 10980 Westdowne Road, Ladysmith, BC V9G 1X3, Canada.

STUART, Steven Lawrence; QC (Scot.) 2008; *b* Dundee, 12 April 1954; *s* of Lawrence and Helen Stuart; *m* 1994, Elizabeth Hayter; one *d*. *Educ:* High Sch. of Dundee; Aberdeen Univ. (LLB Hons). Admitted as Advocate, 1979; Lectr in Scots Private Law, Univ. of Dundee, 1979–86; in practice as Advocate, specialising in valuation for rating, land law, planning law, licensing law, 1986–. *Publications:* (with A. Hajducki) Scottish Civic Government Licensing Law, 1994, 3rd edn 2009. *Recreations:* gardening, walking, horse racing (spectator), film noir. *Address:* Terra Firma Chambers, Advocates Library, Parliament House, Edinburgh EH1 1RF. *T:* (0131) 226 5071. *E:* steven.stuart@terrafirmachambers.com.

STUART, Trevor; *see* Stuart, J. T.

STUART-MENTETH, Sir Charles (Greaves), 7th Bt *cr* 1838, of Closeburn, Dumfriesshire; non-executive director and business angel, since 2000; *b* Cheshire, 25 Nov. 1950; *er s* of Sir James Wallace Stuart-Menteth, 6th Bt, and (Dorothy) Patricia, *d* of late Frank Greaves Warburton; *S* father, 2008; *m* 1976, Nicola St Lawrence; four *d* (one *s* decd). *Educ:* Radley Coll.; Trinity Coll., Oxford (BA Jurisprudence 1972); INSEAD, France (MBA 1977). Worked in banking, 1972–76; venture capital, 1977–85; Founder and CEO, Datavault Ltd, 1985–2000. *Recreations:* classic cars, shooting, grouse moors, scuba. *Heir: b* (William) Jeremy Stuart-Menteth [*b* 31 Jan. 1952; *m* 1983, Rosalind Ann, *e d* of John Stephen Lane; one *s* one *d*]. *Address:* Monkcastle, Kilwinning, Ayrshire KA13 6PN. *T:* 07976 248563. *E:* csmmonkcastle@btinternet.com.

STUART-MOORE, Michael; QC 1990; Vice-President of the Court of Appeal of Hong Kong, 1999–2009; a Deputy Judge of the First Instance of the High Court (part-time), since 2009; *b* 7 July 1944; *s* of (Kenneth) Basil Moore and Marjorie (Elizabeth) Moore; *m* 1973, Katherine Ann, *d* of William and Ruth Scott; one *s* one *d*. *Educ:* Cranleigh School. Called to the Bar, Middle Temple, 1966. A Deputy Circuit Judge, 1981–85; a Recorder of the Crown Court, 1985–2010; a Judge of the High Court, later of the Court of First Instance of the High Court, Hong Kong, 1993–98; a Judge of the Court of Appeal of the High Court, Hong Kong, 1998–99. Chairman: Hong Kong Market Misconduct Tribunal, 2011–15; Hong Kong Securities and Futures Appeals Tribunal, 2011–14; Hong Kong Deposit Protection Appeals Tribunal, 2011–14; Mandatory Provident Fund Schemes Appeal Bd, 2011–14. GBS (Hong Kong), 2009. *Recreations:* photography, travel, music, tennis. *Address:* 2 Hare Court, Temple, EC4Y 7BH. *T:* (020) 7353 5324. *Club:* Hong Kong.

STUART-PAUL, Air Marshal Sir Ronald (Ian), KBE 1990 (MBE 1967); RAF, retired; Chief Executive, British Aerospace, Saudi Arabia, 1997–2001; *b* 7 Nov. 1934; *s* of Dr J. G. Stuart-Paul and Mary (*née* McDonald); *m* 1963, Priscilla Frances (*née* Kay); one *s* one *d*. *Educ:* Dollar Acad.; RAF Coll., Cranwell. Served 14, 19, 56 and 92 Sqns and 11 and 12 Groups, 1957–73; Defence Attaché, Saudi Arabia, 1974–75; Stn Comdr, RAF Lossiemouth, 1976–78; RCDS, 1979; Dep. Comdr, NAEW Force, SHAPE, 1980–82; Dir of Ops Air Defence, RAF, 1982–83; AO Training, RAF Support Command, 1984–85; Dir Gen., Saudi Air Force Project, 1985–92. Freemason (Jun. Grand Warden, 2010–11; Asst Provincial Grand Master, Wilts, 2007–11). *Recreation:* golf. *Address:* Sycamore House, Gaunts Common, Wimborne, Dorset BH21 4JP. *T:* (01258) 840430. *Club:* Royal Air Force.

STUART-SMITH, Rt Hon. Sir Murray, KCMG 2012; Kt 1981; PC 1988; a Lord Justice of Appeal, 1988–2000; *b* 18 Nov. 1927; *s* of Edward Stuart-Smith and Doris Mary Laughland; *m* 1953, Joan Elizabeth Mary Motion, BA, JP, DL (High Sheriff of Herts, 1983); three *s* three *d*. *Educ:* Radley; Corpus Christi Coll., Cambridge (Foundn Scholar; 1st Cl. Hons Law Tripos, Pts I and II; 1st Cl. Hons LLM; MA; Hon. Fellow 1994). 2nd Lieut, 5th Royal Inniskilling Dragoon Guards, 1947. Called to the Bar, Gray's Inn, 1952 (Atkin Scholar), Bencher 1977; Vice-Treas., 1997; Treas., 1998; QC 1970; a Recorder of the Crown Court, 1972–81; a Judge of the High Court of Justice, QBD, 1981–88; Presiding Judge, Western Circuit, 1983–87. Judge of Court of Appeal: Gibraltar, 2001–11 (Pres., 2007–11); Bermuda, 2004. Jt Inspector into Grays Bldg Soc., 1979. Mem., Criminal Injuries Compensation Bd, 1980–81. Commissioner: for the Security Service, 1989–2000; for the Intelligence Services, 1994–2000. Chairman: Proscribed Orgns Appeal Commn, 2001–02; Pathogens Access Appeal Commn, 2002. Pres., Dacorum SO, 1994–. *Recreations:* playing 'cello, shooting, building, playing bridge. *Address:* Serge Hill, Abbots Langley, Herts WD5 0RY.

See also D. Docherty, T. R. S. P. Stuart-Smith.

STUART-SMITH, Thomas Richard Stephen Peregrine; landscape architect; Director, Tom Stuart-Smith Ltd, since 1998; *b* Watford, 14 Feb. 1960; *s* of Rt Hon. Sir Murray Stuart-Smith, *qv*; *m* 1986, Susan Jane Evans; two *s* one *d*. *Educ:* Radley Coll.; Corpus Christi Coll., Cambridge (BA 1981); Manchester Univ. (MLA 1984). Chartered Landscape Architect 1986. Landscape Architect: Colvin and Moggridge, 1985–87; Elizabeth Banks Associates, 1989–98. Major projects include: Broughton Grange, 2001; Queen's Jubilee Gdn, Windsor Castle, 2002; Trentham Gdns, 2004; Bicentenary Glasshouse Gdn, RHS Wisley, 2007. Chelsea Flower Show: Gold Medals 1998, 2000, 2001, 2003, 2005, 2006, 2008, 2010; Best in Show 2005, 2006, 2008. Trustee, Garden Mus., 2009–. *Publications:* The Barn Garden, 2011. *Recreations:* music, gardening. *Address:* Tom Stuart-Smith Ltd, 90–93 Cowcross Street, EC1M 6BF. *T:* (020) 7253 2100. *E:* info@tomstuartsmith.co.uk.

STUART TAYLOR, Sir Nicholas (Richard), 4th Bt *cr* 1917; *b* 14 Jan. 1952; *s* of Sir Richard Laurence Stuart Taylor, 3rd Bt, and of Iris Mary, *d* of Rev. Edwin John Gargery; *S* father, 1978; *m* 1984, Malvena Elizabeth Sullivan, (marr. diss. 1999); two *d*. *Educ:* Bradfield. Admitted Solicitor, 1977. *Recreation:* ski-ing and other sports. *Heir:* none. *Address:* 30 Siskin Close, Bishop's Waltham, Hants SO32 1RQ. *Club:* Ski Club of Great Britain.

STUART-WHITE, Ven. William Robert; Archdeacon of Cornwall, since 2012; *b* Bromsgrove, 21 Jan. 1959; *s* of Sir Christopher Stuart Stuart-White and of Pamela Stuart-White (*née* Grant); *m* 2012, Brenda Susan Venning (*née* Kendall); one *s* two *d* by a previous marriage. *Educ:* Winchester Coll.; Merton Coll., Oxford (BA Lit.Hum.; MA); Trinity Coll., Bristol (BA Theol.). Ordained deacon, 1986, priest, 1987; Asst Curate, Upper Armley, Leeds, 1986–91; Vicar, Austrey and Warton, Birmingham, 1991–98; Rector, Camborne, 1998–2006; Priest-in-charge: Stoke Climsland and Linkinhorne, 2006–09; Wadebridge, 2009–12; Rural Officer, Dio. of Truro, 2006–12. Hon. Canon, Truro Cath., 2009–. *Recreations:* rambling, photography. *Address:* 10 The Hayes, Bodmin Road, Truro TR1 1FY. *T:* (01872) 242374. *E:* billstuartwhite@btinternet.com.

STUBBINGS, Paul John; Headmaster, Cardinal Vaughan Memorial School, since 2011; *b* London, 13 Feb. 1966; *s* of John Stubbings and Moira Hamilton; *m* 1995, Anna Swaebe; one *s* one *d*. *Educ:* Royal Grammar Sch., Worcester; Univ. of Durham (BA Hons Classics); King's Coll. London (PGCE); Inst. of Education, Univ. of London (MA Dist.). Cardinal Vaughan Memorial School: Teacher of Classics, 1989–97; Asst Headmaster, 1997–2004; Dep. Headmaster, 2004–11. *Recreations:* Byzantine Empire, birdwatching. *Address:* Cardinal Vaughan Memorial School, 89 Addison Road, W14 8BZ. *T:* (020) 7603 8478, *Fax:* (020) 7602 3124. *E:* mail@cvms.co.uk. *Club:* National Liberal.

STUBBS, Andrew James; QC 2008; a Recorder, since 2003; *b* York, 16 April 1965; *s* of William Charles Stubbs and Janice Pickles; *m* 1998, Jane Louise; two *s*. *Educ:* Nottingham Univ.; Inns of Court Sch. of Law. Called to the Bar, Lincoln's Inn, 1988; Hd of Chambers, 2012–; Mem., QC Panel of Prosecution Counsel for Serious Fraud Office, 2013–. *Recreations:* golf, theatre, cycling, wine. *Address:* St Paul's Chambers, Trafalgar House, 29 Park Place, Leeds LS1 2SP. *T:* (0113) 245 5866, *Fax:* (0113) 245 5807.

STUBBS, Imogen Mary, (Lady Nunn); actress; *b* 20 Feb. 1961; *d* of late Robin Desmond Scrivener Stubbs and Heather Mary Stubbs (*née* McCracken); *m* 1994, Trevor Robert Nunn (*see* Sir T. R. Nunn); one *s* one *d*. *Educ:* St Paul's Girls' Sch.; Westminster Sch.; Exeter Coll., Oxford (BA 1st cl. Hons); RADA. *Theatre:* Cabaret, Ipswich, 1985; The Rover, 1986, The Two Noble Kinsmen, 1987, Desdemona in Othello, 1989, RSC; Heartbreak House, Theatre Royal, Haymarket, 1992; title rôle, St Joan, Strand, 1994; Uncle Vanya, Chichester Fest., then Albery, 1996; A Streetcar Named Desire, Theatre Royal, Haymarket, 1996; Closer, Lyric, 1998; Betrayal, RNT, 1998; The Relapse, RNT, 2001; Three Sisters, Bath Royal and tour, 2002; Mum's The Word, Albery and tour, 2003; Hamlet, Old Vic, 2004; title rôle, The Duchess of Malfi, W Yorks Playhouse, 2006; Alphabetical Order, Hampstead Th., 2009; The Glass Menagerie, Salisbury Playhouse and tour, 2010; Private Lives, Royal Exchange, Manchester, 2011; Little Eyolf, Jermyn St Th., 2011; Salt, Root and Roe, Trafalgar Studios, 2011; A Marvellous Year for Plums, Chichester Fest., 2012; Orpheus Descending, Royal Exchange, Manchester, 2012; Third Finger, Left Hand, Trafalgar Studios, 2013; Strangers on a Train, Gielgud, 2013; Little Revolution, Almeida, 2014; Communicating Doors, Menier Chocolate Factory, 2015; *play written:* We Happy Few, Gielgud, 2004; *television:* The Rainbow, 1988; Othello, 1990; After the Dance, 1992; Anna Lee, 1994; Big Kids; *films:* Nanou, 1985; Erik the Viking, 1988; Fellow Traveller, 1990; True Colors, 1990; Sandra, c'est la vie; Lucy in Sense and Sensibility, 1995; Viola in Twelfth Night, 1996; Three Guesses; dir, Snow on Saturday (Kino Best British Short Award). *Publications:* (jtly) Amazonians, 1998; regular contribs to Daily Telegraph and Harpers & Queen. *Address:* c/o United Agents, 12–26 Lexington Street, W1F 0LE.

STUBBS, Prof. Michael Wesley, PhD; Professor of English Linguistics, University of Trier, Germany, 1990–2013; *b* 23 Dec. 1947; *s* of late Leonard Garforth Stubbs and Isabella Wardrop (*née* McGavin). *Educ:* Glasgow High Sch. for Boys; King's Coll., Cambridge (MA); Univ. of Edinburgh (PhD 1975). Res. Associate, Univ. of Birmingham, 1973–74; Lectr in Linguistics, Univ. of Nottingham, 1974–85; Prof. of English in Educn, Inst. of Educn, Univ. of London, 1985–90. Vis. Prof. of Linguistics, Univ. of Tübingen, Germany, 1985; Hon. Sen. Res. Fellow, Univ. of Birmingham, 1994–99. Chm., BAAL, 1988–91. Mem., Nat. Curriculum English Working Gp (Cox Cttee), 1988–89. *Publications:* Language, Schools and Classrooms, 1976, 2nd edn 1983; Language and Literacy, 1980; Discourse Analysis, 1983; Educational Linguistics, 1986; Text and Corpus Analysis, 1996; Words and Phrases, 2001; (jtly) Text, Discourse and Corpora, 2007; articles in Lang. and Educn, Applied Linguistics, Jl of Pragmatics, Functions of Lang., Text, Internat. Jl of Corpus Linguistics, Lang. and Lit. *Recreation:* walking. *Address:* FB2 Anglistik, University of Trier, 54286 Trier, Germany. *T:* (651) 2012278.

STUBBS, Rebecca; QC 2012; *b* Barnsley, S Yorks, 1971; *d* of James Stuart Stubbs and Diane Stubbs; *m* 2007, Sharif Asim Shivji; two *s*. *Educ:* Darton High Sch.; Downing Coll., Cambridge (BA Hons Law 1993). Called to the Bar, Middle Temple, 1994 (Harmsworth Entrance Exhibnr, Queen Mother Scholar), Bencher, 2013; called to Supreme Court of

Grenada and WI Associated States, 2005; Jun. Counsel to the Crown, 2000–07. Vice Chm., Access to the Bar Cttee, 2007, Mem., One Case One Fee Wkg Gp, 2008. Bar Council; Mem., Wkg Gp on Alternative Business Structures, Bar Standards Bd, 2008–09. Barrister Rep., Bankruptcy and Companies Court Users' Cttee, 2007–15. Member: Chancery Bar Assoc., 1995– (Mem., Cttee, 2013–); Commercial Bar Assoc., 1995–; Advocates for Internat. Develt, 2009–. Registered to appear in DIFC Court, 2012. FRSA 2004. *Publications:* (contrib.) Butterworths Practical Insolvency, 1999; (contrib.) Mithani on Directors' Disqualification, 2002; (Consultant Ed.) French on Applications to Wind Up Companies, 2007; (contrib.) Butterworths Guide to the Legal Services Act, 2009. *Address:* Maitland Chambers, 7 Stone Buildings, Lincoln's Inn, WC2A 3SZ. *T:* (020) 7406 1200, *Fax:* (020) 7406 1300. *E:* rstubbs@maitlandchambers.com. *Club:* Kandahar.

STUBBS, Sukhvinder K.; *see* Kaur-Stubbs, S.

STUBBS, Thomas, OBE 1980; HM Diplomatic Service, retired; *b* 12 July 1926; *s* of Thomas Stubbs and Lillian Marguerite (*née* Rumball, formerly Bell); *m* 1951, Dorothy Miller (*d* 1997); one *s* one *d*. *Educ:* Heaton Tech. Sch., Newcastle upon Tyne. Served in Army, 1944–48. Joined Min. of Nat. Insce, later Min. of Pensions and Nat. Insce, 1948; transf. to CRO, 1960; New Delhi, 1962; CRO, 1964; Wellington, NZ, 1965; Vice-Consul, Düsseldorf, 1970; seconded to BOTB, 1974; First Sec. (Commercial) and Consul, Addis Ababa, 1977; Consul, Hannover, 1980; Dep. High Comr, Madras, 1983–86. Mayor, Borough of Spelthorne, 1992–93 (Mem. (C) Council, 1987–2003; Vice-Chairman: Leisure and Amenities Cttee, 1987–89; Planning Cttee, 1999–2002; Chairman: Personnel Cttee, 1989–91; Resources Cttee, 1995–96; Finance Sub-Cttee, 1996–98; Dep. Mayor, 1991–92). Chm., SE Employers, 2000–03. Pres., Spelthorne Cons. Constituency Assoc., 2002–05. Hon. Pres., County of Middlesex Trust, 1992–. *Recreation:* reading. *Address:* 17 Chester Close, Ashford, Middx TW15 1PH. *Club:* Sunbury-on-Thames Conservative.

STUBBS, Sir William (Hamilton), Kt 1994; Chairman, Oxford Radcliffe Hospitals NHS Trust, 2003–08; *b* 5 Nov. 1937; *s* of Joseph Stubbs and Mary Stubbs (*née* McNicol); *m* 1963, Marie Margaret Pierce; three *d*. *Educ:* Workington Grammar Sch.; St Aloysius Coll., Glasgow; Glasgow Univ. (BSc, PhD). Res. Associate, Univ. of Arizona, 1963–64; with Shell Oil Co., San Francisco, 1964–67; teaching, 1967–72; Asst Dir of Educn, Carlisle, 1972–74; Asst Dir of Educn, 1974–76, Second Dep. Dir of Educn, 1976–77, Cumbria; Second Dep. Educn Officer, 1977–79, Dir of Educn (Schools), 1979–82, Educn Officer and Chief Exec., 1982–88, ILEA; Chief Exec., PCFC, 1988–93; Chief Exec., FEFC, 1992–96; Rector, The London Inst., 1996–2001. Member: Council, CRAC, 1993–2004; Nat. Cttee of Inquiry into Higher Educn, 1996–97; Bd, NACETT, 1997–2002; Council, Inst. of Employment Studies, 1997–2005; Design Council, 1999–2004; Chairman: CBI Educn Foundn, 1996–99; Qualifications and Curriculum Authority, 1997–2002. Hon. Prof., Dept of Continuing Educn, Univ. of Warwick, 1993. Trustee, Geffrye Mus., 1999–2007; Pres., Assoc. of Colls Trust, 2001–03; Mem., Awards Council, Royal Anniversary Trust, 2002–12. Chancellor, Thames Valley Univ., 2001–04. Chm. Govs, Capel Manor Coll., 2014–; Gov., Birkbeck Coll., London, 1998–2004. CCMI; FRSA. DUniv: Open, 1995; Sheffield Hallam, 1996; Strathclyde, 2004; Hon. DLitt: Exeter, 1996; Bath Spa, 2010; Hon. DSc UWE, 1997; Hon. DEd Greenwich, 2007; Hon. LLD Brighton, 2007. *Address:* Churchill House, 4 Oxford Street, Woodstock, Oxon OX20 1TR.

STUCKEY, Rev. Thomas James; lecturer, preacher and teacher; President of the Methodist Conference, 2005–06; *b* 10 May 1940; *s* of Howard and Pat Stuckey; *m* 1966, Christine Plympton; two *s* one *d*. *Educ:* Yeovil Grammar Sch.; City Univ. (BScEng 1964); Richmond Coll. (BD London Univ. 1967); Edinburgh Univ. (MTh 1972). Engrg appts with Westland Aircraft and Fairey Aviation, 1956–63; theol trng, Richmond Coll., 1964–67; Methodist Circuit appts, Coatbridge, Airdrie and Armadale, Bristol Mission, Exeter, 1967–76; Tutor in Applied Theol., Hartley Victoria Coll., 1982–90; Supt, Reading and Silchester Methodist Circuit, 1990–98; Chair, Southampton Methodist District, 1998–2006; Canon, Salisbury Cathedral, 2002–06. Vis. Scholar, Sarum Coll., 2000–12. *Publications:* Into the Far Country, 2003; Beyond the Box, 2005; The Edge of Pentecost, 2007; The Wrath of God Satisfied?, 2012; (contrib.) As a Fire By Burning, 2013; articles in Worship and Preaching, Epworth Review. *Recreations:* music, theology, theatre, films, watercolour painting, MG club, enjoying the company of my wife. *Address:* 11 The Meadway, Christchurch BH23 4NT.

STUCLEY, Sir Hugh (George Coplestone Bampfylde), 6th Bt *cr* 1859; DL; Lieut Royal Horse Guards, retired; *b* 8 Jan. 1945; *s* of Major Sir Dennis Frederic Bankes Stucley, 5th Bt, and Hon. Sheila Bampfylde (*d* 1996), *o d* of 4th Baron Poltimore; *S* father, 1983; *m* 1969, Angela Caroline, *e d* of Richard Charles Robertson Toller, MC, Theale, Berks; two *s* two *d*. *Educ:* Milton Abbey School; Royal Agricultural College, Cirencester. Chm., Badgworthy Land Co., 1999–2004. Chm., Devon Br., CLA, 1995–97; Pres., Devonshire Assoc., 1997–98. Chm., Wessex Br., Historic Houses Assoc., 2007–12. DL 1998, High Sheriff, 2006–07, Devon. *Heir: s* George Dennis Bampfylde Stucley [*b* 26 Dec. 1970; *m* 1997, Amber (marr. diss. 2013), *yr d* of Thomas Gage; two *s*]. *Address:* Affeton Castle, Worlington, Crediton, Devon EX17 4TU. *Club:* Sloane.

STUDD, Anne Elizabeth; QC 2012; a Recorder, since 2007; *b* London, 1 July 1964; *y d* of Sir (Robert) Kynaston Studd, 3rd Bt and late Anastasia Studd (*née* Leveson-Gower); *m* 2000, Simon Dennis Marsden Freeland, *qv*; one *s* one *d*. *Educ:* Southover Manor Sch., Lewes; Westfield Coll., Univ. of London (BA Hons Hist.); Poly. of Central London (DipLaw). Called to the Bar, Gray's Inn, 1988. *Recreations:* gardening, cooking, family. *Address:* 5 Essex Court, Temple, EC4Y 9AH. *T:* (020) 7410 2000. *E:* studd@5essexcourt.co.uk.

See also Sir E. F. Studd, Bt.

STUDD, Sir Edward (Fairfax), 4th Bt *cr* 1929; *b* 3 May 1929; *s* of Sir Eric Studd, 2nd Bt, OBE, and Stephana (*d* 1976), *o d* of L. J. Langmead; *S* brother, 1977; *m* 1960, Prudence Janet, *o d* of Alastair Douglas Fyfe, OBE, Riding Mill, Northumberland; two *s* one *d*. *Educ:* Winchester College. Lieutenant Coldstream Guards, London and Malaya, 1947–49; Macneill & Barry Ltd, Calcutta, 1951–62; Inchcape & Co. Ltd, London, 1962–86 (Dir, 1974–86). Master, Merchant Taylor's Co., 1987–88 and 1993–94. *Recreation:* rural activities. *Heir: s* Philip Alastair Fairfax Studd [*b* 27 Oct. 1961; *m* 1987, Georgina (marr. diss. 1999), *d* of Sir Roger Neville, VRD; one *s* one *d*].

STUDD, Prof. John William Winston, MD, DSc; FRCOG; Professor of Gynaecology, Imperial College London, 1998–2005, now Emeritus; Consultant Gynaecologist, Chelsea and Westminster Hospital, 1994–2005; *b* 4 March 1940; *s* of late Eric Dacombe Studd and Elsie Elizabeth (*née* Kirby); *m* 1980, Margaret Anne Johnson, *qv*; one *s* two *d*. *Educ:* Royal Hosp. Sch., Holbrook; Univ. of Birmingham (MB ChB 1962; MD 1969; DSc 1995). MRCOG 1967, FRCOG 1982. Res. Fellow, Queen Elizabeth Hosp., Birmingham, 1967–70; Lectr in Obstetrics and Gynaecol., UC of Rhodesia, 1970–71; Consultant and Sen. Lectr, Univ. of Nottingham, 1974–75; Consultant Obstetrician and Gynaecologist, KCH, 1975–94; Dir, Fertility and Endocrine Centre, Lister Hosp., Chelsea, 1987–95. Visiting Professor: Yale Univ., 1982; Duke Univ., 1984; Univ. of Singapore, 1989; Harvard Univ., 1995; Cornell Univ., 2008. Mem. Council, 1980–97, and Pres., Sect. of Obstetrics and Gynaecol., 1994–95, RSocMed. Vice Pres., Nat. Osteoporosis Soc., 1995– (Chm., 1992–95); Pres., Internat. Soc. Reproductive Medicine. Chm., PMS and Menopause Trust. Ed., Yearbook, 1993–97, Publications Officer, 1994–97, RCOG. Editor: Menopause Digest, 1994–; Obstetric and Gynaecol Reviews, 1994–; The Diplomate, 1995–; Member Editorial Board: Brit. Jl Obstetrics and Gynaecol.; Jl RSocMed; N American Jl of Menopause; Eur. Menopause Jl; Brit. Jl Hosp. Medicine; Osteoporosis Internat.; Ed.-in-Chief, Menopause Internat., 2009–. Blair Bell Gold Medal, RSM, 2009. *Publications:* Management of Labour, 1985; Self Assessment in Obstetrics and Gynaecology, 1985; Management of the Menopause, 1988, 4th edn 2003; (ed) Progress in Obstetrics and Gynaecology, Vols 1–18, 1982–2008; Multiple Choice Questions in Obstetrics and Gynaecology, 1993; The Menopause and Osteoporosis, 1993; Annual Progress in Reproductive Medicine, Vols 1 and 2, 1993–94; (with S. S. Sheth) Vaginal Hysterectomy, 2001; contrib. numerous articles on the menopause, osteoporosis, premenstrual syndrome, post-natal depression, labour, sickle cell disease and HIV infection in women. *Recreations:* theatre, opera, history of medicine, collecting antiquarian medical books. *Address:* 27 Blomfield Road, W9 1AA. *T:* (020) 7266 0101; London PMS & Menopause Centre, 46 Wimpole Street, W1G 8SD.

STUDD, Margaret Anne; *see* Johnson, Margaret A.

STUDER, Cheryl Lynn; opera singer, freelance since 1986; Professor of Voice, University of Music, Wuerzburg, since 2003; *b* Midland, USA, 24 Oct. 1955; *m* 1982, G. Marmarides; one *d*; *m* 1992, E. Schwarz; one *d*; *m* 2008, Michalis Doukakis. *Educ:* Interlochen Arts Acad.; Oberlin Coll. Conservatory, Ohio; Univ. of Tennessee; Tanglewood Berkshire Music Center; Hochschule für Musik und darstellende Kunst, Vienna (Masters Degree). First professional recital, Virginia Highlands Fest., 1977; operatic début, Bavarian State Opera, 1980; *débuts:* Lyric Opera, Chicago, 1984; Bayreuth Fest., 1985; La Scala, Milan, 1987; Royal Opera House, Covent Garden, 1987; NY Met, 1988; Vienna State Opera, 1989; has sung at all major opera houses and festivals in the world; regular appearances at Bayreuth and Salzburg Fests; extensive concert tours with all major orchestras and conductors; world-wide recitals. Many recordings, incl. La Traviata, Faust, Salomé, Lohengrin, Figaro, Strauss' Four Last Songs. Franz Schubert Inst. Award, 1979; Grammy Award, 1991, 1994; Internat. Classical Music Award for best female singer, 1992; Furtwängler Preis, 1992; Vocalist of the Year Award, Musical America Directory of Performing Arts, 1994; Terras Sem Sombre, 2011; Ovation Award, 2012.

STUDHOLME, Sir Henry (William), 3rd Bt *cr* 1956, of Perridge, Co. Devon; DL; *b* 31 Jan. 1958; *s* of Sir Paul Henry William Studholme, 2nd Bt and Virginia (*d* 1990), *yr d* of Sir (Herbert) Richmond Palmer, KCMG, CBE; *S* father, 1990; *m* 1988, Sarah Lucy Rosita (*née* Deans); two *s* one *d*. *Educ:* Eton; Trinity Hall, Cambridge (MA). FCA, CTA. Man. Dir, Wood & Wood Internat. Signs Ltd, 1990–92; Chm., Integer plc, 2002–07. Chairman: SW Woodland Show, 1995–2004; SW Regl Adv. Cttee on Forestry, 2000–07; SW Cttee Country Land and Business Assoc., 2001–03; SW Chamber of Rural Enterprise, 2003–09; SW Food and Drink, 2004–08; Member: England Forestry Forum, 2002–07; Bd, SW RDA, 2002–12 (Chm., Rural Adv. Gp and Audit Cttee, 2003–08; Chm., 2009–12). A Forestry Comr, 2007– (Chm., 2013–). Dir, Phaunos Timber Fund Ltd, 2011– (Chm., 2012–). Dir, Assoc. of Lloyd's Members, 2009–. Chm., William Robinson Gravetye Charity, 2009–. Hon. FICFor. DL Devon, 2006. *Heir: s* Joshua Henry Paul Studholme, *b* 2 Feb. 1992. *Address:* Phaunos Timber Fund Ltd, 11 New Street, St Peter Port, Guernsey GY1 2PF. *Clubs:* Brooks's; MCC.

See also J. G. Studholme.

STUDHOLME, Joseph Gilfred, MBE 2015; Chairman and Co-founder, Getmapping (formerly Getmapping.com) plc, 1998–2002; *b* 14 Jan. 1936; *s* of Sir Henry Gray Studholme, 1st Bt, CVO and Judith Joan Mary (*née* Whitbread); *m* 1959, Rachel Fellowes, *d* of Sir William Albemarle Fellowes, KCVO; three *s*. *Educ:* Eton; Magdalen Coll., Oxford (MA). Nat. Service, 2nd Lieut, KRRC (60th Rifles), 1954–56. Man. Dir, King & Shaxson Ltd (Billbrokers), 1961–63; Co-founder, Chm. and Man. Dir, Editions Alecto Gp, 1963–2002. Mem. Council, Byam Shaw Sch. of Art, 1963–94 (Chm., 1988–94). Chm., Wessex Regl Cttee, NT, 1996–2006 (Mem., 1993–2006). Chm., Salisbury and South Wiltshire Mus., 2007–14. Sen. Fellow, RCA, 1999. *Address:* The Court House, Lower Woodford, Salisbury, Wilts SP4 6NQ. *T:* (01722) 782237. *Clubs:* Garrick, Double Crown, MCC.

STUDZINSKI, John Joseph, CBE 2008; Vice Chairman, Blackstone Group International Ltd, since 2006; *b* 19 March 1956; *s* of Alfred Edward Studzinski and Jennie Mary Studzinski (*née* Gaieski). *Educ:* Bowdoin Coll., Maine (AB Biol. and Sociol. 1978); Univ. of Chicago (MBA Finance and Marketing 1980). Morgan Stanley International Ltd: Head: Corporate Finance, Europe, 1989–92; M&A, Europe, 1992–97; Investment Banking, Europe, 1997–2001; Dep. Chm., 2001–03; Chief Exec., Corporate, Investment Banking and Markets, and Mem., Gp Mgt Bd, HSBC, 2003–06. Trustee: Royal Parks Foundn, 1996; Bowdoin College, 1998–; Tate Foundn, 2006–; Internat. Youth Foundn, 2012–; Getty Foundn, 2015–. Founder and Chm., Genesis Foundn, 2000–. Member: Bd of Dirs, Human Rights Watch, 1999– (Vice-Chm., 2005–); Trustees, Passage Day Centre for Homeless, 2000–; Council, Royal Coll. of Art, 2004–. Chairman: Emmaus Revives Lives Campaign, 2006–; Benjamin Franklin House, 2007–. Vice Chair, Atlantic Council. Prince of Wales's Ambassador's Award, 2000; Pres., American Friends of Royal Foundn of Duke and Duchess of Cambridge and Prince Harry, 2013–. KSS, KSG 2001. Prince of Wales Medal for Arts Philanthropy, 2014. *Recreations:* voluntary work with homeless, human rights, nurturing young artists. *Address:* Blackstone Group International Ltd, 40 Berkeley Square, W1J 5AL.

STUNELL, Rt Hon. Sir (Robert) Andrew, Kt 2013; OBE 1995; PC 2012; *b* 24 Nov. 1942; *s* of late Robert George and Trixie Stunell; *m* 1967, Gillian (*née* Chorley); two *s* three *d*. *Educ:* Surbiton Grammar Sch.; Manchester Univ.; Liverpool Poly. Architectural asst, CWS Manchester, 1965–67, Runcorn New Town, 1967–81, freelance, 1981–85; various posts incl. Political Sec., Assoc. of Liberal Democrat Councillors, 1985–97. Member: Chester City Council, 1979–90; Cheshire CC, 1981–91 (Leader, Lib Dem Gp); Stockport MBC, 1994–2002. Vice-Chm., ACC, 1985–90. Contested: (L) 1979, (Lib/Alliance), 1983 and 1987, City of Chester; (Lib Dem) Hazel Grove, 1992. MP (Lib Dem) Hazel Grove, 1997–2015. Lib Dem Chief Whip, 2001–06; Lib Dem front bench spokesman on communities and local govt, 2006–08; Parly Under-Sec. of State, DCLG, 2010–12. Chair, Local Election Campaign Team, 2008–10. *Address:* 84 Lyme Grove, Romiley, Stockport SK6 4DJ.

[Created a Baron (Life Peer) 2015 but title not yet gazetted at time of going to press.]

STURDY, Julian Charles; MP (C) York Outer, since 2010; *b* Yorks, 1971; *s* of Robert William Sturdy, *qv*; *m* Victoria; one *s* one *d*. *Educ:* Harper Adams Univ. Farming and property business. Mem., Harrogate BC, 2002–07. Contested (C) Scunthorpe, 2005. *Address:* House of Commons, SW1A 0AA.

STURDY, Robert William; Member (C) Eastern Region, England, European Parliament, 1999–2014 (Cambridgeshire, 1994–99); *b* 22 June 1944; *s* of late Gordon Sturdy and of Kathleen Sturdy (*née* Wells); *m* 1969, Elizabeth Hommes; one *s* one *d*. *Educ:* Ashville Coll., Harrogate. Partner, G. E. Sturdy & Son. European Parliament: Cons. spokesman on agriculture, 1994–2001, on rural affairs, 2001–04, on internat. trade, 2004–06; Vice-Pres., Delegn to SE Europe, 1994–99; Dep. Leader, Cons. Delegn in Europe, 1999–2001; Chm., Canadian Interparly Delegn, 1999–2002; Chm., Aust. and NZ Interparly Delegn, 2002–04; Mem., ACP-EU Delegn, 2004–14; Mem., Agriculture Cttee, 1994–2004; Substitute Mem., Cttee on Envmt, 1999–2009, on Agriculture, 2004–14; EPP-ED Co-ordinator for Internat. Trade, 2004–09; ECR Co-ordinator for Internat. Trade, 2009–14; Co-Chair, WTO Steering Gp of Parly Assembly, 2004–14; Vice Chm., Internat. Trade Cttee, 2009–14. *Recreations:* fishing, ski-ing, cricket, golf.

See also J. C. Sturdy.

STURGE, Maj.-Gen. (Henry Arthur) John, CB 1978; *b* 27 April 1925; *s* of Henry George Arthur Sturge and Lilian Beatrice Sturge; *m* 1953, Jean Ailsa Mountain; two *s* one *d*. *Educ:* Wilson's Sch., (formerly) Camberwell, London; Queen Mary Coll., London. Commissioned, Royal Signals, 1946; UK, 1946–50; Egypt, 1950–53; UK, incl. psc, 1953–59; Far East, 1959–62; jssc, 1962; BAOR, 1963–64; RMA, Sandhurst, 1965–66; BAOR, incl. Command, 1966–69; UK Comd 12 Sig. Bde, 1970–71; Min. of Defence, 1972–75; Chief Signal Officer, BAOR, 1975–77; ACDS (Signals), 1977–80. Col Comdt, Royal Corps of Signals, 1977–85. Colonel, Queen's Gurkha Signals, 1980–86. Gen. Manager, 1981–84, Dir, 1983–84, Marconi Space and Defence Systems; Man. Dir, 1984–85, Chm., 1985–86, Marconi Secure Radio Systems; Prin. Consultant, Logica Space and Defence Systems, 1986–90; Chm., Logica Defence and Civil Government Ltd, 1991–94. Vice Chm., Governors, Wilson's Sch., 1979–99. *Recreations:* sailing, (formerly) Rugby.

STURGEON, Rt Hon. Nicola; PC 2014; Member (SNP) Glasgow Southside, Scottish Parliament, since 2011 (Glasgow, 1999–2007, Glasgow Govan, 2007–11); First Minister, since 2014 (Deputy First Minister, 2007–14); Leader, Scottish National Party, since 2014; *b* 19 July 1970; *d* of Robert and Joan Sturgeon. *Educ:* Univ. of Glasgow (LLB Hons; Dip. Legal Practice). Trainee Solicitor, McClure Naismith, Glasgow, 1993–95; Asst Solicitor, Bell & Craig, Stirling, 1995–97; Associate Solicitor, Drumchapel Law Centre, Glasgow, 1997–99. Dep. Leader, SNP, 2004–14. Cabinet Sec., for Health and Wellbeing, 2007–12, for Cities Strategy, 2011–12, for Infrastructure, Investment and Cities, 2012–14, Scottish Parlt. *Recreations:* theatre, reading. *Address:* Scottish Parliament, Edinburgh EH99 1SP. *T:* (0131) 348 5695.

STURGIS, Dr Alexander John; Director, Ashmolean Museum, since 2014; Fellow, Worcester College, Oxford, since 2014; *b* London, 6 Nov. 1963; *s* of Tim and Jean Sturgis; *m* 1994, Anna Benn; two *s* one *d*. *Educ:* Marlborough Coll.; University Coll., Oxford (BA Hons Hist.); Courtauld Inst. (PhD Hist. of Art 1990). Educn Officer, 1991–99, Curator, Exhibns and Progs, 1999–2005, National Gall.; Dir, Holburne Mus., Bath, 2005–14. *Publications:* Faces, 1998; Telling the Time, 2000; Understanding Paintings, 2000; Dan's Angel, 2002; Rebels and Martyrs, 2006; Presence: the art of portrait sculpture, 2012. *Recreations:* magic, Arsenal FC. *Address:* Ashmolean Museum, Beaumont Street, Oxford OX1 2PH.

STURKEY, (Robert) Douglas, CVO 1995; AM 1999; PhD; Official Secretary to the Governor-General of Australia, 1990–98; Secretary of the Order of Australia, 1990–98; *b* 7 Sept. 1935; *s* of late James Robert Sturkey and Jessie Grace (*née* Meares). *Educ:* Wesley Coll., S Perth; Univ. of WA (BA Hons); ANU (MA 2000; PhD 2004). Mem., Australian Diplomatic Service, 1957–90: service abroad at Wellington, Lagos, Suva, Malta, Calcutta; Counsellor, later Dep. Perm. Rep., UN, New York, 1974–77; Ambassador to Saudi Arabia (also concurrently to countries of Arabian peninsula), 1979–84; Head, S Asia, Africa and ME Br., Dept of Foreign Affairs, Canberra, 1984–87; Principal Advr, Asia Div., Dept of Foreign Affairs and Trade, Canberra, 1987–90. KStJ 2008 (CStJ 1992). *Publications:* The Limits of American Power: prosecuting a Middle East peace, 2007. *Recreations:* opera, music, theatre. *Address:* PO Box 5562, Hughes, ACT 2605, Australia. *T:* (2) 62324722.

STURLEY, Air Marshal Philip Oliver, CB 2000; MBE 1985; FRAeS; defence adviser and mentor; *b* 9 July 1950; *s* of William Percival Sturley and Delia Agnes Sturley (*née* Grogan); *m* 1972, Micheline Leetch; one *d*. *Educ:* St Ignatius Coll., London; Southampton Univ. (BSc 1971). FRAeS 1993. Pilot trng, RAF Coll., Cranwell, 1971–72; 41 Sqn Coningsby, 1973–76; II (Army Co-operation) Sqn Laarbruch, 1977–80, 1982–84, OC, 1987–89; HQ 1 (British) Corps Bielefeld, 1980–82; jsdc, 1984; Comd Briefing Team, 1984–85, Plans, 1985–86, HQ Strike Comd; Air Plans, 1989–90, Dir of Air Staff Briefing and Co-ordination, 1990–92, MoD; OC RAF Cottesmore, 1992–94; Sec. IMS, HQ NATO, 1994–98; SASO HQ Strike Comd and AOC No 38 Gp, 1998–2000; ACAS, MoD, 2000–03; COS AirNorth Comd, Ramstein, 2003–05; Sen. Mentor, HCSC, Shrivenham, 2006–. Specialist Advr to H of C Defence Cttee, 2006–14. Sen. Military Advr, Shephard Gp, 2006–12; Mil. Advr, Tangent Link, 2012–. Manager, British Gliding Team, 2008–12. Pres., 2005–11, Life Vice Pres., 2011, RAFA. Hon. Air Cdre 4624 Sqdn, RAuxAF, 2012–. CCMI 2010–15. *Recreations:* gliding, golf, ski-ing. *Address:* c/o RAFA Central HQ, 117½ Loughborough Road, Leicester LE4 5ND. *Club:* Royal Air Force.

STURMAN, James Anthony; QC 2002; *b* 19 July 1958; *s* of Gp Capt. Roger Sturman, RAF (retd) and Anne Sturman; *m* 1986, Marcella Mineo; three *s*. *Educ:* Bembridge Sch., Isle of Wight; Reading Univ. (LLB). Called to the Bar, Gray's Inn, 1982, Bencher, 2008; criminal defence, regulatory and sports law barrister. *Recreations:* soccer, cricket, punk rock music, my three children. *Address:* 2 Bedford Row, WC1R 4BU. *T:* (020) 7440 8888, *Fax:* (020) 7242 1738. *E:* jsturman@2bedfordrow.co.uk.

STURRIDGE, Charles; writer and director; *b* 24 June 1951; *s* of Jerome Francis Sturridge and Alyson Sturridge (*née* Burke); *m* 1985, Phoebe Nicholls; two *s* one *d*. *Educ:* Beaumont Coll.; Stonyhurst Coll.; University Coll., Oxford (BA). Mem., NYT, 1967–70; film début as actor, If..., 1968; director: *theatre* includes: The Seagull, Queen's, 1985; *films* include: Runners, 1982; (co-writer) A Handful of Dust, 1988; (co-writer) Where Angels Fear to Tread, 1991; (screenplay) Fairytale—A True Story, 1997 (Best Children's Film, British Acad., 1998); Ohio Impromptu, 2001 (Best TV Drama, LWT Awards); (writer and producer) Lassie, 2005; *television* includes: 16 episodes of Coronation Street; 4 documentary films for World in Action, 1976; Brideshead Revisited, 1981 (Best Series, BAFTA); A Foreign Field, 1993; Gulliver's Travels, 1996 (Best Series, Emmy Awards); (also writer) Longitude, 2000 (Best Series, BAFTA); (also writer) Shackleton, 2002; The No 1 Ladies Detective Agency, 2009; The Road to Coronation Street, 2010; The Scapegoat, 2012. *Address:* c/o United Agents, 12-26 Lexington Street, W1F 0LE. *T:* (020) 3214 0800.

STURRIDGE, Sir Nicholas (Antony), KCVO 2007 (CVO 1986); Surgeon-Dentist to the Queen, 1975–2007; *s* of Frank Sturridge. *Educ:* Royal Dental Hosp., Univ. of London (BDS 1961); Northwestern Univ., Chicago (DDS 1963). LDSRCS. Pt-time clin. teaching post, UCH Dental Sch., 1964–74; in practice with Drs Sturridge & Barrett, later Drs Sturridge, Capp & Barrett, 1964–. Hon. Consultant, King Edward VII Hosp., Sister Agnes. Past President: Amer. Dental Soc. of Europe; Amer. Dental Soc. of London. *Address:* 152 Harley Street, W1G 7LH.

STURROCK, John Garrow; QC (Scot.) 1999; Chief Executive, Core Solutions Group, since 2004; Director, Core Mediation, since 2000; *b* 15 April 1958; *s* of John Chesser Sturrock and Lilian Sturrock; *m* 1984, Fiona Swanson; two *s* one *d*. *Educ:* Univ. of Edinburgh (LLB 1st Cl. Hons 1980); Univ. of Pennsylvania (LLM 1985). MCIArb 2001. Solicitor, 1983–84; Harkness Fellow, 1984–85; admitted Faculty of Advocates, 1986; in practice as advocate, 1986–2002; Dir, Trng and Educn, Faculty of Advocates, 1994–2002. Door Tenant, Brick Court Chambers, 2013–. Standing Jun. Counsel to Dept of Transport in Scotland, 1991–94; Accredited Mediator, CEDR, 1996. Man. Dir, Core Consulting, 2000–04. Vis. Prof. of Advocacy Skills and Conflict Resolution, Univ. of Strathclyde, 1999–. Member: Jt Standing Cttee on Legal Educn, Scotland, 1988–2005; Judicial Studies Cttee, Scotland, 1997–2005; Standards Commn, Internat. Mediation Inst., 2007–; Global Adv. Council, Mediators Beyond Borders, 2008–. Assessor, SHEFC, 1995–96. FRSA 2001. Dist. Fellow, Internat. Acad. of Mediators, 2009–. Hon. LLD Edinburgh Napier, 2010. *Recreations:* family, church, golf, music. *Address:* Core Solutions Group, 10 York Place, Edinburgh EH1 3EP. *E:* John.Sturrock@core-solutions.com.

STURROCK, Philip James, MBE 2014; Chairman, PanCathay Consulting Ltd, since 2004; *b* 5 Oct. 1947; *s* of James Cars Sturrock and Joyce Sturrock (*née* Knowles); *m* 1st, 1972, Susan Haycock (marr. diss. 1995); one *s* two *d*; 2nd, 2000, Madeleine Frances Robinson. *Educ:* Queen Mary's School, Walsall; Trinity College, Oxford (MA); Manchester Business School (MBA). Managing Director: IBIS Information Services, 1972–80; Pitman Books, 1980–83; Group Man. Dir, Routledge & Kegan Paul, 1983–85; Chm., Redwood Publishing Ltd, 1985–86; Chm. and Man. Dir, Cassell, 1986–99; Chm. and Gp Chief Exec., Continuum Internat. Publishing Gp, 1999–2006; Chm., Osprey Publishing, 2007–08. Chm., Wandle Housing Assoc., 2010–13; Dir, The Publishing Partnership, 2010–. Mem., Industrial Develt Adv. Bd, 2009–. Chm., Soc. of Bookmen, 2001–02. Governor, Pusey House, Oxford, 1975–95. Trustee: St Albans Cathedral Educn Trust, 1988–2003; United St Saviour's Charity, 2008–14 (Treas., 2008–10; Chm., Trustees, 2010–14). Gov., Queen Mary's Grammar Sch., Walsall, 2008– (Chm., Finance, 2009–11; Chm., Govs, 2011–); Mem., Southwark Cathedral Fundraising Council, 2012–; Mem. Council and Chm., Finance and Gen. Purposes Cttee, Inst. of Educn, Univ. of London, 2012–; Mem. Council, UCL, 2015–. Chairman: St Albans Internat. Organ Fest., 1983–84; Hatfield Philharmonic Orch., 1988–92. Hon. Vis. Prof., Beijing Normal Univ., 2005–10. FRSA 1992. Liveryman, Glaziers' Co., 1983– (Master's Steward, 2010–11). *Recreations:* reading, walking, music, food and wine. *Address:* 62 Benbow House, New Globe Walk, SE1 9DS. *T:* (020) 3267 1136. *Club:* Athenæum.

STUTTAFORD, Dr (Irving) Thomas, OBE 1996; medical correspondent, The Oldie, since 1992; *b* 4 May 1931; 2nd *s* of late Dr W. J. E. Stuttaford, MC, Horning, Norfolk and Mrs Marjorie Stuttaford (*née* Royden); *m* 1957, Pamela (*d* 2013), *d* of late Col Richard Ropner, TD, DL, Tain; three *s*. *Educ:* Gresham's Sch.; Brasenose Coll., Oxford; West London Hosp. 2nd Lieut, 10th Royal Hussars (PWO), 1953–55; Lieut, Scottish Horse (TA), 1955–59. Qualif. MRCS, LRCP, 1959; junior hosp. appts, 1959 and 1960. Gen. Med. practice, 1960–70. Mem. Blofield and Flegg RDC, 1964–66; Mem., Norwich City Council, 1969–71. MP (C) Norwich S, 1970–Feb. 1974; Mem. Select Cttee Science and Technology, 1970–74. Contested (C) Isle of Ely, Oct. 1974, 1979. Physician, BUPA Medical Centre, 1971–96; Clinical Assistant to: The London Hosp., 1975–93; Queen Mary's Hosp. for East End, 1974–79; Moorfields Eye Hosp., 1975–79. Member: Council, Research Defence Soc., 1970–79; Birth Control Campaign Cttee, 1970–79; British Cancer Council, 1970–79. Vice-Pres., Prostate UK. Medical Adviser: Barclays Bank, 1971–2006 (Sen. Med. Advr, 1987–2001); Rank Organisation, 1980–85; Standard Chartered Bank, Hogg Robinson, Rank Hotels and other cos; Medical Corresp., 1982–91, medical columnist, 1991–2009, The Times. Contributor to: Elle, For Him, Options, etc. *Publications:* To Your Good Health: the wise drinker's guide, 1997; (jtly) In Your Right Mind, 1999; Understanding Your Common Symptoms, 2003; Stress and How to Avoid It, 2004. *Recreation:* country life. *Address:* 36 Elm Hill, Norwich, Norfolk NR3 1HG. *T:* (01603) 615133. *Clubs:* Athenæum, Reform, Cavalry and Guards, Beefsteak, Garrick; Norfolk (Norwich).

STUTTARD, Caroline Anne; *see* Stockmann, C. A.

STUTTARD, David Ashton; freelance writer, lecturer, dramaturg and strategic advisor, since 2004; *b* Perth, Scotland, 1959; *s* of Philip Stuttard and Isobel Stuttard; *m* 2010, Emily Jane Birtwell. *Educ:* Morrison's Acad., Crieff; Univ. of St Andrews (MA Hons Classics); Dundee Coll. of Educn (PGCE). Teacher of Classics, Edinburgh Acad., 1985–87; Curriculum Coordinator, St Leonards Sch., St Andrews, 1987–94; Hd of Classics, Queen Margaret's Sch., Escrick, York, 1994–96; Founder and Jt Artistic Dir, Actors of Dionysus, 1993–2004. Occasional teaching, Madingley Hall, Univ. of Cambridge, 2015. *Publications:* An Introduction to Trojan Women, 2005; (with Sam Moorhead) AD410: the year that shook Rome, 2010; (ed) Looking at Lysistrata, 2010; Power Games, 2012; (with Sam Moorhead) The Romans Who Shaped Britain, 2012; (with Sam Moorhead) 31BC: Antony, Cleopatra and the fall of Egypt, 2012; Parthenon: power and politics on the Acropolis, 2013; A History of Ancient Greece in 50 Lives, 2014; (ed) Looking at Medea, 2014; (ed) Looking at Bacchae, 2016; A Traveller's Guide to Greek Mythology, 2016; articles in Minerva and British Mus. Magazine. *Recreations:* baroque music, spending time in Graeco-Roman theatres, opera, reading detective fiction, making and eating ice cream. *Address:* c/o A. M. Heath & Company Ltd, 6 Warwick Court, Holborn, WC1R 5DJ. *E:* david@davidstuttard.com.

STUTTARD, Sir John (Boothman), Kt 2008; JP; Adviser, PricewaterhouseCoopers, since 2005; Lord Mayor of London, 2006–07; *b* 6 Feb. 1945; *s* of Thomas Boothman Stuttard and Helena Stuttard (*née* Teasdale); *m* 1970, Lesley Sylvia Daish; two *s*. *Educ:* Shrewsbury Sch.; Churchill Coll., Cambridge (BA 1966, MA 1970). FCA 1979. Teacher with VSO, SOAS Coll., Brunei, 1966–67; Coopers & Lybrand, then PricewaterhouseCoopers: articled clerk, then Chartered Accountant, 1970–75; Partner, 1975–2005; Chm., Coopers & Lybrand China, subseq. PricewaterhouseCoopers China, 1994–99; Dep. Chm., Adv. Panel, PricewaterhouseCoopers LLP, 2008–12. Advr, Central Policy Rev. Staff, Cabinet Office, 1981–83. Director: China-Britain Business Council, 2000–06; Finnish-British Chamber of Commerce, 2001–10 (Chm., 2002–06; Life Pres., 2007); Co-Chm., Kazakh-British Trade and Industry Council, 2009–13. Fellow, 48 Gp, 2008. Mem., Fund Raising Adv. Bd, 2000–05, Council, 2006–13, VSO. University of Cambridge: Mem., Appts Bd, 1977–81; Mem. Adv. Cttee, East Asia Inst., Faculty of Oriental Studies, 2001–; By-Fellow, Møller Centre, Churchill Coll., Cambridge, 2008–. Chancellor, City Univ., 2006–07. Mem. Court and Fellow, Bridewell Royal Hosp. and Gov., King Edward VII Sch., Witley, 2002–13. Pres., Shaftesbury Civic Soc., 2013–. Trustee: Lord Mayor of London's Disaster Relief Appeal, 2002–12; Charities Aid Foundn, 2003–09 (Chm., Audit, Risk and Compliance Cttee, 2003–06); Lord Mayor's 800th Anniv. Appeal, 2005–12; Morden Coll., 2005–; St Paul's Cathedral Foundation: Advr, 2005–11; Chm., 2011–13; Fellow, 2013–. Hon. Treas., New Horizon Youth Centre, 1972–77; Dir, Totteridge Manor Assoc., 1980–2005 (Chm., 2002–05); Hon. Vice-President: Totteridge Residents Assoc., 2006–; Cambridge Univ. Land Soc., 2008. Hon. ACCA 2007; Hon. FCSI 2007. Hon. Fellow, Foreign Policy Assoc., USA, 2000; Hon. Member: Maritime London, 2007; GSMD, 2008. Alderman, City of London, Lime Street, 2001–13; Sheriff, City of London, 2005–06; Liveryman: Glaziers' and Painters of Glass Co., 2000– (Ct Asst, 2003–; Master, 2009–10); Chartered Accountants' Co., 2002– (Ct Asst, 2004–; Master, 2011–12); Plumbers' Co., 2005– (Hon. Ct Asst, 2005–); Hon. Liveryman and Ct Asst, Educators' Co., 2014– (Hon. Freeman, 2002–14, Ct Asst, 2002–14, Master, 2013–14, Guild, later Co. of Educators). JP City of London, 2001. Hon. DLitt City, 2006. KStJ 2006. Knight 1st Cl., 1995, Comdr, 2004, Order of the Lion (Finland); Companion, League of Mercy, 2007; Silver Medal, City of Helsinki, 2007; 20th Anniversary Jubilee Medal (Kazakhstan), 2011. *Publications:* The New Silk Road—Secrets of Business Success in China Today, 2000; Whittington to World Financial Centre: the City of London and its Lord Mayor, 2008; Travels in a Lifetime, 2015. *Recreations:* travelling, rallying old cars, theatre, opera, tennis. *Address:* PricewaterhouseCoopers LLP, 1 Embankment Place, WC2N 6RH. *T:* (020) 7213 4590. *Clubs:* Travellers, East India, Walbrook; Rolls-Royce Enthusiasts of Great Britain, 20-Ghost (Chm., 2010–); China (Beijing and Hong Kong).

STUTTLE, Barbara Charmaine, CBE 2004; independent healthcare consultant, specialising in transformation and turn-around, since 2011; Deputy Chief Executive Officer, Chief Nurse and Director of Quality and Nursing, South West Essex Primary Care Trust, 2008–11; *b* 4 May 1952; *d* of Philip George Albert Coote and Edith Marion Coote; two *s*. *Educ:* Hurlingham Sch. for Girls, Fulham; Sweyne Sch., Rayleigh; Southend Hosp.; City Univ., London (MSc Health Mgt 1996). SRN, 1971–73; Staff Nurse, Southend Hosp., 1974–75; Dist Nurse, Southend, 1975–79; Southend Community Care Trust: Dist Nurse, 1981–89; Nursing Officer, 1989–90; Asst Dir of Nursing, 1990–93; Sen. Manager, Thameside

Community Care Trust, 1993–99; Dir of Integrated Care and Exec. Nurse, Castle Point and Rochford PCT, 1999–2005; Dir, Primary Care and Modernisation, Thurrock PCT, 2005–06; Exec. Nurse, SW Essex PCT, 2006–08. Nurse Prescribing Proj. Lead, London and SE Reg., DoH, 1998–2002; Nat. Clinical Lead Nursing and Midwifery, Connecting for Health, NHS, 2005–09. Fellow, Queen's Nursing Inst., 2007. Hon. Dr Health Scis Anglia Ruskin, 2009. *Publications:* Independent and Supplementary Prescribing: an essential guide, 2004, 2nd edn 2009. *Recreations:* going to the gym - reluctantly, reading, eating out, drinking wine, spending time with grandchildren.

STYBELSKI, Peter Stefan; business consultant, since 2010; Chief Executive, Cumbria County Council, 2004–09; *b* 26 Oct. 1952; *s* of Czeslaw and Mary Stybelski; *m* 1980, Lorna Bell; one *s*. *Educ:* Plymouth; Wye Coll., Univ. of London (BSc Hons Geog. 1972; MSc Landscape, Ecol., Design and Maintenance 1976). Dist Grounds Superintendent, Bucks AHA, 1976–78; Parks Superintendent, Oxford CC, 1978–80; Asst Dir (Ops), Blackpool BC, 1980–83; Chief Amenities Officer, RBK&C, 1983–89; Dir, Leisure Services, Bolton MBC, 1989–2000; Town Clerk and Chief Exec., Carlisle CC, 2000–04. Vice Chm., Carlisle Youth Zone Ltd, 2010–12; non-executive Director: Story Homes Ltd, 2012–15; Story Contracting Ltd, 2012–15; Land and Lakes (Anglesey) Ltd, 2014–. Mem. Bd, Sport England, 2010–13. Trustee, Churches Trust for Cumbria, 2010–. *E:* peter@stybelski.com.

STYLE, Vice-Adm. Charles Rodney, CBE 2002; Commandant, Royal College of Defence Studies, 2008–12; Director, White Water Wave Ltd, since 2011; *b* 15 Jan. 1954; *s* of Lt-Comdr Sir Godfrey William Style, CBE, DSC, RN, and Sigrid Elisabeth Julin (*née* Carlberg); *m* 1981, Charlotte Amanda Woodford; three *d*. *Educ:* Eton; St Catharine's Coll., Cambridge (Exhibnr; BA Geog. 1975; MA); BRNC Dartmouth (Queen's Sword, 1976). Served: HMS Endurance, 1977–78; Navigating Officer, HMS Bacchante, 1978–79; Royal Yacht Britannia, 1980–81; Commanding Officer: HMS Sandpiper, 1981–82; HMS Wotton, 1982–83; Ops Officer, HMS Arethusa, 1984–85; Naval Assistant to C-in-C Fleet, 1985–87; CO, HMS Andromeda, 1988–89; Naval Planner, MoD, 1989–92; COS to Comdr UK Task Gp, 1992–93; CO, HMS Campbeltown, 1993–95 (Task Gp Comd, Gulf, 1993–94); Dep. Flag Officer Sea Trng, 1995–96; hcsc 1997; Prin. SO to CDS, 1997–98; rcds 1999; CO, HMS Illustrious, 2000–01 (Task Gp Comd, Arabian Sea, 2001); Capability Manager (Strategic Deployment and Precision Attack), MoD, 2002–04; Comdr UK Maritime Force, 2004–05; DCDS (Commitments) and Dir of Ops, MoD, 2006–07. US Mil. Pinnacle course, 2006. Exec.-in-Residence, Manchester Business Sch., 2009–. Vis. Res. Fellow, Dept of War Studies, KCL, 2012–. Mem. Adv. Gp, Eur. Mentoring and Coaching Council, 2010–12. Mem., Adv. Panel, Concordis Internat., 2012–; Consultant, Veritas Internat., 2012–13. Trustee: Britannia Assoc., 2000–09; Kids4Kids, 2012–15; Queen Elizabeth Foundn, 2013–; Advr, St Martin-in-the-Fields Renewal Proj., 2005–09; Mem. Cttee, Never Such Innocence, 2014–. Mem., Master Mariners' Co., 2003–14. Younger Brother, Trinity House, 1991–. *Publications:* (jtly) In Business and Battle, 2012. *Recreations:* sailing, fishing, reading, music. *E:* charlesstyle.cs@gmail.com. *Club:* Royal Yacht Squadron (Cowes).

STYLE, Christopher John David; QC 2006; *b* 13 April 1955; *s* of David and Anne Style; *m* 1990, Victoria Miles; three *s* one *d*. *Educ:* St Bees Sch.; Trinity Hall, Cambridge (BA Law 1976). Admitted solicitor, 1979; called to the Bar, Lincoln's Inn, 2012. Solicitor with Linklaters, 1977–2012. *Publications:* (with Charles Hollander) Documentary Evidence, 1984, 6th edn 1997. *Recreations:* my family, the country, high mountains. *Address:* One Essex Court, Temple, EC4Y 9AR. *T:* (020) 7583 2000, *Fax:* (020) 7583 0118. *E:* cstyle@oeclaw.co.uk.

STYLE, Sir William Frederick, 13th Bt *cr* 1627, of Wateringbury, Kent; *b* 13 May 1945; *s* of Sir William Montague Style, 12th Bt, and La Verne, *d* of late T. M. Comstock; *S* father, 1981, but his name does not appear on the Official Roll of the Baronetage; *m* 1st, 1968, Wendy Gay (marr. diss. 1971), *d* of Gene Wittenberger, Hartford, Wisconsin, USA; two *d*; 2nd, 1986, Linnea Lorna, *d* of Donn Erickson, Sussex, Wisconsin, USA; one *s* two *d*. *Heir: s* William Colin Style, *b* 1 Sept. 1995.

STYLER, His Honour Granville Charles; a Circuit Judge, 1992–2013; *b* 9 Jan. 1947; *s* of Samuel Charles Styler and Frances Joan Styler (*née* Clifford); *m* 1971, Penelope Darbyshire; three *d*. *Educ:* King Edward VI Sch., Stratford-upon-Avon. Called to the Bar, Gray's Inn, 1970; a Recorder, 1988–92; Resident Judge and Designated Family Judge, Stoke on Trent Combined Court Centre, 1995–2007. *Recreations:* carriage driving, tennis, gardening, horse racing. *Club:* Outer Hebrides Tennis.

STYLES, Amanda Jane; *see* Vickery, A. J.

STYLES, Graham Charles Trayton; HM Diplomatic Service; Head, Kosovo, Albania and Macedonia Team, Foreign and Commonwealth Office, since 2015; *b* Farnborough, 16 April 1958; *s* of Roy Trayton Styles and Audrey Jean Breething (*née* Kelynack); *m* 1984, Rachael Jane Hopkins; two *d*. *Educ:* Sevenoaks Sch.; Orpington Coll. of Further Educn; Birmingham Univ. (BA Hons English 1981). Entered FCO, 1977; Registry Officer, Central and Southern African Dept, FCO, 1977–78; on sabbatical, 1978–81; Registry Officer, Eastern Eur. Soviet Dept, FCO, 1981–85; Registry/Communications Officer, Mauritius, 1985–88; Entry Clearance Officer, Paris, 1989–92; Postings Officer, FCO, 1992–95; Third Sec., UK Delegn to OSCE, Vienna, 1995–98; Desk Officer Sierra Leone, Africa Dept, FCO, 1998–2001; Nat. Contact Point, EU Twinning Prog., EU Dept, FCO, 2001–02; Deptl Report Writer, Directorate for Strategy and Innovation, FCO, 2002–04; Hd, Mekong and Burma Team, SE Asia Dept, FCO, 2004–06; First Sec., UK Mission to UN, Vienna, 2006–11; Ambassador to Rep. of Guinea, 2011–14. *Recreations:* reading, running, disused railways, Arsenal FC, eating rice pudding. *Address:* c/o Foreign and Commonwealth Office, King Charles Street, SW1A 2AH. *E:* graham.styles@fco.gov.uk.

STYLES, Prof. Morag Chrystine Campbell; Professor of Children's Poetry, University of Cambridge, 2011–14; Fellow, Homerton College, Cambridge, until 2014, now Emeritus; *b* Dundee, 19 Sept. 1947; *d* of Ruairidh Ross and Bette McRobb Ross; *m* 1968, Jon Styles (marr. diss. 1983); one *s*. *Educ:* Edinburgh Univ. (BSc Social Sci. 1970); Homerton Coll., Cambridge (PGCE 1971). Primary sch. teacher, Cambridge, 1971–74; Homerton College, Cambridge: Lectr (pt-time) in English and Maths Educn, 1974–84; Dep. Co-ordinator of Curriculum Studies; Homerton College, then Faculty of Education, 1984–2014: Lang. Co-ordinator; Sen. Lectr; Reader. *Publications:* From the Garden to the Street: 300 years of poetry for children, 1998; (with E. Arlzpe) Children Reading Pictures, 2003; (with E. Arlzpe) Reading Lessons from the 18th Century: mothers, children and text, 2006; (ed jtly) Acts of Reading, 2009; (ed jtly) Poetry and Childhood, 2010; (with M. Salisbury) Children's Picturebooks: the art of visual storytelling, 2012. *Recreations:* theatre, music, opera, art, reading, bird-watching, nature, socialising with friends, travelling, miniature glamorous shoe collecting.

STYLES, Prof. Peter, PhD; CGeol, FGS; FRAS; CSci; FIMMM; geophysicist; Professor of Applied and Environmental Geophysics, since 2000, Head of Energy and Sustainability Strategy, since 2009, and Professorial Research Fellow in Applied and Environmental Geophysics, Keele University; *b* 4 Sept. 1950; *s* of Daniel and Alice Styles; *m* 1975, Roslyn Schmeisser; two *s* two *d*. *Educ:* Dukes Grammar Sch., Alnwick; Wadham Coll., Oxford (BA Hons Physics 1972); Univ. of Newcastle upon Tyne (PhD Geophysics 1977). Lectr, 1977–87, Sen. Lectr, 1987–88, in Geophysics, Univ. of Wales, Swansea; Sen. Lectr, 1988–98, Reader, 1998–99, in Geophysics, Univ. of Liverpool; Hd, Sch. of Earth Sci. and Geog., 2001–03, Dir, Envmt, Phys. Scis and Applied Maths Res. Inst., 2005–09, Keele Univ. Chair, Criteria Proposals Gp: Managing Radioactive Waste Safely, DEFRA, 2007–; Member: Geosphere Characterisation Panel, Nuclear Decommissioning Agency, 2009–; Royal Soc. Working Party on Nuclear Non-Proliferation, 2009–11. Pres., Internat. Commn on Hydrocarbon Exploration and Seismicity, 2013–. Mem. Bd, British Geol. Survey, 2001–09. Dist. Vis. Lectr in Near-Surface Geophysics, European Assoc. of Geoscientists and Engrs, 2012. Professional Sec., 1996–99, Pres., 2004–06, Geol Soc. of London; Pres., BAAS (Geol. Section), 2007. Trustee, Underground Coal Gasification Assoc., 2009–. Jt author, report for DECC, Preese Hall Shale Gas Fracturing: review and recommendations for induced seismic mitigation, 2012. William Smith Medal, Geol Soc., 2014. *Recreations:* guitar, singing British folk music, photography, travelling. *Address:* 6 Swan Lane, Bunbury, Cheshire CW6 9RA.

STYLIANIDES, Christos; Member, European Commission, since 2014; European Union Ebola Coordinator, since 2014; *b* Nicosia, Cyprus, 26 June 1958; *m*; one *s*. *Educ:* Aristoteleion Univ., Thessaloniki (Dental Surgeon 1984); JFK Sch. of Govt, Harvard Univ. Govt spokesperson, Cyprus, 1998–99; MHR, Cyprus, 2006–13; Govt spokesperson, 2013–14. Mem., OSCE Parly Assembly, 2006–11. *Address:* European Commission, Rue de la Loi 200, 1049 Brussels, Belgium. *T:* 22954605. *E:* christos.stylianides@ec.europa.eu.

SUÁREZ, Michael Angel; Chief Executive, Cheshire East Council, since 2013; *b* 1 Nov. 1967; *s* of Antonio Suárez and Mary Theresa Suárez; *m* 1996, Jacqueline Elizabeth Bates; two *s* one *d*. *Educ:* Keele Univ. (BSc Jt Hons Biol. and Mgt Sci.). CPFA 1995. Southwark LBC, 1989–98; Asst Dir Finance for Educn, Soc. Services and Housing, Westminster CC, 1998–2002; Strategic Dir of Finance and Property, Slough BC, 2002–05; Exec. Dir of Finance, subseq. Finance and Resources, Lambeth LBC, 2005–13. Non-exec. Dir, London Authorities' Mutual Ltd (Dep. Chm., 2009–); Mem., London Finance Adv. Cttee, 2006–. Member: Soc. of London Treasurers, 2005; Soc. of Municipal Treasurers, 2005. Mem. Bd, CIPFA, 2011–13 (Member: Internat. Strategy Bd; Remuneration Cttee; Chm., Local Govt Policy Panel, 2011–). Treas., Squirrels Day Nursery, 2003–05; non-exec. Dir, Lambeth Coll., 2012–13. Columnist, MJ, 2008–. Public Sector Finance Dir of Yr, Accountancy Age Awards, 2008. *Recreations:* squash, swimming and when I can, scuba diving, five-a-side football.

SUBAK-SHARPE, Prof. John Herbert, CBE 1991; FRSE 1970; Professor of Virology, University of Glasgow, 1968–94, now Emeritus; Hon. Director, Medical Research Council Virology Unit, 1968–94; *b* 14 Feb. 1924; *s* of late Robert Subak and late Nelly (*née* Bruell), Vienna, Austria; *m* 1953, Barbara Naomi Morris; two *s* one *d*. *Educ:* Humanistic Gymnasium, Vienna; Univ. of Birmingham. BSc (Genetics) (1st Cl. Hons) 1952; PhD 1956. Refugee by Kindertransport from Nazi oppression, 1939; farm pupil, 1939–44; HM Forces (Parachute Regt), 1944–47. Asst Lectr in Genetics, Glasgow Univ., 1954–56; Mem. scientific staff, ARC Animal Virus Research Inst., Pirbright, 1956–60; Nat. Foundn Fellow, California Inst. of Technology, 1961; Mem. Scientific staff of MRC, in Experimental Virus Research Unit, Glasgow, 1961–68. Visiting Professor: US Nat. Insts of Health, Bethesda, Md, 1967; US Univ. of Health Services, Bethesda, Md, 1985; Vis. Fellow, Clare Hall, Cambridge, 1986–87. Sec., Genetical Soc., 1966–72, Vice-Pres. 1972–75, Trustee 1971–99. Member: European Molecular Biology Orgn, 1969– (Chm., Course and Workshops Cttee, 1976–78); Genetic Manipulation Adv. Gp, 1976–80; Biomed. Res. Cttee, SHHD Chief Scientist Orgn, 1979–84; British Nat. Cttee of Biophysics, 1970–76; Governing Body, W of Scotland Oncological Orgn, 1974–; Scientific Adv. Body, W German Cancer Res. Centre, 1977–82; Governing Body, Animal Virus Res. Inst., Pirbright, 1986–87; MRC Training Awards Panel, 1985–89 (Chm., 1986–89); Scientific Adv. Gp of Equine Virology Res. Foundn, 1987–98; MRC Cell and Disorders Bd, 1988–92. CIBA Medal, Biochem. Soc., 1993. *Publications:* articles in scientific jls on genetic studies with viruses and cells. *Recreations:* travel, hill walking, bridge. *Address:* 63 Kelvin Court, Glasgow G12 0AG. *T:* (0141) 334 1863. *Club:* Athenæum.

SUBBA ROW, Raman, CBE 1991; Chairman, Test and County Cricket Board, 1985–90; *b* 29 Jan. 1932; *s* of Panguluri Venkata Subba Row and Doris Mildred Subba Row; *m* 1960, Anne Dorothy (*née* Harrison); two *s* one *d*. *Educ:* Whitgift Sch., Croydon; Trinity Hall, Cambridge (MA Hons). Associate Dir, W. S. Crawford Ltd, 1963–69; Man. Dir, Management Public Relations Ltd, 1969–92; internat. cricket match referee, 1993–2002. *Recreations:* sport, bridge. *Address:* Leeward, Manor Way, South Croydon, Surrey CR2 7BT. *T:* (020) 8688 2991. *Clubs:* Royal Air Force, Institute of Directors, MCC, Surrey County Cricket (former Chm.); Bloemfontein (South Africa); Cricket of India (Bombay); Kingston Cricket (Jamaica).

SUBRAMANIAN, Lilian Rachel; *see* Greenwood, L. R.

SUCH, Frederick Rudolph Charles; Immigration Adjudicator, later Immigration Judge, London Region, 2000–06; *b* 19 June 1936; *s* of Frederick Sidney Such and Anne Marie Louise (*née* Martin); *m* 1961, Elizabeth, *d* of late Judge Norman and Mrs Harper, Cloughton, Yorkshire; one *s* one *d*. *Educ:* Mbeya Sch., Tanganyika Territory, E Africa (Tanzania); Taunton Sch.; Keble Coll., Oxford (MA). Called to the Bar, Gray's Inn, 1960; practised: London, 1960–69, then North Eastern Circuit, 1969–2000; a Recorder, 1979–2001. FCIArb 1995. *Recreations:* theatre, opera, Real tennis. *Address:* 38 Church Road, Barnes, SW13 9HN. *Clubs:* Jesters, Queen's; Jesmond Dene Real Tennis.

SUCHET, David, CBE 2011 (OBE 2002); actor; associate artiste, Royal Shakespeare Co., since 1970 (Governor, since 2005); *b* 2 May 1946; *s* of late Jack Suchet and Joan (*née* Jarché); *m* 1976, Sheila Ferris, actress; one *s* one *d*. *Educ:* Wellington Sch.; LAMDA (Best Drama Student, 1968). *Stage:* repertory theatres, incl. Chester, Birmingham, Exeter, Worthing, Coventry, 1969–73; for Royal Shakespeare Co.: Romeo and Juliet (Mercutio and Tybalt), As You Like It (Orlando), Once in a Lifetime (Glogauer), Measure for Measure (Angelo), The Tempest (Caliban), King Lear (The Fool), King John (Hubert), Merchant of Venice (Shylock), Troilus and Cressida (Achilles), Richard II (Bolingbroke), Every Good Boy Deserves Favour, 1983, Othello (Iago), 1986, Timon of Athens (title rôle), 1991; Separation, Comedy, 1988; Oleanna, Royal Court, 1993 (Variety Club Award for Best Actor, 1994); Who's Afraid of Virginia Woolf?, Aldwych, 1996 (Best Actor Award, Critics' Circle and South Bank Awards); Saturday, Sunday, Monday, Chichester, 1998; Amadeus, Old Vic, 1998 (Variety Club Award for Best Actor, 1999), Los Angeles and NY, 1999–2000 (Drama League Award); Man and Boy, Duchess, 2005; Once in a Lifetime, NT, 2006; The Last Confession, Chichester, transf. Th. Royal, Haymarket, 2007; Complicit, Old Vic, 2009; All My Sons, Apollo, 2010; Long Day's Journey into Night, Apollo and tour, 2012; The Last Confession, world tour, Toronto, LA, Perth, Brisbane, Sydney, Melbourne, 2014; The Importance of Being Earnest (Lady Bracknell), Vaudeville, 2015; *films include:* Tale of Two Cities, 1978; The Missionary, 1982; Red Monarch (Best Actor award, Marseilles Film Fest.), 1983; Falcon and the Snowman, 1985; Thirteen at Dinner, 1985; Song for Europe, 1985; Harry and the Hendersons, 1986; When the Whales came, 1990; Deadly Voyage, 1995; Executive Decision, 1996; Sunday, 1996 (winner, Sundance Film Festival); Wing Commander, 1998; A Perfect Murder, 1998; RKO, 2000; Sabotage, 2000; The In-Laws, 2003; Live from Baghdad, 2003; Fool Proof, 2003; The Bank Job, 2007; Diverted, 2008; Effie Gray, 2014; *television includes:* Oppenheimer, 1978; Reilly, 1981; Saigon, 1982; Freud, 1983; Blott on the Landscape, 1984; Oxbridge Blues, 1984; Playing Shakespeare, 1985; Great Writers, 1988; Agatha Christie's Hercule Poirot, 1989–94, 2000–03, 2005, 2007–10, 2013; The Secret Agent, 1992; Solomon, 1997; Seesaw, 1998; National Crime Squad, 2001; Murder in Mind, 2001; Victoria and Albert, 2001; The Way We Live Now, 2001; Henry VIII, 2003; Get Carman, 2003; The Flood, 2006; Dracula, 2006; Maxwell, 2007; Great Expectations, 2011; Richard II, 2012; People I Have Shot, 2012; In the Footsteps of St Paul, 2012; In the Footsteps of St Peter, 2014; *radio:* one-man show, Kreutzer Sonata (Best Radio Actor, Pye Radio Awards, 1979); The Gorey Details, 2003; Einstein in Cromer, 2004; Dracula, 2006; The Last Confession, 2008;

The Willows in Winter, David Golder, 2010; numerous other parts; audio: entire Bible, 2014. Mem. Council, LAMDA, 1985–. Lectr, US univs; Vis. Prof., Univ. of Nebraska, 1975. FRSA 2005. Freeman, City of London, 2008. Hon. Fellow, Chichester Univ., 2008. Hon. DArts Kent, 2010. Numerous awards, incl. Best Actor, RTS, 1986; Best Actor, Critics' Circle Award, 2010. *Publications:* (contrib.) Players of Shakespeare, 2 vols, 1985 and 1988; Poirot and Me, 2013; essays on interpretation of roles. *Recreations:* clarinet, photography, reading, ornithology, theology, narrow boating. *Address:* c/o Gilly Sanguinetti, The Artists Partnership, 101 Finsbury Pavement, EC2A 1RS. *Clubs:* Garrick, St James's.

See also J. A. Suchet.

SUCHET, John Aleck; television and radio broadcaster; author; *b* 29 March 1944; *s* of late Jack and Joan Suchet; *m* 1st, 1968, Moya Hankinson (marr. diss. 1985); three *s*; 2nd, 1985, Bonnie Simonson (*d* 2015). *Educ:* Uppingham; Univ. of St Andrews (MA Hons). Reuters News Agency, 1967–71; BBC TV News, 1971–72; Independent Television News, 1972–2004: reporter, 1976–86; Washington corresp., 1981–83; newscaster, 1986–2004; newscaster, Channel Five, 2006–07; Breakfast prog. presenter, Classic FM, 2011–. Gov., RAM, 2003–07; Pres., Friends of RAM, 1998–2006; Hon. Pres., Dementia UK, 2010–11. Hon. FRAM 2001. Hon. LLD Dundee, 2000; Hon MA Worcester, 2010. TV Journalist of the Year, RTS, 1986; Newscaster of the Year, TRIC, 1996; Lifetime Achievement Award, RTS, 2008; Radio Personality of Year, Assoc. for Internat. Broadcasting, 2013; Gold Award for Best Personality, NY Internat. Radio Awards, 2014. *Publications:* TV News: the inside story, 1989; The Last Master (fictional biography of Ludwig van Beethoven): vol. 1, Passion and Anger, 1996; vol. 2, Passion and Pain, 1997; vol. 3, Passion and Glory, 1998; (with Darren Henley) The Classic FM Friendly Guide to Beethoven, 2006; The Treasures of Beethoven, 2008; My Bonnie, 2010; Beethoven: the man revealed, 2012; The Strauss Dynasty and Vienna, 2015. *Recreations:* classical music, exploring the life, times and music of Beethoven. *Address:* c/o David Foster Management, PO Box 1805, Andover, Hants SP10 3ZN.

See also D. Suchet.

SUCKLING, Prof. Colin James, OBE 2006; PhD, DSc; FRSC, FRSE; Freeland Professor of Chemistry, 1989–2012, Research Professor, since 2012, University of Strathclyde; *b* 24 March 1947; *s* of Dr Charles Walter Suckling, CBE, FRS; *m* 1972, Catherine Mary Faulkner; two *s* one *d*. *Educ:* Univ. of Liverpool (BSc 1967; PhD 1970; DSc 1989). CChem 1977; FRSC 1980. University of Strathclyde: Lectr, 1972–84; Prof. of Organic Chemistry, 1984–89; Dean, Faculty of Sci., 1992–94; Dep. Principal, 1995–98; Vice Principal, 1998–2002. Chairman: West of Scotland Schs Orch. Trust, 1995–; Harmony Music Scotland Trust, 2011–; Scottish Adv. Cttee for Distinction Awards, NHS Scotland, 2002–10; Mem., Jt Cttee on Higher Surgical Trng and Senate of Surgery, 2002–05; Public Partner, Scottish Medicines Consortium, 2011–14 (Chm., Patient and Public Interest Gp, 2012–14). Member: Bd of Govs, Bell Coll. of Technol., 1999–2007; Court, Univ. of Paisley, 2007–08; Court, Univ. of West of Scotland, 2008–13. FRSE 1987; FRSA 1991; FRCSGlas 2004. Hon. FRCSEd 2005; Hon. Life Fellow, Indian Soc. of Chemists and Biologists, 2015. Gold Medal, Lord Provost of Glasgow, 2000; Adrien Albert Medal, RSC, 2009; Gold Medal, Indian Soc. of Chemists and Biologists, 2011; Nexxus Lifetime Career Award, 2011. *Publications:* (with C. W. Suckling and K. E. Suckling) Chemistry through Models, 1978; Biological Chemistry, 1980; Enzyme Chemistry Impact and Applications, 1984, 3rd edn 1998; approx. 200 papers and patents on medicinal and biol chemistry. *Recreations:* horn playing, composing and conducting. *Address:* Department of Pure and Applied Chemistry, University of Strathclyde, 295 Cathedral Street, Glasgow G1 1XL. *T:* (0141) 548 2271, *Fax:* (0141) 548 5473. *E:* c.j.suckling@strath.ac.uk.

SUDBOROUGH, Air Vice-Marshal Nigel John, CB 2002; OBE 1989; FCIPD; JP; Director, Sudborough Investments Ltd, since 2003; non-executive Director, 2007–13 and Deputy Chairman, 2009–13, Leicester Partnership NHS Trust; *b* 23 March 1948; *s* of late Alexander Sudborough and of Beryl Sudborough; *m* 1971, Anne Brown; one *s* one *d*. *Educ:* Oundle Sch. Commnd as navigator, Royal Air Force, 1967; various flying tours, incl. Vulcan, Phantom and Tornado; PSO to Vice-Chief of Air Staff, MoD, 1983–85; i/c 29 (F) sqdn, 1985–87; RAF Mt Pleasant, Falkland Is, 1987–88; DS, RAF Staff Coll., 1988–90; HQ RAF Germany, 1990–93; i/c RAF Leuchars, 1993–95; rcds 1996; AO Plans, HQ Strike Comd, 1997–2000; DCS Ops, Strike Comd, 2000–02. Dir Gen., Winston Churchill Meml Trust, 2002–07. FCIPD 2000; FRAeS 2001. Freeman, City of London, 1985. JP Leicester, 2004. *Recreations:* fly-fishing, philately. *Address:* Knoll House, 5 London Road, Uppingham, Rutland LE15 9TJ. *Club:* Royal Air Force.

SUDBURY, Archdeacon of; *see* Jenkins, Ven. D. H.

SUDBURY, Dr Wendy Elizabeth, (Mrs A. J. Bates); Director: Cambridge Management Group, since 1994; HF Holidays Ltd, since 2012; *b* 14 June 1946; *d* of Clifford Frank Edwards and Betty Edwards (*née* Foster); one *d*; *m* 1st, 1973, R. M. Sudbury (marr. diss. 1980); 2nd, 1993, Alexander John Bates; one step *s* two step *d*. *Educ:* Finchley Co. Grammar Sch.; Lucy Cavendish Coll., Cambridge (MA); Christ Church, Oxford; Cranfield Sch. of Mgt (PhD 1992). Chief Exec., Mus. Documentation Assoc., 1989–97; Dir, Records Centre, C of E, 2001–03. Expert Advr, EC, 1996–. Mem., RCHM, 1997–99. Mem. Adv. Bd, Judge Inst. of Mgt Studies, Cambridge Univ., 1992–94. FRSA 2002. *Publications:* (with A. Fahy) Information: the Hidden Resource, Museums & the Internet, 1995; contrib. to learned jls. *Recreations:* humanities, travel, gardening, hiking, family life.

SUDELEY, 7th Baron *cr* 1838; **Merlin Charles Sainthill Hanbury-Tracy,** FSA; *b* 17 June 1939; *oc* of late Captain Michael David Charles Hanbury-Tracy, Scots Guards, and Colline Ammabel (*d* 1985), *d* of late Lt-Col C. G. H. St Hill and *widow* of Lt-Col Frank King, DSO, OBE; *S* cousin, 1941; *m* 1st, 1980, Hon. Mrs Elizabeth Villiers (marr. diss. 1988; she *d* 2014), *d* of late Viscount Bury (*s* of 9th Earl of Albemarle); 2nd, 1999, Mrs Margarita Kellett (marr. diss. 2006); 3rd, 2010, Dr Tatiana Dudina. *Educ:* Eton; Worcester Coll., Oxford; in the ranks of the Scots Guards. Former Chairman: Monday Club; Constitutional Monarchy Assoc.; Vice-Chancellor, Monarchist League. Pres., Traditional Britain; Vice-Pres., Soc. of Genealogists. Patron, Assoc. of Bankrupts; Lay Patron, Prayer Book Soc. *Publications:* Guide to Hailes Church, 1981, 3rd edn 2013; (jtly) The Sudeleys—Lords of Toddington, 1987; (contrib.) The House of Lords: a thousand years of British tradition, 1994; contribs to Quarterly Review, Contemporary Review, Family History, Trans of Bristol and Gloucestershire Archaeol. Soc., Montgomeryshire Collections, Bull. of Manorial Soc., Die Waage (Zeitschrift der Chemie Grünenthal), Monday Club Jl, London Miscellany. *Recreations:* ancestor worship; cultivating his sensibility. *Heir: kinsman* Nicholas Edward John Hanbury-Tracy, *b* 13 Jan. 1959. *Address:* 25 Melcombe Court, Dorset Square, NW1 6EP. *Club:* Brooks's.

SUDJIC, Deyan, OBE 2000; Director, Design Museum, since 2006; *b* 6 Sept. 1952; *s* of Milivoj Jovo Sudjic and Miroslava Pavlovic; *m* 2002, Sarah Isabel Miller; one *d*. *Educ:* Latymer Upper Sch.; Edinburgh Univ. (BSc Soc. Sci.; DipArch). Founding Ed., Blueprint mag., 1983–94; Architecture Critic: Guardian, 1991–97; Observer, 2000–06; Ed., Domus mag., 2000–04; Dean, Faculty of Art and Design, Kingston Univ., 2005–06; Director: Glasgow 1999 UK City of Architecture and Design, 1996–2000; Venice Architecture Biennale, 2002. Visiting Professor: Acad. for Applied Arts, Vienna, 1993–98; RCA, 2002–. Exhibition Curator: *exhibitions:* Royal Acad., 1986; ICA, 1988; Louisiana Mus., Copenhagen, 1996; McLennan Galls, Glasgow, 1999; BM, 2001. Fellow, Glasgow Sch. of Art, 1999. Hon. FRIAS 2000; Hon. FRIBA 2003. Bicentennial Medal, RSA, 2005. *Publications:* Cult Objects, 1983; Foster, Rogers, Stirling: new British architecture, 1986; Rei Kawskubo and Comme des Garçons, 1991; The Hundred Mile City, 1992; The Architecture Pack, 1996; Ron Arad, 1999; John Pawson: Works, 2000; The Edifice Complex, 2005; The Language of Things, 2009; (ed) Design in Britain: big ideas (small island), 2010; Norman Foster: a life in architecture, 2010; B is for Bauhaus: an A–Z of the modern world, 2014. *Recreation:* looking at buildings. *Address:* Design Museum, Shad Thames, SE1 2YD.

SUE-LING, Henry Michael, MD; FRCS, FRCSGlas; Consultant Gastrointestinal Surgeon and Senior Clinical Lecturer, Leeds General Infirmary, later at St James' University Hospital, since 1995; *b* 3 Feb. 1956; *s* of James and Sheila Sue-Ling; *m* 1979, Susan Marie Lewis; two *s* one *d*. *Educ:* Univ. of Leeds (MB ChB 1980; MD 1986). FRCSGlas 1986; FRCS 1988. Registrar, University Hosp. Wales, Cardiff, 1985–88; Leeds General Infirmary: Lectr in Surgery and Hon. Sen. Registrar, 1988–92; Sen. Lectr in Surgery and Hon. Consultant Surgeon, 1992–95; Lead Clinician in upper gastrointestinal cancer services. Chm., Yorks Cancer Network, 2000–. Silver Scalpel Award for UK Surgical Trainer of the Year, Smith & Nephew Foundn, 2001. *Publications:* contribs to learned jls incl. Lancet, BMJ, Gut and Jl Nat. Cancer Inst. *Recreations:* walking, swimming, tennis, travel. *Address:* St James' University Hospital, Beckett Street, Leeds LS9 7TF. *T:* (0113) 206 8505. *E:* henry.sueling@leedsth.nhs.uk.

SUENSON-TAYLOR, family name of **Baron Grantchester**.

SUFFIELD, 12th Baron *cr* 1786; **Charles Anthony Assheton Harbord-Hamond;** Bt 1745; *b* BMH Hostert, 3 Dec. 1953; *s* of 11th Baron Suffield, MC and Elizabeth Eve (*née* Edgedale); *S* father, 2011; *m* 1999, Emma Louise Royds, *er d* of Sir Lawrence Hugh Williams, Bt, *qv*; two *d*. *Educ:* Eton Coll. Captain, Coldstream Guards, 1972–79; a Temp. Equerry to the Queen, 1977–79. Dir of various Lloyd's of London cos, 1979–. *Recreations:* music, cooking. *Heir: b* Hon. John Edward Richard Harbord-Hamond [*b* 10 July 1956; *m* 1983, Katy Seymour; three *s* one *d*]. *Address:* Dairy Farm, Gunton Park, Norfolk NR11 7HL. *Clubs:* Pratt's; Norfolk (Norwich).

SUFFOLK AND BERKSHIRE, 21st Earl of, *cr* 1603; **Michael John James George Robert Howard;** Viscount Andover and Baron Howard, 1622; Earl of Berkshire, 1626; *b* 27 March 1935; *s* of 20th Earl of Suffolk and Berkshire, GC (killed by enemy action, 1941) and Mimi (*d* 1966), *yr d* of late A. G. Forde Pigott; *S* father, 1941; *m* 1st, 1960, Mme Simone Paulmier (marr. diss. 1967), *d* of late Georges Litman, Paris; (one *d* decd); 2nd, 1973, Anita (marr. diss. 1980), *d* of R. R. Fuglesang, Haywards Heath, Sussex; one *s* one *d*; 3rd, 1983, Linda Viscountess Bridport; two *d*. Owns 5,000 acres. *Heir: s* Viscount Andover, *qv*. *Address:* Charlton Park, Malmesbury, Wilts SN16 9DG.

SUFFOLK, Archdeacon of; *see* Morgan, Ven. I. D. J.

SUFFOLK, John; Global Head of Cybersecurity, Huawei Technologies Co. Ltd, since 2011; *b* 25 Feb. 1958; *s* of Thomas and Elspeth Suffolk; *m* 1989, Julie Davies. *Educ:* Wolverhampton Business Sch. (MBA; DMS). Various tech. roles, Freight Computer Services, 1975–79; Sen. Programmer, TRW Valves, 1979–80; Midshires Building Society: Sen. Designer, 1980–81; Chief Programmer/Programming Manager, 1981–85; Systems Develt Manager, 1985–86; Technical Services Manager, 1986–87; Birmingham Midshires: Planning and Develt Manager, 1987–89; Asst Gen. Manager, Business Systems, 1989–91; Inf. Services Dir, 1991–95; Hd, Customer Services, 1995–98; Britannia Building Society: Dir of Ops, 1998–2001; Ops Dir, 2001–02; Man. Dir, 2002–03; Dir Gen., Criminal Justice IT, Home Office, 2004–06; Govt Chief Information Officer and Sen. Information Risk Officer (formerly Govt Chief Information Officer and Head of e-Govt Unit, then Dir Gen., Transformational Govt), Cabinet Office, 2006–11. Chm., MutualPlus, 2001. Non-exec. Dir, PITO, 2004–. *Recreations:* farming, raising money for charity through challenges. *Address:* Back Forest Farm, Swythamley, Rushton Spencer, Macclesfield, Cheshire SK11 0RF. *T:* (01260) 227643.

SUGAR, family name of **Baron Sugar**.

SUGAR, Baron *cr* 2009 (Life Peer), of Clapton in the London Borough of Hackney; **Alan Michael Sugar,** Kt 2000; Executive Chairman: Amstrad (formerly Betacom) Plc, 1997–2008; Viglen, 1997–2014; Amshold Group; *b* 24 March 1947; *s* of Nathan and Fay Sugar; *m* 1968, Ann Simons; two *s* one *d*. *Educ:* Brooke House School, London. Founder Chm., Amstrad, 1968–97; co. divided into Betacom and Viglen, 1997. Chm., 1991–2001, Chief Exec., 1998–2000, Tottenham Hotspur plc. Non-exec. Chm., YouView Ltd, 2011–13. Presenter: The Apprentice (11 series), BBC TV, 2005–; Junior Apprentice, BBC TV, 2010; Young Apprentice, BBC TV, 2011. Govt Enterprise Champion, 2009–. Hon. DSc City, 1988. *Publications:* The Apprentice: how to get hired not fired, 2005; What You See is What You Get: my autobiography, 2010; The Way I See It: rants, revelations and rules for life, 2011. *Recreations:* tennis, flying (Private Pilot).

SUGAR, Vivienne, FCIH; local government consultant; Member, Board, Consumer Futures, since 2013 (Chair, Consumer Focus Wales (formerly Welsh Consumer Council), 2003–13); *b* Gorseinon, 23 Feb. 1947; *d* of Jack Hopkins and Phyllis Hopkins (*née* Suter); *m* 1972, Adrian Sugar. *Educ:* Mynydd Cynnfig Comprehensive Sch.; Leeds Univ. (BA). Area Improvement Officer, 1979–88, Dir of Housing, 1988–90, Newport BC; Dir of Housing, Cardiff CC, 1990–95; Chief Exec., City and County of Swansea, 1995–2002. Wales Advr to Joseph Rowntree Foundn, 2005–09. Pro Chancellor, Swansea Univ. (formerly Vice Pres., Univ. of Wales, Swansea), 2005–12. *Publications:* various articles in Municipal Jl, Local Govt Chronicle and Inside Housing. *Recreations:* politics and current affairs, walking, birdwatching, cooking. *Address:* Consumer Futures, Room 3.90, 3rd Floor, Companies House, Crown Way, Cardiff CF14 3UZ.

SUGDEN, Prof. David Edward, DPhil; FRSE; Professor of Geography, since 1987, and Head, School of GeoSciences, 2003–06, University of Edinburgh; *b* 5 March 1941; *s* of late John Cyril Gouldie Sugden and of Patricia Sugden (*née* Backhouse); *m* 1966, Britta Valborg, *d* of Harald Stridsberg, Sweden; two *s* one *d*. *Educ:* Warwick Sch.; Jesus Coll., Oxford (BA; DPhil 1965). Scientific officer, British Antarctic Survey, 1965–66; Lectr, then Reader, Univ. of Aberdeen, 1966–87. Vis. Prof., Arctic and Alpine Inst., Boulder, Colo, 1975–76. Pres., IBG, 1995. Member: RSGS; RGS; FRSE 1990. Hon. Dr Stockholm, 1998; Hon. LLB Dundee, 1999. Polar Medal, 2003; Seligman Crystal, Internat. Geological Soc., 2012. *Publications:* Glaciers and Landscape, 1976 (with B. S. John); Arctic and Antarctic, 1982; (jtly) Geomorphology, 1986. *Recreations:* hill-walking, gardening, ski-ing. *Address:* Geography, School of GeoSciences, University of Edinburgh, Drummond Street, Edinburgh EH8 9XP. *E:* david.sugden@ed.ac.uk.

SUGDEN, Prof. Robert, DLitt; FBA 1996; Professor of Economics, University of East Anglia, since 1985; *b* 26 Aug. 1949; *s* of late Frank Gerald Sugden and Kathleen Sugden (*née* Buckley); *m* 1982, Christine Margaret Upton; one *s* one *d*. *Educ:* Eston GS, Cleveland; Univ. of York (BA; DLitt 1988); UC, Cardiff (MSc). Lectr in Econs, Univ. of York, 1971–78; Reader in Econs, Univ. of Newcastle upon Tyne, 1978–85. *Publications:* (with A. Williams) The Principles of Practical Cost-Benefit Analysis, 1978; The Political Economy of Public Choice, 1981; The Economics of Rights, Co-operation and Welfare, 1986; (jtly) The Theory of Choice: a critical guide, 1992; (ed with D. Gauthier) Rationality, Justice and the Social Contract, 1993; (ed with Benedetto Gui) Economics and Social Interaction, 2005; (jtly) Experimental Economics: rethinking the rules, 2009. *Recreations:* family, walking, gardening. *Address:* School of Economics, University of East Anglia, Norwich NR4 7TJ. *T:* (01603) 593423.

SUGHRUE, Dr Cynthia Marie, (Cindy), OBE 2013; freelance theatre producer and consultant; Chief Executive and Executive Producer, Scottish Ballet, 2004–15; *b* Boston, Mass, 30 March 1963; *d* of Robert Emmett Sughrue and Catharine Isabel Sughrue (*née* Guthrie). *Educ:* Boston Univ. (BA *summa cum laude*); Univ. of Sheffield (PhD 1992). Marshall Schol., 1985–88; Dir, Collective Gall., 1990–94; Gen. Manager, Dance Base, 1994–97; Sen. Officer, Performing Arts, 1997–2001, Hd of Dance, 2001–04, Scottish Arts Council. Member, Board of Directors: Benchtours Prodns, 1993–96 (Chm., 1995–96); Dance Base, 2006–08; New Moves Internat., 2006–11. Trustee, Dame Margot Fonteyn Scholarship Fund, 2007–; Chm., Culture Sparks, 2010–14; Mem., Bd of Dirs, Culture Republic, 2013–. Mem., Bd of Govs, Royal Conservatoire of Scotland, 2012–. FRSA 2008. *Recreations:* attending dance and theatre performances, live music events and exhibitions, hill walking, cooking.

SUIRDALE, Viscount; John Michael James Hely Hutchinson; management consultant, since 2007; *b* 7 Aug. 1952; *s* and *heir* of 8th Earl of Donoughmore, *qv*; *m* 1st, 1976, Marie-Claire Carola Etienne van den Driessche (marr. diss. 2006); one *s* two *d*; 2nd, 2008, Nutjarin Photiruk. *Educ:* Harrow. Dep. Man. Dir, Bagajavion, Paris, 1978–89; Purchasing Manager, Alfred Dunhill Ltd, 1989–92; Royalties Dir, Burberry Ltd, 1993–2003; Rep. Dir, Burberry Japan KK, Tokyo, 2003–06; Gp Supply Chain Dir, Lambert Howarth Gp plc, 2007; Man. Dir, DAKS Simpson Gp plc, 2009; Gp CEO, Integrix Sports Gp Ltd, 2011. *Recreations:* golf, ski-ing, fishing, keeping fit, etc. *Heir: s* Hon. Richard Gregory Hely Hutchinson, *b* 3 July 1980. *Address:* 40 Guildford Road, Fleet, Hants GU51 3EY.
See also Hon. T. M. Hely Hutchinson.

SULIVAN, Maj.-Gen. Timothy John, CB 2001; CBE 1991; DL; Vice-President, Customer Relations, General Dynamics (formerly CDC Systems) UK Ltd, 2001–13; *b* 19 Feb. 1946; *s* of late Col John Anthony Sulivan, OBE and Elizabeth Joyce Sulivan (*née* Stevens); *m* 1977, Jane Annette Ellwood; one *s* one *d*. *Educ:* Wellington Coll.; RMCS (BSc); Higher Command and Staff course. Commnd RA, 1966; transf. Blues and Royals, 1980; CO, Blues and Royals, 1987–89; attached US Special Plans Team, C-in-C US CENTCOM, 1990–91; Comd 7 Armd Bde, 1991–93; PSO to CDS, 1993–94; Dir-Gen., Devel t and Doctrine, MoD, 1994–96 (deployed as Jt Force Comd Op. Driver, Kuwait/Saudi Arabia, 1994); COS, HQ ARRC, 1996–98; GOC Fourth Div., 1998–2001; Chief Operating Officer, RICS, 2002–05. Dir, Screen plc, 2002–06; Dir, Customer Relations, Land Securities Trillium, 2006–07. Mem., Ind. Assessment Panel, Army Trng Centre, Pirbright, 2013– (Chm., 2015–). Chm., Surrey Br., ABF. DL Surrey, 2015. Bronze Star, USA, 1991. *Recreations:* shooting, ski-ing, squash, cabinet making. *Club:* Army and Navy.

SULKIN, David Charles Chester, OBE 2014; Executive Director, Help Musicians UK, since 2009; *b* Worthing, 1 Jan. 1949; *s* of Emmanuel Sulkin and Dorothy May Sulkin (*née* Chester); partner, 2010, Geoffrey Milton. *Educ:* St Andrew's High Sch., Worthing; Guildhall Sch. of Music and Drama; Rose Bruford Coll., Sidcup. Partner, Hoxton Th. Trust, 1975–78; Lectr, Rose Bruford Coll., 1978–80; Dir, Royal Court Young People's Th., 1980–85; Co-Dir, Baylis Prog., ENO, 1985–95; Associate Dir, Janáčkovy Hukvaldy, Czech Republic, 1993–97; Lectr, RADA, 1997–2004; Dir of Policy and Progs, Nat. Foundn for Youth Music, 1999–2008. Gov., Cripplegate Foundn, 2004–14; Chair of Govs, Clerkenwell Parochial Sch., 2007–. Chair of Trustees, New London Children's Choir, 2012–. Liveryman, Musicians' Co. *Publications:* (with A. Roth) Gretel and Hansel, 1987; (with K. Duncan) New Old - Thirty Thousand Years of Experience, 1999; Rough Stuff, 2000; (ed) The New River Head, 2012. *Recreations:* motorcycles and motorcyclists, early recording and gramophones, Czech and Russian language and culture, 20th century architecture. *Address:* Help Musicians UK, 7–11 Britannia Street, WC1X 9JS. *T:* (020) 7239 9112. *E:* david.sulkin@helpmusicians.org.uk.

SULLIVAN, Edmund Wendell, FRCVS; Chief Veterinary Officer, Department of Agriculture for Northern Ireland, 1983–90; *b* 21 March 1925; *s* of Thomas Llewellyn Sullivan and Letitia Sullivan; *m* 1957, Elinor Wilson Melville; two *s* one *d*. *Educ:* Portadown College; Queen's University, Belfast; Royal (Dick) Veterinary College. MRCVS 1947, FRCVS 1991. General Veterinary Practice, Appleby, Westmoreland, 1947; joined staff of State Veterinary Service, Dept of Agriculture for N Ireland, 1948; Headquarters staff, 1966–90. *Recreations:* hill walking, wood craft, following rugby and cricket. *Address:* Kinfauns, 26 Dillon's Avenue, Newtownabbey, Co. Antrim BT37 0SX. *T:* (028) 9086 2323.

SULLIVAN, Francis John; Adviser on the Environment, since 2004, and Deputy Head, Global Corporate Sustainability and Head of Europe, since 2012, HSBC Holdings plc; *b* London, 6 March 1963; *s* of Vernon and Shirley Sullivan; *m* 1994, Jackie Nickson; two *d*. *Educ:* Marlborough Coll.; St John's Coll., Oxford (MA Hons Agriculture and Forest Scis; MSc forestry and its reln to land use 1986). Forest officer, WWF-UK, 1987–95; Dir, Forests for Life Campaign, WWF-Internat., 1995–99; Dir of Progs, WWF-UK, 1999–2004. Mem., Adv. Bd, Envmt Change Inst., Univ. of Oxford, 2006–. Member: Internat. Bd, Forest Stewardship Council, 1996–98; Ind. Adv. Gp on Sustainability, Inter-American Develt Bank, 2007–; Corporate Responsibility Expert Adv. Panel, Vodafone, 2007–; Corporate Responsibility Adv. Gp, Centrica, 2011–. Trustee Dir, HSBC Pension Trust (UK), 2009–. Trustee: Baynards Zambia Trust, 2012–; Whitley Fund for Nature, 2012– (Judge, Whitley Awards for Nature Conservation, 2000–12). Gov., St Hilary's Sch., Godalming, 2012–. Freeman, City of London, 2001; Liveryman, Co. of Stationers and Newspaper Makers, 2001. *Recreations:* allotment, sailing, family, running half-marathons. *Address:* HSBC Holdings plc, 8 Canada Square, E14 5HQ. *T:* (020) 7992 3771. *E:* francissullivan@hsbc.com.

SULLIVAN, Jane Teresa; Her Honour Judge Jane Sullivan; a Circuit Judge, since 2009; *b* Bristol, 21 April 1956; *d* of late Timothy Gerard Sullivan and of Margaret Sullivan; *m* 1990, Duncan Macleod. *Educ:* La Retraite High Sch.; University Coll. London (LLB Hons 1977); Univ. of London ext. (BA Hons Eng. 1981). Admitted solicitor, 1980; in practice as a solicitor, 1980–84; called to the Bar, Inner Temple, 1984; in practice as a barrister, 1984–2009; Recorder, 1998–2009. Legal Chm. of Appeals, Postgrad. Med. Educn and Trng Bd, 2005–09; Legal Advr, Royal Pharmaceutical Soc., 2006–09. *Recreations:* travel, arts, reading, swimming. *Address:* Blackfriars Crown Court, 1–15 Pocock Street, SE1 0BJ. *T:* (020) 7922 5800.

SULLIVAN, Rt Hon. Sir Jeremy (Mirth), Kt 1997; PC 2009; a Lord Justice of Appeal, 2009–15; Senior President of Tribunals, 2012–15; *b* 17 Sept. 1945; *s* of late Arthur Brian and Pamela Jean Sullivan; *m* 1st, 1970, Ursula Klara Marie Hildenbrock (marr. diss. 1993); two *s*; 2nd, 1993, Dr Sandra Jean Farmer; two step *s*. *Educ:* Framlingham Coll.; King's Coll., London. LLB 1967, LLM 1968; LAMTPI 1970, LMRTPI 1976. 2nd Lieut, Suffolk & Cambs Regt (TA), 1963–65. Called to the Bar, Inner Temple, 1968, Bencher, 1993; Lectr in Law, City of London Polytechnic, 1968–71; in practice, Planning and Local Govt Bar, Parly Bar, 1971–97; QC 1982; a Recorder, 1989–97; a Dep. High Court Judge, 1993–97; Attorney Gen. to the Prince of Wales, 1994–97; a Judge of the High Court, QBD, 1997–2009. Hon. Standing Counsel to CPRE, 1994–97. Chm., Tribunals Cttee, Judicial Studies Bd, 1999–2007; Dep. Chm., Parly Boundary Commn for England, 2004–09. Mem. Council, RTPI, 1984–87. Gov., Highgate Sch., 1991–2003. *Recreation:* the Wotton Light Railway. *Address:* 50A Montpellier Spa Road, Cheltenham, Glos GL50 1UL. *Club:* Athenæum.

SULLIVAN, Linda Elizabeth, (Mrs J. W. Blake-James); QC 1994; **Her Honour Judge Linda Sullivan;** a Circuit Judge, since 2009; *b* 1 Jan. 1948; *d* of Donal Sullivan and Esmé Beryl Sullivan (*née* McKenzie); *m* 1972, Dr Justin Wynne Blake-James (marr. diss. 1994); one *s* twin *d*. *Educ:* St Leonards-Mayfield Sch.; Univ. of Kent (BA Hons Phil. and English 1969); St Hilda's Coll., Oxford (Cert Ed 1970). Called to the Bar, Middle Temple, 1973, Bencher, 1993; Mem., Western Circuit; Recorder, 1990–2009. Acting Deemster, Isle of Man, 1994. Legal Mem., Mental Health Review Tribunal, 2002–09. *Address:* Portsmouth Combined Court, Winston Churchill Avenue, Portsmouth PO1 2EB.

SULLIVAN, Michael Frederick, MBE 1981; HM Diplomatic Service, retired; Consul-General, Hamburg, 1994–99; *b* 22 June 1940; *s* of late Frederick Franklin Sullivan and Leonora Mary Sullivan; *m* 1967, Jennifer Enid Saunders. *Educ:* King's Sch., Canterbury; Jesus Coll., Oxford (BA). CRO 1962–66; Moscow, 1967; Ulan Bator, Mongolia, 1967–69; Sydney, 1970–74; FCO, 1975–77; First Sec., W Indian and Atlantic Dept, FCO, 1977–79; Consul (Industrial Develt), British Trade Develt Office, NY, 1979–81; Cultural Attaché, Moscow, 1981–85; Assistant Head: Personnel Services Dept, FCO, 1985–86; Energy, Sci. and Space Dept, FCO, 1986–88; Counsellor (Cultural Affairs), Moscow, 1988–89; Counsellor, Export Promotion Policy Unit, DTI, 1989–90; Hd of Nationality, Treaty and Claims Dept, FCO, 1990–93. Res. analyst, FCO, 2000 and 2003. Mem., Panel of Inquiry Secs, Competition Commn, 2004–14. Mem., FCO Assoc., 2007–. *Recreations:* piano playing, music and the arts, tennis, jogging, swimming. *Club:* Übersee.

SULLIVAN, Ven. Nicola Ann, (Mrs T. J. Westwood); Archdeacon of Wells and Canon Residentiary, Wells Cathedral, since 2007; *b* 15 Aug. 1958; *d* of late Peter John Sullivan and Margaret Irene Sullivan (*née* Hancock); *m* 2014, Terence John Westwood. *Educ:* Convent of Jesus and Mary, Ipswich; Mills GS, Framlingham, Suffolk; St Bartholomew's Hosp. (SRN 1981); Bristol Maternity Hosp. (RM 1984); Wycliffe Hall, Oxford (BTh 1995). Various NHS nursing and midwifery posts, 1981–92; Tear Fund UK, in Ethiopia, 1984, Swaziland, 1988. Ordained deacon, 1995, priest, 1996; Asst Curate, St Anne's, Earlham, Norwich, 1995–99; Associate Vicar, Bath Abbey with St James, 1999–2002; Chaplain, Royal Nat. Hosp. for Rheumatic Diseases NHS Trust, 1999–2002; Bishop's Chaplain and Pastoral Asst to Bishop of Bath and Wells, 2002–07; Sub-Dean and Preb., Wells Cathedral, 2003–07; Participating Observer, House of Bishops, 2013–. *Recreations:* reading, theatre (professional and amateur), current affairs, music, walking, relaxing in Suffolk, Bob Dylan. *Address:* 6 The Liberty, Wells, Som BA5 2SU. *T:* (01749) 685147. *E:* adwells@bathwells.anglican.org.

SULLIVAN, Richard Arthur, (9th Bt *cr* 1804, but does not use the title); retired geotechnical engineer; *b* 9 Aug. 1931; *s* of Sir Richard Benjamin Magniac Sullivan, 8th Bt, and Muriel Mary Paget (*d* 1988), *d* of late Francis Charles Trayler Pineo; *S* father, 1977; *m* 1962, Elenor Mary, *e d* of late K. M. Thorpe; one *s* three *d*. *Educ:* Univ. of Cape Town (BSc); Massachusetts Inst. of Technology (SM). Chartered Engineer, UK; Professional Engineer, Ontario, Texas and Louisiana. FASCE 2013. *Publications:* papers and articles to international conferences and technical journals. *Recreation:* tennis. *Heir: s* Charles Merson Sullivan, MA, VetMB Cantab, MRCVS [*b* 15 Dec. 1962; *m* 1993, Helen Mary Alexander; one *s* one *d*]. *Address:* 1 Sea Watch Place, Florence, OR 97439–8967, USA.

SULONG, Datuk Zakaria, PSD 2007; JSM 2005; DIMP 2005; SSA 1998; High Commissioner of Malaysia in the United Kingdom, 2010–13; *b* Kuala Lumpur, 23 Dec. 1952; *s* of Sulong Bin Jawi and Suma Binti Mahatam; *m* 1978, Hazizah Zakaria; two *s* one *d*. *Educ:* Univ. of Malaya (BA Hons). Entered Malaysian Diplomatic Service, 1975; Consul Gen., Hong Kong, 1996–98; Under Sec., Multilateral Dept, 1998–2000; Ambassador to Bosnia and Herzegovina, 2000–04; Chief of Protocol, Min. of Foreign Affairs, 2004–07; Ambassador to Germany, 2007–10. *Recreations:* golf, badminton, reading, music, photography. *Address:* c/o Malaysian High Commission, 45 Belgrave Square, SW1X 8QT. *Clubs:* Travellers; Brocket Hall Golf; Morib Golf, Kelab Golf (Malaysia).

SULSTON, Sir John (Edward), Kt 2001; PhD; FRS 1986; Staff Scientist, MRC Laboratory of Molecular Biology, Cambridge, 1969–2003; Director, The Sanger Centre (for genome research), Hinxton, Cambridge, 1992–2000; Chair, Institute for Science, Ethics and Innovation, University of Manchester, 2007–13; *b* 27 March 1942; *s* of late Rev. Canon Arthur Edward Aubrey Sulston and Josephine Muriel Frearson (*née* Blocksidge); *m* 1966, Daphne Edith Bate; one *s* one *d*. *Educ:* Merchant Taylors' School; Pembroke College, Cambridge (BA, PhD; Hon. Fellow, 2000). Postdoctoral Fellow, Salk Inst., San Diego, 1966–69. Mem., Human Genetics Commn, 2001–09. Mem., EMBO, 1989; MAE 2001. Hon. Member: Biochemical Soc., 2002; RSC, 2003; Acad. of Med. Scis, 2003; Physiol Soc., 2003; Hon. FRSocMed 2015. Hon. Fellow, Cambridge Philosophical Soc., 2008. Freeman, Merchant Taylors' Co., 2004. Hon. ScD: TCD, 2000; Essex, 2002; Cambridge, London, Exeter, 2003; Newcastle, 2004; Hon. LLD Dundee, 2005; Hon. DSc: British Columbia, Liverpool, Manchester, 2009. W. Alden Spencer Award (jtly), Coll. of Physicians and Surgeons, Columbia Univ., 1986; (jtly) Gairdner Foundn Award, 1991, 2002; Darwin Medal, Royal Soc., 1996; (jtly) Rosenstiel Award, Brandeis Univ., 1998; Sir Frederick Gowland Hopkins Medal, Biochemical Soc., 2000; (jtly) George W. Beadle Medal, Genetics Soc. of Amer., 2000; Pfizer Prize for Innovative Sci., 2000; Edinburgh Medal, 2001; (jtly) Prince of Asturias Award, Prince of Asturias Foundn, 2001; Fothergillian Medal, Med. Soc. of London, 2002; (jtly) Dan David Prize, Tel Aviv Univ., 2002; (jtly) Nobel Prize for Physiology or Medicine, 2002; Dawson Prize in Genetics, Trinity Coll., Dublin, 2006. Officier de la légion d'honneur (France), 2004. *Publications:* (with Georgina Ferry) The Common Thread: a story of science, politics, ethics and the human genome, 2002; articles on organic chemistry, molecular and developmental biology in sci. jls. *Recreations:* gardening, walking. *Address:* 39 Mingle Lane, Stapleford, Cambridge CB22 5SY. *T:* (01223) 842248. *E:* jes@sanger.ac.uk.

SUMBERG, David Anthony Gerald; *b* 2 June 1941; *s* of Joshua and Lorna Sumberg; *m* 1972, Carolyn Ann Rae Franks; one *s* one *d*. *Educ:* Tettenhall Coll., Staffs; Coll. of Law, London. Qualified as a Solicitor, 1964. Mem. (C) Manchester City Council, 1982–84. Contested (C) Manchester, Wythenshawe, 1979. MP (C) Bury South, 1983–97; contested (C) same seat, 1997. PPS to: Solicitor-General, 1986–87; Attorney-General, 1987–90. Member: Home Affairs Select Cttee, 1991–92; Foreign Affairs Select Cttee, 1992–97. MEP (C) NW Region, 1999–2009. European Parliament: Member: Cttee on Internat. Trade, 2008–09; Delegn to USA. Mem., Adv. Council on Public Records, 1993–97. *Recreations:* travel, reading, enjoying grandparenthood. *E:* david@sumberg.fsnet.co.uk.

SUMMERFIELD, Prof. (Arthur) Quentin, PhD; Anniversary Professor of Psychology, since 2004, and Head, Department of Psychology, since 2011, University of York; *b* 18 Sept. 1949; *s* of Arthur Summerfield and Aline Summerfield (*née* Whalley); *m* 1989, Diana Lyn Field; two *d*. *Educ:* Tetherdown Primary Sch., Muswell Hill; University Coll. Sch., Hampstead (ILEA Schol.); Corpus Christi Coll., Cambridge (BA 1971, MA Natural Scis); Queen's Univ., Belfast (PhD Psychol. 1975). NATO Postdoctoral Res. Fellow, Haskins Labs, Yale Univ., 1975–77; Speech and Hearing Scientist, 1977–2004, Dep. Dir, 1993–2004, MRC Inst. of Hearing Res.; Special Prof. of Speech and Hearing, Univ. of Nottingham, 1991–2004. Chair: Med. Res. Adv. Panel, RNID, 2003–05; NHS Rev. of cochlear implantation in Scotland, 2005–06. Chief Res. Advr, Deafness Res. UK, 2007–11. Fellow, Acoustical Soc. of America, 1988. Trustee, Action on Hearing Loss, 2013–. *Publications:* (with Dr D. H. Marshall) Cochlear Implantation in the UK 1990–1994, 1995. *Recreation:* repairing and riding bicycles. *Address:* Department of Psychology, University of York, Heslington, York YO10 5DD. *T:* (01904) 432913, 433190, *Fax:* (01904) 433181. *E:* aqs1@york.ac.uk. *Club:* British Cycling.

SUMMERFIELD, Lesley; *see* Regan, L.

SUMMERFIELD, Quentin; *see* Summerfield, A. Q.

SUMMERFIELD, Prof. Rodney John, DSc; JP; Professor of Crop Production, 1995–2001, now Emeritus, and Dean, Faculty of Agriculture and Food, 1998–2001, University of Reading; *b* 15 Nov. 1946; *s* of Ronald John Summerfield and Doris Emily Summerfield (*née* Ellis); *m* 1969, Kathryn Dorothy Olive; one *s* one *d*. *Educ:* Hinckley GS; Univ. of Nottingham (BSc 1st cl. Hons Botany 1968; PhD Eco-Physiol. 1971); Univ. of Reading (DSc 1987); FIBiol 1982–2001. Univ. Demonstr, Univ. of Nottingham, 1969–71; (part-time) Lectr, Trent Poly., 1970–71; University of Reading: Res. Fellow, 1971–73, Lectr in Crop and Plant Physiology, 1973–83, Dept of Agriculture and Horticulture; Dep. Dir, 1979–94, Dir, 1994–99, Plant Envmt Lab.; Reader in Crop Physiology, 1983–90, Prof. of Crop Physiology, 1990–95, Dept of Agriculture; Hd, Dept of Agric., 1992–98. Pres., Eur. Assoc. for Res. in Grain Legumes, 1995–99. EurBiol 1995. JP: Devon and Cornwall, 2004; S and W Devon, 2012. Dr *hc* Debrecen Univ., Hungary, 1999. *Publications:* (ed jtly) Advances in Legume Science, 1980; (ed jtly) Grain Legume Crops, 1985; (ed) World Crops: cool season food legumes, 1988; articles in learned jls. *Recreations:* walking, angling.

SUMMERHAYES, Dr Colin Peter; Emeritus Associate, Scott Polar Research Institute, University of Cambridge, since 2010; *b* 7 March 1942; *s* of late Leonard Percy Summerhayes and Jessica Adelaide (*née* Crump); *m* 1st, 1966 (marr. diss. 1977); one *s* one *d*; 2nd, 1978 (marr. diss. 1979); 3rd, 1981, Diana Ridley (*née* Perry); one step *s* one step *d*. *Educ:* Slough Grammar Sch.; UCL (BSc 1963); Keble Coll., Oxford; Victoria Univ., Wellington, NZ (MSc 1967; DSc 1986); Imperial Coll., London (DIC; PhD 1970). CMarSci; CGeol; FIMarEST; FGS. Scientific Officer, DSIR, NZ Oceanographic Inst., 1964–67; Res. Asst, Geol. Dept, Imperial Coll., London, 1967–70; Sen. Scientific Officer, CSIR, Marine Geosci. Unit, Univ. of Cape Town, 1970–72; Asst Scientist, Geol. and Geophys Dept, Woods Hole Oceanographic Instn, 1972–76; Research Associate/Project Leader: Geochem. Br., Exxon Prodn Res. Centre, Houston, 1976–82; Global Paleoreconstruction Sect., Stratigraphy Br., BP Res. Centre, 1982–85; Manager and Sen. Res. Associate, Stratigraphy Br., BP Res. Centre, 1985–88; Dir, NERC Inst. of Oceanographic Scis Deacon Lab., 1988–95; Dep. Dir, and Hd of Seafloor Processes Div., Southampton Oceanography Centre, 1995–97; Dir, Global Ocean Observing System Project Office, Intergovernmental Oceanographic Commn, Unesco, 1997–2004; Exec. Dir, Scientific Cttee on Antarctic Res., 2004–10; Mem., UK Cttee, Scientific Cttee on Oceanic Res., 2012–15. Chm., Internat. Adv. Bd, Korea Polar Res. Inst., 2011–12. Vis. Prof., UCL, 1987–95. Member: Challenger Soc. for Marine Sci.; RSPB; WWF; Pres., Soc. for Underwater Technol., 2010–11; Vice Pres., Geological Soc., 2010–14. *Publications:* (ed with N. J. Shackleton) North Atlantic Palaeoceanography, 1986; (ed jtly) Upwelling Systems: evolution since the Early Miocene, 1992; (ed jtly) Sequence Stratigraphy and Facies Association, 1993; (ed jtly) Upwelling in the Oceans: Dahlem Conference Report, 1995; (with S. A. Thorpe) Oceanography: an illustrated guide, 1996; (ed jtly) Understanding the Oceans, 2001; (ed jtly) Oceans 2020: science, trends and the challenge of sustainability, 2002; (jtly) Antarctic Climate Change and the Environment, 2009; (ed jtly) Understanding Earth's Polar Challenges: International Polar Year 2007–2008, 2011; (with C. Luedecke) Third Reich in Antarctica, 2012; Earth's Climate Evolution, 2015; 230 papers and abstracts. *Recreations:* birdwatching, jogging, reading, lawn bowls, films and theatre. *Address:* Scott Polar Research Institute, Lensfield Road, Cambridge CB2 1ER.

SUMMERHAYES, Gerald Victor, CMG 1979; OBE 1969; *b* 28 Jan. 1928; *s* of Victor Samuel and Florence A. V. Summerhayes. Administrative Service, Nigeria, 1952–81; Permanent Secretary: Local Govt, North Western State, 1975–76, Sokoto State, 1976–77; Cabinet Office (Political and Trng), 1977–79; Dir of Trng, Cabinet Office, Sokoto, 1979–81. *Address:* Bridge Cottage, Bridge Street, Sidbury, Devon EX10 0RU.

SUMMERS, Alan Andrew; QC (Scot.) 2008; *b* Bridge of Allan, 27 Aug. 1964; *s* of Andrew and Helen Summers; *m* 1990, Rosemary Craig; one *s* four *d*. *Educ:* Dundee Univ. (LLB); Oxford Univ. (BCL); Edinburgh Univ. (DipLP). Admitted as Advocate, 1994; in practice as an Advocate, 1994–; Standing Jun. Counsel to Scottish Exec., 2000–07; Special Counsel to UK Govt, 2008–. Chm., Faculty Services Ltd, 2008–12. Treas., Faculty of Advocates, 2012–. *Recreation:* reading. *Address:* Craigelm, 19 Park Road, Dalkeith EH22 3DH. *T:* (0131) 226 5071. *E:* Alan.summers@advocates.org.uk.

SUMMERS, Andrew William Graham, CMG 2001; Chief Executive, Design Council, 1995–2003; Chairman, Design Partners, since 2004; *b* 19 June 1946; *s* of Basil Summers and Margaret (*née* Hunt); *m* 1971, Frances Halestrap; one *s* two *d*. *Educ:* Mill Hill Sch. (Exhibnr); Fitzwilliam Coll., Cambridge (MA Natural Scis and Econs); Harvard Business Sch. (Internat. SMP). Various mgt rôles, Ranks Hovis McDougall plc, 1968–75; J. A. Sharwood & Co.: Mkting Manager, 1975–78; Mkting Dir, 1978–80; Man. Dir, 1980–85; RHM Foods Ltd: Commercial Dir, 1986; Man. Dir, 1987–90; Chief Exec., Management Charter Initiative, 1991–94; non-executive Director: S. Daniels plc, 1991–2002; Ramboll UK (formerly Whitbybird Ltd), 2005–12. Chairman: Brandsmiths, 2003–06; Creative Connexions, 2007–09. Chm., Companies House, 2007–12. Adjunct Prof., Hong Kong Polytechnic Univ., 2004–. Policy Advr, DTI, later BERR, then BIS, 2003–10. Member: Food from Britain Export Council, 1982–86; DTI European Trade Cttee, 1986–2000 (Chm., 1998–2000); BOTB, 1998–99; British Trade Internat., 1999–2003; Creative Industries Export Promotion Adv. Gp, 1998–2002; Adv. Council, Design Mgt Inst. USA, 1998–2006; Small Business Service Strategy Bd, 2000–07; Bd, QAA, 2005–11; Bd, CRAC, 2008–10; Council, KCL, 2010– (Chm., Audit Cttee, 2011–); Bd, UKTI Olympic Task Force, 2010–12; Bd, Public Data Gp, 2011–12; Chairman: Internat. Adv. Bd, Hong Kong Design Centre, 2004–07; Cala Social Capital, 2011; Adv. Bd, Westminster Business Sch., 2010–; Design Effectiveness Awards, 2010–; Design Jury, Expo 2015 UK Pavilion; Dir, Partners in Quality, 2011–12. Trustee, RSA, 2004–10 (Chm., Migration Commn, 2004–06). Mem., VSO Adv. Bd, 2004–06. Gov., Conservatoire for Dance and Drama, 2005–13. Chairman: Friends of St Mary's, Barnes, 2000–; Barnes Music Fest., 2011–. Stockton Lectr, London Bus. Sch., 2000. Mem., Bd of Companions, Chartered Mgt Inst., 2007–13 (Chm., 2010–13). CCMI (CIMgt 1997). FRSA 1991 (Dep. Pres., 2003–10); Sen. Fellow, Design Mgt Inst., 2003. Hon. DLitt Westminster, 2003. *Publications:* (contrib.) Future Present, 2000; contribs on design to Design Mgt Jl and Sunday Times. *Recreations:* fives (Pres., OM Eton Fives Club, 2004–), theatre, cooking, music, cycling. *Address:* 114 Station Road, SW13 0NB. *E:* andrew@andrewsummers.co.uk.

SUMMERS, Janet Margaret, (Mrs L. J. Summers); *see* Bately, J. M.

SUMMERS, Jonathan; baritone; *b* 2 Oct. 1946; *s* of Andrew James Summers and Joyce Isabel Smith; *m* 1969, Lesley Murphy; three *c*. *Educ:* Macleod High Sch., Melbourne; Prahran Tech. Coll., Melbourne. Professional début, Rigoletto (title rôle), Kent Opera, 1975; performances include: Royal Opera, Covent Garden: début, Der Freischütz, 1977; Samson et Dalila, Don Pasquale, Werther, 1983; Andrea Chénier, A Midsummer Night's Dream, Der Rosenkavalier, 1984; Die Zauberflöte, Le Nozze di Figaro, 1985; Simon Boccanegra, 1986; Falstaff, 1987; Madama Butterfly, 1988; La Bohème, 1990; Fedora, 1994; Nabucco, 1996; The Tempest, 2007; Peter Grimes, 2011; English National Opera: début, I Pagliacci, 1976; Rigoletto, 1982; Don Carlos, 1985; La Bohème, 1986; Simon Boccanegra, 1987; Eugene Onegin, 1989; Macbeth, 1990; Peter Grimes, 1991; The Force of Destiny, 1992; The Pearl Fishers, 1994; Tristan and Isolde, 1996; Figaro's Wedding, 1997; Parsifal, 1999; Billy Budd, 2012; Opera Australia, Sydney: début, La Traviata, 1981; Il Trovatore, 1983; Otello, 1991; Un Ballo in Maschera, 1993; Il Tabarro, 1995; Nabucco, Falstaff, 1996; Wozzeck, 1999; Simon Boccanegra, 2000; Peter Grimes, 2001; Tosca, 2002; Otello, 2003; Der fliegende Holländer, 2004; Rigoletto, 2006; La Traviata, 2012; Metropolitan Opera, NY: début, La Bohème, 1988; has also appeared at Glyndebourne, with Opera North, Welsh National Opera, in Toulouse, Chicago, Lausanne, Paris, Hamburg, Munich etc, and as concert soloist. Numerous recordings. *Address:* c/o Patricia Greenan, 7 White Horse Close, 27 Canongate, Edinburgh EH8 8BU. *T:* (0131) 557 5872.

SUMMERS, Hon. Lawrence H.; Charles W. Eliot University Professor, Harvard University, 2006–09 and since 2010; *b* 30 Nov. 1954; *s* of Robert and Anita Summers; *m* (marr. diss.); one *s* twin *d*; *m* 2005, Prof. Elisa New, PhD. *Educ:* MIT (BS 1975); Harvard Univ. (PhD 1982). Economics Prof., MIT, 1979–82; Domestic Policy Economist, President's Council of Economic Advrs, 1982–83; Prof. of Economics, 1983–93, Nathaniel Ropes Prof., 1987, Harvard Univ.; Vice-Pres., Develt Economics and Chief Economist, World Bank, 1991–93; Under Sec. for Internat. Affairs, 1993–95, Dep. Sec., 1995–99, Sec., 1999–2001, US Treasury; Arthur Okun Dist. Fellow, Brookings Instn, 2001; Pres., Harvard Univ., 2001–06; Dir, Nat. Economic Council and Asst to Pres. of USA for Economic Policy, 2008–10. Alan Waterman Award, 1987; John Bates Clark Medal, 1993. *Publications:* Understanding Unemployment, 1990; (jtly) Reform in Eastern Europe, 1991. *Recreations:* tennis, ski-ing. *Address:* Harvard University, Massachusetts Hall, Cambridge, MA 02138, USA.

SUMMERS, Mark John; QC 2014; *b* Colchester, 17 Dec. 1973; *s* of John and Elspeth Summers; partner, Lindsay Lane; one *s* one *d*. *Educ:* Chantry Sixth Form Coll.; Exeter Univ. (LLB Hons). Called to the Bar, Inner Temple, 1996; in practice as barrister, 1996–. *Publications:* Abuse of Process in Criminal Proceedings, 2000, 4th edn 2014; Human Rights and Criminal Justice, 2001, 3rd edn 2012; The Law of Extradition and Mutual Legal Assistance, 2003, 3rd edn 2013. *Recreations:* travel, American football. *Address:* Matrix Chambers, Griffin Building, Gray's Inn, WC1R 5LN. *T:* (020) 7404 3447, *Fax:* (020) 7404 3448. *E:* marksummers@matrixlaw.co.uk.

SUMMERS, Nicholas; Under Secretary, Department for Education and Employment (formerly of Education and Science, then for Education), 1981–96; *b* 11 July 1939; *s* of Henry Forbes Summers, CB; *m* 1965, Marian Elizabeth Ottley; four *s*. *Educ:* Tonbridge Sch.; Corpus Christi Coll., Oxford. Min. of Educn, 1961–64; DES, 1964–74; Private Sec. to Minister for the Arts, 1965–66; Cabinet Office, 1974–76; DES, subseq. Dept for Educn, 1976–96. Mem., Stevenson Commn on Information and Communications Technol. in Schs, 1996–97. Trustee, Inclusion Trust (formerly TheCademy), 2005–. *Recreations:* family, music.

SUMMERS, William Hay; Sheriff of Grampian, Highland and Islands at Aberdeen, since 2011; *b* Ellon, 18 Dec. 1960; *s* of Joseph B. Summers and Helen B. Summers (*née* Thain); *m* 1990, Gillian E. Craig; two *s* two *d*. *Educ:* Peterhead Acad.; Aberdeen Univ. (LLB, DipLP). Admitted solicitor, 1983; Milne & MacKinnon, 1982–87; Partner: MMP, 1987–94; Davies Wood Summers, 1994–2010; pt-time Sheriff, 2008–10; All-Scotland Floating Sheriff, 2010–11. *Recreations:* golf, ski-ing, walking, reading. *Clubs:* Royal Northern and University (Aberdeen); Royal Aberdeen Golf.

SUMMERSCALE, David Michael, MA; Head Master of Westminster School, 1986–98; *b* 22 April 1937; *s* of late Noel Tynwald Summerscale and Beatrice (*née* Wilson); *m* 1975, Pauline, *d* of late Prof. Michel Fleury, formerly Président de l'Ecole des Hautes Etudes, Paris, and Directeur des Antiquités Historiques de l'Ile-de-France; one *s* one *d*. *Educ:* Northaw; Sherborne Sch.; Trinity Hall, Cambridge. Lectr in English Literature and Tutor, St Stephen's Coll., Univ. of Delhi, 1959–63; Charterhouse, 1963–75 (Head of English, Housemaster); Master of Haileybury, 1976–86. Director: Namdang Tea Co. (India) Ltd, 1991–95; The Education Group Ltd, 1996–98. Oxford and Cambridge Schs Examination Bd Awarder and Reviser in English. Vice-Chm., E-SU Scholarship Cttee, 1982–93; Member: Managing Cttee of Cambridge Mission to Delhi, 1965; C. F. Andrews Centenary Appeal Cttee, 1970; HMC Academic Policy Sub-Cttee, 1982–86; Council, Charing Cross and Westminster Med. Sch., 1986–97. Governor: The Hall Sch., Hampstead, 1986–98; Arnold House Sch., St John's Wood, 1988–98; King's House Sch., Richmond, 1991–98; Hellenic Coll., London, 1996–2006; Shri Ram Sch., Delhi, 1996–2006; Gayhurst Sch., Gerrards Cross, 1998–2002; Solihull Sch., 1998–2006; Step by Step Sch., Noida, India, 2008–; Future Hope Acad., Kolkata, 2009–; Barrett Hodgson Internat. Sch., Karachi, 2010–11. Staff Advisor, Governing Body, Westminster Abbey Choir Sch., 1989–98; Member, Governing Body: Merchant Taylors' Sch., 1996–2001 (Nominated Mem., Sch. Cttee, Merchant Taylors' Co., 1988–96); Haberdashers' Aske's Schs, 2001–06; Consultant and Governor: Assam Valley Sch., India, 1989–; Sagar Sch., India, 2001–11; Exec. Advr, British Sch., Colombo, Sri Lanka, 1999–2011; Adviser: Amman Baccalaureate Sch., Jordan, 2002–04; Al Ain English Speaking Sch., 2006–08; Scholars Internat. Acad., Dubai, 2006–11. Member Council: Queen's Coll., London, 1991–2006 (Vice-Chm., 2000–06); Book Aid Internat. (formerly Ranfurly Library Service), 1992–98. Trustee, Criterion Theatre Trust, 1992–2002. Adviser: Rajiv Gandhi (UK) Foundn, 1999–2002; Pahamune Rehab. Centre, Sri Lanka, 2005–; Ext. Advr, Hong Kong Mgt Assoc. Coll., 1999–2002. Patron, Multi Lang. Acad., Yangon, Myanmar, 1999–2004. FRSA 1984. *Publications:* articles on English and Indian literature; dramatisations of novels and verse. *Recreations:* music, reading, mountaineering, games (squash (Mem. SRA), cricket, tennis, rackets (Mem. Tennis and Rackets Assoc.), golf). *Address:* 4 Ashley Gardens, Ambrosden Avenue, SW1P 1QD. *Clubs:* Athenæum, I Zingari, Free Foresters, Jesters; Club Alpin Suisse.

SUMMERSCALE, Katharine Lucy Claire, (Kate); writer; *b* London, 2 Sept. 1965; *d* of late Peter Wayne Summerscale and Valerie Summerscale; one *s* by Robert Randall. *Educ:* Bedales Sch.; St John's Coll., Oxford (BA Hons English Lang. and Lit.); Stanford Univ., Calif (MA Hons Communication Studies). Sub-Ed. and Commissioning Ed., The Independent Mag., 1989–93; Obituaries Writer, 1993–95, Obituaries Ed., 1995–96, Daily Telegraph; Ed., Sunday Rev., Independent on Sunday, 1998–99; Literary Ed., Daily Telegraph, 1999–2005. *Publications:* The Queen of Whale Cay, 1997 (Somerset Maugham Award, 1998); The Suspicions of Mr Whicher: or, the murder at Road Hill House, 2008 (Samuel Johnson Prize for Non-fiction, BBC Four, 2008; Galaxy Book of Year, 2009; televised, 2011); Mrs Robinson's Disgrace: the private diary of a Victorian lady, 2012. *Address:* c/o David Miller, Rogers, Coleridge & White, 20 Powis Mews, W11 1JN. *T:* (020) 7221 3717.

SUMMERSKILL, Ben Jeffrey Peter, OBE 2009; Director, Criminal Justice Alliance, since 2015; *b* 6 Oct. 1961; *s* of late Michael Brynmôr Summerskill and Florence Marion Johnston Summerskill (*née* Elliott). *Educ:* Sevenoaks Sch.; Merton Coll., Oxford (Exhibnr). Dep. Gen. Manager, Mario & Franco Restaurants, 1983–85; Gen. Manager, Lennoxcourt Ltd, 1985–86; Operations Dir, Kennedy Brookes plc, 1986–90; freelance journalist, Time Out, The Face, etc., 1990; Ed., The Pink Paper, 1992; Deputy Editor: Roof, 1993–96; Londoner's Diary, Evening Standard, 1996–98; Media Ed., Daily Express and Sunday Express, 1998–2000; Society and Policy Ed., 2000, Asst Ed., 2001–03, The Observer; Chief Exec., Stonewall, 2003–14. Mem., Equality and Human Rights Commn, 2006–09 (Mem., Govt Steering Cttee, 2004–06). Mem., Westminster CC, 1994–98. Mem., Parkside CHC, 1993–95; Vice Chm., Kensington Chelsea & Westminster CHC, 1995–96. Trustee, Covent Garden Area Trust, 1995–99. Mem. of Cttee, Queen's Award for Voluntary Service, 2009–. Mem. Exec. Cttee, Fabian Soc., 2004–07. *Publications:* (ed) The Way We Are Now: gay and lesbian lives in the 21st century, 2006.

SUMMERSKILL, Dr the Hon. Shirley Catherine Wynne; Medical Practitioner; Medical Officer in Blood Transfusion Service, 1983–91; *b* London, 9 Sept. 1931; *d* of late Dr E. J. Samuel and Baroness Summerskill, CH, PC. *Educ:* St Paul's Girls' Sch.; Somerville Coll., Oxford; St Thomas' Hospital. MA, BM, BCh, 1958. Treas., Oxford Univ. Labour Club, 1952. Resident House Surgeon, later House Physician, St Helier Hosp., Carshalton, 1959; Partner in Gen. Practice, 1960–68. Contested (Lab): Blackpool North by-election, 1962;

Halifax, 1983. MP (Lab) Halifax, 1964–83; opposition spokesman on health, 1970–74; Parly Under-Sec. of State, Home Office, 1974–79; opposition spokesman on home affairs, 1979–83. Vice-Chm., PLP Health Gp, 1964–69, Chm., 1969–70; Mem., Labour Party NEC, 1981–83. UK delegate, UN Status of Women Commn, 1968 and 1969; Mem. British delegn, Council of Europe and WEU, 1968, 1969. Mem., BMA. *Publications:* A Surgical Affair (novel), 1963; Destined to Love (novel), 1986. *Recreations:* music, reading, attending literature classes.

SUMMERSON, Hugo Hawksley Fitzthomas; Director, Palatine Properties Ltd, since 1983; Director (formerly Principal), Speaker Skills Training, since 1994; *b* 21 July 1950; *s* of late Thomas Hawksley Summerson, OBE and Joan Florence Summerson; *m* 2nd, 1995, Diana, *d* of late Lt-Col T. J. C. Washington, MC; one *s*. *Educ:* Harrow School; Royal Agricultural College. FRICS; MRAC. Land Agent with Knight, Frank and Rutley, 1973–76; travel in S America, 1977; self-employment, 1978–83. Consultant: Amhurst Properties Ltd, 1992–94; Grandfield Public Affairs Ltd, 1996–98; Butler Kelly Ltd, 2001–13; Dir, Meridian Clocks Ltd, 1999–2003. Clerk, Chartered Secretaries' and Administrators' Co., 2011–14. Contested (C): Barking, 1983; Walthamstow, 1992. MP (C) Walthamstow, 1987–92. Mem., Select Cttee on Envmt, 1991–92; Treas., British Latin-American Parly Gp, 1990; Vice-Chm., All-Party Parly Gp on Child Abduction, 1991–92; Sec., Cons. Back Bench Agriculture Cttee, 1991–92. Chm., Greater London Area Adopted Parly Candidates Assoc., 1986; Vice-Pres., Greater London Area, Nat. Soc. of Cons. and Unionist Agents, 1989; Mem. Council, British Atlantic Gp of Young Politicians, 1989; Parly Advr to Drinking Fountain Assoc., 1989; Treas., Assoc. of Cons. Parly Candidates (formerly Westminster Candidates' Assoc.), 1998–2001. Fellow, Industry and Parlt Trust, 1991. Member: Professional Speakers Assoc., 2001–05; Assoc. of Former MPs, 2004–; UK Speechwriters' Guild, 2010–13. Mem., Internat. Bruckner Soc., 2007–. Trustee: Trinity Chapel Site Charity, 1998–2002; Hyde Park Place Estate Charity, 1998–2002; St George's Hanover Sq. Sch., 1998–2002. Churchwarden, St George's, Hanover Sq., 1998–2002; Rep. for St George's, Westminster (St Margaret) Deanery Synod, 2004–07. Sir Anthony Berry Meml Scholar, 1985. Composer, March of the Master Mercer, for piano and two trumpets, dedicated to Mercers' Co., 2013, perf. at Mansion House, 2014. *Recreations:* music, fishing, watching cricket. *Address:* 38 Springfield Avenue, SW20 9JX. *T:* (020) 8543 5550. *Club:* Royal Over-Seas League.

SUMMERTON, Dr Neil William, CB 1997; Secretary, Partnership (UK) Ltd, since 2014 (Chairman and Executive Secretary, 1997–2002, Chairman and Executive Director, 2002–05; Executive Chairman, 2005–07; Chairman, 2007–14); *b* 5 April 1942; *s* of H. E. W. Summerton and Nancy Summerton; *m* 1965, Pauline Webb; two *s*. *Educ:* Wellington Grammar Sch., Shropshire; King's Coll., London (BA History 1963; PhD War Studies 1970). Min. of Transport, 1966–69; PA to Principal, 1969–71, Asst Sec. (Co-ordination), 1971–74, KCL; DoE, 1974–97; Asst Sec., heading various housing Divs, 1978–85; Under Sec., Planning Land-Use Policy Directorate, 1985–87; Under Sec., Planning and Develt Control Directorate, 1987–88; Under Sec., Local Govt Finance Policy Directorate, 1988–91; Under Sec., Water, 1991–95; Dir, Water and Land, 1996–97; Director: Oxford Centre for the Envmt, Ethics and Society, 1997–2002; Oxford Centre for Water Res., 1998–2002; Supernumerary Fellow, Mansfield Coll., Oxford, 1997–2003, now Emeritus Fellow. Attended HM Treasury Centre for Admin. Studies, 1968–69; Civil Service Top Management Programme, 1985. Non-executive Director: Redland Bricks Ltd, 1988–91; Veolia Water Southeast (formerly Folkestone and Dover Water Services Ltd, 1998–2012; North Surrey Water Co. Ltd, 1998–2000; Veolia Water Central plc (formerly Three Valleys Water), 2000–12; Director and Trustee: Partnership (UK) Ltd, 1994–; Christian Impact Ltd, 1989–98; London Christian Housing plc, 1990–98; Christian Research Assoc., 1992–98; George Müller Charitable Trust, 1998–; Church Planting Initiative, 2005–. Member: Cttee of Management, Council on Christian Approaches to Defence and Disarmament, 1983–2014 (Hon. Sec., 1984–91); Evangelical Alliance Council, 1989– (Trustee, 1990–96 and 1997–2000). *Publications:* A Noble Task: eldership and ministry in the local church, 1987, 2nd edn 1994; Learning from the Past, Facing the Future: essays for 'Brethren', 2011; articles and essays on historical, envmtl, theological and ethical matters. *Address:* Mansfield College, Oxford OX1 3TF.

SUMMONS, Roger Everett, PhD; FRS 2008; Professor of Geobiology, Massachusetts Institute of Technology, since 2001; *b* Sydney, NSW, 11 June 1946; *s* of Neil James Summons and Jean Catherine Summons; *m* 1970, Elizabeth Kristine Diment; three *d*. *Educ:* Univ. of New South Wales (BSc Cl. 1 Hons Chem. 1969; PhD Chem. 1972). Fellow in Genetics, Stanford Univ., 1972–73; Australian National University: Postdoctoral Fellow in Chem., 1973–75; Res. Fellow in Chem., 1975–77; Res. Officer in Biol., 1977–83; Sen. Res. Scientist, Baas Becking Geobiological Lab., 1983–87; Principal to Chief Res. Scientist, Geoscience Australia, 1987–2001. Australian Lectr, Petroleum Explorationists Soc. of Australia, 1998. FAA 1998; Fellow: Amer. Geophysical Union, 2006; Hanse-Wissenschaftskolleg, Delmenhorst, 2008. Hon. DSc Wollongong, 2009. Treibs Award, Geochem. Soc., 2003; Halpern Medal, Univ. of Wollongong, 2005. *Publications:* over 320 articles in jls and books. *Recreations:* music, fishing, oenology, gardening. *Address:* Department of Earth, Atmospheric and Planetary Sciences, Massachusetts Institute of Technology, E25–633, 45 Carleton Street, Cambridge, MA 02139, USA. *T:* (617) 4522791, *Fax:* (617) 2538630. *E:* rsummons@mit.edu.

SUMNER, Prof. Ann Beatrice, PhD; Public Art Project Officer, University of Leeds, since 2015; *b* Bath, 1960; *d* of late Tim Sumner and of Rita Sumner; *m* 2009, Martin Johnson; two *d* by a previous marriage. *Educ:* Royal Sch., Bath; Kingswood Sch., Bath; Courtauld Inst. of Fine Art, Univ. of London (BA Hons); Newnham Coll., Cambridge (PhD 1985). Archive asst, NPG, 1981–83; Asst Curator, Holburne Mus., Bath, 1983–88; Res. Asst, Whitworth Art Gall., Manchester, 1988–90; Curator (pt-time), Wilmer Hse, Farnham, 1990–91; Keeper, Dulwich Picture Gall., 1991–95; Keeper, Holburne Mus., Bath, 1996–2000; Hd of Fine Art, Nat. Mus. of Wales, Cardiff, 2000–07; Dir, Barber Inst. of Fine Arts and Prof. of Fine Art and Curatorial Practice, 2007–12, Vis. Prof., 2012–, Univ. of Birmingham; Dir, Birmingham Mus Trust, 2012; Exec. Dir, Brontë Soc., 2012–14. Mem., Steering Cttee, Nat. Inventory of Eur. Paintings, Nat. Gall., 1997–. Mem., Methodist Histl Adv. Gp, Oxford Brookes Univ., 2008–. Trustee, Methodist Collection of Modern Art, 2004–. *Publications:* Death, Passion and Politics: Van Dyck and the Digbys, 1995; (with Greg Smith) Thomas Jones: an artist rediscovered, 2003; Colour and Light: 50 Impressionist paintings, 2004; Gwen John and the Catholic Church, 2008; Court on Canvas: tennis in art, 2011; In Front of Nature: landscapes by Thomas Fearnley, 2012; exhibn catalogues; contrib. articles to jls. *Recreations:* tennis, walking, cinema, theatre, reading, history, family. *Clubs:* Lansdown Tennis; The Priory (Edgbaston).

SUMNER, Gordon Matthew, (Sting), CBE 2003; musician, songwriter and actor; *b* Northumberland, 2 Oct. 1951; *s* of late Ernest and Audrey Sumner; *m* 1st, 1976, Frances Tomelty (marr. diss. 1984); one *s* one *d*; 2nd, 1992, Trudie Styler; two *s* two *d*. *Educ:* St Cuthbert's Grammar Sch., Newcastle; Warwick Coll., Newcastle (BEd 1973). Teacher, St Paul's Primary Sch., Cramlington, Newcastle, 1971–74. Singer, bass-player and songwriter, The Police, 1977–86; tours in UK, Europe and USA; reformed and toured worldwide, 2007–08. Theatre début in The Threepenny Opera, Washington, 1989. *Records include: with The Police: albums:* Outlandos d'Amour, 1978; Regatta de Blanc, 1979; Zenyatta Mondatta, 1980; Ghost in the Machine, 1981; Synchronicity, 1983; *singles:* Roxanne, 1978; Message in a Bottle, 1979; Walking on the Moon, 1979; Every Breath You Take, 1983; *solo: albums:* Dream of the Blue Turtles, 1985; Bring on the Night, 1986 (Grammy Award for Best Male Pop Vocal Perf., 1988); Nothing Like the Sun, 1987; The Soul Cages, 1991; Ten Summoner's Tales, 1993; Mercury Falling, 1996; Brand New Day, 1999 (Grammy Awards for Best Pop Album and Best Male Pop Vocal Perf., 1999); All This Time, 2001; Sacred Love, 2003; Songs from the Labyrinth, 2006; If On A Winter's Night, 2009; Symphonicities, 2010; *singles:* Nothing Like the Sun, 1987; The Soul Cages, 1991 (Grammy Award for Best Rock Song, 1992); Englishman in New York; After the Rain has Gone, 2000. *Film appearances include:* Quadrophenia, 1979; Radio On, 1980; Brimstone and Treacle, 1982; Dune, 1984; The Bride, 1985; Plenty, 1985; Julia and Julia, 1987; Stormy Monday, 1988; The Adventures of Baron von Munchausen, 1989; The Grotesque, 1995; Lock, Stock and Two Smoking Barrels, 1998. Composer and lyricist, musical, The Last Ship, NY, 2014. Co-founder, Rainforest Foundn, 1989. Hon. DMus: Northumbria, 1992; Newcastle, 2006. *Publications:* Jungle Stories: the fight for the Amazon, 1989; Broken Music: a memoir, 2003.

SUMPTION, Rt Hon. Lord; Jonathan Philip Chadwick Sumption, OBE 2003; PC 2012; FRHistS, FSA; a Justice of the Supreme Court of the United Kingdom, since 2012; *b* 9 Dec. 1948; *s* of late Anthony James Chadwick Sumption, DSC; *m* 1971, Teresa Mary (*née* Whelan); one *s* two *d*. *Educ:* Eton; Magdalen College, Oxford (MA). Fellow (in History) of Magdalen College, Oxford, 1971–75; called to the Bar, Inner Temple, 1975, Bencher, 1990; QC 1986; Recorder, 1993–2001; a Judge of the Courts of Appeal of Jersey and Guernsey, 1995–2011. Mem., Judicial Appts Commn, 2006–11. Trustee: RAM, 2002–; Holburne Mus. of Art, Bath, 2008–11; London Library, 2008–12. Sen. Res. Fellow, Inst. of Historical Res., 2009. FRHistS 2006; FSA 2009. Hon. FRAM 2004. *Publications:* Pilgrimage: an image of medieval religion, 1975; The Albigensian Crusade, 1978; The Hundred Years' War, vol. 1, 1990, vol. 2, 1999, vol. 3, 2009 (Wolfson History Prize, 2009), vol. 4, 2015. *Recreations:* music, history. *Address:* Supreme Court of the United Kingdom, Parliament Square, SW1P 3BD.

SUNAK, Rishi; MP (C) Richmond, Yorks, since 2015; *b* 12 May 1980; *m* 2009, Akshatha, *d* of N. R. Narayana Murthy; two *d*. *Educ:* Winchester Coll.; Oxford (BA 1st Cl. Hons PPE 2001); Stanford Univ. (Fulbright Schol.; MBA 2006). Analyst, then Exec. Dir, Merchant Banking, Goldman Sachs, 2001–04; Partner, TCI, London, 2006; Co-Founder, investment firm; Hd, Black and Minority Ethnic Res. Unit, Policy Exchange. Dir, Catamaran Ventures. Mem., Envmt, Food and Rural Affairs Select Cttee, 2015–. *Address:* House of Commons, SW1A 0AA.

SUNDERLAND, Archdeacon of; *see* Bain, Ven. J. S.

SUNDERLAND, (Godfrey) Russell, CB 1991; FCILT; Deputy Secretary, Aviation, Shipping and International, Department of Transport, 1988–94; *b* 28 July 1936; *s* of Allan and Laura Sunderland; *m* 1965, Greta Jones; one *s* one *d*. *Educ:* Heath Grammar Sch., Halifax; The Queen's College, Oxford (MA). Ministry of Aviation: Asst Principal, 1962; Asst Private Sec. to Minister, 1964; Principal, 1965; HM Diplomatic Service: First Sec. (Civil Air), Beirut, and other Middle East posts, 1969; Principal, Board of Trade, 1971; Asst Sec., DTI, 1973; Under Sec., DTI, 1979; Dir of Shipping Policy and Emergency Planning, Dept of Transport, 1984. Chairman: Consultative Shipping Group, 1984–88; Maritime Transport Cttee, OECD, 1992–94. Non-exec. Dir, Air Miles Travel Promotions Ltd, 1995–2001. Advr, Maersk Co. Ltd, 1994–2001. FCILT (FCIT 1995; Vice Pres., CIT, 1997–2001; Chm., Transport Faculty, CILT(UK), 2004–07). FRSA 1991. *Recreations:* garden, piano, amateur theatre. *Address:* Windrush, Silkmore Lane, West Horsley, Leatherhead, Surrey KT24 6JQ. *T:* (01483) 282660.

SUNDERLAND, Sir John (Michael), Kt 2006; Chairman, Cadbury Schweppes plc, 2003–08 (Chief Executive, 1996–2003); *b* 24 Aug. 1945; *s* of Harry Sunderland and Joyce Eileen Sunderland (*née* Farnish); *m* 1966, Jean Margaret Grieve; three *s* one *d*. *Educ:* St Andrews Univ. (MA Hons). Joined Cadbury, 1968. Non-executive Director: Rank Gp plc, 1998–2006; Barclays plc, 2005–; AFC Energy plc, 2012–; Member, Advisory Board: CVC Capital Partners, 2004–; Ian Jones & Partners, 2002–07; Chairman: Merlin Entertainments, 2009–; Cambridge Educn Gp Ltd, 2014–. Dir, Financial Reporting Council, 2004–11 (Chm., Corporate Governance Cttee, 2010); Trinsum (formerly Marakon Associates), 2006–09. President: ISBA, 2002–05; UK Food and Drink Fedn, 2002–04; CBI, 2004–06 (Dep. Pres., 2003–04, 2007–08). Pres., 2006–07, Dep. Pres., 2007–09, Chartered Management Inst. Gov., Council, 2008–11, Chancellor, 2011–, Aston Univ.; Gov., Council, Reading Univ., 2008–. *Address:* Three Barrows, Seale Road, Elstead, Surrey GU8 6LF.

SUNDERLAND, Russell; *see* Sunderland, G. R.

SUNNUCKS, Stephen Richard; Global President, Gap Inc., since 2012; *b* 30 Sept. 1957; *s* of late Richard George Drummond Clitherow Sunnucks and of Hilary Mary Sunnucks; *m* 1993, Louise Anita Marston; three *s*. *Educ:* Dr Challoner's Grammar Sch., Amersham; Sheffield Univ. (BA Hons Econs). Various posts with Marks & Spencer plc, 1979–89 (retail mgt, 1979–84; buying depts, 1984–89); J. Sainsbury plc, 1989–94 (Dir, Non-food, Savacentre, 1989–92; Deptl Dir, J. Sainsbury, 1992–94); Burton Gp plc, subsequently Arcadia Gp plc, 1994–98: Man. Dir, Dorothy Perkins Ltd, 1994–97; Man. Dir, Mergers, Acquisitions and New Business Develt, 1997–98; Man. Dir, Retail, New Look plc, 1998–2000; Chief Exec., New Look Gp plc, 2000–04; Pres., Europe and Strategic Alliances, 2005–11, Internat. Div., 2011–12, Gap Inc. *Recreations:* golf, tennis, ski-ing. *E:* stephen.sunnucks@btinternet.com.

SUPACHAI PANITCHPAKDI, PhD; Secretary-General, UN Conference on Trade and Development, 2005–13; Member, Advisory Board, Institute of Cultural Diplomacy; *b* Bangkok, 30 May 1946; *m* Mrs Sasai; one *s* one *d*. *Educ:* Netherlands Sch. of Econs, Rotterdam (Bank of Thailand Schol.; BA, MA; PhD 1973). Vis. Fellow, Dept of Applied Econs, Univ. of Cambridge, 1973; Bank of Thailand, 1974–86, latterly Dir of Financial Instns Supervision Dept; Pres., Thai Military Bank, 1988–92. MP (Democrat Party) Bangkok, 1986–88, 1992–2002; Dep. Minister of Finance, 1986–88; Mem., Nat. Assembly, 1991; Senator, 1992; Dep. Prime Minister, 1992–95; Dep. Prime Minister and Minister of Commerce, Thailand, 1997–2002; Dir Gen., WTO, 2002–05. Kt Grand Cordon (Special Class), Order of White Elephant (Thailand). *Publications:* Globalization and Trade in the New Millennium, 2001; (with Mark Clifford) China and WTO: changing China changing WTO, 2002.

SUPPERSTONE, Hon. Sir Michael (Alan), Kt 2010; **Hon. Mr Justice Supperstone;** a Judge of the High Court, Queen's Bench Division, since 2010; a Judge of the Employment Appeal Tribunal, since 2011; Liaison Judge (with responsibility for the Administrative Court) for the North and North-East, Queen's Bench Division, since 2013; *b* 30 March 1950; *s* of late Harold Bernard Supperstone and Muriel Supperstone; *m* 1985, Dianne Jaffe; one *s* one *d*. *Educ:* St Paul's School; Lincoln College, Oxford (MA, BCL). Called to the Bar, Middle Temple, 1973, Bencher, 1999; in practice, 1974; QC 1991; Asst Recorder, 1992–96; Recorder, 1996–2010; a Dep. High Ct Judge, 1998–2010. Vis. Scholar, Harvard Law Sch., 1979–80; Vis. Lectr, Nat. Univ. of Singapore, 1981, 1982. Chm., Administrative Law Bar Assoc., 1997–99 (Sec., 1986–91; Treas., 1991–94; Vice-Chm., 1995–96). Consulting Ed., Butterworths Local Government Reports, 1999–2010. *Publications:* Brownlie's Law of Public Order and National Security, 2nd edn 1981; Immigration: the law and practice, 1983, 3rd edn 1994, cons. ed., 4th edn, as Immigration and Asylum, 1996; (contrib.) Halsbury's Laws of England, 4th edn reissue, Administrative Law, 1989, 2001 (Gen. Ed.), Extradition Law, 2000; (ed jtly and contrib.) Judicial Review, 1992, 4th edn 2010; (contrib.) Butterworths Local Government Law, 1998; (jtly) Local Authorities and the Human Rights Act 1998, 1999; (jtly) The Freedom of Information Act 2000, 2001; (Jt Gen. Ed.) Administrative Court Practice,

2002, 2nd edn 2008; (ed) Judicial Review, Halsbury's Laws of England, 5th edn, 2010; articles on public law. *Recreations:* playing tennis, watching cricket, reading history. *Address:* High Court of Justice, Royal Courts of Justice, WC2A 2LL. *Clubs:* MCC, Garrick, Royal Automobile.

SUPPLE, Prof. Barry Emanuel, CBE 2000; FRHistS; FBA 1987; Director, Leverhulme Trust, 1993–2001; Professor of Economic History, University of Cambridge, 1981–93, now Professor Emeritus; *b* 27 Oct. 1930; *s* of Solomon and Rose Supple; *m* 1st, 1958, Sonia (*née* Caller) (*d* 2002); two *s* one *d*; 2nd, 2003, Virginia (*née* McNay). *Educ:* Hackney Downs Grammar Sch.; London Sch. of Econs and Pol Science (BScEcon 1952; Hon. Fellow, 2001); Christ's Coll., Cambridge (PhD 1955); LittD Cantab 1993. FRHistS 1972. Asst Prof. of Business History, Grad. Sch. of Business Admin, Harvard Univ., 1955–60; Associate Prof. of Econ. Hist., McGill Univ., 1960–62; University of Sussex: Lectr, Reader, then Prof. of Econ. and Social Hist., 1962–78; Dean, Sch. of Social Sciences, 1965–68; Pro-Vice-Chancellor (Arts and Social Studies), 1968–72; Pro-Vice-Chancellor, 1978; University of Oxford: Reader in Recent Social and Econ. Hist., 1978–81; Professorial Fellow, Nuffield Coll., 1978–81; Professorial Fellow, 1981–83, Hon. Fellow, 1984, Christ's Coll., Cambridge; Master of St Catharine's Coll., Cambridge, 1984–93 (Hon. Fellow, 1993). Hon. Fellow, Worcester Coll., 1986; Associate Fellow, Trumbull Coll., Yale, 1986. Chm., Consultative Cttee of Assessment of Performance Unit, DES, 1975–80; Member: Council, SSRC, 1972–77; Social Science Fellowship Cttee, Nuffield Foundn, 1974–97. Pres., Econ. Hist. Soc., 1992–95. Foreign Sec., British Acad., 1995–99. Co-editor, Econ. Hist. Rev., 1973–82. Hon. Fellow, Inst. of Historical Res., 2001. Hon. FRAM 2001. Hon. DLitt: London Guildhall, 1993; Sussex, 1998; Leicester, 1999; Warwick, 2000; Bristol, 2001. *Publications:* Commercial Crisis and Change in England, 1600–42, 1959; (ed) The Experience of Economic Growth, 1963; Boston Capitalists and Western Railroads, 1967; The Royal Exchange Assurance: a history of British insurance, 1720–1970, 1970; (ed) Essays in Business History, 1977; History of the British Coal Industry: vol. 4, 1914–46, The Political Economy of Decline, 1987; (ed) The State and Economic Knowledge: the American and British experience, 1990; (ed) The Rise of Big Business, 1992; Doors Open, 2008; Ten Days in Poland, 2010; It Will Go Away: a memoir of the Solovitch family, 1911–2013, 2013; articles and revs in learned jls. *Recreations:* travel, writing. *Address:* 3 Scotts Gardens, Whittlesford, Cambridge CB22 4NR. *T:* (01223) 830606.

See also T. A. Supple.

SUPPLE, Timothy Adam; stage director; *b* 24 Sept. 1962; *s* of Prof. Barry Emanuel Supple, *qv* and late Sonia Caller; one *s* two *d* by Melly Still; *m* 2009, Archana Ramaswamy; one *d*. *Educ:* Lewes Priory Comprehensive Sch.; Gosford Hill Sch.; Gonville and Caius Coll. and Churchill Coll., Cambridge (BA Hist./English). Assistant Director: York Th. Royal, 1985–87; Royal Court Th., 1987; RNT, 1988–89; Associate Dir, Leicester Haymarket, 1989–90; Artistic Dir, Young Vic Th., 1993–2000; estabd Dash Arts, 2005. *Productions include: theatre:* Accidental Death of an Anarchist, NT, 1990; Grimm Tales, Young Vic, 1994, 1998; Spring Awakening, 1995; Comedy of Errors, RSC, 1996; Haroun and the Sea of Stories, NT, 1998; Tales from Ovid, RSC, 1999; A Servant to Two Masters, RSC, Young Vic, 1999; Midnight's Children, RSC, NY, 2003; Cosmonaut's Last Message, Donmar Warehouse, 2005; A Midsummer Night's Dream, Dash Arts/British Council, India, 2005–06, Verona, 2006, Stratford upon Avon, 2006, 2007, London, 2007, UK Tour, 2007, Australia, USA and Canada, 2008; As You Like It, Curve, Leicester, 2009; One Thousand and One Nights, Dash Arts/Luminato, Toronto, Chicago and Edinburgh Internat. Fest., 2011; prodns at Chichester Fest. Th.; Nat. Th. of Norway; Maxim Gorki Th., Berlin; Tel Aviv Opera House; Sheffield Crucible Th.; also tours, British Isles, Europe, USA, Far East, S America, Australia and India; *opera:* Hansel and Gretel, Opera North, 2001; Babette's Feast, Royal Opera, 2002, 2004; The Magic Flute, Opera North, 2003, 2007; *films:* Twelfth Night, 2002; Rockabye, 2004. *Publications:* co-adaptor, theatre adaptations: Dario Fo, Accidental Death of an Anarchist, 1990; Carol Ann Duffy: Grimm Tales, 1994; More Grimm Tales, 1997; Beasts and Beauties, 2004; Salman Rushdie: Haroun and the Sea of Stories, 1998; Midnight's Children, 2003; Ted Hughes, Tales from Ovid, 1999; Hanan al Shaykh, One Thousand and One Nights, 2011. *Recreations:* reading, walking, music, politics, history, yoga, cooking, travel, children. *E:* timsupple@gmail.com.

SUR, Prof. Mriganka, PhD; FRS 2006; Newton Professor of Neuroscience, Department of Brain and Cognitive Sciences, since 1997, and Director, Simons Center for the Social Brain, since 2012, Massachusetts Institute of Technology; *b* Fatehgarh, India, 1953. *Educ:* Indian Inst. of Technol. (BTech 1974); Vanderbilt Univ. (MS 1975; PhD 1978). Postdoctoral res., SUNY Stony Brook; Sch. of Medicine, Yale Univ., 1983–86; joined Dept of Brain and Cognitive Scis, MIT, 1986, Prof., 1993–; Hd of Dept, 1997–2012; Sherman Fairchild Prof. of Neurosci., 1998. *Publications:* articles in jls. *Address:* Mriganka Sur Laboratory, Massachusetts Institute of Technology, 32 Vassar Street, 46–6237, Cambridge, MA 02139, USA.

SURANI, Prof. Azim, PhD; CBE 2007; FRS 1990; Mary Marshall and Arthur Walton Professor of Physiology and Reproduction, 1991–2013, now Emeritus, and Director, Germline and Epigenomics Research, Gurdon Institute, University of Cambridge; Fellow, King's College, Cambridge, since 1994. *Educ:* Univ. of Cambridge (PhD 1976). Sen. Principal Investigator, AFRC Inst. of Animal Physiol., later Inst. of Animal Physiol. and Genetics Res., 1979–91. FMedSci 2001. *Publications:* articles in jls. *Address:* Gurdon Institute, Henry Wellcome Building of Cancer and Developmental Biology, University of Cambridge, Tennis Court Road, Cambridge CB2 1QN.

SURBER, Elizabeth; Headmistress, King's High School for Girls, Warwick, 2001–15; *b* Kingston upon Thames; *d* of George Morphett and Olive Morphett; *m* 1976, Thomas Gordon Surber. *Educ:* Tiffin Girls' Sch., Kingston upon Thames; Univ. of Exeter (BA, MA Hons); Jesus Coll., Oxford (PGCE Dist.). Teacher of French: Tiffin Girls' Sch., Kingston upon Thames, 1979–82; Cheltenham Ladies' Coll., 1982–88; Second Dep. Headmistress, Bedford High Sch., 1988–94; Headmistress, Laurel Park Sch., Glasgow, 1995–2001. *Recreations:* ballet, walking, travel.

SURFACE, Richard Charles; Partner, Oliver Wyman (formerly Oliver, Wyman & Co., then Mercer Oliver Wyman) (Director, 2000–05; Managing Director, 2005). *Educ:* Univ. of Minnesota; Univ. of Kansas (BA Maths); Harvard Grad. Sch. of Business Admin (MBA). Actuarial Asst, Nat. Life & Accident Insce Co., Nashville, Tenn, 1970–72; Corporate Treasury Analyst, Mobil Corp., NY, 1974–77; Dir, Corporate Planning, Northwest Industries Inc., Chicago, 1977–81; American Express Co., London and Frankfurt, 1981–89: Regl Vice-Pres. (Card Strategic Planning), 1981–82; Divisional Vice-President: Business Develt, 1982–86; Card Mkting, 1986–87; and Gen. Manager, Personal Financial Services, 1987–89; Gen. Manager, Corporate Develt, Sun Life, 1989–91; Managing Director: Sun Life Internat., 1991–95; Pearl Group PLC, 1995–99; AMP (UK) PLC, 1995–99.

SURI, Baron *cr* 2014 (Life Peer), of Ealing in the London Borough of Ealing; **Ranbir Singh Suri;** Chairman, Oceanic Jewellers Ltd, since 1991; *b* 1935. Pres., British Asian Conservative Link, 2011– (founding Chm., 1997–2011).

SURREY, Archdeacon of; *see* Beake, Ven. S. A.

SURTEES, John, OBE 2008 (MBE 1961); controls companies in automotive research and development, motorsport and property development; *b* 11 Feb. 1934; *s* of late John Norman and Dorothy Surtees; *m* 1st, 1962, Patricia Phyllis Burke (marr. diss. 1979); 2nd, 1987, Jane A. Sparrow; two *d* (one *s* decd). *Educ:* Ashburton School, Croydon. 5 year engineering apprenticeship, Vincent Engrs, Stevenage, Herts. Motorcycle racing, 1952–60; British Champion, 1954, 1955; World 500 cc Motorcycle Champion, 1956; World 350 and 500 cc Motorcycle Champion, 1958, 1959, 1960. At end of 1960 he retd from motorcycling; motor racing, 1961–72; with Ferrari Co., won World Motor Racing title, 1964; 5th in World Championship, 1965 (following accident in Canada due to suspension failure); in 1966 left Ferrari in mid-season and joined Cooper, finishing 2nd in World Championship; in 1967 with Honda Motor Co. as first driver and develt engr (1967–68); 3rd in World Championship; with BRM as No 1 driver, 1969; designed and built own Formula 1 car, 1970. Team Principal, British A1 Grand Prix Team, 2004–07. Vice-Pres., British Racing Drivers' Club, 1993–2000, 2004– (Dir, 2000–04). Founding Trustee, Henry Surtees Foundn, 2010. Ambassador, Racing Steps Foundn in support of young driver develt prog., 2008. *Publications:* Motorcycle Racing and Preparation, 1958; John Surtees Book of Motorcycling, 1960; Speed, 1963; Six Days in August, 1968; John Surtees—World Champion, 1991; (jtly) The Pirelli Album of Motor Racing Heroes, 1992; Motorcycle Maestro, 2003; John Surtees: my incredible life on two and four wheels, 2014. *Recreations:* period architecture, mechanical restorations; interested in most sports. *Address:* c/o John Surtees Ltd, Monza House, Fircroft Way, Edenbridge, Kent TN8 6EJ. *T:* (01732) 865496.

SUSMAN, Hon. Louis B.; Ambassador of the United States of America to the Court of St James's, 2009–13; non-executive Chairman, DJE Holdings, since 2013; *b* St Louis, Missouri; *m* Marjorie Sachs; one *s* one *d*. *Educ:* Univ. of Michigan (BA 1959); Washington Univ. (LLB 1962). In practice as lawyer, Thompson & Mitchell, St Louis, 1962–89, Sen. Partner, 1981–89; with Salomon Brothers Inc., 1989–98, Vice Chm., Investment Banking, 1996; Chm., N Amer. Customer Cttee, Citibank and Citigroup Inc., 1998–2000; Vice Chm., Citigroup Corporate and Investment Banking, 2000–09; former Mem., Internat. Adv. Bd, Citigroup. Mem., Bd of Dirs and Mgt Cttee, St Louis Cardinals, 1975–89. Mem., Adv. Commn on Public Diplomacy, 1988; Dir, Center for Nat. Policy, Washington, DC. Member: Chm.'s Circle, Chicago Council on Global Affairs; Bd, Art Inst. of Chicago; Bd, Northwestern Children's Meml Hosp.

SUSMAN, Peter Joseph; QC 1997; a Recorder, since 1993; *b* 20 Feb. 1943; *s* of Albert Leonard Susman and Sybil Rebecca Susman (*née* Joseph); *m* 1st, 1966, Peggy Judith Stone (marr. diss. 1996); one *s* one *d*; 2nd, 2006, Belinda Zoe Schwehr; one *s*. *Educ:* Dulwich Coll.; Lincoln Coll., Oxford (Oldfield Open Law Schol.; BA 1964; MA 1970); Law Sch., Univ. of Chicago (British Commonwealth Fellow; Fulbright Schol.; JD 1965). Called to the Bar, Middle Temple, 1966, Bencher, 2005; in practice as a barrister, 1966–70 and 1972–; Associate, Debevoise, Plimpton, Lyons & Gates, NYC, 1970–71; Asst Recorder, 1989–93. Ind. Standing Counsel to Ofcom, 2003–05. *Recreations:* playing the clarinet, windsurfing, ski-ing. *Address:* Henderson Chambers, 2 Harcourt Buildings, Temple, EC4Y 9DB. *T:* (020) 7583 9020.

SUSSKIND, Janis Elizabeth, OBE 2014; Managing Director, Boosey & Hawkes Music Publishers Ltd, London, since 2012; *b* 27 Nov. 1952; *d* of John H. Tomfohrde, Jr, and Ruth Elizabeth Robbins Tomfohrde; *m* 1st, 1973, Walter Susskind (*d* 1980); 2nd, 1993, Antony Fell (*d* 2011). *Educ:* Princeton Univ. (BA *cum laude*). Boosey & Hawkes Music Publishers Ltd: Hd of Promotion, 1984–96; Dir, Composers and Repertoire, 1997–2004; Publishing Dir, 2005–12; Dir, Boosey & Hawkes Hldgs Ltd, 2008–. Director: NMC Record Co., 1991–92; Classic Copyright (Hldgs) Ltd, 2004–08. Chm., SPNM, 1983–88. Arts Council of England, subseq. Arts Council England: Mem., Music Panel, 1993–2001; Mem. and Dep. Chm., Stabilization Adv. Panel, 1996–2006. Mem. Council, RCM, 1996–2005. Member Board: Birmingham Contemporary Music Gp, 1991–2000; English National Opera, 2004–12; Internat. Artist Managers' Assoc., 2012–14. Trustee, Britten-Pears Foundn, 2001–10, 2011–. Hon. RCM 2007. *Recreations:* reading, theatre, contemporary art, ski-ing, tennis, playing chamber music. *Address:* c/o Boosey & Hawkes Music Publishers Ltd, Aldwych House, 71–91 Aldwych, WC2B 4HN.

SUSSKIND, Prof. Richard Eric, OBE 2000; DPhil; FRSE; author and independent consultant, since 1997; Information Technology Adviser to Lord Chief Justice of England, since 1998; *b* 28 March 1961; *s* of Dr Werner and Shirley Susskind; *m* 1985, Michelle Latter; two *s* one *d*. *Educ:* Hutchesons' Grammar Sch., Glasgow; Univ. of Glasgow (LLB Hons 1st class; Dip. Legal Practice); Balliol Coll., Oxford (Snell Exhibnr; DPhil 1986). FRSE 1997. CITP 2004. Tutor in Law, Univ. of Oxford, 1984–86; Head of Expert Systems, Ernst & Young, 1986–89; Special Advr, 1989–94, Mem. of Mgt Bd, 1994–97, Masons. Vis. Prof., 1990–2001, Prof., 2001–, Law Sch., Univ. of Strathclyde; Gresham Prof. of Law, 2000–04; Hon. Prof., 2005, Emeritus Prof. of Law, 2007, Gresham Coll.; Founder Mem., Adv. Bd, 2002–, Vis. Prof. of Internet Studies, 2009–, Oxford Internet Inst., Univ. of Oxford (Chm., Adv. Bd, 2011–); Larry J. Hoffman, Greenberg Traurig Dist. Vis. Prof. in Business of Law, Univ. of Miami Sch. of Law, 2013–14. IT Advr, Lord Woolf's Access to Justice Inquiry, 1995–96. Pres., Soc. for Computers and Law, 2011– (Chm., 1990–92; Hon. Mem., 1992–). Member: Inf. Technol. and the Courts Cttee, 1990– (Co-Chair, 2006–); Court of Appeal (Civil Div.) Review Team, 1996–97; Modernising Govt Project Bd, 1999–2001; Freedom of Inf. Project Bd, 2003–05; Public Legal Educn Strategy Gp, 2008–; Inf. System Improvement Strategy Prog. Bd, Nat. Policing Improvement Agency, 2008–09; Prog. Bd, Making Justice Work, Scottish Govt, 2010–13; Pres. of QBD's Rev. of Efficiency of Criminal Proceedings, 2014–15; Chairman: Adv. Panel on Crown Copyright, subseq. Public Sector Inf., 2003–08; Online Dispute Resolution Adv. Gp, Civil Justice Council, 2014–. IT Advr, Jersey Legal Inf. Bd, 1998–. Mem., Adv. Bd, Lyceum Capital, 2008–; Chm., Client Adv. Bd, Integreon, 2011–12. Expert Consultee: Criminal Courts Rev., 2000–01; Tribunals Rev., 2000–01. Special Advr, Canadian Bar Assoc., 2009–. Mem., Adv. Bd, UCL Judicial Inst., 2011–; Hon. Prof., Faculty of Laws, UCL, 2011–. Gen. Editor, 1992–2014, Founding Ed., 2014–, Internat. Jl of Law and Information Technology; Law columnist, The Times, 1999–2008. Trustee, Lokahi Foundn, 2005–. Freeman, City of London, 1992; Freeman, 1992, Liveryman, 1993, Mem. Court, 1994–2003, Co. of Information Technologists. Member: Council, Gresham Coll., 2002–04; External Adv. Bd, AHRC Res. Centre for Studies in Intellectual Property and Technol. Law, Univ. of Edinburgh, 2002–. Gov., Haberdashers' Aske's Schs, Elstree, 1998–2013; Mem., Balliol Coll. Campaign Bd, 2000–07. FRSA 1992; FBCS 1997. Hon. Fellow, Centre for Law and Computing, Durham Univ., 2001–. George & Thomas Hutcheson Award, 2001. *Publications:* Expert Systems in Law, 1987; (with P. Capper) Latent Damage Law: the expert system, 1988; Essays on Law and Artificial Intelligence, 1993; The Future of Law, 1996; Transforming the Law, 2000; (ed jtly) Essays in Honour of Sir Brian Neill, 2003; (ed) The Susskind Interviews: legal experts in changing times, 2005; The End of Lawyers?, 2008; Tomorrow's Lawyers, 2013; (with D. Susskind) The Future of the Professions, 2015. *Recreations:* running, reading, golf, cinema, ski-ing. *Address:* 67 Aldenham Avenue, Radlett, Herts WD7 8JA. *T:* (01923) 469655. *E:* richard@susskind.com.

SUTCH, Rev. Dom Antony; *see* Sutch, C. T.

SUTCH, Ven. (Christopher) David, TD 1992; Chaplain, St Andrew's, Costa del Sol, 2007–13; Archdeacon of Gibraltar, 2008–13; *b* Oxford, 27 Aug. 1947; *s* of Christopher Lang Sutch and Gladys Ethelwyn Sutch; *m* 1969, Margaret Anne, (Megan); three *s*. *Educ:* King's Coll., London (AKC 1969); DipHE 2000. Ordained deacon, 1970, priest, 1971; Curate, St Andrew's, Hartcliffe, Bristol, 1970–75; Team Vicar, Dorcan, Swindon, 1975–79; Vicar, St Helen's, Alveston, Bristol, 1979–89; Rector, St Mary's, Yate New Town, 1989–99; Vicar, St Matthew's, Cainscross with Selsey, Glos, 1999–2007. Area Dean: Westbury, 1988–89; Stapleton, 1996–99; Stonehouse, 2005–07. Royal Army Chaplains Dept (Volunteers), 1980–2003; Chaplain, RBL, Glos, 2005–07; Hon. Col, N Somerset Yeomanry Sqdn, 2003–09. *Recreations:* digital photography, grandchildren.

SUTCH, Christopher Timothy, (Rev. Dom Antony Sutch); Parish Priest, St Benet, Beccles, 2003–12; *b* 19 June 1950; *s* of late Ronald Antony Sutch and of Kathleen Sutch (*née* Roden). *Educ:* Downside Sch.; Exeter Univ.; St Benet's Hall, Oxford. Chartered Accountant, 1971–75; postulant, 1975, novice, 1977, professed Benedictine monk, 1981; priest, 1981; Housemaster, Caverel House, 1985–95, Headmaster, 1995–2003, Downside Sch. Member: BBC Ind. Assessment Bd on Religious Broadcasting, 1998; Cttee, Catholic Ind. Schs Conf., 2000–03. Mem. (Ind), Beccles Town Council, 2007–10. Mem., Governing Body, Bath Univ., 1995–2002; Governor: All Hallows Prep. Sch., 1996–2004; Sacred Heart Primary, Chew Magna, 1996–2004 (Chm., 1997–99); St Mary's Sch., Woldingham, 2001–04; Moor Park Sch., 2002–09; St Benet's Primary Sch., Beccles (Vice-Chm.), 2003–; Moreton Hall Prep. Sch., 2004–; St Felix Sch., Southwold, 2006–11; Downside Sch., 2006–10; Guardian, St Mary's Sch., Shaftesbury, 1999–2003; Trustee, St Edward's Sch., Cheltenham, 2004–08. Trustee: Jackdaws Educnl Trust, 2003–06; Theodore Trust, 2006–11. Mem. Strategy Bd, Hobsons Guide, 2003–10. Dir, Catholic Herald Ltd, 2003–08. Chair, Adv. Bd, AEGIS, 2008–10. Patron: Dementia UK, 2010–11; Kairos, 2011–. Presenter and contributor, Thought for the Day, BBC Radio 4, 2003–10; TV and radio progs. *Publications:* articles in newspapers, magazines and jls. *Recreations:* gardening, cricket, horse racing. *Address:* Downside Abbey, Stratton-on-the-Fosse, Radstock, Bath BA3 4RJ. *Clubs:* East India, Naval and Military; Emeriti, Ravens Cricket, Stratton Cricket (Pres., 1995–2003).

SUTCH, Ven. David; *see* Sutch, Ven. C. D.

SUTCLIFFE, Allan; a Director, British Gas plc, 1986–91; *b* 30 Jan. 1936; *s* of Bertie and May Sutcliffe; *m* 1983, Pauline, *d* of Mark and Lilian Abrahams; one *s* one *d* by a previous marr. *Educ:* Neath Grammar Sch.; University Coll. London (LLB). FCMA. Graduate trainee, BR, 1957–60; various positions in Finance in Western, Eastern and Southern Regions and at HQ, BR, 1960–70; Wales Gas Board: Chief Accountant, 1970; Dir of Finance, 1972; Deputy Chairman: British Gas W Midlands, 1980; British Gas N Thames, 1983; Man. Dir, Finance, British Gas plc, 1986. Freeman, City of London, 1985. *Publications:* articles on Pepper's Ghost and the Birmingham stage and Dickens in the music hall. *Recreations:* music, pre-1940 entertainment based on Dickens's writings. *Address:* 106 Kenilworth Road, Knowle, Solihull, W Midlands B93 0JD. *T:* (01564) 771538. *Club:* Royal Automobile.

SUTCLIFFE, Andrea Mary; Chief Inspector of Adult Social Care, Care Quality Commission, since 2013; *b* Bradford, 22 March 1964; *d* of David and Rita Sutcliffe; *m* 2008, David Stout. *Educ:* Longfield Sch., Darlington; Queen Elizabeth Sixth Form Coll., Darlington; London Sch. of Econs (BA Hons Medieval and Modern Hist. 1985). Finance Manager, Tower Hamlets HA, 1986–89; Contracting and Policy Manager, Bloomsbury and Islington HA, 1989–92; General Manager: Camden and Islington Community Health Services NHS Trust, 1992–95; St George's Healthcare NHS Trust, 1995–99; Asst Dir, Social Services, London Bor. of Camden, 1999–2000; Planning and Resources Dir, 2000–04, Dep. Chief Exec., 2004–07, NICE; Chief Exec., Appointments Commn, 2007–12; Chief Exec., Social Care Inst. for Excellence, 2012–13. Mem., Audit Commn, 2013–15. *Recreations:* friends and family, quirky films, reading, hiking, Sunderland FC. *Address:* Care Quality Commission, Finsbury Tower, 103–105 Bunhill Row, EC1Y 8TG.

SUTCLIFFE, Andrew Harold Wentworth; QC 2001; a Recorder, since 2000; a Deputy High Court Judge, since 2004; *b* 7 Sept. 1960; *s* of John Harold Vick Sutcliffe, *qv*; *m* 1988, Emma Elisabeth Stirling; three *d* (one *s* decd). *Educ:* Winchester Coll.; Worcester Coll., Oxford (MA). Pres., Oxford Union Soc., 1981. 2nd Lieut, Royal Scots Dragoon Guards, 1978–79. Called to the Bar, Inner Temple, 1983; in practice as barrister, 1983–, specialising in commercial law, esp. banking and entertainment. Chm., Great Fosters (1931) Ltd, 2009–. Mem., Special Project Gp, Duke of Edinburgh's Award, 1986–96. Mem., Cttee, Moorland Assoc., 1996–; Chm., Kildale Agricl and Horticultural Show Cttee, 1988–; Vice Pres., Black Face Sheep Breeders' Assoc., 1989–. Liveryman, Co. of Fishmongers, 1996–. Gov., Fox Primary Sch., Kensington, 1993–. Trustee, Zebra Housing Assoc., 1988–. *Recreations:* walking, bees, listening to music. *Address:* Kildale Hall, Whitby, Yorks YO21 2RQ; 3 Verulam Buildings, Gray's Inn, WC1R 5NT. *T:* (020) 7831 8441. *Clubs:* MCC; Kildale Cricket (Pres.).

SUTCLIFFE, Anne-Marie Christine Elizabeth; Headmistress, Thorpe House School, 2008–10; *b* 24 Jan. 1949; *d* of late Dr Norman Mutton and of Mary Mutton (*née* Dobson); *m* 1970, Victor Herbert Sutcliffe; one *s* one *d*. *Educ:* convent schs; Girton Coll., Cambridge (BA 1st cl. Hons History tripos). Teacher, Stroud Girls' High Sch., 1975–79; Head of History Department: Bishop Thomas Grant Sch., 1979–81; Ursuline Convent High Sch., 1981–86; organising confs, servicing cttees, etc, CAFOD, Council on Christian Approaches to Defence and Disarmament, 1986–88; Teacher, 1988–95, Head of History, 1991–95, St Paul's Girls' Sch.; Dep. Head, Channing Sch., 1995–98; Headmistress, Emanuel Sch., 1998–2004. Mem. Cttee, HMC, 2002–03. Ind. Chm., Cranial Forum, 2004–07. Governor: King's Hse Sch., Richmond, 1999–2004; Hampton Sch., Middx, 2004–10. *Recreations:* theatre, opera, travel, history. *Address:* Mulberry Coach House, The Green, East Rudham, King's Lynn, Norfolk PE31 8RD. *T:* (01485) 528463.

SUTCLIFFE, Gerard; *b* 13 May 1953; *s* of Henry and Margaret Sutcliffe; *m* 1972, Maria Holgate; three *s*. *Educ:* Cardinal Hinsley Grammar Sch.; Bradford Coll. Salesperson, Brown Muff dept store, 1969–71; display advertising clerk, Bradford Telegraph and Argus, 1971–75; Field Printers, 1975–80; Dep. Sec., SOGAT, subseq. GPMU, 1980–94. Bradford Metropolitan District Council: Councillor, 1982–88 and 1990–94; Leader, 1992–94. MP (Lab) Bradford S, June 1994–2015. PPS to Chief Sec., HM Treasury, 1998, to Sec. of State for Trade and Industry, 1998–99; an Asst Govt Whip, 1999–2001; Vice Chamberlain, HM Household, 2001–03; Parly Under-Sec. of State, DTI, 2003–06, Home Office, 2006–07, Ministry of Justice, 2007, DCMS, 2007–10. Chm., Parly Football Team. *Recreations:* sport, music, politics.

SUTCLIFFE, James Harry, FIA; Chairman, Sun Life Financial (Canada), since 2011 (non-executive Director, since 2009); *b* 20 April 1956; *s* of Robert William Sutcliffe and Margaret Sutcliffe; *m* 1977, Esther Sharon Pincus; two *s* (twins). *Educ:* Univ. of Cape Town (BSc). FIA 1979. Chief Operating Officer, Jackson Nat. Life, 1989–92; Chief Exec., Prudential UK plc, 1995–97; Dep. Chm., Liberty Internat., 1998–99; Chief Exec., Life, 2000–01; Gp Chief Exec., Old Mutual plc, 2001–08. Non-executive Director: Lonmin plc, 2007– (Sen. Ind. Dir, 2012–); Liberty Life (S Africa), 2009–; Vice Chm., Gunn Agri Partners, 2014–. Dir, Financial Reporting Council, 2009–15; Chm., Codes and Standards Cttee, 2009–15. Sen. Advr, CVC Capital Partners, 2009–. *Recreations:* golf, bridge. *E:* Jim.Sutcliffe1@gmail.com. *Clubs:* Pinner Hill Golf; Clovelly Golf (S Africa).

SUTCLIFFE, James Thomas, (Tom); critic, dramaturg and author; *b* 4 June 1943; *s* of Lt-Comdr James Denis Sutcliffe, OBE, RN and Rosamund Frances Sutcliffe, *d* of Major T. E. G. Swayne; *m* 1973, Meredith Frances Oakes, playwright, librettist, music critic, translator; one *s* one *d*. *Educ:* Prebendal Sch., Chichester; Hurstpierpoint Coll.; Magdalen Coll., Oxford (MA English 1967). English Teacher, Central Tutorial Sch. for Young Musicians, 1964–65; Manager, Musica Reservata, 1965–69; concert perfs with Musica Reservata, Schola Polyphonica, Pro Cantione Antiqua, Concentus Musicus, Vienna, 1965–70; opera début, Ottone in L'incoronazione di Poppea, Landestheater, Darmstadt, 1970; Countertenor Lay Clerk, Westminster Cathedral, 1966–70; Editor, Music and Musicians, 1970–73; Sub-Editor, Features, Dep. Arts Editor, opera & music critic, and feature writer, Dep. Obituaries Editor, The Guardian, 1973–96; opera, theatre and music critic, Vogue, 1975–87; Opera Critic, Evening Standard, 1996–2002; dramaturg on productions: Turn of the Screw, Brussels, 1998; Macbeth, Brussels, 2001; Ernest Bloch's Macbeth, Vienna, 2003; Don Giovanni, Flammen, Vienna, 2006. Chm., music sect., 1999–2009, Pres., 2010–12, Critics' Circle. Mem., Gen. Synod, C of E, 1990–2015; Member: Exec. Cttee, Affirming Catholicism, 1996–2002; Cathedrals Fabric Commn for England, 2002–11. Leverhulme Fellow, 1991, 2005; Fellow, Rose Bruford Coll., 2006. *Publications:* (contrib.) Theatre 71, 1972, Theatre 72, 1973, and Theatre 74, 1975; (ed) Tracts for our Times, 1983; (ed) In Vitro Veritas, 1984; Believing in Opera, 1996; (ed) The Faber Book of Opera, 2000; (contrib.) The Cambridge Companion to Twentieth-Century Opera, 2005; contrib. San Francisco Opera, Glyndebourne, Brussels, Naples and Vienna opera progs, and in Music and Musicians, Opera News, Musical Times, Opera Now, The Spectator, New Statesman, Prospect, The Times, The Guardian, Wall Street Journal, Financial Times, Opern Welt, New Directions, Le Monde, London Mag., Jl British Cinema and TV. *Address:* 12 Polworth Road, Streatham, SW16 2EU. *T:* (020) 8677 5849. *E:* tomsutcliffe@email.msn.com.

SUTCLIFFE, John Harold Vick, CBE 1994; DL; Chairman, Great Fosters (1931) Ltd, 1958–2009; *b* 30 April 1931; *o s* of late Sir Harold Sutcliffe and Emily Theodora Cochrane; *m* 1st, 1959, Cecilia Mary (*d* 1998), *e d* of Ralph Meredyth Turton; three *s* one *d*; 2nd, 2001, Katherine Fox. *Educ:* Winchester Coll.; New Coll., Oxford (MA). 2nd Lieut RA, 1950–51. Called to Bar, Inner Temple, 1956; practised until 1960, Midland Circuit. Chm., North Housing Association Ltd, 1985–94 (Dir, 1977–86); Director: Allied Investors Trusts Ltd, 1958–69; Norton Junction Sand & Gravel Ltd, 1958–64; Tyne Tees Waste Disposal Ltd, 1964–71. Estate management, Kildale, 1965–95. Member: Housing Corp., 1982–88; Bd, Teesside Develt Corp., 1987–98. Mem. Bd, Civic Trust, 1989–93; Chairman: Northern Heritage Trust, 1981–89; NE Civic Trust, 1989–93 (Vice-Chm., 1977–89). Contested (C): Oldham West, 1959; Chorley, Lancs, 1964; Middlesbrough West, 1966. MP (C) Middlesbrough W, 1970–Feb. 1974. Contested (C) Teesside Thornaby, Oct. 1974. Chairman: Country Endeavour, 1983–88; Bow Street Project, Guisborough, 1988–2008; Pres., N Yorks Youth Clubs, 1984–93 (Chm., 1966–70); Mem., N Yorks Moors Nat. Park Cttee, 1982–88. DL Cleveland, 1983–96, N Yorks, 1996–; High Sheriff, N Yorks, 1987–88. *Recreations:* woodlands, gardening, travel. *Address:* 8 Meadow Road, SW8 1QB. *T:* (020) 7582 9806.

See also A. H. W. Sutcliffe.

SUTCLIFFE, Kevin Anthony; Head of News Programming (EU), Vice Media Group, since 2013; *b* Blackpool, 6 Sept. 1960; *s* of Donald and June Sutcliffe; *m* 2006, Anne-Marie Huby; one *s* one *d*. *Educ:* Arnold Sch., Blackpool; Blackpool Technical Coll.; Hornsey Coll. of Art, London (BA Hons Fine Art). Freelance journalist, 1983–86; Researcher, Watchdog, Asst Prod., Breakfast Time, Prod., Newsnight, BBC TV, 1986–89; Producer: Hard News, Channel 4 TV, 1990; The Late Show, BBC Music and Arts, 1991; Taking Liberties, BBC Documentaries, 1992–94; Public Eye, 1994, Panorama, 1995–99, BBC News and Current Affairs; Exec. Prod., Louis Theroux, MacIntyre Investigates, Anna in Wonderland, BBC Documentaries, 1999–2001; Channel 4 Television: Ed., Dispatches, 2002–12; Commissioning Ed., 2004–06, Dep. Head, 2006–12, News and Current Affairs. *T:* 07903 328171. *E:* kevin.sutcliffe@vice.com, kevinsutcliffekevin@gmail.com.

SUTCLIFFE, Her Honour Linda, (Mrs P. B. Walker); a Circuit Judge, 1993–2006; *b* 2 Dec. 1946; *d* of James Loftus Woodward and Florence Woodward; *m* 1st, 1968 (marr. diss. 1979); 2nd, 1987, Peter Brian Walker. *Educ:* Eccles Grammar Sch.; LSE (LLB Hons 1968); Open Univ. (Dip. French 2007). Called to the Bar, Gray's Inn, 1975; Lectr in Law, Univ. of Sheffield, 1968–76, part-time 1976–81; in practice at the Bar, 1976–93; an Asst Recorder, 1987–91; a Recorder, 1991–93. Part-time Chm., Industrial Tribunals, 1983–92. *Recreations:* music, gardening.

SUTCLIFFE, Margaret Helen; *see* O'Farrell, M. H.

SUTCLIFFE, Tom; *see* Sutcliffe, J. T.

SUTER, Dame Helen Anne; *see* Alexander, Dame H. A.

SUTER, Michael; solicitor in private practice, 1992–2002; Chief Executive, Shropshire County Council, 1987–92; *b* 21 Jan. 1944; *s* of Robert and Rose Suter; *m* 1963, Sandra Harrison; two *s*. *Educ:* Liverpool Collegiate Sch.; Liverpool Univ. (LLB). Solicitor. Dep. Chief Exec., Notts CC, 1980–87. *Recreations:* music, gardening, watching old Hollywood films, visiting Spain. *Address:* 1 Creamore Corner, Wem, Shrewsbury, Shropshire SY4 5YB.

SUTHERELL, Maj.-Gen. John Christopher Blake, CB 2002; CBE 1993 (OBE 1990; MBE 1982); DL; General Secretary (Chief Executive), Officers' Association, 2003–13; *b* 23 Oct. 1947; *s* of Ernest John and Vera Louise Sutherell; *m* 1st, 1979, Stephanie Glover (*d* 1983); 2nd, 1987, Amanda Maxwell-Hudson; one *d*. *Educ:* Christ's Hosp., Horsham; Durham Univ. (BA Hons Geog. 1968); Staff Coll., Camberley. Commnd Royal Anglian Regt, 1968; SO1 DS Staff Coll., 1984–87; CO, 1st Bn, Royal Anglian Regt, 1987–90; Divl Col, Staff Coll., 1990; Comdr, 8th Inf. Bde, 1990–92; Mem., RCDS, 1993; Dep. Mil. Sec. (A), 1994–96; DSF, 1996–99; Comdt, RMCS, 1999–2002. Col Comdt, Queen's Div., 1999–2002; Col, Royal Anglian Regt, 2002–07 (Dep. Col, 1997–2002). Pres., Royal Norfolk Regt Assoc., 2000–12. Mem. Council, Army Records Soc., 2001–05 and 2006–10 and 2011–. Member: Exec. Cttee, COBSEO, 2006–13; British Commn for Mil. Hist., 2014–. Governor: Heathfield Sch., Ascot, 2004–06; Heathfield St Mary's Sch., Ascot, 2006–09. Church Warden, St Peter's, Yoxford, 2009–. Mem., Yoxford Parish Council, 2015–. DL Suffolk, 2006. *Recreations:* family, military history, gardening.

SUTHERLAND, family name of **Countess of Sutherland** and **Baron Sutherland of Houndwood**.

SUTHERLAND, 7th Duke of, *cr* 1833; **Francis Ronald Egerton;** Bt 1620; Baron Gower 1703; Earl Gower, Viscount Trentham 1746; Marquis of Stafford 1786; Viscount Brackley and Earl of Ellesmere 1846; *b* 18 Feb. 1940; *o s* of Cyril Reginald Egerton and Mary, *d* of Rt Hon. Sir Ronald Hugh Campbell, GCMG; *S* cousin, 2000; *m* 1974, Victoria Mary, twin *d* of Maj.-Gen. Edward Alexander Wilmot Williams, CB, CBE, MC; two *s*. *Educ:* Eton; RAC Cirencester. *Heir:* *s* Marquis of Stafford, *qv*. *Address:* Mertoun, St Boswells, Melrose, Roxburghshire TD6 0EA.

SUTHERLAND, Countess of (24th in line), *cr* (*c*) 1235; **Elizabeth Millicent Sutherland;** Lady Strathnaver (*c*) 1235; Chief of Clan Sutherland; *b* 30 March 1921; *oc* of Lord Alistair St Clair Sutherland-Leveson-Gower, MC (*d* 1921; 2nd *s* of 4th Duke), and Hélène Elizabeth (*née* Demarest, later Baroness Osten Driesen) (*d* 1931); *niece* of 5th Duke of Sutherland, KT, PC; *S* (to uncle's Earldom of Sutherland and Lordship of Strathnaver), 1963; *m* 1946, Charles Noel Janson (DL, 1959–93), late Welsh Guards (*d* 2006); two *s* one *d* (and one *s* decd). *Educ:* Queen's College, Harley Street, W1, and abroad. Land Army, 1939–41; Laboratory Technician: Raigmore Hospital, Inverness, 1941–43; St Thomas' Hospital, SE1, 1943–45. Chm., Dunrobin Castle Ltd. *Recreations:* reading, swimming. *Heir:* *e s* Lord Strathnaver, *qv*. *Address:* Dunrobin Castle, Sutherland; House of Tongue, by Lairg, Sutherland; 39 Edwardes Square, W8 6HH.

SUTHERLAND OF HOUNDWOOD, Baron *cr* 2001 (Life Peer), of Houndwood in the Scottish Borders; **Stewart Ross Sutherland,** KT 2002; Kt 1995; FBA 1992; FRSE; President, Royal Society of Edinburgh, 2002–05; *b* 25 Feb. 1941; *s* of late George A. C. Sutherland and of Ethel (*née* Masson); *m* 1964, Sheena Robertson; one *s* two *d*. *Educ:* Woodside Sch.; Robert Gordon's Coll.; Univ. of Aberdeen (MA); Corpus Christi Coll.,

Cambridge (Hon. Schol.; MA; Hon. Fellow, 1989). FRSE 1995. Asst Lectr in Philosophy, UCNW, 1965; Lectr in Philosophy, 1968, Sen. Lectr, 1972, Reader, 1976, Univ. of Stirling; King's College London: Prof. of Hist. and Philos. of Religion, 1977–85, Titular Prof., 1985–94; Vice-Principal, 1981–85; Principal, 1985–90; FKC 1983; Vice-Chancellor, London Univ., 1990–94; Chief Inspector of Schools, 1992–94; Principal and Vice-Chancellor, Univ. of Edinburgh, 1994–2002; Provost, Gresham Coll., 2002–08; Pro-Chancellor, London Univ., 2006–08. Vis. Fellow, ANU, 1974; Gillespie Vis. Prof., Wooster Ohio, 1975. Lectures: Hope, Stirling, 1979; Ferguson, Manchester, 1982; Wilde, Oxford, 1981–84; Boutwood, Cambridge, 1990; F. D. Maurice, KCL, 1993; Drummond, Stirling, 1993; St George's, Windsor, 1993; Debrabant, Southampton, 1994; Ballard Matthews, Bangor, 1994; Cook, St Andrews and Oxford, 1995; Sir Robert Menzies, Melbourne, 1995; T. M. Knox, St Andrews, 2011; Gifford, Edinburgh, 2011. Non-executive Director: NHP, 2001–05; Quarry Products Assoc., 2002–05; Chairman: YTL Education (UK), 2003–; FrogTrade, 2013–. Chairman: British Acad. Postgrad. Studentships Cttee, 1987–95; Royal Inst. of Philosophy, 1988–2006; London Conf. on Overseas Students, 1989–94; Cttee on Appeals Criteria and Procedure (Scotland), 1994–96; Associated Bd of Royal Schs of Music, 2006–; Vice-Chm., CVCP, 1989–92. Member: C of E Bd of Educn, 1980–84; Arts Sub-Cttee, UGC, 1983–85; City Parochial Foundn, 1988–90; Council for Sci. and Technology, 1993–2001; Humanities Res. Bd, Brit. Acad., 1994–95; UGC (Hong Kong), 1995–2003; HEFCE, 1996–2002; Ind. Inquiry into SATS Results, 2008; Chair, Chartered Inst. of Educnl Assessors, 2009–12. Chm., Royal Commn on Long Term Care of the Elderly, 1997–99; Mem., Ind. Review of Care for the Elderly in Scotland, 2007; Member: NW Thames RHA, 1992–94; N Thames RHA, 1994; Chair, Scottish Care, 2003–; Advr, English Community Care, 2004–. President: Soc. for the Study of Theology, 1985, 1986; Saltire Soc., 2002–05; Alzheimer Scotland, 2002–; David Hume Inst., 2005–08. Patron, Centre for Dementia, UCL, 2008–. Chm., Ethiopian Gemini Trust, 1987–92. Editor, Religious Studies, 1984–90; Member, Editorial Board: Scottish Jl of Religious Studies, 1980–95; Modern Theology, 1984–91. Associate Fellow, Warwick Univ., 1986–; Hon. Fellow: UCNW, 1990; Birkbeck Coll., London, 2004; Inst. of Educn, London Univ., 2004. FCP 1994. Hon. FRCGP 2004; Hon. FIA 2007. Hon. LHD: Wooster, Ohio, 1986; Commonwealth Univ. of Virginia, 1992; New York, 1996; Hon. LLD: Aberdeen, 1990; NUI, 1992; St Andrews, 2002; McGill, 2003; Hon. DLitt: Richmond Coll., 1995; Wales, 1996; Glasgow, 1999; Warwick, 2001; Queen Margaret UC, 2004; London, 2004; DUniv Stirling, 1993; Dr *hc*: Uppsala, 1995; Edinburgh, 2004; Hon. DEd: Robert Gordon, 2005; HK Inst. of Educn, 2005. Mem., Ct of Assts, Goldsmiths' Co., 2001– (Prime Warden, 2012–13); Hon. Mem., Merchant Co., Edinburgh, 2008. *Publications:* Atheism and the Rejection of God, 1977, 2nd edn 1980; (ed with B. L. Hebblethwaite) The Philosophical Frontiers of Christian Theology, 1983; God, Jesus and Belief, 1984; Faith and Ambiguity, 1984; (ed) The World's Religions, 1988; (ed with T. A. Roberts) Religion, Reason and the Self, 1989; articles in books and learned jls. *Recreations:* Tassie medallions, theatre, jazz. *Address:* House of Lords, SW1A 0PW. *E:* sutherlands@parliament.uk. *Club:* New (Edinburgh).

SUTHERLAND, Rt Hon. Lord; Ranald Iain Sutherland; PC 2000; a Senator of the College of Justice in Scotland, 1985–2001; *b* 23 Jan. 1932; *s* of J. W. and A. K. Sutherland, Edinburgh; *m* 1964, Janice Mary, *d* of W. S. Miller, Edinburgh; two *s*. *Educ:* Edinburgh Academy; Edinburgh University (MA 1951, LLB 1953). Admitted to Faculty of Advocates, 1956; QC (Scot.) 1969. Advocate Depute, 1962–64, 1971–77; Standing Junior Counsel to Min. of Defence (Army Dept), 1964–69. Mem., Criminal Injuries Compensation Bd, 1977–85. Surveillance Comr, 2001–10. Justice of Appeal, Botswana, 2002–05. *Recreations:* sailing, shooting. *Address:* 1/5 The Cedars, Edinburgh EH13 0PL. *T:* (0131) 667 5280. *Club:* New (Edinburgh).

SUTHERLAND, Alan David Alexander; Chief Executive, Water Industry Commission for Scotland, since 2005 (Water Industry Commissioner for Scotland, 1999–2005); *b* Glasgow, 8 April 1962; *s* of George and Kathleen Sutherland; *m* 1994, Olga Krasnorylkina; one *s* one *d*. *Educ:* Univ. of St Andrews (MA Hons Mod. Russian Studies 1984); Univ. of Pennsylvania (MBA 1993; MA 1993). Mgt trainee, Lloyds Bank, London, 1984; Analyst, Savory Milln & Co., London, 1985; Analyst, 1986–88, Manager, 1988–92, Robert Fleming and Co., London; Consultant, 1992–95, Team Leader, 1995–97, Bain & Co., Moscow, London and Kiev; Man. Dir, Wolverine Russia Ltd, and Gen. Dir, Wolverine CIS, Moscow and Grand Rapids, Mich, 1997–99. Mem., NI Govt Panel of Experts providing advice on reform of water industry in NI, 2001; Advr to Special Secretariat for Water, Greece, under auspices of EU Task Force for Greece, 2014–. Mem., Governing Cttee, UNESCO Centre for Water Law and Policy, Univ. of Dundee, 2008–. Beesley Lect., RA, 2006. *Recreations:* theatre, fine restaurants, family trips to Walt Disney World in Florida. *Address:* 2 Northbank Farm Steadings, Strathkinness High Road, St Andrews, Fife KY16 9TZ. *T:* (01334) 473535, *Fax:* (office) (01786) 462018. *E:* alan.sutherland@watercommission.co.uk, Alan@northbankfarmsteadings.freeserve.co.uk.

SUTHERLAND, Catherine Elizabeth; *see* West, C. E.

SUTHERLAND, Colin John MacLean; *see* Carloway, Rt Hon. Lord.

SUTHERLAND, Duncan; Chairman, Sigma InPartnership Ltd, since 2011; *b* Glasgow, 2 Dec. 1951; *s* of Robert MacKay Sutherland and Margaret Sutherland. *Educ:* Glasgow Sch. of Art (Dip. Town and Country Planning 1976). Planner, Lobban and Mollineux Partnership, Dingwall, 1976–78; Planning Officer, Borders Regl Council, 1978–79; Sen. Planning Officer, 1979–84, Hd of Tourism, 1984–86, Lancs CC; Hd, Implementation, English Tourist Bd, 1986–89; Dir, Inner City Enterprises plc, 1989–92; Dir, City Develt, Coventry CC, 1992–97; Chief Exec., EDI Gp, Edinburgh, 1997–2000; Founder Dir, InPartnership Ltd, 2000–11; Dir, Regeneration, Sigma Capital Gp, 2012–. Non-executive Director: British Waterways Bd, 2006–12; Scottish Canals Bd, 2012–14; HS2 Ltd, 2012–; First Choice Homes, Oldham, 2013–. Dir, Assoc. of Town Centre Mgt, 1995–2002. Director: Cockburn Conservation Trust, 1998–2003; South Bank Sinfonia, 2013–. *Recreations:* music, walking, travel, France, historic cars, buildings and architecture. *Address:* Sigma Inpartnership Ltd, Oxford Place, 61 Oxford Street, Manchester M1 6EQ. *E:* duncanws@me.com.

SUTHERLAND, Euan Ross, CB 1993; Parliamentary Counsel, 1989–2003; *b* 24 Nov. 1943; *s* of Dr Alister Sutherland and Margaret Sutherland; *m* 1st, 1967, Katharine Mary Jenkins, *qv* (marr. diss. 1995); one *s* one *d*; 2nd, 2002, Mary Anne Kenyon. *Educ:* Kingswood Sch., Bath; Balliol Coll., Oxford (BA Hist.). Called to the Bar, Inner Temple, 1969; Office of the Parliamentary Counsel, 1974–2003; seconded to: Govt of Solomon Is, 1979–81; Law Commn, 1986–88. Director: InSpire, St Peter's, Walworth, 2003–; Walter Carrington Educnl Trust, 2010–12. Mem., Ind. Monitoring Bd, HM Prison, Norwich, 2008–09. *Recreations:* choral music, hill-walking, gardening, wildlife, photography, built environment. *Address:* 57 Sutherland Square, SE17 3EL.

SUTHERLAND, Prof. Grant Robert, AC 1998; FRS 1996; FAA; Emeritus Geneticist, Women's and Children's Hospital, Adelaide, since 2007 (WCH Foundation Research Fellow, 2002–07); Affiliate Professor, Department of Paediatrics, University of Adelaide, since 1991; *b* 2 June 1945; *s* of John Sutherland and Hazel Wilson Mason McClelland; *m* 1979, Elizabeth Dougan; one *s* one *d*. *Educ:* Numurkah High Sch.; Univ. of Melbourne (BSc 1967; MSc 1971); Univ. of Edinburgh (PhD 1974; DSc 1984). FAA 1998. Cytogeneticist, Mental Health Authy, Melbourne, 1967; Cytogeneticist i/c, Royal Hosp. for Sick Children, Edinburgh, 1971; Dir, Dept of Cytogenetics and Molecular Genetics, Women's and Children's Hosp., Adelaide, 1975–2002. Internat. Res. Scholar, Howard Hughes Med. Inst., Maryland, 1993–97. President: Human Genetics Soc. of Australasia, 1989–91; Human Genome Orgn, 1996–97. Hon. FRCPA 1994; Hon. Mem., Eur. Cytogeneticists Assoc., 2005. Hon. MD Adelaide, 2013. Australia Prize in Molecular Genetics (jtly), 1998; Thomson ISI Aust. Citation Laureate, 2004. *Publications:* (with F. Hecht) Fragile Sites on Human Chromosomes, 1985; (with R. J. M. Gardner) Chromosome Abnormalities and Genetic Counselling, 1989, 4th edn 2011; over 480 papers in sci. and med. jls. *Recreations:* reading, gardening. *Address:* Women's and Children's Hospital, Adelaide, SA 5006, Australia. *T:* (8) 81617284. *E:* grant.sutherland@adelaide.edu.au; PO Box 1635, Victor Harbor, SA 5211, Australia. *T:* (8) 75163121.

SUTHERLAND, Dr Ian Boyd; Senior Administrative Medical Officer, South Western Regional Hospital Board, 1970–73; Regional Medical Officer, South Western Regional Health Authority, 1973–80; *b* 19 Oct. 1926; *s* of William Sutherland and Grace Alexandra Campbell; *m* 1950, Charlotte Winifred Cordin; two *d*. *Educ:* Bradford Grammar Sch.; Edinburgh Univ. MB, ChB; FRCPE, FFCM, DPH. Medical Officer, RAF, 1950–52; Asst MOH, Counties of Roxburgh and Selkirk, 1953–55; Dep. MOH, County and Borough of Inverness, 1955–59; Dep. County MOH, Oxfordshire CC, 1959–60; Asst SMO, Leeds Regional Hosp. Bd, 1960–63; Dep. Sen. Admin. MO, SW Regl Hosp. Bd, 1963–70; Community Medicine Specialist, Lothian Health Bd, 1980–86. Research Fellow, Dept of Clin. Surgery, Univ. of Edinburgh, 1986–88. *Recreations:* reading, art. *Address:* 8 Chesterfield Road, Eastbourne, E Sussex BN20 7NU.

SUTHERLAND, John Alexander Muir; Chief Executive, Celtic Films Ltd, since 1986; *b* 5 April 1933; *m* 1970, Mercedes Gonzalez; two *s*. *Educ:* India; Trinity Coll., Glenalmond; Hertford Coll., Oxford (MA). 2nd Lieut, HLI, 1952–53. Economist, Fed. Govt of Nigeria, 1957–58; film production, Spain and Portugal, 1958–62; Head of Presentation and Programme Planning, Border TV, 1963–66; Programme Co-Ordinator: ABC TV, 1966–68; Thames TV, 1968–72; Controller of Programme Sales, Thames TV, 1973–74; Man. Dir, 1975–82, Dep. Chm., 1982–86, Thames TV Internat.; Dir of Programmes, Thames TV, 1982–86. Dir, Border TV, 1986–. *Productions include:* The Saint (TV), 1989; The Monk (film), 1990; Red Fox (TV), 1991; Sharpe (TV films), 1992–96; Kiszko (TV film), 1998; Girl from Rio (film), 2000; Sharpe's Challenge (TV film), 2005; Sharpe's Peril, 2008. *Address:* Celtic Films Entertainment Ltd, 1st Floor, 24/25 Bond Street, W1S 2RR.

SUTHERLAND, Prof. John Andrew, PhD; FRSL; Lord Northcliffe Professor of Modern English Literature, University College London, 1992–2004, now Emeritus; *b* 9 Oct. 1938; *s* of Jack Sutherland and Elizabeth (*née* Salter); *m* 1st, 1967, Guilland Watt (marr. diss. 2005); one *s*; 2nd, 2005, Sarah Lee. *Educ:* Colchester Royal Grammar Sch.; Leicester Univ. (BA 1964; MA 1966); Edinburgh Univ. (PhD 1973). FRSL 1991. Nat. Service, 2nd Lieut, Suffolk Regt, 1958–60. Lectr in English, Univ. of Edinburgh, 1965–72; Lectr, then Reader in English, UCL, 1972–84, Fellow, 2004; Prof. of English, CIT, 1984–92. Hon. DLitt: Leicester, 1998; Surrey, 2002. *Publications:* Thackeray at Work, 1974; Victorian Novelists and Publishers, 1976; Fiction and the Fiction Industry, 1978; Bestsellers, 1980; Offensive Literature, 1982; The Longman Companion to Victorian Fiction, 1989; Mrs Humphry Ward, 1992; The Life of Walter Scott: a critical biography, 1995; Victorian Fiction: writers, publishers, readers, 1995; (ed) The Oxford Book of English Love Stories, 1996; Is Heathcliff a Murderer?, 1996; Can Jane Eyre Be Happy?, 1997; Who Betrays Elizabeth Bennet?, 1999; Last Drink to LA, 2001; Reading the Decades, 2002 (televised, 2002); Stephen Spender, 2004; How to Read a Novel: a user's guide, 2006; The Boy Who Loved Books: a memoir, 2007; Bestsellers: a very short introduction, 2007; Curiosities of Literature: a book-lover's anthology of literary erudition, 2008; Magic Moments: life-changing encounters with books, film, music (memoir), 2008; (with Stephen Fender) Love, Death, Sex and Words, 2010; Fifty Literature Ideas, 2010; Lives of the Novelists, 2011; A Little History of Literature, 2013; Jumbo: the unauthorised biography of a Victorian sensation, 2014. *Recreation:* walking. *Address:* Department of English, University College London, Gower Street, WC1E 6BT. *T:* (020) 7679 2000, 07792 587695.

SUTHERLAND, John Brewer; (3rd Bt *cr* 1921, but does not use the title); *b* 19 Oct. 1931; *s* of Sir (Benjamin) Ivan Sutherland, 2nd Bt, and Marjorie Constance Daniel (*d* 1980), *yr d* of Frederic William Brewer, OBE; *S* father, 1980; *m* 1st, 1958, Alice Muireall (*d* 1984), *d* of late W. Stamford Henderson, Kelso; three *s* one *d*; 2nd, 1988, Heather, *d* of late David A. Gray, Chester-le-Street. *Educ:* Sedbergh; St Catharine's Coll., Cambridge. *Heir:* *s* Peter William Sutherland [*b* 18 May 1963; *m* 1988, Suzanna Mary, *d* of R. M. Gledson; one *s* two *d*].

SUTHERLAND, Prof. Kathryn, DPhil; Professor of Bibliography and Textual Criticism, University of Oxford, since 2002; Professorial Fellow, St Anne's College, Oxford, since 1996; *b* 7 July 1950; *d* of Ian Donald Sutherland and Joyce Sutherland (*née* Bartaby). *Educ:* Bedford Coll., Univ. of London (BA 1971); Somerville Coll., Oxford (DPhil 1978; MA 1996). Lectr in English Literature, Univ. of Manchester, 1975–93; Prof. of Modern English Literature, Univ. of Nottingham, 1993–96; Reader in Bibliography and Textual Criticism, 1996–2002. Project Dir and Principal Investigator, Jane Austen's Fiction Manuscripts, 2006–10 (digital edition, 2010). Trustee, Jane Austen's House Mus. and Meml Trust, Chawton, Hampshire, 2013–. *Publications:* Adam Smith: interdisciplinary essays, 1995; Electronic Text: method and theory, 1997; Women Prose Writers 1780–1830, 1998; Jane Austen's Textual Lives: from Aeschylus to Bollywood, 2005; Transferred Illusions: digital technology and the forms of print, 2009; Jane Austen's Fiction Manuscripts, 4 vols, 2016; critical edns; contrib. books and learned jls. *Recreation:* gardening. *Address:* St Anne's College, Oxford OX2 6HS. *T:* (01865) 274893.

SUTHERLAND, Lorraine; Editor, Official Report (Hansard), since 2005; *b* 11 Jan. 1958; *d* of Bunty Sutherland (now Potts); *m* 1982, Robert Kremer. *Educ:* Lybster Primary Sch.; Wick High Sch.; Aberdeen Coll. of Commerce. Official Report (Hansard): Principal Asst Editor, 1994–97; Dep. Editor, 1997–2005. *Recreations:* travelling, planning travel, tennis, cinema, theatre, dreaming on trains. *Address:* Official Report, Department of Chamber and Committee Services, House of Commons, SW1A 0AA. *T:* (020) 7219 3388. *E:* sutherlandl@parliament.uk.

SUTHERLAND, Martin Conrad; Chief Executive Officer, De La Rue plc, since 2014; *b* Aylesbury, 8 Dec. 1968; *s* of Edmond Mackintosh Sutherland and Margaret Hilary Sutherland; *m* Sally Jennifer; two *c*. *Educ:* N Bromsgrove High Sch.; New Coll., Oxford (MA Physics); University Coll. London (MSc Remote Sensing). Andersen Consulting, 1990–92; British Telecom, 1995–96; Detica Ltd, 1996–2008; BAE Systems plc, 2008–14. *Recreations:* cycling, running, golf. *Address:* De La Rue plc, De La Rue House, Jays Close, Basingstoke, Hants RG22 4BS.

SUTHERLAND, Muir; *see* Sutherland, J. A. M.

SUTHERLAND, Peter Denis, Hon. KCMG 2004; SC; non-executive Chairman: Goldman Sachs International, 1995–2015; BP (formerly BP Amoco), 1998–2009 (Chairman, The British Petroleum Co. plc, 1997–98); Special Representative of the UN Secretary-General for Migration and Development, since 2006; President, International Catholic Migration Commission, since 2015; *b* 25 April 1946; *s* of W. G. Sutherland and Barbara Sutherland (*née* Nealon); *m* 1971, Maria Del Pilar Cabria Valcarcel; two *s* one *d*. *Educ:* Gonzaga Coll., Dublin; University Coll. Dublin (BCL). Called to Bar: King's Inns, 1968; Middle Temple, 1976, Bencher, 1981 (Hon. Bencher, 2002); Attorney of New York Bar, 1981; Attorney and Counsellor of Supreme Court of USA, 1986. Tutor in Law, University Coll., Dublin, 1968–71; practising member of Irish Bar, 1968–81, and 1982; Senior Counsel 1980; Attorney General of Ireland, June 1981–Feb. 1982 and Dec. 1982–Dec. 1984; Mem. Council of State,

1981–82 and 1982–84; Comr for Competition and Comr for Social Affairs and Educn, EEC, 1985–86, for Competition and Relns with European Parliament, 1986–88; Chm., Allied Irish Banks, 1989–93; Dir Gen., GATT, later WTO, 1993–95. Director: GPA, 1989–93; CRH plc, 1989–93; James Crean plc, 1989–93; Delta Air Lines Inc., 1990–93; Investor, 1995–2005; Telefonaktiebolaget LM Ericsson, 1996–2004; Royal Bank of Scotland, 2001–09; BW Gp Ltd, 2009–; Koç Hldg AS, 2009–; Mem., Allianz Supervisory Bd, 2010–. Chm., Consultative Bd of Dir Gen., WTO, 2003–05; Foundn Bd Mem., WEF; Consultor, Admin of Patrimony of Holy See, 2007–. Chm. (Europe), Trilateral Commn, 2001–. Pres., Federal Trust. Chairman: Bd of Govs, Eur. Inst. of Public Admin, 1991–96; Council and Ct of Govs, LSE, 2008–15; Pres., Bd of Regents, St Benet's Hall, Oxford, 2015–. Goodwill Ambassador, UNIDO, 2005. MRIA. Hon. Bencher, King's Inns, Dublin, 1995. Hon. LLD: St Louis, 1986; NUI, 1990; Dublin City, 1991; Holy Cross, Mass, 1994; Bath, 1995; Suffolk, USA, 1995; Open, 1995; TCD, 1996; Reading, 1997; Nottingham, 1999; Exeter, 2000; QUB, 2003; Koç, Turkey, 2004; Notre Dame, 2004; Sussex, 2008. Gold Medal, Eur. Parlt, 1988; NZ Commemorative Medal, 1990; David Rockefeller Internat. Leadership Award, 1996; Gold Medal, Royal Dublin Soc., 1996; Eur. Round Table of Industrialists, 2009. KCSG 2008. Grand Cross: King Leopold II (Belgium), 1989; Order of Infante Dom Henrique (Portugal), 1998; Grand Cross of Civil Merit (Spain), 1989; Chevalier, Légion d'Honneur (France), 1993; Comdr, Order of Ouissam Alaouite (Morocco), 1994; Order of Rio Branco (Brazil), 1996; Royal Order of Polar Star (Sweden), 2014. *Publications:* Premier Janvier 1993 ce qui va changer en Europe, 1988; contribs to law jls. *Recreations:* sports generally, reading. *Address:* c/o Goldman Sachs International, Peterborough Court, 133 Fleet Street, EC4A 2BB. *Clubs:* Garrick; Hibernian United Service, Fitzwilliam Lawn Tennis (Dublin); Lansdowne FC.

SUTHERLAND, Ranald Iain; *see* Sutherland, Rt Hon. Lord.

SUTHERLAND, Roderick Henry, (Rory); Vice Chairman and Executive Creative Director, OgilvyOne Worldwide, since 1998; Vice Chairman, Ogilvy & Mather UK (formerly Ogilvy Group), since 2005; *b* Usk, Monmouthshire, 12 Nov. 1965; *s* of James Alan Sutherland and late Florence Mary Sutherland (*née* Townsend); *m* 1989, Sophie Louisa Whitmore; two *d. Educ:* Haberdashers' Monmouth Sch.; Christ's Coll., Cambridge (BA 1987; MA). Joined Ogilvy & Mather Direct as grad. trainee, 1988; Copywriter, 1990–94; Head of Copy, 1994–97; Exec. Creative Dir, 1997–. Columnist, Spectator (Wiki Man), 2008–. Mem., Bd of Trustees, Rochester Cathedral, 2011–. Hon. Prof., Warwick Business Sch., 2012–. Mem., Credos Adv. Bd, Advertising Assoc., 2010–; Pres., Inst. of Practitioners in Advertising, 2009–11. FIPA 2008; FRSA. Hon. DLitt Brunel, 2012. *Recreations:* reading, gadgetry, contrarianism. *Address:* Ogilvy Group, 10 Cabot Square, E14 4GB. *T:* (020) 7345 3000. *E:* rory.sutherland@ogilvy.com. *Clubs:* Walbrook, Ivy.

SUTHERLAND, Prof. Rosamund Jane, PhD; Professor of Education, since 1996, University of Bristol (Head, Graduate School of Education, 2003–06); *b* 19 Jan. 1947; *d* of Percy and Joan Hatfield; *m* 1968, Ian Sutherland; one *s* one *d. Educ:* Monmouth Sch. for Girls; Univ. of Bristol (BSc); Hatfield Poly. (Cert Ed); Inst. of Educn, Univ. of London (PhD 1988). Programmer/Analyst, BAC, 1968–69; Res. Asst, Dept of Physiology, Univ. of Bristol, 1969–71; Tutor, Open Univ., 1975–83; Lectr, De Havilland Further Educn Coll., 1979–83; Lectr and Dir of Res. Projects, 1983–93, Sen. Lectr, 1993–96, Inst. of Educn, Univ. of London. Chm., Jt Mathematical Council of the UK, 2006–10 (Chm., Jt Mathematical Council and Royal Soc. Wkg Gp on Changes to Sch. Algebra, 1997 (report pub. 1997)). *Publications:* (with C. Hoyles) Logo Mathematics in the Classroom, 1989; (with L. Healy) Exploring Mathematics with Spreadsheets, 1990; (ed with J. Mason) Exploiting Mental Imagery with Computers in Mathematics Education, 1995; (with S. Pozzi) The Changing Mathematical Background of Undergraduate Engineers, 1995; (jtly) A Spreadsheet Approach to Maths for GNVQ Engineering, 1996; (ed jtly) Perspectives on School Algebra, 2000; (ed jtly) Learning and Teaching Where Worldviews Meet, 2003; (jtly) Children's Computing in the home (screenplay), 2003; Teaching for Learning Mathematics, 2006; (jtly) Improving Classroom Learning with ICT, 2009; Education and Social Justice in a Digital Age, 2013. *Recreations:* yachting, cycling, dining out, tango, grandchildren. *Address:* 8 Canynge Square, Clifton, Bristol BS8 3LA.

SUTHERLAND, Dame Veronica (Evelyn), DBE 1998; CMG 1988; HM Diplomatic Service, retired; President, Lucy Cavendish College, Cambridge University, 2001–08; *b* 25 April 1939; *d* of late Lt-Col Maurice George Beckett, KOYLI, and of Constance Mary Cavenagh-Mainwaring; *m* 1981, Alex James Sutherland. *Educ:* Royal Sch., Bath; London Univ. (BA); Southampton Univ. (MA); MA Cantab 2001. Joined HM Diplomatic Service, 1965; Second, later First Sec., Copenhagen, 1967–70; FCO, 1970–75; First Sec., New Delhi, 1975–78; FCO, 1978–80; Counsellor, 1981; Perm. UK Deleg. to UNESCO, 1981–84; Counsellor, FCO, 1984–87; Ambassador to Côte d'Ivoire, 1987–90; Asst Under-Sec. of State (Personnel), FCO, 1990–95; Ambassador to Republic of Ireland, 1995–99; Dep. Sec. Gen. (Econ. and Social Affairs), Commonwealth Secretariat, 1999–2001. Chm., Airey Neave Trust, 2000–11; Member: Exec. Cttee, British/Irish Assoc., 2002–13; Cttee, Elizabeth Nuffield Educnl Fund, 2005–08. Hon. LLD TCD, 1998. *Recreations:* theatre, painting (diploma, Society of Botanical Artists, 2010). *Address:* Summer Hill, Robin's Lane, Lolworth, Cambridge CB23 8HH. *Club:* Athenæum.

SUTHERLAND, Sir William (George MacKenzie), Kt 1988; QPM 1981; HM Chief Inspector of Constabulary for Scotland, 1996–98; *b* 12 Nov. 1933; *m* 1957, Jennie Abbott; two *d. Educ:* Inverness Technical High Sch. Cheshire Police, 1954–73; Surrey Police, 1973–75; Hertfordshire Police, 1975–79; Chief Constable: Bedfordshire, 1979–83; Lothian and Borders Police, 1983–96. Hon. Sec., ACPO in Scotland, 1985–96; Chm., British Police Athletic Assoc., 1991–96 (Chm., Squash Section, 1984–96; Chm., Ski Section, 1992–96). *Recreations:* golf, ski-ing, hill walking.

SUTHERLAND, Prof. William James, PhD; Miriam Rothschild Professor of Conservation Biology, University of Cambridge, since 2006; Fellow, St Catharine's College, Cambridge, since 2008; *b* 27 April 1956; *s* of late Alasdair Cameron Sutherland and Gwyneth Audrey Sutherland; *m* 1996, Nicola Jane Crockford; two *d. Educ:* Univ. of East Anglia (BSc); Liverpool Poly. (PhD). NERC Postdoctoral Fellow, Wolfson Coll., Oxford, 1980–82; Lectr, Zoology Dept, Liverpool Univ., 1982–83; University of East Anglia: Demonstrator, Sch. of Envmtl Scis, 1983–85; Lectr, 1985–93, Reader, 1993–96, Prof. of Biology, 1996–2006, Sch. of Biol Scis; Nuffield Fellow, 1992–93; Associate Fellow, Centre for Sci. and Policy, Univ. of Cambridge, 2011–. Trustee, FFI, 1998–. Scientific Medal, Zool Soc., 1997; Marsh Award for Ecology, British Ecol Soc., 2001; Marsh Award for Conservation Biol., Zool Soc., 2005; Ecological Engagement Award, British Ecol Soc., 2012; Dist. Service Award, Soc. for Conservation Biol., 2013; Sir John Burnett Meml Lect. Medal, Nat. Biodiversity Network, 2013. *Publications:* (ed with D. A. Hill) Habitat Management, 1995; From Individual Behaviour to Population Ecology, 1996; (ed) Ecological Census Techniques: a handbook, 1996, 2nd edn 2006; (ed) Conservation Science and Action, 1998; The Conservation Handbook: research, management and policy techniques, 2000; (ed with L. M. Gosling) Behaviour and Conservation, 2000; (ed jtly) Bird Ecology and Conservation: a handbook of techniques, 2004; (jtly) Bee Conservation: evidence for the effects of interventions, 2010; (jtly) Bird Conservation: global evidence for the effects of interventions, 2013; (jtly) Amphibian Conservation: evidence for effectiveness of interventions, 2014; (jtly) Farmland Conservation: evidence for effectiveness of conservation, 2014; (jtly) What Works in Conservation; articles on ecology, behaviour and conservation in scientific jls. *Recreations:* natural history, prehistory, photography, painting, cooking. *Address:* Department of Zoology, Cambridge University, Downing Street, Cambridge CB2 3EJ. *E:* w.sutherland@zoo.cam.ac.uk.

SUTHERLAND-ARDEN, Sian, (Sian Sutherland); Founding Partner and Chief Executive Officer, Mio and Mama Mio Ltd, skincare business, since 2005; Chairman, FilmAid UK, since 2012; *b* Windsor, 29 Jan. 1961; *d* of Hugh Sutherland-Dodd and Molly Sutherland; *m* 1991, Christian Arden; two *s. Educ:* Garth Hill Comp. Sch., Bracknell; Reading Tech. Coll. Founder and Gen. Manager, Sutherlands Restaurant, Soho, London, 1985–91 (Michelin star, 1988); Co-Founding Partner, Miller Sutherland, design and brand creation agency, 1991–2011; Co-Founder and Partner, Arden Sutherland-Dodd, later ASD Lionheart, commercials prodn co., 1994–. *Recreations:* basketball (founded Badabings women's basketball team, 1997, still playing!), sailing, regular mini-breaks in Greek Isles, tennis, mixology. *T:* 07768 385383. *E:* sian@mioskincare.com.

SUTHERS, Martin William, OBE 1988; DL; Consultant, Fraser Brown, Solicitors, 2005–13; *b* 27 June 1940; *s* of Rev. Canon George Suthers and Susie Mary Suthers (*née* Jobson); *m* 1st, 1970, Daphne Joan Oxland (marr. diss. 1988); 2nd, 1990, Philippa Leah Melville la Borde. *Educ:* Dulwich Coll.; Christ's Coll., Cambridge (MA). Admitted Solicitor, 1965. Asst Solicitor, Wells, Hind, 1965–66; Conveyancing Asst, Clerk's Dept, Notts CC, 1966–69; Asst Solicitor, Fishers, 1969–70; Partner, 1971–92, Sen. Partner, 1992–2000, J. A. Simpson & Coulby, then Hopkins (following merger); Consultant, Hopkins, 2000–05. Pres., Notts Law Soc., 1998–99. Chairman: Queen's Med. Centre Nottingham Univ. Hosp. NHS Trust, 1993–2000; Rushcliffe PCT, 2004–06; Notts Shadow Health and Wellbeing Bd, 2011–13. Pres., Notts Valuation Tribunal, 1999–2009. Member (C): Nottingham CC, 1967–69, 1976–95; Notts CC, 2000– (Dep. Leader, 2009–13); Rushcliffe BC, 2015–; Lord Mayor of Nottingham, 1988–89; Hon. Alderman, 1997. DL Notts 1999. Chairman: Notts Wildlife Trust, 2004–09; Operation Wallacea Trust, 2014–. *Recreation:* ornithology. *Address:* The Manor House, Main Street, Flintham, Newark, Notts NG23 5LA. *T:* (01636) 525554.

SUTHIWART-NARUEPUT, Dr Owart, Kt Grand Cordon: Order of Crown of Thailand, 1981; Order of White Elephant, 1985; Hon. CMG 1972; Permanent Secretary for Foreign Affairs, Thailand, 1979–80; *b* 19 Sept. 1926; *s* of Luang Suthiwart-Narueput and Mrs Khae; *m* 1959, Angkana (*née* Sthapitanond); one *s* one *d. Educ:* Thammasat Univ., Thailand (BA Law); Fletcher Sch. of Law and Diplomacy, Tufts Univ., USA (MA, PhD); Nat. Defence Coll. Joined Min. of For. Affairs, 1945; Asst Sec. to Minister, 1958; SEATO Res. Officer, 1959; Protocol Dept, 1963; Econ. Dept, 1964; Counsellor, Thai Embassy, Canberra, 1965; Dir-Gen. of Inf. Dept, 1969; Ambassador to India, Nepal, Sri Lanka, and Minister to Afghanistan, 1972; Ambassador to Poland, E Germany and Bulgaria, 1976; Dir-Gen. of Political Dept, 1977; Ambassador to France and Perm. Representative to UNESCO, 1980; Ambassador: to Switzerland and to Holy See, 1983; to UK, 1984–86, concurrently to Ireland, 1985–86. Mem., Civil Service Bd, Min. of Foreign Affairs, 1994–2006. Commander: Order of Phoenix, Greece, 1963; Order of Orange-Nassau, Netherlands, 1963; Bintang Djasa (1st Cl.), Indonesia, 1970; Order of Merit, Poland, 1979; Grand Officier, l'Ordre Nat. du Mérite, France, 1983. *Publications:* The Evolution of Thailand's Foreign Relations since 1855: from extraterritoriality to equality, 1955. *Recreations:* reading, music. *Address:* 193 Lane 4 Navathanee, Serithai Road, Kannayao, Bangkok 10230, Thailand. *Clubs:* Old England Students' Association, American University Alumni Association (Bangkok).

SUTLIEFF, Barry John; communications consultant, Poland, Macedonia, Kosovo, Georgia, Tanzania and China, 2000–12; Director, Communications and Learning, Civil Contingencies Secretariat, Cabinet Office, 2001–02; *b* 26 Dec. 1942; *s* of Basil Eric and Ruby Ellen Sutlieff; *m* 1967, Linda Valerie Hook; one *s* one *d. Educ:* Brooklands Coll., Weybridge; Coll. for Distributive Trades, London (CAM Dip. PR). Trainee advertising exec., 1961–66; gen. publicity roles, Depts of Trade, Transport and the Envmt, and Price Commn, 1966–75; Chief Press Officer: DoE, 1975–79; Dept of Trade, 1979–83; Dep. Hd of Inf., Home Office, Feb.–July 1985; Dir, Inf. Services, MSC, 1985–87; Director: of Inf., Dept of Employment, 1987–94; of Communication, Cabinet Office, 1994–2000; Fellow, Centre for Management and Policy Studies, Cabinet Office, 2000–01. Non-exec. Dir, Lewis Live Ltd, 2004–06. *Recreations:* travel, reading modern history, lifelong Dickens fanatic, sport, notably football and cricket. *Address:* The Hollies, 26 Hutton Road, Ash Vale, Aldershot, Hants GU12 5HA. *T:* (01252) 654727.

SUTTIE, Baroness *cr* 2013 (Life Peer), of Hawick in the Scottish Borders; **Alison Mary Suttie;** political consultant, since 2012; *b* Hawick, Scotland, 27 Aug. 1968; *d* of late Dr Alastair Suttie and of Gillian Suttie. *Educ:* Hawick High Sch.; Heriot-Watt Univ. (BA Hons Interpreting and Translating (French and Russian)); Univ. of Voronezh, Russia. Teacher of English, St Petersburg, USSR, 1990–91; res. asst to Sir Russell Johnston, MP, 1991–93; Chief Whip's Asst, Lib Dem Whip's Office, H of C, 1993–96; Policy Advr, Eur. Parlt, 1996–99; Press Sec. and Policy Advr to Patrick Cox, MEP as Pres., ELDR, 1999–2002, as Pres. of Eur. Parlt, 2002–04; Hd of Office of Lib Dem Leader, H of C, 2006–10; Dep. COS, Office of the Dep. Prime Minister, 2010–11. *Recreations:* trekking, particularly in the Himalayas, outdoor swimming. *Address:* House of Lords, SW1A 0PW.

SUTTIE, Sir James (Edward) Grant, 9th Bt *cr* 1702, of Balgone, Haddingtonshire; farmer; *b* 29 May 1965; *o s* of Sir Philip Grant-Suttie, 8th Bt and of Elspeth Mary Grant-Suttie (*née* Urquhart); *S* father, 1997; *m* 1st, 1989, Emma Jane Craig (marr. diss. 1996); one *s*; 2nd, 1997, Sarah Jane Smale; two *s. Educ:* Fettes Coll., Edinburgh; Aberdeen Coll. of Agric. *Recreations:* golf, shooting. *Heir: s* Gregor Grant-Suttie, *b* 29 Oct. 1991.

SUTTLE, Stephen John; QC 2003; *b* 28 Sept. 1949; *s* of Ernest Suttle, DMus and Judith Suttle (*née* Gummer); *m* 1984, Rosemary Ann Warren (marr. diss. 2005; remarried 2014); two *s* two *d. Educ:* Westminster Sch.; Christ Church, Oxford (MA Lit.Hum.). Asst classics master, Stowe Sch., 1973–78; called to the Bar, Gray's Inn, 1980; in practice, specialising in defamation, confidence, privacy and media law, until 2010. Pt-time classics teacher, 2011–. *Recreations:* music, cricket. *Address:* c/o 1 Brick Court, Temple, EC4Y 9BY.

SUTTON, Prof. Adrian Peter, PhD; FRS 2003; Professor of Nanotechnology, Department of Physics, Imperial College London, since 2005; *b* 1 July 1955; *s* of Peter Michael Sutton and Beryl Margaret Sutton; partner, 1985, *m* 2003, Patricia Joan White. *Educ:* St Catherine's Coll., Oxford (BA 1st cl. (Metallurgy and Sci. of Materials) 1978; MSc by res. 1978); Univ. of Pennsylvania (PhD 1980). CPhys, FInstP 2000; FIMMM 2000; CEng 2001; CChem, FRSC 2003. Oxford University: SRC postdoctoral researcher, 1981–83; Royal Soc. Res. Fellow, 1983–91; Lectr, 1991–97; Prof. of Materials Science, 1997–2004; Fellow, Linacre Coll., Oxford, 1991–2004; Prof. of Computational Engrg, Helsinki Univ. of Technol., 2002–04; Imperial College London: Head of Condensed Matter Theory, 2005–11; Chm., EPSRC Centre for Doctoral Trng on theory and simulation of materials, 2011– (Dir, 2009–11). *Publications:* Electronic Structure of Materials, 1993 (trans. German 1996); (with R. W. Balluffi) Interfaces in Crystalline Materials, 1995, reissued 2006; numerous scientific papers in physics, materials science and chemistry jls. *Recreations:* cycling, walking, travelling, enthusing children about science. *Address:* 516 Banbury Road, Oxford OX2 8LG.

SUTTON, Alan John; Founder Chairman and Chief Executive, Anglolink Ltd, since 1985; *b* 16 March 1936; *s* of William Clifford Sutton and Emily Sutton (*née* Batten); *m* 1957, Glenis (*née* Henry); one *s* one *d. Educ:* Bristol Univ. BSc (Hons) Elec. Engrg; MIET. Design, Production and Trials Evaluation of Guided Missiles, English Electric Aviation Ltd, 1957–63; Design, Production, Sales and General Management of Scientific Digital, Analogue and

Hybrid Computers, Solartron Electronic Group Ltd, 1963–69; International Sales Manager, Sales Director, of A. B. Electronic Components Ltd, 1969–73; Managing Director, A. B. Connectors, 1973–76; Industrial Dir, Welsh Office, 1976–79; Welsh Development Agency: Exec. Dir (Industry and Investment), 1979–83; Exec. Dir (Marketing), 1983–85; Sen. Vice-Pres., USA W Coast Div., WINvest, 1985–88. CEO, DigiTec Direct Ltd, subseq. Chm., A NOVO Digitec Ltd, 1998–2004; Dir, A NOVO UK Ltd, 2001–05; non-exec. Dir, A NOVO SA, 2003–09; Chm., 2007–09, non-exec. Dir, 2009–10, Conforto Financial Management Ltd. *Recreations:* golf, travel. *Address:* 56 Heol-y-Delyn, Lisvane, Cardiff CF14 0SR. *T:* (029) 2075 3194.

SUTTON, Barry Bridge; JP; MA; Headmaster, Taunton School, 1987–97; *b* 21 Jan. 1937; *s* of Albert and Ethel Sutton; *m* 1961, Margaret Helen (*née* Palmer); one *s* two *d*. *Educ:* Eltham Coll.; Peterhouse, Cambridge (MA Hist. Tripos); Bristol Univ. (PGCE). Asst Master and Housemaster, Wycliffe College, 1961–75; Headmaster, Hereford Cathedral School, 1975–87. Chairman: Cttee, Scout Assoc. Council, 1994–96; Som Co. Scout Council, 1994–; Nat. Scout Awards Bd, 2002–11. Sec., Taunton ESU, 2000– (Chm., 1998–2004). Chm., 1999–2014, Pres., 2014–, Somerton Anglo-Italian Twinning. Churchwarden, 2003–13, Parish Administrator, 2013–, St Andrew's, Compton Dundon. JP Hereford, 1982, Taunton, 1987–2007 (Chm., Taunton Bench, 2005–06). *Recreations:* hill-walking, scouting. *Address:* Burt's Barn, Peak Lane, Dundon, Somerton, Somerset TA11 6NZ.

SUTTON, David Christopher, PhD; Director, Research Projects, University of Reading Library, since 1982; *b* 18 Oct. 1950; *e s* of Derek John Sutton and Sheila Sutton, Bournemouth; *m* 1973, Dr Deborah Jenkins. *Educ:* Leicester Univ. (BA; MA 1973); Sheffield Univ. (MA 1975); Université de Paris VIII; Polytechnic of Central London (PhD 1979). Librarian: Trinity Coll., Dublin, 1973–74; Polytechnic of Central London, 1975–76; BL, 1976–78; Warwick Univ. Library, 1980–82. Mem. (Lab) Reading BC, 1988–2008 (Leader of the Council, 1995–2008); Chm., Reading Miners' Support Cttee, 1984–85; Trustee, Earley Charity, 1987–. Chm. Bd, Reading Buses, 2010–. Chairman: Gp for Literary Archives and Manuscripts, 2010–; Literary Archives Section, Internat. Council of Archives, 2010–. UK Editor, Writers, Artists and Their Copyright Holders, 1994–. FRSA; FRSL 2012. Archivist of Year, Scone Foundn, 2006. Benson Medal for services to literature, RSL, 2002. *Publications:* Points of View in the Writing of History, 1981; (ed) Location Register of Twentieth-Century English Literary Manuscripts and Letters, 1988; (ed) Location Register of English Literary Manuscripts and Letters: eighteenth and nineteenth centuries, 1995; Figs: a global history, 2014; numerous articles on copyright, literary manuscripts, politics and food history. *Recreations:* football, badminton, walking in Dorset, sitting by the Mediterranean. *Address:* The Coach House, 22 Eldon Place, Reading RG1 4ED. *E:* D.C.Sutton@reading.ac.uk.

SUTTON, Dr (Howard) Michael; Principal Research Fellow, University of Warwick, 1999–2003; *b* 12 Nov. 1942; *s* of Albert Sutton and Constance Olive Sutton (*née* Topham); *m* 1967, Diane Cash; one *s* one *d*. *Educ:* Univ. of Edinburgh (BSc 1965; PhD 1968). CChem, FRSC 1977–2008. Res. Fellow, Univ. of Kent at Canterbury, 1968–70; Warren Spring Laboratory: Materials Handling Div., 1970–78; Head, Planning and Marketing, 1978–85; Dep. Dir, 1985–88; Department of Trade and Industry: Head, Shipbuilding and Marine Engineering, 1988–91; Head, Single Market Unit, 1991–93; Head, Mech. Engrg Sponsorship, 1993–94; Dir, Trade and Industry, W Midlands, 1994–98; Hd of Secretariat, W Midlands Regl Develt Agency (in preparation), 1998–99; Advr, Advantage W Midlands—the Develt Agency, 1999–2000. Non-exec. Dir, Manufg Foundn Ltd, 2001–03. Blog, mikesutton161.wordpress.com. *Publications:* contribs to learned jls. *Recreations:* philosophy, music, walking. *E:* mikesutton161@gmail.com. *W:* www.twitter.com/mikesutton161.

SUTTON, Prof. John, PhD; FBA 1996; Sir John Hicks Professor of Economics, London School of Economics and Political Science, since 1998 (Professor of Economics, 1988–98); *b* 10 Aug. 1948; *s* of John Sutton and Marie (*née* Hammond); *m* 1974, Jean Drechsler; one *s* two *d*. *Educ:* University Coll., Dublin (BSc Physics 1969); Trinity Coll., Dublin (MSc Econ. 1973); PhD Sheffield 1978. Voluntary service, UNA, Turkey, 1969–70; Mgt Services, Herbert-BSA, Coventry, 1970–72; Lectr, Sheffield Univ., 1973–77; Lectr, 1977–84, Reader, 1984–88, LSE. Visiting Professor: Tokyo Univ., 1981; Univ. of Calif, San Diego, 1986; Marvin Bower Fellow, Harvard Business Sch., 1990–91; Gaston Eyskens Prof., Leuven Univ., 1996–97; Vis. Prof. of Econs, Harvard Univ., 1998; William Davidson Vis. Prof., Michigan Univ., 2003; Vis. Prof., Graduate Sch. of Business, Univ. of Chicago, 2006. Member: Adv. Council, Japan External Trade Orgn, Tokyo, 1995–2002; Council for Econ. Analysis, EU, 2002–04; Enterprise Policy Gp, Ireland, 2003–04. Pres., REconS, 2004–07. Fellow: Econometric Soc., 1991; European Econ. Assoc., 2004; Dist. Fellow, Industrial Orgn Soc., 2012. Foreign Hon. Mem., AEA, 2007. Hon. DSc(Econ) NUI, 2003; Hon. DSciEcon Lausanne, 2004; Hon. LLD Dublin, 2004. Medal of Franqui Foundn, Belgium, 1992. *Publications:* (jtly) Protection and Industrial Policy in Europe, 1986; Sunk Costs and Market Structure, 1991; Technology and Market Structure: theory and history, 1998; Marshall's Tendencies: what can economists know?, 2000; (jtly) An Enterprise Map of Ethiopia, 2010; (jtly) An Enterprise Map of Ghana, 2012; (jtly) An Enterprise Map of Tanzania, 2012; Competing in Capabilities: the globalization process, 2012. *Address:* London School of Economics, Houghton Street, WC2A 2AE. *T:* (020) 7955 7716.

SUTTON, John Sydney, CBE 1996; education consultant; Director, International Business Education Co-operation Charitable Trust, 1998–2002; General Secretary, Secondary Heads Association, 1988–98; *b* 9 June 1936; *s* of late Sydney and Mabel Sutton; *m* 1961, Carmen Grandoso Martinez; three *s*. *Educ:* King Edward VI Sch., Southampton; Univ. of Keele (BA Hons, MA). Asst Teacher, Christopher Wren Sch., London, 1958–60; Asst Master, later Head of History, Bemrose Sch., Derby, 1960–68; Head, Social Studies Dept, Sir Wilfrid Martineau Sch., Birmingham, 1968–73; Headmaster: Corby Grammar Sch., 1973; Southwood Sch., Corby, 1973–82; Queen Elizabeth Sch., Corby, 1982–88. Mem. Council, Hansard Soc. for Parly Govt, 1973–2000. Trustee, Teaching Awards Trust, 1998–2010. *Publications:* American Government, 1974; Understanding Politics in Modern Britain, 1977; (with L. Robbins and T. Brennan) People and Politics in Britain, 1985; (jtly) School Management in Practice, 1985; (as Archimedes) TES Management Guide for Heads and Senior Staff, 1996; (ed) Learning to Succeed, 2009; A History of the Samuel Lee Charity in Geddington, 2011. *Recreations:* walking, gardening, wine appreciation, Geddington Volunteer Fire Brigade. *Address:* 24 Bright Trees Road, Geddington, Kettering, Northants NN14 1BS. *T:* (01536) 742559. *Club:* Rotary (Kettering Huxloe).

SUTTON, Rt Rev. Keith Norman; Bishop of Lichfield, 1984–2003; *b* 23 June 1934; *s* of Norman and Irene Sutton; *m* 1963, Edith Mary Jean Geldard (*d* 2000); three *s* one *d*. *Educ:* Jesus College, Cambridge (MA 1959). Ordained deacon, 1959, priest, 1960. Curate, St Andrew's, Plymouth, 1959–62; Chaplain, St John's Coll., Cambridge, 1962–67; Tutor and Chaplain, Bishop Tucker Coll., Mukono, Uganda, 1968–73; Principal of Ridley Hall, Cambridge, 1973–78; Bishop Suffragan of Kingston-upon-Thames, 1978–83; Archbp of Canterbury's envoy to Southern Africa, 1986. General Synod: Chairman: Bd for Mission and Unity, 1989–91; Bd of Mission, 1991–94; Member: Standing Cttee, 1989–94; Theol Gp, House of Bishops, 1989–2002. Select Preacher, Univ. of Cambridge, 1987. Pres., Queen's Coll., Birmingham, 1986–94. Entered House of Lords, 1989. Episcopal Visitor, Simon of Cyrene Theol Inst., 1992–. Hon. Vice-Pres., CMS, 1995. Patron: Russian Poets Fund, Keele Univ., 1995–; New Art Gall., Walsall, 1998–. DUniv Keele, 1992; Hon. DLitt Wolverhampton, 1994. *Publications:* The People of God, 1983. *Recreations:* Russian literature, third world issues, music.

SUTTON, Kenneth David, CB 2008; Director, Hillsborough Independent Panel, Home Office, 2010–12; *b* 17 May 1958; *s* of David Vivien Sutton and Audrey Sutton; *m* 1982, Ruth Hopkin; two *s* one *d*. *Educ:* Cefn Hengoed Comprehensive Sch., Swansea; University Coll., Oxford (BA 1st Cl. Hons PPE 1979). Joined Home Office, 1979; Private Sec. to Parly Under Sec. of State, 1983–85; Private Sec. to Permanent Under Sec. of State, 1991–92; Asst Sec., Immigration and Nationality Dept, 1992–95; Principal Private Sec. to Home Secretary, 1995–99; Dir of Regimes, subseq. of Resettlement, HM Prison Service, 1999–2002; Dir, Street Crime Action Team, 2002; Sen. Dir for Asylum Support, Casework and Appeals, 2003–06; Dep. Chief Exec., Border and Immigration Agency (formerly Dep. Dir Gen., Immigration and Nationality), 2006–08. *Recreations:* cycling, holidays in France and Wales. *Address:* c/o Home Office, 2 Marsham Street, SW1P 4DF.

SUTTON, Michael; *see* Sutton, H. M.

SUTTON, Ven. Peter Allerton; Archdeacon of the Isle of Wight, since 2012; *b* Liss, Hants, 18 July 1959; *s* of John and Jean Sutton; *m* 2007, Pippa Dice; two *d*. *Educ:* Warblington Sch.; Exeter Univ. (BA Theol. 1985); Lincoln Theol Coll. Ordained deacon, 1987, priest, 1988; Curate: Holy Trinity and St Columba, Fareham, 1987–90; St Mary, Alverstoke, 1990–93; Chaplain, HM Prison Haslar, 1990–93; Vicar, St Faith, Lee-on-the-Solent, 1993–2012. *Recreations:* music, reading, time in France, time with family. *Address:* 5 The Boltons, Wootton Bridge, Ryde, Isle of Wight PO33 4PB. *T:* (01983) 884432. *E:* adiow@portsmouth.anglican.org.

SUTTON, Philip, CBE 2012; PhD; FREng, FIET, FInstP; Director (formerly Director General), Science and Technology Strategy (formerly Research and Technology), Ministry of Defence, 2004–11; Director, SSES Ltd, since 2011; *b* 28 Nov. 1953; *s* of Percy Ronald and Ivy Nora Sutton; *m* 1974, Kim Cummins; one *s* one *d*. *Educ:* Southampton Univ. (BSc Hons Physics; PhD Electronics 1982). FIET (FIEE 1996); FInstP 1998; FREng 2006. Ministry of Defence: ASWE, Portsdown 1975–83; BAe Dynamics, Bristol, 1983–85; Above Water Sector, ARE, then DRA, Portsdown, 1985–92, Chief Scientist, 1992–94; Hd, Battlefield and Vehicle Systems Dept, DERA, 1994–98; Director: of Corporate Res., 1998–2001; of Technol. Develt, 2001–04. Visiting Professor: Cranfield Univ., 1990–; Loughborough Univ., 1992–2012; Imperial Coll. London, 2006–; UCL, 2011–; Chm., Industrial Adv. Bd, Centre for Secure Information Technols, QUB, 2010–. Dir, Cancer Care Soc., 2000–. Gov., Welbeck Coll., 2005–11; Community Gov., Ampfield Sch., 2013–15. Member: Whiteley Ch Council, 1998–2012; Ampfield Ch Council, 2012–. Member: NT; RNLI (Mem. Council, 2014–). *Publications:* numerous tech. reports and papers; named inventor on 17 patents and patent applications. *Recreations:* sailing, sub-aqua diving, snow-boarding, cycling.

SUTTON, Philip John, RA 1989 (ARA 1977); *b* 20 Oct. 1928; *m* 1954; one *s* three *d*. *Educ:* Slade Sch. of Fine Art, UCL. One-man exhibitions: Roland Browse and Delbanco (now Browse and Darby) Gallery, London, 1958–81; Leeds City Art Gallery, 1960; Newcastle-on-Tyne, 1962; Bradford, 1962; Edinburgh, 1962; Sydney, 1963, 1966, 1970, 1973; Perth, 1963, 1972; Royal Acad. (Diploma Gall.), London, 1977; David Jones Gall., Sydney, 1980; Bonython Art Gall., Adelaide, 1981; Norwich, Bath and New York, 1983; Lichfield Fest., 1985; Beaux Arts Gall., Bath, 1985; Galerie Joël Salaün, Paris, 1988; Gallery 27, and Cork St, London, 2004; Richmond Hill Art Gall., 2006; exhibn of ceramics, Oditte Gilbert Gall., London, 1987; Agnews, London, 1992; touring exhibn, Wales, 1993–94; Shakespeare exhibn, RA, Internat. Shakespeare Globe Centre, RSC Stratford, Royal Armouries Mus., Leeds, Berkeley Square Gall., 1997; Piano Nobile, London 2001; Hay-on-Wye Fest., 2001; exhibn of woodcuts 1962–1976, RA, 2005. Designed Post Office 'Greetings' stamps, 1989. *Recreations:* swimming, running. *Address:* 7 Riverside Court, South Walk, Bridport, Dorset DT6 3XB.

SUTTON, Prof. Richard, DSc (Med); FRCP, FACC, FESC, FAHA; FHRS; Consultant Cardiologist, Imperial College Healthcare NHS Trust (formerly St Mary's Hospital NHS Trust), 2007–11, now Hon. Consultant; Professor of Clinical Cardiology, Imperial College London, 2003–11, now Emeritus; *b* 1 Sept. 1940; *s* of late Dick Brasnett Sutton and Greta Mary (*née* Leadbeater); *m* 1964, Anna Gunilla (*née* Cassö) (marr. diss. 1998); one *s*; *m* 2014, Jeanne-Marie Arrighi. *Educ:* Gresham's Sch.; King's Coll., London; King's Coll. Hosp. (MB, BS 1964); DSc (Med) London 1988. FRCP 1983 (MRCP 1967); FACC 1975; FESC 1990; FAHA 2001; FHRS 2006. Gen. medical trng followed graduation; career in cardiology began at St George's Hosp., London, 1967; Fellow in Cardiol., Univ. of NC, 1968–69; Registrar, Sen. Registrar, then Temp. Consultant, National Heart Hosp., London, 1970–76. Consultant Cardiologist: St Stephen's Hosp., 1976–89; Chelsea and Westminster Hosp. (formerly Westminster Hosp.), 1976–2007; Royal Brompton Nat. Heart and Lung Hosp., subseq. Royal Brompton and Harefield Trust, 1993–2007; Hon. Consultant Cardiologist: Italian Hosp., London, 1977–89; St Luke's Hosp., London, 1980–2011. Chm., Eur. Wkg Gp on Cardiac Pacing, 1998–2000. Exec. Bd Mem., Eur. Heart Rhythm Assoc., 2004–06. Member: British Cardiovascular Soc. (formerly British Cardiac Soc.); Heart Rhythm Soc.; Heart Rhythm UK (formerly British Pacing and Electrophysiology Gp) (Co-Founder, Past Pres. and Hon. Sec.). Governors' Award, Amer. Coll. of Cardiol., 1979 (Scientific Exhibit, Physiol Cardiac Pacing), and 1982 (1st Prize; Scientific Exhibit, 5 yrs of Physiol Cardiac Pacing). Editor in Chief: European Jl of Cardiac Pacing and Electrophysiology, 1991–97; Europace, 1998–2006 (Founding Ed., 2007–). Lifetime Achievement Award, Heart Rhythm UK, 2007. *Publications:* Foundations of Cardiac Pacing, pt 1, 1991, pt 2, 1999; articles on many aspects of cardiology incl. cardiac pacing, syncope, coronary artery disease, left ventricular function, and assessment of pharm. agents, in Nature Cardiol., Circulation, Jl of Amer. Coll. of Cardiol., Amer. Jl of Cardiol., Amer. Heart Jl, Brit. Heart Jl, Heart, Pace, Lancet, BMJ, Europace, and Oxford Textbook of Medicine, 1967–. *Recreations:* opera, foreign travel, walking. *Address:* 9 avenue d'Ostende, Monte Carlo, Monaco, MC 98000.

SUTTON, Richard Lewis; Regional Director, Northern Region, Department of Industry, 1974–81; *b* 3 Feb. 1923; *s* of William Richard Sutton and Marina Susan Sutton (*née* Chudleigh); *m* 1944, Jean Muriel (*née* Turner) (*d* 2014). *Educ:* Ealing County Grammar Sch. Board of Trade, 1939. Served War: HM Forces (Lieut RA), 1942–47. Asst Trade Comr, Port of Spain, 1950–52; BoT, 1953–62; Trade Comr, Kuala Lumpur, 1962–66; Monopolies Commn, 1966; BoT, 1967–68; Dir, British Industrial Develt Office, New York, 1968–71; Regional Dir, West Midland Region, Dept of Trade and Industry, 1971–74. *Recreations:* music, walking, bridge. *Address:* Barton Toft, Dowlish Wake, Ilminster, Somerset TA19 0QG. *T:* (01460) 57127.

SUTTON, Sir Richard (Lexington), 9th Bt *cr* 1772; Director, Sir Richard Sutton's Settled Estates; *b* 27 April 1937; *s* of Sir Robert Lexington Sutton, 8th Bt, and Gwynneth Gwladys, *o d* of Major Arnold Charles Gover, MC; *S* father, 1981; *m* 1959, Fiamma (separated 2000), *o d* of G. M. Ferrari, Rome; one *s* one *d*; partner, 2002, Mrs Anne Schreiber. *Educ:* Stowe. *Recreations:* ski-ing, sailing, swimming, gym. *Heir:* *s* David Robert Sutton [*b* 26 Feb. 1960; *m* 1st, 1992, Annette (marr. diss. 2003), *o d* of B. David; three *d*; 2nd, 2007, Mrs Gay Mary van der Meulen (*née* Luscombe)]. *Address:* Moorhill, Higher Langham, Gillingham, Dorset SP8 5NY. *T:* (01747) 822665.

SUTTON, Richard Patrick; QC 1993; a Recorder, since 1994 (Assistant Recorder, 1991–94); *b* 13 Nov. 1944; *s* of Jack Doherty Sutton and Beryl Clarisse Scholes Sutton (*née* Folkard); *m* 1978, Jean Folley; one *s* one *d*. *Educ:* Culford Sch.; Wadham Coll., Oxford (BA Hons Jurisprudence). Called to the Bar, Middle Temple, 1969, Bencher, 2002. *Recreations:* playing guitar, meeting people.

SUTTON, Robert Hiles; Chairman, Tulchan Communications Group, since 2009; *b* 19 Jan. 1954; *s* of late John Ormerod Sutton and of (Margaret) Patricia Sutton; *m* 1981, Carola, (Tiggy), Dewey; one *s* one *d* (and one *s* decd). *Educ:* Winchester Coll.; Magdalen Coll., Oxford (BA 1st Cl. Hons Modern Hist.). Admitted solicitor, 1979; joined Macfarlanes, Solicitors, 1976: Partner, 1983–2009; Sen. Partner, 1999–2008; Sen. Advr, 2009–13. Chm., OMC Partners, 2009–13; non-exec. Dir, Numis Corp. plc, 2014–. Fellow, Winchester Coll., 2003–. *Recreations:* tennis, wine, family. *Address:* c/o Tulchan Communications, 85 Fleet Street, EC4Y 1AE. *T:* (020) 7353 4200. *E:* robert.manor@virginmedia.com. *Club:* Boodle's.

SUTTON, Prof. Stephen Robert, PhD; Professor of Behavioural Science, University of Cambridge, since 2001; *b* 24 Feb. 1952; *s* of Robert Frank Sutton and Marjorie Sutton (*née* Hook); *m* 1985, Pamela Anne (*née* Stevens). *Educ:* Univ. of Leicester (BA 1973); LSE (MSc 1975); Inst. of Psychiatry, Univ. of London (PhD 1981); City Univ. (MSc 1991). Institute of Psychiatry, University of London: Res. Worker, 1975–90, Lectr, 1980–88, Sen. Lectr, 1988–90, Addiction Res. Unit; Sen. Lectr in Social Psychology, Health Behaviour Unit, 1990–96; Reader in Social/Health Psychology, 1996–2000, Prof. in Social/Health Psychology, 2000–01, Health Behaviour Unit, Dept of Epidemiology and Public Health, UCL. Vis. Prof. of Psychology, Univ. of Bergen, 1996–; Vis. Prof. of Social/Health Psychology, Dept of Psychiatry and Behavioural Scis, UCL, 2000–. *Publications:* numerous papers in learned jls. *Recreations:* walking, bird-watching. *Address:* University of Cambridge, Institute of Public Health, Forvie Site, Robinson Way, Cambridge CB2 0SR. *T:* (01223) 330594, *Fax:* (01223) 762515. *E:* srs34@medschl.cam.ac.uk.

SUZMAN, Dame Janet, DBE 2011; actress and director; *b* 9 Feb. 1939; *d* of Saul Suzman; *m* 1969, Trevor Robert Nunn (*see* Sir T. R. Nunn) (marr. diss. 1986); one *s*. *Educ:* Kingsmead Coll., Johannesburg; Univ. of the Witwatersrand (BA); London Acad. of Music and Dramatic Art. Hon. Associate Artist, RSC, 1980. Vis. Prof of Drama Studies, Westfield Coll., London, 1983–84; Hon. Lectr, Shakespeare Inst., Univ. of Birmingham, 2011–12. Lectures: Spencer, Harvard Univ., 1988; Tanner, Brasenose Coll., Oxford, 1995; Sixth World Shakespeare Congress, LA, 1996; Judith Wilson, Trinity Coll., Cambridge, 1996; Drapers', QMW, 1997; Morrell Meml Address on Toleration, Univ. of York, 1999. Vice-Pres., LAMDA Council, 2002– (Mem., 1978–2002, Vice-Chm., 1992–2002); Pres., Shakespeare Birthday Celebrations, 2010–11. Trustee: The Theatres Trust, 1977–83; Rose of Kingston Th. Trust, 2007–. Hon. Fellow: Shakespeare Birthplace Trust, 2012; British Shakespeare Assoc., 2015. Freeman, City of London, 2015. Rôles played for *Royal Shakespeare Co.* incl.: Joan La Pucelle in The Wars of the Roses, 1963–64; Lulu in The Birthday Party, Rosaline, Portia, 1965; Ophelia, 1965–66; Katharina, Celia, and Berinthia in The Relapse, 1967; Beatrice, Rosalind, 1968–69; Cleopatra and Lavinia, 1972–73; Clytemnestra and Helen of Troy in The Greeks, 1980; The Hollow Crown, 2002, tour of Australia, 2003; Volumnia in Coriolanus, 2007; *other rôles* incl.: Kate Hardcastle, and Carmen in The Balcony, Oxford Playhouse, 1966; Hester in Hello and Goodbye, King's Head Theatre, 1973; Masha in Three Sisters, Cambridge, 1976; Good Woman of Setzuan, Newcastle, 1976, Royal Court, 1977; Hedda Gabler, Duke of York's, 1977; Boo-hoo, Open Space, 1978; The Duchess of Malfi, Birmingham, 1979; Cowardice, Ambassadors, 1983; Boesman and Lena, Hampstead, 1984; Vassa, Greenwich, 1985; Andromache, Old Vic, 1988; Another Time, Wyndham's, 1989; Hippolytus, Almeida, 1991; The Sisters Rosensweig, Greenwich, 1994, Old Vic, 1994–95; The Retreat from Moscow, Chichester, 1999; Cherished Disappointments in Love, Soho, 2001; Whose Life is it Anyway?, Comedy, 2005; Dream of the Dog, Finborough Th., 2010, Trafalgar Studios, 2010; Solomon and Marion, Baxter Th., Cape Town, 2011, Edinburgh Fest., 2013, Kennedy Center, Washington, 2014, Birmingham Rep., 2014; *director:* Othello, Market Theatre, Johannesburg, 1987 (Best Prodn, Vita Awards, 1988); A Dream of People, The Pit, 1990; The Cruel Grasp, Edinburgh Fest., 1991; No Flies on Mr Hunter, Chelsea Centre, 1992; Death of a Salesman, 1993 (Liverpool Echo and Daily Post Arts Awards, Best Production, 1994), The Deep Blue Sea, 1996, Theatr Clywd; The Good Woman of Sharkville, Market Theatre, Johannesburg, 1996, UK tour, 1998; The Free State, Birmingham, 1997, UK tour, 2000 (Barclays Theatrical Managers' Assoc. Award, Best Dir, 1997); The Snow Palace, tour and Tricycle Theatre, 1998, Warsaw Fest., 1999; The Guardsman, Albery, 2000; Measure For Measure, Guildhall Sch., 2004; Hamlet, Cape Town, 2005, Stratford, 2006; Master Harold And the Boys, LAMDA, 2010; Antony and Cleopatra, Liverpool Playhouse, 2010 (Best Prodn, Liverpool Daily Post Awards), Chichester Fest., 2012; Le Nozze di Figaro, RAM, Hackney Empire, 2015. *Films:* A Day in the Death of Joe Egg, 1970; Nicholas and Alexandra, 1971; The Priest of Love, 1980; The Draughtsman's Contract, 1981; E la Nave Va, 1983; A Dry White Season, 1990; Nuns on the Run, 1990; Leon the Pig Farmer, 1993; Max 2001; *television:* plays for BBC and ITV incl.: St Joan, 1968; Three Sisters, 1969; Macbeth, 1970; Hedda Gabler, 1972; Twelfth Night, 1973; Three Men in a Boat, 1973; Antony and Cleopatra, 1974; Miss Nightingale, 1974; Clayhanger, serial, 1975–76; Mountbatten—The Last Viceroy, 1986; The Singing Detective, 1986, The Miser, 1987; dir., Othello, 1988; Cripples, 1989; The Amazon, 1989; master class on Shakespearean comedy, BBC, 1990; White Clouds, 2002; Sinbad, 2012; Labyrinth, 2013. Evening Standard Drama Awards, Best Actress, 1973, 1976; Plays and Players Award, Best Actress, 1976; Pragnell Shakespeare Award, 2012. Hon. Fellow: Sch. of Arts, Liverpool Univ., 2010–May 2016; Liverpool John Moores Univ., 2011. Hon. MA Open, 1984; Hon. DLitt: Warwick, 1990; Leicester, 1992; QMW, 1997; Southampton, 2002; Middx, 2003; Kingston, 2006; Cape Town, 2010; Buckingham, 2014. *Publications:* Acting with Shakespeare: the comedies, 1996; The Free State: a South African response to Chekhov's Cherry Orchard, 2000; (textual commentary) Antony and Cleopatra, 2001; Not Hamlet: meditations on the frail position of women in drama, 2012. *E:* sk@sknco.com. *T:* (020) 7434 9055.

SUZUKI, Prof. Akira, PhD; Professor, Hokkaido University, 1973–94, now Emeritus; *b* Mukawa, Japan, 12 Sept. 1930; *m* Yoko; two *d*. *Educ:* Hokkaido Univ. (PhD 1959). Hokkaido University: Res. Asst, Chem. Dept, 1959–61; Asst Prof., Synthetic Chemical Engrg Dept, 1961; Postdoctoral Res. Associate, Purdue Univ., 1963–65. Professor: Okayama Univ. of Sci., 1994; Kurashiki Univ. of Sci. and the Arts, 1995–2002. Chemical Soc. of Japan Award, 1989; Japan Acad. Prize, 2004; (jtly) Nobel Prize in Chemistry, 2010; H. C. Brown Award, Amer. Chemical Soc., 2011. Order of Culture (Japan), 2010. *Address:* c/o Faculty of Engineering, Hokkaido University, N13, W8, Kita-ku, Sapporo 060–8628, Japan.

SVANBERG, Carl-Henric; Chairman: BP, since 2010 (non-executive Director, since 2009); Volvo, since 2012; *b* Porjus, Sweden; *m* Agneta (marr. diss. 2009); three *c*; *m* 2013, Louise Julian. *Educ:* Linköping Inst. of Technol. (MSc Applied Physics); Univ. of Uppsala (BA Business Admin). With Asea, later Asea Brown Boveri, 1977–86; Securitas, 1986–94, Exec. Vice-Pres., 1990–94; President and Chief Executive Officer: Assa Abloy, 1994–2003; Ericsson, 2003–09 (non-exec. Dir, 2003–12); Chm., Sony Ericsson Mobile Communications AB, 2003–09. King of Sweden's Medal for contrib. to Swedish industry. *Address:* c/o BP plc, 1 St James's Square, SW1Y 4PD.

SVEJSTRUP, Dr Jesper Qualmann, FRS 2009; Senior Scientist, Francis Crick Institute, since 2015 (Principal Scientist, 2005–15, and Head, Mechanisms of Gene Transcription Laboratory, 1996–2015, London Research Institute, Cancer Research UK (formerly Imperial Cancer Research Fund)); *b* 28 March 1963; *s* of Regner and Inga Svejstrup; *m* 1990, A. Barbara Dirac; two *s*. *Educ:* Aarhus Univ. (PhD 1993). Postdoctoral Fellow, Dept of Structural Biology, Stanford Univ. Sch. of Medicine, 1993–96; Res. Scientist, 1996–2000, Sen. Scientist, 2000–05, Imperial Cancer Research Fund, later Cancer Research UK. University College London: Hon. Sen. Res. Fellow, 1996–2000; Hon. Reader, 2000–05; Hon. Prof., 2005–; Adjunct Prof., Novo Nordisk Foundn Center for Protein Res. and Dept of Cellular and Molecular Medicine, Univ. of Copenhagen, 2011–. Mem., EMBO, 2003. *Publications:* articles in jls. *Address:* Mechanisms of Gene Transcription Laboratory, Francis Crick Institute, Clare Hall Laboratories, Blanche Lane, South Mimms, Herts EN6 3LD.

SVENSON, Dame Beryl; *see* Grey, Dame Beryl.

SVENSSON, Lars; author, since 1989; editor; ornithologist; *b* 30 March 1941; *s* of Georg Svensson and Cecilia Svensson (*née* Lovén); *m* 2003, Lena Rahoult; one *s* one *d*. *Educ:* Univ. of Graphic Arts, Stockholm. Graphic designer and publishing editor, 1965–; ornithologist. Swedish Ornithological Society: Mem. Bd, 1971–77; Ed., jl, Vår Fågelvärld, 1971–74; Founder, Swedish Rarities Cttee (Chm., 1971–86); Member: Nomenclature Cttee, 1971–84; Taxonomic Cttee, 2000–14. Mem., BOU Taxonomic Sub-cttee, 2005–11. Hon. Ringer, British Trust for Ornithology, 1985–; Hon. Mem., Spanish Ornithol Soc., 2004–. PhD *hc* Uppsala, 2004. *Publications:* Identification Guide to European Passerines, 1970, 4th edn 1992; (with H. Delin) Birds of Britain and Europe, 1986, 3rd edn 1992; Fågelsång i Sverige (Birdsong in Sweden), 1990; Collins Bird Guide, 1999; (with J. Pedersen and J. Elphick) Birdsong, 2012. *Address:* S:ta Toras väg 28, 269 77 Torekov, Sweden. *T:* and *Fax:* 86632655, 431364022. *E:* lars@lullula.se.

SWABY, Peter; County Treasurer, 1991–2006, Strategic Director, 2006–07, Derbyshire County Council; *b* 8 Oct. 1947; *s* of late Arthur Swaby and Mona Swaby; *m* 1974, Yvette Shann; one *s* one *d*. *Educ:* Longcroft Sch., Beverley; Univ. of Sheffield (BMus (Hons) 2011). CPFA (CIPFA 1973). E Riding CC, 1967; Humberside CC, 1974, Chief Internal Auditor, 1983; Asst County Treasurer, S Glam CC, 1985. Hon. Sec., 2001–04, Vice Pres., 2004–05, Pres., 2005–06, Soc. of Co. Treasurers; Pres., Police Authy Treasurers' Soc., 2003–04. *Recreation:* classical guitarist (ALCM, ALCM(TD)).

SWADE, Doron David, MBE 2009; PhD; FBCS; independent researcher, history of computing; *b* 14 Oct. 1946; *s* of Max Jack Swade and Ruth Leah Swade (*née* Rosenberg). *Educ:* Univ. of Cape Town (BSc Hons 1969; MSc 1971); UCL (PhD 2003). CEng 1994; FBCS 2001. Consultant to computer industry, 1972–96; consultant electronics design engr, UK and USA, 1975–82; Science Museum: Electronics Design Engr, 1982–83; Section Head, audiovisual, electronics and computer-based displays, 1983–85; Sen. Curator, Computing and IT, 1985–99; Asst Dir and Hd of Collections, 1999–2002. Dir, Babbage Proj. and Guest Curator, Computer Hist. Mus., Mountain View, Calif, 2006–08. Visiting Professor: (Interaction Design), RCA, 2004–06; Hist. of Computing, Univ. of Portsmouth, 2005–; Hon. Res. Fellow, Dept of Computer Sci., 2006–, Res. Asst (Computer Sci.), 2014–, Royal Holloway, Univ. of London. Mem., Scientific Cttee, Musée Nat. de la Voiture et du Tourisme, Compiègne, 2002–09. Trustee, Plan 28, 2012–. *Publications:* Charles Babbage and his Calculating Engines, 1991; (jtly) The Dream Machine: exploring the computer age, 1991; The Cogwheel Brain: Charles Babbage and the quest to build the first computer, 2000; popular and scholarly articles. *Recreations:* writing, restoring woodworking machinery, making things. *Address:* 54 Park Road, Kingston upon Thames, Surrey KT2 6AU. *T:* (020) 8392 0072.

SWAFFIELD, Andrew John; Chief Executive Officer, Monarch Group, since 2014; *b* Bournemouth, 27 Sept. 1967; *s* of Derek Edward Swaffield and Jean Margaret Swaffield; civil partnership 2013, William Alexander Low. *Educ:* Bournemouth Grammar Sch.; Wharton Business Sch., IESE Business and China Europe Internat. Business Sch. (Global CEO Prog. in Internat. Business). FRAeS 2015. Thomas Cook, 1984–94; Dept Hd, 1994–98, Jt Man. Dir, 1999–2000, Travel Shops, British Airways; Man. Dir, British Airways Holidays, 2000–01; Hd, UK and Ireland Leisure Sales, British Airways, 2001–05; Man. Dir, Avios Gp Ltd, 2006–13. Vis. Fellow, Kingston Univ., 2012–. Mem., Theosophical Soc., 2010–. *Recreation:* polo player. *Address:* Monarch Group, Prospect House, Prospect Way, London Luton Airport, Luton, Beds LU2 9NU. *Club:* Cowdray Park Polo.

SWAIN, Emma; Controller, Knowledge Commissioning, BBC, since 2011; *b* Fakenham, Norfolk, 10 June 1963; *d* of Anthony Swain and Diana Nurse; partner, Laurence Jack Fitzgerald Martin Bowen; one *s* one *d*. *Educ:* St Martin's Coll. of Art. BBC: Researcher, Dir and Exec. Producer, 1996–2003; Commng Ed., Specialist Factual, 2003–07; Hd, In-house Commng, 2008–09; Hd, Knowledge TV Commng, 2009–11. *Recreations:* shopping for vintage and second-hand clothes, reading science non-fiction.

SWAINSON, Charles Patrick, FRCPE, FRCSE; FFPH; consultant, coach and mentor; Consultant Renal Physician, 1986–2010, and Medical Director, 1999–2010, NHS Lothian (formerly Royal Infirmary of Edinburgh); *b* Gloucester, 18 May 1948; *s* of John Edwin Swainson and Mary Diana Swainson (*née* O'Rourke); *m* 1981, Marie Adele Irwin; one *s*. *Educ:* St Edward's Sch., Cheltenham; Univ. of Edinburgh (MB ChB 1971). FRCPE 1986; FFPH 2004; FRCSE 2007. Sen. Lectr, Univ. of Otago, NZ, 1982–86. Hon. Prof., Univ. of Edinburgh, 2009– (Hon. Sen. Lectr, 2004–09). Convenor, Business Cttee, Gen. Council, Univ. of Edinburgh, 2012–. Treas., RCPE, 2011–. *Publications:* contrib. articles to gen. and med. specialist jls. *Recreations:* ski-ing, golf, wine appreciation. *Address:* 33 Granby Road, Edinburgh EH16 5NP. *T:* (0131) 667 6700. *E:* cpswainson@googlemail.com. *Clubs:* New (Edinburgh); Luffness New Golf.

SWAINSON, Roy; Executive Director, Merseyside Special Investment Fund, since 1998; non-executive Director, St Helens and Knowsley Hospitals NHS Trust, since 2006; *b* 15 April 1947; *s* of William Swainson and Florence Swainson (*née* Moss); *m* 1973, Irene Ann Shearson; one *s* one *d*. *Educ:* Merchant Taylors' Sch., Crosby; Univ. of Manchester (LLB). Southport County Borough Council: Asst Solicitor, 1969–71; Sen. Asst Solicitor, 1971–74; Asst Borough Solicitor and Sec., Sefton MBC, 1974–82; Dep. City Solicitor and Sec., Liverpool CC, 1982–90; Chief Exec. and Dir Gen., Merseytravel, 1990–98. Non-exec. Chm., Air Safety Support Internat. Ltd, 2003–06. *Recreations:* reading, theatre, travel. *Address:* Merseyside Special Investment Fund, Exchange Court, 1 Dale Street, Liverpool L2 2PP. *T:* (0151) 236 4040.

SWAINSTON, Michael George; QC 2002; barrister; *b* 30 Jan. 1961; *s* of George and Ruth Swainston; *m* 1993, Carmita Ferreira Guerreiro; two *s*. *Educ:* Sir William Turner's Grammar Sch.; Downing Coll., Cambridge (MA); University Coll., Oxford (BCL). Called to the Bar: Lincoln's Inn, 1985, Bencher, 2008; California (inactive), 1988. *Address:* Brick Court Chambers, 7-8 Essex Street, WC2R 3LD.

SWALES, Ian Cameron; *b* Leeds, 5 April 1953; *s* of Harry Swales and Elizabeth Adamson Swales (*née* Doig); *m* 1972, Patricia; two *s* one *d*. *Educ:* Manchester Univ. (BSc Chemical Engrg). FCCA 1977. Yorkshire Electricity, 1973–78; ICI, 1978–99: various financial and business mgt roles, then Global Hd, Leadership Develt, 1997–99; trng and consultancy business, 1999–2008. Contested (Lib Dem) Redcar, 2005. MP (Lib Dem) Redcar, 2010–15. Mem., Public Accounts Cttee, H of C, 2010–14; Lib Dem Treasury spokesman, 2013–15. Hon. Life Mem., British Humanist Assoc., 2015. *Address:* 39 Coast Road, Redcar, N Yorks TS10 3NN.

SWALES, Prof. Martin William, PhD; FBA 1999; Professor of German, University College London, 1976–2003, now Emeritus; *b* 3 Nov. 1940; *s* of Percy Johns Swales and Doris (*née* Davies); *m* 1966, Erika Marta Meier; one *s* one *d*. *Educ:* King Edward's Sch., Birmingham; Christ's Coll., Cambridge (BA 1961); Univ. of Birmingham (PhD 1963). Lectr in German, Univ. of Birmingham, 1964–70; Associate Prof. of German, Univ. of Toronto, 1970–72; Reader in German, KCL, 1972–75; Prof. of German, Univ. of Toronto, 1975–76. Hon. Fellow, UCL, 1996; Hon. Sen. Fellow, Inst. of Modern Languages Res., Univ. of London,

2013–. Verdienstkreuz (Germany), 1994. Hon. DLitt Birmingham, 2003. *Publications:* Arthur Schnitzler, 1971; The German Novelle, 1977; The German Bildungsroman, 1978; Thomas Mann, 1980; (with E. M. Swales) Adalbert Stifter, 1984; Goethe's Werther, 1987; Thomas Mann's Buddenbrooks, 1991; Epochenbuch Realismus, 1997; (with E. M. Swales) Reading Goethe, 2007. *Recreations:* music, theatre (incl. amateur dramatics), incompetent house and car maintenance. *Address:* Department of German, University College London, Gower Street, WC1E 6BT. *T:* (020) 7380 7120.

SWALLOW, Prof. Deborah Anne, PhD; Märit Rausing Director, since 2004, and Professor, since 2008, Courtauld Institute of Art; *b* 27 Aug. 1948; *d* of Arnold Birkett Swallow and Denise Vivienne Swallow (*née* Leighton). *Educ:* Perse Sch. for Girls; New Hall, Cambridge (MA); Darwin Coll., Cambridge (PhD). Cambridge University: Asst Curator, Mus. of Archaeology and Anthropology, 1974–83; Lectr, Girton Coll., 1975–80; Fellow, Darwin Coll., 1975–83; Victoria and Albert Museum: Asst Keeper, Indian Dept, 1983–89; Chief Curator, Indian and SE Asian Dept, 1989–2001; Dir of Collections, and Keeper, Asian Dept, 2001–04. *Address:* Courtauld Institute of Art, Somerset House, Strand, WC2R 0RN. *T:* (020) 7848 2687, *Fax:* (020) 7848 2657. *E:* Deborah.Swallow@courtauld.ac.uk.

SWAMINATHAN, Dr Monkombu Sambasivan, FRS 1973; Founder Chairman and Chief Mentor, M. S. Swaminathan Research Foundation, since 2012 (Chairman, 1990–2012, now Emeritus Chairman); Hon. Director, since 1990, and UNESCO Professor in Ecotechnology, since 1996, Centre for Research on Sustainable Agricultural and Rural Development, Madras; Member, Rajya Sabha, India, since 2007; *b* 7 Aug. 1925; *m* Mina Swaminathan; three *d*. *Educ:* Univs of Kerala, Madras and Cambridge. BSc Kerala, 1944; BSc (Agric.) Madras, 1947; Assoc. IARI 1949; PhD Cantab, 1952. Responsible for developing Nat. Demonstration Project, 1964, and for evolving Seed Village concept; actively involved in develt of High Yielding Varieties, Dryland Farming and Multiple Cropping Programmes. Dir, Indian Agricultural Res. Inst., 1961–72; Sec., Dept of Agricultural Res. and Educn, India, 1972–79; Principal Sec., Min. of Agriculture, 1979–80; Acting Dep. Chm. and Mem. (Sci. and Agriculture), Planning Commn, 1980–82; Dir-Gen., Internat. Rice Res. Inst., Manila, 1982–88. Vice-Pres., Internat. Congress of Genetics, The Hague, 1963; Gen. Pres., Indian Science Congress, 1976. President: IUCN, 1984–90; WWF (India), 1989–96; Nat. Acad. of Agricultural Scis, 1991–96, 2005–07; Pugwash Confs on Science and World Affairs, 2002–07. Chairman: UN Science Adv. Cttee, 1980; Nat. Commn on Farmers, 2004–06; Ind. Chm., FAO Council, 1981–85. First Zakir Hussain Meml Lectr, 1970; UGC Nat. Lectr, 1971; lectures at many internat. scientific symposia. Foreign Associate, US Nat. Acad. of Scis; For. Mem., All Union Acad. of Agricl Scis, USSR; Hon. Mem., Swedish Seed Assoc.; Hon. Fellow, Indian Nat. Acad. of Sciences. FNA; Fellow, Italian Nat. Sci. Acad. Hon. DSc from 60 univs. Shanti Swarup Bhatnagar Award for contribs in Biological Scis, 1961; Mendel Centenary Award, Czechoslovak Acad. of Scis, 1965; Birbal Sahni Award, Indian Bot. Soc., 1965; Ramon Magsaysay Award for Community Leadership, 1971; Silver Jubilee Award, 1973, Meghnath Saha Medal, 1981, Indian Nat. Science Acad.; R. B. Bennett Commonwealth Prize, RSA, 1984; Albert Einstein World Science Award, 1986; World Food Prize, 1987; Tyler Prize for Envmtl Achievement, 1991; Honda Prize for Eco-technology, 1991; Jawaharlal Nehru Centenary Award, 1993; Sasakawa Envmt Prize, UN, 1994; Volvo Internat. Envmt Prize, 1999; Indira Gandhi Prize for Peace, Disarmament and Development, 2000; Franklin D. Roosevelt Four Freedoms Medal, 2000; UNESCO Mahatma Gandhi Prize, 2000; Lal Bahadur Sastri Nat. Award, 2007. Padma Shri, 1967; Padma Bhushan, 1972; Padma Vibhushan, 1989. *Publications:* numerous scientific papers. *Address:* 21 Rathna Nagar, Teynampet, Madras 600018, India; M. S. Swaminathan Research Foundation, Third Cross Street, Taramani Institutional Area, Chennai (Madras) 600113, India.

SWAN, Sir Conrad (Marshall John Fisher), KCVO 1994 (CVO 1986 LVO 1978); PhD; Garter Principal King of Arms, 1992–95; Genealogist: Order of the Bath, 1972–95; Grand Priory, OStJ, 1976–95; First Hon. Genealogist, Order of St Michael and St George, 1989–95; *b* 13 May 1924; *yr s* of late Dr Henry Peter Swan, Major RAMC and RCAMC, of BC, Canada and Colchester, Essex, and of Edna Hanson Magdalen (*née* Green), Cross of Honour Pro Ecclesia et Pontifice; *m* 1957, Lady Hilda Susan Mary Northcote (*d* 1995), Dame of Honour and Devotion, SMO Malta, 1979, and of Justice of SMO of Constantine St George, 1975, *yr d* of 3rd Earl of Iddesleigh; one *s* four *d*. *Educ:* St George's Coll., Weybridge; Sch. of Oriental and African Studies, Univ. of London; Univ. of Western Ontario (BA 1949; MA 1951); Peterhouse, Cambridge (PhD 1955). Served Europe and India (Capt. Madras Regt, IA), 1942–47. Assumption Univ. of Windsor, Ont.: Lectr in History, 1955–57; Asst Prof. of Hist., 1957–60; Univ. Beadle, 1957–60. Rouge Dragon Pursuivant of Arms, 1962–68; York Herald of Arms, 1968–92; Registrar and Sen. Herald-in-Waiting, College of Arms, 1982–92. Inspector of Regimental Colours, 1993–95; Knight Principal, Imperial Soc. of Knights Bachelor, 1995–2000. On Earl Marshal's staff for State Funeral of Sir Winston Churchill, 1965 and Investiture of HRH Prince of Wales, 1969. In attendance: upon HM The Queen at Installation of HRH Prince of Wales as Great Master of Order of the Bath, 1975; during Silver Jubilee Thanksgiving Service, 1977; on Australasian Tour, 1977; at Commonwealth Heads of Govt Conf., 1987; Gentleman Usher-in-Waiting to HH the Pope, GB visit, 1982. Woodward Lectr, Yale, 1964; Centennial Lectr, St Thomas More Coll., Univ. of Saskatchewan, 1967; Inaugural Sir William Scott Meml Lectr, Ulster-Scot Hist. Foundn, 1968; 60th Anniv. Lectr, St Joseph's Coll., Univ. of Alberta, 1987; first Herald to execute duties across Atlantic (Bermuda, 1969) and in S Hemisphere (Brisbane, Qld, 1977) (both in tabard) and in Canada in attendance upon the Sovereign (Vancouver, 1987), to visit Australia, 1970, S America, 1972, Thailand, Japan, 1973, NZ, 1976, Poland, 1991, 1995, Lithuania, 1994. World lecture tours, 1970, 1973, 1976. Adviser to PM of Canada on establishment of Nat. Flag of Canada and Order of Canada, 1964–67 and of Canadian Heraldic Authy, 1988; at invitation of Sec. of State of Canada participated in nat. forum on heraldry in Canada, 1987; assisted at the burial of HIM The Emperor Haile Selassie, Addis Ababa, 2000. Co-founder (with Lady Hilda Swan), Heraldic Garden, Boxford, Suffolk, 1983. Hon. Citizen, State of Texas; Freemanships in USA; Freeman: St George's, Bermuda, 1969; City of London, 1974. Fellow, 1976, Hon. Vice-Pres. and a Founder, Heraldry Soc. of Canada; Fellow, Geneal. Soc. of Victoria (Australia), 1970; FSA 1971; FZS 1986. Master, Gunmakers' Co., 1993 (Liveryman and Freeman, 1974; Mem., Ct of Assts, 1983). Hon. LLD Assumption, Ontario, 2006. Heraldic Award, Governor-Gen. of Antigua and Barbuda, 2002. KStJ 1976. Kt of Honour and Devotion, SMO of Malta, 1979 (Kt of Grace and Devotion, 1964) (Genealogist Br. Assoc., 1974–95); Cross of Comdr of Order of Merit, SMO of Malta, 1983; Comdr (with Star), Royal Norwegian Order of Merit, 1995; Cross of Kt Comdr, Order of Merit (Poland), 1995; Grand Cross with collar, Imperial Order of the Holy Trinity (Ethiopia), 1996; Knight's Cross, Order of Grand Duke Gediminas (Lithuania), 2002; Lithuanian Naval Officers' Ring No 107 (Lithuania), 2002; Kt Grand Cross, Order of the Nation (Antigua and Barbuda), 2003. *Publications:* Heraldry: Ulster and North American Connections, 1972; Canada: Symbols of Sovereignty, 1977; (contrib.) The Royal Encyclopedia, 1991; (jtly) Blood of the Martyrs, 1993; A King from Canada (autobiog.), 2005; many articles in learned jls on heraldic, sigillographic and related subjects. *Recreations:* hunting, driving (horse drawn vehicles), rearing ornamental pheasants and waterfowl, marine biology. *Address:* Boxford House, Suffolk CO10 5JT. *T:* (01787) 210872.

SWAN, Jeanna Catherine; Lord Lieutenant for Berwickshire, since 2014; *b* Aldershot, 11 Aug. 1953; *d* of Lt Col John Nevin Agnew and Margaret Scott Agnew (*née* Thomson); *m* 1979, Richard Gilroy Swan; one *s* two *d*. *Educ:* Elmhurst, Camberley, Surrey; St Leonard's, St Andrews; Royal Dick Sch. of Vet. Studies, Univ. of Edinburgh (BVMS). MRCVS 1976. Vet. Asst, Rogerson Baird and Wain, 1976–78; Vet. Partner, Renton Swan and Partners, 1978–2013. Trustee, MacRobert Trust, 2001–. DL Berwickshire, 2014. *Recreations:* socialising, farming, horse riding. *Address:* Blackhouse Farm, Eyemouth, Berwickshire TD14 5LR. *T:* (01361) 882802, 07557 675342. *E:* jeanna.swan@gmail.com.

SWAN, Sir John (William David), KBE 1990; JP; Founder, Chairman, Swan Group of Companies, since 1999; Premier of Bermuda, 1982–95; *b* 3 July 1935; *s* of late John N. Swan and of Margaret E. Swan; *m* 1965, Jacqueline A. D. Roberts; one *s* two *d*. *Educ:* West Virginia Wesleyan Coll. (BA). Salesman, Real Estate, Rego Ltd, 1960–62; Founder, John W. Swan Ltd, 1962 (Chm. and Chief Exec., 1962–2008). MP (United Bermuda Party) Paget E, 1972–95; Minister for: Marine and Air Services; Labour and Immigration, 1977–78; Home Affairs, 1978–82; formerly: Parly Sec. for Finance; Chairman: Bermuda Hosps Bd; Dept of Civil Aviation; Young Presidents' Organization, 1974–86. Member: Chief Execs Orgn; World Business Council, 1986. Mem. and Fellow, Senate, Jun. Chamber Internat., 1992. Hon. Freeman of London, 1985. Hon. LLD: Univ. of Tampa, Fla, 1985; W Virginia Wesleyan Coll., 1987; Atlantic Union Coll., Mass, 1991. Internat. Medal of Excellence (1st recipient), Poor Richard Club of Philadelphia, 1987; Outstanding Learning Disabled Achiever Award, Lab Sch. of Washington, 1992; Eminent Professional Mem., RICS, 2005. *Recreations:* sailing, tennis. *Address:* 11 Grape Bay Drive, Paget PG 06, Bermuda. *T:* 2361303; Challenger Banks Ltd, PO Box HM 2413, Hamilton HM JX, Bermuda. *T:* 2951785, *Fax:* 2991789. *E:* sirjohn@challengerbanks.bm. *Clubs:* Sandys Rotary, Royal Bermuda Yacht (Bermuda); Bohemian (San Francisco); Chevy Chase (Maryland).

SWAN, Robert Charles, OBE 1995; FRGS; polar explorer, since 1980; *b* 28 July 1956; *s* of late Robert Douglas Swan and of Margaret Swan; *m*; one *s*; *m* 2003, Nicole Beyers. *Educ:* Aysgarth Sch.; Sedbergh Sch.; Durham Univ. (BA). With British Antarctic Survey, 1980–81; planning and fund raising, In the Footsteps of Scott, Antarctic Expedn, 1979–84; arrived at South Pole with R. Mear and G. Wood, 11 Jan. 1986; planning and fund raising, Icewalk, North Pole Expedn, 1988–89; Icewalk Internat. Student Expedn (22 participants from 15 nations), 1989; reached North Pole with 8 walkers from 7 nations (first person to have walked to both Poles), 14 May 1989; One Step Beyond (35 young explorers from 25 nations), 1996–97; started Mission Antarctica, ten year challenge dedicated to preservation of Antarctic wilderness, 1997; Internat. Antarctic Expedns, annually, 2003–. Vis. Prof., Sch. of Envmt, Leeds Beckett (formerly Leeds Metropolitan) Univ., 1992–. Founded 2041.com, for promotion of renewable energy and youth and scientific endeavour, 2003; started Voyage for Cleaner Energy with yacht '2041', 2005–. Keynote speaker at first Earth Summit, Rio de Janeiro, 1992. Mem. Council, WWF (UK), 1987; Vice-Pres., Countryside Mgt Assoc., 1995; Pres., Scott Soc., 2000. UN Goodwill Ambassador with special resp. for youth, 1989; Special Envoy to Dir Gen., UNESCO, 1994; EC Goodwill Ambassador for Envmt, 2003. Liveryman, Wheelwright's Co., 2002. FRGS 1987. Hon. LittD Robert Gordon, 1993; Hon. DSc Durham, 2010. Polar Medal, 1988; Global 500 Award, UN, 1989; Paul Harris Fellow, Rotary Internat., 1991; Smithsonian Award, 1998. *Publications:* In the Footsteps of Scott, 1987; A Walk to the Pole, 1987; Antarctic Survival, 1989; Destination South, 1990; Icewalk, 1990; Antarctica 2041, 2009. *Recreations:* yachting, running, tree surgery, road cycling. *Address:* 47 Wood Wharf, Greenwich, SE10 9BB. *T:* 07767 780135. *E:* Robert@RobertSwan.com. *W:* www.2041.com. *Clubs:* Special Forces; Amstel (Netherlands); Explorers (New York).

SWAN, Hon. Wayne Maxwell; MHR (ALP) for Lilley, Queensland, 1993–96 and since 1998; *b* Nambour, Qld, 30 June 1954; *s* of Maurice Roy Swan and Maida Joy Swan; *m* 1984, Kim Williamson; one *s* two *d*. *Educ:* Nambour High Sch.; Queensland Univ. Lectr in Public Admin, Qld Inst. of Technol., 1976–77, 1981–82 and 1985–88; policy analyst, Office of Youth Affairs, 1978; Advr to Leader of Opposition and Opposition spokesperson on industrial affairs and employment, 1978–80; Private Sec. to Minister of State, 1983, to Minister of Foreign Affairs, 1984; Campaign Dir and Asst State Sec., 1988–91, State Sec., 1991–93, ALP, Qld; Advr to Leader of Opposition, 1996–98. Shadow Minister for Family and Community Services, 1998–2000 and 2001–04; Manager of Opposition Business, House of Reps, 2001–03; Shadow Treas., 2004–07; Treas., 2007–13; Dep. Prime Minister, 2010–13. *Address:* 1162 Sandgate Road, Nundah, Qld 4012, Australia.

SWANN, Julian Dana Nimmo H.; *see* Hartland-Swann.

SWANN, Kathryn, (Kate); Chief Executive, SSP, since 2013; *b* 1964; *d* of Ian and Sheila Prior; *m* 1987; two *d*. *Educ:* Bradford Univ. (BSc Hons Business Mgt). Grad. trainee, Tesco, 1986–88; Brand Manager, Homepride Foods, 1988–91; Mktg Controller, Coca Cola Schweppes, 1991; Mktg Dir, Currys, 1992–96; Homebase: Mktg Dir, 1996–99; Man. Dir, 1999; Man. Dir, Argos, 2000–03; CEO, WH Smith, 2003–13. *Address:* SSP, 169 Euston Road, NW1 2AE.

SWANN, Sir Michael (Christopher), 4th Bt *cr* 1906, of Prince's Gardens, Royal Borough of Kensington; TD 1979; Partner, Smith Swann & Co., 1992–99; Payman's, 1999–2006; *b* 23 Sept. 1941; *s* of Sir Anthony Swann, 3rd Bt, CMG, OBE and Jean Margaret, *d* of late John Herbert Niblock-Stuart; *S* father, 1991; *m* 1st, 1965, Hon. Lydia Hewitt (marr. diss. 1985), *e d* of 8th Viscount Lifford; two *s* one *d*; 2nd, 1988, Marilyn Ann Morse (*née* Tobitt). *Educ:* Eton Coll. APMI 1978. Lt KRRC (The Royal Green Jackets), 1960–63; T&AVR 4th Bn The Royal Green Jackets, 1964–79 (Brevet Lt-Col 1979). Director: Wright Deen (Life and Estate Duty), 1964–74; Richards Longstaff (Holdings) Ltd, 1974–86; Richards Longstaff Ltd, 1974–88; Gerrard Vivian Gray (Life & Pensions), 1988–92 (Man. Dir). Trustee, Gabbitas Truman and Thring, 1978–2008 (Chm., 1998–2008). General Comr of Income Tax, 1988–2008. *Recreations:* bridge, golf, ski-ing, gardening, racing. *Heir: s* Jonathan Christopher Swann [*b* 17 Nov. 1966; *m* 1994, Polly, *d* of Comdr David Baston; twin *s*]. *Address:* 38 Hurlingham Road, SW6 3RQ. *Clubs:* Turf, Hurlingham, IZ, MCC; New Zealand Golf.

SWANN, Paul Phillip; Regional Employment Judge, East Midlands Region, since 2012; *b* Birmingham, 24 July 1956.

SWANN, Robert Samuel, (Robin); Member (UU) North Antrim, Northern Ireland Assembly, since 2011; *b* Kells, Co. Antrim, 24 Sept. 1971; *s* of Robert Swann and Ida Swann; *m* 2008, Jennifer McIlroy; one *s* one *d*. *Educ:* Open Univ. (BSc; Professional Cert. Mgt). NI Manager, SGS, 2005–11. Chief Whip (UU), 2012–. Member: Agric. and Rural Develt Cttee, 2011–; Business Cttee, 2011–; Chm., Employment and Learning Cttee, 2013–; Member, All Party Group: on Internat. Develt, 2011–; on Muscular Dystrophy, 2011–; Chm., All Party Gp on Congenital Heart Disease, 2013–. Exec. Mem., Commonwealth Parly Assoc., 2011– (Chm., NI Assembly Br., 2015–). Contested (UU) N Antrim, 2015. Pres., Young Farmers' Clubs, 2005–07; Chm., Rural Youth Europe, 2008–10. Governor: Cambridge House Grammar Sch., 2010–15; Ballee Community High Sch., 2010–15. *Recreation:* Ulster Scots culture and traditions. *Address:* (office) 13–15 Queen Street, Harryville, Ballymena BT42 2BB. *T:* (028) 2565 9595. *E:* robin.swannmla@gmail.com.

SWANNELL, John, FRPS; professional photographer specialising in fashion and portraits; *b* 27 Dec. 1946; *s* of Ted and Lily Swannell; *m* 1982, Marianne Lah; one *s* three *d*. *Educ:* Bishopswood Sch., Highgate. FRPS 1993. Left sch. at 16; Vogue Studios, 1966–69; asst to David Bailey, 1969–74; founded own studio, 1975; worked for Vogue, Harpers & Queen, Sunday Times, Tatler. Exhibitions: show, Royal Acad., Edinburgh, 1989; NPG, Edinburgh, 1990; retrospective of fashion work, RPS, 1990; exhibn of nudes, Hamilton Gall., 1991; exhibn of portraits, NPG, 1996–97, 2011; photographs in permanent collections: V&A; NPG, London and Scotland; RPS. Royal portraits: the Princess Royal, 40th birthday 1992, 50th birthday 2002, 60th birthday, 2010; Diana, Princess of Wales with Princes William and Harry,

1994; the Queen, Queen Mother, Prince of Wales and Prince William, 2001; the Queen and Duke of Edinburgh for Golden Jubilee, 2002; Prince Charles for rainforest project, 2008; the Queen and Duke of Edinburgh for Diamond Jubilee, 2012; Royal Mail stamps: wedding of Duke and Duchess of Wessex, 1999; Queen Mother's 100th birthday; other portraits include: King Hussein of Jordan, King Abdullah and Queen Rania of Jordan, Rowan Atkinson, Helena Bonham Carter, Michael Caine, Joan Collins, Billy Connolly, Dame Judi Dench, Bryan Ferry, Sir Norman Foster, Sir John Gielgud, Gilbert and George, John Hurt, Elton John, Joanna Lumley, Spike Milligan, Roger Moore, Peter O'Toole, Michael Palin, Michael Parkinson, Margaret Thatcher, Tony Blair, Susan Boyle. *Publications:* Fine Lines, 1982; Naked Landscape, 1986; Twenty Years On, 1996; Ten Out of Ten, 2001; I'm Still Standing, 2002; Nudes 1978–2006, 2007; Landscapes, 2009; Highgate Cemetery, 2010; Foxgloves, 2011; Snowdrops, 2012; Daffodils, 2012; Bluebells, 2012. *Recreation:* landscape photography. *Address:* 7 North Road, Highgate, N6 4BD. *T:* (020) 8348 5965. *E:* info@johnswannell.com.

SWANNELL, Nicola Mary, (Mrs Graham Swannell); *see* Pagett, N. M.

SWANNELL, Robert William Ashburnham; Chairman: Marks and Spencer plc, since 2011; Shareholder Executive, Department for Business, Innovation and Skills, since 2014; *b* Nanyuki, Kenya, 18 Nov. 1950; *s* of David William Ashburnham Swannell and Pamela Mary Swannell; *m* 1982, Patricia Ann Ward; one *s* one *d*. *Educ:* Rugby Sch. FCA 1973. Called to the Bar, Lincoln's Inn, 1976. Peat Marwick Mitchell, 1969–73; Investment Banking, Schroders, later Citigroup, 1977–2010: Co-Chm., Citigroup European Investment Bank, 2003–06; Vice Chm., Citigroup Europe, 2006–10. Chm., HMV Gp plc, 2009–11; non-executive Director: British Land Co. plc, 1999–2010; 3i Gp plc, 2006–10. Member: Industrial Adv. Bd, DTI, later BERR, 1999–2008; Regulatory Decisions Cttee, FSA, 2001–05; Takeover Appeal Bd, 2007–. Chm., Governing Body, Rugby Sch., 2009–14. *Recreations:* golf, opera, ballet, theatre. *Address:* Marks and Spencer Group plc, Waterside House, 35 North Wharf Road, W2 1NW. *T:* (020) 8718 9636. *E:* robert.swannell@marks-and-spencer.com. *Club:* Turf.

SWANNEY, Rajni; Sheriff of North Strathclyde at Greenock, 2012–14 (Floating Sheriff, 1999–2012); *b* 27 Aug. 1954; *d* of Sat Dev Dhir and Swarn Lata Dhir; *m* 1981, Robert Todd Swanney; two *s*. *Educ:* Glasgow Univ. (LLB). Court Assistant: MacRoberts, Glasgow, 1978–80; various Glasgow firms, 1982–88; Chm. (pt-time), Child Support Tribunal, 1993–96; Immigration Adjudicator (pt-time), 1995–99. *Recreations:* gardening, reading, jewellery making, enjoying all things French!

SWANSEA, 5th Baron *cr* 1893, of Singleton, co. Glamorgan; **Richard Anthony Hussey Vivian;** Bt 1882; *b* 24 Jan. 1957; *s* of 4th Baron Swansea and Miriam Antoinette Vivian (*née* Caccia-Birch); *S* father, 2005; *m* 1996, Anna Clementine Brooking (*née* Austin); one *s* one *d*. *Educ:* Eton Coll.; Univ. of Durham (BA Hons); City Univ. Business Sch. (MBA). Financial journalist, 1979–97; res. ed., various investment banks, 1998–2006; Investment Research Supervisor: WestLB AG, 2006–10; Nomura International plc, 2010–11; Franchise Partner, Rosemary Bookkeeping, 2013–. Mem. (C) Wandsworth BC, 1994–2006 (Dep. Mayor, 2000–01; Hon. Alderman, 2006). Mem. Sch. Council, Newton Prep. Sch., Battersea, 2001–12. Vice Pres., Morriston RFC Male Choir, 2007–. *Publications:* China's Metals and World Markets, 1992. *Recreations:* racing, Su Doku puzzles, croquet. *Heir: s* Hon. James Henry Hussey Vivian, *b* 25 June 1999. *Address:* 48 Weyside Road, Guildford, Surrey GU1 1HX.

SWANSEA AND BRECON, Bishop of, since 2008; **Rt Rev. John David Edward Davies;** *b* 6 Feb. 1953; *s* of William Howell Davies and Doiran Rallison Davies; *m* 1986, Joanna Lucy Davies (*née* Aulton); one *s* one *d*. *Educ:* Southampton Univ. (LLB 1974); Coll. of Law; St Michael's Coll., Llandaff (DipTh Wales 1984); Univ. of Wales (LLM Canon Law 1995). Admitted Solicitor, 1977; private practice, 1975–82. Ordained deacon, 1984, priest, 1985; Asst Curate, Chepstow, 1984–86; Curate-in-charge, Michaelston-y-Fedw and Rudry, 1986–89; Rector, Bedwas and Rudry, 1989–95; Vicar, St John Evangelist, Newport, 1995–2000; Dean of Brecon, 2000–08. CStJ 2010 (Sub-Prelate, Priory for Wales, 2010–). *Recreations:* cooking, golf, music (wide taste), playing the organ, theatre, opera, reading, current affairs, sport (especially Test Match Special and Peter Alliss), planning walks for the family (and accompanying them when feeling energetic), entertaining my family by trying to convince them of the inestimable benefits of knowing Latin and of appreciating other lost glories of the past. *Address:* Ely Tower, Castle Square, Brecon, Powys LD3 9DJ. *T:* (01874) 622008.

SWANSON, Alayne Elizabeth; Sheriff of Glasgow and Strathkelvin at Glasgow, since 2010; *b* Elgin, 16 April 1959; *d* of David Alan Lawrie and Ethel Lawrie; *m* 1984, Magnus Swanson; three *s*. *Educ:* Elgin Acad.; Univ. of Edinburgh (LLB Hons, DipLP). Trainee, Shepherd & Wedderburn, 1982–84; Asst, McLure Naismith, 1984–86; Foreign Associate, Hughes Hubbard & Reed, 1986–87; Asst and Partner, Bird Semple Fyfe, Ireland, 1987–94; Partner, Dundas & Wilson, 1994–98; Solicitor Advocate, 1996; Partner, Maclay Murray & Spens, 1998–2010. *Recreations:* golf, ski-ing, walking, music. *Address:* Glasgow Sheriff Court, Sheriff's Chambers, 1 Carlton Place, Glasgow G5 9DA. *T:* (0141) 429 8888, *Fax:* (0141) 429 2217. *E:* sheriffaswanson@scotcourts.gov.uk.

SWANSON, His Honour John Alexander; a Circuit Judge, 1996–2012; *b* 31 May 1944; *s* of Sidney Alexander Swanson and Joan Swanson; *m* 1981, Pauline Ann Hearn (*née* Woodmansey) (marr. diss.); two *d*. *Educ:* Giggleswick Sch., Settle; Univ. of Newcastle upon Tyne (LLB 1966). Solicitor, 1970–75; called to the Bar, Inner Temple, 1975; a Recorder, 1994–96. Asst Comr, Boundary Commn for England, 1992–95. *Recreations:* hill-walking, American West, 19th and 20th century music, history of railways, malt whisky. *Clubs:* Bridlington Rugby Union Football; Bridlington Yacht.

SWANSON, Prof. Sydney Alan Vasey, FREng; Professor of Biomechanics, Imperial College, University of London, 1974–97; *b* 31 Oct. 1931; *s* of Charles Henry William Swanson and Hannah Elizabeth Swanson (*née* Vasey); *m* 1956, Mary Howarth; one *s* one *d*. *Educ:* Scarborough Boys' High Sch.; Imperial Coll., London. DSc (Eng), PhD, DIC, FCGI, FIMechE; FREng (FEng 1987). Engineering Laboratories, Bristol Aircraft Ltd, 1955–58; Imperial College, London: Lectr, Mechanical Engineering, 1958–69; Reader in Biomechanics, 1969–74; Dean, City and Guilds Coll., 1976–79; Head of Mechanical Engineering Dept, 1978–83; Pro Rector, 1983–86; Pro Rector (Educnl Quality), 1994–97; Dep. Rector, 1997. *Publications:* Engineering Dynamics, 1963; Engineering in Medicine (with B. M. Sayers and B. Watson), 1975; (with M. A. R. Freeman) The Scientific Basis of Joint Replacement, 1977; papers on bone, cartilage and joints in learned jls. *Recreations:* photography, cycling, fell-walking. *Address:* 12 Holmwood Gardens, Wallington, Surrey SM6 0HN. *Club:* Lyke Wake (Northallerton).

SWANSTON, Roderick Brian, FRCM, FRCO; Reader in Historical and Interdisciplinary Studies, Royal College of Music, 1997–2004; *b* 28 Aug. 1948; *s* of Comdr David Swanston and Sheila Anne Swanston (*née* Lang). *Educ:* Stowe Sch.; Royal Coll. of Music (ARCM 1967; GRSM 1969; FRCM 1994); Pembroke Coll., Cambridge (Organ Schol., 1969; BA 1971, MA 1974; MusB 1975). LRAM 1970; FRCO 1975. Asst Organist, Tower of London, 1967–68; Director of Music: Christ Church, Lancaster Gate, 1972–77; St James, Sussex Gardens, 1977–80; Tutor, Faculty of Contg Educn, Birkbeck Coll., London Univ., 1974–; freelance lectr, 1974–, and broadcaster, 1990–; Prof., RCM, 1976–2004; Lectr in Humanities, Imperial Coll., London Univ., 1996–; Vis. Prof., Dartmouth Coll., NH, 1995, 1999. Artistic Dir, Austro-Hungarian Music Fest., 1994–. *Publications:* A Dictionary of Biblical Interpretation, 1990; Fairest Isle, 1995; Ultimate Encyclopaedia of Instruments, 1996; Collins Encyclopaedia of Music, 2000; contrib. Musical Times, Gramophone, Early Music, Classic CD. *Recreations:* reading, poetry, theatre, thinking. *Club:* Athenæum.

SWANSTON, Roy; Chairman, Shaftesbury Housing Group, 2005–07; *b* 31 Oct. 1940; *s* of Robert Trotter Swanston and Margaret Ann Swanston (*née* Paxton); *m* 1963, Doreen Edmundson; one *s* one *d*. *Educ:* Berwick-upon-Tweed Grammar Sch. FRICS. County Borough of Sunderland, 1958–67; Clasp Develt Gp, Nottingham, 1967–71; Notts CC, 1971–74; Durham CC, 1974–75; Dir of Building Economics, 1975–82, of Dept of Architecture, 1982–87, Cheshire CC; Sen. Management Consultant, Peat Marwick McLintock, 1987–88; Dir of Develt, Bucknall Austin, 1988–90; Dir, Properties in Care, 1990–93, Res. and Professional Services, 1993–95, English Heritage; Chm., Local Govt Residuary Bd (England), 1995–99. Chairman: W Herts HA, 1996–2001; E and N Herts NHS Trust, 2001–02. Chairman: Jones Lang Wootton Educn Trust, 1995–2000; Jt Contracts Tribunal for Standard Form of Building Contract, 1995–2002. Mem., E of England Heritage Lottery Cttee, 2006–12. Pres., RICS, 1994–95 (Pres., QS Div., 1982–83; Hon. Treas., 1987–90; Chm., Bldg Conservation Diploma Adv. Bd, 2000–09); Sec. Gen., Internat. Fedn of Surveyors, 1995–99. Visiting Professor: Liverpool John Moores Univ., 1995–2005; Bedfordshire (formerly Luton) Univ., 1996– (Mem. Court, 1999–); Salford Univ., 1999–2005 (Vis. Fellow, 1986–99). Mem., Yorks Dales Nat. Park Authy, 2001–04. Trustee, NE Civic Trust, 1998–2010 (Chm., 2006–08). Mem., Barnardo's Council, 1989–2005; Chm., Barnardo's Pension Fund, 2003–05 (Trustee, 1998–2002). Governor: Culford Methodist Ind. Sch., 1999–2015 (Chm., 2008–14); Springhill Special Sch., 2001–04 (Chm., 2001–04). Methodist Local Preacher; Chair, Methodist Ch House Mgt Cttee, 2014–. Hon. DSc Salford, 1994. *Recreations:* supporter of Sunderland AFC, fell walking.

SWANTEE, Olaf; Chief Executive Officer, EE (formerly Everything Everywhere) Ltd, since 2011; *b* Netherlands; *m*. *Educ:* BA Econs; European Sch. of Mgt, Paris (MBA 1989). IT industry, Europe and USA, latterly EMEA Sen. Vice Pres. for enterprise sales and software, Hewlett-Packard; former Mem., Exec. Bd, Orange France-Telecom. *Address:* EE Ltd, The Point, 37 North Wharf Road, W2 1AG. *T:* (01707) 315000.

SWANTON, Robert Howard, MD; FRCP; Consultant Cardiologist, University College London Hospitals, since 1979; *b* 30 Sept. 1944; *s* of Robert Neil and Sue Swanton; *m* 1969, Lindsay Ann (*née* Jepson); one *s* one *d*. *Educ:* Monkton Combe Sch.; Queens' Coll., Cambridge (MB BChir 1969; MA; MD 1980); St Thomas's Hosp. Med. Sch. FRCP 1984. Senior Registrar: St Thomas' Hosp., 1975–77; Nat. Heart Hosp., 1977–79; Consultant Cardiologist: Middlesex Hosp., 1979–2005; King Edward VII Hosp. for Officers, 1984–. Mem. Med. Adv. Panel on Cardiology, CAA, 1998–; Chm. Adv. Panel on Cardiology, DVLA, 2002–09. Hon. Sec., 1988–90, Pres., 1998–2001, British Cardiac Soc. FESC 1994; FACC 2005. Mem. Editorial Bd, Hospital Medicine, 1986–. *Publications:* Cardiology, 1984, 6th edn 2008; Essential Angioplasty, 2012; articles in med. literature incl. Heart, American Jl Cardiology, Hospital Medicine, European Heart Jl, etc. *Recreations:* music, photography. *Address:* (home) Kent Lodge, 10 Dover Park Drive, Roehampton, SW15 5BG. *T:* (020) 8788 6920. *E:* howard.swanton@uclh.org; (office) 42 Wimpole Street, W1G 8YF. *T:* (020) 7486 7416, *Fax:* (020) 7487 2569. *Clubs:* Arts; St Albans Medical; Chelsea Clinical.

SWARBRICK, Catherine Marie; Director of Administration, University of London, 2004–11; *b* 25 Nov. 1950; *d* of Hubert Joseph Swarbrick and Margaret Swarbrick. *Educ:* Goldsmiths' Coll., Univ. of London (BA Hons, PGCE). Secondary sch. teacher, 1973–79; Sec., Law Dept, LSE, 1980–82; Exams Officer, British Computer Soc., 1982–85; Sen. Manager, RCGP, 1985–95; Dir, Nat. Childbirth Trust, 1995–99; School Sec., St George's Hosp. Med. Sch., 1999–2004. *Recreations:* reading, art history.

SWARBRICK, Prof. James, PhD, DSc; FRSC, CChem; FRPharmS; President, PharmaceuTech Inc., since 2001; *b* 8 May 1934; *s* of George Winston Swarbrick and Edith M. C. Cooper; *m* 1960, Pamela Margaret Oliver. *Educ:* Sloane Grammar Sch.; Chelsea Coll., Univ. of London (BPharm Hons 1960; PhD 1964; DSc 1972). FRSC (FRIC 1970); FRPharmS (FPS 1978; MPS 1961). Asst Lectr, 1962, Lectr, 1964, Chelsea Coll.; Vis. Asst Prof., Purdue Univ., 1964; Associate Prof., 1966, Prof. and Chm. of Dept of Pharmaceutics, 1969, Asst Dean, 1970, Univ. of Conn; Dir of Product Develt, Sterling-Winthrop Res. Inst., NY, 1972; first Prof. of Pharmaceutics, Univ. of Sydney, 1975–76; Dean, Sch. of Pharmacy, Univ. of London, 1976–78; Prof. of Pharmacy and Chm., Res. Council, Univ. of S California, Los Angeles, 1978–81; Prof. of Pharmaceutics and Chm., Div. of Pharmaceutics, Univ. of N Carolina, 1981–93; Vice-Pres., R&D, 1993–99, Scientific Affairs, 1999–2006, Applied Analytical Industries Inc., subseq. aaiPharma Inc. Vis. Scientist, Astra Labs, Sweden, 1971; Vis. Prof., Shanghai Med. Univ., 1991–92. Indust. Cons., 1965–72, 1975–; Cons., Aust. Dept of Health, 1975–76; Mem., Cttee on Specifications, National Formulary, 1970–75; Chm., Jt US Pharmacopoeia-Nat. Formulary Panel on Disintegration and Dissolution Testing, 1971–75. Member: Cttee on Grad. Programs, Amer. Assoc. of Colls of Pharmacy, 1969–71; Practice Trng Cttee, Pharm. Soc. of NSW, 1975–76; Academic Bd, Univ. of Sydney, 1975–76; Collegiate Council, 1976–78; Educn Cttee, Pharmaceutical Soc. of GB, 1976–78; Working Party on Pre-Registration Training, 1977–78. Pharmaceutical Manufacturers Assoc. Foundation: Mem., Basic Pharmacology Adv. Cttee, 1982–91; Chm., Pharmaceutics Adv. Cttee, 1986–2007; Mem., Scientific Adv. Cttee, 1986–2007; Mem., Generic Drugs Adv. Cttee, Food and Drug Admin, 1992–96 (Chm., 1994–96). FAAAS 1966; Fellow: Acad. of Pharm. Sciences, 1973; Amer. Assoc. of Pharmaceutical Scientists, 1987. Kenan Res. Study Award, 1988. Mem. Editorial Board: Jl of Biopharmaceutics and Pharmacokinetics, 1973–79; Drug Development Communications, 1974–82; Pharmaceutical Technology, 1978–; Biopharmaceutics and Drug Disposition, 1979–; series Editor: Current Concepts in the Pharmaceutical Sciences, Drugs and the Pharmaceutical Sciences. *Publications:* (with A. N. Martin and A. Cammarata) Physical Pharmacy, 2nd edn 1969, 3rd edn 1983; (ed) Encyclopedia of Pharmaceutical Technology, 1988–2010, 4th edn as Encyclopedia of Pharmaceutical Science and Technology, 2013; (ed jtly) Drug Delivery and Targeting, 2001; contributed: American Pharmacy, 6th edn 1966 and 7th edn 1974; Remington's Pharmaceutical Sciences, 14th edn 1970 to 22nd edn 2012; contrib. Current Concepts in the Pharmaceutical Sciences: Biopharmaceutics, 1970; res. contribs to internat. sci. jls. *Recreations:* woodworking, listening to music, golf. *Address:* PharmaceuTech Inc., 180 Doral Drive, Pinehurst, NC 28374–8682, USA. *T:* (910) 2553015. *E:* pharmaceutech@earthlink.net.

SWARUP, Prof. Govind, PhD; FRS 1991; Professor of Eminence, Physics and Radio Astronomy, 1990–94, Professor Emeritus, 1994–99, Homi Bhabha Senior Fellow, 1999–2001, Tata Institute of Fundamental Research, Bombay; *b* 29 March 1929; *m* Bina Jain; one *s* one *d*. *Educ:* Allahabad Univ. (BSc 1948; MSc 1950); Stanford Univ., USA (PhD 1961). Sec., Radio Res. Cttee, CSIR, Nat. Physical Lab., New Delhi, 1950–53; Colombo-Plan Fellowship, CSIRO, Sydney, 1953–55; Res. Associate, Harvard Univ., 1956–57; Grad. Student, Stanford Univ., USA, 1957–60, Asst Prof. 1961–63; Tata Institute of Fundamental Research, Bombay: Reader, 1963–65; Associate Prof., 1965–70; Prof., 1970–79; Sen. Prof., 1979–90; Dir, Giant Metrewave Radio Telescope Project, 1987–96. INSA Hon. Scientist, 2001–05. Visiting Professor: Univ. of Md, USA, 1980; Univ. of Groningen, Netherlands, 1980–81; Univ. of Leiden, Netherlands, 1981. Chm., Indian Nat. Cttee, URSI, 1986–88, 1994–97. Fellow: Indian Nat. Sci. Acad.; Indian Acad. Scis; Nat. Acad. Scis, India; Indian Geophysical Union; Third World Acad. of Scis; Academician: Internat. Acad. of Astronautics; Pontifical Acad. of Scis. Associate, RAS; Member: Astronomical Soc. India (Pres., 1975–77); IAU (Pres., Radio Astronomy Commn, 1979–82); Indian Physics Assoc.; Indian Physical Soc. Member Editorial Board: Indian Jl Radio and Space Physics; Nat. Acad. of Science, India.

Numerous awards, incl. Delinger Award, URSI; S. S. Bhatnager Award, India, 1972; Tsiolkovsky medal, Fedn of Cosmonautics, USSR, 1987; Third World Acad. of Scis Award, Trieste, 1988; R. D. Birla Award, India, 1990; Khwarizmi Award, Iran, 1999; Herschel Medal, RAS, 2006; Grote Reber Medal, Tasmania, 2007. Holder of 2 patents. *Publications:* (ed jtly) Quasars, 1986; (ed jtly) History of Oriental Astronomy, 1987; (ed jtly) Universe at Low Frequency, 2003. *Address:* 10 Cozy Retreat, Road No 3, Sindh Society, Aundh, Pune 411007, India. *T:* (office) (20) 25719000, (home) (20) 25851630.

SWASH, Prof. Michael, MD; FRCP, FRCPath; Hon. Consultant Neurologist: St Bartholomew's and the Royal London Hospitals, since 1972; London Independent Hospital, since 1980; Professor of Neurology, Bart's and the London School of Medicine and Dentistry, Queen Mary (formerly St Bartholomew's and the Royal London School of Medicine and Dentistry, Queen Mary and Westfield College), University of London, 1993–2006, now Emeritus; *b* 29 Jan. 1939; *s* of Edwin Frank Swash and Kathleen Swash; *m* 1966, Caroline Mary Payne; three *s*. *Educ:* Forest Sch., London; London Hosp. Med. Coll., Univ. of London (MB BS 1962; MD 1973); Univ. of Virginia, USA. FRCP 1977; FRCPath 1991. House appts, London and Bath, 1962–63; GP, Westbury, Wilts and Tottenham, 1965; postgrad. trng in neurol. and neurophysiol., Case-Western Reserve Univ., Cleveland, Ohio and Washington Univ., St Louis, Mo, 1965–68; MRC Res. Fellow in Neuropathol., then Sen. Registrar in Neurol., Royal London Hosp., 1968–72; Consultant Neurologist, Newham HA, 1972–91; Sen. Lectr in Neuropathol., London Hosp. Med. Coll., 1976–90; Med. Dir, Royal London NHS Trust, 1990–93. CMO, Swiss Re (formerly Swiss Reinsce) Ltd, 1985–2012. Mem., Med. Adv. Bd, Best Doctors Inc., 2013–. Dir, Medhand Internat. AB, 2002–. Vis. lectr or vis. prof., various univs in Europe, Asia, Australia and N America; Spinoza Vis. Prof., Univ. of Amsterdam, 1999–2000. Hon. Prof. of Neurology, Univ. of Lisbon, 2006–. Ed., Associate Ed. and mem. editl bds, various neurol and other scientific jls. Mem., Neurosci. Bd, MRC, 1987–91. Hon. Secretary: Sect. Neurol., RSocMed, 1977–79; Assoc. of British Neurologists, 1981–87; Motor Neurone Disease Association: Chm., Annual Symposium Cttee, 1991–99; Chm. Trustees, 1998–2001; Chm., World Fedn of Neurol. Res. Gp on MNDs, 1997–2005. Medals and prizes include: Forbes H. Norris Internat. Prize for res. and care in MND/ALS; Medallist, Assoc. of British Neurologists, 2010. *Publications:* (jtly) Colour Guide to Neurology, 1972, 3rd edn 2005; (ed) Hutchison's Clinical Methods, 16th edn, 1975 to 22nd edn, 2007; (jtly) Neuromuscular Disorders: a practical approach to diagnosis and management, 1981, 3rd edn 1999; (jtly) Clinical Neuropathology, 1983; (jtly) Biopsy Pathology of Muscle, 1984, 2nd edn 1991; (jtly) Scientific Basis of Neurology, 1985; (jtly) Coloproctology and the Pelvic Floor, 1985, 2nd edn 1992; (jtly) Neurology: a concise clinical text, 1989; (jtly) Hierarchies in Neurology, 1989; (jtly) Clinical Neurology, 2 vols, 1989; (jtly) Motor Neuron Disease, 1994; Outcomes in Neurology and Neurosurgery, 1998; (jtly) Amyotrophic Lateral Sclerosis, 2000, 2nd edn 2006; (jtly) ALSAQ User Manual, 2001; (jtly) The Pelvic Floor, 2002; (jtly) Neurology in Focus, 2009; contrib. numerous papers to med. and scientific jls. *Recreations:* pianoforte, chamber music and opera, hill walking, Morgan Plus 8. *Address:* London Independent Hospital, E1 4NL. *T:* (020) 7780 2400, *Fax:* (020) 7638 4043. *E:* mswash@btinternet.com. *Clubs:* Athenæum; London Rowing; Rowfant (Cleveland, Ohio).

SWAYNE, Rt Hon. Desmond (Angus), TD 2000; PC 2011; MP (C) New Forest West, since 1997; Minister of State, Department for International Development, since 2014; *b* 20 Aug. 1956; *s* of George Joseph Swayne and Elizabeth McAlister Swayne (*née* Gibson); *m* 1987, Moira Cecily Teek; one *s* two *d*. *Educ:* Bedford Sch.; Univ. of St Andrews (MTh). Schoolmaster: Charterhouse, 1980–81; Wrekin Coll., 1982–87; Systems Manager, Royal Bank of Scotland, 1988–96. Opposition front bench spokesman on health, Jan.–Sept. 2001, on defence, 2001–02, on NI, 2003–04; Opposition Whip, 2002–03; PPS to Leader of the Opposition, 2004–10, to Prime Minister, 2010–12; a Lord Comr of HM Treasury (Govt Whip), 2012–13; Vice Chamberlain of HM Household (Dep. Chief Whip), 2013–14. TA Officer, 1987–. Prison visitor, 1989–. *Address:* House of Commons, SW1A 0AA. *Clubs:* Cavalry and Guards; Serpentine Swimming.

SWAYNE, Giles Oliver Cairnes; composer; *b* 30 June 1946; *s* of Sir Ronald Oliver Carless Swayne, MC and Charmian (*née* Cairnes); *m* 1st, 1972, Camilla Rumbold (marr. diss. 1983); one *s*; 2nd, 1984, Naa Otua Codjoe (marr. diss. 2001); 3rd, 2002, Malu Lin. *Educ:* Ampleforth; Trinity Coll., Cambridge; Royal Acad. of Music. Dir, Gonzaga Music Ltd, 2002–. Composer in Residence, Clare Coll., Cambridge, 2006–14. *Compositions:* Six songs of lust, La rivière, 1966; The kiss, 1967; Sonata for string quartet, 1968; Three Shakespeare songs, 1969; Chamber music for strings, Four lyrical pieces, 1970; The good-morrow, String quartet no 1, Paraphrase, 1971; Trio, Canto for guitar, 1972; Canto for piano, Canto for violin, 1973; Orlando's music, Synthesis, Scrapbook, 1974; Canto for clarinet, Charades, Duo, 1975; Suite for Guitar, Pentecost-music, Alleluia!, 1976; String quartet no 2, 1977; A world within, 1978; Phoenix variations, CRY, 1979; The three Rs, Freewheeling, 1980; Count-down, Canto for cello, 1981; Rhythm-studies 1 and 2, Magnificat I, 1982; Riff-raff, A song for Haddi, 1983; Symphony for small orchestra, Le nozze di Cherubino, NaaOtwa Lala, 1984; Missa Tiburtina, 1985; Into the light, Solo, godsong, Nunc dimittis I, O magnum mysterium, 1986; PP, Tonos, Veni creator I and II, Songlines, The coming of Saskia Hawkins, 1987; The song of Leviathan, Harmonies of Hell, 1988; A memory of sky, 1989; No quiet place, No man's land, 1990; Circle of silence, 1991; Zebra music, The song of the Tortoise, 1992; The Owl and the Pussycat I, String quartet no 3, 1993; Fiddlesticks, Goodnight sweet ladies, Squeezy, 1994; All about Henry, The tiger, Communion service in D, A convocation of worms, 1995; Two romantic songs, The silent land, Ophelia drowning, 1996; Tombeau, Beatus vir, Mr Leary's mechanical maggot, Chinese whispers, Petite messe solitaire, Missa brevissima, Echo, 1997; Winter Solstice carol, Groundwork, Merlis Lied, 1998; The flight of the Swan, HAVOC, 1999; Perturbèd spirit, Canto for flute, The Akond of Swat, 2000; Mancanza, The murder of Gonzago, 2001; Bits and Bobs, Epitaph and refrain, 2002; The Owl and the Pussycat II, Midwinter, Sangre viva, 2003; Stabat Mater, Four Passiontide motets, Ave verum corpus, Stations of the Cross I, Mr Bach's Bottle-bank, Magnificat II, 2004; Four Christmas Carols, Nunc dimittis II, Lonely hearts, Stations of the Cross II, Bits of Mrs Bach, Epithalamium, Elegy for a wicked world, 2005; Sonata for cello and piano, Sinfonietta concertante, Ten Terrible Tunes, A Clare Eucharist, Creepy-crawlies, Two little motets, There is no rose, 2006; Suite for solo cello, Symphony no 1, Threnody, 2007; Leonardo's Dream, Agnes Wisley's Chillout Fantasy, Magnificat III, 2008; The human heart, Bagatelles (Book I) for piano, Toil and trouble, Zig-zag, String quartet No 4, The Joys of Travel, Adam lay ibounden, O mysteria, 2009; Der Wandersmann, Hubbub, The Word, Complaintes, 2010; Dolorosa, Laulu Laulle, Bagatelles for piano (Book 2), 2011; Clare Canticles, Uncommon Prayers, 2012; Strumming, Two Little Prayers, I Do Not Sleep, Double Act, 2013; The Yonghy-Bonghy-Bo, God is gone up, Chansons dévotes et poissonneuses, Our orphan souls, 2014; Kaleidoscope, The Humanity Idea, 2015. *Recreations:* walking, talking and listening. *Address:* c/o Gonzaga Music Ltd, 43 Victor Road, NW10 5XB. *E:* gs@gonzagamusic.co.uk. *W:* www.gilesswayne.com.

SWAYTHLING, 5th Baron *cr* 1907, of Swaythling, co. Southampton; **Charles Edgar Samuel Montagu;** Bt 1894; Director, The Health Partnership; *b* 20 Feb. 1954; *o s* of 4th Baron Swaythling and of Christine Françoise (*née* Dreyfus); *S* father, 1998; *m* 1996, Hon. Angela, *d* of Baron Rawlinson of Ewell, PC, QC; one *d*. Member: Amer. Council of Hypnotist Examiners (Mem. Adv. Bd); British Council of Hypnotist Examiners; Scientific and Medical Network; Adv. Bd, British Council for Complementary Medicine. Trustee, Crossroads Foundn, Antigua. *Heir: cousin* Rupert Anthony Samuel Montagu [*b* 5 Aug. 1965; *m* 2007, Nancy Bondshu, *d* of Donald Wilson; two *s*]. *Address:* c/o The Health Partnership, 12A Thurloe Street, SW7 2ST.

SWEASEY, Peter Duncan; freelance television producer and director, since 1999; *b* Chertsey, Surrey, 14 July 1970; *s* of late Denis Sweasey, OBE, JP, DL and of Diana Sweasey. *Educ:* Fullbrook Secondary Sch., Surrey; St Catherine's Coll., Oxford (BA 1st Cl. English Lang. and Lit. 1993). Television productions include: Petworth House, 2011; Imagine: Dancing with Titian, 2012; David Starkey's Music and Monarchy, 2013; The Brits who Built the Modern World, 2014; How to be Bohemian, 2015; Victorian Bakers, 2015. Hon. FRIBA 2015. *Publications:* From Queer to Eternity: spirituality in the lives of lesbian, gay and bisexual people, 1997. *Recreations:* music, meditation, architecture, pilates, eating (ideally cake). *E:* peters@afterglowtv.co.uk.

SWEENEY, Brendan, MBE 2003; FRCGP; Principal in general practice, Govan, 1975–2010; *b* 11 July 1946; *s* of James and Angela Sweeney; *m* 1973, Dr Rosalie T. Dunn; two *s* three *d*. *Educ:* Univ. of Glasgow (MA 1965; MB ChB 1971). DObstRCOG 1973; MRCGP 1975, FRCGP 1985. McKenzie Lectr, RCGP, 1997. Hon. Sen. Lectr, Dept of Postgrad. Med. Educn, Univ. of Glasgow. Medical Mem., Appeal Tribunal Service, 1995–. Royal College of General Practitioners: Vice-Chm., Council, 1994–97; Chairman: Cttee of Med. Ethics, 1992–98; W of Scotland Cttee on Postgrad. Med. Educn, 1996; Medical and Dental Defence Union of Scotland, 2012– (Treas., 2005–12). *Recreations:* squash, golf, opera, theatre, books. *Address:* 25 Stewarton Drive, Cambuslang, Glasgow G72 8DF. *T:* (0141) 583 1513. *Clubs:* Turnberry Golf, Cathkin Braes Golf, Pollok Golf; Newlands Squash and Tennis.

SWEENEY, Brian Philip, QFSM 2005; Chief Officer/Chief Executive, Strathclyde Fire & Rescue (formerly Strathclyde Fire Brigade), 2004–13; *b* 14 July 1961; *s* of Philip and Mary Sweeney; *m* 1995, Pamela Barratt; three *s*. *Educ:* Holyrood; Coventry Univ. (MA Mgt 2000). Strathclyde Fire Brigade: Firefighter, 1981, Leading Firefighter, 1983; Station Officer, Bde Trng Centre, 1990; Asst Divl Officer, N Glasgow, 1993; Hd of Ops, E Command HQ, Motherwell, 1996; Hd of Personnel and Trng, Central Command, 1997; Dep. Comdr, Central Command, 1998–2000; Dir of Ops, 2000–03; Dep. Chief Officer, 2003; Temp. Firemaster, 2004. MIFireE 1996; Mem., Chief Fire Officers' Assoc., 2000–. Freeman, City of Glasgow, 2004. DUniv Glasgow Caledonian, 2005. *Recreations:* reading, music, accumulating stress.

SWEENEY, Edward, CBE 2014; Chairman, Advisory, Conciliation and Arbitration Service, 2007–14; *b* 6 Aug. 1954; *s* of William Sweeney and Louise Sweeney; *m* 1987, Janet Roydhouse. *Educ:* Warwick Univ. (BA Hons); London Sch. of Economics (MSc Econ.). Banking, Insurance and Finance Union: Research Officer, 1976–79; Negotiating Officer (TSB), 1979–86; National Officer: Scotland, 1986–89; Insurance, 1989–91; Dep. Gen. Sec., 1991–96; Gen. Sec., 1996–99, when BIFU amalgamated with UNIFI; UNIFI: Jt Gen. Sec., 1999–2000; Gen. Sec., 2000–04, when UNIFI merged with Amicus; Dep. Gen. Sec., Amicus, 2004–07. *Recreations:* sport, reading, Egyptology.

SWEENEY, Sir George, Kt 2000; Principal, Knowsley Community College, 1990–2007; *b* 26 Jan. 1946; *s* of George Sweeney and Margaret, (Peggy), Sweeney (*née* Carlin); *m* 1968, Susan Anne Wilson; two *d*. *Educ:* Prescot Boys' GS; Hull Univ. (BA Hons Hist. and Pols 1967; MA 1973). Teacher: Hull Coll. of Technol., 1967–70; Kirby Coll., Teesside, 1970–73; S Trafford Coll., 1973–75 and 1977–83; S Cheshire Coll., 1975–77; Vice Principal, Grimsby Coll. of Technol., 1983–90; Actg Principal, Sheffield Coll., Jan.–Aug. 2000. Hon. DEd Chester, 2008. *Recreations:* painting, drawing, gardening, political biography. *Address:* 12 Red Lane, Appleton, Cheshire WA4 5AD. *T:* (01925) 265113.

SWEENEY, Mark Darren; Constitution Director, Cabinet Office, since 2014; *b* London, 4 June 1974; *s* of Terry Sweeney and Marie Sweeney; *m* 2002, Cheryl Louise Robinson; one *s* one *d*. *Educ:* St Edward's Sch., Oxford; Selwyn Coll., Cambridge (BA Hons Hist. 1995). Cabinet Office: graduate fast stream prog., 1995–99; Govt IT prog. review team, 1999–2000; Desk Officer, Eur. Secretariat, 2000–02; Northern Ireland Office: Hd, Political Develt Unit, 2002–04; Dep. Dir, Rights and Internat. Relns, 2004–07; Dep. Dir, Elections and Democracy, MoJ, 2007–10, Cabinet Office, 2010–11; Principal Private Sec. to the Lord Chancellor and Sec. of State for Justice, 2011–12; Dir, Law, Rights and Internat., MoJ, 2012–14. *Recreations:* family, music, reading, socialising, sport. *Address:* Cabinet Office, 70 Whitehall, SW1A 2AS. *T:* (020) 7276 0535. *E:* mark.sweeney@cabinetoffice.gov.uk.

SWEENEY, Hon. Sir Nigel Hamilton, Kt 2008; **Hon. Mr Justice Sweeney;** a Judge of the High Court of Justice, Queen's Bench Division, since 2008; *b* 18 March 1954; *s* of Alan Vincent Sweeney and Dorothy Sweeney; *m* 1st, 1985, Joanna Clair Slater (marr. diss.); one *s* one *d*; 2nd, 2002, Dr Sheila Theresa Diamond. *Educ:* Wellington Sch., Som; Nottingham Univ. (LLB 1975). Called to the Bar, Middle Temple, 1976 (Harmsworth Schol. 1976), Bencher, 1997. Central Criminal Court: Jun. Prosecuting Counsel to the Crown, 1987–91; First Jun. Prosecuting Counsel, 1991–92; Sen. Prosecuting Counsel, 1992–97; First Sen. Prosecuting Counsel, 1997–2000; Recorder, 1997–2008; QC 2000. *Recreations:* golf, tennis, the arts. *Address:* Royal Courts of Justice, Strand, WC2A 2LL. *Clubs:* Garrick; Wisley Golf.

SWEENEY, Thomas Kevin; Senior Medical Officer, Department of Health and Social Security, 1983–88, retired; *b* 10 Aug. 1923; *s* of John Francis and Mildred Sweeney; *m* 1950, Eveleen Moira Ryan (*d* 2009); two *s* two *d*. *Educ:* O'Connell Sch., Dublin; University Coll., Dublin (MB, BCh, BAO NUI; DTM&H London; TDD Wales). FFPH (FFCM 1983). Principal Med. Officer, Colonial Medical Service, 1950–65, retd; Asst Sen. Med. Officer, Welsh Hosp. Bd, 1965–68; Department of Health and Social Security: Med. Officer, 1968–72; Sen. Med. Officer, 1972–79; SPMO, 1979–83. QHP 1984–87. *Publications:* contrib. BMJ. *Recreations:* gardening, golf, cathedrals. *Address:* Tresanton, Wych Hill Way, Woking, Surrey GU22 0AE. *T:* (01483) 828199.

SWEENEY, Timothy Patrick; Director: Waste Resources Action Programme plc, 2001–11; Cafbank, 2008–10 (Interim Chairman, 2008–09); *b* 2 June 1944; *s* of John Sylvester Sweeney and Olive Bridget (*née* Montgomery-Cunningham); *m* 1965, Carol Ann Wardle; one *s* one *d*. *Educ:* Pierrepont School; Sussex Univ. (MA Philosophy); Surrey Univ. (MSc Econs). With Bank of England, 1967–94; Dir Gen., BBA, 1994–2001. Chm., Amicus Vision, 2001–05. Director: Money Advice Trust, 2000–04; AIB Gp UK, 2001–13. Mem., Better Regulation Commn (formerly Task Force), 2002–06. *Recreations:* music, archery, walking. *Address:* Hollowell Hill House, W Chinnock, Crewkerne, Som TA18 7PS.

SWEENEY, Walter Edward; Solicitor, Yorkshire Law (formerly Walter Sweeney & Co.), 1997–2010; Consultant, Ingrams Solicitors, Hessle, 2010–12; Head of Probate, Williamsons Solicitors, Hull, 2013–14; *b* Dublin, 23 April 1949; *s* of Patrick Anthony Sweeney, retired veterinary surgeon and Jane Yerbury Sweeney, retired head teacher; *m* 1992, Dr Nuala Maire Kennan; three *d*. *Educ:* Church Lawford Primary Sch.; Lawrence Sheriff Sch., Rugby; Univ. of Aix-Marseille; Univ. of Hull (BA Hons; MA); Darwin Coll., Cambridge (MPhil); Cert. Ed. TEFL. Admitted Solicitor, 1976. Mem., Vale of Glam CHC, 1991–92. Joined Cons. Party, 1964; Chairman: Rugby Div. YCs, 1965; Church Lawford Cons. Br., 1969; Rugby Cons. Political Centre, 1970. Member: Church Lawford Parish Council, 1971–74; Rugby BC, 1974–77; Beds CC, 1981–89 (Vice-Chm. and Gp spokesman on Police Cttee). Contested (C) Stretford, 1983. MP (C) Vale of Glamorgan, 1992–97; contested (C) same seat, 1997. Member, Select Committee: on Welsh Affairs, 1992–97; on Home Affairs, 1995–97; on Channel Tunnel Rail Link, 1995–96; Vice Chairman: All-Party Penal Affairs Cttee, 1993–97 (Sec., 1992–93); Cons. back bench Legal Affairs Cttee, 1995–97 (Sec., 1994–95); Sec., Cons. back bench Home Affairs Cttee, 1994–97. Contested (Ind): Haltemprice and Howden, July 2008; Humberside Police and Crime Comr, 2012; contested (UKIP Ind) St Mary's Ward, Beverley, 2015. Pres., Hull Incorp. Law Soc., 2004–05 (Vice-Pres., 2003–04).

Mem., N Cave Parish Council, 2003–07 (Vice-Chm., 2005–07). Owner and proprietor, Newbegin House B&B, 2008– (Visit Hull and E Yorks Award, 2012). Gov., N Cave C of E Primary Sch., 2003–10. *Recreations:* walking, theatre, reading, renovating Georgian house. *Address:* (home) Newbegin House, 10 Newbegin, Beverley HU17 8EG.

SWEENEY, William Martin; Chief Executive Officer, British Olympic Association, since 2013; *b* Calcutta, 10 Oct. 1957; *s* of James Sweeney and Rose Catherine Sweeney; *m* 1984, Elizabeth Anne Smith; one *s* one *d. Educ:* Birkenhead Sch. for Boys; Woking Co. Grammar Sch.; Univ. of Salford (BSc Hons). Shell Internat.; Unilever; Mars; BAT; Reebok International: Pres. and Gen. Manager, Reebok Japan/Asia Pacific; Sen. Vice Pres. and Gen. Manager, N America; Sen. Vice Pres., adidas Reebok Gp, 2003–10; Global Hd, Business Develt, PUMA AG, 2010–13. *Recreations:* golf, ski-ing, roses. *E:* bill.sweeney@teamgb.com. *Club:* Singapore Cricket.

SWEET, Andrew Francis; a District Judge (Magistrates' Courts), since 2004; *b* 12 Nov. 1954; *s* of Rev. Mervyn Thomas Sweet and Joan Myra Dorothy Sweet (*née* Reece); *m* 1980, Fiona (*née* McMurdy); two *d. Educ:* Cordwalles Prep. Sch., SA; Northbrook Secondary Sch., London; South Bank Polytech. (BA Hons Law); Coll. of Law, Guildford. Admitted solicitor of Supreme Court, 1984; solicitor in private practice: Surrey, 1980–90; London, 1992–2004; Crown Prosecutor, 1990–92. Administrator to Richmond Court Duty Solicitor Scheme and Police Station Duty Solicitor Administrator, 1995–2004. Dep. Dist Judge, 1997–2004. LEA Sch. Gov., Grand Avenue Primary Sch., 1994–2004. *Recreations:* reading, motorcycles, mountain trekking. *Address:* Hammersmith Magistrates' Court, 181 Talgarth Road, Hammersmith, W6 8DN. *T:* (020) 8700 9302.

SWEET, Anna Isabel; *see* Poole, A. I.

SWEETBAUM, Henry Alan; Managing Director, PS Capital LLC, since 1997; *b* 22 Nov. 1937; *s* of late Irving and Bertha Sweetbaum; *m* 1st, 1960, Suzanne Milberg (decd); three *s*; 2nd, 1971, Anne Betty Leonie de Vigier; one *s. Educ:* Wharton School, Univ. of Pennsylvania (BS Econ 1959). Underwood Corp., 1960; Exec. Vice-Pres. and Dir, Reliance Corp., 1962–70; Exec. Dir, Plessey Corp., 1970; Chm., Huntingdon Securities, 1973–2006; Data Recording Instrument Co.: non-exec. Dir, 1973–76; Chm., 1976–82; Chm. and Chief Exec., Wickes plc, 1982–96. Non-executive Director: Accelerator Technology Hldgs, 2007–; Law Finance Gp Hldgs Ltd, 2009–; Smart Cube Technologies, 2012–. Founder and Chm., Internat. Centre for the Study of Radicalisation and Political Violence, 2007–. University of Pennsylvania, Wharton School, Board Member: Bd of Overseers, 1994–2005; European Adv. Bd, 1988–2006; SEI Center for Advanced Management Studies, 1989–. Mem., American Bankruptcy Inst. CCMI (CIMgt 1993). Hon. FKC 2013. *Publications:* Restructuring the Management Challenge, 1990; Best Practice, or Just Best People, 1995; (contrib.) Society and Business Review, vol. 3, 2008. *Recreations:* swimming, wine. *Clubs:* Reform; University, Penn (New York).

SWEETING, Col John William Frederick, CBE 2004; Chief Executive, Treloar Trust, 1997–2005; *b* 16 Feb. 1946; *s* of late Quilter William Victor Sweeting and Mary Edith Violet Sweeting (*née* Dewey); *m* 1976, Mary Clark (*née* Millington); two *s* one *d. Educ:* Tonbridge Sch.; Univ. of Bristol (LLB 1967). Commnd RE 1967; Staff Coll., Camberley, 1978; SO1 Defence Commitments (Rest of World), 1985–86; CO 28 Amph. Engr Regt, 1987–89; COS Engr in Chief (Army), 1990–91. Bursar, Lord Mayor Treloar Coll., 1991–97. Founder Mem. and Treas., Nat. Assoc. of Ind. and Non-maintained Special Schs (NASS), 1998–2001; Chm., Assoc. of Nat. Specialist Colls (NATSPEC), 1999–2004; Founder Trustee and Chm., RECOM (nat. org. for recycling computers to disabled), 2000–04; Trustee, Fortune Centre of Riding Therapy, 2005–10. Licensed Lay Minister (formerly Reader), C of E, 1968–; Chaplain to High Sheriff of Hampshire, 2008–09. *Recreations:* choral singing, travel, gardening, golf. *Address:* 17 Lynn Way, Kings Worthy, Winchester, Hants SO23 7TG. *T:* (01962) 884325. *E:* john.sweeting@talktalk.net. *Club:* Rotary (Winchester; Paul Harris Fellow, 2014).

SWEETING, Malcolm; Senior Partner, Clifford Chance LLP, since 2011. Partner, Clifford Chance, 1990–. *Address:* Clifford Chance LLP, 10 Upper Bank Street, Canary Wharf, E14 5JJ. *T:* (020) 7006 2028, *Fax:* (020) 7006 5555. *E:* malcolm.sweeting@cliffordchance.com.

SWEETING, Prof. Sir Martin (Nicholas), Kt 2002; OBE 1996; FRS 2000; FREng, FIET, FRAeS, FInstP; Professor of Satellite Engineering, since 1990, and Director, Surrey Space Centre (formerly Centre for Satellite Engineering Research), since 1996, University of Surrey; Executive Chairman, Surrey Satellite Technology Ltd, since 2008; *b* 12 March 1951; *s* of Frank Morris Sweeting and Dorothy May Sweeting; *m* 1975, Christine Ruth Taplin. *Educ:* Aldenham School, Elstree; University of Surrey (BSc Hons 1974; PhD 1979). Marconi Space & Defence Systems, 1972–73; University of Surrey: Research Fellow, 1978–81; Lectr, 1981–86; Univ. Research Fellow in Satellite Engrg, 1984–87; Dir, Satellite Engrg, 1986–90; Dep. Dir, Centre for Satellite Engrg Res., 1990–96; Distinguished Prof., 2006–. Res. Dir, Satellites Internat., 1983–84; Surrey Satellite Technology: Technical Dir, 1985–94; Acting Man. Dir, 1989–94; CEO, 1995–2008. Member: Internat. Acad. of Astronautics, 1999–; Defence and Aerospace Panel, UK Technology Foresight Cttee, 2003–05; EU Framework Prog. 6 Space Adv. Panel, 2003–06; Aurora Adv. Cttee, 2003–06, Human Spaceflight Microgravity and Exploration Adv. Cttee, 2006–08, ESA; UK Space Leadership Council, 2010–; a Vice-Pres., Internat. Astronautics Fedn, 2000–05. FREng (FEng 1996); FInstP 2001. Hon. Fellow, IED, 2012. Silver Medal, Royal Acad. Engrg, 1995; Gold Medal, UK Engrg Council, 1998; Space Achievement Medal, British Interplanetary Soc., 1998; Mullard Prize, Royal Soc., 2000; Frank Malina Medal, Internat. Acad. of Astronautics, 2003; Gold Medal, Royal Inst. Navigation, 2006; Sir Arthur Clarke Lifetime Achievement Award, UK Space Conf., 2008; Faraday Medal, IET, 2010; Elektra Lifetime Achievement Award, Eur. Electronics Industry, 2010; Guildford Roll of Honour, 2011; Internat. von Karman Wings Award, CIT, 2012. *Publications:* over 200 professional papers and pubns. *Recreations:* amateur radio, photography, travelling, languages, table tennis. *Address:* Surrey Satellite Technology Ltd, Tycho House, 20 Stephenson Road, Surrey Research Park, Guildford, Surrey GU2 7YE.

SWEETMAN, Jennifer Joan, (Mrs Ronald Andrew); *see* Dickson, J. J.

SWEETMAN, John Francis, CB 1991; TD 1964; Clerk Assistant, 1987–90 and Clerk of Committees, 1990–95 of the House of Commons; *b* 31 Oct. 1930; *s* of late Thomas Nelson Sweetman and Mary Monica (*née* D'Arcy-Reddy); *m* 1st, 1959, Susan Margaret Manley; one *s* one *d*; 2nd, 1983, Celia Elizabeth, *yr d* of Sir William Nield, GCMG, KCB; two *s. Educ:* Cardinal Vaughan Sch.; St Catharine's Coll., Cambridge (MA Law). 2nd Lieut, RA, Gibraltar, 1949–51; TA (City of London RA) and AER, 1951–65. A Clerk of the House of Commons, 1954–95: Clerk of Select Cttees on Nationalised Industries and on Sci. and Technol., 1962–65, 1970–73; Second Clerk of Select Cttees, 1979–83; Clerk of the Overseas Office, 1983–87; Clerk of Select Cttee on Sittings of the House, 1991–92. Parly Advr, BBC, 1996–98. Parly missions to Armenia, Croatia, Fiji, Gambia, Kazakhstan, Kyrgyzstan, Moldova, Nigeria, Sierra Leone, Sri Lanka, Uganda, Ukraine and Yemen, 1996–2004. Member: Assoc. of Secs-Gen. of Parliaments, IPU, 1987–; Assoc. of Clerks-at-the-Table, Canada, 1996–. Mem., Oxford and Cambridge Catholic Educn Bd, 1964–84. *Publications:* contrib. to: Erskine May's Parliamentary Practice; Halsbury's Laws of England; parly jls; (ed) Council of Europe, Procedure and Practice of the Parliamentary Assembly. *Address:* 41 Creffield Road, W5 3RR. *T:* (020) 8992 2456. *Clubs:* Garrick, MCC.

SWEETMAN, Stuart John, FCA; Group Managing Director, Royal Mail Group plc (formerly Post Office, then Consignia plc), 1999–2002; *b* 6 Aug. 1948; *s* of Arthur John Sweetman and Joan Sweetman; *m* 1977, Patricia Dean; two *s* one *d. Educ:* University Coll. London (BSc Geog.). FCA 1979. Joined Touche Ross & Co., Chartered Accountants, 1969; held various posts from Articled Clerk to Sen. Manager; Dir, Financial Accounts, PO, 1982–86; Royal Mail: Finance Dir, 1986–92; Business Centres Dir, 1992–94; Service Delivery Dir, 1994–95; Asst Man. Dir, 1995–96; Man. Dir, PO Counters Ltd, 1996–99. Chm. and Dir, Consignia (Customer Mgt) Ltd (formerly Subscription Services Ltd), 1999–2001. Dir, British Quality Foundn, 1998–2002; Mem. Bd, Inst. of Customer Services, 1998–2001. Mem. Adv. Cttee for Business in the Envmt, DTI/DETR, 1997–2001. Pres., Banstead Neville Bowling Club Ltd, 2011–13 (Dir, 2013–; Capt., 2009–10); Chairman: Banstead History Centre, 2010–; Banstead History Research Gp, 2012–; Probus Club of Banstead, 2015–. *Recreations:* family, walking, archaeology, golf, bowls, watercolour painting, cooking and eating. *Address:* 1 Chalmers Road, Banstead, Surrey SM7 3HF.

SWENARTON, Prof. Mark Creighton, PhD; FRHistS; James Stirling Professor of Architecture, University of Liverpool, 2011–15, now Professor Emeritus; *b* India, 1952; *s* of Joseph Swenarton and Mavis Swenarton (*née* Simmonds). *Educ:* Magdalen Coll., Oxford (BA 1973); Univ. of Sussex (MA 1974); University Coll. London (PhD 1979). FRHistS 1987. Lecturer in History of Architecture: Middx Univ., 1975–77; UCL, 1977–89; Founding and Publishing Ed., Architecture Today, 1989–2005; Prof. and Hd, Sch. of Architecture, Oxford Brookes Univ., 2005–10. Special Prof. of Architecture, Univ. of Nottingham, 2003–05; Thank-Offering to Britain Fellow, Royal Acad., 2013–14. Founding Ed., Construction Hist., 1985. Design Review Chair, Cabe at Design Council (formerly CABE), 2008–. Non-exec. Dir, Timber R&D Assoc., 2006–09. FRSA 2004. Hon. FRIBA 2014. *Publications:* Homes fit for Heroes: the politics and design of early state housing in Britain, 1981; Artisans and Architects: the Ruskinian tradition in architectural thought, 1989; Dixon Jones: buildings and projects, 2002; Feilden Clegg Bradley: the environmental handbook, 2007; Building the New Jerusalem: architecture, politics and housing 1900–1930, 2008; Architecture and the Welfare State, 2014; contrib. articles to AA Files, Architectural Hist., Econ. Hist. Rev., Histl Res., Jl Architecture, Planning Perspectives, Town Planning Rev. *Recreations:* tennis, gardening, classical music, opera, theatre, visual arts, travel. *Address:* School of Architecture, University of Liverpool, Leverhulme Building, Abercromby Square, Liverpool L69 7ZN. *T:* (0151) 795 0642. *E:* m.swenarton@liv.ac.uk.

SWIFT, Very Rev. Andrew Christopher; Priest-in-charge, Holy Trinity, Dunoon, and St Paul, Rothesay, since 2010; Dean of Argyll and The Isles, since 2012; *b* Aberdeen, 10 Jan. 1968; *s* of Dr Bernard Swift and Christine Swift; *m* 1991, Mary Calvert; one *s* two *d. Educ:* Univ. of Edinburgh (BEng Electrical and Mech. Engrg 1990); Univ. of Aberdeen (MSc Mech. Engrg 1997); Ripon Coll., Cuddesdon (BTh Theol. 2008). CEng 1995. RAF, 1986–90; Admiralty Res. Scientist, 1991–97; Naval Consultant, YARD Glasgow, 1997–2000; Engrg Manager, Type 45 Destroyer Prime Contract, 2000–03; Business Develt Exec., BAE Systems/Atkins, 2003; Engrg Manager, Aircraft Carrier Alliance, 2003–05; ordained deacon, 2007, priest, 2008; Asst Curate, St Catharine's, Gloucester, 2007–10; Priest-in-charge, St Martin's, Tighnabruaich, 2010–11. Honorary Chaplain: ATC, 2011–; Mission to Seafarers, 2013–. *Recreations:* narrow boating, cartoonist, social media, collie walking, reading, black and white war films. *Address:* The Rectory, 55 Kilbride Road, Dunoon PA23 7LN. *T:* (01369) 702444. *E:* dean@argyll.anglican.org.

SWIFT, Anita; *see* Klein, A.

SWIFT, Hon. Dame Caroline Jane, (Lady Openshaw), DBE 2005; a Judge of the High Court of Justice, Queen's Bench Division, 2005–15; *b* 30 May 1955; *d* of late Vincent Seymour Swift and Amy Ruth Swift; *m* 1979, Charles Peter Lawford Openshaw (*see* Hon. Sir C. P. L. Openshaw); one *s* one *d. Educ:* Lancaster Girls' Grammar Sch.; Univ. of Durham (BA Hons Law). Pres., Durham Union Soc., 1975. Called to the Bar, Inner Temple, 1977, Bencher, 1997; practised on Northern Circuit, 1978–2005; Asst Recorder, 1992–95; QC 1993; a Recorder, 1995–2005; a Dep. High Court Judge, 2000–05. Leading counsel, Shipman Inquiry, 2001–05. *Publications:* (jtly) Ribchester: 100 years in photographs, 1994; Ribchester: a millennium record, 2001. *Recreations:* home and family, cooking, theatre, walking.

SWIFT, Clive Walter; actor, author, teacher; initiator, 1978, now Adviser to the Executive (formerly Board), Actor's Centre; *b* 9 Feb. 1936; *s* of Abram Swift and Lillie (*née* Greenman); *m* 1960, Margaret Drabble (*see* Dame Margaret Drabble) (marr. diss. 1975); two *s* one *d. Educ:* Clifton Coll., Bristol; Caius Coll., Cambridge (MA Hons Eng. Lit.). Teaching at LAMDA and RADA, 1967–79; teaching verse-speaking, 1980–2014, and host of interview series, Voices of Experience, at Actor's Centre, 2012, 2013. *Theatre:* début, Nottingham Playhouse, 1959; RSC, 1960–68; Man and Superman, Arts, Vaudeville, and Garrick, 1965; The Young Churchill, Duchess, 1969; The Hollow Crown, USA tour, 1975; Dirty Linen, Arts, 1976; Inadmissible Evidence, Royal Court, 1978; The Potsdam Quartet, Lyric, Hammersmith, 1980; Messiah, Hampstead, Aldwych, 1982; The Genius, Royal Court, 1983; King Lear, New Vic, 1986; The Sisterhood, New End, 1987; An Enemy of the People, Young Vic, Playhouse, 1988; Othello, Other Place, Young Vic, 1990; Pooter, in Mr and Mrs Nobody, nat. tour, 1993–94; Whittlestaff, in An Old Man's Love, Royal, Northampton, and tour, 1996; Doña Rosita, Almeida, 1997; Higher than Babel, Bridewell, 1999; Hysteria, Minerva Theatre, Chichester, 2000; played Benjamin Jowett, Balliol Coll. 750th Anniv., Sheldonian Th., Oxford, 2013; Richard Bucket Overflows!, Theatre Clwyd, Edinburgh Fringe, 2007; Chichester Festival theatre seasons, 1965 and 1971; *director:* at LAMDA: The Wild Goose Chase, 1969; The Cherry Orchard, 1973; The Lower Depths, 1969; *television:* Love Story, 1961; Dombey & Son, 1968; Waugh on Crime, 1970; The Exorcism, 1972; South Riding, 1974; Clayhanger, 1974; Gibbon, 1975; Barchester Chronicles, 1982; Pickwick Papers, 1984; First Among Equals, 1985; Keeping up Appearances, 5 series, 1990–95; Peak Practice, 1997; Aristocrats, 1998; Born and Bred, 2001–04; The Old Guys, 2009, 2010; Valentine's Kiss, 2014; Suntrap, 2014; *radio:* Radio Rep, 1973; Sword of Honour, 1974; narrator, Babar, 1986; Getting Stratford (monologue), 1987; Heavy Roller, 1988; From the depths of Waters, 1990 (Sony Award Winner); Madame Bovary, 1992; Black Box, 1993; The Double Dealer, 1995; Happy Days, 1995; Everybody Comes to Schicklgruber's, 1996; Altaban the Magnificent, 1999; The Right Time, 2000–04; Poor Pen, 2001; The Go-Between, 2002; Oblomov, 2005; Insane Object of Desire, 2005; Fridays when it Rains, Betjeman's Women, 2006; The Loved One, Dickens Confidential, 2007; Old Spies, 2011; Strangers on a Film, 2011; *films:* Catch us if You Can, 1963; Frenzy, 1971; The National Health, 1972; Excalibur, 1980; A Passage to India, 1984; Sir Horace Jones, in Tower Bridge Permanent Exhibn film, 1994; Gaston's War, 1996; Vacuums, 2001. Mem., BAFTA, 2000–. Hon. Fellow, Liverpool John Moores Univ., 1999. Cyprus Medal, 1956. *Publications:* The Job of Acting, 1976, 2nd edn 1985; The Performing World of the Actor, 1981. *Recreations:* playing and listening to music, writing songs (From the Heart, CD, issued 2009), watching Lancashire CCC and Arsenal. *Address:* c/o Roxane Vacca, Vacca Management, 61 Judd Street, WC1H 9QT. *T:* (020) 7631 5970.

SWIFT, His Honour David Rowland; a Circuit Judge, 1997–2012; *b* 21 April 1946; *s* of James Rowland Swift and Iris Julia Swift; *m* 1974, Josephine Elizabeth Williamson; two *s* two *d. Educ:* Kingsmead Sch., Hoylake; Ruthin Sch.; Liverpool Coll. of Commerce. Admitted Solicitor, 1970; Partner, Percy Hughes and Roberts, Birkenhead, 1971–97; a Recorder, 1993–97. Pres., Liverpool Law Soc., 1995–96. Chairman: Wirral Adult Literacy Project, 1978–84; Liverpool Bd of Legal Studies, 1985–88. Gov., Ruthin Sch., 1988–2005 (Chm.

Govs, 1993–99). *Publications:* Proceedings Before the Solicitors Disciplinary Tribunal, 1996; articles in legal jls. *Recreations:* sailing, walking, history, photography. *Club:* Athenæum (Pres., 2013–14).

SWIFT, Graham Colin, FRSL; author; *b* 4 May 1949; *s* of Sheila Irene Swift and Lionel Allan Stanley Swift. *Educ:* Dulwich Coll.; Queens' Coll., Cambridge (MA; Hon. Fellow, 2005); Univ. of York. Hon. LittD: UEA, 1998; London, 2003; Sussex 2015; DUniv York, 1998. *Publications: novels:* The Sweet Shop Owner, 1980; Shuttlecock, 1981 (Geoffrey Faber Meml Prize, 1983); Waterland, 1983 (Winifred Holtby Award, RSL, 1983; Guardian Fiction Prize, 1983; Premio Grinzane Cavour, 1987); Out of This World, 1988; Ever After, 1992 (Prix du Meilleur Livre Etranger, 1994); Last Orders (Booker Prize, James Tait Black Meml Prize), 1996; The Light of Day, 2003; Tomorrow, 2007; Wish You Were Here, 2011; *short stories:* Learning to swim and other stories, 1982; England and Other Stories, 2014; *non-fiction:* (ed with David Profumo) The Magic Wheel (anthology), 1985; Making an Elephant, 2009. *Recreation:* fishing. *Address:* c/o A. P. Watt, United Agents, 12–26 Lexington Street, W1F 0LE.

SWIFT, John Anthony; QC 1981; Head of Monckton Chambers, 1999–2001; *b* 11 July 1940; *s* of late Jack Swift and Clare Medcalf; *m* 1972, Jane Carol Sharples; one *s* one *d*. *Educ:* Birkenhead Sch.; University Coll., Oxford (MA); Johns Hopkins Univ.; Bologna. Called to the Bar, Inner Temple, 1965, Bencher, 1992. Rail Regulator, 1993–98. Mem., NHS Cooperation and Competition Panel, 2009–14; Chm., Ofgem Enforcement Decision Panel, 2014–; Ind. Mem., Ofwat Casework Cttee, 2014–; Advr, Monitor, regulator of NHS services, 2014–. FCILT (FCIT 1994). *Recreations:* theatre, walking, gardening, golf. *Address:* Monckton Chambers, Gray's Inn, WC1R 5NR. *Clubs:* Reform; Huntercombe Golf.

SWIFT, Jonathan Mark; QC 2010; a Recorder, since 2010; *b* Rochford, Essex, 11 Sept. 1964; *s* of John Christopher Swift and Margaret Fanny Swift (*née* Shead); *m* 2008, Helen Mary Evans; one *s* one *d*. *Educ:* Southend on Sea High Sch. for Boys; New Coll., Oxford (BA 1987); Emmanuel Coll., Cambridge (LLM 1988). Called to the Bar, Inner Temple, 1989, Bencher, 2007; First Treasury Counsel, 2007–14. *Publications:* (contrib.) Judicial Review, 1992, 4th edn 2010; (ed jtly) Employment Court Practice, 2007, 2nd edn 2008; (contrib.) Administrative Court Practice, 2008. *Recreations:* football (Southend United), animal husbandry, playing the ukelele, waiting. *Address:* 11 King's Bench Walk, Temple, EC4Y 7EQ. *T:* (020) 7632 8500.

SWIFT, Malcolm Robin Farquhar; QC 1988; Acting Judge, Grand Court of Cayman Islands, since 2013; *b* 19 Jan. 1948; *s* of late Willie Swift and Heather May Farquhar Swift, OBE (*née* Nield); *m* 1st, 1969, Anne Rachael (marr. diss. 1993), *d* of Ernest Rothery Ayre; one *s* two *d*; 2nd, 2003, Angela, *d* of Reuben Walters. *Educ:* Colne Valley High Sch., Yorks; King's Coll. London (LLB, AKC). Called to the Bar, Gray's Inn, 1970, Bencher, 1998; a Recorder, 1987–2007. Co-opted Mem., Remuneration Cttee of Bar Council, 1978–89 (rep. NE Circuit); Mem., Bar Council, 1995–2001; Leader, NE Circuit, 1998–2001. *Recreations:* cycling, re-cycling. *Address:* Wilberforce Chambers, 7 Bishop Lane, Kingston-upon-Hull HU1 1PA. *T:* (01482) 323264; 2 Hare Court, Temple, EC4Y 7BH. *T:* (020) 7353 5324; Zenith Chambers, 10 Park Square, Leeds LS1 2LH. *T:* (01132) 455438; Silk Road Chambers, 20th Floor, Central Tower, 28, Queens Road, Hong Kong. *T:* 2159 9171.

SWINBURN, Lt-Gen. Sir Richard (Hull), KCB 1991; Deputy Commander-in-Chief, United Kingdom Land Forces, Commander, United Kingdom Field Army, and Inspector General, Territorial Army, 1994–95; *b* 30 Oct. 1937; *s* of late Maj.-Gen. H. R. Swinburn, CB, OBE, MC and Naomi Barbara Swinburn, *d* of late Maj.-Gen. Sir Amyatt Hull, KCB, and *sister* of late Field Marshal Sir Richard Hull, KG, GCB, DSO; *m* 1st, 1964, Jane Elise Brodie (*d* 2001), *d* of late Antony Douglas Brodie and Juliane Chapman (*née* Falk); 2nd, 2012, Susan Rosemary (*née* Deptford), *widow* of late Major Ronald Ferguson; one step *s* two step *d*. *Educ:* Wellington Coll.; RMA Sandhurst. Commnd 17th/21st Lancers, 1957; Adjt, Sherwood Rangers Yeomanry and 17th/21st Lancers, 1963–65; sc 1968–69; MA to VCGS, 1971–72; Instructor, Staff Coll., 1975–76; MA to COS AFCENT, 1976–78; CO 17th/21st Lancers, UK and BAOR, 1979–81; Col ASD 2, MoD, Falklands Campaign, 1982; Comdr, 7th Armoured Bde, BAOR, 1983–84; rcds 1985; Dir Army Plans, 1986–87; GOC 1st Armoured Div., BAOR, 1987–89; ACGS, MoD, 1989–90; Lt-Gen., 1990; GOC SE Dist, 1990–92; GOC Southern Dist, 1992–94; retd. Sheep farmer, Stone Farm, Exmoor, 1994–2010; Dir, Dummer Down Farm, 2013–. Chm., Cavalry Cols, 1997–2001; Col, Queen's Royal Lancers, 1995–2001; Hon. Col, Exeter Univ. OTC, 1994–2003. Dir, Glancal Property Co., 1990–96. President: Somerset Army Benevolent Fund, 1999–2010; Combined Cavalry Old Comrades Assoc., 2003–12 (Vice-Patron, 2014–). Vice-Pres., St Margaret's Hospice, Somerset, 2004–12. Mem. Council, RUSI, 1991–95. Comr, Duke of York's Royal Mil. Sch., 1990–94. Huntsman: RMA Sandhurst Beagles, 1956–57; Dhekelia Draghounds, Cyprus, 1971; (and Master) Staff Coll. Draghounds, 1975–76; Chm., Army Beagling Assoc., 1988–94. Hon. Fellow, Exeter Univ., 2003. *Recreation:* agricultural and country pursuits. *Address:* Dummer Down, Dummer, Hants RG25 2AR. *Clubs:* Cavalry and Guards; Hampshire Hunt.

SWINBURN, Walter Robert John; racehorse trainer, 2004–11; jockey, 1977–2000; *b* 7 Aug. 1961; *s* of Walter Swinburn; *m* 2002, Alison Palmer, *d* of Peter Harris; two *d*, and one step *s* one step *d*. Joined Frenchie Nicholson, 1977; rode 1st winner, Kempton, 1978; first jockey for Michael Stoute, 1981, for Sheikh Maktoum Al Maktoum, 1993. Won on Shergar, 1981, Chester Vase, Derby and King George VI and Queen Elizabeth Diamond Stakes; Irish Derby, 1983, on Shareef Dancer; Derby and Irish Derby, 1986, on Sharastani; Derby, 1995, on Lammtarra; Irish 1,000 Guineas, 1986, on Sonic Lady, 1992, on Marling; Oaks, 1987, on Unite; 2,000 Guineas, 1988, on Doyoun; 1,000 Guineas, 1989, on Musical Bliss, 1992, on Hatoof, 1993, on Sayyedati; Irish 2,000 Guineas, 1989, on Shaadi; Prix de l'Arc de Triomphe, 1983, on All Along.

SWINBURNE, John; Founder and Leader, All Scotland Pensioners Party (formerly Scottish Senior Citizens Unity Party), 2003–13; Member (Scottish Senior Citizens Unity) Scotland Central, Scottish Parliament, 2003–07; *b* 4 July 1930; *s* of Ben and Janet Swinburne; *m* 1953, Mary Hunter Baird; three *s* one *d* (and one *s* decd). *Educ:* Dalziel High Sch., Motherwell. Mechanical engr, 1947–80; apprentice marine engr, Barclay, Curle & Co., Whiteinch, Glasgow and PC&W, Motherwell, 1947–52; freelance journalist, 1980–81; Commercial Manager, 1981–2000, Dir, 2000–15, Motherwell Football and Athletic Club; Co. Sec., ADS Ltd, 2009–. Contested (Scottish Sen. Citizens Unity) Motherwell and Wishaw, Scottish Parlt, 2007. *Publications:* A History of the Steelmen: Motherwell Football Club 1886–1986, 1986; Well Worth the Wait, 1991; Images of Sport: Motherwell Football Club 1886–1999, 1999; The Homecoming (novel), 2012. *Recreation:* Association Football.

SWINBURNE, Dr Kay; Member (C) Wales, European Parliament, since 2009; *b* Aberystwyth, 8 June 1967; *m*; one *c*. *Educ:* Llandysul Grammar Sch.; King's Coll. London (BSc Biochem. and Microbiol.; PhD); Univ. of Surrey (MBA). Work in internat. healthcare and finance; with Deutsche Bank until 1999. Mem. (C) Herefordshire CC, 2007–10. *Address:* European Parliament, Rue Wiertz, 1047 Brussels, Belgium; Rhymney House, Copse Walk, Cardiff Gate Business Park, Cardiff CF23 8RB.

SWINBURNE, Prof. Richard Granville, FBA 1992; Nolloth Professor of Philosophy of Christian Religion, University of Oxford, 1985–2002, now Emeritus; Fellow, Oriel College, Oxford, 1985–2002, now Emeritus; *b* 26 Dec. 1934; *s* of William Henry Swinburne and Gladys Edith Swinburne (*née* Parker); *m* 1960, Monica Holmstrom (separated 1985); two *d*. *Educ:* Exeter College, Oxford (Scholar). BPhil 1959, MA 1961, DipTheol 1960. Fereday Fellow, St John's Coll., Oxford, 1958–61; Leverhulme Res. Fellow in Hist. and Phil. of Science, Univ. of Leeds, 1961–63; Lectr in Philosophy, then Sen. Lectr, Univ. of Hull, 1963–72; Prof. of Philosophy, Univ. of Keele, 1972–84. Vis. Associate Prof. of Philosophy, Univ. of Maryland, 1969–70; Dist. Vis. Schol., Univ. of Adelaide, 1982; Vis. Prof. of Philosophy, Syracuse Univ., 1987; Vis. Lectr, Indian Council for Philosophical Res., 1992; Visiting Professor: Univ. of Rome, 2002; Catholic Univ. of Lublin, 2002; Yale Univ., 2003; St Louis Univ., 2003; Lectures: Wilde, Oxford Univ., 1975–78; Forwood, Liverpool Univ., 1977, 2009; Marrett Meml, Exeter Coll., Oxford, 1980; Gifford, Univ. of Aberdeen, 1982–84; Edward Cadbury, Univ. of Birmingham, 1987; Wade, St Louis Univ., 1990; Dotterer, Pennsylvania State Univ., 1992; Aquinas, Marquette Univ., 1997; Paul Holmer, Univ. of Minnesota, 2006; Sophia Forum, Azusa Pacific Univ., 2013; Gilbert Ryle, Trent Univ., 2014. *Publications:* Space and Time, 1968, 2nd edn 1981; The Concept of Miracle, 1971; An Introduction to Confirmation Theory, 1973; The Coherence of Theism, 1977, rev. edn 1993; The Existence of God, 1979, 2nd edn 2004; Faith and Reason, 1981, 2nd edn 2005; (with S. Shoemaker) Personal Identity, 1984; The Evolution of the Soul, 1986, rev. edn 1997; Responsibility and Atonement, 1989; Revelation, 1992, 2nd edn 2007; The Christian God, 1994; Is There a God?, 1996, rev. edn 2010; Providence and the Problem of Evil, 1998; Epistemic Justification, 2001; The Resurrection of God Incarnate, 2003; Was Jesus God?, 2008; Mind, Brain, and Free Will, 2013; articles and reviews in learned jls. *Address:* 50 Butler Close, Oxford OX2 6JG. *T:* (01865) 514406.

See also D. R. Cope.

SWINBURNE, Prof. Terence Reginald; Professor of Horticultural Development, Wye College, London University, 1994–98, now Emeritus; *b* 17 July 1936; *s* of Reginald and Gladys Swinburne; *m* 1958, Valerie Parkes; two *s*. *Educ:* Imperial Coll., Univ. of London (DSc, ARCS, DIC, PhD); FCIHort. Plant Pathology Res. Div., Min., later Dept, of Agriculture for NI, 1960–80; Scientific Officer, 1960–62; Sen. Scientific Officer, 1962–71; PSO, 1971–79; SPSO, 1979–80; Queen's University, Belfast: Asst Lectr, Faculty of Agriculture, 1961–64; Lectr, 1965–77; Reader, 1977–80; Head of Crop Protection Div., E Malling Res. Stn, 1980–85; Dir, Inst. of Horticl Res., AFRC, 1985–90; Sen. Res. Fellow, Wye Coll., London Univ., 1990–94. Kellogg Fellow, Oregon State Univ., 1964–65; Vis. Prof., Dept of Pure and Applied Biology, Imperial Coll., London, 1986–91. Gov., Hadlow Coll., 2000–06 (Chm., 2003–06). *Publications:* Iron Siderophores and Plant Diseases, 1986. *Recreation:* sailing. *Address:* The Orchard, St Andrews Road, Bridport, Dorset DT6 3BB. *E:* trswinburne@msn.com.

SWINDELLS, Maj.-Gen. (George) Michael (Geoffrey), CB 1985; Controller, Army Benevolent Fund, 1987–97; *b* 15 Jan. 1930; *s* of late George Martyn Swindells and Marjorie Swindells; *m* 1955, Prudence Bridget Barbara Tully; two *d* (and one *s* decd). *Educ:* Rugby School. Nat. Service Commission, 5th Royal Inniskilling Dragoon Guards, 1949; served in Germany, Korea and Canal Zone; Adjutant, Cheshire Yeomanry, 1955–56; Staff Coll., 1960; transfer to 9th/12th Royal Lancers, to command, 1969–71; Comdr 11th Armd Brigade, 1975–76; RCDS course, 1977; Dir of Op. Requirements (3), MoD, 1978–79; Chief of Jt Services Liaison Organisation, Bonn, 1980–83; Dir of Management and Support of Intelligence, 1983–85. Col, 9th/12th Royal Lancers, 1990–95. Chairman: Royal Soldiers' Daughters Sch., 1985–89; BLESMA, 1991–96; Pres., British Korean Veterans Assoc., 2006–15. Mem. Council, Wilts Wildlife Trust, 1998–2004; Trustee, Royal Soc. for Asian Affairs, 1999–2005. *Recreations:* country life, gardening. *Club:* Oriental.

SWINDELLS, Her Honour Heather Hughson, (Mrs R. Inglis); QC 1995; a Circuit Judge, 2005–14; a Deputy High Court Judge, 2000–14; *d* of late Mrs Debra Hughson Swindells; *m* 1976, Richard Inglis, *qv*; one *s*. *Educ:* Nottingham High Sch. for Girls; St Anne's Coll., Oxford (MA Lit.Hum.). Called to the Bar, Middle Temple, 1974, Bencher, 2005; a Recorder, 1994–2005. *Publications:* Family Law and the Human Rights Act 1998, 1999; (contrib.) Family Law: essays for the new millennium, 2000; Adoption: the modern law, 2003; (jtly) Adoption: the modern procedure, 2006. *Recreations:* books, music, art, archaeology.

SWINDELLS, Matthew James; Senior Vice President for Population Health and Global Strategy (formerly Senior Vice President and Managing Director), Cerner Ltd, since 2011 (Vice President, 2010–11); *b* Brighton, 31 Dec. 1964; *s* of Derek and Jacqueline Swindells; *m* 1995, Victoria Rae; two *d*. *Educ:* Blatchington Mill Comp. Sch.; Brighton Hove and Sussex 6th Form Coll.; Univ. of Hull (BSc Hons Econs); Brunel Univ. (MBA). NHS graduate supplies trainee, NW RHA, 1987–89; IT Purchasing Manager, SE Thames RHA, 1989–91; IT Strategy Prog. Manager, St Thomas' Hosp., London, 1991–93; IT Manager, 1993–94, Clin. Ops Manager, 1994–99, Guy's and St Thomas' Hosp., London; Dir of Clin. Services, Heatherwood and Wexham Park Hosp., Slough, 1999–2002; Principal Advr, Prime Minister's Office of Public Service Reform, 2002–03; Chief Exec., Royal Surrey County Hosp., Guildford, 2003–05; Policy Advr to Sec. of State for Health, 2005–07, Dir Gen. for Inf. and Prog. Integration and Chief Inf. Officer, 2007–08, DoH; Gp Man. Dir for Health, Tribal Gp, 2008–10. Chm., BCS, Health, 2009–12. Chm., Charity Trustees, Imperial Coll. Healthcare NHS Trust, 2008–13. Vis. Prof., Sch. of Mgt, Univ. of Surrey, 2005–. *Recreations:* playing football, listening to the poetry of Bob Dylan, supporting Everton, travel, spending time with my wife, enjoying the company of my children. *Address:* Cerner Ltd, 6th Floor, 2800 Rockcreek Parkway, Kansas City, MO 64117, USA. *T:* (816) 5857352. *E:* matthew.swindells@cerner.com.

SWINDELLS, Maj.-Gen. Michael; *see* Swindells, Maj.-Gen. G. M. G.

SWINDELLS, Robert Edward; children's author, since 1973, full-time author, since 1980; *b* 20 March 1939; *s* of Albert Henry Hugh and Alice Alberta Swindells; *m* 1st, 1962, Catherine Hough (marr. diss. 1976); two *d*; 2nd, 1982, Brenda Blamires. *Educ:* Huddersfield Poly. (Teacher's Cert.); Univ. of Bradford (MA Peace Studies). Copyholder, local newspaper, 1954–57; RAF, 1957–60; clerk, local newspaper, 1960–66; engineering inspector, 1966–69; student teacher, 1969–72; teacher, 1972–80. *Publications:* When Darkness Comes, 1973; The Very Special Baby, 1977; Dragons Live Forever, 1978; Moonpath and other stories, 1979; Norah's Ark, 1979; Norah's Shark, 1979; Ghostship to Ganymede, 1980; Norah to the Rescue, 1981; Norah and the Whale, 1981; Science Fiction Stories, 1982; Candle in the Dark, 1983; Weather Clerk, 1983; World Eater, 1983; Brother in the Land, 1984 (Children's Book Award, 1985); Ghost Messengers, 1988; Mavis Davis, 1988; Night School, 1989; A Serpent's Tooth, 1989; Room 13 (Children's Book Award), 1990; Staying Up, 1990; Tim Kipper, 1990; Daz 4 Zoe, 1991; Dracula's Castle, 1991; Follow a Shadow, 1991, 2nd edn 2010; Hydra, 1991; Postbox Mystery, 1991; Go-Ahead Gang, 1992; Ice Palace, 1992; Rolf and Rosie, 1992; You Can't Say I'm Crazy, 1992; Inside the Worm, 1993; Sam and Sue and Lavatory Lou, 1993; Secret of Weeping Wood, 1993, repubd 2014; Siege of Frimly Prim, 1993; Stone Cold (Carnegie Medal), 1993; Thousand Eyes of Night, 1993; We Didn't Mean To, Honest, 1993, repubd 2014; Kidnap at Denton Farm, 1994, repubd 2014; Timesnatch, 1994; Voyage to Valhalla, 1994; Ghosts of Givenham Keep, 1995, repubd 2014; The Muckitups, 1995; Unbeliever, 1995; Jacqueline Hyde, 1996; Last Bus, 1996; Hurricane Summer, 1997, repubd 2015; Nightmare Stairs, 1997; Smash, 1997; Abomination, 1998; Peril in the Mist, 1998, repubd 2014; Strange Tale of Ragger Bill, 1998, repubd 2014; Invisible, 1999; Orchard Book of Vikings, 1999; Roger's War, 1999, repubd 2015; Doodlebug Alley, 2000, repubd 2015; Orchard Book of Egyptian Gods and Pharaohs, 2000; A Wish For Wings, 2001; Wrecked!, 2001; Blitzed, 2002; No Angels, 2003; Ruby Tanya, 2004; Branded, 2005; Snapshot, 2005; Snakebite, 2006; In the Nick of Time, 2007; Burnout, 2007; The Shade of Hettie Daynes, 2008; Knife Edge, 2008; Shrapnel, 2009; A Midsummer Night's Dream (retelling), 2009; The First Hunter, 2009; Just a Bit of Fun, 2009; Henry V (retelling), 2010;

Blackout, 2011; Dan's War, 2012; A Skull in Shadow's Lane, 2012; The Deep End, 2013. *Recreations:* walking, reading, theatre, painting, travel. *Address:* Reservoir Cats, 4 Spring Row, Denholme Road, Oxenhope, Keighley, W Yorks BD22 9NR.

SWINDON, Bishop Suffragan of, since 2005; **Rt Rev. Lee Stephen Rayfield,** PhD; *b* 30 Sept. 1955; *s* of Ronald Reginald Rayfield and Doris Lilian Rayfield; *m* 1978, Elizabeth Vivienne Rundle; two *s* one *d.* *Educ:* Univ. of Southampton (BSc Hons (Biology) 1978); St Mary's Hosp. Med. Sch., Univ. of London (PhD 1981); Ridley Hall, Cambridge. Postdoctoral Res. Fellow, St Mary's Hosp. Med. Sch., Univ. of London, 1981–84; Lectr in Immunology, UMDS, Guy's and St Thomas' Hosps, Univ. of London, 1984–91. Ordained deacon, 1993, priest, 1994; Asst Curate, Woodford Wells, dio. Chelmsford, 1993–97; Priest-in-charge, 1997–2004, Vicar, 2004–05, Furze Platt, dio. Oxford; part-time Chaplain, St Mark's Hosp., Maidenhead, 1997–2005; Area Dean: Maidenhead, 2000–03; Maidenhead and Windsor, 2003–05. Member: UK Gene Therapy Adv. Cttee, 2000–09; HFEA, 2012–. Mem., SOSc, 1995–. *Publications:* contrib. chapters in med. and dental textbks; many scientific papers in immunol jls, incl. Nature, Transplantation, European Jl of Immunology; two papers in theol jls. *Recreations:* cycling, watching athletics and Rugby Union, motor mechanics. *Address:* Mark House, Field Rise, Swindon, Wilts SN1 4HP. *T:* (01793) 538654. *E:* bishop.swindon@bristoldiocese.org. *Club:* Swindon Road.

SWINFEN, 3rd Baron *cr* 1919; **Roger Mynors Swinfen Eady;** *b* 14 Dec. 1938; *s* of 2nd Baron Swinfen and Mary Aline (*née* Farmar, later Siepmann; writer, as Mary Wesley, CBE) (*d* 2002); *S* father, 1977; *m* 1962, Patricia Anne (MBE 2006), *o d* of late F. D. Blackmore, Dundrum, Dublin; one *s* three *d.* *Educ:* Westminster; RMA, Sandhurst. ARICS 1970–99. Mem., Direct Mail Services Standards Bd, 1983–97. Mem., Select Cttee on EC Sub-Cttee C (Envmtl and Social Affairs), 1991–94; elected Mem., H of L, 1999; Member: Select Cttee on Draft Disability Bill, 2004–; Select Cttee on EU Sub-Cttee B, 2004–06; Select Cttee on EU Sub-Cttee C, 2006–10; Hybrid Bill Cttee, 2010–; Jt Cttee on Consolidation Bills, 2010–; Select Cttee on Mental Capacity Act 2005, 2013–14. Chm., Parly Gp, Video Enquiry Working Party, 1983–85. Pres. SE Reg., British Sports Assoc. for the Disabled, 1986–; Dir, Swinfen Charitable Trust, 1998–; Patron: Disablement Income Gp, 1995–; 1 in 8 Gp, 1996–2004; Labrador Rescue SE, 1996–; World Orthopaedic Concern, 2002–; KunDe Foundn, 2007–; Dir, American Telemedicine Assoc., 2009–13; Hon. Res. Fellow, Centre for Online Health, Univ. of Queensland, 2001–10; Hon. Pres., Britain Bangladesh Friendship Soc., 1996–2004. Fellow, Industry and Parlt Trust. Liveryman, Drapers' Co. JP Kent, 1983–85. *Publications:* reports in med. jls. *Heir:* *s* Hon. Charles Roger Peregrine Swinfen Eady, *b* 8 March 1971. *Address:* House of Lords, SW1A 0PW.

SWINGLAND, Prof. Ian Richard, OBE 2007; Founder and Director, Durrell Institute of Conservation and Ecology, 1989–99 and Professor of Conservation Biology, University of Kent, 1994–99, now Emeritus; *b* 2 Nov. 1946; *s* of late Hugh Maurice Webb Swingland and of Flora Mary Swingland (*née* Fernie); *m* 1985, Fiona Mairi Lawson; one *s* one *d.* *Educ:* Haberdashers' Aske's Sch.; QMC, Univ. of London (BSc 1969); Univ. of Edinburgh (Throgmorton Trotman Sen. Exhibn; FCO Schol.; PhD 1974). FZS 1974; FRSB (FIBiol 1993). Res. Scientist, Shell Research, 1969; Wildlife Mgt Biologist, Kafue Nat. Park, Zambia, 1973–74; Vis. Scientist, Royal Soc. Res. Station, Aldabra Atoll, Seychelles, 1974–79; Post-doctoral Fellow and Tutor, St Peter's Hall, St Catherine's Coll., Magdalen Coll., Lady Margaret Hall, Oxford, 1974–79; Lectr, then Sen. Lectr in Natural Scis, Univ. of Kent, 1979–94. Res. Associate, Smithsonian Instn, 1987–2010; Visiting Professor: of Biology, Univ. of Michigan, 1986–87 (Sen. Res. Fellow, Mus. of Zoology, 1986–87); of Conservation, Univ. of Florence, 1996–2000; of Conservation Biology, Univ. of Auckland, 1996–2001; of Conservation Biology, Manchester Metropolitan Univ., 1998–2001; Ext. Examiner in Biodiversity and Conservation, Univ. of Leeds, 1998–2002. Founding Editor, Biodiversity and Conservation, 1989–99. Member: IUCN Species Survival Commn, 1979–; Council, RURAL, 1980– (Founding Mem.); Council, Fauna and Flora Preservation Soc., 1985–91; Council, RSPCA, 1990–96 (150th Anniv. Lecture, 1990); Darwin Initiative, 2000–09; IUCN Nat. Parks Commn, 2000–03; Director: First World Congress of Herpetology, 1984–89; Sustainable Forestry Mgt LLC, 1998–2005. Founder and Vice Pres., Herpetological Conservation Trust, 1989–2009; Pres., British Chelonia Gp, 1989–2005 (Hon. Life Member, 1989–); Chairman: Apple and Pear Res. Council, 1997–2003; Internat. Bd of Trustees, Iwokrama Internat. Centre for Rain Forest Conservation and Develt, 2002–03; Rural Regeneration Unit, 2009–11; Advisor: Swedish Res. Council (Vetenskapsrådet), 2010–12; Swedish Res. Council for Envmt, Agricl Scis and Spatial Planning (Formas), 2010–12; Governor, Powell Cotton Mus., 1984–2006; Trustee: Biodiversity Foundn for Africa, 1992–; Earthwatch, 1999–2009; Operation Wallacea Trust, 1999– (Chm., 2010–14; Patron, 2014–); Durrell Trust for Conservation Biology, 1999– (Chm., 1999–2014; Patron, 2014–); Durrell Wildlife Conservation Trust, 2005–07 (Hon. Life Mem., 2000); Fauna and Flora Internat., 2005–08; Dir, Derwent Forest, 2004–07. Staff Consultant, Asian Develt Bank, 1996–2007; Chief Policy Advr, Countryside Alliance, 1999–2003; Scientific Advr, FCO, 1999–2002; Panel of Experts, World Bank, 1999–2002; Mem. Adv. Bd, Centre for Biodiversity and Restoration Ecology, Victoria Univ. of Wellington, 2006–. Ambassador, Galapagos Conservation Trust, 2008–; Patron, Hadlow Coll., Kent, 2013–. Bioscience Fellow, Commonwealth Agricl Bureau Internat., 2002. Freedom of the City of London, 2001. DSc Kent 2005. *Publications:* *edited jointly:* The Ecology of Animal Movement, 1983; Living in a Patchy Environment, 1990; New Techniques in Integrated Protected Area Management, 1998; Carbon, biodiversity, conservation and income: an analysis of a free-market approach to land-use changes and forestry in developing and developed countries, 2002; Capturing Biodiversity and Conserving Biodiversity: a market approach, 2003; Integrated Wetlands Management, 2012; contrib. books and jls incl. Nature, Phil Trans Royal Soc., Jl Theor. Biology, Jl Zoology, London Jl Animal Ecology, Biodiversity and Conservation, Proc. Biol. Soc. Washington, Applied Animal Behaviour Sci., Animal Behaviour, Can. Jl Zool., Proc. Royal Soc. of London, etc. *Recreations:* growing trees, cooking, being alone in remote wild places, being iconoclastic, losing things. *Address:* Herons Hall, Nash, Kent CT3 2JX. *T:* 07971 669915, *Fax:* (office) (01304) 812099. *Club:* Athenæum.

SWINGLER, Raymond John Peter; editorial and information technology consultant, since 1992; *b* 8 Oct. 1933; *s* of Raymond Joseph and Mary Swingler; *m* 1st, 1960, Shirley (*d* 1980), *e d* of Frederick and Dorothy Wilkinson, Plymouth; two *d*; 2nd, 2008, June, *d* of Thomas James and Irene Morgan, Yorks. *Educ:* St Bede's Coll., Christchurch, NZ; Canterbury Univ. Journalist, The Press, Christchurch, NZ, 1956–57; Marlborough Express, 1957–59; Nelson Mail, 1959–61; freelance Middle East, 1961–62; Cambridge Evening News, 1962–79. Press Council: Mem., 1975–78; Mem., Complaints Cttee, 1976–78; Sec. and conciliator, 1980–91; Asst Dir, 1989–91; Asst Dir, Press Complaints Commn, 1991. Member: Nat. Exec. Council, Nat. Union of Journalists, 1973–75, 1978–79; Provincial Newspapers Industrial Council, 1976–79; Chm., General Purposes Cttee (when journalists' Code of Professional Conduct (revised) introduced), 1974–75. Partner: Haringey Telematics Project, 1995–98; Lee Valley Univ. for Industry, 1997–99; Hon. Sec./Treas., Connexions Project (teaching IT to the disabled), 1994–97. Mem., Metropolitan Police Authy Stop and Search Rev. Bd, 2005–14. Pres., Walthamstow Village Residents' Assoc., 1997–. *Recreation:* horses and horsewomen. *Address:* 11A Church Path, E17 9RQ.

SWINLEY, Margaret Albinia Joanna, OBE 1980; British Council Service, retired; *b* 30 Sept. 1935; *er* twin *d* of late Captain Casper Silas Balfour Swinley, DSO, DSC, RN and Sylvia Jocosa Swinley, 4th *d* of late Canon W. H. Carnegie. *Educ:* Southover Manor Sch., Lewes; Edinburgh Univ. (MA Hons Hist.). English Teacher/Sec., United Paper Mills, Jämsänkoski, Finland, 1958–60; joined British Council, 1960; Birmingham Area Office, 1960–63; Tel Aviv, 1963; Lagos, 1963–66; seconded to London HQ of VSO, 1966–67; New Delhi, 1967–70; Dep. Rep., Lagos, 1970–73; Dir, Tech. Assistance Trng Dept, 1973–76; Rep., Israel, 1976–80; Asst, then Dep., Controller, Educn, Medicine and Science Div., 1980–82; Controller, Africa and Middle East Div., 1982–86; Controller, Home Div., 1986–89. Mem., S Wales Shire Horse Soc., 1993– (Pres., 1998, 2005). Pres., Flaxley WI, 2002–05. Lay Mem., Local Ministry Team, benefice of Westbury-on-Severn with Flaxley and Blaisdon, 1998–. *Recreations:* theatre-going, country life, keeping dogs and Shire horses.

SWINNERTON-DYER, Prof. Sir (Henry) Peter (Francis), 16th Bt *cr* 1678; KBE 1987; FRS 1967; Chief Executive, Universities Funding Council, 1989–91; *b* 2 Aug. 1927; *s* of Sir Leonard Schroeder Swinnerton Dyer, 15th Bt, and Barbara (*d* 1990), *d* of Hereward Brackenbury, CBE; *S* father, 1975; *m* 1983, Dr Harriet Crawford, *er d* of Rt Hon. Sir Patrick Browne, OBE, TD, PC. *Educ:* Eton; Trinity College, Cambridge (Hon. Fellow 1981). University of Cambridge: Research Fellow, 1950–54, Fellow, 1955–73, Dean, 1963–73, Trinity Coll.; Master, St Catharine's Coll., 1973–83 (Hon. Fellow, 1983); Univ. Lectr, 1960–71 (at Mathematical Lab., 1960–67); Prof. of Maths, 1971–88; Vice-Chancellor, 1979–81. Commonwealth Fund Fellow, Univ. of Chicago, 1954–55. Vis. Prof., Harvard Univ., 1971. Hon. Fellow, Worcester Coll., Oxford, 1980. Chairman: Cttee on Academic Organisation, Univ. of London, 1980–82; Meteorological Cttee, 1983–94; UGC, 1983–89; CODEST, 1986–91; European Sci. and Technol. Assembly, 1994–97. Chm., Sec. of State for Nat. Heritage's Adv. Cttee, Liby and Inf. Services Council, 1992–95; Mem., Library and Information Commn, 1995–98. Hon. DSc: Bath, 1981; Ulster, Wales, 1991; Birmingham, Nottingham, 1992; Warwick, 1993; Hon. LLD Aberdeen, 1991. *Publications:* numerous papers in mathematical journals. *Recreation:* gardening. *Heir:* *kinsman* David Dyer-Bennet [*b* 1954; *m* 1982, Pamela Collins Dean]. *Address:* The Dower House, Thriplow, Royston, Herts SG8 7RJ. *T:* (01763) 208220.

SWINNEY, John Ramsay; Member (SNP) Perthshire North, Scottish Parliament, since 2011 (North Tayside, 1999–2011); Deputy First Minister, and Cabinet Secretary for Finance, Constitution and Economy, since 2014; *b* 13 April 1964; *s* of Kenneth Swinney and Nancy Swinney (*née* Hunter); *m* 1st, 1991, Lorna Ann King (marr. diss. 2000); one *s* one *d*; 2nd, 2003, Elizabeth Quigley; one *s.* *Educ:* Univ. of Edinburgh (MA Hons Politics). Sen. Managing Consultant, Developments Options Ltd, 1988–92; Strategic Planning Principal, Scottish Amicable, 1992–97. MP (SNP) North Tayside, 1997–2001. Scottish Parliament: Dep. Leader of the Opposition, 1999–2000, Leader, 2000–04; SNP spokesman for finance and public service reform, 2005–07; Cabinet Sec. for Finance and Sustainable Growth, 2007–14; Convener: Enterprise and Lifelong Learning Cttee, 1999–2000; European Cttee, 2004–05. Scottish National Party: Nat. Sec., 1986–92; Vice Convener for Publicity, 1992–97; Treasury Spokesman, 1995–2000; Dep. Leader, 1998–2000; Leader, 2000–04. *Recreations:* cycling, hill walking. *Address:* 35 Perth Street, Blairgowrie PH10 6DL. *T:* (01250) 876576.

SWINSON, Christopher, OBE 2006; FCA; Comptroller and Auditor General, Jersey, 2005–12; Senior Partner, BDO Stoy Hayward, 1997–2004 (Partner, 1993–97); *b* 27 Jan. 1948; *s* of Arthur Montagu Swinson and Jean Swinson; *m* 1972, Christine Margaret Hallam; one *s.* *Educ:* Wadham Coll., Oxford (MA). FCA 1979 (ACA 1974). Price Waterhouse, 1970–77; Hacker Young, 1977–79; with Binder Hamlyn, 1979–92 (Nat. Man. Partner, 1989–92). Institute of Chartered Accountants in England and Wales: Mem. Council, 1985–2001; Vice-Pres., 1996–97; Dep. Pres., 1997–98; Pres., 1998–99; Chm., Regulation Review Working Party, 1995–2001. Mem., Audit Commn, 2000–03; Chm., Audit Cttee, HM Treasury, 2001–05; Bd Mem., Pensions Regulator, 2005–13. Vis. Prof., Bournemouth Univ., 2006–. Treasurer: Navy Records Soc., 1987–94; Soc. for Nautical Res., 1991–95; NCVO, 1993–97. Trustee: NMSI, 1987–; Greenwich Foundn, RNC, 1997–2002. FRSA 1992. *Publications:* Companies Act 1989, 1990; Regulation of Auditors, 1990; Delivering a Quality Service, 1992; Group Accounts, 1993. *Recreation:* model railway construction. *Address:* No Ways, Frithsden, Hemel Hempstead, Herts HP1 3DD. *T:* (01442) 864640. *E:* chris@swinson.co.uk. *Club:* Athenæum.

SWINSON, Jo; *b* 5 Feb. 1980; *d* of Peter and Annette Swinson; *m* 2011, Duncan John Hames, *qv*; one *s.* *Educ:* London Sch. of Econs (BSc 1st Cl. Hons Mgt 2000). Mktg Exec. then Manager, Viking FM, 2000–02; Mktg Manager, SpaceandPeople Ltd, 2003–04; Scottish Develt Officer, UK Public Health Assoc., 2004–05. Vice Chm., Lib Dem Youth and Students, 1999–2001; Chm., Lib Dem Campaign for Gender Balance (formerly Gender Balance Task Force), 2006–08 (Vice Chm., 2003–06). Contested (Lib Dem): Hull East, 2001; Strathkelvin and Bearsden, Scottish Parlt, 2003. MP (Lib Dem) E Dunbartonshire, 2005–15; contested (Lib Dem) same seat, 2015. Lib Dem Shadow posts: Minister for Culture, Media and Sport, 2005–06; Sec. of State for Scotland, 2006–07; Minister for Women and Equality, 2007; Minister for Foreign Affairs, 2008–10; PPS to Sec. of State, BIS, 2010–12, to Dep. Prime Minister, 2012; Parliamentary Under-Secretary of State: BIS, 2012–15; Women and Equalities, DCMS, then at DFE, 2012–15. *Recreations:* reading, running.

SWINTON, 3rd Earl of, *cr* 1955; **Nicholas John Cunliffe-Lister;** Viscount Swinton, 1935; Baron Masham, 1955; *b* 4 Sept. 1939; *s* of Major Hon. John Yarburgh Cunliffe-Lister (*d* of wounds received in action, 1943) and Anne Irvine (*m* 2nd, 1944, Donald Chapple-Gill; she *d* 1961), *yr d* of late Rev. Canon R. S. Medlicott; *S* brother, 2006; *m* 1st, 1966, Hon. Elizabeth Susan (marr. diss. 1996), *e d* of 1st Viscount Whitelaw, KT, CH, MC, PC; two *s* one *d*; 2nd, 1996, Pamela June Sykes (*née* Wood). *Educ:* Winchester; Worcester Coll., Oxford. *Heir:* *s* Lord Masham, *qv.*

SWINTON, Susan, Countess of; *see* Masham of Ilton, Baroness.

SWINTON, Maj.-Gen. Sir John, KCVO 1979; OBE 1969; Lord-Lieutenant of Berwickshire, 1989–2000; *b* 21 April 1925; *s* of late Brig. A. H. C. Swinton, MC, Scots Guards; *m* 1954, Judith (*d* 2012), *d* of late Harold Killen, Merribee, NSW; three *s* one *d.* *Educ:* Harrow. Enlisted, Scots Guards, 1943, commissioned, 1944; served NW Europe, 1945 (twice wounded); Malaya, 1948–51 (despatches); ADC to Field Marshal Sir William Slim, Governor-General of Australia, 1953–54; Staff College, 1957; DAA&QMG 1st Guards Brigade, 1958–59; Regimental Adjutant Scots Guards, 1960–62; Adjutant, RMA Sandhurst, 1962–64; comd 2nd Bn Scots Guards, 1966–68; AAG PS12 MoD, 1968–70; Lt Col Comdg Scots Guards, 1970–71; Comdr, 4th Guards Armoured Brigade, BAOR, 1972–73; RCDS 1974; Brigadier Lowlands and Comdr Edinburgh and Glasgow Garrisons, 1975–76; GOC London Dist and Maj.-Gen. Comdg Household Div., 1976–79; retired 1979. Mem., Queen's Body Guard for Scotland (Royal Co. of Archers), 1954– (Capt., 2003–07); Hon. Col 2nd Bn 52nd Lowland Volunteers, 1983–90. Pres., Lowland TA & VRA, 1992–96; Nat. Chm., Royal British Legion Scotland, 1986–89 (Nat. Vice-Chm., 1984–86); Mem. Council, British Commonwealth Ex-Services League, 1984–98. Mem., Central Adv. Cttee on War Pensions, 1986–89. Pres., Borders Area SSAFA, 1993–2006. Trustee: Army Museums Ogilby Trust, 1978–90; Scottish Nat. War Meml, 1984–2009 (Vice-Chm., 1987–96; Chm., 1996–2009); Scots at War Trust, 1996–2009; Berwick Mil. Tattoo, 1996–2007; Chm., Thirlestane Castle Trust, 1984–90. Patron, Prosthetic and Orthotic Worldwide Educn and Relief, 1995–2008. Borders Liaison Officer, Duke of Edinburgh's Award Scheme, 1982–84. Chairman: Berwicks Civic Soc., 1982–98 (Pres., 1998–2005); Roxburgh and Berwickshire Cons. Assoc., 1983–85; Jt Management Cttee, St Abb's Head Nat. Nature Reserve, 1991–98; Berwicks Recreation Sports Trust, 1997–2005; Scottish Nat. Motorsport Collection, 1998–2001; Pres.,

Berwickshire Naturalists Club, 1996–97. Pres., RHAS, 1993–94. DL, 1980–89, JP, 1989–2008, Berwickshire. *Address:* Kimmerghame, Duns, Berwickshire TD11 3LU. *T:* (01361) 883277. *E:* kimmerghame@amserve.com.

SWIRE, Sir Adrian (Christopher), Kt 1982; Hon. President, John Swire & Sons Ltd (Chairman, 1987–97 and 2002–04; Deputy Chairman, 1966–87; Director, 1961); Director: Cathay Pacific Airways, 1965–2005; Swire Pacific Ltd, 1978–2008; *b* 15 Feb. 1932; *yr s* of late John Kidston Swire and Juliet Richenda, *d* of Theodore Barclay; *m* 1970, Lady Judith Compton, *e d* of 6th Marquess of Northampton, DSO; two *s* one *d. Educ:* Eton; University Coll., Oxford (MA). Served Coldstream Guards, 1950–52; RAFVR and RAuxAF (AE; Hon. Air Cdre, 1987–2000). Joined Butterfield & Swire in Far East, 1956; Chm., China Navigation Co., 1968–88; Return of SS Great Britain Steering Cttee, 1970–72. Director: Brooke Bond Gp, 1972–82; NAAFI, 1972–87 (Dep. Chm., 1982–85); HSBC Hldgs plc, 1995–2002; Mem., Internat. Adv. Council, CITIC, Beijing, 1995–2004. Mem., Gen. Cttee, Lloyd's Register, 1967–99. Pres., General Council of British Shipping, 1980–81; Chm., Internat. Chamber of Shipping, 1982–87. Elder Brother, Trinity House, 1990. Vis. Fellow, Nuffield Coll., Oxford, 1981–89 (Hon. Fellow, 1998). Chm., RAF Benevolent Fund, 1996–2000. Trustee, RAF Mus., 1983–91. Pres., Spitfire Soc., 1996–2009. Pro-Chancellor, Southampton Univ., 1995–2004. Mem. Council, Wycombe Abbey Sch., 1988–95. Hon. CRAeS 1991. Liveryman: Fishmongers' Co., 1962; Hon. Co. of Air Pilots (formerly GAPAN), 1986. DL Oxon, 1989. Hon. DSc Cranfield, 1995; DUniv Southampton, 2002. Air League Founders' Medal, 2006. *Address:* Swire House, 59 Buckingham Gate, SW1E 6AJ. *Clubs:* White's, Brooks's, Pratt's; Hong Kong (Hong Kong).
See also Sir J. A. Swire, M. B. Swire.

SWIRE, Barnaby Nicholas; Chairman, John Swire & Sons Ltd, since 2015; *b* London, 10 Jan. 1964; *s* of Sir John (Anthony) Swire, *qv*; *m* 1991, Camilla Husband; two *s* two *d. Educ:* Eton Coll.; University Coll., Oxford (BA); INSEAD. John Swire & Sons Ltd, 1985–. *Address:* John Swire & Sons Ltd, Swire House, 59 Buckingham Gate, SW1E 6AJ. *T:* (020) 7834 7717.

SWIRE, Rt Hon. Hugo (George William); PC 2011; MP (C) East Devon, since 2001; Minister of State, Foreign and Commonwealth Office, since 2012; *b* 30 Nov. 1959; *s* of late Humphrey Roger Swire and of Philippa Sophia Montgomerie (she *m* 2004, 7th Marquess Townshend); *m* 1996, Alexandra, (Sasha), Petruška Mina, *d* of Rt Hon. Sir John William Frederic Nott, *qv*; two *d. Educ:* Eton; Univ. of St Andrews; RMA Sandhurst. Lieut, 1 Bn Grenadier Guards, 1980–83; Head, Develt Office, Nat. Gall., 1988–92; Sotheby's, 1992–2001: Dep. Dir, 1996–97; Dir, 1997–2001. Contested (Scottish C and Unionist) Greenock and Inverclyde, 1997. Shadow Minister for the Arts, 2004–05, for Culture, 2005; Shadow Sec. of State for Culture, Media and Sport, 2005–07; Minister of State, NI Office, 2010–12. FRSA 1993. *Address:* House of Commons, SW1A 0AA. *Clubs:* White's, Pratt's, Beefsteak; Exmouth Conservative (Pres., 2005–).

SWIRE, Sir John (Anthony), Kt 1990; CBE 1977; Life President, John Swire & Sons Ltd, since 1997 (Chairman, 1966–87, Executive Director, 1955–92; Hon. President and Director, 1987–97); *b* 28 Feb. 1927; *er s* of late John Kidston Swire and Juliet Richenda, *d* of Theodore Barclay; *m* 1961, Moira Cecilia Ducharne; two *s* one *d. Educ:* Eton; University Coll., Oxford (MA). Served Irish Guards, UK and Palestine, 1945–48. Joined Butterfield & Swire, Hong Kong, 1950; Director: Swire Pacific Ltd, 1965–92; Royal Insurance plc, 1975–80; British Bank of the Middle East, 1975–79; James Finlay plc, 1976–92; Ocean Transport & Trading plc, 1977–83; Shell Transport and Trading Co., 1990–95. Chairman: Hong Kong Assoc., 1975–87; Cook Soc., 1984. Member: London Adv. Cttee, Hongkong and Shanghai Banking Corp., 1969–89; Euro-Asia Centre Adv. Bd, 1980–91; Adv. Council, Sch. of Business, Stanford Univ., 1981–90; Council, Univ. of Kent at Canterbury, 1989–99 (Dep. Pro-Chancellor, 1993–99). KStJ 2014. Hon. Fellow: St Antony's Coll., Oxford, 1987; University Coll., Oxford, 1989. Hon. LLD Hong Kong, 1989; Hon. DCL Kent, 1995. DL Kent, 1996. *Address:* Swire House, 59 Buckingham Gate, SW1E 6AJ. *T:* (020) 7834 7717. *Clubs:* Brooks's, Pratt's, Cavalry and Guards, Flyfishers' (Pres., 1988–89); Hong Kong (Hong Kong).
See also Sir A. C. Swire, B. N. Swire.

SWIRE, Merlin Bingham; Chief Executive, John Swire & Sons Ltd, since 2015; *b* London, 4 Dec. 1973; *s* of Sir Adrian (Christopher) Swire, *qv*; *m* 2014, Laura Carlyn Chisholm; one *d. Educ:* Eton Coll.; University Coll., Oxford (MA Lit.Hum.). Joined John Swire & Sons (Hong Kong) Ltd, 1997; Chief Exec., Taikoo (Xiamen) Aircraft Engrg Co. Ltd, 2006–08; Finance Dir, John Swire & Sons Ltd, 2009–12; Chm., James Finlay Ltd, 2009–; Director: Swire Pacific Ltd, 2009–; Hong Kong Aircraft Engrg Co. Ltd, 2009–; Swire Properties Ltd, 2009–; Cathay Pacific Airways Ltd, 2010–. Dir, United States Cold Storage Inc., 2003–13. *Recreations:* Greece, walking, cricket. *Address:* John Swire & Sons Ltd, Swire House, 59 Buckingham Gate, SW1E 6AJ.

SWITZER, Barbara; Assistant General Secretary, Manufacturing Science Finance, 1988–97; *b* 26 Nov. 1940; *d* of late Albert and Edith McMinn; *m* 1973, John Michael Switzer. *Educ:* Chorlton Central Sch., Manchester; Stretford Technical Coll. City & Guilds Final Cert. for Electrical Technician. Engrg apprentice, Metropolitan Vickers, 1957–62; Draughtswoman: GEC, Trafford Park, 1962–70; Cableform, Romiley, 1970–71; Mather & Platt, 1972–76; Divisional Organiser 1976–79, National Organiser 1979–83, AUEW (TASS); Dep. Gen. Sec., TASS—The Manufacturing Union, 1983–87. President: CSEU, 1995–97; Nat. Assembly of Women, 1999–2009; Mem., TUC Gen. Council, 1993–97. Mem., Employment Appeal Tribunal, 1996–2010. Mem. Council, Women of the Year Lunch and Assembly, 1996–2011. TUC Women's Gold Badge for services to Trade Unionism, 1976. *Address:* 16 Follett Drive, Abbots Langley, Herts WD5 0LP.

SWORD, Dr Ian Pollock, CBE 2002; FRCPE; FRSC; FRSE; Chairman, Inveresk Research Group Inc. (formerly Inveresk Research International Ltd), 1989–2004; *b* 6 March 1942; *s* of John Pollock Sword and Agnes Fyfe; *m* 1967, Flora Collins; two *s* one *d. Educ:* Univ. of Glasgow (BSc; PhD). FRSC 1975; FRSE 1996; FRCPE 1997. Univ. of Princeton, 1967–69; Res. Associate, Univ. of Oxford, 1969–70; Hd of Metabolism, then Chemistry Dept, Huntington Res. Centre, 1970–73; Inveresk Research International Ltd: Dep. Man. Dir, 1973–78; Man. Dir, 1978–89. Sen. Exec. Vice-Pres., Société Générale de Surveillance, 1993–2002. Mem., MRC, 1995–98. Chm., Scottish Stem Cell Network, 2006–08. Dir, Archangel Informal Investment Ltd, 2003–08. Trustee: Carnegie Trust for Univs of Scotland, 2005–; Royal Botanic Garden Edinburgh, 2007–14. Hon. DSc Glasgow, 2008. *Publications:* (ed) Standard Operating Procedures, vol. 3, 1980, vol. 4, 1981. *Recreations:* music, gardening. *Club:* New (Edinburgh).

SYAL, Meera, CBE 2015 (MBE 1998); actress and writer; *b* 27 June 1964; *d* of Surendra Kumar Syal and Surrinder Syal; *m* 2005, Sanjeev Bhaskar, *qv*; one *s*; one *d* from previous marriage. *Educ:* Manchester Univ. (BA Hons English and Drama, double 1st). Various regular appearances on national television and theatre, 1992–; *actress:* television: Goodness Gracious Me, 1998–2001; The Kumars at No. 42, 2001–06, The Kumars, 2014; All About Me, 2002; Life Isn't All Ha Ha Hee Hee (also co-writer), 2005; Murder Investigation Team, 2005; Broadchurch, 2015; theatre: Rafta, Rafta, Nat. Th., 2007; Shirley Valentine, Trafalgar Studios, 2010; The Killing of Sister George, Arts Th., 2011; Much Ado About Nothing, Courtyard Th., Stratford, 2012, transf. Noel Coward Th., 2012; If You Don't Let Us Dream, We Won't Let You Sleep, Royal Court, 2013; Behind the Beautiful Forevers, NT, 2014; *writer:* My Sister Wife (film), 1992; Bhaji on the Beach (film), 1993; Anita and Me (film), 2002; co-writer, Bombay Dreams (musical), Apollo, 2002, transf. Broadway Th., NY, 2004. Cameron Mackintosh Vis. Prof. of Contemporary Th., Oxford Univ., 2011–. Hon. PhD: Wolverhampton, 2000; Leeds, 2002; Birmingham, 2003. *Publications: novels:* Anita and Me, 1997; Life Isn't All Ha Ha Hee Hee, 1999; The House of Hidden Mothers, 2015. *Recreations:* netball, jazz singer. *Address:* c/o Rochelle Stevens, 2 Terretts Place, Islington, N1 1QZ.

SYCAMORE, Phillip; His Honour Judge Sycamore; a Circuit Judge, since 2001; a President, First Tier Tribunal, and a Judge of the Upper Tribunal, since 2008; a Deputy High Court Judge, since 2010; *b* 9 March 1951; *s* of late Frank and Evelyn Martin Sycamore; *m* 1974, Sandra, JP, *d* of late Peter Frederick Cooper and of Marjorie Cooper; two *s* one *d. Educ:* Lancaster Royal Grammar Sch.; Holborn Coll. of Law (LLB London (ext.) 1972). Admitted Solicitor, 1975; in private practice, Lonsdales, solicitors, 1980–2001; Asst Recorder, 1994–99; a Recorder, 1999–2001; Liaison Judge, Mental Health Review Tribunal, 2002–08. Law Society: Mem. Council, 1991–99; Vice-Pres., 1996–97; Pres., 1997–98. Member: Woolf Civil Justice Review (Access to Justice), 1994–96; Criminal Injuries Compensation Panel, 2000–01; Sen. Judicial Appts Comr, 2014–. Gov., Lancaster Royal Grammar Sch., 2001–. Hon. Recorder of Lancaster, 2008–. Hon. LLD: Westminster, 1998; Lancaster, 1999. *Recreations:* family, golf, theatre, travel, ski-ing. *Address:* The Civil Justice Centre, 1 Bridge Street West, Manchester M60 9DJ. *Clubs:* Athenæum; Royal Lytham and St Anne's Golf.

SYDNEY, Archbishop of, and Metropolitan of the Province of New South Wales; since 2013; **Most Rev. Dr Glenn Naunton Davies;** *b* 26 Sept. 1950; *s* of Rodger Naunton Davies and Dorothy Joan Davies; *m* 1979, Dianne Frances Carlisle; two *d. Educ:* Univ. of Sydney (BSc 1972); Westminster Theol Seminary, Philadelphia (MDiv, ThM 1979); Moore Theol Coll. (DipA 1981); Sheffield Univ. (PhD 1988). Ordained deacon, priest, 1981; Asst Minister, St Stephen's, Willoughby, 1981–82; Lectr, Moore Theol Coll., 1983–95; Rector, St Luke's, Miranda, 1995–2001; Asst Bishop, Dio. of Sydney, and Bishop of N Sydney, 2002–13; Archdeacon of N Sydney, 2009–13. Canon Theologian, Dio. of Ballarat, 2000–. Centenary Medal, Australia, 2003. *Publications:* Job, 1989; Faith and Obedience: studies in Romans 1–4, 1990. *Address:* PO Box Q190, QVB Post Office, NSW 1230, Australia.

SYDNEY, SOUTH, Bishop of; *see* Forsyth, Rt Rev. R. C.

SYDNEY, Assistant Bishop of; *see* Forsyth, Rt Rev. R. C.

SYED, Matthew Philip; table tennis player; *b* 2 Nov. 1970; *s* of Abbas Syed and Dilys Syed. *Educ:* Maiden Erleigh Comprehensive Sch.; Balliol Coll., Oxford (MA). Represented GB, Olympic Games, Barcelona, 1992 and Sydney, 2000; British No. 1, 1995–2004; English Men's Singles Champion, 1997, 1998, 2000, 2001; Commonwealth Men's Singles Champion, 1997, 1999, 2001. Sports columnist, The Times, 1999–. Co-founder, TTK Greenhouse (sports charity), 2002–; Trustee, Greenhouse Charity, 2012–. Feature Writer of the Year, Sports Journalists' Assoc., 2007, 2010, 2011; Sports Journalist of the Year, British Press Awards, 2009. *Publications:* Bounce: how champions are made, 2010 (Best New Writer, British Sports Book Awards, 2011); Black Box Thinking, 2015. *Recreations:* walking in Richmond Park, looking at London architecture. *Address:* Dolphin House, Ormond Road, Richmond, Surrey TW10 6TH. *T:* (020) 8948 6050. *E:* matthew@matthewsyed.co.uk.

SYFRET, Nicholas; QC 2008; a Recorder, since 2001; *b* Windlesham, Surrey, 25 Oct. 1954; *s* of Edward Herbert Vyvyan Syfret and Anne Syfret; *m* 1980, Katharine Frances, *d* of Sir (Walter) Leonard Allinson, *qv*; two *s* one *d. Educ:* Winchester Coll.; Emmanuel Coll., Cambridge (BA 1976). Called to the Bar, Middle Temple, 1979; in practice as barrister specialising in criminal law; 6 King's Bench Walk, 1980–93, 13 King's Bench Walk, 1993–2014; Cornwall Street Chambers, Birmingham, 2014–. *Recreations:* countryside, messing about in boats, painting, chess. *Address:* St Margaret's Cottage, 15 The Moors, Pangbourne, Reading RG8 7LP. *T:* (0118) 984 3690. *E:* NSyfret@aol.com.

SYKES, Alastair John, CBE 2011; Chief Executive, 2001–08, and Chairman, 2001–09, Nestlé UK; *b* 25 Jan. 1953; *s* of John and Jackie Sykes; *m* 1982, Kate Rutter; one *s. Educ:* UMIST (BSc Hons Mgt Sci. 1978). Joined Gillette, 1978; held various commercial roles, 1978–89; Eur. Sales and Mktg Dir, 1989–91; Managing Director: McCormick Foods, 1991–95; Spillers UK, 1995–98; Nestlé Rowntree, 1998–2001. Pres., Inst. of Grocery Distribution, 2007–08. *Recreations:* golf, Rugby.

SYKES, Prof. Brian Douglas, PhD; FRS 2000; FRSC 1986; Distinguished University Professor, Department of Biochemistry, University of Alberta, since 1997; *b* Montreal, 30 Aug. 1943; *s* of Douglas Lehman Sykes and Mary Anber Sykes; *m* 1968, Nancy Sengelaub (decd); two *s. Educ:* Univ. of Alberta (BSc 1965); Stanford Univ. (PhD 1969). Asst Prof. of Chemistry, 1969–74, Associate Prof., 1974–75, Harvard Univ.; University of Alberta: Associate Prof., 1975–80, Prof., 1980–97; Mem., 1975–, Dir, 1995–, MRC Gp in Protein Structure and Function; Leader, Alberta Node, 1990–, Dep. Scientific Leader, 1995–98, Protein Engrg Network of Centres of Excellence; Actg Chair, 1998–99, Chair, 1999–2004, Dept of Biochem.; Canada Res. Chair, 2001–08. Pres., Canadian Biochem. Soc., 1989–90. *Publications:* over 510 scientific papers. *Address:* Department of Biochemistry, University of Alberta, Edmonton, AB T6G 2H7, Canada; 11312–37 Avenue, Edmonton, AB T6J 0HS, Canada.

SYKES, Sir David Michael, 4th Bt *cr* 1921, of Kingsknowes, Galashiels, co. Selkirk; Chairman, Bennett Sykes Group (formerly Libra Office Equipment) Ltd, 2000–09; *b* 10 June 1954; *s* of Michael le Gallais Sykes and Joan Sykes (*née* Groome); *S* uncle, 2001; *m* 1st, 1974, Susan Elizabeth Hall (marr. diss. 1987); one *s*; 2nd, 1987, Margaret Lynne McGreavy; one *d. Educ:* Purbrook Park Grammar Sch. Sales Dir, Frank Groome (Nottingham) Ltd, 1974–85; Sen. Partner, Sykes Office Supplies, 1985–2007. Mem., LTA. *Recreations:* travel, food and wine, tennis. *Heir: s* Stephen David Sykes, *b* 14 Dec. 1978.

SYKES, Dr Donald Armstrong; Principal of Mansfield College, Oxford, 1977–86, now Hon. Fellow; *b* 13 Feb. 1930; *s* of late Rev. Leonard Sykes and Edith Mary Sykes (*née* Armstrong); *m* 1st, 1962, Marta Sproul Whitehouse (*d* 2000); two *s*; 2nd, 2002, Sarah Yates. *Educ:* The High Sch. of Dundee; Univ. of St Andrews (MA 2nd cl. Classics 1952; Guthrie Scholar); RAEC, 1952–54; Mansfield Coll., Oxford (BA 1st cl. Theol. 1958; MA 1961; DPhil 1967); Univ. of Glasgow (DipEd). Fellow in Theology, 1959–77, Senior Tutor, 1970–77, and Sen. Res. Fellow, 1986–89, Mansfield Coll., Oxford; retired from tutoring, 2000. Vis. Prof. in Classics and Religion, St Olaf Coll., Northfield, Minn, 1969–70, 1987. Hon. DD St Olaf, 1979. *Publications:* (contrib.) Studies of the Church in History: essays honoring Robert S. Paul, ed Horton Davies, 1983; (introd., trans. and commentary) Gregory of Nazianzus, *Poemata Arcana*, 1997; articles and reviews in Jl Theological Studies, Studia Patristica, Byzantinische Zeitschrift. *Recreations:* miscellaneous reading, recorded music, walking, gardening. *Address:* 52 Pond Bank, Blisworth, Northampton NN7 3EL. *T:* (01604) 859373. *Club:* Oxford and Cambridge.

SYKES, Sir (Francis) John (Badcock), 10th Bt *cr* 1781, of Basildon, Berkshire; Partner, Thring Townsend (formerly Townsends), solicitors, Bath, Swindon and Newbury, 1972–2002, Consultant, 2002–05; *b* 7 June 1942; *s* of Sir Francis Godfrey Sykes, 9th Bt and Lady Eira Betty Sykes (*née* Badcock) (*d* 1970); *S* father, 1990; *m* 1966, Susan Alexandra, *er d* of Adm. of the Fleet Sir E. B. Ashmore, *qv*; three *s. Educ:* Shrewsbury; Worcester Coll., Oxford (MA). Admitted solicitor, 1968; Assistant Solicitor: Gamlens, Lincoln's Inn, 1968–69; Townsends, 1969–71. Hon. Solicitor, 1973–98, Pres., 1981, Swindon Chamber of Commerce. Governor: Swindon Coll., 1982–90; Swindon Enterprise Trust, 1982–89. Vice-Chm., Marlborough Literature Fest., 2010–. Trustee: Roman Research Trust, 1990–2002; Merchant's House (Marlborough) Trust, 1991–; Wilts Community Foundn, 1993–2000; Duchess of Somerset's Hosp., 2003–09. Pres., Nat. Trust Reading Centre, 2008–. Member:

HAC; City Barge Club, Oxford. *Recreations:* local and Anglo-Indian history, Venetian rowing. *Heir: s* Col Francis Charles Sykes, *b* 18 June 1968. *Address:* Kingsbury Croft, Kingsbury Street, Marlborough, Wilts SN8 1HU.

SYKES, Sir Hugh (Ridley), Kt 1997; DL; Chairman, Bamford Group Ltd (formerly Bamford Hall Holdings Ltd, then BHH (Brookfield) Ltd), since 1972; *b* 12 Sept. 1932; *m* 1st, 1957, Norah Rosemary Dougan; two *s*; 2nd, 1978, Ruby Anderson; two *s*. *Educ:* Bristol Grammar Sch.; Clare Coll., Cambridge (MA, LLB). CA 1960. Articled with Thomson McLintock, Chartered Accountants, 1956–61; Treas., 1961–69, Asst Man. Dir, 1969–72, Man. Dir (Finance), 1972–73, Steetley & Co.; Chm. and Chief Exec., Thermal Scientific plc, 1977–88. Non-exec. Dep. Chm., Harris Queensway plc, 1978–83; non-executive Chairman: TCI plc, 1985–88; Harveys Furnishings, 1988–94; Yorkshire Bank plc, 1999–2004 (Dir, 1990–2004); Nat. Australia Gp (Europe) Ltd, 2002–04 (Dir, 1997–2004); non-executive Director: Clydesdale Bank plc, 1999–2004; A4e Ltd, 2005–14. Consultant, Bd, Nat. Australia Bank, 2002–04. Chairman: Sheffield Develt Corp., 1988–97; Renaissance S Yorks, 2004–09; Mid Yorks NHS Trust, 2005–08; SheffCare, 2009–11 (Patron, 2012–); non-exec. Chm., 2000–05, Dir, 2005–07, Sheffield One; Dir, Creative Sheffield, 2007–11; Member of Board: Sheffield TEC, 1990–95; 1NG, 2009–11. Dir, Inst. of Dirs, 2003–09. Chairman: Sir Hugh and Lady Sykes (formerly Hugh and Ruby Sykes) Charitable Trust, 1988–; Sheffield Galleries and Museums Trust, 1998–2008; Industrial Trust, 2001–11 (Trustee, 1998–2011); Mem. Bd, TCV—The Conservation Volunteers, 2008–14 (Mem., Audit Cttee, 2008–); Trustee, Engineering Develt Trust, 2011–12. Life Gov., Royal Humane Soc. Mem. Council, Univ. of Sheffield, 1997–2002 (Treas., 1998–2002). DL S Yorks, 1996. Freeman, City of London, 1990. FCIB 2001. Hon. FInstD 2009. Hon. Fellow, Sheffield Hallam Univ., 1991. Hon. LLD Sheffield, 1996. *Publications:* Working for Benefit, 1997; Welfare to Work: the new deal—maximising the benefits, 1998. *Recreations:* walking, travel, golf, Victorian paintings, helping to find a solution to the problem of unemployment. *Address:* Brookfield Manor, Hathersage, Hope Valley S32 1BR. *T:* (01433) 651190. *Clubs:* Carlton; Lindrick Golf, Sickleholme Golf.

SYKES, Jean Margaret, MBE 2010; Chief Information Officer, London School of Economics and Political Science, 2009–12 (Librarian and Director of IT Services, 1998–2009); *b* 11 April 1947; *d* of David Thomson and Doreen Thomson (*née* Rose). *Educ:* Univ. of Glasgow (MA Hons, MLitt); Liverpool Poly. (DipLib). Actg Hd, Library Services, Middlesex Poly., 1985–87; Dep. Dir, Information Resource Services, Poly. of Central London, subseq. Univ. of Westminster, 1987–97. Chairman: M25 Consortium of Higher Educn Libraries, 1994–96; Soc. of College, Univ. and Nat. Libraries, 2000–02; Nereus Consortium of Eur. Econs Libraries, 2003–12. Mem., various nat. and internat. rev. panels, 2012–. FRSA 2002. *Publications:* contrib. librarianship and IT jls. *Recreations:* theatre, travel, French language and literature, wine.

SYKES, Sir John; *see* Sykes, Sir F. J. B.

SYKES, Rev. Canon John; Vicar, St Mary with St Peter, Oldham and Team Rector, Parish of Oldham, 1987–2004; Chaplain to the Queen, 1995–2009; *b* 20 March 1939; *s* of George Reginald Sykes and Doris Sykes (*née* Briggs); *m* 1967, Anne Shufflebotham; one *s* one *d*. *Educ:* St James C of E Sch., Slaithwaite; Royds Hall Grammar Sch., Huddersfield; W Bridgford Grammar Sch., Nottingham; Manchester Univ. (BA); Ripon Hall, Oxford. Ordained deacon, 1963, priest, 1964; Curate: St Luke's, Heywood, 1963–67; i/c Holy Trinity, Bolton, 1967–71; Lectr, Bolton Inst. of Technol., 1967–71; Chaplain to Bolton Colls of Further Educn, 1967–71; Rector, St Elisabeth, Reddish, 1971–78; Vicar, Saddleworth, 1978–87. Proctor in Convocation and Mem., Gen. Synod of C of E, 1980–90. Council for the Care of Churches: Mem., 1986–90; Vice-Chm., Art and Design Sub-cttee, 1988–90. Mem., various Manchester Diocesan Cttees and Councils, 1968–93. Chaplain to: Coliseum Theatre, Oldham, 1987–2006; eight Mayors of Oldham, 1989–99 and 2011–14; High Sheriff of Gtr Manchester, 1993–94, 1996–97; Gtr Manchester Police, Q Div., 1995–99. Hon. Canon, Manchester Cathedral, 1991–2004, now Canon Emeritus. *Recreations:* architecture, fine arts, music, walking. *Address:* 53 Ivy Green Drive, Springhead, Oldham OL4 4PR. *T:* (0161) 678 6767. *E:* sykesjohn76@gmail.com. *Club:* Manchester Pedestrians.

SYKES, John David; Chairman, Shawspetroleum Ltd, 2008–12 (Director, 1986–2012); Director, Farnley Tyas Estates Ltd, since 1986; *b* 24 Aug. 1956; *m* 1st, 1981, Jane Aspinall (marr. diss. 2003); one *s* two *d*; 2nd, 2006, Vivien Broadbent. *Educ:* St David's Prep. Sch., Huddersfield; Giggleswick Sch., W Riding; Univ. of Sheffield (BA Hons Hist. 2008). Joined Shaws Fuels Ltd (family company), 1974: graduated through every company dept, specialising in sales and transport; Dir, 1978–84; also Dir, subsid. cos. MP (C) Scarborough, 1992–97; contested (C) Scarborough and Whitby, 1997, 2001. PPS to Lord Privy Seal and Leader of H of L, 1995–97. Mem., Select Cttee on Culture and Heritage, 1993–95, on Deregulation, 1995–97; Vice Chm., Backbench Deregulation Cttee, 1995–97 (Sec., 1993–95). *Recreations:* walking, reading, Rugby Union, playing piano, history. *Address:* Wood View Barn, Manor Road, Farnley Tyas, Huddersfield, W Yorks HD4 6UL.

SYKES, Prof. Katharine Ellen, OBE 2009; PhD; CPhys, FInstP; Professor of Sciences and Society, University of Bristol, since 2006 (Collier Professor of Public Engagement in Science and Engineering, 2002–06); *b* 20 Dec. 1966; *d* of Dr John Sykes and Pauline Sykes. *Educ:* Univ. of Bristol (BSc Hons (Physics) 1989; PhD (Physics) 1996). VSO as Hd, Maths Dept and physics teacher, Zhombe High Sch., Zimbabwe, 1989–92; researcher; Hd of Sci., Explore@ Bristol, 1996–2001. Dir, Cheltenham Fest. of Sci., 2001–. Mem., Council for Science and Technology, 2004–11; Trustee, NESTA, 2007–12. Presenter, TV series, incl. Genius of Britain, Hot Planet, Alternative Therapies, Rough Science, Ever Wondered and Mindgames. *Publications:* papers in scientific jls on biodegradable plastic poly hydroxybutyrate; numerous conf. procs on science engagement; contrib. Science. *Recreations:* scuba-diving, mountain-climbing, dancing, singing, good food. *Address:* Royal Fort House, University of Bristol, Bristol BS8 1UJ. *E:* kathy.sykes@bristol.ac.uk.

SYKES, Sir (Malcolm) Keith, Kt 1991; Nuffield Professor of Anaesthetics, University of Oxford, 1980–91, Emeritus Professor since 1991; Hon. Fellow of Pembroke College, Oxford, since 1996 (Fellow, 1980–91, Supernumerary Fellow, 1991–96); *b* 13 Sept. 1925; *s* of Joseph and Phyllis Mary Sykes; *m* 1956, Michelle June (*née* Ratcliffe); one *s* three *d*. *Educ:* Magdalene Coll., Cambridge (MA, MB, BChir); University Coll. Hosp., London (DA; FFARCS). RAMC, 1950–52. House appointments, University Coll. and Norfolk and Norwich Hosps, 1949–50; Sen. House Officer, Registrar and Sen. Registrar in anaesthetics, UCH, 1952–54 and 1955–58; Rickman Godlee Travelling Scholar and Fellow in Anesthesia, Mass. General Hosp., Boston, USA, 1954–55; RPMS and Hammersmith Hosp., 1958–80: Lectr and Sen. Lectr, 1958–67; Reader, 1967–70; Prof. of Clinical Anaesthesia, 1970–80. Vis. Prof., univs in Canada, USA, Australia, NZ, Malaysia, Europe. Eponymous lectures: Holme, 1970; Clover, 1976; Weinbren, 1976; Rowbottom, 1978; Gillespie, 1979; Gillies, 1985; Wesley Bourne, 1986; Husfeldt, 1986; Della Briggs, 1988; E. M. Papper, 1991; BOC Healthcare, 1992; Harold Griffith, 1992; Sir Robert Macintosh, 1992. Mem. Bd, Fac. of Anaesthetists, 1969–85; Pres., Section of Anaesthetics, RSM, 1989–90; Vice Pres., Assoc. of Anaesthetists, 1990–92 (Mem. Council, 1967–70); Senator and Vice Pres., European Acad. of Anaesthesiology, 1978–85. Hon. FANZCA (Hon. FFARACS 1979); Hon. FCA(SA) (Hon. FFA(SA) 1989). Dudley Buxton Prize, Fac. of Anaesthetists, 1980; Fac. of Anaesthetists Medal, 1987; John Snow Medal, Assoc. of Anaesthetists, 1992; Hickman Medal, RSocMed, 2008. *Publications:* Respiratory Failure, 1969, 2nd edn 1976; Principles of Measurement for Anaesthetists, 1970; Principles of Clinical Measurement, 1980; Principles of Measurement and Monitoring in Anaesthesia and Intensive Care, 1991; Respiratory Support, 1995; Respiratory Support in Intensive Care, 1999; Anaesthesia and the Practice of Medicine: historical perspectives, 2007; chapters and papers on respiratory failure, intensive care, respiratory and cardiovascular physiology applied to anaesthesia, etc. *Recreations:* walking, birdwatching, gardening, music. *Address:* Treyarnon, Cricket Field Lane, Budleigh Salterton, Devon EX9 6PB. *T:* (01395) 445884.

SYKES, Sir Richard (Brook), Kt 1994; FRS 1997; Chairman: Royal Institution, since 2010; Imperial College Healthcare NHS Trust, since 2012; *b* 7 Aug. 1942; *s* of late Eric Sykes and of Muriel Mary Sykes; *m* 1969, Janet Mary Norman; one *s* one *d*. *Educ:* Queen Elizabeth Coll., London (1st Cl. Hons Microbiol.); Bristol Univ. (PhD Microbial Biochem.); DSc London, 1993. Glaxo Res. UK (Head of Antibiotic Res. Unit), 1972–77; Squibb Inst. for Med. Res., USA, 1977–86 (Vice-Pres., Infectious and Metabolic Diseases, 1983–86); Glaxo Group Research: Dep. Chief Exec., 1986; Chm. and Chief Exec., 1987–93; Glaxo plc: Group R&D Dir, 1987–93; Dep. Chm. and Chief Exec., 1993–97; Dep. Chm. and Chief Exec., 1993–97, Chm., 1997–2000, Glaxo Wellcome; Chm., GlaxoSmithKline, 2000–02. Dir, British Pharma Gp, 1998–2001. Rector, Imperial Coll. of Sci., Technol. and Med., Univ. of London, 2001–08; Chm., NHS London, 2008–10. Chm., PDS Biotechnol. Corp., 2014–; non-executive Chairman: Merlion Pharmaceuticals Pte Ltd, 2005–09; Circassia Ltd, 2007–13; NetScientific, 2010–; non-executive Director: Rio Tinto plc, 1997–2008; Rio Tinto Ltd, 1997–2008; Lonza, 2003–13; Eurasian Nat. Resources Corp., 2007–11; ContraFect, USA, 2012–14; Mem., Adv. Bd, Virgin Gp, 2010–12. Chairman: Adv. Council, Life Scis Exec. Cttee, EDB, Singapore, 2000–; Healthcare Adv. Gp (Apax Partners Ltd), 2002–; Bioscience Leadership Council, 2004–07; WHO Internat. Adv. Bd overseeing Internat. Clinical Trials Registry Platform, 2005–; CATALYST, 2005–08. Member: Council for Sci. and Technol., 1993–2003; Adv. Council, Save British Science, subseq. Campaign for Sci. and Engrg, 1993–; Foundn for Sci. and Technol. Council, 1994–2000; Trade Policy Forum, 1995–2000; Internat. Adv. Council, Economic Develt Bd, 1995–; Council for Industry and Higher Educn, 1995–2008; Bd, Eur. Fedn of Pharm. Industries and Assocs, 1997–2000; Council, Internat. Fedn of Pharm. Manufrs Assocs, 1998–2001; HEFCE, 2002–08; Engrg & Tech. Bd, 2002–05; DTI Strategy Bd, 2002–04; Temasek Internat. Adv. Panel, Singapore, 2004–. President: BAAS, 1998–99; Res. and Develt Soc., 2002–; Hon. Vice-Pres., Res. Defence Soc., 2004–; Hon. Mem., British Soc. for Antimicrobial Chemotherapy, 2006. Chairman: Business Leader Gp, British Lung Foundn, 1993–2013; Global Business Council on HIV/AIDS, 1997–2000; UK Stem Cell Foundn, 2005–. Vice-Pres., Nat. Soc. for Epilepsy, 1995–. Mem. Council, St George's House, Windsor Castle, 2004–10. Patron, Huddersfield Enterprise Foundn, 2005–. Mem. Bd Trustees, Natural Hist. Mus., 1996–2005; Trustee, Royal Botanic Gardens Kew, 2003–05. Member: Bd of Mgt, LSHTM, 1994–2003; Council, RCM, 2001–; Internat. Adv. Council, King Abdullah Univ. of Sci. and Technol., 2007–; Bd of Trustees, Masdar Inst. of Sci. and Technol., 2008–, Nanyang Technol Univ., Singapore, 2008–; Chancellor, Brunel Univ., 2013–. MInstD 1995. Fleming Fellow, Lincoln Coll., Oxford, 1992; FKC 1997; FIC 1999. Founder FMedSci 1998. Hon. FRCP 1995; Hon. FRSC 1999; Hon. FRPharmS 2001; Hon. FRCPath 2003; Hon. FREng 2004. Hon. Fellow, Univ. of Wales, 1997; Hon. FCGI 2002. Hon. DPharm Madrid, 1993; Hon. DSc: Brunel, Hull, Hertfordshire, 1994; Bristol, Newcastle, 1995; Huddersfield, Westminster, 1996; Leeds, 1997; Edinburgh, Strathclyde, 1998; London, Cranfield, Leicester, Sheffield, Warwick, 1999; Hon. MD Birmingham, 1995; Hon. LLD Nottingham, 1997. *Recreations:* opera, tennis, swimming. *Address:* Flat 11, Hale House, 34 De Vere Gardens, W8 5AQ. *T:* (020) 7937 0742. *Club:* Athenæum.

SYKES, Robert Hedley, OBE 2008; Chief Executive, Worcestershire County Council, 1997–2007; *b* 21 Aug. 1952; *s* of Hedley Sykes and Edith (*née* Oliver); *m* 1987, Jill Frances Brice (marr. diss. 2011); two *d*; *m* 2013, Maureen Gamble. *Educ:* Danum Grammar Sch.; Leeds Univ. (BSc, CQSW); Sheffield Poly. (DMS). Social worker, later Principal Officer (Children's Services), Doncaster MBC, 1975–86; Dep. Divl Dir, Social Services, N Yorks CC, 1986–89; Dep. Dir, Social Services, Oxfordshire CC, 1989–95; Dir, Social Services, Hereford and Worcester CC, 1995–97; non-executive Director: Crown Prosecution Service, 2007–12; Core Assets, 2008–; Nat. Audit Office, 2015–. Sen. Fellow, Univ. of Worcester, 2008–15. CInstLM 2007. FRSA 1999. *Recreations:* family, golf, theatre.

SYKES, Roger Michael Spencer, OBE 2002; HM Diplomatic Service, retired; High Commissioner to Fiji, and concurrently to Tonga, Vanuatu, Tuvalu, Kiribati and Nauru, 2006–09; *b* 22 Oct. 1948; *s* of Kenneth and Joan Sykes; *m* 1976, Anne Lesley Groves Gidney; three *s*. *Educ:* Wintringham Grammar Sch.; John Wilmott Grammar Sch.; Newport Grammar Sch. Entered FCO, 1969; served: Caracas, 1971–72; Freetown, 1972–75; Karachi, 1976–78; Cultural Attaché, Valetta, 1978–81; Press Officer, FCO, 1981–82; Attaché, Lagos, 1982–86; Dep. High Comr, Vila, 1986–90; S Asia Dept, FCO, 1990–93; Political and Econ. Sec., Amman, 1993–97; Hd of Post, Alkhobar, 1997–2001; Dep. Hd of Mission, Karachi, 2002–05. Privy Council Rep., Univ. of S Pacific, 2006–. *Recreations:* golf, game fishing, cricket, social history, National Trust research volunteer, comparing the different attributes of old and new world red wines. *Club:* Weston Park Golf.

SYKES, Sir Tatton (Christopher Mark), 8th Bt *cr* 1783; landowner; *b* 24 Dec. 1943; *s* of Sir (Mark Tatton) Richard Tatton-Sykes, 7th Bt and Virginia (*d* 1970), *d* of late John Francis Grey Gilliat; *S* father, 1978; granted use of additional arms of Tatton, 1980. *Educ:* Eton; Univ. d'Aix-Marseille; Royal Agricl Coll., Cirencester. *Heir: b* Jeremy John Sykes [*b* 8 March 1946; *m* 1st, 1982, Pamela June (marr. diss. 1995; she *m* 2nd, Earl of Swinton, *qv*), *o d* of Thomas Wood; 2nd, 2008, Annabel Celia Dorothy Evans (*d* 2012), *yr d* of Sir Somerled Bosville Macdonald of Sleat, 16th Bt, MC]. *Address:* Sledmere, Driffield, East Yorkshire YO25 3XG.

SYLVA, Prof. Kathleen Danaher, Hon. OBE 2007; PhD; Professor of Educational Psychology, University of Oxford, since 1998; Fellow of Jesus College, Oxford, 1997, now Emeritus. *Educ:* Harvard Univ. (BA 1964; MA 1972; PhD 1974). Lectr in Applied Social Studies, Univ. of Oxford, 1977–88; Fellow of Jesus Coll., Oxford, 1977–88; Prof. of Primary Educn, Univ. of Warwick, 1988–90; Prof. of Child Develt and Primary Educn, Inst. of Educn, Univ. of London, 1990–97; Reader in Educnl Studies, Univ. of Oxford, 1997–98. *Publications:* (ed jtly) Play: its role in development and evolution, 1976; (jtly) Childwatching at Playgroup and Nursery School, 1980; (with I. Lunt) Child Development: a first course, 1982; (ed jtly) Assessing Children's Social Behaviour and Competence, 1997; (jtly) Assessing Quality in the Early Years, 2003; (ed jtly) Early Childhood Matters: evidence from the Effective Pre-school and Primary Education project, 2010; articles in learned jls. *Address:* Department of Education, University of Oxford, 15 Norham Gardens, Oxford OX2 6PY.

SYLVESTER JOHNSON, Anna; Headmistress, Ibstock Place School, since 2000; *m* 1976, Dr Ian Johnson; one *s* one *d*. *Educ:* Pates Grammar Sch.; Kent Univ. (BA Hons); King's Coll. London (PGCE). Teacher, Elliott Sch., Putney, then Bermuda Coll., Bermuda; Head of English: Green Sch. for Girls, Isleworth, 1978–87; Lycée Français, Charles de Gaulle, 1987–97; Headmistress, Arts Educnl Schs, 1997–2000. FRSA. *Recreations:* theatre, opera, art, cinema, antiques (especially 20th century). *Address:* Ibstock Place School, Clarence Lane, Roehampton, SW15 5PY. *E:* head@ibstockplaceschool.co.uk. *Club:* Roehampton.

SYMES, Dr Robert Frederick, OBE 1996; FGS, FMinSoc; Keeper of Mineralogy, Natural History Museum, 1995–96; *b* 10 Feb. 1939; *s* of Alfred Charles Symes and Mary Emily Symes; *m* 1965, Carol Ann Hobbs; two *d*. *Educ:* Birkbeck Coll., London Univ. (BSc Hons); Queen Mary Coll., London Univ. (PhD 1981). FGS 1991. Nat. service, RAF, 1959–61. Natural History Museum, 1957–96: Asst Scientific Officer, 1957–59 and 1961–72; SSO, 1972–81; PSO, 1981–92; Dep. Keeper, 1992–95. Pres., GA, 1996–98. Lay Mem., Exeter Univ.

Council, 2002–06. Hon. Curator, Sidmouth Mus., Devon, 2001–. *Publications:* (jtly) Minerals of Cornwall and Devon, 1987; Rock and Mineral, 1988; (jtly) Crystal and Gem, 1991; Minerals of Northern England, 2008. *Recreations:* countryside, industrial archaeology, local history, tennis, Association Football. *Address:* Violet House, Salcombe Road, Sidmouth, Devon EX10 8PU. *T:* (01395) 578114.

SYMES, Susie; economist; Chairman, Museum of Immigration and Diversity, since 1998; *b* 24 April 1954; *d* of late Oliver Symes and Judith Symes (*née* Blumberg); *m* 1972, Ian Paul Abson (marr. diss. 1977); partner, Philip Jonathan Black; (one *d* decd). *Educ:* Withington Girls' Sch.; Anglo-American Coll.; City Univ., London (Adam Smith Prize 1974); St Antony's Coll., Oxford (Pres., JCR); London Sch. of Econs. Vis. Lectr, Univ. of Buckingham, 1975–77; Lectr and Sen. Res. Officer, Civil Service Coll., 1977–84; Econ. Advr, HM Treasury, 1985–90; Sen. Official, EC, 1990–92; Dir, European Prog., RIIA, 1992–95. Vis. Prof., Nat. Inst. of Defence Studies, Tokyo, 1994. Dir, Charter for Europe, 1997. Fellow, British American Proj., 1993–; Conseiller, Federal Trust, 1996–97; Trustee: Foundn for English Coll. in Prague, 1996–2011; Alzheimer's Soc., 2000–03; Mem. Adv. Council, London East Res. Inst., 2004. Founding Pres., La Légion des Femmes Efficaces, 1998–; Co-Founder, Probo, 2006–. Mem. Adv. Bd, Prospect magazine, 1995; exec. co-producer, Voices (audio anthol.), 1998 (prize for special achievement, Talking Newspaper Assoc. of UK). *Publications:* (jtly) Economics Workbook, 1989; (jtly) European Futures: alternative scenarios, 1998; occasional articles in learned and light jls. *Recreations:* making connections, marmalade and papier mâché. *Address:* The Museum of Immigration and Diversity, c/o 19 Princelet Street, E1 6QH. *T:* (020) 7247 5352. *E:* office@19princeletstreet.org.uk. *Clubs:* Reform, Serpentine.

SYMMONDS, Algernon Washington, GCM 1980; QC (Barbados) 1995; solicitor and attorney-at-law; *b* 19 Nov. 1926; *s* of late Algernon French Symmonds and Olga Ianthe (*née* Harper); *m* 1954, Gladwyn Ward; one *s* one *d*. *Educ:* Combermere Sch.; Harrison Coll.; Codrington Coll., Barbados. Solicitor, Barbados, 1953, enrolled in UK, 1958; in practice as Solicitor, Barbados, 1953–55; Dep. Registrar, Barbados, 1955–59; Crown Solicitor, Barbados, 1959–66; Permanent Secretary: Min. of Home Affairs, 1966–72; Min. of Educn, 1972–76; Min. of External Affairs and Head of Foreign Service, 1976–79; appointed to rank of Ambassador, 1977; High Comr in UK, 1979–83 and non-resident Ambassador to Denmark, Finland, Iceland, Norway and Sweden, 1981–83, and to the Holy See, 1982–83; Perm. Sec., Prime Minister's Office, Barbados, 1983–86; Head of CS, 1986. President: Barbados CS Assoc., 1958–65; Fedn of British CS Assocs in Caribbean, 1960–64; Dep. Mem. Exec., Public Services Internat., 1964–66. Pres., Barbados Bar Assoc., 2001, 2002, 2003 (Chm. Disciplinary Cttee, 1991–97); Vice-Pres., Orgn of Commonwealth Caribbean Bar Assoc., 2001–03; Chm., Barbados Br., WI Cttee, 1992–95; Dep. Chm., Caribbean Examinations Council, 1973–76. Past Pres., Barbados Lawn Tennis Assoc. *Recreations:* tennis, cricket broadcasting (represented Barbados in football, lawn tennis, basketball). *Address:* Melksham, 12 Margaret Terrace, Pine Gardens, St Michael, Barbados, WI; Symmonds, Greene, Reifer, Pinfold Street, Bridgetown, Barbados, WI. *Clubs:* Empire (Cricket and Football) (Life Mem. and Past Vice-Pres.), Summerhayes Tennis (Past Pres.) (Barbados).
See also Dame O. P. Symmonds.

SYMMONDS, Dame (Olga) Patricia, DBE 2000; GCM 1985; Senator, Parliament of Barbados, 1994–2007; Deputy President of the Senate, 2003–07; *b* 18 Oct. 1925; *d* of late Algernon French Symmonds and Olga Ianthe Symmonds (*née* Harper). *Educ:* Queen's Coll., Barbados; Univ. of Reading (BA 2nd Cl. Hons); Inst. of Educn, Univ. of London (PGCE). Teacher, 1945–85, Dep. Principal, 1963–76, Principal, 1976–85, St Michael Sch., Barbados; pt-time Lectr and Tutor, Cave Hill Campus, Univ. of WI, 1963–65. PC (Barbados), 1997–2000. *Publications:* On Language and Life Styles, 1989; (jtly) Caribbean Basic English, 1993; Longer Lasting than Bronze, 1993; Recalling These Things, 2009; contrib. to educnl jls. *Recreations:* reading, music. *Address:* Bank Hall Main Road, St Michael BB11078, Barbados. *T:* 4266470. *Clubs:* Barbados Cricket, Barbados Tennis Association Inc.
See also A. W. Symmonds.

SYMMONS ROBERTS, Michael; *see* Roberts, M. S.

SYMON, Prof. Lindsay, CBE 1994; TD 1967; FRCS, FRCSE; Professor of Neurological Surgery, Institute of Neurology, London University and the National Hospital, Queen Square, 1978–95, now Emeritus; *b* 4 Nov. 1929; *s* of William Lindsay Symon and Isabel Symon; *m* 1954, Pauline Barbara Rowland; one *s* two *d*. *Educ:* Aberdeen Grammar Sch.; Aberdeen Univ. (MB, ChB Hons). FRCSE 1957; FRCS 1959. House Physician and Surgeon, Aberdeen Royal Infirmary, 1952–53; Jun. Specialist in Surgery, RAMC, 1953–55; Surgical Registrar, Aberdeen Royal Infirmary, 1956–58; Neurosurgical Registrar, Middlesex and Maida Vale Hosps, 1958–61, Sen. Neurosurgical Registrar, 1962–65; Mem., External Scientific Staff, MRC, 1965–78; Consultant Neurosurgeon: Nat. Hosp. for Nervous Diseases, Queen Square and Maida Vale, 1965–78; St Thomas' Hosp., 1970–78. Hon. Consultant Neurological Surgeon, St Thomas' Hosp., Hammersmith Hosp., Royal Nose, Throat and Ear Hosp., 1978–95; Hon. Consultant Neurosurgeon, Nat. Hosp. for Neurology and Neurosurgery, 1978–95; Civilian Advr in Neurological Surgery to RN, 1979–95. Hunterian Prof., 1982, Arnott Demonstrator, 1989, RCS. Adjunct Prof., Dept of Surgery, Southwestern Med. Sch., Dallas, 1982–95. Rockefeller Travelling Fellow in Medicine, Wayne State Univ., Detroit, 1961–62. Lectures: Herbert Olivecrona, Karolinska Inst., Sweden, 1980; Mayfield/Aring, Univ. of Cincinatti, 1990; Sir Thomas Willis, Stroke Council of America, 1994. Pres., Harveian Soc., of London, 1998. Hon. Pres., World Fedn Neurosurgical Socs, 1993– (Pres., 1989–93). Mem., Acad. of Scis, Ukraine, 1992. TA, 1955–68, Major i/c Mobile Neurosurgical Team, 1961–68. Freeman, City of London, 1982. Hon. Sen. Fellow, Amer. Neurological Assoc., 1982; Hon. FACS 1994; Hon. FRSocMed 1997. Jamieson Medal, Australasian Neurosurgical Soc., 1982; John Hunter Medal, RCS, 1985; K. J. Zulch Medal, Max Planck Ges., 1993; Otfrid Förster Medal, Deutsche Ges. für Neurochirurgie, 1998; Medal of Honour, Soc. of British Neurol Surgeons, 2008; Samii Medal, WFNS, 2013. *Publications:* Operative Surgery/Neurosurgery, 1976, 2nd edn 1986; Advances and Technical Standards in Neurosurgery, 1972, 18th edn 1991; numerous papers on cerebral circulation and metabolism, brain tumours, general neurosurgical topics, etc. *Recreation:* golf. *Address:* Maple Lodge, Rivar Road, Shalbourne, near Marlborough, Wilts SN8 3QE. *T:* and *Fax:* (01672) 870501. *Clubs:* Caledonian; Royal & Ancient (St Andrews).

SYMON, Rev. Canon Roger Hugh Crispin; Canon Residentiary, Canterbury Cathedral, 1994–2002, now Canon Emeritus; *b* 25 Oct. 1934; *s* of Rev. Alan Symon and Margaret Sarah Symon (*née* Sharp); *m* 1963, Daphne Mary Roberts; two *d*. *Educ:* King's Sch., Canterbury; St John's Coll., Cambridge (MA); Coll. of the Resurrection, Mirfield. Curate, St Stephen's, Westminster, 1961–66; Priest-in-Charge, St Peter's, Hascombe, 1966–68; Chaplain, Univ. of Surrey, Guildford, 1966–74; Vicar, Christ Church, Lancaster Gate, 1974–79, with St James, Sussex Gardens, 1977–79; Home Staff, USPG, 1980–86; Actg Sec. for Anglican Communion Affairs to Archbp of Canterbury, 1987–91, Sec., 1991–94. *Address:* 5 Bath Parade, Cheltenham, Glos GL53 7HL.

SYMONDS, Ann Hazel S.; *see* Spokes Symonds.

SYMONDS, Matthew John; Defence and Diplomatic (formerly Defence and Security) Editor, The Economist, since 2010; *b* 20 Dec. 1953; *s* of Lord Ardwick and Anne Symonds; *m* 1981, Alison Mary Brown; one *s* two *d*. *Educ:* Holland Park, London; Balliol College, Oxford (MA). Graduate trainee, Daily Mirror, 1976–78; Financial Times, 1978–81; economics and defence leader writer, economics columnist, Daily Telegraph, 1981–86; Founding Director, Newspaper Publishing plc, 1986–94; The Independent: Dep. Editor, 1986–94; Exec. Editor, 1989–94; columnist, Sunday Express, 1995; Dir of Strategy, BBC Worldwide Television, 1995–97; The Economist: Technol. and Communications Ed., 1997–2000; Associate Ed., 2001; Political Ed., 2002–07; Industry Ed., 2007–10. Dir, Reach to Teach, 2007–. Sen. Financial Journalist, Wincott Awards, 1999. *Publications:* Softwar, 2003. *Recreations:* walking dog, history, churches, novels, theatre, boating, tennis, Chelsea FC. *Address:* 16 St Peter's Road, St Margarets, Twickenham, Middx TW1 1QX.

SYMONDS, Nicklaus T.; *see* Thomas-Symonds.

SYMONS OF VERNHAM DEAN, Baroness *cr* 1996 (Life Peer), of Vernham Dean in the county of Hampshire; **Elizabeth Conway Symons;** PC 2001; *b* 14 April 1951; *d* of Ernest Vize Symons, CB and Elizabeth Megan Symons (*née* Jenkins); *m* 2001, Philip Alan Bassett; one *s*. *Educ:* Putney High Sch. for Girls; Girton Coll., Cambridge (MA; Hon. Fellow, 2001). Research, Girton Coll., Cambridge, 1972–74; Administration Trainee, DoE, 1974–77; Asst Sec. 1977–88, Dep. Gen. Sec., 1988–89, Inland Revenue Staff Fedn; Gen. Sec., Assoc. of First Div. Civil Servants, 1989–96. Parly Under-Sec. of State, FCO, 1997–99; Minister of State, MoD, 1999–2001; Minister of State (Minister for Trade), FCO and DTI, 2001–03; Minister of State (Minister for ME), FCO, 2003–05. Mem., Employment Appeal Tribunal, 1995. Mem., EOC, 1995–97. Member: Gen. Council, TUC, 1989–96; Council, RIPA, 1989–97; Exec. Council, Campaign for Freedom of Information, 1989–97; Hansard Soc. Council, 1992–97; Council, Industrial Soc., 1994–97; Trustee, IPPR, 1993; Exec. Mem., Involvement and Participation Assoc., 1992. Member: Council, Open Univ., 1994–97; Adv. Council, Civil Service Coll., 1992–97; Governor: Polytechnic of North London, 1989–94; London Business Sch., 1993–97. FRSA. Hon. Associate, Nat. Council of Women, 1989. *Recreations:* reading, gardening, friends.

SYMONS, Christopher John Maurice; QC 1989; a Deputy High Court Judge, 1998–2015; *b* 5 Feb. 1949; *s* of late Clifford Louis Symons and Pamela Constance Symons; *m* 1974, Susan Mary Teichmann; one *s* one *d*. *Educ:* Sherborne Prep. Sch.; Clifton Coll.; Kent Univ. (BA Hons (Law)). Called to the Bar, Middle Temple, 1972, Bencher, 1998 (Treas., 2013); called to the Bar of Gibraltar, 1985, to the Irish Bar, 1988, to the NI Bar, 1990, to the Brunei Bar, 1999. Jun. Crown Counsel (Common Law), 1985–89; an Asst Recorder, 1990–93; a Recorder, 1993–2004. Pres., Lloyd's Appeal Tribunal, 2010–. *Recreation:* hitting balls. *Address:* 3 Verulam Buildings, Gray's Inn, WC1R 5NT. *T:* (020) 7831 8441. *Clubs:* Boodle's; All England Lawn Tennis; Berkshire Golf, Jesters; Royal Sotogrande Golf, Valderrama Golf (Spain).

SYMONS, Sir Patrick (Jeremy), KBE 1986; Chairman, Sussex Weald and Downs (formerly Chichester Priority Care Services) NHS Trust, 1994–98; *b* 9 June 1933; *s* of Ronald and Joanne Symons; *m* 1961, Elizabeth Lawrence; one *s* one *d*. *Educ:* Dartmouth Royal Naval College. Commissioned 1951; in command, HMS Torquay, 1968–70, HMS Birmingham, 1976–77, HMS Bulwark, 1980–81; Naval Attaché, Washington, 1982–84; C of S to Comdr, Allied Naval Forces Southern Europe, 1985–88; SACLANT's Rep. in Europe, 1988–92; retired in rank of Vice-Adm. *Recreation:* swimming.

SYMS, Robert Andrew Raymond; MP (C) Poole, since 1997; *b* 15 Aug. 1956; *s* of Raymond Syms and Mary Syms (*née* Brain); *m* 2000, Fiona Mellersh (separated 2007), *d* of Air Vice-Marshal F. R. L. Mellersh, CB, DFC and bar; one *s* one *d*. *Educ:* Colston's Sch., Bristol. Dir, C. Syms & Sons Ltd, family building and plant hire gp, 1975–. Mem., Wessex RHA, 1988–90. Member (C): N Wilts DC, 1983–87 (Vice Chm., 1984–87; Leader, Cons. Gp, 1984–87); Wilts CC, 1985–97. Contested (C) Walsall N, 1992. PPS to Chm., Conservative Party, 1999; opposition front bench spokesman on the envmt, 1999–2001; an Opposition Whip, 2003; opposition spokesman, DCLG (formerly ODPM), 2003–07; an Asst Govt Whip, 2012–13. Chairman: Regulatory Reform Select Cttee, 2010–12; HS2 (formerly High Speed Rail) Select Cttee, 2014–; Member: Health Select Cttee, 1997–2000 and 2007–10; Procedure Select Cttee, 1998–99; Transport Select Cttee, 2001–03; Liaison Cttee, 2010–12; Vice-Chm., Cons. back bench Constitutional Cttee, 1997–2001. A Vice-Chm., Cons. Party, 2001–03. N Wiltshire Conservative Association: Treas., 1982–83; Dep. Chm., 1983–84; Chm., 1984–96; Vice Pres., 1986–88. FCIOB 1999. *Recreations:* reading, travel, cycling. *Address:* House of Commons, SW1A 0AA; c/o Poole Conservative Association, 38 Sandbanks Road, Poole BH14 8BX. *T:* (01202) 739922.

SYNGE, Sir Allen James Edward, 9th Bt *cr* 1801, of Kiltrough; *b* 15 Jan. 1942; *s* of Neale Francis Synge (*d* 1998), *gs* of Sir Francis Robert Millington Synge, 6th Bt, and Katherine Caroline Bowes; *S* cousin, 2011, but his name does not appear on the Official Roll of the Baronetage.

SZÉLL, Patrick John, CMG 2001; Head, International and EC Environmental Law Division, 1985–2002, and Director (Legal), Department for Environment, Food and Rural Affairs (formerly Department of the Environment, then Department of the Environment, Transport and the Regions), 1992–2002; *b* Budapest, Hungary, 10 Feb. 1942; *s* of Dr János Széll and Vera Széll (*née* Beckett); *m* 1967, Olivia (*née* Brain), JP (*d* 2010); two *s* one *d*. *Educ:* Reading Sch.; Trinity Coll., Dublin (MA, LLB; Julian Prize 1964). Called to the Bar, Inner Temple, 1966. Joined Min. of Housing and Local Govt as Legal Asst, 1969; Department of the Environment: Sen. Legal Asst, 1973–85; Asst Solicitor, 1985–92. Legal Advr to UK Delegns at internat. envmtl negotiations, 1974–2002, including: UN/ECE Convention on Long-Range Transboundary Air Pollution and its protocols, 1979–2002; Vienna Convention for Protection of Ozone Layer and Montreal Protocol, 1982–2002; Basle Convention on Transboundary Movements of Hazardous Wastes, 1988–93; Climate Change Convention and Kyoto Protocol, 1990–2002; Biodiversity Convention and Biosafety Protocol, 1990–2000. Member: Internat. Council of Envmtl Law, Bonn, 1982–; IUCN Commn on Envmtl Law, 1994–2005. Clerk, Lurgashall Parish Council, 2005–11. Global Ozone Award, UNEP, 1995; Elizabeth Haub Prize, Free Univ. of Brussels, 1995; Stratospheric Ozone Protection Award, US Envmtl Protection Agency, 2002; Montreal Protocol Visionaries Award, UNEP, 2007. *Recreations:* travel, hockey, ancient churches. *Address:* Croft's Folly, Windfallwood Common, Haslemere, Surrey GU27 3BX.

SZENTIVÁNYI, Gábor, Hon. GCVO 1999; Ambassador, Ministry of Foreign Affairs, Hungary, 2013–15; *b* 9 Oct. 1952; *s* of József Szentiványi and Ilona Fejes; *m* 1976, Gabriella Gönczi; one *s* one *d*. *Educ:* Budapest Univ. of Economic Scis. Min. of Foreign Affairs, Hungary, 1975; Sec. for Press, Cultural and Educnl Affairs, Baghdad, 1976–81; Protocol Dept, Min. of Foreign Affairs, 1981–86; Counsellor for Press and Media Relations, Washington, 1986–91; Man. Dir, Burson-Marsteller Budapest, 1991–94; Spokesman and Dir Gen., Press and Internat. Information Dept, Min. of Foreign Affairs, 1994–97; Ambassador to UK, 1997–2002; Dep. State Sec., Min. of Foreign Affairs, 2002–04; Ambassador to the Netherlands and to OPCW, 2004–07; State Sec. and Political Dir, Min. of Foreign Affairs, 2007–09; Ambassador to Sweden, 2009–13. Member: Foreign Affairs Soc., Hungary, 1993–; Atlantic Council, Hungary, 1997–. Officer, Order of Prince Henry the Navigator (Portugal), 1983; Grand Cross of Merit (Chile), 2002; Middle Cross, Order of Merit (Hungary), 2004; Knight Grand Cross, Order of Orange-Nassau (Netherlands), 2007; Grand Officer's Cross of Merit, SMO (Malta), 2009. *Recreation:* boating.

SZIRTES, George Gábor Nicholas, PhD; FRSL; FEA; freelance writer; Reader in Creative Writing, University of East Anglia, 2006–13; *b* Budapest, 29 Nov. 1948; *s* of László Szirtes and Magdalena Szirtes (*née* Nussbacher); *m* 1970, Clarissa Upchurch; one *s* one *d*. *Educ:* Leeds Coll. of Art (BA 1st cl. Hons (Fine Art) 1972); Goldsmiths Coll., London (ATC 1973); Anglia

Polytechnic Univ. (PhD by published work 2002). Teacher, Art, Hist. of Art and English, various schs and colls, 1973–91; Dir, Art, St Christopher Sch., Letchworth, 1982–89; Norwich School of Art and Design: Vis. Lectr, 1989–91; estabd Creative Writing course, 1991–94; Co-ordinator of Creative Writing, Norwich Sch. of Art and Design, later Norwich Univ. Coll. of the Arts, 1994–2006. Mem., Hungarian Széchenyi Acad. of Arts and Letters, 2014–. FRSL 1982; FEA 2006. Gold Star, Hungarian Republic, 1991. *Publications: poetry:* Poetry Introduction 4, 1978 (jtly); The Slant Door, 1979 (Faber Meml Prize, 1980); November and May, 1981; Short Wave, 1984; The Photographer in Winter, 1986; Metro, 1988; Bridge Passages, 1991; Blind Field, 1994; Selected Poems, 1996; The Red-All-Over Riddle Book (for children), 1997; Portrait of my Father in an English Landscape, 1998; The Budapest File, 2000; An English Apocalypse, 2001; (with Ana Maria Pacheco) A Modern Bestiary, 2004; Reel, 2004 (T. S. Eliot Prize, 2005); Collected and New Poems, 2008; The Burning of Books, 2009; The Burning of Books and Other Poems, 2009; Shuck, Hick, Tiffey, 2009; Bad Machine, 2013; In the Land of Giants (for children), 2012; Wordless, 2014; Langoustine, 2014; *translations:* Madách, The Tragedy of Man, 1989 (Déry Prize for Translation, 1990); (pt translator) Csoóri, Barbarian Prayer, 1989; (ed and pt translator) Vas, Through the Smoke, 1989; Kosztolányi, Anna Édes, 1991; (ed and translator) Orbán, The Blood of the Walsungs, 1993; (ed and translator) Rakovszky, New Life, 1994 (European Poetry Translation Prize, 1995); (ed jtly and translator) The Colonnade of Teeth: twentieth century Hungarian poetry, 1996; (ed and translator) The Lost Rider: Hungarian poetry 16th–20th century, 1998; Krúdy, The Adventures of Sindbad, 1999; Krasznahorkai, The Melancholy of Resistance, 1999; (ed and translator) The Night of Akhenaton: selected poems of Ágnes Nemes Nagy, 2004; Márai, Casanova in Bolzano, 2004; Krasznahorkai, War and War, 2005; Márai, The Rebels, 2007; Márai, Esther's Inheritance, 2009; Karinthy, Metropole, 2008; Márai, Portraits of a Marriage, 2010; Krasznahorkai, Satantango, 2012; Kiss: the summer my father died, 2012; Szabó, Iza's Ballad, 2014; *other works:* (ed) Birdsuit (nine anthologies), 1991–99; (ed) The Collected Poems of Freda Downie, 1995; (ed with Penelope Lively) New Writing 10, 2001; Exercise of Power: the art of Ana Maria Pacheco, 2001; (ed jtly) An Island of Sound: Hungarian fiction and poetry at the point of change, 2004; Fortinbras at the Fishhouses: responsibility, the Iron Curtain and the sense of history as knowledge (criticism), 2010; (ed) New Order: Hungarian poets of the post-1989 generation, 2010; (ed) In Their Own Words: contemporary poets on poetry, 2012; Uncle Zoltán, 2014; Germania, 2014; Child Helga, 2014. *Recreations:* music, art, some sports, blogging at georgeszirtes.blogspot.com. *Address:* 16 Damgate Street, Wymondham, Norfolk NR18 0BQ. *T:* (01953) 603533, 07752 713533. *E:* georgeszirtes@gmail.com.

SZMUKLER, Prof. George Isaac, MD; FRCPsych, FRANZCP; Professor of Psychiatry and Society, Institute of Psychiatry, Psychology and Neuroscience (formerly Institute of Psychiatry), King's College, London, 2007, now Emeritus; Consultant Psychiatrist, 1993–2010, Honorary Consultant Psychiatrist, 2010–14, South London and the Maudsley NHS Foundation Trust (formerly Maudsley Hospital, South London and Maudsley NHS Trust); *b* 23 April 1947; *s* of Judel Szmukler and Leja Soyka; *m* 1983, Linnet Michele Lee; one *d*. *Educ:* Univ. of Melbourne (MB BS 1970; MD 1984); DPM 1974. MRCPsych 1977, FRCPsych 1989; FRANZCP 1985. Jun. RMO, Royal Melbourne Hosp., 1971–72; SHO, then Registrar in Psychiatry, Royal Free Hosp., 1972–75; Lectr in Psychiatry, Royal Free Hosp. Sch. of Medicine, Univ. of London, 1975–79; Lectr in Psychiatry, Inst. of Psychiatry, Univ. of London, 1980–82; Sen. Lectr, Inst. of Psychiatry, and Hon. Consultant Psychiatrist, Maudsley and Bethlem Royal Hosp., 1982–85; Consultant Psychiatrist, Royal Melbourne Hosp., and Sen. Associate, Univ. of Melbourne, 1985–92; Med. Dir, Bethlem and Maudsley NHS Trust, 1997–99; Jt Med. Dir, S London and Maudsley NHS Trust, 1999–2001; Dean and Hd of Sch., Inst. of Psychiatry, 2001–06, Co-Dir (formerly Chm.), King's Health and Society Centre (formerly Network), 2007–13, KCL. Associate Dir, NIHR-Mental Health Res. Network, 2007–. Vis. Prof., BIOS, LSE, 2007–13. FKC 2008. *Publications:* (jtly) Making Sense of Psychiatric Cases, 1986; (jtly) The Family in the Practice of Psychiatry, 1994; (ed) Eating Disorders: a handbook of theory, practice and research, 1994; (ed) A handbook on Mental Illness for Carers, 2001; (ed with G. Thornicroft) Textbook of Community Psychiatry, 2001; (ed jtly) Oxford Textbook of Community Mental Health, 2010; papers on eating disorders, families, health services res., mental health law and ethics. *Recreations:* music (especially Baroque and opera), art, cinema. *Address:* Institute of Psychiatry, Psychology and Neuroscience, King's College London, De Crespigny Park, Denmark Hill, SE5 8AF. *T:* (020) 7848 0002. *E:* george.szmukler@kcl.ac.uk.

SZOMBATI, Béla; Deputy Head, Delegation of the European Union to Turkey, since 2012; *b* 16 July 1955; *s* of Béla Szombati and Éva Szombati (*née* Herbály); *m* 1978, Zsuzsa Mihályi; two *s*. *Educ:* Eötvös Loránd Univ., Budapest (MA Hist. and French Lang. and Lit.). Joined Hungarian Diplomatic Service, 1980; Dept of Internat. Security, Min. of Foreign Affairs, 1980–82; Third Sec., Hanoi, 1982–85; Dept of W Europe and N America, Min. of Foreign Affairs, 1986–88; Second Sec., Washington, 1988–91; Foreign Policy Advr, Office of Pres. of the Republic, 1991–94; Ambassador, Paris, 1994–99; Dep. Hd, State Secretariat for European Integration, Min. of Foreign Affairs, 1999–2002; Ambassador to UK, 2002–06; Hd, Dept for Strategic Planning and Inf. Mgt, Min. of Foreign Affairs, Hungary, 2006–09; Ambassador to USA, 2009–10. Commander's Cross, Order of Merit (Poland), 2001; Officier, Légion d'Honneur (France), 2002. *Recreations:* music, walking, football. *Address:* Delegation of the European Union to Turkey, Uğur Mumcu Caddesi No. 88, Kat: 4, GOP Ankara, Turkey.

SZOSTAK, Prof. Jack William, PhD; Professor of Genetics, Harvard Medical School, since 1988; Investigator, Howard Hughes Medical Institute, since 1998; Alex Rich Distinguished Investigator, Department of Molecular Biology, Massachusetts General Hospital, since 2000 (Molecular Biologist, since 1988); *b* London, 9 Nov. 1952; *s* of Bill and Vi Szostak. *Educ:* McGill Univ. (BS Cell Biol. 1972); Cornell Univ. (PhD 1977). Res. Associate in Biochem., Cornell Univ., 1977–79; Harvard Medical School: Asst Prof., 1979–83, Associate Prof., 1983–84, Sidney Farber Cancer Inst., subseq. Dana Farber Cancer Inst. and Dept of Biol Chem.; Associate Prof., Dept of Genetics, 1984–87. Co-Chm., Nat. Res. Council Cttee on Origin and Evolution of Life, 2003–. MNAS 1998; Fellow, NY Acad. of Scis, 1999. Medal, Genetics Soc. of America, 2000; (jtly) Nobel Prize in Physiology or Medicine, 2009. *Address:* Department of Genetics, Massachusetts General Hospital, Simches Research Center CPZN# 7320, 185 Cambridge Street, Boston, MA 02114, USA.

T

TAAFFE, Jonathan Paul; a District Judge (Magistrates' Courts), since 2010; *b* Sheffield, 11 June 1961; *s* of Dr John Hilary and Dinah Taaffe; *m* 1989, Louise Frederick; one *s*. *Educ:* Stonyhurst Coll.; Southampton Univ. (LLB Hons Law 1982); Guildford Law Sch. Admitted as solicitor, 1985; Hd of Criminal Defence, Banner Jones Solicitors, 1985–2011; a Dep. Dist Judge, 2006–10. *Recreations:* keen golfer and footballer, avid follower of Chesterfield FC, keen runner. *Address:* c/o Derby Magistrates' Court, St Mary's Gate, Derby DE1 3JR. *E:* DistrictJudge.Taaffe@judiciary.gsi.gov.uk. *Club:* Chesterfield Golf.

TABACHNIK, Eldred; QC 1982; a Recorder, 2000–08; *b* 5 Nov. 1943; *s* of Solomon Joseph Tabachnik and Esther Tabachnik; *m* 1966, Jennifer Kay Lawson; two *s* one *d*. *Educ:* Univ. of Cape Town (BA, LLB); Univ. of London (LLM). Called to the Bar, Inner Temple, 1970, Bencher, 1988. Lectr, UCL, 1969–72. Pres., Bd of Deputies of British Jews, 1994–2000. *Recreation:* reading. *Club:* Reform.

TABBERER, Ralph Edwin, CB 2009; Owner and Chief Executive, BBD Education, since 2012; *b* 5 Aug. 1954; *s* of James William Waring Tabberer and Joyce (*née* Eldered); *m* 1996, Helen Margaret White (*d* 2008); one *s* one *d* (and one *d* decd), and three step *s* two step *d*. *Educ:* Gonville and Caius Coll., Cambridge (BA 1976; MA); Brunel Univ. (PGCE 1977). Sen. Advr, W Sussex LEA, 1989–94; Asst Dir, NFER, 1994–97; Department for Education and Employment: Sen. Educn Advr, Standards and Effectiveness Unit, 1997–99; Hd, Nat. Grid for Learning, 1999–2000; Chief Exec., TTA, subseq. TDA, 2000–06; Dir Gen., Schs, DFES, later DCSF, 2006–09; Chief of School, GEMS, Dubai, 2009–12; consultant-at-large, Dubai, 2012. FRSA 2001.

TABRIZI, Prof. Sarah Joanna, (Mrs M. J. Nath), PhD; FRCP, FMedSci; Professor of Clinical Neurology, Department of Neurodegenerative Disease, University College London Institute of Neurology, since 2009; Hon. Consultant Neurologist, National Hospital for Neurology and Neurosurgery, since 2003; *b* London, 26 Sept. 1965; *d* of Gholam-Reza Sabri-Tabrizi and Jacqueline Sabri-Tabrizi; *m* 2011, Michael John Nath. *Educ:* Heriot-Watt Univ. (BSc 1st Cl. Hons Biochem. 1986); Edinburgh Univ. (MB ChB Hons 1992; Gold Medal); University Coll. London (PhD 2000). MRCP 1995, FRCP 2007; Cert. Completion of Specialist Trng in Neurol. 2003. Jun. Hse Officer, Royal Infirmary Edinburgh, 1992–93; SHO, Hammersmith Hosp. and Nat. Hosp. for Neurol. and Neurosurgery, 1993–94; SHO, St Bartholomew's Hosp., London, 1994–95; Medical Registrar, St Thomas' Hosp., London, 1995–96; MRC Clinical Trng Fellow, UCL, 1996–99; Neurol. Specialist Registrar, Nat. Hosp. for Neurol. and Neurosurgery, 1999–2002; Nat. Clinician Scientist, DoH, 2002–07; Department of Neurodegenerative Disease, UCL Institute of Neurology: Clin. Lectr, 2002; Clin. Sen. Lectr, 2003–07; Reader in Neurol. and Neurogenetics, 2007–09. FMedSci 2014. *Publications:* (ed jtly) Huntington's Disease, 4th edn 2014; contrib. articles to jls incl. Lancet, Nature, Cell and specialist neurol. jls. *Recreations:* working my way through all the classics in literature, walking and swimming in Gower and Mallorca, boxing, attending the theatre, ballet, opera, cinema and musicals, and, above all, spending as much time as I can with my family. *Address:* Department of Neurodegenerative Disease, UCL Institute of Neurology, Box 104, National Hospital for Neurology and Neurosurgery, Queen Square, WC1N 3BG. *T:* (020) 3108 7473, *Fax:* (020) 7676 2180. *E:* s.tabrizi@ucl.ac.uk.

TACK, Dame Louise Agnetha L.; *see* Lake-Tack.

TACKABERRY, John Antony; QC 1982; FCIArb, FFB; a Recorder, 1988–2005; Commissioner, UN Compensation Commission, 1998–2003; *b* 13 Nov. 1939; *s* of late Thomas Raphael Tackaberry and Mary Catherine (*née* Geoghegan); *m* 1st, 1966, Penelope Holt (*d* 1994); two *s*; 2nd, 1996, Kate Jones (*d* 2008); one *d*. *Educ:* Downside; Trinity Coll., Dublin; Downing Coll., Cambridge (MA, LLM). Called to the Bar, Gray's Inn, 1967, Ireland, 1987, California, 1988. FCIArb 1973; FFB 1979. Teacher in China, 1964–65; Lectr, Poly. of Central London, 1965–67. Adjunct Prof. of Law, Qld Univ. of Technology, 1989. Chm., CIArb, 1990–91 (Mem. Council, 1985–94; Vice-Pres., 1988); President: Soc. of Construction Law, 1983–85; Eur. Soc. of Construction Law, 1985–87; Soc. of Construction Arbitrators, 2007–10; Mem., Dispute Bd Register, RICS, 2014–. Registered Arbitrator, 1993; Mem., many panels of internat. arbitrators. Chm., Street UK, 2004–. *Publications:* (contrib.) Bernstein's Handbook of Arbitration and Dispute Resolution, 1st edn 1987, 2nd edn 1993, (Principal Ed.) 3rd edn 1998, 4th edn 2003; (ed jtly) International Dispute Resolution, vol. I, Materials, 2004, (ed) vol. II, Cases, 2004; contrib. numerous articles. *Recreations:* good food, good wine, good company, photography. *Address:* 39 Essex Street, WC2R 3AT. *T:* (020) 7832 1111, *Fax:* (020) 7353 3978; Arbitration Chambers, 22 Willes Road, NW5 3DS. *T:* (020) 7267 2137, *Fax:* (020) 7482 1018. *E:* john.tackaberry@39essex.com, john.tackaberry@arbitration-chambers.com. *Club:* Athenæum.

TACON, Christine Mary, (Mrs William Thomas-Davies), CBE 2004; FIMechE; Groceries Code Adjudicator, Department for Business, Innovation and Skills, since 2013; *b* Eye, Suffolk, 1959; *s* of Peter and Beryl Tacon; *m* 1992, William Thomas-Davies; one *s* one *d*. *Educ:* Wycombe Abbey Sch.; Girton Coll., Cambridge (BA 1981; MEng 1992); Cranfield Univ. (MBA 1986). CEnv 2010; FIMechE 2012; FRAgS 2013. Engrg graduate trainee, then Quality Manager, Coats Viyella, 1982–85; Prodn Planner, then Brand Manager, Mars Confectionery, 1985–92; Mktg Consultant, Vodafone, 1993–94; Mktg Dir, Redland plc, 1994–96; Mktg and Sales Dir, Fonterra, 1996–2000; Man. Dir, Co-operative Farms, 2000–12. Non-executive Director: Anglia Farmers, 2012–; Met Office, 2013–. Mem., NERC, 2013–. Gov., Harper Adams Univ., 2012–. Hon. DSc Cranfield, 2014. Mem., Farmers' Co., 2009–. *Recreations:* narrow-boating, veteran cars, walking, gardening (vegetables) and cooking them. *Address:* (office) Victoria House, Southampton Row, Holborn, WC1B 4DA. *E:* christine.tacon@gca.gsi.gov.uk. *Club:* Farmers.

TADIÉ, Prof. Jean-Yves; Chevalier de la Légion d'honneur, 2002; Chevalier de l'Ordre National du Mérite, 1974; Officier des Palmes académiques, 1988; Commandeur de l'Ordre des Arts et des Lettres, 2011; Professor of French Literature, Université de Paris-Sorbonne, 1991–2005, now Emeritus; Editor, Gallimard, since 1991; *b* 7 Sept. 1936; *s* of Henri Tadié and Marie (*née* Férester); *m* 1962, Arlette Khoury; three *s*. *Educ:* St Louis de Gonzague, Paris; Lycée Louis-le-Grand; Ecole Normale Supérieure (Agrégé de lettres); DèsL Sorbonne 1970; MA Oxford 1988. Lectr, Univ. of Alexandria, 1960–62; Asst Prof., Faculté des Lettres de Paris, 1964; Professor: Univ. de Caen, 1968–69; Univ. de Tours, 1969–70; Univ. de la Sorbonne nouvelle, Paris III, 1970; Hd of French Dept, Cairo Univ., 1972–76; Dir, French Inst., London, 1976–81; Marshal Foch Prof. of French Literature, and Fellow, All Souls Coll., Oxford Univ., 1988–91. Corresp. FBA, 1991. Grand Prix de l'Acad. française, 1988. Officier de l'Ordre de la Couronne de Belgique, 1979. *Publications:* Introduction à la vie littéraire du XIXe Siècle, 1970; Lectures de Proust, 1971; Proust et le Roman, 1971; Le Récit poétique, 1978; Le Roman d'aventures, 1982, 2nd edn 2013; Proust, 1983; La Critique littéraire au XXe Siècle, 1987; (ed) M. Proust, A la Recherche du Temps perdu, 1987–89; Portrait de l'Artiste, 1990; Le Roman au XXe Siècle, 1990; Marcel Proust (biography), 1996, Eng. edn 2000; (ed) N. Sarraute, Oeuvres Complètes, 1996; Le Sens de la Mémoire, 1999; (ed) W. Scott, Romans, 2003; (ed) A. Malraux, Ecrits sur l'art, 2004; Regarde de tous tes yeux - regarde!: Jules Verne, 2005; De Proust à Dumas, 2006; (ed) W. Scott, Romans II, 2007; Le Songe musical: Debussy, 2008; (ed) Proust et ses amis, 2010; (ed) A. Malraux, Essais, 2010; La Création littéraire au XIXe siècle, 2011; Le Lac inconnu: entre Proust et Freud, 2012; Le Roman d'hier à demain, 2012; (ed) Le Cercle de Proust, 2013, vol. II 2015. *Recreations:* opera, cinema. *Address:* 15 rue Raynouard, 75016 Paris, France. *Club:* Athenæum.

TAEL, Dr Kaja; Ambassador of Estonia to Germany, since 2012; *b* 24 July 1960. *Educ:* Tartu Univ., Estonia; Estonian Acad. Scis (PhD 1985). Researcher, 1984–90, Dir, 1991–95, Estonian Inst. for Lang. and Lit.; foreign policy advr to Pres. of Estonia, 1995–98; Ministry of Foreign Affairs, Estonia: Exec. Sec., Estonian-Russian Inter-govtl Commn, 1998–99; Dir Gen., Dept of Policy Planning, 1995–2001; Estonian Ambassador to UK, 2001–05; Under Sec. of EU Affairs, 2006–12. Order of White Star (Estonia), 2000. Order of: Polar Star (Sweden), 1995; Lion (Finland), 1995; Aztec Eagle (Mexico), 1996; Cejalvo Cruz (Spain), 2007; Leopold (Belgium), 2008. *Publications:* translated into Estonian: John Stuart Mills, On Liberty, 1996; Henry Kissinger, Diplomacy, 2002; Eric Hobsbawm, The Age of Extremes, 2002; articles and abstracts for internat. confs. *Address:* Estonian Embassy, Hildebrandstrasse 5, 10785 Berlin, Germany.

TAFFIN de GIVENCHY, Olivier Jean; Managing Director, and Head, United States West Region, JP Morgan Private Bank; *b* Beauvais, France, 27 Aug. 1963; *s* of Jean-Claude Taffin de Givenchy and Patricia Taffin de Givenchy (*née* Myrick); *m* (marr. diss.); one *s* one *d*. *Educ:* Manhattanville Coll., Purchase, NY (BA Internat. Studies 1985). Citibank, 1985–89; Bankers Trust, 1989–93; JP Morgan, 1993–: Dir, 1999, Chm., 2010, JP Morgan Internat. Bank Ltd; Man. Dir, UK, JP Morgan Private Bank, 2005. Trustee, JP Morgan UK Foundn, 2005; Supervisory Cttee, JP Morgan Chase Foundn, 2006. Chm., Children in Crisis, 2006. *Recreations:* tennis, fishing, shooting. *Address:* JP Morgan Private Bank, 2029 Century Park East, Los Angeles, CA 90067, USA. *Club:* Racquet and Tennis (New York).

TAFIDA, Dr Dalhatu Sarki, CFR 2011 (OFR 1983); FNMCP, FWACP; High Commissioner of Nigeria in the United Kingdom, 2008–15; *b* Zaria, Kaduna State, 24 Nov. 1940; *s* of Garba Tafida and Badariyyatu Tafida; *m* Salamatu Ndana Mohammed; six *s* three *d*. *Educ:* Coll. of Medicine, Univ. of Lagos (MB BS 1967); Univ. of Liverpool (Postgrad. Dip. Public Health 1972). MRCP 1971; FNMCP 1975; FWACP 1975. Ahmadu Bello University: House Officer, 1967–68; Sen. House Officer, 1968–69; Registrar, 1969–70; Clin. Asst in Medicine, Royal Victoria Infirmary, Newcastle upon Tyne, 1970–71; Sen. Registrar in Medicine, Katsina Specialist Hosp., 1972–73; Consultant Physician, 1973–76, Perm. Sec., 1976–80, Min. of Health, Kaduna; Chief Physician to Pres. of Nigeria, 1980–83; Comr for Health, Agric. and Educn, Kaduna State, 1984–87; Mem., Constituent Assembly to review Nigerian Constitution, 1988–89; Chm. and Pro Chancellor, Univ. of Agric., Makurdi; Federal Minister of Health, 1993–95. Mem. Kaduna North, Senate, 1999–2003 (Senate Majority Leader, 2003–07). Tafidan Zazzau, 1995. *Publications:* Purple Parliament, 2007. *Recreations:* Scrabble, table tennis.

TAFROV, Stefan Lubomirov; Permanent Representative of Bulgaria to the United Nations, 2001–06 and since 2012; *b* Sofia, 11 Feb. 1958; *s* of Lubomir Tafrov and Nadezhda Tafrova. *Educ:* Sofia Univ. (MA in Journalism). Foreign News Editor, Democratzia, newspaper, Jan. 1990; Chief, Foreign Affairs Dept, Union of Democratic Forces, Feb.–Aug. 1990; Foreign Affairs Advr to Pres. of Bulgaria, 1990–92; First Dep. Minister of Foreign Affairs, 1992–93; Ambassador to Italy, 1993–95, to UK, 1995–98; Ambassador to France, and Perm. Deleg. to UNESCO, 1998–2001. *Recreation:* music. *Address:* United Nations, 11 East 84th Street, New York, NY 10028, USA.

TAFT, William Howard, IV; Of Counsel, Fried, Frank, Harris, Shriver & Jacobson, since 2005 (Partner, 1992–2001); *b* 13 Sept. 1945; *s* of William Howard Taft, III and Barbara Bradfield Taft; *m* 1974, Julia Ann Vadala; one *s* two *d*. *Educ:* St Paul's Sch., Concord, NH; Yale Coll. (BA 1966); Harvard Univ. (JD 1969). Attorney, Winthrop, Stimson, Putnam & Roberts, NY, 1969–70; Attorney Advr to Chm., Federal Trade Commn, 1970; Principal Asst to Dep. Dir, Office of Management and Budget, 1970–72, Exec. Asst to Dir, 1972–73; Exec. Asst to Sec., Health, Educn and Welfare, 1973–76; Gen. Counsel, Dept of Health, Educn and Welfare, 1976–77; Partner, Leva, Hawes, Symington, Martin & Oppenheimer, 1977–81; General Counsel 1981–84, Dep. Sec. of Defense 1984–89, US Dept of Defense; US Perm. Rep. on N Atlantic Council, 1989–92; Legal Advr, US Dept of State, 2001–05. Mem., DC Bar Assoc., Washington. Bd Mem., Washington Opera, 1977–81, 1992–2001. Woodrow Wilson Vis. Teaching Fellow, Woodrow Wilson Foundn, 1977–81. Dir, Atlantic Council, 1993–2001. *Publications:* contrib. Indiana Law Jl. *Recreation:* tennis. *Address:* Fried, Frank, Harris, Shriver & Jacobson, 801 17th Street, NW, Washington, DC 20006, USA. *Clubs:* Cosmos, Leo, Literary Society (Washington, DC).

TAGER, Romie; QC 1995; *b* 19 July 1947; *s* of Osias Tager and Minnie Tager (*née* Mett); *m* 1971, Esther Marianne Sichel; twin *s*. *Educ:* Hasmonean Grammar Sch., Hendon; University Coll. London (Hurst prize; LLB 1st Cl. Hons 1969). Called to the Bar, Middle Temple, 1970; Head of Chambers, Selborne Chambers, 2002–15. Chm., Greenquest Gp, 1998–. Trustee, Jewish Book Council. PhD *hc* Bar Ilan, Israel, 2010. *Recreations:* grandchildren, opera, theatre, travel. *Address:* Selborne Chambers, 10 Essex Street, WC2R 3AA. *T:* (020) 7420 9500.

TAIN, Paul Christopher; His Honour Judge Tain; a Circuit Judge, since 2005; *b* 18 Feb. 1950; *s* of Reginald Tain and Kathleen (*née* Hoffland); *m* 1971, Angela Margaret Kirkup (marr. diss. 2011); four *s*. *Educ:* London Univ. (BA Hist.); Inst. of Judicial Admin, Birmingham Univ. (MJur). Admitted solicitor, 1975; solicitor, Wolverhampton MBC and N Yorks County Council, 1976–80; private practitioner, 1980–92; Dep. Stipendiary Magistrate, 1989–92; Stipendiary Magistrate, subseq. District Judge (Magistrates' Courts), 1992–2005; Asst Recorder, 1996–2000, Recorder, 2000–05. Columnist, Solicitors' Jl, 1998. *Publications:* Local Authority Lawyers and Childcare, 1980; Childcare Law, 1993; Criminal Justice Act, 1994; Public Order Law, 1996; Public Order: the criminal law, 2001. *Recreations:* sailing, sailing and sailing. *Address:* Lewes Crown Court, Lewes, East Sussex BN7 1YB.

TAIT, Andrew Charles Gordon; QC 2003; *b* 18 May 1957; *s* of Adm. Sir (Allan) Gordon Tait, KCB, DSC and of Philippa, *d* of Sir Bryan Todd; *m* 1990, Francesca Sulivan; one *s* three *d*. *Educ:* Eton; Hertford Coll., Oxford (Open Exhibnr; MA Modern History). Called to the Bar, Inner Temple, 1981, Bencher, 2011; in practice as barrister, 1982–; Head of Chambers, 2012–. Asst Comr, Parly Boundary Commn for England (Fifth Review). Liveryman, Gardeners' Co., 2011–. *Address:* Francis Taylor Building, Temple, EC4Y 7BY. *T:* (020) 7353 8415. *Clubs:* White's, Hurlingham.

TAIT, Arthur Gordon; Secretary-General, Institute of Actuaries, 1991–97; *b* 28 July 1934; *s* of George Aidan Drury Tait and Margaret Evelyn Tait (*née* Gray); *m* 1958, Ann Sutcliffe Gilbert; two *s* two *d* (and one *s* decd). *Educ:* Eton Coll.; St John's Coll., Cambridge (BA Hist., MA). FCIPD. Commnd KRRC, 1953–54. Imperial Chemical Industries, 1957–91: Personnel Dir, Mond Div., 1976–82; Internat. Personnel Manager, 1983–91. Chairman: Friends of Brompton Cemetery, 1998–; Nat. Fedn of Cemetery Friends, 2003–15. Church Warden, St Mary, The Boltons, 2005–09. FRSA. *Publications:* A Story of Staple Inn on Holborn Hill, 2001; St Mary, The Boltons: the country church in Kensington and Chelsea, 2004. *Recreations:* family, swimming, travel, friends who visit, following most sports. *Address:* 65 Cheyne Court, SW3 5TT. *T:* (020) 7352 5127.

TAIT, Blyth; *see* Tait, R. B.

TAIT, Eric, MBE 1980; Director of European Operations, 1989–2010, and International Executive Director, 1992–2010, PKF International Ltd (formerly Pannell Kerr Forster, Chartered Accountants); *b* 10 Jan. 1945; *s* of William Johnston Tait and Sarah Tait (*née* Jones); *m* 1st, 1967, Agnes Jean Boag (*née* Anderson) (marr. diss. 1998); one *s* one *d*; 2nd, 1998, Stacey Jane (*née* Todd). *Educ:* George Heriot's Sch., Edinburgh; RMA Sandhurst; Univ. of London (BSc Eng); Churchill Coll., Cambridge (MPhil). 2nd Lieut, Royal Engineers, 1965; despatches 1976; 68 advanced staff course, RAF Staff Coll., Bracknell, 1977; OC 7 Field Sqn, RE, 1979–81; Lt-Col 1982; Directing Staff, Staff Coll., Camberley, 1982–83, retired, at own request, 1983; Sec., Inst. of Chartered Accountants of Scotland, 1984–89. Mem. of Exec., Scottish Council (Develt and Industry), 1984–89. Editor in Chief, The Accountant's Magazine, 1984–89. Chm., European Forum, Nottingham Trent Univ., 1993–98. FRSA 1997. *Recreations:* swimming, hill walking, reading. *Address:* c/o Bank of Scotland, PO Box 17235, Edinburgh EH11 1YH.

TAIT, Fiona; Sheriff of Tayside, Central and Fife at Perth, since 2013; *b* Bridge of Allan, 9 Jan. 1966; *d* of John Paterson and Isabella Wyllie Paterson (*née* Fyfe); *m* 1996, Brian John Tait; two *s*. *Educ:* Lornshill Acad., Alloa; Univ. of Edinburgh (LLB 1st Cl. Hons; DipLP). Admitted as solicitor, 1991; Solicitor, Drummond & Co., later Drummond Miller LLP, 1989–2009 (Partner, 1996–2009); Tutor (pt-time), Univ. of Edinburgh, 1990–97; Sheriff (pt-time), 2006–10; All Scotland Floating Sheriff, 2011–13. *Recreations:* walking, tennis, Dunning. *Address:* Sheriff Court House, Tay Street, Perth PH2 8NL. *E:* sheriff.ftait@scotcourts.gov.uk. *Clubs:* Lomond Tennis, Dunning Tennis.

TAIT, Michael Logan, CMG 1987; LVO 1972; HM Diplomatic Service, retired; Chairman, Oxford and Edinburgh Consultants, 1995–2004; *b* 27 Sept. 1936; *s* of William and Dorothea Tait; *m* 1st, 1968, Margaret Kirsteen Stewart (marr. diss. 1990); two *s* one *d*; 2nd, 1999, Amel Boureghda (marr. diss., 2015); one *d*. *Educ:* Calday Grange Grammar Sch.; New College, Oxford. Nat. service, 2nd Lieut Royal Signals, 1955–57. Foreign Office, 1961; served MECAS, 1961; Bahrain, 1963; Asst Political Agent, Dubai, Trucial States, 1963; FO, 1966; Private Sec. to Minister of State, FO, later FCO, 1968; First Sec. and Hd of Chancery, Belgrade, 1970; First Sec. (Political), Hd of Chancery and Consul, Amman, 1972; FCO, 1975; Counsellor and Hd of Chancery, Baghdad, 1977; Counsellor, FCO, 1978; Dep. Hd of Delegn, CSCE, Madrid, 1980; Dep. Hd of Delegn and Counsellor (Econ. and Finance), OECD, Paris, 1982; Hd of Economic Relns Dept, FCO, 1984; Ambassador to UAE, 1986–89; Asst Under-Sec. of State with responsibility for Soviet Union and Eastern Europe, 1990–92; Ambassador to Tunisia, 1992–95. *Recreations:* languages, mountains, sailing. *Club:* Garrick.

TAIT, Prof. Richard Graham, CBE 2003; DPhil; Professor, School of Journalism, Media and Cultural Studies, Cardiff University, since 2003 (Director, Centre for Journalism (formerly Centre for Journalism Studies), 2003–12); *b* 22 May 1947; *s* of Dr William Graham Tait and Isabella Dempster Tait (*née* Cumiskey); *m* 1st, 1980, Sandra Janine McKenzie McIntosh (marr. diss. 1984); 2nd, 1995, Kathryn Jane Ellison; one *d*. *Educ:* Bradfield Coll.; New Coll., Oxford (BA Mod. Hist.; MA; DPhil 1978). St Edmund Jun. Res. Fellow, St Edmund Hall, Oxford, 1972–74; BBC Television: Researcher, Money Prog., 1974–75; Producer, Nationwide, 1976–82; Editor: People and Power, 1982; Money Prog., 1983–85; Newsnight, 1985–87; General Election Results Prog., 1987; Independent Television News: Editor: Channel Four News, 1987–90; Channel Four progs, 1990–95; Editor-in-Chief, 1995–2002. A Governor, BBC, 2004–06; a Trustee, BBC Trust, 2007–10; Ind. Trustee, Disasters Emergency Cttee, 2014–. Chm., INSIUK, 2012–13 (Treas., 2013–). Member: Internat. Bd, IPI, 1998–2004 (Vice-Chm., 2000–06); Adv. Bd, Internat. News Safety Inst., 2003–. Gov., Kensington Prep. Sch., 2013–. FRTS 1996; Fellow, Soc. of Editors, 2002. Lifetime Achievement Award, RTS, 2013. *Recreations:* history, ballet, opera, tennis, ski-ing. *Address:* Bute Building, Cardiff University, Cardiff CF10 3NB.

TAIT, (Robert) Blyth, MBE 1992; three-day event rider; *b* 10 May 1961; *s* of Robert and Glenise Tait. *Educ:* Whangarei Boys' High Sch., NZ. Individual World Champion: Stockholm, 1990, Rome, 1998; Olympic Games: Individual Bronze, Barcelona, 1992; Individual Gold, Atlanta, 1996; ranked World No 1, 1992, 1994, 1995, 1996, 1998; winner: Burghley Horse Trials, 1998, 2001; Kentucky Horse Trials, 2000. Hon. Dr Essex. *Publications:* Eventing Insights, 1991; Blyth Tait's Cross Country Clinic, 1998; Six of the Best, 1999. *Recreations:* water ski-ing, snow ski-ing, tennis. *E:* blythtait@hotmail.com.

TAJ, Mohammad; President, Trades Union Congress, 2013–14 (Vice-President, 2014–15); *b* Mirpur Azad Kashmir, 7 July 1952; *s* of Mohammed Shafi and Fazal Begum; *m* Naseem; one *s* one *d*. *Educ:* Bradford Coll. Worker Dir, Yorkshire Rider Ltd, 1993–96. Branch Sec., 1981–, Mem., Exec. Council, 1999–, TGWU, later Unite the Union. Mem., Gen. Council, TUC, 2001–. *Recreations:* politics, mountain walking. *Address:* 6 Ederoyd Drive, Pudsey, Leeds LS28 7RB. *T:* 07929 004831. *E:* mohammad.taj@gmail.com.

TAK; *see* Drummond, T. A. K.

TAKOLIA, Museji Ahmed, CBE 2011; Executive Chairman, Intellicomm Solutions Ltd, since 2009; Chairman, Wye Valley NHS Trust, since 2014; *b* Coventry, 10 Dec. 1960; *s* of Ahmed Suleman Takolia and Momin Takolia (*née* Bhunger); *m* 1987, Noorjehan Ebrahim (marr. diss. 2006); one *s* two *d*. *Educ:* John Gulson Jun. Sch., Coventry; Sidney Stringer Sch. and Community Coll., Coventry; Homerton Coll., Cambridge (BEd Hons 1984); Bristol Univ. (MSc Social Scis 1987). Commonwealth Fund Harkness (Exec. Educn) Fellow, Woodrow Wilson Sch. of Public and Internat. Affairs, Princeton Univ., 1993–94; Social Policy Officer, Hackney CRE; sen. rôles with Bristol CC and Gloucester CC; Advr, Coopers & Lybrand, then PricewaterhouseCoopers; Sen. Civil Servant, Cabinet Office. Mem., Commn for Health Improvement; Mem. Bd, OFSTED, 2006–12. Gp Chm., Metropolitan Housing Partnership, 2003–09. Chm., Members' Panel, NEST Corp., 2011–. Non-exec. Dir, Glos Hosps NHS Foundn Trust, 2007–10. Mem. Bd, Ruskin Coll., Oxford. Chm., CEED Charity, St Paul's Bristol. *Recreations:* public policy and current affairs, avid follower of international cricket and football. *Address:* c/o Wye Valley NHS Trust, The County Hospital, Union Walk, Hereford HR1 2ER. *T:* (01432) 364000. *E:* museji.takolia@wvt.nhs.uk.

TALBOT; *see* Chetwynd-Talbot, family name of Earl of Shrewsbury and Waterford.

TALBOT OF MALAHIDE, 10th Baron *cr* 1831 (Ire.); **Reginald John Richard Arundell;** Hereditary Lord Admiral Malahide and Adjacent Seas; Vice Lord-Lieutenant of Wiltshire, 1996–2006; *b* 9 Jan. 1931; *s* of Reginald John Arthur Arundell (*gggs* of 1st Baroness) (who assumed by Royal Licence, 1945, names and arms of Arundell in lieu of Talbot, and *d* 1953), and Winifred (*d* 1954), *d* of R. B. S. Castle; *S* cousin, 1987; *m* 1st, 1955, Laura Duff (*d* 1989), *d* of late Group Captain Edward John Tennant, DSO, MC; one *s* four *d*; 2nd, 1992, Patricia Mary Blundell-Brown, *d* of late J. Riddell, OBE. *Educ:* Stonyhurst. DL Wilts. KStJ 1988 (CStJ 1983; OStJ 1978); Chm., St John Council for Wilts, 1976–97. Knight of Malta, 1977. Hon. Citizen, State of Maryland, USA, 1984. *Heir: s* Hon. Richard John Tennant Arundell [*b* 28 March 1957; *m* 1984, Jane Catherine, *d* of Timothy Heathcote Unwin; one *s* four *d*]. *Address:* Park Gate, Donhead, Shaftesbury, Dorset SP7 9ET. *Clubs:* Pratt's, Farmers.

TALBOT, John Andrew, FCA; Executive Chairman, Johnson Service Group plc, 2008–14 (Chief Executive, 2007–08); *b* 2 Aug. 1949; *s* of Robert Talbot and Lucy E. Talbot (*née* Jarvis); *m* 1st, 1969, Susan Hollingbery (marr. diss.); one *s* one *d*; 2nd, 1983, Jennifer Anne Houghton; one *s* two *d*. *Educ:* Queen's Boys Sch., Wisbech. CA 1971; accountant in manufacturing, 1972–73; Bernard Phillips & Co., Accountants, 1973–75; Spicer & Pegler, 1975–83, Partner, 1979; Partner, Arthur Andersen, 1983–99: Hd, UK Insolvency Practice, 1988; Man. Partner, Worldwide Global Corporate Finance Practice, 1995–99; Administrator, Maxwell Private Cos, 1991; Receiver: Leyland DAF, 1993; Transtec plc, 2000; Sen. Partner, Talbot Hughes, then Talbot Hughes McKillop, LLP, 2001–05; European Chm., Kroll Talbot Hughes, 2005–08; Chief restructuring officer, Marconi PLC, 2002–03. Chm., English Nat. Ballet, 2004–12; Member: Bd, Conservatoire for Dance and Drama, 2001–07; Cttee, Kettles Yard Art Gall., Cambridge, 2003–13. DPhil Archaeol. student, Wolfson Coll., Oxford. *Recreations:* contemporary art, iron age history, modern and classical dance. *E:* john.talbot7@ntlworld.com.

TALBOT, Prof. Michael Owen, FBA 1990; James and Constance Alsop Professor of Music, University of Liverpool, 1986–2003, Emeritus Professor, 2004; *b* 4 Jan. 1943; *s* of Alan and Annelise Talbot; *m* 1970, Shirley Ellen Mashiane; one *s* one *d*. *Educ:* Welwyn Garden City Grammar Sch.; Royal Coll. of Music (ARCM); Clare Coll., Cambridge (Open, later Meml Scholar; MusB Hons 1963; MA; PhD 1968). Lectr in Music, 1968, Sen. Lectr, 1979, Reader, 1983–86, Univ. of Liverpool. Corresp. Mem., Ateneo Veneto, Venice, 1986. Order of Merit (Italy), 1980. *Publications:* Vivaldi, 1978 (Italian, German and Polish edns); Vivaldi, 1979 (Japanese, Brazilian and Spanish edns); Albinoni: Leben und Werk, 1980; Antonio Vivaldi: a guide to research, 1988 (Italian edn); Tomaso Albinoni: the Venetian composer and his world, 1990; Benedetto Vinaccesi: a musician in Brescia and Venice in the age of Corelli, 1994; The sacred vocal music of Antonio Vivaldi, 1995; Venetian Music in the Age of Vivaldi, 1999; The Finale in Western Instrumental Music, 2001; The Chamber Cantatas of Antonio Vivaldi, 2006; Vivaldi and Fugue, 2009; The Vivaldi Compendium, 2011. *Recreations:* chess, reading novels, travel. *Address:* 36 Montclair Drive, Liverpool L18 0HA. *T:* (0151) 722 3328.

TALBOT, Prof. Nicholas José, PhD; FRS 2014; Professor of Molecular Genetics, since 1999 and Deputy Vice Chancellor, since 2010, University of Exeter; *b* Haslemere, Surrey, 5 Sept. 1965; *s* of Ivan Talbot and Rosita Talbot; *m* 1989, Catherine Ann Walsh; two *s* one *d*. *Educ:* Midhurst Grammar Sch.; Univ. of Wales, Swansea (BSc Hons Microbiol.); Univ. of East Anglia (PhD Molecular Genetics 1990). Res. Fellow, Purdue Univ., 1990–93; School of Biosciences, University of Exeter: Lectr, 1993–97; Reader, 1997–99; Hd, 2005–10. Gatsby Plant Sci. Advr, 2009–. Chm., Bd of Govs, Rothamsted Res., 2009–14 (Trustee/Dir, 2006–); Dir/Trustee, 2007–13, Chm., 2013–, Sainsbury Lab., Norwich. Mem., EMBO 2013–. MAE 2014. Ed., The Plant Cell, 2004–10. *Publications:* (ed) Molecular and Cellular Biology of Filamentous Fungi, 2001; (ed) Plant-Pathogen Interactions, 2001; more than 120 scientific articles in learned jls. *Recreations:* walking by the sea, being with my children, looking at the stars. *Address:* University of Exeter, Northcote House, The Queen's Drive, Exeter EX4 4QJ. *T:* (01392) 723006. *E:* N.J.Talbot@exeter.ac.uk.

TALBOT, Patrick John; QC 1990; a Recorder, since 1997; *b* 28 July 1946; *s* of late John Bentley Talbot, MC, and Marguerite Maxwell Talbot (*née* Townley); *m* 1st, 1976, Judith Anne Urwin (marr. diss. 1999); one *s* two *d*; 2nd, 2000, Elizabeth, (Beth), Evans; two *s*. *Educ:* Charterhouse (Foundn Schol.); University Coll., Oxford (MA). Called to Bar, Lincoln's Inn, 1969, Bencher, 1996; in practice at Chancery Bar, 1970–. Member: Senate of Inns of Court and the Bar, 1976–78; Council of Legal Educn, 1977–95 (Vice-Chm., 1992–95). A Judicial Chm., City Disputes Panel, 1997–2000; CEDR Accredited Mediator, 2005–. A Lieut Bailiff of Guernsey, 2000–; a Lieut Seneschal of Sark, 2008–. Member: Ripieno Choir, 2001– (Chm., 2003–07); English Chamber Choir, 2015–. Hon. Life Mem., Nat. Union of Students, 1982. *Recreations:* watching cricket, singing, researching family history. *Address:* Serle Court, 6 New Square, Lincoln's Inn, WC2A 3QS. *T:* (020) 7242 6105; 9 Grove Road, East Molesey, Surrey KT8 9JS. *Clubs:* MCC, Wimbledon Wanderers Cricket, East Molesey Cricket (Chm., 2009–12).

TALBOT, Sarah Patricia; *see* Connolly, S. P.

TALBOT RICE, (Alice) Elspeth (Middleton); QC 2008; barrister; *b* Newcastle upon Tyne, 5 May 1967; *d* of David Middleton Lindsley and Elizabeth Anne Dickinson Lindsley; *m* 1991, Maj. Gen. Robert Harry Talbot Rice, *qv*; three *d*. *Educ:* Queen Mary's Sch., Duncombe Park; Roedean Sch.; Univ. of Durham (BA Hons Law). Called to the Bar, Lincoln's Inn, 1990, Bencher, 2012; in practice as barrister specialising in commercial chancery litigation. *Recreations:* playing polo enthusiastically but badly, playing lacrosse increasingly slowly, playing the French horn occasionally, cooking and eating. *Address:* 24 Old Buildings, Lincoln's Inn, WC2A 3UP. *T:* (020) 7691 2424. *E:* etr@xxiv.co.uk.

TALBOT RICE, Maj. Gen. Robert Harry, FIET; Head, Armoured Vehicles, Defence Equipment and Support, Ministry of Defence, since 2011; *b* London, 19 Aug. 1963; *s* of David Arthur Talbot Rice and Sylvia Dorothea Talbot Rice; *m* 1991, (Alice) Elspeth (Middleton) Lindsley (*see* A. E. M. Talbot Rice); three *d*. *Educ:* Eton Coll.; RMA, Sandhurst; Durham Univ. (BA Hons 1990); Army Staff Coll. and Cranfield Univ. (MA 1995); Saïd Business Sch., Oxford Univ. (Major Projects' Leadership Acad. course); Inst. of Dirs (Cert. 2013, Dip. 2014, in Co. Direction). FIET 2014. Commnd Welsh Guards, 1983; 1st Battalion: Platoon Comdr, 1983–85; Trng Officer, 1986–87; Adjutant, 1990–91; SO3, G3 Ops, HQ 24 Airmobile Bde, 1992–93; sc 1994–95; i/c Prince of Wales's Co., 1st Bn, 1996–98; Military Asst to ACDS OR Land, MoD, 1998–2000; SO1, J5 Plans, HQ KFOR, Kosovo, 2000; Directing Staff, RMCS Shrivenham, 2001–02; i/c 1st Bn, 2002–04; SO1, Plans, Army Resources and Plans, 2004–05; Asst Dir, Equipment Prog., MoD, 2005–08; Chief Liaison Officer to Iraqi MoD, HQ Multi-

Nat. Force, Iraq, 2008; rcds 2009; Dir Equipment, Army HQ, 2009–11. Regtl Lt Col, Welsh Guards, 2010– (Chm., Trustees, 2010–). MInstD 2013. *Recreations:* choral singing, game shooting, polo. *Address:* c/o Regimental Headquarters Welsh Guards, Wellington Barracks, SW1E 6HQ. *T:* (020) 7414 3291. *Club:* Tidworth Polo.

TALIJANCICH, Sir Peter Ivan, (Sir Peter Talley), KNZM 2015 (ONZM 2002); Joint Managing Director, Talley's Group Ltd (formerly Talley's Fisheries), since 1964; *b* Motueka, Nelson, NZ, 11 July 1945; *s* of Ivan and Margaret Talijancich (Talley); *m* 1968, Judith Drummond; one *s* two *d. Educ:* Motueka High Sch. Dir, Sunderland Marine Insce Co., UK. Chm., NZ Seafood Industry Policy Council. Founding Trustee and Mem. Bd, Seafarers Trust. Past Pres., NZ Fishing Industry Assoc. *Recreations:* Rugby, recreational fishing, hunting, motor racing. *Address:* Talley's Group Ltd, PO Box 5, Motueka, New Zealand. *T:* (3) 5282800. *E:* peter.talley@talleys.co.nz.

TALINTYRE, Douglas George; Director, Office of Manpower Economics, 1989–92; *b* 26 July 1932; *o s* of late Henry Matthew Talintyre and Gladys Talintyre; *m* 1st, 1956, Maureen Diana Lyons (*d* 2004); one *s* one *d*; 2nd, 2010, Mrs Audrey Cruse. *Educ:* Harrow County Grammar School; London School of Economics. BSc (Econ.) 1956; MSc (Industrial Relns and Personnel Management) 1983. Joined National Coal Board, 1956: Administrative Assistant, 1956–59; Marketing Officer, Durham Div., 1959–61; Head of Manpower Planning and Intelligence, HQ, 1961–62; Dep. Head of Manpower, HQ, 1962–64; Head of Wages and Control, NW Div., 1964–66. Entered Civil Service, 1966: Principal, Naval Personnel (Pay) Div., MoD, 1966–69; Senior Industrial Relations Officer, CIR, 1969–71; Director of Industrial Relations, CIR, 1971–74; Asst Secretary, Training Services Agency, 1974–75; Counsellor (Labour), HM Embassy, Washington DC, 1975–77; Head of Policy and Planning, Manpower Services Commn, 1977–80; Department of Employment: Hd of Health and Safety Liaison, 1980–83; Asst Sec., Industrial Relations Div., 1983–86; Under Sec., 1986; Dir of Finance and Resource Management, and Principal Finance Officer, 1986–89. Freeman, Co. of Cordwainers, Newcastle upon Tyne, 1952. *Recreations:* travel, wine, walking, short tennis. *Address:* 4 Foxborough Court, Maidenhead SL6 2PX. *Club:* Reform.

See also P. A. Rowan.

TALL, Stephen Joseph Fairweather; Contributing Editor, Liberal Democrat Voice, since 2015 (Editor, 2007–09; Co-Editor, 2009–15); Development Director, Education Endowment Foundation, since 2012; *b* Epsom, 19 March 1977; *s* of John Fairweather Tall and Christine Fairweather Tall; partner, Noa Vázquez Barreiro; one *s. Educ:* St Margaret's C of E High Sch., Aigburth, Liverpool; Mansfield Coll., Oxford (BA Mod. Hist. 1998). University of Oxford: Develt Officer, Mansfield Coll., 1999–2002; Dir, Strategy and Develt, St Anne's Coll., 2002–08; Dir, Develt, Bodleian Libraries, 2008–10; Associate Dir, Develt, 2010–12; Actg Dir, Develt, 2011. Mem. (Lib Dem), Oxford CC, 2000–08 (Dep. Lord Mayor, 2007–08). Res. Associate, CentreForum, 2012. Columnist: ConservativeHome, 2013–15; Total Politics, 2013–; contrib., Times Red Box blog, 2015–. *Publications:* (contrib.) Politico's Guide to Political Blogging, 2007, 2008; (contrib.) Total Politics Guide to Political Blogging, 2010; (ed) Coalition and Beyond: Liberal reforms for the decade ahead, 2013; (contrib.) One Hundred Days for Early Action, 2015. *Recreations:* reading, writing, talking about, listening to and watching politics, failing to go to the gym or learn Spanish. *Address:* 67 Swindon Road, Horsham, W Sussex RH12 2HE. *T:* 07976 629166. *E:* sjftall@gmail.com. *Club:* Everton Football.

TALLEY, Sir Peter (Ivan); *see* Talijancich, Sir P. I.

TALLING, John Francis, DSc; FRS 1978; Research Fellow, Freshwater Biological Association, 1991–2008; *b* 23 March 1929; *s* of Frank and Miriam Talling; *m* 1959, Ida Björnsson; one *s* one *d. Educ:* Sir William Turner's Sch., Coatham; Univ. of Leeds. BSc, PhD, DSc. Lecturer in Botany, Univ. of Khartoum, 1953–56; Visiting Research Fellow, Univ. of California, 1957; Plant Physiologist (SPSO), Freshwater Biological Assoc., 1958–89; Hon. Reader, 1979–84, Vis. Prof., 1992–2001, Univ. of Lancaster. *Publications:* (jtly) Water Analysis: some revised methods for limnologists, 1978; (jtly) Ecological Dynamics of Tropical Inland Waters, 1998; papers in various learned jls. *Address:* Hawthorn View, The Pines, Bongate, Cumbria CA16 6HR. *T:* (017683) 53380.

TALLIS, Prof. Raymond Courteney, FRCP; Professor of Geriatric Medicine, University of Manchester, 1987–2006; Hon. Consultant Physician in Health Care of the Elderly, Salford Royal Hospitals NHS Trust, 1987–2006; *b* 10 Oct. 1946; *s* of Edward Ernest Tallis and Mary Tallis (*née* Burke); *m* 1972, Theresa Bonneywell; two *s. Educ:* Liverpool Coll.; Keble Coll., Oxford (Open schol., 1964; BA 1967; BM BCh 1970); St Thomas' Hosp. Med. Sch. FRCP 1989. Clinical Res. Fellow, Wessex Neurological Centre, 1977–80; Sen. Lectr in Geriatric Medicine, Univ. of Liverpool, 1982–87. Chairman: Cttee on Ethical Issues in Medicine, RCP, 2003–05; Healthcare Professionals for Assisted Dying, 2011–. Numerous vis. professorships, named lectures, etc. Mem., various med. socs. Mem. Bd, Compassion in Dying, 2008–11; Patron, Dignity in Dying. FMedSci 2000. Hon. Vis. Prof. in English Literature, Univ. of Liverpool, 2008–13. Hon. DLitt Hull, 1997; Hon. LittD Manchester, 2002; Hon. DSc St George's, Univ. of London, 2015. *Publications:* Not Saussure, 1988, 2nd edn 1995; In Defence of Realism, 1988, 2nd edn 1998; Clinical Neurology of Old Age, 1988; The Explicit Animal, 1991, 2nd edn 1999; (ed jtly) Brocklehurst's Textbook of Geriatric Medicine and Gerontology, 4th edn 1992, 6th edn 2003; Newton's Sleep, 1995; Epilepsy in Elderly People, 1996; Enemies of Hope, 1997, 2nd edn 1999; Theorrhoea and After, 1998; Increasing Longevity: medical, social and political implications, 1998; On the Edge of Certainty: philosophical explorations, 1999; A Raymond Tallis Reader, 2000; A Conversation with Martin Heidegger, 2002; The Hand: a philosophical inquiry into human being, 2003; I Am: a philosophical inquiry into first-person being, 2004; Hippocratic Oaths: medicine and its discontents, 2004; Why the Mind is Not a Computer: a pocket lexicon of neuromythology, 2004; The Knowing Animal: a philosophical inquiry into knowledge and truth, 2005; The Enduring Significance of Parmenides: unthinkable thought, 2008; The Kingdom of Infinite Space: a fantastical journey around your head, 2008; Hunger: the art of living, 2008; Michelangelo's Finger: an inquiry into everyday transcendence, 2009; Aping Mankind: neuromania, Darwinitis and the misrepresentation of humanity, 2011; In Defence of Wonder and Other Philosophical Reflections, 2012; Reflections of a Metaphysical Flaneur and Other Essays, 2013; (ed jtly) NHS SOS: how the NHS was betrayed and how we can save it, 2013; Epimethean Imaginings, 2014; (with Julian Spalding) Summers of Discontent: the purpose of the arts today, 2014; The Black Mirror: fragments of an obituary for life, 2015; *fiction:* Absence (novel), 1999; short stories; *poetry:* Between the Zones, 1985; Glints of Darkness, 1989; Fathers and Sons, 1993; over 200 scientific papers and articles mainly in the fields of neurology and neurological rehabilitation of older people; numerous pubns in literary criticism, theory and philosophy, especially philosophy of the mind. *Recreations:* thinking, my family, walking, music. *Address:* 5 Valley Road, Bramhall, Stockport, Cheshire SK7 2NH. *T:* (0161) 439 2548. *Club:* Athenæum.

TALLON, John Mark; QC 2000; FCA; *b* 19 March 1948; *s* of late Claude Reginald Tallon and Blanche Mary Tallon; *m* 1st, 1974, Josephine Rowntree (marr. diss.); one *s* one *d*; 2nd, 1988, Patricia Steel. *Educ:* Rugby Sch. FCA 1970. Called to the Bar, Middle Temple, 1975; Mem., Pump Court Tax Chambers, 1976–. *Recreations:* golf, tennis, reading. *Address:* 16 Bedford Row, WC1R 4EF. *T:* (020) 7414 8080. *Clubs:* Huntercombe Golf (Oxfordshire); Berkshire.

TALMON, Prof. Stefan Alexander Gustav, DPhil; barrister; Supernumerary Fellow, St Anne's College, Oxford, since 2011; Professor of Public Law, Public International Law and European Law, and Co-Director of the Institute of Public International Law, University of Bonn, since 2011; *b* Pforzheim, Germany, 22 Jan. 1965; *s* of Roland and Sigrid Talmon; *m* 2008, Bettina Hahn; two *d. Educ:* Neuenbürg Grammar Sch.; Wolfson Coll., Cambridge (LLM 1989); Univ. of Munich; Univ. of Tübingen (First State Exam in Law 1992; Habilitation 2002); Univ. of Oxford (DPhil 1996; MA 2003); Second State Exam in Law, Stuttgart, 1997. Admitted Rechtsanwalt, Germany, 2003; Associate Prof., Univ. of Tübingen, 2002–03; Lectr in Public Internat. Law, 2003–06, Reader, 2006–08, Prof. of Public Internat. Law, Univ. of Oxford, 2008–11; Tutorial Fellow in Law, St Anne's Coll., Oxford, 2003–11; called to the Bar, Lincoln's Inn, 2007; in practice as barrister, 2008–. Visiting Professor: Univ. Aix-Marseille III, 2002, 2003; Yeditepe Univ., Istanbul, 2003; Univ. Panthéon-Assas (Paris II), 2006; Moritz Coll. of Law, Ohio State Univ., 2008; Univ. of Leuven, Belgium, 2010; Xiamen Acad. of Internat. Law, 2012; Centro di Direito Internacional, Belo Horizonte, Brazil, 2013. Dir of Studies, Hague Acad. of Internat. Law, 2011. Erskine Fellow, Univ. of Canterbury, NZ, 2006. *Publications:* (jtly) Alles fließt. Kulturgüterschutz und innere Gewässer im Neuen Seerecht, 1998; (ed jtly) The Reality of International Law, 1998; Recognition of Governments in International Law, 1998; (ed) Recognition in International Law, 2000; Kollektive Nichtanerkennung illegaler Staaten, 2006; La non reconnaissance collective des Etats illégaux, 2007; (ed jtly) The Legal Order of the Oceans, 2009; (ed) The Occupation of Iraq, 2012; (ed) Über Grenzen. Colloquium zum 70 Geburtstag von Wolfgang Graf Vitzthum, 2012; (ed jtly) The South China Sea Arbitration: a Chinese perspective, 2014; contrib. chapters in books; contrib. articles to learned jls, incl. Amer. Jl Internat. Law, British Year Book of Internat. Law, Chinese Jl Internat. Law, Eur. Jl Internat. Law. *Recreation:* walking. *Address:* 20 Essex Street, WC2R 3AL. *T:* (020) 7842 1200, *Fax:* (020) 7842 1270. *E:* stalmon@20essexst.com; Institute for International Law, University of Bonn, Adenauerallee 24–42, 53113 Bonn, Germany. *E:* talmon@jura.uni-bonn.de.

TALWAR, Rana Gurvirendra Singh; Co-founder and Chairman, Sabre Capital Worldwide, since 2003; *b* 22 March 1948; *s* of R. S. and Veera Talwar; *m* 1st, 1970, Roop Som Dutt (marr. diss.); one *s* one *d*; 2nd, 1995, Renuka Singh; one *s. Educ:* Lawrence Sch., Sanawar, India; St Stephen's Coll., Delhi (BA Hons Econs). Citibank, 1969–97: exec. trainee for internat. banking, 1969–70; various operational, corporate and institutional banking assignments, India, 1970–76; Gp Hd for Treasury and Financial Instns, 1976; Regl Manager for Eastern India, 1977; Gp Hd, Treasury and Financial Instns Gp, Saudi American Bank (Citibank affiliate), Jeddah, 1978–80; COS, Asia Pacific Div., 1981; Regl Consumer Business Manager, Singapore, Malaysia, Indonesia, Thailand and India, 1982–88; Div. Exec., Asia Pacific, 1988–91; Exec. Vice Pres. and Gp Exec. responsible for Consumer Bank in Asia Pacific, ME and Eastern Europe, 1991–95; Exec. Vice Pres., Citicorp and principal subsid., Citibank, resp. for US and Europe, 1996–97; Standard Chartered Plc: Gp Exec. Dir, 1997–98; CEO, 1997–2002. Non-executive Director: Pearson plc, 2000–07; Fortis SA, 2004–09; Schlumberger Ltd, 2005–08; Chm., Centurion Bank of Punjab, 2004–08. Governor: Indian Business Sch., 1998–; London Business Sch., 1999. *Recreations:* golf, tennis, bridge, travel. *Address:* Sabre Capital Worldwide, 2/F Berkeley Square House, Berkeley Square, W1J 6BD. *Clubs:* Tanglin (Singapore); Bengal (Calcutta); Delhi Golf (New Delhi).

TAM, Prof. Patrick Ping Leung, FRS 2011; FRSB; FAA; Head, Embryology Research Unit, since 1990, NHMRC Senior Principal Research Fellow, since 2000, and Deputy Director, since 2008, Children's Medical Research Institute; Professor, Discipline of Medicine, Sydney Medical School, University of Sydney, since 2008; *b* 27 Nov. 1952. *Educ:* Univ. of Hong Kong (BSc Hons; MPhil); University Coll. London (PhD 1980). Lectr, 1981–87, Sen. Lectr, 1987–90, Dept of Anatomy, Chinese Univ. of Hong Kong. Croucher Foundn Fellow, Univ. of Oxford, 1986; joined Children's Med. Res. Inst., NSW, 1991. Mok Hing-Yiu Dist. Vis. Prof., Univ. of Hong Kong, 2012–. FRSB (FInstBiol 1989); FAA 2008. Symington Meml Prize, Anatomical Soc. of GB, 1987; President's Medal, Australia and NZ Soc. of Cell and Develtl Biol., 2007. *Publications:* (ed with J. Rossant) Mouse Development, 2002; contribs to scientific jls incl. Develtl Biol., Human Genetics, Develt, Develtl Cell, Internat. Jl Develtl Biol., Eur. Jl Cell Biol. *Address:* Children's Medical Research Institute, Locked Bag 23, Wentworthville, NSW 2145, Australia.

TAM, Robin Bing-Kuen; QC 2006; *b* 1 June 1964; *s* of Sheung Wai Tam and Arleta Yau Ling Tam (*née* Chang); *m* 2007, Rosemary Jane Anger. *Educ:* Leys Sch., Cambridge; St John's Coll., Cambridge (BA 1985); Inns of Court Sch. of Law. Called to the Bar, Middle Temple, 1986; in practice as barrister, 1987–, specialising in admin. and public law, immigration and asylum work; Standing Prosecuting Jun. Counsel to Inland Revenue, 1993; Jun. Counsel to the Crown, 1994–2006 (A Panel, 1999–2006). *Publications:* (jtly) Asylum and Human Rights Appeals Handbook, 2008. *Address:* Temple Garden Chambers, 1 Harcourt Buildings, Temple, EC4Y 9DA. *T:* (020) 7583 1315.

TAMARÓN, 9th Marqués de; **Santiago de Mora-Figueroa;** Spanish Ambassador for Cultural Diplomacy, since 2012; *b* 18 Oct. 1941; *s* of José de Mora-Figueroa, 8th Marqués de Tamarón, and Dagmar Williams; *m* 1966, Isabelle de Yturbe; one *s* one *d. Educ:* Univ. of Madrid; Escuela Diplomática. Lieut, Spanish Marine Corps, 1967; joined Spanish Diplomatic Service, 1968; Secretary: Mauritania, 1968–70; Paris, 1970–73; Banco del Noroeste (on voluntary leave), 1974; Counsellor, Denmark, 1975–80; Minister Counsellor, Ottawa, 1980–81; Private Sec. to Minister of Foreign Affairs, 1981–82; Head of Studies and Dep. Dir, Escuela Diplomática, 1982–88; Dir, Inst. de Cuestiones Internacionales y Política Exterior, 1988–96; Dir, Inst. Cervantes, 1996–99; Spanish Ambassador to the Court of St James's, 1999–2004. Comdr, Orden de Carlos III (Spain), 1982; Gran Cruz, Orden del Mérito Naval (Spain), 1999; Commander: Order of Dannebrog (Denmark), 1980; Order of Merit (Germany), 1981; Officier, Ordre Nat. du Mérite (France), 1974. *Publications:* Pólvora con Aguardiente, 1983; El Guirigay Nacional, 1988, rev. edn 2006; Trampantojos, 1990; El Siglo XX y otras Calamidades, 1993; (jtly) El Peso de la Lengua Española en el Mundo, 1995; El Rompimiento de Gloria, 2003; El Avestruz, Tótem Utópico, 2012. *Recreations:* mountain walking, gardening, philology. *Address:* Castillo de Arcos, 11630 Arcos de la Frontera, Spain.

TAMBINI, Helen; *see* Mountfield, H.

TAMBLING, Pauline Ann, CBE 2014; Chief Executive Officer, Creative and Cultural Skills, since 2011; Managing Director, National Skills Academy for Creative and Cultural Skills, since 2009; *b* 23 April 1955; *d* of James William and Anne Dorling; *m* 1976, Jeremy Tambling; one *s* one *d. Educ:* Ely High Sch. for Girls; Stockwell Coll., Bromley (Cert Ed London); Univ. of Leeds (MA). Teacher, 1976–83; Head of Educn, Royal Opera House, 1983–97; Arts Council of England, subseq. Arts Council England: Dir, Educn and Trng, 1997–99; Exec. Dir, Res. and Develt, 1999–2001; Change Prog. Dir, 2001–03; Exec. Dir, Develt, 2003–07; arts consultant, 2007; Exec. Dir, Progs and Industry, 2007–08, Chief Operating Officer, 2008–09, Creative and Cultural Skills. Chair: Shape, 2007–; Da Vinci Studio Sch. for Creative Enterprise, Letchworth, 2013–. Mem., Strategy Cttee, Clore Leadership Prog., 2003–. Trustee: Shakespeare Schs Fest., 2007–10; Drama UK, 2013–; High House Prodn Park, 2014–. Mem. Bd, Univ. (formerly UC) of the Creative Arts, 2007–13. Deviser/writer, Top Score, TV series, 1996–97; co-dir/researcher, orchestral educn programmes, NFER, 1997–98. FRSA 1990. *Publications:* Performing Arts in the Primary School, 1990; Lessons in Partnership, 1996; articles in Cultural Trends, British Jl Music Educn. *Recreations:* arts, cinema, travel, current affairs. *Address:* (office) The Backstage Centre, High House Production Park, Vellacott Close, Purfleet, Essex RM19 1RJ. *T:* (020) 7015 1800. *E:* pauline.tambling@ccskills.org.uk; 9 Sumburgh Road, SW12 8AJ. *T:* (020) 7228 8089.

TAMEN, (Maria) Isabel (Bénard da Costa); Executive Director, Richard Alston Dance Company, since 2009; *b* Lisbon, 8 July 1963; *d* of Dr Pedro Mário Alles Tamen and Dr Maria Isabel Bénard da Costa Tamen; *m* 1999, Henri Oguike (marr. diss. 2013); one *s* one *d*. *Educ:* Univ. Nova de Lisboa, Lisbon (Modern Langs and Lit. 1982); London Contemp. Dance Sch. (Dip. Contemp. Dance and Choreography 1986). Dancer: Images Dance Co., 1986–88; London Contemp. Dance Th., 1988–94; Richard Alston Dance Co., 1994–99; trainee manager, Independance, 1999–2000; Educn Officer, Sakoba, 2000–02; Gen. Manager, Henri Oguike Dance Co., 1998–2009. *Recreations:* literature, music, theatre and dance.

TAMI, Mark Richard; MP (Lab) Alyn and Deeside, since 2001; *b* 3 Oct. 1962; *s* of Michael John Tami and Patricia Tami; *m* 1992, Sally Daniels; two *s*. *Educ:* Enfield Grammar Sch.; UCW, Swansea (BA Hons). Head of Res. and Communications, 1992–99, Head of Policy, 1999–2001, AEEU. An Asst Govt Whip, 2007–10; an Opposition Whip, 2010–11; Opposition Asst Chief Whip, 2011–15. Chm., Welsh PLP, 2006–. *Publications:* Votes for All: compulsory voting in elections, 2000. *Recreations:* football, cricket, antiques. *Address:* House of Commons, SW1A 0AA.

TAMMADGE, Alan Richard; Headmaster, Sevenoaks School, 1971–81; *b* 9 July 1921; *m* 1950, Rosemary Anne Broadribb; two *s* one *d*. *Educ:* Bromley County Sch.; Dulwich Coll.; Emmanuel Coll., Cambridge. BA (Maths) 1950; MA 1957. Royal Navy Special Entry, 1940; resigned, 1947 (Lt); Cambridge, 1947–50; Lectr, RMA Sandhurst, 1950–55; Asst Master, Dulwich College, 1956–58; Head of Mathematics Dept, Abingdon School, 1958–67; Master, Magdalen College School, Oxford, 1967–71. Royal Instn Mathematics Master Classes, 1982–94. Pres., Mathematical Assoc., 1978–79. FIMA 1965. *Publications:* Complex Numbers, 1965; (jtly) School Mathematics Project Books 1–5, 1965–69; (jtly) General Education, 1969; Parents' Guide to School Mathematics, 1976; articles in Mathemat. Gazette, Mathematics Teacher (USA), Aspects of Education (Hull Univ.). *Recreations:* music, gardens.

TAMWORTH, Viscount; William Robert Charles Shirley; *b* 10 Dec. 1984; *s* and *heir* of Earl Ferrers, *qv*; *m* 2010, Camilla, *d* of late Richard Lutyens. *Educ:* Eton; Christ Church, Oxford (BA 1st cl. Econs and Mgt). Equity Researcher, Liberum, 2009; Fund Manager, Artemis, 2015–.

TAN, Melvyn, FRCM; pianist; *b* 13 Oct. 1956; *s* of Keng Hian Tan and Sov Yuen Wong. *Educ:* Anglo-Chinese Sch.; Yehudi Menuhin Sch.; Royal Coll. of Music. FRCM 2000. Performer of classical piano repertoire on period instruments, 1983–; solo career, 1985–; extended repertoire to include modern piano, 1996–; performs in internat. music festivals, incl. Austria, Germany, Holland, France, Scandinavia, UK, USA, Japan, Australia, in major venues and with leading orchestras worldwide; pioneered interest in keyboard music of 18/19th centuries, incl. tour with Beethoven's own Broadwood piano, 1992; cycle of complete Beethoven sonatas, Japan, 1994–97. Numerous recordings incl. piano sonatas and complete piano concertos of Beethoven and Debussy Preludes Books 1 and 2, and Beethoven and Mozart piano concertos with London Chamber Orch. *Recreations:* swimming, wine, travelling to places where free of performing. *Address:* Dominique Toennesmann Artist Management, Frederikstraat 25B, 1054 LB Amsterdam, Netherlands. *W:* www.melvyntan.com.

TANAKA, Koichi; General Manager, Mass Spectrometry Laboratory, Shimadzu Corporation, Japan, since 2003 (Assistant Manager, Life Science Laboratory, 2002); *b* 3 Aug. 1959; *m* 1995, Yuko Ikegami. *Educ:* Toyama Chubu High Sch.; Tohoku Univ. (BEng). Shimadzu Corporation: joined Central Res. Lab., 1983; Kratos Analytical Ltd, UK, 1992; R&D Dept, Analytical Instruments Div., Japan, 1992–97; Shimadzu Res. Lab. (Europe) Ltd, 1997–99; Kratos Analytical Ltd, UK, 1999–2002. (Jtly) Nobel Prize in Chemistry, 2002. *Address:* Shimadzu Corporation, 1 Nishinokyo-Kuwabara-cho, Nakagyo-ku, Kyoto 604–8511, Japan.

TANBURN, Jennifer Jephcott; research consultant, 1984–94; *b* 6 Oct. 1929; *d* of late Harold Jephcott Tanburn and Elise Noel Tanburn (*née* Armour). *Educ:* St Joseph's Priory, Dorking; Settrington Sch., Hampstead; University Coll. of the South West, Exeter (BSc (Econ)). Market Research Dept, Unilever Ltd, 1951–52; Research and Information, Lintas Ltd, 1952–66, Head of Div., 1962–66, Head of Special Projects, 1966–74; British Airways Board, 1974–76; Head of Res. and Consumer Affairs, 1975–76, a Dir, 1976–83, Booker McConnell Food Distribn Div. Member: Marketing Policy Cttee, 1977–80, and Potato Product Gp, 1980–82, Central Council for Agricl and Horticl Co-operation; Packaging Council, 1978–82; Chm., Consumers' Cttees for GB and England and Wales under Agricl Marketing Act of 1958, 1982–91; Hon. Mem., Marketing Gp of GB, 2000–. Hon. Vis. Academic, Middlesex Univ., 1997–2003. Hon. Fellow, Durham Univ. (Business Sch.), 1991–94. *Publications:* Food, Women and Shops, 1968; People, Shops and the '70s, 1970; Superstores in the '70s, 1972; Retailing and the Competitive Challenge: a study of retail trends in the Common Market, Sweden and the USA, 1974; Food Distribution: its impact on marketing in the '80s, 1981; (with Judy Slinn) The Booker Story, 2004; articles on retailing and marketing subjects. *Recreations:* television viewing, reading. *Address:* 5 Finch Green, Cedars Village, Dog Kennel Lane, Chorleywood, Herts WD3 5GE. *T:* (01923) 497422.

TANCRED, Sir Andrew Peter L.; *see* Lawson-Tancred.

TANDY, Virginia Ann, OBE 2009; Director of Culture, Manchester City Council, 2008–11; *b* 29 Feb. 1956; *d* of William Arthur Francis Tandy and Lucy Tandy (*née* Saunders); *m* 1984, Brian Stephen Fell; one *s*. *Educ:* Newcastle upon Tyne Poly. (BA Hons); Manchester Univ. (Post-grad. Dip. Mus. Studies). Museums Officer, Tameside MBC, 1980–84; Exhibns Officer, Cornerhouse Arts Centre, 1985–87; Visual Arts Officer and Hd, Visual Arts, NW Arts Bd, 1988–94; Dir, Cornerhouse Arts Centre, 1994–98; Dir, Manchester City Galls, 1998–2008. Member: Arts Council Capital Services Adv. Panel, 1998–2001; Creative Industries Develt Service, 2001–09; Commns in the Envmt, 2002–04; Bd, Museums, Libraries and Archives Council, 2004–06 (Mem., Bd of Mgt, NW, 2003–09); Adv. Council, Granada Foundn, 2012–. Museums Association: Mem. Council and Public Affairs Cttee, 2001–10; Professional Vice Pres., 2004–06; Pres., 2006–08. FRSA 2006. Chair, Curious Minds, 2014–; Trustee: Campaign for Museums, 2005–06; Nat. Heritage Meml Fund, 2009– (Mem., NW Cttee, 2009–); Volunteer Centre Glossop, 2013–14. *Recreations:* family, gardening, singing.

TANFIELD, Dr Amanda Susannah; Ambassador to Eritrea, 2012–14; *b* Sutton, Surrey, 12 Dec. 1961; *d* of Maurice and Gillian Pagella; *m* 2003, Matthew Vernon Connolly. *Educ:* Univ. of London (BSc 1st Cl. Genetics 1984; PhD Cytogenetics 1987). Ministry of Defence: various posts, 1988–92; Principal: Directorate of Defence Policy, 1992–95; Resources and Progs (Air), 1995–98; Head: Regl Proliferation, Non Proliferation Dept, FCO, 1998–2001; Iraq Policy, FCO, 2001–03; Pol Counsellor and Dep. Hd of Mission, UK Delegn to OSCE, Vienna, 2003–07; Head: Drugs and Internat. Crime Dept, FCO, 2008–11; Libya Ops, FCO, 2011. *Recreations:* birdwatching and nature, reading, computer games and puzzles, classical music, Daleks.

TANFIELD, Jennifer Bridget, (Mrs J. B. Bannenberg); Librarian, House of Commons, 1993–99; *b* 19 July 1941; *d* of Doylah and Phyllis Tanfield; *m* 2002, Nick Bannenberg, Australia. *Educ:* Abbots Bromley; LSE (BSc Econ 1962). House of Commons: Library Clerk, 1963–72; Head, Econ. Affairs Section, later Statistical Section, 1972–87; Head, Parly Div., 1987–91; Dep. Librarian, 1991–93. Mem., IFLA Sect. on Liby and Res. Services for Parlts (Chm., 1997–99). *Publications:* In Parliament 1939–1951, 1991; (ed) Parliamentary Library, Research and Information Services of Western Europe, 2000. *Recreations:* opera, theatre, travel.

TANG, Sir David (Wing-cheung), KBE 2008 (OBE 1997); Chairman, D. W. C. Tang Development Ltd, since 1990; *b* Hong Kong, 2 Aug. 1954; *s* of late Pak Kan Tang and of Chiu Sim Chan; *m* 1st, 1983, Susanna Cheung Suk-yee (marr. diss. 1994); one *s* one *d*; 2nd, 2003, Lucy Wastnage. *Educ:* La Salle, Hong Kong; The Perse, Cambridge; Univ. of London. Lectr, Peking Univ., 1983–84. Founder: China Club Hong Kong, 1991; Pacific Cigar Co. Ltd, 1992; Shanghai Tang Hong Kong, 1994; Havana House, Canada, 1994; China Club Peking, 1996; China Club Singapore, 2000; Cipriani Hong Kong, 2002; China Tang London, 2005; ICorrect.com, 2011; Tang Tang Tang Tang, 2013. Director: First Pacific Co. Ltd, Hong Kong, 1989–2011; Tommy Hilfiger Inc., USA, 2003–05; Advisor: Asprey and Garrard, London; Blackstone Gp, NY; Savoy Gp of Hotels, London; BA Travel Adv. Bd. Chairman: Asia-Pacific Acquisitions Cttee, Tate Modern; (and Founder) Community English Lang. Lab.; (and Founder) Hong Kong Cancer Fund; Special Fundraising Cttee, Youth Outreach; Prince's Charities Foundn China, 1999; China Exchange, London; Vice Chm., EORTC Foundn; President: London Bach Soc.; Royal Commonwealth Soc., Hong Kong; Hong Kong Down Syndrome Assoc.; Trustee: Royal Acad. of Arts Trust; (and Founder) Anglo-Hong Kong Trust; Mem., Chm.'s Develt Circle, South Bank; Adviser: LSO; Dir, Asia Art Achieve; Patron, Hong Kong Youth Arts Fest. Weekly columnist, Financial Times, 2012–. Chevalier de l'Ordre des Arts et des Lettres (France), 1995. *Publications:* trans. Chinese, Roald Dahl's Charlie and the Chocolate Factory, 1984; An Apple a Week (anthol.), 2006; A Chink in the Armour (anthol.), 2010; Fan cun shi jie (anthol.), 2010. *Recreations:* reading, collecting art, chess, classical music. *Address:* The Penthouse, 24/F Euro Trade Centre, 21–23 Des Voeux Road, Central, Hong Kong. *T:* 25256320, *Fax:* 28101804. *E:* patriciali@dwctang.com. *Clubs:* Beefsteak, Brooks's, Chelsea Arts, Pratt's, White's; Foreign Correspondents', Hong Kong, Hong Kong Jockey (Hong Kong); Brook (NY).

TANKERVILLE, 10th Earl of, *cr* 1714; **Peter Grey Bennet;** Baron Ossulston, 1682; *b* 18 Oct. 1956; *s* of 9th Earl of Tankerville, and Georgiana Lilian Maude (*d* 1998), *d* of late Gilbert Wilson, MA, DD, PhD; *S* father, 1980. *Educ:* Oberlin Conservatory, Ohio (Bachelor of Music); San Francisco State Univ. (Master of Music). Working as musician, San Francisco. *Heir: cousin* Adrian George Bennet [*b* 5 July 1958; *m* 1st, 1984, Lucinda Mary Bell (marr. diss. 1991); 2nd, 1991, Karel Ingrid Juliet Wensby-Scott]. *Address:* 139 Olympia Way, San Francisco, CA 94131, USA.

TANLAW, Baron *cr* 1971 (Life Peer), of Tanlawhill, Dumfries; **Simon Brooke Mackay;** Chairman, Fandstan Electric Group Ltd (formerly Fandstan Ltd), since 1973; *b* 30 March 1934; *s* of 2nd Earl of Inchcape; *m* 1st, 1959, Joanna Susan, *d* of Major J. S. Hirsch; one *s* two *d* (and one *s* decd); 2nd, 1976, Rina Siew Yong Tan, *d* of late Tiong Cha Tan and Mrs Tan; one *s* one *d*. *Educ:* Eton College; Trinity College, Cambridge (MA 1966). Served as 2nd Lt XII Royal Lancers, Malaya. Inchcape Group of Companies, India and Far East, 1960–66; Managing Director, Inchcape & Co., 1967–71, Dir 1971–92; Chm., Thwaites & Reed Ltd, 1971–74; Chm. and Man. Dir, Fandstan Electric Group of private cos, 1973–2014. University of Buckingham (formerly University College at Buckingham): Chm., Building Cttee, 1973–78; Mem. Council of Mgt, 1973–2000; Hon. Fellow, 1981; DUniv 1983; Chancellor, 2010–14; Mem. Ct of Governors, LSE, 1980–96. Mem., Lord Chancellor's Inner London Adv. Cttee on Justices of the Peace, 1972–83. Contested (L) Galloway, by-election and gen. election, 1959, and gen. election, 1964. Mem., EC Cttee Sub-Cttee F (Energy, Transport Technology and Research), H of L, 1980–83; Chairman: Parly Liaison Gp for Alternative Energy Strategies, 1981–83; Parly Astronomy and Space Envmt Gp, 1999–2007 (Pres., 2007); Lighter Evenings All-Party Gp, 2007–. Joint Treasurer, 1971–72, Dep. Chm., 1972, Scottish Liberal Party. Pres., Sarawak Assoc., 1973–75, 1999–2001. Chm., Tanlaw Foundn, 1996–. FBHI 1996; FRAS 2003. *Publications:* Haiku: a journey of perception, 2014; articles and papers on horology in learned jls. *Recreations:* horology, astronomy, piscatorial pursuits. *Address:* Tanlawhill, By Langholm, Dumfriesshire DG13 0PQ; 101 Centurion Building, Chelsea Bridge Wharf, Queenstown Road, SW8 4NZ. *Clubs:* White's, Oriental; Puffin's (Edinburgh).

TANNER, Brian Michael, CBE 1997; DL; Chairman, Taunton and Somerset NHS Trust, 1998–2006; *b* 15 Feb. 1941; *s* of Gerald Evelyn Tanner and Mary Tanner; *m* 1963, June Ann Walker; one *s* one *d*. *Educ:* Acklam Hall Grammar Sch., Middlesbrough; Bishop Vesey's Grammar Sch., Sutton Coldfield; Bristol Univ. (BA 1st class Hons). CIPFA. Trainee Accountant, Birmingham CBC, 1962–66; Economist, Coventry CBC, 1966–69; Chief Accountant, Teesside CBC, 1969–71; Warwickshire County Council: Asst County Treasurer, 1971–73; Asst Chief Exec., 1973–75; Somerset County Council: County Treasurer, 1975–90; Chief Exec., 1990–97; Treasurer, Avon and Somerset Police Authy, 1975–91. Advr, ACC Cttees on agric., educn, nat. parks, finance, policy, police, 1976–92; Mem., Accounting Standards Cttee, 1982–85; Chief Negotiator with Central Govt on Rate Support Grant, 1985–88; Mem., Investment Cttee, Nat. Assoc. of Pension Funds, 1988–91. Director: Avon Enterprise Fund, 1988–97; Somerset TEC, 1990–97; Jupiter Internat. Green Investment Trust, 1997–2001; Somerset Community Foundn, 2002–07; Redstone Trust, 2007–11. Chairman: SW Reg., Nat. Lottery Charities Bd, 1997–2002; Taunton Town Centre Partnership, 1998–2002; Taunton Vision Commn, 2002; Council, Wells Cath., 2007–12; a Comr, Public Works Loan Bd, 1997–2009; Member: SW Regl FEFC, 1997–99; Wessex Ofwat, 1998–99. Trustee: Central Bureau for Educnl Visits and Exchanges, 1981–92; Avon and Somerset Police Trust, 1999–2009; Somerset Crimebeat, 2000–06; St Margaret's Hospice, Somerset, 2005–13. Governor: Millfield Sch., 1989–99; Bridgwater Coll., 1994–2002; Somerset Coll. of Arts and Technol., 2004–12; Queen's Coll., Taunton, 2009–. Pres., Wyvern Sports and Social Club, 2011–. Freeman, City of London, 1990. DL 1998, High Sheriff, 2003–04, Somerset. *Publications:* Financial Management in the 1990s, 1989. *Recreations:* gardening, golf, Rugby, cricket. *Address:* 8 Broadlands Road, Taunton, Somerset TA1 4HQ. *T:* (01823) 337826.

TANNER, Lt-Col Cecil Eustace; Vice Lord-Lieutenant of Bedfordshire, 1998–2005; *b* 14 Oct. 1934. Commnd 2nd Lieut, RASC, 1955; GSO 2, MoD, 1969–71; DAQMG (Logistics), HQ Land SE, 1973–75; Lt-Col 1976; CO 156 Regt, RCT(V), 1977; retd 1987. Formerly Cadet EO for Beds, ACF, TA. *Address:* c/o Lieutenancy Office, Central Bedfordshire Council, Chicksands, Shefford SG17 5TQ.

TANNER, Sir David (Whitlock), Kt 2013; CBE 2009 (OBE 2003); Performance Director, British Rowing (formerly Amateur Rowing Association), since 1996; *b* 29 Dec. 1947; *s* of late Douglas and Connie Tanner. *Educ:* Univ. of Bristol (BA Hons Hist.); Univ. of London (PGCE). Dep. Head, Greenford High Sch., 1985–87; Headmaster, Longford Community Sch., 1987–96. Olympic Rowing Coach, GB Team, Olympic Games: Moscow, 1980; Seoul, 1988; Team Leader, Rowing, Team GB, Olympic Games: Barcelona, 1992; Atlanta, 1996; Sydney, 2000; Athens, 2004; Beijing, 2008; London, 2012. FRSA 1992. Freeman: City of London, 2012; Watermen and Lightermen's Co., 2012. *Recreations:* theatre, classical music, sport, travel, history. *Address:* GB Rowing Team Office, 6 Lower Mall, W6 9DJ. *T:* and *Fax:* (020) 8237 6769. *E:* david.tanner@gbrowingteam.org.uk. *Clubs:* Leander, London Rowing, Molesey Boat, Remenham.

TANNER, David Williamson, DPhil; Under Secretary, Head of Science Branch, Department of Education and Science, 1981–89; *b* 28 Dec. 1930; *s* of late Arthur Bertram Tanner, MBE and of Susan (*née* Williamson); *m* 1960, Glenis Mary (*née* Stringer); one *s* two *d*. *Educ:* Raynes Park County Grammar Sch.; University Coll., Oxford (MA, DPhil); UEA (BA Hons Phil. 1st cl., 1997). Univ. of Minnesota (post-doctoral research), USA, 1954–56; Dept of Scientific and Industrial Research (Fuel Research Station and Warren Spring Lab.),

1957–64; Dept of Educn and Science, 1964–89. *Publications:* papers on physical chem. in Trans Faraday Soc., Jl Applied Chem., Jl Heat and Mass Transfer, etc. *Recreation:* family. *Address:* 72 Highfields Road, Highfields Caldecote, Cambs CB23 7NX. *T:* (01954) 489138.

TANNER, Elizabeth; *see* Tanner, K. E.

TANNER, James Jonathan; Managing Director, since 1999, and Chairman, since 2014, Tanners Wines Ltd (Director, since 1993); *b* Shrewsbury, 5 Jan. 1968; *s* of late Richard Tanner and of Susan Tanner (*née* Mowat); *m* 1994, Katherine Barrett, DL; one *s* two *d. Educ:* Radley Coll., Abingdon; Univ. of Bristol (BSc Hons Geog.); Imperial Coll. Business Sch. (MBA, DIC). Dir, 1993–, Man. Dir, 1999–, Tanners Shrewsbury Ltd. Dir, Merchant Vintners Co. Ltd, 1999–. *Recreations:* hunting, fishing, gardening, travel. *Address:* Tanners Wines Ltd, 26 Wyle Cop, Shrewsbury, Shropshire SY1 1XD. *T:* (01743) 234500, *Fax:* (01743) 234501. *E:* secretarial@tanners-wines.co.uk. *Club:* Flyfishers'.

TANNER, Prof. (Kathleen) Elizabeth, DPhil; CEng, FREng; FRSE; FIMechE, FIMMM; FIPEM; Professor of Biomedical Materials, University of Glasgow, since 2007; *b* 20 March 1957; *d* of late John Darley Tanner and Elizabeth Gordon Tanner (*née* Holmes). *Educ:* Wycombe Abbey Sch.; Lady Margaret Hall, Oxford (MA; DPhil 1985). CEng 1989; FIMechE 1994; FIMMM (FIM 1997); FBSE 2004; CSci 2004; FREng 2006. Queen Mary and Westfield College, subsequently Queen Mary, University of London: Res. Asst, 1983–88; EPSRC Advanced Res. Fellow, 1988–93; Lectr, 1993–95; Reader, 1995–98; Prof. of Biomedical Materials, 1998–2007; Associate Dir of IRC in Biomed. Materials, 1998–2001; Dean of Engrg, 1999–2000. Adjunct Prof., Dept of Orthopaedics, Lund Univ., Sweden, 1998–. Pres., UK Soc. for Biomaterials, 2000. Sec., Eur. Soc. for Biomaterials, 2005–09. Fellow, Eur. Alliance for Med. and Biol Engrg and Sci., 2015; FRSE 2015. Gisela Sturm Prize, Eur. Fedn of Nat. Assocs in Orthopaedics and Traumatol., 1996; Göran Selvik Prize, Eur. Orthopaedics Res. Soc., 1999; President's Prize, UK Soc. for Biomaterials, 2009. *Publications:* (ed jtly) Bioceramics 4, 1991; (ed jtly) Strain Measurement in Biomechanics, 1992; res. papers on biomaterials and biomechanics in learned jls. *Recreations:* riding, tennis, cookery, dress-making. *Address:* School of Engineering, James Watt South Building, University of Glasgow, Glasgow G12 8QQ. *T:* (0141) 330 3733, *Fax:* (0141) 330 4343. *E:* elizabeth.tanner@glasgow.ac.uk.

TANNER, Rev. Mark Simon Austin; Warden of Cranmer Hall, Durham University, since 2011; *b* Canada, Nov. 1970; *s* of Prof. Stuart Tanner and Joy Tanner; *m* 1994; two *c. Educ:* Loughborough Grammar Sch.; Christ Church, Oxford (BA Hons 1992; MA 1997); St John's Coll., Durham Univ. (BA Hons 1998); Liverpool Univ. (MTh 2002). Youth Pastor, Holy Trinity, Coventry, 1992–95; ordained deacon, 1998, priest, 1999; Asst Curate, St Mary's, Upton, 1998–2001; Vicar: St Mary's, Doncaster, 2001–07; Holy Trinity, Ripon, 2007–11; Area Dean of Ripon, 2009–11; Officiating Chaplain to the Military, 2009–. Regl Network Leader, New Wine, 2009–. Series Convenor, Grove Bks, 2005–10. *Publications:* Renewing the Traditional Church, 2002; Developing Visionary Leadership, 2004; How to Write a Good Sermon, 2007; How to Develop Vision in the Local Church, 2009; How to Preach a Good Sermon, 2009; The Introvert Charismatic: the gift of introversion in a noisy Church, 2015. *Address:* Cranmer Hall, St John's College, Durham DH1 3RJ. *T:* (0191) 334 3500, *Fax:* (0191) 334 3501. *E:* m.s.a.tanner@durham.ac.uk. *Club:* Inst. of Advanced Motorists.

TANNER, Dame Mary (Elizabeth), DBE 2008 (OBE 1999); European President, World Council of Churches, 2006–13; *b* 23 July 1938; *d* of Harold Fussell and Marjorie (*née* Teucher); *m* 1961, John Bryan Tanner; one *s* one *d. Educ:* Colston's Girls' Sch., Bristol; Birmingham Univ. (BA Hons). Lecturer in: OT and Hebrew, Hull Univ., 1960–67; OT and Hebrew, Bristol Univ., 1972–75; OT, Westcott House, Cambridge, 1978–82; Theol Sec., Bd for Mission and Unity, C of E, 1982–91; Sec., Council for Christian Unity, General Synod of C of E, 1991–98. Lay Canon, Guildford Cathedral, 2002. Visiting Professor: Gen. Seminary, NY, 1988, 1998; Pontifical Univ. of St Thomas Aquinas, Rome, 2000. Chm., Gov. Council, Cambridge Fedn of Theol Colls, 2015. DD Lambeth, 1988; Hon. DD: General Seminary, NY, 1991; Birmingham, 1997; Virginia Seminary, 1999; Hull, 2010; Liverpool Hope, 2012. Plaque of St Erik, Ch of Sweden, 1997. Officer's Cross, Order of Merit (Germany), 1991; Comdr, Royal Order of the Polar Star (Sweden), 2000. *Publications:* essays in: Feminine in the Church, 1984; The Study of Anglicanism, 1988; Runcie by His Friends, 1989; Women and Church, 1991; Encounters for Living, 1995; Living Evangelism, 1996; Festschrift for Jean Tillard, 1996; The Vision of Christian Unity, 1997; A Church for the 21st Century, 1998; Ecumenical Theology in Worship, Doctrine and Life, 1999; Runcie on Reflection, 2002; The Unity we have and the Unity we seek, 2003; Apostolicity and Unity, 2003; Seeking the Truth of Change in the Church, 2004; Cracks in the Wall, 2005; The Holy Spirit, the Church and Christian Unity, 2005; A Theology for Europe, 2005; One Lord, One Faith, One Baptism, 2006; Who is That Man?: Christ in the renewal of the Church, 2006; BEM at 25: essays in honour of Lukas Vischer, 2007; Inter-Church Relations, Developments and Perspectives: a tribute to Bishop Anthony Farquhar, 2008; Receptive Ecumenism and the Call to Catholic Learning, 2008; Some Implications for a Common Martyrology, 2010; The Ecumenical Patriarch Bartholomew, 2012; Celebrating a Century of Ecumenism, 2012; Unity in Process, 2012; Theological Studies and Ecumene, 2013; Hope of Unity: living ecumenism today, 2013; More Than I Can Say, 2014; articles in Theology, Ecumenical Rev., One in Christ, Ecclesiology, etc. *Recreations:* music, gardening. *Address:* Bainton Farmhouse, Bainton, Stamford, Lincs PE9 3AF. *T:* (01780) 740216.

TANNER, Matthew Richard, MBE 2007; Director and Chief Executive, SS Great Britain Trust, since 2000; *b* Tynemouth, 3 April 1966; *s* of John and Valerie Tanner; *m* 1st, 2000, Rebecca Stevens (marr. diss. 2012); one *s* two *d*; 2nd, 2013, Rhian Tritton. *Educ:* Sevenoaks Sch., Kent; St Andrews Univ. (MA Hons Classics; MPhil Maritime Archaeol.). Curator, Scottish Fisheries Mus., 1990–93; Maritime Curator, Merseyside Maritime Mus., 1993–97; Curator, SS Great Britain Project, 1997–2000. Member: Adv. Cttee on Historic Ships, DCMS, 2006–10; Arts Council SW Area Cttee, 2013–. Chm., Assoc. of Ind. Museums, 2011– (Vice Chm., 2008–11). Trustee: Underfall Restoration Trust, 2007–13 (Hon. Vice Pres., 2013–); Bristol Ensemble (formerly Emerald Ensemble) Ltd, 2008–11; St George's Trust, 2009–15; Black Country Living Mus., 2013–. FRSA. Hon. LLD Bristol 2015. *Publications:* Scottish Fishing Boats, 1995; The Ship and Boat Collection of Merseyside Maritime Museum, 1995; (ed) Manual of Maritime Curatorship, 2003; Royal Yacht Mary: the discovery of the first royal yacht, 2008. *Recreations:* classical music (listening and playing), sailing, scuba diving, popular science writings. *Address:* c/o SS Great Britain Trust, Great Western Dock, Bristol BS1 6TY. *T:* (0117) 926 0680, *Fax:* (0117) 925 5788. *E:* matthewt@ssgreatbritain.org.

TANNER, Meg; *see* Beresford, M.

TANNER, Prof. Roger Ian, PhD; FRS 2001; FAA, FTSE; P. N. Russell Professor of Mechanical Engineering, University of Sydney, since 1975; *b* 25 July 1933; *s* of Reginald Jack Tanner and Ena Maud Tanner (*née* Horsington); *m* 1957, Elizabeth Bogen; two *s*, three *d. Educ:* Univ. of Bristol (BSc 1956); Univ. of California (MS 1958); Manchester Univ. (PhD 1961). FAA 1979; FTSE 1977. Lectr, Manchester Univ., 1958–61; Reader, Univ. of Sydney, 1961–66; Prof. Brown Univ., Providence, USA, 1966–75. *Publications:* Engineering Rheology, 1985, 2nd edn 2000; (with K. Walters) Rheology: an historical perspective, 1998; several hundred jl papers. *Recreations:* tennis, golf. *Address:* School of Aerospace, Mechanical and Mechatronic Engineering, University of Sydney, Sydney, NSW 2006, Australia. *T:* (2) 9351 7153.

TANNER, Simon John, FFPH; Senior Management Adviser to Public Health England, 2013–14; Strategic Adviser to London School of Hygiene and Tropical Medicine, since 2013; *b* 2 Sept. 1957; *s* of John George Tanner and Marianne Tanner; *m* 1982, Katrina Anne Morris; two *d. Educ:* St Olave's and St Saviour's Grammar Sch., Orpington; Univ. of Southampton (BM 1981); London Univ. (MSc 1993); DCH 1983; DRCOG 1984; MRCGP 1985; MFPHM 1997, FFPH 2003. Principal in gen. practice, Alresford, 1986–93; Specialist Registrar in Public Health, 1993–97; Consultant in Public Health Medicine, 1997–99; Director of Public Health: N and Mid Hampshire HA, 1999–2002; Hampshire and IoW Strategic HA, 2002–06; Regl Dir of Public Health, NHS S Central, 2006–07; Regl Dir of Public Health for London, Dir of Public Health, Strategic HA for London, and Health Advr to GLA, 2007–13. Mem., Responsible Gambling Strategy Bd, 2013–. *Recreations:* cycle touring, piano playing, my family.

TANNOCK, Dr (Timothy) Charles Ayrton; Member (C) London, European Parliament, since 1999; *b* 25 Sept. 1957; *s* of Robert Cochrane William Tannock and Anne (*née* England); *m* 1st, 1984, Rosa Maria Vega Pizarro (marr. diss. 1988); one *s*; 2nd, 2007, Dr Silvia Janicinova; twin *d. Educ:* St George's Sch., Rome; St Julian's Sch., Lisbon; Bradfield Coll.; Balliol Coll., Oxford (BA Hons Natural Scis; MA); Middlesex Hosp. Med. Sch. (MB BS). MRCPsych 1988. House surgeon, Middx Hosp., and house physician, Harefield Hosp., 1984–85; W London Psychiatric Registrar Rotation, Charing Cross and Westminster Hosps, 1985–90; Res. Fellow, Charing Cross and Westminster Hosp. Med. Sch., 1988–90; N London Psychiatric Sen. Registrar Rotation, UCH and Middx Hosp., 1990–95; Consultant Psychiatrist and Hon. Sen. Lectr, Camden and Islington NHS Community Trust at UCH and UCL Med. Sch., 1995–99. European Parliament: Member: Economic and Monetary Affairs Cttee, 1999–2001; Foreign Affairs, Human Rights, Common Security and Defence Policy Cttee, 2002– (Vice-Pres., EP-Human Rights Sub-Cttee, 2004–07); Cons. Party Human Rights Commn, 2011–; substitute Member: Envmt, Public Health and Consumer Affairs Cttee, 1999–2004; Develt Cttee, 2000–01; Economic and Monetary Affairs, 2002–08; Conservative delegation: financial services spokesman, 1999–2001, Asst Whip, 2000–03, Dep. Chief Whip, 2003–05; foreign affairs spokesman, 2002–; Foreign Affairs and Human Rights Co-ordinator, ECR Gp, 2009–; Member: EP-Slovakia Jt Parly Cttee, 1999–2004; EP-Ukraine, Belarus and Moldova Delegn, 2002–04 (Vice-Pres., Ukraine Delegn, 2004–09); Vice-Pres., EP Delegn to NATO Parly Assembly, 2009–14. Mem. (C), RBK&C, 1998–2000. Freeman: City of London, 2000; City of Cartagena, Colombia, 2006. Commendatore, Order of St Maurice and St Lazarus, 2000; Order of Merit (Ukraine), 2006; Presidential Medal of Mkhitar Gosh (Armenia), 2009; Gran Official, Order of San Carlos (Colombia), 2010; Medal of Honour, Legislative Yuan of Taiwan, Republic of China, 2011; Presidential Order of Excellence (Georgia), 2013; Order of Brilliant Star (Taiwan), 2014. *Publications: political:* Community Care: the need for action, 1989; A Marriage of Convenience - or reform of the Community Charge, 1991; *medical:* numerous contribs to med. jls in areas of mood disorders and chronic fatigue syndrome; numerous articles in internat. press and for Project Syndicate. *Recreations:* travel, family. *Address:* (office) 44a Southern Row, W10 5AN. *T:* (020) 8962 1286. *E:* charles.tannock@europarl.europa.eu, charles@charlestannock.com. *W:* www.charlestannock.com.

TANNOUDJI, Claude C.; *see* Cohen-Tannoudji, C.

TANSEY, Geoffrey William; freelance writer and consultant, since 1981; *b* 3 June 1950; *s* of William Tansey and Lucy Tansey (*née* Dando); *m* 1973, Kathleen Allan Christie; two *d. Educ:* Prescot Grammar Sch.; Univ. of Aberdeen (BSc Hons Soil Sci); Sussex Univ. (MSc Hist. and Social Studies of Sci.); Case Western Reserve Univ. (Rotary Foundn Grad. Fellow in Hist. of Sci. and Technol.). Editl asst, Energy Policy, 1974–75; Asst Ed., Food Policy, 1975–77; freelance writer, 1977–78; Tech. Co-operation Officer, Ege Univ., Izmir, ODA, 1978–81. Consultant on develt work in Turkey, Albania, Kazakhstan, Mongolia; contributor to BBC, Financial Times and specialist media; advisor on food biodiversity and intellectual property: to Quaker UN Office, Geneva, 2000–07; Quaker Internat. Affairs Prog., Ottawa, 2003–07. Chm., Fabian Commn on Food and Poverty, 2014–15; Curator, Food Systems Acad., 2014–. Hon. Vis. Prof. in Food Policy, Leeds Metropolitan Univ., 1996–99; Hon. Visiting Fellow: Food Policy Res. Unit, Univ. of Bradford, 1990–97; Centre for Rural Econ., Univ. of Newcastle upon Tyne, 2005–; Hon. Vis. Res. Fellow, Dept of Peace Studies, Univ. of Bradford, 2000–. Joseph Rowntree Charitable Trust funded Visionary, working for a fair and sustainable food system, 2006–10. Hon. Campaigns Consultant, World Develt Movt, 1989–94. Derek Cooper Award for best food campaigner/educator, BBC Radio Food and Farming Awards, 2008. *Publications:* (ed jtly) A World Divided: militarism and development after the Cold War, 1994; (with A. Worsley) The Food System: a guide, 1995; (ed with J. D'Silva) The Meat Business: devouring a hungry planet, 1999; (ed jtly) Negotiating Health: intellectual property and access to medicines, 2006; (ed with T. Rajotte) The Future Control of Food: a guide to international negotiations and rules on intellectual property, biodiversity and food security, 2008 (Derek Cooper Award for Campaigning and Investigative Food Writing, Guild of Food Writers, 2009); contrib. various monographs, book chapters and jl articles on food, agriculture, develt and intellectual property. *Recreations:* reading, cinema. *E:* geoff@tansey.org.uk. *W:* www.tansey.org.uk. *Club:* Penn.

TANSEY, Rock Benedict; QC 1990; a Recorder, 1995–2014; *m* 1964, Wendy Carver; one *s* two *d. Educ:* Bristol Univ. (LLB Hons; Dip. Social Studies). Called to the Bar, Lincoln's Inn, 1966, Bencher, 2004. Chm., European Criminal Bar Assoc. of Defence Advocates, 1996–2003. *Recreations:* politics, theatre, opera, football, tennis, golf.

TANSLEY, (Anthony) James (Nicholas); Lead Associate, International Banks Division, Prudential Regulatory Authority, Bank of England, since 2014 (Senior Associate, 2013–14); *b* 19 July 1962; *er s* of late Thomas Anthony Tansley and Marian Tansley; *m* 1998, Bláithín Mary Curran; two *s* one *d* (of whom one *s* one *d* are twins). *Educ:* Tonbridge Sch.; St John's Coll., Oxford (MA); Sch. of Oriental and African Studies, Univ. of London (MSc); London Business Sch. (MSc). Joined FCO, 1984: lang. trng, 1986; Second Secretary (Chancery): Riyadh, 1988–89; Baghdad, 1989–91; First Secretary: FCO, 1991–94; Dublin, 1994–98; Counsellor and Dep. Hd of Mission, Muscat, 1998–2001; Sloan Masters Prog., London Business Sch., 2002–03; Hd, Strategic Planning Team, FCO, 2003–05; Hd, British Office, and Consul-Gen., Basra, 2005–06; Dep. High Comr, Abuja, 2006–08; Hd of Africa Dept (Equatorial), FCO, 2008–09. Associate, Building Societies Div., later UK Banks and Mutuals Dept, FSA, 2010–13. Mem. (C), Kent CC, 2012–. *Recreations:* Islamic architecture, history, cricket, wine. *Address:* c/o Bank of England, 20 Moorgate, EC2R 6DA.

TANSLEY, Mridul; *see* Hegde, M.

TANTUM, Geoffrey Alan, CMG 1995; OBE 1981; Middle East consultant; HM Diplomatic Service, retired; *b* 12 Nov. 1940; *s* of George Frederick Tantum and Margaret Amelia Tantum (*née* Goozée); *m* 1st, 1977, Caroline Kent (marr. diss. 2005); three *d*; 2nd, 2007, Carin Lake (*née* Wood) (marr. diss., 2014); two step *d. Educ:* Hampton Grammar Sch.; RMA Sandhurst; St John's Coll., Oxford (MA 1st Class Hons Oriental Studies (Arabic)). MCIL. HM Forces, 1959–66; joined Diplomatic Service, 1969; Kuwait, 1970–72; Aden, 1972–73; FCO, 1973–76; Amman, 1977–80; FCO, 1980–85; Counsellor, Rome, 1985–88; FCO, 1988–95. Mem. Sen. Adv. Bd, Good Governance Gp, 2008–14. Order of the Star of Jordan, 1995. *Publications:* Muslim Warfare: Islamic arms and armour, 1979. *Recreations:* sailing, oriental studies. *Club:* Travellers.

TANZER, John Brian Camille; His Honour Judge Tanzer; a Circuit Judge, since 2001; *b* 27 Dec. 1949; *s* of late William and Edith Tanzer; *m* 1980, Suzanne Coates, *qv*; two *s. Educ:*

Town Sch., NY; St Faith's Sch., Cambridge; The Leys, Cambridge; Keble Coll., Oxford; Sussex Univ. (BA); Inns of Court Sch. of Law. Teacher, Japan, 1968; engr, Southampton, 1973; called to the Bar, Gray's Inn, 1975; in practice, specialising in criminal and common law, Brighton, 1975–91, London, 1991–2001; involved with eJudiciary and Criminal Justice Efficiency Prog. *Recreations:* sailing, ski-ing, photography, computing. *Address:* Law Courts, Altyre Road, Croydon CR9 5AB; Woodfield House, Isaacs Lane, Burgess Hill, W Sussex RH15 8RA. *E:* john@tanzer.co.uk. *Clubs:* Travellers, Bar Yacht; Royal Gibraltar Yacht.

TAO, Prof. Terence Chi-Shen, PhD; FRS 2007; James and Carol Collins Professor of Mathematics, University of California, Los Angeles, since 2007; *b* Adelaide, 17 July 1975; *s* of Dr Billy Tao and Grace Tao; *m*; one *s*. *Educ:* Flinders Univ., S Australia (BSc Maths 1991; MSc Maths 1992); Princeton Univ. (PhD Maths 1996). Assistant researcher: Flinders Med. Centre, 1992–94; Princeton Univ., 1993–94; University of California, Los Angeles: Hedrick Asst Prof., 1996–98; Actg Asst Prof., 1999; Asst Prof., 2000; Prof., 2000–. Fulbright Postgrad. Schol., 1992–95. Vis. Fellow, 1999, Vis. Prof., 2000, Univ. of NSW; Hon. Prof., ANU, 2001–03; CMI Long-term Prize Fellow, Clay Mathematical Inst., 2001–03; MacArthur Fellow, MacArthur Foundn, 2007–11. Corresp. Mem., Australian Acad. Scis, 2006; For. Mem., NAS, 2008. Salem Prize, 2000; Bôcher Meml Prize, 2002, (jtly) Levi L. Conant Award, 2004, Amer. Math. Soc.; Clay Res. Award, Clay Mathematical Inst., 2003; Australian Mathematical Soc. Medal, 2005; Fields Medal, IMU, 2006; Ramanujan Prize, Shanmugha Arts, Sci., Technol. and Res. Acad., India, 2006; Ostrowski Prize, Ostrowski Foundn, 2007. *Publications:* Solving Mathematical Problems: a personal perspective, 1992; Analysis (2 vols), 2006; (with Van Vu) Additive Combinatorics, 2006; Nonlinear Dispersive Equations: local and global analysis, 2006; contribs to jls incl. Annals Maths, Acta Mathematica, Amer. Jl Maths. *Address:* Department of Mathematics, University of California, Los Angeles, 405 Hilgard Avenue, Los Angeles, CA 90095–1596, USA.

TAPLIN, Prof. Oliver Paul, DPhil; FBA 1995; Professor of Classical Languages and Literature, University of Oxford, 1996–2008; Tutorial Fellow in Classics, Magdalen College, Oxford, 1973–2008; *b* 2 Aug. 1943; *s* of Walter Taplin and Susan (*née* Rosenberg); *m* 1st, 1964, Kim Stampfer (marr. diss. 1996); one *s* one *d*; 2nd, 1998, Beaty Rubens; one *d*. *Educ:* Sevenoaks Sch.; Corpus Christi Coll., Oxford (MA; DPhil 1974; Hon. Fellow 2015). Fellow by Examination, Magdalen Coll., Oxford, 1968–72; Fellow, Center for Hellenic Studies, Washington, 1970–71; Lectr, Bristol Univ., 1972–73; Reader in Greek Lit., Oxford Univ., 1994–96. Visiting Professor: Dartmouth Coll., 1981; UCLA, 1987, 1990. Pres., Classical Assoc., 1999. Dr *hc* Athens, 2013. *Publications:* The Stagecraft of Aeschylus, 1977; Greek Tragedy in Action, 1978; Greek Fire, 1989; (jtly) An Odyssey Round Odysseus, 1990; Homeric Soundings, 1992; Comic Angels, 1993; (ed) Literature in the Greek and Roman Worlds, 2000; Pots and Plays, 2007; (ed jtly) The Pronomos Vase and its Context, 2010; Sophocles, Four Tragedies: a new verse translation, 2015. *Recreations:* theatre, swimming in the Aegean. *Address:* Magdalen College, Oxford OX1 4AU. *T:* (01865) 276000.

TAPOLCZAY, Dr David Joszef, CChem, FRSC; CSci; Chief Executive Officer, Medical Research Council Technology, since 2008; *b* Oldham, Lancs; *s* of Joseph and Mavis Tapolczay. *Educ:* Wallington High Sch. for Boys; Univ. of Southampton (BSc Hons; PhD). Postdoctoral Res. Fellow, Univ. of Oxford; Sen. Vice Pres., Millennium Pharmaceuticals Inc., 2000–03; CSO, Sigma Aldrich Fine Chemicals, 2003–05; Vice Pres., GlaxoSmithKline Pharmaceuticals, 2005–08. FInstD. *Recreations:* sport, weight training. *Address:* Medical Research Council Technology Ltd, 7–12 Lynton House, Tavistock Square, WC1H 9LT. *T:* (020) 7391 2812. *E:* dave.tapolczay@tech.mrc.ac.uk. *Club:* Royal Over-Seas League.

TAPPER, Prof. Colin Frederick Herbert; Professor of Law, Oxford University, 1992–2002; Fellow, Magdalen College, Oxford, 1965–2002, now Emeritus; *b* 13 Oct. 1934; *s* of Herbert Frederick Tapper and Florence Gertrude Tapper; *m* 1961, Margaret White; one *d*. *Educ:* Bishopshalt Grammar Sch.; Magdalen Coll., Oxford. Lectr, LSE, 1959–65; All Souls Reader in Law, Oxford Univ., 1979–92. Special Consultant on Computer Law to Masons (Solicitors), 1990–2002. Visiting Professor, Universities of: Alabama, 1970; NY, 1970; Stanford, 1975; Monash, 1984; Northern Kentucky, 1986; Sydney, 1989; Western Australia, 1991. *Publications:* Computers and the Law, 1973; Computer Law, 1978, 4th edn 1990; (ed) Crime Proof and Punishment, 1981; (ed) Cross on Evidence, 6th edn 1985 to 12th edn (as Cross and Tapper on Evidence) 2010; (ed) Cross and Wilkins Introduction to Evidence, 6th edn 1986; (ed) Handbook of European Software Law, 1993. *Recreations:* reading, computing, writing. *Address:* Corner Cottage, Stonesfield, Oxon OX29 8QA. *T:* (01993) 891284.

TAPPIN, Michael; Lecturer in Politics, School of Politics and the Environment (formerly Department of American Studies), 1974–2010, Fellow, since 2010, University of Keele; Chief Executive, Hartsluz Ltd, since 2009; *b* 22 Dec. 1946; *s* of Thomas and Eileen Tappin; *m* 1971, Angela Florence (*née* Reed); one *s* one *d*. *Educ:* Univ. of Essex; LSE; Strathclyde Univ. Mem. (Lab), Newcastle-under-Lyme BC, 1980–84; Staffordshire County Council: Mem. (Lab), 1981–97; Chairman: Planning Cttee, 1985–89; Enterprise and Econ. Develt Cttee, 1989–94; European Cttee, 1990–94; Mem. (Lab), Stoke-on-Trent CC, 2004–08 (Cabinet Mem. for Resources, 2006–08; Leader, Labour Gp, 2007–08). MEP (Lab) Staffordshire West and Congleton, 1994–99; contested (Lab) W Midlands Reg., 1999. European Parliament: Member: Budget Cttee, 1994–99; Budget Control Cttee, 1994–99; Substitute Mem., Econ. and Monetary Affairs Cttee, 1994–99; Mem., Delegn for relations with USA, 1994–99. Dep. Chm., Staffs Develt Assoc., 1985–94; Chm., N Staffs Steel Partnership Trng, 2000–04; Member: Stoke-on-Trent Local Strategic Partnership, 2000–08 (Chair: Health & Social Care Cttee, 2002–04; Econ. Develt and Enterprise Cttee, 2004–07); Bd, N Staffs Regeneration, 2006–08 (Chm., Employment and Enterprise Sub-Cttee, 2006–08); Stoke-on-Trent Transition Bd, 2008–10. Chm., W Midlands Regl Forum of Local Authorities, 1993–94. Chm., S Stoke Primary Care Trust, 2001–06. Pres., Staffs Ramblers' Assoc., 1998–2000. *Publications:* (jtly) American Politics Today, 1980, 3rd edn 1993. *Recreations:* walking, reading, cinema, theatre. *Address:* 7 Albert Road, Trentham, Stoke-on-Trent, Staffs ST4 8HE. *T:* and *Fax:* (01782) 659554. *E:* michaeltappin@yahoo.com. *Club:* Potters' (Stoke-on-Trent).

TAPPIN, Michael John; QC 2009; DPhil; *b* Cheltenham, 11 Nov. 1964; *s* of Christopher John Tappin and Jean Lee, (Pip), Tappin; *m* 1991, Mary Ruth Clarkson; one *s* three *d*. *Educ:* Cheltenham Grammar Sch.; St John's Coll., Oxford (BA Chem. 1986); Merton Coll., Oxford (DPhil Biochem. 1990). Called to the Bar, Middle Temple, 1991; in practice at the Bar specialising in intellectual property, 1992–; Standing Counsel to Comptroller-Gen. of Patents, Designs and Trade Marks, 2003–08. *Publications:* papers in scientific jls, 1987–91. *Recreations:* family, hockey, cycling, theatre, reading. *Address:* 8 New Square, Lincoln's Inn, WC2A 3QP. *T:* (020) 7405 4321. *E:* michael.tappin@8newsquare.co.uk.

TAPPING, Susan Amanda Mary; Her Honour Judge Tapping; a Circuit Judge, since 2001; *b* 3 Nov. 1953; *d* of Tony and Frankie Tapping; *m* 1988, Michael; one *s* one *d*. *Educ:* Bristol Univ. (LLB). Called to the Bar, Middle Temple, 1975, Bencher, 2010; specialised in criminal law; Asst Recorder, 1995–99; Recorder, 1999–2001. *Address:* Kingston Crown Court, 6–8 Penrhyn Road, Kingston upon Thames, Surrey KT1 2BB.

TAPPS GERVIS MEYRICK; *see* Meyrick.

TAPSELL, Rt Hon. Sir Peter (Hannay Bailey), Kt 1985; PC 2011; *b* Hove, Sussex, 1 Feb. 1930; *s* of late Eustace Bailey Tapsell (39th Central India Horse) and Jessie Maxwell (*née* Hannay); *m* 1st, 1963, Hon. Cecilia Hawke (marr. diss. 1971), 3rd *d* of 9th Baron Hawke; (one *s* decd); 2nd, 1974, Mlle Gabrielle Mahieu, *e d* of late Jean and Bathelde Mahieu, Normandy, France. *Educ:* Tonbridge Sch.; Merton Coll., Oxford (1st Cl. Hons Mod. Hist., 1953; Hon. Postmaster, 1953; MA 1957; Hon. Fellow, 1989). Nat. Service, Subaltern, Royal Sussex Regt, 1948–50 (Middle East). Librarian of Oxford Union, 1953; Rep. Oxford Union on debating tour of United States, 1954 (Trustee, Oxford Union, 1985–93). Conservative Research Department, 1954–57 (Social Services and Agriculture). Personal Asst to Prime Minister (Anthony Eden) during 1955 General Election Campaign. Contested (C) Wednesbury, bye-election, Feb. 1957. MP (C) Nottingham W, 1959–64, Horncastle, Lincs, 1966–83, E Lindsay (Lincs), 1983–97, Louth and Horncastle, 1997–2015. Father of the House, 2010–15. Opposition front bench spokesman on Foreign and Commonwealth affairs, 1976–77, on Treasury and economic affairs, 1977–78. Mem., Trilateral Commn, 1979–98. London Stock Exchange, 1957–90; Partner, James Capel & Co., 1960–90. Internat. investment advr to several central banks, foreign banks and trading cos; Hon. Member: Brunei Govt Investment Adv. Bd, 1976–83; Business Adv. Council, UN, 2001–06; Hon. Dep. Chm., Mitsubishi Trust Oxford Foundn, 1988–; Member: Court, Univ. of Nottingham, 1959–64; Court, Univ. of Hull, 1966–92; Council, Inst. for Fiscal Studies, 1983–2005. Chm., Coningsby Club, 1957–58. Jt Chm., British-Caribbean Assoc., 1963–64. Mem. Organising Cttee, Zaire River Expedn, 1974–75. Vice Pres., Tennyson Soc., 1966–. Hon. Life Mem., 6th Sqdn RAF, 1971. Brunei Dato, 1971. *Recreations:* travel in Third World, walking in mountains, reading history. *Clubs:* Athenæum, Carlton, Hurlingham.

TAPSTER, Caroline Marion, CBE 2013; Chief Executive, Hertfordshire County Council, 2003–12; *b* 9 April 1957. *Educ:* Weymouth Grammar Sch.; Goldsmiths' Coll., London. Social work services: Dorset, 1978–82; E Sussex, 1982–89; NHS, 1989–90; Kent CC, 1990–95; Hertfordshire County Council, 1995–: Asst Dir (Commng) for Social Services, 1995–2000; Dir, Social Services, 2000–01; Dir, Adult Care Services, 2001–03.

TARAR, Muhammad Rafiq; President of Pakistan, 1998–2001; *b* 2 Nov. 1929; *s* of Chaudhry Sardar Tarar; *m* Razia Tarar; three *s* one *d*. *Educ:* Univ. of the Punjab, Lahore (BA, LLB). Pleader, 1951–53; Advocate of the High Court, 1953–66; Additional Dist and Sessions Judge, 1966; Dist and Sessions Judge, 1967–74; Judge, High Court Bench, 1974–89; Chief Justice, Lahore High Court, 1989–91; Judge, Supreme Court of Pakistan, 1991–94. Mem., Senate, 1997–98. *Recreations:* reading, walking. *Club:* Islamabad (Islamabad).

TARASSENKO, Prof. Lionel, CBE 2012; DPhil; FREng; FMedSci; FIET; Professor of Electrical and Electronic Engineering, since 1997, and Head, Department of Engineering Science, since 2014, University of Oxford; Fellow of St John's College, Oxford, since 1997 (Vice-President, 2011–12); *b* 17 April 1957; *s* of Sergei and Rachel Tarassenko; *m* 1st, 1978, Lady Ann Mary Elizabeth (marr. diss. 2001), *d* of 6th Earl of Craven; two *s* one *d*; 2nd, 2001, Anne Elizabeth Le Grice (*née* Moss); two step *s* one step *d*. *Educ:* Keble Coll., Oxford (BA 1978; Edgell Shepee Prize, 1978; MA; DPhil 1985). FIET (FIEE 1996). Electronics Engr, Racal Research Ltd, 1978–81; University of Oxford: Lectr in Engrg Science, 1988–97; Dir, Inst. of Biomed. Engrg, 2008–12; Dir, Centre of Excellence in Med. Engrg, 2008–14; Mem. Council, 2013–; Fellow of St Hugh's Coll., Oxford, 1988–97. Founder Director: Third Phase Ltd, 2000–02; Oxford BioSignals Ltd, 2000–11; t+ Medical (formerly e-San) Ltd, 2002–11; Oxehealth, 2012–; non-exec. Dir, Isis Innovation, 2012–. Scientific co-ordinator, Foresight Project on Cognitive Systems, OST, DTI, 2002–04; Mem. Sub-Panel 13, REF, 2011–. Chm., Biomedical Engr Panel, RAEng, 2010–14. Chm., Oxford Pastorate Trust, 2006–; Lay Canon, Christ Church Cathedral, Oxford, 2012–. Centenary Lectr, Indian Inst. of Sci., 2010. FREng 2000; FMedSci 2013. BCS Medal, 1996; Rolls-Royce Chairman's Award, 2001; Silver Medal, Royal Acad. of Engrg, 2006; Innovation in Engrg IT Award, IET, 2006; Sir Henry Royce Award for High Value Patent, IET, 2008; EPSRC RISE Fellow, 2014. *Publications:* (with A. F. Murray) Analogue Neural VLSI, 1994; A Guide to Neural Computing Applications, 1998; (ed jtly) Cognitive Systems: information processing meets brain science, 2005; contribs to jls on signal processing and biomed. engrg. *Recreations:* Oxford United, cinema. *Address:* Department of Engineering Science, University of Oxford, Parks Road, Oxford OX1 3PJ. *T:* (01865) 273002.

TARBAT, Viscount; Colin Ruaridh Mackenzie; *b* 7 Sept. 1987; *s* and *heir* of Earl of Cromartie, *qv*.

TARGETT, Prof. Geoffrey Arthur Trevor, PhD, DSc; Professor of Immunology of Protozoal Diseases, London School of Hygiene and Tropical Medicine, 1983–2006, now Emeritus; *b* 10 Dec. 1935; *s* of Trevor and Phyllis Targett; *m* 1st, 1958, Sheila Margaret Gibson (*d* 1988); two *s* three *d*; 2nd, 1997, Julie Ann Thompson. *Educ:* Nottingham Univ. (BSc Hons Zool. 1957); London Univ. (PhD 1961; DSc 1982). Research Scientist: MRC Bilharzia Res. Gp, 1957–62; Nat. Inst. for Med. Res., 1962–64; Lectr, Dept of Natural History, St Andrews Univ., 1964–70; London School of Hygiene and Tropical Medicine: Sen. Lectr, 1970–76; Reader, 1976–83; Hd of Dept of Med. Parasitology, 1988–97; Acting Dean, 2000. Develt Ambassador, Gates Malaria Partnership, 2001–08 (Dep. Dir, 2000–07). Ronald Ross Medal, LSHTM, 2010. *Publications:* (ed) Malaria: waiting for the vaccine, 1991; (ed jtly) Prospectus on Malaria Elimination; Shrinking the Malaria Map: a prospectus on malaria elimination, 2009; numerous papers in internat. med. and scientific jls. *Recreations:* golf, music, travel. *Address:* London School of Hygiene and Tropical Medicine, Keppel Street, WC1E 7HT. *T:* (020) 7299 4708.

TARIN, Shaukat Fayaz Ahmed, Quaid-e-Azam Gold Medal 2005; Sitara-e-Imtiaz 2007; Adviser to Prime Minister on Finance, Revenue, Economic Affairs and Statistics, then Minister for Finance, Government of Pakistan, 2008–10; Adviser to Chairman, Silkbank Ltd, since 2010; *b* Multan, Pakistan, 1 Oct. 1953; *s* of Jamshed Ahmed Tarin and Mumtaz Tarin; *m* 1980, Razalia; one *s* two *d*. *Educ:* Punjab Univ., Lahore (MBA Major Finance). Citibank Pakistan: Country Manager, UAE and Oman and Regl Manager, Consumer Business in Gulf and Pakistan, 1985–91; Country Manager, Pakistan, 1991–96, Thailand, 1996–97; Chm. and Pres., Habib Bank, 1997–2000; Chm., 2000–03, Pres. and CEO, 2003–06, Union Bank; Chairman: Karachi Stock Exchange Ltd, 2007–08; Nat. Commodity Exchange Ltd, 2007; Pres. and CEO, Saudi Pak Commercial Bank Ltd, 2008. *Recreations:* golf, sightseeing. *Address:* Silkbank Ltd, 22nd Floor, Centrepoint Building, off Shaheed-e-Millat Expressway, near KPT Interchange, Korangi, Karachi 74900, Pakistan. *Clubs:* Golf, Sind, Boat (Karachi); Punjab, Gymkhana (Lahore).

TARLO, Christine; *see* McCafferty, C.

TARN, Prof. John Nelson, OBE 1992; DL; Professor of Architecture, 1995–99 (Roscoe Professor, 1974–95), and Pro-Vice-Chancellor, 1988–91 and 1994–99, University of Liverpool; *b* 23 Nov. 1934; *s* of Percival Nelson Tarn and Mary I. Tarn (*née* Purvis); unmarried. *Educ:* Royal Grammar Sch., Newcastle upon Tyne; Univ. of Durham (1st cl. hons BArch); Univ. of Cambridge (PhD). FRIBA, FRSA, FRHistS, FSA. Lectr in Architecture, Univ. of Sheffield, 1963–70; Prof. of Architecture, Univ. of Nottingham, 1970–73; Actg Vice-Chancellor, 1991–92, Public Orator, 1994–2002, Liverpool Univ. Member: Professional Literature Cttee, RIBA, 1968–77; RIBA Educn Cttee, 1978–97 (Vice-Chm., 1983–95; Chm., Moderators and Examiners Cttee, 1975–97); Council, RIBA, 1987–93; Council, ARCUK, 1980–90 (Vice-Chm., 1986–87; Chm., 1987–90; Vice-Chm., Bd of Educn, 1981–83, Chm., 1983–86); Technology Sub-Cttee, UGC, 1974–84; Adv. Cttee on Architectural Educn to EEC, Brussels, 1987–90; CNAA Built Environment Bd, 1987–90; Ministerial nominee, Peak Park Jt Planning Bd, 1973–82, a rep. of Greater Manchester Council, PPJPB, 1982–86 (Vice-Chm. of Bd, 1981–86; co-opted Mem., Planning Control Cttee and Park Management Cttee, 1986–97; Chm., Planning Control Cttee, 1979–97); Mem., National Parks Review Cttee, 1990. Trustee, Museums and Art Galls in Merseyside, 1996–2006 (Chm., Building and Design Cttee, 1996–2006). Chm., Art and Architecture

Dept, Liturgy Commn, Archdio. of Liverpool, 1978–; Member: Design and Planning Cttee, Central Council for Care of Churches, 1981–86; Historic Churches Cttee for the NW, 1994– (Vice-Chm., 2009–); DAC for Derby, 1979–93; Liverpool Cathedral Adv. Cttee, 1992–; Sub-cttee for Patrimony, Catholic Bishops' Conf. for England and Wales, 1995–2001. Chm., Riverside Gp (formerly Riverside Housing Assoc.), 1998–2010 (Dep. Chm., 1997–98). Pres., Wirral Soc., 2001–; Vice-President: Peak Dist and S Yorks CPRE, 2002–; Merseyside Civic Soc., 2007–. DL Merseyside, 1999. Hon. Fellow, Chinese Univ. of HK, 2004. DUniv Sheffield Hallam, 1997; Hon. LLD Liverpool, 1999. *Publications:* Working Class Housing in Nineteenth Century Britain, 1971; The Peak District National Park: its architecture, 1971; Five Per Cent Philanthropy, 1974; (adv. ed.) Sir Banister Fletcher's History of Architecture, 19th edn, 1987. *Recreations:* music, cooking. *Address:* 2 Ashmore Close, Barton Hey Drive, Caldy, Wirral CH48 2JX. *Club:* Athenæum.

TARR, Robert James; Principal, The OakVine Consultancy, since 1997; Director, OakVine.net, since 1999; *b* 8 June 1944; *s* of Jack William Tarr; *m* 1966, Linda Andrews. *Educ:* Whytemead and Downsbrook Schools, Worthing; Worthing High Sch. for Boys; BScEcon Hons London, 1977; BA Open Univ., 1979. CPFA (IPFA 1967); FCILT (FCIT 1989). W Sussex CC, Worthing BC, Denbighshire CC, Sunderland Met. BC to 1975; Corporate Planning Co-ordinator and Head of Policy Unit, Bradford Met. Council, 1975–81; Chief Exec., Royal Borough of Kingston upon Thames, 1981–83; Chief Exec. and Town Clerk, Coventry City Council, 1983–87; Dir Gen., Centro (W Midlands PTE), 1987–95; Sec. Gen., Light Rail Transit Assoc., 1997–99. *Publications:* contribs to jls and conf. papers; articles on public transport and light rail transit. *Recreations:* viticulture and wine-making, gardening, art, architecture and history (especially Victorian and industrialisation), soaking up sun and scenery, naturism, running, photography, the internet (blogs and editorial comment on several websites), amateur radio (call sign G3PUR).

TARRANT, Christopher John, OBE 2004; radio and television presenter, producer and writer; *b* 10 Oct. 1946; *s* of late Major Basil Tarrant, MC, and Joan Ellen Tarrant (*née* Cox); *m* 1st, 1977, Sheila Roberton (marr. diss.); two *d*; 2nd, 1991, Ingrid Dupré (marr. diss. 2008); one *s* one *d*. *Educ:* King's Sch., Worcester; Univ. of Birmingham (BA Hons). *Television* includes: presenter and writer, ATV Today, 1972–74; presenter, writer and producer: Tiswas, 1974–82; OTT, 1981–83; presenter: Everybody's Equal, 1989–91; Tarrant on Television, 1989–; Lose a Million, 1993; Pop Quiz, 1994–95; Man o Man, 1996–98; Who Wants to be a Millionaire?, 1998–2014; The Colour of Money, 2009; Chris Tarrant: Extreme Railways, 2012; *radio:* presenter, Breakfast Show, Capital Radio, 1987–2004. Sony Radio Awards: Radio Personality of the Year, 1990; Best Use of Comedy, 1990; Silver Medal, 1992, 1993; Best Breakfast Show, 1995; Gold Award, 2001; Best On-Air Personality, Internat. Radio Fest. of NY, 1987; Radio Personality of the Year, TRIC, 1989; Ind. Radio Personality, Variety Club of GB, 1991; Best Breakfast Show, NY World Awards, 1997; ITV Personality of the Year, Variety Club of GB, 1998; GQ Radio Man of the Year, 1999; Best TV Performer in non-acting role, BPG TV Awards, 1999; Nat. TV Awards Special Recognition, 2000; Lifetime Achievement Award, ITV, 2000; Lifetime Achievement Award, Radio Acad., 2002; Lifetime Achievement Award, British Comedy Awards, 2006. Pres., Anglers' Conservation Assoc., 2002–04. *Publications:* Ken's Furry Friends, 1986; Fishfriar's Hall Revisited, 1987; Ready Steady Go, 1990; Rebel Rebel, 1991; Tarrant off the Record, 1997; The Ultimate Book of Netty Nutters, 1998; Tarrant on Millionaires, 1999; Millionaire Moments, 2002; Tarrant on Top of the World: in search of the polar bear, 2005; Dad's War: father, soldier, hero, 2014. *Recreations:* fishing, cricket. *Clubs:* Lord's Taverners (Pres., 2009–11), White Swan Piscatorials, Red Spinners Fishing, Variety Club of Great Britain.

TARRANT, Prof. John Rex; DL; PhD; Secretary General, Association of Commonwealth Universities, 2007–10; *b* 12 Nov. 1941; *s* of Arthur Rex Tarrant and Joan Mary (*née* Brookes); *m* 1991, Biddy Fisher. *Educ:* Marling Grammar Sch., Stroud; Univ. of Hull (BSc; PhD 1966). Asst Lectr, UC, Dublin, 1966–68; University of East Anglia: Lectr, 1968–74; Sen. Lectr, 1974–82; Dean, Sch. of Envmtl Scis, 1974–77 and 1981–84; Reader, 1982–94; Pro Vice-Chancellor, 1985–88; Dep. Vice-Chancellor, 1989–95; Prof., 1994–95; Hon. Fellow, 1996; Vice-Chancellor and Principal, Univ. of Huddersfield, 1995–2006. Vis. Prof., Dept of Geog., Univ. of Nebraska, 1970; Vis. Lectr, Dept of Geog., Univ. of Canterbury, NZ, 1973; Vis. Res. Associate, Internat. Food Policy Res. Inst., Washington, 1977–78; Vis. Schol., Food Res. Inst., Stanford Univ., USA, 1978; Harris Vis. Prof., Coll. of Geoscis, Texas A&M Univ., 1989. Chm., MLA Yorkshire, 2007–09. DL W Yorks, 2007. Hon. Fellow, Commonwealth of Learning, 2010. Hon. DSc: Hull, 2000; Huddersfield, 2007. *Publications:* Agricultural Geography, 1974; Food Policies, 1980; Food and Farming, 1991; contrib. chapters in books; numerous articles in professional jls. *Recreations:* gliding, motor-cycling. *Address:* Spring Cottage, Leak Hall Lane, Denby Dale, W Yorks HD8 8QU. *T:* (01484) 866697.

TARTAGLIA, Most Rev. Philip; *see* Glasgow, Archbishop of, (RC).

TARUSCHIO, Franco Vittorio, Hon. OBE 2003; chef and restaurateur, Walnut Tree Inn, Abergavenny, 1963–2001; *b* 29 March 1938; *s* of Giuseppe Taruschio and Apina (*née* Cecati); *m* 1963, Ann Forester; one adopted *d* (and one *d* decd). *Educ:* Hotel Sch., Bellagio, Italy. Trainee Chef: Hotel Splendide, Lugano, 1958; Restaurant La Belle Meunière, Clermont-Ferrand, 1959–60; Head Waiter, Three Horseshoes Hotel, Rugby, 1961–63. Pres., St Anne's Hospice, Malpas, Gwent, 2001–13. Patron, Abergavenny Food Fest., 2009–. *Publications:* Leaves from the Walnut Tree: recipes of a lifetime, 1993; Bruschetta, Crostoni and Crostini, 1995; Franco and Friends: Food from the Walnut Tree, 1997; Ice Creams and Semi Freddi, 1997; 100 Great Pasta Dishes, 2002. *Recreations:* funghi and wild food foraging, swimming, walking, teaching cookery, having fun with my grandchildren. *Address:* The Willows, 26 Pen-y-Pound, Abergavenny, Monmouthshire NP7 7RN. *T:* (01873) 859026.

TARVER, Clive Duncan; Director, Intelligence, Surveillance, Target Acquisition and Reconnaissance, Defence Equipment and Support, Ministry of Defence, since 2011; *b* Bromsgrove, Worcs, 30 Nov. 1969; *s* of David Tarver and Diane Tarver; *m* 2004, Dr Kate Rebecca Clemons; one *s* two *d*. *Educ:* Alvechurch Primary and Middle Schs; Abbey High Sch.; Jesus Coll., Cambridge (BA Hons Engrg 1992); Warwick Business Sch. (MBA 2002). CEng 1997; MAPM 1998; ACCA CDipAF 2000; FIMechE 2011; FIET 2014. Ministry of Defence, 1992–: Proj. Manager, Special Projects, 1996–98; Business Manager, Ships Support Agency, 1998–2000; Team Leader, Special Communications, 2000–01; Private Sec. to Chief Defence Procurement, 2003; Team Leader, Marine Electrical Systems, 2004–07; Sen. Civil Service, 2007; Director: Information, Defence Equipment and Support, 2007–08; Infrastructure, 2008–09; Hd, Air Comd and Control Prog. Delivery Gp, 2009–11. FAPM 2015. *Recreations:* family activities with my young children, cricket, football, triathlons (increasingly as spectator). *Address:* Yew 3a #1338, Defence Equipment and Support, Ministry of Defence, Abbey Wood, Bristol BS34 8JH.

TAS, Jacob; Chief Executive, Nacro, since 2014; *b* The Hague, 23 June 1965; *s* of Jan Jacob Tas and Eva Tas-Hueting; partner, Sallyanne Marsh; one *s* three *d*. *Educ:* Haags Montessori Lyceum; Univ. of Amsterdam (MSc Applied Econometrics); Univ. of Oxford (AMP); Regent's Coll. (Accredited Mediator). Royal Nedlloyd, subseq. Royal P&O Nedlloyd: Country/Business Manager, Taiwan, 1995–96; Manager, Merger Office, 1997; Gen. Manager, 1998–2001, Equipment Europe; Global HR & Develt Dir, 2001–05; Ops Dir, 2005–06; Dir England and Hd of Volunteering, The Prince's Trust, 2007–11; Dep. CEO, 2011–13, Interim CEO, 2013–14, Action for Children. Chm. Trustees and Co. Sec., St Paul's Steiner Sch., 2005–13. Trustee: Nedlloyd Pension Fund, 2004–; War Child, 2012–; Dutch Centre, 2014–. Founding Mem., Centre for Narrative Leadership. *Address:* Nacro, First Floor, 46 London Street, SE1 0EH. *T:* (020) 7902 5728. *E:* jacob.tas@nacro.org.uk.

TASKER, Prof. Philip Westerby, PhD; FRSC, FInstP, CPhys; Vice Chancellor, De Montfort University, 1999–2010; Chairman, Leicester Theatre Trust, since 2010; *b* 6 July 1950; *s* of John Westerby Tasker and Alianore Doris Tasker (*née* Whytlaw-Gray); *m* 1974, Alison Helen Davis; one *s* one *d*. *Educ:* King Alfred's Grammar Sch., Wantage; Univ. of Birmingham (BSc Chem. 1971; PhD 1974). CPhys 1989; FInstP 1989; FRSC 1990. Research Fellow: Univ. of Bristol, 1974–75; Theoretical Physics Div., Harwell Lab., UKAEA, 1975–90; Divl Manager, AEA Technol., 1990–93; Chief Exec., Safeguard Internat., 1993–96; Pro-Vice Chancellor, De Montfort Univ., 1996–99. Member: Bd, E Midlands Develt Agency, 2004–12; Midlands Regl Adv. Bd, Nat. Trust, 2012–. Hon. DSc St Petersburg Univ. of Technol. and Design, 2007; DUniv De Montfort, 2011. *Publications:* contribs to Philosophical Mag., Jl Physics, Faraday Trans, Physical Rev., etc.

TATA, Dr Jamshed Rustom, FRS 1973; Head, Division of Developmental Biochemistry, National Institute for Medical Research, 1973–96; *b* 13 April 1930; *s* of Rustom and Gool Tata; *m* 1954, Renée Suzanne Zanetto; two *s* one *d*. *Educ:* Univ. of Bombay (BSc); Univ. of Paris, Sorbonne (DèsSc). Post-doctoral Fellow, Sloan-Kettering Inst., New York, 1954–56; Beit Memorial Fellow, Nat. Inst. for Med. Research, 1956–60; Vis. Scientist, Wenner-Gren Inst., Stockholm, 1960–62; Mem., Scientific Staff, MRC, Nat. Inst. for Med. Research, 1962–96. Visiting Professor: King's Coll., London, 1968–69, and 1970–77; Univ. of California, Berkeley, 1969–70; Vis. Senior Scientist, Nat. Institutes of Health, USA, 1977, 1997; Fogarty Scholar, NIH, USA, 1983, 1986, 1989. The Wellcome Trust: Chm., Cell and Molecular Panel, 1990–92; Mem., Basic Sci. Gp, 1992–93; Mem., Internat. Interest Gp, 1997–2002. Chm., Bd of Trustees, Oxford Internat. Biomed. Centre, 1999–2007 (Trustee, 1996–2008). Non-exec. Dir, Biotech Analytics, 2000–05. Chm., Elections and Awards, Third World Acad. of Sci., 2000–08; Mem., Grants Cttee, Royal Soc., 2005–08. Sci. Advr, EU Nuclear Receptor Consortium, 2006–11. Fellow: Indian Nat. Science Acad., 1978; Third World Acad. of Sci., 1986. Dr *hc* École Normale Supérieure, France, 2009. Van Meter Award, 1954; Colworth Medal, 1966; Medal of Soc. for Endocrinology, 1973; Jubilee Medal, Indian Inst. of Sci., 1985. *Publications:* (jtly): The Thyroid Hormones, 1959; The Chemistry of Thyroid Diseases, 1960; Metamorphosis, 1996; Hormonal Signalling and Postembryonic Development, 1998; papers in jls of: Biochemistry; Developmental Biology; Endocrinology. *Address:* 15 Bittacy Park Avenue, Mill Hill, NW7 2HA. *T:* (020) 8346 6291.

TATA, Ratan Naval, Hon. GBE 2014 (Hon. KBE 2009); Chairman, Tata Sons Ltd, 1991–2012, now Chairman Emeritus; *b* Bombay, 28 Dec. 1937; *s* of Naval H. Tata. *Educ:* Cornell Univ. (BSc Arch. with Structl Engrg, 1962); Harvard Business Sch. (AMP 1975). Joined Tata Steel Ltd, 1962; Dir, National Radio & Electronics Co. Ltd, 1971; Chm., Tata Industries Ltd, 1981–2012; Tata cos incl. Tata Motors, Tata Steel, Tata Consultancy Services, Tata Power, Tata Tea, Tata Chemicals, Indian Hotels, Tata Teleservices. Pres. Court, Indian Inst. of Sci.; Chm. Council, Tata Inst. of Fundamental Res. Chm. Trustees, Sir Dorabji Tata Trust. Hon. FREng 2012. Padma Bhushan, 2000; Padma Vibhushan, 2008. *Address:* c/o Tata Group, Bombay House, 24 Homi Mody Street, Mumbai 400 001, India.

TATCHELL, Peter Gary; lesbian, gay, bisexual and transgender and human rights campaigner; journalist and author; *b* Melbourne, 25 Jan. 1952; *s* of Gordon Basil Tatchell and Mardi Aileen Tatchell (*née* Rhodes, now Nitscke). *Educ:* Mount Waverley High Sch., Melbourne; Polytech. of N London (BSc Hons (Sociol.) 1977). Sec., Christians for Peace, 1970–71; Exec., Vietnam Moratorium Campaign, 1971; Chm., Rockingham Estate Tenants' Assoc., 1980–81; Sec., Southwark and Bermondsey, Labour Party, 1980–85; activist/organiser: Gay Liberation Front London, 1971–73; UK AIDS Vigil Orgn, 1987–89; Green and Socialist Confs, 1987–89; ACT UP London, 1989–91; co-organiser, OutRage!, 1990–2012; spokesperson on human rights, Green Party of England and Wales, 2007–. Dir, Peter Tatchell Foundn, 2011–. Contested (Lab) Bermondsey by-election, 1983; candidate (ind. green left) London Assembly, 2000; Prospective Parly Cand. (Green), Oxford East, 2007–09. Member: NUJ, 1986–; Republic, 2002–; Green Party, 2004–. Ambassador, Make Justice Work, 2010–; Distinguished Supporter, British Humanist Assoc., 2013–; Patron: Pride London, 2010–; Animal Aid, 2011–; Tell Mama, 2014–. Hon. Fellow, Goldsmiths, Univ. of London, 2014. Hon. DLitt Sussex, 2010; Hon. LLD London South Bank, 2011; Hon. DLaw De Montfort, 2014. Blue Plaque erected at residence, Southwark, 2010. Campaigner of the Year, Observer Ethical Awards, 2009; Irwin Prize, Nat. Secular Soc., 2012; Lifetime Achiever Award, Nat. Diversity Awards, 2012; Icon Award for Outstanding Achievement, Attitude Awards, 2012; Lifetime Achievement Award, Out in the City and G3 Awards, 2013. *Publications:* The Battle for Bermondsey, 1983; Democratic Defence: a non-nuclear alternative, 1985; AIDS: a guide to survival, 1986, 3rd edn 1990; Europe in the Pink: lesbian and gay equality in the New Europe, 1992; Safer Sexy: the guide to gay sex safely, 1994; We Don't Want to March Straight: masculinity, queers and the military, 1995; *contributor:* Nuclear-Free Defence, 1983; Into the Twenty-First Century, 1988; Getting There: steps to a green society, 1990; Anti-Gay, 1996; The Penguin Book of Twentieth Century Protest, 1998; Teenage Sex: what should schools teach children?, 2002; The Hate Debate: should hate be punished as a crime?, 2002; Sex and Politics in South Africa, 2005; Good Company: ideas on modern republicanism, 2009; 50 Voices of Disbelief, 2009. *Recreations:* mountain hiking, surfing, art and design, ambushing tyrants and torturers. *Address:* Peter Tatchell Foundation, Studio 5, Disney Place House, 14 Marshalsea Road, SE1 1HL. *E:* Peter@PeterTatchellFoundation.org. *W:* www.twitter.com/PeterTatchell. *Club:* Heaven.

TATE, Ann, CBE 2011; Vice Chancellor, University of Northampton, 2005–10; Chairman, Ipswich Hospital NHS Trust, since 2012; *b* 27 May 1949; *d* of Norman Cooper and Sybil (*née* Judson); *m* 1975, Rodney Tate; one *d*. *Educ:* Queen Elizabeth's Grammar Sch., Middleton; Univ. of London ext. (BSc Hons Sociol. 1970); Bedford Coll., Univ. of London (MSc Sociol. Applied to Medicine 1984). Asst Teacher, Lancs LEA, 1970–71; Lecturer: Belfast Coll. of Business Studies, 1972–74; Ulster Poly., 1974–84; University of Ulster: Sen. Lectr, 1984–95; Pro-Vice-Chancellor, 1995–2002; Rector, UC Northampton, 2002–05. Board Member: HEFCE, 2003–09; W Northants Develt Corp., 2005–10; Mem., Northants LSC, 2003–08. FRSA 1999. DUniv Ulster, 2007. *Recreations:* golf, cooking, walking. *Address:* Two Chimneys, 5 Spencer's Piece, Rattlesden, Suffolk IP30 0SA. *Club:* Reform.

TATE, Prof. Austin, PhD; FREng; FRSE; Professor of Knowledge-Based Systems, since 1995, and Director, Artificial Intelligence Applications Institute, since 1985, University of Edinburgh; *b* Knottingley, W Yorks, 12 May 1951; *s* of Charles Tate and Irene Tate; *m* 1975, Margaret Mowbray. *Educ:* King's Sch., Pontefract; Lancaster Univ. (BA Hons Computer Studies 1972); Univ. of Edinburgh (PhD Machine Intelligence 1975; MSc E-Learning 2012). CEng 1993; FBCS 2000; FREng 2012. University of Edinburgh: Res. Fellow, Dept of Artificial Intelligence, 1975–76; Software Engineer, Data Base Gp, Computer Support Officer and Manager, Microcomputer Support Unit, Edinburgh Regl Computing Centre, 1976–83; Information Technol. Fellow, 1983–84; Asst Dir, Artificial Intelligence Applications Inst., Leader, Knowledge Based Planning Gp and Systems Designers Fellow, 1984–85; Professorial Fellow, 1989–95; Coordinator, Virtual Univ. of Edinburgh, 2005–; Coordinator, Distance Educn, 2012–, Sch. of Informatics. Sen. Res. Scientist, Inst. for Human and Machine Cognition, Florida, 2010–. FRSE 1999. FAAAI 1993; Fellow: Workflow Mgt Coalition, 1998; Soc. for Study of Artificial Intelligence and Simulation of Behaviour, 1999; Eur. Coordinating Cttee on Artificial Intelligence, 1999. *Recreations:* travel, walking, photography, graphic art, space. *Address:* School of Informatics, University of Edinburgh, Crichton Street, Edinburgh EH8 9AB. *T:* (0131) 651 3222. *E:* a.tate@ed.ac.uk.

TATE, Dr (Edward) Nicholas, CBE 2001; Director-General, International School of Geneva, 2003–11; Chairman, International Education Systems, 2011–13; *b* 18 Dec. 1943; *s* of Joseph Edwin Tate and Eva Elsie Tate; *m* 1973, Nadya Grove; one *s* two *d*. *Educ:* Huddersfield New Coll.; Balliol Coll., Oxford (Scholar; MA); Univ. of Bristol (PGCE); Univ. of Liverpool (MA; PhD 1985). Teacher, De La Salle Coll., Sheffield, 1966–71; Lectr, City of Birmingham Coll. of Educn, 1972–74; Lectr, then Sen. Lectr, Moray House Coll. of Educn, Edinburgh, 1974–88; Professional Officer, Nat. Curriculum Council, 1989–91; Asst Chief Exec., Sch. Exams and Assessment Council, 1991–93; Asst Chief Exec., 1993–94, Chief Exec., 1994–97, SCAA; Chief Exec., QCA, 1997–2000; Headmaster, Winchester Coll., 2000–03. Pres., Earth Focus Foundn, 2005–10. Member, Board of Governors: Internat. Schs Assoc., 2005–10; Internat. Baccalaureate, 2009–15. Trustee: Nat. Trust, 1996–99; Richmond, The American Internat. Univ. in London, 2008– (Vice-Chm., 2013–). Hon. DCL Huddersfield, 1998. *Publications:* various history books for schools; articles on history and education. *Recreations:* reading, music. *E:* nick@nicholastate.com. *Club:* Reform.

TATE, Sir Edward Nicholas, 6th Bt *cr* 1898, of Park Hill, Streatham; *b* 2 July 1966; *e s* of Sir (Henry) Saxon Tate, 5th Bt, CBE and Sheila Ann (*née* Robertson); *S* father, 2012, but his name does not appear on the Official Roll of the Baronetage; *m* 1996, Rosalind Susan (*née* Coward); two *d*. *Heir: b* Duncan Saxon Tate [*b* 30 April 1968; *m* 2006, Nicola Stockwell; two *s* one *d* (and one *s* decd)]. *Address:* The Isle, Isle Lane, Bicton, Shrewsbury SY3 8EE.

TATE, Dr Jeffrey Philip, CBE 1990; Chief Conductor, Hamburg Symphoniker, since 2009; *b* 28 April 1943; *s* of Cyril Henry Tate and Ivy Ellen Naylor (*née* Evans). *Educ:* Farnham Grammar Sch.; Christ's Coll., Cambridge (MA; MB, BChir; Hon. Fellow, 1989); St Thomas' Hosp., London. Trained as doctor of medicine, 1961–67; left medicine for London Opera Centre, 1969; joined Covent Garden Staff, 1970; assisted conductors who included Kempe, Krips, Solti, Davies, Kleiber, for performances and recordings; records made as harpsichordist, 1973–77; Assistant to Boulez for Bayreuth Ring, 1976–81; joined Cologne Opera as assistant to Sir John Pritchard, 1977; conducted Gothenberg Opera, Sweden, 1978–80; NY Metropolitan Opera début, USA, 1979; Covent Garden début, 1982; Salzburg Fest. début (world première Henze/Monteverdi), 1985; Principal Conductor, English Chamber Orch., 1985–95; Principal Conductor, 1986–91, Principal Guest Conductor, 1991–94, Royal Opera House, Covent Garden; Chief Conductor and Artistic Dir, Rotterdam Phil. Orch., 1991–94; Chief Guest Conductor, Geneva Opera, 1983–95; Principal Guest Conductor: Orchestre National de France, 1989–98; RAI Nazionale Orch., Turin, 1998–2002 (Hon. Dir, 2002; Hon. Conductor, 2004–); Artistic Dir, Minnesota Orch. Summer Fest., 1997–2000; Musical Dir, Teatro San Carlo, Naples, 2005–10. Appearances with major symph. orchs in Europe and Amer.; numerous recordings with English Chamber Orch. President: ASBAH, 1989–; Music Space Trust, 1991–. Hon. DMus Leicester, 1993. Comdr, Ordre des Arts et des Lettres (France); Chevalier, Légion d'Honneur (France), 1999. *Recreations:* church-crawling, with gastronomic interludes.

TATE, John Richard; Chief Operating Officer, Tamkeen, Abu Dhabi Executive Affairs Authority, since 2014; *b* British Forces, Hanover, 3 Jan. 1975; *s* of Anthony James Tate and Patricia Mary Skipper (*née* McKay); *m* 2003, Fatiha Selmi; one *s* one *d*. *Educ:* Univ. of Essex (BA 1st Cl. Hons 1996); Queen's Coll., Oxford (MPhil 1999). Hd of Res., Eur. Foundn, 1999–2000; Sen. Associate, McKinsey & Co., 2000–03; Hd, Cons. Party Policy Unit, 2003–05; Mgt Consultant, PA Consulting, 2005–07; Dir, Strategic Ops, then Policy and Strategy, BBC, 2007–14; Chm., BBC Studios and Post Production, 2011–14. *Publications:* What's Right Now?, 2006. *Recreations:* aviation, photography, ski-ing. *Address:* Tamkeen, Abu Dhabi Executive Affairs Authority, 10th Floor, Al Mamoura Building, Abu Dhabi, UAE.

TATE, Nicholas; *see* Tate, E. N.

TATE, William John; non-executive Chairman, Your Healthcare CIC, 2010–14; *b* 12 June 1951; *s* of William Kenneth Tate and Dorothy Tate; *m* 1976, Helen Elizabeth Quick; one *s* one *d*. *Educ:* Eastcliffe Grammar Sch., Newcastle upon Tyne; King's Coll., London (LLB 1973). Called to the Bar, Gray's Inn, 1974; Flt Lieut, RAF Directorate of Legal Services, 1976–78; Solicitor's Office, HM Customs and Excise: Legal Asst, 1978–80; Sen. Legal Asst, 1980–86; Sen. Prin. Legal Officer, 1986–88; Asst Dir, Serious Fraud Office, 1988–96; Dep. Parly Comr for Admin, 1996–99; Solicitor to Bloody Sunday Inquiry, 1999–2003; Dir of Legal Services, Ind. Police Complaints Commn, 2004–09. Non-executive Director: Kingston NHS PCT, 2007–10; First Community Health and Care CIC, 2011–12. Lay Mem., Gen. Social Care Council, 2009–12; Chair of Specialist Schs, NHS London Deanery, 2010–14. *Publications:* (Delegated Legislation Ed.) Current Law, annually 1975–95. *Recreations:* reading, music, gardening. *Club:* Royal Air Force.

TATHAM, David Everard, CMG 1991; HM Diplomatic Service, retired; consultant; *b* 28 June 1939; *s* of late Lt-Col Francis Everard Tatham and Eileen Mary Wilson; *m* 1963, Valerie Ann Mylechreest; three *s*. *Educ:* St Lawrence Coll., Ramsgate; Wadham Coll., Oxford (BA History). Entered HM Diplomatic Service, 1960; New York, 1962–63; Milan, 1963–67; ME Centre for Arabic Studies, 1967–69; Jeddah, 1969–70; FCO, 1971–74; Muscat, 1974–77; Asst Head of ME Dept, FCO, 1977–80; Counsellor, Dublin, 1981–84; Ambassador to Yemen Arab Republic, also accredited to Republic of Djibouti, 1984–87; Hd of Falkland Is Dept, FCO, 1987–90; Ambassador to Lebanese Republic, 1990–92; Governor, Falkland Is, and Comr for S Georgia and S Sandwich Is, 1992–96; High Comr, Sri Lanka, also accred to Republic of Maldives, 1996–99. Adviser to Palestinian Authy on Diplomatic Trng, 2000; Census Dist Manager, Ledbury/Ross, 2000–01. Chm., Shackleton Scholarship Fund, 1999–; Vice Pres., Falkland Islands Assoc., 2012– (Chm., 2004–11); President: S Georgia Assoc., 2012–; Friends of Falklands Mus. and Archives, 2013–. Ed., Dictionary of Falklands Biography Project, 2002–08. *Publications:* (ed) The Dictionary of Falklands Biography, 2008. *Recreations:* walking uphill, fishing, historical research. *Address:* South Parade, Ledbury, Hereford HR8 2HA. *T:* (01531) 579090. *E:* d_tatham@hotmail.com. *Clubs:* Athenæum, Geographical.

See also M. H. Tatham.

TATHAM, Michael Harry; HM Diplomatic Service; Director, Eastern Europe and Central Asia, Foreign and Commonwealth Office, since 2015; *b* 2 July 1965; *s* of David Everard Tatham, *qv*; *m* 1998, Belinda Cherrington. *Educ:* Oundle Sch.; Merton Coll., Oxford (BA Hons). Entered FCO, 1987; Third, later Second, Sec., Prague, 1989–93; FCO, 1993–95; Private Sec. to Minister of State, 1995–96; Dep. Hd of Mission, Sofia, 1997–99; on secondment as Private Sec. to Prime Minister, 1999–2002; Dep. Hd of Mission, Prague, 2002–05; Balkans Co-ordinator and Hd, Western Balkans Gp, 2006–08; Ambassador to Bosnia and Herzegovina, 2008–11; Political Counsellor, UK Mission to UN, NY, 2011–15. *Recreations:* mountain hiking, the music of Bob Dylan, cookery. *Address:* c/o Foreign and Commonwealth Office, SW1A 2AH.

TATTEN, Jonathan Altenburger; Consultant, Dentons (formerly Denton Hall, then Denton Wilde Sapte, then SNR Denton), Solicitors, since 2008 (Partner, 1983–2008; Managing Partner, 1993–99; Head of European and Competition Law Department, 2003–07); *b* 17 March 1952; *s* of John Stephenson Tatten and Anna Tatten. *Educ:* Duke of York Sch., Nairobi; Exeter Univ. (LLB); Harvard Business Sch. (AMP). Trainee solicitor, Trower Still & Keeling, 1973–76; solicitor, Holman Fenwick & Willan, Solicitors, 1976–83. *Recreations:* opera, pugs, eating. *Address:* 4 Coutts Crescent, St Albans Road, NW5 1RF.

TATTERSALL, Geoffrey Frank; QC 1992; a Recorder, since 1989; a Deputy High Court Judge, since 2003; *b* 22 Sept. 1947; *s* of late Frank Tattersall and of Margaret (*née* Hassall); *m* 1971, Hazel Shaw; one *s* two *d*. *Educ:* Manchester Grammar Sch.; Christ Church, Oxford (MA Jurisprudence). Called to the Bar, Lincoln's Inn, 1970 (Tancred Studentship in Common Law), Bencher, 1997; in practice, Northern Circuit, 1970–; called to the Bar, NSW, 1992; SC 1995; Judge of Appeal, IOM, 1997–. External Reviewer of Decisions of Dir of Fair Access, 2005–. Lay Chm., Bolton Deanery Synod, 1993–2002; Chm., House of Laity and Vice Pres., Manchester Diocesan Synod, 1994–2003; Mem., Gen. Synod, 1995– (Chm., Standing Orders Cttee, 1999–; Mem., Legislative Cttee, 2010–; Panel of Chairmen, 2011–); Diocesan Chancellor: Carlisle, 2003–; Manchester, 2004–; Dep. Diocesan Chancellor, Durham, 2003–05; Dep. Vicar-Gen., Dio. of Sodor and Man, 2004–08, 2014–; Chairman: Disciplinary Tribunals under Clergy Discipline Measure, 2006–; Revision Cttees for draft C of E Marriage Measure, 2006–07 and draft Ecclesiastical Offices Measure, 2007–08; Synodical Govt Amendment Measure, 2014; Mem., Steering Cttee, Draft Bishops and Priests (Consecration and Ordination of Women) Measure, 2009–. Hon. Lay Canon, Manchester Cathedral, 2003–; Parish Clerk, St George-in-the-East, London, 2008–. Mem., Parish Clerks' Co., 2009–. *Recreations:* family, music, travel. *Address:* 12 Byrom Street, Manchester M3 4PP. *T:* (0161) 829 2100.

TATTERSALL, Jane Patricia; *see* Griffiths, Jane P.

TATTERSFIELD, Prof. Anne Elizabeth, OBE 2005; MD; FRCP, FMedSci; Professor of Respiratory Medicine, University of Nottingham, 1984–2005, now Emeritus; Hon. Consultant Physician, City Hospital, Nottingham, 1984–2005; *b* 13 June 1940; *d* of Charles Percival Tattersfield and Bessie Wharton Tattersfield (*née* Walker). *Educ:* Fairfield High Sch., Manchester; Durham Univ. (MB BS 1963); MD Newcastle 1970. MRCP 1966, FRCP 1979. Jun. hosp. posts, Royal Victoria Infirmary, Newcastle, Leicester Royal Infirmary, Central Middx Hosp. and Brompton Hosp., 1963–66; Medical and Research Registrar posts: Central Middx Hosp., 1966–69; Hammersmith Hosp., 1969–71; Sen. Registrar, London Hosp., 1971–74; Sen. Lectr and Reader in Medicine, Southampton Univ., 1974–83. Sir James Wattie Meml Vis. Prof., NZ, 1987. Altounyan Lectr, British Thoracic Soc., 1995; Philip Ellman Lectr, RCP, 1999. Pres., British Thoracic Soc., 2000 (Gold Medal, 2004). FMedSci 1998. *Publications:* (with M. W. McNicol) Respiratory Disease, 1987; contribs to scientific pubns on asthma, airway pharmacol. and lymphangioleiomyomatosis. *Recreations:* travel, opera, gardening. *Address:* Priory Barn, The Hollows, Thurgarton, Notts NG14 7GY.

TATTERSFIELD, Christian Alexander; Director, Good Soldier Songs and Good Soldier Records; *b* London, 24 Aug. 1967; *s* of Margaret van der Poest Clement; *m* 2003, Eleanor Lewis-Bale; two *s*. *Educ:* King Alfred Sch.; Selwyn Coll., Cambridge (BA Hons Eng. Lit. 1989; MA). London Records, 1990–97 (est. Systematic and Internal labels); BMG, 1997 (Founder, NorthWestSide imprint; signed Jay-Z, Another Level, N Sync); Man. Dir, Eastwest Records (signed David Gray), 2000–03; Founder, 14th Floor, 2003 (signed Biffy Clyro, The Wombats, Damian Rice, Ray Lamontagne); CEO, Warner Music UK and Chm., Warner Bros Records UK, 2009–14. *Recreation:* cricket. *Address:* Good Soldier, Top Floor, Unit 16, Tileyard Studios, N7 9AH. *T:* (020) 3728 9100. *E:* christian@goodsoldiersongs.com.

TATTON-BROWN, Timothy William Trelawny; architectural historian; freelance archaeologist; *b* 3 Feb. 1947; *s* of Robert and Daphne Tatton-Brown; *m* 1979, Veronica Wilson (*d* 2012); two *s* two *d*. *Educ:* Tonbridge Sch., Kent; Inst. of Archaeol., University Coll. London (BA Hons Roman Archaeol.). Dir, Canterbury Archaeological Trust, 1975–85; consultant archaeologist: to Canterbury Cathedral, 1976–87; Rochester Cathedral, 1987–2006; Chichester Cathedral, 1988–93; Salisbury Cathedral, 1990–2011; St George's Chapel, Windsor Castle, 1991–2013; Westminster Abbey, 1998–2004; Lambeth Palace, 1998–2001; Westminster Sch., 2002–. Mem., Adv. Cttee, Historic England (formerly English Heritage), 2012–. Chairman: British Brick Soc., 1981–86; Rescue - British Archaeol Trust, 1983–86. Vice Pres., Royal Archaeol Inst., 2008–14. *Publications:* Great Cathedrals of Britain, 1989; (ed jtly) St Dunstan: his life, times and cult, 1992; Canterbury: history and guide, 1994; Lambeth Palace: a history of the Archbishops of Canterbury and their houses, 2000; The English Cathedral, 2002; (ed with R. Mortimer) Westminster Abbey: the Lady Chapel of Henry VII, 2003; The English Church, 2005; The Abbeys and Priories of England, 2006; (ed with T. Ayers) Medieval Art, Architecture and Archaeology at Rochester, 2006; Salisbury Cathedral: the making of a medieval masterpiece, 2009; (ed with N. Saul) St George's Chapel, Windsor: history and heritage, 2011. *Recreations:* choral singing, canal boating, book collecting, walking and landscape study, church crawling. *Address:* Fisherton Mill House, Mill Road, Salisbury, Wilts SP2 7RZ.

TAUB, Prof. Liba, PhD; FSA; FRHistS; Director and Curator, Whipple Museum of the History of Science, since 1995, and Professor of History and Philosophy of Science, since 2010, University of Cambridge; Fellow, Newnham College, Cambridge, since 1996; *b* NY, 15 Nov. 1954; *d* of Ronald Herbert Taub and Ethel Betty Flecker Taub; *m* 1988, Niall Caldwell. *Educ:* Newcomb Coll., Tulane Univ. (BA 1975); Univ. of Chicago (MA 1978); Univ. of Oklahoma (MA 1981; PhD 1987); Univ. of Texas. Vis. Instructor, Univ. of Kentucky, 1985–87; Mary Isabel Sibley Fellow in Greek Studies, United Chapters of Phi Beta Kappa, 1987–88; Res. Fellow, Amer. Council of Learned Socs, 1988–89; Curator and Hd of Hist. of Astronomy Dept, Adler Planetarium, Chicago, 1991–94; Reader in Hist. and Philosophy of Sci., Univ. of Cambridge, 2003–10. Visiting Scholar: Univ. of Leiden, 2000; Deutsches Mus., 2005; Karman Centre for Advanced Studies in Humanities, Univ. of Bern, 2006; Horning Vis. Schol., Oregon State Univ., 2007; Einstein Foundn Vis. Fellow, TOPOI Excellence Cluster, Berlin, 2010–14. Member: UK Spoliation Adv. Panel, 2000–; Mgt Bd, Cambridge Inst. for Sustainability Leadership, 2009–14; Evaluation Panel, Res. in Museums, VolkswagenStiftung, 2013. Mem., Wissenschaftliche Beirat, Deutsches Mus., 2002–14; Corresp. Mem., Acad. Internat. d'Histoire des Scis, 2012–. Trustee, Freud Mus., 2007–13. Mem., Heritage Cttee, RAS, 2010–. FSA 2007; FRHistS 2014. *Publications:* Ptolemy's Universe: the natural, philosophical and ethical foundations of Ptolemy's astronomy, 1993; Ancient Meteorology, 2003 (trans Greek, 2008); (ed with Frances Willmoth) The Whipple Museum of the History of Science: instruments and interpretations, 2006; Aetna and the Moon: explaining nature in ancient Greece and Rome, 2008; (ed with Aude Doody) Authorial Voices in Greco-Roman Technical Writing, 2009; contrib. articles to books and jls. *Recreations:* opera, the outdoors, cake. *Address:* Whipple Museum of the History of Science, Free School Lane, Cambridge CB2 3RH. *T:* (01223) 334500, *Fax:* (01223) 334554. *Club:* Athenæum.

TAUBE, Prof. (Hirsch) David, FRCP; Professor of Transplant Medicine, Imperial College London, since 2006; Consultant Nephrologist, St Mary's Hospital, London, Northwick Park Hospital, Harrow, and Royal Brompton Hospital, London, since 1990, and Hammersmith Hospital, London, since 2004; Director, Imperial College Academic Health Science Centre, Imperial College Healthcare NHS Trust, since 2012; *b* 4 Oct. 1948; *s* of Ernest and Hilary Taube; *m* 1990, Dr Clare Allen; one *s* one *d*. *Educ:* St Catharine's Coll., Cambridge (BA 1970); Magdalen Coll., Oxford (BM BCh 1970). FRCP 1987. Consultant Nephrologist, King's Coll. Hosp., 1985–90. Chief of Service, W London Renal and Transplant Medicine, St Mary's NHS Trust and Hammersmith Hosps NHS Trust, 2000–04; Hammersmith Hospitals NHS Trust, later Imperial College Healthcare NHS Trust: Clinical Dir, W London Renal and Transplant Centre, 2004–12; Medical Dir, 2007–12. *Publications:* over 145 articles in learned jls, mainly on transplantation and renal medicine. *Recreations:* swimming, digital photography, work. *Address:* Imperial College Academic Health Science Centre, Imperial College Healthcare NHS Trust, Hammersmith Hospital, Du Cane Road, W12 0HS. *T:* (020) 8383 4355, *Fax:* (020) 3313 3100; 66 Harley Street, W1G 7HD. *T:* (020) 7636 6628, *Fax:* (020) 7631 5341. *E:* davidtaube@msn.com.

TAUBE, Simon Axel Robin; QC 2000; *b* 16 June 1957; *s* of late Nils Taube and of Idonea Taube; *m* 1984, Karen Pilkington; three *d. Educ:* Merton Coll., Oxford (BA Hist.). Called to the Bar, Middle Temple, 1980; in practice at Chancery Bar, 1980–. Bencher, Lincoln's Inn, 2008. *Recreations:* singing, tennis, hill-walking. *Address:* 10 Old Square, Lincoln's Inn, WC2A 3SU. *T:* (020) 7405 0758.

TAUNTON, Bishop Suffragan of, since 2015; **Rt Rev. Ruth Elizabeth Worsley;** *b* 1962; *m* Rev. Dr Howard Worsley; three *s. Educ:* Univ. of Manchester; St John's Coll., Nottingham. Ordained deacon, 1996, priest, 1997; Curate, Basford with Hyson Green, 1996–98; Asst Curate, 1998–2001, Priest-in-charge, 2001–08, Hyson Green and Forest Fields; Area Dean, Nottingham N, 2006–08; Dean of Women's Ministry, Dio. of Southwell and Nottingham, 2007–10; Priest-in-charge, St Christopher with St Philip, Sneinton, 2008–10; Parish Develt Officer, Dio. of Southwark, 2010–13; Archdeacon of Wilts, 2013–15. A Chaplain to the Queen, 2009–15. Hon. Canon, Southwell Minster, 2007–10. *Address:* c/o Diocese of Bath and Wells, The Old Deanery, St Andrew's Street, Wells, Som BA5 2UG.

TAUNTON, Archdeacon of; *see* Reed, Ven. J. P. C.

TAUSSIG, Andrew John, PhD; Director of Foreign Language Services, BBC World Service, 1996–2000; *b* 30 March 1944; *s* of Leo Charles Taussig and Magdalene Taussig (*née* Szücs); *m* 1971, Margaret Celia Whines; one *s* two *d. Educ:* Bramcote Sch., Scarborough; Winchester Coll. (Schol.); Magdalen Coll., Oxford (MA Hons Modern History 1962); Harvard Univ. (PhD Pol Sci. 1970). British Broadcasting Corporation, 1971–2000: Gen. Trainee, World Service Talks Dept, BBC North Leeds, and Radio Current Affairs, 1971–72; TV Current Affairs, 1973–80; Special Asst to Dir, News and Current Affairs, 1979–80; Dep. Editor, Nationwide, 1980–81; Chief Asst, TV Current Affairs, 1982–86; Head of Central European Service, 1986–88; Controller, European Services, 1988–94; Regl Head, Europe, 1994–96. Res. Associate (Media Prog.), Centre for Socio-Legal Studies, Univ. of Oxford, 2001–11; Consultant, British Council, World Summit on Inf. Soc., Geneva, 2003; Moderator, Asia-Europe Foundn Colloquium, Larnaca, 2006, Nanjing, 2007; Consultant to UNESCO, New Delhi Internat. Conf. on Disability, 2014–15. Lectr, Cardiff Univ. Sch. of Journalism, Media and Cultural Studies, 2002–03; Consultant, Faculty of Social Scis, Open Univ., 2009–11. Dir, CPTM Ltd (Commonwealth Partners for Technol. Management), 2012– (Mem., 2001–); Member: Council, RIIA (Chatham Hse), 2002–05; Internat. Adv. Council, Asia Media Inf. and Communication Centre, Singapore, 2004–; Trustee, Internat. Inst. of Communications, 2005–14. Trustee, Voice of the Listener & Viewer, 2004–13. MInstD 2002. *Recreations:* photography, travelling. *Address:* 115 Rosebery Road, Langley Vale, Epsom Downs, Surrey KT18 6AB. *T:* (01372) 276257. *Club:* Le Beaujolais.

TAUWHARE, Richard David, MVO 1983; Senior Director, Dechert LLP, since 2015; *b* 1 Nov. 1959; *s* of Albert and Ann Tauwhare; *m* 1985, Amanda; one *s* two *d. Educ:* Abingdon Sch.; Jesus Coll., Cambridge (BA Hist. 1980); Sch. of Oriental and African Studies, London. Joined FCO, 1980; Swahili lang. trng, 1982; Third, then Second Sec., Nairobi, 1982–86; Second, then First Sec., UK Delegn to OECD, 1986–89; FCO, 1989–94; First Sec., then Dep. Perm. Rep., UK Disarmament Delegn, Geneva, 1994–99; FCO, 1999–2005; Gov., Turks and Caicos Islands, 2005–08; FCO, 2008–14; Dir, Green Light Exports Consulting, 2014–15. *Recreations:* tennis, golf, reading, travel.

TAVARÉ, Prof. Simon, PhD; FMedSci; FRS 2011; Professor of Cancer Research (Bioinformatics), Department of Oncology and Professor, Department of Applied Mathematics and Theoretical Physics, since 2003, and Director, Cancer Research UK Cambridge Institute, since 2013, University of Cambridge; Fellow, Christ's College, Cambridge, since 2004; *b* 13 May 1952; *s* of Sir John Tavaré, CBE; *m* 1973, Caroline Jane Page; one *s* one *d. Educ:* Oundle Sch.; Univ. of Sheffield (BSc 1974, MSc 1975; PhD 1979). CStat 1993; CSci 2009. Lectr, Univ. of Sheffield, 1977–78; Res. Fellow, 1978–79, Instructor, 1978–81, Univ. of Utah; Asst and Associate Prof., Colorado State Univ., 1981–85; Associate Prof., Univ. of Utah, 1985–89; Prof., 1989–2014, George and Louise Kawamoto Chair of Biol Scis, 1998–2014, USC. Vis. posts at univs in USA, Australia, England, Sweden, Switzerland and France. Medallion Lectr, Inst. Mathematical Stats, 1993, 2001. Pres., LMS, 2015–. FIMS 1992; FAAAS 1998; FASA 2004; FMedSci 2009; FRSB (FSB 2009); FIMA 2010. Hon. DTech Chalmers Univ. of Technol., 2014. *Publications:* (ed with P. J. Donnelly) Progress in Population Genetics and Human Evolution, 1997; (jtly) Logarithmic Combinatorial Structures: a probabilistic approach, 2003; (with O. Zeitouni) Lectures on Probability and Statistics, Ecole d'Etés de Probabilité de Saint-Flour XXXI, 2004; (jtly) Computational Genome Analysis: an introduction, 2005; numerous articles in learned jls. *Address:* Cancer Research UK Cambridge Institute, University of Cambridge, Li Ka Shing Centre, Robinson Way, Cambridge CB2 0RE. *T:* (01223) 769501. *E:* st321@cam.ac.uk.

TAVERNE, family name of **Baron Taverne**.

TAVERNE, Baron *cr* 1996 (Life Peer), of Pimlico in the City of Westminster; **Dick Taverne;** QC 1965; Chairman, Monitoring Board, AXA Sun Life plc, 2001–11 (Director, 1972–97, Chairman, 1997–2001, AXA Equity & Law Life Assurance Society plc); *b* 18 Oct. 1928; *s* of Dr N. J. M. and Mrs L. V. Taverne; *m* 1955, Janice Hennessey; two *d. Educ:* Charterhouse School; Balliol College, Oxford (First in Greats). Oxford Union Debating tour of USA, 1951. Called to Bar, 1954. MP (Lab) Lincoln, March 1962–Oct. 1972, resigned; MP (Democratic Lab) Lincoln, March 1973–Sept. 1974; Parliamentary Under-Secretary of State, Home Office, 1966–68; Minister of State, Treasury, 1968–69; Financial Secretary to the Treasury, 1969–70. Chm., Public Expenditure (General) Sub-Cttee, 1971–72. Institute for Fiscal Studies: First Dir, 1970; Dir-Gen., 1979–81; Chm., 1981–82; Chm., Public Policy Centre, 1984–87. Non-exec. Dir, BOC Gp, 1975–95; Dir, PRIMA Europe Ltd, 1987–98 (Chm., 1991–93; Pres., 1993–98). Mem., Internat. Ind. Review Body to review workings of European Commn, 1979. Chairman: Alcohol and Drug Prevention and Treatment Ltd, 1996–2008; (and Founder) Sense About Science, 2002–12. Member: Nat. Cttee, SDP, 1981–87; Federal Policy Cttee, Liberal Democrats, 1989–90. Contested (SDP): Southwark, Peckham, Oct. 1982; Dulwich, 1983. Parly Sci. Communicator of the Year, Assoc. of British Sci. Writers, 2006. *Publications:* The Future of the Left: Lincoln and after, 1973; The March of Unreason - Science, Democracy and the New Fundamentalism, 2005; Against the Tide: politics and beyond: a memoir, 2014. *Recreation:* sailing. *Address:* 25 Tufton Court, Tufton Street, SW1P 3QH.

See also M. F. Jermey, S. Taverne.

TAVERNE, Suzanna; Trustee, BBC Trust, since 2012; *b* 3 Feb. 1960; *d* of Baron Taverne, *qv* and Janice Taverne (*née* Hennessey); *m* 1993, Marc Vlessing; one *s* one *d. Educ:* Balliol Coll., Oxford (BA Hons 1982). S. G. Warburg and Co. Ltd, 1982–90; Head, Strategic Planning, 1990–92, Finance Dir, 1992–94, Newspaper Publishing plc; Consultant, Saatchi and Saatchi, 1994–95; Dir, Strategy and Develt, then Man. Dir FT Finance, Pearson plc, 1995–98; Man. Dir, British Museum, 1999–2002; Dir of Ops, Imperial Coll. London, 2003–05; Chm., Gingerbread (formerly NCOPF, then One Parent Families | Gingerbread), 2002–11 (Trustee, 1996–2011). Non-executive Director: Nationwide Building Soc., 2005–12; Ford Financial Europe, 2008–. Trustee: Design Museum, 2007–12; StepChange Debt Charity (formerly Consumer Credit Counselling Service), 2009–; Shakespeare Schools Festival, 2010–. *Address:* 35 Camden Square, NW1 9XA.

TAVERNER, Marcus Louis; QC 2000; *b* 24 April 1958; *s* of Geoffrey Clifford Taverner, DFC and Mildred Taverner (née Thomas); *m* 1983, Dr Deborah Mary Hall; one *s* three *d. Educ:* Monmouth Sch.; Leicester Univ. (LLB Hons); King's Coll. London (LLM). Called to the Bar, Gray's Inn, 1981, Bencher, 2007. Dir, Taverner Develts Ltd, 1996–. *Recreations:* 4 children, opera, guitar, dramatics, theatre, Stevenage FC (Dir, 2008–).

TAVERNOR, Prof. Robert William, PhD; RIBA; Professor of Architecture and Urban Design, London School of Economics, 2005–10, now Emeritus; Founding Director, Professor Robert Tavernor Consultancy Ltd, London and Bath, since 2001; *b* 19 Dec. 1954; *s* of late Michael Frederic Tavernor and of Elisabeth Veronica Tavernor (*née* Hooker); *m* 1976, Denise Alexandra Mackie; one *s* two *d. Educ:* Poly. of Central London (BA 1976; DipArch with Dist. 1979); British Sch. at Rome (Scholar in Arch. 1980); St John's Coll., Cambridge (PhD 1985). RIBA 1985. Lectr in Arch., Univ. of Bath, 1987–92; Forbes Prof. of Arch., Univ. of Edinburgh, 1992–95; University of Bath: Prof. of Arch., 1995–2005; Hd, Dept of Arch. and Civil Engrg, 2003–05; Dir, Cities Prog., LSE, 2005–08. Visiting Professor: UCLA, 1998; Univ. of São Paulo, 2004; Univ. of Bath, 2009–; EU Vis. Scholar, Texas A&M Univ., 2002. *Publications:* Palladio and Palladianism, 1991; (ed) Edinburgh, 1996; On Alberti and the Art of Building, 1998; (ed jtly) Body and Building: essays on the changing relation of body and architecture, 2002; Smoot's Ear: the measure of humanity, 2007; (ed) The London Plan 2000–2010: a decade of transformation, 2010; *translations:* (jtly) Alberti, On the Art of Building in Ten Books, 1988; (jtly) Palladio, The Four Books on Architecture, 1997; (jtly) Vitruvius, On Architecture, 2009. *Recreations:* writing, running with Bertie, watching Bath Rugby. *Address:* Southcot House, 37 Lyncombe Hill, Bath BA2 4PQ. *E:* robert@tavernorconsultancy.co.uk.

TAVINOR, Very Rev. Michael Edward; Dean of Hereford, since 2002; *b* 11 Sept. 1953; *s* of Harold and Elsie Tavinor. *Educ:* Durham Univ. (BA Music 1975); Emmanuel Coll., Cambridge (PGCE 1976); King's Coll., London (AKC, MMus 1977); Ripon Coll., Cuddesdon (BA 1981, MA 1986, Oxon); Univ. of Wales, Lampeter (MTh 2010). ARCO 1977; ARSCM 2015. Ordained deacon, 1982, priest, 1983; Curate, St Peter, Ealing, 1982–85; Precentor, Sacrist and Minor Canon, Ely Cathedral, 1985–90; Priest i/c, Stuntney, 1987–90; Vicar, Tewkesbury Abbey with Walton Cardiff, 1990–2002, also Twyning, 1999–2002. Hon. Canon, Gloucester Cathedral, 1997–2002. Pres., Ch Music Soc., 2003–. Hon. FGCM, 2006. *Publications:* Pilgrim Guide to Tewkesbury Abbey, 1998; Pilgrim Guide to Hereford Cathedral, 2003; (contrib.) Sacred Space: House of God, Gate of Heaven, 2007; Saints and Sinners of the Marches, 2012. *Recreations:* walking, music, gardening, coin collecting. *Address:* The Deanery, College Cloisters, Cathedral Close, Hereford HR1 2NG. *T:* (01432) 374203. *E:* Dean@herefordcathedral.org.

TAVISTOCK, Marquess of; Henry Robin Charles Russell; *b* 7 June 2005; *s* and *heir* of Duke of Bedford, *qv*.

TAVNER, Teresa, (Terry); Editor at large, Woman's Own, since 2012 (Editor, 1998–2002); consultant editor, since 2005; Director, Headztrong Ltd, since 2009; Editor: Chat magazine, 1989–96; She magazine, 2003–05; *b* 18 Jan. 1952; *d* of Bernard Joseph Hayes and Hanorah Hayes; *m* 1972, Barry Tavner (decd); one *s* one *d. Educ:* Notre Dame Grammar Sch., Battersea. Sub Ed. and Fiction Ed., Honey mag., 1981–84; Dep. Chief Sub-Ed., then Chief Sub-Ed., then Asst Ed., She mag., 1984–88; Ed., Eva mag., 1997–98. Editors' Editor, BSME, 1990. *Recreations:* ski-ing, travelling, cinema, reading, socialising. *E:* ttavner@aol.com.

TAYLER, His Honour (Harold) Clive; QC 1979; a Circuit Judge, 1984–99; *b* 4 Nov. 1932; *m* 1959, Catherine Jane (*née* Thomas); two *s* one *d. Educ:* Solihull Sch.; Balliol Coll., Oxford (Eldon Schol.); BCL and BA (Jurisprudence); Inner Temple Entrance Schol. Called to the Bar, Inner Temple, 1956; in practice, Birmingham, 1958–84, and London, 1979–84; a Recorder of the Crown Court, 1974–84; Midland and Oxford Circuit.

TAYLOR; *see* Suenson-Taylor, family name of Baron Grantchester.

TAYLOR, family name of **Barons Kilclooney, Taylor of Blackburn, Taylor of Goss Moor, Taylor of Holbeach** and **Taylor of Warwick,** and **Baroness Taylor of Bolton**.

TAYLOR OF BLACKBURN, Baron *cr* 1978 (Life Peer), of Blackburn in the County of Lancashire; **Thomas Taylor,** CBE 1974 (OBE 1969); JP; *b* 10 June 1929; *s* of James and Edith Gladys Taylor; *m* 1950, Kathleen Nurton; one *s. Educ:* Mill Hill Primary Sch.; Blakey Moor Elementary Sch. Mem., Blackburn Town Council, 1954–76 (Leader, 1972–76; Chm., Policy and Resources Cttee, 1972–76). Chm., Electricity Cons. Council for NW and Mem. Norweb Bd, 1977–80; Former Member: NW Econ. Planning Council; NW AHA (Chm. Brockhall HMC, 1972–74, Vice-Chm. Blackburn HMC, 1964–74); Council for Educational Technology in UK; Nat. Foundn for Educn Research in Eng. and Wales; Schools Council; Regional Rent Tribunal; Nat. Foundn for Visual Aids. Chm., Govt Cttee of Enquiry into Management and Govt of Schools, 1977. Former Mem., Public Schools Commn; past Pres., Assoc. of Educn Cttees. Former Dir, Councils and Education Press. University of Lancaster: Founder Mem. and Mem. Council; author of Taylor Report on problems in univs; Dep. Pro-Chancellor, 1972–95. Former Dep. Dir, Central Lancs Family and Community Project. Non-executive Director: Building Themes Internat. Ltd, 2008–; Pine Mountain Resorts Ltd, 2009–. Vice-Pres., Assoc. of Lancastrians in London. Elder, URC; Pres., Free Church Council, 1962–63. Hon. LLD Lancaster, 1996. JP Blackburn, 1960, DL Lancs, 1994–2009; former Chm., Juvenile Bench. Freeman: Blackburn, 1992; City of London. *Address:* House of Lords, SW1A 0PW. *T:* (020) 7219 5130.

TAYLOR OF BOLTON, Baroness *cr* 2005 (Life Peer), of Bolton in the county of Greater Manchester; **Winifred Ann Taylor;** PC 1997; *b* Motherwell, 2 July 1947; *m* 1966, David Taylor; one *s* one *d. Educ:* Bolton Sch.; Bradford Univ.; Sheffield Univ. Formerly teaching. Past part-time Tutor, Open Univ.; interested in intelligence and security matters, and education. Monitoring Officer, Housing Corp., 1985–87. Member: Association of Univ. Teachers; APEX; Holmfirth Urban District Council, 1972–74. Contested (Lab): Bolton W, Feb. 1974; Bolton NE, 1983. MP (Lab): Bolton W, Oct. 1974–1983; Dewsbury, 1987–2005. PPS to Sec. of State for Educn and Science, 1975–76; PPS to Sec. of State for Defence, 1976–77; an Asst Govt Whip, 1977–79; Opposition front bench spokesman on education, 1979–81, on housing, 1981–83, on home affairs, 1987–90 (Shadow Water Minister, 1988), on environment, 1990–92, on education, 1992–94; Shadow Chancellor of Duchy of Lancaster, 1994–95; Shadow Leader of H of C, 1994–97; Pres. of Council and Leader of H of C, 1997–98; Parly Sec. to HM Treasury (Govt Chief Whip), 1998–2001; Parly Under-Sec. of State, MoD, 2007–10, FCO, 2009–10. Member: Select Cttee on Standards and Privileges, 1995–97; Jt Cttee on Nat. Security Strategy, 2010–14; Chairman: Select Committee: on modernisation, 1997–98; on intelligence and security, 2001–05. Mem. Adv. Bd, Thales Holdings UK plc, 2010–. Hon. Fellow: Birkbeck Coll., 1995; St Antony's Coll., Oxford, 2004. *Address:* House of Lords, SW1A 0PW.

TAYLOR OF GOSS MOOR, Baron *cr* 2010 (Life Peer), of Truro in the County of Cornwall; **Matthew Owen John Taylor;** *b* 3 Jan. 1963; *s* of late Kenneth Heywood Taylor and of Gillian Dorothea Taylor (*née* Black); *m* 2007, Victoria Sophie Garner; three *s. Educ:* Treliske School, Truro; University College School; Lady Margaret Hall, Oxford (Scholar; BA Hons). Pres., Oxford Univ. Student Union, 1985–86. Economic policy researcher to Parly Liberal Party (attached to David Penhaligon, MP), 1986–87. MP Truro, March 1987–1997 (L, 1987–88, Lib Dem, 1988–97); MP (Lib Dem) Truro and St Austell, 1997–2010. Parly spokesman on energy, 1987–88, on local govt, 1988–89, on trade and industry, 1989–90, on educn, 1990–92, on citizen's charter, 1992–94, on environment, 1994–99, and transport, 1997–99, on the economy, 1999–2003, on social exclusion, 2006–10; Special Advr to Govt on sustainable rural communities, 2007–08 (report, Living, Working, Countryside, 2008);

Chm., DCLG Planning Practice Guidance Rev., 2013–14. Liberal Democrats: Communications Chm., 1989–92; Chm. of Campaigns and Communications, 1992–94; Chm., Parly Party, 2003–05. Director: South West Water Ltd, 2010–; Taylor & Garner Ltd, 2010–; Mayfield Market Towns Ltd, 2013–. Chairman: Nat. Housing Fedn, 2009–; Rural Coalition, 2009–12; St Austell Eco-town Strategic Partnership Bd, 2010–; Bridgehall Real Estate Ltd, 2013–. *Address:* House of Lords, SW1A 0PW.

See also V. M. T. Heywood.

TAYLOR OF HOLBEACH, Baron *cr* 2006 (Life Peer), of South Holland in the County of Lincolnshire; **John Derek Taylor,** CBE 1992; PC 2014; Captain of the Honourable Corps of Gentlemen at Arms (Government Chief Whip in House of Lords), since 2014; Deputy Chairman, Conservative Party, and Chairman, National Conservative Convention, 2000–03; *b* 12 Nov. 1943; *s* of late Percy Otto Taylor and Ethel Taylor (*née* Brocklehurst); *m* 1968, Julia Aileen Cunnington, *d* of late Leslie and Evelyn Cunnington, Bedford; two *s*. *Educ:* Holbeach Primary Sch.; St Felix Sch., Felixstowe; Bedford Sch. Dir, family horticultural and farming businesses, 1968–2010. Dir, 1990–2009, Chm., 2000–09, Springfields Horticl Soc. Ltd, and associated cos. Chairman: EC Working Party on European Bulb Industry, 1982; NFU Bulb Sub-cttee, 1982–87. Governor: Glasshouse Crops Res. Inst., 1984–88; Inst. of Horticl Res., 1987–90; Mem., Horticl Develt Council, 1986–91. Member, Minister of Agriculture's Regional Panel: Eastern Reg., 1990–92; E Midlands Reg., 1992–96. Chm., Holbeach and E Elloe Hosp. Charitable Trust, 1989–2006, now Patron; Trustee, Brogdale Horticl Trust, 1998–2005. Mem., Lincoln Diocesan Bd of Finance, 1995–2001 (Mem., Assets Cttee, 1995–2001, 2003–12). East Midlands Conservative Council: Mem., Exec. Cttee, 1966–98; Hon. Treas., 1984–89; Chm., 1989–94; Mem., Cons. Bd of Finance, 1985–89; Mem., Cons. Bd of Mgt, 1996–98; National Union of Conservative Associations: Member: Exec. Cttee, 1966–68 and 1984–98; Gen. Purposes Cttee, 1988–98; Standing Rev. Cttee, 1988–98; Agents Employment Adv. Cttee, 1988–94; Agents Exam Bd, 1994–98; Vice Pres., 1994–97; Pres. and Cons. Conf. Chm., 1997–98; Chairman: Candidates Cttee, Cons. Party, 1997–98, 2002–05; Cons. Party Constitutional Review, 1998–2000; Cons. Agents' Superannuation Fund, 2006–10; Conservatives Abroad, 2001–08. House of Lords: Opposition Whip, 2006–10; Opposition Spokesman: on Envmt, and on Wales, 2006–07; on Work and Pensions, 2006–10; Shadow Minister, Environment, Food and Rural Affairs, 2007–10; govt spokesman for Cabinet Office, for work and pensions and for energy and climate change, 2010–11; a Lord in Waiting (Govt Whip), 2010–11; Parliamentary Under-Secretary of State: DEFRA, 2011–12; Home Office, 2012–14. Chm., Taylor Rev., Sci., Agriculture and Horticulture, 2010–. Founder Chm., local Young Cons. Br., 1964; Mem., Holland with Boston Cons. Assoc., 1964–95 (formerly Treas., Vice Chm., Chm. and Pres.); Pres., S Holland and The Deepings Cons. Assoc., 1995–2001, now Patron. Contested (C): Chesterfield, Feb. and Oct. 1974; Nottingham, EP elections, 1979. President: Lincs Agricl Soc., 2012; E of England Agricl Soc., 2014. FRSA 1994; ARAgS 2012; MIHort, 2013; FCIHort, 2014. Liveryman: Farmers' Co., 2009–; Gardeners' Co., 2010–. Peer of the Year, House Magazine Awards, 2011; Farm Business Personality of the Year, Business Mag., 2012. *Publications:* (ed) Taylor's Bulb Book, 1994. *Recreations:* English landscape and vernacular buildings, France, literature, arts, music. *Address:* House of Lords, SW1A 0PW. *Club:* Farmers.

TAYLOR OF WARWICK, Baron *cr* 1996 (Life Peer), of Warwick in the county of Warwickshire; **John David Beckett Taylor;** barrister-at-law; writer; radio and television presenter; *b* 21 Sept. 1952; *s* of late Derief David Samuel Taylor and Enid Maud Taylor; *m* 1981, Dr Jean Katherine Taylor (*née* Binysh) (marr. diss.); one *s* two *d*. *Educ:* Univ. of Keele (BA Hons Law). Called to the Bar, Gray's Inn, 1978; practised on Midland and Oxford Circuit, 1978–90. Special Advr to Home Sec. and Home Office Ministers, 1990–91. Consultant, Lowe Bell Communications Ltd, 1991–92; Producer/Presenter, BBC Radio and Television, 1994–; Chairman: Warwick Consulting Internat. Ltd, 1997–2000; Warwick Leadership Foundn, 1999–. Member: Solihull FPC, 1986–90; Greater London FEFC Cttee, 1994–96. Non-exec. Dir, NW Thames RHA, 1992–93. Vice-President: Small Business Bureau, 1997–; BBFC, 1998–2008. Dir, City Technology Colls Trust, 1994–95. Mem. (C), Solihull DC, 1986–90. Contested (C): Birmingham, Perry Barr, 1987; Cheltenham, 1992. MInstD 1997. Barker, Variety Club Children's Charity; Patron: Parents for Children, adoption charity; Kidscape, 1997; Mem. Exec. Cttee, Sickle Cell Anaemia Relief. Pres., Ilford Town FC, 1998–; Mem., Aston Villa FC. Freeman: City of London, 1999; Lexington, Ky, USA, 2004. Hon. LLD: Warwick, 1999; Asbury Coll., Ky, USA, 2004. *Recreations:* soccer, cricket, singing, spending time with my lovely family. *Address:* House of Lords, SW1A 0PW. *T:* (020) 7219 3000, *Fax:* (020) 7219 5979. *E:* taylorjdb@parliament.uk. *W:* www.lordtaylor.org, www.twitter.com/lordjohntaylor.

TAYLOR, Alan; *see* Taylor, Robert A.

TAYLOR, His Honour Alan Broughton; a Circuit Judge, 1991–2005; *b* 23 Jan. 1939; *yr s* of Valentine James Broughton Taylor and Gladys Maud Taylor; *m* 1964, Diana Hindmarsh; two *s*. *Educ:* Malvern Coll.; Geneva Univ.; Birmingham Univ. (LLB); Brasenose Coll., Oxford (BLitt, re-designated MLitt 1979). Called to the Bar, Gray's Inn, 1961; barrister on Oxford Circuit, subseq. Midland and Oxford Circuit, 1963–91; a Recorder, 1979–91. A Pres., Mental Health Rev. Tribunal, 2001–09. Gov., St Matthew's Sch., Sandwell, 1988–92. FCIArb 1994; Chartered status, 2005. Lay-reader, Dio. of Carlisle, 2009–13, Reader Emeritus, 2014. *Publications:* (contrib.) A Practical Guide to the Care of the Injured, ed P. S. London, 1967; (contrib.) Crime and Civil Society, ed Green, Grove and Martin, 2005. *Recreations:* philately, fell walking. *Address:* Wetherlam, Wood Close, Grasmere, Cumbria LA22 9SG.

TAYLOR, Andrew David; Partner, Reed Smith (formerly Richards Butler, then Reed Smith Richards Butler), Solicitors, since 1983; *b* 6 March 1952; *s* of Vernon Stephen Taylor and Elizabeth Taylor; *m* 1977, Alison Jane Wright; one *s* two *d*. *Educ:* Magdalen Coll. Sch., Oxford; Lincoln Coll., Oxford (MA). Joined Richards Butler, Solicitors, 1977, Chm., 2000–05; specialises in shipping law. Treas./Sec., British Maritime Law Assoc., 2005–. *Publications:* Voyage Charters, 1993, 4th edn 2014. *Recreations:* ski-ing, walking, opera, wine. *Address:* Reed Smith, The Broadgate Tower, 20 Primrose Street, EC2A 2RS. *Clubs:* Travellers, City Law; Vincent's (Oxford).

TAYLOR, Andrew Dawson, OBE 1999; DPhil; FRSE; FInstP; Executive Director, National Laboratories, Science and Technology Facilities Council, since 2012 (Director, Facility Operations and Development, 2007–12); Head, Rutherford Appleton Laboratory, since 2007; *b* Falkirk, 1 March 1950; *s* of Millar Taylor and Jean Taylor (*née* Dawson); *m* 1973, Elizabeth Slimming; two *s* two *d*. *Educ:* Denny High Sch., Stirlingshire; Univ. of Glasgow (Joseph Black Medal 1969; BSc 1st Cl. Hons 1972); St John's Coll., Oxford (DPhil 1976). FRSE 2006; FInstP 2007. SSO, Rutherford Lab., 1975–80; Vis. Scientist, Los Alamos Nat. Lab., New Mexico, 1980–83; SSO, 1983–85, Excitations Gp Leader, 1985–93, Director, 1993–2012, ISIS Facility, Rutherford Appleton Lab. Dep. Chief Exec., 2000–04, Exec. Dir, CCLRC Facilities, 2005–07, Mem., 2007–, CCLRC. European Spallation Source: Sec., Council, 1992–2000; Mem., Scandinavia Round Table, Sweden, 2007–09; Steering Cttee, Sweden, 2012–. Member: Steering Cttee, Institut Laue Langevin, 1993–2012; Adv. Bd, Los Alamos Neutron Sci. Center, 1994–2004; Neutron Rev. Panel, Univ. of Chicago, 1996–2004; Spallation Neutron Source Adv. Bd, USA, 1998–2008; Internat. Adv. Cttee, Japan Proton Accelerator Res. Complex, 2002–; Chairman: Canadian Foundn for Innovation Spallation Neutron Source Review, 2004; RIKEN Muon Review, 2007–14. Hon. Fellow, Mansfield Coll., 2011. Hon. DSc: Glasgow, 2010; London, 2012. Glazebrook Medal, Inst. of Physics, 2006. *Publications:* articles on develt and exploitation of pulsed neutron sources for condensed matter research. *Recreations:* family, hill walking, ski-ing, gastronomy. *Address:* Rutherford Appleton Laboratory, Harwell Science and Innovation Campus, Chilton, Oxon OX11 0QX. *T:* (01235) 446681. *E:* andrew.taylor@stfc.ac.uk.

TAYLOR, Andrew John, FCA; Chairman: Phantom Music Management Ltd, since 2006; Concept Venues Ltd, since 2006; *b* 23 Feb. 1950; *s* of Thomas Sowler Taylor and Sarah Taylor; *m* 1985, Elizabeth (*née* Robertson); two *d*. *Educ:* Trinity Coll., Cambridge (MA). FCA 1982. Sanctuary Group plc: Founder, 1976; CEO and Chm., 1976–98; CEO, 1998–2002; Chm. and Chief Exec., 2002–06. FRSA. *Recreations:* wine, cinema, books, fell walking, horse racing. *Address:* Bridle House, 36 Bridle Lane, W1F 9BZ. *E:* andy.taylor@phantom-music.com.

TAYLOR, Sir Anthony John N.; *see* Newman Taylor.

TAYLOR, Arthur Robert; President, Muhlenberg College, Pennsylvania, 1992–2002; *b* 6 July 1935; *s* of Arthur Earl Taylor and Marian Hilda Scott; *m* Kathryn Pelgrift; three *d* by previous marriage. *Educ:* Brown Univ., USA (AB, MA). Asst Dir, Admissions, Brown Univ., June 1957–Dec. 1960; Vice-Pres./Dir, The First Boston Co., Jan. 1961–May 1970; Exec. Vice-Pres./Director, Internat. Paper Co., 1970–72; Pres., CBS Inc., 1972–76; Chm., Arthur Taylor & Co., 1977–; Chm. and CEO, Arts Entertainment Network, 1979–83. Dean, Grad. Sch. of Business, Fordham Univ., 1985–92. Director: Louisiana Land & Exploration Co.; Pitney Bowes; Nomura Pacific Basin Fund, Inc.; Trustee, Drucker Foundn; Trustee Emeritus, Brown Univ. Hon. degrees: Dr Humane Letters: Simmons Coll., 1975; Rensselaer Polytechnic Inst., 1975; Fordham, 2003; Dr of Humanities, Bucknell Univ., 1975. *Publications:* contrib. chapter to The Other Side of Profit, 1975; articles on US competitiveness and corporate responsibility in jls. *Recreations:* sailing, tennis, riding. *Address:* 3731 Devonshire Road, Salisbury Township, PA 18103, USA. *Clubs:* Century (New York); Metropolitan (Washington); California (Los Angeles).

TAYLOR, Bernard David, CBE 1993; Director, Cambridge Laboratories Ltd, 2006–11 (Chairman, 1997–2007); *b* 17 Oct. 1935; *s* of Thomas Taylor and Winifred (*née* Smith); *m* 1959, Nadine Barbara; two *s* two *d*. *Educ:* Univ. of Wales, Bangor (BSc Zoology). Science Teacher, Coventry Educn Authority, 1958; Sales and Marketing, SK&F, 1960; Sales and Marketing Manager, Glaxo NZ, 1964; New Products Manager, Glaxo UK, 1967; Man. Dir, Glaxo Australia, 1972; Dir, Glaxo Holdings plc, and Man. Dir, Glaxo Pharmaceuticals UK, 1984; Chief Exec., Glaxo Holdings, 1986–89; Chm., Medeva plc, 1990–96. Councillor and Vice-Pres., Aust. Pharm. Manufrs' Assoc., 1974–79; Councillor, Victorian Coll. of Pharmacy, 1976–82. Member: CBI Europe Cttee, 1987–89; BOTB, 1987–96. Trustee, WWF (UK), 1990–96. CCMI (CBIM 1986). Fellow, London Business Sch., 1988. Hon. Fellow, Bangor Univ., 2015.

TAYLOR, Bernard John; DL; CChem, FRSC; CSci; Chairman and Chief Executive, Evercore Partners Ltd (formerly Braveheart Financial Services Ltd), since 2006; Vice-Chairman, Evercore Partners Inc., since 2007; *b* 2 Nov. 1956; *s* of late John Taylor and Evelyn Frances Taylor; *m* 1984, Sarah Jane, *d* of John Paskin Taylor, Paris; one *s*. *Educ:* Cheltenham Coll.; St John's Coll., Oxford (Schol.; MA; Hon. Fellow 2008). LRPS 1974; CChem, FRSC 1991; CSci 2004. Business Planning and Acquisitions, 1979–82, Dir, Med. Div., 1983–85, Smiths Industries plc; Exec. Dir, Baring Bros & Co. Ltd, 1985–94; Chm. and Chief Exec., Robert Fleming & Co. Ltd, 1994–2001; Dir, Robert Fleming Hldgs Ltd, 1995–2001 (Jt Chief Exec., Investment Banking, 1998–2000); Vice Chm., EMEA, Chase Manhattan, 2000; Vice-Chm., JP Morgan, 2001–06. Non-executive Director: New Focus Healthcare Ltd, 1986–89; Isis Innovation Ltd, 1997– (Chm., 2001–); Ti Automotive Ltd, 2001–07 (Dep. Chm.); Oxford Instruments plc, 2002–. Chm., Bd of Mgt, Royal Commn for Exhibn of 1851, 2012– (Mem., 2005–; Chm., Finance Cttee, 2006–12); Mem., Royal Soc. Investment Adv. Cttee, 2010. Mem. Council, Univ. of Oxford, 2003– (Chm., Audit and Scrutiny Cttee, 2006–; Chm., Remuneration Cttee, 2007–). DL Oxon, 2011. *Publications:* Photosensitive Film Formation on Copper, I, 1974, II, 1976; Synthesis and Mesomorphic Properties of a Liquid Crystal, 1977; Oxidation of Alcohols to Carbonyl Compounds, Synthesis, 1979; Selective Organic Reactions, 1979. *Recreations:* gardening, photography, wine, opera. *Address:* Evercore Partners Ltd, 15 Stanhope Gate, W1K 1LN. *Clubs:* Brooks's, Oxford and Cambridge, Mark's.

TAYLOR, Sir Bill; *see* Taylor, Sir W. G.

TAYLOR, Prof. Brent William, PhD; FRACP, FRCPCH; Professor of Community Child Health, University College London Institute of Child Health (formerly at Royal Free Hospital School of Medicine, then Royal Free and University College Medical School), 1988–2008, now Emeritus; *b* 21 Nov. 1941; *s* of Robert Ernest Taylor and Norma Gertrude Taylor; *m* 1970, Moira Elizabeth Hall; one *s* one *d*. *Educ:* Christchurch Boys' High Sch.; Otago Univ. (MB ChB 1966); Bristol Univ. (PhD 1986). FRACP 1977; FRCPCH 1997. Jun. hosp. posts, Christchurch, NZ, 1967–71; Res. Fellow and Sen. Registrar, Great Ormond Street Hosp. for Sick Children and Inst. of Child Health, 1971–74; Senior Lecturer: in Paediatrics, Christchurch Clin. Sch. of Medicine, 1975–81; in Social Paediatrics and Epidemiology, Bristol Univ., 1981–84; in Child Health, St Mary's Hosp. Med. Sch., 1985–88. Vis. Prof., Tongji Med. Univ., Wuhan, China, 1995–2008. Chm., Nat. Child Health Informatics Consortium, 1995–2008. *Publications:* chapters and papers on child health, social influences, vaccine safety, respiratory problems and informatics. *Recreations:* family, music (Handel), walking. *Address:* General and Adolescent Paediatric Unit, University College London Institute of Child Health, 30 Guilford Street, WC1N 3EH. *E:* brent.taylor@ucl.ac.uk.

TAYLOR, Brian Arthur Edward, CB 2002; Director General, Civilian Personnel (formerly Assistant Under-Secretary of State, Civilian Management), Ministry of Defence, 1996–2001; *b* 10 Jan. 1942; *s* of Arthur Frederick Taylor and Gertrude Maclean Taylor (*née* Campbell); *m* 1967, Carole Ann Smith; three *s* one *d*. *Educ:* St Benedict's Sch., Ealing; Corpus Christi Coll., Oxford (MA Lit.Hum.). Ministry of Defence, 1965–2001: Asst Private Sec. to Sec. of State, 1969–70; Private Sec. to Chief of Air Staff, 1973–75; Head, Management Services Div., 1977–79; Head, Naval Personnel Div., 1979–81; RCDS 1982; Central Policy Review Staff, Cabinet Office, 1983; Head, Civilian Management Div., MoD, 1984–86; Asst Under-Sec. of State (Quartermaster), 1986–88, Air (PE), 1988–91; Head of Personnel Policy Gp (Under Sec.), HM Treasury, 1992–94; Asst Under-Sec. of State (Civilian Mgt (Policy)), MoD, 1994–96. Assessor, Fast Stream Assessment Centre, 2005–11. *Recreations:* sport, music, reading, family. *Club:* Richmond Rugby.

TAYLOR, (Bryan) Hugo M.; *see* Mascie-Taylor.

TAYLOR, Carol Edwina; Regional Employment Judge, London East, since 2011; *b* London, 5 July 1957. Admitted Solicitor, 1985; fee-paid Employment Judge, 1992; full-time Employment Judge, 1996; fee-paid Legal Chm., Reserve Forces Appeal Tribunal, 2003. *Address:* East London Tribunal Service, Anchorage House, 2 Clove Crescent, E14 2BE.

TAYLOR, Catherine Dalling; *see* Stihler, C. D.

TAYLOR, Cavan; Senior Partner, Lovell White Durrant, 1991–96; *b* 23 Feb. 1935; *s* of late Albert William Taylor and Constance Muriel (*née* Horncastle); *m* 1962, Helen Tinling; one *s* two *d*. *Educ:* King's Coll. Sch., Wimbledon; Emmanuel Coll., Cambridge (BA 1958; LLM 1959). 2nd Lieut, RASC, 1953–55. Articled with Herbert Smith & Co., 1958–61; qualified as solicitor, 1961; Legal Dept, Distillers' Co. Ltd, 1962–65; Asst Solicitor, Piesse & Sons, 1965–66, Partner, 1966; by amalgamation, Partner, Durrant Piesse and Lovell White Durrant; Dep. Sen. Partner, Lovell White Durrant, 1990–91. Director: Hampton Gold Mining Areas plc, 1979–86; Ludorum Management Ltd, 1996–2000; Link Plus Corp., 1999–2003. Adjudicator for Investment Ombudsman, 1996–2001. Gov., King's Coll. Sch., Wimbledon, 1970–2004 (Chm., 1973–90, 2000–04; Hon. Fellow, 2004). Vice-Pres., Surrey Co. RFU, 2006–. Trustee, School Fees Charitable Trust, 2000–10. Pres., Old Boys RFC, King's Coll. Sch., Wimbledon, 1997–2002. Pres., Le Cercle Français d'Esher, 2010–. Liveryman, Solicitors' Co., 1983–. *Publications:* articles in legal jls. *Recreations:* reading, gardening, conversation with my children, Rugby football. *Address:* Covenham House, 10 Broad High Way, Cobham, Surrey KT11 2RP. *T:* (01932) 864258. *Club:* Travellers.

TAYLOR, (Charles) Jeremy (Bingham); Chief Executive, Cheshire County Council, 2002–09; *b* 28 Oct. 1947; *s* of Dr Charles Bingham Taylor and Sydna Mary Taylor (*née* Howell); *m* 1972, Rachel Suzanne Hampson; one *d. Educ:* Selwyn Coll., Cambridge (BA, MA 1968). FCIPD 1987. Personnel Manager, ICI Ltd, 1968–72; Sen. Lectr, Univ. of Huddersfield, 1972–79; Cheshire County Council: Director: of Personnel, 1987–91; of Policy, 1991–97; of Community Develt, 1997–2002; Clerk, Cheshire Lieutenancy, 2002–09. Sen. Vice Chm., ACCE, 2008–09 (Hon. Sec., 2006–08). Gov. and Trustee, Brathay Hall Trust, 1987–91; Trustee: Keep Britain Tidy, 2010–11; Ormiston Children and Families, 2010–11. Mem. (C) E Northamptonshire DC, 2011–15. Churchwarden, Nassington, 2011–12. FCMI 1989; FRSA 1990. Hon. MBA Chester, 2009. *Recreations:* gardening, film, theatre, the Greek Islands, opera, cats. *Address:* 2 Homefield, Nassington, Peterborough PE8 6EP. *T:* (01780) 781220. *E:* cjbtaylor@btinternet.com. *Club:* Royal Over-Seas League.

TAYLOR, Prof. Charles Margrave, CC 1996; GOQ 2000; DPhil; FBA 1979; Professor of Political Science, McGill University, 1982–98, now Professor Emeritus of Philosophy; *b* 5 Nov. 1931; *s* of Walter Margrave Taylor and Simone Beaubien; *m* 1st, 1956, Alba Romer (*d* 1990); five *d*; 2nd, 1995, Aube Billard. *Educ:* McGill Univ. (BA History); Oxford Univ. (BA PPE, MA, DPhil). Fellow, All Souls Coll., Oxford, 1956–61; McGill University: Asst Prof., later Associate Prof., then Prof. of Pol Science, Dept of Pol Science, 1961–76; Prof. of Philosophy, Dept of Philos., 1973–76; Chichele Prof. of Social and Political Theory, and Fellow of All Souls Coll., Oxford Univ., 1976–81; Mem., Sch. of Social Science, Inst. for Advanced Study, Princeton, 1981–82. Prof. asst, later Prof. agrégé, later Prof. titulaire, Ecole Normale Supérieure, 1962–64, Dept de Philos., 1963–71, Univ. de Montréal. Vis. Prof. in Philos., Princeton Univ., 1965; Mills Vis. Prof. in Philos., Univ. of Calif, Berkeley, 1974. For. Hon. Mem., Amer. Acad. of Arts and Scis, 1986. *Publications:* The Explanation of Behavior, 1964; Pattern of Politics, 1970; Hegel, 1975; Erklärung und Interpretation in den Wissenschaften vom Menschen, 1975; Social Theory as Practice, 1983; Philosophical Papers, 1985; Negative Freiheit, 1988; Sources of the Self, 1989; The Ethics of Authenticity, 1992; Philosophical Arguments, 1995; Varieties of Religion Today, 2002; Modern Social Imaginaries, 2004; A Secular Age, 2007. *Recreations:* ski-ing, swimming. *Address:* 6603 Jeanne Mance, Montréal, QC H2V 4L1, Canada.

TAYLOR, Very Rev. Charles William; Dean of Peterborough, since 2007; *b* 16 March 1953; *s* of Rev. Preb. Richard John Taylor and Marjorie Taylor; *m* 1983, Catherine Margaret, *d* of Very Rev. Trevor Randall Beeson, *qv*; one *s* one *d. Educ:* Chorister, St Paul's Cathedral Choir Sch.; Marlborough Coll.; Selwyn Coll., Cambridge (BA Hons Theology; MA 1977); Cuddesdon Coll., Oxford; Church Divinity Sch. of the Pacific, Berkeley, Calif, USA. Ordained deacon, 1976, priest, 1977; Curate, Collegiate Church of St Peter, Wolverhampton, 1976–79; Chaplain, Westminster Abbey, 1979–84; Vicar, Stanmore with Oliver's Battery, Winchester, 1984–90; Rector, N Stoneham and Bassett, Southampton, 1990–95; Tutor in Liturgy, Salisbury and Wells Theol Coll., 1992–94; Canon Residentiary and Precentor, Lichfield Cathedral, 1995–2007. Chm., Cathedrals Plus, 2011–. Hon. FGCM 2007. *Publications:* The Word Revealed (with Peter Moger), 2011; numerous papers for Cathedrals' Liturgy and Music Gp. *Recreations:* music, food and wine, hospitality, Black Country humour, classic cars, following sport from a sedentary position, family holidays. *Address:* The Deanery, Minster Precincts, Peterborough PE1 1XS. *T:* (01733) 355315. *E:* dean.pa@peterborough-cathedral.org.uk.

TAYLOR, Christopher Charles, FSA; FBA 1995; Head, Archaeological Survey, Royal Commission on Historical Monuments, 1985–93, retired; *b* 7 Nov. 1935; *s* of Richard Hugh Taylor and Alice Mary Taylor (*née* Davies); *m* 1st, 1961, Angela Ballard (*d* 1983); one *s* one *d*; 2nd, 1985, Stephanie, *d* of Wing Comdr R. J. S. Spooner; one step *d. Educ:* King Edward VI Sch., Lichfield; Univ. of Keele (BA 1958); Inst. of Archaeol., Univ. of London (Dip. Archaeol. 1960). FSA 1966; MCIfA (MIFA 1987). Investigator, Sen. Investigator and Principal Investigator, RCHM, 1960–93. Member: Historic Parks and Gardens Adv. Cttee, 1987–2001, Historic Settlement and Landscape Adv. Cttee, 2001–03, English Heritage. Pres., Cambridge Antiquarian Soc., 1994–96. Hon. DLitt Keele, 1997. John Coles Medal for Landscape Archaeology, British Acad., 2013. *Publications:* Dorset, 1970, 2nd edn 2004; The Making of the Cambridgeshire Landscape, 1973; Fieldwork in Medieval Archaeology, 1974; Fields in the English Landscape, 1975, 3rd edn 1987; Roads and Tracks in Britain, 1979, 2nd edn 1982; The Archaeology of Gardens, 1983; Village and Farmstead, 1983; (ed) W. G. Hoskins, The Making of the English Landscape, rev. edn 1988; Parks and Gardens of Britain, 1998; contrib. to various pubns of RCHM; papers in learned jls on archaeol. and landscape hist. *Recreations:* gardening, garden history. *Address:* 11 High Street, Pampisford, Cambridge CB22 3ES.

TAYLOR, Prof. Christopher John, OBE 2001; PhD; FREng; Professor of Medical Biophysics, since 1990, Director of Manchester Informatics, since 2006, and Associate Vice President for Research, since 2009, University of Manchester; *b* Coventry, 25 Dec. 1945; *s* of Harold Herbert and Gwendoline May Taylor; *m* 1968, Jill Andrea Neal; one *s* one *d. Educ:* Gt Yarmouth Grammar Sch.; Univ. of Manchester (BSc Hons Physics; PhD 1972). FREng 2006. University of Manchester: Lectr in Biophysics, 1974–80; Sen. Lectr, 1980–90; Dir, Wolfson Image Analysis Unit, 1980–93; Head: Sch. of Diagnostic and Investigational Sci., 1993–96; Sch. of Computer Sci., 2003–08. Chair: UK Foresight Health Informatics Wkg Party, 1996–98; UK Inst. for Health Informatics, 1998–2004; Vice Pres., UK Council for Health Informatics Professions, 2002–05. Chm., 1988–91, Dist. Fellow, 2003, British Machine Vision Assoc. (formerly British Pattern Recognition Assoc.). Dist. Fellow, Internat. Assoc. for Pattern Recognition, 2004; Fellow, Med. Image Computing and Computer-Aided Intervention Soc., 2009 (Enduring Impact Award, 2011). *Publications:* (jtly) Statistical Models of Shape: optimisation and evaluation, 2008; contribs to scientific pubns. *Recreations:* mountain biking, running, playing guitar, sky-diving (lapsed). *Address:* Imaging Science, Stopford Building, University of Manchester, Oxford Road, Manchester M13 9PT. *T:* (0161) 275 5403, *Fax:* (0161) 275 5145. *E:* chris.taylor@manchester.ac.uk. *W:* www.manchester.ac.uk/research/chris.taylor.

TAYLOR, Prof. Christopher Malcolm, FREng, FIMechE, FCGI; Vice-Chancellor and Principal, University of Bradford, 2001–07, now Emeritus Professor; *b* 15 Jan. 1943; *s* of William Taylor and Esther Hopkinson; *m* 1st, 1968, Gillian Walton (marr. diss. 1986); one *d*; 2nd, 1994, Diane Shorrocks. *Educ:* King's College London (BScEng); Univ. of Leeds (MSc, PhD, DEng). FIMechE 1986. Research Engineer, English Electric Co.; Sen. Engr, Industrial Unit of Tribology, Leeds, 1968–71; University of Leeds: Lectr, 1971–80; Sen. Lectr, 1980–86; Reader, 1986–90; Prof. of Tribology, 1990–2001; Head of Dept of Mechanical Engrg, 1992–96; Dean of Faculty of Engrg, 1996–97; Pro-Vice-Chancellor, 1997–2001. Vice-Pres., 1997–2001, Dep. Pres., 2001–03, Pres., 2003–04, IMechE. Editor, Part J, Procs IMechE, 1993–2001. FREng (FEng 1995); FCGI 1999. Tribology Trust Silver Medal, 1992; Donald Julius Groen Prize, IMechE, 1993; Jacob Wallenberg Foundn Prize, 1994. *Publications:* numerous contribs to learned jls. *Recreations:* walking, cycling. *Address:* 17 Beech Grove Court, Beech Grove, Harrogate, N Yorks HG2 0EU. *T:* (01423) 701207. *E:* cmtdt@btinternet.com.

TAYLOR, Claire; *see* Taylor, S. C.

TAYLOR, Clifford; Director, Resources Television, BBC, 1988–93 (Deputy Director, 1987–88); *b* 6 March 1941; *s* of Fred Taylor and Annie Elisabeth (*née* Hudson); *m* 1962, Catherine Helen (*née* Green); two *d. Educ:* Barnsley and District Holgate Grammar Sch.; Barnsley College of Mining and Technology. ACMA. NCB, 1957–65; Midlands Counties Dairies, 1965–68; BBC: Radio Cost Accountant, 1968–71; Television Hd of Costing, 1971–76; Chief Accountant, Corporate Finance, 1976–77 and 1982–84; Chief Acct, Engineering, 1977–82; Dep. Dir, Finance, 1984–86. *Recreations:* sport - plays golf, enjoys horse racing. *Address:* 8 Regency Drive, West Byfleet, Surrey KT14 6EN. *Clubs:* MCC, BBC.

TAYLOR, Sir Cyril (Julian Hebden), GBE 2004; Kt 1989; Founder Chairman, American Institute for Foreign Study, since 1964; Chancellor, Richmond, The American International University (formerly School) in London, since 2005 (Chairman, Board of Trustees, 1972–2011); *b* 14 May 1935; *s* of Cyril Eustace Taylor and Margaret Victoria (*née* Hebden); *m* 1965, June Judith Denman; one *d. Educ:* St Marylebone Grammar Sch.; Trinity Hall, Cambridge (MA); Harvard Business Sch. (MBA). National Service, Officer with KAR in Kenya during Mau Mau Emergency, 1954–56 (seconded from E Surrey Regt). Brand Manager in Advertising Dept, Procter & Gamble, Cincinnati, Ohio, 1961–64; Founder Chm., American Institute for Foreign Study, 1964–: group cos include: Amer. Inst. for Foreign Study; Amer. Council for Internat. Studies; Camp America; Au Pair in America. Advr to ten successive Secs of State for Educn on specialist schs and academies initiative, 1987–2007. Mem. for Ruislip Northwood, GLC, 1977–86: Chm., Professional and Gen. Services Cttee, 1979–81; Opposition spokesperson for employment, 1981–82, transport, 1982–85, policy and resources, 1985–86; Dep. Leader of the Opposition, 1983–86; Mem., Wkg Party reviewing legislation to abolish GLC and MCCs, 1983–86. Pres., Ruislip Northwood Cons. Assoc., 1986–97; contested (C): Huddersfield E, Feb. 1974; Keighley, Oct. 1974. Member: Bd of Dirs, Centre for Policy Studies, 1984–98; Council, Westfield Coll., Univ. of London, 1983–89; Council, RCM, 1988–95; Bd of Governors, Holland Park Comprehensive Sch., 1971–74. Trustee, Prince's Charities, 2009–12. Chm., Lexham Gdns Residents' Assoc., 1986–. Pres., Harvard Business Sch. Club, London, 1990–93; Chm., British Friends of Harvard Business Sch., 1991–97, 2001–; Vice Pres., Alumni Council, Harvard Business Sch., 1994–96 (Mem., 1993–96). FRSA 1990. High Sheriff, Greater London, 1996. Hon. LLD: New England, 1991; Richmond, The American Internat. Univ. in London, 1998; DUniv: Open, 2000; Brunel, 2005. *Publications:* (jtly) The New Guide to Study Abroad, USA 1969, 4th edn 1976; Peace has its Price, 1972; No More Tick, 1974; The Elected Member's Guide to Reducing Public Expenditure, 1980; A Realistic Plan for London Transport, 1982; Reforming London's Government, 1984; Quangoes Just Grow, 1985; London Preserv'd, 1985; Bringing Accountability Back to Local Government, 1985; Employment Examined: the right approach to more jobs, 1986; Raising Educational Standards, 1990; The Future of Higher Education, 1996; (jtly) Excellence in Education: the making of great schools, 2004; Education, Education, Education: 10 years on with Tony Blair, 2007; A Good School for Every Child, 2009; How English Universities Could Learn from the American Higher Education System, 2009; Sir Cyril—My Life as a Social Entrepreneur, 2013. *Recreations:* keen swimmer, gardener. *Address:* 1 Lexham Walk, W8 5JD. *T:* (020) 7370 2082; American Institute for Foreign Study, 37 Queen's Gate, SW7 5HR. *T:* (020) 7581 7391, *Fax:* (020) 7581 7388. *E:* ctaylor@aifs.co.uk. *Clubs:* Carlton, Hurlingham, Chelsea Arts; Harvard, Racquet (New York).

TAYLOR, Daria Jean, (Dari); *b* 13 Dec. 1944; *d* of Daniel and Phyllis Jones; *m* 1970, David Taylor; one *d. Educ:* Nottingham Univ. (BA Hons 1970); Durham Univ. (MA 1990). Lectr in Further Educn, Nottingham, 1970–80; part-time Lectr in Sociology and Social Policy, N Tyneside, 1986–90; Regl Educn Officer, GMB, 1990–97. Mem. (Lab) Sunderland CC, 1986–97. MP (Lab) Stockton S, 1997–2010; contested (Lab) same seat, 2010. PPS to Parly Under Sec. of State, MoD, 2001–03, to Minister of State, Home Office, 2003–05. Member: Defence Select Cttee, 1997–99; Intelligence and Security Select Cttee, 2005–10. Member: All Party Cancer Gp, 1998–2010; All Party Parly Gp on Pakistan and Kashmir, 2007–10; Chairman: All Party Gp on Adoption, 2001–10; All Party Parly Gp on Infertility, 2005–08 (Mem., 2008–10); Treasurer: All Party Chemical Industries Gp, 1997–2010; All Party Opera Gp, 1998–2010; Secretary: All Party Parly Gp on Child Abduction; All Party Parly Gp on Cardiac Risk in the Young. Vice Chm., Westbridgford Br., NATFHE, 1970–80. *Recreations:* opera, walking, classical music, travelling.

TAYLOR, Prof. David Samuel Irving, FRCP, FRCS, FRCOphth, FRCPCH; Consultant Ophthalmologist, Great Ormond Street Hospital, London, 1976–2007; Professor, Institute of Child Health, London, University College London, 2003–07, now Emeritus (Senior Lecturer, 1976–2003); Director, International Council of Ophthalmology Examinations (formerly Chairman, Examinations Committee), 2007–14; *b* 6 June 1942; *s* of Samuel Donald Taylor and Winifred Alice May Marker; *m* 1976, Anna (*née* Rhys Jones); two *s. Educ:* Dauntsey's Sch.; Liverpool Univ. (MB ChB 1967); DSc (Med) London 2001. FRCS 1973; FRCP 1984; FRCOphth 1990; FRCPCH 1998. House Surgeon and Physician, Liverpool Royal Infirmary, 1967–68; Registrar, then Sen. Registrar, Moorfields Eye Hosp., 1972–75; Research Fellow: Great Ormond Street Hosp., London, 1975–76; Neuro-ophthalmology Dept, Univ. of California, San Francisco, 1976–77; Consultant Neuro-ophthalmologist, National Hosps, London, 1976–89. Medico-legal expert in med. negligence and child abuse, 2006–. Hon. Mem. Council, Royal London Soc. for the Blind, 1988. Hon. FRSocMed 2005; Hon. FRCOphth 2006. Member, Editorial Board: Brit. Jl of Ophthalmology, 1977–90, 2000–07; European Jl of Ophthalmology, 1998–2007. *Publications:* (ed) Paediatric Ophthalmology, 1990, 4th edn (ed with C. S. Hoyt) 2013; (with C. S. Hoyt) Practical Paediatric Ophthalmology, 1997 (trans. Japanese, Portuguese, Spanish, Russian); 220 other publications as book chapters or in learned jls. *Recreations:* tennis, sailing, forestry, growing vegetables. *Address:* 23 Church Road, Barnes, SW13 9HE. *T:* (020) 8878 0305, 07836 344028. *E:* dsit@btinternet.com.

TAYLOR, David William; educational consultant, since 2004; Director of Inspection, Office for Standards in Education, 1999–2004; *b* 10 July 1945; *s* of Harry William Taylor and Eva Wade Taylor (*née* Day); *m* 1972, Pamela Linda (*née* Taylor); one *s* one *d. Educ:* Bancroft's Sch.; Worcester Coll., Oxford (BA Hons 1967; MA 1972); Inst. of Education, Univ. of London (PGCE, Distinction; Story-Miller Prize, 1968). Watford Grammar School: Classics Teacher, 1968–73; Head of Classics, 1973–78; HM Inspector of Schools, 1978–86; Staff Inspector, 1986–92; seconded to Touche Ross Management Consultants, 1991; Office for Standards in Education: Manager, Work Prog., 1992–93; Head, Strategic Planning, 1993–96; Head, Teacher Educn and Training, 1996–99. Exec. Sec., JACT, 1976–78. Schoolteacher Fellowship, Merton Coll., Oxford, 1978. Mem. Bd, Assoc. of Governing Bodies of Ind. Schs, 2013–. Chair of Govs, St Lawrence Coll., Ramsgate, 2011–. FRSA. Ed., Classical Literature and Society series, Bloomsbury Publishing (formerly Duckworth), 2006–. *Publications:* Cicero and Rome, 1973; Work in Ancient Greece and Rome, 1975; Acting and the Stage, 1978; Roman Society, 1980; The Greek and Roman Stage, 1999; numerous articles in professional jls. *Recreations:* chess, classical (esp. choral) music, cricket, classical literature, theatre, poetry, travel, gardening. *Address:* Firgrove, Seal Hollow Road, Sevenoaks, Kent TN13 3SF. *T:* (01732) 455410. *Club:* Athenæum.

TAYLOR, David William; a District Judge (Magistrates' Courts), Staffordshire, since 2009; *b* 1 March 1957. *Educ:* St Chad's Coll., Wolverhampton; Univ. of Southampton (LLB Hons). Admitted as solicitor, 1982. Recorder, 2002–14. Mem., Mental Health Rev. Tribunal, later Tribunal Judge, Mental Health (pt-time), 1999–. *Address:* North Staffordshire Justice Centre, Rycroft, Newcastle-under-Lyme ST5 2DT.

TAYLOR, David Wilson, CBE 2007; DL; Chairman, David Taylor Partnerships Ltd, since 2000; *b* 9 May 1950; *s* of Eric and Sybil Taylor; *m* 1980, Brenda Elizabeth Birchall; two *s*. *Educ:* Galashiels Acad.; Dundee Univ. Sch. of Architecture; Architectural Assoc. (DipArch, Dip. Urban and Regl Planning). Research and journalism, 1979–81; Advisor on regl policy to John Prescott, MP, 1981–83; Lancashire Enterprises Ltd: Dep. Man. Dir, 1983–85; Man. Dir, 1985–89; AMEC plc: Man. Dir, AMEC Regeneration, 1989–92; Man. Dir, AMEC Develts, 1992–93; Chief Exec., English Partnerships, 1993–96; Gp Chief Exec., Lancs Enterprises, subseq. Enterprise plc, 1996–2000. Director: INWARD, 1996–99; Preston North End plc, 1996– (Dep. Chm.); non-executive Chairman: Vektor Ltd, 1996–2004; Angela Campbell Gp, 1996–98; Era Ltd, 1997–2005; Hull Citybuild Ltd, 2003–09; Elevate East Lancs, 2003–09; Silvertown Quays Ltd, 2003–10; BL-Canada Quays Ltd, 2005–; Parking Eye Ltd, 2005–13; Professional Development TV Ltd, 2005–09; Venture Extreme Ltd, 2006–; Rockpools Resourcing & Consulting Ltd, 2010–; Energy 10 Ltd, 2012–; Allied Lighting Ltd, 2012–; Endo Enterprises (UK) Ltd, 2012–; Momentum + Ltd, 2012–; non-executive Director: John Maunders Gp plc, 1996–98; Central Lancs Develt Agency, 1997–2001; United Waste Services, 1997–2000; Manchester Commonwealth Games Ltd, 1999–2003; London and Southern Ltd, 2000–05; UK Regeneration Ltd, 2004–06. Special Advr to Dep. Prime Minister, 1997–98. Chm., NW Film Commn, 1996–2001; Dir, Olympic Delivery Authy, 2006–14. Chm., Phoenix Trust, 1997–2001; Trustee, Prince's Foundn, 2000–03. Pro-Chancellor and Chm., Univ. of Central Lancashire, 2014–. FRSA 2006. Hon. Fellow, Univ. of Central Lancashire, 1996. DL Lancs, 2014. *Recreations:* football (British and American), Rugby (Union and League). *Address:* (office) 88 Fishergate Hill, Preston PR1 8JD. *T:* (01772) 883888. *Club:* Royal Automobile.

TAYLOR, Deborah Elizabeth; a Judge of the Upper Tribunal (Immigration and Asylum Chamber) (formerly a Senior Immigration Judge, Asylum and Immigration Tribunal), since 2005; *b* Bolton, Lancs, 14 March 1953; *d* of Bernard and Barbara Crossley; *m* 1976, Christopher Marc Taylor; four *s*. *Educ:* Bolton Sch.; York Univ. (BA Hons Hist. 1974); Hughes Hall, Cambridge (Cert Ed 1975). Solicitor, Mary Ward Legal Settlement, 1981–85; teacher, British Sch., New Delhi, 1987–89; solicitor, Stockwell and Clapham Law Centre, 1990–92; Immigration Adjudicator, 1992–97; Centre Adjudicator, Manchester, 1997–2002; Regl Adjudicator, 2002–05. *Recreations:* fell-walking, classical music (listening and playing), family and friends. *Address:* Upper Tribunal (Immigration and Asylum Chamber), Phoenix House, Rushton Avenue, Bradford BD3 7BH. *E:* deborah.taylor@judiciary.gsi.gov.uk.

TAYLOR, Desmond Philip S.; *see* Shawe-Taylor.

TAYLOR, Duncan John Rushworth, CBE 2002; HM Diplomatic Service; Ambassador to Mexico, since 2013; *b* 17 Oct. 1958; *s* of Sir John Lang, (Jock), Taylor, KCMG and of Molly Taylor; *m* 1981, Marie-Beatrice Terpougoff; two *s* three *d*. *Educ:* Trinity Coll., Cambridge (MA Hons Modern Langs 1980). Retail analyst, Gulf Oil GB, 1980–82; entered FCO, 1982; Third Sec., FCO, 1982–83; Third, later Second, Sec., Havana, 1983–87; First Sec., FCO, 1987–92; Hd, Commercial Section, Budapest, 1992–96; on secondment to Rolls Royce plc as Dir, Latin American Affairs, 1996–97; Counsellor, FCO, 1997–2000; Dep. Consul Gen. and Dep. Hd of Mission, New York, 2000–05; High Comr, Barbados and Eastern Caribbean States, 2005–09; Gov., Grand Cayman, 2010–13. *Recreations:* sports, travel, theatre, films, books, food. *Address:* BFPO 5531, HA4 6EP. *E:* duncan.taylor@fco.gov.uk.

TAYLOR, Sir Edward Macmillan, (Sir Teddy), Kt 1991; journalist, consultant and company director; *b* 18 April 1937; *s* of late Edward Taylor and Minnie Hamilton Taylor; *m* 1970, Sheila Duncan; two *s* one *d*. *Educ:* Glasgow High School and University (MA (Hons) Econ. and Politics). Commercial Editorial Staff of Glasgow Herald, 1958–59; Industrial Relations Officer on Staff of Clyde Shipbuilders' Assoc., 1959–64. Director: Shepherds Foods, 1968–; Ansvar (Temperance) Insurance, 1970–98. Advr, Port of Tilbury Police Fedn (formerly Port of London Police Fedn), 1972–2004. MP (C): Glasgow, Cathcart, 1964–79; Southend East, March 1980–1997; Rochford and Southend East, 1997–2005. Parly Under-Sec. of State, Scottish Office, 1970–71, resigned due to opposition to EU membership; Parly Under-Sec. of State, Scottish Office, 1974; Opposition spokesman on Trade, 1977, on Scotland affairs, 1977–79. Vice-Chm., Cons. Parly Party Home Affairs Cttee, 1992–94 (Sec., 1983–92). NZ Commemoration Medal, 1990. *Publications:* Hearts of Stone (novel), 1968; Teddy Boy Blue, 2008; contributions to the press. *Address:* 12 Lynton Road, Thorpe Bay, Southend-on-Sea, Essex SS1 3BE. *T:* (01702) 586282.

TAYLOR, Prof. Edwin William, FRS 1978; Louis Block Professor of Molecular Genetics and Cell Biology, University of Chicago, 1984–99, half-time, 1999, now Emeritus (Professor, Department of Biophysics, 1975–99); part-time Research Professor, Department of Cell and Molecular Biology, Northwestern University Medical School, since 2000; *b* Toronto, 8 June 1929; *s* of William Taylor and Jean Taylor (*née* Christie); *m* 1956, Jean Heather Logan; two *s* one *d*. *Educ:* Univ. of Toronto (BA 1952); McMaster Univ. (MSc 1955); Univ. of Chicago (PhD 1957). Asst Prof., 1959–63, Associate Prof., 1963–67, Prof., 1967–72, Univ. of Chicago; Prof. of Biology, King's College and MRC Unit, London, 1972–74; Associate Dean, Div. of Biol Sci. and Medicine, 1977–79, Prof. and Chm., Dept of Biology, 1979–84, Univ. of Chicago. Rockefeller Foundn Fellow, 1957–58; Nat. Insts of Health Fellow, 1958–59, cons. to NIH, 1970–72, 1976–80. Instructor in Physiology, Marine Biol Lab. summer program, Woods Hole, Ma, 1991–98. Member: Amer. Biochem. Soc.; Biophysical Soc.; Fellow, Amer. Acad. of Arts and Scis, 1991; NAS, USA, 2001. E. B. Wilson Medal, Amer. Soc. for Cell Biology, 1999. *Address:* Cummings Life Sciences Center, University of Chicago, 920 East 58th Street, Chicago, IL 60637, USA. *T:* (773) 7021660; 5805 South Dorchester Avenue, Apt 11C, Chicago, IL 60637, USA. *T:* (773) 9552441.

TAYLOR, Enid, FRCS, FRCOphth; Consultant Ophthalmic Surgeon, North Middlesex Hospital, 1974–98; *b* 18 June 1933; *d* of Joseph William Weldon and Jane Weldon; *m* 1959, Thomas Henry Taylor; two *s*. *Educ:* Girton Coll., Cambridge (MA); London Hosp. Med. Coll. (MB BChir; DO 1963). FRCS 1965; FRCOphth 1988. Consultant Ophthalmic Surgeon, Elizabeth Garrett Anderson Hosp., 1966–73. Chm., NE Thames Ophthalmic Adv. Cttee, DHSS, 1979–86. Member Council: Faculty of Ophthalmologists, 1980–88; Coll. of Ophthalmologists, 1988–90; Sect. Ophthalmol, RSocMed, 1981–85 (Vice-Pres., 1985–88); Mem., Ophthalmic Cttees, BMA, 1982–2000. Liveryman, 1973, Asst, 1989–2008, Master, 2002–03, Soc. of Apothecaries. *Publications:* contrib. papers and presentations on diabetic retinal disease. *Recreations:* cooking, needlework. *Address:* 60 Wood Vale, N10 3DN. *T:* (020) 8883 6146.

See also S. W. Taylor.

TAYLOR, Prof. Eric Andrew, FRCP, FRCPsych, FMedSci; Professor of Child and Adolescent Psychiatry, Institute of Psychiatry, King's College London, 1999–2009, now Emeritus; Hon. Consultant, Maudsley Hospital, since 1978; *b* 22 Dec. 1944; *s* of Dr Jack Andrew Taylor and Grace Taylor; *m* 1969, Anne Patricia Roberts (*d* 2000); two *s*. *Educ:* Trinity Hall, Cambridge (MA); Harvard Univ.; Middx Hosp. Med. Sch. (MB). FRCP 1986; FRCPsych 1988. SHO, Middx Hosp., 1969–71; Res. Fellow, Harvard Univ., 1971; Registrar, then Sen. Registrar, Maudsley Hosp., 1973–76; Institute of Psychiatry: Lectr, then Sen. Lectr, 1976–86; Reader, 1986–93; Prof. of Developmental Neuropsychiatry, 1993–99; Clinical Scientist, MRC, 1990–99. Cantwell Lectr, UCLA, 2004; Emanuel Miller Lectr, Assoc. for Child Psychol. and Psychiatry, 2004. Non-exec. Dir, S London and Maudsley NHS, 2008–10. Trustee: Nat. Acad. of Parenting Practitioners, 2008–10; Place2Be, 2010–. Corresp. Mem., Argentina Acad. of Sci., 2009–. Editor: Jl Child Psychol. and Psychiatry, 1984–95; Eur. Child and Adolescent Psychiatry, 2003–13. FMedSci 2000. Hon. FRCPsych 2012. Hon. Mem., child psychiatry assocs in Germany, Chile and UK. Ruane Prize, Nat. Assoc. for Res. in Schizophrenia and Affective Disorders, 2009; Heinrich Hoffman Medal, World Fedn of Attention Deficit Hyperactivity Disorder, 2011. *Publications:* The Hyperactive Child: a parents' guide, 1985, 3rd edn 1997; The Overactive Child, 1986 (Spanish and Japanese edns 1991); The Epidemiology of Childhood Hyperactivity, 1991; (ed jtly) Child and Adolescent Psychiatry: modern approaches, 3rd edn 1994 to 5th edn (as Rutter's Child and Adolescent Psychiatry) 2009; People with Hyperactivity: understanding and managing their problems, 2009; (with A. Stringaris) Disruptive Mood: irritability in children and adolescents, 2015; contrib. numerous papers to scientific jls on child neuropsychiatry. *Address:* Department of Child and Adolescent Psychiatry, Institute of Psychiatry, Psychology and Neuroscience, King's College London, De Crespigny Park, SE5 8AF. *T:* (020) 7848 0489. *Clubs:* Athenæum, Royal Society of Medicine.

TAYLOR, Dr Frank Henry, CBE 2003; Secretary, Charles Wallace India Trust, 1992–2004; *b* 20 Jan. 1932; *s* of Frank Taylor and Norah (*née* Dunn). *Educ:* Frimley and Camberley Co. Grammar Sch.; King's Coll., London (BSc 1953; PhD 1957). Beit Meml Fellow for Med. Res., Imperial Coll., London and Pasteur Inst., Paris, 1957–60; British Council, 1960–92: Science Officer, 1960–61; Asst Cultural Attaché, Cairo, 1961–64; Asst Regl Rep., Calcutta, 1965–69; Science Officer, Rio de Janeiro, 1970–74; Dir, Science and Technology Dept, 1974–78; Rep., Saudi Arabia, 1978–81; Head Operations, Technical Educn and Trng in Overseas Countries, and Dep. Controller, Science, Technology and Education Div., 1981–84; Counsellor, British Council and Cultural Affairs, Ankara, 1984–87; Dep. Controller, Asia and Pacific Div., then S and W Asia Div., 1987–88; Controller, Africa and ME Div., 1989–90; Dir, Libraries, Books and Inf. Div., 1990–92. *Publications:* articles on surface chemistry and reviews in Proc. Royal Soc., etc. *Recreations:* music, bridge, bookbinding, Middle East. *Address:* 9 Shaftesbury Road, Richmond, Surrey TW9 2TD.

TAYLOR, Prof. Fredric William, DPhil; Halley Professor of Physics, Oxford University, 2000–11, now Emeritus (Head of Department of Atmospheric, Oceanic and Planetary Physics, 1979–2000); Fellow, Jesus College, Oxford, 1979–2011, now Emeritus; *b* 24 Sept. 1944; *s* of William Taylor and Ena Lloyd (*née* Burns); *m* 1969, Doris Jean Buer. *Educ:* Duke of Northumberland's Sch.; Univ. of Liverpool (BSc 1966); Univ. of Oxford (DPhil 1970; MA 1983). Resident Res. Associate, US Nat. Res. Council, 1970–72; Sen. Scientist, 1972–79, Dist. Vis. Scientist, 1996–, Jet Propulsion Lab., CIT; Oxford University: Reader in Atmospheric Physics, 1983–89; Prof. of Atmospheric Physics, 1990–99. *Publications:* Cambridge Atlas of the Planets, 1982, 2nd edn 1986 (trans. German 1984, Italian 1988); Remote Sounding of Atmospheres, 1984, 2nd edn 1987; (with A. Coustenis) Titan, 1999, 2nd edn 2008; (with M. Lopez-Puertas) Non-LTE Radiative Transfer in the Atmosphere, 2001; The Cambridge Guide to the Planets, 2002; Elementary Climate Physics, 2005; (with I. Vardavas) Radiation and Climate, 2007, 2nd edn 2011; The Scientific Exploration of Mars, 2009; Planetary Atmospheres, 2010; The Scientific Exploration of Venus, 2014; contrib. to learned jls. *Recreations:* walking, motoring, watching sport, literature, history, railways. *Address:* Clarendon Laboratory, Oxford OX1 3PU. *T:* (01865) 272903; Jesus College, Oxford OX1 3DW.

TAYLOR, Geoffrey Keith, CB 2007; PhD; Director (part-time), External Relations, Government Communications Headquarters, since 2001; *b* 1 March 1948; *s* of Wilfred Taylor and Irene Isobel Taylor (*née* Smith); *m* 1969, Patricia Anne Angell; two *s*. *Educ:* Nottingham High Sch.; Queens' Coll., Cambridge (BA 1970); Univ. of Leicester (PhD 1973). Res. Demonstrator, Univ. of Leicester, 1970; Government Communications Headquarters: joined, 1973, Asst Deptl Specialist; Principal, 1978; Sen. Civil Service, 1987; Dir, Special Progs, 1999–2001. Mem., Croquet Assoc. *Publications:* papers on quantum molecular dynamics in Physical Rev., etc. *Recreations:* croquet, buying, selling and mending anything, foreign travel, playing 1930s popular piano music poorly, mooching. *Address:* c/o Government Communications Headquarters, Hubble Road, Cheltenham GL51 0EX. *Clubs:* Nottingham Croquet, Cheltenham Croquet.

TAYLOR, Gordon, OBE 2008; Chief Executive, Professional Footballers' Association, since 1981; *b* 28 Dec. 1944; *s* of Alec and Mary Taylor; *m* 1968, Catharine Margaret Johnston; two *s*. *Educ:* Ashton-under-Lyne Grammar Sch.; Bolton Technical Coll.; Univ. of London (BScEcon Hons (ext.)). Professional footballer with: Bolton Wanderers, 1960–70; Birmingham City, 1970–76; Blackburn Rovers, 1976–78; Vancouver Whitecaps (N American Soccer League), 1977; Bury, 1978–80, retd. Professional Footballers Association: Mem., Management Cttee, 1971; Chm., 1978–80; (full-time) Asst Sec., 1980; Sec./Treasurer, 1981; Pres., Internat. Assoc. of Professional Footballers Unions, 1994–2005 (Hon. Pres., 2005–). Hon. MA Loughborough Univ. of Technol., 1986 (for services to football); Hon. DArts De Montfort, 1998. *Recreations:* theatre, dining-out, watching football, reading. *Address:* (office) 20 Oxford Court, Bishopsgate, off Lower Mosley Street, Manchester M2 3WQ. *T:* (0161) 236 0575.

TAYLOR, Dr Gordon William; Managing Director, Firemarket Ltd, since 1988; *b* 26 June 1928; *s* of William and Elizabeth Taylor; *m* 1954, Audrey Catherine Bull; three *s* two *d*. *Educ:* J. H. Burrows Sch., Grays, Essex; Army Technical Sch.; London Univ. (BScEng Hons, PhDEng). MICE, MIMechE, MIET. Kellogg Internat. Corp., 1954–59; W. R. Grace, 1960–62; Gen. Man., Nalco Ltd, 1962–66; BTR Industries, 1966–68; Managing Director: Kestrel Chemicals, 1968–69; Astral Marketing, 1969–70; Robson Refractories, 1970–87. Greater London Council: Alderman, 1972–77; Mem. for Croydon Central, 1977–80; Chairman: Public Services Cttee, 1977–78; London Transp. Cttee, 1978–79. Chm., W London Residents' Assoc., 2003–. *Recreations:* theatre, reading, tennis, croquet. *Club:* Holland Park Lawn Tennis.

TAYLOR, Graham, OBE 2002; football summarizer, Radio Five Live, since 2003; freelance football media correspondent, since 2003; *b* Worksop, Notts, 15 Sept. 1944; *s* of Tommy Taylor; *m* 1965, Rita Cowling; two *d*. *Educ:* Scunthorpe Grammar Sch. Professional football player: Grimsby Town, 1962–68; Lincoln City, 1968–72; Manager: Lincoln City, 1972–77; Watford, 1977–87 and 1996–2001; Aston Villa, 1987–90 and 2002–03; England Football Team, 1990–93; Wolverhampton Wanderers, 1994–95.

TAYLOR, Hamish Wilson; Chief Executive, Hamish Taylor Skills Exchange Network, since 2004; *b* Kitwe, N Rhodesia, 18 June 1960; *s* of late Dr Douglas James Wilson Taylor and of Mairi Helen Taylor (*née* Pitt); *m* 1984, Fiona Marion Darroch; three *s*. *Educ:* Skinners' Sch., Tunbridge Wells; Univ. of St Andrews (Pres., Athletic Union, 1981–82; MA Hons Econs 1982); Emory Univ., Atlanta (Robert T. Jones Schol., 1983; Business Sch. Fellow; St Andrews Soc. of Washington Schol., 1983–84; MBA 1984). FCILT (FCIT 1999); FCIB 2001. Brand Manager, Procter and Gamble Ltd, 1984–90; Mgt Consultant, Price Waterhouse, 1990–93; Gen. Manager, Brands, British Airways, 1993–97; Man. Dir, Eurostar (UK) Ltd, 1997–99; Chief Exec., Eurostar Gp, 1999; Chief Executive: Sainsbury's Bank, 2000–02; Vision UK, 2002–04. Non-exec. Dir, Chartered Brands, 2003–08; Mem., Adv. Panel, Bright Grey, 2003–08. Chm., Europe, Middle East and Africa Adv. Bd, Emory Univ., 2006–08. Trustee, Robert T. Jones Meml Trust, 2005–. Mem. Bd, Edinburgh Rugby, 2010–14. Mentor, BBC TV series, Teen Canteen, 2013. FRSA 1999. Freeman, City of Glasgow, 1979.

Rail Professional Business Manager of the Year, Rail Professional Magazine, 1998; Sheth Dist. Internat. Alumni Award, Emory Univ., 2004. *Recreations:* athletics (Scottish Junior international, 1979), football, Rugby, piano. *E:* hamish@hamishtaylor.com.

TAYLOR, Dr Hilary Anne, (Mrs Peter Vickers); Director, Hilary Taylor Landscape Associates Ltd, since 1998; Partner, Howgill Tattershall Fine Art, since 2012; *b* Spital, Cheshire, 16 March 1948; *d* of Derek George Dawson Taylor and Dorothy Taylor (*née* Fullerton); *m* 1992, Peter Vickers; one *s*. *Educ:* Wycombe High Sch. for Girls, High Wycombe; Univ. of E Anglia (BA Hons Art/Architecture Hist. 1969); Univ. of Nottingham (PhD 1974). Hd, Art and Design Hist., Trent Poly., 1974–88; freelance lectr, researcher and campaigner, historic public parks and gardens, 1988–94; Dir, Dawson Taylor Landscapes, 1990–96. England-wide survey of public parks, English Heritage, 1994–95. Churchill Fellow, 1994. Member: Expert Panel on Historic Bldgs and Land, Heritage Lottery Fund, 2001–08; Church Bldgs Council and Statutory Adv. Cttee, 2008–. Work on conservation mgt plans for English landscapes for Nat. Trust incl. Studley Royal and Fountains Abbey, Calke Abbey, Kedleston and Lyveden New Bield. Trustee, Horniman Mus. and Gardens, 2009–14. FRSA. *Publications:* James McNeill Whistler, 1976; British Impressionism, 1989; (contrib.) The Regeneration of Public Parks, 2000; (contrib.) Encyclopedia of Gardens: history and design, 2001; contrib. articles to Art Hist., Garden Hist. *Recreations:* Pembrokeshire coast, churches, gardening, reading, art galleries, sharing my husband's and my son's love of cricket. *Address:* 1 Scotsmansfield, Burway Road, Church Stretton, Shropshire SY6 6DP. *T:* (01694) 723273. *E:* hilary-taylor@htla.co.uk.

TAYLOR, Sir Hugh (Henderson), KCB 2009 (CB 2000); Permanent Secretary, Department of Health, 2006–10; Chairman, Guy's and St Thomas' NHS Foundation Trust, since 2011; *b* 22 March 1950; *s* of late Leslie Henderson Taylor and Alison Taylor; *m* 1989, Diane Bacon; two *d*. *Educ:* Brentwood Sch.; Emmanuel Coll., Cambridge (BA). Joined Home Office, 1972; Private Sec. to Minister of State, 1976–77; Principal Private Sec. to Home Sec., 1983–85; Asst Sec., 1984; Prison Service, 1985–88 and 1992–93; seconded to Cabinet Office, 1988–91; Under Sec., 1993–96, and Dir, Top Mgt Prog., 1994–96, Cabinet Office; Dir of Services, Prison Service, 1996–97; Dir of Human Resources, NHS Exec., 1998–2001; Dir Gen. of Ext. and Corporate Affairs, then Corporate Affairs, subseq. of Deptl Mgt, DoH, 2001–06. Chm., Nat. Skills Acad. for Health, 2013–. Trustee: Macmillan Cancer Support, 2011–; Nuffield Trust, 2011–; RCP, 2011–14; Cicely Saunders Inst., 2011–. Trustee, James Allen's Girls Sch., 2008– (Chm., 2014–). *Recreations:* arts, sport. *Club:* MCC.

TAYLOR, Hugo M.; *see* Mascie-Taylor.

TAYLOR, Rt Rev. Humphrey Vincent; Bishop Suffragan of Selby, 1991–2003; an Hon. Assistant Bishop, Diocese of Worcester, since 2004; *b* 5 March 1938; *s* of late Maurice Humphrey Taylor and Mary Patricia Stuart Taylor (*née* Wood, later Pearson); *m* 1965, Anne Katharine Dart; two *d*. *Educ:* Harrow School; Pembroke College, Cambridge (MA); London University (MA). Nat. Service Officer, RAF, 1956–58; Cambridge 1958–61; College of the Resurrection, Mirfield, 1961–63; Curate in London, 1963–66; Rector of Lilongwe, Malaŵi, 1967–71; Chaplain, Bishop Grosseteste Coll., Lincoln, 1971–74; Sec. for Chaplaincies in Higher Education, Gen. Synod Bd of Education, 1974–80; Mission Programmes Sec., USPG, 1980–84; Sec., USPG, 1984–91. Hon. Canon of Bristol Cathedral, 1986–91; Provincial Canon of Southern Africa, 1989. Moderator, Conf. for World Mission, BCC, 1987–90; Chairman: Internat. and Develt Affairs Cttee, Archbps' Council, 1996–2003; Northern and Yorkshire Adv. Cttee on Spiritual Care and Chaplaincy, 1997–2003. *Recreations:* music, gardening. *Address:* 10 High Street, Honeybourne, Worcs WR11 7PQ.

See also R. M. Thornely-Taylor.

TAYLOR, Ian Colin, MBE 1974; Managing Director, Fentiman Consultants Ltd; *b* 18 April 1945; *s* of late Horace Stanley Taylor and Beryl Taylor (*née* Harper); *m* 1974, Hon. Carole Alport, *d* of Baron Alport, PC, TD; two *s*. *Educ:* Whitley Abbey Sch., Coventry; Keele Univ. (BA); London School of Economics (Res. Schol.). Corporate financial adviser; Director: Mathercourt Securities Ltd, 1980–90; Petards Gp (formerly Screen plc), 1999–2009 (Dep. Chm., 2003); Next Fifteen Group plc, 1999–2011; Speed-Trap Ltd, 1999–. Mem. Council, STFC, 2011–. Nat. Chm., Fedn of Cons. Students, 1968–69; Chm., Eur. Union of Christian Democratic and Cons. Students, 1969–70; Hon. Sec., Brit. Cons. Assoc. in France, 1976–78; Chairman: Commonwealth Youth Exchange Council, 1980–84; Cons. Foreign and Commonwealth Council, 1990–96; Nat. Chm., Cons. Gp for Europe, 1985–88 and 2007–. Contested (C) Coventry SE, Feb. 1974. MP (C) Esher, 1987–97, Esher and Walton, 1997–2010. Parliamentary Private Secretary: FCO, 1990; to Sec. of State for Health, 1990–92; to Chancellor of Duchy of Lancaster, 1992–94; Parly Under-Sec. of State, DTI (Minister for Sci. and Technol.), 1994–97; opposition front bench spokesman on NI, 1997. Member, Select Committee on: Foreign Affairs, 1987–90; Science and Technol., 1998–2001. Chm., Parly and Scientific Cttee, 2009–10; Vice Chm., Parly Information Technol. Cttee. Chairman: Cons. Parly European Affairs Cttee, 1988–89; Cons. Policy Taskforce on Sci., 2006–10. Chairman: European Movement, 2000–04; Cuba Initiative, 2008–; Mem., IPPR Commn on Nat. Security; Dir, EURIM. Chm., Tory Europe Network, 2002–10. Vice-Chm., Assoc. of Cons. Clubs, 1988–92. Gov., Research into Ageing, 1997–2001; Centre of Cell, 2004–. Liveryman, Co. of Information Technologists, 1998–. *Publications:* various pamphlets; contrib. to various jls, etc, on politics and business. *Recreations:* opera, cigars, shooting. *Club:* Buck's.

TAYLOR, Prof. Irving, MD; FRCS; Professor of Surgery, since 1993, and Vice Dean, UCL Medical School (formerly University College London Medical School, then Royal Free and University College Medical School), since 2002, University College London (Chairman, Academic Division of Surgical Specialties and Head of Department, 1993–2004); *b* 7 Jan. 1945; *s* of Sam and Fay Taylor; *m* 1969, Berenice Penelope Brunner; three *d*. *Educ:* Roundhay Sch., Leeds; Sheffield Univ. Med. Sch. (MB ChB 1968; MD 1973; ChM 1978). FRCS 1972. Royal Infirmary, then Royal Hospital, Sheffield: House Officer, 1968; SHO, 1969–70; Surg. Registrar, 1971–73; Sen. Registrar in Surgery, 1973–77; Sen. Lectr and Consultant Surgeon, Liverpool Univ., 1977–81; Prof. of Surgery, Univ. of Southampton, 1981–93. Hunterian Prof., RCS, 1981 (Jacksonian Award, 1996; Stanford Cade Medal, 2000; Bradshaw Medal, 2012); Bennett Lectr, TCD, 1990; Gordon Bell Lectr, RACS, 1996. Mem. Council, RCS, 2004–13 (Examr, 2000–01); Chm., MRC Colorectal Cancer Cttee, 1990–95; President: British Assoc. of Surgical Oncology, 1995–98; Soc. of Academic and Res. Surgeons, 2005–; Eur. Soc. of Surgical Oncology, 2006–08 (Vice-Pres., 2004–06); Sec., Surgical Res. Soc., 1988–90; Editorial Sec., Assoc. of Surgeons, 1988–91. Case Examiner, Fitness to Practise Directorate, GMC, 2003–. Editor-in-Chief: Eur. Jl of Surgical Oncology, 1995–2003; Annals of RCS, 2004–09. FRSocMed 1983; FMedSci 2000; FRCPSGlas 2001. *Publications:* Progress in Surgery, 1985, 3rd edn 1989; Complications of Surgery of the Gastrointestinal Tract, 1985; Benign Breast Disease, 1990; Essential General Surgical Oncology, 1995; Surgical Principles, 1996; Recent Advances in Surgery, annually, 1991–; Fast Facts: colorectal cancer, 1999, 3rd edn 2010; Mind Maps in Surgery, 2008; articles and papers on gen. surgery, surgical educn, surgical oncology, breast, colorectal and liver cancer in med. jls. *Recreations:* bridge, swimming, rambling, watching cricket, travel, supporting Leeds United. *Address:* 43 Francklyn Gardens, Edgware HA8 8RU. *T:* (020) 8958 8364.

TAYLOR, Dr James; Geographical Director, Africa, Middle East and South Asia, British Council, 2000–03; *b* 22 April 1951; *s* of George Thomson Taylor and Elizabeth Gibson Taylor (*née* Dunsmore); *m* 1986, Dianne Carol Cawthorne; one *s*. *Educ:* Cumnock Acad.; Strathclyde Univ. (BSc 1973; PhD 1977). ACS Petroleum Res. Fellow, Bristol Univ., 1977–78; von Humboldt Fellow, Univ. des Saarlandes, Germany, 1978–79; Res. Chemist, Procter & Gamble, 1979–80; SSO, Scottish Marine Biol Assoc., 1980–84; British Council: Asst Dir, Kuwait, 1984–86; First Sec. (Sci. and Develt), British High Commn, Calcutta, 1986–88; Head, Tech. Adv. Service, Sci. and Technol. Dept, 1988–90; Asst Registrar, Res. Support Unit, Leeds Univ., 1990–92; Development and Training Services, British Council: Contract Dir, Central and Eastern Europe, 1992–93; Head, Europe Gp, 1993–95; Head, Africa and ME Gp, 1995–97; Dir, Zimbabwe and Head, Africa Gp, 1997–2000. *Publications:* contribs on marine sediment chem. to sci. jls. *Recreations:* gardening, TV soaps, walking.

TAYLOR, James Alastair; Sheriff Principal of Glasgow and Strathkelvin, 2005–11; *b* 21 Feb. 1951; *s* of Alastair and Margaret Taylor; *m* 1980, Lesley Doig Macleod; two *s*. *Educ:* Nairn Acad.; Univ. of Aberdeen (BSc; LLB). Partner, A. C. Morrison & Richards, Solicitors, Aberdeen, 1980–87; Partner, 1988–98, Hd of Litigation Dept, 1992–98, McGrigor Donald, Solicitors, Glasgow; Sheriff: of Lothian and Borders, 1998–99; of Glasgow and Strathkelvin, 1999–2005. Chm., Disciplinary Tribunal, ICAS, 2000–. Mem. Bd, Civil Justice Review, 2007–09; Chm., Review into the Expenses and Funding of Civil Litigation in Scotland, 2011–13. Dir, Lodging House Mission, 2002–12. Hon. LLD Glasgow, 2013. *Publications:* (contrib.) International Intellectual Property Litigation, 1998; (contrib.) Sentencing Practice, 2000; (contrib.) Macphail Sheriff Court Practice, 3rd edn, 2006. *Recreations:* golf, wine, good food, jazz. *Address:* Tyninghame, Albert Street, Nairn IV12 4HQ. *Clubs:* Nairn Golf; Nairn Dunbar Golf; Royal Aberdeen Golf.

TAYLOR, Jeremy; *see* Taylor, C. J. B.

TAYLOR, Jeremy Paul; Chief Executive, National Voices, since 2009; *b* Leeds, 30 Dec. 1962; *s* of David Taylor and late Rosalind Taylor (*née* Sacks); *m* 1999, Meriel Schindler; one *s* two *d*. *Educ:* Gonville and Caius Coll., Cambridge (BA Social and Pol Scis 1985; MA). Res. Asst, Univ. of Glasgow, 1985–87; Res. Officer, Scottish Consumer Council, 1987–89; civil servant, Scottish Office, incl. Hd, Perm. Sec.'s Office, and Hd, London Office, Locate in Scotland, 1989–97; civil servant, then sen. civil servant, HM Treasury, incl. Sec., Lyons relocation review, and Hd, Performance and Efficiency Team, 1997–2007; Exec. Dir, Groundwork E London, 2007–09. *Recreations:* running, walking, ski-ing, theatre, family. *Address:* c/o National Voices, 1st Floor, Bride House, 18–20 Bride Lane, EC4Y 8EE. *T:* (020) 3176 0738. *E:* jeremy.taylor@nationalvoices.org.uk.

TAYLOR, Jessie; *see* Taylor, Margaret J.

TAYLOR, Rt Rev. John Bernard, KCVO 1997; Bishop of St Albans, 1980–95; Lord High Almoner to HM the Queen, 1988–97; Hon. Assistant Bishop: diocese of Ely, since 1995; diocese of Europe, 1998–2013; *b* 6 May 1929; *s* of George Ernest and Gwendoline Irene Taylor; *m* 1956, Linda Courtenay Barnes; one *s* two *d*. *Educ:* Watford Grammar Sch.; Christ's Coll., Cambridge; Jesus Coll., Cambridge. MA Cantab. Vicar of Henham and Elsenham, Essex, 1959–64; Vice-Principal, Oak Hill Theological Coll., 1964–72; Vicar of All Saints', Woodford Wells, 1972–75; Archdeacon of West Ham, 1975–80. Examining Chaplain to Bishop of Chelmsford, 1962–80. Hon. Chaplain, Jesus Coll., Cambridge, 1997–. Chm., Gen. Synod's Cttee for Communications, 1986–93. Member: Churches' Council for Covenanting, 1978–82; Liturgical Commn, 1981–86; Doctrine Commn, 1989–95. Chairman Council: Haileybury Coll., 1980–95; Wycliffe Hall, Oxford, 1985–99; Tyndale House, Cambridge, 1997–2004. President: Hildenborough Evangelistic Trust, 1985–99; Garden Tomb Assoc., Jerusalem, 1986–2010; Church's Ministry among Jewish People, 1996–2010; Bible Soc., 1997–2004. Took his seat in House of Lords, 1985. Hon. LLD Hertfordshire, 1995. *Publications:* A Christian's Guide to the Old Testament, 1966; Evangelism among Children and Young People, 1967; Tyndale Commentary on Ezekiel, 1969; Preaching through the Prophets, 1983; Preaching on God's Justice, 1994. *Address:* 22 Conduit Head Road, Cambridge CB3 0EY. *T:* (01223) 313783. *Club:* National.

TAYLOR, Rev. John Brian, PhD; President, Methodist Conference, 1997–98; Chairman, Liverpool District, Methodist Church, 1995–2003; *b* 3 July 1937; *s* of Frank and Alice Taylor; *m* 1959, Patricia Margaret Lord; two *s*. *Educ:* Buxton Coll.; Durham Univ. (BA, DipEd); Hartley Victoria Coll. and Manchester Univ. (BD); PhD Open Univ. 1992. Headmaster, Cours Secondaire Protestant de Dabou, Côte d'Ivoire, 1961–64; Methodist Minister, 1964–; Chaplain, Univ. of Sheffield, 1976–79; Tutor, Queen's Coll., Birmingham, 1979–88 (Hon. Fellow, 2001); Gen. Sec., Methodist Church Div. of Ministries, 1988–95. Commandeur: l'Ordre National (Côte d'Ivoire), 1997; l'Ordre du Mono (Togo), 2000. *Publications:* Preaching as Doctrine, 2001; various articles in learned jls. *Recreations:* genealogy, gardening, music, cooking. *Address:* 7 Mordaunt Drive, Four Oaks, Sutton Coldfield B75 5PT.

TAYLOR, Prof. John Bryan, FRS 1970; Fondren Professor of Plasma Theory, University of Texas at Austin, 1989–94; Chief Physicist, 1981–89, Consultant, 1994–2008, UKAEA Culham Laboratory; *b* 26 Dec. 1928; *s* of Frank and Ada Taylor, Birmingham; *m* 1951, Joan M. Hargest; one *s* one *d*. *Educ:* Oldbury Grammar Sch.; Birmingham Univ., 1947–50 and 1952–55. RAF, 1950–52. Atomic Weapons Research Establishment, Aldermaston, 1955–59 and 1960–62; Harkness Fellow, Commonwealth Fund, Univ. of California (Berkeley), 1959–60; Culham Laboratory (UKAEA), 1962–69 and 1970–89 (Head of Theoretical Physics Div., 1963–81); Inst. for Advanced Study, Princeton, 1969. FInstP 1969. Fellow, Amer. Phys. Soc., 1984. Maxwell Medal, IPPS, 1971; Max Born Medal, German Phys. Soc., 1979; Award for Excellence in Plasma Physics Res., 1986, James Clerk Maxwell Prize, 1999, Amer. Phys. Soc.; Dist. Career Award, Fusion Power Associates, 1999; Hannes Alfven Prize, Eur. Phys. Soc., 2004. *Publications:* contribs to scientific learned jls. *Address:* Radwinter, Winterbrook Lane, Wallingford OX10 9EJ. *T:* (01491) 837269.

TAYLOR, John Clayton, PhD; FRS 1981; FInstP; Professor of Mathematical Physics, Cambridge University, and Fellow of Robinson College, Cambridge, 1980–95, now Professor and Fellow Emeritus; *b* 4 Aug. 1930; *s* of Leonard Taylor and Edith (*née* Tytherleigh); *m* 1959, Gillian Mary (*née* Schofield); two *s*. *Educ:* Selhurst Grammar Sch., Croydon; Peterhouse, Cambridge (MA). Lectr, Imperial Coll., London, 1956–60; Lectr, Cambridge Univ., and Fellow of Peterhouse, 1960–64; Reader in Theoretical Physics, Oxford Univ., and Fellow of University Coll., Oxford, 1964–80 (Hon. Fellow, 1989). *Publications:* Gauge Theories of Weak Interactions, 1976; Hidden Unity in Nature's Laws, 2001; Gauge Theories in the Twentieth Century, 2001. *Address:* 9 Bowers Croft, Cambridge CB1 8RP.

TAYLOR, John Crawshaw, OBE 2011; FREng; inventor; Chairman: Sterna Aviation, since 1993; John C Taylor Ltd, since 1997; Auctor Ltd, since 2000; Fromanteel Ltd, since 2003; Arragon Mooar Estate Ltd, since 2004; *b* Buxton, Derbys, 25 Nov. 1936; *s* of Eric Hardman Taylor and Gwendolen Majorie Taylor (*née* Jones); *m* 1964, Heather Patricia Anderson (marr. diss. 1979); one *s* one *d*; partner, 1989, Valerie Whiteway (separated 1991); one *d*; *m* 1993, Jean Kathleen Turley; two step *c* (and one step *c* decd). *Educ:* King William's Coll., I of M; Corpus Christi Coll., Cambridge (BA Nat. Sci. Tripos 1959; Hon. Fellow 2002). Otter Controls Ltd: graduate trainee, 1959; Develt Manager, 1961; Dir, 1962; Chm., 1971–76; Dir, 1976–99, Chm., 1980–99, Castletown Thermostats, later Strix Ltd. Mem. Bd, Manx Electricity Authy, 2000–05. Visiting Professor: Manchester Sci. Enterprise Centre, UMIST, 2001; Physics Dept, Durham Univ., 2006–. Fellow, Inst. of Patentees and Inventors, 1965; FREng 2011. Mem., RYA. Hon. DEng UMIST, 2000. Percy Dawson Medal, Antiquarian Horol Soc., 2004; Master's Medal, Clockmakers' Co., 2009; Chancellor's 800th Anniversary Medal for Outstanding Philanthropy, Univ. of Cambridge, 2009. *Publications:* (contrib.)

Horological Masterworks, 2003; (contrib.) Huygen's Legacy, 2004; (jtly) The Excitement of Time, 2006. *Recreations:* flying (TBM 850 and glider), rock climbing and mountaineering, skiing, photography, yachtmaster ocean instructor. *E:* john@johnctaylor.com. *Clubs:* Air Squadron; Scottish Gliding.

TAYLOR, John D.; *see* Debenham Taylor.

TAYLOR, John Edward, CBE 2013; Chief Executive, Advisory, Conciliation and Arbitration Service, 2001–13; *b* 14 Nov. 1949; *s* of Thomas Taylor and Margaret Jane Taylor (*née* Renwick). *Educ:* Chester-le-Street Grammar Sch.; Durham Univ. (BA Gen. Arts). Grad. Trainee, Littlewoods Orgn, 1971–72; Department of Employment: various posts as Exec. Officer, 1972–79; Private Sec. to Minister of State, 1979–80; Head: of Personnel, 1980–83; of Res. Br., 1983–84; Regl Employment Manager, Midlands, 1984–86; Hd, Overseas Labour Div., 1986–88; Dep. Chief Exec., Rural Develt Commn, 1988–95; Chief Executive: Develt Bd for Rural Wales, 1995–98; SE Wales TEC, 1998–2001. German Marshall Fellowship Schol., USA, 1986. Vis. Prof. for Employment Relns, Glamorgan Univ., 2001–10. Public Sector examiner, Inst. of Dirs, 2006–10. UK Advr to Botswana on public sector unionisation, 2011; Expert Advr to Internat. Labour Orgn, 2012–; Olympic Legacy Advr to Rio, 2012–. Member: UK Delegn to USSR on SME Develt, 1991; NHS Partnership Forum (formerly NHS Partnership Bd), 2001–13; Employment Tribunal System Taskforce, 2003–06; Learning and Skills Develt Agency, 2004–06; Central Govt Sector Skills Council, 2005–10; Employment Tribunal System Steering Bd, 2006–10; Quality Improvement Agency, 2006–08; Adv. Bd, unionlearn, 2006–; UK Delegn to Colombia on industrial relns, 2008; Skills Strategy Delivery Bd, 2009–10; Chartered Mgt Inst. Skills Acad., 2010–13; Skill Exchange UK (formerly Skill Exchange Partnership), 2010–; Chm., Careers Services Wales, 2013–. Non-exec. Dir, Employee Relations Inst., 2012–. Chm. Trustees, WEA, 2013–. Governor: Univ. of W London (formerly Thames Valley Univ.), 2005– (Dep. Chm., 2010–14); Reading Further Educn Coll., 2007–10. CCMI 2003. Hon. DLitt W London, 2014. *Recreations:* Sunderland AFC, all sport, CAMRA, travel, conservation. *Address:* Careers Services Wales, Brecon Court, William Brown Close, Llantarnam Industrial Park, Cwmbran NP44 3AB. *Club:* Durham County Cricket.

TAYLOR, John H.; *see* Hermon-Taylor.

TAYLOR, John Mark; *b* 19 Aug. 1941; *s* of Wilfred and Eileen Martha Taylor. *Educ:* Eversfield Prep. School; Bromsgrove School and College of Law. Admitted Solicitor, 1966; Senior Partner, John Taylor & Co., 1983–88. Member: Solihull County Borough Council, 1971–74; W Midlands Metropolitan County Council, 1973–86 (Opposition (Conservative) Leader, 1975–77; Leader, 1977–79). Mem., W Midlands Economic Planning Council, 1978–79. Mem. (C) Midlands E, European Parlt, 1979–84; EDG spokesman on Community Budget, 1979–81, Group Dep. Chm., 1981–82. Contested (C): Dudley East, Feb. and Oct. 1974; Solihull, 2005. MP (C) Solihull, 1983–2005. PPS to Chancellor of Duchy of Lancaster and Minister for Trade and Industry, 1987–88; an Asst Govt Whip, 1988–89; a Lord Comr of HM Treasury (Govt Whip), 1989–90; Vice Chamberlain of HM Household, 1990–92; Parly Sec., Lord Chancellor's Dept, 1992–95; Parly Under-Sec. of State for Competition and Consumer Affairs, DTI, 1995–97; an Opposition Whip, 1997–99; Opposition spokesman on NI, 1999–2003. Mem., Select Cttee on the Environment, 1983–87, on modernisation, 2001–02; Sec., Cons. Back bench Cttee on Eur. Affairs, 1983–86 (Vice-Chm., 1986–87); Vice-Chm., Cons. Back bench Cttee on Sport, 1986–87, on Trade and Industry, 1997, on Legal Affairs, 1997. Mem., Parly Assembly, Council of Europe and WEU, 1997. Vice-Pres., AMA, 1979–86 (Dep. Chm., 1978–79). Governor, Univ. of Birmingham, 1977–81. *Publications:* Please Stay to the Adjournment, 2003. *Recreations:* fellowship, cricket, golf, reading. *Address:* Apartment 8, Blossomfield Gardens, 34 Blossomfield Road, Solihull, West Midlands B91 1NZ. *T:* (0121) 705 5467. *Club:* MCC.

TAYLOR, (John) Martin; Vice-Chairman, RTL Group SA, since 2004 (Director, since 2000); *b* 8 June 1952; *m* 1st, 1976, Janet Davey (marr. diss. 2002); two *d*; 2nd, 2008, Pippa Wicks; one *s*. *Educ:* Eton; Balliol Coll., Oxford. Reuters, 1974–78; Financial Times, 1978–82; Courtaulds plc, 1982–90 (Dir, 1987–90); Courtaulds Textiles plc, 1990–93 (Chief Exec., 1990–93; Chm., 1993); Chief Exec., Barclays plc, 1994–98; Chairman: W. H. Smith Gp plc, 1999–2003; Syngenta AG, 2005–13 (Dir, 2000–13; Vice-Chm., 2004–05). Dir, Antigenics Inc., 1999–2003; advr, Goldman Sachs Internat., 1999–2005. Govt advr on tax and welfare issues. Ext. Mem., Bank of England Financial Policy Cttee, 2013–. Sec.-Gen., Bilderberg Gp, 1999–2005.

TAYLOR, (John) Maxwell (Percy); Chairman, Mitsui Sumitomo (London) Ltd, since 2008 (non-executive Director, since 2006); *b* 17 March 1948; *s* of Harold Guy Percy Taylor and Anne Katherine Taylor (*née* Stafford); *m* 1970, Dawn Susan Harling; one *s* one *d*. *Educ:* Haileybury; ISC. Joined Willis Faber & Dumas, 1970; Dir, Willis Faber, then Willis Corroon Gp plc, 1990–97; Chm., Lloyd's, 1998–2000. Chm., Lloyd's Insce Brokers Cttee, 1997. Dep. Chm., Aon Ltd, 2001–08; Director: Henderson Smaller Companies Investment Trust plc, 1997–2008; Qatar Insce Services, 2009–13. Dir, Financial Services Compensation Scheme, 2007–13. Chairman: BIIBA, 2004–07; BIPAR, 2004; ANV Syndicates (formerly Jubilee Managing Agency) Ltd, 2011–; Pioneer Underwriters, 2013–. Pres., Insurance Inst. of London, 2001. Pro-Chancellor, Univ. of Surrey, 2015– (Chm. Council, 2007–13). *Recreations:* music, travel, classic cars. *Clubs:* Royal Automobile, City.

TAYLOR, Sir John (Michael), Kt 2004; OBE 1994; PhD; FRS 1998; FREng; Chairman, Web Science Trust, 2009–14; *b* 15 Feb. 1943; *s* of Eric and Dorothy Taylor; *m* 1965, Judith Moyle; two *s* two *d*. *Educ:* Emmanuel Coll., Cambridge (MA; PhD 1969; Hon. Fellow, 2000). FIET (FIEE 1985); FBCS 1986; FREng (FEng 1986). Supt, Communication Systems Div., 1977–79, Computer Applications Div., 1979–81, RSRE; Head, Command, Control and Communications Dept, ARE, 1981–84; Dir, Hewlett-Packard Labs, Europe, 1984–98; Dir Gen. of Res. Councils, OST, DTI, 1999–2004; Chm., Roke Manor Research Ltd, 2004–10. Non-exec. Dir, Rolls Royce, 2004–07. Pres., IEE, 1998–99; Mem. Council, Royal Acad. Engrg, 2004–07. Vis. Prof., Univ. of Oxford, 2003–09. FInstP. Hon. Fellow, Cardiff Univ., 2002. Hon. DEng: Bristol, 1998; UWE, 1999; Surrey, 1999; Exeter, 2000; Brunel, 2000; Birmingham, 2002. *Recreations:* family, sailing and boating, photography, music. *E:* john@taylorfamily.tv.

TAYLOR, Rt Rev. John Mitchell; Bishop of Glasgow and Galloway, 1991–98; Assistant Bishop of Glasgow and Galloway, 2000–09; *b* 23 May 1932; *m* 1959, Edna Elizabeth (*née* Maitland); one *s* (one *d* decd). *Educ:* Banff Acad.; Aberdeen Univ. (MA 1954); Edinburgh Theol Coll. Ordained deacon, 1956, priest, 1957; Asst Curate, St Margaret, Aberdeen, 1956–58; Rector: Holy Cross, Glasgow, 1958–64; St Ninian, Glasgow, 1964–73; St John the Evangelist, Dumfries, 1973–91; Chaplain: Crichton Royal Hospital; Dumfries and Galloway Royal Infirmary, 1973–91; Canon, St Mary's Cathedral, 1979–91, Hon. Canon, 1999–. *Recreations:* angling, hill walking, music, ornithology. *Address:* 85 Lord Lyell Drive, Kinnordy View, Kirriemuir DD8 4LF. *T:* (01575) 573132. *E:* j.taylor897@btinternet.com.

TAYLOR, John Russell; Art Critic, The Times, 1978–2005; *b* 19 June 1935; *s* of Arthur Russell and Kathleen Mary Taylor (*née* Picker); civil partnership 2006, Ying Yeung Li. *Educ:* Dover Grammar Sch.; Jesus Coll., Cambridge (MA); Courtauld Inst. of Art, London. Sub-Editor, Times Educational Supplement, 1959; Editorial Asst, Times Literary Supplement, 1960; Film Critic, The Times, 1962–73. Dir of Film Studies, Tufts Univ. in London, 1970–71; Prof., Div. of Cinema, Univ. of Southern California, 1972–78. Editor, Films and Filming, 1983–90. *Publications:* Anger and After, 1962; Anatomy of a Television Play, 1962; Cinema Eye, Cinema Ear, 1964; Penguin Dictionary of the Theatre, 1966; The Art Nouveau Book in Britain, 1966; The Rise and Fall of the Well-Made Play, 1967; The Art Dealers, 1969; Harold Pinter, 1969; Look Back in Anger: a casebook, 1969; The Hollywood Musical, 1971; The Second Wave, 1971; David Storey, 1974; Directors and Directions, 1975; Peter Shaffer, 1975; Hitch, 1978; The Revels History of Drama in English, vol. VII, 1978; Impressionism, 1981; Strangers in Paradise, 1983; Ingrid Bergman, 1983; Alec Guinness, 1984; Vivien Leigh, 1984; Portraits of the British Cinema, 1985; Hollywood 1940s, 1985; Orson Welles, 1986; Edward Wolfe, 1986; Great Movie Moments, 1987; Post-war Friends, 1987; Robin Tanner, 1989; Bernard Meninsky, 1990; John Copley 1875–1950, 1990; Impressionist Dreams, 1990; Liz Taylor, 1991; Ricardo Cinalli, 1993; Igor Mitoraj, 1993; Muriel Pemberton, 1993; Claude Monet, 1995; Michael Parkes: the stone lithographs, 1996; Bill Jacklin, 1997; Antonio Saliola, 1998; The Sun is God, 1999; Roberto Bernardi, 2001; The Ben Uri Story, 2001; Peter Coker, 2002; Philip Sutton Printmaker, 2005; Roboz, 2005; Skrebneski: moving pictures!, 2005; Adrian George, 2005; Donald McGill, 2006; The Art of Michael Parkes, 2006; The Painter's Quarry, 2006; Carl Laubin, 2007; The Art of Jeremy Ramsay, 2007; Philip Sutton, 2008; Glamour of the Gods, 2008; Exactitude, 2009; Kurt Jackson, 2010; Face to Face, 2011; David Breuer-Weil: radical visionary, 2011; Philip Hicks, 2013. *Address:* c/o The Times, 1 London Bridge Street, SE1 9GF.

TAYLOR, Jonathan Francis, CBE 2005; Chairman: Booker Prize Foundation, since 2001; Booker plc, 1993–98 (Chief Executive, 1984–93); *b* 12 Aug. 1935; *s* of Sir Reginald Taylor, CMG and Lady Taylor; *m* 1965, Anthea Gail Proctor; three *s*. *Educ:* Winchester College; Corpus Christi College, Oxford (Schol.; BA Mod. Hist.; MA; Hon. Fellow 1996). Joined Booker, 1959; Chm., Agricultural Div., 1976–80; Dir, Booker plc, 1980; Pres., Ibec Inc. (USA), 1980–84; Dir, Arbor Acres Farm Inc., 1980–98 (Dep. Chm., 1985–90; Chm., 1990–95). Director: Sifida Investment Bank, Geneva, 1978–90; Tate & Lyle, 1988–99; MEPC, 1992–2000; Equitable Life Assurance Soc., 1995–2001; Chm., Ellis & Everard, 1993–99. Mem., Adv. Council, UNIDO, 1986–93; Director: Foundn for Develt of Polish Agric., 1991–99 (Chm., 1992–99); Internat. Agribusiness Management Assoc., 1991– (Pres., 1993–94); Winrock Internat. Inst. for Agricl Develt (US), 1991–2001. Chm., Marshall Aid Commemoration Commn, 2000–07. Chm., Governing Body, SOAS, London Univ., 1999–2005 (Gov., 1988–2005; Hon. Fellow, 2010); Governor: RAC, Cirencester, 1995–2010; Commonwealth Inst., 1998–2005. Co-opted Curator, Bodleian Library, 1989–97; Chairman: Bodleian Liby Develt Bd, 1989–2000; Paintings in Hosps, 1996–2006. Chairman: Council, Caine Prize for African Writing, 1999–; Trustees, Internat. Prize for Arabic Fiction, 2006–13. *Recreations:* collecting water colours, travel, reading, grandchildren. *Address:* 48 Edwardes Square, W8 6HH. *Club:* Brooks's.

TAYLOR, Jonathan McLeod Grigor; Vice-President and Member, Management Committee, European Investment Bank, since 2013; *b* 5 March 1955; *s* of John Grigor Taylor and Dorothy Jean Taylor (*née* McLeod); *m* 1984, Stella Schimmel; one *s* one *d*. *Educ:* Bedales Sch.; New Coll., Oxford (MA PPE). HM Treasury, 1977–2002: Admin. trainee, 1977–79; Private Sec. to Perm. Sec., 1979–81; Principal, 1981; First Sec. (Budget), UK Perm. Rep., Brussels, 1982–84 (on secondment); Private Sec. to Chancellor of Exchequer, 1987–89; Asst Sec., 1990; Counsellor (Econ. and Financial), UK Perm. Rep., Brussels, 1994–98 (on secondment); Dir, Macroeconomic Policy and Internat. Finance Directorate, 1998–2002; Man. Dir and Hd of Public Policy, Internat., UBS AG, 2002–05; Dir Gen., London Investment Banking Assoc., 2005–09; CEO, Assoc. for Financial Markets in Europe, 2009; Man. Dir, Internat. and Finance Directorate, then Dir Gen., Financial Services, HM Treasury, 2010–12. *Address:* European Investment Bank, 98–100 Boulevard Konrad Adenauer, L-2950, Luxembourg.

TAYLOR, Jonathan Peter; Partner, Bird & Bird Solicitors, since 2007; *b* Bristol, 6 Nov. 1967; *s* of Gavin and Louise Taylor; *m* 1994, Kate Thefaut; two *d*. *Educ:* University Coll., Oxford (BA 1st Cl. Hons Juris. 1989); Univ. of Virginia (LLM 1990). Called to the Bar, NY, 1991; admitted solicitor, England and Wales, 1997; Associate, Schulte Roth & Zabel, NYC, 1990–97; Solicitor, Townleys, 1997–2001; Partner, Hammonds, 2001–07. Stipendiary Lectr in Law, University Coll., Oxford, 1992–93; Dir of Studies in Sports Law, KCL, 2000–08. Member: Anti-Doping Panel, Internat. Baseball Fedn, 2008–; Ethics Cttee, British Horseracing Authy, 2009–; Panel of Arbitrators, Sports Resolutions, 2012–; World Anti-Doping Agency Ind. Observer Mission, Asian Games, 2014. *Publications:* (ed jtly) Sport: law & practice, 2003, 3rd edn 2014; (contrib.) The New Oxford Companion to Law, 2008. *Recreations:* family, Fulham FC. *Address:* c/o Bird & Bird LLP, 15 Fetter Lane, EC4A 1JP. *E:* jonathan.taylor@twobirds.com.

TAYLOR, Prof. Joseph Hooton, Jr, PhD; James S. McDonnell Distinguished University Professor of Physics, Princeton University, 1986–2006, now Emeritus (Professor of Physics, 1980–86; Dean of the Faculty, 1997–2003); *b* 29 March 1941; *s* of Joseph Taylor and Sylvia Taylor (*née* Evans); *m* 1st, 1963, Alexandra Utgoff (marr. diss. 1975); one *s* one *d*; 2nd, 1976, Marietta Bisson; one *d*. *Educ:* Haverford Coll. (BA Physics 1963); Harvard Univ. (PhD Astronomy 1968). Res. Fellow and Lectr, Harvard Univ., 1968–69; University of Massachusetts, Amherst: Asst Prof. of Astronomy, 1969–72; Associate Prof., 1973–77; Prof., 1977–81. Wolf Prize in Physics, Wolf Foundn, 1982; Einstein Prize, Albert Einstein Soc., 1991; (jtly) Nobel Prize in Physics, 1993. *Publications:* (with R. N. Manchester) Pulsars, 1977; over 200 articles in jls. *Recreations:* sailing, ham radio, golf. *Address:* Department of Physics, Princeton University, PO Box 708, Princeton, NJ 08544, USA.

TAYLOR, Judy, (Julia Marie), (Judy Hough), MBE 1971; writer and publisher; *b* 12 Aug. 1932; adopted *d* of Gladys Spicer Taylor; *m* 1980, Richard Hough, writer (*d* 1999). *Educ:* St Paul's Girls' Sch. Joined The Bodley Head, 1951, specialising in children's books; Director: The Bodley Head Ltd, 1967–84 (Dep. Man. Dir, 1971–80); Chatto, Bodley Head & Jonathan Cape Ltd, 1973–80; Chatto, Bodley Head & Jonathan Cape Australia Pty Ltd, 1977–80. Publishers Association: Chm., Children's Book Gp, 1969–72; Mem. Council, 1972–78; Member: Book Develt Council, 1973–76; Unicef Internat. Art Cttee, 1968–70, 1976, 1982–83; UK Unicef Greeting Card Cttee, 1982–85. Consultant to Penguin (formerly to Frederick Warne) on Beatrix Potter, 1981–87, 1989–92; Associate Dir, Weston Woods Inst., USA, 1984–2003; Consulting Ed., Reinhardt Books, 1988–93. Chm., Beatrix Potter Soc., 1990–97, 2000–03, 2006–09 (Vice-Pres., 2012); Volunteer Reading Help: Mem., 1993–99, Chm., 1989–99, London, subseq. Inner London, Cttee; Trustee, 2000–05. *Publications: children's:* Sophie and Jack, 1982; Sophie and Jack Help Out, 1983; Sophie and Jack in the Snow, 1984; Dudley and the Monster, 1986; Dudley Goes Flying, 1986; Dudley in a Jam, 1986; Dudley and the Strawberry Shake, 1986; My Dog, 1987; My Cat, 1987; Dudley Bakes a Cake, 1988; Sophie and Jack in the Rain, 1989; *non-fiction:* My First Year: a Beatrix Potter baby book, 1983; Beatrix Potter: artist, storyteller and countrywoman, 1986, 3rd edn 2002; That Naughty Rabbit: Beatrix Potter and Peter Rabbit, 1987, 2nd edn 2002; Beatrix Potter and Hawkshead, 1988; Beatrix Potter and Hill Top, 1989; (ed) Beatrix Potter's Letters: a selection, 1989; (ed) Letters to Children from Beatrix Potter, 1992; (ed) So I Shall Tell You a Story: encounters with Beatrix Potter, 1993; (ed) The Choyce Letters: Beatrix Potter to Louie Choyce 1916–1943, 1994; (ed) Beatrix Potter: a holiday diary, 1996; (ed) Beatrix Potter's Farming Friendship, 1998; (ed) Sketches for Friends, by Edward Ardizzone, 2000; *play:* (with Patrick Garland) Beatrix, 1996; numerous professional articles. *Recreations:* collecting early children's books, growing things. *Address:* 31 Meadowbank, Primrose Hill Road, NW3 3AY.

TAYLOR, Julie; Director General, Transformation, Home Office, since 2015; *b* London, 26 March 1968; *d* of Robert John Taylor and Virginia Taylor; *m* 1999, David Lawrence. *Educ:*

Forest Sch., London; Lady Margaret Hall, Oxford (BA Hons Maths 1989). Qualified Accountant 1992; Psychotherapist, Human Givens Inst., 2011. Dir, Sevice Develt, E London and City HA, 1998–2000; Department of Health: Hd, Planning and Progs, 2000–02; Director: Corp. Services, 2002–04; System Reform, 2005–06; Dir, Offender Mgt Strategy, MoJ, 2006–11; Dep. Chief Exec., London Bor. of Barnet, 2011–13; Dir, Strategy and Change, UK Border Force, Home Office, 2013–15. *Recreations:* ski-ing, sailing, walking, bridge. *Address:* 4th Floor, Seacole Building, Home Office, 2 Marsham Street, SW1P 4DF. *T:* (020) 7035 5245. *E:* julie.taylor19@homeoffice.gsi.gov.uk.

TAYLOR, Prof. Kenneth MacDonald, MD; FRCSE, FRCSGlas; FSAScot; Professor and Chief of Cardiac Surgery, Imperial College School of Medicine (formerly Royal Postgraduate Medical School), Hammersmith Hospital, 1983–2007, now Emeritus; British Heart Foundation Professor of Cardiac Surgery, University of London, 1983–2007; Deputy Head, National Heart & Lung Institute (formerly Division of Heart, Lung and Circulation), Imperial College Faculty of Medicine, 1997–2007; Clinical Director of Cardiac Sciences, Imperial College Healthcare NHS Trust (formerly Hammersmith Hospitals NHS Trust), 2003–07; *b* 20 Oct. 1947; *s* of late Hugh Baird Taylor and Mary Taylor; *m* 1971, Christine Elizabeth (*née* Buchanan) (*d* 2010); one *s* one *d*. *Educ:* Jordanhill College School; Univ. of Glasgow (MB ChB, MD; Cullen Medal, 1968; Gairdner Medal, 1969; Allan Hird Prize, 1969). Univ. of Glasgow: Hall Fellow in Surgery, 1971–72, Lectr and Sen. Lectr in Cardiac Surgery, 1975–83; Consultant Cardiac Surgeon, Royal Infirmary and Western Infirmaries, Glasgow, 1979–83. Vis. Prof., Dept of Bio-engineering, Univ. of Strathclyde, 1997–2007. Chm., Specialist Adv. Cttee in Cardiothoracic Surgery, 1992–95 (Mem., 1986–92); Dir, UK Heart Valve Registry, 1986–2007; Clin. Dir, UK Sch. of Perfusion Science, 1987–97. Member: Exec. Cttee, Soc. of Cardiothoracic Surgeons of GB and Ire., 1992–95; Wkg Gp on Cardiac Waiting Times, DoH, 1994–95; Central R & D Cttee, Acute Sector Panel, DoH, 1996–2007; Reference Gp, Nat. Service Framework, Coronary Heart Disease, DoH, 1999–2002; Chairman: Database Cttee, European Assoc. for Cardiothoracic Surgery, 1994–2000; UK Cardiac Audit Steering Gp, 1994–2001. FESC 1995; FECTS 1998 (Mem., 1988); Member: British Cardiac Soc., 1983–; Amer. Soc. of Thoracic Surgeons, 1984–; Council and Exec. Cttee, BHF, 2001–10 (Trustee, 2006–10); Hon. Member: Amer. Acad. of Cardiovascular Perfusion, 1993; Amer. Assoc. for Thoracic Surgery, 1998 (Mem., 1988–98; Honoured Guest, 1998); Soc. of Perfusionists of GB and Ire., 1998 (Pres., 1989–93; Hon. Life Mem., 1999). Trustee: Garfield Weston Trust, 1998–; European Soc. of Perfusion, 2002–. Hon. Alumnus, Cleveland Clinic, USA, 2000. Governor, Drayton Manor High Sch., London, 1989–96. Pres., Friends of Hammersmith Hosp., 2007–. Church Warden, St Stephen's C of E, Ealing, 2010–. Editor, Perfusion, 1986–2008; Member, Advisory Editorial Board: Annals of Thoracic Surgery, 1990–2000; Jl of Cardiovascular Anaesthesia, 1993–2000; Jl of Heart Valve Disease, 1993–2000. Peter Allen Prize, Soc. of Thoracic and Cardiovascular Surgeons, 1975; Patey Prize, Surgical Res. Soc., 1977; Fletcher Prize, RCSG, 1977; Watson Prize, RCSG, 1982. *Publications:* Pulsatile Perfusion, 1979, 2nd edn 1982; Handbook of Intensive Care, 1984; Cardiopulmonary Bypass, 1986; Cardiac Surgery, 1987; Principles of Surgical Research, 1989, 2nd edn 1995; The Brain and Cardiac Surgery, 1992; numerous articles on cardiac surgery. *Recreations:* family, church, music. *Address:* 129 Argyle Road, Ealing, W13 0DB.

TAYLOR, Prof. Kevin Michael Geoffrey, PhD; FRPharmS; Professor of Clinical Pharmaceutics, UCL School of Pharmacy, University College London (formerly School of Pharmacy, University of London), since 2006; Chair, British Pharmacopoeia Commission, since 2013; *b* Dartford, 8 June 1961; *s* of Geoffrey and Janet Taylor; *m* 1984, Pauline McBride; one *s* one *d*. *Educ:* Chislehurst and Sidcup Grammar Sch.; Welsh Sch. of Pharmacy, Univ. of Wales Inst. of Sci. and Technol. (BPharm 1982; PhD 1987). MRPharmS 1983, FRPharmS 2013. Pre-registration pharmacist, Boots the Chemist, Lewisham, 1982–83; School of Pharmacy, University of London: Teaching and Res. Fellow, 1986–88; Lectr, 1988–94; Sen. Lectr, 1994–2002; Reader, 2002–04; Prof. of Clin. Pharmaceutics, UCL Hosps and Sch. of Pharmacy, 2004–06; Hd, Dept of Pharmaceutics, Sch. of Pharmacy, Univ. of London, later UCL Sch. of Pharmacy, University Coll. London, 2006–13. Hon. Prof., Inst. of Nanotechnol. and Bioengrg, Univ. of Central Lancs, 2012–. Member: Commn on Human Medicines, 2012– (Mem., 2006–, Chm., 2013–, Chem., Pharmacy and Standards Expert Adv. Gp); UK Delegn to Eur. Pharmacopoeia Commn, 2014–; Inhalanda Wkg Party, Eur. Pharmacopoeia, 2014–; Pharmacy Expert Adv. Gp, British Pharmacopoeia Commn, 2015–. Mem., Chem., Pharmacy and Standards Sub-cttee, Cttee on Safety of Medicines, 2002–06. Freeman, City of London, 1987. *Publications:* (jtly) Sociology for Pharmacists: an introduction, 1990, 2nd edn 2003; (ed jtly) Social Pharmacy: innovation and development, 1994; (ed jtly) Pharmacy Practice, 2001; (jtly) Nanocarrier Systems for Drug Delivery for the Treatment of Asthma, 2011; (ed jtly) Aulton's Pharmaceutics: the design and manufacture of medicines, 4th edn 2013; (ed jtly) Integrated Pharmacy Case Studies, 2015. *Recreations:* travel, vegetable growing, humming. *Address:* UCL School of Pharmacy, 29–39 Brunswick Square, WC1N 1AX. *T:* (020) 7753 5853. *E:* kevin.taylor@ucl.ac.uk.

TAYLOR, Prof. Laurence John, (Laurie); Professor of Sociology, University of York, 1974–93; *s* of Stanley Douglas Taylor and Winifred Agnes (*née* Cooper); marr. diss.; one *s*; *m* 2010, Sally Joy Feldman, *qv*. *Educ:* St Mary's Coll., Liverpool; Rose Bruford College of Drama, Kent; Birkbeck Coll., Univ. of London (BA); Univ. of Leicester (MA). Librarian, 1952–54; Sales Asst, 1954–56; Professional Actor, 1960–61; English Teacher, 1961–64; Lectr in Sociology, 1965–73, Reader in Sociology, 1973–74, Univ. of York. Vis. Prof., 1994–, Fellow, 1996–, Birkbeck Coll., Univ. of London. *Publications:* Deviance and Society, 1971; (jtly) Psychological Survival, 1972; (jtly) Crime, Deviance and Socio-Legal Control, 1972; (ed jtly) Politics and Deviance, 1973; Man's Experience of the World, 1976; (jtly) Escape Attempts, 1976, 2nd edn 1992; (jtly) Prison Secrets, 1978; (jtly) In Whose Best Interests?, 1980; In the Underworld, 1984; (jtly) Uninvited Guests, 1986; Professor Lapping Sends His Apologies, 1987; The Tuesday Afternoon Time Immemorial Committee, 1989; Laurie Taylor's Guide to Higher Education, 1994; (jtly) What Are Children For?, 2003; In Confidence: talking frankly about fame and fortune, 2014; articles, reviews, broadcasts, TV series. *E:* lolsoc@dircon.co.uk.

See also Matthew Taylor.

TAYLOR, Louise Méarie; Relationship Partner, Rockpool Investments, since 2013; writer and curator; *b* 8 Sept. 1967; *d* of Prof. A. Taylor and J. M. Taylor; *m* 2000, Jason Brooks (separated 2009); one *d*. *Educ:* Univ. of Warwick (BA Hons (Hist. of Art) 1988); Staffordshire Univ. (PhD (Design Hist.) 1995). Craftspace Touring: Exhibns Dir, 1991–95; Actg Dir, 1995–96; Crafts Council: Hd, Exhibns and Collection, 1996–99; Dir, Artistic Programming and Information, 1999–2002; Dir, 2002–05; arts consultant, writer and mentor, 2006–14; Associate, Modus Operandi, 2012–15. Trustee, Craft Pottery Charitable Trust, 2003–. Hon. FRCA 2004. *Publications:* editor and joint author: Recycling: forms for the next century, 1996; Handmade in India, 1998; Satellites of Fashion, 1998; No Picnic, 1998; (ed and introd.) Contemporary International Basketmaking, 1999; (ed and introd.) Contemporary Japanese Jewellery, 2000; (ed jtly and introd.) Wendy Ramshaw: rooms of dreams, 2012; (ed jtly and introd.) Necklace for an Elephant and Other Stories: the working lives of David Poston, 2014. *Recreations:* tennis, dance, fashion. *Address:* 2 Testers Close, Oxted, Surrey RH8 0HW. *E:* louisembtaylor@yahoo.co.uk.

TAYLOR, Malcolm; *see* McDowell, M.

TAYLOR, (Margaret) Jessie, OBE 1989; piano teacher, since 2001; Headmistress, Whalley Range High School for Girls, 1976–88; *b* 30 Nov. 1924; *d* of Thomas Brown Gowland and Ann Goldie Gowland; *m* 1958, Eric Taylor (*d* 2010). *Educ:* Queen Elizabeth's Grammar Sch., Middleton; Manchester Univ. (BA Hons, DipEd). Jun. Classics Teacher, Cheadle Hulme Sch., 1946–49; North Manchester Grammar School for Girls: Sen. Classics Teacher, 1950; Sen. Mistress, 1963; Actg Headmistress, Jan.–July 1967; Dep. Head Teacher, Wright Robinson Comprehensive High Sch., 1967–75. Voluntary worker, UNICEF, 1988–97. Dir, Piccadilly Radio, 1979–2000. Chm., Manchester High Sch. Heads Gp, 1984–88; Member: Council and Exams Cttee, Associated Lancs Schs Examining Bd, 1976–91 (Mem. Classics Panel, 1968–72); Exams Cttee, Northern Exams Assoc., 1988–92; Nursing Educn Cttee, S Manchester Area, 1976–84; Home Office Cttee on Obscenity and Film Censorship, 1977–79; Consultant Course Tutor, NW Educnl Management Centre, Padgate, 1980–82. Mem. Court, Salford Univ., 1982–88; Gov., William Hulme's Grammar Sch., 1989–. FRSA 1980. *Recreations:* music, riding. *Address:* 10 Mercers Road, Hopwood, Heywood, Lancs OL10 2NP. *T:* (01706) 366630.

TAYLOR, Mark Christopher; Chief Executive, Society of Homeopaths, since 2015; *b* 24 Nov. 1958; *s* of Norman and June Taylor; *m* (marr. diss.); two *s* one *d*. *Educ:* Loughborough Grammar Sch.; Birmingham Univ. (BA Medieval and Modern Hist.); Leeds Poly. (postgrad. Hotel Management qualification). Hotel Management, Norfolk Capital Hotels, 1981–84; Conf. Manager, 1984–89, Dir, 1989–2014, Museums Assoc.; Chief Exec., VocalEyes, 2014–15. Chairman: Network of Eur. Museum Orgns, 1998–2001; Campaign for Learning through Museums, 1998–2003; Cultural Tourism and Heritage Export Cttee, 2003–05; Board Member: Nat. Campaign for Arts, 1999–2008; Bedfordshire Music Trust, 2003–; Creative and Cultural Industries Sector Skills Council, 2004–05. Trustee: Museum Prize Trust, 2002–14; Campaign for Museums, 2004–09; Culture Unlimited, 2008–12. *Recreations:* sport, films, food. *E:* taylors.bedford@ntlworld.com.

TAYLOR, Prof. Mark Peter, PhD, DSc; FCIPD; Dean, Warwick Business School, since 2010, and Professor of International Finance and Macroeconomics (formerly of Macroeconomics), since 1999, University of Warwick; *b* 17 May 1958; *s* of Arthur Leslie Taylor and Lorna Kathleen Taylor; *m* 1980, Anita Margaret Phillips; two *s* one *d*. *Educ:* St John's Coll., Oxford (BA (PPE) 1980; MA 1984); Birkbeck Coll., London (MSc (Econs) 1982; PhD (Econs) 1984); Liverpool Univ. (MA (Eng. Lit.) 2001); Inst. of Educn, Univ. of London (MBA (HE Mgt) 2010); Warwick Univ. (DSc (Finance) 2012). Foreign exchange dealer, Citibank, London, 1980–82; Lectr in Econs, Univ. of Newcastle upon Tyne, 1984–86; Res. Economist, Bank of England, 1986–87; Professor of Economics: Dundee Univ., 1987–88; City Univ. Business Sch., 1988–90; Sen. Econ. Advr, IMF, Washington, 1990–94; Prof. of Econs, Univ. of Liverpool, 1994–97; Fellow in Econs, University Coll., Oxford, 1997–99. Consultant, IMF, 1999–2005; Managing Director: Barclays Global Investors Ltd, 2006–09; BlackRock, 2009–10. Res. Fellow, Centre for Econ. Policy Res., 1987–. Councillor, REconS, 2002–09. FRSA 1995; FAcSS (AcSS 2009); FCIPD 2013. *Publications:* Macroeconomic Systems, 1987; The Balance of Payments: new perspectives on open economy macroeconomics, 1990; Money and Financial Markets, 1991; Applied Econometric Techniques, 1992; Policy Issues in the Operation of Currency Unions, 1993; Modern Perspectives on the Gold Standard, 1996; Speculation and Financial Markets, 2001; The Economics of Exchange Rates, 2002; Economics, 2006, 3rd edn 2014; Macroeconomics, 2007, 2nd edn 2014; numerous articles in learned jls. *Recreations:* horology, antique clocks, languages, literature, wine. *Address:* Dean's Office, Warwick Business School, University of Warwick, Coventry CV4 7AL. *T:* (024) 7652 4534, *Fax:* (024)7652 4170. *E:* mark.taylor@wbs.ac.uk. *Club:* Reform.

TAYLOR, Martin; *see* Taylor, John M.

TAYLOR, Sir Martin (John), Kt 2009; PhD; FRS 1996; Warden, Merton College, Oxford, since 2010; *b* 18 Feb. 1952; *s* of John Maurice Taylor and Sheila Mary Barbara Taylor (*née* Camacho); *m* 1973, Sharon Lynn Marlow; two *s* two *d*. *Educ:* St Clare's Prep. Sch., Leicester; Wyggeston Boys' Sch., Leicester; Pembroke Coll., Oxford (BA 1st Class; Hon. Fellow, 2012); King's College, London (PhD). Res. Assistant, KCL, 1976–77; Jun. Lectr, Oxford Univ., 1977–78; Lectr, QMC, 1978–81; Fellow, Trinity Coll., Cambridge, 1981–85; Univ. Asst Lectr, Cambridge, 1984–85; Prof. of Pure Maths, UMIST, later Univ. of Manchester, 1986–2010. Associate Researcher, CNRS, Besançon, 1979–80; NSF Researcher, Univ. of Illinois, Urbana, 1981; Royal Soc. Leverhulme Sen. Res. Fellowship, 1991–92; CNRS Poste Rouge, Bordeaux, 1996; EPSRC Sen. Res. Fellow, 1999–2004; Royal Soc. Wolfson Res. Fellow, 2002–07. Pres., London Mathematical Soc., 1998–2000; Mem. Council, 2000–01, Vice-Pres. and Physical Sec., 2004–09, Royal Soc.; Mem. Council, EPSRC, 2004–09. Trustee: Mitsubishi UFJ Trust Oxford Foundn, 2014–; Dame Kathleen Ollerenshaw Trust, 2015–. Hon. DSc: Leicester, 2006; Bordeaux, 2009; UEA, 2012. *Publications:* Class Groups of Group Rings, 1984; (with Ph. Cassou-Noguès) Elliptic Functions and Rings of Integers, 1987; (with J. Coates) L-functions and Arithmetic, 1991; (with A. Fröhlich) Algebraic Number Theory, 1991; (with K. Roggenkamp) Group Rings and Class Groups, 1992. *Recreations:* fly fishing, hill walking. *Address:* Merton College, Oxford OX1 4JD.

TAYLOR, Matthew; Chief Executive, Royal Society for the Encouragement of Arts, Manufactures and Commerce, since 2006; *b* 5 Dec. 1960; *s* of Prof. Laurence John Taylor, *qv* and Jennifer Howells; two *s* one *d*. *Educ:* Southampton Univ. (BA Sociol.); Warwick Univ. (MA Industrial Relns). Set up Res. Unit, NAS/UWT, 1985–88; Dir, W Midlands Health Service Monitoring Unit, 1988–90; Sen. Res. Fellow, Univ. of Warwick, 1990–93; Asst Gen. Sec., Labour Party, 1994–98; Dir, IPPR, 1998–2003; Chief Advr on Political Strategy to Prime Minister, 2003–06. Chm., Social Integration Commn, 2014–. Regular contributor on public service reform, political strategy and communities to newspapers and jls. *Publications:* (with L. J. Taylor) What Are Children For?, 2003. *Recreations:* running, learning the guitar, West Bromwich Albion. *Address:* Royal Society for the Encouragement of Arts, Manufactures and Commerce, 8 John Adam Street, WC2N 6EZ. *T:* (020) 7451 6883.

TAYLOR, Rt Rev. Maurice, DD; Bishop of Galloway, (RC), 1981–2004, now Emeritus; *b* 5 May 1926; *s* of Maurice Taylor and Lucy Taylor (*née* McLaughlin). *Educ:* St Aloysius Coll., Glasgow; Our Lady's High School, Motherwell; Pontifical Gregorian Univ., Rome (DD). Served RAMC in UK, India, Egypt, 1944–47. Ordained to priesthood, Rome, 1950; lectured in Philosophy, 1955–60, in Theology 1960–65, St Peter's Coll., Cardross; Rector, Royal Scots Coll., Valladolid, Spain, 1965–74; Parish Priest, Our Lady of Lourdes, East Kilbride, 1974–81. Vice-Pres., Progressio (formerly Catholic Inst. for Internat. Relations), 1985–; Episcopal Sec., Bishops' Conf. of Scotland, 1987–2004; Chm., Internat. Commn on English in the Liturgy, 1997–2002. *Publications:* The Scots College in Spain, 1971; Guatemala: a bishop's journey, 1991; El Salvador: portrait of a parish, 1992; (with Ellen Hawkes) Opening Our Lives to the Saviour, 1995; (with Ellen Hawkes) Listening at the Foot of the Cross, 1996; (compiled) Surveying Today's World, 2003; Being a Bishop in Scotland, 2006; It's the Eucharist, Thank God, 2009; Life's Flavour: a variety of experiences, 2014. *Address:* 41 Overmills Road, Ayr KA7 3LH. *T:* (01292) 285865. *W:* www.bishopmauricetaylor.org.uk.

TAYLOR, Maxwell; *see* Taylor, J. M. P.

TAYLOR, Rev. Prof. Michael Hugh, OBE 1998; Professor of Social Theology, University of Birmingham, 1999–2004, now Emeritus; Director, World Faiths Development Dialogue, 2002–04; *b* 8 Sept. 1936; *s* of Albert Ernest and Gwendoline Louisa Taylor; *m* 1960, Adèle May Dixon; two *s* one *d*. *Educ:* Northampton Grammar School; Univ. of Manchester (BA, BD, MA); Union Theological Seminary, NY (STM). Baptist Minister, N Shields, 1961–66, Birmingham Hall Green, 1966–69; Principal, Northern Baptist Coll., Manchester, 1970–85; Lectr, Univ. of Manchester, 1970–85; Dir, Christian Aid, 1985–97; Pres. and Chief Exec., Selly Oak Colls, 1998–99. Mem. Council, ODI, 1989–2000; Chairman: Assoc. of Protestant

Develt Agencies in Europe, 1991–94; The Burma Campaign UK, 2000–10; Health Unlimited, 2002–10; Member: WCC Commn on Sharing and Service, 1991–98; Adv. Bd, High Pay Commn, 2012– (Comr, 2010–11). Trustee: Mines Adv. Gp, 1998– (Chm., 2000–13); Responding to Conflict, 2004–09 (Chm., 2007–09); St Philip's Centre, Leicester, 2006–. Gov., Fircroft Coll., Birmingham, 1998– (Chm., 2006–). Hon. Canon, Worcester Cathedral, 2002–07. JP Manchester, 1980–85. DLitt Lambeth, 1997. *Publications:* Variations on a Theme, 1973; Sermon on the Mount, 1982; (ed) Christians and the Future of Social Democracy, 1982; Learning to Care, 1983; Good for the Poor, 1990; Christianity and the Persistence of Poverty, 1991; Not Angels But Agencies, 1996; NGOs and their Future in Development, 1997; Poverty and Christianity, 2000; Christianity, Poverty and Wealth, 2003; Eat, Drink and Be Merry for Tomorrow We Live, 2005; Border Crossings: social theology in Christianity and Islam, 2006; Sorting out Believing, 2011; Christ and Capital, 2015; contribs to books and jls. *Recreations:* walking, cooking, music, cinema, theatre. *Address:* 128 Springfield Road, Kings Heath, Birmingham B14 7DX.

TAYLOR, Michael John; His Honour Judge Michael Taylor; a Circuit Judge, since 1996; *b* 28 Feb. 1951; *m* 1973, Pamela Ann Taylor. *Educ:* Hull Univ. (LLB). Called to the Bar, Inner Temple, 1974; in practice, 1974–96. *Address:* Teesside Combined Court Centre, Russell Street, Middlesbrough TS1 2AE.

TAYLOR, Michael John Ellerington, CBE 1992; TD 1972; DL; Chairman, Cumbria Partnership NHS Foundation Trust, since 2011; *b* 15 Sept. 1937; *s* of Leonard George Taylor and Marjorie Ellerington Taylor. *Educ:* Harrow Sch.; Emmanuel Coll., Cambridge (BA Hons 1962; LLB Hons 1963; MA 1967). Shell UK and Shell Internat., 1969–91; Chief Exec., Mgt Charter Initiative, 1990–91; Investors in People: Nat. Assessor, 1991–96; Chief External Verifier, 1996–2001; Regl Comr, NW, 2001–06, NW and W Mids, 2006–10, Appts Commn (formerly NHS Appts Commn); Chm., NHS Cumbria, 2010–11. Chairman: NW TAVRA, 1995–2000; Council, RFCA, 2000–04; Nat. Artillery Assoc., 1988–2003 (Vice Pres., 2004–); W Chester Regeneration Bd, 2000–05; Chester Aid to the Homeless, 2001–09; Council, Cumbria, St John Ambulance, 2009–12; Pres., Nat. Home Service Force Assoc., 2004–12 (Patron, 2012–). Vice-Chm., W. Cheshire Coll., 2001–04. Col, TA, 1982–93; ADC to the Queen, 1988–92; Hon. Col Comdt, RA, 1994–2005. DL Cheshire, 1998. *Recreations:* Territorial Army, walking the dogs. *Address:* Lowther House, Clifton, Penrith, Cumbria CA10 2EG. *Club:* Army and Navy.

TAYLOR, Prof. Miles, PhD; FRHistS; Professor of Modern History, University of York, since 2004; *b* Farnham Common, Bucks, 19 Sept. 1961; *s* of late Geoffrey Peter Taylor and of Dorothy Pearl Taylor (*née* Weaver, later Irish); *m* 2012, Dr Shalini Sharma; one *s*; one *s* two *d* by a previous marriage. *Educ:* Tapton Sch., Sheffield; Queen Mary Coll., Univ. of London (BA 1st Cl. Hist. and Politics 1983); Harvard Univ. (Kennedy Scholar); St John's Coll., Cambridge (PhD 1989). FRHistS 1997. Eugenie Strong Res. Fellow in Hist., Girton Coll., Cambridge, 1988–91; Fellow and Dir of Studies in Hist., Christ's Coll., Cambridge, 1991–95; Lectr in Mod. Hist., KCL, 1995–2001; Prof. of Mod. British Hist., Univ. of Southampton, 2001–04; Prof. of Hist. and Dir, Inst. of Historical Res., Univ. of London, 2008–14; Leverhulme Major Res. Fellow, 2014–. *Publications:* (ed) The European Diaries of Richard Cobden, 1846–1849, 1994; The Decline of British Radicalism, 1847–1860, 1995; (ed jtly) Party, State and Society: electoral behaviour in Britain since 1820, 1997; (ed) Bagehot's The English Constitution, 2001; Ernest Jones, Chartism and the Romance of Politics, 1819–69, 2003; (ed jtly) The Victorians since 1901: histories, representations and revisions, 2004; (ed jtly) Palmerston Studies, 2 vols, 2007; (ed) Southampton: gateway to the British Empire, 2007; (ed) The Victorian Empire and Britain's Maritime World, 1837–1901: the sea and global history, 2013; articles in Past and Present, Histl Jl, Hist. Workshop Jl, Jl of Imperial and Commonwealth Hist., Social Hist., etc. *Recreations:* tennis, long-distance running, crosswords. *Address:* Department of History, University of York, Vanbrugh College, Heslington, York YO10 5DD.

TAYLOR, Miranda; *see* Haines, M.

TAYLOR, Neil; *see* Taylor, Richard N.

TAYLOR, Neville, CB 1989; Director-General, Central Office of Information and Head of Government Information Service, 1985–88; *b* 17 Nov. 1930; *y s* of late Frederick Taylor and Lottie Taylor (*née* London); *m* 1954, Margaret Ann, *y d* of late Thomas Bainbridge Vickers and Gladys Vickers; two *s*. *Educ:* Sir Joseph Williamson's Mathematical Sch., Rochester; Coll. of Commerce, Gillingham, Kent. Junior Reporter, Chatham News Group, 1947; Royal Signals, 1948–50; Journalism, 1950–58; Asst Information Officer, Admiralty, 1958; Information Officer (Press), Admiralty, 1960; Fleet Information Officer, Singapore, 1963; Chief Press Officer, MoD, 1966; Information Adviser to Nat. Economic Develt Office, 1968; Dep. Dir, Public Relns (Royal Navy), 1970; Head of Information, Min. of Agriculture, Fisheries and Food, 1971; Dep. Dir of Information, DoE, 1973–74, Dir of Information, 1974–79; Dir of Information, DHSS, 1979–82; Chief of Public Relations, MOD, 1982–85. Hon. Vice Pres., Pen and Sword Club, 2011–. *Recreation:* fishing. *Address:* Crow Lane House, 11 Crow Lane, Rochester, Kent ME1 1RF. *T:* (01634) 842990.

TAYLOR, Sir Nicholas Richard S.; *see* Stuart Taylor.

TAYLOR, Nicola Jane N.; *see* Nelson-Taylor.

TAYLOR, Prof. Pamela Jane, (Mrs J. C. Gunn), FRCPsych; FMedSci; Professor of Forensic Psychiatry, Cardiff University (formerly University of Wales College of Medicine), since 2004; Hon. Consultant Psychiatrist, Bro Morgannwg NHS Trust, since 2004; *b* 23 April 1948; *d* of Philip Geoffrey Taylor and Joan Taylor (*née* Alport); *m* 1989, John Charles Gunn, *qv*. *Educ:* Merchant Taylors' Girls' Sch., Liverpool; Guy's Hosp. Med. Sch. and King's Coll. Hosp. Med. Sch. (MB BS 1971). MRCP 1974; MRCPsych 1976, FRCPsych 1989. Gen. prof. trng in psychiatry, Guy's Hosp., 1972–74; Teaching Fellow in Psychiatry, Univ. of Vermont, 1975; clin. res., Guy's Hosp. Trustees, 1976–79; MRC res. scientist, Inst. of Psychiatry, 1979–81; Sen. Lectr in Forensic Psychiatry, and Hon. Cons. Psychiatrist, 1982–89, Dir of Medium Secure Service, 1988–89, Inst. of Psychiatry and Bethlem Royal and Maudsley Hosp.; Hd of Med. Services, Special Hosps' Service Authy, 1990–95; Prof. of Special Hosp. Psychiatry, Inst. of Psychiatry, KCL, 1995–2004; Hon. Consultant Psychiatrist: Broadmoor Hosp., 1995–2005; Bethlem Royal and Maudsley Hosp., 1995–2005. Vis. Prof., Inst. of Psychiatry, KCL, 2004–. Advr on Forensic Psychiatry to CMO, Welsh Assembly Govt. Member: Inner London Probation Bd, 1990–2001; DoH and Home Office Steering Gp, Review of Health and Social Services for Mentally Disordered Offenders and other requiring similar services, 1990–94 (Chm., Res. Sub Gp, 1990–91); Wkg Party on Genetics of Mental Disorders, Nuffield Council on Bio-Ethics, 1996–98. Member: RSocMed, 1972–; British Soc. of Criminology, 1980–; Mental Health Foundn, 1990–94; Howard League for Penal Reform, 1990–; Council, RCPsych, 2003– (Mem., various cttees and wkg parties, 1982–). Jt Founder and Jt Editor, Criminal Behaviour and Mental Health, 1991–; Internat. Ed., Behavioral Scis and the Law, 2003–. FMedSci 2004. Gaskell Gold Medal and Prize, RCPsych, 1978. *Publications:* (ed jtly) Forensic Psychiatry: clinical, legal and ethical issues, 1993; (ed) Violence in Society, 1993; Couples in Care and Custody, 1999; Personality Disorder and Serious Offending, 2006; numerous sci. papers, editorials, reviews and contribs to books. *Recreations:* family, friends, an acre of previously neglected garden and, in every spare moment, a book. *Address:* Institute of Psychological Medicine and Clinical Neurosciences, Cardiff University, Hadyn Ellis Building, Maindy Road, Cathays, Cardiff CF24 4HQ.

TAYLOR, Pamela Margaret, OBE 2004; Chief Executive, Water UK, since 1998; *b* 25 March 1949; *d* of late Geoffrey Higgins and of Elena Higgins; *m* 1972, John Marc Taylor. Hd of Public Affairs, BMA, 1977–92; Dir, Corporate Affairs, BBC, 1992–94; mgt consultant, 1994–95; Chief Exec., Water Companies Assoc., 1995–98. President: IPR, 1993; Eur. Union of Nat. Assocs of Water Suppliers and Waste Water Services, 2002. Member Board: PHLS, 1998–2003; Health Protection Agency, 2002–13. Trustee, Wateraid, 2003– (Vice Chm., 2008–). Trustee and Treas., RSA, 2000–; Mem. Council, RSPH (formerly Trustee, RIPH). MInstD. *Publications:* (ed) Smoking Out the Barons, 1986; articles in BMJ and Jl of American Med. Assoc. *Recreations:* running, working out, wines, ballet, football, cricket. *Address:* Water UK, 3rd Floor, 36 Broadway, Westminster, SW1H 0BH. *T:* (020) 7344 1800, *Fax:* (020) 7344 1853. *E:* ptaylor@water.org.uk. *Clubs:* Mosimann's, Annabel's.

TAYLOR, Paul B.; choreographer; Artistic Director, Paul Taylor Dance Company, since 1954; President, Paul Taylor Dance Foundation (Board Chairman, 1966); Founder, Paul Taylor's American Modern Dance, 2014; *b* 29 July 1930; *s* of Paul B. Taylor and Elizabeth P. Rust. *Educ:* Virginia Episcopal Sch.; Syracuse Univ.; Juilliard Sch.; Metropolitan Sch. of Ballet; Martha Graham Sch. of Contemporary Dance. Former dancer with companies of Martha Graham, George Balanchine, Charles Weidman, Anna Sokolow, Merce Cunningham, Katherine Litz, James Waring and Pearl Lang; Paul Taylor Dance Company, 1954–: dancer, 1954–75, choreographer and dir; co. has performed in over 500 cities in more than 62 countries; formed Taylor 2, 1993; choreographed 136 dances including: Three Epitaphs, 1956; Junction, 1961; Aureole, 1962; From Sea to Shining Sea, 1965; Big Bertha, 1970; Esplanade, 1975; Runes, 1975; Cloven Kingdom, 1976; Images, 1976; Dust, 1977; Airs, 1978; Profiles, 1979; Le Sacré du Printemps (The Rehearsal), 1980; Arden Court, 1981; Lost, Found and Lost, 1982; Mercuric Tidings, 1982; Sunset, 1983; Last Look, 1985; Musical Offering, 1986; Speaking in Tongues, 1988 (Emmy Award, 1991); Company B, 1991; Fact and Fancy, 1991; Piazzolla Caldera, 1997; Black Tuesday, 2001; Promethean Fire, 2002; Dante Variations, 2004; Klezmerbluegrass, 2004; Spring Rounds, 2005; Banquet of Vultures, 2005; Lines of Loss, 2007; Three Dubious Memories, 2010; House of Joy, 2012. Guggenheim Fellow, 1961, 1965, 1983. Hon. Mem. American Acad. and Inst. of Arts and Letters, 1989. Hon. DFA: Connecticut Coll.; Duke Univ., 1983; Syracuse, 1986; Juilliard Sch.; Skidmore Coll.; State Univ. of NY, Purchase; Calif. Inst. of Arts. Centennial Achievement Award, Ohio State Univ., 1970; Creative Arts Award Gold Medal, Brandeis Univ., 1978; Dance Magazine Award, 1980; American Dance Fest. Award, Samuel H. Scripps, 1983; MacArthur Foundn Fellow, 1985; NY State Governor's Award, 1987; NY City Mayor's Award of Honor for Arts and Culture, 1989; Kennedy Center Honor, 1992; Nat. Medal of Arts, 1993; Award, Chicago Internat. Film Fest., 1993; Award for Excellence in the Arts, Algur H. Meadows, 1995. Chevalier, 1969, Officier, 1984, Commandeur, 1990, de l'Ordre des Arts et des Lettres (France); Légion d'Honneur (France), 2000. *Publications:* Private Domain (autobiog.), 1987. *Recreations:* gardening, snorkelling. *Address:* Paul Taylor's American Modern Dance, 551 Grand Street, New York, NY 10002, USA.

TAYLOR, Ven. Paul Stanley; Archdeacon of Sherborne, and Canon and Prebendary of Salisbury Cathedral, since 2004; *b* 28 March 1953; *s* of Stanley and Beryl Taylor; *m* 1984, Janet Wendy Taylor (*née* Harris); three *s*. *Educ:* Westminster Coll., Oxford (BEd 1975; MTh 1998); Westcott House, Cambridge. Ordained deacon, 1984, priest, 1985; Curate, St Stephen, Bush Hill Park, 1984–88; Asst Dir, 1987–94, Dir, 1994–2000 and 2002–04, Post Ordination Trng, Dio. London; Vicar: St Andrew, Southgate, 1988–97; St Mary, Hendon, 1997–2001; Priest-in-charge, Christ Ch, Hendon, 1997–2001; Vicar, St Mary and Christ Ch, Hendon, 2001–04; Area Dean, W Barnet, 2000–04. *Recreations:* golf, fell walking, running, Rugby Union, sailing, football. *Address:* Aldhelm House, West Stafford, Dorchester DT2 8AB. *T:* and *Fax:* (01305) 269074. *E:* adsherborne@salisbury.anglican.org. *Club:* Dorset Golf and Country (Bere Regis).

TAYLOR, Ven. Peter Flint; Archdeacon of Harlow, 1996–2009; *b* 7 March 1944; *s* of late Alan Flint Taylor and Josephine Overbury Taylor (*née* Dix); *m* 1971, Joy M. Sampson; one *d*. *Educ:* Clifton Coll., Bristol; Queens' Coll., Cambridge (MA); London Coll. of Divinity (BD ext. London Univ.). Ordained deacon, 1970, priest, 1971; Assistant Curate: St Augustine's, Highbury, 1970–73; St Andrew's, Plymouth, 1973–77; Vicar, Christ Church, Ironville, Derbys, 1977–83; Priest-in-charge, St James, Riddings, 1982–83; Rector, Holy Trinity, Rayleigh, Chelmsford, 1983–96. Part-time Chaplain, Bullwood Hall Prison and Youth Custody Centre, 1986–90; Rural Dean of Rochford, 1989–96. *Recreations:* walking, electronics and computing, astronomy, archaeology of Jerusalem, Dartmoor and its history. *Address:* 5 Springfield Terrace, Springfield Road, South Brent, Devon TQ10 9AP. *T:* (01364) 73427. *E:* peterftaylor@lineone.net.

TAYLOR, Prof. Peter James, PhD; FBA 2004; Professor of Geography, Loughborough University, 1995–2010, now Emeritus, and founding Director, Globalization and World Cities Research Network; Professor of Human Geography, Northumbria University, since 2010; *b* 21 Nov. 1944; *s* of Peter Taylor and Margaret Alice Taylor; *m* 1965, Enid; one *s* one *d*. *Educ:* Univ. of Liverpool (BA Hons; PhD). Lectr, Sen. Lectr, Reader, then Prof., Univ. of Newcastle upon Tyne, 1971–95. Visiting positions: Univ. of Iowa, 1970–71; Univ. of Alberta, 1976; Clark Univ., 1978–79; Univ. of Illinois, 1985; Binghamton Univ., 1990; Univ. of Amsterdam, 1991; Virginia Tech, 1992–93, 2002, 2003; Univ. of Paris, 1995; Ghent Univ., 2004–05. Francqui Medal, Francqui Foundn, Brussels, 2005; Ghent Univ. Medal, 2005. *Publications:* (with Colin Flint) Political Geography: world-economy, nation-state, locality, 1985, 6th edn 2011; Britain and the Cold War: 1945 as geopolitical transition, 1990; The Way the Modern World Works, 1996; Modernities: a geohistorical introduction, 1999; World City Network, 2004; (ed jtly) Cities in Globalization, 2006; (ed jtly) Global Urban Analysis: a survey of cities in globalization, 2010; (ed jtly) The Globalization of Advertising: agencies, cities and spaces of creativity, 2010; (ed jtly) International Handbook of Globalization and World Cities, 2011. *Recreations:* watching sport, collecting postcards, playing with grandchildren. *Address:* 33 Percy Park, Tynemouth NE30 4JZ. *T:* (0191) 259 1113, *Fax:* (01509) 223930.

TAYLOR, Peter William Edward; QC 1981; *b* 27 July 1917; *s* of late Peter and Julia A. Taylor; *m* 1948, Julia Mary Brown (*d* 1997), *d* of Air Cdre Sir Vernon Brown, CB, OBE; two *s*. *Educ:* Peter Symonds' Sch., Winchester; Christ's Coll., Cambridge (MA; Wrangler, Math. Tripos, Part II; 1st Class, Law Tripos, Part II). Served RA, 1939–46: France and Belgium, 1939–40; N Africa, 1942–43; NW Europe, 1944–45 (mentioned in dispatches); Actg Lt-Col 1945; transferred to TARO as Hon. Major, 1946. Called to the Bar, Inner Temple, 1946; Lincoln's Inn, *ad eundem*, 1953 (Bencher, 1976); practice at the Bar, 1947–94; Occasional Lectr, LSE, 1946–56; Lectr in Construction of Documents, Council of Legal Educn, 1952–70; Conveyancing Counsel of the Court, 1974–81. Member: General Council of the Bar, 1971–74; Senate of Inns of Court and the Bar, 1974–75; Inter-Professional Cttee on Retirement Provision, 1974–92; Land Registration Rule Cttee, 1976–81; Standing Cttee on Conveyancing, 1985–87; Incorporated Council of Law Reporting, 1977–91 (Vice-Chm., 1987–91); Council, Selden Soc., 1977–. Bar Musical Society: Hon. Sec., 1952–61; Treas. and External Sec., 1961–80; Chm., 1980–86; Vice-Pres., 1986–. *Recreations:* sailing, shooting, music. *Address:* 46 Onslow Square, SW7 3NX. *T:* (020) 7589 1301.

TAYLOR, Philippe Arthur; Managing Director, SeaTrain Sailing, 1993–99; *b* 9 Feb. 1937; *s* of Arthur Peach Taylor and Simone Vacquin; *m* 1973, Margaret Nancy Wilkins; two *s*. *Educ:* Trinity College, Glenalmond; St Andrews University. Procter & Gamble, 1963; Masius International, 1967; British Tourist Authority, 1970; Chief Executive, Scottish Tourist Board, 1975–80; Man. Dir, Taylor and Partners, 1980–92; Chief Exec., Birmingham Convention and Visitor Bureau Ltd, 1982–94. Vice-Chm., Ikon Gall., 1982–92; Chm., British Assoc. of

Conf. Towns, 1987–90. *Publications:* children's books; various papers and articles on tourism. *Recreations:* sailing, making things, tourism, reading. *Address:* The Granary, Theberton, Suffolk IP16 4RR. *Clubs:* Royal Northumberland Yacht (Blyth); Orford Sailing.

TAYLOR, Rebecca; Project Manager, Macmillan Cancer Support, since 2014; *b* Todmorden, W Yorks, 10 Aug. 1975. *Educ:* Univ. of Leeds (BA Japanese and Mgt Studies 1997); Univ. of Kent (MA Internat. Relns 2001); Open Univ. (Human Biol. 2010); King's Coll. London (Master in Public Health 2014). Public affairs asst, Plasma Protein Therapeutics Assoc. Europe, 1998–2000; web ed. and journalist, IMS Health, Brussels, 2000–01; Information and Communications Officer, Pharmaceutical Gp of EU, Brussels, 2002–05; Ext. Communications Manager, Internat. Fedn of Animal Health, Brussels, 2005–06; consultant, Food, Health and Retail team, Fleishman-Hillard, Brussels, 2006–09; Stakeholder Relns Manager, NHS Commng Support for London, 2009–10; Sen. Researcher, Internat. Longevity Centre-UK, 2010–11; Account Dir, Healthcare team, Hanover Communications, 2011–12. Mem. (Lib Dem) Yorks and the Humber, Eur. Parlt, 2012–14. Contested (Lib Dem): Rotherham, 2010; Morley and Outwood, 2015. *W:* www.twitter.com/RTaylor_LibDem.

TAYLOR, Prof. Richard Edward, CC (Can.) 2005; FRS 1997; Professor, Stanford Linear Accelerator Center, Stanford University, 1968–2003, now Emeritus; *b* 2 Nov. 1929; *s* of Clarence Richard Taylor and Delia Alena Taylor (*née* Brunsdale); *m* 1951, Rita Jean Bonneau; one *s*. *Educ:* Univ. of Alberta (BS 1950; MS 1952); Stanford Univ. (PhD 1962). Boursier, Lab. de l'Accélérateur Linéaire, France, 1958–61; physicist, Lawrence Berkeley Lab., Berkeley, Calif., 1961–62; staff mem., 1962–68, Associate Dir, 1982–86, Stanford Linear Accelerator Center. Distinguished Prof., Univ. of Alberta, 1992–2003, now Emeritus. Fellow: Guggenheim Foundn, 1971–72; Amer. Phys. Soc. (W. K. H. Panofsky Prize, Div. of Particles and Fields, 1989); FRSC; Fellow, Amer. Acad. of Arts and Scis, 1992. Foreign Associate, NAS, USA. Hon. DSc: Paris-Sud, 1980; Alberta, 1991; Lethbridge, 1993; Victoria, 1994; Blaise Pascal, 1997; Carleton, Ottawa, 1999; Liverpool, 1999; Queen's, Kingston, Ont., 2000; Hon. LLD Calgary, 1993. Von Humboldt Award, 1982; Nobel Prize in Physics, 1990. *Address:* SLAC National Accelerator Laboratory, 2575 Sand Hill Road, M/S 43, Menlo Park, CA 94025, USA. *T:* (650) 9262417.

TAYLOR, Prof. Richard Kenneth Stanley, PhD; Professor and Director of Continuing Education and Lifelong Learning, University of Cambridge, 2004–09; Fellow, Wolfson College, Cambridge, 2004–09, now Emeritus Professorial Fellow; *b* 18 Nov. 1945; *s* of Jeanne Ann Taylor and Kenneth Charles Taylor; *m* 1967, Jennifer Teresa Frost (marr. diss. 2004); one *s* two *d*. *Educ:* Merchant Taylors' Sch., Northwood; Exeter Coll., Oxford (MA 1967); PhD Leeds 1983. Admin. Asst, Univ. of Lancaster, 1967–70; University of Leeds: Admin. Asst, Dept of Adult and Continuing Educn, 1970–73; Warden, Non-Residential Centre for Adult Educn, Bradford, 1973–83; Dir of Extramural Studies, 1985–88; Head, Dept of Adult and Continuing Educn, 1988–91; Prof. and Dir of Continuing Educn, 1991–2004. Sec., Univs Assoc. for Continuing Educn, 1994–98, 2002–03; Chairman: Nat. Inst. for Adult Continuing Educn, 1999–2006 (Vice Chm., 1996–99); Trustees, WEA, 2006–13. Trustee, Acid Survivors' Trust Internat., 2008–13. *Publications:* (with Colin Pritchard) Social Work: reform or revolution?, 1978; (with Colin Pritchard) The Protest Makers, 1980; (jtly) Adult Education in England and the USA, 1985; (with Kevin Ward) Adult Education and the Working Class, 1986, 2nd edn 2012; Against the Bomb: the British peace movement 1958–65, 1988; (with Nigel Young) Campaigns for Peace, 1988; (with Tom Steele) Learning Independence, 1995; Beyond the Walls, 1996; (with David Watson) Lifelong Learning and the University: a post-Dearing agenda, 1998; (with Tom Steele and Jean Barr) For a Radical Higher Education: after postmodernism, 2002; (with Tom Steele) British Labour and Higher Education, 1945–2000: ideologies, policies and practice, 2011; (with Roger Fieldhouse) E. P. Thompson and English Radicalism, 2013. *Recreations:* mountain walking and climbing, cricket, politics, pubs. *Address:* Bowerbank Cottage, Pooley Bridge, Penrith, Cumbria CA10 2NG. *Club:* Yorkshire County Cricket.

TAYLOR, Prof. Richard Lawrence, PhD; FRS 1995; Robert and Luisa Fernholz Professor, Institute for Advanced Study, Princeton, since 2013 (Professor of Mathematics, 2012–13); *b* 19 May 1962; *s* of John Clayton Taylor and Gillian Mary Taylor (*née* Schofield); *m* 1995, Christine Jiayou Chang; one *s* one *d*. *Educ:* Magdalen Coll. Sch., Oxford; Clare Coll., Cambridge (BA); Princeton Univ. (PhD). Fellow, Clare Coll., Cambridge, 1988–95; Asst Lectr, 1989–92, Lectr, 1992–94, Reader, 1994–95, Cambridge Univ.; Savilian Prof. of Geometry, and Fellow of New Coll., Oxford Univ., 1995–96; Prof. of Mathematics, 1996–2002, Herchel Smith Prof. of Maths, 2002–12, Harvard Univ. *Publications:* (with M. Harris) The Geometry and Cohomology of Some Simple Shimura Varieties, 2001. *Recreation:* hill walking. *Address:* Institute for Advanced Study, Einstein Drive, Princeton, NJ 08540, USA. *T:* (609) 7348189.

TAYLOR, Sir Richard (Leslie), KNZM 2010 (ONZM 2003); Managing Director, Weta Workshop, since 1994; *b* Cheadle, Staffs, UK, 8 Feb. 1965; *s* of Norman Taylor and Jean Taylor; *m* 2010, Tania Rodger; one *s* one *d*. *Educ:* Wesley Coll., Auckland; Wellington Poly. (Dip. Visual Communication and Design 1987). Design and Effect Supervisor, RT Effects Ltd, 1987–94. Films contributed to include: The Fellowship of the Ring, 2001 (jtly) Best Special Visual Effects, and Best Make up and Hair, BAFTA, 2002; (jtly) Best Visual Effects and Make up, Academy Awards, 2002); The Two Towers, 2002 (jtly) Best Costume Design, BAFTA, 2003); The Return of the King, 2003 (jtly) Best Costume Design, and Best Make up, Academy Awards, 2004); King Kong, 2005 (jtly) Best Special Visual Effects, BAFTA, 2006; (jtly) Best Visual Effects, Academy Awards, 2006). New Zealander of the Year Award, 2012. *Recreations:* sculpting, 7¼ inch trains, family, art, sculpture. *Address:* PO Box 15208, Miramar, Wellington 6243, New Zealand. *T:* (4) 9094000, *Fax:* (4) 3889722.

TAYLOR, Prof. R(ichard) Neil, PhD; Professor of Geotechnical Engineering, City University London, since 1996; *b* 14 May 1955; *s* of Charles L. Taylor and Mary Taylor. *Educ:* Emmanuel Coll., Cambridge (BA 1976; MPhil 1979; MA 1980; PhD 1984). MICE 1990. Lectr in Geotechnical Engrg, 1984–91, Sen. Lectr, 1991–96, City Univ. London. Associate, Geotechnical Consulting Gp, 1990–. Sec. Gen., Internat. Soc. for Soil Mechanics and Geotechnical Engrg, 1999–. *Publications:* (ed) Geotechnical Centrifuge Technology, 1995; contrib. papers to jls and confs mainly associated with ground movements caused by tunnels and excavations incl. geotechnical centrifuge modelling and analysis. *Recreations:* running (5km+), walking. *Address:* Research Centre for Multi-scale Geotechnical Engineering, City University London, Northampton Square, EC1V 0HB. *T:* (020) 7040 8157.

TAYLOR, Richard Thomas, MBE 2014; FRCP; *b* 7 July 1934; *s* of Thomas Taylor and Mabel (*née* Hickley); *m* 1st, 1962, Ann Brett (marr. diss.); one *s* two *d*; 2nd, 1990, Christine Miller; one *d*. *Educ:* Leys Sch.; Clare Coll., Cambridge (BA); Westminster Med. Sch. (MB, BChir). FRCP 1979. Jun. hosp. doctor trng posts, Westminster Hosp. and other London hosps, 1959–72; MO, RAF, 1961–64; Consultant Physician, Kidderminster Gen. Hosp., 1972–95 (Chm., Hosp. Med. Staff Cttee, 1975–77 and 1986–90). Consultant Rep., Kidderminster DHA, 1982–86. MP (Ind) Wyre Forest, 2001–10; contested (Ind) same seat, 2010; contested (Nat. Health Action) same seat, 2015. Mem., Select Cttee on Health, 2001–10. Chairman: Kidderminster Hosp. League of Friends, 1996–2001; Save Kidderminster Hosp. Campaign Cttee, 1997–2001. President: Kidderminster Civic Soc., 2010–; Leukaemia CARE, 2010–. *Publications:* articles on drug treatment and rheumatic diseases in med. jls. *Recreations:* family, ornithology, gardening, classic cars. *Address:* 11 Church Walk, Kidderminster, Worcs DY11 6XY. *Club:* Royal Society of Medicine.

TAYLOR, (Robert) Alan; Chief Executive and Town Clerk, Royal Borough of Kensington and Chelsea, 1990–2000; *b* 13 Sept. 1944; *s* of Alfred Taylor and Hilda Mary (*née* Weekley); *m* 1st, 1965, Dorothy Joan Walker (*d* 1986); two *s*; 2nd, 1987, Margaret Susanne Barnes. *Educ:* Thornbury Grammar Sch., Thornbury, Glos; King's Coll., Univ. of London (LLB). Solicitor. Asst Solicitor, Plymouth CBC, 1970–74; Plymouth City Council: Dep. City Solicitor and Sec., 1974–76; Asst Town Clerk, 1976–81; Chief Exec., London Borough of Sutton, 1981–90. Lay Mem., Investigation Cttee, CIMA, 2002–05. Pres., SOLACE, 1998–99 (Hon. Sec., 1992–95; Sen. Vice-Pres., 1997–98); Trustee, Voluntary Reading Help, 2001–07. Chm., Dartmoor Local Access Forum, 2003–06; Mem., Devon and Cornwall Regl Cttee, NT, 2004–13. *Recreations:* theatre, books, walking, choral singing. *Address:* Catkins, Green Lane, Exton, Devon EX3 0PW. *T:* (01392) 873850.

TAYLOR, Robert Bruce; Head of Wealth Management and Private Banking, Financial Conduct Authority, since 2014; *b* London, 4 Jan. 1960; *s* of Robert Wilson Taylor and Joy Rosina Taylor; partner, Michael David Julius Kallenbach. *Educ:* Sam Barlow High Sch.; Lewis & Clark Coll. (BA Internat. Affairs 1982); Columbia Univ. (MS Journalism 1986). Congressional Aide to Congressman Les AuCoin, 1982–85; Editor, Bond Buyer, 1987–90; Vice Pres., Merrill Lynch, 1990–98; Man. Dir, SG Hambros Bank & Trust, 1998–2000; Hd, Private Banking, Coutts & Co., 2000–04; CEO, Kleinwort Benson, 2004–11. Mem., Jury, Turner Prize, Tate Britain, 2004; Chm., Trustees, Whitechapel Gall., 2005–. Gov., Charlotte Sharman Sch., 2001–08; Chm., Bd of Govs, Univ. for Creative Arts, 2012–. *Recreations:* reading, theatre, Rugby, tennis, music, opera. *Club:* Royal Automobile.

TAYLOR, His Honour Robert Carruthers; a Circuit Judge, 1984–2004; *b* 6 Jan. 1939; *o s* of late John Taylor, CBE and Barbara Taylor; *m* 1968, Jacqueline Marjorie, *er d* of Nigel and Marjorie Chambers; one *s* one *d*. *Educ:* Wycliffe Coll.; St John's Coll., Oxford. MA 1967; Open Univ. (BA 2011). Called to Bar, Middle Temple, 1961; practised NE Circuit, 1961–84; a Recorder, 1976–84. Chm., Agricl Land Tribunal, Yorks and Humberside Areas, 1979–2013; Mem., Mental Health Tribunal, 2001–12. *Recreations:* reading, music, gardening, walking, family. *Address:* Abbotsview, 59 King's Road, Ilkley, W Yorks LS29 9BZ. *T:* (01943) 607672.

TAYLOR, Prof. Robert Henry, PhD; Vice-Chancellor, University of Buckingham, 1997–2001; *b* 15 March 1943; *s* of Robert E. Taylor and Mabelle L. Taylor (*née* Warren), Greenville, Ohio; *m* 1st (marr. diss.); one *s* one *d*; 2nd, 2000, Ingrid Porteous. *Educ:* Ohio Univ. (BA 1965); Antioch Coll. (MA 1967); Cornell Univ. (PhD 1974). Social Studies Teacher, Cardozo High Sch., Washington DC, 1965–67; Instructor in Pol Sci., Wilberforce Univ., Ohio, 1967–69; Lectr in Govt, Univ. of Sydney, 1974–79; School of Oriental and African Studies, University of London: Lectr, 1980–88, Sen. Lectr, 1988–89, in Politics (with ref. to SE Asia); Prof. of Politics, 1989–96; Pro-Dir, 1991–96; Professorial Res. Associate, 2003–. Associate Sen. Fellow, 2003–12, Vis. Professorial Res. Fellow, 2012–14, Vis. Sen. Res. Fellow, 2014–15, Inst. of Southeast Asian Studies, Singapore; Visiting Professor: Univ. of Buckingham, 2007–; City Univ. of Kong Kong, 2010–12. Lay Mem., Asylum and Immigration Tribunal, 2004–11. *Publications:* Marxism and Resistance in Burma, 1985; The State in Burma, 1987; (contrib.) In Search of Southeast Asia: a modern history, 1987; (ed) Handbooks of the Modern World: Asia and the Pacific, 2 vols, 1991; (ed) The Politics of Elections in Southeast Asia, 1996; (ed) Burma: political economy under military rule, 2001; (ed) The Idea of Freedom in Asia and Africa, 2002; (contrib.) The Emergence of Southeast Asia, 2005; (ed jtly) Myanmar: beyond politics to societal imperatives, 2005; (ed) Dr Maung Maung: gentleman, scholar and patriot, 2008; The State in Myanmar, 2009; General Ne Win: a political biography, 2015; numerous articles in books and learned jls. *T:* (020) 8361 4002. *E:* dr.tinhla@gmail.com. *Club:* Travellers.

TAYLOR, Dr Robert Thomas, CBE 1990; Chairman, Management Interviewing and Research Institute, 1993–2004; *b* 21 March 1933; *s* of George Taylor and Marie Louise Fidler; *m* 1st, 1954, Ina Wilson (marr. diss. 1965); one *s*; 2nd, 1965, Rosemary Janet Boileau; two *s* one *d*. *Educ:* Boteler Grammar Sch., Warrington; University Coll., Oxford (Open Exhibnr; BA 1954, MA 1957; DPhil 1957). Fulbright Scholar. Research Associate, Randall Lab. of Physics, Univ. of Michigan, USA, 1957–58; ICI Research Fellow, 1958–59, Lectr, Physics Dept, 1959–61, Univ. of Liverpool; Chief Examr for NUJMB, GCE Physics (Scholarship Level), 1961; British Council: Asst Regional Rep., Madras, 1961–64; Science Officer, Madrid, 1964–69; Dir, Staff Recruitment Dept, 1969–73; Regional Educn Advr, Bombay, 1973–77; Rep., Mexico, 1977–81; Controller, Personnel, 1981–86; Rep., Greece, 1986–90; Asst Dir-Gen., British Council, 1990–93. Mem. (C), Weald Central Ward, Ashford BC, 2003–15. Vis. Sen. Fellow, Manchester Business Sch., 1993–99. *Publications:* contrib. to Chambers Encyclopaedia, 1967 edn; papers in scientific jls. *Recreations:* computers, war and war gaming. *Address:* Mark Haven, Ashford Road, High Halden, Kent TN26 3LJ. *T:* (01233) 850994.

TAYLOR, Prof. Rodney Hemingfield, MD; FRCP; Consultant Physician and Gastroenterologist, Ealing Hospital, 2001–07 (Medical Director, 2001–03); Visiting Professor, School of Arts and Humanities (formerly of Theology, Philosophy and History), St Mary's University (formerly University College), Twickenham, since 2009; *b* London, 21 Dec. 1942; *s* of late (Alfred) Alan Taylor, PhD and Margaret Taylor (*née* Paine); *m* 1st, 1965, Jean Williams (marr. diss. 1972); 2nd, 1972, Dr Janet Mary Baldwin, FRCP, FRCOG; one *s* two *d*. *Educ:* The Grammar Sch., Enfield; Univ. of Bristol (BSc Psychol. 1965); University Coll., London and UCH Med. Sch., London (MB BS 1972; MD 1984); Open Univ. Business Sch. (MBA 1996); King's Fund Top Manager Prog., 1997; Univ. of Surrey (MA Bioethics 2008). MRCS 1972; LRCP 1972, MRCP 1976, FRCP 1987; DHMSA 1992; DPMSA 1994; FRSPH 2001. Clin. Psychologist, Harperbury and Cell Barnes Hosps, 1965–67; trng posts in medicine at UCH, W Middx, Whittington, London Chest and Central Middx Hosps, 1972–78; Res. Fellow, Univ. Lab. of Physiol., Oxford and Central Middx Hosp., 1978–80; Wellcome Sen. Res. Fellow in Clin. Sci. and Hon. Sen. Lectr, Middx Hosp. Med. Sch., London, 1980–84; Hon. Consultant Physician and Gastroenterologist, Central Middx Hosp., 1980–94; Hd, Human Pharmacol., Res. Div., Beecham Pharmaceuticals, Harlow, 1984–86. Commnd RNR (London Div.), 1977–86; commnd RN, 1986–2002 (Surgeon Captain); sea service in Mediterranean, Iberian waters, N and S Atlantic; active service in Gulf War, 1990–91, Kosovo, Bosnia and NI; shore based, Akrotiri and Gibraltar; Consultant Physician, 1986–2001, Med. Dir, 1997–2001, Royal Naval Hospital, Haslar; RCP Prof. of Naval Medicine, 1988–94; Clin. Teacher, Univ. of Southampton Med. Sch., 1987–2001; Associate Postgrad. Dean, Royal Defence Med. Coll., 1997–2001; Defence Consultant Advr in Medicine to Surgeon Gen., 2000–01. Tutor in Med. Ethics and Law, ICSM, 2007–. Osler Lectr, 1994, Gideon de Laune Lectr, 2004, Soc. of Apothecaries; Inaugural Charles Bernard Lectr, Barbers' Co., 2001. Associate and Assessor: Commn for Health Improvement, 1998–2002; Healthcare Commn, 2002–08; Associate and Professional Performance Assessor, GMC, 2000– (PLAB Examr, 2000–05); Professional Perf. Assessor, Nat. Clin. Assessment Service, 2001–. Surveyor, Healthcare Accreditation and Quality Unit, King's Fund Organisational Audit, then Health Quality Service, later CHKS, 1998– (Vice Chair, Accreditation Council and Panel, 2007–11; Chm., Accreditation Council, 2011–). Mem., Mgt Bd, Haemato-Oncology Tissue Bank, KCL, 2012–. British Society of Gastroenterology: Mem., 1976–2011 (Hon. Mem., 2011); Mem. Council, 1989–98; Treas., Chair of Trustees and Chair of Dirs, 1992–98; Treas., United Eur. Gastroenterol. Week, 1997. Trustee, 1996–2004, Hon. Med. Dir, 1996–2001, Digestive Disorders Foundn; Foundn Trustee, Mulberry Centre, 2004– (Chm. Trustees, 2008–12). Chm., Patient Support Gp, MDS UK, 2011– (Dep. Chm., 2009–11). Fellow, Med. Soc. of London, 1976; Faculty of History and

Philosophy of Medicine and Pharmacy, Society of Apothecaries: Fellow, 1992–2009; Hon. Fellow, 2009; Sec., 1996–2000; Dep. Pres., 2000–04; Pres., 2004–08; Convenor of Examrs in Hist. of Medicine, 2000–04 and 2008–; Freeman, Soc. of Apothecaries, 1997 (Liveryman, 2001; Asst, 2006–; Jun. Warden, 2010; Sen. Warden, 2011; Master, 2012); Freeman, 2006, Liveryman, 2008, Barbers' Co. Parish Church of St James, Hampton Hill: Mem., PCC, 1996–2010; Churchwarden, 2002–07 (interregnum, 2006–07); Mem., Deanery Synod, 2008–10. Wandsman, St Paul's Cathedral, 2010–. Mem., RNSA. Errol Eldridge Prize, RN, 1995. *Publications:* (jtly) Gastroenterology - Pocket Consultant, 1991, 2nd edn 1998; contribs on carbohydrate absorption, dietary fibre, glycaemic index, gut hormones, enzyme inhibitors, clin. gastroenterol. and hist. of medicine. *Recreations:* choral singing, opera, fine arts, medical history, messing about in boats (RYA Yachtmaster), English churches, choral Evensong. *Address:* 29 Park Road, Hampton Hill, Middx TW12 1HG. *T:* (020) 8979 0046. *E:* RodnTayl@aol.com. *Club:* Royal Society of Medicine.

TAYLOR, Roger Miles Whitworth; Director, London's Growth Boroughs Unit (formerly Olympic Host Boroughs Unit), 2008–13; *b* 18 May 1944; *s* of Richard and Joan Taylor; *m* 1969, Georgina Lucy Tonks (marr. diss. 2003); two *s* two *d*; *m* 2003, Gabriele Eva Bock. *Educ:* Repton School; Birmingham University (LLB). Solicitor, admitted 1968; Asst Solicitor, Cheshire CC, 1969–71; Asst County Clerk, Lincs parts of Lindsey, 1971–73; Dep. County Secretary, Northants CC, 1973–79; Dep. Town Clerk, 1979–85, Town Clerk and Chief Exec., 1985–88, City of Manchester; Chief Exec., Birmingham CC, 1988–94; Dir, 1994–2000, Chm., 1997–2000, Newchurch and Co.; Man. Dir, Pinnacle Consulting, 2000–06; Dir, Pinnacle Public Services Gp (formerly Pinnacle PSG), 2000–10; Chief Exec., Waltham Forest LBC, 2007–08. Dir, Fermosa Consulting Ltd, 2011–15. Mem., Farrand Cttee on Conveyancing, 1983–84; Clerk, Greater Manchester Passenger Transport Authy, 1986–88. Sec., W Midlands Jt Cttee, 1988–94. Chairman: Birmingham Marketing Partnership, 1993–94; Birmingham Common Purpose, 1994; Local Govt Television Adv. Bd, 1994–95; Dir, Birmingham TEC, 1990–93. Mem., Standards Bd for England, 2001–07. Dir, Ex Cathedra Chamber Choir, 1996–98. Mancunian of the Year, Manchester Jun. Chamber of Commerce, 1988; SOLACE Interim Manager of the Year, 2009. *Publications:* contribs to Local Govt Chronicle, Municipal Review, Municipal Jl. *Recreations:* sailing, walking, organic olive farming and olive oil making. *Address:* Codigo Postal SP 10170, Montanchez, Caceres, Extremadura, Spain. *T:* 07967 057054. *E:* rogermwt@gmail.com.

TAYLOR, Prof. Ronald Wentworth, MD; FRCOG; Professor Emeritus of Obstetrics and Gynaecology, United Medical and Dental Schools of Guy's and St Thomas' Hospitals, since 1989; *b* 28 Oct. 1932; *s* of George Richard and Winifred Taylor; *m* 1962, Mary Patricia O'Neill; three *s* one *d*. *Educ:* St Mary's Coll., Crosby; Liverpool Univ. (MB ChB 1958; MD 1972). MRCOG 1965, FRCOG 1975. Jun. House Officer posts, Liverpool, 1958–59; Sen. House Officer posts, Preston, 1960, Manchester, 1962; GP, Ormskirk, Lancs, 1962–63; Registrar, Whittington Hosp., London, 1963–64; St Thomas' Hospital: Lectr, 1965–67; Sen. Lectr, 1968–76; Prof., 1977–89, subseq. at UMDS of Guy's and St Thomas' Hosps. Founder Mem., Expert Witness Inst., 1995– (Fellow, 2000). *Publications:* Gynaecological Cancer, 1975; "Ten Teachers" Obstetrics and Gynaecology, 14th edn 1985; (ed) Confidential Enquiry into Perinatal Deaths, 1988; Endometrial Cancer, 1988. *Recreations:* sailing, silversmithing, restoration of furniture, photography. *Address:* Keld Head, Keld Shap, Penrith, Cumbria CA10 3QF. *T:* (01931) 716553.

TAYLOR, Rupert Maurice T.; *see* Thornely-Taylor.

TAYLOR, Russell Philip, MBE 2003; writer, cartoonist and composer; *b* 8 July 1960; *s* of Captain Hal Taylor and Iona Taylor (*née* Mackenzie); *m* 1990, Anne-Frederique Dujon (marr. diss. 2007). *Educ:* St Anne's Coll., Oxford (BA Russian and Philosophy). Freelance writer and journalist, 1984–87; writer of Alex cartoon (with Charles Peattie) in: London Daily News, 1987; The Independent, 1987–91; Daily Telegraph, 1992–; writer of Celeb cartoon (with Charles Peattie and Mark Warren), Private Eye, 1987–; Alex (stage play), Arts Th., 2007; composer of film and TV music, 1991–. *Publications:* The Looniness of the Long Distance Runner, 2001; (with Marc Polonsky) USSR from an original idea by Karl Marx, 1986; with Charles Peattie: Alex, 1987; The Unabashed Alex, 1988; Alex II: Magnum Force, 1989; Alex III: Son of Alex, 1990; Alex IV: The Man with the Golden Handshake, 1991; Celeb, 1991; Alex V: For the Love of Alex, 1992; Alex Calls the Shots, 1993; Alex Plays the Game, 1994; Alex Knows the Score, 1995; Alex Sweeps the Board, 1996; Alex Feels the Pinch, 1997; The Full Alex, 1998; The Alex Technique, 1999; The Best of Alex, 1998–2001, 2001; The Best of Alex, annually 2002–11. *Recreations:* playing piano, running, perudo, time-wasting. *Address:* PO Box 39447, London, N10 3WA. *T:* (020) 8374 1225. *E:* alex@alexcartoon.com. *Clubs:* Groucho, Soho House.

TAYLOR, (Samantha) Claire, MBE 2010; cricketer; Member, England Women's cricket team, 1998–2011; *b* Amersham, 25 Sept. 1975; *d* of Frederick Roger Taylor and Barbara Taylor (*née* MacDonald). *Educ:* Kendrick Sch., Reading; Queen's Coll., Oxford (BA Maths 1997). Procter and Gamble, 1998–2001; semi-professional cricketer, 2002–05; Mgt Consultant, Sums Consulting, 2006–. One-day internat. début, Australia, 1998, England Women's Test cricket début, India, 1999; Mem., winning team: Ashes, 2005 and 2008; Women's World Cup, 2009; Women's ICC World Twenty20, 2009; Member of team: Reading CC, 1989– (Capt., 2007–12); Berks Cricket, 1992–2012. (Jtly) Wisden Cricketer of the Year, 2009; Women's Cricketer of the Year, ICC, 2009. *Recreations:* reading, playing the violin for Aldworth Philharmonic, dog walking, cooking. *Address:* c/o Sums Consulting, Science and Technology Centre, University of Reading, Earley Gate, Whiteknights Road, Reading RG6 6BZ.

TAYLOR, Sandra Anne; independent consultant, writer; Chief Executive, Barnsley Hospital NHS Foundation Trust, 2007–10; *b* 5 Sept. 1953; *d* of Harold E. Taylor and May Taylor (*née* Draper). *Educ:* Portsmouth Poly. (BA Hons); Essex Univ. (MA). Lectr and Tutor, Hull Univ., 1977–80; Res. Fellow and Lectr, UCL, 1981–82; Nottinghamshire County Council: Community Develt Officer, 1982–86; Principal Officer, 1986–88, Principal Asst, 1988–89, Asst Dir, 1990–96, Social Services Dept; Dir, Social Services, Leics City Council, 1996–99; Dir of Social Services, Birmingham CC, 1999–2002. Social Services expert consultant, Capita Business Services, 2003; Advr, Vertex Customer Services, 2003; interim Dir of Policy, 2003–04, interim Exec. Dir of Develt, 2004–05, Surrey and Sussex Strategic HA; Project Dir, Health Reconfiguration, E Berks Health Economy/Slough BC, 2006–07. *Publications:* (ed) Nottinghamshire Labour Movement, 1986; (jtly) Housing Futures: housing policy, management and practice, 1992; (ed) Managing Housing in a larger authority, 1993. *Recreations:* swimming, gardening, walking.

TAYLOR, Simon Wheldon; QC 2003; a Recorder, since 2002; *b* 4 July 1962; *s* of Thomas Henry Taylor and Enid Taylor, *qv*; *m* 1990, Elizabeth Lawes Paine; one *s* two *d*. *Educ:* Trinity Coll., Cambridge (BA Hons); London Hosp. Med. Coll. (MB BChir); Inns of Court Sch. of Law. Called to the Bar, Middle Temple, 1984; qualified doctor, 1987; pupillage, 1988; tenancy, 1989; in practice as barrister, 1989–. Ordained deacon, 2012, priest, 2013; Curate (pt-time), St Philip's, Tunbridge Wells, 2013–. *Address:* Cloisters, 1 Pump Court, Temple, EC4Y 7AA. *T:* (020) 7827 4000. *E:* st@cloisters.com.

TAYLOR, Ven. Stephen Ronald, MBE 2009; Archdeacon of Maidstone, since 2011; *b* Bradford, 2 May 1955; *s* of Ronald Taylor and Joyce Taylor; *m* 1981, Julie Anderson; three *d* (one *s* decd). *Educ:* Durham Univ. (MA 1999). Community Recreation Officer, Bradford, 1978; ordained deacon, 1983, priest, 1984; Curate, Chester le Street, 1983; Vicar: Newbottle, 1988–93; Stranton, Hartlepool, 1993–2000; Canon Provost, Sunderland, 2000–11. Hon. Chaplain, Frankland Prison, 1989–93; Hon. Canon, dio. of Rift Valley, Tanzania, 1999–. Chm., Sunderland Partnership, 2007–11. Founder, Kilimatinde Trust, Tanzania, 1997. Hon. Fellow, Univ. of Sunderland, 2009. *Recreations:* Isles of Scilly holidays, supports Maidstone FC, walking, bird photography. *Address:* The Archdeaconry, 4 Redcliffe Lane, Penenden Heath, Maidstone ME14 2AG. *T:* 07944 680855. *E:* staylor@archdeacmaid.org.

TAYLOR, Sir Teddy; *see* Taylor, Sir E. M.

TAYLOR, Thomas William; Director, Corporate Operations and Organisational Development, Office of Rail and Road (formerly Office of Rail Regulation), since 2013; *b* London, 19 Oct. 1971; *s* of Sidney Taylor and Catherine Taylor (*née* Hewitt); *m* 2000, Jayne Marie Priddin; one *s*. *Educ:* Highbury Grove Sch., Islington; Girton Coll., Cambridge (BA 1993); Sch. of Oriental and African Studies, Univ. of London (MSc Econs); Univ. of Warwick (Post Grad. Dip. Finance). CPFA 2011. Department of Social Security, then Department for Work and Pensions: Econ. Advr, Welfare Benefits, 1994–2001; Deputy Director: Child Poverty, 2001–04; Housing Benefits, 2004–06; on loan as Dep. Dir, Analytical Audit, Office of Climate Change, 2006–07; Dep. Dir, Corporate Performance, 2007–09, Dir, Finance and Performance, 2009–13, DEFRA. *Recreations:* motorcycles, cabinet making. *Address:* Office of Rail and Road, 1 Kemble Street, WC2B 4AN.

TAYLOR, Timothy Hugh Christian; QC 2011; Partner, King & Wood Mallesons (formerly SJ Berwin) LLP, since 1988; *b* Barton, 22 June 1956; *s* of Hugh Garner Taylor and Doreen May Taylor; *m* 2010, Jessica Yao Affi; four *s* one *d*, and one step *d*. *Educ:* King's Sch., Canterbury; St John's Coll., Oxford (BA Juris.). Solicitor Advocate. Solicitor, Herbert Smith, 1980–87. Founder Dir, Internat. Lawyers for Africa, 2007–. *Recreations:* carousing, laughter and reflection. *Address:* King & Wood Mallesons Dubai, Suite 303, Level 3, Park Place, Sheikh Zayed Road, PO Box 24482, Dubai, UAE. *T:* 07775 681391, (50) 2485354. *E:* timtaylorqc@gmail.com.

TAYLOR, Victoria Mary; *see* Edwards, V. M.

TAYLOR, Wendy Ann, CBE 1988; FRBS 1995; sculptor; Member, Royal Fine Art Commission, 1981–99; *b* 29 July 1945; *d* of late Edward Philip Taylor and Lilian Maude Wright; *m* 1982, Bruce Robertson; one *s*. *Educ:* St Martin's School of Art. LDAD (Hons). One-man exhibitions: Axiom Gall., London, 1970; Angela Flowers Gall., London, 1972; 24th King's Lynn Fest., Norfolk, and World Trade Centre, London, 1974; Annely Juda Fine Art, London, 1975; Oxford Gall., Oxford, 1976; Oliver Dowling Gall., Dublin, 1976 and 1979; Building Art—the process, Building Centre Gall., 1986; Austin, Desmond and Phipps, 1992; Nature and Engineering, Osborne Gp, London, 1998; Cass Gall., London, 2005; Seed Series, Canary Wharf, London, 2009. Shown in over 100 group exhibitions, 1964–82. Represented in collections around the world. Major commissions: The Travellers 1970, London; Gazebo (edn of 4) 1970–71, London, New York, Suffolk, Oxford; Triad 1971, Oxford; Timepiece 1973, London (Grade II listed, 2004); Calthae 1978, Leicestershire; Octo 1980, Milton Keynes; Counterpoise 1980, Birmingham; Compass Bowl 1980, Basildon; Sentinel 1981, Reigate; Bronze Relief 1981, Canterbury; Equatorial Sundial 1982, Bletchley; Essence 1982, Milton Keynes; Opus 1983, Morley Coll., London; Gazebo 1983, Golder's Hill Park, London; Network, 1985, London; Roundacre Improvement Scheme Phase I, 1985–88, Phase II, 1989–90, Basildon; Geo I & Geo II 1986, Stratford-Upon-Avon; Landscape, and Tree of the Wood 1986, Fernhurst, Surrey; Pharos 1986, Peel Park, E Kilbride; Ceres 1986, Fernhurst, Surrey; Nexus 1986, Corby, Northants; Globe Sundial 1987, Swansea Maritime Quarter; Spirit of Enterprise 1987, Isle of Dogs, London; Silver Fountain 1988, Continuum 1990, Guildford, Surrey; The Whirlies 1988, Pharos II 1989, Phoenix 1989–90, E Kilbride; Pilot Kites 1988, Norwich Airport; Fireflow 1988, Strathclyde Fire Brigade HQ, Hamilton; Armillary Sundial 1989, The New Towns, Essex; Globe Sundial II 1990, London Zool Gdns; Butterfly Mosaic 1990, Barking and Dagenham Council; Square Piece 1991, Plano, Ill; Sundial Meml 1991, Sheffield; Anchorage 1991, Salford Quays, Manchester; Wyvern 1992, Leics; stained glass window, St George's Church, Sheffield Univ., 1994; The Jester, Emmanuel Coll., Cambridge, 1994; Challenge, Stockley Park, Middx, 1995; Equilibrium, Coopers & Lybrand, London, 1995; Spirit, Vann, Guildford, 1996; Rope Circle, Hermitage Waterside, London, 1997; Waves, Berners Mews, London, 1998; Dancer, Chelsea and Westminster Hosp., 1998; Dung Beetles, Millennium Conservation Bldg, Zool Soc., Regent's Park, 1999; Mariner's Astrolabe, Virginia Settlers Meml, Brunswick Quay, 1999; Globe View, Blackfriars, 2000; Millennium Fountain, Chase Gardens, Enfield, 2000 (Civic Trust Award, 2002); Voyager, Cinnabar Wharf, London, 2001; Three Reclining Rope Figures, and Conqueror, GlaxoSmithKline, Middx, 2001; Through the Loop, and Around the Square, Pacific Place, HK, 2002; Hunters Square, Chain Piece, Warren, Ohio, 2002; Knowledge, Library Sq., Queen Mary, Univ. of London, 2003; Acorn Wall Relief, Switch House, Brunswick Wharf, London, 2003; Anchor Iron, Anchor Iron Wharf, Greenwich, 2004; Feather Piece, Capital East, Royal Victoria Docks, 2005; Gravesend Heritage, Gravesham, 2005; Silver Fountain II, Bryn Mawr, Penn, 2006; Square Chain Piece, Bartlesville, Oklahoma, 2007; WW II Meml to civilians of E London, Hermitage Meml Gdn, Wapping, 2007; Spirit I, Royal Docks, London, 2008; Running Hares, Gravesham, 2009; Unity, Unison Centre, Euston, 2011; Swirl, Park Rd, London, 2013. Mem., CNAA, 1980–85 (Specialist Advr, 1985–93; Mem., Cttee for Art and Design, 1987–91); Consultant, New Town Commn (Basildon) (formerly Basildon Develt Corp.), 1985–88; Design Consultant, London Borough of Barking and Dagenham, 1989–93 and 1997–2003; LDDC Mem., Design Adv. Panel, 1989–98; Mem., Design Panel, Kent N, 2005–09. Mem., Adv. Gp, PCFC, 1989–90. Examiner, Univ. of London, 1982–83; Mem. Court, RCA, 1982–; Mem. Council, Morley Coll., 1984–88. Trustee, Leicestershire's Appeal for Music and the Arts, 1993–2010. FZS 1989; Fellow, QMW, 1993; FRSA 2004. Awards: Walter Neurath, 1964; Pratt, 1965; Sainsbury, 1966; Arts Council, 1977; Duais na Riochta (Kingdom Prize), 1977; Gold Medal, Eire, 1977; 1st Prize Silk Screen, Barcham Green Print Comp., 1978. *Recreation:* gardening. *Address:* 73 Bow Road, Bow, E3 2AN. *T:* (020) 8981 2037. *W:* www.wendytaylorsculpture.co.uk.

TAYLOR, Sir William, Kt 1990; CBE 1982; *b* 31 May 1930; *s* of Herbert and Maud E. Taylor, Crayford, Kent; *m* 1954, Rita, *d* of Ronald and Marjorie Hague, Sheffield; one *s* two *d*. *Educ:* Erith Grammar Sch.; London Sch. of Economics (BSc Econ 1952); Westminster Coll., Oxford (Hon. Fellow, 1990); Univ. of London Inst. of Educn (PhD 1960). Teaching in Kent, 1953–56; Deputy Head, Slade Green Secondary Sch., 1956–59; Sen. Lectr, St Luke's Coll., Exeter, 1959–61; Head of Educn Dept, Bede Coll., Durham, 1961–64; Tutor and Lectr in Educn, Univ. of Oxford, 1964–66; Prof. of Educn and Dir of Sch. of Educn, Univ. of Bristol, 1966–73; Dir, Univ. of London Inst. of Educn, 1973–83; Principal, Univ. of London, 1983–85; Vice-Chancellor: Univ. of Hull, 1985–91; Univ. of Huddersfield, 1994–95; Thames Valley Univ., 1998–99. Hd, Winchester Sch. of Art, Univ. of Southampton, 2004. Visiting Professor of Education: Oxford Univ., 1991–97; Southampton Univ., 1998–2012; Commonwealth Vis. Fellow, Australian States, 1975; NZ UGC Prestige Fellowship, 1977; Hon. Vis. Fellow, Green Coll., Oxford, 1991–97; Hon. Prof., Univ. of Winchester, 2010–. Academic Adviser: States of Jersey Educn Cttee, 2000–05; SE Essex Coll., 2001–03; Special Advr, H of C Cttee on Educn and Skills, 2000–07. Research Consultant, Dept of Educn and Science (part-time), 1968–73; Chairman: European Cttee for Educnl Research, 1969–71; UK Nat. Commn for UNESCO Educn Cttee, 1975–83 (Mem., 1973–83); Educnl Adv. Council, IBA, 1974–82; UCET, 1976–79; Cttee on Training of Univ. Teachers, 1981–88; NFER, 1983–88; CATE, 1984–93; Univs Council for Adult and Continuing Educn, 1986–90; N of England Univs Management and Leadership Prog., 1987–91; Studies in Education, 1991–95; Convocation of Univ. of London, 1994–97; UUK Higher Educn Funding Review Gp,

2000–01; IoW Tertiary Strategy Gp, 2002–03; Southampton Travel-to-learn Review, 2002–04; Strategic Area Rev. of 16+ educn and trng, Hants and IoW, 2002–05; Skills Commn Inquiry into Apprenticeship, 2008–09. Member: UGC Educn Cttee, 1971–80; British Library Res. and Develt Cttee, 1975–79; Open Univ. Academic Adv. Cttee, 1975–82; SSRC Educnl Research Board, 1976–80 (Vice-Chm., 1978–80); Adv. Cttee on Supply and Training of Teachers, 1976–79; Working Gp on Management of Higher Educn, 1977–78; Steering Cttee on Future of Examinations at 16+, 1977–78; Cttee of Vice-Chancellors and Principals, 1980–91; Adv. Cttee on Supply and Educn of Teachers (Sec. of State's nominee), 1980–83. UK Rep., Permanent Educn Steering Cttee, Council of Europe, 1971–73; Rapporteur, OECD Review of Educn in NZ, 1982–83. Member: Senate, Univ. of London, 1977–85; Cttee of Management, Inst. of Advanced Legal Studies, 1980–83; Council, Open Univ., 1984–88; Council, Coll. of Preceptors, 1987–89; Editl Adv. Bd, World Book Internat., 1989–2007; CBI Educn Foundn, 1993–98. President: Council for Educn in World Citizenship, 1979–90; English New Educn Fellowship, 1979–86; Comparative Educn Soc. of GB, 1981–84; Assoc. of Colls of Further and Higher Educn, 1984–88; European Assoc. for Instnl Res., 1990–92; Univs of N of England Consortium for Internat. Develt, 1991–94; N of England Educn Conference, 1992; Inst. of Educn Soc., 1990–93; Soc. for Res. in HE, 1996–2001; Vice President: British Educnl Admin, and Management Soc., 1985–; Council for Internat. Educn, 1992–; Soc. for Res. in Higher Educn, 2002–. Chm., NFER/Nelson Publishing Co., 1985–86, 1987–99; Dir, Fenner plc, 1988–93. Trustee, Forbes Trust, 1987–88. Governor: Wye Coll., 1981–83; Hymers Coll., Hull, 1985–91; Westminster Coll., Oxford, 1991–96; Univ. of Glamorgan (formerly Poly. of Wales), 1991–2002; Sevenoaks Sch., 1994–97; Christ Church UC, Canterbury, 1996–2004; Mem. Council, Hong Kong Inst. of Educn, 1998–2004. Freeman, City of London, 1985. Yeoman, 1982–87, Liveryman, 1988–, Worshipful Soc. of Apothecaries of London. Hon. FCP 1977; Hon. FCCEA 1980. Hon. Fellow: Thames Polytechnic, 1991; Inst. of Educn, Univ. of London, 1995; Christ Church Canterbury UC, 2005. Hon. DSc Aston (Birmingham), 1977; Hon. LittD Leeds, 1979; Hon. DCL Kent, 1981; DUniv: Open, 1983; Ulster, 2000; Glamorgan, 2004; Hon. DLitt: Loughborough, 1984; Southampton, 1998; London, 1999; Leicester, 2004; Essex, 2004; Hon. LLD: Hull, 1992; Huddersfield, 1996; Bristol, 2001; Hon. DEd: Kingston, 1993; Oxford Brookes, 1993; Plymouth, 1993; UWE, 1994; Hong Kong Inst. of Educn, 2004; Hon. DSc (Educ) QUB, 1997. *Publications:* The Secondary Modern School, 1963; Society and the Education of Teachers, 1969; (ed with G. Baron) Educational Administration and the Social Sciences, 1969; Heading for Change, 1969; Planning and Policy in Post Secondary Education, 1972; Theory into Practice, 1972; Research Perspectives in Education, 1973; (ed with R. Farquhar and R. Thomas) Educational Administration in Australia and Abroad, 1975; Research and Reform in Teacher Education, 1978; (ed with B. Simon) Education in the Eighties: the central issues, 1981; (ed) Metaphors of Education, 1984; Universities Under Scrutiny, 1987; Policy and Strategy for Higher Education: collaboration between business and higher education, 1989; articles and papers in professional jls. *Recreations:* books, music, walking. *E:* william.taylor@btinternet.com.

TAYLOR, William, CBE 2001; QPM 1991; HM Chief Inspector of Constabulary for Scotland, 1999–2001; *b* 25 March 1947; *s* of late William Taylor and Margaret Taylor; *m* 1978, Denise Lloyd; two step *s*. *Educ:* Blairgowrie High Sch.; Nat. Police Coll. (8th Special Course and 16th Sen. Command Course). Joined Metropolitan Police Service, 1966; served Central London locations as Det. Constable, Sergeant and Inspector, and Chief Inspector, 1966–76; New Scotland Yard: Community Relations Branch, 1976–78; Det. Supt, Central Drugs Squad, 1978–79; Staff Officer to Comr of Police, 1980–82 (Det. Chief Supt); Comdr CID NE London, then Uniform Comdr, Hackney; Comdr Robbery Squad (Flying Squad) and Regional Crime Squad, 1982–85; Asst Comr, City of London Police, 1985–89; Dep. Chief Constable, Thames Valley Police, 1989–90; Asst Comr, Specialist Ops, Metropolitan Police, 1990–94; Comr, City of London Police, 1994–98; HM Inspector of Constabulary, 1998. Chm., Crime Cttee, ACPO, 1994–98; Mem. Exec. Cttee, Interpol, 1995–98; Dir, Police Extended Interviews, 1996–98. Police Long Service and Good Conduct Medal, 1988. *Recreations:* reading (travel, management and historical), hill walking, horse riding, collecting some Dalton ware.

TAYLOR, His Honour William Edward Michael; a Circuit Judge, Western Circuit, 1989–2006; Resident Judge for Plymouth, 1990–2006; *b* 27 July 1944; *s* of William Henry Taylor and Winifred Mary (*née* Day); *m* 1969, Caroline Joyce Gillies; two *d*. *Educ:* Denstone Coll., Uttoxeter, Staffs; Council of Legal Educn. Called to the Bar, Inner Temple, 1968; practised from 2 Harcourt Bldgs, Temple; a Recorder, 1987–89; Liaison Judge for Devon and Cornwall, 1999–2006; Hon. Recorder of Plymouth, 2004. Lectr, Council of Legal Educn, 1976–89. Chairman: Criminal Justice Strategy Cttee for Devon and Cornwall, 2000–06; Area Judicial Forum, 2004–06. Mem., Probation Cttees for Devon and Cornwall, 1995–2006. Hon. Pres., Univ. of Plymouth Law Soc., 1994–. Governor: Blundell's Sch., Tiverton, 2000–15; Plymouth Univ., 2006–14 (Chm., 2012–14); Chairman: Blundell's Prep. Sch. Cttee, 2000–09; Hamoaze House, 2009–. Chm., River Yealm and Dist Assoc., 2008–11; Pres., Devon Safer Communities Trust. Patron, Twelve's Co. charity, Plymouth; Vice Patron, Drake Foundn, Plymouth. Hon. LLD Plymouth, 2005. *Recreations:* music, opera, fishing, vintage cars, wine. *Address:* Combined Court Service, Armada Way, Plymouth, Devon PL1 2ER. *Clubs:* Athenæum; English XX.

TAYLOR, Sir William George, (Sir Bill), Kt 2003; Managing Director, Improve Your Council consultancy, since 2006; *b* 10 April 1952; *s* of late Colin Frey Taylor and of Isobel Lauder Yule Taylor (now Allsopp); *m* 1978, Anne Charles; one *s* one *d*. *Educ:* Church Road (Yardley) Primary Sch., Birmingham; Sheldon Heath Comprehensive Sch., Birmingham; Univ. of Lancaster (BA Hons 1973, MA 1985); Manchester Poly. (Advanced Cert Ed 1976). Detached Youth Worker, Young Unemployed People, Blackburn, 1973–74; Area Worker, Audley and Centre Manager, Accrington Rd, Youth Centre, Blackburn, 1974–77; Youth Tutor, Shadsworth HS, Blackburn, 1977–83; Youth Work Trainer Co-ordinator, Lancs, 1984–85; Youth Work Trainer/Manager, Blackburn, 1985–95; Youth Work Dist Team Manager, Ribble Valley, 1995–2006. Member: Bd, City Challenge, 1994–98; Bd, Elevate E Lancs Housing Mkt Restructuring Pathfinder, 2002–04; Chairman: Strategic Partnership Bd with Capita, 2001–04; Blackburn and Darwen Strategic Partnership Exec. (Local Strategic Partnership), 2002–04; E Lancs Partnership Forum, 2003–04; Chm. and Dir, NHS Healthwatch Blackburn with Darwen, 2013–. Associate Consultant: IDeA; Solace Enterprises; Nat. Youth Agency; Warwick Business Sch. Local Govt Centre. Member: NW Unitary Councils and Assoc. of Gtr Manchester Authorities, 2001–04; NW Regl Assembly and NW Constitutional Convention, 2001–04. Blackburn with Darwen Borough Council: Mem. (Lab), 1980–2004; Mayor, 1989–90, Dep. Mayor, 1990–91, of Blackburn; Dep. Leader, 1994–2001; Leader, 2001–04; Exec. Mem. for Educn and Lifelong Learning, 2000–01; Chairman of Committees: Recreation, 1984–86; Community and Leisure Services, 1986–89; Urban Prog., 1990–93; Urban Regeneration, 1993–94; Mgt and Finance, 1994–97; City Challenge, 1994; Educn and Trng, 1997–2000; Chairman: Early Years Sub-cttee, 1997–98; Ethnic Minorities Consultative Panel, 1990–91 and 1992–96; Vice-Chm., Exec. and Forum, Educn Action Zone, 1999–2001. Chairman: Mentor Enterprise for All, 2009–; Third Sector Lancashire, 2009–10; Blackburn with Darwen NHS Teaching Health Care Trust Plus, 2010–13; Blackburn with Darwen NHS Healthwatch, 2013–. Non-executive Director: Vision Twenty One, 2006–09; Blackburn Community Business Partnership, 2006–14. Assoc. Lectr, Univ. of Cumbria (formerly St Martin's Coll.), 2006–. Mem., 1995–2001, Chm., 1996–2001, Prince's Trust Volunteers Bd, Lancs; Vice-Chm., Prince's Trust Strategic Forum, Lancs, 2000–01. Governor, Blackburn Coll., 1981–93 and 2002– (Chm., 2008); Mem. Court, Lancaster Univ., 2008–; Trustee and Vice Chm., Lancaster Univ. Students Union, 2008–13. *Publications:* various in youth and community work, education, regeneration, leadership and local govt jls; regular blogger and occasional columnist in Lancashire Telegraph, Local Government Chronicle, Health Service Jl. *Recreations:* golf (off 20), sampling good wines and food, trying to engage with the world of digital technology, photography. *Address:* Arden House, Eden Park, Blackburn, Lancs BB2 7HJ. *T:* (01254) 668404. *E:* sirbilltaylor@btinternet.com, sirbill@improveyourcouncil.co.uk. *Club:* Blackburn Golf.

TAYLOR, Rev. Canon Dr William Henry; Vicar, St John's, Notting Hill, since 2002; *b* 23 Dec. 1956; *s* of Thomas Mather Taylor and Barbara Taylor (*née* Pitt). *Educ:* Westcott House, Cambridge. BA, MTh, MPhil; Sch. of Oriental and African Studies, Univ. of London (DPhil 2010). Ordained deacon, 1983, priest, 1984; Asst Curate, All Saints and St Philip with Tovil, Canterbury, 1983–86; Archbp's Advisor on Orthodox Affairs, Lambeth Palace, 1986–88; Sen. Curate, All Saints, Margaret St, London, 1986–88; Chaplain, Guy's Hosp., 1988; CMS 1988–91; Chaplain, Jordan Chaplaincy, 1988–91; Vicar, St Peter, Ealing, 1991–2000; Area Dean, Ealing, 1993–98; Provost, subseq. Dean, of Portsmouth, 2000–02. Chm., Anglican and Eastern Churches Assoc., 2001–; Mem., Internat. Commn of Anglican-Oriental Orthodox Dialogue, 2001–. Ecumenical Canon, Cath. of Holy Child, Manila. FRAS 1982. Freeman, City of London, 1997. *Publications:* (ed) Christians in the Holy Land, 1994; Antioch and Canterbury, 2005; Narratives of Identity, 2013. *Recreations:* good wine, challenging travel. *Address:* 25 Ladbroke Road, W11 3PD. *T:* (020) 7727 3439, *T:* and *Fax:* (office) (020) 7727 4262. *Club:* Nikaean.

TAYLOR, William James; QC (Scot.) 1986; QC 1998; *b* 13 Sept. 1944; *s* of Cecil Taylor and Ellen Taylor (*née* Daubney). *Educ:* Robert Gordon's College, Aberdeen; Aberdeen Univ. (MA Hons 1966; LLB 1969); Glasgow Univ. (Cert. in European Law (French) 1990). Admitted Faculty of Advocates, 1971; called to the Bar, Inner Temple, 1990. Standing Junior Counsel to DHSS, 1978–79, to FCO, 1979–86; Temp. Sheriff, 1997–99; part-time Sheriff, 2003–. Member: Criminal Injuries Compensation Bd, 1997–; Scottish Criminal Cases Review Commn, 1999–. Former Chairman: Traverse Th., Edinburgh; Fedn of Scottish Theatres; former Mem., TMA; former Member, Board: Scottish Ballet; Scottish Opera (Chm., 2004–07). Contested (Lab) Edinburgh W, Feb. and Oct. 1974; Regional Councillor (Lab), 1973–82. FRSA. *Recreations:* the arts, ski-ing, sailing, Scottish mountains, swimming, travel, restoring a garden, cooking. *Address:* Duirnish Lodge, Duirnish, by Kyle of Lochalsh, Ross-shire IV40 8BE. *T:* (01599) 544278; (office) Parliament House, Parliament Square, Edinburgh EH1 1RF. *T:* (0131) 226 2881, *Fax:* (0131) 225 3642; Carmelite Chambers, 9 Carmelite Street, EC4Y 0DR. *T:* (020) 7936 6300. *E:* qc@wjt.org.uk. *Clubs:* Scottish Arts, Traverse Theatre (Edinburgh); Royal Highland Yacht (Oban), Plockton Sailing.

TAYLOR, William McCaughey; Chief Executive, Northern Ireland Police Authority, 1979–86; *b* 10 May 1926; *s* of William and Georgina Lindsay Taylor; *m* 1955, June Louise Macartney; two *s* two *d*. *Educ:* Campbell College, Belfast; Trinity College, Oxford (MA 1950). Lieut, Royal Inniskilling Fusiliers, 1944–47. International Computers Ltd, 1950–58; Lobitos Oilfields Ltd, 1958–60; HM Vice Consul, New York, 1960–63, HM Consul, 1963–65; NI Dept of Commerce, 1965–79. Chm., NI Coal Importers Assoc., 1986–91. *Recreations:* golf, bridge, gardening, piano, musical compositions. *Address:* 1 Knocktern Gardens, Belfast BT4 3LZ. *Club:* Royal Belfast Golf.

TAYLOR, William Rodney E.; *see* Eatock Taylor.

TAYLOR BRADFORD, Barbara; *see* Bradford.

TAYLOR-GOOBY, Prof. Peter Frederick, OBE 2012; PhD; FBA 2009; FAcSS; Professor of Social Policy, University of Kent, since 1990; *b* Watford, 5 March 1947; *s* of John and Irene Taylor-Gooby; *m* 1999, Susan Lakeman; two *s* one *d*. *Educ:* Watford Grammar Sch.; Univ. of Bristol (BA Philos. and Eng. Lit. 1969); Univ. of York (Dip. Soc. Admin (with dist.) 1972; MPhil Soc. Admin 1974; PhD Soc. Policy 1984). Lectr in Social Admin, Univ. of Manchester, 1974–79; Lectr, Sen. Lectr, then Reader in Social Policy, Univ. of Kent, 1979–89. Chairman: Social Work Social Policy Panel, RAE 2008; Social Work Social Policy Panel, REF 2014. Pres., Sociol. and Social Policy Section, BAAS, 2005–06. Co-Dir, Risk Res. Centre, Beijing Normal Univ., 2008–. FAcSS (AcSS 2001). FRSA 2005. Lifetime Achievement Award, Social Policy Assoc., 2013. *Publications:* (jtly) Political Philosophy and Social Welfare, 1980, 2nd edn 2009; (with Jen Dale) Social Theory and Social Welfare, 1981; From Butskellism to the New Right, 1983; Public Opinion, Ideology and the Welfare State, 1985; (with Elim Papadakis) The Private Provision of Public Welfare, 1987; Social Change, Social Welfare and Social Science, 1991; (with Hartley Dean) Dependency Culture, 1992; (ed jtly) Markets and Managers, 1993; (ed jtly) European Welfare Policy: squaring the welfare circle, 1996; (ed) Choice and Public Policy: the limits to welfare markets, 1998; (ed jtly) The End of the Welfare State?: responses to retrenchment, 1999; (jtly) European Welfare Futures, 2000 (rev. edn Korean, 2004); (ed) Risk, Trust and Welfare, 2000; (ed) Welfare States under Pressure, 2001; (ed) Making a European Welfare State?: convergences and conflicts over European social policy, 2004; (ed) New Risks, New Welfare: the transformation of the European welfare state, 2004 (trans. Chinese 2009); (ed) Ideas and Welfare State Reform in Western Europe, 2005; (ed jtly) Learning about Risk, 2006; (ed jtly) Risk in Social Science, 2006; Reframing Social Citizenship, 2009; (ed) New Paradigms in Public Policy, 2013; The Double Crisis of the Welfare State and What We Can Do About It, 2013; (ed jtly) The British Growth Crisis, 2015; A Perfect World (novel), 2015; over 150 articles in jls and 112 book chapters. *Recreations:* hill-walking, cycling, socialism, children. *Address:* School of Social Policy, Sociology and Social Research, University of Kent CT2 7NF. *E:* p.f.taylor-gooby@kent.ac.uk.

TAYLOR-JOHNSON, Samantha, OBE 2011; artist; *b* 4 March 1967; formerly Taylor-Wood; *m* 1997, Jeremy Michael Neal, (Jay), Jopling, *qv* (marr. diss. 2009); two *d*; *m* 2012, Aaron Johnson; two *d*. *Educ:* Goldsmiths' Coll., London (BA Hons Fine Art 1990; Hon. Fellow 2008). *Solo exhibitions include:* Sam Taylor-Wood: Killing Time, Showroom, London, 1994; Travesty of a Mockery, White Cube, London, 1995; Pent-Up, Chisenhale Gall., London, and Sunderland City Art Gall., 1996; 16mm, Ridinghouse Editions, London, 1996; Sam Taylor-Wood: Five Revolutionary Seconds, Barcelona, 1997; Sustaining the Crisis, LA, 1997; Milan, Seattle, 1998, Stuttgart, 1999, Warsaw, Madrid and NY, 2000; Directions, Washington, 1999; Mute, White Cube, London, 2001; Sam Taylor-Wood: Films and Photographs, Paris, 2001, Amsterdam, 2002; Hayward Gall., Montreal and Tokyo, 2002, Vienna, 2003, St Petersburg and Moscow, 2004; The Passion, NY, 2002; David, Nat. Portrait Gall., 2004; Strings, Edinburgh, 2004; Sorrow, Suspension, Ascension, NY, 2004; New Work, White Cube, 2004; Ascension, Chicago, 2004; Sex and Death and a Few Trees, Rome, 2005; Still Lives, Baltic, Gateshead, 2006; Yes I No, White Cube, 2008; Saatchi Gall., 2014; *group exhibitions include:* General Release, Venice Biennale, 1995; Brilliant! New Art from London, Walker Art Centre, Minneapolis, and Contemporary Art Mus., Houston, 1995; Sensation, RA, Hamburger Bahnhof, Berlin, and Brooklyn Mus., NY, 1997; work in public collections including: British Council, Contemp. Art Soc., Nat. Portrait Gall., Saatchi Collection, Tate Gall., London; Stedelijk Mus., Amsterdam; Bangkok Mus. of Contemp. Art; Fundacio "la Caixa", Barcelona; Royal Mus. of Fine Arts, Copenhagen; Collection Lambert, Geneva; Israel Mus., Jerusalem; Inst. d'Arte Contemporanea, Lisbon; Walker Art Centre, Minneapolis; New Orleans Mus.; Guggenheim, NY; Robert Shiffler Collection, Ohio; Astrup Fearnley Mus., Oslo; Caldic Collection, Rotterdam; San Francisco Mus. of Mod. Art; Samsung Mus., Seoul. Director of films: Love You More, 2008; Nowhere Boy, 2009; Fifty

Shades of Grey, 2015. Illy Cafe Prize for most promising young artist, Venice Biennale, 1997. *Publications:* Unhinged, 1996; Sam Taylor-Wood: third party, 1999; Contact, 2001; Sam Taylor-Wood, 2001; Sam Taylor-Wood: crying men, 2004; Second Floor, 2014. *Address:* White Cube, 144–152 Bermondsey Street, SE1 3TQ.

TAYLOR-SMITH, David James Benwell, MBE 2003; FRGS; Regional Managing Director, Europe, Middle East and Africa, Aggreko plc, 2013–15; *b* Winchester, 16 Oct. 1961; *s* of Maj. (retd) Alan Taylor-Smith and Joy Taylor-Smith; *m* 1990, Jacqueline Ann Hunter Fletcher; two *d*. *Educ:* Tunbridge Wells Grammar Sch.; Southampton Univ. (BSc Hons Geog.); RMC Sandhurst. Pres., Student Union, Southampton Univ., 1984–85. Captain, 4th/7th Royal Dragoon Guards, 1985–89; Royal Dragoon Guards TA Officer, 1989–92. Director: Operation Raleigh, Zimbabwe, Botswana and Chile, 1989–94; Project Orbis, 1994–96; Corporate Affairs Dir, Jardine Pacific, 1996–98; Managing Director: Jardine Securicor Hong Kong, 1998–2002; Group 4 Securicor Justice Services, 2002–06; CEO, G4S (formerly Group 4 Securicor) UK and Ireland, 2006–10; Regl CEO, UK and Africa, 2010–12, Gp Chief Operating Officer, 2012, G4S plc. Mem. Bd, Hong Kong Business Envmt Council, 1998–2002. Mem. Council, Scientific Exploration Soc., 2006–08. Chm., RGS Hong Kong, 1995–2002. Trustee: WWF Hong Kong, 2001–02; WWF UK, 2005–11. Chm., Westerham Soc., 2006–10. MInstD 2002. FRGS 1985. *Recreations:* walking, conservation, bee keeping, ski-ing.

TAYLOR-WOOD, Samantha; *see* Taylor-Johnson, S.

TAYLORSON, John Brown, OBE 2007; Managing Director: John Taylorson Associates, 1990–2001; Inflight Marketing Services, 1990–2001; *b* 5 March 1931; *s* of John Brown Taylorson and Edith Maria Taylorson; *m* 1st, 1960, Barbara June (*née* Hagg) (marr. diss.); one *s* one *d*; 2nd, 1985, Helen Anne (*née* Parkinson); one *s*. *Educ:* Forest School, Snaresbrook; Hotel School, Westminster. Capt., Essex, Squash Racquets, 1955–65. Sales Director, Gardner Merchant Food Services Ltd, 1970–73; Managing Director: International Division, Gardner Merchant Food Services, 1973–77; Fedics Food Services, 1977–80; Chief Executive, Civil Service Catering Organisation, 1980–81; Hd of Catering Servs, British Airways, 1981–89; Chief Exec., Inflight Catering Services, 1990–96. Dir, Internat. Service Industry Search, 1990–97. DebRA: Corporate Appeals Dir, 1993–2007; Dir, Internat. Res. Appeal, 2007–08; Dir, Special Projects, 2009–10. Pres., Internat. Flight Catering Assoc., 1983–85; Chm., Inflight Services Gp, Assoc. of European Airlines, 1983–85. Catey Special Award, Caterer and Hotelkeeper, 1988. *Recreations:* golf, theatre, crossword puzzles. *Address:* Deer Pond Cottage, Highfields, East Horsley, Surrey KT24 5AA. *Clubs:* Old Foresters; Burhill Golf.

TAYLOUR, family name of **Marquess of Headfort**.

TAYTON, Lynn Margaret; QC 2006; **Her Honour Judge Tayton;** a Circuit Judge, since 2011; *b* 5 Feb. 1959; *d* of Gerald and Margaret Tayton; *m*; one *s*. *Educ:* Barr's Hill Sch., Coventry; University Coll. London (LLB Hons 1980); Council of Legal Educn. Called to the Bar, Gray's Inn, 1981; barrister, Nottingham, 1982–89; Sen. Lectr in Law, Nottingham Trent Poly., 1990–91; barrister, London, 1995–2011; a Recorder, 2009–11. Legal Assessor, GMC, 2010–11. Chair, Herts and Beds Bar Mess, 2007–11. Associate Lectr, OU, 2006; Mem., OU Law Prog. Cttee, 2007–. *Recreations:* going to the theatre, cookery, variety of not too energetic physical pursuits, spending time with my family and other people who make me laugh. *Address:* Northampton Combined Court, 85–87 Lady's Lane, Northampton NN1 3HQ.

TCHALENKO, Janice Anne, FRCA; potter, since 1964; Chief Designer, Dartington Pottery, since 1984; *b* 5 April 1942; *d* of late Eric Cooper and Marjorie Cooper (*née* Dodd); *m* 1964, Dr John Stephen Tchalenko; one *s*. *Educ:* Barr's Hill Grammar Sch., Coventry. FRCA 1987. Clerical Officer, PO Telephones, Coventry and FO, London, 1958–60; Art Therapist, The Priory, Roehampton, 1965–69; studio pottery course, Harrow Sch. of Art, 1969–71; travelled extensively in Soviet Union and Middle East, 1965–77; set up workshop, London, 1971; pt-time Tutor, Camberwell Sch. of Art and Crafts, 1972–86; Tutor, RCA, 1981–96; Curator: Colours of the Earth exhibn, British Council, 1989–92 (toured India, 1991–92); British Ceramics for Brazil, British Council, 2000 (touring). Mem., Crafts Council, 1994–2000. Consultant: Goa You Porcelain Factory, China, 1991; Blue Factory, China, 1991–92. *Works* include: (with Spitting Image Workshop) Seven Deadly Sins, 1993, Modern Antiques, 1996; pottery designs for Dartington range, 1984–2006, Designers Guild, 1985, Next Interiors, 1986, and Poole Pottery, 1994–; exhibits in major public collections, including: Helsinki Mus. of Decorative Art; Los Angeles County Mus. of Art; Mus. für Kunst und Gewerbe, Hamburg; Nat. Mus. of Modern Art, Kyoto; Stockholm Nat. Mus.; V&A Mus.; Sèvres Mus., Paris; Limoges Mus., France; Ashmolean Mus.; Fitzwilliam Mus.; Contemp. Arts Soc.; Ulster Mus.; Walker Mus., Liverpool; *solo exhibitions* include: Sideshow, ICA, 1980; Craftshop, V&A Mus., 1981; Scottish Gall., Edinburgh, 1989, 2001, 2011; Stockholm Nat. Mus., 1990; retrospective, Ruskin Gall., Sheffield, and tour, 1992; Beaux Arts, Bath, 1997; *group exhibitions* include: Summer Exhibn, RA, 2010; Gall. Paul Fort, Paris, 2012; Contemp. Applied Arts, 2014. Laura Ashley Fellowship, Laura Ashley Foundn, 2001. Manchester Prize for Art in Producn, Coloroll Gp and Manchester City Galls, 1988; Enterprise Award, Radio 4, 1988. *Recreations:* gardening, reading. *Address:* 47A Chevening Road, Crystal Palace, SE19 3TD.

TCHURUK, Serge; President and Chief Executive Officer, Joule Unlimited, Inc., since 2014; *b* 13 Nov. 1937; *s* of Georges Tchuruk and Mathilde (*née* Dondikian); *m* 1960, Héléna Kalfus; one *d*. *Educ:* Ecole Nationale Supérieure de l'Armement; Ecole Polytechnique. With Mobil Oil in France, USA and Netherlands, 1968–80; Head, Mobil Oil BV, Rotterdam, 1979–80; with Rhône-Poulenc, 1980–86: Gen. Manager, Fertilizer Div., 1980–82; Mem., Exec. Cttee, 1981; Dep. Man. Dir, 1982–83; Man. Dir, 1983–86; Chm. Mgt Bd, 1986–87, Chm. and CEO, 1987–90, CDF Chimie, later ORKEM; Chm. and CEO, Total SA, Paris, 1990–95 (non-exec. Dir, 1995–2010); Dir, Thales, 1998–2009; Chm. and CEO, 1995–2006, Chm., 2006–08, Alcatel Alsthom, then Alcatel, later Alcatel-Lucent. Officier de la Légion d'Honneur, 1998. *Recreations:* music, ski-ing, tennis.

TE PAA-DANIEL, Dr Jennifer Louise Plane; JP; educational consultant, Auckland, since 2013; Senior Research Scholar, College of St John the Evangelist, Auckland, 2013 (Lecturer in Global Anglican Studies, Race Politics and Theological Education, 1992–2012, and Ahorangi (Principal), 1995–2012); Lay Canon, Holy Trinity Cathedral, Auckland, since 2005; *b* 19 Oct. 1953; *d* of Theodore Malcolm Plane and Wirihita (Zita) Te Paa; *m* (marr. diss.); one *s* one *d*; *m* 2012, Dr Roro Mana Daniel. *Educ:* Coll. of St John the Evangelist, Auckland (Dip. in Social Services 1990); Univ. of Auckland (BTh 1992; MEd Hons 1994); Graduate Theol Union, Berkeley (PhD 2001). Special Employment Liaison Officer, Auckland, 1981; Social Worker, Auckland, 1983–86; Sen. Vocational Trng Officer, Auckland, 1986–88; Tertiary Student Counsellor and Teacher, Auckland Inst. of Technol., 1988–90; Sen. Local Govt Policy Advr, 1990–92. Member: Internat. Anglican Indigenous Peoples Network, 1994–; Gen. Synod, 1998–2011; Social Justice Commn of Anglican Church, 2000–08; Inter-Anglican Internat. Theol Doctrinal Commn, 2001–08; Lambeth Commn, 2001–04; Archbishop of Canterbury's Commn on Theol Educn, 2001–; Internat. Anglican Women's Network, 2004–; Council, Internat. Women, Develt and Faith Alliance, 2007–; Nat. Complaints Assessment Cttee, NZ Teachers' Council, 2012–; Moderator, Working Gp on Ecumenical Theol Educn, WCC, 2000–06; Mem., 1995, Global Convenor, 2001–12, Internat. Anglican Peace and Justice Network; Convenor, Nat. Anglican Church Centre for Women's Studies, 2005–11. Maori/Moriori Res. Fellow, 2013, Res., Affiliate, 2013–, Nat. Centre for Peace and Conflict Studies, Univ. of Otago; St Margaret's Vis. Prof. of Women in Ministry, Church Divinity Sch. of Pacific, Berkeley, Calif., 2014. Member: NZ Arts Council, 2007–09; South Pacific Assoc. of Theol Schs, 2008–. Member: Nat. Women's Adv. Cttee to Govt, 1981–86; Nat. Lotteries Distribution Cttee, 1981–86; Nat. Govtl Rev. Cttee on Tertiary Educn, 1986–88; Prisons Bd, 1987–97; Nat. Govtl Rev. Cttee on Prison Reform (Women), 1990; Human Rights Adv. Cttee, 1992–93. Cultural Advr to NZ Spirit of Adventure Trust, 2010. JP NZ, 2014. Hon. DD: Episcopal Divinity Sch., Cambridge, 2003; Virginia Theol Seminary, Alexandria, 2008; Hon. Dr Humane Letters, Church Divinity Sch. of Pacific, Univ. of Calif, Berkeley, 2014. Winston Churchill Fellowship Award, 1990; Distinguished Alumni Award, Univ. of Auckland, 2010; Alumni of Year Award, Grad. Theol. Union, Berkeley, 2010. *Publications:* What is the Family? A Cross Cultural Perspective, 1996; (contrib.) Growing Up Maori, 1999; (contrib.) Leadership Formation for a New World: an emergent indigenous Anglican Theological College, 2001; (contrib.) Thinking Outside the Square: church in Middle Earth, 2003; (contrib.) Theology Today, 2005; (contrib.) The Oxford Guide to the Book of Common Prayer Worldwide, 2005; (contrib.) Challenging Christian Zionism: theology, politics and the Israel-Palestine conflict, 2005; (contrib.) Other Voices, Other Worlds, 2006; (contrib.) Pursuing the Mind of Christ in Faith and Action: Njongonkulu Ndungane. Archbishop for the Church and the world, 2008; (jtly) Lifting Women's Voices: prayers to change the world, 2009; (jtly) In the Beginning was the Word: group bible studies on the Gospel of John, 2009; (contrib.) To the Church, To the World: Ki te Hahi, Ki te Ao, 2010; (contrib.) The Handbook of Theological Education in World Christianity, 2010; (contrib.) Tolerance - Respect - Trust, 2010; (ed with E. Fairbrother and contrib.) Our Place, Our Voice: explorations in contextual theology, 2012; (ed jtly and contrib.) Anglican Women on Church and Mission, 2013; (ed jtly and contrib.) Canterbury Studies in Anglicanism: Anglican women on Church and mission, 2013; (contrib.) The Reemergence of Liberation: models for the Twenty-First century, 2013; Whispers, Whisperers, Whispering in Whispers and Vanities: Samoan indigenous knowledge and religion, 2014; (contrib.) Wisdom and Imagination: religious progressives and the search for meaning, 2014; contribs to jls incl. Anglican Theol Rev., Circle, First Peoples Theology Jl, NZ Herald, Pacific Jl of Theology, Stimulus. *Recreations:* grandchildren, fishing, living into retirement in Aitutaki, Cook Islands! *E:* jenzat1@gmail.com.

TEACHER, Michael John, FCA; Chairman: Avgol, since 2013; Jeyes Holdings Ltd, since 2014; Chief Executive, Ontex NV, 2006–13; *b* 2 June 1947; *s* of Charles and Ida Teacher; *m* 1972, Sandra Posner; three *s*. *Educ:* City Univ. (MSc Financial Mgt 1972). FCA 1969. Articled Clerk, Abey, Lish & Co., 1964–69; Audit Senior, Deloitte & Co., 1969–71; Corporate Finance Exec., Corinthian Holdings, then Welbeck Investment, 1973–76; Man. Dir, Holding Co. Ltd, Welbeck Investment Plc, 1976–82; Exec. Dir, Sir Joseph Causton Plc, 1983–84; Man. Dir, Pointon York Ltd, Venture Capital Co., 1984–87; Hillsdown Holdings PLC: Man. Dir, HIT Plc (Venture Capital subsid.), 1987–93; Exec. Dir, 1993–98; Chief Exec., 1998–99; Chief Executive: Unipoly Hldgs, 2001–06; Peek Hldgs, 2005–07. Dir, PPF Ltd, 2015–. *Recreations:* tennis, soccer, running, charitable work.

TEAGLE, Vice-Adm. Sir Somerford (Francis), KBE 1994; Chief of Defence Force, New Zealand, 1991–95; *b* 9 June 1938; *s* of Leonard Herbert Teagle and Muriel Frances Teagle; *m* 1961, Leonie Marie Maire; one *s* one *d*. *Educ:* Christ's Coll., Christchurch, NZ; Royal Naval Coll., Dartmouth. Royal New Zealand Navy: Sea and Staff appts, 1958–85: Commanding Officer HMNZS: Manga, 1962–64; Taranaki, 1977; jssc, Canberra, 1977; CO HMNZS Canterbury, 1978–79; Captain, Naval Trng, 1981–84; ndc, Canada, 1983; Cdre, Auckland, 1986–87; Dep. Chief of Naval Staff, 1988–89; Chief of Naval Staff, 1989–91. *Recreation:* wine growing. *Address:* Omarere, Ponatahi Road, PO Box 84, Martinborough, New Zealand. *Club:* Wellington (Wellington).

TEAGUE, David Norman, CMG 2011; Technical Lead, Foreign and Commonwealth Office, since 2008; *b* Liverpool, 21 Aug. 1958; *s* of Norman Francis Teague and Patricia Teague; *m* 1982, Elizabeth Anne Kain; two *s*. *Educ:* Liverpool Blue Coat Sch.; Brasenose Coll., Oxford (BA Hons 1983). Various technical and leadership posts, FCO, 1983–. *Publications:* (jtly) papers on group theory. *Recreations:* vintage wireless—late valve, early transistor, British light music, cookery.

TEAGUE, (Edward) Thomas (Henry); QC 2000; **His Honour Judge Teague;** a Circuit Judge, since 2006; *b* Weymouth, 21 May 1954; *s* of Harry John Teague and Anne Elizabeth Teague (*née* Hunt); *m* 1980, Helen Mary Howard; two *s*. *Educ:* St Francis Xavier's Coll., Liverpool; Christ's Coll., Cambridge (MA). Called to the Bar, Inner Temple, 1977; Mem., Wales and Chester Circuit, 1978–2006, Western Circuit, 2002–06; Asst Recorder, 1993–97; a Recorder, 1997–2006; Hon. Mem., Northern Circuit, 2007–. Legal Assessor, GMC, 2002–06. FRAS 1991. *Recreations:* music, fly-fishing, astronomy. *Address:* Queen Elizabeth II Law Courts, Derby Square, Liverpool L2 1XA. *T:* (0151) 473 7373.

TEAPE, Angela Dawn; *see* Hatton, A. D.

TEAR, Rebecca, MA; Headmistress, Badminton School, since 2012; *b* Plymouth, 15 Nov. 1972; *d* of B. Warlow; *m* 1998, Richard Frederick John Tear; two *s*. *Educ:* Kelly Coll., Tavistock; Univ. of Exeter (BSc Chem. 1995); Inst. of Educn, Univ. of London (PGCE 1996; MA 2012). Hd, Jun. Sci., Hd of Lower Sixth, and Hd, Becket House, St George's, Ascot, 1998–2005; Hd of Sixth Form, 2005–08, Dep. Hd, 2008–12, Wycombe Abbey. *Recreations:* cooking, jogging, keeping fit with family, sailing, moorland walking, pilates, music (singing with choirs when possible). *Address:* Badminton School, Westbury Road, Westbury on Trym, Bristol BS9 3BA.

TEARE, Andrew Hubert; Chief Executive, Rank Group (formerly Rank Organisation) plc, 1996–98; *b* 8 Sept. 1942; *s* of late Arthur Hubert Teare and Rosalind Margaret Baker; *m* 1964, Janet Nina Skidmore; three *s*. *Educ:* Kingswood School, Bath; University College London (BA Hons Classics 1964). Turner & Newall, 1964–72; CRH, 1972–83 (Gen. Manager Europe, 1978–83); Rugby Group, 1983–90 (Asst Man. Dir, 1983–84; Man. Dir, 1984–90); Gp Chief Exec., English China Clays plc, 1990–95. Non-executive Director: Heiton Holdings, 1984–90; NFC, 1989–96; Prudential Corp., 1992–98. Pres., Nat. Council of Building Material Producers, 1990–92. CCMI. *Publications:* The Chairman (novel), 2005. *Recreations:* ski-ing, mountain walking, reading. *Address:* Turleigh Down House, Bradford-on-Avon BA15 2HF. *Club:* Hibernian United Service (Dublin).

TEARE, His Honour Jonathan James; a Circuit Judge, 1998–2014; Presiding Senior Judge, Sovereign Base Areas, Cyprus, 2007–14 (Deputy Senior Judge, 2001–06); *b* 13 Dec. 1946; *y s* of Prof. Donald Teare, MD, FRCP, FRCPath, DMJ and Kathleen Teare; *m* 1972, Nicola Jill, 2nd *d* of Lt-Col Peter Spittall, RM, CP and Peggy Spittall; two *d*. *Educ:* Pinewood Sch.; Rugby Sch. Called to the Bar, Middle Temple, 1970; practised, Midland and Oxford Circuit, 1971–98; Asst Recorder, 1985–90; Recorder, 1990–98. Member: Mental Health Review Tribunal, 2002–; Notts Probation Bd, 2004–11. Dir and Trustee, Egalitarian Trust, 2014–. Served TA, HAC, 1965–69, RRF, 1970–72. Freeman, City of London, 1981; Liveryman, Soc. of Apothecaries, 1980–. *Recreations:* gardening, shooting, travel, wine.

TEARE, Hon. Sir Nigel (John Martin), Kt 2006; **Hon. Mr Justice Teare;** a Judge of the High Court of Justice, Queen's Bench Division, since 2006; a Presiding Judge, Western Circuit, since 2013; *b* 8 Jan. 1952; *s* of Eric John Teare and Mary Rackham Teare; *m* 1975, Elizabeth Jane Pentecost; two *s* one *d*. *Educ:* King William's Coll., Isle of Man; St Peter's Coll., Oxford (BA 1973; MA 1975; Hon. Fellow, 2010). Called to the Bar, Lincoln's Inn, 1974, Bencher, 2004; practising barrister, 1975–2006; Jun. Counsel to Treasury in Admiralty matters, 1989–91; QC 1991; Asst Recorder, 1993–97; a Recorder, 1997–2006; a Dep. High Court Judge, 2002–06. Acting Deemster, IOM, 2000–06. Lloyd's Salvage Arbitrator,

1994–2000, Lloyd's Salvage Appeal Arbitrator, 2000–06. *Recreations:* collecting Manx paintings, tennis, golf. *Address:* Royal Courts of Justice, Strand, WC2A 2LL. *Club:* Royal Automobile.

TEARLE, Katharine, (Katie), (Mrs Mark Pappenheim), MBE 2012; Head of Opera and Dance, Edition Peters Group, music publishers, since 2012; *b* Cheltenham, 12 Sept. 1961; *d* of Michael Victor Tearle and Sadie Catherine Tearle (*née* Bonstow); *m* 1988, Mark Pappenheim, *qv*; two *s*. *Educ:* Coloma Convent Girls Sch., Croydon; Univ. of Birmingham (BA 1st Cl. Hons Music, Drama and Dance 1983); Guildhall Sch. of Music and Drama and City Univ., London (MA Performance Studies (Vocal) 1985). Mktg Asst, Opera North, 1983–84; professional singer, contemp. repertoire, 1985–93; Hd of Educn, Glyndebourne Prodns Ltd, 1986–2011. Visiting Lecturer: Royal Holloway Coll., Univ. of London, 1984–87; City Univ., 1985–86. Mem., Arts Council England, SE, 2003–08. Chair, Eur. Network of Opera and Dance Educn, 2005–08. Mem. Council, Spitalfields Music, 2013–. Trustee, Michael Tippett Musical Foundn, 1998–. FRSA 2005. *Recreations:* singing, swimming, walking. *Address:* Peters Edition Ltd, 2–6 Baches Street, N1 6DN. *T:* (020) 7553 4003. *E:* katie.tearle@editionpeters.com.

TEASDALE, Sir Graham (Michael), Kt 2006; FRCP, FRCSE, FRCSGlas; Professor and Head of Department of Neurosurgery, University of Glasgow, 1981–2003; *b* 20 Sept. 1940; *s* of Thomas Teasdale and Eva Teasdale (*née* Elgey); *m* 1971, Dr Evelyn Muriel Arnott; two *s* one *d* (and one *s* decd). *Educ:* Johnston Grammar Sch., Durham; Durham Univ. Med. Sch. (MB BS 1963). MRCP 1966, FRCP 1988; FRCSE 1970; FRCSGlas 1981. Trng in medicine, surgery and specialisation in neurosurgery, 1963–75; University of Glasgow: Sen. Lectr in Neurosurgery, 1975–79; Reader in Neurosurgery, 1979–81; Associate Dean for Med. Res., 1999–2003. Pres., RCPSG, 2003–06. Chm. Bd, NHS Quality Improvement Scotland, 2006–10. President: Internat. Neurotrauma Soc., 1994–98; Eur. Brain Injury Consortium, 1993–2003; Soc. of British Neurological Surgeons, 2000–02. FMedSci 1999; FRSE 2001. Hon. FACS 2002; Hon. FRCS 2008. Hon. DM Athens 2002; Hon. DSc Sunderland, 2013. *Publications:* (jtly) Management of Head Injuries, 1982; (jtly) Current Neurosurgery, 1992; articles and papers on med. res., particularly on head injuries, in med. jls. *Recreations:* water sports, hill walking and midge dodging in the West of Scotland, ski-ing, fly fishing. *Address:* Ardgryffe, Duchal Road, Kilmacolm PA13 4AY.

TEASDALE, John Douglas, PhD; FBA 2000; Special Scientific Appointment, MRC Cognition and Brain Sciences (formerly Applied Psychology) Unit, 1991–2004; *b* 1 Sept. 1944; *s* of George Eric Teasdale and Vera Joan Teasdale; *m* 1969, Jacqueline Blackburn; two *s*. *Educ:* Emmanuel Coll., Cambridge (BA 1965, MA); Inst. of Psychiatry, Univ. of London (Dip. Psych. 1966; PhD 1971). Lectr, Psychology Dept, Inst. of Psychiatry, Univ. of London, 1967–71; Principal Clin. Psychologist, University Hosp. of Wales, Cardiff, 1971–74; Sen. Res. Worker, Dept of Psychiatry, Univ. of Oxford, 1974–85; Sen. Scientist, MRC Applied Psychol. Unit, 1985–91. Vis. Prof., Inst. of Psychiatry, Univ. of London, 1995–2004. FMedSci 2000. *Publications:* (with P. J. Barnard) Affect, Cognition and Change, 1993; (with Z. V. Segal and J. M. G. Williams) Mindfulness-Based Cognitive Therapy for Depression, 2002, 2nd edn 2013; (jtly) The Mindful Way through Depression, 2007; (jtly) The Mindful Way Workbook, 2014; approx. 100 articles in books and learned jls. *Recreations:* sitting quietly, doing nothing. *Address:* 15 Chesterford House, Southacre Drive, Cambridge CB2 7TZ.

TEATHER, Sarah Louise; *b* 1 June 1974. *Educ:* Leicester Grammar Sch.; St John's Coll., Cambridge (BA 1996). Policy analyst, Macmillan Cancer Relief, until 2003. Mem. (Lib Dem), Islington LBC, 2002–03. Contested (Lib Dem) Finchley & Golders Green, 2001. MP (Lib Dem) Brent E, Sept. 2003–2010, Brent Central, 2010–15. Lib Dem spokesman: on mental health, 2003–04; on London, 2004–05; on communities and local govt, 2005–06; on educn and skills, 2006–07; on innovation, univs and skills, 2007; on business, enterprise and regulatory reform, 2007–08; on housing, 2008–10; Minister of State, DFE, 2010–12. Chair, All Party Parliamentary Group: on Guantanamo Bay, 2006–10; on Refugees, 2012–15; Mem., Jt Cttee on Human Rights, 2014–15. FRSA 2007.

TEBBIT, family name of **Baron Tebbit**.

TEBBIT, Baron *cr* 1992 (Life Peer), of Chingford, in the London Borough of Waltham Forest; **Norman Beresford Tebbit,** CH 1987; PC 1981; Director: Sears (Holdings) PLC, 1987–99; British Telecommunications plc, 1987–96; BET, 1987–96; Spectator (1828) Ltd, 1989–2004; *b* 29 March 1931; 2nd *s* of Leonard and Edith Tebbit, Enfield; *m* 1956, Margaret Elizabeth Daines; two *s* one *d*. *Educ:* Edmonton County Grammar Sch. Embarked on career in journalism, 1947. Served RAF: commissioned GD Branch; qualif. Pilot, 1949–51; Reserve service RAuxAF, No 604 City of Middx Sqdn, 1952–55. Entered and left publishing and advertising, 1951–53. Civil Airline Pilot, 1953–70 (Mem. BALPA; former holder various offices in that Assoc.). Active mem. and holder various offices, Conservative Party, 1946–. MP (C) Epping, 1970–74, Chingford, 1974–92; PPS to Minister of State, Dept of Employment, 1972–73; Parly Under Sec. of State, Dept of Trade, 1979–81; Minister of State, Dept of Industry, 1981; Secretary of State for: Employment, 1981–83; Trade and Industry, 1983–85; Chancellor of the Duchy of Lancaster, 1985–87; Chm., Conservative Party, 1985–87. Former Chm., Cons. Members Aviation Cttee; former Vice-Chm. and Sec., Cons. Members Housing and Construction Cttee; Sec. House of Commons New Town Members Cttee. Dir, J. C. Bamford Excavators, 1987–91. Co-presenter, Target, Sky TV, 1989–98; columnist: The Sun, 1995–97; The Mail on Sunday, 1997–2001; blogger, Daily Telegraph, 2010–. *Publications:* Upwardly Mobile (autobiog.), 1988; Unfinished Business, 1991; The Game Cook, 2009; Ben's Story, 2014. *Address:* c/o House of Lords, SW1A 0PW.

TEBBIT, Sir Kevin (Reginald), KCB 2002; CMG 1997; company director and strategic adviser; Permanent Secretary, Ministry of Defence, 1998–2005; *b* 18 Oct. 1946; *s* of R. F. J. Tebbit and N. M. Tebbit (*née* Nichols); *m* 1969, Elizabeth Alison, *d* of John and Elizabeth Tinley; one *s* one *d*. *Educ:* Cambridgeshire High Sch.; St John's Coll., Cambridge (Schol.; BA Hons 1969). Asst Principal, MoD, 1969–72; Asst Private Sec. to Sec. of State for Defence, 1973–74; Principal, MoD, 1974–79; First Sec., UK Delegn to NATO, 1979–82; transferred to FCO, 1982; E European and Soviet Dept, 1982–84; Hd of Chancery, Ankara, 1984–87; Dir, Cabinet of Sec. Gen. of NATO, 1987–88; Counsellor (Politico-Mil.), Washington, 1988–91; Hd, Econ. Relns Dept, FCO, 1992–94; Dir (Resources) and Chief Inspector, FCO, 1994–97; Dep. Under-Sec. of State, FCO, 1997; Dir, GCHQ, 1998. Exec. Vice Pres. (UK Defence and Govt), AECOM, 2015–. Chm., Finmeccanica UK, 2007–12; Senior Adviser: URS Corp., 2012–; Hewlett Packard, 2013–15; non-exec. Dir, Smiths Gp plc, 2006–. Visiting Professor: QMUL, 2006–14; KCL, 2015–. Chm., Lifeboat Fund, 2004–10. Gov., Ditchley Foundn, 2004–; Member, Advisory Board: Centre for Social Justice, 2010–; Inst. for Security Sci. and Technol., Imperial Coll. London, 2009–; Sen. Associate Fellow, RUSI, 2012–. Trustee: British Friends of Aphrodisias, 1997–; Airey Neave Trust, 2006–. *Recreations:* music, countryside, archaeology, West Ham Utd. *Club:* Savile.

TECKMAN, Jonathan Simon Paul; Director, Fletcher Teckman Consulting Ltd, since 2002; *b* 27 May 1963; *s* of Sidney Teckman and late Stephanie Audrey Teckman (*née* Tresman); *m* 1997, Anne Caroline Fletcher; two *s*. *Educ:* Weston Favell Upper Sch., Northampton; Univ. of Warwick (BSc Hons Mgt Scis). Admin. trainee, 1984–86, HEO (Develt), 1986–90, DoE; Gp Finance Manager, Historic Royal Palaces Agency, 1990–93; Department of National Heritage, subsequently Department for Culture, Media and Sport: Principal, Nat. Lottery Div., 1993–95; Films Div., 1995–98 (Sec. to Adv. Cttee on Film Finance); Dep. Dir, 1998, Dir, 1999–2002, BFI; Public Sector Tutor, Ashridge Business Sch., 2004–09, Associate Tutor, 2009–; Chief Exec., Phoenix Educn Trust, 2011–13. Mem., BAFTA. Treas., BBFC, 2011–. *Recreations:* cinema, reading, cricket, Rugby Union. *Clubs:* Bold Dragoon Cricket (Northampton); Aylesbury Rugby Football.

TEDDER, family name of **Baron Tedder**.

TEDDER, 3rd Baron *cr* 1946, of Glenguin, Co. Stirling; **Robin John Tedder;** Chairman, Vintage Capital Pty Ltd; Proprietor, Glenguin Wine Co.; *b* 6 April 1955; *er s* of 2nd Baron Tedder and of Peggy Eileen Growcott; *S* father, 1994; *m* 1st, 1977, Jennifer Peggy (*d* 1978), *d* of John Mangan, NZ; 2nd, 1980, Rita Aristeia, *yr d* of John Frangidis, Sydney, NSW; two *s* one *d*. MW. Director: Pelorus Property Gp; Italtile Australia; Glenguin Estate. Australian Ambassador, Singularity Univ., Calif; Mentor, INCUBATE, Sydney Univ. Fellow: Securities Inst. of Australia, 1992 (Associate 1981); Financial Services Inst. *Heir:* *s* Hon. Benjamin John Tedder, *b* 23 April 1985. *Address:* 11 Kardinia Road, Clifton Gardens, Sydney, NSW 2088, Australia.

TEGNER, Ian Nicol, CA; Chairman, Control Risks Group, 1992–2000; *b* 11 July 1933; *s* of Sven Stuart Tegner, OBE, and Edith Margaret Tegner (*née* Nicol); *m* 1961, Meriel Helen, *d* of Brig. M. S. Lush, CB, CBE, MC; one *s* one *d*. *Educ:* Rugby School. CA. Clarkson Gordon & Co., Toronto, 1958–59; Manager 1959–65, Partner 1965–71, Barton Mayhew & Co., Chartered Accts; Finance Dir, Bowater Industries, 1971–86; Chm., Cayzer Steel Bowater, 1981–86; Dir, Gp Finance, Midland Bank, 1987–89. Chm., Crest Packaging, 1993–99; Director: Wiggins Teape Appleton, subseq. Arjo Wiggins Appleton, 1990–2000; Opera 80, subseq. English Touring Opera, 1991–99; TIP Europe plc, 1992–93; Teesside Power Ltd, 1993–2001; Coutts & Co., 1996–98. Institute of Chartered Accountants of Scotland: Mem. Council 1981–86; Pres., 1991–92; Mem., Accounting Standards Cttee of CCAB, 1984–86; Chm., Hundred Gp of Finance Dirs, 1988–90. Chm., Children of the Andes, 2001–03; Trustee, ClementJames Centre, 1996–2013. *Publications:* articles on accountancy in various jls and pubns. *Recreations:* book collecting, travel, hill-walking, choral singing, family life. *Address:* 44 Norland Square, W11 4PZ.

TEHRANI, Joanna Elizabeth; *see* Glynn, J. E.

TEIKMANIS, Andris; Ambassador of the Republic of Latvia to the Court of St James's, since 2013; *b* Rīga, Latvia, 29 Nov. 1959; *s* of Gunārs Teikmanis and Veronika Teikmane; *m* 1990, Inguna Peniķe; one *s* one *d*. *Educ:* Riva High Sch. No 5; Latvian Univ. (MA Law). Investigator, Police Bd, Riga City, 1983–88; Judge, Court of Kirov Dist, Riga City, 1988–90; Chm., Riga City Council, 1990–94; Mem., Supreme Council, Latvia, 1990–93, signed Declaration on Restoration of Independence of Republic of Latvia, 1990; Ambassador: to Council of Europe, 1994–98; to Germany, 1998–2002; Under-Sec. of State, Min. of Foreign Affairs, 2002–05; Ambassador to Russian Fedn, 2005–08; Sec. of State, Min. of Foreign Affairs, 2008–13. Commemorative Medal for participation in barricades of 1991 (Latvia), 1996; Comdr, Order of Three Stars (Latvia), 2000; Hon. Medal, 2002, Commemorative Medal, 2004, Min. of Defence (Latvia); Cross of Recognition (Latvia), 2007; Commander: Prince Don Enrique Order (Portugal), 2003; Order of Merit (Italy), 2004; Grand Cross, Order of Merit (Germany), 2004; Grand Decoration of Honour in Gold with Star (Austria), 2013. *Recreations:* opera, classical music, jogging, cycling. *Address:* Embassy of the Republic of Latvia, 45 Nottingham Place, W1U 5LY. *T:* (020) 7312 0041. *E:* andris.teikmanis@mfa.gov.lv. *W:* www.twitter.com/teikmanis. *Club:* Travellers.

TE KANAWA, Dame Kiri (Jeanette Claire), ONZ 1995; DBE 1982 (OBE 1973); opera singer; *b* Gisborne, New Zealand, 6 March 1944; *m* 1967, Desmond Stephen Park (marr. diss. 1997); one *s* one *d*. *Educ:* St Mary's Coll., Auckland, NZ; London Opera Centre. Major rôles at Royal Opera House, Covent Garden, include: the Countess, in Marriage of Figaro; Elvira, in Don Giovanni; Mimi, in La Bohème; Desdemona, in Otello; Marguerite, in Faust; Amelia, in Simon Boccanegra; Fiordiligi, in Così Fan Tutte; Tatiana, in Eugene Onegin; title rôle in Arabella; Rosalinde, in Die Fledermaus; Violetta, in La Traviata; Manon, in Manon Lescaut. Has sung leading rôles at Metropolitan Opera, New York, notably, Desdemona, Elvira, and Countess; also at the Paris Opera, Elvira, Fiordiligi, and Pamina in Magic Flute, title rôle in Tosca; at San Francisco Opera, Amelia and Pamina; at Sydney Opera House, Mimi, Amelia, and Violetta in La Traviata; Elvira, with Cologne Opera; Amelia at La Scala, Milan; Countess in Le Nozze di Figaro at Salzburg Fest. Many recordings, incl. Maori songs. Estabd Kiri Te Kanawa Foundn, 2004. Hon. DMus: Oxford, 1983; Cambridge, 1997. Classical Brit Lifetime Achievement Award, 2010. Hon. AC 1990. *Publications:* Land of the Long White Cloud, 1989; Opera for Lovers, 1997. *Recreations:* golf, swimming, tennis. *Address:* c/o Michael Storrs Music Ltd, 211 Piccadilly, W1J 9HF.

TELFER, Robert Gilmour Jamieson, (Rab), CBE 1985; PhD; Executive Chairman, BSI Standards, 1989–92; Director, Manchester Business School, 1984–88; *b* 22 April 1928; *s* of late James Telfer and Helen Lambie Jamieson; *m* 1953, Joan Audrey Gunning; three *s*. *Educ:* Bathgate Academy (Dawson Trust Bursary); Univ. of Edinburgh (Mackay-Smith Prize; Blandfield Prize; BSc (Hons 1st cl.) 1950, PhD 1953). Shift Chemist, AEA, 1953–54; Chem. Lectr (pt-time), Whitehaven Tech. Coll., 1953–54; Imperial Chemical Industries Ltd: Res. Chemist, Billingham Div., 1954–58; Chem. Lectr (pt-time), Constantine Tech. Coll., Middlesbrough, 1955–58; Heavy Organic Chemicals Div., 1958–71; Fibre Intermediates Dir and R & D Dir, 1971–75; Div. Dep. Chm., 1975–76, Div. Chm., 1976–81, Petrochemicals Div.; Chm. and Man. Dir, 1981–84, Dir, 1984, Mather & Platt Ltd; Chm., European Industrial Services Ltd, 1988–89. Mem. Bd, Philips-Imperial Petroleum Ltd, 1975–81; Director: Renold PLC, 1984–98 (Chm., Audit Cttee, 1993–98); Volex PLC, 1986–98 (Chm., Audit Cttee, 1993–98); Teesside Hldgs Ltd, 1993–95. Sen. Vis. Fellow, Manchester Business Sch., 1988–. Group Chm., Duke of Edinburgh's Study Conf., 1974; Mem., ACORD for Fuel and Power, 1981–87; Chm., Adv. Council on Energy Conservation, 1982–84. Personal Adviser to Sec. of State for Energy, 1984–87. British Standards Institution: Mem. Main Bd, and Mem. Finance Cttee, 1988–92; non-exec. Chm., Standards Bd and Testing Bd, 1988–89. Member: Civil Service Coll. Adv. Council, 1986–89; HEFCE, 1992–97 (Chairman: Audit Cttee, 1993–97; Quality Assessment Cttee, 1996–98); Dir, Quality Assurance Agency for Higher Educn, 1997–98. Governor, Univ. of Teesside (formerly Teesside Polytechnic), 1989–97 (Chm., Govs, 1992–97; Chm., Resources Cttee, 1989–92). CCMI. Hon. MBA Manchester, 1989; Hon. LLD Teesside, 1998. *Publications:* papers in Jl Chem. Soc. and Chemistry and Industry. *Recreations:* walking, gardening, fossil hunting, decorative egg collecting, supporting Middlesbrough FC. *Address:* Downings, Upleatham Village, Redcar, Cleveland TS11 8AG.

TELIČKA, Pavel; Member (Alliance of Liberals and Democrats for Europe), European Parliament, since 2014; *b* 24 Aug. 1965; *s* of František Telička and Marie Teličková; *m* 1990, Eva Pašková; one *s* one *d*. *Educ:* Charles Univ., Prague (Dr of Law). Dir Gen. for Integration (EU, NATO and UN), 1996–98; Dep. Minister of Foreign Affairs, 1998–2000; State Sec. for European Affairs and 1st Dep. Minister of Foreign Affairs, 2000–03; Ambassador of Czech Republic to the EU, 2003–04; Mem., EC, 2004; Eur. Coordinator TEN-T: Rail Baltic(a), 2005–13; North Sea Baltic Corridor, 2014. Co-founder and Partner, BXL Consulting Ltd, 2005–13. President's Medal for contribn to integration process of Czech Republic into EU, 2003. *Publications:* How We Entered the EU, 2003. *Address:* European Parliament, Rue Wiertz, 1047 Brussels, Belgium.

TELLER, Sadie; *see* Coles, S.

TEMIRKANOV, Yuri; Music Director and Principal Conductor, St Petersburg (formerly Leningrad) Philharmonic Orchestra, since 1988; Music Director, Teatro Regio di Parma, since 2009; *b* 10 Dec. 1938. *Educ:* Leningrad Conservatory (graduated violinist, 1962, conductor, 1965). Musical Dir, Leningrad Symphony Orch., 1969–77; Artistic Dir and Chief Conductor, Kirov Opera, Leningrad, 1977–88; Principal Conductor, Royal Philharmonic Orch., 1978–98, now Conductor Laureate; Music Dir, Baltimore SO, 2000–06, now Emeritus. Principal Guest Conductor: Dresden Philharmonic Orch., 1994–98; Danish Nat. SO, 2004–08. Has conducted: Boston Symphony; Dresden Philharmonic; Danish Nat. Radio Symphony; Orch. of Santa Cecilia, Rome; Orch. Nat. de France; La Scala, Milan; Philadelphia Orch.; San Francisco Symphony; New York Philharmonic, etc. Recordings of major orchestral works of Tchaikovsky, Stravinsky, Prokofiev, Mussorgsky and Shostakovich. Abbiati Prize for best conductor, Italian Critics' Assoc., 2002. *Address:* c/o IMG Artists Europe, The Light Box, 111 Power Road, Chiswick, W4 5PY. *T:* (020) 7957 5800.

TEMKIN, Prof. Jennifer, (Mrs G. J. Zellick); Professor of Law, City University London, since 2012; *b* 6 June 1948; *d* of late Michael Temkin and Minnie Temkin (*née* Levy); *m* 1975, Prof. Graham Zellick, *qv*; one *s* one *d*. *Educ:* S Hampstead High Sch. for Girls; LSE (LLB, LLM (Dist.), LLD); Inns of Court Sch. of Law. Called to the Bar, Middle Temple, 1971, Bencher, 2009; Lectr in Law, LSE, 1971–89; Prof. of Law and Dean, Sch. of Law, Univ. of Buckingham, 1989–92; Prof. of Law, 1992–2012, now Emeritus, and Dir, Centre for Legal Studies, 1994–96, Univ. of Sussex. Vis. Prof., Univ. of Toronto, 1978–79. Mem., Cttee of Heads of Univ. Law Schs, 1989–92, 1994–96. Member: Scrutiny Cttee on Draft Criminal Code, CCC, 1985–86; Home Sec's Adv. Gp on Use of Video Recordings in Criminal Proceedings, 1988–89; NCH Cttee on Children Who Abuse Other Children, 1990–92; External Reference Gp, Home Office Sex Offences Review, 1999–2000; Cttee of Experts on Treatment of Sex Offenders, Council of Europe, 2003–05; Expert Gp on Rape and Sexual Assault, Victims of Violence and Abuse Prevention Prog., DoH and Nat. Inst. for Mental Health in England, 2005–07; Nat. DNA Database Ethics Gp, 2014–. Patron, Standing Cttee on Sexually Abused Children, 1993–96. Gov., S Hampstead High Sch. for Girls, 1991–99. FRSA 1989. FAcSS (AcSS 2009). Member: Editl Adv. Gp, Howard Jl of Criminal Justice, 1984–; Editl Bd, Jl of Criminal Law, 1986–2005. *Publications:* Rape and the Legal Process, 1987, 2nd edn 2002; Rape and Criminal Justice, 1995; (with Barbara Krahe) Sexual Assault and the Justice Gap: a question of attitude, 2008; articles in Mod. Law Rev., Criminal Law Rev., Cambridge Law Jl, Law Qly Rev., Internat. and Comparative Law Qly and other learned and professional jls. *Address:* City University London, Northampton Square, EC1V 0HB.

TEMKO, Edward James, (Ned); writer, journalist and political analyst; Chief Political Correspondent, The Observer, 2005–08; *b* 5 Nov. 1952; *s* of late Stanley L. Temko and Francine Temko (*née* Salzman); *m* 1st, 1980, Noa Weiss (marr. diss. 1984); 2nd, 1986, Astra Bergson Kook; one *s*. *Educ:* Williams Coll., USA (BA Hons Pol Sci. and Econs). Reporter, Associated Press, Lisbon, 1976; United Press International: Europe, ME and Africa Editl Desk, Brussels, 1977; Correspondent, ME Office, Beirut, 1977–78; Christian Science Monitor: Chief ME Correspondent, Beirut, 1978–80; Moscow Correspondent, 1981–83; ME Correspondent, Jerusalem, 1984–85; SA Correspondent, Johannesburg, 1986–87; Sen. TV Correspondent for Europe, ME and Africa in London, World Monitor TV, 1989–90; Editor, Jewish Chronicle, 1990–2005. Regular appearances as political and current affairs analyst on UK and US television. *Publications:* To Win or To Die: a biography of Menachem Begin, 1987. *Recreations:* tennis, travel, technology, reading, writing, supporting perennially frustrating sports teams (the Washington Redskins and Tottenham Hotspur). *Address:* c/o The Observer, Kings Place, 90 York Way, N1 9GU.

TEMPEST, Annie; cartoonist; sculptor; *b* 22 Aug. 1959; *d* of Henry and Janet Tempest; *m* 1991, James McConnel, composer (marr. diss. 2006); one *d* (one *s* decd). *Educ:* Rye St Anthony Sch., Oxford; St Mary's Sch., Ascot. Cartoonist: The Yuppies, Daily Mail, 1985–93; Tottering-by-Gently, Country Life Magazine, 1994–; Senior Moments, WI Home & Country, 2005–06. Strip Cartoonist of the Year, Cartoonists' Club of GB, 1989; Pont Award for drawing the British Character, Cartoon Art Trust, 2009. *Publications:* Turbocharge Your Granny!, 1985; How Green are your Wellies?, 1985; Hooray Henry, 1986; Henry on Hols, 1987; Westenders, 1988; Tottering-by-Gently, vol. I, 1996, vol. II, 1998, vol. III, 2003; Tottering Hall, 2001; Lady Tottering's Journal, 2002; At Home with the Totterings, 2007; Out and About with the Totterings, 2010; The Tottering Annual, 2010; Drinks with the Totterings, 2010; In the Garden with the Totterings, 2011; She talks Venus, He talks Mars, 2011; Tottering Life, 2012; Tails of Tottering Hall, 2012; Tottering-by-Gently: the first twenty years, 2013; Lord Tottering: an English gentleman, 2013; *illustrator/contributor:* Publish and Be Damned!, 1988; Best Cartoons of the Year, 1988; Anneka Rice, The Recycled Joke Book, 1989; Mary Killen, Best Behaviour, 1991; Michael Seed, I Will See You in Heaven Where Animals Don't Bite..., 1991; Crime–check!, 1992; R. Rushbrooke, Where Did I Go Wrong?, 1992; Jonathan Ray, Berry's Best Cellar Secrets, 1998; Michael Seed, Will I See You in Heaven?, 1999; Alistair Sampson, The Guest from Hell, 2000; Robin Page, Why the Reindeer has a Velvet Nose, 2002. *Recreations:* inventing labour-saving devices, gardening, sculpting in all media, music, people watching, good wine, gory medical documentaries. *Address:* Tylers Barn, Wood Norton Road, Stibbard, Norfolk NR21 0EX; The O'Shea Gallery, No 4 St James's Street, SW1A 1EF. *E:* daffy@tottering.com. *Clubs:* British Cartoonists' Association, Sloane, Naval and Military; Muthaiga (Nairobi).

TEMPEST, Kate; *see* Calvert, K.

TEMPIA, Nina Giuseppina; a District Judge (Magistrates' Courts), since 2009; *b* London, 6 Aug. 1959; *d* of Orlando Tempia and Rina Angela Tempia (*née* Necchi-Ghiri). *Educ:* Sarah Siddons Comp. Sch., London; Univ. of Warwick (LLB); Guildford Coll. of Law. Admitted solicitor, 1987; Solicitor: Hogan Harris & Co., 1986–88; Jepson Goff & Co., 1988–89; Good Good & Co., 1989–98; Mackesys, 1998–2009; a Dep. Dist Judge (Magistrates' Courts), 2003–09. Member: Costs Cttee, Legal Services Commn, 1990–2009; Cttee, London Criminal Courts Solicitors' Assoc., 1998–2000. Chm., Soho Soc., 1998–2004. *Recreations:* theatre, cinema, reading, travelling, eating Italian food, drinking Merlot, walking Cassie. *Address:* Hammersmith Magistrates' Court, 181 Talgarth Road, W6 8DN.

TEMPLE OF STOWE, 9th Earl *cr* 1822; **James Grenville Temple-Gore-Langton;** Partner, Slade & Cooper, since 2002; *b* 11 Sept. 1955; *er s* of 8th Earl Temple of Stowe and Zilla Ray Temple-Gore-Langton (*née* Boxall) (*d* 1966); *S* father, 2013; *m* 2008, Julie Christine Mainwaring; one *s* one *d*. FCCA. Joined Slade & Cooper, 1994. *Heir: b* Hon. Robert Chandos Temple-Gore-Langton [*b* 22 Nov. 1957; *m* 1985, Susan Penelope Cavender; three *s* one *d*].

TEMPLE, Anthony Dominic Afamado; QC 1986; a Recorder, since 1989; *b* 21 Sept. 1945; *s* of Sir Rawden John Afamado Temple, CBE, QC and late Margaret Jessie Temple; *m* 1st, 1975 (marr. diss.); 2nd, 1983, Suzie Bodansky; two *d*. *Educ:* Haileybury and ISC; Worcester College, Oxford (Hon. Sec., OU Modern Pentathlon Assoc.). Called to the Bar, Inner Temple, 1968, Bencher, 1995; Crown Law Office, Western Australia, 1969; Assistant Recorder, 1982; a Dep. High Ct Judge, 1994–2014. Chm., Modern Pentathlon Assoc. of GB, 2004–; Mem. Bd, Eur. Confedn Modern Pentathlon, 2012–. *Recreations:* modern pentathlon, travel, history. *Address:* 4 Pump Court, EC4Y 7AN.

See also V. B. A. Temple.

TEMPLE, Jane Rosemary; *see* Ray, J. R.

TEMPLE, Jill; *see* Stansfield, J.

TEMPLE, Prof. Sir John (Graham), Kt 2003; FRCSE, FRCS, FRCPE, FRCP; FMedSci; Professor of Surgery, University of Birmingham, 1995–2003, now Emeritus; President, Royal College of Surgeons of Edinburgh, 2000–03; Chair, Research Council, Healing Foundation, since 2002; *b* 14 March 1942; *s* of Joseph Henry Temple and Norah Temple; *m* 1966, Margaret Jillian Leighton Hartley; two *s* one *d*. *Educ:* William Hulme's Grammar Sch., Manchester; Liverpool Univ. Med. Sch. (MB ChB Hons; ChM). FRCSE 1969; FRCS 1970 (Hon. FRCS 2004); FRCP, FRCPE 1999; FRCPSGlas (*ad eundem*) 2003; FRCGP 2003; FRCEM (FFAEM 2003); FRCA 2005. Consultant Surgeon, Queen Elizabeth Hosp., Birmingham, 1979–98; Regl Postgrad. Dean, W Midlands, 1991–2000. Chm., Conf. Postgrad. Med. Deans UK, 1995–2000. Mem. Council, RCSE, 1997–2003. Mem., Specialist Trng Authy, 1996–2006 (Chm., 2001–08); Hon. Col, 202 Field Hospital (V), 2004–09. FMedSci 1998; Fellow, Polish Soc. Surgeons, 1997; FFICM 2014. Hon. FHKCS 2001; Hon. FRACS 2002; Hon. FRCSI 2004. Hon. DSc Bristol, 2014. *Publications:* papers on postgraduate education and training. *Recreations:* off-shore sailing and racing, ski-ing. *Address:* Wharncliffe, 24 Westfield Road, Edgbaston, Birmingham B15 3QG.

TEMPLE, Mark Howard; QC (Jersey) 2015; Solicitor General, Jersey, since 2015; *b* London, 28 Aug. 1966; *s* of John and Julienne Temple; *m* 1993, Silvia; one *s* one *d*. *Educ:* King's Coll. Sch., Wimbledon; Selwyn Coll., Cambridge (BA Hist. 1988; MA 1992); Westminster Univ. (DipLaw). Admitted as solicitor, 1994; Solicitor Advocate, 2002. Solicitor: Ashurst Morris Crisp, 1992–2003; Mourant Ozannes, 2003–15 (Partner, 2007–15); Advocate, Royal Court of Jersey, 2005. *Recreations:* ski-ing, tennis, walking, family, Church (Anglican). *Address:* Law Officers' Department, Morier House, St Helier, Jersey, Channel Islands JE1 1DD. *T:* (01534) 441233, *Fax:* (01534) 441299. *E:* m.temple@gov.je. *Club:* Hurlingham.

TEMPLE, Martin John, CBE 2005; Chairman: EEF Ltd (formerly Engineering Employers Federation), since 2008 (Director General, 1999–2008); Design Council, since 2011 (Board Member, since 2009); *b* 30 Aug. 1949; *s* of John Douglas Temple and Kathleen Temple; *m* 1972, Lesley Imeson; one *s* one *d*. *Educ:* Bridlington Sch.; Univ. of Hull (BSc Hons 1970); Newcastle Poly. (Dip Mktg 1972); INSEAD (AMP 1991). Gen. Manager, British Steel Corp. Refractories Gp, 1979–85; Works Dir, GR-Stein Refractories, 1985–87; Dir, Sales and Mktg, British Steel Stainless, 1987–92; Avesta Sheffield: Dir, Mktg and Sales, 1992–95; Vice Pres., 1995–98. Bd Mem., Namtec Ltd, 2004–09; Dir, Vestry Court Ltd, 2000–; Chm., 600 Gp plc, 2007–11. Chm., Transition Mgt Bd, Business Support Simplification Prog., BERR, later BIS, 2008–11. Chm., Warwick Business Sch., 2014–. Board Member: Council of Eur. Employers of Metal, Engrg and Technology-based Industries, 1999– (Chm., 2005–08); Women in Sci. and Engrg, 2001–08 (former Chm.); Engrg Develt Trust, 2000–07; Sci. Engrg Manufacturing Technol. Alliance, 2000–09; Engrg and Technol. Bd, 2002–08; Sheffield Teaching Hosp. Foundn Trust, 2013–; Mem. Supervisory Bd, Sci., Engrg, Technol. and Maths Network, 2001–07. Mem. Council, Univ. of Warwick, 2011–. Hon. FFOM 2008. Freeman, Co. of Cutlers, 1998. Hon. DSc Hull, 2011; Hon. Dr Sheffield Hallam, 2014. *Recreations:* Rugby, music, countryside, current affairs. *E:* mtemple@eef.org.uk.

TEMPLE, Nicholas John; Chairman, Intela, since 2009; *b* 2 Oct. 1947; *s* of late Leonard Temple and of Lilly Irene Temple (*née* Thornton); *m* 1st; one *s* two *d*; 2nd, 2004, Lucinda (*née* Westmacott). *Educ:* King's Sch., Glos. Joined IBM, 1965; Chief Exec., 1992–94, Chm., 1994–96, IBM UK; Vice Pres., Industries, IBM Europe, 1995–96; mgt consultant, N. M. Rothschild & Sons, 1996. Chm., Hotelscene, 2008–13; non-executive Director: Electrocomponents PLC, 1996–2007; Blick plc, 1999–2004; Datacash, 2000–10; Datatec, 2002–. Council Mem., Foundn for Mfg and Ind., 1993–96. Chm., Action: Employees in the Community, 1993–96. Mem., President's Adv. Gp, Spastics' Soc., 1993–95. *Recreations:* rowing, ski-ing, opera. *Address:* 10 Markham Square, SW3 4UY. *T:* (020) 7581 2181.

TEMPLE, Sir Richard (Carnac Chartier), 5th Bt *cr* 1876, of The Nash, Kempsey, co. Worcester; Founder and Director, The Temple Gallery, since 1959; *b* 17 Aug. 1937; *er s* of Sir Richard Temple, 4th Bt, MC and Lucy Geils de Lotbinière; *S* father, 2007; *m* 1964, Emma Rose, 2nd *d* of Maj.-Gen. Sir Robert Laycock, KCMG, CB, DSO; three *d*. *Educ:* Stowe. PhD. Lieut, Royal Horse Guards (The Blues), 1958 (Gen. Service Medal, 1958). Lectr, Sch. of Traditional Arts, The Prince's Foundation, 1997–. *Publications:* Icons and the Mystical Origins of Christianity, 1991, 2nd edn 2001; Icons: divine beauty, 2004; numerous scholarly articles and catalogues. *Recreations:* music, travel, philosophy. *Heir: nephew* Nicholas Christopher Lee Temple, *b* 3 Nov. 1986]. *E:* richard@templegallery.com. *T:* (020) 7727 3809.

TEMPLE, Victor Bevis Afoumado; QC 1993; a Recorder of the Crown Court, since 1989; *b* 23 Feb. 1941; *s* of Sir Rawden John Afamado Temple, CBE, QC and Margaret Jessie Temple; *m* 1974, Richenda Penn-Bull; two *s*. *Educ:* Shrewsbury Sch.; Inns of Court Sch. of Law. TA, Westminster Dragoons, 1960–61. Marketing Exec., 1960–68. Called to the Bar, Inner Temple, 1971, Bencher, 1996; Jun. Prosecuting Counsel to the Crown, 1985–91, Sen. Treasury Counsel, 1991–93, CCC. DTI Inspector into Nat. Westminster Bank Ltd, 1992. Mem. Panel of Chairmen, Police Discipline Tribunals, 1993–. *Recreations:* rowing, carpentry. *Address:* 21 College Hill, EC4R 2RP. *T:* (020) 3301 0910. *Club:* Thames Rowing (Pres., 2009–).

See also A. D. A. Temple.

TEMPLE COX, Richard, CBE 2002; Chairman: Birmingham and Solihull NHS Local Improvement Finance Trust, 2004–07; Community Regeneration Partnership, 2005–09; *b* 25 Dec. 1937; *s* of Richard G. Cox and Marianne A. Cox (*née* Ladbrook); *m* 1990, Caroline Mary Fauset Jefferson (*née* Welsh); one *s* two *d* from previous marriage. *Educ:* King Edward's Sch., Birmingham; Birmingham Sch. of Architecture (DipArch 1963). RIBA 1964. Secretary: Birmingham Civic Soc., 1964–71; Victorian Soc. W Midlands, 1969–71; Chm., Temple Cox Nicholls Architects, 1970–2000. Pres., Birmingham Architectural Assoc., 1983–84; Royal Institute of British Architects: Council Mem., 1987–93; Sen. Vice Pres., 1989–91; Chm., Educn Cttee, 1989–91. Mem., Construction Industry Council, 1991–94. Chm., Castle Vale HAT, 1992–2005. Mem., Community, Voluntary and Local Services, Cabinet Honours Selection Cttee, 2005–10. Trustee: Birmingham Pub Bombing Lord Mayor's Appeal, 1974; Sense in Midlands, 1988–92; Nat. Council, Deaf Blind Rubella Assoc., 1991–93; Birmingham Dogs Home, 2008–15 (Chm. Trustees, 2010–15); Chm., Birmingham Inst. for Deaf, 1976–94; Founder Chm., Access for Disabled, Birmingham, 1986. *Publications:* occasional contribs to RIBA Jl and Regeneration and Renewal. *Recreations:* travel, music, golf, gardening, after-dinner speaking, model railways, military history. *Clubs:* Aberdovey Golf; Droitwich Golf.

TEMPLE-GORE-LANGTON, family name of **Earl Temple of Stowe**.

TEMPLE-MORRIS, family name of **Baron Temple-Morris**.

TEMPLE-MORRIS, Baron *cr* 2001 (Life Peer), of Llandaff in the County of South Glamorgan and of Leominster in the County of Herefordshire; **Peter Temple-Morris;** *b* 12 Feb. 1938; *o s* of His Honour Sir Owen Temple-Morris, QC and Lady (Vera) Temple-Morris (*née* Thompson); *m* 1964, Taheré, *e d* of late HE Senator Khozeimé Alam, Teheran; two *s* two *d*. *Educ:* Hillstone Sch., Malvern; Malvern Coll.; St Catharine's Coll., Cambridge (MA). Chm., Cambridge Univ. Conservative Assoc., 1961; Mem. Cambridge Afro-Asian Expedn, 1961. Called to Bar, Inner Temple, 1962. Judge's Marshal, Midland Circuit, 1958; Mem., Young Barristers' Cttee, Bar Council, 1962–63; in practice on Wales and Chester Circuit, 1963–66; London and SE Circuit, 1966–76; 2nd Prosecuting Counsel to Inland Revenue, SE Circuit, 1971–74; admitted a solicitor, 1989. Contested (C): Newport (Mon), 1964 and 1966;

Norwood (Lambeth), 1970; MP Leominster, Feb. 1974–2001 (C, Feb. 1974–1997, Ind., 1997–98, Lab, 1998–2001). PPS to Minister of Transport, 1979. Member: Select Cttee on Agriculture, 1982–83; Select Cttee on Foreign Affairs, 1987–90. Chairman: British-Lebanese Parly Gp, 1983–94 (Vice-Chm., 1994–97); British-Netherlands Parly Gp, 1988–2001 (Sec., 2001–08); British-Iranian Parly Gp, 1989–2005 (Sec., 1974–89); British-South Africa (formerly British-Southern Africa) All-Party Gp, 1992–95 (Vice-Chm., 1995–2001); British-Russian All-Party Gp, 1992–94; British-Spanish All-Party Gp, 1994–2001 (Treas., 2001–05); House of Lords and Commons Solicitors Gp, 1992–97; H of L Cttee on Delegated Legislation and Regulatory Powers, 2002–06; Co-Chm., Working Party to establish British-Irish Inter-Parly Body, 1988–90, first British Co-Chm., 1990–97, Mem., 1997–2005; Mem., H of L Eur. Cttee, Sub-Cttee E (Justice and Instns, 2010–13; Secretary: Conservative Parly Transport Cttee, 1976–79; Cons. Parly Legal Cttee, 1977–78; Vice-Chairman: Cons. Parly Foreign and Commonwealth Affairs Cttee, 1982–90 (Sec., 1979–82); Cons. Parly NI Cttee, 1989–92; British-Argentina Parly Gp, 1990–94; European-Atlantic Gp, 1991–97. Member: Exec. British Branch, IPU, 1977–97 (Chm., 1982–85; British delegate, fact-finding mission on Namibia, 1977); Exec. Cttee, UK Br., CPA, 1993–98; Mem., 1980, Leader, 1984, Parly Delegation to UN Gen. Assembly; Mem., Argentine-British Conf., 1991. Chm., Hampstead Conservative Political Centre, 1971–73; Society of Conservative Lawyers: Mem. Exec., 1968–71, 1990–97 (Chm., 1995–97); Vice-Chm., Standing Cttee on Criminal Law, 1976–79; Chm., F&GP Cttee, 1992–95. Chm., Bow Gp Standing Cttee on Home Affairs, 1975–79. Chm., Afghanistan Support Cttee, 1981–82; Vice-Chm., GB-Russian Centre (formerly GB-USSR Assoc.), 1993–98 (Mem. Council, 1982–92); Pres., Iran Soc., 1995–2009 (Mem. Council, 1968–80); Chm. Bd, British Iranian Chamber of Commerce, 2002–04; Mem. Adv. Council, British Inst. of Persian Studies, 1997–2008. Mem., RIIA. Nat. Treas., UNA, 1987–97 (Hon. Vice Pres., 1997–). Mem., Lord Chancellor's Adv. Cttee, Nat. Records Office and Archives, Kew, 2008–09. Freeman, City of London; Chief Steward, City of Hereford, 2009–. Gov., Malvern Coll., 1975– (Council Mem., 1978–2002); Mem. Council, Wilton Park Conf. Centre, (FCO), 1990–97. Pres., St Catharine's Coll., Cambridge Soc., 2003–04. Fellow, Industry and Parlt Trust, Barclays Bank, 1988. Hon. Associate, BVA, 1976. Hon Citizen: New Orleans; Havana, Cuba. Chevalier du Tastevin, 1991; Jurade de St Emilion, 1999. Knight, Order of Orange-Nassau (Netherlands), 2007. *Recreations:* wine and food, family, biographies, cinema and theatre. *Address:* House of Lords, SW1A 0PW. *Clubs:* Reform; Cardiff and County.

TEMPLEMAN, Miles Howard; Director General, Institute of Directors, 2004–11; *b* 4 Oct. 1947; *s* of Robert James and Margot Elizabeth Templeman; *m* 1970, Janet Elizabeth Strang; two *s* one *d. Educ:* Haberdashers' Aske's Boys' Sch.; Jesus Coll., Cambridge (BA 1969, MA). Young & Rubicam, 1970–73; Beecham Foods, 1973–79; Levi Strauss, 1979–85; Whitbread, 1985–2000; Chief Exec., Bulmers, 2002–03; Eldridge Pope, 2002–04. Non-executive Director: Ben Sherman, 2000–03; Royal Mail, 2001–03; Shepherd Neame, 2002– (Chm., 2005–); Portman Gp, 2003; non-exec. Chm., YO! Sushi, 2003–08. *Recreations:* tennis, golf, reading, opera. *Address:* Shepherd Neame, The Faversham Brewery, 17 Court Street, Faversham, Kent ME13 7AX. *Club:* Queen's.

TEMPLER, Maj.-Gen. James Robert, CB 1989; OBE 1978 (MBE 1973); Managing Director, Templers Gardening (formerly Templers Flowers), since 1990; *b* 8 Jan. 1936; *s* of Brig. Cecil Robert Templer, DSO and Angela Mary Templer (*née* Henderson); *m* 1963 (marr. diss. 1979); two *s* one *d*; 2nd, 1981, Sarah Ann Evans (*née* Rogers). *Educ:* Charterhouse; RMA Sandhurst. RCDS, psc. Commissioned Royal Artillery, 1955; Instructor, Staff Coll., 1974–75; Comd 42nd Regt, 1975–77; Comd 5th Regt, 1977–78; CRA 2nd Armd Div., 1978–82; RCDS 1983; ACOS Training, HQ UKLF, 1983–86; ACDS (Concepts), MoD, 1986–89. Mem., British Cross Country Ski Team, 1958; European 3 Day Event Champion, 1962; Mem., British Olympic 3 Day Event Team, 1964. FCMI (FBIM 1988). *Recreations:* sailing, ski-ing, gardening, fishing, DIY. *Address:* c/o Lloyds Bank, Crediton, Devon EX17 3HL.

TEMPLETON, Prof. (Alexander) Allan, CBE 2009; FRCOG, FRCP, FRCPE, FMedSci; Professor of Obstetrics and Gynaecology, University of Aberdeen, 1985–12, now Emeritus (Regius Professor of Obstetrics and Gynaecology, 1985–2007); Clinical Director, Office of Research and Clinical Audit, Royal College of Obstetricians and Gynaecologists, 2007–14; *b* 28 June 1946; *s* of Richard and Minnie Templeton; *m* 1980, Gillian Constance Penney; three *s* one *d. Educ:* Aberdeen Grammar School; Univ. of Aberdeen (MB ChB 1969; MD Hons 1982). MRCOG 1974, FRCOG 1987; FRCPE 2005; FRCP 2006. Resident and Registrar, Aberdeen Hosps, 1969–75; Lectr and Sen. Lectr, Dept of Obst. and Gyn., Univ. of Edinburgh, 1976–85; Hd, Dept of Obst. and Gyn., Univ. of Aberdeen, 1985–2007. Chm., Soc. for the Study of Fertility, 1996–99; Mem., HFEA, 1995–2000. Hon. Sec., 1998–2004, Pres., 2004–07, RCOG. FMedSci 2002. *Publications:* The Early Days of Pregnancy, 1988; Reproductive Medicine and the Law, 1990; (ed jtly) Infertility, 1992; The Prevention of Pelvic Infection, 1996; Evidence-based Fertility Treatment, 1998; Management of Infertility, 2000; Models of Care in Women's Health, 2009; clinical and sci. articles on human infertility and *in vitro* fertilisation. *Recreations:* west coast of Scotland, mountains, photography. *Address:* Oak Tree Cottage, Leacnasaide, Gairloch, Wester Ross IV21 2AP. *T:* (01445) 741354.

TEMPLETON, Darwin Herbert, CBE 1975; Senior Partner, Price Waterhouse Northern Ireland (formerly Ashworth Rowan Craig Gardner), 1967–82; *b* 14 July 1922; *s* of Malcolm and Mary Templeton; *m* 1950; two *s* one *d. Educ:* Rocavan Sch.; Ballymena Academy. FICAI. Qualified as Chartered Accountant, 1945. Partner, Ashworth Rowan, 1947. Chm., Ulster Soc. of Chartered Accountants, 1961–62; Pres., ICAI, 1970–71. Mem., Royal Commn on Legal Services, 1976–79. *Recreations:* music, golf, motor racing. *Address:* 4 Cashel Road, Broughshane, Ballymena, Co. Antrim, Northern Ireland BT42 4PL. *T:* (028) 2586 1017.

TEMPLETON, Dr Ian Godfrey; Warden, Glenalmond College, Perth, 1992–2003; *b* 1 Feb. 1944; *s* of late Anthony Godard Templeton and Mary Gibson Templeton (*née* Carrick Anderson); *m* 1970, Elisabeth Aline Robin; one *s* one *d. Educ:* Gordonstoun Sch.; Edinburgh Univ. (MA); Bedford Coll., London Univ. (BA 1st cl. Hons Philosophy); Univ. of Edinburgh (PhD Simon Somerville Laurie 2010). Asst Master, 1969–71, Housemaster, 1971–73, Melville Coll.; Housemaster, Daniel Stewart's and Melville Coll., 1973–78; Asst Headmaster, Robert Gordon's Coll., Aberdeen, 1978–85; Headmaster, Oswestry Sch., 1985–92. FRSA. *Recreations:* golf, choral singing, travel. *Address:* 18 Craigleith Crescent, Edinburgh EH4 3JL. *T:* (0131) 332 2449. *Clubs:* Royal & Ancient; Bruntsfield Links Golfing Society.

TENBY, 3rd Viscount *cr* 1957, of Bulford; **William Lloyd-George;** *b* 7 Nov. 1927; 2nd *s* of 1st Viscount Tenby, TD, PC, and Edna Gwenfron (*d* 1971), *d* of David Jones, Gwynfa, Denbigh; *S* brother, 1983; *m* 1955, Ursula Diana Ethel, *y d* of late Lt-Col Henry Edward Medlicott, DSO; one *s* two *d. Educ:* Eastbourne College; St Catharine's Coll., Cambridge (Exhibnr; BA 1949). Captain, Royal Welch Fusiliers, TA. Consultant, Williams Lea & Co., 1988–93; Chm., St James Public Relations, 1990–93; non-exec. Dir, Ugland Internat. plc, 1993–96. House of Lords: Member: Cttee on Procedure, 1995–98; Cttee of Selection, 1998–2010; Sub-Cttee on Admin and Works, 1992–95; All Party Media Gp; elected Mem., H of L, 1999–2015. JP Hants (Chm., NE Hants (formerly Odiham) Bench, 1990–94). *Heir: s* Hon. Timothy Henry Gwilym Lloyd-George, *b* 19 Oct. 1962. *Address:* The White House, Dippenhall Street, Crondall, Farnham, Surrey GU10 5PE.

TENCH, Leslie Owen; Chairman, SIG plc, 2004–11 (Deputy Chairman, 2003–04). *Educ:* Univ. of Nottingham (BSc Metallurgy). Steetley plc; Twyfords Bathrooms; Reed International; Procter & Gamble; Managing Director: CRH UK, 1992–98; CRH Europe - Building Products, 1998–2002. Non-executive Director: Shepherd Bldg Gp, 1994–2004; Norcros plc, 2007–12; Tyman plc (formerly Lupus Capital plc), 2009–. *Recreations:* walking, theatre, music, travelling to unusual places.

TENDLER, Prof. Saul Jonathan Benjamin, PhD, DSc; Deputy Vice-Chancellor and Provost, University of York, since 2015; *b* Watford, 26 May 1961; *s* of Arnold Tendler and Maxine Tendler; *m* 1991, Katherine Kraven; two *s* one *d. Educ:* Kingsbury High Sch.; Univ. of Manchester (BSc Pharmacy 1982); Aston Univ. (PhD 1986); Univ. of Nottingham (DSc 2007). MRPharmS 1983, FRPharmS 2000; FRSC 1993. Pre-registration Pharmacist, Westminster Hosp., London, 1982–83; MRC Trng Fellow, NIMR, Mill Hill, 1986–88; University of Nottingham: Lectr in Medicinal Chem., 1988–95; Reader in Biophysical Chem., 1995–98; Prof. of Biophysical Chem., 1998–2015; Dean, Graduate Sch., 1999–2003; Hd, Sch. of Pharmacy, 2003–09; Pro-Vice-Chancellor, 2009–15. Director: Nottingham Univ. Industrial and Commercial Enterprise Ltd, 2006–11; Biocity Ltd, 2006–12. Chairman: MRC/EPSRC/BBSRC Discipline Hopping Panel, 2005–12; EPSRC Analytical Sci. Rev., 2006; Member: Biological Methods Gp Cttee, RSC, 1990–96; BBSRC/EPSRC Biomolecular Scis Cttee, 1994–97; BBSRC Engrg and Physical Scis Cttee, 1995–97; BBSRC Engrg and Biological Systems Cttee, 1998–2001; Royal Soc./Royal Acad. of Engrg Nanotechnol. Wkg Gp, 2002–04; HEFCE Strategy Cttee for Res., 2003–08; BBSRC Tools and Resources Strategy Panel, 2006–10; BBSRC Biosci. Skills and Careers Strategy Panel, 2009–10; HEFCE/UUK/Dept for Employment and Learning, NI/GuildHE Quality in Higher Educn Gp, 2010–; UK Healthcare Educn Adv. Cttee, 2013–. UK Rep., Nanosci. Cttee, 1999–2006, Domain Cttee: Materials, Physical and Nanoscis, 2006–09, EU COST. Non-exec. Dir, Notts Healthcare NHS Trust, 2010–15. Nuffield Foundn Sci. Res. Fellow, 1996–97. Theophilus Redwood Lectr, RSC, 2003. Lilly Prize for Pharmaceutical Excellence, 1994; Sci. Medal, British Pharmaceutical Conf., 1994; SAC Silver Medal, RSC, 1997; Pfizer Prize, 1998; GlaxoSmithKline Internat. Achievement Award, 2003. *Publications:* over 200 papers in learned jls. *Recreations:* sailing, walking the dog. *Address:* University of York, Heslington, York YO10 5DD. *T:* (01904) 322055. *E:* saul.tendler@york.ac.uk. *Club:* Attenborough Sailing.

TENDULKAR, Sachin Ramesh, Bharat Ratna 2013; Padma Vibhushan 2008 (Padma Shri 1999); Member, Rajya Sabha, India, since 2012; Indian Test cricketer, 1989–2013; *b* Mumbai, 24 April 1973. Youngest cricketer (aged 14) to play in Mumbai team in Ranji Trophy 1st cl. cricket tournament; youngest player (aged 15) to score a century in Ranji Trophy; only player to have scored a century on début in all of India's 1st cl. cricket tournaments - Ranji Trophy, Duleep Trophy and Irani Trophy; Test Cricket debut for India against Pakistan, 1989 (aged 16); 2nd youngest player to captain India in Test Cricket (aged 23); captained India in 17 Test matches and 54 limited overs Internats, 1996–97, 1999–2000; second youngest cricketer to have scored a century against England, 1990; first overseas player to play for Yorkshire CCC, 1992; highest aggregate run scorer (1796 runs) in World Cup cricket tournaments; leading run scorer in limited over internat. cricket (17,598 runs by Sept. 2010); in 2010 was highest run scorer in one-day internats (200) (18,426 runs in 463 one-day internats); highest century scorer and leading run scorer in Test Cricket (15,921 runs in 200 Tests by Nov. 2013, and in 2010 became first player to score 50 Test centuries); first player to score 100 internat. centuries, 2012. Chatrapati Shivaji Award, 1990–91, Maharashtra Bhushan, 2001, Maharashtra State. Arjuna Award (India), 1994; Rajiv Gandhi Khel Ratna Award (India), 1998. *Publications:* Playing it My Way (autobiog.), 2014. *Address:* 10th Floor, La Mer, Mistry Park, Kadeshwari Road, Bandra Reclamation, Mumbai 400 050, India.

TENENBAUM, Jane Elaine; *see* Lush, J. E.

TENET, George John; Managing Director, Allen & Company LLC, since 2007; *b* 5 Jan. 1953; *m* A. Stephanie Glakas; one *s. Educ:* Georgetown Univ., Washington; Columbia Univ., NY (MIA 1978). Legislative Asst specialising in nat. security and energy issues, then Legislative Dir to Senator H. John Heinz, III; Designee to Vice Chm., Senator Patrick J. Leahy, 1985–86; Dir, Oversight of Arms Control Negotiations between Soviet Union and US, then Staff Dir, Senate Select Cttee on Intelligence, 1986–93; National Security Council: Mem., Presidential Transition Team, 1993; Special Asst to Pres. and Sen. Dir for Intelligence Programs, 1993–95; Dep. Dir, CIA, 1995–97; Dir, CIA, 1997–2004; Prof. of Diplomacy, Georgetown Univ., Washington, DC, 2004–07. Non-executive Director: Guidance Software, 2005–08; L-1 Identity Solutions, 2005–08; QinetiQ, 2006–08; QinetiQ North America, 2008. Presidential Medal of Freedom, USA, 2004. *Publications:* The Ability of US Intelligence to Monitor the Intermediate Nuclear Force Treaty; At the Center of the Storm: my years at the CIA (memoirs), 2007.

TENISON; *see* Hanbury-Tenison.

TENISON; *see* King-Tenison.

TENNANT, family name of **Baron Glenconner**.

TENNANT, Bernard; Director of Retail, British Chambers of Commerce, 1993–95; *b* 14 Oct. 1930; *s* of Richard and Phyllis Tennant; *m* 1956, Marie (*née* Tonge); two *s* one *d. Educ:* Farnworth Grammar Sch.; Open Univ. (BA Hons Govt and Modern European Hist.). Nat. Service, RAF, 1949. Local authority admin, Worsley and Bolton, 1950; Secretary: Bolton Chamber of Trade, 1960–74; Bolton Chamber of Commerce and Industry, and numerous trade associations, 1968–74; National Chamber of Trade, 1975–92, Dir Gen., 1987–92. Member: British Retail Consortium Council, 1986–95; Home Office Standing Cttee on Crime Prevention, 1986–92; Dept of Employment Retail Price Index Adv. Cttee, 1988–92. Magistrate, Bolton, 1968–75; Reading, 1975–78. Founder Sec., Moorside Housing Gp of charitable housing assocs, 1964–75. Editor, NCT News, 1986–92. *Publications:* (contrib.) Chambers' Book of Days, 2004; articles in professional and trade jls, historical and lifestyle magazines. *Recreations:* music, photography, collating historical chronology.

TENNANT, David; *see* McDonald, D. J.

TENNANT, Lady Emma; Chairman, National Trust Gardens Advisory Panel, 1984–2001; Member, Council, National Trust, 1990–2002; *b* 26 March 1943; *d* of 11th Duke of Devonshire, KG, MC, PC and Dowager Duchess of Devonshire, DCVO; *m* 1963, Hon. Tobias William Tennant, *y s* of 2nd Baron Glenconner; one *s* two *d. Educ:* St Elphin's Sch., Darley Dale; St Anne's Coll., Oxford (BA History 1963). *Publications:* Rag Rugs, 1992. *Recreations:* gardening, painting. *Address:* Shaws, Newcastleton, Roxburghshire TD9 0SH. *T:* (01387) 376241.

TENNANT, Emma Christina, FRSL 1982; writer; *b* 20 Oct. 1937; *d* of 2nd Baron Glenconner and Elizabeth Lady Glenconner; one *s* two *d. Educ:* St Paul's Girls' School. Freelance journalist to 1973; became full time novelist, 1973; founder Editor, Bananas, 1975–78; general editor: In Verse, 1982–; Lives of Modern Women, 1985–. TV film script, Frankenstein's Baby, 1990. Hon. DLitt Aberdeen, 1996. *Publications:* The Colour of Rain (pseud. Catherine Aydy), 1963; The Time of the Crack, 1973; The Last of the Country House Murders, 1975; Hotel de Dream, 1976; (ed) Bananas Anthology, 1977; (ed) Saturday Night Reader, 1978; The Bad Sister, 1978; Wild Nights, 1979; Alice Fell, 1980; Queen of Stones, 1982; Woman Beware Woman, 1983; Black Marina, 1985; Adventures of Robina by Herself, ed Emma Tennant, 1986; Cycle of the Sun: The House of Hospitalities, 1987, A Wedding of Cousins, 1988; The Magic Drum, 1989; Two Women of London, 1989; Sisters and Strangers, 1990; Faustine, 1991; Tess, 1993; Pemberley, 1993; An Unequal Marriage, 1994; Elinor and Marianne, 1996; Emma in Love, 1996; Strangers: a family romance, 1998; Girlitude: a memoir of the 50s and 60s, 1999; Burnt Diaries, 1999; The Ballad of Sylvia and Ted, 2001;

A House in Corfu, 2001; Felony: the private history of the Aspern Papers, 2002; Corfu Banquet, 2004; Heathcliff's Tale, 2005; The Harp Lesson, 2005; The French Dancer's Bastard, 2006; Confessions of a Sugar Mummy, 2007; The Autobiography of the Queen, 2007; Seized, 2008; Waiting for Princess Margaret, 2009; The Beautiful Child, 2012; (as Isabel Vane, jtly) Balmoral, 2004; (contrib.) Novelists in Interview (ed John Haffenden), 1985; (contrib.) Women's Writing: a challenge to theory (ed Maria Monteith), 1986; *for children:* The Boggart (with Mary Rayner), 1979; The Search for Treasure Island, 1981; The Ghost Child, 1984. *Recreation:* walking about. *Address:* c/o Jonathan Cape, Random House, 20 Vauxhall Bridge Road, SW1V 2SA.

TENNANT, Helen Anne, (Lena); Lecturer, Faculty of Education, University of Glasgow (formerly St Andrew's College, Glasgow), 1989–2004; *b* 15 Dec. 1943; *d* of late Joseph Dawson and Anna Dawson (*née* Giavarini); *m* 1975, Gerard E. Tennant; three *s* one *d*. *Educ:* St Mary's Acad., Bathgate; Notre Dame Coll. of Education, Glasgow (DipCE); RSAMD (Dip. Speech and Drama). Lectr in Speech and Drama, Notre Dame Coll. of Educn, Glasgow, 1969–75; extra-mural Lectr, St Peter's Seminary, Cardross, subseq. Glasgow, 1972–92; part-time Lectr, Coatbridge Coll., 1983–89. Member: Viewer's Consultative Council (Scotland), 1989–94; Radio Authy, 1995–2000. *Recreations:* theatre-going, playing church organ.

TENNANT of Balfluig, Mark Iain; Master of the Supreme Court, Queen's Bench Division, 1988–2005; Baron of Balfluig; *b* 4 Dec. 1932; *s* of late Major John Tennant, TD, KStJ and Hon. Antonia Mary Roby Benson, *d* of 1st Baron Charnwood and later Viscountess Radcliffe; *m* 1965, Lady Harriot Pleydell-Bouverie, *y d* of 7th Earl of Radnor, KG, KCVO; one *s* one *d*. *Educ:* Eton College; New College, Oxford (MA 1959). Lieut, The Rifle Brigade (SRO). Called to the Bar, Inner Temple, 1958, Bencher, 1984; Recorder, 1987–96. Restored Balfluig Castle (barony of Balfluig *cr* of Charles II, 1650), dated 1556 in 1967 (the first to obtain a grant from Historic Bldgs Council for Scotland for bldg not inhabited or inhabitable). Chm., Royal Orchestral Soc. (formerly for Amateur Musicians), 1989–2009 (Pres., 2009–). *Recreations:* music, architecture, books, shooting. *Address:* Balfluig Castle, Aberdeenshire AB33 8EJ; 30 Abbey Gardens, NW8 9AT. *T:* (020) 7624 3200. *Club:* Brooks's.

TENNANT, Michael Humphrey; a District Judge, 1992–2008; President, Association of District Judges, 2007–08; *b* 11 Sept. 1942; *s* of Norman Humphrey Tennant and Marjorie Lillian Tennant (*née* Coles); *m* 1st, 1965, Kathleen Nicolette Chapman (marr. diss. 1998); two *d*; 2nd, 1998, June Mary Dixon. *Educ:* Bedford Modern Sch.; University College London (LLB Hons 1963). Admitted solicitor, 1966; Partner, Damant & Sons, 1969–84; High Court District Registrar and County Court Registrar, 1984; Asst Recorder, 1989; a Recorder, 1992. *Recreations:* music—listening to classical (mostly instrumental) and jazz and playing piano (classical), sailing—racing own National Sonata nationally and internationally, defending occasional hard-won sailing trophies, cruising wherever possible when time permits. *Address:* Chazey House, Salisbury Road, Sherfield English, Hants SO51 6FQ. *T:* (01794) 323344. *Clubs:* Sloane; Island Sailing (Cdre, 1989–92).

TENNANT, Maj.-Gen. Michael Trenchard, CB 1994; Army Adviser, British Aerospace, 1998–2001; *b* 3 Sept. 1941; *s* of Lt-Col Hugh Trenchard Tennant, MC and Mary Isobel Tennant (*née* Wilkie); *m* 1st, 1964, Susan Daphne (*d* 1993), *d* of late Lt-Col Frank Beale, LVO; three *s*; 2nd, 1996, Jacqueline Mary Parish (*née* ap Ellis), *widow* of David Parish; two step *d*. *Educ:* Wellington College. psc†. Commissioned RA 1961; served Bahrain, Aden, BAOR, Hong Kong, UK, 1962–71; Staff College, 1972–73; MoD, 1974–75; Bty Comdr, 127 (Dragon) Bty, BAOR, 1976–78; Directing Staff, Staff Coll., 1978–80; CO, 1 RHA, UK and BAOR, 1980–83; Comdr British Training Team, Nigeria, 1983–85; CRA 3 Armd Div., BAOR, 1985–87; CRA UKLF, 1988–91; Dir, RA, 1991–94. Hd of External Commns, Royal Ordnance Div., BAe, 1994–98. Col Comdt, RA, 1994–2005; Hon. Col, 1 RHA, 1994–99. Chm., CCF Assoc., 1996–2003. President: Army Cricket, 1992–93; RA Golf Soc., 1998–2012. *Recreations:* bridge, golf. *Clubs:* Fadeaways; Denham Golf, Rye Golf, Senior Golfers.

TENNANT, Teresa Mary; President and non-executive Director, Ice Organisation, since 2011 (Founder Executive Chairman, 2006–11); *b* Surrey, 29 May 1959; *d* of John McRae Cormack and late Hon. (Gwendoline Rita) Jean Cormack, *d* of 1st Baron Davies; *m* 1st, 1983, Hon. Henry Lovell Tennant (*d* 1990); one *s*; 2nd, 2007, William A. Staempfli. *Educ:* Priorsfield Sch.; Beech Lawn Coll.; King's Coll. London (BSc Human Envmtl Studies). Special Projs Officer (pt-time), Green Alliance, 1983–87; internship, Franklin Research and Development Corp., 1987; Hd, Socially Responsible Investment, Merlin Fund Mgt Ltd, 1988–94; Hd, Socially Responsible Investment, NPI, 1994–2000; Co-Founder and Exec. Chm., Assoc. for Sustainable and Responsible Investment in Asia, Hong Kong, 2000–05 (Member: Exec. Bd, 2005–06; Bd, 2006–15). Lead Trustee, Glen Settlement, 1990–; Disinterested Dir, World Values Fund, Calvert Gp, 1993–2005, Calvert Social Fund Bd, 2005–09; non-exec. Dir, 1999–2005, Former Dir Advr, 2005–, Solar Century UK; Co-Founder and Exec. Chm., 2000–02, Trustee, 2009–, Carbon Disclosure Proj.; Advr, Robeco Sustainable Private Equity Fund, 2004–06; non-exec. Dir, UK Green Investment Bank, 2012–. Originator, OurVoices.net, 2014–. Mem., Adv. Cttee on Business and the Envmt, 1994–97; informal advr, UNEP Finance Initiative, 1994–2005. Founder Mem., Prince of Wales's Envmtl Adv. Cttee, 1989–97; Co-Founder and Chm., UK Social Investment Forum, 1993–97; Mem. Bd, Friends of the Earth UK Trust, 1999–2003; Ambassador, WWF UK, 2000–09; Mem., Jury Panel, FT-IFC Sustainable Banking Awards, 2005–09; Chm., Bd of Trustees, Global Cool Foundn, 2008–; External Advr, Socially Responsible Investment Cttee, Univ. of Oxford, 2009–15. Fellow, Schumacher Soc., 1994. Hon. Fellow, Centre for Social and Envmtl Accounting and Reporting, Dundee Univ., 1992. *Publications:* numerous contribs to specialist jls related to responsible investment. *Recreations:* walking, riding, reading, painting, cooking. *Address:* Glen House, Innerleithen, Borders, Scotland EH44 6PX. *E:* tt@tessatennant.net.

TENNANT, Veronica, CC 2003 (OC 1975); ballet dancer, broadcaster and writer; *b* London, 15 Jan. 1947; *d* of Harry Tennant and Doris Tennant (Bassous); *m* 1969, Dr John Robert Wright; one *d*. *Educ:* Bishop Strachan Sch., Toronto; National Ballet Sch., Toronto. Prima Ballerina, Nat. Ballet of Canada, 1965–89; major performances include: début, Juliet in Romeo and Juliet, with Earl Kraul, 1965; Pulcinella, Triptych; Les Rendezvous; Solitaire; Swan Lake; The Lesson; Cinderella; Kraanerg (created leading rôle); Le Loup; La Sylphide; première perf. as Princess Aurora with Rudolf Nureyev in his Sleeping Beauty, 1972; La Sylphide, with Mikhail Baryshnikov, 1974; Giselle, with Rudolf Nureyev, 1974; Swanhilda in Coppelia, 1975; Washington Square, with Peter Schaufuss, 1978; La Fille Mal Gardée, 1979, and Le Corsaire Pas de Deux, 1980, with Peter Schaufuss; Napoli; The Dream, with Anthony Dowell, 1981; début, Tatiana in Onegin, with Raymond Smith, 1985; farewell perfs, Romeo and Juliet, with Raymond Smith and A Passion for Dance: Celebrating the Tennant Magic (gala tribute), 1989; film maker and writer, 1989–; host and consultant/writer, Sunday Arts Entertainment CBC TV, 1989–92; producer and dir for CBC Television and Bravo!FACT; founded Veronica Tennant Prodns, 1998; television producer: Salute to Dancers for Life, 1994; Margie Gillis: Wild Hearts in Strange Times, 1996; Governor General's Performing Arts Awards Gala, 2000; The Four Seasons, 2000; television producer and director: Mavis Staines—"Courage…", 1998; Karen Kain: Dancing in the Moment, 1999 (Internat. Emmy Award for Perf. Arts); Song of Songs, 1999; The Dancers' Story: the National Ballet of Canada, 2002; Northern Light: Visions and Dreams, 2003; A Pairing of SwanS, 2004; Shadow Pleasures, 2004; A Pair of RED Shorts, 2005; Celia Franca: Tour de Force, 2006; Vida y Danza, Cuba, 2008; Finding Body & Soul, 2009; conceived and Dir, Niágara: a Pan-American Story, 2015. Dancers' Rep., Bd of Dirs, Nat. Ballet Co., 1972, 1984; Director: Ontario Arts Council, 1975–78; Toronto Arts Awards Foundn, 1988–90; Glenn Gould Foundn, 1989–92; Dancer Transition Centre, 1992–95; Governor General's Performing Arts Awards, 1992–95; Mem. Bd of Dirs, City of Toronto Olympic Bid 2008, 1998 (Chm., Arts and Culture Cttee, 1998–2000). Adjunct Prof., Fine Arts, 1989–2004, Fellow, Winters Coll., 1991–99, York Univ. FRSC 2006. Hon. DLitt: Brock, 1985; McGill, 2005; Hon. LLD: York, 1987; Simon Fraser, 1992; Toronto, 1992. Walter Carsen Prize for Excellence in the Performing Arts, 2004; Queen's Diamond Jubilee Medal, 2012. *Publications:* On Stage, Please, 1977; The Nutcracker, 1986; articles in Toronto Star, Dance International, Saturday Night Mag. and The Globe and Mail.

TENNET, Michael John; QC 2006; barrister; *b* 18 Jan. 1963; *s* of Brian and Margaret Tennet; *m* 1998, Jessica; two *s*. *Educ:* Solihull Sixth Form Coll.; New Coll., Oxford (MA 1st cl. Law 1984). Called to the Bar, Inner Temple, 1985; barrister, 1986–. *Publications:* (contrib.) Professional Negligence and Liability; (contrib.) International Trust Laws. *Recreations:* golf, tennis, Tottenham Hotspur Football Club. *Address:* Wilberforce Chambers, 8 New Square, Lincoln's Inn, WC2A 3QP. *T:* (020) 7306 0802. *E:* mtennet@wilberforce.co.uk.

TENNYSON, family name of **Baron Tennyson**.

TENNYSON, 6th Baron *cr* 1884; **David Harold Alexander Tennyson;** *b* 4 June 1960; *s* of James Alfred Tennyson, *ggs* of 1st Baron Tennyson, and of Beatrice Aventon (*née* Young); *S* cousin, 2006. *Educ:* Univ. of Canterbury, NZ (ME). *Heir: b* Alan James Drummond Tennyson [*b* 28 Jan. 1965; *m* 1998, Susanna Ruth Brow (marr. diss. 2006); one *s*; one *s* by Maria Elizabeth Walker].

TENNYSON, Prof. (Charles) Jonathan (Penrose), DPhil; FRS 2009; Massey Professor of Physics, University College London, since 2005 (Head, Department of Physics and Astronomy, 2004–11); Chief Scientist, Quantemol Ltd, since 2004; Chairman, European Task Force for Laboratory Astrophysics, since 2012; *b* Hitchin, 11 May 1955; *s* of late (Beryl) Hallam (Augustine) Tennyson and Margot Tennyson (*née* Wallach); *m* 1983, Janice Hopson; three *s* one *d*. *Educ:* Bootham Sch., York; King's Coll., Cambridge (BA 1977); Univ. of Sussex (DPhil 1980). Royal Soc. W Eur. Exchange Fellow, Univ. of Nijmegen, 1980–82; SO, SERC Daresbury Lab., 1982–85; University College London: Lectr, 1985–91; Reader, 1991–94; Prof., 1994–. Vis. Scientist, Inst. for Theoretical Atomic Molecular and Optical Physics, Harvard Univ., 1995–96. JILA Fellow, 1996. Dir, Blue Skies Space Ltd, 2014–. Chm., Hackney Chess Club, 2007–. *Publications:* Astronomical Spectroscopy, 2005, 2nd edn 2011; approx. 600 scientific papers. *Recreations:* chess, Tottenham Hotspurs. *Address:* Department of Physics and Astronomy, University College London, WC1E 6BT. *T:* (office) (020) 7679 7809, (home) (020) 8341 0923, *Fax:* (020) 7679 7145. *E:* j.tennyson@ucl.ac.uk.

TENNYSON, Prof. Jonathan; *see* Tennyson, Prof. C. J. P.

TENNYSON-d'EYNCOURT, Sir Mark (Gervais), 5th Bt *cr* 1930, of Carter's Corner Farm, Herstmonceux; *b* 12 March 1967; *o s* of Sir Giles Gervais Tennyson-d'Eyncourt, 4th Bt and of Juanita, *d* of late Fortunato Borromeo; *S* father, 1989. *Educ:* Charterhouse; Kingston Polytechnic (BA Hons Fashion). Freeman, City of London, 1989. *Heir:* none.

TENZIN GYATSO; The Dalai Lama XIV; spiritual and temporal leader of Tibet, since 1940; *b* 6 July 1935; named Lhamo Thondup; *s* of Chokyong Tsering and Diki Tsering. *Educ:* Monasteries of Sera, Drepung and Gaden, Lhasa; traditional Tibetan degree equivalent to Dr in Buddhist philosophy, 1959. Enthroned Dalai Lama, Lhasa, 1940; given name Jetsun Jampel Ngawang Losang Yeshi Tenzin Gyatso Sisum Wang-gyur Tsungpa Mepai De Pel Sangpo. Fled to Chumbi, South Tibet, on Chinese invasion, 1950; negotiated with China, 1951; fled to India after abortive revolt of Tibetan people against Communist Chinese, 1959, and established govt-in-exile in Dharamsala; stood down as political leader, 2011. Awards include: Magsaysay, Philippines, 1959; Lincoln, USA, 1960; Albert Schweitzer Humanitarian, USA, 1987; Congressional Gold Medal, USA, 2006; Templeton Prize, 2012; numerous other awards, hon. doctorates, hon. citizenships from France, Germany, India, Mongolia, Norway, USA; Nobel Peace Prize, 1989. *Publications:* My Land and My People (autobiog.), 1962; The Opening of the Wisdom Eye, 1963; An Introduction to Buddhism, 1965; Key to the Middle Way, 1971; Universal Responsibility and Good Heart, 1977; Four Essential Buddhist Commentaries, 1982; A Human Approach to World Peace, 1984; Kindness, Clarity and Insight, 1987; Freedom in Exile (autobiog.), 1990; The Good Heart, 1996; Ethics for the New Millennium, 1998; Ancient Wisdom, Modern World, 1999; A Simple Path, 2000; Advice on Dying, 2002; (jtly) The Art of Happiness at Work, 2003; (jtly) The Wisdom of Forgiveness, 2005. *Address:* Thekchen Choeling, PO Mcleod Ganj, Dharamsala, HP 176219, India.

TEO Eng Cheng, Michael; High Commissioner of Singapore to Australia, 2011–14; *b* 19 Sept. 1947; *m* Joyce; one *s* one *d*. *Educ:* Auburn Univ., USA (BSc Business Admin); Fletcher Sch. of Law and Diplomacy, Tufts Univ., USA (MA). Joined Republic of Singapore Air Force, 1968: Comdr, 1985; Dist. Grad., USAF War Coll., 1985; Brig.-Gen., 1987; Chief of Air Force, 1990; High Comr to NZ, 1994–96; Ambassador, Republic of Korea, 1996–2001; High Comr to UK, and concurrently Ambassador to Ireland, 2001–11. FRAeS 2008. Gold Public Admin Medal (Mil.) (Singapore), 1989; Most Noble Order of Crown (Thailand), 1981; Outstanding Achievement Award (Philippines), 1989; Bintang Swa Bhuana Paksa Utama (Indonesia), 1991; Comdr, Legion of Merit (USA), 1991; Gwanghwa Medal (Korea), 2002. *Recreations:* golf, hiking, reading.

TEPARAK, Pasan; Ambassador of Thailand to the Court of St James's, 2012–14; *b* 30 Jan. 1961; *m* 1991, Paradee Tesavibul; two *s*. *Educ:* Satit Pathumwan Sch., Bangkok; Carlsbad High Sch., Carlsbad, Calif; Thammasat Univ., Bangkok (BA Internat. Relns; MA Public Admin). Joined Thai Foreign Service, 1984; Consul-Gen. of Thailand, Dubai, 2006–11; Minister, Royal Thai Embassy, Canberra, 2011; Ambassador attached to Min. of Foreign Affairs and assigned to the Prime Minister, 2011–12. Member, Board of Directors: Government Savings Bank, 2011–12; Krungthai Bank Public Co., 2012 (Mem., Bd of Exec. Dirs, 2012); EGCO Public Co., 2012–13 (Mem., Audit Cttee, 2012–13). Silver Medal (7th Class), Direkgunabhorn (Thailand), 2005; Kt Grand Cross (1st Class), Order of the White Elephant (Thailand), 2006; Chakrabarti Mala Medal (Thailand), 2009; Kt Grand Cordon (Special Class), Order of the Crown of Thailand, 2011; decorations from the Netherlands, Sweden, Brunei Darussalam and Denmark. *Recreations:* golf, reading. *Club:* Brocket Hall Golf.

TERESHKOVA, Valentina Vladimirovna; Russian cosmonaut; Chairman, Russian Association of International Co-operation, 1992–95; Head, Russian Centre for International Scientific and Cultural Co-operation, Russian Federation, 1994–2004; Deputy Chairman, Committee on International Affairs, State Duma, Russian Federation, since 2011; *b* Maslennikovo, 6 March 1937; *d* of late Vladimir Aksyonovich Tereshkov and of Elena Fyodorovna Tereshkova; *m*; one *d*. Formerly textile worker, Krasny Perekop mill, Yaroslavl; served on cttees; Sec. of local branch, Young Communist league, 1960; Member: CPSU, 1962–91; Central Cttee, CPSU, 1971–90; Deputy, 1966–90, Mem. of Presidium, 1970–90, USSR Supreme Soviet; Chairperson: Soviet Women's Cttee, 1968–87; Union of Soviet Societies for Friendship and Cultural Relns with Foreign Countries, 1987–92. Joined Yaroslavl Air Sports Club, 1959, and started parachute jumping; joined Cosmonaut Training Unit, 1962; became first woman in the world to enter space when she made 48 orbital flights of the earth in spaceship Vostok VI, 16–19 June 1963. Hero of the Soviet Union; Order of Lenin; Gold Star Medal; Order of October Revolution; Joliot-Curie Peace Medal; Nile Collar (Egypt), 1971; holds honours and citations from other countries. *Address:* 10 Granatny Pereulok, 123001 Moscow, Russia.

TERFEL, Bryn; *see* Jones, B. T.

ter HAAR, Rev. Roger Eduard Lound; QC 1992; a Recorder, and Deputy High Court Judge, since 2003; *b* 14 June 1952; *s* of late Dirk ter Haar and Christine Janet ter Haar; *m* 1977, Sarah Anne Martyn (marr. diss. 2012); two *s* one *d*; *m* 2014, Charlotte Mary Elizabeth Barney (*née* Raeburn). *Educ:* Felsted Sch.; Magdalen Coll., Oxford (BA 1973). Called to the Bar, Inner Temple, 1974, Bencher, 1992. Ordained deacon, 2006, priest, 2007; OLM, Bramley and Graffham, 2006–07; Asst Priest, Hascombe and Dunsfold, 2007–13. *Publications:* (ed jtly) Construction Insurance and UK Construction Contracts, 2nd edn, 2008; (jtly) Remedies in Construction Law, 2010. *Recreations:* gardening, reading. *Address:* Crown Office Chambers, 2 Crown Office Row, Temple, EC4Y 7HJ. *T:* (020) 7797 8100. *Clubs:* Brooks's, Garrick.

TERRACCIANO, Pasquale; Ambassador of Italy to the Court of St James's, since 2013; *b* Naples, 4 May 1956; *s* of late Silvio Terracciano and of Maria Terracciano (*née* Racana); *m* 1991, Karen Lawrence; two *s* one *d*. *Educ:* Univ. of Naples (law degree). Entered Italian Diplomatic Service, 1981; Second Sec., HR Directorate, Min. of Foreign Affairs, 1982–85; Consul, Rio de Janeiro, 1985–89; First Sec., later Counsellor, Perm. Repn of Italy to NATO, Brussels, 1989–93; Counsellor, Econ. Affairs Directorate, Min. of Foreign Affairs, 1993–95; Counsellor and Private Sec. to Foreign Minister, 1995–96; Counsellor, later First Counsellor, London and Alt. Exec. Dir for Italy, EBRD, 1996–2000; First Counsellor, Perm. Repn to Atlantic Council, Brussels, 2000–01; Dep. Hd of Cabinet to Foreign Minister, 2001–04; Hd, Inf. and Press Office, Min. of Foreign Affairs and spokesman for Foreign Minister, 2004–06; Ambassador to Madrid, also Andorra, 2006–10; Hd, Cabinet of Foreign Minister, 2010–11; Diplomatic Advr to Prime Minister and Prime Minister's G6 and G20 Sherpa Rep., 2011–13. Cavaliere: Gran Croce di Giustizia Sacro Militare Ordine Costantiniano di San Giorgio, 2007; Gran Croce dell'Ordine al Merito della Repubblica Italiana, 2013. Gran Cruz, Orden de Isabel la Católica (Spain), 2011. *Recreations:* going to the opera, classical music. *Address:* Italian Embassy, 14 Three Kings Yard, W1K 4EH. *T:* (020) 7312 2200, *Fax:* (020) 7312 2217. *E:* ambasciata.londra@esteri.it. *Clubs:* Athenæum, Travellers, Royal Automobile, Beefsteak.

TERRELL, Prof. (Richard) Deane, AO 2002; PhD; Vice-Chancellor, 1994–2000, now Emeritus Professor and Visiting Fellow, College of Business and Economics, Australian National University; *b* 22 April 1936; *s* of Norman Walter Terrell and Dorothy Ismay Terrell; *m* 1961, Jennifer Anne Kathleen, *d* of Leonard Spencer and Margaret Rose Doman; two *s* one *d*. *Educ:* St Peter's Coll., Adelaide; Adelaide Univ. (Joseph Fisher Medal, 1958; Rhodes Scholar, 1959; BEc Hons); Oxford Univ.; ANU (PhD). Teaching appts, Univ. of Adelaide and MIT, 1959–64; Australian National University: Lectr, 1964–70; Sen. Lectr, Stats, 1970; Prof. of Econometrics, 1971–89; Dean, Faculty of Econs and Commerce, 1975–77, 1982–89; Head, Dept of Stats, 1979–82, 1989–91; Chm., Bd of Faculties, 1989–92; Acting Dep. Vice-Chancellor, and Dep. Vice-Chancellor, 1991–93; Mem., Adv. Bd, Centre for Arab Islamic Studies, 2001–. Visiting Professor: Pennsylvania, 1969; Princeton and LSE, 1972–73. Chm., Bd of Mgt, AARNet Pty Ltd, 2002–11; Vice-Pres., IDP Educn Australia, 1995–2004. Chm. Bd, IELTS (Aust.) Pty Ltd, 2002–07; Bd Mem., Gen. Sir John Monash Foundn, 2002–13 (Mem., Awards Cttee, 2002–13; Chm., Investment Cttee, 2002–13). Chm. and Principal Dir, Canberra Sch. of Music Foundn, 2004–; Chm., Canberra Symphony Orch., 2008–13 (Dep. Chm., 2006–08). Mem. Adv. Bd, Aust. Defence Coll., 2004–09. *Publications:* numerous articles in professional jls. *Recreations:* farming and grape growing, football, cricket. *Address:* c/o School of Finance, Actuarial Studies and Applied Statistics, Australian National University College of Business and Economics, CBE Building 26C, Kingsley Street, Canberra, ACT 0200, Australia. *Club:* Commonwealth (Canberra).

TERRINGTON, 6th Baron *cr* 1918, of Huddersfield, co. York; **Christopher Richard James Woodhouse,** FRCS; Professor of Adolescent Urology, University College London, 2005–11, now Emeritus; Consultant Urologist, Royal Marsden Hospital, 1981–2014; *b* 20 Sept. 1946; *s* of 5th Baron Terrington, DSO, OBE and Lady Davina Woodhouse (*née* Lytton), *widow* of 5th Earl of Erne; *S* father, 2001; *m* 1975, Hon. Anna Philipps, *d* of 3rd Baron Milford; one *s* one *d*. *Educ:* Winchester; Guy's Hosp. Med. Sch. (MB, BS 1970). FRCS 1975. Sen. Registrar in Urology, Inst. of Urology and St Peter's Hosps, 1977–81; Sen. Lectr in Urology, Inst. of Urology, 1981–97; Reader in Adolescent Urology, UCL, 1997–2005. Consultant Urologist, St George's Hosp., 1985–95; Clin. Dir of Urology, UCL Hosps, 2001–03. Hon. Consultant Urologist: Inst. of Urology, University Coll. London Hosps (formerly St Peter's Hosps), 1981–2012; Hosp. for Children, Great Ormond Street, 1981–2012. Vis. Professorships in Europe, USA and Australasia. Fellow, European Bd of Urology, 1993. Pres., Soc. of Genito-Urinary Reconstructive Surgeons, USA, 2002–03. Corresp. Member: German Assoc. of Urology, 2004; American Assoc. of Genito-Urinary Surgeons, 2005; Special Internat. Mem., Amer. Urological Assoc., 2012; Hon. Mem., Urological Soc. of Australia and NZ (formerly Australasian Urological Assoc.), 1999. *Publications:* (with F. D. Thompson) Physiological Basis of Medicine: disorders of the kidney and urinary tract, 1987; Long Term Paediatric Urology, 1991; (jtly) Management of Urological Emergencies, 2004; Adolescent Urology and Long Term Outcomes, 2015; contrib. to learned jls. *Recreations:* gardening, walking. *Heir:* *s* Hon. Jack Henry Lehmann Woodhouse, *b* 7 Dec. 1978. *Address:* Chelsea Urology, Lister House, Chelsea Bridge Road, SW1W 8RH. *T:* (020) 3701 7025. *E:* c.terrington@btinternet.com. *Club:* Leander (Henley-on-Thames).

See also Earl of Erne, Hon. N. M. J. Woodhouse.

TERRY, Air Marshal Sir Colin George, KBE 1998 (OBE 1983); CB 1995; DL; CEng, FREng; FRAeS; FCGI; FCILT; FIC; aerospace consultant; Chairman, Meggitt plc, 2004–15; *b* 8 Aug. 1943; *e s* of late George Albert Terry and Edna Joan Terry (*née* Purslow); *m* 1966, Gillian, *d* of late Conrad Glendor Grindley and Muriel Grace Grindley (*née* Duffield); two *s* one *d*. *Educ:* Bridgnorth Grammar Sch.; RAF Coll.; Imperial Coll., London (BScEng (Hons) 1965; FIC 2005). CEng; FRAeS 1986; FCGI 1997; FREng 2001. Commnd, Engr Br., RAF, 1962; served Abingdon, RAF Coll., Church Fenton, Leeming, Oakington, Finningley, RNAY Belfast, Laarbruch, Wildenrath, HQ Strike Comd; Student, RAF Coll., 1979; OC Eng Wing, RAF Coltishall, 1979–82; Eng Authy Staff, HQ Strike Comd, 1982–84; OC Eng Wing, RAF Stanley, 1982–83; Dep. Comd Engr, HQ Strike Comd, 1985–86; Station Comdr, RAF Abingdon, 1986–88; RCDS 1989; Dir, Support Management and Sen. Dir, MoD Harrogate, 1990–92; Dir Gen., Support Management, RAF, 1993–95; COS and Dep. C-in-C, Logistics Comd, RAF, 1995–97; AOC-in-C, Logistics Comd and Air Mem. for Logistics, RAF, 1997–99; Chief Engr (RAF), 1996–99. Chm., Safety Advisory Cttee, Military Aviation Authy, MoD, 2011–. Gp Man. Dir, Inflite Engrg Services Ltd, 1999–2001; Adv. Bd, Kingfisher Airlines, Mumbai, 2006–10; non-exec. Chm., Avia Media Tech Ltd, 2013–; non-exec. Director: Fox Marble Plc, 2011–; Aveillant Ltd, 2014–. Advr to Bd, Horton Internat., 2010–12. Chm., Engineering Council, 2002–06 (Mem. of Senate, 1999–2002); President: RAeS, 2005–06 (Mem. Council, 1999–2007; Chm., Learned Soc. Bd, 2003–06); Council of European Aerospace Socs, 2006–07; Member: ETB, 2002–06; Queen's Awards for Enterprise Cttee, 2002–06. FRSA; FILog. Commodore, RAF Sailing Assoc., 1994–99; Pres., Assoc. of Service Yacht Clubs, 1997–99; Flying Officer, RAFVR(T), 1999–2008. Pres., SSAFA Bucks, 2006–. Member, Council: CGLI, 2004–08; Cranfield Univ., 2005–08 (Mem. Court, 1997–); Pres., C & G Coll. Assoc., 2003–04. Freeman, City of London, 2004. DL Bucks, 2005. *Recreations:* sailing, flying, ski-ing, modern languages, music, field sports. *Address:* c/o Royal Air Force Club, 128 Piccadilly, W1J 7PY. *Club:* Royal Air Force.

TERRY, Ian Keith; Partner, Freshfields Bruckhaus Deringer (formerly Freshfields), since 1986; *b* 26 July 1955; *s* of late Keith Harold Terry and Shirley Margaret Terry; *m* 1993, Dr Elizabeth Ann Fischl; one *d*. *Educ:* Leeds Grammar Sch.; Keble Coll., Oxford (MA, BCL). Freshfields: trainee solicitor, 1978–80; admitted solicitor, 1980; Partner (Commercial Litigation), 1986–96; Managing Partner, worldwide, 1996–2001; Practice Gp Leader, Dispute Resolution, 2006–09. *Recreations:* shooting, ski-ing, theatre, opera. *Address:* (office) 65 Fleet Street, EC4Y 1HS. *T:* (020) 7936 4000.

TERRY, John George; professional footballer; Captain, Chelsea Football Club, since 2004; *b* Barking, 7 Dec. 1980; *s* of Ted and Sue Terry; *m* 2007, Toni Poole; one *s* one *d* (twins). Chelsea Football Club: mem., Youth Team, 1995–98, First Team, 1998–99 and 2000–; member, winning team: FA Cup, 2000, 2007, 2009, 2010, 2012; Premier League, 2005, 2006, 2010; League Cup, 2005, 2007; UEFA Champions League, 2012; UEFA Europa League, 2013; team mem., Nottingham Forest FC, 1999–2000; Capt., England Under 21s, 2001–02; team mem., England, 2003–12 (Captain, 2007–10 and 2011–12); Mem., England squad, Eur. Championships, 2004, 2012, World Cup, 2006, 2010. Player of Year, PFA, 2005. *Publications:* John Terry: my winning season, 2005. *Address:* c/o Chelsea Football Club, Stamford Bridge, Fulham Road, SW6 1HS.

TERRY, (John) Quinlan, CBE 2015; FRIBA 1962; architect in private practice, since 1967; *b* 24 July 1937; *s* of Philip and Phyllis Terry; *m* 1961, Christine de Ruttié; one *s* four *d*. *Educ:* Bryanston School; Architectural Association; Rome Scholar. Assistant to Raymond Erith, RA, FRIBA, 1962, Partner 1967–, Erith & Terry, subseq. Quinlan & Francis Terry; work includes: new Infirmary, Royal Hospital Chelsea; offices, shops and flats at Richmond Riverside; 20–32 Baker Street; 264–7 Tottenham Court Road; new retail bldgs in historic centre of Colonial Williamsburg, Va; six classical Villas in Regent's Park for Crown Estate Comrs; new Library, Lecture Theatre, and Residential Bldg, Downing Coll., Cambridge; new Brentwood Cathedral; restoration of the three State Drawing Rooms, 10 Downing Street; restoration of St Helen's, Bishopsgate, and Castletown Cox, Co. Kilkenny; Queen Mother Sq., Poundbury for Duchy of Cornwall. Mem., Royal Fine Art Commn, 1994–97. *Publications:* Architects Anonymous, 1994; Radical Classicism, 2006; The Practice of Classical Architecture, 2015. *Recreation:* the Pauline epistles. *Address:* Old Exchange, High Street, Dedham, Colchester, Essex CO7 6HA. *T:* (01206) 323186.

TERRY, Sir Michael Edward Stanley I.; *see* Imbert-Terry.

TERRY, Air Chief Marshal Sir Peter (David George), GCB 1983 (KCB 1978; CB 1975); AFC 1968; QCVSA 1959 and 1962; *b* 18 Oct. 1926; *s* of James George Terry and Laura Chilton Terry (*née* Powell); *m* 1946, Betty Martha Louisa Thompson; one *s* one *d* (and one *s* decd). *Educ:* Chatham House Sch., Ramsgate. Joined RAF, 1945; commnd in RAF Regt, 1946; Pilot, 1953. Staff Coll., 1962; OC, No 51 Sqdn, 1966–68; OC, RAF El Adem, 1968–70; Dir, Air Staff Briefing, MoD, 1970–71; Dir of Forward Policy for RAF, 1971–74; ACOS (Policy and Plans), SHAPE, 1975–77; VCAS, 1977–79; C-in-C RAF Germany and Comdr Second Allied Tactical Air Force, 1979–81; Dep. C-in-C, Allied Forces Central Europe, Feb.–April 1981; Dep. Supreme Allied Commander, Europe, 1981–84; Governor and C-in-C, Gibraltar, 1985–89. Vice-Pres., Re-Solv, 1985–. KStJ 1986. *Recreation:* golf. *Club:* Royal Air Force.

TERRY, Quinlan; *see* Terry, J. Q.

TERZOPOULOS, Prof. Demetri, PhD; FRS 2014; FRSC; Distinguished Professor, since 2012, and Chancellor's Professor of Computer Science, since 2005, University of California, Los Angeles. *Educ:* McGill Univ. (BEng Hons 1978; MEng 1980); Massachusetts Inst. of Technol. (PhD 1984). Res. Scientist, Artificial Intelligence Lab., MIT, 1984–85; Prog. Leader, Schlumberger Res., Palo Alto, 1985–89; University of Toronto: Associate Prof. of Computer Sci. and Associate Prof. of Electrical and Computer Engrg, 1989–95; Prof. of Computer Sci. and Prof. of Electrical and Computer Engrg, 1995–2005; Lucy and Henry Moses Prof. of Sci., and Prof. of Computer Sci. and Maths, Courant Inst., New York Univ., 2000–05. Consultant to: Hughes Aircraft Co.; Schlumberger Lab. for Computer Sci.; Ont. Hydro; Digital Equipment Corp.; NEC Res. Inst.; Intel Corp.; Almaden Res. Center, IBM; Honda R&D Americas. AI and Robotics Fellow, Canadian Inst. for Advanced Res., 1989–95; E. W. R. Steacie Meml Fellow, NSERC, 1996–98; Killam Res. Fellow, Canada Council for Arts, 1998–2000; Guggenheim Fellow, 2009–10; Okawa Fellow, 2011–12. FIEEE 2001; Mem., Eur. Acad. of Scis, 2002; FRSC 2006; Fellow, Assoc. for Computer Machinery, 2008. Gov. Gen.'s Academic Medal, 1973; Internat. Digital Media Award, 1994; Computer Animation Hon. Award, Prix Ars Electronica, 1995; Investigator Award, Canadian Image Processing and Pattern Recognition Soc., 1998; Tech. Achievement Award, Acad. of Motion Picture Arts and Scis, 2005; Computer Vision Dist. Researcher Award, IEEE, 2007; (jtly) Helmholtz Prize, IEEE Computer Soc., 2013. Founder Mem. of Editl Bds of eight sci. jls. *Publications:* (ed jtly) Real-Time Computer Vision, 1994; (ed jtly) Computer Animation and Simulation, 1995; (ed jtly) Deformable Models in Medical Image Analysis, 1998; (ed jtly) Distributed Video Sensor Networks, 2011; articles in sci. jls. *Address:* UCLA Computer Science Department, Boelter Hall, Los Angeles, CA 90095, USA. *W:* www.terzopoulos.com.

TESLER, Brian, CBE 1986; Deputy Chairman, LWT (Holdings) plc, 1990–94; Chairman: London Weekend Television Ltd, 1984–92 (Managing Director, 1976–90; Deputy Chairman, 1982–84; Deputy Chief Executive, 1974–76); The London Studios Ltd (formerly LWT Production Facilities Ltd), 1989–92; LWT International Ltd, 1990–92; LWT Programmes Ltd, 1990–92; *b* 19 Feb. 1929; *s* of late David Tesler and of Stella Tesler; *m* 1959, Audrey Mary Maclean; one *s*. *Educ:* Chiswick County School for Boys; Exeter Coll., Oxford (State Schol.; MA). Theatre Editor, The Isis, 1950–51; Pres., Oxford Univ. Experimental Theatre Club, 1951–52. British Forces Broadcasting Service, 1947–49; Producer/Director: BBC Television, 1952; ATV, 1957; ABC Television: Head of Features and Light Entertainment, 1960; Programme Controller, 1961; Dir of Programmes, 1962; Dir of Programmes, Thames Television, 1968. Chairman: ITV Superchannel Ltd, 1986–88; ITCA, 1980–82; Ind. TV Network Prog. Cttee, 1976–78, 1986–88; LWT Programme Adv. Bd, 1990–92; ITCA Cable and Satellite Television Wkg Party, 1981–88; ITV Film Purchase Cttee, 1989–90; The Magazine Business Ltd, 1992–96. Director: ITN Ltd, 1979–90; Channel Four Television Ltd, 1980–85; Oracle Teletext Ltd, 1980–92; Services Sound and Vision Corp. (formerly Services Kinema Corp.), 1981–2004. Chm., Lord Chancellor's Adv. Cttee on JPs, 1993–96 (Mem., 1991–96); Lay Interviewer for Judicial Appts, 1994–99; Ind. Assessor, OCPA, 2001–10. Member: British Screen Adv. Council, 1985–94 (Wkg Party on Future of British Film Industry, 1975–77; Interim Action Cttee on Film Industry, 1977–85); TRIC, 1979– (Pres., 1979–80; Companion, 1986); Vice-Pres., RTS, 1984–94 (FRTS 1992). Governor: Nat. Film and TV Sch. (formerly Nat. Film Sch.), 1977–95; BFI, 1986–95 (Dep. Chm., 1993–95). Daily Mail Nat. TV Award, 1954; Guild of Television Producers and Directors Award, 1957; Lord Willis Trophy for Outstanding Services to Television, Pye Television Award, 1986; Presidential Award, TRIC, 1991. *Recreations:* books, theatre, cinema, music.

TESORIÈRE, (Harcourt) Andrew (Pretorius), FRGS; HM Diplomatic Service; Deputy Head, European Union Border Assistance Mission to Moldova and Ukraine, since 2014; *b* 2 Nov. 1950; *s* of Pieter Ivan Tesorière and Joyce Margaret Tesorière (*née* Baxter); *m* 1987, Dr Alma Gloria Vasquez. *Educ:* Nautical Coll., Pangbourne; Britannia Royal Naval Coll., Dartmouth; University Coll. of Wales, Aberystwyth (BScEcon Hons); Ecole Nat. d'Admin, Paris. RNR, 1964–68; RN Officer, 1969–73; joined FCO, 1974; Persian lang. student, SOAS and Iran, 1975–76; Oriental Sec., Kabul, 1976–79; Third Sec., Nairobi, 1980–81; Second Sec., Abidjan (also accredited to Ouagadougou and Niamey), 1981–84; First Sec. and Hd of Chancery, later Chargé d'Affaires, Damascus, 1987–91; Hd, Field Ops, UN Office for Co-ordination of Humanitarian Assistance to Afghanistan, Afghanistan, 1994–95; Ambassador to Albania, 1996–98; Actg Hd of Mission and Sen. Pol Advr, UN Special Mission to

Afghanistan, 1998–2000 (on secondment); Chargé d'Affaires *ai*, Kabul, 2001–02; Ambassador to Latvia, 2002–05; Ambassador to Algeria, 2005–07; Sen. Policy Advr to Internat. Security Assistance Force Comdr S, Afghanistan, 2007–08; OSCE Ambassador to Kyrgyzstan, 2008–12; FCO, 2012–14. Chm., Bd of Trustees, OSCE Acad., Bishkek, Kyrgyzstan, 2008–. FRGS 1993. NATO Medal, ISAF, 2007; HM Operational Service Medal, Afghanistan, 2008; Sherektesh (Concord) Medal, Kyrgyz Republic, 2008. *Recreations:* travel, sport, foreign languages, art, countryside. *Address:* c/o Foreign and Commonwealth Office, King Charles Street, SW1A 2AH.

TESSIER-LAVIGNE, Dr Marc, FMedSci; FRS 2001; FRSC; President, and Carson Family Professor, Laboratory of Brain Development and Repair, Rockefeller University, since 2011; *b* 18 Dec. 1959; *s* of Sheila and Jacques Tessier-Lavigne; *m* 1989, Mary Alanna Hynes; two *s* one *d*. *Educ:* McGill Univ., Montreal (BSc 1st Cl. Hons Physics 1980); New Coll., Oxford (BA 1st Cl. Hons Phil. and Physiol., 1982; Hon. Fellow 2011); University Coll. London (PhD 1987; Schaffer Prize). FRSC 1999. University of California, San Francisco: Asst Prof., Dept of Anatomy, 1991–95; Associate Prof., 1995–97; Prof., Depts of Anatomy and Biochem. and Biophysics, 1997–2001; Asst Investigator, 1994–97, Investigator, 1997–2003, Howard Hughes Med. Inst.; Prof. of Biol Scis and Susan B. Ford Prof., Sch. of Humanities and Scis, Stanford Univ., 2001–03; Genentech Inc.: Sen. Vice-Pres., 2003–08; Exec. Vice-Pres., Research Drug Discovery, 2008–09; Exec. Vice-Pres., Research, and Chief Scientific Officer, 2009–11. Member: NAS, USA, 2005; Inst. of Medicine, NAS, USA, 2011. FAAAS 2001; FMedSci 2004. Hon. Dr Medicine and Surgery, Pavia, Italy, 2006; Hon. DSc McGill, 2011. McKnight Investigator Award, 1994; Charles Judson Herrick Award in Comparative Neurol., Amer. Assoc. Anatomists, 1995; Ameritec Foundn Prize, 1995; (jtly) Fondation IPSEN Prize for Neuronal Plasticity, 1996; Viktor Hamburger Award, Internat. Soc. for Develtl Neurosci., 1997; Young Investigator Award, Soc. for Neurosci., USA, 1997; (jtly) Wakeman Foundn Award for contribs in field of neuronal regeneration, 1998; Robert Dow Neurosci. Award, Oregon Health Sci. Univ., 2003; Reeve-Irvine Res. Medal, Univ. of Calif, Irvine, 2007; Ferrier Prize Lect., Royal Soc., 2007; Gill Dist. Award, Univ. of Indiana, Bloomington, 2010; (jtly) Alden Spencer Award, Columbia Univ., 2010; Meml Sloan-Kettering Medal for outstanding contribs to biomed. res., Meml Sloan-Kettering Cancer Center, 2011; W. Maxwell Cowan Award for outstanding achievement in develtl neurosci., Cajal Club, 2011; Henry G. Friesen Internat. Prize in Health Res., Canadian Acad. Health Scis and Friends of Canadian Insts Health Res., 2012. *Publications:* contribs in physiol. and develtl neurobiol. to scientific jls. *Recreations:* family, history. *Address:* Rockefeller University, 1230 York Avenue, New York, NY 10065, USA.

TESTINO, Mario, Hon. OBE 2013; fashion photographer; *b* Lima, 1954. *Educ:* American Sch. of Lima; Univ. del Pacífico; Pontificia Univ. Católica del Perú; Univ. of San Diego, Calif. Photograph subjects include Naomi Campbell, Diana, Princess of Wales, Cameron Diaz, Elizabeth Hurley, Janet Jackson, Keira Knightley, Madonna, Kate Moss, Gwyneth Paltrow, Julia Roberts, Catherine Zeta-Jones, Prince Harry, Prince Charles and Duchess of Cornwall. Exhibitions include: NPG, 2002; Kensington Palace, 2005. *Publications:* Any Objections?, 1998; Front Row/Backstage, 1999; Alive, 2001; Portraits, 2002; Kids, 2003; Let Me In, 2007; (ed) Lima Peru, 2007; Kate Moss, 2011. *Address:* c/o Art Partner, 1 Dekalb Avenue, 4th Floor, Brooklyn, NY 11201, USA.

TETLEY, Air Vice-Marshal John Francis Humphrey, CB 1987; CVO 1978; *b* 5 Feb. 1932; *s* of Humphrey and Evelyn Tetley; *m* 1960, Elizabeth, *d* of Wing Comdr Arthur Stevens; two *s*. *Educ:* Malvern College. RAF Coll., Cranwell, 1950–53; served No 249 Sqn, No 204 Sqn and HQ Coastal Command, 1955–64; RAF Staff Coll., 1964; HQ Middle East Command, 1965–67; OC No 24 Sqn, 1968–70; JSSC 1970; MoD (Air), 1971–72; RAF Germany, 1973–75; Dir Air Staff Briefing, MoD (Air), 1975–76; Silver Jubilee Project Officer, 1977; RCDS, 1978; SASO HQ 38 Group, 1979–82; Dir of Ops (Air Support), RAF, 1982–83; AO Scotland and NI, 1983–86; Sen. Directing Staff (Air), RCDS, 1986–87; retired 1987. Mem. Exec. Cttee, RNLI, 1993–2002 (Vice-Pres., 1996; Dep. Chm., 2000–02). *Recreations:* gardening, photography, boating. *Club:* Royal Air Force.

TETLEY, Ven. Joy Dawn, PhD; Archdeacon of Worcester and Canon Residentiary of Worcester Cathedral, 1999–2008; Area Director of Ordinands, Diocese of Oxford, 2009–10 and 2012–13; *b* 9 Nov. 1946; *d* of Frederick and Mary Payne; *m* 1980, Rev. Brian Tetley, BA, FCA. *Educ:* Durham Univ. (BA 1968; PhD 1988); Leeds Univ. (CertEd 1969); St Hugh's Coll., Oxford (BA 1975; MA 1980); NW Ordination Course. Ordained deaconess 1977, deacon 1987, priest 1994; Deaconess: Bentley, 1977–79; St Aidan, Buttershaw, 1979–80; Durham Cathedral, 1980–83; Lectr, Trinity Coll., Bristol, and Deaconess, Chipping Sodbury and Old Sodbury, 1983–86; Deacon, 1987–89, Hon. Canon, 1990–93 (Canon Emeritus, 1993–), Rochester Cathedral, and Dio. Dir, Post-Ordination Trng, 1988–93; Principal, E Anglian Ministerial Trng Course, 1993–99; Actg Chaplain, Wadham Coll., Oxford, 2010. Lay Assessor, NHS, 2009–13. Columnist, Church Times, 1993–95. FRSA 2006. *Publications:* Encounter with God in Hebrews, 1995; Sunday by Sunday, 1995; A Way into Hebrews, 1998; Jonah, 2003; (jtly) Renewing the Eucharist, vol. 2: word, 2009; (contrib.) Apostolic Women, Apostolic Authority, 2010; (contrib.) Facing the Issues, 2012; (contrib.) Sermons on Difficult Subjects, 2013; (contrib.) Faith Matters, 2013; (contrib.) And With All Your Mind, 2015; God Speaking, 2015. *Address:* 23 Cripley Road, Oxford OX2 0AH. *T:* (01865) 250209. *E:* briantetley@btinternet.com. *Club:* National Liberal.

TETLOW, Bernard Geoffrey; QC 2011; *b* London, 31 July 1957; *s* of Brian and Agnes Tetlow; *m* 1991, Claire Hanika (marr. diss. 2008); two *s*. *Educ:* Thornleigh Salesian Coll.; S Bank Poly. (BA Hons Law); Hughes Hall, Cambridge (LLM 1983). Called to the Bar, Middle Temple, 1984; Lead Counsel, Lebanon Tribunal, 2010–. Legal Advr to Elgin and Arundel Garden Cttee, 2008–. *Recreations:* cricket, football, tennis, ski-ing, walking, reading, theatre, poker. *Address:* Garden Court Chambers, 57–60 Lincoln's Inn Fields, WC2A 3LJ. *E:* b_tetlow@hotmail.com. *Clubs:* Drones; Bolton Wanderers, South Bank Cricket, Holland Park Lawn Tennis.

TETLOW, His Honour Christopher Bruce; a Circuit Judge, 1992–2010; *b* 27 Feb. 1943; *s* of George Wilfred Tetlow and Betty Tetlow; *m* 1981, Rosalind Jane Cope; two *s* one *d*. *Educ:* Stowe Sch.; Magdalene Coll., Cambridge (MA). Called to the Bar, Middle Temple, 1969. *Clubs:* St James's (Manchester); Manchester Tennis and Racquet.

TETT, Gillian Romaine; US Managing Editor, Financial Times, 2010–12 and since 2014; *b* 10 July 1967. *Educ:* Clare Coll., Cambridge (BA 1989; PhD Social Anthropol.). Financial Times, 1993–: Bureau Chief, Tokyo, 1997–2003; Dep. Hd, Lex Column, 2003; Asst Ed., 2012–14. Mem., Amer. Anthropological Assoc. Sen. Financial Journalist of Year, Wincott Awards, 2007; Business Journalist of Year, 2008, Journalist of Year, 2009, BPA; President's Medal, British Acad., 2011; Columnist of Year, Press Awards, 2014; Marsh Award for Anthropol. in World, RAI, 2014. *Publications:* Saving the Sun: a Wall Street gamble to rescue Japan from its trillion dollar meltdown, 2003; Fool's Gold: how unrestrained greed corrupted a dream, shattered global markets and unleashed a catastrophe, 2009; The Silo Effect: ordered chaos, the peril of expertise, and the power of breaking down barriers, 2015. *Address:* Financial Times, 330 Hudson Street, 8th Floor, New York, NY 10013, USA. *T:* (212) 6416503. *E:* Gillian.Tett@ft.com. *Club:* Overseas Press (New York).

TETTAMANZI, His Eminence Cardinal Dionigi; Archbishop of Milan, (RC), 2002–11; Administrator, Diocese of Vigevano, Lombardy, since 2012; *b* 14 March 1934. Ordained priest, 1957; Bishop of Ancona-Osimo, 1989–91; Gen. Sec., Italian Episcopal Conf., 1991–95; Archbishop of Genoa, 1995–2002; apptd Cardinal, 1998; Cardinal-Priest, SS Ambrose and Charles, 1998.

TEULINGS, Prof. Coenraad Nicolaas, (Coen), PhD; Montague Burton Professor of Industrial Relations and Labour Economics, University of Cambridge, since 2013; *b* Rijswijk, 13 Dec. 1958; *m* 1988, Salomé Bentinck; one *s* one *d*. *Educ:* Gymnasium β, Fons Vitae, Amsterdam; Univ. of Amsterdam (Master Econs cum laude 1985; PhD 1990). Jun., later Sen. Researcher, SEO Economic Res., 1985–91; Res. Fellow, Royal Dutch Acad. of Arts and Scis, 1991–95; Hd, Dept of Income Policy, Min. of Social Affairs, 1995–98; Prof. of Labour Econs, Univ. of Amsterdam, 1997–98; Dir, Tinbergen Inst., 1998–2004; Prof. of Labour Econs, Erasmus Univ., Rotterdam, 1998–2004; CEO, SEO Economic Res., 2004–06; Pres., CPB Netherlands Bureau for Econ. Policy Analysis, 2006–13. Pt-time Prof., Univ. of Amsterdam, 2004–. Fellow, Tinbergen Inst., 1996; Member: CEPR, London; CES-IFO, Munich; IZA, Bonn. *Recreations:* sailing, cooking. *Address:* Faculty of Economics, University of Cambridge, Sidgwick Avenue, Cambridge CB3 9DD. *T:* (01223) 335203. *E:* cnt23@cam.ac.uk.

TEVERSON, family name of **Baron Teverson**.

TEVERSON, Baron *cr* 2006 (Life Peer), of Tregony, in the County of Cornwall; **Robin Teverson;** *b* 31 March 1952; *s* of Dr Crofton Teverson and Joan Teverson; *m* 1st, 1975, Rosemary Anne Young (marr. diss. 2005); two *d*; *m* 2nd, 2006, Terrye Lynn Jones. *Educ:* Exeter Univ. (BA Hons Econs). Managing Director: SPD Ltd and Dir, Exel Logistics, 1987–89; Supply Chain Consultancy (Rationale Ltd), 1989–94; Chm., Finance SW Ltd, 1999–2002; Chief Exec., Finance Cornwall, 2002–06. MEP (Lib Dem) Cornwall and West Plymouth, 1994–99; contested (Lib Dem) SW Reg., 1999. Chair: H of L EU Select Cttee on Foreign Affairs, Defence and Develt, 2008–12; H of L Select Cttee on Arctic, 2014–15; Lib Dem spokesman on Energy and Climate Change, H of L, 2009–. *Recreations:* history, riding, astronomy, travel, music. *Address:* House of Lords, SW1A 0PW.

TEVERSON, Paul Richard; Master of the Senior (formerly Supreme) Court, Chancery Division, since 2005; *b* 1 May 1953; *s* of late George Eric Teverson and Ailsa Betty Teverson (*née* Moor); *m* 1978, Hon. Joanna Rosamund Georgina, *d* of Baron Gore-Booth, GCMG, KCVO; two *s* one *d*. *Educ:* St Paul's Sch., London (Sen. Schol.); Corpus Christi Coll., Cambridge (Exhibnr; BA 1975). Called to the Bar, Inner Temple, 1976; in practice at Chancery Bar, 1978–2005. Dep. Chancery Master, 2000–05. *Publications:* (contrib.) The White Book, 2008–. *Recreations:* reading, cycling (Mem., Barnes Bikers), theatre, opera. *Address:* Rolls Building, 110 Fetter Lane, EC4A 1BR. *Club:* Hurlingham.

TEVIOT, 2nd Baron *cr* 1940, of Burghclere; **Charles John Kerr;** genealogist; *b* 16 Dec. 1934; *s* of 1st Baron Teviot, DSO, MC, and Florence Angela (*d* 1979), *d* of late Lt-Col Charles Walter Villiers, CBE, DSO; *S* father, 1968; *m* 1965, Patricia Mary Harris; one *s* one *d*. *Educ:* Eton. Bus Conductor and Driver; genealogical and historical record agent. Director: Debrett's Peerage Ltd, 1977–83; Burke's Peerage Research, 1983–85; Burke's Peerage Ltd, 1984–85. Mem., Adv. Council on Public Records, 1974–83. Pres., Assoc. of Genealogists and Record Agents, 1997–2011. Fellow, Soc. of Genealogists, 1975. *Recreations:* reading, walking. *Heir: s* Hon. Charles Robert Kerr [*b* 19 Sept. 1971; *m* 1st, 2000, Yamaleth Molina Guillen (marr. diss.); one *d* (and one *d* decd); 2nd, 2012, Fiona, *d* of David Parry-Jones; one *d*]. *Address:* 28 Hazel Grove, Burgess Hill, West Sussex RH15 0BY. *T:* (01444) 242605.

TEWKESBURY, Bishop Suffragan of, since 2013; **Rt Rev. Martyn James Snow;** *b* 1968. *Educ:* Sheffield Univ. (BSc 1989); Wycliffe Hall, Oxford (BTh 1995). Ordained deacon 1995, priest 1996; Asst Curate, St Andrew's, Brinsworth with Catcliffe and Treeton, 1995–97; with CMS, Guinea, 1998–2001; Vicar, Christ Ch, Pitsmoor, Sheffield, 2001–10; Priest-in-charge, St Mathias', Stockbridge, 2007–08; Area Dean, Ecclesfield, 2007–10; Archdeacon of Sheffield and Rotherham, 2010–13. *Address:* The Bishop's House, Church Road, Staverton, Cheltenham GL51 0TW.

TEWSON, Jane, (Mrs C. Lane), CBE 1999; Founder and Director, Igniting Change (formerly Pilotlight Australia), since 2000; *b* 9 Jan. 1958; *d* of Dr Tim Tewson, Oxford, and Dr Blue Tewson (*née* Johnston); *m* 1992, Dr Charles Lane; two *s*. *Educ:* Headington Sch., Oxford; Lord Williams' Sch., Thame. Project Co-ordinator, MENCAP, 1979–83; Founder: and Chief Exec., Charity Projects and Comic Relief, 1984–96; Pilotlight UK, 1996–99; TimeBank, 1999. Trustee: Media Trust, 1996–99; Oxfam, 1996–99; Camelot Foundn, 1997–2000; Diana, Princess of Wales Meml Cttee, 1997–2000; St James Ethics Centre, 2000–; Reichstein Foundn, 2000–; Virgin Unite, 2005–. *Publications:* Dying to Know: bringing death to life, 2010 (Australian edn 2008). *Recreations:* travel, walking, gardening. *Address:* 35 Cressy Street, Malvern, Melbourne, Vic 3144, Australia.

TEYNHAM, 20th Baron *cr* 1616; **John Christopher Ingham Roper-Curzon;** *b* 25 Dec. 1928; *s* of 19th Baron Teynham, DSO, DSC, and Elspeth Grace (who *m* 2nd, 1958, 6th Marquess of Northampton, DSO, and *d* 1976), *e d* of late William Ingham Whitaker; *S* father, 1972; *m* 1964, Elizabeth, *yr d* of Lt-Col the Hon. David Scrymgeour-Wedderburn, DSO, Scots Guards (killed on active service 1944), and of Patricia, Countess of Dundee; five *s* five *d* (of whom one *s* one *d* are twins). *Educ:* Eton. A Land Agent. Late Captain, The Buffs (TA), formerly Coldstream Guards; active service in Palestine, 1948. ADC to Governor of Bermuda, 1953 and 1955; ADC to Governor of Leeward Islands, 1955; Private Secretary and ADC, 1956; ADC to Governor of Jamaica, 1962. Pres., Inst. of Commerce, 1972–; Vice Pres., Inst. of Export. Member of Council, Sail Training Association, 1964–69. OStJ. Lord of the Manors of South Baddesley and Sharpricks. *Recreations:* shooting, fishing. *Heir: s* Hon. David John Henry Ingham Roper-Curzon [*b* 5 Oct. 1965; *m* 1st, 1985, Lydia Lucinda (marr. diss. 2003), *d* of Maj.-Gen. Sir Christopher Airy, *qv*; two *s* one *d*; 2nd, 2003, Melanie Hayward; one *s* one *d* (twins)]. *Address:* Pylewell Park, Lymington, Hants SO41 5SJ. *Clubs:* Turf; House of Lords Yacht; Ocean Cruising; Puffin's (Edinburgh).

THACKER, Prof. David Thomas; theatre, film and television director; Associate Artistic Director, Octagon Theatre, Bolton, since 2015 (Artistic Director, 2009–15); Professor of Theatre, University of Bolton, since 2015; *b* 21 Dec. 1950; *s* of Thomas Richard Thacker and Alice May (*née* Beaumont); *m* 1983, Margot Elizabeth Leicester; three *s* one *d*. *Educ:* Wellingborough Grammar Sch.; Univ. of York (BA English and Related Lit.; MA Shakespeare). Theatre Royal, York: Asst Stage Manager, Dep. Stage Manager and Stage Manager, 1974–75; Asst Dir, 1975–76; Gateway Theatre, Chester: Arts Council Asst Dir, 1975–76; Associate Dir, 1977–78; Duke's Playhouse, Lancaster: Arts Council Associate Dir, 1978–79; Dir, 1980–84; Dir, Young Vic Theatre, 1984–93; Dir-in-Residence, RSC, 1993–95. Vis. Prof. of Dramatic Arts, Univ. of Bolton, 2009–15. *Theatre productions:* over 100 including: Young Vic: Ghosts, 1987; Who's Afraid of Virginia Woolf?, 1987; A Touch of the Poet, An Enemy of the People, 1989; The Winter's Tale, 1991; The Last Yankee, 1993; RSC: Pericles (Dir of the Year and Best Revival, Laurence Olivier Awards, 1991), The Two Gentlemen of Verona, 1991; As You Like It, 1992; The Merchant of Venice, 1993; Julius Caesar, Coriolanus, 1995; Bingo, The Tempest, 1995; Broken Glass, RNT, 1994, transf. Duke of York's, 1995; A View from the Bridge, Bristol Old Vic, 1994, transf. Strand, 1995; Death of a Salesman, RNT, 1996; The Price, Scarborough, 2011; Octagon: All My Sons, 2009; A Midsummer Night's Dream, Comedians, The Hired Man, A Streetcar Named Desire, Love on the Dole, 2010; Romeo and Juliet, The Price, Who's Afraid of Virginia Woolf?, Habeas Corpus, 2011; Alfie, The Winslow Boy, Lighthearted Intercourse, 2012; Of Mice and Men, Tull, The Glass Menagerie, An Inspector Calls, Long Day's Journey Into Night, 2013; Hobson's Choice, Twelfth Night, Journey's End, Early One Morning, 2014; A View from the Bridge, Hindle Wakes, The Ancient Secret of Youth and the Five Tibetans,

Noises Off, 2015. *Television:* over 30 productions including: A Doll's House, 1992; Measure for Measure, 1994; Death of a Salesman, 1996; Broken Glass; The Scold's Bridle, 1998; Grafters; Kavanagh QC; The Vice; Waking the Dead; Murder in Mind; Blue Dove; The Mayor of Casterbridge, 2003; Faith, 2005. *Recreations:* sport, family, film and television, reading, politics. *Address:* 84 Ferme Park Road, N8 9SD.

THAKKER, Prof. Rajesh Vasantlal, MD, ScD; FRCP, FRCPE, FRCPath, FMedSci; FRS 2014; May Professor of Medicine, and Fellow of Somerville College, University of Oxford, since 1999; *b* 27 Aug. 1954; *s* of late Vasantlal Gordhandas Thakker and of Indira Vasantlal Thakker; *m* 1980, Julie Clare Magee; one *d. Educ:* Pembroke Coll., Cambridge (MA, MB BChir, MD; ScD 2010); Middlesex Hosp. Med. Sch. MRCP 1983, FRCP 1993; FRCPE 1997; FRCPath 1998. Middlesex Hospital: House Physician, 1980–81; Registrar, 1983–85; MRC Trng Fellow and Hon. Sen. Registrar, 1985–88; Sen. House Physician, Northwick Park Hosp. and Hammersmith Hosp., 1981–83; MRC Clin. Scientist and Consultant Physician, Northwick Park Hosp., 1988–92; Sen. Lectr and Consultant Physician, 1988–94, Reader of Medicine, 1994–95, RPMS; Hd of MRC Molecular Endocrinology Gp, 1994–99, and Prof. of Medicine, 1995–99, RPMS, then ICSM, Univ. of London. Jack W. Coburn Endowed Lectr, Amer. Soc. Nephrology, 2012. NIHR Sen. Investigator, 2015–. Chm., Efficacy, Mechanisms and Evaluations Bd, NIHR/MRC, 2008–. Gov., Oxford High Sch. (GDST), 2013–. Mem., Amer. Assoc. Physicians, 2013. Hon. Sen. Fellow, Harris Manchester Coll., Oxford, 2010. FMedSci 1999. Soc. for Endocrinol. Medal, 1995; Eur. Fedn of Endocrine Socs Prize, 1998; Graham Bull Prize, RCP, 1999; Louis V. Avioli Founders Award, Amer. Soc. for Bone and Mineral Res., USA, 2009; Parathyroid Medal, Fondazionefirmo, Florence, 2012. *Publications:* (ed) Genetic and Molecular Biological Aspects of Endocrine Disease, 1995; (ed) Molecular Genetics of Endocrine Disorders, 1997; (ed) Transitional Endocrinology and Metabolism: neoplasia update, 2011; (ed) Genetics of Bone Biology and Skeletal Disease, 2013; articles in jls. *Recreations:* running, rambling, reading. *Address:* Somerville College, Oxford OX2 6HD.

THAKSIN SHINAWATRA, PhD; Prime Minister of Thailand, 2001–06; *b* 26 July 1949; *m* Khunying Potjaman Shinawatra (marr. diss. 2008). *Educ:* Police Cadet Acad., Thailand; Eastern Kentucky Univ., USA (MA Criminal Justice 1975); Sam Houston State Univ., Texas (PhD Criminal Justice 1978). Royal Thai Police Department, 1973–87: Dep. Supt, Policy and Planning Subdiv.; Police Lt Col, 1987. Founder and Chm., Shinawatra Computer and Communications Gp, 1987–94. Minister of Foreign Affairs, Thailand, 1994–95; Leader, Palang Dharma Party, 1995–96; Dep. Prime Minister i/c of traffic and transportation, Bangkok, 1995–96; Dep. Prime Minister, 1997; MP (party list), 1998–2001; Founder and Leader, Thai Rak Thai Party, 1998–2006. Founder and Vice Chm., Thaicom Foundn, 1993–; Chm. Adv. Cttee, Pre-Cadet Class 10 and Police Cadet Class 26, 1994–; Honorary Member: Council, Police Cadet Acad.; Assoc. of Ex-Military Officers; President: Northerners' Assoc. of Thailand, 1998; Professional Golf Assoc. of Thailand; Honorary Advisor: Bangkok Club; Thai Northerners' Assoc. of Illinois, 1999; Northerners Club of Nontaburi. ASEAN Businessman of the Year Award, Asian Inst., Indonesia, 1992; Kiattiyod Jakdao Award in Economical Develt, Cttee of Armed Forces Prep. Sch. Foundn, 1992; 1993 Outstanding Telecom Man of Year Award, 1994; Outstanding Criminal Justice Alumnus Award, Sam Houston State Univ., 1996; Hon. Award, Mass Media Photographer Assoc. of Thailand, 1997. Kt Grand Cordon (Special Cl.), Order of Crown (Thailand), 1995, Order of White Elephant (Thailand), 1996; Kt Grand Cross (First Cl.), Order of Direkgunabhorn (Thailand), 2001; Grand Cross, Order of Sahametrei (Cambodia), 2001.

THALMANN, Anton Meinrad Friedrich; Ambassador of Switzerland to the Court of St James's, 2010–13; *b* Berne, 28 May 1948; *s* of Dr Ernesto Thalmann and Paula Thalmann (*née* Degen); *m* 1975, Dominique Andrée Schnyder-von-Wartensee; two *d. Educ:* Univ. of Geneva; Univ. of Berne (PhD 1975); Graduate Inst. for Advanced Internat. Studies, Geneva. Asst to gen. mgt, Swiss Bank Corp., Basle, 1974–77; diplomatic trainee, Swiss Mission to EC, Brussels, 1978–79; Legal Affairs Directorate, Fed. Dept of Foreign Affairs, 1979–83; Econ. Counsellor, Tokyo, 1983–87; Counsellor, Perm. Delegn of Switzerland to OECD, Paris, 1987–90; Hd, UN and Internat. Orgns Section, Fed. Dept of Foreign Affairs, 1990–95; Ambassador and Dep. Sec. Gen., Fed. Dept of Defence, Civil Protection and Sport, 1995–99; Ambassador: to Belgium and Hd, Mission to NATO, Brussels, 1999–2003; to Canada and the Bahamas, 2003–06; Ambassador and Dep. State Sec. and Political Dir, Fed. Dept of Foreign Affairs, 2006–10. Chm., UN Open-ended Wkg Gp on Marking and Tracing of Small Arms and Light Weapons, NY, 2004–05; Co-Chair, Geneva process on armed violence and develt, 2006–10. *Recreations:* ski-ing, windsurfing, golf, jogging, horse riding, classical music and jazz. *Clubs:* Athenæum, Travellers, London Capital.

THANE, Prof. Patricia Mary, PhD; FBA 2006; FRHistS; Leverhulme Professor of Contemporary British History, Institute of Historical Research, University of London, 2001–10, now Professor Emerita; Research Professor in Contemporary History, King's College London, since 2010; *b* 17 Aug. 1942; *d* of John Lawrence Williams, RAF (killed in action, 1944) and of Violet (*née* Beckett); *m* 1966, John Sutherland Thane (separated 1982); one *d. Educ:* Convent of the Holy Family, Birkenhead; St Anne's Coll., Oxford (BA, MA Mod. Hist. 1964); LSE (DSA 1965; PhD 1970). FRHistS 1985. Asst Lectr, Lectr, Sen. Lectr, then Reader in Social Hist., Dept of Social Sci. and Admin, Goldsmiths' Coll., Univ. of London, 1967–94; Prof. of Contemp. Hist., Univ. of Sussex, 1994–2001. Hon. Treas., 1992–96, Vice-Pres., 2006–09, RHistS; Vice-Pres., Internat. Econ. Hist. Assoc., 1998–2001; Chair, Social Hist. Soc., UK, 2001–08. Mem., Fawcett Soc., 2000–. *Publications:* (ed and contrib.) The Origins of British Social Policy, 1978; The Foundations of the Welfare State, 1982 (trans. Japanese), 2nd edn 1996 (trans. Japanese); (ed jtly and contrib.) The Power of the Past: essays for Eric Hobsbawm, 1984; (ed jtly) Essays in Social History, vol. 2, 1986; (ed with Gisela Book) Maternity and Gender Policies: women and the rise of the European welfare states 1880s–1950s, 1991; (ed with Paul Johnson) Old Age from Antiquity to Post-Modernity, 1998; (ed jtly) Labour's First Century: the Labour Party 1900–2000, 2000; Old Age in English History: past experiences, present issues, 2000; (ed with Lynn Botelho) Women and Ageing in British Society since 1500, 2001; Companion to Twentieth Century British History, 2001; (ed) The Long History of Old Age, 2005; (ed) Unequal Britain: equalities in Britain since 1945, 2010; (ed with E. Breitenbach) Women and Citizenship in Britain and Ireland in the Twentieth Century: what difference did the vote make?, 2010; (with Tanya Evans) Sinners? Scroungers? Saints?: unmarried motherhood in twentieth-century England, 2012; numerous articles in learned jls and contribs to edited vols. *Recreation:* cooking. *Address:* 5 Twisden Road, NW5 1DL. *T:* (office) (020) 7848 7042.

THANE, Sarah Ann, (Mrs S. A. Wenban), CBE 2003; JP; FRTS; Member, National Lottery Commission, 2005–13; *b* 21 Sept. 1951; *d* of John and Winifred Thane; *m* 1996, Peter Wenban; three step *s* two step *d. Educ:* Sutton Coldfield Grammar Sch. for Girls; Co. High Sch., Stourbridge; City of Birmingham Poly. (Dip. Communication Studies). Independent Television Commission: Dir of Public Affairs, 1990–96; Dir of Progs and Cable, 1996–2001; Dir of Progs and Advertising, 2001–03; Advisor: Content and Standards, Ofcom, 2004–05; (pt-time) to BBC Governors, 2005–06, to BBC Trust, 2007–08; Mem., Bd of Govs, Teachers' TV, 2008–10. Conducted exploratory review of the system of regulating child performances (reported, 2010). Non-exec. Dir, Films of Record, 2005–08. Vice-Chm., 1998–2000, Chm., 2000–02, RTS. Chm., Suffolk Craft Soc., 2014–. FRTS 1994. JP Suffolk, 2005 (Dep. Chm., W Suffolk Bench, 2012–14). DUniv Birmingham City, 2010. *Recreations:* music, visual arts and crafts, cooking, gardening, time with friends and family. *E:* sarahwenban@hotmail.com, chair@suffolkcraftsociety.org. *Club:* Reform.

THANKI, Bankim; QC 2003; *b* 19 April 1964; *s* of late B. D. Thanki and of Vijayalaxmi Thanki (*née* Modha); *m* 1988, Catherine Jane Margaret Spotswood (*d* 2015); three *s* one *d. Educ:* Owen's Sch., Herts (Hd of Sch.); Balliol Coll., Oxford (BA 1st cl. Hons Ancient and Modern History, 1986; MA 1989). Called to the Bar, Middle Temple, 1988 (Harmsworth Schol.), Bencher, 2008; in practice as barrister, specialising in commercial law, 1989–. Mem., Commercial Bar Assoc., 1989–. *Publications:* (jtly) Carriage by Air, 2000; (ed jtly) Commercial Court Procedure, 2001; (contrib.) Brindle & Cox, Law of Bank Payments, 2004, 4th edn 2010; (ed) Law of Privilege, 2006, 2nd edn 2011; (contrib.) Coppel, Information Rights, 4th edn 2014. *Recreation:* Manchester United FC. *Address:* (chambers) Fountain Court, Temple, EC4Y 9DH. *T:* (020) 7583 3335, *Fax:* (020) 7353 0329. *Clubs:* Athenæum, Royal Automobile.

THANKI, (Frances) Jane; *see* McIvor, F. J.

THAPAR, Prof. Romila, PhD; Professor of History, Jawaharlal Nehru University, New Delhi, 1970–91, now Professor Emeritus; *b* 30 Nov. 1931; *d* of Daya Ram Thapar and Kaushalya Khosla. *Educ:* Punjab Univ. (BA Hons Lit. 1952); Sch. of Oriental and African Studies, Univ. of London (BA Hons Hist. 1955; PhD Hist. 1958). Reader in Ancient Indian Hist., Delhi Univ., 1963–70. Kluge Vis. Prof., Library of Congress, 2003–04. Corresp. FBA 1999; Corresp. Fellow, RSE, 2006. Mem., Amer. Acad. of Arts and Scis, 2009. Hon. Fellow: Lady Margaret Hall, Oxford, 1986; SOAS, 1991. Hon. DLitt: Chicago, 1992; Oxford, 2002; Hon. DSc Edinburgh, 2004. Kluge Prize for Lifetime Achievement in the Humanities, 2008. *Publications:* Asoka and the Decline of the Mauryas, 1961, 3rd edn 2013; History of India, Vol. 1, 1966; Ancient Indian Social History: some interpretations, 1978, 2nd edn 2009; From Lineage to State, 1984, 2nd edn 2000 (14th impression 2013); Cultural Pasts, 2000 (9th impression 2010); Sakuntala, 2001 (3rd impression 2008); Early India, 2002 (2nd impression 2004); Somanatha, 2004 (3rd impression 2008); (ed) India: historical beginnings and the concept of the Aryan, 2006; The Aryan: recasting constructs, 2008 (3rd impression 2011); The Past Before Us: historical traditions of early North India, 2013; Readings in Early Indian History, 2013; The Past as Present, 2014; for children: Indian Tales, 1961, 2nd edn 1993. *Recreations:* music, poetry, searching for unusual finger rings. *Address:* 23 B Road, Maharani Bagh, New Delhi 110065, India.

THAROOR, Shashi, PhD; Member (Congress) Thiruvananthapuram, Kerala, Lok Sabha, since 2009; *b* 9 March 1956; *s* of Chandran Tharoor and Lily Tharoor; *m* 1st, 1977, Tilottama Mukherji (marr. diss. 2000); two *s* (twins); 2nd, 2007, Christa Giles (marr. diss. 2010); 3rd, 2010, Sunanda Pushkar (*d* 2014). *Educ:* St Stephen's Coll.; Delhi Univ. (BA Hons); Fletcher Sch. of Law and Diplomacy, Tufts Univ. (MA 1976; MALD 1977; PhD 1978). United Nations High Commissioner for Refugees: Asst to Dir for External Affairs, 1978–81; Rep., Singapore, 1981–84; Dep. Chief of Secretariat, 1984–87; Exec. Asst to Dep. High Comr, 1987–89; United Nations Headquarters: Special Asst to Under-Sec.-Gen. for Peacekeeping, 1989–96; Exec. Asst to Sec.-Gen., 1997–98; Dir, Communications and Special Projs, 1998–2001; Under Sec.-Gen. for Commns and Public Inf., 2001–07. Chm., Afras Ventures, 2007–09. Union Minister of Ext. Affairs, India, 2009–10; Union Minister of State for Human Resource Develt, 2012–14. Chm., Parly Standing Cttee on Ext. Affairs, 2014–. Member Advisory Board: ICRC, Geneva; Indo-American Arts Council; Virtue Foundn; Breakthrough: the Vijay Amritraj Foundn. Fellow, NY Inst. of the Humanities. Bd of Overseers, Fletcher Sch. of Law and Diplomacy. Columnist: The Times of India; The Hindu; The Asian Age; Deccan Chronicle; The Mail Today; former Contrib. Editor, Newsweek Internat. Pravasi Bharatiya Samman, 2004. *Publications:* Reasons of State, 1982; The Great Indian Novel (novel), 1989; The Five-Dollar Smile and Other Stories, 1990; Show Business (novel), 1992; India: from midnight to the millennium, 1997, rev. edn as India: from midnight to the millennium and beyond, 2006; Nehru: the invention of India, 2003; Riot (novel), 2001; Bookless in Baghdad and Other Reflections on Literature, 2005; The Elephant, the Tiger and the Cellphone: reflections on India in the 21st century, 2007; (with Shaharyar Khan) Shadows Across the Playing Field: 60 years of India-Pakistan cricket, 2009; Pax Indica: India and the world in the 21st century, 2012; India Shastra: reflections on the nation in our time, 2015. *Recreations:* cricket, theatre, reading. *E:* office@tharoor.in. *Club:* India International Centre (New Delhi).

THARP, Kenneth Olumuyiwa, OBE 2003; Chief Executive, The Place, since 2007; *b* Croydon, 11 Feb. 1960; *s* of Prof. Gabriel O. Esuruoso and Pamela Tharp; partner, Luca Silvestrini. *Educ:* Perse Sch., Cambridge; Cambridge Coll. of Arts and Technol.; London Contemp. Dance Sch. (Professional Dip. Contemp. Dance; BA 1st Cl. Hons Contemp. Dance, Univ. of Kent, 1987). Dancer, London Contemp. Dance Th., 1981–94; freelance dancer, choreographer, teacher and dir, 1994–2007; dancer, rehearsal dir, Educn Co-ordinator, Arc Dance Co., 1994–2005; Artistic Dir, Sadler's Wells Youth Dance Co., 1994–2000; Dancer in Residence and Dir of Dance, Queens' Coll., Cambridge, 1998–2006; Asst to Dir and Hd of Contemp. Dance, Millennium Performing Arts, 1999–2007; Associate Artistic Dir, then Artistic Dir Designate, Nat. Youth Dance Co., 2002–04; Artistic Advr and Lead Artist, Royal Ballet Sch. Dance Partnership and Access Prog., 2005–07. Vis. Prof. in Dance: Choreog. and Perf., Univ. of Lincoln, 2009–12. Member: Exec., Dance UK, 1995–2001; Adv. Bd, Royal Ballet, 1998–99; Dancers Career Develt, 2002–06; London 2012 Culture and Creativity Adv. Forum, 2006–08; Steering Gp, Cultural Learning Alliance; Adv. Council, Creative Industries Fedn. Trustee: Jazz Xchange Music and Dance Co., 1996–98; Creative Dance Artists Trust, 1999–2006; Royal Opera Hse, 2002–10 (Trustee, Benevolent Fund, 2009–); Phoenix Dance Th., 2006–07. Patron, Akademi, 2014–. Finalist Judge, BBC Young Dancer 2015. FRSA. *Publications:* contrib. articles to Dancing Times, Dance UK mag., Animated mag., Queens' Coll. Record, Arts Professional mag. *Recreations:* music, listening and playing (especially piano, Javanese gamelan, mbira), swimming, cycling, walking, nature, Buddhist studies, tennis, sea-kayaking. *Address:* The Place, 17 Duke's Road, WC1H 9PY. *T:* (020) 7121 1072. *E:* kenneth.tharp@theplace.org.uk.

THARP, Lars Broholm; ceramics historian; broadcaster, since 1986; Director, Lars Tharp Ltd, ceramics and fine arts consultants, since 1993; Hogarth Curator, Foundling Museum, since 2010 (Director, 2008–10); *b* Copenhagen, 27 March 1954; *s* of Harry Tharp and Anne Marie Broholm; *m* 1983, Gillian Block; two *d. Educ:* Wyggeston Grammar Sch. for Boys, Leicester; Gonville and Caius Coll., Cambridge (BA Hons Archaeol. and Anthropol. 1976). Sotheby's, 1977–93: auctioneer, oriental and Eur. ceramics specialist; Hd, Ceramics, Oriental Works of Art; Dir, 1983–93. Freelance broadcaster; TV series include: The Antiques Roadshow, 1986–; presenter: Inside Antiques, 2004; Treasures of Chinese Porcelain, 2011; (and devisor) China in Six Easy Pieces, 2013; radio includes: chm. and writer, Hidden Treasures, 1998–2002; presenter, Out of the Fire, 2000, On the China Trail, 2007; columnist: Scandinavian Mag., 2010–; Ceramic Review, 2011–; The Spanner, 2011–. Guest Curator, York Mus, 2005–06. Vis. Prof. of Humanities, De Montfort Univ., 2008–. Judge, Art Fund Prize, 2010, 2011. Listed NADFAS speaker; Guest Lecturer: Australia (ADFAS), 2010; NZ (NZDFAS), 2013. Chm., Hogarth Gp, 2004–. Patron: Leicester Internat. Music Festival, 2006–; Framework Knitters' Mus., Wigston, 2007–. Trustee: Mus. of Worcester Porcelain, 1994–2000; William Hogarth Trust, 2009–. Freeman, City of London, 2003; Liveryman, Weavers' Co., 2005 (Mem., Ct of Assts, 2011). FSA 2011; FRSA 2000–11. Hon. DArt De Montfort, 2007. *Publications:* The Little Brown Illustrated Encyclopaedia of Antiques (ed with Paul Atterbury), 1994; China in Hogarth's England, 1997; How to Spot a Fake, 1999; (ed) A-Z of 20th Century Antiques, 2000; contribs to various jls and newspapers. *Recreations:* 'cellist, choir, travel (Europe and China), museums. *T:* (office) (0116) 244 8788. *E:* lars@tharp.co.uk. *W:* www.tharp.co.uk. *Club:* Blacks.

THARP, Twyla; American dancer and choreographer; *b* 1 July 1941; *m* Peter Young (marr. diss.); *m* Robert Huot (marr. diss.); one *s*. *Educ:* Pomona Coll.; American Ballet Theatre Sch.; Barnard Coll. (BA Art History 1963). With Paul Taylor Dance Co., 1963–65; Founder, 1965, choreographer, 1965–87, Twyla Tharp Dance Foundn; Artistic Associate Choreographer, American Ballet Theatre, 1988–91; regrouped Twyla Tharp Dance, 1991; *modern dances/ballets* choreographed include: Tank Dive, 1965; Re-Moves, 1966; Generation, 1968; Medley, 1969; The One Hundreds, 1970; Eight Jelly Rolls, 1971; Deuce Coupe, Joffrey Ballet, 1973; As Time Goes By, Joffrey Ballet, 1973; Sue's Leg, 1975; Push Comes to Shove, American Ballet Theatre, 1976; Mud, 1977; Baker's Dozen, 1979; The Catherine Wheel, 1981; The Little Ballet, American Ballet Theatre, 1984; In the Upper Room, 1986 (Olivier Award, 1991); Everlast, 1989; The Rules of the Game, 1989; (with Mikhail Baryshnikov) Cutting Up, 1993; Demeter and Persephone, 1993; Mr Wordly Wise, Royal Ballet, Covent Garden, 1995; Heroes, Sweet Fields, 66, 1997; Known By Heart, 1998; The Beethoven Seventh, 2000; also dir., Movin' Out (Tony Award for best choreography), 2003; also dir, Come Fly Away (Drama Desk Award for outstanding choreography), 2010; *films* choreographed: Hair, 1978; Ragtime, 1980; Amadeus, 1984; White Nights, 1985; I'll Do Anything, 1994; *television* includes directing: Making Television Dance; The Catherine Wheel; Baryshnikov by Tharp. Hon. Mem., Amer. Acad. Arts and Letters, 1997. Creative Arts Award, Brandeis Univ., 1972; Astaire Award, 2003; Drama League Award for Sustained Achievement in Musical Theater, 2003; Nat. Medal of Arts, 2004; Jerome Robbins Award, 2008. *Publications:* Push Comes to Shove (autobiog.), 1992; The Creative Habit: learn it and use it for life, 2003; The Collaborative Habit: life lessons for working together, 2009.

THATCHER, Anthony Neville, CEng, FIMechE; Vice Chairman, Thyssen-Bornemisza SAM, 1993–2007 (President and Chief Executive Officer, Thyssen-Bornemisza Group, 1991–92); *b* 10 Sept. 1939; *s* of Edwin Neville Thatcher and Elsie May Webster; *m* 1968, Sally Margaret Clark. *Educ:* Sir John Lawes Sch., Harpenden; Luton Tech. Coll.; Manchester Univ. (MSc). Student apprentice, Haywards Tyler & Co., Luton, 1956–64; Project Engineer, Smiths Industries, 1964–67; Ultra Electronics: Operations Res. Asst, Acton, 1967–69; Vice-Pres., Sales, USA, 1970–73; Marketing Dir, Acton, 1973–77; Managing Dir, Ultra Electronic Controls, 1977; Managing Director: Dowty Electronic Controls, 1978–82; Electronics Div., Dowty Gp, 1982; Dir, 1983–91, Chief Exec., 1986–91, Dowty Gp. Member: Avionics Cttee, Electronics and Avionics Requirements Bd, DTI, 1981–85; Council, Electronics Engineering Assoc., 1983–91 (Pres., 1986–87); RARDE Management Bd (Indust.), 1986–91; Council, SBAC, 1986–91; Innovation Adv. Bd, DTI, 1988–91; Engrg Markets Adv. Bd, DTI, 1988–90; Engrg Council, 1989–91. Council Mem., Cheltenham Ladies' Coll., 1988–91. Freeman, City of London; Liveryman and Trustee, Glass Sellers' Co. *Recreations:* art, jazz piano, opera, fishing, gardening, bird watching. *Clubs:* Athenæum, Carlton; Georgetown (Washington).

THATCHER, Hon. Sir Mark, 2nd Bt *cr* 1991, of Scotney in the County of Kent; *b* 15 Aug. 1953; *s* of Sir Denis Thatcher, 1st Bt, MBE, TD and Baroness Thatcher, LG, OM, PC, FRS; *S* father, 2003; *m* 1st, 1987, Diane Bergdorf (marr. diss. 2007), Dallas, Texas; one *s* one *d*; 2nd, 2008, Sarah-Jane (*née* Clemence), former wife of Lord Francis Russell; two step *s*. *Educ:* Harrow. *Heir: s* Michael Thatcher, *b* 28 Feb. 1989.

THAW, Sheila, (Mrs John Thaw); *see* Hancock, S.

THEAKSTON, John Andrew; Director, Black Sheep Brewery, since 1992; *b* 23 May 1952; *s* of late Robert Francis Theakston and Jane Hawley; *m* 1977, Elizabeth Jane Morgan; one *s* one *d*. *Educ:* Sedbergh Sch., Yorks; Worcester Coll., Oxford (MA Mod. History); Durham Univ. (MSc). Trainee, T. & R. Theakston, Brewers, 1975–77; Donald Macpherson Group: Corporate Planning Manager, 1977–81; Overseas Div. Manager, 1981–84; Higgs & Hill, subseq. Swan Hill Group, plc: Business Develt Manager, 1985–87; Gp Finance Dir, 1987–89; Jt Gp Man. Dir, 1989–90; Chief Exec., 1991–2004. Non-executive Director: ARCO Ltd, 2005– (non-exec. Chm., 2006–); Halcrow Ltd, 2006–11. *Recreations:* sailing, walking, trout fishing, golf.

THEIS, Hon. Dame Lucy (Morgan), DBE 2010; **Hon. Mrs Justice Theis;** a Judge of the High Court of Justice, Family Division, since 2010; *b* 6 Nov. 1960; *d* of Michael and Jill Theis; *m* 1991, Andrew Firrell; one *s* one *d*. *Educ:* Birmingham Univ. (LLB 1981). Called to the Bar, Gray's Inn, 1982, Bencher, 2007; Asst Recorder, 1998–2000; Recorder, 2000–10; QC 2003; a Dep. High Ct Judge, Family Div., 2009–10. Hd, Field Court Chambers, 1995–2010. Mem., Gen. Council of the Bar, 2010–; Vice-Chm., 2006–07, Chm., 2008–09, Family Law Bar Assoc. *Recreations:* gardening, riding, farming. *Address:* Royal Courts of Justice, Strand, WC2A 2LL.

THELLUSSON, family name of **Baron Rendlesham**.

THEOCHAROUS, Archbishop Gregorios; His Eminence The Most Rev. Gregorios; Greek Orthodox Archbishop of Thyateira and Great Britain, since 1988; *b* 2 Jan. 1929. *Educ:* High Sch., Lefkoniko, Famagusta; Pan Cyprian Gymnasium, Nicosia; Theol Faculty, Univ. of Athens. Monk in the Sacred Monastery, Stavrovouni, Cyprus; ordained: deacon, 1953; presbyter, 1959; asst parish priest and later parish priest, All Saints, Camden Town, 1959–69; Archdiocese of Thyateira: Chancellor, 1965–79; Asst Bishop of Tropaeou, 1970–88; locum tenens on death of Archbishop Athenagoras, 1979; spiritual oversight of Community of St Barnabas, Wood Green, 1970–88. Dr *hc* North London, 1993. *Address:* Thyateira House, 5 Craven Hill, W2 3EN. *T:* (020) 7723 4787, *Fax:* (020) 7224 9301. *E:* mail@thyateira.org.uk.

THERBORN, Prof. Göran, PhD; FAcSS; Professor of Sociology, 2006–08, now Emeritus, and Director of Research, Department of Sociology, 2008–10, University of Cambridge; Affiliated Professor of Sociology, Linnaeus University, Sweden, since 2011; *b* 23 Sept. 1941; *s* of Ragnar and Karin Therborn; *m* 1982, Sonia Piña; one *s* one *d*. *Educ:* Lund Univ. (PhD 1974). Reader in Sociol., Lund Univ., 1975–81; Professor: of Political Sci., Catholic Univ., Nijmegen, Netherlands, 1981–87; of Sociol., Gothenburg Univ., Sweden, 1987–2003; Dir, Swedish Collegium for Advanced Study in the Social Scis, Uppsala, 1996–2006. Eur. Prof. of Social Policy, Budapest, 1996; Visiting Professor: FLACSO Mexico, and ANU, 1978; Sorbonne, 1980; UCLA, 1991; Buenos Aires, 1992; L'Institut des scis politiques, Paris, 2004. FAcSS (AcSS 2010). Hon. DPhil Roskilde, 2007; Hon. FilDr Linnaeus, Sweden, 2010; Hon. Dr Pols Helsinki, 2011; Dr *hc* Nacional de Educación a Distancia Madrid, 2014. *Publications:* Science, Class and Society, 1976; What Does the Ruling Class Do When It Rules?, 1978; The Ideology of Power and the Power of Ideology, 1980; Why Some Peoples are More Unemployed than Others, 1986; European Modernity and Beyond, 1995; Between Sex and Power: family in the world 1900–2000, 2004; (ed jtly) Asia and Europe in Globalization, 2006; (ed) Inequalities of the World, 2006; From Marxism to Post-Marxism?, 2008; Les sociétés d'Europe au XXe au XXIe siècle, 2009; (ed jtly) Handbook of European Societies, 2010; The World, 2011; The Killing Fields of Inequality, 2013. *Recreations:* travelling, arts, country house. *Address:* Byvägen 4, 38892 Ljungbyholm, Sweden. *T:* (480) 30613. *E:* gt274@cam.ac.uk.

THÉRIAULT, Hon. Camille Henri; President and Chief Executive Officer, Mouvement des Caisses Populaires Acadiennes, since 2004; *b* 25 Feb. 1955; one *s* one *d*. *Educ:* Baie-Sainte-Anne High Sch.; Université de Moncton (BSocSc Political Sci.). Formerly: Vice-Pres., Corporate Affairs, United Maritime Fisherman's Co-operative; Manager, Kent Industrial Commn. Government of New Brunswick: MLA (L) Kent South, 1987–March 2001; Minister of: Fisheries and Aquaculture, 1991–94; Advanced Educn and Labour, 1994–95; Economic Develt and Tourism, 1995–98; Premier, 1998–99; Leader of the Opposition, 1999–2001. Chair: Public Accounts Cttee, 1987; Select Cttee on Representation and Electoral Boundaries; Jt Chair, Ministerial Cttee on Creating New Options; Member: Standing Cttee on Estimates, 1987; Cabinet Cttee on Policy and Priorities, 1994. Leader, NB Liberal Party, 1998–2001. Mem., 2001–, Chm., 2002–, Transportation Safety Bd. *Address:* (office) Place de l'Acadie, 295 Boulevard St-Pierre Ouest, CP 5554, Caraquet, NB E1W 1B7, Canada.

THEROUX, Louis Sebastian; journalist; writer, documentary maker and presenter, BBC, 1996–2003 and since 2006; *b* Singapore, 20 May 1970; *s* of Paul Edward Theroux, *qv*; *m* 2012, Nancy Strang; two *s*. *Educ:* Westminster Sch.; Magdalen Coll., Oxford (BA 1st Cl. Hons Mod. Hist.). BBC documentary series include: Weird Weekends, 1998–2000; When Louis Met…, 2000–02; Louis Theroux's LA Stories, 2014; programmes include: Gambling in Las Vegas, 2006; Under the Knife, 2007; Behind Bars, 2008; By Reason of Insanity, Transgender Kids, 2015. *Publications:* The Call of the Weird, 2005. *Address:* c/o Anita Land Ltd, 10 Wyndham Place, W1H 2PU.

THEROUX, Paul Edward, FRSL; FRGS; writer; *b* 10 April 1941; *s* of Albert Eugene Theroux and Anne Dittami Theroux; *m* 1st, 1967, Anne Castle (marr. diss. 1993); two *s*; 2nd, 1995, Sheila M. L. Donnelly. *Educ:* Univ. of Massachusetts (BA). Lecturer: Univ. of Urbino, 1963; Soche Hill Coll., Malawi, 1963–65; Makerere Univ., Kampala, Uganda, 1965–68; Univ. of Singapore, 1968–71; Writer-in-Residence, Univ. of Virginia, 1972. Mem., AAAL (formerly AAIL), 1984. Hon. DLitt: Trinity Coll., Washington DC, 1980; Tufts Univ., Mass, 1980; Univ. of Mass, 1988. Patrons Gold Medal, RGS, 2015. *Publications: novels:* Waldo, 1967; Fong and the Indians, 1968; Girls at Play, 1969; Murder in Mount Holly, 1969; Jungle Lovers, 1971; Sinning with Annie, 1972; Saint Jack, 1973 (filmed, 1979); The Black House, 1974; The Family Arsenal, 1976; Picture Palace, 1978 (Whitbread Award, 1978); A Christmas Card, 1978; London Snow, 1980; The Mosquito Coast, 1981 (James Tait Black Prize, 1982; filmed, 1987); Doctor Slaughter, 1984 (filmed as Half Moon Street, 1987); O-Zone, 1986; My Secret History, 1989; Chicago Loop, 1990; Doctor de Marr, 1990; Millroy the Magician, 1993; My Other Life, 1996; Kowloon Tong, 1997; The Collected Short Novels, 1998; Hotel Honolulu, 2001; Blinding Light, 2005; The Elephanta Suite, 2007; A Dead Hand, 2009; The Lower River, 2012; *short stories:* The Consul's File, 1977; World's End, 1980; The London Embassy, 1982 (televised, 1987); The Collected Stories, 1997; The Stranger at the Palazzo d'Oro and Other Stories, 2003; Mr Bones: twenty stories, 2014; *play:* The White Man's Burden, 1987; *criticism:* V. S. Naipaul, 1972; *memoir:* Sir Vidia's Shadow, 1998; *travel:* The Great Railway Bazaar, 1975; The Old Patagonian Express, 1979; The Kingdom by the Sea, 1983; Sailing through China, illus. Patrick Procktor, 1983; Sunrise with Seamonsters: travels and discoveries 1964–84, 1985; The Imperial Way, 1985; Riding the Iron Rooster, 1988; Travelling The World, 1990; The Happy Isles of Oceania, 1992; The Pillars of Hercules, 1995; Fresh-Air Fiend, 2000; Dark Star Safari, 2002; Ghost Train to the Eastern Star: on the tracks of The Great Railway Bazaar, 2008; The Tao of Travel, 2011; The Last Train to Zona Verde, 2013; Deep South, 2015; *screenplay:* Saint Jack, 1979; reviews in New York Times, etc. *Recreation:* paddling. *Address:* c/o Hamish Hamilton Ltd, 80 Strand, WC2R 0RC.
See also L. S. Theroux.

THESIGER, family name of **Viscount Chelmsford**.

THETFORD, Bishop Suffragan of, since 2009; **Rt Rev. Alan Peter Winton;** *b* London, 4 Sept. 1958; *s* of David John Winton and June Winton; *m* 1982, Philippa Mary Harrold; two *d*. *Educ:* Sheffield Univ. (BA Hons Biblical Studies 1983; PhD 1987); Lincoln Theol Coll. Ordained deacon, 1991, priest, 1992; Asst Curate, Christchurch, Southgate, 1991–95; Priest-in-charge, St Paul's, Walden with Preston, and Continuing Ministerial Educn Officer, Dio. of St Albans, 1995–99; Rector, Welwyn, 1999–2005; Team Rector, Welwyn Team Ministry, 2005–09. Hon. Canon, Cathedral and Abbey Church of St Alban, 2007–09. *Publications:* The Proverbs of Jesus, 1990. *Recreations:* reading, cricket. *Address:* The Red House, 53 Norwich Road, Stoke Holy Cross, Norfolk NR14 8AB. *T:* (01508) 491014. *E:* bishop.thetford@dioceseofnorwich.org.

THEW, Rosemary Constance Evelyn; Chief Executive, Driving Standards Agency, 2005–13; *b* 3 Nov. 1949; *d* of John Henry Thew and Enid Thew. *Educ:* Preston Manor County Grammar Sch. Civil Service: County Court Clerk, Lord Chancellor's Dept, 1967–70; Exec. Officer, IR, 1970–79; Manpower Services Commn, 1979–86; Regl Employment Manager, W Midlands, Dept of Employment, 1986–89; Implementation and Policy Manager, 1989–96, W Midlands Regl Dir, 1996–2001, Employment Service, Employment Dept Gp, then DfEE; Field Dir, W Midlands Jobcentre Plus, 2001–05. *Recreations:* gardening, walking, golf.

THEWLES, Col (Francis) Edmund, OBE 1989; Vice Lord-Lieutenant of Shropshire, since 2007; *b* 11 Nov. 1942; *s* of Wing Comdr H. J. A. Thewles, OBE and Rhoda Frances Thewles (*née* Hulme); *m* 1969, Caroline, *y d* of Col R. W. B. Simonds, CBE and Laetitia (*née* Melsome); one *s* two *d*. *Educ:* Berkhamsted Sch.; RMA, Sandhurst. Commnd Worcestershire Regt, later Worcs and Sherwood Foresters Regt, 1964–93. Comdt, Shropshire ACF, 1997–2000; Chm., Shropshire AFC Trust, 2000–. *Recreations:* mountaineering, theatre, travel, classic cars. *Address:* 45 Bishop Street, Shrewsbury SY2 5HD. *T:* (01743) 353424, 07817 757835.

THEWLIS, Sarah Anne; Managing Director, Thewlis Graham Associates, since 2010; *b* 12 May 1958; *d* of Geoffrey Frank Bennett and Mollie Bennett (*née* Bates); *m* 1983, Rev. Canon Dr John Charles Thewlis. *Educ:* Dartford Grammar Sch. for Girls; Univ. of Hull (BA Hist. 1979); Relate Cert. in Marital and Couple Counselling; Univ. of Glasgow (MML 2008). MIPD 1991, FCIPD 1998. Marks and Spencer, 1979–91, Divl Personnel Controller for Distribution Centres; Dep. Sec., RCP, 1991–94; Chief Exec., RCGP, 1994–2002; Chief Exec. and Registrar, NMC, 2002–08; Principal Consultant, 2008–09, Man. Dir, 2009–10, GBR Search, subseq. Gundersen Partners. Lay Mem., Employment Tribunal Panel, 1999–2008. Member: Bishops' Equal Opportunities Cttee, 2001–09; Deployment, Remuneration and Conditions of Service Cttee, subseq. Remuneration and Conditions of Service Cttee, Archbishops' Council, 2006–11; Home Office Database Ethics Gp, 2007–; Audit Cttee, RCGP, 2010–; Bd, Recruitment and Employment Confedn, 2013–. Non-exec. Dir, Phoenix Futures, 2007– (Mem., Audit Cttee, 2007–11; Vice Chm., 2011–). Chm., Assoc. of Exec. Recruiters, 2014–. Mem. Bd, Internat. Women's Forum (UK), 2014–. Governor: Deansfield Sch., Eltham; Horne Park Sch., Eltham; Queen Anne's Sch., Caversham, 2012– (Chm., Personnel Cttee, 2014–). Liveryman, Needlemakers' Co., 2010. FRSA 2001; FRSocMed 2006. Hon. FRCGP 2002. *Recreations:* horses, cats, people, current affairs. *Address:* The Rectory, 2 Talbot Road, Carshalton, Surrey SM5 3BS. *T:* (020) 8647 2366. *E:* sat@thewlisgraham.com; Thewlis Graham Associates, Portland House, Bressenden Place, SW1E 5RS. *T:* (020) 7850 4781. *Club:* Royal Society of Medicine.

THEWLISS, Alison Emily; MP (SNP) Glasgow Central, since 2015; *b* 13 Sept. 1982; *m*; two *c*. *Educ:* Univ. of Aberdeen. Mem. (SNP), Glasgow CC, 2007–15. SNP spokesperson on cities, 2015–. Mem., Communities and Local Govt Select Cttee, 2015–. Mem., Scottish CND. *Address:* House of Commons, SW1A 0AA.

THIAM, (Cheick) Tidjane; Chief Executive, Credit Suisse, since 2015; *b* Abidjan, Côte d'Ivoire, 29 July 1962; *s* of Amadou Thiam and Marietou Sow; *m* 1991, Annette April Anthony; two *s*. *Educ:* Ecole Polytechnique de Paris (Engrg 1984); École Nationale Supérieure des Mines de Paris (Civil Engrg 1986); INSEAD (MBA 1988). McKinsey & Co.: internat. consultant, Paris, NY, EU, 1986–89; Young Professionals Prog., World Bank, Washington, DC (on sabbatical), 1989–90; Associate Dir, Financial Services Practice, Paris,

1991–94; CEO, 1994–98, Chm., 1998–99, Nat. Bureau for Tech. Studies and Develt, Côte d'Ivoire; Partner, McKinsey & Co., Paris, 2000–02; Aviva plc: Gp Strategy and Develt Dir, 2002–06; Man. Dir, Aviva Internat., 2006; CEO, Aviva Europe, 2006–07; Gp Chief Financial Officer, 2008–09, Gp Chief Exec., 2009–15, Prudential plc. Non-executive Director: Arkema, 2006–09; 21st Century Fox, 2014–. Member: Africa Progress Panel, 2007–; ODI, 2011–; Internat. Business Council, WEF; Prime Minister's Business Adv. Gp, 2012–; European Financial Round Table, 2013–; UK-ASEAN Business Council; Chairman: G20 High Level Panel for Infrastructure Investment, 2011; Assoc. of British Insurers, 2012–14; UKTI Strategic Adv. Gp; UKTI British Business Ambassador, 2014–. Chevalier, Legion d'Honneur (France), 2011; Les Echos Grand Prix de l'Economie, 2013.

THIAN, Robert Peter; Reforming, Performance-enhancing Chairman; *b* 1 Aug. 1943; *s* of Clifford Peter Thian and Frances Elizabeth (*née* Stafford-Bird); *m* 1964, Liselotte von Borges; two *d*. *Educ:* Geneva Univ. (Lic. en Droit 1967). Called to the Bar, Gray's Inn, 1971. Glaxo Group plc: Legal Advr, 1967–71; Man. Dir, Portugal, 1972–80; Abbott Laboratories (USA): European Business Develt Dir, 1981–84; Regional Dir, Europe, 1985–87; Vice Pres., Internat. Operations, Novo Industri A/S (Denmark), 1987–89; Gp Chief Exec., North West Water Group, 1990–93; Founder and Chief Exec., Renex Ltd, 1993–; Chief Exec., The Stationery Office Gp, 1996–99; Chairman: IMO Gp, 1999–2000; Tactica Solutions Ltd, 1999–2001; Astron Gp, 2001–05; Orion Gp, 2001–04; Whatman Plc, 2002–07; Southern Water Gp (formerly Southern Water Services Ltd), 2003–07; Cardpoint plc, 2006–08; Equiniti Ltd (formerly Lloyds TSB Registrars), 2007–09; Dep. Chm., Lansen Pharmaceutical Hldgs Ltd (Hong Kong), 2010–11. Mem., Mgt Adv. Bd, TowerBrook Capital Partners (UK) LLP, 2010–. Non-executive Director: Celltech Gp, 1992–99; Medeval Ltd, 1995–98. *Recreations:* horses, golf, reading. *Address:* 15 Princes Gate Mews, SW7 2PS. *E:* bob.thian@renex.net. *Clubs:* Lansdowne; Chantilly Golf, Monte Carlo Golf; Black Diamond Golf (Fla).

THICKNESSE, Cdre Philip John; Clerk to Worshipful Company of Haberdashers, since 2013; *b* London, 6 June 1959; *s* of John D. Thicknesse and Anne M. Thicknesse (*née* Hardie); *m* 1985, Jane Elizabeth Bryant; three *s*. *Educ:* Downside Sch.; BRNC Dartmouth; Lancaster Univ. (BA Hons Hist. 1981); Royal Naval Coll., Greenwich (MA 1993). Joined RN 1978; Bridge Watch Keeper, HMS Fearless, Falklands War, 1982; Helicopter pilot, Fleet Air Arm, 1985–2011; 820 Naval Air Sqdn/HMS Ark Royal, 1986–87; Anti Submarine Warfare Officer, 1989; Principal Warfare Officer, HMS Birmingham, 1989–91; 829 Naval Air Sqdn/HMS Norfolk, 1991–93; 1st Lt, HM Yacht Britannia, 1993–95; CO, HMS Leeds Castle, 1996; Directing Staff, RMCS, 1997–99; CO, HMS Westminster, 2000–01; MA to 2nd Sea Lord, 2001–03; MoD Staff, 2003–06; Commanding Officer: Naval Transition Team, Iraq, 2006; Royal Naval Air Stn, Culdrose, 2006–08; Dir, Maritime Warfare Centre, 2009; Comdr, British Forces S Atlantic Is, 2009–11. Vis. Schol., Wolfson Coll., Oxford, 2012–13. Mem., Internat. Adv. Gp, Project for Study of 21st Century, 2014–. FCMI 2012. Trustee, Royal Humane Soc., 2013–. Bronze Star (US), 2006. *Publications:* (jtly) Brassey's Military Rotorcraft, 2nd edn 1999. *Recreations:* windsurfing, sailing, Real tennis, writing. *Address:* Haberdashers' Hall, 18 West Smithfield, EC1A 9HQ. *T:* (020) 7246 9988, *Fax:* (020) 7246 9989. *E:* clerk@haberdashers.co.uk. *Clubs:* Royal Navy of 1765 and 1785; Goldfish, Amphibians.

THIELEMANN, Christian; Principal Conductor, Sächsische Staatskapelle Dresden, since 2012; *b* Berlin, 1 April 1959. *Educ:* Orchestra Acad. of Berlin Philharmonic Orch. (violist). Rehearsal pianist, Deutsche Oper, Berlin, 1978; positions in Gelsenkirchen, Karlsruhe and Hanover; joined conducting staff of Rhine Opera, Dusseldorf, 1985; Generalmusikdirector: Nuremburg, 1988–97; Deutsche Oper, Berlin, 1997–2004; Munich Philharmonic, 2004–11. Conductor, Bayreuth Fest., 2000–; Artistic Dir, Salzburg Easter Fest., 2013–. Hon. RAM. Hon. Dr: Franz Liszt Coll. of Music, Weimar; Catholic Univ., Leuven. Conductor of the Year, Opernwelt mag., 2011. *Publications:* Christian Thielemann: Mein Leben mit Wagner, 2012. *Address:* Sächsische Staatskapelle Dresden, Theaterplatz 2, 01067 Dresden, Germany.

THIESSEN, Gordon, OC 2002; PhD; Chair, Canadian Public Accountability Board, 2002–07; *b* 14 Aug. 1938; *m* 1964, Annette Hillyar; two *d*. *Educ:* Univ. of Saskatchewan (BA 1960; MA 1961); London School of Economics (PhD 1972). Lectr in Economics, Univ. of Saskatchewan, 1962; joined Bank of Canada, 1963; Res., and Monetary and Financial Analysis Depts, 1963–79; Advr to Gov., 1979–84; Dep. Gov. (Econ. Res. and Financial Analysis), 1984–87; Sen. Dep. Gov., 1987–94; Gov., 1994–2001; Mem., Exec. Cttee, 1987–2001; Mem., 1987–2001, Chm., 1994–2001, Bd of Dirs. Vis. Economist, Reserve Bank of Australia, 1973–75.

THIN, Andrew, OBE 2014; Chairman, Scottish Canals, since 2014; *b* Edinburgh, 21 Jan. 1959; *s* of James and Marjorie Thin; *m* 1985, Frances Elizabeth Clark; one *s* one *d*. *Educ:* Edinburgh University (BSc Hons 1982; MBA 1988; DipM 1991). Team leader, Highlands and Is Develt Bd, 1989–91; Chief Exec., Caithness and Sutherland Enterprise, 1991–95; Chm., John Muir Trust, 1997–2003; Convener, Cairngorms Nat. Park Authy, 2003–06; Chm., Scottish Natural Heritage, 2006–14. Mem. Bd, Crofters Commn, 2001–06. Non-exec. Dir, Scottish Govt, 2010–. Mem. Bd, Children's Hearings Scotland, 2011–14. *Recreations:* long-distance running, canoeing, hill walking, climbing. *Address:* Wester Auchterflow Cottage, Munlochy, Ross-shire IV8 8PQ. *T:* (01463) 811632. *E:* andrew.thin@hotmail.co.uk.

THIRD, Rt Rev. Richard Henry McPhail; an Assistant Bishop, Diocese of Bath and Wells, since 1992; *b* 29 Sept. 1927; *s* of Henry McPhail and Marjorie Caroline Third; *m* 1966, Helen Illingworth; two *d*. *Educ:* Alleyn's Sch.; Reigate Grammar Sch.; Emmanuel Coll., Cambridge (BA 1950, MA 1955); Lincoln Theological Coll. Ordained deacon 1952, priest 1953, Southwark; Curate: St Andrew, Mottingham, 1952–55; Sanderstead (in charge of St Edmund, Riddlesdown), 1955–59; Vicar of Sheerness, 1959–67; Vicar of Orpington, 1967–76; RD of Orpington, 1973–76; Hon. Canon of Rochester, 1974–76; Proctor in Convocation, 1975–76 and 1980–85; Bishop Suffragan: of Maidstone, 1976–80; of Dover, 1980–92. Hon. DCL Kent, 1990. *Recreations:* music, walking, reading, gardening.

THIRLWALL, Prof. Anthony Philip, PhD; Professor of Applied Economics, University of Kent, 1976–2004, now Emeritus; *b* 21 April 1941; *s* of Isaac Thirlwall and Ivy Florence Ticehurst; *m* 1st, 1966, Gianna Paoletti (marr. diss. 1986); one *s* one *d* (and one *s* decd); 2nd, 2011, Dr Penélope Pacheco-López; one *s*. *Educ:* Harrow Weald County Grammar Sch.; Univ. of Leeds (BA 1962; PhD 1967); Clark Univ. (MA 1963). Teaching Fellow, Clark Univ., 1962–63; Tutor, Cambridge Univ., 1963–64; Asst Lectr, Univ. of Leeds, 1964–66; Lectr and Reader, Univ. of Kent, 1966–76. Economic Adviser: ODM, 1966; Dept of Employment, 1968–70. Res. Associate, Princeton Univ., 1971–72; Visiting Professor: West Virginia Univ., 1967; Melbourne Univ., 1981, 1988; Vis. Scholar, King's Coll., Cambridge, 1979; Bye-Fellow, Robinson Coll., Cambridge, 1985–86; Dist. Vis. Fellow, La Trobe Univ., 1994. Consultant: Pacific Islands Develt Program, 1989–90, 1996; African Develt Bank, 1993–94 and 1999; Asian Develt Bank, 2003; UNCTAD, 2004–. Member: Council and Exec. Cttee, Royal Econ. Soc., 1979–89; Council, Business for Sterling, 1999–2006. Governor, NIESR, 1979–. Trustee, New Europe Res. Trust, 1999–2006. Member, Editorial Board: Jl of Develt Studies, 1979–2008; Jl of Post Keynesian Econs, 1998–; African Develt Review, 1999–; Series Ed., Great Thinkers in Econs, 2007–. *Publications:* Growth and Development, 1972, 9th edn as Economics of Development, 2011 (trans. Chinese and Greek 2002); Inflation, Saving and Growth in Developing Economies, 1974 (trans. Spanish 1978); (with R. Dixon) Regional Growth and Unemployment in the UK, 1975; Financing Economic Development, 1976 (trans. Greek 1977, Spanish 1978, Turkish 1980); (with H. Gibson) Balance of Payments Theory and the UK Experience, 1980, 4th edn 1992; Nicholas Kaldor, 1987; (with S. Bazen) Deindustrialisation, 1989, 3rd edn 1997; Performance and Prospects of the Pacific Island Economies in the World Economy, 1991; (with J. McCombie) Economic Growth and the Balance of Payments Constraint, 1994; Economics of Growth and Development: selected essays, vol. 1, 1995; Macroeconomic Issues from a Keynesian Perspective: selected essays, vol. 2, 1997; The Euro and Regional Divergence in Europe, 2000; The Nature of Economic Growth: an alternative framework for understanding the performance of nations, 2002 (trans. Spanish and Japanese, 2003, Portuguese, 2005); Trade, the Balance of Payments and Exchange Rate Policy in Developing Countries, 2003; (with J. McCombie) Essays on Balance-of-Payments Constrained Growth: theory and evidence, 2004; (with P. Pacheco-López) Trade Liberalisation and The Poverty of Nations, 2008 (trans. Turkish 2010, Spanish 2011); Economic Growth in an Open Developing Economy: the role of structure and demand, 2013; Essays on Keynesian and Kaldorian Economics, 2015; numerous edited books, esp. on Lord Keynes and Lord Kaldor; articles in professional jls; *festschrift* Growth and Economic Development: essays in honour of A. P. Thirlwall, 2006. *Recreations:* athletics (rep. GB, European Veterans Athletics Champs (400m, 800m), 1982), tennis, gardening, travel. *Address:* 14 Moorfield, Canterbury, Kent CT2 7AN. *T:* (01227) 769904. *E:* at4@kent.ac.uk. *Club:* Royal Over-Seas League.

THIRLWALL, Hon. Dame Kathryn (Mary), DBE 2010; **Hon. Mrs Justice Thirlwall;** a Judge of the High Court of Justice, Queen's Bench Division, since 2010; *b* 21 Nov. 1957; *d* of Brian Edward Thirlwall and Margaret Thirlwall (*née* Earl); *m* 1984, Prof. Charles Kelly; one *s* one *d*. *Educ:* St Anthony's Sch., Sunderland; Bristol Univ. (BA Hons 1980); Newcastle Poly. (CPE 1981). Called to the Bar, Middle Temple, 1982; QC 1999; Recorder, 2000–10. *Address:* Royal Courts of Justice, Strand, WC2A 2LL.

THIRSK, Amanda Jane, LVO 2013; Private Secretary and Comptroller to the Duke of York, since 2012; *b* London, 4 July 1965; *d* of Michael Emanuel Reynolds, CBE and Susan Geraldine Reynolds (now Smith); *m* 1991, Jeremy David Thirsk (*d* 2007); three *d*. *Educ:* St Paul's Girls' Sch.; Selwyn Coll., Cambridge (BA Law 1987). Guinness Mahon & Co. Ltd: graduate trainee, 1987–88; Manager, Syndications Dept, 1988–91; COS to Dep. Chief Exec., 1991–94; Dep. Hd of Treasury, 1994–96; Dir, Banking Dept, 1996–98; Asst Private Sec., 2005–06, Dep. Private Sec., 2006–12, to the Duke of York. *Address:* Buckingham Palace, SW1A 1AA. *T:* (020) 7024 4227. *E:* amanda.thirsk@royal.gsx.gov.uk.

THIRUNAMACHANDRAN, Prof. Rama Shankaran, FRGS; Vice-Chancellor and Principal, and Professor of Higher Education Policy, Canterbury Christ Church University, since 2013; *b* London, 26 Sept. 1966; *s* of Dr T. Thirunamachandran and S. Thirunamachandran; *m* 1994, Rachel Cottrell; one *s*. *Educ:* Downing Coll., Cambridge (BA 1989). Researcher, KCL, 1990–92; Sen. Asst Registrar, Univ. of Bristol, 1992–95; Hd of Res., Enterprise and Ext. Relns, Royal Holloway, Univ. of London, 1996–99; Regl Dir (SE), 1999–2001, Dir (Res., Innovation and Skills), 2002–08, HEFCE; Dep. Vice-Chancellor and Provost, Keele Univ., 2008–13. Director and Trustee: Higher Educn Acad., 2010–; UCAS, 2010–13. FRGS 2013. *Recreations:* cricket, bridge, travel. *Address:* Vice-Chancellor's Office, Canterbury Christ Church University, Canterbury, Kent CT1 1QU. *T:* (01227) 782915. *E:* vc@canterbury.ac.uk.

THISELTON, Prof. Rev. Canon Anthony Charles, PhD, DD; FBA 2010; Professor of Christian Theology, University of Nottingham, 1992–2001 and 2006–11, now Emeritus (Head, Department of Theology, 1992–2001; Professor Emeritus in Residence, 2001–06); Canon Theologian: Leicester Cathedral, 1994–2011, now Emeritus; Southwell Minster, 2000–10, now Emeritus; *b* 13 July 1937; *s* of Eric Charles Thiselton and Hilda Winifred (*née* Kevan); *m* 1963, Rosemary Stella Harman; two *s* one *d*. *Educ:* City of London School; King's Coll., London (BD 1959; MTh 1964; FKC 2010); PhD Sheffield 1977; DD Durham 1993. Curate, Holy Trinity, Sydenham, 1960–63; Lectr and Chaplain, Tyndale Hall, Bristol, 1963–67, Sen. Tutor, 1967–70; Recognised Teacher in Theology, Univ. of Bristol, 1965–71; University of Sheffield: Sir Henry Stephenson Fellow, 1970–71; Lectr in Biblical Studies, 1971–79; Sen. Lectr, 1979–86; Principal, St John's Coll., Nottingham and Special Lectr in Theology, Univ. of Nottingham, 1986–88; Principal, St John's Coll. with Cranmer Hall, Univ. of Durham, 1988–92; Public Orator, Nottingham Univ., 1999–2001. British Acad. Res. Leave Award, 1995–96. Visiting Professor: Calvin Coll., Grand Rapids, USA, 1982–83; Regent Coll., Vancouver, 1983; Fuller Theolog. Seminary, Pasadena, Calif, 1984 and 2002; North Park Coll. and Seminary, Chicago, 1984; Res. Prof. of Christian Theology, Univ. of Chester (formerly Chester UC), 2003–; Scottish Jl of Theol. Lectures, 1994. Exam. Chaplain to Bishop of Sheffield, 1977–80, to Bishop of Leicester, 1979–89 and 1993–. Member: C of E Faith and Order Adv. Group, 1971–81, 1987–90; Doctrine Commn, 1977–90, 1996–2005 (Vice-Chm., 1987–90); Wkg Pty on Revised Catechism, 1988–89; Steering Gp, Revised Weekday Lectionary, 2004–05; Gen. Synod of C of E, 1995– (Mem., Theol. Educn and Trng Cttee, 1999–2005; Chm., Evangelical Gp, 1999–2004; Mem., Appts Cttee, 2005–); Crown Nominations (formerly Appts) Commn, 2000–10; Wkg Pty on Women in the Episcopate, 2001–06; C of E Evangelical Council, 2001–04; C of E Bd of Educn, 2005–10. Consultant, Clergy Discipline (Doctrine) Gp, 2000–04; Mem., Task Gp for Theol Educn in the Anglican Communion, 2003–06. Mem., HFEA, 1995–99. Council for National Academic Awards: Vice-Chm., Bd of Theol and Religious Studies, 1984–87; Mem., Cttee for Humanities, 1987–89. Pres., Soc. for the Study of Theology, 1998–2000. Adv. Editor, Jl for Study of NT, 1981–91; Editl Consultant, Ex Auditu (Princeton and Chicago), 1985–2010; Mem. Editl Bd, Biblical Interpretation (Brill, Leiden), 1992–2003, Internat. Jl Systematic Theol., 1999–2010. DD Lambeth, 2002; Hon. DTheol Chester, 2012. *Publications:* The Two Horizons: New Testament Hermeneutics and Philosophical Description, 1980; (with C. Walhout and R. Lundin) The Responsibility of Hermeneutics, 1985; New Horizons in Hermeneutics: theory and practice of transforming biblical reading, 1992; Interpreting God and the Postmodern Self, 1995; (with C. Walhout and R. Lundin) The Promise of Hermeneutics, 1999; First Corinthians: a commentary on the Greek text, 2000; Concise Encyclopedia of Philosophy of Religion, 2002; (ed jtly) Reading Luke: interpretation, reflection, formation, 2005; Thiselton on Hermeneutics: collected works, 2006; Shorter Exegetical and Pastoral Commentary on 1 Corinthians, 2006; The Hermeneutics of Doctrine, 2007; Hermeneutics, 2009; The Living Paul, 2009; Blackwell Commentary on 1 and 2 Thessalonians, 2010; The Last Things: a new approach, 2012; The Holy Spirit in Biblical Teaching: through the centuries, and today, 2012; The Thiselton Companion to Christian Theology, 2015; Systematic Theology, 2015; Discovering Romans, 2016; contribs to learned jls and other books on New Testament, doctrine, and philosophical hermeneutics. *Recreation:* choral and organ music. *Address:* South View Lodge, 390 High Road, Chilwell, Nottingham NG9 5EG. *E:* thiselton@ntlworld.com.

THISTLETHWAITE, Rev. Canon Dr Nicholas John; Precentor, since 1999, and Sub Dean, since 2006, Guildford Cathedral; a Chaplain to the Queen, since 2014; *b* Mansfield, Notts, 23 Oct. 1951; *s* of Peter and Joan Thistlethwaite; *m* 1980, Tessa North; one *s*. *Educ:* Brunts Grammar Sch., Mansfield; Selwyn Coll., Cambridge (MA 1977; PhD 1981); Ripon Coll., Cuddesdon, Oxford (MA 1982). Ordained deacon, 1979, priest, 1980; Asst Curate, St Gabriel's, Heaton, 1979–82; Chaplain, 1982–90, Fellow, 1986–90, Gonville and Caius Coll., Cambridge; Vicar, Trumpington, Cambridge, 1990–99. Member: Cathedrals Fabric Commn for Eng., 2001–11; Fabric Adv. Cttee, Canterbury Cathedral, 2011–; Fabric Adv. Commn, Westminster Abbey, 2012–. Chm., British Inst. of Organ Studies, 1992–97. Medal, RCO, 2015. *Publications:* The Organs of Cambridge, 1983, 2nd edn 2008; (contrib.) The New Grove Dictionary of Music and Musicians, 1985; The Making of the Victorian Organ, 1990; (ed jtly) The Cambridge Companion to the Organ, 1998; (contrib.) The Organ: an encyclopedia,

2006, 2nd edn 2015; (contrib.) Die Musik in Geschichte und Gegegwart, 2007. *Recreations:* political history, architecture and art, theatre, opera. *Address:* 3 Cathedral Close, Guildford, Surrey GU2 7TL. *T:* (01483) 547865. *Club:* Royal Over-Seas League.

THOBURN, Prof. June, CBE 2002; LittD; Professor of Social Work, University of East Anglia, Norwich, 1994–2004, now Emeritus; *b* 17 May 1939; *d* of late William Shuttleworth Bailey and Elizabeth Anne Bailey; *m* 1965, John Thomas Thoburn; two *s*. *Educ:* Univ. of Reading (BA Hons French); Oxford Univ. (Dip. Public and Soc. Admin); Univ. of East Anglia (MSW; LittD). Social worker, Social Services Depts of Leicester CC, RBK&C and Norfolk CC, 1964–79; University of East Anglia: Lectr in Social Work, 1979–94; Dean, Sch. of Social Work, 1998–2001. Non-exec. Dir, E Norfolk HA, 1994–98; Member: Pres. of Family Division's Adv. Gp, 1998–2004; Gen. Social Care Council, 2001–08; Advr on child protection and adoption to DoH, 1995–2004; Chairman: Jersey Child Protection Cttee, 2007–09; Norfolk Family Justice Bd, 2012–; Bd Mem., CAFCASS, 2009–12. FRSA 2001; AcSS 2002–06. Editor, Child and Family Social Work, 2002–04. *Publications:* Permanence in Child Care, 1986; Child Placement: principles and practice, 1988, 2nd edn 1994; Safeguarding Children with the Children Act 1989, 1999; Permanent Family Placement for Children of Minority Ethnic Origin, 2000; Family Support in Cases of Emotional Maltreatment and Neglect, 2000; Child Welfare Services for Minority Ethnic Families, 2004. *Recreations:* dinghy sailing, films, travel. *Address:* School of Social Work, University of East Anglia, Norwich NR4 7TJ. *T:* (01603) 593566, *Fax:* (01603) 573552. *E:* j.thoburn@uea.ac.uk.

THODAY, Jonathan Murray; Joint Managing Director, Avalon Entertainment Ltd, since 1998; *b* 7 May 1961; *s* of Prof. John Marion Thoday, FRS and of Doris Joan Thoday; *m* 1996, Leanne Newman; one *s* one *d*. *Educ:* Corpus Christi Coll., Cambridge (BA Natural Scis 1983; MSc Biotechnol. and Genetic Engrg 1984). Co-founding Managing Director: Avalon Promotions; Avalon Public Relns; Avalon Motion Pictures; Avalon Television. *Address:* Avalon, 4A Exmoor Street, W10 6BD. *T:* (020) 7598 8000.

THOM, Dr Gordon; Director, Nobasu Consulting Ltd, since 2014; *b* 18 May 1953; *m* 1977, Margaret Pringle; one *s* one *d*. *Educ:* Univ. of Aberdeen (PhD 1978). DoE, 1978; joined FCO, 1979; Second, subseq. First Sec., Tokyo, 1981; FCO, 1985–89; First Sec., New Delhi, 1989–93; Economic Counsellor, Tokyo, 1994–98; Man. Dir, Dyson Japan, 1998–2001; Internat. Man. Dir, Dyson Ltd, 2001–04; Chm., Dyson Japan, 2004–05; Pres., Dyson US, 2006–08; Dir, Thom Consulting, 2009–10; Man. Dir, Floor Care and Small Appliances, Electrolux Japan, 2009–12; Pres., Bodum Japan, 2012–14.

THOM, James Alexander Francis; QC 2003; a Recorder, since 2002; *b* 19 Oct. 1951; *s* of James Flockhart Thom and Elspeth Margaret Thom (*née* Macnaughton); *m* 1st, 1974, Theresa Lindsie Hawkins (marr. diss. 1997); two *s* one *d*; 2nd, 1999, Elisabeth Jane Campbell Mardall. *Educ:* Corpus Christi Coll., Oxford (MA, BCL). Called to the Bar, Middle Temple, 1974; admitted to Bar: of St Vincent and Grenadines, 1997; of British Virgin Islands, 2005. *Recreations:* walking, reading, cooking, wine. *Address:* New Square Chambers, 12 New Square, Lincoln's Inn, WC2A 3SW. *T:* (020) 7419 8000, *Fax:* (020) 7419 8050. *E:* james.thom@newsquarechambers.co.uk.

THOM, Kenneth Cadwallader; HM Diplomatic Service, retired; *b* 4 Dec. 1922; *m* 1948, Patience Myra (*née* Collingridge); three *s* one *d*. *Educ:* University College School, London; St Andrews Univ. (MA (Hons)). Army Service, 1942–47; Assistant District Officer, then District Officer, Northern Nigerian Administration, 1950–59; 1st Secretary: FO, 1959; UK Mission to UN, NY, 1960–63; FO, 1963–66; Budapest, 1966–68; FCO, 1968–72; Counsellor, Dublin, 1972–74; Counsellor, FCO, 1974–78; Consul-General: Hanover, 1978–79; Hamburg, 1979–81; retired, and re-employed, FCO, 1981–85. *Address:* Heybrook, Lower Backway, Bruton, Somerset BA10 0EA.

THOMAS; *see* Elis-Thomas.

THOMAS, family name of **Barons Thomas of Cwmgiedd, Thomas of Gresford, Thomas of Macclesfield** and **Thomas of Swynnerton,** and **Baroness Thomas of Walliswood.**

THOMAS OF CWMGIEDD, Baron *cr* 2013 (Life Peer), of Cwmgiedd in the County of Powys; **Roger John Laugharne Thomas,** Kt 1996; PC 2003; Lord Chief Justice of England and Wales, since 2013; *b* 22 Oct. 1947; *s* of Roger Edward Laugharne Thomas and Dinah Agnes Thomas, Cwmgiedd; *m* 1973, Elizabeth Ann, *d* of S. J. Buchanan, Ohio, USA; one *s* one *d*. *Educ:* Rugby School; Trinity Hall, Cambridge (BA; Hon. Fellow, 2004); Univ. of Chicago (Commonwealth Fellow; JD). Called to Bar, Gray's Inn, 1969, Bencher, 1992; QC 1984; a Recorder, 1987–96; a Judge of the High Court of Justice, QBD, 1996–2003; Judge of the Commercial Court, 1996–2003; Judge i/c Commercial Court List, 2002–03; a Lord Justice of Appeal, 2003–11; Vice-Pres., 2008–11, Pres., 2011–13, QBD; Dep. Hd of Criminal Justice, 2008–13. Presiding Judge, Wales and Chester Circuit, 1998–2001; Sen. Presiding Judge for England and Wales, 2003–06. Asst Teacher, Mayo College, Ajmer, India, 1965–66; Lord Morris of Borth-y-Gest Lectr, Univ. of Wales, 2000. Faculty Fellow, Law Sch., Univ. of Southampton, 1990. DTI Inspector, Mirror Gp Newspapers plc, 1992. Vice Pres., British Maritime Law Assoc., 1996–; President: British Insurance Law Assoc., 2004–06; Eur. Network of the Councils of the Judiciary, 2008–10. Hon. Fellow: Univ. of Wales, Aberystwyth, 2002; Univ. of Wales, Swansea, 2003; Cardiff, 2005; Bangor, 2008. Hon. LLD: Glamorgan, 2003; UWE, 2008. *Publications:* papers and articles on commercial, maritime and insurance law, the Welsh courts and devolution, constitutional law. *Recreations:* gardens, walking, travel. *Address:* Royal Courts of Justice, Strand, WC2A 2LL.

THOMAS OF GRESFORD, Baron *cr* 1996 (Life Peer), of Gresford in the co. borough of Wrexham; **Donald Martin Thomas,** OBE 1982; QC 1979; a Recorder of the Crown Court, 1976–2002; *b* 13 March 1937; *s* of Hywel and Olwen Thomas; *m* 1st, 1961, Nan Thomas (*née* Kerr) (*d* 2000); three *s* one *d*; 2nd, 2005, Baroness Walmsley, *qv*. *Educ:* Grove Park Grammar Sch., Wrexham; Peterhouse, Cambridge (MA, LLB). Solicitor at Wrexham, 1961–66; Lectr in Law, 1966–68; called to the Bar, Gray's Inn, 1967, Bencher, 1989; Barrister, Wales and Chester Circuit, 1968–; Dep. Circuit Judge, 1974–76; Dep. High Court Judge, 1985–. Mem., Criminal Injury Compensation Bd, 1985–93. Contested (L): W Flints, 1964, 1966, 1970; Wrexham, Feb. and Oct. 1974, 1979, 1983, 1987; Vice Chm., Welsh Liberal Party, 1967–69, Chm. 1969–74; President: Welsh Liberal Party, 1977, 1978, 1979; Welsh Liberal Democrats, 1993–97 (Vice-Pres., 1991–93). Lib Dem Shadow Attorney Gen., 2004–06 and 2007–10, Shadow Lord Chancellor, 2006–07. Chairman: Marcher Sound, 1991–2000 (ind. local radio for NE Wales and Cheshire) (Vice Chm., 1983–91); Southbank Sinfonia Develt Council, 2003–08. President: London Welsh Choral, 2002–; Sirenian Singers, 2003–; Friends of Gresford Church, 1998–; Patron, Hong Kong Welsh Male Voice Choir, 2005–. *Recreations:* Rugby football, rowing, golf, choral singing, harp and piano playing, fishing, cooking. *Address:* Glasfryn, Gresford, Wrexham, Clwyd LL12 8RG. *T:* (01978) 852205. *Club:* Reform.

THOMAS OF MACCLESFIELD, Baron *cr* 1997 (Life Peer), of Prestbury in the co. of Cheshire; **Terence James Thomas,** CBE 1997; Managing Director, The Co-operative Bank, 1988–97; Chairman, Internexus, 2002–04; *b* 19 Oct. 1937; *s* of late William Emrys Thomas and Mildred Evelyn Thomas; *m* 1963, Lynda, *d* of late William John Stevens; three *s*. *Educ:* Queen Elizabeth Grammar Sch., Carmarthen; Univ. of Bath (Postgrad. Dip. Business Admin); INSEAD (AMP). FCIB. Nat. Provincial, later Nat. Westminster Bank, 1962–71; Joint Credit Card Co., 1971–73; The Co-operative Bank: Mkting Manager, 1973–77; Asst Gen. Manager, then Jt Gen. Manager, 1977–83; Dir, 1984; Exec. Dir, Gp Develt, 1987. Director: Stanley Leisure Organisation plc, 1994–98; Capita Gp, 1998–99; Rathbone CI, 1998–99. Chm., Venture Technic (Cheshire) Ltd, 1984–97. Director: English Partnerships (Central), 1998–99; Commn for the New Towns, 1998–99; CDA; Chairman: NW Partnership, 1994–97; Northwest Develt Agency, 1998–2002. Mem., Regl Economic Develt Commn. Mem., Gen. Council, CIB, until 1997; Pres., Internat. Co-operative Banking Assoc., 1988–95. Chm., NW Media Charitable Trust, 1998–99. Vis. Prof., Univ. of Stirling, 1988–91. Mem., Ct of Governors, UMIST, 1996–2004. Mem. Bd Trustees, UNICEF, 1998–99. FRSA; CCMI. Hon. Fellow, Univ. of Central Lancs, 2000. Hon. DLitt Salford, 1996; Hon. DBA Manchester Metropolitan, 1998; DUniv UMIST, 1999. Mancunian of the Year, 1998. *Publications:* An Inclusive Community with Integrity (memoir), 2008. *Address:* 51 Willowmead Drive, Prestbury, Cheshire SK10 4DD.

THOMAS OF SWYNNERTON, Baron *cr* 1981 (Life Peer), of Notting Hill in Greater London; **Hugh Swynnerton Thomas,** FRSL, FRHistS; historian; *b* 21 Oct. 1931; *s* of Hugh Whitelegge Thomas, CMG, sometime Sec. for Native Affairs, Gold Coast (Ghana) and late Margery Swynnerton, sometime Colonial Nursing Service; *m* 1962, Vanessa Jebb, *d* of 1st Baron Gladwyn, GCMG, GCVO, CB; two *s* one *d*. *Educ:* Sherborne; Queens' Coll., Cambridge (Scholar; Hon. Fellow 2008); Sorbonne, Paris. Pres. Cambridge Union, 1953. Foreign Office, 1954–57; Sec. to UK delegn to UN Disarmament Sub-Cttee, 1955–56; Lectr at RMA Sandhurst, 1957; Prof. of History, 1966–76, and Chm., Grad. Sch. of Contemp. European Studies, 1973–76, Univ. of Reading. Anshen Lectr, Frick Mus., NY, 1991; Yaseen Lectr, Met. Mus. of Art, NY, 1995. King Juan Carlos I (Vis.) Prof., New York Univ., 1995; Vis. Prof. of History, Univ. of Boston, 1996; Univ. Prof., Boston Univ., 1997–. Chm., Centre for Policy Studies, 1979–90. Trustee, Fundación Medinaceli, 1996–. Caballero, Maestranza of Ronda, 2011–. Corresp. Mem., Real Acad. de la Historia, Madrid, 1994; Académico, Categoría de Honor, Real Acad. Hispano Americana, 2004; Mem., Real Academia Sevillana de Bellas Letras, 2013. Somerset Maugham Prize, 1962; Arts Council prize for History (1st Nat. Book Awards), 1980; Gabarrón Prize, Gabarrón Foundn, Valladolid, 2005; Calvo Serer Prize, Diario Madrid Foundn, 2009; Nonino Prize, Udine, 2009; Boccaccio Prize, Giovanni Boccaccio Literary Assoc., Italy, 2009; PEN Mexico Prize, 2011; Joaquín Romero Morube Prize, ABC newspaper, Seville, 2013. Order of Aztec Eagle (Mexico), 1994; Knight Grand Cross, Order of Isabel la Católica (Spain), 2001; Commandeur, Ordre des Arts et des Lettres (France), 2008. *Publications:* (as Hugh Thomas) The World's Game, 1957; The Spanish Civil War, 1961, rev. edn 1977, rev. illustrated edn, Spain, 1979; The Suez Affair, 1967; Cuba, or the Pursuit of Freedom, 1971; (ed) The selected writings of José Antonio Primo de Rivera, 1972; Goya and The Third of May 1808, 1972; Europe, the Radical Challenge, 1973; John Strachey, 1973; The Cuban Revolution, 1977; An Unfinished History of the World, 1979, rev. edn 1982 (US 1979, A History of the World); The Case for the Round Reading Room, 1983; Havannah (novel), 1984; Armed Truce, 1986; A Traveller's Companion to Madrid, 1988; Klara (novel), 1988; Ever Closer Union: Britain's destiny in Europe, 1991; The Conquest of Mexico, 1993; The Slave Trade: the history of the Atlantic slave trade 1440–1870, 1997; The Future of Europe, 1997; Who's Who of the Conquistadors, 2000; Rivers of Gold, 2003; Letter from Asturias, 2006; Beaumarchais in Seville, 2006; Don Eduardo, 2008; The Golden Age: the Spanish Empire of Charles V, 2010; World without End: the Spanish Empire of King Philip II, 2013. *Address:* 29 Ladbroke Grove, W11 3BB.

THOMAS OF WALLISWOOD, Baroness *cr* 1994 (Life Peer), of Dorking in the County of Surrey; **Susan Petronella Thomas,** OBE 1989; DL; a Deputy Speaker, House of Lords, 2002–07; Chairman, Surrey County Council, 1996–97 (Member (Lib Dem), 1985–97; Vice Chairman, 1993–96); *b* 20 Dec. 1935; *m* 1958, David Churchill Thomas, *qv*; one *s* two *d*. *Educ:* Cranborne Chase Sch.; Lady Margaret Hall, Oxford. NEDO, 1971–74; Chief Exec., British Clothing Industries Council for Europe, 1974–78. Chm. and Treas., Richmond Liberal Assoc., 1974–77; former Pres., Women Lib Dems. Chm., Highways and Transport Cttee, Surrey CC, 1993–96; Member: Surrey Probation Cttee, 1997–2001; Surrey Area Probation Bd, 2001–04. Contested: (Lib Alliance) Mole Valley, 1983 and 1987; (Lib Dem) Surrey, Eur. Parly elecns, 1994. Lib Dem spokesman, H of L, on transport, 1994–2001, on women, 2001–06, on Equality, 2007–09. Chm., Associate (formerly All-Party) Parly Gp on Sex Equality, 1998–2001; Mem., H of L European Select Cttee on EU, 2005–07 (Mem., Law and Instns Sub-Cttee, 2003–05; Chm., Social and Consumer Affairs Sub-Cttee, 2005–07). DL Surrey, 1996. *Address:* Hidden House, 15 Guilden Road, Chichester, W Sussex PO19 7LA. *T:* (01243) 780096.

See also Hon. D. W. P. Thomas.

THOMAS OF WINCHESTER, Baroness *cr* 2006 (Life Peer), of Winchester in the County of Hampshire; **Celia Marjorie Thomas,** MBE 1985; Head, Liberal Democrat (formerly Liberal) Whips' Office, House of Lords, 1977–2006; *b* 14 Oct. 1945; *d* of David and Marjorie Thomas. *Educ:* St Swithun's Sch., Winchester. Winchester Diocesan Bd of Finance, 1963–65; Winchester Cathedral Appeal, 1965–66; The Pilgrims' Sch., Winchester, 1967–72; Christ Church Cathedral Sch., Oxford, 1972–74; Asst in office of Rt Hon. Jeremy Thorpe, MP, 1975–76. Party Agent: (Lib) Winchester, Oct. 1974; (Lib/SDP Alliance, later Lib Dem) Brecon and Radnor, 1987 and 1992. House of Lords: Lib Dem spokesman for Work and Pensions, 2007–10. Chm., Delegated Powers and Regulatory Reform Cttee, 2010–15; Member: Merits of Statutory Instruments Select Cttee, 2006–10; Procedure Select Cttee, 2007–12; Liaison Select Cttee, 2007–10; Refreshment Select Cttee, 2007–12. Vice-Pres., Lloyd George Soc., 2005–; Pres., Winchester Lib Dems, 2007–. Trustee, Muscular Dystrophy UK (formerly Campaign), 2010– (Vice Pres., 2008–). Patron: Winchester Churches Nightshelter, 2008–; Avonbrook Projects Abroad, 2008–; Thrive, 2011–; Pinotage Youth Develt Acad., 2012–. *Recreations:* music, theatre, gardening, butterfly conservation, watching cricket. *Address:* House of Lords, SW1A 0PW. *T:* (020) 7219 3586. *E:* thomascm@parliament.uk. *Club:* Two Brydges.

THOMAS, Abraham, FSA; Director, Sir John Soane's Museum, since 2013; *b* Sunderland, 17 Oct. 1977; *s* of Dr Thomas Mathew and Dr Elizabeth Thomas. *Educ:* Tiffin Sch.; Univ. of Leicester (BSc Computer Sci.). Analyst, Deutsche Bank, 2000–05; Curator, Designs, V&A Mus., 2005–13. Trustee, Blue Elephant Th., 2003–05. Gov., Newham Sixth Form Coll., 2003–05. FSA 2014. *Publications:* Owen Jones, 2009; 1:1 - Architects Build Small Spaces, 2010. *Address:* Sir John Soane's Museum, 13 Lincoln's Inn Fields, WC2A 3BP.

THOMAS, Prof. Adrian Tregerthen; Professor of Music: Cardiff University (formerly University of Wales, Cardiff), 1996–2010, now Emeritus; Gresham College, 2003–06, Professor Emeritus, 2008; *b* 11 June 1947; *s* of Owen George Thomas and Jean Tregerthen. *Educ:* Univ. of Nottingham (BMus 1969); University Coll., Cardiff (MA 1971). Lectr in Music, 1973–82, Sen. Lectr, 1982–85, Hamilton Harty Prof. of Music, 1985–96, QUB. Hd of Music, BBC Radio 3, 1990–93. Medal of Polish Composers' Union, for Distinguished Service to Contemporary Polish Music, 1989; Order of Merit for Polish Culture, 1996; Lutoslawski Medal, Lutoslawski Soc., 2005; Gloria Artis Gold Medal, Polish Min. of Culture and Nat. Heritage, 2013. *Publications:* Grazyna Bacewicz: chamber and orchestral music, USA 1985; (contrib.) Cambridge Companion to Chopin, 1992; (contrib.) New Grove Dictionary of Opera, 1993; (contrib.) New Grove Dictionary of Women Composers, 1994; Górecki, 1997; (contrib.) New Grove Dictionary of Music and Musicians, 2nd edn 2000; Polish Music since Szymanowski, 2005; contrib. Music Rev., THES, Contemp. Music Rev., Music and Letters. *Recreations:* visual arts, poetry, oriental arts, entomology, Cornish landscape and history. *E:* adrianthomasmusic@me.com.

THOMAS, Sir Alan; *see* Thomas, Sir J. A.

THOMAS, Andrew Martin; QC 2008; a Recorder, since 2008; a Deputy High Court Judge, since 2013; *b* Wrexham, 18 Oct. 1965; *s* of Martin and Nan Thomas; *m* 1995, Jodie Swallow; one *s* one *d*. *Educ:* Darland Comp. Sch., Rossett; Yale Sixth Form Coll., Wrexham; Peterhouse, Cambridge (BA 1987); Inns of Court Sch. of Law. Called to the Bar, Gray's Inn, 1989; barrister, 1990–. Judge of First-tier Tribunal (Restricted Patient Panel) (pt-time), 2012–. *Recreations:* family, running, ski-ing. *Address:* c/o Lincoln House Chambers, Tower 12, The Avenue North, Spinningfields, 18–22 Bridge Street, Manchester M3 3BZ. *T:* (0161) 832 5701. *E:* andrew.thomas@lincolnhousechambers.com.

THOMAS, (Anthony) Richard, CMG 1995; HM Diplomatic Service, retired; High Commissioner, Jamaica, and non-resident Ambassador to Haiti, 1995–99; *b* 11 July 1939; *s* of Frederick James Thomas and Winifred Kate Apthorpe Webb; *m* 1976, Ricky Parks Prado, London and Lima; one *s* one *d*. *Educ:* Ampleforth; Peterhouse, Cambridge (MA). FO 1962; served Caracas, Budapest, Washington, Madrid and FCO; Counsellor, Dep. Consul-Gen., Johannesburg, 1981; Minister Counsellor and Consul-Gen., Brasilia, 1985; FCO 1989; Ambassador to Angola, São Tomé and Príncipe, 1993. *Recreations:* listening to music, reading, theatre, visual arts, cooking. *Address:* c/o 83 Broxash Road, SW11 6AD.

THOMAS, Prof. (Antony) Charles, CBE 1991; DL; DLitt; FSA; FRHistS; FBA 1989; Professor of Cornish Studies, University of Exeter, 1971–91, Professor Emeritus, 1993; Director, Institute of Cornish Studies, 1971–91; *b* 24 April 1928; *s* of late Donald Woodroffe Thomas and Viva Warrington Thomas; *m* 1959, Jessica Dorothea Esther, *d* of late F. A. Mann, CBE, FBA, Hon. QC; two *s* two *d*. *Educ:* Winchester; Corpus Christi Coll., Oxon (BA Hons Jurisp.); Univ. of London (Dipl. Prehist. Archaeol.; Fellow, UCL, 1993); DLitt Oxon, 1983. FSA 1960; FRHistS 1983. Lectr in Archaeology, Univ. of Edinburgh, 1957–67; Prof. of Archaeology, Univ. of Leicester, 1967–71. Leverhulme Fellowship, 1965–67; Sir John Rhys Fellow, Univ. of Oxford, and Vis. Sen. Res. Fellow, Jesus Coll., 1985–86; Emeritus Leverhulme Fellowship, 1993–95. Hon. Prof., UCL, 2013. Lectures: Dalrymple, Univ. of Glasgow, 1991; (first) Whithorn Trust, 1992; (first) John Jamieson, Scottish Church History Soc., 1997; Rhind, Edinburgh, 1999. President: Council for British Archaeology, 1970–73; Royal Instn of Cornwall, 1970–72; Cornwall Archaeol. Soc., 1984–88; Soc. for Medieval Archaeology, 1986–89; Soc. for Landscape Studies, 1993–; Cornwall Methodist History Soc., 2003–; John Harris Soc., 2010–. Chairman: BBC SW Reg. Adv. Council, 1975–80; DoE Area Archaeol Cttee, Cornwall and Devon, 1975–79; Cornwall Cttee Rescue Archaeol., 1976–88; Soc. for Church Archaeol., 1995–98; Mem., Royal Commn on Historical Monuments (England), 1983–97 (Acting Chm., 1988–89; Vice Chm., 1991–97). DL Cornwall, 1988. Hon. MRIA 1973; Hon. Fellow: RSAI, 1975; St David's UC Lampeter, 1992; Hon. FSAScot 2000. Hon. DLitt NUI, 1996. William Frend Medal, Soc. of Antiquaries, 1982; Jenner Medal, Royal Instn of Cornwall, 2008. *Publications:* Christian Antiquities of Camborne, 1967; The Early Christian Archaeology of North Britain, 1971; Britain and Ireland in Early Christian Times, 1971; (with A. Small and D. Wilson) St Ninian's Isle and its Treasure, 1973; (with D. Ivall) Military Insignia of Cornwall, 1974; Christianity in Roman Britain to AD 500, 1981; Exploration of a Drowned Landscape, 1985; Celtic Britain, 1986; Views and Likenesses: photographers in Cornwall and Scilly 1839–70, 1988; Tintagel, Arthur and Archaeology, 1993; And Shall These Mute Stones Speak?: post-Roman inscriptions in Western Britain, 1994; Christian Celts, Messages and Images, 1998; Silent in the Shroud, 1999; The Penzance Market Cross, 1999; Whispering Reeds, 2002; (with D. R. Howlett) Vita Sancti Paterni, 2003; Badges of Cornwall's Home Guard 1941–1944, 2007; (as 'Cornubiensis') Cornish Chapel Stories, 2008; Real Cornish Humour, 2008; Greg McGrath, 2011; Fletcher's Lane, 2012; Gathering the Fragments, 2012. *Recreations:* military history, archaeological fieldwork. *Address:* Lambessow, St Clement, Truro, Cornwall TR1 1TB.
See also M. N. C. Thomas.

THOMAS, Hon. Barbara; *see* Thomas Judge, Hon. Barbara Singer.

THOMAS, Catherine; Member (Lab) Llanelli, National Assembly for Wales, 2003–07; *b* 1963. *Educ:* Llanelli Girls' Grammar Sch.; Univ. of Glamorgan; Univ. of Wales, Cardiff (MSc). Formerly press and PR officer, Wales gp, Tidy Britain. Mem., Children in Wales. Contested (Lab) Llanelli, Nat. Assembly for Wales, 2007. *Address:* c/o National Assembly for Wales, Cardiff CF99 1NA.

THOMAS, Charles; *see* Thomas, A. C.

THOMAS, Ven. Charles Edward; Archdeacon of Wells, 1983–93; *b* 30 Dec. 1927. *Educ:* St David's College, Lampeter (BA 1951); College of the Resurrection, Mirfield. Deacon 1953, priest 1954; Curate of Ilminster, 1953–56; Chaplain and Asst Master, St Michael's Coll., Tenbury, 1956–57; Curate of St Stephen's, St Albans, 1957–58; Vicar, St Michael and All Angels, Boreham Wood, 1958–66; Rector, Monksilver with Elworthy, 1966–74, with Brompton Ralph and Nettlecombe, 1969–74 (Curate-in-charge of Nettlecombe, 1968–69); Vicar of South Petherton with the Seavingtons, 1974–83. RD of Crewkerne, 1977–82. *Address:* Geryfelin, Pentre, Tregaron, Ceredigion SY25 6ND. *T:* (01974) 298102.

THOMAS, Prof. Christian David, PhD; FRS 2012; Professor, Department of Biology, University of York, since 2004; *b* Croydon, 9 Sept. 1959; *s* of Ambler Thomas and Diana Thomas; *m* 1985, Dr Helen Billington; one *s* three *d*. *Educ:* Bradfield Coll.; Corpus Christi Coll., Cambridge (BA Natural Scis 1981); University Coll. of North Wales, Bangor (MSc Ecol. 1984); Univ. of Texas at Austin (PhD Zool. 1988). Scientist: Ecol. Div., DSIR, NZ, 1988–89; Dept of Conservation, Christchurch, NZ, 1989; Post-doctoral work, NERC Centre for Population Biol., Imperial Coll. London at Silwood Park, 1990–92; Lectr, Sch. of Biol Scis, Univ. of Birmingham, 1992–95; Res. Fellow, Dept of Biol., 1995–99, Prof., Sch. of Biol., 1999–2004, Univ. of Leeds. Hon. PhD Helsinki, 2014. *Publications:* over 225 articles in scientific jls, edited book chapters. *Recreations:* wildlife gardening, natural history. *Address:* Department of Biology, University of York, York YO10 5DD. *T:* (01904) 328646. *E:* chris.thomas@york.ac.uk.

THOMAS, (Christopher) Paul; Deputy Chief Executive, Manchester Enterprises (formerly Manchester Training and Enterprise Council), 1998–2006; consultant, 2006–11; *b* 9 Feb. 1951; *s* of Donald Thomas and Rita Thomas (*née* Kershaw); *m* 1981, Colleen Doey. *Educ:* Hutton Grammar Sch.; Bridlington Sch.; Keble Coll., Oxford (MA PPE). Civil Service, 1973–97: Customs & Excise, HM Treasury, Cabinet Office, Dept of Employment, and DfEE; Regl Policy Advr, Yorks and Humberside TECs, 1997–98. Director: Sheffield Jazz, 2008–; Jobsteps Employment Services Ltd, 2011–14 (Chm., 2012–14); Adsetts Partnership, 2012–14; Chevin Housing Assoc. Ltd, 2013–. Gov., Hope Valley Coll., 2006–11 (Chm. Govs, 2009–11). *Recreations:* cricket, jazz, walking, sailing, ski-ing, reading, theatre. *Address:* 11 Dore Road, Dore, Sheffield, S Yorks S17 3NA.

THOMAS, Christopher Sydney; QC 1989; PhD; FCIArb; a Recorder, since 2000; *b* 17 March 1950; *s* of late John Raymond Thomas and of Daphne May Thomas; *m* 1979, Patricia Jane Heath; one *s* one *d*. *Educ:* King's Sch., Worcester; Univ. of Kent at Canterbury (BA Hons, 1st Cl.); Faculté International de Droit Comparé, Paris (Diplôme de Droit Comparé (avec mérite), 1972); King's Coll., London (PhD 1994). FCIArb 1994. Hardwick Scholar and Jenkins Scholar, Lincoln's Inn; called to the Bar, Lincoln's Inn, 1973; Asst Recorder, 1994–2000. Called to Gibraltar Bar, 1989. CEDR accredited Mediator, 1999. Dep. Hd, Keating Chambers, 2008–. *Recreations:* farming, sailing. *Address:* Keating Chambers, 15 Essex Street, WC2R 3AA. *T:* (020) 7544 2600.

THOMAS, Claire C.; *see* Curtis-Thomas.

THOMAS, Clarence; Associate Justice of the Supreme Court of the United States, since 1991; *b* 23 June 1948. *Educ:* Yale Univ. (JD). Asst to Attorney Gen., State of Missouri, 1974–77; attorney in private practice, 1977–79; Legislative Asst, US Senate, 1979–81; Asst Sec. for Civil Rights, Dept of Educn, Washington, 1981–82; Chm., Equal Employment Opportunity Commn, Washington, 1982–90; Judge, US Court of Appeals, 1990–91. *Publications:* My Grandfather's Son: a memoir, 2007. *Address:* United States Supreme Court, 1 First Street NE, Washington, DC 20543, USA.

THOMAS, David; *see* Thomas, W. D.

THOMAS, Rt Rev. David; Provincial Assistant Bishop, Church in Wales, 1996–2008; *b* 22 July 1942; *s* of late Rt Rev. John James Absalom Thomas; *m* 1967, Rosemary Christine Calton; one *s* one *d*. *Educ:* Christ College, Brecon; Keble College, Oxford; St Stephen's House, Oxford. MA Oxon. Curate of Hawarden, 1967–69; Tutor, St Michael's College, Llandaff, Cardiff, 1969–70, Chaplain 1970–75; Secretary, Church in Wales Liturgical Commn, 1970–75; Vice-Principal, St Stephen's House, Oxford, 1975–79; Vicar of Chepstow, 1979–82; Principal, St Stephen's House, Oxford, 1982–87; Vicar of St Peter's, Newton, Swansea, 1987–96; Residentiary Canon, Brecon Cathedral, 1994–96. Mem., Standing Doctrinal Commn, 1975–93, Standing Liturgical Adv. Commn, 1987–2008, Church in Wales. *Publications:* (contrib.) The Ministry of the Word (ed G. J. Cuming), 1979. *Recreations:* music, walking. *Address:* 65 Westland Avenue, West Cross, Swansea SA3 5NR.

THOMAS, Prof. David; Professor of Geography, University of Birmingham, 1978–95, now Professor Emeritus; *b* 16 Feb. 1931; *s* of William and Florence Grace Thomas; *m* 1955, Daphne Elizabeth Berry; one *s* one *d*. *Educ:* Bridgend Grammar School; University College of Wales, Aberystwyth (BA, MA); PhD London. Asst Lectr, Lectr, Reader, University College London, 1957–70; Prof. and Head of Dept, St David's University College, Lampeter, 1970–78; Birmingham University: Head of Dept of Geography, 1978–86; Head of Sch. of Geog., 1991–93; Pro Vice-Chancellor, 1984–89. Pres., IBG, 1988 (Hon. Sec., 1976–78); Mem., Council, RGS, 1988–91. *Publications:* Agriculture in Wales during the Napoleonic Wars, 1963; London's Green Belt, 1970; (ed) An Advanced Geography of the British Isles, 1974; (with J. A. Dawson) Man and his world, 1975; (ed) Wales: a new study, 1977; (with P. T. J. Morgan) Wales: the shaping of a nation, 1984; articles in learned jls. *Recreations:* music, wine, spectating. *Address:* 3 Is-y-Coed, Wenvoe, Cardiff CF5 6DL. *T:* (029) 2059 2861.

THOMAS, David; strategy consultant, since 2012; Principal Ombudsman, Financial Ombudsman Service, 2000–12 (interim Chief Ombudsman, 2009–10); *b* 7 Nov. 1945; *s* of late Harold Bushell Thomas and Margaret Thomas; *m* (marr. diss.); three *s* one *d*; partner, Jane Bibby. *Educ:* St Anselm's Coll., Birkenhead; Liverpool Univ. (LLB Hons 1966). Admitted Solicitor, England and Wales, 1969, Ireland, 1991; with F. S. Moore & Price, subseq. Lees Moore & Price, Birkenhead, then Lees Lloyd Whitley, Liverpool and London: Solicitor, 1969–71; Partner, 1971–84; Managing Partner, 1984–93; Chm., 1993–96; Banking Ombudsman, 1997–2000. Member: Accountancy and Actuarial Discipline (formerly Accountancy Investigation and Discipline) Bd, 2001–09; Bd, Office of Legal Complaints, 2009–15; Mem., Audit Adv. Cttee, 2007–11, Ind. Service Delivery Reviewer, 2012–, Scottish Public Services Ombudsman; Chm., CI Financial Ombudsman, 2014–. Financial Redress Consultant, World Bank, 2011–. Mem., Regulatory Bd, ACCA, 2013–. Member: Steering Cttee, FIN-NET, 2006–11; Cttee, Internat. Network of Financial Services Ombudsmen, 2009–. Sec., 1981–86, Vice-Pres., 1986–87, Pres., 1987–88, Liverpool Law Soc.; Member: Council, Law Soc., 1987–96; Cttee, City of London Law Soc., 2005–09. Mem., Council, QMUL, 2006–14. *Recreations:* modern history, theatre, naval aviation, walking. *Address:* PO Box 256, Totnes, Devon TQ9 9FE.

THOMAS, David Bowen, PhD; Keeper, Department of Physical Sciences, Science Museum, 1984–87 (Keeper, Department of Physics, 1978–84); *b* 28 Dec. 1931; *s* of Evan Thomas and Florence Annie Bowen. *Educ:* Tredegar Grammar Sch.; Manchester Univ. (BSc). Research Fellow, Wayne Univ., Detroit, USA, 1955–57; Research Scientist, Min. of Agriculture, Fisheries and Food, Aberdeen, 1957–61; Asst Keeper, Science Museum, Dept of Chemistry, 1961–73; Keeper, Dept of Museum Services, 1973–78. Hon. FRPS 1985. *Publications:* The First Negatives, 1964; The Science Museum Photography Collection, 1969; The First Colour Motion Pictures, 1969. *Recreation:* country walking. *Address:* Tanglewood, Moushill Lane, Milford, Godalming, Surrey GU8 5BQ.

THOMAS, David Churchill, CMG 1982; HM Diplomatic Service, retired; Assistant Under Secretary of State, Foreign and Commonwealth Office, 1984–86; *b* 21 Oct. 1933; *o s* of late David Bernard Thomas and Violet Churchill Thomas (*née* Quicke); *m* 1958, Susan Petronella Arrow (*see* Baroness Thomas of Walliswood); one *s* two *d*. *Educ:* Eton Coll.; New Coll., Oxford (Exhibnr). Mod. Hist. 1st Cl., 1957. Army, 2nd Lieut, Rifle Brigade, 1952–54. Foreign Office, 1958; 3rd Sec., Moscow, 1959–61; 2nd Sec., Lisbon, 1961–64; FCO, 1964–68; 1st Sec. (Commercial), Lima, 1968–70; FCO, 1970–73; Head of South West European Dept, 1974; Asst Sec., Cabinet Office, 1973–78; Counsellor (Internal Affairs), Washington, 1978–81; Ambassador to Cuba, 1981–84. Advr on Overseas Scholarships Funding, FCO, 1989–2000. Mem., Marshall Aid Commemoration Commn, 1999–2005. Mem. Council, RIIA, 1988–94. Mem. Bd, Inst. of Latin American Studies, Univ. of London, 1988–93. Associate Fellow, Centre for Caribbean Studies, Warwick Univ., 1990–96. *Publications:* essays and review articles on Latin American affairs. *Recreations:* photography, listening to music. *Address:* Hidden House, 15 Guilden Road, Chichester, W Sussex PO19 7LA. *T:* (01243) 780096.
See also Hon. D. W. P. Thomas.

THOMAS, David (Edward); *b* 12 Jan. 1955; *m* 1975, Janet Elizabeth Whatrup; one *s* one *d*. *Educ:* Univ. of East Anglia (BA). Served RN, 1972–80; Suffolk Constabulary, 1980–88. Mem. (Lab), Suffolk CC, 1993–95, 2000–09; Mem., Police Authy. MEP (Lab) Suffolk and SW Norfolk, 1994–99; contested (Lab) Eastern Reg., 1999.

THOMAS, David Emrys, OBE 1998; management and personnel consultant, 1991–2001; Member, Local Government Commission for England, 1992–98; *b* Ewell, 9 July 1935; *s* of Emrys and Elsie Florence Thomas; *m* 1957, Rosemary, *d* of Alexander and Kathleen De'Ath of Hampton, Middx; two *s* one *d*. *Educ:* Tiffin Grammar Sch., Kingston upon Thames. Dip. Mun. Admin; FCIPD. Local Govt Administrator, 1951–63; Indust. Relations Officer, LACSAB, 1963–68; Chief Admin. Officer, LGTB, 1968–69; Dep. Estab. Officer, Surrey CC, 1969–70; County Personnel Officer, Surrey, 1970–77; Under-Sec. (Manpower), AMA, 1977–81; Dep. Sec., 1981–87, Sec., 1987–91, LACSAB; Employers' Sec. to nat. jt negotiating councils in local govt, 1987–91; Official Side Sec., Police Negotiating Bd, 1987–91; Sec., UK Steering Cttee on Local Govt Superannuation, 1987–91. Founder Pres., Soc. of Chief Personnel Officers in Local Govt, 1975. *Recreations:* unskilled gardening, the musical theatre (Mem., Olivier Awards panel, 1998; Sec., Stage Musical Appreciation Soc., 1996–2006). *Address:* The White House, Three Pears Road, Merrow, Guildford, Surrey GU1 2XU. *T:* (01483) 569588. *E:* DEThomas41@aol.com.

THOMAS, Prof. David Glyndor Treharne, FRCSE, FRCP, FRCPG, FRCS; Professor of Neurosurgery, 1992–2006, Professor of Neurological Surgery, 2006, now Professor Emeritus, Institute of Neurology, University of London; Honorary Consultant Neurosurgeon, National Hospital for Neurology and Neurosurgery, Queen Square, since 1977; *b* 14 May 1941; *s* of Dr John Glyndor Treharne Thomas, MC and Ellen Thomas (*née*

Geldart); *m* 1970, Dr Hazel Agnes Christina Cockburn, FFARCS; one *s*. *Educ:* Perse Sch., Cambridge; Gonville and Caius Coll., Cambridge (BA, MA); St Mary's Hosp. Med. Sch.; MB BChir Cantab. Hosp. appts at St Mary's to 1969 and Asst Lectr in Anatomy, 1967–68; Sen. House Officer in Surgery, 1970, Registrar in Cardio-Thoracic Surgery, 1970–71, RPMS; Registrar, Sen. Registrar and Lectr in Neurosurgery, Inst. of Neur. Scis, Glasgow, 1972–76; Sen. Lectr, 1976–92, Hd, Gough Cooper Dept of Neurological Surgery, 1995–2006, Inst. of Neurology; Consultant Neurosurgeon: Nat. Hosp. for Neurology and Neurosurgery and Northwick Park Hosp., Harrow, 1976–2006; St Mary's Hosp., 1994–2006. Vice-President: Eur. Assoc. of Neurosurgical Socs, 1991–95; Eur. Soc. for Stereotactic and Functional Neurosurgery, 1994–98; World Fedn of Neurosurgical Socs, 1995–99, 1999–2003 (Parliamentarian, 2010); Pres., Academia Neuroeurasiana, 1999–2003. Member: Medical Soc. of London; Harveian Soc. (Pres., 2013). *Publications:* (ed with D. I. Graham) Brain Tumours, 1980; (ed with M. D. Walker) Biology of Brain Tumour, 1986; (ed) Neuro-oncology: primary brain tumours, 1989; (ed) Stereotactic and Image Directed Surgery of Brain Tumours, 1993; (ed with D. I. Graham) Malignant Brain Tumours, 1995. *Recreation:* military and naval history. *Address:* Box 147, The National Hospital for Neurology and Neurosurgery, Queen Square, WC1N 3BG. *T:* (020) 3448 8993; 106 Globe Wharf, 205 Rotherhithe Street, SE16 5XX. *T:* (020)7237 0024. *Clubs:* Athenæum, Royal Society of Medicine.

THOMAS, David Hugh; Chief Executive, 1997–2002, non-executive Chairman, 2002–04, Morgan Grenfell & Co. Ltd, later DB UK Bank Ltd; *b* 6 Dec. 1951; *s* of late John William Hugh Thomas and Joyce Thomas (*née* Fox); *m* 1978, Frances Mary Brown; one *s* one *d*. *Educ:* Hertford GS; Corpus Christi Coll., Oxford (BA 1st cl. Hons Lit. Hum. 1974; Sec., then Librarian, Oxford Union Soc., 1973); St John's Coll., Oxford (MA; DPhil 1978). Joined Morgan Grenfell & Co. Ltd, 1978: Italian Export Credits, 1978–83; Eurobonds, 1983–84; Interest Rate and Currency Swaps, 1984–87; Dir, 1988–March 2002, Nov. 2002–2004; Market and Credit Risk Mgt, 1988–97; Global Head of Risk, Investment Banking Activities, Deutsche Bank Gp, 1995–98; Chief Exec., Bankers Trust Internat. PLC, 1999–2002 (non-exec. Chm., 2002–04); non-exec. Chm. and Partner, Altima Partners LLP, 2004–10; non-exec. Dir, Schroder & Co. Ltd, 2005–. Mem. Council, 2008–09, Hon. Treas., 2009–15, Soc. for Promotion of Hellenic Studies. Trustee, Oxford Lit. and Debating Union Trust, 2003–08. Gov., 1999–2009, Vice-Chm., 2002–09, Abbot's Hill Sch. *Publications:* (introd.) The Landmark Xenophon's Hellenika, 2009. *Recreations:* classical studies, especially Greek history, playing the piano (very badly).

THOMAS, Prof. David (John), MD; FRCP; Professor Emeritus of Clinical Neurosciences, Imperial College London, 2007 (Professor of Stroke Medicine, 2005–06); Chairman, St Mary's Therapy & Imaging Ltd, since 2006; *b* 7 Dec. 1943; *s* of Jack and Rachel Lloyd Thomas, Cwmgorse; *m* 1966, Celia Margaret Barratt, *d* of Sir Charles and Lady Barratt; two *s* three *d*. *Educ:* Alleyn's Sch.; Clare Coll., Cambridge (BA Nat. Sci. 1966; BChir 1969; MA, MB 1970); Univ. of Birmingham Med. Sch. (MD 1977). MRCP 1972, FRCP 1985. Consultant Neurologist: King Edward VII Hosp., Windsor, Heatherwood Hosp., Ascot, Wexham Park Hosp., Slough and St Mark's Hosp., Maidenhead, 1978–2000; Sen. Consultant Neurologist, St Mary's Hosp., London, 1978–2006; Sen. Lectr in Neurology, Inst. of Neurology and Hon. Consultant Neurologist, Nat. Hosp. for Neurology and Neurosurgery, 1979–2006, and Chalfont Centre for Epilepsy, 1995–2006. Dir, D-Gen Ltd, 2000–. Sec. and Chm., Special Adv. Cttee on Neurology to RCP, 1985–91. Member: Council, Stroke Assoc., 1992–2008; Stroke Council, Amer. Heart Assoc., 1992–; European Stroke Council, 1993–. Chm., Charitable Assoc. Supplying Hosps, 1984–99 (Life Pres., 1999–). Governor, Nat. Soc. for Epilepsy, 2001–04; Trustee, Assoc. of British Neurologists, 2005–08. *Publications:* Strokes and their Prevention, 1988; The Eye and Systemic Disease, 1989; Neurology: what shall I do?, 1990, 2nd edn 1997; papers on cerebrovascular disease and other neurological subjects. *Recreation:* photography. *Address:* 14 Queen Court, Queen Square, WC1N 3BG. *Club:* Royal Society of Medicine.

THOMAS, Sir David (John Godfrey), 12th Bt *cr* 1694, of Wenvoe, Glamorganshire; *b* 11 June 1961; *o s* of Sir Michael Thomas, 11th Bt and of Margaret Greta Thomas (*née* Cleland); *S* father, 2003; *m* 2004, Nicola Jane Lusty. *Educ:* Harrow; Ealing Coll. Health club owner. *Recreations:* squash, tennis. *Heir:* none. *Address:* 1 Waters Edge, Eternit Walk, SW6 6QU. *T:* and *Fax:* (020) 7381 4078. *Clubs:* Hurlingham, MCC, Escorts, Jesters.

THOMAS, David Malcolm, CBE 2000; LVO 2007; Chairman, In Kind Direct, 2004–07; *b* 20 Feb. 1944; *s* of Edward Reginald Thomas and Edna Thomas (*née* Lowcock); *m* 1969, Ursula Maria Brinkbaumer; one *s* one *d*. *Educ:* Burnage Grammar Sch.; Univ. of Manchester (BA Hons 1965); Manchester Business Sch. (Dip. Advanced Studies in Business Mgt); Harvard Business Sch. (AMP 1988). Mktg Controller, CWS, 1965–71; Regl Gen. Manager, Finefare, 1971–73; Regl Dir, Linfood, 1973–82; Regl Man. Dir, Grand Metropolitan, 1982–84; Whitbread: Regl Dir, 1984–89; Man. Dir, Whitbread Inns, 1989–91; Man. Dir, Restaurants and Leisure, 1991–97; Chief Exec., 1997–2004. Non-executive Director: Xansa, 2000–07; Sandown Park, 2004–14. Mem., Honours Selection Cttee (Economy), 2005–12. Trustee, Kids in Sport, 2009–. *Recreations:* opera, ballet, gardening, horse racing, golf, wine, foreign travel. *E:* dmthomas44@gmail.com. *Clubs:* Sloane; Woking Golf.

THOMAS, (David) Roger, CMG 2000; HM Diplomatic Service, retired; Senior Consultant, MEC International Ltd, since 2003; Partner, Cley Energy Consultants, since 2003; Director, Eurasia Energy Ltd, since 2006; *b* 1 Jan. 1945; *s* of late Alun Beynon Thomas, FRCS, and Doreen Thomas. *Educ:* Leys Sch., Cambridge; Sch. of Oriental and African Studies, London Univ. (BA Hons Turkish). Entered Foreign Office, 1968: FO, 1968–71; Third Sec. (Chancery), Cairo, 1971–74; Second Sec. (Envmt), UK Repn to EEC, Brussels, 1974–78; Consul, Ankara, 1979–82; UN and EC Dept, FCO, 1982–86; Consul (Commercial), Frankfurt, 1986–90; Consul-Gen., Stuttgart, 1990–93; Non-Proliferation, FCO, 1993–97; Ambassador to Azerbaijan, 1997–2000; Consul-Gen., San Francisco, 2001–03. *Recreations:* gardening, ski-ing, sailing, photography. *E:* roger@drthomas.f2s.com.

THOMAS, Prof. David Stephen Garfield, DPhil; Professor of Geography, University of Oxford, since 2004 (Head, School of Geography and Environment, 2008–12); Fellow of Hertford College, Oxford, since 2004; *b* Dover, 2 Oct. 1958; *s* of late Frederick Garfield Thomas and Ruth Muriel Thomas; *m* 1st, 1987, (Helen) Elizabeth Martin (*d* 1990); 2nd, 1992, Lucy Marie Heath; two *d*. *Educ:* Dover Grammar Sch. for Boys; Hertford Coll., Oxford (BA Hons 1980; PGCE 1981; DPhil 1984). Department of Geography, University of Sheffield: Lectr, 1984–93; Sen. Lectr, 1993–94; Prof., 1994–2004; Chm., 1997–2000; Dir, Sheffield Centre of Internat. Drylands Res., 1994–2004. Hon. Professor: Univ. of Cape Town, 2006–; Univ. of Witwatersrand, 2013–. Occasional Consultant, UNEP, 1990–; Lead Expert, UK Govt Foresight Project, Envmtl Drivers of Migration, 2009–12. Mem. Council, RGS, 2001–05 and 2011–July 2016 (Hon. Sec., 2001–02; Vice Pres., 2002–05; Vice Pres., Res. and Higher Educn, 2013–July 2016); Chm., British Geomorphological Res. Gp, 2002–03. Res. into long and short term envmtl change in drylands, dry land geomorphology, human-envmt interactions in drylands, esp. in Southern Africa. El-Baz Award for advances to desert sci., Geol Soc. of Amer., 2011. Editor, Jl of Arid Envmt, 1990–. *Publications:* Arid Zone Geomorphology, 1989, 3rd edn 2011; (with P. Shaw) The Kalahari Environment, 1991; (with N. Middleton) World Atlas of Desertification, 1992, 2nd edn 1997; (ed with R. Allison) Landscape Sensitivity, 1993; (with N. Middleton) Desertification: exploding the myth, 1995; (ed with A. Goudie) Dictionary of Physical Geography, 4th edn 2015; (with D. Sporton) Sustainable Livelihoods in Kalahari Environments, 2002. *Recreations:* Africa, Dover Athletic FC, running, gardening. *Address:* School of Geography and Environment, Oxford University Centre for the Environment, Dyson-Perrins Building, South Parks Road, Oxford OX1 3QY.

THOMAS, David W.; *see* Wynford-Thomas.

THOMAS, Hon. David (William Penrose); author, journalist; *b* 17 Jan. 1959; *s* of David Churchill Thomas, *qv* and Baroness Thomas of Walliswood, *qv*; *m* 1986, Clare Jeremy; one *s* two *d*. *Educ:* Eton; King's College, Cambridge (BA History of Art). Freelance journalist, 1980–84; Editor, The Magazine, 1984–85; Editor, Extra Magazine, Sunday Today, 1986; Asst Editor and Chief Feature Writer, You Magazine, Mail on Sunday, 1986–89; Ed., Punch, 1989–92; TV Critic, Sunday Express, 1991–96. Young Journalist of the Year (British Press Awards), 1983; Columnist of the Year (Magazine Publishing Awards), 1989. *Publications:* Not Guilty: in defence of the modern man, 1993; Great Sporting Moments, 1990; Girl (novel), 1995; Show Me The Money, 2000; Foul Play, 2003; Blood Relative (novel), 2011; Ostland, 2013; as Tom Cain: The Accident Man, 2007; The Survivor, 2008; Assassin, 2009; Dictator, 2010; Carver, 2011; Revenger, 2012; as David Churchill: Devil (The Leopards of Normandy), Vol 1, 2015; with Ian Irvine: Bilko: the Fort Baxter Story, 1985; Fame and Fortune, 1988; Sex and Shopping, 1988. *Recreations:* gardening, singing, manically competitive quizzing. *Address:* c/o LAW Ltd, 14 Vernon Street, W14 0RJ. *T:* (020) 7471 7900.

THOMAS, Derek Gordon; MP (C) St Ives, since 2015; *b* 20 July 1972; *m*; two *s*. Apprentice Cornish mason; community worker, Chapel St Methodist Ch, Penzance and Mustard Seed, Helston; proprietor, construction business. Founder, Survivealive, outdoor adventure project, 1997–. Former Mem. (C), Penwith DC. Mem., Sci. and Technol. Select Cttee, 2015–. *Address:* House of Commons, SW1A 0AA.

THOMAS, Derek John, CBE 1996; DL; CPFA; Chief Executive, Surrey County Council, 1988–95; *b* 3 Dec. 1934; *s* of late James Llewellyn Thomas and Winifred Mary Thomas; *m* 1st (marr. diss.); three *d*; 2nd, 1978, Christine (*née* Brewer); one *s*. *Educ:* Hele's Sch., Exeter. Formerly: Treasurer's Depts: Devon CC; Corby Development Corporation; Bath CC; Taunton Bor. Council; Sen. Asst Bor. Treasurer, Poole Bor. Council; Asst County Treasurer, Gloucestershire CC; Principal Asst County Treasurer, Avon CC; County Treasurer, Surrey CC. Mem. Council, CIPFA, 1977–78, 1985–87; Mem. Cttee of Mgt, Schroder Exempt Property Unit Trust, 1981–2001. Chm., Local Management in Schools Initiative, 1988–93. Mem. Bd, Surrey TEC, 1990–95; Chm., Surrey First, 1996–2002. Chm., Disability Initiative, 1996–2011. Surrey University: Mem. Council, 1994–2004; Chm., F and GP Cttee, 1995–2004; Treas., 1997–2004; Mem., Finance Cttee, UCL, 2006–10. CCMI. DL Surrey, 1996. *Publications:* (ed jtly) A Fresh Start for Local Government, 1997. *Address:* Squirrels Leap, 14 Lime Avenue, Camberley, Surrey GU15 2BS. *T:* (01276) 684433.

THOMAS, Sir Derek (Morison David), KCMG 1987 (CMG 1977); HM Diplomatic Service, retired; *b* 31 Oct. 1929; *s* of K. P. D. Thomas and Mali McL. Thomas; *m* 1956, Lineke van der Mast; two *c*. *Educ:* Radley Coll., Abingdon; Trinity Hall, Cambridge (Mod. Langs Tripos; MA; Hon. Fellow, 1997). Articled apprentice, Dolphin Industrial Developments Ltd, 1947. Entered HM Foreign Service, 1953; Midshipman 1953, Sub-Lt 1955, RNVR; FO, 1955; 3rd, later 2nd, Sec., Moscow, 1956–59; 2nd Sec., Manila, 1959–61; UK Delegn to Brussels Conf., 1961–62; 1st Sec., FO, 1962; Sofia, 1964–67; Ottawa, 1967–69; seconded to HM Treasury, 1969–70; Financial Counsellor, Paris, 1971–75; Head of N American Dept, FCO, 1975–76; Asst Under Sec. of State, FCO, 1976–79; Minister Commercial and later Minister, Washington, 1979–84; Dep. Under Sec. of State for Europe and Political Dir, FCO, 1984–87; Amb. to Italy, 1987–89. European Advr to N. M. Rothschild & Sons, 1990–2004; Director: N. M. Rothschild & Sons, 1991–99; Nexus Marketing Consultancy, 1991–92. Chm., Liberalisation of Trade in Services Cttee, BI, 1992–96; Mem., Export Guarantees Adv. Cttee, 1992–97. Member, Council: RIIA, 1994–97; Reading Univ., 1991–99. Chm., British Inst. of Florence, 1987–89 and 1997–2002. Hon. LLD Leicester, 2003. *Recreations:* listening to people and music; being by, in or on water; grandfathering, gardening. *Address:* Flat 1, 12 Lower Sloane Street, SW1W 8BJ; Ferme l'Epine, 14490 Planquery, France. *Clubs:* Oxford and Cambridge; Leander.

See also Sir E. W. Gladstone, Bt.

THOMAS, Donald Michael; poet and novelist; *b* Redruth, Cornwall, 27 Jan. 1935; *s* of Harold Redvers Thomas and Amy (*née* Moyle); two *s* one *d*. *Educ:* Redruth Grammar Sch.; Univ. High Sch., Melbourne; New Coll., Oxford (BA 1st cl. Hons in English; MA). School teacher, Teignmouth Grammar Sch., 1959–63; Lectr, Hereford Coll. of Educn, 1964–78; full-time author, 1978–. *Publications: poetry:* Penguin Modern Poets 11, 1968; Two Voices, 1968; Logan Stone, 1971; Love and Other Deaths, 1975; The Honeymoon Voyage, 1978; Dreaming in Bronze, 1981; Selected Poems, 1983; Dear Shadows, 2004; Not Saying Everything, 2006; Unknown Shores, 2009; Flight & Smoke, 2009; Two Countries, 2011; Vintage Ghosts (verse novel), 2012; Mrs English and Other Women, 2014; *novels:* The Flute-Player, 1979; Birthstone, 1980; The White Hotel, 1981; Russian Nights, a quintet (Ararat, 1983; Swallow, 1984; Sphinx, 1986; Summit, 1987; Lying Together, 1990); Flying in to Love, 1992; Pictures at an Exhibition, 1993; Eating Pavlova, 1994; Lady with a Laptop, 1996; Charlotte, 2000; Hunters in the Snow, 2015; *play:* Hell Fire Corner, 2004; *translations:* Requiem and Poem without a Hero, Akhmatova, 1976; Way of All the Earth, Akhmatova, 1979; Bronze Horseman, Pushkin, 1982; Onegin, Pushkin, 2011; *memoirs:* Memories and Hallucinations, 1988; Bleak Hotel, 2008; *biography:* Alexander Solzhenitsyn: a century in his life, 1998. *Recreations:* travel, Russia and other myths, the culture and history of Cornwall, the life of the imagination. *Address:* The Coach House, Rashleigh Vale, Truro, Cornwall TR1 1TJ. *W:* www.dmthomasonline.net.

THOMAS, Dudley Lloyd; a District Judge (Magistrates' Courts) (formerly Stipendiary Magistrate), Somerset and Avon, 1999–2008, and Gloucestershire, 2004–08; Member: Family Proceedings Court Panel, 1991–2008; Youth Court Panel, 1994–2008; *b* 11 Jan. 1946; *s* of late Myrddin Lloyd Thomas and Marjorie Emily (*née* Morgan); *m* 1970, Dr Margaret Susan Early; two *s* (and one *s* decd). *Educ:* King Edward's Sch., Bath; Coll. of Law, London. Justices Clerk's Asst, 1966–71; admitted as solicitor, 1971; Partner, Trump & Partners, Bristol, 1973–88; called to the Bar, Gray's Inn, 1988; Metropolitan Stipendiary Magistrate, 1990–99. Formerly Mem., Western Circuit. Mem., Heritage in Wales. Friend, Royal Acad. of Arts. *Recreations:* Rugby football, cricket, music, theatre, travel, walking.

THOMAS, Edward Stanley, FIA; Pension Director, Law Debenture Corporation plc, 2002–08; *s* of Stanley Frederick Thomas and Kate Dickason Thomas; *m* 1974, Elizabeth Mary Helen Casson; three *s* one *d*. *Educ:* King Edward VI Grammar Sch., Stourbridge; Slough Grammar Sch.; Clare Coll., Cambridge (MA). FIA 1974; ACII. Teacher, Sherwood Coll., Naini Tal, India, 1965; Actuarial trainee, Prudential, 1968–70; joined Bacon & Woodrow, 1970, Partner, 1978–98; Nat. Sec., Nat. Council of YMCAs, 1998–2002. Treas., Scripture Union. Liveryman, Actuaries' Co. *Club:* Royal Automobile.

THOMAS, Elizabeth; *see* Thomas, M. E.

THOMAS, Emyr, CBE 1980; DL; LLB, LMRTPI; General Manager, Telford New Town Development Corporation, 1969–80; Chairman, Telford Community Council, 1980–84; *b* 25 April 1920; *s* of late Brinley Thomas, MA, Aldershot; *m* 1947, Barbara J. May; one *d*. *Educ:* Aldershot County High School. Served War of 1939–45, RASC. Admitted Solicitor, 1947. Asst Solicitor, Exeter City Council, 1947–50; Sen. Asst Solicitor, Reading County Borough Council, 1950–53; Dep. Town Clerk, West Bromwich County Borough Council, 1953–64; Sec. and Solicitor, Dawley (later Telford) Development Corp., 1964–69. First Hon. Sec., 1968–89, Hon. Curator and Vice-Pres., 1989–, Ironbridge Gorge Museum Trust. DL Salop, 1979. *Publications:* Coalbrookdale and the Darby Family, 1999; Coalbrookdale in the 18th

Century, 2001; (ed) Private Journal of Adelaide Darby of Coalbrookdale, 2004. *Recreation:* industrial archaeology. *Address:* 8 Vixen Walk, New Milton, Hampshire BH25 5RU. *T:* (01425) 628826.

THOMAS, Sir Eric (Jackson), Kt 2013; DL; MD; Vice-Chancellor, University of Bristol, 2001–15; *b* 24 March 1953; *s* of late Eric Jackson Thomas and Margaret Mary Thomas (*née* Murray); *m* 1976, Narell Marie Rennard; one *s* one *d*. *Educ:* Ampleforth Coll.; Univ. of Newcastle upon Tyne (MB BS 1976; MD 1987). MRCOG 1983, FRCOG 2001; FRCP 2004. Jun. hosp. posts, 1976–87; Res. Fellow, and Lectr, Univ. of Sheffield, 1984–87; Sen. Lectr, Univ. of Newcastle upon Tyne, 1987–90; Consultant Obstetrician and Gynaecologist: Newcastle Gen. Hosp., 1987–2000; Princess Anne Hosp., Southampton, 1991–2001; Southampton University: Prof. of Obstetrics and Gynaecol., 1991–2001; Hd of Sch. of Medicine, 1995–98; Dean, Faculty of Medicine, Health and Biol Scis, 1998–2000. Mem., Medicines Commn, 2002–03. Chm., 7th World Congress of Endometriosis, 2000. Mem. Council, RCOG, 1995–2001 (Chm. Scientific Adv. Cttee, 1998–2000). Non-executive Director: Southampton Univ. Hosps NHS Trust, 1997–2000; Southampton and SW Hampshire HA, 2000–01. Dir, 2001–15, Chm., 2003–07, Worldwide Univs Network Ltd; Universities UK: Mem. Bd, 2006–11; Chm., Res. Policy Strategy Cttee, 2006–11; Chm., England and NI Council, 2009–11; Vice Pres., 2009–11; Pres., 2011–13. Mem. Bd, CASE (US), 2010–14; Chm., CASE Europe, 2010–14. Member: Bd, SW RDA, 2003–08; Regl Sports Bd, 2003–06; Bd, W of England Local Enterprise Partnership, 2014–; Chairman: HERDA-SW, 2002–04; DfES Taskforce on Increasing Voluntary Giving in Higher Educn, 2003–04; ERIC (formerly Educn and Resources for Improving Childhood Continence), 2007–12 (Patron, 2013–); Marshall Aid Commn, 2010–13. Trustee: Nat. Endometriosis Soc., 1998–2000; RCOG, 2013–; IntoUniversity, 2013–. William Blair Bell Meml Lectr, RCOG, 1987. Founder FMedSci 1998. FRSA 1998. Mem., Soc. of Merchant Venturers, 2008. DL Bristol, 2005. Hon. LLD Bristol, 2004; Hon. DSc: Southampton, 2006; Teesside, 2008; UWE, 2010. *Publications:* (ed jtly) Modern Approaches to Endometriosis, 1991; articles on endometriosis and reproductive biology. *Recreations:* Newcastle United, golf. *Address:* Abbey Farm House, Oakley Road, Mottisfont, ROMSEY, Hants SO51 0LQ. *E:* Eric.Thomas@bristol.ac.uk. *Club:* Athenæum.

THOMAS, Franklin Augustine; lawyer, consultant; *b* 27 May 1934; *s* of James Thomas and Viola Thomas (*née* Atherley); *m* (marr. diss.); two *s* two *d*. *Educ:* Columbia College, New York (BA 1956); Columbia Univ. (LLB 1963). Admitted to NY State Bar, 1964; Attorney, Fed. Housing and Home Finance Agency, NYC, 1963–64; Asst US Attorney for Southern District, NY, 1964–65; Dep. Police Comr, charge legal matters, NYC, 1965–67; Pres., Chief Exec. Officer, Bedford Stuyvesant Restoration Corp., Brooklyn, 1967–77; Pres., Ford Foundn, 1979–96. Dir, Alcoa, 1977–2010. Chm., September 11th Fund, 2001–06. Hon. LLD: Yale, 1970; Fordham, 1972; Pratt Institute, 1974; Pace, 1977; Columbia, 1979. *Address:* 380 Lexington Avenue, New York, NY 10168, USA.

THOMAS, Gareth; barrister; *b* 25 Sept. 1954; *s* of William and Megan Thomas; *m*; one *s* one *d*. *Educ:* Rockferry High Sch., Birkenhead; UCW, Aberystwyth (LLB). ACII. Worked in insurance industry. Called to the Bar, Gray's Inn, 1977. Member (Lab), Flints CC, 1995–97. MP (Lab) Clwyd West, 1997–2005. Contested (Lab) Clwyd West, 2005. PPS to Sec. of State for Wales, 2001–02, to Sec. of State for NI, 2002–05. Member: Social Security Select Cttee, 1999–2001; Jt Human Rights Cttee, 2000–01. Bd Mem., N Wales Housing Assoc., 2006–. *Recreations:* walking, theatre, music. *Address:* Pine Lodge, Llanfwrog, Rhuthun, Denbighshire LL15 2LN; Atlantic Chambers, 4–6 Cook Street, Liverpool L2 9QU.

THOMAS, Gareth Richard; MP (Lab) Harrow West, since 1997; *b* 15 July 1967; *s* of Howard and Susan Thomas. *Educ:* UCW, Aberystwyth (BScEcons Hons Politics 1988); Univ. of Greenwich (PGCE 1991); KCL (MA Imperial and Commonwealth Hist. 1997). Teacher, 1992–97. Mem. (Lab) Harrow BC, 1990–97. PPS to Minister Without Portfolio and Party Chairman, 2001–02, to Sec. of State for Educn and Skills, 2002–03; Parly Under-Sec. of State, 2003–08, Minister of State, 2008–10, DFID; Parly Under-Sec. of State, 2007–08, Minister of State, 2008–09, BERR. Chm., Parly Renewable and Sustainable Energy Gp, 1998–2003. Chm., Co-op Party, 2000–. *Recreations:* arts (member of the Tate, theatre, etc.), road running, supporting Arsenal, Swansea City FC and Harrow Borough FC, watching London Welsh RFC. *Address:* House of Commons, SW1A 0AA.

THOMAS, Gareth Vaughan; Director: Total Retail Concepts, since 2010; Nature Paint Ltd, since 2011; *b* Belfast, 24 April 1957; *s* of Griff and Esther Thomas; *m* 1983, Sallie Campbell (marr. diss. 2013); two *s* one *d*. *Educ:* Royal Belfast Academical Instn; University Coll. of Wales, Aberystwyth (LLB Hons). Joined John Lewis as graduate trainee, 1979: Managing Director: Norwich, 1991–96; Bristol, 1996–98; Cribbs Causeway, 1998–2000; Director: Retail Ops, 2000–07; Design and Develt, 2007–08; Retail Dir, 2009–10. Non-exec. Dir, Share PLC Gp, 2014–; non-exec. Dir and Ind. Dir, Shoppers Stop India, 2014–. Trustee: Save the Children, 2005–13; Tate, 2010–; American Mus. in Britain, 2012–. *Recreations:* playing tennis, running, swimming, bodyboarding, watching live Rugby and F1. *Address:* 1 Nugent Hill, Cotham, Bristol BS6 5TD. *E:* garethvthomas@me.com. *Club:* Bath Rugby.

THOMAS, Dr Geoffrey Price; Director, University of Oxford Department for Continuing Education, 1986–2007; President, Kellogg College (formerly Rewley House), 1990–2007, now President Emeritus (Hon. Fellow, 2008); *b* 3 July 1941; *s* of Richard Lewis Thomas and Aerona (*née* Price); *m* 1965, Judith Vaughan, *d* of Arsul John Williams; two *d*. *Educ:* Maesteg Grammar Sch.; UC of Swansea (BSc 1st Cl. Hons Physics); Churchill Coll., Cambridge (PhD 1966); Univ. of Oxford (MA). Post-doctoral res., Cavendish Lab., Univ. of Cambridge, 1966–67; Staff Tutor, UC of Swansea, 1967–78; Dep. Dir, Dept of Ext. Studies, Univ. of Oxford, 1978–86; Fellow, Linacre Coll., Oxford, 1978–90, Hon. Fellow, 1990. Co-Chm., Council on Scientific Literacy, Chicago Acad. of Sci., 1993–. Mem., HEFCW, 2000–08. Visiting Scholar: Smithsonian Instn, 1986; Northern Illinois Univ., 1986; Univ. of Calif, Berkeley, 1993; Univ. of Washington, 1993; Harvard Univ., 1993; Univ. of Georgia, 1999. Gov., Univ. of Glamorgan, 2009–11; Chair, Univ. of Wales Trinity St David, 2010–14. Patron, David Mather Foundn, 2011–. Aelod, Gorsedd Beirdd Ynys Prydain, 2014. FLSW 2014. Hon. Fellow: Trinity Coll., Carmarthen, 2007; Swansea Metropolitan Univ., 2009. Paul Harris Fellow, Rotary Internat., 2007. Hon. DSc Wales Trinity St David, 2014. *Publications:* (ed jtly) The Nuclear Arms Race, 1982; (ed jtly) Science and Sporting Performance, 1982; (ed jtly) University Continuing Education 1981–2006, 2010; numerous articles on public understanding of science, and on continuing educn policy. *Address:* 102 Old Road, Headington, Oxford OX3 8SX.

THOMAS, Prof. Geraint Wynn, DPhil; Professor of Equity and Property Law, Queen Mary School of Law, University of London, 1999–2013, now Emeritus; *b* 10 Aug. 1948; *s* of David and Mair Thomas; *m* 1972, Janice Lilian Tilden; one *s* one *d* (and one *d* decd). *Educ:* Ardudwy Sch., Harlech; University Coll. of Swansea (BA 1969); Balliol Coll., Oxford (DPhil 1974). Called to the Bar, Inner Temple, 1976; in practice as barrister, specialising in trusts, estate, planning and pensions, 1981–2002; Lectr in Law, Univ. of Kent, 1976–91; Sen. Lectr in Law, QMW, 1995–99. Hon. QC 2015. *Publications:* Taxation and Trusts, 1981; Powers, 1998, 2nd edn 2010; (with A. Hudson) The Law of Trusts, 2004, 2nd edn 2010; (contrib.) International Trust Laws, ed J. Glasson, 2006. *Address:* School of Law, Queen Mary University of London, E1 4NS. *T:* (020) 7882 3603. *E:* g.w.thomas@qmul.ac.uk.

THOMAS, Sir (Gilbert) Stanley, Kt 2006; OBE 1994; Co-Founder and Chairman, TBI, airport owner and operator, 1993–2005; *b* 20 Sept. 1941; *s* of Thomas Stanley Thomas, MBE and Connie Thomas; *m* 1962, Shirley Mary Powell; two *s* one *d*. Food manufacturer; founder and Jt Man. Dir, Peter's Savoury Products Ltd, 1970–88, when co. sold. President: Boys' and Girls' Clubs of Wales, 1991–; Royal Welsh Agricl Soc., 2001–02; Cancer Aid Merthyr Tydfil, 2007; Pres., Noah's Ark Appeal, 2007– (Chm., 1999–2007); Chm., fund raising for NSPCC in Wales (Chm., Full Stop Campaign, Wales, 2005–08); Nat. Vice Pres., NSPCC, 2015–. Patron, Merthyr Tydfil Rugby Club, 2009–. Freeman of Merthyr Tydfil, 2000. Hon. Fellow, Cardiff Univ., 2011. OStJ 1996. *Recreations:* Rugby, golf, sailing. *Address:* The Paddocks, Druidstone Road, St Mellons, Cardiff CF3 6XD. *T:* (029) 2079 5840. *Clubs:* Cardiff Rugby; La Moye Golf (Jersey); Aloha Golf (Marbella).

THOMAS, Gwenda; Member (Lab) Neath, National Assembly for Wales, since 1999; *b* 22 Jan. 1942; *d* of Hermas and Menai Evans (*née* Parry); *m* 1963, Morgan Thomas; one *s*. *Educ:* Pontardawe Grammar Sch. Clerical Officer, County Courts Br., LCD; Exec. Officer, Benefits Agency. Member: Gwaun Cae Gurwen Community Council, 1986–99 (Chm., 1988–89); Llanguicke Community Council, 1981–86; W Glamorgan CC, 1989–96 (Chm., Social Services Cttee); Neath Port Talbot CBC, 1996–99 (Chm., Social Services Cttee). Chm., review into services for vulnerable children, 2003–06 (report, Keeping Us Safe, 2006). Dep. Minister for Social Services, 2011–, and for Children, 2011–, Nat. Assembly for Wales. Mem., CPSA (Br. Chm., 1974–84). *Address:* National Assembly for Wales, Cardiff Bay, Cardiff CF99 1NA.

THOMAS, Gwyn; *see* Thomas, R. G.

THOMAS, Gwyn Edward Ward, CBE 1973; DFC; Chairman and Chief Executive, Yorkshire-Tyne Tees Television Holdings plc, 1993–99; Chairman, Irving International, since 2005; *b* 1 Aug. 1923; *o s* of William J. and Constance Thomas; *m* 1st, 1945, Patricia Cornelius (marr. diss. 1989); one *d*; 2nd, 1991, Janice Thomas; one *s*. *Educ:* Bloxham Sch.; The Lycée, Rouen. Served RAF, 1 Group Bomber Command and 229 Group Transport Command, 1941–46. Swissair, 1947–53; Granada Television, 1955–61; Man. Dir, Grampian Television, 1961–67; Man. Dir, 1967–73, Dep. Chm., 1973–81, Yorkshire Television; Man. Dir, 1970–84, Chm., 1976–84, Trident Television. Chairman: Castlewood Investments Ltd, 1969–83; Don Robinson Holdings Ltd, 1969–83; Watts & Corry Ltd, 1969–83; Trident Casinos, 1982–84. British Bureau of Television Advertising: Dir, 1966; Chm., 1968–70; Mem. Council, Independent Television Companies Assoc., 1961–76 (Chairman: Labour Relations Cttee, 1967; Network Programme Cttee, 1971). Croix de Guerre, 1945. *Recreations:* ski-ing, boats, photography. *Address:* Autumn House, Broomfield Park, Sunningdale, Berks SL5 0JT. *Clubs:* British Racing Drivers', Travellers.

THOMAS, Harvey, CBE 1990; international public relations consultant, since 1976; Director of Presentation (formerly Director of Press and Communications), Conservative Party, 1985–91; Executive Director, African Enterprise UK, since 2011; *b* 10 April 1939; *s* of John Humphrey Kenneth Thomas and Olga Rosina Thomas (*née* Noake); *m* 1978, Marlies (*née* Kram); two *d*. *Educ:* Westminster School; Northwestern Bible College, Minneapolis; Univs of Minnesota and Hawaii. Billy Graham Evangelistic Assoc., 1960–75; Producer, Jeddah Economic Forum, 2006–07. Chm., Trans World Radio UK, 2005–; Member, Board of Directors: London Cremation Co. plc, 1984–2014 (Chm., 2014–); Cameo Ltd, 2011–. Chm., Cremation Soc. of GB, 2009–. FCIPR, FCIJ, FRSA. *Publications:* In the Face of Fear, 1985; Making an Impact, 1989; If they haven't heard it—you haven't said it, 1995, 2nd edn 2000. *Recreations:* travel, family, trains. *Address:* 23 The Service Road, Potters Bar, Herts EN6 1QA. *T:* (01707) 649910. *E:* harvey@hthomas.net. *Club:* Institute of Directors.

THOMAS, Heidi-Louise; playwright and screenwriter, since 1986; *b* Liverpool, 13 Aug. 1962; *d* of Frederick Thomas and Marie-Louise Thomas; *m* 1990, Stephen McGann; one *s*. *Educ:* St Edmund's College Sch., Liverpool; Univ. of Liverpool (BA Hons Eng. Lang. and Lit.). Playwright: Shamrocks and Crocodiles, Liverpool Playhouse, 1986; Indigo, RSC, 1987; Some Singing Blood, Royal Court, 1992; The House of Special Purpose, Chichester Fest., 2009; Gigi, Neil Simon Th., NY, 2015; screenwriter: Madame Bovary, 1999; I Capture the Castle, 2002; Cranford, 2007; Return to Cranford, 2009; writer and executive producer for television: Lilies, 2006; Ballet Shoes, 2007; Upstairs Downstairs, 2010–12; Call the Midwife, 2012–. *Publications:* Shamrocks and Crocodiles, 1988; Indigo, 1988; The Life and Times of Call the Midwife, 2012, 2nd edn 2013. *Recreations:* reading, theatre, cinema, ballet, Viennese art, English seaside, antique diamonds, new technology. *Address:* c/o The Agency, 24 Pottery Lane, Holland Park, W11 4LZ. *T:* (020) 7727 1346.

THOMAS, Prof. Howard, DSc; LKCSB Distinguished Professor of Strategic Management and Management Education, and Director, Academic Strategy and Consulting Unit, Singapore Management University, since 2015 (Professor of Strategic Management, and Dean, Lee Kong Chian School of Business, 2010–14); *b* 31 Jan. 1943; *m* 1978. *Educ:* LSE (BSc 1964, MSc 1965); Univ. of Chicago (MBA 1966); Edinburgh Univ. (PhD 1970; DSc 2007). First Internat. Business Prog. Fellow, Grad. Sch. of Business, Univ. of Chicago, 1965–66; Lectr in Stats and Operational Res., Univ. of Edinburgh, 1966–69; Lectr, Sen. Lectr, then Adjunct Prof., London Business Sch., 1969–77; Foundn Prof. of Mgt, Australian Grad. Sch. of Mgt, Sydney, 1977–80; University of Illinois, Urbana-Champaign: James F. Towey Prof. of Strategic Mgt, Coll. of Business Admin, 1980–2000; Dean, Coll. of Business Admin, 1991–2000; Prof. Emer. and Dean Emer., 2000; Dean, Warwick Business Sch., 2000–10; Prof. Emeritus, Univ. of Warwick, 2010. Visiting Professor: Harvard Business Sch., 1970; USC, 1975; UBC, 1979; Sloan Sch. of Mgt, MIT, 1987; Kellogg Sch. of Mgt, Northwestern Univ., 1990. *Publications:* (with H. Behrend) Incomes Policy and the Individual, 1967; Decision Theory and the Manager, 1972; (with P. G. Moore) Case Studies in Decision Analysis, 1976; (with P. G. Moore) Anatomy of Decisions, 1976, 2nd edn 1988; (with G. M. Kaufman) Modern Decision Analysis, 1977; (with D. W. Bunn) Formal Methods in Policy Formulation, 1978; (with D. B. Hertz) Risk Analysis and its Applications, 1983; (with D. B. Hertz) Practical Risk Analysis, 1984; (with J. McGee) Strategic Management Research: an European perspective, 1986; (jtly) Managing Ambiguity and Change, 1988; (with R. Bettis) Risk and Strategy, 1990; (with H. Daems) Strategic Groups, Strategic Moves and Performance, 1994; (jtly) Building the Strategically-Responsive Organization, 1995; (jtly) Strategic Renaissance and Business Transformation, 1995; (jtly) Entrepreneurship: perspectives on theory building, 1995; (with W. C. Bogner) Drugs to Market, 1996; (with D. O'Neal) Strategic Integration, 1996; (jtly) Dynamics of Competence-Based Competition: theory and practice of competence-based competition, 1996; (jtly) Strategy, Structure and Style, 1997; (jtly) Strategic Discovery: competing in new arenas, 1997; (jtly) Auditing Organizations Through a Strategic Systems Lens, 1997; (jtly) Strategic Flexibility: managing in a turbulent environment, 1998; (jtly) Handbook of Strategy and Management, 2001; (jtly) Strategy: analysis and practice, 2005; (jtly) Strategic Leadership Processes in Business Schools, 2011; numerous articles in Jl Business Venturing, Jl Mgt Studies, Strategic Mgt Jl, Acad. of Mgt Jl, Acad. of Mgt Rev., Admin. Sci. Qly. *Recreations:* golf, Rugby (spectating), reading, swimming. *Address:* Lee Kong Chian School of Business, Singapore Management University, 50 Stamford Road, Singapore 178899. *T:* (65) 68280535, *Fax:* (65) 68280107. *E:* howardthomas@smu.edu.sg.

THOMAS, Prof. Howard Christopher, PhD; FRCP, FRCPGlas, FRCPath, FMedSci; Professor of Medicine, 1987–2011, now Emeritus Professor of Hepatology, Department of Medicine, Vice Chairman, Division of Medicine, 1997–2004, and Clinical Dean, 2001–04, Imperial College Faculty of Medicine (formerly St Mary's Hospital Medical School), London University; *b* 31 July 1945; *s* of Harold Thomas and Hilda Thomas; *m* 1975, Dilys Ferguson; two *s* one *d*. *Educ:* Univ. of Newcastle (BSc Physiol; MB, BS); PhD Glasgow. MRCPath 1983, FRCPath 1992; MRCP 1969, FRCP 1983; FRCPGlas 1984. Lectr in Immunology,

Glasgow Univ., 1971–74; Royal Free Hospital Medical School, London: Lectr in Medicine, 1974–78; Sen. Wellcome Fellow in Clin. Sci., 1978–83; Reader in Medicine, 1983–84; Titular Prof. of Medicine, 1984–87; Chm., Dept of Medicine, St Mary's Hosp. Med. Sch., London Univ., 1987–97; Consultant Physician and Hepatologist, St Mary's Hosp., 1987–2011; Hd, Section (formerly Dept) of Hepatol. and Gastroenterol., Imperial Coll. Faculty of Medicine, Univ. of London, 2004–11. Non-exec. Dir, Riotech Pharmaceuticals, 2004– (Chm., 2009–). Member: Scientific Cttee, European Assoc. for Study of Liver, 1983–86; DoH Adv. Gp on Infected Health Care Personnel, 1994–2000; Australian Cttee to Review Nat. Hepatitis C Strategy, 2002–03; Nat. Expert Panel on New and Emerging Infections, 2003–09; Adv. Bd, German Network of Competence in Medicine (viral hepatitis) (Hep-Net), 2003–10; British Liver Disease Clinical Interest Gp, 2007–10; RCP/DoH Ad Hoc Hepatology Expert Gp, 2007; Comprehensive UK Clinical Res. Network (Hepatology Nat. Specialist Gp), NIHR, 2009–11; 4th Internat. Adv. Cttee, Univ. of Mauritius, 2009; Service Configuration and Workforce Gp preparing Nat. Plan for Liver Services, 2010–11; Chairman: DoH Adv. Gp on Hepatitis, 1999–2009 (Mem., 1987–99); DoH Strategy Cttee on Hepatitis C, 2001–02; NW Thames Hepatology Network, 2004–08; Pan-London Hepatitis Commissioning Gp, 2004–06; Clinical Guidelines Gp for Chronic Hepatitis B, NICE, 2011–13; Co-Chm., Blood Borne Viruses Gp preparing Nat. Plan for Liver Services, 2010–11. Vice Pres., British Liver Trust, 2000– (Mem., Med. Adv. Cttee, 1990–96); Pres., British and Eur. Assocs for Study of the Liver, 1996–97; Mem., Assoc. of Physicians of GB and Ireland, 1983–; Member Council: RCP, 2002–04 (Mem., Nominations Cttee, 2002–07); British Soc. of Gastroenterol., 2002–05. Chm. of Trustees, Liver Res. Trust, 1987–; Trustee: Hepatitis B Foundn, 2007–; Caxton Trust, 2011–; Mem., Liver Alliance, 2011–. Dir, Skipton Fund Ltd, 2013–. Founder and Editor, Jl of Viral Hepatitis, 1993–. Lectures: Humphry Davy Rolleston, 1986; Cohen, Israel, 1988; Bushell, Australia, 1990; Hans Popper, Internat. Assoc. for Study of Liver, S Africa, 1996; Ralph Wright, Southampton, 1999; Sheila Sherlock, British Soc. of Gastroenterol., 2005. FMedSci 1999. British Soc. of Gastroenterol. Res. Medal, 1984; Hans Popper Internat. Prize for Distinction in Hepatology, 1989; Ivanovsky Medal of Russian Acad. of Med. Scis, 1997; Lifetime Recognition Award: British Assoc. for Study of the Liver, 2010; Eur. Assoc. for Study of the Liver for clin. and scientific contrib. in field of liver diseases, 2010; Kowsar Award, Univ. of Tehran, Iran, 2011; Imperial Coll. Medal, 2013. *Publications:* Clinical Gastrointestinal Immunology, 1979; (ed jtly) Recent Advances in Hepatology, vol. 1, 1983, vol. 2, 1986; (ed jtly) Viral Hepatitis, 1996, 4th edn 2013; (ed jtly) Hepatitis C, 2009; pubns on oral tolerance and in Hepatology. *Recreations:* fishing, golf. *Address:* Department of Medicine, Imperial College Faculty of Medicine, St Mary's Hospital, Praed Street, W2 1PG. *T:* (020) 7725 6454. *Club:* Athenæum.

THOMAS, Hugh; *see* Thomas of Swynnerton, Baron.

THOMAS, Prof. Huw Jeremy Wyndham, PhD; FRCP; Consultant Physician and Gastroenterologist, St Mary's Hospital, London, since 1994; Professor of Gastrointestinal Genetics, Imperial College London, since 2007; Physician to the Queen and Head of HM Medical Household, since 2014; *b* London, 25 Feb. 1958; *s* of late William John Thomas and of Enid Thomas (*née* James); *m* 1986, Caroline Susan Sayer; two *s* one *d*. *Educ:* Harrow Sch.; Trinity Coll., Cambridge (BA 1979; MA); London Hosp. Med. Coll. (MB BS 1982); University Coll. London (PhD 1991). FRCP 1997. Jun. appts, London Hosp., 1982–86; Registrar, Liver Unit, Royal Free Hosp., 1986–88; Clin. Res. Fellow, Imperial Cancer Res. Fund, 1988–91; Sen. Registrar, St Mary's Hosp., 1991–94; Physician, King Edward VII Hosp. for Officers, later King Edward VII Hosp. Sister Agnes, 1997–; Physician to Royal Household, 2005–14. Hon Consultant Physician, St Mark's Hosp., 1994–. *Publications:* contrib. chapters, reviews and papers to med. jls. *Address:* 5 Devonshire Place, W1G 6HL. *E:* huw.thomas@imperial.ac.uk.

THOMAS, Huw Vaughan; Auditor General for Wales, since 2010; *b* 23 Nov. 1948; *s* of Idris Thomas and Winifred Thomas; *m*; two *s*. *Educ:* Durham Univ. (BA Hons Mod. Hist. 1970); City Univ., London (MSc Admin. Scis 1971). Initial mgt postings, Dept of Employment, 1971–74; Manager, London Office, Professional and Exec. Recruitment, 1974–76; Private Sec. to Parly Under Sec. of State for Employment, 1976–77; Manpower Services Commission: Principal, Employment Rehabilitation Service, 1978–81; Industrial Relns Manager, 1982–83; Department of Employment: Regl Dir, SW England, 1984–88; Dir for Wales, 1988–91; Chief Executive: Gwynedd CC, 1991–96; Denbighshire CC, 1995–2001; Dir, Taro Consultancy Ltd, 2001–10. Dir, N Wales Trng and Enterprise Councils, 1991–98; Member: New Deal Adv. Taskforce for Wales, 1997–2000; HEFCW, 1998–2002; Commn on Powers and Electoral Arrangements of Nat. Assembly of Wales, 2002–04; Consumer Mem., Hearing Aid Council, 2000–10; Ind. Mem., Parole Bd of England and Wales, 2005–11; Chm., Nat. Registers of Communication Professionals working with Deaf and Deafblind People, 2010–15. Chm., Wales, Big Lottery Fund, 2004–10; Interim Mem. Bd, Olympic Lottery Distributor, 2005–06. Mem., Nat. Exec., Soc. of Local Authy Chief Executives, 1995–2001; Lay Mem. Council, Law Soc., 2001–05. Dir, Inst. of Welsh Affairs, 1994–97; Chm., Plas Glyn y Weddw Arts Centre, 1995–96; Member: Cttee for Wales, Nat. Trust, 1996–2000; Council for Wales, Prince's Trust, 2000–02; Trustee, RNID, 2000–06. FCIPD; CCMI. Hon. Mem. CIPFA. *Recreations:* cinema, art, travelling. *Address:* Wales Audit Office, 24 Cathedral Road, Cardiff CF11 9LJ. *T:* (029) 2032 0510, *Fax:* (029) 2032 0555. *E:* huw.vaughan.thomas@wao.gov.uk.

THOMAS, Rev. (Hywel) Rhodri Glyn; Member (Plaid Cymru) Carmarthen East and Dinefwr, National Assembly for Wales, since 1999; *b* 11 April 1953; *s* of late Thomas Glyn Thomas and Eleanor Glyn Thomas; *m* 1975, Marian Gwenfair Davies; two *s* one *d*. *Educ:* Ysgol Morgan Llwyd, Wrexham; UCW, Aberystwyth, Bangor and Lampeter. Minister of Religion, St Clears Area, 1978–89 and 1992–; Man. Dir, Cwmni'r Gannwyll Cyf, 1989–95; Welsh Spokesman, Forum of Private Business, 1992–99; Dir, "Sgript" Cyf, 1992–. National Assembly for Wales: Shadow Minister for Agricl and Rural Affairs, 2002–03, for Envmt, Planning and the Countryside, 2003, for Health and Social Services, 2004–05; Minister for Heritage, 2007–08; Chairman: Agricl and Rural Affairs Cttee, 1999–2000; Culture Cttee, 2000–03; SW Wales Regl Cttee, 2001–02; HSS Cttee, 2006–07; Dep. Ldr, Plaid Cymru Assembly Gp, 2003–. *Address:* National Assembly for Wales, Cardiff Bay, Cardiff CF99 1NA; Llanddwyn, Llangynin, St Clears, Carmarthenshire SA33 4JY; (office) 37 Wind Street, Ammanford, Carmarthenshire SA18 3DN.

THOMAS, Prof. Hywel Rhys, PhD; Professor of the Economics of Education, University of Birmingham, 1993–2015, now Emeritus; *b* 11 Jan. 1947; *s* of John Howard Thomas and Eva Beryl Thomas (*née* James); *m* 1st, 1968, Patricia Anne Beard (marr. diss.); 2nd, 1980, Christine MacArthur; one *s* two *d*. *Educ:* Llanelli Boys' Grammar Sch.; Univ. of Manchester (BA, MEd, PGCE); Univ. of Birmingham (PhD 1988). Parkinson Cowan Ltd, 1968–69; teacher: New Mills Sch., Derbys, 1970–73; Kersal High Sch., Salford, 1974–79; University of Birmingham: Lectr, 1979–89; Sen. Lectr, 1989–91; Reader, 1991–93; Hd, Sch. of Educn, 1993–2003; Dir of Lifelong Learning, 2000–02; Dir, Centre for Res. in Med. and Dental Educn, 2001–15. Sen. Educn Advr, British Council, 1997–2000. Hon. FRCGP 2006. *Publications:* Managing Education: the system and the institution, 1985; Economics and Education Management, 1986; Education Costs and Performance, 1990; Financial Delegation and Local Management of Schools, 1990; Managing Resources for School Improvement, 1996; Schools at the Centre?, 1997; National Evaluation of Specialty Selection, 2010. *Address:* 30 Linden Road, Bournville, Birmingham B30 1JU.

THOMAS, Prof. Hywel Rhys, PhD, DSc; FRS 2012; CEng, FREng; FICE; FGS; FLSW; Professor of Civil Engineering, since 1995, Director, Geoenvironmental Research Centre, since 1996, and Pro Vice-Chancellor, Research, Innovation and Enterprise, since 2013, Cardiff University (formerly University of Wales College of Cardiff); *b* 20 April 1951; *s* of Howard Lionel Thomas and Elizabeth Sybil Thomas; *m*; one *s* two *d*. *Educ:* UC, Swansea (BSc 1st cl. Hons (Civil Engrg); PhD 1980); Imperial Coll., London (MSc (Soil Mechanics) 1973; DIC); Univ. of Wales (DSc 1994). CEng 1977; FICE 2000. Grad. engr, 1973–76, then Asst Resident Engr, 1976–78, Scott Wilson Kirkpatrick and Partners; Sen. Res. Asst, UC, Swansea, 1978–80; University College Cardiff, later University of Wales College of Cardiff, then Cardiff University: Lectr in Civil Engrg, 1980–90; Sen. Lectr, Sch. of Engrg, 1990–92; Reader, 1992–95; Cardiff School of Engineering: Dir, Geoenvmtl Res. Centre, 1996–; Sen. Dep. Hd, 1999–2002, Hd, 2002, Div. of Civil Engrg; Dir, 2002–10; Dep. Pro Vice-Chancellor, Innovation and Engagement, 2007–10; Pro Vice-Chancellor, Engagement and Internationalisation, 2010–12. MAE 2012. FGS 2001; FREng 2003; FLSW 2011. *Publications:* The Finite Element Method in Heat Transfer Analysis, 1996; numerous contribs to learned jls. *Address:* Cardiff University, Main Building Room 0.46, Park Place, Cardiff CF10 3AT. *T:* (029) 2087 0650, *Fax:* (029) 2087 0689. *E:* thomashr@cardiff.ac.uk.

THOMAS, James Bowen, CMG 1989; Senior Director, Global Security, Pfizer Inc., New York, 1999–2004; *b* 3 July 1942; *s* of William George Thomas and Rose Thomas (*née* Bowen); *m* 1966, Gaynor Margaret Wilkins (*d* 2005); one *s* one *d*. *Educ:* Queen Elizabeth I Grammar Sch., Carmarthen; University Coll. of Wales, Aberystwyth (BA Hons; MSc Econ. Internat. Politics). Lectr in Modern Chinese Hist., Oxford Poly., 1968–71; MoD, 1971–99; attached to FCO as First Sec., Washington, 1979–81. Trustee, Surrey Care Trust, 2008–09. *Recreations:* Rugby (Welsh), travel, the visual arts, giving TLC to old properties.

THOMAS, Jane Elizabeth G.; *see* Garland-Thomas.

THOMAS, Dame Jean Olwen, DBE 2005 (CBE 1993); ScD; FMedSci; FLSW; FRS 1986; Master of St Catharine's College, Cambridge, since 2007; Professor of Macromolecular Biochemistry, University of Cambridge, 1991–2010, now Emeritus; *b* 1 Oct. 1942; *oc* of John Robert Thomas and Lorna Prunella Thomas (*née* Harris). *Educ:* Llwyn-y-Bryn High School for Girls, Swansea; University Coll., Swansea, Univ. of Wales (BSc and Ayling Prize, 1964; PhD and Hinkel Research Prize, 1967 (Chem.)); MA Cantab 1969; ScD Cantab 1985. Beit Meml Fellow, MRC Lab. of Molecular Biology, Cambridge, 1967–69; Cambridge University: Demonstrator in Biochemistry, 1969–73; Lectr, 1973–87; Reader in the Biochemistry of Macromolecules, 1987–91; New Hall, Cambridge: Fellow, 1969–91, Professorial Fellow, 1991–2006; Coll. Lectr, 1969–91; Tutor, 1970–76; Vice-Pres., 1983–87; Hon. Fellow, 2007. Chm., Cambridge Centre for Molecular Recognition, 1993–2002. Member: SERC, 1990–94; Council, Royal Soc., 1990–92, 2007–13 (Biol Sec. and Vice Pres., 2008–13); EPSRC, 1994–97; Council and Scientific Adv. Cttee, ICRF, 1994–2001; Scientific Adv. Cttee, Lister Inst., 1994–2000. President: Biochemical Soc., 2001–05 (Hon. Mem., 2007); Soc. of Biol., later Royal Soc. of Biol., 2014– (Hon. Fellow, 2013). Trustee: BM, 1994–2004; Wolfson Foundn, 2013–. Gov., Wellcome Trust, 2000–07; Pres., Techniquest, 2005–08. Mem., EMBO, 1982; MAE 1991; FMedSci 2002; FLSW 2010. Hon. Fellow: UCW, Swansea, 1987; Univ. of Wales, Cardiff, 1998; Darwin Coll., Cambridge, 2007; Worcester Coll., Oxford, 2008; Aberystwyth Univ., 2009; Swansea Metropolitan Univ., 2011. Hon. Mem., Biophys. Soc., 2009. Hon. Bencher, Middle Temple, 2009. Hon. DSc: Wales, 1992; UEA, 2003; London, 2007. K. M. Stott Research Prize, Newnham Coll., Cambridge, 1976. *Publications:* Companion to Biochemistry: selected topics for further study, vol. 1, 1974, vol. 2, 1979 (ed jtly and contrib.); papers in sci. jls, esp. on chromatin structure and DNA-binding proteins. *Recreations:* reading, music, walking. *Address:* Department of Biochemistry, 80 Tennis Court Road, Cambridge CB2 1GA. *T:* (01223) 333670; Master's Lodge, St Catharine's College, Cambridge CB2 1RL. *T:* (01223) 338349.

THOMAS, Jenkin; HM Diplomatic Service, retired; Deputy UK Permanent Representative and Counsellor (Economic and Financial), OECD, Paris, 1990–94; *b* 2 Jan. 1938; *s* of late William John Thomas and of Annie Muriel (*née* Thomas). *Educ:* Maesydderwen Sch.; University Coll. London (BA Hons); Univ. of Michigan, Ann Arbor (MA). Joined HM Foreign (subseq. Diplomatic) Service, 1960; Foreign Office, 1960–63; Pretoria/Cape Town, 1963–66; Saigon, 1966–68; FCO, 1968–73; Washington, 1973–77; FCO, 1977–79; Cabinet Office, 1979–80; Tokyo, 1980–82; Athens, 1982–87; FCO, 1987–90. Mem., Council, Cymmrodorion Soc. *Recreations:* reading, music, amateur musical comedies, active Anglican Church member. *Address:* 43 Charleville Mansions, Charleville Road, W14 9JA.

THOMAS, Sir Jeremy (Cashel), KCMG 1987 (CMG 1980); HM Diplomatic Service, retired; *b* 1 June 1931; *s* of Rev. H. C. Thomas and Margaret Betty (*née* Humby); *m* 1957, Diana Mary Summerhayes (*d* 2009); three *s*. *Educ:* Eton; Merton Coll., Oxford. 16th/5th Lancers, 1949–51. Entered FO, 1954; served Singapore, Rome and Belgrade; Dep. Head, Personnel Ops Dept, FCO, 1970–74; Counsellor and Head of Chancery, UK Mission to UN, NY, 1974–76; Head of Perm. Under-Sec.'s Dept, FCO, 1977–79; Ambassador to Luxembourg, 1979–82; Asst Under-Sec. of State, FCO, 1982–85; Ambassador to Greece, 1985–89. Chm., Chichester Harbour Trust, 2002–13. *Publications:* The Rhythm of the Tide: tales through the ages of Chichester Harbour, 1999. *Recreations:* sailing, fishing. *Address:* East Manor Farm, Pook Lane, East Lavant, near Chichester, West Sussex PO18 0AH. *T:* (01243) 531661. *Clubs:* Oxford and Cambridge; Itchenor Sailing, Bosham Sailing.

THOMAS, Maj. Gen. Jeremy Hywel, CB 2012; DSO 2007; security sector consultant (part-time), since 2012; Assistant Chief of Defence Staff (Intelligence Capability), Ministry of Defence, 2009–12; *b* 12 April 1957; *s* of Brian and Eslie Thomas; *m* 1978, Oenone French; one *s* one *d*. *Educ:* Worthing High Sch. for Boys; Worthing Sixth Form Coll.; Univ. of St Andrews (MLitt 2013). Royal Marines: joined, 1975; Army Staff Coll., Camberley, 1989; OC L Company, 42 Commando, 1993–95; COS 3 Commando Bde, 1995–97; Comdr 45 Commando Gp, 1997–99; COS Jt Force HQ, 1999–2001; HCSC 2000; Dir Intelligence Ops, Defence Intelligence Staff, 2003–05; Commanded: 3 Commando Bde, 2006–07; UK Task Force in Afghanistan, Oct. 2006–April 2007; Sen. British Mil. Advr to HQ US Central Comd, Tampa, 2007–09. Rep. Col Comdt, RM, 2012–. Chm. Trustees, RM Charitable Trust Fund, 2013–. Hon. Fellow, Univ. of Exeter Strategy and Security Inst., 2012. PhD student, Univ. of Exeter, 2013–. *Recreations:* keeping fit, history and current affairs, gardening, active family holidays.

THOMAS, Jeremy Jack, CBE 2009; film producer; Chairman, Recorded Picture Co., since 1973; *b* 26 July 1949; *s* of late Ralph Philip Thomas, MC and Joy Thomas; *m* 1st, 1977, Claudia Frolich (marr. diss. 1981); one *d*; 2nd, 1982, Vivien Coughman; two *s*. *Educ:* Millfield. Has worked in most aspects of film prodn, esp. in editing dept before becoming a producer. Chm., BFI, 1993–97. Producer: Mad Dog Morgan, 1974; The Shout, 1977; Bad Timing, 1980; Merry Christmas, Mr Lawrence, 1982; Eureka, 1982; The Hit, 1984; Insignificance, 1985; The Last Emperor, 1987 (9 Acad. Awards incl. Best Film); Everybody Wins, 1990; The Sheltering Sky, 1990; The Naked Lunch, 1991; Little Buddha, 1992; Stealing Beauty, 1996; Blood and Wine, 1997; Brother, 1999; Sexy Beast, 2001; Young Adam, 2003; The Dreamers, 2003; Tideland, 2006; Fast Food Nation, 2007; Franklyn, 2008; Creation, 2009; Hara-Kiri: Death of a Samurai, 2011; A Dangerous Method, 2011; Dom Hemingway, 2013; Only Lovers Left Alive, 2014; High Rise, 2015; Tale of Tales, 2015; Executive Producer: The Great Rock 'n Roll Swindle, 1979; Let Him Have It, 1991; Crash, 1995; The Brave, 1996; The Cup, 1999; Gohatto, 1999; Triumph of Love, 2001; Rabbit Proof Fence, 2002; Heimat 3 (TV series), 2004; Promised Land Hotel, 2004; Dreaming Lhasa, 2004; Don't Come Knocking, 2004; Glastonbury, 2005; Joe Strummer: the future is unwritten, 2007; Essential Killing, 2010; Thirteen Assassins, 2010; Pina, 2011; Prod./Dir, All

The Little Animals, 1998. Special Award for Outstanding Contribn to Cinema, Evening Standard, 1990; Michael Balcon Award for Outstanding Contribn to Cinema, BAFTA, 1991; European Achievement in World Cinema, European Film Awards, 2006; Life Fellow, BFI, 1998. *Clubs:* Garrick, Royal Automobile.

THOMAS, Sir (John) Alan, Kt 1993; Chairman, Hyder Consulting plc, 2002–14; *b* 4 Jan. 1943; *s* of late Idris Thomas and Ellen Constance Thomas (*née* Noakes); *m* 1966, Angela Taylor; two *s*. *Educ:* Dynevor Sch.; Nottingham Univ. (Richard Thomas & Baldwin's Industrial Schol.; BSc Mech. Engrg). FCMA (First Prizewinner); CEng; FIET. Chief Exec., Data Logic, 1973–85; Vice Pres., Raytheon Co. (US), 1985–89; Pres. and Chief Exec. Officer, Raytheon Europe, 1985–89; Chm., Tag Semi-Conductors (US), 1985–89; Dir, Eur. subsids, 1978–89; seconded to MoD as Head of Defence Export Services Orgn, 1989–94. Chairman: Micro Quoted Growth Trust plc, 1997–2001; Chelverton Asset Mgt, 1997–2005; Global Design Technologies LLC, 2005–07; Three Valleys Water plc, 2000–09; Director: Powergen plc, 1996–99; Radstone Technology plc, 2004–06; Sen. Industrial Advr, OFWAT, 1997–2000. Member: Defence Industries Council, 1990–94; Engrg Council, 1994–96. Dir, Centre for Policy Studies, 1996–2003. University of Westminster (formerly Polytechnic of Central London): Vis. Prof., 1981–; Gov., 1989–2005, Chm., Ct of Govs, 1999–2005. Dir, London Welsh RFC, 1997–2008. Pres., Computing Services Assoc., 1980–81. Liveryman, Co. of Information Technologists, 1988–. Hon. DSc Westminster, 2005. *Recreations:* music, sport. *Club:* Athenæum.

THOMAS, Dr John Anthony Griffiths; Director and Trustee, Relate Avon, since 2004 (Counsellor and Tutor, 1999–2004; Vice Chair, since 2009); *b* 28 Aug. 1943; *s* of late William and Bernice Thomas; *m* 1965, Sylvia Jean Norman; two *d*. *Educ:* Leeds Univ. (BSc Chem. 1965); Univ. of Keele (PhD 1968); Open Univ. Mem., BPsS 2004. Teacher of Chemistry, Leeds Grammar Sch., 1968–69; Reed Business Publishing Ltd: Editor, 1969–75; Editorial Dir, 1975–77; Publishing Dir, 1977–84; Divisional Man. Dir, Med. Div., 1984–86; BBC Enterprises Ltd: Dir, BBC Magazines and Electronic Publishing Gp, 1986–93; Man. Dir, 1993–94; Managing Director: BBC Worldwide Television Ltd, 1994–95; BBC Worldwide Learning, 1995–97; Dep. Chm., BBC Worldwide Publishing, 1994–97; Dir, BBC Worldwide Ltd, 1994–97. Chairman: Redwood Publishing Ltd, 1988–93; Frontline Ltd, 1990–94; BBC Haymarket Exhibns Ltd, 1992–94; Galleon Ltd, 1993–94; Dir, Periodicals Publishing Assoc., 1989–94. Dir and Trustee, Bath Fests, 2007–13. Stanford Univ. Alumni, 1991. *Publications:* (ed) Energy Modelling, 1974; Energy Today, 1977; (ed) Energy Analysis, 1977; The Quest for Fuel, 1978. *Recreations:* psychology, reading, music, dance, walking, reading, jazz guitar.

THOMAS, Prof. John David, PhD; FBA 1989; Professorial Fellow in Papyrology, University of Durham, 1990–92, now Emeritus Professor; *b* 23 June 1931; *s* of Henry Thomas and Elsie Thomas (*née* Bruin); *m* 1st, 1956, Marion Amy Peach (*d* 2011); two *s*; 2nd, 2014, Angela Shaw. *Educ:* Wyggeston Grammar Sch., Leicester; Worcester Coll., Oxford (MA); PhD Wales. Lectr in Classics, UCW, Aberystwyth, 1955–66; University of Durham: Lectr, then Sen. Lectr in Palaeography, 1966–77; Reader in Papyrology, 1977–90. Vis. Fellow, Wolfson Coll., Oxford, 1981 (Life Mem. of Common Room, 2014). Member: Inst. for Advanced Study, Princeton, 1972; Comité Internat. de Papyrologie, 1983–95. *Publications:* Greek Papyri in the Collection of W. Merton III, 1967; The Epistrategos in Ptolemaic and Roman Egypt, Pt I 1975, Pt II 1982; (with A. K. Bowman) Vindolanda: the Latin writing tablets, 1983; (with A. K. Bowman) The Vindolanda writing-tablets: Tabulae Vindolandenses II, 1994, III, 2003; contribs to the Oxyrhynchus Papyri XXXVIII, XLIV, XLVII, L, LVII, LXV–LXVII, LXX, LXXII, LXXIII, LXVIII (Gen. Ed., Oxyrhynchus Papyri, LXVI, LXVII; Adv. Ed., LXVIII); articles and reviews in learned jls. *Recreations:* music, bird watching, walking. *Address:* 43 Orchard House, New Elvet, Durham DH1 3DB. *T:* (0191) 386 1723.

THOMAS, Sir John Meurig, Kt 1991; MA, PhD, DSc, ScD; FRS 1977; Distinguished Research Fellow, Department of Materials Science and Metallurgy, University of Cambridge, 1993–2002, now Hon. Professor in Solid State Chemistry; Master of Peterhouse, Cambridge, 1993–2002, Hon. Fellow, 2002; *b* Llanelli, Wales, 15 Dec. 1932; *s* of David John and Edyth Thomas; *m* 1st, 1959, Margaret (*née* Edwards) (*d* 2002); two *d*; 2nd, 2010, Prof. Jehane Ragai, Cairo. *Educ:* Gwendraeth Grammar Sch. (State Scholar); University College of Swansea (Hon. Fellow, 1985); Queen Mary Coll., London; DSc Wales, 1964; ScD Cantab, 1994. Scientific Officer, UKAEA, 1957–58; Asst Lectr 1958–59, Lectr 1959–65, Reader 1965–69, in Chemistry, UCNW, Bangor; Prof. and Head of Dept of Chemistry, UCW, Aberystwyth, 1969–78 (Hon. Fellow, 1996); Prof. and Head of Dept of Physical Chemistry, and Fellow of King's Coll., Univ. of Cambridge, 1978–86; Dir, Royal Instn of GB, and Davy Faraday Res. Lab., 1986–91; Resident Prof. of Chemistry, 1986–88, Fullerian Prof. of Chemistry, 1988–94, Prof. of Chemistry, 1994–2002, Emeritus Prof., 2002, Royal Instn of GB; Dep. Pro-Chancellor, Univ. of Wales, 1991–94. Visiting appointments: Tech. Univ. Eindhoven, Holland, 1962; Penna State Univ., USA, 1963, 1967; Tech. Univ. Karlsruhe, Germany, 1966; Weizmann Inst., Israel, 1969; Univ. of Florence, Italy, 1972; Amer. Univ. in Cairo, Egypt, 1973; IBM Res. Center, San José, 1977; Harvard, 1983; Ecole Nat. Sup. de Chimie de Paris, 1991; Scuola Normale Superiore, Pisa, 2003; USC, 2005–11; Cardiff, 2005–; Southampton, 2006–09; York, 2008–; Monchot Prize Vis. Prof., Technische Universität, München, 2009; Vis. Prof., Hokkaido Univ., Japan, 2010; Adv. Prof., Jiao Tong Univ., Shanghai, 2010–; Dist. Vis. Lectr in Chem., NY Univ., 2014. Ind. Mem., Radioactive Waste Management Cttee, 1978–80; Member: Chem. SRC, 1976–78; SERC, 1986–90; Adv. Cttee, Davy-Faraday Labs, Royal Instn, 1978–80; Scientific Adv. Cttee, Sci. Center, Alexandria, 1979–2005; ACARD (Cabinet Office), 1982–85; COPUS, 1986–92; Bd of Governors, Weizmann Inst., 1982–2006; Academia Europaea, 1989. Mem., Royal Commn for Exhibn of 1851, 1995–2006 (Chm., Scientific Res. Cttee, 1996–2006). Chm., Chemrawn (Chem. Res. Applied to World Needs), IUPAC, 1987–93; Member, International Advisory Board: NSF Lab. of Molecular Scis, CIT, 1999; Nat. Inst. of Informatics, Tokyo, 2000–; President: Chem. Section, BAAS, 1988–89; London Internat. Youth Sci. Fortnight, 1989–93. Trustee: BM (Natural Hist.), 1987–92; Science Mus., 1990–95. Vice-President: Cambridge Univ. Musical Soc., 1994–; Cambridge Philosophical Soc., 1994–2000. Hon. Visiting Professor: in Physical Chem., QMC, 1986–2006; of Chem., Imperial Coll., London, 1986–91; Academia Sinica, Beijing; Inst. of Ceramic Sci., Shanghai, 1986; Hon. Prof., Dalian Inst. Chem. Physics, Chinese Acad. of Scis, 2010. Pres., Nat. Eisteddfod of Wales, 2014. New mineral, meurigite, named in his honour, 1995. Lectures: BBC Welsh Radio Annual, 1978; Gerhardt Schmidt Meml, Weizmann Inst., 1979; Baker, Cornell Univ., 1982–83; Hund-Klemm, Max Planck Ges., Stuttgart, 1987; Christmas Lectures, Royal Instn, 1987 (televised, 1988); First Kenneth Pitzer, Coll. of Chem., Univ. of Calif, Berkeley, 1988; Van't Hoff, Royal Dutch Acad. of Arts and Scis, 1988; Bakerian, Royal Soc., 1990; Bruce Preller Prize, RSE, 1990; Sir Krishnan Meml, Delhi, 1991; Watson Centennial, CIT, 1991; Birch, ANU Canberra, 1992; Liversidge, Univ. of Sydney, 1992; Sir Joseph Larmor, Cambridge Philos. Soc., 1992; Patten, Indiana Univ., 1993; François Gault, Eur. Fedn of Catalyst Socs, 1995; Prettre, Lyons, 1996; Rutherford Meml (presented at seven locations in NZ), Royal Soc., 1997; Tetelman, Yale Univ., 1997; Pollack, Technion Haifa, 1998; Ziegler Centenary, Max Planck Inst., Mülheim, 1998; Linus Pauling, CIT, 1999; Taylor, Penn State, 1999; Major, Univ. of Connecticut, 2000; Miller, Univ. of Calif., Berkeley, 2000; Linus Pauling, Oregon State, 2000; John C. Polanyi Nobel Laureate Series Speaker, Univ. of Toronto, 2000; Griffiths Meml (250th anniv.), Hon. Soc. of Cymmrodorion, London, 2001; Debye, Univ. of Utrecht, 2001; Plenary Speaker, World Congress of Chemistry, Brisbane, 2001; Annual Public, Univ. of Surrey, 2002; Inst. of Appl. Catalysis Annual, UK, 2002; Linus Pauling (and Gold Medallist), Stanford Univ., 2003; Eyring, Arizona State Univ., 2003; Guggenheim, Reading Univ., 2003; Giulio Natta Centenary (and Centenary Gold Medallist), Italian Chem. Soc., 2003; Barrer, Penn State Univ., 2004; Ipatieff, Northwestern Univ., 2004; Discours Éminents, Geneva, 2005; David Lloyd George Meml, Criccieth Fest., 2005; Woodward, Yale, 2006; Golden Jubilee Dist., Hong Kong Baptist Univ., 2006; Max T. Rogers Dist., Michigan State Univ., 2007; Pirkey, Texas A & M Univ., 2007; A. S. Williams Dist., Univ. of S Carolina, 2007; Oersted, Danish Tech. Univ., 2007; Annual, Welsh Centre for Internat. Affairs, Cardiff, 2008; Solvay, Free Univ. of Brussels, 2009; English Public Lee, Amer. Univ., Cairo, 2009; Bragg Prize Lectr, British Crystallographic Assoc., 2010; Hassel, Univ. of Oslo, 2010; Sven Breggen Prize Lectr, Royal Lund Acad. of Sci. and Technol., 2010; Gerhard Ertl Prize Lectr, Fritz-Haber Inst., Berlin, 2010; Areces Foundn Dist., Royal Acad. of Spain, 2011; J. J. Hermans, State Univ., N Carolina, 2011; Willard Gibbs Medal Centenary, Amer. Chem. Soc., 2011; Shipley, Clarkson Univ., NY, 2011; Waterloo Inst. of Nanosci., Canada, 2011; Stoner, Univ. of Leeds and Literary and Philos. Soc. of Leeds, 2011; Chemical Heritage Foundn, Philadelphia, 2011; 600th Anniv., Univ. of St Andrews, 2012; Jayne Prize, Amer. Philos. Soc., 2012. Founder FLSW 2010. Hon. FRSE 1993; Hon. FInstP 1999; Hon. FREng 1999. Hon. Fellow: Indian Acad. of Science, 1980; UMIST, 1984; UCNW, Bangor, 1988; RMS, 1989; Queen Mary and Westfield Coll., London, 1990; Foreign Fellow, INA, 1985; Hon. Foreign Member: Amer. Acad. of Arts and Scis, 1990; Venezuelan Acad. of Scis, 1994; Hon. For. Assoc., Engrg Acad. of Japan, 1991; Internat. Mem. (formerly Foreign Mem.), Amer. Philosophical Soc., 1993; Hon. Foreign Fellow: Russian Acad. of Scis, 1994; Hungarian Acad. of Sci., 1998; Polish Acad. of Arts and Scis, 1999; Amer. Carbon Soc., 1999; Göttingen Acad. of Natural Scis, 2003; Russian Chem. Soc., 2004; Accademia Nazionale dei Lincei, Rome, 2004; Royal Swedish Acad. Scis, 2013. Hon. Bencher, Gray's Inn, 1987. Hon. LLD Wales, 1984; Hon. DLitt CNAA, 1987; Hon. DSc: Heriot-Watt, 1989; Birmingham, 1991; Complutense, Madrid, 1994; Western Ontario, Glamorgan, 1995; Hull, 1996; Aberdeen, 1997; Hong Kong Baptist, 2008; DUniv: Open, 1991; Surrey, 1997; Dr *hc*: Lyon, 1994; Eindhoven, 1996; American Univ., Cairo, 2002; Turin, 2004; Clarkson, NY, 2005; Sydney, 2005; Osaka Prefecture Univ., 2006; Bangor, 2009; St Andrews, 2012; S Carolina, 2013. Corday Morgan Silver Medal, Chem. Soc., 1967; first Pettinos Prize, American Carbon Soc., 1969; Tilden Medal and Lectr, Chem. Soc., 1973; Chem. Soc. Prizewinner in Solid State Chem., 1978; Hugo Müller Medal, RSC, 1983; Faraday Medal and Lectr, RSC, 1989; Messel Medal, SCI, 1992; Davy Medal, Royal Soc., 1994; Gibbs Gold Medal, ACS, 1995; Longstaff Medal, RSC, 1996; Hon. Medal, Polish Acad. of Scis, Warsaw, 1996; Semenov Centenary Medal, Russian Acad. of Sci., 1996; ACS Award for creative res. in homogeneous or heterogeneous catalysis (first recipient), 1999; Hon. Soc. of Cymmrodorion Medal, 2003; Sir George Stokes Gold Medal for innovation in analytical chem., RSC, 2005; Silver Medal for services to sci., Univ. of Siena, 2005; Dist. Achievement Award, Internat. Precious Metal Inst., 2007; Ahmed Zewail Gold Medal, Wayne State Univ., 2009; Kapitsa Gold Medal, Russian Acad. of Natural Scis, 2011; Blaise Pascal Medal for Material Sci., Eur. Acad. Scis, 2014; Menelaus Prize, Learned Soc. Wales, 2015; Ahmed Zewail Gold Medal and Prize for Molecular Scis, Elsevier, 2015. Crystals and Lasers, TV series, 1987; Dylanwadau, radio series, 1990. Founding Editor: (jtly), Catalysis Letters, 1988; (jtly) Topics in Catalysis, 1992; (jtly) Current Opinion in Solid State and Materials Sci., 1996. *Publications:* (with W. J. Thomas) Introduction to the Principles of Heterogeneous Catalysis, 1967 (trans. Russian 1970); Pan edrychwyf ar y nefoedd, 1978; Michael Faraday and the Royal Institution: the genius of man and place, 1991 (trans. Japanese 1994, Italian 2007, Chinese 2013); (with K. I. Zamaraev) Perspectives in Catalysis, 1992; (with W. J. Thomas) Heterogeneous Catalysis: theory and practice, 1997, 2nd edn as Heterogeneous Catalysis: principles and practice, 2015; (with A. Zewail) 4D Electron Microscopy: imaging in space and time, 2010 (trans. Chinese 2013); Design and Applications of Single-Site Heterogeneous Catalysts: contributions to green chemistry, green technology and sustainability, 2012 (trans. Chinese 2013); numerous articles on solid state materials and surface chemistry, catalysis and influence of crystalline imperfections, in Proc. Royal Soc., Jl Chem. Soc., etc. *Recreations:* ancient civilizations, bird watching, hill walking, Welsh literature, music, reading other people's recreations in Who's Who. *Address:* Department of Materials Science and Metallurgy, University of Cambridge, 27 Charles Babbage Road, Cambridge CB3 0FS. *T:* (01223) 334300, *Fax:* (01223) 334567.

THOMAS, Prof. Jonathan Paul, DPhil; FBA 2002; Professor of Economics, University of Edinburgh, since 2002; *b* 28 May 1957; *s* of Berwyn Harold Thomas and Christine Erica Thomas (*née* Foden); *m* 1992, Ruth McFadyen; one *s*. *Educ:* Llanishen High Sch., Cardiff; St John's Coll., Cambridge (BA); MPhil 1981, DPhil 1989, Oxon. Res. Officer, Dept of Applied Econs, Univ. of Cambridge, 1982–84; temp. Lectr in Econs, Univ. of Bristol, 1984–85; Lectr, 1985–93, Sen. Lectr, 1993–96, Prof. of Econs, 1996–99, Univ. of Warwick; Prof. of Econs, Univ. of St Andrews, 1999–2002. Professorial Fellow, Univ. of Edinburgh, 2001–02. Hon. Prof., Univ. of Warwick, 1999. *Publications:* contribs to Econometrica, Rev. of Econ. Studies, Jl of Econ. Theory, American Econ. Review, etc. *Recreations:* tennis, golf, ski-ing. *Address:* School of Economics, University of Edinburgh, 31 Buccleuch Place, Edinburgh EH8 9JT. *E:* Jonathan.Thomas@ed.ac.uk.

THOMAS, Julian Paul; Master, Wellington College, since 2015; *b* Redbridge, 30 Dec. 1966; *s* of Ronald Norman and Sylvia Elsie Thomas; *m* 2001, Julia Wade; two *s*. *Educ:* Bancroft Sch.; King's Coll. London (BSc Hons Computer Sci.); Queens' Coll., Cambridge (PGCE Maths); Univ. of Hull (MBA Educnl Leadership). Teacher of Maths, Forest Sch., 1995–97; Hd of Year and Second in Charge of Maths, St Dunstan's Coll., 1997–2000; Dir of Studies, Portsmouth GS, 2000–03; Second Master, Hampton Sch., 2003–07; Headmaster, Caterham Sch., 2007–15. FRSA 2007. Gov., London Acad. of Excellence, 2012–. *Publications:* Foundation Mathematics Teacher's Resource, 1998; Intermediate Mathematics 2, 1998; Mathematics GCSE in a Year, 1999; Formula One Maths B1, 2001; Formula One Maths B2, 2001. *Recreations:* trekking/climbing (expedition to S Pole, Nov. 2014–Jan. 2015), running, guitar, Leyton Orient FC. *Address:* Master's Lodge, Wellington College, Crowthorne, Berks RG45 7PU. *Clubs:* East India; Hawks' (Cambridge).

THOMAS, Kathrin Elizabeth, (Mrs E. V. Thomas), CVO 2002; JP; Lord-Lieutenant of Mid Glamorgan, since 2003 (Vice Lord-Lieutenant, 1994–2002); *b* 20 May 1944; *d* of Dillwyn Evans and Dorothy Nelle (*née* Bullock); *m* 1967, Edward Vaughan Thomas (*d* 2006); two *s*. *Educ:* Cheltenham Ladies' Coll. Chairman: Mid Glamorgan FHSA, 1990–94; Mid Glamorgan HA, 1994–96; Bro Taf HA, 1996–99; Prince's Trust, Cymru, 1999–2001; Mem., Prince's Trust Council, 1996–2001; Pres., Royal Welsh Agricl Show, 2009. Hon. Col 203 (Welsh) Field Hosp. (V), 1998–2006 (Hon. Patron, 2008–). Mid Glamorgan: JP 1983; High Sheriff 1986–87; DL 1989. *Recreations:* family, travel, reading. *Address:* c/o 14 de Londres Close, Porthcawl CF36 3JE. *Club:* Army and Navy.

THOMAS, Keith Garfield; His Honour Judge Keith Thomas; a Circuit Judge, since 2004; *b* 10 Aug. 1955; *s* of Howard and Shirley Thomas; *m* 2003, Melinda Jane (*née* Vaughan). *Educ:* Mill Hill Sch.; Bristol Polytech. (LLB). Called to the Bar, Gray's Inn, 1977; Asst Provincial Stipendiary Magistrate, 1995; Asst Recorder, 1996–2000; Recorder, 2000–04; Resident Judge, Swansea Crown Court, 2011–. Hon. Recorder, City and Co. of Swansea, 2011–. *Recreations:* Rugby Union, cricket. *Address:* c/o Crown Court, St Helens Road, Swansea SA1 4PF. *Club:* Glamorgan Wanderers Rugby Football (Vice Chm., 1999–2008; Trustee, 2004–).

THOMAS, Keith Henry Westcott, CB 1982; OBE 1962; FREng, FRINA; RCNC; Chief Executive, Royal Dockyards, and Head of Royal Corps of Naval Constructors, 1979–83; *b* 20 May 1923; *s* of Henry and Norah Thomas; *m* 1946, Brenda Jeanette Crofton; two *s*. *Educ:* Portsmouth Southern Secondary Sch.; HM Dockyard Sch., Portsmouth; RNC, Greenwich.

Asst Constructor, Admiralty Experiment Works, Haslar, 1947–49; Constructor: Admty, London, 1949–56; Large Carrier Design Section, Admty, Bath, 1956–60; Submarines and New Construction, HM Dockyard, Portsmouth, 1960–63; Project Leader, Special Refit HMS Hermes, Devonport, 1963–66; Dep. Planning Manager, HM Dockyard, Devonport, 1966–68; Project Manager, Ikara Leanders, MoD(N), 1968–70; Dir-Gen. of Naval Design, Dept of Navy, Canberra, Aust. (on secondment), 1970–73; Planning Manager, 1973–75, Gen. Manager, 1975–77, HM Dockyard, Rosyth; Gen. Manager, HM Dockyard, Devonport, 1977–79. Member: Portsmouth Royal Dockyard Historical Trust, 1995– (Chm., 1995–2006; Pres., Portsmouth Royal Dockyard Historical Soc., 1988–95); Nat. Historic Ships Cttee, 1996–2000. *Recreations:* music, lapidary, painting. *Address:* 6 Wyborn Close, Hayling Island, Hants PO11 9HY. *T:* (023) 9246 3435.

THOMAS, Sir Keith (Vivian), Kt 1988; FBA 1979; FLSW; Fellow of All Souls College, Oxford, 1955–57 and 2001–15, now Hon. Fellow; President of Corpus Christi College, Oxford, 1986–2000 (Hon. Fellow, 2000); *b* 2 Jan. 1933; *s* of late Vivian Jones Thomas and Hilda Janet Eirene Thomas (*née* Davies); *m* 1961, Valerie Little; one *s* one *d*. *Educ:* Barry County Grammar Sch.; Balliol Coll., Oxford (Brackenbury Schol.; 1st Cl. Hons Mod. History, 1955; Hon. Fellow 1984). Oxford University: Senior Scholar, St Antony's Coll., 1955; Fellow of St John's Coll., 1957–86 (Tutor, 1957–85; Hon. Fellow, 1986); Reader in Modern Hist., 1978–85; Prof. of Modern Hist., Jan.–Sept. 1986; Pro-Vice-Chancellor, 1988–2000; Mem., Hebdomadal Council, 1988–2000. Vis. Professor, Louisiana State Univ., 1970; Vis. Fellow, 1978, Lawrence Stone Vis. Prof., 2001, Princeton Univ.; Kratter Univ. Prof., Stanford Univ., 2004; Vis. Fellow, Heyman Center for the Humanities, Columbia Univ., 2008. Joint Literary Director, Royal Historical Soc., 1970–74, Mem. Council, 1975–78, Vice-Pres., 1980–84, Hon. Vice-Pres., 2001; Pres., British Acad., 1993–97. Member: ESRC, 1985–90; Reviewing Cttee on Export of Works of Art, 1989–92; Royal Commn on Historical Manuscripts, 1992–2002; Trustee: Nat. Gall., 1991–98; British Museum, 1999–2008; Chairman: British Liby Adv. Cttee for Arts, Humanities and Social Scis, 1997–2002; Adv. Council, Warburg Inst., Univ. of London, 2000–08; Supervisory Cttee, Oxford DNB, 1992–2004. Delegate, OUP, 1980–2000 (Chm., Finance Cttee, 1988–2000). Judge, Wolfson Hist. Prize, 1975–2015 (Chm., 1996–2015). Lectures: Stenton, Univ. of Reading, 1975; Raleigh, British Acad., 1976; Neale, University Coll. London, 1976; G. M. Trevelyan, Univ. of Cambridge, 1978–79; Sir D. Owen Evans, University Coll. of Wales, Aberystwyth, 1980; Kaplan, Univ. of Pennsylvania, 1983; Creighton, Univ. of London, 1983; Ena H. Thompson, Pomona Coll., 1986; Prothero, RHistS, 1986; Merle Curti, Univ. of Wisconsin-Madison, 1989; Spinoza, Univ. of Amsterdam, 1992; Ford's in British History, Univ. of Oxford, 2000; British Acad., 2001; Menahem Stern, Jerusalem, 2003; Leslie Stephen, Univ. of Cambridge, 2004. FLSW 2010. MAE 1993 (Trustee, 1997–2001); For. Hon. Mem., Amer. Acad. of Arts and Scis, 1983; Hon. Mem., Japan Acad., 2009. Hon. Fellow: Univ. of Wales Coll. of Cardiff, 1995; Warburg Inst., Univ. of London, 2008. Hon. DLitt: Kent, 1983; Wales, 1987; Hull, 1995; Leicester, 1996; Sussex, 1996; Warwick, 1998; London, 2006; Hon. LLD: Williams Coll., Mass, 1988; Oglethorpe Univ., Ga, 1996; Hon. LittD: Sheffield, 1992; Cambridge, 1995; Columbia, 2011; Hon. PhD Uppsala, 2014. Norton Medlicott Medal, Histl Assoc., 2003; Lifetime Achievement Award, All-Party Parly Gp on Archives and Hist., 2015. Cavaliere Ufficiale, Ordine al Merito della Repubblica Italiana, 1991. Gen. Editor, Past Masters Series, OUP, 1979–2000. *Publications:* Religion and the Decline of Magic, 1971 (Wolfson History Prize, 1972); Rule and Misrule in the Schools of Early Modern England, 1976; Age and Authority in Early Modern England, 1977; (ed with Donald Pennington), Puritans and Revolutionaries, 1978; Man and the Natural World, 1983; (ed) The Oxford Book of Work, 1999; (ed with Andrew Adonis) Roy Jenkins: a retrospective, 2004; Changing Conceptions of National Biography, 2005; The Ends of Life, 2009; The Wolfson History Prize 1972–2012: an informal history, 2012; contribs to historical books and jls. *Recreation:* looking for secondhand bookshops. *Address:* All Souls College, Oxford OX1 4AL; The Broad Gate, Broad Street, Ludlow, Shropshire SY8 1NJ.

THOMAS, Dame Kristin S.; *see* Scott Thomas.

THOMAS, Prof. Lancelot, FInstP; Professor of Physics, University of Wales, Aberystwyth, 1981–95, Research Professor, 1995–97, now Emeritus Professor (Head of Department, 1981–94); *b* 4 Aug. 1930; *s* of Evan Lancelot Redvers Thomas and Olive Margaretta Thomas; *m* 1955, Helen McGraith Reilly; two *s* one *d*. *Educ:* Port Talbot Secondary Grammar Sch.; University College of Swansea (BSc, PhD, DSc). Nat. Service Trng, Flying Officer, RAF, Bomber Comd, 1954–56; Royal Soc. post-doctoral appt, UC of Swansea, 1956–58; SSO, PSO, then Individual Merit SPSO, SERC Appleton Lab., 1959–65, 1966–81; Guest Worker, Envmtl Res. Labs, Nat. Oceanic and Atmospheric Admin, Boulder, Colorado, 1965–66; Principal Investigator, SERC/NERC VHF Radar Facility, 1981–97. Chm., British Nat. Cttee for Solar Terrestrial Physics, Royal Soc., 1982–87; Member: Adv. Cttee on Solar Systems, ESA, 1973–76; Royal Soc. Study Gp on Pollution in the Atmosphere, 1975–77; Wkg Gp for Scientific Definition of Spacelab Missions, NASA, 1975–77; Solar System Cttee, Astronomy, Space and Radio Bd, SERC, 1975–79; Scientific Adv. Cttee, British Antarctic Survey, 1983–86; Earth Observation Prog. Bd, BNSC, 1987–88; Astronomy and Planetary Sci. Bd, SERC, 1989–93; Royal Soc. Interdisciplinary Sci. Cttee on Space Res., 1990–93; Astronomy Cttee, PPARC, 1994–97; Council, Inst. of Physics, 1994–98. Hon. Fellow, Univ. of Wales, Swansea, 1998. Charles Chree Medal and Prize, Inst. of Physics, 1991. *Publications:* (ed with T. M. Donahue and P. A. Smith) COSPAR: Space Research X, 1970; papers in learned journals on theoretical studies of the upper atmosphere and ionosphere with related experimental work using laser radar techniques, VHF radar facility and rocket soundings. *Recreations:* music, modern history, golf, lifelong interest in Rugby (played for Aberavon, Neath and Doncaster).

THOMAS, Leslie Letchworth; QC 2014; *b* London, 1965; *s* of Godfrey and Sheila Thomas; one *s* one *d*. *Educ:* Kingston Univ. (LLB Hons 1987). Called to the Bar, Inner Temple, 1988, Bencher, 2015; barrister, specialising in public and administrative law, claims against the police and inquests: Wellington St Chambers, 1989–90; Garden Court Chambers, 1990– (Treas., 2012–). Lectr in Law, Westminster and Kingston Univs, 1988–92. Mem., Mgt Cttee, Central London Law Centre, 1989–2014 (Chair, 1999–2007). Mem., Standards Cttee for Public Life, Lewisham Council, 2008–. Mem., Mgt Cttee, Liberty, 1988–98. Hon. LLD Kingston, 2013. Legal Aid Barrister of Year, Legal Aid Practitioners' Gp, 2012. *Publications:* (jtly) Inquests: a practitioner's guide, 2002, 3rd edn 2014; contrib. articles on develts in inquest law. *Recreations:* motorcycles, playing the tenor saxophone, jazz, conversing in Russian and French, travel. *Address:* Garden Court Chambers, 57–60 Lincoln's Inn Fields, WC2A 3LJ. *T:* (020) 7993 7600, *Fax:* (020) 7993 7700. *E:* info@gclaw.co.uk.

THOMAS, Margaret, Women's International Art Club, 1940; RBA 1947; NEAC 1950; Contemporary Portrait Society, 1970; practising artist (painter); *b* 26 Sept. 1916; *d* of late Francis Stewart Thomas and Grace Whetherly. *Educ:* privately; Slade Sch.; RA Schools. Slade Scholar, 1936. Hon. Sec. Artists International Assoc., 1944–45; FRSA 1971. Group exhibitions, Wildensteins, 1946, 1949 and 1962; First one-man show at Leicester Galls, 1949, and subsequently at same gallery, 1950; one-man shows in Edinburgh (Aitken Dotts), 1952, 1955, 1966, and at Outlook Tower, Edinburgh, during Internat. Fest., 1961; RBA Galleries, London, 1953; at Canaletto Gall. (a barge, at Little Venice), 1961; Exhibition of Women Artists, Wakefield Art Gall., 1961; Howard Roberts Gallery Cardiff, 1963, The Minories, Colchester, 1964, QUB, 1967, Mall Galls, London, 1972; Octagon Gall., Belfast, 1973; Court Lodge Gallery, Kent, 1974; Gallery Paton, Edinburgh, 1977; Scottish Gall., Edinburgh (major retrospective), 1982; Sally Hunter, London, 1988, 1991, 1995 and 1998; RWA, 1992; Messum Gall., London, 2001, 2003; Strand Gall., Aldeburgh, 2006, 2007, 2008, 2010, 2011; Cork Brick Gall., Bungay, 2008, 2010; regular exhibitor Royal Academy and Royal Scottish Academy. Official purchases: Prince Philip, Duke of Edinburgh; Chantrey Bequest; Arts Council; Exeter College, Oxford; Min. of Education; Min. of Works; Wakefield, Hull, Paisley and Carlisle Art Galleries; Edinburgh City Corporation; Nuffield Foundation Trust; Steel Co. of Wales; Financial Times; Mitsukoshi Ltd, Tokyo; Scottish Nat. Orchestra; Robert Flemming collection; Lloyd's of London; Sock Shop Internat.; Mercury Asset Mgt; Nat. Library of Wales; GLC and county education authorities in Yorks, Bucks, Monmouth, Derbyshire, Hampshire and Wales. Coronation painting purchased by Min. of Works for British Embassy in Santiago. Winner, Hunting Gp Award for best oil painting of the year, 1981 and 1996. *Publications:* work reproduced in: Daily Telegraph, News Chronicle, Listener, Studio, Scottish Field, Music and Musicians, The Lady, Arts Review, Western Mail, Illustrated London News, The Artist, The Spectator, Eastern Daily Press, Country Life. *Recreations:* antique collecting, gardening, vintage cars. *Address:* Ellingham Mill, Mill Pool Lane, near Bungay, Suffolk NR35 2EP. *T:* (01508) 518656.

THOMAS, Mark David; Owner and founder, TM Media, media consultancy, since 2007; *b* 1 March 1967; *s* of Rick and Jennie Thomas; *m*; two *s* two *d*; *m* 2009, Helen Morgan; one *s* one *d*. *Educ:* Rutlish Sch., London. News reporter, The People, 1988–94; News reporter, then Chief Reporter, News of the World, 1994–97; Features Ed., then Asst Ed., Daily Mirror, 1997–2001; Dep. Ed., Sunday Mirror, 2001–03; Ed., The People, 2003–07. *Address:* TM Media PR, 25 Frith Street, W1D 5LB. *T:* 07710 740468, (020) 7437 0474. *E:* mark@tm-media.co.uk.

THOMAS, Martin Nicholas Caleb; Chairman, Lancashire Holdings Ltd, since 2007; Partner, Board Member and Head, Unlisted Investments, Altima Partners LLP, since 2008; *b* Edinburgh, 1 June 1963; *s* of Prof. (Antony) Charles Thomas, *qv*; *m* 1990, Miranda Jane Brett, *d* of Viscount Esher, *qv*; two *s* three *d*. *Educ:* Winchester Coll., Hants; St Anne's Coll., Oxford (BA Lit.Hum.; MA). Solicitor, Travers Smith and Clifford Chance; Sen. Legal Counsel, European Central Bank, 1996–2000; Dep. Chief Exec., Financial Law Panel, 2000–02; Sec., Financial Markets Law Cttee, Bank of England, 2002–06; Sec., Legal Certainty Gp, EC (on secondment), 2004–06. Dir, BACIT Ltd, 2012–; Chm., BACIT (UK) Ltd, 2014–. Chm., BACIT Foundn, 2012–; Trustee, Forward Arts Foundn, 2013–. *Address:* Ark Farm, Old Wardour, Tisbury, Wilts SP3 6RP. *T:* (020) 7968 6460.

THOMAS, Martyn Charles, CBE 2007; FREng; Director and Principal Consultant, Martyn Thomas Associates Ltd, IT consultancy and expert witness services, since 1998; *b* 13 Aug. 1948; *s* of late Leslie and Ruth Thomas; *m* 1980, Anne Rogers; one *s* one *d*. *Educ:* University Coll. London (BSc Biochem. 1969). FBCS 1980; CEng 1993; FIET (FIEE 1994); FREng 2007. Researcher, 1969–70, Systems Programmer, 1970–73, UCL; Designer, Standard Telephones & Cables, 1973–75; South West Universities Regional Computer Centre: Team Ldr, 1975–79; Systems Manager, 1979–83; Dep. Dir, 1980–83; Founder and Chm., Praxis plc, 1983–92; Partner, Deloitte & Touche, 1992–98. Visiting Professor: Univ. of Wales, Aberystwyth, 1993–2008; Bristol Univ., 1994–; Oxford Univ., 1999–; Livery Co. Prof. of Inf. Technol., Gresham Coll., 2015–. Ind. Mem., EPSRC, 2002–05; Member: Defence Scientific Adv. Council, 2010–; Expert Gp, Identity and Passport Service, 2010; Exec. Cttee, UK Computing Res. Cttee, 2013–; non-executive Director: Office of the Ind. Adjudicator for Higher Educn, 2010–; SOCA, 2011–13; Health and Safety Lab., 2012–14; Health and Safety Exec., 2014–; consultant, Nat. Crime Agency, 2013–15. Mem., Engrg Policy Cttee, 2008–12, Vice-Pres., 2012–14, Chm., Ext. Affairs Cttee, 2012–15, Trustee, 2012–, RAEng; Chm., IT Strategic Panel, IET, 2010–14. Assce and Innovation Dir, Aspect Assce Ltd, 2001–03. Chm., First Earth Ltd, 2001–03. Mem., Longitude Prize Cttee, 2013–. FRSA 1987. Hon. DSc: Hull, 1994; Edinburgh, 2004; City, 2005. Achievement Medal in Computing and Control, IEE, 1993. *Publications:* (with M. Ould) The Fell Revival, 2000; (jtly) Harry Carter - Typographer, 2005; (with A. Rogers) Three Pieces, 2005; (ed jtly) Software for Dependable Systems: sufficient evidence?, 2007; (ed with A. Romanovsky) Industrial Deployment of System Engineering Methods, 2013; numerous papers, lectures and broadcasts. *Recreations:* researching and writing about typography and printing, art, backgammon, watching cricket at the Oval, walking, reading, theatre. *Address:* 72 Fentiman Road, SW8 1LA. *T:* (020) 7582 7169. *E:* martyn@thomas-associates.co.uk.

THOMAS, (Mary) Elizabeth; with Shropshire Music Service (part-time), 1993–98; Director, West Midlands Board, Central Television plc, 1982–92 (Member, Regional Advisory Council, 1993); *b* 22 March 1935; *d* of Kathleen Mary Thomas (*née* Dodd) and David John Thomas; *m* 1962, Brian Haydn Thomas; two *d*. *Educ:* Dr Williams' School, Dolgellau; Talbot Heath School, Bournemouth; Royal Acad. of Music. ARCM, GRSM. Head of Music, High Sch., Totnes, 1958–61; Music Lectr, Ingestre Hall, Stafford, 1962; Berkshire Music Schs, 1964–66; Adult Educn Lectr, Bridgnorth Coll. of Further Educn, 1966–69. Chm., Pentabus Arts Ltd, 1983–87. Arts Council of Great Britain: Member, 1984–88; Chm., Regl Adv. Cttee, 1984–86; Chm., Planning and Develt Bd, 1986–88. Chairman: W Midlands Arts, 1980–84; Council, Regional Arts Assocs, 1982–85; Nat. Assoc. of Local Arts Councils, 1980–82 (Vice-Pres., 1982); City of Birmingham Touring Opera, 1987–92. Chairman: Shropshire Schs Forum, 2003–06; Standards Cttee, Bridgnorth DC, 2004–07 (Vice-Chm., 2003–04). Mem., Much Wenlock Town Council, 1995–2007 (Mayor, 2000–01, 2004–05). Member: W Midlands Cultural Olympiad, 2010–12; Mgt Bd, Shropshire Hills Area of Outstanding Natural Beauty, 2010–14; Shropshire, Telford and Wrekin STW 2012 Gp, 2012. *Recreation:* gardening.

THOMAS, Mervyn; Group Human Resources Director, Ministry of Justice, since 2014; *b* Cardiff, 8 May 1965; *s* of Richard Thomas and Hazel Thomas; civil partnership 2006, Malcolm Collingwood (*d* 2006). *Educ:* Open Univ. (MBA). Hd, Human Resources, European Investment Banking, Citigroup, 1998–2002; Hd, Human Resources, Corporate Banking Div., Royal Bank of Scotland, 2002–07; Director: Human Resources, DfT, 2007–12; Civil Service Resourcing, 2012–13. *Recreations:* running, gym. *Address:* Richmond upon Thames, Surrey.

THOMAS, Prof. (Meurig) Wynn, OBE 2007; FBA 1996; FLSW, FEA; Professor of English, 2009–10, now Emeritus, and Emyr Humphreys Chair of Welsh Writing in English, since 2009, Swansea University (formerly University College of Swansea, then University of Wales, Swansea) (Director, Centre for Research into the English Literature and Language of Wales, 1998–2008); *b* 12 Sept. 1944; *s* of William John Thomas and Tydfil Thomas (*née* Rees); *m* 1975, Karen Elizabeth Manahan; one *d*. *Educ:* Gowerton Boys' Grammar Sch.; UCW, Swansea (BA 1965). University College of Swansea: Asst Lectr, 1966–69; Lectr in English, 1969–88; Sen. Lectr, 1988–94. Mem., British Library Adv. Cttee, Arts, Humanities and Social Scis, 2000–. Visiting Professor: Harvard, 1991–92; Univ. of Tübingen, 1994–95; Obermann Fellow, Univ. of Iowa, 1992. Mem., Welsh Arts Council and Chm., Literature Cttee, 1985–91; Vice-Chm., Welsh Language Section, Welsh Acad., 1996–97; Chairman: Univ. of Wales Press, 1998–2005; Welsh Books Council, 2005–; Mem., Wales Arts Review Panel, 2006. Sec., Univ. of Wales Assoc. for Study of Welsh Writing in English, 1983–96; Adjudicator, David Cohen Prize, 1996–97. Founding FLSW 2010 (Vice Pres., Arts, Humanities and Social Scis, 2010–). Hon. Mem., Nat. Eisteddfod Gorsedd of Bards, 2000. Hon. Fellow, Coleg Cymraeg Cenedlaethol, 2012. Literary Executor, R. S. Thomas (unpublished work), 2000–; Chm., Saunders Lewis Meml Trust, 2008–. FEA 2005. *Publications:* Morgan Llwyd, 1984; The Lunar Light of Whitman's Poetry, 1987; (ed) Morgan Llwyd, Llyfr y Tri Aderyn, 1988; Emyr Humphreys, 1989; (ed) Emyr Humphreys, A Toy Epic, 1989; (ed) R. S. Thomas: y cawr awenydd, 1990; (ed) Wrenching Times: Whitman's

Civil War poetry, 1991; Morgan Llwyd: ei gyfeillion a'i gyfnod, 1991 (Welsh Arts Council Prize, Vernam Hull Meml Prize, Ellis Griffith Meml Prize); Internal Difference: literature in twentieth-century Wales, 1992; (ed) The Page's Drift: R. S. Thomas at eighty, 1993; (ed) DiFfinio Dwy Lenyddiaeth Cymru (essays), 1995; (trans.) Dail Glaswellt, 1995; John Ormond, 1997; Corresponding Cultures: the two literatures of Wales, 1999; (ed) Gweld Sêr: Cymru a chanrif America, 2001; (ed) Emyr Humphreys: conversations and reflections, 2002; Kitchener Davies, 2002; (ed jtly) James Kitchener Davies: detholion o'i waith, 2002; (ed) R. S. Thomas, Residues, 2002; (ed) Welsh Writing in English, 2003; Transatlantic Connections: Whitman US-Whitman UK, 2005; In the Shadow of the Pulpit: literature and nonconformist Wales, 2011; R. S. Thomas: serial obsessive, 2013; contrib. to jls and books. *Recreations:* reading, music, televiewing sport. *Address:* Department of English, Swansea University, Singleton Park, Swansea SA2 8PP. *T:* (01792) 295926.

THOMAS, Michael Christopher Pryce; Legal Adviser to the European Union Committee, House of Lords, 2008–14; *b* 31 Oct. 1949; *s* of late David Hamilton Pryce Thomas, CBE and Eluned Mair Thomas (*née* Morgan); *m* 1978, Pauline Marie Buckman. *Educ:* St John's Coll., Oxford (BA); Univ. of Sussex (MA). Admitted solicitor, 1976; in private practice as asst solicitor, 1976–79; Legal Dept, MAFF, 1980–86; Law Officers' Dept, 1986–88; Grade 5, Legal Dept, MAFF, 1988–92; Legal Adviser: Dept of Transport, later DETR, 1993–97; European Secretariat, Cabinet Office, 1997–2004; Dir, Legal Services A, DTI, 2004–06; Legal Counsellor, FCO, 2006–07. *Recreations:* music, theatre. *E:* Michael.thomas10@which.net.

THOMAS, Michael David, CMG 1985; QC 1973; barrister in private practice, 1958–2013; Attorney-General of Hong Kong, 1983–88; Member, Executive and Legislative Councils, Hong Kong, 1983–88; Chairman, Law Reform Commission, Hong Kong, 1983–88; Chairman, Qatar Regulatory Tribunal, 2011–13; *b* 8 Sept. 1933; *s* of late D. Cardigan Thomas and Kathleen Thomas; *m* 1st, 1958, Jane Lena Mary (marr. diss. 1978), *e d* of late Francis Neate; two *s* two *d*; 2nd, 1981, Mrs Gabrielle Blakemore (marr. diss. 1986); 3rd, 1988, Hon. Lydia Dunn (*see* Baroness Dunn). *Educ:* Chigwell Sch., Essex; London Sch. of Economics. LLB (Hons) 1954. Called to Bar, Middle Temple, 1955 (Blackstone Entrance Schol., 1952; Harmsworth Schol., 1957); Bencher, 1981. Nat. Service with RN, Sub-Lt RNVR, 1955–57. In practice at Bar from 1958. Junior Counsel to Minister of Defence (RN) and to Treasury in Admty matters, 1966–73. Wreck Commissioner under Merchant Shipping Act 1970; one of Lloyd's salvage arbitrators, 1974. Governor: Chigwell Sch., 1971–83; LSE, 2001–11. *Publications:* (ed jtly) Temperley: Merchant Shipping Acts, 6th edn 1963 and 7th edn 1974. *Recreations:* music, travel, tennis. *Address:* Essex Court Chambers, 24 Lincoln's Inn Fields, WC2A 3EG; 19 Cadogan Square, SW1X 0HU. *Clubs:* Garrick, Queen's; Hong Kong (Hong Kong).

THOMAS, Col Michael John Glyn; private consultant in transfusion medicine, since 1995; Clinical Director, Blood Care Foundation, since 1995; Director, MG & SJ Enterprises, since 1995; *b* 14 Feb. 1938; *s* of Glyn Pritchard Thomas and Mary Thomas (*née* Moseley); *m* 1969, Sheelagh Thorpe; one *d*. *Educ:* Haileybury and ISC; Trinity College, Cambridge; St Bartholomew's Hosp. MA, MB, BChir, LMSSA, DTM&H. FRCPEd 1997. Qualified 1962; House Surgeon, Essex County Hosp. and House Physician, St James, Balham, 1963; Regtl MO, 2nd Bn The Parachute Regt, 1965; Trainee Pathologist, BMH Singapore, 1968; Specialist in Pathology, Colchester Mil. Hosp., 1971; Senior Specialist in Pathology, Army Blood Supply Depot, 1977; Exchange Pathologist, Walter Reed Army Inst. of Research, 1982–84; Officer in Charge of Leishman Lab., Cambridge Mil. Hosp., 1985–87; CO, Army Blood Supply Depot, 1987–95. Hon. Consultant Haematologist, UCH/Middlesex Hosp., 1987. Member: Council, BMA, 1974–82 (Chm., Junior Mems Forum, 1974–75; Chm., Central Ethical Cttee, 1978–82; Mem., expert panel on AIDS, 1986–; Mem., Bd of Sci. and Educn, 1987–93; Fellow, 1995); Cttee on Transfusion Equipment, BSI; Economic and Social Cttee, EEC, 1989–; Council, British Blood Transfusion Soc., 1998–2001 (Founder Chm., 1992–98, Sec., 1998–2004, Autologous Transfusion Special Interest Gp). Congress Pres., XXVIIIth Congress of Internat. Soc. of Blood Transfusion, 2004. *Publications:* contribs to ref. books, reports and jls on Medical Ethics, Haematology and Blood Banking, Malariology and subjects of general medical interest. *Recreations:* sailing, travel, photography, philately. *Address:* 8 Aveley Way, Maldon, Essex CM9 6YQ. *Club:* Tanglin (Singapore).

THOMAS, Rear-Adm. Michael Richard, BSc (Eng); CEng, FIET. RN, 1960–96: served HMS Lincoln, Dido, and Andromeda; subseq. HM Dockyards Devonport and Portsmouth; Naval Sec's Dept, MoD; Naval Asst to Chief of Fleet Support; Supt Ships, Devonport; comd HMS Drake, 1992; Pres., Ordnance Bd, and DG Technical Services, 1994–96. Comdr 1977; Capt. 1985; Cdre 1993. Dir, Electrical Contractors' Assoc., 1996; Man. Dir, Penzance Drydock Co. Ltd, 1997–2008; Trustee, Royal Fleet Club, 2002–; Chm. Trustees, Devonport Field Gun Assoc. Ltd, 2010–13 (Patron, 2013–). Chm., Penzance Arts Club Ltd, 2009–11. President: Plymouth Scouts; Sea Cadet Corps. Gov., Plymouth Univ., 2000–05. *Address:* Millstone, Links Lane, Yelverton, Devon PL20 6BZ.

THOMAS, Michael Stuart, (Mike); management consultant; Chairman, Corporate Communications Strategy, since 1988; Consultant to the King Abdullah Fund for Development (Jordan) and Inspirational Development Group, since 2009; *b* 24 May 1944; *s* of Arthur Edward Thomas. *Educ:* Latymer Upper Sch.; King's Sch., Macclesfield; Liverpool Univ. (BA). Pres., Liverpool Univ. Guild of Undergraduates, 1965–66; Past Mem. Nat. Exec., NUS. Head of Research Dept, Co-operative Party, 1966–68; Sen. Res. Officer, Political and Economic Planning (now PSI), 1968–73; Dir, Volunteer Centre, 1973–74; Dir of Public Relations and Public Affairs, Dewe Rogerson, 1984–88; Mem., BR Western Reg. Bd, 1985–92; Chairman: Media Audits, 1990–2001; Fotorama (Holdings) Ltd, 1995–2000; Atalink Ltd, 1998–2001; SMF International, subseq. SMFI Ltd, 2000–12; Music Choice Europe, 2000–05; 422 Ltd, 2001–02; WAA Ltd, 2003–08; H. K. Wentworth Ltd, 2005–08; Utarget plc, 2007–08; Ad. IQ Global Ltd, 2008–10; VRL Financial News Publishing Ltd, 2011–12; Industrial Engrg Plastics Gp, 2014–; Director: Lopex plc, 1998–2000; Metal Bulletin plc, 2000–02; Finance South East, 2008–10. Site Moderator/Ed.-in-Chief, www.charter2010.co.uk, 2009–10. MP (Lab and Co-op 1974–81, SDP 1981–83) Newcastle upon Tyne E, Oct. 1974–1983. Mem., Select Cttee on Nationalised Industries, 1975–79; Chm., PLP Trade Gp, 1979–81; SDP spokesman on health and social services, 1981–83; Member: SDP Nat. Cttee, 1981–90; SDP Policy Cttee, 1981–90; Chairman: Organisation Cttee of SDP, 1981–88; By-election Cttee, SDP, 1984–88; SDP Finance Working Gp, 1988–90; a Vice-Pres., SDP, 1988–90; Mem., Alliance Strategy Cttee, 1983–87. Contested: (Lab and Co-Op) E Herts, 1970; (SDP) Newcastle upon Tyne East, 1983; (SDP/Alliance) Exeter, 1987. Founder of parly jl The House. *Publications:* Participation and the Redcliffe Maud Report, 1970; (ed) The BBC Guide to Parliament, 1979, 1983; various PEP pamphlets, contribs, etc, 1971–; various articles, reviews, etc. *Recreations:* collecting pottery, medals and ephemera relating to elections (1750–), architectural and garden history, gardening, garden design, theatre, opera, music, cooking. *Address:* 57 Syke Ings, Ritchings Park, Bucks SL0 9ES. *E:* mikethomas77@virginmedia.com. *Club:* Reform.

THOMAS, Michael T.; *see* Tilson Thomas.

THOMAS, Neil, RDI 2014; CEng; Chairman and Director, Atelier One Structural Engineers, since 1989; *b* Fordingbridge, 11 March 1959; *s* of Derek Francis Thomas and Rita Emily Thomas; *m* 2005, Sonia Pabla; one *s* three *d*. *Educ:* Rugeley Grammar Sch., Staffs; Univ. of Leeds (BSc Hons); Penn State Univ. CEng 1987; MIStructE 1987. Graduate Engr to Sen. Engr, Buro Happold, 1980–86; Resident Engr, Kuwait (on secondment), 1984–86; Associate, Anthony Hunt Associates, 1986–88; Founder and Dir, Hunt Projects, 1988–89; Co-founder, Atelier Ten, 1991. Visiting Professor: Yale Univ., 2010–14; MIT, 2015–. Ext. Examr, AA, 2012–. Mem., Steering Gp, Architectural Engrg course, Leeds Univ., 2015–. *Publications:* Super Sheds, 1991; Remarkable Structures, 2002; Support and Resist, 2007; Liquid Threshold, 2009. *Recreations:* reading, swimming, scientific research, family. *Address:* Atelier One, 3 Charlotte Mews, W1T 4DZ. *T:* (020) 7323 3350. *E:* mail@atelierone.com.

THOMAS, Neville; *see* Thomas, R. N.

THOMAS, Prof. Nicholas Jeremy, PhD; FBA 2005; Professor of Historical Anthropology, and Director, Museum of Archaeology and Anthropology, University of Cambridge, since 2006; Fellow of Trinity College, Cambridge, since 2007; *b* 21 April 1960; *s* of Keith James Thomas and Sylvia Lawson; *m* 2004, Prof. Annie Coombes. *Educ:* Australian National Univ. (BA 1982; PhD 1986). Res. Fellow, King's Coll., Cambridge, 1986–89; Australian National University: Queen Elizabeth II Res. Fellow, 1990–92; Sen. Res. Fellow, 1993–96; Dir, Centre for Cross-Cultural Res., 1997–99; Prof. of Anthropology, Goldsmiths Coll., London, 1999–2006. Iris Foundn Award, 2015. *Publications:* Out of Time: history and evolution in anthropological discourse, 1989; Marquesan Societies: inequality and political transformation in eastern Polynesia, 1990; Entangled Objects: exchange, material culture and colonialism in the Pacific, 1991; Colonialism's Culture: anthropology, travel, and government, 1994; Oceanic Art, 1995; In Oceania: visions, artefacts, histories, 1997; Possessions: indigenous art/colonial culture, 1999; Discoveries: the voyages of Captain James Cook, 2003; Islanders: the Pacific in the age of empire, 2010 (Wolfson History Prize, 2010); (ed jtly) Art in Oceania: a new history, 2012 (Art Book Prize, 2014); many articles in jls. *Address:* Museum of Archaeology and Anthropology, University of Cambridge, Downing Street, Cambridge CB2 3DZ. *T:* (01223) 333516.

THOMAS, Nick; Chairman, Qdos Entertainment Group, since 1999; *b* Blandford Forum, Dorset, 16 Dec. 1959; *y s* of Douglas William and Mona Ellen Thomas; *m* 1985, Sandra Jane Finnigan; two *d*. *Educ:* Gladstone Rd Jun. Sch.; Scarborough Boys High Sch.; Graham Sch., Scarborough. Creator, Tommer Puppets (winner of ITV New Faces), 1975–80; owner, Nick Thomas Enterprises Ltd, 1981–91; CEO, Artist Mgt Gp Ltd, 1992–99. Vice Pres., Entertainment Artistes Benevolent Fund, 2010–. *Recreations:* family, theatre, restaurants, motor cars, theatre memorabilia, fund raising for Great Ormond Street Hospital. *Address:* Qdos Entertainment Ltd, Queen Margaret's Road, Scarborough YO11 2YH. *T:* (01723) 500038. *E:* nthomas@qdosentertainment.co.uk.

THOMAS, Norman, CBE 1980; HM Chief Inspector of Schools (Primary Education), 1973–81; Specialist Professor in Primary Education, University of Nottingham, 1987–88; *b* 1 June 1921; *s* of Bowen Thomas and Ada Thomas (*née* Redding); *m* 1942, Rose Henshaw (*d* 2005); two *d*. *Educ:* Latymer's Sch., Edmonton; Camden Coll. Qual. Teacher, 1948. Commerce and Industry, 1937–47. Teacher, primary schs in London and Herts, 1948–56; Head, Longmeadow Jun. Mixed Sch., Stevenage, 1956–61; HM Inspector of Schools, Lincs and SE England, 1962–68; HMI, Staff Inspector for Primary (Junior and Middle) Schs, 1969–73. Chm., Cttee of Enquiry on Primary Educn in ILEA, 1983–84. Adviser to Parly Cttee on Educn, Science and Art, 1984–86, on Educn, 1994–97. Visiting Professor: NE London Polytechnic, 1984–86; Univ. of Herts (formerly Hatfield Poly.), 1991–; Hon. Prof., Univ. of Warwick, 1986–94. Hon. FCP 1988. Hon. DLitt Hertfordshire, 1998. *Publications:* Primary Education from Plowden to the 1990s, 1990; chapters in books and articles in professional jls. *Recreations:* photography, reading. *Address:* Kingsbury Manor, St Michael's, St Albans, Herts AL3 4SE.

THOMAS, Owen John; Member (Plaid Cymru) Central South Wales, National Assembly for Wales, 1999–2007; *b* 3 Oct. 1939; *s* of late John Owen Thomas and Evelyn Jane Thomas; *m* 1985, Siân Wyn Evans; twin *s*; three *s* one *d* by a previous marriage. *Educ:* Glamorgan Coll. of Educn (Cert Ed 1971); UC, Cardiff (MA 1990). Tax Officer, Inland Revenue, 1956–61; Chemical Analyst, 1961–68; Primary Sch. Teacher, 1971–78; Dep. Headteacher, 1979–99. Shadow Minister for Culture, Sport and Welsh Lang., Nat. Assembly for Wales, 2001–07. Mem., Gorsedd of Bards, Royal Nat. Eisteddfod, 2001. *Recreations:* reading, socialising. *Address:* 4 Llwyn y Grant Place, Penylan, Cardiff CF23 9EX. *T:* (029) 2049 9868. *Club:* Ifor Bach (Cardiff).

THOMAS, Patricia Ann; environmental campaigner, author and journalist; *b* Los Angeles, Calif, 27 Oct. 1959; *d* of late William Shows and Patricia Gayle Thomas; *m* 1992, Jonathan Ralph Althelstan Savage (marr. diss. 1995); one *s*. *Educ:* Thousand Oaks High Sch., Calif; Centre for Counselling and Psychotherapy Educn, London (Dip. Psychotherapy and Counselling 1991). Record Sales Analyst, Record Business Mag., 1979–83; Asst Res. Manager, Music Div., Gallup Poll Ltd, 1983; Asst Producer, DJ Show, TVS, Southampton, 1984; freelance journalist and broadcaster, 1984–91; feature writer, Number One Mag., 1984–89; Editor: Insight mag., 1990–91; AIMS Jl, 1994–2004; Contrib. Editor, Wallace Press, 1994–2004; Editor, Proof!, 2003; Health Editor, 2004–07, Editor, 2007–09, Ecologist Mag.; Campaign Dir, Meat Free Monday, 2009–10 (Scientific Advr, 2010–); Campaign Manager, Cows Belong in Fields Campaign, Compassion in World Farming, 2010–11; Hd, Sustainability, 2011–12, Consultant, campaigns and sustainability projects, 2012–, Neal's Yard Remedies. Editor, NYR Natural News online, 2011–. Dir, Beyond GM Ltd, 2014–. Host: British Airways in-flight entertainment, 1987–91; Deep Fried Planet, Resonance FM, London, 2010; reporter/interviewer: Capital Radio, London, 1989–90; Westwood One Radio Network, NY, 1989–90. Trustee: Soil Assoc., 2012–14; Eyewitness Investigative Agency, 2013–; Organic Res. Centre, 2015–. Consultant, organic toiletries range, Stella McCartney Care, 2009. Mem., Guild of Health Writers, 2011. *Publications:* Every Woman's Birthrights, 1996; Every Birth is Different, 1997; The PROOF! Guide to Alternative First Aid, 1998; Choosing a Home Birth, 1998; Headaches: the common sense approach, 1999; Pregnancy: the common sense approach, 1999; You Can Prevent Cancer, 1999; Alternative Therapies for Pregnancy and Birth, 2000; Cleaning Yourself to Death: how safe is your home?, 2001; Living Organic, 2001; Your Birth Rights, 2002; What Works, What Doesn't: the guide to alternative healthcare, 2002; (contrib.) Failure to Progress: the contraction of midwifery, 2002; Living Dangerously: are everyday toxins making you sick?, 2003; Under the Weather: how weather and climate affect our health, 2004; What's in This Stuff?: the essential guide to what's really in the products you buy, 2006; (contrib.) A Slice of Organic Life, 2007; The 21st Century is Making You Fat, 2008; Skin Deep, 2008; Healthy, Happy Baby, 2008; Stuffed: positive action to prevent a global food crisis, 2010; Healing Foods: eat your way to a healthier life, 2013; Neal's Yard Remedies Beauty Book, 2015; *for children:* First Look series: My Amazing Journey, 1998; My Family's Changing, 1998; My Brother, My Sister and Me, 2000; Stop Picking on Me!, 2000; I Miss You, 2000; My Friends and Me, 2000; Don't Call Me Special!, 2001; My Amazing Body, 2001; The Skin I'm In, 2003; I Can Be Safe, 2003; Is it Right to Fight?, 2003; My New Family!, 2003; Do I Have to Go to School?, 2006; My Manners Matter, 2006; Do I Have to Go to Hospital?, 2006; I'm Telling the Truth, 2006; Why Am I So Tired?, 2008; I Think I'm Going to Sneeze, 2008; Do I Have to Go to the Dentist?, 2008; Why is it So Hard to Breathe, 2008; I Can Make a Difference, 2010; Everyone Matters, 2010; Why Do I Feel Scared?, 2010; I Can Do It!, 2010; I Miss My Pet, 2012; Come Home Soon, 2012; This is My Family, 2012. *Recreations:* cooking, foraging, photography, reading, music, walking, film, watersports, family. *Address:* c/o MBA Literary Agents, 62 Grafton Way, W1T 5DW. *T:* (020) 7387 2076. *E:* laura@mbalit.co.uk. *W:* www.howlatthemoon.org.uk.

THOMAS, Patricia Anne, CBE 2006; Commissioner for Local Administration in England, 1985–2005; Vice-Chairman, Commission for Local Administration in England, 1994–2005; *b* 3 April 1940; *d* of Frederick S. Lofts and Ann Elizabeth Lofts; *m* 1968, Joseph Glyn Thomas; one *s* two *d*. *Educ:* King's College London. LLB, LLM. Lectr in Law, Univ. of Leeds, 1962–63, 1964–68; Teaching Fellow, Univ. of Illinois, 1963–64; Sen. Lectr, then Principal Lectr, Head of Sch. of Law and Prof., Lancashire Polytechnic, 1973–85. Mem., Administrative Justice & Tribunals Council (formerly Council on Tribunals), 2005–10. Mem., 1976–84, Vice-Pres., 1984, Pres., 1985, Greater Manchester and Lancashire Rent Assessment Panel; Chm., Blackpool Supplementary Benefit Appeal Tribunal, 1980–85. Non-exec. Dir, Univ. Hospitals of Morecambe Bay NHS Trust, subseq. Foundn Trust, 2009–12. Hon. Fellow, Lancashire Polytech., 1991. *Publications:* Law of Evidence, 1972.

THOMAS, Patrick Anthony; QC 1999; **His Honour Judge Patrick Thomas;** a Circuit Judge, since 2008; *b* 30 Oct. 1948; *s* of Basil and Marjorie Thomas; *m* 1978, Sheila Jones; two *d*. *Educ:* Rugby Sch.; Lincoln Coll., Oxford (BA). Called to the Bar, Gray's Inn, 1973, Bencher, 2005; Recorder, 1992–2008. *Recreations:* reading, theatre, walking, France. *Address:* Birmingham Crown Court, Queen Elizabeth II Law Courts, 1 Newton Street, Birmingham B4 7NA.

THOMAS, Paul; *see* Thomas, C. P.

THOMAS, Rear Adm. Paul Anthony Moseley, CB 1998; FREng, FIMechE; Director, Environment, Health, Safety and Quality, British Nuclear Fuels plc, 2001–08; *b* 27 Oct. 1944; *s* of Glyn Pritchard Thomas and Mary (*née* Moseley); *m* 1972, Rosalyn Patricia Lee; one *s* two *d*. *Educ:* Haileybury; London Univ. (BSc(Eng) 1969); MSc CNAA 1971. CEng 1985, FREng (FEng 1998); FIMechE 1993; FCGI 2011. Joined RN, 1963; Asst Marine Engr Officer, HMS Renown, 1971–77; Sen. Engr Officer, HMS Revenge, 1977–82 (mentioned in despatches, 1979); Asst Dir, Reactor Safety, 1982–84; Naval Superintendent, Vulcan Naval Reactor Test Estabt, Dounreay, 1984–87; Chm., Naval Nuclear Technical Safety Panel, 1987–90; Dir, Nuclear Propulsion, 1990–94; Captain, RNEC Manadon, 1994–95; Chief Strategic Systems Exec., MoD (PE), 1995–98; AEA Technology Nuclear Engineering: Dir, Engrg Projects, 1999–2000; Dir, Strategic Develt, 2000–01. Chairman: Rail Safety and Standards Bd, 2008; Process Safety Forum, 2008–; Hazards Forum, 2009–. Non-executive Director: NNB GenCo, 2011–; Magnox Ltd, 2013–. Pres., Nuclear Inst., 2008–10. Hon. FNucI (Hon. FINucE 2005); Hon. FSaRS 2011. *Recreations:* cycling, sailing, ballooning, railways. *Address:* Byway, Chapel Lane, Box, Corsham, Wilts SN13 8NU.

THOMAS, Paul Huw; QC 2003; **His Honour Judge Paul Thomas;** a Circuit Judge, since 2009; *b* 25 June 1957; *s* of Hubert and Joan Thomas; *m* 1984, Mayda Elisabeth Jones; one *s* one *d*. *Educ:* Gowerton Sch.; Fitzwilliam Coll., Cambridge (MA). Called to the Bar, Gray's Inn, 1979, Bencher, 2008; Barrister, Iscoed Chambers, Swansea, 1980–2009; Jt Hd of Chambers, 2006–09; Asst Recorder, 1996–2000; Recorder, 2000–09. Asst Boundary Comr for Wales, 2003–09. Mem., Dermatology Council for Wales, 2005–10; Chm., Skin Care Cymru, 2006–. Trustee: Swansea Rugby Foundn, 1996–; Assoc. of Friends of Glynn Vivian Art Gall., 2006–10, 2012–; Changing Faces, 2008–. *Recreations:* sport, especially Rugby, history, the arts, Rhossili. *Address:* Swansea Crown Court, St Helen's Road, Swansea SA1 4PF. *Clubs:* Swansea Rugby Football; Gowerton Cricket.

THOMAS, Paul Roger; Vice-President of Marketing, Ford of Europe, 2006–12; *m* Karen; two *c*. *Educ:* City Univ. (BSc). Joined Ford as trainee, 1974; sales and mktg posts with Ford of Britain, Ford Credit and Ford of Europe; Manager of Business Planning, Ford Credit, 1987–89; Gen. Field Manager, 1989–90, Mktg and Product Plans Manager, 1990–93, Ford of Britain; Vehicle and Derivative Progs Manager, Ford of Europe, 1993–95; Dist Manager, Midlands, Ford of Britain, 1995–99; Mktg Plans and Brand Develt Manager, Ford Product Develt Europe, 1999–2000; European Brand Manager, 2000–01; Dir of Sales, 2001–02, Man. Dir, 2002–06, Ford of Britain.

THOMAS, Ven. Paul Wyndham; Archdeacon of Salop, since 2011; Priest-in-charge, Forton, since 2011; *b* Llantwit Major, Vale of Glamorgan, 22 April 1955; *s* of Wyndham Ernest Clifford Thomas and Kathleen Mary Thomas; *m* June Garfield; three *s* two *d*. *Educ:* Cardiff High Sch. for Boys; Oriel Coll., Oxford; Wycliffe Hall, Oxford (BA Modern Hist. 1976; MA 1978; BA Theol. 1978; CTh 1979). Ordained deacon, 1979, priest, 1980; Curate, Llangynwyd with Maesteg, 1979–85; Team Vicar, Langport Area Churches, 1985–90; Priest-in-charge, Thorp Arch and Walton, 1990–93; Clergy Trng Officer, 1990–93; Vicar, Nether with Upper Poppleton, York, 1993–2004; Priest-in-charge, Doxey Stafford and Parish Develt Advr, 2004–11. *Recreations:* walking, theatre, music. *Address:* Archdeacon's House, The Vicarage, Tong, Shifnal, Shropshire TF11 8PW. *T:* (01902) 372622. *E:* paul.thomas@lichfield.anglican.org.

THOMAS, Sir Philip (Lloyd), KCVO 2003; CMG 2001; HM Diplomatic Service, retired; Senior Advisor, Shell International Ltd, 2006–09; *b* 10 June 1948; *s* of Gwyn Thomas and Eileen Thomas (*née* Jenkins); one *s*. *Educ:* Dulwich Coll.; St John's Coll., Cambridge (MA). Joined HM Diplomatic Service, 1972; Third Sec., FCO, 1972–74; Second Sec., Belgrade, 1974–77, FCO, 1977–80; First Secretary: (Commercial), Madrid, 1981–87; UK Perm. Representation to EU, Brussels, 1987–89; Cabinet Office, 1989–91; Counsellor (Politico-Military), Washington, 1991–96; Head, Eastern Dept, FCO, 1996–98; Consul Gen., Düsseldorf, and Dir-Gen. for Trade and Investment Promotion in Germany, 1999–2000; High Comr, Nigeria, 2001–04; Consul-Gen., New York, and Dir Gen., Trade and Investment in US, 2004–06.

THOMAS, Prof. Phillip Charles, FRSE; FRSB; FRAgS; Managing Director, Artilus Consultancy and Research, 1999–2010; Principal, 1990–99, now Emeritus Professor of Agriculture, Scottish Agricultural College; *b* 17 June 1942; *s* of William Charles Thomas and Gwendolen (*née* Emery); *m* 1967, Pamela Mary Hirst; one *s* one *d*. *Educ:* University College of North Wales, Bangor (BSc, PhD). FRSB (FIBiol 1983); FRSE 1993; FRAgS 1997. Lectr in animal nutrition and physiology, Univ. of Leeds, 1966–71; progressively, SSO to SPSO, Hannah Research Inst., 1971–87; Principal, West of Scotland Coll., 1987–90; Prof. of Agriculture, Univ. of Glasgow, 1987–99. Hon. Prof., Edinburgh Univ., 1990–; Vis. Prof., Univ. of Glasgow, 1999–2001. Chairman: Govt Adv. Cttee on Animal Feedingstuffs, 1999–2001; Animal Medicines Trng Regulatory Authy, 1999; Cumbria Foot and Mouth Disease Inquiry, 2002; Scottish Salmon Producers' Orgn, 2008–; Tenant Farming Forum, Scottish Govt, 2010–; Member: Scottish Food Adv. Cttee, 2000–05; Scottish Natural Heritage Bd, 2005–11; Quality Meat Scotland Bd, 2008–14. Chm., Central Scotland Forest Trust, 2001–08. *Publications:* (with J. A. F. Rook) Silage for Milk Production, 1982; (with J. A. F. Rook) Nutritional Physiology of Farm Animals, 1983. *Club:* Farmers.

THOMAS, Sir Quentin (Jeremy), Kt 1999; CB 1994; President, British Board of Film Classification, 2002–12; Head of Constitution Secretariat, Cabinet Office, 1998–99; *b* 1 Aug. 1944; *s* of late Arthur Albert Thomas and Edith Kathleen Thomas (*née* Bigg); *m* 1969, Anabel Jane, *d* of late J. H. Humphreys; one *s* two *d*. *Educ:* Perse School, Cambridge; Gonville and Caius College, Cambridge. Home Office, 1966; Private Sec. to Perm. Under-Sec. of State, 1970; Crime Policy Planning Unit, 1974–76; Sec. to Royal Commn on Gambling, 1976–78; Civil Service (Nuffield and Leverhulme) Travelling Fellowship, 1980–81; Head, Broadcasting Dept, Home Office, 1984–88; Under Sec., 1988–91, Dep. Sec., then Political Dir, 1991–98, NI Office. Led Cabinet Office Review of BBC Monitoring, 2004–05; Chm., BBC Governors' Impartiality Review of BBC coverage of Israeli-Palestinian Conflict, 2005–06.
See also R. C. Thomas.

THOMAS, Rachel Mary S.; *see* Sandby-Thomas.

THOMAS, Dr Raymond Tudor, OBE 1994; Director, Brussels, British Council, 2003–06; *b* 19 May 1946; *s* of Edgar William Thomas and Lilian Phylis Thomas; *m* 1973, Gloria Forsyth; two *s*. *Educ:* King's Sch., Macclesfield; Jesus Coll., Oxford (BA Modern Hist. 1968); Inst. of Internat. Relns, Univ. of WI (Dip. 1970); Univ. of Sussex (DPhil 1976). Tutor, Davies's Ltd, 1969–70; Lectr, Inst. of Internat. Relns, Trinidad, 1970–71; British Council: Assistant Representative: Morocco, 1974–77; Pakistan, 1977–80; Malaysia, 1980–82; Regl Rep., Sabah, Malaysia, 1982–84; Projects Officer, London, 1984–85; Dep. Dir 1985–88, Dir 1988–90, Educnl Contracts Dept; Dir, EC Relns, Brussels, 1990–95; Regl Dir, subseq. Policy Dir, Middle East and N Africa, 1995–2000; Dir, Turkey, 2000–03. Chm., Renewable World (formerly Koru Foundn), 2010–12 (Trustee, 2008–12). *Publications:* Britain and Vichy: the dilemma of Anglo-French relations 1940–42, 1979. *Recreations:* family life, travel, reading, fly-fishing. *Address:* 52 St Anne's Crescent, Lewes, East Sussex BN7 1SD.

THOMAS, Rev. Rhodri Glyn; *see* Thomas, Rev. H. R. G.

THOMAS, Richard; *see* Thomas, A. R.

THOMAS, Richard, CMG 1990; HM Diplomatic Service, retired; *b* 18 Feb. 1938; *s* of late Anthony Hugh Thomas, JP and Molly Thomas, MBE; *m* 1966, Catherine Jane Hayes, Sydney, NSW; one *s* two *d*. *Educ:* Leighton Park; Merton Coll., Oxford (MA). Nat. Service, 2nd Lt, RASC, 1959–61. Entered CRO, later FCO, 1961; Accra, 1963–65; Lomé, 1965–66; UK Delegn NATO, Paris and Brussels, 1966–69; FCO, 1969–72; New Delhi, 1972–75; FCO, 1976–78; FCO Visiting Res. Fellow, RIIA, 1978–79; Counsellor, Prague, 1979–83; Ambassador, Iceland, 1983–86; Overseas Inspector, 1986–89; Ambassador to Bulgaria, 1989–94; High Comr, Eastern Caribbean, 1994–98. Trustee: Leonard Cheshire Disability (formerly Leonard Cheshire), 1999–2005 (Internat. Chm., 2000–05; Vice Pres., 2005–14); Rye Arts Fest., 2003–10 (Chm., 2006–10); Mem. Adv. Bd, Peasmarsh Chamber Music Fest., 2012–. *Publications:* India's Emergence as an Industrial Power: Middle Eastern Contracts, 1982. *Recreations:* foreign parts, music, sketching. *Address:* 4 Hiham Green, Winchelsea, E Sussex TN36 4HB. *Club:* Oxford and Cambridge.

THOMAS, (Richard) Gwyn, PhD; Chief Information Officer for Wales, and Director, Informatics for Health and Social Services, Welsh Government, 2009–13; Managing Director, Cogan Hall Consultancy, since 2013; *b* Treorchy, Rhondda, 14 Sept. 1949; *s* of Richard Lewis Thomas and Catherine Thomas; *m* 1971, Eirwen Birney; one *s* one *d*. *Educ:* Cowbridge Grammar Sch.; Univ. of Sheffield (BMet; PhD Metallurgy 1974); Univ. of Stirling (MSc Public Relns). Various sen. mgt posts and specialist positions, electricity supply industry, UK and Australia, 1974–92; Exec. Dir, Nottingham City Hosp., 1994–2000; Chief Executive Officer: NHS Information Authy, 2000–05; Informing Healthcare Prog., NHS Wales, 2005–09. Chm., Health Data Insight CIC, 2012–; Dir, Strategy GPC plc, 2013–. Vis. Prof., Sch. of Information Systems and Computing, Brunel Univ., 2003–06; Hon. Prof., Sch. of Medicine, Swansea Univ., 2013–. Chm., UK Council for Health Informatics Professionals, 2013–. Sec., BCS Health, 2014–. Life FBCS. *Recreations:* West Wales in general and Aberystwyth in particular, springer spaniels, walking (see previous entry), Wales Rugby team. *E:* rgwyn.thomas@gmail.com.

THOMAS, Richard James, CBE 2009; LLB; Chairman, Administrative Justice and Tribunals Council, 2009–13; *b* 18 June 1949; *s* of Daniel Lewis Thomas, JP, and Norah Mary Thomas; *m* 1974, Julia Delicia, *d* of Dr E. G. W. Clarke; two *s* one *d*. *Educ:* Bishop's Stortford Coll.; Univ. of Southampton (LLB Hons); College of Law. Admitted Solicitor, 1973. Articled clerk and Asst Solicitor, Freshfields, 1971–74; Solicitor, CAB Legal Service, 1974–79; Legal Officer and Hd of Resources Gp, Nat. Consumer Council, 1979–86; Under Sec. and Dir of Consumer Affairs, OFT, 1986–92; Dir, Public Policy, Clifford Chance, 1992–2002; Information Comr, 2002–09. Vis. Prof., Northumbria Univ., 2007–13. Chm., British Univs N America Club, 1970–71; Member: Management Cttee, Royal Courts of Justice CAB, 1992–98; London Electricity Cons. Council, 1979–84; European Consumer Law Gp, 1981–86; European Commn Working Party on Access to Justice, 1981–82; Lord Chancellor's Adv. Cttee on Civil Justice Rev., 1985–88; Council, Office of Banking Ombudsman, 1992–2001; Adv. Cttee, Oftel, 1995–98; Advertising Adv. Cttee, ITC, 1996–2002; Bd, Financial Ombudsman Service, 1999–2002; Bd, NCC, 2001–02; Bd, Consumers Assoc., 2008–13 (Dep. Chm., 2009–13); Bd, Whitehall and Industry Gp, 2008–14; Cttee on Standards in Public Life, 2012–. Advr, Centre for Information Policy Leadership, 2009–. FRSA 1992. Hon. LLD Southampton, 2007. Internat. Privacy Leadership Award, Internat. Assoc. of Privacy Professionals, 2008. *Publications:* reports, articles and broadcasts on range of legal, consumer, privacy, data protection and freedom of information issues. *Recreations:* family, maintenance of home and garden, travel. *Address:* 36 Park Lane, Reigate, Surrey RH2 8JX.

THOMAS, Dr Robert Kemeys, FRS 1998; Aldrichian Praelector and Reader in Physical Chemistry, University of Oxford, 2002–08, now Emeritus; Fellow, University College, Oxford, 1978–2008, now Emeritus; *b* 25 Sept. 1941; *s* of Preb. H. S. G. Thomas and Dr A. P. Thomas; *m* 1968, Pamela Woods; one *s* two *d*. *Educ:* Radley Coll., Abingdon; St John's Coll., Oxford (MA, DPhil 1968). Royal Soc. Pickering Fellow, 1970–75; Fellow, Merton Coll., Oxford, 1975–78; Lectr in Physical Chemistry, Univ. of Oxford, 1978–2002. Hon. Professor: Inst. of Chemistry, Chinese Acad. of Scis, Beijing, 1999–; China Petroleum Univ., Huangdao, 2005–. Dr *hc* Lund, 2012. *Publications:* contribs to chemical jls. *Recreations:* flora, funghi, music, Chinese language. *Address:* Physical and Theoretical Chemistry Laboratory, South Parks Road, Oxford OX1 3QZ.

THOMAS, (Robert) Neville; QC 1975; barrister-at-law; a Recorder of the Crown Court, 1975–82; *b* 31 March 1936; *s* of Robert Derfel Thomas and Enid Anne Thomas; *m* 1970, Jennifer Anne Brownrigg; one *s* one *d*. *Educ:* Ruthin Sch.; University Coll., Oxford (MA, BCL). Called to Bar, Inner Temple, 1962, Bencher, 1985. *Recreations:* fishing, walking, gardening, reading. *Address:* Milford Hall, Newtown, Powys SY16 3HF. *Club:* Garrick.

THOMAS, Rt Rev. Roderick Charles Howell; *see* Maidstone, Bishop Suffragan of.

THOMAS, Roger; *see* Thomas, D. R.

THOMAS, Roger, CBiol; Chief Executive, Countryside Council for Wales, 2002–13; *b* 26 Jan. 1953; *s* of Gerwyn and Daphne Thomas; *m* 1988, Jan Tyrer; one *s* twin *d*. *Educ:* NE London Poly. (BSc Hons); Henley Coll. of Mgt (MBA). MRSB; CBiol 1978. Various posts, incl. Lab. Manager, Welsh Water Scientific Directorate, 1976–92; Area Manager, NRA, 1992–95; Regl Gen. Manager, NRA Wales, 1995–96; Area Manager, 1996–98, Dir, 1998–2002, Envmt Agency Wales. Ind. Chair, Sci. and Liaison Gps, Skerries Tidal Turbine Array for SeaGen Wales, Marine Current Turbines Siemens, 2013–. Associate, Welsh Inst. for Natural Resources, Bangor Univ., 2013–. Chairman: Coed Cymru, 2010–; Tir Coed, 2012–; N Wales Wildlife Trust, 2014–; Dir, Canolfan Beaumaris, 2014–. Trustee, Freshwater Habits (formerly Ponds Conservation) Trust, 2006–. *Recreations:* cycling, walking, junior Rugby coach, music, reading, sailing. *Club:* Bangor Rugby.

THOMAS, Prof. Roger Christopher, FRS 1989; Professor of Physiology, University of Cambridge, 1996–2006, now Emeritus (Head of Department, 1996–2006); Fellow, Downing College, Cambridge, 1996–2006; *b* 2 June 1939; *e s* of late Arthur Albert Thomas and Edith Kathleen (*née* Bigg); *m* 1964, Monica Mary, *d* of late Lt-Comdr William Peter Querstret, RN; two *s*. *Educ:* Perse Sch., Cambridge; Univ. of Southampton (BSc, PhD). Res. Associate,

Rockefeller Univ., NY, 1964–66; Hon. Res. Asst, Biophysics, UCL, 1966–69; Bristol University: Lectr, 1969–77; Reader in Physiology, 1977–86; Prof. of Physiol., 1986–96; Hd of Dept of Physiol., 1985–90; Dean, Faculty of Science, 1990–93. Visiting Professor: Yale Univ., 1979–80; SISSA, Trieste, 2002–03. Ed.-in-Chief, Physiology News, 2015–. *Publications:* Ion-Sensitive Intracellular Microelectrodes, 1978; many papers on ion transport in learned jls. *Recreations:* cooking, walking, entertaining grandchildren. *Address:* Department of Physiology, Development and Neuroscience, University of Cambridge, Cambridge CB2 3EG. *T:* (01223) 333869, *Fax:* (01223) 333840. *E:* rct26@cam.ac.uk.

See also Sir Q. J. Thomas.

THOMAS, Roger Christopher; QC 2014; *b* Singapore, 1955; *s* of Victor Thomas and Rosina Thomas; *m* 1981, Jocelyn Anne Stoddard; one *s*. *Educ:* Portsmouth Grammar Sch.; St John's Coll., Oxford (MA; BCL). Called to the Bar, Lincoln's Inn, 1979; in practice as a barrister, 11 New Square, 1979–91, Pump Court Tax Chambers, 1991–. *Publications:* (ed) Halsbury's Laws of England, VAT, 4th edn, 1996, Customs and Excise, 4th edn, 1999; (ed jtly) Hill and Redman's Law of Landlord and Tenant, Stamp Taxes, 2013. *Recreations:* ski-ing, scuba diving, theatre. *Address:* 16 Bedford Row, WC1R 4EF. *T:* (020) 7414 8080. *E:* clerks@pumptax.com.

THOMAS, Roger Geraint, OBE 1997; DL; Chairman, Higher Education Funding Council for Wales, 2008–14; *b* Cardiff, 22 July 1945; *s* of Geraint Phillips Thomas and Doreen Augusta Thomas (*née* Cooke); *m* 1971, Rhian Elisabeth Kenyon Thomas. *Educ:* Univ. of Birmingham (LLB 1966). Admitted solicitor, 1969; Phillips & Buck, later Eversheds solicitors: Partner, then Jt Sen. Partner, 1969–87; Jt Regl Sen. Partner, 1987–95; Regl Sen. Partner, 1995–2000; consultant, 2000–06. Business partnership advr, Nat. Assembly for Wales, 1999–2002; Welsh Assembly: Mem., Ministerial Adv. Gp, Dept for Educn and Skills (formerly Dept for Children, Educn, Lifelong Learning and Skills), 2008–14; Mem., Rev. of Higher Educn in Wales, 2008–09. Chm., Chairs of Higher Educn Wales, 2004–08; Member: Gen. Adv. Council, BBC, 1992–95; Prog. Monitoring Cttee for Industrial S Wales Objective 2 Eur. Structural Funds, 1995–99; Chm.'s Gp, Cttee of Univ. Chairmen, 2003–08; Jt Negotiating Cttee for Higher Educn Staff, 2004–08; Wales Cttee, Leadership Foundn for Higher Educn, 2004–08; Dir, Univs and Colls Employers' Assoc., 2004–08. Mem., Welsh Council, CBI, 1987–97, 1998–2004, 2005–11. Vice Chairman: Techniquest, 1988–2010; Business in Focus Ltd, 1998–2014. Mem. Court and Council, Nat. Mus. of Wales, 1983–2002 (Vice Pres., 2000–02); Director: Wales Millennium Centre, 1996–98; Welsh Nat. Opera Ltd, 2000–10 (Actg Chm., 2006). University of Glamorgan: Mem. Bd of Govs, 1994–2008; Chm., Audit Cttee, 1998–2001; Dep. Chm., 2001–02; Chm. and Pro-Chancellor, 2002–08; Mem. Council, Cardiff Univ., 2000–02. Judge, Provincial Court, Church in Wales, 2006–. CCMI 1996; FRSA 2000. High Sheriff, 2011–12, DL 2013, S Glamorgan. DUniv Glamorgan, 2008. OStJ 2003. *Recreations:* hill walking, music, travel. *E:* rgt@rgtpenarth.co.uk. *Clubs:* Cardiff and County; Penarth Yacht; Glamorganshire Golf.

THOMAS, Roger Humphrey; Chairman, Raymarine plc (formerly Raymarine Group Ltd), 2001–05; Chairman and Managing Director, Black & Decker, 1983–96; *b* 12 April 1942; *s* of Cyril Lewis Thomas and Phyllis Amy Thomas; *m* 1962, Myfanwy Ruth, (Nikki), Nicholas; three *s*. *Educ:* Slough Grammar School. FCCA. Black & Decker, 1970–96. *Recreations:* theatre, DIY, golf. *Address:* Stayes Wood, Northend, nr Henley-on-Thames, Oxon RG9 6LH. *T:* (01491) 638676.

THOMAS, Roger Lloyd; QC 1994; a Recorder, since 1987; *b* 7 Feb. 1947; *s* of David Eyron Thomas, CBE and Marie Lloyd Thomas; *m* 1974, Susan Nicola Orchard; one *s* one *d*. *Educ:* Cathays High Sch., Cardiff; University Coll. of Wales Aberystwyth (LLB). Called to the Bar, Gray's Inn, 1969. *Recreations:* tennis, music, reading. *Address:* 9 Park Place, Cardiff CF10 3DP. *T:* (029) 2038 2731. *Club:* Cardiff Lawn Tennis.

THOMAS, Roger Martin; QC 2000; **His Honour Judge Thomas;** a Circuit Judge, since 2004; *b* 18 Aug. 1954; *s* of Donald Thomas and Jessie Thomas (*née* Attwood); *m* 1981, Vanessa Julia Valentine Stirum; one *s* two *d*. *Educ:* Worksop Coll., Notts; Univ. of Hull (LLB). Called to the Bar, Inner Temple, 1976. Hon. Recorder of Bradford, 2013–. *Recreation:* sport. *Address:* Bradford Combined Court, The Law Courts, Exchange Square, Drake Street, Bradford BD1 1JA.

THOMAS, Roger R.; *see* Ridley-Thomas.

THOMAS, Ronald Richard; *b* 16 March 1929; *m* Lilian Audrey Jones; two *s*. *Educ:* Ruskin Coll. and Balliol Coll., Oxford (MA). Sen. Lectr, Econ. and Indust. Studies, Univ. of Bristol. Contested (Lab): Bristol North-West, Feb. 1974; Bristol East, 1987; MP (Lab) Bristol NW, Oct. 1974–1979. Former Mem., Bristol DC. Mem. UNITE (formerly ASTMS). *Address:* 64 Morris Road, Lockleaze, Bristol BS7 9TU.

THOMAS, Rosemary, OBE 2009; HM Diplomatic Service; Deputy Director, Eastern Europe and Central Asia, Foreign and Commonwealth Office, since 2014; *b* Liverpool, 17 July 1964; *d* of James and Madeleine O'Brien; *m* 1990, Alan Howard Thomas. *Educ:* Bellerive Convent Grammar Sch. for Girls, Toxteth, Liverpool; Univ. of Leeds (BA Hons Russian). Foreign and Commonwealth Office: joined 1990; Overseas Visits Sect., 1990–94; Research Analysts, 1994–97; Desk Officer: Asia-Europe Meeting Summit, 1997–98; Russian Sect., Eastern Dept, 1998–2001; Hd, Council of Europe Sect., OCSE/Council of Europe Dept, 2001–03; Hd, War Crimes Sect., Internat. Orgns Dept, 2003–05; Hd of Communications, EU Border Assistance Mission to Moldova and Ukraine, 2006–07; First Sec., Counter Narcotics, Kabul, 2007–08; Ambassador to Belarus, 2009–12; First Sec., Mexico, 2013. *Recreations:* ski-ing, walking, reading, music. *Address:* c/o Foreign and Commonwealth Office, King Charles Street, SW1A 2AH. *Club:* National Liberal.

THOMAS, Prof. Sandra Mary, OBE 2013; PhD; Director, Global Panel on Agriculture and Food Systems for Nutrition, since 2015; Professor of Science Policy, University of Sussex, 2005–06, Hon. Professor, since 2006; *b* 1 June 1951; *d* of late Alan Wallace Thomas and Josette Charlotte Jeanne Thomas (*née* Costa); *m* 1983 (marr. diss. 1993); one *s* one *d*. *Educ:* Dunsmore Sch. for Girls, Rugby; Westfield Coll., London (BSc 1971; PhD 1980); Brunel Univ. (MSc 1975). Tutor, Open Univ., 1978–90; Lectr, Goldsmiths' Coll., London, 1979–82, 1985–87; University of Sussex: Res. Fellow, 1987–94; Sen. Res. Fellow, 1994–2005; Professorial Fellow, 2005–06; Hon. Professorial Fellow, 2007–; Dir, Nuffield Council on Bioethics, 1997–2006; Dep. Dir, Govt Office for Sci. and Hd (formerly Dir) of Foresight, DTI, subseq. DIUS, later BIS, 2006–14; Dep. Dir, UK Space Agency, 2014–15. Member: Econ. and Social Cttee of EU, 1998–2002; Expert Adv. Gp on Genomes, DTI, 1999–2000; DFID Commn on IP Rights, 2000–02; UK Intellectual Adv. Cttee, 2000–05; Foresight Adv. Gp, 2000–02; Expert Adv. Gp on Clinical Res., Acad. Med. Scis, 2002–03; Expert Adv. Gp, MHRA, 2003–04; Ethics and Governance Council, UK Biobank, 2004–06; Sci. and Soc. Cttee, Royal Soc., 2004–06; Human Remains Adv. Gp, 2006–09; Vice Chm., Cttee on IP, Human Genome Orgn, 2003–08. Trustee: Centre for Mgt of IP in Health R&D, 2003–07. *Address:* Global Panel on Agriculture and Food Systems for Nutrition, 36 Gordon Square, WC1H 0PD.

THOMAS, Sarah Joan; Head of Bryanston School, since 2005; *b* 5 Sept. 1961; *d* of Raymond John Peter Thomas and Joan Mary Thomas (*née* Day); *m* 1985, Adrian Boote; two *d*. *Educ:* Birkenhead High Sch., GDST; Hertford Coll., Oxford (BA Lit.Hum. 1984); King's Coll. London (PGCE 1986). Classics Teacher, Sevenoaks Sch., 1986–99; Dep. Hd, Uppingham Sch., 1999–2005. *Recreations:* family, food, friends. *Address:* Bryanston School, Blandford, Dorset DT11 0PX. *T:* (01258) 452411.

THOMAS, Simon; Member (Plaid Cymru) Wales Mid and West, National Assembly for Wales, since 2011; *b* Aberdare, 28 Dec. 1963; *m* 1997, Gwen Lloyd Davies; one *s* one *d*. *Educ:* UCW, Aberystwyth (BA Hons Welsh 1985); Coll. of Librarianship, Aberystwyth (Post-grad. DipLib 1988). Asst Curator, Nat. Liby of Wales, Aberystwyth, 1986–92; Policy and Res. Officer, Taff-Ely BC, 1992–94; Develt Officer, 1994–97, Manager, Jigso, 1997–2000, Wales Council for Voluntary Action. Mem. (Plaid Cymru) Ceredigion CC, 1999–2000. MP (Plaid Cymru) Ceredigion, Feb. 2000–2005. Contested (Plaid Cymru) Ceredigion, 2005. Mem., Standards and Privileges Cttee, H of C, 2003–05; Vice Chairman: Parly Envmt Gp, 2000–05; PRASEG, 2002–05; Mem., Envmtl Audit Cttee, 2000–05. Plaid Cymru: Member: Nat. Exec., 1995–98; Nat. Assembly Policy Gp, 1997–99; Policy Forum, 1999– (Policy Co-ordinator for the Envmt); special advr on econ. develt and rural affairs, 2007–11. Vice-Chm., Global Legislators for a Better Environment, 2003–05. *Publications:* As Good as Our Words: guidelines for the use of Welsh by voluntary organisations, 1996; Plaid Cymru election manifestos, 1997, 1999; contrib. numerous articles in Welsh and English lang. jls. *Recreations:* culture and literature, cycling, family life. *Address:* (office) Ty Bres, Bres Road, Llanelli SA15 1UA.

THOMAS, Sophie Lysandra; Director of Design, Useful Simple Ltd, since 2012; Director of Circular Economy, Royal Society of Arts, since (Co-Director of Design, 2012–15); *b* Oxford, 25 June 1973; *d* of late Michael Thomas and of Pamela Thomas; *m* 2001, Daniel Epstein; one *s* one *d*. *Educ:* Oxford Brookes Univ. (Foundn in Art and Design); Central St Martin's Sch. of Art and Design (BA Hons Graphic Design 1995); Royal Coll. of Art (MA Communication Design 1997). Designer, Body Shop Internat., 1997–98; Founding Dir, Thomas.Matthews Ltd, 1998–. Co-Founder: Three Trees Don't Make a Forest, 2007; Greengaged, 2008; Mem., London United. Trustee: Design Council, 2009–11; Useful Simple Trust, 2010–. Friend, St Bride's Liby. MCIWM, 2014. FRSA. *Publications:* regular contribs to UK and internat. design press. *Recreations:* collecting plastic flotsam, screen printing, growing vegetables, cheating at crosswords, choral singing (Hackney Singers). *Address:* Useful Simple Ltd, First Floor, Morley House, 320 Regent Street, W1B 3BB. *T:* (020) 7307 9292. *E:* sophie@usefulsimple.co.uk.

THOMAS, Sir Stanley; *see* Thomas, Sir G. S.

THOMAS, Rt Hon. Sir Swinton (Barclay), Kt 1985; PC 1994; a Lord Justice of Appeal, 1994–2000; *b* 12 Jan. 1931; *s* of late Brig. William Bain Thomas, CBE, DSO, and Mary Georgina Thomas; *m* 1967, Angela, Lady Cope; one *s* one *d*. *Educ:* Ampleforth Coll.; Lincoln Coll., Oxford (Scholar; MA; Hon. Fellow, 1995). Served with Cameronians (Scottish Rifles), 1950–51, Lieut. Called to Bar, Inner Temple, 1955 (Bencher, 1983; Reader, 2000; Treas., 2001); QC 1975; a Recorder of the Crown Court, 1975–85; a Judge of the High Court of Justice, Family Div., 1985–90, QBD, 1990–94. A Presiding Judge, Western Circuit, 1987–90. Member: General Council of the Bar, 1970–74; Criminal Injuries Compensation Bd, 1984–85; Vice-Chairman: Parole Bd, 1994 (Mem., 1992–95); Review on Child Protection in Catholic Church in England and Wales, 2000–01; Comr for the Interception of Communications, 2000–06. Chm., Assoc. of Papal Orders in GB, 2005–. KCSG 2002. *Recreations:* reading, travel, theatre, bridge. *Address:* 53 Wynnstay Gardens, Allen Street, W8 6UU. *Club:* Garrick.

THOMAS, Sybil Milwyn; Her Honour Judge Thomas; a Circuit Judge, since 2005; a Senior Circuit Judge, since 2014; Designated Family Judge for Birmingham; *d* of late Terence Barrington Thomas and Ann Veronica Thomas. *Educ:* Edgbaston High Sch. for Girls, Birmingham; Univ. of Bristol (LLB Hons 1975). Called to the Bar, Gray's Inn, 1976; in practice, Midland and Oxford Circuit, 1977–2005; Asst Recorder, 1993–97; a Recorder, 1997–2005. Dep. Chancellor, Dio. of Lichfield, 2006–. *Address:* c/o Birmingham Family Court, 33 Bull Street, Birmingham B4 6DS.

THOMAS, Trevor Anthony, FRCA; Emeritus Consultant Anaesthetist, United Bristol Healthcare NHS Trust (formerly United Bristol Hospitals), since 2002 (Consultant Anaesthetist, 1972–2002); *b* 16 March 1939; *s* of Arthur William Thomas and Gladys Mary Gwendoline Thomas (*née* Hulin); *m* 1965, Yvonne Louise Mary Branch; one *s*. *Educ:* Bristol Grammar Sch.; Univ. of St Andrews (MB ChB 1964). FRCA (FFARCS 1969). Chm., Dept of Anaesthesia, United Bristol Hosps, 1977–80; Hon. Clin. Sen. Lectr, Bristol Univ., 1980–2002. SW Regl Assessor in Anaesthesia, 1978–2000, Central Assessor, 1999–2003, Confidential Enquiries into Maternal Deaths in UK (formerly Confidential Enquiry into Maternal Deaths in England and Wales). Chm., Med. Cttee, Bristol and Weston DHA, 1988–90. Mem. Council, 1989–96, Hon. Sec., 1994, Sect. of Anaesthetists, RSocMed; Obstetric Anaesthetists Association: Mem. Cttee, 1978–85; Minute Sec., 1980–81; Hon. Sec., 1981–85; Mem. Cttee and Pres. Elect, 1994–95; Pres., 1995–99; Society of Anaesthetists, SW Region: Mem. Cttee, 1975–85; Hon. Sec., 1985–88; Pres., 1997–98. Examr, Fellowship Exams, RCAnaes, 1985–96. Trustee, Special Trustees for United Bristol Hosps, 1992–99; Trustee and Mem. Council, St Peter's Hospice, 1996–2012. Asst Ed., 1975–76, Ed., 1976–80, Anaesthesia Points West. *Publications:* (with A. Holdcroft) Principles and Practice of Obstetric Anaesthesia and Analgesia, 2000; contrib. chapters to textbooks; contribs to learned jls, mainly on matters related to obstetric anaesthesia. *Recreations:* music, theatre, Tai Chi, genealogy, history relating to Spain and Spanish artists. *Address:* 14 Cleeve Lawns, Downend, Bristol BS16 6HJ.

THOMAS, Victor Gerald B.; *see* Bulmer-Thomas.

THOMAS, Vivian Elliott Sgrifan, CBE 1998 (OBE 1992); Chairman, British Standards Institution, 1992–2002; *b* 13 March 1932; *s* of William Edward Thomas and Cicely (*née* Elliott); *m* 1962, Valerie Slade Thomas; one *s* one *d*. *Educ:* Swindon High Sch.; Southampton Univ. (1st Class Marine Engrg). Engr Officer, Union Castle Line, 1953–58; with British Petroleum plc, 1959–92; Chief Exec. Officer, BP Oil UK Ltd, 1989–92. Director: Southern Water plc, 1992–96; Jaguar Ltd, 1993–2006; Gowrings Plc, 1992–2001. *Recreations:* golf, music, theatre. *Address:* Camelot, Bennett Way, West Clandon, Guildford, Surrey GU4 7TN. *T:* (01483) 222665. *Club:* Royal Automobile.

THOMAS, Maj.-Gen. Walter Babington, CB 1971; DSO 1943; MC and Bar, 1942; Commander, HQ Far East Land Forces, Nov. 1970–Nov. 1971 (Chief of Staff, April–Oct. 1970); retired Jan. 1972; *b* Nelson, NZ, 29 June 1919; *s* of Walter Harington Thomas, Farmer; *m* 1947, Iredale Edith Lauchlan (*née* Trent); three *d*. *Educ:* Motueka Dist High Sch., Nelson, NZ. Clerk, Bank of New Zealand, 1936–39. Served War of 1939–45 (despatches, MC and Bar, DSO): 2nd NZEF, 1940–46, in Greece, Crete, Western Desert, Tunis and Italy; Comd 23 (NZ) Bn, 1944–45; Comd 22 (NZ) Bn, in Japan, 1946; transf. to Brit. Army, Royal Hampshire Regt, 1947; Bde Major, 39 Inf. Bde Gp, 1953–55 (despatches); GSO2, UK JSLS, Aust., 1958–60; AA&QMG, HQ 1 Div. BAOR, 1962–64; Comd 12 Inf. Bde Gp, 1964–66; IDC, 1967; GOC 5th Div., 1968–70. Silver Star, Medal, 1945 (USA). *Publications:* Dare to be Free, 1951; Touch of Pitch, 1956; (with Denis McLean) Pathways to Adventure, 2004. *Recreation:* riding. *Address:* Kambellan, 986 Kerry Road, Beaudesert, Qld 4285, Australia.

THOMAS, (William) David; a District Judge (Magistrates' Courts) (formerly Stipendiary Magistrate), South Yorkshire, 1989–2010; *b* 10 Oct. 1941; *s* of Arnold and Ada Thomas; *m* 1st, 1966, Cynthia Janice Jackson (marr. diss. 2000); one *s* two *d*; 2nd, 2000, Mrs Muriel

Hainsworth. *Educ:* Whitcliffe Mount Grammar Sch., Cleckheaton; LSE (LLB Hons 1963); Part II, Law Society Finals, 1964. Admitted Solicitor, 1966. Asst Solicitor 1966, Partner, 1967–89, Finn Gledhill & Co., Halifax. Ind. adjudicator for prisons, 2003–12. *Publications:* contribs to Yorkshire Ridings Magazine and Pennine Radio, Bradford. *Recreations:* amateur dramatics, theatre, ballet, gardening.

THOMAS, (William) David; QC 2002; *b* 20 Dec. 1958; *s* of John Lloyd Thomas and Kathleen Thomas; *m* 1987, Victoria Susan Cochrane; one *s* one *d*. *Educ:* The Heights; Midhurst Grammar Sch.; Wadham Coll., Oxford (MA). Called to the Bar, Middle Temple, 1982; in practice as barrister, 1983–. *Publications:* (contrib.) Keating on Construction Contracts, 8th edn 2006; (ed) Keating on NEC3, 2012. *Recreations:* gardening, cricket, wine, tennis. *Address:* Keating Chambers, 15 Essex Street, WC2R 3AA. *E:* dthomas@keatingchambers.com. *Clubs:* MCC; Kirdford Cricket.

THOMAS, William Ernest Ghinn, FRCS; Consultant Surgeon, Sheffield Teaching Hospitals NHS Foundation Trust, 1986–2010, now Consultant Surgeon Emeritus (Clinical Director of Surgery, 1989–2008); Senior Vice President, Royal College of Surgeons of England, 2008–10; *b* London, 13 Feb. 1948; *s* of late Kenneth Dawson Thomas and of Monica Isobel Thomas; *m* 1973, Grace Violet Samways; two *s* three *d*. *Educ:* Dulwich Coll.; King's Coll. London (BSc 1969); St George's Hosp. Med. Sch., London (MB BS 1972); MS London 1980. MRCS 1972, FRCS 1976; LRCP 1972; ECFMG 1972. Consultant Surgeon, Royal Hallamshire Hosp., Sheffield, 1986–2010; Hon. Sen. Lectr in Surgery, Univ. of Sheffield, 1986–. Phase 2 Assessor, GMC, 1999–2003. Royal College of Surgeons of England: Bernard Sunley Fellow, 1977; Arris and Gale Lect., 1981–82; Hunterian Prof., 1986–87; Mem., Court of Examrs, 1992–2000; Surgical Skills Tutor, 1994–2004; Mem., Council, 2002–12; Internat. Dir, 2002–08; Chm., Educn, 2003–08; Zachary Cope Meml Lect., 2005; Chm., Editl Bd, 2008–12. Member: Surgical Cttee, British Soc. of Gastroenterology, 1991–95; Intercollegiate Panel of Examrs, Gen. Surgery, 1995–2002; Internat. Bd of Dirs, Gastrointestinal Workshop, 2000–; Pres., Surgical Section, RSocMed, 2000–01; Permanent Dean, Acad. of Educn, Internat. Soc. of Surgery, 2011–13. Hon. Sec., E Midlands Surgical Soc., 1994–99. Pres., Gideons Internat., 2013–. Hon. FSACS 2006; Hon. Fellow, German Surgical Soc., 2010. Mem., Editl Bd, Hospital Doctor, 1987–2001; Chm. and Exec. Ed., Current Practice in Surgery, 1988–97; Series Ed. and Chm., Editl Bd, Surgery, 2000–; Ed., Bulletin, RCS, 2002–08. Lectures: State of the Art, British Soc. of Gastroenterology, 1986; Martin Allgöwer, Internat. Soc. of Surgery, 2005; Heyendael Prize, Nijmegen, 2006. Award for bravery, Royal Humane Soc., 1974; Eur. Soc. for Surgical Res. Prize, 1981; Dr of the Year Award, BUPA Med. Foundn, 1985. *Publications:* Preparation and Revision for the FRCS, 1986; Self-Assessment Exercises in Surgery, 1986; (with E. Rhys Davies) Nuclear Medicine: applications in surgery, 1988; (with J. H. F. Smith) Colour Guide to Surgical Pathology, 1992; Basic Surgical Skills, 1996, 4th edn 2007; Preparation and Revision for MRCS, 1999, 2nd edn 2004; Specialist Registrar Skills in General Surgery, 1999; (with A. Aluwihare) Introduction to Surgical Skills, 2001; (with A. Wyman) The Abdomen, STEP Course Module VII, 2001; MCQs and Extended Matching Questions for the MRCS, 2002; (jtly) An Introduction to the Symptoms and Signs of Surgical Disease, 4th edn 2005 (1st Prize, BMA Med. Book Competition, 2006); (ed jtly) Anastomosis Techniques in the Gastro-Intestinal Tract, 2007; Short Stay Surgery, 2008; An Introduction to the Diagnosis and Management of Surgical Disease, 2010; over 200 articles in learned jls. *Recreations:* ski-ing, oil painting, photography. *Address:* Ash Lodge, 65 Whirlow Park Road, Whirlow, Sheffield S11 9NN. *T:* (0114) 262 0852, *Fax:* (0114) 236 3695. *E:* wegthomas@btinternet.com. *W:* www.wegthomas.com.

THOMAS, Ven. William Jordison; Archdeacon of Northumberland, 1983–92, Archdeacon Emeritus 1993; *b* 16 Dec. 1927; *s* of Henry William and Dorothy Newton Thomas; *m* 1954, Kathleen Jeffrey Robson, *d* of William Robson, Reaveley, Powburn, Alnwick. *Educ:* Holmwood Prep. School, Middlesbrough; Acklam Hall Grammar School, Middlesbrough; Giggleswick School; King's Coll., Cambridge (BA 1951, MA 1955); Cuddesdon College. National Service, RN, 1946–48. Assistant Curate: St Anthony of Egypt, Newcastle upon Tyne, 1953–56; Berwick Parish Church, 1956–59; Vicar: Alwinton with Holystone and Alnham and the Lordship of Kidland, 1959–70; Alston with Garrigill, Nenthead and Kirkhaugh, 1970–80, i/c Knaresdale, 1973–80; Industrial Chaplain, 1972–80; Team Rector of Glendale, 1980–82; RD of Bamburgh and Glendale, 1980–82. Travel leader, chaplain and lectr with leading pilgrimage, tour and cruise cos, 1992–2008. Hon. Chaplain: Actors' Church Union, 1953–56; Northumberland County NFU, 1978–2000. Harbour Comr, N Sunderland, 1990–92. *Recreations:* sailing own dinghy and other people's yachts, making pictures, travelling and making magic. *Club:* Victory Services.

THOMAS, Sir William Michael, 3rd Bt *cr* 1919, of Ynyshir, co. Glamorgan; *b* 5 Dec. 1948; *er s* of Sir William James Cooper Thomas, 2nd Bt, TD, and Freida Dunbar Thomas (*née* Whyte); *S* father, 2005. *Educ:* Harrow; Christ Church, Oxford. *Heir: brother* Stephen Francis Thomas [*b* 13 April 1951; *m* 1986, Hon. Jane Ridley, *e d* of Baron Ridley of Liddesdale, PC; two *s*].

THOMAS, Wyndham, CBE 1982; Chairman, Cambridge New Town Corporation PLC, 1999–2008; *b* 1 Feb. 1924; *s* of Robert John Thomas and Hannah Mary; *m* 1947, Elizabeth Terry Hopkin; one *s* three *d*. *Educ:* Maesteg Grammar School. Served Army (Lieut, Royal Welch Fusiliers), 1943–47. Schoolmaster, 1950–53; Director, Town and Country Planning Association, 1955–67; Gen. Manager, Peterborough New Town Develt Corp., 1968–83; Chm., Inner City Enterprises, 1983–92. Member: Land Commission, 1967–68; Commission for the New Towns, 1964–68; Property Adv. Gp, DoE, 1978–90; London Docklands Develt Corp., 1981–88. Chm., House Builders' Fedn Commn of Inquiry into Housebuilding and the Inner Cities, 1986–87 (report published 1987). A Vice-Pres., TCPA, 1992–. Mayor of Hemel Hempstead, 1958–59. Contested (Lab) SW Herts, 1955. Hon. MRTPI 1979 (Mem. Council, 1989–98). Freedom, City of Peterborough, 2012. Officer of the Order of Orange-Nassau (Netherlands), 1982. *Publications:* many articles on town planning, housing, etc, in learned jls. *Recreations:* collecting/restoring old furniture, writing. *Address:* 8 Westwood Park Road, Peterborough PE3 6JL. *T:* (01733) 564399.

THOMAS, Wynn; *see* Thomas, M. W.

THOMAS, Zoë Siobhan; *see* O'Sullivan, Z. S.

THOMAS-DAVIES, Christine Mary; *see* Tacon, C. M.

THOMAS-SYMONDS, Nicklaus, FRHistS; MP (Lab) Torfaen, since 2015; *b* Panteg, Torfaen, 26 May 1980; *s* of Jeffrey and Pamela Symonds; *m* 2006, Rebecca Thomas; two *d*. *Educ:* St Alban's RC High Sch., Pontypool; St Edmund Hall, Oxford (MA PPE); Univ. of Glamorgan (DipLaw); Cardiff Univ. (BVC). FRHistS 2012. Tutor and Lectr in Politics, St Edmund Hall, Oxford, 2002–15; called to the Bar, Lincoln's Inn, 2004; in practice as barrister, 2004–15. Secretary: Blaenavan Lab. Party, 2004–15; Torfaen CLP, 2009–15. *Publications:* Attlee: a life in politics, 2010; Nye: the political life of Aneurin Bevan, 2014; contrib. articles to British Hist., Llafur: Jl of Welsh People's Hist. Soc., Parly Affairs. *Recreations:* reading, watching football and Rugby. *Address:* House of Commons, SW1A 0AA. *T:* (020) 7219 4294. *E:* nick.thomassymonds.mp@parliament.uk. *Club:* Elgan Working Men's (Blaenavon).

THOMAS JUDGE, Hon. Barbara Singer, (Lady Judge), CBE 2010; Chairman, UK Pension Protection Fund, since 2010; Deputy Chairman, Financial Reporting Council, 2003–07; Chairman, UK Atomic Energy Authority, 2004–10, now Emeritus; *b* 28 Dec. 1946; *d* of Jules Singer and Marcia Bosniak; *m* 1978, Allen Lloyd Thomas (marr. diss. 2002); one *s*; *m* 2003, Sir Paul Rupert Judge, *qv*. *Educ:* Univ. of Pennsylvania (BA 1966); New York Univ. Sch. of Law (JD with Hons 1969). Partner, Kaye Scholer, Fierman, Hays & Handler, 1973–80; Comr, US Securities and Exchange Commn, 1980–83; Exec. Dir, Samuel Montagu & Co. Ltd, 1984–86; Sen. Vice Pres. and Gp Hd, Bankers Trust Co., 1986–90; Dir, News International plc, 1993–94; Chairman: Whitworths Gp Ltd, 1996–2000; Private Equity Investor plc, 2000–04 (Dir, 2004–); Dep. Chm., Friends Provident plc, 2001–09; non-executive Director: NV Belaert SA, 2007–; Magna International Inc., 2007–; Statoil, 2010–. Non-exec. Dir, DCA, 2004–06. Mem., Trilateral Commn, 2007–; Chm., Task Force on Nuclear Safety, 2014– (Dep. Chm., Tokyo Electric Power Co. Nuclear Reform Monitoring Cttee, 2014–); Mem., UAE Adv. Bd for Develt of Peaceful Nuclear Energy, 2012–. Mem. Bd of Dirs, Lauder Inst. of Internat. Mgt, Wharton Sch., Univ. of Pennsylvania; Chm., Inst. of Dirs, 2015–; Chm., Energy Inst., UCL, 2010–. Chm. Benjamin West Gp and Mem. Corporate Develt Bd, RA; Mem., Council of Mgt, Ditchley Foundn, 2006–. Trustee: Wallace Collection, 2004–07; RA, 2005–. Governor, SOAS, 1997–2005 (Chm., 2006–10). *Recreations:* food, oriental porcelain. *Address:* c/o Eversheds, 1 Wood Street, EC2V 7WS. *T:* (020) 7919 0623. *Clubs:* Reform; Metropolitan (New York).

THOMASON, Prof. George Frederick, CBE 1983; Montague Burton Professor of Industrial Relations, University College, Cardiff, 1969–85, now Emeritus; *b* 27 Nov. 1927; *s* of George Frederick Thomason and Eva Elizabeth (*née* Walker); *m* 1953, Jean Elizabeth Horsley; one *s* one *d*. *Educ:* Kelsick Grammar Sch.; Univ. of Sheffield (BA); Univ. of Toronto (MA); PhD (Wales). University College, Cardiff: Research Asst, 1953; Asst Lectr, 1954; Research Associate, 1956; Lectr, 1959; Asst Man. Dir, Flex Fasteners Ltd, Rhondda, 1960; University College, Cardiff: Lectr, 1962; Sen. Lectr, 1963; Reader, 1969; Dean, Faculty of Economics, 1971–73; Dep. Principal (Humanities), 1974–77. Member: Doctors' and Dentists' Pay Review Body, 1979–95; Pay Rev. Body for Nurses, Midwives, Health Service Visitors and Professions allied to Medicine, 1983–95. Chm., Prosthetic and Orthotic Worldwide Educn and Relief, 1995–2002. *Publications:* Welsh Society in Transition, 1963; Personnel Manager's Guide to Job Evaluation, 1968; Professional Approach to Community Work, 1969; The Management of Research and Development, 1970; Improving the Quality of Organization, 1973; Textbook of Personnel Management, 1975, 5th edn as Textbook of Human Resource Management, 1988; Job Evaluation: Objectives and Methods, 1980; Textbook of Industrial Relations Management, 1984. *Recreation:* gardening. *Address:* Ty Gwyn, 149 Lake Road West, Cardiff CF23 5PJ. *T:* (029) 2075 4236.

THOMASON, (Kenneth) Roy, OBE 1986; Chairman, Charminster Estates Ltd, since 1998; director of other property companies; solicitor; *b* 14 Dec. 1944; *s* of Thomas Roger and Constance Dora Thomason; *m* 1969, Christine Ann (*née* Parsons); two *s* two *d*. *Educ:* Cheney Sch., Oxford; London Univ. (LLB). Admitted Solicitor, 1969; Partner, 1970–91, Sen. Partner, 1979–91, Horden & George, Bournemouth. Mem., Bournemouth Council, 1970–92 (Leader, 1974–82; past Chm. Policy, Ways and Means, and Finance Cttees). Association of District Councils: Mem. Council, 1979–91; Leader, 1981–87; Chm., 1987–91; Chm., Housing and Environmental Health Cttee, 1983–87. Mem., Cons. Nat. Local Govt Adv. Cttee, 1981–97; various Cons. Party positions at constituency and area level, 1966–97 (Constituency Chm., 1981–82); contested (C) Newport E, 1983. MP (C) Bromsgrove, 1992–97. Member: Envmt Select Cttee, 1992–97; Jt Statutory Instrument Cttee, 1992–97; Chm., All-Party Export Gp, 1996–97 (Sec., 1993–96); Vice Chm., Cons. Parly Envmt Cttee, 1993–97. Fellow, Industry and Parlt Trust, 1996. Mem. Bd, London Strategic Housing, 2001–06 (Chm., 2002–06). Office holder, Dodford PCC, 2000–14. FRSA. Hon. Alderman, Bournemouth BC, 1993. Bailiff of the Court Leet and Court Baron of Bromsgrove, 2012–13 (Reeve, 2011–12). *Recreations:* walking, reading, architectural history, local activities. *Address:* The Old Chapel, Station Road, Middleton St George, Darlington DL2 1JG.

THOMÉ, David Geoffrey C.; *see* Colin-Thomé.

THOMLINSON, Nicholas Howard, FRICS; Chairman, Knight Frank Group, 2004–13; *b* 9 Jan. 1953; *s* of John and Lorna Thomlinson; *m* 2001, Lucy Joly de Lotbinière; two *s*, and three step *s*. *Educ:* Stowe Sch.; Keble Coll., Oxford (MA). FRICS 1978. With Knight Frank & Rutley, subseq. Knight Frank, then Knight Frank LLP, 1974–2013. Non-exec. Dir, Develt Securities plc, 2012–. Trustee, Hft (formerly Home Farm Trust), 2012–. *Recreations:* making marmalade and chutney, bee-keeping, tennis. *E:* nick.thomlinson@gmail.com. *Clubs:* Hurlingham; Wimbledon.

THOMPSON; *see* Grey-Thompson.

THOMPSON, Prof. Alan Eric; A. J. Balfour Professor of the Economics of Government, 1972–84, Professor Emeritus, since 1984, Heriot-Watt University; *b* 16 Sept. 1924; *oc* of late Eric Joseph Thompson and Florence Thompson; *m* 1960, Mary Heather Long; three *s* one *d*. *Educ:* Kingston-upon-Hull GS; University of Edinburgh (MA 1949, MA (Hons Class I, Economic Science), 1951, PhD 1953, Carnegie Research Scholar, 1951–52). FSAScot 1995. Served army (including service with Central Mediterranean Forces), World War II. Asst in Political Economy, 1952–53, Lectr in Economics (formerly Political Economy), 1953–59, and 1964–71, Univ. of Edinburgh. Parly Adviser to Scottish Television, 1966–76; Scottish Governor, BBC, 1976–79. Visiting Professor: Graduate School of Business, Stanford Univ., USA, 1966, 1968; Marmara Univ., Istanbul, 1982. Contested (Lab) Galloway, 1950 and 1951; MP (Lab) Dunfermline, 1959–64. Mem., Speaker's Parly Delegn to USA, 1962. Chm., Adv. Bd on Economics Educn (Esmée Fairbairn Research Project), 1970–76; Jt Chm., Scottish-USSR Co-ordinating Cttee for Trade and Industry, 1985–90; Member: Scottish Cttee, Public Schools Commn, 1969–70; Cttee enquiring into conditions of service life for young servicemen, 1969; Scottish Council for Adult Educn in HM Forces, 1973–98; Jt Mil. Educn Cttee, Edinburgh and Heriot-Watt Univs, 1975–; Local Govt Boundary Commn for Scotland, 1975–82; Royal Fine Art Commn for Scotland, 1975–80; Adv. Bd, Defence Finance Unit, Heriot-Watt Univ., 1987–90; Chm., Northern Offshore (Maritime) Resources Study, 1974–77; Chm., Edinburgh Cttee, Peace Through NATO, 1984–95. Parly Adviser, Pharmaceutical Gen. Council (Scotland), 1984–2000. Hon. Vice-Pres., Assoc. of Nazi War Camp Survivors, 1960–; Pres., Edinburgh Amenity and Transport Assoc., 1970–75; Dir, Scottish AIDS Res. Foundn, 1988–97. Chm. of Governors, Newbattle Abbey Coll., 1980–82 (Governor, 1975–82); Governor, Leith Nautical Coll., 1981–85; Trustee, Bell's Nautical Trust, 1981–85. Has broadcast and appeared on TV (economic and political talks and discussions) in Britain and USA. FRSA 1972. *Publications:* Development of Economic Doctrine (jtly), 1980; contribs to learned journals. *Address:* 11 Upper Gray Street, Edinburgh EH9 1SN.

THOMPSON, Prof. Alan James, MD; FRCP, FRCPI, FMedSci; Consultant Neurologist, National Hospital for Neurology and Neurosurgery, Queen Square, since 1990; Garfield Weston Professor of Clinical Neurology and Neurorehabilitation, since 1998, and Dean, Faculty of Brain Sciences, since 2011, University College London; Chair, Neuroscience Programme, University College London Partners Academic Health Science Centre, since 2014; Senior Investigator, National Institute for Health Research, since 2008; *b* Dublin, 29 Aug. 1955; *s* of Frank and Maureen Thompson. *Educ:* Terenure Coll., Dublin; Trinity Coll. Dublin (MB BCh, BAO, BA 1979; MD 1985). FRCP 1994; FRCPI 1995. Hse officer, Meath Hosp., Dublin, 1979–80; SHO, then Registrar, Trinity Coll. and Dublin Hosps, 1980–82; Registrar in Neurol., 1982–83, Res. Registrar in Neurol., 1983–85, St Vincent's and Adelaide Hosps Dublin; Registrar in Neurol., London Hosp., 1985–87; Sen. Registrar in Neurol., Nat. Hosp. for Nervous Diseases, UCH, 1987–89; National Hospital for Neurology and Neurosurgery: Scarfe Lectr and Sen. Registrar, Dept of Clin. Neurol., 1989–90; Clin. Dir of Neurorehabilitation and Therapies, 1993–98; Dir, R&D, 1998–2006; Divl Clin. Dir, 2003–07; Consultant Neurologist, Whittington Hosp., London, 1990–98; Hd, Dept of Brain Repair and Rehabilitation, Inst. of Neurol., UCL, 2006–08; Dep. Dir, R&D Unit, 2006–08, Comprehensive Biomedical Res. Centre, 2006–10, Jt UCLH/UCL; Dir, Inst. of Neurol., 2008–11, and Vice-Dean and Dep. Hd, Faculty of Biomed., 2009–11, UCL; Clin. Lead for Neurol Diseases, Central and E London Clin. Res. Network, 2013–14. Series Ed., Queen Square Neurol Rehabilitation Series, 2003–; Ed.-in-Chief, Multiple Sclerosis Jl, 2006–; Member: Editl Bd, Lancet Neurol., 2003–; Adv. Bd, Current Med. Lit.: Multiple Sclerosis, 2009–11. Chairman: Internat. Med. and Scientific Bd, MS Internat. Fedn, 2005–; Scientific Adv. Cttee, Internat. Progressive MS Alliance, 2012–; Member: Adv. Cttee for revision of ICD-10-neurol diseases, WHO, 2009–12; Res. Adv. Cttee, Nat. MS Soc., USA, 2009–. FAAN 2009; FANA 2013; FMedSci 2015. Corresp. Mem., Amer. Neurol Assoc., 1997–2013. Guarantor, Brain, 2005–; Trustee: Nat. Hosp. Develt Foundn, subseq. Nat. Brain Appeal, 1998–; Patrick Berthoud Trust, 2004–09; Pewterers' Co. 500th Anniv. Trust, 2010–. Friend: Almeida Th.; Wexford Opera Fest.; RA. Hon Dr Hasselt, Belgium, 2008. Pioneer of the Nation, 2003. *Publications:* (ed jtly) Multiple Sclerosis: clinical challenges and controversies, 1997 (trans. Russian 2000); (ed jtly) Magnetic Resonance in Multiple Sclerosis, 1997 (trans. German 1998); (ed with I. McDonald) Key Advances in the Effective Management of Multiple Sclerosis, 1999; (jtly) Frontiers in Multiple Sclerosis, vol. 2, 1999; (ed) Neurological Rehabilitation of Multiple Sclerosis, 2006; (jtly) Multiple Sclerosis: the guide to treatment and management, 6th edn 2006; (jtly) Atlas of Multiple Sclerosis: multiple sclerosis resources in the world, 2008; (jtly) Multiple Sclerosis: recovery of function and neurorehabilitation, 2010; contrib. chapters in books and articles on MS, MRI, neurorehabilitation and outcome measurement to scientific jls. *Recreations:* music, theatre, reading, wine, Irish art. *Address:* UCL Institute of Neurology, Box 9, Queen Square, WC1N 3BG. *T:* (020) 3448 4152. *E:* alan.thompson@ucl.ac.uk. *Clubs:* Garrick; Trinity College Dublin Sports.

THOMPSON, Amanda, OBE 2012; Managing Director, Blackpool Pleasure Beach, since 2004 (Director, since 1988); President, Stageworks Worldwide Productions, since 1982; *b* 2 Sept. 1962; *d* of William Geoffrey Thompson, OBE, DL and Barbara Thompson; *m* 2003, Stephen Thompson. *Educ:* Badminton Sch., Bristol; Dover Brooks, Oxford. Ran dance studio; worked for Disney, Florida; produced first ice shows in Myrtle Beach, USA, 1982; Dep. Man. Dir, Blackpool Pleasure Beach, 2000–04. Producer/Dir of UK shows: Hot Ice Show; Mystique; Eclipse; Forbidden. Former Mem., Bd of Dirs, Internat. Assoc. of Amusement Parks and Attractions. *Recreations:* shows, cinema, ski-ing, travel, fashion and interior design. *Address:* Blackpool Pleasure Beach, Ocean Boulevard, Blackpool FY4 1EZ. *T:* 0870 444 5588, *Fax:* (01253) 343958.

THOMPSON, Prof. Andrew Stuart, DPhil; Professor of Modern History, University of Exeter, since 2011; *b* Mansfield, Notts, 3 June 1968; *s* of John and June Thompson; *m* 1998, Sarah Jane Lenton; two *d.* *Educ:* Loughborough Grammar Sch.; Regent's Park Coll., Oxford (BA Modern Hist. 1990; MA 1991); Nuffield Coll., Oxford (DPhil Modern Hist. 1994). Fixed-term Tutorial Fellow in Modern Hist., Corpus Christi Coll., Oxford, 1993–97; University of Leeds: Lectr, 1997–2001; Sen. Lectr, 2001–05; Prof. of Imperial and Global Hist., 2005–11; Dean, Faculty of Arts, 2007–09; Pro-Vice Chancellor for Res., 2009–11. Hon. Prof., Univ. of S Africa, 2014–. Mem., AHRC, 2010–. Gen. Ed., Studies in Imperialism series, 2014– (Co-Ed., 2011–14). *Publications:* Imperial Britain: the Empire in British politics, *c* 1880–1932, 2000; The Empire Strikes Back?: the impact of Imperialism on Britain from the mid-nineteenth century, 2005; Empire and Globalisation: networks of people, goods and capital in the British world, *c* 1850–1914, 2010; (ed) Britain's Experience of Empire in the Twentieth Century, 2011; Writing Imperial Histories, 2013. *Recreations:* distance running, Nottingham Forest FC, my Reliant Sabre sports car, Hanna-Barbera cartoons. *Address:* Department of History, Amory Building, Rennes Drive, University of Exeter, Exeter EX4 4RJ. *T:* (01392) 724 297. *E:* A.S.Thompson@exeter.ac.uk. *Club:* East India.

THOMPSON, His Honour Anthony Arthur Richard; QC 1980; a Circuit Judge, 1992–2003; Designated Civil Judge for Hampshire and Dorset, 1999–2003; *b* 4 July 1932; *s* of late William Frank McGregor Thompson and Doris Louise Thompson (*née* Hill); *m* 1958, Françoise Alix Marie Reynier; two *s* one *d* (and one *s* decd). *Educ:* Latymer Upper Sch.; University Coll., Oxford; La Sorbonne. FCIArb 1991. Called to the Bar, Inner Temple, 1957, Bencher, 1986; admitted to Paris Bar, 1988; a Recorder, 1985–92; Liaison Judge for Cornwall, 1993–99; Resident Judge for Cornwall, 1993–99. Chm., Bar European Gp, 1984–86 (Vice-Chm., 1982–84); Mem., Internat. Relations Cttee, Bar Council, 1984–86. QC: Singapore, 1985; Hong Kong, 1986; St Vincent and the Grenadines, 1986. Vice Pres., Cornwall Magistrates' Assoc., 1995–2005. Contested (Lab) Arundel and Shoreham, Oct. 1964. *Recreations:* food and wine, croquet, theatre, cinema, 19th century music, 20th century painting. *Clubs:* Garrick, Roehampton.

See also R. P. R. Thompson.

THOMPSON, Barnaby David Waterhouse; film and television director and producer; Partner, Ealing Studios, since 2001 (Head of Studios, 2001–14); *b* London, 29 March 1961; *s* of John Brian Thompson, *qv*; *m* 1991, Christina Robert; one *s* one *d.* *Educ:* St Paul's Sch., London; Regent's Park Coll., Oxford (MA Hons Theol. and Philosophy). Producer and Dir, Refugees of Faith, 1984; Asst to Producer, Number One, 1985; Asst Producer, Witness in the War Zone, 1986; Man. Dir, World's End Prodns, 1987–90; Vice Pres., Creative Affairs, Broadway Video, NY, 1990–96; Chief Exec., Fragile Films, 1996–2001. Dir, Thin Blue Line, 1988; director and producer: Singing for Your Supper, 1988; Jimi Hendrix, 1989; producer: The Money Slaves, 1987; The Forgotten Holocaust, 1989; Dear Rosie, 1990; Spice World, 1997; An Ideal Husband, 1999; High Heels and Low Lifes, 2001; Lucky Break, 2001; The Importance of Being Earnest, 2002; Hope Springs, 2003; Imagine Me & You, 2005; Alien Autopsy, 2006; Fade to Black, 2006; I Want Candy, 2007; St Trinian's (also co-dir), 2007; Easy Virtue, 2008; St Trinian's 2: the Legend of Fritton's Gold (also co-dir), 2009; Dorian Gray, 2009; Burke and Hare, 2010; The D Train, 2015; Associate Producer, Wayne's World, 1992; Co-Producer: Coneheads, 1993; Wayne's World 2, 1993; Lassie, 1994; Tommy Boy, 1995; Kids in the Hall: Brain Candy, 1996; Executive Producer: Kevin & Parry Go Large, 2000; Valiant, 2005; From Time to Time, 2009. Member: BAFTA; Acad. of Motion Picture Arts and Scis. *Recreations:* swimming, music, cycling. *Address:* Ealing Studios, Ealing Green, W5 5EP. *T:* (020) 8567 6655. *Clubs:* Groucho, Soho House; Serpentine Swimming; Maidstone.

THOMPSON, Bruce Kevin, MA; Head, Strathallan School, since 2000; *b* 14 Nov. 1959; *s* of Keith Bruce Thompson, *qv*; *m* 1993, Fabienne Goddet; two *d.* *Educ:* Newcastle High Sch., Newcastle-under-Lyme; New Coll., Oxford (MA Lit.Hum.). Asst Master, 1983–86, Head of Classics, 1986–94, Cheltenham Coll.; Dep. Rector, Dollar Acad., 1994–2000. Chm., Scottish HMC, 2010–11. Schs' Rep., Scottish Rugby Council, 2010–. *Recreations:* weight training, rowing, cycling, literature, music. *Address:* c/o Strathallan School, Forgandenny, Perth PH2 9EG. *T:* (01738) 815000. *Club:* Leander (Henley-on-Thames).

THOMPSON, Catriona Helen Moncrieff; *see* Kelly, C. H. M.

THOMPSON, Prof. Christopher, MD; FRCP, FRCPsych; Chief Executive, Chris Thompson Consultants Ltd, since 2014; *b* 23 Sept. 1952; *s* of Derek and Margaret Thompson; *m* 1976, Celia Robertson; three *d.* *Educ:* Lincoln Grammar Sch.; Strode's Sch., Egham; University Coll. London (BSc 1974; MB BS 1977; MD 1987). FRCPsych 1991; FRCP 1995; MRCGP 2000. Registrar in Psychiatry, Maudsley Hosp., 1978–81; Res. Fellow and Lectr, Inst. of Psychiatry, 1981–84; Sen. Lectr, Charing Cross Hosp. Med. Sch., 1984–88; University of Southampton: Prof. of Psychiatry, 1988–2003; Hd, Sch. of Medicine, 2000–03; CMO (formerly Dir of Healthcare), 2004–14, Dir of Public Affairs, 2012–14, Priory Gp. Royal College of Psychiatrists: Registrar, 1993–97; Vice Pres., 1997–99; Pres., Internat. Soc. for Affective Disorders, 2000–06. Mem. Bd, Depression Alliance, 2007–. Mem. Council, UCL, 2007–. FRSA. Gold Medal, RCPsych, 1983. *Publications:* (ed and contrib.) Research Instruments in Psychiatry, 1989; (jtly) Caring for a Community, 1995; edited jointly and contributed: Psychological Applications in Psychiatry, 1985; The Origins of Modern Psychiatry, 1987; Learning Psychiatry through MCQ, 1988; Melatonin: clinical perspectives, 1988; Seasonal Affective Disorders, 1989; Violence: basic and clinical science, 1993; 3 official govt reports; over 100 scientific articles in learned jls. *Recreation:* enthusiastic amateur of the classical guitar. *Address:* Priory Group, 21 Exhibition House, Addison Bridge Place, W14 8XP.

THOMPSON, Lt-Col Sir Christopher (Peile), 6th Bt *cr* 1890; Equerry to HRH Prince Michael of Kent, since 1989 (Private Secretary, 1990–92); non-executive Chairman, Nuclear Decommissioning Ltd, 1995–2000 (Director, 1994–2000); *b* 21 Dec. 1944; *s* of Lt-Col Sir Peile Thompson, 5th Bt, OBE, and Barbara Johnson (*d* 1993), *d* of late H. J. Rampling; *S* father, 1985; *m* 1st, 1969, Anna Elizabeth (marr. diss. 1997), *d* of Major Arthur Callander; one *s* one *d*; 2nd, 2001, Penelope (*née* Allin), *widow* of 9th Viscount Portman. *Educ:* Marlborough; RMA Sandhurst. Commnd 11th Hussars (PAO), 1965; Tank Troop Leader and Reconnaissance Troop Leader, 11th Hussars, 1965–69; Gunnery Instructor, RAC Gunnery Sch., 1970–72; Sqdn Second i/c, A Sqdn, Royal Hussars, 1972–75; GSO 3 Intelligence, Allied Staff, Berlin, 1975–76; RMCS Shrivenham, 1977; Staff Coll., Camberley, 1978; DAAG (a) M2 (A) (Officer Manning), MoD, 1978–81; C Sqdn Ldr, Royal Hussars, 1981–83; GSO 2 (Operational Requirements), HQ DRAC, 1983–85; CO, Royal Hussars (PWO), 1985–87; SO1, Sen. Officers Tactics Div., 1987–90, retd. Director: Logical Security Ltd, 1996–98; Falcon Security Control (Overseas) Ltd, 2000–04; Nuclear Decommissioning Services Ltd, 2007–13 (Chm., 2006–11). Dir, Hyde Park Appeal, 1990–96; Trustee: Bike Aid, 1990–94; Queen Elizabeth Gate Appeal, 1990–96; Tusk, 1994–2002 (Patron, 2002–); Antigua Heritage Trust (UK), 1997–2000. Mem., Standing Council of the Baronetage, 2001–10. Patron, Earth 2000, 1997–2002. *Recreations:* travel, fishing, reading, golf, tennis. *Heir:* *s* Peile Richard Thompson, *b* 3 March 1975. *Clubs:* Cavalry and Guards; Mill Reef (Antigua).

THOMPSON, Clive Hepworth, CBE 1998; Director, Sustainable Governance Ltd, since 2009; *b* 7 July 1937; *s* of late Sidney Hepworth Thompson and Vera Wynne; *m* 1962, Joan Mary Kershaw; two *s.* *Educ:* Holywell Grammar Sch.; Manchester Univ. (BTech, MSc); Harvard Business Sch. BP Chemicals: Technical and Management appts; Works Gen. Manager, Barry Plant, 1975–78, Baglan Bay Plant, 1978–82; Gen. Manager, later Dir, Worldwide Petrochemicals, Production and Human Resources, 1982–90; Vice-Pres., Ops and Supply, Arco Chemical Europe, 1990–95. Mem., Audit Commn, 1990–97 (Dep. Chm., 1995–97). Creator, Science Opens Doors Project. Chm., Polymer Industry Skills Council, 2009–. Member: Welsh Water Authy, 1980–82; Chem. Industries Assoc. Cttees, 1985–; Chm., Inter-Company Productivity Group, 1987–90 (Mem., 1983–90). Non-exec. Dir, Frimley Park Hosp. NHS Trust, 1999–2002; Chm., Ashford and St Peter's Hosps NHS Trust, 2002–08. Hon. FRSocMed 2008. Liveryman, Horners' Co. (Mem., Ct of Assts, 1995–). *Publications:* contribs to newspapers and learned jls, incl. Corporate Governance, on petrochemicals, environment policy and costs, management; articles on governance. *Recreations:* hill walking, opera, music, golf, reading history. *Address:* Dwr Golau, 13 Heronscourt, Lightwater, Surrey GU18 5SW. *T:* (01276) 476410. *Clubs:* Harvard Business School; Windlesham Golf.

THOMPSON, Sir Clive (Malcolm), Kt 1996; Deputy Chairman, Strategic Equity Capital plc, since 2005; *b* 4 April 1943; *s* of Harry Louis Thompson and Phyllis Dora Thompson; *m* 1968, Judith Howard; two *s.* *Educ:* Clifton Coll.; Univ. of Birmingham (BSc). Marketing Executive: Royal Dutch Shell Gp, 1964–67; Boots Co. plc, 1967–70; Gen. Manager, Jeyes Gp Ltd, 1970–73; Managing Director: Aerosols Internat. Ltd, 1973–75; Jeyes Ltd, 1975–78; Health and Hygiene Div., Cadbury Schweppes, 1978–82; Gp Chief Exec. Designate, 1982, Gp Chief Exec., 1983–2003, Chm., 2002–04, Rentokil Initial (formerly Rentokil Gp) plc. Chm., Farepak, then Kleeneze, subseq. European Home Retail plc, 2001–06 (Dir, 1988–2006); Director: Caradon plc, 1986–96; Wellcome plc, 1993–95; Sainsbury plc, 1995–2001; BAT Industries plc, 1995–98; Seeboard plc, 1995–96. Member: BOTB, 1997–99; Cttee on Corporate Governance, 1996–98; Dep. Chm., Financial Reporting Council, 1999–2001. Vice Pres., Chartered Inst. of Marketing, 1996–; Pres., CBI, 1998–2000 (Dep. Pres., 1997–98 and 2000–01). Hon. DSc Birmingham, 1999. *Recreations:* current affairs, stockmarket, golf, walking. *Address:* Strategic Equity Capital plc, 25 North Road, W1K 6DJ. *Clubs:* Royal Cinque Ports; Wildernesse (Sevenoaks).

THOMPSON, Collingwood Forster James; QC 1998; a Recorder, since 1997; *b* 19 Dec. 1952; *s* of Collingwood Forster James Thompson and Lillian Thompson; *m* 1985, Valerie Joyce Britchford. *Educ:* Merchiston Castle Sch., Edinburgh; University Coll. London (LLB Hons 1974). Called to the Bar, Gray's Inn, 1975; in practice at the Bar, 1977–. *Recreations:* fly-fishing (badly), hill walking (slowly), wine tasting (frequently), music, reading. *Address:* 7 Bedford Row, WC1R 4BS. *T:* (020) 7242 3555.

THOMPSON, Damian Mark, PhD; journalist and author; Editor-in-Chief, 2003–09, and Director, since 2003, The Catholic Herald; *b* 24 Jan. 1962; *s* of late Leonard Gilbert Thompson and of Pamela Mary Thompson. *Educ:* Presentation Coll., Reading; Mansfield Coll., Oxford (MA); London Sch. of Econs (PhD). Religious Affairs Corresp., Daily Telegraph, 1990–94; freelance feature writer and television critic, 1994–; leader writer, 2003–14, Saturday columnist, 2011–14, Daily Telegraph; Ed., Telegraph Blogs, 2009–14; Associate Ed., Spectator. Mem., Adv. Panel, INFORM, 2013– (Gov., 2003–13). *Publications:* The End of Time: faith and fear in the shadow of the millennium, 1996; (ed) Loose Canon: a portrait of Brian Brindley, 2004; Waiting for Antichrist: charisma and apocalypse in a Pentecostal Church, 2005; Counterknowledge: how we surrendered to conspiracy theories, quack medicine, bogus science and fake history, 2008; The Fix: how addiction is invading our lives and taking over your world, 2012. *Recreation:* playing the piano. *Address:* 19 Moorhouse Road, W2 5DH. *T:* 07968 119540. *Club:* Brooks's.

THOMPSON, Sir David (Albert), KCMG 2002; Vice-President, Royal Commonwealth Society for the Blind, since 2002 (Chairman, 1991–2001); *b* 28 Jan. 1932; *s* of Frederick Thompson and Mildred (*née* Dennis); *m* 1956, Doreen Jo Pryce (*d* 2014); one *s* one *d.* *Educ:* various UK schs. Nat. Service, Military Police, Germany, 1950–52. Served Northern Rhodesia Colonial Police, then with copper mining gp, Southern Rhodesia, 1953–58; sales and mktg posts with IBM UK, 1959–63; new product planning, IBM World Trade Corp., Ky, 1963–65; Rank Xerox, 1965–93: Sen. Mktg posts, London, 1965–67; Man. Dir, Rank Xerox Holland, Amsterdam, 1967–69; Sen. Mktg Exec., UK, 1969–72; Regl Dir for Australia, NZ, Hong Kong and Singapore, Sydney, 1972–74; Main Bd Dir, 1975–79; Pres., Xerox Latin America, 1979–83; Main Bd Dir, Rank Xerox Ltd, 1984–90; Chairman: Rank Xerox Pensions Ltd, 1989–93; Rank Xerox (UK) Ltd, 1990–93; Xerox Engrg Systems (Inc.), USA, 1990–93; Dir, Lyell Hldgs (Inc.) USA, 1990–93; non-exec. Chm., Gestetner Hldgs Plc, 1993–95. Mem., Internat. Adv. Bd, Bank Austria Vienna, 1993–95. London Transport: Mem. (pt-time), London Transport Property Bd, 1991–95 (Vice Chm., 1993–95); Chm., London Buses, 1992–93; Mem., Audit, Safety, Remuneration and Design Cttees, 1992–95. Vice Chm., 1989–94, Chm., 1994–2001, Bd of Govs, Commonwealth Inst. Pres., Inst. Trng and

Develt, 1992–94. Mem., President's Council, 1990–93, Overseas Trade Cttee, 1990–93, CBI. *Recreations:* reading, voluntary work. *Address:* 2 Ravenscroft Road, Henley-on-Thames, Oxon RG9 2DH. *Clubs:* Reform; Phyllis Court (Henley on Thames).

THOMPSON, David Anthony Roland, FCA; Deputy Chief Executive, Boots Co. plc, 2000–02; *b* 4 Sept. 1942; *s* of Harold Alfred Thompson and Olive Edna (*née* Marlow); *m* 1966, Stella Eunice Durow; two *s*. *Educ:* Burton Grammar Sch. FCA 1964. Joined Boots Co. plc, 1966: Gp Mgt Accountant, 1973–77; Vice-Pres. Finance, Boots Drug Stores, Canada, 1977–80; Finance Dir, Retail Div., 1980–89; Gp Financial Controller, 1989–90; Gp Finance Dir, 1990–2002; Jt Gp Man. Dir, 1997–2000. Non-executive Director: E Midlands Electricity, 1996–97; Cadbury Schweppes, 1998–2008; Nottingham Building Soc., 2002–14 (Chm., 2004–14). Chairman: Reach Learning Disability (formerly Southwell Care Project), 2002–; Nottingham Positive Futures Healthy Living Centre, 2003–05. *Recreations:* all sports (especially football), music, cinema, theatre.

THOMPSON, David Brian; Director, Cheveley Park Stud Ltd, since 1975; Chairman, Union Square plc, 1987–91; *b* 3 April 1936; *s* of Bernard Thompson and Rosamund Dee; *m* 1962, Patricia Henchley; one *s* two *d*. *Educ:* Haileybury and ISC. Jt Man. Dir, B. Thompson Ltd, 1960–70; Chm. and co-founder, 1974–84, Jt Chm., 1984–87, Dir, 1987–89, Hillsdown Holdings plc. *Recreations:* family, business, breeding and racing of bloodstock, swimming.

THOMPSON, David George; Member (SNP) Skye, Lochaber and Badenoch, Scottish Parliament, since 2011 (Highlands and Islands, 2007–11); *b* 20 Sept. 1949; *s* of John Thompson and Doreen Thompson; *m* 1969, Veronica Macleod; one *s* three *d*. *Educ:* Lossiemouth High Sch.; Cert. in Legal Metrol., Dept of Trade, 1971; Dip. in Consumer Affairs, Trading Standards Inst., 1976; Inverness Coll. (HNC Gaelic 2004). Apprentice mechanic, Avery Scales, 1965–67; Trainee, then Trading Standards Officer, Banff, Moray and Nairn CC, 1967–73; Asst Chief Trading Standards Officer, Ross and Cromarty CC, 1973–75; Chief Trading Standards Officer, Comhairle Nan Eilean Siar, 1975–83; Dep. Dir of Trading Standards, 1983–86, Dir of Trading Standards, 1986–95, Highland Regl Council; Dir of Protective Services, Highland Council, 1995–2001. Contested (SNP): Inverness, Nairn, Badenoch and Strathspey, 2005; Ross, Skye and Inverness W, Scottish Parlt, 2003. *Recreations:* DIY, hill walking. *Address:* Skye, Lochaber and Badenoch Constituency Office, Thorfin House, Bridgend Business Park, Dingwall IV15 9SL. *T:* (01349) 864701, *Fax:* (01349) 866327. *E:* dave.thompson.msp@scottish.parliament.uk.

THOMPSON, David George Fossett; Chief Executive, Anglia Maltings (Holdings) Ltd, since 2005; *b* 4 July 1954; *s* of late Edwin John and Helen Wilson Thompson; *m* 1980, Marika Ann Moran Davies; one *s* three *d*. *Educ:* Winchester Coll.; Magdalene Coll., Cambridge (Exhibnr; Schol.; BA 1975). Cons. Research Dept, 1975–76; Whitbread plc, 1976–77; Wolverhampton & Dudley Breweries, subseq. Marston's plc: various posts, 1977–86; Man. Dir, 1986–2001; Chm., 2001–13. Chm., Smiths Flour Mills, 2007–12; non-executive Director: Income & Growth Trust plc, 1994–2006 (Chm., 2005–06); Persimmon plc, 1999–2012; Warburtons Ltd, 2002–05; Caledonia Investments plc, 2003–13; Tribal Gp plc, 2004–09. Chm., Wolverhampton TEC, 1990–95; Dir, W Midlands Regl Develt Agency, 1998–2001.

THOMPSON, David John; economic consultant, since 2009; *b* 22 Nov. 1951; *s* of Cyril Thompson and Doris (*née* Savage). *Educ:* Beverley Grammar Sch.; Manchester Univ. (BA Econs 1973); London Sch. of Economics (MSc Econs 1977). Economist: DoE and Dept of Transport, 1973–83; Monopolies and Mergers Commn, 1984; Dir of Res. on Regulation, IFS, 1985–86; Economist: Dept of Transport, 1987–88; HM Treasury, 1989–91; Sen. Economic Advr, DfEE, 1992–98; Hd of Econs and Stats, MAFF, 1998–2001, DEFRA, 2001–04; Director: Central Analytical Directorate, DEFRA, 2004–05; Analysis and Strategy, later Analysis and Econs, DfT, 2005–09. Sen. Res. Fellow, London Business Sch., 1989–91. Dir, Economics Plus, 1996–98. *Publications:* contribs to books, articles in learned jls. *Recreations:* watching soccer, Rugby League and the Tour de France, rock and roll. *E:* david.jthompson@ntlworld.com, 14thompson@14 thompson.karoo.co.uk. *T:* (020) 8863 9471, 07985 450157.

THOMPSON, David Marcus; Director, Origin Pictures Ltd, since 2008; *b* London, 18 July 1950; *s* of Louis and Cynthia Thompson. *Educ:* St Catharine's Coll., Cambridge (BA Hons English). English and Gen. Studies teacher, Bedales Sch.; joined BBC, 1975: Documentary Producer, Open Univ. Prodns, 1975–79; Producer, Everyman, 1979–85 (incl. first drama, Shadowlands (BAFTA and Emmy Awards)); BBC Drama, 1985–94 (created Screenplay series focusing on new talent); Exec. Producer, Single Drama, 1994–97; Hd of Films and Single Drama, BBC, 1997–2008. Exec. producer of films for cinema and TV incl. Shadowlands, 1985; Road, 1987; The Firm, 1988; Safe, 1993; Captives, 1994; Face, Woman in White, 1997; A Rather English Marriage, 1998; Wonderland, Mansfield Park, Ratcatcher, 1999; Nice Girl, Maybe Baby, Born Romantic, Last Resort, Liam, Billy Elliot, Madame Bovary, 2000; When I Was 12, Perfect Strangers, Iris, 2001; Conspiracy, The Gathering Storm, Dirty Pretty Things, In this World, Morvern Callar, Out of Control, Tomorrow La Scala!, 2002; Heart of Me, The Lost Prince, I Capture the Castle, 2003; Mrs Henderson Presents, 2005; The History Boys, 2006; Miss Potter, Notes on a Scandal, 2007; Miss Austen Regrets, The Other Boleyn Girl, Brideshead Revisited, The Duchess, 2008; Freefall, Revolutionary Road, 2009. *Recreations:* family life, tennis.

THOMPSON, (David) Robin (Bibby), CBE 1997; TD 1987; DL; Director, Bibby Line Ltd, 1974–87; Deputy Chairman, Rural Development Commission, 1992–96 (Member, 1986–96); *b* 23 July 1946; *s* of Noel Denis Thompson and Cynthia Joan (*née* Bibby); *m* 1971, Caroline Ann Foster (marr. diss. 1998); one *s* one *d*; *m* 1999, Jane Craddock; one *d*. *Educ:* Uppingham Sch.; Mons Officer Cadet Sch. Short service commn, QRIH, 1965; comd Queen's Own Yeomanry (TA), 1984–87; Hon. ADC to the Queen, 1987–90. Member: Council, Royal Agricl Soc. of England, 1985–91; Bd, Housing Corp., 1989–98; Chm., S Shropshire Housing Assoc., 1991–2000. Vice Chm., Pony Club, 2008–13. Shropshire: High Sheriff, 1989; DL, 2004. *Recreations:* ski-ing, horses, conservation. *Address:* Holly Bank Hadnall, Shrewsbury, Shropshire SY4 3DH. *Club:* Cavalry and Guards.

THOMPSON, Dame Dianne; *see* Thompson, Dame I. D.

THOMPSON, Dr Dorothy Joan, FBA 1996; Fellow, since 1968 and Lecturer in Classics and History, 1968–2006, Girton College, Cambridge; Isaac Newton Trust Lecturer in Classics, University of Cambridge, 1992–2005; *b* 31 May 1939; *d* of late Frank William Walbank, CBE, FBA and Mary Woodward (*née* Fox); *m* 1st, 1966, Michael Hewson Crawford, *qv* (marr. diss. 1979); 2nd, 1982, John Alexander Thompson. *Educ:* Birkenhead High Sch.; Girton Coll., Cambridge (BA 1961; MA 1965; PhD 1966); Bristol Univ. (CertEd 1962). Girton College, Cambridge: Research Fellow, 1965–68; Grad. Tutor (Arts), 1971–81 and 1995–96; Sen. Tutor, 1981–92; Dir of Studies in Classics, 1983–2006; Clare College, Cambridge: Lectr in Classics, 1973–2006; Bye-Fellow, 2006–. Vis. Mem., IAS, Princeton, 1982–83; Vis. Prof., Princeton Univ., 1986; Fellow, Nat. Humanities Center, N Carolina, 1993–94; Leverhulme Trust Major Res. Fellowship, 2002–04. President: Assoc. Internationale de Papyrologues, 2001–07 (Hon. Pres., 2007–); Cambridge Philological Soc., 2002–04. James H. Breasted Prize, American Historical Assoc., 1989. Hon. DLitt Liverpool, 2013. *Publications:* Kerkeosiris: an Egyptian village in the Ptolemaic period, 1971; (jtly) Studies on Ptolemaic Memphis, 1980; Memphis under the Ptolemies, 1988, 2nd edn 2012; (with W. Clarysse) Counting the People in Hellenistic Egypt, 2 vols, 2006; numerous articles and reviews in learned jls. *Recreations:* reading, walking. *Address:* Girton College, Cambridge CB3 0JG. *T:* (01223) 338999.

THOMPSON, Emma; actor; *b* 15 April 1959; *d* of late Eric Norman Thompson and of Phyllida Ann Law; *m* 2003, Greg Wise; one *d*. *Educ:* Newnham College, Cambridge (MA; Hon. Fellow, 1996). *Stage:* Footlights, Australia, 1982; Me and My Girl, Adelphi, 1984; Look Back in Anger, Lyric, 1989; King Lear, and A Midsummer Night's Dream, Renaissance Th. Co. world tour, 1989; Sweeney Todd, NY, 2014, Coliseum, 2015; *films:* Henry V, 1988; The Tall Guy, 1988; Impromptu, 1989; Dead Again, 1990; Howards End, 1992 (BAFTA Best Actress, Academy Award, Golden Globe Award, 1993); Peter's Friends, 1992; Much Ado About Nothing, 1993; The Remains of the Day, 1993; In the Name of the Father, 1993; Junior, 1994; Carrington, 1995; Sense and Sensibility (also wrote screenplay; BAFTA Best Actress; awards for screenplay incl. Academy Award), 1996; The Winter Guest, 1997; Judas Kiss, 1997; Primary Colors, 1998; Wit, 2001; Imagining Argentina, 2003; Love Actually, 2003; Harry Potter and the Prisoner of Azkaban, 2004; Nanny McPhee (also wrote screenplay), 2005; Stranger than Fiction, 2006; Harry Potter and the Order of the Phoenix, 2007; The Boat that Rocked, 2009; Last Chance Harvey, 2009; An Education, 2009; Nanny McPhee and the Big Bang, 2010; Harry Potter and the Deathly Hallows, Pt 2, 2011; Brave, 2012; Beautiful Creatures, Saving Mr Banks, 2013; Love Punch, Walking on Sunshine, Effie Gray (also wrote screenplay), 2014; A Walk in the Woods, The Legend of Barney Thomson, Adam Jones, 2015; *television:* Alfresco, 1983; Tutti Frutti, 1986 (BAFTA Best Actress); Fortunes of War, 1986 (BAFTA Best Actress); Thompson, 1987; Angels in America, 2004. Chm., Helen Bamber Foundn, 2007–. *Publications:* The Further Tale of Peter Rabbit, 2012; The Christmas Tale of Peter Rabbit, 2013; The Spectacular Tale of Peter Rabbit, 2014. *Recreations:* reading, walking, cooking, acting. *Address:* c/o Hamilton Hodell Ltd, 20 Golden Square, W1F 9JL.

THOMPSON, Prof. Francis Michael Longstreth, CBE 1992; FBA 1979; Director, Institute of Historical Research, and Professor of History in the University of London, 1977–90, now Emeritus Professor; *b* 13 Aug. 1925; *s* of late Francis Longstreth-Thompson, OBE; *m* 1951, Anne Challoner; two *s* one *d*. *Educ:* Bootham Sch., York; Queen's Coll., Oxford (Hastings Schol.; MA, DPhil; Hon. Fellow 2011). MRICS (ARICS 1968). War service, with Indian Artillery, 1943–47; James Bryce Sen. Schol., Oxford, 1949–50; Harmsworth Sen. Schol., Merton Coll., Oxford, 1949–51; Lectr in History, UCL, 1951–63; Reader in Economic History, UCL, 1963–68; Prof. of Modern Hist., Univ. of London, and Head of Dept of Hist., Bedford Coll., London, 1968–77. Joint Editor, Economic History Review, 1968–80. Sec., British Nat. Cttee of Historical Scis, 1978–94; British Mem., Standing Cttee for Humanities, European Sci. Foundn, 1983–93; President: Economic Hist. Soc., 1983–86; RHistS, 1988–92 (Fellow, 1964); British Agricl Hist. Soc., 1989–92; Hon. Treas., Internat. Econ. History Assoc., 1986–94. Member: Senate and Academic Council, Univ. of London, 1970–78; Senate and Collegiate Council, 1981–89. Ford's Lectr, Oxford Univ., 1994. Fellow, RHBNC, 1992. DUniv York, 1995; Hon. DLitt Hertfordshire, 2006. *Publications:* English Landed Society in the Nineteenth Century, 1963; Chartered Surveyors: the growth of a profession, 1968; Victorian England: the horse-drawn society, 1970; Countrysides, in The Nineteenth Century, ed Asa Briggs, 1970; Hampstead: building a borough, 1650–1964, 1974; introd. to General Report on Gosford Estates in County Armagh 1821, by William Greig, 1976; Britain, in European Landed Elites in the Nineteenth Century, ed David Spring, 1977; Landowners and Farmers, in The Faces of Europe, ed Alan Bullock, 1980; 2 chapters in The Victorian Countryside, ed G. E. Mingay, 1981; (ed) The Rise of Suburbia, 1982; (ed) Horses in European Economic History, 1983; Towns, Industry and the Victorian Landscape, in The English Landscape, ed S. R. J. Woodell, 1985; Private Property and Public Policy, in Salisbury: The Man and his Policies, ed Lord Blake and Hugh Cecil, 1987; Rise of Respectable Society: a social history of Victorian Britain, 1988; (ed) The Cambridge Social History of Britain 1750–1950, vol. 1 Regions and Communities, vol. 2 People and their Environment, vol. 3 Social Agencies and Social Institutions, 1990; (ed) The University of London and the World of Learning 1836–1986, 1990; (ed) Landowners, Capitalists, and Entrepreneurs: essays for Sir John Habakkuk, 1994; Gentrification and the Enterprise Culture: Britain 1780–1980, 2001; numerous articles in Economic History Review, History, English Historical Review, etc. *Recreations:* gardening, walking, carpentry. *Address:* Holly Cottage, Sheepcote Lane, Wheathampstead, Herts AL4 8NJ. *T:* (01582) 833129.

THOMPSON, Geoffrey Austin; Head, Mill Hill County High School, since 2004; *b* Belfast, 23 July 1952; *s* of Herbert, (Tommy), and Patricia Thompson; *m* 2000, Sally Mary (*née* Pulford); two step *s* one step *d*. *Educ:* Campbell Coll., Belfast; St Catharine's Coll., Cambridge (BA 1974); Stockwell Coll. (PGCE London 1978); South Bank Univ. (MBA Educn 1994). Teacher of English and Hist., Cannock Sch., 1974–77; Asst Dir of Music, Dir of Music, then Hd of Yr, Langley Park Boys' Sch., Beckenham, 1978–93; Dep. Hd, Downham Market High Sch., 1993–97; Hd, The Duchess's Community High Sch., Alnwick, 1997–2003. FCMI. *Recreations:* pianist, classical music, theatre, mountain sports, modern history. *Address:* Mill Hill County High School, Worcester Crescent, Mill Hill, NW7 4LL. *T:* (020) 8238 8184. *E:* geoffreyandsally@btinternet.com.

THOMPSON, Rt Rev. (Geoffrey) Hewlett; an Hon. Assistant Bishop, Diocese of Carlisle, since 1999; *b* 14 Aug. 1929; *o s* of late Lt-Col R. R. Thompson, MC, RAMC; *m* 1954, Elisabeth Joy Fausitt, MA (Oxon), *d* of late Col G. F. Taylor, MBE and Dr Frances Taylor; two *s* two *d*. *Educ:* Aldenham Sch.; Trinity Hall, Cambridge (MA); Cuddesdon Theol College. 2nd Lieut, Queen's Own Royal West Kent Regt, 1948–49 (Nat. Service). Ordained deacon, 1954, priest, 1955; Curate, St Matthew, Northampton, 1954–59; Vicar: St Augustine, Wisbech, 1959–66; St Saviour, Folkestone, 1966–74; Bishop Suffragan of Willesden, 1974–79, Area Bishop of Willesden, 1979–85; Bishop of Exeter, 1985–99. Chairman: Community and Race Relations Unit, BCC, 1980–84 (Vice-Chm., 1976–80); Hospital Chaplaincies Council, 1991–97. Introduced into House of Lords, 1990. *Recreations:* fell walking, reading, gardening, music. *Address:* Low Broomrigg, Warcop, Appleby, Cumbria CA16 6PT. *T:* (017683) 41281. *Club:* Oxford and Cambridge.

THOMPSON, Rev. George H.; Parish Priest, St Peter's, Dalbeattie, 1995–2004; *b* 11 Sept. 1928. *Educ:* Dalry Sch.; Kirkcudbright Acad.; Edinburgh Univ. Teacher, modern languages, Kirkcudbright Academy; Principal Teacher of French, 1979–85, Principal Teacher of Modern Languages, 1985–86, Annan Acad., Dumfriesshire. Contested (SNP): Galloway, Feb. 1974, 1979; Galloway and Upper Nithsdale, 1983. Former SNP Asst Nat. Sec.; MP (SNP) Galloway, Oct. 1974–1979; SNP Spokesman: on health, Oct. 1974–1979; on forestry, 1975. Deacon, RC dio. of Galloway, 1989, priest 1989; Asst Priest, St Teresa's, Dumfries, 1989–93; Administrator, St Margaret of Scotland's, Irvine, 1993–95. *Address:* 53 Kirkland Street, Dalry, Castle Douglas DG7 3UX. *T:* (01644) 430254.

THOMPSON, Glenn; *see* Thompson, J. McM. S. H. G.

THOMPSON, Rt Rev. Gregory Edwin; *see* Newcastle, NSW, Bishop of.

THOMPSON, (Henry) Antony Cardew W.; *see* Worrall Thompson.

THOMPSON, Rt Rev. Hewlett; *see* Thompson, Rt Rev. G. H.

THOMPSON, Howard; *see* Thompson, James H.

THOMPSON, (Hugh) Patrick; *b* 21 Oct. 1935; *s* of late Gerald Leopold Thompson and Kathleen Mary Lansdown Thompson; *m* 1962, Kathleen Howson. *Educ:* Felsted Sch., Essex; Emmanuel Coll., Cambridge (MA). Nat. Service, 2nd Lieut, KOYLI, 1957–59; TA, Manchester, 1960–65; Gresham's Sch., CCF, 1965–82 (CFM 1980); Major, retd. Engr, English Electric Valve Co., Chelmsford, 1959–60; Sixth Form Physics Master: Manchester Grammar Sch., 1960–65; Gresham's Sch., Holt, 1965–83. MP (C) Norwich North, 1983–97. Parliamentary Private Secretary: to Minister of State for Transport, 1987–88; to Minister of State, Dept of Social Security, 1988–89; to Minister for Health, 1992–94. Member: Parly and Scientific Cttee, 1983–97; Select Cttee, Educn, Science and the Arts, 1991–92; Select Cttee, Sci. and Technol., 1995–97; Speaker's Panel of Chairmen, 1994–97; Founder Mem., All Party Gp for Engrg Develt, 1985–97; Secretary: Cons. Back Bench Energy Cttee, 1986–87; Cons. Back Bench European Cttee, 1991–92. *Publications:* Elementary Calculations in Physics, 1963. *Recreations:* travel, music, gardening. *Club:* Norfolk (Norwich).

THOMPSON, Ian; Director, IKT Consulting Ltd, 2003–09; *b* 20 May 1951; *s* of Eber Edward Thompson and Edith (*née* Gilchrist); *m* 1st, 1972, Anne Rosalind Clouston (marr. diss. 1995); one *d*; 2nd, 1998, Karin Bell. *Educ:* Workington Grammar Sch.; Univ. of Hull (BSc); St Martin's Coll., Lancaster (PGCE). IPFA. VSO, Nigeria, 1973–74; with Humberside CC, 1974–80; Northamptonshire County Council, 1980–89: Chief Acct, 1986–88; Sen. Asst Educn Officer, 1988–89; Berkshire County Council: Sen. Asst Co. Treas., 1989–93; Co. Treas., 1993–96; Chief Finance and Property Officer, subseq. Dir of Finance and Property, then Dir of Resources, Swindon BC, 1997–2003. *Recreations:* playing guitar, playing squash, playing trains. *Address:* Snowberry House, Hinton Parva, Swindon SN4 0DW. *T:* (01793) 790970.

THOMPSON, Dr (Ian) McKim; Vice President, British Medical Association, since 1998; *b* 19 Aug. 1938; *s* of late J. W. Thompson and Dr E. M. Thompson; *m* 1962, Dr Veronica Jane Richards (marr. diss. 1988); two *s* one *d*. *Educ:* Epsom Coll.; Birmingham Univ. (MB, ChB 1961). Lectr in Pathology, Univ. of Birmingham, 1964–67; Sen. Registrar, Birmingham RHB, 1967–69; Sen. Under Sec., 1969–85, Dep. Sec., 1985–96, BMA. Consulting Forensic Pathologist to HM Coroner, City of Birmingham, 1966–97. Part time Tutor, Dept of Adult and Continuing Educn, Keele Univ., 1985–2009; Tutor, Wedgwood Meml Coll., Barlaston, 1990–2009. Member: GMC, 1979–94; Royal Medical Foundn, 1998–2009 (Life Gov., 2009); Pres., Birmingham Med. Inst., 2003–10 (Fellow, 2010); Chm., Retired Members Forum, BMA, 2009–11 (Dep. Chm., 2007–09). Hon. MO, Inland Waterways Assoc., 1976– (Richard Bird Medallist, 2008). President: Sands Cox Soc., Univ. of Birmingham, 2006–07 (Vice-Pres., 2005–06); Russell Newbery Register, 2011–; Dudley Canal Trust, 2014–. FRSocMed 1987. Hon. Collegian, Med. Colls of Spain, 1975. *Publications:* (ed) The Hospital Gazeteer, 1972; (ed) BMA Handbook for Hospital Junior Doctors, 1977, 5th edn 1990; (ed) BMA Handbook for Trainee Doctors in General Practice, 1982, 3rd edn 1985; various medical scientific papers. *Recreations:* inland waterways, rambling. *Address:* Canal Cottage, Hinksford Lane, Kingswinford DY6 0BH. *T:* (01384) 294131.

THOMPSON, Dame (Ila) Dianne, DBE 2015 (CBE 2006); Chief Executive, Camelot Group plc, 2000–14 (Commercial Director, 1997–2000); *b* 31 Dec. 1950; *d* of Ronald Wood and Joan Wood (*née* Pinder); *m* 1972, Roger Thompson (marr. diss. 1992); one *d*. *Educ:* Batley Girls' Grammar Sch.; Manchester Poly. (BA Hons ext. London). Product Manager, CWS, 1972–74; Mktg Manager, ICI, 1974–79; Lectr, Manchester Poly., 1979–86; Mktg Dir, Sterling Roncraft, 1986–88; Man. Dir, Sandvik Saws & Tools, 1988–92; Marketing Director: Woolworths plc, 1992–94; Signet Gp, 1994–97. Mem., Mktg Gp of GB, 1993. Mem., Press Complaints Commn, 2003–08. Chancellor, Manchester Metropolitan Univ., 2011–. Pres., Mkt Res. Soc., 2014–. FCIM 1988; Fellow, Mktg Soc., 1998; FRSA 2000; CCMI 2001. Veuve Cliquot Businesswoman of the Year, 2000; Marketer of the Year, Mktg Soc., 2001; Gold Medal, Chartered Mgt Inst., 2006. *Recreations:* theatre, cinema, entertaining, travel. *Address:* The George Hotel, Yarmouth, Isle of Wight PO41 0PE.

THOMPSON, (James) Howard, OBE 1984; Programme Manager, Schistosomiasis Control Initiative, Imperial College London, 2002–08; *b* 26 March 1942; *s* of James Alan Thompson and Edna (*née* Perkins); *m* 1965, Claire Marguerite Dockrell; one *s* one *d*. *Educ:* Northampton Grammar Sch.; Magdalene Coll., Cambridge (BA); Stanford Univ. (MA). English Language Officer, British Council, Yugoslavia, 1966–69; Associate Prof., Punjab Univ., 1970–73; Dep. Representative, British Council, Kenya, 1974–78; Advr, Schs and Further Educn Dept, 1978–80; Educn Attaché, British Embassy, Washington, 1980–84; Dep. Controller, 1984–87, Controller, 1987–89, Science, Technology and Educn Div., British Council; Chm., Educn and Trng Export Cttee, 1988–89; British Council Director: Indonesia, 1989–92; Egypt, 1993–96; Brazil, 1997–2002. Vice Chm., Govs, Bentworth Prim. Sch., Hammersmith, 2008–12; Volunteer, Prison Advice and Care Trust, 2009–. *Publications:* Teaching English, 1972. *Recreations:* photography, travel. *Address:* 1 Homefield Road, W4 2LN.

THOMPSON, Jan, OBE 2005; HM Diplomatic Service; Ambassador to the Czech Republic, since 2013; *b* Bexleyheath, 25 Aug. 1965; *d* of late Thomas Henry Thompson and of Jean Thompson. *Educ:* Durham Univ. (BA Hons French and German); Postgrad. Dip. Interpreting and Translating. BBC World Service, 1989–90; joined FCO, 1990; Desk Officer, El Salvador, Honduras and Costa Rica, Latin Amer. Dept, 1990–91; German Min. of For. Affairs (on secondment), 1991–92; Second Sec. (Pol), Bonn, 1992–94; Hd of Section, E Adriatic Dept, FCO, 1994–97; First Sec. (Security Council), UK Mission to UN, NY, 1997–2000; Dep. Hd, UN Dept, FCO, 2000–02; Hd, Afghanistan Dept, FCO, 2002–05; Hd, British Embassy Office, Phuket, 2005; Sen. FCO Rep. in Scotland for G8 Summit, FCO, 2005; Dir, Comprehensive Spending Review Prog., FCO, 2005–07; UK Lead Negotiator, Internat. Climate Negotiations, DECC (on secondment), 2007–10; Head: Strategic Defence and Security Rev. Team, FCO, 2010; Libya Unit, FCO, 2011; Proj. Leader, Future of FCO Climate Diplomacy, FCO, 2012; lang. trng, 2012–13. *Recreations:* theatre, travel. *Address:* c/o Foreign and Commonwealth Office, King Charles Street, SW1A 2AH.

THOMPSON, Janet, CB 2000; DPhil; Chief Executive, Forensic Science Service, 1988–2001; *b* 23 Oct. 1941; *d* of late Arthur Hugh Denison Fairbarns and Eleanor Mary Fairbarns (*née* Cattel); *m* 1999, Elliot Grant; one *s* one *d*, and one *s* from a former marriage. *Educ:* North London Collegiate Sch.; Brighton Coll. of Technol. (BSc 1963); Univ. of Oxford (DPhil 1968). CPhys, FInstP 1999. Chm., Science, Technol. and Mathematics Council, 1999–2001. Chm., European Network of Forensic Insts, 1997–99.

THOMPSON, Jeff; *see* Thompson, John J.

THOMPSON, Jeremy Gordon; Presenter, Live at Five, Sky News, since 1999; *b* 23 Sept. 1947; *s* of Gordon and Betty Thompson; *m* 1st, Nicky Wood (marr. diss. 1979); two *s*; 2nd, 1986, Lynn Bowland. *Educ:* Sevenoaks Prep. Sch.; Sevenoaks Sch.; King's Sch., Worcester. Reporter: Cambridge Evening News, 1967–71; BBC Radio Sheffield, 1971–74; BBC TV Look North, Leeds, 1974–77; N of England corresp., BBC TV News, 1977–82; ITN: Chief Sports Corresp., 1982–86; Asia Corresp., 1987–90; Africa Corresp., 1991–93; Sky News: Africa Corresp., 1993–95; USA Corresp., 1995–98; presenter, 1998–. Gold Award for Best Internat. Reporter, NY Fest., 1992; Emmy Awards, 1992 and 1994 for reporting in Africa; Presenter of the Yr, RTS, 2005. *Recreations:* travelling, safaris, walking, golf, watching sport. *Address:* c/o Sky News, British Sky Broadcasting, Grant Way, Isleworth, Middx TW7 5QD. *T:* 0870 240 3000. *E:* jeremy.thompson@bskyb.com. *Clubs:* Cricket Writers', Rugby Writers'; Surrey CC; Harlequins Rugby; Hampton Court Palace Golf; Los Arqueros Golf (Spain).

THOMPSON, John, MBE 1975; senior archival consultant, Foreign and Commonwealth Office; HM Diplomatic Service, retired; Ambassador to Angola, and St Thomas and Prince, 2002–05; *b* 28 May 1945; *s* of late Arthur Thompson and Josephine (*née* Brooke); *m* 1966, Barbara Hopper; one *d*. *Educ:* Whiteheath County Primary Sch., Ruislip, Middx; St Nicholas Grammar Sch., Northwood, Middx; Polytechnic of Central London (DMS 1975). Joined FO, 1964; Vice-Consul, Düsseldorf, 1966–69; Consular Officer, later Vice-Consul, Abu Dhabi, 1969–72; Vice-Consul, Phnom Penh, 1972–74; seconded to DTI, 1975–77; First Sec., FCO, 1977–79; First Sec., Hd of Chancery and Consul, Luanda, 1979–81; Consul (Commercial), São Paulo, 1981–85; Assistant Head: S Pacific Dept, FCO, 1985–87; Aid Policy Dept, FCO, 1987–88; High Comr to Vanuatu, 1988–92; Dep. Consul-Gen. and Dir of Trade, NY, 1992–97; Hd of Inf. Systems Dept and Library and Records Dept, FCO, 1997–99; Hd of Inf. Mgt Gp, FCO Services, FCO, 1999–2001. *Recreations:* philately, walking, reading, bridge.

THOMPSON, Sir John; *see* Thompson, Sir T. d'E. J.

THOMPSON, John Brian, CBE 1980; Director of Radio, Independent Broadcasting Authority, 1973–87; *b* 8 June 1928; *y s* of late John and Lilian Thompson; *m* 1957, Sylvia, *d* of late Thomas Waterhouse, CBE, and of Doris Waterhouse (*née* Gough); two *s* one *d*. *Educ:* St Paul's; Pembroke College, Oxford (BA; MA). Eileen Power Studentship, LSE, 1950; Glaxo Laboratories Ltd, 1950–54; Masius & Fergusson Ltd, 1955; Asst Editor, Truth, 1956–57; Daily Express, 1957–59 (New York Correspondent; Drama Critic); ITN, 1959–60 (Newscaster/Reporter); Editor, Time and Tide, 1960–62; News Editor, The Observer, 1962–66; Editor, Observer Colour Magazine, 1966–70; Publisher and Editorial Dir, BPC Publishing Ltd, 1971; Editor, The Viewer, 1988–90. Vis. Prof., Sch. of Media, Lancashire Poly., 1987–90. Sen. Advr on Radio to Minister of Posts and Telecommunications, 1972; Mem., MoD Study Group on Censorship, 1983. Director: Worlds End Productions Ltd, 1987–91; The Observer, 1989–93; Dep. Chm., Zabaxe Gp, 1988–90. Vice-Chm. (radio), EBU, 1986–88. Mem. Delegacy, Goldsmiths' Coll., London, 1986–96. Associate Mem., Nuffield Coll., Oxford, 1988–90. Judge, Booker Fiction Prize, 1987; Panel of Selection Bd Chairmen, CS Commn/RAS, 1988–93. Sony Radio special award, 1983. *Address:* 1 Bedwyn Common, Great Bedwyn, Marlborough, Wilts SN8 3HZ. *T:* (01672) 870641. *Clubs:* Garrick, Groucho.
See also B. D. W. Thompson.

THOMPSON, Prof. John Griggs, PhD; FRS 1979; Rouse Ball Professor of Mathematics, University of Cambridge, 1971–93, now Professor Emeritus; Fellow of Churchill College, Cambridge, since 1968; Graduate Research Professor, Department of Mathematics, University of Florida, since 1983; *b* Kansas, 13 Oct. 1932; *s* of John and Eleanor Thompson; *m* 1960, Diane Oenning (*d* 2013); one *s* one *d*. *Educ:* Yale (BA 1955); Chicago (PhD 1959); MA Cantab 1972. Prof. of Mathematics, Chicago Univ., 1962–68; Vis. Prof. of Mathematics, Cambridge Univ., 1968–70. Hon. DSc Oxon, 1987. Cole Prize, 1966; Field Medal, 1970; Berwick Prize, London Math. Soc., 1982; Sylvester Medal, Royal Soc., 1985; Wolf Prize, 1992; Poincaré Medal, 1992; (jtly) Abel Prize, Norwegian Acad. of Sci. and Letters, 2008. *Address:* 16 Millington Road, Cambridge CB3 9HP.

THOMPSON, John Handby, CB 1988; CVO 1994; Ceremonial Officer, Cabinet Office, and Secretary, Political Honours Scrutiny Committee, 1988–94; *b* 21 Feb. 1929; *s* of late Rev. John Thomas Thompson and Clara Handby; *m* 1st, 1957, Catherine Rose Heald (*d* 2014); two *s* one *d*; 2nd, 2015, Petra Laidlaw. *Educ:* Silcoates Sch., Wakefield; St John's Coll., Oxford (MA); Sheffield Univ. (PhD 1991). Served Intell. Corps, 1947–49. HM Inspector of Taxes, 1953–63; Dept of Educn and Science, 1964–88: Schs Council, 1971–73; Asst Sec., 1973; Mem., Prep. Cttee of European Univ. Inst., 1973–75; Dep. Accountant-Gen., 1976–78; Under Sec., 1978; Head of Schs Br. 1, 1978–80; Head of Further and Higher Educn Br. 1, 1980–84; Dir of Estabts and Orgn, 1985–88. Gov., Univ. (formerly Poly.) of N London, 1989–98 (Hon. Fellow, 1999). Pres., Chapels Soc., 1998–2001. Chm., Friends of the Congregational Library, 2001–06; Trustee: Congregational Meml Hall Trust, 2003–14; Lord Wharton's Charity, 2005–13. *Publications:* A History of the Coward Trust 1738–1988, 1998; Highgate Dissenters: their history since 1660, 2001; (contrib.) Modern Christianity and Cultural Aspirations, 2003; (contrib.) Who They Were in the Reformed Churches of England and Wales 1901–2000, 2007; The Free Church Army Chaplain 1830–1930, 2012; (contrib.) The Clergy in Khaki, 2013; (contrib.) Protestant Nonconformity and Christian Missions, 2014. *Recreations:* reading about Albania, Nonconformist history. *Address:* 2 Alwyne Villas, N1 2HQ. *Club:* Reform.

THOMPSON, Air Marshal John Hugh, CB 2000; FRAeS; farmer, Lincolnshire, 2006–14; *b* 18 Sept. 1947; *m* 1969, Mary Elizabeth Emerson; two *s* one *d*. *Educ:* Fielding High Sch., NZ; RAF Coll., Cranwell. Hunter pilot, Bahrain, 1970–71; Harrier pilot, weapons instructor and Sqdn Comdr; Army Staff Coll., 1982; Station Comdr, Wittering, 1988–90; RCDS, 1991; Higher Comd and Staff Course, 1992; SASO, Rheindahlen, 1993–96; Office of the High Rep., Sarajevo, 1996; AOC and Comdt, RAF Coll., Cranwell, 1997–98; AOC No 1 Gp, 1998–2000; Defence Attaché and Head of British Defence Staff, Washington, 2000–02; Dir Gen., Saudi Armed Forces Project, 2002–06. FRAeS 2007. *Recreations:* golf, reading. *Club:* Royal Air Force.

THOMPSON, Prof. John Jeffrey, (Jeff), CBE 1989; PhD; CChem, FRSC; Professor of Education, 1979–2005, and Director, Centre for the Study of Education in an International Context, 1992–2005, University of Bath, now Professor Emeritus; *b* 13 July 1938; *s* of late John Thompson and Elsie May Thompson (*née* Wright); *m* 1963, Kathleen Audrey Gough; three *d*. *Educ:* King George V Sch., Southport; St John's Coll., Cambridge (MA); Balliol Coll., Oxford (MA); PhD (CNAA); DipEd (Oxon). Asst Master, Blundell's Sch., 1961–65; Head of Chemistry, Watford Grammar Sch., 1965–69; Lectr in Educn, KCL, 1968–69; Shell Fellow, UCL, 1969–70; Lectr and Tutor, Dept of Educnl Studies, Oxford Univ., 1970–79; Lectr in Chemistry, Keble Coll., Oxford, 1970–76; Pro-Vice-Chancellor, Univ. of Bath, 1986–89. Chief Examr, Internat. Baccalaureate, 1970–89 (Chm., Bd of Chief Examnrs, 1985–89); International Baccalaureate Organisation: Chm. Res. Cttee, 1998–2004; Dir for Internat. Educn, 2000–02; Academic Dir, 2003–04; Hd of Res. Unit, 2000–05; Chm., Examination Appeals Bd, 2003–13 (Dep. Chm., 1999–2003). Chairman: Assoc. for Science Educn, 1981; Nat. Curriculum Science Working Gp, 1987–88; Adv. Bd, Total Science Solutions, 2003–05; Chair: Alliance for Internat. Educn, 2001–09, 2011–; Curriculum Adv. Bd, Internat. Primary Curriculum and Internat. Middle Years Curriculum, 2002–; Adv. Bd, Internat. Teacher Educn for Primary Schs, 2013–. Mem., Council, 1988–92, Dep. Chm., 1989–92, School Exams and Assessment Council; Member: Nat. Commn on Educn, 1991–93; English Nat. Bd for Nursing, Midwifery and Health Visiting, 1993–2002. Pres., Educn Div., Royal Soc. of Chemistry, 1983–85; Dep. Chm., Educn Cttee, Royal Soc., 1995–98; British Association for the Advancement of Science: Vice Pres., 1996–2001; Vice Pres. and Gen. Sec., 1985–91; Chm. Council, 1991–96. Dir, Internat. Bd, United World Colls, 2005–11; Gov. and Mem. Council, United World Coll. of the Atlantic, 1992–2009; Governor: UWC Mostar, 2005–10; UWC Council of Admin, UWC Duino, Italy, 2009–; Chm., Bd of Govs, Oaktree Internat. Sch., Kolkata. Hon. Mem., ASE, 1994; Hon. Fellow, British Sci. Assoc. (Hon. Fellow, BAAS, 2006). Mem. Council, Wildfowl Trust, 1981–91. FRSA 1983. Freeman, 1992, Liveryman, 1995, Goldsmiths' Co., 1992; Freeman, City of London, 1992. Gen. Editor, Bath Science series, age gps 16–19 (12 titles), and 5–16 (78 titles), 1990–2000; Ed.-in-Chief, Jl for Res. in Internat. Educn, 2002–06; Co-Ed., Internat. Sch. mag., 2014–. Hon DLitt Hertfordshire, 2000; Hon. EdD Bath, 2014. Distinguished Service Award: Internat. Schs Assoc., 2005; Eur. Council for Internat. Schs, 2005. *Publications:* Introduction to Chemical Energetics, 1967; European Curriculum Studies; Chemistry, 1972; (ed) Practical Work in Sixth Form Science, 1976; Foundation Course in Chemistry, 1982; Modern Physical Chemistry, 1982; (ed)

Dimensions of Science (9 titles), 1986; The Chemistry Dimension, 1987; International Education: Principles and Practice, 1998; (ed) International Schools and International Education, 2000; (ed) International Education in Practice, 2002; (ed) A Handbook of Research in International Education, 2006, 2nd edn 2015; (jtly) International Schools: growth and influence, 2008; (ed) Taking the MYP Forward, 2011; (ed) Taking the DP Forward, 2011; (ed) Forward with the IPC, 2012; (ed) Taking the IB Continuum Forward, 2013; contrib. articles to res. jls and chapters in books on internat. educn. *Recreations:* music (brass bands and blue grass), North Country art, collecting sugar wrappers. *Address:* University of Bath, Claverton Down, Bath BA2 7AY.

THOMPSON, (John McMaster Samuel Hugh) Glenn, CB 2001; Business Consultant, g thompson consulting, since 2001; *b* 11 Nov. 1949; *s* of Hugh Glenn Thompson and Sarah (*née* McMaster); *m* 1971, Elizabeth McClements; two *d. Educ:* Regent House Grammar Sch., Newtownards. Clerk to Principal, NICS, 1967–86; Asst Sec., Industrial Develt Bd for NI, 1986–89; Regl Manager, 1989–92, Exec. Dir, 1992–96, Crestacare plc; Under-Sec., Civil Service, 1996–2001. *Recreations:* travel, Rugby Union.

THOMPSON, John Michael Anthony, FMA; museums and heritage consultant, since 1991; Associate Director, Barker Langham, 2007–12; *b* 3 Feb. 1941; *s* of George Thompson and Joan Smith; *m* 1965, Alison Sara Bowers; two *d. Educ:* William Hulme's Grammar Sch., Manchester; Univ. of Manchester. BA, MA; FMA 1980. Research Asst, Whitworth Art Gall., 1964–66; Keeper, Rutherston Collection, City Art Gall., Manchester, 1966–68; Director: North Western Museum and Art Gall. Service, 1968–70; Arts and Museums, Bradford City Council, 1970–74; Chief Arts and Museums Officer, Bradford Metropolitan Council, 1974–75; Dir, Art Galls and Museums, Tyne and Wear County Museums, 1975–91. Sen. Consultant, Prince Research Consultants Ltd, 1995–2007. Museums Association: Councillor, 1977–80, 1984–87 (Chm., Accreditation Cttee, 1978–80); Mentor and Reviewer, 1995–; Advisor to Arts and Recreation Cttee, AMA, 1981–91; Pres., Museums North, 1977, and 1991–92; Chm., Soc. of County Museum Dirs, 1982–86; Founder Mem. and Hon. Sec., Gp of Dirs of Museums in the British Isles, 1985–91. Dir, Museums and Galleries Consultancy Ltd, 1992–95; Mem. Bd, Jarrow 700 AD Ltd, 1992–2006. External Verifier: Museum Trng Inst., 1996–99; Qualifications for Industry, 1999–2006. Advr to UNESCO, 2001–06; Educn and Access Advr to Heritage Lottery Fund, 2005–. Chairman: Gosforth Adult Educn Assoc., 1994–2006; Friends of Shipley Art Gall., Gateshead, 2009–14. Vice Chm. Governors, Gosforth High Sch., 1997–99. Mem. Council, Tyne and Wear Building Preservation Trust, 2008– (Vice Chm., 2013–). Attender, Newcastle Local Meeting, Soc. of Friends, 2009–. *Publications:* (ed) The Manual of Curatorship: a guide to museum practice, 1984, 2nd edn 1993; Contracting Culture: museums and local government, 1994; articles in Museums Jl, Penrose Annual, Connoisseur, Printmaking Today, Quaker Voices. *Recreations:* classical guitar, running, walking. *Address:* 21 Linden Road, Gosforth, Newcastle upon Tyne NE3 4EY. *T:* and *Fax:* (0191) 284 2797.

THOMPSON, Prof. (John) Michael (Tutill), FRS 1985; Professor of Nonlinear Dynamics, Department of Civil and Environmental Engineering, and Director, Centre for Nonlinear Dynamics and Its Applications, University College London, 1991–2002, now Emeritus Professor; a Sixth Century Professor in Theoretical and Applied Dynamics (part-time), University of Aberdeen, since 2006; Chairman, ES-Consult (Consulting Engineers), Copenhagen, since 1995; *b* 7 June 1937; *s* of John Hornsey Thompson and Kathleen Rita Thompson (*née* Tutill); *m* 1959, Margaret Cecilia Chapman; one *s* one *d. Educ:* Hull Grammar Sch.; Clare Coll., Cambridge (MA, PhD, ScD). FIMA; CMath. Research Fellow, Peterhouse, 1961–64; Vis. Res. Associate, Stanford (Fulbright grant), 1962–63; Lectr, 1964–68, Reader, 1968–77, Prof. of Structural Mechanics, 1977–91, UCL; Chm., Bd of Studies in Civil and Mech. Eng., Univ. of London, 1984–86. Vis. Prof., Faculté des Sciences, Univ. Libre de Bruxelles, 1976–78; Vis. Mathematician, Brookhaven Nat. Lab., 1984; Vis. Res. Fellow, Centre for Nonlinear Studies, Univ. of Leeds, 1987–97; Sen. Fellow, SERC, 1988–93; Hon. Fellow, Dept of Applied Maths and Theoretical Physics, Univ. of Cambridge, 2003–. Hon. Prof., Aberdeen Univ., 2004 (R. V. Jones Lectr, 2011). Organizer and Editor, IUTAM Symposium: on Collapse: the buckling of structures in theory and practice, 1982; on non-linearity and chaos in engrg dynamics, 1993; Ed., Phil. Trans Royal Soc., Series A, 1998–2007 (Actg Ed., 1990; Ed. and Organizer, first Theme Issue, 1990 and three Millennium Issues, 2000; Mem. Editl Bd, 2008–10); Chm. and Exec. Ed., Royal Soc. Trailblazing Project, 2008–10; sci. contribs to radio and TV, 1975–; Member Council: IMA, 1989–92 (Organizer, Conf. on Chaos, UCL, 1990); Royal Soc., 2002–03. MAE 2010. Hon. Mem., Hungarian Acad. Scis, 2010. Hon. DSc Aberdeen, 2004. Cambridge University Prizes: Rex Moir, 1957; Archibald Denny, 1958; John Winbolt, 1960; OMAE Award, 1985, Lyapunov Award, 2013, ASME; James Alfred Ewing Medal, ICE, 1992; Gold Medal for Mathematics, IMA, 2004. *Publications:* (with G. W. Hunt) A general theory of elastic stability, 1973; Instabilities and catastrophes in science and engineering, 1982; (with G. W. Hunt) Elastic instability phenomena, 1984; (with H. B. Stewart) Nonlinear dynamics and chaos, 1986, 2nd edn 2002; (ed) Localisation and solitary waves in solid mechanics, 1999; Visions of the Future, vol. I, Astronomy and Earth Science, vol. II, Physics and Electronics, vol. III, Chemistry and Life Science, 2001; (ed) Advances in Astronomy: from big bang to the solar system, 2005; (ed) Advances in Earth Science: from earthquakes to global warming, 2007; Advances in Nanoengineering: electronics, materials and assembly, 2007; (ed with B. E. Launder) Geo-Engineering Climate Change: environmental necessity or Pandora's Box?, 2010; 200 articles in learned jls (and mem., editl bds). *Recreations:* walking, wildlife photography, badminton, tennis, astronomy with grandchildren. *Address:* 33 West Hill Road, Foxton, Cambs CB22 6SZ. *T:* (01223) 704354.

THOMPSON, Jonathan Michael; Permanent Secretary, Ministry of Defence, since 2012; *b* 29 Dec. 1964; *s* of John and Jenny Thompson; *m* 1987, Dawn Warnes; three *s. Educ:* Earlham High Sch.; Norwich City Coll.; Suffolk Coll.; Anglia Poly. CIPFA 1989; CIMA 2014. Audit and accountancy posts, Norfolk CC, 1983–91; Superintendent, Eagle Star Gp, 1991–93; Manager, 1993–95, Sen. Manager, 1995–97, Ernst & Young; North Somerset Council: Finance Strategy Advr, 1997–2001; Hd, Corporate Finance, 2001–02; Dir, Finance and Resources, 2002–04; Dir of Finance, Ofsted, 2004–06; Dir Gen., Finance, DfES, May–July 2006; Dir Gen., Corporate Services, DfES, later DCSF, 2006–09; Hd, Govt Finance Profession, HM Treasury, 2008–11; Dir Gen. Finance, MoD, 2009–12. *Recreations:* Church, community activities, movies, reading, cooking, wood-turning. *Address:* Ministry of Defence, Main Building, Whitehall, SW1A 2HB.

THOMPSON, Maj.-Gen. Julian Howard Atherden, CB 1982; OBE 1978; Visiting Professor, Department of War Studies, King's College London, since 1997; *b* 7 Oct. 1934; *s* of late Major A. J. Thompson, DSO, MC and Mary Stearns Thompson (*née* Krause); *m* 1960, Janet Avery, *d* of late Richard Robinson Rodd; one *s* one *d. Educ:* Sherborne School. 2nd Lieut RM, 1952; served 40, 42, 43, 45 Commandos RM, 1954–69; Asst Sec., Chiefs of Staff Cttee, 1970–71; BM, 3 Cdo Brigade, 1972–73; Directing Staff, Staff Coll., Camberley, 1974–75; CO 40 Cdo RM, 1975–78; Comdr 3 Cdo Brigade, 1981–83, incl. Falklands campaign (CB); Maj.-Gen. Comdg Trng Reserve Forces and Special Forces RM, 1983–86, retired. Sen. Res. Fellow in Logistics and Armed Conflict in the Modern Age, KCL, 1987–97. Chm., Idarat Maritime Ltd, 2010–. Life Vice-Pres., British Assoc. for Physical Training, 1998 (Pres., 1988–98). *Publications:* No Picnic: 3 Commando Brigade in the South Atlantic 1982, 1985; Ready for Anything: The Parachute Regiment at War 1940–1982, 1989; (contrib.) Military Strategy in a Changing Europe, 1991; (contrib.) Fallen Stars, 1991; The Lifeblood of War, 1991; (contrib.) The Observer at 200, 1992; The Imperial War Museum Book of Victory in Europe: North West Europe 1944–45, 1994; The Imperial War Museum Book of the War at Sea: the Royal Navy in the Second World War, 1996; (contrib.) Leadership and Command, 1997; The Imperial War Museum Book of War Behind Enemy Lines, 1998; (contrib.) Dimensions of Sea Power, 1998; The Royal Marines: from Sea Soldiers to a Special Force, 2000; (contrib.) Lightning Strikes Twice: the Great World War 1914–1945, 2000; (ed) The Imperial War Museum Book of Modern Warfare, 2002; The Imperial War Museum Book of the War in Burma 1942–1945, 2002; The Imperial War Museum Book of the War at Sea: 1914–1918, 2004; The Victory in Europe Experience, 2004; The 1916 Experience: Verdun and the Somme, 2006; (contrib.) Amphibious Assault: manoeuvre from the sea, 2007; Masters of the Battlefield, 2007; Dunkirk: retreat to victory, 2008; Call to Arms: great military speeches, 2009; Forgotten Voices of Burma, 2009; Forgotten Voices Desert Victory, 2011; The Second World War in 100 Objects, 2012; Gallipoli, 2015. *Recreations:* sailing, shooting, history, cross-country ski-ing, ballet, opera, jazz. *Address:* c/o Lloyds Bank, Royal Parade, Plymouth, Devon PL1 1HB. *Clubs:* Army and Navy; Royal Marines Sailing.

THOMPSON, Julian O.; *see* Ogilvie Thompson.

THOMPSON, Keith Bruce; Vice-Chancellor, Staffordshire University, 1992–95, now Emeritus; *b* 13 Sept. 1932; *m* 1956, Kathleen Reeves; one *s* one *d. Educ:* Bishopshalt School, Hillingdon; New College, Oxford (Sec./Librarian, Oxford Union). PPE 1955, Dip Educn (distn), 1956, MA 1959; MEd Bristol, 1968. Schoolmaster, City of Bath Boys' School, 1956–62; Lectr, Newton Park Coll., Bath, 1962–67; Head of Dept, Philippa Fawcett Coll., Streatham, 1967–72; Principal, Madeley Coll. of Educn, 1972–78; Dep. Dir, 1978–86, Dir, 1987–92, N Staffs, later Staffs Poly. Chairman: Standing Conf. on Studies in Educn, 1980–82; Undergraduate Initial Training Bd (Educn), CNAA, 1981–85; Polytechnics Central Admissions System, 1989–93; Dep. Chm., UCAS, 1993–95; Mem. Bd, Nat. Adv. Body for Public Sector Higher Educn, 1983–88 (Chm., Teacher Educn Gp, 1983–85). Sec., British Philos. of Sport Assoc., 2002–05. Editor, Educn for Teaching, 1968–74. *Publications:* Education and Philosophy, 1972; (jtly) Curriculum Development, 1974; articles on educn, philosophy, physical educn, sport. *Recreations:* sport, music, books. *Address:* 3 Swindon Manor, Swindon Village, Cheltenham GL51 9TP. *T:* (01242) 698554.

See also B. K. Thompson.

THOMPSON, McKim; *see* Thompson, I. McK.

THOMPSON, Marjorie Ellis; Senior Adviser, Media and Major Gifts, Mental Health Foundation, since 2014; Director, C_3I (Campaigns, Communications, Cause-related marketing and Imagination), since 2002; *b* St Louis, Mo, 8 June 1957; *d* of John William Thompson, III and Janet Ann (*née* Neubeiser). *Educ:* Woodrow Wilson High Sch., Long Beach, California; Colorado Coll., Colorado Springs (BSc Hons 1978); LSE (MSc Econ 1979). Parly Officer, 1983–87, Vice Chm., 1987–90, Chm., 1990–93, Campaign for Nuclear Disarmament; Researcher for Ann Clwyd, MP, 1987; Royal College of Nursing, 1988–93; Dir, Communications and Res., CRE, 1993–97; Dir, Cause Connection, Saatchi & Saatchi, 1997–2001; Dir, Cause Related Marketing, Octagon Marketing, 2001–02. Associate, Brands & Values, Bremen, 2008–13. Chair, 2009–10, Exec. Mem., 2010–, Cons. Cooperative Movt; Exec. Mem., Camberwell and Peckham Cons. Party, 2007– (Dep. Chm., 2014–). Fellow: British-American Project, 1990–2012; Davos World Econ. Forum, 2000. Trustee: S London Maudsley Charitable Trust, 2006–07; Stand to Reason, 2008–10; Project Pressure, 2010–; Why Me?, 2011–. *Publications:* (contrib.) Nursing: the hidden agenda, 1993; (with Hamish Pringle) Brand Spirit: how cause-related marketing builds brands, 1999; (with Christian Conrad) The New Brand Spirit: how communicating sustainability builds brands, reputations and profits, 2013; contrib. Market Leader, and Spectator and Guardian blogs. *Recreations:* watching Wales play Rugby, African safaris, entertaining, reading, historic homes, convertibles, beaches.

THOMPSON, Mark; *see* Thompson, O. M.

THOMPSON, Mark John Thompson; President and Chief Executive, The New York Times Company, since 2012; *b* 31 July 1957; *s* of late Duncan John Thompson and Sydney Columba Corduff; *m* 1987, Jane Emilie Blumberg; two *s* one *d. Educ:* Stonyhurst Coll.; Merton Coll., Oxford (BA; Violet Vaughan Morgan English Prize; MA; Hon. Fellow, 2006). BBC Television: Research Asst Trainee, 1979–80; Asst Producer, Nationwide, 1980–82; Producer, Breakfast Time, 1982–84; Output Editor: London Plus, 1984–85; Newsnight, 1985–87; Editor: Nine O'Clock News, 1988–90; Panorama, 1990–92; Head of Features, 1992–94; Head of Factual Progs, 1994–96; Controller, BBC2, 1996–98; Dir of Nat. and Regl Broadcasting, 1998–2000; Dir of Television, 2000–01; Chief Exec., Channel Four, 2002–04; Dir Gen., BBC, 2004–12. Chm., Edinburgh Internat. TV Fest., 1996. Vis. Fellow, Nuffield Coll., Oxford, 2005. FRTS 1998; FRSA 2000. *Recreations:* walking, cooking. *Address:* The New York Times Company, 620 Eighth Avenue, New York, NY 10018, USA. *Club:* Reform.

THOMPSON, Michael, FRAM; Professor of Horn, Royal Academy of Music, since 1985; Principal Horn, London Sinfonietta, since 1986; *b* 4 Jan. 1954; *s* of Ronald and Joan Thompson; *m* 1975, Valerie Botwright; two *s* one *d. Educ:* Royal Acad. of Music. FRAM 1988. Principal Horn: BBC Scottish SO, 1972–75; Philharmonia Orch., 1975–85; internat. soloist and recording artist, 1985–. *Publications:* Warm-up Exercises, 1986; Schumann, Konzertstück: performing edition, 1988; Cadenzas for Haydn and Mozart Horn Concerti, 1990. *Recreations:* reading, walking, cooking. *Address:* 26 Presburg Road, New Malden, Surrey KT3 5AH. *T:* (020) 8241 8585.

THOMPSON, Michael; *see* Thompson, J. M. T.

THOMPSON, Michael Harry Rex, OBE 1992; FCIB; Director: Wellington Underwriting plc, 1996–2001; Wellington Underwriting Agencies Ltd, 1995–2001; Deputy Chairman, Lloyds Bank Plc, 1991–95 (Director, 1986–95); *b* 14 Jan. 1931; *s* of late William Henry Thompson and Beatrice Hylda Thompson (*née* Heard); *m* 1958, Joyce (*née* Redpath); one *s* one *d. Educ:* St John's Sch., Leatherhead, Surrey. Joined Lloyds Bank, 1948; Dep. Chief Exec., 1987–91; Director: National Bank of New Zealand, 1978–82, 1991–95. Financial Advr to Dean and Chapter, 1995–2001, Lay Canon, 1996–2001, Salisbury Cathedral. Trustee, Bankers Club, 1995–2001. *Recreation:* Rugby football.

THOMPSON, Michael Jacques, CMG 1989; OBE 1977; HM Diplomatic Service, retired; *b* 31 Jan. 1936; *s* of late Christopher Thompson and of Colette Jeanne-Marie Thompson; *m* 1967, Mary Susan (*née* Everard); one *s* one *d. Educ:* Uppingham; Christ's Coll., Cambridge (Law Tripos, 1956–60; MA). National Service, Kenya, Aden and Cyprus, 1954–56. HMOCS, Kenya, 1960–63; FCO, 1964; served Kuala Lumpur, Saigon, Lusaka and FCO, 1965–79; Counsellor, Kuala Lumpur, 1979–82; seconded to Comdr, British Land Forces, Hong Kong, 1982–85; Counsellor, FCO, 1985. Mem., Royal Asia Soc. Mem., Co. of Barbers. *Recreations:* tennis, golf, gardening. *Clubs:* Oxford and Cambridge; Huntercombe Golf.

THOMPSON, Sir Michael (Warwick), Kt 1991; DSc; FInstP; Deputy Chairman, Alliance & Leicester PLC, 1997–2000; Vice-Chancellor and Principal, University of Birmingham, 1987–96, Emeritus Professor, since 1996; *b* 1 June 1931; *s* of Kelvin Warwick Thompson and Madeleine Thompson; *m* 1st, Sybil (*née* Spooner) (*d* 1999); two *s*; 2nd, 2000, Jennifer (*née* Mitchell). *Educ:* Rydal Sch.; Univ. of Liverpool (BSc, DSc). Research scientist, AERE, Harwell, 1953–65; Sussex University: Prof. of Experimental Physics, 1965–80; Pro-Vice-Chancellor, 1973–77, actg Vice-Chancellor, 1976; Vis. Prof., 1980–86; Vice-Chancellor, UEA, 1980–86. Chairman: Physics Cttee, SRC, 1975–79; British Council Cttee for

Academic Res. Collaboration with Germany, 1989–2000; Review of ISIS Neutron Source for Central Lab. of Res. Councils, 1997–98. Member: E Sussex Educn Cttee, 1973–78; E Sussex AHA, 1974–79; non-exec. Dir, W Midlands RHA, 1987–96; Chm., Review of London SHAs, 1993. Member: Council, Birmingham Chamber of Industry and Commerce, 1987–96; Council, CNAA, 1989–91; Council for Internat. Co-operation in Higher Educn, 1989–91; Council, CVCP, 1990–93, 1994–96 (Chm. Med. Cttee, 1994–96); Council for Industry and Higher Educn, 1991–96; Council, ACU, 1991–95; Standing Gp of Depts of Health and Educn on Undergrad. Med. and Dental Educn and Res., 1994–96. Director: Alliance & Leicester PLC (formerly Alliance Bldg Soc., then Alliance & Leicester Bldg Soc.), 1979–2000; Cobuild Ltd, 1987–96. Member Council: Eastbourne Coll., 1977–2000; QMW, 1996–2000 (Chm., Med. Sub-Cttee, 1996–2000). Trustee: Barber Inst. of Fine Arts, 1987–2007; St Bartholomew's Hosp. Med. Coll., 1998–2000. Mem., Birmingham Lunar Soc., 1991–96. President: Bodmin DFAS, 2000–11; Fowey River Assoc., 2001–07; Chm., Fowey Harbour Comrs Consultation Gp, 2010–13. Hon. Fellow, Univ. of Sussex, 2012. Hon. LLD Birmingham, 1997; Hon. DSc Sussex, 1998. Oliver Lodge Prizewinner, Univ. of Liverpool, 1953; Prizewinner, Materials Science Club, 1970; C. V. Boys Prizewinner, Inst. of Physics, 1972. Officer's Cross, Order of Merit (Germany), 1997. *Publications:* Defects and Radiation Damage in Metals, 1969; (jtly) Channelling, 1973; over 100 papers in sci. jls. *Recreations:* the arts, walking, sailing, fly fishing. *Address:* Readymoney Cottage, 3 Tower Park, Fowey, Cornwall PL23 1JD. *Clubs:* Athenæum; Royal Fowey Yacht.

See also P. Warwick Thompson.

THOMPSON, Nathan James; Chief Executive and Clerk of the Council, Duchy of Lancaster, since 2013; *b* Colwyn Bay, 15 June 1964; *s* of John Baragwanath Thompson and Helen Mary Saunders; *m* 1993, Lara; three *c. Educ:* Stonyhurst Coll.; Sheffield Hallam Univ. (BSc Urban Land Econs). MEPC plc, 1986–2000; JER Partners, 2000–04; Forth Ports plc, 2004–11, Man. Dir, Property Div., 2006–11. Trustee, Duke of Lancaster Housing Trust, 2013–. Mem., Assoc. of Lancastrians, 2013–. *Recreations:* family, sailing, golf, tennis. *Address:* Duchy of Lancaster, 1 Lancaster Place, Strand, WC2E 7ED. *T:* (020) 7269 1700, *Fax:* (020) 7269 1710. *E:* nthompson@duchyoflancaster.co.uk.

THOMPSON, Neil; *see* Thompson, R. N.

THOMPSON, Nicholas, RIBA; theatre architect in private practice; Director, 1974–2005, Leader, Arts Team, 1998–2005, Consultant, 2005–07, Renton Howard Wood Levin LLP; *b* 25 Feb. 1936; *s* of Eric Thompson and Dorothy (*née* Lake); *m* 1966, Clare Ferraby; two *s. Educ:* Christ's Hosp., Horsham; Oxford Sch. of Architecture (DipArch). RIBA 1961. Specialist in building design for performing arts, including: Crucible Th., Sheffield, 1971; Univ. of Warwick Arts Centre, 1973; Th. Royal and Royal Concert Hall, Nottingham, 1978–82; Old Vic, 1984; Alhambra, Bradford, 1986; Th. Royal, Newcastle, 1988; Lyceum Th., Sheffield, 1990; New Victoria Th., Woking, 1992; Donmar Warehouse, 1992; Anvil Concert Hall, Basingstoke, 1994; Bridgewater Concert Hall, Manchester, 1996; Sadler's Wells Th., 1998; masterplan and boarding houses for Christ's Hosp. Sch., 1998–2001; renovation of London Coliseum for ENO, 1999–2004; Dome Concert Hall and Mus., Brighton, 2002; theatre renovations for Sir Cameron Mackintosh, incl. Prince Edward Th., 1993 and 2004, Prince of Wales Th., 2004; refurbishment of Wigmore Hall, 2004; Wells Cathedral Sch., 2006–; *overseas projects* include: Concert Hall and Acad. of Music for Sultan of Oman, 1992; National Th., Damascus, 1993; Musik Th., Stuttgart, 1995; Musik Th., Duisburg, 1996; design consultant, Lazaristes Th. and Art Gall., Thessalonika, 1996; consultant: Athens Opera House, 1997–2004; Gennadius Lecture Th., American Sch. of Classical Studies, Athens, 2000; Montecasino Th., Johannesburg, 2005–07; (in association with Daniel Libeskind) interior architect, Grand Canal Th., Dublin, 2010. Dir, Paxos Fest. Trust, 1998–. FRSA 1999. Goodwin & Wimperis Silver Medal, RIBA, 1964. *Publications:* articles in architectural press and lectures. *Recreations:* outdoors and active by day (travel, sailing, painting, making gardens), watching performances by night, collecting modern art. *Address:* 22 Lichfield Road, Richmond, Surrey TW9 3JR. *T:* and *Fax:* (020) 8948 0645. *E:* thomferr60@gmail.com. *Club:* Garrick.

THOMPSON, Sir Nicholas (Annesley Marler), 2nd Bt *cr* 1963, of Reculver, co. Kent; solicitor with CMS Cameron McKenna LLP (formerly Cameron McKenna), 1997–2008; *b* 19 March 1947; *s* of Sir Richard Hilton Marler Thompson, 1st Bt and of Anne Christabel de Vere Marler Thompson (*née* Annesley); *S* father, 1999; *m* 1982, Venetia Catherine, *yr d* of Mr and Mrs John Heathcote; three *s* one *d. Educ:* King's Sch., Canterbury; Univ. of Kent at Canterbury (BA Law 1969). Admitted a solicitor, 1973. Mem. (C) Westminster City Council, 1978–86; Dep. Lord Mayor of Westminster, 1983–84. Contested (C) Newham South, 1983. Mem. Exec. Cttee, Standing Council of the Baronetage, 2003–12, 2014–. *Recreations:* foreign travel, cycling, walking, theatre, reading, visiting historic houses and museums. *Heir: s* Simon William Thompson, *b* 10 June 1985. *Clubs:* Carlton (Member: Political Cttee, 2008–; Gen. Cttee, 2011–14), United and Cecil (Mem., Cttee, 2008–).

THOMPSON, Sir Nigel (Cooper), KCMG 2002; CBE 1996; CEng, FICE, FIStructE; Chairman, Campaign to Protect Rural England, 2003–08; Director, Trevor Estate, 1985–2011; *b* 18 June 1939; *s* of Henry Cooper Thompson and Beatrix Mary Cooper Thompson; *m* 1965, Nicola Jane Bonnett; one *s* two *d. Educ:* St Paul's Sch. CEng 1967; FIStructE 1985; FICE 2000. Joined Ove Arup and Partners, Consulting Engrs, 1960: Main Bd Dir, 1986; Dep. Chm., 1998–2005. Chm., St Helena Leisure Co., 2002–. Chm., British Consulting Bureau, 1993–94. Chm., Construction Procurement Gp, DoE, 1993–96; Dep. Chm., British Airports Gp, DTI, 1996–98. Chairman: Govt/Private Sector Task Force for Kosovo, 1999–2000; Govt Task Force for Serbia and Montenegro, 2000–02. Mem., Business Adv. Council for Stability Pact for SE Europe, 2001. Founder Mem. Council, British Council of Offices, 1994; Mem. Council, CBI, 1993–96. Chm., BUILD - Building Understanding through Internat. Links for Devlt, 2008–12. Major, Logistics Staff Corps, RE, 2001. Mem. Cttee, Kennet Gp, CPRE; Chm., Action for the River Kennet, 2003–12. Chm., Parish Council, Mildenhall, Wilts, 2004– (Vice-Chm., 2000–04). Liveryman, Engrs' Co., 2002–. Hon. Vice-Pres., Cambridge Univ. Land Soc., 2005. Gov., St Paul's Sch., 2007–11. Pres., Old Pauline Club, 2015–. Internat. Medal, ICE, 2000; Outstanding Contribn Award, ACE, 2001. *Recreations:* cricket, Rugby, landscape/estate gardening, farmer of pedigree Hampshire Down sheep. *Address:* Grove House, Stitchcombe, Marlborough, Wilts SN8 2NG. *Club:* Boodle's.

THOMPSON, Nimble; *see* Thompson, P. J. S.

THOMPSON, Owen; MP (SNP) Midlothian, since 2015; *b* Glasgow; *s* of late Robert Thompson and of Margaret Thompson. *Educ:* Napier Univ. (BA Hons Accounting and Finance). Work for financial service cos. Mem. (SNP) Midlothian Council, 2005–15 (Dep. Leader, 2012–13; Leader, 2013–15). *Recreations:* football, computer games. *Address:* House of Commons, SW1A 0AA. *E:* owen.thompson.mp@parliament.uk.

THOMPSON, (Owen) Mark; theatre designer; *b* 12 April 1957; *s* of late Owen Edgar Thompson and of Barbara Adele (*née* Lister). *Educ:* Radley Coll.; Birmingham Univ. (BA Hons Drama and Theatre Arts). Worked in rep. at Worcester, Exeter, Sheffield and Leeds; designs for: The Scarlet Pimpernel, Chichester, 1985 (transf. Her Majesty's); Cabaret, Strand, 1986; The Sneeze, Aldwych, 1988; Ivanov, and Much Ado About Nothing, Strand, 1989; A Little Night Music, Piccadilly, 1989; Shadowlands, Queen's, 1989 (transf. NY); Joseph and the Amazing Technicolor Dreamcoat, Palladium and Canadian, Australian and American tours, 1991 (Set Design Olivier Award, 1992); Company, Albery, 1996; Art, Wyndhams and NY, 1997; The Blue Room, Donmar Warehouse and NY, Dr Dolittle, Apollo Labbatts, 1998; Mamma Mia!, Prince Edward, 1999, Toronto, 2000, US tour, Australia, NY 2001; Blast!, Apollo, 1999, NY, 2001; Lady in the Van, Queen's, 1999; (set only) Follies, NY, 2001; Bombay Dreams, Apollo Victoria, 2002, NY 2004; And Then There Were None, Gielgud, 2005; Kean, Apollo, 2007; God of Carnage, Gielgud, 2008, NY 2009; The Female of the Species, Vaudeville, 2008; Funny Girl, Chichester Festival Th., 2008; The Fastest Clock in the Universe, Hampstead, 2009; La Bête, Comedy, 2010, NY 2010; The Children's Hour, Comedy, 2011; One Man Two Guvnors, NY, 2012; Charlie and the Chocolate Factory, Th. Royal, 2013 (Best Costume Olivier Award, 2014); (set only) A Raisin in the Sun, NY, 2014; Electra, Old Vic, 2014; *for Royal Exchange Manchester:* Jumpers, 1984; The Country Wife, Mumbo Jumbo, 1986; The School for Scandal, 1990; *for RSC:* Measure for Measure, 1987; The Wizard of Oz, Much Ado About Nothing, 1988; The Comedy of Errors, 1990 (Set Design and Costume Design Olivier Awards, 1992); The Unexpected Man, 1998, NY 2001; *for Almeida:* Volpone, 1990; Betrayal, Party Time, 1991; Butterfly Kiss, 1992; Rope, 2009; *for National Theatre:* The Wind in the Willows, 1990 (Olivier Award, Plays and Players Award, Critics Circle Award, 1991); The Madness of George III, 1991 (costume design for film, 1994); Arcadia, 1993; Pericles, 1994; What the Butler Saw, 1997; The Day I Stood Still, 1998; Life x 3, 2000, also NY 2003; The Duchess of Malfi, 2003; Henry IV parts 1 and 2, 2005; The Alchemist, 2006; The Rose Tattoo, 2007; England People Very Nice, 2009; London Assurance, 2010; One Man Two Guvnors, 2011; She Stoops to Conquer, 2012; NT 50th, 2013; *for Royal Court:* Six Degrees of Separation, 1992 (transf. Comedy); Hysteria, 1994 (Olivier Award for Set Design); The Kitchen, 1995 (Critics' Circle Award); Mouth to Mouth, 2001; The Woman Before, 2005; Piano/Forte, 2006; Tribes, 2010; Birthday, 2012; *opera:* Montag aus Licht, La Scala, 1989 (costume design only); Falstaff, Scottish Opera, 1991; Peter Grimes, Opera North, 1989; Ariadne auf Naxos, Saltzburg, 1991; Il Viaggio a Reims, Royal Opera, 1992; Hansel and Gretel, Sydney, 1992; The Two Widows, ENO, 1993; Queen of Spades, 1995, Macbeth, 2007, Metropolitan Opera, NY; Carmen, Opera Comique, Paris, 2009; The Mikado, Chicago Lyric Opera, 2010; *ballet:* Don Quixote, Royal Ballet, 1993. *Recreations:* cooking, gardening. *Address:* c/o Annette Stone, Arthouse B7–3, 1 York Way, N1C 4AT. *T:* (020) 3725 6893.

THOMPSON, Patrick; *see* Thompson, H. P.

THOMPSON, Sir Paul (Anthony), 2nd Bt *cr* 1963; company director; *b* 6 Oct. 1939; *s* of Sir Kenneth Pugh Thompson, 1st Bt, and Nanne (*d* 1994), *yr d* of Charles Broome, Walton, Liverpool; *S* father, 1984; *m* 1971, Pauline Dorothy, *d* of Robert O. Spencer, Bolton, Lancs; two *s* two *d. Educ:* Aldenham School, Herts. *Heir: s* Richard Kenneth Spencer Thompson [*b* 27 Jan. 1976; *m* 2008, Hayley Watts, Auckland, NZ; one *s* one *d*]. *Address:* Woodlands Farmhouse, Ruff Lane, Ormskirk, Lancs L39 4UL.

THOMPSON, Prof. Paul Richard, DPhil; social historian; Research Professor in Social History, University of Essex, 1988–2008, now Emeritus Professor; Founder, National Life Stories, 1987; *b* 1935; *m* 1st, Thea Vigne; one *s* one *d*; 2nd, Natasha Burchardt; one *d*; 3rd, Elaine Bauer. *Educ:* Bishop's Stortford Coll.; Corpus Christi Coll., Oxford (MA); The Queen's Coll., Oxford (Junior Research Fellow, 1961–64); DPhil Oxon 1964. University of Essex: Lectr in Sociology, 1964–69; Sen. Lectr, 1969–71; Reader, 1971–88; Sen. Res. Fellow, Nuffield Coll., Oxford, 1968–69; Vis. Prof. of Art History, Johns Hopkins Univ., 1972; Hoffman Wood Prof. of Architecture, Univ. of Leeds, 1977–78; Benjamin Meaker Prof., Univ. of Bristol, 1987. Dir, Qualidata, 1994–2001. Editor: Victorian Soc. Conf. Reports, 1965–67; Oral History, 1970–; Life Stories, 1985–89; International Yearbook of Oral History and Life Stories, 1992–96; Memory and Narrative, 1996–2002. Hon. DLitt: Aberdeen, 2007; Sussex, 2013; Essex, 2015. *Publications:* History of English Architecture (with Peter Kidson and Peter Murray), 1965, 2nd edn 1979; The Work of William Morris, 1967, 3rd edn 1991; Socialists, Liberals and Labour: the struggle for London 1880–1914, 1967; The Edwardians: the remaking of British Society, 1975, 2nd edn 1992; The Voice of the Past: Oral History, 1978, 3rd edn 2000; Living the Fishing, 1983; I Don't Feel Old: the experience of later life, 1990; (with Raphael Samuel) The Myths We Live By, 1990; (with Gloria Wood) The Nineties, 1993; (with Hugo Slim) Listening for a Change, 1993; (with Cathy Courtney) City Lives, 1996; (with Daniel Bertaux) Pathways to Social Class, 1997; (jtly) Growing Up in Stepfamilies, 1997; (with Mary Chamberlain) Narrative and Genre, 1998; (with Daniel Bertaux) On Living Through Soviet Russia, 2004; (with Elaine Bauer) Jamaican Hands Across the Atlantic, 2006; Sea-change: Wivenhoe remembered, 2006. *Recreations:* cycling, drawing, music, friendship, travel. *Address:* 154 Clark Street, Stepney, E1 3HD. *T:* (020) 7790 9556. *E:* paulth_wivenhoe@yahoo.co.uk.

THOMPSON, Paul W.; *see* Warwick Thompson.

THOMPSON, Sir Peter (Anthony), Kt 1984; FCILT; President, Goldcrest Land PLC (formerly Goldcrest Homes plc), since 2014 (Chairman, 1998–2014); Chairman: Green Energy plc, since 2001; Mill Manor Properties Ltd, since 2003; *b* 14 April 1928; *s* of late Herbert Thompson and Sarah Jane Thompson; *m* 1st, 1958, Patricia Anne Norcott (*d* 1983); one *s* two *d*; 2nd, 1986, Lydia Mary Kite (*née* Hodding); two *d. Educ:* Royal Drapers Sch.; Bradford Grammar Sch.; Leeds Univ. (BA Econ). Unilever, 1952–62; GKN, 1962–64; Transport Controller, Rank Organisation, 1964–67; Head of Transport, BSC, 1967–72; Group Co-ordinator, BRS Ltd, 1972–75; Exec. Vice-Chm. (Operations), Nat. Freight Corp., 1975–77; Chief Exec., Nat. Freight Corp., later Nat. Freight Co., 1977–80; Dep. Chm. and Chief Exec., 1980–82, Chm. and Chief Exec., 1982–84, Exec. Chm., 1984–90, Pres., 1991–93, NFC. Dir, 1989–90, Dep. Chm., 1989–90, Chm., March–July 1990, British & Commonwealth Hldgs; Chairman: Community Hospitals plc, 1981–96; Child Base Ltd, 1989–2005 (Pres., 2006–); FI Group plc, 1990–99; Douglas Stewart Ltd, 1992–2004; Phoenix Asset Mgt Ltd, 1998–2003, 2004–09; Stocktrade, 2000–01; Durabuild, 2001–02; OMG Ltd, 2001–02; Goodnights Entertainments, 2003–13; Milton Keynes Theatre Prodn Co. Ltd, 2004–08; Dep. Chm., Wembley plc, 1991–95; Director: Granville & Co. Ltd, 1984–90; Pilkington plc, 1985–93; Kenning Motor Group, 1985–86; Smiths Industries PLC, 1986–98; Meyer International, 1988–92; Aegis plc, 1993–99; Brewin Dolphin Gp, 1994–2000; Legal Document Co., 2001–07; Ecorider Ltd, 2006–07; Image Analysis, 2010–13; Pres., ProShare, 1994–99 (Chm., 1992–94). Mem., Nat. Trng Task Force, 1989–93. President: Inst. of Freight Forwarders, 1982–83; Inst. of Logistics and Distribn Management (formerly Inst. of Physical Distribn Management), 1988–93 (Chm., 1985–88); Vice-Pres., CIT, 1982–85; Chm., CBI Wider Share Ownership Task Force, 1990. Chm., Milton Keynes Theatre Gall. Trust, 1995–2003. CCMI. Hon. LLD: Leeds, 1991; Nottingham, 1991; Hon. DTech Bradford, 1991; Hon. DSc Cranfield Inst. of Technol., 1992. Hambro Businessman of the Year, 1983; BIM Gold Medal, 1991. *Publications:* Sharing the Success: the story of the NFC, 1990. *Recreations:* golf, walking, shooting, theatre, music. *Address:* The Mill House, Mill Street, Newport Pagnell, Bucks MK16 8ER. *Clubs:* Garrick, Royal Automobile.

THOMPSON, Peter James; Owner, Peter Thompson Associates, since 1970; *b* Sheffield, 23 Feb. 1945; *s* of Andrew and Janet Thompson. *Educ:* Hurstpierpoint Coll.; Sussex Univ. (BA Hons). Founder, Peter Thompson Associates, PR agency, 1970. *Recreations:* food, drink, travel.

THOMPSON, Peter John; education and training consultant; *b* 17 April 1937; *s* of late George Kenneth Thompson and Gladys Pamela (*née* Partington), W Midlands; *m* 1961, Dorothy Ann Smith; one *s* three *d. Educ:* Aston Univ. (BSc 1st Cl. Hons MechEngrg; MSc); CNAA (DTech). Whitworth Soc. Prize. CEng, FIET; FIPD. With Tube Investments, 1952–61; Lectr 1961, Sen. Lectr 1968–70, Harris Coll., Preston; Sen. Sci. Officer, UKAEA, Preston, 1965–68; Prin. Lectr, Sheffield City Poly., 1970–77; Hd of Dept and Dean of Engrg,

Trent Poly., Nottingham, 1977–83; Pro Rector, then Dep. Rector, Poly. of Central London, 1983–86; Professor: Trent Poly., 1980–83; Poly. of Central London, 1983–86; Chief Exec., NCVQ, 1986–91; Vis. Prof., Sch. of Mgt, Open Univ., 1991–94. School Inspector, OFSTED, 1984–2012. Partner, P & D Medallions, 1986–; Consultant, HR Services, 1997–. Mem., then Chm., Manufacturing Bd, CNAA, 1978–86; Mem., Cttee for Sci. and Technology, CNAA, 1982–86; Mem. then Chm., Cttee for Engrg in Polytechnics, 1981–86; Member: Engrg Adv. Cttee, NAB, 1980–84; Engrg Scis Divl Bd of IMechE, 1984–86; Chm., Materials Tech. Activities Cttee, IMechE, 1984–86; Mem., Council, Open Coll., 1987–90. Sen. Awards Consultant, C&G, 1992–95. Hon. Mem., C&G, 1991. FRSA. *Publications:* numerous papers on engrg manufacture and vocational educn and trng, 1968–, incl. papers on hydrostatic extension, lubrication, cutting tool wear and mechanics and metal forming; patents. *Recreations:* genealogy, numismatics, golf. *Address:* Berkhamsted, Herts HP4 3JJ. *T:* (01442) 865127.

THOMPSON, His Honour Peter John; a Circuit Judge, 1998–2013; *b* 30 Dec. 1943; *s* of late Eric Thompson and Olive Ethel Thompson (*née* Miskin); *m* 1969, Elizabeth Anne Granger Rees; one *s* two *d.* *Educ:* Glyn Grammar Sch., Epsom; St Catherine's Coll., Oxford (MA Jurisp.). Admitted Solicitor, 1970; Solicitor and Barrister, Supreme Court of Vic., Australia, 1972; Partner: Turner Martin & Symes, Solicitors, Ipswich, 1976–91; Eversheds, Solicitors, Ipswich, 1991–98. *Recreations:* jazz, playing and listening, soccer, playing and watching, jogging and walking in English and French countryside, family, literature, travel. *E:* pjthompson1943@gmail.com.

THOMPSON, Peter John Stuart, (Nimble); Chairman, N. G. Bailey Ltd, 2001–13; *b* 28 Sept. 1946; *s* of Douglas Thompson and Rene Thompson, OBE; *m* 1970, Morven Mary Hanscomb; one *s* one *d* (and one *s* decd). *Educ:* Rossall Sch.; Univ. of Leeds (LLB). MCIArb. Admitted solicitor, 1971; Managing Partner, Hepworth & Chadwick, 1989–94; Eversheds: Sen. Partner, Leeds and Manchester, 1994–99; Dep. Chm., 1995–98. Non-executive Director: TEP Electrical Distributors, 1975–; S. Lyles plc, 1994–99; Denney O'Hara Ltd, 1999–2011; Judicium plc, 2000–14; Rushbond plc, 2002–; Scarborough Building Soc., 2005–09; Institute of Dirs, 2008– (Regl Chm., Yorks, 2005–09; Dep. Chm., 2013–); Skipton Building Soc., 2009– (Dep. Chm., 2013–; Chm., Remuneration Cttee, 2013–); Henderson Insurance Brokers Ltd, 2011–14. Chairman: Bd, Leeds Metropolitan Univ., 2000–06; Eureka!, the Mus. for Children, Halifax, 2003–07; Gov., Giggleswick Sch., 1998– (Vice Chm., 2002–07). Hon. DLaws Leeds Metropolitan, 2006. *Recreations:* fishing, wine, family, friends, stalking. *Address:* The Grange, Kirkby Malzeard, Ripon, N Yorks HG4 3RY. *T:* (01765) 658398. *E:* nimble@nimble.entadsl.com. *Club:* Royal Automobile.

THOMPSON, Peter Kenneth James; Solicitor to Departments of Health and of Social Security, 1989–97; *b* 30 July 1937; *s* of Kenneth George Thompson and Doreen May Thompson; *m* 1970, Sandy Lynne Harper; two *d.* *Educ:* Worksop Coll.; Christ's Coll., Cambridge (MA, LLB). Called to the Bar, Lincoln's Inn, 1961; practised at Common Law Bar, 1961–73; Lawyer in Govt Service: Law Commission, 1973–78; Lord Chancellor's Dept, 1978–83; Under Sec., DHSS, 1983. General Editor: The County Court Practice, 1991–98; The Civil Court Practice, 1999–. Hon. QC 1997. *Publications:* The Unfair Contract Terms Act 1977, 1978; The Recovery of Interest, 1985; *radio plays:* A Matter of Form, 1977; Dormer and Grand-Daughter, 1978. *Recreation:* running a free legal advice service.

THOMPSON, Raymond, CBE 1988; PhD; FRSC; FREng; Deputy Chairman, Borax Research Ltd, 1986–90 (Managing Director, 1980–86); Director: RTZ Chemicals (formerly Borax Consolidated) (Borides) Ltd, 1986–89; Boride Ceramics and Composites Ltd, 1990–92; Azmat Ltd, 1993–2001; *b* 4 April 1925; *s* of late William Edward Thompson and Hilda Thompson (*née* Rowley). *Educ:* Longton High Sch.; Univ. of Nottingham (MSc 1950, PhD 1952); Imperial Coll., Univ. of London (DIC 1953). Research Manager, Borax Consolidated, 1961; Res. Dir, 1969–86, Business Develt Dir, 1986–87, Scientific Advr, 1987–95, Borax Hldgs Ltd, later RTZ Borax and Minerals Ltd. Consultant: RTZ Chemicals Ltd, 1988–89; CRA Ltd, 1988–91; Rhône-Poulenc, 1989–92. Special Professor of Inorganic Chemistry, Univ. of Nottingham, 1975–96; Hon. Prof., Molecular Sciences, Univ. of Warwick, 1975–94. Member Council: Royal Inst. of Chemistry, 1969–72; Chemical Soc., 1977–80 (Chm., Inorganic Chemicals Gp, 1972–83); RSC, 1983–88 (Vice-Pres., Industrial Div., 1981–83, Pres., 1983–85 and 1988–89). Governor, Kingston-upon-Thames Polytechnic, 1978–88. Hon. Associate, RHC, London Univ., 1984. Freeman, City of London. FREng (FEng 1985). Industrial Chemistry Award, Chem. Soc., 1976. *Publications:* (ed) The Modern Inorganic Chemicals Industry, 1977; (ed) Mellors Comprehensive Treatise, Boron Supplement, Part A, 1979, Part BI, 1981; (ed) Speciality Inorganic Chemicals, 1981; (ed) Energy and Chemistry, 1981; (ed) Trace Metal Removal From Aqueous Solution, 1986; (ed) The Chemistry of Wood Preservation, 1991; Industrial Inorganic Chemicals: production and uses, 1995; various papers on inorganic boron and nitrogen chemistry. *Address:* 10 Waldorf Heights, Hawley Hill, Camberley, Surrey GU17 9JH. *T:* (01276) 32900.

THOMPSON, Rhodri William Ralph; QC 2002; a Recorder, since 2010; *b* 5 May 1960; *s* of Ralph Kenneth Thompson and Dilys Grace Thompson (*née* Hughes); *m* 1989, Paula Mary Donaghy; one *s* two *d.* *Educ:* Eastbourne Coll.; University Coll., Oxford (BPhil, MA); City Univ. (Dip. Law). Called to the Bar, Middle Temple, 1989; in practice as barrister, 1989–; Monckton Chambers, 1990–2000 (Brussels, 1990–92, London, 1993–2000); Founder Mem., Matrix Chambers, 2000– (Chm., Mgt Cttee, 2004–06, 2014–). Jt Chm., Jt Wkg Party of Bars and Law Socs of UK on Competition Law, 2012–; Hon. Treas., UK Assoc. of European Law, 2012–. *Publications:* (contrib.) Bellamy & Child, EC Law of Competition, 4th edn 1993 to 7th edn 2013; Single Market for Pharmaceuticals, 1994. *Recreations:* walking, golf, tennis, philosophy. *Address:* Matrix Chambers, Griffin Building, Gray's Inn, WC1R 5LN. *T:* (020) 7611 9316. *E:* rhodrithompson@matrixlaw.co.uk.

THOMPSON, (Richard) Neil; Vice President, Retail Sales and Category Management, Europe, Middle East and Africa, Microsoft Corporation, since 2013; *b* Swansea, 23 Sept. 1966; *s* of Melvin and Joan Thompson; *m* 1994, Sarah Bruce; two *d.* *Educ:* Dwr-y-Felin Comprehensive Sch.; Loughborough Univ. (BSc Econs). Graduate trainee, Sea Containers Ltd, 1989–90; Direct Mktg Manager, Stena Line, 1990–92; Microsoft, 1992–: Mktg Manager, 1994–97, Hd of Communications, 1994–97, Microsoft UK; Eur. Communications Dir, 1997–2000; Eur. Mktg Dir, Xbox, 2000–03; Regl Dir, EMEA, 2003–05; General Manager: Entertainment Div., 2005–10; Consumer Channels Gp, 2011–13. Mem. Bd, Entertainment and Leisure Software Publishers Assoc., 2007–. *Recreations:* ski-ing, golf, travel. *Address:* Microsoft Ltd, Thames Valley Park, Reading RG6 1WG. *E:* neilt@microsoft.com.

THOMPSON, Sir Richard (Paul Hepworth), KCVO 2003; DM; FRCP; Physician to the Queen and Head of HM Medical Household, 1993–2005 (Physician to the Royal Household, 1982–93); Consultant Physician, St Thomas' Hospital, 1972–2005, now Emeritus Consultant, and Governor, since 2007, Guy's and St Thomas' NHS Trust; President, Royal College of Physicians, 2010–14; *b* 14 April 1940; *s* of Stanley Henry and Winifred Lilian Thompson; *m* 1974, Eleanor Mary Hughes. *Educ:* Epsom Coll.; Worcester Coll., Oxford (MA, DM; Hon. Fellow, 2010); St Thomas's Hosp. Med. Sch. MRC Clinical Res. Fellow, Liver Unit, KCH, 1967–69; Fellow, Gastroenterology Unit, Mayo Clinic, USA, 1969–71; Lectr, Liver Unit, KCH, 1971–72; Physician, King Edward VII Hosp. for Officers, 1982–2005. Mem., Lambeth, Southwark and Lewisham AHA, 1979–82. Examiner in Medicine: Soc. of Apothecaries, 1976–80; Faculty of Dental Surgery, RCS, 1980–86; Examr, 1991–2003, Censor, 1998–2000, Treas., 2003–10, RCP. Governor, Guy's Hosp. Med. Sch., 1980–82; Member Cttee of Management: Inst. of Psychiatry, 1981–95; King Edward VII Hosp. Fund, 1985–89, 1992–96 (Mem., Gen. Council, 1985–); Mem Council, Royal Med. Foundn of Epsom Coll., 2003–10. Member, Council: BHF, 2001–08 (Vice-Chm., 2001–08); British Cardiovascular Soc., 2008–14; Trustee: Thrive, 2001–10; Henry Smith Charity, 2007–15; Quit, 2011–; Wellbeing of Women, 2014; Nat. Garden Scheme, 2014–. Hon. Associate Nightingale Fellow, 2004. *Publications:* Physical Signs in Medicine, 1980; Lecture Notes on the Liver, 1986; papers and reviews in med. jls. *Address:* 36 Dealtry Road, SW15 6NL. *T:* (020) 8789 3839.

THOMPSON, Richard Paul Reynier, OBE 2001; Chief Executive Officer, Facewatch Ltd, since 2014; Director: Elvaston Global Ltd, since 2012; Advanced Laser Imaging, since 2013; *b* 17 Aug. 1960; *s* of His Honour Anthony Arthur Richard Thompson, *qv*; *m* 1991, Louisa (*née* Yeates) (marr. diss.); two *s* one *d.* *Educ:* St Paul's Sch.; Exeter Univ. (LLB); Harvard Business Sch. Served Army, RGJ, 1978–88. Entered FCO, 1989; Second, later First Sec., Stockholm, 1991–93; First Secretary: FCO, 1993–96; UK Mission to UN, Geneva, 1996–99; Counsellor: Pristina, 1999–2000; FCO, 2000–04; Baghdad, 2004–05; FCO, 2006–07; Chief Constable, Civil Nuclear Constabulary, 2007–12. Vis. Fellow, KCL. Hon. Fellow, Strategy and Security Inst., Univ. of Exeter, 2013–. Lay Mem., Bar Standards Bd. *Recreations:* keeping fit, reading (politics and history).

THOMPSON, Robert; *see* Thompson, W. R.

THOMPSON, Robin; *see* Thompson, D. R. B.

THOMPSON, Dr Ruth; Chief Executive, Partnerships for Schools, 2011–12; Director General, Higher Education, Department for Innovation, Universities and Skills (formerly Department for Education and Skills), 2007–09 (Acting Director General, 2006–07); *b* 4 July 1953; *d* of late Arthur Frederick (Pat) Thompson and Mary Thompson (*née* Barritt); *m* 2004, Hon. Sir David Michael Bean, *qv.* *Educ:* Somerville Coll., Oxford (MA Modern Hist.; Hon. Fellow, 2010); St Antony's Coll., Oxford and Instituto di Tella, Buenos Aires (DPhil Econ. Hist. 1978). Depts of Industry, Trade and Prices and Consumer Protection, 1978–90; Private Sec. to Parly Under-Sec., Dept of Trade and successive Secs of State for Trade and Industry, 1982–84; Cabinet Office (on secondment), 1987; Asst Sec., DTI, 1990–92; HM Treasury, 1992–98; DSS, 1999–2000; Dir of Finance, DfEE, then DfES, 2000–03; Dir, Higher Educn Strategy and Implementation Gp, DfES, 2003–06. Director: Fusion Lifestyle, 2011–; Moat Homes Ltd, 2012–. Member: Adv. Bd, Higher Educn Policy Inst., 2009–; Bd, London TravelWatch, 2013– (Vice Chm., 2013–); Audit Commn, 2013–15; Ind. Mem., Audit Cttee, HEFCE, 2012–. Co-Chm., Higher Educn Commn Inquiry into financial sustainability of English higher educn, 2014. Governor: Birkbeck, Univ. of London, 2009–; Staffordshire Univ., 2009– (Chair, Educn Cttee, 2010–). *Recreations:* walking, swimming, gardening, books, Latin America. *E:* ruththompson7794@btinternet.com.

THOMPSON, Simon Robert; Chairman: Tullow Oil plc, since 2012; 3i plc, since 2015; *b* Bramhall, 16 June 1959; *s* of Robert Thompson and Patricia Thompson; *m* 1986, Fiona Graham-Bryce. *Educ:* Manchester Grammar Sch.; University Coll., Oxford (BA Geol. 1981). Lloyds Bank Internat., 1981–85; N. M. Rothschild & Sons Ltd, 1985–94; Dir, S. G. Warburg & Co. Ltd, 1994–95; Minorco SA: Hd, Project Finance, 1995–97; Pres., Minorco Brasil, 1997–99; Anglo American plc: Hd, Zinc, 1999–2001; CEO, 2001–05, Chm., 2003–07, Base Metals Div.; Chm., Exploration Div., 2003–07; Chm., Tarmac, 2003–07; Exec. Dir, 2005–07. Non-executive Director: AngloGold Ashanti, 2004–08; UC Rusal, 2007–09; Sandvik AB, 2008–15; Newmont Mining Corp., 2008–14; Amec Foster Wheeler plc, 2009–15; Rio Tinto plc, 2014–; Rio Tinto Ltd, 2014–. *Publications:* Unjustifiable Risk?: the story of British climbing, 2010; A Long Walk with Lord Conway, 2013. *Recreations:* mountaineering, writing. *Address:* Tullow Oil plc, 9 Chiswick Park, 566 Chiswick High Road, W4 5XT. *Clubs:* Athenæum, Alpine.

THOMPSON, Steven Lim; QC 2015; *b* London, 1969; *s* of John Quentin Thompson and Miao-Ling Thompson; *m* (marr. diss.); one *s* one *d.* *Educ:* Westminster Sch., London; St John's Coll., Cambridge (BA Hons 1990). Called to the Bar, Inner Temple, 1996. *Address:* XXIV Old Buildings, Lincoln's Inn, WC2A 3UP. *T:* (020) 7691 2424. *E:* clerks@xxiv.co.uk.

THOMPSON, Sir (Thomas d'Eyncourt) John, 6th Bt *cr* 1806, of Hartsbourne Manor, Hertfordshire; Director, Rockspring Iberia, Madrid, since 2006; *b* 22 Dec. 1956; *o s* of Sir (Thomas) Lionel Tennyson Thompson, 5th Bt and of Margaret Thompson (*née* Brown); *S* father, 1999; *m* 2002, Tanya, *d* of Michael Willcocks; one *s* two *d.* *Educ:* Eton; King's Coll., London (BA; MSc). MRICS (ARICS 1993). Associate Partner, Folkard & Hayward, London, 1984–90; Investment Surveyor, King Sturge, London, 1991–93, Brussels, 1994; Dir, Weatherall Green & Smith, Madrid, 1995–97; Partner, King Sturge, Madrid, 1997–2006. *Heir: s* Thomas Boulden Cameron Thompson, *b* 31 Jan. 2006. *Club:* East India.

THOMPSON, (William) Robert; freelance cartoonist and illustrator, since 1992; *b* 21 July 1960; *s* of Wildon and Eileen Thompson; *m* 1993, Siobhán Maria Doyle; one *s* one *d.* *Educ:* Leeds Polytechnic (BA Hons Graphic Design). Art Dir, Camden Graphics, 1985–92. Contrib. cartoons/illustrations to The Guardian, The Times, Private Eye, The Spectator, The Oldie, FT, Mail on Sunday, Metro, Decanter, Radio Times, New Statesman, Real Deals. *Publications:* Pointless Things to Do, 1995; illustrator: Private Eye's Cutting Humour, 1993; Can They Do That?, 2003; The Origins of Words and Phrases, 2007; QI Annual, 2009, 2010; Eyeballs, 2012. *Recreations:* walking my Jack Russell, growing vegetables, eating dark chocolate, drinking red wine, having heart palpitations. *E:* rtcartoonist@btinternet.com. *W:* www.robertthompsoncartoons.com.

THOMPSON, Willoughby Harry, CMG 1974; CBE 1968 (MBE 1954); *b* 3 Dec. 1919; *m* 1963, Sheelah O'Grady; no *c.* Served War: RA, and E African Artillery, 1939–47. Kenya Govt Service, 1947–48; Colonial Administrative Service, Kenya, 1948–63; Colonial Sec., Falkland Islands, 1963–69 (Actg Governor, 1964 and 1967); Actg Judge, Falkland Islands and Dependencies Supreme Court, 1965–69; Actg Administrator, British Virgin Islands, May–July 1969; HM Comr in Anguilla, July 1969–1971; Governor of Montserrat, 1971–74.

THOMPSON, Yvonne, CBE 2003; Managing Director, ASAP Communications Ltd, 1995–2010; *b* 1957; one *d.* Phonogram; CBS; Founder: Positive Publicity, 1983–89; WM&P, 1990–94. Dir, Choice FM Radio. Member: Bd, Britain in Europe, 1999; Bd, London Develt Agency, 2000–07; Small Business Council, DTI, 2000–02; Economy Honours Cttee, 2013–; Comr, Local Govt Inf. Unit; Chairman: London Central LSC, 2000–08; Ethnic Minority Business Forum, DTI, 2000–06. Mem. Council, City & Guilds, 2013–16. Founder and Pres., Eur. Fedn of Black Women Business Owners, 1996–2011. Hon. DPhil London Metropolitan, 2005.

THOMPSON-McCAUSLAND, Benedict Maurice Perronet; Partner: Temax Associates, since 1991; Thompson Best, since 2008; Group Chief Executive, National & Provincial Building Society, 1987–90; *b* 5 Feb. 1938; *s* of late Lucius P. Thompson-McCausland, CMG and Helen Laura McCausland; *m* 1964, Frances Catherine Fothergill Smith; three *d.* *Educ:* Eton Coll.; Trinity Coll., Cambridge (MA; Rowing Blue). FCA 1974–2003. Articled to Coopers & Lybrand, Chartered Accountants, 1961–64; Arbuthnot Latham & Co. Ltd, 1964–80: Asst to Dirs, 1964; Banking Manager, 1967; Dir, 1968; Dep. Chm., 1978; London Life Association Ltd: Dir, 1976–81; Vice-Pres., 1979–87; Chief Exec., 1981–87. Dir, Advanced Personnel Technology, 1993–2001; formerly Director: Western Trust & Savings Ltd; Concord Internat.; First National Finance Corp. plc. Chm., Lombard Assoc., 1979–81. Director: British Sch. of Osteopathy, 1991–2000 (Chm., 1996–2000); Harefield Hosp. NHS Trust, 1992–98. Mem. Council, 1987–2000, and Mem. Exec. Cttee, 1988–91, Industrial Soc.

Mem., Council of Management, Arnolfini Gall., 1983–86. John Loxham Lectr, Inst. of Quality Assurance, 1997. *Publications:* (with Derek Biddle) Change, Business Performance and Values, 1985; (with J. Bergwerk) Leading to Success: how leaders unlock energy, 1994; articles in business jls. *Recreations:* rough gardening, military history. *Address:* 14 Alexander Street, W2 5NT. *T:* (020) 7221 7549. *Clubs:* Leander (Henley-on-Thames); Hawks (Cambridge).

THOMSEN, Kim Stuart L.; *see* Lerche-Thomsen.

THOMSON, family name of **Baron Thomson of Fleet**.

THOMSON OF FLEET, 3rd Baron *cr* 1964; **David Kenneth Roy Thomson;** Chairman: Thomson Reuters (formerly The Thomson Corporation), since 2002 (Director, since 1988); Woodbridge Co. Ltd; *b* 12 June 1957; *s* of 2nd Baron Thomson of Fleet and of Nora Marilyn (*née* Lavis); *S* father, 2006; *m* 1st, 1988, Mary Lou La Prairie (marr. diss. 1997); two *d*; 2nd, 2000, Laurie Ludwick (marr. diss.); one *s*. *Educ:* Upper Canada Coll.; Selwyn Coll., Cambridge (MA). Chm., The Globe and Mail Inc. *Heir: s* Hon. Benjamin James Ludwick Thomson, *b* 10 March 2006. *Address:* Thomson Reuters, 333 Bay Street, Suite 400, Toronto, ON M5H 2R2, Canada.

THOMSON, Sir Adam (McClure), KCMG 2014 (CMG 2009); HM Diplomatic Service; UK Permanent Representative, UK Delegation to NATO, since 2014; *b* 1 July 1955; *e s* of Sir John Thomson, *qv*; *m* 1984, Fariba Shirazi; one *s* two *d*. *Educ:* Westminster Sch.; Trinity Coll., Cambridge (MA); Harvard Univ. (MPP). Joined FCO, 1978; Third, later Second Sec., Moscow, 1981–83; Second, later First Sec., UK delegn to NATO, Brussels, 1983–86; First Sec., FCO, 1986–89; Cabinet Office, 1989–91; First Sec. (Politico-Military), Washington, 1991–95; Counsellor (Political), New Delhi, 1995–98: Counsellor, Security Policy Dept, FCO, 1998–2002; Ambassador and Dep. Perm. Rep., UK Mission to UN, NY, 2002–06; Dir, South Asia and Afghanistan, FCO, 2006–09; High Comr to Pakistan, 2010–13. *Address:* c/o Foreign and Commonwealth Office, King Charles Street, SW1A 2AH. *Club:* Athenæum.

THOMSON, Alan Matthew, CA; President, Institute of Chartered Accountants of Scotland, 2010–11; *b* Lennoxtown, 6 Sept. 1946; *s* of George Kerr Thomson and Jean Lees Thomson (*née* Gemmell); *m* 2005, Angela Georgina Manuello; two *s* two *d*. *Educ:* Eastwood Sch., Renfrewshire; Glasgow Univ. (MA 1967). CA 1970. Audit Manager, Price Waterhouse, 1971–75; Finance Director: Rockwell Internat., 1975–82; Raychem Ltd, 1982–84; Divl Finance Dir, Courtaulds plc, 1984–92; Gp Financial Dir, Rugby Gp plc, 1992–95; Gp Finance Dir, Smiths Gp plc, 1995–2006. Chairman: Hamsard Ltd, 2007–; Bodycote plc, 2008–; Hays plc, 2010–; Sen. Independent Dir, Johnson Matthey plc, 2008–11. Non-exec. Dir, Alstom SA, 2007–. *Recreations:* golf, opera. *Club:* Caledonian.

THOMSON, Andrew Francis; Chairman and Joint Managing Director, D. C. Thomson & Co. Ltd, since 2005 (Director, since 1974); *b* Dundee, 14 Aug. 1942; *s* of C. Howard and Frances H. Thomson; *m* 1970, Bridget Ivory; two *s* one *d*. *Educ:* Ardvreck Sch.; Glenalmond Coll.; Churchill Coll., Cambridge (BA 1964). Dir, Alliance Trust plc, 1989–2001. Hon. LLD Dundee, 2006. *Recreations:* golf, travel, theatre. *Address:* 22 Meadowside, Dundee DD1 1LN. *T:* (01382) 223131.

THOMSON, Prof. Andrew James, OBE 2008; DPhil; FRS 1993; CChem, FRSC, FRSocMed; Professor of Chemistry, University of East Anglia, 1985–2007, Emeritus Professor of Chemistry and Biology, 2008; *b* 31 July 1940; *s* of late Andrew Henderson Thomson and Eva Frances Annie (*née* Moss); *m* 1966, Anne Marsden; two *s*. *Educ:* Steyning Grammar Sch.; Wadham Coll., Oxford (MA, DPhil; Hon. Fellow, 2012). FRSC 1990; FRSocMed 2008. Res. Asst Prof., Dept of Biophysics, Michigan State Univ., 1967; School of Chemical Sciences, University of East Anglia: Demonstrator, 1967–68; Lectr, 1968–77; Sen. Lectr, 1977–83; Reader, 1983–85; Hd of Inorganic Chem. Sector, 1984–97; Norwich Res. Park Prof., 1995–2007; Dean, Sch. of Chemical Scis and Pharmacy, 1999–2004; Dean, Faculty of Sci., 2004–07. Royal Society of Chemistry: Silver Medal for analytical chemistry, 1991; Hugo Muller Lectureship, 1997; Interdisciplinary Award, 2000; Chatt Lectureship, 2004. *Publications:* papers in scientific jls. *Recreations:* walking, ballroom dancing, choral singing. *Address:* 12 Armitage Close, Cringleford, Norwich NR4 6XZ. *T:* (01603) 504623. *E:* a.thomson@uea.ac.uk, andrew33thomson@btinternet.com.

THOMSON, Benjamin John Paget, FRSE; Chairman: National Galleries of Scotland, since 2009; Reform Scotland, since 2008; Barrington Stoke Ltd, since 2008; Inverleith LLP (formerly Inverleith Capital LLP), since 2010; Antonine Asset Mgt LLP, since 2010; Urbicus Ltd, since 2011; Castle Capital Ltd, since 2013; *b* London, 8 April 1963; *s* of David Paget Thomson, *qv*; *m* 1993, Lucy Juckes; two *s* two *d*. *Educ:* Bradfield Coll., Berks; Edinburgh Univ. (MA Hons Physics 1985); INSEAD. Researcher, H of C, 1981–82; Kleinwort Benson Ltd, 1985–90; Noble Group Ltd, 1990–2010: Dir, 1993; Chief Exec., 1997–2007; led mgt buy-out, 2000; Chm., 2007–10 (non-exec., 2008–10). Non-executive Director: Wellington Underwriting plc, 1993–97; Canmore Partnership, 1995–2003; CBS Private Capital SLP Ltd, 1996–2004; Roberts & Hiscox Gen. Partners Ltd, 1996–2011; PFI (NT) Ltd, 2001–05; Martin Currie Global Portfolio Trust (formerly Martin Currie Portfolio Investment Trust) plc (Sen. Ind. Dir), 2001–13; Oval Insce, 2003–06; Fidelity Special Values plc (Sen. Ind. Dir), 2008–; Scotch Malt Whisky (Hldgs) Ltd, 2015–. Non-executive Director: Scottish Financial Enterprise, 2001–08; Patrons of Nat. Galls of Scotland, 2003–09; Edinburgh Internat. Sci. Fest., 2008–. Mem., Speculative Soc. FRSE 2014. *Publications:* Higher Education Financial Yearbook, 1993; Further Education Financial Yearbook, 1993. *Recreations:* athletics, tennis, ski-ing, art, opera. *Address:* 33 Inverleith Terrace, Edinburgh EH3 5NU. *Clubs:* New (Edinburgh); Edinburgh Athletics.

THOMSON, Caroline, (Lady Liddle); Chair, Digital UK, since 2013 (non-executive Director, 2006–12); Executive Director, English National Ballet, since 2013; *b* 15 May 1954; *d* of Baron Thomson of Monifieth, KT, PC; *m* 1st, 1977, Ian Bradley (marr. diss. 1980); 2nd, 1983, Roger John Liddle (*see* Baron Liddle); one *s*. *Educ:* Mary Datchelor Grammar Sch.; Univ. of York (BA Hons). BBC trainee, 1975–77; producer: Analysis, BBC Radio, 1978–81; Panorama, 1982; Political Advr to Rt Hon. Roy Jenkins, 1983; Commng Ed., Business and Sci., 1984–90, Hd, Corporate Affairs, 1991–95, Channel 4; Dep. Chief Exec., BBC World Service, 1995–2000; Dir, Public Policy, 2000–04, Strategy, 2004–06, Chief Operating Officer, 2007–12, BBC. Non-executive Director: Pensions Regulator, 2005–09; CN Gp, 2013–; NHS Trust Develt Authy, 2013–; Shareholder Exec., BIS, 2014–. Trustee: One World Broadcasting Trust, 2001–08; National Gall., 2008– (Dep. Chair, 2012–); Tullie Hse Mus. and Gall., Carlisle, 2010–. Pres., Prix Italia, 2005–08. FRTS, 2007. DUniv York, 2013. *Recreations:* Italy, Cumbria, domesticity.

THOMSON, Rev. Canon Celia Stephana Margaret; Canon Residentiary, Gloucester Cathedral, since 2003; *b* Ripon, N Yorks, 19 Dec. 1955; *d* of late Duncan Thomson and Stephana Thomson. *Educ:* St Swithun's, Winchester; Lady Margaret Hall, Oxford (BA Modern History 1977); Birkbeck Coll., London (MA Renaissance Studies 1987); King's Coll., London (MA Religious Studies 1994); Salisbury and Wells Theol Coll. Eur. Res. Manager, Franklin Mint, 1978–85; self-employed in res. and public relns, 1985–89; ordained deacon, 1991, priest, 1994; Curate, St Barnabas, Southfields, 1991–95; Vicar, Christ Church, W Wimbledon, 1995–2003. Tutor in Ethics, SE Inst. of Theol Educn, 1995–2000; Vocations Advr, Lambeth Archdeaconry, 1995–2000. Mem., Gen. Synod, 2008– (Member: Clergy Discipline Commn, 2011–; Cathedrals Fabric Commn for England, 2011–). *Publications:* The Book of Ripon, 1978; (jtly) Gloucester Cathedral—Faith, Art and Architecture: 1000 years, 2010. *Recreations:* classical music especially opera and chamber music, singing, playing chamber music, walking, gardening, reading. *Address:* 3 Miller's Green, Gloucester GL1 2BN. *T:* (01452) 415824. *E:* cthomson@gloucestercathedral.org.uk.

THOMSON, Sir David; *see* Thomson, Sir F. D. D.

THOMSON, Rt Rev. David; *see* Huntingdon, Bishop Suffragan of.

THOMSON, David; writer and film critic; *b* London, 1941; *m* Lucy Gray; two *s*. *Educ:* Dulwich Coll.; London Sch. of Film Technique. Film studies teacher, then Hd, Film Studies, Dartmouth Coll., New Hants; Hd of Film, then Feature Producer, subseq. writer, BBC; various posts with Penguin. Contribs to Independent on Sunday, New York Times, New Republic, Sight and Sound, Film Comment, Movieline, Salon. *Publications:* Wild Excursions: the life and fiction of Laurence Sterne, 1972; A Biographical Dictionary of the Cinema, 1975, 5th edn, as The New Biographical Dictionary of Film, 2010; Suspects (novel), 1985; Warren Beatty and Desert Eyes: a life and a story, 1987; Silver Light (novel), 1990; Showman: life of David O. Selznick, 1993; Rosebud: the story of Orson Welles, 1996; 4–2, 1996; Big Sleep, 1997; Alien Quartet, 1998; Beneath Mulholland: thoughts on Hollywood and its ghosts, 1998; (with Lucy Gray) In Nevada: the land, the people, God and chance, 2000; Hollywood: a celebration!, 2001; The Whole Equation: a history of Hollywood, 2005; Nicole Kidman, 2006; Have You Seen…?, 2008; The Moment of Psycho: how Alfred Hitchcock taught America to love murder, 2010; The Big Screen: the story of the movies and what they did to us, 2012; Why Acting Matters, 2015.

THOMSON, David Paget, RD 1969; *b* 19 March 1931; *s* of Sir George Paget Thomson, FRS, Nobel Laureate, and Kathleen Buchanan Smith; *m* 1959, Patience Mary, *d* of Sir William Lawrence Bragg, CH, OBE, MC, FRS, Nobel Laureate; two *s* two *d*. *Educ:* Rugby Sch.; Grenoble Univ.; Trinity Coll., Cambridge (MA). Nat. Service, RN (Sub-Lieut), 1953–55; subseq. Lieut-Comdr RNR. Lazard Bros & Co., 1956, Director, 1965–86; seconded to HM Diplomatic Service, 1971–73, as Counsellor (Economic), Bonn. Dir Gen., BIEC, 1987–90. Chairman: Kleinwort, subseq. Dresdner RCM, Emerging Markets Trust, 1993–2002; Medical Sickness Annuity and Life Assce Soc. Ltd, 1995–97; Dep. Chm., Permanent Insce Co., 1995–97; Director: Finance Co. Viking, Zurich, 1969–87; Richard Daus & Co., bankers, Frankfurt, 1974–81; Applied Photophysics, 1976–87; Wesleyan Assce Soc. Ltd, 1997–2000; Foreign & Colonial European Investment Trust, 1998–2002. Mem., Monopolies and Mergers Commn, 1984–94. Member: Council, Brunel Univ., 1974–85; Court of Governors, Henley Management Coll., 1979–94. Hon. Treasurer, British Dyslexia Assoc., 1984–86. Chairman: Fitzwilliam Mus. Trust, Cambridge, 1988–93; Portsmouth Naval Base Property Trust, 1992–98; Royal Institution: Treasurer, 1976–81; Chm. Council, 1985. CC Oxon 1985–89. Master, Plumbers' Co., 1980–81. *Recreations:* hill-walking, gardening, real tennis. *Address:* Queens Croft, 16a Castle Street, Wallingford, Oxon OX10 8DW. *T:* (01491) 837161. *Club:* Athenæum (Chm., 1995–98).

See also B. J. P. Thomson, Sir J. A. Thomson.

THOMSON, Maj.-Gen. David Phillips, CB 1993; CBE 1989; MC 1965; Senior Army Member, Royal College of Defence Studies, 1992–95; *b* 30 Jan. 1942; *s* of Cyril Robert William Thomson and Louise Mary Thomson (*née* Phillips). *Educ:* Eastbourne Coll.; RMA Sandhurst. Commnd, Argyll and Sutherland Highlanders, 1962; despatches, 1968; Bde Major, 6th Armd Bde, 1975; Instr, Staff Coll., 1980; CO, 1st Bn, A and SH, 1982; Chief of Staff: RMCS, 1985; 1st Armd Div., 1986; Comdr, 1st Inf. Bde/UK Mobile Force, 1987; despatches, 1992. Col, Argyll and Sutherland Highlanders, 1992–2000. Captain, Royal Castle of Tarbert, 1992–2000. Chm., Sussex Combined Services Museum Trust, 1995–2007. FRGS 1993. *Recreations:* golf, historical research. *Address:* Home HQ, Argyll and Sutherland Highlanders, The Castle, Stirling FK8 1EH. *T:* (01786) 475165.

THOMSON, Dick; HM Diplomatic Service, retired; Consul General, Barcelona, 1999–2002; *b* 18 Dec. 1942; *s* of Adam and Janet Alexander Thomson; *m* 1972, Jacqueline Margaret Dunn (*d* 2003); one *s* one *d*. *Educ:* Port Glasgow High Sch.; Greenock High Sch. With Ministry of Transport, 1961–66; entered FCO, 1966; served: Havana, 1969–70; Athens, 1970–71; Rome, 1971–72; Warsaw, 1972–73; Personnel Dept, FCO, 1973–76; San Francisco, 1976–80; Consul, Algiers, 1980–83; Near East and N Africa Dept, FCO, 1984–87; First Sec., Copenhagen, 1988–92; Head of Parly Relns Unit, FCO, 1992–95; Ambassador to Dominican Republic, 1995–98. *Recreations:* mainly sport—soccer, tennis, swimming. *Address:* 202 Chesterfield Drive, Sevenoaks, Kent TN13 2EH.

THOMSON, Duncan, PhD; Keeper, Scottish National Portrait Gallery, 1982–97; *b* 2 Oct. 1934; *s* of Duncan Murdoch Thomson and Jane McFarlane Wilson; *m* 1964, Julia Jane Macphail; one *d*. *Educ:* Airdrie Acad.; Univ. of Edinburgh (MA 1956, PhD 1970; Hon. Fellow, 1998); Edinburgh Coll. of Art (Cert. of Coll.; Post-Dip. Scholarship); Moray House Coll. of Educn. Teacher of Art, 1959–67; Asst Keeper, Scottish National Portrait Gall., 1967–82. Scottish Arts Council: Mem., Art Cttee, 1983–89; Chm., Exhibn Panel, 1985–89. Chm., Mansfield Traquair Trust, 1996–. Vice-Pres., Art in Healthcare, 2007–14 (Mem. Bd, 2014–). Mem., Editl Bd, Scottish Cultural Resources Access Network, 1998–2004. *Publications:* The Life and Art of George Jamesone, 1974; Sir Henry Raeburn, 1994; Arikha, 1994; (jtly) The Skating Minister, 2004; A History of the Scottish National Portrait Gallery, 2011; *exhibition catalogues:* A Virtuous and Noble Education, 1971; Painting in Scotland 1570–1650, 1975; Eye to Eye, 1980; (jtly) John Michael Wright, 1982; (jtly) The Queen's Image, 1987; Raeburn: the art of Sir Henry Raeburn 1756–1823, 1997; (jtly) Avigdor Arikha From Life, 2006. *Recreation:* reading poetry (and thinking about writing it). *Address:* 3 Eglinton Crescent, Edinburgh EH12 5DH. *T:* (0131) 225 6430. *Club:* Scottish Arts (Edinburgh).

THOMSON, Elaine Margaret; Bid Manager, Absoft Ltd, since 2014 (Logistics SAP Consultant, 1995–99; Support Centre Manager, 2003–09; Senior Public Sector Specialist, 2009–14); *b* 10 Aug. 1957; *d* of Dr Charles Thomson and Moira Thomson; partner, Archie Flockhart. *Educ:* Aberdeen Univ. (BSc Pure Sci.); Robert Gordon Univ. (Postgraduate Cert. in Corporate Communications and Public Affairs). Analyst/Programmer, ABB Vetco Gray UK Ltd, 1982–94. MSP (Lab) Aberdeen N, 1999–2003; contested same seat, 2003, 2007. Chair, Cornerstone (formerly Cornerstone Community Care), 2005–12 (non-exec. Dir, 2003–); Dir, Corners Turned, social enterprise co., 2008–12. *Recreations:* ski-ing, walking, reading. *E:* elaine.thomson@talk21.com.

THOMSON, Sir (Frederick Douglas) David, 3rd Bt *cr* 1929; Chairman: S. A. Meacock, since 1996; The Investment Co., since 2005; *b* 14 Feb. 1940; *s* of Sir James Douglas Wishart Thomson, 2nd Bt, and of Evelyn Margaret Isabel, (Bettina), *d* of Lt-Comdr D. W. S. Douglas, RN; *S* father, 1972; *m* 1st, 1967, Caroline Anne (marr. diss. 1994), *d* of Major Timothy Stuart Lewis; two *s* one *d*; 2nd, 2003, Hilary Claire, *d* of Sidney Paul Youldon, MC. *Educ:* Eton; University College, Oxford (BA Agric). Ben Line, 1961–89; Chairman: Through Transport Mutual Insce Ltd, 1983–2008 (Dir, 1973–2013); Britannia Steam Ship Insurance Assoc. Ltd, 1986–2008 (Dir, 1965–2008). Mem., Queen's Body Guard for Scotland, Royal Company of Archers. *Recreations:* shooting, ski-ing, music. *Heir: s* Simon Douglas Charles Thomson, *b* 16 June 1969. *Address:* Holylee, Walkerburn, Peeblesshire EH43 6BD. *T:* 07831 355691. *E:* sirdthomson@holylee.go-plus.net. *Club:* Boodle's.

THOMSON, James Phillips Spalding; Consultant Surgeon, St Mark's Hospital, 1974–99, now Emeritus (Clinical Director, 1990–97); Administrator, Priory Church of St Bartholomew the Great, 2000–02; Master, Sutton's Hospital in Charterhouse, 2001–12; *b* 2 Oct. 1939; *s* of late Peggy Marion Thomson (*née* Phillips) and James Laing Spalding Thomson, MB ChB,

MRCGP; *m* 1968, Dr Anne Katharine (*née* Richards), MB BS, MRCP, DCH; one *s* three *d*. *Educ:* Haileybury and Imperial Service Coll.; Middlesex Hosp. Med. Sch., Univ. of London (MB BS 1962; MS 1974). LRCP, MRCS, 1962, FRCS 1969; DObst RCOG 1964. Jun. med. and surgical appts, 1962–71; Demonstrator, Dept of Anatomy, 1964–66, Lectr, Dept of Surgery, 1971–74, Middlesex Hosp. Med. Sch.; Consultant Surgeon: Royal Northern Hosp., 1975–77; Hackney Hosp., 1977–86; Homerton Hosp., 1986–90. Hon. Consultant Surgeon: St John's Hosp. for Diseases of the Skin, 1973–75; St Mary's Hosp., 1982–99; St Luke's Hosp. for the Clergy, 1976–99; Civil Cons. in Surgery, RAF, 1984–99, now Hon. Civil Cons.; Civilian Cons. in Colorectal Surgery, RN, 1986–99, now Emeritus Cons. in Surgery; Hon. Lectr in Surgery, Bart's Hosp. Med. Coll., 1977–94; Hon. Clin. Sen. Lectr in Surgery, Imperial Coll. Sch. of Medicine at St Mary's (formerly St Mary's Hosp. Med. Sch., Imperial Coll.), London, 1994–99. Hon. Cons. Advr in Surgery, Ileostomy Assoc., 1986–99. Examr in Surgery, Univs of Cambridge, Liverpool and London; Mem., Court of Examrs, RCS, 1986–92. Mem., UK Develt Cttee, Anglican Centre in Rome, 2013–. President: Section of Coloproctology, RSocMed, 1994–95; Travelling Surgical Soc., 1998–2001; St Mark's Assoc., 1999; Hunterian Soc., 2001–02; Friends of St Mark's Hosp., 2006–; Haileybury Soc., 2006–07; Patron and Fellow, Burgon Soc., 2002– (Pres., 2011–); Patron, Walbrook Music Trust, 2011–. Chm., Notarial Adv. Bd, 2008–10. Vice-Chm. of Council and Trustee, St Luke's Hosp. for the Clergy, 1992–2004; Trustee: Med. Coll. of St Bartholomew's Hosp. Trust, 2002–11; St Andrew Holborn Church Foundn, 2003–11; Rev. Dr George Richards Charity, 2001–11; Tancred's Charities, 2001–11. Governor, Corp. of Sons of the Clergy, 1988–. Liveryman: Apothecaries' Soc., 1980–; Barbers' Co., 1992–; Merchant Taylors' Co., 2014–. Hon. Fellow, Queen Mary, Univ. of London, 2007. Frederick Salmon Medal, RSocMed, 1996; William Harvey Medal, QMUL, 2012. DM Lambeth, 1987. *Publications:* (jtly) Colorectal Disease, 1981; (jtly) Frontiers in Colorectal Disease, 1986; (jtly) Updates in Coloproctology, 1992; contribs to books and learned jls. *Recreations:* church music and architecture, heraldry, railways, canals, guide at Lambeth Palace. *Address:* Gallery House, 13 New Street, Holt, Norfolk NR25 6JJ. *T:* (01263) 711214, 07550 079522; 15 Nelson Terrace, N1 8DG. *T:* (020) 7253 1052. *E:* JamesPSThomson@aol.com. *Clubs:* Athenæum, Royal Society of Medicine.

THOMSON, Sir John (Adam), GCMG 1985 (KCMG 1978; CMG 1972); MA; HM Diplomatic Service, retired; *b* 27 April 1927; *s* of late Sir George Thomson, FRS, Master of Corpus Christi Coll., Cambridge, 1952–62 (*s* of Sir J. J. Thomson, OM, FRS, Master of Trinity Coll., Cambridge, 1919–40), and late Kathleen, *d* of Very Rev. Sir George Adam Smith, DD, LLD, Principal of Aberdeen Univ., 1909–35; *m* 1st, 1953, Elizabeth Anne McClure (*d* 1988), *d* of late Norman McClure, Pres. of Ursinus Coll., Penn, USA; three *s* one *d*; 2nd, 1992, Judith Ogden Bullitt, *d* of late John Stanley Ogden, NY, and Olga Geddes Bradshaw, Melbourne. *Educ:* Phillips Exeter Acad., USA; Univ. of Aberdeen; Trinity Coll., Cambridge. Foreign Office, 1950; Third Sec., Jedda, 1951; Damascus, 1954; FO, 1955; Private Sec. to Permanent Under-Secretary, 1958–60; First Sec., Washington, 1960–64; FO, 1964; Acting Head of Planning Staff, 1966; Counsellor, 1967; Head of Planning Staff, FO, 1967; seconded to Cabinet Office as Chief of Assessments Staff, 1968–71; Minister and Dep. Permanent Rep. to N Atlantic Council, 1972–73; Head of UK Delegn to MBFR Exploratory Talks, Vienna, 1973; Asst Under-Sec. of State, FCO, 1973–76; High Comr to India, 1977–82; UK Perm. Rep. to UN, 1982–87. Chm., Fleming Emerging Markets Investment Trust, 1991–98; Internat. Advr, ANZ Grindlays Bank, 1996–97 (Dir, 1987–96). Mem., Howie Cttee on Scottish Secondary Educn, 1990–93. Trustee, Nat. Museums of Scotland, 1991–99. Principal Dir, 21st Century Trust, 1987–90; Dir, Minority Rights Gp, USA, 1993–99; Chm., Minority Rights Gp Internat., 1991–99. Member: Council, IISS, 1987–96; Council, ODI, 1987–96; Governing Body, IDS, 1987–96. Director's Visitor, IAS, Princeton, 1995–96. Trustee, Indian Nat. Trust, 1989–2009. Associate Mem., Nuffield Coll., Oxford, 1987–91; Res. Associate, MIT, 2005–. Hon. Foreign Mem., American Acad. of Arts and Scis, 2010. Hon. LLD: Ursinus Coll., Penn, 1984; Aberdeen, 1986; Hon. DHL Allegheny Coll., Penn, 1985. *Publications:* Crusader Castles (with R. Fedden), 1956. *Recreations:* carpets, castles, walking. *Clubs:* Athenæum; Century (New York).

See also Sir A. McC. Thomson, D. P. Thomson.

THOMSON, Rt Rev. John Bromilow; *see* Selby, Bishop Suffragan of.

THOMSON, Prof. Joseph McGeachy, FRSE; Commissioner, Scottish Law Commission, 2000–09; *b* 6 May 1948; *s* of James Thomson and Catherine (*née* McGeachy); *m* 1999, Marilyn Ann Iverson. *Educ:* Keil Sch., Dumbarton; Univ. of Edinburgh (LLB 1970). FRSE 1996. Lectr in Law, Univ. of Birmingham, 1970–74; Lectr in Laws, King's Coll., London, 1974–84; Prof. of Law, Univ. of Strathclyde, 1984–90; Regius Prof. of Law, Glasgow Univ., 1991–2005. Vis. Prof., Glasgow Caledonian Univ., 2005–09. Dep. General Editor, Stair Meml Encyclopaedia of Laws of Scotland, 1984–96; Ed., Juridical Rev., 2009–. Dir, Scottish Universities Law Inst., 2000–09. Pres., SPTL, 2000–01; Hon. Vice-Pres., Assoc. of Law Teachers, 2003–. Hon. Sheriff, 2015–. Hon. Fellow, Soc. for Advanced Legal Studies, 2001. *Publications:* Family Law in Scotland, 1987, 7th edn 2014; Delictual Liability, 1994, 5th edn 2014; (with H. MacQueen) Contract Law in Scotland, 2000, 3rd edn 2012; Scots Private Law, 2006; contribs to Law Qly Review, Modern Law Review, Juridical Review, Scots Law Times, etc. *Recreations:* bridge, wine and food. *Address:* Askomel End, Low Askomil, Campbeltown, Argyll PA28 6EP. *T:* (01586) 554930.

THOMSON, Kenneth Andrew Lyons; Director-General, Strategy and External Affairs, Scottish Government, since 2011; *b* 18 Oct. 1962; *s* of Andrew Leslie Thomson and Jennifer Thomson (*née* Lyons); *m* 1986, Ursula Schlapp; one *s* one *d*. *Educ:* Inch and Cramond Prim. Schs; Royal High Sch., Edinburgh; Univ. of St Andrews (MA Hons Music); Open Univ. (MBA). Supernumerary Lightkeeper, Northern Lighthouse Bd, 1980–83; Admin. Trainee, Civil Service, Scottish Office, 1988; Higher Exec. Officer (Develt) 1988–90; Pvte Sec. to Minister of State, Scottish Office, 1990–91; Principal Officer, 1991; Asst Dir, Scottish Financial Enterprise, 1991–93; project team, Setting Forth, 1993–96; Bill Manager, Crime and Punishment (Scotland) Act, 1996–97; work on white paper, 'Scotland's Parliament', 1997; Asst Sec., 1997; Principal Pvte Sec. to Sec. of State for Scotland, 1997–99, to First Minister of Scotland, 1999; Dir, Corporate Develt, 1999–2000, Hd, Health Improvement Strategy Div., 2000–02, Scottish Exec.; Dir, Corporate Services, Scottish Prison Service, 2002–05; Dir, Constitutional and Parly Secretariat, Scottish Exec., 2005–07; Dir, Constitution Law and Cts, 2007–10, Dir, Constitution, subseq. International and Constitution, 2010–11, Scottish Govt. Trustee, Dunedin Concerts Trust, 2007–12. *Recreations:* cooking, consort music, crosswords, cycling. *Address:* c/o Scottish Government, St Andrew's House, Edinburgh EH1 3DG.

THOMSON, Malcolm George; QC (Scot.) 1987; *b* 6 April 1950; *s* of late George Robert Thomson, OBE, and Daphne Ethel Thomson; *m* 1st, 1978, Susan Gordon Aitken (marr. diss. 2001); two *d*; 2nd, 2008, Maybel Hutton. *Educ:* Edinburgh Acad.; Edinburgh Univ. (LLB). Advocate 1974; called to the Bar, Lincoln's Inn, 1991. Standing Junior Counsel to Dept of Agriculture and Fisheries for Scotland and Forestry Commn in Scotland, 1982–87. Chm., NHS Tribunal (Scotland), 1995–2005; Mem., Scottish Legal Aid Bd, 1998–2006; Temp. Judge, Court of Session, 2002–. Trustee, Nat. Liby of Scotland, 1995–2013. *Recreations:* sailing, ski-ing. *Address:* 12 Succoth Avenue, Edinburgh EH12 6BT. *T:* (0131) 337 4911. *Club:* New (Edinburgh).

THOMSON, Mark Cameron Angus, CMG 2015; OBE 2004; Secretary General, Association for the Prevention of Torture, since 2001; *b* Redhill, 21 May 1956; *s* of Sir John Sutherland, (Sir Ian), Thomson, KBE, CMG, MBE (mil.) and Nancy Marguerite Thomson; *m* 1992, Catherine Girod; two *s* one *d*. *Educ:* Drasa Avenue Sch., Lautoka, Fiji; Grenville Coll., Bideford; Univ. of Essex (BA Latin Amer. Studies 1979); University Coll. London (MA Rural Develt in Latin America 1982). Coordinator, Nicaragua Solidarity Campaign, 1982–84; Community Educn Officer, Tower Hamlets Internat. Solidarity, 1984–88; Latin America and Caribbean Prog. Officer, World Univ. Service, 1988–91; Inter-govtl Orgns Coordinator, Amnesty Internat., 1991–92; Dep. Dir, Internat. Service for Human Rights, 1992–2001. *Recreation:* trying to keep my wife happy. *Address:* Association for the Prevention of Torture, Centre Jean-Jacques Gautier, 10 route de Ferney, PO Box 137, 1211 Geneva 19, Switzerland. *T:* (22) 9192170. *E:* mthomson@apt.ch. *Club:* Mosquito Coasters Football.

THOMSON, Sir Mark (Wilfrid Home), 3rd Bt *cr* 1925, of Old Nunthorpe, Co. York; *b* 29 Dec. 1939; *s* of Sir Ivo Wilfrid Home Thomson, 2nd Bt and Sybil Marguerite, *yr d* of C. W. Thompson; *S* father, 1991; *m* 1st, 1976, Lady Jacqueline Rufus Isaacs (marr. diss. 1997), *o d* of 3rd Marquess of Reading, MBE, MC; three *s* one *d* (incl. twin *s*); 2nd, 2002, April MacKenzie Russell (*née* Arbon). *Heir: s* Albert Mark Home Thomson [*b* 3 Aug. 1979; *m* 2012, Olivia J. Hill].

THOMSON, Michelle Rhonda; MP for Edinburgh West, since 2015 (SNP, May–Oct. 2015, Ind, since Oct. 2015); *b* 11 March 1965; *m*; two *c*. *Educ:* Royal Scottish Acad. of Music and Drama; Abertay Univ. (MSc IT). Professional musician, 1985; Prog. Manager and Project Manager, Standard Life, 1991–2006; Prog. Manager and Portfolio Manager, Royal Bank of Scotland Gp, 2006–08; Dir, Your Property Shop, 2009–15. Founder Mem. and Exec. Bd Mem., Business for Scotland, 2012–14. Mem., Business, Innovation and Skills Select Cttee, 2015–. *Address:* House of Commons, SW1A 0AA.

THOMSON, Peter Alexander Bremner, CVO 1986; HM Diplomatic Service, retired; *b* 16 Jan. 1938; *s* of Alexander Thomson, financial journalist, and Dorothy (*née* Scurr); *m* 1965, Lucinda Sellar; three *s*. *Educ:* Canford School; RN College, Dartmouth; Sch. of Oriental and African Studies, London (BA 1970; MPhil 1975; MA 1991). Sub Lieut and Lieut RN in HM Ships Albion, Plover, Tiger, Ark Royal, Eagle; Lt Comdr ashore in Taiwan and Hong Kong; joined Diplomatic Service, 1975; First Sec., FCO, Lagos, Hong Kong, 1975–84; Counsellor, Peking, 1984–87; High Comr, Belize, 1987–90; Counsellor, FCO, 1991–95; High Comr, Seychelles, 1995–97. *Publications:* Belize: a concise history, 2005. *Recreations:* sailing, walking. *Address:* The Red House, Charlton Horethorne, near Sherborne DT9 4NL.

THOMSON, Prof. Richard Geoffrey, FRCP, FFPH; Professor of Epidemiology and Public Health, Institute of Health and Society, since 1999, and Associate Dean for Patient and Public Engagement, Faculty of Medical Sciences, Newcastle Medical School, since 2010, University of Newcastle upon Tyne; *b* 2 May 1958; *s* of Lesley Bambridge and Honor Thomson (*neé* Gooding); *m* 1989, Tracy Robson; two *d*. *Educ:* Stamford Sch., Stamford; St Edmund Hall, Oxford (BA Physiol. 1979; BM BCh 1982); Univ. of Newcastle upon Tyne (MD 1990). FRCP 1996; FFPH 1996. Sen. House Officer, Medicine, Freeman Hosp., Newcastle upon Tyne, 1983–85; Res. Fellow, Newcastle upon Tyne Univ., 1985–88; Registrar, then Sen. Registrar in Public Health, 1988–89, Dir, Service Quality and Standards, 1989–92, Northern RHA; Sen. Lectr and Consultant in Public Health, Medical Sch., Newcastle upon Tyne Univ., 1992–99. Director: UK Quality Indicator Proj., 1997–2007; Epidemiology and Res., Nat. Patient Safety Agency, 2004–07. Mem., Steering Gp on Internat. Patient Safety Classification, WHO, 2005–07. Mem., 13th Club. Associate Editor, Quality and Safety in Health Care, 1991–2010. *Publications:* numerous articles in professional jls on risk communication and decision making, stroke epidemiology, health care quality and safety, and health services research. *Recreations:* tennis, literature, theatre, good food, fine wine, sitting with a fishing rod contemplating. *Address:* Institute of Health and Society, Newcastle University, Baddiley-Clark Building, Richardson Road, Newcastle upon Tyne NE2 4AX. *T:* (0191) 208 8760, *Fax:* (0191) 208 8422. *E:* richard.thomson@newcastle.ac.uk.

THOMSON, Prof. Richard Ian, PhD; FRSE; Watson Gordon Professor of Fine Art, University of Edinburgh, since 1996; *b* 1 March 1953; *s* of late Rev. George Ian Falconer Thomson and Mary Josephine Lambart Thomson (*née* Dixon); *m* 1978, Belinda Jane Greaves; two *s*. *Educ:* Shrewsbury Sch.; St Catherine's Coll., Oxford (Exhibnr; BA); Univ. of Oxford (Dip. Hist. of Art); Courtauld Inst. of Art, Univ. of London (MA; PhD 1989). FRSE 1998. Lectr, 1977–88, Sen. Lectr, 1988–95, Reader, 1995–96, in History of Art, Univ. of Manchester. Guest Scholar, J. Paul Getty Mus., Malibu, 1993; Van Gogh Vis. Fellow, Univ. of Amsterdam, 2007; Slade Prof. of Fine Art, Univ. of Oxford, 2008–09. Trustee, Nat. Galls of Scotland, 2002–10; Member, Comité Scientifique: Institut National d'Histoire de l'Art, Paris, 2008–; Musée d'Orsay, Paris, 2010–. Exhibitions curated or co-curated: Harold Gilman, 1981–82; Impressionist Drawings, 1986; The Private Degas, 1987; Camille Pissarro: impressionism, landscape and rural labour, 1990; Toulouse-Lautrec, 1991–92; Monet to Matisse: landscape painting in France 1874–1914, 1994; Seurat and the Bathers, 1997; Theo van Gogh, 1999; Monet 1878–1883: the Seine and the Sea, 2003; Toulouse-Lautrec and Montmartre, 2005; Degas, Sickert and Toulouse-Lautrec: London and Paris 1870–1910, 2005; Monet, 1840–1926, 2010–11; Dreams of Nature: Symbolist landscape from Van Gogh to Kandinsky, 2012–13. Officier, l'Ordre des Arts et des Lettres, 2012. *Publications:* Toulouse-Lautrec, 1977; French Nineteenth Century Drawings in the Whitworth Art Gallery, 1981; Seurat, 1985; Degas, the Nudes, 1988; Edgar Degas, Waiting, 1995; (ed) Framing France, 1998; (ed jtly) Soil and Stone: impressionism, urbanism, environment, 2003; The Troubled Republic: visual culture and social debate in France 1889–1900, 2004; Vincent van Gogh: Starry Night, 2008; Art of the Actual, Naturalism and Style in Early Third Republic France 1880–1900, 2012. *Recreations:* gardening, jazz, hill walking. *Address:* School of Arts, Culture and the Environment, University of Edinburgh, Minto House, 20 Chambers Street, Edinburgh EH1 1JZ. *T:* (0131) 650 4124, *Fax:* (0131) 650 6638. *E:* R.Thomson@ed.ac.uk.

THOMSON, Robert James; Chief Executive Officer, News Corporation, since 2013; *b* 11 March 1961; *s* of Jim and Gen Thomson; *m* 1992, Wang Ping; two *s*. *Educ:* Royal Melbourne Inst. of Technol. (BA Journalism). Finance and gen. affairs reporter, The Herald, Melbourne, then Sydney, 1979–83; Sen. Feature Writer, Sydney Morning Herald, 1983–85; Financial Times: Beijing corresp., 1985–89; Tokyo corresp., 1989–94; Foreign News Ed., 1994–96; Asst Ed., and Ed., Weekend FT, 1996–98; Man. Ed., based in NY, 1998–2002; Ed., The Times, 2002–07; Publisher, 2007–08, Ed.-in-Chief, 2008–12, Dow Jones & Co.; Man. Ed., Wall Street Journal, 2008–12. Chm., Arts Internat., 2001–02. Dir, Soc. of Amer. Business Editors and Writers, 2001–02. *Publications:* The Judges: a portrait of the Australian judiciary, 1986; (jtly) The Chinese Army, 1990; (ed) True Fiction, 1998. *Recreations:* reading, tennis, cinema. *Address:* News Corporation, 1211 Avenue of Americas, New York, NY 10036, USA.

THOMSON, Prof. Robert William, PhD; FBA 1995; Calouste Gulbenkian Professor of Armenian Studies, University of Oxford, 1992–2001, now Professor Emeritus; Fellow of Pembroke College, Oxford, 1992–2001, now Supernumerary Fellow; *b* 24 March 1934; *s* of late David William Thomson and Lilian (*née* Cramphorn); *m* 1963, Judith Ailsa Cawdry; two *s*. *Educ:* George Watson's Boys' Coll., Edinburgh; Sidney Sussex Coll., Cambridge (BA 1955); Trinity Coll., Cambridge (PhD 1962). Halki Theol Coll., Istanbul, 1955–56; Jun. Fellow, Dumbarton Oaks, Washington, 1960–61; Louvain Univ., 1961–62; Harvard University: Instructor, then Asst Prof. of Classical Armenian, Dept of Near Eastern Langs, 1963–69; Mashtots Prof. of Armenian Studies, 1969–92; Chm., Dept of Near Eastern Langs, 1973–78, 1980–81. Dir, Dumbarton Oaks, Washington DC, 1984–89. Hon. PhD Tübingen, 2003. *Publications:* (ed with J. N. Birdsall) Biblical and Patristic Studies in Memory of Robert Pierce Casey, 1963; Athanasiana Syriaca, 4 parts, 1965–77; Athanasius: Contra Gentes and De Incarnatione, 1971; The Teaching of Saint Gregory, 1971, 2nd edn 2001; Introduction to

Classical Armenian, 1975; Agathangelos: history of the Armenians, 1977; (with K. B. Bardakjian) Textbook of Modern Western Armenian, 1977; Moses Khorenatsi: history of the Armenians, 1978, 2nd edn 2006; Elishe: history of Vardan, 1982; (ed with N. G. Garsoian and T. J. Mathews) East of Byzantium, 1982; (with B. Kendall) David the Invincible Philosopher, 1983; Thomas Artsruni: history of the Artsruni House, 1985; The Armenian Version of Dionysius the Areopagite, 2 vols, 1987; Lazar Parpetsi: history of the Armenians, 1991; Studies in Armenian Literature and Christianity, 1994; The Syriac Version of the Hexaemeron by Basil of Caesarea, 1995; A Bibliography of Classical Armenian Literature, 1995; Rewriting Caucasian History: the Armenian version of the Georgian Chronicles, 1996; (ed with J.-P. Mahé) From Byzantium to Iran: Armenian studies in honour of Nina G. Garsoian, 1997; (with J. Howard-Johnston) The Armenian History of Sebeos, 1999; The Lawcode of Mxit'ar Gosh, 2000; The Armenian Adaptation of the Ecclesiastical History of Socrates Scholasticus, 2001; Hamam: commentary on Proverbs, 2005; Nerses of Lambron: commentary on Revelation, 2007; The Lives of Saint Gregory, 2010; Saint Basil and Armenian Cosmology, 2012; Nonnus of Nisibis: commentary on Gospel of St John, 2014; contribs to Jl Theol Studies, Le Muséon, Revue des études arméniennes, Dumbarton Oaks Papers, Oxford Dictionary of Byzantium, Encyclopedia Iranica, The Cambridge History of the Byzantine Empire. *Address:* Oriental Institute, Pusey Lane, Oxford OX1 2LE.

THOMSON, Roderick Nicol; QC (Scot.) 2008; *b* Paisley, Scotland, 25 Aug. 1959; *s* of Frank William Thomson and Mabel Cockburn Thomson (*née* Nicol); *m* 1989, Catriona Mary McCraw; one *s* one *d*. *Educ:* Hitchin Boys' Grammar Sch.; Morrison's Acad.; Edinburgh Univ. (BCom 1980; LLB 1982; DipLP 1983). Admitted Advocate, 1990; Standing Junior Counsel in Scotland: to FCO, 2002–08; to HMRC, 2006–08. *Recreations:* fine art, painting, photography, cinema, fishing, golf, travel. *Address:* 142 East Trinity Road, Edinburgh EH5 3PR. *T:* (0131) 552 5965; Advocates' Library, Parliament House, Edinburgh EH1 1RF. *E:* rntadvocate1@aol.com.

THOMSON, Prof. Wendy, CBE 2005; PhD; Managing Director, Norfolk County Council, since 2014; *b* Montreal, 28 Oct. 1953; *d* of Shirley and Grace Thomson; *m* 1995, David Dorne (*d* 1999); two step *s*; one *d*. *Educ:* McGill Univ. (BSW; Masters of Social Work); Univ. of Bristol (PhD 1989). Asst Chief Exec., Islington BC, 1987–93; Chief Executive: Turning Point, 1993–96; Newham BC, 1996–99; Dir of Inspection, Audit Commn, 1999–2001; Prime Minister's Advr on Public Services Reform, Cabinet Office, 2001–05; Prof. and Dir, Sch. of Social Work, McGill Univ., Montreal, 2005–14. Adviser: Office of Pres., Republic of Ghana, 2006–09; UNDP, 2006–08; Internat. Advr, Global Forum on Re-inventing Govt, 2007. Comr, Ontario Commn on Child Welfare, 2009–12; Chm., Expert Panel on Health Care Financing, Quebec Govt, 2012–14. *Recreations:* yoga, gardening, theatre, travel, shopping, ski-ing. *Address:* Norfolk County Council, County Hall, Martineau Lane, Norwich, Norfolk NR1 2DH.

THOMSON, William Oliver, MD, DPH, DIH; Chief Administrative Medical Officer, Lanarkshire Health Board, 1973–88; *b* 23 March 1925; *s* of William Crosbie Thomson and Mary Jolie Johnston; *m* 1956, Isobel Lauder Glendinning Brady; two *s*. *Educ:* Allan Glen's Sch., Glasgow; Univ. of Glasgow (MB ChB, MD). DPA; FFCM; FRCPGlas 1988 (MRCPGlas 1986). Chronic student of Gray's Inn, London. Captain, RAMC, 1948–50. Hospital appointments, 1951–53; appointments in Public Health, Glasgow, 1953–60; Admin. MO, Western Regional Hospital Bd, 1960–70; Group Medical Superintendent, Glasgow Maternity and Women's Hospitals, 1970–73; Mem., Health Services Ind. Adv. Cttee, 1980–86. Visiting Lecturer: Univ. of Michigan, Ann Arbor; Ministry of Health, Ontario; Hon. Lectr, Univ. of Glasgow. Med. Advr, Scottish TV, 1992–98. Diploma of Scottish Council for Health Educn (for services to health educn), 1979. *Publications:* (jtly) In England Now, 1989; articles on clinical medicine, community medicine, general practice, occupational health and health education, in various medical jls; humorous pieces in The Lancet, BMJ, etc. *Recreations:* walking, talking, writing. *Address:* Flat 7, Silverwells Court, Bothwell, Glasgow G71 8LT. *T:* (01698) 852586.

THONEMANN, Peter Clive, MSc, DPhil; Professor Emeritus, University of Wales, Swansea; *b* 3 June 1917; *m*; one *s* one *d*. *Educ:* Melbourne Church of England Grammar Sch., Melbourne; Sydney and Oxford Univs. BSc Melbourne, 1940; MSc Sydney, 1945; DPhil Oxford, 1949. Munition Supply Laboratories, Victoria, Australia, 1940; Amalgamated Wireless, Australia, 1942; University of Sydney, Commonwealth Research Fellow, 1944; Trinity Coll. and Clarendon Laboratory, Oxford, ICI Research Fellow, 1946; initiated research for controlled fusion power, 1947–49; United Kingdom Atomic Energy Authority: Head of Controlled Fusion Res., 1949–60; designed and built prototype fusion reactor, ZETA, 1954–57; with Res. Unit, 1960–64, Head of B Div., 1964–67, Dep. Dir, 1967–68, Culham Laboratory; Prof. and Hd of Dept of Physics, UC, Swansea, 1968–84. *Publications:* many contributions to learned journals. *Address:* 130 Bishopston Road, Bishopston, Swansea SA3 3EU.

't HOOFT, Prof. Dr Gerardus; Professor of Theoretical Physics, Utrecht University, 1977–2011; *b* 5 July 1946; *s* of H. 't Hooft and M. A. van Kampen; *m* 1972, Albertha A. Schik, MD; two *d*. *Educ:* Dalton Lyceum Gymnasium beta, The Hague; Utrecht Univ. (PhD). Fellow, Theoretical Physics Div., CERN, Geneva, 1972–74; Asst Prof., Univ. of Utrecht, 1974–77. Heineman Prize, APS, 1979; Wolf Prize, Wolf Foundn, Israel, 1982; Franklin Medal, Franklin Inst., Philadelphia, 1995; (jtly) Nobel Prize for Physics, 1999; several decorations and 11 hon. doctorates. Commandeur in de Orde van de Nederlandse Leeuw, 1999. *Publications:* De bouwstenen van de Schepping, 1992 (In Search of the Ultimate Building Blocks, 1996); Under the Spell of the Gauge Principle, 1994; Playing with Planets, 2008; (with S. Vandoren) Tijd in Machten van Tien, 2011; over 200 scientific pubns. *Address:* Spinoza Institute, Leuvenlaan 4, PO Box 80.195, 3508 TD Utrecht, Netherlands. *T:* 302531863. *W:* www.staff.science.uu.nl/~thooft101.

THORBURN, Andrew, BSc; FRTPI; Principal, Thorburns, since 1990; Chairman, Bow Street Partners, 1999–2005; Founder Chairman, Ringstall Ltd, since 2011; *b* 20 March 1934; *s* of James Beresford Thorburn and Marjorie Clara Burford; *m* Margaret Anne Crack; one *s* two *d*. *Educ:* Bridport Grammar Sch.; Univ. of Southampton (BSc). MRTPI 1959, FRTPI 1969. National Service, RN, 1954–56. Planning Asst, Kent CC, 1957–59; Planning Officer, Devon CC, 1959–63; Asst County Planning Officer, Hampshire CC, 1963–68; Dir, Notts and Derbyshire Sub-Region Study, 1968–70; Dep. County Planning Dir, Cheshire CC, 1970–73; County Planning Officer, E Sussex CC, 1973–83; Chief Exec., English Tourist Bd, 1983–85; Head of Tourism and Leisure Div., Grant Thornton, 1986–90. Pres., RTPI, 1982; Mem. Exec., Town and Country Planning Assoc., 1969–81; Founder Trustee, Sussex Heritage Trust, 1978–99. Fellow, Tourism Soc., 1983–2008. *Publications:* Planning Villages, 1971; The Missing Museum, 2006. *Recreation:* thinking. *Club:* Fareham Sailing and Motor Boat.

THORLEY, Giles Alexander; Operating Partner, TDR Capital LLP, since 2010; *b* 29 June 1967; *s* of Hugh A. Thorley and Jillian E. Thorley; *m* 1993, Michelle Britt; three *s*. *Educ:* Hereford Cathedral Sch.; QMC, Univ. of London (LLB); Inns of Court Sch. of Law. Called to the Bar, Inner Temple, 1990. Director: Nomura Internat. plc, 1990–98; Inntrepreneur Pub Co., 1998–99; Chief Exec., Unique Pub Co. plc, 1999–2001; Exec. Chm., 2001–03, Chief Exec., 2003–10, Punch Taverns plc; Chm., Tragus Hldgs, 2005–12. Dir and Supervisory Bd Mem., Brewers and Licensed Retailers Assoc., subseq. British Beer and Pub Assoc., 1998–2010. *Recreations:* ski-ing, water sports, the family.

THORLEY, Simon Joe; QC 1989; International Judge, Singapore International Commercial Court, since 2015; *b* 22 May 1950; *s* of Sir Gerald Bowers Thorley, TD and of Beryl, *d* of G. Preston Rhodes; *m* 1983, Jane Elizabeth Cockcroft (*d* 2007); two *s* one *d*. *Educ:* Rugby Sch.; Keble Coll., Oxford (MA Jurisprudence). Called to the Bar, Inner Temple, 1972, Bencher, 1999 (Reader, 2012; Treas., 2013); pupilled to William Aldous; in practice at Intellectual Property Bar (formerly Patent Bar), 1972–2014; apptd by Lord Chancellor to hear Trade Mark Appeals, 1996–2003; Dep. High Court Judge, 1998–2014. Dep. Chm., Copyright Tribunal, 1998–2006. Chm., IP Bar (formerly Patent Bar) Assoc., 1995–99; Member: Gen. Council of the Bar, 1995–99; Council, British Gp, Internat. Assoc. for Protection of Industrial Property, 1993–95; Disciplinary Cttee, Eur. Patent Orgn, 2015–. Arbitrator and Mediator, 2014–. Trustee, Addenbrooke's Charitable Trust, 2015–. *Publications:* (co-ed) Terrell on The Law of Patents, 13th edn 1982 to 16th edn 2005. *Recreations:* family, shooting, opera. *Address:* Brick Court Chambers, 7–8 Essex Street, WC2R 3LD. *T:* (020) 7379 3550.

THORN, John Leonard, MA; writer and educational consultant; Headmaster of Winchester College, 1968–85; *b* 28 April 1925; *s* of late Stanley and Winifred Thorn; *m* 1955, Veronica Laura (*d* 1999), *d* of late Sir Robert Maconochie, OBE, QC; one *s* one *d*. *Educ:* St Paul's School; Corpus Christi College, Cambridge. Served War of 1939–45, Sub-Lieutenant, RNVR, 1943–46. Asst Master, Clifton Coll., 1949–61; Headmaster, Repton School, 1961–68. Dir, Winchester Cathedral Trust, 1986–89. Dir, Royal Opera House, Covent Garden, 1971–76. Chm., Headmasters' Conference, 1981. Member: Bd, Securities Assoc., 1987–91; Exec. Cttee, Cancer Res. Campaign, 1987–90; Chm., Hants Bldgs Preservation Trust, 1992–96 (Vice-Chm., 1989–92); Trustee: British Museum, 1980–85; Oakham Sch., 1985–89. Governor, Stowe Sch., 1985–90; Chm. of Governors, Abingdon Sch., 1991–94. *Publications:* (joint) A History of England, 1961; The Road to Winchester (autobiog.), 1989; various articles. *Address:* 6 Chilbolton Avenue, Winchester SO22 5HD. *T:* (01962) 855990. *Club:* Garrick.

THORN, His Honour Roger Eric; QC 1990; a Circuit Judge, 2004–14; *b* 23 March 1948; twin *s* of late James Douglas 'Pat' Thorn and of Daphne Elizabeth (*née* Robinson); *m* 2005, Clare, *d* of late George Lillywhite, OBE and of Maureen Lillywhite. *Educ:* Mill Hill Sch.; Newcastle Univ. (LLB Hons). Called to the Bar, Middle Temple, 1970 (Harmsworth Schol. and Major Exhibn; Bencher, 1999); NE Circuit, 1970–2014; Asst Recorder, 1995–99; Recorder, 1999–2004; Dep. High Ct Judge, 1999–2014. Member: Bd of Faculty of Law, Newcastle Univ., 1990–94; Advocacy Studies Bd, Bar Council, 1996–2002; Panel of Arbitrators, Bar Council, 1999; Restricted Patients Panel, Mental Health Rev. Tribunal, 2000–11; Faculty, Middle Temple Advocacy, 2004–06. Hd of Mission to Kosovo, Bar Human Rights Cttee, 2000. Liaison Judge to Law Sch., 2004–10, Mem. Ct, 2006–10, Univ. of Hull. Life Gov., Mill Hill Sch., 1994. *Publications:* A Practical Guide to Road Traffic Accident Claims, 1987, 2nd edn 1991; legal contributor to Negotiating Better Deals, by J. G. Thorn (twin *b*), 1988; (jtly) Kosovo 2000: justice not revenge, 2000. *Recreations:* theatre, music, walking, local Amenity Society (Chairman, 1986–99). *Address:* Holly House, Main Street, Corbridge, Northumberland. *Clubs:* National Liberal; Old Millhillians; Durham County.

THORNBERRY, Emily; MP (Lab) Islington South and Finsbury, since 2005; *b* 27 July 1960; *d* of late Sallie Thornberry; *m* 1991, Christopher George Nugee (*see* Hon. Sir C. G. Nugee); two *s* one *d*. *Educ:* Univ. of Kent (BA 1982). Called to the Bar, Gray's Inn, 1983; in practice, specialising in criminal law, 1985–. Shadow Energy and Climate Change Minister, 2010; Shadow Health and Social Care Minister, 2010–11; Shadow Attorney Gen., 2011–14. *Address:* (office) 65 Barnsbury Street, N1 1EK; House of Commons, SW1A 0AA. *E:* thornberrye@parliament.uk. *W:* www.emilythornberry.com.

THORNBERRY, Prof. Patrick, CMG 2006; PhD; Professor of International Law, Keele University, now Emeritus; *b* Middlesbrough, 4 Dec. 1944. *Educ:* Univ. of London (LLB); Univ. of Keele (LLM; PhD). Called to the Bar, Lincoln's Inn. Vis. Fellow, Kellogg Coll., Oxford. Mem., UN Cttee on Elimination of Racial Discrimination, 2001– (Rapporteur, 2002–08). Former Chm., Monitoring Rights Gp Internat. *Publications:* International Law and the Rights of Minorities, 1991; Indigenous Peoples and Human Rights, 2002; (with M. A. Estebanez) Minority Rights in Europe, 2004; (contrib.) The Rights of Minorities, 2005; (contrib.) Universal Minority Rights, 2007; The International Convention on the Elimination of All Forms of Racial Discrimination: a legal commentary, 2010; contribs to Human Rights Law Rev. *Address:* School of Politics, International Relations and Philosophy, Keele University, Keele, Staffs ST5 5BG.

THORNBURGH, Richard Lewis; Counsel, K&L Gates (formerly Kirkpatrick & Lockhart Nicholson Graham, then Kirkpatrick & Lockhart Preston Gates Ellis) LLP, since 1994; *b* 16 July 1932; *s* of Charles G. and Alice S. Thornburgh; *m* 1955, Virginia Hooton (decd); *m* 1963, Virginia Judson; four *s*. *Educ:* Yale Univ. (BEng 1954); Univ. of Pittsburgh Sch. of Law (LLB 1957). Staff Counsel, Aluminum Co. of America, 1957–59; Associate, Kirkpatrick, Pomeroy, Lockhart & Johnson, 1959–69; US Attorney, Western District, Pennsylvania, 1969–75; Asst Attorney General, Criminal Div., US Dept of Justice, 1975–77; Partner: Kirkpatrick Lockhart, Johnson & Hutchison, 1977–79; Kirkpatrick & Lockhart LLP, 1987–88 and 1991–92; Governor, Commonwealth of Pennsylvania, 1979–87; Attorney Gen. of the USA, 1988–91; Under-Sec.-Gen. for Admin and Management, UN, 1992–93. Dir, Inst. of Politics, John F. Kennedy Sch. of Govt, 1987–88. Numerous hon. degrees. *Publications:* Where the Evidence Leads (autobiog.), 2004, rev. edn 2010; Puerto Rico's Future: a time to decide, 2007; articles in professional jls. *Address:* 2540 Massachusetts Avenue NW, Washington, DC 20008, USA; K&L Gates LLP, 1601 K Street NW, Washington, DC 20006–1600, USA.

THORNE, Benjamin, CMG 1979; MBE 1966; *b* 19 June 1922; *m* 1949, Sylvia Una (*née* Graves); one *s* two *d*. *Educ:* St Marylebone Grammar Sch.; Regent Street Polytechnic. Served War, RAF, 1940–46. Joined Civil Service, 1946; British Trade Commission: India, 1950–54; Ghana, 1954–58; Nigeria, 1958–61; Hong Kong, 1964–68; Dir, British Week in Tokyo, 1968–69; Commercial Counsellor, Tokyo, 1973–79, retd. Life Vice Pres., Japan Soc., 1998. Japanese Order of the Sacred Treasure, 3rd cl., 1975. *Recreations:* cricket, travel, gardening, reading. *Address:* 34 Quarry Hill Road, Borough Green, Sevenoaks, Kent TN15 8RH. *T:* (01732) 882547. *Clubs:* Civil Service; Hong Kong (Hong Kong); Foreign Correspondents' (Tokyo); Yokohama Country and Athletic.

THORNE, Prof. Michael Philip, PhD; Vice Chancellor, Anglia Ruskin University, since 2007; *b* 19 Oct. 1951; *m* 1975, Val Swift (*d* 2011); three *s*. *Educ:* Queen Mary Coll., Univ. of London (BSc Hons); Univ. of Birmingham (PhD 1979). Lecturer: SE Derbyshire Coll., 1973–75; UCL, 1978–79; UC Cardiff, 1979–88; Hd, Sch. of Computing, 1989–93, Pro Vice Chancellor, 1993–97, Univ. of Sunderland; Vice Principal, Napier Univ., 1998–2001; Vice Chancellor, Univ. of E London, 2001–06. Member: Foresight Panel (Leisure and Learning), OST, 1998–2001; Scottish Further Educn Funding Council, 1999–2003; Bd, Learning and Skills Network, 2006–11; Bd, Office of the Ind. Adjudicator, 2007–; Sci. and Res. Adv. Bd, DCMS, 2009–10; Bd of Trustees, Sir John Cass Foundn, 2009–. Member, Board: London Thames Gateway Develt Corp., 2004–07; Gtr Cambridge and Gtr Peterborough Local Enterprise Partnership, 2012–. Non-exec. Dir, Scottish Univ. for Industry, 1998–2004. Formerly Chair: Open Learning Foundn; Lead Scotland; Chm., Adv. Council on Libraries, 2007–10; Mem., Adv. Council, British Library, 2008–10. Formerly Member Board: Northern Sinfonia; Northern Jun. Philharmonic; Learning World; Northern Informatics Applications Agency; Council of Administrators, Eur. Lifelong Learning Initiative. Radio and TV progs. FIMA; FBCS. FRSA. *Publications:* contrib. acad. papers and articles. *Recreations:*

music (bassoon and conducting), theatre, hill-walking, reading Funding Council circulars. *Address:* Anglia Ruskin University, Bishop Hall Lane, Chelmsford, Essex CM1 1SQ. *T:* 0845 196 4221, *Fax:* (01245) 495419. *E:* michael.thorne@anglia.ac.uk. *Club:* Reform.

THORNE, Sir Neil (Gordon), Kt 1992; OBE 1980; TD 1969; DL; *b* 8 Aug. 1932; *s* of late Henry Frederick Thorne and Ivy Gladys Thorne. *Educ:* City of London Sch.; Coll. of Estate Mgt (BSc London Univ.). FCGI; FRICS. Asst Adjt, 58 Med. Regt, RA, BAOR, 1957–59. Sen. Partner, Hull & Co., Chartered Surveyors, 1962–76. Mem. Bd, Jt Docklands Develt Corp., 1973–76. Councillor, London Borough of Redbridge, 1965–68, Alderman, 1975–78; Mem., GLC and Chm., Central Area Bd, 1967–73. MP (C) Ilford South, 1979–92; contested (C) same seat, 1992, 1997. Founder and first Chm., Unpaired Members Gp, 1982–85; Chairman: British Nepalese Parly Gp, 1983–92; British Korean Parly Gp, 1988–92; Vice Chm., UK Br., IPU, 1987–90; Member: Defence Select Cttee, 1983–92; Court of Referees, 1987–92. Chm., H of C Motor Club, 1985–91; Founder and Chairman: Armed Forces Parly Scheme, 1988–2015 (now Life Pres., Armed Forces Parly Trust); Police Service Parly Scheme, 1996–; Fire Service Parly Scheme, 2010–. Jt Chm., World War II Widows Pension Gp, 1989. Chm., Britain-Nepal Soc., 1992–98 (Vice Pres., 1998–); Mem. Bd, British Chinese Armed Forces Heritage Project, 2015–. Fellow, Industry and Parliament Trust, 1980 and 1990; Pres., Inst. of Civil Defence and Disaster Studies, 1996–2007; Chairman: Nat. Council for Civil Defence, 1982–86; St Edward's Housing Assoc., 1986–93; Ilford Age Concern, 1984–87, 1990–93; President: Redbridge Parkinson's Disease Soc., 1982–2001; Ilford Arthritis Care, 1986–2001; Gtr London Dist, St John Ambulance, 1992–2003; Redbridge Age Concern, 1993–2008; N and E London REME Assoc., 2000–; Vice President: Ilford Tuberculosis and Chest Care Assoc., 1987–2000; Royal Soc. of St George, Chigwell, 2007–14; Royal British Legion, GLA City Hall, 2008–; Patron: Jubilee Club for Visually Handicapped, 1986–2000; Benevolent Fund for W Essex Hospices, 2001–06; Health Aid for Africa, 2008–; Trustee: Children In Distress, 1986– (Life Pres., 2011); Meml Gates Trust, 1999–2009 (Dir of Develt for Constitution Hill Commonwealth War Meml); Amb., Girl Guiding, 2002–08. Chairman: Lord Mayor's £5 million Appeal for St Paul's Cathedral, 1993–94; Whitefriars Club, 2014–. Founder Mem., Royal Artillery Firepower Mus., 2001–16. Mem., Mil. Educn Cttee, 1994–, and Court, 1995–2001, Univ. of Leeds. Prime Warden, Blacksmiths' Co., 2000–01. Member: TA, 1952–82; Metropolitan Special Constab. (HAC), 1983–92; Hon. Vice Comdt, HAC Specials, City of London Police, 2007–; CO, London Univ. OTC, 1976–80; Hon. Col, Leeds Univ. OTC, 1999–2007. DL Greater London, 1991; Rep. DL London Bor. of Brent, 2001–07. KStJ 1995 (Mem., Chapter Gen., 1989–97; Almoner, 1995–97). HQA (Pakistan), 1991; GDB (Nepal), 1991. *Publications:* Pedestrianised Streets: a study of Europe and America, 1973; Highway Robbery in the Twentieth Century: policy reform for compulsory purchase, 1990. *Address:* 13 Cowley Street, Westminster, SW1P 3LZ. *T:* (020) 7222 0480. *Clubs:* Honourable Artillery Company, Royal Air Force.

THORNE, Nicholas Alan, CMG 2002; HM Diplomatic Service, retired; International Relations Adviser to the Chief Executive Officer, Internet Corporation for the Assignment of Names and Numbers, California, 2008–11; consultant on issues related to governance of the Internet, since 2011; International Organisations Adviser to British Red Cross, since 2008; *b* 31 March 1948; *s* of late James Leslie Thorne and Grace Agnes Thorne; *m* 2003, Kristina Tronningsdal; one *s* one *d* by previous marriage. *Educ:* Chatham House Grammar Sch.; Westminster Univ. Joined HM Diplomatic Service, 1965; Yaoundé, 1971; UK Repn to EC, Brussels, 1974–78; UKMIS, UN, NY, 1980–83; Hd of Chancery, Manila, 1983–87; Dep. Hd, UN Dept and Hd, Human Rights, FCO, 1987–89; on secondment to Thorn/EMI, 1989–91; Counsellor and Dep. Hd of Mission, Helsinki, 1991–95; UKMIS, UN, NY, 1995–2003; Ambassador and UK Permanent Rep. to UN and other internat. orgns, Geneva, 2003–08. Mem., UN Adv. Cttee on finance and mgt issues, 1998–2003. *Recreations:* travel, flying light aircraft, cooking. *Address:* Les Augers, 16700 St Gourson, France. *E:* nicktny@aol.com. *Club:* Royal Over-Seas League.

THORNE, Rosemary Prudence; non-executive Director: Santander UK plc, since 2006; Smurfit Kappa Group plc, since 2008; Solvay SA, since 2014; *b* Bristol, 12 Feb. 1952; *d* of Arnold Rex and Brenda Prudence Bishop. *Educ:* St Ursula's High Sch. for Girls; Warwick Univ. (BSc Hons Maths and Econs). FCMA 1984; FCT 1993. Finance Dir and Co. Sec., Harrods Ltd, 1986–90; Gp Financial Controller, Grand Metropolitan plc, 1990–92; Group Finance Director: J Sainsbury plc, 1992–99; Bradford & Bingley plc, 1999–2005; Ladbrokes plc, 2006–07. Non-executive Director: Royal Mail plc, 1998–2004; Cadbury Schweppes plc, 2004–07. Member: Financial Reporting Rev. Panel, 1996–2006; Financial Reporting Council, 1998–2007. CCMI 1996; CGMA 2012. *E:* rosemary_thorne@btinternet.com.

THORNELY-TAYLOR, Rupert Maurice; Consultant in Noise, Vibration and Acoustics, since 1968; Director: Rupert Taylor Ltd, since 1993; Saxtead Livestock Ltd, since 2013; farmer and bloodstock breeder; *b* Whalton, Northumberland, 21 May 1946; *s* of late Maurice Humphrey Taylor and Mary Patricia Stuart Taylor (*née* Wood); surname changed to Thornely-Taylor by Deed Poll, 1988; *m* 1st, 1964, Alison Grant, *d* of late Alistair Grant Saunders (marr. diss. 1987, she *d* 1999); 2nd, 1988, Frances Marion, *d* of late William John Lindberg. *Educ:* Harrow Sch. Acoustical engr, Burgess Products Co. Ltd, 1964–68; Dir, Rupert Taylor and Partners Ltd, 1970–81; Consultant to: London Underground, 1984–2001 and 2014–; LDDC, 1984–98; Crossrail, 1991–; Railtrack, 1999–2003; Associated British Ports, 2000–06; Network Rail, 2003–05; Transport for London, 2004–; Heathrow Airport Ltd (formerly BAA), 2007–13; HS2 Ltd, 2013–; res. contract, DoE, 1996. Consultant: New Victoria Th., N Staffs, 1984–2011; Railway Procurement Agency, Dublin, 2008–12; Shell E&P Ireland Ltd, 2010–; ITV, 2015; Manchester Univ., 2015. Breeder, Rumsden Herd of Pedigree Charolais Cattle (King's Trophy, Royal Smithfield Show, 2002; Reserve Breed Champion, Royal Show, 2009; Jun. Champion, Perth, 2010; Sen. Champion, Carlisle, 2010; Female Champion, Carlisle, 2011; Breed Champion and Interbreed Jun. Champion, Royal Welsh Show, 2011; Breed Champion and Interbreed Male Champion, S of England Show, 2011; Male Champion, Royal Highland Show, 2011, herd dispersed, 2012). Conservator, Ashdown Forest, 1997–2003 and 2006–13 (Chm., Finance and Gen. Purposes Cttee, 2007–09; Vice Chm., 2009–10, Chm., 2010–13, Bd of Conservators). Member: Noise Adv. Council, 1970–80 (Chm., Wkg Gp on Noise Monitoring); ISO Wkg Gp on Groundborne Noise and Vibration from Rail Systems, 1998–; Project Bd, DEFRA, 2004–11. Mem. Council, British Acoustical Soc., 1968–71; Founder Member and Hon. Treasurer: Assoc. Noise Consultants, 1970–74 (Vice Chm., 2001–03; Chm., 2003–05; Pres., 2006–11; Hon. Mem., 2011; Outstanding Contribn Award, 2013); Inst. Acoustics, 1971–74 (Fellow, 1981; Dip. Examiner, 2010–). Dir, Internat. Inst. Acoustics and Vibration, 2007–11, 2012– (Chm., Membership Cttee, 2011–). Mem. (C) Wealden DC, 1995–2003 (Leader, 1999–2003). Member: E Sussex Econ. Partnership, 1999–2003; Inter-reg. Jt Monitoring Cttee, 1999–2001; SE England Regl Assembly, 1999–2003; Mem., Exec. Cttee, Wealden Constituency Cons. Assoc., 1993–2003; Chm., Wealden Constituency Business Gp, 2007–12. Trustee, Ashdown Forest Conservation Trust, 2010–13. Mem., PCC, All Saints, Saxtead, 2013– (Churchwarden, 2015–). Churchill Fellow, USA, 1972. Hon. Treas., Nat. Pony Soc., 1991–97. Winner (with F. M. Thornley-Taylor) of Best in Show: S Western Tibetan Spaniel Club Open Show, 2013; SE and E Anglia Tibetan Spaniel Club Open Show, 2014; Reserve Best of Breed Midland Counties Canine Soc., 2014; Northern Tibetan Spaniel Club Championship Show, 2014 and Open Show, 2015; Tibetan Spaniel Assoc. Open Show, 2015. *Publications:* Noise, 1970, 4th edn 2001; Le Bruit et ses Méfaits, 1972; (ed) Noise Control Data, 1976; (jtly) Handbook of Noise Assessment, 1978; Electricity, 1979; (jtly) Measurement and Assessment of Groundborne Noise and Vibration, 2002, 2nd edn 2012; (illustrator) Perry the Perfect Puppy, 2000; contrib. papers to Proc. Inst. Acoustics, Internat. Inst. Acoustics and Vibration, Internat. Inst. Noise Control Engrg. *Recreations:* painting, music, gardening, Tibetan Spaniels. *Address:* Saxtead Hall, Saxtead, Woodbridge, Suffolk IP13 9QT. *T:* (01728) 621521.

See also Rt Rev. H. V. Taylor.

THORNEYCROFT, Rev. Prebendary Pippa Hazel Jeanetta; Prebendary of Lichfield Cathedral, 2000–09, now Prebendary Emeritus; Chaplain to the Queen, 2001–14; *b* 18 Feb. 1944; *d* of Philip Fitzgerald Mander and Priscilla Patricia (*née* Waller); *m* 1965, John Patrick Thorneycroft; two *s* two *d*. *Educ:* Cheltenham Ladies' Coll.; Exeter Univ. (BA Hons French 1965); W Midlands Ministerial Trng Course, Queen's Coll., Birmingham (GOE 1988). Ordained deacon, 1988, priest, 1994; Curate (non-stipendiary), St Mary Magdalene, Albrighton, 1988–90; asst deacon/priest (non-stipendiary), Badger, Beckbury, Kemberton, Ryton, Stockton and Sutton Maddock, 1990–96; Advr for Women in Ministry, Lichfield Dio., 1993–99; Priest-in-Charge: Shareshill, 1996–2009; Essington, 2006–09; Rural Dean of Penkridge, 2001–05; Interim Minister: Tettenhall Wood, Wolverhampton, 2010–12; Wellington and Hadley, 2012–13; Actg Team Rector, Central Telford, 2013–14; Associate Priest, Shifnal (Tong), 2014–. Mem., Skinners' Co., 1966–. *Recreations:* walking, cycling, bee-keeping. *Address:* Manor Cottage, High Street, Albrighton, nr Wolverhampton WV7 3JB. *T:* (01902) 375523.

THORNHILL, Alan Russell, PhD; Associate Director, Market Development, Reproductive and Genetic Health, Illumina Inc., since 2013; *b* Portsmouth, 12 Nov. 1966; *s* of John Roger Thornhill and Zandra Mary Knight (*née* Edwards); *m* 1999, Vikki Isobel Cookson (*d* 2014); one *s* two *d*. *Educ:* Royal Hospital Sch.; University Coll. London (BSc Hons Biol. 1989); Univ. of London (PhD Genetics 1996). High-complexity Clin. Lab. Dir, Amer. Bd of Bioanalysis, 2003; State Registered Clinical Scientist, 2005; Eur. Soc. of Human Reprodn and Embryol. Certified Sen. Clin. Embryologist, 2008. Res. Fellow, Molecular Embryology Unit, Inst. of Child Health, London, 1993–96; Clinical Embryologist, Assisted Conception Unit, King's Coll. Sch. of Medicine and Dentistry, London, 1996–98; Postdoctoral Res. Fellow, Dept of Obstetrics and Gynaecol., St Thomas' Hosp., London, 1999; IVF Lab. Dir, Mayo Clinic, Rochester, Minn, 2000–04; Scientific Dir, London Fertility Centre, 2005–06; Scientific Dir, 2007–13 and HFEA Person Responsible, 2010–13, London Bridge Fertility, Gynaecology and Genetics Centre, London; Consultant Clin. Res. Scientist, Assisted Conception Unit, Guy's Hosp., London, 2013. Hon. Sen. Lectr, UCL, 2004–08; Hon. Reader in Reproductive Genetics, Dept of Bioscis, Univ. of Kent, Canterbury, 2008–. Sec., Alpha Scientists in Reproductive Medicine, 2004–13 (Chair, 2012–13). Mem., HFEA, 2009–. *Publications:* (ed) Single Cell Diagnostics: methods and protocols, 2007; over 100 articles on assisted reproduction and genetics. *Recreations:* amateur dramatics, choral singing. *Club:* Victory Services.

THORNHILL, Andrew Robert; QC 1985; a Recorder, 1997–2004; *b* 4 Aug. 1943; *s* of Edward Percy Thornhill and Amelia Joy Thornhill; *m* 1971, Helen Mary Livingston; two *s* two *d*. *Educ:* Clifton Coll. Prep. Sch.; Clifton Coll.; Corpus Christi Coll., Oxford. Called to the Bar, Middle Temple, 1969, Bencher, 1995; entered chambers of H. H. Monroe, QC, 1969. Chm. Council, Clifton Coll., 1994–2010. *Publications:* (ed) Potter & Monroe: Tax Planning with Precedents, 7th edn 1974, to 9th edn 1982; (jtly) Tax Planning Through Wills, 1981, 1984; (jtly) Passing Down the Family Farm, 1982; (jtly) Passing Down the Family Business, 1984. *Recreations:* wooden boats, dinghy sailing, squash, Real tennis, walking. *Address:* 37 Canynge Road, Clifton, Bristol BS8 3LD. *T:* (0117) 974 4015. *Clubs:* Oxford and Cambridge, Bar Yacht.

THORNHILL, Dorothy, MBE 2012; Elected Mayor (Lib Dem) of Watford, since 2002; *m* 1st, Andrew Thornhill; one *s* one *d*; 2nd, Dr Iain Sharpe. Teacher, schools in Herts incl. Asst Hd, Queens Sch., Bushey. Spokesman on communities and local govt, H of L, 2015–. Mem. (Lib Dem), Watford BC, 1992–2002. Contested (Lib Dem) Watford, 2015. *Recreations:* avid Wales Rugby supporter and aficionado, Coronation Street. *Address:* House of Lords, SW1A 0PW.

[Created a Baroness (Life Peer) 2015 but title not yet gazetted at time of going to press.]

THORNHILL, John Joseph Andrew; President, National Council of Independent Monitoring Boards, since 2013; Chairman, Magistrates' Association, 2008–11; *b* Liverpool, 1 July 1945; *s* of Walter Thornhill and Anne Margaret Thornhill; unmarried. *Educ:* St Francis Xavier's Coll., Liverpool; Univ. of Hull (BA Hons Classics 1967); Univ. of Edinburgh (Dip Ed Psych 1968); Manchester Metropolitan Univ. (Grad. Dip. Law 2001); Univ. of Wales, Aberystwyth (MPhil Law 2007). Teacher of Classics, Madras Coll., St Andrews, 1968–70; Hd, Classics, 1970–72, Dir of Studies, 1972–78, Notre Dame High Sch., Liverpool; Curriculum Develt Officer, ICT, Liverpool Poly., 1978–82; Sen. Lectr in IT, Liverpool Hope Univ., 1982–85; Teacher/Advr, ICT, Liverpool Educn Authy, 1985–94; Dir of ICT, Calderstones Sch., 1994–97. Ofsted Inspector, 1997–; consultant to DCSF, then DFE, 2007–; Nat. Leader of Governance, 2014–. Called to the Bar, Middle Temple, 2002. Mem., Judicial Appts Commn, 2012–14. E and W Rep., Eur. Network of Councils for Judiciary, 2010–15. Chm., Nat. Mock Trial Competition for Schs, 2013–. Chm. Govs, Sudley Sch., Liverpool. FRSA. Hon. LLD Manchester Metropolitan, 2013. JP Liverpool 1983–2015. *Publications:* (with D. A. Brodie) Microcomputing in Sport and Education, 1982; (contrib.) The Analysis of Practical Skills, 1985. *Recreations:* former professional referee Football and Rugby League, international athletics official, ski-ing, Scottish culture and country dancing, classical music (listening), spending time with sister Monica, niece Lucy and their families. *Address:* 5 Lynnbank Road, Calderstones, Liverpool L18 3HE. *T:* (0151) 722 1813, 07714 759466. *E:* johnjp@blueyonder.co.uk. *Clubs:* Army and Navy; Athenæum (Liverpool).

THORNICROFT, Prof. Graham John, PhD; FRCPsych, FMedSci; Professor of Community Psychiatry, since 1996, and Director, WHO Collaborating Centre for Research and Training in Mental Health, Institute of Psychiatry, Psychology and Neuroscience (formerly Institute of Psychiatry), King's College London; Consultant Psychiatrist, South London and Maudsley NHS Foundation Trust, since 1991; Director: King's Improvement Science, since 2013; NIHR Collaboration for Leadership in Applied Health Research and Care South London, since 2013. *Educ:* Queens' Coll., Cambridge (BA 1st cl. Hons Soc. and Pol Sci. 1977); Guy's Hosp. Med. Sch., London (MB BS 1984); London Sch. of Hygiene and Tropical Medicine (MSc Epidemiol. 1989); Univ. of London (PhD 1995). MRCPsych 1988, FRCPsych 2000; MFPHM 1999. Mem., Health Services and Population Res. Dept, Inst. of Psychiatry, KCL, 1999–. Sen. Investigator, NIHR, 2007–. Vis. Scientist, Dept of Psychiatry, Univ. of Verona, 2000–; Vis. Prof., Dept of Epidemiol., Columbia Univ., NY, 2002–. FMedSci 2005. *Publications:* (ed jtly) Measuring Mental Health Needs, 1992, 2nd edn 2001; (jtly) Emergency Mental Health Services in the Community, 1995; (with H. Knudsen) Mental Health Service Evaluation, 1996 (trans. Italian); (with G. Strathdee) Commissioning Mental Health Services, 1996; (jtly) London's Mental Health, 1997; (with D. Goldberg) Mental Health in Our Future Cities, 1998; (jtly) Camberwell Assessment of Need (CAN), 1999; (with M. Tansella) Common Mental Disorders in Primary Care: essay in honour of Professor Sir David Goldberg, 1999; (with M. Tansella) The Mental Health Matrix: a manual to improve services, 1999 (trans. Italian, Romanian, Russian, Spanish); (with A. Reynolds) Managing Mental Health Services, 1999 (trans. Italian, Portuguese); (with G. Szmukler) Textbook of Community Psychiatry, 2001; (with M. Tansella) Mental Health Outcome Measures, 1996, 2nd edn 2001; (jtly) Camberwell Assessment of Need for Adults with Developmental and Intellectual Disabilities (CANDID), 2003; (ed jtly) The Forensic CAN: a needs assessment for forensic mental health service users, 2006; (jtly) International Outcome Measures in Mental Health, 2006; Shunned: discrimination against people with mental illness, 2006 (Book of the

Yr Award, Mental Health, BMA, 2007); Actions Speak Louder: tackling discrimination against people with mental illness, 2006; (ed jtly) Mental Health Policy and Practice Across Europe (Baxter Award, Eur. Health Mgt Assoc.), 2007; (ed jtly) Home Treatment Teams, 2008; (with M. Tansella) Better Mental Health Care, 2008; (jtly) Camberwell Assessment of Need: mother's version (CAN-M), 2008; over 397 peer-reviewed papers on stigma and discrimination, mental health needs assessment, the development of outcome scales, cost-effectiveness evaluation of mental health treatments, and global mental health. *Address:* Health Service and Population Research Department P029, Institute of Psychiatry, Psychology and Neuroscience, King's College London, De Crespigny Park, SE5 8AF. *T:* (020) 7848 0736, *Fax:* (020) 7277 1462. *E:* graham.thornicroft@kcl.ac.uk.

THORNTON, Baroness *cr* 1998 (Life Peer), of Manningham in the co. of West Yorkshire; **Dorothea Glenys Thornton;** *b* 16 Oct. 1952; *e c* of Peter and Jean Thornton; *m* 1977, John Carr; one *s* one *d. Educ:* Thornton Secondary Sch., Bradford; LSE (BSc Econ 1976). Nat. Organiser, Gingerbread, 1976–78; N London Area Officer, Greater London CABx, 1978–79; Projects Dir, Inst. of Community Studies, 1979–81; Political Sec., Royal Arsenal Co-op. Soc., 1981–86; Public and Political Affairs Advr, CWS, 1986–92. Chm., Pall Mall Consult, 2001–07. Chm., Social Enterprise Coalition, 2001–07. A Baroness in Waiting (Govt Whip), 2008–10; Parly Under-Sec. of State, DoH, 2010. Fabian Society: Gen. Sec., 1993–94; Develt Dir, 1994–96; Mem., Nat. Exec. Cttee, 1997–2000. Chm., Greater London Labour Party, 1986–91. Director: Labour Women's Network, 1990–; EMILY's List UK, 1993–; Improvement and Develt Agency, 1999–2007; Training for Life, 2003–07. Trustee, Fifteen Foundn, 2003–10. Gov., LSE, 2000–. FRSA 1999. *Recreations:* canoeing, hill-walking, Star Trek. *Address:* House of Lords, SW1A 0PW.

THORNTON, Allan Charles, OBE 2004; Chairman, Environmental Investigation Agency, since 1988 (Co-Founder and Director, 1984–86); *b* 17 Nov. 1949; *s* of Robert Charles Antoine Thornton and Jessie (Waldram) Thornton; *m* 1995, Polly Ghazi, journalist and author; two *d. Educ:* Banff Centre of Fine Art, Banff, Canada. Co-ordinator of Banff Centre Creative Writing Programme, 1976, 1977; established Greenpeace UK, 1977; Exec. Dir, 1977–81 and 1986–88; co-founder of Greenpeace vessel, Rainbow Warrior, 1978; co-founder, Greenpeace International, 1980; Internat. Project Co-ordinator with Greenpeace International, 1981. Albert Schweitzer Award, 1991; BBC TV Lifetime Achievement Award, 2000. *Publications:* To Save an Elephant, 1990. *Recreation:* viewing elephants and other wildlife in their natural habitat. *Address:* c/o Environmental Investigation Agency, 62–63 Upper Street, N1 0NY. *T:* (020) 7354 7960.

THORNTON, His Honour Anthony Christopher Lawrence; QC 1988; a Senior Circuit Judge, 1994–2015; a Deputy Judge of the Administrative Court and Queen's Bench Division, since 2009; Judge of the Crown Court and of the First-tier (Mental Health) Tribunal, since 2010; *b* 18 Aug. 1947; *s* of Richard Thornton and Margery Alice (*née* Clerk); *m* 1st, 1983, Lyn Christine Thurlby (marr. diss. 1998); one *s*; 2nd, 2006, Dawn Elisabeth Collins. *Educ:* Eton Coll.; Keble Coll., Oxford (BCL, MA). Called to the Bar, Middle Temple, 1970, Bencher, 1992. A Recorder, 1992–94; Judge of the Technology and Construction Court of the High Court, 1998–2009. Mem. (pt-time), Parole Bd, 2002–10. Chairman: Fulham Legal Advice Centre, 1973–78; Hammersmith and Fulham Law Centre, 1975–78. External Moderator, Centre of Construction and Project Management, KCL, 1987–; Hon. Sen. Vis. Fellow, Centre for Commercial Law Studies, QMC, 1987–92. Mem., Gen. Council of the Bar, 1988–94 (Treas., 1990–92; Chm., Professional Standards Cttee, 1992–93). Dir, Apex Trust, 1991–94. Gov., Colfe's Sch., Lewisham, 2000–12. Liveryman, Leathersellers' Co., 1976– (Mem. Ct, 2002–). Jt Editor, Construction Law Jl, 1984–94. *Publications:* (ed jtly) Building Contracts, in Halsbury's Laws of England, vol. 4, 1972; (contrib.) Construction Disputes: liability and the expert witness, 1989; contribs to Construction Law Jl. *Recreations:* football, opera, legal history, walking in Orkney, companionship. *Club:* South Ronaldsay Golf.

THORNTON, Air Marshal Sir Barry (Michael), KCB 2007 (CB 2004); CEng, FIMechE; FRAeS; engineering, aerospace and safety consultant; Chairman, SQEP Ltd, since 2014; *b* 19 Nov. 1952; *s* of Ronald Thornton and Enid Margaret Thornton (*née* Baxendale); *m* 1977, Delia Brown, barrister; two *s. Educ:* Baines Grammar Sch.; Nottingham Univ. (BSc); RMCS, Cranfield Univ. (MSc). CEng 1981; FIMechE 1994; FRAeS 2002. Joined RAF, 1971; initial and professional trng, 1974–75; aircraft and weapon systems appts at RAF Waddington, RAF Lyneham, RAF Abingdon and HQ RAF Germany, 1975–87; Advanced Staff Trng, 1988; OC Engrg and Supply Wing, RAF Honington, 1988–90; OC Engrg Wing, RAF Detachment Tabuk, Gulf War; Weapons Support Authy and Standardization, MoD, 1991–93; Combat Aircraft Test and Evaluation, DERA, MoD, 1994–96; rcds 1997; Dir Maritime Projects, MoD PE, 1998; Nimrod MRA4 Integrated Project Team Leader, Defence Procurement Agency, MoD, 1998–2000; Controller Aircraft RAF, and Exec. Dir, Defence Procurement Agency, MoD, 2000–03; Dir-Gen. Equipment Support (Air), 2003–04, Air Mem. for Logistics and Dir Gen. Logistics (Strike), 2004–06, Defence Logistics Orgn, MoD; Air Mem. for Personnel and C-in-C PTC, 2006–07; Air Mem. for Materiel and Chief of Materiel (Air), Defence Equipment and Support, 2007–09. Man. Dir, Ascent Flight Training Ltd, 2009–12. FCMI (FIMgt 1995). *Recreations:* golf, gardening, ski-ing. *Club:* Royal Air Force.

THORNTON, Clive Edward Ian, CBE 1983; FInstLEx, FCIB; corporate consultancy services, since 2003; Chairman: Melton Mowbray Building Society, 1991–2003 (Director, 1988–2003; Hon. President, 2003–09); Armstrong Capital Holdings Ltd, 1988–98; *b* 12 Dec. 1929; *s* of Albert and Margaret Thornton; *m* 1956, Maureen Carmine (*née* Crane); one *s* one *d. Educ:* St Anthony's Sch., Newcastle upon Tyne; Coll. of Commerce, Newcastle upon Tyne; College of Law, London; LLB 1977, BA Hons 1996, MA 1999, DipTh 2001, LLM 2005, London Univ. (ext.); Open Univ. (BSc Hons 1998, Dip. Geog. 1998); Heythrop Coll., Univ. of London (BD Hons (ext.) 2008; MTh 2010); Oxford Univ. (AdvDip English Local Hist. 2011); Univ. of Dundee (Postgrad. Cert. Family and Local Hist. 2013). FInstLEx 1958; FCIB (FCBSI 1970). Solicitor. Associate, Pensions Management Inst., 1978. Articled to Kenneth Hudson, solicitor, London, 1959; admitted solicitor of Supreme Court, 1963. Asst Solicitor, Nationwide Building Soc., 1963; Solicitor, Cassel Arenz Ltd, Merchant Bankers, 1964–67; Abbey National Building Society: Chief Solicitor, 1967; Dep. Chief Gen. Man., 1978; Chief Gen. Manager, 1979–83; Dir, 1980–83; Partner, Stoneham Langton and Passmore, Solicitors, 1985–88. Chm., Metropolitan Assoc. of Building Socs, 1981–82. Chairman: Mirror Group Newspapers, 1984; Financial Weekly, 1985–87; Thamesmead Town Ltd, 1986–90; Gabriel Communications (formerly Universe Publications) Ltd, 1986–96; Dir, Investment Data Services Ltd, 1986–90. Proprietor, Thorndale Devon Cattle, 1983–2007; President: Devon Cattle Breeders Soc., 1997–98; Midland Columbarian Soc., 2011–13. Member: Law Soc. (Chm., Commerce and Industry Gp, 1974); Council, Chartered Bldg Socs Inst., 1973–81; Council, Building Socs Assoc., 1979–83; Bd, Housing Corp., 1980–86. Chairman: SHAC, 1983–86; Belford Hall Management Co. Ltd, 1990–93. Member: Council, St Mary's Hosp. Med. Sch., 1984–96; St Mary's Develt Trust, 1984–98. Freeman, City of London; Liveryman, Worshipful Co. of Bakers. *Publications:* Building Society Law, Cases and Materials, 1969, 3rd edn 1988; History of Devon Cattle, 1994. *Recreations:* music, reading, Modena pigeons, English local history, painting. *Address:* The Manor, The Green, Woughton on the Green, Milton Keynes MK6 3BE.

THORNTON, Daniel; Programme Director, Institute for Government, since 2015; *b* Leeds, 6 Aug. 1969; *s* of Vernon and Frances Thornton; *m* 1998, Tasja Dorkofikis; one *s* one *d. Educ:* Wadham Coll., Oxford (BA PPE); London Sch. of Econs (MA Internat. Hist.). Oxford Analytica, 1990–91; FCO, 1991–97; Enron Europe, 1998; Cttee Specialist, Foreign Affairs Cttee, H of C, 1999–2001; HM Treasury, 2001–04; Private Sec. to Prime Minister, 2004–06; Principal Private Sec. to Sec. of State for Communities and Local Govt, 2006–07; Dir, Local Economic Develt and Renewal, DCLG, 2007–09; COS, 2009–13, Dir, Strategic Initiatives, 2013–15, GAVI Alliance.

THORNTON, Sir (George) Malcolm, Kt 1992; Chairman: Value Based Solutions, since 2006; Birmingham Local Education Partnership, 2009–13; *b* 3 April 1939; *s* of George Edmund and Ethel Thornton; *m* 1st, 1962; (one *s* decd); 2nd, 1972, Shirley Ann, (Sue) (*née* Banton) (*d* 1989); 3rd, 1990, Rosemary (*née* Hewitt). *Educ:* Wallasey Grammar Sch.; Liverpool Nautical Coll. Liverpool Pilot Service, 1955–79 (Sen. 1st cl. Licence holder). Chairman: Keene Public Affairs Consultants Ltd, 1997–2009; Broadskill Ltd (formerly Intuition Gp Ltd), 2002–08; non-executive Director: Stack Computer Solutions, 2000–; HB Villages Ltd, 2011–. Member: Wallasey County Borough Council, 1965–74 (Chm., Transport Cttee, 1968–69); Wirral Metropolitan Council, 1973–79 (Council Leader, 1974–77); Chairman: Merseyside Metropolitan Districts Liaison Cttee, 1975–77; Educn Cttee, AMA, 1978–79 (Mem., 1974–79); Council of Local Educn Authorities, 1978. Mem., Burnham (Primary and Secondary) Cttee, 1975–79. MP (C) Liverpool, Garston, 1979–83, Crosby, 1983–97; contested Crosby, 1997. PPS to Sec. of State for Industry, 1981–83, for the Environment, 1983–84. Chairman: Select Cttee on Educn, Sci. and the Arts, 1989–96 (Mem., 1985–96); Select Cttee on Educn and Employment, 1996–97. Pro Chancellor and Chm., Liverpool John Moores Univ., 2007–13 (Mem. Bd, 2001–13; Chm., Audit Cttee, 2003–07; Hon. Ambassador Fellowship, 2013). Trustee, Mersey Mission to Seafarers, 1999–2010 (Chm., 2002–10). Chm. Govs, Liscard Primary Sch., Wallasey, 1974–2011. Hon. Col 156 (NW) Transport Regt, RLC (V), 2000–05. FRSA. Hon. DEd De Montfort, 1994. *Recreations:* fishing, walking, golf, cooking, boating. *Address:* Meadow Brook, 79 Barnston Road, Heswall, Wirral CH60 1UE. *Club:* Heswall Golf.

THORNTON, Helen Ann Elizabeth, (Mrs J. E. C. Thornton); *see* Meixner, H. A. E.

THORNTON, James Kevin; Chief Executive Officer, ClientEarth, since 2006; *b* New York, 14 Feb. 1954; *s* of Peter William Thornton and Catherine Marion Thornton; partner, Martin John Goodman. *Educ:* Yale Univ. (BA Philos. *magna cum laude* 1976; Phi Beta Kappa); New York Univ. Sch. of Law (Juris Dr 1979). Member of the Bar, NY, 1981, US Supreme Court, 1987, Calif, 1989. Law Clerk, Judge John Wisdom, US Court of Appeals for 5th Circuit, New Orleans, 1979–80; Legal Fellow, Natural Resources Defense Council, NY, 1980–81; Lawyer, Paul, Weiss, Rifkind, Wharton and Garrison, NY, 1981–83; Lawyer, then Sen. Lawyer, Natural Resources Defence Council, 1983–91 (Founder: Citizen Enforcement Proj.; Los Angeles Office); Executive Director: Positive Futures, Santa Fe, 1992–99; Heffter Res. Inst., 1999–2006. Dir, Barbican Press, 2009–. Dir, Fundacja ClientEarth Poland, 2010–. Advr, Stranded Assets Prog., Smith Sch. of Enterprise and Envmt, Univ. of Oxford, 2014–. Mem., Task Force on Rule of Law and Ecol Civilization, China Council for Internat. Cooperation and Develt, 2015–. Mem., Law Soc., 2008; Mem., Wkg Gp on Model Statute Climate Change Remedies, Internat. Bar Assoc., 2015–. FZS; FRSA. Fellow, Ashoka, 2013–. Ordained Zen Buddhist priest, Soto sect, 2009. Editor in Chief, New York Univ. Law Rev., 1978–79. Business Green Leader of Year, 2014. *Publications:* A Field Guide to the Soul, 1999; Immediate Harm (novel), 2010; (jtly) Environmental and Social Transparency under the Companies Act 2006: digging deeper, 2010; Sphinx: the second coming (novel), 2014. *Recreations:* natural history of Pyrenees, playing the violin, composing poetry, koan practice, photographing London, wines of the Côtes du Rousillon Villages in situ. *Address:* ClientEarth, The Hothouse, 274 Richmond Road, E8 3QW. *T:* (020) 7749 5970. *E:* jthornton@clientearth.org. *W:* www.jamesthornton.org. *Club:* Yale (New York).

THORNTON, James Sebastian; HM Diplomatic Service; Ambassador to Bolivia, since 2015; *b* Farnborough, Kent, 2 Nov. 1964; *s* of late Edward Alfred Thornton and of Mary Thornton (now Howard); *m* 1999, Anne Fiona Scrase; two *d. Educ:* Hampton Sch., Middx; Lycée Internat. de St Germain-en-Laye, France; King Edward VI Sch., Southampton; Lincoln Coll., Oxford (MA). UKAEA, 1986–89; entered FCO, 1989; Officer, Envmt, Sci. and Energy Dept, 1990–91; Desk Officer, UKMIS to UN, NY, 1991; Second Sec., Algiers, 1992–94; Desk Officer, Near East and N Africa Dept, FCO, 1994–95; Perm. Under-Sec.'s Dept, FCO, 1995–96; Hd of War Crimes, Sect., UN Dept, FCO, 1997–99; Hd, Pol Sect., Mexico City, 2000–03; Dep. Hd of Mission, Abidjan, 2003–04; Dep. Hd, FCO/DFID Sudan Unit, 2005–07; Dep. Perm. Rep. to OECD, Paris, 2007–11; High Comr to Zambia, 2012–15. *Recreations:* running, hill walking, visiting art galleries. *Address:* c/o Foreign and Commonwealth Office, King Charles Street, SW1A 2AH. *E:* james.thornton@fco.gov.uk.

THORNTON, Dame Janet (M.), DBE 2012 (CBE 2000); PhD; FRS 1999; Director, European Bioinformatics Institute, European Molecular Biology Laboratory, since 2001 (on secondment from University College London and Birkbeck College, London); *b* 23 May 1949; *d* of James Stanley McLoughlin and Kathleen McLoughlin (*née* Barlow); *m* 1970, Alan D. Thornton; one *s* one *d. Educ:* Nottingham Univ. (BSc 1st Cl. Hons Physics); King's Coll. London and NIMR (PhD 1973). Research Assistant: Lab. of Molecular Biophysics, Oxford, 1973–78; Molecular Pharmacol., NIMR, 1978; Crystallography Department, Birkbeck College, London: SERC Advanced Fellow, 1979–83; Lectr, 1983–89; Sen. Lectr, 1989–90; Tutor, Open Univ., 1976–83; Prof. of Biomolecular Structure, and Dir, Biomolecular Structure and Modelling Unit, UCL, 1990–2001; Bernal Prof. of Crystallography, Birkbeck Coll., London, 1996–2001; Hd, Jt Res. Sch. in Molecular Scis, UCL and Birkbeck Coll., 1996–2001. Extraordinary Fellow, Churchill Coll., Cambridge, 2002–. For. Associate, NAS, USA, 2003. FMedSci 2014. *Publications:* contrib. numerous articles to jls incl. Jl Molecular Biol., Structure, Nature, Trends in Biochemical Scis, Proc. Nat. Acad. Sci., Protein Science. *Recreations:* reading, music, gardens, home. *Address:* European Bioinformatics Institute, European Molecular Biology Laboratory, Wellcome Trust Genome Campus, Hinxton, Cambridge CB10 1SD. *T:* (01223) 494648.

THORNTON, John Henry, OBE 1987; QPM 1980; Deputy Assistant Commissioner, Metropolitan Police, 1981–86; *b* 24 Dec. 1930; *s* of late Sidney Thornton and Ethel Thornton (*née* Grinnell); *m* 1st, 1952, Norma Lucille (marr. diss. 1972; she *d* 1999), *d* of late Alfred and Kate Scrivenor; two *s*; 2nd, 1972, Hazel Ann (marr. diss. 1996), *d* of late William and Edna Butler; one *s* one *d* (and one *s* decd); 3rd, 1996, Mary Elizabeth, *d* of late John Patrick and Elizabeth Unity Jackson. *Educ:* Prince Henry's Grammar Sch., Evesham. RN 1949–50. Metropolitan Police, 1950; Comdr, 1976; Head of Community Relations, 1977–80; RCDS, 1981; Dep. Asst Commissioner, 1981; Dir of Information, 1982–83; Hd of Training, 1983–85; NW Area, 1985–86. Vice-Pres., British Section, Internat. Police Assoc., 1969–79. Chm., Breakaway Theatre Co., St Albans, 1987–94; Chm., St Albans Internat. Organ Fest., 1988–91. Chm. of Govs, Townsend C of E Sch., St Albans, 1990–96. Lay Canon and Cathedral Warden, St Albans, 1988–94; Churchwarden, St Leonard's, Bretforton, Worcs, 2002–. Volunteer, Broadway Police Station, W Mercia Constabulary, 2005–14. CStJ 1984. *Recreations:* music, gardening, horses. *Address:* c/o Barclays Bank, PO Box 300, St Albans, Herts AL1 3EQ.

THORNTON, Prof. John Lawson; Chairman: Barrick Gold Corporation, since 2014 (Director, since 2012; Co-Chairman, 2012–14); PineBridge Investments, since 2014; Professor and Director of Global Leadership, Tsinghua University, China, since 2003; Senior Adviser, Goldman Sachs Group, Inc., since 2003; *b* 2 Jan. 1954; *s* of John and Edna Thornton; *m* 1990, Margaret Bradham; two *s* one *d. Educ:* Hotchkiss Sch.; Harvard Coll. (AB); Oxford Univ. (MA); Yale Sch. of Mgt. Joined Goldman Sachs, 1980: Gen. Partner, 1988; Co-CEO, Goldman Sachs Internat. (Europe, ME and Africa), 1995–96; Chm., Goldman Sachs-Asia,

1996–98; Pres., and co-Chief Operating Officer, 1999–2003; Dir, Mem. Mgt Cttee, and Co-Chm., Partnership Cttee until 2003. Director: Laura Ashley plc, 1995–2003 (Chm., 1996–99); Ford Motor Co., 1996–; Sky (formerly BSkyB) Gp plc; Pacific Century Gp, Inc., 2003–; Intel, 2003–; News Corp., 2004–12; China Unicom Ltd, 2008–. Mem., Council on Foreign Relns. Dir, Goldman Sachs Foundn. Member, Board of Trustees: Brookings Instn, 2000– (Chm., 2003–); Hotchkiss Sch.; Asia Soc.; Morehouse Coll.; Member: Investment Cttee, Yale Univ.; Adv. Bd, Yale Sch. of Mgt. *Address:* Tsinghua University, 1 Qinghuayuan, Beijing 100084, China.

THORNTON, Sir Malcolm; *see* Thornton, Sir G. M.

THORNTON, Michael Douglas; *b* Farnham, Surrey, 1 May 1952; *s* of Sir Peter Eustace Thornton, KCB and of Rosamond Hobart Thornton; *m* 1989, Peta Mary; one *d*. *Educ:* Charterhouse. FPC; CeMAP. Mktg manager, wholesale news and magazines, 1988–93; ind. financial advr and mortgage advr, 1993–2001; business develt manager, mortgage industry, 2001–08; local business bank manager, 2008–11; business develt manager for tax specialists, 2013. MP (Lib Dem) Eastleigh, March 2013–2015; contested (Lib Dem) same seat, 2015. *Recreations:* tennis, table tennis, country walks, squash, cricket, pubs.

THORNTON, Neil Ross; Director, Food and Green Economy, Department for Environment, Food and Rural Affairs, 2012–14; *b* 11 Feb. 1950; *s* of late George and Kay Thornton; *m* 1977, Christine Anne Boyes (marr. diss. 2006); two *d*; *m* 2009, Rachel Mary Haywood. *Educ:* Sedbergh Sch.; Pembroke Coll., Cambridge (BA Eng. 1971). Private Sec. to Perm. Sec., DoI, 1975; HM Treasury, 1979; Asst Sec., DTI, 1984; Principal Private Sec. to Sec. of State for Trade and Industry, 1988–90; Under Sec., 1990, Head, Europe Div., 1990–93, Exports to Europe and the Americas Div., 1993–96, DTI; Hd of Food, Drink and Marketing Policy Gp, 1996–99, Hd of Food Industry Competitiveness and Consumers, 1999–2000, MAFF; Hd of Animal Health Gp, MAFF, then Dir, Animal Health, DEFRA, 2000–03; Dir, Sustainable Consumption and Prodn and Waste (formerly Envmt Quality and Waste), DEFRA, 2003–09; Dir, Waste and Resources, and Dir, Delivery Transformation, DEFRA, 2009–12. *Recreations:* literature, choral singing, golf.

THORNTON, Peter Anthony, CEng; FRICS; FICE; Chief Executive, since 1994, and Chairman, since 2008, Greycoat Real Estate LLP (formerly Greycoat Estates Ltd); *b* 8 May 1944; *s* of Robert and Freda Thornton; *m* 1st, 1969, Patricia Greenwood (marr. diss. 1987); one *s* two *d*; 2nd, 1997, Susan Harris. *Educ:* Bradford Grammar Sch.; Manchester Univ. (BSc). CEng 1971; FRICS 1984; FICE 1990. Engineer, Binnie & Partners (Consulting Engrs), 1967–71; self-employed, 1972–75; Commercial Manager, Sears Hldgs plc, 1975–79; Greycoat Plc, subseq. Greycoat Estates Ltd, then Greycoat Real Estate LLP, 1979–: Dir, 1981–99; Jt Man. Dir, 1986–94. *Recreations:* cars, tennis, water ski-ing. *Address:* Van Buren Cottage, Queen's Ride, Barnes Common, SW13 0JF. *T:* (020) 8788 1969. *Clubs:* Harbour; Riverside Health and Racquet (Chiswick).

THORNTON, Peter Ribblesdale; QC 1992; **His Honour Judge Peter Thornton;** a Specialist Circuit Judge, since 2007; Chief Coroner, since 2012; *b* 17 Oct. 1946; *s* of late Robert Ribblesdale Thornton, CBE; *m* 1981, Susan Margaret Dalal; one *s* one *d*. *Educ:* Clifton Coll.; St John's Coll., Cambridge (BA). Called to the Bar, Middle Temple, 1969, Bencher, 2001; Asst Recorder, 1994–97; Recorder, 1997–2007; Dep. High Ct Judge, 2003–; Co-Hd, Doughty St Chambers, 2005–07. Chair, Fitness to Practise Appeals Panel, Royal Free and UC Med. Sch., 2003–; Chairperson Arbitrator, Sports Dispute Resolution Panel, 2004–. Mem., Editl Bd, Criminal Law Review, 1997–. Chairman: NCCL, 1981–83; Civil Liberties Trust, 1991–95. Trustee, Howard League for Penal Reform, 2004–. *Publications:* (contrib.) Civil Liberties 1984, 1984; We Protest: Public Order Debate, 1985; The Civil Liberties of the Zircon Affair, 1987; Public Order Law, 1987; (contrib.) The Polygraph Test, 1988; Decade of Decline: Civil Liberties in the Thatcher Years, 1989; (ed jtly) Penguin Civil Liberty Guide, 1989; (jtly) Justice on Trial, 1992; (ed jtly) Archbold's Criminal Pleadings, Evidence and Practice, 1992–; (contrib.) Analysing Witness Testimony, 1999. *Address:* Central Criminal Court, Old Bailey, EC4M 7EH.

THORNTON, Sally; *see* Burgess, Sally.

THORNTON, Sara Joanne, CBE 2011; QPM 2006; Chair, National Police Chiefs' Council, since 2015; *b* Poole, 27 Dec. 1962; *d* of Kenneth and Margreta Thornton; *m* 1st, 1986, Ewan McPhie (marr. diss. 1995); one *s*; 2nd, 1996, Daniel Haigh (marr. diss. 2004); one *s*. *Educ:* Durham Univ. (BA Philos. and Pols); Univ. of Cambridge (Dip. Applied Criminol.; MSt Applied Criminol., 2011). Metropolitan Police Service, 1986–2000; Thames Valley Police: Asst Chief Constable, 2000–03; Dep. Chief Constable, 2003–07; Chief Constable, 2007–15. Dir, Police Nat. Assessment Centre, 2010–15. Vice Pres., ACPO, 2011–15. Hon. LLD Oxford Brookes, 2010; Hon. PhD Bucks New Univ., 2010. *Publications:* articles in Policing jl. *Recreations:* reading, dancing, keeping fit. *Address:* National Police Chiefs' Council, 1st Floor, 10 Victoria Street, SW1H 0NN. *T:* (020) 7084 8976. *E:* sara.thornton@npcc.pnn.police.uk.

THORNTON, Stephen, CBE 2002; Chair, East of England Collaboration for Leadership in Applied Health Research and Care, since 2014; *b* 23 Jan. 1954; *s* of Harry Thornton and Alice Thornton (*née* Ainsworth); *m* 1976, Lorraine Anne Cassells; one *s* one *d*. *Educ:* Paston Sch., N Walsham, Norfolk; Manchester Univ. (BA Hons Politics and Mod. Hist.). DipHSM. NHS Nat. Mgt Trng scheme, 1979; Administrator: Prestwich Hosp., Manchester, 1980–82; Salford Royal Hosp., 1982–83; Fulbourn Hosp., Cambridge, 1983–85; Gen. Manager, Community Health Services, Cambs, 1985–89; Dir of Planning, E Anglia RHA, 1989–93; Chief Exec., Cambridge and Huntingdon HA, 1993–97; Cabinet Office Top Mgt Programme, 1996; Chief Executive: NHS Confedn, 1997–2002; The Health Foundn (formerly PPP Foundn), 2002–13. Member: NHS Modernisation Bd, 2000–01; Healthcare Commn (formerly Commn for Healthcare Audit and Inspection), 2002–06; NHS Nat. Quality Bd, 2009–; NMC, 2013–. Non-executive Director: Monitor, 2006–14 (Dep. Chair, 2012–14); Eastern Academic Health Sci. Network, 2013–; The Pathology Partnership, 2013–. Mem. Council, Open Univ., 2003–06. Dir, Christian Blind Mission (UK), 2002–04. Trustee, Aquaid Lifeline Fund, 2001–. FRSocMed 1998. Hon. FRCP 2010. *Publications:* articles in Health Service Jl.

THORNTON, Prof. Steven, DM; FRCOG; Dean, University of Exeter Medical School, since 2012 (Dean, Peninsula College of Medicine and Dentistry, 2010–12); *b* Lincoln, 4 Nov. 1959; *s* of Harry and Connie Thornton; *m* Georgina Hesling; one *s* one *d*. *Educ:* N Kesteven Comprehensive Sch.; Univ. of Southampton (BM 1983; DM 1989). MRCOG 1989, FRCOG 2004. MRC clinician scientist, Univ. of Cambridge, 1992–96; Prof. of Obstetrics, 1998–2010, Associate Dean (Res.), 2005–10, Univ. of Warwick. Hon. Consultant Obstetrician, Royal Devon and Exeter Hosp., 1996–. R&D Dir, Univ. Hosp. Coventry and Warwickshire NHS Trust, 2005–10; Clin. Dir, Comprehensive Local Res. Network, W Midlands (S), 2007–10; Res. Lead, W Midlands SHA, 2008–10. *Publications:* (ed) Pain in Obstetrics and Gynaecology, 2001; (ed) Hypertension in Pregnancy, 2003; (ed) Pre-term Labour, 2004; (ed) Pre-term Labour: best practice and research in clinical obstetrics and gynaecology, 2007; papers, research findings, letters and book chapters. *Recreations:* squash, running, motor sports. *Address:* Barford House, 4 Fieldgate Lane, Kenilworth, Warks CV8 1BT. *T:* 07771 747277; University of Exeter Medical School, Medical School Building, St Luke's Campus, Heavitree Road, Exeter EX1 2LU. *E:* s.thornton@exeter.ac.uk. *Clubs:* Lansdowne, Gynaecological Travellers.

THORNTON, Rt Rev. Timothy Martin; *see* Truro, Bishop of.

THORNTON, Victoria Jane Dianne, OBE 2012; Founding Director, Open-City, and Open House concept, since 1992; *b* Rochford, 12 Jan. 1953; *d* of Bill Thornton and Marianne Thornton (*née* Elliott); *m* 2007, Ken Allinson. *Educ:* Birkbeck, Univ. of London (MA 2009). Dir., Architectural Dialogue, 1983–; estabd RIBA Architecture Centre, 1994–98; Architecture Consultant to British Council VAD, 1998–2000; Architectural Advr to Scottish Arts Council, 2000. Judge, RIBA Awards, 2003. Member, Board: Irish Architecture Foundn, 2005–; Architecture Centre Network, 2006–. FRSA. Hon. FRIBA 2003. Hon. MA Metropolitan, 2005. *Publications:* Open House London: 100 buildings, 2012; (with K. Allinson) London's Contemporary Architecture: an explorer's guide, 2014. *Recreations:* architecture, hiking. *Address:* Open-City, 18 Ensign Street, E1 8JD. *T:* (020) 7383 0782. *E:* vthornton@open-city.org.uk.

THORNTON, Dr William Dickson, CB 1990; Deputy Chief Medical Officer, Department of Health and Social Services, Northern Ireland, 1978–90, retired; *b* 9 July 1930; *s* of late William J. Thornton and Elfreda Thornton (*née* Dickson); *m* 1957, Dr Maureen Gilpin; one *s* three *d*. *Educ:* Portora Royal School; Trinity College Dublin (BA, MD). FFPH. General medical practitioner, 1955–65; NI Hospitals Authy, 1966–72; Dept of Health and Social Services (NI), 1973–90. Civil QHP, 1990–92. Chm., 1993–97, Vice-Pres., 2001–, Age Concern (NI). *Recreations:* boating, reading, gardening. *Address:* 54 Deramore Park South, Belfast BT9 5JY. *T:* (028) 9066 0186.

THOROGOOD, Alfreda, (Mrs D. R. Wall), ARAD (PDTC); Artistic Director of Dance, Elmhurst School for Dance and the Performing Arts (formerly Elmhurst Ballet School), 1994–2004 (Senior Teacher, 1992–94); *b* Westminster, England, 17 Aug. 1942; *d* of Alfreda and Edward Thorogood; *m* 1967, David Richard Wall, CBE (*d* 2013); one *s* one *d*. *Educ:* Lady Eden's Sch.; Royal Ballet Sch., Jun. and Sen. Royal Ballet Company, 1960–80: Soloist, Aug. 1965; Principal Dancer, 1968; Bush Davies School: Sen. Teacher, 1982–84; Dep. Ballet Principal, 1984–89; Dir, 1988–89; Artistic Advr, Royal Acad. of Dancing, 1989–92. Guest Repetiteur, English Nat. Ballet Co., 2006–13; dance consultant and assessor. Gov., English Nat. Ballet Sch., 2012–. *Recreations:* listening to music, cooking, interior design, art, painting, gardening. *Address:* 34 Croham Manor Road, S Croydon CR2 7BE.

THOROGOOD, Rev. Bernard George, OBE 1992; General Secretary, United Reformed Church, 1980–92; *b* 21 July 1927; *s* of Frederick and Winifred Thorogood; *m* 1952, Jannett Lindsay Paton (*née* Cameron) (*d* 1988); two *s*; *m* 1991, Joan Tierney. *Educ:* Glasgow Univ. (MA); Scottish Congregational College. Ordained in Congregational Church, 1952; missionary appointment under London Missionary Society in South Pacific Islands, 1953–70; Gen. Sec., Council for World Mission, 1971–80. Moderator, Exec. Cttee, BCC, 1984–90; Mem., Central Cttee, WCC, 1984–91. DD Lambeth 1992. *Publications:* Not Quite Paradise, 1960; Guide to the Book of Amos, 1971; Our Father's House, 1983; Risen Today, 1987; The Flag and The Cross, 1988; No Abiding City, 1989; On Judging Caesar, 1990; One Wind Many Flames, 1991; Looking at Leisure: a European view, 1991; (ed) Gales of Change, 1994; Letters to Paul, 1999; Reef Passage, 2014; A Minister's Minutes, 2015. *Recreation:* sketching. *Address:* Unit 1/12 Congham Road, West Pymble, NSW 2073, Australia. *T:* (2) 94987069.

THOROLD, Sir (Anthony) Oliver, 16th Bt *cr* 1642, of Marston, Lincolnshire; *b* 15 April 1945; *o s* of Captain Sir Anthony Thorold, 15th Bt, OBE, DSC and Jocelyn Elaine Laura Thorold (*née* Heathcote-Smith); *S* father, 1999, but his name does not appear on the Official Roll of the Baronetage; *m* 1977, Genevra Mercy Richardson, *qv*; one *s* one *d*. *Educ:* Winchester; Lincoln Coll., Oxford. Called to the Bar, Inner Temple, 1971. *Heir:* *s* Henry Lowry Thorold, *b* 6 Aug. 1981. *Address:* (chambers) 53–54 Doughty Street, WC1N 2LS; 8 Richmond Crescent, N1 0LZ.

THORP, David; Consultant, Livingbridge VC LLP (formerly ISIS Capital plc, then ISIS EP LLP), since 2014 (Director, since 1995; Chairman, 2001–04; Partner, 2005–14; Managing Director, Friends Ivory & Sime Private Equity (formerly Ivory & Sime Baronsmead) plc, 1997–2001); Chairman, Sussex Place Ventures Ltd, since 2004; *b* 22 July 1945; *s* of late John and Kathleen Mary Thorp; *m* 1969, Christine Janice Kenyon; three *s*. *Educ:* Portsmouth Grammar Sch.; Queens' College, Cambridge (MA Natural Scis); London Business School (MBA). Alcan (UK), 1967–69; ICFC, then FFI, subseq. 3i plc, 1971–91, Dir, 1985–91; Dir-Gen., ESU, 1991–94. Chairman: Unipalm Ltd, 1992–94; Unipalm Gp plc, 1994–95; non-executive Director: Baronsmead VCT plc, 1995–2005; Patientline plc (formerly Patientline Ltd), 1998–2001 (Chm., Patientline Ltd, 1994–98); Job Opportunities Ltd, 2000–04; Assoc. of Investment Cos, 2007– (Dep. Chm., 2013–14). Mem. Council, 1997–2002, Chm., 2000–01, BVCA (formerly British Venture Capital Assoc.); Chm., AIC VCT Forum, 2006–. Non-exec. Dir, Royal Surrey County Hosp., 1990–97. Liveryman, Glovers' Co., 2013–. *Recreations:* tennis, walking. *Address:* Larks Hill, 16 Longdown, Guildford, Surrey GU4 8PP. *T:* (01483) 561016.

THORP, (Ian) Simon; His Honour Judge Thorp; a Circuit Judge, since 2013. Called to the Bar, Inner Temple, 1988; a Recorder, 2002–13; a District Judge, 2008–13. *Address:* Worthing County Court, The Law Courts, Christchurch Road, Worthing, W Sussex BN11 1JD.

THORP, Jeremy Walter, CMG 2001; HM Diplomatic Service, retired; a Director, British Bankers' Association, and Secretary, Joint Money Laundering Steering Group, 2002–06; *b* 12 Dec. 1941; *s* of Walter and Dorothy Bliss Thorp; *m* 1973, Estela Lessa Guyer. *Educ:* King Edward VII Sch., Sheffield; Corpus Christi Coll., Oxford (MA). HM Treasury, 1963–67; DEA, 1967–69; HM Treasury, 1969–71; First Sec. (Financial), HM Embassy, Washington, 1971–73; HM Treasury, 1973–78; FCO, 1978–82; Head of Chancery, Lima, 1982–86; FCO, 1986–88; Dep. Hd of Mission, Dublin, 1988–92; Head of Resource and Finance, then Resource Planning, Dept, FCO, 1993–97; with Unilever PLC, 1997–98; Ambassador to Colombia, 1998–2001. Dir, British and Colombian Chamber of Commerce, 2003–; Mem., Exec. Cttee, Anglo-Colombian Soc., 2002– (Dep. Chm., 2004–06; Chm., 2006–10). Mem. Adv. Council, Farnham Castle Briefing and Conf. Centre, 2002–06. Trustee, Children of the Andes, 2002–. *Recreations:* music, travel, looking at paintings, modern Irish history, walking, Latin America, Germany. *Address:* 9 Coutts Crescent, St Albans Road, NW5 1RF.

THORP, Nicola Jayne Maria Louise, FRCR; Consultant Clinical Oncologist, and Associate Medical Director, Clatterbridge Cancer Centre NHS Foundation Trust (formerly Clatterbridge Centre for Oncology NHS Foundation Trust), since 2001; *b* Shrewsbury, 11 April 1967; *d* of John Thorp and Elaine Thorp; *m* 1997, John Brennan; one *s* two *d*. *Educ:* Edgbaston High Sch. for Girls; Univ. of Leicester (MB ChB 1990). MRCP 1994; FRCR 1998. Junior doctor in Leicester, Liverpool and Clatterbridge. Chm., Brain Tumour Gp, and Mem. Exec., Children's Cancer and Leukaemia Gp. Trustee, Nat. Mus Liverpool, 2011–. Gov., Belvedere Sch. GDST, 2006–09. *Recreations:* family, fell walking, Burgundy wine. *Address:* Clatterbridge Cancer Centre NHS Foundation Trust, Bebington, Wirral CH63 4JY. *T:* (0151) 334 1155, ext. 4859. *E:* nicky.thorp@clatterbridgecc.nhs.uk.

THORP, Simon; *see* Thorp, I. S.

THORPE, Adrian Charles, CMG 1994; MA; HM Diplomatic Service, retired; Ambassador to Mexico, 1999–2002; *b* 29 July 1942; *o s* of late Prof. Lewis Thorpe and Dr Barbara Reynolds; *m* 1968, Miyoko Kosugi. *Educ:* The Leys Sch., Cambridge; Christ's Coll., Cambridge (MA). HM Diplomatic Service, 1965–2002: Tokyo, 1965–70; FCO, 1970–73; Beirut, 1973–76 (Head of Chancery, 1975–76); FCO, 1976; Tokyo, 1976–81; FCO, 1981–85, Hd of IT Dept, 1982–85; Counsellor (Econ.), Bonn, 1985–89; Dep. High Comr,

Kuala Lumpur, 1989–91; Minister, Tokyo, 1991–95; Ambassador to the Philippines, 1995–98. Man. Dir, Traviata Books Ltd, 2004–13. FRSA. *Publications:* articles in journals. *Recreations:* opera, travel, bookshops, comfort. *Address:* The Cider House, Compton Park, Sherborne, Dorset DT9 4QU. *Club:* Oxford and Cambridge.

THORPE, Prof. Alan John, PhD; Director General, European Centre for Medium-Range Weather Forecasts, since 2011; Visiting Professor of Meteorology, University of Reading, since 2006; *b* 15 July 1952; *s* of Jack Fielding Thorpe and Dorothy Kathleen Thorpe (*née* Davey); *m* 1979, Helen Elizabeth Edgar; one *s* one *d*. *Educ:* Univ. of Warwick (BSc Physics); Imperial Coll., London (PhD). Res. Asst, Imperial Coll., London, 1976–81; Scientist, Met. Office, 1981–82; University of Reading: Lectr, 1982–88, Reader, 1988–92, Prof., 1992–2006, Dept of Meteorol; on leave of absence as Dir, Hadley Centre, Met. Office, 1999–2001; Dir, NERC Centres for Atmospheric Sci., 2001–05; Chief Exec., NERC, 2005–11. *Publications:* over 100 papers in atmospheric sci. jls. *Recreation:* art appreciation. *Address:* European Centre for Medium-Range Weather Forecasts, Shinfield Park, Reading RG2 9AX. *T:* (0118) 949 9001. *E:* alan.thorpe@ecmwf.int.

THORPE, His Honour Anthony Geoffrey Younghusband; a Circuit Judge, 1990–2008; *b* 21 Aug. 1941; *s* of G. J. Y. Thorpe, MBE; *m* 1966, Janet Patricia; one *d* (one *s* decd). *Educ:* Highgate School; Britannia Royal Naval College (scholarship); King's College London. Royal Navy: served HM Ships Hermes, Ark Royal, Vidal, Blake; Captain 1983; Chief Naval Judge Advocate, 1983–86; retired from RN 1990. Called to the Bar, Inner Temple, 1972 (Treasurer's Prize); Asst Recorder, 1984–89, Recorder, 1989–90; Resident Judge, Chichester Crown Ct, 2000–08. Pres., Ind. Tribunal Service, 1992–94 (Social Security, Medical, Disability, and Vaccine Damage Appeals, Child Support Appeals). Judicial Mem., Parole Bd for England and Wales, 2008–10. *Publications:* articles in learned jls incl. Ocean Develt and Internat. Law. *Recreation:* sailing. *Address:* 79 Bishopsgate Walk, Chichester, W Sussex PO19 6FQ. *Club:* Victory Services.

THORPE, Brian Russell, CBE 1987; Deputy Chairman, Southern Water PLC (formerly Southern Water Authority), 1983–93 (Chief Executive, 1973–88); *b* 12 July 1929; *s* of late Robert and Florrie Thorpe; *m* 1955, Ann Sinclair Raby; three *d*. *Educ:* Rastrick Grammar Sch.; LLB London, LLM Leeds. Solicitor, 1952. Asst Prosecuting Solicitor, Bradford CC, 1954–55; Asst Solicitor, later Asst Town Clerk, Southampton CC, 1955–61; Dep. Town Clerk, Blackpool, 1961–65; Gen. Manager, Sussex River Authority, 1965–73. Churchill Fellow, 1972. *Recreations:* golf, gardening, foreign travel. *Club:* Worthing Golf.

THORPE, Ian James, OAM 2001; swimmer; *b* Sydney, 13 Oct. 1982; *s* of Kenneth William and Margaret Grace Thorpe. *Educ:* East Hills Boys High Sch. Founder, Ian Thorpe's Fountain for Youth, charity, 2000–14. World Championships: Perth, 1998: Gold Medal: 400m freestyle; 4 x 200m freestyle relay; Fukuoka, 2001: Gold Medal: 200m freestyle; 400m freestyle; 800m freestyle; 4 x 100m freestyle relay; 4 x 200m freestyle relay; 4 x 100m medley relay; Barcelona, 2003: Gold Medal: 200m freestyle; 400m freestyle; 4 x 200m freestyle relay; Silver Medal, 200m individual medley; Bronze Medal, 100m freestyle; Commonwealth Games: Kuala Lumpur, 1998: Gold Medal: 200m freestyle; 400m freestyle; 4 x 100m freestyle relay; 4 x 200m freestyle relay; Manchester, 2002: Gold Medal: 100m freestyle; 200m freestyle; 400m freestyle; 4 x 100m freestyle relay; 4 x 200m freestyle relay; 4 x 100m medley relay; Silver Medal, 100m backstroke; Pan Pacific Championships: Sydney, 1999: Gold Medal: 200m freestyle; 400m freestyle; 4 x 100m freestyle relay; 4 x 200m freestyle relay; Yokohama, 2002: Gold Medal: 100m freestyle; 200m freestyle; 400m freestyle; 4 x 100m freestyle relay; 4 x 200m freestyle relay; Silver Medal, 4 x 100m medley relay; Olympic Games: Sydney, 2000: Gold Medal: 400m freestyle; 4 x 100m freestyle relay; 4 x 200m freestyle relay; Silver Medal: 200m freestyle; 4 x 100m medley relay; Athens, 2004: Gold Medal: 200m freestyle; 400m freestyle; Silver Medal, 4 x 200m freestyle relay; Bronze Medal, 100m freestyle. Aust. Male Athlete of the Year, 1999, 2000, 2001, 2004; Young Australian of the Year, 2000; American Internat. Athlete Trophy, 2001; Telstra People's Choice Award, 2001, 2002; Centenary Medal, 2003. *Publications:* The Journey, 2000; Live Your Dreams, 2002; This Is Me (autobiog.), 2012. *Recreations:* surfing, movies, going out with friends, charity work. *Address:* c/o Grand Slam International Pty Ltd, Pacific Point Arcade level 1, Suite 11, 4–10 Sydney Road, Manly, NSW 2095, Australia. *Club:* SLC Aquadot (Sydney).

THORPE, Rt Hon. Sir Mathew Alexander, Kt 1988; PC 1995; a Lord Justice of Appeal, 1995–2013; Deputy Head, Family Justice, and Head of International Family Justice, 2005–13; *b* 30 July 1938; *s* of late Michael Alexander Thorpe and Dorothea Margaret Lambert; *m* 1st, 1966, Lavinia Hermione Buxton (marr. diss. 1989); two *s* (and one *s* decd); 2nd, 1989, Mrs Carola Millar (marr. diss. 2013). *Educ:* Stowe; Balliol Coll., Oxford. Called to the Bar, Inner Temple, 1961, Bencher, 1985; QC 1980; a Recorder, 1982–88; a Judge of the High Court, Family Div., 1988–95. *Address:* 1 Hare Court, Temple, EC4Y 7BE.

THORPE, Nigel James, CVO 1991; HM Diplomatic Service, retired; Secretary, Friends of the Connection, St Martin in the Fields, since 2014; *b* 3 Oct. 1945; *s* of Ronald Thorpe and Glenys (*née* Robilliard); *m* 1969 (marr. diss. 1976); two *s*; *m* 1978 (marr. diss. 2001); three *d*. *Educ:* East Grinstead Grammar Sch.; University Coll. of S Wales and Monmouthshire (BA Hons). Joined HM Diplomatic Service, 1969; Warsaw, 1970–72; Dacca, 1973–74; FCO, 1975–79; Ottawa, 1979–81; seconded to Dept of Energy, 1981–82; Asst Hd of Southern Africa Dept, FCO, 1982–85; Counsellor, Warsaw, 1985–88; Dep. High Comr, Harare, 1989–92; Head, Central European Dept, FCO, 1992–96; Sen. Directing Staff, RCDS (on secondment), 1996–97; Ambassador to Hungary, 1998–2003. Chm., Vodafone Hungary Foundn, 2003; acting Dir, Vodafone Gp Foundn, 2005–06; Dir, Corporate Affairs, Vodafone Hungary, 2004–07. Pres., Friends of Hungarian Fine Arts Mus., 2007–08. Trustee: Liszt Acad. Network, 2001–; Personal Support Unit, 2010–13; Chm., Respond, 2011–14 (Trustee, 2009–14). *Publications:* Harmincad Utca 6, a 20th Century History of Budapest, 1999. *Recreations:* gardening, carpentry, tennis.

THORPE, Phillip Andrew; Chairman and Chief Executive Officer, 2005–12, Advisor to Chairman, since 2012, Qatar Financial Centre Regulatory Authority; Advisor to Governor, Qatar Central Bank, since 2012; *b* 26 Aug. 1954; *s* of late Reginald Thorpe, OBE and of Fay Eglantine Thorpe; *m* 1st, 1976, Isabell Hanna Henkel (marr. diss. 1989); one *s* two *d*; 2nd, 1990, Melinda Kilgour Lowis (marr. diss. 1997); one *s* one *d*; 3rd, 1998, Jane Chunhae Kang. *Educ:* Victoria Univ., Wellington, NZ (BA Pol Sci., LLB); Univ. of Hong Kong (MSocSc Dist.). Admitted Barrister and Solicitor of Supreme Court of NZ and as Solicitor and Notary Public, Republic of Nauru. Solicitor, Beyer Christie O'Regan & Partners, Wellington, NZ, 1976–79; Legal Officer and Public Prosecutor, Govt of Republic of Nauru, 1979–81; Solicitor, Registrar-General's Dept, Hong Kong Govt, 1981–83; Hong Kong Securities Commission: Sen. Legal Advr, 1983–86; Asst Comr, 1986–88; Dep. Comr, 1988–89; Exec. Vice-Chm. and Chief Exec., Hong Kong Futures Exchange, 1987–89; Chief Exec., Assoc. of Futures Brokers and Dealers Ltd, 1989–91; Exec. Dir and Dep. Chief Exec., SFA Ltd, 1991–93; Exec. Dir and Chief Exec., London Commodity Exchange (1986) Ltd, 1991–92; Chief Exec., IMRO, 1993–98; Man. Dir, Authorisations, Enforcement, and Consumer Relns, FSA, 1998–2001; Pres., Futures Industry Inst., Washington, 2001–02; Chief Comr, Regulatory Agency, Dubai, then Chief Exec., Dubai Financial Services Authy, 2002–04. *Publications:* (Country Editor for Hong Kong) International Securities Regulation, 1986. *Recreations:* fishing, flying. *Address:* PO Box 22989, Doha, Qatar. *E:* p.thorpe@qfcra.com.

THORPE, Rt Rev. Richard Charles; *see* Islington, Bishop Suffragan of.

THORPE, Prof. Stephen Austen, PhD; FRS 1991; Professor of Oceanography, University of Southampton, 1986–2003, now Emeritus. *Educ:* Rutherford Coll., Newcastle (BSc London 1958); Trinity Coll., Cambridge (BA 1961; PhD 1966). SPSO, Inst. of Oceanographic Scis, NERC, until 1986. Mem., NERC, 1991–94 (Mem., Marine Scis Cttee). Hon. Prof., Sch. of Ocean Scis, Univ. of Wales, Bangor, 2001–. Pres., RMetS, 1990–92; Vice-Pres., Scottish Assoc. for Marine Sci., 1993–2009, 2011–15. Walter Munk Medal, US Office of Naval Res. and Oceanography Soc., 1998; Fridtjof Nansen Medal, Eur. Geophysical Soc., 2000. *Publications:* (ed jtly) Oceanography, 1996; (ed jtly) Encyclopedia of Oceanography, 2001, 2nd edn 2009; The Turbulent Ocean, 2005; An Introduction to Ocean Turbulence, 2007; contribs to learned jls. *Address:* 1A Green Edge, Beaumaris, Anglesey LL58 8BY. *T:* (01248) 209579.

THORPE-TRACEY, Stephen Frederick; Controller, Newcastle Central Office, Department of Social Security (formerly of Health and Social Security), 1986–89, retired; *b* 27 Dec. 1929; *s* of Rev. and Mrs J. S. V. Thorpe-Tracey; *m* 1955, Shirley Byles; one *s* two *d*. *Educ:* Plymouth Coll. Emergency Commn, 1948; Short Service Commn, 1950; Regular Commn, DLI, 1952; Staff Coll., Camberley, 1960 (psc); GSO2, Defence Operational Res. Estabt, 1961–64; Training Major, 8 DLI (TA), 1964–65; Major, 1 DLI, 1965–66; GSO2, MoD, 1966–70; direct entry, Home Civil Service, 1970; Principal, DHSS, 1970; Asst Sec., 1977; Under Sec., 1986. Mem., Prescription Pricing Authy, 1990–93. Hon. Secretary: Mid Devon Div., SSAFA (formerly SSAFA and FHS, then SSAFA Forces Help), 1992–99; Uffculme Br., RBL, 1995–2013 (Chm., 2013–). Mem., Uffculme Parish Council, 1995–2003. Chm., Uffculme Soc., 1994–2002. Chairman: Trustees, Coldharbour Mill, 1996–2006 (Hon. Sec., 1994–96); Coldharbour Mill Ltd, 1998–2006. Chm., Tiverton Chess Club, 1994–; Pres., Devon County Chess Assoc., 2003–05, 2007–11. *Recreation:* chess. *Address:* 9 Grantlands, Uffculme, Cullompton, Devon EX15 3ED. *T:* (01884) 841864.

THOULD, Anthony Julian, MA; Head Master, King Edward VI School, Southampton, since 2002; *b* 16 June 1958; *s* of late Dr Anthony Keith Thould and of Bernine Thould; *m* 1984, Susan Jane Isabelle Rentoul; three *s* one *d*. *Educ:* King's Coll., Taunton; Pembroke Coll., Oxford (MA Hist.). Distribn Manager, H. P. Bulmer Plc, 1981–84; asst teacher, Westminster Sch., 1984–88; Hd of Hist., 1988–91, Dir of Studies, 1991–97, Cranleigh Sch.; Dir of Studies, King's Sch., Worcester, 1997–2002. *Recreations:* classical guitar, fencing. *Address:* King Edward VI School, Southampton SO15 5UQ. *E:* headmaster@kes.hants.sch.uk.

THOULESS, Prof. David James, FRS 1979; Professor of Physics, University of Washington, 1980–2003, now Emeritus; *b* 21 Sept. 1934; *s* of late Robert Henry Thouless; *m* 1958, Margaret Elizabeth Scrase; two *s* one *d*. *Educ:* Winchester Coll.; Trinity Hall, Cambridge (BA; Hon. Fellow, 2014); Cornell Univ. (PhD). Physicist, Lawrence Radiation Laboratory, Berkeley, Calif, 1958–59; ICI Research Fellow, Birmingham Univ., 1959–61; Lecturer, Cambridge Univ., and Fellow of Churchill Coll., 1961–65; Prof. of Mathematical Physics, Birmingham Univ., 1965–78; Prof. of Applied Science, Yale Univ., 1979–80; Royal Soc. Res. Prof., and Fellow of Clare Hall, Cambridge Univ., 1983–86. Mem., US Nat. Acad. Scis, 1995. Wolf Prize for Physics, Wolf Foundn, Israel, 1990; Dirac Prize, Inst. of Physics, 1993; Onsager Prize, Amer. Physical Soc., 1999. *Publications:* Quantum Mechanics of Many-Body Systems, 1961, 2nd edn 1972, repubd 1990; Topological Quantum Numbers in Non-Relativistic Physics, 1998; (contrib.) 40 Years of Berezinskii-Kosterlitz-Thouless Theory, 2013. *Address:* Department of Physics, Box 351560, University of Washington, Seattle, WA 98195–1560, USA.

THRASHER, Prof. Adrian James, PhD; FRCP; FRCPCH; FRCPath; FRSB; FMedSci; Professor of Paediatric Immunology, since 2002, and Lead for Programme of Infection, Immunity, Inflammation and Physiological Medicine, since 2013, Institute of Child Health, University College London; *b* Shoreham-by-Sea, W Sussex, 27 May 1962; *s* of Paul and Isobel Thrasher; *m* 1991, Kanchan Pandurang Rege; two *s* one *d*. *Educ:* Brighton Coll.; St George's Hosp. Med. Sch. (MB BS 1986); PhD London 1995. MRCP 1989, FRCP 2004; MRCPCH 1998, FRCPCH 2011; FRCPath 2009; FRSB (FSB 2011). Hse physician, St Helier Hosp., Carshalton, 1986–87; hse surgeon, Ashford Hosp., Middx, 1987; Senior House Officer in Medicine: Broomfield Hosp., Chelmsford, 1987–88; Royal Surrey Co. Hosp., Guildford, 1988–89; Locum Registrar in Medicine, Royal Surrey Co. Hosp., then Dulwich Hosp., 1989; SHO in Thoracic Medicine, Brompton Hosp., 1989; University College Hospital: Registrar in Gen. Medicine, 1989–90; Sen. Registrar, 1992–93; University College London: Lectr in Molecular Medicine and Hon. Sen. Registrar in Medicine, 1990–91; Wellcome Clin. Trng Fellow and Hon. Sen. Registrar in Medicine, 1991–94; Lectr, Molecular Immunology Unit, Inst. of Child Health, 1994–98; Wellcome Trust Clin. Sci. Fellow, 1995–99, Sen. Fellow, 1999–2009; Sen. Lectr in Paediatric Immunol., 1998–2002; Dir, Centre for Immunodeficiency, Inst. of Child Health, 2006–13; Dir, Clin. Gene Therapy Prog., Gt Ormond St Hosp., 2001–. NIHR Sen. Investigator, 2008–. Hon. Consultant: Gt Ormond St Hosp. for Children NHS Trust, 1998–; UCL Hosps, 2000–; Vis. Specialist in Paediatric Immunol., Addenbrooke's Hosp. NHS Trust, 2004–. Mem., Editl Bd, 2005–, Associate Ed., 2011–, Human Gene Therapy; Mem. Editl Bd, 2007–, Associate Ed., 2008–, Molecular Therapy. Member: British Soc. of Immunol., 1997–; Sci. Adv. Panel, Neuroblastoma Soc., 2003–11; Exec. Mem. Cttee, British Soc. for Cell and Gene Therapy (formerly British Soc. for Gene Therapy), 2004– (Pres., 2009–13). Gov., London Acad. of Excellence, 2012–. FMedSci 2005. Descartes Prize for Res. and Sci., EU, 2005; Outstanding Achievement Award, Eur. Soc. of Gene and Cell Therapy, 2011; Gene Therapy Pioneer Award, 2014. *Publications:* contrib. chapters in books including: Oxford Textbook of Medicine, 3rd edn 1995; Clinical Studies in Medical Biochemistry, 2nd edn 1998; Concise Oxford Textbook of Medicine, 2000; Encyclopedia of Life Sciences, 2001; Gene Therapy: the use of DNA as a drug, 2002; Blood and Bone Marrow Pathology, 2002; contrib. articles to jls incl. Jl Biol. Chem., Lancet, Qly Jl Medicine, Immunodeficiency, Nature, Biochem. Jl, Gene Therapy, Blood, British Jl Haematol., Eur. Jl Haematol.; Human Gene Therapy, British Jl Immunol., BMJ, Leukemia. *Recreations:* astronomy, cycling, cricket, photography. *Address:* Blaysworth Manor, Colmworth, Beds MK44 2LD. *E:* a.thrasher@ucl.ac.uk.

THRELFALL, David; actor; *b* 12 Oct. 1953. *Educ:* Wilbraham Comprehensive Sch.; Sheffield Art Coll.; Manchester Polytechnic Sch. of Theatre. Associate Artistic Dir, Royal Exchange Theatre, Manchester, 1998–2001. *Stage:* Bed of Roses, Royal Court; 3 years with RSC, incl. Savage Amusement, Nicholas Nickleby, 1980 (Clarence Derwent Award, British Theatre Assoc., SWET Award); Not Quite Jerusalem, Royal Court, 1982; Hamlet, Edinburgh Fest., 1986; Bussy D'Ambois, Old Vic, 1988; Wild Duck, Phoenix, 1990; Count of Monte Cristo, Royal Exchange, 1994; Richard II, Cottesloe, RNT, 1995; Hedda Gabler, Chichester, 1996; Present Laughter, Royal Exchange, 1997; The Rehearsal, NY, 1997; Peer Gynt, Royal Exchange, 1999; Tartuffe, RNT, 2002; The Entertainer, Derby Playhouse, 2003; Skellig, Young Vic, 2003; Someone Who'll Watch Over Me, New Ambassadors, 2005; *television:* The Kiss of Death, 1976; Jumping the Queue, 1989; Clothes in the Wardrobe, 1993; Mary and Jesus, 1999; In the Beginning, 2000; series: Nicholas Nickleby, 1984; Paradise Postponed, 1985; The Marksman, 1988; Nightingales, 1990; Titmuss Regained, 1991; Statement of Affairs, Diana: Her True Story, 1993; Men of the World, 1994; Sex & Chips & Rock-'n'-Roll, 1999; Dinner of Herbs, 2000; Shameless (10 series; also dir 11 episodes), 2004–13 (North West Comedy Award, 2004; RTS Award, 2004, 2007, 2009, 2012); The Queen's Sister, 2005 (RTS Award); Constantine, Housewife 49 (BAFTA Award, 2007), 2006; Whistleblower, 2007; What Remains, 2013; Tommy Cooper: Not Like That, Like This, 2014; The Ark, Code of a Killer, Midwinter of the Spirit, 2015; *radio:* three series of

Baldi; John Gabriel Borkman, 2015; *films:* When the Whales Came, 1989; The Russia House, 1990; Patriot Games, 1992; Master and Commander, 2003; Alien Autopsy, 2006; Elizabeth: The Golden Age, Hot Fuzz, 2007; Black Sea, 2014. Hon. DArt: Manchester, 2013; Sheffield, 2014. Plays and Players Promising Newcomer, 1978. *Recreations:* motor bike, friends. *Address:* c/o Independent Talent Group Ltd, 40 Whitfield Street, W1T 2RH.

THRIFT, Sir Nigel (John), Kt 2015; PhD, DSc; DL; FBA 2003; Vice-Chancellor, University of Warwick, since 2006; *b* 12 Oct. 1949; *s* of Leonard John Thrift and Joyce Mary Wakeley; *m* 1978, Lynda Jean Sharples; two *d*. *Educ:* UCW, Aberystwyth (BA Hons); Univ. of Bristol (PhD 1979; DSc 1992); MA Oxon 2004. Research Fellow: Dept of Architecture, Univ. of Cambridge, 1975–76; Dept of Geog., Univ. of Leeds, 1976–78; Dept of Human Geog., ANU, 1979–81 (Sen. Res. Fellow, 1981–83); Lectr, 1984–86, Reader, 1986–87, St David's UC, Lampeter; Bristol University: Lectr, 1987–88; Reader, 1988–90; Prof. of Geography, 1990–2003, now Emeritus; Head, Dept of Geog., 1995–99; University of Oxford: Prof. of Geography, 2003–06; Hd, Div. of Life and Envmtl Scis, 2003–05; Student of Christ Church, 2004–06; Pro-Vice-Chancellor (Res.), 2005–06; Vis. Prof. of Geog., 2006–. Visiting Professor: Macquarie Univ., 1989; UCLA, 1992; Univ. of Vienna, 1998; Nat. Univ. of Singapore, 2002. Mem., Geography Res. Assessment Panel, HEFCE RAE, 1997–2003; Chair, Main Panel H, 2008 RAE, 2004–06. FCO Marshall Fund Comr, 2010–. Member: Bd, Higher Educn Stats Agency, 2008–; Adv. Panel, Nat. Curriculum Rev., 2010–; Governing Body, Eur. Inst. of Innovation and Technol., 2012–; Bd, Univ. Develt Trust, Univ. of Warwick; Chair: IPPR Commn on Future of HE, 2011–; Russell Gp A-level Content Adv. Bd, 2012–13. Dir, Nat. Centre for Univs and Business (formerly Trustee, Council for Industry and HE), 2012–; Trustee: Liverpool Sch. of Tropical Medicine, 2013–; Higher Educn Policy Inst. Fellow: Netherlands Inst. Advanced Study, 1993; Swedish Collegium for Advanced Study in Social Scis, 1999. FAcSS (AcSS 2001). DL W Midlands, 2014. Hon DLaws Bristol, 2010; Hon. LLD Monash, 2013. Heath Award, 1988, Victoria Medal, 2003, RGS; Medal, Univ. of Helsinki, 1999; Dist. Scholarship Honors, Assoc. of Amer. Geographers, 2007; Gold Medal, RSGS, 2009. *Publications:* (with D. N. Parkes) Times, Spaces, Places, 1980; (with D. K. Forbes) The Price of War, 1986; Spatial Formations, 1996; (with A. Leyshon) Money/Space, 1997; (jtly) Shopping, Place and Identity, 1998; (with A. Amin) Cities, 2002; Knowing Capitalism, 2005; Non-Representational Theory, 2007; (with P. Glennie) Shaping the Day, 2009; (with A. Amin) Arts of the Political, 2013; numerous ed volumes; contrib. chapters in ed vols, and papers in learned jls. *Recreations:* reading, writing. *Address:* University of Warwick, Kirby Corner Road, Coventry CV4 8UW.

THROCKMORTON, Clare McLaren, (Mrs Andrew McLaren); *see* Tritton, E. C.

THROUP, Margaret Ann; MP (C) Erewash, since 2015; *b* W Yorks, 27 Jan. 1957. *Educ:* Univ. of Manchester (BSc Hons Biol.). Biomed. scientist, Calderdale HA; sales exec., product manager, mktg manager, business devel; Dir, In-Vitro Diagnostic Div., pharmaceutical co.; business consultant. Member: Health Select Cttee, 2015–; Scottish Affairs Select Cttee, 2015–. *Address:* House of Commons, SW1A 0AA.

THRUSH, Prof. Brian Arthur, FRS 1976; Professor of Physical Chemistry, University of Cambridge, 1978–95, now Emeritus; Fellow, Emmanuel College, Cambridge, since 1960; *b* Hampstead Garden Suburb, 23 July 1928; *s* of late Arthur Albert Thrush and late Dorothy Charlotte Thrush (*née* Money); *m* 1958, Rosemary Catherine Terry, *d* of late George and Gertrude Terry, Ottawa; one *s* one *d*. *Educ:* Haberdashers' Aske's Sch.; Emmanuel Coll., Cambridge (Schol. 1946–50). BA 1949, MA, PhD 1953, ScD 1965. University of Cambridge: Demonstrator in Physical Chemistry, 1953; Asst Dir of Research, 1959; Lectr in Physical Chemistry, 1964, Reader, 1969; Hd of Dept of Physical Chemistry, 1986–88; Head of Dept of Chemistry, 1988–93; Tutor, 1963–67, Dir of Studies in Chemistry, 1963–78, Vice-Master, 1986–90 and Acting Master, 1986–87, Emmanuel Coll. Consultant Physicist, US Nat. Bureau of Standards, Washington, 1957–58; Sen. Vis. Scientist, Nat. Res. Council, Ottawa, 1961, 1971, 1980. Tilden Lectr, Chem. Soc., 1965; Vis. Prof., Chinese Acad. of Science, 1980–; Member: Faraday Council, Chem. Soc., 1976–79; US Nat. Acad. of Scis Panel on Atmospheric Chemistry, 1975–80; Lawes Agric. Trust Cttee, 1979–89; NERC, 1985–90; Council, Royal Soc., 1989–91; NATO Panel on Global Change, 1989–92. Pres., Chemistry Sect., BAAS, 1986. Mem., Academia Europaea, 1990 (Mem., Council, 1992–98). M. Polanyi Medal, RSC, 1980; Rank Prize for Opto-Electronics, 1992. *Publications:* papers on gas kinetics and spectroscopy in Proc. Royal Soc., Trans Faraday Soc., etc. *Recreations:* wine, gardening. *Address:* Brook Cottage, Pemberton Terrace, Cambridge CB2 1JA. *T:* (01223) 357637.

THUBRON, Colin Gerald Dryden, CBE 2007; travel writer and novelist, since 1966; *b* 14 June 1939; *s* of late Brig. Gerald Ernest Thubron, DSO, OBE, and Evelyn (*née* Dryden); *m* 2011, Margreta de Grazia. *Educ:* Eton Coll. Editorial staff, Hutchinson & Co., 1959–62; freelance television film maker, Turkey, Japan, Morocco, 1962–64; Editorial staff, Macmillan Co., New York, 1964–65. FRSL 1969 (Vice-Pres., 2003–09; Pres., 2010–); FRAS 1991. Hon. DLitt Warwick, 2002. Mungo Park Medal, RSGS, 2000; Lawrence of Arabia Meml Medal, RSAA, 2001; Travel Award, Soc. of Authors, 2008; Ness Award, RGS, 2011; Internat. Prize, Spanish Geographical Soc. *Publications: non-fiction:* Mirror to Damascus, 1967; The Hills of Adonis, 1968; Jerusalem, 1969; Journey into Cyprus, 1975; The Royal Opera House, 1982; Among the Russians, 1983; Behind the Wall, 1987 (Thomas Cook Award, Hawthornden Prize, 1988); The Lost Heart of Asia, 1994; In Siberia, 1999 (Prix Bouvier, Fest. Saint-Malo, 2010); Shadow of the Silk Road, 2006; To a Mountain in Tibet, 2011; *novels:* The God in the Mountain, 1977; Emperor, 1978; A Cruel Madness, 1984 (Silver Pen Award, 1985); Falling, 1989; Turning Back the Sun, 1991; Distance, 1996; To The Last City, 2002; contribs The Times, TLS, NY Rev. of Books. *Address:* 28 Upper Addison Gardens, W14 8AJ. *T:* (020) 7602 2522.

THURLEY, Anna Julia; *see* Keay, A. J.

THURLEY, Dr Simon John, CBE 2011; FSA; Senior Research Fellow, Institute of Historical Research, since 2015; *b* 29 Aug. 1962; *s* of late Thomas Manley Thurley and of Rachel Thurley (*née* House); *m* 1st, 1998, Katharine (*née* Goodison) (marr. diss. 2007); 2nd, 2008, Anna Julia Keay, *qv*; one *s* one *d* (twins). *Educ:* Kimbolton Sch., Cambs; Bedford Coll., London (BA Hist.; Hon. Fellow, RHBNC, 2003); Courtauld Inst., London (MA, PhD Art Hist.). Inspector of Ancient Monuments, Crown Buildings and Monuments Gp, English Heritage, 1988–90; Curator, Historic Royal Palaces, 1990–97; Dir, Mus. of London, 1997–2002; Chief Exec., English Heritage, 2002–15. Vis. Prof. of Medieval London History, Royal Holloway, Univ. of London, 2000–06; Vis. Prof. of the Built Envmt, Gresham Coll., 2009–. Member: Cttee, Soc. for Court Studies, 1996– (Chm., 2005–11); Council, St Paul's Cathedral, 2001–15; Bd, British Liby, 2015–. President: City of London Archaeol Soc., 1997–2002; Huntingdonshire Local Hist. Soc., 2004–; London and Middlesex Archæol Soc., 2006–08; Vice-Pres., NADFAS, 2000–08. Trustee, Dickens House Museum, 1998–2002; Patron, London Parks and Gardens Trust, 2001; Trustee, Canal and River Trust, 2011–. FSA 2004; MCIfA (MIFA 1998); FRHistS 2006. Hon. RIBA 2006; Hon. RICS 2008. Writer and Presenter, TV series: The Lost Buildings of Britain, 2004; Buildings that Shaped Britain, 2006. *Publications:* (jtly) Henry VIII: images of a Tudor King, 1989; The Royal Palaces of Tudor England, 1993; Whitehall Palace, 1999; Hampton Court Palace: a social and architectural history, 2003; The Lost Buildings of Britain, 2004; Whitehall Palace, 2008; Somerset House, 2009; Men from the Ministry: how Britain saved its heritage, 2013; The Building of England: how the history of England has shaped our buildings, 2013; contribs to books and jls. *Recreation:* ruins. *E:* simon@kingstaithe.com.

THURLOW, 9th Baron *cr* 1792; **Roualeyn Robert Hovell-Thurlow-Cumming-Bruce;** chartered surveyor; Principal, RCB Advisors, since 2007; *b* London, 13 April 1952; *s* of 8th Baron Thurlow, KCMG and Yvonne Hovell-Thurlow-Cumming-Bruce (*née* Wilson); *S* father, 2013; *m* 1980, Bridget Anne Julia Ismay Cheape; two *s* two *d*. *Educ:* 13 schs in Africa, Canada, NZ and UK. MRICS 1979. Partner, 1985–99, Man. Dir, 1999–2007, Jones Lang Wootton, later Jones Lang LaSalle. Elected Mem., H of L, 2015. *Recreations:* shooting, golf, Real tennis. *Heir:* *s* Hon. Nicholas Edward Decimus Hovell-Thurlow-Cumming-Bruce, *b* 16 Feb. 1986. *Address:* Killiechronan, Isle of Mull, Argyll PA72 6JU; The Old Vicarage, Mapledurham, Oxon RG4 7TP. *Clubs:* White's, Pratt's.

THURLOW, Alan John, FRCO; FRSCM; Organist and Master of the Choristers, Chichester Cathedral, 1980–2008; *b* 18 May 1947; *s* of John Edward Thurlow and Mary Bruce Thurlow (*née* Bennallack); *m* 1974, Christina Mary Perren. *Educ:* Bancroft's Sch., Woodford; Sheffield Univ. (BA 1st cl. Hons 1968); Emmanuel Coll., Cambridge. FRCO 1972; FRSCM 2007. Sub Organist, Durham Cathedral, 1973–80. Chairman: Friends of Cathedral Music, 1990–2002; Organs Adv. Cttee, Council for the Care of Churches, 1997–2006; Chichester Diocesan Adv. Cttee, 2011–; British Inst. of Organ Studies, 2011–; President: Cathedral Organists Assoc., 1995–96; IAO, 2009–13. DMus Lambeth, 2005. *Recreations:* walking, cycling. *Address:* 8 Old Bakery Gardens, Chichester, W Sussex PO19 8AJ. *T:* (01243) 533092. *Club:* Chichester City (Pres., 2004–11).

THURSO, 3rd Viscount *cr* 1952, of Ulbster; **John Archibald Sinclair;** Bt 1786; PC 2014; *b* 10 Sept. 1953; *er s* of 2nd Viscount Thurso and of Margaret Beaumont Sinclair (*née* Robertson); *S* father, 1995; *m* 1976, Marion Ticknor (*née* Sage); two *s* one *d*. *Educ:* Summerfields; Eton Coll. FIH (FHCIMA 1991); Master Innholder 1991. Savoy Hotel plc: Trainee, 1972; Gen. Manager and Dir, Lancaster Hotel, Paris, 1981–85; Gen. Manager and Dir, Cliveden, 1985–92; Chief Executive Officer: Granfel Hldgs, 1992–95; Champneys Gp Ltd, 1995–2001; Chm., Scrabster Harbour, 1997–2001; non-executive Director: Savoy Hotel plc, 1993–98; Lochdhu Hotels Ltd, 1975– (Chm., 1995–); Sinclair Family Trust Ltd, 1976– (Chm., 1995–); Thurso Fisheries Ltd, 1979– (Chm., 1995–); Ulbster Hldgs Ltd, 1994– (Chm., 1994–); Profile Selection and Recruitment Ltd, 1995–2002; Walker Greenbank PLC, 1997–2002 (Chm., 1999–2002); Royal Olympic Cruise Lines Inc. (USA), 1997–99; Mosimann's Ltd, 1998–2002. President: Licensed Victuallers Schs, 1997–98; Acad. of Food and Wine Service, 1998–. Patron: HCIMA, 1998–2003; IMS, 1998–. Lib Dem Spokesman on tourism, 1997–99, on food, 1998–99, H of L. MP (Lib Dem) Caithness, Sutherland and Easter Ross, 2001–15; contested (Lib Dem) same seat, 2015. Lib Dem Spokesman on Scottish matters, 2001–06, on transport, 2003–05, on business, innovation and skills (formerly business, enterprise and regulatory reform), 2009–10, H of C. Mem., H of C Commn, 2010–15; Chair, Finance and Services Cttee, H of C, 2010–15. FInstD 1997. *Recreations:* shooting, fishing, food and wine. *Heir:* *s* Hon. James Alexander Robin Sinclair [*b* 14 Jan. 1984; *m* 2010, Claire Rebecca, *e d* of John Schofield; one *s*]. *Address:* Thurso East Mains, Thurso, Caithness KW14 8HW. *Clubs:* Brooks's; New (Edinburgh).

THUYSBAERT, Jonkheer Prosper; Ambassador of Belgium to the Court of St James's, 1994–97; *b* 7 Dec. 1931; *s* of Prosper Thuysbaert and Marguerite Levie; *m* 1957, Marie-Claire Vuylsteke; two *s*. *Educ:* Leuven Univ. (grad. in Law and Notarial Scis; BA Thomistic Philosophy). Entered Belgian Diplomatic Service, 1957: Attaché, Luxembourg, 1960–61; Economic Attaché, Paris, 1961–62; 1st Sec., Tel Aviv, 1963–64; Advr to Minister for Foreign Trade, 1964–65; Counsellor, Perm. Repn to EC, 1965–70; European Adviser to: Minister for Foreign Affairs, 1970–77; Prime Minister, 1977–80; Dir, European Orgns, Ministry for Foreign Affairs, 1980–81; Chef de Cabinet to Minister for External Relns, 1981–83; Political Dir, Ministry for Foreign Affairs, 1983–85; Ambassador: Perm. Repn to UN, Geneva, 1985–87; Perm. Repn to NATO, Brussels, 1987–93; EC Consultant for European Stability Pact, 1993–94. University of Leuven, Belgium: Prof. Emeritus, 1977; Guest Prof., 1977–79; Special Guest Prof., 2005–08. President: Euro-Atlantic Assoc. of Belgium, 2002–14; Assoc. of former officials of Belgian Foreign Service, 2010–14. Officer 1978, Comdr 1987, Order of Leopold (Belgium); Comdr 1987, Grand Officer, 1995, Order of Crown (Belgium). Grand Officer, Order of Leopold II (Belgium), 1991. *Publications:* La Diplomatie Multilatérale, 1991; Multilateraal Kunst en Vliegwerk, 1991; Het Belgisch Buitenlandse Beleid, 1995; Diplomatic Skating on Thin Multilateral Ice, 2006. *Recreations:* art, tennis, ski-ing, swimming, golf. *Address:* Clos d'Orleans 12, 1150 Brussels, Belgium. *Club:* Anglo-Belgian.

THWAITE, Ann Barbara, DLitt; FRSL; writer; *b* London, 4 Oct. 1932; *d* of A. J. Harrop, LittD, PhD and H. M. Valentine of New Zealand; *m* 1955, Anthony Simon Thwaite, *qv*; four *d*. *Educ:* Marsden School, Wellington, NZ; Queen Elizabeth's Girls' Grammar Sch., Barnet; St Hilda's Coll., Oxford (MA 1959); DLitt Oxford 1998. FRSL 1987. Contributing Ed. and Mem., Editl Bd, Cricket Mag. Gp (US), 1974–2000. Vis. Prof., Tokyo Women's Univ., 1985–86; Helen Stubbs Meml Lectr, Toronto Public Library, 1990; Ezra Jack Keats Meml Lectr, Univ. of Southern Mississippi, 1992. Churchill Travelling Fellowship, 1993; Gladys Krieble Delmas Fellowship, British Library, 1998–99. Hon. Fellow, Univ. of Surrey Roehampton (Nat. Centre for Res. in Children's Literature), 2001. Regular reviewer of children's books: TLS, 1963–85; Guardian; TES. Vice-Pres., Tennyson Soc., 1997–. Governor: St Mary's Middle Sch., Long Stratton, Norfolk, 1990–2002; Hapton VC Primary Sch., Norfolk, 1995–2006. Hon. DLitt UEA, 2007. *Publications:* Waiting for the Party: the life of Frances Hodgson Burnett, 1974, reissued as Frances Hodgson Burnett: beyond the Secret Garden, 2007; (ed) My Oxford, 1977; Edmund Gosse: a literary landscape, 1984 (Duff Cooper Meml Prize, 1985); A. A. Milne: his life, 1990 (Whitbread Biography Award); (ed) Portraits from Life: essays by Edmund Gosse, 1991; The Brilliant Career of Winnie-the-Pooh, 1992; Emily Tennyson: the poet's wife, 1996; Glimpses of the Wonderful: the life of Philip Henry Gosse, 2002; Passageways: the story of a New Zealand family, 2009; Running in the Corridors: seven stories, 2014; *children's books include:* The Camelthorn Papers, 1969; Tracks, 1978; (ed) Allsorts 1–7, 1968–75; (ed) Allsorts of Poems, 1978; The Ashton Affair, 1995; The Horse at Hilly Fields, 1996. *Recreations:* other people's lives, messing about on the river. *Address:* The Mill House, Low Tharston, Norfolk NR15 2YN. *T:* (01508) 489569. *Clubs:* Society of Authors, Royal Over-Seas League.

THWAITE, Anthony Simon, OBE 1990; FRSL; FSA; poet; Editorial Consultant, André Deutsch Ltd, 1992–95 (Director, 1986–92); *b* 23 June 1930; *s* of late Hartley Thwaite, JP, FSA, and Alice Evelyn Mallinson; *m* 1955, Ann Barbara Harrop (*see* A. B. Thwaite); four *d*. *Educ:* Kingswood Sch.; Christ Church, Oxford (MA). Vis. Lectr in English, Tokyo Univ., 1955–57; Producer, BBC, 1957–62; Literary Editor, The Listener, 1962–65; Asst Prof. of English, Univ. of Libya, 1965–67; Literary Editor, New Statesman, 1968–72; co-editor, Encounter, 1973–85. Henfield Writing Fellow, Univ. of East Anglia, 1972; Vis. Prof., Kuwait Univ., 1974; Japan Foundn Fellow, Tokyo Univ., 1985–86; Poet-in-Residence, Vanderbilt Univ., 1992. Member: Literature Adv. Cttee (formerly English Teaching Adv. Cttee), British Council, 1978–2002; Cttee, Royal Literary Fund, 1993–2014; Council, RSL, 2003–08. Chm. of Judges, Booker Prize, 1986. Pres., Philip Larkin Soc., 1995–. FRSL 1978; FSA 2000. Hon. Lay Canon, Norwich Cathedral, 2005–. Hon. Fellow, Westminster Coll., Oxford, 1990. Hon. DLitt: Hull, 1989; UEA 2007. Cholmondeley Poetry Award, 1983. *Publications: poetry:* Home Truths, 1957; The Owl in the Tree, 1963; The Stones of Emptiness, 1967 (Richard Hillary Memorial Prize, 1968); Penguin Modern Poets 18, 1970; Inscriptions, 1973; New Confessions, 1974; A Portion for Foxes, 1977; Victorian Voices, 1980; Poems 1953–1983, 1984; Letter from Tokyo, 1987; Poems 1953–1988, 1989; The Dust of the World, 1994; Selected Poems 1956–1996, 1997; A Different Country, 2000; A Move in the Weather, 2003; Collected Poems, 2007; Late Poems, 2010; Going Out, 2015; *criticism:*

Contemporary English Poetry, 1959; Poetry Today, 1973, rev. and expanded, 1985, 1996; Twentieth Century English Poetry, 1978; Six Centuries of Verse, 1984 (companion to Thames TV/Channel 4 series); Anthony Thwaite in Conversation with Peter Dale and Ian Hamilton, 1999; *travel:* (with Roloff Beny) Japan, 1968; The Deserts of Hesperides, 1969; (with Roloff Beny and Peter Porter) In Italy, 1974; (with Roloff Beny) Odyssey: Mirror of the Mediterranean, 1981; *editor:* (with Geoffrey Bownas) Penguin Book of Japanese Verse, 1964, rev. and expanded, 1998 and 2009; (with Peter Porter) The English Poets, 1974; (with Fleur Adcock) New Poetry 4, 1978; Larkin at Sixty, 1982; (with John Mole) Poetry 1945 to 1980, 1983; Collected Poems of Philip Larkin, 1988, rev. edn 2003; Selected Letters of Philip Larkin, 1992; Further Requirements: Philip Larkin, 2001; The Ruins of Time, 2006; Poet-to-Poet: John Skelton, 2008; Philip Larkin: letters to Monica, 2010; *for children:* Beyond the Inhabited World, 1976. *Recreations:* archaeology, antiquarian beachcombing, pottery. *Address:* The Mill House, Low Tharston, Norfolk NR15 2YN. *T:* (01508) 489569.

THWAITES, Prof. Sir Bryan, Kt 1986; MA, PhD; CMath, FIMA; Hon. Professor, Southampton University, since 1983; *b* London, 6 Dec. 1923; *e s* of late Ernest James and Dorothy Marguerite Thwaites; *m* 1948, Katharine Mary (*d* 1991), 4th *c* of late H. R. Harries and late Mrs L. Harries, Longhope, Glos; four *s* two *d. Educ:* Dulwich College (Fellow, 2006); Winchester College; Clare College, Cambridge (Wrangler, 1944). Scientific Officer, National Physical Laboratory, 1944–47; Lecturer, Imperial College, London, 1947–51; Assistant Master, Winchester College, 1951–59; Professor of Theoretical Mechanics, Southampton Univ., 1959–66; Principal, Westfield Coll., London, 1966–83 (Hon. Fellow, 1983; Hon. Fellow, QMW, 1990). Gresham Prof. in Geometry, City Univ., 1969–72. Co-founder and Co-Chm., Education 2000, 1982–86. Hon. Sec. and Treas., Dulwich College Mission, 1946–57; inventor of the Thwaites Flap, 1947. Chm. and Mem. ARC Cttees, 1948–69. Mem. Exec. Cttee, Internat. Commn on Math. Instruction, 1967–70. Special Lecturer, Imperial College, 1951–58. Chm., Southampton Mathematical Conf., 1961. Founding Director of the School Mathematics Project, 1961–75, Chm. of Trustees, 1966–83, Life Pres., 1984; Chm. of Internat. Mathematical Olympiad, first in UK, 1979; Chm. Adv. Council, ICL/CES, 1968–84. Member: Approved Sch. Cttee, Hampshire CC, 1954–58, 1961–66; US/UK (Fulbright) Commn, 1966–76; Davies Cttee on CSSB, 1969–70; Council, Kennedy Inst. of Rheumatology, 1969–71; Ct of London Univ., 1975–81; Council, Middlesex Hosp. Med. Sch., 1975–83; Court, Southampton Univ., 1981–94; Council, European Atlantic Gp, 2004–10. Chm., Collegiate Council, London Univ., 1973–76; Chm., Delegacy, Goldsmiths' Coll., 1975–80. Mem. Acad. Advisory Committee: Univ. of Bath, 1964–71; Open Univ., 1969–75. Chairman of: Council of C of E Colleges of Education, 1969–71; Church of England Higher Educn Cttee, 1974–76; Northwick Park Hosp. Management Cttee, 1970–74; Brent and Harrow AHA, 1973–82; Wessex RHA, 1982–88; King's Fund Enquiry into Sen. Management Trng in NHS, 1975–76; Nat. Staff Cttee for Admin. and Clerical Staff, NHS, 1983–86; Enquiry into Radiotherapy Incident, Exeter Hosp., 1988. Founding Chm., British False Memory Soc., 1993. Chairman: Govs, Heythrop Coll., 1978–82; Friends of Winchester Coll., 1989–91; Govs, More House, 1993–96; Trustee: Westfield Coll. Develt Trust, 1979–83; Southampton Med. Sch. Trust, 1982–88; Richmond Coll., 1987–93 (Academic Gov., 1992–2000); City Tech. Colls Trust, 1987–97; Forbes Trust, 1987–2009; Patron, Winchester Detached Youth Project, 1990–96. Pres., Dulwich Prep Old Boys, 2012–15. Mercier Lectr, Whitelands Coll., 1973; Foundn Lectr, Inst. of Health Policy Studies, Southampton Univ., 1987; 25th Anniv. Lectr, Nuffield Inst., Leeds Univ., 1988. Shadow Vice-Chancellor, Independent Univ., July–Nov. 1971. Hon. Life Mem., Math. Assoc., 1962. JP, Winchester City Bench, 1963–66. A Vice-Pres., Friends of GPDST, 1975–95. Mem. Council, 1964–94, Pres., 1966–67, Hon. Fellow, 2004, Institute of Mathematics and its Applications. Sponsor, Family and Youth Concern (formerly The Responsible Society), 1979–98 (Trustee, 1992–98). Founding Chm., 2001–04, Life Pres., 2004, Soc. of Our Lady at Winton; Founder, Millstream Forum, Bosham, 2009–. *Publications:* (ed) Incompressible Aerodynamics, 1960; (ed) On Teaching Mathematics, 1961; The SMP: the first ten years, 1973; (ed) Hypotheses for Education in AD 2000, 1983; (ed) A Contemporary Catholic Commentary, 1998; numerous contributions to Proc. Royal Soc., Reports and Memoranda of Aeronautical Research Council, Quart. Jl of Applied Mech., Jl of Royal Aeronautical Soc., etc. *Recreations:* music, sailing, writing letters to The Times. *Address:* The Byre, Salthill Park, Fishbourne, W Sussex PO19 3PS. *T:* (01243) 790142. *E:* bryan.thwaites@btinternet.com. *Club:* Athenæum.

THWAITES, Jacqueline Ann; *see* Duncan, J. A.

THWAITES, Ronald; QC 1987; *b* 21 Jan. 1946; *e s* of Stanley Thwaites and Aviva Thwaites; *m* 1972, Judith Myers; three *s* one *d. Educ:* Richard Hind Secondary Tech. Sch.; Grangefield Grammar Sch., Stockton-on-Tees; Kingston Coll. of Technol. (subseq. Polytechnic, now Univ.); LLB London (external) 1968. Called to the Bar, Gray's Inn, 1970. *Recreations:* swimming, lighting bonfires. *Address:* (chambers) Ely Place Chambers, 30 Ely Place, EC1N 6TD. *T:* (020) 7400 9600.

THWAITES, Roy; Deputy Director, South Yorkshire Branch, British Red Cross Society, 1990–96; *b* 13 Aug. 1931; *s* of Walter and Emily Alice Thwaites; *m* 1st, 1954, Margaret Anne (*née* Noble) (marr. diss.); one *s*; 2nd, 1991, Mary (*née* Appleby). *Educ:* Southey Green Secondary Sch.; Sheffield Central Technical Sch. City Councillor, Sheffield, 1965–74, Chief Whip and Chm. of Transport Cttee, 1969–74; South Yorkshire County Council: Councillor, 1973–86; Chief Whip and Chm. Passenger Transport Authority, 1973–78; Dep. Leader, 1978–79; Leader, and Chm. of Policy Cttee, 1979–86. Dep. Chm. and Dir, SYT Ltd, 1986–93. Member: E Midlands Airport Consultative Gp, 1982–86; Industrial Tribunals, 1987–2001. Vice-Chm., 1979–84, Dep. Chm., 1984–86, AMA; Member: Local Authorities' Conditions of Service Adv. Bd, 1979–86; Yorks and Humberside County Councils Assoc., 1983–86; Vice-Chm., 1982–85, Chm., 1985–86, NJC Local Govt Manual Workers Employers. Mem., Special Employment Measures Adv. Gp, MSC, 1983–86. Dep. Chm., Nat. Mining Mus. Trust (formerly Yorks Mining Mus. Trust), 1984–93 (Dir, 1986–92). Dep. Pres., Northern Racing Coll. (formerly Northern Racing Sch. Trust), 2004– (Dep. Chm., 1986–2004). Hon. Fellow, Sheffield City Poly., 1982. *Recreations:* walking, reading, photography.

THYATEIRA AND GREAT BRITAIN, Archbishop of; *see* Theocharous, Archbishop Gregorios.

THYKIER, Claudia; *see* Winkleman, C.

THYNE, Malcolm Tod, MA; FRSE; Headmaster, Fettes College, Edinburgh, 1988–98; *b* 6 Nov. 1942; *s* of late Andrew Tod and Margaret Melrose Thyne; *m* 1969, Eleanor Christine Scott; two *s. Educ:* The Leys Sch., Cambridge; Clare Coll., Cambridge (MA Nat. Scis with Pt II in Chem.; Cert. of Educn). FRSE 1994. Asst Master, Edinburgh Acad., 1965–69; Asst Master, Oundle Sch., 1969–72, Housemaster, 1972–80; Headmaster, St Bees School, 1980–88. Develt Dir, Arkwright Scholarship Trust, 1999–2000. Gov., St Bees Sch., Cumbria, 2000–05; Dir, Edinburgh Acad., 2000–07. Trustee: CLIC, 2000–03; Cumbria Cerebral Palsy, 2003–10. *Publications:* Periodicity, Atomic Structure and Bonding (Revised Nuffield Chemistry), 1976. *Recreations:* hillwalking, organic gardening, watercolours. *Address:* Tofts Close, 37 Uppleby, Easingwold, York YO61 3BD. *T:* (01347) 823063.

THYNN, family name of **Marquess of Bath**.

THYNN, Alexander; *see* Bath, Marquess of.

THYNNE, John Corelli James, CB 1990; PhD, DSc; Adviser to the Chairman, Wesley Clover Corporation, since 2006; *b* 27 Nov. 1931; *s* of Corelli James Thynne and Isabel Ann (*née* Griffiths); *m* 2008, Barbara Elizabeth Huemer. *Educ:* Milford Haven Grammar Sch.; Nottingham Univ. (BSc, PhD); Edinburgh Univ. (DSc). Res. Chemist, English Electric Co. (Guided Missile Div.), 1956–58; Fellow: Nat. Res. Council, Ottawa, 1958–59; UCLA, 1959–60; Univ. of Leeds, 1960–63; Lectr in Chemistry and Dir of Studies, Univ. of Edinburgh, 1963–70; Principal, DTI, 1970–73; Counsellor (Scientific), British Embassy, Moscow, 1974–78; Asst Sec., IT Div., DoI, 1978–83; Department of Trade and Industry: Under Sec., 1983; Regl Dir, NW Reg., 1983–86; Electronic Applications Div., 1986–87; IT Div., 1987–89; Dir, Information Engrg Directorate, 1989–90. Dir Gen., Electronic Components Industry Fedn, 1991–94. Chm., ComCare Systems Ltd, 1992–94; Deputy Chairman: Celtic Manor Resort, 1994–; nCipher Corp. Ltd, 1996–99; Newport Networks Corp. Ltd, 2000–03; Dir, Camrose Consultancy Services, 1991–99; Sen. Advr, InterMatrix Gp, 1991–98; Director: Newbridge Networks Corp., 1992–2000; LTW Ltd, 1993–95; Celtic House Investment Partners Ltd, 1993–2002; Nolton Consultancy Services Ltd, 1995–2002; Spikes Cavell Ltd, 1996–99; UWS Ventures, 1998–2000; Enfis Ltd, 2001–10; Wesley Clover Corp. Ltd, 2002–; InUK Ltd, 2005–08. Member: Exec. Cttee, Nat. Electronics Council, 1986–90; NEDO Electronics Industries Sector Gp, 1986–90; Welsh Funding Councils Res. Gp, 1992–94; Radiocommunications Agency Bd, 1994–99. Mem. Council, Salford Univ., 1984–87; Gov., Univ. of Glamorgan (formerly Poly. of Wales), 1991–95. Vice Chm. Trustees, Mus. of Sci. and Industry, 1991–97. Hon. Fellow, Univ. of Wales Swansea, 1998. Hon. DSc Glamorgan, 1996. *Publications:* contribs on physical chemistry to scientific journals. *Recreation:* cricket. *Address:* 1021 Laguna Street, #3, Santa Barbara, CA 93101, USA. *E:* jthynne@wesleyclover.com. *Clubs:* Athenæum, MCC.

THYSSEN, Marianne Leonie Petrus; Member, European Commission, since 2014; *b* Sint-Gillis-Waas, Belgium, 24 July 1956. *Educ:* Catholic Univ. of Leuven (law degree 1979). Res. asst, Faculty of Law, Catholic Univ. of Leuven, 1979–80; legal advr, Union of Self-employed Entrepreneurs and to Markant, 1980–88; Dir, Res. Dept, Union of Self-employed Entrepreneurs, 1988–91; Legal Associate, Sec. of State for Public Health, Belgium, 1986–88. MEP, 1991–2014. Pres., Christen-Democratisch en Vlaans Party, 2008–10. *Address:* European Commission, Rue de la Loi 200, 1049 Brussels, Belgium. *T:* 22955491. *E:* marianne.thyssen@ec.europa.eu.

TIBBER, His Honour Anthony Harris; a Circuit Judge, 1977–99; *b* 23 June 1926; *s* of Maurice and Priscilla Tibber; *m* 1954, Rhona Ann Salter; three *s. Educ:* University College School, London; Magdalen College School, Brackley. Served in Royal Signals, 1945–48; called to the Bar, Gray's Inn, 1950; a Recorder of the Crown Court, 1976. Member: Matrimonial Causes Rule Cttee, 1980–84; Matrimonial Causes Procedure Cttee (Booth Cttee), 1983–85. Arbitrator and mediator, 2002–. *Recreations:* cultivating, idling, pottering. *Address:* 2 Osprey Court, 256 Finchley Road, NW3 7AA. *T:* (020) 7433 3234.

See also P. H. Tibber.

TIBBER, Peter Harris, DPhil; HM Diplomatic Service; Ambassador to Colombia, since 2015; *b* 7 Sept. 1956; *s* of His Honour Anthony Harris Tibber, *qv*; *m* 1983, Eve Levy-Huet, MSc (Oxon); three *s. Educ:* Haberdashers' Aske's Sch.; University Coll., Oxford (MA; DPhil 1983). FCO, 1984–86; Paris, 1986–88; First Sec., FCO, 1988–90; Private Sec. to Minister of State, FCO, 1990–92; Ankara, 1993–96; Dep. Hd of Mission, Mexico City, 1996–2000; Trade Partners UK, subsequently UK Trade & Investment: Dir, Africa and ME, 2000–01; Internat. Mgt Directorate, 2001–02; Dir, Internat. Sectors (formerly Business) Gp, 2002–04; Consul-Gen., Dusseldorf, and Dir Gen., Trade and Investment, Germany, 2005–09; Dep. High Comr, Islamabad, Pakistan, 2009–11; Interim High Comr, Kenya, 2011–12; Ambassador to Sudan, 2012–15. *Recreations:* choral singing, piano, tennis, swimming, fiction. *Address:* c/o Foreign and Commonwealth Office, King Charles Street, SW1A 2AH.

TIBBITT, Rear Adm. Ian Peter Gordon, CBE 2007; FRAeS; FIET; defence management consultant, since 2009; Managing Director, TDHB Ltd, since 2009; *b* 22 Oct. 1954; *s* of Peter Tibbitt and Daphne Tibbitt; *m* 1980, Marion Diane Lyons; two *d. Educ:* Arnold Sch.; Sidney Sussex Coll., Cambridge (BA 1976). MIET, CEng 1984; FRAeS 2003; FIET 2009. Joined RN as Air Engr Officer, 1973; Commando Helicopter and Sea Harrier Sqdns; acquisition, logistics and change mgt specialist, Merlin Mk 1 Project Manager, 1996–99; on staff of C-in-C Fleet, 2000–02; Dir Logistic Support (Air), 2002–03; Defence Logistics Orgn Restructuring Team Leader, 2003–04; Dir Logistics Rotary Wing, 2004–07; Dir Gen. Safety and Engrg, Defence Equipment and Support, MoD, 2007–09. Trustee, Fly Navy Heritage Trust, 2011–. *Recreation:* hockey (qualified hockey umpire). *T:* 07854 219409. *E:* mail@tdhb.co.uk.

TIBBS, (Geoffrey) Michael (Graydon), OBE 1987; Secretary of the Royal College of Physicians, 1968–86 (Secretary of Joint Faculty of Community Medicine, 1971–72, of Joint Committee in Higher Medical Training, 1972–86, and of Faculty of Occupational Medicine, 1978–86); *b* 21 Nov. 1921; *s* of Rev. Geoffrey Wilberforce Tibbs, sometime Chaplain RN and Vicar of Lynchmere, Sussex, and Margaret Florence Tibbs (*née* Skinner); *m* 1951, Anne Rosemary Wortley; two *s. Educ:* Berkhamsted Sch.; St Peter's Hall, Oxford. BA Hons Geography, 1948; MA 1952. FInstAM; MCIPD; FRGS. Served RNVR, Ordinary Seaman/Lieut, 1940–46 (despatches), HMS Cottesmore, HMS Sheffield, HM S/M Tantalus, HM S/M Varne. Sudan Political Service, Kordofan Province, 1949–55: seconded to MECAS, 1950; Dist Comr, Dar Messeria District, 1953. Various appointments in personnel, organisation and overseas services depts, Automobile Assoc., 1955–68. Hon. Mem., Soc. of Occupational Medicine, 1983; Hon. FRCP 1986; Hon. FFOM 1986; Hon. FFCM 1987. Freeman, City of London, 1986. *Publications:* Hello Lad, Come to join the Navy?, 2013; (with Anne Tibbs): A Look at Lynchmere, 1990; A Sudan Sunset, 2000; Another Look at Lynchmere, 2004. *Recreations:* producing pantomimes, parish affairs, preserving lowland heath, making bonfires. *Address:* Bunchfield, Lynchmere Ridge, Haslemere, Surrey GU27 3PP. *T:* (01428) 643120, 642176. *Club:* Naval.

TICEHURST, David Keith; His Honour Judge Ticehurst; a Circuit Judge, since 1998; *b* 1 May 1950; *s* of Frederick John and Barbara Elisabeth Ticehurst; *m* 1972, Gillian Shepherd; two *s* one *d. Educ:* Taunton's Grammar Sch., Southampton; Keynsham Grammar Sch., Bristol; Kingston Poly. (BA). Admitted solicitor, 1975; articled clerk, 1971–73, Solicitor, 1975–78, Lawrence & Co., Bristol; Solicitor, Osborne Clarke, Bristol, 1978–98 (Partner, 1980–98); Asst Recorder, 1991–94; Recorder, 1994–98. Founder Mem., Employment Lawyers' Assoc., 1992. Judicial Studies Board: Mem., Equal Treatment Adv. Cttee, 2002–06; Tutor Judge, 2004–. Gov., Sidcot Sch., 2002–07. Chm., Winscombe Youth Club, 2008–. Trustee, Fly 2Help, 2006–13. *Recreations:* cricket, watching Rugby, painting, reading. *Address:* Taunton Crown Court, Shire Hall, Taunton, Som TA1 4EU. *Clubs:* Winscombe Rugby Football (Vice-Pres.); Gloucestershire County Cricket (Life Mem.), Old Herpesians Cricket (Pres., 1998–).

TICKELL, Maj. Gen. Christopher Linley, CBE 2011 (OBE 2003; MBE 2001); Director General Army Recruiting and Training Division, since 2013; *b* Epsom, 17 March 1964; *s* of Richard Tickell and Angela Tickell; *m* 1995, Fiona Gifford; two *d. Educ:* Wellington Coll.; Cranfield Univ. (MA Military Studies). Joined Army, 1983; Troop Comdr, Germany, NI, GB, Norway and Botswana, 1984–91; Adjt 39 Engr Regt, 1992–93; SO3 5 Airborne Bde, 1993–94; sc 1995; SO2 Operational Requirements, MoD, 1996–98; OC 9 Parachute Sqn, 1998–2000; Co. Comdr, RMA Sandhurst, 2001; SO1 Ops, HQ Land, 2002; CO 23 Engr Regt (Air Assault), 2003–05; Col Trng, Directorate of Trng, 2005–07; Comdr 8 Force Engr

Bde, 2007–09; Dir, Army Div., 2010–12. *Recreations:* walking, swimming, cycling, family. *Address:* Army Recruiting and Training Division, Trenchard Lines, Upavon, Wilts SN9 6BE.

TICKELL, Dame Clare; *see* Tickell, Dame O. C.

TICKELL, Sir Crispin (Charles Cervantes), GCMG 1989 KCVO 1983 (MVO 1958); HM Diplomatic Service, retired; Warden, Green College, Oxford, 1990–97 (Hon. Fellow, 1997); *b* 25 Aug. 1930; *s* of late Jerrard Tickell and Renée (*née* Haynes); *m* 1st, 1954, Chloë (marr. diss. 1976), *d* of late Sir James Gunn, RA, PRP; two *s* one *d*; 2nd, 1977, Penelope, *d* of late Dr Vernon Thorne Thorne. *Educ:* Westminster (King's Schol.; Hon. Fellow, 1993); Christ Church, Oxford (Hinchliffe and Hon. Schol.; 1st Cl. Hons Mod. Hist. 1952). FZS 2014. Served with Coldstream Guards, 1952–54; entered HM Diplomatic Service, 1954. Served at: Foreign Office, 1954–55; The Hague, 1955–58; Mexico, 1958–61; FO (Planning Staff), 1961–64; Paris, 1964–70; Private Sec. to successive Ministers responsible for British entry into the European Community, 1970–72; FCO, 1972–75; Fellow, Center for Internat. Affairs, Harvard Univ., 1975–76; Chef de Cabinet to Pres. of Commn of European Community, 1977–81; Vis. Fellow, All Souls Coll., Oxford, 1981; Ambassador to Mexico, 1981–83; Dep. Under-Sec. of State, FCO, 1983–84; Perm. Sec., ODA, 1984–87; British Perm. Rep. to UN, 1987–90. Director: IBM (UK), 1990–95 (Mem. IBM Adv. Bd, 1995–2000); BOC Envmtl Foundn, 1990–2003; Govett Mexican Horizons, 1991–96; Govett American Smaller Cos Trust, 1996–98; Govett Enhanced Income Investment Trust, 1999–2004. Member, Environment Committee: Friends Provident, 1995–99; F&C Asset Mgt, 1999–2007. Chairman: Internat. Inst. for Envmt and Develt, 1990–94; Climate Inst. of Washington, 1990–2002, 2012–; Earthwatch (Europe), 1990–97; Adv. Cttee on the Darwin Initiative for the Survival of Species, 1992–99. Director: Green Coll. Centre for Envmtl Policy & Understanding, Oxford, 1992–2006; Policy Foresight Prog., James Martin Inst. for Sci. and Civilisation, later James Martin 21st Century Sch., Univ. of Oxford, 2006–10. Sen. Vis. Fellow, Center for Envmt, Harvard Univ., 2002–03. Advr-at-Large to Pres., Arizona State Univ., 2004–. Chm., St Andrews Prize for Envmt, 1999–2015. Trustee: Baring Foundn, 1992–2002; Natural Hist. Mus., 1992–2001; WWF (UK), 1993–99; Royal Botanic Garden, Edinburgh, 1997–2001; Thomson Reuters (formerly Reuters) Foundn, 2000–14; Foundn for the Future, 2007–. President: Marine Biol. Assoc., 1990–2001; RGS, 1990–93; Nat. Soc. for Clean Air and Envmtl Protection, 1997–99; Gaia Soc., 1998–2001; Tree Aid, 2007–14. Convenor, Govt Panel on Sustainable Develt, 1994–2000; Member, Government Task Force: on Urban Regeneration, 1998–99; on Near Earth Objects, 2000. Chancellor, Univ. of Kent, 1996–2006. Mem., Global 500 (UN Roll of Honour for Envmtl Achievement), 1991. Minor planet named No 5971 Tickell, 2006. FLS 2008. Hon. Fellow: St Edmund's Coll., Cambridge, 1995; Royal Instn, 2002; Hon. FRIBA 2000. Mem. (Dr *hc*), Mexican Acad. of Internat. Law, 1983 (Orden Académico del Derecho, de la Cultura y de la Paz, 1989). Hon. LLD: Massachusetts, 1990; Bristol, Birmingham, 1991; Kent, 1996; Nottingham, 2003; Hon. DSc: UEA, 1990; Sussex, 1991; Cranfield, 1992; Loughborough, 1995; Exeter, 1999; Hull, Plymouth, 2001; St Andrews, Southampton, Oxford Brookes, Univ. du Littoral, 2002; Brighton, 2006; Dr *hc*: Central London Poly., Stirling, 1990; Sheffield Hallam, 1996; E London, 1998; Amer. Univ. of Paris, 2003; Univ. Juarez Autonoma de Tabasco, 2011; DUniv Open, 2006. Global Envmtl Leadership Award, Climate Inst., 1996; Patron's Medal, RGS, 2000. Officer, Order of Orange Nassau (Netherlands), 1958; Order of Aztec Eagle with sash (Mexico), 1994; Friendship Award (China), 2004. *Publications:* Climatic Change and World Affairs, 1977, 2nd edn 1986; Mary Anning of Lyme Regis, 1996; *contributed to:* The Evacuees, 1968; Life After Death, 1976; The United Kingdom/The United Nations, 1990; Sustaining Earth, 1990; Sir Francis Galton, 1991; Monitoring the Environment, 1992; Threats Without Enemies, 1993; Science for the Earth, 1995; The Changing World, 1996; Managing the Earth, 2002; Remaking the Landscape, 2002; Johannesburg Summit, 2002; A Parliament of Sciences, 2003; Roy Jenkins: a retrospective, 2004; Environmental Stewardship, 2005; China and Britain, 2005; Making the Difference: essays for Shirley Williams, 2011. *Recreations:* climatology; palæohistory; art, especially pre-Columbian and African. *Address:* Ablington Old Barn, Ablington, Cirencester, Glos GL7 5NU. *Clubs:* Brooks's, Garrick.

TICKELL, Kathryn Derran, OBE 2015; DL; musician, composer and educator; *b* Staffordshire, 8 June 1967; *d* of Michael Scott Tickell and Kathleen Tickell; two *d*. Professional musician, specialising in Northumbrian pipes and violin, 1986–; Leader, Kathryn Tickell Band. Lectr, Newcastle Univ., 2000–; Artistic Dir, Folkworks, 2009–. Recordings include 14 CDs. DL Northumberland, 2015. Hon. DCL Northumbria, 2007. Queen's Medal for Music, 2008. *Recreations:* playing music, reading, cooking. *W:* www.kathryntickell.com.

TICKELL, Dame (Oriana) Clare, DBE 2010; Chief Executive, Hanover Housing Association, since 2014; *b* 25 May 1958; *d* of Patrick and Diana Tickell; *m* 1997, Edward Andres; two *s*. *Educ:* Bristol Univ. (CQSW 1986). Dep. Chief Exec., Centrepoint, 1986–89; Dir, Riverpoint, 1989–92; Chief Executive: Phoenix House, 1992–97; Stonham Housing Assoc., 1997–2004; Chief Exec., Nat. Children's Homes, then NCH, the children's charity, later Action for Children, 2004–13. Non-executive Director: Information Commn, 2003–10; Guinness Trust, 2010–14. Chair, Help the Hospices Commn into the Future of Hospice Care, 2011–13; Mem., Community, Voluntary and Local Services Honours Cttee, 2011– (Chair, 2012–). Mem. Bd, IPSO, 2014–15. Chm., Early Intervention Foundn, 2015–. FRSA. Hon. FCGI. Hon. DLaws Bristol, 2012; DUniv Bishop Grosstesste, 2013. *Publications:* Tickell Review on the Early Years Foundation Stage, 2011. *Recreations:* cycling, art, literature, photography. *Address:* Hanover Housing Association, Hanover House, 1 Bridge Close, Staines TW18 4TB. *E:* clare.tickell@hanover.org.uk.
See also S. M. Tickell.

TICKELL, Sophia Mary; Founder and Director, Meteos Ltd, since 2009; *b* London, 7 Oct. 1960; *d* of Patrick Tickell and Diana Tickell; *m* 1989, James Painter; two *d*. *Educ:* Univ. of Birmingham (BA Hons 1983). Project Asst, Christian Aid, 1985–88; journalist, CEDOIN, Bolivia, 1988–92; Project Manager, Christian Aid, 1992–94; Advocacy Trainer, 1994–97, Hd, Private Sector Team, 1997–2003, Oxfam; Dir, 2004–05, Chm. Bd, 2005–09, Sustainability Ltd; Founder and Dir, PharmaFutures, 2003–. Member, Advisory Committee: Aviva Global Responsible Investments, 2007–; Doughty Centre, Cranfield, 2008–; Advisor: Bd Cttee on Corporate Social Responsibility, GlaxoSmithKline, 2008–10, 2013–; Alliance Trust Sustainable Futures Funds, 2013–. Trustee, Green Alliance, 2008–. *Publications:* (jtly) Mugged: poverty in your coffee cup, 2002; PharmaFutures reports. *Recreations:* singing, walking, gardening, literature. *Address:* Meteos Ltd, Suite 3, 16/17 Hollybush Row, Oxford OX1 1JH.
See also Dame O. C. Tickell.

TICKLE, Prof. Cheryll Anne, CBE 2005; PhD; FRS 1998; FRSE; Royal Society Foulerton Research Professor at University of Dundee, 2001–07, at University of Bath, 2007–10, now Professor Emeritus; *b* 18 Jan. 1945; *d* of Lewis Sidney Tickle and Gwendoline Muriel Tickle; *m* 1979, John Gray. *Educ:* Girton Coll., Cambridge (MA); Glasgow Univ. (PhD 1970). NATO Fellowship, Yale Univ., 1970–72; Middlesex Hospital Medical School, subseq. University College London Medical School: Research Fellow, Lectr, Sen. Lectr, 1972–87; Reader, 1987–91; Prof. of Developmental Biology, 1991–98; Prof. of Developmental Biology, Univ. of Dundee, 1998–2001. Mem. Council, BBSRC, 2001–07. FRSE 2000. *Address:* Department of Biology and Biochemistry, University of Bath, Bath BA2 7AY.

TICKNER, Prof. Sylvia Elizabeth, (Lisa), PhD; FBA 2008; Honorary Professor, Courtauld Institute of Art, University of London, since 2014 (Visiting Professor, 2007–14); *b* London, 21 Dec. 1944; *d* of Horace and Doris Warton; *m* Clive Tickner (marr. diss. 1981); partner, 1981, *m* 2006, Alexander Robert, (Sandy), Nairne, *qv*; one *s* one *d*. *Educ:* Wembley Co. Grammar Sch.; Hornsey Coll. of Art (BA Hons Fine Art); Univ. of Reading (PhD). Hornsey College of Art, later Middlesex Polytechnic, then Middlesex University: Lectr (pt-time), 1968–73; Sen. Lectr, then Principal Lectr, 1973–88; Reader, 1988–92; Prof., 1992–2007, now Emeritus. Vis. Fellow, Yale Centre for British Art, 1990; Kreeger Wolf Dist. Vis. Prof., Northwestern Univ., 1991; Leverhulme Res. Fellow, 1992–93; Vis. Fellow, Sterling and Francine Clark Inst., 2007. Paul Mellon Lectures, 1996. Mem., English Heritage Blue Plaques Panel, 2007–15; Trustee, The Art Fund, 2010–. Hon. DArt Kingston, 2005. *Publications:* The Spectacle of Women: imagery of the Suffrage Campaign 1907–1914, 1988; Modern Life and Modern Subjects: British art in the early twentieth century, 2000; Dante Gabriel Rossetti, 2003; Hornsey 1968: the art school revolution, 2008; *co-edited*: Mapping the Futures: local cultures, global change, 1993; Travellers' Tales: narratives of home and displacement, 1994; Future/Natural: nature, science, culture, 1996; The Block Reader in Visual Culture, 1996; British Art in the Cultural Field 1939–1969, 2012; catalogue essays, articles in acad. press and broadcasts. *Recreations:* gardening, Association Croquet. *E:* Lisa.Tickner@courtauld.ac.uk.

TIDMARSH, Christopher Ralph Francis, QC 2002; *b* 11 Dec. 1961; *s* of late Peter Francis Charles Tidmarsh and of Mary Elizabeth Tidmarsh; *m* 1992, Lorna Clare Johnson; three *s* one *d*. *Educ:* Merton Coll., Oxford (BA Hons Physics); Poly. of Central London (Dip. Law). Called to the Bar, Lincoln's Inn, 1985; Jun. Counsel to Inland Revenue, 1993. *Publications:* contrib. to various jls. *Recreations:* family, garden, surfing. *Address:* 5 Stone Buildings, Lincoln's Inn, WC2A 3XT. *T:* (020) 7242 6201.

TIDMARSH, Prof. David H., PhD; CEng, FIMechE; Vice-Chancellor, Birmingham City University (formerly University of Central England), 2007–12. *Educ:* Lanchester Poly. (BSc, PhD). Joined Chrysler as grad. engr; British Leyland Technology; Head of Mech. Engrg, 1988, then Dir, Sch. of Engrg, Sheffield City Poly.; Dean of Engrg, 1993, Pro-Vice-Chancellor, 1998, Univ. of Central England; Vice-Chancellor, Anglia Poly. Univ., subseq. Anglia Ruskin Univ., 2004–07. FCMI.

TIDMARSH, Sir James (Napier), KCVO 2008; MBE 1989; Pro Chancellor, University of Bristol, 2007–14; Chairman, SouthWest One, 2008–11; Lord-Lieutenant, County and City of Bristol, 1996–2007; *b* 15 Sept. 1932; *yr s* of late Edward and Madeline Tidmarsh; *m* 1967, Virginia, *y d* of late Robin and Audrey Warren; two *s*. *Educ:* Taunton Sch. National Service: 1st Bn Duke of Cornwall's LI, 1952–54; TA 4/5 Bn Somerset LI, 1955–60. Factory manager, Dir, and Man. Dir, footwear industry, UK and Australasia, 1955–72; Man. Dir, Dycem Ltd, 1972–96; Director: Radio Avonside, 1979–83; Radio West, 1983–85; Founder Dir, GWR Radio plc, 1985–89. Director: Bristol Chamber of Commerce and Initiative, 1992–2015; Learning Partnership West (formerly Western Educn and Trng Partnership), 1995–99. Mem. Council, Royal Bath & West, 2012–. Vice-Chm., Nat. Assoc. Prison Visitors, 1966–69; Chm., Lord Chancellor's Adv. Cttee for Magistrates, 1997–2007. Patron: Young Bristol, 1999–; Avon Youth Assoc., 2000–; Bristol Dist, Merchant Navy Assoc., 2005–; Teenage Parents (Bristol), 2007–; West Country Br., Britain-Australia Soc., 2008–; Pres., Avon and Bristol Fedn of Clubs for Young People, 1994–98 (Chm., 1982–94). Mem. Council, Bristol Univ., 1994–2000. Governor, Colston's Collegiate Sch., 1986–94. Mem., Cook Soc., 1999–; Trustee, British Empire and Commonwealth Mus., 2003–14. Hon. Col, RM Reserve, SW England, 1998–2005. Mem., Soc. of Merchant Venturers, 1979– (Master, 1994–95). JP Bristol, 1977; High Sheriff, Avon, 1995–96. FRSA 2000. Hon. LLD: Bristol, 2002; UWE, 2003. KStJ 1997 (Pres., St John in Avon, 1998–2007). *Address:* 8 Prince's Buildings, Clifton, Bristol BS8 4LB. *T:* (0117) 973 0462. *Clubs:* Army and Navy, Saintsbury; Clifton (Bristol).

TIDMARSH, Janet; *see* Legrand, J.

TIDY, Morley David; Assistant Under-Secretary of State (Personnel) (Air), Ministry of Defence, 1990–92; *b* 23 April 1933; *s* of James Morley and Winnie Tidy; *m* 1957, Wendy Ann Bennett; one *s* two *d*. *Educ:* Hove County Grammar School; Magdalene College, Cambridge (MA). National Service, RAF, 1951–53. Dept of Employment, 1956–57; HM Inspector of Taxes, Inland Revenue, 1957–66; MoD, 1966; Manchester Business School, 1967; First Sec. (Defence), UK Delegn to NATO, 1969–72; MoD, 1973; RCDS, 1977; Chief Officer, SBAA, Cyprus, 1980–83; Asst Under-Sec., Air Staff, MoD, 1984; Asst Under-Sec. (Ordnance), MoD, 1985; Asst Under-Sec., Defence Export Services, Administration, MoD, 1988. *Recreations:* cricket, golf, jigsaw puzzles.

TIDY, William Edward, (Bill), MBE 2001; freelance cartoonist, since 1958; writer, playwright, television and radio presenter; *b* 9 Oct. 1933; *s* of William Edward Tidy and Catherine Price; *m* 1960, Rosa Colotti; one *s* one *d* (and one *s* decd). *Educ:* Anfield Road Jun. Sch., Liverpool; St Margaret's Sen. Sch., Anfield, Liverpool. Shipping office boy, R. P. Houston, Liverpool, 1950–51. Served RE, 1952–55. Layout artist, Pagan Smith Advertising Agency, 1956–58. Cartoon strips: The Fosdyke Saga, Daily Mirror; The Cloggies, Private Eye; Gimbledon Down, New Scientist; Kegbuster, CAMRA; Dr Whittle, Gen. Practitioner. Presented for BBC TV: Tidy Up Walsall; Tidy Up Naples; My City; Draw Me; radio broadcasting includes: The News Quiz (also Guest Presenter); Midweek (also Guest Presenter); I'm Sorry I Haven't a Clue; Back to Square One; The Law Game; Trivia Test Match; Down Your Way; radio adaptation, The Fosdyke Saga (with John Junkin). After dinner speaker for many major cos; regular cruise lectr and after dinner entertainer, P&O. *Publications: (written and illustrated):* Sporting Chance, 1961; O Cleo, 1962; Laugh with Bill Tidy, 1966; Up the Reds, Up the Blues, 1968; Tidy's World, 1969; The Cloggies, 1969; Tidy Again, 1970; The Fosdyke Saga (14 vols), 1972–85; The Cloggies Dance Back, 1973; The Great Eric Ackroyd Disaster, 1976; The Cloggies Are Back, 1977; Mine's a Pint, What's Yours (The Kegbuster Story), 1981; Robbie and the Blobbies, 1982; Bill Tidy's Little Rude Book, 1984; A Day at Cringemound School, 1985; Bill Tidy's Book of Classic Cockups, 1985; The World's Worst Golf Club, 1987; The Incredible Bed, 1990; Draw me 387 Baked Beans in 10 seconds, 1991; Save Daring Waring with a pencil, 1993; Is there any news of the Iceberg? (autobiog.), 1995; (with P. Bahn) Disgraceful Archaeology, 1999; Bill Tidy's Book of Quotations, 1999, 2011; has also illustrated over seventy other books; contrib. to What's Brewing?, Classic FM Magazine, British Archaeology, Archaeology (USA). *Recreation:* cricket. *Address:* Terry Meadow Farm, Boylestone, Derbyshire DE6 5AB. *T:* (01335) 330858. *E:* bill@billtidy.com. *Clubs:* Cartoonist of Great Britain; Lord's Taverners (Pres., 2007–09).

TIECH, Andrew C.; *see* Campbell-Tiech.

TIERNEY, Darren Christopher; Director of Civil Service Strategy and Efficiency, Cabinet Office, since 2015; *b* Belfast, 29 Jan. 1975; *s* of Patrick Tierney and Margaret Tierney; *m* 2001, Martha, *d* of Sir Louis Jacques Blom-Cooper, *qv*. *Educ:* St Columb's Coll., Derry; Queen's Univ., Belfast (BA Hons Business Admin and Mod. Langs 1997). Advertising sales exec., Daily Mail and Gen. Trust Gp, 1998–2000; Department of the Environment, Transport and the Regions, then Department of Transport, Local Government and the Regions, later Office of the Deputy Prime Minister: jun. policy roles in aviation, housing and land law, 2000–04; Bill Manager for Mental Capacity Bill, 2004–06; Private Sec. to Minister of State, MoJ, 2006–07; Dep. Principal Private Sec., 2007–09, Principal Private Sec., 2010–11, to the Lord Chancellor; Policy Manager for Legal Aid, Sentencing and Punishment of Offenders Act 2012, 2011–12; Dir of Youth Justice Policy (formerly of Strategy), MoJ, 2012–15. *Recreations:* cooking, cycling to burn the calories created by the cooking, reading contemporary fiction and political biographies. *Address:* Studio 44b, Limehouse Cut, 46 Morris Road, E14 6NQ. *T:* (020) 7517 9234. *E:* darren.tierney@hotmail.com.

TIERNEY, James Kevin; Sheriff of Grampian, Highland and Islands at Aberdeen, 2003–11; Consultant, Burness Paull (formerly Paull & Williamsons, then Burness Paull & Williamsons), since 2011; *b* 5 Oct. 1947; *s* of Edward Bird Tierney, schoolmaster, and Catherine Scanlan or Tierney; *m* 1971, Susan Mary Hubb; one *s* two *d*. *Educ:* St Aloysius' Coll., Glasgow; Edinburgh Univ. (LLB 1969). Admitted Law Soc. of Scotland, 1971; Partner: Littlejohns, Solicitors, Stirling, 1976–82; Paull & Williamsons, Advocates, Aberdeen, 1982–2000; Temp. Sheriff, 1987–92 and 1998–99; Sheriff of Tayside, Central and Fife at Perth, 2000. *Recreations:* golf, walking, gardening, European history, spectator sports. *Address:* Ardbeck, Banchory, Aberdeenshire AB31 4FE.

TIERNEY, John; caseworker, SDLP constituency office, Foyle, since 2003; *b* 9 Dec. 1951; *s* of Paddy and Catherine Tierney; *m* 1972, Bernie Harkin; two *s* one *d*. *Educ:* St Joseph's, Derry. Mem. (SDLP), Derry City Council, 1981–2003, 2007–13; Mayor of Derry, 1984–85. Member: NI Forum, 1996–98; (SDLP) Foyle, NI Assembly, 1998–2003; SDLP Dep. Whip, 1999–2002, Whip, 2002–03. *Address:* 72 William Street, Derry BT48 9AD. *T:* (028) 7136 0700, *Fax:* (028) 7136 0808.

TIETJEN, Tina, (Mrs G. R. Robertson), OBE 2010; Chairman: East Thames Group, since 2010; Billing Board, Energy UK, since 2014; *b* 10 June 1947; *d* of Arthur Tietjen and Mary Alice (*née* Storey); *m* 1972, Gordon R. Robertson. *Educ:* Coloma Convent Grammar Sch. Jt Man. Dir, Video Arts Gp Ltd; Dir, MediaKey Gp, 1996–98; Chairman: WRVS, 1999–2005; Air Transport Users Council, 2003–11; Willow Foundn, 2008–10. Former non-executive Director: Phoenix Business Consultants; Michael Davey Financial Management. Mem. Bd, BITC, 1992–97. Membership Consultant, Business in the Community. Gov., Thames Valley Univ., 1999–2008. *Recreations:* travel, theatre, opera, gardening.

TIETMEYER, Dr Hans; President, Deutsche Bundesbank, 1993–99 (Vice-Governor, 1991–93); *b* 18 Aug. 1931; *s* of Bernhard and Helene Tietmeyer; *m* 1st, Marie-Luise Floßdorf (*d* 1978); one *s* one *d*; 2nd, 1980, Maria-Therese Kalff. *Educ:* Univs of Münster, Bonn and Cologne (Dr rer. pol.). Sec., Bischöfliche Studienförderung Cusanuswerk, 1959–62; Fed. Min. of Economics, 1962–82, Head of Div. of Gen. Economic Policy, 1973–82; Mem. and Chm., Econ. Policy Cttees of EC and OECD, 1972–82; Sec. of State, Min. of Finance, 1982–89; Mem., Bd of Dirs, Deutsche Bundesbank, 1990–99. Vice-Chm., BIS, Basel, 2003–10. Chm. Bd, German Fed. Foundn for the Envmt, 1990–2003; Chm. of Govs, G–10 Central Bank, 1994–99. Hon. Prof., Faculty of Econ. Scis, Martin Luther Univ., Halle-Wittenberg, 1996–. President: European Centre for Financial Studies, Mercator Sch. of Mgt, Univ. of Duisburg-Essen, 1993–2005; European Business Sch., Oestrich Winkel, 2000–10. Five hon. drs. Grand Cross, Order of Merit with Star and Sash (Germany). *Publications:* numerous articles on economics and especially on Euro. *Recreation:* sport. *Address:* c/o Deutsche Bundesbank, Wilhelm-Epstein Strasse 14, 60431 Frankfurt, Germany.

TIKOISUVA, Pio Bosco; High Commissioner of Fiji in the United Kingdom, also accredited to the Republic of Ireland, Denmark, Germany, Israel, Egypt and the Holy See, 2008–11; Director, Catholic Education, Archdiocese of Suva, since 2014; *b* 13 March 1947; *m* 1973, Seniana Coalala; two *s* two *d*. *Educ:* St John's Coll., Fiji; Twickenham Coll. of Technol. (Dip. Printing 1976); Western Sydney Univ. (Postgrad. Cert. Mgt 2001). Government Printing Office, Fiji: apprentice, 1967–73; Tech. Asst, 1973–76; Sen. Tech. Asst, 1976–77; Fiji Institute of Technology: Hd, Sch. of Printing, 1977–82; Vice Principal, 1982–87; Dir, Min. of Youth and Sports, 1987–95; Regl Youth Develt Advr for S Pacific Commn, Noumea, New Caledonia, 1989–95; Govt Printer, Govt Printing Office, 1996–2000; Comr E Div., Min. of Regl Develt, 2000–02; CEO, Fiji Rugby Union, 2002–05, Acting CEO, 2011. Rugby: Vice Capt., Fiji Sec. Schs XV against NZ Vikings, 1966; Capt., St John's Coll. 1st XV team, 1966; Mem. Fiji Nat. rep. team, 1968–79; Internat. Invitation XV in NZ, 1972, in Tonga, 1972; played for: Harlequins Rugby Club, Surrey Dist Side, and British Barbarians Team, UK, 1973–76; Steel Bodgers XV v Cambridge, 1973–76; Steel Bodgers XV and Carwyn James XV, Newport Rugby Club Special Centenary Match, 1975; Capt., Fiji Nat. Team, 1977; Manager/Coach, Fiji Rugby 7s Team to Hong Kong, 1978–79; Coach, Nat. Juniors and Colts Team, 1983–84; Chm., Nat. Rugby Selectors, Fiji, 1989; Manager: Fiji XV Rugby Team, World Cup, France, 2007, NZ, 2011; Flying Fijians, Pacific Nations Cup, Fiji, 2007.

TILBIAN, Lorna Mona; Executive Director, Numis Corporation plc, since 2001 (Member, Board, since 2005); *b* Nicosia; *d* of Berdge Tilbian and Mayda Tilbian (*née* Ouzounian); *m* 1992, Paul Dezelsky (marr. diss.). *Educ:* Cheltenham Ladies' Coll.; Univ. of Southampton (BA Jt Hons English and Hist.; PGCE). Agencies analyst, Sheppards and Chase, 1984–88; Dir, S. G. Warburg Securities, 1988–95; Exec. Dir, Panmure Gordon, 1995–2001. Non-executive Director: Jupiter Primadona Growth Trust plc, 2001–; ProVen VCT plc, 2013–. *Recreations:* jewellery design, flower arrangement, Near Eastern cookery. *Address:* Numis Corporation plc, 10 Paternoster Square, EC4M 7LT. *T:* (020) 7260 1234. *E:* l.tilbian@numiscorp.com. *Club:* Addison.

TILBROOK, Richard James; Head of Honours and Appointments Secretariat, Cabinet Office, and Prime Minister's Appointments Secretary, since 2011; Deputy Appointments Secretary to the Prime Minister for senior ecclesiastical appointments, since 2014; Clerk of the Privy Council, since 2012; *b* 11 April 1962; 2nd *s* of late Dennis Frederick Tilbrook and Ann Elizabeth Tilbrook (*née* Knight). *Educ:* Royal Grammar Sch., Guildford; Queens' Coll., Cambridge (BA Classics 1983; MA 1987). Government Communications Headquarters, 1983–99: on secondment to Cabinet Office, 1995–98; Hd, London Office and Private Sec. to Perm. Sec., 1993–95; Department for International Development: Hd, Policy Coordination Unit, 1999–2000; Programme Manager: for Ukraine, Moldova and Belarus, 2000–01; for Afghanistan, 2002; policy posts, incl. secondment to Cabinet Office, 2002–08; Dep. Dir for Burma and corporate business, 2008; Dep. Chief of Assessments Staff, Cabinet Office, 2008–11. *Recreations:* singing (counter-tenor), gardening, village life, theatre, reading, writing pub reviews. *Address:* Honours and Appointments Secretariat, Cabinet Office, 1 Horse Guards Road, SW1A 2HQ. *Club:* Scribes.

TILBY, Rev. Canon Angela Clare Wyatt; Diocesan Canon, Christ Church Cathedral, Oxford, since 2011; Adviser for Continuing Ministerial Development, Diocese of Oxford, since 2011; *b* 6 March 1950; *d* of Julian George Wyatt Tilby and Constance Mary (*née* Collier). *Educ:* North London Collegiate Sch.; Girton Coll., Cambridge (MA). Producer, Religious Programmes, BBC Radio, 1973–79, BBC TV 1979–94; Sen. Producer, Religious Programmes, BBC North, 1994–97. Ordained deacon, 1997, priest, 1998; NSM, St John the Evangelist, Cherry Hinton, 1997–2006. Tutor, 1997–2007, and Vice Principal, 2001–06, Westcott House, Cambridge; Vicar, St Benedict's, Cambridge, 2007–11. Lectr in Spirituality and Early Ch History, Cambridge Theological Fedn, 1997–2011. Consultant, C of E Liturgical Commn, 2006– (Mem., 1998–2005). *Publications:* Teaching God, 1978; Won't You Join the Dance, 1984; Let There be Light, 1989; Science and the Soul, 1992; The Little Office Book, 1997; Son of God, 2001; God Before Breakfast, 2005; The Seven Deadly Sins: their origin in the spiritual teaching of Evagrius the Hermit, 2009. *Recreations:* science and crime fiction, history, psychology, cooking, wine. *Address:* 33a Vicarage Road, Oxford OX1 4RD. *T:* (01865) 286876.

TILGHMAN, Prof. Shirley Marie, OC 2014; PhD; FRS 1995; Professor of Molecular Biology, Princeton University (President, 2001–13, now President Emerita); *b* 17 Sept. 1946; *d* of Henry W. Caldwell and Shirley P. Carre; *m* (marr. diss.); one *s* one *d*. *Educ:* Queen's Univ., Kingston, Canada (BSc Hons 1968); Temple Univ., Philadelphia (PhD Biochem. 1975). Fogarty Internat. Fellow, NIH, Bethesda, 1975–77; Asst Prof., Temple Univ., 1978–79; Mem., Inst. for Cancer Res., Pa, 1979–86; Princeton University: Howard A. Prior Prof. of Life Scis, 1986–2001; Investigator, Howard Hughes Med. Inst., 1988–2001; Trustee, Jackson Lab., 1994–. Adjunct Associate Prof. of Human Genetics, Biochem. and Biophysics, Univ. of Pa, 1980–86; Adjunct Prof., Dept of Biochem., Univ. of Medicine and Dentistry of New Jersey-Robert Wood Johnson Med. Sch., NJ, 1988–2001. Ed. and Mem., Editl Bd, Molecular and Cell Biol., 1985–94; Member, Editorial Board: Jl Cell Biol., 1988–91; Genes and Develt, 1990–2001. Fellow, Inst. of Medicine, USA, 1995; Foreign Associate, Nat. Acad. of Scis, USA, 1996; Amer. Acad. of Arts and Scis, 1990; Amer. Phil Soc., 2000. Hon. DSc: Mt Sinai Coll. of Med., City Coll. of NY, 1994; Oxford, 2002; British Columbia, 2002; Dickenson Coll., 2002; Bard Coll., 2002; Queen's Univ., Kingston, Ont, 2002; Yale, 2002; Toronto, 2003; Western Ont, 2003; New York, 2005; Columbia, 2005; Univ. of Medicine and Dentistry of NJ, 2005; Rutgers, 2006; Rockefeller, 2006; Washington, 2007; Ryerson, 2007; Memorial Univ. of Newfoundland, 2007; Mills Coll., 2007; Amherst Coll., 2008; Rensselaer Polytechnic Inst., 2008; Hon. DLaws: Westminster Choir Coll., Rider Univ., 2002; Simon Fraser, 2002; Harvard, 2004; Hon. DHL Drew Univ., 2004. *Publications:* (ed with K. E. Davies) Genome Analysis: Vol. I 1990, Vols II and III 1991, Vol. IV 1992, Vols V and VI 1993; contrib. chapters in books; contrib. numerous articles and papers in Proc. Nat. Acad. Scis, USA, Jl Biol. Chem., Science, Nature, Genes Develt, Jl Cell Biol., Molecular Cell Biol. and others. *Recreations:* ski-ing, tennis, gardening, reading. *Address:* c/o Molecular Biology Faculty, Princeton University, 119 Lewis Thomas Laboratory, Washington Road, Princeton, NJ 08544–1014, USA.

TILL, Prof. Geoffrey, PhD; Professor of Maritime Studies, since 1990, and Chairman, Corbett Centre for Maritime Policy Studies, since 2014 (Director, 2007–14), King's College London; *b* 14 Jan. 1945; *s* of Arthur Till and Violet Dorothy Till (*née* Beech); *m* 1968, Cherry (*née* Austin); two *s* one *d*. *Educ:* King's Coll. London (BA Hons Mod. Hist. 1966; PGCE 1967; MA War Studies 1968; PhD 1976; FKC 2006). Lectr, then Sen. Lectr, Britannia RNC, 1968–72; Royal Naval College, Greenwich: Sen., then Prin., Lectr, 1972–89; Prof. of Hist. and Internat. Affairs, 1989–97; Dean of Academic Studies, JSCSC, Shrivenham, 1997–2006. Vis. Lectr, City Univ., 1973–85; Vis. Prof. in Maritime Studies, Nanyang Tech. Univ., Singapore, 2009–. Hon. Capt., RNR, 2009–14. *Publications:* Airpower and the Royal Navy, 1979; Maritime Strategy and the Nuclear Age, 1982; The Sea in Soviet Strategy, 1983; Naval Warfare and Policy, 1984; The Future of British Seapower, 1984; Modern Seapower, 1987; East-West Relations in the 1990s, 1990; Seapower: theory and practice, 1994; Seapower in the Millennium, 2001; Seapower: a guide for the 21st century, 2004, 3rd edn 2013; The Development of British Naval Thinking, 2006; Seapower and the Asia Pacific, 2011; Asian Naval Expansion, 2013; Understanding Victory: naval operations from Trafalgar to the Falklands, 2014. *Recreations:* visiting country churches, bird watching, travel, extreme gardening. *Address:* Wansdyke Cottage, Allington, Devizes, Wilts SN10 3NL. *T:* (01380) 860176. *E:* geofftill45@gmail.com.

TILL, Prof. James Edgar, OC 1994; OOnt 2006; PhD; FRS 2000; FRSC; University Professor, University of Toronto, 1984–97, now Professor Emeritus; Senior Scientist, Ontario Cancer Institute, 1957–96, Emeritus, since 1997; *b* 25 Aug. 1931; *s* of William Till and Gertrude Ruth Till (*née* Isaac); *m* 1959, Marion Joyce Sinclair; one *s* two *d*. *Educ:* Univ. of Saskatchewan (BA Arts and Sci. 1952; MA Physics 1954); Yale Univ. (PhD Biophysics 1957). Postdoctoral Fellow, Connaught Med. Res. Labs, 1956–57; University of Toronto: Asst Prof., 1958–62, Associate Prof., 1962–65, Dept of Med. Biophysics; Prof., 1965–97; Associate Dean, Life Scis, Sch. of Grad. Studies, 1981–84; Hd, Div. of Biol Res., Ont. Cancer Inst., 1969–82. Sen. Fellow, Massey Coll., Toronto, 1985–2009. FRSC 1969. Internat. Award, Gairdner Foundn, 1969; Thomas W. Eadie Medal, RSC, 1991; Robert L. Noble Prize, 1993, R. M. Taylor Medal, 2001, Nat. Cancer Inst. of Canada; Canadian Medical Hall of Fame, 2004; Centenary Medal, RSC, 2005; (jtly) Albert Lasker Award, Lasker Foundn, 2005; Canadian Sci. and Engrg Hall of Fame, 2010. *Publications:* contrib. chapters in books and conf. proceedings; numerous contribs to refereed jls. *Address:* Ontario Cancer Institute, University Health Network, 610 University Avenue, Room 9–416, Toronto, ON M5G 2M9, Canada. *T:* (416) 9462948.

TILL, Prof. Jeremy William, RIBA; Head, Central St Martins, and Pro Vice-Chancellor, University of the Arts London, since 2012; *b* 5 April 1957; *s* of late Barry Dorn Till; partner, Prof. Sarah Heath Wigglesworth, *qv*. *Educ:* Peterhouse, Cambridge (BA 1979); Poly. of Central London (DipArch 1983); Middlesex Univ. (MA 1999). RIBA 1995. Sen. Lectr and Sub-Dean, Bartlett Sch. of Architecture, UCL, 1991–99; University of Sheffield: Prof. of Architecture, 1999–2008; Head, Sch. of Architecture, 1999–2005; Dir of Architecture, 2005–08; Dean, Sch. of Architecture and the Built Envmt, Univ. of Westminster, 2008–12. Partner, Sarah Wigglesworth Architects, 1996–. Vis. Prof., Technical Univ., Vienna, 1995. *Publications:* (ed jtly) The Everyday and Architecture, 1998; (ed jtly) Architecture and Participation, 2005; Echo City, 2006; (jtly) Flexible Housing, 2007; Architecture Depends, 2009; (jtly) Spatial Agency, 2011; (jtly) The Design of Scarcity, 2014; numerous articles on architectl theory and educn. *Recreations:* growing, cooking and eating food. *Address:* Central St Martins, Granary Building, 1 Granary Square, N1C 4AA. *T:* (020) 7514 7444. *E:* jeremy@jeremytill.net.

TILL, Stewart Myles, CBE 2000; Director, Sonar Entertainment (Chief Executive, 2012–14); *b* 24 April 1951; *s* of Ronald Leslie and Olive Till; *m* 1986, Lynda Helen Jones; one *s* one *d*. *Educ:* Dulwich Coll.; Univ. of Bath (BSc Hons Business Studies); Essex Univ. (MA American Politics). Account Executive: Leo Burnett Ltd, 1974–76; Saatchi & Saatchi, 1976–78; Marketing Dir, WEA Records, 1978–83; Vice-Pres., N Europe CBS/Fox Video, 1983–88; Dep. Managing Dir, Sky TV, 1988–92; President: International Polygram Filmed Entertainment, 1992–99; Universal Pictures Internat., 1999–2000; Pres. and Chief Exec., Signpost Films, 2001–02; Chm. and Chief Exec., United Internat. Pictures, 2002–06; Pres., Stadium Films, 2007–10; Chief Exec., 2009–11, Chair, 2011–12, Icon UK Gp. Chm., UK Film Council, 2004–09 (Dep. Chm., 1999–2004); non-exec. Chair, Picture Prodn Co., 2011–; non-exec. Dir, Mediamorph, 2012–. Chm., Skillset, 2011– (Dep. Chm., 2002–10); Chm., Skills Action Gp, 2003–04. Trustee, Nat. Film and TV Sch., 1998–2005. Chm., Silverfish, 2009–. Chm., Fife, 1997–. Mem., Develt Bd, Henley River and Rowing Mus., 2000–05. Mem., Adv. Bd, Sch. of Mgt, Univ. of Bath, 2002–06. Chm., 2006–08, Vice Chm., 2008–09, Millwall FC; Mem., Commercial Cttee, Football League, 2008–09. Gov., Dulwich Coll., 2005–09. Hon. Mem., Women in Film and TV, 2004–; Hon. Fellow, Goldsmiths, Univ. of London, 2006 (Vis. Prof., 2011–). FRSA 2001. DU Essex, 2006. *Recreations:* most sports, family. *Address:* Highfield House, Mill Lane, Shiplake RG9 3ND.

TILLER, Ven. John; Archdeacon of Hereford, 2002–04, now Emeritus; *b* 22 June 1938; *s* of Harry Maurice Tiller and Lucille Maisie Tiller; *m* 1961, Ruth Alison (*née* Watson); two *s* one *d*. *Educ:* St Albans Sch.; Christ Church, Oxford (MA, 2nd Cl. Mod. Hist.); Bristol Univ. (MLitt). Ordained deacon 1962, priest 1963, St Albans; Assistant Curate: St Cuthbert, Bedford, 1962–65; Widcombe, Bath, 1965–67; Chaplain and Tutor, Tyndale Hall, Bristol, 1967–71; Lectr in Church History and Worship, Trinity Coll., Bristol, 1971–73; Priest-in-Charge, Christ Church, Bedford, 1973–78; Chief Sec., ACCM, 1978–84; Chancellor and Canon Residentiary, Hereford Cathedral, 1984–2002; Diocesan Dir of Trng, Hereford, 1991–2000. Non-stipendiary Local Ministry and Mission Advr, Shrewsbury Episcopal Area, dio. Lichfield, 2005–10; Asst Chaplain, Meole Brace Holy Trinity, 2009. Hon. Canon of St Albans Cathedral, 1979–84. *Publications:* The Service of Holy Communion and its Revision (with R. T. Beckwith), 1972; A Modern Liturgical Bibliography, 1974; The Great Acquittal, 1980; Puritan, Pietist, Pentecostalist, 1982; A Strategy for the Church's Ministry, 1983; The

Gospel Community, 1987; contribs to: The New International Dictionary of the Christian Church, 1974; Anglican Worship Today, 1980; New Dictionary of Christian Theology, 1988; The Parish Church?, 1988; (ed with G. E. Aylmer) Hereford Cathedral: a history, 2000. *Recreations:* walking, bird-watching, spuddling. *Address:* 2 Pulley Lane, Bayston Hill, Shrewsbury SY3 0JH. *T:* (01743) 873595. *E:* canjtiller@btinternet.com.

TILLETT, Michael Burn; QC 1996; a Recorder, since 1989; *b* 3 Sept. 1942; *s* of late Cyril Vernon Tillett and Norah Phyllis Tillett; *m* 1977, Kathryn Ann Samuel (marr. diss. 2008); two *d*; *m* 2011, Mary Kathleen Merrill. *Educ:* Marlborough Coll.; Queens' Coll., Cambridge (MA (Hons) Law). Called to the Bar, Inner Temple, 1965; in practice, 1966–2010; Asst Recorder, 1984–89. Legal Mem., Mental Health Rev. Tribunal, 2000–12. *Recreations:* golf, sailing, ski-ing. *Clubs:* Royal Automobile, Hurlingham, Royal Thames Yacht; Downhill Only; Seaview Yacht; Richmond Golf.

TILLEY, Charles Basil, FCA, FCMA, CGMA; Chief Executive, Chartered Institute of Management Accountants, since 2001; *b* 22 Dec. 1950; *s* of Basil and Irene Tilley; *m* 1983, Sarah Anne Morgan; one *s* one *d*. CA 1973, FCA 2012; FCMA 2012; CGMA 2012. KPMG, 1974–88, Partner, 1986–88; Gp Finance Dir, Hambros plc, 1989–96; Hd of Finance and Ops, Granville Baird, 1997–2001. Mem. Bd, 2004–07, Chm., Professional Accountants in Business Cttee, 2014–, Internat. Fedn of Accountants; Mem. Bd, Gt Ormond St Hosp. Foundn Trust (formerly Gt Ormond St Hosp.), 2007– (Dep. Chm., 2012–; Chm., Audit Cttee, 2008–; Mem., Remuneration Cttee, 2007–). Member: Accounting 4 Sustainability Project, 2008–; Internat. Integrated Reporting Council (formerly Cttee), 2010–. CCMI. FRSA 2004. Hon. Dr BPP University Coll., 2011. *Recreations:* sailing, tennis, cycling, ski-ing, walking. *Address:* The Chartered Institute of Management Accountants, The Helicon, One South Place, EC2M 2RB. *E:* charles.tilley@cimaglobal.com. *Clubs:* Sea View Yacht; Telford Park Tennis.

TILLING, George Henry Garfield; Chairman, Scottish Postal Board, 1977–84, retired; *b* 24 Jan. 1924; *s* of late Thomas and Anne Tilling; *m* 1956, Margaret Meriel, MStJ, *d* of late Rear-Adm. Sir Alexander McGlashan, KBE, CB, DSO; two *s* two *d*. *Educ:* Hardye's Sch., Dorchester; University Coll., Oxford (Open Exhibnr, Kitchener Schol., Farquharson Prizeman, MA). Served War of 1939–45, NW Europe: Captain, Dorset Regt, 1943–46. Post Office: Asst Principal, 1948; Principal, 1953; Private Sec. to Postmaster General, 1964; Dep. Dir of Finance, 1965; Dir, Eastern Postal Region, 1967; Sec. of the Post Office, 1973–75; Dir of Postal Ops, 1975–77. Mem. Council, Lord Kitchener Nat. Meml Fund, 1979–90. Order of St John: Mem. Council, London, 1975–77; Mem. Cttee of the Order for Edinburgh, 1978–87; Mem., Scottish Priory Chapter, 1993–99. Trustee, Bield Retirement Housing Trust, 1988–98. Hon. Mem., St Andrew's Ambulance Assoc., 1980. KStJ. FSAScot. *Recreations:* orders and medals, heraldry, uniforms. *Address:* 4 Fountain Place, Loanhead, Midlothian EH20 9EA. *T:* (0131) 440 1433.

TILLMAN, Harold Peter, CBE 2010; entrepreneur; Chairman, British Fashion Council, 2008–12; *b* 15 Oct. 1945. CEO, Lincroft Kilgour, 1969–74; Vice Chm., Sumrie Clothes plc, 1979–82; non-executive Chairman: Honorbilt plc; BMB Menswear; Jaeger Ltd, 2003–12; Allders Croydon Ltd, 2005; First Restaurant Gp, 2006–; Complete Leisure Gp, 2007–10; Aquascutum, 2009. Chm., Fashion Matters, Univ. of the Arts London (Chm., Alumni Bd, 2008). Trustee, V&A Mus., 2012–14. Barker, Variety, the Children's Charity (formerly Variety Club), 2009–14; Chm. and Founder, Patrons of Variety, the Children's Charity, 2014.

TILLMANN, Prof. Ulrike Luise, PhD; FRS 2008; Professor of Mathematics, University of Oxford, since 2000; Fellow of Merton College, Oxford, since 1992; *b* Rhede, FRG, 12 Dec. 1962; *d* of Ewald and Marie-Luise Tillmann; *m* 1995, Jonathan Morris; three *d*. *Educ:* Gymnasium Georgianum, Vreden; Brandeis Univ. (BA 1985); Stanford Univ. (MA 1987; PhD 1990); Bonn Univ. (Habilitation 1996). SERC Res. Asst, Univ. of Cambridge, 1990–92; Jun. Res. Fellow, Clare Hall, Cambridge, 1990–92; CUF Lectr, Univ. of Oxford, 1992–2010; Tutor, 1992–2010, Subwarden, 2012–14, Merton Coll., Oxford. Member: Prog. Cttee, Internat. Centre for Mathematical Studies Edinburgh, 2005–; Council, LMS, 2008–14 (Chm., Res. Meetings Cttee, 2011–14); Section Cttee, Internat. Congress of Mathematicians, 2000, 2014; Vice Chair: Sci. Adv. Bd, Courant Res. Centre, Göttingen, 2007–; Scientific Adv. Bd, Oberwolfach, 2013–; Chair, Internat. Rev. Cttee, Mathematical Res. in Norwegian Univs, 2012. Chaire de la Vallée Poussin, UCL Louvain, 2006–07. Lectures: ICM, 2002; Emmy Noether, Deutsch Mathematiker Vereinigung, 2009; Ladyzhenskaya Vorlesung, Leipzig, 2011. Ed., Topology, 2002–07; Founding and Man. Ed., Jl of Topology, 2008–; Member, Editorial Board: LMS Pubns, 2007–11; Qly Jl of Mathematics, 2000–; AGT, 2000–; Ergebnisse der Mathematik, 2015–. Whitehead Prize, 2004; Bessel Forschungspreis, 2007. *Recreations:* singing, baking. *Address:* Mathematical Institute, University of Oxford, Andrew Wiles Building, Radcliffe Observatory Quarter, Woodstock Road, Oxford OX2 6GG.

TILLMANS, Wolfgang; artist and photographer; Professor of Fine Art, Städelschule, Frankfurt, 2003–09; *b* 16 Aug. 1968; *s* of Karl A. and Elisabeth Tillmans. *Educ:* Bournemouth & Poole Coll. of Art & Design. Guest Prof., Sch. of Fine Arts, Hamburg, 1998–99. Hon. Fellow, Arts Inst., Bournemouth, 2001. *Solo exhibitions* include: Kunsthalle, Zurich, 1995, 2012; Galerie Daniel Buchholz, Cologne, 2001, 2013; Andrea Rosen Gall., NY, Deichtorhallen Hamburg, and touring, Mus. Ludwig, Cologne, 2001; Regen Projects, LA, Maureen Paley Interim Art, London, 2002; Tate Britain, 2003; P.S.1 Contemp. Art Center, NY, 2006; Mus. of Contemp. Art, Chicago, 2006; Hamburger Bahnhof Mus. für Gegenwart, Berlin, 2008; Maureen Paley, London, 2008, 2013; Serpentine Gall., London, 2010; Walker Art Gall., London, 2010; Nat. Kunstgalerie Zachęta, Warsaw, 2011; Moderna Museet, Stockholm, and touring, Westfalen, Dusseldorf, 2012; Common Guild, Glasgow, 2012; Mus. de Arte Moderna, São Paulo, and touring, Bogatá, Lima and Santiago de Chile, 2012; Rencontres d'Arles, Arles, 2013; Wako Works of Art, Tokyo, 2014; Metropolitan Mus. of Art, NY, 2015; *retrospective exhibition:* Tate Britain, 2003; *group exhibitions* include: MOMA, NY, 1996; Berlin Biennale, 1998; Castello di Rivoli, Turin, Royal Acad. of Art, Tate Britain, 2000; Tate Modern, 2001; Tate Liverpool, 2002; Tokyo Opera City Art Gall., 2004; 53rd Venice Biennale, 2009; Fondation Beyeler, Riehen, Switzerland (also curator), 2014. Member: Akademie der Künste, Berlin, 2012; Royal Acad. of Arts, 2013. Trustee, Tate Gall., 2009–14. Ars viva Prize, Bundesverband der Deutschen Industrie, 1995; Böttcherstrasse Prize, Bremen, 1995; Turner Prize, 2000; Kulturpreis der Deutschen Gesellschaft für Photographie, Germany, 2009; Wollaston Award, Royal Acad., 2014; Internat. Award in Photography, Hasselblad Foundn, Sweden, 2015. *Publications: monographs:* Concorde, 1995; Burg, 1997; View from Above, 2001; Wolfgang Tillmans, 2002; (jtly) truth study center, 2005; Manual, 2007; Lighter, 2008; Abstract Pictures, 2011; FESPA Digital - Fruit Logistica, 2012; Neue Welt, 2012; Utoquai, 2013; Wako Book 5, 2014; Wolfgang Tillmans, 2014; The Cars, 2015; exhibn catalogues. *Address:* c/o Maureen Paley, 21 Herald Street, E2 6JT. *T:* (020) 7729 4112, *Fax:* (020) 7729 4113.

TILLOTSON, Maj.-Gen. (Henry) Michael, CB 1983; CBE 1976 (OBE 1970, MBE 1956); writer; *b* 12 May 1928; *er s* of late Henry and May Elizabeth Tillotson; *m* 1st, 1956, Angela Wadsworth Shaw (marr. diss.; she *d* 2012); two *s* one *d*; 2nd, 2006, Sybil Osborne. *Educ:* Chesterfield Sch.; RMA Sandhurst. Professional soldier, 1948–83: commnd E Yorks Regt, 1948; served: Austria, 1948–50; Germany and Berlin, 1951–52; Indo-China (attached French Union Forces), 1953 (Croix de Guerre with Palm); Malayan Emergency, 1953–55; Indonesian Confrontation, 1964–65; S Arabia, 1965–67 (despatches); MoD Intelligence, 1967–69; Inf. Bn Comdr, Cyprus, 1969–71; Col GS, Hong Kong, 1974–76; Chief of Staff UN Force, Cyprus, and Comdr British Contingent, 1976–78; research mission for UN Sec.-Gen. to UN Forces, Israel, Lebanon, Syria and Sinai, 1978; Dep. Dir, Army Staff Duties, and MoD rep., Cabinet Civil Contingencies Cttee, 1978–79; Chief of Staff (Maj.-Gen.) to C-in-C UKLF, 1980–83. Regl Dir SE Asia, Internat. Mil. Services Ltd, 1983–86. Col, PWO Regt of Yorks, 1979–86. Hon. Life Fellow, RSPB, 1993. *Publications:* Finland at Peace and War 1918–1993, 1993, 2nd edn 1996 (Finnish Gold Medal of Merit, 1996); With the Prince of Wales's Own, 1995; Dwin Bramall: the authorised biography of Field Marshal the Lord Bramall, 2005, rev. and reissued as The Fifth Pillar, 2006; (ed with Ian Brunskill and Guy Liardet) Great Military Lives in Obituaries, 2008; (ed) SOE and The Resistance as told in The Times Obituaries, 2011; occasional columnist in The Times, 2000–. *Recreations:* abroad, birds, listening to music. *Address:* West End House, Wylye, Wilts BA12 0QT. *Club:* Army and Navy.

TILLSLEY, Gen. Bramwell Harold; General of the Salvation Army, 1993–94; *b* 18 Aug. 1931; *s* of Harold Tillsley and Doris Tillsley (*née* Lawrence); *m* 1953, Maude Pitcher (*d* 2014); two *s* one *d*. *Educ:* Kitchener-Waterloo Collegiate; Univ. of Western Ontario (BA); Wycliffe Coll., Toronto; Salvation Army Trng Coll., Toronto. Social worker, Children's Aid Soc., Kitchener, Ont., 1952–55; Salvation Army: Windsor, Nova Scotia, 1956–58; Oakville, Ont., 1958–59; on staff, Salvation Army Coll., Toronto, 1959–65; Divl Youth Sec., Saskatchewan, 1965–66; N Toronto Congregation, 1966–71; Training Principal: Newfoundland, 1971–74; NY, 1974–77; Provincial Comdr, Newfoundland, 1977–79; Divl Comdr, Metro-Toronto, 1979–81; Trng Principal, London, 1981–85; Chief Sec., USA, South, 1985–89; Territorial Comdr, Australian Southern Territory, 1989–91; COS, Internat. HQ, London, 1991–93. Mem., Rotary Club, Toronto, Melbourne and London. Queen's Medal (Canada), 1978. *Publications:* Life in the Spirit, 1966; Life More Abundant, 1968; Manpower for the Master, 1970; This Mind in You, 1989. *Recreations:* music, golf, sports (ice hockey in youth). *Address:* 65 Spring Garden Avenue, Unit 604, North York, ON M2N 6H9, Canada.

TILLYARD, James Henry Hugh, QC 2002; a Recorder, since 1998; a Deputy High Court Judge, since 2004; *b* 7 March 1955; *s* of William Stephen Tillyard and Margaret Diana Tillyard; *m* 2000, Helen Patricia Scott; two *d*, and one *s* one *d* by a previous marriage. *Educ:* Sherborne Sch., Dorset; Leeds Univ. (BSc Chem. Eng). Called to the Bar, Middle Temple, 1978; Wales and Chester Circuit; specialises in family law. *Recreations:* boating, spending time with my wife and children. *Address:* 30 Park Place Chambers, Cardiff CF10 3BS. *T:* (029) 2039 8421. *E:* clerks@parkplace.co.uk. *Club:* Cardiff and County.

TILSON, Joseph Charles, (Joe), RA 1991 (ARA 1985); painter, sculptor and printmaker; *b* 24 Aug. 1928; *s* of Frederick Albert Edward Tilson and Ethel Stapley Louise Saunders; *m* 1956, Joslyn Morton; one *s* two *d*. *Educ:* St Martin's School of Art; Royal Coll. of Art (ARCA); British School at Rome (Rome Scholar). RAF, 1946–49. Worked in Italy and Spain, 1955–59; Vis. Lectr, Slade Sch., Univ. of London and King's Coll., Univ. of Durham, 1962–63; taught at Sch. of Visual Arts, NY, 1966; Vis. Lectr, Staatliche Hochschule für Bildende Kunste, Hamburg, 1971–72. Mem., Arts Panel, Arts Council, 1966–71. Exhib. Venice Biennale, 1964; work at Marlborough Gall., 1961–77, later at Waddington Galls; retrospective exhibitions: Boymans Van Beuningen Mus., Rotterdam, 1973; Vancouver Art Gall., 1979; Volterra, 1983; Castelbasso, 2001; RA, 2002. Biennale Prizes: Krakow, 1974; Ljubljana, 1985, 1995. Subject of TV films, 1963, 1968, 1974. *Recreation:* planting trees.

TILSON THOMAS, Michael; Music Director, San Francisco Symphony Orchestra, since 1995; Principal Guest Conductor, London Symphony Orchestra, since 1995 (Principal Conductor, 1988–95); Artistic Director (formerly Artistic Adviser), New World Symphony, since 1988; concert pianist; *b* 21 Dec. 1944; *s* of Theodor and Roberta Thomas; *g s* of Boris and Bessie Thomashefsky, founders of Yiddish Theater, United States. *Educ:* Univ. of Southern California (Master of Music). Conductor, Young Musicians' Foundn Orchestra, LA, and conductor and pianist, Monday Evening Concerts, 1963–68; musical asst, Bayreuth, 1966–67; Koussevitzky Prize, Tanglewood, 1968; Asst then Principal Guest Conductor, Boston Symphony, 1969–74; NY début, 1969; London début, with LSO, 1970; Music Director: Buffalo Philharmonic, 1971–79; televised NY Philharmonic Young People's Concerts, 1971–77; Principal Guest Conductor, LA Philharmonic, 1981–85; Music Dir, Great Woods Festival, 1985; Co-Artistic Dir, Pacific Music Fest., Sapporo, Japan, 1990–; guest conductor with orchestras and opera houses in US and Europe; numerous recordings. Grammy Award: best orchestral recording, 1997, for Prokofiev's Romeo and Juliet with San Francisco SO; best classical album of the year, 1999, for Stravinsky's Firebird and Rite of Spring with San Francisco SO. *Address:* MTT Inc., 1745 Broadway, 18th Floor, New York, NY 10019, USA. *Club:* St Botolph (Boston).

TILT, Sir (Robin) Richard, Kt 1999; Social Fund Commissioner for UK, 2000–09; Director General, HM Prison Service, 1995–99; *b* 11 March 1944; *s* of late Francis Arthur Tilt and Mary Elizabeth (*née* Ashworth); *m* 1966, Kate Busby; two *s* one *d*. *Educ:* King's Sch., Worcester; Univ. of Nottingham (BA Hons); Open Univ. (Dip). HM Prison Service: Asst Governor, HM Borstal, Wellingborough, 1968–71; Tutor, Prison Service Staff Coll., 1971–74; Governor, HM Borstal, Pollington, 1974–75; Deputy Governor: Ranby, 1975–78; Gartree, 1978–80; Governor, Bedford, 1980–82; Hd, Manpower Section, HQ, 1982–84; Governor, Gartree, 1984–88; Dep. Regl Dir, Midlands, 1988–89; Hd, Industrial Relns, HQ, 1989–92; Hd of Finance, Police Dept, 1992–94; Dir of Services, 1994; Dir of Security and Progs, 1995. Chairman: Kettering Gen. Hosp. NHS Trust, 1999–2000; Northants HA, 2000–02; Leics, Northants and Rutland Strategic HA, 2002–06. Mem., Sentencing Adv. Panel, 1999–2002; Chairman: Social Security Adv. Cttee, 2005–11; Ind. Complaints Panel, Portman Gp, 2007–; Internet Watch Foundn, 2012–. Churchill Fellow, 1991. Friend of RA. *Recreations:* walking, reading, theatre, art. *Address:* First Floor Building 7300, Cambridge Research Park, Waterbeach, Cambridge CB25 9TN.

TILTMAN, Sir John H.; *see* Hessell Tiltman.

TIMBURY, Morag Crichton, MD, PhD; FRSE; FRCP, FRCPGlas, FRCPath; Director, Central Public Health Laboratory, Public Health Laboratory Service, 1988–95; *b* 29 Sept. 1930; *d* of William McCulloch and Dr Esther Sinclair McCulloch (*née* Hood); *m* 1954, Dr Gerald Charles Timbury, FRCPE, FRCPGlas, FRCPsych (decd); one *d*. *Educ:* St Bride's Sch.; Univ. of Glasgow (MB ChB; MD; PhD); Univ. of Edinburgh (MSc). MRCPath 1964, FRCPath 1976; MRCPGlas 1972, FRCPGlas 1974; FRCP 1994; FRSE 1979. University of Glasgow: Maurice Bloch Res. Fellow in Virology, 1960–63; Lectr in Bacteriology, 1963–65; Sen. Lectr in Virology, 1966–76; Reader, 1976–78; Prof. of Bacteriology and William Teacher Lectr, 1978–88. Hon. Cons. in Bacteriology and Virology, 1966–88. Member Council: RCPSG, 1985–88; RCPath, 1987–90. External examiner in med. microbiol., at various univs, 1973–88. Vis. Associate Prof. in Virology, Baylor College of Medicine, Houston, Texas, 1975; Vis. Mayne Guest Prof., Univ. of Queensland, Brisbane, 1990; Hon. Vis. Prof. of Virology, ICSM, 1997–99. Chm., Ind. Rev. Gp, Rev. of Food-Related Scientific Services in Scotland, 1998. *Publications:* Notes on Medical Virology, 1967, 11th edn 1997; (with J. D. Sleigh) Notes on Medical Bacteriology, 1981, 5th edn 1998; (co-ed) vol. 4, Virology, Topley and Wilson's Principles of Bacteriology, Virology and Immunity, 8th edn 1990; (jtly) Notes on Medical Microbiology, 2002; sci. papers on bacterial and viral infections, genetics of herpes simplex virus type 2. *Recreations:* military history, theatre.

TIMMER, Damien Gerard; Joint Managing Director, Mammoth Screen Ltd, since 2007; *b* London, 20 Oct. 1968; *s* of Maarten Timmer and Ann Timmer; *m* 1998, Rebecca Keane; two *s*. *Educ:* New Coll., Oxford (BA Mod. Hist. 1991). Script Editor, Central Films, 1994–95; Drama Develt Exec./Producer, Carlton TV, 1995–98; Exec. Producer, United Film and TV

Prodns, 1998–2001; Hd of Drama, ITV Prodns, 2001–06. *Recreations:* piano, knitting. *Address:* Mammoth Screen Ltd, Third Floor, 142–144 New Cavendish Street, W1W 6YF. *T:* (020) 7268 0050.

TIMMINS, Col Sir John (Bradford), KCVO 2002; OBE (mil.) 1973; TD 1968 (1st Clasp 1974); JP; Lord Lieutenant of Greater Manchester, 1987–2007; Chairman, Warburton Properties Ltd, since 1973; *b* 23 June 1932; *s* of John James Timmins and Janet Gwendoline (*née* Legg); *m* 1956, Jean Edwards; five *s* one *d*. *Educ:* Dudley Grammar Sch.; Wolverhampton Technical Coll.; Univ. of Aston-in-Birmingham (MSc). Building and Civil Engrg Industry, 1949–80; NW Regional Pres., Nat. Fedn of Building Trade Employers, 1974–75. Commnd RE, 1954; National Service, 1954–56; TA, 1956–80; comd 75 Eng. Regt(V), 1971–73, Hon. Col of the Regt, 1980–90; Hon. Colonel: Manchester and Salford Univ. OTC, 1990–98; Gtr Manchester ACF, 1991–2007. President: TA&VRA for NW England, 1994–99 (Vice-Chm., 1983–87; Vice-Pres., 1987–94, 1999–2007); EC&SM Wing ATC, 2007–12. ADC to the Queen, 1975–80. DL, 1981, High Sheriff, 1986–87, Gtr Manchester; JP Trafford, 1987. President, Greater Manchester: Order of St John, 1987–2007 (Chapter Gen., 1993–99); Royal Soc. of St George, 1988–2008 (Fellow, 2009). FRSA 1996. Hon. RNCM 1994. Hon. DSc Salford, 1990; Hon. LLD Manchester, 2001. KStJ 1988; KLJ 1990. *Recreations:* sailing, gardening. *Address:* 7 Little Heath Lane, Dunham Massey, Cheshire WA14 4TS. *Club:* Army and Navy.

TIMMINS, Nicholas James Maxwell-; chronicler and author; Public Policy Editor, Financial Times, 1996–2011; *b* 7 Sept. 1949; *s* of Rev. Leslie James and Audrey Maxwell-Timmins; *m* 1981, Elaine Barbara Brown; two *s* (twins) one *d*. *Educ:* Galleywall Road Prim. Sch., Bermondsey; Priors Court, Newbury; Kingswood Sch., Bath; Regent's Park Coll., Oxford (BA English Lang. and Lit. 1971). Reporter, Nature, 1971–74; Sci. and Medicine Corresp., 1974–78, Chief Labour and Industrial Corresp., 1978–79, Press Assoc.; gen. reporter, 1980, Health and Social Services Corresp., 1983–86, The Times; Health and Social Services Corresp., 1986–90, Political Corresp., 1990–95, The Independent; Public Policy Ed., 1995–96. Dist. Vis. Fellow, 1993, Mem. Adv. Council, 2001–03, Policy Studies Inst. Advr, Work, Income and Social Protection Cttee, Joseph Rowntree Foundn, 1994–98; Member Advisory Board: ESRC Centre for Analysis of Social Exclusion, 1997–2008; ESRC Centre for Market and Public Orgn, 2005–; Mem. Council, Pensions Policy Inst., 2001–; Mem., Phillis Cttee on Govt Communications, 2003–04. Visiting Professor: of Public Mgt, KCL, 2006–; in Social Policy, LSE, 2012–. Sen. Associate, Nuffield Trust, 2008–; Senior Fellow: Inst. for Govt, 2011–; King's Fund, 2011–. Pres., Social Policy Assoc., 2008–11. Mem. Adv. Bd, Social Dimensions of Health Inst., Dundee and St Andrews Univs, 2005–11. Hon. FRCP. *Publications:* The Five Giants: a biography of the welfare state, 1995, 2nd edn 2001; NHS 50th Anniversary: a history of the NHS, 1998; Rejuvenate or Retire?: views of the NHS at 60, 2008; Never Again: how and why the 2012 Health Act happened, 2012; The Wisdom of the Crowd: 65 views of the NHS at 65, 2013; Dying to Improve: the demise of the Audit Commission, 2014; (contrib.) The Coalition Effect, 2015; (jtly) Glaziers and Window Breakers: the role of the Secretary of State for Health, 2015. *Recreation:* kitchen talks. *T:* 07771 898094. *E:* nicholas.timmins@gmail.com.

TIMMIS, Prof. Adam David, MD; FRCP; Professor of Clinical Cardiology, Queen Mary (formerly Queen Mary and Westfield College), University of London, since 2002; Deputy Director, NIHR Cardiovascular Biomedical Research Unit; Consultant Cardiologist, Barts Health NHS Trust (formerly Barts and the London NHS Trust), and Newham University Hospital, since 1987; *b* Harpenden, Herts, 3 July 1949; *s* of late Peter Timmis and of Kathreen Timmis; *m* 1989, Naureen Bhatti; three *d*. *Educ:* Berkhamsted Sch.; Gonville and Caius Coll., Cambridge (BA 1970, MB BChir 1973; MD 1983); St Bartholomew's Hosp. Med. Coll. MRCP 1976, FRCP 1993. Res. and Clinical Fellow in Cardiol., Massachusetts Gen. Hosp., Boston, 1980–82; Sen. Registrar, Cardiol., Guy's Hosp., London, 1983–87. Mem., Post-AMI, Chm., Chest Pain, Chm., Angina, Guideline Develt Gps, NICE, 2004–11. Member, Executive Committee: Nat. Inst. of Cardiovascular Outcomes Res., 2011–15; Farr Inst., 2013–15. Asst Sec., then Sec., 2002–04, Mem. Council, 2006–13, British Cardiac Soc. FESC 1994. Editor: Heart, 2006–13; Eur. Heart Jl: Quality of Care and Clin. Outcomes, 2015–. *Publications:* (contrib.) Hutchison's Clinical Methods, 20th edn 1995 to 22nd edn 2007; (contrib.) Oxford Textbook of Medicine, 5th edn 2010; over 200 papers in cardiovascular literature, major interests being cardiovascular outcomes research. *Recreations:* family and friends, cardiology, Arsenal FC, tennis. *Address:* NIHR Cardiovascular Biomedical Research Unit, Barts Health, West Smithfield, EC1A 7BE. *T:* (020) 7377 7000. *E:* a.d.amtimmis@qmul.ac.uk.

TIMMIS, Prof. Kenneth Nigel, PhD; FRS 2008; Professor, Institute of Microbiology, Technical University of Braunschweig, since 1988; *b* Blackpool, 16 Feb. 1946; *s* of Ernest Charles Timmis and Edith Primrose Timmis (*née* Holland); *m* 1964, Joan Kathleen Chalkley; one *s*. *Educ:* Kings Norton Grammar Sch., Birmingham; Univ. of Bristol (BSc Hons Microbiol.; PhD Microbiol. 1971); Free Univ. of Berlin (Habilitation in Microbiol. and Molecular Biol.). Postdoctoral posts, Yale Univ., 1972–73, Stanford Univ., 1973–76; Hd, Res. Gp, Max-Planck Inst. for Molecular Genetics, Berlin, 1976–81; Prof., Univ. of Geneva Med. Sch., 1981–88; Hd, Div. of Microbiol., Nat. Res. Centre for Biotechnol., Braunschweig, 1988–2011; Hd, Envmtl Microbiol. Lab., Helmholtz Centre for Infection Res., Braunschweig, 2006–11. Founding Editor: Envmtl Microbiol., 1999–; Microbial Biotechnol., 2008–; Envmtl Microbiol. Reports, 2009–. Mem., EMBO. Member: Amer. Acad. Microbiol.; Eur. Acad. Microbiol. Erwin Schrödinger Prize, German Assoc. for Promotion of Scis and Humanities, 2001. *Publications:* Handbook of Hydrocarbon and Lipid Microbiology, 2009; contrib. res. papers to learned jls. *Recreations:* family, reading, cooking, walking, gardening, cinema. *Address:* Institute of Microbiology, Technical University Braunschweig, Spielmannstrasse 7, 38106 Braunschweig, Germany. *E:* kntimmis@gmail.com.

TIMMS, Prof. Edward Francis, OBE 2005; PhD; FBA 2006; Research Professor in History, University of Sussex, since 2003; *b* 3 June 1937; *s* of Rev. John Timms and Joan Timms; *m* 1966, Saime Göksu; two *s* one *d*. *Educ:* Christ's Hosp.; Gonville and Caius Coll., Cambridge (MA 1963; PhD 1967). Asst Lectr in German, Univ. of Sussex, 1963–65; Cambridge University: Lectr in German, 1965–91; Fellow, Gonville and Caius Coll., 1965–91, Life Fellow, 1992–; University of Sussex: Prof. of German, 1992–99; Founder and Dir, Centre for German-Jewish Studies, 1994–2003. Lectr, Middle East Technical Univ., Ankara, 1970. Austrian State Prize for History of the Soc. Scis, 2002; Austrian Cross of Honour for Arts and Scis, 2008; Decoration of Honour in Gold for Services to Province of Vienna, 2013. *Publications:* Karl Kraus—Apocalyptic Satirist, Part 1: Culture and Catastrophe in Habsburg Vienna, 1986, Part 2: The Post-War Crisis and the Rise of the Swastika, 2005; (ed with Ritchie Robertson) Vienna 1900: from Altenberg to Wittgenstein (Austrian Studies 1), 1990; Freud and the Child Woman: the memoirs of Fritz Wittels, 1995; (with Saime Göksu) Romantic Communist: the life and work of Nazim Hikmet, 1999, 2nd edn 2006; Taking up the Torch: English institutions, German dialectics and multicultural commitments, 2011; Dynamik der Kreise, Resonanz der Räume: die schöpferischen impulse der wiener moderne, 2013; (trans. with Fred Bridgham) Karl Kraus, The Last Days of Mankind, 2015; Anna Haag and her Secret Diary of the Second World War, 2016. *Recreations:* exploring archives, compiling memoirs. *E:* eftimms@gmail.com.

TIMMS, Kate; *see* Gordon, V. K.

TIMMS, Prof. Noel Walter; Professor of Social Work and Director, School of Social Work, University of Leicester, 1984–89, now Emeritus Professor; *b* 25 Dec. 1927; *s* of Harold John Timms and Josephine Mary Cecilia Timms; *m* 1956, Rita Caldwell; three *s* three *d*. *Educ:* Cardinal Vaughan School; Univ. of London (BA Hons History; MA Sociology); Heythrop Coll., Univ. of London (MA Theology); Birkbeck, Univ. of London (Cert. Religious Studies). Social Worker, Family Service Units, 1952–54; Psychiatric social worker, 1955–57; Lectr, Dept of Social Science, Cardiff University Coll., 1957–61; Lectr, LSE, 1963–69; Prof. of Applied Social Studies, Bradford Univ., 1969–75; Prof. of Social Work Studies, Newcastle upon Tyne Univ., 1975–84. *Publications:* Social Casework, Principles and Practice, 1964; Language of Social Casework, 1968; (with John Mayer) The Client Speaks, 1970; (with Rita Timms) Dictionary of Social Welfare, 1982; Social Work Values: an enquiry, 1983; Family and Citizenship, 1992; (jtly) Secure Accommodation in Child Care, 1993; (jtly) Mediation: the making and remaking of co-operative relationships, 1994; In Pursuit of Quality, 1995; Authority in the Catholic Priesthood, 2001; (jtly) Diocesan Dispositions and Parish Voices in the Roman Catholic Church, 2001; A Sociological Approach to a Social Problem, 2015. *Recreations:* Evensong, looking at old furniture and at performances of Don Giovanni. *Address:* 157 Kingsway, Orpington, Kent BR5 1PP. *T:* (01689) 877982.

TIMMS, Rt Hon. Stephen (Creswell); PC 2006; MP (Lab) East Ham, since 1997 (Newham North East, June 1994–1997); *b* 29 July 1955; *s* of late Ronald James Timms and of Margaret Joyce Timms (*née* Johnson); *m* 1986, Hui-Leng Lim. *Educ:* Farnborough Grammar Sch.; Emmanuel Coll., Cambridge (MA, MPhil). Consultant, Logica, 1978–86; Ovum: Principal Consultant, 1986–94; Manager, Telecommunications Reports, 1994. Sec., Newham NE Labour Party, 1981–84. Newham Borough Council: Councillor (Lab), 1984–97; Chm., Planning Cttee, 1987–90; Leader, 1990–94. PPS to Minister of State, DFEE, 1997–98, to Sec. of State for NI, 1998; Parly Under-Sec. of State, DSS, 1998–99; Minister of State (Minister for Pensions), DSS, 1999; Financial Sec., HM Treasury, 1999–2001, 2004–05 and 2008–10; Minister of State: (Minister for School Standards), DFES, 2001–02; (Minister for e-commerce and Competitiveness, then for Energy, e-Commerce and Postal Services), DTI, 2002–04; (Minister for Pensions), DWP, 2005–06; Chief Sec. to HM Treasury, 2006–07; Minister of State: BERR, 2007–08; DWP, 2008; Parly Under-Sec. of State, BIS, 2009–10; Shadow Minister for Employment, 2010–15. Mem., H of C Treasury Select Cttee, 1996–97; Mem. Council, 1996–98, Hon. Treas., 1997–98, Parly IT Cttee. Mem., Plaistow Christian Fellowship; Chm., Christians on the Left (formerly Christian Socialist Movement), 2012– (Vice-Chm., 1996–99); Vice-Chm., Labour Party Faith Gps, 2007–. Trustee, Traidcraft Foundn, 2011–. Mem., Ramblers' Assoc. Hon. Pres., Telecommunications Users' Assoc., 1995–99. Hon. DEd E London, 2002. *Publications:* Broadband Communications: the commercial impact, 1986; ISDN: customer premises equipment, 1988; Broadband Communications: market strategies, 1992. *Address:* House of Commons, SW1A 0AA. *T:* (020) 7219 4000.

TIMMS, Stephen John, OBE 1997; CEng, CMarEng; Chief Operating Officer, Engineering and Technology Board, 2006–09; Trustee, Engineering Council UK, 2006–09; *b* Bristol, 25 March 1951; *s* of Ray Timms and Jean Timms; *m* 1973, Rosemary Kennedy; two *s*. *Educ:* Ashford Boys' Grammar Sch.; BRNC Dartmouth; RNEC Manadon (BSc Hons Mech. Engrg; MSc Marine Engrg); RNC Greenwich (Postgrad. Dip. Nuclear Reactor Technol.); Open Univ. (MBA). CEng 1982; MIMechE 1989; CMarEng 2007; FIMarEST 2007. Engineer Officer: HM Submarines Renown, Resolution, Repulse, 1976–79; HM Submarine Turbulent, 1984–88; Proj. Manager, Sub-surface Ballistic Nuclear reactor instrumentation and future Sub-surface Nuclear propulsion plant, 1988–91; Principal Lectr, Dept of Nuclear Sci. and Technol., 1991–93; JSDC, 1993–94; Dep. Captain Fleet Maintenance, Faslane, 1994–96; UK Mil. Rep. NATO HQ, Brussels, SO for Partnership for Peace, Mediterranean Dialogue, NATO-Russia, NATO-Ukraine, NATO enlargement, Arms Control and Peacekeeping, 1996–99; CSO (Support), British Forces Gibraltar and CO RN Gibraltar, 1999–2000; Naval Attaché, Brasília, 2001–04; Dir, RNR and RN Youth Orgns, 2004–06. UK Rep. on wkg gp of Internat. Arctic Seas Assessment Proj., IAEA, Vienna, 1993–97. Mem. Bd, Naval Recruiting and Trng Agency, 2004–06. Mem. Cttee, Benelux Br., IMechE, 1997–99. Mem. Bd, Women in Sci., Engrg and Construction (formerly Women in Sci. and Engrg), 2008–09. Mem., RN Sailing Assoc. *Publications:* co-author of tech. papers for Internat. Arctic Seas Assessment Proj., IAEA, Vienna. *Recreations:* house renovation (of necessity), golf (for the walk), sailing. *E:* sj_timms@hotmail.com.

TIMMS, (Vera) Kate; *see* Gordon, V. K.

TIMNEY, Jacqueline Jill; *see* Smith, Rt Hon. J. J.

TIMPERLEY, Prof. Stuart Read; Chairman: Stuart Timperley Associates, since 2002; GFM Ltd, since 2010; Partner, Stuart Slatter and Co., since 2002; Professor, Istituto Studi Direzionali, University of Milan, since 1998; *b* 30 July 1943; *s* of late Kenneth Read Timperley and Florence Timperley (*née* Burgess); *m* 1967, Veronica Parke; two *d*. *Educ:* Birkenhead Sch.; Univ. of Strathclyde (BA 1967; MBA 1968); Univ. of London (BSc 1967); Univ. of Liverpool (Shell Mex Res. Fellow, 1968; PhD 1971). Lectr, Univ. of Liverpool, 1970–72; London Business School: Lectr, 1972–80; Sen. Lectr, 1980–89; Dir, Sloan Fellows Prog., 1976–80; Dir, Centre for Mgt Develt, 1984–91; Associate Prof., 1989–95; Sen. Associate, Judge Inst., Univ. of Cambridge, 1998–2002. Chm., Slatter Timperley Associates, 1990–2002. Vis. Prof., European Inst. for Advanced Studies in Mgt, Brussels, 1973–85. Chairman: Freightliner Ltd, 1988–91 (Dir, 1979); GSM Hldgs Ltd, 2009–; Director: Jermyn Hldgs Ltd, 1978–80; Intasun Ltd, 1983–87; ILG Ltd, 1986–89; Communisis plc, 2000–03; Pres., Consulteque.com SpA, 2000–03. Mem., Arts Council England, 2002–08; Chairman: Arts Council England, East (formerly Eastern Arts Bd), 1998–2008; English Regl Arts Bds, 2000–01. Chm., Watford FC, 1993–97, 2010– (Dir, 1990–97, 2009–10). Gov., London Business Sch., 1991–94. *Publications:* Personnel Planning and Occupational Choice, 1974; Humanisation of Work, 1982. *Recreations:* performing arts, football. *Address:* Stuart Timperley Associates, 3 Dorset Street, W1U 4EF. *T:* (020) 7486 1585.

TIMPSON, (Anthony) Edward; MP (C) Crewe and Nantwich, since May 2008; Minister of State, Department for Education, since 2015; *b* Knutsford, Cheshire, 26 Dec. 1973; *s* of John Timpson, CBE and Alex Timpson, MBE; *m* 2002, Julia Helen Still; one *s* two *d*. *Educ:* Pownall Hall Sch.; Alderley Edge Co. Prim. Sch.; Stockport Grammar Jun. Sch.; Terra Nova Sch.; Uppingham Sch.; Durham Univ. (BA Hons Politics); Coll. of Law, London (LLB). Called to the Bar, Inner Temple, 1998; non-practising family law specialist. PPS to Home Secretary, 2010–12; Parly Under-Sec. of State, DfE, 2012–15. *Recreations:* football (watching and playing), cricket, marathon running, travel, playing with my children. *Address:* House of Commons, SW1A 0AA.

TIMS, Sir Michael (David), KCVO 1992 (CVO 1984; LVO 1973 MVO 1963); Serjeant-at-Arms to HM The Queen, 1987–92, retired; *b* 14 Sept. 1931; *s* of late William Edward Tims and Eva Ida Tims; *m* 1959, Jacqueline Lily Clark; one *s*. *Educ:* Christ's Hosp.; Westminster Coll. Nat. Service Commn, Army Catering Corps, 1950–52. The Queen's Household: Dep. Comptroller of Supply, 1953–68; Asst to the Master of the Household, 1968–92. Mem., Bd of Green Cloth, 1988–. FRSA 1992. Donation Gov., Christ's Hosp., 2008–. JP Inner London, 1984–91. Freeman, City of London, 1986; Liveryman, Co. of Cooks, 1993–. Various hon. foreign awards. *Publications:* articles on fishing in national magazines. *Recreations:* battling with and painting big game fish, illustrated maps for anglers, also wildlife and Venice watercolours (exhibitor, Venice in Peril exhibns, London). *Address:* Clock Tower House, The Royal Paddocks, Hampton Court Road, E Molesey, Surrey KT8 9DA.

TIMSON, Dame Penelope Anne Constance; *see* Keith, Dame P. A. C.

TIMSON, Dr Simon Edward; Director of Performance, UK Sport, since 2013; *b* Leicester, 8 Dec. 1970; *s* of Frank and Margaret Timson; *m* 2007, Joanne Clarke; one *s* one *d*. *Educ:* Univ. of Exeter (BA(Ed) Hons Physical Educn); Univ. of Leeds (PhD Psychol. 2002). Accredited Sport and Exercise Scientist, BASES, 1999. Mem., British Bobsleigh Team, 1990–97; Teacher of PE, Richard Huish Coll., Taunton, 1994–96; Manager, Somerset CCC and SW Tennis Academies, 1996–2000; Performance Dir, British Skeleton, 2000–06; Hd, England Develt Prog. and Sci. Medicine, ECB, 2006–12. *Publications:* contribs to Sport and Exercise Psychol. Rev. *Recreations:* ski-ing, sport. *Address:* UK Sport, 21 Bloomsbury Street, WC1B 3HF. *E:* Simon.timson@uksport.gov.uk.

TINCKNELL, Amanda Margaret, CBE 2015; Chief Executive, Cranfield Trust, since 2000; *b* Uckfield, 12 July 1961; *d* of Dr Ray Tincknell and Margaret Tincknell; *m* 1997, Christopher Barrington Brown; one *s*. *Educ:* Beaconsfield High Sch.; Wycombe High Sch.; Leicester Univ. (BSc Hons); Cranfield Univ. (MBA 1989). Mkt Researcher, HR & H Market Res., 1984–85; Mkt Researcher, Lopex plc, 1985–86; Researcher, Bull Thompson Exec. Search, 1986–88; ind. consultant and researcher, 1989–2000. Volunteer Consultant and Trustee, Cranfield Trust, 1993–99. *Recreations:* family, gardening, books, sailing. *Address:* Cranfield Trust, Court Room Chambers, 1 Bell Street, Romsey, Hants SO51 8GY.

TINCKNELL, Robert George; Chief Executive Officer, Battersea Power Station Development Co., since 2012; *b* 2 April 1967; *m* 1996, Rachel; one *s* one *d*. *Educ:* Allhallows Sch., Lyme Regis; De Montfort Univ., Leicester. MRICS 1997–2000. Commercial Manager, Connaught Gp plc, 1992–95; Man. Dir, Commercial, Berkeley Gp plc, 1995–2001; Develt Dir, Treasury Hldgs, 2002–05; Man. Dir, Treasury Hldgs (China) Ltd, 2006–08; Dir, China Real Estate Opportunities plc, 2006–08; CEO, Treasury Hldgs, 2008–12; Dir, Real Estate Opportunities plc, 2008–12. *Publications:* Battersea Power Station Community Charter: building a real place, brick by brick, 2014; (contrib.) Battersea Power Station: the placebook, 2014. *Recreations:* sailing, horse racing, music, practising Anglican. *Address:* Battersea Power Station, 188 Kirtling Street, SW8 5BN. *T:* (020) 7501 0734.

TINDALE, Gordon Anthony, OBE 1983; Director of Government and Public Affairs, WH Smith (USA) Inc., 1995–99; *b* 17 March 1938; *s* of George Augustus Tindale and Olive Sarah Collier; *m* 1960, Sonia Mary Soper; one *s* one *d*. *Educ:* Highgate Sch.; Trinity Coll., Oxford (BA (Mod. Hist)); Birkbeck Coll., London (MA (Internat. Relations)). Nat. Service, 1956–58. Joined British Council, 1961; postings in Iraq, Jordan, London and Egypt; Representative: Lesotho, Botswana and Swaziland, 1975–78; Zambia, 1979–83; Controller, Management Div., 1984–87; Representative, Egypt, 1987–89; Cultural Counsellor (formerly Cultural Attaché), Washington, 1989–94. *Recreations:* music, golf. *Address:* 26 Oppidans Road, Primrose Hill, NW3 3AG. *T:* (020) 7722 9343. *Club:* Hendon Golf.

TINDALE, Stephen Christopher; Director, Weinberg Foundation, since 2015; climate and energy consultant, since 2009; *b* 29 March 1963; *s* of Gordon Anthony Tindale and Sonia Mary Tindale; *m* 1995, Katharine Quarmby; one *s* one *d*. *Educ:* St Anne's Coll., Oxford (BA Politics, Philosophy, Econs); Birkbeck Coll., Univ. of London (MSc Politics and Admin). FCO, 1986–89; Friends of the Earth, 1989–90; Fabian Soc., 1990–92; Advr to Rt Hon. Christopher Smith, MP, 1992–94; IPPR, 1994–96; Dir, Green Alliance, 1996–97; Advr to Minister for the Environment, 1997–2000; Chief Policy Advr, Greenpeace UK, 2000–01; Exec. Dir, Greenpeace UK, 2001–06; Hd of Communications and Public Affairs, npower renewables, 2008–09. Vis. Res. Fellow, Policy Studies Inst., 2008–12; Associate Fellow, Centre for European Reform, 2010–15. Lectr in Politics, Birkbeck Coll., Univ. of London, 1994–2000. *Publications:* Green Tax Reform, 1996; (ed) The State and the Nations, 1996; (jtly) Repowering Communities: small-scale solutions for large-scale energy problems, 2011. *Recreations:* walking, hockey, football.

TINDALL, Gillian Elizabeth, FRSL; novelist, biographer, historian; *b* 4 May 1938; *d* of D. H. Tindall and U. M. D. Orange; *m* 1963, Richard G. Lansdown; one *s*. *Educ:* Univ. of Oxford (BA 1st cl., MA). Freelance journalism: occasional articles and reviews for Observer, Guardian, London Evening Standard, The Times, Independent, Daily Telegraph and New York Times. Occasional broadcasts, BBC. JP (as Gillian Lansdown), Inner London, 1980–98. Chevalier de l'Ordre des Arts et des Lettres (France), 2001. *Publications: novels:* No Name in the Street, 1959; The Water and the Sound, 1961; The Edge of the Paper, 1963; The Youngest, 1967; Someone Else, 1969, 2nd edn 1975; Fly Away Home, 1971 (Somerset Maugham Award, 1972); The Traveller and His Child, 1975; The Intruder, 1979; Looking Forward, 1983; To the City, 1987; Give Them All My Love, 1989; Spirit Weddings, 1992; *short stories:* Dances of Death, 1973; The China Egg and Other Stories, 1981; Journey of a Lifetime and Other Stories, 1990; *biography:* The Born Exile (George Gissing), 1974; *other non-fiction:* A Handbook on Witchcraft, 1965; The Fields Beneath, 1977, 3rd edn 2011; City of Gold: the biography of Bombay, 1981, 2nd edn 1992; Rosamond Lehmann: an Appreciation, 1985; (contrib.) Architecture of the British Empire, 1986; Countries of the Mind: the meaning of place to writers, 1991; Célestine: voices from a French village, 1995 (Franco-British Soc. Award, 1996); The Journey of Martin Nadaud, 1999; The Man Who Drew London: Wenceslaus Hollar in reality and imagination, 2002; The House by the Thames and the People Who Lived There, 2006; Footprints in Paris: a few streets, a few lives, 2009; Three Houses, Many Lives, 2012. *Recreations:* keeping house, foreign travel. *Address:* c/o Curtis Brown Ltd, 28/29 Haymarket, SW1Y 4SP.

TINDLE, David, RA 1979 (ARA 1973); painter; *b* 29 April 1932. *Educ:* Coventry Sch. of Art. MA Oxon 1985. Worked as scene painter and commercial artist, 1946–51; subseq. taught at Hornsey Coll. of Art; Vis. Tutor, Royal Coll. of Art, 1972–83, Fellow, 1981, Hon. FRCA, 1984; Ruskin Master of Drawing, Oxford Univ., and Professorial Fellow, St Edmund Hall, Oxford, 1985–87 (Hon. Fellow, 1988). RE, 1988–91. Hon. RBSA 1989. First showed work, Archer Gall., 1952 and 1953; regular one-man exhibns, Piccadilly Gall., from 1954; one-man exhibns at many public and private galleries in Gt Britain incl. Fischer Fine Art, 1985, 1989, 1992; Redfern Gall., London, 1994, 1996, 1998, 2000, 2001, 2003, 2004, 2005, 2007, 2009; Galerie du Tours, San Francisco and Los Angeles, 1964; Galleria Vinciana, Milan, 1968; Galleria Carbonesi, Bologna, 1968; Gallery XX, Hamburg, 1974, 1977, 1980; rep. in exhibns at: Piccadilly Gall., 1954–; Royal Acad.; Internat. Biennale of Realist Art, Bruges, 1958 and Bologna, 1967; British Exhibn Art, Basel, 1958; John Moores, 1959 and 1961; Arts Council Shows: British Self-Portraits; Painters in East Anglia; Thames in Art; The British Art Show, 1979–80; Salon de la Jeune Peinture, Paris, 1967; Mostra Mercato d'Arte Contemporanea, Florence, 1967; British Painting 1974, Hayward Gall.; British Painting 1952–77, RA; Six English Painters—Eros in Albion, Arezzo, Italy, 1989; Portrait of the Artist, Tate Gall., 1989. Set of 3 Mural decorations for Open Univ., Milton Keynes, 1977–78. Designed sets for Iolanta, Aldeburgh Fest., 1988. Work rep. in numerous public and private collections, incl. Nat. Portrait Gall.; Chantrey Bequest purchases, 1974 and 1975, now in Tate Gall. Critic Prize, 1962; Europe Prize for Painting, 1969; Critics' Choice, Tooths, 1974; Waddington Prize, Chichester Nat. Art Exhibn, 1975; Johnson Wax Award, RA, 1983. *Address:* c/o Redfern Gallery, 20 Cork Street, W1S 3HL.

TINDLE, Sir Ray (Stanley), Kt 1994; CBE 1987 (OBE 1973); DL; Chairman: Tindle Newspapers Ltd, since 1972; Tindle Radio Ltd, since 1998; *b* 8 Oct. 1926; *s* of late John Robert Tindle and Maud Tindle; *m* 1949, Beryl Julia (*née* Ellis), MBE 2008, MA, DipEd; one *s*. *Educ:* Torquay Grammar Sch.; Strand Sch. FCIS; FCIArb. War service, Devonshire Regt (Captain), 1944–47. Asst to Dir, Newspaper Soc., 1952–58; Managing Director: Surrey Mirror Newspapers, 1959–63; Surrey Advertiser Newspapers, 1963–78 (Chm., 1978–97). Pres., Newspaper Soc., 1971–72; Vice Pres. and Chm. of Appeal, Newspaper Press Fund, 1990; Member: Newspaper Panel, Monopolies and Mergers Commn, 1987–93; Council, CPU, 1987–; Press Bd of Finance, 1990–. Founder, Tindle Enterprise Centres for the Unemployed, 1984–. Master, Stationers' and Newspaper Makers' Co., 1985–86. DL Surrey, 1989. Hon. DLitt Buckingham, 1999; DUniv Surrey, 2008. *Publications:* The Press Today and Tomorrow, 1975. *Recreations:* veteran cars, newspapers, boating. *Address:* Tindle Newspapers Ltd, Old Court House, Union Road, Farnham, Surrey GU9 7PT. *Clubs:* Royal Automobile, Veteran Car, City Livery Yacht.

TINER, John Ivan, CBE 2008; non-executive Chairman, Towergate Insurance Group, since 2015; Partner, Resolution Operations LLP, 2008–13; *b* 25 Feb. 1957; *s* of Kenneth Tiner and late Joan Tiner; *m* 1978, Geraldine Kassell; two *s* one *d*. *Educ:* St Peter's Sch., Guildford; Kingston Poly. ACA 1980. Joined Arthur Andersen, 1976: Partner, 1988–2001; Managing Partner, Global Financial Services, 1997–2001; Financial Services Authority: Man. Dir, Consumer, Insce and Investment Directorate, 2001–03; Chief Exec., 2003–07. Director: Henderson New Star (formerly New Star Asset Management) Gp plc, 2008–09; Lucida plc, 2008–; Credit Suisse Gp, 2009–; Resolution Ltd (formerly Friends Provident, then Friends Life Gp plc), 2009–14. Dir, Financial Services Skills Council, 2008–10. Trustee, Urological Foundn, 2009–. Vis. Fellow, Oxford Univ., 2008. Hon. DLitt Kingston, 2011. *Publications:* Accounting for Treasury Products, 1987, 2nd edn 1990. *Recreations:* family, tennis, sailing, golf, watching football and Rugby.

TING, Prof. Samuel Chao Chung; Thomas D. Cabot Institute Professor, Massachusetts Institute of Technology, since 1977; *b* 27 Jan. 1936; *s* of K. H. Ting and late T. S. Wang; *m*; two *d*; *m* 1985, Susan Carol Marks; one *s*. *Educ:* Univ. of Michigan (PhD). Ford Fellow, CERN, Geneva, 1963; Asst Prof. of Physics, Columbia Univ., 1965; Prof. of Physics, MIT, 1969–. Assoc. Editor, Nuclear Physics B, 1970; Mem. Editorial Board: Nuclear Instruments and Methods, 1977; Mathematical Modeling, 1980. Hon. Professor: Beijing Normal Coll., 1984; Jiatong Univ., Shanghai, 1987. Member: US Nat. Acad. of Science, 1976; European Physical Soc.; Italian Physical Soc.; Foreign Member: Pakistan Acad. of Science, 1984; Academia Sinica (Republic of China), 1975; Soviet Acad. of Science, 1988; Russian Acad. of Sci.; Hungarian Acad. of Sci.; Deutsche Akad. Naturforscher Leopoldina; For. Corresp. Mem., Royal Spanish Acad. of Sci., 2003. Fellow, Amer. Acad. of Arts and Science, 1975. Hon. Fellow, Tata Inst. of Fundamental Res., Mumbai, 2004. Hon. ScD: Michigan, 1978; Chinese Univ. of Hong Kong, 1987; Bologna, 1988; Columbia, 1990; Univ. of Sci. and Technol. of China, 1990; Moscow State Univ., 1991; Bucharest, 1993; Nat. Tsinghua Univ., Taiwan, 2002; Nat. Jiatong Univ., Taiwan, 2003; Hon. Dr: HK Baptist, 2003; Rheinisch Westfälische Technische Hochschule, 2004; Dr *hc*: Nat. Central Univ., Taiwan, 2005; Hong Kong Univ. of Sci. and Technol., 2005. Nobel Prize for Physics (jt), 1976; Ernest Orlando Lawrence Award, US Govt, 1976; A. E. Eringen Medal, Soc. of Engineering Science, USA, 1977; Gold Medal in Science, City of Brescia, Italy, 1988; De Gasperi Prize, Italian Republic, 1988; Forum Engelberg Prize, 1996; Public Service Medal, NASA, 2001. *Publications:* articles in Physical Review and Physical Review Letters. *Address:* Department of Physics, Massachusetts Institute of Technology, 77 Massachusetts Avenue, Cambridge, MA 02139–4307, USA. *Club:* Explorers (New York).

TINKER, Prof. Andrew, PhD; FRCP, FMedSci; Professor of Cardiac Electrophysiology and Hon. Consultant, William Harvey Research Institute, Barts and the London and Queen Mary University of London, since 2011; *b* 12 June 1963; *s* of late Dr Jack Tinker, FRCP, FRCSGlas; *m* 1987, Janet Elizabeth Sweetnham (*née* Fricker); three *s* one *d*. *Educ:* Queen's Coll., Oxford (BA 1984); Royal Free Hosp., Univ. of London (MB BS Dist. 1987; PhD 1993). MRCP 1990, FRCP 2004. MRC Trng Fellow, Nat. Heart and Lung Inst., 1990–93; Postdoctoral Res. Fellow, UCSF, 1994–96; University College London: Wellcome Trust Sen. Res. Fellow, 1996–2001; Reader, 2001–04; Prof. of Molecular Medicine, 2004–; Hon. Consultant, Dept of Medicine, 2001–. FMedSci 2006. *Publications:* articles on ion channels, in particular in relation to their function in the heart and blood vessels. *Recreations:* running, chess, bridge. *Address:* Room 1.02, The Heart Centre, William Harvey Research Institute, Charterhouse Square, EC1M 6BQ. *T:* (020) 7882 5783. *E:* a.tinker@qmul.ac.uk.

TINKER, Prof. Anthea Margaret, CBE 2000; PhD; FAcSS; Professor of Social Gerontology, since 1988, Director, Age Concern Institute of Gerontology, 1988–98, King's College London; *b* 24 Oct. 1932; *d* of Lt-Comdr James Collins and Margaret Collins (*née* Herring); *m* 1956, Rev. Preb. Dr Eric Tinker, OBE (*d* 2011); two *s* one *d*. *Educ:* Univ. of Birmingham (BCom Econs, Pol., Sociol. 1953); City Univ. (PhD 1976). Asst Buyer, then Buyer, Boxfoldia Ltd, 1953–54; Res. Officer, BoT, 1954; HM Insp. of Factories, Min. of Labour, 1954–58; (pt-time) Res. Asst to Dir, Inst. of Local Govt Studies, and Lectr in Public Admin, Univ. of Birmingham, 1958–65; (pt-time) Lectr in Public Admin, Birmingham Sch. of Planning, 1958–65; (pt-time) Lectr in Social Policy, Extra-Mural Dept, Univ. of London, 1965–75; engaged in res., Royal Commn on Local Govt, 1967; Res. Fellow, City Univ., 1975–77; Sen., then Principal Res. Officer, DoE, 1977–88. Consultant: OECD, 1989–90; EU, 1991–2001; WHO, 2003–04. Exec. Mem., 1987–93, Fellow, 2008, British Soc. of Gerontology. Member: Cttee on Ageing, C of E Bd of Social Responsibility, 1988–89; Cttee on Long Term Care, Joseph Rowntree Foundn, 1995–96; Council, Assoc. of Res. Ethics Cttees, 2008–12; Chm., Res. Ethics Cttee, KCL, 2001–11; Chm. and Mem. of nat. and internat. adv. gps on ageing. Gov., Centre for Policy on Ageing, 1988–94. FRSocMed 1995 (Pres., Sect. of Geriatrics and Gerontology, 1998–2000); FKC 1998; FAcSS (Founder AcSS 1999). *Publications:* The Elderly in Modern Society, 1981, 4th edn as Older People in Modern Society, 1997; Staying at Home: helping elderly people, 1984; The Telecommunication Needs of Disabled and Elderly People, 1989; An Evaluation of Very Sheltered Housing, 1989; *jointly:* Women in Housing: access and influence, 1980; Families in Flats, 1981; A Review of Research on Falls among Elderly People, 1990; Falls and Elderly People: a study of current professional practice in England and innovations abroad, 1991; Life After Sixty: a profile of Britain's older population, 1992; Caring: the importance of third age carers, 1992; Homes and Travel: local life in the third age, 1992; The Information Needs of Elderly People, 1993; The Care of Frail Elderly People in the UK, 1994; Difficult to Let Sheltered Housing, 1995; Alternative Models of Care for Older People, Research Vol. 2, Royal Commn on Long Term Care, 1999; Home Ownership in Old Age, 1999; To Have and to Hold: the bond between older people and the homes they own, 1999; Eighty-five Not Out, 2001; University Research Ethics Committees: their role, remit and conduct, 2004; Facts and Misunderstandings about Pension and Retirement Ages, 2004; Improving the Provision of Information about Assistive Technology, 2005; UK Study of Elder Abuse and Neglect of Older People, 2008; pamphlets and booklets; numerous papers in learned and other jls. *Recreations:* family, houses. *Address:* 35 Theberton Street, N1 0QY. *T:* (020) 7359 4750.

TINKER, Prof. Philip Bernard Hague, OBE 2000; PhD, DSc; FRSB, FRSC, FRGS; FLS; Director of Terrestrial and Freshwater Science, Natural Environment Research Council, 1985–92; *b* 1 Feb. 1930; *s* of Philip and Gertrude Tinker; *m* 1955, Maureen Ellis (*d* 2005); one *s* one *d*. *Educ:* Rochdale High Sch.; Sheffield Univ. (BSc); PhD 1955; MA, DSc 1984, Oxon. FRSB (FIBiol 1974); FRSC 1985; FRGS 1989; FLS 1992. Overseas Res. Service, 1955–62; Sen. Scientific Officer, Rothamsted Experimental Stn, 1962–65; Lectr, Oxford Univ., 1965–71; Prof. of Agricultural Botany, Leeds Univ., 1971–77; Head of Soils Div., 1977–85, and Dep. Dir, 1981–85, Rothamsted Experimental Stn; Fellow, 1969–72, Sen. Res. Fellow, 1988–96, St Cross Coll., Oxford. Hon. Vis. Prof., Imperial Coll., 1992–95; Sen. Vis. Fellow, Plant Scis Dept, Oxford Univ., 1995–. Lectures: Regents, Univ. of California, 1979; Hannaford Meml, Adelaide, 1990; Francis New Meml and Medal, Fertilizer Soc., 1991.

Chairman: UK Man and Biosphere Cttee, 1990–93; UK Cttee for Internat. Geosphere-Biosphere Prog., 1992–98; Biology Cttee, Palm Oil Res. Inst., Malaysia, 1995–98 (Mem., 1987–98). Member: UNESCO Adv. Cttee for Biosphere Reserves, 1992–96; IGBP Scientific Cttee, 1992–98. Pres., British Soil Sci. Soc., 1983–84; Gov., Macaulay Land Use Res. Inst., Aberdeen, 1990–2001. Fellow, Norwegian Acad. of Science and Letters, 1987; Hon. FRASE 1990; Hon. Mem., Internat. Union of Soil Scis, 2002. Busk Medal, RGS, 1994. *Publications:* (with F. E. Sanders and B. Mosse) Endomycorrhizas, 1975; (with P. H. Nye) Solute Movement in the Soil-root System, 1977; Soil and Agriculture—Critical Reviews, 1980; (with L. Fowden and R. M. Barrer) Clay Minerals, 1984; (with A. Läuchli) Advances in Plant Nutrition, vol. I, 1984, vol. II, 1986, vol. III, 1988; (with P. H. Nye) Solute Movement in the Rhizosphere, 2000; Shades of Green: a review of UK farming systems, 2000; (with R. H. V. Corley) The Oil Palm, 2003; *c* 175 papers. *Recreations:* reading, gardening, map collecting. *Address:* The Glebe House, Broadwell, Lechlade, Glos GL7 3QS. *T:* (01367) 860436. *Club:* Farmers.

TINNISWOOD, Peter Maurice; Head Master, Lancing College, 1998–2005; *b* 30 May 1951; *s* of late Maurice Owen Tinniswood; *m* 1975, Catharina Elizabeth Oeschger. *Educ:* Charterhouse; Magdalen Coll., Oxford (MA); INSEAD (MBA 1981). Assistant Master: Repton Sch., 1974–76; Marlborough Coll., 1976–80; Sec. Gen., Franco-British Chamber of Commerce and Industry, Paris, 1981–83; Marlborough College: Asst Master, 1983–91; Head of Dept, 1983–86; Housemaster, 1985–91; Master, Magdalen Coll. Sch., Oxford, 1991–98. Governor: Dorset House Sch., 2000–06; Mowden Sch., 2002–05; St Paul's Sch., São Paulo, 2007–. *Publications:* Marketing Decisions, 1981; Marketing and Production Decisions, 1991. *Address:* Samvara, Les Girvaysses, 81170 Noailles, France.

TINSON, Dame Susan (Myfanwy), DBE 1990; media consultant; Associate Editor and Director, External Relations, Independent Television News, 1989–2003; *b* 15 Jan. 1943; *d* of John and Kathleen Thomas; *m* 1968, Trevor James Tinson (marr. diss. 1979). *Educ:* South Hampstead High Sch.; Hull Univ. (BA Hons Social Studies). Independent Television News: Senior Editor, News at Ten and Asst Editor, ITN, 1982; consultant: ITV, 2003–06; ITN, 2003–. Non-executive Director: Asda plc, 1997–99; Yorkshire Building Soc., 1999–2006; Chime Communications plc, 2001–06; St Ives plc, 2004–07. Trustee, Heritage Lottery Fund, 1996–2001; Comr, Commonwealth War Graves Commn, 1999–2004; Mem. Cttee, Queen's Diamond Jubilee Pageant, 2012–13. Mem., Adv. Bd, Pagefield Ltd, 2010–. Mem., Archbishop of Canterbury's Media Adv. Gp, 2014–. FRTS 1996. *Address:* 170 Ebury Street, SW1W 8UP.

TIPLER, Laura; *see* Drysdale, L.

TIPPER, Prof. Steven Paul, DPhil; FBA 2007; Professor of Cognitive Psychology, University of York, since 2013; *b* 12 Sept. 1956; *s* of Malcolm Tipper and June Tipper; *m* 1987, Alison Warner; two *s* one *d*. *Educ:* Wolfson Coll., Oxford (BSc 1980; MSc 1981; DPhil 1985). Asst Prof., Mount Allison Univ., Canada, 1985–89; Associate Prof., McMaster Univ., Canada, 1989–93; Prof. of Cognitive Sci., 1993–2012, Dir, Wolfson Centre of Clinical and Cognitive Neurosci., 2004–12, Univ. of Wales, Bangor, later Bangor Univ. *Publications:* over 140 articles in learned jls, incl. Qly Jl of Exptl Psychology. *Recreations:* spending time with my family, discovering the history of York. *Address:* Department of Psychology, University of York, Heslington, York YO10 5DD. *T:* (01904) 323162.

TIPPING, Rt Hon. Sir Andrew (Patrick Charles), KNZM 2009 (DCNZM 2006); PC 1998; a Judge of the Supreme Court of New Zealand, 2004–12; *b* 22 Aug. 1942; *s* of Wing Comdr Patrick Alexander Tipping, RAF retd and Elizabeth Ayliffe Tipping; *m* 1st, 1967, Judith Ann Oliver (*d* 2010); two *s* one *d*; 2nd, 2012, Mary Jo Nicholson. *Educ:* Christ's Coll., Christchurch; Univ. of Canterbury (BA, LLB 1965; LLM 1st Cl. Hons 1966). Canterbury Dist Law Soc. Gold Medal, 1966; Sir Timothy Cleary Meml Prize, NZ Law Soc., 1967. Partner, Wynn Williams & Co., Barristers and Solicitors, 1967–86; Judge, High Court of NZ, 1986–97; Judge, Ct of Appeal of NZ, 1997–2004. Member of Council: Canterbury Dist Law Soc., 1976–84 (Pres., 1984); NZ Law Soc., 1982–84 (Mem., 1979–86, Chm., 1985–86, Courts and Tribunals Cttee). *Recreations:* gardening, fishing, tramping. *Address:* 256 Matapaua Bay Road, Opito RD 2, Whitianga 3592, New Zealand; 136 Confederation way, Thornhill, ON L3T 5R5, Canada. *Clubs:* Christchurch (Christchurch); Wellington (Wellington).

TIPPING, Sir David Gwynne E.; *see* Evans-Tipping.

TIPPING, Simon Patrick, (Paddy); Police and Crime Commissioner (Lab) for Nottinghamshire, since 2012; *b* 24 Oct. 1949; *m* 1970, Irene Margaret Quinn (decd); two *d*. *Educ:* Hipperholme Grammar Sch.; Nottingham Univ. (BA 1972; MA 1978). Social Worker, Notts, 1972–79; Project Leader, C of E Children's Soc., Nottingham, 1979–83. Mem. (Lab) Notts CC, 1981–93 (Chm., Economic Develt and Finance Cttees); Director: Notts Co-op. Develt Agency, 1983–92; Nottingham Develt Enterprise, 1987–93; REalliance, 2010–; Chm., Notts Lift Cos, 2008–. MP (Lab) Sherwood, 1992–2010. Dep. Leader, H of C, 2007. Contested (Lab) Rushcliffe, 1987. Chm., Notts Community Foundn, 2010–. Vice Pres., Ramblers Assoc., 1995–. Trustee: Under One Roof, 2000–; Gedling Conservation Trust, 2010–; Rural Community Action Notts, 2013–. Gov., Notts Healthcare Trust, 2014–. *Recreations:* running, walking, gardening. *Address:* 14 Jarvis Avenue, Nottingham NG3 7BH.

TIPPLER, John; Director, Network, and Management Board Member, British Telecom, UK Communications Division, 1986–89, retired; *b* 9 Aug. 1929; *s* of George Herbert and Sarah Tippler, Spalding, Lincs; *m* 1st, 1952, Pauline Taylor (marr. diss. 1983); two *s*; 2nd, 1992, Martha Elisabet Berg (*d* 2014), psychoanalyst, Stockholm. *Educ:* Spalding Grammar School. Architect's Dept, Spalding RDC, 1945; Post Office Telephone Service, 1947; Royal Signals, 1949–50; Staff Mem., PO Central Engineering Sch., 1954–59; PO Engineering Develt, electronic and digital switching systems, 1959–80; Dep. Dir, System X Digital Exchange Develt, 1979–80; Dir, Exchange and Data Systems Op. and Develt, 1980; Dir of Engrg, BT, 1982–86. Dir, IT Inst., 1986–88. Mem., Youth Offending Community Panel, 2002–06. Mem., Exec. Cttee, 1997–2004, Trustee, 2004–08, Friends of Birzeit Univ. Advr, CAB, 1995–2002. *Recreations:* music, country walking, travel, cinema, theatre.

TIPPLES, Amanda Jane; QC 2011; a Recorder, since 2009; a Deputy High Court Judge, since 2013; *b* Pembury, 18 Dec. 1966; *d* of Bernard Sidney Tipples and Gillian Molly Tipples. *Educ:* Roedean Sch.; Gonville and Caius Coll., Cambridge (BA Zool. (Molecular Biol.) 1989); Council of Legal Educn. Called to the Bar, Gray's Inn, 1991; Bencher, Lincoln's Inn, 2014. *Address:* Maitland Chambers, 7 Stone Buildings, Lincoln's Inn, WC2A 3SZ. *T:* (020) 7406 1200, *Fax:* (020) 7406 1300.

TIRAMANI, Jennifer Jane; theatre designer and dress historian; Director, The School of Historical Dress, since 2009; *b* 16 Aug. 1954; *d* of Fredo Paulo Tiramani and Barbara Doreen Tiramani (*née* King); one *s* with Alastair Brotchie. *Educ:* Dartford Grammar Sch. for Girls; Central Sch. of Art and Design, London (Foundn course); Trent Poly., Nottingham (1st Cl. Dip. Theatre Design 1976). Designer, 7:84 England and 7:84 Scotland Th. Cos, 1978–84; Associate Designer, Theatre Royal, Stratford East, 1980–97; Designer, Renaissance Th. Co., 1988–90; Shakespeare's Globe: Associate Designer, 1997–2002; designs include: Henry V, 1997; Hamlet, 2000; Dir, Th. Design, 2003–05; designs include: Twelfth Night, 2003 (Olivier Award for Best Costume Design), 2012, transf. NY, 2013 (Tony Award for Best Costume Design of a Play, 2014); Measure for Measure, The Tempest, 2005; Richard III, 2012; West End prodns include: Steaming, Comedy, 1981; Much Ado About Nothing, Phoenix, 1988; designs for opera include: (stage and costume) Orlando, Opera Lille, 2010; La Clemenza di Tito, Aix-en-Provence Fest., 2011; (costume) Anna Bolena, Metropolitan Opera, NY, 2011; (costume) André Chenier, Royal Opera Hse, Covent Gdn, 2015. Advr and contrib., Searching for Shakespeare exhibn, NPG, 2006. Vis. Prof., Sch. of Art and Design, Nottingham Trent Univ., 2008–11. Sam Wanamaker Award (jtly), Shakespeare's Globe, 2007. *Publications:* (contrib.) Shakespeare's Globe: a theatrical experiment, 2008; (jtly) Patterns of Fashion 4: the cut and construction of linen shirts, smocks, neckwear, headwear and accessories for men and women *c*1540–1660, 2008; (jtly) Seventeenth Century Women's Dress Patterns, Book 1, 2011, Book 2, 2012; (contrib.) Netherlandish Fashion in the Seventeenth Century, 2012; contribs to Costume. *Address:* 47 Charles Square, N1 6HT. *T:* and *Fax:* (020) 7490 0987. *E:* jtiramani@theschoolofhistoricaldress.org.uk.

TIRVENGADUM, Sir Harry (Krishnan), Kt 1987; Chevalier, Ordre National de la Légion d'Honneur 1986; Chairman and Managing Director, Air Mauritius, 1981–97, 2000–01; Managing Director, Air Afrique, 1997–99; *b* 2 Sept. 1933; *s* of late Govinden Tirvengadum and Meenatchee Sangeelee; *m* 1970, Elahe Amin Amin (*d* 2012); three *d*. *Educ:* Royal College, Mauritius; Oxford Univ. Asst Sec., Min. of Works, 1952–67; Principal Assistant Secretary: Min. of Communications, in charge of Depts of Civil Aviation, Telecommunications, Marine Services, Posts & Telegraphs and Meteorological Services, 1968–72; Min. of Commerce and Industry, 1970; Air Mauritius: Gen. Manager, 1972–78; Dep. Chm. and Dep. Man. Dir, 1978–81. Chairman: Rodrigues Hotel, 1981–; New Airport Catering Services, 1988–; Mauritius Shopping Paradise Ltd, 1984–93; Director: Mauritius Hotels Gp, 1973–81; Plaisance Airlift Catering Unit, 1980–92; Mauritius Telecom, 1984–; Mauritius Estate Development & Co., 1986–; Mauritius Commercial Bank, 1989; State Bank Internat., 1990–. Chm., Municipal Commn, Quatre-Bornes, 1974–77. Chief delegate of Mauritius, Triennial Assemblies, ICAO, 1971–; Rep. of Employers on Employment of Disabled Persons Bd, 1988–. Member: Exec. Cttee, IATA, 1988–91 (Chm., 1992–93); Nat. Educn Award Panel, 1988; Pres., African Airlines Assoc., 1995–96; Chm., Indian Ocean Regl Fund, 1999–2001. FCIT; FInstD. Citoyen d'Honneur, Town of Beau Bassin/Rose Hill, Mauritius, 1986. *Recreations:* bridge, swimming, walking. *Address:* Dr Arthur De Chazal Lane, Floréal, Mauritius. *T:* 6964455. *Club:* Mauritius Gymkhana.

TISDALL, Caroline Croft; author; film maker; countryside campaigner and conservationist; racehorse owner; *b* Stratford-upon-Avon, 14 Dec. 1945; *d* of Frederick Mackenzie Tisdall and Elisabeth Croft Tisdall; *m* 1971, Angelo Bozzolla. *Educ:* Tiffin Girls' Sch.; Courtauld Inst. of Art, Univ. of London (BA Hons). Lectr in 20th Century Art Hist., Univ. of Reading, 1968–77; Art Critic, 1971–82, Corresp., Europe and Arab World, 1979–82, The Guardian. Ind. film writer and dir, 1982–, films include: The Last Post Run, Channel 4, 1982; Joseph Beuys, BBC, 1986; Marakele, The Making of a National Park, African Parks Foundn, 2001. Exhibns of photography incl. Mus. of Modern Art, NY, 1979, and Tate Modern, 2005. Vis. Prof., Oxford Brookes Univ., 2001. Member: Bd, Countryside Alliance, 1997–; Council, Nat. Trust, 2007–13; UK Chm., African Parks Foundn, 2005–14. Trustee, John Muir Trust, 1994–2002; Trustee, Chiswick House and Gardens Trust, 2008–. MRHS (Founder FRHS, 2011). Mem., Internat. Dendrology Soc. Master of Hounds, 2006. Hon. DArt Oxford Brookes, 1998. *Publications:* (with Angelo Bozzolla) Futurism, 1977, 4th edn 2006; Joseph Beuys: Coyote, 1976, 6th edn 2008; Joseph Beuys, 1979; (with Selim Nessib) Beirut: front-line story, 1983; (with Paul van Vlissingen) Witches Point, 1987; Joseph Beuys: we go this way, 1998. *Recreations:* National Hunt racing, scuba diving and marine research, dendrology, gardening, fishing, shooting, stalking, beagling. *Address:* Red Lion House, Chiswick Mall, W4 2PJ. *T:* 07792 930297. *E:* ctisdall@aol.com. *Clubs:* Kimbridge Fly Fishing; Silkie Scuba Diving and Fly Fishing.

TISHLER, Gillian; Director, Oxford Citizens' Advice Bureau, since 2010; *b* 27 March 1958; *d* of Harry and Joyce Tishler. *Educ:* King Edward VI Sch., Morpeth; St Anne's Coll., Oxford (BA Hons Mod. Langs). Ministry of Agriculture, Fisheries and Food: fast stream trainee, 1979; Private Office (Private Sec. to Parly Sec.), 1986–87; Royal National Institute for the Blind: Parly Officer, 1987–89; Head of Public Affairs, 1989–93; Chief Exec., YWCA of GB, 1993–2007; Dir, Plymouth CAB, 2007–10. *Recreations:* theatre, singing, walking.

TITCHENER, Alan Ronald, CB 1993; Managing Director, Resource (Science and Technology Expertise) Ltd, 1993–96; *b* 18 June 1934; *s* of Edmund Hickman Ronald Titchener and Minnie Ellen Titchener; *m* 1959, Joyce Blakesley; two *s*. *Educ:* Harrow County Grammar Sch.; London School of Economics (BScEcon 1962). RAF, 1952. Colonial Office, 1954; Min. of Transport, 1962; Board of Trade, 1964; HM Consul New York, 1969; Dept of Trade, 1973; HM Consul-Gen., Johannesburg, 1978; Under Secretary, Department of Trade and Industry, 1982–93: Overseas Trade Div., 1982; Enterprise Initiative Div., 1987; Head of Personnel, 1991. *Club:* Royal Air Force.

TITCHMARSH, Alan Fred, MBE 2000; VMH; DL; writer and broadcaster; *b* 2 May 1949; *s* of Alan Titchmarsh and Bessie Titchmarsh (*née* Hardisty); *m* 1975, Alison Margaret Needs; two *d*. *Educ:* Ilkley County Secondary Sch.; Shipley Art and Tech. Inst.; Herts Coll. of Agric. and Hort. (Nat. Cert. Hort.); Royal Botanic Gardens, Kew (DipHort). FCIHort (FIHort 1998). Apprentice gardener, Parks Dept, Ilkley UDC, 1964–68; Supervisor, Staff Trng, Royal Botanic Gardens, 1972–74; Asst Editor, gardening books, Hamlyn Publishing, 1974–76; Asst Editor and Dep. Editor, Amateur Gardening, 1976–79; freelance writer and broadcaster, 1979–; gardening correspondent: Woman's Own, 1980–85; Daily Mail, 1985–99; Daily Express, and Sunday Express, 1999–; Radio Times, 1996–2001, 2004–07; gardening editor, Homes & Gardens, 1985–89; contrib. to BBC Gardeners' World Magazine, 1992–, Gardenlife, 2004–06; Country Life, 2011–; Sunday Telegraph, 2013–. *BBC radio series include:* You and Yours, Down to Earth, A House in a Garden, Alan Titchmarsh Show; numerous other progs incl. Alan Titchmarsh, Classic FM, 2012–; *BBC TV:* Nationwide, Breakfast Time, Open Air, Daytime Live; Chelsea Flower Show, 1983–97, 2001–13; Songs of Praise, 1989–94; Pebble Mill, 1991–96; Sweet Inspiration, 1993–94; Gardeners' World, 1995–2002; Ground Force, 1997–2003; How to be a Gardener, 2002–03; The Royal Gardeners, 2003; British Isles: a natural history, 2004; BBC Proms, 2004–08; 20th Century Roadshow, 2005; The Gardener's Year, 2006; The Great British Village Show, 2007; The Nature of Britain, 2007; Saving Planet Earth, 2007; *other TV includes:* Britain's Best, 2007; The Alan Titchmarsh Show, 2007–14; All the Queen's Horses, 2009; The Seasons, 2010; All the Queen's Men, 2010; Highgrove, 2010; Love Your Garden, 2011–; Prince Philip at 90, 2011; A Royal Year to Remember, 2011; Royal Windsor Jubilee Pageant, 2012; Prince Charles at Dumfries House, 2012; The Queen's Garden, 2014; Britain's Best Back Gardens, 2015; Titchmarsh on Capability Found, 2015; *theatre:* (narrator) The Wind in the Willows, Vaudeville, 2014. Founder, Alan Titchmarsh's Gardens for Schools, 2001–11. Chancellor, Univ. of Winchester, 2015–. Vice-President: Wessex Cancer Trust, 1988–2013; Butterfly Conservation, 2000–; Arboricultural Assoc., 2000–; Patron: Rainbow Trust, 1993–2012; Kaleidoscope Theatre, 1995–; Seeds for Africa, 1999–; Treloar Trust, 1999–; Henry Spink Foundn, 2000–; Country Holidays for Inner City Kids, 2000–; Cowes Inshore Lifeboat, 2000–10; Writtle Coll., 2001–; Horticap, 2002–; Hampshire and Wight Trust for Maritime Archaeology, 2005–; Royal Fund for Gardeners' Children (formerly Royal Gardeners' Orphan Fund), 2006–; Child Bereavement Charity, 2011–; Hon. Patron, Friends of the Castle of Mey, 2005–; Vice Patron, Jubilee Sailing Trust, 2000–12; Trustee: Nat. Maritime Mus., 2004–08; Garden Mus., 2008–; President: Gardening for Disabled Trust, 1989–; Telephones for the Blind, 1993–; London Children's Flower Soc., 2001–; Perennial (Gardeners' Royal Benevolent Soc.), 2005–; Plant Heritage, Nat. Council for the Conservation of Plants and Gardens, 2010–; Vice Pres., RHS, 2009–; Ambassador: Prince's Trust, 2003–; Prince's Countryside Fund, 2012–; RHS, 2013–. Mem., Consultative Cttee, Nat. Pinetum, 1996–2004. Comr, Royal Hosp., Chelsea,

2010–16. Freeman, City of London; Liveryman, Gardeners' Co. DL Hants, 2001; High Sheriff, IoW, 2008. Hon. FCGI 2000. Hon. DSc Bradford, 1999; DUniv: Essex, 1999; Leeds Metropolitan, 2003; Winchester, 2007. Gardening Writer of the Year, 1980, 1983; RHS Gold Medal, Chelsea Flower Show, 1985; Television Broadcaster of the Year, Garden Writer's Guild, 1997, 1998, 1999, 2000; Yorks Man of the Year, 1997, 2007; Lifetime Achievement Award, Garden Writers' Guild, 2004; Special Award, TRIC, 2004. VMH 2004. *Publications:* Starting With House Plants, 1976; Gardening Under Cover, 1979, 2nd edn 1985; Guide to Greenhouse Gardening, 1980; Climbers and Wall Plants, 1980; Everyone's Book of House Plants, 1981; (with R. C. M. Wright) Complete Book of Plant Propagation, 1981; Gardening Techniques, 1981; Pocket Indoor Gardener, 1982; Hamlyn Guide to House Plants, 1982; Pest-Free Plants, 1982; The Allotment Gardener's Handbook, 1982, 2nd edn 1993; The Rock Gardener's Handbook, 1983; How to be a Supergardener, 1983, 3rd edn 1999; (ed) 1,000 Handy Gardening Hints, 1983; Alan Titchmarsh's Avant Gardening, 1984, 2nd edn 1994; Alan Titchmarsh's Gardening Guides, 1984; The Gardener's Logbook, 1985; (ed) A–Z of Popular Garden Plants, 1985; Pocket Guide to Gardening, 1987; (cons. ed.) All Your Gardening Questions Answered, 1988; Daytime Live Gardening Book, 1990; The English River, 1993; Alan Titchmarsh's Favourite Gardens, 1995; (cons. ed) Ground Force Weekend Workbook, 1999; Gardeners' World Complete Book of Gardening, 1999; How to be a Gardener, 2001; Trowel and Error (memoirs), 2002; How to be a Gardener, Book 2, 2003; The Royal Gardeners, 2003; British Isles: a natural history, 2004; (ed and contrib.) Fill My Stocking (anthology), 2005; The Gardener's Year, 2005; Nobbut A Lad (memoir), 2006; The Nature of Britain, 2007; England, Our England (anthology), 2007; The Kitchen Gardener, 2008; Alan Titchmarsh's How to Garden: Vegetables and Herbs, 2009, Garden Design, 2009, Lawns, Paths and Patios, 2009, Pruning and Training, 2009, Container Gardening, 2009, Gardening in the Shade, 2009, Flowering Shrubs, 2010, Growing Fruit, 2010, Perennial Garden Plants, 2010, Climbers and Wall Shrubs, 2010, Greenhouse Gardening, 2010, Small Gardens, 2011, Pests and Problems, 2011, Growing Roses, 2011, Growing Bulbs, 2011, Small Trees, 2012, Allotment Gardening, 2012, Instant Colour, 2012, Weekend Gardening, 2012; Grow Your Own Plants, 2013; Water Gardening, 2013; Flowers and Foliage For Cutting, 2013; Knave of Spades (memoir), 2009; When I Was a Nipper (memoir), 2010; Tales from Titchmarsh, 2011; The Complete Countryman, 2011; Elizabeth: her life, our times, 2012; Love Your Garden, 2012; My Secret Garden, 2012; The Queen's Houses, 2014; *novels:* Mr MacGregor, 1998; The Last Lighthouse Keeper, 1999; Animal Instincts, 2000; Only Dad, 2001; Rosie, 2004; Love and Dr Devon, 2006; Folly, 2008; The Haunting, 2011; Bring Me Home, 2014. *Recreations:* art, music, boating, theatre, books. *Address:* c/o Arlington Enterprises, 1–3 Charlotte Street, W1P 1HD. *T:* (020) 7580 0702. *Clubs:* Athenæum, Lord's Taverners, Royal Automobile.

TITCHMARSH, Prof. John Michael, DPhil; Royal Academy of Engineering Research Professor in Microanalytical Techniques for Structural Integrity Problems, University of Oxford, 1998–2005; Fellow, St Anne's College, Oxford, 1998–2005, now Emeritus; *b* 4 Sept. 1944; *s* of late Harold Titchmarsh and of Ada Titchmarsh; *m* 1967, Elaine Joy Knightley; two *d. Educ:* Christ's Coll., Cambridge (BA Nat. Sci. 1966; MA 1970); Wadham Coll., Oxford (DPhil 1969). Res. Asst, Univ. of Oxford, 1969–74; UKAEA, 1974–94; Philips Prof. in Materials Analysis, Sheffield Hallam Univ., 1994–98. Member of Committee: Inst. of Physics; RMS. Birks Award, Microbeam Analysis Soc., USA, 1995. *Publications:* papers in learned jls on electron microscopy. *Address:* Department of Materials, University of Oxford, Parks Road, Oxford OX1 3PH; St Anne's College, Oxford OX2 6JF.

TITCOMB, Lesley Jane; Chief Executive, Pensions Regulator, since 2015; *b* Farnham Royal, Bucks, 16 June 1961; *d* of late Roy Thomas Titcomb and Claire Titcomb (*née* Belcher); *m* 1989, (Michael) Mark Prisk, *qv. Educ:* Oxford High Sch. GDST; St Anne's Coll., Oxford (MA Lit. Hum.). ACA 1990. Financial Services Authority: Dir of Authorisations, 2007–08; Dir, Small Firm Supervision, 2008–10; Actg Chief Operating Officer, 2010–13; Chief Operating Officer and Exec. Bd Mem., Financial Conduct Authy, 2013–15. Mem., Diocesan Bd of Finance and Diocesan Synod, Dio. of St Albans, 2010–. *Recreations:* singing, cooking, watching Rugby, theatre, ballet. *Address:* Pensions Regulator, Napier House, Trafalgar Place, Brighton BN1 4DW. *T:* (01273) 648448. *E:* lesley.titcomb@thepensionsregulator.gov.uk.

TITE, Prof. Michael Stanley, DPhil; FSA; Edward Hall Professor of Archaeological Science and Director of Research Laboratory for Archaeology and History of Art, University of Oxford, 1989–2004, now Emeritus; Fellow of Linacre College, Oxford, 1989–2004, now Emeritus; *b* 9 Nov. 1938; *s* of late Arthur Robert Tite and Evelyn Frances Violet Tite (*née* Endersby); *m* 1967, Virginia Byng Noel; two *d. Educ:* Trinity Sch. of John Whitgift, Croydon; Christ Church, Oxford (MA, DPhil). FSA 1977. Research Fellow in Ceramics, Univ. of Leeds, 1964–67; Lectr in Physics, Univ. of Essex, 1967–75; Keeper, Dept of Scientific Res. (formerly Res. Lab.), British Museum, 1975–89. Pomerance Award for Sci. Contribs to Archaeol., Archaeol Inst. of America, 2008; Costa Navarino Internat. Archaeometry Award, Univ. of Peloponnese, Kalamata, 2013–14. *Publications:* Methods of Physical Examination in Archaeology, 1972; (with A. J. Shortland) Production Technology of Faience and Related Vitreous Materials, 2008; papers on scientific methods applied to archaeology in various jls. *Recreations:* travelling with "The Buildings of England", gardening. *Address:* 7 Kings Cross Road, Oxford OX2 7EU. *T:* (01865) 558422.

TITFORD, Jeffrey William; Member (UK Ind) Eastern Region, England, European Parliament, 1999–2009; *b* 24 Oct. 1933; *s* of Guy Frederick Titford and Queta Mehalah (*née* D'Wit); *m* 1956, Margaret Cheeld; one *s* three *d.* DipFD. Titford Funeral Service Ltd, 1954–89, Man. Dir, 1970–89. Pres., Nat. Assoc. Funeral Dirs, 1975–76. UK Independence Party: Leader, 2000–02, 2010–11; Whip, 2004–09; Life Pres., 2011. Contested: (Referendum) Harwich, 1997; (UKIP) Harwich, 2005. *Recreations:* fishing, walking, golf. *Address:* Bratton House, Charlton Gardens, Ditchling, E Sussex BN6 8WA.

TITLEY, Gary; Member (Lab) North West Region, England, European Parliament, 1999–2009 (Greater Manchester West, 1989–99); Leader, European Parliamentary Labour Party, 2002–09; Senior Consultant, Hume Brophy, since 2011; *b* 19 Jan. 1950; *s* of Wilfred James and Joyce Lillian Titley; *m* 1975, Rosario, (Charo); one *s* one *d. Educ:* York Univ. (BA Hons Hist./Educn, 1973; PGCE 1974). TEFL, Bilbao, 1973–75; taught History, Earls High Sch., Halesowen, 1976–84; Personal Assistant to MEP, 1984–89. Mem., W Midlands CC, 1981–86 (Vice-Chair: EDC, 1981–84; Consumer Services Cttee, 1984–86). Dir, W Midlands Enterprise Bd, 1982–89; Chairman: W Midlands Co-op Finance Co., 1982–89; Black Country Co-op Develt Agency, 1982–88. Non-exec. Dir, Bolton PCT, 2009–12. Contested (Lab): Bromsgrove, 1983; Dudley W, 1987. Pres., Eur. Parlt delegn for relations with Finland, 1992–94; rapporteur, accession of Finland to EU. President: European Economic Area Jt Parly Assembly, 1994–95; Jt Parly Cttee for relns with Lithuania, 1999–2001; Cttee of Jt Parly Assembly and delegn presidents, 2001–02. Commander, White Rose (Finland), 1995; Golden Cross (Austria), 1996; Order of Grand Duke Gediminas (Lithuania), 2003. *Recreations:* family, reading, sport.

TITLEY, Commandant Nursing Officer Jane, CBE 1995; RRC 1990 (ARRC 1986); Director of Defence Nursing Services, 1992–95; *b* 22 April 1940; *d* of Louis and Phyllis Myra (Josephine) Titley. *Educ:* St Catherine's Convent, Nottingham; St Bartholomew's Hosp.; Sussex Maternity Hosp. SRN 1962; SCM 1963. Joined QARNNS, 1965; served in Naval hosps and estabts in UK, Malta, Singapore, Naples and Gibraltar; Matron, 1986; Dep. Matron-in-Chief, 1988; Matron-in-Chief, 1990–94; QHNS, 1990–94. OStJ 1990. *Recreations:* 'to stand and stare', narrow-boating, genealogy. *Address:* Flat 10, 28 Pembridge Square, W2 4DS.

TITTERINGTON, Prof. David Michael; Professor of Organ, since 1991, and Head, Organ Studies, since 1996, Royal Academy of Music, University of London; concert organist, since 1986; *b* 10 Jan. 1958; *s* of Geoffrey Bridge Titterington and Claire Elizabeth Titterington (*née* Parsons). *Educ:* Pembroke Coll., Oxford (Organ Schol.; BA Hons 1980, MA 1984); Conservatoire de Rueil-Malmaison, Paris (1st Prize 1984, Prix d'Excellence 1985). Dir of Music, Dutch Ch, London, 1992–; Organ Consultant: Pembroke Coll., Oxford, 1993–95; Chapel Royal, HM Tower of London, 1997–2000; St Catharine's Coll., Cambridge, 2000–01; Sidney Sussex Coll., Cambridge, 2007–; Canterbury Cathedral, 2007–; Organ Curator, St John's Smith Square, 2012–. Vis. Prof. of Organ, Liszt Ferenc Acad. of Music, Budapest, 1997–; Hon. Prof., Liszt Ferenc State Univ., 1999. Gen. Ed., Organ Repertoire Series, 1987–97. Artistic Director: European Organ Fest. and Comp. (for FCO), 1992; Internat. Organ Fest., St Albans, 2007–. Solo recital début, RFH, 1986; *festival performances* include: Bicentennial Fest., Sydney, 1988; Hong Kong, Adelaide, NZ, Israel, Guelph, Prague Spring, Schleswig Holstein, Lahti, Granada, León, Brezice, BBC Proms, Cheltenham, City of London, Dartington, Belfast; *concerto performances* include: Berlin SO; BBC SO; Lahti SO; BBC Scottish SO; City of London Sinfonia; Britten Sinfonia; Guildhall String Ensemble; Allegri String Quartet. Hon. Fellow, Bolton Inst. of Higher Educn, 1992; Hon. FRCO 1999. Hon. RAM 2008. Hon. DMus Liszt Ferenc State, Budapest, 1999; DUniv Huddersfield, 2010. Arts Council of GB Award, 1984. *Publications:* (with J. Wainright) History of Pembroke College, Organs, 1995; (contrib.) Organs of Britain 1990–1995, 1996; (contrib.) New Grove Dictionary of Music and Musicians, 2000; article in RCO Jl. *Recreations:* silence, the sea, reading, friends. *Address:* Royal Academy of Music, Marylebone Road, NW1 5HT. *T:* (020) 7873 7339, *Fax:* (020) 7873 7439. *E:* d.titterington@ram.ac.uk. *Clubs:* Travellers; Noblemen and Gentlemen's Catch.

TIWARI, Narayan Datt; Governor, Andhra Pradesh, 2007–09; Chief Minister, Uttaranchal, 2002–07 (Chief Minister, Uttar Pradesh, 1976–77, 1984–85, March–Sept. 1985 and 1988–89); *b* Balyuti, UP, 18 Oct. 1925; *s* of Poorna Nand Tiwari and Chandrawati Devi Tiwari; *m* 1954, Dr Sushila Tiwari (*d* 1993). *Educ:* Allahabad Univ., UP (Golden Jubilee Schol. 1948; MA Diplomacy and Internat. Affairs; LLB; Pres., Students' Union). Studied Scandinavian Econ. and Budgetary Systems in Sweden, 1959; Congressional Practices and Procedures in USA, 1964; Whitley Council System, UK, and Co-op. Banking System in Germany, Dairy Develt in Denmark. Joined Freedom Movement, 1938, and Quit India Movement, 1942, resulting in 15 months in jail, 1942. MLA (Socialist) UP, 1952, re-elected nine times. State Govt appts, 1969–77: Chm., Public Accts Cttee; Minister for Finance, Heavy Industry, Sugar Cane Develt; Dep. Chm., State Planning Commn, 1980. Leader of Opposition in UP, 1977–79, 1991. MP: Nainital, Lok Sabha, 1980–84, 1995–98 and 1999–2002; Rajya Sabha, 1985–88; Union Minister for Planning and Labour and Dep. Chm., Planning Commn, India, 1980; Union Minister: for Industry and Steel and Mines, 1981–84; of Industry, Petroleum and Natural Gas, Ext. Affairs, Finance and Commerce, 1985–87; of Finance and Commerce, India, 1987–88; Leader of House, Rajya Sabha, 1986–88. Mem., Nat. Working Cttee, Indian Nat. Congress, 1993. Editor, Prabhat (a Hindi Monthly magazine). *Publications:* European Miscellany, 1964; hundreds of articles as a journalist. *Recreations:* playing cricket, hockey, chess; reading. *Address:* Village Padampuri, PO Padampuri, Dist Nainital, UP, India; B 315, Sector B, Dr Sushila Tiwari Marg, Mahanagar, Lucknow, UP, India. *T:* (522) 384859, (522) 239398, (11) 3382259, (11) 3382218.

TIZARD, Dame Catherine (Anne), ONZ 2002; GCMG 1990; GCVO 1995; DBE 1985; QSO 1996; Governor-General of New Zealand, 1990–96; *b* 4 April 1931; *d* of Neil Maclean and Helen Montgomery Maclean; *m* 1951, Rt Hon. Robert James Tizard, *qv* (marr. diss. 1983); one *s* three *d. Educ:* Matamata College; Auckland University (BA). Tutor in Zoology, Univ. of Auckland, 1967–84. Member: Auckland City Council, 1971–83 (Mayor of Auckland, 1983–90); Auckland Regional Authy, 1980–83. Chair, NZ Historic Places Trust, 1996–2002; Trustee, NZ SO Foundn, 1996–; Trustee, Kiri te Kanawa Trust, 2004–14 (Dep. Chair, 2004–12); Trustee and Patron, Howard League for Penal Reform NZ, 2012–. *Recreations:* music, reading, drama, cryptic crosswords. *Address:* 12A Wallace Street, Herne Bay, Auckland 1011, New Zealand.

TIZARD, John Nigel; independent strategic advisor and commentator on public policy and public services, since 2009; Director, John Tizard Ltd, since 2009; *b* Colchester, 16 Nov. 1954; *s* of Rodger Tizard and Angela Tizard; *m* 1995, Glenda Walker; one *s* one *d. Educ:* Colchester Royal Grammar Sch.; London Sch. of Econs (BScEcon). Spastics Soc., later Scope, 1977–97, Dir, Policy and Strategy, 1994–97; Gp Dir, Govt and Business Engagement, Capita Gp plc, 1997–2007; Dir, Centre for Public Services Partnerships, Univ. of Birmingham, 2008–10; Dir, Centre for Public Service Partnerships, Local Govt Inf. Unit, 2010–11. Founder and Convener, Voluntary Orgns Disability Gp, 1990–95; Exec. Advr to Public Services Strategy Bd, CBI, 2002–07 (seconded as Dir of Public Services (pt-time), 2005); Member: HM Treasury adv. panel on public sector perf. mgt, 2007; Adv. Panel, Govt's Rev. of Public Service Industry, 2008; Policy Adv. Bd, Social Market Foundn, 2008–; Adv. Bd, Centre for Public Scrutiny, 2008–; CLG/LGA Local Innovations Awards Adv. Panel, 2009–10; non-executive Director: Social Investment Business, 2008–13; Resultsmark, 2014–. Interim Dir, 2012–13, Mem. Adv. Council, 2013–, Collaborate, London S Bank Univ.; Chm. Govs, Aldridge Portland Community Acad., 2013–. Contested (Lab): Arundel, 1979; Mid Beds, 1983. Mem., Beds CC, 1981–99 (Jt Leader, 1985–96). Non-exec. Dir, S Beds Community NHS Trust, 1990–94; Mem., Beds Police Authy, 1996–98. Mem., Council, Assembly of Eur. Regions, 1993–99 (Chm., Social Affairs Gp, 1993–99). Trustee: Adventure Capital Fund, 2007–; Nat. Assoc. for Voluntary and Community Action, 2010– (Vice Chm., 2012–13); Action Space, 2011– (Chm., 2015–); Tomorrow's People, 2011–. Sen. Hon. Fellow, Univ. of Birmingham, 2010. Vis. Fellow, London S Bank Univ., 2012–. FRSA. Mem., Guardian Local Govt Editl Bd, 2010–. *Publications:* regular contribs to nat. and internat. media. *Recreations:* cooking, reading, holidays in France and Europe. *Address:* John Tizard Ltd, 50 Ampthill Road, Shefford, Beds SG17 5BB. *E:* john@johntizard.com.

TIZARD, Rt Hon. Robert James, CNZM 2000; PC (NZ) 1985; MP for Tamaki, Otahuhu, Pakuranga, and Panmure, New Zealand, 1957–90; Minister of Defence, Science and Technology, 1987–90; *b* 7 June 1924; *s* of Henry James and Jessie May Tizard; *m* 1951, Catherine Anne Maclean (*see* Dame Catherine Tizard) (marr. diss. 1983); one *s* three *d*; *m* 1983, Mary Christina Nacey; one *s. Educ:* Auckland Grammar Sch.; Auckland Univ. MA, Hons Hist., 1949. Served War: RNZAF, 1943–46, incl. service in Canada and Britain; (commnd as a Navigator, 1944). Pres., Students' Assoc., Auckland Univ., 1948; Lectr in History, Auckland Univ., 1949–53; teaching, 1954–57 and 1961–62. MP 1957–60 and 1963–90; Minister of Health and State Services, 1972–74; Dep. Prime Minister and Minister of Finance, 1974–75; Dep. Leader of the Opposition, 1975–79; Minister of Energy, Science and Technol., and Statistics, and Minister i/c Audit Dept, 1984–87. Mem., Auckland District Health Bd, 2007–10. *Recreation:* golf. *Address:* 3/131 Grafton Road, Auckland 1010, New Zealand.

TJOENG, Sir James Nang Eng, KBE 2007 (CBE 2002); Director, and Deputy Chairman, since 2014, Air Niugini Ltd (Chairman, 2003); *b* Sarmi Irian Jaya, Indonesia; *s* of Sick Jong Tjoeng and Man Moi Leo; *m* 1980, Judith Ann; two *s* two *d. Educ:* St Peter's Lutheran Coll., Brisbane. Man. Dir, Garamut Enterprises Pty Ltd, 1974; Director: Mineral Resources Develt Corp., 2003; Central Bank PNG, 2008. *Recreations:* Rugby Union fan, swimming. *Address:* PO Box 88, Gordons, NCD, Papua New Guinea. *T:* 3250729, *Fax:* 3257096. *E:* jtjoeng@hotmail.com. *Clubs:* Tattersalls (Brisbane); Port Moresby Yacht.

TOAL, Rt Rev. Mgr Joseph; *see* Motherwell, Bishop of, (RC).

TOAL, Patrick Thomas, CB 2007; Permanent Secretary, Department of Agriculture and Rural Development, Northern Ireland, 2003–07; *b* 8 March 1944; *s* of late Edward and Brigid Toal; *m* 1969, Bridget Macklin; one *s*. *Educ:* Abbey Grammar Sch., Newry; QUB. Appointed NI Civil Service, 1968; Department of Agriculture: admin trainee, 1976; various posts in Animal Health, Fisheries, Agricl Mktg and Co-opn, Horticulture, and Milk and Eggs Divs, 1976–83; Princ. Officer, Milk and Eggs Div., 1983–86; Head of Finance, 1986–89; Asst Sec., Hd of Animal Health and Welfare and Agric. Policy Divs, 1989–98; Dep. Sec., Agric. Policy, 1998–2003. Mem. Bd, Intervention Agency for Agricl Produce, 1998–2002. Mem. Council, Royal Ulster Agricl Soc., 2003–07. *Recreations:* golf (playing and admin), theatre, reading, amateur dramatics, gardening, Gaelic football, Rugby Union. *Clubs:* Fortwilliam Golf (Belfast) (Hon. Sec., 2007–12; Captain, 2013), Rosapenna Golf (Co. Donegal).

TOASE, Philip Cursley, CBE 2004; QFSM 2009; DL; Chief Fire Officer and Chief Executive, West Yorkshire Fire & Rescue Service, 2000–08; *b* 26 Sept. 1953; *s* of Gordon and Ray Toase; *m* 2003, Lorraine Robertson; one *s* one *d*, and one step *s*. *Educ:* Queen Elizabeth Grammar Sch., Wakefield; South Bank Univ. (BSc 1996). MCGI 1996. Joined W Yorks Fire Service as Fire fighter, Dewsbury, 1974; Station Officer, 1981; Asst Divl Officer, 1985; Divl Officer, 1987; Sen. Divl Officer, 1990; Asst Chief Fire Officer, 1995–99; Dep. Chief Fire Officer, 1999–2000. DL W Yorks, 2008. Long Service and Good Conduct Medal, 1994. *Recreations:* Manchester United season ticket holder, cricket, Rugby, keeping fit. *Address:* Huddersfield, W Yorks.

TOBIAS, Prof. Jeffrey Stewart, MD; FRCP, FRCR; Consultant in Radiotherapy and Oncology, University College and Middlesex Hospitals, since 1981; Professor of Cancer Medicine, University College London, since 2002; *b* 4 Dec. 1946; *s* of late Gerald Joseph Tobias and of Sylvia Tobias (*née* Pearlberg); *m* 1st, 1973, Dr Gabriela Jill Jaecker (*d* 2008); two *s* one *d*; 2nd, 2011, Dr Susan Jacqueline Rachel Kiernan. *Educ:* Hendon Grammar Sch.; Gonville and Caius Coll., Cambridge (MA, MD, BChir); St Bartholomew's Hosp. Med. Sch. Junior hosp. posts, St Bartholomew's, Whittington, UCH and Hammersmith Hosps, 1971–74; Research Fellow in Oncology, Harvard Med. Sch., 1975–76; Fellow in Oncology, St Bartholomew's and Royal Marsden Hosps, 1976–80; Clinical Dir, Meyerstein Inst. of Oncology, Middlesex Hosp., 1992–97. Chairman: CRC New Studies Breast Cancer Working Party, 1990–2000; UK Co-ordinating Cttee for Cancer Research Head and Neck Working Party, 1990–2000; CRC Educn Cttee, 2000–02; Cancer Res. UK Tobacco Adv. Gp, 2003–06; Member: Nat. Adv. Gp for Screening in Oral Cancer, 1994–97; various MRC Adv. Gps. Advr, Audit Commn for Nat. Cancer Services, 2000. Founder Sec., British Oncological Assoc., 1986; Member Council: RCR, 1992–94; Cancer Res. UK (formerly CRC UK), 2000–12 (Trustee, 2002–12); Pres., British Assoc. of Head and Neck Oncologists, 1996–98; Chm., Annual British Cancer Res. Meeting, 2004. Lectures include: BAAS, 1997, 2006; Natalie Shipman, RCP, 2006; Centenary, RSocMed, 2011. *Publications:* (with M. J. Peckham) Primary Management of Breast Cancer, 1985; (with R. L. Souhami) Cancer and its Management, 1986, 6th edn (with D. Hochhauser) 2010; (with C. J. Williams) Cancer, a Colour Atlas, 1993; (with P. R. Thomas) Current Radiation Oncology, 3 vols, 1994, 1995, 1997; Cancer: what every patient needs to know, 1995, rev. edn 1999; (with A. C. Silverstone) Gynecologic Oncology, 1997; (with J. Houghton) Breast Cancer—New Horizons in Research and Treatment, 2000; (with L. Doyal) Informed Consent in Medical Research, 2001; (with K. Eaton) Living with Cancer, 2001; Clinical Governance and Revalidation: a practical guide, 2003; many contribs to newspapers and learned jls about cancer management and medical ethics. *Recreations:* nothing too strenuous: music, cycling, skiing, reading, writing. *Address:* Department of Oncology, University College Hospital, NW1 2BU. *T:* (020) 3447 9088, *Fax:* (020) 3447 9055; 4 Canonbury Place, N1 2NQ. *E:* j.tobias@uclh.org, j.tobias100@btinternet.com. *Clubs:* Garrick, Royal Society of Medicine, Les Six; Albatross Wind and Water.

TOBIN, Hon. Brian Vincent, OC 2012; PC (Can.) 1993; Vice Chairman, BMO Capital Markets, since 2013; *b* 21 Oct. 1954; *s* of Patrick Vincent Tobin and Florence Mary Tobin (*née* Frye); *m* 1977, Jodean Smith; two *s* one *d*. *Educ:* Meml Univ. of Newfoundland. MP (L): Humber-St Barbe-Baie Verte, 1980–96; Bonavista-Trinity-Conception, 2000–02; Parly Sec. to Minister of Fisheries and Oceans, 1981; Minister: of Fisheries and Oceans, 1993–96; of Industry, 2000–02; MHA (L) Bay of Islands, 1996–99, Straits and White Bay North, 1999–2000; Premier of Newfoundland and Labrador, 1996–2000. Leader, Liberal Party of NF, 1996–2000; Chair, Nat. Liberal Caucus, 1989. Sen. Business Advr, Dentons Canada (formerly Fraser Milner Casgrain) LLP, 2004–13; Exec. Chm., Consolidated Thompson Iron Mines Ltd, 2009–11. *Publications:* (jtly) All in Good Time (memoirs), 2002. *Recreations:* reading, music, sports.

TOBIN, Patrick Francis John; Administrator, Headmasters' and Headmistresses' Conference Projects in Central and Eastern Europe, 2003–12; *b* 4 Oct. 1941; *s* of Denis George and Una Eileen Tobin; *m* 1970, Margery Ann Sluce; one *s* three *d*. *Educ:* St Benedict's Sch., Ealing; Christ Church, Oxford (MA in Modern Hist.); London Univ. (PGCE). Head: of Econs, St Benedict's Sch., Ealing, 1963–71; of History, Christ Coll., Brecon, 1971–75; of History, Tonbridge Sch., 1975–81; Headmaster, Prior Park Coll., Bath, 1981–89; Principal, Mary Erskine Sch. and Daniel Stewart's and Melville Coll., Edinburgh, 1989–2000. Member: HMC, 1981– (Chm., 1998; Vice-Chm., 1999; Chm., Professional Develt Cttee, 1991–95); Governing Council, Scottish Council of Ind. Schs, 1990–94; Scottish Consultative Council for the Curriculum, 1991–95; Assessor, SHA Educnl Assessment Centres, 1991–95. Governor: Bryanston Sch., 2000–06; Portsmouth Grammar Sch., 2001–13; Ryde Sch., 2001–11; Magdalen Coll. Sch., Oxford, 2001–05; Our Lady's Convent Sen. Sch., Abingdon, 2004–11 (Chm., 2004–11); Bede's Sch., E Sussex, 2011–; Advisory Governor: Ampleforth Coll., 2000–10; St Benedict's Ealing, 2000–06 (Chm., 2001–06); Downside Sch., 2001–03. Chm., Lower Park (Putney) Ltd, 2013–. *Publications:* Sweet Wells, 1998; Making Good Teachers Better, 1994; Portrait of a Putney Pud: an unpredictable career in teaching (memoir), 2004. *Recreations:* reading, travelling, canal boats. *Address:* Glentruim, Ashlake Copse Lane, Kite Hill, Wootton, Ryde, Isle of Wight PO33 4LG. *Club:* East India.

TOD, John Mackenzie, OBE 1987; Director, France, British Council, and Cultural Counsellor, British Embassy, Paris, 1998–2004; *b* 24 Oct. 1944; *s* of John Alexander Tod and Eleanor May Tod (*née* Darrah); *m* 1970, Christiane Teytaud; two *s* one *d*. *Educ:* Calday Grange GS; King's Coll., Cambridge (BA English); Leeds Univ. (postgrad. Dip. TESL 1969); Inst. of Educn, London Univ. (MA Ed 1983). VSO, Malaita, Solomon Is, 1963–64; teacher, Ruffwood Comp. Sch., Kirby, 1965; joined British Council, 1968: Ghana, 1969–72; Brazil, 1972–74; Asst Dir (Educn), Kano, Nigeria, 1975–78; Asst Dir, Overseas Educnl Appts Dept, 1978–82; Rep., Senegal, 1983–88; Regl Dir and Supt Gen., Sociedade Brasileira de Cultura Inglesa, São Paulo, 1988–93; Dir of Arts, 1993–98. *Recreations:* choral music, literature, theatre, travel. *Address:* 35 rue du Tabellion, 1050 Brussels, Belgium. *T:* (2) 5340715.

TOD, Vice-Adm. Sir Jonathan (James Richard), KCB 1996; CBE 1982; Deputy Commander Fleet, 1994–97; *b* 26 March 1939; *e s* of late Col Richard Logan Tod and Elizabeth Allan Tod; *m* 1962, Claire Elizabeth Russell Dixon (*d* 2015); two *s*. *Educ:* Gordonstoun Sch. BRNC, Dartmouth, 1957–59; Flying trng, 1961; Hal Far (Malta), 1963; HM Ships: Ark Royal, Hermes, Eagle, RNAS, Lossiemouth, 1962–70; BRNC, Dartmouth, 1970–72; Exec. Officer, HMS Devonshire, 1972–74; Naval Staff, 1975–77; Comd HMS Brighton, 1978–80; Cabinet Office, 1980–82; RCDS 1983; Comd HMS Fife, 1984–85; Dir, Defence Programme, 1986–88; Comd HMS Illustrious, 1988–89; Flag Officer Portsmouth and Naval Base Comdr Portsmouth, 1989–90; ACDS (Policy and Nuclear), MoD, 1990–94. Chm., Sea Cadet Assoc., 1998–2005; Vice Chm., Marine Soc. and Sea Cadets, 2004–05 (Vice Pres., 2005); Mem. Council, RNLI, 2005–09 (Vice-Pres., 2009–). *Recreations:* electric boating, gardening. *Address:* c/o Naval Secretary, Fleet Headquarters, Whale Island, Portsmouth PO2 8BY.

TODD, Prof. Christopher James, PhD; Professor of Primary Care and Community Health, University of Manchester, since 2001 (Director of Research, School of Nursing, Midwifery and Social Work, 2003–13); *b* Bournemouth, 1 Dec. 1956; *s* of Ernest James Todd and late Pamela Mary Todd (*née* Bramley); *m* 2001, Victoria Jane Brandon. *Educ:* Epsom Coll.; Univ. of Durham (BA Hons Psychol. 1978; MA 1980; PhD 1987). CPsychol 1989, AFBPsS 1990. Temp. Lectr in Psychol., Dept of Soc. Scis, Sunderland Poly., 1980; Interviewer, PSI, London, 1986; Res. Officer, Centre for Applied Health Studies, Univ. of Ulster, Coleraine, 1987–90; University of Cambridge: Res. Associate, 1990–92, Sen. Res. Associate, 1992–93, Dir, 1993–2001, Health Services Res. Gp, Dept of Public Health and Primary Care; Affiliate Lectr, Fac. of Soc. and Pol Scis, 1994–2000; Co-Dir, Cambridge Res. Develt Support Gp, Inst. of Public Health, 1997–2001; Wolfson College, Cambridge: Fellow, 1995–2001; Members' Steward, 1996–2000; Dir of Studies in Soc. and Pol Scis, 1999–2000. Director: EC Prevention of Falls Network Europe, 2003–11; EC Prevention of Falls Network for Dissemination, 2013–. Associate Fellow, BPsS, 1990; Regl Fellow, RSM, 2009. *Publications:* contrib. to papers on palliative care, epidemiology of osteoporosis, falls prevention and health psychol. in jls. *Recreations:* sculling, walking, wine tasting. *Address:* School of Nursing, Midwifery and Social Work, University Place, University of Manchester, Oxford Road, Manchester M13 9PL. *T:* (0161) 306 7865, *Fax:* (0161) 306 7894. *E:* chris.todd@manchester.ac.uk. *Club:* Agecroft Rowing.

TODD, Damian Roderic, (Ric); HM Diplomatic Service; High Commissioner, Cyprus, since 2014; *b* 29 Aug. 1959; *s* of late George Todd and of Annette Todd. *Educ:* Lawrence Sheriff Grammar Sch., Rugby; Worcester Coll., Oxford (BA Hons History). Joined HM Diplomatic Service, 1980; Third Sec., then Second Sec., Pretoria and Cape Town, 1981–84; FCO, 1984–87; HM Consul and First Sec., Prague, 1987–89; FCO, 1989–91; First Sec. (Econ.), Bonn, 1991–95; on secondment to HM Treasury, 1995–97, Hd of Agric. Team, 1996–97; FCO, 1997–98; on loan to HM Treasury as Hd of EU Co-ordination and Strategy Team, 1998–2001; Amb. to the Slovak Republic, 2001–04; Finance Dir, FCO, 2004–07; Ambassador to Poland, 2007–11; Gov., Turks and Caicos Is, 2011–13. *Address:* c/o Foreign and Commonwealth Office, King Charles Street, SW1A 2AH.

TODD, Daphne Jane, (Mrs P. R. T. Driscoll), OBE 2002; PPRP (RP 1985); NEAC; artist; President, Royal Society of Portrait Painters, 1994–2000; *b* 27 March 1947; *d* of Frank Todd and Annie Mary Todd (*née* Lord); *m* 1984, Lt-Col (Patrick Robert) Terence Driscoll; one *d*. *Educ:* Simon Langton Grammar Sch. for Girls, Canterbury; Slade Sch. of Fine Art, UCL (DFA 1969; HDFA 1971). Vis. Lectr, Byam Shaw Sch. of Art, 1971–75 and 1978–80; Dir of Studies, Heatherley Sch. of Fine Art, 1980–86. NEAC 1984; Royal Society of Portrait Painters: Mem. Council, 1986–90; Hon. Sec., 1990–91. Hon. Mem., Soc. of Women Artists, 1995. Tour Artist with TRH Prince of Wales and Duchess of Cornwall, S Africa and Tanzania, 2011. Judge, Big Painting Challenge, BBC TV, 2015. Work in exhibitions, including: Royal Acad. Summer Exhibns, 1969–; Critic's Choice, Tooth's, 1972; Slade Centenary, 1972; Slade Ladies, Mall Gall., 1991; President's Exhibn, Birmingham, 1995; solo retrospective exhibn, Morley Gall., London, 1989; solo exhibn, Messum's Gall., 2001, 2004, 2008, 2009, 2015; solo exhibn, Threadneedle Space, Mall Galleries, 2012. Work in private and public collections including: Royal Acad. (Chantrey Bequest); Lady Margaret Hall, UC, St Anne's Coll., Lincoln Coll. and Rhodes House, Oxford; Pembroke, St Catharine's, Girton, Clare and Sidney Sussex Colls, Cambridge; UCL; St David's Univ., Lampeter; De Montfort Univ.; Royal Holloway Mus. and Art Gall.; Bishop's Palace, Hereford; Wellington Barracks; BMA; ICE; NUMAST; Science Mus.; Nat. Portrait Gall.; Chapter House, St Paul's Cath.; Windsor Castle. Portrait commissions include: Grand Duke of Luxembourg; Lord Adrian; Dame Janet Baker; Spike Milligan; Sir Neil Cossons; Baron Klingspor; Sir Kirby and Lady Laing; Dr Stephen Spurr; Rt Rev. Graeme Knowles; Christopher Ondaatje; Dame Anne Mueller; Lord Sainsbury of Preston Candover; Lord Sharman; Prof. Marilyn Strathern; Lord Morris of Castle Morris, Sir Tom Stoppard; Lord Tugendhat; Lord Ashburton; Lord Armstrong of Ilminster; Lord and Lady Tebbit; Bill Packer; Lord Bledisloe; Viscount Mackintosh; Peter Scott; Lord Fellowes of West Stafford; Lady Armstrong; Sir Peter Gwynn-Jones, Garter King of Arms; Viscount Gage; HRH the Prince of Wales. Governor: Thomas Heatherley Educnl Trust, 1987–2014; FBA, 1994–2000. Treas., Friends of Argos Hill Windmill, 2009–11; Mem. Honour Cttee, Friends of Canterbury Mus, 2011–14. Freeman, Painter-Stainers' Co., 1997 (Hon. Liveryman, 2004). FRSA 1996. Ambassador for E Sussex, 2004–09. Hon. DArts: De Montfort, 1998; Kent, 2014. 2nd Prize, John Player Award, Nat. Portrait Gall., 1983 (Special Commendation, 1984); First Prize, Oil Painting of Year, Hunting Gp Nat. Art Prize, 1984; GLC Prize, Spirit of London, RFH, 1985; Ondaatje Prize for Portraiture, and RP Gold Medal, 2001; 1st Prize, BP Portrait Award, Nat. Portrait Gall., 2010. *Publications:* contribs to The Artist. *Recreation:* gardening. *Address:* Salters Green Farm, Mayfield, E Sussex TN20 6NP. *T:* and *Fax:* (01892) 852472. *E:* daphne.todd@btinternet.com. *W:* www.daphnetodd.com. *Clubs:* Athenæum, Arts, Chelsea Arts.

TODD, Prof. Sir David, Kt 1995; CBE 1990 (OBE 1982); FRCP, FRCPE, FRCPGlas, FRACP, FRCPath; Professor of Medicine, University of Hong Kong, 1972–96, now Emeritus; *b* 17 Nov. 1928; *s* of Paul J. Todd and Margaret S. Todd. *Educ:* Univ. of Hong Kong (MB BS, MD). FRCPE 1966; FRACP 1974; FRCP 1976; FRCPGlas 1979; FRCPath 1992. University of Hong Kong: Lectr, Sen. Lectr and Reader, 1958–72; Head of Dept, 1974–89; Sub-Dean of Medicine, 1976–78; Pro-Vice-Chancellor, 1978–80. Hong Kong Government: Consultant in Medicine, 1974–89; Chm., Research Grants Council, Hong Kong, 1991–93. President: Hong Kong Coll. of Physicians, 1986–92; Hong Kong Acad. of Medicine, 1992–96; Chm., Council for Aids Trust Fund, Hong Kong, 1993–96. Hon. FAMS Singapore, 1986; Hon. Mem., Chinese Med. Assoc., 1995. Hon. DSc: Chinese Univ. of Hong Kong, 1990; Univ. of Hong Kong, 1992; Hon. LLD Lingnan, 1997. *Publications:* articles on: haematological disorders in liver disease and splenomegaly; thalassaemia; G6PD deficiency; lymphoma; leukaemia; med. educn and physician training. *Recreations:* swimming, travelling, classical music. *Address:* D12 Breezy Court, 2A Park Road, Mid-levels, Hong Kong. *Clubs:* Hong Kong Golf, Hong Kong Country.

TODD, Jane Clare, OBE 2013; DL; Chief Executive, Nottingham City Council, 2008–12; *b* 26 March 1951; *d* of Norman Henry Todd and Joyce Mary Todd; *m* (marr. diss.); two *s* one *d*. *Educ:* Nottingham Univ. (BA Social Policy). Nottingham City Council: Asst Chief Exec., Policy, 1992–97; Dir, Develt, 1997–2000; Dir, Develt and Envmtl Services, 2000–02; Regional Dir, Govt Office for the E Midlands, 2002–07. DL Notts, 2013. *Recreations:* walking, reading.

TODD, Prof. Janet Margaret, OBE 2013; PhD; President, Lucy Cavendish College, Cambridge, 2008–15; Professor of English Literature, University of Aberdeen, 2004–12; *b* 10 Sept. 1942; *d* of George and Elizabeth Dakin; *m* 1st, 1966 (marr. diss. 1983); one *s* one *d*; 2nd, 2001, Prof. D. W. Hughes. *Educ:* Newnham Coll., Cambridge (BA 1964; Hon. Fellow 2015); Univ. of Leeds; Univ. of Florida (PhD). Lectr, Univ. of Cape Coast, Ghana, 1966–67; Asst Prof. of English, Univ. of Puerto Rico, 1972–74; Asst, Associate, Full Prof. of English, Rutgers Univ., NJ, 1974–83; Fellow in English, Sidney Sussex Coll., Cambridge, 1983–89; Prof. of English Lit., UEA, 1990–2000; Francis Hutcheson Prof. of English Lit., Univ. of Glasgow, 2000–04. Vis. Prof. Univ. of Southampton, 1982–83. Bye-Fellow, Newnham Coll., Cambridge, 1998; Hon. Fellow, Lucy Cavendish Coll., Cambridge, 2000. General Editor: Complete Works of Jane Austen, 9 vols, 2005–06; Cambridge edn of Works of Jane Austen,

2005–09. Numerous awards. *Publications:* In Adam's Garden: a study of John Clare, 1973; Mary Wollstonecraft: an annotated bibliography, 1976; Women's Friendship in Literature, 1980; (jtly) English Congregational Hymns in the 18th Century, 1983; Sensibility, 1986; Feminist Literary History, 1988; The Sign of Angellica: women writing and fiction 1660–1800, 1989; (ed jtly) The Complete Works of Mary Wollstonecraft, 1989; (ed) A Dictionary of British Women Writers, 1989; (ed) The Works of Aphra Behn, 7 vols, 1992–96; (ed) Aphra Behn's Oroonoko, The Rover and Other Works, 1993; Gender, Art and Death, 1993; (ed) Aphra Behn Studies, 1996; The Secret Life of Aphra Behn, 1996; (ed) Female Education, 6 vols, 1996; The Critical Fortunes of Aphra Behn, 1998; Mary Wollstonecraft: a revolutionary life, 2000; Rebel Daughters: Ireland in conflict 1798, 2003; (ed) Collected Letters of Mary Wollstonecraft, 2003; (ed) Oroonoko, 2003; (ed jtly) Cambridge Companion to Aphra Behn, 2004; (ed) Jane Austen in Context, 2005; Cambridge Introduction to Jane Austen, 2006; Death and the Maidens: Fanny Wollstonecraft and the Shelley Circle, 2007; (ed jtly) Jane Austen: the later manuscripts, 2008; Pride and Prejudice, 2011; (ed) Cambridge Companion to Pride and Prejudice, 2013; Jane Austen, Her Life, Times and Novels, 2013; Lady Susan Plays the Game, 2013. *Address:* Grange House, Selwyn Gardens, Cambridge CB3 9AX.

TODD, Prof. John Andrew, PhD; FRS 2009; Professor of Medical Genetics, and Fellow of Gonville and Caius College, University of Cambridge, since 1998; *b* 23 June 1958; *s* of William and Elizabeth Todd; *m* 1988, Anne Nicola Roberts (marr. diss. 2012); two *s* one *d*. *Educ:* Coleraine Academical Instn; Edinburgh Univ. (BSc 1st cl. Hons 1980); Gonville and Caius Coll., Cambridge (PhD Biochemistry 1983). Research Fellow: Dept of Biochemistry, Cambridge Univ., 1983–85; MRC Molecular Biology Lab., Cambridge, 1984; SERC/NATO Res. Fellow, Dept of Microbiology and Immunology, Stanford Univ., Calif, 1985–88; Career Develt Award Fellow, Juvenile Diabetes Foundn Internat., 1988–90 (Grodsky Prize, 1998); University of Oxford: Sen. Scientist, Nuffield Dept of Surgery, 1988–98; Mem., Faculty of Medicine, 1989–98; Wellcome Trust Sen. Fellow in Basic Biomed. Sci., 1990–93; Univ. Res. Lectr, 1992–98; Wellcome Trust Prin. Res. Fellow, 1993–98; Prof. of Human Genetics, 1996–98. Wellcome Vis. Prof., Louisiana State Univ., 1997. NIHR Sen. Investigator, 2009. Lectures: Balfour, Genetical Soc., 1994; Lilly, QUB, 1995; Dorothy Hodgkin, Diabetes UK, 2001. FMedSci 1998. Hon. MRCP 2000. Minkowski Prize, Eur. Assoc. for Study of Diabetes, 1995; Res. Prize, Boehringer Mannheim and Juvenile Diabetes Res. Foundn Internat., 1995; Biennial Biochem. Soc. Medal, Wellcome Trust, 1998; R. and B. Sackler Res. Award, 1998; Carter Medal and Lecture, Clin. Genetics Soc., 1999; NDRI Distinguished Scientist Award, 2008; David Rumbough Award for Scientific Excellence, Juvenile Diabetes Res. Foundn, 2011. *Publications:* articles in learned jls. *Recreations:* lateral thinking, study of natural selection and evolution, fly fishing, cycling, ski-ing, swimming, child minding. *Address:* JDRF/Wellcome Trust Diabetes and Inflammation Laboratory, Cambridge Institute for Medical Research, Wellcome Trust/MRC Building, Hills Road, Cambridge CB2 0XY. *T:* (01223) 762101.

TODD, Sir John (Desmond), KNZM 2012 (CNZM 2009); Chairman, Todd Corporation Ltd, 1987–2011; Founder Trustee, since 1972, Chairman, since 1987, Todd Foundation; *b* Wellington, NZ, 12 Feb. 1927; *s* of Sir Desmond Henry Todd and Rita Todd (*née* Edmonds); *m* 1st, 1950, Angela Beverly Stock (marr. diss. 1986); one *s* three *d*; 2nd, 1986, Christina Grant Bamber. *Educ:* St Patrick's Coll., Silverstream, Wellington; Victoria Univ., Wellington. Todd Motors Ltd: various positions, 1946–68; Man. Dir, 1968–87. Former Non-executive Director: AGC (NZ); General Finance Ltd; Mitsubishi Motors New Zealand; Shortland Properties Ltd; Adv. Bd, Westpac Banking Corp. Former Mem., Overseas Investment Commn. Former Pres., Wellington Manufacturers Assoc. Former Chairman: Gen. Cttee, NZ Lottery Grants Bd; NZ Sch. of Dance Trust; NZ Ballet Foundn; Duke of Edinburgh's Award NZ Foundn; Founder and former Trustee, Arts Foundn of NZ; former Trustee: Royal NZ Ballet; Queen Elizabeth II Arts Council; Volunteer Service Abroad; Mem., Supporters Council, Enterprize NZ Trust. Dist. Fellow, Inst. of Dirs, 2001. Court of Honour, Royal Australasian Soc. of Surgeons, 1989; Wellington Icon, Wellington Gold Awards, 2009; NZ Business Hall of Fame, 2011; Petroleum Exploration and Prodn Assoc. of NZ Hall of Fame, 2015. *Recreations:* boating, golf, reading, music, performing and visual arts. *Address:* 7/254 Oriental Parade, Oriental Bay, Wellington 6011, New Zealand. *Clubs:* Wellington, Rotary (Wellington) (Chm., 1979–80); Royal Wellington Golf.

TODD, Prof. John Francis James, PhD; CEng, FInstMC; CChem, FRSC; Professor of Mass Spectroscopy, University of Kent at Canterbury, 1991–2000, now Emeritus; *b* 20 May 1937; *o s* of late Eric Todd and Annie Lewin Todd (*née* Tinkler); *m* 1963, Mavis Georgina Lee; three *s*. *Educ:* Leeds Grammar Sch.; Leeds Univ. (BSc, Ph.D. 1 Hons Chem.). Research Fellow: Leeds Univ., 1962–63; Yale Univ., USA, 1963–65; University of Kent at Canterbury: Asst Lectr in Chemistry, 1965–66; Lectr in Chemistry, 1966–73; Sen. Lectr, 1973–89; Reader in Physical Chemistry, Faculty of Natural Scis, 1990; Dir, Univ. Chemical Lab., 1991–94; Dep. Head, Chemistry Dept (Finance), 1996–97; Master of Rutherford Coll., 1975–85. CIL Distinguished Vis. Lectr, Trent Univ., Canada, 1988. J. B. Cohen Prizeman, Leeds Univ., 1963; Fulbright Research Scholar, 1963–65. Chm., Canterbury and Thanet HA, 1982–86. Chairman: Kent Section of Chem. Soc., 1975; British Mass Spectroscopy Soc., 1980–81 (Treas., 1990–93); Titular Mem., IUPAC Commn on Molecular Structures and Spectroscopy, 1979–91; Nat. Mem. Council, RSC, 1993–95. Mem., Kent Educn Cttee, 1983–88. Member: Clergy Orphan Corp., 1985–96; Council, Strode Park Foundn for the Disabled, 1986–90. Governor: S Kent Coll. of Technology, 1977–89; Canterbury Christ Church Univ. (formerly Canterbury Christ Church Coll., later UC), 1994–2007; Chm. of Govs, St Edmund's Sch., Canterbury, 1996–2006. Mem., Amer. Soc. of Sigma Xi, Yale Chapter. Jt Editor, Internat. Jl of Mass Spectrometry and Ion Processes, 1985–98. Hon. Life Mem., RSC, 2009. Hon. Fellow, Canterbury Christ Church Univ., 2008. Thomson Gold Medal, Internat. Mass Spectrometry Soc., 1997; Aston Medal, British Mass Spectrometry Soc., 2006. *Publications:* Dynamic Mass Spectrometry, vol. 4, 1975, vol. 5, 1978, vol. 6, 1981; Advances in Mass Spectrometry 1985, 1986; Practical Aspects of Ion Trap Mass Spectrometry, vols 1–3, 1995; Quadrupole Ion Trap Mass Spectrometry, 2005; Practical Aspects of Trapped Ion Mass Spectrometry, vol. 4, 2010, vol. 5, 2009; reviews and papers, mainly on mass spectrometry, in Jl of Chem. Soc. and Jl of Physics, etc. *Recreations:* music, travel, genealogy. *Address:* Ingram Building, School of Physical Sciences, University of Kent, Canterbury, Kent CT2 7NH; West Bank, 122 Whitstable Road, Canterbury, Kent CT2 8EG. *T:* (01227) 769552.

TODD, Keith; *see* Todd, T. K.

TODD, Sir Mark James, KNZM 2013; CBE 1995 (MBE 1984); equestrian rider; *b* 1 March 1956; *s* of Norman Edward Todd and Lenore Adele Todd; *m* 1986, Carolyn Faye Berry; one *s* one *d*. *Educ:* Cambridge High Sch., NZ; Hamilton Tech. Inst. (Dip. Agric.). Three-day event wins: Badminton, 1980 (Southern Comfort), 1994 (Horton Point), 1996 (Bertie Blunt), 2011 (Land Vision); Burghley, 1987 (Wilton Fair, also runner up, on Charisma), 1990 (Welton Greylag), 1991 (Face the Music), 1997 (Broadcast News), 1999 (Diamond Hall Red); Olympic Games: Individual Gold Medal, 1984 (Charisma), 1988 (Charisma); Individual Bronze Medal, 2000 (Eye Spy II); NZ Team Bronze Medal, 2012; World Championships: NZ Team Gold Medal, 1990; Individual Silver Medal, 1998 (Broadcast News). New Zealand Sportsman of the Year, 1988; Event Rider of the Century, Internat. Equestrian Fedn, 1999; Equestrian Personality of the Century, Horse & Hound, 2000; Sportsman of the Century, Waikato, NZ, 2000; New Zealander of the Year, NZ Soc., 2000. *Publications:* Charisma; Mark Todd's Cross-Country Handbook, 1991; One Day Eventing, 1996; So Far, So Good, 1998; Second Chance (autobiog.), 2012. *Recreations:* ski-ing, swimming, tennis, squash, horse racing, music.

TODD, Mark Wainwright; Chair, Derbyshire Healthcare NHS Foundation Trust, since 2014; *b* 29 Dec. 1954; *s* of Matthew and Viv Todd; *m* 1979, Sarah Margaret (*née* Dawson); one *s*. *Educ:* Sherborne Sch.; Emmanuel Coll., Cambridge (BA History 1976; MA). Longman Group, later Addison Wesley Longman, 1977–96: Man. Dir, Longman Industry and Public Service Mgt, 1988–92, Longman Cartermill, 1990–92; Dir, IT, 1992–94, Ops, 1994–96. MP (Lab) S Derbyshire, 1997–2010. Chair: NHS Derby City, 2010–13; NHS Derbyshire County, 2011–13. Chair of Trustees, Motor Neurone Disease Assoc., 2010–14.

TODD, Michael Alan; QC 1997; *b* 16 Feb. 1953; *y s* of Charles Edward Alan Todd and late Betty Todd (*née* Bromwich); *m* 1976, Deborah Collett. *Educ:* Kenilworth Grammar Sch.; Keele Univ. (BA 1976). Called to the Bar, Lincoln's Inn, 1977, Bencher, 2006; Jun. Counsel to the Crown, Chancery Div., 1992–97. Chm., Chancery Bar Assoc., 2007–10. Mem., Bar Council, 2007– (Vice-Chm., 2011; Chm., 2012). *Recreation:* equestrianism. *Address:* Erskine Chambers, 33 Chancery Lane, WC2A 1EN. *T:* (020) 7242 5532.

TODD, Ric; *see* Todd, D. R.

TODD, Richard Frazer; QC 2009; a Recorder, since 2010; *b* Gosport, 21 Jan. 1965; *s* of late Alan Todd, RN and of Gillian Todd; *m* 1995, Elisabeth MacBean; two *s* two *d*. *Educ:* Royal Hosp. Sch.; Trinity Coll., Oxford (MA); Inns of Court Sch. of Law. Called to the Bar, Middle Temple, 1988; in practice as barrister specialising in high value matrimonial finance cases; called (*ad hoc*) to the Bar: Cayman Islands, 2009; Hong Kong SAR, 2014. Member: Family Law Bar Assoc., 1988–; Gen. Council of the Bar, 1998–2002; Prosecuting Counsel, Bar Standards Bd, 2002–. Mem., Royal Artillery Assoc., 1983–. Fellow, Internat. Acad. of Matrimonial Lawyers, 2009. Chambers and Partners Family Law Silk of the Year, 2010 and 2013; Family Law QC of Year, Economist/Law Monthly, 2011, 2012, 2014. *Publications:* (ed jtly) Practical Matrimonial Precedents, 2 vols, 1989, 44th edn 2015; At Court, 2000; The Essential Family Practice, 2 vols, 2000, 3rd edn 2003; (ed jtly) Jowitt's Dictionary of English Law, 2010; (ed with Elisabeth Todd) Todds' Relationship Agreements, 2013. *Recreations:* laws, wars and the great indoors. *Address:* 1 Hare Court, Temple, EC4Y 7BE. *T:* (020) 7797 7070, *Fax:* (020) 7797 7435. *E:* RT@1hc.com; Temple Chambers, 16/F One Pacific Place, Central, Hong Kong. *T:* 25232003, *Fax:* 28100302. *E:* todd@templechambers.com. *Club:* Athenæum.

TODD, (Thomas) Keith, CBE 2004; FCMA; Executive Chairman, ION Agency Business, since 2015; Chairman: FFastFill plc, since 2002; Amino Technologies, since 2007; Magic Lantern Productions Ltd, since 2006; *b* 22 June 1953; *s* of Thomas William Todd and Cecilie Olive Todd; *m* 1979, Anne Elizabeth Hendrie; two *s* two *d*. FCMA 1985. Chief Accountant, Marconi Co. Ltd, 1978–81; Chief Financial Officer, Cincinnati Electronics, USA, 1981–86; Financial Dir, Marconi Co. Ltd, 1986–87; Dir, Finance and Business Strategy, 1987–96, Chief Exec., 1996–2000, ICL plc; Chm. and CEO, Dexterus Ltd, 2001; Chairman: Ecsoft, plc, 2002–03; Broad Band Stakeholder Gp, 2002–05; Easynet plc, 2002–06. Mem. Board, Camelot Gp plc, 1994–2000. Mem. Council, Open Univ., 1992–2000 (Hon. Treas., 1992–97). Life Mem., BAFTA, 2000. FRSA 1996. DUniv Open, 1999. *Recreation:* sports. *Address:* Granchester House, Manor Close, Penn, Bucks HP10 8HZ. *Clubs:* Royal Automobile; Beaconsfield Golf.

TODHUNTER, Michael John Benjamin, MBE 2011; DL; Director, 1977–2009, Chairman, 2002–09, James Finlay Ltd; Director, 1989–2005, Chairman, 1999–2005, Kleinwort Capital Trust plc; *b* 25 March 1935; *s* of late Brig. Edward Joseph Todhunter and Agnes Mary (*née* Swire); *m* 1959, Caroline Francesca (MVO 2003), *d* of Maj. William Walter Dowding; one *s* two *d*. *Educ:* Eton Coll.; Magdalen Coll., Oxford (MA). 2nd Lieutenant, 11 Hussars, PAO, 1953–55. Banker; with Jessel Toynbee & Co. Ltd, 1958–84 (Dir, 1962, Dep. Chm., 1977): Chief Exec., Alexanders Discount plc, 1984–86; Dir, Mercantile House Hldgs plc, 1984–86; Man. Dir, PK English Trust Co. Ltd, 1986–89; London Advr, Yasuda Trust Banking Co. Ltd, 1989–98. Chm., Clyde Shipping Co. Ltd, 1978–2000. Dir, Newbury Racecourse plc, 1983–2004. Special Trustee, Gt Ormond St Hosp., 1979–96; Trustee: Missions to Seamen, 1980–96; Gift of Thomas Pocklington, 1990–99; Trustee and Gov., 2000–10, Fund Raiser, 2005–13, Prior's Court Foundn. High Sheriff, 1999, DL, 2005, Berks. Hon. Fellow, Inst. of Child Health, 1994. *Recreations:* travel, shooting. *Address:* The Old Rectory, Farnborough, Wantage OX12 8NX. *T:* (01488) 638298; (office) Swire House, 59 Buckingham Gate, SW1E 6AJ. *T:* (020) 7834 7717. *Clubs:* White's, Pratt's.

TODIWALA, Cyrus Rustom, OBE 2010 (MBE 2000); DL; Chef Patron, since 1995, and Co-owner, since 2004, Café Spice Namasté; Chef Patron: Mr Todiwala's Kitchen, since 2011; The Park Café, since 2013; Assado, since 2014; *b* Bombay, 16 Oct. 1956; *s* of Rustom Todiwala and Dowlat Todiwala; *m* 1984, Pervin Talati; two *s*. *Educ:* St Mary's Byculla, Bombay; Barnes High Sch., Bombay; Basant Kumar Somani Poly., Bombay (Dip. Hotel Admin and Food Technol. 1976). Commis Chef, 1976–78, Demi Chef, 1978–80, Chef de Partie, 1980–82, Taj Mahal Hotel, Bombay; Chef de Cuisine, Taj Holiday Village, Goa, 1982–84; Exec. Chef, Fort Aguada Beach Resort, 1984–86; Corporate Exec. Chef, Fort Aguada Beach Resort, Taj Holiday Village and Aguada Hermitage, 1986–89; The Place, Poona, 1989–91; Chef/Manager, 1991–95, Chef Patron, 1993–95, Namasté Indian Restaurant. Presenter, TV series, The Incredible Spice Men, 2013. Former Member: NACETT; NHS Better Hosp. Food Prog. Panel. Director: Asian and Oriental Sch. of Catering, 1999–; London Food Bd, 2008–; Hospitality Skills Acad., 2008–; non-exec. Mem. Bd, Investors in People UK, 2004–10; Member: British Hospitality Assoc., 1995– (former Mem., Steering Cttee); Guild of Fine Food Retailers, 2002–; Campaign for Real Food, 2003–; Steering Cttee, Mutton Renaissance Movement, 2003–; Steering Cttee, Greener Food Britain, 2004–; Craft Guild of Chefs, 2004–; Royal Acad. (formerly Acad.) of Culinary Arts, 2004–; Scotch Beef Club, 2004–; London Adv. Bd, Springboard UK, 2006–; Chm., London Food Waste Cttee, 2008–. Pres., Time and Talents Assoc., 2000; Trustee, Learning for Life, 2000; Chef Ambassador, the Clink, 2013–. Hon. Prof., Univ. of W London (formerly Thames Valley Univ.), 2002–; Enterprise Champion, LeSoCo, 2013. FIH (FHCIMA 2007); Fellow: Epicurean World Master Chefs Soc., 1996; Master Chefs of GB, 2006; FRSA 2004. DL Gtr London, 2009. Hon. DBA London Metropolitan, 2009. Food Personality of the Year, BBC Radio 4 Food and Farming Awards, 2014. *Publications:* New Wave Indian Cooking, 1998; International Cuisine India, 2005; Indian Summer, 2008; Mr Todiwala's Bombay, 2013; (with Tony Singh) The Incredible Spice Men, 2013. *Recreations:* travel, reading, cooking for friends, Zoroastrian history, animals and animal welfare, environment, sustainability all encompassing. *Address:* Café Spice Namasté, 16 Prescot Street, E1 8AZ. *T:* (020) 7488 9242. *E:* ctodiwala@yahoo.co.uk.

TODNER, Karen Elizabeth; Managing Director, Kaim Todner Ltd, since 1990; *b* Sunderland, 10 April 1962; *d* of Urias Todner and Lilian Todner; *m* 1996, Ian Jobling; three *s*. *Educ:* Higham Lane Sch., Nuneaton; King Edward VI Sch., Nuneaton; Univ. of Exeter (LLB); Coll. of Law, Chester. Admitted solicitor, 1987. Dir, Solicitors Disciplinary Tribunal, 2002– (Vice Pres., 2009–); Pres., Mental Health Rev. Tribunal, 2003–. *Recreations:* eating out, cinema, family, travel. *Address:* Kaim Todner Ltd, 11 Bolt Court, EC4A 3DQ. *T:* (020) 7353 6660, *Fax:* (020) 7353 6661. *E:* karentodner@kaimtodner.com.

TODOLÍ, Vicente; Artistic Advisor, HangarBicocca Foundation, since 2013; *b* 31 May 1958; *s* of Vicente and Julia Todolí; *m* 1998, Cristina Gimenez. *Educ:* Univ. of Valencia (Master of

Geog. and Hist. 1980); Yale Univ. and CUNY (Fulbright Schol.; grad. studies in art). ISP Fellow, Whitney Mus. of American Art, NY, 1985; Chief Curator, 1986–88, Artistic Dir, 1988–96, Inst. Valenciano de Arte Moderno; Director: Museu Serralves, Porto, Portugal, 1996–2002; Tate Modern, 2002–10. Member, Advisory Boards: Museu d'Art Contemporani de Barcelona, 1998–; Manifesta Internat. Foundn, 2002–07; Serralves Foundn, 2003–; Botin Foundn, 2003–; Contemp. Art Soc., 2003–07; La Caixa Foundn, 2003–. Member: Adv. Cttee for Reina Sofia Nat. Mus. of Art, Madrid, 1993–96; Jury and Adv. Cttee, Carnegie Internat., 1995; Advr, for Future, Past, Present, Venice Biennale, 1997. Comendador, Orden de Santiago (Portugal), 2002.

TODT, Jean Henri; President, Fédération Internationale de l'Automobile, since 2009; *b* Pierrefort, Cantal, France, 25 Feb. 1946; *s* of Emmanuel Todt and Hilda Todt (*née* Benoliel); partner, Michelle Yeoh; one *s* by a previous marriage. *Educ:* Ecole des Cadres Sch. of Econs and Business, Paris. Rally co-driver, 1966–81. Dir, Peugeot Racing Activities, then PSA Peugeot-Citroën Sporting Activities, 1982–93; Team Principal, Scuderia Ferrari, 1993–2004; Mem., Bd of Dirs, 2001–09, Gen. Manager, 2004–06, CEO, 2006–08, Ferrari SpA. Member, Board of Directors: Edmond de Rothschild SA, 2008–; Gaumont, 2004–; Groupe Lucien Barriere, 2004–; Internat. Peace Inst., 2015; Chm., Bd of Dirs, SUU Foundn, 2014–. Special Envoy of UN Sec. Gen. for Road Safety, 2015–. Mem., Internat. Adv. Bd, Sotheby's, 2013–. Founder Mem., ICM Brain & Spine Inst. (formerly Inst. for Brain and Spinal Cord Disorders Foundn), 2002– (Vice Pres., 2007–). Member: Académie des Technologies, 2004–; Académie des Sports, 2011–. Pres., E Safety Aware, 2009–. Mem., Bd of Trustees, Fedn Internat. de l'Automobile Foundn for the Automobile and Society, 2008–. Commendatore (Italy), 2002; Dato Seri (Malaysia), 2006; Grand Croix, Légion d'Honneur (France), 2011; Mem., Order of Prince Yaroslav the Wise (Ukraine), 2011; Grand Officer, Ordre de Sainte Agathe (San Marino), 2012; Comdr, Nat. Order of Merit (Senegal), 2013; First Class Order Medal (Bahrain), 2014; Medal, Order of Friendship (Russia), 2015. *Publications:* 205: l'histoire d'un défi, 1985. *Recreation:* backgammon. *Address:* Fédération Internationale de l'Automobile, 8 Place de la Concorde, 75008 Paris, France, and 2 Chemin de Blandonnet, 1215 Genève 15, Switzerland. *T:* (1) 43124455. *E:* jtodt@fia.com. *Clubs:* Automobile Club de France, Polo de Paris.

TOFFOLO, Rt Rev. Mgr Adrian Titian; Parish Priest, The Sacred Heart, Kingsbridge, since 2012; Episcopal Vicar for Safeguarding, since 2013; *b* 22 Sept. 1944; *s* of Sante Battista Toffolo and Ethel Elizabeth (*née* Hannaford-Hill). *Educ:* St Boniface's Coll., Plymouth; Gregorian Univ., Rome (PhL, STL). Asst Priest, Penzance, 1969–72; Prof. of Theology, Oscott Coll., 1972–76; Assistant Priest: Torquay, 1976–80; Plymouth, 1980–84; Parish Priest: St Austell, 1984–85; Truro, 1985–91; Rector, Venerable English College, Rome, 1991–99; Parish Priest, Bovey Tracey and Chudleigh, 1999–2003; Episcopal Vicar for Formation, Dio. of Plymouth, 1999–2009; Parish Priest, Barnstaple, 2003–13. Prelate of Honour, 1992. *Recreations:* mountain walking, music, DIY. *Address:* 19 Fosse Road, Kingsbridge, Devon TQ7 1NG. *T:* (01548) 852670.

TOFT, Dr Anthony Douglas, CBE 1995; LVO 2010; FRCPE; Consultant Physician, Royal Infirmary, Edinburgh, 1978–2009; Physician to the Queen in Scotland, 1996–2009; *b* 29 Oct. 1944; *s* of William Vincent Toft and Anne Laing; *m* 1968, Maureen Margaret Darling; one *s* one *d*. *Educ:* Perth Academy; Univ. of Edinburgh (BSc Hons, MD). FRCPE 1980; FRCP 1992; FRCPI 1993; FRCPGlas 1993; FRCSE (*ad hominem*), 1994. House Physician and House Surgeon, 1969–70, jun. med. posts, 1970–78, Royal Infirmary, Edinburgh. Chief Medical Adviser, Aegon (formerly Scottish Equitable Life Assurance Soc.), 1984–2015. Mem., Health Appointments Adv. Cttee, 1994–2000. Royal Coll. of Physicians of Edinburgh: Chm., Collegiate Members' Cttee, 1977; Mem. Council, 1986–88; Vice-Pres., 1990–91; Pres., 1991–94; Chm. Trustees, 1999–. Chairman: Scottish Royal Colls, 1993–94; Jt Cttee on Higher Med. Trng, 1994–96; Vice-Chm., UK Conf. of Med. Royal Colls, 1993–94. General Medical Council: Mem., 1999–2003; Occasional Chm., Professional Conduct Cttee, 1999–2004; Chm., Prof. and Linguistic Assessments Bd, 1999–2006. Pres., British Thyroid Assoc., 1997–99; Mem., Assoc. of Physicians of GB and Ireland, 1983–; Sec., Harveian Soc., 1980–94. Hon. Mem., Acad. of Medicine of Malaysia, 1993. Hon. FCPS (Pak) 1990; Hon. FACP 1993; Hon. FRACP 1993; Hon. FRCPC 1994; Hon. FRCGP 1994; Hon. FFPM 1994; Hon. Fellow, Acad. of Medicine of Singapore, 1994; Hon. FCPS (Bangladesh) 1995; Hon. FRCEM (Hon. FFAEM 1997). *Publications:* Diagnosis and Management of Endocrine Diseases, 1982; papers on thyroid disease. *Recreations:* gardening, collecting art. *Address:* 41 Hermitage Gardens, Edinburgh EH10 6AZ. *T:* (0131) 447 2221.

TÓIBÍN, Colm; writer; Mellon Professor, Department of English and Comparative Literature, Columbia University, since 2012; *b* 30 May 1955; *s* of Micheál Tóibín and Bríd O'Rourke. *Educ:* University Coll., Dublin (BA). Features Ed., In Dublin mag., 1981–82; Ed., Magill mag., 1982–85. Leonard Milberg Vis. Lectr in Irish Letters, Princeton Univ., 2009–11; Prof. of Creative Writing, Manchester Univ., 2011–12. *Publications: novels:* The South, 1990; The Heather Blazing, 1992; The Story of the Night, 1996; The Blackwater Lightship, 1999; The Master, 2004; Brooklyn, 2009; Testament of Mary (novella), 2012 (stage version, 2013); Nora Webster, 2014 (Hawthornden Prize, 2015); *short stories:* Mothers and Sons, 2006; The Empty Family, 2010; *non-fiction:* Walking Along the Border, 1987, reissued as Bad Blood, 1994; Homage to Barcelona, 1990; The Trial of the Generals: selected journalism 1980–90, 1990; The Sign of the Cross: travels in Catholic Europe, 1994; Love in a Dark Time: gay lives from Wilde to Almodovar, 2001; (jtly) The Irish Famine: a documentary, 2001; Lady Gregory's Toothbrush, 2002; (ed) Synge: a celebration, 2005; New Ways to Kill Your Mother: writers and their families, 2012; Colm Tóibín on Elizabeth Bishop, 2015. *T:* (1) 6768383. *E:* ctoibin@eircom.net.

TOKSVIG, Sandra Birgitte, (Sandi), OBE 2014; writer and comedian; *b* 3 May 1958; *d* of late Claus Bertel Toksvig and of Julie Anne Toksvig; one *s* two *d*. *Educ:* Mamaroneck High Sch., NY; Tormead, Guildford; Girton Coll., Cambridge (MA Hons). *Television* includes: No 73, 1980–86; Whose Line Is It Anyway?; Behind the Headlines, 1993; Great Journeys, 1993; The Big One, 1993; Island Race, 1995; Call My Bluff, 1996–; *stage* includes: (performer) Nottingham Playhouse Rep., 1980; Open Air Theatre, Regent's Park, 1980; (jt writer) The Pocket Dream, 1993; (performer and writer) Big Night Out at the Little Sands Picture Palace, 1995; (writer and performer) Sandi Toksvig's Christmas Cracker, Festival Hall, 2009; Sandi Toksvig Live (touring), 2012; *radio* includes: Loose Ends, 1994–; I'm Sorry I Haven't a Clue, 1998–; Presenter: Midweek, 1996; Excess Baggage; Chair, The News Quiz, R4, 2006–15. Chancellor, Univ. of Portsmouth, 2012–. *Publications: for children:* Tales from the Norse's Mouth, 1994; Unusual Day, 1997; If I Didn't Have Elbows, 1998; Super-saver Mouse, 1999; Super-saver Mouse to the Rescue, 2000; The Troublesome Tooth Fairy, 2001; Hitler's Canary, 2005; Girls Are Best, 2008; A Slice of the Moon, 2015; *plays:* The Pocket Dream, 1994; Bully Boy, 2011; *travel books:* Great Journeys of the World, 1994; (with John McCarthy) Island Race, 1995; *novels:* Whistling for the Elephants, 1999; Flying Under Bridges, 2001; Melted Into Air, 2006; Valentine Grey, 2012; *non-fiction:* The Chain of Curiosity, 2009; Peas and Queues: the minefield of modern manners, 2013. *Recreations:* golf, ski-ing, scuba diving, sewing. *Club:* Ivy.

TOLAND, Prof. John Francis, FRS 1999; FRSE; N. M. Rothschild & Sons Professor of Mathematical Sciences and Director, Isaac Newton Institute for Mathematical Sciences, University of Cambridge, since 2011; Fellow, St John's College, Cambridge, since 2011; *b* 28 April 1949; *s* of late Joseph Toland and Catherine Toland (*née* McGarvey); *m* 1977, Susan Frances Beck, *d* of late (James Henry) John Beck. *Educ:* St Columb's Coll., Derry (Alumnus Illustrissimus 2007); Queen's Univ., Belfast (BSc 1970, DSc 1993); Univ. of Sussex (MSc 1971, DPhil 1973). Batelle Advanced Studies Centre, Geneva, 1973; Lectr in Maths and Fellow of Fluid Mechanics Res. Inst., Univ. of Essex, 1973–79; Lectr in Maths, UCL, 1979–82; Prof. of Maths, Univ. of Bath, 1982–2011; EPSRC Sen. Res. Fellow, 1997–2002. Scientific Dir, Internat. Centre for Math. Scis, Edinburgh, 2002–10; Hon. Professor of Mathematics: Univ. of Edinburgh, 2003–; Heriot-Watt Univ., 2003–. Vis. lectr, Europe, Australia, USA. Chm., Mathematical Scis sub-panel, REF 2014. Pres., LMS, 2005–07. FRSE 2003. Hon. Fellow, UCL, 2008. Hon. DSc: QUB, 2000; Edinburgh, 2007; Heriot-Watt, 2007; DUniv Essex, 2009. Sen. Berwick Prize, LMS, 2000; Wolfson Res. Merit Award, 2008, Sylvester Medal, 2012, Royal Soc. *Publications:* mathematical research papers, mainly in nonlinear analysis. *Recreations:* horses, walking the dog. *Address:* Isaac Newton Institute for Mathematical Sciences, 20 Clarkson Road, Cambridge CB3 0EH. *T:* (01223) 335999. *E:* director@newton.ac.uk.

TOLEDANO, Daniel Ze'ev; QC 2009; *b* London, 2 Nov. 1969; *s* of Pinchas and Cynthia Toledano; *m* 1998, Dr Jan Raeburn; two *s* one *d*. *Educ:* Haberdashers' Aske's Sch., Elstree; Jesus Coll., Cambridge (BA 1st Cl. Hons 1992; MA). Called to the Bar, Inner Temple, 1993; in practice as barrister, specialising in commercial law, 1993–. *Recreations:* music and opera, theatre, running, ski-ing. *Address:* One Essex Court, Temple, EC4Y 9AR. *T:* (020) 7583 2000, *Fax:* (020) 7583 0118. *E:* dtoledano@oeclaw.co.uk.

TOLER; *see* Graham-Toler, family name of Earl of Norbury.

TOLHURST, Rear Adm. John Gordon, CB 1995; FRAeS; defence consultant, retired; *b* 22 April 1943; *s* of Cdre Virgil George Tolhurst, CBE, VRD, RNR, and Elizabeth Mary Tolhurst. *Educ:* Sevenoaks Sch. Joined RN 1961; Commanding Officer: HMS Berwick, 1977; HMS Exeter, 1984; Asst Dir, Naval Warfare, 1986; Commodore, HMS Nelson, 1988; CO HMS Invincible, 1990; ADC to the Queen, 1990; Flag Officer: Sea Trng, 1992–96; Scotland, Northern England and NI, 1996–97; Mil. Dep. to Head of Defence Export Services, MoD, 1997–2002. Man. Dir, JGT Associates Ltd, 2006–12. Chm., Aerospace & Defence Bd, Reed Exhibns, 2005–08. Chm., Clarion Defence and Security Ltd, 2008–12. Trustee: RNLI, 2002–12 (Chm., Ops Cttee, 2002–12); RNLI Heritage Trust, 2012–15. Dir, Royal Naval Club and Royal Albert Yacht Club, 2014–. Younger Brother, Trinity House. FRAeS 2004. *Recreations:* motor boating, classic cars, travelling, gardening. *E:* jgtolhurst2@gmail.com.

TOLHURST, Kelly Jane; MP (C) Rochester and Strood, since 2015; *b* Borstal, Rochester, 23 Aug. 1978; *d* of Morris and Christine Tolhurst. *Educ:* Chapter High Sch. Dir, Skipper UK Ltd, Rochester, 2002–. Mem. (C) Medway Council, 2011–. Member: Eur. Scrutiny Select Cttee, 2015–; Business, Innovation and Skills Select Cttee, 2015–. *Address:* House of Commons, SW1A 0AA. *T:* (020) 7219 5387. *E:* kelly.tolhurst.mp@parliament.uk.

TOLLEMACHE, family name of **Baron Tollemache**.

TOLLEMACHE, 5th Baron *cr* 1876; **Timothy John Edward Tollemache,** KCVO 2015; Lord-Lieutenant of Suffolk, 2003–14 (Vice Lord-Lieutenant, 1994–2003); farmer and landowner; *b* 13 Dec. 1939; *s* of 4th Baron Tollemache, MC, DL, and Dinah Susan (*d* 1998), *d* of late Sir Archibald Auldjo Jamieson, KBE, MC; *S* father, 1975; *m* 1970, Alexandra Dorothy Jean, *d* of late Col Hugo Meynell, MC; two *s* one *d*. *Educ:* Eton. Commissioned into Coldstream Guards, 1959; served Kenya, Persian Gulf and Zanzibar, 1960–62; Course of Estate Management at Sandringham, Norfolk, 1962–64. President: E Anglian Productivity Assoc., 1984–88; Suffolk Agricl Assoc., 1988; Chm., CLA, Suffolk, 1990–93; Vice Pres., Suffolk Assoc. of Local Councils, 1996–2003 (Pres., 1978–96). Mem., Firearms Consultative Cttee, 1995–98. Chairman, Lord Chancellor's Advisory Committee: on JPs, 2003–14; on Gen. Comrs for Income Tax, 2003–10. Vice President: Cheshire Red Cross, 1980–; Suffolk Horse Soc., 2009–14; President: Friends of Ipswich Museums, 1980–96; CAB, Ipswich & dist, 1998–2005; Suffolk Historic Churches Trust, 2003– (Chm., 1996–2003); Music for Country Churches, Suffolk, 2003–14; Army Benevolent Fund, Suffolk, 2003–14; Suffolk Co. Scout Council, 2003–14; RLSS, Suffolk, 2003–14; Friends of Suffolk Record Office, 2003–14; Britain Australia Soc., Suffolk, 2003–14; E Anglia Reserve Forces and Cadets Assoc., 2003–; Suffolk Reserve Forces and Cadets Assoc., 2006–14; Jt Pres., NORCAS, 2006–14. Chairman: HHA (E Anglia), 1979–83; Bury St Edmunds Cathedral Appeal, 1986–90; Suffolk Family History Soc., 1988–2003; Suffolk Lieutenancy Honours Cttee, 2006–. Patron: Suffolk Accident Rescue Service, 1983–2014; E Suffolk Assoc. for the Blind, 1992–2006; Suffolk, BRCS, 2003–14; NSPCC, Suffolk, 2003–14; ACRE, Suffolk, 2003–14; Magistrates' Assoc., Suffolk, 2003–14; Suffolk Wildlife Trust, 2003–; Disability Care Enterprise, 2003–11; Help the Aged, Suffolk, 2003–14; Gainsborough House Mus., 2003–14; Friends of St Edmundsbury Cathedral, 2003–14; Suffolk Preservation Soc., 2003– (Vice Patron, 1992–2003); SSAFA (formerly SSAFA Forces Help), 2003– (Pres., 1996–2003); E Anglia Children's Hospices, 2005–14; St Matthew's Housing, 2005–14; Friends of Royal Hosp. Sch., 2006–14; St Nicholas Hospice, Bury St Edmunds, 2006–14; Suffolk Community Foundn, 2006–14; E Anglian Air Ambulance, 2006–14; Soc. of E Anglia Watercolourists (formerly RWS, E Anglia), 2006–14; Flatford Mill Campaign, 2007–14; Red Lodge Marine Detachment, 2009–14; East Coast Hospice, 2009–14; Suffolk Heraldry Soc., 2011–14; Guildhall Project, 2011–14; Ipswich Sch. Music Appeal, 2012–. Vice-Patron: Just 42, 2005–14; Almshouse Assoc., 2009–14; Ipswich Umbrella Trust, 2009–14. Gov., Framlingham Coll., 2003–14. Mem., 1996–2010, Trustee, 2000–10, SAS Regtl Assoc. DL Suffolk, 1984. KStJ 2004 (CStJ 1988) (Chm., 1982–89, Pres., 2003–13, St John's Council for Suffolk). *Recreations:* shooting, fishing, natural history. *Heir: s* Hon. Edward John Hugo Tollemache [*b* 12 May 1976; *m* 2007, Sophie, *d* of Iain Johnstone, *qv*; two *s*]. *Address:* Helmingham Hall, Stowmarket, Suffolk IP14 6EF. *Clubs:* White's, Pratt's, Special Forces.

TOLLEMACHE, Sir Lyonel (Humphry John), 7th Bt *cr* 1793, of Hanby Hall; JP, DL; *b* 10 July 1931; *s* of Maj.-Gen. Sir Humphry Tollemache, 6th Bt, CB, CBE, DL and Nora Priscilla (*d* 1990), *d* of John Taylor; *S* father, 1990; *m* 1960, Mary Joscelyne, *d* of late Col William Henry Whitbread, TD; one *s* two *d* (and one *s* decd). *Educ:* Uppingham Sch.; RMA Sandhurst; RAC Cirencester. FRICS. Major, Coldstream Guards, retd 1963. Member: Melton and Belvoir RDC, 1969–74, Melton BC, 1974–87 (Mayor, 1981–82); Leics CC, 1985–97. Gov., Royal Star and Garter Home, Richmond, 1985–2001. High Sheriff 1978–79, JP 1978, DL 1980, Leics. *Heir: s* Richard John Tollemache, JP [*b* 4 May 1966; *m* 1992, Amanda, *er d* of Gordon Phillips; one *s* two *d*]. *Address:* The Old Vicarage, Buckminster, Grantham NG33 5RT.

TOLLERVEY, Prof. David, PhD; FRS 2004; FRSE; Wellcome Trust Principal Research Fellow, since 1997, Professor of Cell Biology, since 2008, and Director, Wellcome Trust Centre for Cell Biology, since 2011, University of Edinburgh; *b* 19 Sept. 1955; *s* of Robert Muirhead Tollervey and late Isabella Stewart Tollervey (*née* Davidson); partner, Dr Hildegard Tekotte; three *s* one *d*. *Educ:* George Heriot's Sch., Edinburgh; Univ. of Edinburgh (BSc Hons 1977); Darwin Coll., Cambridge (PhD 1981). Postdoctoral Fellow, Univ. of Calif, San Francisco, 1980–83; Charge de Recherche, Institut Pasteur, Paris, 1984–88; Gp Leader, EMBL, Heidelberg, 1988–97. FRSE 2004. *Publications:* over 200 papers and reviews in scientific jls. *Recreations:* sailing, hill-walking. *Address:* Wellcome Trust Centre for Cell Biology, University of Edinburgh, King's Buildings, Edinburgh EH9 3JR. *T:* (0131) 650 7092, *Fax:* (0131) 650 7040. *E:* d.tollervey@ed.ac.uk. *Club:* Fisherrow Yacht.

TOLLEY, Carole Anne Bennett; Director of Resources Head Office and Corporate Finance, Ministry of Defence, 2011–15; *b* 4 May 1955; *d* of Sidney and Monica Cox; *m* 1982, Graeme Neil Tolley; two *s*. *Educ:* Lady Margaret Hall, Oxford (BA Hons PPE 1977); University Coll. London (MSc Econs of Public Policy 1978). ACCA 1998. Joined MoD as admin trainee, 1978; Private Secretary: to Chief Scientific Advr, 1983; to Under-Sec. of State for Armed Forces, 1984–85; Assistant Director: Finance and Admin (Nuclear), 1985–86; Naval Pay and Conditions, 1987–88; Financial Mgt Develt Unit, 1988–89; Secretariat (Air Staff), 1989–92; Civilian Mgt, 1992–95; Dir, Intelligence Progs and Resources, 1995–97; rcds 1998; Director: Defence Mgt Trng, 1999–2001; Resources and Plans (Centre), 2001–04; Dir Gen., Financial Mgt, 2004–07; Dir Gen., subseq. Dir, Scrutiny, 2007–11. *Recreations:* music, hiking, wind-surfing, gardening, su doku.

TOLLEY, David Anthony, FRCS, FRCSEd; Consultant Urological Surgeon, and Director, Scottish Lithotriptor Centre, Western General Hospital, Edinburgh, 1980–2012; President, Royal College of Surgeons of Edinburgh, 2009–12; *b* Warrington, 29 Nov. 1947; *s* of Frank Stanley Tolley and Elizabeth Tolley (*née* Dean); *m* 1970, Judith Finn; three *s* one *d*. *Educ:* Manchester Grammar Sch.; King's Coll. Hosp. Med. Sch. (MB BS 1970). FRCS 1975; FRCSEd 1983; FRCPE 2006; FDSRCSE (*ad hominem*) 2007. House Surgeon and Physician, 1970–71, Sen. Surgical Registrar (Urol.), 1976–77, King's Coll. Hosp.; Sen. Urol Registrar, Yorks Regl Trng Scheme, 1977–80. Lectr in Human Morphol., Southampton Univ., 1971–72; Lectr in Anatomy and Fulbright Fellow, Univ. of Texas at Houston, 1972. Past Pres., Endourol. Soc. Mem. Council, 2000–05, Hon. Treas., 2006–09, RCSEd; Mem. Council, British Assoc. of Urological Surgeons, 1978–79, 1995–2000. Hon. FCSHK 2010; Hon. FCSSL 2010. *Publications:* Urinary Stones, 2002; contrib. *c* 150 articles on kidney stone disease, urinary tract cancer and urology. *Clubs:* New (Edinburgh); Luffness New Golf.

TOLLEY, Rev. Canon George, SOSc; Hon. Canon, 1976–98, Hon. Assistant, 1990–2007, now Canon Emeritus and Dean's Chaplain, since 2007, Sheffield Cathedral; *b* 24 May 1925; *s* of George and Elsie Tolley, Old Hill, Staffordshire; *m* 1947, Joan Amelia Grosvenor; two *s* one *d*. *Educ:* Halesowen Grammar Sch.; Birmingham Central Tech. Coll. (part-time); Princeton Univ., USA; Lincoln Theol Coll., 1965–67; Sheffield Univ. (MA). BSc, MSc, PhD (London); FRSC; FIMMM. Rotary Foundation Fellow, Princeton Univ., 1949–50. Head, Department of Chemistry, College of Advanced Technology, Birmingham, 1954–58; Head of Research and Experimental Dept, Allied Ironfounders Ltd, 1958–61; Principal, Worcester Tech. College, 1961–65; Senior Director of Studies, Royal Air Force Coll., Cranwell, 1965–66; Principal, Sheffield Coll. of Technology, 1966–69, Sheffield City Polytechnic, 1969–82; Manpower Services Commission: Dir, Open Tech Unit, 1983–84; Head, Quality Branch, 1984–85; Chief Officer, Review of Vocational Qualifications, 1985–86; Advr, NCVQ, 1986–88; Advr, Trng Commn, then Trng Agency, 1988–90. Ordained deacon, 1967, priest, 1968; Curate, St Andrew's, Sharrow, 1967–90. Chairman: Council, Plastics Inst., 1959–61; Further Educn Adv. Cttee, Food, Drink and Tobacco Ind. Trng Bd, 1974–78; Bd, Further Educn Curriculum Unit, 1978–82; BTec Continuing Educn Cttee, 1983–85; Council of the Selly Oak Colls, Birmingham, 1984–92; Adv. Bd, Pitman Exams Inst., 1987–92; Central Sheffield Univ. Hosps NHS Trust, 1992–95; Pres., Inst. of Home Economics, 1987–90; Vice-Pres., Educn 2000, 1990–92; Hon. Sec., Assoc. of Colleges of Further and Higher Educn, 1975–82; Member: CNAA (Chm., Cttee for Business and Management Studies, 1972–83); Yorks and Humberside Economic Planning Council, 1976–79; RAF Trng and Educn Cttee, 1975–80; Governing Body, Derbyshire Coll. of Higher Educn, 1984–87. Member Council: PSI, 1981–89; RSA, 1983–92. Dep. Chm., S Yorks Foundn, 1986–90. Hon. Treas., SOSc, 1995–2010. Sheffield Church Burgess. CCMI. Hon. FCP; Hon. Fellow: Sheffield City Polytechnic, 1982; CGLI, 1984; Inst. of Trng and Develt, 1989. Hon. DSc: Sheffield, 1984; CNAA, 1986; DUniv Open, 1984. *Publications:* Meaning and Purpose in Higher Education, 1976; A History of the Sheffield Church Burgesses, 1998; Bringing Prayer to Life, 2001; Julian of Norwich: saying 'yes' to God, 2010; many papers relating to plastics and education in British and foreign journals. *Recreation:* savouring remembered sounds. *Address:* 74 Furniss Avenue, Dore, Sheffield S17 3QP.

TOLPUTT, John Nigel, MA; Head, The Purcell School, 1999–2007; *b* 1 May 1947; *s* of Basil Tolputt and Betty Durrant; *m* 1971, Patta Davis; one *s* one *d*. *Educ:* St John's Coll., Cambridge (MA); Bristol Univ. (Cert Ed 1969). Teacher, Bromsgrove Sch., 1969–74; Head of English and Drama, Cranleigh Sch., 1974–87; Head, Rendcomb Coll., 1987–99. Chm., Nat. Schs' SO, 2009– (Trustee, 2008–). FRSA 1994. Hon. ARAM 2005. *Recreation:* theatre. *Address:* Mill End, Sir George's Place, Steyning, Sussex BN44 3LS.

TOLSON, James; Member (Lib Dem) Dunfermline West, Scottish Parliament, 2007–11; *b* 26 May 1965; *s* of Robert Archibald Tolson and Jane Wallace Tolson; *m* 1996, Alison Patricia Lord. *Educ:* Napier Univ., Edinburgh (BSc Hons Network Computing). Fitter/turner, Babcock Rosyth Defence Ltd, 1981–2000; Sales Advr, British Sky Broadcasting, 2003–07. Member (Lib Dem): Dunfermline DC, 1992–96; Fife Council, 1995–2007. Scottish Parliament: Lib Dem Shadow Minister for Communities and Sport, 2007–08; Mem., Local Govt and Communities Cttee, 2007–11; Lib Dem spokesperson on Local Govt and Transport, 2008–11. Contested (Lib Dem) Dunfermline West, Scottish Parlt, 2011. *Recreations:* gardening, travel, cycling.

TOLSON, Robin Stewart; QC 2001; **His Honour Judge Tolson;** a Circuit Judge, since 2014; *b* 21 June 1958; *s* of Trevor and Vivian Tolson; *m* 1987, Carol Atkinson (*d* 2011); two *d*. *Educ:* Hull Grammar Sch.; Jesus Coll., Cambridge (MA). Called to the Bar, Inner Temple, 1980; in practice as barrister, 1980–2014, specialising in family law and local govt admin. law; Asst Recorder, 1998–2000; Recorder, 2000–14; Dep. High Court Judge, 2004–14. *Publications:* Care Plans and the Human Rights Act, 1998. *Recreation:* tennis. *Address:* Oxford Combined Court Centre, St Aldates, Oxford OX1 1TL.

TOM, Peter William Gregory, CBE 2006; Chairman, Breedon Aggregates (formerly Marwyn Materials) Ltd, since 2008; *b* 26 July 1940; *s* of late John Gregory Tom and Barbara Tom (*née* Lambden); one *s* three *d* (and one *s* decd). *Educ:* Hinckley Grammar Sch. Joined Bardon Hill Quarries Ltd, 1956: Man. Dir, 1977; Chm. and Chief Exec., 1985; merged with: Evered plc, 1991, to form Evered Bardon; CAMAS, 1997, to form Aggregate Industries plc, Chief Exec., 1997–2005, non-exec. Chm., 2006–07. Director: Leicester FC plc, 1997–; Leicester Rugby Club Ltd, 1997–; Leicester Tigers Ltd, 1997–; Bardon Mill House Co., 2003–; Tigers Events Ltd, 2003–; Aga Foodservice Gp plc, 2004–; Rise Rocks Ltd, 2005–; Global Botanical Research Ltd, 2006–; Nature's Defence (UK) Ltd, 2006–; Nature's Defence Investments Ltd, 2006–; Macquarie Growth Income Group, 2006–; Mayven UK plc, 2006–; Mayven International Ltd, 2006–. Chm., Quarry Products Assoc., 1997. *Address:* Breedon Aggregates Ltd, Breedon Quarry, Main Street, Breedon on the Hill, Derby DE73 8AP.

TOMALIN, Claire; writer; *b* 20 June 1933; *d* of late Emile Delavenay and of Muriel Herbert; *m* 1st, 1955, Nicholas Osborne Tomalin (*d* 1973); one *s* two *d* (and one *s* one *d* decd); 2nd, 1993, Michael Frayn, *qv*. *Educ:* Hitchin Girls' Grammar Sch.; Dartington Hall Sch.; Newnham Coll., Cambridge (MA). Publishers' reader and editor, Messrs Heinemann, Hutchinson, Cape, 1955–67; Evening Standard, 1967–68; New Statesman: Asst Literary Editor, 1968–70; Literary Editor, 1974–77; Literary Editor, Sunday Times, 1979–86. Stage play, The Winter Wife, Nuffield, Southampton, 1991; CD, Songs of Muriel Herbert, 2009. Curator: Mrs Jordan, The Duchess of Drury Lane, Kenwood, 1995; Hyenas in Petticoats, Grasmere and NPG, 1997. Trustee, Nat. Portrait Gallery, 1992–2002. Registrar, Royal Literary Fund, 1984– (Mem. Cttee, 1974–99; Life Vice-Pres., 2000). Vice-Pres., English PEN, 1997–. Trustee, Wordsworth Trust, 2001–03 (Fellow, 2003–). FRSL 1974 (Mem. Council, 1993–2000; Vice-Pres., 2003–). Freeman, City of London, 2012. Hon., Mem., Magdalene Coll., Cambridge, 2003; Hon. Fellow: Lucy Cavendish Coll., Cambridge, 2003; Newnham Coll., Cambridge, 2004. Hon. LittD: UEA, 2005; Birmingham, 2005; Greenwich, 2006; Cambridge, 2007; Open, 2008; Goldsmiths, 2009; Roehampton, 2011; Portsmouth, 2012. *Publications:* The Life and Death of Mary Wollstonecraft, 1974; Shelley and his World, 1980; Parents and Children, 1981; Katherine Mansfield: a secret life, 1987; The Invisible Woman: the story of Nelly Ternan and Charles Dickens, 1990 (NCR, Hawthornden, and James Tait Black Prizes, 1991; filmed 2014); Mrs Jordan's Profession, 1994; Jane Austen: a life, 1997; (ed) Mary Shelley, Maurice, 1998; Several Strangers: writing from three decades, 1999; Samuel Pepys: the unequalled self, 2002 (Whitbread Prize, 2002; Samuel Pepys Award, 2003; Rose Mary Crawshay Prize, 2003); Thomas Hardy: the time-torn man, 2006; (ed) Selected Poems of Thomas Hardy, 2006; (ed) Selected Poems of John Milton, 2008; (ed) Selected Poems of John Keats, 2009; Charles Dickens: a life, 2011; literary journalism. *Recreations:* walking, gardening, music. *Address:* c/o David Godwin, 55 Monmouth Street, WC2H 9DG.

TOMALIN, Michael Hardwick, CMG 2014; OBE 1990; non-executive Director, National Bank of Abu Dhabi, since 2013 (Group Chief Executive, 1999–2013; Executive Director, 2012–13); *b* London; *s* of Edward Thomas Tomalin and Florence Mary Tomalin; *m* 1980, Carolyn Anne Rowe; one *s* one *d*. *Educ:* Univ. of the Witwatersrand (BA Hons); Harvard Business Sch. (SMP). Investment Manager, N. M. Rothschild, London, 1972–76; Barclays Group: Hd, Planning, Johannesburg, 1976, London, 1977–80; Caribbean Dir, Barbados, 1980–82; Exec. Dir, Hong Kong, 1982–84; Man. Dir, Wellington, NZ, 1984–85; Country Manager, Tokyo, 1985–90; Chief Exec., Barclays Private Banking, London, 1992–99. Chm., Nat. Bank of Abu Dhabi Private Bank Suisse SA, Geneva. Advr, Abdul Lateef Jameel Gp, Jeddah. Hon. DSc Banking and Finance, Sch. of Finance, IFS, 2015. *Recreations:* golf, bridge, travel. *Address:* Vinnicks, Highclere, Hants RG20 9SB; Trafalgar Gardens, W8. St Regis, Saadiyat, Abu Dhabi, UAE. *E:* mhtomalin@gmail.com. *Clubs:* Brooks's, Hurlingham; Thurlestone Golf; Saadiyat Golf.

TOMBS, family name of **Baron Tombs**.

TOMBS, Baron *cr* 1990 (Life Peer), of Brailes in the county of Warwickshire; **Francis Leonard Tombs,** Kt 1978; FREng; Chairman: Rolls-Royce, 1985–92 (Director, 1982–92); Old Mutual South Africa Trust, 1994–98; *b* 17 May 1924; *s* of Joseph and Jane Tombs; *m* 1949, Marjorie Evans (*d* 2008); three *d*. *Educ:* Elmore Green Sch., Walsall; Birmingham Coll. of Technology; BSc (Econ) Hons, London. GEC, 1939–45; Birmingham Corp., 1946–47; British Electricity Authority, Midlands, then Central Electricity Authority, Merseyside and N Wales, 1948–57; Gen. Manager, GEC, Erith, 1958–67; Dir and Gen. Man., James Howden & Co., Glasgow, 1967–68; successively Dir of Engrg, Dep. Chm., Chm., South of Scotland Electricity Bd, 1969–77; Chm., Electricity Council, 1977–80. Chairman: Weir Group, 1981–83; Turner & Newall, subseq. T & N, 1982–89; Director: N. M. Rothschild & Sons, 1981–94; Shell-UK, 1983–94. Pres., Molecule Theatre Ltd, 1993–96 (Chm., 1985–92). Member: Nature Conservancy Council, 1978–82; Standing Commn on Energy and the Environment, 1978–; SERC, 1982–85; Chairman: Engrg Council, 1985–88; ACARD, 1985–87 (Mem., 1984–87); ACOST, 1987–90. Mem., H of L, 1990–2015; Chm., H of L Select Cttee on Sustainable Develt, 1994–95; Mem., H of L Select Cttee on Sci. and Technol., 1997–2005. Pres., IEE, 1981–82; Vice-Pres., Fellowship of Engrg, 1982–85; Vice-Pres., Engineers for Disaster Relief, 1985–94. Chm., Assoc. of British Orchestras, 1982–86. FREng (FEng 1977); FRAeS 1994, Hon. FRAeS 1995; Hon. FIChemE 1985; Hon. FICE 1986; Hon. FIProdE 1986; Hon. FIMechE 1989; Hon. FIET (Hon. FIEE 1991); Hon. FRSE 1996; Hon. Mem., British Nuclear Energy Soc. Pro-Chancellor and Chm. Council, Cranfield Inst. of Technol., 1985–91; Chancellor, Strathclyde Univ., 1991–97 (Hon. LLD 1976; DUniv 1991). Freeman, City of London, 1980; Liveryman, 1981–, and Prime Warden, 1994–95, Goldsmiths' Co. Hon. DTech Loughborough, 1979; Hon. DSc: Aston, 1979; Lodz, Poland, 1980; Cranfield, 1985; Bradford, 1986; City, 1986; Surrey, 1988; Nottingham, 1989; Warwick, 1990; Cambridge, 1990; DSc(Eng) QUB, 1986; DEd CNAA, 1989. KSG 2002. *Publications:* Power Politics, 2011. *Recreation:* music. *Address:* Honington Lodge, Honington, Shipston-upon-Stour, Warwickshire CV36 5AA.

TOMBS, Sebastian Martineau, FRIAS; Chief Executive, Architecture and Design Scotland, 2005–09; *b* 11 Oct. 1949; *s* of late Dr David M. Tombs and Joan (*née* Parley); *m* 1988, Eva Heirman; four *s* two *d*. *Educ:* Bryanston; Corpus Christi Coll., Cambridge (BArch, DipArch). ACIArb 1977, MCIArb 2002; FRIAS 1992. RMJM, Edinburgh, 1975–76; Roland Wedgwood, Edinburgh, 1976–77; Fountainbridge Housing Assoc., Edinburgh, 1977–78; Housing Corp., 1978–81; Housing Dept, Edinburgh DC, 1982–86; Depute Sec., 1986–94, Sec., 1995–2005, RIAS. Founder and first Sec., Scottish Ecological Design Assoc., 1991–94 (Chm., 1994–97); Founder and first Chm., Assoc. Planning Supervisors, 1995–97. Co-chair, Anthroposophical Soc. in GB, 2011–13. Contested (Lib Dem): Edinburgh N and Leith, Scottish Parlt, 1999, 2003; Edinburgh N and Leith, 2001; Kilmarnock and Loudoun, 2010. *Recreations:* designing cartograms, choral music, doggerel, sketching, reverse cycling, house building (www.lismoreislandhome.com). *Address:* Baile Geamhraidh, Isle of Lismore, Argyll PA34 5UL.

TOMEI, Anthony Laurence, CBE 2013; Director, Nuffield Foundation, 1995–2012; *b* 1 June 1949; *s* of late Laurence Stephen Tomei and Dora Tomei (*née* Myring); *m* 1977, Nicola Bourn; one *s* two *d*. *Educ:* St Joseph's Coll., London; Univ. of Sussex (BSc); Univ. of Manchester (MSc). Physics teacher, VSO, Johore, Malaysia, 1970–72; teacher, William Ellis Sch., London, 1972–74; Nuffield Foundation: Research Grants Officer, 1977–82; Asst Dir, 1982–95; on secondment to DCSF, 2007. Vis. Prof., Dept of Educn, KCL, 2012–. Trustee: Bristol Exploratory, 1983–86; Rutherford Trust, 1992–96; Integrated Educn Fund (NI), 1992–97. Governor: Nuffield Chelsea Curriculum Trust, 1980–88; Pensions Policy Inst., 2005– (Mem. Council, 2012–). Trustee: Bell Educnl Trust, 2012–; DEBRA, 2012–14; Assoc. of Charitable Foundns, 2015–. Governor: Parliament Hill Sch., London, 1992–2000; City and Islington Coll., 2013–. *Recreations:* tennis, family life, reading, walking. *Club:* MCC.

TOMES, Susan Mary; musician (pianist) and writer; *b* 26 May 1954; *d* of Albert Henry Tomes and Catherine Mary Tomes (*née* Brodie); one *d*; *m* 2004, Dr Robert Philip. *Educ:* RSAMD; King's Coll., Cambridge (BA 1975 (first woman to read Music), MA 1978). ARCM 1970. Solo recitalist and concerto soloist, 1979–; Founder Member: Domus Piano Quartet, 1979–95 (Gramophone Awards, 1985, 1995); Florestan Trio, 1995–2012 (Gramophone Award, Classic CD Award, 1999; Royal Philharmonic Soc. Award, 2000); Pianist, Gaudier Ensemble, 1993–. Prof., GSMD, 1995–; Guest Prof., Eur. Chamber Music Acad., 2013–. Mem., internat. music competition juries, 2011–. Affiliate Artist, Centre for Musical Perf. and Creative Practice, Univ. of Cambridge, 2010–; presents annual masterclasses, London, 2010–. Contributor: The Guardian, 2000–; Financial Times, 2002–; book reviewer: The Independent, 2006–; The Guardian, 2008–. Writer and presenter of talks on music, BBC Radio 3 and Radio 4. Mem., Acad. Adv. Bd, Centre for Hist. and Analysis of Recorded Music, 2005–09. Cobbett Medal, Musicians' Co., 2013. *Publications:* Beyond the Notes: journeys with chamber music, 2004; A Musician's Alphabet, 2006; (contrib.) Cambridge Companion to Recorded Music, 2009; Out of Silence, 2010; Sleeping in Temples, 2014. *Recreations:* reading, letter-writing, walking. *E:* susan@susantomes.com. *W:* www.susantomes.com.

TOMIĆ, Dr Ivica; Ambassador of the Republic of Croatia to the Court of St James's, 2009–12; *b* Split, Croatia, 13 March 1941; *s* of Jakov and Marija Tomić; *m* 1964, Jasna Berković; two *s*. *Educ:* Coll. of Maritime Studies, Univ. of Rijeka (Master Mariner 1966); Coll. of Foreign Trade, Univ. of Zagreb; Univ. of Wales Inst. of Sci. and Technol. (OECD Schol. 1974); Dept of Economy, Univ. of Zagreb (MBA 1977); Univ. of Oregon (Fulbright Schol. 1977); Faculty of Marine and Transportation Studies, Univ. of Rijeke (PhD 1983). Cadet, third, second and Chief Officer, Adriatic Shipping Co., Split, 1960–71; University of Zagreb: Institute of Transportation Studies: Res. Fellow and Project manager, 1972–83;

teaching asst, Intercollegiate Transportation Studies, 1974–76; Hd, Transportation Technol., 1978–80; Asst Prof., Faculty of Maritime and Transportation Studies, Univ. of Rijeka, 1987. Asst Minister, Min. of Transportation and Maritime Affairs (Maritime sect.), 1983–93; Nat. Coordinator for Adriatic Danube Initiative, Min. of Foreign Affairs and Eur. Integration, 1993; Ambassador to: Slovakia, 1993–96; to Turkey, 1996–2000; Nat. Coordinator for Adriatic-Ionian Initiative, Min. of Foreign Affairs, 2000–01; Ambassador to Egypt, 2001–05; Asst Minister of Foreign Affairs, 2005–09; Perm. Rep. of Croatia to IMO, 2009–12. White Double Cross Order, 2nd class (Slovakia), 1997; Order of Prince of Branimir with Necklace (Croatia), 1998. *Publications:* Transportation Technology of Ports, 1986. *Recreations:* sailing, swimming, tennis, art, reading.

TOMKA, Dr Peter; Judge, International Court of Justice, since 2003 (Vice-President, 2009–12; President, 2012–15); *b* Banská Bystrica, 1 June 1956; *s* of Ján Tomka and Kornélia Tomková; *m* 1990, Zuzana Halgašová; one *s* one *d*. *Educ:* Charles Univ. Law Sch., Prague (LLM 1979; DJur 1981; PhD Internat. Law 1985). Lectr, Charles Univ., 1984–91; Asst Legal Advr, Min. of Foreign Affairs, Czechoslovakia, 1986–91; Legal Advr, Perm. Mission of Czechoslovakia to UN, NY, 1991–92; Ambassador and Dep. Perm. Rep., 1993–94, Actg Perm. Rep., 1994–97, of Slovakia to UN; Dir for Legal Affairs, 1997–98 and Dir-Gen. for Legal and Consular Affairs, 1998–99, Min. of Foreign Affairs, Slovakia; Ambassador and Perm. Rep. of Slovakia to UN, NY, 1999–2003; Agent of Slovakia before Internat. Court of Justice, 1993–2003. United Nations: Chm., Sixth (Legal) Cttee, Gen. Assembly, 1997; Mem., Internat. Law Commn, 1999–2003; Chm., Cttee of Legal Advrs on Public Internat. Law, Council of Europe, 2001–02; Member: Perm. Court of Arbitration, 1994–; American Soc., 2000–; Eur. Soc. Internat. Law, 2004–; Panel of Arbitrators, Annex VII, UN Law of the Sea Convention, 2004–; Panel of Arbitrators, Internat. Center for Settlement of Investment Disputes, 2005–; Curatorium, Hague Acad. of Internat. Law, 2013–. Associate Mem., Inst. de droit internat., 2011–. Hon. Bencher, Middle Temple, 2012. *Recreations:* chess, ski-ing, art, history. *Address:* International Court of Justice, Peace Palace, Carnegieplein 2, 2517 KJ The Hague, Netherlands. *T:* 703022468, *Fax:* 703022420. *E:* p.tomka@icj-cij.org.

TOMKINS, Patrick Lindsay, QPM 2006; HM Chief Inspector of Constabulary for Scotland, 2007–09; *b* 20 Aug. 1960; *m* Susan; one *s* one *d*. *Educ:* Hastings Grammar Sch.; King's Coll., London (BA Hons); Royal Coll. of Defence Studies; Open Univ. (MA 2012). With Sussex Police, 1979–93; Chief Superintendent, 1993–97, Comdr, 1997–99, Metropolitan Police; Asst Inspector of Constabulary, 1999–2002; Chief Constable, Lothian and Borders Police, 2002–07. *Recreations:* fly fishing, reading. *Club:* New (Edinburgh).

TOMKYS, Sir (William) Roger, KCMG 1991 (CMG 1984); DL; HM Diplomatic Service, retired; Master of Pembroke College, Cambridge, 1992–2004; *b* 15 March 1937; *s* of late William Arthur and Edith Tomkys; *m* 1963, Margaret Jean Abbey; one *s* one *d*. *Educ:* Bradford Grammar Sch.; Balliol Coll., Oxford (Domus Scholar; 1st cl. Hons Lit.Hum.). Entered Foreign Service, 1960; MECAS, 1960; 3rd Sec., Amman, 1962; 2nd Sec., FCO, 1964; 1st Sec., Head of Chancery, Benghazi, 1967; Planning Staff, FCO, 1969; Head of Chancery, Athens, 1972; Counsellor, seconded to Cabinet Office, 1975; Head of Near East and North Africa Dept, FCO, 1977–80; Counsellor, Rome, 1980–81; Ambassador: to Bahrain, 1981–84; to Syria, 1984–86; Asst Under Sec. of State and Principal Finance Officer, FCO, 1987–89; Dep. Under Sec. of State, FCO, 1989–90; High Comr, Kenya, 1990–92. Chm., Arab-British Chamber of Commerce, 2004–10. DL Cambridgeshire, 1996. Liveryman: Drapers' Co., 2003–; Merchant Taylors' Co., 2004–. Commendatore dell'Ordine al Merito, 1980; Order of Bahrain, 1st cl., 1984. *Address:* Croydon House Farm, Lower Road, Croydon, Royston, Herts SG8 0EF. *Clubs:* Royal & Ancient Golf (St Andrews); Royal Worlington and Newmarket Golf.

TOMLIN, Rt Rev. Graham Stuart; *see* Kensington, Area Bishop of.

TOMLINSON, Baron *cr* 1998 (Life Peer), of Walsall in the co. of West Midlands; **John Edward Tomlinson;** *b* 1 Aug. 1939; *s* of Frederick Edwin Tomlinson, headmaster, and Doris Mary Tomlinson. *Educ:* Westminster City Sch.; Co-operative Coll., Loughborough; Nottingham Univ. (Dip. Polit. Econ. Social Studies); MA (Industrial Relations) Warwick, 1982. Sec., Sheffield Co-operative Party, 1961–68; Head of Research Dept, AUEW, 1968–70; Lectr in Industrial Relations, 1970–74. MP (Lab) Meriden, Feb. 1974–1979; PPS to Prime Minister, 1975–76; Parly Under-Sec. of State, FCO, 1976–79, and ODM, 1977–79. Sen. Lectr in Industrial Relations and Management, later Hd of Social Studies, Solihull Coll. of Tech., 1979–84. MEP (Lab) Birmingham W, 1984–99; Eur. PLP spokesman on budgetary control, 1989–99. Member: EU Select Cttee, H of L, 1999–2002 and 2005–; Audit Cttee, H of L, 2009–12; H of L Rep., Convention on the Future of Europe, 2002–03; Mem., Jt Cttee on Conventions, 2006–. Chairman: Adv. Cttee, London Sch. of Commerce, 2004–; Assoc. of Ind. HE Providers, 2006–12; Bd, Anglia Ruskin Univ., 2010–; Assoc. Business Executives, 2011–. Mem., Council of Europe. Trustee, Industry and Parlt Trust, 1988–2007 (Pres., 2002–07). Pres., British Fluoridation Soc., 1998–2011. Contested (Lab) Warwicks N, 1983. *Publications:* Left, Right: the march of political extremism in Britain, 1981. *Address:* House of Lords, SW1A 0PW. *Club:* West Bromwich Labour.

TOMLINSON, Sir Bernard (Evans), Kt 1988; CBE 1981; DL; MD; FRCP, FRCPath; Chairman, Northern Regional Health Authority, 1982–90; Emeritus Professor of Pathology, University of Newcastle upon Tyne, since 1985; Consultant Neuropathologist, Newcastle upon Tyne Hospitals NHS Trust (formerly Newcastle Area Health Authority, then Newcastle Health Authority), since 1976; *b* 13 July 1920; *s* of James Arthur Tomlinson and Doris Mary (*née* Evans); *m* 1944, Betty Oxley; one *s* one *d*. *Educ:* Brunts Sch., Mansfield; University Coll. and University Coll. Hosp., London (MB BS 1943, MD 1962). FRCP 1965; FRCPath 1964. Trainee Pathologist, EMS, 1943–47; served RAMC as Specialist Pathologist, 1947–49 (Major). Newcastle upon Tyne General Hospital: Sen. Registrar, Pathology, 1949–50; Consultant Pathologist, 1950–53; Sen. Consultant Pathologist, 1953–82; Hon. Lectr in Path., Univ. of Newcastle upon Tyne, 1960–71, Hon. Prof., 1972–85. Hon. Mem. Scientific Staff, MRC Neurochemical Pathology Unit, 1987–; Founding Chm., Res. Gp on Dementia, World Fedn of Neurology, 1984–87. Chm., Jt Planning Appts Cttee, DHSS, 1986–90; Mem., Disablement Services Authority, 1987–91. Leader of ind. enquiry into London's health services, 1991–92; non-exec. Dir, Newcastle City Health Trust, 1994–95. Mem. Council, Assoc. of Clinical Pathologists, 1965–68; Privy Council Mem., RPharmS, 1990–95 (Hon. Mem., 1997). President: British Neuropathol Soc., 1979–81; NE Alzheimer Disease Soc., 1985–. Hon. Mem., Amer. Neurol Assoc., 1997. Hon. MD Newcastle upon Tyne, 1993. Chm., Friends of Durham Cathedral, 1991–94. DL Tyne and Wear 1988. Dorothy Russell Lectr and Medallist, British Neuropathol Soc., 1989; Gold Medal Sci. Award, 3rd Internat. Conf. on Alzheimer's Disease, Padua, 1992. *Publications:* articles and book chapters on neuropath., partic. on path. of brain injury, brain changes in old age and on dementia. *Recreations:* gardening, golf, music, walking. *Address:* Greyholme, Wynbury Road, Low Fell, Gateshead, Tyne and Wear NE9 6TS.

TOMLINSON, David Redvers; His Honour Judge Tomlinson; a Circuit Judge, since 2010; *b* Aylesbury, 6 April 1954; *s* of David Cecil Macalister Tomlinson and Audrey Tomlinson (*née* Freeman); *m* 1988, Jane Packer; one *s* two *d*. *Educ:* Lord Williams' Sch., Thame; Univ. of Leeds (LLB). Called to the Bar, Inner Temple, 1977; Asst Recorder, 1997–2000; Recorder, 2000–10. Gov., Waldegrave Sch., 2003–. *Recreations:* tennis, ski-ing, gardening, theatre, cinema. *Address:* Southwark Crown Court, English Grounds, Battlebridge Lane, SE1 2HU. *Club:* Garrick.

TOMLINSON, Heather Ann; International Associate, Saudi Arabia, National College for Teaching and Leadership, 2013–14; *b* 23 June 1953; *d* of Kenneth and Joan Veneear; two *d*; *m* Charles George Sisum. *Educ:* Cheshunt Grammar Sch.; Univ. of Sheffield (BEd Hons; MEd; DPSE). Teacher, Rotherham LEA, 1976–80; Teacher, 1981–88, Educn Advr, 1988–98, Sheffield LEA; Regl Advisory Teacher, S Yorks and Humberside LEAs, 1988–90; Asst Dir of Educn, Nottingham City LEA, 1998–2001; Corporate Dir of Educn, Nottingham CC, 2001–04; Dir of Educn and Lifelong Learning, 2004–05, Corporate Dir of Children and Young People's Services, 2005–09, Bristol CC; Interim Dir of Educn, Birmingham CC, 2009–10; Interim Strategic Dir, Children and Young People, Derby CC, 2011; Interim Exec. Dir, Brighton and Hove CC, 2012–13; Interim Asst Dir of Educn, Merton LBC, 2015. *Recreations:* sailing, photography, running. *Club:* St Mawes Sailing (Cornwall).

TOMLINSON, Sir John (Rowland), Kt 2005; CBE 1997; operatic bass; *b* 22 Sept. 1946; *s* of Rowland and Ellen Tomlinson; *m* 1969, Moya (*née* Joel); one *s* two *d*. *Educ:* Accrington GS; Manchester Univ. (BSc Civil Engrg); Royal Manchester Coll. of Music. Since beginning career with Glyndebourne in 1970, has sung over 150 operatic bass roles with ENO, Royal Opera, Covent Garden, Opera North, Scottish Opera, and in Geneva, Lisbon, Bologna, Florence, Milan, Copenhagen, Amsterdam, Stuttgart, Bayreuth, Berlin, Dresden, Madrid, Santiago, Tokyo, Vienna, Paris, Bordeaux, Avignon, Aix-en-Provence, Orange, San Diego, San Francisco, Pittsburgh, Vancouver, NY, Munich, Chicago, Salzburg, Hamburg, Boston, Frankfurt, Barcelona, Rome and Antwerp; also broadcasts and recordings; best known for interpretations of Wagner bass and bass-baritone rôles, incl. Hans Sachs, Wotan (Bayreuth, 1988–98), Wanderer, Hagen, Gurnemanz and The Flying Dutchman (Bayreuth, 2003, 2004, 2006), König Marke, König Heinrich; other rôles include: Boris Godunov, Figaro, Leporello, Sarastro, Fiesco, Arkel, Balstrode, Kingfisher, Dosifey, four villains in Hoffman, Méphistophélès, Zaccharia, Claggart, Bluebeard, Baron Ochs, Rocco, Golaud, Moses, Philip II, Attila, Oberto, Green Knight, The Minotaur and Borromeo. Hon. FRNCM 1996; Hon. FGS 2011. Hon. Dr: Sussex, 1997; Manchester, 1998; Hon. DMus: Nottingham, 2004; Birmingham, 2004. Singer of the Year, Royal Philharmonic Soc., 1991, 1998, 2007; Grammy Award (for Bartok, Cantata Profana), 1993; Reginald Goodall Award, Wagner Soc., 1996; Evening Standard Opera Award, 1998; Southbank Show Opera Award, 1999; Society's Special Award, Laurence Olivier Awards, 2007; Gold Medal, Royal Philharmonic Soc., 2014. *Address:* c/o Music International, 13 Ardilaun Road, Highbury, N5 2QR. *T:* (020) 7359 5183. *W:* www.johntomlinson.org.

TOMLINSON, Justin Paul; MP (C) North Swindon, since 2010; Parliamentary Under-Secretary of State, Department for Work and Pensions, since 2015; *b* 1976; *m* 2012, Joanne Wheeler. *Educ:* Harry Cheshire High Sch., Kidderminster; Oxford Brookes Univ. (BA Business and Mktg 1999). Sales and Mktg Manager, First Leisure, 1999–2000; Mktg Exec., Point to Point, 2000; Dir, TB Mktg Solutions Ltd, 2000–10. Mem. (C), Swindon BC, 2000–10. Mem., Public Accounts Cttee, 2012–14. Contested (C) N Swindon, 2005. *Address:* House of Commons, SW1A 0AA.

TOMLINSON, Lindsay Peter, OBE 2005; Director, Legal and General Investment Management, since 2012; *b* Derby, 7 Oct. 1951; *s* of Dr Peter and Dr Jean Tomlinson; *m* 1973, Sarah Caroline Anne Martin; four *s* one *d*. *Educ:* Clifton Coll.; St John's Coll., Cambridge (BA 1972). FIA 1975. Asst Actuary, Commercial Union, 1973–77; Sen. Consultant, Metropolitan Pensions Assoc., 1977–81; Sen. Investment Manager, Provident Mutual, 1981–87; Dir, BZW Investment Mgt, 1987–94; Chief Exec., BZW Asset Mgt, 1994–95; Barclays Global Investors: Jt Chief Exec., 1995–97; Chief Exec., Europe, 1997–2005; Vice Chm., 2005–09; Man. Dir, BlackRock, 2009–11. Chairman: FTSE Policy Gp, 1997–2009; Investment Mgt Assoc., 2003–05; Code Cttee, Takeover Panel, 2006–14; Nat. Assoc. of Pension Funds, 2009–11 (Dir, 2007–13); Dir, Financial Reporting Council, 2007–11. Non-exec. Dir, Legal and General plc, 2013–15. Chm., Handcross Park Sch., 2011–. *Recreations:* ballet, opera, football, Rugby, cricket. *Address:* Beacon Hall, Slough Green Lane, Warninglid, W Sussex RH17 5SL. *T:* (01444) 461308.

TOMLINSON, Michael James; MP (C) Mid Dorset and North Poole, since 2015; *b* Wokingham, 1 Oct. 1977; *s* of Howard and Heather Tomlinson; *m* 2000, Frances Mynors; one *s* two *d*. *Educ:* Univ. of London (BA Hons Classics). Called to the Bar, Middle Temple, 2002 (Queen Mother's Schol.). *Recreations:* all sports, reading, going to the beach with my family. *Address:* House of Commons, SW1A 0AA. *Clubs:* Hamworth Cricket, Poole Hockey.

TOMLINSON, Sir Michael (John), Kt 2005; CBE 1997; Chairman, Myscience Ltd, since 2008; *b* 17 Oct. 1942; *s* of Edith Cresswell and Jack Tomlinson; *m* 1965, Maureen Janet; one *s* one *d*. *Educ:* Oakwood Technical High Sch., Rotherham; Bournemouth Boys' Sch.; Durham Univ. (BSc Hons Chem.); Nottingham Univ. (post-grad. Cert Ed (First Div.)). Chemistry teacher, Henry Mellish GS, Nottingham, 1965–69; Head of Chemistry, Ashby-de-la-Zouch GS, 1969–77; on secondment to ICI, 1977; Chief Inspector (Schools), HM Inspectorate of Schs, 1989–92; Dep. Dir, 1992–95, Dir of Inspection, 1995–2000, Office for Standards in Education; HM Chief Inspector of Schs, 2000–02; Chm., Hackney Educn Trust, 2002–07; Chief Advr for London Schs, DCSF, 2008–09. Educn Comr for Birmingham, 2014–. Non-executive Director: RM plc, 2004–13; Piscari Ltd, 2008–10. Chair, 14–19 Govt Working Gp, 2003–04. Director: Sci. Yr 2002; Planet Science, 2003. Pres., ASE, 2005. Mem., Adv. Educn Bd, LSO, 2008–. Chm., Basildon Excellence Panel, 2014–. Trustee: Comino Foundn, 2002–11; Industrial Trust, 2003–07; Business Dynamics, 2004–07; Farming and Countryside Educn, 2008–13; Baker-Dearing Trust, 2010–; Oxford Trust, 2010–14. Chm. Govs, RSA Acad., 2008–12; Governor: Merchant Taylors' Sch., Northwood, 2007–12, 2014–; Mem. Ct, Univ. of Herts, 2009–14 (Gov., 2004–09). Pres., RASE, 2010–12. FRSA. Hon. FCGI 2009. Freeman, City of London, 2013; Liveryman, Merchant Taylors' Co., 2014. Hon. DEd: Wolverhampton, 2004; De Montfort, Nottingham Trent, 2005; Durham, 2007; Manchester Metropolitan, 2008; Hon. DLitt Warwick, 2011; Hon. DCL: UEA, Northumbria, 2005; Leicester, 2006; Hon. Dr: Middlesex, 2005; York, 2012; Buckinghamshire, 2012. Chem. Soc. Award in Chem. Educn (Bronze Medal), 1975. Silver Jubilee Medal, 1977. *Publications:* New Movements in the Study and Teaching of Chemistry, 1975; Organic Chemistry: a problem-solving approach, 1977; Mechanisms in Organic Chemistry: case studies, 1978; BP educn service contribs, 1974–78; 14–18: a new vision for secondary education, 2013; articles in professional jls. *Recreations:* gardening, fishing, food and wine, reading. *Address:* Brooksby, Mayhall Lane, Chesham Bois, Amersham, Bucks HP6 5NR. *T:* (01494) 726967.

TOMLINSON, Prof. Richard Allan, FSA; Director, British School at Athens, 1995–96; *b* 25 April 1932; *s* of James Edward Tomlinson and Dorothea Mary (*née* Grellier); *m* 1957, Heather Margaret Murphy (*d* 2009); three *s* one *d*. *Educ:* King Edward's Sch., Birmingham; St John's Coll., Cambridge (BA, MA). FSA 1970. Asst, Dept of Greek, Univ. of Edinburgh, 1957; University of Birmingham: Asst Lectr 1958, Lectr 1961, Sen. Lectr 1969, Prof., 1971–95, now Emeritus, Dept of Ancient History and Archaeology; Head of Sch. of Antiquity, 1988–91. British School at Athens: Editor, Annual, 1978–91; Chm. Managing Cttee, 1991–95; Vice-Pres., 2001–. *Publications:* Argos and the Argolid, 1972; Greek Sanctuaries, 1976; Epidaurus, 1983; (ed) Greek Architecture, by A. W. Lawrence, 5th edn 1996; (contrib.) Sir Banister Fletcher, A History of Architecture, 20th edn, 1996; Greek Architecture, 1989; The Athens of Alma-Tadema, 1991; From Mycenae to Constantinople, 1992; Greek and Roman Architecture, 1995; (jtly) A Gazetteer of the Cyrene Necropolis, 2009; articles in Annual of British Sch. at Athens, Jl of Hellenic Studies, Amer. Jl of Archaeology, etc. *Recreations:* architecture, walking. *Address:* 15 Eymore Close, Birmingham B29 4LB.

TOMLINSON, Prof. Sally, PhD; Goldsmiths Professor of Policy and Management in Education, Goldsmiths College, London University, 1992–98, now Emeritus; Senior Research Fellow, Department of Education, University of Oxford, since 1998; *b* 22 Aug. 1936; *d* of Clifford Gilmore Entwistle and Alice Nora Stubbs; *m* 1957, Brian Joseph Tomlinson, Sqdn Ldr, RAF (retd); one *s* two *d*. *Educ:* Macclesfield Grammar Sch.; Liverpool Univ. (BA Hons); Birmingham Univ. (MSocSci); Warwick Univ. (PhD); Manchester Univ. (PGCE). Lectr and Sen. Lectr, West Midlands Coll. of Educn, 1970–74; Sen. Res. Fellow, Warwick Univ., 1974–78; Lectr, then Sen. Lectr, later Prof. of Educn, Lancaster Univ., 1978–91; Prof. of Educn, UC Swansea, 1991–92; Dean, Faculty of Educn, 1992–95, Pro Warden, 1994–97, Goldsmiths' Coll., London Univ. Sen. Associate Mem., St Antony's Coll., Oxford, 1984–85; Res. Associate, Centre for Res. in Ethnic Relns, 2002–10, Associate Fellow, Dept of Sociol., 2014–, Univ. of Warwick. Vis. Prof., Univ. of Wolverhampton, 2008–11. Leverhulme Emeritus Fellow, 2009. Member: Court, Univ. of Bradford, 2001–04; Council, Univ. of Glos, 2001–09; Council, S Worcestershire Coll., 2011–15. Mem., Commn on Future of Multi-ethnic Britain, 1998–2000. Trustee: Africa Educational Trust, 1992–2012 (Vice-Chair, 2003–04; Chair, 2005–09); Learning from Experience Trust, 1992–99; Educn Extra, 1992–2000. *Publications:* (with John Rex) Colonial Immigrants in a British City, 1979; Educational Subnormality, 1981; A Sociology of Special Education, 1982, repr. 2012; Ethnic Minorities in British Schools, 1983; Home and School in Multicultural Britain, 1984; (ed with Len Barton) Special Education and Social Interests, 1984; (with David Smith) The School Effect, 1989; Multicultural Education in White Schools, 1990; Educational Reform and its consequences, 1994; (jtly) The Assessment of Special Educational Needs: whose problem?, 1994; (ed with Maurice Craft) Ethnic Relations and Schooling, 1995; Education 14–19: critical perspectives, 1997; (ed jtly) School Effectiveness for Whom?, 1998; (jtly) Hackney Downs: the school that dared to fight, 1999; Education in a Post-Welfare Society, 2001, 2nd edn 2005; (with Tony Edwards) Selection isn't Working, 2002; Race and Education: policy and politics in Britain, 2008; (ed with T. Basit) Social Inclusion and Higher Education, 2012; Ignorant Yobs? Low Attainers in a Global Knowledge Economy, 2013; The Politics of Race, Class and Special Education, 2014; many contribs to books and learned jls. *Recreations:* walking, politics. *Address:* Department of Education, University of Oxford, 15 Norham Gardens, Oxford OX2 6PY.

TOMLINSON, Prof. Stephen, CBE 2007; MD; FRCP; FMedSci; Provost, Cardiff University, 2006–10, now Professor Emeritus of Medicine; Hon. Consultant Physician, Cardiff and Vale NHS Trust, since 2001; *b* 20 Dec. 1944; *s* of Frank Tomlinson and Elsie Tomlinson (*née* Towler); *m* 1970, Christine Margaret Hope; two *d*. *Educ:* Hayward GS, Bolton; Univ. of Sheffield (MB ChB Hons 1968; MD 1976). FRCP 1982. SHO and Registrar, Sheffield Royal Infirmary, 1969–72; Registrar, Middlesex Hosp., 1972–73; MRC Clin. Res. Fellow, 1973–75, Hon. Lectr, 1974–76, Middlesex Hosp. Med. Sch.; Sen. Registrar, Middlesex Hosp., 1975–76; Sir Henry Wellcome Travelling Fellow, MIT, 1976–77; Sheffield University: Wellcome Trust Sen. Res. Fellow in Clin. Sci., 1977–80; Wellcome Sen. Lectr, 1980–85; Hon. Reader in Medicine, 1982–85; Hon. Cons. Physician, Sheffield HA, 1977–85; Manchester University: Prof. of Medicine, 1985–2001; Dean of Med. Sch. and Faculty of Medicine, 1993–97, of Faculty of Medicine, Dentistry and Nursing, 1997–99; Hon. Consultant Physician, Manchester Royal Infirmary, 1985–2001; Vice-Chancellor, UWCM, 2001–04; Provost, Wales Coll. of Medicine, Biol., Life and Health Scis and Dep. Vice-Chancellor, Cardiff Univ., 2004–06. Mem., Ind. Rev. of Modernising Med. Careers (Tooke Inquiry), 2006. Mem. Bd, UK Res. Integrity Office, 2008–12. Chairman: Assoc. of Clin. Profs of Med., 1996–99; Fedn of Assocs of Clin. Profs, 1997–2000; Tropical Health and Educn Trust, 2007–10; ASH Wales, 2007–13; R&D Cttee, Velindre NHS Trust, 2002–12 (Mem. Bd, 2002–12); Wales for Africa Health Links Network, 2012–14 (Vice-Chm., 2011–12); Founder Chm., Vale for Africa, 2009–13. Pres., Assoc. of Physicians, 2002–03 (Hon. Sec. and Treas., 1988–98); Exec. Sec., Council of Heads of Med. Schs, 1997–99; Mem., GMC, 2001–03 (Mem., Educn Cttee, 1999). Member: Bd, QAA, 2003–07 (Chm., Wales Adv. Cttee, 2003–07); Bd, Nat. Coordinating Centre for Cancer, 2008–12 (Dep. Chm., 2010–12); HEFC Wales, 2013– (Mem., Res., Innovation and Educn Cttee, 2013–); Adv. Council, UWC Atlantic Coll., 2013–; Council, Univ. of Exeter, 2013–. Founder FMedSci, 1998. Hon. DSc Sheffield, 2012. *Publications:* papers on stimulus-response coupling and intracellular signalling in endocrine tissues; the orgn of health services for people with diabetes; international health. *Recreations:* arts and health, history of medicine, good food and wine (mine and others!). *Address:* Cardiff University, Room 0.46, Main Building, Park Place, Cardiff CF10 3AT. *Club:* Medical Pilgrims (Hon. Sec., 1995–2012).

TOMLINSON, Rt Hon. Sir Stephen (Miles), Kt 2000; PC 2011; **Rt Hon. Lord Justice Tomlinson;** a Lord Justice of Appeal, since 2010; *b* 29 March 1952; *s* of Enoch Tomlinson and Mary Marjorie Cecilia Tomlinson (*née* Miles); *m* 1980, Joanna Kathleen Greig; one *s* one *d*. *Educ:* King's Sch., Worcester (schol.); Worcester Coll., Oxford (schol.; Eldon Law Schol.; MA; Hon. Fellow, 2012). Called to the Bar, Inner Temple, 1974, Bencher, 1990 (Treas., 2014). Lectr in Law, Worcester Coll., Oxford, 1974–76. QC 1988; a Recorder, 1995–2000; a Dep. High Court Judge, 1996–2000; a Judge of the High Ct of Justice, QBD, 2000–10; Judge in Charge of Commercial Court, 2003–04. Chm., Assoc. of Average Adjusters, 2009. Gov., Shrewsbury Sch., 2003–12. *Recreations:* gardening, family, walking, ski-ing, cricket. *Address:* Royal Courts of Justice, Strand, WC2A 2LL. *Clubs:* Garrick, MCC.

TOMOS, Linda; Director, CyMAL: Museums Archives and Libraries Wales, Welsh Government (formerly Welsh Assembly Government), since 2003; *b* Llanelli, 1 April 1952; *d* of Arthur Horatio Williams and Mary Eileen Williams; *m* 1974, Merfyn Wyn Tomos; two *s*. *Educ:* Didcot Girls' Grammar Sch.; Univ. of Wales, Aberystwyth (BLib Hist. and Librarianship). MCLIP 1975. Librarian: Coll. of Librarianship, Wales, 1974–76; Clwyd CC, 1976–79; Dir, Wales Information Network, 1990–2003. Chairman: BBC Educn Broadcasting Council Wales, 1999–2003; Liby and Information Services Council Wales, 2000–03; Mem., Welsh Adv. Council on Telecommunications, 1999–2003; Dir, Careers Wales NW, 2001–03. *Publications:* numerous reports and articles relating to electronic information management. *Recreation:* researching Welsh history and culture. *Address:* Welsh Government, Aberystwyth SY23 3UR. *T:* 0300 062 2098. *E:* Linda.Tomos@wales.gsi.gov.uk.

TOMPKINS, Hon. Sir David (Lance), KNZM 1999; Judge of the High Court of New Zealand, 1983–97, Acting Judge, 1998–2003; Judge, Court of Appeal of Kiribati, since 2001, of Vanuatu, since 2002, and of Tuvalu, since 2009; *b* 26 July 1929; *s* of Arthur Lance Tompkins, Judge, Supreme Court of NZ, and Marjorie Rees Tompkins (*née* Manning); *m* 1956, Erica Lya Felicity Ann Faris; two *s* one *d*. *Educ:* Whitiora Primary Sch.; Southwell Sch., Hamilton; King's Coll., Auckland; Auckland University Coll. (LLB 1951). Served 1st Field Regt, RNZA, TA, 1949–59 (Capt. 1958). Partner, Tompkins & Wake, Hamilton, 1953–71; Barrister, 1971; QC (NZ) 1974; Courts Martial Appeal Court Judge, 1982–83; Exec. Judge, Auckland High Court, 1989–92; Judge of the Privy Council and Court of Appeal of Tonga, 1995–; Judge, Criminal Appeal Div., Court of Appeal of NZ, 1996–97; Justice of Appeal, Court of Appeal of Fiji, 1997–2005; Judge, Supreme Court of Vanuatu, 1998–. Chairman: Council of Legal Educn, 1992–97; Nat. Case Mgt Cttee, 1994–97; Electricity Mkt Appeal, 1998–. Pres., Hamilton Dist Law Soc., 1969–71; Mem. Council, 1969–71, Vice Pres., 1979–81, NZ Law Soc.; Mem. Council, 1976–83, Life Mem., 1987, Law Asia; Pres., Auckland Medico-Legal Soc., 1994–95. Associate, Arbitrators' and Mediators' Inst., 1997; Mem., LEADR, 1997–. Pro-Chancellor, 1979–80, Chancellor, 1980–85, Waikato Univ. Outward Bound Trust: Vice-Pres., 1981–83; Pres., 1983–84; Guardian, 1992–. Chm., Chelsea Park Trust, 2002–. Hon. Dr Waikato Univ., 1986. Silver Jubilee Medal, 1977; Commemoration Medal (NZ), 1990. *Recreations:* sailing, croquet, ski-ing, computers, trout fishing, cooking. *Address:* PO Box 25 153, St Heliers, Auckland, New Zealand. *Clubs:* Hamilton (Life Mem.), Northern (Auckland).

TOMPKINS, Steven Charles, RIBA; Director, Haworth Tompkins Architects Ltd, since 1991; *b* 5 Oct. 1959; *s* of Keith and Patricia Tompkins; *m* 1986, Katherine Claire Tyndall; two *s*. *Educ:* Wellingborough Grammar Sch.; Univ. of Bath (BSc, BArch 1983). RIBA 1992. Arup Associates, London, 1984–86; Bennetts Associates, London, 1987–90. Major commissioned projects include: Royal Court Th., 2000; Coin St Housing, London, 2001; Regent's Park Open Air Th., 1998–2000; Almeida Th. at Gainsborough Studios, 2000, at King's Cross, 2001; Hayward Gall., 2005; Young Vic Th., 2006; Egg Th., Bath, 2006; Nat. Theatre Studio, 2008; Snape Maltings, 2009; London Liby, 2010; RCA, 2013; Everyman Th., Liverpool, 2014 (RIBA Stirling Prize); Chichester Fest. Th., 2014; NT Future project, 2015; other Haworth Tompkins clients include: RCA; Aldeburgh Music; Donmar Th.; Grosvenor Estates; AXA; Peabody Trust; Chichester Fest. Th.; London Film Sch. Trustee, Young Vic Th. *Recreations:* painting, theatre, mountain walking. *Address:* Haworth Tompkins Ltd, 33 Greenwood Place, NW5 1LB. *T:* (020) 7250 3225, *Fax:* (020) 7267 1391. *E:* steve.tompkins@haworthtompkins.com.

TOMPKINSON, Stephen Philip Patrick; actor; *b* 15 Oct. 1965; *s* of Brian and Josephine Tompkinson; one *d* by former marriage. *Educ:* St Bede's RC High Sch., Lytham St Anne's; Central Sch. of Speech and Drama. *Theatre* includes: No One Sees the Video, Royal Court, 1990; Across the Ferry, Bush, 1991; Love's Labours Lost, Women Laughing, Manchester Royal Exchange, 1992; Tartuffe, nat. tour, 1997; Art, Wyndham's, 2000; Arsenic and Old Lace, Strand, 2003; Rattle of a Simple Man, Comedy Th., 2004; Cloaca, Old Vic, 2004; Charley's Aunt, nat. tour, 2007; The Revenger's Tragedy, Manchester Royal Exchange, 2008; Sign of the Times, nat. tour, 2009; Faith and Cold Reading, Live Th. Newcastle, 2011; Spamalot, Playhouse, 2012; *films* include: Treacle, 1987; Brassed Off, 1996; Hotel Splendide, 2000; Tabloid TV, 2001; *television* includes: And a Nightingale Sang, 1989; The Deep Blue Sea, 1994; A Very Open Prison, 1995; First Signs of Madness; Flint Street Nativity, 1999; Lucky Jim, In Denial of Murder, 2003; Murder at the Vicarage, 2004; The Last Detective; New Tricks; Taming of the Shrew; Marian Again; DCI Banks, 2010, 2011, 2014; *series:* Drop the Dead Donkey, 1990; All Quiet on the Preston Front, 1994 and 1995; Ballykissangel, 1996–98; Grafters, 1998; In Deep, 2001 and 2003; Bedtime, 2001; Ted and Alice; Wild at Heart, 2005, 2006, 2007, 2008, 2009, 2010, 2011; Stephen Tompkinson's African Balloon Adventure, 2009; Stephen Tompkinson's Australian Balloon Adventure, 2010; Truckers, 2013. Hon. Fellow, Univ. of Central Lancashire, 1998. *Recreations:* cricket, snooker. *Address:* c/o Conway van Gelder Grant, Third Floor, 8/12 Broadwick Street, W1F 8HW. *T:* (020) 7287 0077. *E:* nick@conwayvg.co.uk. *Club:* Gerry's.

TOMS, Edward Ernest; Director, Studio Gallery, London, 1983–2002; Partner, Studio Gallery and Picture Framers, since 2003; *b* 10 Dec. 1920; *s* of Alfred William and Julia Harrington Toms; *m* 1946, Veronica Rose (*d* 2003), Dovercourt, Essex; three *s* one *d*. *Educ:* St Boniface's Coll.; Camel's Head 6th Form; HM Dockyard Sch., Devonport; Staff Coll., Camberley (psc), Nat. Defence Coll. (jssc). Electrical Engrg apprentice, HM Dockyard, Devonport, 1937–41; war service 1941–45; Trooper, Royal Tank Regt, Western Desert, PAIFORCE, Egypt, 1943; Captain Seaforth Highlanders; Special Forces, W Desert, Italy, Balkans, NW Europe; Regular Army, 1946, Seaforth Highlanders and QO Highlanders; Brigade Major, Berlin, 1959–61; Trng Major, 8th Bn Argyll and Sutherland Highlanders, 1961–63; CO QO Highlanders Depot, 1963–65; CO 3rd Bn Gordon Highlanders, 1965–67; Col GS (UK Cs-in-C Cttee), 1967–69. Principal, Home Civil Service, 1969; Asst Sec., Dept of Employment, 1973; seconded to Diplomatic Service as Counsellor, Bonn and Vienna, 1977–81; Internat. Labour Advr, FCO, 1981–83. Dir, Porcelain & Pictures Ltd, 1983–2002. *Recreations:* reading, writing, hill-walking (founder Mem., Aberdeen Mountain Rescue Assoc., 1964). *Address:* 25 Spanton Crescent, Hythe, Kent CT21 4SF. *Clubs:* Special Forces, Chelsea Arts, Army and Navy.

TOMSETT, Alan Jeffrey, OBE 1974; Director, Associated British Ports Holdings PLC, 1983–92 (Finance Director, 1983–87); chartered accountant; *b* 3 May 1922; *s* of Maurice Jeffrey Tomsett and Edith Sarah (*née* Mackelworth); *m* 1948, Joyce May Hill; one *s* one *d*. *Educ:* Trinity School of John Whitgift, Croydon; Univ. of London (BCom). JDipMA. Hodgson Harris & Co., Chartered Accountants, London, 1938. Served War, with RAF, 1941–46 (Middle East, 1942–45). Smallfield Rawlins & Co., Chartered Accountants, London, 1951; Northern Mercantile & Investment Corp. Ltd, 1955; William Baird & Co. Ltd, 1962–63. British Transport Docks Board, later Associated British Ports: Dep. Chief Accountant, 1963; Chief Accountant, 1964; Financial Controller, 1970; Bd Mem., 1974–87 (Finance Dir, 1974–85). Churchwarden, St John's, Shirley, 1988–92. FCA, FCMA, CPFA, FCIS, FCILT (Vice-Pres., 1981–82, Hon. Treasurer, 1982–88, CIT); FRSA 1969. *Address:* 14 Colts Bay, Craigwell on Sea, Bognor Regis, W Sussex PO21 4EH. *T:* (01243) 267211.

TONBRIDGE, Bishop Suffragan of; *no new appointment at time of going to press.*

TONBRIDGE, Archdeacon of; *see* Mansell, Ven. C. N. R.

TONEGAWA, Prof. Susumu, PhD; Picower Professor of Biology and Neuroscience, Department of Biology, Massachusetts Institute of Technology, since 2002; Director: RIKEN-MIT Center for Neural Circuit Genetics, since 2008; RIKEN Brain Science Institute, Japan, since 2009; *b* Nagoya, 5 Sept. 1939; *s* of Tsutomo and Miyoko Tonegawa; *m* 1985, Mayumi Yoshinari; one *s* one *d* (and one *s* decd). *Educ:* Kyoto Univ. (BS); Univ. of San Diego (PhD 1968). Postgraduate work: Univ. of California, San Diego, 1968–69; Salk Inst., San Diego, 1969–70; Mem., Basel Inst. of Immunology, 1971–81; Prof. of Biology and Neurosci., Center for Cancer Res., Dept of Biol., MIT, 1981–; Investigator, Howard Hughes Med. Inst., 1988–; Dir, Picower Center for Learning and Memory, MIT, 1994–2006. Avery Landsteiner Prize, Ges. für Immunologie, 1981; Gairdner Foundn Internat. Award, 1983; Nobel Prize for Physiology or Medicine, 1987. *Address:* Department of Biology, Massachusetts Institute of Technology, 77 Massachusetts Avenue, 46–5285, Cambridge, MA 02139–4307, USA.

TONER, Charles Gerard; Group Chairman, Barratt Developments PLC, 2002–08; *b* 20 Jan. 1942; *s* of Hugh and Sally Toner; *m* 1967, Valerie Anne Metcalfe; one *s* one *d*. *Educ:* Holy Cross Acad., Edinburgh. Mgt trainee in industry, 1959–64; Abbey National Plc, 1964–99: various mgt posts in branch network, 1969–86; Gen. Manager, branches and agencies, 1986–88; Ops Dir, 1988–92; Dir, Plc Bd and Man. Dir, New Business Div., 1992–93; Man. Dir, Retail Bank Div., 1993–96; Dep. Gp CEO, 1996–99, retd. Non-executive Director: NHBC, 1996–2002 (Dep. Chm., 1999–2002); MSB Internat. (Sen. non-exec. Dir), 1999–2002; FCE Bank Plc (Ford), 1999–2007. Trustee, Hospice of St Francis, Berkhamsted, 2009– (Chm., 2010–). *Recreations:* golf, tennis, travel. *Address:* Trundles, Crossfield Close, Shootersway, Berkhamsted, Herts HP4 3NT. *T:* (01442) 862985. *E:* charles.toner@btinternet.com. *Clubs:* Rotary (Berkhamsted Bulbourne); Berkhamsted Golf.

TONEY, Terence; Regional Director, East Asia, British Council, since 2011; *b* 23 Aug. 1952; *s* of Norman Toney and Margaret Toney (*née* Taglione); *m* 1977, Young Hae Kim; one *s*. *Educ:* Cardinal Hinsley Grammar Sch.; King's Coll. London (BA Hons German and Philosophy); Inst. of Educn, Univ. of London (PGCE); Univ. of Lancaster (MA). Lectr in English, British Centre, Sweden, 1975–76; English teacher, Dortmund, 1976–78; Lectr in English, Hokkaido Univ., Japan, 1980–82; British Council, 1983–: Asst Consultant, English Lang., London, 1983–85; Asst English Lang. Officer, Tokyo, 1985–87; English Lang. Officer,

Colombia, 1987–90; Acad. Dir, Cultura Inglesa, São Paulo, 1990–94; Director: Korea, 1994–99; Japan, 1999–2002; Educnl Enterprises, 2002–04; Customer Services, 2004–06; Regl Dir, SE Europe, 2006–09; Hd of Business Transformation, 2009–11. *Recreations:* travelling, reading, foreign languages, walking, swimming, cycling. *Address:* British Council, 10 Spring Gardens, SW1A 2BN.

TONGA, HM the King of; **King Lavaka Tupou VI;** *b* 12 July 1959; *s* of HM the King of Tonga, King Taufa'ahau Tupou IV and Halaevalu Mata'aho 'Ahome'e; *S* brother, 2012; *m* 1982, Heuifanga Nanasipau'u Vaea; two *s* one *d. Educ:* Leys Sch., Cambridge. Tongan Defence Services, 1982–98. Minister of Foreign Affairs and of Defence, 1998–2004; Prime Minister of Tonga, 2000–06; High Comr of Tonga to Australia, 2008–12. Former Chm., Tonga Communications Corp. *Heir:* HRH Prince 'Ukukalala [*b* 1985; *m* 2012, Hon. Sinaitakala Fakafanua; one *s* one *d*]. *Address:* The Palace, Nuku'alofa, Tonga.

TONGE, family name of **Baroness Tonge**.

TONGE, Baroness *cr* 2005 (Life Peer), of Kew in the London Borough of Richmond upon Thames; **Jennifer Louise Tonge,** FRSPH; *b* 19 Feb. 1941; *d* of late Sidney Smith and Violet Smith (*née* Williams); *m* 1964, Dr Keith Angus Tonge (*d* 2013); two *s* (one *d* decd). *Educ:* Dudley Girls' High Sch.; University Coll. London (MB BS 1964). FRSPH (FRIPHH 1997). GP and family planning doctor, 1964–96; Hd, Women's Services, Ealing HA, 1983–89. Mem. (Lib Dem), Richmond on Thames LBC, 1981–90 (Chm., Social Services, 1983–89). Contested (Lib Dem) Richmond and Barnes, 1992. MP (Lib Dem) Richmond Park, 1997–2005. Lib Dem spokesman on internat. develt, 1997–2003, for children, 2003–04, for health, 2007–10. Hon. FFSRH (Hon. FFFP 2002). *Address:* House of Lords, SW1A 0PW.

TONGE, Dr Gary James, FREng, FIET; consultant in electronic communications, since 2004; *b* 5 Sept. 1957; *s* of Dennis and Dorothy Tonge; *m* 1978, Fiona Margaret Mackintosh; two *s* two *d. Educ:* Univ. of Southampton (BSc 1st Cl. Hons Electronics; PhD Maths 1981). FREng 2001; FIET (FIEE 1993). Independent Broadcasting Authority: jun. engr, rising to Principal Engr, 1980–87; Hd, Engrg Secretariat, 1987–90; Independent Television Commission: Controller of Engrg, 1990–95; Dir, Engrg, 1995–2000; Dir, Technology, 2000–03. FRTS 1995. *Publications:* contrib. to IEEE Trans, RTS Jl, SMPTE Jl, Physics Rev. *Recreations:* Christian work, humanitarian projects. *E:* garytonge@yahoo.co.uk.

TONGE, Very Rev. Lister; Dean of Monmouth, since 2012; *b* Oldham, 23 Dec. 1951; *s* of Edward Tonge and Dorothy Tonge (*née* Clough). *Educ:* Heywood Grammar Sch.; Salford Grammar Sch.; King's Coll. London (AKC 1974); Loyola Univ., Chicago (Master of Pastoral Studies 1995). Ordained deacon, 1975, priest, 1976; Curate, Liverpool Parish Church, 1975–78; Precentor, Johannesburg Cathedral, SA, 1978–79; Community of the Resurrection, Mirfield, 1979–91; Chaplain: Community of St John the Baptist, Windsor, then Oxford, 1996–2012; Ripon Coll., Cuddesdon, 2005–09. *Address:* The Deanery, 105 Stow Hill, Newport NP20 4ED. *T:* (01633) 259627. *E:* listertonge@gmail.com.

TONGE, Simon David; HM Diplomatic Service; High Commissioner to Papua New Guinea, since 2014; *b* Oldham, Lancs, 18 Sept. 1969; *s* of Kenneth Tonge and Andrea Tonge (*née* Latchford); *m* 2012, Hera Lutsenko. *Educ:* Oldham Hulme Grammar Sch. for Boys; Lancaster Univ. (BSc Hons Mktg); Sheffield Univ. (MBA); Open Univ. (MA Envmt, Policy and Society; BSc Hons Geoscis). Entered FCO, 1996; Res. Analyst for SE Asia, FCO, 1996–97; Cttee Support Officer, UKMIS to UN, NY, 1997–98; Second Sec. (Political), Jakarta, 1998–2002; Regl Security Policy Advr, S Asia Gp, FCO, 2002–04; Hd of Section, Press Office, FCO, 2004; Hd, Governor's Office, Cayman Is, 2004–08; Dep. Hd of Mission, Baku, 2008–11; French lang. trng, 2012; Hd of Mission, Abidjan, 2012–14. Comdr, Nat. Order (Côte d'Ivoire), 2014. *Recreations:* hiking, photography, kitesurfing. *Address:* British High Commisssion, Locked Bag 212, Waigani, Port Moresby, Papua New Guinea. *T:* 3251677, *Fax:* 3253547. *E:* simondtonge@gmail.com.

TONGUE, Carole; adviser and lecturer on the media, broadcasting, culture and European affairs, since 1999; artistic producer; Founder and Chair, UK Coalition for Cultural Diversity, since 2005; Chair, European Coalitions for Cultural Diversity, since 2015; *b* 14 Oct. 1955; *d* of Muriel Esther Lambert and Walter Archer Tongue; *m* 1990, Chris Pond, *qv* (marr. diss. 1999); one *d. Educ:* Brentwood County High School; Loughborough University of Technology (BA Govt (Hons) and French). Asst Editor, Laboratory Practice, 1977–78; courier/guide in France with Sunsites Ltd, 1978–79; Robert Schuman scholarship for research in social affairs with European Parlt, Dec. 1979–March 1980; sec./admin. asst, Socialist Group of European Parlt, 1980–84. Consultant, Citigate Public Affairs, 2001–03; Associate Dir, Sovereign Strategy, 2003–10; Partner, CSPH Internat., 2010–. Advr, EUTOP, 2012–. MEP (Lab) London E, 1984–99; contested (Lab) London Reg., 1999. Dep. Leader, Eur. PLP, 1989–91. Bd Mem., Westminster Foundn for Democracy, 1990–93. Sen. Vis. Lectr, Dept European Studies, Loughborough Univ., 1995; Vis. Prof., Media Sch., Univ. of the Arts, London (formerly London Inst.), 2000–. Hon. Vice Pres., Professional Land Reform Gp, 2005–. Member: Adv. Bd, Eur. Media Forum, 1996–99; Bd, London Film and Video Develt Agency, 1999–2003; Chair, UK Ind. Film Parlt, 2003–. Mem., Professional Conduct Cttee, GMC, 2000–06. Pres., Cities and Cinemas Europe, 1997–2000. Trustee and Vice Chair, Couper Art Collection, 2010–; Co-producer, The Fleeting Opera, 2000. Patron, Federal Trust, 1997–. Member: Fabian Soc.; BECTU. Trustee, CSV, 1995–. FRSA 2000. Hon. Dr Lincoln, 2005. *Publications:* chapters in books on European media; EP reports; articles on culture, film, citizenship, European affairs. *Recreations:* piano, cello, painting, horse riding, cinema, theatre, opera. *Address:* 246 Caledonian Road, N1 0NG. *T:* (020) 7278 1344. *E:* tonguec@btinternet.com.

TONKIN, Boyd Miles; Senior Writer, The Independent, since 2013 (Literary Editor, 1996–2013); *b* 7 April 1955; *s* of Douglas George Marcus Tonkin and Joan Yvonne Tonkin (*née* Collis). *Educ:* Haberdashers' Aske's Sch., Elstree; Trinity Coll., Cambridge (MA English). Res. Student and pt-time Tutor, Univ. of Cambridge, 1978–81; Adult Educn Lectr, City Univ., 1981–83; Lecturer in English: Manchester Poly., 1983–84; West Sussex Inst., 1984–85; Staff Writer and Features Editor, Community Care mag., 1986–89; Social Affairs Editor, 1989–91, Literary Editor, 1991–96, New Statesman. Broadcaster, BBC Radio arts progs, 1995–. Judge: Whitbread Biography award, 1997; Booker Prize, 1999; Foreign Fiction Award, Independent, 2000– (also Convenor); David Cohen Prize for Literature, 2007. *Publications:* (contrib.) Oxford Readers' Guide to Fiction, 2000; contribs to lit. guides and ref. works; essays in lit. jls in UK, US, France and Germany; articles in jls. *Recreations:* music, cinema, cricket, walking. *Address:* 104 Islington High Street, N1 8EG. *T:* (020) 7005 2656.

TONKIN, Derek, CMG 1982; HM Diplomatic Service, retired; *b* 30 Dec. 1929; *s* of Henry James Tonkin and Norah Wearing; *m* 1953, Doreen Rooke; one *s* two *d* (and one *s* decd). *Educ:* High Pavement Grammar Sch., Nottingham; St Catherine's Society, Oxford (MA). HM Forces, 1948–49; FO, 1952; Warsaw, 1955; Bangkok, 1957; Phnom Penh, 1961; FO, 1963; Warsaw, 1966; Wellington, 1968; FCO, 1972; East Berlin, 1976; Ambassador to Vietnam, 1980–82; Minister, Pretoria, 1983–86; Ambassador to Thailand, and concurrently to Laos, 1986–89. Chairman: Beta Viet Nam Fund Ltd, 1993–99; Beta Mekong Fund Ltd, 1994–2000; Network Myanmar, 2007–14. Director: Palais Angkor SA, 1998–2006; Euro-Thai Investments Ltd, 1999–2007. Chairman: Adv. Bd, Centre for SE Asia Studies, SOAS, 1990–93; Thai-British Business Assoc., 1991–93; Vietnam-Britain Business Assoc., 1993–94. Dir, Ockenden Internat. Bd of Trustees, 1990–2003. *Recreations:* tennis, music, linguistics. *Address:* Heathfields, Berry Lane, Worplesdon, Guildford, Surrey GU3 3PU. *Club:* Royal Over-Seas League.

TONKING, His Honour (Russel) Simon (William Ferguson); DL; a Circuit Judge, 1997–2015; *b* 25 March 1952; *s* of John Wilson Tonking and Mary Oldham Tonking (*née* Ferguson); *m* 1976, (Sylvia) Mithra McIntyre; one *s* one *d. Educ:* King's Sch., Canterbury; Emmanuel Coll., Cambridge (MA). Called to the Bar, Inner Temple, 1975, Bencher, 2011; barrister, Midland and Oxford Circuit, 1976–97; Asst Recorder, 1991–94; Recorder, 1994–97; Resident Judge at Stafford, 2006–15; Hon. Recorder of Stafford, 2008–15. Mem., Criminal Cttee, 2005–08, Jt Course Dir, 2008–, Judicial Coll. (formerly Judicial Studies Bd). Lichfield Cathedral: Steward, 1978– (Head Steward, 1985–87, Pres. of Stewards, 2003–04); Mem., 2000–, Chm., 2009–, Cathedral Council (Mem. Transitional Council, 1998–2000); Dep. Chancellor, Diocese of Southwell, 1997–2005. DUniv Staffs, 2009. DL Staffs, 2006. *Recreations:* many! *Address:* c/o Stafford Combined Court Centre, Victoria Square, Stafford ST16 2QQ. *T:* (01785) 610730. *Club:* Outer Hebrides Tennis.

TONRY, Prof. Michael; McKnight Presidential Chair in Law and Public Policy, since 2010, and Director, Institute on Crime and Public Policy, since 2005, University of Minnesota (Sonosky Professor of Law and Public Policy, 1990–2006; Bennett University Chair of Excellence, 2006–10); Senior Fellow, Netherlands Institute for the Study of Crime and Law Enforcement, Leiden, since 2003; *b* 9 June 1945; *s* of J. Richard Tonry and Frances Zimmerman Tonry (*née* Keedy); *m* 1st, 1966, Penelope Tyson (*d* 2010); two *s* two *d*; 2nd, 2012, Rossella Selmini. *Educ:* Univ. of N Carolina (AB Hist. 1966); Yale Univ. (LLB). Admitted to legal practice: Illinois, 1970; Pennsylvania, 1975; Maine, 1982. Lecturer in Law: Univ. of Chicago, 1971–73; Univ. of Birmingham, 1973–74; Dechert Price & Rhodes, Esqs, 1974–76; Prof. of Law, Univ. of Md, 1976–83; Pres., Castine Res. Corp., 1983–; Prof. of Law and Public Policy, and Dir, Inst. of Criminology, Univ. of Cambridge, 1999–2004. Vis. Prof. (Prof. avec indemnité), Univ. of Lausanne, 2001–. President: Amer. Soc. of Criminology, 2005–08; Eur. Soc. of Criminology, 2012–15. Scientific Mem., Max-Planck Soc., 2012–. Ed. and Publisher, The Castine Patriot, 1987–90. PhD *hc* Free Univ. Amsterdam, 2011. *Publications:* Sentencing Reform Impacts, 1987; Malign Neglect: race, crime and punishment in America, 1994; Sentencing Matters, 1996; Confronting Crime, 2003; Punishment and Politics: evidence and emulation in the making of English crime control policy, 2004; Thinking About Crime: sense and sensibility in American Penal Policy, 2004; Thinking About Punishment, 2009; Punishing Race, 2011; Why Punish? How Much?, 2011; *jointly:* Hypnotically Refreshed Testimony, 1985; Human Development and Criminal Behavior, 1991; *edited:* Ethnicity, Crime and Immigration, 1997; Intermediate Sanctions in Sentencing Guidelines, 1997; Handbook of Crime and Punishment, 1998; Penal Reform in Overcrowded Times, 2001; Crime, Punishment and Politics, 2007; The Oxford Handbook of Crime and Public Policy, 2009; The Oxford Handbook of Crime and Criminal Justice, 2011; Recidivism Has a Past—Has It A Future?, 2011; Politics and Prosecutors in Comparative Perspective, 2012; *edited jointly:* Reform and Punishment: essays on criminal sentencing, 1983; Communities and Crime, 1986; The Sentencing Commission: guidelines for criminal sanctions, 1987; Prediction and Classification, 1987; Managing Appeals in Federal Courts, 1988; Family Violence, 1990; Between Prison and Probation, 1990; Drugs and Crime, 1990; Modern Policing, 1992; Beyond the Law: crime in complex organisations, 1993; Intermediate Sanctions in Overcrowded Times, 1995; Building a Safer Society, 1995; Sentencing Reform in Overcrowded Times, 1997; Youth Violence, 1998; Prisons, 1999; Sentencing and Sanctions in Western Countries, 2001; Ideology, Crime and Criminal Justice, 2002; Reform and Punishment, 2002; Cross-national Studies in Crime and Justice, 2003; Youth Crime and Youth Justice, 2004; Crime and Justice in the Netherlands, 2007; Crime and Justice in Scandinavia, 2011; Crime and Justice in America, 1975–2025, 2013; Why Crime Rates Fall and Why They Don't, 2014. *Address:* University of Minnesota, Law School, 312 Mondale Hall, 229–19th Avenue South, Minneapolis, MN 55455, USA.

TOOBY, Michael Bowen; curator, writer and researcher; *b* 20 Dec. 1956; *s* of Leslie and Jill Tooby; *m* 1980, Jane Pare; one *s* one *d. Educ:* King Henry VIII Sch., Coventry; Magdalene Coll., Cambridge. Asst Curator, Kettle's Yard, Cambridge, 1978–80; Exhibns Orgnr, Third Eye Centre, Glasgow, 1980–84; Keeper, Mappin Art Gall., Sheffield, 1984–92; Founding Curator, Tate Gall. St Ives, and Curator, Barbara Hepworth Mus. and Sculpture Gdn, 1992–99; Dir, Nat. Mus. and Gall., Cardiff, 2000–04; Dir, Learning, Progs and Develt, Nat. Museums Wales, 2004–11. Chm., engage, (nat. assoc. for visual arts educn), 1999–2004. Vis. Prof. in Contemp. Curatorial Practice, Univ. of S Wales (formerly Univ. of Glamorgan), 2007–; Res. Prof., Bath Sch. of Art and Design, Bath Spa Univ., 2012– (Dean, Sch. of Art and Design, 2012–13); Sen. Res. Fellow, Henry Moore Inst., Leeds, 2014–15. Macready Lectr in Canadian Art, Art Gall. of Ontario, 1997. Trustee, Artes Mundi Internat. Art Prize, 2014–. *Publications:* The True North: Canadian painting 1896–1939, 1988; monograph studies of: Lois Williams, 1996; Iwan Bala, 1999; David Nash, 2000; Trevor Bell, 2003; (contrib.) Kurt Jackson, 2010. *Address:* c/o Bath School of Art and Design, Sion Hill, Bath BA1 5SF. *E:* mike.tooby@gmail.com.

TOOHEY, Mrs Joyce, CB 1977; Under-Secretary, Department of the Environment, 1970–76; *b* 20 Sept. 1917; *o d* of Louis Zinkin and Lena Zinkin (*née* Daiches); *m* 1947, Monty I. Toohey, MD, MRCP, DCH (*d* 1960); two *d. Educ:* Brondesbury and Kilburn High Sch.; Girton Coll., Cambridge (BA 1938, MA 1945); London Sch. of Economics. Asst Principal, Min. of Supply, 1941; transferred to Min. of Works, 1946; Principal, 1948; Asst Secretary, MPBW, 1956; Under-Secretary, 1964. Harvard Business Sch., 1970. *Recreations:* reading, walking. *Address:* 11 Kensington Court Gardens, W8 5QE.

TOOK, John Michael Exton, (James), MBE 1964; Controller, Europe and North Asia Division, British Council, 1983–86, retired; *b* 15 Sept. 1926; *s* of late George Took, Dover, and Ailsa Clowes (*née* Turner); *m* 1964, Judith Margaret, *d* of late Brig. and Mrs W. J. Birkle; two *d. Educ:* Dover Coll.; Jesus Coll., Cambridge. Served Indian Army, 1944–47. HM Colonial Admin. Service (later HMOCS), N Rhodesia, 1950–57; Min. of External Affairs, Fedn of Rhodesia & Nyasaland, 1957–63; Min. of External Affairs, Republic of Zambia, 1964–65; joined British Council, 1965; Asst Reg. Dir, Frankfurt, 1965–67; Reg. Dir, Cape Coast, 1967–69; Rep., Cyprus, 1971–74; Cultural Attaché, British Embassy, Budapest, 1974–77; Dep. Controller, European Div., 1977–80; Rep., Greece, 1980–83. Dir, UK Cttee, Eur. Cultural Foundn, 1992–94. Chm., Romney Marsh Historic Churches Trust, 2001–05. *Publications:* Common Birds of Cyprus, 1973, 4th edn 1986; Birds of Cyprus, 1992; contribs to ornithological jls. *Recreations:* ornithology, fishing, natural history. *Address:* Downgate Lodge, Silverden Lane, Sandhurst, Cranbrook, Kent TN18 5NU. *T:* (01580) 851050. *Club:* Oxford and Cambridge.

TOOKE, Sir John (Edward), Kt 2007; DM, DSc; FRCP, FRCPI, FRCGP, FMedSci; Vice-Provost (Health), 2010–15, Head, School of Life and Medical Sciences and Head, Medical School, 2010–14, University College London; President, Academy of Medical Sciences, since 2012; *b* 4 March 1949; *s* of Thomas Edward Tooke and Edna (*née* Wilgose); *m* 1972, Elizabeth Moore; one *s* one *d. Educ:* St John's Coll., Oxford (MA 1970; MSc 1972; BM BCh 1974; DM 1982; DSc 1998); King's Coll. Hosp. Med. Sch. FRCP 1993. Lectr in Medicine, Leeds Univ., 1979–82; BHF Res. Fellow, Karolinska Inst. Dept of Medicine, Sweden, 1982–83; Wellcome Trust Sen. Lectr in Medicine and Physiol., Charing Cross and Westminster Med. Sch., 1984–87; Sen. Lectr, 1987–92, Prof. of Vascular Medicine, 1992–2009, Univ. of Exeter; Inaugural Dean, Peninsula Med. Sch., 2000–09, Exec. Dean, Peninsula Coll. of Medicine and Dentistry, Univs of Exeter and Plymouth. Chm., Med. Schs Council (formerly Council of Hds of Med. Schs), 2006; former Chm., UK Healthcare Educn Adv. Cttee. Hon. Consultant Physician in diabetes and vascular medicine, Royal Devon and Exeter Healthcare NHS Trust, 2000–. Chm., Ind. Inquiry into Modernising Med. Careers, 2007–08. Hon. FMedSci 2000;

Hon. FAcadMed. Camillo Golgi Award, Eur. Assoc. for Study of Diabetes, 1994. *Publications:* (ed with G. D. Lowe) A Textbook of Vascular Medicine, 1996; (ed) Diabetic Angiopathy, 1999. *Recreations:* angling, golf, sailing, le bricolage. *Address:* University College London, Gower Street, WC1E 6BT.

TOOKEY, Angela Mary, (Jill), (Mrs Christopher Fone), MBE 2004; Founder and Artistic Director, National Youth Ballet of Great Britain, since 1988; *b* London, 18 March 1937; *d* of Alan and Freda Tookey; *m* 1961, Christopher Fone (*d* 2004); one *s* three *d*. *Educ:* Bromley High Sch.; Alice Ottley Sch., Worcs; Arts Educnl Sch., London. Fashion journalist, incl. Woman & Beauty and Honey mags, 1959–64. FRSA. *Publications:* Pedro the Parrot, 1983. *Recreations:* water colour painting, photography, theatre, travel, family. *Address:* 9 The Green, Westerham, Kent TN16 1AS. *T:* (01959) 569291. *E:* jilltookey@tiscali.co.uk, jill@nyb.org.uk.

TOOKEY, Richard William, CBE 1984; Director and Group Public Affairs Co-ordinator, Shell International Petroleum Co. Ltd, 1984–93; *b* 11 July 1934; *s* of Geoffrey William Tookey, QC and Rosemary Sherwell Tookey (*née* Clogg); *m* 1st, 1956, Jill (*née* Ransford) (marr. diss. 1994); one *s* one *d* (and one *s* decd); 2nd, 1994, Colleen (*née* Channon) (*d* 2002); 3rd, 2006, Zoë (*née* Lambiris). *Educ:* Charterhouse. National Service, 2nd Lieut, 1st King's Dragoon Guards, 1952–54; Lanarkshire Yeomanry (TA), 1954–56; Inns of Court Regt/Inns of Court and City Yeomanry (TA), 1957–64. Joined Royal Dutch/Shell Group, 1954; posts in internat. oil supply and trading, 1954–73; Head of Supply Operations, 1973–75; Vice-Pres., Shell Internat. Trading Co., 1975–77; Man. Dir, Shell Tankers (UK) Ltd, 1978–79, Chm., 1980–84; Man. Dir, Shell Internat. Marine Ltd, 1980–84; Marine Co-ordinator, Shell Internat. Petroleum Co. Ltd, 1980–84. Part-time Mem., BRB, 1985–90; Mem., Gen. Cttee, Lloyd's Register of Shipping, 1978–85; Pres., Gen. Council of British Shipping, 1983–84. Liveryman, Shipwrights' Co., 1983–, Mem. Ct of Assts, 1987–96. *Recreation:* home. *Address:* 38 Mill Park Road, Mill Park, Port Elizabeth, 6001, South Africa. *T:* (41) 3745025. *E:* rwtookey@iafrica.com.

TOOLEY, Prof. James Nicholas, PhD; Professor of Education Policy, University of Newcastle upon Tyne, since 1998 (on leave of absence as President, Education Fund, Orient Global, 2007–09); *b* 21 July 1959; *s* of Arthur Henry Tooley and Barbara May Tooley (*née* Tubby). *Educ:* Kingsfield Sch., Bristol; Univ. of Sussex (BSc 1983; MSc 1986); PhD London 1994. Mathematics Teacher, Zimbabwe, 1983–86; Sen. Res. Officer, NFER, 1988–91; Res. Fellow, Univ. of Oxford, 1994–95; Sen. Res. Fellow, Univ. of Manchester, 1995–98. Member, Academic Advisory Council: IEA, 2005– (Dir, Educn Prog., 1995–2002); Centre for Market Reform of Educn, 2015–. Chairman: Omega Schs Franchise Ltd, Ghana, 2008–; Empathy Learning Systems Pvt Ltd, India, 2009–. Trustee, Omega Schs Foundn, Ghana, 2009–; Patron: Wilderspin Nat. Sch., 2010–; Assoc. of Formidable Educnl Develt, Nigeria, 2011–; Ind. Private Schs Assoc., Sierra Leone, 2014–; Chief Mentor, Nat. Ind. Schs Alliance, 2014–. Adjunct Scholar, Cato Inst., 2009–; Visitor, Ralston Coll., 2013–; Vis. Prof., Beijing Normal Univ., 2013–. *Publications:* Disestablishing the School, 1995; Education without the State, 1996; Educational Research: a critique, 1998; The Global Education Industry, 1999; The Seven Habits of Highly Effective Schools, 1999; Reclaiming Education, 2000; The Miseducation of Women, 2001; The Enterprise of Education, 2001; (ed) Buckingham at 25, 2002; (jtly) HIV and AIDS in Schools, 2002; (jtly) Private Schools for the Poor: a case study from India, 2003; (jtly) Delivering Better Education, 2003; (jtly) Government Failure: E. G. West on education, 2004; Could the Globalisation of Education Benefit the Poor?, 2004; (jtly) What Americans Can Learn from School Choice in Other Countries, 2005; (jtly) Private Education is Good for the Poor: a study of private schools serving the poor in low-income countries, 2005; E. G. West: economic liberalism and the role of government in education, 2008; The Beautiful Tree: a personal journey into how the world's poorest people are educating themselves, 2009; Educational Equality: key debates in education policy, 2010; (jtly) The Private Schools Revolution in Bihar, 2012; From Village School to Global Brand: changing the world through education, 2012; Gandhi, RTE and the Denial of the Right to Education, 2014; (jtly) The Role and Impact of Private Education in Developing Countries: a response to the DFID-commissioned "rigorous literature review", 2015. *Recreation:* walking in the foothills of Simonside. *Address:* King George VI Building, Newcastle University, Newcastle NE1 7RU. *T:* (0191) 208 6374. *E:* james.tooley@newcastle.ac.uk. *Clubs:* Athenæum, Royal Over-Seas League.

TOOLEY, Sir John, Kt 1979; Arts consultant, since 1988; General Director, Royal Opera House, Covent Garden, 1980–88; *b* 1 June 1924; *yr s* of late H. R. Tooley; *m* 1st, 1951, Judith Craig Morris (marr. diss., 1965); three *d*; 2nd, 1968, Patricia Janet Norah Bagshawe (marr. diss. 1990), 2nd *d* of late G. W. S. Bagshawe; one *s*; 3rd, 1995, Jennifer-Anne Shannon (marr. diss. 2003). *Educ:* Repton; Magdalene Coll., Cambridge (Hon. Fellow, 2005). Served The Rifle Brigade, 1943–47. Sec., Guildhall School of Music and Drama, 1952–55; Royal Opera House, Covent Garden: Asst to Gen. Administrator, 1955–60; Asst Gen. Administrator, 1960–70; Gen. Administrator, 1970–80. Chairman: Nat. Music Council Executive, 1970–72; HEFCE Music Conservatories Adv. Gp, 1993–97. Director: Britten Estate Ltd, 1989–97; South Bank Bd, 1991–97; Compton Verney Opera Project, 1991–97; WNO, 1992–2000; David Gyngell & Co. Ltd, 1995–97; Almeida Th., 1997–2002 (Chm., 1990–97); LPO, 1998–2010 (Mem., Adv. Council, 2014–); Chm., Monument Insurance Brokers Ltd, 1997–2002; Consultant: Internat. Management Gp, 1988–97; Ballet Opera House, Toronto, 1989–90; Trustee: Wigmore Hall, 1987–2001; SPNM; Australian Music Foundn, 1986–; Walton Trust, 1988–2000; Britten Pears Foundn, 1989–99; Dartington Summer Sch., 1989–2000; Purcell Tercentenary Trust, 1991–97; Performing Arts Labs, 1993–97; Sidney Nolan Trust, 1996– (Chm., 2005–14; Jt Pres., 2014–). Pres., Salisbury Festival, 1988–2005; Chairman: Salisbury Cathedral Fabric Cttee, 1990–2005; Salisbury Cathedral Girl Choristers' Trust, 1995–2005; Chm., Rudolf Nureyev Foundn, 1995–2008. Gen. Advr, Istanbul Foundn for Culture and Arts, 1993–2008; Advr, Borusan Chamber Orch., Istanbul, 2005–08. Governor, Repton Sch., 1984–94. FGS. Hon. FRAM; Hon. RNCM. DUniv UCE, 1996. Queen Elizabeth II Coronation Award, RAD, 2005. Commendatore, Italian Republic, 1976. *Publications:* In House, 1999. *Recreations:* walking, theatre. *Address:* 18 Grange Court, Pinehurst, Grange Road, Cambridge CB3 9BD. *T:* (01223) 358737. *E:* tooley@btinternet.com.

TOOLEY, Dr Peter John Hocart; pharmaceutical physician, since 1990; Director, PT Pharma Consultancy Ltd, Guernsey, since 1998; *b* St Helens, Lancs, 28 Feb. 1939; *s* of Dr Patrick Hocart Tooley and Margaret Brenda Tooley (*née* Williams); *m* 1st, 1966, Elizabeth Monica Roche (marr. diss. 1983); one *s* two *d*; 2nd, 1987, Diana Edith (*née* Sturdy); two step *d*. *Educ:* Elizabeth Coll., Guernsey; St George's Sch., Harpenden; London Hospital Med. Coll., Univ. of London (MB BS 1964; DObstRCOG 1965; DMJ (Clin.) 1981; DFFP 1993); Univ. of Wales Coll., Cardiff (LLM 1994). MRCS 1963; LRCP 1963; MRCGP 1971; MFPM (Dist.) 2012. HO Surgery, Connaught Hosp., London, 1963; HO Medicine, 1963–64, Resident Accoucheur, 1964, London Hosp.; SHO Gen. Surgery, Royal Sussex County Hosp., 1965; Jun. Registrar, Dept of Obstetrics and Gynaecol., London Hosp., 1966; Principal in Gen. Practice, 1966–90; Asst Dep. Coroner, Reading, 1984–89; Sen. Med. Advr and Med. Dir (Ireland), Janssen Pharmaceuticals, 1990–98. Consultant Med. Advr, Daiichi Sankyo (formerly Sankyo Pharma, 1998–. Member: Berks Local Med. Cttee, 1975–85; Berks Family Practitioner Cttee, 1975–85. FRSocMed 1990. Member: BMA, 1965–; Reading Pathol. Soc., 1967–; British Acad. of Forensic Sci., 1981–; Medico-legal Soc., 1982–2015; British Assoc. of Pharmaceutical Physicians, 1990–; Bolam Soc., 1996–. Freeman, City of London; Mem., Apothecaries' Soc., 1965 (Livery Cttee, 1994–2005; Sen. Warden, 2012; Master, 2013–14). Hon. Medical Officer: Oxfordshire RFU, 1970–97; Henley Rugby Club, 1970–97; Wasps RFC, 1993–98. Member: Vale Douzaine Council, 2005–; Vale Commons Council, 2007–. *Recreations:* Rugby, gardening, boating, family history, Guernsey history. *Address:* Les Mielles, Les Mielles Road, Vale, Guernsey GY3 5AZ. *T:* (01481) 244543, 07781 105664. *E:* peter@pjtpharma.co.uk. *Clubs:* Royal Channel Islands Yacht; Guernsey Rugby Football.

TOOTH, Sir (Hugh) John L.; *see* Lucas-Tooth.

TOOZE, Dr John, FRS 1994; Vice President, Scientific and Facility Operations, Rockefeller University, 2005–13; *b* 16 May 1938; *s* of Reginald John Tooze and Doris Edith Tooze (*née* Bull); *m* 1st, 1962, Sarah Margaret Wynn (marr. diss.); two *s* one *d*; 2nd, 1983, Sharon Ann Queally; one *s* one *d*. *Educ:* Handsworth Grammar Sch., Birmingham; Jesus Coll., Cambridge (BA 1961); King's Coll. London (PhD 1965); Harvard Univ. Served Army, 1956–58. King's College London: Asst Lectr in Biophysics, 1961–65; Lectr, 1965–68; Wellcome Res. Fellow, Harvard Univ., 1965–67; Dep. Editor, Nature, 1968–70; Res. Administrator, ICRF, 1970–73; Exec. Sec., EMBO, Heidelberg, 1973–94; Associate Dir, EMBL, 1993–94; Dir, Support Services, ICRF, subseq. Res. Services, CRUK, 1994–2005. Editor: Trends in Biochemistry, 1979–85; EMBO Jl, 1982–2003. Trustee, Darwin Trust of Edinburgh, 1991–. EMBO Medal, 1986. *Publications:* Molecular Biology of Tumor Viruses, 1973; DNA Tumor Viruses, 1980; (with J. D. Watson) The DNA Story, 1982; (with C. I. Branden) Introduction to Protein Structure, 1991, 2nd edn 1999. *Recreations:* numismatics, English history, gardening. *Club:* Athenæum.

TOPE, family name of **Baron Tope**.

TOPE, Baron *cr* 1994 (Life Peer), of Sutton in the London Borough of Sutton; **Graham Norman Tope,** CBE 1991; Member (Lib Dem) London Assembly, 2000–08; *b* 30 Nov. 1943; *s* of late Leslie Tope, Plymouth and Winifred Tope (*née* Merrick), Bermuda; *m* 1972, Margaret East; two *s*. *Educ:* Whitgift Sch., S Croydon. Company Sec., 1965–72; Insce Manager, 1970–72; Dep. Gen. Sec., Voluntary Action Camden, 1975–90. Pres., Nat. League of Young Liberals, 1973–75 (Vice-Chm., 1971–73); Mem., Liberal Party Nat. Council, 1970–76; Exec. Cttee, London Liberal Party, 1981–84. Sutton Council: Councillor 1974–2014; Leader, Lib Dem (formerly Soc & Lib Dem) Group, 1974–99 (Liberal Gp, 1974–83, Liberal/SDP Alliance Gp, 1983–88); Leader of Opposition, 1984–86; Leader of Council, 1986–99; spokesperson on libraries, heritage, economic develt and community safety, arts and culture, 1999–2006, on community safety and cultural services, 2006–12; Vice Chm., Envmt and Neighbourhoods Cttee, 2012–14; Chm., Nonsuch Park Jt Mgt Cttee, 2012–13. Greater London Authority: Member: Metropolitan Police Authy, 2000–08; Mayor's Adv. Cabinet, 2000–04; Chm., Finance Cttee, 2000–08; Leader, Lib Dem Gp, 2000–06. MP (L) Sutton and Cheam, 1972–Feb. 1974; Liberal Party spokesman on environment, Dec. 1972–1974; contested (L) Sutton and Cheam, Oct. 1974. Lib Dem spokesman, H of L, on educn, 1994–2000, on communities and local govt, 2008–15; Mem., Select Cttee on Public Services and Demographic Change, 2012–13; Co-Chair, Lib Dem Communities and Local Govt Parly Cttee, 2010–15; Vice-Chm., All Party Parly Gp on Libraries, 1998–2014 (Chm., 2014–). President: London Lib Dems, 1991–2000; Sutton Bor. Lib Dems, 2015–; Lib Dem European and Internat. spokesperson, 1997–2014, Vice Pres., 2013–, Local Govt Assoc. Mem., Policy Cttee, AMA, 1989–97; Chm., Policy and Finance Cttee, London Boroughs Assoc., 1994–95. EU Committee of the Regions: UK Rep., 1994–2014; Mem. Bureau, 1996–2014; Vice Chm., UK Delegn, 1996–2014; Pres., European Lib Dem Reform Gp, 1998–2002; Chm., Constitutional Affairs Cttee, 2002–04 (First Vice Chm., 2004–06); Mem. Council of Europe, CLRAE, 1996–2004. Vice Chm., 1997–2000, Mem. Leaders' Cttee, 1995–2000, Assoc. of London Govt. Chm., Local Govt Gp for Europe, 2005–. Trustee, Wandle Valley Regl Park, 2012–14. Pres., Save the Children, Sutton, 2009–; Patron, Arts Network Sutton, 2014–. Freeman: City of London, 1998; London Bor. of Sutton, 2014; Liveryman, Needlemakers' Co., 1999–. *Publications:* (jtly) Liberals and the Community, 1974; (with Andrew Tope) A Life in Politics, 2010. *Address:* 88 The Gallop, Sutton, Surrey SM2 5SA. *T:* (020) 8642 5292; House of Lords, SW1A 0PW. *T:* (020) 7219 3098. *E:* topeg@parliament.uk.

TÖPFER, Dr Klaus; Member, Advisory Board, Holcim Foundation for Sustainable Construction, since 2003; Founding Director, Institute for Advanced Sustainability Studies, since 2009; *b* Waldenburg, Silesia, 29 July 1938; *m* Mechthildis; three *c*. *Educ:* König-Wilhelm-Gymnasium, Höxter, Weser; Univ. of Münster (DipEcon 1964; PhD 1968). Lectr, Econ. Acad., Hagen and Univ. of Bielefeld, 1965–71; Asst to Dir of Econ. Res., 1965–71, Hd, Econs Dept, 1970–71, Central Inst. for Regl Planning, Univ. of Münster; Lectr, Coll. of Admin. Scis, Speyer, 1971–78; Consultant in field of develt policy, Egypt, Malaŵi, Brazil and Jordan, 1971–78; Prof. and Dir, Inst. for Regl R&D, Univ. of Hanover, 1978–79; Associate Lectr in Envmtl and Resource Econs, Univ. of Mainz, 1985–86. Hd, Dept for Planning and Inf., State Chancellery of Saarland, 1971–78; State Sec., Min. for Social Affairs, Health and Envmt, 1978–85, Minister for Envmt and Health, 1985–87, Rhineland-Palatinate; Federal Minister for Envmt, Nature Conservation and Nuclear Safety, 1987–94; Mem. (CDU) Bundestag, 1990–98; Federal Minister for Regl Planning, Building and Urban Develt, and Co-ordinator for Transfer of Parlt and Federal Govt to Berlin and Compensation for Bonn Reg., 1994–98. Chm., UN Commn on Sustainable Develt, 1994–95; Under-Sec.-Gen., UN, 1998–2006; Dir-Gen., UN Office, Nairobi, 1998; Actg Exec. Dir, UN Centre for Human Settlements (Habitat), 1998–2000; Exec. Dir, UNEP, 1998–2006. Joined Christian Democratic Union, 1972: Dist Chm., Saarbrücken and Mem., State Exec. Cttee, Saarland, 1977–79; Vice-Chm., Fed. Exec. Cttee on Envmtl Questions, 1983–87; Dist Chm., Rhine-Hunsrück, 1987–89; State Chm., Saarland, 1990–95; Mem., Presiding Cttee, 1992. Hon. Prof., Tongji Univ., Shanghai, 1997. Hon Dr: Free Univ., Berlin, 2002; Essen, 2002; Hannover, 2003. TÜV Rheinland Pfalz Envmt Award, 2000; Bruno H. Schubert Envmt Prize, 2002; German Envmt Prize, 2002; Wilhelm Weber Prize, 2003; Golden Steering Wheel Internat. Prize (Russia), 2003. OM (FRG), 1986; Comdr's Cross, 1989, Grand Cross, 1997, OM (FRG); Order of Southern Cross (Brazil), 2002; Danaker Order (Kyrgyz Republic), 2003. *Publications:* Die Beeinflussbarkeit privater Pläne dargestellt unternehmerischen Standortentscheidung, 1968; Regionalpolitik und Standort-entscheidung, 1969; Standortentscheidung und Wohnortwahl, 1974; Die europäische Dimension der Umweltpolitik, 1989; Internationaler Umweltschutz, 1989; numerous contribs to books and to learned jls. *Recreations:* avid fan of card games, including Skat, football, fine wine. *Address:* c/o Holcim Foundation for Sustainable Construction, Hagenholzstrasse 85, 8050 Zurich, Switzerland.

TOPP, Air Commodore Roger Leslie; AFC 1950 (Bar 1955, 2nd Bar 1957); independent consultant, aviation and defence, 1988–99; *b* 14 May 1923; *s* of William Horace Topp and Kathleen (*née* Peters); *m* 1945, Audrey Jane Jeffery (*d* 1999); one *s* one *d*. *Educ:* North Mundham Sch.; RAF, Cranwell. Served War: Pilot trng, Canada, 1943–44, commissioned 1944; 'E' Sqdn Glider Pilot Regt, Rhine Crossing, 1945. Nos 107 and 98 Mosquito Sqdns, Germany, 1947–50; Empire Test Pilots' Sch. and RAE Farnborough, 1951–54; Commanded No 111 Fighter Sqdn (Black Arrows) Aerobatic Team, 1955–58; Allied Air Forces Central Europe, Fontainebleau, 1959; Sector Operational Centre, Brockzetel, Germany, 1959–61; jssc, Latimer, 1961–62; commanded Fighter Test Sqdn, Boscombe Down, 1962–64; Station Comdr, RAF Coltishall, 1964–66; Nat. Def. Coll., Canada, 1966–67; Opl Requirements, MoD (Air), London, 1967–69; Multi-role Combat Aircraft Project, Munich, 1969–70; HQ No 38 Gp, Odiham, 1970; Commandant, Aeroplane and Armament Experimental Estabt, Boscombe Down, 1970–72; Dep. Gen. Man., Multi-role Combat Aircraft Develt and

Production Agency, Munich, 1972–78; retd from RAF, 1978. Consultant to Ferranti Defence Systems Ltd, Scotland (Aviation and Defence, FRG), 1978–88. *Recreations:* golf, sailing. *Club:* Royal Air Force.

TOPPIN, Gilbert Anthony Lester; independent advisor and non-executive director specialising in business issues, strategy and mergers and acquisitions, since 2010; *b* Barbados, 6 Nov. 1952; *s* of Herbert Lester Toppin and Betty Joan Toppin (*née* Mayers); *m* 2008, Donna Louise Reed; two *s* by a previous marriage. *Educ:* Univ. of Edinburgh (BSc Hons Civil Engrg 1975); Univ. of Southampton (MSc Irrigation Engrg 1976). MICE 1980; CEng 1981; MIStructE 1986; MCIWEM 1987; ACMA 1990; CGMA 2012. Researcher, Hydraulics Res. Station, 1976–77; Engineer: Binnie Black & Veatch, 1977–84; Stewart Lyons Partnership, 1984–86; Consultant, then Partner, Deloitte Consulting, 1986–2003; independent advr, 2004–07; CEO, EEF, 2008–09. Chm., ContactPartners Ltd, 2011–. FRSA 2009. *Publications:* (with Fiona Czerniawska) Business Consulting, 2005. *Recreations:* diving, family interests. *Address:* Old Potters, Pitch Place, Thursley, Godalming GU8 6QW. *T:* 07831 101144. *E:* gilbert@toppin.net.

TOPPING, Rev. Frank; actor, author, broadcaster and Methodist minister; Warden, John Wesley's Chapel (The New Room), Bristol, 2000–07; *b* 30 March 1937; *s* of late Frank and Dorothy Topping; *m* 1958, June Berry; two *s* one *d*. *Educ:* St Anne's Convent Sch., Birkenhead; St Anselm's Christian Brothers' Coll., Birkenhead; North West School of Speech and Drama; Didsbury Methodist Theol Coll., Bristol. Served RAF, Cyprus, 1955–57. Leatherhead Rep. Th., 1957–59; Royal Court, Chelsea, 1959; Wolverhampton Rep. Th., 1959; Granada TV, 1960–64; minister, Brighton, and Chaplain, Sussex Univ., 1967–70; freelance broadcaster, BBC Radio Brighton, 1967–70; ordained 1970; staff producer, BBC, 1970–80; Supt Methodist Minister, Barnet Circuit, 1997–2001. Song-writing partnership with Donald Swann, 1973–81; two-man show, Swann with Topping, Opera House, Jersey, fringe theatre, then at Ambassadors, London; presented three one-man plays, Edinburgh Fest. Fringe, 1986. TV series: Sunday Best, 1981; Topping on Sunday, 1982–84; The 5 Minute Show, TVS, 1989–90. Author of radio plays: On the Hill, 1974 (Grace Wyndham Goldie UNDA Dove award, 1975); A Particular Star, 1977. Formed Emmaus, later Topping Theatre Prodns with wife, 1985. *Publications:* Lord of the Morning, 1977; Lord of the Evening, 1979; Lord of my Days, 1980; Working at Prayer, 1981; Pause for Thought with Frank Topping, 1981; Lord of Life, 1982; The Words of Christ: forty meditations, 1983; God Bless You—Spoonbill, 1984; Lord of Time, 1985; An Impossible God, 1985, new edns 1997, 2011; Wings of the Morning, 1986; Act Your Age, 1989; Laughing in my Sleep (autobiog.), 1993; All the Days of my Life, 1994; Here I Stand…, 1997; Grappling with God on the M25, 1998; (ed) Daily Prayer, 2nd edn, 2003; Splinters of Light, 2008. *Recreations:* gardening, photography, travel. *Address:* Lamb Cottage, The Cross, Clearwell, Coleford, Glos GL16 8JU. *T:* and *Fax:* (01594) 834278.

TORDOFF, family name of **Baron Tordoff**.

TORDOFF, Baron *cr* 1981 (Life Peer), of Knutsford in the County of Cheshire; **Geoffrey Johnson Tordoff;** Lib Dem Chief Whip, House of Lords, 1988–94 (Liberal Chief Whip, 1984–88; Deputy Chief Whip, 1983–84); an Extra Lord in Waiting to the Queen, since 2004; *b* 11 Oct. 1928; *s* of Stanley Acomb Tordoff and Annie Tordoff (*née* Johnson); *m* 1953, (Mary) Patricia (*née* Swarbrick) (*d* 2013); two *s* three *d*. *Educ:* North Manchester School; Manchester Grammar School; Univ. of Manchester. Contested (L), Northwich 1964, Knutsford 1966, 1970. Chairman: Liberal Party Assembly Cttee, 1974–76; Liberal Party, 1976–79 (and its Campaigns and Elections Cttee, 1980, 1981); Member, Liberal Party Nat. Executive, 1975–84; Pres., Liberal Party, 1983–84. Chm. of Cttees, H of L, 2001–02 (Principal Dep. Chm. of Cttees, 1994–2001); Chm., H of L Select Cttee on the EC, 1994–2001. Chm., ME Cttee, Refugee Council, 1990–95. Mem., Press Complaints Commn, 1995–2002. *Address:* House of Lords, SW1A 0PW.

TORLOT, Timothy Achille; HM Diplomatic Service; Head, Delegation to Bolivia, European External Action Service (on secondment), since 2012; *b* 17 Sept. 1957; *s* of Sidney Achille Hodgson Torlot and Margaret Jane Torlot (*née* Read); *m* 1986, Bridie Morton (marr. diss. 2011); one *d*; partner, Jennifer Steil; one *d*. *Educ:* Worcester Coll., Oxford (BA Hons Modern Langs). Joined FCO, 1981; Arabic lang. trng, SOAS, 1982–84; Third Sec. (Pol/Inf./Aid), Muscat, 1984–87; Second Sec. (Political), Wellington, 1987–92; Head: of Section, Personnel Mgt Dept, FCO, 1992–95; Commonwealth Section, SE Asian Dept, FCO, 1995–97; Commercial Section, Santiago, 1997–2001; Multilateral Section, Counter-Terrorism Policy Dept, FCO, 2001; Dir, Advanced Technologies, UK Trade & Investment, 2002–05; Dep. Hd of Mission, Baghdad, 2005–06; Advr to Dir, Internat. Security, FCO, 2006; Leader, Rev. of FCO's Afghanistan Ops, 2006–07; Ambassador to Yemen, 2007–10. *Address:* c/o Foreign and Commonwealth Office, King Charles Street, SW1A 2AH.

TORO-HARDY, Alfredo; Ambassador of Venezuela to Singapore, since 2009; *b* Caracas, 22 May 1950; *s* of Fernando Toro and Ofelia Toro (*née* Hardy); *m* 1st, 1972, Dinorah Carnevali (marr. diss. 1998); two *s* one *d*; 2nd, 2001, Gabriela Gaxiola. *Educ:* Central Univ. of Venezuela (LLB 1973; LLM Internat. Trade Law 1977); Univ. of Paris II (Comparative Law 1974); Internat. Inst. of Public Admin, Paris (Diplomatic Studies 1974); Univ. of Pennsylvania (LLM Corporate Law 1979). Simón Bolívar University, Caracas: Associate Prof., 1989–92; Co-ordinator, Latin American Studies Inst., and Dir, N American Studies Centre, 1989–91; Dir, Diplomatic Acad., with rank of Ambassador, Foreign Affairs Ministry, 1992–94; Ambassador: to Brazil, 1994–97; to Chile, 1997–99; to USA, 1999–2001; to the Court of St James's and concurrently to Republic of Ireland, 2001–07; to Spain, 2007–09. Advr to Minister of Foreign Affairs, 1992–94; Mem., Consultative Bd, Nat. Security and Defence Council, 1988–2000. Mem., Academic Bd on Social Responsibility, Univ. of Barcelona, 2003–; External Adviser, Univ. of Westminster Review Panel, 2004–. Vis. Schol. and Sen. Fulbright Schol., Princeton Univ., 1986–87; Hon. Prof., Univ. of Brasilia, 1996–97; Resident Schol., Rockefeller Foundn Bellagio Center, Sept. 2011; prof. and guest speaker in several univs and acad. instns in Venezuela, USA, Chile, Brazil, UK and others. Member: Inter-American Peace and Justice Commn, Santiago, 1997–; Windsor Energy Gp, London, 2002–; Global Dimensions, London, 2002–; RIIA, 2003–. Mem., Chairmans Club, 2003–. Weekly columnist and collaborator in numerous media publications, in Venezuela, Mexico, Brazil, Chile and Spain, including: El Universal, Caracas, 1994–; El Globo, Caracas, 1989–97. Holds several Venezuelan and foreign decorations. *Publications:* include: Los Libertadores de Venezuela, 1982; Rafael Caldera, 1982; Para qué una Política Exterior?, 1984; Venezuela, Democracia y Política Exterior, 1986; El Desafío Venezolano: Como Influir las Decisiones Políticas Estadounidenses, 1988; La Maldición de Sísifo: quince años de política exterior Venezolana, 1991; Bajo el Signo de la Incertidumbre, 1992; Las Falacias del Libre Comercio, 1993; De Yalta a Sarajevo: de la guerra fría a la paz caliente, 1993; Del Descalabro Mexicano a la Crisis Venezolana, 1995; El Desorden Global, 1996; The Age of Villages: the small village *vs* the global village, 2002; Iraky la Reconfiguración del Orden Mundial, 2003; La Guerra en Irak: causas y consecuencias, 2003; Tiene Futuro América Latina?, 2004; Los Estadounidenses, 2005; Hegemonía e Imperio, 2007; The World Upside Down: the complex partnership between China and Latin America, 2013. *Address:* 9 Ardmore Park #04-02, Singapore 259955. *T:* 68360872. *E:* alfredotorohardy@hotmail.com.

ToROBERT, Sir Henry Thomas, KBE 1981; Governor and Chairman of the Board of the Bank of Papua New Guinea since its formation, 1973–93; Partner, Deloitte Touche Tohmatsu, PNG, since 1993; Chairman, Credit Corporation (PNG) Ltd, 1993–2007; *b* Kokopo, 1942. *Educ:* primary educn in East New Britain; secondary educn in Qld, Australia; Univ. of Sydney, Aust. (BEcon. 1965). Asst Research Officer, Reserve Bank of Australia, Port Moresby, 1965 (one of first local officers to join the bank); Dep. Manager, Port Moresby Branch, 1971; Manager of the Reserve Bank, 1972 (the first Papua New Guinean to hold such a position at a time when all banks were branches of the Aust. commercial banks). Member of the cttee responsible for working out a PNG banking system which came into effect by an act of parliament in 1973; Chairman: Management Bd, PNG Bankers' Coll., 1973–; PNG Currency Working Group advising the Govt on arrangements leading to the introduction of PNG currency, the Kina; ToRobert Cttee to look into problems of administration in PNG Public Service, 1979 (ToRobert Report, 1979); Council, PNG Inst. of Applied Social and Econ. Res., 1975–82; Govt Super Task Force on project implementation, 1994–. Pres., PNG Amateur Sports Fedn and PNG Olympic and Commonwealth Games Cttee, 1980–2012. *Address:* PO Box 898, Port Moresby, Papua New Guinea.

TORONTO, Archbishop of, since 2010; **Most Rev. Colin Robert Johnson;** Bishop of Toronto, since 2004; Metropolitan of Ontario, since 2010; *b* 6 Nov. 1952; *s* of John McLellan Johnson and Marie Lynn (*née* Johnston); *m* 1976, (Margaret) Ellen Johnson (*née* Smith); one *s* two *d*. *Educ:* Univ. of Western Ont (BA 1974); Trinity Coll., Toronto (MDiv 1977; DD 2005). Ordained deacon, 1977, priest, 1978; Asst Curate, Ch of St Simon-the-Apostle, Toronto, 1977–78; Incumbent, Parish of Georgina, 1978–83; Regional Dean, Deanery of the Holland, 1980–83; Incumbent, Ch of the Holy Trinity, Ajax, 1983–92; Exec. Asst to Archbishop of Toronto, and Hon. Asst, St Martin's Bay Ridges, Pickering, and Assisting Priest, St James' Cathedral, Toronto, 1992–2003; Archdeacon of York, 1994–2003; Acting Dir of Communications, Dio. Toronto, 1994–97 and 2001–03; a Bp Suffragan of Toronto, and Area Bp of Trent Durham, 2003–04. *Recreations:* music, mystery novels, movies, cooking, computers. *Address:* (office) 135 Adelaide Street East, Toronto, ON M5C 1L8, Canada. *T:* (416) 3636021. *E:* cjohnson@toronto.anglican.ca.

TORONTO, Archbishop of, (RC), since 2007; **His Eminence Cardinal Thomas Collins,** STD; *b* 16 Jan. 1947. *Educ:* St Jerome's Coll., Waterloo, Ont. (BA 1969); St Peter's Seminary, London, Ont. (BTh 1973); Univ. of Western Ontario (MA 1973); Pontifical Biblical Inst., Rome (SSL 1978); Gregorian Univ., Rome (STD 1986). Ordained deacon, 1972, priest, 1973; Associate Pastor, Holy Rosary Parish, Burlington, Ont., and Christ the King Cath., Hamilton, Ont., and teacher and Chaplain, Cathedral Boys' High Sch., Hamilton, Ont., 1973–75; Lectr, Dept of English, King's Coll., Univ. of Western Ontario, 1978–84; St Peter's Seminary: Lectr in Scripture, 1978–84; Gp Leader and Spiritual Dir, 1981–95; Associate Prof. of Scripture, 1985–97; Dean of Theol. and Vice-Rector, 1992–95; Rector, 1995–97; Bishop of St Paul, Alberta, 1997–99; Archbishop of Edmonton (Alberta), (RC), 1999–2007. Cardinal, 2012. President: Alberta Conf. of Catholic Bishops, 1999–2007; Assembly of Catholic Bishops of Ontario (formerly Ontario Conf. of Catholic Bishops), 2008–; Mem., Permt Council, Canadian Conf. of Catholic Bishops, 1999–2003, 2007– (Chm., Nat. Commn of Theol., 1999–2001; Chm., 2001–03, Mem., 2003–05, Nat. Commn on Christian Unity); Member: Vatican Pontifical Council for Social Communications, 2010–; Vatican Congregation for Catholic Educn, 2012–; Commn of Cardinals for oversight of Inst. for Works of Religion, 2014–. Member, Board of Directors: Caritas Health Gp, Edmonton, 1999–2007; Alberta Catholic Health Corp., 1999–2007; Chm., Bd of Dirs, Catholic Charities, Archdiocese of Toronto, 2007–; Trustee, Adv. Bd, Sharelife, 2007–. Chairman, Board of Governors: Newman Theol Coll., Edmonton, 1999–2007; St Joseph's Coll., Edmonton, 1999–2007; St Augustine's Seminary, Toronto, 2007–; Chancellor: Univ. of St Michael's Coll., Univ. of Toronto, 2007–; Pontifical Inst. of Mediaeval Studies, Toronto, 2007–; Chair, Bd of Dirs, Redemptoris Mater Missionary Seminary, Toronto, 2007–. Associate Ed., Discover the Bible, 1989–94; columnist, Bread of Life mag., 1987–89. *Publications:* The Eucharist: It is the Lord!, 2000; Reconciliation: Go in Peace, 2003; Pathway to Our Hearts: a simple approach to Lectio Divina with the Sermon on the Mount, 2011; Cornerstones of Faith: reconciliation, Eucharist and stewardship, 2012; contrib. to Journey, Emmanuel, and Canadian Catholic Review. *Address:* 1155 Yonge Street, Toronto, ON M4T 1W2, Canada.

TORONTO, Area Bishops of; *see* Nicholls, Rt Rev. L. C.; Yu, Rt Rev. P. T.-S.

TORPHICHEN, 15th Lord *cr* 1564; **James Andrew Douglas Sandilands;** *b* 27 Aug. 1946; *s* of 14th Lord Torphichen, and Mary Thurstan, *d* of late Randle Henry Neville Vaudrey; *S* father, 1975; *m* 1976, Margaret Elizabeth, *o d* of late William A. Beale and of Mrs Margaret Patten Beale, Peterborough, New Hampshire, USA; four *d*. *Heir: cousin* Robert Powell Sandilands, Master of Torphichen [*b* 10 Dec. 1950; *m* 1974, Cheryl Lynn Watson; one *s* one *d*]. *Address:* Calder House, Mid-Calder, West Lothian EH53 0HN.

TORPY, Air Chief Marshal Sir Glenn (Lester), GCB 2008 (KCB 2005); CBE 2000; DSO 1991; Senior Military Advisor, BAE Systems, since 2011; *b* 27 July 1953; *s* of Gordon Torpy and Susan Torpy (*née* Lindsey); *m* 1977, Christine Jackson. *Educ:* Imperial Coll., London (BSc Eng). OC No 13 Sqn, 1989–92; PSO to AOC-in-C STC, 1992–94; Stn Comdr, RAF Bruggen, 1994–96; rcds 1997; ACOS Ops, Permanent Jt HQ, 1998–99; Dir Air Ops, MoD, 1999–2000; ACDS (Ops), 2000–01; AOC No 1 Gp, 2001–03; Dep. C-in-C Strike Command, 2003–04; Chief of Jt Ops, MoD, 2004–06; CAS, 2006–09; Air ADC to the Queen, 2006–09. Chm., Trustees, RAF Mus., 2013–. Liveryman, Haberdashers' Co., 2006. FRAeS 2003; FCGI 2007. Officer, Legion of Merit (USA), 2003. *Recreations:* golf, hill walking, military history, cabinet making. *T:* (01252) 384880. *E:* glenn.torpy@btinternet.com.

TORRANCE, Very Rev. Prof. Iain Richard, TD 1995; DPhil; FRSE; a Chaplain-in-Ordinary to the Queen in Scotland, since 2001; Pro-Chancellor, University of Aberdeen, since 2013; Dean, Chapel Royal in Scotland, since 2013; Dean of the Order of the Thistle, since 2014; Hon. Professor of Early Christian Doctrine and Ethics, University of Edinburgh, since 2013; *b* 13 Jan. 1949; *yr s* of Very Rev. Prof. Thomas Forsyth Torrance, MBE, FBA and of Margaret Edith Spear; *m* 1975, Morag Ann MacHugh, *er d* of Francis John MacHugh and Wendy Anne Lang; one *s* one *d*. *Educ:* Edinburgh Acad.; Monkton Combe Sch., Bath; Edinburgh Univ. (MA Mental Philosophy, 1971); St Andrews Univ. (BD New Testament Langs and Lit., 1974); Oriel Coll., Oxford (DPhil 1980). Chaplain to the Moderator, Gen. Assembly of Church of Scotland, 1976–77; ordained, 1982; Minister, Northmavine, Shetland, 1982–85; Lecturer: in NT and Christian Ethics, Queen's Coll., Birmingham, 1985–89; in NT and Patristics, Birmingham Univ., 1989–93; Aberdeen University: Lectr in Divinity, 1993–97; Sen. Lectr, 1997–99; Prof. in Patristics and Christian Ethics, 1999–2004; Prof. Emeritus, 2004; Senate Assessor to Univ. Court, 1999–2003; Head, Dept of Divinity and Religious Studies, 2000–01; Dean, Faculty of Arts and Divinity, 2001–03; Master, Christ's Coll., Aberdeen, 2001–04; Pres., 2004–12, now Pres. Emeritus, and Prof. of Patristics, 2004–12, now Prof. Emeritus, Princeton Theological Seminary, New Jersey; Trustee, Center for Theological Inquiry, Princeton, 2004–12. Moderator, Gen. Assembly of Church of Scotland, 2003–04. TA Chaplain, 1982–97; ACF Chaplain, 1996–2000; Convener: Cttee on Chaplains to HM Forces, Gen. Assembly of C of S, 1998–2002; Theological Forum, Gen. Assembly of C of S, 2013–. Select Preacher: Univ. of Oxford, 2004; Princeton Univ., 2005; Univ. of Aberdeen, 2009, 2013; St Andrews Univ., 2013; Lectures: Willard, Charlotte, 2005; W. G. A. Wright, Sandhurst, 2005; Berger, Potomac, 2006; Stoner, Pittsburgh, 2008; Hoon-Bullock, San Antonio, 2009; Henderson, Pittsburgh Theological Seminary, 2013. Member: Dialogue between World Alliance of Reformed Churches and the Orthodox Church, 1992–2010 (Co-Chm., 2005–10); Acad. Internat. des Sciences Religieuses, 1997–; Benchmarking Panel for Degrees in Theology and Religious Studies, QAA, 1999–2000; Dialogue between World Communion of Reformed Churches and Anglican Communion,

2015–. Sec., Soc. for Study of Christian Ethics, 1995–98; Hon. Sec., 1995–98, Hon. Pres., 1998–99, Aberdeen AUT. Judge, Templeton (UK) Award, 1994–99; Mem. Adv. Bd, Templeton Foundn, 2008–10. Trustee, Aberdeen Univ. Develt Trust, 2013–; Patron, Assoc. of Univ. Depts of Theol. and Religious Studies, 2013–. Co-ed., Scottish Jl of Theol., 1982–2015; Mem., Editl Bd, Ecclesiology, 2015–. Burgess of Guild, City of Aberdeen, 2004. Corresp. FRSE 2007, FRSE 2013. OStJ 2015. Hon. DD: Aberdeen, 2005; St Andrews, 2005; Edinburgh, 2012; Hon. DTheol Reformed Theol Univ., Debrecen, Hungary, 2006; Hon. LHD King Coll., Tennessee, 2007. Friend for Life Award, Equality Network, 2004; Hon. Dist. Alumnus, 2012, Medal of Commendation for Christian Leadership, 2012, Princeton Theological Seminary; James I. McCord Award for Outstanding Contrib. to Ecumenical Scholarship, Center for Theological Inquiry, Princeton, 2012. *Publications:* Christology after Chalcedon, 1989; (jtly) Human Genetics: a Christian perspective, 1995; Ethics and the Military Community, 1998; (ed jtly) To Glorify God: essays on modern reformed liturgy, 1999; (ed) Bioethics for the New Millennium, 2000; (ed jtly) The Oxford Handbook of Systematic Theology, 2007; (ed jtly) The Cambridge Dictionary of Christian Theology, 2011; The Correspondence of Severus and Sergius, 2011; many articles. *Recreation:* historical Scottish culture (buildings, literature, art). *Address:* (home) 25 The Causeway, Duddingston Village, Edinburgh EH15 3QA. *T:* (0131) 661 3092. *E:* irt@ptsem.edu. *Clubs:* New, Royal Scots (Edinburgh); Pilgrims (NY); Duddingston Golf (Edinburgh).

TORRANCE, Madeline Mary; *see* Drake, M. M.

TORRANCE, Monica; *see* Ali, Monica.

TORRANCE, Samuel Robert, OBE 2003 (MBE 1995); professional golfer; *b* Largs, 24 Aug. 1953; *s* of late Robert Torrance and of June Torrance; *m* 1995, Suzanne Danielle; one *s* two *d.* Winner: Under-25 Match Play tournament Radici Open, 1972; Zambian Open, 1975; Martini Internat., Wales, 1976; Scottish PGA Championship, 1978, 1980, 1985, 1991, 1993, 1995; Colombian Open, 1979; Australian PGA Championship, 1980; Irish Open, 1981, 1995; Spanish Open, 1982; Portuguese Open, 1982, 1983; Scandinavian Open, 1983; Tunisian Open, 1984; Benson & Hedges Internat., England, 1984; Sanyo Open, Spain, 1984; Monte Carlo Open, 1985; Italian Open, 1987, 1995; German Masters, 1990; Jersey Open, 1991; Catalan Open, 1993; Kronenbourg Open, Italy, 1993; Honda Open, Germany, 1993; British Masters, 1995; French Open, 1998; Travis Perkins Senior Masters, 2004; European Senior Tour Order of Merit, 2005, 2006. Member: Dunhill Cup team, 1985–95 (winners, 1995); World Cup team, 1976–95; Mem., 1981–95, Captain, 2001–02, Ryder Cup team (winners, 1985, 1995, 2002). *Publications:* Sam (autobiog.), 2003. *Recreations:* snooker, tennis, all sport.

TORRAVILLE, Rt Rev. David; *see* Newfoundland, Central, Bishop of.

TORRENTS, Deborah Jane; *see* Bronnert, D. J.

TORRINGTON, 11th Viscount *cr* 1721; **Timothy Howard St George Byng;** Bt 1715; Baron Byng of Southill, 1721; *b* 13 July 1943; *o s* of Hon. George Byng, RN (*d* on active service, 1944; *o s* of 10th Viscount) and Anne Yvonne Wood (she *m* 2nd, 1951, Howard Henry Masterton Carpenter; 3rd, 1990, Michael Ingram Bostock); *S* grandfather, 1961; *m* 1973, Susan, *d* of late Michael George Thomas Webster; three *d. Educ:* Harrow; St Edmund Hall, Oxford. Mem., Select Cttee on EEC, H of L, 1984–87 (Chm., Sub-Cttee B (Energy, Transport and Broadcasting), 1985–87). Chm., Baltic Mills Ltd, 1995–; Dir, Lansdowne Oil & Gas plc, 2005–. *Recreation:* travel. *Heir: kinsman* Colin Hugh Cranmer-Byng [*b* 10 Sept. 1960; *m* 1984, Lisa Anne Dallimore; two *s* four *d*]. *Address:* Belbins House, Whitehill, Mere, Wilts BA12 6BL. *Clubs:* White's, Pratt's; Muthaiga (Nairobi).

TORRY, Sir Peter (James), GCVO 2004; KCMG 2003; HM Diplomatic Service, retired; consultant; *b* 2 Aug. 1948; *m* 1979, Angela Wakeling Wood, *d* of late Joseph Neville Wood, CBE; three *d. Educ:* Dover Coll.; New Coll., Oxford (Open Schol.; BA 1970; Irvine Award, 1968; Rugby Blue, 1968, 1969). Joined FCO, 1970; Third Sec., Havana, 1971; Second Sec., Jakarta, 1974; First Sec., FCO, 1977; Bonn, 1981; First Sec., subseq. Counsellor, FCO, 1985; Washington, 1989; FCO, 1993–98, Dir (Personnel and Security), 1995–98; Ambassador: to Spain, 1998–2003; to the FRG, 2003–07. Senior Adviser: Celesio AG, 2007–10; Centrica PLC, 2008–; STAR Capital, 2009–; Cairn Capital, 2013–; Mem., Supervisory Bd, Blohm and Voss AG. Member, Advisory Board: Kiel World Economic Forum, 2007–; Betfair plc, 2011–. Policy Fellow, Bonn Inst. for Employment, 2009–. *Recreations:* golf, walking, ski-ing, books, antique furniture. *Address:* c/o Peter Torry Consultancy, 192 Emery Hill Street, SW1P 1PN. *Clubs:* Oxford and Cambridge; Vincent's (Oxford).

TORTELIER, Yan Pascal; Principal Conductor, São Paulo Symphony Orchestra, 2009–11, now Guest Conductor of Honour; *b* 19 April 1947; *s* of late Paul Tortelier and of Maud (*née* Martin); *m* 1970, Sylvie Brunet-Moret; two *s. Educ:* Paris Conservatoire; general musical studies with Nadia Boulanger; studied conducting with Franco Ferrara in Sienna. Leader and Associate Conductor, Orchestre du Capitole de Toulouse, 1974–82; Principal Conductor and Artistic Dir, Ulster Orchestra, 1989–92; Principal Conductor, BBC Philharmonic, 1999–2002, now Conductor Emeritus. Principal Guest Conductor, Pittsburgh SO, 2005–. Has conducted all major British orchestras and toured extensively in USA, Canada, Japan, Australia, Scandinavia, E and W Europe. Numerous recordings incl. complete symphonic works of Debussy and Ravel with Ulster Orch., and Hindemith and Dutilleux series with BBC Philharmonic. Hon. DLitt Ulster, 1992. *Publications:* Première orchestration of Ravel's Piano Trio, 1992. *Recreations:* ski-ing, windsurfing, scuba diving, nature. *Address:* c/o IMG Artists Europe, The Light Box, 111 Power Road, Chiswick, W4 5PY.

TORVILL, Jayne, (Mrs P. L. Christensen), OBE 2000 (MBE 1981); professional ice skater; *b* 7 Oct. 1957; *d* of George Henry Torvill and Betty (*née* Smart); *m* 1990, Philip Lee Christensen; one adopted *s* one adopted *d. Educ:* Clifton Hall Grammar Sch. for Girls, Nottingham. Ice dancer, with Christopher Dean, *qv*; British Champions, 1978, 1979, 1980, 1981, 1982, 1983 and 1994; European Champions, 1981, 1982, 1984 and 1994; World Champions, 1981, 1982, 1983 and 1984; World Professional Champions, 1984, 1985, 1990, 1995 and 1996; Olympic Champions, 1984; Olympic Bronze Medallists, 1994. Trainer, choreographer and performer: Stars on Ice, USA, 1998–99, 1999–2000; Dancing on Ice, ITV, 2006, 2007, 2008, 2009, 2010, 2011, 2012, 2013, 2014; trainer, Ice Rink on the Estate, ITV, 2015. Hon. MA Nottingham Trent, 1994. *Publications:* (with Christopher Dean) Facing the Music, 1995; (with Christopher Dean) Our Life on Ice, 2014. *Recreations:* dance, theatre. *Address:* PO Box 32, Heathfield, E Sussex TN21 0BW. *T:* (01435) 867825.

TOSELAND, Ronald James, OBE 1991; Deputy Controller, National Air Traffic Services, 1988–91, retired; *b* 7 March 1933; *s* of W. M. and E. Toseland; *m* 1954, Joan Mary (*d* 2002), *d* of A. R. and D. M. Pickett; two *s. Educ:* Kettering Central School. RAF Navigator, 1951–61; Air Traffic Control Officer, 1961–91; i/c Heathrow ATC, 1981–83; Dir, Civil Air Traffic Ops, 1983–87; Joint Field Commander, NATS, 1987–88. *Recreations:* music, walking. *Address:* 1 Marshall Place, Oakley Green, Windsor SL4 4QD. *T:* (01753) 863313.

TOSH, (Neil) Murray, MBE 1987; Member (C) Scotland West, Scottish Parliament, 2003–07 (Scotland South, 1999–2003); *b* 1 Sept. 1950; *s* of late Neil Ferguson Tosh and of Mary Drummond Tosh (*née* Murray); *m* 1970, Christine Hind (*d* 2007); two *s* one *d. Educ:* Kilmarnock Acad.; Univ. of Glasgow (MA 2nd Cl. Hons); Jordanhill Coll. of Educn (Secondary Teaching Qualif.). Teacher of history, Ravenspark Acad., Irvine, 1975–77; principal teacher of history: Kilwinning Acad., 1977–84; Belmont Acad., Ayr, 1984–99. Mem. (C) Kyle and Carrick DC, 1987–96 (Convener, Housing Cttee and Vice Convener, Planning and Develt Cttee, 1992–96). Contested (C) Dumfries, Scottish Parlt, 2007. Scottish Parliament: Convener, Procedures Cttee, 1999–2003; Member: Transport and Envmt Cttee, 1999–2001; Subordinate Legislation Cttee, 2003–07; Dep. Presiding Officer, 2001–07. *Recreations:* hill-walking, reading (historical, political), historic buildings, touring holidays. *Address:* 14 Harleyburn Avenue, Melrose, Roxburghshire TD6 9JZ.

TOTARO, Prof. Burt James, PhD; FRS 2009; Professor of Mathematics, University of California, Los Angeles, since 2012; *b* 8 Aug. 1967. *Educ:* Princeton Univ. (AB 1984); Univ. of Calif at Berkeley (PhD 1989). Mathematical Scis Res. Inst., Berkeley, 1989–90; Dickson Instructor, 1990–93, Asst Prof., 1993–99, Dept of Maths, Univ. of Chicago; Mem., Inst. for Advanced Study, Princeton, 1994–95; Lectr, Dept of Pure Mathematics and Mathematical Statistics, 1999, Lowndean Prof. of Astronomy and Geometry, 2000–13, Univ. of Cambridge. Eisenbud Prof., Mathematical Scis Res. Inst., Berkeley, 2009. Mem. Council, LMS, 2007–12. Ed., Proc. of LMS, 2003–08; Mem., Mgt Cttee, Jl of K-Theory, 2007–09; Man. Ed., Compositio Mathematica, 2008–. Whitehead Prize, LMS, 2000; Prix Franco-Britannique, Acad. des Scis, 2001. *Recreation:* cats. *Address:* Mathematics Department, University of California, Los Angeles, PO Box 951555, Los Angeles, CA 90095–1555, USA.

TOTNES, Archdeacon of; *see* Dettmer, Ven. D. J.

TOTTEN, William John; Sheriff of Glasgow and Strathkelvin at Glasgow, since 1999; *b* 11 Sept. 1954; *s* of David and Sarah Totten; *m* 1985, Shirley Ann Morrison; one *s. Educ:* John Neilson Instn, Paisley; Univ. of Glasgow (LLB Hons 1977). Apprentice, Tindal, Oatts & Rodger, 1977–79; admitted solicitor, 1979; Procurator Fiscal Service, 1979–83; Asst, then Partner, Beltrami & Co., 1983–88; admitted to Faculty of Advocates, 1989; Advocate-Depute, 1993–96; Temp. Sheriff, 1998–99. *Recreations:* cycling, ski-ing, walking, reading, foreign travel. *Address:* Sheriff's Chambers, Sheriff Court House, 1 Carlton Place, Glasgow G5 9DA. *T:* (0141) 429 8888.

TOTTENHAM, family name of **Marquess of Ely**.

TÖTTERMAN, Richard Evert Björnson, Kt Comdr, Order of the White Rose of Finland; Hon. GCVO 1976 (Hon. KCVO 1969); Hon. OBE 1961; Finnish Ambassador, retired; *b* 10 Oct. 1926; *s* of Björn B. Tötterman and Katharine C. (*née* Wimpenny); *m* 1953, Camilla Susanna Veronica Huber; one *s* one *d. Educ:* Univ. of Helsinki (Jur. lic.); Brasenose Coll., Oxford (DPhil; Hon. Fellow, 1982). Entered Finnish Foreign Service, 1952: served Stockholm, 1954–56; Moscow, 1956–58; Min. for For. Affairs, Finland, 1958–62; Berne, 1962–63; Paris, 1963–66; Dep. Dir, Min. for For. Affairs, Helsinki, 1966; Sec.-Gen., Office of the President of Finland, 1966–70; Sec. of State, Min. for For. Aff., 1970–75; Ambassador: UK, 1975–83; Switzerland, 1983–90, and (concurrently) to the Holy See, 1988–90. Chm. or Mem. of a number of Finnish Govt Cttees, 1959–75, and participated as Finnish rep. in various internat. negotiations; Chm., Multilateral Consultations preparing Conf. on Security and Co-operation in Europe, 1972–73. Holds numerous foreign orders (Grand Cross, Kt Comdr, etc). *Recreations:* music, outdoor life, international relations. *Address:* Parkgatan 9 A 11, 00140 Helsinki, Finland.

TOUCHE, Sir Anthony (George), 3rd Bt *cr* 1920; Deputy Chairman, Friends' Provident Life Office, 1983–96; *b* 31 Jan. 1927; *s* of Donovan Meredith Touche (*d* 1952) (2nd *s* of 1st Bt) and of Muriel Amy Frances (*d* 1983), *e d* of Rev. Charles R. Thorold Winckley; *S* uncle, 1977; *m* 1961, Hester Christina, *er d* of Dr Werner Pleuger; two *s* one *d* (and one *s* decd). *Educ:* Eton College. FCA. Partner in George A. Touche & Co. (later Touche Ross & Co.), 1951; Director of investment trust companies, 1952–90; retired from Touche Ross & Co., 1968; Touche, Remnant Holdings Ltd, 1965–89. Dir, 1968–90, Dep. Chm., 1977–87, National Westminster Bank. Chairman, Assoc. of Investment Trust Companies, 1971–73. Prime Warden, Goldsmiths' Co., 1987. *Recreations:* music, reading, walking. *Heir: s* William George Touche [*b* 26 June 1962; *m* 1987, Elizabeth Louise, *y d* of Allen Bridges; three *s* one *d*]. *Address:* Stane House, Ockley, Dorking, Surrey RH5 5TQ. *T:* (01306) 627397.

TOUCHE, Sir Rodney (Gordon), 2nd Bt *cr* 1962; *b* 5 Dec. 1928; *s* of Rt Hon. Sir Gordon Touche, 1st Bt, and Ruby, Lady Touche (formerly Ruby Ann Macpherson) (*d* 1989); *S* father, 1972; *m* 1955, Ouida Ann (*d* 2009), *d* of F. G. MacLellan, Moncton, NB, Canada; one *s* two *d* (and one *d* decd). *Educ:* Marlborough; University Coll., Oxford. *Heir: s* Eric MacLellan Touche [*b* 22 Feb. 1960; *m* 1990, Leeanne Marie Stringer (marr. diss. 1998); one *s* one *d*; *m* 2005, Catherine Parenteau]. *Address:* 2403 Westmount Place, 1100 8th Avenue SW, Calgary, AB T2P 3T9, Canada. *T:* (403) 2338800.

TOUHIG, family name of **Baron Touhig**.

TOUHIG, Baron *cr* 2010 (Life Peer), of Islwyn and Glansychan in the County of Gwent; **James Donnelly, (Don), Touhig;** PC 2006; *b* 5 Dec. 1947; *s* of Michael Touhig and Catherine Touhig (*née* Corten); *m* 1968, Jennifer Hughes (*d* 2014); two *s* two *d. Educ:* St Francis Sch., Aberyschan; E Monmouth Coll., Pontypool. Journalist, 1968–95; Editor, Free Press of Monmouthshire, 1976–90; General Manager: Free Press Gp, 1988–92; (Business Develt) Bailey Gp, 1992–93; Bailey Print, 1993–95. MP (Lab and Co-op) Islwyn, 1995–2010. PPS to Chancellor of the Exchequer, 1997–99; an Asst Govt Whip, 1999–2001; Parly Under-Sec. of State, Wales Office, 2001–05, MoD, 2005–06. Member: Welsh Select Cttee, 1996–97; Public Accounts Cttee, 2006–10; Chm., Members' Allowances Cttee, 2009–10 (Mem., Liaison Cttee, 2009–10); Chm., All-Party Alcohol Abuse Gp, 1996–99; Jt Sec., All-Party Police Gp, 1996–97; Hon. Sec., Welsh Gp, 1995–99, Mem., Backbench Cttee, 2007–10, PLP. Lab. Party Parly Advr to Police Fedn of Eng. and Wales, 1996–98. KSS 1991. *Recreations:* reading, cooking for family and friends, walking. *Address:* House of Lords, SW1A 0PW.

TOULMIN, (Ann) Camilla, DPhil; Director, International Institute for Environment and Development, since 2003; *b* Melbourne, 12 Aug. 1954; *d* of late Prof. Stephen Edelston Toulmin and Margaret Alison Toulmin (*née* Coutts); *m* 1983, Mark Ellis Powell Jones (*see* Sir Mark Jones); two *s* one *d. Educ:* English Sch., Addis Ababa; Oxford High Sch.; New Hall, Cambridge (BA Econs 1975); Sch. of Oriental and African Studies, Univ. of London (MSc Econs 1976); Somerville Coll., Oxford (DPhil Econs 1987). Lectr, Ahmadu Bello Univ., Zaria, 1977–79; Researcher: Internat. Livestock Centre for Africa, 1980–82; ODI, 1985–87; International Institute for Environment and Development: Prog. Dir, 1987–2002; Sen. Fellow, 2002–03. Member: French Min. of Foreign Affairs Steering Cttee on Land Tenure, 1996–; UK Govt Foresight Lead Expert Gp, Global Food and Farming Futures, 2009–11; Royal Soc. Wkg Gp on Reaping the Benefits, 2008–09, on Resilience, 2013–14; Adv. Council, Grantham Inst. for Climate Change Res., 2009–; Adv. Council, Envmtl Change Inst., Univ. of Oxford, 2013–. Trustee: Oxfam, 1986–88; WWF, 2004–10; Internat. Center for Agricl Res. in Dry Areas, 2008– (Chair, 2012–); Franco-British Council, 2008–. Mem. Council, Royal Africa Soc., 2003–. *Publications:* Cattle, Women and Wells, 1992; Sustaining the Soil, 1996; Evolving Land Rights, Policy and Tenure in Africa, 2000; Dynamics of Resource Tenure, 2002; Towards a New Map of Africa, 2005; Climate Change in Africa, 2009. *Recreations:* walking, family and friends. *Address:* International Institute for Environment and Development, 80–86 Gray's Inn Road, WC1X 8NH. *T:* (020) 3463 7399, *Fax:* (020) 3514 9055. *E:* camilla.toulmin@iied.org.

TOULMIN, Timothy James; Founder and Managing Director, Alder Media Ltd, since 2010; Specialist Partner, Issues and Crisis Management, Pagefield, since 2013; *b* 19 Jan. 1975; *s* of Michael Toulmin and Sandy Toulmin (*née* Rawkins). *Educ:* Repton Sch.; Peterhouse, Cambridge (MA (Hist.)). Press Complaints Commission, 1996–2009: Dep. Dir, 2000–03; Acting Dir, 2004; Dir, 2004–09. Mem. Council, Friends of Peterhouse, 2005–09. Trustee:

Parents and Abducted Children Together, 2013–; Stonewall, 2015–. *Recreations:* sailing, hill walking, watching cricket. *Address:* Alder Media Ltd, 25 Sackville Street, W1S 3AX. *E:* tim.toulmin@aldermedia.co.uk.

TOULSON, Rt Hon. Lord; Roger Grenfell Toulson, Kt 1996; PC 2007; a Justice of the Supreme Court of the United Kingdom, since 2013; *b* 23 Sept. 1946; *s* of late Stanley Kilsha Toulson and Lilian Mary Toulson; *m* 1973, Elizabeth Chrimes (*see* E. Toulson); two *s* two *d*. *Educ:* Mill Hill School; Jesus College, Cambridge (MA, LLB; Hon. Fellow 2007). Called to the Bar, Inner Temple, 1969, Bencher, 1995; QC 1986; a Recorder, 1986–96; a Judge of the High Court of Justice, QBD, 1996–2007; Presiding Judge, Western Circuit, 1997–2002; a Lord Justice of Appeal, 2007–13. Chm., Law Commn, 2002–06; Mem., Judicial Appts Commn, 2007–12. Hon. LLD: UWE, 2002; Bradford, 2008. *Publications:* (with C. M. Phipps) Confidentiality, 1996, 3rd edn 2012. *Recreations:* ski-ing, tennis, gardening. *Address:* Supreme Court of the United Kingdom, Parliament Square, SW1P 3BD. *Club:* Old Millhillians.

TOULSON, Elizabeth, (Lady Toulson), CBE 1999; DL; *b* 10 Nov. 1948; *d* of late Henry Bertram Chrimes and of Suzanne Isabel Chrimes (*née* Corbett-Lowe); *m* 1973, Roger Grenfell Toulson (*see* Rt Hon. Lord Toulson); two *s* two *d*. *Educ:* Liverpool Univ.; Clare Hall, Cambridge (LLB). Called to the Bar, Inner Temple, 1974. Women's Royal Voluntary Service: Trustee, 1981–; Vice-Chm., 1989–93; Nat. Chm., 1993–99. Director: Queen Elizabeth Foundn for Disabled People, 1999–; Surrey Voluntary Service Council, 1999–2002; Chm., Children's Soc., 2001–04. Chm. Council, 2011–, Lay Canon, 2013–, Guildford Cathedral. Trustee, Elizabeth Finn Trust, 2002–05. Vice-Patron: Guildford Choral Soc., 2001–; Vocaleyes, 2004–; Patron: Marriage Foundn, 2012–; Surrey Assoc. for Visual Impairment, 2013–; Pres., Surrey St John Ambulance, 2010–12. Advr, CAB, 2002–. Chairman: Nyika Vwaza Trust, 2003–08; Music of Life Foundn, 2003–04; Time for Families, 2006–10; Trustee, Guildford Community Family Trust, 2004–06. Governor: Charterhouse Sch., 1998–; Suttons Hosp., 2004–08. FRSA 2006. High Sheriff, 2009–10, DL 2009, Surrey. *Recreations:* reading, music, walking, tennis, swimming, ski-ing. *Address:* Billhurst Farm, White Hart Lane, Wood Street Village, Guildford, Surrey GU3 3DZ; 201 Rowan House, 9 Greycoat Street, SW1P 2QD.

TOULSON, Roger Grenfell; *see* Toulson, Rt Hon. Lord.

TOUMAZOU, Prof. Christofer, PhD; FRS 2008; FREng, FMedSci; Regius Professor of Engineering, since 2013 and Chief Scientist and Director, Institute of Biomedical Engineering, since 2003, Imperial College London; *b* Cheltenham, 5 July 1961; *s* of Markos and Andriana Toumazou; *m* 2003, Melanie Anne Joyce; two *s*; one *s* one *d* by previous marriage to Ann Mackenzie. *Educ:* Oxford Brookes Univ. (BSc Hons 1st Cl. 1983; PhD; Hon. DEng 2010). FIEEE 2002; FIET 2005; FREng 2008. Imperial College London: Lectr, 1986–92; Prof. of Circuit Design, 1992–2013; Hd, Bioengrg Dept, 1999–2004; Winston Wong Prof. of Biomedical Circuits, 2005–13. Chairman and Chief Technology Officer: Toumaz Technology, 2000–; Future Waves Ltd, 2003–; Chm. and CEO, DNA Electronics Ltd, 2004–. MAE 2007. FCGI 2009; FMedSci 2013. Eur. Patent of Year Award, Eur. Patent Office, 2014. *Publications:* Analogue IC Design: the current-mode approach, 1990; (ed jtly) Switched-Currents: an analogue technique for digital technology, 1993; (ed jtly) Trade-Offs in Analog Circuit Design, 2004. *Recreations:* travelling, kendo, classical music. *Address:* 19 Ravenscourt Road, W6 0UH. *T:* (020) 8743 2037. *E:* c.toumazou@ic.ac.uk.

TOUT, Paul Edward H.; *see* Hill-Tout.

TOVEY, Sir Brian (John Maynard), KCMG 1980; independent art history scholar; Visiting Research Fellow, British Institute of Florence, since 2003; *b* 15 April 1926; *s* of Rev. Collett John Tovey (Canon, Bermuda Cathedral, 1935–38) and Kathleen Edith Maud Tovey (*née* Maynard); *m* 1989, Mary Helen (*née* Lane); one *s* three *d* by previous marriage. *Educ:* St Edward's Sch., Oxford; St Edmund Hall, Oxford, 1944–45; School of Oriental and African Studies, London, 1948–50. BA Hons London. Service with Royal Navy and subseq. Army (Intelligence Corps and RAEC), 1945–48. Joined Government Communications Headquarters as Jun. Asst, 1950; Principal, 1957; Asst Sec., 1967; Under Sec., 1975; Dep. Sec., 1978; Dir, 1978–83, retired. Defence Systems Consultant, 1983–85, and Defence and Political Adviser, 1985–88, Plessey Electronic Systems Ltd; Dir, Plessey Defence Systems Ltd, 1983–85. Chairman: IES Gp PLC, 1993–98; Cresswell Associates Ltd, 1988–2001; Fujitsu Europe Telecoms R & D Centre Ltd, 1990–2001. Vice-Pres. (Information and Communications Technology), Fedn of Electronics Industry, 1995–97. *Publications:* The Pouncey Index of Baldinucci's Notizie, 2005; contrib. Gazette des Beaux-Arts, Art Newspaper, Jl of Soc. for Renaissance Studies, Bull. of Soc. for Renaissance Studies. *Recreations:* music, history of art (espec. 16th and 17th Century Italian, and historical methodology of Filippo Baldinucci). *Club:* Naval and Military (Vice-Pres., 1995–2005).

TOVUE, Sir Ronald, Kt 1987; OBE 1981; Commissioner, Constitution Review Commission, Papua New Guinea, 1995–97; Premier, Provincial Government of East New Britain Province, Papua New Guinea, 1981–87; Member of Provincial Assembly, 1979–87; *b* 14 Feb. 1933; *s* of Apmeledi ToPalanga and Rachael Waruruai; *m* 1971, Suluet Tinvil; two *s* one *d*. *Educ:* Pilapila Community Sch.; Kerevat High Sch. Teacher, 1957–65; Magistrate, 1965–74; Commissioner, 1974–76; businessman, 1977–. *Recreations:* golf, reading, gardening, fishing, church activities. *Address:* Ratavul, PO Box 354, Rabaul, Papua New Guinea. *Club:* Rabaul Golf (Rabaul).

TOWE, Stewart Ronald, CBE 2008; DL; Chairman and Managing Director, Hadley Industries plc, since 2006; *b* Birmingham, 2 Aug. 1951; *s* of Ronald Towe and Margaret Towe; *m* 1978, Anne Westley; one *s* one *d*. *Educ:* Bromsgrove Sch. Accountant, Farmiloe & Co., 1972–76; Gp Accountant, 1976–78, Finance Dir, 1978–2006, Hadley Gp. Chairman: W Midlands Reg., Business in the Community, 2009–14; Black Country Local Enterprise Partnership, 2010–. Pro-Chancellor, Wolverhampton Univ., 2014– (Gov., 2008–14); Gov., Aston Univ., 2009–14; Chair of Governors: Ace Acad., Tipton, 2009–; Bromsgrove Sch., 2010–; Sandwell Acad., 2013–. Patron, Prince's Trust, 2012–. High Sheriff 2012, DL 2013, W Midlands. *Recreations:* equestrian centre management, dressage, Rugby, endurance motorsport. *Address:* Hadley Industries plc, PO Box 92, Downing Street, Smethwick, W Midlands B66 2PA. *T:* (0121) 555 1300, *Fax:* (0121) 555 1301. *E:* stewart.towe@hadleygroup.com.

TOWERS, John, CBE 1995; FREng, FIMechE; Chairman, Phoenix Venture Holdings Ltd, 2000–11; Chairman, Rover Group Ltd, 2000–05; *b* 30 March 1948; *s* of Jack Towers and Florence Towers (*née* Abley); *m* 1990, Bethanie Williams; one *s* one *d*. *Educ:* Durham Johnston Sch.; Univ. of Bradford (BSc Hons Mech. Engrg). CEng 1974; FREng (FEng 1992); FIMechE 1992; FIIM 1989. Joined Perkins Engines as student apprentice, 1966: Quality Engr, later Mfg Dir and Gen. Manager, 1983–86; Vice-Pres., Internat. Services, Varity Corp. (Canada), 1986–87; Man. Dir, Massey Ferguson Tractors, 1987–88; Rover Group, 1988–96: Mfg Dir, Land Rover, 1988–89; Product Develt Dir, 1989–90; Dir, 1990–91, Man. Dir, Jan.–Dec. 1991, Product Supply; Gp Man. Dir, 1991–94; Gp Chief Exec., 1994–96; Chief Exec., Concentric Gp, 1996–2000. Director: Midland Bank, 1995–96; B. Elliott, 1996–2000; HatWel Ltd, 1996–2011. Vis. Prof., Warwick Univ., 1993. Mem., Council for Sci. and Technol., 1993–97. DUniv Central England in Birmingham, 1994. *Recreations:* golf, music, shooting.

TOWL, Prof. Graham John, DSc; FBPsS; FAcSS; Principal, St Cuthbert's Society and Professor of Psychology, since 2008, and Pro-Vice-Chancellor and Deputy Warden, since 2011, Durham University; *b* Boosbeck, 13 Aug. 1961; *s* of John Bruce Towl and Barbara Towl (*née* Moore); *m* 1993, Jacqueline Marie Walton. *Educ:* St Martin's Comp. Sch., Caerphilly; Durham Univ. (BA 1988; DSc 2008); Birkbeck Coll., Univ. of London (MSc 1990); Univ. of Birmingham (MBA 2000). FBPsS 2009; FAcSS (AcSS 2010). Psychologist, HM Prison Service, 1988–92; Hd, Psychology Dept, HMP and YOI Highpoint, 1992–95; Area Psychologist, East Anglia, 1995–98, Kent, 1998–2000, HM Prison Service; Hd, Psychological Services, Prisons and Probation, 2000–05; Chief Psychologist, Home Office, later MoJ, 2005–08. Visiting Professor: Univ. of Birmingham, 2000–08; Univ. of Portsmouth, 2001–08. Member: Health and Care Professions Council, 2014–; Ind. Adv. Panel, Deaths in Custody, 2014–; Audit Cttee, Acad. of Social Scis; Nat. Advr on Mental Health, Nightline. FRSA 2010. Member: British Tang Sou Dao Fedn (3rd Dan Mem.); Zi Shiying Tang Sou Dao (studied Shotokan and Kyokushinkai). *Publications:* The Handbook of Psychology for Forensic Practitioners, 1996; Suicide in Prisons, 2000; Psychology in Prisons, 2003, 2nd edn 2008; Applying Psychology to Forensic Practice, 2004; Psychology in Probation Services, 2005; Psychological Research in Prisons, 2006; Dictionary of Forensic Psychology, 2008; Forensic Psychology, 2010, 2nd edn 2015. *Recreations:* walking (our beauceron on the beach), watching films, martial arts, eating good food. *Address:* Psychology Department, Durham University, Science Laboratories, South Road, Durham DH1 3LE.

TOWLE, Bridget Ellen, CBE 2001; DL; Chair, Council, University of Leicester, since 2013 (Member, since 2000); *b* 19 April 1942; *d* of late William Henry Towle and Marjorie Louisa (*née* Hardstaff). *Educ:* Westonbirt Sch.; Univ. of Exeter (BA Gen. Hons, BA Hons); Leicester Poly. (Post Grad. Courses in Textile Technol. and Business Mgt). Teacher, VSO, Uganda, 1965–66; Towles plc: marketing mgt roles, 1966–94; Dir, 1972–94; Jt Man. Dir, 1980–94. Guide Association, later Girlguiding UK: various appts, incl. County Comr, Leics, 1985–92; Chief Guide, UK, and Chief Comr, Commonwealth Girl Guide Assocs, 1996–2001; Vice Pres., 2003–. Treas., Univ. of Leicester, 2009–13. Trustee: Coll. of Optometrists, 2004–10 (Chm., Lay Adv. Panel, 2007–10); Friends of Nyakasura Sch., Uganda, 2005–12; RAF Benevolent Fund, 2005–13. Mem. Council, Leicester Literary and Philosophical Soc., 2014–. FRSA 1999. Hon. FCOptom 2013. Hon. LLD Exeter, 2000; Hon. DLitt Loughborough, 2002. Charity Trustee of the Year, Charity Times, 2000. DL Leics, 2013. *Recreations:* decorative arts, walking. *Address:* c/o University of Leicester, University Road, Leicester LE1 7RH. *Club:* Royal Air Force.

TOWNELEY, Sir Simon (Peter Edmund Cosmo William), KCVO 1994; Lord-Lieutenant and Custos Rotulorum of Lancashire, 1976–96; *b* 14 Dec. 1921; *e s* of late Col A. Koch de Gooreynd, OBE and Baroness Norman, CBE; assumed surname and arms of Towneley by royal licence, 1955, by reason of descent from *e d* and senior co-heiress of Col Charles Towneley of Towneley; *m* 1955, Mary, MBE (*d* 2001), 2nd *d* of Cuthbert Fitzherbert; one *s* six *d*. *Educ:* Stowe; Worcester Coll., Oxford (MA, DPhil; Ruffini Scholar). Served War of 1939–45, KRRC. Lectr in History of Music, Worcester Coll., Oxford, 1949–55. Mem., Agricultural Lands Tribunal, 1960–92. Dir, Granada Television, 1981–92. CC Lancs, 1961–64; JP 1956; DL 1970; High Sheriff of Lancashire, 1971. Mem. Council, Duchy of Lancaster, 1986–96. Patron: Nat. Assoc. for Mental Health (North-West); Emmaus Burnley, 2009–. Pres., NW of England and IoM TA&VRA, 1987–92; Chm., Northern Ballet Theatre, 1969–86; Member: Bd of Governors, Royal Northern Coll. of Music, 1961–98; Council, 1971–97, Court, 1971–98, Univ. of Manchester; Trustee: Historic Churches Preservation Trust, 1984–93; British Museum, 1988–93. Hon. Col, Duke of Lancaster's Own Yeomanry, 1979–88. CRNCM 1990; Hon. Fellow, Lancashire Polytechnic, 1987. Hon. DMus Lancaster, 1994. KStJ; KCSG. *Publications:* Venetian Opera in the Seventeenth Century, 1954 (repr. 1968); contribs to New Oxford History of Music. *Address:* Dyneley, Burnley, Lancs BB11 3RE. *T:* (01282) 423322. *Clubs:* Boodle's, Pratt's, Beefsteak.

See also Sir P. G. Worsthorne.

TOWNEND, Ian Howard, CEng, FREng; independent consultant, since 2014; Research Director, HR Wallingford Ltd, 2006–14; *b* Wolverhampton, 28 Feb. 1954; *s* of Gordon and Peggy Townend; *m* 1980, Mary Cranston; one *s* one *d*. *Educ:* Regis Sch., Wolverhampton; Exeter Univ. (BSc Engrg Sci. 1975). CEng 1980; CMarSci 2002. Joined Halcrow as Graduate Engr, 1975; Design Engr, 1975–81; Project Engr, 1981–91; Chief Coastal Engr, 1991–93; Man. Dir, ABPmer, 1993–2006. Visiting Professor: Univ. of Southampton, 2006–; East China Normal Univ., Shanghai, 2014–; Nanjing Hydraulic Res. Inst., Nanjing, 2014–. FREng 2010. *Recreations:* sailing, walking, music, sculpture, family. *Club:* Royal Southampton Yacht (Southampton).

TOWNEND, James Barrie Stanley, QC 1978; an Assistant Boundary Commissioner, since 2000; *b* 21 Feb. 1938; *s* of late Frederick Stanley Townend and Marjorie Elizabeth Townend (*née* Arnold); *m* 1st, 1970, Airelle Claire (*née* Nies) (marr. diss. 2005); one step *d*; 2nd, 2008, Marleen Marie Lucie (*née* Deknudt). *Educ:* Tonbridge Sch.; Lincoln Coll., Oxford (MA). National Service in BAOR and UK, 1955–57: 2nd Lieut, 18th Medium Regt, RA. Called to Bar, Middle Temple, 1962, Bencher, 1987; Head of Chambers, 1982–99; a Recorder, 1979–2003. Chairman: Sussex Crown Court Liaison Cttee, 1978–89; Family Law Bar Assoc., 1986–88; Member: Kingston and Esher DHA, 1983–86; Bar Council, 1984–88; Supreme Court Procedure Cttee, 1986–88. *Recreations:* sailing, fishing, writing verse. *Address:* Glenside, 69 Liverpool Road, Walmer, Deal, Kent CT14 7NN. *T:* (01304) 362723.

TOWNEND, John Coupe; Director for Europe, Bank of England, 1999–2002; *b* 24 Aug. 1947; *s* of Harry Norman Townend and Joyce Dentith (*née* Coupe); *m* 1969, Dorothy Allister; three *s*. *Educ:* Liverpool Inst. High Sch. for Boys; London Sch. of Economics (BSc Econ; MSc). With Bank of England, 1968–2002: First Head, Wholesale Markets Supervision Div., 1986–90; Head, Gilt-Edged and Money Markets Div., 1990–94; Dep. Dir, 1994–98. Non-executive Director: LCH.Clearnet Ltd, 2004–12; LCH.Clearnet Gp, 2008–12; LCH.Clearnet SA, 2008–12. *Publications:* articles in econ. jls. *Recreations:* running, trekking, opera, birds, grandchildren.

TOWNEND, John Ernest; *b* 12 June 1934; *s* of Charles Hope Townend and Dorothy Townend; *m* 1963, Jennifer Ann; two *s* two *d*. *Educ:* Hymers Coll., Hull. FCA (Plender Prize). Articled Clerk, Chartered Accountants, 1951–56; National Service: Pilot Officer, RAF, 1957–59; J. Townend & Sons Ltd (Hull) Ltd: Co. Sec./Dir, 1959–67; Man. Dir, 1967–77; Chm., 1977–; Vice-Chm., Surrey Building Soc., 1984–93; Dir, AAH Hldgs, 1989–94. Mem., Hull City Council, 1966–74 (Chm., Finance Cttee, 1968–70); Chm., Humber Bridge Bd, 1969–71; Mem., Yorks and Humberside Econ. Planning Council, 1970; Member, Humberside County Council, 1973–79: Cons. Leader of Opposition, 1973–77; Leader, 1977–79; Chm., Policy Cttee, 1977–79. Mem., Policy Cttee, Assoc. of County Councils, 1977–79. MP (C) Bridlington, 1979–97, E Yorks, 1997–2001. PPS to Minister of State for Social Security, 1981–83. Mem., Treasury and Civil Service Select Cttee, 1983–92; Chm., Cons. Small Business Cttee, 1988–92; Vice Chm., Cons. back bench Finance Cttee, 1983–91, 1997–2001 (Chm., 1993–97). Member: Council of Europe, 1992–2001; WEU, 1992–2001. Life Gov., Hymers Coll., Hull, 1965. Chm., Merchant Vintners Co., 1964–2000 (Life Pres., 2000); Liveryman, Distillers' Co., 1998–; Liveryman, Woolmen's Co., 1984– (Master, 2004–05). *Recreations:* swimming, tennis. *Address:* Little Acorns, 2 Brimley Green, Beverley, E Yorks HU17 7BU. *Club:* Carlton.

TOWNEND, His Honour John Philip; a Circuit Judge, 1987–2001; *b* 20 June 1935; *o s* of Luke and Ethel Townend; *m* 1st, 1959; two *s* one *d*; 2nd, 1981, Anne Glover; one step *s* one step *d*. *Educ:* St Joseph's Coll., Blackpool; Manchester Univ. (LLB). National Service, 1957–58. Called to the Bar, Gray's Inn, 1959; Lectr in Law, Gibson and Weldon College of

Law, 1960–65; Asst Legal Advr, Pilkington Bros, 1966–68; Legal Advr, Honeywell Ltd and G. Dew Ltd, 1968–70; joined chambers of Mr Stewart Oakes, Manchester, 1970. *Publications:* articles in various jls on legal topics. *Recreations:* classical music, jazz, food and wine, a decreasing number of active games, mountain walking. *Address:* c/o Preston Crown Court, Openshaw Place, Preston PR1 2LL. *Club:* Silverdale Golf.

TOWNEND, Warren Dennis; HM Diplomatic Service, retired; *b* 15 Nov. 1945; *s* of Dennis Jennings Townend and Mary Elizabeth Townend (*née* Knowles); *m* 1978, Ann Mary Riddle; three *s* one *d*. *Educ:* Netheredge Grammar Sch.; Abbeydale Grammar Sch. Joined Diplomatic Service, 1964; FO 1964–69; Vice Consul, Hanoi, 1969–70; Vice Consul (Commercial), Hamburg, 1970–73; Second Sec. (Commercial), Dacca, 1973–75; FCO, 1976–79; Second, later First, Sec., Bonn, 1979–84; First Sec. (Commercial), Bangkok, 1984–87; FCO, 1987–91; Dep. Consul-Gen. and Dep. Dir-Gen. for Trade and Investment Promotion in Germany, Düsseldorf, 1991–96; Consul-General: Shanghai, 1996–2000; Washington, 2001–04. *Recreations:* DIY, travel. *E:* WDTownend@gmail.com.

TOWNER, Neena; *see* Gill, N.

TOWNLEY, Ven. Peter Kenneth; Archdeacon of Pontefract, since 2008; *b* Manchester, 16 Nov. 1955; *s* of David Townley and Elsie Townley; *m* 1981, Moira Margaret Whitehorn; three *s*. *Educ:* Crab Lane Co. Primary Sch., Manchester; Moston Brook High Sch., Manchester; Univ. of Sheffield (BA 1978); Ridley Hall, Cambridge; Univ. of Manchester (Dip. Social and Pastoral Theol. 1986). Ordained deacon, 1980, priest, 1981; Asst Curate, Christ Church, Ashton-under-Lyne, 1980–83; Priest-in-charge, St Hugh's, Holts, Oldham, 1983–88; Rector, All Saints', Stretford, 1988–96; Vicar, St Mary-le-Tower, Ipswich, 1996–2008; Rural Dean, Ipswich, 2001–08. Member: Meissen Commn, 1991–2001; Gen. Synod, C of E, 1992–95, 2000–08; Porvoo Panel, 2003–. Hon. Canon, Dio. of St Edmundsbury and Ipswich, 2003–08. *Publications:* (contrib.) Spiritualitaet und innovative Unternehmensfuehrung, 2011; (contrib.) Prayer for the Day: 365 inspiring daily reflections, 2014; various newspaper articles and obituaries. *Recreations:* the arts, travel, fun, still supporting The Tractor Boys. *Address:* The Vicarage, Kirkthorpe, Wakefield, W Yorks WF1 5SZ. *T:* and *Fax:* (01924) 896327. *E:* archdeacon.pontefract@westyorkshiredales.anglican.org. *Clubs:* Lansdowne, Nikaean.

TOWNSEND, Prof. Alain Robert Michael, PhD; FRS 1992; Professor of Molecular Immunology, since 1992, and Fellow of New College, since 1998, University of Oxford. *Educ:* St Mary's Hosp. Med. Sch., London Univ. (MB BS 1977); PhD London 1984; MA Oxon. MRCP 1979. Oxford University: Lectr in Clin. Immunology, 1985–92; Fellow, Linacre Coll., 1985–98. *Address:* Weatherall Institute of Molecular Medicine, John Radcliffe Hospital, Headington, Oxford OX3 9DS. *T:* (01865) 222328; New College, Oxford OX1 3BN.

TOWNSEND, Antony John; Financial Services Complaints Commissioner, since 2014; *b* London, 24 April 1957; *s* of Paul and Molly Townsend; *m* 1st, 1984, Jill Grice; two *s* two *d*; 2nd, 2006, Katherine Carter; two *s*. *Educ:* Bedales Sch.; Merton Coll., Oxford (MA English Lang. and Lit.). Civil Servant, Home Office, 1980–90; Hd of Conduct, then Dir, Standards and Educn, GMC, 1990–2001; Chief Executive: GDC, 2001–06; Solicitors' Regulation Authy, 2006–14. Chair: UK and Ireland Regulatory Bd, RICS, 2013–; Regulatory Bd, ACCA, 2014–; Mem. Bd, Professional Standards Authy for Health and Social Care, 2015–. Trustee, Warwick Dist CAB, 2014–. *Recreation:* singing. *Address:* Office of the Complaints Commissioner, 3rd Floor, 48–54 Moorgate, EC2R 6EJ. *T:* (020) 7562 5530. *E:* complaintscommissioner@fscc.gov.uk.

TOWNSEND, Bryan Sydney, CBE 1994; Chairman, Midlands Electricity plc (formerly Midlands Electricity Board), 1986–96 (Chief Executive, 1990–92); *b* 2 April 1930; *s* of Sydney and Gladys Townsend; *m* 1951, Betty Eileen Underwood; one *s* two *d*. *Educ:* Wolverton Technical Coll. CEng, FIET; FIMgt. Trainee, Northampton Electric Light & Power Co., 1946–50; successive appts, E Midlands, Eastern and Southern Electricity Bds, 1952–66; Southern Electricity Board: Swindon Dist Manager, 1966–68; Newbury Area Engr, 1968–70; Asst Chief Engr, 1970–73; Dep. Chief Engr, SE Electricity Bd, 1973–76; Chief Engr, S Wales Electricity Bd, 1976–78; Dep. Chm., SW Electricity Bd, 1978–86. Chm., Applecourt Develt. *Recreation:* golf.

TOWNSEND, Dr Christina; JP; Chief Executive, Valuation Tribunal Service, 2007–09; *b* 10 Jan. 1947; *d* of Sidney Townsend and Vera (*née* Wallis). *Educ:* Dursley Grammar Sch., Glos; Leeds Univ. (BSc Psychol.); Birmingham Univ. (MSc); UWIST (PhD). Lectr, UWIST, 1973–75; Sen. Res. Officer, MSC, 1976–78; Asst Dir, Ashridge Mgt Coll., 1978–80; Hd of Div., Inst. of Manpower Studies, 1981–84; NHS Training Authority, subseq. Directorate: Dir, Res. Educn and Trng, 1984–88; Chief Exec., 1988–91; Nat. Trng Dir and Chief Exec., 1991–93; Chief Executive: Business & Technol. Educn Council, subseq. Edexcel Foundn, 1994–2002; Soc. of Chiropodists and Podiatrists, 2002–03; Appeals Service, 2003–06; Efficiency Dir, Tribunals Service, 2006–07. Dep. Chm., Personnel Standards Lead Body, 1991–94; Director: City Technol. Colls Trust, 1994–95; Mgt Charter Initiative, 1994–95; Further Educn Develt Agency, 1994–97; Member Council: Nat. Forum for Mgt Educn and Develt, 1994–99; Inst. for Employment Studies, 1998–; Mem. Bd, British Trng Internat., 1999–2001. Mem., Southwark PCT, 2007; Chm., Patient Participation Gp, Surrey Docks Health Centre, 2012–. Gov., Corp. of Cambridge Regl Coll., 1997–2003. Chm., Housing for Women, 2007–11. Trustee: Volunteer Reading Help, 2002–08; Age UK, 2015–; Ind. Trustee, Police Dependants' Trust, 2015–. MInstD 1991 (Mem., Nat. Employment Cttee, 1991–97); CCMI (CIMgt 1994). JP City of Westminster, 2006. *Recreations:* travelling, hill-walking, theatre, bird watching. *Address:* 173 Rotherhithe Street, SE16 5QY.

TOWNSEND, Christopher Peter, OBE 2013; Executive Director, and Chief Executive Officer, Broadband Delivery UK, Department for Culture, Media and Sport, since 2014; *b* Salisbury, Rhodesia, 25 May 1956; *s* of Gordon H. Townsend and Jean D. Townsend; *m* 1986, Michelle Jane; two *s*. *Educ:* St Wilfrid's RC Secondary Sch.; Newcastle Univ. (BSc Hons Geog. 1977); Nottingham Trent Univ. (MSc Mktg Mgt 1997). Grad. trainee and Sales Manager, EMI Records, 1977–80; Sales and Mktg Manager, Riva Computers, 1980–84; Mktg Controller, Laskys, 1984–86; Jt Man. Dir, DMB & B Direct, 1986–90; Marketing Director: BBC Subscription TV, BBC Enterprises, 1990–92; BSkyB, 1992–98; Dir, Interactive Services & Ecommerce, Telewest Broadband, 1999–2003; Gp Mktg Dir, TfL, 2003–06; Commercial Dir, LOCOG, 2006–12. Associate Fellow, Green Templeton Coll., Oxford, 2006–; Vis. Fellow, Newcastle Univ. Business Sch., 2012–. Dir, Invictus Games, 2014–. Mem., Develt Bd, Tusk, 2015–. *Recreations:* road cycling, circuit training, motor sport, rock concerts, classical concerts, ballet, collecting art, Manchester United. *Address:* Department for Culture, Media and Sport, 100 Parliament Street, SW1A 2BQ. *T:* (020) 7211 6000. *E:* chris.townsend@culture.gov.uk.

TOWNSEND, Brig. Ian Glen, CBE 2006; Director (formerly Secretary) General, Royal British Legion, 1996–2006; *b* 7 Feb. 1941; *s* of Kenneth Townsend and Irene (*née* Singleton); *m* 1st, 1964, Loraine Jean (marr. diss. 1988), *d* of late William A. H. Birnie, USA; twin *d*; 2nd, 1989, Susan Natalie, *d* of late Comdr Frank A. L. Heron-Watson, Dalbeattie; two step *s*. *Educ:* Dulwich Coll.; RMA, Sandhurst (psc †). Commnd RA, 1961; served UK, Norway, Singapore, Brussels and Germany, 1961–71; RMCS, 1971–72; Staff Coll., Camberley, 1972–73; MoD, BAOR and NATO, 1973–85; Comdr Artillery, 1st Armd Div., BAOR, 1986–88; ACOS, Trng, HQ UKLF, 1988–91. Hon. Col, 27 Field Regt, 1988–92. Dir, Sales and Marketing, Land Systems, 1991–93, Mil. Advr, 1993–96, VSEL; Director: Townsend Associates, 1993–96; Legion Enterprise Ltd, 1999; RBL Training Coll., 2000–; NMA Enterprise, 2004–08; Nat. Meml Arboretum, 2004–08. Mem., Nat. Meml Cttee for NI, 2004–08. Trustee: Officers' Assoc., 1996–2006; Mil. Mus. of the Pacific, 1997–; Desert Rats 7th Armd Div. Commemoration Fund, 1998–2008; Armed Forces Meml Trust, 2003–; Chm., Confedn of Service and Ex-Service Orgns, 2002–03; Vice-Pres., World Veterans' Fedn, 2006– (Chm., World Veterans' Fedn, Europe, 2002–09). Freeman, City of London, 1999. CCMI 2004 (FCMI) (FInstM 1988); FRSA 2006. Mem., ACEVO (formerly ACENVO), 1997–2006. Gov., Salisbury Coll., 2001–03. *Publications:* articles in professional jls. *Recreations:* walking, painting, music, theatre. *Clubs:* Army and Navy, Royal Over-Seas League.

TOWNSEND, Mrs Joan, MA, MSc; Headmistress, Oxford High School, GPDST, 1981–96; *b* 7 Dec. 1936; *d* of Emlyn Davies and Amelia Mary Davies (*née* Tyrer); *m* 1960, William Godfrey Townsend, Prof. Emeritus, Cranfield Univ.; two *d*. *Educ:* Somerville Coll., Oxford (Beilby Schol.; BA (Cl.I), MA); University College of Swansea, Univ. of Wales (MSc). School teaching and lecturing of various kinds, including: Tutor, Open University, 1971–75; Lectr, Oxford Polytechnic, 1975–76; Head of Mathematics, School of S Helen and S Katharine, Abingdon, 1976–81. FRSA 1986. *Publications:* paper in Qly Jl Maths and Applied Mech., 1965. *Address:* Silver Howe, 62 Iffley Turn, Oxford OX4 4HN. *T:* (01865) 715807.

TOWNSEND, Martin; Editor, Sunday Express, since 2001; *b* 11 July 1960; *s* of Ronald Norman Townsend and Margaret Annie Townsend (*née* Pattrick); *m* 1989, Jane O'Gorman; two *s* one *d*. *Educ:* Harrow Co. Grammar Sch.; London Coll. of Printing. Staff writer: Do It Yourself, 1979–81; Caravan, 1981–82; Sen. Writer, No 1, 1983–85; Co-creator, The Hit, 1985; Pop Ed., Today newspaper, 1986–87; freelance journalist, 1987–94; Showbusiness Ed., You mag., 1994–96; Ed., OK! mag., 1998–2001. *Publications:* The Father I Had, 2007 (Mind Book of the Year, 2008). *Recreations:* listening to music, cycling, architecture, football, conversation. *Address:* Sunday Express, The Northern and Shell Building, Number 10, Lower Thames Street, EC3R 6EN. *E:* martin.townsend@express.co.uk.

TOWNSEND, Michael John, OBE 2003; Principal Advisor, Conservation Advocacy, since 2013 (Senior Advisor, 2006–13); *b* 12 July 1957; *s* of John and Kathleen Townsend; *m* 1991, Amanda Adkins; two *s*. *Educ:* University Coll. of N Wales (BSc Hons Forestry 1986); Open Univ. (MA Envmt, Policy and Society 2007). MICFor 1990, FICFor 2002. Project leader, VSO, Kenya, 1980–83; Regl Manager, EFG plc, 1986–92; Michael Townsend Forestry & Landscapes, 1992–95; Woodland Trust: Woodland Ops Dir, 1995–97; Chief Exec., 1997–2004; Special Advr, 2006–. Trustee, Tree Aid, 2003–05. *Recreations:* hill-walking, gardening. *Address:* The Woodland Trust, Kempton Way, Grantham, Lincs NG31 6LL.

TOWNSEND, Prof. Paul Kingsley, PhD; FRS 2000; Professor of Theoretical Physics, University of Cambridge, since 1998; *b* 3 March 1951; *m* Fátima Azpiroz; one *d*. *Educ:* Queens' Coll., Cambridge (BA 1972; MA); Brandeis Univ., Mass (PhD 1976). Postdoctoral Fellow, SUNY, 1976–79; UK Fellow, CERN, Geneva, 1980–81; Curie-Joliot Fellow, subseq. CNRS Vis. Fellow, Lab. de Physique Théorique, Ecole Normale Supérieure, Paris, 1982–83; Lectr, 1984–96, Reader, 1996–98, Dept of Applied Maths and Theoretical Physics, Univ. of Cambridge. *Address:* Department of Applied Mathematics and Theoretical Physics, Centre for Mathematical Sciences, Wilberforce Road, Cambridge CB3 0WA.

TOWNSEND, Dr Ralph Douglas; Headmaster, Winchester College, since 2005; *b* 13 Dec. 1951; *s* of Harry Douglas Townsend and Neila Margaret McPherson; *m* 1973, Cathryn Julie Arnold; one *s* one *d*. *Educ:* Scotch Coll., WA; Univ. of Western Australia (BA 1973); Univ. of Kent at Canterbury (MA 1975); Keble Coll., Oxford (MA 1983; DPhil 1981). Assistant Master: Dover Coll., 1975–77; Abingdon Sch., 1977–78; Sen. Scholar, Keble Coll., Oxford, 1978–81; Jun. Res. Fellow and Dean of Degrees, Lincoln Coll., Oxford, 1983–85; Asst Master, then Head of English, Eton Coll., 1985–89; Head Master, Sydney Grammar Sch., Australia, 1989–99; Headmaster, Oundle Sch., 1999–2005. Governor: Mowden Hall Sch., Northumberland, 1999–2007; Old Buckenham Hall Sch., Suffolk, 1999–2006; Ardvreck Sch., Perthshire, 2001–06; Bramcote Lorne Sch., Notts, 2003–06; Ampleforth Coll., Yorks, 2003–06; Worth Sch., Sussex, 2004–10; St Swithin's Sch., Winchester, 2005–14; The Pilgrim's Sch., Winchester, 2005–14; Church Schs Co., 2005–11; Ct, Univ. of Southampton, 2005–14; St John's Sch., Old Windsor, 2008–; Midhurst Rother Coll., W Sussex, 2008–. Dir, 2012–14, Chm., 2014–, Educn Fellowship; Adviser: United Learning Trust, 2005–11; African Leadership Acad., 2005–; Nat. Coll. of Music, London, 2005–; Special Advr, World Leading Schs Assoc., 2015–. Trustee: Cothill Educn Trust, 2007–; St George's House, Windsor, 2015–. Hon. Liveryman, Grocers' Co., 2005. KHS 2011. *Recreations:* music, reading, walking. *Address:* Winchester College, Winchester, Hants SO23 9NA. *Club:* Savile.

TOWNSEND, Valerie Carol Marian; *see* Vaz, V. C. M.

TOWNSHEND, family name of **Marquess Townshend**.

TOWNSHEND, 8th Marquess *cr* 1787; **Charles George Townshend;** Bt 1617; Baron Townshend, of Lynn Regis 1661; Viscount Townshend, of Raynham 1682; *b* 26 Sept. 1945; *s* of 7th Marquess Townshend and Elizabeth (*née* Luby, later Gault); *S* father, 2010; *m* 1st, 1975, Hermione (*d* 1985), *d* of Lt-Cdr R. M. D. Ponsonby and Mrs Dorothy Ponsonby; one *s* one *d*; 2nd, 1990, Mrs Alison Marshall, *yr d* of Sir Willis Combs, KCVO, CMG. *Educ:* Eton; Royal Agricultural College, Cirencester. Chm. and Dir, AIMS Ltd, 1977–87; Man. Dir, Raynham Workshops Ltd, 1986–94; Chm., Pera International, 1988–96. Gen. Comr, Income Tax, Norwich, 1989–97. Mem. Council, Design Gp Great Britain Ltd, 1984–90 (Chm., 1988); Mem. Council for Norfolk and Chief Steward, Royal Show, RASE, 1982–94. Patron: Gen. Townshend Club, Fakenham, 2004–; Upper Wensum Benefice, 2008–; Coxford Gp of Churches, 2008–. Churchwarden, St Mary's, East Raynham, and St Margaret's, West Raynham, 1991–. *Heir:* *s* Viscount Raynham, *qv*. *Address:* Raynham Hall, Fakenham, Norfolk NR21 7EP. *E:* townshend@raynhamhall.com.

TOWNSHEND, Prof. Charles Jeremy Nigel, DPhil; FBA 2008; Professor of International History, University of Keele, 1987–2012, now Emeritus; *b* Nottingham, 27 July 1945; *s* of John Walter Henwood Townshend and Helen Betty Townshend; *m* 1978, Katherine Jane Lawley; two *s*. *Educ:* Oriel Coll., Oxford (BA 1967; DPhil 1973). Lectr in Hist., 1973–81, Sen. Lectr, 1981–87, Keele Univ. Olin Fellow, Nat. Humanities Center, N Carolina, 1987–88; Fellow, Woodrow Wilson Internat. Center for Scholars, Washington, 1991–92. *Publications:* The British Campaign in Ireland, 1975; Political Violence in Ireland: government and resistance since 1848, 1983; Britain's Civil Wars: counter insurgency in the twentieth century, 1986; Consensus in Ireland: approaches and recessions, 1988; Making the Peace: public order and public security in modern Britain, 1993; The Oxford Illustrated History of Modern War, 1997; Ireland: the 20th century, 1998; The State: historical and political dimensions, 1999; Terrorism: a very short introduction, 2002; Easter 1916: the Irish Rebellion, 2005; When God Made Hell: the British invasion of Mesopotamia and the creation of Iraq 1014–1921, 2010; The Republic: the fight for Irish independence 1918–1923, 2013. *Recreation:* mountain biking. *Address:* 5 Church Plantation, Keele, Staffs ST5 5AY. *E:* c.j.n.townshend@keele.ac.uk.

TOWNSHEND, Peter Dennis Blandford; composer, performer, publisher, author; *b* London, 19 May 1945; *s* of Clifford and Betty Townshend; *m* 1968, Karen Astley (marr. diss. 2010); one *s* two *d*. *Educ:* Acton County Grammar Sch.; Ealing Art Coll. Mem., The Who, rock group, 1963–; Editor, Faber & Faber, 1983–90s; *recordings* include: with The Who: Tommy, 1969 (musical, filmed 1975, Grammy Award 1993, staged NY (Tony Award for best score), 1993, Toronto (Dora Mavor Moore Award), 1994, London, 1996 (Olivier Award, 1997)); Quadrophenia, 1973 (Classic Rock Award, 2011); Endless Wire, 2006; Quadrophenia: The Director's Cut, 2011; singles: My Generation; I Can See For Miles; Can't Explain; Substitute; Pinball Wizard; solo: Empty Glass, 1980; Iron Man, 1989; Psychoderelict, 1993. Hon. DLitt W London, 2010. Ivor Novello Award, 1981; British Phonographic Industry Lifetime Achievement Award, 1983. BRIT Award for contribn to British Music, 1988; Living Legend Award, Internat. Rock Awards, 1991; Q Lifetime Achievement Award, 1997; Ivor Novello Lifetime Achievement Award, 2001; (jtly) Kennedy Center Honor, John F. Kennedy Center for Performing Arts, 2008; (jtly) Rock Honor, VH1, 2008; Les Paul Award, TEC Foundn, 2012. *Publications:* Horse's Neck, 1986; Who I Am (autobiog.), 2012. *Recreation:* sailing.

TOY, Rev. Canon John, PhD; FSA; Chancellor of York Minster, 1983–99 (also Librarian and Guestmaster); Residentiary Canon, York Minster, 1983–99, now Emeritus; Prebendary of Laughton-en-le-Morthen, 1994–99; *b* 25 Nov. 1930; *e s* of late Sidney Toy, FSA and late Violet Mary (*née* Doudney); *m* 1963, Mollie, *d* of Eric and Elsie Tilbury; one *s* one *d*. *Educ:* Epsom County Grammar Sch.; Hatfield Coll., Durham (BA 1st cl. Hons Theol. 1953, MA 1962); PhD Leeds 1982. FSA 2013. FSA 2013. Ordained deacon, 1955, priest, 1956; Curate, St Paul's, Lorrimore Sq., Southwark, 1955–58; Student Christian Movement Sec. for S of England, 1958–60; Chaplain: Ely Theol Coll., 1960–64; St Andrew's Church, Gothenburg, Sweden, 1965–69; St John's College, York: Lectr in Theology, 1969; Sen. Lectr, 1972; Principal Lectr, 1979–83; Prebendary of Tockerington, 1983–94. FSA 2013. Kt, Royal Order of Polar Star (Sweden), 2002. *Publications:* Jesus, Man for God, 1988; (jtly) A Pilgrim Guide to York, 1997; English Saints in the Medieval Liturgies of Scandinavian Churches, 2009; contrib. to learned jls and cathedral booklets. *Recreations:* Scandinavia, history, architecture. *Address:* Dulverton Hall, Esplanade, Scarborough, N Yorks YO11 2AR. *T:* (01723) 340115. *E:* jtoy19@talktalk.net.

TOYE, Bryan Edward; JP; Chairman, Toye & Co. and associated companies, since 1969; *b* 17 March 1938; *s* of Herbert Graham Donovan Toye and late Marion Alberta Toye (*née* Montignani); *m* 1982, Fiona Ann, *d* of G. H. J. Hogg, Wellington, NZ; three *s* one *d*. *Educ:* St Andrew's Prep. Sch., Eastbourne; Stowe Sch. Joined Toye & Co., 1956; Dir, Toye Kenning & Spencer, 1962–; Dir, Toye & Co., 1966; Dep. Chm., Futurama Sign Gp Ltd, 1992–96; Mem. Adv. Bd, The House of Windsor Collection Ltd, 1994–95; non-executive Director: Trehaven Trust Ltd, 1990–97; DG HR (Navy) (formerly Naval Manning Agency), 1999–2005. Mem., Lloyd's, 1985–91. Member: Council, Advancing UK Aerospace Defence and Security Industries (formerly Defence Manufacturers Assoc.), 2005–10 (Chm., Clothing Interest Gp; Dep. Chm., Commercial Gp); Defence Sector Bd, 2010–. Alderman, Ward of Lime Street, City of London, 1983–96 (Past Pres., Lime St Ward Club); Master, Gold and Silver Wyre Drawers' Co., 1984; Liveryman, Goldsmiths' Co., 1985– (Prime Warden, 2004–05); Member, Court of Assistants: Broderers' Co. (Master, 1996–97); Guild of Freemen of City of London, 1986–97 (Mem., 1983–). Member: United Wards Club, City of London; Tower Ward Club; Dowgate Ward Club. Pres., Royal Warrant Holders' Assoc., 1991–92 (Mem. Council, 1983–; Hon. Auditor, 1998–). Mem. Council, NSPCC, London, 1966–69; Chm., Greater London Playing Fields Assoc., 1988–90; Mem. Council, London Playing Fields Soc., 1990–92; Policy and Resources Cttee, King George's Fund for Sailors, 1990–92. Mem., W Midlands Council, CBI, 2010–. Trustee: (founder Mem.) Queen Elizabeth Scholarship Trust, 1990–96; Britain-Australia Bicentennial Trust; Black Country Museum (London Gp), 1991–97; British Red Cross, 1993– (Vice Pres. London Br., 1993–). Governor: City of London Sch., 1985–88; King Edward's Sch., Witley, 1988–93; Bridewell Royal Hosp., 1989–96; Christ's Hosp., 1989–96; City of London Freemen's Sch., 1993–96. Mem. Ct, RCA, 1983–86. Hon. Mem., Ct of Assts, HAC, 1983–96; Hon. Col 55 Ordnance Co. RAOC (V), 1988–93; Hon. Col, 124 Havering Petroleum Sqdn RLC (V), 1994–2000; Hon. Ordnance Officer, Tower of London, 1994–2008. Member: TA&VRA for Gtr London, 1992–99; City of London TA&VRA, 1992–99. Member: Royal Soc. of St George, London Br., 1981–; Huguenot Soc., 1985–; Cttee, Old Stoic Soc., 1985–92; Stewards' Enc., Henley Royal Regatta, 1980–. FInstD 1966; FCMI (FIMgt 1983); FRSA 1985; MCIPS 1991. JP: City of London, 1983–96 (Chm. Bench, 1990–96); Hereford & Worcs, Supplemental list, 1996. OStJ 1980. *Recreations:* cricket, squash, shooting, sailing, swimming, tennis, gardening, classical music, Rugby, entertaining. *Address:* Toye & Co., 19/21 Great Queen Street, WC2B 5BE. *T:* (020) 7242 0471, *Fax:* (020) 7831 8692. *Clubs:* Royal Automobile, City Livery (Pres., 1988–89), MCC; Middlesex Co. RFC; Wasps FC (Trustee and Vice-Pres.); Leander (Henley).

TOYE, Prof. John Francis Joseph; Chairman, Advisory Council, Department of International Development, University of Oxford, since 2010; *b* 7 Oct. 1942; *s* of late John Redmond Toye and Adele Toye (*née* Francis); *m* 1967, Janet Reason; one *s* one *d*. *Educ:* Christ's Coll., Finchley; Jesus Coll., Cambridge (schol.; MA); Harvard Univ. (Frank Knox Vis. Fellow); Sch. of Oriental and African Studies, Univ. of London (MScEcon; PhD). Asst Principal, HM Treasury, 1965–68; Res. Fellow, SOAS, Univ. of London, 1970–72; Fellow (later Tutor), Wolfson Coll., Cambridge, 1972–80, and Asst Dir of Develt Studies, Cambridge Univ., 1977–80; Dir, Commodities Res. Unit Ltd, 1980–85; Prof. of Develt Policy and Planning and Dir, Centre for Develt Studies, University Coll. of Swansea, 1982–87; Dir, 1987–97, Fellow, 1987–98, Inst. of Develt Studies, Univ. of Sussex; Dir, Globalisation and Develt Strategies Div., UN Conf. on Trade and Develt, Geneva, 1998–2000; Dir, Centre for Study of African Economies, Oxford, 2000–03; Sen. Res. Associate, Queen Elizabeth Hse, Oxford, 2003–09. Hon. Fellow, Univ. of Birmingham, Inst. of Local Govt Studies, 1986. Member: Council, ODI, 1988–96; Adv. Cttee on Econ. and Social Res., ODA, 1989–95. Dir, Penn Club, 2010–12. *Publications:* (ed) Taxation and Economic Development, 1978; (ed) Trade and Poor Economies, 1979; Public Expenditure and Indian Development Policy 1960–70, 1981; Dilemmas of Development, 1987; (jtly) Does Aid Work in India?, 1990; (jtly) Aid and Power, 1991; Structural Adjustment and Employment Policy, 1995; Keynes on Population, 2000; (jtly) The UN and Global Political Economy, 2004; UNCTAD at Fifty: a short history, 2014; numerous articles in acad. jls. *Recreations:* walking, music. *Address:* 31 Riverside Road, Oxford OX2 0HT. *W:* www.johntoye.net.

TOYN, His Honour Richard John; a Circuit Judge 1972–92; *b* 24 Jan. 1927; *s* of Richard Thomas Millington Toyn and Ethel Toyn; *m* 1955, Joyce Evelyn Goodwin (*d* 2014); two *s* two *d*. *Educ:* Solihull Sch.; Bristol Grammar Sch.; Bristol Univ. (LLB). Royal Army Service Corps, 1948–50. Called to the Bar, Gray's Inn, 1950. Mem., Parole Bd, 1978–80. Contributing Ed., Butterworths County Court Precedents and Pleadings, 1985. *Recreations:* music, drama, photography.

TOYNBEE, Polly; columnist, The Guardian, 1977–88 and since 1998; writer; *b* 27 Dec. 1946; *d* of late Philip Toynbee, and of Anne Powell; *m* 1970, Peter Jenkins (*d* 1992); one *s* two *d*, and one step *d*. *Educ:* Badminton Sch.; Holland Park Comprehensive; St Anne's Coll., Oxford. Reporter, The Observer, 1968–71; Editor, The Washington Monthly, USA, 1972–73; Feature Writer, The Observer, 1974–76; Social Affairs Editor, News and Current Affairs, BBC, 1988–95; Associate Editor and columnist, The Independent, 1995–97. Vis. Fellow, Nuffield Coll., Oxford, 2004–12. Contested (SDP) Lewisham E, 1983. Gov., LSE, 1988–99. Member: Home Office Cttee on Obscenity and Censorship, 1980; DoH Adv. Cttee on the Ethics of Xenotransplantation, 1996; DoH Nat. Screening Cttee, 1996–2003; Mitochondria Consultation Gp, HFEA, 2012. Mem. Bd, Political Qly, 2003–. Pres., Social Policy Assoc., 2005–09. Chm. of Judges, Orange Prize, 2002; Chair, Brighton Dome and Fest., 2005–. Dir, Wise Gp, 2005–10; Trustee, Social Mobility Foundn, 2007–15. Hon. LLD: Essex, 2001; South Bank, 2002; Hon. DLitt: Loughborough, 2004; Sussex, 2006; DUniv: Stafford, 2004; Open, 2005; Kent, 2007; Hon. DLaws Leeds, 2004. Catherine Pakenham Award for Journalism, 1975; British Press Award, 1977, 1982, 1986, Columnist of the Year, 2007; BBC What the Papers Say Award, 1996 (Commentator of the Year); Magazine Writer of the Year, PPA, 1996; George Orwell Prize, 1997. *Publications:* Leftovers, 1966; A Working Life, 1970 (paperback 1972); Hospital, 1977 (paperback 1979); The Way We Live Now, 1981; Lost Children, 1985; Hard Work: life in low-pay Britain, 2003; with David Walker: Did Things Get Better? an audit of Labour's successes and failures, 2001; Better or Worse? Has Labour Delivered?, 2005; Unjust Rewards, 2008; The Verdict: did Labour change Britain?, 2010; Dogma and Disarray: Cameron at half time, 2012; Cameron's Coup: how the Tories took Britain to the brink, 2015. *Address:* The Guardian, Kings Place, 90 York Way, N1 9LG. *T:* (020) 7239 9556.

TOYNE, Prof. Peter, CBE 2009; Chairman, Friends of Cathedral Music, since 2002; *b* 3 Dec. 1939; *s* of Harold and Doris Toyne; *m* 1969, Angela Wedderburn; one *s*. *Educ:* Ripon Grammar Sch.; Bristol Univ. (BA); The Sorbonne. Res. Asst, Univ. of Lille, 1964; Univ. of Exeter: Lectr in Geography, 1965–76; Sen. Lectr in Geography and Sub Dean of Social Studies, 1976–78; Dir, DES Credit Transfer Feasibility Study, 1978–80; Hd of Bishop Otter Coll., Chichester, and Dep. Dir (Academic), W Sussex Inst. of Higher Educn, 1980–83; Dep. Rector, NE London Polytechnic, 1983–86; Rector, Liverpool Poly., 1986–92, then Vice-Chancellor and Chief Exec., Liverpool John Moores Univ., 1992–2000 (Hon. Fellow, 2000). Sen. Inspector, Theol Colls, 1980–. Chm., Guidance Accreditation Bd, 1999–2002; Member: Council, Industrial Soc., 1997–2000; C of E Archbishops' Council, 1999–2006; Merseyside Bd, Nat. Probation Service, 2004–08. Chairman: Trustees, Rodolfus Choir, 1995–2001; Trustees, Liverpool St George's Hall, 1996–2000; Groundwork St Helens, Knowsley, Sefton & Liverpool, 1997–2001; Royal Liverpool Philharmonic Soc., 2000–03; Liverpool Culture Co., 2000–03; Liverpool Cathedral Develt Trust, 2002–08; Choirbook Trust, 2010–; Thames Youth Orch., 2010–; Trustee, Southwark Cathedral Educn Centre, 2012–. Chm., Woodlands Hospice, 2005–. Governor: Glyndŵr Univ., 2008–13; Liverpool Inst. of Performing Arts, 2008–13. Pres., Liverpool YMCA, 1997–. Hon. Life Pres., Liverpool Organists' Assoc., 2000–. DL 1990–2009, High Sheriff 2001, Merseyside. Hon. Col, 33 Signal Regt (V), 1999–2006. Hon. Freeman, City of Liverpool, 2010. FRSA; CCMI; FICPD; Fellow, Eton Coll., 1996–2001. Hon. Fellow, Glyndŵr Univ., 2013. Hon. DEd CNAA, 1992. *Publications:* World Problems, 1970; Techniques in Human Geography, 1971; Organisation, Location and Behaviour, 1974; Recreation and Environment, 1974; Toyne Report: Credit Transfer, 1979; Toyne Report: Environmental Education, 1993; numerous articles in geographical, educnl jls, festschriften and popular press. *Recreations:* railways (model and real), liturgy, music (especially sacred). *Address:* 50 Commodore House, Juniper Drive, SW18 1TW. *E:* p.toyne@btinternet.com.

TOYNE SEWELL, Maj.-Gen. Timothy Patrick; DL; Director, Goodenough College (formerly The London Goodenough Trust for Overseas Graduates), 1995–2006; *b* 7 July 1941; *s* of late Brig. E. P. Sewell, CBE and E. C. M. Sewell, MBE (*née* Toyne); *m* 1965, Jennifer Lesley Lunt; one *s* one *d*. *Educ:* Bedford Sch.; Royal Military Acad., Sandhurst. Commnd KOSB, 1961; ADC to Governor of Aden, 1962–63; helicopter pilot, 2 RGJ and 2 Para, 1966–69; psc 1973; GSO 1, staff of CDS, 1979–81; CO, 1 KOSB, 1981–83; COS, British Forces Falkland Is, 1983–84; Sen. Directing Staff (Army), JSDC, 1984–85; Comdr, 19 Infantry Bde, 1985–87; rcds 1988; Comdr, British Mil. and Adv. Team, Zimbabwe, 1989–91; Comdt, RMA, 1991–94. Team Ldr, Tri Service Study into Services Recruiting Orgns, 1994–95. Col, KOSB, 1995–2001. Chairman: Exec. Cttee, Disability Sport England, 1998–99; Internat. Bd, United World Colls, 2006–12. Non-exec. Dir, Catalyst Investment Gp Ltd, 2007–12. Chm., Benjamin Britten Internat. Violin Competition, 2002–. Life Gov., Haileybury, 1993; Chm. of Govs, Lambrook Haileybury Sch., 2003–08; Mem. Council, QMW, 1996–2005; Trustee: Med. Coll. of St Bartholomew's Hosp. Trust, 2000–05; Bedford Sch. Foundn, 2006–09; North-West Univ. (SA) Trust UK, 2004–08; Trichord Abrahamic Foundn, Poland, 2014–; Mem. Bd, UWC Dilijan, Armenia, 2013–; Chm., Supervisory Bd, Seeb Sch., Oman, 2011–. Chm., Nether Wallop New Village Hall Trust, 2014–. DL Greater London, 1999. Freeman, City of London, 2006. *Recreations:* racquet sports, golf, fishing, music. *Club:* Royal Over-Seas League (Mem. Council, 2002–09).

TOZZI, Keith, CEng, FICE; Executive Director: Tozzi Ltd, since 2011; The Bodyworks Ltd, since 2014; *b* 23 Feb. 1949; *s* of late Edward Thomas Tozzi and Winifred Tozzi (*née* Killick); *m* 2013, Fiona Begley; two *s* one *d* by a former marriage. *Educ:* Dartford Grammar Sch.; City Univ. (BSc Hons); Univ. of Kent (MA); Harvard Business Sch. (Internat. SMP). Civil Engr, Thames Water, 1973–75; Southern Water plc: Water Manager, 1975–81; Ops Manager, 1981–86; Engrg Manager, 1986–88; Divl Dir, 1988–92; Gp Technical Dir, 1992–96; Chm., Nat. Jt Utilities Gp, 1993–96; Chief Exec., BSI, 1997–2000; Gp Chief Exec., Mid-Kent Hldgs, subseq. Swan Gp plc, 2000–03; Chief Exec., Clifton Capital Investments, 2003–06; Chief Exec., 2005–06, Chm., 2006–10, Concateno plc; Dir, Ingemino Ltd, 2011–14. Chairman: RSVP.i (formerly IPID.com), 2000–; Inspicio plc, 2005–08; Kane Insce Gp, 2011–14; non-executive Director: Legal & General UK Select Investment Trust, 2000–03; Seal Analytical Ltd, 2004–09. Mem., CBI Southern Regl Council, 2000–04. *Publications:* articles in newspapers and technical jls. *Recreations:* gardening, reading, classic cars. *Address:* The Top House, Chalfont Heights, Gerrards Cross, Bucks SL9 9TD. *T:* (01753) 889497.

TOZZI, Nigel Kenneth; QC 2001; *b* 31 Aug. 1957; *s* of Ronald Kenneth Tozzi and Doreen Elsie Florence Tozzi; *m* 1983, Sara Louise Clare Cornish; two *s* one *d*. *Educ:* Hitchin Boys' Grammar Sch.; Exeter Univ. (LLB 1st Cl. Hons); Inns of Court Sch. of Law (1st Cl.). Called to the Bar, Gray's Inn, 1980; in practice as Barrister and Arbitrator, specialising in commercial, insce and professional negligence litigation and internat. arbitration, 1980–. *Recreations:* playing hockey, watching cricket, theatre, cinema. *Address:* 4 Pump Court, Temple, EC4Y 7AN. *T:* (020) 7842 5555. *Clubs:* MCC; Sevenoaks Hockey.

TRACE, Anthony John; QC 1998; *b* 23 Oct. 1958; *s* of late Comdr Peter Trace, RD and bar, RNR, and Anne Trace (*née* Allison-Beer); *m* 1986, Caroline Tessa Durrant, *e d* of His Honour A. H. Durrant, *qv*; three *s* one *d*. *Educ:* Vinehall Prep. Sch.; Uppingham Sch.; Magdalene Coll., Cambridge (MA 1st Cl. Hons). Called to the Bar, Lincoln's Inn, 1981, Bencher, 2006. Dep. Managing Ed., Receivers, Administrators and Liquidators' Qly, 1993–2002. Vice-Chm., Chancery Bar Assoc., 2001–04 (Hon. Sec., 1997–2001). Mem., Internat. Editl Bd, Briefings in Real Estate Finance, 2000–02. Trustee, Uppingham Sch., 1999–2014. Churchwarden, St Helen's, Saddington, 2009–. Jt Organiser, Saddington Aid, 2013. Founder Member: Campaign for Real Gin, 1978; Plodda Falls Swimming Club, 2004; Friends of Turkey, 2006; CRAFT, Salcombe, 2013. Freeman, City of London, 1981; Liveryman, Musicians' Co., 1982. Jt Winner, Observer Mace Debating Championship, 1981. *Publications:* (contrib.) Butterworths European Law Service (Company Law), 1992; (contrib.) Butterworths Practical Insolvency, 1999. *Recreations:* stalking, shooting, fishing, the Turf, music, messing about in boats. *Address:* Maitland Chambers, 7 Stone Buildings, Lincoln's Inn, WC2A 3SZ. *T:* (020) 7406 1200. *Clubs:* Athenæum, Garrick, Beefsteak; Pitt (Cambridge).

TRACEY, Craig Paul; MP (C) North Warwickshire, since 2015; *b* Durham, 21 Aug. 1974; *s* of Edward and Joyce Tracey; *m* 2014, Karen. *Educ:* Framwellgate Moor Comprehensive Sch. Owner, Dunelm Insce Brokers, 1996–2015. Dir, Dunelm Business Consultants, 2014–. Member: Southern Staffs Employment and Skills Bd, 2014–. Founder Trustee, Lichfield Garrick Th., 2012–. *Recreations:* local football, ski-ing. *Address:* House of Commons, SW1A 0AA. *T:* (020) 7219 5646. *E:* craig.tracey.mp@parliament.uk.

TRACEY, Prof. Ian Graham; DL; Organist and Master of the Choristers, 1980–2007, Organist Titulaire, since 2008, Liverpool Cathedral; Professor, Fellow and Organist, Liverpool John Moores University (formerly Liverpool Polytechnic), since 1988; *b* 27 May 1955; *s* of William Tracey and Helene Mignon Tracey (*née* Harris). *Educ:* Trinity Coll. of Music, London (FTCL); St Katharine's Coll., Liverpool (PGCE). FRSCM 2008; FGCM 2009. Chorus Master, Royal Liverpool Philharmonic Soc., 1985–; Liverpool City Organist (formerly Consultant Organist, City of Liverpool), 1986–; Guest Dir of Music, BBC Daily Service, 1998–. Pres., Incorp. Assoc. of Organists of GB, 2001–03. Gov., Liverpool Coll., 1993–. DL Merseyside, 2015. FRSA 1988. Hon. FRCO 2004. Hon. DMus Liverpool, 2006. NW Arts Award for Classical Music, 1994. *Address:* Mornington House, Mornington Terrace, Upper Duke Street, Liverpool L1 9DY. *T:* and *Fax:* (0151) 708 8471. *E:* iantraceyenquiries@hotmail.co.uk. *W:* www.iantracey.com. *Club:* Artists' (Liverpool).

TRACEY, Richard Patrick; JP; Member (C) Merton and Wandsworth, London Assembly, Greater London Authority, since 2008; strategic marketing and public affairs consultant, since 1997; *b* 8 Feb. 1943; *o s* of late P. H. (Dick) Tracey and Hilda Tracey; *m* Katharine Gardner; one *s* three *d*. *Educ:* King Edward VI Sch., Stratford-upon-Avon; Birmingham Univ. (LLB Hons). Leader Writer, Daily Express, 1964–66; Presenter/Reporter, BBC Television and Radio, 1966–78: internat. news and current affairs (The World at One, PM, Today, Newsdesk, 24 Hours, The Money Prog.); feature programmes (Wheelbase, Waterline, Motoring and the Motorist, You and Yours, Checkpoint); also documentaries (Colossus, Me and My Migraine); Public Affairs Consultant/Advisor, 1978–83. Non-executive Director: Tallack Golf Course Construction Ltd, 1987–91; Ranelagh Ltd, 1992–96. Member: Econ. Res. Council, 1981–2000; ISIS Assoc., 1981–92. Various Conservative Party Offices, 1974–81; Dep. Chm., Greater London Cons. Party, 1981–83; Mem., Cons. National Union Exec. Cttee, 1981–83. Contested (C) Northampton N, Oct. 1974. MP (C) Surbiton, 1983–97; contested (C) Kingston and Surbiton, 1997. PPS to Min. of State for Trade and Industry (IT), 1984–85; Parly Under Sec. of State, DoE (with special responsibility for sport), 1985–87. Member: Select Cttee on Televising H of C, 1988–92; Selection Cttee, 1992–94; Public Accounts Cttee, 1994–97. Chm., Cons. Parly Greater London MPs' Cttee, 1990–97 (Jt Sec., 1983–84); Sec., Cons. Parly Media Cttee, 1983–84. Mem., Exec. Cttee, Assoc. of Former MPs, 2007–. Member: Metropolitan Police Authy, 2008–10; London Fire and Emergency Planning Authy, 2010–12 (Vice-Chm., 2010–12); Chm., London Waste and Recycling Bd, 2012–. Community Relns Advr, Battersea Power Station Proj., 2004–08; Chm., Pro-Active S London, Sport England, 2006–08; London Mayor's Ambassador for River Transport, 2009–. Fellow, Industry and Parlt Trust, 1984. JP SW London (Wimbledon PSD), 1977. Freeman, City of London, 1984. Mem., Inst. of Advanced Motorists, 1993. *Publications:* (with Richard Hudson-Evans) The World of Motor Sport, 1971; (with Michael Clayton) Hickstead—the first twelve years, 1972; articles, pamphlets. *Recreations:* riding, boating, debating. *Address:* Greater London Authority, City Hall, The Queen's Walk, SE1 2AA. *E:* richard.tracey@london.gov.uk.

TRACEY, Stephen Frederick T.; *see* Thorpe-Tracey.

TRACY; *see* Hanbury-Tracy, family name of Baron Sudeley.

TRAEGER, Tessa; photographer of still life portraiture and landscape; *b* 30 April 1938; *d* of Thomas Cecil Grimshaw and Hannah Joan (*née* Dearsley); *m* 1st, 1965, Ronald S. Traeger (*d* 1968); 2nd, 2006, Patrick C. Kinmonth. *Educ:* Guildford High Sch. for Girls; Guildford Sch. of Art. Freelance photographer of private and commissioned work, 1975–91, incl. Vogue UK food series; 50 portraits of leading horticulturists commnd by NPG for main collection, 2000. *Solo exhibitions:* Photographers' Gall., 1978; Gall. Ratié, Paris, 1979; Neal St Gall., 1980; John Hansard Gall., Southampton, 1983; Sheffield Fine Art, 1988; M Gall., Hamburg, 1993; Ardèche Fest. des Arts, France, annually, 1994–98, 2003; Michael Hoppen Gall., London, 1997; Witkin Gall., NY, 1997; James Danziger Gall., NY, 1999; Association Gall., London, 2000; Foto Fest., Naarden, Holland, 2001; A Gardener's Labyrinth, NPG, 2003, Bradford, Hove and Scarborough, 2004, Bowes Mus., 2005, Port Eliot Fest., 2011; Voices of Vivarias, Purdy Hicks Gall., London, 2010, Oklahoma City Arts Centre, 2011; Chemistry of Light, 2013, Chemistry of Light Pt II, 2016, Purdy Hicks Gall., London; Calligraphy of Dance, Boughton House, 2014, Purdy Hicks Gall., London, 2015; Water Tank project, New York City, 2014–15; *group exhibitions:* Seeing Things, V&A, 2002; Credit Suisse Gall., Zürich, 2005; Garden of the Year, Christie's, London, 2010; L'Arbre et le photographe, Beaux-arts de Paris, 2012; Ardèche Fest. des Arts, 2013; *collections:* V&A Mus.; Bibliothèque National, Paris; Metropolitan Mus. of Art, NY; Citibank Private Bank, London; NPG, London; Buhl Collection, USA; New Hall, Cambridge; RHS, London, and many private collections. Contrib. to Oral Hist. of British Photography for Nat. Sound Archive, British Liby, 1996. Silver Award, 1979, Gold Award, 1982, DAAD; Lion d'Or, Cannes Advertising Fest., 1994; Silver Award, Assoc. of Fashion, Advertising and Editorial Photographers, 1997 and 1998; Pink Lady Photographer of the Year Lifetime Achievement Award, 2014. *Publications:* (with A. Boxer) Summer Winter Cookbook, 1978; (with A. Boxer) A Visual Feast, 1991 (Andre Simon Award); (with M. Harrison) Ronald Traeger New Angles: a memoir (to accompany exhibn at V&A Mus.), 1999; (with P. Kinmonth) A Gardener's Labyrinth (to accompany exhibn at NPG), 2003; (with Lora Zarubin) I'm almost always hungry, 2003 (Gourmand World Cookbook Award; Best Cookbook Photography and Internat. Assoc. of Culinary Professionals awards, USA; Julia Child Award); (with Stewart Grimshaw) A Garden in Sussex, 2009; Voices of the Vivarais, 2010 (Photographic Book Prize, British Book Design and Prodn Awards); Fern Verrow, 2015; Sally Clarke: 30 Ingredients, 2015; The Loveliest Valley, 2015. *Recreations:* gardening, walking in N Devon, restoring 16th century manor house. *Address:* 7 Rossetti Studios, 72 Flood Street, SW3 5TF.

See also Sir N. T. Grimshaw.

TRAFFORD, Dr Bernard St John; Headmaster, Newcastle upon Tyne Royal Grammar School, since 2008; *b* 23 May 1956; *s* of Peter and Josephine Trafford; *m* 1981, Katherine Potts; two *d*. *Educ:* All Hallows Prep. Sch.; Downside Sch.; St Edmund Hall, Oxford (BA Music, MA); Westminster Coll., Oxford (PGCE); Univ. of Birmingham (MEd; PhD; George Cadbury Prize). Teacher, Royal GS, High Wycombe, 1978–81; Wolverhampton Grammar School: Dir of Music, 1981–90; Hd of Sixth Form, 1987–90; Head, 1990–2008. Chair of Trustees, Sch. Councils UK, 2006–09; Equal Opportunities Officer, 2001–03, Pubns Officer, 2003–05, Assoc. of Sch. and Coll. Leaders. Chm., HMC, 2007–08 and 2008–09. Trustee, youngchoirs, 1984–2006 (Chm., 1998–2006); Trustee and Dir, Nat. Schs SO, 1998–2006. FRSA. Freedom, City of London, 2009; Liveryman, Merchant Taylors' Co., 2009. *Publications:* Sharing Power in Schools: raising standards, 1993; Participation, Power-sharing and School Improvement, 1997; (ed) Diversity, Inclusivity and Equal Opportunities, 2002; (ed) Making the Most of It: management in schools and colleges, 2002; (jtly) What's It All About?, 2002; (ed) Two Sectors, One Purpose: independent schools in the system, 2002; School Councils, School Democracy, School Improvement: why, what, how, 2003; Raising the Student Voice, 2006; (jtly) The Personal Touch, 2006; (ed) i^2=Independent and Innovative: examples of innovation in HMC schools, 2006; (jtly) Democratic Governance of Schools, 2007; contribs to educn books and jls. *Recreations:* playing jazz, writing music, walking in Northumberland, running and cycling, trying to get thinner and fitter. *Address:* Royal Grammar School, Eskdale Terrace, Newcastle upon Tyne NE2 4DX. *T:* (01912) 815711, *Fax:* (01912) 120392. *E:* b.trafford@rgs.newcastle.sch.uk.

TRAFFORD, Hon. Mark Russell; QC 2015; *b* Brighton, 27 July 1966; *s* of Baron Trafford and Helen Trafford (*née* Chalk); *m* 1995, Brigitte Anne Howe; two *s* two *d*. Called to the Bar, Lincoln's Inn, 1992 (Megarry Schol. 1992); in practice as barrister, 1992–. Associate Lectr, Oxford Inst. of Legal Practice, 1996–2013. *Publications:* contribs to Jl Internat. Banking and Financial Law. *Address:* 23 Essex Street, WC2R 3AA. *T:* (020) 7413 0353.

TRAHAIR, John Rosewarne, CBE 1990; DL; Chairman, Plymouth District Health Authority, 1981–90; *b* 29 March 1921; *s* of late Percy Edward Trahair and Edith Irene Trahair; *m* 1948, Patricia Elizabeth (*née* Godrich) (*d* 2015); one *s* one *d*. *Educ:* Leys Sch.; Christ's Coll., Cambridge (MA). FCIS. Served with Royal Artillery, 1941–46 (Captain). Finance Dir, Farleys Infant Food Ltd, 1948–73; Dir 1950–74, Dep. Chm. 1956–74, Western Credit Holdings Ltd. Chairman: Moorhaven HMC, 1959–66; Plymouth and District HMC, 1966–74; Member: SW Regional Hosp. Bd, 1965–74 (Vice-Chm. 1971–73, Chm. 1973–74); South Western RHA, 1974–81. Mem., Devon CC, 1977–81. Pres., Devon County Agricl Assoc., 1993–. High Sheriff, Devon, 1987–88; DL Devon, 1989. *Recreations:* sailing, walking. *Address:* West Park, Ivybridge, South Devon PL21 9JP. *T:* (01752) 892466.

TRAHAR, Anthony John; Chairman, Bartlett Resources LLP, since 2007; *b* 1 June 1949; *s* of Thomas Walter Trahar and Thelma Trahar (*née* Ashmead-Bartlett); *m* 1977, Patricia Jane; one *s* one *d*. *Educ:* St John's Coll., Johannesburg; Witwatersrand Univ. (BComm). Chartered Accountant (South Africa) 1973. Anglo American: joined as mgt trainee, Anglo American Corp. of S Africa Ltd, 1974; PA to Chm., 1976–77; Financial Dir, Anglo American Industrial Corp., 1982–86; Man. Dir, 1986–89, Exec. Chm., 1989–2000, Mondi Paper Co.; Exec. Dir, Anglo American Corp., 1991; Dep. Chm., Anglo American Industrial Corp., 1992–99; Exec. Dir, 1999–2007, CEO, 2000–07, Anglo American plc; Chm., Mondi Europe, 1993–2003. Chairman: S African Motor Corp., 1996–2000; AECI Ltd, 1999–2001; Senior Adviser: Barclays Natural Resources, 2007–13; Macquarie Capital, 2013–. Chm., Paleo-Anthropological Scientific Trust, 1999–2007. Hon. PhD Pretoria, SA, 2007. Gold Cross with Star, 1st cl. (Austria), 2004. *Recreations:* trout fishing, shooting, classic cars, music. *Clubs:* Royal Automobile; Rand, (Johannesburg).

TRAILL, Sir Alan (Towers), GBE 1984; QSO 1990; arbitrator, expert witness and insurance consultant; Lord Mayor of London, 1984–85; *b* 7 May 1935; *s* of George Traill and Margaret Eleanor (*née* Matthews); *m* 1964, Sarah Jane (*née* Hutt); one *s*. *Educ:* St Andrew's Sch., Eastbourne; Charterhouse; Jesus Coll., Cambridge (MA). Underwriting Member of Lloyd's, 1963–89; Man. Dir, Colburn Traill Ltd, 1989–96; Divl Dir, First City Insurance Brokers Ltd, 1996–2000. Dir, Cayman Is Monetary Authy, 2003–06. British Insurance Brokers Association: Mem. Council, 1978–79; Chairman: Reinsurance Brokers Cttee, 1978–79; UK/NZ 1990 Cttee, 1989–90; Founder Mem. Cttee, ARIAS (Insce Arbitration Soc.), 1997–2012. Mem., Court of Common Council, City of London, 1970–2005; Alderman for Langbourn Ward, 1975–2005; Sheriff, City of London, 1982–83. Master: Cutlers' Co., 1979–80; Musicians' Co., 1999–2000. Vice-Pres., City Arts Trust, 2010– (Dir, 1980–2010). Trustee, Morden Coll., 1995–. Mem. Adv. Cttee, 1995–, Educn Cttee, 1998–, LSO. Patron, Treloar Coll. (Gov., 1986–2002); Hon. Gov., Christ's Hosp. Foundn, 2005–; Gov., Menuhin Sch., 2000–11 (Chm., 2006–11). KStJ 1985. *Recreations:* DIY, travel, opera, assisting education. *Address:* Wheelers Farm, Thursley, Godalming, Surrey GU8 6QE.

TRAINOR, Sir Richard (Hughes), KBE 2010; DPhil; FRHistS; FAcSS; Rector, Exeter College, Oxford, since 2014; *b* 31 Dec. 1948; *s* of late William Richard Trainor and Sarah Frances (*née* Hughes); *m* 1980, Prof. Marguerite Wright Dupree; one *s* one *d*. *Educ:* Brown Univ. (BA); Princeton Univ. (MA); Merton Coll., Oxford (Rhodes Scholar; MA; Hon. Fellow, 2004); Nuffield Coll., Oxford (DPhil 1982). FRHistS 1990. Jun. Res. Fellow, Wolfson Coll., Oxford, 1977–79; Lectr, Balliol Coll., Oxford, 1978–79; University of Glasgow: Lectr in Econ. Hist., 1979–89; Sen. Lectr in Econ. and Social Hist., 1989–95; Prof. of Social Hist., 1995–2000; Dir, Design and Implementation of Software in Hist. Project, 1985–89; Co-Dir, Computers in Teaching Initiative Centre for Hist., Archaeol. and Art Hist., 1989–99; Dean, Faculty of Social Sci., 1992–96; Vice-Principal, 1996–2000; Vice-Chancellor and Prof. of Social Hist., Greenwich Univ., 2000–04; Principal and Prof. of Social History, KCL, 2004–14 (Fellow, 2004). Member: Jt Inf. Systems Cttee, 2001–05; HEFCE Cttee on Quality Assessment, Learning and Teaching, 2003–06; HEFCE Cttee on Leadership, Governance and Mgt, 2006–07; AHRC, 2006–11; HEFCE Rev. of Philanthropy in UK Higher Educn, 2012 (Mem., Implementation Gp, 2013); Commn on Future of Higher Educn, 2012–13. Universities UK: Mem. UK Bd, 2000–05, 2009–11; Treas., 2005–06; Pres., 2007–09; Co-Chm., UK/US Study Gp, 2008–09; Chm., Steering Gp, UUK/DfES Review of Student Services, 2002; Convenor, Steering Gp, Learning and Teaching Support Network, 2000–04. Chairman: London Metropolitan Network, 2002–06; Adv. Council, Inst. of Histl Res., 2004–09 (Hon. Fellow, 2009); Member: US-UK Fulbright Commn, 2003–09 (Patron, 2010); Bd, Higher Educn Acad., 2004–07. Governor: Henley Mgt Coll., 2003–05; St Paul's Sch., 2012–14; RAM, 2013–. Mem., Bd of Trustees, Univ. of London, 2010–13; Trustee, Museum of London, 2014–. Mem., Exec. Cttee, Pilgrims Soc. of GB, 2004–10. President: Glasgow and W of Scotland Br., HA, 1991–93; Econ. Hist. Soc., 2013– (Hon. Sec., 1998–2004). FAcSS (AcSS 2001). FRSA 1995. Hon. FTCL 2003. Hon. DCL Kent, 2009; Hon. DHL Rosalind Franklin Univ. of Medicine and Sci., 2012; DUniv Glasgow, 2014. Leadership Award, CASE Europe, 2011. *Publications:* (ed jtly) Historians, Computers and Data: applications in research and teaching, 1991; (ed jtly) Towards an International Curriculum for History and Computing, 1992; (ed jtly) The Teaching of Historical Computing: an international framework, 1993; Black Country Elites: the exercise of authority in an industrialised area 1830–1900, 1993; (ed with R. Morris) Urban Governance: Britain and beyond since 1750, 2000; (jtly) University, City and State: the University of Glasgow since 1870, 2000; contrib. numerous articles to books and jls. *Recreations:* parenting, observing politics, tennis. *Address:* Exeter College, Oxford OX1 3DP. *T:* (01865) 279605. *Club:* Athenæum.

TRAPIDO, Barbara Louise; freelance writer, since 1982; novelist; *b* Cape Town, 5 Nov. 1941; *d* of Frits Johan Schuddeboom and Anneliese Schuddeboom (*née* Jacobsen); *m* 1963, Stanley Trapido (*d* 2008); one *s* one *d*. *Educ:* Natal Univ., Durban (BA Hons English); London Univ. Inst. of Educn (PGCE). Teacher: schs, London, 1964–67; Coll. of Further Educn, Sunderland, and Remand Centre for Young Offenders, Co. Durham, 1967–70; Supervisor, Jericho Pre-School Playgroup, Oxford, 1970–82. *Publications:* Brother of the More Famous Jack, 1982; Noah's Ark, 1985; Temples of Delight, 1990; Juggling, 1994; The Travelling Hornplayer, 1999; Frankie & Stankie, 2003; Sex and Stravinsky, 2010. *Recreations:* concerts, opera, ballet, theatre, trawling fine art galleries (all spectator activities), cycling, dogs, family and friends. *Address:* c/o Victoria Hobbs, A. M. Heath & Co., 6 Warwick Court, WC1R 5DJ.

TRAVERS, David; QC 2010; *b* Durham City, 19 March 1957; *s* of late George Bowes Travers and of Gertrude Colbert Travers (*née* Churnside); *m* 1984, Sheila Mary Killoran; one *s* two *d*. *Educ:* Spennymoor Sch.; King's Coll., London (Royal Instn Australian Sci. Schol., 1975; LLB; AKC 1979; LLM 1980); Regent's Coll.; Inns of Court Sch. of Law. Accredited Mediator 2000. Sabbatical Pres., Union of Students, KCL, 1979–80. Called to the Bar, Middle Temple, 1981 (Harmsworth Scholar 1982); in practice as a barrister, Manchester, 1981–88, Birmingham, 1988–2001, Temple, London, 2001–; Mem., Midland Circuit. Mem., Attorney Gen.'s Panel of Counsel (List A), 2002–10. Member: Bar Council, 1995–2000 (Member: IT Cttee, 1996–98; Law Reform Cttee, 1996–98); Planning and Envmt Bar Assoc., 1997–. Legal Assessor: Fitness to Practise Cttees (formerly Professional Conduct Cttees), GDC; Fitness to Practise Cttees, GMC, 2003–. Lecturer: Accountancy Tuition Centre, Manchester and Liverpool, 1982–84; Sch. of Mgt Scis, UMIST, 1986–87; professional confs, 1992–; Central Law Trng, 1996–; Tutor, Dept of Biomed. Scis and Biomed. Ethics, Univ. of Birmingham, 1998–99. Vis. Prof. of Business Accountability, Newport Business Sch., Univ. of Wales, 2011–13; Vis. Prof., Univ. of South Wales, 2013–. Libel Reader, Daily Star and Daily Express,

1987–88. Member: Assoc. of Regulatory and Disciplinary Lawyers; Food Law Gp; Planning and Envmt Bar Assoc. Gov., Highclare Sch., 2004–10 (Chm., 2006–07). Student Mem., Gov. Body, KCL, 1977–78; Sabbatical Pres., Union of Students, KCL, 1978–79 (Hon. Life Mem., 1980). Hon. Fellow, Soc. of Food Hygiene and Technol., 2012. Editor, King's Counsel, jl of Sch. of Law, KCL, 1978. *Publications:* (jtly) Planning Law and Practice, 2013; (jtly) Planning Enforcement, 2015. *Recreation:* 'finding the great in the small and the many in the few and practising difficult things while they are easy'. *Address:* 6 Pump Court, Temple, EC4Y 7AR. *T:* (020) 7797 8400. *E:* davidtravers@6pumpcourt.co.uk.

TRAVERS, William Morell Lindon, OBE 2012; President, Born Free Foundation (UK), since 2014 (Chief Executive Officer, 1991–2013); *b* London, 4 Nov. 1958; *s* of late William, (Bill), Travers, MBE and of Virginia Travers (*née* McKenna), (Virginia McKenna, OBE); *m* 1989, Carolyne Baird (marr. diss. 2004); one *s* one *d*. *Educ:* Cranleigh Sch. Dir, Swan Productions, documentary films, 1979–86; Founder and Dir, Zoo Check Trust, 1984–90; Pres., Born Free USA, 2004–. Pres. and Chm. Bd, Species Survival Network, USA, 1994–; Mem., Species Survival Commn Reintroduction Specialist Gp, IUCN. FRGS. *Publications:* (ed jtly) Beyond the Bars, 1987. *Recreations:* travel, photography, wildlife, writing. *Address:* Born Free Foundation, Broadlands Business Campus, Langhurstwood Road, Horsham, W Sussex RH12 4QP. *T:* (01403) 240170. *E:* will@bornfree.org.uk. *W:* www.twitter.com/willtravers. *Club:* Special Forces.

TRAVERSE-HEALY, Prof. Thomas Hector, (Tim), OBE 1989; FCIPR, FPA; Director, Centre for Public Affairs Studies, since 1969; Senior Partner, Traverse-Healy Ltd, 1947–93; *b* 25 March 1923; *s* of John Healy, MBE, and Gladys Traverse; *m* 1946, Joan Thompson; two *s* three *d*. *Educ:* Stonyhurst Coll.; St Mary's Hosp., London Univ. DipCAM. Served War, Royal Marines Commandos and Special Forces, 1941–46. Chairman: Traverse-Healy & Regester Ltd, 1985–87; Charles Barker Traverse-Healy, 1987–89; non-exec. Dir, Charles Barker Hldgs, 1990–92. Mem., Public and Social Policy Cttee, National Westminster Bank, 1974–92; Professional Advr, Corporate Communications, 1990–92; Specialist Advr, CNAA, 1990–92. Prof. of Public Relns, Univ. of Stirling, 1988–97; Visiting Professor: Baylor Univ., Texas, 1988–97; Univ. of Wales, 1990–97; Advisor: Ball State Univ., USA; Westminster Univ. President: Internat. PR Res. and Educn Foundn, 1983–86; Internat. Foundn for PR Studies, 1987–89; Chm., (UK) PR Educn Trust, 1990–92; Mem., Professional Practices Cttee, PR Consultants Assoc., 1987–91; Sec., PR Res. Network, 1994–97. Institute of Public Relations, later Chartered Institute of Public Relations: Mem. 1948, Fellow 1956; Pres. 1967–68; Tallents Gold Medal, 1985; Hon. Fellow 1988; Campbell-Johnson Medal, 2005; European PR Federation: Vice-Pres. 1965–69; International PR Association: Sec. 1950–61, Pres. 1968–73, Mem. Emeritus, 1982; Presidential Gold Medal, 1985; Chm., Coll. Emeriti, 2006–07. FRSA 1953; FIPA 1957. Member, US Public Affairs Council, 1975–91; Pres., World PR Congress: Tel Aviv, 1970; Geneva, 1973. Congress Foundn Lecture: Boston, 1976; Bombay, 1982; Melbourne, 1988; Istanbul, 2006. PR News Award, 1983; PR Week Award, 1987; Page Soc. Award, 1990; IPRA Award, 2008. *Publications:* numerous published lectures and articles in professional jls. *Recreations:* French politics, Irish Society. *Address:* 2 Henman Close, Devizes, Wilts SN10 1HD. *T:* (01380) 724940. *Clubs:* Athenæum; Philippics.

TREACHER, Adm. Sir John (Devereux), KCB 1975; Chairman, CNIguard (formerly Hatchguard) Ltd, 2005–11; Member, Advisory Board, London Technology Fund, 2007–11; *b* Chile, 23 Sept. 1924; *s* of late Frank Charles Treacher, Bentley, Suffolk; *m* 1st, 1953, Patcie Jane (marr. diss. 1968), *d* of late Dr F. L. McGrath, Evanston, Ill; one *s* one *d*; 2nd, 1969, Kirsteen Forbes, *d* of late D. F. Landale; one *s* one *d*. *Educ:* St Paul's School. Joined RN, 1942; war service in HM Ships Nelson, Glasgow, Keppel and Mermaid in Mediterranean, Normandy, Atlantic, D-Day, Omaha Beach, Russian convoys; qual. Fleet Air Arm pilot, 1947; Korean War, 800 Sqdn HMS Triumph; CO, 778 Sqdn 1951, 849 Sqdn 1952–53 (Flag Lieut and personal pilot to Adm.); British Services Mission to Washington, 1954–55; Exec. Officer, HMS Protector, S Atlantic Guardship, 1956–57; Naval Asst to Controller of Navy, 1961–63; CO, HMS Lowestoft, 1964–66; Dir, Naval Air Warfare, MoD, 1966–68; CO, HMS Eagle, 1968–70; Flag Officer Carriers and Amphibious Ships and Comdr Carrier Striking Gp 2, 1970–72; Flag Officer, Naval Air Comd, 1972–73; Vice-Chief of Naval Staff, 1973–75; C-in-C Fleet, and Allied C-in-C Channel and Eastern Atlantic, 1975–77. Chief Exec., 1977–81, and Dir, 1977–85, Nat. Car Parks; CEO and Chm., Playboy Clubs Internat., 1981–82; Chairman: R. L. Glover Ltd, 1985–87; Westland Inc., 1983–89; Dep. Chm., Westland Gp, 1986–89 (Dir, 1978–89); Director: Contipark GmbH, 1978–2001; Meggitt PLC, 1989–95; Chairman: Interparking Hispania SA, 1995–2005; Interoute Telecommunications plc, 1996–98. Non-press Mem., Press Council, 1978–81; Dir, SBAC, 1983–89. Pres., Fly Navy (formerly Swordfish) Heritage Trust, 1994–. FRAeS 1973. *Publications:* Life at Full Throttle, 2004. *Recreations:* family, travel, boating. *Address:* 59 St Mary Abbot's Court, W14 8RB. *Club:* Boodle's.

TREACY, Rt Hon. Sir Colman Maurice, Kt 2002; PC 2012; **Rt Hon. Lord Justice Treacy;** a Lord Justice of Appeal, since 2012; *b* 28 July 1949; *s* of Dr Maurice Treacy and Mary Treacy; *m* (marr. diss.); one *s* one *d*; *m* 2002, Jane Ann, *d* of Edwin and Maureen Hooper; one step *d*. *Educ:* Stonyhurst Coll.; Jesus Coll., Cambridge (Open Scholar in Classics; MA; Hon. Fellow 2014). Called to the Bar, Middle Temple, 1971, Bencher, 1999; QC 1990; an Asst Recorder, 1988–91; a Recorder, 1991–2002; Head of Chambers, 1994–2000; a Judge of the High Court, QBD, 2002–12; a Presiding Judge, Midland Circuit, 2006–10. Mem., Mental Health Rev. Tribunal, 1999–2002; Asst Boundary Comr, 2000–02; Chm., Sentencing Council for England and Wales, 2013– (Mem., 2010–). *Address:* Royal Courts of Justice, Strand, WC2A 2LL.

TREACY, Philip Anthony, Hon. OBE 2007; milliner; *b* Ballinasloe, Co. Galway, Ireland, 26 May 1967; *s* of late James Vincent Treacy and Katie Agnes Treacy. *Educ:* Nat. Coll. of Art and Design, Dublin (BA); Royal Coll. of Art (MDes; Sen. Fellow, 2002). Worked for designers incl. Rifat Ozbek, John Galliano and Victor Edelstein; former House Milliner to Marc Bohan and Victor Edelstein. Founder, Philip Treacy Ltd, 1990; first show in London, 1993, in New York, 1997, in Paris, 2000; hat manufacturer to designers incl. Karl Lagerfeld, Gianni Versace, Valentino, Rifat Ozbek, Givenchy, Alexander McQueen; designer for Debenhams, 1997–2001; launched accessory range, 1997; Design Dir, interiors, The G, Monogram Hotels, 2005; sports wear range for Umbro, 2006. Hon. DFA NUI, 2006. Accessory Designer of the Year, British Fashion Awards, 1991, 1992, 1993, 1996, 1997; Irish Fashion Oscar, 1992. *Address:* (office) 1 Havelock Terrace, SW8 4AS; (store) 69 Elizabeth Street, SW1W 9PJ.

TREACY, Hon. Sir Séamus, Kt 2007; **Hon. Mr Justice Treacy;** a Judge of the High Court of Justice of Northern Ireland, since 2007; *b* 22 March 1956; *s* of late Joseph Treacy and Rose Veronica Treacy; *m* 1976, Viviane Jones; one *s* two *d*. *Educ:* St Malachy's Coll., Belfast; Queen's Univ., Belfast (LLB Hons). Called to the Bar: NI, 1979; Ireland (King's Inns), 1990; Inner Bar of Ireland, 2000; QC (NI) 1999. Mem., Panel of Arbitrators, Motor Insurers Bureau, 2005–07. *Recreations:* cycling, running, the arts. *Address:* Royal Courts of Justice, Belfast BT1 3JF.

TREADELL, Victoria Marguerite, CMG 2010; MVO 1989; HM Diplomatic Service; High Commissioner to Malaysia, since 2014; *b* 4 Nov. 1959; *née* Jansz; *m* 1985, Alan Treadell. Entered FCO, 1978; Econ. Relns Dept, FCO, 1979–81; Visa Support Officer, Islamabad, 1981–83; Diary Sec., Perm. Under Sec.'s Office, 1983–85, Desk Officer, Western Europe Dept, 1985, FCO; Asst Mgt Officer, 1986–89, Commonwealth Heads of Govt Meeting and State Visits Officer, 1989–90, Kuala Lumpur; Asst Desk Officer, Resource Policy Dept, 1990–92, British Council Quinquennial Rev. Team, 1992–93, FCO; Dep. Hd, Export Services Section, FCO/DTI, 1993–96; Desk Officer, Latin America Dept, FCO, 1996–98; Hd, Professionalism in Trade Unit, FCO/DTI, 1998–99; Dep. Dir, Corporate Resources Gp, British Trade Internat., 1999–2002; Dir, NW of England, UK Trade and Investment, 2002–05; Dep. High Comr, Mumbai, 2006–10; High Comr, New Zealand, 2010–14. *Address:* c/o Foreign and Commonwealth Office, King Charles Street, SW1A 2AH.

TREADGOLD, Hazel Rhona; Central President of the Mothers' Union, 1983–88; *b* 29 May 1936; *m* 1959, Very Rev. John David Treadgold, LVO (*d* 2015); two *s* one *d*. Mothers' Union: has held office, Dioceses of Southwell, Durham and Chichester, and at HQ; Chm., Central Young Families Cttee, 1971–76; a Central Vice-Pres., 1978–83; Life Vice-Pres., Chichester Dio., 2003. Archbishop of Canterbury's Co-ordinator, Bishops' Wives Conf., Lambeth, 1988; Member: Women's Nat. Commn, 1980–83; Exec., Women's Council, 1989–91. Gov., Bishop Luffa C of E Comprehensive Sch., 1990–2010. JP Chichester, 1991–2006. *Recreations:* travel, reading, flower arranging, swimming, theatre. *Address:* 43 Prior's Acre, Boxgrove, W Sussex PO18 0ER. *T:* (01243) 782385. *E:* jandh@skymarket.org.

TREADGOLD, Sydney William, CBE 1999; FCA; Secretary: Financial Reporting Council, 1990–98; Financial Reporting Review Panel, 1991–98; Accountancy Foundation, 2000–01; *b* 10 May 1933; *s* of Harold and Gladys Treadgold; *m* 1961, Elizabeth Ann White; two *s*. *Educ:* Larkmead Sch., Abingdon. Chartered accountant (ACA 1960, FCA 1970). Served RAF, 1951–53 (Navigator). Wenn Townsend, Chartered Accountants, 1954–62; Asst Finance Officer, Univ. of Liverpool, 1963–65; Principal: Min. of Aviation, 1965–67; Min. of Technol., 1967–71; Asst Sec., DTI, 1972–78; Under Secretary: Price Commn, 1978–79; Depts of Industry and Trade, 1979–83; DTI, 1983–89; Mem., Accounting Standards Task Gp, 1989–90; Secretary: Accounting Standards Bd, 1990–93; Regulation of Accountancy Profession Implementation Gp, 1999–2001. Mem., Certified Accountants' Disciplinary Panel, 1999–2003, Appointments Cttee, 2004–08. FRSA 1988. *Recreations:* Shakespeare, theatre, film, bridge. *Address:* 23 Sturges Road, Wokingham, Berks RG40 2HG.

TREANOR, Most Rev. Noel; *see* Down and Connor, Bishop of, (RC).

TREDINNICK, David Arthur Stephen; MP (C) Bosworth, since 1987; *b* 19 Jan. 1950; *m* 1983, Rebecca Jane Shott (marr diss. 2008); one *s* one *d*. *Educ:* Ludgrove Sch., Wokingham; Eton; Mons Officer Cadet Sch.; Graduate Business Sch., Cape Town Univ. (MBA); St John's Coll., Oxford (MLitt 1987). Trainee, E. B. Savoury Milln & Co., Stockbrokers, 1972; Account Exec., Quadrant International, 1974; Salesman, Kalle Infotec UK, 1976; Sales Manager, Word Processing, 1977–78; Consultant, Baird Communications, NY, 1978–79; Marketing Manager, Q1 Europe Ltd, 1979–81; Res. asst to Kenneth Warren, MP, and Angela Rumbold, CBE, MP, 1981–87; Dir, Malden Mitcham Properties (family business), 1985–. Contested (C) Cardiff S and Penarth, 1983. PPS to Minister of State, Welsh Office, 1991–94. Chm., Select Cttee on Statutory Instruments, 1997–2005; Member: Select Cttee on Health, 2010–15; Select Cttee on Sci. and Technol., 2013–15; Chairman: Jt Cttee on Statutory Instruments, 1997–2005; All-Party Parly Gp for Integrated Healthcare (formerly for Alternative and Complementary Medicine, then for Complementary and Integrated Medicine), 2006– (Treas., 1991–2002; Jt Chm., 2002–06); Treas., Parly Gp for World Govt, 1991–95; Secretary: Cons. backbench Defence Cttee, 1990–91; Cons. backbench Foreign Affairs Cttee, 1990–91. Chm., British Atlantic Gp of Young Politicians, 1989–91; Co-Chm., Future of Europe Trust, 1991–94; Chairman: Anglo East European Trade Co., 1990–97; Ukraine Business Agency, 1992–97. *Address:* House of Commons, SW1A 0AA. *T:* (020) 7219 4514.

TREES, family name of **Baron Trees**.

TREES, Baron *cr* 2012 (Life Peer), of The Ross in Perth and Kinross; **Alexander John Trees,** PhD; Professor of Veterinary Parasitology, University of Liverpool, 1994–2011, now Emeritus (Dean, Faculty of Veterinary Science, 2001–08); *b* 12 June 1946; *s* of John Trees and Margaret Trees (*née* Bell); *m* 1970, Frances Ann McAnally; one *d*. *Educ:* Univ. of Edinburgh (BVM&S 1969; PhD 1976). MRCVS 1969. Asst in gen. veterinary practice, Derby, 1970–71; Res. Asst, Univ. of Edinburgh, 1971–76; Elanco Products Ltd: Veterinary Advr for ME in Rome, 1977–80; Hd, Animal Sci., Rome (ME/N Africa), 1980; Liverpool School of Tropical Medicine, University of Liverpool: Lectr, Dept of Veterinary Parasitol., 1980–91; Sen. Lectr, 1991–94; Head: Veterinary Parasitol., 1992–2001; Parasite and Vector Biol. Div., 1994–97; Mem. Council, 1995–2004. Chm. Bd, Moredun Res. Inst., Edinburgh, 2011–. Member Council: RCVS, 2000–15 (Jun. Vice-Pres., 2008–09; Pres., 2009–10; Sen. Vice-Pres., 2010–11); RSTM&H, 1997–2000. Pres., Assoc. Veterinary Teachers and Res. Workers, 1996–97. Founding DipEVPC, 2003 (Vice-Pres., EVPC, 2006–09). Hon. Fellow, Myerscough Coll., 2009. McCall Lect., 2011, Vis. Prof., 2012, Univ. of Glasgow. Hon. DVetMed London. Selborne Medal for vet. res., Assoc. of Vet. Teachers and Res. Workers, 2005; Wooldridge Meml Medal and Lecture, BVA, 2009; Amoroso Award, British Small Animal Vet. Assoc., 2011. Member, Editorial Board: Res. in Vet. Sci., 1991–2001; Trends in Parasitol. (formerly Parasitol. Today), 1992–2007; Vet. Ed.-in-Chief, Veterinary Record, 2011–. *Publications:* numerous peer-reviewed scientific papers and book chapters. *Recreations:* mountaineering, natural history, living life while I'm alive. *Address:* House of Lords, SW1A 0PW. *Club:* Farmers.

TREFETHEN, Prof. Lloyd Nicholas, (Nick), PhD; FRS 2005; Professor of Numerical Analysis, Oxford University, since 1997; Fellow, Balliol College, Oxford, since 1997; *b* 30 Aug. 1955; *s* of Lloyd McGregor Trefethen and Florence Newman Trefethen; *m* 1st, 1988, Anne Elizabeth Daman (marr. diss. 2008); one *s* one *d*; 2nd, 2011, Kate McLoughlin. *Educ:* Harvard Coll. (AB 1977); Stanford Univ. (MS Computer Sci./Numerical Analysis 1980; PhD 1982). NSF Post-doctoral Fellow and Adjunct Asst Prof., Courant Inst. of Mathematical Scis, New York Univ., 1982–84; Massachusetts Institute of Technology: Asst Prof. of Applied Maths, 1984–87; Associate Prof., 1987–91; Cornell University: Associate Prof., 1991–93; Prof. of Computer Sci., 1994–97. Pres., SIAM, 2011–12. Mem., NAE (US), 2007. *Publications:* Numerical Conformal Mapping, 1986; Numerical Linear Algebra, 1997; Spectral Methods in MATLAB, 2000; Schwarz-Christoffel Mapping, 2002; Spectra and Pseudospectra, 2005; Trefethen's Index Cards, 2011; Approximation Theory and Approximation Practice, 2013; numerous technical articles. *Address:* Mathematical Institute, Oxford University, Woodstock Road, Oxford OX2 6GG.

TREFGARNE, family name of **Baron Trefgarne**.

TREFGARNE, 2nd Baron *cr* 1947, of Cleddau; **David Garro Trefgarne;** PC 1989; *b* 31 March 1941; *s* of 1st Baron Trefgarne and Elizabeth (*d* 2007), *d* of Charles Edward Churchill (she *m* 2nd, 1962, Comdr A. T. Courtney, from whom she obt. a divorce, 1966; 3rd, 1971, H. C. H. Ker (*d* 1987), Dundee); *S* father, 1960; *m* 1968, Rosalie, *d* of Baron Lane of Horsell; two *s* one *d*. *Educ:* Haileybury; Princeton University, USA. Opposition Whip, House of Lords, 1977–79; a Lord in Waiting (Govt Whip), 1979–81; Parly Under Sec. of State, DoT, 1981, FCO, 1981–82, DHSS, 1982–83, (Armed Forces) MoD, 1983–85; Minister of State: for Defence Support, 1985–86; for Defence Procurement, 1986–89; DTI, 1989–90; elected Mem., H of L, 1999. Chm., Assoc. of Cons. Peers, 2000–04. Dir of various companies. Chm., Sci., Engrg, Manufacturing Technologies Alliance (formerly Engrg Trng Authority), 1994–2006. Dir, UK Skills, 1999–2005. Chm., Libyan British Business Council, 2003–13; Dep. Chm., Arab British Chamber of Commerce, 2004–. President: Popular Flying Assoc., 1992–97, 2000–03; Air Safety Gp, 2012–; Hon. President: British Assoc. of Aviation Consultants, 1994–; IEE, 2003–06; Welding Inst., 2006–08; Mem. Council, Air League,

1996–2006. Chm., Fairoaks Airport Consultative Cttee, 2009–. Vice Chm., ACF Assoc., 1992–2000. Gov., Guildford Sch. of Acting, 1992–2000; Life Gov., Haileybury, 1992. Trustee, Mary Rose Trust, 1994–2001; Chm., Brooklands Mus. Trust, 2001–14. Patron, Catering Equipment Suppliers Assoc., 2005–. Hon. Fellow, Univ. of Central Lancs, 2004. DUniv Staffs, 2004. Awarded Royal Aero Club Bronze Medal (jointly) for flight from England to Australia and back in light aircraft, 1963. *Recreation:* photography. *Heir: s* Hon. George Garro Trefgarne [*b* 4 Jan. 1970; *m* 2007, Camilla D'Arcy-Irvine; one *s* one *d*]. *Address:* House of Lords, SW1A 0PW.

TREFUSIS; *see* Fane Trefusis, family name of Baron Clinton.

TREGEAR, Francis Benedict William; QC 2003; a Recorder, since 2004; *b* 18 May 1957; *s* of late (George Herbert) Benjamin Tregear and of (Elisabeth) Bridget Tregear; *m* 1984, Elizabeth Anne Burke; one *s* one *d*. *Educ:* Lycée Français de Londres; Colet Court; St Paul's Sch.; St John's Coll., Cambridge (BA); Inns of Court Sch. of Law. Called to the Bar, Middle Temple, 1980; Mem., Lincoln's Inn, 1993, Bencher, 2010; called to the Bar, Eastern Caribbean Supreme Ct, 2004; Commercial Chancery practice. *Recreations:* running, music, London. *Address:* 24 Old Buildings, Lincoln's Inn, WC2A 3UP. *T:* (020) 7404 0946, *Fax:* (020) 7405 1360. *E:* francis.tregear@xxiv.co.uk.

TREGEAR, (Vyvyan Alexander) Gordon; Vice Lord-Lieutenant of West Sussex, 2009–14; *b* Karachi, 28 April 1944; *s* of Lt Col Vivian William Tregear and Virginia Doris Tregear (*née* Shrapnel-Smith); *m* 1981, Susan Alexandra Symington; three *d*. *Educ:* Cheltenham Coll.; Trinity Coll., Cambridge (BA Hons 1966; MA 2001). Admitted solicitor, 1970; Partner: Field Fisher & Martineau, 1974–76; Elbourne Mitchell & Co., 1976–82; est. own firm, Tregear & Co., 1982, merged with Bentleys Stokes & Lowless, 1986: Partner, 1986–95; Consultant, 1995–97. Owner and manager, S Lodge Estate, Horsham, 1982–. Mem., Legal and Parly Cttee, 1998–2003, Chm., Sussex Br., 1999–2001, CLA. Dir, Highland Soc. of London, 1980–82. Vice Pres., W Sussex Co. Scout Council, 2006–. High Sheriff, 2005–06, DL, 2008, W Sussex. *Publications:* (contrib.) Butterworth's Encyclopaedia of Forms and Precedents, 5th edn, 1989. *Recreations:* music (piano, bagpipes), shooting, family. *Address:* Long House, Long House Lane, Cowfold, W Sussex RH13 8AR. *T:* (01403) 864966, *Fax:* (01403) 865355. *E:* s.lodge.estate@btconnect.com. *Club:* Boodle's.

TREGLOWN, Prof. Jeremy Dickinson; Professor of English, University of Warwick, 1993–2013, now Emeritus (Chairman, Department of English and Comparative Literary Studies, 1995–98); Senior Research Fellow, Institute of English Studies, School of Advanced Studies, University of London, since 2014; *b* 24 May 1946; *s* of late Rev. Geoffrey and Beryl Treglown; *m* 1st, 1970, Rona Bower (marr. diss. 1982); one *s* two *d*; 2nd, 1984, Holly Eley (*née* Urquhart) (*d* 2010); one *d* by Jennifer Lewis; 3rd, 2013, Maria Alvarez. *Educ:* Bristol Grammar Sch.; St Peter's Coll. and Hertford Coll., Oxford (MA, BLitt); PhD London. Lecturer: Lincoln Coll., Oxford, 1974–77; University College London, 1977–80; Times Literary Supplement: Asst Editor, 1980–82; Editor, 1982–90. Vis. Fellow: All Souls Coll., Oxford, 1986; Huntington Library, San Marino, Calif, 1988; Mellon Vis. Associate, Calif Inst. of Technol., 1988; Hon. Res. Fellow, UCL, 1991–; Ferris Vis. Prof., Princeton Univ., 1991–92; Jackson Brothers Fellow, Beinecke Liby, Yale, 1999; Leverhulme Res. Fellow, 2001–03; Mellon Fellow, Harry Ransom Humanities Res. Center, Univ. of Texas at Austin, 2002; Sokol Fellow, Cullman Center for Scholars and Writers, NY Public Liby, 2002–03; Fellow in Hist., Bogliasco Foundn, 2011; Fellow, Rockefeller Foundn Bellagio Center, 2011; Donald C. Gallup Fellow in Amer. Lit., Beinecke Liby, Yale, 2014; Leverhulme Emeritus Fellow, 2014–15. Mem. Council, RSL, 1989–96 and 2011–13; FRSL 1991; FRSA 1990; FEA 2001. Chairman of Judges: Booker Prize, 1991; Whitbread Book of the Year Award, 1998. Contributing Editor, Grand Street, NY, 1991–98. *Publications:* Roald Dahl, 1994; Romancing: the life and work of Henry Green, 2000; V. S. Pritchett: a working life, 2004; Franco's Crypt: Spanish culture and memory since 1936, 2013; edited: The Letters of John Wilmot, Earl of Rochester, 1980; Spirit of Wit: reconsiderations of Rochester, 1982; The Lantern Bearers, Essays by Robert Louis Stevenson, 1988; (with B. Bennett) Grub Street and the Ivory Tower: literary journalism and literary scholarship from Fielding to the Internet, 1998; (with D. McVea) Contributors to The Times Literary Supplement 1902–74: a biographical index, 2000; V. S. Pritchett: essential stories, 2005; Roald Dahl: collected stories, 2006; various articles and book introductions. *Address:* Gardens Cottage, Ditchley Park, Enstone, Chipping Norton, Oxon OX7 4EP.

TREISMAN, Prof. Anne Marie, DPhil; FRS 1989; Professor of Psychology, 1993, James S. McDonnell Distinguished Professor of Psychology, 1995, now Emeritus, Princeton University; *b* 27 Feb. 1935; *d* of Percy Strawson Taylor and Suzanne (*née* Touren); *m* 1st, 1960, Michel Treisman (marr. diss.); two *s* two *d*; 2nd, 1978, Prof. Daniel Kahneman, *qv*. *Educ:* Newnham Coll., Cambridge (BA 1956); DPhil Oxon 1962. University of Oxford: Res. Asst, 1961–63, Mem., MRC Psycholinguistics Res. Unit, 1963–66, Dept of Experimental Psychol.; Lectr in Psychol., 1968–78; Fellow, St Anne's Coll., Oxford, 1967–78; Professor of Psychology: Univ. of BC, 1978–86; Univ. of Calif, Berkeley, 1986–94. Member: US Nat. Acad. of Scis, 1994; Amer. Acad. Arts and Scis, 1995; Amer. Philosophical Soc., 2005. Corresp. FBA 2009. Hon. DSc: British Columbia, 2004; UCL, 2006. Dist. Scientific Contribn Award, Amer. Psychological Assoc., 1990; Grawemeyer Award in Psychol., Univ. of Louisville, 2009; Nat. Medal of Sci. (USA), 2012. *Publications:* contrib. chapters in books and articles in learned jls. *Address:* Department of Psychology, Princeton University, Princeton, NJ 08540–1010, USA; 70 East 19th Street, PHD, New York, NY 10003, USA.

TREISMAN, Dr Richard Henry, FRS 1994; Head, Signalling and Transcription Laboratory, since 1988, and Research Director, since 2015, Francis Crick Institute (formerly Imperial Cancer Research Fund Laboratories, later Cancer Research UK London Research Institute) (Director, 1999–2015); *b* 7 Oct. 1954; *s* of Woolf Benjamin Treisman and Marjorie Elizabeth (*née* Grounsell); *m* 1993, Kathleen Mary Weston; one *s* one *d*. *Educ:* Haberdashers' Aske's Sch.; Christ's Coll., Cambridge (BA 1977); ICRF/UCL (PhD 1981). Postdoctoral Fellow, Harvard Univ., 1981–84; Mem., Scientific Staff, Lab. of Molecular Biol., Cambridge, 1984–88. Mem., EMBO, 1987. Mem., Festiniog Railway Soc., Porthmadog, 1967–. EMBO Medal, 1995; Louis Jeantet Prize for Medicine, 2002. *Publications:* papers in scientific jls. *Recreations:* piano playing, fell-walking. *Address:* Signalling and Transcription Laboratory, Room 401, Francis Crick Institute, 44 Lincoln's Inn Fields, WC2A 3PX. *T:* (020) 7269 3271.

TREITEL, Sir Guenter (Heinz), Kt 1997; QC 1983; DCL; FBA 1977; Vinerian Professor of English Law, Oxford University, 1979–96, now Emeritus; Fellow of All Souls College, Oxford, 1979–96, now Emeritus; *b* 26 Oct. 1928; *s* of Theodor Treitel and Hanna Lilly Treitel (*née* Levy); *m* 1957, Phyllis Margaret Cook; two *s*. *Educ:* Kilburn Grammar School; Magdalen College, Oxford. BA 1949, BCL 1951, MA 1953, DCL 1976. Called to the Bar, Gray's Inn, 1952, Hon. Bencher, 1982. Asst Lectr, LSE, 1951–53; Lectr, University Coll., Oxford, 1953–54; Fellow, Magdalen Coll., Oxford, 1954–79, Fellow Emeritus, 1979; All Souls Reader in English Law, Univ. of Oxford, 1964–79. Vis. Lectr, Univ. of Chicago, 1963–64; Visiting Professor: Chicago, 1968–69 and 1971–72; W Australia, 1976; Houston, 1977; Southern Methodist, 1978, 1988–89, 1994 (Dist. Vis. Prof., 2000, 2003); Virginia, 1978–79 and 1983–84; Santa Clara, 1981; Vis. Scholar, Ernst von Caemmerer Gedächtnisstiftung, 1990; Clarendon Lectr in Law, Oxford Univ., 2001. Trustee, British Museum, 1983–98; Mem. Council, National Trust, 1984–93. *Publications:* The Law of Contract, 1962, 11th edn 2003; An Outline of the Law of Contract, 1975, 6th edn 2004; Remedies for Breach of Contract: a comparative account, 1988; Unmöglichkeit, "Impracticability" und "Frustration" im anglo-amerikanischen Recht, 1991; Frustration and Force Majeure, 1994, 3rd edn 2014; (jtly) English Private Law, 2000, 2nd edn 2007; (jtly) Carver on Bills of Lading, 2001, 3rd edn 2011; Some Landmarks of Twentieth Century Contract Law, 2002 (trans. Chinese, 2010); edited jointly: Dicey's Conflict of Laws, 7th edn 1958; Dicey and Morris, Conflict of Laws, 8th edn 1967; Chitty on Contracts, 23rd edn 1968 to 31st edn 2012; Benjamin's Sale of Goods, 1974, 9th edn 2014. *Recreations:* music, reading.

TRELAWNY, (James Edward) Petroc; broadcaster, BBC Radio and Television; *b* Worcester, 27 May 1971; *s* of late Richard Trelawny and Jennifer Ann Trelawny (*née* Blackwood). *Educ:* Helston Sch. Presenter and reporter, BBC Radio Devon, 1989–91; presenter: British Forces Radio Hong Kong, 1991–92; Classic FM Radio, 1992–94; London Radio and LBC Radio, 1994–96; BBC Manchester, 1997; BBC Radio Three, 1998–; Cardiff Singer of the World, Leeds Piano Comp., BBC Proms and other progs, BBC TV, 1999–; contrib. to From Our Own Correspondent, BBC Radio 4, 2010–. Chm., 2005–15, Pres., 2015–, Lennox Berkeley Soc. President: Three Spires Singers, 2009–; Luton Music, 2015–; Vice Pres., London Cornish Soc., 1994–. Trustee, British Friends of Zimbabwe Acad. of Music, 2011–. *Publications:* occasional contribs to Spectator, Catholic Herald, Irish Times, Evening Standard, BBC Music Mag., Daily Telegraph. *Recreations:* music, theatre, travel, food, Zimbabwe, unusual rail journeys. *Address:* c/o BBC Radio Three, Broadcasting House, W1A 1AA. *E:* petroc.trelawny@bbc.co.uk. *Clubs:* Brydges Place, Savile.

TRELAWNY, Sir John William Richard Salusbury-, 14th Bt *cr* 1628, of Trelawny, Cornwall; *b* 30 March 1960; *o s* of Sir John Barry Salusbury-Trelawny, 13th Bt and of Carol Knox (*née* Watson); *S* father, 2009; *m* 1st, 1980, Anita Snelgrove (marr. diss. 1986); one *s* one *d*; 2nd, 1987, Sandra Thompson (marr. diss. 1993); one *s*; 3rd, 2001, Laurian, *d* of Rev. Peter Adams; two *s*. *Heir: s* Harry John Salusbury-Trelawny, *b* 10 Dec. 1982.

TRELAWNY, Petroc; *see* Trelawny, J. E. P.

TRELEAVEN, Prof. Philip Colin, PhD; Professor of Computing, University College London, since 1985 (Pro-Provost, 1994–2008); *b* 15 March 1950; *s* of Frederick Colin and Evelyn Treleaven; *m* 1981, Isabel Gouveia-Lima. *Educ:* Brunel Univ. (BTech); Manchester Univ. (MSc, PhD). Research Fellow, Univ. of Newcastle upon Tyne, 1979–83; Sen. Res. Fellow, Reading Univ., 1983–85. Contested (C): Ealing Southall, 1992; SW London, Eur. Parly elecns, 1994. *Recreation:* politics. *Address:* Department of Computer Science, University College London, Gower Street, WC1E 6BT. *T:* (020) 7679 7288.

TRELFORD, Prof. Donald Gilchrist; journalist; Emeritus Professor in Journalism Studies, Sheffield University, since 2007; Editor, The Observer, 1975–93; *b* 9 Nov. 1937; *s* of late Thomas and Doris Trelford (*née* Gilchrist); *m* 1st, 1963, Janice Ingram; two *s* one *d*; 2nd, 1978, Kate Mark; one *d*; 3rd, 2001, Claire Bishop; one *s* one *d*. *Educ:* Bablake Sch., Coventry (School Captain, 1956); Selwyn Coll., Cambridge (Open exhibnr in English, MA; University Rugby and cricket). Pilot Officer, RAF, 1956–58. Reporter and Sub-Editor, Coventry Standard and Sheffield Telegraph, 1960–63; Editor, Times of Malawi, 1963–66; Correspondent in Africa for The Observer, The Times, and BBC, 1963–66; The Observer: Dep. News Editor, 1966; Asst Man. Editor, 1968; Dep. Editor, 1969; Chief Exec., The Observer Ltd, 1992–93; Prof. and Hd of Dept of Journalism Studies, 1994–2000, Vis. Prof., 2000–04, Sheffield Univ. Acting Editor, The Oldie, 1994; Sports columnist, Daily Telegraph, 1993–2008; columnist, Majorca Daily Bulletin, 2010–. Chm., The Baby Channel, 2000–01; Director: Optomen Television, 1988–97; Observer Films, 1989–93; Central Observer TV, 1990–93; Nat. Acad. of Writing, 2000–03; London Press Club, 2001–09 (Chm., 2002–07, Pres., 2007–12). Ind. Assessor, BBC TV Regl News, 1997. Member: British Executive Cttee, IPI, 1976–2000; Soc. of Editors, 1984–93; Guild of British Newspaper Editors, 1985–2000 (Mem., Parly and Legal Cttee, 1987–91); Council, Media Soc., 1981–2003 (Pres., 1999–2002); Defence, Press and Broadcasting Cttee, 1986–93; Competition Commn (newspaper panel), 1999–2006; Council, ASA, 2002–08; Vice-Pres., Newspaper Press Fund, 1992– (Appeals Chm., 1991). Chm., Eur. Fedn of Press Clubs, 2005–06; Pres., Internat. Assoc. of Press Clubs, 2006–07. Member, judging panel: British Press Awards, 1981–2002 (Chm., 2002); Scottish Press Awards, 1985; London Press Club Awards, 2002–12 (Chm., 2007–12); Mem., Olivier Awards Cttee, SWET, 1984–93; Judge: Whitbread Prize, 1992; Sony Radio Awards, 1994; George Orwell Prize, 1998. Mem. Adv. Bd, London Choral Soc., 1991–98; Chm., Soc. of Gentlemen, Lovers of Musick, 1996–2001. Vice-Pres., British Sports Trust, 1988–2002; Hon. Advr, NPFA, 1996–2004. Mem., Jurade de St Emilion, 1997–2003. Liveryman, Worshipful Co. of Stationers and Newspaper Makers, 1986; Freeman, City of London, 1986. FRSA 1988. Hon. DLitt Sheffield, 1990. Granada Newspaper of the Year Award, 1983, 1993; commended, Internat. Editor of the Year, World Press Rev., NY, 1984. Frequent broadcasts (writer, interviewer and panellist) on TV and radio; presenter: Running Late (C4); LBC Morning Report; TV interviews include: Rajiv Gandhi, Lord Goodman, Sir Leonard Hutton, Gromyko; speaker at internat. media confs in Spain, Egypt, W Germany, Italy, USA, India, Turkey, S Africa, Argentina, Kenya, Trinidad, Lebanon, Canada, Russia, Korea, Peru, Belgium, Singapore, Ethiopia and Dubai. *Publications:* Siege, 1980; (ed) Sunday Best, 1981, 1982, 1983; (contrib.) County Champions, 1982; Snookered, 1986; (contrib.) The Queen Observed, 1986; (with Garry Kasparov) Child of Change, 1987; (contrib.) Saturday's Boys, 1990; (contrib.) Fine Glances, 1991; Len Hutton Remembered, 1992; (contrib.) One Over Par, 1992; (ed) The Observer at 200, 1992; (with Daniel King) World Chess Championship, 1993; (contrib.) Animal Passions, 1994; W. G. Grace, 1998. *Recreations:* snooker, tennis, watching Rugby and cricket. *Address:* 2 Queen Street, Henley-on-Thames RG9 1AP. *T:* 07850 131742. *E:* donaldtrelford@yahoo.co.uk; Apartado 146, 07460 Pollenca, Majorca, Spain. *T:* (971) 535117, 663453506. *Clubs:* Garrick, London Press, MCC (Mem., Cttee, 1988–91).

TREMAIN, Rose, CBE 2007; FRSL; novelist and playwright; *b* 2 Aug. 1943; *d* of late Viola Mabel Thomson and Keith Nicholas Home Thomson, MBE; *m* 1st, 1971, Jon Tremain (marr. diss.); one *d*; 2nd, 1982, Jonathan Dudley (marr. diss.); partner, Richard Gordon Heath Holmes, *qv*. *Educ:* Sorbonne, Paris; Univ. of East Anglia (BA Hons Eng. Lit.). Part-time Lectr, UEA, 1988–94, Chancellor, 2013–, UEA. FRSL 1983. Dylan Thomas Prize, 1984; Giles Cooper Award, Best Radio Play, 1984. *Publications: novels:* Sadler's Birthday, 1976; Letter to Sister Benedicta, 1978; The Cupboard, 1981; The Swimming Pool Season, 1984; Restoration, 1989 (Sunday Express Book of the Year Award; filmed, 1996); Sacred Country, 1992 (James Tait Black Meml Prize, 1993; Prix Femina Etranger (France), 1994); The Way I Found Her, 1997; Music and Silence, 1999 (Whitbread Novel Award); The Colour, 2003; The Road Home, 2007 (Orange Broadband Prize for Fiction, Good Housekeeping Fiction of the Year Award, 2008); Trespass, 2010; Merivel: a man of his time, 2012; *short stories:* The Colonel's Daughter, 1982; The Garden of the Villa Mollini, 1986; Evangelista's Fan, 1994; The Darkness of Wallis Simpson, 2005; The American Lover, 2014; *for children:* Journey to the Volcano, 1985. *Recreations:* gardening, swimming, yoga. *Address:* 2 High House, South Avenue, Thorpe St Andrew, Norwich NR7 0EZ.

TREMAINE, Prof. Scott Duncan, PhD; FRS 1994; FRSC 1994; Richard Black Professor of Astrophysics, Institute for Advanced Study, Princeton, since 2007; *b* 25 May 1950; *s* of Vincent Joseph Tremaine and Beatrice Delphine (*née* Sharp). *Educ:* McMaster Univ. (BSc); Princeton Univ. (MA, PhD). Postdoctoral Fellow, CIT, 1975–77; Res. Associate, Inst. of Astronomy, Cambridge, 1977–78; Long-term Mem., Inst. for Advanced Study, Princeton, 1978–81; Associate Prof., MIT, 1981–85; University of Toronto: Prof. of Physics and Astronomy, 1985–97; Dir, Canadian Inst. for Theoretical Astrophysics, 1985–96; Prof. and Chm., Dept of Astrophysical Scis, Princeton Univ., 1998–2006, now Prof. Emeritus. Dir, Prog. in Cosmology and Gravity, Canadian Inst. for Advanced Res., 1996–2002. Foreign

Hon. Mem., Amer. Acad. of Arts and Scis, 1992; Mem., US NAS, 2003. *Publications:* (with J. J. Binney) Galactic Dynamics, 1987, 2nd edn 2008; papers in jls of physics and astronomy. *Address:* School of Natural Sciences, Institute for Advanced Study, Einstein Drive, Princeton, NJ 08540, USA. *T:* (609) 7348191.

TREMBATH, Graham Robert; QC 2003; *b* 18 May 1952; *s* of late Robert Edward George Trembath, MBE and Gladys Booth Trembath; *m* 1981, Ulrika Lillie Maria; one *s* one *d. Educ:* Cambusdoon Prep. Sch.; Fettes Coll.; Southampton Univ. (LLB Hons). Called to the Bar, Middle Temple, 1978; in practice specialising in serious crime defence. *Recreations:* golf, lifelong supporter of Chelsea Football Club, general sports fan. *Address:* 5 Paper Buildings, Temple, EC4Y 7HB. *T:* (020) 7583 6117, *Fax:* (020) 7353 0075. *E:* clerks@5pb.co.uk.

TREMBERG, David; His Honour Judge Tremberg; a Circuit Judge, since 2007; *b* London, 7 July 1961; *s* of late Philip Tremberg and of Sally Tremberg (now Firth); *m* 1987, Alison Jones; one *s. Educ:* Craven Park Prim. Sch.; JFS Sch.; Univ. of Hull (LLB Hons); Coll. of Europe, Bruges (Dip. Adv. Eur. Studies); Inns of Court Sch. of Law. Called to the Bar, Lincoln's Inn, 1985; Recorder, 2001–07. *Recreations:* watching and playing sport, spending time with family and friends, reading, cars. *Address:* Great Grimsby Combined Court Centre, Town Hall Square, Grimsby, Lincs DN31 1HX.

TREMLETT, Ven. Andrew; Sub-Dean and Archdeacon, Westminster Abbey, since 2014; Canon of Westminster, and Rector of St Margaret's, Westminster, since 2010; *b* Plymouth, 9 March 1964; *s* of Ven. Anthony Frank Tremlett, *qv*; *m* 1988, Alison Louise Hills; two *s* one *d. Educ:* Plymouth Coll.; Pembroke Coll., Cambridge (BA 1986); Wycliffe Hall and Queen's Coll., Oxford (BA 1988); Exeter Univ. (MPhil 1996); University Coll., Chester (Postgrad. Cert. Church Sch. Educn 2003); Hebrew Univ., Jerusalem (Arabic Immersion 2014). Ordained deacon, 1989, priest, 1990; Asst Curate, St Matthias, Torquay, 1989–92; Asst Chaplain, Mission to Seamen and St Mary's, Rotterdam, 1992–95; Team Vicar, St Columba's, Fareham, 1995–98; Chaplain to the Bishop of Portsmouth, 1998–2003; Vicar, St Mary's, Goring-by-Sea, 2003–08; Residentiary Canon, Bristol Cath., 2008–10. Chairman: Field Lane Foundn, 2012–; Westminster Abbey Inst., 2013–. Vice-Chm., Govs, Westminster City Sch., 2012–. *Recreations:* running, playing the piano, learning Arabic. *Address:* 5 Little Cloister, Westminster, SW1P 3PL. *T:* (020) 7654 4806. *E:* andrew.tremlett@westminster-abbey.org.

TREMLETT, Ven. Anthony Frank; Archdeacon of Exeter, 1994–2002; *b* 25 Aug. 1937; *s* of Frank and Sally Tremlett; *m* 1958, Patricia Lapthorn; two *s* one *d. Educ:* Plymouth College. Clerk, Management Trainee (Traffic Apprentice), Area Manager, 1953–68, British Rail; Traffic Manager, District Manager, Operations Director, 1968–80, National Carriers (Nat. Freight Corporation). Asst Curate, 1981–82, Priest-in-Charge, 1982–84, Vicar, 1984–88, Southway, Plymouth; RD of Moorside, Plymouth, 1986–88; Archdeacon of Totnes, 1988–94. *Recreations:* music, travel, political and economic affairs. *Address:* 57 Great Berry Road, Crownhill, Plymouth, Devon PL6 5AY. *T:* (01752) 240052.

See also Ven. A. Tremlett.

TREMLETT, George William, OBE 1981; author, journalist and bookseller; Director, Corran Books Ltd, since 1981; Founder Chairman, George Tremlett Ltd, since 1965; *b* 5 Sept. 1939; *s* of late Wilfred George and of Elizabeth Tremlett; *m* 1971, Jane, *oc* of late Benjamin James Mitchell and Mrs P. A. Mitchell; three *s. Educ:* Taunton School; King Edward VI School, Stratford upon Avon. Member of Richmond upon Thames Borough Council, 1963–74; Chairman: Further Education Cttee, 1966–68; Barnes School Governors, 1967–73; Schools Cttee, 1972–73; Shene VIth Form Coll. Governors, 1973–74; Housing Cttee, 1972–74; Thames Water Authority, 1973–74. Greater London Council: Mem. (C) for Hillingdon, 1970–73, for Twickenham, 1973–86; Opposition Housing Spokesman, 1974–77; Leader of Housing Policy Cttee, 1977–81. Consultant: Nat. Assoc. of Voluntary Hostels, 1980–84; Local Govt Inf. Unit, 1985–86; Appeal Dir, SHAC and Help the Homeless National Appeal, 1985–87. Member: Housing Minister's Adv. Cttee on Co-operatives, 1977–79; Housing Consultative Council for England, 1977–81; Northampton Develt Corp., 1979–83; Stonham Housing Assoc., 1978–92; Chiswick Family Rescue Appeal Fund, 1979–80; Bd, Empty Property Unit, 1985–86; Adv. Panel, BBC Community Prog. Unit, 1985–87. Founder Chm., Dylan Thomas Meml Trust, 1985–90. Governor, Kingston Polytechnic and Twickenham Coll. of Technology, 1967–70; Court of City Univ., 1968–74. *Publications:* 17 biographies of rock musicians, 1974–77—on John Lennon, David Bowie, 10cc, Paul McCartney, The Osmonds, Alvin Stardust, Cat Stevens, Cliff Richard, Slade, The Who, David Essex, Slik, Gary Glitter, Marc Bolan, Rod Stewart, Queen and the Rolling Stones (published in many different countries); Living Cities, 1979; (with Caitlin Thomas) Life with Dylan Thomas, 1986; Clubmen, 1987; Homeless but for St Mungo's, 1989; Little Legs, 1989; Rock Gold, 1990; Dylan Thomas: in the mercy of his means, 1991; Gadaffi: the desert mystic, 1993; David Bowie, 1995; (with James Nashold) The Death of Dylan Thomas, 1997. *Recreations:* ornithology, exploring old churches, local history, rock 'n' roll music. *Address:* The Ship and Castle, King Street, Laugharne, Carmarthenshire SA33 4RY. *T:* (01994) 427444. *Club:* Laugharne RFC.

TRENCH; *see* Le Poer Trench, family name of Earl of Clancarty.

TRENCH, family name of **Baron Ashtown**.

TRENCH, John; Master of the Supreme Court, Queen's Bench Division, 1986–2002; *b* 15 Sept. 1932; *s* of late Prince Constantine Lobanow-Rostovsky and Princess Violette Lobanow-Rostovsky (*née* Le Poer Trench); *m* 1st, 1955, Roxane Bibica-Rosetti (marr. diss.); two *s* (one *d* decd); 2nd, 1980, Patricia Margaret Skitmore. *Educ:* Oundle; Christ's College, Cambridge (MA). Nat. Service, 1950–52; commissioned The Duke of Wellington's Regt. Called to the Bar, Lincoln's Inn, 1956, practised at the Bar, in London and on the Oxford Circuit, 1956–86. *Recreations:* painting, collecting antique handwriting equipment. *Address:* c/o Royal Courts of Justice, Strand, WC2A 2LL.

TRENCH, Jonathan Charles Stewart C.; *see* Chenevix-Trench.

TRENCHARD, family name of **Viscount Trenchard**.

TRENCHARD, 3rd Viscount *cr* 1936, of Wolfeton; **Hugh Trenchard;** DL; Bt 1919; Baron 1930; Consultant, Simon Robertson Associates (formerly Robertson Robey Associates) LLP, since 2013; *b* 12 March 1951; *s* of 2nd Viscount Trenchard, MC and of Patricia, *d* of Admiral Sir Sidney Bailey, KBE, CB, DSO; *S* father, 1987; *m* 1975, Fiona Elizabeth Morrison, *d* of 2nd Baron Margadale, TD, DL; two *s* two *d. Educ:* Eton; Trinity Coll., Cambridge (BA 1973). Captain, 4th Royal Green Jackets, TA, 1973–80. Entered Kleinwort Benson Ltd, 1973; Chief Rep. in Japan, 1980–85; Gen. Man., Kleinwort Benson Internat. Inc., Tokyo Br., 1985–88; Dir, Kleinwort Benson Ltd, 1986–96; Pres., 1988–95, Rep. in Japan, 1993–95, Dep. Chm., 1995–96, Kleinwort Benson Internat. Incorporated; Director: Robert Fleming & Co. Ltd, 1996–98; Robert Fleming Internat. Ltd, 1998–2000. Chm., Dejima Fund Ltd, 2001–09; Man. Dir, Mizuho Internat. plc, 2007–12; Director: KB Berkeley Japan Development Capital Ltd, 1987–97; Dover Japan Inc., 1985–87; ACP Hldgs Ltd, 1990–94; Berkeley Technology (formerly London Pacific Gp) Ltd, 1999–2011; AC European Finance Ltd, subseq. Westhall Capital Ltd, 2001–03; Dryden Wealth Mgt Ltd, 2004–05; Stratton Street PCC Ltd, 2006– (Chm., 2009–); Bache Global Series, 2008–; Lotte Chemical UK Ltd, 2010–; Senior Adviser: Prudential Financial Inc., 2002–08; Rolls-Royce Power Engrg plc, 2014–15; Optum Health Solutions (UK) Ltd, 2014–; Adamas Asset Mgt (HK) Ltd, 2014–; Consultant and Sen. Advr, Mizuho Corporate Bank Ltd, 2013–14. Dir Gen., European Fund and Asset Mgt Assoc., 2006. Chm., Securities Cttee, 1993–95, Vice Chm. Council, 1995, European Business Community (Japan); Director: Japan Securities Dealers' Assoc., 1994–95; Bond Underwriters' Assoc. of Japan, 1994–95; Member: Japan Assoc. of Corporate Executives, 1987–95; Council, Japan Soc., 1992–93 and 1995–2004 (Vice-Chm., 1996–2000; Jt Chm., 2000–04; Hon. Vice Pres., 2013–). Vice-Chm., British-Japanese Parly Gp, 1997–99 and 2004–; Hon. Treas., H of L All-Party Defence Study Gp, 1992–93; elected Mem., H of L, 2004–. Mem. Council, RAF Benevolent Fund, 1991–2003, 2006– (Chm., 2006–13; Dep. Chm., 2014–). Hon. Air Cdre, 600 (City of London) Sqn, RAuxAF, 2006–. DL Herts, 2008. Lieut, City of London, 2015. Order of the Rising Sun, Gold and Silver Star (Japan), 2014. *Heir: s* Hon. Alexander Thomas Trenchard [*b* 26 July 1978; *m* 2007, Mira, *d* of late Rainer Ostendorf; two *s*]. *Address:* Standon Lordship, Ware, Herts SG11 1PR. *Clubs:* Brooks's, Pratt's, Cavalry and Guards; Tokyo (Tokyo).

TREND, Hon. Michael (St John), CBE 1997; Executive Director, Relationships Foundation, since 2008; *b* 19 April 1952; *e s* of Baron Trend, PC, GCB, CVO and Patricia Charlotte, *o d* of Rev. Gilbert Shaw; *m* 1987, Jill Elizabeth Kershaw; one *s* two *d. Educ:* Tormore Sch., Upper Deal, Kent; Westminster; Oriel Coll., Oxford; Greek Govt Scholar. Toynbee Hall, 1975–76; Sub-Editor, then Managing Editor, TLS, 1976–81; Editor: History Today, 1981–82; Parliamentary House Magazine, 1984–87; Home Editor, Spectator, 1987–90; Chief Leader Writer, Daily Telegraph, 1990–92. MP (C): Windsor and Maidenhead, 1992–97; Windsor, 1997–2005. PPS to Minister of State, DoH, 1993–94, to Sec. of State for Transport, 1994–95; Dep. Chm. and Dir Gen., Conservative Party, 1995–98; Chm., Cons. Party Internat. Office, 2000–05; Opposition frontbench spokesman on European affairs, 1998–99, on pensions, 1999–2000. Member: Select Cttee on Health, 1992–93, on Public Admin, 2000–05; Speaker's Adv. Cttee on Works of Art, 1993–2005. Asst Chm., Internat. Democrat Union, 1999–2005; Gov. and Vice-Chm., Westminster Foundn for Democracy, 1999–2005. Mem. Council of Reference, Zane. Mem. Bd, Victoria County History, 1992–98. *Publications:* The Music Makers, 1985. *Recreations:* music, hill walking.

TRENTHAM, Dr David Rostron, FRS 1982; Hon. Professor, Randall Division of Cell and Molecular Biophysics, King's College London, since 2003; *b* 22 Sept. 1938; *s* of John Austin and Julia Agnes Mary Trentham; *m* 1966, Kamalini; two *s. Educ:* Univ. of Cambridge (BA Chemistry, PhD Organic Chemistry). Biochemistry Dept, University of Bristol: Jun. Research Fellow (Medical Research Council), 1966–69; Research Associate, 1969–72; Lectr in Biochemistry, 1972–75; Reader in Biochemistry, 1975–77; Edwin M. Chance Prof., Biochemistry and Biophysics Dept, Univ. of Pennsylvania, 1977–84; Hd of Physical Biochem. Div., NIMR, Mill Hill, 1984–2003. Colworth Medal, Biochemical Soc., UK, 1974; Wilhelm Feldberg Prize, Feldberg Foundn Bd for Anglo-German Scientific Exchange, 1990. *Publications:* numerous research papers in scientific jls. *Address:* Randall Division of Cell and Molecular Biophysics, New Hunt's House, King's College London, Guy's Campus, SE1 1UL. *T:* (020) 7848 6434.

TREPTE, Paul, FRCO; Organist and Master of the Choristers, Ely Cathedral, since 1990; *b* 24 April 1954; *s* of Harry and Ruth Trepte; *m* 1981, Sally Lampard; one *d. Educ:* New College, Oxford (MA). Asst Organist, Worcester Cathedral, 1976; Dir of Music, St Mary's, Warwick, 1981; Organist and Master of the Choristers, St Edmundsbury Cathedral, 1985. Hon. FRSCM 2012; Hon. FGCM 2012. *Publications:* choral works. *Address:* 14b Back Hill, Ely CB7 4BZ. *T:* (01353) 660336.

TRESCOWTHICK, Sir Donald (Henry), AC 1991; KBE 1979; Chairman, Signet Group Holdings Pty Ltd, 1978–2005; Executive Director, Australian Olympic Committee, 1992–2001; *b* 4 Dec. 1930; *s* of Thomas Patrick and Elsie May Trescowthick; *m* 1952, Norma Margaret Callaghan; two *s* two *d.* FCPA. Chairman: Charles Davis Ltd, later Harris Scarfe Holdings Ltd, 1972–98; Harris Scarfe, 1976–93. Founder Chm., Victorian Div., Aust. Olympic Team Fund; Emeritus Chm., Sport Australia Hall of Fame, 1996–99; Chairman: Minus Children's Fund, 1975–98; Sir Donald and Lady Trescowthick Foundn; Inaugural Chm., 1972–88, Patron, 1972–, Melbourne to Hobart Yacht Race Cttee; Dir, Aust. Ballet Develt, 1978–93. Pres., Peter MacCallum Cancer Inst. Appeal, 1991–94; Patron: DOXA Youth Welfare Foundn; Special Olympics Australia, 1992–98; Team Equestrian Australia, 1993–2001. Olympic OM, 1981; CLJ 1982; Knight of Magistral Grace, SMO, Malta, 1984; KCSHS 1995. *Recreations:* golf, travel, reading, painting. *Address:* PO Box 93, Toorak, Vic 3142, Australia. *T:* (3) 98266933. *Clubs:* Athenæum, Victoria Racing (Melbourne); Geelong Football.

TRESEDER, Sarah Louise; Chief Executive Officer, Royal Yachting Association, since 2010; *b* 1969; *d* of Hugh and Anna Treseder. *Educ:* Magdalen Coll., Oxford (BA Hons PPE 1991). Business Analyst, McKinsey & Co., 1991–93; Strategic Analyst, SEGA Europe, 1993–95; Gp Controller, Westminster Press, 1995–96; Man. Dir, Newsquest Buckinghamshire, 1996–99; Lead Strategist, Diageo, 2000–02; Man. Dir, Diageo Canaries, 2002–05; Global Dir, Diageo Reserve Brands, 2005–07; Man. Dir, The Admirable Crichton, 2008–10. Mem., Oxford and Cambridge Sailing Soc. *Recreations:* sailing (racing and cruising), cooking, reading, travel, dancing, seeing friends. *Address:* Royal Yachting Association, RYA House, Ensign Way, Hamble, Southampton SO31 4YA. *T:* (023) 8060 4102. *E:* sarah.treseder@rya.org.uk. *Clubs:* Royal Thames Yacht, Royal Southampton Yacht, Royal Southern Yacht, Oxford University Yacht.

TRETHEWEY, Ven. Frederick Martyn; Priest-in-charge, Christ Church, Brittany, since 2013; *b* 24 Jan. 1949; *s* of Kendall and Winifred Trethewey; *m* 1971, Margaret (*née* Davidson); one *s* three *d. Educ:* Bedford Coll., London Univ. (BA (Hons) English, 1970); Inst. of Educn, London Univ. (PGCE 1971); Oak Hill Theol Coll. (DipTh 1977). Ordained deacon, 1978, priest 1979; Curate: St Mark with St Anne, Tollington Park, London, 1978–82; St Andrew, Whitehall Park, London, 1982–87; Team Vicar, Hornsey Rise, Whitehall Park Team, 1987–88; Vicar, Brockmoor, W Midlands, 1988–2001; Chaplain, Dudley Gp of Hosps, 1988–2000; RD, Himley, 1996–2001; Archdeacon of Dudley, 2001–13. *Recreations:* sport, walking. *Address:* 4 Rue des Bandes Mavieux, 56460 La Chapelle Caro, France.

TREUHERZ, Julian Benjamin; art historian and curator; Keeper of Art Galleries, National Museums Liverpool (formerly National Museums and Galleries on Merseyside) (Walker Art Gallery, Lady Lever Art Gallery and Sudley), 1989–2007; *b* 12 March 1947; *s* of late Werner Treuherz and Irmgard (*née* Amberg). *Educ:* Manchester Grammar Sch.; Christ Church, Oxford (MA); Univ. of East Anglia (MA). Dip. Museums Assoc. 1974. Manchester City Art Gallery: Trainee, 1971; Asst Keeper, 1972–74, Keeper, 1974–89, of Fine Art. Member: Victorian Soc. (Hon. Sec., Manchester Gp, 1972–79, Chm., 1980–83); Cttee, Whitworth Art Gall., 1993–2004; Cttee, Lakeland Arts (formerly Lake District Art Gall. and Mus.) Trust, 1997–2010; Burlington Mag. Consultative Cttee, 2003–. Hon. DLaws Liverpool, 2009. *Publications:* Pre-Raphaelite Paintings from the Manchester City Art Gallery, 1981; Hard Times: social realism in Victorian art, 1987; (with Peter de Figueiredo) Country Houses of Cheshire, 1988; Victorian Painting, 1993; (jtly) Dante Gabriel Rossetti, 2003; (jtly) The Railway: art in the age of steam, 2008; Ford Madox Brown, Pre-Raphaelite Pioneer, 2011; articles in art-historical jls. *Recreations:* playing the piano, cooking, opera, Sicily. *Address:* 1 Ingestre Road, Oxton, Wirral CH43 5TZ.

TREVELYAN, Anne-Marie Belinda; MP (C) Berwick-upon-Tweed, since 2015; *b* London, 6 April 1969; *d* of (Donald) Leonard Beaton and Katherine Beaton; *m* 1998, John Henry Thornton Trevelyan; one *s* one *d. Educ:* St Paul's Girls' Sch., London; Oxford Poly. (BSc Hons Maths 1990). CA 1993. Contested (C) Berwick-upon-Tweed, 2010.

Recreations: walking, cooking, tennis, tapestry, Berwick Rangers Football Supporters Club. *Address:* House of Commons, SW1A 0AA. *T:* (020) 7219 4437. *E:* annemarie.trevelyan.mp@parliament.uk.

TREVELYAN, Dennis John, CB 1981; FCIPD; Principal, Mansfield College, Oxford, 1989–96, Hon. Fellow, 1997; *b* 21 July 1929; *s* of John Henry Trevelyan; *m* 1959, Carol Coombes; one *s* one *d*. *Educ:* Enfield Grammar Sch.; University Coll., Oxford (Scholar; MA). Entered Home Office, 1950; Treasury, 1953–54; Sec. to Parly Under-Sec. of State, Home Office, 1954–55; Principal Private Sec. to Lord President of Council and Leader of House, 1964–67; Asst Sec., 1966; Asst Under-Sec. of State, NI Office, 1972–76; Home Office: Asst Under-Sec. of State, Broadcasting Dept, 1976–77; Dep. Under-Sec. of State and Dir-Gen., Prison Service, 1978–83; First CS Comr and Dep. Sec., Cabinet Office, 1983–89, retd. Secretary: Peppiatt Cttee on a Levy on Betting on Horse Races, 1960; Lord Radcliffe's Cttee of Privy Counsellors to inquire into D Notice Matters, 1967. Vice-Chm., CS Sports Council, 1980–; Vice-Pres., Industrial Participation Assoc., 1987–98; Member: Bd of Management, Eur. Inst. of Public Admin, Maastricht, 1984–89; Council, City Univ. Business Sch., 1986–89; ECCTIS Adv. Group, 1990–98; Governor: Ashridge Management Coll., 1985–89; Contemporary Dance Trust, 1986–89; Oxford Centre for Hebrew and Jewish (formerly for Postgraduate Hebrew) Studies, 1992–2008 (Emeritus Gov., 2008); Mem., Philharmonia Chorus Adv. Develt Bd, 2004–; Trustee, Dancers Resettlement Fund, 1987–91. FRSA 1986. *Recreation:* music. *Address:* Lindfield, 1 Begbroke Lane, Begbroke, Oxon OX5 1RN. *Clubs:* Athenæum, MCC; Vincent's (Oxford).

TREVELYAN, Edward Norman; Statistician - Demographer, Population Division, Demographic Directorate, US Bureau of the Census, 2006–13; *b* 14 Aug. 1955; *er s* of Norman Irving Trevelyan, and of Jennifer Mary Trevelyan, *d* of Arthur E. Riddett; *m* 1993, Debbie Mullin-Trevelyan; one *s* one *d*. *Educ:* Univ. of Calif, San Diego (BA History 1981); Univ. of Calif, Santa Barbara (MA Political Sci. 1986; PhD Political Sci. 1998). Admissions Asst, Graduate Div., UCSB, 1990–99; Survey Statistician, Governments Div., Economic Directorate, US Census Bureau, 1999–2006. *Recreation:* sailing (Gold Medal, Soling Class, Olympic Games, 1984). *Address:* 25028 Maplewood Drive, St Michaels, MD 21663, USA. *T:* (410) 7452975.

TREVELYAN, George Macaulay, CB 2005; Chief Executive, Intervention Board, Ministry of Agriculture, Fisheries and Food, 1995–2001; *b* 1 April 1944; *s* of late (Charles) Humphry Trevelyan and Molly Trevelyan (*née* Bennett); *m* 1st, 1966, Susan Pearson; one *s* two *d*; 2nd, 1980, Valerie Preston; one *s*; 3rd, 2002, Julia Barker (*née* McDonald). *Educ:* Queen's Coll., Oxford (BA Mod. Hist.). Joined MAFF, 1967: Principal, 1971; UK spokesman on numerous agricl mgt cttees under Common Agricl Policy, 1973–81; Mem. of Cabinet, EC Commn for Social Affairs, Brussels, 1981–84; Head, Pesticides Safety, Plant Health, and Cereals/Set Aside Divs, 1984–95; Regl Dir (SE), 1989–91; Dir of Ops, Foot and Mouth Disease, MAFF, subseq. DEFRA, 2001–02; Dir, Delivery Strategy Team, DEFRA, 2002–04; Managing Consultant, Hedra plc, 2005–06; Finance and Performance Manager, New Forest Nat. Park Authy, 2006–08. Pt-time Conciliator, EC Directorate Gen. for Agriculture, 2008–13. Councillor (Lab), London Borough of Camden, 1971–74 (Alderman; Chm., Planning and Communications, 1975–76). *Recreations:* sailing, cycling, walking, singing, reading. *Address:* 19 Leelands, Lymington, Hants SO41 8EY.

See also L. K. Trevelyan.

TREVELYAN, Laura Kate; anchor, BBC World News America, since 2012; *b* 21 Aug. 1968; *d* of George Macaulay Trevelyan, *qv* and Susan (*née* Pearson); *m* 1998, James Goldston; three *s*. *Educ:* Parliament Hill Sch., London; Bristol Univ. (BA); Univ. of Wales Coll. of Cardiff (dip. newspaper journalism). Reporter, London Newspaper Gp, 1991; Researcher, A Week in Politics, Channel 4, 1991–92; BBC: Researcher, Breakfast News, 1993; Asst Producer, Newsnight, 1994; Reporter: On the Record, 1994–98; Today Prog., Radio 4, 1998–99; Political Corresp., 1999–2004; Political Corresp., Newsnight, 2000–01; Correspondent: N America, 2004–06; UN, 2006–09; BBC World Affairs Corresp., NY, 2009–12. Mem. Bd, City Squash, Brooklyn. *Publications:* A Very British Family: the Trevelyans and their world, 2006; The Winchester: an American icon, 2016. *Recreations:* hill-walking, tennis. *Address:* BBC News, 450 W 33rd Street, New York, NY 10001, USA. *Club:* Heights Casino (New York).

TREVELYAN, Sir Peter (John), 6th Bt *cr* 1874, of Wallington, Northumberland; *b* 11 Sept. 1948; *o s* of Sir Geoffrey Washington Trevelyan, 5th Bt and Gillian Isabel (*née* Wood), MBE; *S* father, 2011; also the rightful claimant to Trevelyan Baronetcy of Nettlecombe, Somerset, *cr* 1662, but claim not proven; *m* 1996, Diane Christine Terry; one *s*. *Educ:* Oundle; Trinity Coll., Cambridge (BA 1969; MA 1973). *Heir:* *s* Julian Miles Trevelyan, *b* 29 Oct. 1998.

TREVELYAN, Rupert; Regional Director, London, Jockey Club Racecourses, since 2012; *b* Salisbury, Rhodesia, 20 July 1963; *s* of John and Patricia Trevelyan; *m* 1987, Sara; one *s* three *d*. *Educ:* Guinea Fowl Sch., Gweru, Rhodesia; Felsted Sch., Essex; Univ. of Westminster (MBA). Various posts with Centrica, 2000–04; Mktg and Passenger Services Dir, I of M Steampacket Co., 2004–08; Consultant, RHS, 2008–09; Man. Dir, Epsom Downs Racecourse, 2009–12. MCIM. *Address:* Weybrook, 51 Station Road, Gomshall, Guildford, Surrey GU5 9NP. *T:* 07826 050690.

TREVELYAN, Vanessa Mary; museum consultant and adviser, since 2013; Director, Norfolk Museums and Archaeology Service, 1999–2013; President, Museums Association, 2010–13; *b* London, 29 Sept. 1952; *d* of Frederick Cheetham and Ann Cheetham; *m* 1977, John Trevelyan. *Educ:* Notting Hill and Ealing High Sch. for Girls, London; Univ. of East Anglia (BA Hons); City Univ. (Dip. Arts Admin). Victoria and Albert Museum: Mus. Asst, 1975–79; Manager, Purchase Grant Fund for the Regions, 1979–89; Mus. Develt Officer, South Eastern Mus Service, 1989–94; Hd, Public Services and Registration, Mus and Galls Commn, 1994–98. Convenor, Ethic Cttee, Museums Assoc., 2001–09. Gov., Norwich University of the Arts (formerly Norwich University Coll. of the Arts), 2008–. Pres., Norfolk Costume and Textiles Assoc., 2013–. Mem., E of England Regl Adv. Bd, Nat. Trust, 2013–; Trustee, Mus. of East Anglian Life, 2013–. Member: Women Leaders in Mus Network, 2004–; Norwich Soc., 2013– (Exec. Cttee Mem., 2015–). *Publications:* (ed) Dingy Places with Different Kinds of Bits: an attitudes survey of London museums amongst non-visitors, 1991; articles relating to museum standards and operations. *Recreations:* cross-country ski-ing, gardening, early musicals, sketching, jogging, singing, visiting museums.

TREVERTON-JONES, Gregory Dennis; QC 2002; *b* 23 Nov. 1954; *s* of Paul and Margaret Treverton-Jones; *m* 1990, Tamsin Thomas; one *s* two *d*. *Educ:* Malvern Coll.; New Coll., Oxford (MA). Called to the Bar, Inner Temple, 1977. *Publications:* Imprisonment: the legal status of prisoners, 1989. *Recreations:* most sports including cricket, golf and tennis. *Address:* 39 Essex Street, WC2R 3AT. *T:* (020) 7832 1111, *Fax:* (020) 7353 3978. *E:* gregtj@39essex.com. *Club:* MCC.

TREVES, Vanni Emanuele, CBE 2012; Chairman: Intertek Group plc, 2001–11; Korn/Ferry Whitehead Mann, since 2004; *b* 3 Nov. 1940; *s* of Giuliano Treves (partisan, killed in action, 1944), and of Marianna Treves (*née* Baer); *m* 1971, Angela Veronica Fyffe; two *s* one *d*. *Educ:* St Paul's Sch. (Foundn Scholar); University Coll., Oxford (MA); Univ. of Illinois (LLM; Fulbright Scholar). Res. Fellow, Univ. of Illinois, 1961–62. Macfarlanes: articled clerk and Solicitor, 1963–68; Partner, 1970–2002; Sen. Partner, 1987–99. Vis. Attorney, White & Case, New York, 1968–69. Director: Oceonics Group, 1984–96; Saatchi & Saatchi, 1987–90; Chairman: BBA Gp plc, 1989–2000; McKechnie plc, 1991–2000; Fledgeling Equity and Bond Funds, 1992–2000; Dennis Gp (formerly Trinity Holdings) PLC, 1996–99; Channel 4 Television, 1998–2004; Equitable Life Assurance Soc., 2001–09; Director: Amplifon SpA, 2000–11; Amplifin SpA, 2000–; non-exec. Dir, Homerton Univ. Hosp. NHS Foundn Trust, 2011– (Chm., Risk Cttee, 2012–). Mem., Council for Industry and Higher Educn, 2003–06. Solicitor to Royal Acad., 1992–. Chm., Develt Cttee, Nat. Portrait Gall., 1991–99. Chairman: NSPCC Justice for Children Appeal, 1997–2000; NSPCC Organised Abuse Appeal, 2004–08; Fellow, NSPCC, 2009. Trustee: J. Paul Getty Jr Charitable Trust, 1985–; 29th May 1961 Charitable Trust, 1970–; Prisoners Educn Trust, 2010–. Vice-Pres., London Fedn of Clubs for Young People (formerly of Boys' Clubs), 1991– (Hon. Treas., 1976–95). Gov., Sadler's Wells Foundn, 1999–2008. Chairman: Governors, London Business Sch., 1998–2006 (Gov., 1996–2006); Nat. Coll. of Sch. Leadership, 2004–12; Governor: Coll. of Law, 1999–2006; Hall Sch., Hampstead, 1983–94. Hon. Fellow, London Business Sch., 2006. Fellow, St Paul's Cathedral, 2012–. Mem., Editl Adv. Bd, Corporate Governance, 2001–. Knight, Order of Star (Italy), 2014. *Recreation:* epicurean pursuits. *Address:* Ryder Court, 14 Ryder Street, SW1Y 6QB. *Club:* Boodle's.

TREVETHIN, 5th Baron *cr* 1921, **AND OAKSEY,** 3rd Baron *cr* 1947; **Patrick John Tristram Lawrence;** QC 2002; *b* 29 June 1960; *s* of 4th Baron Trevethin and Oaksey, (known as Lord Oaksey) and Victoria Mary (*née* Dennistoun); *S* father, 2012; *m* 1987, Lucinda, *e d* of Demetri Marchessini and Mrs Nicholas Peto; one *s* two *d*. *Educ:* Christ Church, Oxford. Called to the Bar, Inner Temple, 1985. *Heir:* *s* Hon. Oliver John Tristram Lawrence, *b* 17 May 1990. *Address:* 4 New Square, Lincoln's Inn, WC2A 3RJ. *T:* (020) 7822 2000.

TREVETT, Peter George; QC 1992; *b* 25 Nov. 1947; *s* of late George Albert Trevett and Janet Trevett; *m* 1972, Vera Lucia dos Santos Ferreira; two *s* one *d*. *Educ:* Kingston Grammar Sch.; Queens' Coll., Cambridge (MA, LLM). Called to the Bar, Lincoln's Inn, 1971 (Mansfield Schol.), Bencher, 2000; in practice at Revenue Bar, 1973–. *Publications:* contribs to legal pubns. *Recreations:* golf, reading, collecting succulent plants, gardening.

TREVIS, Diane Ellen; theatre director; *b* 8 Nov. 1947; *d* of late Joseph Trevis and of Marjorie Trevis; *m* 1986, Dominic John Muldowney, *qv*; one *d*. *Educ:* Waverley Grammar Sch., Birmingham; Sussex Univ. Actress and dir, Glasgow Citizens' Theatre, 1972–80; Arts Council Associate Dir, Palace Theatre, Westcliff, 1982; Founder, The Workshop, Jerwood Studios, 2001, Dir, Jerwood Workshop, 2001–; Head of Directing, Drama Centre, Univ. of the Arts London, 2003–07; Artistic Dir, Rough Classics Th. Co., 2005–. Director: Royal Shakespeare Company: Taming of the Shrew, Happy End, 1985–86; The Revenger's Tragedy, 1987; Much Ado About Nothing, 1988; Elgar's Rondo, 1993; Royal National Theatre: Irish-Hebrew Lesson, 1981; The Mother, Yerma, School for Wives, A Matter of Life and Death, 1985–86; The Resistible Rise of Arturo Ui, 1991; Inadmissible Evidence, 1993; Happy Birthday Brecht, 1998; Remembrance of Things Past (adapted with Harold Pinter), 2000; Gawain, Royal Opera House, 1991; The Daughter in Law, 1996, The House of Bernarda Alba, 1997, Theatr Clwyd; Human Cannon, Ballad of California, 1997, Awake and Sing, Happy Birthday Brecht, 1998, Univ. of California; Masterclass, Th. Royal, Bath, 1999; Death of a Salesman, Birmingham Rep., 2000; The Voluptuous Tango, Pirate Jenny, Almeida Fest., 2000; Duchess of Malfi, 2005, Fears and Miseries of the Third Reich, 2006, Cochrane Th.; The Voluptuous Tango, As You Like It, 2006, Le Grand Meaulnes, 2007, Pittsburgh; Silverland, NY, 2007; An English Tragedy, The Dresser, Palace Th., Watford, 2008; London Cries, NY, 2008; Beaux Stratagem, Penn State Univ., 2011; Dracula, Cochrane Th., 2011; Romeo and Juliet, Akzent Th., Vienna, 2012. *Publications:* Remembrance of Things Proust, 2001; Being a Director: a life in the theatre, 2011. *Recreations:* Morocco, movies, mountain walks. *Address:* c/o National Theatre, South Bank, SE1 9PX.

TREVOR, 5th Baron *cr* 1880, of Brynkinalt, co. Denbigh; **Marke Charles Hill-Trevor;** *b* 8 Jan. 1970; *s* of 4th Baron Trevor and of Susan Janet Elizabeth, *o d* of Dr Ronald Bence; *S* father, 1997. *Educ:* Rannoch Sch., Perthshire. *Heir:* *b* Hon. Iain Robert Hill-Trevor [*b* 12 June 1971; *m* 1998, Kate, *yr d* of David Lord; one *s* one *d*]. *Address:* Brynkinalt Hall, Brynkinalt, Chirk, Wrexham LL14 5NS.

TREVOR, Thomas Henry Llewellyn; curator and writer on contemporary art; Artistic Director, Dojima River Biennale, Osaka, 2014–15; Guest Curator, Whitechapel Gallery, London, 2015; *b* 22 Nov. 1962; *s* of Tudor and Jean Trevor; *m* 1996, Zoë Shearman. *Educ:* Exeter Sch.; Exeter Coll.; Exeter Coll. of Art (Foundn); Pembroke Coll., Oxford (Ruskin Sch. Prize for Painting 1983); Goldsmiths' Coll., London (BA Hons 1986). Artist, musician and music producer for TV, 1986–94; independent curator, 1994–99, incl. projs at Inst. of Internat. Visual Arts, Wellcome Trust, UCL, Camden Arts Centre and Freud Mus.; Dir, Spacex Gall., Exeter, 1999–2005, incl. two projs as part of Liverpool Biennial and Frieze Art Fair; Dir, Arnolfini, Bristol, 2005–13, incl. projects in Belgium, Germany, Italy, S Korea and Sweden; Associate Curator, Art Fund Internat. collection, Bristol Mus., 2008–12; Guest Curator, Devi Art Foundn, Delhi, India, 2013–14; Curatorial Consultant, ARos Mus., Aarhus, Denmark, 2014. Hon. Res. Fellow, Univ. of Exeter, 2014–. Founder Chair, Visual Arts South West (formerly Turning Point SW), 2010–13. Member: Internat. Assoc. of Curators of Contemp. Art, 2008–; Internat. Assoc. of Art Critics, 2010–; Steering Gp, Contemp. Visual Arts Network, 2010–13; Adv. Cttee, Gwangju Biennale, South Korea, 2012–14; Jury, Korea Artist Prize, South Korea, 2014; Internat. Biennial Assoc., 2014–. Hon. DLitt Exeter, 2014. *Recreations:* reading, walking, swimming. *E:* mail@tomtrevor.net. *W:* www.tomtrevor.net.

TREVOR, William, (William Trevor Cox), Hon. KBE 2002 (Hon. CBE 1977); CLit 1994; writer; *b* 24 May 1928; *er s* of J. W. Cox; *m* 1952, Jane, *yr d* of C. N. Ryan; two *s*. *Educ:* St Columba's College, Co. Dublin; Trinity College, Dublin. Mem., Irish Acad. Letters. Television plays include: The Mark-2 Wife; O Fat White Woman; The Grass Widows; The General's Day; Love Affair; Last Wishes; Matilda's England; Secret Orchards; Autumn Sunshine. Radio plays include: The Penthouse Apartment; Beyond the Pale (Giles Cooper award, 1980); Travellers; Autumn Sunshine (Giles Cooper award, 1982); Events at Drimaghleen. Hon. Mem., Amer. Acad. of Arts and Letters, 2004. Hon. DLitt: Exeter, 1984; TCD, 1986; Cork, 1990; Hon. DLit Belfast, 1989; DUniv Open, 2011. Allied Irish Banks Award for Literature, 1976; Bennett Award, Hudson Review, USA, 1990; David Cohen British Literature Prize, 1999; Ireland Funds' Literary Prize, 2005; Nonino Internat. Prize, 2008. *Publications:* A Standard of Behaviour, 1956; The Old Boys, 1964 (Hawthornden Prize; as play, produced Mermaid, 1971); The Boarding-House, 1965; The Love Department, 1966; The Day We Got Drunk on Cake, 1967; Mrs Eckdorf in O'Neill's Hotel, 1969; Miss Gomez and the Brethren, 1971; The Ballroom of Romance, 1972 (adapted for BBC TV, 1982); Going Home (play), 1972; A Night with Mrs da Tanka (play), 1972; Marriages (play), 1973; Elizabeth Alone, 1973; Angels at the Ritz, 1975 (RSL award); The Children of Dynmouth, 1976 (Whitbread Novel Award; televised, 1987); Lovers of Their Time, 1978; Other People's Worlds, 1980; Beyond the Pale, 1981 (televised, 1989); Scenes from an Album (play), 1981; Fools of Fortune, 1983 (Whitbread Novel Award); A Writer's Ireland, 1984; The News from Ireland and other stories, 1986; Nights at the Alexandra, 1987; The Silence in the Garden, 1988; (ed) The Oxford Book of Irish Short Stories, 1989; Family Sins and other stories, 1989; Two Lives, 1991; Juliet's Story (for children), 1992; Excursions in the Real World, 1993; Felicia's Journey, 1994 (Whitbread Book of the Year Award; Sunday Express Book of the Year Award; filmed 1999); After Rain and other stories, 1996; Death in Summer, 1998; The Hill Bachelors, 2000 (PEN/Macmillan award for short stories, Irish Times Irish Lit. award); The Story of Lucy Gault, 2002 (Listowel Prize for Irish fiction, 2003); A Bit on the Side, 2004; Cheating at Canasta, 2007; Love and Summer, 2009.

TREVOR-JONES, Robert David; His Honour Judge Trevor-Jones; a Circuit Judge, since 2008; *b* Bangor, N Wales, 29 March 1955; *s* of Robert Trevor-Jones and Elizabeth Trevor-Jones; *m* 1981, Elizabeth Anne Cheetham; three *d*. *Educ:* Shrewsbury Sch.; Southampton Univ. (LLB); Coll. of Law. Called to the Bar, Gray's Inn, 1977; Asst Recorder, 2000; Recorder, 2000–08. *Recreations:* rowing, sailing, hill walking. *Address:* Liverpool Crown Court, Queen Elizabeth II Law Courts, Derby Square, Liverpool L2 1XA. *T:* (0151) 473 7373. *Clubs:* City; Royal Chester Rowing.

TREW, Peter John Edward, MICE; Director, Rush & Tompkins Group plc, 1973–90 (Chairman of Executive Committee, 1986–87); *b* 30 April 1932; *s* of late Antony Trew, DSC and Nora Trew (*née* Houthakker); *m* 1st, 1955, Angela (marr. diss. 1985; she *d* 1991), *d* of Kenneth Rush, CBE; two *s* one *d*; 2nd, 1985, Joan (*d* 2005), *d* of Allan Haworth; 3rd, 2011, Kuki Hahndel, *d* of Zevi Gregor Bielsky. *Educ:* Diocesan Coll., Rondebosch, Cape. Royal Navy, 1950–54; served HMS Devonshire, Unicorn and Charity. Chartered Inst. of Secretaries Sir Ernest Clarke Prize, 1955. Contested (C) Dartford, 1966; MP (C) Dartford, 1970–Feb. 1974; Jt Sec., Cons. Parly Finance Cttee, 1972–74; Mem., Select Cttee on Tax Credits, 1972–73. Chm., Kent West Cons. European Constituency Council, 1978–80. Mem. Council, CBI, 1975–83 (Mem., Econ. and Fin. Policy Cttee, 1980–86). *Publications:* The Boer War Generals, 1999; Rodney and the Breaking of the Line, 2006. *Address:* 1 Painshill House, Cobham, Surrey KT11 1DL. *T:* (01932) 863315.

TREWAVAS, Prof. Anthony James, PhD; FRS 1999; FRSE; Professor of Plant Biochemistry, Edinburgh University, 1990–2004, now Emeritus; *b* 17 June 1939; *s* of Clifford John Trewavas and Phyllis (*née* Timms); *m* 1963, Valerie Leng; one *s* two *d*. *Educ:* Roan Grammar Sch.; University Coll. London (BSc 1961; PhD 1964). Sen. Res. Fellow, Univ. of East Anglia, 1964–70; University of Edinburgh: Lectr, 1970–84; Reader, 1984–90. Visiting Professor: Michigan State Univ., 1973; Univ. of Illinois, 1980; Univ. of Alberta, 1983; Univ. of Calif, Davis, 1985; Univ. of Mexico City, 1987; Univ. of Bonn, 1989; Univ. of Milan, 1996. Mem., Scottish Cttee, LEAF. Mem., Most Highly Cited Researcher gp, Inst. of Scientific Inf.; MAE 2002; Life Mem., Amer. Soc. of Plant Physiologists, 1999; Fellow, World Innovation Foundn, 2001; FRSE 1993. *Publications:* Molecular and Cellular Aspects of Calcium in Plant Development, 1985; (with David Jennings) Plasticity in Plants, 1986; Plant Behaviour and Intelligence, 2014; 250 res. papers. *Recreations:* music, reading, thinking, good wine. *Address:* Old Schoolhouse, Croft Street, Penicuik, Midlothian EH26 9DH. *T:* (01968) 673372.

TREWEEK, Rt Rev. Rachel; *see* Gloucester, Bishop of.

TREWIN, Simon Courtenay; literary agent, since 1993; Head, London Office (Literary), and Partner, WME (William Morris Endeavour Entertainment Ltd), since 2012; *b* Highgate, 24 May 1966; *s* of late Ion Courtenay Gill Trewin and of Susan Harriet Trewin; *m* 1992, Helen Adie; one *s*. *Educ:* Highgate Sch.; Univ. of Kent (BA Hons Drama and Theatre Studies 1988). Mem., Equity, 1989–; actor and on prodn teams, Chichester Festival Th., Birmingham Rep Th., Royal Alexandra Th., Toronto and in West End; Literary Agent: Sheil Land Associates, 1993–99; Peter Fraser & Dunlop Ltd, 1999–2009; Hd of Literary, and Dir, United Agents Ltd, 2009–12. Vis. Lectr, Southampton Univ., 2010–12. Trustee: Salisbury Playhouse Trust Ltd, 2011–14; Arun Foundn, 2011–. *Recreations:* mid-life crisis, classic cars, theatre, collecting emerging artists, new experiences. *Address:* 110 Venner Road, SE26 5HR. *E:* simon.trewin@gmail.com; c/o WME, 5th Floor, 100 New Oxford Street, WC1A 1HB. *Clubs:* Soho House, Ivy, Hospital, Library, Old Cholmelians.

TREWSDALE, Janet Margaret, OBE 2000; CStat, FSS; Senior Lecturer in Economics, Queen's University of Belfast, 1995–2004; *b* 8 May 1944; *d* of Keith and Joan Crush; *m* 1970, Dr John M. Trewsdale (*d* 1990). *Educ:* Univ. of York (BA Econs and Stats 1967). FSS 1969; CStat 1993. Lecturer in Economic Statistics: Univ. of Kent, 1969–70; Trent Poly., 1970–71; Lectr in Econs, QUB, 1972–95. Chm., NI Econ. Council, 1998–2006; Mem., Statistics Commn, 2000–08. Vice-Pres., Royal Statistical Soc., 1983–84. *Publications:* numerous contribs to books and learned jls. *Address:* 1 Belair Avenue, Newtownards, Co. Down, Northern Ireland BT23 4UD. *T:* (028) 9181 3542. *E:* j.trewsdale@gmail.com.

TRIBE, Geoffrey Reuben, OBE 1968; Controller, Higher Education Division, British Council, 1981–83, retired; *b* 20 Feb. 1924; *s* of late Harry and Olive Tribe; *m* 1st, 1946, Sheila Mackenzie (marr. diss. 1977); 2nd, 1978, Malvina Anne Butt. *Educ:* Southern Grammar Sch., Portsmouth; University Coll. London (BA). Served War, Royal Hampshire Regt (Lieut), 1942–45. Teaching, 1948–58. Appointed to British Council, 1958; Asst Regional Rep., Madras, 1958–63; Regional Dir, Mwanza, 1963–65; Regional Rep., E Nigeria, 1965–67; Asst Controller, Personnel and Staff Recruitment, 1968–73; Controller, Arts Div., 1973–79; Representative, Nigeria, 1979–81. *Recreations:* walking, writing. *Address:* 26 Lambourne Chase, Chelmsford, Essex CM2 9FF.

TRICHET, Jean-Claude Anne Marie Louis; Chairman and Chief Executive Officer, Group of Thirty, since 2011; Chairman: Bruegel, since 2012; Trilateral Commission Europe, since 2012; *b* 20 Dec. 1942; *s* of Jean Trichet and Georgette (*née* Vincent-Carrefour); *m* 1965, Aline Rybalka; two *s*. *Educ:* Ecole Nationale des Mines, Nancy; Inst. d'Etudes Politiques, Paris; Ecole Nationale d'Admin; Univ. de Paris (LèsSc Econ). Inspector of Finances, 1971–76; Sec.-Gen., Business Restructuring Interministerial Cttee, 1976–78; Advr, Ministry of Finance, 1978; counsellor on industry, energy and res. to the President (Valéry Giscard d'Estaing), 1978–81; Dep. Asst Sec., later Asst Sec., Treasury, 1981–86; Chief of Staff to Minister of Finance (Edouard Balladur), 1986–87; Under-Sec., Treasury, 1987–93; Governor, Bank of France, 1993–2003 (Hon. Gov., 2012–). Chairman: Paris Club (sovereign debt rescheduling), 1985–93; EC Monetary Cttee, 1992–93; Member, Board of Directors: BIS, 1993–2003, 2006–11; Eur. Central Bank (formerly Eur. Monetary Inst.), 1994–2011 (Pres., 2003–11); Airbus, 2012–; Gov., IBRD, 1993–95; Pres., Global Economy Meeting of Governors (formerly Gp of 10 Governors), 2003–11. Mem., Supervisory Bd, EADS, 2012–. Mem., Acad. des Scis Morales et Politiques, 2010–. Hon. doctorates from Liège, Tel Aviv, Montréal and Stirling Univs. Policy-maker of the Year, Internat. Economy, 1991, 2007; Zerilli Marimo Prize, Acad. des Scis Morales et Politiques, 1999; Pico della Mirandola Prize, 2002; Franco-German Cultural Prize, 2006; Person of the Year, FT, 2007; Ludwig Erhard Meml Coin in Gold, 2007; Central Banker of the Year: Euromoney, 2008; The Banker, 2008; Internat. Charlemagne Prize of Aachen, 2011. Commandeur, Légion d'honneur (France); Officier, Ordre National du Mérite (France); many foreign decorations, including Grand Cross in the orders of The Netherlands, Germany, Austria, and Commander in the Orders of Belgium, Brazil, Argentina, Portugal. *Publications:* articles on monetary policy, finance and economy. *Recreation:* poetry. *Address:* 7 Rue Rembrandt, 75008 Paris, France.

TRICKER, Prof. Robert Ian, DLitt; FCMA; Hon. Professor: Hong Kong Open University, since 2006; Director, International Corporate Policy Group (formerly Corporate Policy Group, Oxford), since 1979; *b* 14 Dec. 1933; *m* 1st, 1958, Doreen Murray (marr. diss. 1982); two *d*; 2nd, 1982, Gretchen Elizabeth Bigelow. *Educ:* King Henry VIII Sch., Coventry; Harvard Business Sch., USA; DLitt CNAA, 1983. FCA 1955–2002; FCMA 1959. Articled Clerk, Daffern & Co., 1950–55; Sub-Lt, RNVR, 1956–58; Controller, Unbrako Ltd, 1959–64; Directing Staff, Iron & Steel Fedn Management Coll., 1965; Barclays Bank Prof. of Management Information Systems, Univ. of Warwick, 1968–70; Director, Oxford Centre for Management Studies, 1970–79, Professorial Fellow, 1979–84 (P. D. Leake Res. Fellow, 1966–67); Res. Fellow, Nuffield Coll., Oxford, 1979–84 (Vis. Fellow, 1971–79); Dir, Management Develt Centre of Hong Kong, 1984–86; Prof. of Finance and Accounting, Univ. of Hong Kong, 1986–96. Hon. Professor: Univ. of Hong Kong, 1996–2006; Warwick Univ., 1996–2000. Institute of Chartered Accountants in England and Wales: Mem. Council, 1979–84; Mem. Educn and Trng Directorate, 1979–82; Chairman: Examination Cttee, 1980–82; Tech. and Res. Cttee, 1982–84. Member: Council, ICMA, 1969–72; Management and Industrial Relations Cttee, SSRC, 1973–75; Chm., Independent Inquiry into Prescription Pricing Authority for Minister for Health, 1976. Member: Nuffield Hosp. Management Cttee, 1972–74; Adv. Panel on Company Law, Dept of Trade, 1980–83; Company Affairs Cttee, Inst. of Directors, 1980–84; Standing Commn on CS Salaries and Conditions of Service, Hong Kong, 1989–96. Dep. Launching Authy, Torbay Lifeboat, 2001–05. Editor, Corporate Governance—an international review, 1992–2000 (Mem., Editl Bd, 2001–). CGMA 2012. *Publications:* The Accountant in Management, 1967; Strategy for Accounting Research, 1975; Management Information and Control Systems, 1976, 2nd edn 1982; The Independent Director, 1978; Effective Information Management, 1982; Governing the Institute, 1983; Corporate Governance, 1984; The Effective Director, 1986; The Director's Manual, 1990; International Corporate Governance, 1993; Harnessing Information Power, 1994; The Economist Pocket Director, 1996, 3rd edn 1999; The Economist Essential Director, 2003 (trans. Chinese and Russian 2003); Corporate Governance: principles, policies and practises, 2009, 3rd edn 2015; Directors: an A–Z guide, 2009; (with Gretchen Tricker) Business Ethics: a stakeholder, governance and risk approach, 2014. *Address:* The Hill House, 22/23 St Peter's Hill, Brixham, Devon TQ5 9TE. *E:* BobTricker@aol.com. *W:* www.bobtricker.com. *Club:* Naval.

TRICKETT, Jon Hedley; MP (Lab) Hemsworth, since Feb. 1996; *b* 2 July 1950; *s* of Lawrence and Rose Trickett; *m* 1969 (marr. diss.); one *s* one *d*; *m* 1994, Sarah Balfour; one *d*. *Educ:* Hull Univ. (BA Politics); Leeds Univ. (MA Pol Sociol). Builder/plumber, to 1985. Joined Labour Party, 1971; Leeds City Council: Councillor, Beeston Ward, 1985–96; Chair: Finance Cttee, 1986–89; Housing Cttee, 1988–89; Leader, 1989–96. Chm., Leeds City Development Co., 1989–96; Member of Board: Leeds Development Corp., 1992–96; Leeds Health Care, 1992–96; Director: Leeds/Bradford Airport, 1988–96; Leeds Playhouse, 1988–96; Leeds Theatre Co., 1988–96. PPS to Minister Without Portfolio, 1997–98, to Sec. of State for Trade and Industry, 1998, to the Prime Minister, 2008–10; Shadow Minister of State, Cabinet Office, 2010–11; Shadow Minister for the Cabinet Office, 2011–13; Shadow Minister without Portfolio and Dep. Chair, Labour Party, 2013–15; Shadow Sec. of State for Communities and Local Govt, and Shadow Minister for Constitutional Convention, 2015–. Mem., Public Accounts Select Cttee, 2001–06. Mem., GMBATU. *Recreations:* cycling, sailboarding. *Address:* Ground Floor, Moorthorpe Railway Station, Barnsley Road, South Kirkby, Pontefract, W Yorks WF9 3AT. *T:* (01977) 655695; House of Commons, SW1A 0AA. *Club:* Cyclists' Touring.

TRICKEY, Very Rev. (Frederick) Marc; Dean of Guernsey, 1995–2003; Rector of St Martin de la Bellouse, Guernsey, 1977–2002; Priest-in-charge of Sark, 1996–2003; *b* 16 Aug. 1935; *s* of Alan Paul Trickey and Isabella Livingston (*née* Gunn); *m* 1963, Elisabeth Marriette Plummer; one *s* one *d*. *Educ:* Bristol Grammar Sch.; St John's Coll., Univ. of Durham (BA (Hons) Psychol. 1962; DipTh 1964). Commercial trainee, Nat. Smelting Co. Ltd, Avonmouth, Bristol, 1954–59. Ordained deacon, 1964, priest, 1965; Asst Curate, St Lawrence, Alton, Hants, 1964–68; Rector of St John with Winnall, Winchester, 1968–77. Mem., General Synod of C of E, 1995–2000. Hon. Canon of Winchester Cathedral, 1995–2003, Canon Emeritus, 2003. States of Guernsey: Pres., Ecclesiastical Cttee, 1995–2003; Chairman: Panel of Appeal, Public Assistance Authy, 1985–96; RPI Steering Gp, 1996–; Member: Broadcasting Cttee, 1977–2004; Bd of Industry, 1982–95; Housing Appeal Tribunal, 2005–15; States of Deliberation Code of Conduct Panel, 2007–. Chairman: Guernsey Hard of Hearing Assoc., 1983–95 (Pres., 1995–); MIND, Guernsey, 1985–2002 (Pres., 2002–). Chaplain: Guernsey Assoc. RN and RM, 1977–; St John Ambulance, Guernsey, 2004–. *Publications:* Your Marriage, 1987. *Recreations:* singing, embroidery, walking, photography, philately (GB and Guernsey), saxophone. *Address:* L'Espérance, La Route des Camps, St Martin's, Guernsey GY4 6AD. *T:* (01481) 238441, *Fax:* (01481) 231018. *E:* fmt@cwgsy.net.

TRICKEY, Jane Elizabeth; *see* Hutt, J. E.

TRIESMAN, Baron *cr* 2004 (Life Peer), of Tottenham in the London Borough of Haringey; **David Maxim Triesman;** Director: Salamanca Group, since 2013; One Ocean Ventures Ltd, since 2015; *b* 30 Oct. 1943; *s* of Michael Triesman and Rita (*née* Lubran); *m* 2004, Lucy Hooberman; one *d*. *Educ:* Stationers' Co. Sch., London; Univ. of Essex (BA Hons, MA Philosophy); King's Coll., Cambridge. FSS 1984. Res. Officer in Addiction, Inst. of Psychiatry, 1970–74; ASTMS secondment, 1974–75; Sen. Lectr and co-ord. postgrad. res., Poly. of S Bank, 1975–84; Dep. Sec. Gen. (Nat. Negotiating Sec.), NATFHE, 1984–93; General Secretary: AUT, 1993–2001; Lab. Party, 2001–03. Chairman: FA, 2008–10; England 2018 FIFA World Cup Bid, 2009–10. Chm. and Man. Dir, Triesman Associates, 2011–. A Lord in Waiting (Govt Whip) and govt spokesman on energy, higher educn, transport and Europe, 2004–05; Parliamentary Under-Secretary of State: FCO, 2005–07; DIUS, 2007–08; Opposition Spokesman: for Business, 2010–11; for FCO, 2011–15. Co-Chm., British-St Lucia All-Party Parly Gp, 2012–; Vice Chm., All-Party Parly Gp on Chinese in Britain, 2012–; Member: All-Party Parly Univ. Gp, 2004–; All-Party Parly Gp on EU-US Trade and Investment, 2013–; EU Ext. Affairs Sub-cttee, 2015–. Vis. Prof. in Social Econ., S Lawrence Univ., 1977; Vis. Fellow, Univ. of London Inst. of Educn, 1993–96; Visiting Fellow: in Econs, Wolfson Coll., Cambridge, 2000–; in Govt, LSE, 2005–; Sen. Associate Fellow, Sch. of Engrg, Warwick Univ., 2004–. Member: Greater London Manpower Bd, 1981–86; Home Office Consultative Cttee on Prison Educn, 1980–83; Burnham Further and Higher Educn Cttee, 1980–84; Univ. Entrance and Schs Exams Bd for Soc. Sci., 1980–84; Standing Cttee on Business and the Community, HEFCE, 1999–2002. Mem., Kensington, Chelsea and Westminster AHA, 1976–82. Member: Industrial Relns Public Appointments Panel, DTI, 1996–2001; Ind. Review of Higher Educn Pay and Conditions, 1998–99; Cabinet Office Better Regulation Task Force, 2000–01; Treasury Public Services Productivity Panel, 2000–02; British N American Cttee, 1999–2013. Non-executive Chairman: Mortgage Credit Corp., 1978–2001; Victoria Mgt Ltd, 2000–01; Templewood Student Investments, 2012–13; Chm., ReGen World Develt, 2012–13; non-exec. Dir, Havin Bank Ltd, 2013–; Chm., Bd of Advrs, Templewood Merchant Bank LLP, 2010–13; Member: Bd, Augur Buchler Partners, 2011–13; Advisory Board: UBS, 1987–2001; Joule Africa, 2011–; NextEnergy, 2012–13; Dir, Funding Affordable Homes Housing Assoc. (formerly Funding Affordable Homes Investment Fund), 2014–. Chm., Usecolor Foundn, 2001. Member: Fabian Soc., 1974–; Charles Rennie Mackintosh Soc., Glasgow, 1986–; Highgate Literary and Scientific Inst., 1990–; Bd, Chester Art Collections, 2012–13. Treas., Public Sector Reform Gp, 2007–09. Mem. Council, Ruskin Coll., Oxford, 2000–02; Mem. Governing Council and Hon. Fellow, Univ. of Northampton (formerly Nene Coll. of Higher Educn, then UC Northampton), 1996–; Chm., Internat. Bd, Hibernia Coll., 2012–. Patron, Tottenham Hotspur Foundn, 2007–; Trustee, Football Foundn, 2008–10. Mem. Bd, Wembley Nat. Stadium Ltd, 2008–10. FRSA 1990. Hon. DLaws South Bank, 2009; DUniv Essex, 2010. *Publications:* The Medical and Non-Medical Use of Drugs, 1969; (with G. Viani) Football Mania, 1972; Football in London, 1985; (jtly) College Administration, 1988; Managing Change, 1991; Can Unions Survive (Staniewski Meml Lect.), 1999; Higher Education for the New Century, 2000. *Recreations:* football, art, reading, walking, blues and rock guitar, family. *Address:* House of Lords, SW1A 0PW. *Clubs:* Middlesex CC; Tottenham Hotspurs' Supporters.

TRIFFITT, Jayne; Head, Woldingham School, since 2007; *b* Newquay, 14 June 1957; *d* of Kenneth and Margaret Woolcock. *Educ:* Truro High Sch.; St Hilda's Coll., Oxford (BA Chem. 1980; PGCE 1981). Teacher of Chemistry and Science: King Alfred's Sch., Wantage, 1981–85; St Michael's Grammar Sch., Finchley, 1985–86; Hd of Chem., St Angela's Sch., Palmer's Green, 1986–88; Hd of Sci., La Sainte Union Sch., London, 1988–98; Head of Sixth Form, St Mary's Sch., Ascot, 1998–2001; Headmistress, St Mary's Sch., Cambridge, 2001–07. Member: Nat. Catholic Ind. Schs Conf. Cttee, 2007–10; GSA Council, 2009–12; ASCL Council, 2014–. *Recreations:* family, swimming, Cornwall. *Address:* Woldingham School, Marden Park, Woldingham, Surrey CR3 7YA. *T:* (01883) 654205, *Fax:* (01883) 348653. *E:* triffittj@woldinghamschool.co.uk.

TRIGGER, His Honour Ian James Campbell; a Circuit Judge, 1993–2014; *b* 16 Nov. 1943; *s* of late Walter James Trigger and Mary Elizabeth Trigger; *m* 1971, Jennifer Ann Downs; two *s*. *Educ:* Ruthin Sch.; UCW, Aberystwyth (LLB); Downing Coll., Cambridge (MA, LLM). Called to the Bar, Inner Temple, 1970 (major scholarship, 1967); Lectr in Law, UWIST, 1967–70; practice on Northern Circuit, 1970–93. Pt-time Pres., Mental Health Review Tribunal, 1995–2014; pt-time Chm., Immigration Appeal Tribunal, 1999–2005; pt-time Immigration Judge, 2005–08. Church in Wales: Lay Reader, 2005–; Judge, Provincial Court, 2006–. Chm., Standards Cttee, Denbighshire CC, 2012–. Gov., Ruthin Sch., 2008–; Pres., Old Ruthinian Assoc., 2014–. *Recreations:* gardening, walking, spending time with family. *Address:* Alyn Bank, Llanarmon-yn-lal, Denbighshire CH7 4QX.

TRIMBLE, family name of **Baron Trimble**.

TRIMBLE, Baron *cr* 2006 (Life Peer), of Lisnagarvey in the County of Antrim; **William David Trimble;** PC 1997; Member (UU) Upper Bann, 1998–2007, and First Minister, 1998–2002, Northern Ireland Assembly; *b* 15 Oct. 1944; *s* of William and Ivy Trimble; *m* 1978, Daphne Orr; two *s* two *d*. *Educ:* Bangor Grammar Sch.; Queen's University Belfast (LLB). Called to the Bar of Northern Ireland, 1969; Lectr, 1968, Sen. Lectr, 1977, Faculty of Law, QUB. Mem., Constitutional Convention, 1975–76. MP (UU) Upper Bann, May 1990–2005; contested (UU) same seat, 2005. Leader, Ulster Unionist Party, 1995–2005. Joined Cons. Party, 2007. (Jtly) Nobel Peace Prize, 1998. *Publications:* Northern Ireland Housing Law, 1986; To Raise up a new Northern Ireland, 2001; NI Law Reports, 1975–90. *Recreations:* music, reading. *Address:* House of Lords, SW1A 0PW.

TRIMBLE, Dame Jenifer; *see* Wilson-Barnett, Dame J.

TRIMLESTOWN, 21st Baron *cr* 1461 (Ire.), of Trimlestown, co. Meath; **Raymond Charles Barnewall;** *b* 29 Dec. 1930; *yr s* of 19th Baron Trimlestown and Muriel (*d* 1937), *d* of Edward Oskar Schneider; *S* brother, 1997. *Educ:* Ampleforth.

TRIMMER, Sir Jon (Charles), KNZM 1999; MBE 1974; Senior Artiste, Royal New Zealand Ballet, since 1993; *b* 18 Sept. 1939; *s* of Charles Trimmer and Lily Pamela (*née* Arrowsmith); *m* 1963, Jacqui de Joux Oswald. *Educ:* Wellington Tech. Coll. Art Sch., NZ. Joined Royal NZ Ballet, 1958; with Sadler's Wells, London, 1960–61; Australian Ballet, 1965–66; Royal Danish Ballet, 1969–71; has performed in 5 Royal Command Performances in NZ and overseas; rôles in dramatic plays on stage and TV. Patron, several arts and dance socs in NZ. Fulbright Scholar, NY, 1981. Turnovsky Award, NZ, 1986. Commemoration Medal (NZ), 1990. *Recreations:* pottery, gardening, writing short stories, painting. *Address:* 29 Ocean Road, Paekakariki, Kapiti Coast, New Zealand.

TRIMMER, Stuart Alan; QC 2006; a Recorder, since 2009; *b* 5 Oct. 1954; *s* of Alan and Vera Trimmer; *m* 1982, Fiona Hester; two *s* one *d*. *Educ:* Yeovil Sch.; Poly. of North London (LLB London 1976). Called to the Bar, Gray's Inn, 1977; Hd of Chambers, 4 Breams Buildings, 2010– (Jt Hd, 2006–10). *Recreations:* active church leader, youth activities organiser. *Address:* 4 Breams Buildings, Chancery Lane, EC4A 1HP. *T:* (020) 7092 1900, *Fax:* (020) 7092 1999. *E:* stuart.trimmer@4bb.co.uk.

TRINDER, Frederick William; Charity Commissioner, 1984–85; *b* 18 Nov. 1930; *s* of Charles Elliott Trinder and Grace Johanna Trinder (*née* Hoadly); *m* 1st, 1964, Christiane Friederike Brigitte Dorothea (*née* Hase) (*d* 1994); one *s*; 2nd, 2010, Vivien Margaret Neville (*née* Cox). *Educ:* Ruskin Coll., Oxford (Dip. Pols and Econs); LSE, Univ. of London (BSc). Admitted Solicitor, 1966; Legal Asst/Sen. Legal Asst, Charity Commn, 1966–74; Dep. Charity Comr, 1974–84. Mem., BBC and IBA Central Appeals Adv. Cttees, 1986–92. Trustee, Charities Official Investment Fund, 1988–2002. Mem. (Lab), Wandsworth BC, 1953–56, 1959–62. *Recreations:* travel, gardening, music. *Address:* 37 The Common, West Wratting, Cambridge CB21 5LR. *T:* (01223) 290469.

TRINICK, Christopher John; DL; Chairman, Qualifications and Curriculum Development Agency (formerly Qualifications and Curriculum Authority), 2008–12; Chief Executive, Lancashire County Council, 2002–08; *b* 26 Dec. 1948; *s* of George Herbert Trinick and Mary Elizabeth Trinick (*née* Burton); *m* 1976, Pamela May Hall; three *d*. *Educ:* Northumberland Coll. of Educn (Teacher's Cert. 1971); Univ. of Newcastle (BPhil 1980); Brunel Univ. (MA 1984). Teacher, Kelvin Hall, Hull, 1971–75; Head of House, Seaton Burn High Sch., N Tyneside, 1975–79; Professional Asst, Ealing LBC, 1979–82; Special Educnl Needs Prin. Officer, Bradford MBC, 1982–87; Dep. Chief Educn Officer, Salford City Council, 1987–91; Dir of Educn, Solihull MBC, 1991–96; Chief Educn Officer, then Dir of Educn and Cultural Services, 1996–2001, Exec. Dir for Change, 2001–02, Lancs CC. Clerk, Lancs Lieutenancy, 2002–08; Sec., Lancs Adv. Cttee, 2002–08. Director: E Lancs TEC, 1996–99; Adult Learning Inspectorate, 2001–07 (Vice Chm., 2005); Excellence NW, 2001–05. Mem. Bd, OFSTED, 2007–12 (Chm., Audit Cttee, 2007–12). Mem., All Souls Gp, 2002–04. Treasurer: Soc. of Educn Officers, 1997–2002; Schs Curriculum Award, 1997–2002; Sec., Primary Educn Study Gp, 1997–2002. Mem. Bd, Foundn for IT in Local Govt, 1992–2004; Chm., ACCE, 2007–08 (Vice Chm., 2006–07). Sec., Lord Chancellor's Adv. Cttee on Gen. Comrs of Income Tax, 2002–08. Pro-Chancellor, Edge Hill Univ., 2008–12. DL Lancs, 2008. *Recreations:* gardening, outdoors, fly fishing.

TRINICK, (George) Marcus (Arthur); QC 2010; Partner, Eversheds LLP, since 2008; *b* Redhill, 11 June 1952; *s* of Michael Trinick and Elizabeth Trinick; *m* 2009, Geraldine Mortimore; one *s* one *d*. *Educ:* Haileybury; Queen's Univ., Belfast (BA 1976). Bond Pearce, 1979–83; admitted solicitor, 1983; Coodes, solicitors, 1983–90; Bond Pearce, 1990–2008. Member: Royal Instn of Cornwall, 1974–; Trevithick Soc., 1977–. Mem., Rockbourne Wine Club. *Recreations:* cricket, Roman history, sailing, walking. *Address:* Crendell Cottage, Crendell, Fordingbridge, Hants SP6 3EB. *T:* (01725) 517091. *E:* mtrinick6@aol.com. *Club:* Lobster Cricket.

TRIPP, Alan Charles Macdonald; chartered accountant; *b* Edinburgh, 3 Feb. 1951; *s* of Charles Taylor Tripp and Agnes Tripp (*née* Macdonald); *m* 1974, Kathryn Margaret Morgan; two *s*. *Educ:* George Watson's Coll., Edinburgh; Univ. of Edinburgh (BCom Hons 1973). Chartered Accountant 1976. Student, then qualified Accountant, Deloitte & Co., 1973–77; Financial, then Chief Accountant, Vickers Oceanics Ltd, 1977–79; Hughes Microelectronics Ltd: Chief Accountant, 1979–83; Financial Controller, 1983–88; Co. Sec., 1985–91; Ops Dir, 1988–90; Dir and Gen. Manager, 1990–91; Man. Dir (EMEA), Hughes Identification Devices Inc., 1991–93; Gp Finance Dir, then Man. Dir (Customer Product Services), McQueen International Ltd, 1993–97; Man. Dir (CPS) and Sen. Vice Pres., Sykes Enterprises Inc., 1997–2000. Mem., Scottish Econ. Council, 1991–98; Member Board: Scottish Council for Res. in Educn, 1991–98; Scottish Further Educn Unit, 1994–2000; Scottish Higher Educn Funding Council, 2000–05; Vice Chairman: Scottish Further Educn Funding Council, 1999–2005; Scottish Further and Higher Educn Funding Council, 2005–09. Member: Criminal Injuries Compensation Appeals Panel, later First Tier Tribunal, Criminal Injuries Compensation, 2000–; Social Security and Child Support Tribunal, 2011–. Mem. Bd, Glenrothes Coll., 1986–96. *Recreations:* Heart of Midlothian FC, golf, theatre, walking, history, cinema, reading, opera. *Address:* 66 Craigleith Road, Edinburgh EH4 2DU. *T:* (0131) 332 1983, *Fax:* (0131) 332 9831. *E:* alantripp@atripp.fsnet.co.uk.

TRIPP, Prof. Charles Rees Howard, PhD; FBA 2012; Professor of Politics with reference to the Middle East, School of Oriental and African Studies, University of London, since 2007; *b* Lui, Sudan, 8 March 1952; *s* of Peter Tripp and Rosemary Tripp; *m* 1991, Venetia Porter; two *d*. *Educ:* Winchester Coll.; New Coll., Oxford (BA); Sch. of Oriental and African Studies, Univ. of London (MSc; PhD 1984). Res. Associate, IISS, 1981–83; Dep. Dir, Prog. for Strategic and Internat. Security Studies, Institut Universitaire de Hautes Études Internationales et du Développement, Geneva, 1983–86; Lectr, 1986–92, Sen. Lectr, 1992–2001, Reader in Middle East Politics, 2001–07, SOAS, Univ. of London. *Publications:* Iran and Iraq at War (with S. Chubin), 1988; A History of Iraq, 2000, 3rd edn 2007; Islam and the Moral Economy: the challenge of capitalism, 2006; The Power and the People: paths of resistance in the Middle East, 2013. *Recreations:* reading, drawing. *Address:* School of Oriental and African Studies, University of London, Thornhaugh Street, WC1H 0XG. *T:* (020) 7898 4748, *Fax:* (020) 7898 4559. *E:* ct2@soas.ac.uk.

TRIPP, Rt Rev. Howard George; an Auxiliary Bishop in Southwark, (RC), 1980–2004, now Emeritus; Titular Bishop of Newport, since 1980; *b* 3 July 1927; *s* of late Basil Howard Tripp and Alice Emily Tripp (*née* Haslett). *Educ:* John Fisher School, Purley; St John's Seminary, Wonersh. Priest, 1953; Assistant Priest: Blackheath SE3, 1953–56; East Sheen, 1956–62; Asst Diocesan Financial Sec., 1962–68; Parish Priest, East Sheen, 1965–71; Dir, Southwark Catholic Children's Soc., 1971–80; VG, 1980–2006. Chm., London Churches Gp, 1993–98. *Recreation:* vegetable gardening. *Address:* 35 St Catherine's Close, SW20 9NL. *T:* (020) 8542 4886. *E:* howardtripp@outlook.com.

TRIPPIER, Sir David (Austin), Kt 1992; RD 1983; JP; DL; Chairman, W. H. Ireland PLC, Stockbrokers, 1994–2008; *b* 15 May 1946; *s* of late Austin Wilkinson Trippier, MC and Mary Trippier; *m* 1975, Ruth Worthington, Barrister; three *s*. *Educ:* Bury Grammar School. Commnd Officer, Royal Marines Reserve, 1968 (qualif. parachutist, 1970; sc 1982). Member of Stock Exchange, 1968–; Chairman: Murray VCT, 1995–2005; Cambridgeshire Horizons Ltd, 2004–11. Mem., Rochdale Council, 1969–78, Leader Cons. Gp, 1974–76. MP (C) Rossendale, 1979–83, Rossendale and Darwen, 1983–92; contested (C) Rossendale and Darwen, 1992. Sec., Cons. Parly Defence Cttee, 1980–82; PPS to Minister for Health, 1982–83; Parliamentary Under-Secretary of State: (Minister for Small Firms and Enterprise) DTI, 1983–85; Dept of Employment, 1985–87; DoE, 1987–89; Minister of State (Minister for the Envmt and Countryside), DoE, 1989–92. Dep. Chm., Cons. Party, 1990–91. Nat. Vice Chm., Assoc. of Cons. Clubs, 1980–84. Chairman: Tepnel Diagnostics PLC, 1992–94; Envirosystems Ltd, 1992–99; Davenham Gp, 1994–96; Marketing Manchester Ltd, 1996–99; Vector Investments Ltd, 1996–2000; Director: Dunlop Heywood & Co., 1992–99; St Modwen Properties, 1992–2004; Sir David Trippier & Associates, 1992–; Murray Income plc, 1996–2005; Nord Anglia Educn PLC, 1996–2007; Camfil Air Filters Ltd, 1998–2000; UCG Ltd, 2001–03; ITV Granada (formerly Granada) Television Ltd, 2002–07; Consultant: Halliwell Landau, 1992–2006; Waste Management, 1992–97; Halliday Meecham, 1992–99. President: Manchester Chamber of Commerce and Industry, 1999–2000; Royal Lancs Agricl Soc., 1999–2000. Chm., Tidy Britain Gp, 1996–98. Governor, Manchester Grammar Sch., 1992–2005. President: Northern Reg., RM Assoc., 1988–93; Lancs, RBL, 2004–07; Gtr Manchester, SSAFA, 2012–; Chm., NW of England Reserve Forces and Cadets Assoc., 2000–08; Vice-Chm., Council, RFCA (RM), 1999–2008. Hon. Col, RM Reserve, Merseyside, 1996–2010. Provincial Grand Master and Grand Superintendent for E Lancs, 2011–. FRSA 2006. JP Rochdale, 1975; DL Lancs, 1994, High Sheriff, Lancs, 1997–98. OStJ 2000. *Publications:* Defending the Peace, 1982; New Life for Inner Cities, 1989; Lend Me Your Ears (autobiog.), 1999. *Recreation:* gardening. *Address:* Dowry Head, Helmshore, Rossendale, Lancs BB4 4AE.

TRITTON, Alan George, CBE 1999; DL; Director, Barclays Bank Ltd, 1974–91; *b* 2 Oct. 1931; *s* of George Henton Tritton, Lyons Hall, Essex, and Iris Mary Baillie, Lochloy, Nairn; *m* 1st, 1958, Elizabeth Clare d'Abreu (marr. diss.); two *s* one *d*; 2nd, 1972, Diana Marion Spencer. *Educ:* Eton. Member of British Schools Exploring Soc. Expedn, Arctic Norway, 1949. Lt, 1st Batt. Seaforth Highlanders, active service Pahang, Malaya, 1950–52. Leader, S Orkneys Antarctic Survey Station, 1952–54, and Antarctic Relief Voyage, 1954, Falkland Islands Dependencies Survey; entered Barclays Bank Ltd, 1954; local Dir, 54 Lombard Street, 1964; Dir, Barclays Bank UK Management Ltd, 1972; India Adv., Barclays Bank, 1992–95. Dir, 1976–99, a Vice-Pres., 1983–99, Equitable Life Assce Soc.; Chairman: Plantation and Gen. Investments, 1994–96; University Life Assce Soc., 1994–99; Permanent Insurance Co. Ltd, 1995–99. A Vice-Pres., Royal Geographical Soc., 1983–86 (Mem. Council, 1975–96, Hon. Treas., 1984–96). Member: Cttee, British Trans-Arctic Expedn, 1966–69; Cttee, British Everest SW Face Expedn, 1974–75; Cttee of Management, Mount Everest Foundn, 1976–80; Friends' Cttee, Scott Polar Research Inst., 1976–80. Chairman: Westminster Abbey Investment Cttee, 1976–94; Calcutta Tercentenary Trust, 1989–2004; Member: Council, Internat. Chamber of Commerce, 1975–90 (Hon. Treas. 1985); Council, Foundn for Aviation and Sustainable Tourism, New Delhi, 1994–2005; Finance Cttee, 1997–, Council, 1999–2004, 2006–10, Royal Asiatic Soc.; Court, Essex Univ., 1995–2005. Pres., BACSA, 2010–. Trustee: Brentwood Cathedral Trust, 1996–2010; Falkland Is Conservation Trust, 1998–2003. High Sheriff, 1992, DL 1993, Essex. *Publications:* This Half-Closed Door, 2009; When the Tiger fought the Thistle: the tragedy of Colonel William Baillie of the Madras Army, 2013. *Recreations:* travelling, writing. *Clubs:* Boodle's, Antarctic (Pres., 2012; Mem. Cttee, 2012–), Geographical, Essex (Pres., 2001); Tollygunge (Calcutta).

TRITTON, (Elizabeth) Clare, (Clare McLaren-Throckmorton; Mrs Andrew McLaren); QC 1988; Chief Executive, Throckmorton Estates; *b* 18 Aug. 1935; *d* of Prof. Alfonsus d'Abreu and Elizabeth d'Abreu (*née* Throckmorton); *m* 1st, 1958, Alan Tritton, *qv* (marr. diss. 1971); two *s* one *d*; 2nd, 1973, Andrew McLaren (*d* 2007); name changed to McLaren-Throckmorton by deed poll, 1991, following death of uncle, Sir Robert Throckmorton, 11th Bt. *Educ:* Convent of the Holy Child Jesus, Mayfield, St Leonards; Univ. of Birmingham (BA Hons English). Called to the Bar, Inner Temple, 1968. Lived and worked in USA, France, Germany and Italy, intermittently, 1952–86; Centre Organiser, WVS, 1963–64; Charlemagne Chambers, Brussels, 1985–87; founded European Law Chambers, 1987. Chm., Bar European Group, 1982–84; Vice Chm., Internat. Practice Cttee, Gen. Council of the Bar, 1988–91; Chm., Sub Cttee on Eur. Legislation, Hansard Commn on Legislative Reform, 1991–93. Member: Council, Bow Gp, 1963–65; Eur. Cttee, British Invisible Exports Council, 1989–93; Monopolies and Mergers Commn, 1993–97. Dir, Severn Trent plc, 1991–2003. Ind. Mem., Council, FIMBRA, 1991–98. Mem. Cttee, Warwicks CLA, 2004–. Trustee Dir, Birmingham Royal Ballet Trust Co. Ltd, 1996–99. Chm., Primary Immunodeficiency Assoc., 2002–05. Founder, Bar European News, 1983. *Publications:* articles in law magazines on EEC and private internat. law. *Recreations:* reading, gardening, children, travel. *Address:* Coughton Court, Alcester, Warwicks B49 5JA. *T:* (01789) 762542. *E:* secretary@throckmortons.co.uk; Estate Office, Molland, South Molton, North Devon EX36 3ND. *T:* (01769) 550325.

TRITTON, Sir Jeremy Ernest, 5th Bt *cr* 1905, of Bloomfield, Lambeth; *b* 6 Oct. 1961; *o s* of Major Sir Anthony John Ernest Tritton, 4th Bt and of Diana, *d* of Rear-Adm. St John

Aldrich Micklethwait, CB, DSO; *S* father, 2012; *m* 2007, Mary Catherine Claydon; one *d. Educ:* Eton; Bristol Univ. (BSc). *Heir:* none. *Address:* 183 Old Brompton Road, SW5 0AN. *Club:* Boodles.

TROLLOPE, Andrew David Hedderwick; QC 1991; a Recorder of the Crown Court, since 1989; *b* 6 Nov. 1948; *s* of late Arthur George Cecil Trollope and Rosemary (*née* Hodson); *m* 1978, Anne Forbes; two *s. Educ:* Charterhouse; Univ. of Nancy. Called to the Bar, Inner Temple, 1971, Bencher, 2002; Asst Recorder, 1985–89. Hd of Chambers, 1991–. Special Advr, NI Affairs Select Cttee, H of C, 2014–15. Chm., N London Bar Mess, 1998–2001. Member: South Eastern Circuit Cttee, 1990–93, 1994–97, 2006–09, 2013–; Cttee, Criminal Bar Assoc., 1991–2001; Internat. Relns Cttee, Bar Council, 2001–08; Mem. Council of Mgt, 2001–06, Mem. Adv. Council, 2006–, British Inst. of Internat. and Comparative Law. Fellow, Soc. of Advanced Legal Studies, 1998. *Recreations:* opera, jazz, swimming, tennis, sailing, travel. *Address:* 187 Fleet Street, EC4A 2AT. *T:* (020) 7430 7430, *Fax:* (020) 7430 7431. *Clubs:* Garrick, Hurlingham.

See also J. Trollope.

TROLLOPE, Sir Anthony (Simon), 17th Bt *cr* 1642, of Casewick, Lincolnshire; *b* 31 Aug. 1945; *s* of Sir Anthony Owen Clavering Trollope, 16th Bt and of Joan Mary Alexis, *d* of Alexis Robert Gibbs; *S* father, 1987; *m* 1969, Denise, *d* of Trevern and Vida Thompson; two *d. Educ:* Univ. of Sydney (BA 1969); Univ. of New England (MBA 1998); Univ. of Western Sydney (BTeaching 2002). Worked in mktg mgt in major mgt positions for food producing companies, 1977–99; schoolteacher, retired. Breeder, in partnership with his wife, of Anglo-Arabian horses and Rhodesian Ridgeback dogs. Mem., Australian Marketing Inst., 1988–2002. *Heir: b* Hugh Irwin Trollope [*b* 31 March 1947; *m* 1971, Barbara Anne, *d* of William Ian Jamieson; one *s* two *d*]. *Address:* 116 Midson Road, Oakville, NSW 2765, Australia. *Clubs:* Gordon Rugby, Arabian Horse Society of Australia (Sydney).

TROLLOPE, Joanna, OBE 1996; writer; *b* 9 Dec. 1943; *er d* of late Arthur George Cecil Trollope and Rosemary Trollope (*née* Hodson); *m* 1st, 1966, David Roger William Potter, *qv* (marr. diss. 1983); two *d*; 2nd, 1985, Ian Bayley Curteis, *qv* (marr. diss. 2001); two step *s. Educ:* Reigate County Sch. for Girls; St Hugh's Coll., Oxford (Gamble Scholar; MA 1972). Inf. and Research Dept, Foreign Office, 1965–67; teaching posts, 1967–79, incl. Farnham Girls' Grammar Sch., adult educn, English for foreigners and at Daneshill Sch. Writer in Residence, Victoria Magazine, USA, 1999. Chm., DNH Adv. Cttee on Nat. Reading Initiative, 1996–97; Member: Govt Adv. Body, Nat. Year of Reading, 1998; Adv. Bd, Costa Awards; Adv. Body, Sieghart Ind. Review of E-Lending in Public Libraries in England, DCMS, 2012; Govt Adv. Panel on public library service in England, 2014–. Judge: Melissa Nathan Awards, 2005–11; Sunday Times EFG Private Bank Short Story Award, 2012; Chief Judge, Orange Prize for Fiction, 2012. Vice President: Trollope Soc., 1995–; West Country Writers' Assoc., 1998–; Mem. Council, Soc. of Authors, 1997–. Member: Internat. PEN; Romantic Novelists Assoc. Trustee, Joanna Trollope Charitable Trust, 1995–. Patron: Glos Community Foundn, 1994–2006; Mulberry Bush Sch., Witney, 2006–; Dementia UK (formerly for dementia); March Foundn; Ambassador: Meningitis Trust; RNIB (esp. Talking Books); Children's Reading Fund, Nat. Literary Trust, 2012–. DL Glos, 2002–06. *Publications:* Eliza Stanhope, 1978; Parson Harding's Daughter, 1979 (reissued under pseudonym Caroline Harvey, 1995); Leaves from the Valley, 1980; The City of Gems, 1981; The Steps of the Sun, 1983 (reissued under pseudonym Caroline Harvey, 1996); Britannia's Daughters: a study of women in the British Empire, 1983; The Taverners' Place, 1986 (reissued under pseudonym Caroline Harvey, 2000); The Choir, 1988 (televised, 1995); A Village Affair, 1989 (televised, 1994); A Passionate Man, 1990; The Rector's Wife, 1991 (televised, 1994); The Men and the Girls, 1992; A Spanish Lover, 1993; (ed) The Country Habit: an anthology, 1993; The Best of Friends, 1995; Next of Kin, 1996; Other People's Children, 1998 (televised, 2000); Marrying the Mistress, 2000 (dramatised for stage, 2005); Girl from the South, 2002; Brother and Sister, 2004; The Book Boy, 2006; Second Honeymoon, 2006; Friday Nights, 2008; The Other Family, 2010; Daughters-in-Law, 2011; The Soldier's Wife, 2012; Sense and Sensibility, 2013; Balancing Act, 2014; *as Caroline Harvey:* Legacy of Love, 1992; A Second Legacy, 1993; A Castle in Italy, 1993; The Brass Dolphin, 1997; contribs to newspapers and magazines. *Recreations:* reading, conversation, very long baths. *Address:* c/o United Agents, 12–26 Lexington Street, W1F 0LE. *W:* www.joannatrollope.com.

See also A. D. H. Trollope.

TROMANS, Stephen Richard; QC 2009; *b* Birmingham, 2 Feb. 1957; *s* of Henry and Dorothy Tromans; *m* 1981, Caroline Frances Power; three *d. Educ:* Rowley Regis Grammar Sch.; Selwyn Coll., Cambridge (BA Law 1978). Admitted as solicitor, 1981; Lectr in Law, Dept of Land Econ., Univ. of Cambridge, and Fellow, Selwyn Coll., Cambridge, 1981–87; Partner: Wild Hewitson & Shaw, 1987–90; Simmons & Simmons, 1990–99; called to the Bar, Inner Temple, 1999; Jt Hd of Chambers, 39 Essex St, 2011–. Chm., Environmental Law Foundn, 2010–14. Mem. Council, English Nature, 1994–2000. Mem. Council, Ridley Hall, Cambridge, 2008–. *Publications:* Commercial Leases, 1987, 2nd edn 1997; Planning Law, Practice and Precedents, 1990; The Environment Acts 1990–1995, 1991, 3rd edn 2003; The Law of Nuclear Installations, 1997, 2nd edn as Nuclear Law, 2010; Environmental Impact Assessment, 2003, 2nd edn 2012; Contaminated Land, 1994, 2nd edn 2008. *Recreations:* social tennis, industrial history, the great conductors, drawing, oil painting. *Address:* 39 Essex Street, WC2R 3AT. *T:* (020) 7832 1111, *Fax:* (020) 7353 3978. *E:* stephen.tromans@39essex.com.

TRONCHETTI PROVERA, Marco; Chairman, Pirelli & Co. Real Estate SpA, Milan, since 1991; Chairman, since 2003, and Managing Director, since 2011, Pirelli & Co. SpA, Milan; *b* Milan, 1948; *m*; three *c. Educ:* Bocconi Univ., Milan (grad. 1971). Founder, holding co. in field of maritime transportation, 1973–86; joined Pirelli Gp, 1986; Partner, Pirelli & Co., 1986–; Man. Dir and Gen. Manager, Société Internationale Pirelli SA, Basle, 1988–92; Pirelli SpA: Man. Dir and Gen. Manager, Finance and Admin and Gen. Affairs, 1991–92; Exec. Dep. Chm. and Man. Dir, 1992–96; Dep. Chm., 1995–99, Chm., 1999–2003, Pirelli & Co.; Chm. and CEO, Pirelli SpA, 1996–2003; Chairman: Olimpia SpA, 2001–07; Telecom Italia SpA, 2001–06; Dep. Chm. and Man. Dir, Olivetti SpA, 2001–08. Chm., CAMFIN SpA, Milan. Member: Internat. Adv. Bd, Allianz; Internat. Council, JP Morgan; European Adv. Cttee, NY Stock Exchange. Dep. Chm., Confindustria (Confedn of Italian Industries), 2000–. Board Member: Teatro alla Scala Foundn, 2001–05; Univ. Commerciale Luigi Bocconi; FC Internazionale SpA. Italian Chm., Council for US and Italy. Member: Assonime Steering Cttee; European Round Table of Industrialists; Italian Gp, Trilateral Commn. *Address:* Pirelli & Co. SpA, Viale Sarca 222, 20126 Milan, Italy.

TROOP, Patricia Ann, (Mrs P. A. Dittner), CBE 2001; FRCP, FFPH; Deputy Chairman, Cambridge University Hospitals Foundation Trust, since 2013 (non-executive Director, 2009–10; Senior Independent non-executive Director, 2010–13); independent consultant on public health and health policy, since 2005; *b* 5 April 1948; *d* of John Ronald Troop and Phoebe Margaret Troop; *m* 1979, Michael Dittner; one *s* one *d. Educ:* Manchester Univ. Med. Sch. (MB ChB 1971; MSc Community Medicine 1979); MA Cantab 1988. MFCM 1980, FFPHM (FFCM 1986); FRCP 2001. Dir of Public Health, Cambridge HA, 1988–91; Associate Lectr, Faculty of Medicine, Cambridge Univ., 1988–; Chief Executive: Cambridge HA, 1990–93; Cambs Family Health Services, 1992–93; Director of Public Health: East Anglia RHA, 1993–95; Anglia and Oxford, then Eastern, Regl Office, NHS Exec., DoH, 1995–99; Dep. CMO, DoH, 1999–2003; Chief Exec., HPA, 2003–08. Work for DoH, ECDC, WHO, 2008–. Chm., Ind. Rev. of Incidents of Pseudomonas Infection in Neonatal Units in NI, 2012. Mem. and Vice-Chm., Cambs TEC, 1992–93. Chairman: Intercollegiate Gp on Nutrition, 2006–; Internat. Cttee, Faculty of Public Health, 2011–13; Mem., Internat. Health Regulation Rev. Cttee, WHO, 2010–11. Vis. Prof., LSHTM, 2000–08; Hon. Prof., City Univ., 2003–14. Mem., Lucy Cavendish Coll., Cambridge, 1990–99. Hon. DSc: East Anglia, 2005; Cranfield, 2006. *Publications:* chapters and articles in various med. jls. *Recreations:* painting, yachting, golf. *Address:* 47a Lode Way, Haddenham, Ely, Cambs CB6 3UL. *T:* (01353) 741087.

TROSS, Jonathan Edward Simon, CB 2004; non-executive Director: National Institute for Health and Care (formerly Clinical) Excellence, since 2007; UK Biobank, since 2013; *b* 21 Jan. 1949; *s* of late Francis Tross and Audrey (*née* Payne); *m* 1972, Ann Humphries; one *s* one *d. Educ:* Chislehurst and Sidcup Grammar Sch.; University Coll., Oxford (BA Hons Modern Hist., 1970). Teacher in Kenya, 1971; Department of Health and Social Security: grad. trainee, 1972; Principal, 1977–84; Asst Sec., Supplementary Benefits Review, 1984–87; Asst Dir, Corporate Div., Barclays Bank, on secondment, 1987–90; Pharmaceutical Industry Br., DoH, 1990–91; G3, Head of Planning and Finance Div., 1991–94, G2, Dir of Corporate Mgt, 1994–99, DSS; G2, Head of Constitution Secretariat, Cabinet Office, 1999–2001; Chief Exec., CAFCASS, 2001–04; Collaboration Proj. Dir, LGA, 2004–06. Comr, IPCC, 2009–15. Trustee and Treas., Citizens Advice, 2005–11. *Recreations:* football, reading, theatre, walking, allotment. *Club:* Fulham Football.

TROTMAN, Andrew Frederick, MA; educational consultant and leadership coach, since 2011; *b* 9 Dec. 1954; *s* of late Campbell Grant Trotman and Audrey Trotman (*née* Simpson); *m* 1980, Mary Rosalind Spencer; one *s* one *d. Educ:* Alleyne's Grammar Sch., Stevenage; Balliol Coll., Oxford (MA English Language and Lit. 1977); Cert Ed Oxon 1978; Oxford Brookes Univ. (MA Coaching and Mentoring Practice 2013). Asst Master, Radley Coll., 1978–84; Housemaster, Abingdon Sch., 1984–90; Dep. Rector, Edinburgh Acad., 1991–95; Head Master, St Peter's School, York, 1995–2004; Warden, St Edward's Sch., Oxford, 2004–11; Acting Headmaster, Repton Sch., 2012. Governor: Cheam Sch., 2005–12; St Hugh's Sch., 2009–. Dir, Aspirance Leadership Services, 2013–. Educnl Advr, Sons and Friends of Clergy, 2013–. MInstD 1997. JP City of York, 1998–2004. *Recreations:* walking, rowing, music, bagpiping. *Address:* The Grey House, Grump Street, Ilmington, Shipston-on-Stour, Warwicks CV36 4LE. *E:* andrew@aspirance.co.uk.

See also J. G. Trotman.

TROTMAN, John Grant; Headmaster, Bishop's Stortford College, 1997–2011; *b* Silloth, Cumberland, 19 Sept. 1952; *s* of late Campbell Grant Trotman and Audrey Trotman (*née* Simpson); *m* 1st, 1977, Alexandra Kitchener-Payne (marr. diss. 2003); two *s*; 2nd, 2011, Melanie Carruthers (*née* Crawford). *Educ:* Alleyne's Grammar Sch., Stevenage; St Edmund Hall, Oxford (BA, PGCE). Asst Master, Kent Coll., Canterbury, 1976–83; Head of English: Newcastle-under-Lyme Sch., 1983–85; St Edward's Sch., Oxford, 1985–92; Dep. Hd, The Leys, Cambridge, 1992–97. Chair, Isle of Wight Samaritans, 2015–. *Recreations:* writing poetry, birds, wild places, school fiction of 1920s and 1930s, trees, trying to draw. *Address:* Brantwood House, 8 Pomona Road, Shanklin Old Village, Isle of Wight PO37 6PF. *T:* (01983) 863799. *E:* john.g.trotman@gmail.com.

See also A. F. Trotman.

TROTMAN-DICKENSON, Sir Aubrey (Fiennes), Kt 1989; Principal, University of Wales College of Cardiff, 1988–93; Vice-Chancellor, University of Wales, 1975–77, 1983–85 and 1991–93; *b* 12 Feb. 1926; *s* of late Edward Newton Trotman-Dickenson and Violet Murray Nicoll; *m* 1953, Danusia Irena Hewell; two *s* one *d. Educ:* Winchester Coll.; Balliol Coll., Oxford (MA, BSc); PhD Manchester; DSc Edinburgh. Fellow, National Research Council, Ottawa, 1948–50; Asst Lecturer, ICI Fellow, Manchester Univ., 1950–53; E. I. du Pont de Nemours, Wilmington, USA, 1953–54; Lecturer, Edinburgh Univ., 1954–60; Professor, University College of Wales, Aberystwyth, 1960–68; Principal; UWIST, Cardiff, 1968–88; UC Cardiff, 1987–88. Chm., Job Creation Programme, Wales, 1975–78. Member: Welsh Council, 1971–79; Planning and Transport Res. Adv. Council, DoE, 1975–79. Tilden Lectr, Chem. Soc., 1963. Hon. LLD Wales, 1995. *Publications:* Gas Kinetics, 1955; Free Radicals, 1959; Tables of Bimolecular Gas Reactions, 1967; (ed) Comprehensive Inorganic Chemistry, 1973; contrib. to learned journals. *Address:* Siston Court, Bristol BS16 9LU. *T:* (0117) 937 2109.

TROTT, Andrew James, FRICS; Surveyor Member, Upper Tribunal (Lands Chamber) (formerly Lands Tribunal), since 2006; *b* 24 Dec. 1953; *s* of John and Lydia Trott; *m* 1981, Fiona Jane Maynard; three *s. Educ:* Sir Antony Browne's Sch., Brentwood; Poly. of South Bank (BSc Hons Estate Mgt); Open Univ. (BA, MBA). ARICS 1977, FRICS 1992. RICS Res. Fellow, Poly. of South Bank, 1979–80; Partner, John Trott and Son, 1980–82; Hd of Property Consultancy, London Transport, subseq. Transport for London, 1982–2005. *Recreations:* flying (private pilot's licence), football, golf, collecting modern first editions, Globe Theatre. *Address:* Upper Tribunal (Lands Chamber), Royal Courts of Justice, Strand, WC2A 2LL. *T:* (020) 7612 9725. *E:* andrew.trott@justice.gsi.gov.uk.

TROTT, Christopher John; HM Diplomatic Service; High Commissioner to Solomon Islands, Vanuatu and Nauru, from Jan. 2016; *b* 14 Feb. 1966; *s* of John and Averil Trott; *m* 1992, Sunna Park; one *s* one *d. Educ:* Hawthorns Sch., Blechingley; Whitgift Sch., S Croydon; Bristol Univ. (BA Hons Hist. 1988); Sch. of Oriental and African Studies, Univ. of London (MA SE Asian Area Studies 1991). Entered FCO, 1991; Dep. Hd of Mission, Rangoon, 1993–96; First Secretary: (Commercial), 1996–99, (Political), 1999–2002, Tokyo; Dep. Hd of Mission, Kabul, 2002; FCO, 2003–07; Ambassador to Senegal and concurrently to Guinea-Bissau and Cape Verde, 2007–11, and concurrently to Mali, 2007–10; Consul Gen., Cape Town, 2011–15; Dean, Consular Corps, Cape Town, 2014–15. Vice Pres., Whitgiftian Assoc., 2012–. Citizen of Honour, Commune of Timbuktu, 2010. *Recreations:* travel, reading, ski-ing, scuba-diving, season ticket holder at Crystal Palace FC. *Address:* Foreign and Commonwealth Office, King Charles Street, SW1A 2AH. *E:* Chris.Trott@fco.gov.uk.

TROTT, Philip David Anthony; Partner, Bates Wells & Braithwaite London LLP, since 1992; *b* Exeter, 5 June 1952; *s* of Sydney Harold Trott and Ruth Lotte Trott; partner, Kate Edwards. *Educ:* Portsmouth Grammar Sch.; Oxford Poly. (HND Business Studies 1973); University Coll. London (LLB Hons 1976). Admitted solicitor, 1979; Partner: Lawford & Co., 1982–89; Thomson Snell & Passmore, 1989–92. Hon. Legal Advr, Holborn CAB, 1979–96; Advr, ArtLaw, 1983–84; Mem., Adv. Panel, Office of the Immigration Services Comr, 2001–06. Immigration Law Practitioners' Association: Co-Founder, 1984; Mem., Exec. Cttee, 1984–90, 1994–95, 2001–02; Convenor, Econ. Migration Sub-Cttee, 1984–; Chm., 1986–88. Editor, Immigration and Internat. Employment Law Jl, 1999–2000; Mem., Editl Bd and contrib., Lexis Nexis Immigration PSL, 2012–. *Publications:* (contrib.) Macdonald's Immigration Law and Practice, 3rd edn, 1991 to 7th edn, 2008; (contrib.) Jackson's Immigration Law and Practice, 2nd edn, 1999, 3rd edn, 2002. *Recreations:* sailing, cycling, walking, rowing, Southern Italian cookery, benefactor to the arts, VW Campervan enthusiast (Member, VW Owners' Club). *Address:* Bates Wells & Braithwaite London LLP, 10 Queens Street Place, EC4R 1BE. *T:* (020) 7551 7722, *Fax:* (020) 7551 7800. *E:* p.trott@bwbllp.com. *Clubs:* Lensbury, House of St Barnabus.

TROTTER, Major Alexander Richard, CVO 2013; JP; Lord-Lieutenant of Berwickshire, 2000–14; Chairman, Meadowhead Ltd (formerly Mortonhall Park Ltd), since 1974; *b* 20 Feb. 1939; *s* of late Major H. R. Trotter, TD, and of Rona Trotter (*née* Murray); *m* 1970, Julia Henrietta, *d* of Capt. Sir Peter McClintock Greenwell, 3rd Bt, TD; three *s. Educ:* Eton Coll.; City of London Tech. Coll. Served Royal Scots Greys, 1958–68; Manager, Charterhall Estate and Farm, 1969–; Vice Chm., Border Grain, Ltd, 1984–2003. Dir, Timber Growers GB Ltd, 1977–82. Scottish Landowners' Federation: Mem. Council, 1975–2004; Convener, 1982–85;

Vice Pres., 1986–96; Pres., 1996–2001; Mem., NCC and Chm., Scottish Cttee, 1985–90; Mem., UK Cttee, Euro Year of the Envmt, 1986–88. Gen. Comr for Income Tax, Berwickshire, 1973–2010. Mem. (Ind.), Berwickshire CC, 1969–75 (Chm., Roads Cttee, 1974–75). Chm., Thirlstane Castle Trust, 1996–2007. Officer, Royal Co. of Archers. FRSA. DL 1987, JP 2000, Berwickshire. OStJ 2005. *Recreations:* golf, bridge, country sports. *Address:* Whinkerstones House, Duns, Berwickshire TD11 3RE. *T:* (home) (01890) 840555, (office) (01890) 840301. *E:* alex@charterhall.net. *Clubs:* Turf, Pratt's; New (Edinburgh).

TROTTER, David; *see* Trotter, W. D.

TROTTER, Dame Janet (Olive), DBE 2001 (OBE 1991); Lord-Lieutenant for Gloucestershire, since 2010; *b* 29 Oct. 1943; *d* of Anthony George Trotter and Joyce Edith Trotter (*née* Patrick). *Educ:* Derby Lonsdale Coll. of Educn (Cert Ed); BD (ext.) London Univ.; Inst. of Educn, London Univ. (MA); Henley Mgt Coll. (MSc Brunel Univ.). Teacher: St Leonards Secondary Sch., 1965–67; Chartham Secondary Sch., 1967–69; Rochester Grammar Sch. for Girls, 1969–73; Lectr, King Alfred's Coll., Winchester, 1973–84; Vice Principal, St Martin's Coll., Lancaster, 1985–86; Principal, St Paul and St Mary's Coll., Cheltenham, 1986–90; Principal, 1990–2006, Vice-Chancellor, 2002–06, Univ. of Gloucestershire (formerly Cheltenham and Gloucester Coll. of Higher Educn). Mem. and Chm., Glos HA, 1991–96; Chairman: S and W Reg., NHS Exec., DoH, 1996–2001; Glos Hosps NHS Foundn Trust (formerly NHS Trust), 2002–10. Member: HEFCE, 1992–97; TTA, 1994–99. DL Glos, 2006. Hon. Freeman, Cheltenham, 2002. Hon. DTech Pecs, Hungary, 1996; Hon. DEd: UWE, 2001; Brunel, 2004; Hon. DHum Elizabethtown Coll., Pa, 2002; Hon. DLaws Bristol, 2002. *Publications:* various articles. *Recreations:* cycling, music. *Address:* Shire Hall, Gloucester GL1 2TG.

TROTTER, Sir Neville (Guthrie), Kt 1997; JP; DL; FCA; FRAeS, FCIT; Consultant, Thornton Baker, 1974–83, Grant Thornton, Chartered Accountants, 1983–2005; *b* 27 Jan. 1932; *s* of Captain Alexander Trotter and Elizabeth Winifred Trotter (*née* Guthrie); *m* 1983, Caroline, *d* of late Captain John Farrow, OBE, RN and Oona Farrow (*née* Hall); one *d*. *Educ:* Shrewsbury; King's Coll., Durham (BCom). Short service commn in RAF, 1955–58. Partner, Thornton Baker & Co., Chartered Accountants, 1962–74. Former Director: MidAmerican Energy Hldgs Co.; Wm Baird plc; Darchem Ltd; Romag plc. Mem. Council, NE Chamber of Commerce, 1998–2014; Regl Ambassador of NE in N America, UKTI and One Northeast, 2008–11; Chm., British-American Chamber of Commerce, NE of England, 1999–2014; Pres., 2000–12, Mem. Adv. Bd, 2012–, Northern Defence Industries; Vice Pres., Soc. of Maritime Industries, 1996–. Former Member: East Coast Main Line (formerly Great North Eastern Railway, later National Express East Coast Main Line) Business Forum; Council, European Atlantic Gp. Mem., Newcastle City Council, 1963–74 (Alderman, 1970–74; Chm., Finance Cttee, Traffic Highways and Transport Cttee, Theatre Cttee). Mem., CAA Airline Users Cttee, 1973–79. Mem., Tyne and Wear Metropolitan Council, 1973–74; Vice-Chm., Northumberland Police Authority, 1970–74. MP (C) Tynemouth, Feb. 1974–1997. Chm., Cons. Party Shipping and Shipbuilding Cttee, 1979–85, 1994–97 (Vice-Chm., 1976–79); Secretary: Cons. Party Industry Cttee, 1981–83; Cons. Party Transport Cttee, 1983–84; Mil. Sec., Cons. Party Aviation Cttee, 1976–79; Member: Industry Sub-Cttee, Select Cttee on Expenditure, 1976–79; Select Cttee on Transport, 1983–92; Select Cttee on Defence, 1993–97; Parly Defence Study Group, 1980–97; Armed Forces Parly Scheme (RAF), 1990–91; formerly Chm., All-Party Gp for Prevention of Solvent Abuse. Private Member's Bills: Consumer Safety, 1978; Licensing Amendment, 1980; Intoxicating Substances Supply (Glue Sniffing), 1985. Pres., North Area Cons. Party, 1996–2003. Vice Pres., Soc. for Prevention of Solvent and Volatile Substance Abuse, 1989–. Former Parliamentary Consultant: British Transport Police Fedn; Go Ahead Gp; Bowrings. Former Member: Northern Economic Planning Council; Tyne Improvement Commn; Tyneside Passenger Transport Authority; Industrial Relations Tribunal; UK Defence Forum; Steering Cttee, Parly Maritime Gp; Member: Defence and Security Forum; Atlantic Council; Air League; RUSI (formerly Council Mem.); NE RFCA (formerly TAVRA), 1997–; US Naval Inst.; USAF Assoc.; US Navy League; Assoc. of US Army; Railway Studies Assoc. Pres., Tyneside Br., RM Assoc., 2001–. Hon. Colonel: Royal Marine Reserve, 1998–2003; Durham ACF, 2003–05. Pres., TS Dauntless (formerly TS Rodney) Gosforth Sea Cadets, 2006–. Pres., Whitley Bay and Dist Scout Council, 2004–12. Council Member: Northumbria, Order of St John, 2005–12; High Sheriff's Assoc. of England and Wales, 2005–11. FRAeS 1998; FCIT 1998. Freeman, City of London, 1978; Member: Co. of Chartered Accountants, 1978; Hon. Co. of Air Pilots (formerly GAPAN), 2006–. JP Newcastle upon Tyne, 1973; DL 1997, High Sheriff, 2004–05, Tyne and Wear. *Recreations:* aviation, gardening, fell-walking, study of foreign affairs, defence and industry. *Clubs:* Royal Air Force; Northern Counties (Newcastle upon Tyne).

TROTTER, Thomas Andrew, FRCO; Organist, St Margaret's Church, Westminster Abbey, since 1982; Organist to the City of Birmingham, since 1983; *b* 4 April 1957; *s* of late His Honour Richard Stanley Trotter and Ruth Elizabeth Trotter. *Educ:* Malvern Coll.; Royal Coll. of Music, 1974–76 (schol.; ARCM) (organ schol., St George's Chapel, Windsor, 1975–76); King's Coll., Cambridge (organ schol., 1976–79; MA). John Stewart of Rannock Schol. in Sacred Music, Cambridge Univ., 1979; Countess of Munster schol. for further organ studies with Marie-Claire Alain in Paris. Début at Royal Fest. Hall, 1980; Prom. début, 1986; regular broadcasts for Radio 2 and Radio 3; has performed at fests throughout UK and in Europe; concert tours to Australia, USA and Far East; organ recordings. DUniv UCE, 2003; Hon. DMus Birmingham, 2006. Walford Davies Prize, RCM, 1976; First prize and Bach prize, St Albans Internat. Organ Competition, 1979; Prix de Virtuosité, Conservatoire Rueil-Malmaison, 1981; Instrumental Award, Royal Philharmonic Soc., 2001; Internat. Performer of the Year, NY Chapter, Amer. Guild of Organists, 2012. *Address:* c/o The Town Hall, Birmingham B3 3DQ.

TROTTER, Prof. (Wilfred) David, PhD; FBA 2004; King Edward VII Professor of English Literature, University of Cambridge, since 2002; Fellow, Gonville and Caius College, Cambridge, since 2002; *b* 25 July 1951; *s* of late Wilfred Robert Trotter and Enid Beatrice Trotter (*née* Roulston). *Educ:* Gonville and Caius Coll., Cambridge (BA, PhD). Res. Fellow, Magdalene Coll., Cambridge, 1975–77; University College London: Lectr in English, 1977–87; Reader, 1987–90; Prof. of English, 1990–91; Quain Prof. of English Lang. and Lit., 1991–2002. Vis. Prof., CIT, 1988–89. *Publications:* The Poetry of Abraham Cowley, 1979; The Making of the Reader, 1984; Circulation: Defoe, Dickens and the economies of the novel, 1988; The English Novel in History 1895–1920, 1993; (jtly) A Companion to Edwardian Fiction, 1997; Cooking with Mud: the idea of mess in nineteenth century art and fiction, 2000; Paranoid Modernism, 2001; Cinema and Modernism, 2007; The Uses of Phobia: essays on literature and film, 2010; Literature in the First Media Age: Britain between the Wars, 2013. *Address:* Faculty of English, 9 West Road, Cambridge CB3 9DP.

TROUBRIDGE, Sir Thomas (Richard), 7th Bt *cr* 1799, of Plymouth; FCA; Partner, PricewaterhouseCoopers (formerly Price Waterhouse), 1989–2015; *b* 23 Jan. 1955; *s* of Sir Peter Troubridge, 6th Bt and of Hon. Venetia Daphne (who *m* 2nd, Captain W. F. E. Forbes, *qv*), *d* of 1st Baron Weeks; *S* father, 1988; *m* 1984, Hon. Rosemary Douglas-Pennant, *yr d* of 6th Baron Penrhyn, DSO, MBE; two *s* one *d*. *Educ:* Eton College; Durham Univ. (BSc Eng). ACA 1980, FCA 1991. Joined Price Waterhouse, 1977. *Recreations:* sailing, ski-ing. *Heir:* *s* Edward Peter Troubridge, *b* 10 Aug. 1989. *Address:* The Manor House, Elsted, Midhurst, W Sussex GU29 0JY. *T:* (01730) 825286. *Clubs:* White's, Hurlingham; Itchenor Sailing.

TROUGHTON, James Michael; Chairman, Tulliemet Ltd, since 1999; *b* Hambleden, 8 Nov. 1950; *s* of Sir Charles Hugh Willis Troughton, CBE, MC, TD and (Constance) Gillean (*née* Mitford), DL; *m* 1973, Sarah Campbell-Preston; one *s* two *d*. *Educ:* Radley Coll.; Trinity Coll., Cambridge (BA 1972; DipArch). RIBA 1975; ARIAS 1999. With Foster Associates, 1975–78; Richard Rogers and Partners, 1978–82; Founder Partner, Troughton McAslan, 1983–96; Chm., John McAslan and Partners, 1996–98. Troughton McAslan Architects completed works include: Derwent Valley Properties; Apple Computer Stockley Park; FC3 Canary Wharf; Jubilee line Stations, Canning Town and Stratford; Delawarr Pavilion, Bexhill; Yapi Kredi Bankasi HQ, Gebze, Istanbul; North End, Blair Castle, 1999 (jtly RIBA award). Trustee: Dunkeld Chapter House Mus., 2001–; Nat. Mus of Scotland, 2011–. *Recreations:* hydro electric power generation, boats, art. *Address:* Blair Castle, Blair Atholl, Pitclochry PH18 5TJ. *T:* (01796) 481355. *Club:* Royal Highland Yacht.

TROUGHTON, Peter, PhD; Chairman, 4RF Ltd, 1999–2012; *b* 26 Aug. 1943; *s* of late Frank Sydney Troughton and of Joan Vera Troughton (*née* Root); *m* 1967, Joyce Uncles; two *s*. *Educ:* City Univ. (BSc Eng); University College London (PhD). Technical apprentice, Plessey Co., then Post Office apprentice, 1959; PO scholarship, 1964; research for PhD, 1967; develt of microprocessor techniques for control of telephone switching systems, 1970; Dep. Gen. Manager, South Central Telephone Area, 1977; Head of Ops, Prestel, 1979; Gen. Manager, City Telephone Area, 1980; Regional Dir, British Telecom London, 1983; Man. Dir, British Telecom Enterprises, 1984–86; Dir and Partner, Alan Patricof Associates, 1986–88, non-exec. Dir, 1988–90; Man. Dir and Chief Exec. Officer, Telecom Corp. of NZ, 1988–92; Chairman: Trans Power (NZ National Power Grid) Estabt Bd, 1990–92; Marine Air Systems, then MAS Technology Ltd, 1993–98; Troughton, Swier and Associates, 1996–99. Director: Crown Health Enterprise Develt Unit, NZ, 1992–93; Electricity Supply Industry Reform Unit, Vic, Australia, 1993–95. Advr to NZ govt, 1993–94; Special Advr to Vic. Govt on reform and privatisation of electricity, gas and aluminium industries, 1995–99; Advr to Australian Davos Connection, World Econ. Forum, for conf. on energy in 21st century, 1998–2000. Mem., State Owned Enterprises Steering Cttee, 1992–93. Mem., NZ Business Round Table, 1988–92; Chm., Twyford and Dist Round Table, 1981–82. NZ Chief Exec. of the Year Award, 1991. NZ Commemoration Medal, 1990. *Publications:* articles and papers on microwave systems, computers, communications, and on restructuring, regulation and privatisation of utility industries. *Recreations:* travel, archaeology, bridge. *Club:* Wellington (NZ).

TROUGHTON, Peter John Charles, CBE 2015; Chairman, Lowland Investment Co. plc, since 2012 (non-executive Director, since 1990); *b* 18 June 1948; *s* of Sir Charles Hugh Willis Troughton, CBE, MC, TD and (Constance) Gillean (*née* Mitford), DL; *m* 1977, Sarah Rose Colman (*see* S. R. Troughton); one *s* two *d*. *Educ:* Radley Coll.; Trinity Coll., Cambridge (MA Hons); Harvard Business Sch. (AMP 1987). Joined HM Diplomatic Service 1970; FCO, 1970–72; Jakarta, 1972–75; First Sec., FCO, 1975–79; W. H. Smith Gp plc, 1979–95: Managing Director: News, 1988–91; Retail, 1991–95; Dir, 1991–95; Chief Executive: Rothschild Asset Mgt Internat. Ltd, 1995–99; First Arrow Investment Mgt Ltd, 2000–04; Dir, J. Rothschild Services Ltd, 2005–10. Non-executive Director: Archant Ltd (formerly Eastern Counties Newspaper Gp), 1991– (Vice-Chm., 2006–); Waverton Global Investments plc (formerly JOHIM Global Funds plc), 2011–; Waverton Global Funds plc, 2011–; Waverton Investment Management Ltd, 2014–. Partner, Spencer Hse Capital Mgt LLP, 2008–11. Trustee: Nat. Gall., 1988–96 (Mem., Publications Cttee, 1982–88); Nat. Gall. Trust, 1996–2007 (Hon. Treas., 2001–07); Rothschild Foundn, 2004–11; Royal Opera House Endowment Fund, 2005–; Royal Collection Trust, 2007– (Chm., Audit Cttee, 2007–); Butrint Foundn, 2008–11; Chm., National Gallery Publications Ltd, 1988–96. Mem. Council, 2005– (Chm., 2006–14), Pro Chancellor, 2013–, Univ. of Bath. Gov., St Mary's Sch., Calne, 1992–2002. Mem., Soc. of Dilettanti, 2008–. *Recreations:* reading, walking. *Address:* The Lynch House, Upper Wanborough, near Swindon, Wilts SN4 0BZ. *T:* (01793) 790385. *Clubs:* Brooks's, Pratt's.

TROUGHTON, Sarah Rose; Lord-Lieutenant of Wiltshire, since 2012; *b* London, 3 May 1953; *d* of Sir Timothy (James Alan) Colman, *qv*; *m* 1977, Peter John Charles Troughton, *qv*; one *s* two *d*. Lady-in-Waiting to Duchess of Kent, 1992–99. Member, Council: Friends of Tate Gall., 1983–89; Tate Patrons of British Art, 1985–90; American Mus. in Britain, 2001–09; Trustee, Chelsea Physic Garden, 2003–15 (Chm., 2009–15). Trustee, Wilts and Swindon Community Foundn, 2001–. Mem., Wiltshire House Hostel, 1989–2004. President or Patron, 2012–: Wilts Community Foundn; Naomi House; Community First; Youth Action Wilts; Friends of Salisbury Cathedral; Wilts Victoria Co. Hist.; Wessex MS Centre; Relate; Mediation Plus; ABF the Soldiers' Charity; CPRE; Wilts Historic Churches Trust; Order of St John; Merchant's House, Marlborough; Wilts Mus., Devizes. DL Wilts, 2006. *Recreations:* painting, gardening, grandchildren, Scotland. *Address:* The Lynch House, Upper Wanborough, Swindon, Wilts SN4 0BZ. *T:* (01793) 790385.

TROUP, (John) Edward (Astley); Tax Assurance Commissioner and second Permanent Secretary, HM Revenue and Customs, since 2012; *b* 26 Jan. 1955; *s* of Vice-Adm. Sir (John) Anthony (Rose) Troup, KCB, DSC, and of Cordelia Mary Troup; *m* 1978, Siriol Jane Martin; three *s* one *d*. *Educ:* Oundle Sch.; Corpus Christi Coll., Oxford (BA Maths 1976, MA; MSc Applied Maths 1977). ATII 1983. Admitted solicitor, 1981; joined Simmons & Simmons, 1979, Partner, 1985–95, 1997–2004; HM Treasury: Special Advr on Tax, 1995–97; Dir, Business and Indirect Tax, 2004–10; Dir-Gen., Tax and Welfare, 2010–12. *Recreations:* cinema, cycling, Beethoven, birdwatching, art, astronomy, the Anglo-Saxons and the landscape, buildings and history of the British Isles. *Address:* HM Revenue and Customs, 100 Parliament Street, SW1A 2BQ.

TROUSDELL, Lt Gen. Sir Philip (Charles Cornwallis), KBE 2004; CB 2000; General Officer Commanding Northern Ireland, 2003–05; *b* 13 Aug. 1948; *s* of late Col Philip James Cornwallis Trousdell, OBE and Doreen Mary Trousdell (*née* Durdle); *m* 1986, Sally Caroline Slade Parker; one *s* two *d*. *Educ:* Berkhamsted; RMA, Sandhurst. Commnd Royal Irish Rangers, 1968: CO, 1st Bn, 1989–91; commanded 48 Gurkha Bde, 1992–93; Dir, Public Relns (Army), 1994–97; COS, HQ Land Comd, 1997–2000; Dep. Comdr (Ops) Stabilisation Force, Bosnia Herzegovina, 2000; Comdt, RMA Sandhurst, 2001–03. Col, Queen's Own Gurkha Transport Regt, 1993–2003; Dep. Col, 1996–2001, Col, 2001–13, Royal Irish Regt; Colonel Commandant: Media Ops Gp (Vol.), 2001–06; Bde of Gurkhas, 2003–07. Chm., Civil Nuclear Police Authy, 2011–. Chm., Corporate Battlefields, 2007–13. Chairman: Gurkha Welfare Trust, 2003–07; Army Mus Ogilby Trust, 2012–; Help for Heroes Recovery Centres, 2014– (Trustee, 2012–). *Recreations:* reading, bicycling, wine. *Address:* Riverside House, Fordingbridge SP6 2JS. *Club:* Army and Navy.

TROWELL, Prof. Brian Lewis, PhD; Heather Professor of Music and Fellow of Wadham College, University of Oxford, 1988–96, now Emeritus; *b* 21 Feb. 1931; *s* of Richard Lewis and Edith J. R. Trowell; *m* 1958, Rhianon James; two *d*. *Educ:* Christ's Hospital; Gonville and Caius Coll., Cambridge. MA 1959; PhD 1960. Asst Lectr, later Lectr, in Music, Birmingham Univ., 1957–62; freelance scholar, conductor, opera producer, lecturer and editor, 1962–67; Head of BBC Radio opera, 1967–70; Reader in Music, 1970, Professor of Music, 1973, King Edward Prof. of Music, 1974–88, KCL. Regents' Prof., Univ. of California at Berkeley, 1970; Vis. Gresham Prof. of Music, City Univ., 1971–74. Pres., Royal Musical Assoc., 1983–88. Hon. RAM 1972; Hon. FGSM 1972; FRCM 1977; FTCL 1978; Fellow: Curwen Inst., 1987; KCL, 1997. Chm., Editorial Cttee, Musica Britannica, 1983–93. *Publications:* The Early Renaissance, Pelican History of Music vol. ii, 1963; Four Motets by John Plummer, 1968; (ed jtly) John Dunstable: Complete Works, ed M. F. Bukofzer, 2nd edn, 1970; (ed) Invitation to

Medieval Music, vol. 3 1976, vol. 4 1978; Elgar Complete Edition, vol. 16: solo songs with piano, 1901–1934, 2010; opera translations; contrib. dictionaries of music and articles in learned journals. *Recreations:* theatre, reading, gardening. *Address:* 5 Tree Lane, Iffley Village, Oxford OX4 4EY.

TROWELL, Stephen Mark; QC 2015; *b* Hemel Hempstead, 5 Oct. 1967; *s* of Peter Trowell and Judith Trowell; *m* 1997, Leila; two *s* one *d. Educ:* Dame Alice Owens Sch.; Keble Coll., Oxford (BA 1989); Wolfson Coll., Oxford (DPhil 1992). Called to the Bar, Middle Temple, 1995. *Recreations:* family, theatre, reading. *Address:* 1 Hare Court, Temple, EC4Y 7BE. *T:* (020) 1797 7070. *E:* clerks@1hc.com.

TROWER, William Spencer Philip; QC 2001; a Deputy High Court Judge (Chancery Division), since 2007; *b* 28 Dec. 1959; *s* of late Anthony Gosselin Trower and Catherine Joan Trower (*née* Kellett); *m* 1986, Mary Louise Chastel de Boinville; four *d. Educ:* Eton Coll.; Christ Church, Oxford (MA); City Univ. (Dip. Law). Called to the Bar, Lincoln's Inn, 1983, Bencher, 2009. Mem., Insolvency Rules Cttee, 2000–11. Mem. Council, Insolvency Lawyers' Assoc., 2005–. *Publications:* (ed jtly) The Law and Practice of Corporate Administrations, 1994, 2nd edn as Corporate Administrations and Rescue Procedures, 2004; (contrib.) Montgomery and Ormerod on Fraud: Criminal Law and Procedure, 2008; (consulting ed.) Parry on Transaction Avoidance in Insolvencies, 2011; (consulting ed.) O'Dea on Schemes of Arrangement: law and practice, 2012. *Recreations:* family, gardening, countryside, theatre. *Address:* 3–4 South Square, Gray's Inn, WC1R 5HP. *T:* (020) 7696 9900. *Club:* Garrick.

TROWLER, Isabelle; Chief Social Worker for England (Children and Families), since 2013; *b* Nantwich, Cheshire, 10 Oct. 1967; *d* of Dr Eric Trowler and Pat Trowler (*née* Fairclough, now Paxton); two *s. Educ:* Poly. of North London (BSc Sociol.); London Sch. of Econs and Pol Sci. (MSc Social Policy and Social Work). Social Worker, London Bor. of Lewisham, 1996–98; Commng Manager, London Bor. of Hackney, 1998–2001; Hd, Youth Support Develt, Royal Bor. of Kensington and Chelsea, 2001–05; Asst Dir, Children's Social Work, London Bor. of Hackney, 2005–11; Dir, Morning Lane Associates, 2010–13. *Publications:* (ed jtly) Social Work Reclaimed, 2011. *Recreations:* reading, writing and arithmetic.

See also R. Trowler.

TROWLER, Rebecca; QC 2012; *b* Nantwich, Cheshire, 20 Oct. 1965; *d* of Dr Eric Trowler and Pat Trowler (*née* Fairclough, now Paxton); civil partnership 2008, Dr Alison Mears; one *d. Educ:* Manchester High Sch.; London Guildhall Univ. (BSc 1st Cl. Hons Psychol.). Called to the Bar, Gray's Inn, 1995; in practice as a barrister, specialising in criminal law, 1999–. *Publications:* (contrib.) Taylor on Criminal Appeals, 2nd edn 2012. *Recreations:* music, art, food, film, football. *Address:* Doughty Street Chambers, 53–54 Doughty Street, WC1N 2LS. *E:* r.trowler@doughtystreet.co.uk.

See also I. Trowler.

TROWSDALE, Prof. John, PhD; FMedSci; Professor of Immunology, and Head of Division of Immunology, Department of Pathology, University of Cambridge, since 1997; *b* 8 Feb. 1949; *s* of Roy R. Trowsdale and Doris Trowsdale (*née* Graham); *m* 1971, Susan Price; two *s* one *d. Educ:* Beverley Grammar Sch.; Univ. of Birmingham (BSc 1970; PhD 1973). European Fellow, Biochemical Soc., Gif-sur-Yvette, France, 1973–75; Res. Fellow, Scripps Clinic and Res. Foundn, Calif, 1975–78; SRC Res. Fellow, Genetics Lab., Univ. of Oxford, 1978–79; Imperial Cancer Research Fund: ICRF Fellow, 1979–82; Res. Scientist, 1982–85; Sen. Scientist, 1986–90; Prin. Scientist, 1990–97. Member: Council, European Fedn of Immunogenetics, 1995–98; Sci. Adv. Bd, Onyvax, 1997–; Chm., Histocompatibility and Immunogenetics Affinity Gp, British Soc. of Histocompatibility and Immunogenetics, 1996–99. FMedSci 2000. *Publications:* (jtly) Advanced Immunology, 1996; res. papers in science jls. *Recreations:* playing rock, jazz and classical music, painting. *Address:* Department of Pathology, Tennis Court Road, Cambridge CB2 1QP. *T:* (01223) 333711.

TROY, Jill Mary; Her Honour Judge Troy; a Circuit Judge, since 2013. *Educ:* Ralph Thoresby High Sch., Leeds; Lady Margaret Hall, Oxford (MA Juris.). Called to the Bar, Middle Temple, 1986; in practice as barrister, 1986–2013; a Dep. Dist Judge, 2008–13; a Recorder, 2008–13.

TRUDGILL, Prof. Peter John, FBA 1989; Professor of English Linguistics, University of Fribourg, 1998–2005, now Emeritus; Hon. Professor of Sociolinguistics, University of East Anglia, since 2005; Professor of Sociolinguistics, Agder University, Norway, since 2006; *b* 7 Nov. 1943; *s* of John Trudgill and Hettie Jean Trudgill (*née* Gooch); *m* 1980, Jean Marie Hannah. *Educ:* City of Norwich Sch.; King's Coll., Cambridge (BA; MA 1966); Edinburgh Univ. (Dip Gen Linguistics 1967; PhD 1971). Asst Lectr, Lectr, Reader, Prof., Dept of Linguistic Sci., Univ. of Reading, 1970–86; Reader, 1986–87, Prof. of Sociolinguistics, 1987–92, Essex Univ.; Prof. of English Linguistics, Univ. of Lausanne, 1993–98. Vis. Prof. at Univs of Hong Kong, Bergen, Aarhus, Illinois, Stanford, Osmania, Tokyo International Christian, ANU, Texas Austin, Toronto, Canterbury (NZ). Fellow: Norwegian Acad. of Sci and Letters, 1995; Royal Norwegian Acad. of Scis, 1996. Lifetime Hon. Mem., Linguistic Soc. of America, 2011. Hon. PhD: Uppsala, 1995; UEA, 2002; La Trobe, 2005. *Publications:* The Social Differentiation of English in Norwich, 1974; Sociolinguistics: an introduction, 1974, 4th edn 2000; Accent, Dialect and the School, 1975; Sociolinguistic Patterns in British English, 1978; (with A. Hughes) English Accents and Dialects, 1979; (with J. K. Chambers) Dialectology, 1980; (with J. M. Hannah) International English, 1982, 3rd edn 1994; On Dialect, 1983; Coping with America, 1983, 2nd edn 1985; Language in the British Isles, 1984; Applied Sociolinguistics, 1984; Dialects in Contact, 1986; The Dialects of England, 1990; (with J. K. Chambers) English Dialects: studies in grammatical variation, 1991; (with L. Andersson) Bad Language, 1991; Introducing Language and Society, 1992; Dialects, 1994; (with L. Bauer) Language Myths, 1998; Sociolinguistic Variation and Change, 2002; New Dialect Formation, 2004; Sociolinguistic Typology: social determinants of linguistic complexity, 2011. *Recreation:* Norwich City FC. *Address:* School of Language and Communication Studies, University of East Anglia, Norwich NR4 7TJ.

TRUDINGER, Prof. Neil Sidney, PhD; FRS 1997; FAA; Professor of Mathematics, Australian National University, since 1973; *b* 20 June 1942; *s* of Laurence Robert Trudinger and Dorothy Winifred Trudinger; *m* 1st, 1964, Patricia Robyn Saunders; one *s* one *d*; 2nd, 1991, Tess Rosario Valdez. *Educ:* Univ. of New England, Australia (BSc Hons 1962); Stanford Univ., USA (MS 1965; PhD 1966). FAA 1978. Courant Instructor, New York Univ., 1966–67; Lectr, then Sen. Lectr, Macquarie Univ., Australia, 1967–70; Reader, then Prof., Univ. of Qld, 1970–73; Australian National University: Head, Dept of Pure Maths, 1973–78; Director: Commonwealth Special Res. Centre for Mathematical Analysis, 1982–96; Centre for Maths and its Applications, 1991–93; Dean, Sch. of Math. Scis, 1992–2000; Prof., Northwestern Univ., 1989–93. *Publications:* Elliptic Partial Differential Equations of the Second Order, 1977, 2nd edn 1983. *Address:* Mathematical Sciences Institute, Australian National University, Canberra, ACT 0200, Australia. *T:* (2) 62492957.

TRUE, family name of **Baron True**.

TRUE, Baron *cr* 2010 (Life Peer), of East Sheen in the County of Surrey; **Nicholas Edward True,** CBE 1993; Private Secretary to Leader of the Opposition, and Director, Opposition Whips' Office, House of Lords, 1997–2010; *b* 31 July 1951; *s* of Edward Thomas True and Kathleen Louise True (*née* Mather); *m* 1979, Anne-Marie Elena Kathleen Blanco Hood; two *s* one *d. Educ:* Nottingham High Sch.; Peterhouse, Cambridge (BA Hons 1973; MA 1978). Mem., Cons. Res. Dept, 1975–82; Asst to Cons. Party Dep. Leader, 1978–82; Special Advr to Sec. of State for Health and Social Security, 1982–86; Dir, Public Policy Unit, 1986–90; Dep. Head, Prime Minister's Policy Unit, 1991–95; Special Advr, Prime Minister's Office, 1997. Councillor (C), Richmond-upon-Thames, 1986–90, 1998– (Dep. Leader, 2002–06; Leader of Opposition, 2006–10; Leader, 2010–). Mem., Leaders' Cttee, London Councils, 2010–. Member: House Cttee, H of L, 2012–15; Procedure Cttee, H of L, 2015–. Mem. Bd, Royal Parks Agency, 2012–. Trustee: Olga Havel Foundn, 1990–94; Sir Harold Hood's Charitable Trust, 1996–; Richmond Civic Trust, 2006–10. *Publications:* articles in newspapers, jls etc; pamphlets and papers on policy matters. *Recreations:* Byzantium, Italy, gardens, books. *Address:* 114 Palewell Park, East Sheen, SW14 8JH. *T:* (020) 8876 9628; Contrada Salino 15, San Ginesio, Macerata, Italy. *Clubs:* Beefsteak, Brooks's, Travellers.

TRULUCK, Maj. Gen. Ashley Ernest George, CB 2001; CBE 1997; Managing Director, Kerykeion Services (formerly Ashley Truluck Associates), since 2003; *b* 7 Dec. 1947; *s* of Maj. George William Truluck, RA and Elizabeth Truluck (*née* Kitchener); *m* 1976, Jennifer Bell; one *s* one *d. Educ:* Harvey's Sch.; RMA Sandhurst; BA. Regtl duty, Bde of Gurkhas, Malaysia, Hong Kong, Nepal, 1969–74; ADC to Maj. Gen., Bde of Gurkhas, and Comdr FARELF, 1974–75; Commns Officer, Guards Armoured Bde, 1976–77; sc, 1978–79; GSO2, MoD, 1980–81; Sqn Comdr, BAOR, UK, 1982–84; Dir, Staff RMCS, 1984–86; Regt Comdr, BAOR, 1986–88; Col Army Staff Duties, 1989–90; HCSC, 1990; Comdt, Royal Sch. of Signals, 1991–92; RCDS, 1993; Brig. Gen. Staff, UK Land Comd, 1994–96; Dir, Attack Helicopter, 1997–98; ACOS, SHAPE, 1998–2000. Chief Exec., Gtr London Magistrates' Courts Authy, 2001–03. Leader, MoD Information Mgt Study, 2004–05. Nat. Project Manager, Fire and Rescue Services Communications, 2005–10. Strategic Defence Advr, IBM i2, 2010–14. Col Comdt, RCS, 2001–07; Adm., Royal Signals Yacht Club, 2003–12. Chairman: Defence Housing Review, 2001; London Criminal Justice Bd, 2001–03. Dir, The Cultural Experience, 2012–. Chairman: Royal Signals Benevolent Fund, 2002–12; Gurkha Welfare Trust (Wessex and S), 2010–; Royal Signals Trustee Ltd, 2012–14; Chalke Valley Community Hub Ltd, 2013–; Soc. for Army Historical Res., 2014–. FInstD 2002; MRUSI 2004. *Recreations:* offshore sailing, country pursuits, sketching, military history. *Clubs:* Army and Navy, Ocean Cruising; Cape Horners.

TRUMP, Donald John; Chairman and President, Trump Organization; *b* New York, 14 June 1946; *s* of Fred C. Trump and Mary Trump; *m* 1st, 1977, Ivana Zelnicek (marr. diss. 1991); two *s* one *d*; 2nd, 1993, Marla Maples (marr. diss. 1999); one *d*; 3rd, 2005, Melania Knauss; one *s. Educ:* New York Military Acad.; Wharton Sch. of Finance, Univ. of Pennsylvania (BS 1968). Joined father's co., Trump Organization; Chm. and CEO, Trump Hotels & Casino Resorts, 1995–2004; Chm., Trump Entertainment Resorts Inc., 2005–; holdings include: Trump Tower, Trump Palace, Trump Plaza, Trump World Tower, Trump International Hotel and Tower, New York; Trump Plaza, Mar-A-Lago, Florida; Trump Plaza Hotel Casino, Trump Castle Casino, Trump Taj Mahal Casino Resort, Atlantic City; acquired 50% stake in Empire State Bldg, 1994. Co-Exec. Prod., TV series, The Apprentice, 2004–. Launched Trump World Magazine, 2004. *Publications:* Trump: the way to the top, 2004; *jointly:* Trump: the art of the deal, 1988; Trump: surviving at the top, 1990; The Art of Survival, 1991; The Art of the Comeback, 1997; The America We Deserve, 2000; Trump: how to get rich, 2004; Trump: think like a billionaire, 2004; Trump Strategies for Real Estate, 2005; Why We Want You to Be Rich: two men - one message, 2006; Take Command, 2006; Trump University Real Estate 101, 2006; Trump University Marketing 101, 2006; Trump 101: the way to success, 2006; Trump University Entrepreneurship 101, 2007; Think Big and Kick Ass: in business and life, 2007; Trump - Never Give Up: how I turned my biggest challenges into success, 2008; Think Like a Champion: an informal education in business and life, 2009. *Address:* Trump Organization, 725 Fifth Avenue, New York, NY 10022, USA.

TRUMPINGTON, Baroness *cr* 1980 (Life Peer), of Sandwich in the County of Kent; **Jean Alys Barker,** DCVO 2005; PC 1992; an Extra Baroness in Waiting to the Queen, since 1998; *d* of late Arthur Edward Campbell-Harris, MC and late Doris Marie Robson; *m* 1954, William Alan Barker (*d* 1988); one *s. Educ:* privately in England and France. Land Girl to Rt Hon. David Lloyd George, MP, 1940–41; Foreign Office, Bletchley Park, 1941–45; European Central Inland Transport Orgn, 1945–49; Sec. to Viscount Hinchingbrooke, MP, 1950–52. Conservative Councillor, Cambridge City Council, Trumpington Ward, 1963–73; Mayor of Cambridge, 1971–72; Deputy Mayor, 1972–73; Conservative County Councillor, Cambridgeshire, Trumpington Ward, 1973–75; Hon. Councillor of the City of Cambridge, 1975–. A Baroness in Waiting (Government Whip), 1983–85 and 1992–97; Parly Under-Sec. of State, DHSS, 1985–87, MAFF, 1987–89; Minister of State, MAFF, 1989–92. UK Delegate to UN Status of Women Commn, 1979–82. Member: Air Transport Users' Cttee, 1972–80 (Dep. Chm. 1978–79, Chm. 1979–80); Bd of Visitors to HM Prison, Pentonville, 1975–81; Mental Health Review Tribunal, 1975–81. Gen. Commissioner of Taxes, 1976–83. Pres., Assoc. of Heads of Independent Schs, 1980–89. Steward, Folkestone Racecourse, 1980–92. Hon. Fellow, Lucy Cavendish Coll., Cambridge, 1980. Hon. FRCPath 1992; Hon. ARCVS 1994; Hon. Mem., BVA, 1995. JP Cambridge, 1972–75, South Westminster, 1976–82. Officier, Ordre de la Mérite (France), 2005. *Publications:* Coming up Trumps: a memoir, 2014. *Recreations:* bridge, racing, collecting antiques, needlepoint. *Address:* House of Lords, SW1A 0PW. *Clubs:* Farmers, Grillions.

TRUNDLE, Shirley Jean, CBE 2004 (OBE 1999); Director, Countryside and Nature, Department for Environment, Food and Rural Affairs, since 2015; *b* 28 Feb. 1958; *d* of Derek and Jean Hayles; *m* 1979, John Malcolm Trundle; one *s* two *d. Educ:* Guildford High Sch.; Newnham Coll., Cambridge (MA); St Catharine's Coll., Cambridge (MPhil). Entered DES, 1981, subseq. DFE, then DFEE; Private Sec. to Sec. of State for Educn and Sci., 1986–87; Principal, 1987–93; Divl Manager, Higher Educn Policy and Funding, 1993–96; Sec. to Nat. Cttee of Inquiry into Higher Educn (Dearing Cttee), 1996–97; Head, Childcare Unit, 1998–99; Dir, Opportunity and Diversity Gp, 1999–2001; Department for Work and Pensions: Dir, Universal Banking Prog., 2001–03; Dir, Welfare Strategy and Performance, 2003–06; Dir, Benefit Strategy, 2006–08; Dir, Families, 2008–13, Care and Adoption, 2013–14, DCSF, subseq. DFE; Dir, Sustainable Land Mgt and Livestock Farming, DEFRA, 2014–15. *Recreations:* family, music, food. *Address:* Department for Environment, Food and Rural Affairs, Nobel House, 17 Smith Square, SW1P 3JR.

TRURO, Bishop of, since 2008; **Rt Rev. Timothy Martin Thornton;** DL; *b* 14 April 1957; *s* of John and Mary Thornton; *m* 1978, Siân Evans; one *s* one *d. Educ:* Southampton Univ. (BA Theol. 1978); St Stephen's House, Oxford (Cert. Theol.); KCL (MA Ecclesl Hist. 1997). Ordained deacon, 1980, priest, 1981; Asst Curate, Todmorden, Dio. Wakefield, 1980–83; Priest i/c, Walsden, 1983–85; Chaplain, UC Cardiff, 1985–87; Bishop's Chaplain: Wakefield, 1987–91; London, 1991–94; Principal, N Thames Ministerial Trng Course, 1994–98; Vicar of Kensington, 1998–2001; Area Bishop of Sherborne, 2001–08. DL Dorset, 2007. *Address:* Lis Escop, Truro, Cornwall TR3 6QQ.

TRURO, Dean of; *see* Bush, Very Rev. R. C.

TRUSCOTT, Baron *cr* 2004 (Life Peer), of St James's in the City of Westminster; **Peter Derek Truscott;** parliamentarian, businessman, author and political analyst; *b* 20 March 1959; *s* of late Derek Truscott and of Dorothy Truscott; *m* 1991, Svetlana, *d* of late Col Prof. Nicolai Chernikov and Svetlana Chernikova. *Educ:* Newton Abbot Grammar Sch.; Exeter Coll., Oxford (History Prize; BA 1981, MA 1985, DPhil 1985, Modern History). Labour Party Organiser, 1986–89; NACRO, 1989–94. Councillor, Colchester Borough Council, 1988–92; contested (Lab) Torbay, 1992. Member: TGWU, 1986–2009; Co-op Party,

1987–2009; posts in Trade Union and Labour movements. MEP (Lab) Hertfordshire, 1994–99; contested (Lab) Eastern Reg., 1999. European Parliament: Labour spokesman on foreign affairs and defence, 1997–99; Vice-Pres., Cttee on Security and Disarmament, 1994–99; Mem., Foreign Affairs Cttee, 1994–99; Substitute Member: Regl Policy Cttee, 1994–97; Economic, Monetary and Industrial Policy Cttee, 1997–99. Deptl liaison peer, MoD, 2004–05; Mem., Select European Sub-Cttee C, H of L, 2005–06, 2007–09; Parly Under-Sec. of State for Energy, DTI, and DTI spokesman in H of L, 2006–07. Dir, Energy Enterprises Ltd, 2008–; non-executive Director: Gulf Keystone Petroleum, 2008–12 (Member: Remuneration Cttee, 2008–12; Nomination Cttee, 2012; Audit Cttee, 2012 (Chm., 2010–12)); Eastern Petroleum Corp., 2008–11; African Minerals Ltd, 2008–09 (Consultant, 2009–12); 25 Jermyn Street St James's (RTM) Co. Ltd, 2012–; Chm., 9 Lansdown Place West Ltd, 2014–; Member, Advisory Board: OPUS Exec. Partners, 2008–11 (Chm., 2008–11); VAL Energy, 2009–11; Advr, Japan Bank for Internat. Cooperation, 2009–10. Associate Res. Fellow, IPPR, 2000–06; Associate Fellow, RUSI, 2005–06, 2008– (Mem., Internat. Adv. Bd, 2011–). Fellow, Industry and Parlt Trust. Mem., Internat. and Domestic Sub-Cttee, Labour Party NEC, 1996–97. Sch. governor, 1988–92. *Publications:* Russia First, 1997; European Defence, 2000; Kursk, 2002; Putin's Progress, 2004; The Ascendancy of Political Risk Management, 2006; European Energy Security, 2009; numerous articles. *Recreations:* walking, music, theatre, swimming, travel. *Address:* House of Lords, SW1A 0PW. *Club:* Ritz.

TRUSCOTT, Ian Derek, PhD; QC (Scot.) 1997; *b* 7 Nov. 1949; *s* of Derek and Jessie Truscott; *m* 1972, Julia Elizabeth Bland; four *s*. *Educ:* Edinburgh Univ. (LLB Hons 1971); Leeds Univ. (LLM 1974); Strathclyde Univ. (PhD 2004). Solicitor, 1973–87, 2013–; Faculty of Advocates, 1988–2013; called to the Bar, Gray's Inn, 1995. Pt-time Judge (formerly Chm.), Employment Tribunals, England and Wales, 2002–. Vis. Prof. of Law, Strathclyde Univ., 1999–2010. *Recreations:* walking, snow dome collecting. *Address:* Albany House, Albany Street, Edinburgh EH1 3QR. *T:* (0131) 557 1545. *Club:* Royal Northern and University (Aberdeen).

TRUSCOTT, Sir Ralph (Eric Nicholson), 4th Bt *cr* 1909, of Oakleigh, East Grinstead, Sussex; *b* 21 Feb. 1966; *o s* of Sir George James Irving Truscott, 3rd Bt and of Yvonne Dora Truscott (*née* Nicholson); *S* father, 2001, but his name does not appear on the Official Roll of the Baronetage. *Educ:* Sherborne Sch. *Heir:* none.

TRUSS, Rt Hon. Elizabeth (Mary); PC 2014; MP (C) South West Norfolk, since 2010; Secretary of State for Environment, Food and Rural Affairs, since 2014; *b* Oxford, 26 July 1975; *d* of John Kenneth Truss and Priscilla Mary Truss; *m* 2000, Hugh O'Leary; two *d*. *Educ:* Roundhay Sch., Leeds; Merton Coll., Oxford (MA PPE). Commercial Analyst, Shell International, 1996–2000; Commercial Manager and Regulatory Econs Dir, Cable & Wireless, 2000–05; Divl Man. Dir, Communication Gp, 2005–07; Dep. Dir, Reform, 2007–09. Parly Under-Sec. of State, DFE, 2012–14. Contested (C): Hemsworth, 2001; Calder Valley, 2005. *Recreations:* food, design, cinema. *Address:* House of Commons, SW1A 0AA. *T:* (020) 7219 7151. *E:* elizabeth.truss.mp@parliament.uk.

TRUSS, Lynne; writer; *b* 31 May 1955; *d* of Ernest Edward Truss and Joan Dorothy Truss. *Educ:* UCL (BA 1st cl. Hons (English Lang. and Lit.) 1977; Fellow 2004). Literary Ed., The Listener, 1986–90; columnist, TV Critic and Sports Columnist, The Times, 1990–2000. Writer, BBC drama series: Acropolis Now, 2000, 2002; A Certain Age, 2002, 2005; Inspector Steine, 2007, 2008, 2009, 2011. FRSL 2004. Hon. DLitt Brighton, 2005; DUniv Open, 2006; Hon. DFA, New York Sch. of Visual Arts, 2006. *Publications: novels:* With One Lousy Free Packet of Seed, 1994; Making the Cat Laugh, 1995; Tennyson's Gift, 1996; Going Loco, 1999; Cat Out of Hell, 2014; *non-fiction:* Tennyson and his Circle, 1999, rev. edn 2014; Eats, Shoots & Leaves, 2003 (Book of the Year, British Book Awards, and USA Today, 2004); Talk to the Hand, 2005; Get Her Off the Pitch, 2009; *drama scripts:* A Certain Age, 2007; Hell's Bells, 2012. *Address:* c/o David Higham Associates, 7th Floor, Waverley House, 7–12 Noel Street, W1F 8GQ. *T:* (020) 7434 5900, *Fax:* (020) 7437 1072. *E:* dha@davidhigham.co.uk, info@lynnetruss.com. *W:* www.lynnetruss.com.

TRUSTRAM EVE; *see* Eve, family name of Baron Silsoe.

TRUSWELL, Prof. (Arthur) Stewart, AO 2001; MD, DSc, FRCP, FRACP; Professor of Human Nutrition, University of Sydney, 1978–99, now Emeritus; *b* 18 Aug. 1928; *s* of George Truswell and Molly Truswell (*née* Stewart-Hess); *m* 1st, 1956, Sheila McGregor (marr. diss. 1983); four *s*; 2nd, 1986, Catherine Hull; two *d*. *Educ:* Ruthin Sch., Clwyd; Liverpool Univ.; Cape Town Univ. (MB, ChB 1952, MD 1959); DSc Sydney 1998. FRCP 1975; FRACP 1980. Registrar in Pathology, Cape Town Univ., 1954; Registrar in Med., Groote Schuur Hosp., 1955–57; Research Bursar, Clin. Nutrition Unit, Dept of Med., Cape Town Univ., 1958 and 1959; Adams Meml Trav. Fellowship to London, 1960; Sen. Fellow, Clin. Nutrition, Tulane Univ., USA, 1961; Res. Officer, Clin. Nutrition Unit, Cape Town Univ., 1962; Sen. Mem., Scientific Staff, MRC Atheroma Research Unit, Western Infirmary, Glasgow, 1963 and 1964; full-time Lectr, then Sen. Lectr in Med. and Consultant Gen. Physician, Cape Town Univ. and Groote Schuur Hosp., 1965–71; Warden of Med. Students' Residence, Cape Town Univ., 1967–69; Prof. of Nutrition and Dietetics, Queen Elizabeth Coll., London Univ., 1971–78. Vice-Pres., Internat. Union of Nutritional Sciences, 1985–93; Member, numerous cttees, working parties, editorial bds and socs related to nutrition. *Publications:* Human Nutrition and Dietetics, 7th edn (with S. Davidson, R. Passmore, J. F. Brock), 1979; ABC of Nutrition, 1986, 4th edn 2003; (with J. I. Mann) Essentials of Human Nutrition, 1998, 4th edn 2012; History of Research on Diet and Coronary Heart Disease, 2010; numerous research papers in sci. jls on various topics in human nutrition. *Recreations:* gardening, walking. *Address:* 23 Woonona Road, Northbridge, NSW 2063, Australia; Human Nutrition Unit, School of Molecular Bioscience, Building G08, Sydney University, Sydney, NSW 2006, Australia. *T:* (2) 93513726. *E:* stewart.truswell@sydney.edu.au.

TRUSWELL, Paul Anthony; *b* 17 Nov. 1955; *s* of John and Olive Truswell; *m* 1981, Suzanne Clare Evans; two *s*. *Educ:* Firth Park Comprehensive Sch., Sheffield; Leeds Univ. (BA Hons 1977). Journalist, Yorkshire Post newspapers, 1977–88; Local Govt Officer, Wakefield MDC, 1988–97. Member: Leeds HA, 1982–90; Leeds FHSA, 1992–96. Mem. (Lab) Leeds CC, 1982–97, 2012–. MP (Lab) Pudsey, 1997–2010. Mem., Envmtl Audit Select Cttee, 1997–99. Hon. Vice Pres., Trading Standards Inst., 2008–13. *Club:* Belle Isle Working Men's.

TRUSWELL, Stewart; *see* Truswell, A. S.

TRYON, family name of **Baron Tryon**.

TRYON, 3rd Baron *cr* 1940, of Durnford; **Anthony George Merrik Tryon,** OBE 2001; DL; *b* 26 May 1940; *s* of 2nd Baron Tryon, PC, GCVO, KCB, DSO, and Etheldreda Josephine, *d* of Sir Merrik Burrell, 7th Bt, CBE; *S* father, 1976; *m* 1973, Dale Elizabeth (*d* 1997), *d* of Barry Harper; two *s* two *d* (of whom one *s* one *d* are twins). *Educ:* Eton. Page of Honour to the Queen, 1954–56. Captain Wessex Yeomanry, 1972. Dir, Lazard Bros & Co. Ltd, 1976–83; Chairman: English & Scottish Investors Ltd, 1977–88; Swaine Adeney Brigg, 1991–93. Chm., Salisbury Cathedral Spire Trust, 1985–2000. Pres., Anglers Conservation Assoc., 1985–2000. DL Wilts, 1992. *Recreations:* fishing, shooting. *Heir:* *s* Hon. Charles George Barrington Tryon [*b* 15 May 1976; *m* 2011, Dr Katherine Anne Lyon Carroll; one *s* two *d*]. *Address:* The Mill House, Chilton Foliat, Hungerford, Berks RG17 0TG. *T:* (01488) 680738. *Clubs:* White's, Pratt's.

TSANG, Sir Donald Yam-kuen, KBE 1997 (OBE 1993); GBM 2002; Chief Executive, Hong Kong Special Administrative Region, 2005–12; *b* 7 Oct. 1944; *m* 1969, Selina Pou; two *s*. *Educ:* Harvard Univ. (MPA). Joined Govt of Hong Kong, 1967: Dep. Dir of Trade, responsible for trade with N America, 1984; Dep. Sec., Gen. Duties, responsible for Sino-British Jt Declaration, 1985; Dir of Admin, Office of Chief Sec., 1989–91; Dir-Gen. of Trade, 1991–93; Sec. for Treasury, 1993–95; Financial Sec., Hong Kong, 1995–2001; Chief Sec. for Admin, HKSAR, 2001–05. Grand Bauhinia Medal (HKSAR), 2002. *Recreations:* hiking, swimming, birdwatching. *Address:* c/o Office of Former Chief Executives, 28 Kennedy Road, Hong Kong.

TSE, Simon; Director, Contracted Customer Services, Department for Work and Pensions, since 2013; *b* Swansea, 30 May 1962; *s* of Phillip and Carol Ann Tse; *m* 1991, Elizabeth Ann Evans; two *s*. *Educ:* Bishopsgore Comprehensive Sch.; Halesowen Coll. (HND Mech. Engrg). Draughtsman, Unit Superheater Engrg, 1980–84; Dir, Welshglass Works Ltd, 1984–94; Man. Dir, MPlan Software Ltd, 1994–96; Man. Dir, 1996–2001, Business Services Dir, 2001–05, Virgin Media; mgt consultant, 2005–08; Chief Operating Officer, 2008–10, CEO, 2010–13, DVLA. Non-executive Director: Ty Hafan, 1998–2005; Phoenix, 2004–14; Maggie's Cancer Care Centre, 2008–14; Hill Community Develt Trust, Swansea, 2006–. *Address:* Department for Work and Pensions, Caxton House, Tothill Street, SW1H 9NA.

TSELENTIS, Michael; QC 2003; *b* 4 Nov. 1948; *s* of Anastasios and Helen Tselentis; *m* 1975, Jacqueline de Mowbray Niehaus; two *s*. *Educ:* Univ. of Cape Town (BA 1969; LLB 1971); Magdalen Coll., Oxford (Rhodes Schol. 1972; BCL 1975). Advocate, Supreme Court of South Africa, 1978; SC South Africa, 1989; Acting Judge, Supreme Court of South Africa, 1992; called to the Bar, Gray's Inn, 1995, Bencher, 2008; in practice at the Bar, specialising in international commercial law and arbitration, 1996–; Chartered Arbitrator, 2008. Chm., Johannesburg Bar Council, 1993–94. FCIArb. *Recreations:* squash, swimming, running, golf, reading, music, travelling. *Address:* 20 Essex Street, WC2R 3AL. *T:* (020) 7583 9294, *Fax:* (020) 7583 1341. *E:* mtselentis@20essexst.com. *Clubs:* Oxford and Cambridge; Rand (Johannesburg).

TSIEN, Prof. Roger Yonchien, PhD; Professor of Pharmacology, Professor of Chemistry and Biochemistry, and Investigator, Howard Hughes Medical Institute, University of California, San Diego, since 1989; *b* New York, 1 Feb. 1952; *s* of late Hsue Chu Tsien and Yi Ying Li; *m* 1982, Wendy Globe. *Educ:* Livingston High Sch.; Harvard Univ. (BS Chem. and Physics 1972); Churchill Coll., Cambridge (PhD 1978). Postdoctoral Res. Fellow, Gonville and Caius Coll., Cambridge, 1977–81; Asst Prof., then Associate Prof., later Prof., Univ. of Calif, Berkeley, 1982–89. MNAS; Member: Inst. of Medicine; EMBO; Foreign Mem., Royal Soc., 2006. (Jtly) Wolf Foundn Prize in Medicine, 2004; (jtly) Nobel Prize in Chemistry, 2008. *Publications:* articles in jls. *Address:* Department of Pharmacology, University of California, San Diego, 9500 Gilman Drive, La Jolla, CA 92093–0647, USA.

TS'ONG, Fou; *see* Fou Ts'ong.

TSUI, Prof. Daniel C., PhD; Arthur LeGrand Doty Professor, Department of Electrical Engineering, Princeton University, since 1982; *b* Henan, China, 1939; US citizen; *m* Linda Varland. *Educ:* Pui Ching Middle Sch., Hong Kong; Augustana Coll., Rock Island, Ill; Univ. of Chicago (PhD 1967). Res. Associate, Univ. of Chicago, 1967–68; Mem. Technical Staff, Bell Labs, Murray Hill, NJ, 1968–82. Fellow, AAAS; Mem., US NAS, 1987. Nobel Prize for Physics (jtly), 1998; Benjamin Franklin Award in Physics, 1998. *Publications:* contribs to jls. *Address:* Department of Electrical Engineering, Princeton University, Princeton, NJ 08544, USA.

TSUI, Prof. Lap-Chee, OC 1991; OOnt 2000; PhD; FRS 1991; FRSC 1989; President, Victor and William Fung Foundation; Director, Qiushi Academy for Advanced Studies, Zhejiang University; Emeritus University Professor, University of Toronto, since 2006; *b* 21 Dec. 1950; *s* of Jing-Lue Hsue and Hui-Ching Wang; *m* 1977, Lan Fong (Ellen); two *s*. *Educ:* Chinese Univ. of Hong Kong (BSc Biol. 1972; MPhil 1974); Univ. of Pittsburgh (PhD Biol Scis 1979). University of Toronto: Asst Prof. 1983–88, Associate Prof. 1988–90, Depts of Med. Genetics and Med. Biophysics; Prof., Dept of Molecular and Med. Genetics, 1990–2002, Univ. Prof., 1994–2006; Hospital for Sick Children, Toronto: Sen. Res. Scientist, 1983–2002; Sellers Chair in Cystic Fibrosis Res., 1989–2002; Dir, Cystic Fibrosis Res. Prog., 1995–99; Geneticist-in-Chief, 1996–2002; Dir, Centre for Applied Genomics, 1998–2002; Vice-Chancellor, 2002–14, Sen. Advr to the Pres., 2014, Univ. of Hong Kong. Mem. of team which identified first DNA marker linked to cystic fibrosis on chromosome 7, 1985; led team which isolated the gene responsible for cystic fibrosis and defined the principal mutation, 1989. Chairman: Gordon Res. Conf. on Human Molecular Genetics, 1995; Genome Canada Task Force, 1998–99; Internat. Sci. Prog. Cttee, Human Genome Meeting 2000, 1999–2000. Trustee, Educn Foundn, Fedn of Chinese Canadian Professionals, Ontario. Hon. Fellow, World Innovation Foundn, 2001. For. Associate, NAS, USA, 2004; For. Mem., Chinese Acad. of Scis, 2009. Hon. FRCP 2005. Hon. Fellow, Hughes Hall, Cambridge, 2012. Hon. DCL: Univ. of King's Coll., Halifax, 1991; St Francis Xavier, Antigonish, NS, 1994; Hon. DSc: New Brunswick, Fredericton, 1991; Chinese Univ. of Hong Kong, 1992; York Univ., Toronto, 2001; Tel Aviv, 2005; Toronto, 2007; Aberdeen, 2007; KCL, 2009; Edinburgh, 2010; Fudan, 2013; Western, 2013. Paul di Sant'Agnese Distinguished Scientific Achievement Award, Cystic Fibrosis Foundn, USA, 1989; Gold Medal of Honor, Pharmaceutical Manufacturers' Assoc., Canada, 1989; Centennial Award, RSCan, 1989; Maclean's Honor Roll, 1989; Award of Excellence, Genetic Soc. Canada, 1990; Courvoisier Leadership Award, 1990; Gairdner Internat. Award, 1990; Cresson Medal, Franklin Inst., 1992; Mead Johnson Award, 1992; Sarsdedt Res. Prize, 1993; Sanremo Internat. Award, 1993; Lecocq Prize, Acad. des Scis, Inst de France, 1994; Henry Friesen Award, 1995; Medal of Honour, Canadian Med. Assoc., 1996; Community Service Award, Toronto Biotechnol. Initiative, 1998; Distinguished Scientist Award, MRC (Canada), 2000; Zellers Sen. Scientist Award, 2001; Killam Prize Award, Canada Council, 2002; Henry G. Friesen Internat. Prize, Friends of Canadian Inst. of Health Res., 2014. Gold Bauhinia Star (HKSAR), 2011. *Publications:* numerous papers in learned jls and invited papers and reviews. *Recreations:* cooking, travel, sightseeing. *Address:* Victor and William Fung Foundation, 33rd Floor, Alexandra House, 18 Chater Road, Central, Hong Kong. *T:* 28441051, *Fax:* 28441019.

TUAM, Archbishop of, (RC), since 1995; **Most Rev. Michael Neary;** *b* 15 April 1946. Ordained priest, 1971; Titular Bishop of Quaestoriana and Auxiliary Bishop of Tuam, 1992–95. *Address:* Archbishop's House, Tuam, Co. Galway, Ireland. *T:* (93) 24166, *Fax:* (93) 28070.

TUAM, KILLALA AND ACHONRY, Bishop of, since 2011; **Rt Rev. Patrick William Rooke;** *b* 12 April 1955; *s* of late Rev. William Warburton Lloyd Rooke and Lucy Gwendoline Rosemary Rooke; *m* 1979, Alison Isobel Forsythe; one *s* two *d*. *Educ:* Sandford Park Sch., Dublin; Gurteen Agricl Coll., Roscrea; Salisbury and Wells Theol Coll.; Open Univ. (BA); Irish Sch. of Ecumenics, Trinity Coll. Dublin (MPhil). Ordained deacon 1978, priest 1979; Curate, Mossley, 1978–81; Ballwillan, Portrush, 1981–83; Rector: Craigs, Dunaghy and Killagan, 1983–88; Ballymore, Tandragee, 1988–94; Agherton, Portstewart, 1994–2006; Canon Preb., Lisburn Cathedral, 2001–05; Archdeacon of Dalriada, 2005–06; Dean of Armagh, and Keeper of the Robinson Public Library, 2006–11. Chm., Hard Gospel Cttee, Church of Ireland, 2005–09. *Recreations:* gardening, swimming, supporting Rugby. *Address:* Bishop's House, Breaffy Woods, Cottage Road, Castlebar, Co. Mayo, Ireland. *T:* (94) 9035703. *E:* bishop@tuam.anglican.org.

TUCK, Anne Victoria, (Vicky); Director-General, International School of Geneva, since 2011; *b* 9 Jan. 1953; *m* 1977, Peter John Tuck; two *s*. *Educ:* Univ. of Kent (BA Hons French and Italian); Univ. of London Inst. of Educn (PGCE); Univ. de Lille et de Paris (Dip. Supérieur de Droit et de français des Affaires); Univ. of South Bank (MA). French and Italian teacher, Putney High Sch., 1976–81; Hd of Mod. Langs, Bromley High Sch., 1981–86; Lectr, Inst. of Educn, London Univ., 1991–94; Dep. Hd, City of London Sch. for Girls, 1994–96; Principal, Cheltenham Ladies' Coll., 1996–2011. Vice-Chm., ISC, 2009–10 (Chm., Educn Cttee, 2009–10). Pres., GSA, 2008. *Address:* International School of Geneva, 62 route de Chêne, 1208 Geneva, Switzerland.

TUCK, Anthony; *see* Tuck, J. A.

TUCK, Sir Bruce (Adolph Reginald), 3rd Bt *cr* 1910; *b* 29 June 1926; *o s* of Major Sir (William) Reginald Tuck, 2nd Bt, and Gladys Emily Kettle (*d* 1966), *d* of late N. Alfred Nathan, Wickford, Auckland, New Zealand, and *widow* of Desmond Fosberry Kettle, Auckland Mounted Rifles; *S* father, 1954; *m* 1st, 1949, Luise (marr. diss., in Jamaica, 1964), *d* of John C. Renfro, San Angelo, Texas, USA; two *s*; 2nd, 1968, Pamela Dorothy Nicholson, *d* of Alfred Nicholson, London; one *d*. *Educ:* Canford School, Dorset. Lieutenant, Scots Guards, 1945–47. *Heir: s* Richard Bruce Tuck, *b* 7 Oct. 1952. *Address:* Clopton House, 39 Mill Road, Ashley, Newmarket, Cambs CB8 9EE.

TUCK, Prof. (John) Anthony, MA, PhD; FRHistS; Professor of Medieval History, University of Bristol, 1990–93, now Emeritus; *b* 14 Nov. 1940; *s* of late Prof. John Philip Tuck and Jane Adelaide Tuck; *m* 1976, Amanda (marr. diss. 2003), *d* of late Dr L. J. Cawley, Carlton Husthwaite, near Thirsk, Yorks; two *s*. *Educ:* Newcastle upon Tyne Royal Grammar Sch.; Jesus Coll., Cambridge (BA, MA, PhD). FRHistS 1987. Lecturer in History, 1965–75, Sen. Lectr, 1975–78, Univ. of Lancaster; Master of Collingwood Coll., and Hon. Lectr in History, Univ. of Durham, 1978–87; Reader in Medieval History, Univ. of Bristol, 1987–90. Res. Associate, Oxford DNB, 1998–. Hon. Life Fellow, Collingwood Coll., Durham Univ., 1998. Clerk, Stapleford Parish Council, 2000–03. *Publications:* Richard II and the English Nobility, 1973; Crown and Nobility 1272–1461, 1985, 2nd edn 1999; (contrib.) Oxford DNB, 2004; (jtly) History of Newport, Victoria County History of Essex, 2015; contribs to various acad. jls and vols of essays. *Recreations:* walking, gardening, local history. *Address:* 8 Cherry Garden Lane, Newport, Saffron Walden, Essex CB11 3PZ.
See also R. F. Tuck.

TUCK, Jonathan Philip; Director of Library Services, Royal Holloway, University of London, since 2008; *b* 6 Sept. 1952; *s* of Philip Charles Tuck and Janetta Margaret Tuck; *m* 1982, Ann Lambert; one *s*. *Educ:* Portsmouth Grammar Sch.; Univ. of Manchester (MA); MA Oxon 1998. MCLIP (ALA 1981). John Rylands University Library of Manchester: Asst Librarian, 1978–90; Sub-Librarian, 1990–94; Asst Dir and Head of Admin, 1994–96; Asst Dir and Dep. Univ. Librarian, 1996–97; Dep. to Dir, Univ. Liby Services, and to Bodley's Librarian, Oxford Univ., 1998–2002; Fellow, Wolfson Coll., Oxford, 1998–2002; Hd, British Collections, BL, 2002–08. Chm., M25 Consortium of Academic Libraries, 2010–14. Trustee, Egham Mus., 2013–. *Publications:* contrib. articles on aspects of librarianship, library collections, web archiving and e-books. *Recreations:* book collecting, sport, especially cricket, football, Portsmouth Football Club and Forest Green Rovers. *Address:* Royal Holloway, University of London, Founder's Library, Egham, Surrey TW20 0EX. *T:* (01784) 443330.

TUCK, Prof. Richard Francis, PhD; FBA 1994; Frank G. Thomson Professor of Government, Harvard University, since 2002 (Professor of Government, 1995–2002); *b* 9 Jan. 1949; *s* of late Prof. John Philip Tuck and Jane Adelaide Tuck; *m* 1st, 1970, Mary Polwarth (marr. diss. 1993); two *s*; 2nd, 1993, Anne Malcolm; one *d*. *Educ:* Royal Grammar Sch., Newcastle upon Tyne; Jesus Coll., Cambridge (BA 1970; PhD 1976; Hon. Fellow 1997). Cambridge University: Research Fellow, 1970, Fellow, 1971–97, Jesus Coll.; Univ. Asst Lectr in History, 1973–77; Lectr in History, 1977–95; Reader in Political Theory, 1995. Vis. Fellow, Princeton Univ., 1989; Carlyle Lectr, Oxford, 1991. Foreign Hon. Mem., Amer. Acad. of Arts and Scis, 1992. *Publications:* Natural Rights Theories, 1979; Hobbes, 1989; Hobbes' Leviathan, 1991; Philosophy and Government 1572–1651, 1993; Hobbes on the Citizen, 1998; The Rights of War and Peace, 2001; Free Riding, 2008. *Recreations:* repairing houses, looking after children. *Address:* Department of Government, 1737 Cambridge Street, CGIS Knafel Building 404, Harvard University, Cambridge, MA 02138–3001, USA; 9 Park Terrace, Cambridge CB1 1JH.
See also J. A. Tuck.

TUCK, Vicky; *see* Tuck, A. V.

TUCKER, Andrew Victor Gunn; independent consultant, political analyst, since 2009; *b* 20 Dec. 1955; *s* of Kenneth Gunn Tucker and Megan Tucker; *m* 1986, Judith Anne Gibson. *Educ:* Calday Grange Grammar Sch., Wirral; University Coll., Oxford (BA Hons 1978; MA 1986). MCIL (MIL 1988). Jt Tech. Lang. Service, 1978–81; joined HM Diplomatic Service, 1981; lang. trng, SOAS, 1982; Second Sec., Dar es Salaam, 1982–85; First Secretary: on loan to Cabinet Office, 1985–87; and Press Attaché, Moscow, 1987–90; Dep. Hd, CSCE Unit, FCO, 1991–93; on loan to Auswärtiges Amt, 1993–94; Bonn, 1994–97; Dep. High Comr, Nairobi, and concurrently Alternate Perm. Rep. to UNEP and UN Centre for Human Settlements (Habitat), 1997–2000; Ambassador to Azerbaijan, 2000–03; Manager, Prism Prog., FCO, 2003–05; on interchange at GCHQ, 2005–09. Member: Friends of RSC; Winchester Russian Circle; Central Brittany Integration Assoc. *Recreations:* theatre, long walks, music, crosswords, cooking, general knowledge quizzes (finalist, BBC Brain of Britain, 2011; runner-up, BBC Mastermind, 2011; finalist, BBC Only Connect, 2012). *E:* andrewtucker@orange.fr.

TUCKER, Clive Fenemore, CB 1996; international education consultant; Director, International Affairs, Department for Education and Skills (formerly Department for Education and Employment), 1995–2006, and Department for Work and Pensions, 2001–06; *b* 13 July 1944; *s* of William Frederick Tucker and Joan Tucker; *m* 1978, Caroline Elisabeth Macready; two *d*. *Educ:* Cheltenham Grammar Sch.; Balliol Coll., Oxford (BA). Entered Ministry of Labour, 1965; Private Sec. to Perm. Sec., 1968–70; Department of Employment, later Department for Education and Employment: Principal, 1970; Asst Sec., 1978; Grade 4, 1986; Under Sec., 1987. Chm., EU Employment Cttee, 2001–03. Mem., Security Vetting Appeals Panel, 2009–15. Non-exec. Dir, RTZ Chemicals, 1987–90. Mem., Fulbright Commn, 1998–2006. Associate Dir, Specialist Schs and Acads Trust, 2006–12. *Publications:* (with C. Macready) Who Goes Where and Why: an overview and analysis of global education mobility, 2011. *Recreations:* opera, looking at pictures, tennis.

TUCKER, Elizabeth Mary; Head Mistress, Headington School, Oxford, 1982–96; *b* 20 July 1936; *d* of late Harold and Doris Tucker. *Educ:* Cheltenham Ladies' College; Newnham College, Cambridge (BA Classical Tripos 1958); King's College London (PGCE). Assistant Mistress, Queen Anne's School, Caversham, 1959–64; Head of Classics, Notting Hill and Ealing High School, GPDST, 1964–72; Head Mistress, Christ's Hospital, Hertford, 1972–82. Associate, Newnham Coll., Cambridge, 1986–99. Corporate Mem., Cheltenham Ladies' Coll., 1994. Trustee, Bloxham Project, 1982–2005; Mem., Channing Sch., Highgate, 2001– (Mem. Council, 1995–2000); Donation Gov., Christ's Hosp., 2002–. Eye-opener guide, Greeks, BM, 1997–. Commissary for Rt Rev. Dinis Sengulane, retired Bishop of Lebombo, Mozambique, 2010–. Chair, Enfield Chamber Orch., 2006–12. *Recreations:* music (piano, cello, church choir), friends and family. *Address:* 78 Manor Drive, N20 0DU. *Club:* University Women's.

TUCKER, His Honour (Henry John) Martin; QC 1975; DL; a Circuit Judge, 1981–99; Resident Judge, Winchester Combined Court Centre, 1994–99; *b* 8 April 1930; *s* of late P. A. Tucker, LDS, RCS and Mrs Dorothy Tucker (*née* Hobbs); *m* 1957, Sheila Helen Wateridge, LRAM; four *d* (one *s* decd). *Educ:* St Peter's Sch., Southbourne; Downside Sch.; Christ Church, Oxford (MA). Called to Bar, Inner Temple, 1954; Dep. Chm., Somerset QS, 1971; a Recorder of the Crown Court, 1972–81. Pres., Council of HM Circuit Judges, 1993. DL Hampshire, 1996. *Publications:* The Chingri Khal Chronicles, 2006. *Recreations:* walking occasionally; gardening gently; listening to music. *Address:* Chingri Khal, Sleepers Hill, Winchester, Hants SO22 4NB. *T:* (01962) 853927.

TUCKER, Jon(athan Leslie Tucker); Faculty Operating Officer (formerly Director of Operations), Imperial College Business School, Imperial College London, since 2009; *b* 13 Oct. 1961; *s* of Leslie Harold Tucker and Marilyn Alice Tucker; *m* 1991, Janette Roe; one *s* one *d*. *Educ:* Fitzwilliam Coll., Cambridge (MA Sci. Tripos 1984). ACIB 1987. Lloyds Bank, subseq. Lloyds TSB: various managerial appts, Retail and Commercial Banking, 1984–96; Sen. Manager, Exec. Develt, 1997–98; Asst Dir, 1999–2002, Head, 2002–07, Science Mus.; Dir, Corporate Services, Nat. Mus. of Sci. and Industry, 2007–09. *Recreations:* science, museums and heritage, gardening, wildlife, military history. *Address:* Imperial College Business School, Imperial College London, Tanaka Building, South Kensington Campus, SW7 2AZ. *T:* (020) 7594 1246. *E:* j.tucker@imperial.ac.uk.

TUCKER, Katherine Jane Greening; Her Honour Judge Tucker; a Circuit Judge, since 2014; *b* Durham; *d* of Ian and Caroline Tucker; *m* 1997, Dr Julian Paul; three *d*. *Educ:* Framwellgate Moor Comprehensive Sch.; Leicester Univ. (LLB 1st Cl. French with Dist. in spoken French). Called to the Bar, Lincoln's Inn, 1993; fee-paid Employment Judge, 2004–09; full-time Employment Judge, 2009–14. *Publications:* (ed with S. George) Discrimination in Employment (looseleaf), 2006–. *Recreations:* family, riding, cycling, sailing, walking, literature, community, school governor (primary). *E:* katherine.tucker1@judiciary.gsi.gov.uk.

TUCKER, Martin; *see* Tucker, His Honour H. J. M.

TUCKER, Prof. Maurice Edwin, PhD; FGS; Professor of Geological Sciences, Durham University, 1993–2011, now Emeritus; Hon. Professor of Earth Sciences, University of Bristol, since 2011; *b* 6 Nov. 1946; *s* of Edwin Herlin and Winifred Tucker; *m* 1970, Vivienne; one *s* one *d*. *Educ:* Wanstead High Sch., Redbridge; Durham Univ. (BSc 1st cl. Hons Geol. 1968); Reading Univ. (PhD Sedimentol. 1971). CGeol; FGS 1973. Lecturer: Univ. of Sierra Leone, 1971–72; UC Cardiff, Univ. of Wales, 1973–74; Univ. of Newcastle, 1975–82; Lindemann Trust Fellow, Univ. of Calif, Berkeley, 1980–81; Durham University: Lectr, 1983–86; Sen. Lectr, 1986–88; Reader, 1988–93; Master, University Coll., 1998–2001. Pres., Internat. Assoc. of Sedimentologists, 1998–2002 (Hon. Mem., 2010); Hon. Fellow, Acad. of Scis and Arts, Croatia, 2009. Geological Society: Moiety of Lyell Fund, 1983; Coke Medal, 1994; Percy Allen Award, British Sedimentological Res. Gp, 2008; André Dumont Medal, Geol Soc. of Belgium, 2009; Jean-Baptiste Lamarck Medal, Eur. Union of Geoscis, 2009. *Publications:* Sedimentary Petrology, 1981, 3rd edn 2001; Field Description of Sedimentary Rocks, 1982; Carbonate Sedimentology, 1990; Sedimentary Rocks in the Field, 1996, 4th edn 2011; *edited:* Modern and Ancient Lake Sediments, 1978; Techniques in Sedimentology, 1988; Carbonate Platforms, 1990; Carbonate Diagenesis, 1990; Calcretes, 1991; Dolomites, 1994; res. papers in carbonate sedimentol. and limestones. *Recreations:* tennis, ski-ing, sailing, scuba diving, modern art, North American auto licence plates. *Address:* School of Earth Sciences, University of Bristol, Bristol BS8 1RJ. *T:* (0117) 954 5400; Department of Earth Sciences, Durham University, Durham DH1 3LE.

TUCKER, Michael Edward George; self-employed farmer; equestrian consultant, since 1986; equestrian commentator: BBC, since 1990; Sky TV, since 2004; *b* Chipping Sodbury, 30 Nov. 1944; *s* of Herbert George Tucker and Margaret Betty Tucker; *m* 1972, Angela Sowden; one *s* one *d*. *Educ:* Wycliffe Coll., Stonehouse, Stroud; Royal Agricultural Coll., Cirencester (NDA). Farmer, 1961–, Partner, H. G. Tucker and Son, 1976; equestrian commentator, 1969–. Local Steward for Jockey Club, then British Horseracing Authy, Bath, Ffos Las, Chepstow and Cheltenham, 2000–. Chm., British Eventing, 2004–05. Gov., RAU (formerly RAC), Cirencester, 2012–. Professional rider: winner, Tidworth Horse Trials, 1970, 1971; Mem., British squad, Eur. Championships, Burghley, 1971. *Address:* Church Farm, Long Newnton, Tetbury, Glos GL8 8RS. *T:* (01666) 502352. *E:* meg.tucker@virgin.net.

TUCKER, Paul Geoffrey; QC 2010; *b* Scarborough, 6 March 1967; *s* of late Geoffrey William Tucker and of Janet Victoria Tucker (*née* Nevitt); *m* 1993, Ursula McCormack; three *s*. *Educ:* Raincliffe Comp. Sch.; Scarborough Sixth Form Coll.; Selwyn Coll., Cambridge (BA Hons Law 1988). Called to the Bar, Gray's Inn, 1990; in practice as a barrister, specialising in planning and envmt, Kings Chambers, Manchester, 1991–; Associate Mem., Landmark Chambers, 2011–. Attorney Gen.'s Regl Panel, 2008–10. *Recreations:* guitar, archaeology, ski-ing, hill walking, travel, reading. *Address:* Kings Chambers, 36 Young Street, Manchester M3 3FT. *T:* (0161) 832 9082, *Fax:* (0161) 835 2139. *E:* ptucker@kingschambers.com.

TUCKER, Sir Paul (Michael William), Kt 2014; Deputy Governor, Bank of England, 2009–13; *b* 24 March 1958; *s* of Brian William Tucker and late Helen May Tucker (*née* Lloyd). *Educ:* Trinity Coll., Cambridge (BA Maths, and Philosophy). Joined Bank of England, 1980; Bank Supervisor, 1980–84, and 1987; seconded to merchant bank as corporate financier, 1985–86; seconded to Hong Kong Govt as Advr to Hong Kong Securities Review Cttee, 1987–88; Mkts Area, 1988–89; Private Sec. to Gov., 1989–92; Gilt-Edged and Money Mkts Div., 1993–96 (Hd of Div., 1994–96); Hd of Monetary Assessment and Strategy Div., 1997–98; Dep. Dir, Financial Stability, 1999–2002; Exec. Dir, Markets, 2002–09; Member: Monetary Policy Cttee Secretariat, 1997–2002; Monetary Policy Cttee, 2002–13; Financial Policy Cttee (formerly Interim Financial Policy Cttee), 2011–13; Bd, Prudential Regulatory Authy, 2013; Bd, Bank for Internat. Settlements, 2009–13. Chairman: Basel Cttee on Payment and Settlement Systems; Resolution Gp, G20 Financial Stability Bd (Mem., Steering Gp). Vis. Fellow, Nuffield Coll., Oxford, 2010–; Sen. Fellow, Mossavar-Rahmani Center for Business and Govt, Harvard Kennedy Sch. and Harvard Business Sch., 2013–. Gov., Ditchley Foundn. *Club:* Athenæum.

TUCKER, Peter Louis; Chairman, Sierra Leone Law Reform Commission, 2003–08; *b* 11 Dec. 1927; *s* of Peter Louis Tucker and Marion Tucker; *m* 1st, 1955, Clarissa Mary Harleston; three *s* one *d* (and one *d* decd); 2nd, 1972, Teresa Josephine Ganda; one *s*. *Educ:* Fourah Bay Coll., Sierra Leone (MA Latin, Dunelm); Jesus Coll., Oxford (MA Jurisp.); DipEd. Called to Bar, Gray's Inn, 1970; practised as barrister, Sierra Leone, 1983–84. Teacher, 1952–57; Education Officer, 1957–61; Secretary, Training and Recruitment, Sierra Leone Civil Service, 1961–63; Establishment Sec., 1963–66; Sec. to the Prime Minister and Head of Sierra Leone Civil Service, 1966–67; Asst Director, UK Immigrants Advisory Service, 1970–72; Principal Admin. Officer, Community Relations Commn, 1972–74, Dir of Fieldwork and Admin, 1974–77; Dir of Legal and Gen. Services, and Sec., 1977, Chief Exec., 1977–82, CRE; Comr and Chm., Sierra Leone Population Census, 1984; Special Envoy on Foreign Aid to Sierra Leone and Chm., Nat. Aid Co-ordinating Cttee, 1986–90; Chairman: National Constitutional Review Commn, 1990–91; Nat. Policy Adv. Cttee, 1998–99; Advr to Pres., Sierra Leone, 1998–99. DCL (*hc*) Sierra Leone. Papal Medal Pro Ecclesia et Pontifice, 1966. *Publications:* The Tuckers of Sierra Leone 1665–1914, 1997; Origin and Philosophy of the

Sierra Leone People's Party, 2001; miscellaneous booklets, articles and reports for Community Relations Commission and Govt of Sierra Leone. *Recreations:* photography, listening to music, the internet.

TUCKER, Sir Richard (Howard), Kt 1985; a Judge of the High Court of Justice, Queen's Bench Division, 1985–2000; *b* 9 July 1930; *s* of Howard Archibald Tucker (His Honour Judge Tucker), and Margaret Minton Tucker; *m* 1st, 1958, Paula Mary Bennett Frost (marr. diss. 1974); one *s* two *d*; 2nd, 1975, Wendy Kate Standbrook (*d* 1988); 3rd, 1989, Jacqueline Suzanne Rossvell Thomson, *widow* of William Thomson, artist. *Educ:* Shrewsbury Sch.; The Queen's Coll., Oxford (MA; Hon. Fellow, 1992). 2nd Lieut, RAOC, 1948–50. Called to Bar, Lincoln's Inn, 1954; Bencher, 1979; Treasurer, 2002. QC 1972; a Recorder, 1972–85; Mem. Senate, Inns of Court and the Bar, 1984–86; Dep. Leader, 1984–85, and Presiding Judge, 1986–90, Midland and Oxford Circuit. Member: Employment Appeal Tribunal, 1986–2000; Parole Bd, 1996–2003 (Vice-Chm., 1998–2000); Comr, Royal Ct of Jersey, 2003–10. Mediator, 2004–. Comr, Commn of Enquiry, Grand Cayman, 2008. *Recreations:* gardening, model railways, wood-turning. *Address:* Treasury Office, Lincoln's Inn, WC2A 3TL. *Clubs:* Garrick, Bean.

TUCKER, William; Lord-Lieutenant of Derbyshire, since 2009; *b* Port Glasgow, 28 July 1945; *s* of William Tucker and Mary Tucker; *m* 1976, Jill Stanton; two *d*. *Educ:* Port Glasgow High Sch.; Co-operative Coll., Loughborough. Co-operative Movement, 1960–2005: non-exec. Chm., Co-operative Insce, 1994–2000; non-exec. Dir, Co-operative Bank, 1994–2000; Chief Exec., Midlands Co-operative Soc., 2000–05. Non-exec. Dir, Derby Hosps Foundn Trust, 2005–11. *Recreations:* gardening, reading, walking, travel. *Address:* Acacia House, Rectory Gardens, Aston on Trent, Derby DE72 2AZ. *T:* (01332) 792792. *E:* wtucker28@gmail.com.

TUCKETT, William Jonathan; Principal Guest Artist, Royal Ballet; Creative Associate, Royal Opera House (ROH2); freelance choreographer and director of theatre, film and opera, since 2005; *b* 3 Feb. 1969; *s* of John Tuckett and Gillian Gould; *m* Caro Howell; one *s*. *Educ:* Bristol Cathedral Sch.; Royal Ballet Upper Sch. Dancer and Choreographer: Sadler's Wells Royal Ballet, 1988–90; Royal Ballet, Covent Garden, 1990–2005; freelance, 2005–, working for orgns incl. Royal Ballet, Channel Four, BBC, Vertigo Films, Almeida Th., Opera North, Iford Arts, Sage Gateshead, KAAT Th., Japan, Sarasota Ballet, Florida. *Recreations:* flying kites on Blackheath, gardening, imagining unfundable projects, ignoring hideous DIY imperatives. *Address:* c/o Royal Opera House, Covent Garden, WC2E 9DD.

TUCKEY, Andrew Marmaduke Lane; Senior Adviser, Quayle Munro, since 2012 (Chairman, 2010–12); Chairman: Teraco Data Environments, South Africa, since 2008; Energy Works, since 2013; *b* 28 Aug. 1943; *s* of late Henry Lane Tuckey and Aileen Rosemary Newsom Tuckey; *m* 1st, 1967, Margaret Louise (*née* Barnes) (marr. diss. 1998); one *s* two *d*; 2nd, 1998, Tracy Elisabeth (*née* Long); two *d*. *Educ:* Plumtree Sch., Zimbabwe. Chartered Accountant, 1966. Dixon Wilson, Chartered Accountants, 1962–66; British American Tobacco, 1966–68; Baring Brothers & Co., Ltd, 1968–95: Dir, 1973–81; Man. Dir, 1981–89; Chm., 1989–95; Dep. Chm., Barings plc, 1989–95; Adviser: Baring Brothers Ltd, 1995–96; Phoenix Securities Ltd, 1996–97; Senior Adviser: Donaldson, Lufkin & Jenrette, 1997–2000; Credit Suisse First Boston, 2000–01; Bridgewell, 2001–07 (Dir, 2003–05; Man. Dir, 2005–07); Academic Partnerships Internat., 2012–14; Vice Chm., Corporate Finance, Landsbanki Securities (UK) Ltd, 2007–08; Dep. Chm., Corporate Finance, 2008–09, Chief Exec., 2009–10, Quayle Munro. Director: Dillon, Read Holding Inc., 1991–95; Morris Homes Ltd, 2009–; Soak and Sleep, 2013–. Member: Federal Reserve Bank of New York Internat. Capital Markets Adv. Cttee, 1992–95; Financial Law Panel, 1993–97; Council, Baring Foundn, 1994–96. Director: Friends of Covent Garden, 1981–98 (Treas., 1981–96); Royal Opera House, 1992–95; City of London Fest., 2004–11; Watermill Th., 2005–. Gov., 2005–, Chm., 2007–, Central Sch. of Ballet (Chm., Develt Bd, 2002–05; Dep. Chm., 2008–). Trustee: Esmée Fairbairn Charitable Trust, 1986–99; Classic FM Charitable Trust, 1992–99. *Recreations:* opera, ballet, theatre. *Address:* Quayle Munro, 22 Berners Street, W1T 3LP. *Club:* White's.

See also Rt Hon. Sir S. L. Tuckey.

TUCKEY, Rt Hon. Sir Simon (Lane), Kt 1992; PC 1998; a Lord Justice of Appeal, 1998–2009; international arbitrator and mediator, since 2009; Judge of Appeal, Gibraltar, 2010–12; *b* 17 Oct. 1941; *s* of late Henry Lane Tuckey and Aileen Rosemary Newsom Tuckey; *m* 1964, Jennifer Rosemary (*née* Hardie); one *s* two *d*. *Educ:* Plumtree School, Zimbabwe. Called to Bar, Lincoln's Inn, 1964, Bencher, 1989; QC 1981; a Recorder, 1984–92; a Judge of the High Court of Justice, QBD, 1992–98; a Judge, Employment Appeal Tribunal, 1993–98; Presiding Judge, Western Circuit, 1995–97; Judge in Charge, Commercial List, 1997–98. Chm., Review Panel, Financial Reporting Council, 1990–92. Mem., Judicial Studies Bd, 1993–95 (Chm., Civil and Family Cttee, 1993–95). *Recreations:* sailing, tennis. *Address:* 20 Essex Street, WC2R 3AL.

See also A. M. L. Tuckey.

TUCKMAN, Frederick Augustus, (Fred), OBE 1990; FCIS, FCIPD; *b* 9 June 1922; *s* of Otto and Amy Tina Tuchmann (*née* Adler); *m* 1966, Patricia Caroline Myers; two *s* one *d*. *Educ:* English and German schools; London School of Economics, 1946–49 (BScEcon). Served RAF, 1942–46. Commercial posts, 1950–65; Management Consultant and Partner, HAY Gp, 1965–85; Managing Director, HAY GmbH, Frankfurt, 1970–80; Partner, HAY Associates, 1975–85; Chm., Suomen HAY, OY, Helsinki, 1973–81; consultant assignments in Europe, Africa and N America. Hon. Sec., Bow Gp, 1958–59; Councillor, London Borough of Camden, 1965–71 (Chm., Library and Arts, 1968–71). Mem. (C) Leicester, European Parliament, 1979–89; contested (C) Leicester, Eur. Parly elecn, 1989. Mem. Council, Inst. of Personnel Management, 1963–70. Chm., Greater London Area, CPC, 1968–70. European Parliament: Budget Cttee, 1979–81; Social and Employment Cttee, 1981–89 (Cons. spokesman, 1984–89); substitute Mem., Economic and Monetary Cttee, 1979–87; substitute Mem., Budgetary Control Cttee, 1984–87; First Vice Pres., Latin American Delegn, 1982–85; Mem., Israel Delegn, 1987–89; Chm., Internat. Gp on Small Business, 1985–86. UK Chm., European Year of Small Business, 1983; Vice Chm., Small Business Bureau, London, 1985–89. Pres., Anglo-Jewish Assoc., 1989–95 (Vice-Pres., 1995–2003); Vice Pres., Eur. Medium and Small Units, 1985–90. Cross, Order of Merit (FRG), 1989. *Recreations:* reading, arguing, travel, swimming; priority—family. *Address:* 6 Cumberland Road, Barnes, SW13 9LY. *T:* (020) 8748 2392. *Club:* Athenæum.

TUCKNOTT, John Anthony, MBE 1990; HM Diplomatic Service; Deputy High Commissioner, Karachi, and UK Trade and Investment Director for Pakistan, since 2013; UK Government Trade Champion for Pakistan, since 2014; *b* 2 Jan. 1958; *s* of late Eric Tucknott and Ethel Tucknott (*née* Holland); *m* 2000, Riitta-Leena Irmeli Lehtinen; one *s*. *Educ:* Bournemouth Sch.; King's Coll. London (MA). Dept of Employment, 1975–77; joined HM Diplomatic Service, 1977; Communications Ops Dept, FCO, 1977–78; Lord Privy Seal's Office, 1978–80; Archivist, Rome, 1980–82; Cairo, 1982–85; N American Dept, 1985–87, W African Dept, 1987–88, FCO; Dep. Hd of Mission, Beirut, 1988–93; Hd of Section, Security Policy Dept, FCO, 1993–95; First Sec., UKMIS to UN, NY, 1995–98; Dep. Hd, Non-proliferation Dept, 1998–2000, UK Co-ordinator for War Crimes Issues, 2000–01, FCO; Counsellor (Trade and Investment Develt), Stockholm, 2002–05; Sen. Directing Staff (Civilian), RCDS, 2005–07; Dep. Hd of Mission, Baghdad, 2007–09; FCO, 2009–10; Ambassador to Nepal, 2010–13. *Recreations:* walking, reading, music, travel. *Address:* c/o Foreign and Commonwealth Office, King Charles Street, SW1A 2AH.

TUCKWELL, Anthony David, MA; National Director, National Educational Assessment Centre, 2000–10; Headmaster, King Edward VI Grammar School, Chelmsford, 1984–99; *b* 4 July 1943; *s* of Alec William Tuckwell and Muriel Florence Tuckwell (*née* Green); *m* 1967, Kathleen Olivia Hatton. *Educ:* St Peter's Coll., Oxford (MA); Oxford Univ. Dept of Educn (DipEd); Leeds Metropolitan (MBA 1995); Essex Univ. (Cert. in Local History 2004). History Master, Southern Grammar Sch. for Boys, Portsmouth, 1966–69; St John's College, Southsea: Hd of Hist., 1970–73; Sen. Teacher (Curriculum Co-ordinator), 1973–78; Dep. Headmaster, Sale Co. Grammar Sch. for Boys, 1979–83. Headship Appt Consultant, ASCL, 1999–2009. Mem., Essex Rural Commn, 2008–09. Mem. Bd of Dirs, Chelmsford Cathedral Fest. Ltd, 1999–2008. Governor: Cobham Hall Sch., 2003–14; New Hall Sch., 2010–. *Publications:* (contrib.) School Leadership in the 21st Century, 1996; (contrib.) Living Headship: voices, value, vision, 1999; That Honourable and Gentlemanlike House: a history of King Edward VI Grammar School, Chelmsford 1551–2001, 2000, 2nd edn, 2008; New Hall and its School: 'a true school of virtuous demeanour', 2006; Coming of Age: the life and times of Chelmsford Cathedral 1914–2014, 2013; (contrib.) New Hall's Catholic Heritage in South Eastern Catholic History. *Recreations:* choral singing, literature, walking, travel. *Address:* 28 Oaklands Crescent, Chelmsford, Essex CM2 9PP.

TUCKWELL, Barry Emmanuel, AC 1992; OBE 1965; horn soloist, retired; conductor; Conductor and Music Director, Maryland Symphony Orchestra, 1982–98; *b* 5 March 1931; *s* of late Charles and Elizabeth Tuckwell, Australia; *m* 1st, 1958, Sally Eelin Newton; one *s* one *d*; 2nd, 1971, Hilary Jane Warburton; one *s*; 3rd, 1992, Susan Terry Levitan. *Educ:* various schs, Australia; Sydney Conservatorium. FRCM 1993. Melbourne Symph. Orch., 1947; Sydney Symph. Orch., 1947–50; Hallé Orch., 1951–53; Scottish Nat. Orch., 1953–54; Bournemouth Symphony Orch., 1954–55; London Symph. Orch., 1955–68; founded Tuckwell Wind Quintet, 1968; Chief Conductor, Tasmanian Symphony Orch., 1979–83; Guest Conductor, Northern Sinfonia, 1993–97. Mem. Chamber Music Soc. of Lincoln Center, 1974–81; Horn Prof., Royal Academy of Music, 1963–74; Pres., Internat. Horn Soc., 1969–77, 1992–94. Has played and conducted annually throughout Europe, GB, USA and Canada; has appeared at many internat. festivals, incl. Salzburg and Edinburgh; took part in 1st Anglo-Soviet Music Exchange, Leningrad and Moscow, 1963; toured: Far East, 1964 and 1975; Australia, 1970–95; S America, 1976; USSR, 1977; People's Republic of China, 1984. Many works dedicated to him; has made numerous recordings. Editor, complete horn literature for G. Schirmer Inc. Professorial Fellow, Univ. of Melbourne, 2005. Hon. RAM 1966; Hon. GSM, 1967. Hon. DMus Sydney. Harriet Cohen Internat. Award for Solo Instruments, 1968; George Peabody Medal, 1997; Andrew White Medal, Loyola Coll., 1998. *Publications:* Playing the Horn, 1978; The Horn, 1981. *Club:* Athenæum.

TUDGE, Colin Hiram; author; *b* 22 April 1943; *s* of late Cyril Tudge and Maisie Tudge; *m* 1st, 1966, Rosemary Shewan (marr. diss. 2001); one *s* two *d*; 2nd, 2001, Ruth West. *Educ:* Dulwich Coll.; Peterhouse, Cambridge (MA 1966). Writer on various magazines, 1965–80; staff writer, Farmers' Weekly, 1970–72; Features Ed., New Scientist, 1980–85; presenter, BBC Radio 3, 1985–90; freelance author and broadcaster, 1990–. Res. Fellow, Centre for the Philosophy of Social and Natural Scis, LSE, 1995–2005. Co-founder: Campaign for Real Farming, 2009; Oxford Real Farming Conf., 2010; Funding Enlightened Agriculture, 2012. *Publications:* The Famine Business, 1977; (with M. Allaby) Home Farm, 1977; Future Cook, 1980; The Food Connection, 1985; Food Crops for the Future, 1988; Global Ecology, 1991; Last Animals at the Zoo, 1991; The Engineer in the Garden, 1993; The Day Before Yesterday, 1995; Neanderthals, Bandits and Farmers, 1998; The Second Creation, 2000; The Variety of Life, 2000; In Mendel's Footnotes, 2001; So Shall We Reap, 2003; The Secret Life of Trees, 2005; Feeding People is Easy, 2007; Consider the Birds, 2008; (with J. Young) The Link: uncovering our early ancestors, 2009; Good Food for Everyone Forever, 2011; Why Genes are Not Selfish and People are Nice, 2013. *Recreation:* working with farmers and activists to bring about a people's takeover of the world's food supply chain via the Campaign for Real Farming. *Address:* 20 Dove House Close, Wolvercote, Oxon OX2 8BQ. *E:* colin@colintudge.co.uk. *W:* www.colintudge.com.

TUDOR, (Fiona) Philippa, DPhil; Clerk of Committees, House of Lords, since 2011; *b* Shrewsbury, 15 Feb. 1958; *d* of (James) Brian Tudor and Rosaleen Tudor (*née* O'Connor); *m* 1989, David Richard Beamish, *qv*; one *d*. *Educ:* Sch. of SS Mary and Anne, Abbots Bromley; Somerville Coll., Oxford (MA; DPhil). FCIPD 2005; Dip. Corporate Governance, ACCA, 2006. House of Lords: Clerk, 1982; Sen. Clerk, 1986; Chief Clerk, 1993; seconded to Scotland Office as Hd, Party and Constitl Div., 2001–03; Hd, Human Resources, 2003–07; Finance Dir, 2007–11. *Recreations:* historical research, classical music, walking. *Address:* House of Lords, SW1A 0PW. *T:* (020) 7219 3130. *E:* tudorfp@parliament.uk.

TUDOR-CRAIG, Pamela; *see* Wedgwood, Pamela Lady.

TUDOR JOHN, William; DL; Deputy Chairman, Nationwide Building Society, 2007–11; *b* 26 April 1944; *s* of Tudor and Gwen John; *m* 1st, 1967, Jane Clark (*d* 2007); three *d*; 2nd, 2014, Joanna Clayton. *Educ:* Cowbridge Sch., S Wales; Downing Coll., Cambridge (MA). Asst Solicitor, Allen & Overy, 1969–71; Banker, Orion Bank Ltd, 1971–72; Allen & Overy: Partner, 1972–2001; Head of Banking Dept, 1972–92; Man. Partner, 1992–94; Sen. Partner, 1994–2000; Chm. and Man. Dir, European Commitment Cttee, Lehman Brothers, 2000–08; Director: Lehman Brothers Europe Ltd, 2000–08; Lehman Brothers Internat. (Europe), 2000–08; Lehman Brothers European Mezzanine; SICAV, 2004–10; Man. Dir, Nomura Internat. plc, 2008–12. Non-executive Chairman: Sutton Seeds (Hldgs) Ltd, 1978–93; Horticultural & Botanical Hldgs Ltd, 1985–93; non-executive Director: Woolwich plc, 2000; Portman Bldg Soc., 2001–07 (Dep. Chm., 2004–06; Chm., 2006–07); Sun Bank plc, 2001–04; Grainger plc, 2005–10. Associate Fellow, Downing Coll., Cambridge, 1985–92, 1997–. Member: Law Soc., 1969–; City of London Solicitors' Co., 1974–; IBA, 1978–; Financial Law Panel, 1996–2002; Financial Mkts Law Cttee, 2002–09 (Vice-Chm., 2002–09); Chm., Wales in London, 2002–06. Chm., Law Foundn Adv. Council, Oxford Univ., 1998–2003; Member: Adv. Bd, Oxford Univ. Develt Prog., 1999–; Develt Bd, Nat. Mus. of Wales, 2007–; Develt Bd, WNO, 2012–; Trustee, St Albans Abbey Fabric Trust, 2005–. Non-exec. Dir, Nat. Film and Television Sch., 2000–; Mem. Court, Univ. of Hertfordshire, 2006–. Steward of Appeal, BBB of C, 1978–. Freeman, City of London, 1994; Liveryman, Co. of Gunmakers, 1994–. High Sheriff, Herts, 2006–07; DL Herts, 2007. *Recreations:* Rugby football as an observer, music as a listener, shooting and reading as a participant, daughters' banker. *Address:* Willian Bury, Willian, Herts SG6 2AF. *T:* (01462) 683532. *E:* tjwillian@btinternet.com. *Club:* Cardiff and County (Cardiff).

TUFFIN, Alan David, CBE 1993; General Secretary, Union of Communication Workers, 1982–93; *b* 2 Aug. 1933; *s* of Oliver Francis and Gertrude Elizabeth Tuffin; *m* 1957, Jean Elizabeth Tuffin; one *s* one *d*. *Educ:* Eltham Secondary Sch., SE9. Post Office employment, London, 1949–69; London Union Regional Official for UCW, 1957–69; National Official, 1969; Deputy General Secretary, 1979. Member: TUC Gen. Council, 1982–93 (Pres., 1992–93); HSC, 1986–96; Employment Appeal Tribunal, 1995–2000. Dir, Trade Union Fund Managers Ltd (formerly Trade Union Unit Trust), 1985–2011; non-exec. Dir, Remploy Ltd, 1999–2006. FRSA 1990. *Recreations:* reading, squash, West Ham United FC. *Address:* c/o TUFM Ltd, Congress House, Great Russell Street, WC1B 3LQ.

TUFFIN, David William, FRICS; Consultant: Tuffin Ferraby Taylor LLP, since 2009; St Brides Fund Managers, since 2011; President, Royal Institution of Chartered Surveyors, 2007–08; *b* 11 June 1948; *s* of Reginald and Dorothy Tuffin; *m* 1968, Brenda King; one *s* one *d*. *Educ:* Portsmouth Northern Grammar Sch.; Raynes Park Co. Grammar Sch. FRICS 1979;

FBEng 1998; MCIArb 1999. Founding Partner, 1973–2004, Man. Partner, 2004–08, Tuffin Ferraby Taylor LLP. Royal Institution of Chartered Surveyors: Chairman: RICS Awards, 2012–; Dispute Resolution Appts Bd, 2013–; Mem., Business Develt Bd, 2011–. *Recreations:* shooting, socialising, unsuccessful angling. *Address:* Tuffin Ferraby Taylor LLP, 2 Throgmorton Avenue, EC2N 2DG. *T:* 07768 648266. *E:* dtuffin@tftconsultants.com.

TUFFREY, Michael William; Founder and Director, Corporate Citizenship Company, since 1997; *b* 30 Sept. 1959; *m*; one *s* two *d*. *Educ:* Douai Sch., Woolhampton; Durham Univ. (BA Hons Econ. Hist. and Econs 1981). ACA 1984. Accountant, Peat Marwick Mitchell & Co., London, 1981–84; Res. and Parly Officer, Lib/SDP whips office, H of L, 1984–87; Dir, Finance and Admin, Action Resource Centre, London, 1987–90; Community Affairs Consultant, Prima Europe, London, 1990–97. Mem. for Vauxhall: GLC, 1985–86 (Mem., Industry and Employment, Housing and Planning Cttees); ILEA, 1985–86; Mem. (Lib Dem), Lambeth LBC, 1990–2002 (Gp Leader, Lib Dem, 1990–98; de facto Jt Leader, Council, 1994–98). Contested: (L) Streatham, 1987; (Lib Dem) Vauxhall, June 1989, 1992. London Assembly, Greater London Authority: Mem. (Lib Dem), Feb. 2002–2012; Leader, Lib Dem Gp, 2006–10; Member: London Fire and Emergency Planning Authy, 2002–08 and 2010–12 (Leader, Lib Dem Gp, 2006–08); Budget Cttee, 2002–12; Envmt Cttee, 2004–12. Mem., Assoc. of London Govt Leaders Cttee, 1994–2000 (Dep. Lib Dem Leader, 1994–2000); Lambeth Representative: AMA; LGA; Board Member: Business Link London, 1994–2000; London Develt Partnership, 1998–2000; 1994–98: Brixton City Challenge; Cross River Partnership; Central London Partnership; South Bank Partnership. Chm., Parly Lib Party Staff Assoc., 1986–87. Formerly: Nat. Treas., Gingerbread; Treas., then Chm., L'Arche Lambeth (former Nat. Bd Mem., L'Arche); founding Bd Mem., Vauxhall St Peter's Heritage Centre; Bd Mem., Vauxhall Cross Amenity Trust. Editor, Corporate Citizen Briefing, 1991–. *Recreation:* licensed radio amateur. *Address:* 50 Lynette Avenue, SW4 9HD.

TUFNELL, Col Greville Wyndham, CVO 2002; DL; Development Officer, National Star Centre for Disabled Youth, 1982–95; Lieutenant, Queen's Body Guard of the Yeomen of the Guard, 1993–2002; *b* 7 April 1932; *s* of K. E. M. Tufnell, MC and E. H. Tufnell (*née* Dufaur); *m* 1st, 1962, Hon. Anne Rosemary Trench (*d* 1992), *d* of 5th Baron Ashtown, OBE and *widow* of Capt. Timothy Patrick Arnold Gosselin; three *d*, and one step *d*; 2nd, 1994, Susan Arnot Burrows. *Educ:* Eton; RMA, Sandhurst. Commnd Grenadier Guards, 1952; Adjt, 2nd Bn, 1959–61; GSO 3, War Office, 1962–63; Staff Coll., 1964; Maj. 1965; DAQMG, London Dist, 1966–67; GSO 2, HQ 2 Div., 1969–71; Lt Col 1971; comdg 1st Bn, 1971–73 (despatches, 1972); Bde Maj., Household Div., 1974–76; Col 1976; Lt Col comdg Grenadier Guards, 1976–78; retd 1979. Queen's Body Guard of Yeomen of the Guard: Exon, 1979; Ensign, 1985; Clerk of the Cheque and Adjutant, 1987. Freeman, City of London, 1961; Liveryman, Grocers' Co., 1965–. DL Glos, 1994. *Recreations:* shooting, fishing, gardening. *Address:* Arrow House, Church Road, Quenington, Glos GL7 5BN. *Clubs:* Cavalry and Guards, Sloane, Pitt, MCC.

TUFTON, family name of **Baron Hothfield**.

TUGE-ERECIŃSKA, Barbara; Ambassador of Poland to Cyprus; *b* 24 March 1956; *d* of Janusz Tuge and Jadwiga Duchnowska; one *s* by Andrzej Ereciński. *Educ:* Gdańsk Univ. (MA Scandinavian Studies). Staff mem., Foreign Dept, Nat. Bureau of Solidarity, 1981; Mem., Primate's Cttee for Assistance to Repressed Persons, 1982–87; Hon. Sec., Consular Agency of Sweden, Denmark and Norway, Gdynia, 1987–90; Plenipotentiary of City Bd for foreign contacts, Municipal Office to Gdańsk, 1990–91; Ambassador of Poland to Sweden, 1991–97; Ministry of Foreign Affairs: Dir, Europe-West Dept, 1997–98; Dir, Eur. Policy Dept, 1998–99; Under-Sec. of State, 1999–2001; Ambassador of Poland to Denmark, 2001–05; Sec. of State, Min. of Foreign Affairs, 2005–06; Ambassador of Poland to UK, 2006–12. Golden Cross, Order of Merit (Poland), 1997; Commander's Cross: Order of Merit (Italy), 2000; Order of Merit (Hungary), 2001; Order of the Dannebrog (Denmark), 2005. *Recreations:* reading books, walking (especially along the seashore). *Club:* Athenæum.

TUGENDHAT, family name of **Baron Tugendhat**.

TUGENDHAT, Baron *cr* 1993 (Life Peer), of Widdington in the County of Essex; **Christopher Samuel Tugendhat,** Kt 1990; *b* 23 Feb. 1937; *er s* of late Dr Georg Tugendhat; *m* 1967, Julia Lissant Dobson; two *s*. *Educ:* Ampleforth Coll.; Gonville and Caius Coll., Cambridge (Pres. of Union; Hon. Fellow 1998). Financial Times leader and feature writer, 1960–70. MP (C) City of London and Westminster South, 1974–76 (Cities of London and Westminster, 1970–74); Mem., 1977–85, a Vice-Pres., 1981–85, EEC Commn. Director: Sunningdale Oils, 1971–76; Phillips Petroleum International (UK) Ltd, 1972–76; National Westminster Bank, 1985–91 (Dep. Chm., 1990–91); The BOC Group, 1985–96; Commercial Union Assce, 1988–91; LWT (Hldgs), 1991–94; Eurotunnel plc, 1991–2003; Rio Tinto plc, 1997–2004; Chairman: Abbey National plc, 1991–2002; Blue Circle Industries PLC, 1996–2001; Eur. Adv. Bd, Lehman Brothers, 2002–07. Chm., Imperial Coll. Healthcare NHS Trust, 2006–11. Member: Econ. Affairs Cttee, H of L, 2009–; EU Select Cttee, H of L, 2013– (Chm., Sub-Cttee on EU External Affairs, 2013–). Chm., CAA, 1986–91. Chairman: RIIA (Chatham House), 1986–95; Adv. Council, European Policy Forum, 1998–; Governor, Council of Ditchley Foundn, 1986–2010; Vice-Pres., British Lung Foundn, 1986–2014. Chancellor, Univ. of Bath, 1998–2013. Hon. LLD Bath, 1998; Hon. DLitt UMIST, 2002. *Publications:* Oil: the biggest business, 1968; The Multinationals, 1971 (McKinsey Foundn Book Award, 1971); Making Sense of Europe, 1986; (with William Wallace) Options for British Foreign Policy in the 1990s, 1988; various pamphlets and numerous articles. *Recreations:* being with his family, reading, conversation. *Address:* 35 Westbourne Park Road, W2 5QD. *Club:* Athenæum.

See also Hon. Sir M. G. Tugendhat.

TUGENDHAT, Hon. Sir Michael (George), Kt 2003; a Judge of the High Court of Justice, Queen's Bench Division, 2003–14; Judge in charge of Queen's Bench jury and non-jury lists, 2010–14; *b* 21 Oct. 1944; *s* of late Georg Tugendhat and Maire Littledale; *m* 1970, Blandine de Loisne; four *s*. *Educ:* Ampleforth Coll.; Gonville and Caius Coll., Cambridge (Scholar; MA); Yale Univ. Henry Fellowship. Called to the Bar, Inner Temple, 1969, Bencher, 1988; QC 1986; a Recorder, 1994–2003; a Dep. High Court Judge, 1995–2003; a Judge of the Courts of Appeal in Jersey and Guernsey, 2000–03. Mem., Bar Council, 1992–94. Chm., Civil Law Working Party on Corruption, 1999. Member, Mgt Cttee, Advice on Individual Rights in Europe Centre, 2000–03. Pres., Franco-British Lawyers Soc., 2011–14. Chm., Investment Cttee, Inner Temple, 2011–14. Fellow, Inst. Advanced Legal Studies, 1999–. Hon. Prof., Sch. of Law, Univ. of Leicester, 2013–Aug. 2016. *Publications:* (contrib.) Restitution and Banking Law, 1998; (contrib.) Yearbook of Copyright and Media Law, 2000; (ed jtly) The Law of Privacy and the Media, 2002, 2nd edn as Tugendhat and Christie: The Law of Privacy and the Media, 2011, 3rd edn 2015; (consulting ed.) Commercial Fraud Civil Liability, Human Rights, and Money Laundering, 2006; (contrib.) Halsbury's Laws of England, 4th edn; (contrib.) Thomas More's Trial by Jury, 2011; (consulting ed.) The Illicit Trade in Art and Antiquities, 2012; occasional contribs to legal jls. *E:* mt312@le.ac.uk. *Clubs:* Brooks's, Royal Automobile.

See also Baron Tugendhat, T. G. J. Tugendhat.

TUGENDHAT, Thomas Georg John, MBE 2010; MP (C) Tonbridge and Malling, since 2015; *b* 27 June 1973; *s* of Hon. Sir Michael George Tugendhat, *qv*; *m* Anissia; one *s*. *Educ:* Bristol Univ. (BA Theol. 1995); Gonville and Caius Coll., Cambridge (MPhil Islamic Studies 1996). Volunteer, CSV, 1991–92; freelance journalist, Beirut, 1997–99; Founder and Manager, Fortune Promoseven, PR co., Lebanon, 1997–99; Mgt Consultant, First Consulting Ltd, 2000–01; Energy Analyst, Bloomberg LP, 2001–03; Dir, Lashkar & Co., 2013–. Officer, Territorial Army, 2003–: with RM, Iraq War as Intelligence Officer, 2003; Advr to Nat. Security Advr, Office of Nat. Security Council, Afghanistan, 2005–06; Advr to Gov., Helmand Province, 2006–07; with Army Strategy Br., 2009–10; MA to CDS, 2010–13. Mem., Admin and Constitutional Affairs Cttee, 2015–. *Address:* House of Commons, SW1A 0AA.

TUGHAN, John Charles Ronald; QC 2015; *b* Belfast, 9 Dec. 1968; *s* of Kenneth and Carole Tughan; *m* 2000, Louise Haddleton; two *d*. *Educ:* Campbell Coll., Belfast; Liverpool Univ. (LLB Hons). Called to the Bar, Inner Temple, 1991. *Address:* 4 Paper Buildings, Temple, EC4Y 7EX. *E:* jt@4pb.com.

TUGWELL, Very Rev. Simon Charles ffoster, DD, STD; OP; Fellow, Dominican Historical Institute, Rome, since 1987 (President, 1992–97); *b* 4 May 1943; *s* of Major Herbert Frederick Lewen Tugwell and Mary Brigit (*née* Hutchinson). *Educ:* Lancing Coll.; Corpus Christi Coll., Oxford (DD 1993); STD (Angelicum, Rome) 1987, STM (Dominican Order) 1993. Entered English Province of Dominican Order, 1965, ordained priest, 1971; Lectr and Tutor, Blackfriars, Oxford, 1972–92; Regent of Studies, English Dominicans, 1976–90; Mem., Faculty of Theol., Univ. of Oxford, 1982–92. Vis. Lectr, Angelicum, Rome, 1977–92; Flannery Prof. of Theol., Gonzaga Univ., Spokane, WA, 1982–83; Read-Tuckwell Lectr on human immortality, Bristol Univ., 1988. Has lectured and preached in many parts of the world. Founding Ed., Dominican Hist. Newsletter, 1992–97. *Publications:* The Way of the Preacher, 1979; Early Dominicans, 1982; Ways of Imperfection, 1984; Albert and Thomas, 1988; The Apostolic Fathers, 1989; (ed) Letters of Bede Jarrett, 1989; Human Immortality and the Redemption of Death, 1990; (ed) Miraculi sancti Dominici mandato magistri Berengarii collecta, Petri Calo legendae sancti Dominici, 1997; (ed) Bernardi Guidonis scripta de sancto Dominico, 1998; (ed) Humberti de Romanis legendae sancti Dominici, 2008; Pelagius Parvus and his Summa, 2012; (ed) Petri Ferrandi legenda sancti Dominici, 2015; contribs to books and dictionaries; articles and reviews in learned jls. *Recreations:* teddy bears, writing silly verses. *Address:* Istituto Storico Domenicano, Largo Angelicum 1, 00184 Roma, Italy. *Fax:* 066702270.

TUITE, Sir Christopher (Hugh), 14th Bt *cr* 1622; Senior Advisor, Carbon Fund, Conservation International, since 2008; *b* 3 Nov. 1949; *s* of Sir Dennis George Harmsworth Tuite, 13th Bt, MBE, and Margaret Essie, *d* of late Col Walter Leslie Dundas, DSO; *S* father, 1981; *m* 1976, Deborah Ann, *d* of A. E. Martz, Punxsutawney, Pa; two *s*. *Educ:* Univ. of Liverpool (BSc Hons); Univ. of Bristol (PhD). Research Officer, The Wildfowl Trust, 1978–81; Controller, The Nature Conservancy, Washington, DC, 1987–99; Director: Wildlife and Habitat Prog., IFAW, 1999–2004; USA, Green Belt Movement Internat., 2005–08. *Publications:* contribs to Jl of Animal Ecology, Jl of Applied Ecology, Freshwater Biology, Wildfowl. *Heir: s* Thomas Livingstone Tuite, *b* 24 July 1977. *Address:* c/o HSBC, 33 The Borough, Farnham, Surrey GU9 7NJ.

TUIVAGA, Sir Timoci (Uluiburotu), Kt 1981; CF 1995; Chief Justice of Fiji, 1980–87, and 1988–2002; *b* 21 Oct. 1931; *s* of Isimeli Siga Tuivaga and Jessie Hill; *m* 1st, 1958, Vilimaina Leba Parrott Tuivaga (*d* 2000); three *s* one *d*; 2nd, 2002, Raijeli Vasakula. *Educ:* Univ. of Auckland (BA). Called to Bar, Gray's Inn, 1964, and NSW, 1968. Native Magistrate, 1958–61; Crown Counsel, 1965–68; Principal Legal Officer, 1968–70; Acting Director of Public Prosecutions, 1970; Crown Solicitor, 1971; Puisne Judge, 1972; Acting Chief Justice, 1974; sometime Acting Gov.-Gen., 1983–87. *Recreations:* golf, gardening. *Address:* 1 Newboult Place, Suva, Fiji. *T:* 3316619. *Club:* Fiji Golf (Suva).

TULETT, Louise Wendy, (Mrs J. L. W. Lee-Emery), CBE 2010; Director General, Finance, Ministry of Defence, since 2015; *b* Dorking, 12 March 1960; *d* of Anthony and Valerie Linfield; *m* 1st, Barry Tulett; two *s*; 2nd, 2005, Jason L. W. Lee-Emery. *Educ:* Raleigh Primary Sch.; Howard of Effingham Co. Secondary Sch.; Southampton Inst. Higher Educn. CIPFA 1989. Clerical asst, Surrey CC, 1976–78; finance trainee, Waverley DC, 1978–87; trainee accountant, Woking BC, 1987–90; Asst Dir, Finance, NW Surrey HA, 1990–94; Dep. Dir, Finance, Frimley Park Hosp., 1994–2000; HM Treasury: Accountant, 2000–04; Team Leader, 2004–07; Gp Dir, Finance and Procurement, 2007–10; Finance Dir, MoD, 2010–15. Mem. Bd, UK Financial Investments Ltd, 2009–10. *Recreations:* relaxing with family and friends, walking the dogs, reading. *Address:* Ministry of Defence, Main Building, Whitehall, SW1A 2HB.

TULLIBARDINE, Marquess of; Michael Bruce John Murray; Project Manager, Client Services, Oktra; *b* 5 March 1985; *s* and *heir* of Duke of Atholl, *qv*.

TULLO, Carol Anne; Director: The National Archives, since 2006; Office of Public Sector Information, since 2005; Controller of HM Stationery Office, Queen's Printer of Acts of Parliament and Government Printer for Northern Ireland, since 1997; Queen's Printer for Scotland, since 1999; *b* 9 Jan. 1956; *d* of Edward Alan Dodgson and late Patricia Dodgson; *m* 1979, Robin Brownrigg Tullo; one *s* one *d*. *Educ:* Hull Univ. (LLB Hons 1976); Inn of Courts Sch. of Law, City Univ. Called to the Bar, Inner Temple, 1977; Publishing Dir, Sweet & Maxwell Ltd, 1990–96; Consultant, Thomson Legal and Professional Gp, 1996–97. Chair, Law Publishers' Exec., 1995–2004, Bd Mem., Council of Acad. and Professional Publishers, 1996–2005, Publishers Assoc.; Mem., Exec. Cttee, Internat. Govt Printers and Publishers' Assoc., 1999–2009. Mem., Jt Cttee on Legal Deposit, 2012–. Vis. Prof., 2000–, Mem., Ext. Adv. Panel, Centre for Inf. Leadership, 2009–, Cass Business Sch., City Univ. Liveryman, Stationers' and Newspaper Makers' Co., 2015– (Mem., Masters and Wardens Cttee, 2015). *Address:* National Archives, Kew, Richmond, Surrey TW9 4DU.

TULLY, Sir (William) Mark, KBE 2002 (OBE 1985); freelance journalist and broadcaster, since 1994; *b* 24 Oct. 1935; *s* of late William Scarth Carlisle Tully, CBE and Patience Treby Tully; *m* 1960, Frances Margaret (*née* Butler); two *s* two *d*; partner, Gillian Wright. *Educ:* Twyford School, Winchester; Marlborough College; Trinity Hall, Cambridge (MA; Hon. Fellow, 1994). Regional Dir, Abbeyfield Soc., 1960–64; BBC, 1964–94: Asst, Appointments Dept, 1964–65; Asst, then Actg Rep., New Delhi, 1965–69; Prog. Organiser and Talks Writer, Eastern Service, 1969–71; Chief of Bureau, Delhi, 1972–93; South Asia Correspondent, 1993–94. Presenter: Something Understood, BBC Radio 4, 1995–; The Lives of Jesus, BBC TV series, 1996. Padma Shri (India), 1992. *Publications:* (with Satish Jacob) Amritsar: Mrs Gandhi's last battle, 1985; (with Z. Masani) From Raj to Rajiv, 1988; No Full Stops in India, 1991; The Heart of India (short stories), 1995; The Lives of Jesus, 1996; (with Gillian Wright) India in Slow Motion, 2002; India's Unending Journey, 2007; India: the road ahead, 2011. *Recreations:* fishing, bird watching, reading. *Address:* B26 Nizamuddin West, Delhi 110013, India. *T:* (11) 41033839. *Clubs:* Oriental; India International Centre, Gymkhana (Delhi), Bengal (Calcutta).

TULVING, Prof. Endel, OC 2006; PhD; FRS 1992; FRSC; Anne and Max Tanenbaum Chair in Cognitive Neuroscience, Rotman Research Institute, Baycrest Centre, Toronto and University of Toronto, 1992–2010, Scientist Emeritus, 2012; University Professor Emeritus in Psychology, University of Toronto, since 1992; *b* 26 May 1927; *s* of Juhan Tulving and Linda (*née* Soome); *m* 1950, Ruth Mikkelsaar; two *d*. *Educ:* Hugo Treffner Gymnasium; Univ. of Heidelberg; Univ. of Toronto (BA, MA); Harvard Univ. (Foundn Fellow, 1954–55; PhD). FRSC 1979. Teaching Fellow, Harvard Univ., 1955–56; University of Toronto: Lectr, 1956–59; Asst Prof. of Psychol., 1959–62; Associate Prof., 1962–65; Prof., 1965–70; Prof. of Psychol., Yale Univ., 1970–75; University of Toronto: Prof. of Psychol., 1972–92; Chm., Dept of Psychol., 1974–80; Univ. Prof., 1985–92. Vis. Scholar, Univ. of Calif., Berkeley,

1964–65; Fellow, Center for Advanced Study in Behavioural Scis, Stanford, Calif., 1972–73; Commonwealth Vis. Prof., Univ. of Oxford, 1977–78; Distinguished Res. Prof. of Neurosci., Univ. of Calif., Davis, 1993–98; Clark Way Harrison Dist. Vis. Prof. of Psychology and Cognitive Neurosci., Washington Univ., 1996–2007. Izaak Walton Killam Meml Scholarship, 1976; Guggenheim Fellow, 1987–88; William James Fellow, Amer. Psychol Soc., 1990; Montgomery Fellow, Dartmouth Coll., 1999. For. Hon. Mem., Amer. Acad. Arts and Scis, 1986; For. Associate, Nat. Acad. Scis, USA, 1988; Foreign Member: Royal Swedish Acad. Scis, 1991; Academia Europaea, 1996; Estonian Acad. of Scis, 2002. Hon. MA Yale, 1969; Hon. PhD: Umeå, Sweden, 1982; Haifa, Israel, 2003; Hon. DLitt: Waterloo, Canada, 1987; Laurentian, Canada, 1988; Hon. DPsych Tartu, Estonia, 1989; Hon. ScD: Queen's Univ., Ontario, 1996; Univ. of Toronto, 2002; Columbia Univ., NY, 2005. Warren Medal, Soc. of Exptl Psychologists, 1982; Dist. Scientific Contrib. Award, Amer. Psychol Assoc., 1983; Award for Dist. Contribs to Psychol. as a Science, Canadian Psychol Assoc., 1983; Izaak Walton Killam Prize in Health Scis, Canada Council, 1994; Gold Medal Award, Amer. Psychol Foundn, 1994; McGovern Award in the behavioral scis, AAAS, 1996; Wilhelm Wundt-William James Prize, Eur. Fedn of Psychologists' Assocs, 2003; Gairdner Internat. Award, Gairdner Foundn, 2005; Canadian Medical Hall of Fame, 2007; Pasteur-Weizmann/Servier Internat. Prize, 2009. *Publications:* Elements of Episodic Memory, 1983; (ed jtly) Organization of Memory, 1972; Memory Systems 1994, 1994; (ed) Memory, Consciousness, and the Brain: the Tallinn Conference, 1999; Oxford Handbook of Memory, 2000; articles in scientific jls. *Recreations:* golf, walking, chess, bridge. *Address:* 45 Bâby Point Crescent, Toronto, ON M6S 2B7, Canada. *T:* (416) 7623736.

TUMPEL-GUGERELL, Gertrude; Member, Executive Board, European Central Bank, 2003–11; *b* Kapelln, Austria, 11 Nov. 1952. *Educ:* grammar sch.; Univ. of Vienna (MSc Hons Econs and Soc. Scis 1975; Doctorate in Econs and Soc. Scis 1981). Economist, Econs Div., Oesterreichische Nationalbank, 1975–81; Econ. Policy Advr to Minister of Finance, and Mem. Supervisory Bd, Oesterreichische Laenderbank AG, 1981–84; Oesterreichische Nationalbank: Dep. Hd, Econs Div., 1985–86; Comptroller Gen. in charge of developing strategic planning and auditing, 1986–92; Dir, Area Corporate Planning and Mgt, 1992–97; Exec. Dir, Econs and Financial Markets Dept, 1997–2003; Vice-Gov., 1998–2003. Alternate Gov. of Austria to IMF, 1997–2003; European Union: Mem., Econ. and Finance Cttee, 1997–2003; Chm., Banking Adv. Cttee, 2002–03; European Central Bank: Member: Internat. Relns Cttee, 1999–2003; Banking Supervision Cttee, 1999–2003; Mem., Supervisory Bd, Financial Market Authy, Austria, 2002–03. Non-executive Director: Vienna Insurance Gp, 2012–; Commerzbank AG, 2012–; ÖBB Hldg AG, 2011–; Chm., Supervisory Bd, Austrian Res. Promotion Agency, 2011–. Consultant, Austrian Inst. of Econ. Res. Mem. Council, Univ. of Vienna, 2003–; Mem. Bd, Montanuniversität Leoben, 2013–. *Publications:* numerous articles and essays.

TUNBRIDGE, William Michael Gregg, MD; FRCP; Director of Postgraduate Medical Education and Training, Oxford University, 1994–2003; Professorial Fellow of Wadham College, Oxford, 1994–2003, now Fellow Emeritus; *b* 13 June 1940; *s* of Sir Ronald Ernest Tunbridge, OBE and of Dorothy (*née* Gregg); *m* 1965, Felicity Katherine Edith Parrish; two *d. Educ:* Kingswood Sch., Bath; Queens' Coll., Cambridge (MA, MD); University Coll. Hosp. House appointments: UCH, 1964–65; Mpilo Hosp., Bulawayo, 1965–66; Manchester Royal Infirmary, 1967–68; Tutor in Medicine, Univ. of Manchester, 1969–70; Registrar, Hammersmith Hosp., 1970–72; Sen. Res. Associate, Univ. of Newcastle, 1972–75; Sen. Registrar in Medicine, Durham, 1975–76; MRC Travelling Fellow, Liège, 1976–77; Consultant Physician, Newcastle Gen. Hosp. and Sen. Lectr in Medicine, Univ. of Newcastle upon Tyne, 1977–94; Consultant Physician, Radcliffe Infirmary, then Oxford Radcliffe Hosps, 1994–2005; Physician Emeritus, Nuffield Dept of Medicine, Oxford Univ., 2005–. President: Thyroid Club, 1994–96; Endocrine Section, Union of European Med. Specialists, 1994–98. *Publications:* (with P. D. Home) Diabetes and Endocrinology in Clinical Practice, 1991; Thyroid Disease: the facts, 3rd edn (with R. I. S. Bayliss) 1998, 4th edn (with M. P. J. Vanderpump) 2008; (ed) Rationing of Health Care in Medicine, 1993. *Recreations:* walking, golf. *Address:* Millstone, Ranmoor Lane, Hathersage, Hope Valley, Derbys S32 1BW. *T:* (01433) 650765. *Club:* Athenæum.

TUNG Chee Hwa; Chief Executive, Hong Kong Special Administrative Region, 1997–2005; Vice-Chairman, National Committee, Chinese People's Political Consultative Conference, since 2005; *b* 29 May 1937; *er s* of Tung Chao Yung and Koo Lee Ching; *m* 1961, Betty Tung Chiu Hung Ping; two *s* one *d. Educ:* Liverpool Univ. (BSc Marine Engrg 1960). Chm. and CEO, Orient Overseas (International) Ltd, 1986–96. Advr, Hong Kong Affairs, 1992–96; Member: Basic Law Consultative Cttee, 1985–90; Exec. Council, Hong Kong Govt, 1992–96; 8th Cttee, Chinese People's Political Consultative Conf., 1993–98, 10th Cttee, 2005–08, 11th Cttee, 2008–; Vice-Chm., Prep. Cttee, HKSAR, 1995–96. Member: Hong Kong/Japan Business Co-operation Cttee, 1991–96; Chm., Hong Kong/US Economic Co-operation Cttee, 1993–96; Founding Chm., China-US Exchange Foundn, 2008–. Hon. LLD Liverpool, 1997. *Recreations:* hiking, Tai Chi, swimming, reading.

TUNNICLIFFE, family name of **Baron Tunnicliffe**.

TUNNICLIFFE, Baron *cr* 2004 (Life Peer), of Bracknell in the County of Berkshire; **Denis Tunnicliffe,** CBE 1993; an Opposition Whip, House of Lords, since 2010; *b* 17 Jan. 1943; *s* of Harold Arthur and Nellie Tunnicliffe; *m* 1968, Susan Dale; one *s* (and one *s* decd). *Educ:* Henry Cavendish Sch., Derby; University Coll. London (State Schol.; BSc (Special)); College of Air Training, Hamble. Pilot, BOAC, 1966–72; British Airways, 1972–86; Chief Exec., International Leisure Group, Aviation Div., 1986–88; Man. Dir, London Underground Ltd, 1988–98; Mem. of Bd, 1993–2000, Chief Exec., 1998–2000, London Transport. Chairman: UKAEA, 2002–04; Rail Safety and Standards Bd, 2003–08; non-exec. Dir, Defence Equipment and Support (formerly Defence Logistics Orgn and Defence Procurement Agency), MoD, 2006–08. A Lord in Waiting (Govt Whip), 2008–10. Councillor, Royal Bor. of New Windsor, 1971–75; Councillor, Royal County of Berkshire, 1974–77; Dist Councillor, Bracknell, 1979–83. *Recreations:* flying, boating, church, travelling. *Address:* House of Lords, SW1A 0PW. *Clubs:* Royal Air Force, Royal Automobile.

TUNSTALL, Sir Craig, Kt 2014; Executive Headteacher, Gipsy Hill Federation, Lambeth, since 2007; *b* Workington, Cumbria, 8 March 1971; s of Tom and Sarah Jane Tunstall; partner, Jeffrey Michael. *Educ:* Broughton Moor Primary Sch.; Netherhall Secondary Sch.; University Coll. of Ripon and York St John, Univ. of Leeds (BEd Hons); Greenwich Univ. (MA); Leicester Univ. (MBA). NPQH 2000. Teacher, Ayresome Jun. Sch., Middlesbrough, 1993–95; Torridon Jun. Sch., Lewisham, 1995–97; Sen. Teacher, Kender Primary Sch., Lewisham, 1997–99; Dep. Hd, Wyborne Primary Sch., Greenwich, 1999–2002; Headteacher: Kingswood Primary Sch., Lambeth, 2002–; Executive Headteacher: Elm Wood Primary Sch., Lambeth, 2007–; Paxton Primary Sch., Lambeth, 2009–; Crawford Primary Sch., Southwark, 2011–; Fenstanton Primary Sch., Lambeth, 2012–; Mayflower Fedn, Southwark, 2013–; Glenbrook Primary Sch., Lambeth, 2013–. *Recreations:* classical music, theatre. *Address:* Kingswood Primary School (Lower Site), 55 Gipsy Road, SE27 9NP. *T:* (020) 8761 4827. *E:* execheadteacher@gipsyhillfederation.org.uk.

TUNSTALL, Kathryn; Strategic Director for Services to Children and Young People, Bradford Metropolitan District Council, 2007–13; *b* St Helens, Merseyside, 26 Nov. 1953; *d* of Eric Thomas Tunstall and Majorie Naomi Tunstall (*née* Guest); *m* 1992, Keith McKay Watson; one *s* one *d*, and two step *d. Educ:* Rivington Road Prim. Sch., St Helens; Cowley Girls' Grammar Sch., St Helens (Hd Girl); Univ. of Leeds (BA Hons Psychol./Sociol. 1975); Univ. of Hull (DipASS 1978; CQSW 1978). Qualified Social Worker, 1978, specialising in child protection; Sen. Manager, responsible for Community Social Work Services, Leeds CC, 1998–2002; Bradford Metropolitan District Council: Asst Dir for Children's Services, Social Services, 2002–05; Dir, Social Services, 2005–07. Chairman: Bradford Area Child Protection Cttee, 2002–06; Bradford Safeguarding Children Bd, 2006–13; Bradford Youth Offenders Services Bd, 2007–13; Bradford Children and Young People's Strategic Partnership, 2007–13. *Recreations:* spending time with my own family, worldwide travel, understanding how families tick, indulging in quality food and wine, gardening, bird watching, Coronation Street, supporting St Helens Rugby League Football Club.

TUOHY, Denis John; broadcaster, writer and actor; *b* 2 April 1937; *s* of late John Vincent Tuohy and Anne Mary, (Nan), Tuohy (*née* Doody); *m* 1st, 1960, Moya McCann (marr. diss. 1988); two *s* two *d*; 2nd, 1998, Elizabeth Moran (marr. diss. 2007). *Educ:* Clongowes Wood Coll., Co. Kildare; Queen's Univ., Belfast (BA Hons Classics). Eisenhower Fellow, USA, 1967. BBC: Newscaster and Reporter, NI, 1960–64; Presenter, Late Night Line Up, 1964–67; Reporter and Presenter: 24 Hours, 1967–71; Panorama, 1974–75; Reporter, Man Alive, 1971–72; Presenter, Tonight, 1975–79; Thames Television: Reporter, This Week, 1972–74; Presenter, People and Politics, 1973–74; Presenter and Reporter: TV Eye, 1979–86; This Week, 1986–92; Newscaster, ITN, 1994–2001; Presenter: Something Understood, BBC Radio 4, 1995–99; Cards of Identity, RTE, 2002; A Living Word, RTE, 2003; Thought for the Day, BBC Radio Ulster, 2013–15; reporter/presenter on numerous documentaries, incl. for BBC and ITV: A Life of O'Reilly, 1974; Mr Truman, why did you drop the second bomb?, 1975; Do You Know Where Jimmy Carter Lives?, 1977; To Us a Child (prod jtly by Thames TV and UNICEF), 1986; The Blitz, 1991; The Real Dad's Army, 1998; The Law and the "Lunatic", 1999; for UTV: The Troubles I've Seen, 2008, 2012, 2014, 2015; UTV at Fifty, 2009; Belfast Blitz Anniversary, 2011; Thatcher's Ireland, 2013. Actor: Fair City, and The Clinic, RTE TV series, 2003; Fallout, RTE TV drama, 2006; The Tempest, Cork Midsummer Fest., 2006; Strength and Honour (film), 2007; Killinaskully, RTE TV series, 2007–08; Scapegoat, 2009, Betrayal of Trust, 2011, BBC NI TV drama; Blackness After Midnight, Belfast City Hall, 2012. *Publications:* Wide-eyed in Medialand (memoirs), 2005; articles in Irish Times, Sunday Independent, Belfast Telegraph, Irish News, Scotsman, Independent, New Statesman, The Tablet, The Oldie, etc. *Recreations:* walking in the Mournes, theatre, cinema, watching Rugby and cricket. *Address:* 16 Aurora na Mara, Shore Road, Rostrevor, Co. Down BT34 3UP.

TUPPER, Sir Charles Hibbert, 6th Bt *cr* 1888, of Armdale, Halifax, Nova Scotia; *b* 10 July 1964; *o s* of Sir Charles Hibbert Tupper, 5th Bt and of Bernice Yvonne (*née* Quinn, now Elderkin); *S* father, 2008, but his name does not appear on the Official Roll of the Baronetage; *m* 1987, Elizabeth Ann Heaslip; one *d. Heir: cousin* Charles Reginald Hibbert Tupper, *b* 20 Dec. 1947.

TURBOTT, Sir Ian (Graham), Kt 1968; AO 1997; CMG 1962; CVO 1966; Foundation Chancellor, University of Western Sydney, 1989–2001, Emeritus Chancellor, since 2001; *b* Whangarei, New Zealand, 9 March 1922; *s* of late Thomas Turbott and late E. A. Turbott, both of New Zealand; *m* 1952, Nancy Hall Lantz (*d* 1999), California, USA; three *d. Educ:* Takapuna Grammar School, Auckland, NZ; Auckland University; Jesus College, Cambridge; London University; Harvard Univ. NZ Forces (Army), 1940–46: Solomon Is area and 2 NZEF, Italy. Colonial Service (Overseas Civil Service): Western Pacific, Gilbert and Ellice Is, 1948–56; Colonial Office, 1956–58; Administrator of Antigua, The West Indies, 1958–64; also Queen's Representative under new constitution, 1960–64; Administrator of Grenada and Queen's Representative, 1964–67; Governor of Associated State of Grenada, 1966–68. Partner, Spencer Stuart and Associates Worldwide, 1973–84; Chairman: Spencer Stuart and Associates Pty Ltd, 1970–84; Chloride Batteries Australia Ltd, 1978–85; I. T. Graham Investments plc, 1982–; TNT Security Pty Ltd; Stuart Brooke Consultants Pty Ltd, Sydney, 1974–82; 2MMM Broadcasting Co. Pty Ltd; Melbourne F/M Radio Pty Ltd, 1986–93; Penrith Lakes Develt Corp., 1980–2007; Essington Ltd, 1984–89; New World Pictures (Aust.) Ltd, 1986–89; Triple M FM Radio Group, 1986–93; Cape York Space Agency Ltd, 1987–89; Hoyts Media Ltd, 1991–93; Dir, Hoyts Entertainment Ltd, 1990–93; Dep. Chm., Adv. Bd, Amer. Internat. Underwriting (Aust.) Ltd; Director: Standard Chartered Bank Australia Ltd, 1980–91; Capita Financial Gp, 1979–91; Newcastle F/M P/L, 1983–94. Chairman: Internat. Piano Competition Ltd, Sydney, 1977–84; Duke of Edinburgh's Award Scheme, NSW, 1984–95; Australia Youth Trust, 2001–; Dir, Ted Noffs Foundn, 2000–. Chm., Japan Entrepreneurs and Presidents Assoc., Australia, 1996–2005. Dir, Commonwealth Council, 2001–. Governor, NSW Conservatorium of Music, 1974–89. Inaugural Patron, Hawkesbury Foundn, Univ. of Western Sydney, 2010. FRSA; FAIM; FAICD. Hon Consul for Cook Is in Australia, 1995. JP 1972. Hon. DLitt Western Sydney, 1993. CStJ 1964. Silver Jubilee Medal, 1977; Guadalcanal Medal (Solomon Is), 1998. Holds 1939–45 Star, Pacific Star, Italy Star, Defence Medal, War Medal, New Zealand Service Medal. *Publications:* Lands of Sun and Spice, 1996; Nancy - my beloved, 2000; For My Children and Grandchildren - a war record, 2002; Masters of Survival, 2006; various technical and scientific, 1948–51, in Jl of Polynesian Society (on Pacific area). *Recreations:* watching cricket, fishing. *Address:* 8/8 Lauderdale Avenue, Fairlight, NSW 2094, Australia; 38 MacMasters Parade, MacMasters Beach, NSW 2251, Australia. *Clubs:* Australian (Sydney); Royal Sydney Yacht.

TURCAN, Henry Watson; a Recorder of the Crown Court, 1985–2013; *b* 22 Aug. 1941; *s* of late Henry Hutchison Turcan and Lilias Cheyne; *m* 1969, Jane Fairrie Blair; one *s* one *d. Educ:* Rugby School; Trinity College, Oxford (BA, MA). Called to the Bar, Inner Temple, 1965, Bencher, 1992. Legal Assessor to General Optical Council, 1983–2003. Special Adjudicator, Immigration Appeals, 1998–2005; an Immigration Judge, 2005–11. *Recreations:* shooting, fishing, golf. *Address:* Cairney Hall, Newburgh, Fife KY14 6JB. *T:* (01337) 810302. *Clubs:* New (Edinburgh); Royal and Ancient Golf (St Andrews); Hon. Company of Edinburgh Golfers (Muirfield).

TURCAN, William James; Chief Executive, Elementis (formerly Harrisons & Crosfield plc), 1994–98; *b* 4 Jan. 1943; *m* 1967, Elisabeth Margaret Stewart; three *s* one *d. Educ:* Rugby Sch.; Trinity Coll., Oxford (MA). Binder Hamlyn, 1965–70; Pauls Malt, 1970–86; Finance Dir, Pauls plc, 1986–88; Finance Dir, Harrisons & Crosfield, 1988–94. Bd Mem., Glenrothes New Town Develt Corp., 1983–86.

TUREI, Most Rev. William Brown; *see* Aotearoa, Archbishop of.

TURING, Sir John Dermot, 12th Bt *cr* 1638 (NS), of Foveran, Aberdeenshire; Partner, Clifford Chance, Solicitors, since 1999; *b* 26 Feb. 1961; *s* of John Ferrier Turing (*d* 1983) and of Beryl Mary Ada, *d* of late Herbert Vaughan Hann; *S* kinsman, Sir John Leslie Turing, 11th Bt, 1987; *m* 1986, Nicola J., *er d* of M. D. Simmonds; two *s. Educ:* Sherborne Sch., Dorset; King's Coll., Cambridge (BA 1982; MA 1986); New Coll., Oxford (DPhil 1986). Admitted solicitor, 1991. Trustee, Bletchley Park Trust, 2012–. *Heir: s* John Malcolm Ferrier Turing, *b* 5 Sept. 1988. *Address:* 68 Marshalswick Lane, St Albans AL1 4XF.

TÜRK, Dr Danilo; President, Republic of Slovenia, 2007–12; *b* Maribor, 19 Feb. 1952; *m* 1976, Barbara Miklič; one *d. Educ:* elementary and grammar sch., Maribor; Univ. of Ljubljana (law degree 1975; Dr 1982); Univ. of Belgrade (LLM 1979). Prof. of Internat. Law, 1981–92, Hd, Inst. of Internat. Law and Internat. Relns, 1983–92, Univ. of Ljubljana; Ambassador of Slovenia to UN, 1992–2000; Rep. of Slovenia on UN Security Council, 1998–99; Asst of UN Sec.-Gen. for Political Affairs, 2000–05; Prof. of Internat. Law, 2005–08, Vice-Dean, 2006–07, Univ. of Ljubljana. Mem., UN Sub-Commn on Prevention of Discrimination and Protection of Minorities, 1984–92; UN Special Rapporteur on Realization of Econ., Social and Cultural Rights, 1986–92; Mem., Slovene Delegn at Conf. of Yugoslavia, 1991–92. *Publications:* Načelo neintervencije v mednarodnih odnosih in v mednarodnem pravu (The Principle of Non-intervention), 1984; Temelji mednarodnega prava (Foundations of International Law), 2007; contrib. articles to law jls. *Recreations:* nordic walking, cross-country ski-ing, ski-ing.

TURLEY, Anna Catherine; MP (Lab Co-op) Redcar, since 2015; *b* Dartford, 9 Oct. 1978. *Educ:* Ashford Sch., Kent; Greyfriars Hall, Oxford (BA Hons Hist.). Civil Servant, Home Office, 2001–05; Special Adviser: to Sec. of State for Work and Pensions, 2005; to Chancellor of Duchy of Lancaster, 2006–07; Dep. Dir, New Local Govt Network, 2007–10. *Address:* House of Commons, SW1A 0AA. *T:* (020) 7219 5441. *E:* anna.turley.mp@parliament.uk.

TURMEAU, Prof. William Arthur, CBE 1989; PhD; FRSE; CEng, FIMechE; Chairman, Scottish Environment Protection Agency, 1995–99; Principal and Vice-Chancellor, Napier University, 1992–94 (Principal, Napier College, subseq. Napier Polytechnic of Edinburgh, 1982–92); *b* 19 Sept. 1929; *s* of Frank Richard Turmeau and Catherine Lyon Linklater; *m* 1957, Margaret Moar Burnett, MA, BCom; one *d. Educ:* Stromness Acad., Orkney; Univ. of Edinburgh (BSc); Moray House Coll. of Educn; Heriot-Watt Univ. (PhD). FIMechE, CEng, 1971; FRSE 1990. Royal Signals, 1947–49. Research Engr, Northern Electric Co. Ltd, Montreal, 1952–54; Mechanical Engr, USAF, Goose Bay, Labrador, 1954–56; Contracts Manager, Godfrey Engrg Co. Ltd, Montreal, 1956–61; Lectr, Bristo Technical Inst., 1962–64; Napier College: Lectr and Sen. Lectr, 1964–68; Head, Dept of Mechanical Engrg, 1968–75; Asst Principal and Dean, Faculty of Technology, 1975–82. Member: CICHE, British Council, 1982–92; CVCP, 1992–94 (Mem., Cttee of Dirs of Polytechnics, 1982–92); Standing Conf. of Rectors and Vice-Chancellors of European Univs, 1990–94; Cttee of Scottish Univ. Principals, 1992–94; Scottish Div. Cttee, Inst. of Dirs, 1992–94; Acad. Standards Cttee, IMechE, 1994–2004. Dir, ASH Scotland, 1996–. Trustee, Dynamic Earth Charitable Trust, 1994–2000. Mem. Court, Edinburgh Acad., 1993–99. Dr *hc* Edinburgh, 1992; DEd *hc* Napier, 1995. *Publications:* various papers relating to higher educn. *Recreations:* modern jazz, Leonardo da Vinci. *Address:* 132 Victoria Street, Stromness, Orkney KW16 3BU. *T:* (01856) 850500. *E:* profwaturmeau@aol.com.

TURNAGE, Mark-Anthony, CBE 2015; composer; *b* 1960. *Educ:* Royal College of Music. Mendelssohn Scholar, Tanglewood, USA, 1983. Composer in Association: City of Birmingham Symphony Orchestra, 1989–93; ENO, 1995–2000; Associate Composer, BBC SO, 2000–03; Mead Composer in Residence, Chicago SO, 2006–10; Composer in Residence, LPO, 2006–11. *Compositions include: stage:* Greek, 1988 (BMW prizes for best opera and best libretto, Munich Biennale, 1988); The Silver Tassie (opera), 2000 (Outstanding Achievement in Opera (jtly), Laurence Olivier Awards, and South Bank Show Award for opera, 2001); Anna Nicole (opera), 2011; *vocal:* Lament for a Hanging Man, 1983; Greek Suite, 1989; Some Days, 1989; Twice Through The Heart, 1997; A Relic of Memory, 2003; The Torn Fields, 2004; Two Baudelaire Songs, 2004; About Water, 2007; At Sixes and Sevens, 2013; *orchestral:* Night Dances, 1981; Three Screaming Popes, 1989; Momentum, 1991; Drowned Out, 1993; Your Rockaby (saxophone concerto), 1994; Dispelling the Fears, 1995; Silent Cities, 1998; Evening Songs, 1999; Another Set To, 2000; Dark Crossing, 2001; Etudes and Elegies, 2002; On Opened Ground (viola concerto), 2002; Scherzoid, 2005; Yet Another Set To (trombone concerto), 2005; From All Sides, 2006; Chicago Remains, 2007; Mambo, Blues and Tarantella (violin concerto), 2008; Five Views of a Mouth, 2009; Texan Tenebrae, 2010; Hammered Out, 2010; Undance (ballet score), 2011; Canon Fever, 2012; Cello Concerto, 2012; Trespass (ballet score), 2012; Speranza, 2013; Frieze, 2013; Piano Concerto, 2013; Erskine, 2013; Passchendale, 2014; *ensemble:* On All Fours, 1985; Kai, 1990; Three Farewells, 1990; Blood on the Floor, 1996; About Time, 1999; Bass inventionS, 2000; Slide Stride, 2002; Eulogy, 2003; No Let Up, 2004; Crying Out Loud, 2004; A Prayer Before Stillness, 2007; A Constant Obsession, 2009; *instrumental:* Sleep on, 1992; Two Elegies framing a Shout, 1994; True Life Stories, 1995–99; Two Memorials, 1995–2000; Riffs and Refrains (solo clarinet), 2003; A Few Serenades, 2004; A Slow Pavane, A Fast Stomp, A Short Procession (piano trios), 2005; Twisted Blues with Twisted Ballad, 2008; Contusion, 2014. *Relevant publication:* Mark-Anthony Turnage, by Andrew Clements, 2000. *Address:* c/o Cathy Nelson Artists and Projects, The Court House, Dorstone, Herefordshire HR3 6AW. *T:* (01981) 551903.

TURNBERG, family name of **Baron Turnberg**.

TURNBERG, Baron *cr* 2000 (Life Peer), of Cheadle in the county of Cheshire; **Leslie Arnold Turnberg,** Kt 1994; MD; FRCP, FMedSci; Chairman: National Centre for Replacement, Refinement and Reduction of Animals in Research, 2004–07; Medical Advisory Board, Nations Health Care, 2004–07; *b* 22 March 1934; *s* of Hyman and Dora Turnberg; *m* 1968, Edna Barme; one *s* one *d. Educ:* Stand Grammar Sch., Whitefield; Univ. of Manchester (MB, ChB 1957, MD 1966). MRCP 1961, FRCP 1973; FRCPE 1993; FRCP(I) 1993; FRCPSGlas 1994; FRCS 1996; FCPS (Pak). Junior medical posts: Manchester Jewish Hosp.; Northern Hosp.; Ancoats Hosp.; Manchester Royal Infirmary, 1957–61 and 1964–66; Registrar, UCH, 1961–64; Lectr, Royal Free Hosp., 1967; Res. Fellow, Univ. of Texas South-Western Med. Sch., Dallas, Texas, 1968; University of Manchester: Lectr, then Sen. Lectr, 1968–73; Dean, Fac. of Medicine, 1986–89; Prof. of Medicine, 1973–97. Chm., Specialist Training Authy, 1996–98. Hon. Consultant Physician, Salford HA, 1973–97. Member: Salford HA, 1974–81 and 1990–92; NW RHA, 1986–89. Chairman: PHLS Bd, 1997–2002; Health Quality Service, 2000–04; Mem. Bd, Renovo Gp, 2005–11. Mem., Select Cttee on sci. and technol., H of L, 2001–05. Scientific Advr, Assoc. Med. Res. Charities, 1997–. Royal College of Physicians: Mem. Council, 1989–92; Pres., 1992–97; Chairman: Educn Cttee, 1990–92; Wkg Gp on Communication, 1991–92; British Society of Gastroenterology: Mem. Council, 1989–92; Chm., Res. Cttee, 1991–92; Pres., 1999–2000; President: Med. Section, Manchester Med. Soc., 1992–93; Medical Protection Soc., 1997–2007. Trustee: Wolfson Foundn, 1997–; Hadassah UK, 2000–12; Ovarian Cancer Action, 2008–; Weizmann UK, 2010–. Founder FMedSci 1998 (Vice Pres., 1998–2004). Hon. FFOM 1993; Hon. FRACP 1994; Hon. FRCOphth 1996; Hon. FRCOG 1996; Hon. FFPM 1997; Hon. Fellow: Acad. of Medicine, Singapore, 1994; Coll. of Medicine, S Africa, 1994. Hon. DSc: Salford, 1996; Manchester, 1998; Imperial Coll. London, 2000; Keele, 2008. *Publications:* Electrolyte and Water Transport Across Gastro-intestinal Epithelia, 1982; Clinical Gastroenterology, 1989; Forks in the Road, 2014; pubns on mechanisms of intestinal absorption and secretion in health and disease and on clinical gastroenterology. *Recreations:* reading, antiquarian books, painting, walking, talking. *Address:* House of Lords, SW1A 0PW.

TURNBULL, family name of **Baron Turnbull**.

TURNBULL, Baron *cr* 2005 (Life Peer), of Enfield in the London Borough of Enfield; **Andrew Turnbull,** KCB 1998 (CB 1990); CVO 1992; Secretary of the Cabinet and Head of the Home Civil Service, 2002–05; *b* 21 Jan. 1945; *s* of Anthony and Mary Turnbull; *m* 1967, Diane Clarke; two *s. Educ:* Enfield Grammar Sch.; Christ's Coll., Cambridge (BA). ODI Fellow working as economist, Govt of Republic of Zambia, Lusaka, 1968–70; Asst Principal, HM Treasury, 1970; Principal, 1972; on secondment to staff of IMF, 1976–78; Asst Sec., HM Treasury, 1978; Private Sec. to the Prime Minister, 1983–85; Under Sec., 1985; Hd of Gen. Expenditure Policy Gp, HM Treasury, 1985–88; Principal Private Sec. to Prime Minister, 1988–92; Dep. Sec. (Public Finance), 1992, Second Permanent Sec. (Public Expenditure), 1993–94, HM Treasury; Permanent Secretary: DoE, later DETR, 1994–98; HM Treasury, 1998–2002. Chair, BH Global Ltd, 2008–12; non-executive Director: Prudential plc, 2006–15; British Land Co. plc, 2006–; Frontier Economics Ltd, 2006–. Trustee, Global Warming Policy Foundn, 2009–. Chair of Govs, Dulwich Coll., 2009–15. *Recreations:* walking, sailing, opera, golf. *Address:* House of Lords, SW1A 0PW. *Club:* Tottenham Hotspur.

TURNBULL, Hon. Lord; Alan D. Turnbull; a Senator of the College of Justice in Scotland, since 2006. *Educ:* Univ. of Dundee (LLB 1979). Admitted to Faculty of Advocates, 1982; in practice at the Bar; Advocate Depute, 1995–97; QC (Scot.) 1996; Principal Advocate Depute, 2001–06. *Address:* Court of Session, Parliament House, Edinburgh EH1 1RQ.

TURNBULL, Alan, PhD; FRS 2013; FREng; Senior Fellow, National Physical Laboratory, since 2011 (Fellow, since 1989); *b* Glasgow, 4 Sept. 1949; *s* of Alexander Stewart Turnbull and Mary Turnbull; *m* 1971, Ruth Jane Bolton (*d* 2009); two *d. Educ:* St Augustine's Sch., Glasgow; Univ. of Strathclyde (BSc 1st Cl. Hons 1970); Univ. of Bristol (PhD 1974). FICorr 1986; FIMMM 1999; FREng 2011. Joined Materials Div., NPL, 1973. Vis. Scientist, MIT, 1989. Fellow, 2008, Whitney Award, 2009, Nat. Assoc. of Corrosion Engrs Internat.; T. P. Hoar Prize, ICorr, 1987 and 2011; Bengough Prize and Medal, Inst. of Materials, 1994; Cavallaro Medal, Eur. Fedn of Corrosion, 2002; U. R. Evans Award, ICorr, 2004; Alec Hough-Grassby Award, Inst. of Measurement and Control, 2013. *Publications:* scientific papers in Corrosion, Corrosion Sci., Materials Sci. and Engrg. *Recreations:* golf, hiking, gardening, watching football. *Address:* 1 Kingsmead Avenue, Sunbury TW16 5HW. *T:* (work) (020) 8943 7115. *E:* alan.turnbull@npl.co.uk.

TURNBULL, Alan D.; *see* Turnbull, Hon. Lord.

TURNBULL, Rt Rev. (Anthony) Michael (Arnold); *see* Turnbull, Rt Rev. M.

TURNBULL, Charles Emerson Lovett; an Upper Tribunal Judge (Administrative Appeals Chamber) (formerly a Social Security and Child Support Commissioner), since 2000; *b* Windlesham, 14 Jan. 1952; *s* of Muir Turnbull and Joan Turnbull (*née* Lovett); *m* 1990, Judith Mason; one *s* one *d. Educ:* Charterhouse; Worcester Coll., Oxford (BA 1st Cl. Hons Juris. 1973; Eldon Law Scholar). Called to the Bar, Inner Temple, 1975; in practice as a barrister, specialising in Chancery law, Wilberforce Chambers, Lincoln's Inn, 1976–2000. *Recreations:* tennis, ringing church bells, classical music, walking, cross-country ski-ing. *Address:* Upper Tribunal, Administrative Appeals Chamber, 5th Floor, Rolls Building, 7 Rolls Buildings, Fetter Lane, EC4A 1NL. *E:* charles.turnbull@judiciary.gsi.gov.uk.

TURNBULL, David Knight Thomas, FCA; Director: Worldbeater Solutions Ltd, since 2000; XXX Building Ltd, since 1999; *b* 13 Dec. 1948; *s* of Stanley Thomas Turnbull and Lalla Turnbull (*née* Knight); *m* 1972, Monica Belton; one *s* one *d. Educ:* Stationers' Co. Sch.; Westfield Coll., London Univ. (BSc). FCA 1975. With Coopers & Lybrand, Sheffield and Iran, 1972–79; Amalgamated Metal Corporation plc: Gp Chief Acct, 1980–84; Corporate Controller, 1984–86; Gen. Manager, Business Develt, 1986–89; Finance Director: PO Counters Ltd, 1989–94; British Council, 1994–2000; Army Benevolent Fund, 2001–06. Sec., Interstate Programmes Ltd, 2000–. *Recreations:* anything old, watching Rugby. *Address:* Halfway Grange, Chantry View Road, Guildford, Surrey GU1 3XR. *T:* (01483) 569285.

TURNBULL, Hon. Malcolm Bligh; MHR (L) Wentworth, New South Wales, since 2004; Prime Minister of Australia, since 2015; Leader of the Liberal Party, Australia, since 2015; *b* 24 Oct. 1954; *s* of late Bruce Bligh Turnbull and Coral (*née* Lansbury); *m* 1980, Lucinda Mary Forrest Hughes, AO, *d* of Hon. Thomas Hughes, AO, QC; one *s* one *d. Educ:* Sydney Grammar Sch.; Sydney Univ. (BA, LLB); Brasenose Coll., Oxford (Rhodes Schol. (NSW) 1978, BCL 1980). Journalist, Nation Review, 1975; Political Correspondent: TCN–9, Sydney, 1976; The Bulletin, 1977–78; Journalist, Sunday Times, London, 1979; admitted to NSW Bar, 1980; Barrister, Sydney, 1980–83; Gen. Counsel and Secretary, Consolidated Press Holdings Ltd, 1983–86; Partner: Turnbull McWilliam, Solicitors, Sydney, 1986–87; Turnbull & Co., Solicitors, 1987–90; Jt Man. Dir, Whitlam Turnbull & Co. Ltd, Investment Bankers, Sydney, 1987–90; Man. Dir, Turnbull & Partners Pty Ltd, Investment Bankers, 1987–97; Man. Dir and Chm., Goldman Sachs Australia, 1997–2001; Partner, Goldman Sachs & Co., 1998–2001. Chm., Australian Republican Movement, 1993–2000 (Dir, 1991–2002); Deleg., Constitutional Convention, 1998; Hon. Federal Treas., Liberal Party of Australia, 2002–03. Parly Sec. to PM of Australia, 2006–07; Minister for the Envmt and Water Resources, 2007; Federal Shadow Treas., 2007–08; Leader, Parly Liberal Party and Leader of the Opposition, 2008–09; Shadow Minister for Communications and Broadband, 2010–13; Minister for Communications, 2013–15. Chairman: FTR Holdings, then WebCentral Gp, Ltd, 1995–97, 2001–04 (Dir, 1995–2004); OzEmail Ltd, 1995–99 (Dir, 1995–99); Dir, Reach Ltd, 2001–04. Chm., Menzies Res. Centre, 2002–04. Centenary Medal, Australia, 2003. *Publications:* The Spycatcher Trial, 1988; The Reluctant Republic, 1993; Fighting for the Republic, 1999. *Recreations:* walking, swimming, sailing. *Address:* PO Box 545, Edgecliff, NSW 2027, Australia. *T:* (2) 93273988, *Fax:* (2) 93272533; 46 Wunulla Road, Point Piper, NSW 2027, Australia. *Clubs:* Athenæum (Philadelphia); Australian, Tattersall's (Sydney); Royal Prince Edward Yacht, Royal Motor Yacht; North Bondi Surf Life Saving (Sydney).

TURNBULL, Mark; *see* Turnbull, W. M.

TURNBULL, Rt Rev. Michael, CBE 2003; DL; Bishop of Durham, 1994–2003; an Honorary Assistant Bishop: Diocese of Canterbury, since 2003; Diocese of Europe, since 2003; Diocese of Rochester, since 2010; *b* 27 Dec. 1935; *s* of George Ernest Turnbull and Adeline Turnbull (*née* Awty); *m* 1963, Brenda Susan Merchant; one *s* two *d. Educ:* Ilkley Grammar Sch.; Keble Coll., Oxford (MA); St John's Coll., Durham (DipTh). Deacon, 1960; priest, 1961; Curate: Middleton, 1960–61; Luton, 1961–65; Domestic Chaplain to Archbishop of York, 1965–69; Rector of Heslington and Chaplain, York Univ., 1969–76; Chief Secretary, Church Army, 1976–84; Archdeacon of Rochester, also Canon Residentiary of Rochester Cathedral and Chm., Dio. Bd for Mission and Unity, 1984–88; Bishop of Rochester, 1988–94. Entered H of L, 1994. Mem., General Synod, C of E, 1970–75, 1987–2003; Vice-Chm., Central Bd of Finance, C of E, 1990–98; Member: Bd, Church Commissioners, 1989–98; Archbishops' Council, 1998–2000 (Chm., Ministry Div., 1999–2000); Archbps' Commn on Cathedrals, 1992–93; Chairman: Archbps' Commn on orgn of C of E, 1994–96; Foundn for Church Leadership, 2003–07. Chairman: NE Constitutional Convention, 1999–2003; Campaign for English Regs, 2000–03. Chairman: Bible Reading Fellowship, 1985–94; Coll. of Preachers, 1990–98. Lectr, Swan Hellenic, 2003–15; Pilgrimage Leader, 2003–15. DL Kent, 2005. Hon. Fellow, St Chad's Coll., Durham, 2002. Hon. DLitt Greenwich, 1994; Hon. DD Dunelm, 2003. *Publications:* (contrib.) Unity: the next step?, 1972; God's Front Line, 1979; Parish Evangelism, 1980; Learning to Pray, 1981; 100 Minute Bible Reflections, 2007; The State of the Church and the Church of the State, 2012. *Recreations:* cricket, family life, allotment. *Address:* 3 Gardners Quay, Upper Strand Street, Sandwich, Kent CT13 9DH. *T:* (01304) 611389. *E:* amichaelturnbull@yahoo.co.uk. *Club:* MCC.

TURNBULL, Rev. Dr Richard Duncan, PhD; FRHistS; Director, Centre for Enterprise, Markets and Ethics, since 2012; *b* 17 Oct. 1960; *s* of Alan Allgood Turnbull and late Kathleen Turnbull; *m* 1986, Caroline Andrew; one *s* three *d. Educ:* Moseley Grammar Sch.; Normanton High Sch.; Univ. of Reading (BA 1982); Univ. of Durham (BA 1992; PhD 1997); Univ. of Oxford (MA 2005). CA 1985. Supervisory and trng posts, 1982–87, Manager, 1987–90, Ernst and Young, chartered accountants; ordination trng, Cranmer Hall, Durham, 1990–94; ordained deacon, 1994, priest, 1995; Curate, Christ Church, Portswood, Southampton, 1994–98; Vicar, Christ Church, Chineham, Basingstoke, 1998–2005; Principal, Wycliffe Hall, Oxford, 2005–12 (Hon. Res. Fellow, 2012–); Mem., Faculty of Theology, Univ. of

Oxford. Member: Gen. Synod, 1995–2005 (Chm., Business Cttee, 2004–05); Archbishops' Council, 2003–05. *Publications:* Anglican and Evangelical?, 2007; Shaftesbury: the great reformer, 2010; Reviving the Heart, 2012; A Passionate Faith, 2012; Quaker Capitalism: lessons for today, 2014; articles on Evangelicalism in Churchman and Anvil; contrib. dictionary entry on 7th Earl of Shaftesbury to Theologische Realenzyklopädie, 1999. *Recreations:* walking, reading, visiting historic houses, Real tennis. *Address:* Centre for Enterprise, Markets and Ethics, 1st Floor, 31 Beaumont Street, Oxford OX1 2NP. *T:* (01865) 513453. *E:* richard.turnbull@theceme.org.

TURNBULL, (Wilson) Mark, RIBA; FRIAS, FLI; Principal, Mark Turnbull Landscape Architect, since 1999; Chairman, Envision 3D (formerly TJP Envision, then Envision), since 1999; *b* 1 April 1943; *s* of Wilson and Margaret Turnbull. *Educ:* Edinburgh Coll. of Art (Andrew Grant scholar, 1964, 1965, 1967, 1968; DipArch (distinction in Design) 1968); Univ. of Pennsylvania (Fulbright scholar, 1968–74; Faculty Medal, Dept of Landscape Arch. and Regl Planning, 1970; MLA summa cum laude 1970). RIBA 1977; MBCS 1984; FLI 1989; FRIAS 1991. John D. Carnagie, Architect, 1962–63; Reiach and Hall, Architects and Planners, 1965–66; Chartered Architect, Landscape Architect and IT Professional, Wallace, McHarg, Roberts and Todd, Landscape Architects and Regl Planners, Philadelphia, 1968–70; Asst Prof., Dept of Architecture, Univ. of S Calif, LA, 1970–74; Envmtl Consultant: Union Carbide; US Atomic Energy Commn, 1970, 1974; Kamnitzer, Marks, Lappin and Vreeland, Architects and Regl Planners, LA, 1973–74; Associate, 1974–77, Partner, 1977–82, W. J. Cairns and Partners, Envmtl Consultants, Edinburgh; Partner, Design Innovations Res., 1978–82; Principal, 1982–99, Chm., 1999–2001, Turnbull Jeffrey Partnership, Landscape Architects. Comr, Royal Fine Art Commn for Scotland, 1996–2005. Mem. Council, Cockburn Assoc., Edinburgh Civic Trust, 1984–95; Landscape Institute: Mem., Tech. Cttee, 1996– (Chm., 2013–); Mem., Guidelines for Landscape and Visual Impact Assessment Panel, 2010–; Bd Mem., 2013–; Chair, Landscape Inst. Scotland, 2011–; Comr, Countryside Commn for Scotland, 1988–92; Chm., Edinburgh Green Belt Initiative, 1988–92; Vice-Chm., 1992–2002, Dir, 2002–, Edinburgh and Lothians Greenspace (formerly Edinburgh Green Belt) Trust. Edinburgh Corp. Medal for Civic Design, 1970. *Publications:* numerous articles on landscape architecture, computer visualisation and design methods in jls. *Recreation:* sailing. *Address:* Mark Turnbull Landscape Architect, Creag an Tuirc House, Balquhidder, Lochearnhead, Perthshire FK19 8NY. *T:* (01877) 384728.

TURNER, family name of **Barons Netherthorpe**, **Turner of Ecchinswell** and **Baroness Turner of Camden**.

TURNER OF CAMDEN, Baroness *cr* 1985 (Life Peer), of Camden in Greater London; **Muriel Winifred Turner;** *b* 18 Sept. 1927; *m* 1955, Reginald Thomas Frederick Turner (*d* 1995), MC, DFC. Asst Gen. Sec., ASTMS, 1970–87. Member: Occupational Pensions Board, 1978–93; Central Arbitration Cttee, 1980–90; TUC General Council, 1981–87; Equal Opportunities Commission, 1982–88. Junior Spokesperson on Social Security, 1986–96, Principal Opposition Spokesperson on Employment, 1988–96, H of L. Chm., Ombudsman Council, PIA, 1994–97. Hon. LLD Leicester, 1991. *Address:* House of Lords, SW1A 0PW.

TURNER OF ECCHINSWELL, Baron *cr* 2005 (Life Peer), of Ecchinswell in the County of Hampshire; **(Jonathan) Adair Turner;** Chairman, Governing Board, Institute for New Economic Thinking, since 2015 (Senior Fellow, 2013–15); *b* 5 Oct. 1955; *s* of Geoffrey Vincent Turner and Kathleen Margaret (*née* Broadhurst); *m* 1985, Orna Ní Chionna, *qv*; two *d*. *Educ:* Gonville and Caius Coll., Cambridge (MA Hist. and Econs 1978; Hon. Fellow, 2011). Chm., Cambridge Univ. Cons. Assoc., 1976; Pres., Cambridge Union Soc., 1977. BP, 1979; with Chase Manhattan Bank, 1979–82; McKinsey & Co., 1982–95: Principal, 1988; Dir, 1994–95; Dir Gen., CBI, 1995–99; Vice Chm., Merrill Lynch Europe, 2000–06. Mem., Ct of Dirs, 2008–13, Interim Financial Policy Cttee, 2011–13, Bank of England. Non-executive Director: United Business Media, 2000–08; Siemens plc, 2006–08; Paternoster UK Ltd, 2006–08; Standard Chartered plc, 2006–08; Prudential, 2015–; Ind. Dir, Oak North, 2014–. Chairman: Low Pay Commn, 2002–06; Pension Commn, 2003–06; ESRC, 2007–08 (Mem., 2003–08); Climate Change Cttee, 2008–12; Standing Cttee on Supervisory and Regulatory Cooperation, Financial Stability Bd, 2009–13. Vis. Prof., 1999–, and Chair, Policy Cttee, Centre for Economic Performance, 1999–2007, LSE; Vis. Prof., Cass Business Sch., 2004–. Vis. Fellow, Nuffield Coll., Oxford, 2008–; Sen. Fellow, Centre for Financial Studies, Frankfurt, 2013–. Mem., Adv. Council, Bank of China's Sch. of Finance, Tsinghua Univ., 2015–. Trustee: Cambridge Foundn, 2002–08; WWF, 2001–07; Save the Children, 2006–08; BM, 2012– (Chm., Audit Cttee, 2013–). Hon. FRSE 2010. Hon. DSc City, 2002. *Publications:* Just Capital: the liberal economy, 2001; Economics after the Crisis: objectives and means, 2012; Between Debt and the Devil: money, credit and fixing global finance, 2015. *Recreations:* ski-ing, opera. *Address:* House of Lords, SW1A 0PW.

TURNER OF ECCHINSWELL, Lady; *see* Ní Chionna, O.

TURNER, Amédée Edward; QC 1976; *b* 26 March 1929; *s* of Frederick William Turner and Ruth Hempson; *m* 1960, Deborah Dudley Owen; one *s* one *d*. *Educ:* Temple Grove, Heron's Ghyll, Sussex; Dauntsey's Sch., Wilts; Christ Church, Oxford (MA). Called to Bar, Inner Temple, 1954; practised patent bar, 1954–57; Associate, Kenyon & Kenyon, patent attorneys, NY, 1957–60; London practice, 1960–2009; Senior Counsel: APCO Europe, Brussels, 1995–98; WorldSpace Ltd, 1999–2001; of Counsel, Oppenheimer Wolff and Donnelly, Brussels, 1994–2003. Dir, CJA Consultants Ltd, 1999– (Chm., 2004–). Hon. Sec., ME Gp, Cons. Commonwealth Council, 1954–57, 1960 and 1979. Contested (C) Norwich N, gen. elections, 1964, 1966, 1970. European Parliament: MEP (C) Suffolk, 1979–94; contested (C) Suffolk and SW Norfolk, 1994; Hon. MEP, 1994; EDG spokesman on energy res. and technol., 1984–89; Chief Whip, EDG, 1989–92; joined EPP Gp, 1992; Mem., EPP Gp Bureau, 1992–94; Chm., Civil Liberties and Internal Affairs Cttee, 1992–94; Vice Chm., Legal Cttee, 1979–84; Member: Economic and Monetary Cttee, 1979–84; ACP Jt Assembly, 1980–94; Transport Cttee, 1981–84; Energy Cttee, 1984–94; Legal Affairs Cttee, 1984–89. PHARE Advr to Macedonian Parlt on improving legislature and democratic effectiveness, 2001–02 (manual, The Approximation of EU Law, 2002). Mem., Exec. Cttee, European League for Econ. Co-operation, 1996–2000. Mem., Adv. Council to Anglican Observer, UN, 2002–06; organised and prepared report, Muslim Grass-roots in the West Discuss Democracy, 2007, campaign of over 140 speaking engagements on report, Britain, USA, Canada, Brussels and Istanbul, 2007–13; Lay Muslims roundtable discussions on compatibility of Islam and democracy, Canada, Italy, France, Germany and Spain, 2009–14; Founder and Mem., IDDEX, Innovation Mgt, speaking engagements on patent litigation insurance, 2012. Mem., Soc. of Cons. Lawyers, 1960–. Mem., Salzburg Global Fellowship, 2008–. *Publications:* The Law of Trade Secrets, 1962, supplement, 1968; The Law of the New European Patent, 1979; many Conservative Party study papers, 1950–70, on defence, oil and Middle East; reports on patent litigation insce for EC, 2003, 2006; A Qur'an Paper: everything in the Qur'an as described by a Non-Muslim Westerner for Non-Muslims, 2014. *Recreations:* designing historical themes in 13 acre garden at Westleton, Suffolk, art deco collection, oil painting. *Address:* Penthouse 7, Bickenhall Mansions, 63–104 Bickenhall Street, W1U 6BS. *T:* (020) 7935 2949, *Fax:* (020) 7935 2950; 5 New Square, Lincoln's Inn, WC2A 3RJ. *T:* (020) 7404 0404; The Barn, Westleton, Saxmundham, Suffolk IP17 3AN. *T:* (01728) 648235; La Combe de la Boissière, St Maximin, Uzès 30700, France. *T:* 466220393; 15 La Bastide d'Uzes, Chemin de l'Escalette, 30700 Uzes (2720), France. *T:* 466372567. *E:* amedee.turner@btinternet.com. *Club:* Coningsby.

TURNER, Andrew John; MP (C) Isle of Wight, since 2001; *b* Coventry, 24 Oct. 1953; *s* of late Eustace Albert Turner and Joyce Mary Turner (*née* Lowe); partner, Carole Dennett. *Educ:* Rugby Sch.; Keble Coll., Oxford (BA 1976, MA 1981); Birmingham Univ. (PGCE 1977); Henley Mgt Centre. Teacher of Econs and Geog., Rushden Boys' Comp. Sch., 1977, Lord Williams's Sch., Thame, 1978–84; Res. Officer, Cons. Central Office, 1984–86; Special Advr to Sec. of State for Social Services, 1986–88; Dir, Grant-maintained Schools Foundn, 1988–97; Dep. Dir, Educn Unit, IEA, 1998–2000; Head of Policy and Resources, Educn Dept, Southwark BC, 2000–01. Educn Consultant, 1997–2001, Dir, 2000–02, Empire Packet Co. A Vice-Chm., Conservative Party, 2003–05; Opposition front bench spokesman on charities, 2005–06. FRSA. *Recreations:* walking, the countryside, old movies, avoiding gardening. *Address:* House of Commons, SW1A 0AA; (home) Seal House, Sea Street, Newport, Isle of Wight PO30 5BW; (constituency office) Riverside Centre, The Quay, Newport, Isle of Wight PO30 2QR. *T:* (01983) 530808.

TURNER, Prof. (Andrew) Neil, PhD; FRCP, FRCPE; Professor of Nephrology, since 1998, and Head, Undergraduate Medical Education, since 2012, University of Edinburgh; Hon. Consultant Nephrologist, Edinburgh Royal Infirmary, since 1998; *b* 28 April 1956; *s* of Rodney Turner and Eileen (*née* Wade); *m* 1984, Helen Cameron; three *s*. *Educ:* Downing Coll., Cambridge (MA 1977); Lincoln Coll., Oxford (BM BCh 1980); PhD London 1992. FRCP 1996; FRCPE 1997. Med. trng in Oxford, Croydon, Northampton, Liverpool, Norwich and York, 1980–85; renal trng, Oxford, 1983, and Hammersmith, 1985–92; NKRF Sen. Res. Fellow, 1990; Hon. Consultant, Hammersmith Hosp. and Sen. Lectr, RPMS, 1993; Sen. Lectr in Medicine and Nephrology, Univ. of Aberdeen and Aberdeen Royal Hosp., 1994–98. Chm., Kidney Res. UK, 2008–. ILTM 2000. Editor: www.edren.org, 2000–; www.patientview.org, 2005–. *Publications:* (contrib.) Oxford Textbook of Medicine, 4th edn 2005, 5th edn 2010; (contrib.) Oxford Textbook of Clinical Nephrology, 4th edn 2015; (contrib.) Davidson's Principles and Practice of Medicine, 22nd edn 2014; papers in learned jls on autoimmunity, antigen processing, renal disease, teaching, information technology and health. *Recreations:* art, the outdoors, music. *Address:* Renal Medicine, Royal Infirmary, Little France, Edinburgh EH16 4SA. *T:* (0131) 242 9167. *E:* neil.turner@ed.ac.uk.

TURNER, Ven. Antony Hubert Michael; Archdeacon of the Isle of Wight, 1986–96, now Archdeacon Emeritus; *b* 17 June 1930; *s* of Frederick George and Winifred Frances Turner; *m* 1956, Margaret Kathleen (*née* Phillips); one *s* two *d*. *Educ:* Royal Liberty Grammar School, Romford, Essex; Tyndale Hall, Bristol. FCA 1963 (ACA 1952); DipTh (Univ. of London), 1956. Deacon, 1956; Priest, 1957; Curate, St Ann's, Nottingham, 1956–59; Curate in Charge, St Cuthbert's, Cheadle, Dio. Chester, 1959–62; Vicar, Christ Church, Macclesfield, 1962–68; Home Sec., Bible Churchmen's Missionary Soc., 1968–74; Vicar of St Jude's, Southsea, 1974–86; RD of Portsmouth, 1979–84; Priest i/c, St Mary, Rotterdam, 1999–2000. Church Commissioner, 1983–93. Vice Chm., C of E Pensions Bd, 1988–97. *Recreations:* photography, caravanning. *Address:* 15 Avenue Road, Hayling Island, Hants PO11 0LX. *T:* (023) 9246 5881.

TURNER, Barry Horace Page, PhD; writer and editor; *b* 4 Oct. 1937; *o s* of Laurence and Esther Turner; *m* 1st, 1965, Sandra Hogben (marr. diss. 1972); 2nd, 1974, Gunilla Nordquist (marr. diss. 1986); one *s* one *d*; 3rd, 1997, Mary Elizabeth Fulton. *Educ:* King Edward VII Grammar Sch., Bury St Edmunds; London School of Economics (BSc Econs 1961; PhD 1966); Inst. of Educn, London Univ. (DipEd 1962). Dep. Editor, New Education, 1966–68; Educn Corresp., Observer, 1969–71; Reporter and Presenter, BBC Current Affairs, Thames TV, Yorkshire TV, Granada TV, 1969–77; Mktg Dir, Macmillan Press, 1977–81. Chm., Nat. Acad. of Writing, 2003–09. Vis. Prof., Birmingham City Univ. (formerly UCE), 2006–13. Editor: The Writer's Handbook, annually 1988–2011; The Statesman's Yearbook, annually 1997–2014. *Plays:* (jtly) Henry Irving, 1995; Agate, 1997; Novello, 2011. *Publications:* (jtly) Adventures in Education, 1969; Free Trade and Protection, 1971; Equality for Some, 1974; A Place in the Country, 1974; Sweden, 1976; The Other European Community, 1982; (jtly) The Playgoer's Companion, 1983; A Jobbing Actor, 1984; Richard Burton, 1987; East End, West End, 1990; Marks of Distinction, 1988; …And the Policeman Smiled, 1991; The Long Horizon, 1993; Quest for Love, 1994; (jtly) When Daddy Came Home, 1995; The Writer's Companion, 1996; One Small Suitcase (for children), 2003; Countdown to Victory, 2004; Suez 1956: the inside story of the first oil war, 2006; Outpost of Occupation: how the Channel Islands survived Nazi rule, 1940–45, 2010; Beacon for Change: how the Festival of Britain shaped the modern age, 2011; The Victorian Parson, 2015; contribs to The Times, Daily Mail. *Recreation:* revisiting old books and movies. *Address:* 34 Ufton Road, N1 5BX. *T:* (020) 7241 0116; Le Bernet, 32480 La Romieu, France. *T:* 562288841. *Clubs:* Garrick, Chelsea Arts.

TURNER, Brian James, CBE 2002; chef, restaurateur; *b* 7 May 1946; *s* of Lawrence and Lily Turner; *m* 1973, Denise Parker; two *s*. *Educ:* Morley Grammar Sch.; Leeds Coll. of Food Technol. Chef: Simpson's, Strand, 1963–65; Savoy Grill, 1965–68; Beau Rivage Palace, Lausanne, 1969; Claridge's, London, 1970–71; Capital Hotel/Restaurant, London, 1971–86; Turner's Restaurant, London, 1986–2001; Brian Turner's Restaurant, Crowne Plaza Hotel, NEC Birmingham, 2001–05; Turner's Grill, Slough, 2006–08; Turner's Grill, Birmingham, 2006–08; Chef/Patron, Brian Turner Mayfair, 2003–08; Dir, Foxtrot Oscar, 2001–03. *Television* includes: This Morning, 1992–2000 and 2003–; Food and Drink, 1992–2000; Ready Steady Cook, 1992–; Great Food Live, 2003–; Saturday Kitchen, 2005–; Saturday Cooks, 2006–; Daily Cooks, 2007–; A Taste of Britain, 2014. Member: Royal Acad. (formerly Acad.) of Culinary Arts, 1987– (Chm., 1993–2004; Pres., 2004–); Hospitality Skills, 2001–; UK Skills, 2002–; Prince's Trust, 2002–; Les Disciples D'Auguste Escoffier, 2010–. Hon. Prof., Thames Valley Univ., 2001. FCGI 2005; FRSA 2006. Hon. DSc Leeds Metropolitan, 2006; DUniv Sheffield Hallam, 2008. Chef of Year Award, 1997, Special Award, 2004, Caterer and Hotelkeeper; Special Award, Craft Guild of Chefs, 1997; Wedgwood Award, 1997; Nestlé Toque d'Or, 2003; Ambassadorial Award, Yorks Life Food and Drink Awards, 2004; Special Award, Springboard Awards for Excellence, 2004; Lifetime Achievement Award, Yorks TV Awards, 2005; British Hospitality Assoc. Award, 2006; Award for Outstanding Contrib. to British Food Industry, Nat. Assoc. of Catering Butchers, 2007; Hon. Apprenticeship Award, Apprenticeship Ambassadors Network, 2009. *Publications:* Campaign for Great British Food, 1990; Sunday Best, 1995; Out to Lunch, 2 vols, 1996 and 1997; (with A. Worrall Thompson) Ready Steady Cook, Book 1, 1997; The Big Ready Steady Cookbook, 1997; Grills and Barbecues, 1997; A Yorkshire Lad: my life with recipes, 2000; Brian Turner's Favourite British Recipes, 2003; Ready Steady Cook: the top 100 recipes, 2003; Great British Grub, 2009; A Taste of Summer, 2011. *Recreations:* sport, brass band music, opera, travel. *Address:* 212 Central Meat Market, Smithfield, EC1A 9LH. *T:* (020) 7248 1005, *Fax:* (020) 7248 1006. *E:* turnerrest@aol.com. *W:* www.brianturner.co.uk.

TURNER, Prof. Bryan Stanley, PhD, DLitt, LittD; Presidential Professor of Sociology, Graduate Center, City University of New York, since 2010 (Director, Committee on Religion, since 2010); Professor of Sociology of Religion, Australian Catholic University, Melbourne, since 2013; *b* 14 Jan. 1945; *s* of Stanley W. Turner and Sophie (*née* Brooks); *m* 2008, Nguyen Kim Hoa. *Educ:* Univ. of Leeds (BA 1966; PhD 1970); Flinders Univ. (DLitt 1976); Univ. of Cambridge (MA 2002; LittD 2009). Lecturer: Univ. of Aberdeen, 1969–74; Univ. of Lancaster, 1974–78; Sen. Lectr, 1979–80, Reader, 1980–82, Univ. of Aberdeen; Prof. of Sociology, Univ. of Flinders, 1982–88; Prof. of Gen. Social Sci., Univ. of Utrecht, 1988–90; Professor of Sociology: Univ. of Essex, 1990–92; Deakin Univ., 1992–98; Cambridge Univ., 1998–2005; Fellow of Fitzwilliam Coll., Cambridge, 2002–05; Prof. of Sociology and Res. Leader, Asia Res. Inst., Nat. Univ. of Singapore, 2005–09; Prof. of Social and Political Thought, Univ. of Western Sydney, 2009; Alona Evans Dist. Vis. Prof. of

Sociology, Newhouse Center for Humanities, Wellesley Coll., Mass, 2009–10. FASSA 1988. Editor: (jtly) Body & Society, 1994–; Citizenship Studies, 1997–; (jtly) Jl of Classical Sociology, 2001–. *Publications:* Weber and Islam, 1974; For Weber, 1981; Religion and Social Theory, 1983; The Body and Society, 1984; Citizenship and Capitalism, 1986; Medical Power and Social Knowledge, 1987; Regulating Bodies, 1992; Orientalism, Postmodernism and Globalism, 1994; (ed) The Blackwell Companion to Social Theory, 1996; Classical Sociology, 1999; Islam: critical concepts in sociology, 2003; The New Medical Sociology, 2004; (ed jtly) International Handbook of Sociology, 2005; The Cambridge Dictionary of Sociology, 2006; Vulnerability and Human Rights, 2006; (ed with Patrick Baert) Pragmatism and European Social Theory, 2007; Rights and Virtues: political essays on citizenship and social justice, 2008; (ed) The Routledge International Handbook of Globalization Studies, 2010; (with Habibul Haque Khondker) Globalization East and West, 2010; Religion and Modern Society, 2011; (with Anthony Elliott) On Society, 2012; The Religious and the Political, 2013; (with Kamaludeen M. Nasr) The Future of Singapore, 2014; (with Oscar Salemink) The Routledge Handbook of Religions in Asia, 2015. *Recreations:* gardening, tourism, walking, collecting books. *Address:* Graduate Center, City University of New York, 365 Fifth Avenue, New York, NY 10016–4309, USA.

TURNER, Dr Christian Philip Hollier, CMG 2012; HM Diplomatic Service; High Commissioner, Kenya, since 2012; *b* Crawley, 19 Aug. 1972; *s* of Andrew and Caroline Turner; *m* 2003, Claire Barber; one *s* one *d*. *Educ:* Marlborough Coll.; Univ. of Manchester (BA Hons English Lang. and Lit. 1994); Univ. of York (DPhil English and Related Lit. 1998). Tutor, Univ. of York, 1996–98; researcher, Videotext Communications, 1998; Cabinet Office: Sec. to Better Regulation Taskforce, 1998–99; Sec. to Econ. and Domestic Cttees of Cabinet, 1999–2000; Private Sec. to Minister of State, 2001–02; Dep. Team Leader, Prime Minister's Strategy Unit, 2002–03; First Sec., Washington, 2003–06; entered FCO, 2005; Private Sec. to Prime Minister, 2007; Dep. Dir, 2008–09, Dir, 2009–12, Middle East and N Africa, FCO. Trustee, Latitude Global Volunteering, 2009–12. *Recreations:* choral singing, walking, opera, family, medieval history. *Address:* Foreign and Commonwealth Office, King Charles Street, SW1A 2AH. *E:* christian.turner@fco.gov.uk.

TURNER, Rev. Christopher Gilbert; Minister with permission to officiate, Oxford Diocese, since 2000; Headmaster, Stowe School, 1979–89; *b* 23 Dec. 1929; *s* of late Theodore F. Turner, QC; *m* 1961, Lucia, *d* of late Prof. S. R. K. Glanville (Provost of King's Coll., Cambridge); one *s* one *d* (and one *d* decd). *Educ:* Winchester Coll. (Schol.); New Coll., Oxford (Exhibnr, MA); Oxford Ministry Course. Asst Master, Radley Coll., 1952–61; Senior Classics Master, Charterhouse, 1961–68; Headmaster, Dean Close Sch., 1968–79. Schoolmaster Student at Christ Church, Oxford, 1967. Foundation Member of Council, Cheltenham Colleges of Educn, 1968. Mem., HMC Cttee, 1974–75, 1987–88; Chm., Common Entrance Cttee, 1976–80; Gov., Chipping Norton Sch., 1996–2006. Ordained deacon, 1992, priest, 1993. *Publications:* chapter on History, in Comparative Study of Greek and Latin Literature, 1969; chapter on Dean Close in the Seventies, in The First Hundred Years, 1986; (contrib.) Encounters, 2007. *Recreations:* music (violin-playing), reading, walking, different forms of manual labour; OUBC 1951. *Address:* Rosemullion, High Street, Great Rollright, near Chipping Norton, Oxon OX7 5RQ. *T:* (01608) 737359.

See also Sir M. J. Turner.

TURNER, Colin Francis; Senior District Judge (formerly Senior Registrar), Family Division of High Court, 1988–91, retired (Registrar, 1971–88); *b* 11 April 1930; *s* of Sidney F. and Charlotte C. Turner; *m* 1951, Josephine Alma Jones (*d* 2013); two *s* one *d*. *Educ:* Beckenham Grammar Sch.; King's Coll., London. LLB 1955. Entered Principal Probate Registry, 1949; District Probate Registrar, York, 1965–68. MBOU. Hon. Mem., London Nat. History Soc., 1998. *Publications:* (ed jtly) Rayden on Divorce, 9th, 11th, 12th and 13th edns, consulting editor to 14th edn; an editor of Supreme Court Practice, 1972–90; (jtly) Precedents in Matrimonial Causes and Ancillary Matters, 1985. *Recreations:* birding, fishing, entomology. *Address:* Lakers, Church Road, St Johns, Redhill, Surrey RH1 6QA. *T:* (01737) 761807.

TURNER, Colin William; Rector, Glasgow Academy, 1983–94; *b* 10 Dec. 1933; *s* of William and Joyce Turner; *m* 1958, Priscilla Mary Trickett; two *s* two *d*. *Educ:* Torquay Grammar Sch.; King's Coll., London (BSc; AKC). Edinburgh Academy: Asst Master, 1958–82; OC CCF, 1960–74; Head, Maths Dept, 1973–75; Housemaster, 1975–82. *Recreations:* mountaineering, gardening, local history. *Address:* Leat, Lowerdown, Bovey Tracey, Devon TQ13 9LF. *T:* (01626) 832266.

TURNER, David Andrew; QC 1991; a Recorder of the Crown Court, since 1990; *b* 6 March 1947; *s* of late James and Phyllis Turner; *m* 1978, Mary Christine Moffatt (*d* 2012); two *s* one *d*. *Educ:* King George V Sch., Southport; Queens' Coll., Cambridge (MA, LLM). Cambridge Footlights, 1967–69. Called to the Bar, Gray's Inn, 1971, Bencher, 2001; Asst Recorder, 1987–90; Panel Deemster, 2008–, Dep. High Bailiff, 2012–, IOM. *Recreation:* music.

TURNER, David George Patrick; QC 2000; **His Honour Judge Turner;** a Circuit Judge, since 2004; Deputy Designated Family Judge for London, 2005–13; *b* 11 July 1954; *s* of George P. Turner and Elsie B. Turner (*née* McClure); *m* 1978, Jean Patricia Hewett; two *s*. *Educ:* Foyle Coll., Londonderry; King's Coll. London (LLB, AKC 1975). Called to the Bar, Gray's Inn, 1976, Bencher, 2015; in practice at the Bar, 1976–2004; Asst Recorder, 1997–2000; a Recorder, 2000–04; Head of Chambers, 2003–04. Judicial Member: Essex Courts Bd, 2004–07; Beds, Essex, Herts Courts Bd, 2007–09; Magistrates' Area Trng Cttee for London, 2006–13. Chancellor, dio. of Chester, 1998–; Dep. Chancellor, dio. of Liverpool, 2001–02, and of London, 2002–; Mem., Legal Adv. Commn, C of E, 2007–10. Reader, 1981–, Churchwarden, 1983–2006, All Souls, Langham Place. Trustee: Langham Partnership, 1978–; London Lectures Trust, 1990–; Vice-Pres., Nature in Art Trust, 2010–. Mem., Patron's Circle, Sir John Soane's Mus., 2009–. *Address:* c/o Crown Court, New Street, Chelmsford, Essex CM1 1EL.

TURNER, David John; Chairman, Commonwealth Bank of Australia, since 2010 (non-executive Director, since 2006); *b* 7 Feb. 1945; *s* of late Frederick and Sheila Margaret Turner; *m* 1991, Julia Anne Thompson; two *s* three *d*. FCA 1969. Cook & Co., Liverpool, 1963–67; Touche Ross & Co., London, 1967–69; Mgt Auditor, Mobil Oil Corp., 1969–71; Chief Accountant, Mobil Servs Ltd, 1971–73; Special Projects Co-ordinator, Mobil Europe Inc., 1973–74; Finance Director: Booker Agriculture, 1975–84; Booker McConnell Ltd, subseq. Booker plc, 1984–93; GKN plc, 1993–2001; Chief Financial Officer, 2001–03, CEO, 2003–07, Brambles Industries plc. Dep. Chm., 2007–08, Chm., 2008–10, Cobham plc; non-exec. Dir, Whitbread plc, 2001–06. Dir, O'Connell Street Associates Pty Ltd, 2007–; Ind. Mem. Bd, Ashurst, 2013–. Dir, Great Barrier Reef Foundn, 2007–. *Recreations:* tennis, fishing, ski-ing, opera. *Address:* Commonwealth Bank of Australia, Ground Floor, Tower 1, 201 Sussex Street, Sydney, NSW 2000, Australia. *Clubs:* Boodle's; Elanora Country.

TURNER, Prof. David Warren, FRS 1973; Fellow of Balliol College, Oxford, 1967–94, now Emeritus Fellow; Professor of Electron Spectroscopy, Oxford, 1985–94, now Emeritus Professor; *b* 16 July 1927; *s* of Robert Cecil Turner and Constance Margaret (*née* Bonner); *m* 1954, Barbara Marion Fisher; one *s* one *d*. *Educ:* Westcliff High Sch.; Univ. of Exeter. MA, BSc, PhD, DIC. Lectr, Imperial Coll., 1958; Reader in Organic Chemistry, Imperial Coll., 1965; Oxford University: Lectr in Physical Chem., 1968; Reader in Physical Chemistry, 1978; Reader in Electron Spectroscopy, 1984. Lectures: Kahlbaum, Univ. of Basle, 1971; Van Geuns, Univ. of Amsterdam, 1974; Harkins, Chicago Univ., 1974; Kistiakowsky, Harvard, 1979; Liversidge, RSC, 1981–82. Tilden Medal, Chemical Soc., 1967; Harrison Howe Award, Amer. Chem. Soc., 1973. Hon. DTech, Royal Inst., Stockholm, 1971; Hon. DPhil Basle, 1980; Hon. DSc Exeter, 1999. *Publications:* Molecular Photoelectron Spectroscopy, 1970; contrib. Phil. Trans Royal Soc., Proc. Royal Soc., Jl Chem. Soc., etc. *Recreations:* music, gardening, tinkering with gadgets. *Address:* Balliol College, Oxford OX1 3BJ.

TURNER, Prof. Denys Alan, DPhil; Horace Tracy Pitkin Professor of Historical Theology, and Professor of Religious Studies, Yale University, 2005–14; *b* 5 Aug. 1942; *s* of Alan Turner and Barbara Turner (*née* Mason); two *s* one *d*; *m* 2015, Courtney Palmbush. *Educ:* Nat. Univ. of Ireland (BA 1962; MA 1965); St Edmund Hall, Oxford (DPhil 1975). Asst Lectr, 1967–74, Coll. Lectr, 1974–76, in Philosophy, UC, Dublin; Lectr, 1976–89, Sen. Lectr, 1989–95, in Philosophy of Religion, Dept of Theology and Religious Studies, Univ. of Bristol; H. G. Wood Prof. of Theology, Univ. of Birmingham, 1995–99; Norris Hulse Prof. of Divinity, Cambridge Univ., and Fellow of Peterhouse, Cambridge, 1999–2005 (Emeritus Fellow, 2005–). Hon. DLitt UCD, 2011; Hon. DHumLit Albertus Magnus Coll., 2014. *Publications:* Marxism and Christianity, 1983; Eros and Allegory: medieval exegesis of the Song of Songs, 1995; The Darkness of God: negativity in Christian mysticism, 1995; Faith Seeking, 2002; Faith, Reason and the Existence of God, 2004; Julian of Norwich, Theologian, 2011; Thomas Aquinas: a portrait, 2013. *Recreations:* mediaeval church architecture, classical music from Ockeghem to Mahler, gardens. *Address:* Yale Divinity School, 409 Prospect Street, New Haven, CT 06511, USA.

TURNER, Derek, CBE 2003; FREng, CEng; FICE, FCILT; consultant, since 2013; Director, Network Delivery and Development (formerly Traffic Operations, then Network Operations Director), 2005–13, and Deputy Chief Executive, Highways Agency, 2009–13; *b* 8 May 1953; *s* of Edgar and Maud Turner; *m* 1977, Maggy Sporne (marr. diss. 2005); one *d*, and one step *s*. *Educ:* Hinchley Wood Co. Secondary Sch.; Sheffield Univ. (BEng Hons). CEng 1979; FICE 1991; FCIHT (FIHT 1991); FCILT (FILT 1995); FREng 2005. Asst Engr, Herts CC, 1974–80; Professional Officer, GLC, 1980–82; Principal Engr, Hackney, 1982–85; Gp Planner, Islington, 1985–86; Dep. Asst Bor. Engr, Wandsworth, 1986–90; Bor. Engr and Surveyor, Haringay, 1990–91; Traffic Dir for London, 1991–2000; Man. Dir, Street Mgt, Transport for London, 2000–03; Principal, Derek Turner Consultancy, 2003–05. Vis. Prof. of Civil and Envmtl Engrg, UCL, 2003–. Non-executive Director: Infocell Hldgs Ltd, 2003–05; EGS Ltd, 2007–08; Bd Dir, Colin Buchanan and Partners, 2004–05; Co-Chair, Highways UK Adv. Bd, 2015–. MCIM 1985; FRSA 1993. AA Award for Red Route 2000; European Transport Planner of Year, European Transport Cttee (ETC), 2003; Transport Planner of Year, Transportation Planning Soc., 2003. *Publications:* contribs to Jl ICE (Webb Prize 1997), Traffic Engrg and Control, Amer. Soc. of Civil Engrs. *Recreations:* classical music, walking, countryside, travel. *T:* 07920 096150. *E:* derek-turner@hotmail.co.uk.

TURNER, Dr Desmond Stanley; *b* 17 July 1939; *s* of Stanley and Elsie Turner; *m* 1st, 1966, Lynette Gwyn-Jones (marr. diss. 1987); one *d*; 2nd, 1997, Lynn Rogers. *Educ:* Luton Grammar Sch.; Imperial Coll., London (BSc); University Coll. London (MSc); PhD London; Brighton Univ. (PGCE). ARCS. Junior posts, Royal Free and St Mary's Hosps Schs of Medicine, 1963–67; Research Associate and Hon. Lectr, Guy's Hosp. Med. Sch., 1967–71; Research Fellow and Hon. Lecturer: Univ. of Surrey, 1971–76; Univ. of Sussex, 1974–78; Chm. and Man. Dir, Martlet Brewery, 1979–83; science teacher, 1984–95. MP (Lab) Brighton Kemptown, 1997–2010. R. D. Lawrence Meml Fellowship, British Diabetes Assoc., 1970–72. *Publications:* research papers and reviews. *Recreations:* sailing, fencing. *Address:* 49 Queen's Park Terrace, Brighton BN2 2YZ. *T:* (01273) 687732.

TURNER, Geoffrey Howard; Chief Executive, Securities Institute, 1997–2003; *b* 1945; *s* of Charles William Turner and Evelyn Doris; *m* 1975, Margaret Linda Donaldson; two *d*. *Educ:* King's Sch., Chester; St Edmund Hall, Oxford (BA, MA; Special Dip. Social Studies). With Simon & Coates, stockbrokers, 1968–70; British India Steam Navigation Co., 1970–73; Stock Exchange, 1973–90: Asst Manager, 1973–75, Manager, 1975–78, Membership Dept; Secretary: Wilson Evidence Cttee, 1978; Planning Cttee, 1977–78; Restrictive Practices Case Cttee, 1978–83; Head of Membership, 1983–86; Dir of Membership, 1986–90; Dir of Authorisation, Securities Assoc., 1986–92; Dir of Public Affairs, SFA, 1993–94; Chief Exec., Assoc. of Private Client Investment Managers and Stockbrokers, 1994–97. External Examr, London Guildhall Univ., 1996–2000. Mem. (C), St Albans DC, 2006–. Mem., Harpenden Village Rotary Club. *Recreations:* visiting country churches, collecting prints and ephemera. *Clubs:* Vincent's (Oxford); Leander (Henley).

TURNER, Rt Rev. Geoffrey Martin; Bishop Suffragan of Stockport, 1994–2000; an Hon. Assistant Bishop, Diocese of Chester, since 2002; *b* 16 March 1934; *s* of Ernest Hugh Turner and Winifred Rose Turner (*née* Martin); *m* 1959, Gillian Chope; two *s* one *d*. *Educ:* Bideford Grammar Sch.; Sandhurst; Oak Hill Theol Coll. Commnd RA, 1954; 25 Field Regt, 1954–57; Trucial Oman Scouts, 1957–59; Jun. Leader Regt RA, 1959–60. Ordained deacon, 1963, priest, 1964; Assistant Curate: St Stephen, Tonbridge, 1963–66; St John, Heatherlands, dio. of Salisbury, 1966–69; Vicar: St Peter, Derby, 1969–73; Christ Church, Chadderton, dio. of Manchester, 1973–79; Rector of Bebington, 1979–93; Rural Dean, Wirral North, 1989–93; Hon. Canon, Chester Cathedral, 1989–93; Archdeacon of Chester, 1993–94. *Recreations:* sport, literature. *Address:* 23 Lang Lane, West Kirby, Wirral CH48 5HG. *T:* (0151) 625 8504.

See also M. Turner.

TURNER, George, PhD; *b* 9 Aug. 1940; *s* of late George and Jane Turner; *m* Lesley Duggan; two *d*, and one step *s* one step *d*. *Educ:* Laxton Grammar Sch.; Imperial Coll., London (BSc Hons); Gonville and Caius Coll., Cambridge (PhD Physics 1967). Formerly Lectr in electronic engrg, Univ. of E Anglia. Mem. (Lab) Norfolk CC, 1977–97. Contested (Lab) Norfolk NW, 1992; MP (Lab) Norfolk NW, 1997–2001; contested same seat, 2001. Founding Man. Dir, 2001–10, Chm., 2010–, Cranberry Commns Ltd (formerly Datasharp Telecom Ltd); Chm., Oxicoco Ltd, 2011–. *Address:* 35 Chapel Street, Barford, Norwich NR9 4AB.

TURNER, Prof. Grenville, FRS 1980; Professor of Isotope Geochemistry, 1988–2002, Research Professor, 2002–12, Manchester University, now Professor Emeritus; *b* 1 Nov. 1936; *o s* of Arnold and Florence Turner, Todmorden, Yorks; *m* 1961, Kathleen, *d* of William and Joan Morris, Rochdale, Lancs; one *s* one *d*. *Educ:* Todmorden Grammar Sch.; St John's Coll., Cambridge (MA); Balliol Coll., Oxford (DPhil). Asst Prof., Univ. of Calif at Berkeley, 1962–64; Lectr, Sheffield Univ., 1964–74, Sen. Lectr, 1974–79, Reader, 1979–80, Prof. of Physics, 1980–88. Vis. Associate in Nuclear Geophysics, 1970–71, Vis. Associate in Geochem., 2013, Calif Inst. of Technol. Mem. Council, Royal Soc., 1990–92. Fellow: Meteoritical Soc., 1980 (Leonard Medal, 1999); American Geophysical Union, 1998; Geochemistry Fellow, Geochemical Soc. and European Assoc. of Geochemistry, 1996. Rumford Medal, Royal Soc. 1996; Urey Medal, Eur. Assoc. of Geochemistry, 2002; Gold Medal for Geophysics, RAS, 2004. Hon. Citizen, Todmorden, 2013. *Publications:* scientific papers on applications of isotope geochem. to understanding the evolution of the earth and solar system, and on earliest development of the widely used Ar-Ar dating method. *Recreations:* photography, walking, theatre. *Address:* 42 Edgehill Road, Sheffield S7 1SP. *T:* (office) (0161) 275 0401. *E:* grenville.turner@manchester.ac.uk.

TURNER, Harry Edward; Chairman, Amcom Resources plc, 1995–2000; *b* 28 Feb. 1935; *s* of Harry Turner and Bessie Elizabeth Jay; *m* 1956, Carolyn Bird; one *s* one *d*. *Educ:* Sloane Grammar Sch., Chelsea. Served Middlesex Regt, Austria, 2nd Lieut, 1953–55. Sales Representative, Crosse & Blackwell Foods, 1955–56; Advertising Executive: Daily Herald, 1956–58; Kemsley Newspapers, 1958–60; Feature Writer and Advtsg Manager, TV

International Magazine, 1960–62; Sales Dir, Westward Television, 1962–80; Dir of Marketing, 1980–85, Man. Dir, 1985–92, Television South West; Dir, ITN, 1987–92. Dir, Prince of Wales Trust, 1988–. FRSA 1986. Mem., Middx Regtl Assoc., 1955–. Mem., Solus Club, 1986–. *Publications:* The Man Who Could Hear Fishes Scream (short stories), 1978; The Gentle Art of Salesmanship, 1985; So You Want To Be a Sales Manager, 1987; Innocents in the Boardroom, 1991; The Venetian Chair, 1998; Poems of the Peninsular, 2001; Poems of Nelson's Navy, 2002; Wrapped in Whirlwinds, 2005; Growing Up in Fulham, 2005; Urban Legends, 2006; Zen and the Art of Gentle Retirement, 2009; Heaven's Anvil, 2010. *Recreations:* tennis, riding, ski-ing, literature, travel. *Address:* Old Boathouse View, 5 Admiral Stirling Court, Weybridge, Surrey KT13 8XX. *T:* (01932) 821465. *Clubs:* Garrick; Ackosando (NY).

TURNER, James; QC 1998; *b* 23 Nov. 1952; *s* of late James Gordon Melville Turner, GC and of Peggy Pamela Hare (*née* Masters); *m* 1979, Sheila Green (separated); three *s* two *d*. *Educ:* Robertsbridge Co. Secondary Modern Sch.; Bexhill Grammar Sch.; Univ. of Hull (LLB Hons). Called to the Bar, Inner Temple, 1976, Bencher, 2006. *Publications:* (contrib. editor) Archbold: Criminal Pleading, Evidence and Practice, annually, 1992–. *Recreations:* eating, reading, cinema, soul music. *Address:* 1 King's Bench Walk, Temple, EC4Y 7DB. *T:* (020) 7936 1500, *Fax:* (020) 7936 1590. *E:* jturner@1kbw.co.uk.

TURNER, Prof. James Johnson, FRS 1992; Research Professor in Chemistry, University of Nottingham, 1995–97, now Emeritus (Professor of Inorganic Chemistry, 1979–95); *b* 24 Dec. 1935; *s* of Harry Turner and Evelyn Turner (*née* Johnson); *m* 1961, Joanna Margaret Gargett; two *d*. *Educ:* Darwen Grammar Sch.; King's Coll., Cambridge (MA, PhD 1960; ScD 1985). CChem; FRSC. Research Fellow, King's Coll., Cambridge, 1960; Harkness Fellow, Univ. of Calif, Berkeley, 1961–63; University of Cambridge: Univ. Demonstrator, 1963–68; Univ. Lectr, 1968–71; College Lectr, 1963–71, Admissions Tutor, 1967–71, King's Coll.; Prof. and Head of Dept of Inorganic Chemistry, Univ. of Newcastle upon Tyne, 1972–78; Nottingham University: Hd of Chem. Dept, 1982–85, 1991–93; Pro-Vice-Chancellor, 1986–90. Science and Engineering Research Council (formerly SRC): Mem., 1974–77, Chm., 1979–82, Chemistry Cttee; Mem., Science Bd, 1979–86; Mem. Council, 1982–86. Royal Society of Chemistry: Mem., 1974–77, Vice-Pres., 1982–84 and 1991–93, Pres., 1993–95, Dalton Council; Tilden Lectr, 1978; Liversidge Lectr, 1991; Mem. Council, Royal Soc., 1997–99. *Publications:* papers mainly in jls of Chem. Soc. and Amer. Chem. Soc. *Recreations:* walking, cycling, music. *Address:* 7 Hallams Lane, Chilwell, Nottingham NG9 5FH. *T:* (0115) 917 0353.

TURNER, James Michael; QC 2013; *b* London, 28 Sept. 1967; *s* of Sir Michael John Turner, *qv* and (Frances) Deborah Turner; *m* 1994, Franca Edelaar; three *s* one *d*. *Educ:* Radley Coll.; Univ. of Durham (BA Law); Tübingen Univ. (LLM). Called to the Bar, Inner Temple, 1990; in practice as a barrister, specialising in internat. commercial and shipping law, 1992–. *Publications:* (with Sarah Derrington) Law and Practice of Admiralty Matters, 2007. *Recreations:* photography, wine, music.

TURNER, Janet Mary, (Mrs Paul Griffin); QC 1996; barrister; Head of Not for Profit Solutions, Berwin Leighton Paisner LLP, since 2012; *b* 16 Nov. 1957; *d* of Cecil Sidney Turner and Gwendoline Joyce Turner (*née* Loseby); *m* 1983, Paul Griffin; one *s* one *d*. *Educ:* Wycombe Abbey Sch.; Bristol Univ. (LLB 1st cl. Hons). Called to the Bar, Middle Temple, 1979 (Harmsworth Schol.); practising in field of commercial litigation, 1979–2000; legal consultant, 2000–07; partner (charities and not for profit), Taylor Vinters, 2007–12. Member: London Common Law and Commercial Bar Assoc., 1986–99 (Sec., 1990–97); Commercial Bar Assoc., 1989–99; Charity Law Assoc., 2007–. Non-exec. Dir, Norwich and Peterborough Building Soc., 2007–11. Trustee: Wothorpe Towers Preservation Trust, 2005–; Cambridge Union Soc., 2010–; Norfolk Hospice, 2011–14. *Recreations:* heritage conservation, food and wine, collecting ephemera, landscape gardening. *E:* jmtqc@btconnect.com.

TURNER, Jean McGiven; Executive Director, Scotland Patients Association, 2007–14; *b* Glasgow, 1939. *Educ:* Hillhead High Sch., Glasgow; Aberdeen Univ. (MB ChB 1965; DA 1970). Anaesthetist: Aberdeen Royal Infirmary; Southern Gen. Hosp., Glasgow; GP, Springburn, Glasgow, 1975–2000. Vocational Studies Tutor (pt-time) on gen. practice, Glasgow Univ., 1999–2003. MSP (Ind) Strathkelvin and Bearsden, 2003–07; contested same seat, 2007. Mem., Health Cttee, Scottish Parlt, 2003–07.

TURNER, John, CB 1999; Under Secretary, Department for Education and Employment (formerly Department of Employment), 1988–99; Member, Civil Service Appeal Board, 2000; *b* 22 April 1946; *s* of late William Cecil Turner and Hilda Margaret Turner; *m* 1971, Susan Georgina Kennedy; two *s* one *d*. *Educ:* Ramsey Abbey Grammar Sch.; Northwood Hills Grammar Sch. Entered Civil Service, 1967; Principal, DoI, 1979; MSC, 1981–84; Asst Sec., Dept of Employment, 1985; Prin. Pvte Sec. to Rt Hon. Lord Young of Graffham and Rt Hon. Norman Fowler, 1986–87; Small Firms and Tourism Div., Dept of Employment, 1989; Dep. Chief Exec., Employment Service, 1989–94; Govt Regl Dir for Eastern Reg., 1994–96; Dir of Jobcentre Services, Employment Service, 1997–99. Trustee, Rathbone Trng, 2001. Non-exec. Dir, Sheffield Children's NHS Trust, 2002–12. *Recreations:* music, reading, the outdoors.

TURNER, Rt Hon. John Napier; PC (Can.) 1965; CC (Can.) 1995; QC (Can.); Leader of the Liberal Party of Canada, and Leader of the Opposition, 1984–90; Partner, Miller Thomson, Toronto, 1990–2013; *b* 7 June 1929; *s* of Leonard Turner and Phyllis Turner (*née* Gregory); *m* 1963, Geills McCrae Kilgour; three *s* one *d*. *Educ:* Normal Model Public Sch., Ottawa, Ont.; Ashbury Coll., 1939–42; St Patrick's Coll., 1942–45; Univ. of BC (BA Hons Pol Sci. 1949); Oxford Univ. (Rhodes Scholar; BA Juris. 1951; BCL 1952; MA 1957). Joined Stikeman, Elliott, Tamaki, Mercier & Turner, Montreal, Quebec; practised with them after being called to English Bar, 1953, Bar of Quebec, 1954 and Bar of Ont., 1968; QC (Ont and Que) 1968; with McMillan Binch, Toronto, 1976–84. MP for Montreal-St Lawrence-St Georges, 1962–68, Ottawa-Carleton, 1968–76, Vancouver Quadra, 1984–93; Parly Sec. to Minister of Northern Affairs and Nat. Resources, 1963–65; Minister without Portfolio, Dec. 1965–April 1967; Registrar-Gen. of Canada, April 1967–Jan. 1968; Minister of Consumer and Corporate Affairs, Dec. 1967–July 1968; Solicitor-Gen., April–July 1968; Minister of Justice and Attorney-Gen. of Canada, July 1968–Jan. 1972; Minister of Finance, Jan. 1972–Sept. 1975; resigned as MP, Feb. 1976; Prime Minister of Canada, June–Sept. 1984. Barbados Bar, 1969; Yukon and Northwest Territories, 1969; Trinidad Bar, 1969; British Columbia, 1969. Hon. LLD: Univ. of New Brunswick, 1968; York Univ., Toronto, 1969; Univ. of Toronto, 1996; Hon. DCL Mt Allison Univ., NB, 1980. *Publications:* Senate of Canada, 1961; Politics of Purpose, 1968. *Recreations:* tennis, canoeing, ski-ing; Canadian Track Field Champion 1948, Mem. English Track and Field Team. *Address:* 59 Oriole Road, Toronto, ON M4V 2E9, Canada.

TURNER, Prof. (John) Stewart, FAA 1979; FRS 1982; Foundation Professor of Geophysical Fluid Dynamics, Australian National University, 1975–95, now Emeritus; *b* Sydney, Aust, 11 Jan. 1930; *s* of Ivan Stewart Turner and Enid Florence (*née* Payne); *m* 1959, Sheila Lloyd Jones; two *s* one *d*. *Educ:* North Sydney Boys' High Sch.; Wesley Coll., Univ. of Sydney (BSc, MSc); Trinity Coll., Univ. of Cambridge (PhD). FInstP 1969. Research Officer, CSIRO cloud physics group, 1953–54 and 1960–61; 1851 Exhibition Overseas Schol., 1954–57; postdoctoral research post, Univ. of Manchester, 1958–59; Rossby Fellow, then Associate Scientist, Woods Hole Oceanographic Instn, 1962–66; Asst Director of Research, then Reader, Dept of Applied Mathematics and Theoretical Physics, Univ. of Cambridge, 1966–75; Fellow of Darwin Coll., Cambridge, 1974; Overseas Fellow, Churchill Coll., Cambridge, 1985; Fairchild Scholar, CIT, 1993. Matthew Flinders Lectr, Aust. Acad. of Science, 1990. Member, Australian Marine Sciences and Technologies Adv. Cttee (AMSTAC), 1979–84. Associate Editor, Journal of Fluid Mechanics, 1975–95; Mem. Editorial Adv. Board, Deep-Sea Research, 1974–84. *Publications:* Buoyancy Effects in Fluids, 1973, paperback 1979; papers in various scientific jls. *Recreations:* reading, photography. *Address:* c/o Research School of Earth Sciences, Australian National University, Canberra, ACT 0200, Australia.

TURNER, Jonathan Chadwick; QC 2003; a Recorder, 2000–06; *b* 10 Feb. 1951; *s* of David and Joyce Turner. *Educ:* Hindley and Abram Grammar Sch.; University Coll. London (LLB Hons). Called to the Bar, Gray's Inn, 1974; in practice, specialising in criminal law, prosecuting and defending; Asst Recorder, 1997–2000. *Recreations:* golf, cricket, football, Rugby League. *Address:* 21 College Hill, EC4R 2RP. *T:* (020) 3301 0910, *Fax:* (020) 3301 0911. *E:* jonathan.turner@6kbw.com, jctqc@aol.com. *Clubs:* Reform; Denham Golf.

TURNER, Jonathan Richard; QC 2006; *b* 13 Sept. 1963; *s* of Norman Asher Turner and Annette Suzanne Turner; *m* 1991, Manuela Grayson; three *d*. *Educ:* Trinity Coll., Cambridge (BA 1986); Harvard Law Sch. (LLM 1987); Inns of Court Sch. of Law. Called to the Bar, Middle Temple, 1988; Mem., NY Bar, 1988; in practice, 1988–, specialising in competition, European, public and admin., envmtl, and commercial law. Standing Counsel, OFT, 1997–2006; Crown A Panel of Treasury Counsel, 2001–06. *Publications:* (contrib.) Bellamy & Child Common Market Law of Competition, 3rd edn 1987, 4th edn 1993, 7th edn as Bellamy & Child, European Union Law of Competition, 2013, (consultant ed) Supplement to 7th edn, 2014. *Recreations:* squash, literature, social and political theory, family. *Address:* Monckton Chambers, 1 Raymond Buildings, Gray's Inn, WC1R 5NR. *T:* (020) 7405 7211, *Fax:* (020) 7405 2084. *E:* jturner@monckton.com.

TURNER, Karl; MP (Lab) Kingston upon Hull East, since 2010; *b* East Hull, 15 April 1971; *s* of Ken Turner and Pat Turner. *Educ:* Bransholme High Sch.; Hull Coll.; Hull Univ. YTS, Hull CC; self-employed antiques dealer; called to the Bar, Middle Temple, 2005; in practice as a barrister, Max Gold Partnership, Hull, 2005–09, Wilberforce Chambers, Hull, 2009–. *Address:* House of Commons, SW1A 0AA.

TURNER, Kerry; *see* Turner, R. K.

TURNER, Leigh; *see* Turner, R. L.

TURNER, Mark; Headmaster, Shrewsbury School, since 2010; *b* Hampstead, 19 Sept. 1961; *s* of Rt Rev. Geoffrey Martin Turner, *qv*; *m* 1987, Elizabeth Jane Gugan; two *s*. *Educ:* Rossall Sch.; Mansfield Coll., Oxford (BA 1984); RMA Sandhurst; Hughes Hall, Cambridge (PGCE 1987). Short service commn RA, 1984–87. Asst Master, 1988–89, Hd of Dept, 1989–90, Housemaster, Laxton House, 1990–95, Oundle Sch.; Headmaster: Kelly Coll., Tavistock, 1995–2001; Abingdon Sch., 2002–10. Inspector, ISI, 1997–. Governor: Packwood Haugh Sch., 2010–; Abberley Hall Sch., 2010–; Prestfelde Sch., 2010–. *Recreations:* deer stalking, fly fishing. *Address:* Headmaster's House, Shrewsbury School, Shropshire SY3 7BA. *E:* hm@shrewsbury.org.uk. *Club:* East India.

TURNER, Hon. Sir Mark (George), Kt 2013; **Hon. Mr Justice Turner;** a Judge of the High Court of Justice, Queen's Bench Division, since 2013; a Presiding Judge, Northern Circuit, since 2013; *b* 27 Aug. 1959; *s* of Jeffrey Turner and Joyce Turner; *m* 1988, Caroline Sophia Bullock; three *d*. *Educ:* Sedbergh Sch.; Queen's Coll., Oxford (BA). Called to the Bar, Gray's Inn, 1981, Bencher, 2004; in practice as barrister, Northern Circuit, 1982–2013; Asst Recorder, 1997–2000; QC 1998; a Recorder, 2000–13; a Dep. High Ct Judge, 2007–13. Patron, New Beginnings charity for homeless children, 1999–. *Publications:* Occupational Rhinitis, 1998; Occupational Asthma, 1998; Occupational Stress, 2007. *Recreations:* quizzes, computers, classical music, history. *Address:* Royal Courts of Justice, Strand, WC2A 2LL. *T:* (020) 7947 6955.

TURNER, Rev. Martin Hugh; Supernumerary Methodist Minister, St Michael's Whaddon, Cheltenham, since 2015; *b* Loughton, Essex, 13 July 1948; *s* of Percy and Dorothy Turner; *m* 1976, Biddy Bazlinton; one *s* two *d*. *Educ:* Brentwood Coll. of Educn (Cert Ed); Wesley Coll., Bristol; West Hill, Birmingham (Postgrad. Cert. Youth and Community Work). Ordained Methodist Minister, 1978; Methodist Chaplain, Bradford Univ., and Asst Minister, Bradford Mission, 1977–80; Minister: St Andrew's Church and Community Centre, Halifax, 1980–86; St Albans Circuit, and Regl Chaplain, NCH, 1986–97; Superintendent Minister, Hemel Hempstead Circuit, and Methodist Chaplain, HM Prison Bovington (Mount Prison), 1997–2001; Superintendent Minister and Team Leader, Methodist Central Hall, Westminster, 2001–15. Member: Methodist Conference, 1982, 1984, 1988, 1990–91, 1993–2008, 2010–14; Methodist Council, 2000–06; Methodist Strategy and Resources Cttee, 2000–06; Mem. College, Westminster Abbey, 2008–15. *Publications:* (contrib.) Digging for Treasure, 2009; (contrib.) As a Fire by Burning, 2013; contrib. to Scripture Union Bible notes. *Recreations:* antiques, fishing, gardening, West Ham Utd, friends and family. *Address:* 22 Noverton Lane, Prestbury, Cheltenham GL52 5BB. *T:* (01242) 300761. *E:* mhturner@talk21.com.

TURNER, Sir Michael (John), Kt 1985; a Judge of the High Court of Justice, Queen's Bench Division, 1985–2002; *b* 31 May 1931; *s* of late Theodore F. Turner, QC; *m* 1st, 1956, Hon. Susan Money-Coutts (marr. diss. 1965); one *s* one *d*; 2nd, 1965, (Frances) Deborah (marr. diss.), *d* of Rt Hon. Sir David Croom-Johnson, DSC, VRD, PC; two *s*; 3rd, 1995, Ingrid Maria Fear (*née* Ortner). *Educ:* Winchester; Magdalene Coll., Cambridge (BA). Called to Bar, Inner Temple, 1954 (Bencher 1981); a Recorder, 1972–85; QC 1973–85. Additional Judge, Supreme Court of Gibraltar, 2006–13. Chm., E Mids Agricultural Tribunal, 1979–82. Mem., Judicial Studies Bd, 1988–93 (Co-Chm., Civil and Family Cttee, 1988–93). Chm., Disciplinary Cttee, British Eventing, 2006–11. FRGS 2002. *Recreations:* horses, walking, listening to music, shooting. *Address:* c/o Royal Courts of Justice, Strand, WC2A 2LL.

See also C. G. Turner, J. M. Turner.

TURNER, Michael John, CBE 1999; FRAeS; Chairman: Babcock International Group plc, since 2008 (non-executive Director, 2008); GKN plc, since 2012 (Senior Independent non-executive Director, 2009–12); *b* 5 Aug. 1948; *s* of Thomas Turner and Hilda Turner (*née* Pendlebury); *m* 1st, 1972, Rosalind Thomas (marr. diss.); two *s*; 2nd, 1985, Jean (*née* Crotty); two step *d*. *Educ:* Didsbury Tech. High Sch.; Manchester Poly. (BA). ACIS 1973; FRAeS 1991. With British Aerospace, subsequently BAE SYSTEMS, 1966–2008: undergrad. apprentice, Hawker Siddeley Aviation, Manchester, 1966; Contracts Manager (Mil.), 1978–80; Exec. Dir, Admin, 1981–84, Manchester Div.; Division Director and General Manager: Kingston and Dunsfold, 1984–86; Weybridge, Kingston and Dunsfold, 1986–87; Exec. Vice-Pres., Defence Mktg, 1988–92; Chm. and Man. Dir, Regl Aircraft, 1992–99; Main Bd Dir, 1994; Gp Man. Dir, 1997–98; Exec. Dir, 1998–99; Chief Operating Officer, 1999–2002; Chief Exec., 2002–08; Mem., Supervisory Bd, Airbus, 1998–2006. Chairman: Aerospace Innovation and Growth Team, DTI, 2005–; Defence Industries Council, 2007–10; Jt Chm., Nat. Defence Industries Council, 2007–10. Non-exec. Dir, Lazard Ltd, 2006–. President: SBAC, 1996–97; AeroSpace and Defence Industries Assoc. of Europe, 2003–04. Hon. DAdmin Manchester Metropolitan, 2006; Hon. DSc: Cranfield, 2007; Loughborough, 2007. *Recreations:* golf, cricket, Rugby, Manchester United. *Address:* Babcock International Group plc, 33 Wigmore Street, W1U 1QX.

TURNER, Neil; Chair, Wigan and Leigh Housing Company, since 2011; non-executive Director, Wrightington, Wigan and Leigh Hospital Foundation Trust, since 2010; *b* 16 Sept.

1945; *m* 1971, Susan Beatrice; one *s*. Quantity surveyor, AMEC Construction, 1963–92. Member (Lab): Wigan CBC, 1972–74; Wigan MBC, 1975–2000 (Chairman: Highways and Works Cttee, 1980–97; Best Value Rev. Panel, 1998–2000). MP (Lab) Wigan, Sept. 1999–2010. Sec., All Party Parly Gp on Rugby League, 2005–10; founder and Vice-Chair, All Pty Orthopaedic Alliance of MPs, 2004–10; Chair, SIGOMA Gp of MPs, 2005–10. Chairman: Public Services Cttee, AMA, 1995–97; Quality Panel, LGA, 1997–99. *Club:* Marsh Green Labour (Marsh Green, Wigan).

TURNER, Neil; *see* Turner, A. N.

TURNER, Pamela Ann; *see* Major, P. A.

TURNER, Peter; *see* Turner, T. P.

TURNER, Ven. (Peter) Robin, CB 1999; DL; Hon. Canon of Southwell Minster, 2002–12, now Canon Emeritus; Chaplain to Sector Ministries, Diocese of Southwell and Nottingham, 2004–12; *b* 8 March 1942; *s* of late Ronald James Turner and Irene Bertha (*née* Stocker); *m* 1967, Elizabeth Mary Kennen; two *s*. *Educ:* Dulwich Coll.; King's Coll. London (AKC); St Luke's Coll., Exeter (PGCE); Open Univ. (BA); Westminster Coll., Oxford (MTh). Ordained deacon, 1966, priest, 1967; Asst Curate, Crediton, 1966–69; Chaplain, RAF: Locking, 1970; Waddington, 1971–72; Nicosia, 1972–74; Little Rissington, 1975–76; Coltishall, 1976–78; Chaplains' Sch., 1978–81; Religious Progs Advr, British Forces Broadcasting Service, Germany, 1981–84; Chaplain, RAF: Odiham, 1984–85; Gutersloh, 1985–88; RAF Coll., Cranwell, 1988–89; Assistant Chaplain-in-Chief: RAF, Germany, 1989–91; RAF Strike Command, 1991–93; QHC, 1991–98; Principal, RAF Chaplains' Sch., 1993–95; Chaplain-in-Chief and Archdeacon, RAF, 1995–98, now Archdeacon Emeritus; non-residentiary Canon, Lincoln, 1995–98; Chaplain: Dulwich Coll., 1998–2002; to Bp of Southwell, subseq. Bp of Southwell and Nottingham, 2002–07; Notts Fire and Rescue Service, 2008–. Freeman, City of London, 2001; Liveryman, Musicians' Co., 2003–. President: Friends of St Clement Danes Ch (Central Ch of RAF), 2005–13; Notts, RBL, 2007–; Alleyn Club, 2007–08. Trustee, Dulwich Estate, 2005–15; Chairman: St Boniface Trust, 2005–; Bereavement Trust, 2012–. FRSA 2000. DL Notts, 2007. *Recreations:* choral singing, classical music, reading history and biography, armchair cricket, wine and its enjoyment. *Address:* 12 Chimes Meadow, Southwell, Notts NG25 0GB. *T:* (01636) 812250, 07890 633137. *E:* pr.turner@lineone.net. *Clubs:* Royal Air Force, Victory Services.

TURNER, Phil; Member, 1971–2006, and Executive Member, Culture, 2005–06, Camden Borough Council; *b* 7 June 1939; *s* of William Morris Turner and Eileen Lascelles Turner; *m* 1st, 1963, Gillian Sharp (*d* 1988); one *s* two *d* (and one *s* decd); 2nd, 2007, Maureen Alcock; two step *s* (and one step *s* decd). *Educ:* Beckenham and Penge Grammar School for Boys; University Coll. London (BScEcon). National Coal Board, later British Coal: Management Trainee, 1961–63; Hd of Information, Purchasing and Stores, 1963–65; O & M Officer, 1965–66; Hd of Admin, R & D Dept, 1966–68; Hd of Manpower Planning, 1968–73; Staff Manager, Opencast Exec., 1973–78; Hd of Conditions of Service, 1978–80; Dep. Dir of Staff Pay and Conditions, 1980–86; Head of Employment Policy, 1986–89. Joined Labour Party, 1963; Chair, Hampstead Labour Party, 1968–70; Camden Borough Council, 1971–2006: Chair: Building Works and Services Cttee, 1978–80 and 1986–89; Staff and Management Services Cttee, 1990–93; Leisure Services Cttee, 1993–97, 1998–2001; Corporate Services Cttee, 1997–98; Exec. Mem., Leisure and Community Services, 2001–05; Leader of Council, 1982–86, Dep. Leader, 1992–93, 1994–95 and 2003–06. Member: Assoc. of London Authorities, 1983–86; Policy Cttee, AMA, 1984–86; Vice Chair, Assoc. of London Govt Arts and Leisure Cttee, 1995–2000; Chair: London Steering Gp, Euro '96, 1995–96; London Sport Bd, 1996–2000. Contested (Lab): Cities of London and Westminster South, Feb. and Oct. 1974; (Lab) Hampstead and Highgate, 1987. Board Member: Kingsgate Community Assoc., 2006–10; Winchester Project, 2006–15 (Chair, Bd of Trustees, 2009–15). Sec., Camden Co-op. Party, 2009–. *Recreations:* family, travelling, book collecting. *Address:* 33 Minster Road, NW2 3SH. *T:* (020) 7692 0439.

TURNER, Richard Keith, OBE 2007; CEng, FCIHT; Chief Executive, Freight Transport Association, 2001–07; *b* 2 Oct. 1944; *s* of Richard Louis Turner and Queenie Kate Turner; *m* 1968, Jenny Georgina Whitehead; two *s* one *d*. *Educ:* E Barnet Grammar Sch.; Leeds Univ. (BSc Civil Engrg 1965); Bradford Univ. (MSc Traffic Engrg Planning 1972). CEng 1972. Grad. Engr, Herts CC, 1965–67; Sen. Engr, Leeds CC, 1967–73; Freight Transport Association: Highways and Traffic Advr, 1973–83; Dir of Planning, 1983–95; Dep. Dir Gen., 1995–2000. Member: Commn for Integrated Transport, 2004–10; Planning Cttee, London Thames Gateway Develt Corp., 2007–12. FCIHT (FIHT 1980); FCILT (FILT 1993); MICE 1972. *Publications:* numerous papers on transport planning and freight. *Recreations:* big DIY, cycling, swimming.

TURNER, Richard Timmis, CMG 2002; OBE 1978; FRAeS; Group Marketing Director, 1991–2002, Director, 1992–2002, Rolls-Royce plc; *b* 17 Aug. 1942; *s* of late Dr John Richard Timmis Turner and of Alison Elizabeth Turner; *m* 1982, Margaret Corbett; two *d*. *Educ:* Shrewsbury Sch.; Univ. of Manchester (BA Politics and Mod. Hist.). FRAeS 1993. Joined Rolls-Royce Ltd, 1965; Commercial Manager, NY, 1971–74; Mktg Exec., Civil Engines, 1977–88; Commercial Dir, Civil Engines, Rolls-Royce plc, 1988–89; Gp Mktg Dir, 1988–91, Dir, 1989–91, STC plc; rejoined Rolls-Royce plc, 1991. Non-executive Director: British Steel, 1994–99; Corus Gp plc, 1999–2004; Senior plc, 1996–2004. Member: BOTB, 1997–99; Bd, British Trade Internat., 1999–2003 (Chm., Business Adv. Panel, 1999–2003). Member: Council, SBAC, 1992–2002 (Pres., 1994–95); Ext. Affairs Bd, Royal Aeronautical Soc., 2006–13. Dep. UK Chm., Singapore British Business Council, 1996–2002; Mem., Indonesian British Business Council, 1997–2002. Mem. Adv. Council, British Expertise (formerly British Consultants and Contractors Bureau), 2001–14. Board Member: Nat. Campaign for Arts, 2006–13; Bath Fests, 2009–; Manning Camerata, 2013–. Trustee, Swordfish Heritage Trust (RN), 1998–2002. *Recreations:* music, opera, Rugby football. *Address:* 6 Widcombe Terrace, Bath BA2 6AJ. *T:* 07770 442333. *E:* Richardturner45@yahoo.co.uk. *Club:* Athenæum.

TURNER, Robert Edward, (Ted); American broadcasting company executive; Chairman and President, Turner Broadcasting System Inc., 1970–96; Founder and Chairman, Turner Foundation Inc., since 1991; *b* 19 Nov. 1938; *s* of Robert Edward Turner and Florence Turner (*née* Rooney); *m* 1st, Judy Nye (marr. diss.); one *s* one *d*; 2nd, 1965, Jane Shirley Smith (marr. diss. 1988); one *s* two *d*; 3rd, 1991, Jane Fonda (marr. diss. 2001). *Educ:* Brown Univ. Gen. Manager, Turner Advertising, 1960–63; Pres. and Chief Exec. Officer, various Turner cos, 1963–70; founded Turner Enterprises, 1976; Dir, 1996–2006, Vice Chm., 1996–2003, Time Warner Inc., then AOL Time Warner, subseq. Time Warner; launched Ted's Montana Grill, 2002. Pres., Atlanta Braves, 1976–96; Chm. of Bd, Atlanta Hawks, 1977–96. Won America's Cup in yacht Courageous, 1977. Pres.'s Award, 1979, 1989, Ace Special Recognition Award, 1980, Nat. Cable TV Assoc.; Special Award, Edinburgh Internat. TV Fest., 1982; Lifetime Achievement Award, NY Internat. Film and TV Fest., 1984; Tree of Life Award, Jewish Nat. Fund, 1985. *Publications:* (jtly) The Racing Edge, 1979.

TURNER, Prof. (Robert) Kerry, CBE 2000; Professorial Research Fellow, University of East Anglia, since 2010 (Professor of Environmental Sciences, 1991–2010); *b* 10 Aug. 1948; *s* of Ben Rees Turner and Eunice Ann Turner; *m* 1971, Merryl Noreen Eborne; one *s*. *Educ:* UC, Swansea (BSc Econs 1970); UC, Cardiff (Cert Ed 1971); Leicester Univ. (MA (Dist) 1972). Lectr in Econs, Coventry Poly., 1974–76; Sen. Res. Fellow, Dept of Econs, Leicester Univ., 1976; Lectr, 1977–88, Sen. Lectr, 1989–91, Sch. of Envmtl Scis, UEA. Chair, Foresight Panel on Natural Resources and the Envmt, OST/DTI, 1995–99; Co-Chair, UK Nat. Ecosystem Assessment, 2012–; Member: Bd, NRA, 1991–96; Regl Envmtl Protection Agency Cttee (Anglian Reg.), Envmt Agency, 1996–2002; Chair, Broads Authy, 2003–08 (Mem., 1996–2008, Vice Chair, 1996–2000, Chair, 2000–02, Envmt Cttee; Chm., Standards Cttee, 2002–03). Ed.-in-Chief, Envmtl and Resource Econs Jl, 1999–2012; Jt Ed., Regl Envmtl Change Jl, 1999–2002. FRSA 1991. Hon. FCIWEM. Hon. DSc Hull, 2014. *Publications:* Household Waste: separate collection recycling, 1983; *jointly:* Economics of Planning, 1977; Environmental Planning and Management, 1983; Economics of Natural Resources and the Environment, 1990 (trans. Italian 1992, Spanish 1995); Elementary Environmental Economics, 1994; Blueprint III, 1993; *edited:* Sustainable Environmental Management: principles and practice, 1988, 2nd edn 1993; *edited jointly:* Bibliography of Environmental Economics, vols 1 and 2, 1976; Progress in Resource Management and Environmental Planning, vol. 2, 1980, vol. 3, 1981, vol. 4, 1983; Wetlands: market and intervention failure, 1991; Economic Incentives and Environmental Policy, 1994; Ecosystems and Nature, 1999; Perspectives on Integrated Coastal Zone Management, 1999; Economics of Coastal and Water Resources, 2000; Managing a Sea: the ecological economics of the Baltic Sea, 2000; Managing Wetlands: an ecological economics approach, 2003; Managing European Coasts: past, present and future, 2005; Valuing Ecosystem Services: the case of multifunctional wetlands, 2008; over 300 contribs to books, articles in jls and reports. *Recreations:* outdoor environment, tennis. *Address:* School of Environmental Sciences, University of East Anglia, Norwich NR4 7TJ. *T:* (01603) 592551.

TURNER, (Robert) Leigh, CMG 2014; HM Diplomatic Service; Consul General, Istanbul, and Director-General of Trade and Investment for Turkey, South Caucasus and Central Asia (formerly Director of Trade for Turkey and Central Asia), since 2012; *b* 13 March 1958; *s* of late John Turner and of Susan Turner; *m* 1992, Pamela Ann Major, *qv*; one *s* one *d*. *Educ:* Downing Coll., Cambridge (BA Geog. 1979). Admin. Trainee, Freight Central Div., Dept of Transport, 1979; Asst to Regl Dir, Germany, PSA, 1980; HEO (Develt), Housing Policy, Pvte Rented Sector, DoE, 1981; IC2/IA3 Div., Supply Side Policy, HM Treasury, 1982; entered FCO, 1983; Second Sec., Vienna, 1984–87; FCO, 1987–92; First Sec., Moscow, 1992–95; FCO, 1995–98; Counsellor, EU and Econ., Bonn and Berlin, 1998–2002; special unpaid leave, 2002–06: writer, 2002–06; freelance journalist, FT, Boston Globe, Die Welt, Berliner Morgenpost, Philadelphia Inquirer, 2003–06; Dir, Overseas Territories, FCO, 2006–08; Ambassador to Ukraine, 2008–12. *Recreations:* writing, travel journalism, Lundy Island. *Address:* c/o Foreign and Commonwealth Office, King Charles Street, SW1A 2AH. *W:* http://blogs.fco.gov.uk/leighturner, www.twitter.com/LeighTurnerFCO.

TURNER, Robert Lockley; Senior Master of the Supreme Court, Queen's Bench Division, and Queen's Remembrancer, 1996–2007; *b* 2 Sept. 1935; *s* of James Lockley Turner, OBE and Maud Beatrice Turner; *m* 1963, Jennifer Mary Leather; one *s* one *d*. *Educ:* Clifton Coll.; St Catharine's Coll., Cambridge (BA 1957, MA 1973). Called to the Bar, Gray's Inn, 1958, Bencher, 2000. Commnd Gloucestershire Regt (28th/61st), 1959 (2nd Lieut); transf. to Army Legal Services, 1960 (Captain); Major 1962; retd from Army, 1966 (GSM with clasp South Arabia, 1966). Practised at Common Law Bar in London and on Midland and Oxford Circuit, 1967–84; a Recorder of the Crown Court, 1981–84; Master of Supreme Court, QBD, 1984–96. Prescribed Officer for Election Petitions, 1996–2007. Advisor to Law Reform Commn, Malta, 1993–99. Assessor, Access to Justice Inquiry, 1994–96. Mem., Notarial Bd, 1999–2012. President: Inst. of Credit Mgt, 2003–10 (Hon. FICM 1997); High Court Enforcement Officers Assoc., 2007–10. Chm., Sherbert Foundn, 2008–15. Vis. Fellow, Inst. of Internat. Maritime Law, Malta, 1998–99; Vis. Prof., Univ. of Glos, 2007–. Hon. Sen. Steward, Westminster Abbey, 2003–07 (Hon. Steward, 1985–2003); Churchwarden, St Matthew's, Midgham, 1990–92. Freeman, City of London, 1997; Liveryman: Scriveners' Co., 1999–2010; Goldsmiths' Co., 2007–. Warden, Hon. Co. of Glos, 2010–11. Trustee: Glos Regt, 2005–11; Soldiers of Gloster Mus., 2005–11. Chief Advisory Ed., Atkin's Court Forms, 1997–2009; Sen. Ed., Civil Procedure, 1999–2007. Hon. LLD West of England, 2006. *Publications:* (ed jtly) Supreme Court Practice, 1988–99; The Office of the Queen's Bench Master, 1990; (ed jtly) Chitty and Jacob, Queen's Bench Forms, 1992; (ed jtly) High Court Litigation Manual, 1992; Annual Practice, 1995; Queen's Bench Guide, 2000; Within the Permitted Variation, 2007; (jtly) Awards to Children and Protected Parties, 2007; Civil Procedure Rules 10 Years On, 2009; Recollections of a Remembrancer, 2010; Of Pennies and the Pyx, 2010; Civil Justice, 2011; Improving Quality of Civil Justice, 2013; The English Notary: his place in history, 2013; Medieval Shields of Westminster Abbey, 2014. *Recreation:* Drosselmeyer to grandchildren. *E:* robertturner1935@gmail.com. *Club:* Army and Navy.

TURNER, Ven. Robin; *see* Turner, Ven. P. R.

TURNER, Stephen Edward; HM Diplomatic Service, retired; Consul General, Auckland, and Director, Trade Development, New Zealand, 2002–05; *b* 25 March 1946; *s* of Leslie and Kathleen Turner; *m* 1966, Maureen Ann Dick; two *s* two *d*. *Educ:* John Ruskin Grammar Sch., Croydon. Entered FCO, 1963; served: Jakarta, 1968–72; Kuala Lumpur, 1972–75; FCO 1975–78; Malta, 1978–83; Jakarta, 1983–87; FCO, 1987–90; Consul, Seattle, 1990–95; Dep. Hd of Mission and Consul Gen., Hanoi, 1995–98; Dep. High Comr, Dhaka, 1998–2002. *Recreations:* entomology, ornithology, gardening, travel, the study of the life of Alfred Russel Wallace. *Address:* PO Box 1319, Mossman, Qld 4873, Australia.

TURNER, Stephen Gordon; Life President, British Association of Journalists, since 2009 (General Secretary, 1992–2013); *b* 27 July 1935; *s* of John Turner and Lillian Turner (*née* Wiseman); *m* 1st, 1955, Jean Florence Watts (marr. diss. 1978); two *s* one *d*; 2nd, 1979, Deborah Diana Thomas; one *d*. *Educ:* Triptons Secondary Modern Sch., Dagenham; Royal Liberty Grammar Sch., Romford. Royal Signals radio mechanic, 1953–55. Reporter: Romford Times, 1955–56; Ilford Recorder, 1956; Bristol Evening World, 1957; freelance journalist, 1958–68; News sub-editor: Ipswich Evening Star, 1969; Daily Mail, 1969–71; Features sub-editor, 1971–73, Public Opinion Editor, 1973–90, Daily Mirror; Gen. Sec., NUJ, 1990–92. Independent Councillor, Colchester BC, 1967–68. Mem., NUJ, 1955–92; Father of the Chapel, Daily Mirror, 1976–78, 1986–90. *Address:* 3 Stanley Road, Deal, Kent CT14 7BT.

TURNER, Stewart; *see* Turner, J. S.

TURNER, Ted; *see* Turner, R. E.

TURNER, (Thomas) Peter; Evaluation Consultant, since 1985; *b* 8 May 1928; *s* of Thomas Turner and Laura Crawley; *m* 1952, Jean Rosalie Weston; one *s* one *d*. *Educ:* Ilford County High Sch.; London University. BSc (1st Class Hons), Maths and Physics. GEC, North Wembley, 1947–50; Armament Design Establishment, 1950–54; Air Ministry (Science 3), 1954–58 and 1962–63; Chief Research Officer, RAF Maintenance Command, 1958–62; Police Research and Development Branch, Home Office, 1963–68; Civil Service Dept (OR), 1968–73; Head of Treasury/CSD Joint Operational Research Unit, 1973–76; Head of Operational Res., CSD, 1977–81, HM Treasury, 1981–84. *Address:* 8 Waring Drive, Green St Green, Orpington, Kent BR6 6DW. *T:* (01689) 851189.

TURNER, Dr William; Regional Medical Officer, Yorkshire Regional Health Authority, 1976–86, retired; *b* 23 Feb. 1927; *s* of Clarence and Mabel Turner; *m* 1950, Patricia Bramham Wilkinson; one *s* two *d*. *Educ:* Prince Henry's Grammar Sch., Otley, Yorks; Leeds Univ. MB, ChB; DPH, FFCM; LLB. House Officer, Leeds Gen. Infirmary, 1950–51; RAMC, 1951–53; Gen. Practitioner, 1953–55; Public Health Trng, 1955–60; Medical Officer of Health: Hyde, 1960–63; Huddersfield, 1963–67; Bradford, 1967–74; Area MO, Bradford, 1974–76.

Member: Standing Med. Adv. Cttee, 1978–82; NHS Steering Gp on Health Services Inf., 1979–84. *Publications:* contrib. BMJ, Medical Officer. *Address:* Bentcliffe, 1 Premiere Park, Ilkley, West Yorks LS29 9RQ. *T:* (01943) 600114.

TURNER LAING, Sophie Henrietta, (Mrs C. Comninos); Chief Executive Officer, Endemol Shine Group, since 2014; *b* 7 Sept. 1960; *d* of late Graham Turner Laing and of Gillian Vera Turner Laing (*see* G. V. Drummond); *m* 1987, Carlo Comninos; one *s* one *d*. *Educ:* Oakdene Sch., Bucks. Variety Club of GB, 1979–80; KM Campbell Pty Ltd, Australia, 1980–82; Sales Exec., 1982–85, Sales Dir, 1986–89, Henson Internat. TV; Jt Founder and Dep. Man. Dir, Hit Entertainment, 1989–95; Vice Pres., Broadcasting, Flextech TV, 1995–98; BBC: Controller, Programme Acquisition, 1998–2003; Acting Dir, Marketing and Communications, 2001; Acting Dir, BBC TV, 2002; British Sky Broadcasting Ltd: Dir, Film Channels and Acquisitions, 2003–04; Dep. Man. Dir, Sky Networks, 2004–07; Man. Dir, Content (formerly Entertainment, News and Broadcast Ops), 2007–14. Non-exec. Dir, Debenhams plc, 2009–. Gov., Nat. Film and TV Sch., 2004–. Mem., BAFTA, 2000– (Trustee, 2006–10; Vice Pres., TV, 2010–); Trustee, Media Trust, 2010–14. *Recreations:* film, theatre, ski-ing.

TURNER-SAMUELS, David Jessel; QC 1972; barrister; *b* 5 April 1918; *s* of late Moss Turner-Samuels, QC, MP, and Gladys Deborah Turner-Samuels (*née* Belcher); *m* 1939, Norma Turner-Samuels (*née* Verstone) (marr. diss. 1975); one *s* one *d*; *m* 1976, Norma Florence Negus (*d* 2009). *Educ:* Westminster Sch. Called to Bar, Middle Temple, 1939 (Bencher 1972); admitted to Trinidad Bar, 1976, Antigua Bar, 1997, St Lucia Bar, 1998. Served War of 1939–45, in Army, 1939–46. *Publications:* (jointly) Industrial Negotiation and Arbitration, 1951. *Recreation:* getting away from it all. *Address:* 4E Oak Lodge, Lythe Hill Park, Haslemere, Surrey GU27 3TF. *T:* (01428) 651970.

TURNER-WARWICK, Prof. Dame Margaret (Elizabeth Harvey), DBE 1991; MA, DM, PhD; FRCP; Chairman, Royal Devon and Exeter Health Care NHS Trust, 1992–95; President, Royal College of Physicians, 1989–92; Consultant Physician, Brompton Hospital, since 1965 (Professor of Medicine (Thoracic Medicine), 1972–87, Dean, 1984–87, Cardiothoracic Institute, now Emeritus Professor); *b* 19 Nov. 1924; *d* of William Harvey Moore, QC, and Maud Baden-Powell; *m* 1950, Richard Trevor Turner-Warwick, *qv*; two *d*. *Educ:* Maynard Sch., Exeter; St Paul's Girls' Sch.; Lady Margaret Hall, Oxford (Open Schol. 1943; Hon. Fellow, 1990). DM Oxon, 1956; PhD London, 1961; FRCP 1969; FFOM 1983; FRACP 1983; FRCPE 1990; FFPH (FFPHM 1990); FRCPGlas 1991; FRCGP 1991; FRCPI 1992. University Coll. Hosp., 1947–50: Tuke silver medal, Filliter exhibn in Pathology, Magrath Schol. in Medicine, Atchison Schol.; Postgrad. trng at UCH and Brompton Hosp., 1950–61; Cons. Physician: (Gen. Med.), Elizabeth Garrett Anderson Hosp., 1961–67; Brompton and London Chest Hosps, 1967–72. Sen. Lectr, Inst. of Diseases of the Chest, 1961–72. Lectures: Marc Daniels, 1974, Phillip Ellman, 1980, Tudor Edwards, 1985, Harveian, 1994, RCP; Lettsomian, Med. Soc. of London, 1982. Pres., British Thoracic Soc., 1982–85; Chairman: Central Academic Council, BPMF, 1982–85; Asthma Res. Council (Chm., Med. Res. Cttee, 1982–87); Conf. of Colleges and their Faculties in UK, 1990–92; UKCCCR, 1991–97; Member: MRC Systems Bd (DHSS nomination), 1982–85; Council, British Lung Foundn, 1984–90; Gen. Council, King's Fund, 1991; Council, BHF, 1994–; Mem. Council and Vice-Pres., ASH, 1990–. University of London: Mem. Senate, 1983–87; Mem., Academic Council, 1983–87; Mem., Scholarships Cttee, 1984–87; Mem., Cttee of Extramural Studies, 1984–87. Member: Nuffield Bioethics Council, 1993–2007; Round Table on Sustainable Develt, 1995–98. Fellow, UCL, 1991; FIC 1996. Founder FMedSci 1998. Hon. Fellow: Girton Coll., Cambridge, 1993; Green Coll., Oxford, 1993; Imperial Coll., London, 1996. Hon. FACP 1988; Hon. FRCP&S (Canada) 1990; Hon. FRCAnaes 1991; Hon. FCMSA 1991; Hon FRCPath 1992; Hon. FRCS 1993; Hon. FRCR 1994. Hon. Bencher, Middle Temple, 1990. Hon. Member: Assoc. of Physicians of GB and Ireland, 1991; S German and Australasian Thoracic Socs; Member; Alpha Omega Alpha, USA, 1987; Acad. of Malaysia, 1991. Hon. DSc: New York, 1985; Exeter, 1990; London, 1990; Hull, 1991; Sussex, 1992; Oxford, 1992; Cambridge, 1993; Leicester, 1998. Osler Meml Medal, Univ. of Oxford, 1995; President's Award, Eur. Respiratory Soc., 1997; President's Medal, British Thoracic Soc., 1999. *Publications:* Immunology of the Lung, 1978; (jtly) Occupational Lung Diseases: research approaches and methods, 1981; Living Medicine: recollections and reflections, 2005; chapters in various textbooks on immunology and thoracic medicine, particularly fibrosing lung disorders and asthma; contrib. original articles: Lancet, BMJ, Quarterly Jl Med., Thorax, Tubercle, Jl Clin. Experimental Immunology, etc. *Recreations:* her family and their hobbies, gardening, country life, watercolour painting, violin playing. *Address:* Pynes House, Thorverton, Exeter EX5 5LT.

TURNER-WARWICK, Richard Trevor, CBE 1991; MA, MSc, DM Oxon, MCh; Hon. DSc; FRCP, FRCS, FRCOG, Hon. FACS; Hon. FRACS; specialist in reconstruction and functional restoration of the urinary tract; Emeritus Surgeon and Urologist to the Middlesex Hospital (Senior Surgeon, 1969–90); Hon. Senior Lecturer, London University Institute of Urology, since 1962; Hon. Consultant Urologist, Royal Prince Alfred Hospital, Sydney, since 1980; Robert Luff Foundation Fellow in Reconstructive Surgery, 1990; *b* 21 Feb. 1925; *s* of W. Turner Warwick, FRCS; *m* 1950, Margaret Elizabeth Harvey Moore (*see* Dame Margaret Turner-Warwick); two *d*. *Educ:* Bedales School; Oriel Coll., Oxford; Middlesex Hosp. Medical School. Pres. OUBC, 1946; Mem. Univ. Boat Race Crew, Isis Head of River crew and Univ. Fours, 1946; Winner OU Silver Sculls, 1946; BSc thesis in neuroanatomy, 1946. Sen. Broderip Schol., Lyell Gold Medallist and Freeman Schol., Middx Hosp., 1949; surgical trng at Middx Hosp. and St Paul's Hosp., London, and Columbia Presbyterian Med. Centre, NY, 1959. Hunterian Prof. of RCS, 1957, 1976; Comyns Berkeley Travelling Fellowship to USA, 1959. British Assoc. of Urological Surgeons: Mem. Council, 1975–78 and 1982–92; Pres., 1988–90; Fellow, 1961; St Peter's Medal, 1978; Member: Council, Royal Coll. of Surgeons, 1980–92; RCOG, 1990–92; Internat. Soc. of Urology, 1966–; European Soc. of Urology; Soc. of Pelvic Surgeons, 1963; Founder Mem., 1969, Pres., 1985, Internat. Continence Soc.; Corresp. Member: Amer. Assoc. of Genito Urinary Surgeons, 1972 (Harry Spence Medal, 1998); American and Australasian Urological Assocs. Fellow UCL, 1992. Fellow: Assoc. of Surgeons of GB and Ireland, 1960; Australasian Soc. Urology, 1989; Hon. FRACS 1981; Hon. FACS 1997; Hon. FRSocMed 2003. Hon. DSc New York, 1985. Moynihan Prize of Assoc. of Surgeons, 1957; Victor Bonney Prize, RCOG, 1987; Valentine Medal, NY Acad. of Medicine, 1992. *Publications:* various articles in scientific jls, contributing to surgery, to develt of operative procedures for the reconstruction and restoration of function of the urinary tract, and to design of surgical instruments. *Recreations:* water, family, fishing, gardening. *Address:* Pynes House, 9 Silver Street, Thorverton, Exeter EX5 5LT. *T:* (01392) 861173, *Fax:* (01392) 860940. *Clubs:* Vincent's (Oxford); The Houghton (Stockbridge); Leander (Henley); Ottery St Mary Fly Fishers.

TURNOCK, Graham, PhD; Chief Executive, Better Regulation Executive, Department for Business, Innovation and Skills, since 2011; *b* Aberdeen, 30 July 1968; *s* of David Turnock and Edith Marion Turnock; *m* 2002, Cheryl Smith. *Educ:* St Catharine's Coll., Cambridge (BA 1989; PhD 1993); Ecole Nationale d'Administration (Diplôme d'Admin Publique 1997). HM Treasury: fast stream trainee, 1992–97; Principal, European Communities Budget, 1997–99, Public Enterprise Partnerships, 1999–2002; Dir, British Energy Team, DTI, 2002–03; Dir, Gershon Efficiency Rev., Cabinet Office, 2003–04; Leader, Transport Team, HM Treasury, 2004–08; Dir, Programmes, DCMS, 2008–11. *Publications:* papers on particle physics. *Recreations:* cycling, exploring France, music (listening and playing). *Address:* Department for Business, Innovation and Skills, 1 Victoria Street, SW1H 0ET. *Club:* Finsbury Park Cycling.

TURNOUR, family name of **Earl Winterton**.

TURNQUEST, Sir Orville (Alton), GCMG 1995; QC (Bahamas) 1992; Governor-General of the Bahamas, 1995–2001; *b* 19 July 1929; *y s* of late Robert Turnquest and Gwendolyn Turnquest; *m* 1955, Edith Louise Thompson; one *s* two *d*. *Educ:* Govt High Sch.; Univ. of London (LLB). Articled 1947–53; called to Bahamas Bar, 1953; called to the Bar, Lincoln's Inn, 1960 (Hon. Bencher); Counsel and Attorney of Supreme Ct; Notary Public; private practice, 1953–92; stipendiary and circuit magistrate and coroner, 1959; law tutor and Mem., Exam. Bd, Bahamas Bar, 1965–92. Chancellor, Dio. of Nassau and Bahamas. Sec.-Gen., Progressive Liberal Party, 1960–62; MP South Central, Nassau, 1962–67, Montagu, 1982–94; Opposition Leader in Senate, 1972–79; Dep. Leader, Free Nat. Movement, 1987–94; Attorney-Gen., 1992–94; Minister of Justice, 1992–93, of Foreign Affairs, 1992–94; Dep. Prime Minister, 1993–94. Pres., Bahamas Bar Assoc.; Chm., Bahamas Bar Council, 1970–72. Pres., CPA, 1992–93. Chm., One Bahamas Foundn. Member: Anglican Central Educnl Authy; Nat. Cttee of United World Colls; Bd of Govs, St John's Coll. and St Anne's High Sch. Trustee, Governor-General's Youth Award (Bahamas). *Recreations:* swimming, music, reading. *Address:* Kalamalka, Skyline Drive, PO Box N–8181, Nassau, Bahamas.

TUROK, Prof. Neil Geoffrey, PhD; Executive Director, Perimeter Institute of Theoretical Physics, Canada, since 2008; *b* 16 Nov. 1958; *s* of Benjamin and Mary Turok; *m* 1992, Corinne Francesca Squire; one *d*. *Educ:* Churchill Coll., Cambridge (BA); Imperial Coll., London (PhD). Postdoctoral Fellow, Univ. of California, Santa Barbara, 1983–85; Advanced Res. Fellow, 1985–87, Reader in Theoretical Physics, 1991–92, Imperial Coll.; Associate Scientist, Fermilab, Ill, 1987–88; Asst Prof., 1988–91, Associate Prof., 1992–95, David and Lucile Packard Fellow, 1992–97, Prof., 1995, Princeton Univ.; Prof. of Math. Physics, Univ. of Cambridge, 1996–2008. Founder, African Inst. for Mathematical Scis, 2003. James Clerk Maxwell Prize, Inst. of Physics, 1992. *Publications:* over 100 articles in Nuclear Physics B, Phys. Review, Phys. Review Letters, New Scientist, Scientific American. *Recreations:* jazz, nature, playing with Ruby. *Address:* Perimeter Institute for Theoretical Physics, 31 Caroline Street North, Waterloo, ON N2L 2Y5, Canada.

TURRELL, David Geoffrey, CBE 2009; Executive Headteacher, Sir Bernard Lovell School, since 2009 (Headteacher, 1995–2009); *b* 6 Feb. 1951; *s* of Stuart Turrell and Catherine Turrell; *m* 2013, Jane Gardner; one *s* one *d*, and two step *d*. *Educ:* Univ. of London (BA, MA). *Publications:* (contrib.) Developing Quality Schools, 1994. *Recreations:* walking, theatre, politics, travelling, family. *Address:* The Sir Bernard Lovell School, North Street, Oldland Common, Bristol BS30 8TS. *T:* (01454) 868023. *E:* dturrell@sblonline.org.uk.

TURTON, Eugenie Christine, (Genie), CB 1996; *b* 19 Feb. 1946; *d* of late Arthur Turton and Georgina (*née* Fairhurst). *Educ:* Nottingham Girls' High Sch. (GPDST); Girton Coll., Cambridge (schol.; MA). Research student (G. C. Winter Warr Studentship), Univ. of Cambridge, 1967–70; joined CS as Asst Principal, MoT, later DoE, 1970; Private Sec. to Parly Under Sec. of State, 1973–74; Principal, 1974–80; Prin. Private Sec. to successive Secretaries of State for Transport, 1978–80; Asst Sec., 1980–86; seconded to Midland Bank International, 1981–82, and to Cabinet Office/MPO (Machinery of Govt Div.), 1982–85; Under Sec., DoE, 1986–91; Director: Heritage and Royal Estate (formerly Ancient Monuments and Historic Bldgs), 1987–90; Inner Cities, 1990–91; Dep. Sec., DoE, 1991–94; Dir, Citizen's Charter Unit, Cabinet Office, 1994–97; Dir, Govt Office for London, 1997–2000; a Director General: DETR, then DTLR, 2000–02; ODPM, 2002–04. Non-executive Director: Woolwich Building Soc., 1987–91; Wates Gp, 2004–13; Rockpools Ltd, 2005–; Cognatum Trust, 2011–13; Mem. Bd, Genesis Housing Gp, 2009–; Associate, Critical Eye, 2009–. Advr to Min. of Public Admin, Govt of Trinidad and Tobago, 2010–. Trustee: Pilgrim Trust, 1991–2008; Horniman Mus., 2002–12; Dulwich Picture Gall., 2004–15; AA Motoring Trust, 2005–07: Sir Edward Heath Charitable Foundn, 2007–; Wessex Archaeology, 2008– (Chm., 2013–). Mem. Council, City Univ., 2000–04. Mem. Chapter, Salisbury Cath., 2007–. *Recreations:* books, music, painting, gardening.

TURVEY, Garry, CBE 1991; Director-General, Freight Transport Association, 1984–93; *b* 11 Oct. 1934; *s* of Henry Oxley Turvey and Annie Maud Braley; *m* 1960, Hilary Margaret Saines; three *s*. *Educ:* Morecambe Grammar School. FCIS. Metropolitan Vickers Ltd, Manchester, 1956–58; AEI Manchester Ltd, 1958–60; Asst Sec., 1960–67, Sec., 1967–69, Traders' Road Transport Assoc.; Sec., 1969–84 and Dep. Dir-Gen., 1974–84, Freight Transport Assoc. Freeman, City of London, 1994; Liveryman, Carmen's Co., 1994. *Recreations:* cricket, fly-fishing, gardening. *Address:* 139 Imberhorne Lane, East Grinstead, West Sussex RH19 1RP. *T:* (01342) 325829. *Club:* MCC.

TUSA, Sir John, Kt 2003; Managing Director, Barbican Centre, 1995–2007; Chair, Clore Leadership Foundation, 2009–14; *b* 2 March 1936; *s* of late John Tusa, OBE and Lydia Sklenarova; *m* 1960, Ann Hilary Dowson; two *s*. *Educ:* Trinity Coll., Cambridge (BA 1st Cl. Hons History). BBC general trainee, 1960; Producer, BBC External Services, 1962; freelance radio journalist, 1965; Presenter: BBC Radio 4 The World Tonight, 1968; BBC2 Newsnight, 1979–86; Man. Dir, World Service, BBC, 1986–92; Presenter, One O'Clock News, BBC TV, 1993–95. Chm., London News Radio, 1993–94. Pres., Wolfson Coll., Cambridge, 1993. Chairman: Adv. Cttee, Govt Art Collection, 1993–2003; BBC Marshall Plan of the Mind Trust, 1992–99; Wigmore Hall Trust, 1999–2011 (Trustee, 1993–95); Dep. Chm. Trustees, BM, 2004–09 (Trustee, 2000–04); Member: Council, RIIA, 1984–90, 1991–95; Board, Public Radio Internat. (formerly American Public Radio), 1990–99; Adv. Cttee, London Internat. String Quartet Competition, 1991–2009 (Vice-Chm. of Board, 1995–2009); Board, ENO, 1996–2003; Trustee: Nat. Portrait Gall., 1988–2000; Thomson Foundn, 1992–95; Design Mus. Trust, 1999–2000; Somerset House Trust, 2004–06; Turquoise Mountain Trust, 2006–; New Deal of the Mind, 2009–12; EU Youth Orch., 2014–; Hon. Chm., www.theartsdesk.com, 2009–13. Chm. of Govs, Univ. of the Arts, London, 2007–13. Hon. FRIBA 2001; Hon. RAM 1999; Hon. GSMD 1999; Hon. Mem., ISM, 2001; Hon. FRA, 2011. Hon. LLD London, 1993; DUniv Heriot-Watt, 1993; Hon. DLitt City, 1997; DU: Essex, 2006; Kingston, 2007; Kent, 2008; Hon. Dr Univ. of the Arts, London, 2014. TV Journalist of the Year, RTS 1983; Richard Dimbleby Award, BAFTA, 1984; BPG Award for outstanding contribn to radio, 1991; Presenter of the Year, RTS, 1995. Knight First Class, Order of the White Rose (Finland), 1998. *Publications:* Conversations with the World, 1990; A World in Your Ear, 1992; (with Ann Tusa): The Nuremberg Trial, 1983; The Berlin Blockade, 1988; Art Matters: reflecting on culture, 1999; On Creativity, 2003; The Janus Aspect: artists in the twenty first century, 2005; Engaged with the Arts: writings from the front line, 2007; Pain in the Arts, 2014. *Recreations:* tennis, chamber music, listening, travel. *Address:* 16 Canonbury Place, N1 2NN. *T:* (020) 7704 2451.

TUSHINGHAM, Rita; actress; *b* 14 March 1942; *d* of John Tushingham; *m* 1962, Terence William Bicknell (marr. diss. 1976); two *d*; *m* 1981, Ousama Rawi (marr. diss. 1996). *Educ:* La Sagesse Convent, Liverpool. Student, Liverpool Playhouse, 1958–60. Associate, London Film Sch., 2011. Hon. Fellow, Liverpool John Moores Univ., 2009. BBC Personality of the Year, Variety Club of GB, 1988. *Stage appearances:* Royal Court Theatre: The Changeling, 1960; The Kitchen, 1961; A Midsummer Night's Dream, 1962; Twelfth Night, 1962; The Knack, 1962; other London theatres: The Giveaway, 1969; Lorna and Ted, 1970; Mistress of Novices, 1973; My Fat Friend, 1981; Children, Children, 1984; Vagina Monologues, 2003. *Films:* A Taste of Honey, 1961 (Brit. Film Acad. and Variety Club awards for Most Promising

Newcomer, 1961; NY Critics, Cannes Film Festival and Hollywood Foreign Press Assoc. awards); The Leather Boys, 1962; A Place to Go, Girl with Green Eyes (Variety Club award), 1963; The Knack, 1964 (Silver Goddess award, Mexican Assoc. of Film Corresps); Dr Zhivago, 1965; The Trap, 1966; Smashing Time, Diamonds For Breakfast, 1967; The Guru, 1968; The Bed-Sitting Room, 1970; Straight on till Morning, 1972; Situation, 1972; Instant Coffee, 1973; Rachel's Man, 1974; The Human Factor, 1976; Pot Luck, State of Shock, 1977; Mysteries, 1978; Incredible Mrs Chadwick, 1979; The Spaghetti House Siege, 1982; Flying, 1984; A Judgement in Stone, Single Room, 1986; Resurrected, Dante and Beatrice in Liverpool, 1989; Hard Days' Hard Nights, 1990; Paper Marriage, Rapture of Deceit, 1991; Desert Lunch, 1992; An Awfully Big Adventure, 1994; The Boy from Mercury, 1995; Under The Skin, 1996; Swing, Out of Depth, 1998; Home Ground, 2000; Being Julia, 2003; Loneliness and the Modern Pentathlon, 2004; The Hideout, 2006; Puffball, Come Here Today, 2008; Telstar, Broken Lines, The Calling, 2009; One of the Things that makes me Doubt (film art installation), Seamonsters, 2011; Outside Bet, The Wee Man, 2012. *TV appearances include:* Red Riding Hood (play), 1973; No Strings (own series), 1974; Don't Let Them Kill Me on Wednesday, 1980; Confessions of Felix Krull, 1980; Seeing Red, 1983; Pippi Longstocking, 1984; The White Whale—The Life of Ernest Hemingway (film), 1987; cameo appearance in Bread, 1988; Sunday Pursuit; Gütt, Ein Journalist, 1991; Hamburg Poison, 1992; Family Secrets (film), 1995; I Was Eddie Mostyn, 1995; Shadow Play, 2001; Margo beyond the Box, 2003; New Tricks, 2005; Miss Marple: The Sittaford Mystery, 2005; Angel Cake, 2006; Bedlam, 2011; In the Flesh, 2013–14; Patty and Chips with Scraps (BBC radio play), 1997; voiceover for documentary celebrating 50th anniversary of 'A Hard Day's Night', 2014. *Recreations:* interior decorating, cooking, watercolour painting. *Address:* c/o Michele Milburn, Milburn Browning Associates, The Old Truman Brewery, 91 Brick Lane, E1 6QL.

TUSK, Donald Franciszek; President of the European Council, since 2014; *b* Gdańsk, Poland, 22 April 1957; *s* of late Donald and Ewa Tusk; *m* Małgorzata; one *s* one *d*. *Educ:* Univ. of Gdańsk. Manual labourer, Świetlik co-operative; journalist, Maritime Publishing House; Dep. Ed., Gazeta Gdańska, 1989; Founder and Ed., Przeglad Polityczny. Mem., Solidarity Trade Union, 1980–89. Leader, 1989, Chair, 1991–94, Congress of Liberals, later Liberal-Democratic Congress; Vice-Chair, Freedom Union, 1994. MP (Freedom Union), 1991–93, 2001–14; Dep. Marshal of Sejm, 2001–05; Senator and Vice Marshal of Senate, 1997–2001; Leader of Opposition, 2001–07; Prime Minister of Poland, 2007–14. Co-Founder, 2001, Leader, 2003–14, Civic Platform. *Publications:* Kashubian Lake District, 1985; Once There Was Gdańsk, 1996; Gdańsk 1945, 1998; Old Sopot, 1998; Ideas of Gdańsk's Liberalism, 1998. *Address:* Council of the European Union, Wetstraat 175, 1048 Brussels, Belgium.

TUSTIN, Rt Rev. Dr David; Hon. Assistant Bishop of Lincoln, since 2001; Bishop Suffragan of Grimsby, 1979–2000; *b* 12 Jan. 1935; *s* of John Trevelyan Tustin and Janet Reynolds; *m* 1964, Mary Elizabeth (*née* Glover) (*d* 2014); one *s* one *d*. *Educ:* Solihull School; Magdalene Coll., Cambridge (MA Hons); Geneva Univ. (Cert. in Ecumenical Studies); Cuddesdon Coll., Oxford. Philip Usher Memorial Scholar (in Greece), 1957–58; deacon 1960, priest 1961; Curate of Stafford, 1960–63; Asst Gen. Sec., C of E Council on Foreign Relations and Curate of St Dunstan-in-the-West, Fleet St, 1963–67; Vicar of S Paul's, Wednesbury, 1967–71; Vicar of Tettenhall Regis, 1971–79; RD of Trysull, 1977–79. Canon and Prebendary of Lincoln Cathedral, 1979–2000. Co-Chm., Anglican/Lutheran Internat. Commn, 1986–98; Pres., Anglican/Lutheran Soc., 1986–99; Mem., Gen. Synod of C of E, 1990–2000 (Chm., Council for Christian Unity, 1993–98). Trustee, British Horological Inst. Mus., Upton Hall, 2015–. DD Lambeth 1998. Comdr, Royal Order of Polar Star (Sweden), 2000. *Publications:* A Bishop's Ministry: reflections and resources for church leadership, 2013. *Recreations:* music, family life, languages, travel, horology. *Address:* The Ashes, Tunnel Road, Wrawby, Brigg, N Lincs DN20 8SF.

TUTT, Prof. Norman Sydney, OBE 2002; Executive Director of Housing and Social Services, London Borough of Ealing, 2001–03 (Director of Social Services, 1999–2001); *b* 8 June 1944; *s* of Sydney Robert Tutt and Stella May Tutt; *m* 1966, Diana Patricia Hewitt; two *s*. *Educ:* Chislehurst and Sidcup Grammar Sch.; Univ. of Keele (BA); Univ. of Leeds (MSc); Univ. of Nottingham (PhD). Clin. Psychologist, Nottingham, 1966–69; Resident Psychologist, St Gilbert's Approved Sch., 1969–73; Professional Advr, Northampton Social Services, 1973–74; Sen. Develt Officer, London Boroughs Children Reg. Planning Cttee, 1974–75; Principal Social Work Services Officer, DHSS, 1975–79; Prof. of Applied Social Studies, 1979–92 (on leave of absence, 1989–92), and Hon. Prof., 1992–95, Lancaster Univ.; Dir of Social Services, Leeds CC, 1989–93; Exec. Dir, Social Information Systems, 1993–98. Man., Gulbenkian Commn on Violence to Children, 1995–96. Vis. Prof., Faculty of Community Health Scis, Univ. of Wales Inst. at Cardiff (formerly Cardiff Inst.), 1994–2000. Mem. Council, ASA, 1996–2002. Mem. Bd, Hanover Housing Assoc., 1996–99. *Publications:* Care or Custody, 1975; (ed) Violence, 1975; (ed) Alternative Strategies for Coping with Crime, 1978; (ed) A Way of Life for the Handicapped, 1983; Children in Custody, 1987; (ed) Children and Homicide, 1996; contributor to other pubns. *Recreations:* work, wine, walks, cracking jokes. *Address:* Chateau Milhau, 34620 Puisserguier, France. *T:* (4) 67893275. *Club:* as with Groucho Marx he would not join a club which would have him as a member.

TUTT, Roger Clive, CMG 1994; MBE 1966; HM Diplomatic Service, retired; *b* 22 March 1939; *s* of Clive Pritchard Tutt and Ada (*née* Kyle); *m* 1963, Gwen Leeke; two *s* one *d*. *Educ:* Bristol GS; Ledbury GS; Bristol Univ. (BA Econ). Bristol Univ. expedn to India and S America, 1960–61; Asst Administrator, Turks and Caicos Is, 1963–66; joined HM Diplomatic Service, 1966; Second Secretary: Copenhagen, 1967–69; Lusaka, 1969–71; First Secretary: FCO, 1971–74; Regl Inf. Officer, Barbados, 1974–79; FCO, 1979–87; Counsellor: UKMIS NY, 1987–89; FCO, 1989–94, 1995–2005. *Recreations:* stewardship of a small piece of rural Gloucestershire, fishing, sailing, travel.

TUTTLE, Hon. Robert Holmes; Joint Managing Partner, Tuttle-Click Automotive Group, 1989–2005 and since 2009; *b* 1944; *s* of Holmes Tuttle; *m* Maria Denise Hummer; two *d* from former marr. *Educ:* Stanford Univ. (BA 1965); Univ. of Southern Calif (MBA 1968). Special Asst to President of USA, 1982–85, Dep. Asst, 1985–88, Asst, 1988–89; Dir, Presidential Personnel, 1985–89; Ambassador of USA to the Court of St James's, 2005–09. Director: Arizona Bank, 1989–99 (Chm., Exec. Cttee, 1994–98); City Nat. Corp., 2002–05, 2010–.

TUTU, Most Rev. Desmond Mpilo; Archbishop of Cape Town and Metropolitan of Southern Africa, 1986–96, now Archbishop Emeritus; Chair, Truth and Reconciliation Commission, 1995–99; Co-Founder, Desmond Tutu Peace Centre, 1998; *b* Klerksdorp, Transvaal, 7 Oct. 1931; *s* of Zachariah and Aletta Tutu; *m* 1955, Leah Nomalizo Shenxane; one *s* three *d*. *Educ:* Johannesburg Bantu High Sch.; Bantu Normal Coll., Pretoria (Higher Teachers' Dip. 1953); Univ. of S Africa (BA 1954); St Peter's Theol Coll., Johannesburg (LTh 1960); King's Coll. London (BD 1965, MTh 1966; FKC 1978). Schoolmaster: Madibane High Sch., Johannesburg, 1954; Munsieville High Sch., Krugersdorp, 1955–57. Theological coll. student, 1958–60; deacon 1960, priest 1961, St Mary's Cathedral, Johannesburg. Curate: St Alban's Church, Benoni, 1960–61; St Philip's Church, Alberton, 1961–62; St Alban's, Golders Green, London, 1962–65; St Mary's, Bletchingley, Surrey, 1965–66; Lecturer: Federal Theol Seminary, Alice, CP, 1967–69; Univ. of Botswana, Lesotho and Swaziland, Roma, Lesotho, 1970–72; Associate Dir, Theol Education Fund (WCC) based in Bromley, Kent, and Hon. Curate, St Augustine's, Grove Park, 1972–75; Dean of Johannesburg, 1975–76; Bishop of Lesotho, 1976–78; Gen. Sec., South African Council of Churches, 1978–85; Rector, St Augustine's Parish, Soweto, 1981–85; Bishop of Johannesburg, 1985–86. Woodruff Vis. Prof., Emory Univ., 1998–2000. Chancellor, Univ. of Western Cape, Cape Town, 1988–2010. Pres., All Africa Conference of Churches, 1987–97. Mem., The Elders. Trustee, Phelps Stoke Fund, New York. Holds over fifty hon. degrees from academic institutions in UK, Europe and USA. Athena Prize, Onassis Foundation, 1980; Nobel Peace Prize, 1984; Albert Schweitzer Humanitarian Award, Emmanuel Coll., Boston, 1988; Mo Ibrahim Foundn Award, 2012; Templeton Prize, Templeton Foundn, 2013. Order of Meritorious Service, Gold (S Africa), 1996; Order of Southern Cross (Brazil), 1987; Order of Merit of Brasilia (Brazil), 1987; Grand Cross of Merit (Germany), 1996; Presidential Medal of Freedom (USA), 2009. *Publications:* Crying in the Wilderness, 1982; Hope and Suffering, 1983; The Words of Desmond Tutu, 1989; The Rainbow People of God, 1994; No Future Without Forgiveness, 1999; God Has a Dream: a vision of hope for our time, 2004; Made for Goodness: and why this makes all the difference, 2010; God Is Not a Christian: speaking truth in times of crisis, 2011; (with M. Tutu) The Book of Forgiving: the fourfold path for healing ourselves and our world, 2014; In God's Hands, 2014; articles and reviews. *Recreations:* music, reading, jogging.

TUYMANS, Luc; artist; *b* Belgium, 14 July 1958. Solo exhibitions worldwide, 1985–, including: Zeno X Gall., Antwerp; White Cube, London, 1999, 2001; Tokyo Opera Art Gall., 2000; Venice Biennale, 2001; Helsinki Kunsthalle, 2003; Pinakothek der Moderne, Munich, 2003; Tate Modern, 2004; Fundação de Serralves, 2006; Kunsthalle Budapest, 2007; Haus der Kunst, Munich, 2008; Wiels, Brussels, 2008; Wexner Center for the Arts, Ohio, 2008; Baibakov Art Projects, Moscow, 2009; Moderna Museet, Malmö, 2009; San Francisco Mus. of Modern Art, 2010; Dallas Mus. of Art, 2010; Mus. of Contemporary Art, Chicago, 2010; Paleis voor Schone Kunsten, Brussels, 2011; Kunsthalle Bremerhaven, 2012; Menil Collection, Houston, 2013. *Address:* c/o Zeno X Gallery, Godtsstraat 15, 2140 Antwerp Borgerhout, Belgium. *E:* info@zeno-x.com.

TVEIT, Rev. Dr Olav Fykse; General Secretary, World Council of Churches, since 2010. *Educ:* Norwegian Sch. of Theol., Oslo (MTh 1986; Practicum 1987; DTh 2002). Army chaplain, Sessvollmoen (nat. service), 1987–88; parish priest, Haram, Møre dio., 1988–91; Consultant and Sen. Consultant for theol issues, Ch of Norway Council on Ecumenical and Internat. Relns, 1991–96; res. schol., Res. Council of Norway and Norwegian Sch. of Theol., 1996–2001; Church of Norway: Sec., Doctrinal Commn, 1999–2000; Sec., Commn on Church-State Relns, 2001–02; Gen. Sec., Council on Ecumenical and Internat. Relns, 2002–09. Moderator: Ecumenical Mt of Olive Foundn, Norway, 2002; Ch of Norway-Islamic Council of Norway contact gp, 2005–09; Ch of Norway-Jewish Congregation in Norway contact gp, 2005–09. Member: Bd of Dirs and Exec. Cttee, Christian Council of Norway, 2002–09; Exec. Cttee, Commn for Cooperation between parishes and missionary orgns, 2005–09; Inter-Faith Council of Norway, 2006–09; Faith and Order Plenary Commn, WCC, 2007–09; Mt of Olive Land Develt Cttee, Jerusalem, 2008–09; Mem. and Moderator, Palestine-Israel Ecumenical Forum Core Gp, WCC, 2007–09. Mem., Bd of Trustees, Norwegian Ch Aid, 2007–09. *Recreation:* ski-ing. *Address:* World Council of Churches, PO Box 2100, 1211 Geneva 2, Switzerland. *T:* (22) 79162885, *Fax:* (22) 7916535. *E:* dcb@wcc-coe.org.

TWEEDALE, (John) Christopher; Chief Executive Officer and Schools Director, CfBT Schools Trust, since 2014 (UK Director, 2013); *b* Rochdale, 15 Dec. 1956; *s* of late Austen Tweedale and of Bernadette Tweedale; *m* 1985, Jacqueline Sullivan; two *s*. *Educ:* Bishop Henshaw High Sch., Rochdale; Univ. of Leicester (BSc Hons Geol. 1978; PGCE 1979); Keele Univ. (MBA 2000). Teacher: Cardinal Wiseman High Sch., Ealing, 1979–82; John F. Kennedy High Sch., Herts, 1982–86; Sen. Teacher, Therfield Sch., 1986–89; Dep. Principal, Okehampton Coll., 1989–96; Headteacher, John Masefield High Sch., Herefordshire, 1996–2004; Sen. Policy Advr, 2004–07, Dep. Dir, 14–19 Educn, 2007–09, DfES, later DCSF; Dir, Schs and Young People (formerly Children, Young People and School Effectiveness), Welsh Govt (formerly Welsh Assembly Govt), 2009–13. FRSA. *Recreations:* golf, walking, sport, arts, travel. *Address:* CfBT Schools Trust, 60 Queens Road, Reading RG1 4BS. *T:* (0118) 902 1080. *E:* ctweedale@cfbt.com. *Clubs:* Royal Over-Seas League; Ross-on-Wye Golf; Wormcatchers Golf Soc. (Glos).

TWEEDDALE, 14th Marquis of, *cr* 1694; **Charles David Montagu Hay;** Lord Hay of Yester, 1488; Earl of Tweeddale, 1646; Viscount Walden, Earl of Gifford, 1694; Baron Tweeddale (UK), 1881; Hereditary Chamberlain of Dunfermline; *b* 6 Aug. 1947; *yr* twin *s* of 12th Marquis of Tweeddale, GC and of Hon. Sonia Mary, *d* of 1st Viscount Ingleby, PC; *S* brother, 2005. *Educ:* Milton Abbey, Blandford, Dorset; Trinity Coll., Oxford. *Heir:* *b* (Lord) Alistair James Montagu Hay, DPhil, *b* 4 Nov. 1955; does not use courtesy title.

TWEEDIE, Prof. Sir David (Philip), Kt 1994; Chairman, International Valuation Standards Board, since 2012; President, Institute of Chartered Accountants of Scotland, 2012–13 (Senior Vice-President, 2011–12; Junior Vice-President, 2010–11); *b* 7 July 1944; *s* of Aidrian Ian Tweedie and Marie Patricia Tweedie (*née* Phillips); *m* 1970, Janice Christine Brown; two *s*. *Educ:* Grangemouth High Sch.; Edinburgh Univ. (BCom, PhD). CA 1972. Accountancy trng, Mann, Judd, Gordon (Glasgow), 1969–72; Edinburgh University: Lectr in Accounting, 1973–78; Associate Dean, Fac. of Social Scis, 1975–78; Technical Dir, Inst. of Chartered Accountants, Scotland, 1978–81; Nat. Res. Partner, KMG Thomson McLintock, 1982–87; Nat. Tech. Partner, KPMG Peat Marwick McLintock, 1987–90; Chairman: Accounting Standards Bd, 1990–2000; Internat. Accounting Standards Bd, 2000–11. Visiting Professor of Accounting: Univ. of Lancaster, 1978–88; Univ. of Bristol, 1988–2000; Edinburgh Univ., 1999–. UK and Irish Representative: Internat. Auditing Practices Cttee, 1983–88; Internat. Accounting Standards Cttee, 1995–2000; Auditing Practices Committee, Consultative Committee of Accountancy Bodies: Mem., 1985–90; Vice-Chm., 1986–88; Chm., 1989–90. Institute of Chartered Accountants in England and Wales: Mem. Council, 1989–91; Mem., Financial Reporting Council, 1990–2000; Chm., Urgent Issues Task Force, 1990–2000. FRSE 2001. Hon. FIA 1999; Hon. FSIP 2004; Hon. FCCA 2005; Hon. CPA (Aust.) 2012. Freeman, City of London, 2014. Hon. DSc (Econ) Hull, 1993; Hon. LLD: Lancaster, 1993; Exeter, 1997; Dundee, 1998; Hon. DLitt Heriot-Watt, 1996; Hon. DBA: Napier, 1999; Oxford Brookes, 2004; Lincoln, 2012; Hon. DSc (SocSci) Edinburgh, 2001. Centenary Award, Chartered Accountants Founding Socs, 1997; CIMA Award, 1998; IFAC Internat. Gold Service Award, 2011; Accounting Hall of Fame, 2013. *Publications:* (with T. A. Lee) The Private Shareholder and the Corporate Report, 1977; Financial Reporting, Inflation and the Capital Maintenance Concept, 1979; (with T. A. Lee) The Institutional Investor and Financial Information, 1981; (with G. Whittington) The Debate on Inflation Accounting, 1984; contribs to professional and acad. accounting jls and books. *Recreations:* athletics and Rugby (watching, not participating, sadly), walking, gardening. *Address:* International Valuation Standards Council, 1 King Street, EC2V 8AU.

TWEEDSMUIR, 4th Baron *cr* 1935, of Elsfield, Oxford; **John William Howard de l'Aigle, (Toby), Buchan;** *b* 25 May 1950; *s* of 3rd Baron Tweedsmuir and Barbara, 2nd *d* of Ernest Nash Ensor; *S* father, 2008; *m* 1st, 1977, Amanda Jocelyn, *d* of Sir Gawain Westray Bell, KCMG, CBE; two *s*; 2nd, 2001, Dominique, *d* of late Dennis Joseph Enright, OBE; one *s* two *d*. *Educ:* Magdalen Coll. Sch., Oxford. *Heir:* *s* Hon. John Alasdair Gawain Buchan, *b* 20 Nov. 1986.

TWEEDY, Colin David, LVO 2003; OBE 2000; Chief Executive: The Building Centre, since 2012; Built Environment Trust, since 2015; *b* 26 Oct. 1953; *s* of late Clifford Harry Tweedy, of Abbotsbury, Dorset and Kitty Audrey (*née* Matthews); *m* 2008, Campbell Guthrie Gray. *Educ:* City of Bath Boys' Sch.; St Catherine's Coll., Oxford (MA). Manager, Thorndike Theatre, Leatherhead, 1976–78; Corporate Finance Officer, Guinness Mahon, 1978–80; Asst

Dir, Streets Financial PR, 1980–83; Dir Gen., Assoc. for Business Sponsorship of the Arts, later Chief Exec., Arts & Business, 1983–2012. Chm., Comité Européen pour le Rapprochement de l'Economie et de la Culture; Mem. Council, Japan Festival, 1991; Director: Covent Garden International Festival, 1995–2001; Headlong Th. Co. (formerly Oxford Stage Co.), 1985–2012; Crusaid, 1987–2004; Mariinsky Theatre Trust, 1999–; Mem. Council, Nat. Musicians' Symphony Orch., 2001–; Member: UK Nat. Cttee, European Cinema and TV Year, 1988–89; Council for Charitable Support, 1998–2008; Design Council Sounding Bd, 2013–. Co-Founder, Stonewall Equality Trust, 1989; Founder, 2002, and Trustee, Prince's Foundn for Children and the Arts (formerly Prince of Wales Arts & Kids Foundn), 2000–15; Trustee: Serpentine Gall., 1990–; The Ideas Foundn, 2003–; Next Generation Foundn, 2003–08. Selector, Discerning Eye 2000 exhibn; a Judge: PR Week Awards, 2000; Art & Work Awards, 2002; Mem. Adv. Panel, Costa (formerly Whitbread) Bk Awards, 1998–. Gov., Univ. of Creative Arts, 2009–. Freeman, City of London, 1978. CCMI 2002; FRSA. Hollis Sponsorship Personality of the Year, 2003. *Publications:* A Celebration of Ten Years' Business Sponsorship of the Arts, 1987. *Recreations:* the arts in general, opera, theatre and contemporary art in particular, Italy, food, travel. *Address:* The Building Centre, 26 Store Street, WC1E 7BT. *T:* (020) 7692 4000. *E:* c.tweedy@buildingcentre.co.uk. *Club:* Groucho.

TWELFTREE, Dame Marcia (Anne), DBE 2010; part-time education consultant, since 2009; *b* Walsall Wood, 31 March 1950; *d* of Bernard Harold Daffern and Sylvia May Daffern (*née* Booth); *m* 1983, Michael Richard Twelftree; one *s* one *d*. *Educ:* King Edward VI High Sch. for Girls, Birmingham; Bristol Univ. (BSc Hons Chem. 1971); St John's Coll., Oxford (PGCE 1972). Teacher: Oxford Sch., 1972–73; Burford Sch., 1973–74; Lectr, Swindon Coll., 1979–84; Sen. Teacher, Ridgeway Sch., Wroughton, 1984–90; Dep. Headteacher, Sheldon Sch., Chippenham, 1990–93; Head Teacher: John O'Gaunt Sch., Hungerford, 1993–97; Charters Sch., Sunningdale, 1997–2009. Association of School and College Leaders: Salaries Condition of Service Officer, 1995–97; Mem., Nat. Council, 1999–2009. Mem., Implementation Rev. Unit, 2003–09. Mem. Bd, Sch. Food Trust, 2007–11. Trustee, Prince Philip Trust, 2011–. Chair: Govs, Burnham Park Acad., 2012–15; Interim Exec. Bd, Wye Valley Sch., 2013–14; Interim Exec. Bd, Parker EACT Acad., Daventry, 2014. Secondary Head, CfBT Educn Trust, 2015–. *Recreations:* being a 'mad' grandma to 6 grandsons, travel to far-flung places, touring Europe in a camper-van, theatre, cinema, walking. *Address:* Rose Cottage, 117 Rowtown, Addlestone, Surrey KT15 1HQ. *T:* (01932) 888908. *E:* twelftree@gmail.com.

TWELVETREE, Eric Alan; County Treasurer, Essex County Council, 1974–87; *b* 26 Dec. 1928; *m* 1953, Patricia Mary Starkings; two *d*. *Educ:* Stamford Sch., Lincs; qualif. IPFA and ACCA. Served with Borough Councils: Gt Yarmouth, Ipswich, Stockport, Southampton; County Councils: Gloucestershire, Kent. Pres., Soc. of County Treasurers, 1986–87. Dir, Chelmsford Hospice, then Farleigh Hospice, Chelmsford, 1991–99. Mem., Exec. Cttee, Field Studies Council, 1978–2001. *Recreations:* watercolours, history of Tetbury Society. *Address:* 12 Cherry Orchard Road, Tetbury, Glos GL8 8HX.

TWIGG, (John) Derek; MP (Lab) Halton, since 1997; *b* 9 July 1959; *s* of Kenneth and Irene Twigg; *m* 1988, Mary Cassidy; one *s* one *d*. *Educ:* Bankfield High Sch., Widnes; Halton Coll. of Further Educn. Civil service posts, Department of Employment, and DFE, then DFEE, 1975–96; political consultant, 1996–97. Member (Lab): Cheshire CC, 1981–85; Halton DC, 1983–97. PPS to Minister of State, DTI, 1999–2001, to Sec. of State, DTLR, 2001–02; an Asst Govt Whip, 2002–03; a Lord Comr of HM Treasury (Govt Whip), 2003–04; Parliamentary Under-Secretary of State: DFES, 2004–05; DfT, 2005–06; MoD, 2006–08; Shadow Health Minister, 2010–11. Mem., Public Accounts Cttee, 1998–99. *Recreations:* hill walking, reading military history. *Address:* House of Commons, SW1A 0AA. *T:* (020) 7219 3000.

TWIGG, Stephen; MP (Lab and Co-op) Liverpool West Derby, since 2010; *b* 25 Dec. 1966; *s* of Ian David Twigg and late Jean Barbara Twigg. *Educ:* Southgate Comprehensive Sch.; Balliol Coll., Oxford (BA Hons). Pres., NUS, 1990–92; Parliamentary Officer: British Sect., Amnesty Internat., 1992–93; NCVO, 1993–94; researcher, office of Margaret Hodge, MP, 1994–96. Mem. (Lab), Islington LBC, 1992–97. Gen. Sec., Fabian Soc., 1996–97 (Mem. Exec., 1997–). MP (Lab) Enfield, Southgate, 1997–2005; contested (Lab) same seat, 2005. Parly Sec., Privy Council Office, 2001–02; Parly Under-Sec. of State, DfEE, 2002–04, Minister of State, DfES, 2004–05; Shadow Sec. of State for Educn, 2011–13. Member: Select Cttee on Modernisation of H of C, 1998–2000; Select Cttee on Educn and Employment, 2000–01; Chm., Select Cttee on Internat. Develt, 2015–. Dir, Foreign Policy Centre, 2005–10 (Bd Mem., 1998–2005). Chairman: Labour Campaign for Electoral Reform, 1998–2001; Lab. Friends of Israel, 1998–2001. Dir, Crime Concern, 1997–2000. Dir, Special Projects, AEGIS Charitable Trust, 2005–10; Chm., Young People Now Foundn, 2006–08. Trustee, WEA, 2006–08 (Patron, 2008–); Chair of Trustees, Merseyside Domestic Violence Services, 2008–. Patron: Merseyside Motor Neurone Disease Assoc., 2011–; Amputees and Carers Support In Liverpool, 2011–. Mem., USDAW. Gov., Jubilee Primary Sch., 2006–07. *Address:* House of Commons, SW1A 0AA.

TWIGGER, Andrew Mark; QC 2011; *b* Cuckfield, 23 Oct. 1968; *s* of Alan and Gillian Twigger; *m* 1997, Harriet Leeper; two *s* one *d*. *Educ:* Aylesbury Grammar Sch.; St John's Coll., Oxford (BA Lit.Hum. 1991); City Univ. (DipLaw). Called to the Bar, Inner Temple, 1994; in practice as barrister, specialising in chancery and commercial litigation, esp. banking and finance; Hd of Chambers, 2012–. *Recreations:* music, history. *Address:* 3 Stone Buildings, Lincoln's Inn, WC2A 3XL. *T:* (020) 7242 4937. *E:* atwigger@3sb.law.co.uk.

TWIGGER, Robert James; Secretary, House of Commons Commission, since 2012; *b* Hornchurch, 27 July 1958; *s* of late Ernest Twigger and of Marion Twigger (*née* Riley); *m* 1990, Corinne Lethieullier (*d* 1996); one *s* one *d*. *Educ:* Royal Liberty Sch., Romford; Univ. of Birmingham (BSocSc Mathematical Econs). House of Commons Library: Statistician, 1979–93; Hd, Econ. Policy and Statistics Section, 1993–2000; House of Commons: Dir, Parly and Reference Services, 2000–04; Hd, Office of the Clerk, 2004–08; Dir, Information Services for Members, 2008–12; Associate Serjeant at Arms, 2008–. *Recreations:* family, church, sailing, railways. *Address:* House of Commons, SW1A 0AA. *E:* twiggerrj@parliament.uk.

TWIGGER, Terence; Chief Executive, Meggitt plc, 2001–13 (Finance Director, 1993–2000); *b* 21 Nov. 1949; *s* of Gilbert and Elizabeth Twigger; *m* 1973, Elizabeth Kimberley; two *d*. *Educ:* King Edward VI Grammar, Nuneaton; Bristol Univ. (BSc). FCA; FRAeS. Touche Ross & Co., 1971–76; various appts, 1977–90, Finance Dir, 1990–93, Lucas Aerospace. *Recreations:* reading, shooting, fishing. *Address:* The Walled Garden, Holly Hill Lane, Sarisbury Green, Southampton SO31 7AH.

TWIGGY; *see* Lawson, Lesley.

TWIN, Prof. Peter John, OBE 1991; FRS 1993; Professor of Experimental Physics, University of Liverpool, 1987–2001, Emeritus Professor and Senior Fellow, since 2001; *b* 26 July 1939; *s* of Arthur James and Hilda Ethel Twin; *m* 1963, Jean Esther Leatherland; one *s* one *d*. *Educ:* Sir George Monoux Grammar Sch., Walthamstow; Univ. of Liverpool (BSc Hons, PhD). University of Liverpool: Lectr, 1964–73; Sen. Lectr, 1973–79; Reader, 1979–85; Head, Nuclear Structure Facility, Daresbury Lab., SERC, 1983–87. Vis. Prof., Univ. of Alberta, 1968–69. Reader, dio. of Chester, 1991–. Tom Bonner Prize, APS, 1991; John Price Wetherill Medal, Benjamin Franklin Inst., USA, 1991; Lisa Meitner Prize, Eur. Physical Soc., 2004. *Publications:* numerous papers in learned jls. *Address:* Oliver Lodge Laboratory, University of Liverpool, Liverpool L69 3BX. *T:* (0151) 794 3378.

TWINE, Derek Milton, CBE 2007; FCIPD; Chief Executive, Scout Association, 1996–2013; *b* 1 May 1951; *s* of late Edward Montague Twine and Winifred May Twine (*née* Milton); *m* 1974, Rhoda, *d* of Very Rev. R. J. N. Lockhart; one *s* one *d*. *Educ:* Reigate GS; UCNW, Bangor (BA Hons Educn 1st cl.). FCIPD (FITD 1987). Researcher, 1973–75, Lectr in Education, 1975–76, Univ. of Wales; Scout Association: Dir, Venture Scout Trng, 1976–79; Dir of Programme, 1979–85; Exec. Comr (Programme and Trng), 1985–96. Member: Youth Panel, Nat. Trust, 1978–85; Voluntary Sector Panel, RSA, 1990–96; Mgt Cttee, Educn and Standards, Nat. Youth Agency, 1991–95 (Chm., 1993–95); Strategic Adv. Panel, British Youth Council, 2007–; Council, Nat. Trust, 2013–; Council, Bradford Cathedral, 2013– (Chm., 2014–); National Society for Voluntary Youth Service: Mem., Exec. Cttee, 1979–82; Chm., Develt Project, 1979–82; Chm., Trng Managers' Gp, 1990–96. Trustee: Whitechapel Foundn, 1996–2012; Croatia Sunrise City Support, 1996–99; Church Urban Fund, 2008– (Vice Chm., 2009–). Gov., Davenant Foundn Sch., 1994–2012. FRSA 2002. *Publications:* various articles in youthwork and educnl jls. *Recreations:* church activities, theatre, cooking. *Address:* 14 Rose Bank, Burley-in-Wharfedale, W Yorks LS29 7PQ.

TWINING, Alexandra Mary; *see* Hall Hall, A. M.

TWINING, James Douglas Robert; Group Commercial Director, Jardine Lloyd Thompson plc, since 2011; *b* Watford, 13 Dec. 1972; *s* of Robert Ernest Twining and Ann Carolyn Twining; *m* 2002, Victoria Laura Toft; one *s* two *d*. *Educ:* Merchant Taylors' Sch., Northwood; Christ Church, Oxford (MA). Associate Dir, UBS Warburg, 1995–99; Finance Dir, grouptrade.com, 1999–2002; Man. Dir, Se7en Mile Ltd, 2002–04; Associate Principal, McKinsey & Co., 2004–11. Chm., English Heritage Foundn, 2011–15; Trustee, English Heritage Trust, 2015–. Gov., St Christopher's Sch., 2010–. *Publications: novels:* The Double Eagle, 2005; The Black Sun, 2006; The Gilded Seal, 2007; The Geneva Deception, 2009. *Recreations:* the past, collecting safe plates, trivia. *Address:* c/o Curtis Brown, 28–29 Haymarket, SW1Y 4SP. *E:* mail@jamestwining.com.

TWINING, Prof. William Lawrence, FBA 1997; Quain Professor of Jurisprudence Emeritus, University College London, since 2004 (Quain Professor of Jurisprudence, 1983–96; Research Professor of Law, 1996–2004); *b* 22 Sept. 1934; *s* of Edward Francis Twining and Helen Mary Twining (*née* Dubuisson); *m* 1957, Penelope Elizabeth Wall Morris; one *s* one *d*. *Educ:* Charterhouse School; Brasenose College, Oxford (BA 1955; MA 1960; DCL 1990); Univ. of Chicago (JD 1958). Lectr in Private Law, Univ. of Khartoum, 1958–61; Sen. Lectr in Law, University Coll., Dar-es-Salaam, 1961–65; Prof. of Jurisprudence, The Queen's Univ., Belfast, 1965–72; Prof. of Law, Univ. of Warwick, 1972–82. Mem., Cttee on Legal Educn in N Ireland, 1972–74; President: Soc. of Public Law Teachers of Law, 1978–79; UK Assoc. for Legal and Social Philosophy, 1980–83; Chairman: Bentham Cttee, 1982–2000; Commonwealth Legal Educn Assoc., 1983–93; vis. appts in several Univs. Foreign Mem., Amer. Acad. of Arts and Scis, 2007. Hon. QC 2002. Hon. LLD: Univ. of Victoria, BC, 1980; Edinburgh, 1994; QUB, 1999; Southampton Inst., 2000; York Univ., Toronto, 2002; Windsor, Ont, 2009; Coll. of Law, London, 2011. General Editor: Law in Context series, 1966–; Jurists series, 1979–. *Publications:* The Karl Llewellyn Papers, 1968; Karl Llewellyn and the Realist Movement, 1973, 2nd edn 2012; (with David Miers) How to Do Things with Rules, 1976, 5th edn 2010; (with J. Uglow) Law Publishing and Legal Information, 1981; (ed) Facts in Law, 1983; Theories of Evidence, 1985; (ed) Legal Theory and Common Law, 1986; (ed with R. Tur) Essays on Kelsen, 1986; (ed jtly) Learning Lawyers' Skills, 1989; (ed jtly) Access to Legal Education and the Legal Profession, 1989; Rethinking Evidence, 1990, 2nd edn 2006; (ed) Issues of Self-determination, 1991; (with T. Anderson) Analysis of Evidence, 1991, 2nd edn (with T. Anderson and D. Schum) 2005; (with E. Quick) Legal Records in the Commonwealth, 1994; Blackstone's Tower: the English Law School, 1994; Law in Context: enlarging a discipline, 1997; Globalisation and Legal Theory, 2000; The Great Juristic Bazaar, 2002; (ed jtly) Evidence and Inference in History and Law, 2003; General Jurisprudence, 2009; (ed) Human Rights: southern voices, 2009; (with P. Dawid and M. Vasilaki) Evidence, Inference and Enquiry, 2011; Globalisation and Legal Scholarship, 2011; (ed jtly) Legal Fictions in Theory and Practice, 2015. *Address:* 10 Mill Lane, Iffley, Oxford OX4 4EJ.

TWINN, Ian David, PhD; Director of Public Affairs, Incorporated Society of British Advertisers, since 1998; *b* 26 April 1950; *s* of late David Twinn and of Gwynneth Irene Twinn; *m* 1973, Frances Elizabeth Holtby; two *s*. *Educ:* Netherhall Secondary Modern School, Cambridge; Cambridge Grammar School; University College of Wales, Aberystwyth (BA hons); University of Reading (PhD). Senior Lecturer in Planning, Polytechnic of the South Bank, 1975–83. MP (C) Edmonton, 1983–97; contested (C) same seat, 1997. PPS to Minister of State for Industry, 1985–86, to Dep. Chm. of Cons. Party, 1986–88, to Minister of State for Energy, 1987–90, to Minister of State for the Environment, 1990–92, to Paymaster Gen., 1992–94. MEP (C) London Reg., Oct. 2003–2004; contested (C) London Reg., EP elecns, 1999, 2004, 2009. Chm., London Reg., Cons. Party, 2014–. Vice Chm., British Caribbean Assoc., 1986–. FRSA 1989; FRGS (MIBG 1972). Comdr, Order of Honour (Greece), 2000. *Recreations:* collecting secondhand books, renovating antique furniture. *Address:* 85 Calton Avenue, SE21 7DF. *T:* (020) 8299 4210.

TWISLETON-WYKEHAM-FIENNES; *see* Fiennes.

TWIST, Kenneth Lyndon; HM Chief Inspector of Mines, 1992–96; *b* 13 Jan. 1938; *s* of Joseph and Sarah Ellen Twist; *m* 1959, Emily Owens; three *s*. *Educ:* Wigan and Dist Mining & Technical Coll. (Dip. Mining Engrg). Colliery Manager's Cert., 1963. FIMinE 1979. Dep. General Manager, Agecroft, 1969–76; Health and Safety Executive: Inspector of Mines, 1976–87; Principal Dist Inspector of Mines, 1987–91; Dep. Chief Inspector of Mines, 1991–92. Chm., Safety in Mines Res. Adv. Bd, HSC, 1992–96. *Publications:* papers in Mining Engineer, Jl of Instn of Mining Engrs. *Recreations:* gardening, reading, photography, computing, golf. *Address:* Ridgeway, Sunnyridge Avenue, Marford, Wrexham LL12 8TE. *T:* (01978) 855638.

TWITE, Robin, OBE 1982; Director, Environmental Program, Israel-Palestine Center for Research and Information, Jerusalem, since 1997; *b* 2 May 1932; *s* of Reginald John Twite and May Elizabeth Walker; *m* 1st, 1958, Sally Randall (marr. diss.); 2nd, 1980, Sonia Yaari; one *s* three step *d*. *Educ:* Lawrence Sheriff School, Rugby; Balliol College, Oxford (BA History 1955). Asst Editor, Schoolmaster, weekly jl of NUT, 1956–58; British Council, 1958–73: served in Israel and London as Sec., Overseas Students Fees Awards Scheme; Sec., Open Univ. of Israel, 1973–76; British Council, 1976–88: adviser on adult and further educn, 1977–79; regional rep., Calcutta, 1980–84; Controller, Books, Libraries and Inf. Div., 1984–88. Hebrew University, Jerusalem: Advr to Chm., Res. Authy, 1988–91; Develt Advr, Truman Res. Inst. for Peace, 1991–93; Dir, Conflict Resolution Project, Leonard Davis Inst. for Internat. Relns, 1994–97. *Publications:* (ed) The Future of Jerusalem, 1993; (ed) Israeli-Arab Negotiations, 1993; (ed) Our Shared Environment: environmental problems of Israel, the West Bank and Gaza, 1994. *Recreations:* travel, music making, local history. *Address:* 10 Noah Emmanuel Street, Jerusalem 93105, Israel. *T:* (2) 5665378.

TWOMLOW, Richard William; His Honour Judge Twomlow; a Circuit Judge, since 2011; *b* Loughborough, 19 Nov. 1953; *s* of William Henry and Mavis Millicent Twomlow; *m* 1995, Laura Jane; one *d*. *Educ:* Whitchurch High Sch., Cardiff; Trinity Coll., Cambridge (BA 1975). Called to the Bar, Gray's Inn, 1976; Recorder, 1997–2011. *Recreations:* reading, travel, music, watching sport (especially cricket and Association Football), military history. *Address:* Merthyr Tydfil Combined Court Centre, Globeland Street, Merthyr Tydfil CF47 8BH.

TWYCROSS, Fiona Ruth, PhD; Member (Lab), London Assembly, Greater London Authority, since 2012; *b* London, 29 May 1969; *d* of Robert Geoffrey Twycross, *qv*. *Educ:* Cheney Sch., Oxford; Univ. of Edinburgh (MA Hons Scandinavian Studies 1992; PhD 1997); Birkbeck Coll., Univ. of London (MSc Public Policy and Mgt 2004). Labour Party: Cttee Officer, 1998–2001; Regl Organiser, 2001–03; Dep. Regl Dir, 2003–05; Regl Dir, 2005–08; Diabetes UK: Hd, Campaigns and Volunteer Develt, 2008–09; Hd, Governance, 2009–12. *Address:* Greater London Authority, City Hall, The Queen's Walk, More London, SE1 2AA. *T:* (020) 7983 5545. *E:* fiona.twycross@london.gov.uk.

TWYCROSS, Dr Robert Geoffrey, FRCP, FRCR; Macmillan Clinical Reader in Palliative Medicine, Oxford University, 1988–2001, now Emeritus; Director, palliativedrugs.com, since 2000; *b* 29 Jan. 1941; *s* of Jervis and Irene Twycross; *m* 1964, Deirdre Maeve, *d* of John Richard Campbell; two *s* three *d*. *Educ:* St John's Sch., Leatherhead; St Peter's Coll., Oxford (BA 1962; BM BCh 1965; MA 1965; DM 1977). MRCP 1969, FRCP 1980; FRCR 1996. Hosp. appts, Oxford, Lancaster, Epsom and Manchester, 1966–71; Res. Fellow, St Christopher's Hospice, London, 1971–76; Vis. MO, St Joseph's Hospice, London, 1971–76; Consultant Physician, Sir Michael Sobell House, Churchill Hosp., Oxford, 1976–2001; Fellow of St Peter's Coll., Oxford, 1987–2001, now Emeritus; Hd, WHO Collaborating Centre for Palliative Care, 1988–2005; Academic Dir, Oxford Internat. Centre for Palliative Cancer Care, 1992–2005. Visiting Professor: RSocMed of USA Foundation, 1979; Sir Ernest Finch, Sheffield, 1994; Univ. del Salvador, Buenos Aires, 1999–2005; Amrita Inst. of Med. Scis, Kochi, India, 2003–06. Mem., WHO Expert Adv. Panel on Cancer, 1985–2005. Hon. Life Mem., British Lymphology Soc., 2004; Hon. Member: Polish Soc. of Palliative Medicine, 2011; Paliativos Sin Fronteras, Spain, 2011. Aid and Co-operation Medal, Poland, 1993; Founder's Award, Nat. Hospice Orgn, USA, 1994; Serturner Prize, Serturner Soc., 1995; Vittorio Ventafridda Award, Internat. Assoc. for Hospice and Palliative Care, 2006; Lifetime Achievement Award: Amer. Acad. of Hospice and Palliative Medicine, 2008; Indian Assoc. for Palliative Care, 2008; Plaque of Honour, Indian Assoc. of Palliative Care, 2012. *Publications:* The Dying Patient, 1975; (ed) Pain Relief in Cancer, vol. 3 No 1, 1984; A Time to Die, 1984; (ed) Edinburgh Symposium on Pain Control and Medical Education, 1989; Pain Relief in Advanced Cancer, 1994; Introducing Palliative Care, 1995, 4th edn 2003; Symptom Management in Advanced Cancer, 1995, 4th edn (with A. Wilcock and C. Stark Toller) 2009; (jtly) Palliative Care Formulary, 1998, 5th edn 2014 (ed jtly, Italian edn 2004, German edn 2005, USA edn, as Hospice and Palliative Care Formulary, 2006, 2nd edn 2008, Canadian edn 2010, Polish edn 2011); (ed jtly) Lymphoedema, 2000; with S. A. Lack: Symptom Control in Far-Advanced Cancer: pain relief, 1983; Therapeutics in Terminal Cancer, 1984; Oral Morphine in Advanced Cancer, 1984, (sole author) 5th edn 2009; Control of Alimentary Symptoms in Far-Advanced Cancer, 1986; Oral Morphine: information for patients, families and friends, 1987, (sole author) 2nd edn, as Morphine and the relief of cancer pain, 1999; (ed jtly) Pruritus in advanced disease, 2004; (jtly) Palliative Medicine (Chinese edn), 2005; (with J. Li) Palliative Medicine: cancer pain and symptom management (Chinese edn), 2009; contribs to learned jls. *Recreations:* gardening, walking, reading. *Address:* Tewsfield, Netherwoods Road, Oxford OX3 8HF. *E:* robtwy@yahoo.com.
See also F. R. Twycross.

TWYFORD, Donald Henry, CB 1990; Under Secretary, Export Credits Guarantee Department, 1981–89, Director and Chairman of Project Group Board, 1986–89; *b* 4 Feb. 1931; *s* of Henry John Twyford and Lily Hilda (*née* Ridler); *m* 2006, Maria Dolores Quintero Hernández. *Educ:* Wembley County School. Joined Export Credits Guarantee Dept, 1949; Principal, 1965; seconded to Dept of Trade: Principal (Commercial Relations with East Europe), 1972–75; Asst Secretary (Country Policy), 1976; Establishment Officer, 1979–81; Under Secretary, Head of Services Group (internat. and country policy), ECGD, 1981–85; Hd of Project Underwriting Gp, 1985–89. Chairman, European Policy Co-ordination Group, 1981. President: Jávea Fest. Cttee, 2000; Jávea Internat. Civic Soc., 2001–02. Mem. Founding Cttee, Nueva Jávea party, 2006. *Recreations:* gardening, music, travel. *Address:* Cami de la Sabatera 33, Jávea 03739, Alicante, Spain.

TWYMAN, Paul Hadleigh; management consultant; Director: Nationwide (formerly Nationwide Anglia) Building Society, 1987–2002 (Anglia Building Society, 1983–87); Connex Transport UK Ltd, 1999–2002; *s* of late Lawrence Alfred Twyman and Gladys Mary (*née* Williams). *Educ:* Leyton County High Sch.; Chatham House Sch., Ramsgate; Univ. of Sheffield (BAEcon); London Sch. of Econs and Pol Science (MScEcon). Schoolteacher, 1964; Asst Principal, BoT, 1967; Secretariat, Commn on Third London Airport, 1969; Private Sec. to Sec. of State for Trade and Industry, 1971; Dept of Industry, 1975; Anti-Dumping Unit, Dept of Trade, 1976; Asst Sec., and Head of Overseas Projects Group, Dept of Trade, 1978; Dept of Transport, 1983; Cabinet Office, 1984; Under Sec., and Dir, Enterprise and Deregulation Unit, Dept of Employment, 1985. Econ. Adviser to Chm. of Conservative Party, and Head of Econ. Section, Cons. Res. Dept, 1987. Chm., Policy Strategy Ltd, 1988–2006. Contested (C) Greater Manchester W, European Parly elecn, 1989. Dir, D'Arcy Masius Benton & Bowles, 1990–96; Corporate Strategy Dir, Bates Dorland Ltd, later Bates UK, 1996–99. Mem., Central London LSC, 2001–05. Chm., Consultative Cttee, Kent Internat. Airport, 2006–14; Member: Thanet Dist Police Adv. Cttee, 1989–99; Thanet DC, 1991–95. Mem., Lambeth Community Police Consultative Gp, 1996–2002 (Hon. Comptroller, 1998–99; Vice-Chm., 1999–2001). Associate Mem., Kensington, Chelsea and Westminster HA, 1996–2002. Trustee, Opportunity Internat. (UK), 1995–2002. Gov., City of Westminster Coll., 1999–2002. Member: RIIA; FRSA. Mem., Royal African Soc. *Recreations:* family and friends, gardening, hill walking, observing gorillas.

TYACKE, Sarah Jacqueline, (Mrs Nicholas Tyacke), CB 1998; FSA; FRHistS; Chief Executive, National Archives (formerly Chief Executive and Keeper of Public Records, Public Record Office), 1992–2005 and Historical Manuscripts Commissioner, 2003–05; *b* 29 Sept. 1945; *d* of late Colin Walton Jeacock and Elsie Marguerite Stanton; *m* 1971, Nicholas, *s* of Maj.-Gen. David Noel Hugh Tyacke, CB, OBE; one *d*. *Educ:* Chelmsford County High Sch.; Bedford Coll., London (BA Hons History). FSA 1985; FRHistS 1994. Asst Keeper, Map Room, BM, 1968; Dep. Map Librarian, British Liby, 1973–85; undertook govt scrutiny of BL preservation (under Efficiency Unit, Cabinet Office), 1985–86; Director of Special Collections, British Library, 1986–91. Chm., European Co-ordinating Bd, 1992–96, a Vice-Pres., 1996–2000, Internat. Council on Archives; Vice-Chm., Professional Bd, IFLA, 1987–89. Vice Pres., 1995–97 and 2002–, Trustee, 2004–, Hakluyt Soc. (Jt Hon. Sec., 1984–95; Pres., 1997–2002); a Vice-Pres., RHistS, 2000–03 (Hon. Vice-Pres., 2004–). Dir, Imago Mundi, 1987–; Trustee, Mappa Mundi, 1989–96; Chm. Trustees, Internat. Records Mgt Trust, 2004–; Chm., Harley Trustees, 2007–; Chair: Mount Everest Foundn, 2009–13 (Trustee, 2011–12); Fund for Internat. Develt of Archives/Internat. Council on Archives, 2010–. Mem. Council, RHBNC, 2003–13 (Hon. Fellow, 1999); Gov., London Metropolitan Univ., 2004–09. Mem., Hillsborough Ind. Panel, 2010–12. Sandars Lectures, Cambridge, 2007; Leverhulme Emeritus Fellowship, 2005–07. Sen. Res. Fellow, Sch. of Advanced Study, Univ. of London, 2005–. Hon. DPhil: Guildhall, 1996; Essex, 2005; Hon. DLitt London, 2006. President's Medal, British Acad., 2010. *Publications:* Copernicus and the New Astronomy (with H. Swiderska), 1973; (ed jtly with H. M. Wallis) My Head is a Map: essay and memoirs in honour of R. V. Tooley, 1973; London Map-Sellers 1660–1720, 1978; (with John Huddy) Christopher Saxton and Tudor map-making, 1980; (ed) English map-making 1500–1650: historical essays, 1983; Catalogue of maps, charts and plans in the Pepys Library, Magdalene College, Cambridge, 1989; The History of Cartography, vol. 3 (contrib.), 2007; contribs to archival, library and cartographic jls, incl. The Library, Imago Mundi, Cartographic Jl. *Recreations:* the sea, travel, hill-walking, painting. *Address:* 1a Spencer Rise, NW5 1AR.

TYDEMAN, John Peter, OBE 2003; Head of BBC Radio Drama, 1986–94; *b* 30 March 1936; *s* of George Alfred Tydeman and Gladys (*née* Johnson). *Educ:* Feltonfleet; Hertford GS; Trinity Coll., Cambridge (MA). Nat. Service, 2 Lieut RA, 1954–56. Joined BBC, 1959; producer, 1962–80; Asst Head, Radio Drama, 1980–86. Dir of stage, radio and television plays. Prix Italia, 1970; Prix Futura, 1979 and 1983; Broadcasting Press Guild Award, 1983; Sony Special Award for Services to Radio, 1994; Lifetime Achievement Award, Radio Acad., 2010. *Recreations:* theatre, travel, reading, the company of friends. *Address:* Bay Tree Cottage, 23 The Street, North Lopham, Diss, Norfolk IP22 2NB. *T:* (01379) 687339, 07931 547070. *Club:* Garrick.

TYE, Alan Peter, RDI 1986; Partner, Tye Design (formerly Alan Tye Design (Industrial & Product Designers)), since 1962; *b* 18 Sept. 1933; *s* of Chang Qing Tai and Emily Tai (*née* Thompson); *m* 1966, Anita Birgitta Göethe Tye; three *s* two *d*. *Educ:* Regent Street Polytechnic Sch. of Architecture. RIBA 1959; FCSD (FSIAD 1979). Qualified as architect, 1958; with Prof. Arne Jacobsen, Copenhagen, 1960–62; formed Alan Tye Design, 1962; incorporated HID Ltd, 1977; launched Healthy Individual Design Practice Method (HID), 1992. Mem., Selection Cttee, Council of Industrial Design, 1967; Civic Trust Award Assessor, 1968, 1969; Vis. Tutor, RCA, 1978–83, External Examr, 1987–90; Specialist Adviser on Industrial Design, CNAA, 1980; London Region Assessor, RIBA, 1981 and 1988; RSA Bursary Judge, 1983–; External Examr, Design Res. for Disability, London Guildhall Univ., 1998–2002. Convenor, Faculty of RDI, RSA, 1991–. Guest Prof., Royal Danish Acad. of Fine Arts, 1996. Hon. FRCA 2012. Internat. Design Prize, Rome, 1962; Council of Industrial Design Award, 1965, 1966, 1981; British Aluminium Design Award, 1966; 1st Prize, GAI Award, 1969; Observer (London) Design Award, 1969; Ringling Mus. of Art (Fla) Award, 1969; Gold Medal, Graphic Design, 1970; 1st Prize, GAI Award, Internat. Bldg Exhibn, 1971; British Aluminium Eros Trophy, 1973; 4 Awards for Design Excellence, Aust., 1973; Commendation for Arch., 1977; Internat. Award, Inst. of Business Designers (NY), 1982; Internat. Bldg Exhibits Top Design Award, 1983, 1985; Resources Council of America Design Award, 1987; Prince Philip Duke of Edinburgh Designer of the Year Finalist, 1993, 1999; RIBA Regl Design Award, 1995; other design awards. *Publications:* (with Dermot O'Flynn) Healthy Industrial Design, 1995. *Recreations:* tai chi, aikido. *Address:* The Red House, Great West Plantation, Tring, Herts HP23 6DA. *T:* (01442) 823325.

TYLER, family name of **Baron Tyler**.

TYLER, Baron *cr* 2005 (Life Peer), of Linkinhorne in the county of Cornwall; **Paul Archer Tyler,** CBE 1985; PC 2014; journalist and public affairs consultant; *b* 29 Oct. 1941; *s* of Oliver Walter Tyler and Ursula Grace Gibbons Tyler (*née* May); *m* 1970, Nicola Mary Ingram; one *s* one *d*. *Educ:* Mount House Sch., Tavistock; Sherborne Sch.; Exeter Coll., Oxford (MA). Pres., Oxford Univ. Liberal Club, 1962. Royal Inst. of British Architects: Admin. Asst, 1966; Asst Sec., 1967; Dep. Dir Public Affairs, 1971; Dir Public Affairs, 1972. Man. Dir, Cornwall Courier newspaper gp, 1976–81; Exec. Dir, Public Affairs Div., 1982–84, Dir, 1985–88, Good Relations plc; Chief Exec., 1984–86, Chm., 1986–87, Good Relations Public Affairs Ltd; Sen. Consultant, Good Relations Ltd, 1987–92; Dir, 1987–95, Man. Dir, 1987–92, Western Approaches Public Relns Ltd, Launceston, Cornwall. County Councillor, Devon, 1964–70; Mem., Devon and Cornwall Police Authority, 1965–70; Vice-Chm., Dartmoor Nat. Park Cttee, 1965–70; Chm., CPRE Working Party on the Future of the Village, 1974–81; Mem. Bd of Shelter (Nat. Campaign for the Homeless), and rep. in Devon and Cornwall, 1975–76; Advr to Bd, SW Ambulance Service NHS Trust, 2014–. Chm., Faiths and Civil Soc. Unit, Anglia Ruskin Univ., then at Goldsmiths, Univ. of London, 2006–. Sec., L/SDP Jt Commn on Employment and Industrial Recovery, 1981–82. Chm., Devon and Cornwall Region Liberal Party, 1981–82; Chm., Liberal Party NEC, 1983–86. Campaign Adviser to Rt Hon. David Steel, and Mem., Alliance Campaign Planning Gp, 1986–87. Contested (L): Totnes, 1966; Bodmin, 1970, 1979; Beaconsfield, 1982; contested (Soc & Lib Dem) Cornwall and Plymouth, European Parly Election, 1989. MP: (L) Bodmin, Feb.–Sept. 1974; (Lib Dem) North Cornwall, 1992–2005. Parly Liberal spokesman on housing and transport, 1974; Parly adviser to RIBA, 1974; Lib Dem spokesman on agriculture and rural affairs, 1992–97, on transport, 1994–95, on food, 1997–99, on constitutional affairs, 2001–05; Lib Dem Chief Whip, 1997–2001; Shadow Leader of House, 1997–2005. Member: Select Cttee on Modernisation of H of C, 1997–2005; Jt Select Cttee on Parly Privilege, 1997–99, on H of L Reform, 2002–05, on Conventions, 2006–07, on Draft Constitutional Renewal Bill, 2008, on Draft Lords Reform Bill, 2011–12. Lib Dem Spokesman on constitutional affairs, H of L, 2006–. Dir, Make Votes Count, 2006–; Vice Chm., Hansard Soc., 2008–. DL Cornwall, 2005–10. *Publications:* A New Deal for Rural Britain (jtly), 1978; Country Lives, Country Landscapes, 1996; Parliament's Last Chance, 2003; Britain's Democratic Deficit: constitutional reform – unfinished business, 2003; (jtly) Reforming the House of Lords: breaking the deadlock, 2005; (jtly) Funding Democracy: breaking the deadlock, 2013; Who Decides?, 2014. *Recreations:* gardening, walking, Cornish ancestry. *Address:* House of Lords, SW1A 0PW.

TYLER OF ENFIELD, Baroness *cr* 2011 (Life Peer), of Enfield in the London Borough of Enfield; **Claire Tyler;** Chairman, Children and Family Court Advisory and Support Service, since 2012; *b* 4 June 1957. *Educ:* Latymer Grammar Sch.; Univ. of Southampton (BSc Law and Politics); South Bank Poly. (Postgrad. Dip. Mgt Studies). With GLC/ILEA, 1978–88; mgt posts, Dept of Employment, 1988–92; Divl Manager, DFES, 1992–97; Hd, Connexions Unit, 1998–2000; Dep. Chief Exec., Connexions Nat. Unit, 2000–02; Dir, Social Exclusion Unit, Cabinet Office, then OPDM, subseq. DCLG, 2002–06; Dir, Vulnerable Children Gp, DFES, 2006–07; CEO, Relate, 2007–12 (Vice Pres., 2012). Mem., H of L Select Cttee on Public Service and Demography; Vice-Chair: Associate Parly Gp for Parents and Families; All Party Parly Gp on Social Mobility, on Wellbeing, on Sustainable Relationships; Chair, Lib Dem Policy Working Gp on Balanced Working Life, 2012–13; Co-Chair, Growing Giving Parly Inquiry. Co-Chair, Social Policy Forum, 2005–10; Chair, Making Every Adult Matter Coalition of Charities, 2013–. Mem., Exec. Bd, Public Mgt and Policy Assoc., 2005–10. Pres., Nat. Children's Bureau, 2012–; Vice-Pres., Liberal Internat. GB. *Address:* House of Lords, SW1A 0PW.

TYLER, Andrew Oliver, CBE 2012; PhD; CMarSci, CEng; FIMarEST, FREng, FRAeS, RCNC; Chief Executive, UK and Europe, Northrop Grumman, since 2013; Director, Ancient Horse Ltd, since 2013; *b* 22 June 1967; *s* of Thomas Tyler and Patricia Tyler; *m* 1995, Emma Tyler (marr. diss. 2008); two *s* two *d*; partner, Mrs Jennifer Parker. *Educ:* Univ. of Plymouth (BSc 1st cl. Hons Nautical Studies 1989; PhD Marine Sci. 1999); London Business Sch. (MBA Distn 2001). MRICS 1991; FIMarEST 2002; CMarSci 2003; RCNC 2007; CEng, FREng 2010. British Maritime Technology Group: oceanographer and marine scientist, 1989–96; Man. Dir, BMT Marine Information Systems, 1996–2001; Man. Dir, BMT Defence Services, 2001–05; Chief Exec., BMT Defence, 2005–06; Dir Land and Maritime, Defence Procurement Agency, 2006–07; Dir Gen. Ships, 2007–08, Chief Operating Officer, 2008–11, Defence Equipment and Support, MoD; Chief Exec., Marine Current Turbines, 2001–13. *Publications:* several papers in field of marine pollution science. *Recreations:* coasteering, windsurfing, running (for waist control), progressive/heavy rock and ecclesiastical choral music, bass guitar, hill walking, supporting England's great test cricket team. *Address:* Ancient Horse Ltd, Bakers Orchard, 7 Huntingdon Street, Bradford-on-Avon, Wilts BA15 1RF.

TYLER, Anne; writer; *b* 25 Oct. 1941; *d* of Lloyd Parry Tyler and Phyllis Mahon Tyler (*née* Mahon); *m* 1963, Taghi M. Modarressi, MD (*d* 1997); two *d. Educ:* Duke Univ. (BA). Mem., AAIL. AAIL Award for Literature, 1977; Nat. Book Critics Circle Award for fiction, 1985; Sunday Times Award for Literary Excellence, 2012. *Publications:* If Morning Ever Comes, 1964; The Tin Can Tree, 1965; A Slipping Down Life, 1970; The Clock Winder, 1972; Celestial Navigation, 1974; Searching for Caleb, 1976; Earthly Possessions, 1977; Morgan's Passing, 1980; Dinner at the Homesick Restaurant, 1982; The Accidental Tourist, 1985; Breathing Lessons, 1988 (Pulitzer Prize for fiction, 1989); Saint Maybe, 1991; Tumble Tower (for children), 1993; Ladder of Years, 1995; A Patchwork Planet, 1998; Back When We Were Grownups, 2001; The Amateur Marriage, 2004; Timothy Tugbottom Says No (for children), 2005; Digging to America, 2006; Noah's Compass, 2010; The Beginner's Goodbye, 2012; A Spool of Blue Thread, 2015. *Address:* 8 Roland Green, Baltimore, MD 21210, USA.

TYLER, Antony Nigel; Director General and Chief Executive Officer, International Air Transport Association, since 2011; *b* Moascar, Egypt, 27 April 1955; *s* of Maj.-Gen. Sir Leslie Norman Tyler, KBE, CB and late Sheila Tyler (*née* Field); *m* 1st, 1980, Jane Douglas Blackley (marr. diss. 2008); two *s* one *d*; 2nd, 2012, Charlotte Andsager. *Educ:* Worth Sch.; Brasenose Coll., Oxford (BA Juris. 1977). FRAeS 2012. John Swire & Sons Ltd, 1977–2011; Chief Operating Officer, 2005–07, Chief Exec., 2007–11, Cathay Pacific Airways; Chm., Dragonair, 2007–11. Non-exec. Dir, NATS, 2013–. Mem., Hong Kong Develt Commn, 2012–15. *Recreations:* ski-ing, scuba diving, music. *Address:* International Air Transport Association, Route de l'Aeroport 33, Geneva 2015, Switzerland. *Clubs:* Royal Automobile; Hong Kong, Hong Kong Country, Hong Kong Foreign Correspondents' (Hong Kong).

See also Maj.-Gen. C. Tyler, Maj.-Gen. T. N. Tyler.

TYLER, Maj.-Gen. Christopher, CB 1989; Secretary, Royal Humane Society, 1995–2004; *b* 9 July 1934; *s* of Maj.-Gen. Sir Leslie Norman Tyler, KBE, CB, and late Louie Teresa Tyler (*née* Franklin); *m* 1958, Suzanne, *d* of late Eileen Whitcomb and Patrick Whitcomb; one *s* three *d. Educ:* Beaumont College; RMA Sandhurst; Trinity Coll., Cambridge (MA). Commissioned REME, 1954; served UK and BAOR, 1959–65; Army Staff Course, 1966–67; Weapons Staff, 1968–70 and 1972–74; CO 1st Parachute Logistic Regt, 1974–76; MoD, 1976–80; Chief Aircraft Engineer, Army Air Corps, 1980–82; DEME (Management Services), Logistic Exec., 1982–83; Comd Maint., HQ 1 (BR) Corps, 1983–85; Dep. Comdt, RMCS, 1985–87; DCOS (Support), HQ Allied Forces N Europe, 1987–89. Resident Gov. and Keeper of the Jewel House, HM Tower of London, 1989–94. Col Comdt, REME, 1989–94; Hon. Col, REME (V), 1994–2000. External Mem. of Council, Parachute Regt, 1993–98; Trustee: Tower Hill Trust (formerly Tower Hill Improvement Trust), 1990–2009; Ulysses Trust, 1992–94. Governor: St Mary's Sch., Ascot, 1995–2003; St John's, Beaumont, 1996–2007. Liveryman, Turners' Co., 1979– (Master, 2000–01). *Recreation:* Rugby football (RFU Panel Referee, 1957–59 and 1967–73 and Chm., Army and Combined Services, 1985–86). *Address:* 22 Seymour Place, Odiham, Hook, Hants RG29 1AY. *T:* (01256) 704993. *Club:* Hawks (Cambridge).

See also Maj.-Gen. T. N. Tyler.

TYLER, David Alan; Chairman: J. Sainsbury plc, since 2009; Hammerson plc, since 2013; Hampstead Theatre, since 2012; *b* Woking, 23 Jan. 1953; *s* of Alan and Jill Tyler; *m* 1977, Sharon Lantin (marr. diss. 2011); one *s* one *d. Educ:* Trinity Hall, Cambridge (BA Econs 1974). FCMA 1983; MCT 1991. Unilever plc, 1974–86; County NatWest Ltd, 1986–89; Finance Director: Christie's International plc, 1989–96; GUS plc, 1997–2007. Chairman: 3i Quoted Private Equity plc, 2007–09; Logica plc, 2007–12; non-executive Director: Burberry Gp plc, 2002–; Experian plc, 2006–12; Reckitt Benckiser Gp plc, 2007–09. *Recreations:* enjoying barn in Sussex, family, friends, theatre, current affairs, jogging, cycling, listening to music, washing up. *Address:* Sainsbury's plc, 33 Holborn, EC1N 2HT.

TYLER, Ian Paul; Chairman: Bovis Homes, since 2013; Cairn Energy PLC, since 2014 (non-executive Director, since 2013); *b* 7 July 1960; *s* of Ray and Peggy Tyler; *m* Janet; two *d. Educ:* Univ. of Birmingham (BCom). ACA. Arthur Andersen & Co., 1982–88; Gp Treas./Financial Controller, Storehouse Plc, 1988–91; Financial Comptroller, Hanson Plc, 1991–93; Finance Dir, ARC Ltd, 1993–96; Finance Dir, 1996–2002, Chief Operating Officer, 2002–05, Chief Exec., 2005–13, Balfour Beatty plc. Non-executive Director: Cable & Wireless Communications plc, 2011; BAE Systems, 2013–. Chm., Al Noor Hospitals, 2013–. *Recreations:* private pilot, keeping fit.

TYLER, Prof. Lorraine Komisarjevsky, PhD; FBA 1995; MRC Professor of Cognitive Neuroscience, University of Cambridge, since 1998, and Director (formerly Co-Director), Centre for Speech, Language and the Brain, since 1990; Fellow, Clare College, Cambridge, since 2000; *b* 11 Jan. 1945; *d* of James and Anne Komisarjevsky; *m* 1982, William D. Marslen-Wilson, *qv*; one *s* one *d. Educ:* Leicester Univ. (BA); Chicago Univ. (PhD 1977). Sen. Res. Fellow, Max Planck Inst. for Psycholinguistics, 1977–85; Lectr, Dept of Psychology, Cambridge Univ., 1985–90; Prof. of Psychology, Birkbeck Coll., Univ. of London, 1990–98. *Publications:* Spoken Language Comprehension, 1992; contrib. Brain and Lang., Jl of Cognitive Neurosci., Cerebral Cortex, Psychological Rev., Cognition, etc. *Address:* Department of Experimental Psychology, University of Cambridge, Downing Street, Cambridge CB2 3EB. *T:* (01223) 766457.

TYLER, Prof. Nicholas Andrew, CBE 2011; PhD; FREng; Chadwick Professor of Civil Engineering, University College London, since 2003; *b* Harrow, Middx, 3 Sept. 1954; *s* of Douglas Eric Rhodes Tyler and Joan Priscilla Tyler (*née* Hill); *m* 1988, Katrina Hoogendam. *Educ:* University College Sch.; Royal Coll. of Music (ARCM 1975); Poly. of Central London (MSc 1987); University Coll. London (PhD 1992). FREng 2014. Freelance musician, 1975–82; Mgt Trainee, BEREC Gp, 1982–84; Ops Manager, Unichem Ltd, 1984–85; Mentor, Community Aid, 1985–86; University College London: Res. Asst, 1987–92, Lectr, 1992–97, Sen. Lectr, 1997–99, Reader, 1999–2002, in Transport Studies; Prof. of Communities and Transport, 2002–03; Hd of Dept, Civil, Envmtl and Geomatic Engrg, 2003–13; Pro Provost, E and S Asia, 2011–. Prof. Honorario de Ingeniería, Pontificia Universidad Católica del Peru, 2008–. *Publications:* (ed) Accessibility and the Bus System, 2002; articles in New England Jl of Medicine, Transportation Res., Transportation Planning and Technol. *Recreation:* music (oboe playing). *Address:* Department of Civil, Environmental and Geomatic Engineering, University College London, Gower Street, WC1E 6BT. *T:* (020) 7679 1562. *E:* n.tyler@ucl.ac.uk.

TYLER, Paula Margot; Her Honour Judge Tyler; a Circuit Judge, since 2012; *b* Manchester, 18 Sept. 1961; *d* of Joseph Paul Tyler and Margaret Tyler; partner, Jai Penna, *qv. Educ:* Stand Grammar Sch. for Girls; University Coll. London (BSc Hons Anthropol.). Admitted solicitor, 1989; transferred to the Bar, Middle Temple, 1997; a Recorder, 2005–12. *Recreations:* crime fiction, film, a range of sports, all things Italian.

TYLER, Richard Herbert; executive coach and business consultant; Senior Partner, 2011–14, Consultant, 2014–15, CMS Cameron McKenna LLP; *b* Cheltenham, 19 Feb. 1959; *s* of Peter Anthony Tyler and Barbara Margaret Tyler (*née* Wilson); *m* 1985 (marr. diss. 2011); two *d. Educ:* Cheltenham Grammar Sch.; Fitzwilliam Coll., Cambridge (BA 1982; MA 1985). Admitted solicitor, 1985; McKenna & Co., later CMS Cameron McKenna LLP: joined 1983; Partner, 1992–2014; Man. Partner, 2000–08; Exec. Partner, CMS Legal Services EEIG, 2008–11. Mem. Bd, London Legacy 2020, 2006–12. Faculty Mem., Meyler Campbell Ltd, 2011–; Dir/Trustee, PRIME, 2012–15. Dir, Varsity Match Co. Ltd, 2015–. President: Old Patesians RFC, 2006–; Fitzwilliam Soc., 2012–13. Member: Cttee, City of London Law Soc., 2012–; Develt Cttee, Fitzwilliam Coll., Cambridge, 2014–. *Recreations:* watching Rugby and other sport, fitness, performing arts, choral singing (Barts Choir). *Address:* c/o Dick Tyler Ltd, First Floor, York House, 74–82 Queen Victoria Street, EC4N 4SJ. *T:* (020) 7282 0101. *E:* dick@dicktyler.com. *Club:* Hawks' (Cambridge).

TYLER, Maj.-Gen. Timothy Nicholas, CB 2008; Director, Kilmeston Consulting, since 2012; *b* 15 Dec. 1953; *s* of Maj.-Gen. Sir Leslie Norman Tyler, KBE, CB and late Sheila Tyler; *m* 1976, Johanna Lee Weston; three *s* six *d. Educ:* Worth Sch.; Christ's Coll., Cambridge (MA 1979). Commnd REME, 1972; Commander: Equipment Support, 1st Armoured Div., 1992–93; REME Trng Gp, 1997–99; Director: Army Staff Duties, 1999–2001; Army Resources and Plans, 2001–02; rcds 2002; COS HQ Adjt Gen., 2003; Dep. Adjt Gen., 2004–05; Quartermaster Gen., 2006–07; Dir Gen. Logistics (Land), 2006–07; Dir Gen. Land Equipment, 2007–08. Dir, Serco Gp plc, 2009–12. Asst Col Comdt, AGC, 2004–05; Colonel Commandant: REME, 2005–12; Corps of Army Music, 2005–09. *Recreations:* singing, sailing.

See also A. N. Tyler, Maj.-Gen. C. Tyler.

TYLER, William John; QC 2014; a Recorder, since 2012; *b* Northampton, 25 May 1974; *s* of late John Douglas Tyler and of Gillian Mary Tyler (*née* Haig); *m* 1999, Charlotte Taylor-Hunt; one *s* two *d. Educ:* Stoneygate Sch., Leicester; Oundle Sch.; Worcester Coll., Oxford (BA Hons Juris. 1995; MA). Called to the Bar, Inner Temple, 1996; in practice as a barrister, specialising in children's law, 1996–. *Recreations:* family, gardening, cycling, opera. *Address:* 36 Bedford Row, WC1R 4JH. *T:* (020) 7421 8000.

TYLER-HAYWOOD, (June) Sandra; HM Diplomatic Service; Head of Governor's Office, Falkland Islands, since 2012; *b* Nuneaton, 5 March 1957; *d* of late Herbert Sidney Kirk and of Cynthia Ruby Kirk (*née* Hartshorn); *m* 1991, Ian Haywood; one *s* one *d. Educ:* Manor Park Grammar Sch.; Open Univ. (BSc). Entered FCO, 1989; Admin. Officer, FCO, 1989–92; Third Secretary: FCO, 1992–94; Beijing, 1994–97; Lisbon, 1998–2002; Second Sec., FCO, 2002–05; First Secretary: Eastern Caribbean, 2005–07; Basra, 2008–09; Ambassador to Eritrea, 2010–12. *Recreations:* photography, golf. *Address:* c/o Foreign and Commonwealth Office, King Charles Street, SW1A 2AH.

TYMKEWYCZ, Stefan; Member (SNP) Edinburgh City Council, since 2007; *b* 18 Sept. 1959; *s* of Bohdan and Jean Tymkewycz. *Educ:* St David's Primary and Secondary Schs, Dalkeith; Esk Valley Coll., Dalkeith. Apprentice engr, 1976–80; traveller, 1980–84; Metropolitan Police Officer, 1984–2001; property landlord, 2001–07. MSP (SNP) Lothians, May–Aug. 2007. *Recreations:* travelling, keeping fit, cycling, theatre and cinema, hill walking, football (season ticket holder at Hibernian FC), Scrabble. *Address:* City of Edinburgh Council, City Chambers, High Street, Edinburgh EH1 1YJ. *E:* stymkewycz@btinternet.com.

TYNAN, Prof. Michael John, MD, FRCP; Professor of Paediatric Cardiology, Guy's Hospital, 1982–99; *b* 18 April 1934; *s* of late Jerry Joseph Tynan and Florence Ann Tynan; *m* 1958, Eirlys Pugh Williams. *Educ:* Bedford Modern School; London Hospital. MD, BS. Senior Asst Resident, Children's Hosp., Boston, Mass, 1962; Registrar, Westminster Hosp., 1964; Registrar, later Lectr, Hosp. for Sick Children, Great Ormond St, 1966; consultant paediatric cardiologist, Newcastle Univ. Hospitals, 1971, Guy's Hosp., 1977. *Publications:* (jtly) Paediatric Cardiology, a textbook, 1983; articles on nomenclature and classification of congenital heart disease and on heart disease in children. *Recreations:* singing, watching cricket, playing snooker. *Address:* 5 Ravensdon Street, SE11 4AQ. *T:* (020) 7735 7119. *Clubs:* Athenæum; Borth and Ynyslas Golf.

TYNAN, William; part-time researcher for John Robertson, MP, 2005–15; *b* 18 Aug. 1940; *s* of late James and Mary Tynan; *m* 1964, Elizabeth Mathieson; three *d. Educ:* St Joseph's Sch.; St Mungo's Acad.; Stow Coll. Press toolmaker, 1961–88. Joined AEU (subseq. AEEU), 1966: shop steward and convener, 1966; Member: Mid Lanark Dist Cttee, 1969; Divl Cttee, 1976; Nat. Cttee, 1977–88; full-time Union Official, 1988–99: Dist Sec., 1988–96; Regl Officer, 1996–99; Political Officer, 1991; Scottish Political Sec., 1993. MP (Lab) Hamilton South, Sept. 1999–2005. Member: Parly Select Cttee on NI, 2001–05; European Scrutiny Cttee, 2001–05; Convenor, Scottish Gp of MPs, 2001–02; Special Advr, All Party Parly Gp on Nuclear Energy, 2005– (Chm., 2001–05). Joined Labour Party, 1969: Mem. Exec. and Gen. Mgt Cttee, Hamilton N and Hamilton S Constituency Parties, 1979–2005; Chm., Hamilton S CLP, 1987; Member: Scottish Labour Policy Forum, 1998; Scottish Exec., 1982–88. Nat. Coordinator, Trade Unions for Safe Nuclear Energy, 2006–. Board Member: SoLVE, S Lanarkshire, 2006–; VASLAN, 2011–. *Recreations:* golf, swimming, gardening, DIY. *Address:* 6 East Scott Terrace, Hamilton ML3 6SF. *T:* (01698) 421660.

TYNDALL, Rev. Canon Timothy; Chief Secretary, Advisory Council for the Church's Ministry, 1985–90; *b* 24 April 1925; *s* of Rev. Denis Tyndall and Nora Tyndall; *m* 1953, Dr Ruth Mary Turner (*d* 1998); two *s* twin *d. Educ:* Jesus Coll., Cambridge (BA). Parish Incumbent: Newark, 1955; Nottingham, 1960; Sunderland, 1975. *Address:* Flat 16, 2B Bollo Lane, Chiswick, W4 5LE. *T:* (020) 8994 4516.

TYRE, Hon. Lord; Colin Jack Tyre, CBE 2010; a Senator of the College of Justice in Scotland, since 2010; *b* 17 April 1956; *s* of James Harrison Tyre and Lilias Carmichael Tyre (*née* Kincaid); *m* 1982, Elaine Patricia Carlin (*d* 2010); one *s* two *d. Educ:* Dunoon Grammar Sch.; Univ. of Edinburgh (LLB Hons); Université d'Aix-Marseille (DESU). Admitted Solicitor, 1980; admitted to Faculty of Advocates, 1987; QC (Scot.) 1998. Lectr in Law, Univ. of Edinburgh, 1980–83; Tax Editor, CCH Editions Ltd, 1983–86; Standing Junior Counsel: MoD (PE), 1991–95; Scottish Office Envmt Dept (in planning matters), 1995–98; Comr (pt-time), Scottish Law Commn, 2003–09. Pres., CCBE, 2007 (Hd, UK Delegn, 2004). Chm., Bd of Govs, Fettes Coll., Edinburgh, 2012–. Grand Decoration of Honour, Austria, 2009. *Publications:* CCH Inheritance Tax Reporter, 1986; (jtly) Tax for Litigation Lawyers, 2000; contrib. Stair Memorial Encyclopaedia, learned jls. *Recreations:* mountain walking, golf, orienteering, music (especially popular). *Address:* Parliament House, Edinburgh EH1 1RQ. *T:* (0131) 225 2595.

TYRELL-KENYON; *see* Kenyon.

TYRER, His Honour Christopher John Meese; DL; a Circuit Judge, 1989–2011; Resident Judge, Aylesbury Crown Court, 2005–11; *b* 22 May 1944; *s* of late Jack Meese Tyrer and of Margaret Joan Tyrer (*née* Wyatt); *m* 1974, Jane Beckett, JP, LLB, MA, barrister; one *s* one *d. Educ:* Wellington College; Bristol University. LLB Hons. Called to the Bar, Inner Temple, 1968. Asst Recorder, 1979–83; a Recorder, 1983–89; Designated Family Judge, Bucks 1991–97, London 1998–2005. Governor: St John's Sch., Lacey Green, 1984–92; Speen Sch., 1984–96 (Chm., 1989–91 and 1995–96); Misbourne Sch., 1993–2007 (Vice Chm., 1995–2000, Chm., 2000–07). Mem., Bucks Assoc. of Govs of Primary Schs, 1989–90. Patron, Law Soc., Buckinghamshire New Univ. (formerly Buckinghamshire Chilterns University Coll.), 2002–12; Vice Patron, Oasis Partnership, 2014–. Chair, New Leaf Charity for supporting ex-offenders, 2011–. Trustee, Thames Valley Partnership, 2011–. Hon. Recorder of Aylesbury, 2010–11. DL Bucks, 2008. Hon. Dr Bucks New, 2010. Ed., Clarke Hall and Morrison on Children, 2003–07. *Recreations:* grandchildren, sponsored children in Nicaragua and The Philippines, music, boating, following Wycombe Wanderers Football Club. *Address:* Randalls Cottage, Loosley Row, Princes Risborough, Bucks HP27 0NU. *T:* (01844) 344650.

TYRER, Prof. Peter Julian, MD; Professor of Community Psychiatry, Imperial College of Science, Technology and Medicine, since 1991; *b* 13 Aug. 1940; *s* (identical twin) of Frank Herbert Tyrer and Mary (May) Jane Tyrer; *m* 1st, 1967, Ann Anderson (marr. diss. 2003); one *s* two *d*; 2nd, 2010, Helen Seivewright (*née* Bown). *Educ:* King Edward Sch., Birmingham; Gonville and Caius Coll., Cambridge (BA 1962; MB, BChir 1966; MD 1975); St Thomas's Hosp. Med. Sch., London. FRCPsych 1979, Hon. FRCPsych 2014; FRCP 1993; FFPH (FFPHM 1999). House Officer in Psychological Medicine, St Thomas' Hosp., 1966–67; Sen. House Officer in Medicine, Burton-on-Trent Gen. Hosp., 1967–68; Registrar in Psychiatry: St John's Hosp., Aylesbury, 1968–69; Maudsley Hosp., 1969–70; MRC Clin. Res. Fellow, 1970–73; Sen. Lectr in Psychiatry, Univ. of Southampton, 1973–79; Cons. Psychiatrist, Mapperley Hosp., Nottingham, 1979–88; Sen. Lectr in Community Psychiatry, St Mary's Hosp. Med. Sch., 1988–91; Hd, Dept of Public Mental Health, 1997–2002, Dept of Psychol Medicine, 2002–05, ICSTM. Andrew Woods Prof., Univ. of Iowa, 1986. Milroy Lectr, RCP, 2007. Ed., British Jl of Psychiatry, 2003–13. European Pres., Internat. Soc. for Study of Personality Disorders, 1995–98; Founding Pres., British and Irish Gp for the Study of Personality Disorders, 1999; Chairman: Sect. on Personality Disorders, World Psychiatric Assoc., 2008– (Co-Chm., 2002–08); Working Gp for Revision of Personality Disorders, WHO, 2010–15. FMedSci 1999. Gaskell Bronze Medal and Res. Prize, 1973, Lifetime Achievement Award, 2015, RCPsych. *Publications:* The Role of Bodily Feelings in Anxiety, 1976; Insomnia, 1978; Stress, 1980, 2nd edn 2003; (ed) Drugs in Psychiatric Practice, 1982, 2nd edn 1997; How to Stop Taking Tranquillisers, 1986; Models for Mental Disorder (with D. Steinberg), 1987, 5th edn (sole author) 2013; Personality Disorders: diagnosis, management and course, 1988, 2nd edn 2000; (ed) Psychopharmacology of Anxiety, 1989; Classification of Neurosis, 1989; (with C. Freeman) Research Methodology in Psychiatry: a beginner's guide, 1989, 3rd edn 2006; (with B. Puri) Sciences Basic to Psychiatry, 1992, 2nd edn 1998; (with P. Casey) Social Function in Psychiatry: the hidden axis of classification exposed, 1993; Anxiety: a multidisciplinary review, 1999; (with K. Silk) Cambridge Textbook of Effective Treatments in Psychiatry, 2008; Nidotherapy: harmonising the environment with the patient, 2009; (with K. R. Silk) Effective Treatments in Psychiatry, 2011. *Recreations:* jousting with social workers, anthropophytomorphy, doggerel, composing operettas. *Address:* The Poplars, Cotham Lane, Hawton, Newark, Notts NG24 3RL. *T:* (01636) 679245.

TYRIE, Rt Hon. Andrew (Guy); PC 2015; MP (C) Chichester, since 1997; *b* 15 Jan. 1957; *s* of late Derek and of Patricia Tyrie. *Educ:* Felsted Sch.; Trinity Coll., Oxford (MA); Coll. of Europe, Bruges; Wolfson Coll., Cambridge (MPhil). BP, 1981–83; Cons. Res. Dept, 1983–84; Special Adviser: to Sec. of State for the Envmt, 1985; to Minister for Arts, 1985–86; to Chancellor of the Exchequer, 1986–90; Fellow, Nuffield Coll., Oxford, 1990–91; Woodrow Wilson Scholar, Washington, 1991; Sen. Economist, EBRD, 1992–97. Contested (C) Houghton and Washington, 1992. Shadow Financial Sec., 2003–04; Shadow Paymaster Gen., 2004–05. Chairman: Treasury Select Cttee, 2010– (Mem., 2001–03, 2009–10); Parly Commn on Banking Standards, 2012–13; Member: Select Cttee on Public Admin, 1997–2001; Justice Cttee (formerly Constitutional Affairs Select Cttee), 2005–10; Public Accounts Commn, 1997–; Exec. Cttee, 1922 Cttee, 2005–06. *Publications:* The Prospects for Public Spending, 1996; Sense on EMU, 1998; Reforming the Lords, 1998; (jtly) Leviathan at Large, 2000; Mr Blair's Poodle, 2000; (jtly) Statism by Stealth, 2002; Mr Blair's Poodle Goes to War, 2004; (jtly) Account Rendered, 2011; many pamphlets on econ. and parly issues. *Recreation:* golf. *Address:* House of Commons, SW1A 0AA. *Clubs:* Garrick, MCC, Royal Automobile.

TYRIE, Peter Robert, MBE 2010; Managing Director, Eton Group, 1999–2009; *b* 3 April 1946; *m* 1972, Christine Mary Tyrie; three *s* (and one *d* decd). *Educ:* Westminster College Hotel Sch. (BSc Hotel Admin). Manager, Inverurie Hotel, Bermuda, 1969–71; Resident Manager, Portman Hotel, London, 1971–73; Project Dir, Pannell Kerr Forster, 1973–77; Operations Dir, Penta Hotels, 1977–80; Managing Director: Gleneagles Hotels plc, 1980–86; Mandarin Oriental Hotel Gp, 1986–89; Balmoral Internat. Hotels, 1989–98. Director: Bell's Whisky, 1983; Dragon Trust, Edinburgh Fund Managers, 1989–2010; Aberdeen Asset Managers Dragon Fund, 1989–2010. FIH (FHCIMA 1977). *Recreations:* squash, shooting, fishing, Rugby, classic cars. *Address:* Popple Meadows, Graffham, Petworth, W Sussex GU28 0QF.

TYRONE, Earl of; Richard John de la Poer Beresford; *b* 19 Aug. 1987; *er s* and *heir* of Marquess of Waterford, *qv. Educ:* Harrow.

TYROR, John George, OBE 1999; JP; Director of Safety, United Kingdom Atomic Energy Authority, 1990–92, retired; *b* 5 Nov. 1930; *s* of John Thomas Tyror and Nora Tyror (*née* Tennant); *m* 1956, Sheila Wylie; one *s* one *d*. *Educ:* Manchester Univ. (BSc 1st cl. Hons Maths, MSc); Trinity Hall, Cambridge. FInstP. Asst Lectr, Univ. of Leeds, 1955–56; AEA Harwell, 1956–59; Atomic Energy Estabt, Winfrith, 1959–63; Reactor Develt Lab., Windscale, 1963–66; Winfrith, 1966–87 (Asst Dir, 1979–87); Dir, Safety and Reliability Directorate, Culcheth, 1987–90. Member: Eur./Amer. Cttee on Reactor Physics, 1960–72; Adv. Cttee for Transport of Radioactive Materials, 1981–84; Adv. Cttee on Safety of Nuclear Installations, HSC, 1992–95; Nuclear Safety Adv. Cttee, HSC, 1995–98. Chm., Compensation Scheme for Radiation-Linked Diseases, 2001–07. JP Poole, 1976, Macclesfield, 1988. *Publications:* An Introduction to the Neutron Kinetics of Nuclear Power Reactors, 1970. *Recreations:* bridge playing and teaching, food and wine, grandfather.

TYRRELL, Prof. (Henry John) Valentine, FRSC; Vice-Principal, King's College London (KQC), 1985–87, retired; *b* 14 Feb. 1920; *s* of John Rice Tyrrell and Josephine (*née* McGuinness); *m* 1st, 1947, Sheila Mabel (*née* Straw) (*d* 1985); two *s* two *d* (and one *s* one *d* decd); 2nd, 1986, Dr Bethan Davies. *Educ:* state schools; Jesus Coll., Oxford. DSc. Chemical Industry, 1942–47; Sheffield Univ., 1947–65; Chelsea College: Professor of Physical and Inorganic Chemistry, 1965–84; Head of Dept, 1972–82; Vice-Principal, 1976–84; Principal, 1984–85. Royal Institution of Great Britain: Sec., 1978–84; Vice-Pres., 1978–84, 1987–89, 1991–94; Chm. Council, 1987–89. *Publications:* Diffusion and Heat Flow in Liquids, 1961; Thermometric Titrimetry, 1968; Diffusion in Liquids, 1984; papers in chemical and physical jls. *Recreation:* gardening. *Address:* 5 Chapel Lane, Wilmslow, Cheshire SK9 5HZ. *Clubs:* Athenæum, Royal Institution.

TYRRELL, Prof. John, DPhil; Honorary Professor, School of Music, Cardiff University, since 2008 (Professorial Research Fellow in Music, 2000–03; Professor, 2003–08); *b* Salisbury, Southern Rhodesia, 17 Aug. 1942; *s* of Henry John Ranger Tyrrell and Florence Ellen Tyrrell (*née* Wright). *Educ:* St John's Coll., Johannesburg; Univ. of Cape Town (BMus); Lincoln Coll., Oxford (DPhil 1969). FRCM 2009. Associate Ed., Musical Times, 1972–76; Desk Ed., Grove's Dictionary of Music, 1973–76; University of Nottingham: Lectr in Music, 1976–89; Reader in Opera Studies, 1989–96; Prof., 1996–97; Exec. Ed., The New Grove Dictionary of Music and Musicians, 1997–2000 (Dep. Ed., 1996–97). British Acad. Res. Reader in the Humanities, 1992–94. Chm., Music Libraries Trust, 1999–2005. Dr *hc*: Masaryk Univ., 2002; Janáček Acad. of Performing Arts, Brno, 2011. *Publications:* (with R. Wise) A Guide to International Congress Reports in Music 1900–1975, 1979; Leoš Janáček: Kát'a Kabanová, 1982; Czech Opera, 1988 (Czech trans. 1992); Janáček's Operas: a documentary account, 1992; (ed and trans.) Intimate Letters: Leoš Janáček to Kamila Stösslová, 1994; (ed with Charles Mackerras) Janáček's Jenůfa, 1996; (jtly) Janáček's Works: a catalogue of the music and writings of Leoš Janáček, 1997; (ed and trans.) Zdenka Janáčková: my life with Janáček, 1998; Janáček: years of a life: Vol. 1, The Lonely Blackbird, 2006, Vol. 2, Tsar of the Forests, 2007; (ed with N. Simeone) Charles Mackerras, 2015. *Recreations:* gardening, bread-making.

TYRRELL, Robert James; Principal, Bob Tyrrell and Co., since 2000; Chairman, Demos, 2002–06 (Member, Advisory Council, since 1992); *b* 6 June 1951; *s* of Peter John Tyrrell and Mair (*née* Harries); *m* 1983, Jean Linda McKerrow; two *d*. *Educ:* St Peter's Coll., Oxford (MA, PPE), LSE (MSc Phil with dist.). Academic research, Sussex and Glasgow Univs, 1972–74; joined James Morrell & Associates, 1974; Perkins Engines, 1977; Futures Group, USA, 1980; Man. Dir, 1986–92, Chief Exec., 1992–95, Exec. Chm., 1995–96, Henley Centre for Forecasting. Develt Partner, Cognosis Strategy Consultants, 1999–2003. Chm., Global Future Forum Europe, 2001–03. Vis. Prof., City Univ. Business Sch., 1994–2001. Director: New Solutions, 1997–2000; La Table du Pain, Luxembourg, 1999–2007; Archial (formerly SMC) Gp plc, 2005–09; non-exec. Dir, Trajectory Ltd, 2011–; Chm., Sociovision, UK, 2001–03. Associate and Consultant, Milligan Retail, 2005–. Member: Steering Cttee, Econ. Beliefs and Behaviour Prog., ESRC, 1994–99; Council, Conservative Party Policy Forum, 1999–2002. Assoc. Mem., BUPA, 2004–. Trustee and Dir, Golden Oldies, 2007–09. Presenter: Opinions, C4, 1994; Analysis, BBC Radio, 1997–. FRSA. *Publications:* (ed jtly) Britain in the 1980s, 1974; (ed jtly) Britain 2001, 1977; (ed jtly) Planning for Social Change, 1991; Things Can Only Get... Different, 2001. *Recreations:* reading, sailing, fly-fishing, cycling, walking, theatre. *Address:* Warberry Lodge, Lansdown Road, Bath BA1 5RB.

TYRRELL, Valentine; *see* Tyrrell, H. J. V.

TYRWHITT, Sir Reginald (Thomas Newman), 3rd Bt *cr* 1919; DL; *b* 21 Feb. 1947; *er s* of Admiral Sir St John Tyrwhitt, 2nd Bt, KCB, DSO, DSC and Bar (*d* 1961), and Nancy (Veronica) Gilbey (who *m* 1965, Sir Godfrey Agnew, KCVO, CB; she *d* 2010); *S* father, 1961; *m* 1972, Sheila Gail (marr. diss. 1980 and annulled 1984), *d* of William Alistair Crawford Nicoll, Liphook, Hants; *m* 1984, Charlotte, *o d* of late Captain and the Hon. Mrs Angus Hildyard, Goxhill Hall, Goxhill, N Lincs; one *s* one *d*. *Educ:* Downside. Served in Royal Artillery 1966–69. Career spent subseq. in UK paper industry. DL Lincs, 2014. *Recreations:* shooting, fishing, drawing. *Heir: s* Robert St John Hildyard Tyrwhitt, *b* 15 Feb. 1987.

TYSON, Prof. Laura D'Andrea, PhD; Dean of London Business School, 2002–06; S. K. and Angela Chan Chair in Global Management, Haas School of Business, University of California at Berkeley, since 2008; *b* 28 June 1947; *m* Erik Tarloff; one *s*. *Educ:* Smith Coll. (BA 1969); MIT (PhD 1974). Asst Prof., Dept of Econs, Princeton Univ., 1974–77; University of California, Berkeley: Prof. of Econs, 1977–2002; Prof., 1990–2002, Dean, 1998–2002, Prof. of Econs and Business Admin, 2007–08, Haas Sch. of Business; Dir, Inst. of Internat. Studies, 1990–92; Dir of Res., Berkeley Roundtable on Internat. Economy, 1988–92; Dist. Teaching Award, 1982. Chairman: US President's Council of Econ. Advrs, 1993–95; Nat. Econ. Council, 1995–96; Principal, Law and Econs Consulting Gp, 1997–2000; Mem., Council on Foreign Relations, 1997–. Member Board: Eastman Kodak Co., 1997–; Morgan Stanley Co., 1998–; SBC Communications, 1999–; Bruegel, 2005–. Columnist, Business Week. Fellow, Nat. Fellows Prog., Hoover Inst., 1978–79. *Publications:* The Yugoslav Economic System and its Performance in the 1970s, 1980; (ed with Egon Neuberger) The Impact of External Economic Disturbances on the Soviet Union and Eastern Europe, 1980; (ed with John Zysman) American Industry in International Competition: political and economic perspectives, 1983; Economic Adjustment in Eastern Europe, 1984; (ed with Ellen Comisso) Power, Purpose and Collective Choice: economic strategy in socialist states, 1986; (ed with William T. Dickens and John Zysman) The Politics of Productivity: the real story of why Japan works, 1989; Who's Bashing Whom? trade conflict in high technology industries, 1992; articles in professional jls. *Address:* Haas School of Business, 545 Student Services #1900, University of California at Berkeley, Berkeley, CA 94720–1900, USA.

TYSZKIEWICZ, Zygmunt Jan Ansgary, CMG 1998; President, Lanckoronski Foundation, 1996–2014; *b* 4 Feb. 1934; *s* of Count Jan Michal Tyszkiewicz and Anna Maria Tyszkiewicz (*née* Princess Radziwill); *m* 1958, Kerstin Barbro Ekman; two *s* two *d*. *Educ:* Downside Sch.; Sidney Sussex Coll., Cambridge (BA Hons Mod. and Medieval Langs). Officer, XII Royal Lancers, 1956–57. Joined Shell International Petroleum, 1957: Man. Dir, Shell-BP Tanzania, 1970–73; Gen. Manager, Shell Hellas, 1979–85; Sec. Gen., UNICE, Brussels, 1985–98. Member: Bd, Eur. Foundn for Mgt Develt, Brussels, 1985–98; Adv. Council, Involvement and Participation Assoc., London, 1998–2005. Gov., Eur. Policy Forum, London, 1998–2011. Hon. DBA Robert Gordon Univ., 2000. KM 1994; Grand Cross ad Merito Melitensi, SMO Malta, 2002; Kt, Order of Dannebrog (Denmark), 1997; Comdr, Order of Leopold (Belgium), 1998. *Publications:* contrib. numerous articles on European and business issues in UK and European jls. *Recreations:* family holidays with grandchildren, European Union and Polish politics. *Address:* 5 Champneys Walk, Cambridge CB3 9AW. *T:* (01223) 302816, *Fax:* (01223) 368596. *E:* zygmunttysz@hotmail.co.uk. *Clubs:* Cavalry and Guards; Cercle Royal Gaulois Artistique et Littéraire (Brussels).

TYTE, David Christopher, CB 1997; PhD; Director Rationalisation, Defence Evaluation and Research Agency, Ministry of Defence, 1991–97; *b* 19 Aug. 1937. *Educ:* Dulwich Coll.; Imperial Coll., London (PhD, BSc). CEng, FInstP, MIET. NRC Post Doctoral Fellow, Univ. of Western Ontario, 1962–65; Asst Prof., York Univ., Toronto, 1965–67; joined MoD, 1967; Dep. Dir (Underwater), Admiralty Res. Estabt, 1987–89; Technical Dir, DRA, 1989–91.

TYZACK, His Honour David Ian Heslop; QC 1999; a Circuit Judge, 2000–14; Designated Family Judge, Exeter, 2010–14; Nominated Judge of the Court of Protection, 2011–14; *b* 21 March 1946; *s* of late Ernest Rudolf Tyzack and Joan Mary Tyzack (*née* Palmer); *m* 1973, Elizabeth Anne Cubitt; one *s* one *d*. *Educ:* Allhallows Sch., Rousdon; St Catharine's Coll., Cambridge (MA 1969). Called to the Bar, Inner Temple, 1970, Bencher, 2007; in practice at the Bar, Western Circuit, 1971–2000; Asst Recorder, 1996–2000; Recorder, 2000; a Dep. High Ct Judge, 2000–14; Designated Family Judge, Plymouth, 2003–09. Chm., Devon and Cornwall Br., Family Law Bar Assoc., 1992–2000. Mem., Devonshire Assoc. Churchwarden, Farringdon Ch, Devon, 1992–2010. *Publications:* (contrib.) Essential Family Practice, 2001. *Recreations:* gardening, ski-ing, church, house in France. *Address:* Magdalen Chambers, Victory House, Dean Clarke Gardens, Exeter EX2 4AA. *Club:* Devon and Exeter Institution.

U

UCHIDA, Dame Mitsuko, DBE 2009 (CBE 2001); pianist; *b* 20 Dec. 1948; *d* of Fujio and Yasuko Uchida. *Educ:* Hochschule für Musik, Vienna. First recital at age of 14 in Vienna; performs regularly with orchestras worldwide incl. Berlin Philharmonic, Vienna Philharmonic, Cleveland, etc.; performed complete Mozart piano sonatas in London, 1982, Tokyo, 1983, and NY, 1991; Schubert and Schoenberg recitals in Salzburg, London, Vienna, NY, Tokyo, etc, 1994–96; complete Mozart piano concertos with Cleveland Orch., 2003–08; five Beethoven piano concertos with Berlin Philharmonic, 2010; repertoire ranges from Bach to Boulez. Co-Dir, Marlboro Music Fest., Vermont, USA, 2000–; Founder Mem., Borletti-Buitoni Trust, 2003–. Mem., American Philosophical Soc. Recordings include: complete piano sonatas and concertos of Mozart; Beethoven's piano concertos; Debussy's Etudes; Schumann's Carnaval; Schoenberg piano concerto; Beethoven's last five piano sonatas. Has won many prizes for recordings. Hon. DMus: Oxford, 2009; Cambridge, 2014. *Recreations:* sleeping, listening to music. *Address:* c/o Victoria Rowsell Artist Management, 34 Addington Square, SE5 7LB. *T:* (020) 7701 3219. *E:* management@victoriarowsell.co.uk.

UDAL, Rev. Canon Joanna Elizabeth Margaret; Archbishop of Canterbury's Secretary for Anglican Communion Affairs, 2009–14; Chaplain, Southwark Cathedral, since 2011; *b* London, 27 Dec. 1964; *d* of John Udal and Ann Hopkins-Clarke. *Educ:* Sherborne Sch. for Girls; Univ. of Durham (BSc Maths 1986; PGCE 1987); Ripon Coll., Cuddesdon (BTh Theol. Oxon 1997). Admin. Asst, Internat. Chamber of Shipping, 1987–89; Chamber of Shipping: Admin. Asst, 1989–91; Asst Manager, 1991–94; Manager, Internat. Policy, 1994. Ordained deacon, 1997, priest, 1998; Asst Curate, St Augustine of Canterbury, Whitton, London, 1997–2000; Asst to Archbishop of Sudan, 2001–09. Provincial Canon, All Saints' Cathedral, Juba, Sudan, 2007–. *Publications:* contrib. article in Ecumenical Rev. *Recreations:* choral singing, opera, Sudan Archaeology Society (Sec., 2005–09).

UDALL, Jan; *see* Beaney, J.

UDDIN, family name of **Baroness Uddin**.

UDDIN, Baroness *cr* 1998 (Life Peer), of Bethnal Green in the London Borough of Tower Hamlets; **Pola Manzila Uddin;** *b* Bangladesh, 17 July 1959; *m* 1976, Komar Uddin; four *s* one *d*. Youth and Community Worker, YWCA, 1980–82; Liaison Officer, Tower Hamlets Social Services, 1982–84; Manager: Women's Health Project, 1984–88; Asian Family Counselling Service, 1989–90; Social Worker, Manager and subseq. Mgt Consultant, London Borough of Newham Social Services, 1993–98. Mem. (Lab), Tower Hamlets LBC, 1990–98 (Dep. Leader, Lab Gp, 1993–94; Dep. Leader, Council, 1994–96). House of Lords: former Chairman: Home Office Wkg Gp; Wkg Gp on Pol and Community Leadership; European Select Cttee; Chair, Govt Cttee on Forced Marriage; Mem., Community Cohesion Bd. Non-exec. Dir, Carlton TV (Chm., London Licensing Bd). Member: CPA; IPU; former Mem., CETSW. Member, Board: Autism Speak UK; St Katharine and Shadwell Trust. Patron: Bethnal Green and Victoria Park Housing Assoc.; Orbis International; Tower Hamlets Women's Aid; Royal Coll. of Speech and Language Therapy; Disability Trust; Attlee Foundn; Social Action for Health. *Address:* House of Lords, SW1A 0PW. *T:* (020) 7219 8506.

UDEN, Martin David; HM Diplomatic Service; Deputy High Commissioner, Lagos, since 2015; *b* 28 Feb. 1955; *s* of late Rodney Frederick Uden and Margaret Irene Uden (*née* Brunt); *m* 1982, Fiona Jane Smith; two *s*. *Educ:* Ravensbourne Sch. for Boys; Queen Mary Coll., London Univ. (LLB). Called to the Bar, Inner Temple, 1977; joined FCO, 1977; Second Sec., Seoul, 1978–81; Second, later First Sec., FCO, 1981–86; First Sec., Bonn, 1986–90; FCO, 1990–93; Dep. Head, CSCE Unit, FCO, 1993–94; Pol Counsellor and Consul-Gen., Seoul, 1994–97; Econ., then Trade/Econ., Counsellor, Ottawa, 1997–2001; Internat. Dir, Invest-UK, 2001–03; Consul-Gen., San Francisco, 2003–07; Ambassador to South Korea, 2008–11; Man. Dir, British Business Embassy, UK Trade & Investment, 2012; Coordinator, Security Council Panel of Experts on the Democratic People's Rep. of Korea, UN, 2012–14. Mem. Bd, Human Liberty, 2014–. *Publications:* (with T. Bennett) Korea: caught in time, 1997; Times Past in Korea, 2003. *Address:* c/o Foreign and Commonwealth Office, King Charles Street, SW1A 2AH.

UDNY-LISTER, Sir Edward Julian; *see* Lister, Sir E. J. U.

UFF, Prof. John Francis, CBE 2002; QC; PhD; FREng, FICE; FCIArb; international arbitrator, advocate and engineer; Nash Professor of Engineering Law, University of London, 1991–2003, now Emeritus Professor; a Recorder, 1998–2005; *b* 30 Jan. 1942; *s* of Frederick and Eva Uff; *m* 1967, Diana Muriel Graveson; two *s* one *d*. *Educ:* Stratton Sch.; King's College London (BSc (Eng), PhD; FKC 1997). Asst engineer, Rendel Palmer & Tritton, 1966–70; Vis. Lectr in civil engineering, 1963–68; called to the Bar, Gray's Inn, 1970, Bencher, 1993 (Vice-Treas., 2010; Treas., 2011); practice at Bar, Keating Chambers, 1970–, Head of Chambers, 1992–97; Asst Recorder, 1993–98; a Dep. Judge, Technology and Construction Court, 1999–2005. Dir, Centre of Construction Law and Management, KCL, 1987–99; arbitrator in construction disputes; lectr to professional bodies in engineering law and arbitration. Vice-Pres., London Court of Internat. Arbitration, 2003–08. Member: Standing Cttee on Structural Safety, 1984–90; Bldg Users Insurance against Latent Defects Cttee, DoE, 1986–88; Adv. Cttee on arbitration law, DTI, 1993–95. Chairman: Ind. Commn of Inquiry into Yorks Water, 1996; Public Inquiry into Southall Rail Accident, 1997–99; Commn of Enquiry into Public Construction Sector, Trinidad and Tobago, 2008–10; Jt Chm., Public Inquiry into Rail Safety Systems, 1999–2000. Mem. Council, ICE, 1982–85; Mem. and Trustee, Bd of Trustees, Engrg Council, 2012–; President: Engrg Section, BAAS, 2003–04; Soc. of Construction Arbitrators, 2004–07; Bar Music Soc., 2008–. Vice-Pres., KCL Assoc., 1993–95. FREng (FEng 1995). Master, Arbitrators' Co., 2014–15. Prin. Ed., book series of Centre of Construction Law and Mgt, KCL, on construction law, management, environment law and dispute resolution, 1988–. President's Medal, Soc. Construction Law, 2000; Gold Medal, ICE, 2002. *Publications:* Construction Law, 1974, 11th edn 2013; (contrib.) Keating on Building Contracts, 4th edn 1978 to 9th edn 2012; (jtly) ICE Arbitration Practice, 1986; (jtly) Methods of Procurement in Ground Investigation, 1986; (principal draftsman) Construction Industry Model Arbitration Rules, 1998; (contrib.) Chitty on Contracts, 28th edn 1999, 31st edn 2012; (principal draftsman) ICC Form of Contract, 2014; technical papers in civil engineering; papers and articles in engineering law and procedure. *Recreations:* playing with violins, painting, walking. *Address:* 15 Essex Street, WC2R 3AU. *T:* (020) 7544 2600; Pale Farm, Chipperfield, Herts WD4 9BH. *Clubs:* Athenæum, Ronnie Scott's.

UFFEN, Kenneth James, CMG 1977; HM Diplomatic Service, retired; Ambassador and UK Permanent Representative to OECD, Paris, 1982–85; *b* 29 Sept. 1925; *s* of late Percival James Uffen, MBE, former Civil Servant, and late Gladys Ethel James; *m* 1954, Nancy Elizabeth Winbolt; one *s* two *d*. *Educ:* Latymer Upper Sch.; St Catharine's Coll., Cambridge. HM Forces (Flt-Lt, RAFVR), 1943–48; St Catharine's Coll., 1948–50; 3rd Sec., FO, 1950–52; Paris, 1952–55; 2nd Sec., Buenos Aires, 1955–58; 1st Sec., FO, 1958–61; 1st Sec. (Commercial), Moscow, 1961–63; seconded to HM Treasury, 1963–65; FCO, 1965–68; Counsellor, Mexico City, 1968–70; Economic Counsellor, Washington, 1970–72; Commercial Counsellor, Moscow, 1972–76; Res. Associate, IISS, 1976–77; Ambassador to Colombia, 1977–82. *Recreations:* music, gardens. *Address:* 40 Winchester Road, Walton-on-Thames, Surrey KT12 2RH.

UGANDA, Archbishop of, since 2012; **Most Rev. Stanley Ntagali;** *b* Kabale, Uganda, 1 March 1955; *s* of late Ernest Ntagali and of Molly Ntagali; *m* 1978, Beatrice; four *s* one *d*. *Educ:* Bishop Turker Theol Coll. (CTh 1981); Kilimanjaro Christian Med. Centre, Moshi, Tanzania (CertCPE 1983); St Paul's Univ., Limuru, Kenya (BD 1993); Oxford Centre for Mission Studies (MA Theol. and Devlt 2000). Missionary, Karamoja, 1977–86; Archdeacon of Masindi, 1994–99; Diocesan Sec., Dio. of Bunyoro-Kitara, 2000–02; Provincial Sec., Church of Uganda, 2003–04; Bishop, Dio. of Masindi-Kitara, 2004–12. *Publications:* More than One Wife: polygamy and grace, 2012. *Address:* Church of Uganda, PO Box 14123, Kampala, Uganda. *E:* bishopntagali@yahoo.com.

UIST, Hon. Lord; Roderick Francis Macdonald; a Senator of the College of Justice in Scotland, since 2006; *b* 1 Feb. 1951; *s* of late Finlay Macdonald and Catherine Maclean. *Educ:* St Mungo's Acad., Glasgow; Glasgow Univ. (LLB Hons). Admitted advocate, 1975; Advocate-Depute (Crown Counsel), 1987–93; QC (Scot.) 1988; Home Advocate-Depute (Sen. Crown Counsel), 1990–93; called to the Bar, Inner Temple, 1997. Legal Chm., Pension Appeal Tribunals for Scotland, 1995–2001; Member: Criminal Injuries Compensation Bd, 1995–2000; Criminal Injuries Compensation Appeals Panel, 1997–99. *Recreations:* walking, Provence. *Address:* Court of Session, Parliament House, Edinburgh EH1 1RQ. *T:* (0131) 225 2595.

ULLMAN, Jennifer Margaret; landscape management consultant, since 2009; *b* Boston, Mass, 19 Dec. 1964; *d* of Richard Ullman and Yoma Ullman; *m* 1994, John G. Curtin. *Educ:* Oberlin Coll. (BA Hons Hist. of Art); Yale Univ. (Master and MPhil Hist. of Art); Inchbald Sch. of Design (Dip. Garden Design 1994). Manager, Historic Morven, New Jersey, 1995–97; Wandsworth Council: Manager, Battersea Park, 1998–2000; Asst Chief Parks Officer, 2000–02; Chief Parks Officer, 2002–08. Chm., Bd of Dirs, Greenspace, 2001–03; Member: Managing Cttee, London Parks and Gardens Trust, 2003–09; London Cttee, Heritage Lottery Fund, 2012–; Council, RSPB, 2014–. Trustee, Royal Botanic Garden, Kew, 2008–. Judge, Green Flags Awards, 2001–. *Recreations:* gardening, cycling, birdwatching, walking. *Address:* Hill Cottage, Sutton Place, Abinger Hammer, Surrey RH5 6RL. *T:* (01306) 730270. *E:* jennifer@jenniferullman.com.

ULLMANN, Sir Anthony James, Kt 2015; Chairman and Managing Director, Autofil Worldwide Ltd, since 1998; *b* London, 15 June 1954; *s* of Jean-Jacques and Bella Ullmann; *m* 1983, Riva; two *s* one *d*. *Educ:* Bradford Grammar Sch. Chm., Ullmann Internat. Ltd, 1980–2005. Advr to Rt Hon. Nicholas Clegg, MP, 2000–. Mem., Lib Dem Business Adv. Gp, 2014–. *Recreations:* family, travel, theatre, golf. *Address:* Autofil Worldwide Ltd, Sherwood Park, Annesley Woodhouse, Nottingham NG15 0RS. *Club:* Ivy.

ULLMANN, Liv (Johanne); actress; *b* Tokyo, 16 Dec. 1938; *d* of late Viggo Ullmann and of Janna (*née* Lund), Norway; *m* 1st, 1960, Dr Gappe Stang (marr. diss. 1965); 2nd, 1985, Donald Saunders (marr. diss. 1995). *Educ:* Norway; London (dramatic trng). Stage début, The Diary of Anne Frank (title role), Stavanger, 1956; major roles, National Theatre and Norwegian State Theatre, Oslo; Amer. stage début, A Doll's House, New York Shakespeare Festival, 1974–75; Anna Christie, USA, 1977; The Bear, La Voix humaine, Australia, 1978; I Remember Mama, USA, and Ghosts (Ibsen), Broadway, 1979; British theatre début, Old Times, Guildford, 1985; dir, A Streetcar Named Desire, Sydney Th. Co., Sydney and NY, 2009. Wrote and dir. short film, Parting, 1981. Twelve hon. doctorates, including Brown, Smith Coll., Tufts and Haifa. *Films:* Pan, 1965; The Night Visitor, 1971; Pope Joan, 1972; The Emigrants, 1972 (Golden Globe Award); The New Land, 1973 (Best Actress, Nat. Soc. of Film Critics, USA); Lost Horizon, 1973; 40 Carats, 1973 (Golden Globe Award); Zandy's Bride, 1973; The Abdication, 1974; The Wild Duck, 1983; The Bay Boy, 1985; Let's Hope it's a Girl, 1987; Mosca Addio, 1987; Time of Indifference, 1987; La Amiga, 1987; The Ox, 1993; *director:* Sophie, 1993; Kristin Lavrandsdatter (also wrote screenplay), 1995; Private Confessions, 1996; Faithless, 2000; (*dir. by Ingmar Bergman*): Persona, 1966; The Hour of the Wolf, 1968 (Best Actress, Nat. Soc. of Film Critics, USA); Shame, 1968 (Best Actress, Nat. Soc. of Film Critics, USA); The Passion of Anna, 1969; Cries and Whispers, 1972; Scenes from a Marriage, 1974; Face to Face, 1976; The Serpent's Egg, 1977; The Autumn Sonata, 1978 (5 NY Film Critics awards); Saraband, 2005. Goodwill Ambassador, UNICEF, 1980–; Vice Pres., Internat. Rescue Cttee. Peer Gynt Award, Norway (1st female recipient). Commander, Order of St Olav (Norway), 1994. *Publications:* (autobiog.) Changing, 1977; Choices, 1984.

ULLRICH, Kay Morrison; Member (SNP) West of Scotland, Scottish Parliament, 1999–2003; *b* 5 May 1943; *d* of John Dallas Morrison and Charlotte McMillan Morrison (*née* Neil); *m* 1st, 1964, Andrew Jofre (marr. diss.); one *s* one *d*; 2nd, 1976, Grady Ullrich. *Educ:* Ayr Acad.; Queen's Coll., Glasgow (CQSW). Butlin's Redcoat, 1961–64; schools swimming instructor, N Ayrshire, 1973–81; sch. social worker, 1984–86, hosp. social worker, 1986–92, Strathclyde; sen. court social worker, E Ayrshire, 1992–97. Scottish Parliament: Spokesperson on health and community care, 1999–2000; SNP Chief Whip, 2000–03; Mem., Standards and Equal Opportunities Cttees, 2000–03. Vice-Pres., SNP,

1997–99. Contested (SNP): Cunninghame S, 1983 and 1987; Motherwell S, 1992; Monklands E, June 1994. *Recreations:* swimming, travel, meeting friends. *Address:* Tulsa, Montgomeryfield, Dreghorn, Irvine KA11 4HB. *T:* (01294) 213331.

ULLSTEIN, Augustus Rupert Patrick Anthony; QC 1992; a Recorder, since 1999; *b* 21 March 1947; *s* of late Frederick Charles Leopold Ullstein and Patricia (*née* Guinness); *m* 1970, Pamela Margaret Wells; two *s* two *d*. *Educ:* Bradfield Coll., Berks; LSE (LLB Hons). Called to the Bar, Inner Temple, 1970, Bencher, 2006; in practice as barrister, 1970–; an Asst Recorder, 1993–99. Liveryman, Bowyers' Co., 1980–2009. *Publications:* (Supervising Editor) Pelling and Purdie, Matrimonial Injunctions, 1982; Compensation for Personal Injury in England, Germany and Italy, 2005. *Recreations:* my children, after dinner speaking. *Address:* 39 Essex Street, WC2R 3AT. *T:* (020) 7832 1111.

ULLSWATER, 2nd Viscount *cr* 1921, of Campsea Ashe, Suffolk; **Nicholas James Christopher Lowther,** LVO 2002; PC 1994; Private Secretary, Comptroller and Equerry to Princess Margaret, Countess of Snowdon, 1998–2002; *b* 9 Jan. 1942; *s* of Lieut John Arthur Lowther, MVO, RNVR (*d* 1942), and Priscilla Violet (*d* 1945), *yr d* of Reginald Everitt Lambert; *S* great-grandfather, 1949; *m* 1967, Susan, *d* of James Howard Weatherby; two *s* two *d*. *Educ:* Eton; Trinity Coll., Cambridge. Captain, Royal Wessex Yeomanry, T&AVR, 1973–78. A Lord in Waiting (Govt Whip), H of L, 1989–90; Parly Under-Sec. of State, Dept of Employment, 1990–93; Capt. of Corps of Gentlemen at Arms (Govt Chief Whip), H of L, 1993–94; Minister of State (Minister for Construction and Planning), DoE, 1994–95; elected Mem., H of L, 2003. *Heir: s* Hon. Benjamin James Lowther [*b* 26 Nov. 1975; *m* 2007, Theresa Schoeman; one *s* one *d*]. *Address:* Whiteacres, Cross Lane, Brancaster, King's Lynn, Norfolk PE31 8AE. *T:* (01485) 210488.

ULPH, Prof. David Tregear, FRSE; Professor of Economics, University of St Andrews, since 2006 (Head, School of Economics and Finance, 2006–10); Director, Scottish Institute for Research in Economics, since 2010; *b* 26 Oct. 1946; *s* of late Cyril Ulph and Myra Ulph; *m* 1971, Elizabeth Mackie; two *d*. *Educ:* Univ. of Glasgow (MA); Balliol Coll., Oxford (BLitt). FRSE 2010. Lectr in Econs, Univ. of Stirling, 1971–78; Lectr, then Reader in Econs, UCL, 1978–84; Professor of Economics: Univ. of Bristol, 1984–92; UCL, 1992–2001; Chief Economist and Dir, Analysis and Res., subseq. Analysis, HM Inland Revenue, then HMRC, 2001–06. FRSA 2001. *Publications:* over 90 articles in refereed jls and books. *Recreations:* bridge, cinema, travel. *Address:* School of Economics and Finance, The Scores, University of St Andrews, St Andrews, Fife KY16 9AL. *T:* (01334) 462420.

ULRICH, Walter Otto; Deputy Secretary, Department of Education and Science, 1977–87; *b* 1 April 1927. Ministry of Works: Asst Principal, 1951; Principal, 1955; Treasury 1958–60; Principal Private Sec. to Minister of Public Building and Works, 1963–65; Asst Sec., 1965; Min. of Housing and Local Govt, 1966; DoE, 1970; Under-Sec., 1972; Cabinet Office, 1974–76. *Address:* 46 Grinstead Lane, Lancing, W Sussex BN15 9DZ. *T:* (01903) 762169.

ULSTER, Earl of; Alexander Patrick Gregers Richard Windsor; *b* 24 Oct. 1974; *s* of HRH The Duke of Gloucester and HRH The Duchess of Gloucester; *m* 2002, Dr Claire Alexandra, *d* of Mr and Mrs Robert Booth; one *s* one *d*. *Educ:* Eton Coll.; King's Coll., London Univ. (BA War Studies 1996); RMA, Sandhurst. Commnd King's Royal Hussars, 1998; Captain, 2000. *Heir: s* Lord Culloden, *qv*.
See under Royal Family.

UMUNNA, Chuka; MP (Lab) Streatham, since 2010; *b* 17 Oct. 1978. *Educ:* St Dunstan's Coll., Catford; Univ. of Manchester (LLB English and French Law); Univ. of Burgundy; Nottingham Law Sch. Admitted Solicitor, 2004; with Herbert Smith, London, 2002–06, Rochman Landau, 2006–10. Shadow Sec. of State for Business, Innovation and Skills, 2011–15. Mem., Treasury Select Cttee, 2010–11; Vice Chairman, All Party Parliamentary Group: on Nigeria, 2010–15; on Thameslink, 2010–15. Member: GMB; Unite; Fabian Soc.; Compass. *Publications:* (ed) Owning the Future: how Britain can make it in a fast-changing world, 2014. *Address:* House of Commons, SW1A 0AA.

UNDERHILL, Prof. Allan Edward, PhD, DSc; CChem, FRSC; Professor of Inorganic Chemistry, University College of North Wales, then University of Wales, Bangor, 1983–99, now Emeritus; *b* 13 Dec. 1935; *s* of Albert Edward Underhill and Winifred Underhill (*née* Bailey); *m* 1960, Audrey Jean Foster; one *s* one *d*. *Educ:* Univ. of Hull (BSc 1958; PhD 1962); DSc Wales 1983. Res. Chemist, ICI Ltd, 1961–62; Lectr, Loughborough CAT, 1962–65; University College of North Wales (Bangor): Lectr, 1965–74; Sen. Lectr, 1974–83; Dean, Faculty of Sci., 1985–87, 1994–95; Pro-Vice-Chancellor, 1995–99. Restoration Project Coordinator, St George's Ch, Shrewsbury. *Publications:* over 250 res. papers in RSC jls, Nature, etc. *Recreations:* theatre, bridge, walking, photography.

UNDERHILL, Prof. Michael James, PhD; FREng; Professor of Electronics, 1992–2004, part-time Lecturer, since 2004, University of Surrey; Chief Executive Officer, Underhill Research Ltd, since 2007; *b* 22 March 1939; *s* of Gp Capt. (retd) Rev. Wilfrid Underhill, DSC and Barbara Nowell Underhill (*née* James); *m* 1977, Gillian Brown; two *s*. *Educ:* St John's Sch., Leatherhead; Oriel Coll., Oxford (Schol.; Bible Schol.; Capt. of Boats, 1959–60; BA Physics 1960; MA); Univ. of Surrey (PhD Electronics 1972). FIET (FIEE 1982); FREng (FEng 1982). Philips Res. Labs (formerly Mullard Res. Labs), 1960–84 (Head of Systems Div., 1982–84); Tech. Dir, MEL (Philips), 1984–90; Engrg Dir, Thorn EMI Sensors Div., 1990–91; Head of Dept, Electronic and Electrical Engrg, 1992–96, Dean of Engrg, 1996–97, Univ. of Surrey (Vis. Lectr on Systems Engrg, 1968–82; Vis. Prof., 1984–90). Chm., European Frequency and Time Forum, 1996. Member: NATS Res. Adv. Council, 1996–99; Defence Science Adv. Council, 1982–96 (Chm., various bds and cttees). Founder and Res. Dir, Toric Ltd, 2001–10. Chm., Sussex IET, 2007–09. Institution of Electrical Engineers, subseq. of Engineering and Technology: Mem. Council, 1992–2007; Chm., Electronics Div., 1993–94; Chm., Surrey Centre, 1996–97; P. Perring Thoms Award, 1981; J. J. Thomson Award, 1993. Parish Councillor, Rusper, 1977–83. FRSA 1992. *Publications:* 50 patents; 85 papers on frequency control, phase noise, time jitter, electronics, antennas and propagation, and an electromagnetic theory of everything. *Recreations:* licensed radio amateur and Member of Radio Society of Great Britain since 1956, amateur dramatics (Holding Trustee and Pres., Ifield Barn Theatre Club), playing jazz piano, ski-ing, travel, hack and bash gardening. *Address:* Hatchgate, Tandridge Lane, Lingfield, Surrey RH7 6LL. *T:* (01342) 892154.

UNDERHILL, Rt Hon. Sir Nicholas Edward, Kt 2006; PC 2013; **Rt Hon. Lord Justice Underhill;** a Lord Justice of Appeal, since 2013; *b* 12 May 1952; *s* of late Judge Underhill, QC and Rosalie Jean Underhill (who *m* 1989, William Anderson Beaumont, *qv*); *m* 1987, Nina Grunfeld; two *s* two *d*. *Educ:* Winchester Coll.; New Coll., Oxford (MA Hons). Called to the Bar, Gray's Inn, 1976, Bencher, 2000. QC 1992; a Recorder, 1994–2006; Attorney Gen. to the Prince of Wales, 1998–2006; a Dep. High Court Judge, 1998–2006; a Judge of the High Ct of Justice, QBD, 2006–13; a Judge of the Employment Appeal Tribunal, 2000–03 and 2006–13; Pres. of the Employment Appeal Tribunal, 2009–11. Chm., Bar Pro Bono Unit, 2002–05. Trustee: St John's Smith Square, 1996–2014 (Chm., 2010–13); London Library, 2008–12 (Vice-Chm., 2011–12). *Publications:* The Lord Chancellor, 1978. *Address:* Royal Courts of Justice, Strand, WC2A 2LL.

UNDERWOOD, Ashley Grenville; QC 2001; *b* 28 Dec. 1953; *s* of Dennis William Underwood and Brenda Margarita Underwood; *m* 1982, Heather Kay Leggett; one *d*. *Educ:* London Sch. of Econs (LLB Hons). Called to the Bar, Gray's Inn, 1976; Hd of Chambers, 1999–2006. *Recreations:* motorcycling, classic cars, conversation. *Address:* 5 Essex Court, Temple, EC4Y 9AH.

UNDERWOOD, Prof. Graham James Charles, DPhil; Professor of Marine and Freshwater Biology, since 2004, and Executive Dean, Faculty of Science and Health, since 2013, University of Essex; *b* Leicester, 31 March 1964; *s* of John Underwood and Valerie Underwood; *m* 1990, Dr Nicola Jane Durward Slee; one *s* one *d*. *Educ:* Beauchamp Coll., Oadby; Univ. of Reading (BSc Zool. 1986); Univ. of Sussex (DPhil 1989). Department of Biological Sciences, University of Essex: Lectr, 1992–98; Sen. Lectr, 1998–2002; Reader, 2002–04. Natural Environment Research Council: Member: Panel of Chairs, 2009–14; Sci. and Innovation Strategy Bd, 2011–14; Chm., Strategic Progs Adv. Gp, 2015–; Mem., Marine Protected Areas Sci. Adv. Panel, DEFRA, 2009–12. Adjunct Prof., Michigan Technol Univ., 2001–. Gov., N Essex Partnership Foundn Trust, 2013–. *Publications:* contribs to Limnology and Oceanography, Procs of NAS, Jl of Phycology. *Recreations:* gardening, morris dancing, history, sailing, natural history. *Address:* Faculty of Science and Health, University of Essex, Wivenhoe Park, Colchester, Essex CO4 3SQ. *T:* (01206) 873337. *E:* gjcu@essex.ac.uk.

UNDERWOOD, Sir James (Cresseé Elphinstone), Kt 2005; MD; FRCP, FRCPath, FMedSci; Joseph Hunter Professor of Pathology, University of Sheffield, 1984–2006, now Emeritus Professor (Dean, Faculty of Medicine, 2006); *b* 11 April 1942; *s* of John and Mary Underwood; *m* 1st, 1966 (marr. diss. 1986); one *s* one *d*; 2nd, 1989, Alice Cameron Underwood; one *s*. *Educ:* Downside Sch.; St Bartholomew's Hosp. Med. Coll. (MB BS 1965; MD 1973). MRCS, LRCP 1965; MRCPath 1972, FRCPath 1984; FRCP 2004; FRCPI 2004. SHO, then Registrar in Pathology, St Bartholomew's Hosp., London, 1966–69; University of Sheffield: Lectr in Pathology, 1969–73; Sen. Lectr, 1974–82; Reader, 1983. MRC Clinical Res. Fellow, Chester Beatty Res. Inst., London, 1973–74; Wellcome-Ramaciotti Res. Fellow, Univ. of Melbourne, 1981. Consultant Histopathologist, Sheffield AHA(T), subseq. Central Sheffield Univ. Hosps NHS Trust, later Sheffield Teaching Hosps NHS Foundn Trust, 1974–2006; Hon. Civilian Consultant Histopathologist, RAF, 2002–09. President: RCPath, 2002–05 (Vice-Pres., 1999–2002); British Div., Internat. Acad. Pathology, 2000–02. Ed., Histopathology, 1995–2002. FMedSci 2005. Hon. Member: Japanese Soc. Pathology, 1996; Hungarian Soc. Pathologists, 1996. Hon. FCPath: Hong Kong, 2001; S Africa, 2006. Cunningham Medal, British Div., Internat. Acad. of Pathology, 2005; Doniach Award, Pathol Soc., 2008. *Publications:* Introduction to Biopsy Interpretation and Surgical Pathology, 1981, 2nd edn 1987; General and Systematic Pathology, 1992, 5th edn 2009; papers on tumour pathology, chronic liver disease and the autopsy. *Recreations:* music, art, photography, fell-walking, local history. *Address:* Cliburn Mill, Cliburn, Cumbria CA10 3AW. *Club:* Athenæum.

UNDERWOOD, John Morris; Deputy Chief Executive, Freshwater Group, since 2009; Director, Centre for Health Communication Research and Excellence, and Visiting Professor, Buckinghamshire New University, since 2011; *b* 8 Nov. 1953; *s* of John Edward Underwood and Ella Lillian Morris Underwood; *m* 1987, Susan Clare Inglish; two *s*. *Educ:* Univ. of Sheffield (BSc Hons); University Coll., Cardiff (Graduate Dip. in Journalism). BBC trainee journalist, 1976–78; regional TV reporter, 1978–80; TV reporter, ITN, 1980–82; home affairs corresp., ITN, 1982–83; freelance TV producer and presenter, 1983–89; Exec. Producer, House of Commons Cttee TV, 1989–90; Dir of Campaigns and Communications, Labour Party, 1990–91; Partner, subseq. Dir, Clear Communication, 1991–2006. Mem., Mgt Bd, Catalyst think tank, 1998–2005 (Chm., 2001–05). Trustee, Alcohol Research UK, 2013–. Hon. Prof., Univ. of Glasgow, 2006–. Editor, New Century, 1993–95. *Publications:* The Will to Win: John Egan and Jaguar, 1989. *Recreations:* theatre, walking. *Address:* 10 Percival Road, SW14 7QE. *T:* (020) 8876 8884.

UNDERWOOD, Susan Lois, OBE 2006; FMA; Director, Qatar Children's Museum, since 2009; *b* 6 Aug. 1956; *d* of John and Lois Underwood; two *s* one *d*. *Educ:* Univ. of St Andrews (MA Hons); Univ. of Leicester (Mus. Studies Grad. Cert.). FMA 1994. Curator, Nat. Railway Mus., York, 1983–85; Keeper of Local Hist., Scunthorpe Mus. and Art Gall., 1985–88; Dep. Dir, N of England Museums Service, 1989–90; Dir, N of England Museums Service, subseq. NE Museums, then Chief Exec., NE MLA, 1990–2005; Dir, Sharjah Mus, 2005–08; Advr for Mus to Ruler of Sharjah, UAE, 2008–09. Comr, English Heritage, 1997–2003. Mem. Bd, One NorthEast, 2005. *Recreations:* my children, my grandson, the arts. *Address:* Qatar Museums Authority, PO Box 2777, Qatar. *E:* sunderwood@qma.org.qa.

UNERMAN, Sandra Diane, CBE 2002; Solicitor and Legal Adviser, Department for Communities and Local Government (formerly Office of the Deputy Prime Minister), 2004–08; Lawyer (part-time), Treasury Solicitor's Department, 2008–10; *b* 23 Aug. 1950; *d* of Cecil Unerman and Renee Unerman (*née* Goldberg). *Educ:* Gartlett Sch.; Orange Hill Grammar Sch.; Bristol Univ. (BA Hons History); Middx Univ. (MA Creative Writing 2013). Called to the Bar, Inner Temple, 1973; Legal Dept, DoE, later DETR, then DTLR, subseq. ODPM, now DCLG, 1974–2010; Dep. Solicitor, 1992–2004. UK Civil Service Fellow, Humphrey Inst., Univ. of Minnesota, 1989–90. *Publications:* Trial of Three (novel), 1979. *Recreations:* writing, reading, listening to music, theatre going, folklore, conversation.

UNGER, Michael Ronald; Chief Executive, Roy Castle Lung Cancer Foundation, 2002–08; Chairman, Piccadilly Radio Ltd, 2006–08; *b* 8 Dec. 1943; *s* of Ronald Unger, CBE and Joan Maureen Unger; *m* 1st, 1966, Eunice Dickens (marr. diss. 1992); one *s* (one *d* decd); 2nd, 1993, Noorah Ahmed (marr. diss. 2005; she *d* 2013). *Educ:* Wirral Grammar School. Trainee journalist, Thomson Regional Newspapers, Stockport, 1963; Reading Evening Post, 1965–67; Perth Daily News, W Australia, 1967–71; Daily Post, Liverpool, 1971, Editor, 1977–82; Editor: Liverpool Echo, 1982–83; Manchester Evening News, 1983–97; Gen. Manager, Jazz FM (NW), 2000–02. Dir, Guardian Media Gp plc (formerly Guardian and Manchester Evening News plc), 1983–97; non-executive Director: Kenyon Fraser PR Ltd, 2009–11; HM Partnerships Ltd, 2009–13. Chm., NW Arts Bd, 1991–93; Mem., Broadcasting Standards Commn, 1999–2000. Chm., Eternal Forest Trust, 2005–10; Trustee: Scott Trust, 1986–97; The Lowry, 1994–; Youth Charter for Sport, 1994–2000; NW Film Archives, 1998–2004; All Together Now, 2005–; Hoylake Cottage Trust, 2010–13; Cheshire W CAB, 2012–. *Publications:* (ed) The Memoirs of Bridget Hitler, 1979; The Hitlers of Liverpool, 2011. *Recreations:* art, reading, walking, gardening.

UNGERER, Jean Thomas, (Tomi); writer and graphic artist; Ambassador for Childhood and Education, Council of Europe, since 2000; *b* Strasbourg, 28 Nov. 1931; *s* of Theo Ungerer and Alice (*née* Essler); *m* 1970, Yvonne Wright; two *s* one *d*. *Educ:* Strasbourg; Ecole Municipale des Arts Décoratifs, Strasbourg. Moved to USA, 1956; joined Harper's, 1957; worked for Amer. magazines and in advertising; moved to Nova Scotia, 1971, to Ireland, 1976; exhibitions: (first) Berlin, 1962; Strasbourg, 1975; Louvre, Paris, 1981; RFH, London, 1985. Chargé de Mission, Jack Lang, Ministre de la Culture, commission inter-ministérielle Franco-Allemande, 1987–94; Pres. and Founder, Culture Bank, Strasbourg, 1990; Founder, European Centre of Yiddish Cultures, 1999. Hon. Dr Karlsruhe, 2004. Burckhardt Prize, Goethe Foundn, 1983; Andersen Prize, Denmark, 1998; French culture prize, 1998, European culture prize, 1999; Berlin Academy prize, 2008. Commandeur des Arts et des Lettres (France), 1985; Officier, Légion d'Honneur (France), 2001 (Chevalier, 1990); Cross of Merit (Germany), 1992; Chevalier, Ordre des Palmes Académiques (France), 2009; numerous other prizes and awards. *Films include:* The Three Robbers, 1972; The Beast of

Monsieur Racine, 1975; Moon Man, 2013. *Publications:* over 130 books in English, French and German, including: Horrible, 1958; Inside Marriage, 1960; The Underground Sketchbook, 1964; The Party, 1966; Fornicon, 1970; Compromises, 1970; The Poster Art of Tomi Ungerer, 1971; Once in a Lifetime, 1985; Far Out is not Far Enough, 1985; Joy of Frogs, 1985; Testament, 1985; Cats As Cats Can, 1997; Tomi: a Nazi childhood, 1998; Tortoni Tremolo, 1998; Otto, 1999; Europolitan, 1998; S & M, 2000; Vracs, 2000; Erotoscope: the art of Tomi Ungerer, 2001; Tomi Ungerer et New York, 2001; From Father to Son, 2003; Mes Cathédrales, 2007; *for children:* The Mellops series: The Mellops go Diving for Treasure; Crictor, 1958; Adelaide, 1959; Christmas Eve at the Mellops', 1960; Emile, 1960; Rufus, 1961; The Three Robbers, 1962; Snail, Where Are You?, 1962; One, Two, Where's My Shoe?, 1964; The Brave Vulture Orlando, 1966; Moon Man, 1967; Zeralda's Ogre, 1967; Ask Me a Question, 1968; The Hat, 1970; The Beast of Monsieur Racine, 1971; I am Papa Snap and These are My Favourite No Such Stories, 1971; No Kiss for Mother, 1973; Allumette, 1974; Flix, 1997; The Blue Cloud, 2000; Ami-Amies, 2007. *Address:* Diogenes Verlag AG, Sprecherstrasse 8, 8032 Zürich, Switzerland; Tomi Ungerer Museum, Villa Greiner, 2 avenue de la Marseillaise, 67076 Strasbourg Cedex, France.

UNGLEY, John Guilford Gordon; Master of the Supreme Court, Queen's Bench Division, 1997–2008; Master assigned to clinical negligence cases, 1999–2008; *b* 30 Jan. 1939; *s* of Harold Gordon Ungley and Ella Gwyneth Reay Ungley (*née* Heslop); *m* 1976, Elizabeth Metcalfe (*née* Mayall); one *d*, and two step *d*. *Educ:* Charterhouse. Queen's Royal Irish Hussars, 1960–61. Called to the Bar, Gray's Inn, 1965; in practice at the Bar, Western Circuit, 1966–97; Asst Recorder, 1986–89, Recorder, 1989–2004. *Recreations:* sailing, learning to garden and cook in retirement, bellringing. *Clubs:* Cavalry; Bar Yacht, Royal Solent Yacht.

UNRUH, Prof. William George, PhD; FRS 2001; FRSC 1984; Professor of Physics, University of British Columbia, since 1984; Fellow, Canadian Institute for Advanced Research, since 1987; *b* 28 Aug. 1945; *s* of Benjamin Unruh and Anne Unruh (*née* Janzen); *m* 1974, Patricia Truman; one *s*. *Educ:* Univ. of Manitoba (BSc Hons 1967); Princeton Univ. (MA 1969; PhD 1971). FAPS 2000. NSERC (Rutherford) Post Doctoral Fellow, Birkbeck Coll., 1971–72; Miller Fellow, Univ. of Calif, Berkeley, 1973–74; Asst Prof., McMaster Univ., 1974–76; Asst Prof., Univ. of BC, 1976–81; Dir, Cosmology Prog., Canadian Inst. for Advanced Res., 1987–97. Hon. Foreign Mem., American Assoc. of Arts and Scis, 2003. Hon. DSc McMaster, 2008. Sloan Medal, Sloan Foundn, 1978; Rutherford Medal, RSC, 1982; Herzberg Medal, 1983, Medal of Achievement, 1996, Canadian Assoc. of Physicists; Steacie Prize, Steacie Foundn, 1984; Sci. and Engrg Gold Medal, Sci. Council of BC, 1990; Killam Prize in Natural Scis, Canadian Council, 1995; Mathematical Physics Prize, Canadian Assoc. of Physicists and Centre Recherche du Mathématique, 1996. *Publications:* (ed with G. Semenoff) The Early Universe, 1987; contrib. numerous papers to scientific jls. *Address:* Department of Physics and Astronomy, University of British Columbia, Vancouver, BC V6T 1Z1, Canada. *T:* (604) 8223273.

UNSWORTH, Prof. Anthony, PhD, DEng; CEng, FREng, FIMechE; Professor of Engineering, since 1989, Director, Centre for Biomedical Engineering, 1989–2012, Durham University; *b* 7 Feb. 1945; *s* of late James Unsworth and Annie Unsworth (*née* Halliwell); *m* 1967, Jill Chetwood. *Educ:* Salford Univ. (BSc 1967); Leeds Univ. (MSc 1968; PhD 1972; DEng 1990). CEng 1972; FIMechE 1984; FREng 1996. Res. Engr, David Brown Industries, 1967–69; University of Leeds: Res. Fellow, 1969–71; Lectr, 1971–76; University of Durham: Lectr, 1976–79; Sen. Lectr, 1979–84; Reader, 1984–89; Hd, Sch. of Engrg and Applied Sci., then Sch. of Engrg and Computer Sci., 1990–94; Dep. Dean of Sci., 1994–97; Dean of Sci., 1997–2000; Hd, Sch. of Engrg, 2000–06; Dir of Res., Faculty of Sci., 2006–10. Vis. Scientist, Cornell Univ., 1981. Dir, Action Research, 1992–95; non-exec. Dir, S Durham HA, 1993–96. Chm., NHS Res. Ethics Cttee, 1995–96; Chm., Engrg in Medicine Gp, 1989–92, Vice-Pres., 2008–11, Chair, Pubns Bd, 2010–, IMechE; Member: Panel 30, 2001 RAE; Panel 28, 2008 RAE; Bd, Engrg Council, 2008–13. Editor: Pt H, Proc. IMechE; Jl Engrg in Medicine. Hon. Lifetime Mem., Internat. Soc. for Technol. in Arthroplasty, 2013. Silver Medal in Tribology, 1972, Donald Julius Groen Prize in Tribology, 1991, James Clayton Prize, 1999, IMechE; James Alfred Ewing Medal, ICE, 2005; Best Paper Prize, Professional Engrg Publishing, 2009; Lifetime Achievement Award, Internat. Soc. for Technol. in Arthroplasty, 2011. *Publications:* (contrib.) Tribology of Natural and Artificial Joints, 1981; (contrib.) Introduction to Biomechanics, 1981; (contrib.) Mechanics of Joints, 1993; (contrib.) Oxford Textbook of Rheumatology, 2001; over 325 papers in internat. jls in tribology and biomed. engrg; numerous presentations at internat. confs. *Recreation:* singing sacred music and light opera. *Address:* School of Engineering and Computing Sciences, University of Durham, Science Laboratories, South Road, Durham DH1 3LE. *T:* (0191) 334 2521. *E:* tony.unsworth@durham.ac.uk.

UNSWORTH, Ian Stephen; QC 2010; *b* Billinge, Lancs, 7 Dec. 1966; *s* of William Unsworth and Jean Unsworth; *m* 1996, Michelle Cown; two *s* one *d*. *Educ:* Ashton-in-Makerfield Grammar Sch.; Alsager Sch.; Univ. of Huddersfield (LLB Hons Business Law). Called to the Bar, Lincoln's Inn, 1992; in practice as barrister, specialising in criminal law: Exchange Chambers, 2000–10; 7 Harrington Street Chambers, 2010–; apptd to Attorney Gen.'s A List, 2007. Chm., Disciplinary Appeals Panel, RFU, 2010–; Judicial Officer, 6 Nations Rugby Championship, 2014–. *Recreations:* golf, running, triathlon, Rugby Union, family life, concerts, debating. *Address:* 7 Harrington Street Chambers, 7 Harrington Street L2 9YH. *T:* (0151) 242 0707, *Fax:* (0151) 236 2800. *E:* ian.unsworth@7hs.co.uk; Farrars Building, Temple, EC4Y 7BD. *T:* (020) 7583 9241, *Fax:* (020) 7583 0090. *Club:* Royal Liverpool Golf.

UNWIN, Sir Brian; *see* Unwin, Sir J. B.

UNWIN, David Charles; QC 1995; *b* 12 May 1947; *s* of Peter Unwin and Rosemary (*née* Locket); *m* 1969, Lorna Bullivant; one *s* one *d*. *Educ:* Clifton Coll.; Trinity Coll., Oxford. Called to the Bar, Middle Temple, 1971; Jun. Counsel to Attorney Gen. in charity matters, 1987–95. Charity Comr, 2002–07. *Recreations:* music, mountaineering, windsurfing. *Club:* Climbers'.

UNWIN, Eric Geoffrey; Chairman, Advisory Board, Palamon Capital Partners, since 2015; Chairman: Xchanging plc, since 2012; Tryzens Holdings Ltd, since 2014; *b* 9 Aug. 1942; *s* of Maurice Doughty Unwin and Olive Milburn (*née* Watson); *m* 1967, Margaret Bronia Element; one *s* one *d*. *Educ:* Heaton Grammar School, Newcastle upon Tyne; King's College, Durham Univ. (BSc Hons Chemistry). Cadbury Bros, 1963–68; joined John Hoskyns & Co., 1968; Managing Dir, Hoskyns Systems Development, 1978; Dir, 1982, Man. Dir, 1984, Exec. Chm., 1988–93, Hoskyns Group; Chief Operating Officer, 1993–2000, and Vice Chm., Exec. Bd, 1996–2000, Cap Gemini Sogeti, then Cap Gemini; CEO, Cap Gemini, then Cap Gemini Ernst and Young, 2000–01. Chairman: Cap Programmator AB, 1993–2000; United Business Media, 2002–07; Halma plc, 2003–13 (Dep. Chm., 2002–03); Cloud Networks Ltd, 2005–06; Liberata, 2003–11; Omnibus Systems Ltd, 2005–10; Taptu Ltd, 2007–12; Alliance Medical, 2008–10; ReD, 2011–14; OpenCloud, 2011–14; non-executive Director: Volmac Software Groep NV, 1992–; Gemini Consulting Hldg SA, 1994–2000; United News & Media plc, 1995–2002; Towry Hldgs Ltd, 2014–; Mem. Bd, Cap Gemini SA, 2000–. Pres., Computing Services Assoc., 1987–88. Mem., ITAB, 1988–91. CCMI (CBIM 1984; Mem. Bd, 1990–94). Freeman, City of London, 1987; Founder Mem., and Liveryman, Co. of Information Technologists, 1987. *Recreations:* golf, riding, ski-ing. *Address:* 17 Park Village West, NW1 4AE. *Clubs:* Royal Automobile; Hendon Golf, Hunstanton Golf, Royal West Norfolk Golf, Morfontaine Golf (France).

UNWIN, Sir (James) Brian, KCB 1990 (CB 1986); President, European Investment Bank, 1993–99, now Hon. President; President, European Centre for Nature Conservation, 2001–13, now Hon. President; *b* 21 Sept. 1935; *s* of Reginald Unwin and Winifred Annie Walthall; *m* 1964, Diana Susan, *d* of Sir David Aubrey Scott, GCMG; three *s*. *Educ:* Chesterfield School; New College, Oxford (MA; Hon. Fellow, 1997); Yale University (MA). Asst Principal, CRO, 1960; Private Sec. to British High Commissioner, Salisbury, 1961–64; 1st Secretary, British High Commission, Accra, 1964–65; FCO, 1965–68; transferred to HM Treasury, 1968; Private Sec. to Chief Secretary to Treasury, 1970–72; Asst Secretary, 1972; Under Sec., 1976; seconded to Cabinet Office, 1981–83; Dep. Sec., HM Treasury, 1983–85; Dir, Eur. Investment Bank, 1983–85; Dep. Sec., Cabinet Office, 1985–87; Chm., Bd of HM Customs and Excise, 1987–93. Chm., Supervisory Bd, European Investment Fund, 1994–99; Gov., EBRD, 1993–99; Chm., European Task Force on Banking and Biodiversity, 2002–10. Dir, Dexia SA, 2000–10; Chairman: Asset Trust Housing Ltd, 2003–12; Asset Trust Housing Assoc., 2012–14. Pres., Customs Co-operation Council, 1991–92. Chm., Civil Service Sports Council, 1989–93. Member: IMPACT Adv. Bd, 1990–93; Bd of Dirs, ENO, 1993–94, 2000–08 (Sec., 1987–93); Bd, Centre d'Etudes Prospectives, 1996–2000; Bd, Foundation Pierre Werner, 1998–2000. Mem. Council, Federal Trust for Educn and Res., 2003–. Pres., New Coll. Soc., 2003–08. Hon. Pres., Euronem, Athens, 2000–10. Gold Medal, Fondation du Mérite Européen, 1995. Comdr, Order of Ouissam Aloui (Morocco), 1998; Grand Officier, Ordre de la Couronne (Belgium), 2001; Grand Croix, Ordre Grand-Ducal de la Couronne de Chêne (Luxembourg), 2002. *Publications:* Terrible Exile: the last days of Napoleon on St Helena, 2010; (jtly) Financial Regulation: Britain's next European challenge, 2010; A Tale in Two Cities: Fanny Burney and Adele, Comtesse de Boigne, 2013. *Recreations:* opera, bird watching, Wellingtoniana, cricket. *Club:* Reform.

UNWIN, Julia, CBE 2006 (OBE 2000); Chief Executive (formerly Director), Joseph Rowntree Foundation, since 2007; *b* 6 July 1956; *d* of Peter William Unwin, *qv*; partner, Patrick Kelly; two *d*. *Educ:* Univ. of Liverpool (BA 1978); London Sch. of Econs (MSc 1991). Dir, Homeless Network, 1986–92; consultant, 1992–2006. Member: Bd, Housing Corporation, 1992–2001; Charity Commn, 1998–2003; Dep. Chm., Food Standards Agency, 2003–06. Chairman, Committee of Reference: ISIS Asset Mgt, 2004–06; Friends Provident, 2004–06. Lectures: York Ebor, 2011; Gresham Coll., 2012; CREW Regeneration Wales and Univ. of Glamorgan, 2013; Beveridge, Toynbee Hall, 2013. Mem. Council, Univ. of York, 2009–. FRSA; FCGI 2012. Hon. DLaws York St John, 2012; DUniv S Wales, 2014. *Publications:* The Grant Making Tango, 2004; Fruitful Funding, 2005; Why Fight Poverty, 2013. *Address:* c/o Joseph Rowntree Foundation, The Homestead, 40 Water End, York YO30 6WP. *T:* (01904) 629241, *Fax:* (01904) 620072. *E:* julia.unwin@jrf.org.uk.

UNWIN, Ven. Kenneth; Archdeacon of Pontefract, 1981–92, now Emeritus; *b* 16 Sept. 1926; *s* of Percy and Elsie Unwin; *m* 1958, Beryl Riley; one *s* four *d*. *Educ:* Chesterfield Grammar School; St Edmund Hall, Oxford (MA Hons); Ely Theological Coll. Assistant Curate: All Saints, Leeds, 1951–55; St Margaret, Durham City (in charge, St John's, Neville's Cross), 1955–59; Vicar: St John Baptist, Dodworth, Barnsley, 1959–69; St John Baptist, Royston, Barnsley, 1969–73; St John's, Wakefield, 1973–82. Hon. Canon, Wakefield Cathedral, 1980–92. RD of Wakefield, 1980–81. Proctor in Convocation, 1972–82. *Address:* 2 Rockwood Close, Skipton, Yorks BD23 1UG. *T:* (01756) 791323.

See also Sir D. D. Acland, Bt.

UNWIN, Nigel; *see* Unwin, P. N. T.

UNWIN, Peter Francis, CB 2011; Chief Executive, Whitehall and Industry Group, since 2015; *b* 8 June 1954; *s* of Francis Charles Unwin, MBE and Margaret (Marjorie) Unwin (*née* Caskey); *m* 1978, Margaret Elizabeth Wiseman; two *s* one *d*. *Educ:* George Watson's Coll., Edinburgh; Pembroke Coll., Cambridge (BA Hons Maths 1975; Dip. Mathematical Stats 1976). Asst Statistician, Capital and Co. Taxation, Inland Revenue, 1976–79; Private Sec. to Hd, Govt Statistical Service, 1979–81; Principal, Gen. Finance Div., MoD, 1981–84; Statistician, Local Authy Statistics Div., 1984–87; Principal, Local Authy Capital Finance Div., 1987–90; Hd, Inner Cities Policy Unit, 1990–93, Internat. Envmt Div., 1993–97, DoE; Hd, Global Atmosphere Div., DoE, then DETR, 1997–98; Principal Private Secretary: to Dep. Prime Minister, 1998–2001; to Sec. of State for Local Govt, Transport and the Regions, 2001; Director: Central Policy Gp, Cabinet Office, 2001–02; Corporate Strategy and Resources, ODPM, 2002–04; Dir Gen., Corporate Strategy and Resources Gp, ODPM, 2004–06; Corporate Delivery Gp, DCLG, 2006–07; Department for Environment, Food and Rural Affairs: Dir Gen., Natural Envmt Gp, later Envmt and Rural Gp, 2007–12; Acting Perm. Sec., 2011; Dir Gen., Policy Delivery Gp, 2012–15. *Recreations:* golf, ski-ing, travel, hill walking, wine. *Address:* Whitehall and Industry Group, 80 Petty France, SW1H 9EX. *Club:* Chislehurst Golf.

UNWIN, Dr (Peter) Nigel (Tripp), FRS 1983; Scientist, Medical Research Council Laboratory of Molecular Biology, Cambridge, 1968–80 and since 1987; Senior Research Fellow, Trinity College, Cambridge, since 1988; *b* 1 Nov. 1942; *s* of Peter Unwin and Cara Unwin (*née* Pinckney); *m* 1968, Janet Patricia Ladd; one *s* one *d*. *Educ:* Univ. of Otago, NZ (BE); Univ. of Cambridge (PhD 1968). Prof. of Structural Biol., then Cell Biol., Stanford Univ. Sch. of Medicine, Calif, 1980–87. Founder FMedSci 1998. Hon. FRMS 1989. Ernst Ruska Award, Ernst Ruska Foundn, 1980; Rosenstiel Award, Brandeis Univ., Mass, 1991; Louis Jeantet Prize for Medicine, Jeantet Foundn, Geneva, 1996; Gregori Aminoff Prize, Royal Swedish Acad. of Scis, 1999. *Recreation:* mountaineering. *Address:* 19/20 Portugal Place, Cambridge CB5 8AF.

UNWIN, Prof. (Peter) Timothy (Holt), PhD; UNESCO Chair in Information and Communication Technologies for Development, Royal Holloway and Bedford New College, University of London, since 2007 (Professor of Geography, 1999–2011, now Emeritus); *b* 11 July 1955; *s* of Thomas Peter Farrer Unwin and Rhoda Patricia Unwin (*née* Vare); *m* 1981, Pamela Julie Cottam; one *s* two *d*. *Educ:* St John's Coll., Cambridge (BA 1976, MA 1980); Univ. of Durham (PhD 1980). Bedford College, subseq. Royal Holloway and Bedford New College, University of London: Lectr, 1981–92; Sen. Lectr, 1992–93; Reader in Geog., 1993–99; Hd, Dept of Geog., 1999–2001; on secondment as Leader, Imfundo: Partnership for Inf. Technol. in Educn, DFID, 2001–04. CEO, 2011–12, Sec. Gen., 2012–15, Commonwealth Telecommunications Orgn. Prog. Dir, 2007, Sen. Advr, 2008–11, Partnerships for Educn, World Economic Forum; Chair, Commonwealth Scholarship Commn in UK, 2009–14 (Commonwealth Scholarship Comr, 2004–14). Member, Advisory Board: Internat. Multilateral Partnership Against Cyberthreats, 2012–; m-Powering Develt, ITU, 2013–; Mem., Digital Adv. Panel, DFID, 2013–. Vis. Scholar, Peking Univ., 2011; Hon. Prof., Lanzhou Univ., 2011–. Hon. Sec., RGS (with IBG), 1995–97. Academic Advr and Ext. Examiner, Inst. of Masters of Wine, 2004–12. Hon. Mem., Estonian Geographical Soc., 2002. Cuthbert Peek Award, RGS, 1992. *Publications:* Wine and the Vine: an historical geography of viticulture and the wine trade, 1991 (trans. Italian, Greek and Spanish); The Place of Geography, 1992 (trans. Spanish); (ed) Atlas of World Development, 1996; (ed jtly) Environmental Management, 1997; (ed) A European Geography, 1998; (ed jtly) European Landscapes, 2003; (ed) Information and Communication Technology for Development, 2009. *Recreations:* wine, photography, walking, gardening. *Address:* Department of Geography, Royal Holloway, University of London, Egham, Surrey TW20 0EX. *W:* http://unwin.wordpress.com. *Clubs:* Athenæum, Geographical.

UNWIN, Peter William, CMG 1981; HM Diplomatic Service, retired; writer; Chairman, David Davies Memorial Institute of International Studies, 2001–07 (Director, 1995–2001); *b* 20 May 1932; *s* of Arnold and Norah Unwin; *m* 1955, Monica Steven; two *s* two *d*. *Educ:* Ampleforth; Christ Church, Oxford (history scholar). Army, 1954–56; FO, 1956–58; British Legation, Budapest, 1958–61; British Embassy, Tokyo, 1961–63; FCO, 1963–67; British Information Services, NY, 1967–70; FCO, 1970–72; Bank of England, 1973; British Embassy, Bonn, 1973–76; Head of Personnel Policy Dept, FCO, 1976–79; Fellow, Center for Internat. Affairs, Harvard, 1979–80; Minister (Economic), Bonn, 1980–83; Ambassador to: Hungary, 1983–86; Denmark, 1986–88; a Dep. Sec. Gen. of the Commonwealth, 1989–93. Chairman: British-Hungarian Soc., 1993–2000 (Pres., 2000–04); Abbeyfield Internat., 1996–2002; Vice Chm., UK Cttee, UNICEF, 1996–2000. Order of Merit (Hungary), 1996. *Publications:* Voice in the Wilderness: Imre Nagy and the Hungarian Revolution, 1991; Baltic Approaches, 1996; Hearts, Minds & Interests: Britain's place in the world, 1998; Where East Met West: a Central European journey, 2000; The Narrow Sea: the history of the English Channel, 2003; 1956: power defied, 2006; (ed) Newcomers' Lives: the story of immigrants as told in obituaries from The Times, 2013; contrib. The European, Evening Standard, Guardian, Independent, Independent on Sunday, International Affairs, International Relations, The Observer, The Times and The Tablet. *Address:* 4 Airedale Road, SW12 8SF. *T:* (020) 8675 6629. *Club:* Oxford and Cambridge.
See also J. Unwin.

UNWIN, Timothy; *see* Unwin, P. T. H.

UPPAL, Paul Singh; *b* Birmingham, 14 June 1967; *s* of Surjit and Balbir Uppal; *m* 1991, Kashmir Matto; one *s* two *d*. *Educ:* Harborne Hill State Sch.; Warwick Univ. (BA Pol. 1st cl.). Owner of own business. MP (C) Wolverhampton SW, 2010–15; contested (C) same seat, 2015. *Recreations:* running, reading, theatre and, very rarely, cooking.

UPRICHARD, Dame Mary (Elizabeth), DBE 1998 (OBE 1983); President, UK Central Council for Nursing, Midwifery and Health Visiting, 1993–98 (Member of Council, 1980–93); *b* 23 March 1938; *d* of late Norman Uprichard and Rebecca Uprichard (*née* Gracey). *Educ:* Grosvenor Grammar Sch., Belfast. RSCN, RGN, RM, MTD. Sch. of Midwifery, Belfast, 1974–83; Dir of Midwifery Educn, NI Coll. of Midwifery, 1983–97. Chairman: Nat. Bd for Nursing, Midwifery and Health Visiting, 1988–93 (Mem. Bd, 1980–93); Nurses Welfare Service, 1999; Member: EC Adv. Cttee on Training of Midwives, 1984–98; Council for Professions Supplementary to Medicine, 1997; Council on Social Responsibility, Methodist Church in Ireland, 1994. *Address:* 29 Glenview Avenue, Belfast BT5 7LZ. *T:* (028) 9079 1466.

UPSHAW, Dawn; American soprano; Charles Franklin Kellogg and Grace E. Ramsey Kellogg Professor of the Arts and Humanities, and Artistic Director, Graduate Vocal Arts Program, Bard College Conservatory of Music, since 2004; *b* 17 July 1960; *m* Michael Nott; two *c*. *Educ:* Illinois Wesleyan Univ. (BA Music 1982); Manhattan Sch. of Music (MA 1984). Joined NY Metropolitan Opera, 1984; début, Rigoletto, 1984; other productions include: Magic Flute, Wolf Trap Fest., 1985, Aix-en-Provence Fest., 1988; Death in the Family, Opera Co. of St Louis, 1986; Béatrice et Bénédict, 1993, Theodora, 1996, Glyndebourne Fest.; The Rake's Progress, Stravinsky Fest., Paris, 1996; El Niño, Châtelet, Paris, 2000; Cunning Little Vixen, Royal Opera House, Covent Garden, 2003; numerous recitals and concerts with major orchestras and chamber gps. Numerous recordings (Grammy Awards). (Jtly) Winner, Naumburg Competition, 1985. *Address:* c/o IMG Artists, The Light Box, 111 Power Road, Chiswick, W4 5PY.

UPTON, Prof. Graham, PhD; DL; educational consultant; Director, GU Consultants Ltd, since 2009; Vice Chancellor, Glyndŵr University, since 2015; *b* 30 April 1944; *m* 1st, 1966, Jennifer Ann Clark (marr. diss. 1984); one *s* one *d*; 2nd, 1986, Bebe Speed; one *s* one *d*. *Educ:* Univ. of Sydney (BA, Dip Educn 1966; MA 1969); Univ. of New South Wales (MEd 1973); UC Cardiff, Univ. of Wales (PhD 1978). CPsychol 1988; FBPsS 1996. Teacher, New South Wales, 1966–70; Lectr in Educn, Sydney Teachers' Coll., 1970–71; Lectr in Special Educn, Leeds Poly., 1972–74; University College, Cardiff, 1974–88: Lectr; Sen. Lectr; Reader; Hd of Dept of Educn; Dean, Collegiate Faculty of Educn; Dean, Faculty of Educn and Prof. Studies; University of Birmingham: Prof. of Educnl Psychology and Special Educn and Hd, Sch. of Educn, 1988–93; Pro-Vice-Chancellor, 1993–97; Vice-Chancellor: Oxford Brookes Univ., 1997–2007; Univ. of Cumbria, 2010–11. Oxford Playhouse: Mem. Bd, 2001–09; Chm., 2004–09; Pres., 2009–. Chm., Oxford Expression Technologies, 2009– (non-exec. Dir, 2008–). Mem. Adv. Council, Oxford Trust, 2001–07. Chairman: Oxford Community Partnership, 2002–07; Experience Oxfordshire, 2013–. Governor, Headington Sch., 1999–2007; Mem., Bd of Govs, UWE, 2009–15. Internat. Assoc., UK Leadership Foundn for Higher Educn, 2009–11. AcSS 2000. FRSA 1999. Hon. Fellow: Birmingham Coll. of Food, Tourism and Leisure Studies, 1997; Univ. of Cumbria, 2012. DUniv Oxford Brookes, 2009. Under Sheriff, 2012–13, High Sheriff, 2013–14, DL 2014, Oxfordshire. *Publications:* Physical and Creative Activities for the Mentally Handicapped, 1979; Behaviour Problems in the Comprehensive School, 1980; Educating Children with Behaviour Problems, 1983; Staff Training and Special Educational Needs, 1991; Special Educational Needs, 1992; Special Education in Britain After Warnock, 1993; Emotional and Behavioural Difficulties in Schools, 1994; The Voice of the Child, 1996; Pupils with Severe Learning Difficulties who Present Challenging Behaviour, 1996; Stresses in Special Educational Needs Teachers, 1996; Sound Practice, 1997; Effective Schooling for Pupils with Emotional and Behavioural Difficulties, 1998. *Recreations:* good food, DIY, cycling.

UPTON, Robert Ian William, CBE 2009; strategic policy and planning consultant, since 2014; Senior Examining Inspector, National Infrastructure Division, Planning Inspectorate, 2012–14; *b* 20 Aug. 1951; *s* of late Ronald Alfred Upton and of Iris Eveline Upton; *m* 1987, Mary Faith Higgins; two *d*. *Educ:* Dulwich Coll.; Magdalene Coll., Cambridge (MA); Harvard Business Sch. Hong Kong Government, 1972–91: Clerk of Councils, 1982–84; Sec., Educn Commn, 1985–86; Dep. Sec. for Security, 1986–89; Dir of Planning, 1989–91. Chief Exec., Rushmoor BC, 1992–96; Sec.-Gen., Royal Town Planning Inst., 1996–2009; Jt Deputy Chair, Infrastructure Planning Commn, 2009–12. Vis. Prof., Sheffield Univ., 2003–. FAcSS (AcSS 2010). Hon. MRTPI 2006; Hon. Mem., HK Inst. of Planners, 2014. Hon. LittD Sheffield, 2011. Jt Ed., Planning Theory & Practice, 1999–; Series Ed., RTPI Library Series, 1999–. *Recreations:* reading, walking, book-hunting, Newfoundland dogs.

UPTON, Rt Hon. Simon (David); PC 1999; FRSNZ 1999; Director, Environment, Organisation for Economic Co-operation and Development, since 2010 (Chairman, Round Table on Sustainable Development, 1998–2015); *b* 7 Feb. 1958; *s* of Thomas Wilson Upton and Dorothy Vernon Upton (*née* Hosking); *m* 1984, Bhaady Jane Miller; one *s* one *d*. *Educ:* Southwell Prep. Sch., Hamilton, NZ; St Paul's Collegiate Sch.; Auckland Univ. (BA, LLB Hons); Wolfson Coll., Oxford (Rhodes Schol.; MLitt). MHR (Nat.): Waikato, then Raglan, 1981–96; party list, 1996–99; Minister: for the Envmt, 1990–91 and 1993–99; of Res., Sci. and Technol., 1990–96; of Health, 1990–93; for Crown Res. Insts, 1991–99; of Biosecurity, 1996–97; of State Services, 1998–99; of Cultural Affairs, 1998; Associate Minister of Foreign Affairs, 1996–99; Dir, Global Subsidies Initiative, Internat. Inst. for Sustainable Develt, 2007–08. Dir, Holcim (NZ) Ltd, 2007–10. Advr on climate change to PricewaterhouseCoopers (NZ). Chm., 7th Session of UN Commn on Sustainable Develt, 1999. *Publications:* The Withering of the State, 1986. *Recreations:* gardening and landscaping, NZ geology and botany, music, ski-ing, running, roller-blading. *Address:* Environment Directorate, OECD, 2 rue André-Pascal, Paris 75775 Cedex 16, France. *Club:* Wellington (Wellington, NZ).

UPWARD, Mrs Janet; Chair, Birmingham and Solihull Mental Health Patients' Forum, 2007–08 (Member, 2004–08). *Educ:* Newnham College, Cambridge (BA (Geog. Hons) 1961; MA 1966); Univ. of Birmingham (MSocSci 1993). Sec., Nat. Fedn of Consumer Gps, 1972–82; Mem., 1978–84, Dep. Chm., 1978–83, Domestic Coal Consumers' Council; Chm., Nat. Consumer Congress, 1981–83; Chief Officer, S Birmingham CHC, 1982–90; Project Manager, Birmingham FHSA, 1991–96. Chair, Bromsgrove Concert Club, 2010–.

URBAN, Mark Lee; Diplomatic and Defence Editor, BBC Newsnight, since 1999; *b* London, 26 Jan. 1961; *s* of Harry and Josephine Urban; *m* 1993, Hilary Jane Rosen; one *s* two *d*. *Educ:* King's College Sch., Wimbledon; London Sch. of Economics (BSc (Econ) Internat. Relns). Asst producer, BBC TV, 1983–86; Defence Corresp., Independent, 1986–90; BBC Television: reporter, Newsnight, 1990–93; Middle East Corresp., 1993–94; Diplomatic Corresp., Newsnight, 1995–98. Trustee, Royal Armouries, 2012–. *Publications:* Soviet Land Power, 1983; War in Afghanistan, 1987; Big Boys' Rules: the secret struggle against the IRA, 1992; UK Eyes Alpha: the inside story of British Intelligence, 1996; The Illegal, 1996; The Linguist, 1998; The Man Who Broke Napoleon's Codes, 2001; Rifles: six years with Wellington's legendary sharpshooters, 2003; Generals: ten British commanders who shaped the world, 2005; Fusiliers: eight years with the Redcoats in America, 2007; Task Force Black: the explosive true story of the SAS and the secret war in Iraq, 2010; The Edge: is the military dominance of the West coming to an end?, 2015. *Recreations:* good food, reading, trying to keep fit. *Address:* c/o Newsnight, BBC News Centre, Broadcasting House, Portland Place, W1A 1AA.

URCH, Maj. Gen. Tyrone Richard, CBE 2011 (OBE 2005; MBE 2000); General Officer Commanding Force Troops Command, since 2015; *b* Malta, 12 June 1965; *s* of Christopher Urch and Carole Urch; *m* 1987, Gillian Elizabeth Tidd; one *s* one *d*. *Educ:* Warminster Sch.; Wellbeck Coll.; Cranfield Univ. (BEng Civil Engrg); King's Coll. London (MA). CEng 1997; FICE 2005; FInstRE 2010. Commnd RE, 1984; Regtl duty and on Army Staff, 1984–2003; CO 22 Engr Regt, 2003–05; Comdr, 1st Mechanized Bde, 2008–10; ACOS Ops PJHQ, 2010–12; operational deployments to NI, Bosnia, Iraq; COS Land Forces, Army HQ, 2012–15. *Recreations:* spending time with family, squash, Rugby, mountaineering, dog walking, staying fit, reading, travel. *Address:* HQ Force Troops Command, Building 19A, Trenchard Lines, Upavon, Pewsey, Wilts SN9 6BE.

URE, James Mathie, OBE 1969; British Council Representative, India, and Minister (Education), British High Commission, New Delhi, 1980–84; *b* 5 May 1925; *s* of late William Alexander Ure, and Helen Jones; *m* 1950, Martha Walker Paterson; one *s* one *d*. *Educ:* Shawlands Acad., Glasgow; Glasgow Univ. (MA); Trinity Coll., Oxford (BLitt). Army Service, 1944–47. Lectr, Edinburgh Univ., 1953–59; British Council: Istanbul, 1956–57; India, 1959–68; Dep. Controller, Arts Div., 1968–71; Rep., Indonesia, 1971–75; Controller, Home Div., 1975–80. *Publications:* Old English Benedictine Office, 1952; (with L. A. Hill) English Sounds and Spellings, 1962; (with L. A. Hill) English Sounds and Spellings—Tests, 1963; (with J. S. Bhandari and C. S. Bhandari) Read and Act, 1965; (with C. S. Bhandari) Short Stories, 1966.

URE, Sir John (Burns), KCMG 1987 (CMG 1980); LVO 1968; HM Diplomatic Service, retired; author; *b* 5 July 1931; *s* of late Tam Ure; *m* 1972, Caroline, *d* of late Charles Allan, Roxburghshire; one *s* one *d*. *Educ:* Uppingham Sch.; Magdalene Coll., Cambridge (MA); Harvard Business Sch. (AMP). Active Service as 2nd Lieut with Cameronians (Scottish Rifles), Malaya, 1950–51; Lieut, London Scottish (Gordon Highlanders) TA, 1952–55. Book publishing with Ernest Benn Ltd, 1951–53; joined Foreign (subseq. Diplomatic) Service, 1956; 3rd Sec. and Private Sec. to Ambassador, Moscow, 1957–59; Resident Clerk, FO, 1960–61; 2nd Sec., Leopoldville, 1962–63; FO, 1964–66; 1st Sec. (Commercial), Santiago, 1967–70; FCO, 1971–72; Counsellor, and intermittently Chargé d'Affaires, Lisbon, 1972–77; Head of South America Dept, FCO, 1977–79; Ambassador to Cuba, 1979–81; Asst Under-Sec. of State for the Americas, FCO, 1981–84; Ambassador to Brazil, 1984–87, to Sweden, 1987–91. UK Comr Gen., Expo 92, 1990–92. Director: Thomas Cook Group, 1991–99; Sotheby's Scandinavia AB, 1991–99; CSE Aviation, 1992–94; Consultant: Robert Fleming & Co. (merchant bankers), 1995–98; Ecosse Films, 1997–99; European Risk Mgt Consultants, 1997–2000; Sotheby's Scandinavia, 1999–. Chairman: panel of judges, Thomas Cook Travel Book of the Year Award, 1991–2000; Anglo-Swedish Soc., 1992–96; Anglo-Brazilian Chamber of Commerce, 1994–96. Pres., Weald of Kent Protection Soc., 2005–11. Trustee, Leeds Castle Foundn, 1995–2006. Life Fellow and Mem. Council, RGS, 1982–84. Comdr, Mil. Order of Christ, Portugal, 1973. *Publications:* Cucumber Sandwiches in the Andes, 1973 (Travel Book Club Choice); Prince Henry the Navigator, 1977 (History Guild Choice); The Trail of Tamerlane, 1980 (Ancient History Club Choice); The Quest for Captain Morgan, 1983; Trespassers on the Amazon, 1986; Central and South America sections, in RGS History of World Exploration, 1990; A Bird on the Wing: Bonnie Prince Charlie's flight from Culloden retraced, 1992; Diplomatic Bag, 1994; The Cossacks, 1999; In Search of Nomads, 2003; Pilgrimage: the great adventure of the Middle Ages, 2006; (contrib.) The Seventy Great Journeys in History, 2006; Shooting Leave: spying out Central Asia in the Great Game, 2009; (contrib.) The Great Explorers, 2010; Sabres on the Steppes, 2012; travel articles in Daily and Sunday Telegraph; book reviews in TLS and Country Life; biographies for Oxford DNB. *Recreation:* travelling uncomfortably in remote places and writing about it comfortably afterwards. *Address:* Netters Hall, Hawkhurst, Kent TN18 5AS. *T:* (01580) 752191. *Clubs:* White's, Beefsteak, Pilgrims.

URQUHART, Sir Brian (Edward), KCMG 1986; MBE 1945; Scholar-in-Residence, Ford Foundation, 1986–96; an Under-Secretary-General, United Nations, 1974–86; *b* 28 Feb. 1919; *s* of Murray and Bertha Urquhart; *m* 1st, 1944, Alfreda Huntington (marr. diss. 1963); two *s* one *d*; 2nd, 1963, Sidney Damrosch Howard; one *s* one *d*. *Educ:* Westminster; Christ Church, Oxford (Hon. Student, 1985). British Army: Dorset Regt and Airborne Forces, N Africa, Sicily and Europe, 1939–45; Personal Asst to Gladwyn Jebb, Exec. Sec. of Preparatory Commn of UN, London, 1945–46; Personal Asst to Trygve Lie, 1st Sec.-Gen. of UN, 1946–49; Sec., Collective Measures Cttee, 1951–53; Mem., Office of Under-Sec.-Gen. for Special Political Affairs, 1954–71; Asst Sec.-Gen., UN, 1972–74; Exec. Sec., 1st and 2nd UN Conf. on Peaceful Uses of Atomic Energy, 1955 and 1958; active in organization and direction of UN Emergency Force in Middle East, 1956; Dep. Exec. Sec., Preparatory Commn of Internat. Atomic Energy Agency, 1957; Asst to Sec.-Gen.'s Special Rep. in Congo, July–Oct. 1960; UN Rep. in Katanga, Congo, 1961–62; responsible for organization and direction of UN peace-keeping ops and special political assignments. Hon. LLD: Yale, 1981; Tufts, 1985; Grinnell, 1986; State Univ. NY, 1986; Warwick, 1989; DUniv: Essex, 1981; City Univ. NY, 1986; Hon. DCL Oxford, 1986; Hon. DHL Colorado, 1987; Hon. DLitt: Keele, 1987; Cambridge, 2005; Brown, 2006, Amherst, 2008. *Publications:* Hammarskjold, 1972; A Life in Peace and War (autobiog.), 1987; Decolonization and World Peace, 1989; (with Erskine Childers) A World in Need of Leadership: tomorrow's United Nations, 1990; Ralph Bunche: an American life, 1993; (with Erskine Childers) Renewing the United Nations System, 1994; A World in Need of Leadership: tomorrow's United Nations, a fresh appraisal, 1996; various articles and reviews on internat. affairs. *Address:* 50 West 29th Street, Apt 11E, New York, NY 10001, USA; PO Box 384, Tyringham, MA 01264, USA. *T:* (212) 6796358. *Club:* Century (New York).

URQUHART, Rt Rev. David Andrew; *see* Birmingham, Bishop of.

URQUHART, Lawrence McAllister, CA; Chairman, BAA plc, 1998–2002 (Director, 1993–2002); *b* 24 Sept. 1935; *s* of Robert and Josephine Urquhart; *m* 1961, Elizabeth Catherine Burns; three *s* one *d*. *Educ:* Strathallan; King's Coll., London (LLB). CA 1961. Price Waterhouse & Co., 1957–62; Shell International Petroleum, 1962–64; P. A. Management Consultants, 1964–68; Charterhouse Gp, 1968–74; TKM Gp, 1974–77; Burmah Oil, subseq. Burmah Castrol, 1977–99: Gp Man. Dir, 1985–88; Chief Exec., 1988–93; Chm., 1990–98; non-exec. Dir, 1998–99. Chairman: English China Clays, 1995–99 (Dir, 1991–99); Scottish Widows plc (formerly Scottish Widows' Fund and Life Assurance Soc.), 1995–2001 (non-exec. Dir, 1992–2001); non-executive Director: Imerys SA, 1999–2002; Lloyds TSB Bank plc, 2000–02; Lloyds TSB Group plc, 2000–02. *Recreations:* golf, music. *Club:* Royal Mid-Surrey Golf.

URQUHART, Linda Hamilton, (Lady Burns), OBE 2012; Chairman, Morton Fraser, since 2011; *b* Edinburgh, 21 Sept. 1959; *d* of Douglas Hamilton Urquhart and Ina Allan Urquhart; *m* 1988, David Spencer Burns, (Hon. Lord Burns, a Senator of the College of Justice in Scotland); two *d*. *Educ:* James Gillespie's High Sch.; Univ. of Edinburgh (LLB, DipLP). Admitted as solicitor, 1982; Partner, 1985–99, Chief Exec., 1999–2011, Morton Fraser. Non-executive Director: ESPC Gp of cos, 2005–09; Investors in People Scotland, 2011– (Chm., 2011–). Mem. Bd, Scottish Enterprise, 2011–. Chm., CBI Scotland, 2009–11; Mem. Bd, CBI, 2011–. Non-executive Director: Adam Bank, 2012–; Edinburgh Airport Ltd, 2013–. Mem., Develt Bd, Prince's Trust Scotland, 2011–13. Trustee: Royal Scottish Acad. Foundn, 2013–; Marie Curie Cancer Care, 2014–. Mem., Soc. of WS, 1985. Ambassador, Girlguiding UK, 2008–. Co-Ed., Green's Property Law Bulletin, 1997–. *Recreations:* sailing, walking, ski-ing, golf, singing. *Address:* Morton Fraser, Quartermile Two, 2 Lister Square, Edinburgh EH3 9GL. *T:* (0131) 247 1020, *Fax:* (0131) 247 1007. *E:* linda.urquhart@morton-fraser.com. *Club:* Royal Highland Yacht.

URQUHART, His Honour Peter William Gordon; a Circuit Judge, 1992–2001; *b* 18 March 1934; *s* of Gordon Eldridge Urquhart and Constance Margaret (*née* Taylor); *m* 1965, Carolyn Hemingway Hines; one *s* one *d*. *Educ:* Liverpool Coll.; Peterhouse, Cambridge (MA, LLB). Admitted solicitor, 1960. Member: Lord Chancellor's Legal Aid Adv. Cttee, 1974–80; Equal Opportunities Commn, 1977–82. *Recreations:* book collecting, reading, gardening, early music, jazz. *Address:* Braehead, 19 Poplar Road, Prenton, Merseyside CH43 5TB. *T:* (0151) 652 4043. *Club:* Athenæum (Liverpool).

URQUHART IRVINE, Oliver Henry, FSA, FRAS; Librarian, Royal Library, and Assistant Keeper, Royal Archives, since 2014; *b* Carlisle, 11 Jan. 1974; *s* of Robert John Macferson Irvine and Lesley Marion Irvine (*née* Urquhart); *m* 2002, Elizabeth Jane Over; one *s* one *d*. *Educ:* Ampleforth Coll.; Courtaulds Inst., Univ. of London (BA 1966); Univ. of Amsterdam (MA 1997); Coll. of Law (Grad. Dip. Law); Inst. of Art Law (Postgrad. Dip. Art Law 2007; Dip. Art Profession Law and Ethics 2008). Specialist, Books and MSS Dept, Christie's, 1997–99; antiquarian bookseller, Maggs Bros Ltd, 1999–2005; British Library: Cultural Property Manager, 2005–10; Hd, Asian Middle Eastern and African Dept, 2010–12; Hd, BL Qatar Foundn Partnership, 2011–14. Sen. Associate Mem., Hughes Hall, Cambridge, 2012–. Gov., Tottenhall Infants Sch., 2012–14. FSA 2008; FRAS 2011. *Recreations:* reading, music, wine, outdoors, cycling, photography. *Address:* Royal Library, Windsor Castle, Windsor SL4 1NJ. *T:* (01753) 868286. *E:* oliver.urquhartirvine@royalcollection.org.uk. *Clubs:* Athenæum, Savile.

URSELL, Rev. Canon Philip Elliott; Principal, Pusey House, Oxford, 1982–2003 (Governor, 2006–13); Fellow, St Cross College, Oxford, 1982–2003; Warden, Society of The Most Holy Trinity, Ascot Priory, 1984–2013; *b* 3 Dec. 1942; *o s* of late Clifford Edwin Ursell and Hilda Jane Ursell (*née* Tucker). *Educ:* Cathays High Sch.; University Coll. Cardiff (Craddock Wells Exhibnr; BA); St Stephen's House, Oxford. MA Oxon. DD Nashotah House, Wisconsin. Curate of Newton Nottage, Porthcawl, 1968–71; Asst Chaplain of University Coll. Cardiff, 1971–77; Chaplain of Polytechnic of Wales, 1974–77; Chaplain, Fellow and Dir of Studies in Music, Emmanuel Coll., Cambridge, 1977–82. Bishop's Commissary for Province of Canterbury, and Canon of Rio Grande, 2005–. Select Preacher, Harvard Univ., 1982, 1983, 1996, 1997; Univ. Preacher, Harvard Summer Sch., 1985. Examining Chaplain to the Bishop of London, 1987–2010. Chairman: Number One Trust Fund, 1991–; Soc. for Maintenance of the Faith, 1995–; Anglo-Catholic Ordination Candidates Fund, 2003–. Gov., Heathfield Sch., 2008–. Mem. Governing Body, Church in Wales, 1971–77. *Recreations:* fine wines, opera, championing lost causes. *Address:* 273 Hayes Apartments, Cardiff CF10 1BZ. *T:* (029) 2132 8359.

URWICK, Sir Alan (Bedford), KCVO 1984; CMG 1978; Serjeant at Arms, House of Commons, 1989–95; *b* 2 May 1930; *s* of late Col Lyndall Fownes Urwick, OBE, MC and Joan Wilhelmina Saunders (*née* Bedford); *m* 1960, Marta, *o d* of Adhemar Montagne; three *s*. *Educ:* Dragon Sch.; Rugby (Schol.); New Coll., Oxford (Exhibnr). 1st cl. hons Mod. History 1952. Joined HM Foreign (subseq. Diplomatic) Service, 1952; served in: Brussels, 1954–56; Moscow, 1958–59; Baghdad, 1960–61; Amman, 1965–67; Washington, 1967–70; Cairo, 1971–73; seconded to Cabinet Office as Asst Sec., Central Policy Review Staff, 1973–75; Head of Near East and N Africa Dept, FCO, 1975–76; Minister, Madrid, 1977–79; Ambassador to Jordan, 1979–84; Ambassador to Egypt, 1985–87; High Comr to Canada, 1987–89. Chm., Anglo-Jordanian Soc., 1997–2001. KStJ 1982. Grand Cordon, first class, Order of Independence (Jordan), 1984. *Address:* The Moat House, Slaugham Place, near Haywards Heath, Sussex RH17 6AL. *Club:* Garrick.

URWIN, Rt Rev. Lindsay Goodall, OGS; Rector, Christ Church, Brunswick, since 2015; Bishop with responsibility for the care of Anglican Schools, Diocese of Melbourne, since 2015; Hon. Assistant Bishop of Norwich, since 2009; *b* 13 March 1956. *Educ:* Camberwell GS, Australia; Ripon Coll., Cuddesdon; Heythrop Coll., Univ. of London (MA 2003). Ordained deacon, 1980, priest, 1981; Curate, St Peter, Walworth, 1980–83; Vicar, St Faith, N Dulwich, 1983–88; Diocesan Missioner, Chichester, 1988–93; Area Bishop of Horsham, 1993–2009; Guardian, 2006–15, Administrator, 2009–15, Shrine of Our Lady of Walsingham, Norfolk, now Guardian Emeritus. Honorary Assistant Bishop: Dio. of Chichester, 2009–15; Dio. of Peterborough, 2011–15; Dio. of Ely, 2011–15. Nat. Chm., Church Union, 1995–98. Member: OGS, 1991– (UK Provincial, 1996–2005); Coll. of Evangelists, 1999–. Provost, Southern Region, Woodard Corp. of Schs, 2006–15. Hon. DD Nashotah House, Wisconsin, 2011. *Publications:* (ed jtly) Youthful Spirit, 1999. *Address:* Christ Church, 8 Glenlyon Road, Brunswick, Vic 3056, Australia. *T:* (3) 93801064.

URWIN, Peter; *see* Urwin, T. P.

URWIN, Roger John, CBE 2007; PhD; FREng, FIET; Chairman, Utilico Investments Ltd (formerly Utilico Ltd), since 2010; *b* 8 Feb. 1946. *Educ:* Watford Grammar Sch.; Weston-super-Mare Grammar Sch.; Southampton Univ. (BSc 1964; PhD 1971). CEng; FIET (FIEE 1990). Various appts with CEGB, 1971–85; Dir of Engrg, Midlands Electricity Bd, 1985–90; Man. Dir, subseq. Chief Exec., London Electricity, 1990–95; Dir, 1995–2001, Chief Exec., 2001–02, Nat. Grid Gp; Chief Exec., Nat. Grid Transco plc, 2002–06. Chm., Alfred McAlpine plc, 2007–08 (non-exec. Dir, 2006–08); non-executive Director: Special Utilities Investment Trust plc, 1993–2003; TotalFinaElf Exploration UK plc, 1996–2003; Utilico Investment Trust plc, 2003–10; Canadian Utilities Ltd, 2007–. FREng (FEng 1998).

URWIN, (Terence) Peter; public sector consultant, since 2001; Director of Administration and County Solicitor, Northumberland County Council, 1990–2000; *b* 28 Oct. 1948; *s* of John Robson Urwin; *m* 1971, Mary Theresa Smith; one *d*. *Educ:* Durham Johnston Sch.; Liverpool Univ. (LLB Hons). Solicitor. Durham County Council: Asst Solicitor, 1973–74; Asst Clerk of the Council, 1974–86; Dep. County Solicitor, 1986–90. Clerk to the Lieutenancy, Northumberland, 1990–2000. Secretary, Northumberland Advisory Committee: Justices of the Peace, 1990–2000; Gen. Comrs of Income Tax, 1990–2000. Mem. Council, Law Soc., 1997–2001. *Recreations:* Rugby, walking, crosswords, motorcycling. *Address:* Buckburns, Brancepeth Village, Durham City DH7 8DT. *T:* (0191) 378 3086.

USBORNE, (Thomas) Peter, MBE 2011; Founder and Managing Director, Usborne Publishing Ltd, since 1973; *b* 18 Aug. 1937; *s* of Thomas George Usborne and Gerda (*née* Just); *m* 1964, Cornelie Tücking; one *s* one *d*. *Educ:* Summer Fields Sch., Oxford; Eton Coll.; Balliol Coll., Oxford (BA); INSEAD, Fontainebleau, France (MBA 1966). Co-Founder and Man. Dir, Private Eye mag., 1962–65; Sen. Scientist, Metra Sigma Martech, 1967–68; Asst to Chm., BPC Publishing Ltd, 1969–70; Publishing Dir, Macdonald Educnl, 1970–73. *Recreations:* flying, gardening, France. *Clubs:* Garrick, Groucho.

USHER, Sir Andrew (John), 8th Bt *cr* 1899, of Norton, Ratho, Midlothian and of Wells, Hobkirk, Roxburghshire; interior decorator and builder; *b* 8 Feb. 1963; *er s* of Sir John Usher, 7th Bt and of Rosemary Margaret, *d* of Col Sir Reginald Houldsworth, 4th Bt, OBE, TD; *S* father, 1998; *m* 1987, Charlotte Louise Alexandra, *o d* of R. B. Eldridge; two *s*. *Educ:* Hilton Coll., S Africa. *Recreations:* golf, fishing. *Heir:* *s* Rory James Andrew Usher, *b* 11 June 1991.

USHER, Rt Rev. Graham Barham; *see* Dudley, Bishop Suffragan of.

USSHER, Kitty; Managing Director, Tooley Street Research, since 2014; Chief Economic Adviser, Portland Communications, since 2013; *b* 18 March 1971; *d* of Patrick Ussher and Susan (*née* Bottomley, now Whitfield); *m* 1999, Peter Colley; one *s* one *d*. *Educ:* Balliol Coll., Oxford (PPE 1993); Birkbeck Coll., London (MSc Econs 1998). Researcher, Labour Party, 1994–97; Economist: EIU, 1997–98; Centre for European Reform, 1998–2000; Chief Economist, Britain in Europe Campaign, 1999–2001; Special Advr to Rt Hon. Patricia Hewitt, MP, at DTI, 2001–04. Mem., Lambeth LBC, 1998–2002. MP (Lab) Burnley, 2005–10. Economic Sec., 2007–08, Exchequer Sec., 2009, HM Treasury; Parly Under-Sec. of State, DWP, 2008–09. Dir, Demos, 2010–11. Chair, Labour in the City, 2012–; Member: Ind. Economists Gp, TheCityUK, 2012–; Financial Services Consumer Panel, 2015–. *Publications:* pamphlets for Demos, Centre for European Reform, Smith Inst., Social Market Foundn, Centre for London. *Recreations:* hill walking, supporting Burnley Football Club. *Address:* c/o Tooley Street Research Ltd, Renaissance Works, 120–122 Bermondsey Street, SE1 3TX.

UTEEM, Cassam; President, Republic of Mauritius, 1992–2002; *b* 22 March 1941; *s* of Omar and Aisha Uteem; *m* 1967, Zohra Uteem; one *s* one *d* (and one *s* decd). *Educ:* Univ. of Mauritius (Dip. Soc. Work); Univ. of Paris VII (LèsL, MPsychol). Mem., Municipal Council, Port Louis, 1969, 1977–79, 1986–88 (Lord Mayor, 1986); MLA Port Louis East/Maritime, 1982–92; Minister of Employment, Social Security and National Solidarity, 1982–83; Opposition Whip, 1983–87; Chm., Public Accounts Cttee, 1988–90; Dep. Prime Minister and Minister of Industry and Industrial Technol., 1990–92. Mem. Bd, Internat. Inst. for Democracy and Electoral Assistance. Hon. DCL Mauritius, 1994; Dr *hc* Aix Marseilles III, 1994. Grand Commander, Order of Star and Key of the Indian Ocean (Republic of Mauritius), 1993. *Recreations:* reading, walking. *Address:* c/o State House, Le Reduit, Mauritius. *T:* 4543021.

UTLEY, Prof. James Henry Paul; Professor of Organic Chemistry, Queen Mary and Westfield College (formerly at Queen Mary College), University of London, 1983–2001, now Emeritus; *b* 11 Sept. 1936; *s* of Victor Eric Utley and Lena Beatrice Utley; *m* 1959, Hazel Wendler (*née* Brown); two *s* two *d*. *Educ:* E. P. Collier Sch., Reading; Univ. of Hull (BSc, PhD); Technische Hogeschool, Delft; University College London; DSc London. CChem, FRSC. NATO Research Fellowships, 1961–62; Queen Mary, later Queen Mary and Westfield College, London: Lectr, 1963–76; Reader in Organic Chemistry, 1976–83; Head of Chemistry, 1987–91, 1997–99; Dean, Faculty of Natural Scis, 1991–94; Mem. Council, 1991–94. Guest Professor: Univ. of Aarhus, 1973; Univ. of Münster, 1985; Ecole Normale Supérieure, Paris, 1994; Univ. of Texas at Austin, 1995. M. M. Baizer Award, Electrochem. Soc., USA, 2000. *Publications:* research and review articles in internat. learned jls on physical-organic chemistry, organic electrochemistry and conversion of biomass. *Recreations:* talking about former activity in walking, bowls and other sports; jazz. *Address:* School of Biological and Chemical Sciences, Queen Mary, University of London, Mile End Road, E1 4NS. *Club:* Heathfield (Wandsworth Common).

UTTERSON, Joanna; *see* Mackle, J.

UTTING, Sir William (Benjamin), Kt 1991; CB 1985; President, Mental Health Foundation, 1999–2014 (Trustee, 1988–97; Vice-President, 1997–99); *b* 13 May 1931; *s* of John William Utting and Florence Ada Utting; *m* 1954, Mildred Jackson; two *s* one *d*. *Educ:* Great Yarmouth Grammar Sch.; New Coll., Oxford (Exhibnr; MA; Hon. Fellow, 1996); Barnett House, Oxford. Probation Officer: Co. Durham, 1956–58; Norfolk, 1958–61; Sen. Probation Officer, Co. Durham, 1961–64; Principal Probation Officer, Newcastle upon Tyne, 1964–68; Lectr in Social Studies, Univ. of Newcastle upon Tyne, 1968–70; Dir of Social Services, Kensington and Chelsea, 1970–76; Chief Social Work Officer, DHSS, 1976–85; Chief Inspector, Social Services Inspectorate, DHSS, subseq. DoH, 1985–91. Member: Chief Scientist's Res. Cttee, DHSS, 1973–76; SSRC, 1979–83; ESRC, 1984; Cttee on Standards in Public Life, 1994–2001. Chm., 1991–97, Pres., 1997–2002, NISW. Chairman: Mary Ward House Trust, 1997–2006; Forum on Children and Violence, 1997–2000; Vice-Pres., Nat. Children's Bureau, 2002–07; Member of Council: Caldecott Foundn, 1998–2002; Goldsmiths Coll., London Univ., 1993–2006 (Chair, 2000–06, Hon. Fellow, 2007); Trustee: Joseph Rowntree Foundn, 1991–2006 (Dep. Chm., 2001–05; Chm., 2005–06); CSV, 1991–97; Family Fund Trust, 1996–2000. Pres., New Coll. Soc., 2002–03. Fellow, Centre for Social Policy, Dartington, 2001. Hon. DLitt: UEA, 1992; East London, 1998; Hon. DCL Northumbria, 1997; Hon. DSc Kingston, 2000. *Publications:* Children in the Public Care, 1991; People Like Us, 1997; contribs to professional jls. *Recreations:* literature, music, art. *Address:* 76 Great Brownings, SE21 7HR. *T:* (020) 8670 1201.

UXBRIDGE, Earl of; Benedict Dashiel Thomas Paget; *b* 11 April 1986; *s* and *heir* of Marquess of Anglesey, *qv*.

V

VADERA, Baroness *cr* 2007 (Life Peer); **Shriti Vadera;** PC 2009; Director, Shriti Vadera Ltd, since 2010; Chair, Santander UK, since 2015; *b* Uganda. *Educ:* Somerville Coll., Oxford. With S. G. Warburg, later UBS, 1984–99; Advr to Chancellor of Exchequer and Mem. Council of Econ. Advrs, HM Treasury, 1999–2007; Parliamentary Under-Secretary of State: DFID, 2007–08; BERR, later BIS, and in Cabinet Office, 2008–09. Advr to S Korean Presidency of G20 Gp of Nations, 2009–10. Non-executive Director: BHP Billiton, 2011–15 (Sen. Ind. Dir, 2015–); Astra Zeneca, 2011–. Trustee, Oxfam, 2000–05. *Address:* House of Lords, SW1A 0PW.

VADGAMA, Prof. Pankaj Maganlal, PhD; FRCPath; FRSC; FInstP; FIMMM; FRSB; Professor of Clinical Biochemistry, and Director, Interdisciplinary Research Centre in Biomedical Materials, Queen Mary University of London, since 2000; *b* 16 Feb. 1948; *s* of Maganlal Vadgama and Champaben Vadgama (*née* Gajjar); *m* 1977, Dixa Bakrania; one *s* two *d*. *Educ:* Orange Hill Co. Grammar Sch.; Univ. of Newcastle upon Tyne (MB BS, BSc 1st cl. Hons; PhD 1984). FRCPath 1989; FRSC 1996; FInstP 2000; FIMMM 2001; FRSB (FSB 2012). MRC Trng Fellow, Newcastle Univ., 1978–81; Sen. Registrar in Clin. Biochem., Newcastle Gen. Hosp., 1981–83; Dir, Biosensor Gp, Newcastle Univ., 1983–88; Manchester University: Prof. of Clin. Biochem., 1988–2000; Prof. of Biomed. Materials, 1999–2000. Hon. Consultant Chemical Pathologist: Royal Victoria Infirmary, Newcastle, 1983–88; Hope Hosp., Salford, 1988–2000; Barts Health NHS Trust (formerly Barts and the London NHS Trust), 2000–15. *Publications:* (ed) Surfaces and Interfaces for Biomaterials, 2005; contribs on biosensors, *in vivo* monitoring, biomaterials, biocompatibility and membrane technol. *Recreations:* reading, walking. *Address:* 16 Wellfields, Loughton, Essex IG10 1NX. *T:* (office) (020) 7882 5151, *Fax:* (020) 7882 3390. *Club:* Athenæum.

VAILE, Hon. Mark Anthony James, AO 2012; Chairman: CBD Energy Ltd, 2008–13; Whitehaven Coal, since 2012; *b* 18 April 1956; *s* of George and Sue Vaile; *m* 1976, Wendy Duff; three *d*. *Educ:* Taree High Sch., NSW. Jackaroo, 1973–75; farm machinery retailer, 1975–78; stock, station and real estate agent and auctioneer, 1978–92. Greater Taree City Council: Alderman, 1985–93; Dep. Mayor, 1986–87, 1991–92, 1992–93. Mem., National Party, 1978– (Chm., Wingham Br., 1982–86); Sec., Lyne Electorate Council, 1984–90. MP (National) Lyne, NSW, 1993–2008. Minister: for Transport and Regl Develt, 1997–98; for Agric., Fisheries and Forestry, 1998–99; for Trade, 1999–2006; for Transport and Regl Services, 2006–07; Dep. Prime Minister, 2005–07. Asst Nat. Party Whip, 1994–96; Nat. Party Whip, 1996–97; Dep. Leader, 1999–2005, Leader, 2005–07, Fed. Parly Nat. Party, Australia. Palisade Investment Partners: Chm., Regl Infrastructure Fund, 2008–; Chm., Investor Adv. Gp, 2008–; Mem., Adv. Bd, 2014–. Chm., Aston Resources Ltd, 2009–12; non-executive Director: Virgin Australia (formerly Blue) Hldgs Ltd, 2008–; Stamford Land Ltd, 2009–; Servcorp Ltd, 2011–; HostPlus Investments Pty Ltd, 2012–. *T:* (4) 18229227. *E:* mav@vaileassoc.com.

VAISEY, David George, CBE 1996; FSA; FRHistS; Bodley's Librarian, Oxford, 1986–96, now Emeritus; Keeper of the Archives, Oxford University, 1995–2000; Professorial Fellow then Fellow by Special Election, Exeter College, Oxford, 1975–2000, now Emeritus; *b* 15 March 1935; *s* of William Thomas Vaisey and Minnie Vaisey (*née* Payne); *m* 1965, Maureen Anne (*née* Mansell); two *d*. *Educ:* Rendcomb Coll., Glos (schol.); Exeter Coll., Oxford (Exhibnr; BA Mod. Hist., MA). 2nd Lieut, Glos Regt and KAR, 1955–56. Archivist, Staffordshire CC, 1960–63; Asst then Sen. Asst Librarian, Bodleian Liby, 1963–75; Dep. Keeper, Oxford Univ. Archives, 1966–75; Keeper of Western Manuscripts, Bodleian Liby, 1975–86. Vis. Prof., Liby Studies, UCLA, 1985. Hon. Res. Fellow, Dept of Library, Archive and Information Studies, UCL, 1987–. Member: Royal Commn on Historical Manuscripts, 1986–98; Adv. Council on Public Records, 1989–94; Expert Panel on Museums, Libraries and Archives, Heritage Lottery Fund, 1999–2005; Archive, Libraries and Information Adv. Cttee, English Heritage, 1999–2002; Chm., Nat. Council on Archives, 1988–91. Vice-Pres., British Records Assoc., 1998–2006; Pres., Soc. of Archivists, 1999–2002. FRHistS 1973; FSA 1974. Hon. Fellow, Kellogg Coll., Oxford, 1996. Encomienda, Order of Isabel the Catholic (Spain), 1989. *Publications:* Staffordshire and The Great Rebellion (jtly), 1964; Probate Inventories of Lichfield and District 1568–1680, 1969; (jtly) Victorian and Edwardian Oxford from old photographs, 1971; (jtly) Oxford Shops and Shopping, 1972; (jtly) Art for Commerce, 1973; Oxfordshire: a handbook for students of local history, 1973, 2nd edn 1974; The Diary of Thomas Turner 1754–65, 1984; Bodleian Library Treasures, 2015; articles in learned jls and collections. *Address:* 3 Stonehill Lane, Southmoor, Oxon OX13 5HU.

VAITILINGAM, Adam Skanda; QC 2010; a Recorder, since 2004; *b* Clevedon, 29 Nov. 1963; *s* of Skanda Vaitilingam and Angela Vaitilingam; *m* 2012, Sarah Gibson; one *d*. *Educ:* Bristol Grammar Sch.; King's Coll., Cambridge (BA 1986). Called to the Bar, Middle Temple, 1987. *Publications:* (jtly) The Rough Guide to Jamaica, 1995. *Recreations:* ski-ing, cricket, Bristol City FC. *Address:* Albion Chambers, Broad Street, Bristol BS1 1DR. *T:* (0117) 927 2144.

VAIZEY, Lady; Marina Vaizey, CBE 2009; writer, lecturer and art critic; Editor, National Art Collections Fund Publications, 1991–94 (Editorial Consultant, 1994–98); *b* 16 Jan. 1938; *o d* of late Lyman and Ruth Stansky; *m* 1961, Lord Vaizey (*d* 1984); two *s* one *d*. *Educ:* Brearley Sch., New York; Putney Sch., Putney, Vermont; Radcliffe Coll., Harvard Univ. (BA Medieval History and Lit.); Girton Coll., Cambridge (BA, MA). Art Critic: Financial Times, 1970–74; Sunday Times, 1974–92; Dance Critic, Now!, 1979–81. Member: Arts Council, 1976–79 (Mem. Art Panel, 1973–79, Dep. Chm., 1976–79); Advisory Cttee, DoE, 1975–81; Paintings for Hospitals, 1974–90; Cttee, Contemporary Art Soc., 1975–79, 1980–94 (Hon. Sec., 1988–94); Hist. of Art and Complementary Studies Bd, CNAA, 1978–82; Photography Bd, CNAA, 1979–81; Fine Art Bd, CNAA, 1980–83; Passenger Services Sub-Cttee, Heathrow Airport, 1979–83; Visual Arts Adv. Cttee, British Council, 1987–2004; Crafts Council, 1988–94; Art Wkg Gp, National Curriculum, DES, 1990–91; Cttee, 20th Century Soc., 1995–98; Gov., South Bank Bd, 1993–2003; Trustee: Nat. Mus and Galls on Merseyside, 1986–2001; Geffrye Mus., London, 1990–2010; Imperial War Mus., 1991–2003 (Mem. Council, Friends of Imperial War Mus., 2003–); London Open House, 1996–2008; Internat. Rescue Cttee UK, 1997–2007; The Musical Brain, 2010–; Contemp. Applied Arts, 2014–; Mem. Council, Friends of the V&A, 2001–13 (Chm., 2006–13); Gov., Nat. Army Mus., 2001–08 (Mem. Council, Friends of Nat. Army Mus., 2003–06); Exec. Dir, Mitchell Prize for the Hist. of Art, 1976–87. Governor: Camberwell Coll. of Arts and Crafts, 1971–82; Bath Acad. of Art, Corsham, 1978–81. Curated: Critic's Choice, Tooth's, 1974; Painter as Photographer, touring exhibn, UK, 1982–85; Shining Through, Crafts Council, 1995. Turner Prize Judge, 1997. *Publications:* 100 Masterpieces of Art, 1979; Andrew Wyeth, 1980; The Artist as Photographer, 1982; Peter Blake, 1985; Christiane Kubrick, 1990; Christo, 1990; Sorensen, 1994; Picasso's Ladies, 1998; Sutton Taylor, 1999; Felim Egan, 1999; (with Charlotte Gere) Great Women Collectors, 1999; (ed) Art, the Critics' Choice, 1999; Magdalene Odundo, 2001; The British Museum Smile, 2002; Colin Rose, 2003; Wendy Ramshaw, 2004; Andrew Logan, 2009; Room of Dreams, 2012; Being Tracey, 2012; Lucian Freud: mapping the human, 2012; Documents and Dreams, 2013; Between Dream and Nightmare: a view of modern German art, 2014. *Address:* 41 Brackley Road, Chiswick, W4 2HW. *T:* (020) 8994 7994. *E:* marinavaizey@virginmedia.com. *Club:* Athenæum.

See also Hon. E. H. B. Vaizey.

VAIZEY, Hon. Edward Henry Butler, (Ed); MP (C) Wantage, since 2005; Minister of State, Department for Culture, Media and Sport and Department for Business, Innovation and Skills, since 2014; *b* 5 June 1968; *s* of Baron Vaizey and of Lady Vaizey, *qv*; *m* 2005, Alexandra Mary Jane Holland; one *s* one *d*. *Educ:* St Paul's Sch., London; Merton Coll., Oxford (BA 1989, MA 2004); City Univ. (Dip. Law 1992). Desk Officer, Conservative Res. Dept, 1989–91; called to the Bar, Middle Temple, 1993, practised as barrister, 1993–96; Director: Public Policy Unit, 1996–97; Politics Internat., 1997–98; Consolidated Communications, 1998–2003; Chief Speech Writer to Leader of the Opposition, 2004. Opposition frontbench spokesman on the arts, 2006–10; Parliamentary Under-Secretary of State: BIS, 2010–11; DCMS, 2010–14. Contested (C) Bristol East, 1997. Exec. Dir, Edexcel Ltd, 2007–10. Vice-Chm., National Churches Trust, 2008–10; Trustee, Heritage of London Trust, 2009–10. Mem. Bd, Bush Th., 2009–10. Pres., Didcot Town FC, 2005–. Fellow, Radio Acad., 2015. Hon. FRIBA 2010. *Publications:* (ed with M. Gove and N. Boles) A Blue Tomorrow, 2001; (ed with M. McManus) The Blue Book on Transport, 2002; (ed) The Blue Book on Health, 2002. *Address:* House of Commons, SW1A 0AA. *T:* (020) 7219 3000. *E:* vaizeye@parliament.uk. *Club:* Soho House.

VAJDA, Christopher Stephen; a Judge of the Court of Justice of the European Union, since 2012; *b* 6 July 1955; *s* of late Stephen Vajda and of Heidi Vajda (*née* Schmalhorst); *m* 2012, Brenda Wing-Yin Chow; one *s*. *Educ:* Winchester Coll.; Corpus Christi Coll., Cambridge (MA); Inst d'Etudes Européennes, Brussels (Licence spéciale en droit européen). Called to the Bar, Gray's Inn, 1979 (Bencher 2004), NI, 1996; QC 1997; a Recorder, 2002–12. Mem., Supplementary Panel, Treasury Counsel, 1993–97. *Publications:* (contrib.) Bellamy & Child, Common Market Law of Competition, 3rd edn 1987 to 6th edn 2008. *Recreations:* architecture, opera, theatre, tennis. *Address:* Court of Justice of the European Union, L-2925 Luxembourg. *Club:* Royal Automobile.

VAJPAYEE, Atal Bihari; Member, Lok Sabha, 1957–62, 1967–84 and 1991–2009; Prime Minister of India, May 1996 and 1998–2004; Leader, Bharatiya Janata Party Parliamentary Party, 1980–84, 1986–91 and 1993–2004; *b* Gwalior, Madhya Pradesh, 25 Dec. 1926; *s* of Shri Krishna Bihari; unmarried. *Educ:* Victoria Coll., Gwalior; D.A.V. Coll., Kanpur (MA). Journalist and social worker. Arrested in freedom movement, 1942; Founder Mem., Jana Sangh, 1951–77; Leader, Jana Sangh Parly Party, 1957–77; Pres., Bharatiya Jana Sangh, 1968–73; detained 26 June 1975, during Emergency; Founder Member: Janata Party, 1977–80; Bharatiya Janata Party, 1980– (Pres., 1980–86). Mem., Rajya Sabha, 1962–67 and 1986–91; Minister of External Affairs, 1977–79; Leader of the Opposition, Lok Sabha, 1993–98; Chairman: Cttee on Govt Assurances, 1966–67; Public Accounts Cttee, 1969–70, 1991–92; Cttee on Petitions, 1990–91. Member: Parly Goodwill Mission to E Africa, 1965; Parly Delegns to Australia, 1967, Eur. Parlt, 1983; Member: Indian Delegation: to CPA meetings in Canada, 1966, Zambia, 1980, IOM, 1984; to IPU Confs in Japan, 1974, Sri Lanka, 1975, Switzerland, 1984; to UN Gen. Assembly, 1988, 1989, 1990, 1991. Mem., Nat. Integration Council, 1958–62, 1967–73, 1986, 1991. President: All India Station Masters and Asst Station Masters Assoc., 1965–70; Pandit Deen Dayal Upadhyay Smarak Samiti, 1968–84; Pandit Deen Dayal Upadhyaya Janma Bhumi Smarak Samiti, 1979–. Formerly Editor: Rashtra-dharma; Panchajanya; Veer Arjun. *Publications:* Lok Sabha Mein Atalji (collection of speeches); Qaidi Kavirai ki Kundaliyan; New Dimensions of India's Foreign Policy; Sansad Mein Teen Dashak (collection of speeches). *Address:* Shinde ki Chhawni, Gwalior, MP, India.

VALE, Brian, CBE 1994 (OBE 1977); Regional Director for Middle East and North Africa, British Council, 1995; retired; *b* 26 May 1938; *s* of Leslie Vale and May (*née* Knowles); *m* 1966, Margaret Mary Cookson; two *s*. *Educ:* Sir Joseph Williamson's Mathematical Sch., Rochester; Keele Univ. (BA, DipEd); King's Coll., London (MPhil). HMOCS, N Rhodesia, 1960–63; Assistant to Comr for N Rhodesia, London, 1963–64; Educn Attaché, Zambia High Commn, London, 1964–65; British Council: Rio de Janeiro, 1965–68; Appts Div., 1968–72; Educn and Sci. Div., 1972–75; Rep., Saudi Arabia, 1975–78; Dep. Controller, Educn and Sci. Div., 1978–80; Dir Gen., Tech. Educn and Trng Orgn for Overseas Countries, 1980–81; Controller, Sci., Technol. and Educn Div., 1981–83; Rep. in Egypt, and Cultural Counsellor, British Embassy, Cairo, 1983–87; Asst Dir Gen., 1987–90; Dir, Spain, and Cultural Attaché, British Embassy, Madrid, 1991–95. Chm., Internat. Family Health, 1998–2005; Vice Pres., Navy Records Soc., 2009–13 (Mem. Council, 2005–09, 2013–). Chm., St Alfege Develt Cttee, Greenwich, 2004–10. Medalha Merito Tamandaré (Brazil), 1997. *Publications:* Independence or Death: British sailors and Brazilian independence, 1996; A War Betwixt Englishmen: Argentina versus Brazil in the River Plate 1825–30, 1999; A Frigate of King George: life and duty on HMS Doris 1807–1829, 2001; The Audacious Admiral Cochrane, 2004; Cochrane in the Pacific: fortune and freedom in Spanish America, 2007; (with Prof. Griffith Edwards) Physician to the Fleet: the life and times of Thomas Trotter, 1760–1832, 2011; contribs to specialist jls on naval hist. *Recreations:* reading, talking, naval history. *Address:* 40 Gloucester Circus, SE10 8RY. *T:* (020) 8858 6233.

VALENTIA, 16th Viscount *cr* 1622 (Ire.); **Francis William Dighton Annesley;** Bt 1620; Baron Mountnorris 1628; *b* 29 Dec. 1959; *s* of 15th Viscount Valentia and of Anita Phyllis Annesley (*née* Joy); *S* father, 2005; *m* 1982, Shaneen Therese Hobbs; two *d*. *Educ:* Falcon Coll., Bulawayo (DipAgr; BCom (Mktg)). *Recreations:* golf, scuba diving. *Heir: b* Hon. Peter John Annesley [*b* 18 Dec. 1967; *m* 1997, Deborah Ann Coelen; five *s*]. *Address:* 3 Ruby Close, Wokingham, Berks RG41 3TX. *T:* (0118) 989 0258. *E:* fwd.annesley@live.co.uk.

VALENTINE, Baroness *cr* 2005 (Life Peer), of Putney in the London Borough of Wandsworth; **Josephine Clare Valentine;** Chief Executive, London First, since 2003; *b* 8 Dec. 1958; *d* of Michael and Shirley Valentine; *m* 1990, Simon Acland; two *d*. *Educ:* St Hugh's Coll., Oxford Univ. (BA Hons Maths and Philosophy). Manager, Corporate Finance, Barings, 1981–88; Chief Exec., Blackburn Partnership, 1988–90; Sen. Manager, Planning and Corporate Finance, BOC Gp, 1990–95; Chief Exec., Central London Partnership, 1995–97; London First, 1997–. Comr, Nat. Lottery, 2001–05. Mem. Bd, Peabody, 2012–. *Recreations:* piano, bridge, travel. *T:* (020) 7665 1513, *Fax:* (020) 7665 1537.

VALENTINE, Caroline, (Mrs Malcolm Valentine); *see* Charles, Caroline.

VALIANT, Prof. Leslie Gabriel, FRS 1991; T. Jefferson Coolidge Professor of Computer Science and Applied Mathematics, Harvard University, since 2001; *b* 28 March 1949; *s* of Leslie Valiant and Eva Julia (*née* Ujlaki); *m* 1977, Gayle Lynne Dyckoff; two *s*. *Educ:* Tynemouth High Sch.; Latymer Upper Sch.; King's Coll., Cambridge (MA; Hon. Fellow, 2013); Imperial Coll., London (DIC); Warwick Univ. (PhD). Vis. Asst Prof., Carnegie Mellon Univ., Pittsburgh, 1973–74; Lecturer: Leeds Univ., 1974–76; Edinburgh Univ., 1977–81, Reader 1981–82; Gordon McKay Prof. of Computer Sci. and Applied Maths, Harvard Univ., 1982–2001. Vis. Prof., Harvard Univ., 1982; Vis. Fellow, Oxford Univ. Computing Lab. and Merton Coll., Oxford, 1987–88; Guggenheim Fellow, 1985–86. Fellow, Amer. Assoc. for Artificial Intelligence, 1992; Mem., US NAS, 2001. Dr *hc* École Normale Supérieure, Lyon, 2012; Hon. DSc Warwick, 2013; DMath Waterloo, 2013. Nevanlinna Prize, IMU, 1986; Knuth Prize, ACM/IEEE, 1997; Eur. Assoc. for Theoretical Comp. Sci. Award, 2008; A. M. Turing Award, 2010. *Publications:* Circuits of the Mind, 1994; Probably Approximately Correct, 2013; research papers in scientific jls. *Address:* School of Engineering and Applied Sciences, Harvard University, 33 Oxford Street, Cambridge, MA 02138, USA. *T:* (617) 4955817.

VALIN, Reginald Pierre; business consultant; *b* 8 March 1938; *s* of Pierre Louis Valin and Molly Doreen Valin; *m* 1960, Brigitte Karin Leister; one *d*. *Educ:* Emanuel School. Bank of America, 1959–60; Charles Barker & Sons Ltd, later Charles Barker City, 1960–79: Dir, 1971–73; Man. Dir, 1973–76; Chief Exec., 1976–79; Founder Dir, Valin Pollen, subseq. The VPI Gp: Chm. and Chief Exec., 1979–89, Dep. Chm., 1989–90. *Address:* 38 Monckton Court, Melbury Road, W14 8NF. *T:* (020) 7371 1872.

VALIOS, Nicholas Paul; QC 1991; a Recorder of the Crown Court, since 1986; *b* 5 May 1943; *s* of Nicholas William and Elizabeth Joan Valios; *m* 1967, Cynthia Valerie Horton; one *s* one *d*. *Educ:* Stonyhurst Coll., Lancs. Called to the Bar, Inner Temple, 1964; Mem., SE Circuit. *Recreations:* windsurfing, golf, reading, computers, scuba diving. *Address:* 4 Breams Buildings, EC4A 1HP. *T:* (020) 7092 1900.

VALLANCE, family name of **Baron Vallance of Tummel**.

VALLANCE OF TUMMEL, Baron *cr* 2004 (Life Peer), of Tummel in Perth and Kinross; **Iain David Thomas Vallance,** Kt 1994; Chairman, Royal Conservatoire of Scotland (formerly Royal Scottish Academy of Music and Drama), since 2006; *b* 20 May 1943; *s* of late Edmund Thomas Vallance and Janet Wright Bell Ross Davidson; *m* 1967, Elizabeth Mary McGonnigill (*see* E. M. Vallance); one *s* one *d*. *Educ:* Edinburgh Acad.; Dulwich Coll.; Glasgow Acad.; Brasenose Coll., Oxford (Hon. Fellow, 1997); London Grad. Sch. of Business Studies (MSc). FCIBS 2002. Joined Post Office, 1966; Director: Central Finance, 1976–78; Telecommunications Finance, 1978–79; Materials Dept, 1979–81; British Telecommunications: a Corp. Dir, 1981–2001; Board Mem. for Orgn and Business Systems, 1981–83; Man. Dir, Local Communications Services Div., 1983–85; Chief of Operations, 1985–86; Chief Exec., 1986–95; Chm., 1987–2001 (part-time 1998–2001); Pres. Emeritus, 2001–02. Dir, 1993–2005, Vice-Chm., 1994–2005, Royal Bank of Scotland; Dir, Mobil Corp., 1996–99. Chairman: Nations Healthcare Ltd, 2005–07; Amsphere Ltd, 2006–. Pres., CBI, 2000–02 (Mem., Pres.'s Cttee, 1988–2008); Member, President's Committee: (also Adv. Council), BITC, 1988–2002; Eur. Foundn for Quality Management, 1988–96. Chairman: Eur. Adv. Cttee, New York Stock Exchange, 2000–02 (Mem., 1995–2005); European Services Forum, 2003–07; Dep. Chm., Financial Reporting Council, 2001–02. Member: Internat. Adv. Bd, British-American Chamber of Commerce, 1991–2002; Bd, Scottish Enterprise, 1998–2001; Internat. Adv. Bd, AllianzSE, 1998–; Supervisory Bd, Siemens AG, 2003–13; European Adv. Council, Rothschild Gp, 2003–09. Chm., H of L Econ. Affairs Cttee, 2008–10 (Mem., 2005–07); Mem., H of L Sub Cttee A, Econ. and Financial Affairs and Internat. Trade, 2010–. Vice Pres., Princess Royal Trust for Carers, 1999–2012 (Chm., 1991–98); Trustee, Monteverdi Trust, 1993–2001; Patron, Loughborough Univ., 1996–. Freeman, City of London, 1985; Liveryman, Wheelwrights' Co., 1986–. Hon. Gov., Glasgow Acad., 1993–. Fellow, London Business School, 1989. Hon. DSc: Ulster, 1992; Napier, 1994; City, 1996; Hon. DTech: Loughborough, 1992; Robert Gordon, 1994; Hon. DBA Kingston, 1993; Hon. DEng Heriot-Watt, 1995. *Recreations:* hill walking, music. *Address:* House of Lords, SW1A 0PW.

VALLANCE OF TUMMEL, Lady; *see* Vallance, E. M.

VALLANCE, Air Vice-Marshal Andrew George Buchanan, CB 2003; OBE 1987; FRAeS; Secretary, Defence Press and Broadcasting Advisory Committee, since 2004; *b* 7 April 1948; *s* of George Charles Buchanan Vallance and Dorothy Mabel Vallance (*née* Wooton); *m* 1972, Katharine Ray Fox; one *s* one *d*. *Educ:* RAF Coll., Cranwell; RAF Staff Coll. (psa 1980); Queens' Coll., Cambridge (MPhil Internat. Relns 1988). Commnd RAF, 1969; sqdn pilot with Nos 9, 617 and 27 Sqdns; Flight Comdr, No 50 Sqdn, 1977–79; Personal SO to Air Mem. for Personnel, 1981; OC No 55 Sqdn, 1982–84; Personal SO to CAS, 1984–87; Dir of Defence Studies, 1988–90; Chief of Mil. Co-op., SHAPE, 1991–93; OC RAF Wyton, 1993–95; Dep. Dir, Nuclear Policy, MoD, 1995; Chief, Special Weapons Br., SHAPE, 1996–98; COS, Reaction Forces Air Staff, NATO, 1998–2000; COS and Dep. C-in-C, RAF Personnel Trng Comd, 2000; Exec. Asst to COS, Comd Gp, SHAPE, 2000–04. Chm., Services Sound and Vision Corp., 2009–. FRAeS 1999. Member: RUSI, 1988–; IISS, 1988–. *Publications:* Air Power, 1989; RAF Air Power Doctrine, 1990; The Air Weapon, 1995; contrib. numerous articles to various defence jls. *Recreations:* military history, classical music, structural gardening, strategic studies. *Address:* Ministry of Defence, Main Building, Whitehall, SW1A 2HB. *Club:* Royal Air Force.

VALLANCE, Dr Elizabeth Mary, (Lady Vallance of Tummel); JP; Founder and Chairman, me too, since 1999; Chairman: I CAN, since 2007; Centre for Mental Health, since 2010; Centre for Effective Dispute Resolution, since 2011; National Autism Project, since 2015; *b* 8 April 1945; *e d* of William Henderson McGonnigill and Hon. Jean, *d* of 1st Baron Kirkwood; *m* 1967, Iain David Thomas Vallance (*see* Baron Vallance of Tummel); one *s* one *d*. *Educ:* Univ. of St Andrews (MA Philosophy and Politics (1st Cl. Hons)); London Sch. of Econs and Pol Sci. (MSc Dist.); Univ. of London (PhD); London Business Sch. (Sloan Fellow; sen. mgt course); Harvard Business Sch. (sen. mgt course). Queen Mary College, later Queen Mary and Westfield College, University of London: Asst Lectr, Lectr, Sen. Lectr, Reader in Govt and Politics, 1968–85; Head, Dept of Politics, 1985–88; Vis. Prof., 1990–96; Hon. Fellow, 1997. Chm., St George's Healthcare NHS Trust, 1993–99; Director: HMV Group, 1990–97; Norwich Union plc, 1995–2000; Charter European Trust (formerly Charter Pan-European Trust) plc, 1998–2012 (Sen. Ind. Dir, 2006–12); Health Foundn (formerly PPP Healthcare Medical Trust), 1999–2008 (Vice-Chm., 2003–08); Aviva plc (formerly CGNU) plc, 2000–05; Medical Protection Soc., 2005–. Chm., NHS Adv. Cttee on Distinction, then Clin. Excellence, Awards, 2000–05; Mem., Cttee on Standards in Public Life, 2004–11. Chm. of Govs, James Allen's Girls' Sch., 1991–94; Chm. Council, Inst. of Educn, Univ. of London, 2000–09; Gov., Sutton Valence Sch., 2006–. Member: Adv. Council, Citizenship Foundn, 1988–; Council, Dulwich Picture Gallery Trust, 1995–2000; Council, RSA, 1997–2002; Adv. Council, NCVO, 1998–; Press Complaints Commn Appts Commn, 2009–11. Vice-Pres., Autistica, 2010–. Trustee: Royal Anniversary Trust, 1994–2004; St George's Hosp. Special Trustees, 1999–2001; Playing Alive Foundn, 2004–08; Autism Speaks, 2006–10. Patron: Donaldson Coll., Edinburgh, 1998–2004; Marlow Theatre Develt Trust, 2007–; Sheriffs' and Recorders' Fund, 2008–; Pitlochry Fest. Th., 2011–. Kent Ambassador, 2012–. FRSA 1991; FCGI 2004; Hon. Fellow, Inst. of Educn, 2010; Hon. FCollT 2010. JP Inner London, 1993; High Sheriff, Greater London, 2008–09. Hon. DCL Kent, 2013. Carrington Award, Hon. Co. of Educators, 2014. *Publications:* (ed) The State, Society and Self-destruction, 1975; Women in the House, 1979; (with Davies) Women of Europe, 1982; (with Radice and Willis) MP: the job of a backbencher, 1988; (with Mahoney) Business Ethics in a New Europe, 1992; Business Ethics at Work, 1995; contribs to other books, academic articles, journalism. *Recreations:* writing, reading novels, ski-ing, opera. *Address:* Centre for Mental Health, Maya House, 134–138 Borough High Street, SE1 1LB. *T:* (020) 7827 8362.

VALLANCE, Prof. Patrick John Thompson, MD; FRCP; FMedSci; President, Pharmaceutical R&D, GlaxoSmithKline, since 2012 (Head of Drug Discovery, 2006–10; Senior Vice-President and Head of Medicines Discovery and Development, 2010–12); *b* 17 March 1960; *s* of Peter John Vallance and Barbara Bickford Vallance (*née* Thompson); *m* 1986, Sophia Ann Dexter; two *s* one *d*. *Educ:* Truro Sch.; St George's Hosp. Med. Sch., Univ. of London (BSc 1981; MB BS with Dist. 1984; MD 1990). MRCP 1987, FRCP 1995. Lectr, 1986–90, Sen. Lectr and Consultant Physician, 1990–95, St George's Hosp. Med. Sch.; Prof. of Clin. Pharmacol. and Consultant Physician, 1995–2002, Prof. of Medicine and Hd, Div. of Medicine, 2002–06, UCL. Goulstonian Lectr, RCP, 1996. Chm., Wellcome Trust Pharmacol. and Physiology Panel, 2002–05. FMedSci 1999 (Registrar, 2003–06). Hon. Fellow: Faculty of Medicine, Imperial Coll. London, 2006; UCL, 2007. Hon. DSc London, 2007. Graham Bull Prize, RCP, 2002. *Publications:* (ed jtly) Endothelial Function in Hypertension, 1987; (ed jtly) Endothelium in Human Physiology and Pathophysiology, 1989; contribs to learned jls on pharmacol., vascular biol., and exptl and clin. medicine. *Recreations:* mushrooming, cooking, gardening, playing tennis badly. *Address:* GlaxoSmithKline, GSK House, Brentford, Middx TW8 9GS.

VALLANCE, Philip Ian Fergus; QC 1989; in-house counsel, BLM (formerly Berrymans Lace Mawer), since 2002; *b* 20 Dec. 1943; *o s* of Aylmer Vallance and Helen Gosse; *m* 1973, Wendy, *d* of J. D. Alston; one *s* one *d*. *Educ:* Bryanston; New Coll., Oxford (BA Mod. Hist). Called to the Bar, Inner Temple, 1968. *Recreation:* dining on trains. *Address:* BLM, Plantation Place, 30 Fenchurch Street, EC3M 3BL. *Club:* Travellers (Chm., 2006–10).

VALLANCE WHITE, James Ashton, CB 1997; Fourth Clerk at the Table and Clerk of the Judicial Office, House of Lords, 1983–2002; Clerk to Committee for Privileges (Peerage Claims) 1983–2002; Registrar of Lords' Interests, 1996–2002; *b* 25 Feb. 1938; *s* of Frank Ashton White and Dieudonnée Vallance; *m* 1987, Anne O'Donnell. *Educ:* Allhallows School; Albert Schweitzer College, Switzerland; St Peter's College, Oxford (MA). Clerk, House of Lords, 1961; Clerk of Committees, 1971–78; Chief Clerk, Public Bill Office, 1978–83. *Address:* 14 Gerald Road, SW1W 9EQ. *T:* (020) 7730 7658; Biniparrell, San Luis, Menorca. *T:* (971) 151476. *Clubs:* Brooks's, Beefsteak.

VALLELY, Paul, CMG 2006; writer, broadcaster and consultant; Visiting Professor in Public Ethics and Media, University of Chester, since 2013; Senior Honorary Fellow, Brooks World Poverty Institute, University of Manchester, since 2013; Managing Director, Paul Vallely Consulting Ltd, since 2013; *b* 8 Nov. 1951; *s* of late Victor Terence Vallely and Mary Frances Mannion; *m* 1st, 1972, Heather Cecilia Neil (marr. diss.); one *d*; 2nd, 2000, Christine Lesley Morgan, *qv*; one *s*. *Educ:* St Mary's Coll. Grammar Sch., Middlesbrough; Univ. of Leeds (BA Philosophy and English). Reporter, Feature Writer, Theatre Critic, Yorkshire Post, 1974–80; Asst Features Editor, Sunday Telegraph Magazine, 1980–82; Radio Critic, The Listener, 1980–82; Feature Writer, Mail on Sunday, 1982–84; Home News Reporter and Corresp. in Africa, Belfast and NY, The Times, 1984–89; Sen. Foreign Writer, Religious Affairs Editor, News Editor and Asst Editor, Sunday Correspondent, 1989–90; Land Reform Study, Philippines, Brazil, Eritrea, Christian Aid, 1990; Editor of Irish edn, Sunday Times, 1991–92; Oped Feature Writer, Daily Telegraph, 1992–94; Dep. Editor, The European, 1994; Editor, News Review, Sunday Times, 1994–95; Feature Writer and Leader Writer, The Independent, 1995–2013 (Associate Editor, 2000–13); Exec. Editor, Independent on Sunday, 1999–2000; seconded to PM's Commn for Africa, 2004–05 (co-author report, Our Common Interest, 2005). Columnist: The Tablet, 1996–99 (Dir, 2006–); Third Way, 1995–; Church Times, 2002–; Independent on Sunday, 2008–. Editl Advr, Catholic Bishops' Conf. of England and Wales, 2004, 2011. Lectures: La Casas, Blackfriars, Oxford, 2000; Gilpin, Durham, 2004; Newman, London, 2008; Anthony Storey Meml, 2008, 2014; Greenbelt, 2013, 2015; Ushaw, 2013; Patrick Finn, Dublin, 2014; Fisher, Cambridge, 2014; Seattle, 2015; Inaugural, Chester, 2015. Chair, Catholic Inst. for Internat. Relations, 1995–2001 (Trustee, 1993–2001). Mem., Bd of Corporate Social Responsibility, Waitrose, 2014–. Media Adviser: Christian Aid, 1990–92; CAFOD, 1993–2001; Trustee, Traidcraft, 1992–95; Chair, Traidcraft Exchange, 1995–99. FRSA 1996. Hon. Res. Fellow, Univ. of Manchester, 2009–. Gov., St Joseph's RC Primary Sch., Sale, 2005–09 (Chair, 2006–09). *Publications:* (with David Blundy) With Geldof in Africa, 1985; (with Bob Geldof) Is That It?, 1986; Bad Samaritans: First World ethics and Third World debt, 1990; Promised Lands: stories of power and poverty in the Third World, 1992; (for children) Daniel and the Mischief Boy, 1993; (ed) The New Politics: Catholic social teaching for the 21st century, 1999; The Church and the New Age, 2000; (ed) A Place of Redemption: a Christian approach to punishment and prison, 2004; The Fifth Crusade: George Bush and the Christianisation of the war in Iraq, 2004; (with Bob Geldof) Geldof in Africa, 2005; Hello World: the official Live8 book, 2005; New Labour and the New World Order in Remoralising Britain, 2008; Catholic Social Teaching and The Big Society, 2011; Pope Francis: untying the knots, 2013; Pope Francis: the struggle for the soul of Catholicism, 2015. *Recreation:* Thomas. *Address:* Paul Valley Consulting Ltd, PO Box 165, Sale, Cheshire M33 2YA. *T:* (0161) 973 3456. *E:* paul@paulvallely.com. *W:* www.paulvallely.com. *Club:* Manchester United Football.

van ANDEL, Dr Katharine Bridget, (Mrs T. H. van Andel); *see* Pretty, Dr K. B.

van BESOUW, Jean-Pierre William Gerard, FRCA; FRCPE; President, Royal College of Anaesthetists, 2012–15; *b* Dublin, 20 April 1957; *s* of late Jos van Besouw and of Anne van Besouw; *m* 1987, Dr Liliane Field; one *s* twin *d*. *Educ:* Wyggeston Boys' Grammar Sch., Leicester; Medical Coll. of St Bartholomew's Hosp., Univ. of London (BSc Hons 1978; MB BS 1981). FRCA 1985. Hse Surgeon, Royal Berks Hosp., 1981–82; Hse Physician, 1982, SHO in Anaesthesia, 1982–83, St Bartholomew's Hosp.; SHO in Medicine, Intensive Therapy Unit and Anaesthesia, Whittington Hosp., 1983–84; Registrar in Anaesthesia, St George's Hosp. Gp, 1985–87; Senior Registrar in Anaesthesia: Royal Perth Hosp., Australia,

1986; St Bartholomew's Hosp., Hosp. for Sick Children, Gt Ormond St, Whipps Cross Hosp., Homerton Hosp., 1987–90; Consultant Anaesthetist, St George's Hosp. NHS Trust, 1990–. Hon. Sen. Lectr, St George's Hosp. Med. Sch., later St George's, Univ. of London, 1990–; Hd, St George's Sch. of Anaesthesia, 2002–08. Co-Chm., Med. Adv. Bd, Health Educn England, 2014–; Mem., Adv. Bd, Centre for Workforce Intelligence, 2015–. Mem. Council, RCAnaes, 2008– (Vice Pres., 2010–12). Chm., Assoc. of Cardiothoracic Anaesthetists, 2009–11; Chm., Trustees, Faculty of Intensive Care Medicine, 2012–; Vice Chm., Acad. of Med. Royal Colls, 2013–15. Gov., St George's Hosp., 2014–. FRCPE 2013. Hon. FRCS 2014; Hon. FCAI 2015. Mem. Bd, British Jl of Anaesthesia, 2010–. *Publications:* (contrib.) Guide to the FRCA Examination: the primary, 2001, (ed) 3rd edn 2010. *Recreations:* family, gardening, Rugby (spectator), travel (particularly in SW France). *Address:* Royal College of Anaesthetists, Churchill House, 35 Red Lion Square, WC1R 4SG. *T:* (020) 7092 1500, *Fax:* (020) 7092 1730. *E:* president@rcoa.ac.uk.

van BEURDEN, Bernardus Cornelis Adriana Margriet, (Ben); Chief Executive Officer, Royal Dutch Shell, since 2014; *b* Roosendaal, 23 April 1958; *m* 2008, Stacey Dickson; one *s* three *d*. *Educ:* Delft Univ. of Technol. (Masters degree Chem. Engrg). Royal Dutch Shell: joined 1983; Private Asst to Chm., 2002; Vice Pres., Manufacturing Excellence, 2005–06; Exec. Vice Pres., Chemicals, 2006–12; Downstream Dir, 2013. *Recreations:* reading, running. *Address:* Royal Dutch Shell, Carel van Bylandtlaan 16, 2596 HR The Hague, The Netherlands. *T:* (70) 3779111, *Fax:* (70) 3772780.

VAN BUEREN, Prof. Geraldine; Professor of International Human Rights Law, School of Law, Queen Mary (formerly Queen Mary and Westfield College), University of London, since 1998; *b* Hackney, London, 1955; *d* of Sidney and Ann Van Bueren; *m* 1995, James Michael. *Educ:* LLB Wales; University Coll. London (LLM). Called to the Bar, Middle Temple, Bencher, 2012. WP Schreiner and Internat. Human Rights Law Prof., Univ. of Cape Town, 2002–06. Fellow, Goodenough Coll., London. Visiting Professor: Univ. of Cape Town, 1999; Northwestern Univ., 2005; Vis. Fellow, Kellogg Coll., Oxford, 2005–; Vis. Schol., Baldy Center, SUNY, 1995. Associate Tennant, Doughty St Chambers. Mem., Equality and Human Rights Commn, 2009–12. Non-exec. Dir and Trustee, Save the Children, 2005–09. Co-founder, INTERIGHTS (represented Amnesty Internat. at UN during drafting of Convention on Rights of the Child and UN Rules for Protection of Juveniles Deprived of their Liberty). Member, Advisory Board: Human Rights Watch (Children's Rights Project); British Inst. of Human Rights; René Cassin. Hon. QC 2013. Child Rights Lawyer Award, UNICEF, 2003. *Publications:* The International Law on the Rights of the Child, 1995; Child Rights in Europe, 2008; Law's Duty to the Poor, 2010. *Recreations:* breakfasts in bed, tracking wildlife in the bush. *Club:* Athenæum.

VAN CAENEGEM, Baron Raoul Charles Joseph; Ordinary Professor of Medieval History and of Legal History, University of Ghent, Belgium, 1964–92, now Emeritus; *b* 14 July 1927; *s* of Joseph Van Caenegem and Irma Barbaix; created Baron, 1994; *m* 1954, Patricia Mary Carson; two *s* one *d*. *Educ:* Univ. of Ghent (LLD 1951; PhD 1953); Univ. of Paris; London Univ. Ghent University: Assistant to Prof. of Medieval Hist., 1954; Lectr, 1960. Vis. Fellow, UC, Cambridge, 1968; Arthur L. Goodhart Prof. in Legal Science, and Vis. Fellow of Peterhouse, Cambridge Univ., 1984–85; Erasmus Lectr on the History and Civilization of the Netherlands, Harvard Univ., 1991. Corresp. Fellow, Medieval Acad. of Amer., 1971; Corresp. FBA 1982; Sir Henry Savile Fellow, Merton Coll., Oxford, 1989. Mem. Acad. of Scis, Brussels, 1974; For. Mem., Acad. of Scis, Amsterdam, 1977. Hon. Dr: Tübingen, 1977; Catholic Univ., Louvain, 1984; Paris, 1988. Francqui Prize, Brussels, 1974; Solvay Prize, Brussels, 1990. *Publications:* Royal Writs in England from the Conquest to Glanvill: studies in the early history of the common law, 1959; The Birth of the English Common Law, 1973, 2nd edn 1988; Geschiedenis van Engeland (History of England), 1982, 2nd edn 1997; Judges, Legislators and Professors: chapters in European legal history, 1987; An Historical Introduction to Private Law, 1992; An Historical Introduction to Western Constitutional Law, 1995; Introduction aux sources de l'histoire médiévale, 1997; European Law in the Past and Future: unity and diversity over two millennia, 2002; Historical Considerations on Judicial Review and Federalism in the United States of America, 2003; Engeland Wonderland, 2005; (contrib.) International Encyclopaedia of Comparative Law, 1973. *Recreations:* wine (Bordeaux, Alsace), swimming, classical music, bridge. *Address:* Veurestraat 47, 9051 Afsnee, Belgium. *T:* (9) 2226211. *Club:* Universitaire Stichting (Brussels).

VANCOUVER, Archbishop of, (RC), since 2009; **Most Rev. John Michael Miller,** CSB; *b* Ottawa, 9 July 1946; *s* of Albert Henry Miller and Katharine Beatrice Miller (*née* Robb). *Educ:* Univ. of Toronto (BA 1969); Univ. of Wisconsin (MA 1970); Univ. of St Michael's Coll., Toronto (MDiv 1974); Pontifical Gregorian Univ., Rome (STL 1976; STD 1979). Ordained priest, 1975; Prof. of Theol., Univ. of St Thomas, Houston, 1979–90; Vice Pres., Academic Affairs, Univ. of St Thomas, Houston, 1990–92; Asst, Secretariat of State, Holy See, 1992–97; Pres., Univ. of St Thomas, Houston, 1997–2003; apptd Archbishop, 2003; Sec., Congregation of Catholic Educn, Holy See, 2003–07; Coadjutor Archbishop of Vancouver, 2007–09. *Publications:* The Divine Right of the Papacy in Recent Ecumenical Theology, 1980; What Are They Saying about Papal Primacy?, 1983; Life's Greatest Grace: why I belong to the Catholic Church, 1993; The Shepherd and the Rock: origin, development and mission of the papacy, 1995; (ed) The Encyclicals of John Paul II, 1996, 2nd edn 2001; (ed) The Post-Synodal Apostolic Exhortations of John Paul II, 1998; contribs to jls incl. Seminarium, America, Catholic Higher Education in Europe, Crisis, Canadian Catholic Review, Current Issues in Catholic Higher Education. *Address:* Chancery Office, Archdiocese of Vancouver, 150 Robson Street, Vancouver, BC V6B 2A7, Canada. *T:* (604) 4433240, *Fax:* (604) 6818355. *E:* chancery@rcav.org.

VAN CULIN, Rev. Canon Samuel; Residentiary Canon, Washington National Cathedral; Secretary General, Anglican Consultative Council, 1983–94; Organising Secretary, Lambeth Conference of Anglican Bishops, 1988; *b* 20 Sept. 1930; *s* of Samuel Van Culin and Susie (*née* Mossman). *Educ:* High School, Honolulu; Princeton University (AB); Virginia Theological Seminary (BD). Ordained 1955; Curate, St Andrew's Cathedral, Honolulu, 1955–56; Canon Precentor and Rector, Hawaiian Congregation, 1956–58; Asst Rector, St John, Washington DC, 1958–60; Gen. Sec., Laymen International, Washington, 1960–61; Asst Sec., Overseas Dept, Episcopal Church, USA, 1962–68; Sec. for Africa and Middle East, Episcopal Church, USA, 1968–76; Executive, World Mission, 1976–83. Hon. Canon: Canterbury Cathedral, 1983; Ibadan, Nigeria, 1983; Jerusalem, 1984; Southern Africa, 1989; Honolulu, 1991. Hon. DD: Virginia Seminary, 1977; Gen. Theol Seminary, 1983. *Recreations:* music, swimming. *Address:* 3900 Watson Place, NW, #5D–B, Washington, DC 20016, USA. *Clubs:* Athenæum, Huguenot Society; Princeton (New York).

VandeLINDE, Prof. (Vernon) David, PhD; Vice-Chancellor, 2001–06, Vice-Chancellor Emeritus, 2011, University of Warwick; *b* Charleston, W Virginia, 9 Aug. 1942; *s* of Vernon Geno VandeLinde and Ava Mae (*née* Scott); *m* 1964, Marjorie Ann Park; two *s*. *Educ:* Carnegie Mellon Univ. (BS 1964; MS 1965; PhD 1968). Johns Hopkins University: Asst Prof., Elec. Engrg, 1967–74; Associate Prof., 1974–77; Prof., 1977–92; Dean, Sch. of Engrg, 1978–92; Vice-Chancellor, Univ. of Bath, 1992–2001. Chairman: Overseas Res. Students Awards Scheme Cttee, UUK (formerly CVCP), 1993–2005; Better Regulation Review Gp, DfES, 2003–04; Mem., Council for Science and Technology, 2000–03. Non-exec. Dir, W Midlands S Strategic HA, 2003–06. Hon. LLD Bath, 2001; Hon. DEd West of England, 2001; Hon. LLD Warwick, 2007. Distinguished Alumni Award, Carnegie Mellon Univ., 2008. *Address:* 2180 Waterview Drive, Unit 721, North Myrtle Beach, SC 29582, USA.

VANDEN-BEMPDE-JOHNSTONE; *see* Johnstone.

van den BERGH, Maarten Albert; Chairman, Supervisory Board, Akzo Nobel nv, 2006–09 (Deputy Chairman, 2005–06); *b* 19 April 1942; *s* of Sidney James van den Bergh and Maria van den Bergh (*née* Mijers); *m* 1965, Marjan Désirée Kramer; two *d*. *Educ:* Univ. of Groningen (Drs Econs). Joined Shell Gp, 1968; East and Australasia Area Co-ordinator, 1981–84; Dep. Gp Treas., Shell Internat., 1984–86; Chm., Shell cos in Thailand, 1987–89; Regl Co-ordinator, Western Hemisphere and Africa, Shell Internat., 1989–92; Royal Dutch/Shell Group plc: Gp Man. Dir, 1992–2000; Dir of Finance, 1994–98; Vice-Chm., Cttee of Man. Dirs, and Pres., Royal Dutch Petroleum Co., 1998–2000; non-exec. Dir, 2000–09. Dep. Chm., 2000–01, Chm., 2001–06, Lloyds TSB Gp plc; non-executive Director: British Telecommunications plc, 2000–01; BT Group plc, 2001–09 (Dep. Chm., 2006–09); British Airways Plc, 2002–11. Advr to Chief Exec., HKSAR, 1998–2002. Member: Internat. Bd of Advisers to Pres. of Philippines, 2001–05; Adv. Council, Amsterdam Inst. of Finance, 2001–05. Mem., Steering Bd, and Dutch Co-Chm., Apeldoorn Conf., 2003–09. Advr, Rembrandt Soc., 2001–05. Fellow and Vice-Pres., Inst. of Financial Services, 2001–06; Mem., Guild of Internat. Bankers, 2001–06. *Recreation:* European history. *Club:* Soc. De Witte (The Hague).

van den BERGH, Prof. Sidney, OC 1994; FRS 1988; astronomer, Dominion Astrophysical Observatory, Victoria, British Columbia, 1977–2012; *b* 20 May 1929; *s* of S. J. van den Bergh and S. M. van den Berg; *m* 1st, 1957, Roswitha Koropp (marr. diss.); one *s* two *d*; 2nd, 1978, Gretchen Krause (*d* 1987); 3rd, 1990, Paulette Brown. *Educ:* Princeton Univ. (AB); Ohio State Univ. (MSc); Göttingen Univ. (Dr rer. nat.). Asst Prof., Ohio State Univ., 1956–58; progressively, Asst Prof., Associate Prof., Prof., Univ. of Toronto, 1958–77; Dir, Dominion Astrophys. Observatory, 1977–86. Adjunct Prof., Univ. of Victoria, 1978–2009. Res. Associate, Mt Wilson and Palomar Observatories, 1967–68. ARAS 1984. Hon. DSc: St Mary's Univ., 1995; Univ. of Victoria, 2001. NRCC President's Research Medal, 1988; Killam Laureate, Killam Trust, 1990; Henry Norris Russel Prize Lecture, Amer. Astron. Soc., 1990; Carlyle S Beals Award, 1998, R. M. Petrie Prize, 1999, Can. Astron. Soc.; Catherine Wolfe Bruce Gold Medal, Astron. Soc. Pacific, 2008; Canadian Hall of Fame for Sci. and Technol., 2012; Gruber Cosmology Prize, Peter Gruber Foundn, 2014. *Publications:* approx. 900 articles in various scholarly jls. *Recreation:* archaeology.

van den BROEK, Hans, Grand Cross Order of Oranje Nassau; Hon. GCMG; President, Netherlands Institute for International Relations, 2000–07; Honorary Minister of State, Netherlands, since 2005; *b* 11 Dec. 1936; *m* 1965, Josephine van Schendel; two *d*. *Educ:* Univ. of Utrecht (Law degree). Lawyer, Rotterdam, 1965–68; Enka Bv., Arnhem: Sec., Mgt Bd, 1969–73; Commercial Manager, 1973–76. Member: Lower House of Parliament, Netherlands, 1976–78; Exec., Catholic People's Party, 1978–81; State Sec. for Foreign Affairs, 1981–82; Minister for Foreign Affairs, 1982–93. Mem., CEC, later EC, 1993–99. Chm., Radio Netherlands Internat., 2000–; Member: Supervisory Bd, Schiphol Gp, 2000–; Supervisory Council, Utrecht Univ., 2000–07. Pres., Carnegie Foundn, 2000–07; Founding Mem., Global Leadership Foundn, 2000–. Grand Cross: Order of Merit (Italy); Order of Isabel la Católica (Spain); Nat. Order of Merit (France); Order of Merit (Germany); Order of the Rising Sun (Japan). *Address:* Zwiepseweg 158, 7241 PV Lochem, The Netherlands.

VAN DEN HOVEN, Helmert Frans; *see* Hoven.

VAN der BIJL, Nigel Charles; His Honour Judge Van der Bijl; a Circuit Judge, since 2001; *b* 28 April 1948; *s* of late Nicholas Alexander Christian Van der Bijl and of Mollie Van der Bijl; *m* 1974, Loba Nassiri; one *s* one *d*. *Educ:* Trinity Coll., Dublin (MA Classics, LLB). Called to the Bar, Inner Temple, 1973; Co. Sec., Internat. Div., Beecham Pharmaceutical, 1973–74; Legal Manager, Shahpur Chemical Co. Ltd and Nat. Iranian Oil Co., Tehran, 1974–77; in private practice as barrister, specialising in crime and in European and human rights law, 1977–2001; a Recorder, 1996–2001. Recorder of the City of Canterbury, 2004–. Friend, British Sch. of Athens, 1996–. *Recreation:* cycling. *Address:* c/o The Law Courts, Chaucer Road, Canterbury, Kent CT1 1ZA.

VANDERMARK, Simone; *see* Hochgreb, S.

VANDERMEER, (Arnold) Roy, OBE 2009; QC 1978; a Recorder of the Crown Court, 1972–97; a Deputy High Court Judge, 1989–99; *b* London, 26 June 1931; *o s* of late William Arnold Vandermeer and Katherine Nora Vandermeer; *m* 1964, Caroline Veronica (*née* Christopher); one *s* two *d*. *Educ:* Dame Alice Owen's Sch., Islington; King's Coll., London (LLB). Called to Bar, Gray's Inn, 1955, Bencher, 1988. Flt-Lt, RAF, 1955–58. Chairman: Greater Manchester Structure Plan Examination in Public, 1978; County of Avon Structure Plan Examination in Public, 1983. Inspector, Heathrow Terminal 5 and associated enquiries, 1995–2000. Non-exec. Dir, Majestic Wine plc, 1996–99. *Recreations:* reading, watching cricket, golf. *Address:* The Dower House, Cheverells Green, Markyate, Herts AL3 8BH. *T:* (01582) 849458. *Club:* MCC.

VANDERMERWE, Prof. Sandra, DBA; Associate Fellow, and Visiting Professor, since 2006 (Professor, 1996–2005) specializing in Customer Focused Transformation, Imperial College (formerly Tanaka) Business School, Imperial College of Science, Technology and Medicine; Adjunct Professor, European School of Management and Technology, Germany, since 2006; Extraordinary Professor, Gordon Institute of Business Science, South Africa, since 2011; *b* 8 Aug. 1946; *d* of late David Fortes and Myra Fortes; two *d*. *Educ:* Univ. of Cape Town (BA 1966); Grad. Sch. of Business, Univ. of Cape Town (MBA 1972); Grad. Sch. of Business, Univ. of Stellenbosch (DBA 1974). Senior Lecturer: Dept of Business Sci., Univ. of Cape Town, 1973–76; Grad. Sch. of Business, Univ. of Stellenbosch, 1976–79; Prof., and Head of Mktg Dept, Univ. of Witwatersrand, 1979–82; Vis. Prof. of Mktg, Internat. Mgt Inst., Geneva, 1983–85; Prof. of Internat. Mktg and Services, IMD-Internat. Inst. for Mgt Develt, Lausanne, 1985–96 (also Dir, several exec. progs). Mem. Bd, Internat. Health Insurance, 2000–05. Sen. Associate, Deloitte Consulting, 2014–. Consultant on implementing customer-focused growth and transformation, major internat. cos; speaker on Executive progs for business schs incl. INSEAD, London Business Sch., and Templeton Coll., Oxford. Board Member: Internat. Women's Forum, 2010–13; Handspring Puppet Trust, 2011–. Trustee, Wendy Appelbaum Foundn, 2009–. Mem., editl bds, and reviewer for internat. academic and mgt jls. FRSA 1996. Several awards. *Publications:* From Tin Soldiers to Russian Dolls: creating added value through services, 1993; (jtly) Cases in European Marketing Management, 1994; (jtly) Competing Through Services, 1994; The 11th Commandment: transforming to 'own' customers, 1995; Customer Capitalism: getting increasing returns in new market spaces, 1999; Breaking Through: implementing customer focus in enterprises, 2004 (trans. Japanese 2009), 2nd edn as Implementing Disruptive Customer Centricity, 2014; numerous articles in prof. jls. *Recreations:* animal healing, hiking, arts. *Address:* 4 Jasper Lane, St Quinton's Road, Oranjezicht, Cape Town 8001, South Africa.

VANDERSTEEN, Martin Hugh; Chairman, Bart's and The London NHS Trust, 2001–03; *b* 9 Aug. 1935; *s* of William Martin Vandersteen and Dorothy Margaret Vandersteen (*née* Leith); *m* 1967, Catherine Susan Mary Webb; two *s*. *Educ:* Harrow Co. Grammar Sch. for Boys; Open Univ. (BSc 2004). Chartered Accountant, 1957; Allen, Attfield & Co. Chartered Accountants, 1951–57; Andersen Consulting, 1957–97: Partner, 1968; Man. Partner UK, 1973–86; Man. Partner Regl, 1989–94; Man. Partner Resources and Quality, 1994–97. Non-exec. Dir, 1999–, Chm., 2000, Kingston Hosp. NHS Trust. *Recreations:* sailing, fishing, golf, swimming, science. *Address:* 2 Bristol Gardens, Putney Heath, SW15 3TG. *T:* (020) 8788 9026. *E:* mvanderstn@aol.com. *Clubs:* Royal Ocean Racing; Royal Southern Yacht; Otter Swimming.

van der VEEN, Air Vice-Marshal Marten; Senior Bursar, 2000–05 (Bursar, 1998–2000) and Fellow, 1999–2005, Balliol College, Oxford; *b* 22 Jan. 1946; *s* of late Lourens Jan van der Veen and Esmé Lily van der Veen (*née* Edwards); *m* 1968, Susan Mary Wallers; two *s*. *Educ:* King's Coll. Sch., Wimbledon; Magdalen Coll., Oxford (MA Engrg Sci. and Econs); RAF Coll., Cranwell (Aerosystems course). Exchange Officer with French Air Force, Paris, 1978–79; RAF Staff Coll., 1980; Dir of Defence Studies, RAF, 1985–88; Station Comdr, RAF Cosford, 1989–90; Dir, Support Policy, RAF, 1991–93; Station Comdr, RAF St Athan and Air Officer, Wales, 1994–95; last Commandant, RAF Staff Coll., Bracknell, 1996; DG Support Mgt, RAF, 1997. Gov., Stowe Sch., 2002–12 (Vice-Chm., 2007–12). Chm., RAF Oxford and Cambridge Soc., 2009–12. *Recreations:* travel, classical music, opera, social tennis, inevitable DIY. *Clubs:* Royal Air Force; Phyllis Court (Henley).

VAN der VEER, Jeroen; Chairman and Member, Supervisory Board: ING, since 2009; Philips, since 2009; President, Royal Dutch Petroleum NV, 2000–09; a Group Managing Director, 1997–2009, Chairman, Committee of Managing Directors, 2004–09, and Chief Executive, 2004–09, Royal Dutch/Shell Group (Vice-Chairman, 2000–04; non-executive Director, 2009–13); *b* 1947; *m*; three *d*. *Educ:* Delft Univ. (MMechE 1971); Rotterdam Univ. (MEcons 1976). Joined Shell Internat. BV, 1971; Refining, Curaçao, 1978; Marketing, UK, 1981; Corporate Planning, UK, 1984; Area Officer, 1990; Pres. and CEO, Shell Chemicals Co., Houston, 1995–97; Gp Res. Advr, 1997. Vice Chm., Unilever, 2009–11 (non-exec. Dir, 2002–09). *Recreations:* golf, sailing, ski-ing, visiting museums. *Address:* c/o ING, PO Box 180, 1000 AV Amsterdam, The Netherlands.

van der WATEREN, Jan Floris, FCLIP; Keeper and Chief Librarian, National Art Library, 1988–2000; *b* 14 May 1940; *s* of late Jacob van der Wateren and Wilhelmina (*née* Labuschagne). *Educ:* Potchefstroom Univ., S Africa (MA); University Coll. London (Postgrad. Dip. Librarianship). ALA 1971, FCLIP (FLA 1995). Lectr in Philosophy, Potchefstroom Univ., 1962–64; Asst Librarian, Univ. of London Inst. of Educn, 1967–71; Dep. Librarian, Sir Banister Fletcher Liby, RIBA, 1971–78; British Architectural Library: Managing Librarian, 1978–83; Dir and Sir Banister Fletcher Librarian, 1983–88. Sec., British Architectural Liby Trust, 1983–88. Hon. FRIBA 1995. FRSA 1994. *Publications:* articles, reviews for librarianship jls. *Address:* 52 Blenheim Crescent, W11 1NY. *T:* (020) 7221 6221.

van der WERFF, His Honour Jonathan Ervine; a Circuit Judge, 1986–2007; Resident Judge, Inner London Crown Court, 1993–2007; *b* 23 June 1935; *s* of H. H. J. van der Werff; *m* 1968, Katharine Bridget (*d* 2014), *d* of Major J. B. Colvin, Withypool, Som; two *d*. *Educ:* St Piran's Sch., Maidenhead; Harrow; RMA, Sandhurst. Commnd in Coldstream Guards, 1955; Adjt 1st Bn, 1962–63; Major 1967, retired 1968. Called to Bar, Inner Temple, 1969; a Recorder, 1986; Resident Judge, Croydon Law Courts, 1989–93; Sen. Circuit Judge, 1993. *Clubs:* Boodle's, Pratt's, Something.

VANDER ZALM, Hon. William N.; Premier of the Province of British Columbia, 1986–91; MLA (Social Credit Party) for Richmond, British Columbia; *b* Noordwykerhout, Holland, 29 May 1934; *s* of Wilhelmus Nicholaas van der Zalm and Agatha C. Warmerdam; *m* 1956, Lillian Mihalic; two *s* two *d*. *Educ:* Phillip Sheffield Sen. Secondary Sch., Abbotsford, BC. Purchased Art Knapp Nurseries Ltd, and became Co. Pres., 1956. Alderman 1965, Mayor 1969, Surrey Municipal Council. Minister of Human Resources, BC, 1975; Minister of Municipal Affairs and Minister responsible for Urban Transit Authority, 1978; Minister of Educn and Minister responsible for BC Transit, 1982; Leader, BC Social Credit Party, 1986–. Established Fantasy Garden World, major tourist attraction in Richmond, BC, 1983–. Hon. Dr Law Univ. of the North, Prince George, BC, 2004. *Publications:* The Northwest Gardener's Almanac, 1982; Bill Vander Zalm For the People: hindsight, insight, foresight (autobiog.), 2008; HST—The People for Democracy, 2013. *Recreations:* gardening, fishing, soccer. *Address:* 3553 Arthur Drive, Ladner, BC V4K 3N2, Canada. *Clubs:* Union (Victoria, BC); Hon. Member: Victoria Golf, Royal Vancouver Yacht, Royal Victoria Yacht.

VANDEVELDE, Luc Emile; Founder and Managing Director, Change Capital Partners, since 2002; *b* Belgium, 26 Feb. 1951; *s* of Emile Vandevelde and Sylvie Vandevelde (*née* Jacobs); *m* Monique Sapin; one *s*. Administrator, Kraft NV SA, Brussels, 1971–80; Finance Dir, Kraft Leonesas SA, Madrid, 1980–83; Vice-Pres. of Develt and Planning, Kraft Europe, Lausanne, 1983–86; Dir of Finance and Admin, Kraft GmbH, Germany, 1986–88; Vice-Pres. of Finance and Admin, Kraft Internat., USA, 1988–90; Vice-Pres. of Admin and Develt, Kraft General Foods Internat., NY, 1989–90; CEO, France, 1989–93, Italy, 1994–95, Kraft Jacobs Suchard; Pres. and Chief Operating Officer, 1995–99, Chm., 1999–2000, Promodès; Chief Exec., 2000–02, Chm., 2000–04, Marks and Spencer plc; Dir, 2004–07, Chm., 2005–07, Carrefour. Non-exec. Dir, Société Générale, 2006–; Sen. non-exec. Dir, Vodafone, 2012–15 (non-exec. Dir, 2003–12). *Address:* Change Capital Partners, 2nd Floor, College House, 272 Kings Road, SW3 5AW.

van de VEN, Prof. Johan Jacob, (Hans), PhD; FBA 2013; Professor of Modern Chinese History, University of Cambridge, since 2004; Fellow of St Catharine's College, Cambridge, since 1988; *b* The Hague, 10 Jan. 1958; *s* of Henk van de Ven and Reina van de Ven (*née* Jonker Roelants); *m* 1983, Susan Kerr; three *s*. *Educ:* Leiden Univ. (BA 1980); Harvard Univ. (PhD 1987). University of Cambridge: Lectr, 1988–2000; Sen. Lectr, 2000–02; Reader, 2002–04. Dir, Melbourn Village College Acad., 2011–13. *Publications:* From Friend to Comrade: the founding of the Chinese Communist Party, 1991; (ed) Warfare in Chinese History, 2000; War and Nationalism in China, 2003; (ed jtly) The Battle for China, 2010; Breaking with the Past, 2014. *Recreations:* sailing, tennis. *Address:* St Catharine's College, Trumpington Street, Cambridge CB2 1RL. *Club:* Royal Harwich Yacht.

VAN de WALLE, Leslie; Chairman: SIG plc, since 2011 (non-executive Director, since 2010); Robert Walters plc, since 2012; Chief Executive, Rexam PLC, 2007–09; *b* 27 March 1956; *s* of Philippe Van de Walle and Luce Van de Walle; *m* 1982, Domitille Noel; two *d*. *Educ:* Hautes Etudes Commerciales, Paris. Managing Director: Schweppes Benelux, 1990–92; Schweppes France and Benelux, 1992–93; Schweppes Spain and Portugal, 1993–94; Snacks Div., Continental Europe UB, 1994–95; Chief Executive Officer: UB Continental Europe, 1996–97; McVitie's Gp, 1998; Chief Exec., United Biscuits Gp, 1999–2000; CEO, Shell South America and Africa, 2001; Pres., Shell Europe Oil Products; Exec. Vice-Pres., Global Retail, Royal Dutch Shell, 2004–06. Non-executive Director: Aegis Gp plc, 2003–09; Aviva plc, 2009–12; DCC plc, 2010–; La Seda de Barcelona, 2011–; Cape plc, 2012–. *Recreations:* golf (handicap 4), travel. *Address:* 65 Rose Square, Fulham Road, SW3 6RS. *Club:* Lambourne Golf.

VANE; *see* Fletcher-Vane, family name of Baron Inglewood.

VANE, family name of **Baron Barnard**.

VANE, Amber; *see* Feldman, S. J.

VANE-TEMPEST-STEWART, family name of **Marquess of Londonderry**.

VANE-WRIGHT, Richard Irwin; Keeper of Entomology, 1998–2004, Scientific Associate, since 2004, Natural History Museum; *b* 26 July 1942; *s* of late Gerald, (James), Vane Wright, and Jessie Margaret (*née* Baldwin); *m* 1987, Hazel June Whitehead; two *d*. *Educ:* University Coll. London (BSc 1st Cl. Hons Zool. 1967). British Museum (Natural History), subseq. Natural History Museum: Asst (Scientific), 1961–63; SO, Dept Entomology, 1967–84; Dep. Keeper of Entomology, 1984–90; Individual Merit Researcher (Band 2), 1990–98. Chair: Scientific Names Cttee, N Amer. Butterfly Assoc., 2011–; Friends of Westgate Parks (Canterbury), 2012–14; Hon. Curator, Westgate Parks Invertebrate Resource, 2011–. Fellow: Wissenschaftskolleg, Berlin, 1993–94; NESTA, 2005–08; Vis. Sen. Res. Fellow, Ecol. Res. Gp, Sch. of Human and Life Scis, Canterbury Christ Church Univ., 2010–. Hon. Prof. of Taxonomy, Univ. of Kent, Canterbury, 2006–. Hon. Fellow, Royal Entomol Soc. of London, 2004. Sec., South Canterbury Residents Assoc., 2009–14. Hon. DSc Copenhagen, 2003. Karl Jordan Medal, Lepidopterists' Soc., USA, 1989; Jacob Hübner Award, Assoc. for Tropical Lepidoptera, 2005. *Publications:* (with P. R. Ackery) The Biology of Butterflies, 1984, 2nd edn 1989; (with P. R. Ackery) Milkweed Butterflies, 1984; (ed jtly) Phylogenetics and Ecology, 1994; (ed jtly) Systematics and Conservation Evaluation, 1994; (jtly) Carcasson's African Butterflies, 1995; Butterflies, 2003, 2nd edn 2015; (with Harold Hughes) The Seymer Legacy: Henry Seymer and Henry Seymer Jnr of Dorset, and their entomological paintings, 2005; (ed and contrib.) The Role of Behaviour in Evolution, 2014; numerous contribs to books and science jls. *Recreations:* jazz, walking, woodwork, books, clocks, craneflies, butterflies, conservation. *Address:* Department of Life Sciences, Natural History Museum, Cromwell Road, SW7 5BD. *Club:* Tetrapods (Chair, 2002–).

VANEZIS, Prof. Peter Savvas, OBE 2001; MD, PhD; FRCPath, FRCPGlas, FFFLM, FCSFS, FAFMS; Director, Cameron Forensic Medical Sciences, Barts and the London School of Medicine and Dentistry, Queen Mary University of London, since 2006; Chief Medical Officer, iGene London Ltd, since 2013; *b* 11 Dec. 1947; *s* of Savvas Vanezis and Efrosini Vanezis; *m* 1981, Maria Galatariotis; one *s* one *d*. *Educ:* Wanstead High Sch.; Bristol Univ. (MB ChB, MD); PhD London; DMJ Path; MRCPGlas. FFFLM 2006; FCSFS (FFSSoc 2011); FAFMS 2011. Jun. appt, St Olave's Hosp. (Guy's), 1973–74; Jun. Lectr, Lectr and Sen. Lectr in Forensic Medicine, London Hosp. Med. Coll., 1974–90; Reader and Head of Dept of Forensic Medicine and Toxicology, Charing Cross and Westminster Med. Sch. and Hon. Consultant, Riverside AHA, 1990–93; Regius Prof. of Forensic Medicine and Sci., 1993–2003, and Dir, Human Identification Centre, 1994–2003, Univ. of Glasgow; Dir Gen., Centre for Internat. Forensic Assistance, 2001–03; Chief Forensic Med. Officer, Forensic Sci. Service, 2003–06. External Examiner in Forensic Pathology: Postgrad. Med. Inst., Sri Lanka, 1995–; Coll. of Pathologists, Hong Kong, 1999–; Ext. Examiner in Forensic Medicine, Univ. of Malaysia, 2001–. Visiting Professor: Inst. of Forensic Medicine, Singapore, 2000–; London South Bank (formerly S Bank) Univ., 2001–; Univ. of Glasgow, 2003–; Leicester Univ., 2010–12; UCL, 2015–; Vis. Prof. Laureate, European Univ. of Cyprus, 2014–; Hon. Prof., Dept of Pathology, Univ. of HK, 2003–. Hon. Consultant: Tower Hamlets AHA, 1982–90; the Armed Forces, 1992–; Gtr Glasgow Health Bd, 1993–; Medico-legal Inst., Santiago, 1994–; Govt of Republic of Cyprus, 1984–. Advr in Forensic Medicine to: ICRC, 2006–; Govt of Malaysia, 2009–. President: British Acad. of Forensic Scis, 1996–97; British Assoc. in Human Identification, 2001–03; Pres. and Dir, Acad. of Forensic Med. Scis, 2011–; mem., numerous forensic science socs, UK and USA. Mem. Adv. Cttee, Action Against Medical Accidents, 2010–. Mem., Editl Bds (Path), Science and Justice, Jl of Clinical Path, Amer. Jl Forensic Medicine & Path; Ed.-in-Chief, Medicine, Science and the Law, 2009–. *Publications:* Pathology of Neck Injury, 1989; Suspicious Death-Scene Investigation, 1996; articles on forensic medicine and science in learned jls. *Recreations:* painting, golf. *Address:* Cameron Forensic Medical Sciences, Clinical Pharmacology, Barts and the London School of Medicine and Dentistry, Charterhouse Square, EC1M 6BQ.

VAN GELDER, Daniel Nathan; Co-Founder and Director, Exemplar Properties, since 2003; *b* London, 4 July 1973; *s* of Stanley Malcom Van Gelder and Beverley Anne Van Gelder; *m* 1994, Daniela Davidson; two *d*. *Educ:* Harrow Sch. (Scholar); Univ. of Bristol (BSc Hons Valuation and Estate Mgt). Director: CB Richard Ellis, 1993–95; Development Securities plc, 1995–2003. *Recreations:* sailing, shooting, backgammon. *Address:* Exemplar Properties, Kent House, Market Place, W1W 8AJ. *T:* (020) 7299 0800, *Fax:* (020) 7299 0801. *E:* dvg@exemplar.co.uk. *Clubs:* Royal Thames Yacht, Royal Southern Yacht.

van GELDER, Prof. Gerard Jan Henk, PhD; FBA 2005; Laudian Professor of Arabic, University of Oxford, 1998–2012, now Emeritus; Fellow, St John's College, Oxford, 1998–2012, now Emeritus; *b* 10 June 1947; *s* of Gerard Jan van Gelder and Hendrika Venmans; *m* 1973, Sheila Maureen Ottway; two *d*. *Educ:* Univ. of Amsterdam (doctoral); Univ. of Leiden (PhD 1982). Librarian, Inst. for Modern Near East, Univ. of Amsterdam, 1973–75; Lectr in Arabic, Univ. of Groningen, 1975–98. Mem., Royal Netherlands Acad. of Arts and Scis, 1997. *Publications:* Beyond the Line: classical Arabic literary critics on the coherence and unity of the poem, 1982; Two Arabic Treatises on Stylistics, 1987; The Bad and the Ugly: attitudes towards invective poetry (Hijā') in classical Arabic literature, 1989; Of Dishes and Discourse, 2000; Close Relationships: incest and inbreeding in classical Arabic literature, 2005; (with Marlé Hammond) Takhyīl: the imaginary in classical Arabic poetics, 2008; Sound and Sense in Classical Arabic Poetry, 2012; Classical Arabic Literature: a library of Arabic literature anthology, 2013; (ed and trans. with G. Schoeler) al-Ma'arri, Risalat al-ghufran, 2014; books in Dutch; contrib. articles in learned jls and encyclopaedias. *Recreations:* music and musicology, especially early music. *Address:* Middelhorsterweg 40, 9751 TG Haren, The Netherlands.

van GRIETHUYSEN, Dr (Willem) John, CEng, FREng; FRINA; RCNC; Chief Engineer (Submarines), Defence Equipment and Support, Ministry of Defence, 2009–14; *b* 14 May 1953; *s* of Jean-Pierre van Griethuysen and Margaret Emily (*née* Williams); *m* 1983, Zaida Katharine Gibbs; three *d*. *Educ:* Haberdashers' Aske's Boys' Sch., Elstree; UCL (BSc (Mech. Engrg) 1975; MSc (Nav. Arch.) 1976; PhD 1989). Mem., Type 23 Design Team, 1981–83; Lectr in Naval Architecture, UCL, 1983–86; In-Service Submarine Project, 1986–91; Project Manager, Minehunters, 1991–93; Ship Design Manager, Horizon Jt Project Office, 1993–96; Hd, Business Improvement, DG Surface Ships, 1996–98; Prof. of Naval Architecture, UCL, 1998–2003; Chief Naval Architect, MoD and Dir Sea Systems (formerly Dir Sea Technol., then Sea Systems Gp Leader), Defence Equipment and Support (formerly Defence Procurement Agency), MoD, 2003–09. Technical Advr to Judge in re-opened formal investigation into loss of MV Derbyshire, 2000. Member: Council, RINA, 1998–2002; Court, Imperial Coll., London, 2001–07. Dep. Hd, RCNC, 2003–14. FREng 2003. *Publications:* papers on naval engrg and design.

VAN HAEFTEN, John Henry; Chairman and Managing Director, Johnny Van Haeften Ltd, since 1977; *b* London, 22 June 1952; *s* of John Francis Henry Van Haeften and Barbara Joan Van Haeften; *m* 1977, Sarah Anne Rowley; one *d*. *Educ:* Eton. Liaison, Postage Stamp Dept, later Asst Press Officer, Christie's, 1969–77. Mem., Reviewing Cttee on Export of Works of Art and Objects of Cultural Interest, 2001–11. Mem. Council, British Antique Dealers Assoc., 1989–92; Vice Chm., Soc. of London Art Dealers, 1998–2000, 2001–02. Mem., Exec. Cttee, Eur. Fine Art Foundn, 1989–; Trustee, Dulwich Picture Gall., 2010–. *Recreations:* philately, pop music. *Address:* Johnny Van Haeften Ltd, 13 Duke Street, St James's, SW1Y 6DB. *T:* (020) 7930 3062, *Fax:* (020) 7839 6303. *Club:* Carlton.

VANHANEN, Matti; Executive Director, Finnish Family Firms Association, since 2010; *b* Jyväskylä, Finland, 4 Nov. 1955; *s* of Tatu and Anni Vanhanen; *m* (marr. diss.); one *s* one *d*. *Educ:* Helsinki Univ. (Master Soc. Scis). Journalist, 1985–88, Ed.-in-Chief, 1988–91, Kehäsanomat (local newspaper). MP (Centre Party) Uusimaa, Finland, 1991–2010. Vice Chairman: Parly Envmt Cttee, 1991–95; Parly Gp, Centre Party, 1994–2001; Chm., Parly Grand Cttee, 2000–01; Rep. of Parlt, European Convention on Future of EU, 2002–03; Minister of Defence, 2003; Prime Minister, 2003–10. Centre Party: Mem. or Dep. Mem.,

Party Delegn, 1976–2000; Chm., Youth League, 1980–83; Bd Mem., 1980–83; Vice Chm., 2000–03; Chm., 2003–10. Espoo City Council, 1981–84; Nurmijärvi Municipal Council, 1989–; Board Member: Helsinki Met. Area Council YTV, 1983–84; Uusimaa Regl Council, 1997–2000. Member Supervisory Board: Neste/Fortum, 1991–2003; Helsingin Osuuskauppa (Cooperative), 2002–03. Chairman: State Youth Council, 1987–90; Housing Foundn for the Young, 1998–2003 (Vice Chm., 1981–97); Union for Rural Educn, 1998–2003; Vice Chairman: Housing Council, 1991–2003; Pro Medi-Heli Assoc., 1995–2003.

van HASSELT, Marc; Headmaster, Cranleigh School, 1970–84; *b* 24 April 1924; *s* of Marc and Helen van Hasselt; *m* 1st, 1949, Geraldine Frances Sinclair (marr. diss. 1976); three *s* one *d*; 2nd, 1989, Tessa Carolyn, *d* of Mrs B. Gofton-Salmond. *Educ:* Sherborne; Selwyn Coll., Cambridge (MA); Corpus Christi Coll., Oxford (DipEd). Served War of 1939–45 (despatches): commissioned in Essex Yeomanry, RHA, 1944; served North-West Europe (D-day). Lecturer in Commonwealth Studies, RMA, Sandhurst, 1950–58; Asst Master, Oundle School, 1959–70 (Housemaster, Sanderson House, 1963–70). Member: Admiralty Interview Bd, 1972–86; Army Scholarship Bd, 1972–86. Chairman: Castle Court Sch., 1988–95; Walhampton Sch., 1990–97; Gov., Canford Sch., 1985–95. *Publications:* occasional articles and reviews. *Recreations:* cruising under sail, governing schools. *Address:* Carrick Corner, New Road, Keyhaven, Lymington, Hants SO41 0TN. *T:* (01590) 644690; rue Lyvet, 22690 Vicomte-sur-Rance, France. *Clubs:* Royal Cruising; Royal Lymington Yacht; Keyhaven Yacht.

VANHEGAN, Joanna Angela; *see* Smith, J. A.

VANHEGAN, Mark James; QC 2009; barrister, since 1990; *b* Oxford, 27 March 1966; *s* of Dr Robert Ian Vanhegan and late Valerie Vanhegan; *m* 1994, Joanna Angela Smith, *qv*; two *d*. *Educ:* Abingdon Sch.; Trinity Coll., Cambridge (BA Nat. Sci. and Law 1989). Called to the Bar, Lincoln's Inn, 1990. *Recreations:* walking, tennis, gardening, travel. *Address:* 11 South Square, Gray's Inn, WC1R 5EY. *T:* (020) 7405 1222, *Fax:* (020) 7242 4282. *E:* mark@vanhegan.org. *Club:* TSSC.

van HEYNINGEN, Joanna; architect; Consultant, van Heyningen and Haward Architects, since 2012 (Joint Principal, then Partner, 1982–2012); *b* 22 July 1945; *d* of William Edward Kits van Heyningen and Ruth Eleanor van Heyningen (*née* Treverton); *m* 1977, Birkin Anthony Christopher Haward, *qv*; one *s* one *d*. *Educ:* Oxford High Sch. for Girls; St Anne's Coll., Oxford (BA (French and Russian) 1967); New Hall, Cambridge (BA (Architecture) 1971); Darwin Coll., Cambridge (Dip Arch 1973). RIBA 1981. Estab. private practice, 1977; formed van Heyningen and Haward Architects, 1982. RIBA: Member: Awards Gp, 2000–04. Co-Chair, Oxford Design Rev. Panel, Design Council CABE, 2014–; Mem., New Bermondsey Quality Team, 2011–. Governor: Building Centre Trust, 1998–; Purcell Sch. of Music, 2012– (Chair, Bldg Cttee, 2012–). Trustee, Find Your Feet, 2013–; Founder, CoHo (Dartmouth Park Co-housing). BDA Assessor, 2007–; External Examiner: Cambridge Univ. Sch. of Architecture, 2009–11; Cardiff Sch. of Architecture, 2014–; Stirling Prize Assessor, 2012. Award winning buildings include: Haward House, London, 1976; Newnham Coll. Rare Books Liby, Cambridge, 1981; 2nd Haward House, London, 1986; Clovelly Visitor Centre, 1989; Wilson Court, Cambridge, 1994; Jacqueline du Pré Music Building, Oxford, 1995; King Alfred's Sch., London, 1997; Gateway to the White Cliffs (NT), Dover, 1999; West Ham Station, Jubilee Line Extension, 1999; Nat. Centre for Early Music, York, 2000; Polhill Information Centre, Bedford, 2000; Khoan & Michael Sullivan Chinese Painting Gall., Ashmolean Mus., Oxford, 2001; Sutton Hoo Visitor Centre (NT), 2002; RSPB Envmt and Educn Centre, Rainham, 2006; Lewisham Children and Young People's Centre, 2006; Centre for Classical and Byzantine Studies, Oxford Univ., 2006; Trinity Events Centre, Suffolk Showground, 2006; Ysol Ifor Bach, Caerphilly, 2007; Performing Arts Centre, Latymer Sch., 2008; Dennis Sciama Building, Portsmouth Univ., 2008; Gillespie Court, Clare Coll., Cambridge, 2008; Market Hall, Bolton, 2008; Corfield Court, St John's Coll., 2009; National Museums at Chatham, 2009; Edward Alleyn Bldg, Alleyn's Sch., 2010; Latymer Sci. and Library Building, 2010; New N London Synagogue, 2011; Performance Buildings, Hornsey, 2011. Exhibitions: Kent Design, Maidstone, 2000; University Challenge: buildings for higher educn, Building Centre, 2001; New Connections, Municipal Arts Soc. of NY, NY, 2001; Winning Designs, Bristol Arch. Centre, RIBA, and Cube Gall., Manchester, 2002; Diverse City, RIBA, 2003; Celebration of Architectural Competitions, Cube Gall., Manchester, 2003, RIAS, Edinburgh, 2004; Women in Architecture, Paris, 2004. *Recreations:* visiting buildings and places, making things, painting, seeing friends. *Address:* 1c Laurier Road, NW5 1SD. *T:* (020) 7482 5146. *E:* joannavanh@gmail.com.

van HEYNINGEN, Prof. Veronica, CBE 2010; DPhil; FRS 2007; FRSE; FMedSci; research scientist in human genetics, retired; Group Leader and Section Head, MRC Human Genetics Unit, Edinburgh, 1992–2012; Hon. Professor: University of Edinburgh; Institute of Ophthalmology, University College London, since 2012; *b* 12 Nov. 1946; *d* of Laszlo and Anna Daniel; *m* 1968, Simon van Heyningen; one *s* one *d*. *Educ:* Girton Coll., Cambridge (BA 1968, MA 1971); Northwestern Univ. (MS 1970); DPhil Oxon 1973. Beit Meml Fellow, Oxford and Edinburgh Univs, 1973–76; MRC Human Genetics Unit: postdoctoral scientist, 1977–81; Scientist with tenure, 1981–86; Sen. Scientist, 1986–91; Special Appt grade, 1991. President: Eur. Soc. of Human Genetics, 2003; Genetics Soc., 2009–12. Mem., Human Genetics Commn, 2000–06. Trustee, Nat. Museums of Scotland, 1994–2000; Trustee Dir, Genome Analysis Centre, 2013–. Patron, Aniridia Network UK, 2013–. Pres., Galton Inst., 2014–. Mem., EMBO, 2002. FRSE 1997; FMedSci 1999. *Publications:* contribs to scientific jls. *Recreations:* museums, theatre, feeding people, travelling, novels. *Address:* 51 Rectory Grove, SW4 0DS. *E:* veronica.vanheyningen@igmm.ed.ac.uk.

VAN KLAVEREN, Adrian; Head, Strategic Change, BBC News, since 2014; *b* 31 Dec. 1961; *s* of late Arthur Van Klaveren and Thelma Van Klaveren; *m* 1990, Julie Stringer; two *s*. *Educ:* Bristol Grammar Sch.; St John's Coll., Oxford (BA Modern Hist.). Joined BBC, 1983; news trainee, 1983–85; producer, TV News, 1985–90; Sen. Producer, Panorama, 1990–91; Deputy Editor: Nine O'Clock News, 1992–94; Newsnight, 1994; Hd, Local Progs, BBC W Midlands, 1995–96; News Ed., 1996–2000, Hd, 2000–05, Newsgathering, Dep. Dir and Controller of Prodn, 2005–08, BBC News; Controller, BBC Radio 5 Live and 5 Live Sports Extra, 2008–12; Controller, World War One Centenary, BBC, 2013–14. *Recreations:* football (especially Spurs), cricket, political biography. *Address:* BBC, New Broadcasting House, Portland Place, W1A 1AA. *T:* (020) 7224 3064.

van KUFFELER, John Philip de B.; *see* de Blocq van Kuffeler.

van LEUVEN, (John) Nikolas; QC (Guernsey) 2002; Director General, Guernsey Financial Services Commission, 2009–13; *b* 17 July 1947; *s* of John van Leuven and Catherine van Leuven; *m* 1990, Wendy Sheppard (decd); two *s* one *d*. *Educ:* Elizabeth Coll., Guernsey; Trinity Hall, Cambridge (MA); Caen Univ. (Cert. d'Etudes Juridiques Françaises et Normandes). NP 1989. Called to the Bar, Inner Temple, 1970; called to the Guernsey Bar, 1971; Batonnier, Guernsey Bar, 1994–96; in private practice, Guernsey, 1971–2002; Sen. Partner, Ozannes, 1983–2002; HM Procureur (Attorney Gen.) and HM Receiver Gen., Guernsey, 2002–09. Mem., Chief Pleas of Sark, 1997–2002; Mem., Guernsey States of Deliberation, 2002–09. Mem., British Acad. of Forensic Sci., 1981. FCIArb 1999. Chm., Council, 2001–08, Knight Comdr, 2013, Order of St John, Bailiwick of Guernsey. KStJ 2012 (CStJ 2010; OStJ 2000). Mem., Editl Bd, Jersey and Guernsey Law Rev., 2006–. *Recreations:* book collecting, local history. *Address:* Portland, Domaine de Beauport, Hauteville, St Peter Port, Guernsey GY1 1DL. *Clubs:* Royal Automobile; Sark Yacht; Royal Guernsey Golf.

van LINT, Prof. Theo Maarten, PhD; Calouste Gulbenkian Professor of Armenian Studies, University of Oxford, and Fellow, Pembroke College, Oxford, since 2002; *b* 15 June 1957; *s* of Henk and Coby van Lint. *Educ:* Leiden Univ. (MA Slavic Langs and Lits, 1988; MA Indo-European Comparative Linguistics 1988; PhD Armenian Studies 1996). Researcher: Netherlands Orgn for Scientific Res., 1996–99; Deutsche Forschungsgemeinschaft, Westfälische Wilhelms-Universität, Münster, 1999–2001. Mem., Assoc. Internat. des Études Arméniennes, 1986–. *Publications:* articles in Revue des Études Arméniennes. *Recreations:* volleyball, literature. *Address:* The Oriental Institute, University of Oxford, Pusey Lane, Oxford OX1 2LE.

VANN, Ven. Cherry Elizabeth; Archdeacon of Rochdale, since 2008; Prolocutor of the Lower House, Convocation of York, since 2013; *b* Whetstone, Leicester, 29 Oct. 1958; *d* of Maurice and Jean Vann. *Educ:* Lutterworth Upper Sch.; Royal Coll. of Music (ARCM 1978; GRSM 1980); Westcott House. Ordained deacon, 1989, priest, 1994; Parish Deacon, St Michael, Flixton, 1989–92; Parish Deacon, 1992–94, Asst Curate, 1994–98, Bolton-le-Moors; Team Vicar, 1998–2004, Incumbent, 2004–08, E Farnworth and Kearsley; Area Dean, Farnworth, 2005–08. Chaplain: Colleges of Higher Educn and Further Educn, Bolton, 1992–98; Deaf Community, 1998–2004. Hon. Canon, Manchester Cathedral, 2007–. *Recreations:* music, gardening, hill-walking. *Address:* 57 Melling Road, Oldham OL4 1PN. *T:* (0161) 678 1454. *E:* archrochdale@manchester.anglican.org.

VANNECK, family name of **Baron Huntingfield**.

VANNET, Alfred Douglas; Sheriff of South Strathclyde, Dumfries and Galloway at Airdrie, 2003–09, part-time, since 2009; Senior Tutor in Criminal Litigation, and Hon. Professorial Teaching Fellow, School of Law, University of Glasgow, since 2010; *b* 31 July 1949; *s* of William Peters Vannet and Jean Farquhar Low or Vannet; *m* 1979, Pauline Margaret Renfrew; one *s* one *d*. *Educ:* High Sch. of Dundee; Univ. of Dundee (LLB 1973). Solicitor in private practice, Oban, 1973–76; Procurator Fiscal Depute, Dundee, 1976–77; Procurator Fiscal Depute, then Sen. Procurator Fiscal Depute, Glasgow, 1977–84; Crown Office, Edinburgh: Head of Appeals Section, 1984–87; Asst Solicitor, Law Officers' Secretariat, 1987–88; Dep. Crown Agent, 1990–94; Solicitor to Public Inquiry into Piper Alpha Disaster, 1988–90; Regional Procurator Fiscal: Grampian Highland and Islands, 1994–97; Glasgow and Strathkelvin, 1997–2000; floating Sheriff, all Scotland, 2000–01; Sheriff at Airdrie and Lanark, 2001–03. Mem., Criminal Courts Rules Council, 1997–2000. Member: Forensic Sci. Soc., 1985–2000; Internat. Assoc. of Prosecutors, 1997–2000; Council, Scottish Medico-Legal Soc., 1997–2000. Hon. Mem., Royal Faculty of Procurators in Glasgow, 1997. FRSA 1995. *Recreations:* music, dog walking, curling. *Address:* Sheriff Court House, Graham Street, Airdrie ML6 6EE. *T:* (01236) 751121. *E:* sheriff.advannet@scotcourts.gov.uk.

VAN ORDEN, Brig. Geoffrey Charles, MBE 1973; Member (C) Eastern, European Parliament, since 1999; *b* 10 April 1945; *s* of Thomas and Mary Van Orden; *m* 1974, Frances Elizabeth Weir; three *d*. *Educ:* Sandown Sch.; Mons OCS; Univ. of Sussex (BA Hons Pol Sci.); Indian Defence Services Staff Coll. (psc). Commnd Intelligence Corps, 1964; operational service in Borneo, NI and BAOR; Directing Staff, Führungs Akademie der Bundeswehr, 1985–88; COS and ACOS, G2 Berlin (British Sector), 1988–90; Assessment Staff, Cabinet Office, 1990; Res. Associate, IISS and Service Fellow, Dept of War Studies, KCL, 1990–91; Head, Internat. Mil. Staff Secretariat, NATO HQ, 1991–94; retd and trans. to Regular Reserve, 1994; Sen. Official, EC (Directorate-Gen. Ext. Relations), 1995–99. European Parliament: Cons. Defence Spokesman, 1999–; Mem., Foreign Affairs Cttee, 1999– (Vice-Chm., 2002–06). Vice Chm., ECR, 2009–. Mem., IISS, 1991–. Founder Mem., Anglo-German Officers' Assoc., 1991. Chairman: Europe-India Chamber of Commerce, 2010–; Friends of Sri Lanka, 2010–; Pres., New Direction - The Foundn for Eur. Reform, 2010–; Member: Friends of the Union, 1997–; Countryside Alliance, 1999–; Bow Gp, 1999–; Founder Mem., Friends of India, 2003–. Freeman, City of London, 1991; Freeman, Co. of Painter-Stainers, 1991. *Publications:* various articles on foreign and security policy issues. *Address:* 88 Rectory Lane, Chelmsford, Essex CM1 1RF; European Parliament, Rue Wiertz, 1047 Brussels, Belgium. *T:* (2) 2847332. *Club:* Army and Navy.

van OSS, Angela Ruth; *see* McLean, A. R.

VAN REENEN, Prof. John Michael, PhD; FBA 2010; Director, Centre for Economic Performance, since 2003; Professor, Department of Economics, London School of Economics and Political Science, since 2003; *b* 26 Dec. 1965; *s* of Lionel and Anne Van Reenen; *m* 2001, Sarah Chambers; one *d*. *Educ:* Queens' Coll., Cambridge (BA 1988; Joshua King Prize, 1988); LSE (MSc 1989; Automation Prize, 1989); University Coll. London (PhD 1992). Res. Fellow, Inst. for Fiscal Studies, 1993–95; Prof., Dept of Econs, UCL, 1995–2003. Visiting Professor: Univ. of Calif, Berkeley, 1998–99; Stanford Univ., 2008–09; Harvard Univ., 2013–14. Sen. Policy Advr to Sec. of State, DoH, 2000–01. Research Fellow: Centre for Econ. Policy Res., 1996–; Nat. Bureau of Econ. Res., 2006–; Inst. for the Study of Labor, 2010–. Fellow: Econometric Soc., 2012; Soc. for Labor Economists, 2013. Yrjö Jahnsson Award, 2009; Arrow Prize, Internat. Assoc. of Health Econs, 2011; (jtly) EIB Prize for Excellence in Econ. and Social Res., 2014. *Publications:* over 100 articles in American Econ. Rev., Qly Jl of Econs, Rev. of Econ. Studies and many others. *Recreations:* music, cooking, film, reading, arguing, politics. *Address:* 161 Fentiman Road, SW8 1JZ. *T:* (020) 7955 6976. *E:* j.vanreenen@lse.ac.uk. *Clubs:* Black's, Tuesday.

VAN ROMPUY, Herman; President of the European Council, 2009–14; *b* Etterbeek, Belgium, 31 Oct. 1947; *s* of Prof. Vic Van Rompuy and Germaine Geens; *m* Geertrui Windels; two *s* two *d*. *Educ:* St-Jan Berchmanscollege, Brussels; Katholieke Universiteit Leuven (Bachelor of Philos. 1968; Master Applied Econs 1971). Attaché Internal Affairs, Nat. Bank of Belgium, 1972–75; Adviser to Cabinet of Prime Minister of Belgium, 1975–78, of Minister of Finance, 1978–80; Dir, Centrum voor Politieke, Economische en Sociale Studies, 1980–88; Lecturer: Handelshogeschool, Antwerp, 1980–87; Vlaamse Economische Hogeschool, Brussels, 1982–2008. Vice-Prime Minister and Minister of Budget, 1993–99; MP (Christian Democratic and Flemish), 1995–2009; Speaker, House of Representatives, 2007–08; Royal Explorer, 2007; Royal Conciliator, 2007; Prime Minister, 2008–09. Grootlint in de Leopoldsorde (Belgium), 2009. *Publications:* De kentering der tijden, 1979; Hopen na 1984, 1984; Het christendom: een moderne gedachte, 1990; Vernieuwing in hoofd en hart: een tegendraadse visie, 1998; De binnenkant op een kier: avonden zonder politiek, 2000; Dagboek van een vijftiger, 2004; Op zoek naar wijsheid, 2007; Haiku, 2010; In de wereld van Herman Van Rompuy, 2010; Haiku 2, 2014.

van SCHOONHETEN, Baron Willem Oswald B.; *see* Bentinck van Schoonheten.

VÄNSKÄ, Osmo; Music Director, Minnesota Symphony Orchestra, since 2003; *b* Finland, 1953. *Educ:* trained as clarinettist; Sibelius Acad., Helsinki (conducting, under Jorma Panula). Formerly co-principal clarinettist, Helsinki Philharmonic Orch.; Music Dir, 1988–2008, Conductor Laureate, 2008–, Lahti SO; Chief Conductor: Icelandic SO, 1993–96; BBC Scottish SO, 1996–2002; Guest Conductor of orchestras in Europe, USA, Australia and Japan. First Prize, Internat. Young Conductors' Competition, Besançon, 1982. *Address:* c/o HarrisonParrott Ltd, 5–6 Albion Court, Albion Place, W6 0QT.

van STEENIS, Camilla Hilary; *see* Cavendish, C. H.

van WACHEM, Lodewijk Christiaan; Knight, Order of the Netherlands Lion, 1981; Commander, Order of Orange-Nassau, 1990; Hon. KBE 1988 (Hon. CBE 1977); *b* Pangkalan Brandan, Indonesia, 31 July 1931; *m* 1958, Elisabeth G. Cristofoli; two *s* one *d*.

Educ: Univ. of Technol., Delft (mech. engr). Joined Royal Dutch/Shell Gp, 1953; worked in Latin America, Africa, FE and Europe; Royal Dutch Petroleum Co.: Man. Dir, 1976–82; Pres., 1982–92; Chm., Supervisory Bd, 1992–2002. Member, Supervisory Board: Akzo Nobel NV, 1992–2002; BMW AG, 1994–2002; Bayer AG, 1997–2002; Chm., Bd of Dirs, Global Crossing Ltd, 2003–11; Member, Board of Directors: Credit Suisse Hldg, 1992–96; IBM Corp., 1992–2002; Philips Electronics NV, 1993–2005 (Chm., 1999–2005); Atco Ltd, 1993–09; Zurich Financial Services, 1993–2005 (Vice-Chm., 2001–02; Chm., 2002–05). Hon. Citizen, Singapore, 2004.

van ZWANENBERG, Zoë; Management Consultant: Zwan Consulting, since 2008; Associate Centre for Confidence and Well-Being, since 2008; research consultant, Churches Together in Britain and Ireland, 2011; *b* Ipswich, 20 Dec. 1952; *d* of David Francis and Aldyth Vincent van Zwanenberg; *m* 1986, Stephen Thompson (marr. diss. 1995); two step *d*. *Educ:* Univ. of Birmingham (BA Eng. Lang. and Lit.); Univ. of Sussex (MA Hist. of Art). MCIPD 1987; MIHM 1984. Gen. mgt, NHS, 1979–86; Force Personnel Officer, Suffolk Constabulary, 1987–90; Dir, Personnel and Trng, Life Span Healthcare, 1990–92; Mgt and Employee Develt Advr, InterCity, 1992–93; Dir, HR, Anglia Railways, 1993–96; Orgn Develt Advr, EA, 1996–99; Hd, Strategic Change Unit, NHS in Scotland, 1999–2001; Chief Exec., Scottish Leadership Foundn, 2001–08. Non-exec. Dir, Scottish Prison Service, 2009–. Chairman: Scottish Youth Dance, 2000–06, 2010– (Dir, 2007); Scottish Ballet, 2004–13; Lamp of Lothian, 2013–; Diocesan Standing Cttee, 2013–; Dir, Scottish Sculpture Trust, 2001–04. Hon. Professor: Queen Margaret Univ., 2007–12; De Montfort Univ., 2007–13. *Recreations:* arts and culture, European travel, ballet, opera, reading, gardens. *Address:* 10 Bielside Gardens, West Barns, Dunbar, Scotland EH42 1WA. *E:* zoe_van_zwanenberg@hotmail.com.

VARA, Shailesh Lakhman; MP (C) North West Cambridgeshire, since 2005; Parliamentary Under-Secretary of State: Ministry of Justice, since 2013; Department for Work and Pensions, since 2015; *b* 4 Sept. 1960; *s* of Lakhman Arjan Vara and Savita Vara (*née* Gadher); *m* 2002, Beverley Deanne Fear; two *s*. *Educ:* Aylesbury Grammar Sch.; Brunel Univ. (LLB; Hon. Fellow, 2010). Admitted Solicitor, 1990; articled, Richards Butler, 1988–90; Crossman Block, 1991–92; Payne Hicks Beach, 1992–93; CMS Cameron McKenna, 1994–2001. Shadow Dep. Leader of the H of C, 2006–10; an Asst Govt Whip, 2010–12. Mem., Select Cttee on Envmt, Food and Rural Affairs, 2005–06, on Admin, 2010–11, on Finance and Services, 2011–13. Chm., Cons. Parly Friends of India, 2008–10; Vice Chm., Cons. China Parly Gp, 2009–10. A Vice-Chm., Cons. Party, 2001–05. Contested (C): Birmingham Ladywood, 1997; Northampton S, 2001. Treas., 2001–04, Vice Chm., 2006–09, Exec. Cttee, Soc. of Cons. Lawyers. Mem., Campaign Exec. Gp, Great Fen Project, 2005–10. Gov., Westminster Kingsway Coll., 2002–05. Vice-Pres., Huntingdonshire CCC, 2007–. *Recreations:* travel, cricket, tae kwon do. *Address:* House of Commons, SW1A 0AA. *T:* (020) 7219 3000. *E:* varas@parliament.uk.

VARADHAN, Prof. Srinivasa, PhD; FRS 1998; Professor of Mathematics, Courant Institute of Mathematical Sciences (formerly Courant Institute), New York University, since 1972; *b* 2 Jan. 1940; *s* of S. V. Rangaiyengar and S. R. Janaki; *m* 1964, Vasundara Narayanan; two *s*. *Educ:* Madras Univ. (BSc Hons, MA); Indian Statistical Inst. (PhD 1963). Courant Institute, New York University: Vis. Member, 1963–66; Asst Prof., 1966–68; Associate Prof., 1968–72; Dir, 1980–84 and 1992–94. Fellow, Amer. Acad. Arts and Sci., 1988; Associate Fellow, Third World Acad. Scis, 1988; Mem., NAS, 1995. *Publications:* Multi-dimensional Diffusion Processes, 1979; On Diffusion Problems and Partial Differential Equations, 1980; Large Deviations and Applications, 1984; Probability Theory, 2001; Stochastic Processes, 2007. *Recreations:* travel, tennis, squash, bridge. *Address:* Courant Institute of Mathematical Sciences, New York University, 251 Mercer Street, New York, NY 10012, USA. *T:* (212) 9983334.

VARCOE, (Christopher) Stephen; baritone; *b* 19 May 1949; *s* of Philip William and Mary Northwood Varcoe; *m* 1972, Melinda Davies; two *s* two *d* (and one *s* decd). *Educ:* King's School, Canterbury; King's College, Cambridge (MA); University of York (PhD). Freelance concert and opera singer, 1970–; on teaching staff, Royal Coll. of Music, 2003–, Clare Coll., Cambridge, 2007–; Robinson Coll., Cambridge, 2011–. Fellow, Murray Edwards Coll., Cambridge, 2009–10. Calouste Gulbenkian Foundation Fellowship, 1977. *Publications:* Sing English Song: a practical guide to the language and repertoire, 2000; (contrib.) Cambridge Companion to Singing, 2000; (contrib.) New Percy Grainger Companion, 2010. *Recreations:* painting, gardening, building. *Address:* c/o Caroline Phillips, 11 Pound Pill, Corsham, Wilts SN13 9HZ.

VARCOE, Jeremy Richard Lovering Grosvenor, CMG 1989; HM Diplomatic Service, retired; part-time Immigration Judge (formerly Adjudicator), 1995–2007; *b* 20 Sept. 1937; *s* of late Ronald A. G. Varcoe and Zoe E. Varcoe (*née* Lovering); *m* 1st, 1961, Wendy Anne Moss (*d* 1991); two *d*; 2nd, 1995, Ruth Murdoch (*née* Wallis). *Educ:* Charterhouse; Lincoln Coll., Oxford (MA). National Service, Royal Tank Regt, 2nd Lieut, 1956–58. HMOCS: District Officer, Swaziland, 1962–65. Called to the Bar, Gray's Inn, 1966; Lectr in Law, Univ. of Birmingham, 1967–70; joined HM Diplomatic Service, 1970; FCO, 1970–72; Dep. Secretary General, Pearce Commn on Rhodesian Opinion, 1972; First Sec., Ankara, 1972–74, Lusaka, 1974–78; FCO, 1978–79; Counsellor, Kuala Lumpur, 1979–82; Head of Southern African Dept, FCO, 1982–84; Counsellor, Ankara, 1984–85; on special leave with Standard Chartered Bank, Istanbul, 1985–87; Ambassador to Somalia, 1987–89; Minister/Dep. High Comr, Lagos, 1989–90; Asst Under-Sec. of State, FCO, 1990–92. Co-ordinator, London Economic Summit, 1991. Dir Gen., United World Colls, 1992–94; Dep. Dir, Develt Office, Oxford Univ., 1995–96. *Publications:* Legal Aid in Criminal Proceedings—a Regional Survey, 1970. *Recreations:* walking, golf, local issues in Cornwall, tilting at wind turbines. *Address:* Dozmary, Rock Road, Rock, Wadebridge, Cornwall PL27 6PW. *Club:* St Enodoc Golf.

VARCOE, Stephen; *see* Varcoe, C. S.

VARDAXOGLOU, Prof. John Costas, (Yiannis), PhD; CEng, FIET, FREng, FIEEE; Professor of Wireless Communications, Loughborough University, since 1998 (Dean, School of Electronic, Electrical and Systems Engineering, 2006–12); *b* Athens, 3 Sept. 1959; *s* of Costas and Evangelia Vardaxoglou; *m* 1987, Rachel McQuail; two *s*. *Educ:* First Sch. of Kalamaki, Alimos, Athens; Univ. of Kent (BSc Math. Physics 1982; PhD Electronics 1985). CEng 2011; FIET 2011; FREng 2011; FIEEE 2012. Res. Asst, Univ. of Kent, 1985–88; Lectr, 1988–92, Sen. Lectr, 1992–98, Loughborough Univ. of Technol., later Loughborough Univ. Founder Dir, Antrum Ltd, 2011–. *Publications:* Frequency Selective Surfaces: analysis and design, 1997. *Address:* 38 Fairmount Drive, Loughborough, Leics LE11 3JR. *T:* (01509) 560625, (office) (01509) 227001, *Fax:* (01509) 227008. *E:* j.c.vardaxoglou@lboro.ac.uk.

VARDY, Prof. Alan Edward, PhD, DEng, DSc; FREng, FICE; FRSE; Research Professor of Civil Engineering (part-time), University of Dundee, since 1995 (Professor of Civil Engineering, 1979–95); Engineering Consultant, Dundee Tunnel Research, since 1995; *b* Sheffield, 6 Nov. 1945; *s* of John Moreton Vardy and Margaret Vardy (*née* Thompson); *m* 1991, Susan Janet Upstone; two *s* one *d*. *Educ:* Univ. of Leeds (BSc 1st Cl. Hons Civil Engrg 1967; PhD Civil Engrg 1971; DEng Tunnel Safety 1997); Univ. of Dundee (DSc Transient 1-D Flows 2007). FICE 1989 (MICE 1975); Eur Ing 1989; FRSE 2002; FREng 2007. Res. Officer, 1971–72, Lectr in Civil Engrg, 1972–75, Univ. of Leeds; Royal Soc. Warren Res. Fellow, Univ. of Cambridge, 1975–79; University of Dundee: Hd, Dept of Civil Engrg, 1979–85; Dir, Wolfson Bridge Res. Unit, 1980–90; Dep. Principal, 1985–88; Dep. Principal and Vice Principal, 1988–89; Royal Soc./SERC Industrial Fellow, 1990–94; Dir, Lightweight Structures Unit, 1998–2004. FASCE 1995 (MASCE 1980). FRSA 1980; FHEA 2007. *Publications:* Fluid Principles, 1990; 190 papers in jls and confs. *Recreations:* wine, wife, walking. *Address:* Dundee Tunnel Research, Kirkton, Abernyte, Perthshire PH14 9SS. *T:* (01828) 686241.

VARDY, Sir Peter, Kt 2001; DL; Chairman, Vardy Group of Companies (incorporating The Vardy Foundation, Vardy Property Group and Peter Vardy Ltd), since 2006; *b* 4 March 1947; *s* of late Reginald Vardy and of Sarah Vardy; *m* 1971, Margaret; two *s* one *d* (and one *s* decd.). *Educ:* Chorister Sch.; Durham Sch. Began work in family business, Reg Vardy Ltd (motor dealership), at age of 16; built co. to become one of largest UK motor retail gps; CEO, 1982–2006; floated on Stock Exchange, 1989; sold to Pendragon Plc, 2006. Sponsor Chairman: Emmanuel Coll., Gateshead (City Tech. Coll.), 1990–2010; Kings Acad. (City Acad.), Middlesbrough, 2003–10; Trinity Acad. (City Acad.), Doncaster, 2005–10; Chm., Bede Acad., Blyth, 2009–10. Founder, Safe Families for Children in the UK, 2013–. DL Tyne and Wear, 2002. Freedom of the City of Sunderland, 2011. Hon. DBA Sunderland, 1995; Hon. DLaws Pennsylvania, 2009. Beacon Award for Philanthropy, 2015. *Address:* (office) Venture House, Aykley Heads, Durham DH1 5TS.

VARDY, Peter Christian, PhD; Vice-Principal, Heythrop College, London, 1999–2011; *b* 29 July 1945; *s* of Mark and Christa Vardy; *m* 1st, 1974, Anne Moore (marr. diss. 2004); two *s* four *d*; 2nd, 2009, Charlotte Vardy (*née* Fowler); two *d*. *Educ:* Charterhouse; Univ. of Southampton (BA 1979); W Sussex Inst. of Higher Educn (PGCE 1980); KCL (MTh 1982; PhD 1985). FCA 1967. Chm., H. Young Holdings plc, 1979–83. Chm., Bd of Theology, Univ. of London, 1990–93. Pres., London Soc. for the Study of Religion, 1996–98. Ed., Dialogue Australasia, 1997–2009; Mem. Bd, Dialogue Australasia Network, 2001–13. *Publications:* The Puzzle of God, 1989, 4th edn 1999; (jtly) The Puzzle of Ethics, 1990, 4th edn 1999; The Puzzle of Evil, 1991, 2nd edn 1997; The Puzzle of Sex, 1993, 2nd edn 2009; (jtly) The Puzzle of the Gospels, 1994; (ed) Great Christian Thinkers, 1995; What is Truth, 1999, 2nd edn 2003; (jtly) The Thinker's Guide to Evil, 2003; (jtly) The Thinker's Guide to God, 2003; Being Human, 2003; Kierkegaard, 2008; Good and Bad Religion, 2010; (jtly) Ethics Matters, 2012; (jtly) God Matters, 2013; (jtly) Bible Matters, 2014. *Recreations:* reading, writing, stillness and preparing for death. *T:* (01423) 755048. *E:* petervardy@ymail.com.

VARGAS LLOSA, Mario; writer; *b* Arequipa, Peru, 28 March 1936; *m* 1st, 1955, Julia Urquidi (marr. diss. 1964); 2nd, 1965, Patricia Llosa Urquidi; two *s* one *d*. *Educ:* Univ. Nacional Mayor de San Marcos, Lima (BA); Univ. of Madrid (PhD 1971). Journalist and broadcaster, Lima and Paris; Lectr, QMC, 1967; Writer in Residence, Wilson Center, Smithsonian Instn, 1980; Vis. Fellow, Wissenschaftskolleg, Berlin, 1991–92; Dist. Writer-in-Residence, Georgetown Univ., Washington DC, 2003; Visiting Professor: Washington State Univ., 1968; KCL, 1969; Univ. de Puerto Rico, 1969; Columbia Univ., 1975; Cambridge Univ., 1977; Syracuse Univ., 1988; Florida Internat. Univ., 1991; Harvard Univ., 1992–93; Princeton Univ., 1993; Georgetown Univ., 1994, 1999; Oxford Univ., 2000. Founder of political party, Movimiento Libertad, 1988; Presidential candidate, Peru, 1990. Pres., PEN Club Internat., 1976–79. Member: Acad. Peruana de la Lengua, 1975; Royal Spanish Acad., 1994; Internat. Acad. of Humanism, 1996. Hon. FKC 2007. Holds numerous honorary doctorates. Biblioteca Breve prize (Spain), 1963; Rómulo Gallegos Internat. Literature prize (Venezuela), 1967; Ritz Paris Hemingway prize (France), 1985; Asturias prize (Spain), 1986; Planeta prize (Spain), 1993; Cervantes prize (Spain), 1994; Jerusalem prize (Israel), 1995; Pluma de Oro Award, Club de la Escritura, Madrid, 1997; Crystal Award, World Econ. Forum, 2001; Americas Award, Americas Foundn, 2001; Nabokov Prize, PEN American Center, 2002; Budapest Prize (Hungary), 2003; Premio Mercosur a las Letras, Konex Foundn (Argentina), 2004; Premio a la libertad, Friedrich Naumann Foundn (Germany), 2009; Nobel Prize in Literature, 2010. Congressional Medal of Honour (Peru), 1981; Gran Cruz, Orden El Sol (Peru), 2001; Medal of Honor of Peruvian Culture (Peru), 2004; Légion d'honneur (France), 1985; Commandeur, Ordre des Arts et des Lettres (France), 1993; Gran Cruz, Order of Rubén Dario (Nicaragua), 2006. *Publications:* Los jefes (short stories), 1959; Mario Vargas Llosa: obras completas, vol. I Narraciones y novelas (1959–1967), 2004, vol. II Novelas (1969–1977), 2004, vol. III Novelas y Teatro (1981–1986), 2005; Diálogo de damas (poems), 2007; Fonchito y la luna (children's story), 2010; *novels:* La ciudad y los perros, 1963; La casa verde, 1966; Los cachorros, 1967; Conversación en la Catedral, 1969; Historia secreta de una novela, 1971; Pantaleón y las visitadoras, 1973; La tía Julia y el escribidor, 1977 (filmed as Tune in Tomorrow, 1990); La guerra del fin del mundo, 1981; La historia de Mayta, 1984; ¿Quién mató a Palomino Molero?, 1986; El hablador, 1987; Elogio de la madrastra, 1988; Lituma en los Andes, 1993; Los cuadernos de Don Rigoberto, 1997; La fiesta del chivo, 2000 (filmed as The Feast of the Goat, 2006); El paraíso en la otra esquina, 2003; Travesuras de la niña mala, 2006; El sueño del celta, 2010; El Héroe Discreto, 2015; *plays:* La señorita de Tacna, 1981; Kathie y el hipopótamo, 1983; La Chunga, 1986; El loco de los balcones, 1993; Odiseo y Penélope, 2007; Al pie del Támesis, 2008; Las mil noches y una noche, 2009; *non-fiction:* Contra viento y marea (essays), vols I and II, 1986, vol. III, 1990; La verdad de las mentiras (essays), 1990, new edn 2002; El pez en el agua (autobiog.), 1993; Desafíos a la libertad (essays), 1994; Making Waves (essays), 1996; Touchstones: essays on literature, art and politics, 2007; Wellsprings (essays), 2008; Sables y utopías: visiones de América Latina (essays), 2009; Notes on the Death of Culture, 2015; articles for El País and Letras Libres. *Address:* Las Magnolias 295-6° Piso, Barranco, Lima 04, Peru. *Fax:* (1) 4773518; c/o Faber & Faber Ltd, Bloomsbury House, 74–77 Great Russell Street, WC1B 3DA. *Fax:* (020) 7927 3801.

VARLEY, Dame Joan (Fleetwood), DBE 1985 (CBE 1974); Director, Local Government Organisation, Conservative Central Office, 1976–84; *b* 22 Feb. 1920; *d* of late F. Ireton and Elizabeth Varley. *Educ:* Cheltenham Ladies' College; London School of Economics (BSc Econ). Section Officer, WAAF, 1944–46. Conservative Agent, Shrewsbury, 1952–56; Dep. Central Office Agent, NW Area, 1957–65; Dep. Dir Orgn, 1966–74, Dir, Central Admin, 1975–76, Cons. Central Office. Chm., Friends of St James Norlands Assoc., 1986–95; Pro Chancellor, Univ. of Greenwich Court of Governors, 1992–94 (Vice-Chm., 1986–91, Chm., 1991–92, Thames Polytechnic Court of Governors); pt-time Mem., Panel of VAT Tribunals, 1986–94. DUniv Greenwich, 1995. *Recreations:* gardening, walking. *Address:* 21 Chartwell House, 12 Ladbroke Terrace, W11 3PG. *T:* (020) 7727 9005.

VARLEY, John Christian, TD 1991, and bar 1997; FRAgS; FCIM; Estates Director, Clinton Devon Estates, since 2000; *b* Leeds, 5 Oct. 1960; *s* of late Maurice Varley and of Audrey Varley; *m* 1995, Rebecca Warner; one *s* two *d*. *Educ:* Leeds Grammar Sch.; Univ. of Leeds (BA Hons); McGill Univ., Montreal (MBA). Mktg Exec., Dunlop Hldgs, 1982–84; Product Manager, Gestetner Internat., 1984–86; British Telecom: Mktg Manager, IDD, 1986–90; Manager: IDD Strategy, 1990–92; Internat. Telephony, 1992–95; Sen. Customer and Field Ops Manager Scotland, 1995–98; Gen. Manager, Corporate Clients, 1998; Prog. Dir, AT&T/BT Global Venture, 1998–99; Dir, Project Heritage, 1999–2000. Chm., Rural Cttee, 2008–14, Gp Chm., 2015–, Estates Business Gp. Member, Board: Countryside Agency, 2002–06; Commn for Rural Communities, 2006–09; Envmt Agency, 2009– (Chm., Envmt Agency Pension Fund, 2012–); Govt Wildlife Network Rev. Panel, 2009–10; Govt Ind. Forestry Panel, 2011–12; Natural England, 2015–. Officer, RA, TA, 1978–2000. FCIM 2004; FRAgS 2014. *Recreations:* walking, travel, family, keeping a global perspective. *Address:* c/o Clinton Devon Estates, Bicton Arena, East Budleigh, Budleigh Salterton, Devon EX9 7BL. *T:* (01395) 441141/2. *E:* mail@clintondevon.com. *Clubs:* Farmers, Cavalry and Guards.

VARLEY, John Silvester; Group Chief Executive, Barclays Bank plc, 2004–11; *b* 1 April 1956; *m* 1981, Carolyn Thorn Pease; one *s* one *d*. *Educ:* Downside Sch.; Oriel Coll., Oxford (MA 1st cl. Hons History). Admitted Solicitor, 1979; Commercial Law Dept, Frere Cholmeley, Solicitors, 1979–82; Asst Dir, Corporate Finance Dept, Barclays Merchant Bank, 1982–86; Barclays de Zoete Wedd: Corporate Finance Div., 1986–89; Man. Dir, BZW Asia, 1989–91; Dep. Chief Exec., Global Equities Div., 1991–94; Dir, Odey Asset Management, 1994–95; Chairman: BZW Asset Management, 1995–96; BZW Property Investment Management, 1995–96; Dir, Barclays Global Investors, 1995–96; Chm., Barclays Asset Management Gp, 1996–98; Barclays Bank plc: Dir, 1998–; Chief Exec., Retail Finance Services, Barclays Bank plc, 1998–2000; Gp Finance Dir, 2000–03. Non-executive Director: BlackRock; AstraZeneca (Sen. Ind. Dir, 2012–15); Rio Tinto, 2011– (Sen. Ind. Dir, 2012–). Chm., Marie Curie Cancer Care, 2011–. *Clubs:* Brooks's, Army and Navy, White's.

VARLEY, Rosemary Margaret, (Rosie), OBE 2007; Chairman: Public Guardian Board, 2007–12; General Social Care Council, 2008–12; *b* 22 Dec. 1951; *d* of late Ratcliffe Bowen Wright, MD, FRCOG and of Dr Margaret Bowen Wright (*née* Williams); *m* 1976, Andrew Iain Varley (*d* 2005); one *s* one *d*. *Educ:* New Hall, Chelmsford; Durham Univ. (BA Hons); Manchester Univ. (MA Econ). Various acad. posts, Manchester Univ., 1978–83; Mem., W Suffolk HA, 1984–92; Chairman: Mid Anglia Community NHS Trust, 1992–97; Anglia and Oxford, then Eastern, Reg., NHS Exec., DoH, 1997–2001; NHS Appointments Comr, Eastern Reg., 2001–06. Ind. Mem., E of England Regl Assembly, 1999–2001. Non-exec. Dir, W Suffolk Hospital NHS Trust, 2011–. Member: Mental Health Rev. Tribunal, 1995–; Disability Appeal Tribunal, 1992–. Chm., General Optical Council, 1999–2009; Mem., Council for Healthcare Regulatory Excellence (formerly Council for the Regulation of Healthcare Professionals), 2002–08 (Actg Chm., 2007–08); Mem., NMC Appts Bd, 2007–09; Ind. Public Appts Assessor, 2012–. Governor: Priory Sch., Bury St Edmunds, 2007–; St Benedict's RC Sch., Bury St Edmunds, 2011–. FRSocMed 1999; Hon. Fellow, Coll. of Optometrists, 2009. Freeman, City of London, 2005; Liveryman, Co. of Spectacle Makers, 2006–. DUniv: East Anglia, 2009; Essex, 2009. *Publications:* contrib. various articles in health jls and mgt textbooks. *Recreations:* walking, all things Italian, bridge, extended family. *Address:* 72 Southgate Street, Bury St Edmunds, Suffolk IP33 2BJ. *T:* (01284) 753135. *E:* rosievarley@btinternet.com.

VARMUS, Prof. Harold Eliot, MD; Director, National Cancer Institute, Maryland, since 2010; *b* 18 Dec. 1939; *s* of Frank Varmus and Beatrice Barasch Varmus; *m* 1969, Constance Louise Casey; two *s*. *Educ:* Freeport High Sch., NY; Amherst Coll., Mass (BA 1961); Harvard Univ. (MA 1962); Columbia Univ., NY (MD 1966). Surgeon, US Public Health Service, 1968–70; Dept of Microbiology, Univ. of California Medical Center, San Francisco: Lectr, 1970–72; Asst Prof., 1972–74; Associate Prof., 1974–79; Prof. of Microbiology and Immunology, 1979–93 (Dept of Biochem. and Biophys, 1982–93); Amer. Cancer Soc. Prof. of Molecular Virology, 1984–93; Dir, NIH, Bethesda, Md, 1993–99; Pres. and CEO, Memorial Sloan-Kettering Cancer Center, NY, 2000–10. Scientific Consultant, Chiron Corp., 1982–87; Member, Scientific Adv. Bd: Merck Corp., 1985–88; Gilead Corp., 1988–. Co-Chm., US President's Council of Advrs on Sci. and Technol., 2009–. Associate Editor: Cell, 1974–78, 1979–; Virology, 1974–84; Genes and Develt, 1986–; Editor, Molecular and Cellular Biol., 1984–88; Mem., Editl Bd, Trends in Genetics, 1989–. Member: Special Grants Cttee, Calif. Div., Amer. Cancer Soc., 1973–76; Breast Cancer Virus Wkg Gp, Virus Cancer Program, 1973–74. Bd of Scientific Counselors, Div. of Cancer Biol. and Diagnosis, 1983–87, Nat. Cancer Inst.; Virology Study Section, NIH, 1976–80. Member: AAAS; Amer. Soc. Microbiology; Amer. Soc. Biochem. and Molecular Biol; Amer. Soc. Virology; Nat. Acad. Scis, 1984; Amer. Acad. Arts and Scis, 1988. Foreign Mem., Royal Soc., 2005. Hon. DSc: Amherst Coll., 1984; Columbia Univ., 1990. Numerous awards and prizes incl. (jtly) Nobel Prize for Physiology or Medicine, 1989. *Publications:* The Art and Politics of Science (memoirs), 2009. *Address:* National Cancer Institute, 9000 Rockville Pike, Bethesda, MD 20892–9760, USA.

VARNEY, Sir David (Robert), Kt 2006; Chairman, Packt Ltd, since 2012; *b* 11 May 1946; *s* of Robert Kitchener Frederick Varney and Winifred Gwendoline Williams; *m* 1971, Patricia Ann Billingham; one *s* one *d*. *Educ:* Brockley County Grammar Sch.; Surrey Univ. (BSc); Manchester Univ. (MBA; Alumnus of the Year, 2005). Joined Shell Refining Co., 1968; various appts in UK, Australia, Holland and Sweden, 1968–90; Head of Mkting, Branding and Product Develt, SIPCO, 1990–91; Man. Dir, Downstream Oil, Shell UK, 1991–95; Dir (responsible for Shell's oil products business in Europe), Shell Internat. Petroleum Co., 1996; Chief Exec., BG Group plc, 1997–2000; Chairman: BT Wireless, subseq. mmO_2, 2001–04; HM Revenue and Customs, 2004–06. Non-executive Director: Cable and Wireless, 1999–2000; HM Treasury, 2004–07; Civil Service Steering Bd, 2007–09. PM's Advr on Public Service Transportation, 2007–09. Member: Bd, Oil, Gas and Petrochemicals Supplies Office, 1997–99; Public Service Productivity Panel, 2000–01; Policy Commn on Future of Farming and Food, 2001–02. Chm., BITC, 2002–04. President: Inst. of Employment Studies, 2003–07; Chartered Mgt Inst., 2005–06. Interim Chm., Barking, Havering and Redbridge Univ. Hosps NHS Trust, 2010. Chm., Annual Fund Disbursement Cttee, Univ. of Surrey, 2012– (Mem., 1994–2002, Vice-Chm., 2001–02, Council). Chm., Stroke Assoc., 2013–. Hon. DTech London Metropolitan, 2005; Hon. LLD Bath, 2006; DUniv Surrey, 2007. *Recreations:* opera, Formula 1 motor racing, Rugby. *Address:* Suite 215, Butlers Wharf Building, 36 Shad Thames, SE1 2YE. *Clubs:* Athenæum, Royal Society of Medicine (Mem. Council, 2003–05).

VARNISH, Peter, OBE 1982; FREng, FIET; Director, since 2001, and Chief Executive, since 2006, Geopolitical (formerly International Geopolitical) Solutions Ltd; *b* 30 May 1947; *s* of John Varnish and Ilma Varnish (*née* Godfrey); *m* 1968, Shirley-Anne Bendelow; two *s*. *Educ:* Warwick Sch.; UCNW, Bangor (BSc Hons 1968). CEng 1987; FIET (FIEE 1989); FREng (FEng 1995). Res., Services Electronics Res. Lab., Baldock, 1968–75; Scientific Advr to MoD, British Embassy, Washington, 1975–79; Res. Area Co-ordinator for Electrical Warfare in UK, ASWE Portsdown, 1979–81; Officer i/c, ASWE Funtington, 1981–84; Head: Radar Div., ASWE Portsdown, 1984–86; Signature Control, ARE Funtington, 1986–88; Electronic Warfare and Weapons Dept, ARE Portsdown, 1988–90; Dir, Above Water Weapons, DRA, 1990–92; RCDS 1992; Dir, SDI Participation Office, 1993; Dir of Sci. for Ballistic Missile Defence, MoD, 1993–95; Defence Evaluation and Research Agency: Dir, Internat. Business Develt, 1995–98; Dir, Business Develt, 1998–2000; Dir of Technology (Partnership), 2000–01; Chief Exec., S3T Ltd, 2001–05. Chairman: Definition International Ltd, 2002–09; Wrightson Gp, 2002–11; AeroGB Ltd, 2010; Director: CMB Ltd, 2001–04; Sparks Technology Ltd, 2001–06; Charteris, Mackie, Baillie, 2001–05; Closed Solutions Ltd, 2002–; CMBIE Ltd, 2003–04; ITAG Ltd, 2003–06; Evesham Ltd, 2004–06; Table 27 Ltd, 2004–07; Ipsotek Ltd, 2005; QTEL Europe Plc, 2005–06; Consols Ltd, 2006–08; WPM Ltd, 2008–12; Blue Star Capital, 2008–13; Trango Ltd, 2009–11; 1SH Division, 2003–11; Tridex Ltd, 2010–11; Halcyon LLP, 2010–12; Deep Secure, 2011; Cambridge Global Capital UK Ltd. Mem., Defence Scientific Adv. Council, 1991–99; Adviser: Home Office, 2003–11; MoD Faraday Initiative, 2004–; FBM Babcock, 2005–08; to Shadow Minister for Defence Procurement, 2007–11; Aerospace Resources, 2008–; Foreign and Commonwealth Office, 2009–14; Northrop Grumman, 2009–14; Lockheed Martin, 2009–15; Algero Capital, 2010–12; Broadcast Networks Ltd, 2012–14; Risk Engineering Bulgaria, 2012–; BN Homeland Security and Defence, 2013–14; Cambridge Global Capital LLC, 2014–; Sen. Advr, Tayrona UK Ltd. Chairman: Common Defence Forum, 1988–2004; Military Microwaves, 1990; Stealth Conf., 1990, 2003, 2004; Milcon, Abu Dhabi, biennially, 1995–; Singapore Internat. Defence Conf., 1997, 1999, 2005; Air Missile Conf., 2001, 2002, 2003, 2004, 2005; Global Security Conf., 2002; Interoperability Conf., 2002, 2003, 2004, 2005; Air Launched Weapons Conf., 2002, 2003, 2004, 2005; Military Aviation Repair and Maintenance, 2004, 2005; Asymmetric Warfare, 2004, 2005, 2006; Homeland Defence Conf., Dubai, 2005, 2006; Internat. Security Nat. Resilience, London, 2007; EW-AOC, Interlaken, 2007; Networked Public Safety, London, 2008; Owning the Night, Bisley, 2009, 2011; CNi, Expo London, 2010; Vice-Chm., Global Security, Asia Conf., Singapore, 2005, 2007; Mem., Judging Panel, IFSEC Internat., 2011. Mem., Cttee, RN Seamore Appeal. Faculty Mem., Duke Univ., Durham, NC, 2013–. Mem., Sainsbury Award Cttee, Royal Acad. of Engrg, 2010–. Mem. Assoc. of Old Crows, later Assoc. of Electronic Warfare, 1978–. TV appearances, Horizon and Discovery. Liveryman, Coachmakers' and Coach Harness Makers' Co., 2008–; Freeman, City of London, 2009. SMIEE; MInstD 1995. FRSA 1996. Several patents on stealth technology, electronic devices, radar. *Publications:* numerous papers on electron bombarded semiconductor devices, radar, electronic warfare, Stealth, SDI, ballistic missile defence and res. policy, engrg higher educn, defence globalisation, technol. of modern warfare, homeland defence, novel threats. *Recreations:* Rugby football, classical music, cyber-security, furtherance of science in UK, travelling, being a grandparent. *Address:* 1 Greatfield Way, Rowlands Castle, Hants PO9 6AG. *T:* (023) 9241 2440. *E:* peter.varnish@btinternet.com. *Clubs:* Army and Navy, Brooks's, Savage.

VÁSÁRY, Tamás; pianist and conductor; Principal Conductor, Budapest Symphony Orchestra, 1993–2004, now Lifetime Hon. Chief Conductor; Music Director and Conductor, Kodály-Bartók World Youth Orchestra, since 2006; *b* 11 Aug. 1933; *s* of Jozsef Vásáry and Elizabeth (*née* Baltazàr); *m* 1967, Ildiko (*née* Kovàcs). *Educ:* Franz Liszt Acad. of Music, Budapest. First concert at age of 8 in Debrecen, Hungary; First Prize, Franz Liszt Competition, Budapest, 1947; prizes at internat. competitions in Warsaw, Paris, Brussels, Rio de Janeiro; Bach and Paderewski medals, London, 1961; début in London, 1961, in Carnegie Hall, NY, 1961; plays with major orchestras and at festivals in Europe, USA, Australasia and Far East; 3 world tours. Conducting debut, 1970; Musical Dir, Northern Sinfonia Orch., 1979–82; Principal Conductor, 1989–97, Conductor Laureate, 1997–98, Bournemouth Sinfonietta; conducts worldwide. Records Chopin, Debussy, Liszt, Rachmaninov (in Germany), Brahms, Mozart, Honegger, Respighi, Martinu, Beethoven. *Recreations:* yoga, writing, sports. *Address:* c/o Magyar Rádió Zenekari Iroda, Bródy Sándor u. 5–7, 1800 Budapest, Hungary.

VASELLA, Dr Daniel L.; Chairman, Novartis AG, 1999–2013 (President and Head of Executive Committee, 1996–99; Chief Executive Officer, 1999–2010); *b* 15 Aug. 1953; *m*; two *s* one *d*. *Educ:* Univ. of Berne (MD 1979). Former resident physician: Waid Hosp., Zurich; Univ. Hosp., Berne; Inst. of Pathology, Univ. of Berne; attendant physician, C. L. Lory Haus, Univ. Hosp., Berne, 1984–88; Sandoz Group: consecutively, mkt res. and sales, Product Manager for Sandostatin, then Dir of special project mkting, Sandoz Pharmaceuticals Corp., USA, 1988–92; Asst Vice-Pres., 1992; Head of Corp. Mkting, 1993; Sandoz Pharma Ltd: Sen. Vice-Pres. and Hd of Worldwide Develt, 1994; Chief Operating Officer, 1994; CEO, 1995–96. Member, Board of Directors: PepsiCo, Inc., 2002–; American Express Co., 2012–; XBiotech, 2014–. Member: Internat. Bd of Govs, Peres Center for Peace in Israel; Bd of Trustees, Carnegie Endowment for Internat. Peace; Internat. Business Leaders Adv. Council for Mayor of Shanghai.

VASEY, Terence, CMG 2004; Chief Executive, British Leprosy Relief Association, 1991–2010; *b* 5 Sept. 1944; *s* of Thomas William Vasey and Hannah Mary Vasey (*née* Wilkinson); *m* 1976, Margarita Pradera de Mendivil. *Educ:* Heythrop Coll., London (BA (Philos. and Theol.) 1968); Southampton Univ. (Dip. Social Work). CQSW 1976. Principal Social Worker, Emergency Services, London Borough of Hackney, 1969–82; Hd of Therapy and Social Work Co-ordinator, Dartmouth House Centre, London, 1982–85; Country Co-ordinator, Bolivia and Brazil, UNA Internat. Service, 1985–90. KLJ 2005 (CLJ 1998). *Recreation:* diving. *Address:* 4 Irvine Road, Colchester, Essex CO3 3TR. *T:* 07709 955412. *Club:* New Cavendish.

VASSAR-SMITH, Sir John (Rathborne), 4th Bt *cr* 1917, of Charlton Park, Charlton Kings, Co. Gloucester; Headmaster, St Ronan's Preparatory School, 1972–97; *b* 23 July 1936; *o s* of Major Sir Richard Rathborne Vassar-Smith, 3rd Bt and Mary Dawn, *d* of Sir Raymond Woods, CBE; *S* father, 1995; *m* 1971, Roberta Elaine, *y d* of Wing Comdr N. Williamson; two *s*. *Educ:* Eton. *Heir:* *s* Richard Rathborne Vassar-Smith [*b* 29 Dec. 1975; *m* 2013, Lydia Newhouse; one *d*]. *Address:* 24 Haywards Close, Wantage, Oxon OX12 7AT.

VASSILIOU, Androulla; Member, European Commission, 2008–14; *b* Pafos, Cyprus, 30 Nov. 1943; *d* of Evelthon and Lucia Géorgiades; *m* 1966, Dr George Vassos Vassiliou, *qv*; one *s* two *d*. *Educ:* London Inst. of World Affairs (Dip. Internat. Affairs 1966). Called to the Bar, Middle Temple, 1964; in practice as a barrister, 1968–88; Legal Advisor: Standard Chartered Bank, 1970–80; Bank of Cyprus, 1980–93. President: UN Assoc. of Cyprus, 1978–92; World Fedn of UN Assocs, 1991–95 (Hon. Pres., 1995); Mem., Select Internat. Gp on occasion of 50th Anniv. of UN, 1995. Pres., Cyprus Fedn of Business and Professional Women, 1996–2000. MP (United Democrats), Cyprus, 1996–2006; Alternate Rep. of Cyprus Parlt to Convention on Future of Europe, 2001–03. Vice Pres., ELDR, 2001–06. Chm., Eur. Liberal Women's Network, 2001–06. Chm., Bd of Trustees, Bank of Cyprus Oncology Centre, 2002–08. *Recreations:* listening to music, walking, swimming, reading, travelling.

VASSILIOU, Dr George Vassos; President of Cyprus, 1988–93; *b* 20 May 1931; *s* of Vassos Vassiliou and Fofo Vassiliou; *m* 1966, Androulla Georgiades (*see* A. Vassiliou); one *s* two *d*. *Educ:* Univs of Geneva, Vienna and Budapest (DEcon). Market researcher, Reed Paper Group, UK; Founder: Middle East Marketing Research Bureau, 1963 (Chm., 1963–); Ledra Advertising Agency, 1967 (Chm., 1967–); Middle East Centre for Management and Computing Studies, 1984; Cyprus Branch, Inst. of Directors (Hon. Sec.). Vis. Prof., Cranfield School of Management, 1985–2012. Leader, Free Democrats Movt, later United Democrats, Cyprus, 1993–2005. MP (United Democrats), Cyprus, 1993. Head, Cyprus negotiating team for accession to EU, 1998–2003. Member: Bd and Exec. Cttee, Bank of Cyprus, 1981–88; Econ. Adv. Council, Church of Cyprus, 1982–88; Educn Adv. Council, 1983–88; Inter Action Council, 1994–; Club de Monaco, 1995–2012; Trilateral Commn, 2000–. Chm. Bd, World Inst. for Develt Econ. Res. of UN Univ., Helsinki, 1999–2000 (Mem., 1995–). Mem., Bd of Govs, Shimon Peres Inst. for Peace, 1997–. Dr *hc:* Univ. of Athens; Univ. of Econs, Budapest; Univ. of Salonica; Univ. of Cyprus; Cyprus Inst. of Internat. Mgt. Grand Cross of Order of Merit (Cyprus), 2002. Grand Cross: Legion of Honour (France); Order of the Saviour (Greece); Order of Republic of Italy; Standard (Flag) Order (Hungarian People's Republic); Grand Collar, Order of Austria. *Publications:* Marketing in the Middle East, 1976; The Middle East Markets up to 1980, 1977; Towards the Solution of the Cyprus Problem, 1992; Modernisation of the Civil Service, 1992; (with Klaus Schwab) Overcoming Indifference, 1994; Towards a larger, yet more effective European Union, 1999; Cyprus—European Union: from the first steps to the accession, 2004; The Accession Story: the enlargement of the EU from 15 to 25 members, 2007; Pragmatism vs Popularism: the vision and the performance of the government (1988–1993), 2007; From the President's Office: a journey towards reconciliation in a divided Cyprus, 2010; Responsibilities Ahead: a collection of articles, speeches and interviews (1998–2009), 2010; A Contemporary Odyssey (autobiog.), 2013; numerous articles and contribs in internat. media. *Address:* 21 Academia Avenue, Aglandjia, PO Box 22098, Nicosia 1583, Cyprus.

VASSYLENKO, Volodymyr; Professor of International Public Law, Diplomatic Academy, Ministry of Foreign Affairs, Ukraine and National University of Kyiv-Mohyla Academy, since 2010; Member, Constitutional Commission, since 2015; Chairman, Presidential Selection Commission for High Council of Justice of Ukraine, since 2015; *b* Kyiv, Ukraine, 16 Jan. 1937; *m*; one *s* one *d*. *Educ:* Kyiv State Univ. (PhD 1964; LLD 1977). Teaching Public Internat. Law, Human Rights Law, Internat. Humanitarian Law and Law of Internat. Orgn, Ukrainian Inst. Internat. Relns, Kyiv State Univ., 1964–93 (Prof. 1978); Legal Advr to Min. of Foreign Affairs, Ukraine, 1972–93; Sen. Legal Advr to Parliament of Ukraine and Mem., Constitutional Commn, 1991–93; Ambassador to Belgium, The Netherlands and Luxembourg, and Rep. to EU and N Atlantic Co-operation Council, 1993–95; Ambassador-at-Large, Min. of Foreign Affairs, 1995–98; Ambassador to UK and (non-resident) to Ireland, 1998–2002; Permanent Rep. to IMO, 1999–2002; Judge *ad litem*, Internat. Criminal Tribunal for Former Yugoslavia, 2002–05; Advr, Minister of Foreign Affairs, Ukraine, 2005–10. Rep. of Ukraine to internat. confs; Rep. to UN Commn on Human Rights, 1989–91, 1996–98, 2005; Rep. to UN Human Rights Council, 2006–10; Mem., Ukrainian Delegn to CIS summits, 1991, 1992; Agent of govt of Ukraine, UN Internat. Court of Justice (maritime delimitation in Black Sea), 2007–09. Member: Consultative Council to Min. of Justice, Ukraine; Supervisory Bd, Ukrainian Legal Foundn. Sec., Adv. and Governing Councils, 1972–78, Mem., 1978–92, Inst. Internat. Relns, Kyiv State Univ. Mem., Grand Council, Popular Democratic People's Movement of Ukraine, 1969–91. Vice-President: Ukrainian Assoc. for UN, 1989–98; For Ukraine in NATO, 2015–. *Publications:* International Law, 1971; *monographs:* (jtly) State Responsibility for International Offences, 1976; Sanctions in International Law, 1982; Legal Aspects of Participation of the Ukrainian SSR in International Relations, 1985; Protection Mechanisms for International Law and Order, 1986; (jtly) Fundamentals of International Law, 1988; The Ukrainian Holodomor of 1932–1933 as a Crime of Genocide: a legal assessment, 2009; Main Trends in the Development of International Human Rights Law, 2013; The Geopolitical and National Dimensions of the Language Situation in Ukraine, 2013; A War Against the Ukrainian Language, 2013; The 2014 Russo-Ukrainian War, 2014; contrib. numerous articles in public internat. law and constitutional protection of human rights. *Address:* 4/6 Antonovych St, Apt 23, 01004 Kyiv, Ukraine. *T:* (050) 3859453, (44) 5262774, 4256073.

VATER, John Alistair Pitt; QC 2012; *b* Wallasey, 23 July 1971; *s* of Gordon Vater and Joan Vater; *m* 2002, Chloe Hubbert; one *s*. *Educ:* Birkenhead Sch.; St Peter's Coll., Oxford (Domus Scholar; BA Juris. 1993). Called to the Bar, Gray's Inn, 1995 (Lord Justice Holker Scholar); in practice as a barrister, Harcourt Chambers, specialising in family law, 1995–. Member: Midland Circuit; Family Law Bar Assoc. *Publications:* (jtly) Contact: the new deal, 2006; (jtly) The Public Law Outline: a case management compendium, 2008. *Recreations:* playing it by ear, keeping my head down, game fishing, shooting, travelling, Liverpool FC. *Address:* Harcourt Chambers, 2 Harcourt Buildings, Temple, EC4Y 9DB. *T:* (020) 7353 6961, *Fax:* (020) 7353 6968. *E:* jvater@harcourtchambers.law.co.uk.

VAUGHAN, family name of **Earl Lisburne**.

VAUGHAN, David Arthur John, CBE 2002; QC 1981; QC (NI) 1981; a Deputy High Court Judge, since 1997; a Judge of the Courts of Appeal of Jersey and Guernsey, since 2000; *b* 24 Aug. 1938; *s* of late Captain F. H. M. Vaughan, OBE, RN and J. M. Vaughan; *m* 1st, 1967, (marr. diss.); 2nd, 1985, Leslie Anne Fenwick Irwin; one *s* one *d*. *Educ:* Eton Coll.; Trinity Coll., Cambridge (MA). 2nd Lieut, 14th/20th King's Hussars, 1958–59. Called to the Bar, Inner Temple, 1962, Bencher, 1988; a Recorder, 1994–2001. Vis. Prof., 1989–2000, Hon. Vis. Prof., 2000–, European Law, Durham Univ. Leader, European Circuit, Bar of England and Wales, 2001–03. Member: Bar Council, 1968–72, 1984–86; Bar Cttee, 1987–88; International Relations Committee of Bar Council, 1968–86 (Chm., 1984–86); Bar/Law Soc. Working Party on EEC Competition Law, 1977–88 (Chm., 1978–88); UK Delegation to Consultative Committee of the Bars and Law Societies of the European Communities, 1978–81 (Chm., Special Cttee on EEC Competition Law, 1978–88); Law Adv. Cttee, British Council, 1982–85; Bar European Gp, 1978– (Founder and Chm., 1978–80, Hon. Vice-Pres., 1990–); EEC Section, Union Internationale des Avocats, 1987–91 (Chm., 1987–91); Adv. Bd, Centre for Eur. Legal Studies, Cambridge Univ., 1991–; Council of Management, British Inst. of Internat. and Comparative Law, 1992–2004; Chm., Mgt Cttee, Lord Slynn of Hadley Eur. Law Foundn, 1999–2014 (Man. Trustee, 2004–10). Trustee, Wye Foundn, 1997–2000 (Chm., Steering Gp, Wye Habitat Improvement Project, 1999–2000). Chm. Editl Bd, European Law Reports, 1997–2012; Member, Editorial Board: Eur. Business Law Review, 1998–2002; Cambridge Yearbook of European Legal Studies, 1999–; Welsh Law Jl, 2001–05; Consulting editor for numerous pubns on EC Law. FRSA 1997. Bronze Medal, Bar of Bordeaux, 1985; Lifetime Achievement Award, Chambers UK Bar Awards, 2014. *Publications:* co-ordinating editor, vols on European Community Law, Halsbury's Laws of England, 1986; (ed) Vaughan on Law of the European Communities, 2 vols, 1986, 2nd edn 1993–98; Vaughan and Robertson's Law of the European Union, 2003–. *Recreation:* fishing. *Address:* 50 Oxford Gardens, W10 5UN. *T:* (020) 8960 5865, (020) 8969 0707; Brick Court Chambers, 7–8 Essex Street, WC2R 3LD. *T:* (020) 7379 3550. *Clubs:* Brooks's, Pratt's.

VAUGHAN, Derek; Member (Lab) Wales, European Parliament, since 2009; *b* 2 May 1961; *s* of Ivor and Marlene Vaughan; *m* 1998, Eirly Herbert; one *s* one *d*. *Educ:* Swansea Univ. (BSc Econ. Hons). Engr, Hoover Ltd, 1977–81; civil servant, Valuation Office Agency, 1981–92; official, Public Services, Tax and Commerce Union, later PCS trade union, 1992–2004. Mem. (Lab) Neath Port Talbot BC, 1995–2010 (Leader, 2004–09). Leader, Welsh LGA, 2005–08. *Recreation:* sport (obtained 5 Welsh schoolboy caps at football). *Address:* (office) 4th Floor, Transport House, 1 Cathedral Road, Cardiff CF11 9SD. *T:* (029) 2022 7660. *E:* derek.vaughan@europarl.europa.eu. *Clubs:* Neath Cricket, Cimla Cricket; Port Talbot Town Football.

VAUGHAN, Elizabeth, (Mrs Ray Brown), FRAM, FRWCMD; international operatic mezzo-soprano (formerly soprano); *b* Llanfyllin, Montgomeryshire; *m* 1968, Ray Brown (former Gen. Manager, D'Oyly Carte Opera); one *s* one *d*. *Educ:* Llanfyllin Grammar Sch.; RAM (ARAM, LRAM); Kathleen Ferrier Prize. Joined Royal Opera House; rôles in: Benvenuto Cellini; La Bohème; Midsummer Night's Dream; Madama Butterfly; Rigoletto; Simon Boccanegra; La Traviata; Il Trovatore; Turandot; Don Giovanni; Un Ballo in Maschera; Ernani; Nabucco; Aida; Cassandra; La Forza del Destino; Tosca; Idomeneo; Macbeth; Gloriana; Salome; Katya Kabanova; Hansel and Gretel; The Carmelites; Suor Angelica. Frequent appearances with: ENO; WNO; Opera North; Scottish Opera; Vienna State Opera; Deutsche Oper, Berlin; Hamburg State Opera; Metropolitan Opera, NY; Paris Opera. Professor of Singing: Guildhall School of Music, 1989–; RNCM, 1994–96. Has toured in: Europe; USA; Australia; Canada; Japan; S America. Hon. DMus Wales, 1989. *Recreations:* tapestry, antiques, cookery. *Address:* c/o IMG, The Light Box, 111 Power Road, W4 5PY.

VAUGHAN, Prof. John Patrick, CBE 1998; MD; FRCPE, FFPH; Professor of Epidemiology and Public Health (formerly Health Care Epidemiology), London School of Hygiene and Tropical Medicine, University of London, 1987–2000, now Emeritus; consultant in international health; *b* 27 Dec. 1937; *s* of Thomas Frances Gerald Vaughan and Ellaline (*neé* Norwood); *m* 1st, 1960, Patricia Elspeth Pooley; two *s*; 2nd, 1975, Pauline Winifred Macaulay; two step *s* one step *d*. *Educ:* Bishop Wordsworth GS, Salisbury (Holgate and Folliott Prizes); Guy's Hosp. Med. Sch. (MB BS 1961; MD 1978); London Sch. of Hygiene and Tropical Medicine (Dip. Clin. Tropical Med. 1964; Dip. Tropical Public Health (Dist.) 1969). FRCPE 1982; FFPH (FFPHM 1988). Specialist physician, Papua New Guinea, 1966–68; Head, Dept of Epidemiology and Biostats, Univ. of Dar es Salaam, 1969–73; Sen. Lectr in Epidem. and Public Health, Med. Sch., Nottingham, 1973–75; London School of Hygiene and Tropical Medicine: Sen. Lectr, 1975–83; Director: Trop. Epidem. Unit, 1975–79; Evaluation and Planning Centre, 1980–89; Reader, 1983–87; Head of Dept of Public Health and Policy, 1989–93; on secondment as Dir, Public Health Scis Div., Internat. Centre for Diarrhoeal Disease Res., Dhaka, 1995–98. Visiting Professor: Pelotas Fed. Univ., Brazil, 1986–90 (Hon. Prof. 2013); Andalucian Sch. of Public Health, Spain, 1994. Specialist Advr in Public Health to World Bank, 1989; hon. consultancies include: NHS, 1975–; MRC; WHO, in foreign countries; Sen. Health and Population Advr, DFID, 1998–99; Adviser in Public Health: Perf. and Innovation Unit, Cabinet Office, 2000–01; WHO Geneva staff, 2001–02. Member: Amnesty Internat.; WWF; Dorset Trust for Nature Conservation; Trustee: Malaria Consortium (UK), 2002–07; BBC World Service Trust (UK), 2003–10; BRAC UK, 2006–10; HealthProm, 2012–. Founder and Editor, Health Policy and Planning Jl, 1985–93. Okeke and William Simpson Prizes for best student, LSHTM, 1969. *Publications:* (jtly) Community Health, 1981; (ed jtly and contrib.) Refugee Community Health Care, 1983; (jtly) Community Health Workers: the Tanzanian experience, 1987; (jtly) In the Shadow of the City: community health and the urban poor, 1988; (with R. Morrow) Manual of Epidemiology for District Health Management, 1989 (trans. French, Portuguese, Spanish, Turkish); (jtly) Health System Decentralization: concepts, issues and country experience, 1990 (trans. French, Spanish, Indonesian); (ed with C. Normand) Europe without Frontiers: the implications for health, 1993; (contrib.) Disease Control Priorities in Developing Countries, 1993; monographs on health and medicine; over 120 contribs to learned jls on internat. health and epidemiology. *Recreations:* travel, yachting, reading, art history, wild life, natural history. *Address:* Department of Public Health and Policy, London School of Hygiene and Tropical Medicine, Keppel Street, WC1E 7HT. *T:* (020) 7636 8636. *E:* jpatrickvaughan@aol.com.

VAUGHAN, Jonathan Randal, (Johnny); broadcaster; presenter: Capital Breakfast, London, Capital FM radio, 2004–11; X Radio, since 2015; *b* Barnet, 16 July 1966; *s* of Randal John Vaughan and Lilius Fay Vaughan; *m* 1999, Antonia Davies (marr. diss.); one *s* one *d*. *Educ:* Uppingham Sch., Rutland. *Television:* presenter: Moviewatch, 1994; Here's Johnny, 1997; The Big Breakfast, 1997–2001; Johnny Vaughan Film Show, 1999; helped launch BBC 3, 2003–04; Superstars, 2003; Johnny Vaughan Tonight, 2003; Live at Johnny's, 2004; Johnny and Denise, 2004; Passport to Paradise, 2004; My Kind of Town, 2005; Space Cadets, 2005; Car of the Year, 2008; Mud Men, 2011–13; writer: Orrible (also actor), 2001; Dead Casual, 2002; Top Buzzer, 2004; *radio:* presenter: Fighting Talk, 2003; The Warm Up with Johnny Vaughan, 2013–15. *Publications:* (with C. Murray) Fighting Talk, 2008. *Address:* c/o Independent Talent Group Ltd, 40 Whitfield Street, W1T 2RH. *T:* (020) 7636 6565. *E:* jessicastone@independenttalent.com. *Club:* Coombe Hill Golf.

VAUGHAN, Karen; *see* Vaughan, M. K.

VAUGHAN, Kieran Patrick; QC 2012; *b* Birmingham, 13 March 1970; *s* of Carmel and Damzen Vaughan; *m* 2001, Barbara; two *d*. *Educ:* St Patrick's Coll., Armagh; Univ. of Kent at Canterbury (LLB Hons). *Recreations:* Gaelic football, ski-ing. *Address:* Garden Court Chambers, 57–60 Lincoln's Inn Fields, WC2A 3LJ. *E:* Kieranv@gclaw.co.uk.

VAUGHAN, Prof. Megan Anne, PhD; FBA 2002; Smuts Professor of Commonwealth History, University of Cambridge, since 2003; Fellow of King's College, Cambridge, since 2003; *b* 1 May 1954; *d* of late Albert Edward Vaughan and of Winifred Margaret Vaughan (*née* Breaman); one *d*. *Educ:* United World College of the Atlantic; Univ. of Kent (BA Hons); PhD London 1981. Lectr, Univ. of Malaŵi, 1978–83; Smuts Res. Fellow, Univ. of Cambridge, 1984–86; Rhodes Lectr in Commonwealth Studies, 1986–96, Prof. of Commonwealth Studies, 1996–2003, Univ. of Oxford; Fellow, Nuffield Coll., Oxford, 1986–2003. *Publications:* The Story of an African Famine, 1987; Cutting Down Trees: gender, nutrition and agricultural change in northern Zambia, 1994 (Herskovits Award, 1995); Curing Their Ills: colonial power and African illness, 1991; Creating the Creole Island: slavery in eighteenth century Mauritius, 2005; articles in learned jls. *Recreations:* cooking, dancing, running, writing. *Address:* History Faculty, West Road, Cambridge CB3 9EF.

VAUGHAN, Michael Paul, OBE 2006; cricketer; *b* 29 Oct. 1974; *s* of Graham Vaughan and Deirdre Vaughan (*née* Greenhaugh); *m* 2003, Nichola Shannon; one *s* one *d*. *Educ:* Silverdale Comprehensive Sch., Sheffield. Cricketer (right-handed batsman): Yorks CCC, 1993–2009; England: début, 1999; apptd Captain, One Day Internat. and Test teams, 2003, World Cup team, 2007; won Test series: *v* Bangladesh, 2003, 2005; *v* W Indies (home and away), 2004; *v* NZ, 2004; *v* S Africa, 2004–05; *v* Australia, 2005; resigned as Test Captain, 2008. Ranked world number one batsman, 2003. *Publications:* A Year in the Sun, 2003; Calling the Shots: the Captain's story, 2005. *Address:* Yorkshire County Cricket Club, Headingley Cricket Ground, Leeds LS6 7QE; c/o International Sports Management Ltd, Cherry Tree Farm, Cherry Tree Lane, Rostherne, Cheshire WA14 3RZ.

VAUGHAN, (Moira) Karen, FRAM; Co-principal harp, London Symphony Orchestra, 1984–2015; Professor, since 2004, and Head of Harp, since 2010, Royal Academy of Music; Associate Artistic Director, World Harp Congress, since 2011; *b* Kirkby Lonsdale, 18 March 1950; *d* of (Douglas) Brian Vaughan and (Ethel) Moira Vaughan (*née* Kneale); *m* 1979, Adrian Evett (marr. diss. 1989); one *s*. *Educ:* James Allen's Girls' Sch., Dulwich; Alice Ottley Sch., Worcester; Royal Acad. of Music (LRAM; Performance Dip.). FRAM 2014. Harpist: Scottish Chamber Orch., 1974–78; Scottish Nat. Orch., 1978–84; Prof., RSAMD, 1999–2008. Mem., Bd of Dirs, 2002–, Corp., 2011–, World Harp Congress. *Publications:* contrib. articles to UK Harp Assoc. mag. *Recreations:* theatre, opera, home, family, friends. *Address:* Royal Academy of Music, Marylebone Road, NW1 5HT. *E:* k.vaughan@ram.ac.uk.

VAUGHAN, Peter James, QPM 2013; DL; Chief Constable, South Wales Police, since 2010; *b* Merthyr Tydfil, 7 Sept. 1962; *s* of Cyril and June Vaughan; *m* 1986, Suzanne Journeaux; one *s* one *d*. *Educ:* Univ. of Wales, Swansea (BSc Hons); Fitzwilliam Coll., Cambridge (Dip. Applied Criminol.). Joined S Wales Police, 1984; Sgt, 1990; Insp., 1992; Chief Insp., 1996; Supt, 1997; Chief Supt, 2001; Asst Chief Constable, Wilts Police, 2003–07; Asst Chief Constable, 2007, Dep. Chief Constable, 2007–09, S Wales Police. Chm., Acquisitive Crime Cttee, 2010, Vice Pres., 2013–15, ACPO; Vice Pres., Nat. Police Chiefs Council, 2015–. Mem. Council, Prince's Trust, Cymru, 2010–. Chairman: Jt Emergency Services Gp Wales, 2013–; All Wales Criminal Justice Bd, 2012–. Ind. Trustee, St John's Cymru, 2014–. OStJ 2013. DL Mid Glamorgan, 2013. Hon. Fellow, Cardiff Univ., 2014. Hon. Dr S Wales, 2015. *Recreations:* fitness, surfing, holidays, family. *Address:* South Wales Police Headquarters, Cowbridge Road, Bridgend, Glam CF31 3SU. *T:* (01656) 869200. *E:* peter.vaughan@south-wales.pnn.police.uk.

VAUGHAN, Rt Rev. Peter St George; Area Bishop of Ramsbury, 1989–98; Hon. Assistant Bishop, Dioceses of Gloucester and Bristol, 2002–11; *b* 27 Nov. 1930; *s* of late Dr Victor St George Vaughan and Dorothy Marguerite Vaughan; *m* 1961, Elisabeth Fielding Parker; one *s* two *d*. *Educ:* Charterhouse; Selwyn Coll., Cambridge (MA Theology 1959); Ridley Hall, Cambridge; MA Oxon (by incorporation) 1963. Nat. Service, 1949–51, Lt RAPC. Ordained deacon 1957, priest 1958; Asst Curate, Birmingham Parish Church, 1957–62; Chaplain to Oxford Pastorate, 1963–67; Asst Chaplain, Brasenose Coll., Oxford, 1963–67; Vicar of Christ Church, Galle Face, Colombo, 1967–72; Precentor of Holy Trinity Cathedral, Auckland, NZ, 1972–75; Principal of Crowther Hall, CMS Training Coll., Selly Oak Colleges, Birmingham, 1975–83; Archdeacon of Westmorland and Furness, 1983–89. Hon. Asst Bishop, Dio. of Bradford, 1998–2001; Hon. Canon: Carlisle Cathedral, 1983–89; Salisbury Cathedral, 1989–98, now Emeritus; Bradford Cathedral, 1998–2001. Commissary for Bishop of Colombo, 1984–2011. Mem., Third Order Of St Francis, 2006. *Recreations:* gardening, reading, people. *Address:* Willowbrook, Downington, Lechlade-on-Thames, Glos GL7 3DL. *T:* (01367) 252216. *E:* e.vaughan786@btinternet.com.

VAUGHAN, Prof. Robert Charles, FRS 1990; Professor of Mathematics, Pennsylvania State University, since 1999; *b* 1945. Imperial College, London, 1972–97: Prof. of Pure Maths, 1980–97; EPSRC (formerly SERC) Senior Fellow, 1992–96; Vis. Prof. of Maths, Univ. of Michigan, Ann Arbor, 1997–98; Dist. Vis. Prof., Univ. of York, 2008; Frederick W. and Lois B. Gehring Vis. Prof. of Maths, Univ. of Michigan, 2013–14. *Publications:* The Hardy-Littlewood Method, 1981, 2nd edn 1997; (with H. L. Montgomery) Multiplicative Number Theory I: classical theory, 2006. *Address:* Department of Mathematics, McAllister Building, Pennsylvania State University, University Park, PA 16802–6400, USA.

VAUGHAN, Roger, PhD; FREng; FRINA; Chairman, Safinah Ltd, since 1998; *b* 14 June 1944; *s* of late Benjamin Frederick Vaughan and Marjorie (*née* Wallace); *m* 1st, 1968 (marr. diss.); three *s* two *d*; 2nd, 1987, Valerie (*née* Truelove); one step *s* (and one step *s* decd). *Educ:* Newcastle Univ. (BSc Hons Naval Architecture and Shipbuilding 1966, PhD 1971). FREng (FEng 1990). Student apprentice, Vickers Gp, 1962; Shipbuilding Develt Engr, Swan Hunter Shipbuilders Ltd, 1970–71; Dir, 1971–81, Man. Dir, 1978–81, A&P Appledore Ltd; Dir, Performance Improvement and Productivity, British Shipbuilders, 1981–86; took part in privatisation of Swan Hunter, 1986; Joint Chief Exec., Swan Hunter, 1988–93; Chief Exec., Sch. of Mgt, Newcastle Univ., 1995–99. Non-exec. Dir, Newcastle City Health NHS Trust, 1996–2001; Dir, Northern Sinfonia Concert Soc. Ltd, 1996–2002. Vis. Prof., 2000–01, 2005–10, Res. Fellow, 2001–05, Business Sch. (formerly Sch. of Mgt), Univ. of Newcastle. Member: Nat. Curriculum Council, 1992–94; Council, Newcastle Univ., 1992–95 (Chm., Engrg Design Centre, 1990–94). Dir, Three Rivers Learning Trust, 2011– (Chm., 2011–14). Pres., Shipbuilders and Shiprepairers Assoc., 1991–93. FRSA 1993. Shipbuilding Gold Medal, NECInst, 1969. *Recreations:* music, theatre, ballet, opera, sailing, walking, reading. *Address:* Correslaw, Netherwitton, Morpeth, Northumberland NE61 4NW.

VAUGHAN, Roger Davison, OBE 1986; FREng; General Manager, Fast Reactor Projects, National Nuclear Corporation Ltd, 1977–88, retired; Director, Fast Reactor Technology Ltd, 1984–88; *b* 2 Oct. 1923; *s* of late David William and Olive Marion Vaughan; *m* 1951, Doreen Stewart; four *s*. *Educ:* University High Sch., Melbourne; Univ. of Melbourne, Aust. (BMechE). Engineer Officer, RAAF, 1945–46. Chemical Engr, Commonwealth Serum Laboratories, 1946–47; Works apprenticeship, C. A. Parsons & Co., 1948–49; Chief Engr, C. A. Parsons Calcutta, 1950–53; AERE, Harwell, 1954; Chief Engineer: Nuclear Power Plant Co., 1955–59 (Director, 1958); The Nuclear Power Group, 1960–75 (Dir, 1960–75); Manager, Technology Div., Nuclear Power Co., 1976–77. Chairman: Gas-cooled Breeder Reactor Assoc., Brussels, 1970–78; Forum on Cabinet Office Energy Review, 2002; Member: Bd, BSI, 1989–92 (Chm., BSI Engineering Council, 1983–88); BSI Standards Bd, 1992–96. FIMechE (Mem. Council, 1977–81, 1985–89; Chairman: Power Industries Div., 1985–89; Energy Jt Venture Study Gp, Engrg Council, 1996–98); FREng (FEng 1981). *Publications:* papers in jls of IMechE, Brit. Nuc. Energy Soc., World Energy Conf. *Recreations:* ski-ing, mountain walking; questionable performer on piano and clarinet. *Address:* Otterburn House, Manor Park South, Knutsford, Cheshire WA16 8AG. *T:* (01565) 632514. *Club:* Himalayan (Bombay).

VAUGHAN, Tom; *see* Phillips, Sir T. R. V.

VAUGHAN JONES, Sarah Jane, (Mrs Julian O'Halloran); QC 2008; a Recorder, since 2004; *b* London, 20 July 1961; *d* of Dr Ronald Vaughan Jones and Pamela Vaughan Jones; *m* 1986, Julian O'Halloran; three *d*. *Educ:* Trinity Hall, Cambridge (BA Law 1982). Called to the Bar, Middle Temple, 1983; in practice as barrister specialising in clinical negligence and medical law. *Recreation:* walking the Cornish cliffs. *Address:* 2 Temple Gardens, EC4Y 9AY. *T:* (020) 7822 1200. *E:* svj@2tg.co.uk.

VAUX OF HARROWDEN, 12th Baron *cr* 1523; **Richard Hubert Gordon Gilbey;** Managing Director, Corporate Development, Sungard, since 2004; *b* London, 16 March 1965; *s* of 11th Baron Vaux of Harrowden and of Beverley Anne Gilbey (*née* Walton); *S* father, 2014; *m* 1996, Elizabeth Frances Worsley; two *s*. *Educ:* Ampleforth Coll.; Univ. of Aberdeen (MA Hons). ACA 1991. Sen. Manager, Price Waterhouse; Sen. Investment Officer, Indochina Asset Mgt; Chief Financial Officer, Reech Capital plc. *Recreations:* ski-ing, walking, fishing, shooting, dogs. *Heir:* *s* Hon. Alexander John Charles Gilbey, *b* 17 June 2000. *Address:* 46 Lavender Gardens, SW11 1DN. *T:* (020) 7228 3273. *E:* r_gilbey@yahoo.com. *Club:* Kandahar Ski.

VAUX, John Esmond George, CBE 2009; Speaker's Counsel, House of Commons, 2000–08; *b* 3 Sept. 1948; *s* of Arthur Ernest Vaux and Marjory May Vaux; *m* 1980 Jenny Lennox; one *s* one *d*. *Educ:* Gosport Co. Grammar Sch.; Selwyn Coll., Cambridge (MA). Legal Dept, MAFF, 1979–90 (on secondment to EC, 1983–85); Cabinet Office Legal Advr, and Hd, European Div., Treasury Solicitor's Dept, 1990–97; Speaker's Counsel (European Legislation), H of C, 1997–2000.

VAUX, Maj.-Gen. Nicholas Francis, CB 1989; DSO 1982; DL; Major General Royal Marines Commando Forces, 1987–90, retired; *b* 15 April 1936; *s* of late Harry and Penelope Vaux; *m* 1966, Zoya Hellings (*d* 2012); one *s* two *d*. *Educ:* Stonyhurst College. Commissioned RM, 1954; served Suez, 1956; Far East, 1958–61; West Indies Frigate, 1962–64; Staff Coll., Camberley, 1969; MoD (Army), 1975–77; Special Advisor, USMC, 1979–81; CO 42 Commando RM, 1981–83; Falklands, 1982; RCDS, 1985. Consultant and Man. Dir, UK-Russia Security Gp, subseq. Internat. Security Co., 1993. Chm., Exeter Racecourse, 2003–11. DL Devon, 2003. *Publications:* March to the South Atlantic, 1986. *Recreation:* field sports. *Address:* National Westminster Bank, Old Town Street, Plymouth PL1 1DG. *Club:* Farmers.

VAVALIDIS, Barbara Joan; *see* Donoghue, B. J.

VAVASOUR, Sir Eric (Michel Joseph Marmaduke), 6th Bt *cr* 1828, of Haslewood, Yorkshire; Managing Director, Hilltop Design Ltd, since 2009; *b* 3 Jan. 1953; *s* of Hugh Bernard Moore Vavasour (*d* 1989) and Monique Pauline Marie Madeleine (*née* Beck) (*d* 1982); *S* kinsman, 1997; *m* 1976, Isabelle Baudouin Françoise Alain Cécile Cornelie Ghislaine (*née* van Hille); two *s* one *d*. *Educ:* St Joseph's Coll., Stoke-on-Trent; Manchester Univ. (BSc). MIET. BCRA, 1977; Matthey Printed Products Ltd, 1979; BAL (UK) Ltd, 1985–2009: Sen. Engr, then Chief Engr, 1997–2009, Tech. Consultant, 2009, BAL Broadcast Ltd (Dir, 2001–08); Dir, Faraday Technol. Hldgs Ltd, 2001–08. *Heir:* *s* Joseph Ian Hugh André Vavasour, *b* 22 Jan. 1978. *Address:* 15 Mill Lane, Earl Shilton, Leicester LE9 7AW.

VAVER, Prof. David, JD; Professor of Intellectual Property Law, Osgoode Hall Law School, York University, Canada, since 2009; *b* 28 March 1946; *s* of Ladislav and Pola Vaver; *m* 1978, Judith Maxine McClenaghan; one *s* one *d*. *Educ:* Auckland Grammar Sch.; Univ. of Auckland (BA French 1969; LLB Hons 1970); Univ. of Chicago (JD 1971); MA Oxon 1998. Called to the Bar, NZ, 1970; Asst Prof. of Law, Univ. of BC, 1971; Lectr, 1972–74, Sen. Lectr in Law, 1974–78, Univ. of Auckland; Res. Dir, later Dir, Legal Res. Foundn, Auckland, 1972–78; Associate Prof. of Law, Univ. of BC, 1978–85; Prof. of Law, Osgoode Hall Law Sch., York Univ., Toronto, 1985–98; Reuters Professor of Intellectual Property and Inf. Technol. Law, Univ. of Oxford, 1998–2008, now Emeritus; Fellow, St Peter's Coll., Oxford, 1998–2008, now Emeritus; Dir, Oxford Intellectual Property Res. Centre at St Peter's Coll., 1998–2008. Assoc. Mem., Chambers of Michael Silverleaf, QC, 11 South Square, 2008–. NZ Law Foundn Dist. Vis. Fellow, 2000. Editor-in-Chief, Intellectual Property Jl, 1984–98, 2010–. Consultant on copyright law reform to Dept of Canadian Heritage, 1989–98; Mem., Intellectual Property Adv. Cttee to Minister of Trade and Industry, 2001–08. Pattishall Medal, Internat. Trademark Assoc., 2012. *Publications:* Intellectual Property Law: copyright, patents, trade-marks, 1997, 2nd edn 2011; Copyright Law, 2000; numerous contribs to edited books and legal jls on intellectual property and contract law. *Recreations:* music, art, wine.

VAZ, Rt Hon. (Nigel) Keith (Anthony Standish); PC 2006; MP (Lab) Leicester East, since 1987; *b* Aden, 26 Nov. 1956; *s* of late Anthony Xavier Vaz and Merlyn Verona Vaz; *m* 1993, Maria Fernandes; one *s* one *d*. *Educ:* St Joseph's Convent, Aden; Latymer Upper Sch., Hammersmith; Gonville and Caius Coll., Cambridge (BA 1979); Coll. of Law, Lancaster Gate. Solicitor, Richmond-upon-Thames BC, 1982; Senior Solicitor, Islington BC, 1982–85; Solicitor, Highfields and Belgrave Law Centre, Leicester, 1985–87. Contested (Lab): Richmond and Barnes (gen. election), 1983; Surrey W (European Parlt election), 1984. Opposition front bench spokesman on inner cities and urban areas, 1992–97; PPS to Attorney Gen. and Solicitor Gen., 1997–99; Parly Sec., Lord Chancellor's Dept, 1999; Minister of State (Minister for Europe), FCO, 1999–2001. Member: Home Affairs Select Cttee, 1987–92 (Chm., 2007–); Constitutional Affairs Select Cttee, 2002–07. Chairman: All Party Hosiery and Knitwear Gp, 1987–92; Unison Gp of MPs, 1996–99; Indo-British Parly Gp, 1997–99 (Vice Pres., 1999–); Yemen Parly Gp, 1997–99, 2001–; Vice Chairman: Tribune Gp of MPs, 1992 (Treas., 1994); PLP Internat. Develt Gp, 1997–99; All Party Parly Gp to Holy See, 2006; Treas., All Party Parly Race and Community Gp, 2006. Labour Party: Mem., Regl Exec., 1994–96; Chm., Ethnic Minority Taskforce, 2006–; Vice Chm., Women's Race and Equality Cttee; Mem., NEC, 2007–; Trustee, Pension Regulator, 2008. Pres., India Develt Gp (UK) Ltd, 1992–. Chm., City 2020, Urban Policy Commn, 1993–99; Mem., Nat. Adv. Cttee, Crime Concern, 1989–93; Vice Chm., British Council, 1998–99. Mem., Clothing and Footwear Inst., 1988–94. Vice Pres., Assoc. of Dist Councils, 1993–97. Patron: Gingerbread, 1990–; Labour Party Race Action Gp, 2000–. Founder Patron: Naz Project London, 1999–; Next Steps Foundn, 2003; Silver Star Appeal, 2006. Jt Patron, UN Year of Tolerance, 1995; EU Ambassador, Year of Intercultural Dialogue, 2008. President: Leicester and S Leics RSPCA, 1988–99; Leicester Kidney Patients Assoc., 2000. Former Columnist: Tribune; Catholic Herald; New Life (Gujarat Samachar). *Address:* 144 Uppingham Road, Leicester LE5 0QF. *T:* (0116) 212 2028. *Clubs:* Safari (Leicester); Scraptoft Valley Working Men's.
See also V. C. M. Vaz.

VAZ, Valerie Carol Marian; MP (Lab) Walsall South, since 2010; *b* Aden, 7 Dec. 1954; *d* of late Anthony Xavier Vaz and Merlyn Verona Vaz (*née* Pereira); *m* 1992, Paul John Townsend; one *d*. *Educ:* Twickenham Co. Grammar Sch.; Bedford Coll., Univ. of London (BSc); Coll. of Law (CPE and Law Soc. final exam.). Articled clerk, Herbert Smith, 1982–84; admitted solicitor, 1984; local govt solicitor, London Bors of Brent and Hammersmith and Fulham, 1985–92; Townsend Vaz Solicitors, 1992–2001; Dep. Dist Judge, 1996–2000; Treasury Solicitor's Dept, 2001–10; MoJ, 2008–09 (on secondment). Mem. (Lab) Ealing LBC, 1986–90 (Dep. Leader, 1988–89). Member: Health Select Cttee, 2010–15; Regulatory Reform Cttee, 2010–15; Panel of Chairs, 2015–; All Party Parly Gp on Burma; Vice-Chair, Parly Labour Party. Mem., Lay Adv. Panel, Coll. of Optometrists, 2007. Presenter, Network East, BBC TV, 1987. Mem., Law Soc. *Recreations:* music, playing piano and guitar, gardening, member of National Trust and Kew Gardens. *Address:* House of Commons, SW1A 0AA. *T:* (020) 7219 7176, *Fax:* (020) 7219 5045. *E:* valerie.vaz.mp@parliament.uk.
See also Rt Hon. N. K. A. S. Vaz.

VEAL, Kevin Anthony; Sheriff of Tayside Central and Fife, 1993–2014; *b* 16 Sept. 1946; *s* of George Algernon Veal and Pauline Grace Short; *m* 1969, Monica Flynn; two *s* two *d*. *Educ:* St Joseph's Primary Sch., Dundee; Lawside Acad., Dundee; Univ. of St Andrews (LLB 1966). Partner, Burns Veal & Gillan, Dundee, 1971–93; Temp. Sheriff, 1984–93. Dean, Faculty of Procurators and Solicitors in Dundee, 1991–93; part-time Tutor, Dept of Law, Univ. of Dundee, 1978–85. Mem., Court, Abertay Dundee Univ., 1998–2009 (Hon. Fellow, 2010). Musical Dir, Cecilian Choir, Dundee, 1975–; Hon. Pres., Dundee Operatic Soc., 2003–14. KC*HS 2007 (KCHS 1998; KHS 1989); KSG 1993. *Recreations:* choral music, organ playing, classical music, hill-walking. *Address:* Viewfield, 70 Blackness Avenue, Dundee DD2 1JL. *T:* (01382) 668633.

VEALE, Sarah, CBE 2006; Head, Equality and Employment Rights, Trades Union Congress, since 2003; *b* Oxford, 6 June 1953; *d* of John Veale and Diana Veale; *m* 1989, Roy Collins; two *d*. *Educ:* Milham Ford Sch.; Oxford Brookes Univ. (BA Hons Eng.); Goldsmiths' Coll., London (PGCE). Vice Pres., NUS, 1982–84; various policy positions, 1985–93, Sen. Employment Rights Officer, 1994–2003, TUC. Member: Council, ACAS, 2004–11; Regulatory Policy Cttee, 2009–; Bd, HSE, 2012–; Bd, Equality and Human Rights Commn, 2013–. FRSA. Hon. LLD Oxford Brookes, 2011. *Publications:* (contrib.) Adding Value Through Information and Consultation, 2005; (jtly) Statutory Regulation and Employment Relations, 2013. *Recreations:* reading, music, politics, art. *Address:* Trades Union Congress, Congress House, Great Russell Street, WC1B 3LS. *T:* (020) 7467 1326. *E:* sveale@tuc.org.uk.

VEASEY, Josephine, CBE 1970; opera singer (mezzo soprano), retired; teaching privately, since 1982; vocal consultant to English National Opera, 1985–94; *b* London, 10 July 1930; *m* (marr. diss.); one *s* one *d*. Joined chorus of Royal Opera House, Covent Garden, 1948; a Principal, on tour, in opera, for Arts Council; a Principal, Royal Opera House, Covent Garden, 1955–. Teacher of voice production, RAM, 1983–84. Has sung at Royal Opera House, Glyndebourne, Metropolitan (NY), La Scala, and in France, Germany, Spain, Switzerland, South America; operatic Roles include: Octavian in Der Rosenkavalier; Cherubino in Figaro; name role in Iphigénie; Dorabella in Così fan Tutte; Amneris in Aida, Fricka in Die Walküre; Fricka in Das Rheingold; name role in Carmen; Dido and Cassandra in the Trojans; Marguerite in The Damnation of Faust; Charlotte in The Sorrows of Werther; Eboli, Don Carlos; name role, Orfeo; Adalgisa in Norma; Rosina in The Barber of Seville; Kundry in Parsifal; Gertrude in Hamlet, 1980. Concerts, 1960–70 (Conductors included Giulini, Bernstein, Solti, Mehta, Sargent). Verdi's Requiem; Monteverdi's Combattimento di Tancredi e Clorinda, Aix Festival, 1967; various works of Mahler; two tours of Israel (Solti); subseq. sang in Los Angeles (Mehta); then Berlioz: Death of Cleopatra, Royal Festival Hall, and L'enfance du Christ, London and Paris; Rossini's Petite Messe Solennelle, London and Huddersfield (with late Sir Malcolm Sargent); Handel's Messiah, England, Munich, Oporto, Lisbon; Berlioz's Romeo and Juliette, London, and Bergen Festival; Rossini's Stabat Mater, Festival d'Angers and London, 1971; Berlioz's Beatrice and Benedict, NY, and London; Emperor in 1st perf. Henze's We Come to the River, Covent Garden, 1976. Has sung Elgar's Dream of Gerontius all over England. Hon. RAM 1972. *Recreations:* grandchildren, gardening. *Address:* 99 Micheldever Road, Whitchurch, Hants RG28 7JH.

VEAZEY, Janis Mary; *see* Kelly, J. M.

VEDERAS, Prof. John Christopher, PhD; FRS 2009; FRS(Can) 1997; University Professor of Chemistry, University of Alberta, since 2000; *b* Detmold, Germany, 19 Feb. 1947; *s* of Joseph and Irene Vederas; *m* 1991, Andrea A. Opgenorth; one *s*. *Educ:* Stanford Univ. (BSc); Massachusetts Inst. of Technol. (PhD). Postdoctoral Fellow: Univ. of Basel, 1973–76; Purdue Univ., 1976–77; Asst Prof., 1977–82, Associate Prof., 1982–87, Prof., 1987–, Univ. of Alberta; Canada Res. Chair in Bioorganic and Medicinal Chem., 2001–. Pres., Canadian Soc. for Chem., 2002–03. Mem. Council, NSERC, 2001–04. *Publications:* contribs to Desktop Edns in Chem., Topics in Current Chem., and major scientific jls; 16

patents. *Recreations:* music, film, travel, literature. *Address:* Department of Chemistry, University of Alberta, Edmonton, AB T6G 2G2, Canada. *T:* (780) 4925475, *Fax:* (780) 4928231. *E:* john.vederas@ualberta.ca.

VEDI, Anu Kiran, CBE 2005; strategic and property consultant, since 2009; Group Chief Executive, Genesis Housing Group, 1999–2009; *b* 10 Feb. 1955; *s* of late Jagjeet Singh Vedi and Bimla Vedi; *m* 1980, Shobhana Chadha; two *s*. *Educ:* Duke of Gloucester Sch., Nairobi; Cranford Sch., Middlesex. Chartered Accountant, 1980; Director of Finance: Ealing Family Housing Assoc., 1982–86; Sanctuary Housing Assoc., 1986–88; Paddington Churches Housing Assoc., 1988–99. Member: Adv. Bd, Relationships Foundn, 2005–; Bd, Dolphin Square Foundn, 2005–10. Trustee, World Child Cancer, 2010–. *Recreations:* sports, reading, family. *Address:* Silver Springs, Over The Misbourne, Denham UB9 5DR. *E:* a1akv@hotmail.co.uk.

VEDRINE, Hubert Yves Pierre; Managing Partner, Hubert Vedrine Conseil, since 2003; *b* 31 July 1947; *s* of Jean and Suzanne Vedrine; *m* 1974, Michèle Froment; two *s*. *Educ:* Lycée Albert-Camus; Univ. of Nanterre; Institut d'Etudes Politiques; Ecole Nationale d'Administration. Chargé de mission, Min. of Culture, 1974–78; Head, Dept of Architecture, Min. of the Envmt, 1978–79; Co-ordinator, Cultural Relations, Near and Middle East, Min. of Foreign Affairs, 1979–81; Head, Dept for Technical Co-operation on Health, Housing, Public Admin and Human Science, 1979–81; Technical Advr on External Affairs (diplomatic and visa), Office of Sec.-Gen. of the Pres., 1981–86; Maître des requêtes, Conseil d'Etat, 1986; Advr and Spokesman, 1988–91, Sec.-Gen., 1991–95, Office of the Pres.; Partner, Jeantet & Associés, barristers, 1996–97; Minister of Foreign Affairs, 1997–2002. *Publications:* Mieux aménager sa ville, 1979; Les Mondes de François Mitterand, 1996; (with D. Moïsi) Les Cartes de la France à l'Heure de la Mondialisation, 2000; Face à l'hyperpuissance, 2003; François Mitterand: un dessein, un destin, 2005; Continuer l'Histoire, 2007; Le temps des chimères, 2010; Dans la mêlée mondiale: 2009–12, 2012; La France au défi, 2014; with P. Boniface: Atlas du Monde Global, 2008; Atlas des crises et des conflits, 2009; Atlas de la France, 2011. *Address:* 21 rue Jean Goujon, 75008 Paris, France.

VEEDER, Van Vechten; QC 1986; *b* 14 Dec. 1948; *s* of John Van Vechten Veeder and Helen Letham Townley; *m* 1st, 1970; one *s* one *d*; 2nd, 1991, Marie Lombardi; one *d*. *Educ:* Ecole Rue de la Ferme, Neuilly, Paris; Clifton College, Bristol; Jesus College, Cambridge. Called to the Bar, Inner Temple, 1971, Bencher, 2000; a Recorder, 2000–06. *Recreations:* sailing, travelling, reading. *Address:* Essex Court Chambers, 24 Lincoln's Inn Fields, WC2A 3EG. *T:* (020) 7813 8000, *Fax:* (020) 7813 8080. *Clubs:* Garrick; Myopia (Mass).

VEIL, Simone Annie, Hon. DBE 1998; Chevalier de l'Ordre national du Mérite; Grand Officier de la Légion d'Honneur, 2009; Member, Constitutional Council, 1998–2007; Magistrate; *b* Nice, 13 July 1927; *d* of André Jacob and Yvonne (*née* Steinmetz); *m* 1946, Antoine Veil (*d* 2013), Inspecteur des Finances, President, A. V. Consultants; three *s*. *Educ:* Lycée de Nice; Lic. en droit, dipl. de l'Institut d'Etudes Politiques, Paris; qualified as Magistrate, 1956. Deported to Auschwitz and Bergen-Belsen, March 1944–May 1945. Ministry of Justice, 1957–69; Technical Advr to Office of Minister of Justice, 1969; Gen.-Sec., Conseil Supérieur de la magistrature, 1970–74. Minister of Health, France, 1974–76; Minister of Health and Social Security, 1976–79; Minister of Social Affairs, Health and Urban Develt, 1993–95. European Parliament: Member, 1979–93; Pres., 1979–82; Chm., Liberal and Democratic Reformist Gp, 1984–89. President: Haut Conseil à l'Intégration, 1997–99; Trust Fund for Victims, Internat. Criminal Court, 2003–09. Mem., Académie Française, 2008. Monismanien Prize, 1978; Onassis Foundn Prize, Athens, 1980; Charlemagne Prize, Prix Louise Weiss, 1981; Louise Michel Prize, 1983; Jabotinsky Prize, 1983; Prize for Everyday Courage, 1984; Special Freedom Prize, Eleanor and Franklin Roosevelt Foundn, 1984; Fiera di Messina Prize, 1984; Living Legacy Award, San Diego, Univ. d'Acadie, 1987; Johanna Löwenherz Prize, Neuwied, 1987; Thomas Dehler Prize, Munich, 1988. Dr *hc*: Princeton, 1975; Institut Weizmann, 1976; Yale, Cambridge, Edinburgh, Jerusalem, 1980; Georgetown, Urbino, 1981; Yeschiva, Sussex, 1982; Free Univ., Brussels, 1984; Brandeis, 1989; Glasgow, 1995; Pennsylvania, 1997; Montreal, 2007; Netanya, 2008; Bologna, 2009; Ben Gurion, 2010. *Publications:* (with Prof. Launay and Dr Soulé) Les Données psycho-sociologiques de l'Adoption, 1969; Les hommes aussi s'en souviennent, 2004; Une Vie (memoir), 2007. *E:* dorothee.guerrin@orange.fr.

VEITS, Peter John; a District Judge (Magistrates' Courts), since 2011; *b* Liverpool, 18 July 1958; *s* of Arthur and Patricia Veits; *m* 1976, Catherine Fabian; two *d*. *Educ:* Litherland High Sch., Liverpool; Manchester Poly. (Dip. Magisterial Law 1982). Called to the Bar, Gray's Inn, 1985; Magistrates' Court Clerk, Liverpool, Ripon, S Sefton and Nottingham, 1977–89; Dep. Justices' Clerk, 1989–91, Justices' Clerk, 1991–2011, Lincoln; a Dep. Dist Judge, 2000–11. Pres., Justices' Clerks' Soc., 2007–08. Asst Ed., Wilkinson's Road Traffic Offences, 2011–. *Recreations:* hill-walking, family, grandchildren. *Address:* Norwich Magistrates' Court, Bishopgate, Norwich NR3 1UP. *T:* (01603) 679575. *E:* DistrictJudge.veits@judiciary.gsi.gov.uk.

VEL, Mary Elaine; *see* Hammond, M. E.

VELTMAN, Prof. Dr Martinus Justinus Godefridus; McArthur Professor of Physics, University of Michigan, 1981–97, Emeritus Professor, since 1997; *b* Netherlands, 27 June 1931; *s* of Gerard P. H. Veltman and Goverdina Veltman; *m* 1960, Anna M. M.; two *s* one *d*. *Educ:* Univ. of Utrecht (PhD 1963). Fellow and Staff Mem., CERN, Geneva, 1961–66; Prof. of Theoretical Physics, Univ. of Utrecht, 1966–81. High Energy Physics Prize, Eur. Physics Soc., 1993; Nobel Prize for Physics, 1999. Comdr, Order of Dutch Lion (Netherlands), 1999; Officier, Légion d'Honneur (France), 2000. *Publications:* Diagrammatica, 1994; Facts and Mysteries in Particle Physics, 2002. *Recreation:* billiards. *Address:* Nikhef, PO Box 41882, 1009 DB Amsterdam, Netherlands. *Club:* Probus '83 (Bilthoven, Netherlands).

VENABLES, Prof. Anthony James, CBE 2009; DPhil; FBA 2005; BP Professor of Economics and Director, Oxford Centre for the Analysis of Resource Rich Economies, University of Oxford, since 2007; Fellow of New College, Oxford, since 2007; *b* 25 April 1953; *s* of John Stuart Venables and Phyllis (*née* Cox); *m* 1983, Patricia Rice, *qv*; one *s* one *d*. *Educ:* Clare Coll., Cambridge (MA); St Antony's Coll., Oxford (BPhil); Worcester Coll., Oxford (DPhil 1984). Lecturer in Economics: Univ. of Essex, 1978–79; Univ. of Sussex, 1979–88; Eric Roll Prof. of Econ. Policy, Univ. of Southampton, 1988–92; Prof. of Internat. Econs and Dir, Globalization Prog., Centre for Econ. Perf., LSE, 1992–2007. Ed., Eur. Econ. Rev., 1991–95. Res. Manager, Trade Gp, World Bank, Washington, 1998–99; Chief Economist, DFID, 2005–08. Res. Fellow, 1984–, Co-Dir, Internat. Trade Prog., 1994–2003, Trustee, 2013–, Centre for Econ. Policy Res., London. Specialist Advr, H of L Select Cttee on Econ. Affairs, 2001–02; Advr, HM Treasury, 2001–02. Member: Econs Res. Adv. Bd, GLA, 2003–; Adv. Bd, Regl Growth Fund, 2011–; Council, British Acad., 2013–. Fellow: Econometric Soc., 2003; Regl Sci. Assoc. Internat., 2009. *Publications:* (jtly) The Spatial Economy: cities, regions and international trade, 1999; (jtly) Multinational Firms in the World Economy, 2004; contrib. acad. jls in internat. econs, econ. geography, develt econs and resource econs. *Address:* Department of Economics, Manor Road, Oxford OX1 3UQ.

VENABLES, Rt Rev. Cameron David; an Assistant Bishop, Diocese of Brisbane, since 2014; *b* Bangor, NI, 15 March 1965; *s* of Peter Arthur Goode Venables and Jennifer Anne Venables (*née* Davidson); *m* 1998, Katharine Rebecca Doulin; one *s* two *d*. *Educ:* Wilson's Grammar Sch.; Wolverhampton Poly (BA Hons); Brisbane Coll. of Theology (BTh). Ordained deacon, 1993, priest, 1995; Asst Curate, Bundaberg, 1994–95; Foundn Chaplain, St Luke's Anglican Sch., 1994–95; PNG-Popondota Diocesan Youth Co-ordinator, 1996–2000; Associate Priest, Lismore, 2000–03; Anglican Chaplain, Lismore Campus, Southern Cross Univ., 2001–03; Ministry Co-ordinator, Fitzroy Ministry Cluster, 2004–05; Rector, All Saints' Community, Anglican Parish of N Rockhampton, 2005–14; Canon, St Paul's Cathedral, Rockhampton, 2008–12; Chaplain, Rockhampton Grammar Sch., 2010–14; Archdeacon and Vicar Gen., Dio. of Rockhampton, 2012–14. Mem., Anglican Bd of Mission-Community Develt Cttee, 2002–14. Dir, Anglicare, Central Queensland, 2010–13; Pres., Sanctuary, Central Queensland, 2005–14. Chair, Oro Provincial AIDS Cttee, PNG, 1998–2000. *Recreations:* piano, guitar, reading, gardening, walking. *Address:* PO Box 2600, Toowoomba, Qld 4350, Australia. *T:* (7) 46391875, 0419784456. *E:* cvenables@anglicanchurchsq.org.au. *Club:* United Service (Brisbane).

VENABLES, Most Rev. Gregory James; *see* Argentina, Bishop of.

VENABLES, Jean, CBE 2010 (OBE 2004; MBE 1997); CEng, FREng; FICE; Chairman, Crane Environmental, since 1994; Chief Executive, Association of Drainage Authorities, 2003–15; *b* 11 June 1948; *d* of Denis and Zena Edwards; *m* 1970, Roger Kendrick Venables; two *s*. *Educ:* Imperial College, London (BSc(Eng); MSc). CEng 1974, FREng 2006; MCIWEM 1995; FICE 1998; CEnv 2004. Sen. Lectr in Civil Engrg, Kingston Poly., 1975–94; Chm., Venables Consultancy Services Ltd, 1988–. Non-exec. Dir, HR Wallingford, 2011–. Visiting Lecturer: Southampton Univ., 2006–; Imperial Coll., London, 2007–; Strathclyde Univ., 2008–11. Chairman: Thames Regl Flood Defence Cttee, 1994–2003; Thames Estuary Partnership, 2003–10; Customer Challenge Gp, Sutton and E Surrey Water, 2012–; Nuclear Liabilities Fund, 2014–. Mem., Technical Commn, 2010–, Council, 2013–, RNLI. Vice Pres., 2007–08, Pres., 2008–09, Chair, Professional Conduct Panel, ICE, 2010–; Mem. Council, RAEng, 2010–14. FCGI 2002. Foundn Gov., Tiffin Sch., Kingston upon Thames, 2010–. Liveryman, Co. of Engrs, 2006– (Mem., Ct of Assts, 2009–). Hon. DSc: Nottingham, 2005; Kent, 2012; Hon. DEng Kingston, 2006. *Publications:* Preparing for the Professional Reviews of the ICE, 1995. *Recreations:* walking, gardening, seeing friends and family, travelling. *Address:* c/o Institution of Civil Engineers, 1 Great George Street, SW1P 3AA.

VENABLES, Patricia; *see* Rice, P.

VENABLES, Robert; QC 1990; *b* 1 Oct. 1947; *s* of Walter Edwin Venables, MM, and Mildred Daisy Robson Venables. *Educ:* Merton Coll., Oxford (MA); London School of Economics (LLM). FTII. Called to Bar, Middle Temple, 1973, Bencher, 1999; private practice as barrister, 1976–. Lecturer: Merton Coll., Oxford, 1972–75; UCL, 1973–75; Official Fellow and Tutor in Jurisprudence, St Edmund Hall, Oxford, and CUF Lectr, Oxford Univ., 1975–80; Fellow, St Edmund Hall, Oxford, 1992–. Chartered Institute of Taxation: Council Mem., 1999–2011; Chartered Tax Adviser, 1999. Chm., Revenue Bar Assoc., 2001–05. Pres., Key Haven Pubns Ltd (formerly Key Haven Pubns plc), 1990–. Treasurer, CRUSAID, 1991–96 (Pres. Council, 1996–); Director: Yves Guihannec Foundn, 1992–; Temple Music Foundn, 2004–; Trustee, Morris Venables Charitable Foundn, 2004–. Consulting Editor: Personal Tax Planning Review; Corporate Tax Review; Offshore and Internat. Taxation Review; EC Tax Jl; Taxation Ed., Charities Law and Practice Review. *Publications:* Inheritance Tax Planning, 1986, 4th edn 2000; Preserving the Family Farm, 1987, 2nd edn 1989; Non-Resident Trusts, 1988, 8th edn 2000; Tax Planning and Fundraising for Charities, 1989, 3rd edn 2000; Hold-Over Relief, 1990; The Company Car, 1990; Tax Planning Through Trusts—Inheritance Tax, 1990; National Insurance Contributions Planning, 1990; Capital Gains Tax Planning for Non-UK Residents, 1991, 3rd edn 1999; The Family Home, 2002; The Taxation of Trusts, 2006, 3rd edn 2009; The Taxation of Foundations, 2010; The Taxation of Trusts, 2010. *Recreation:* music making. *Address:* Tax Chambers, 15 Old Square, Lincoln's Inn, WC2A 3UE. *T:* (020) 7242 2744, *Fax:* (020) 7831 8095. *E:* taxchambers@15oldsquare.co.uk. *Clubs:* Athenæum, Travellers.

VENABLES, Robert Michael Cochrane; Consultant, Bircham Dyson Bell (formerly Bircham & Co.), Solicitors, 1997–2007; *b* 8 Feb. 1939; *s* of late Cdre Gilbert Henry Venables, DSO, OBE, RN and Muriel Joan Haes; *m* 1972; two *s* two *d*. *Educ:* Portsmouth Grammar Sch. Admitted solicitor, 1962; in private practice, London, Petersfield and Portsmouth, 1962–70; Treasury Solicitor's Department: Legal Asst, 1970; Sen. Legal Asst, 1973; Asst Treasury Solicitor, 1980; Charity Comr, 1989–97. Adminr, Cobbe Collection Trust, 1997–99. Mem. Council, Law Soc., 1993–2001; Pres., City of Westminster Law Soc., 1997–98. Trustee: Incorp. Council of Law Reporting for Eng. and Wales, 1999–2010; LawCare (formerly SolCare), 1997– (Chm., 1998–2003, 2005–07); Old Portmuthian Charity, 1999–. Mem., FDA, 1974–97 (Chm., Legal Sect., 1981–83; Mem., Exec. Cttee, 1981–83, 1987–92). Ind. Co-opted Mem., Standards Cttee, E Hants DC, 2002–12 (Chm., 2004–12). Vis. Prof. of Charity Law, London S Bank Univ., 2005–08. Pres., Petersfield Dist, Scout Assoc., 2013– (Dist Sec., 2009–11). Trustee: Helios Foundn for Sustainable Energy, 2010–; Winton House Trust, 2011–; Steep Allotments Charity, 2012–. FRSA 1995. *Recreations:* opera, theatre, collecting domestic anachronisms. *Address:* c/o Bircham Dyson Bell LLP, 50 Broadway, SW1H 0BL.

VENABLES, Terence Frederick; Owner, Hotel La Escondida, Alicante; Assistant Coach, England football team, 2006–07; *b* 6 Jan. 1943; *m* Yvette; two *d*. *Educ:* Dagenham. Played at football clubs: Chelsea, 1958–66 (Captain, 1962); Tottenham Hotspur, 1966–68 (winners FA Cup 1967); Queen's Park Rangers, 1968–73; represented England at all levels; Club Manager: Crystal Palace, 1976–80 (took club from 3rd Div. to top of 1st Div.); QPR, 1980–84 (won 2nd Div. title, 1980); Barcelona, 1984–87 (won Spanish championship, 1984); Tottenham Hotspur, 1987–93 (won FA Cup, 1991; Chief Exec., 1991–93); Coach: England football team, 1994–96; Australian football team, 1996–98; Chm., Portsmouth FC, 1996–98; Head Coach, Crystal Palace FC, 1998–99; Coach, Middlesbrough FC, 2000–01; Manager, Leeds Utd FC, 2002–03. Chm., Acad. of Dreams, 2012. *Publications:* They Used to Play on Grass, 1971; (with Gordon Williams) TV detective series Hazell: Hazell plays Solomon, 1974; Hazell and the Three Card Trick, 1975; Hazell and the Menacing Jester, 1976; (with Neil Hanson) Terry Venables: the Autobiography, 1994; (with Jane Nottage) Venables' England, 1996; The Best Game in the World, 1996; Born to Manage, 2014.

VENABLES-LLEWELYN, Sir John (Michael) Dillwyn-, 4th Bt *cr* 1890; farmer, since 1975; *b* 12 Aug. 1938; *s* of Sir Charles Michael Dillwyn-Venables-Llewelyn, 3rd Bt, MVO, and Lady Delia Mary Dillwyn-Venables-Llewelyn, *gd* of 1st Earl St Aldwyn; *S* father, 1976; *m* 1st, 1963, Nina (marr. diss. 1972), *d* of late Lt J. S. Hallam; two *d*; 2nd, 1975, Nina Gay Richardson Oliver (*d* 1995); one *d* decd; 3rd, 2005, Carolyn I'Anson. *Recreation:* racing vintage cars. *Address:* Llysdinam, Newbridge-on-Wye, Llandrindod Wells, Powys LD1 6NB.

VENDLER, Helen Hennessy, PhD; author and poetry critic; Porter University Professor, Harvard University, since 1990; *b* Boston, Mass, 30 April 1933; *d* of George and Helen Hennessy (*née* Conway); one *s*. *Educ:* Emmanuel Coll., Boston, Mass (AB 1954); Harvard Univ. (PhD 1960). Instructor, Cornell Univ., 1960–63; Lectr, Swarthmore Coll. and Haverford Coll., Pa, 1963–64; Asst Prof., Smith Coll., Northampton, Mass, 1964–66; Associate Prof., 1966–68, Prof., 1968–85, Boston Univ.; Harvard University: Kenan Prof., 1985–90; Associate Acad. Dean, 1987–92; Sen. Fellow, Harvard Soc. Fellows, 1981–93. Fulbright Lectr, Univ. of Bordeaux, 1968–69; Vis. Prof., Harvard Univ., 1981–85. Poetry Critic, New Yorker, 1978–95. Member: Educnl Adv. Bd, Guggenheim Foundn, 1991–2001; Pulitzer Prize Bd, 1991–2000. Jefferson Lectr, NEH, 2004. Overseas Fellow, Churchill Coll., Cambridge, 1980; Stewart Parnell Fellow, Magdalene Coll., Cambridge, 1996, Hon. Fellow, 1996. Holds numerous hon. degrees, including: DLitt: Columbia, 1987; Washington, 1991;

DHL: Toronto, 1992; TCD, 1993; Cambridge, 1997; NUI, 1998; QUB, 2010. Awards include: Nat. Book Critics Award, 1980; Keats-Shelley Assoc. Award, 1994; Truman Capote Award, 1996; Jefferson Medal, APS, 2000. *Publications:* Yeats's Vision and the Later Plays, 1963; On Extended Wings: Wallace Stevens' longer poems, 1969; The Poetry of George Herbert, 1975; Part of Nature, Part of Us, 1980; The Odes of John Keats, 1983; Wallace Stevens: words chosen out of desire, 1984; (ed) Harvard Book of Contemporary American Poetry, 1985; Voices and Visions: the poet in America, 1987; The Music of What Happens, 1988; Soul Says, 1995; The Given and the Made, 1995; The Breaking of Style, 1995; Poems, Poets, Poetry, 1995; The Art of Shakespeare's Sonnets, 1997; Seamus Heaney, 1998; Coming of Age as a Poet, 2003; Poets Thinking, 2004; Invisible Listeners, 2005; Our Secret Discipline, 2007; Last Looks, Last Books, 2010; Dickinson: selected commentaries, 2010; The Ocean, the Bird, and the Scholar, 2015. *Address:* Department of English, Harvard University, Barker Center, 12 Quincy Street, Cambridge, MA 02138–3929, USA.

VENESS, Sir David (Christopher), Kt 2005; CBE 2000; QPM 1994; Under-Secretary-General for Safety and Security, United Nations, 2005–09; *b* 20 Sept. 1947; *m*; three *c*. *Educ:* Raynes Park Co. Grammar Sch.; Trinity Coll., Cambridge (BA 1975; LLB 1976). Joined Metropolitan Police, 1966; CID officer, 1969; detective in N, E and Central London; Detective Chief Supt in Fraud Squad and Crime Ops Gp; Comdr, 1987, served with Royal and Diplomatic protection, until 1990; rcds, 1990; Comdr, Public Order, Territorial Security and Operational Support; a Dep. Asst Comr, 1991–94; an Asst Comr, 1994–2005. Chm., Adv. Bd, Security and Resilience Network, London First, 2009–.

VENGEROV, Maxim; violinist, conductor and teacher; Menuhin Professor of Music, Royal Academy of Music, since 2012; *b* 1974; *s* of Alexander Vengerov, oboist, and Larissa Vengerov; studied with Galina Turtschaninova, then Zakhar Bron; *m* 2011, Olga Gringolts; two *d*. Has performed in recitals worldwide; has appeared with major orchestras throughout the world, including: NY Philharmonic, 1991; Berlin Philharmonic; LSO; Chicago SO; LA Philharmonic; Vienna Philharmonic; San Francisco SO; Concertgebouw. Ambassador for UNICEF, 1997–. Numerous recordings. First Prize: Jun. Wieniawski Competition, Lublin, 1985; Carl Flesch Internat. Violin Competition, London, 1990; Grammy Award, best instrumental soloist, 2004.

VENKITARAMAN, Prof. Ashok, FMedSci; Ursula Zoellner Professor of Cancer Research, University of Cambridge, since 1998; Fellow, Pembroke College, Cambridge, since 2007; Director, Medical Research Council Cancer Cell Unit, Cambridge, since 2006 (Deputy Director, 2001–06); *s* of Prof. Avittathur R. Venkitaraman and Vasanti Venkitaraman; *m* 1984, Dr Rajini Ramana; one *s* one *d*. *Educ:* Christian Med. Coll., Vellore, India (MB BS 1984); University Coll. London (PhD 1988); MA Cantab 1993. House Physician, Christian Med. Coll. Hosp., Vellore, India, 1983–84; Fellow, Lady Tata Meml Trust, UCL and Charing Cross and Westminster Med. Sch., 1985–88; MRC Laboratory of Molecular Biology, Cambridge: Fellow, Beit Meml Trust, 1988–91; Mem., Scientific Staff, 1991–98; Fellow, New Hall, Cambridge, 1991–2007, now Emeritus. Mem., EMBO European Acad., 2004–. FMedSci 2001. *Publications:* numerous contribs to scientific and med. jls. *Address:* University of Cambridge, Hutchison/MRC Research Centre, Hills Road, Cambridge CB2 0XZ. *T:* (01223) 336901.

VENNE, Roger André; Queen's Coroner and Attorney, Master of the Crown Office, Registrar of Criminal Appeals, Registrar of the Courts-Martial Appeal Court and a Master of the Queen's Bench Division, 2003–11; *b* 11 June 1946; *s* of Georges and Rose Ellen Venne; *m* 1970, Katherine Winter; one *s* one *d* (and one *d* decd). *Educ:* St Mary's Coll., Southampton; Inns of Court Sch. of Law. Called to the Bar, Gray's Inn, 1972, Bencher, 2000; Legal Asst, Criminal Appeal Office, 1973–78; Sen. Legal Asst and Legal Sec. to Lord Chief Justice, 1978–80; Crown Office, 1980; Asst Registrar, Criminal Appeal Office, 1981–87; Hd, Crown Office, 1987–89; Sen. Lawyer, Civil Appeals Office, and Legal Sec. to Master of the Rolls, 1989; Lord Chancellor's Department: Head: Law Reform and Adv. Div., 1990–93; Judicial Appts Div. 2, 1993–96; Dep. Sec. of Commns, 1996–99; Hd, Civil Appeals Office, and Master, 1999–2003. Mem., Criminal Cttee, Judicial Studies Bd, 2003–08. Dep. Ed.-in-Chief, Administrative Court Digest (formerly Crown Office Digest), 1988–; an Ed., Civil Procedure (formerly Supreme Court Practice), 1989–2011. Hon. QC 2011. *Publications:* (jtly) Alderney Annals, 1992; contribs to legal jls. *Recreations:* sailing, book-collecting. *Address:* 14 St James Terrace, Winchester SO22 4PP. *Clubs:* Royal Cruising, Bar Yacht; Alderney Sailing.

VENNER, Rt Rev. Stephen Squires; DL; Bishop for the Falkland Islands, 2007–14; Bishop to the Forces, 2009–14; an Honorary Assistant Bishop: Diocese of Rochester, since 2010; Diocese of Europe, since 2011; Diocese of St Albans, since 2013; *b* 19 June 1944; *s* of Thomas Edward Venner and Hilda Lester Venner; *m* 1972, Judith Sivewright Johnstone; two *s* one *d*. *Educ:* Hardyes Sch., Dorchester; Birmingham Univ. (BA); Linacre Coll., Oxford (MA); London Univ. (PGCE). Curate, St Peter, Streatham, 1968–71; Hon. Curate: St Margaret, Streatham Hill, 1971–72; Ascension, Balham, 1972–74; Head of RE, St Paul's Girls' Sch., Hammersmith, 1972–74; Vicar, St Peter, Clapham and Bishop's Chaplain to Overseas Students, 1974–76; Vicar: St John, Trowbridge, 1976–82; Holy Trinity, Weymouth, 1982–94; RD of Weymouth, 1988–94; Canon and Prebendary of Salisbury Cathedral, 1989–94; Bishop Suffragan of Middleton, 1994–99; Bishop Suffragan of Dover and Bishop in Canterbury, 1999–2009. Chaplain to Lord Warden of Cinque Ports, 2004–09. Pro-Chancellor, Canterbury Christ Church Univ., 2005–09. Vice Pres., Woodard Corp., 1995–98 (Pres., 1999–2002); Co-Chm., Church of England/Moravian Contact Gp, 1996–99. Non-exec. Dir, Abbeyfield Soc., 2015–. Ambassador, Chatham Historic Dockyard, 2013–. DL Kent, 2009. Mem. Council, Greater Manchester, 1996–99, Kent, 2000–09, Order of St John. Hon. DD Birmingham Univ., 2009; DUniv Canterbury Christ Church, 2010. *Recreations:* being a grandfather, playing organ and piano, computing, reading and friends. *Address:* 81 King Harry Lane, St Albans AL3 4AS. *T:* (01727) 831704. *E:* stephen@venner.org.uk.

VENNING, Philip Duncombe Riley, OBE 2003; FSA; Secretary, Society for the Protection of Ancient Buildings, 1984–2012; *b* 24 March 1947; *s* of late Roger Venning and of Rosemary (*née* Mann); *m* 1987, Elizabeth Frances Ann, *d* of M. A. R. Powers; two *d*. *Educ:* Sherborne Sch.; Trinity Hall, Cambridge (MA). Times Educational Supplement, 1970–81 (Asst Editor, 1978–81); freelance journalist and writer, 1981–84. Mem., Westminster Abbey Fabric Commn, 1998–. Member: Council, Nat. Trust, 1992–2001; Expert Panel, 2005–11, E of England Cttee, 2013–, Heritage Lottery Fund. Vice-Pres., Nat. Churches Trust (formerly Historic Churches Preservation Trust), 2005–08; Founder Trustee, Heritage Link, 2002–03. Accredited lectr, NADFAS, 2013–. FSA 1989; FRSA 1990. Queen Mother Meml Medal for Contribution to Craftmanship, SPAB, 2011. *Publications:* contribs to books and other pubns on educn and on historic buildings. *Recreations:* exploring Britain, book collecting. *Address:* Wyke House, Mill Lane, Docking, Norfolk PE31 8NX.

VENNING, Robert William Dawe; Principal Establishment and Finance Officer, Cabinet Office, 1993–96; *b* 25 July 1946; *s* of Tom William Dawe and Elsie Lillian Venning; *m* 1969, Jennifer Mei-Ling Jackson; one *s* one *d*. *Educ:* Midhurst Sch.; Univ. of Birmingham (BA Special Hons Philosophy 1968). Tutor in Philosophy, Univ. of Birmingham, 1968; Lectr in Logic and Scientific Method, Lanchester Polytechnic, 1969; Department of Health and Social Security: Admin. Trainee, 1971; Private Sec. to Minister for Disabled, 1974; Principal, 1975; Private Sec. to Minister for Health, 1981; Asst Sec., 1983; Under Sec., HA Personnel Div., DoH, 1990–93. Non-exec. Dir, Compel plc, 1990–93. *Recreations:* playing classical and flamenco guitar; electronics and computing. *Address:* 85 Oaks Avenue, Shelly Beach, NSW 2261, Australia.

VENTER, J. Craig, PhD; Founder, Chairman and Chief Executive Officer, J. Craig Venter Institute, since 2006; Co-Founder, Chairman and Co-Chief Scientist, Synthetic Genomics, since 2005; Co-founder, Chairman and Chief Executive Officer, Human Longevity Inc., since 2014; *b* 14 Oct. 1946; *m* Claire Fraser. *Educ:* UCSD (BS; PhD 1975). Served US Navy, Vietnam, 1967. Asst Prof., subseq. Prof., of Pharmacol. and Therapeutics, SUNY, 1976–84; Section and Lab. Chief, NIH, 1984–92; Founder, Chm. and Chief Scientist, Inst. for Genomic Res., 1992–2006; President and Chairman: Inst. for Biol Energy Alternatives, 2002–06; Center for the Advancement of Genomics, 2002–06; J. Craig Venter Sci. Foundn, 2002–06; Founder, 1998, Pres. and CSO, 1998–2002, Chm., Scientific Adv. Bd, 2002, Celera Genomics Corp. *Publications:* A Life Decoded (autobiog.), 2007; Life at the Speed of Light: from the double helix to the dawn of digital life, 2013; articles in learned jls. *Address:* J. Craig Venter Institute, 9704 Medical Center Drive, Rockville, MD 20850–3343, USA.

VENTERS, Ewan Andrew; Chief Executive Officer, Fortnum & Mason plc, since 2012; *b* Dunfermline, Fife, 24 Aug. 1972; *s* of Alexander Venters and Josephine Venters; *m* 1998, Jane Houghton; two *d*. *Educ:* St Serf's Sch., Edinburgh. Sainsbury's Supermarkets Ltd: Mgt trainee to Dept Manager, Fresh Produce, 1989–91; New Store Logistics Controller, 1991–92; PA to Northern Regl Dir, 1992–94; PA to Dep. Chm., J. Sainsbury plc, 1994–97; Food Buyer, Sainsbury's Supermarkets Ltd, 1997–99; Brake Bros Ltd, later Brakes: Buying Controller, 1999–2001; Commercial Dir, 2001–03; Sales Ops Dir, 2003; UK Nat. Account Dir, 2003–04; Man. Dir, White Tablecloths, 2005; Dir, Food and Restaurants, Selfridges, 2005–12. *Recreations:* food and entertaining, theatre, shooting. *Address:* Fortnum & Mason plc, 181 Piccadilly, W1A 1ER. *T:* (020) 7973 5619. *E:* Ewan.Venters@FortnumandMason.co.uk.

VENTERS, June Marion, (Mrs R. P. Brown); QC 2006; Senior Partner, Venters Solicitors, since 1991; a Recorder, since 1998; *b* 25 March 1957; *o d* of Douglas William Walter Venters and Lily Lydia Venters (*née* Grimwood); *m* 1994, Robin Perry Brown; one *d*. *Educ:* Honor Oak Grammar Sch.; College of Law. Admitted solicitor, 1984. Family and Civil Mediator, 2007; Resolution Accredited Specialist—domestic abuse and children advocacy, 2010–, and internat. child abduction, 2011–. Mem., Family Law Cttee, Law Soc., 2013–. Legal Business Woman of the Year, Law Soc. and Assoc. of Women Solicitors, 2009. *Publications:* Standard Letters and Forms, 1995; (contrib.) Child Care Management Practice, 2009. *Recreation:* my family. *Address:* Venters Solicitors, 7a West Street, Reigate, Surrey RH2 9BL. *T:* (01737) 229610, *Fax:* (01737) 244520. *E:* j.ventersqc@venters.co.uk.

VENTRESS, Peter John; Chief Executive Officer, Berendsen plc (formerly Davis Service Group plc), since 2010; *b* England, 3 Dec. 1960; *s* of Gordon Denis and Pauline Marie Ventress; *m* 1988, Karen Morris; three *d*. *Educ:* St Joseph's Coll., Beulah Hill, London; Greyfriars, Oxford (BA Modern Hist. and Modern Langs 1983; MA); Open Univ. (MBA 1993). Exec., NatWest Internat., 1984–86; Mktg Dir, McNaughton Paper Gp, 1986–93; Sales and Mktg Dir, Guppy Paper plc, 1993–95; Business Develt Dir, UK Paper plc, 1995–97; Man. Dir, Guppy Paper plc 1997–99; President: Buhrmann France, 1999–2002; Corporate Express Canada, 2003–05; Corporate Express Europe, 2005–07; CEO, Corporate Express NV, 2007–08; Pres., Staples Internat., 2008–09. Non-exec. Dir, Premier Farnell plc, 2013–. *Recreations:* golf, theatre, opera, tennis. *Address:* Berendsen plc, 4 Grosvenor Place, SW1X 7DL. *T:* (020) 7259 6663. *E:* ventress@berendsen.eu. *Clubs:* Oxford and Cambridge, Farmers.

VENTRY, 8th Baron *cr* 1800 (Ire.); **Andrew Wesley Daubeny de Moleyns;** Bt 1797; Marketing Manager, Unico (UK) Ltd, 1994; *b* 28 May 1943; *s* of Hon. Francis Alexander Innys Eveleigh Ross de Moleyns (*d* 1964) (2nd *s* of 6th Baron) and Joan (later Joan Springett), *e d* of Harold Wesley; assumed by deed poll, 1966, surname of Daubeny de Moleyns; *S* uncle, 1987; *m* 1st, 1963, Nelly Renée (marr. diss. 1979), *d* of Abel Chaumillon; one *s* two *d*; 2nd, 1983, Jill Rosemary, *d* of C. W. Oramon; one *d*. *Educ:* Edge Grove; Aldenham. Farmer, 1961–; Dir, Burgie Lodge Farms Ltd, 1970–95; in electronics, 1986–. *Recreations:* shooting, stalking, photography, sailing, ski-ing. *Heir:* *s* Hon. Francis Wesley Daubeny de Moleyns, *b* 1 May 1965.

VENTURI, Robert; architect; Principal, Venturi, Scott Brown and Associates, Inc., 1989–2012 (Venturi, Rauch and Scott Brown, 1980–89); *b* 25 June 1925; *s* of Robert Charles Venturi and Vanna Venturi (*née* Lanzetta); *m* 1967, Denise Scott Brown; one *s*. *Educ:* Princeton Univ. (AB 1947, MFA 1950). Designer, Oskar Stonorov, 1950, Eero Saarinen & Assoc., 1950–53; Rome Prize Fellow, Amer. Acad. in Rome, 1954–56; designer, Louis I Kahn, 1957; Principal: Venturi, Cope and Lippincott, 1958–61; Venturi and Short, 1961–64; Venturi and Rauch, 1964–80. Associate Prof., Univ. of Pennsylvania, 1957–65; Charlotte Shepherd Davenport Prof. of Architecture, Yale, 1966–70. Works include: Vanna Venturi House, 1961, Guild House, 1961, Franklin Court, 1972, Inst. for Sci. Inf. Corp. HQ, 1978 (all Philadelphia); Allen Meml Art Museum Addition (Oberlin, Ohio), 1973; Gordon Wu Hall (Princeton), 1980; Seattle Art Mus., 1984; Sainsbury Wing, Nat. Gall., London, 1986; Fisher and Bendheim Halls, 1986, Princeton Campus Center, 1996, Princeton Univ.; Gordon and Virginia MacDonald Med. Res. Labs (with Payette Associates), 1986, Gonda (Goldschmied) Neuroscience and Genetics Res. Center (with Lee, Burkhart, Liu Inc.), 1993, UCLA; Charles P. Stevenson Jr Library, Bard Coll., 1989; Roy and Diana Vagelos Labs (with Payette Associates), Univ. of Penn, 1990; Regl Govt Bldg, Toulouse, France, 1992; Kirifuri resort facilities, Nikko, Japan, 1992; Perelman Quadrangle, Univ. of Pennsylvania, 1995; Frist Campus Center, Princeton Univ., 1996; Baker/Berry Liby, Dartmouth Coll., 1996; Master Plan and buildings for Univ. of Michigan, 1997–; Congress Ave Bldg, Yale Univ. Sch. of Medicine (with Payette Associates), 1998; Woodmere Art Mus., Philadelphia, 2000; Biomed. Res. Bldg, Univ. of Kentucky, 2000; Dumbarton Oaks Liby Expansion, Washington, 2001; Stuart Country Day Sch. Theater, Auditorium and Sanctuary, Princeton, 2001; Lehigh Valley Hosp., Muhlenberg, Allentown, Pennsylvania, 2002. Fellow: Amer. Inst. of Architects; Amer. Acad. in Rome; Accad. Nazionale di San Luca; Amer. Acad. of Arts and Letters; Amer. Acad. of Arts and Scis; Hon. FFRIAS; Hon. RIBA. Hon. DFA: Oberlin Coll., 1977; Yale, 1979; Univ. of Pennsylvania, 1980; Princeton Univ., 1983; Philadelphia Coll. of Art, 1985; Hon. LHD NJ Inst. of Technology, 1984. James Madison Medal, Princeton Univ., 1985; Thomas Jefferson Meml Foundn Medal, Univ. of Virginia, 1983; Pritzker Architecture Prize, Hyatt Foundn, 1991; US Nat. Medal of Arts, 1992; Benjamin Franklin Medal, RSA, 1993. Comdr, Order of Arts and Letters (France), 2000. *Publications:* A View from the Campidoglio: selected essays, 1953–84 (with Denise Scott Brown), 1984; Complexity and Contradiction in Architecture, 1966, 2nd edn 1977 (Classic Book Award, AIA, 1996); Learning from Las Vegas (with Denise Scott Brown and Steven Izenour), 1972, 2nd edn 1977; Iconography and Electronics upon a Generic Architecture, 1996; (with D. Scott Brown) Architecture as Signs and Systems for a Mannerist Time, 2004; articles in periodicals. *Recreation:* travel.

VENUGOPAL, Dr Sriramashetty, OBE 1992; FRCGP; Principal in General Practice, Aston, Birmingham, 1967–99; *b* 14 May 1933; *s* of Satyanarayan and Manikyamma Sriramashetty; *m* 1960, Subhadra Venugopal; one *s* one *d*. *Educ:* Osmania Univ., Hyderabad, India (BSc, MB BS); Madras Univ. (DMRD). MRCGP 1990, FRCGP 1997; MFPHM 1998. Medical posts, Osmania Hosp., State Med. Services, Hyderabad, Singareni Collieries, 1959–65; Registrar, Radiology, Selly Oak Hosp., Birmingham, 1965–66; Registrar, Chest Medicine, Springfield Hosp., Grimsby, 1966–67; Hosp. Practitioner, Psychiatry, All Saints Hosp., Birmingham, 1972–94. Member: Working Group, DHSS, 1984–94; Local Med.

Cttee, 1975–99; Dist Med. Cttee, 1978–88; GMC, 1984–99; West Birmingham HA, 1982–87 (Chm., sub-cttee on needs of ethnic minorities, 1982–85); Birmingham FPC, 1984–88; Birmingham Community Liaison Adv. Cttee, 1985–87. Vice-Chm., Birmingham Div., BMA, 1986–87 (Chm., 1985–86). Mem., Local Review Cttee for Winson Green Prison, 1981–83. Founder Mem., Overseas Doctors' Assoc., 1975–81 (Dep. Treasurer, 1975–81; Nat. Vice-Chm., 1981–87; Inf. and Adv. Service, 1981–99; Nat. Chm., 1987–93; Pres., 1993–99); Founder Mem. and Chm., Link House Council, 1975–89. Founder Mem., Osmania Grad. Med. Assoc. in UK, 1984–99. Vice-Chm., Hyderabad Charitable Trust, 1985–99. Involved in rotary charities, arranging eye camps and supporting educn at sch. in Phagwada, Punjab, India; help to run charitable out-patient clinics at Viveka Nanda dispensary, Ramakrishna Mutt, Hyderabad, India. FRSocMed 1986; FRSPH (FRIPHH 1988; FRSH 1997). Paul Harris Fellow, Rotary Internat., 2005. *Publications:* contribs to learned jls on medico-political topics. *Recreations:* medical politics, music, gardening. *Address:* 24 Melville Road, Edgbaston, Birmingham B16 9JT. *T:* (0121) 454 1725. *Club:* Aston Rotary (Pres., 1984–85).

VERANNEMAN de WATERVLIET, Jean-Michel; Ambassador of Belgium to Portugal, 2010–12; *b* Bruges, 11 July 1947; *s* of Raymond Veranneman de Watervliet and Manuela van den Bogaerde de Terbrugge; *m* 1981, Maria do Carmo; three *s*. *Educ:* Paris Inst d'Etudes Politiques; Army Reserve Officers course, Chasseurs Ardennais Regt; Univ. Libre de Bruxelles (Soc. Scis degree); Vrije Univ. Brussel (Press and Communication Scis degree). Intern, EC, Brussels, 1976; joined Diplomatic Service, 1976; trng, Foreign Min., Brussels, 1976–77 and 1977–78; Third Sec., Bonn, 1977; Dep. Hd of Mission, Brasilia, 1978–80 and 1980–81; Chargé d'Affaires, La Paz, 1980; Dep. Hd, Pol Mil. Desk, 1981–83; Ambassador, Mozambique and Swaziland, 1983–86; First Secretary: UN, NY, 1986–89; EC, Brussels, 1989–91; Consul Gen., São Paulo, 1991–94; Minister Plenipotentiary and Dep. Hd of Mission, London, 1994–97; Africa Dir, 1997–2000; Ambassador: Brasilia, 2000–03; Tel Aviv, 2003–06; Court of St James's, 2006–10. Professor: Univ. Católica de Lisboa, 2012–; Univ. Nova de Lisboa, 2013–. Grand Officier, Ordre de Léopold II; Commandeur: Ordre de Léopold; Ordre de la Couronne; Croix Civique de Première Classe; Grand Cross, Order of Southern Cross (Brazil); Grand Cross, Order of Merit (Portugal). *Publications:* Is the Sovereign Nation State Obsolete?, 1997; History of Africa, 2003; The Ally We All Forgot: Brazil in World War Two, 2011; Belgium in the Second World War, 2014. *Recreations:* reading history books, archery, ship models, yachting. *Address:* Rua Joseph Bleck 48–2A, 1494–724 Dafundo-Oeiras, Portugal; Château de Wodémont, 4607 Dalhem-Neufchateau, Belgium. *Clubs:* Royal Anglo-Belgian; Prince Albert, Cercle Gaulois (Brussels).

VERCOE, Miranda Lucy Mary; *see* Carruthers-Watt, M. L. M.

VERDAN, (Hilaire) Alexander; QC 2006; a Recorder, since 2004; a Deputy High Court Judge (Family Division), since 2009; *b* 24 May 1963; *s* of Jean Pierre Verdan and late Sonya de Vries (*née* Beasley); *m* 1987, Alexandra Mutch; three *s*. *Educ:* W London Inst. of Higher Educn (BA Hons); Poly. of Central London (Dip. Law). Called to the Bar, Inner Temple, 1987; in practice as a barrister, 1987–, specialising in family law (children). *Recreations:* cycling, ski-ing, reading, theatre, cinema, eating and drinking. *Address:* 4 Paper Buildings, Temple, EC4Y 7EX.

VERDI, Prof. Richard Frank, OBE 2007; PhD; Professor of Fine Art, 1989–2007, and Director, Barber Institute of Fine Arts, 1990–2007, University of Birmingham; *b* 7 Nov. 1941; *s* of Frank and Anne Verdi. *Educ:* Univ. of Michigan (BA 1963); Univ. of Chicago (MA 1966); Courtauld Inst. of Art, Univ. of London (PhD 1976). Lectr in Hist. of Art, Univ. of Manchester, 1969–71; Lectr, 1971–81, Sen. Lectr, 1981–89, in Hist. of Art, Univ. of York. FRSA 1999. *Publications:* Klee and Nature, 1984; Cézanne and Poussin: the classical vision of landscape, 1990; Cézanne, 1992; Nicolas Poussin 1594–1665, 1995. *Recreations:* music, literature, natural history. *Address:* 42 Upland Road, Selly Park, Birmingham B29 7JS.

VERE OF HANWORTH, Lord; James Malcolm Aubrey Edward de Vere Beauclerk; *b* 2 Aug. 1995; *s* and *heir* of Earl of Burford, *qv*. *Educ:* Uppingham Sch.; Univ. of Kent. Model, represented by Next Models, London.

VERE-HODGE, Michael John Davy; QC 1993; a Recorder, since 1989; *b* 2 July 1946; *s* of late Nicholas and Ann Vere-Hodge; *m* 1st; one *s* one *d*; 2nd, 2004, Nicola Anne Heron. *Educ:* Winchester Coll.; Grenoble Univ. Called to the Bar, Gray's Inn, 1970, Bencher, 2005. Head of Chambers, 2001–05. *Recreations:* shooting (GB Helice Shooting team, 2006), fishing. *Address:* 3 Paper Buildings, Temple, EC4Y 7EU.

VEREKER, family name of **Viscount Gort**.

VEREKER, Sir John (Michael Medlicott), KCB 1999 (CB 1992); Independent Director: XL Group plc, since 2007; XL Insurance Company Ltd, since 2008; MWH Global, since 2009; *b* 9 Aug. 1944; *s* of late Comdr C. W. M. Vereker and M. H. Vereker (*née* Whatley); *m* 1971, Judith Diane, *d* of Hobart and Alice Rowen, Washington; one *s* one *d*. *Educ:* Marlborough Coll.; Keele Univ. (BA Hons 1967). Asst Principal, ODM, 1967–69; World Bank, Washington, 1970–72; Principal, ODM, 1972; Private Sec. to successive Ministers of Overseas Devełt, 1977–78; Asst Sec., 1978; Prime Minister's Office, 1980–83; Under Sec., 1983–88, and Principal Finance Officer, 1986–88, ODA, FCO; Dep. Sec., DES, then DFE, 1988–93; Perm.-Sec., ODA, subseq. DFID, 1994–2002; Gov. and C-in-C of Bermuda, 2002–07. Chm., Students Loans Co. Ltd, 1989–91. Mem. Council, Inst. of Manpower Studies, 1989–92; Member Board: British Council, 1994–2002; IDS, 1994–2001; VSO, 1994–2002; Mem. Adv. Council, British Consultants and Construction Bureau, 2000–05; Mem., Volcker Commn on World Bank, 2007–. Gov., Ditchley Foundn for Internat. Relations, 2007–. Hon. Vice-Pres., Raleigh Internat., 2002–. Trustee, Internat. Assoc. for Digital Pubns, 2004–09. CCMI (CIMgt 1995). FRSA 1999. KStJ 2002. Hon. DLitt Keele, 1997. *Publications:* Blazing the Trail, 2002; tech. papers for Commonwealth Secretariat and World Bank.

VEREY, Sir David (John), Kt 2015; CBE 2004; Chairman, The Art Fund, 2004–14; *b* 8 Dec. 1950; *s* of late Michael John Verey, TD and Sylvia Mary Verey; *m* 1st, 1974, Luise Jaschke (marr. diss. 1990); two *s* one *d*; 2nd, 1990, Emma Katharine Broadhead (*née* Laidlaw). *Educ:* Eton College; Trinity College, Cambridge (MA). Lazard Brothers: joined 1972; Dir, 1983–2001; Dep. Chief Exec., 1985–90; Chief Exec., 1990–2001; Chm., 1992–2001; Dep. Chm., Cazenove Gp Plc, 2001–02. Chairman: Blackstone Gp UK, 2004–08; Thames River Capital Ltd, 2009–10. Director: Pearson plc, 1996–2000; Daily Mail and Gen. Trust plc, 2004–; Sofina S.A., 2004–; Mem., Supervisory Bd, Bank Gutmann AG, 2002–; Sen. Advr, Lazard & Co. Ltd, 2010–. Lead non-exec. Dir, DCMS, 2011–. Mem., Financial Services Practitioner Panel, 2002–05. Special Advr, Fresh Minds Ltd, 2004–10. Trustee: Tate Gall., 1992–2004 (Chm., Bd of Trustees, 1998–2004); Pilgrim Trust, 2008–14; Teaching Awards Trust, 2009–14; British Council, 2014–; Chm., Adv. Bd, Govt Art Collection, 2013–. Fellow, Eton Coll., 1997–2012. *Recreations:* stalking, bridge, gardening, travel.

VERHAGEN, Maxime Jacques Marcel; Chairman, Bouwend Nederland, since 2013; *b* Maastricht, 14 Sept. 1956; *m* Annemieke Beijlevelt; three *c*. *Educ:* Univ. of Leiden (degree in History 1986). Christian Democratic Alliance: Asst to an MP, 1984–87; joined parly staff with responsibility for Eur. affairs, devełt cooperation and trade policy. Mem. (CDA) Oegstgeest Municipal Council, 1986–90 (Leader, CDA Gp, 1986). Mem., European Parlt, 1989–94. Mem., House of Representatives, Netherlands, 1994–2007 (Leader, CDA Parly Party, 2002–07). Minister of Foreign Affairs, Netherlands, 2007–10; Dep. Prime Minister and Minister of Economic Affairs, Agriculture and Innovation, Netherlands, 2010–12. Vice Chairman: ACP-EU Jt Assembly; Perm. Parly Cttee on Foreign Affairs. Member Board: Eduardo Frei Foundn; Netherlands Atlantic Assoc., 1996–2003; European Movement, 1996–2003; Parly Hist. Foundn, Nijmegen Univ.; Member, Supervisory Board: Free Voice; Chemelot Campus BV, 2013–. Grand Officer, Order of the Legion of Merit of O'Higgins (Chile); Grand Cross: Order of Merit (Germany), 2007; Order of the Southern Cross (Brazil), 2008.

VERHEUGEN, Günter, Hon. GCVO 1998; non-executive Managing Director, European Experience GmbH, since 2010; Board Member: Ford Otosan, Turkey; Löwen Entertainment, Germany; Honorary Professor, Viadrina University, Frankfurt; *b* Bad Kreuznach, 28 April 1944; *s* of Leo Verheugen and Leni (*née* Holzhäuser); *m* 1st, Helga (*d* 1983); 2nd, 1987, Gabriele (*née* Schäfer) (marr. diss. 2011). *Educ:* studied history, sociol. and politics in Cologne and Bonn. Trainee, Neue Rhein-Neue Ruhr Zeitung, 1963–65; Head: Public Relns Div., Min. of Interior, W Germany, 1969–74; Analysis and Inf. task force, Foreign Office, 1974–76; Federal Party Manager, 1977–78, Gen. Sec., 1978–82, FDP. Mem. (SPD) Bundestag, 1983–99 (Mem., Foreign Affairs Cttee, 1983–99; Chm., EU special cttee, 1992). Chm., Socialist Internat. Peace, Security and Disarmament Council, 1997–99. Chm., Radio Broadcasting Council, Deutsche Welle, 1990–99. Joined SPD, 1982: spokesman of Nat. Exec., 1986–87; Editor-in-Chief, Vorwärts (SPD newspaper), 1987–88; Dep. foreign policy spokesman and Chm., UN wkg gp of parly gp, 1991–93; Chm., Bavarian SPD gp in Bundestag, 1993–95; Sec., parly gp, 1993; Fed. Party Manager, 1993–95; Dep. Chm., parly gp for foreign, security and devełt policy, 1994–97; Chm., Kulmbach-Lichtenfels dist, 1996–99; Mem., Upper Franconia regl exec., 1996–99; Co-ordinator for internat. relns of SPD and SPD parly gp, 1997–99; Mem., Nat. Exec., 1997–. European Commission: Mem., 1999–2010; Vice-Pres., 2004–10; Co-chair, Trans Atlantic Econ. Council, 2007–10. Mem., Cttee for Envmt and Devełt, Protestant Ch, Germany, 1998–. Dr *hc*: Vilnius; Szczecin; Wroclaw; Bratislava; Prague; Ljubljana; Cluj; Timisoara. Prizes: Schumpter, 2004; Hoegner, 2005; Polish Business Oscar, 2011; German SME, 2011; Jadwiga of Silesia, 2013. Officer's Cross, Order of Merit (Germany), 1994; Order of Merit (Bavaria), 1997; Kt Comdr's Cross, Order of Merit (Italy), 1982; Commandeur de la Légion d'Honneur (France). *Publications:* Zukunft für Deutschland, 1980; Der Ausverkauf: Macht und Verfall der FDP, 1984; (jtly) Halbzeit in Bonn: die BRD zwei Jahre nach der Wende, 1985; Apartheid, Südafrika und die deutschen interessen am Kap, 1986; Europa in der Krise, 2005; and numerous others.

VERHOFSTADT, Guy; Member (Lib Dem), European Parliament, since 2009; Leader, Alliance of Liberals and Democrats for Europe, since 2009; Prime Minister of Belgium, 1999–2008; *b* 11 April 1953; *s* of Marcel Verhofstadt and Gaby (*née* Stockmans); *m* 1981, Dominique Verkinderen; one *s* one *d*. *Educ:* Koninklijk Atheneum, Ghent; Univ. of Ghent (LLM 1975). Attorney, Ghent Bar, 1975–94. Pol Sec. to Nat. Pres., Party for Freedom and Progress, 1977–81; Mem. (Party for Freedom and Progress) Ghent-Ekklo, House of Reps, Belgium, 1978–84, 1985–95; Dep. Prime Minister and Minister for the Budget, Scientific Res. and the Plan, 1985–88; Pres., shadow cabinet, 1988–91; Minister of State, 1995–2008; Senator (Flemish Liberals and Democrats), and Vice Pres., Senate, 1995–99. Mem., City of Ghent Council, 1976–82, 2007–. Nat. Pres., Party for Freedom and Progress, 1982–85, 1989–92; Nat. Pres., Flemish Liberals and Democrats, 1992–95, 1997–99. Vice-Pres. and Rapporteur, Rwanda Investigation Commn, Senate, 1996–97. *Publications:* Angst, afgunst en het algemeen belang, 1994; De Belgische ziekte, 1997; De Vierde Golf, 2002; De Verenigde Staten van Europa, 2005; Het Vierde Burgermanifest, 2006; pamphlets, articles, contribs to books. *Address:* European Parliament, 60 rue Wiertz, 1047 Brussels, Belgium.

VERITY, Anthony Courtenay Froude, MA; Master, Dulwich College, 1986–95; *b* 25 Feb. 1939; *s* of Arthur and Alice Kathleen Verity; *m* 1962, Patricia Ann Siddall; one *s* one *d*. *Educ:* Queen Elizabeth's Hosp., Bristol; Pembroke Coll., Cambridge (MA). Assistant Master: Dulwich Coll., 1962–65; Manchester Grammar Sch., 1965–69; Head of Classics, Bristol Grammar Sch., 1969–76; Headmaster, Leeds Grammar Sch., 1976–86. Educnl Advr to Emir of Qatar, 1996. Chm., Schools' Arabic Project, 1988–96. Trustee, Dulwich Picture Gallery, 1994–96. Gov., Stonyhurst Coll., 2004–. Editor, Greece and Rome, 1971–76. *Publications:* Latin as Literature, 1971; (trans.) The Idylls of Theocritus, 2002; (trans.) The Odes of Pindar, 2007; (trans.) Homer, The Iliad, 2011; contribs to Jl of Arabic Lit. *Recreations:* music, fell-walking, classics, the Middle East. *Address:* 14 Duncombe Hill, SE23 1QB. *Club:* Athenæum.

VERJEE, Baron *cr* 2013 (Life Peer), of Portobello in the Royal Borough of Kensington and Chelsea; **Rumi Verjee,** CBE 2009; Owner and Chairman, Thomas Goode & Co., since 1995; *b* Uganda, 1957. *Educ:* Haileybury Sch.; Downing Coll., Cambridge (BA Law 1978; Hon. Fellow). Called to the Bar, Middle Temple, 1979. Founder in UK, Domino's Pizza, 1985–89. Co-Owner, Watford FC, 1993–97. Chairman: Brompton Capital Ltd, 1996–; Ipanema Properties, Brazil. Mem., Adv. Bd for 2012 London Olympic Games, British Olympic Assoc., 2007–12. Member: World Presidents' Orgn, 2008–; Chief Executives' Foundn, 2011–; Global Leadership Foundn, 2013–. Founder, Rumi Foundn, 2006. *Address:* Rumi Foundation, 19 South Audley Street, W1K 2BN.

VERMA, Baroness *cr* 2006 (Life Peer), of Leicester in the County of Leicestershire; **Sandip Verma;** Parliamentary Under-Secretary of State, Department for International Development, since 2015; *b* 30 June 1959; *d* of S. S. and R. Rana; *m* 1977, Ashok Kumar Verma; one *s* one *d*. *Educ:* locally. Senior Partner, Domiciliary Care Services, 2000. Contested (C): Hull E, 2001; Wolverhampton SW, 2005. House of Lords: Opposition spokesperson on health, educn and skills, 2006–07, on innovation, univs and skills, 2007–10, on children, schs and families, 2007–08, 2009–10; an Opposition Whip, 2006–10; a Baroness in Waiting (Govt Whip), 2010–12; govt spokesman for Cabinet Office, 2010–12, internat. devełt, 2010–11, women and equalities, 2010–12, business, innovation and skills, 2011–12; Parly Under-Sec. of State, DECC, 2012–15. Advr, Bright Distributors Ltd, 2006–. Exec. Mem., Ethnic Diversity Council, 2005–. Chm. (Political), Leics South Cons Assoc., 2006–08; Pres., City of Leics Cons. Assoc., 2008–09, 2010–11. Champion, Roko Breast Cancer, 2006–; Patron: Tory Reform Group, 2006–; Cons. British Asian Link, 2006–; Pakistan-India Friendship Soc., 2006–; Bucks Punjabi Internat. Soc., 2006–. *Recreations:* socialising, reading, walking, going to different parts of the world, arranging events, watching cricket. *Address:* House of Lords, SW1A 0PW. *T:* (office) (020) 7219 5216, (home) (0116) 270 1686, *Fax:* (0116) 270 1603. *E:* Vermas@parliament.uk.

VERMONT, Christopher John; Managing Director, GuarantCo (formerly Head, Debt Capital Markets, then Head of GuarantCo), Frontier Markets Fund Managers, since 2007; *b* London, 16 Dec. 1959; *s* of David Neville Vermont and Ann Marion Vermont (*née* Wilson); *m* 1987, Sarah Webster; one *s* three *d*. *Educ:* St Paul's Sch., Barnes; Magdalene Coll., Cambridge (BA Social and Pol Scis 1982; MA). Manager, Internat., ANZ Grindlays Bank, London, Calcutta, Delhi, 1982–90; Head: Origination and Syndication, ANZ Bank Ltd, 1991–2000; Primary Mkts, 2001, Project and Structured Finance, 2002–03, Debt Solutions, 2003–04, ANZ Investment Bank. Non-exec. Dir, BPL Global Ltd, 2008–; Dir, Long Acre Estates Ltd, 2013–. Dir, Charity Bank Ltd, 2010– (Trustee, 2010–; Chm., Assets and Liabilities Cttee, 2010–13). Dir, Art Circuit, 2007–. Gov., St Paul's Sch., Barnes, 2010– (Member: Educn Cttee, 2011–14; Investment Sub-Cttee, 2013–; Finance Cttee, 2014–). Mem., Finance Cttee, 2007–, Mem. Ct, 2014–, Mercers' Co (Mem., Investment Sub-Cttee, 2009–13). *Recreations:* gardening (vegetables), log splitting, tennis, swimming, classic cars. *Address:* Frontier Markets Fund Managers, 100 Cannon Street, EC4N 6EU. *T:* (020) 3696 1862, *Fax:* (020) 3696 1875. *E:* chris.vermont@fmfml.com.

VERMUNT, Prof. Jan Dominicus Hyacinthus, PhD; Professor of Education, University of Cambridge, since 2012; Fellow, Wolfson College, Cambridge, since 2013; *b* Breda, Netherlands, 16 Feb. 1957; *s* of Kees and Corrie Vermunt; *m* 1984, Margaret Hylkema; one *s* one *d*. *Educ:* Tilburg Univ. (MSc Psychol. and Educn (*cum laude*) 1984; PhD Psychol. (*cum laude*) 1992). Tilburg University: Res. Asst, 1984–86; Asst Prof., 1986–95; Associate Prof., Leiden Univ., 1995–99 and 2002–04; Professor: Maastricht Univ., 1999–2002; Utrecht Univ., 2004–12. Vis. Prof., Hasselt Univ., Belgium, 2002–03; Res. Fellow, Univ. of Amsterdam, 1992–95. *Publications:* (ed jtly) Learning Patterns in Higher Education, 2014; contribs to learned jls incl. Learning and Instruction, British Jl Educnl Psychol., Learning and Individual Differences, Studies in Higher Educn, Teaching and Teacher Educn, Internat. Jl Sci. Educn, Educnl Psychol. Rev. *Recreations:* travel, cycling, music, chess. *Address:* Faculty of Education, University of Cambridge, 184 Hills Road, Cambridge CB2 8PQ. *T:* (01223) 767600, *Fax:* (01223) 767602. *E:* jdhv2@cam.ac.uk.

VERNEY, family name of **Baron Willoughby de Broke**.

VERNEY, Sir Edmund Ralph, 6th Bt *cr* 1818, of Claydon House, Buckinghamshire; *b* 28 June 1950; *o s* of Sir Ralph Bruce Verney, 5th Bt, KBE and Mary (*née* Vestey); *S* father, 2001; *m* 1982, Daphne Fausset-Farquhar; one *s* one *d*. *Educ:* Harrow; York Univ. FRICS. Mem., Nat. Council, CLA, 1990–2001 (Chm., Bucks Br., 1996–99). Prime Warden, Dyers' Co., 2001–02. High Sheriff, Bucks, 1998–99. *Heir: s* Andrew Nicholas Verney [*b* 9 July 1983; *m* 2013, Alexandra Edwina Luttrell, *d* of Ronald Munro Ferguson; one *s*]. *Address:* Claydon House, Middle Claydon, Bucks MK18 2EX.

VERNEY, (Sir) (John) Sebastian, (3rd Bt *cr* 1946, of Eaton Square, City of Westminster; *S* father, 1993, but does not use the title and his name does not appear on the Official Roll of the Baronetage). *Heir: cousin* Christopher Ralph Evelyn Verney [*b* 4 Oct. 1948; *m* 1976, Madeliene Lindberg].

VERNON, family name of **Baron Lyveden**.

VERNON, 11th Baron *cr* 1762; **Anthony William Vernon-Harcourt;** founder and Chairman, Monks Partnership Ltd, 1980–2002; *b* 29 Oct. 1939; *s* of William Ronald Denis Vernon-Harcourt, OBE and Nancy Everil (*née* Leatham); *S* kinsman, 2000; *m* 1966, Cherry Stanhope, *er d* of T. J. Corbin; three *s* one *d*. *Educ:* Eton; Magdalene Coll., Cambridge. *Publications:* Archibald Sturrock: pioneer locomotive engineer, 2007; Yorkshire Engine Company: Sheffield's locomotive manufacturer, 2008; Leveson Francis Vernon-Harcourt, Civil Engineer, 2012. *Recreations:* Church of England, railway history, cycling, gardening. *Heir: s* Hon. Simon Anthony Vernon-Harcourt [*b* 24 Aug. 1969; *m* 1999, Jessica Jane, *e d* of William Eric Faber; two *d*]. *Address:* Monks Farm, Debden Green, Saffron Walden, Essex CB11 3LX.

VERNON, Annette; *see* Sharkey, A.

VERNON, David Bowater; Under Secretary, Inland Revenue, 1975–84; *b* 14 Nov. 1926; *s* of Lt-Col Herbert Bowater Vernon, MC, and Ivy Margaret Vernon; *m* 1954, Anne de Montmorency Fleming, *d* of late John and Margaret Fleming; three *s* three *d*. *Educ:* Marlborough Coll.; Oriel Coll., Oxford (MA). RA, 1945–48 (Lieut). Inland Revenue, 1951–84. *Recreation:* gardening. *Address:* 6 Hurstwood Park, Tunbridge Wells, Kent TN4 8YE.

VERNON, Diana Charlotte; Principal, Methodist Ladies' College, Melbourne, since 2014; *b* 30 April 1961; *d* of Roderick W. P. Vernon and late Jennifer F. F. Vernon (*née* Tyrrell). *Educ:* St Michael's, Burton Park; Durham Univ.; King's Coll., London (PGCE). Editl Asst, John Wiley & Sons Ltd, 1982–84; Account Executive: Business Image PR, 1984–85; Grayling, 1985–87; Corporate Communications Executive: Thorn EMI, 1987–89; London Internat. Gp, 1989–93; Housemistress and Dir of PR, Downe House, Newbury, 1994–2000; Headmistress: Woldingham Sch., 2000–07; City of London Sch. for Girls, 2007–14. Governor: Lilian Baylis, London, 1985–2002; Flexlands Sch., Chobham, 1994–2003; St Christopher's, Hampstead, 2003–14; Conifers, Sussex, 2003–06; Notting Hill Prep Sch., 2007–14. *Recreations:* theatre, cookery, travel, swimming. *Address:* Methodist Ladies' College, 207 Barkers Road, Kew, Vic 3101, Australia.

VERNON, Sir James (William), 5th Bt *cr* 1914, of Shotwick Park, Chester; business consultant; *b* 2 April 1949; *s* of Sir Nigel Vernon, 4th Bt and Margaret Ellen Vernon (*née* Dobell); S father, 2007; *m* 1981, Davinia Elizabeth Howard; two *s* one *d*. *Educ:* Shrewsbury. FCA. *Recreations:* shooting, fishing, vintage cars, gardening. *Heir: s* George William Howard Vernon, *b* 25 July 1987. *Address:* The Hall, Lygan-y-Wern, Pentre Halkyn, Holywell, Flintshire CH8 8BD. *Clubs:* Army and Navy, Honourable Artillery Company; Liverpool Artists; Chester City; Bentley Drivers, Vintage Sports Car.

VERNON, Kenneth Robert, CBE 1978; Deputy Chairman and Chief Executive, North of Scotland Hydro-Electric Board, 1973–88; *b* 15 March 1923; *s* of late Cecil W. Vernon and Jessie McGaw, Dumfries; *m* 1946, Pamela Hands, Harrow; one *s* three *d* (and one *d* decd). *Educ:* Dumfries Academy; Glasgow University. BSc, FREng, FIET, FIMechE. BTH Co., Edinburgh Corp., British Electricity Authority, 1948–55; South of Scotland Electricity Bd, 1955–56; North of Scotland Hydro-Electric Bd, 1956: Chief Electrical and Mech. Engr, 1964; Gen. Man., 1966; Bd Mem., 1970. Dir, British Electricity International Ltd, 1976–88; Mem. Bd, Northern Ireland Electricity Service, 1979–85. *Publications:* various papers to technical instns. *Recreations:* fishing, gardening. *Address:* 10 Keith Crescent, Edinburgh EH4 3NH. *T:* (0131) 332 4610.

VERNON-HARCOURT, family name of **Baron Vernon**.

VERPLAETSE, Viscount Alfons Remi Emiel; Governor, National Bank of Belgium, 1989–99, now Hon. Governor; *b* Zulte, Belgium, 19 Feb. 1930; created Viscount, 1999; *s* of Leon Verplaetse and Alida Baert; *m* 1954, Odette Vanhee; three *s* two *d*. *Educ:* Catholic Univ. of Louvain (Licentiate of Commercial and Consular Scis). Joined National Bank of Belgium, 1953: Attaché, 1960–62; Asst Advr, 1962–66; Advr, 1966–74; Inspector Gen., 1974–80; Sen. Economist, 1980–82; on secondment to Social and Econ. Cabinet of Prime Minister as Dep. Chief of Cabinet, 1982–83, Chief of Cabinet, 1983–88; Dir, 1985–88; Vice-Governor, 1988–89. Gov., IMF, 1989–99; Deputy Governor: IBRD, 1989–99; IFC, 1989–99; IDA, 1989–99. Dir, European Fund for Monetary Co-operation, 1989–94; Mem. Council, European Monetary Inst., 1994–99. Grand Officier, Ordre de la Couronne (Belgium), 1991; Grande Ufficiale, Ordine al Merito (Italy), 1986; Officier de la Légion d'Honneur (France), 1994. *Address:* National Bank of Belgium, Boulevard de Berlaimont 14, 1000 Bruxelles, Belgium. *T:* (2) 2214777.

VERSACE, Donatella; Vice-President and Creative Director, Gianni Versace Group, since 1997; *b* 2 May 1955; *d* of Antonio Versace and Francesca Versace; *m* Paul Beck (marr. diss.); one *s* one *d*. *Educ:* Univ. of Florence. Joined Versace, 1978; designer: Versace Young, 1993; Versus; Isante; launched fragrance, Versace Woman, 2001. *Address:* Gianni Versace SpA, Via Borgospesso 15/A, 20121 Milan, Italy.

VERTOVEC, Prof. Steven Allen, DPhil; Director, Max Planck Institute for the Study of Religious and Ethnic Diversity, Göttingen, since 2007; Hon. Joint Professor of Sociology and Ethnology, University of Göttingen, since 2007; *b* 2 July 1957; *s* of Frank J. Vertovec and Dorothea M. Vertovec; *m* 1994, Astrid Gräfe; one *s* one *d*. *Educ:* Immaculate Conception High Sch., Elmhurst, Ill; Univ. of Colorado, Boulder (BA); Univ. of Calif, Santa Barbara (MA); Nuffield Coll., Oxford (DPhil 1988). Res. Fellow, Sch. of Geography, Oxford Univ., 1991–93; Principal Res. Fellow, Centre for Res. in Ethnic Relns, Univ. of Warwick, 1994–97; Dir, ESRC Transnat. Communities Res. Prog., 1997–2003; University of Oxford: Res. Reader in Anthropology, 1997–2002; Prof. of Transnational Anthropology, 2002–07; Dir, Centre on Migration, Policy and Society, 2003–07; Jt Dir, Internat. Migration Inst., 2006–07; Sen. Res. Fellow, Linacre Coll., Oxford, 1997–2007. Regents' Fellow, Univ. of Calif, 1980–82; Overseas Res. Student Award, CVCP, 1983–86; Res. Fellow, Alexander von Humboldt-Stiftung, 1993–94; Vis. Fellow, Inst. Ethnology, Free Univ., Berlin, and Inst. Eur. Ethnology, Humboldt Univ., Berlin, 1993–94. *Publications:* (jtly) South Asians Overseas: migration and ethnicity, 1990; Aspects of the South Asian Diaspora, 1991; Hindu Trinidad: religion, ethnicity and socio-economic change, 1992; (with A. Rogers) The Urban Context: ethnicity, social networks and situational analysis, 1995; (with C. Peach) Islam in Europe: the politics of religion and community, 1997; (with A. Rogers) Muslim European Youth: reproducing religion, ethnicity and culture, 1998; Migration and Social Cohesion, 1999; (with R. Cohen) Migration, Diasporas and Transnationalism, 1999; The Hindu Diaspora: comparative patterns, 2000; (with R. Cohen) Conceiving Cosmopolitanism, 2002; (with B. Parekh) Culture and Economy in the Indian Diaspora, 2003; (with D. Posey) Globalization, Globalism, Environments and Environmentalism, 2004; (with W. Schiffauer) Civil Enculturation, 2004; (jtly) Citizenship in European Cities, 2004; Transnationalism, 2008; contrib. articles to Religion, Ethnic and Racial Studies, Social and Economic, Ethnology, New Community, Etnolog, Contribs to Indian Sociology, Social Compass, Internat. Social Sci. Jl; Jl of Ethnic and Migration Studies; Internat. Migration Review. *Address:* Max Planck Institut zur Erforschung multireligiöser und multiethnischer Gesellschaften, Hermann Foge Weg 11, 37073 Göttingen, Germany.

VERULAM, 7th Earl of, *cr* 1815; **John Duncan Grimston;** Bt 1629; Baron Forrester (Scot.), 1633; Baron Dunboyne and Viscount Grimston (Ire.), 1719; Baron Verulam (Gt. Brit.), 1790; Viscount Grimston (UK), 1815; *b* 21 April 1951; *s* of 6th Earl of Verulam and Marjorie Ray (*d* 1994), *d* of late Walter Atholl Duncan; *S* father, 1973; *m* 1976, Dione Angela (*see* Countess of Verulam), *e d* of Jeremy Fox Eric Smith, *qv*; three *s* one *d*. *Educ:* Eton; Christ Church, Oxford (MA 1976). Dir, Baring Brothers, 1987–96; Man. Dir, ABN-AMRO Bank, 1996–2000; Dir, Kleinwort Benson Private Bank, 2001–08. Chm., Grimston Trust Ltd, 1982–. *Heir: s* Viscount Grimston, *qv*. *Clubs:* White's, Beefsteak.

VERULAM, Countess of; Dione Angela Grimston; Lord Lieutenant of Hertfordshire, since 2007; artist; *b* 19 July 1954; *d* of Jeremy Fox Eric Smith, *qv*; *m* 1976, Earl of Verulam, *qv*; three *s* one *d*. *Educ:* Benenden Sch.; Exeter Univ. (BA Hons Hist. and Archaeol.). Stencilling commns, 1981–2001; solo exhibitions: Fleming Collection, 2007; Sladmore Gall., 2010; Mount St Gall., 2013; Rebecca Hossack Art Gall., 2015. Mem., Panel of Acceptance in Lieu, DCMS, 2001–06. Mem., Regl Cttee, NT, 1991–98. Liveryman, Goldsmiths' Co., 2005–. High Sheriff, 2002–03, DL 2003–07, Herts. Trustee, St Albans Cathedral Fabric Trust, 1995–2004. Pres. or Patron of various orgns in Herts. *Publications:* (ed) Memories of Strathvaich, 1992; Gorhambury Gardens Guide, 1993. *Recreations:* ski-ing, golf, theatre, opera, reading, sewing, painting, Gorhambury. *Clubs:* Boodle's Ladies' Side; Northern Meeting (Inverness).

VESEY, family name of **Viscount de Vesci**.

VESSEY, Prof. Martin Paterson, CBE 1994; FRS 1991; FMedSci; Professor of Public Health (formerly Social and Community Medicine), University of Oxford, 1974–2000, now Emeritus; Fellow of St Cross College, Oxford, since 1973; *b* 22 July 1936; *s* of Sidney J. Vessey and Catherine P. Vessey (*née* Thomson); *m* 1959, Anne Platt; two *s* one *d*. *Educ:* University College Sch., Hampstead; University Coll. London (Fellow, 1992); University Coll. Hosp. Med. Sch., London. MB, BS London 1959; MD London 1971; FFCM RCP 1972; MA Oxon 1974; MRCPE 1978; FRCPE 1979; FRCGP 1983; FRCP 1987; FRCOG 1989; FFSRH (FFFP 1995). Scientific Officer, Dept of Statistics, Rothamsted Exper. Stn, 1960–65; House Surg. and House Phys., Barnet Gen. Hosp., 1965–66; Mem. Sci. Staff, MRC Statistical Research Unit, 1966–69; Lectr in Epidemiology, Univ. of Oxford, 1969–74. Advr to WHO Human Reproduction Prog., 1972–96; Chairman: Adv. Cttee on Breast Cancer Screening, DHSS, subseq. DoH, 1987–99; Adv. Cttee on Cervical Cancer Screening, DoH, 1996–2006; Adv. Cttee on Bowel Cancer Screening, DoH, 2008–11; Member: Cttee on Safety of Medicines, 1980–92, 1996–98; Royal Commn on Environmental Pollution, 1984–89. Founder FMedSci 1998. *Publications:* many sci. articles in learned jls, notably on med. aspects of fertility control, safety of drugs, epidemiology of cancer and women's health. *Recreations:* fine arts, conservation, model engineering. *Address:* Clifden Cottage, Burford Road, Fulbrook, Burford OX18 4BL.

VESTEY, family name of **Baron Vestey**.

VESTEY, 3rd Baron *cr* 1922, of Kingswood; **Samuel George Armstrong Vestey,** KCVO 2009; DL; Bt 1913; Master of the Horse, since 1999; *b* 19 March 1941; *s* of late Captain the Hon. William Howarth Vestey (killed in action in Italy, 1944; *o s* of 2nd Baron Vestey and Frances Sarah Howarth) and Pamela Helen Fullerton, *d* of George Nesbitt Armstrong; *S* grandfather, 1954; *m* 1st, 1970, Kathryn Mary (marr. diss. 1981), *er d* of John Eccles, Moor Park, Herts; two *d*; 2nd, 1981, Celia Elizabeth, *d* of late Major Guy Knight, MC, Lockinge Manor, Wantage, Oxon; two *s* one *d*. *Educ:* Eton. Lieut, Scots Guards. Chairman: Steeplechase Co. (Cheltenham), 1990–2011; Vestey Group Ltd, 1995–. Chm., Meat Training Council, 1991–95. President: London Meat Trade and Drovers Benevolent Assoc., 1973; Inst. of Meat, 1978–83; Three Counties Agricl Soc., 1978; Royal Bath and W of England Soc., 1994; BHS, 1994–97. Chm., Royal Agricl Soc. of the Commonwealth, 1998–. Patron, Glos CCC, 1997–2014. Liveryman, Butchers' Co. DL Glos, 1982. Queen's Golden Jubilee Medal, 2002; Queen's Diamond Jubilee Medal, 2012. GCStJ 1987 (Chancellor of the Order, 1988–91, Lord Prior, 1991–2002). *Recreations:* racing, shooting, cricket. *Heir: s* Hon. William Guy Vestey [*b* 27 Aug. 1983; *m* 2012, Violet Gwyneth, *o d* of late Gavin Henderson; one *d*. Page of Honour to the Queen, 1995–97]. *Address:* Stowell Park, Northleach, Glos GL54 3LE. *Clubs:* White's, Turf; Jockey (Newmarket); I Zingari; Melbourne (Melbourne); South Cerney Golf.

VESTEY, Sir Paul (Edmund), 3rd Bt *cr* 1921, of Shirley; *b* 15 Feb. 1944; *s* of Sir (John) Derek Vestey, 2nd Bt and Phyllis Irene Vestey (*née* Brewer); *S* father, 2005; *m* 1971, Victoria Anne Scudamore, *d* of John Salter; three *d*. *Educ:* Radley. *Heir: cousin* James Patrick Vestey [*b* 13 April 1954; *m* 1981, Nicola Jane Knight]. *Address:* Manor House Farm, Bishops Sutton, Alresford, Hants SO24 0BA.

VETTRIANO, Jack, OBE 2003; artist, since 1988; Co-Founder, Heartbreak Publishing Ltd, since 2008; *b* Fife, 17 Nov. 1951; *s* of William and Catherine Hoggan; *né* Jack Hoggan. Mining engr, 1966–70; variety of middle mgt posts, 1970–88. Self-taught artist; solo exhibitions: Edinburgh, London, Hong Kong, Johannesburg; Portland Gall., London, 2004, 2006; Homage a Tuiga, Monaco Yacht Club, 2009; Days of Wine and Roses, Kirkcaldy Mus., Fife and Heartbreak Gall., London, 2010; The Ballroom Spy, Heartbreak Gall., London, and Royal West Acad., Bristol, 2011; retrospective, Kelvingrove Art Gall. and Mus., Glasgow, 2013. Represented by Portland Gall., 1994–2007, by Heartbreak Gall., London, 2009–. Hon. DLitt St Andrews, 2003; DUniv Open, 2004. *Publications:* (with W. Gordon Smith) Fallen Angels, 1996; Man's World, 2009; Women in Love, 2009; (with Anthony Quinn): Lovers and Other Strangers, 2000; Jack Vettriano: a life, 2004; Studio Life, 2008; Jack Vettriano: a retrospective, 2013. *Recreations:* music, film, ballroom dancing. *E:* nathalie@jackvettriano.com.

VIALA, Prof. Alain Bernard Jean; Professor of French Literature and Fellow of Lady Margaret Hall, University of Oxford, since 2002; Professor of French Literature, University of Paris III, Sorbonne Nouvelle, since 1985; *b* 20 Nov. 1947; *s* of Ernest and Marie Viala. *Educ:* Ecole Normale Supérieure, Cachan; (Agrégé des lettres; DèsL). Lecturer: Ecole Nationale de Chimie, 1972–78; Ecole d'Artillerie, 1973–74; Asst Prof., Univ. Sorbonne Nouvelle, 1978–84; Prof. of French Studies and Fellow, Wadham Coll., Univ. of Oxford, 1997–2002. Guest Professor: Univ. of Liège, 1988; Univ. of Tel Aviv, 1996. Pres., Commn des Programmes de Lettres, Min. of Educn, France, 1993–2002. Member: Lit. Cttee, Presses Universitaires de France, 2007–; Steering Cttee, Agence Nat. de la Recherche, France. Chevalier des Palmes Académiques (France), 1988; Chevalier, Ordre National du Mérite (France), 2006. *Publications:* Savoir-lire, 1982; Naissance de l'écrivain, 1985; Racine: la stratégie du caméléon, 1990; Approches de la réception, 1993; Le théâtre en France, 1996, new edn 2008; Le Dictionnaire du Littéraire, 2002; Le Tragique, 2002; De la Publication, 2002; Lettre à Rousseau sur l'intérêt littéraire, 2005; Histoire du théâtre, 2006, 4th edn 2012; La France galante, 2008 (R. H. Gapper Prize, Soc. for French Studies, 2009); La culture littéraire, 2009; (with Daniel Mesguich) Le Theatre, 2011. *Address:* Lady Margaret Hall, Oxford OX2 6QA.

VICARY-SMITH, Peter David; Chief Executive, Which?, since 2004; *b* 31 May 1962; *s* of James David Smith and Valerie Ann Smith; changed name by deed poll to Vicary-Smith on marriage, 1991; *m* 1991, Susan Joy Vicary; two *d*. *Educ:* Dulwich Coll.; Queen's Coll., Oxford (BA PPE 1984). Various mktg appts, Procter and Gamble, Mars Confectionery and Kenner Parker, 1984–88; McKinsey & Co., 1988–91; Hd of Appeals, Oxfam, 1991–96; Dir of Fundraising and Communications, ICRF, 1996–2002; Commercial Dir, Cancer Research UK, 2002–04. Non-exec. Dir, Oxfordshire Learning Disabilities NHS Trust, 1994–96. Member: Fundraising Standards Bd, 2006–08; Commercial Panel, Nat. Trust Enterprises, 2007–. Pres., BEUC, Eur. Consumers' Orgn, 2012–14. Trustee: Methodist Homes for the Aged, 2003–06; Marie Curie Cancer Care, 2012–13. *Recreations:* gardening, golf. *Address:* Which?, 2 Marylebone Road, NW1 4DF. *T:* (020) 7770 7000. *Club:* Lansdowne.

VICK, Graham, CBE 2009; Founder, 1987, and Artistic Director, Birmingham Opera Company (formerly City of Birmingham Touring Opera); *b* 30 Dec. 1953. Trained as a singer and conductor. Associate Dir, English Music Theatre; Director of Productions: Scottish Opera, 1984–87; Glyndebourne Fest. Opera, 1994–2000. Hambro Vis. Prof. of Opera Studies, Oxford Univ., 2002–03; Hon. Prof. of Music, Univ. of Birmingham. Work in a wide repertoire from Monteverdi to Berio includes productions for: Royal Opera House, Covent Garden; ENO; Glyndebourne Fest. Opera; Opera North; Scottish Opera; Metropolitan Opera, NY; Chicago Lyric Opera; San Francisco Opera; La Scala, Milan; Opéra Nationale de Paris; Vienna State Opera; Bavarian State Opera; Maggio Musicale, Florence; Netherlands Opera; Deutsche Oper, Berlin; Teatro Real, Madrid; Gran Teatre del Liceu, Barcelona; Mariinsky Theatre, St Petersburg. *Address:* Birmingham Opera Company, 205 The Argent Centre, 60 Frederick Street, Birmingham B1 3HS; c/o Ingpen & Williams, 7 St George's Court, 131 Putney Bridge Road, SW15 2PA.

VICKERMAN, Jill Margaret; Scottish Secretary, British Medical Association, since 2013; *b* Edinburgh, 18 June 1965; *d* of William Justice Vickerman and Seonaid Mairi Grant Vickerman. *Educ:* Edinburgh Univ. (BSc Maths and Stats). Statistician, Scottish Office, 1987–2004; Scottish Government: Hd, Analytical Services for Health and Social Care, 2004–09; Dep. Dir for Healthcare Planning, 2009–10; Policy Dir for Health and Social Care, 2010–13. Trustee, Erskine Hosp., 2012–. *Recreations:* golf, ski-ing, hill-walking, piano, fiddle. *Address:* 14 Queen Street, Edinburgh EH2 1LL. *T:* (0131) 247 3016, *Fax:* (0131) 247 3001. *E:* jvickerman@bma.org.uk.

VICKERMAN, Prof. Keith, FRS 1984; FRSE 1971; FMedSci; Regius Professor of Zoology, University of Glasgow, 1984–98; *b* 21 March 1933; *s* of Jack Vickerman and Mabel Vickerman (*née* Dyson); *m* 1961, Moira Dutton, LLB; one *d*. *Educ:* King James' Grammar School, Almondbury; University College London (BSc 1955; PhD 1960; DSc 1970; Fellow, 1985). Wellcome Trust Lectr, Zoology Dept, UCL, 1958–63; Royal Soc. Tropical Res. Fellow, UCL, 1963–68; Glasgow University: Reader in Zoology, 1968–74; Prof., 1974–98; Head of Dept of Zoology, 1979–85. Leeuwenhoek Lectr, Royal Soc., 1994. Mem., WHO Panel of Consultant Experts on Parasitic Diseases, 1973–98. Mem. Council, Royal Soc., 1996–97. Founder FMedSci 1998. Gold Medal for Zoology, Linnean Soc., 1996. *Publications:* The Protozoa (with F. E. G. Cox), 1967; numerous publications on protozoa and parasites. *Recreations:* sketching, gardening. *Address:* Institute of Biodiversity, Animal Health and Comparative Medicine, Graham Kerr Building, University of Glasgow, Glasgow G12 8QQ. *T:* (0141) 330 5157; 16 Mirrlees Drive, Glasgow G12 0SH. *T:* (0141) 586 7794.

VICKERS, Andrew Julian; Associate Attending Research Methodologist, Memorial Sloan-Kettering Cancer Center, New York, since 2007 (Assistant Attending Research Methodologist, 1999–2007); *b* 11 Feb. 1967; *s* of Jeffrey Vickers and Angela Vickers; *m* 1996, Caroline Batzdorf; one *s* one *d*. *Educ:* Girton Coll., Cambridge; Green Coll., Oxford. Joined Res. Council for Complementary Medicine, 1993; Dir of Res., 1997–99; estabd registry of randomised trials in complementary medicine for Cochrane Collaboration, 1995. Ed., Complementary Therapies in Medicine, 1996–99. Principal investigator, NHS funded trial of acupuncture for headache, 1998. Mem., R&D Cttee, Prince of Wales initiative for Integrated Medicine, 1996–98. *Publications:* Complementary Medicine and Disability, 1993; Health Options: complementary therapies for cerebral palsy and related conditions, 1994; Massage and Aromatherapy: a guide for health professionals, 1996; (ed) Examining Complementary Medicine: the sceptical holist, 1998; (jtly) ABC of Complementary Medicine, 2000; What is a p value anyway?, 2010; contrib. numerous papers to peer-reviewed health-related jls. *Recreations:* cooking, Ultimate Frisbee, running, guitar. *E:* andrewline@earthlink.net.

VICKERS, Andrew Robert; a District Judge (Magistrates' Courts), since 2004; *b* 18 Jan. 1951; *s* of late Francis Albert Vickers and Barbara Winifred Vickers (*née* Tappenden); *m* 1973, Alison Ayres; one *s* two *d*. *Educ:* Windsor Grammar Sch.; Univ. of London (ext. BA 1976). Called to the Bar, Gray's Inn, 1987. Assistant: Chamberlain's Dept, City of London Corp., 1977–78; Mansion House and Guildhall Justice Rooms, 1978–83; PSDs, Slough and Windsor, 1983–86; Principal Court Clerk, Hounslow PSA, 1986–89; Dep. Justices' Clerk, Enfield PSA, 1989–92; Clerk to the Justices, Kingston upon Thames PSA, 1992–2004; Justices' Chief Exec., Kingston upon Thames MCC, 1995–2001; Regl Justices' Clerk for Hounslow, Ealing, Richmond, Wimbledon, W London and S Western PSAs, 2003–04. *Recreations:* avid supporter of Brentford FC, reading, music. *Address:* Maidenhead Magistrates' Court, Bridge Road, Maidenhead, Berks SL6 8PB.

VICKERS, Sir Brian (William), Kt 2008; PhD, LittD; FBA 1998; Professor of English Literature, and Director, Centre for Renaissance Studies, ETH Zürich, 1975–2003, now Emeritus Professor; *b* 13 Dec. 1937; *s* of William Morgan Davies and Josephine Davies (*née* Grant); *m* 1st, 1962, Ilse-Renate Freiling (marr. diss. 1989); two *d*; 2nd, 1989, Sabine Köllmann; one *s* one *d*. *Educ:* St Marylebone Grammar Sch.; Trinity Coll., Cambridge (BA 1st Cl. Hons English 1962; Charles Oldham Shakespeare Schol., 1961; Sen. Schol., 1962); PhD 1967, LittD 1996 Cantab. Cambridge University: Res. Fellow, Churchill Coll., 1964–65; Asst Lectr in English, 1964–68; Fellow and Dir of Studies in English, Downing Coll., 1966–71; Univ. Lectr in English, 1968–72; Prof. of English Lit., Univ. of Zürich, 1972–75. Vis. Fellow, All Souls Coll., Oxford, 1980–81; Fellow, Wissenschaftskolleg zu Berlin, 1986–87; Vis. Prof. of English Lit., UCL, 2012–. Lectures: Shakespeare, British Acad., 1992; John Coffin, London Univ., 2001; Sam Wanamaker Fellowship, Shakespeare's Globe, 2015. Pres., Internat. Soc. for History of Rhetoric, 1977–79; Chm., Soc. for Renaissance Studies, 2004–07. Dist. Sen. Fellow, Sch. of Advanced Study, Univ. of London, 2003–; Sen. Res. Fellow, Inst. of English Studies, 2004–. Hon. Fellow, Downing Coll., Cambridge, 2008. Hon. Foreign Mem., Amer. Acad. of Arts and Scis, 2007. Hon. Pres., Old Philologians Assoc., 2004–. Member of Editorial Board: Renaissance Studies, 1994–98; Annals of Science, 1995–; Isis, 1999–2002; Early Science and Medicine, 2009–; Interdisciplinary Science Reviews, 2011–. Dir, The Oxford Francis Bacon, 2009– (Chm. Adv. Bd, 2005–09); Gen. Ed., The Complete Works of John Ford, 2005–. Dr *hc* Fribourg, 2003; Hon. DLit London, 2009. *Publications:* (ed) Henry Mackenzie, The Man of Feeling, 1967, 2nd edn 2001; Francis Bacon and Renaissance Prose, 1968; The Artistry of Shakespeare's Prose, 1968, rev. edn 1979; (ed) Essential Articles for the Study of Francis Bacon, 1968; (ed) The World of Jonathan Swift, 1968; (ed) Seventeenth Century Prose, 1969; Classical Rhetoric in English Poetry, 1970, rev. edn 1989 (trans. German 2008); Towards Greek Tragedy, 1973; (ed) Shakespeare: the critical heritage, 6 vols, 1623–1692, 1974, 1693–1733, 1974, 1733–1752, 1975, 1753–1765, 1976, 1765–1774, 1979, 1774–1801, 1981; (ed jtly) Hooker: the laws of ecclesiastical polity, 1976; Shakespeare's Coriolanus, 1976; (ed) Rhetoric Revalued, 1982; (ed) Occult and Scientific Mentalities in the Renaissance, 1984 (trans. Spanish 1980); (ed) Arbeit, Musse, Meditation: Betrachtungen zur Vita activa und Vita contemplativa, 1985, rev. edn 1991; (ed) Public and Private Life in the Seventeenth Century: the Mackenzie-Evelyn debate, 1986; (ed) English Science: Bacon to Newton, 1987; In Defence of Rhetoric, 1988 (trans. Italian 1994), rev. edn 1997; Returning to Shakespeare, 1989; Appropriating Shakespeare: contemporary critical quarrels, 1993; (ed) Francis Bacon: the major works, 1996, 2nd edn 2002; (ed) Francis Bacon: history of the reign of King Henry VII, 1998; (ed) Francis Bacon: the essays and counsels, civil and moral, 1999; (ed) English Renaissance Literary Criticism, 1999; Counterfeiting Shakespeare: evidence, authorship and John Ford's Funerall Elegye, 2002; Shakespeare, Co-Author: a historical study of five collaborative plays, 2002; Shakespeare, A Lover's Complaint, and John Davies of Hereford, 2007; (with S. Köllmann) Mächtige Worte—Antike Rhetorik und europäische Literatur, 2008; (jtly) The Collected Works of John Ford, vol. I, 2011; (Gen. Ed.) series, Shakespeare: the critical tradition: King John, 1996; Richard II, 1998; A Midsummer Night's Dream, 1999; Measure for Measure, 2001; Coriolanus, 2004; The Merchant of Venice, 2005; articles and reviews in learned jls. *Recreations:* music, sport, film. *Address:* 7 Abbot's Place, NW6 4NP. *T:* (020) 7624 7217.

VICKERS, Hilary Anne; *see* Taylor, H. A.

VICKERS, Hugo Ralph; DL; author, lecturer and broadcaster; Chairman, Outdoor Trust, since 2012; *b* 12 Nov. 1951; *s* of late Ralph Cecil Vickers, MC, and Dulcie (*née* Metcalf); *m* 1995, Elizabeth Anne Blyth Vickers (marr. diss. 2015), *y d* of late (Dennis) Michael Vickers, Montaillac, France; two *s* one *d*. *Educ:* Eton; Strasbourg Univ. St George's Chapel, Windsor Castle: Lay Steward, 1970–; Capt., 2015–; Mem., Adv. Council, later Mgt Cttee, Friends of St George's, 2001–04, 2005–11. Worked with London Celebrations Cttee, Queen's Silver Jubilee, 1977; Administrator, Great Children's Party, Hyde Park, 1979. Chm., Jubilee Walkway Trust, 2002–12; Member: Prince of Wales' Royal Parks Tree Appeal, 1987–2003; Council of Mgt, Windsor Fest., 1999–. Broadcaster including: studio guest, weddings of Prince of Wales and Duke of York, funeral of Diana, Princess of Wales; asstd with commentaries: wedding of Earl of Wessex, Queen Mother's 100th birthday and funeral. Producer and writer, one-man play, The Immortal Dropout, Jermyn St Th., 2008; Historical Adviser: The King's Speech (film), 2010; Titanic (TV), 2012. Golo Mann Dist. Lectr, Claremont McKenna Coll., 2007. Trustee, Age Unlimited, 2010–. Patron, Me2 Club, 2012–. Liveryman, Co. of Musicians, 1978. DL Berks, 2010. *Publications:* We Want the Queen, 1977; Gladys, Duchess of Marlborough, 1979; Debrett's Book of the Royal Wedding, 1981; (ed) Cocktails and Laughter, 1983; Cecil Beaton, 1985; Vivien Leigh, 1988; Royal Orders, 1994; Loving Garbo, 1994; The Private World of the Duke and Duchess of Windsor, 1995; The Kiss (Stern Silver Pen for non-fiction), 1996; Alice, Princess Andrew of Greece, 2000; (ed) The Unexpurgated Beaton, 2002; (ed) Beaton in the Sixties, 2003; (ed) Alexis: the memoirs of the Baron de Redé, 2005; Elizabeth, The Queen Mother, 2005; (ed) The Rich Spoils of Time, 2006; (ed) Horses and Husbands, 2007; St George's Chapel, Windsor Castle, 2008; Behind Closed Doors, 2011; A Walk for the Queen, 2012; Coronation, 2013; (ed) Cecil Beaton: portraits and profiles, 2014. *Recreations:* reading, travel, photography, walking. *Address:* 62 Lexham Gardens, W8 5JA. *T:* (020) 7373 2695, 07774 671540; The Manor House, East Chisenbury, Wilts SN9 6AQ; 62 Frances Road, Windsor, Berks SL4 3AJ. *E:* hugovickers@wyeford.co.uk. *W:* www.hugovickers.co.uk. *Club:* Beefsteak.

VICKERS, Sir John (Stuart), Kt 2005; DPhil; FBA 1998; Warden, All Souls College, Oxford, since 2008 (Fellow, 1991–2008); *b* 7 July 1958; *s* of Aubrey and late Kay Vickers; *m* 1991, Maureen Freed; one *s* two *d*. *Educ:* Eastbourne Grammar Sch.; Oriel Coll., Oxford (BA PPE 1979; Hon. Fellow 2005); MPhil Econs Oxon 1983; DPhil Econs Oxon 1985. Financial Analyst, Shell UK, 1979–81; Fellow, All Souls Coll., Oxford, 1979–84; Roy Harrod Fellow in Economics of Business and Public Policy, Nuffield Coll., Oxford, 1984–90; Drummond Prof. of Political Economy, Univ. of Oxford, 1991–2008 (on leave, 1998–2005); Exec. Dir, Chief Economist, and Mem. Monetary Policy Cttee, Bank of England, 1998–2000; Dir Gen., 2000–03, Chm., 2003–05, OFT. Chm., Ind. Commn on Banking, 2010–11. Vis. Fellow, Princeton, 1988; Vis. Lectr, Harvard, 1989, 1990; Vis. Prof., London Business Sch., 1996. President: Inst. for Fiscal Studies, 2003–07; REconS, 2007–10. Rhodes Trustee, 2006–11. Fellow, Econometric Soc., 1998. Hon. DLitt UEA, 2001. *Publications:* (jtly) Privatization: an economic analysis, 1988; (jtly) Regulatory Reform, 1994; articles in econ. jls on industrial organisation, regulation, competition, monetary policy. *Address:* All Souls College, Oxford OX1 4AL. *T:* (01865) 279379.

VICKERS, Martin John; MP (C) Cleethorpes, since 2010; *b* Cleethorpes, 13 Sept. 1950; *m* 1981, Ann Gill; one *d*. *Educ:* Havelock Sch.; Grimsby Coll.; Univ. of Lincoln (BA Hons Politics 2004). In printing industry, 1967–78; in retail trade, 1978–94; Constituency Agent to Edward Leigh, MP, 1994–2010. Member (C): Great Grimsby BC, 1980–94; NE Lincs Council, 1999–2011 (Cabinet Mem., 2003–09). Contested (C) Cleethorpes, 2005. *Address:* House of Commons, SW1A 0AA.

VICKERS, Rt Rev. Michael Edwin; Area Bishop of Colchester, 1988–94; an Assistant Bishop, Diocese of Blackburn, 1994–2013; *b* 13 Jan. 1929; *s* of William Edwin and Florence Alice Vickers; *m* 1960, Janet Cynthia Croasdale; three *d*. *Educ:* St Lawrence Coll., Ramsgate; Worcester Coll., Oxford (BA Mod. History 1952; MA 1956); Cranmer Hall, Durham (DipTheol with distinction, 1959). Company Secretary, Hoares (Ceylon) Ltd, 1952–56; Refugee Administrator for British Council for Aid to Refugees, 1956–57; Lay Worker, Diocese of Oklahoma, 1959; Curate of Christ Church, Bexleyheath, 1959–62; Sen. Chaplain, Lee Abbey Community, 1962–67; Vicar of St John's, Newland, Hull, 1967–81; Area Dean, Central and North Hull, 1972–81; Archdeacon of E Riding, 1981–88. Chm., York Diocesan House of Clergy, 1975–85; Canon and Prebendary of York, 1981–88. Mem., Gen. Synod, 1975–88 (Proctor in Convocation, 1975–85). *Recreations:* gardening, walking, travel, drama. *Address:* 137 Canalside, Redhill, Surrey RH1 2FH. *T:* (01737) 642984.

VICKERS, Prof. Michael John, DLitt; FSA 1978; Professor of Archaeology, University of Oxford, 2002–10, now Emeritus (Reader in Archaeology, 1996–2002); Dean of Degrees, Jesus College, Oxford, since 2002 (Garden Master, 2002–08; Senior Research Fellow in Classical Studies, 1996–2010, now Emeritus Fellow); Senior Assistant Keeper, Department of Antiquities, Ashmolean Museum, 1988–2010 (Assistant Keeper, 1971–88); *b* 17 Feb. 1943; *s* of late John Fletcher and Agnes Mary Vickers; *m* 1st, 1966, Marie Moley (marr. diss. 1982); one *s* one *d*; 2nd, 1982, Susan Brandes (*d* 1998); two *s*; 3rd, 2001, Manana Odisheli. *Educ:* St

Bede's Coll., Manchester (jun. high jump champion, Lancs, 1960); UCNW Bangor (BA (Classics) 1964); Corpus Christi Coll., Cambridge (Dip. Classical Archaeol. 1965); Univ. of Wales (DLitt 1999). Asst Lectr in Ancient Hist. and Classical Archaeol., University Coll., Dublin, 1966–69; Lectr in Archaeol., Univ. of Libya, Benghazi, 1969–70. Vis. Mem., University Coll., Cambridge, 1970–71; Mem., Inst. for Advanced Study, Princeton, 1976; Vis. Lectr, Univ. of Texas, 1979–80; George Tait Meml Lectr, Eton Coll., 1987; Visiting Scholar: Inst. for Advanced Studies, Hebrew Univ., Jerusalem, 1993; Getty Villa, Malibu, 2013; Visiting Professor: Univ. of Catania, 2002; Univ. of Colorado at Boulder, 2003 and 2013; Tbilisi State Univ., 2012; Kress Lectr, Archaeol Inst. of America, 2002–03. Co-Dir, excavations at Pichvnari, Georgia, 1998–2010. Chm., Friends of Academic Res. in Georgia, 2005–10. Corresponding Member: German Archaeol Inst., 1978; Archaeol Inst. of America, 2010; Hon. Mem., Vani Expedn, Centre for Archaeol Studies, Georgian Acad. of Scis, 1995. Hon. Dr Batumi State Univ., 2008. *Publications:* The Roman World, 1977, 2nd edn as Ancient Rome, 1989; Greek Vases, 1978, 3rd edn 1989; Greek Symposia, 1978; Scythian Treasures in Oxford, 1979; (with K. Branigan) Hellas, 1980; (jtly) From Silver to Ceramic: the potter's debt to metalwork in the Greco-Roman, Chinese and Islamic worlds, 1986; (ed) Pots and Pans, 1986; The Ancient Romans, 1992; (ed with M. Henig) Cameos in Context: the Benjamin Zucker lectures 1990, 1993; (with D. W. J. Gill) Artful Crafts: Ancient Greek silverware and pottery, 1994, 2nd edn 1996; Pericles on Stage: political comedy in Aristophanes' early plays, 1997; Ancient Greek Pottery, 1998; Images on Textiles: the weave of fifth-century Athenian art and society, 1999; Skeuomorphismus, oder die Kunst aus wenig viel zu machen, 1999; Scythian and Thracian Antiquities in Oxford, 2002; (with A. Kakhidze) Pichvnari I, Pichvnari 1998–2002: Greeks and Colchians on the East Coast of the Black Sea, 2004; Oedipus and Alcibiades in Sophocles, 2005; The Arundel and Pomfret Marbles in Oxford, 2006; Sophocles and Alcibiades: Athenian politics in Ancient Greek literature, 2008; Aristophanes and Alcibiades: echoes of contemporary history in Athenian comedy, 2015; articles in jls. *Recreation:* classical philology. *Address:* 20 Stone Meadow, Oxford OX2 6TQ. *E:* michael.vickers@jesus.ox.ac.uk. *Club:* Athenæum.

VICKERS, Lt-Gen. Sir Richard (Maurice Hilton), KCB 1983; CVO 1998 (LVO 1959); OBE 1970 (MBE 1964); an Extra Gentleman Usher to the Queen, since 1998 (a Gentleman Usher, 1986–98); *b* 21 Aug. 1928; *s* of Lt-Gen. W. G. H. Vickers, CB, OBE; *m* 1957, Gaie, *d* of Maj.-Gen. G. P. B. Roberts, CB, DSO, MC; three *d*. *Educ:* Haileybury and Imperial Service Coll.; RMA. Commissioned Royal Tank Regt, 1948; 1st RTR, BAOR, Korea, Middle East, 1948–54; Equerry to HM The Queen, 1956–59; Brigade Major, 7 Armd Bde, 1962–64; 4th RTR, Borneo and Malaysia, 1964–66; CO The Royal Dragoons, 1967–68, The Blues and Royals, 1968–69; Comdr, 11th Armd Brigade, 1972–74; Dep. Dir of Army Training, 1975–77; GOC 4th Armoured Div., 1977–79; Comdt, RMA, 1979–82; Dir-Gen. of Army Training, 1982–83. Dir Gen., Winston Churchill Meml Trust, 1983–93. *Recreation:* flyfishing.

VICKERS, Sir Roger (Henry), KCVO 2010; FRCS; Orthopaedic Surgeon, 1992–2010, and Serjeant Surgeon, 2006–10, to the Queen; Consultant Orthopaedic Surgeon: St George's Hospital, 1980–2008; King Edward VII's Hospital Sister Agnes (formerly King Edward VII Hospital for Officers), 1992–2011; Civilian Consultant Orthopaedic Surgeon to the Army, 1992–2008; *b* 26 July 1945; *s* of late Dr H. Renwick Vickers, FRCP and of Penelope Evelyn (*née* Peck); *m* 1972, Joanna, *d* of late John Francis Mordaunt; two *s* two *d*. *Educ:* Winchester Coll.; Magdalen Coll., Oxford (MA); St Thomas's Hosp. (BM, BCh 1970). FRCS 1975. Sen. Orthopaedic Registrar, Charing Cross, St Mary's and Royal Nat. Orthopaedic Hosps, 1977–80; Consultant Orthopaedic Surgeon, St James' Hosp., London, 1980–88. Mem. Council, Med. Defence Union, 1983–; Mem., Adv. Bd, Med. Sickness Soc., subseq. Wesleyan Med. Sickness, 1998–2011. Trustee, RNLI, 2006–13. Master, Barbers' Co., 2014–15. *Recreations:* sailing, Real tennis. *Address:* Creek Cottage, Woodgaston Lane, Hayling Island PO11 0RL. *Clubs:* Garrick, Hurlingham; Royal Yacht Squadron.

VICKERS, Dr Tony; Project Manager, UK Human Genome Mapping Project, 1990–92; *b* 6 July 1932; *s* of Harry and Frances Vickers; *m* 1964, Anne Dorothy Wallis (marr. diss. 1986); two *d*. *Educ:* Manchester Grammar Sch.; Sidney Sussex Coll., Cambridge (MA, PhD). University of Cambridge: Demonstrator, 1956–61; Lectr in Physiology, 1961–72; Fellow, Sidney Sussex Coll., 1956–70; Headquarters Office, MRC, 1972–84 (Head of Medical Div., 1980–84); UK Administrator, Ludwig Inst. for Cancer Res., 1985–89. Member of Council: BAAS, 1969–72, 1982–85 (Pres., Biomed. Scis Sect., 1977); Cancer Res. Campaign, 1980–85 (Mem., Scientific Cttee, 1979–85); Paterson Labs, Manchester, 1984–85. Chm., Tenovus Sci. Adv. Cttee, 1987–91; Mem. Res. Cttee, Clatterbridge Centre for Oncology and Cancer Res. Trust, 1994–99. Governor, Beatson Inst., Glasgow, 1983–85. *Address:* 42 Bengeo Street, Hertford, Herts SG14 3ET.

VICKERY, Prof. Amanda Jane, PhD; Professor of Early Modern History, Queen Mary University of London, since 2011; *b* Preston, Lancs, 8 Dec. 1962; *d* of Derek Vickery and Renée Grant; *m* 1994, Prof. John Styles; three *d*. *Educ:* Penwortham Girls Grammar Sch., Preston; Bedford Coll., Univ. of London (BA 1984); Royal Holloway and Bedford New Coll., Univ. of London (PhD 1991). Res. Fellow, Churchill Coll., Cambridge, 1989; Royal Holloway, University of London: Lectr in Mod. Brit. Women's Hist., 1992–99, Reader, 1999–2009; Prof. in Mod. Brit. Hist., 2009–10. Leverhulme Major Res. Fellow, 2004–07. Vis. Prof., Historicum, Ludwig Maximilians Univ., Munich, 2007; Kratter Prof., Stanford Univ., 2010. Writer and presenter: television: The Trouble with Love, 2002; At Home with the Georgians, 2010; The Many Lovers of Jane Austen, 2011; The Story of Women and Art, 2014; Suffragettes Forever, 2015; La Traviata: Love, Death and Divas, 2015; radio: A History of Private Lives, 2009; Voices from the Old Bailey, 2010, 2011; A History of Men, 2012. *Publications:* The Gentleman's Daughter: women's lives in Georgian England (Longman-History Today Prize; Whitfield Prize, RHistS; Wolfson Prize), 1998; (ed) Women, Privilege and Power: British politics, 1750 to the present, 2001; (ed jtly) Gender, Taste and Material Culture in Britain and North America, 1700–1830, 2006; Behind Closed Doors: at home in Georgian England, 2009. *Recreations:* culture, clothes, chat. *Address:* School of History, Queen Mary University of London, Mile End Road, E1 4NS.

VICTOR, Ed; Chairman, Ed Victor Ltd, since 1977; *b* 9 Sept. 1939; *s* of late Jack Victor and Lydia Victor; *m* 1st, 1963, Michelene Dinah Samuels (marr. diss.); two *s*; 2nd, 1980, Carol Lois Ryan; one *s*. *Educ:* Dartmouth Coll. USA (BA *summa cum laude* 1961); Pembroke Coll., Cambridge (MLitt 1963). Began as art books editor, later editorial Dir, Weidenfeld & Nicolson, 1964–67; editorial Dir, Jonathan Cape Ltd, 1967–71; Senior Editor, Alfred A. Knopf Inc., NY, 1972–73; literary agent and Dir, John Farquharson Ltd (lit. agents), 1974–76; founded Ed Victor Ltd (lit. agency), 1977. Council Mem., Aids Crisis Trust, 1986–98. Vice-Chm., Almeida Theatre, 1994–2002 (Dir, 1993–). Trustee: The Arts Foundn, 1991–2004; Hay Literary Fest., 2002–14. *Publications:* The Obvious Diet, 2001. *Recreations:* golf, travel, opera. *Address:* 10 Cambridge Gate, Regent's Park, NW1 4JX. *T:* (020) 7224 3030. *Club:* Garrick.

VICTORY, Louis Eamonn Julian; artist, photographer and designer; community activist; consultant, public interest consultancy, since 2004; *b* 14 Feb. 1948; *s* of Gerald Louis Victory and Doris Mabel Victory; *m* 1st, 1969, Sian Anne Bees Davies (marr. diss. 1996; she *d* 2002); three *d*; 2nd, 2004, Mary Reville. *Educ:* Cambridge Grammar Sch.; Christ's Coll., Cambridge (MA). DipArch; RIBA 1974. Architect in public and private practice, Birmingham, Oxon and Dyfed, 1972–90; Nottinghamshire County Council: Dep. Co. Architect, 1990; Dep. Dir, 1991, Dir, 1992–95, Construction and Design; Dir, Envmt, 1995–2000; Chief Exec., Cumbria CC, 2000–04. Chm., Avon Ambulance NHS Trust, 2005–06. Trustee: Portland Coll.; Totnes Trust. *Recreations:* observing, enhancing and commenting creatively on the visual world.

VICUÑA, Francisco O.; *see* Orrego-Vicuña.

VIDYASAGAR, Prof. Mathukumalli, PhD; FRS 2012; Cecil and Ida Green Professor of Systems Biology Science, since 2009, and Founder Head, Department of Bioengineering, 2010, University of Texas, Dallas; *b* Guntur, India, 29 Sept. 1947; *s* of late Mathukumalli Venkata Subbarao. *Educ:* Univ. of Wisconsin, Madison (BS Electrical Engrg 1965; MS 1967; PhD 1969). Assistant Professor of Electrical Engineering: Marquette Univ., Milwaukee, 1969–70; Concordia Univ., Montreal, 1970–80; Prof. of Electrical Engrg, Univ. of Waterloo, 1980–89; Dir, Centre for Artificial Intelligence and Robotics, Bangalore, 1989–2000; Exec. Vice Pres., Tata Consultancy Services, Hyderabad, 2000–09. FIEEE 1983; FIASc 1992; Fellow: Indian Nat. Acad. of Engrg, 1992; Indian Nat. Acad. of Sci., 1994; FInstP 2012. Control Systems Award, IEEE, 2008; Rufus Oldenburger Medal, ASME, 2012. *Publications:* ten books; articles in jls. *Address:* Department of Bioengineering, University of Texas at Dallas, 800 W Campbell Road, Richardson, TX 75080–3021, USA.

VIGARS, Della, (Mrs Paul Vigars); *see* Jones, Della.

VIGARS, Robert Lewis; *b* 26 May 1923; *s* of late Francis Henry Vigars and Susan Laurina May Vigars (*née* Lewis); *m* 1962, Margaret Ann Christine, *y d* of late Sir John Walton, KCIE, CB, MC, and Lady Walton; two *d*. *Educ:* Truro Cathedral Sch.; London Univ. (LLB (Hons)). Served War of 1939–45: RA and Royal Corps of Signals, 1942–47; attached Indian Army (Captain), 1944–47; Captain, Princess Louise's Kensington Regt, TA, 1951–54. Qualified as solicitor (Hons), 1948. Partner, Simmons & Simmons, London, EC2, 1951–75. Member: Kensington Borough Council, 1953–59; London and Home Counties Traffic Adv. Cttee, 1956–58; London Roads (Nugent) Cttee, 1958–59; LCC and GLC Kensington (formerly South Kensington), 1955–86; Environmental Planning Cttee, GLC, 1967–71 (Chm.); Strategic Planning Cttee, GLC, 1971–73 (Chm.); Leader of Opposition, ILEA, 1974–79; Chm. of the GLC, 1979–80; Mem., Standing Conf. on London and SE Regional Planning and SE Economic Planning Council, 1968–75. Gen. Comr of Income Tax (Highbury), 1988–98; Mem., Central London Valuation Tribunal, 1989–95. Dir, Heritage of London Trust, 1985–2008; Mem., Historic Buildings and Monuments Commn for England, 1986–88 (Mem., London Adv. Cttee, 1986–92 (Chm. 1986–88)); Trustee, Historic Chapels Trust, 1993–2008. Mem. Court, London Univ., 1977–82. Chm., Kensington Soc., 1994–99. *Recreation:* dreaming of past mountain walking. *Club:* Hurlingham.

VIGGERS, Lt-Gen. Sir Frederick (Richard), KCB 2007; CMG 2004; MBE 1988; DL; Gentleman Usher of the Black Rod and Serjeant-at-Arms, House of Lords, and Secretary to the Lord Great Chamberlain, 2009–11; *b* 29 June 1951; *m* Jane; one *s* one *d*. Commnd RA, 1972; served in Germany and UK; psc 1983; Comdr, Gun Battery, 3rd Regt, RHA, 1984–85; COS, 1st Infantry Bde, UK Mobile Force, 1986; Staff Coll. Directing Staff, Camberley, 1988; Comdr, 3 RHA, Germany, 1989; 19 Infantry Bde, Colchester, 1990; Central Staff Directorate of Defence Policy, MoD, 1991–93; Defence Costs Study Secretariat, MoD, 1993; Comdr Artillery, 3rd UK Div., 1994; hcsc; Dir of Manning (Army), 1997; Comdr, Multi-Nat. Div. (SW), Stabilisation Force, Bosnia Herzegovina, 1999–2000; COS, HQ Land Comd, 2000–03; Dep. Comdg Gen., Combined Jt Task Force 7, and Sen. British Mil. Rep., Iraq, 2003; Mil. Sec. and Chief Exec., Army Personnel Centre, 2003–05; Adjutant Gen., 2005–08. DL Hants, 2008. *Address:* c/o NatWest, 12 Fore Street, Wellington, Somerset TA21 8AL.

VIGGERS, Sir Peter (John), Kt 2008; *b* 13 March 1938; *s* of late J. S. Viggers and E. F. Viggers (later Mrs V. E. J. Neal), Gosport; *m* 1968, Jennifer Mary McMillan, MB, BS, LRCP, MRCS, DA, *d* of late Dr R. B. McMillan, MD, FRCP, Guildford, and late Mrs J. T. C. McMillan, MA, MIB; two *s* one *d*. *Educ:* Portsmouth Grammar Sch.; Trinity Hall, Cambridge (MA 1961). Chm., Cambridge Univ. Cons. Assoc., 1960. Solicitor 1967. Royal Canadian Air Force (pilot), 1956–58; commnd 457 (Wessex) Regt, RA (TA), 1963. MP (C) Gosport, Feb. 1974–2010. PPS to Solicitor-General, 1979–83, to Chief Sec. of HM Treasury, 1983–85; Parly Under-Sec. of State (Industry Minister), NI Office, 1986–89. Chm., Select Cttee on Armed Forces Bill, 1986, 1996; Member: Select Cttee on Members' Interests, 1991–93; Select Cttee on Defence, 1992–97, 2000–01, 2003–05 (Vice-Chm., 2000–01, 2003–05); Exec., British-American Parly Gp, 2000–10 (Jt Treas., 2003–09); Vice-Chm., British-Japanese Parly Gp, 1999–2010 (Chm., 1992–99); UK Delegate: Jt IPU and UN Conf. on Conventional Disarmament, Mexico City, 1985; N Atlantic Assembly, 1981–86, 1992–2010 (Vice-Chm., Political Cttee, 1995–97; Chm., 2000–04). Chm. and dir of public and private cos, 1972–. Underwriting Member of Lloyd's (Council Mem., 1992–96); Chm. Trustees, Lloyd's Pension Fund, 1996–2010. Mem., Management Cttee, RNLI, 1979–89, Vice-Pres., 1989–2008. Dir and Trustee, HMS Warrior 1860, 1995–2004. *Recreations:* opera, travel, trees, Burgundy. *Address:* 30 Smith Square, SW1P 3HF. *T:* (020) 7222 2775. *E:* peter@viggers.com. *Club:* Boodle's.

VIGNOLES, Prof. Anna Frances, PhD; Professor of Education (1938), University of Cambridge, since 2012; *b* 1969; *d* of Phil and Lucy Vignoles; *m* Robin Griffiths; one *s* one *d*. *Educ:* Sch. of Oriental and African Studies, Univ. of London (BA 1st Cl. Econs with Politics 1991); Univ. of Newcastle upon Tyne (PhD Econs 1998). Res. Fellow, LSE, 1998–2003; Prof. of Econs of Educn, Inst. of Educn, Univ. of London, 2003–12; Res. Fellow, IFS, 2011–. Economist Mem., NHS Pay Rev. Body. Mem., Evaluation Cttee, ESRC, 2013–. *Publications:* (with S. Machin) What's the Good of Education?: the economics of education in the UK, 2005; contribs to Jl Royal Statistical Soc., Series A, Oxford Rev. of Educn, Oxford Econ. Papers, Economica, Econs of Educn Rev. *Recreations:* sailing, travel. *Address:* Faculty of Education, University of Cambridge, 184 Hills Road, Cambridge CB2 8PQ. *T:* (01223) 767600, *Fax:* (01223) 767602. *E:* av404@cam.ac.uk.

VIGNOLES, Roger Hutton, ARCM; pianoforte accompanist; *b* 12 July 1945; *s* of late Keith Hutton Vignoles and of Phyllis Mary (*née* Pearson); *m* 1st, 1972, Teresa Ann Elizabeth Henderson (marr. diss. 1982); 2nd, 1982, Jessica Virginia, *d* of late Prof. Boris Ford; one *s* one *d*. *Educ:* Canterbury Cathedral Choir Sch.; Sedbergh Sch.; Magdalene Coll., Cambridge (BA, BMus; Hon. Fellow, 2009); Royal College of Music, London (ARCM). Accompanist of internat. reputation, regularly appearing with the most distinguished internat. singers and instrumentalists (Sir Thomas Allen, Dame Kiri te Kanawa, Dame Felicity Lott, Sarah Walker, etc.), both in London and provinces and at major music festivals (e.g. Aldeburgh, Cheltenham, Edinburgh, Brighton, Bath, Salzburg, Prague, etc.) and broadcasting for BBC Radio 3 and television. International tours incl. USA, Canada, Australia-New Zealand, Hong Kong, Scandinavia, and recitals at Opera Houses of Cologne, Brussels, Frankfurt, Lincoln Center, NY, San Francisco, Tokyo, Carnegie Hall, NY, Venice, Paris, Munich, Berlin, etc. Repetiteur: Royal Opera House, Covent Garden, 1969–71; English Opera Group, 1968–74; Australian Opera Company, 1976. Professor of Accompaniment, 1974–81, Prince Consort Prof. of Piano Accompaniment, 1996–, RCM; Consultant Prof. of Accompaniment, RAM, 1989–. Masterclasses for singers and pianists in Aarhus, Amsterdam, Barcelona, Copenhagen, Stockholm, Vienna, Toronto, Montreal, Ravinia Fest., Santa Fe Opera, Britten-Pears Sch., Snape. Extensive discography of vocal and chamber music. Hon. RAM 1984; Hon. FRCM 1997. *Recreations:* drawing, painting, looking at pictures, swimming, sailing. *Address:* 130 Mercers Road, N19 4PU. *T:* (020) 7272 5325, *Fax:* (020) 7281 1840.

VIJAYRAGHAVAN, Prof. Krishnaswamy, PhD; FRS 2012; Secretary, Department of Biotechnology, Ministry of Science and Technology, India, since 2013; Distinguished Professor, National Centre for Biological Sciences, Tata Institute of Fundamental Research, Bangalore, since 2012; *b* 3 Feb. 1954; *m* Usha; one *s*. *Educ:* Indian Inst. of Technol., Kanpur (BTech Chem. Engrg 1975; MTech); Bombay Univ. (PhD Molecular Biol.). Res. Fellow, 1984–85, Sen. Res. Fellow, 1986–88, Calif Inst. of Technol.; joined Tata Inst. of Fundamental Res., 1988, joined Nat. Centre for Biol Scis, Bangalore, 1992, Sen. Prof. and Dir, 1998–2012. Mem., Sci. Adv. Council to Prime Minister of India, 2005–. Mem., Adv. Cttee, Howard Hughes Med. Inst. Janelia Farm Res. Campus, 2009–. Mem., Bd of Govs, Okinawa Inst. of Sci. and Technol. Sch. Corp., 2011–. FASc 1997; FNA 1999. Foreign Associate: EMBO; NAS, USA, 2014. Shanti Swarup Bhatnagar Prize, 1998; Infosys Prize in Life Scis, 2009. Padma Shri (India), 2013. *Address:* Department of Biotechnology, Ministry of Science and Technology, 6–8th Floor, Block 2, CG0 Complex, Lodhi Road, New Delhi 110003, India.

VILE, Prof. Maurice John Crawley; Professor Emeritus of Political Science, University of Kent; *b* 23 July 1927; *s* of Edward M. and Elsie M. Vile; two *s*; *m* Nancy Gaffield. *Educ:* London Sch. of Economics (BSc (Econ) 1951); PhD London, 1954; MA Oxford, 1962. FRHistS 1989. Lectr in Politics, Univ. of Exeter, 1954–62; Fellow of Nuffield Coll., Oxford, 1962–65; Lectr in Politics, Magdalen Coll., Oxford, 1963–64; University of Kent: Reader in Politics and Govt, 1965–68; Prof. of Political Sci., 1968–84; Dir of Internat. Progs, 1984–87; Dean of Faculty of Social Scis, 1969–75; Pro-Vice-Chancellor, 1975–81; Dep. Vice-Chancellor, 1981–84; Dir of British Progs, Boston Univ., 1989–94; Dir of Res., Canterbury Christ Church Coll., 1994–99. Visiting Professor: Univ. of Massachusetts, 1960; Smith College, Mass., 1961. Royer Lectr, Univ. of Calif., Berkeley, 1974. Hon. Fellow, Canterbury Christ Church UC, 2003. Hon. DCL Kent, 1993. *Publications:* The Structure of American Federalism, 1961; Constitutionalism and the Separation of Powers, 1967, 2nd edn 1998; Politics in the USA, 1970, 6th edn 2007; Federalism in the United States, Canada and Australia (Res. Paper No 2, Commn on the Constitution), 1973; The Presidency (Amer. Hist. Documents Vol. IV), 1974.

VILIKOVSKÝ, Ján, PhD; Head: Slovak Centre for Literary Translation, 1997–2002; Centre for Information on Literature, 2001–02; Dean, Philological Faculty, Matej Bel University, Banská Bystrica, 2001–04; *b* 13 July 1937; *s* of late Prof. Ján Vilikovský and Dr Júlia Vilikovská (*née* Bárdošová); *m* 1st, 1962, Božica Štúrová (*d* 1985); two *d*; 2nd, 1992, Mária Horváthová. *Educ:* Comenius Univ., Bratislava (BA 1959; MA 1975; PhD 1982). Editor, Slovak Writers' Publishing House, 1959–70; Asst Prof., Inst. of Translators, 1970–74; Asst Prof., Dept of English and American Studies, Comenius Univ., 1974–90; Sec.-Gen., Slovak Translators' Assoc., 1986–90; Dir, Tatran Publishers, 1990–92; Ministry of Foreign Affairs, 1992–96; Ambassador of Czechoslovakia, 1992; Ambassador of Slovak Republic to UK, 1993–96. Asst Gen. Sec., RECIT (European Network of International Centres of Literary Translators), 2000–04. Hon. Dr Constantine the Philosopher Univ., Nitra, 2007. Ján Hollý Prize for Translation, 1969, 1980, 2003. *Publications:* Slovak-English Dictionary, 1959, 5th edn 1992; Preklad ako tvorba (Translation as a creative process), 1984; Shakespeare u nás, 2014; contribs to learned jls; translations from English and American literature. *Recreations:* classical music, reading, talking. *Address:* Zálužická 7, 821 01 Bratislava, Slovakia.

VILJOEN, His Honour (Theo) Leon; a Circuit Judge, 1992–2007; *b* 25 Aug. 1937; *s* of Robert Bartlett Viljoen and Cecilia Jacoba Viljoen (*née* van der Walt); *m* 1967, Dorothy Nina Raybould (*d* 2014), *d* of late Prof. S. G. Raybould; two *d*. *Educ:* Afrikaanse Hoër Seunskool; Univ. of Pretoria. Called to the Bar, Middle Temple, 1972; a Recorder, 1991–92; a Deputy High Court Judge, 1993–2010. Legal Assessor, UKCC, 1987–92. Mem., 1997–2003, 2004–10, Appraiser, 2005–10, Parole Bd. Life Pres., Les Planes Tractor Co-op., Gard, France. *Recreations:* walking, gardening, wine. *Address:* c/o 2 Harcourt Buildings, Temple, EC4Y 9DB. *T:* (020) 7583 9020.

VILLAGE, Peter Malcolm; QC 2002; *b* 3 Feb. 1961; *s* of late Malcolm Rowland Village and of Margaret Village; *m* 1992, Alison Helen Wallis; one *s* two *d*. *Educ:* Repton Sch.; Univ. of Leeds (LLB Hons); Inns of Court Sch. of Law. Called to the Bar, Inner Temple, 1983, Bencher, 2011, NI, 1997; barrister specialising in planning, compulsory purchase and judicial review, 1985–. Gov., Repton Sch., 1998–. *Recreations:* salmon fishing, shooting, ski-ing, walking the dog, clubbing. *Address:* 39 Essex Street, WC2R 3AT. *T:* (020) 7832 1111. *E:* peter.village@39essex.com. *Club:* Brooks's.

VILLIERS; *see* Child Villiers, family name of Earl of Jersey.

VILLIERS; *see* de Villiers.

VILLIERS, family name of **Earl of Clarendon**.

VILLIERS, Viscount; George Henry William Child-Villiers; *b* 1 Sept. 2015; *s* and *heir* of Earl of Jersey, *qv*.

VILLIERS, Charles Nigel, FCA; Deputy Chairman, Abbey National plc, 1999–2001; *b* 25 Jan. 1941; *s* of Robert Alexander and Elizabeth Mary Villiers; *m* 1970, Sally Priscilla Magnay; one *s* one *d*. *Educ:* Winchester Coll.; New Coll., Oxford (MA German and Russian); Harvard Business Sch. (AMP). Arthur Andersen & Co., 1963–67; ICFC, 1967–72; County Bank Ltd, 1972–86; Dir, 1974; Dep. Chief Exec., 1977; Chm. and Chief Exec., 1984–85; Exec. Chm., 1985–86; Exec. Dir, National Westminster Bank, 1985–88; Chief Exec., NatWest Investment Bank Ltd (estab. June 1986 incorporating the business of County Bank Ltd), 1986–88; Chm., County NatWest Ltd, 1986–88; Man. Dir of Corporate Develt, then Abbey Nat. Building Soc.), Abbey National plc, 1988–99. Non-exec. Dir, DTZ Hldgs, 1997–2004. Treas., E Thames Housing Gp, 2001–08. *Recreations:* opera, ski-ing, European history, tennis. *Club:* Reform.

VILLIERS, Rt Hon. Theresa (Anne); PC 2010; MP (C) Chipping Barnet, since 2005; Secretary of State for Northern Ireland, since 2012; *b* 5 March 1968; *d* of late George Villiers and of Virginia Villiers; *m* 1999, Sean David Henry Wilken, *qv*. *Educ:* Univ. of Bristol (LLB Hons 1990); Jesus Coll., Oxford (BCL Hons 1991). Called to the Bar, Inner Temple, 1992; Barrister specialising in chancery, insolvency and entertainment law, 1994–95; Lectr in Law, King's Coll., London, 1995–99. MEP (C) London Region, 1999–2005. Treas. and economic spokesman, 1999–2004, Dep. Leader, 2001–02, Cons. delegn to EP; EP Rapporteur for Investment Services Directive, 2002–05. Shadow Chief Sec. to HM Treasury, 2005–07; Shadow Sec. of State for Transport, 2007–10; Minister of State, DfT, 2010–12. *Publications:* (with Sean Wilken) Waiver, Variation and Estoppel, 1998; Tax Harmonisation: the impending threat, 2001; various articles in legal jls, incl. Lloyd's Maritime and Commercial Law Qly. *Address:* House of Commons, SW1A 0AA. *Club:* Middlesex CC.

VINCENT, family name of **Baron Vincent of Coleshill**.

VINCENT OF COLESHILL, Baron *cr* 1996 (Life Peer), of Shrivenham, in the County of Oxfordshire; **Field Marshal Richard Frederick Vincent,** GBE 1990; KCB 1984; DSO 1972; FIMechE; FRAeS; *b* 23 Aug. 1931; *s* of late Frederick Vincent and Frances Elizabeth (*née* Coleshill); *m* 1955, Jean Paterson, *d* of Kenneth Stewart and Jane (*née* Banks); one *s* one *d* (and one *s* decd). *Educ:* Aldenham Sch.; RMCS. Commnd RA, National Service, 1951; Germany, 1951–55; Gunnery Staff, 1959; Radar Res. Estabt, Malvern, 1960–61; BAOR, 1962; Technical Staff Training, 1963–64; Staff Coll., 1965; Commonwealth Bde, Malaysia, 1966–68; MoD, 1968–70; Comd 12th Light Air Def. Regt, Germany, UK and NI, 1970–72; Instr, Staff Coll., 1972–73; Greenlands Staff Coll., Henley, 1974; Mil. Dir of Studies, RMCS, 1974–75; Comd 19 Airportable Bde, 1975–77; RCDS, 1978; Dep. Mil. Sec., 1979–80; Comdt, Royal Military College of Science, 1980–83; Master-Gen. of the Ordnance, MoD, 1983–87; VCDS, 1987–91; CDS, 1991–92; Chm. of Mil. Cttee, NATO, 1993–96. Master Gunner, St James's Park, 1996–2000. Dir, 1996–2001, Chm., 1998–2001, Hunting Engrg Ltd; Chairman: Hunting Defence Ltd, 1996–2003; Hunting Brae, 1997–2003; non-executive Director: Vickers Defence Systems Ltd, 1997–2002; INSYS Ltd, 2001–05. Mem., Commn on Britain and Europe, RIIA, 1996. Col Commandant: REME, 1981–87; RA, 1983–2000; Hon. Colonel: 100 (Yeomanry) Field Regt RA, TA, 1982–91; 12th Air Defence Regt, 1987–91. Vice Pres., Forces' (formerly Officers') Pension Soc., 1997–2005. President: Combined Services Winter Sports Assoc., 1983–90; Army Ski-ing Assoc., 1983–87. Patron, Nat. Service Veterans Assoc., 2007–. Kermit Roosevelt Lectr, 1988; Vis. Fellow, Australian Coll. of Defence and Strategic Studies, 1995–99. Vice-Pres., 1996–2000, Pres., 2000–05, Defence Manufacturers Assoc. Chancellor, Cranfield Univ., 1998–2010 (Sen. Fellow, 2010–); Member: Court, Cranfield Inst. of Technol., 1981–83; Court, Greenwich Univ., 1997–2001; Adv. Council, RMCS, 1983–91; Governor: Aldenham Sch., 1987–2009; Imperial Coll., London (formerly ICSTM), 1995–2004 (Chm., 1996–2004; Fellow, 1996). Freeman: City of London, 1992; Wheelwrights' Co., 1997; Mem., Guild of Freemen, 1992. FRAeS 1990; FIMechE 1990. Hon. DSc Cranfield, 1985. Order of Merit (1st cl.) (Jordan), 1991; Commander, Legion of Merit (USA), 1993. *Publications:* contrib. mil. jls and pubns. *Recreation:* seven grandchildren. *Address:* c/o House of Lords, SW1A 0PW.

VINCENT, Prof. Angela Carmen, FRS 2011; Professor of Neuroimmunology, University of Oxford, 1998–2008, now Emeritus; Fellow, Somerville College, Oxford, 1992–2008, now Emeritus; *b* Woking, Surrey, 30 Sept. 1942; *d* of Sir Joseph Molony, KCVO and Carmen Mary Molony (*née* Dent); *m* 1967, Philip Vincent; two *s* two *d*. *Educ:* St Mary's Convent, Ascot; Westminster Hosp. Med. Sch., London Univ. (MB BS 1966); University Coll. London (MSc Biochem. 1969). MRCPath 1991. Lectr in Clin. Neuroimmunol., Univ. of Oxford, 1992–98; Hon. Consultant in Immunol., John Radcliffe Hosp., Oxford, 1992–. FMedSci 2002. Hon. PhD Bergen, 2004. *Publications:* (ed jtly) Clinical Neuroimmunology, 2005; (ed with R. C. Dale) Inflammatory and Autoimmune Disorders of the Nervous System in Children, 2010; contrib. articles and chapters on autoimmune diseases of the nervous system. *Recreation:* children and grandchildren. *Address:* Taverners, Woodeaton, Oxon OX3 9TH. *T:* (01865) 559636. *E:* angela.vincent@ndcn.ox.ac.uk.

VINCENT, Anthony Lionel; Legal Adviser, Department of Foreign Affairs and Trade, Canberra, 1993–97; *b* 18 Oct. 1933; *s* of Harold Francis Vincent and Lesley Allison Vincent; *m* 1958, Helen Frances Beasley; one *s* one *d*. *Educ:* Univ. of Western Australia, Perth (LLB); Univ. of Oxford (BCL). Joined Dept of Foreign Affairs, Aust., 1958; served: Karachi, 1959–61; Hong Kong, 1963–66; Singapore, 1966–69; Belgrade, 1972–74; Paris, 1977–80; Australian Ambassador to: Iraq, 1981–83; GDR, 1984; Dep. High Comr in London, 1984–87; Asst Sec., Treaties and Sea Law Br., 1987–89, Intelligence and Defence Br., 1989–90, Dept of Foreign Affairs and Trade, Canberra; Ambassador to Czech and Slovak Federal Republic, subseq. to Czech and Slovak Republics, 1990–93. *Recreations:* drawing, painting, reading. *Address:* 56 Blackwall Reach Parade, Bicton, WA 6157, Australia.

VINCENT, Catherine Beatrice Margaret, (Katie); *see* Derham, C. B. M.

VINCENT, Prof. Colin Angus, OBE 2003; Professor of Electrochemistry, 1989–2003, Master of the United College, 1996–2003 and Deputy Principal, 2001–03, University of St Andrews; *b* 4 March 1938; *s* of Harold Frederick Vincent and Helen McEachern Vincent; *m* 1964, Doris Susan Cole; one *s* one *d*. *Educ:* Oban High Sch.; Univ. of Glasgow (BSc 1960; PhD 1963; DSc 1987); Univ. of St Andrews (MA 2008). MIEE; CChem, FRSC 1976; FRSE 1992. Assistant, Univ. of Glasgow, 1963–65; Lectr, Univ. of Illinois, 1965–67; University of St Andrews: Lectr, 1967–76; Sen. Lectr; 1976–84; Reader, 1984–89; Head, School of Chemistry, 1990–97; Vice-Principal, 1996–2001; Vice-Chancellor and Acting Principal, 2000. Hon. LLD St Andrews, 2003. Galvani Medal, Italian Chem. Soc., 1998. *Publications:* (jtly) Alkali Metal, Alkaline Earth Metal and Ammonium Halides in Amide Solvents, 1980; Modern Batteries, 1984, 2nd edn 1997; Polymer Electrolyte Reviews, vol. 1, 1987, vol. 2, 1989; more than 120 papers in learned jls. *Recreations:* squash, hill walking, opera. *Address:* 1 Station Brae, Newport-on-Tay, Fife DD6 8DQ. *T:* (01382) 543156.

VINCENT, Rev. Dr John James; writer and lecturer; Methodist Minister, Sheffield Inner City Ecumenical Mission (Superintendent, 1970–97); Director, Urban Theology Unit, 1969–97, Director Emeritus, since 1997; President of the Methodist Conference, 1989–90; *b* 29 Dec. 1929; *s* of late David Vincent and Ethel Beatrice Vincent (*née* Gadd); *m* 1958, Grace Johnston, *d* of late Rev. Wilfred Stafford, Bangor, Co. Down; two *s* one *d*. *Educ:* Manchester Grammar Sch.; Richmond Coll.; London Univ. (BD 1954); Drew Univ., USA (STM 1955); Basel Univ., Switzerland (DTheol 1960). Sgt, RAMC, 1948–49. Minister, Manchester and Salford Mission, 1956–62; Supt, Rochdale Mission, 1962–69; Founder and Leader, The Ashram Community, 1967–. Visiting Professor of Theology: Boston Univ., and New York Theol Seminary, 1969–70; Drew Univ., 1977; Adjunct Prof. of Theol., New York Theol Seminary, 1979–88. Hon. Lectr in Biblical Studies, 1990–; supervisor, doctoral prog. in Contextual, Urban and Liberation Theologies, 1993–, Sheffield Univ.; Hon. Lectr in Theol. and doctoral supervisor, Birmingham Univ., 2003–. Chairman: NW Campaign for Nuclear Disarmament, 1957–63; Alliance of Radical Methodists, 1970–76; Urban Mission Trng Assoc., 1982–90; Trustee Savings Bank Depositors Assoc. (also litigant in High Court and H of L, TSB *v* Vincent), 1986; Jt Co-ordinator, British Liberation Theol. Inst., 1990–; Co-Chair, Urban Theologians Internat., 1993–; Member: Studiorum Novi Testamenti Societas, 1961–; Council, Christian Orgns for Social, Political and Econ. Change, 1981–91; Exec., Assoc. of Centres of Adult Theol. Educn, 1984–90. Fellow, St Deiniol's Library, Hawarden, 2003. Jt Ed., British Liberation Theology series, 1995, 1997, 1999, 2001. Centenary Achievement Award, Sheffield Univ., 2005. *Publications:* Christ in a Nuclear World, 1962; Christian Nuclear Perspective, 1964; Christ and Methodism, 1965; Here I Stand, 1967; Secular Christ, 1968; The Race Race, 1970; The Jesus Thing, 1973; Stirrings: essays Christian and Radical, 1975; Alternative Church, 1976; Disciple and Lord: discipleship in the Synoptic Gospels, 1976; Starting All Over Again, 1981; Into the City, 1982; OK, Let's Be Methodists, 1984; Radical Jesus, 1986, 2nd edn 2004; Mark at Work, 1986; Britain in the Nineties, 1989; Discipleship in the Nineties, 1991; A Petition of Distress from the Cities (to the Queen and Govt), 1993; (ed jtly) The Cities: Methodist report, 1997; Hope from the City, 2000; (ed jtly) Bible and Practice, 2001; (ed jtly) Methodist and Radical, 2003; (ed) Faithfulness in the City, 2003; (ed) Mark: gospel of action, 2006; (ed) Primitive Christianity, 2007; (jtly) The City in Biblical Perspective, 2009; A Lifestyle of Sharing, 2009; (jtly) The Drama of Mark, 2010; (ed) Stilling the Storm, 2011; (ed) Christian Communities, 2011; (ed) Acts in Practice, 2012; (ed) British Liberation Theology: for Church and Nation, 2012; Christ in the City: the dynamics of Christ in urban theological practice, 2013; Methodism Unbound: Christ and Methodism for the 21st century, 2015; (ed) Radical Christianity: roots and fruits, 2015; *relevant publication:* Urban Christ: responses to John Vincent, ed I. K. Duffield, 1997. *Recreations:* jogging, writing. *Address:* 178 Abbeyfield Road, Sheffield S4 7AY. *T:* (0114) 243 6688, *T:* and *Fax:* (Urban Theology Unit) (0114) 243 5342. *E:* john@utu.sheffield.fsnet.co.uk.

VINCENT, Prof. John Russell; Professor of History, University of Bristol, 1984–2002, now Emeritus Professor; *b* 20 Dec. 1937; *s* of late Prof. J. J. Vincent and M. Monica Vincent, MSc, PhD (*née* Watson); *m* 1972, Nicolette Elizabeth Kenworthy; one *s* (and one *s* decd). *Educ:* Bedales Sch.; Christ's Coll., Cambridge. Fellow, Peterhouse, Cambridge, 1962–70; Lectr in Modern British History, Cambridge Univ., 1967–70; Prof. of Modern History, Univ. of

Bristol, 1970–84. Vis. Prof., UEA, 2003–08. Chm., Bristol Br., NCCL, 1972–74. *Publications:* The Formation of the Liberal Party, 1966 (2nd edn as The Formation of the British Liberal Party 1857–68, 1980); Poll Books: How Victorians voted, 1967; (ed with A. B. Cooke) Lord Carlingford's Journal, 1971; (ed with M. Stenton) McCalmont's Parliamentary Poll Book 1832–1918, 1971; (with A. B. Cooke) The Governing Passion: Cabinet Government and party politics in Britain 1885–86, 1974; (ed) Disraeli, Derby and the Conservative Party: the political journals of Lord Stanley 1849–69, 1978; Gladstone and Ireland (Raleigh Lecture), 1979; (ed) The Crawford Papers: the journals of David Lindsay, Twenty-Seventh Earl of Crawford and Tenth Earl of Balcarres during the years 1892 to 1940, 1984; Disraeli, 1990; (ed) The Derby Diaries 1869–1878, 1995; (contrib.) Twentieth-Century Britain: an encyclopaedia, 1995; An Intelligent Person's Guide to History, 1995; (contrib.) Why Tory Governments Fall, 1996; (ed) The Derby Diaries 1878–1893, 2003. *Recreation:* journalism. *Address:* University of Bristol, Senate House, Bristol BS8 1TH.

VINCENT, Matthew Philip Jude; Deputy Companies Editor, Financial Times, since 2014 (UK Companies Editor, 2012–14); *b* 28 Oct. 1966; *s* of Dudley Joseph and Claire Vincent. *Educ:* Salvatorian Coll., Harrow Weald; Univ. of Manchester (BA Hons English Lang. and Lit.). Prodn asst, BBC TV, 1988–89; staff writer: Stately Homes and Gardens mag., 1989–90; Money mag., 1990; Moneywise magazine: staff writer, 1990–92; Chief Sub-ed./Associate Ed., 1992–95; Ed., 1995–2000; Hd of Content, Investors Chronicle Online and FT Business, 2000–02; Editor: Investors Chronicle, 2002–07; FT Business, 2002–07; FT Personal Finance, 2007–12. BBC TV: reporter, Short Change, 1994; presenter, Pound For Pound, 1998. *Publications:* contrib. articles to various financial jls. *Recreations:* poetry, cricket, sherry. *Address:* Financial Times, 1 Southwark Bridge Road, SE1 9HL. *Club:* Blackheath Cricket.

VINCENT, Prof. Nicholas Charles, DPhil; FBA 2010; Professor of Medieval History, University of East Anglia, since 2003; *b* Sittingbourne, 20 Oct. 1961; *s* of Roy Charles Vincent and Joan Mary Vincent (*née* Biart); *m* Juliet Tyson; one *s* two *d*. *Educ:* Borden Sch.; Kent Jun. Music Sch.; St Peter's Coll., Oxford (BA Hons 1st Cl. 1983; MPhil 1987; DPhil 1993). House Tutor, Clifton College Prep. Sch., 1983–84; History Master: Stowe Sch., Buckingham, 1986; Gstaad Internat. Sch., 1986–87; William Stone Res. Fellow, 1990–95, Bye Fellow, 1994, Peterhouse, Cambridge; Reader, 1995–99, Prof., 1999–2003, Christ Church Coll., Canterbury. Visiting Fellow: All Souls Coll., Oxford, 1999–2000; Peterhouse, Cambridge, 2000–01; École Nationale des Chartes, Paris, 2002; Université de Poitiers, 2009. FRHistS 1995; FSA 1999. Hon. Sec., Pipe Roll Soc., 1994. Mem., Adv. Bds incl. English Historical Review, Cahiers de Civilisation Médiévale, Annales du Midi. *Publications:* (trans. with A. Alikhani) Asadollah Alam, The Shah and I: the confidential diary of Iran's Royal Court, 1969–1977, 1991; English Episcopal Acta IX: Winchester 1205–1238, 1994; Peter des Roches, 1996; The Letters and Charters of Cardinal Guala Bicchieri, 1996; Acta of Henry II and Richard I, 1996; The Holy Blood, 2001; The Magna Carta, 2007; (ed with C. Harper-Bill) Henry II: new interpretations, 2007; (ed) Records, Administration and Aristocratic Society in the Anglo-Norman Realm, 2009; A Brief History of Britain 1066–1485, 2011; Magna Carta: a very short introduction, 2012; Norman Charters from English Sources, 2013; Magna Carta: the foundation of freedom, 2014; Magna Carta: making and legacy, 2015; approx. 60 academic articles. *Recreations:* music, 19th century literature. *Address:* School of History, University of East Anglia, Norwich NR4 7TJ. *T:* (01603) 592745. *E:* n.vincent@uea.ac.uk.

VINCENT, Prof. Nigel Bruce, FBA 2006; Mont Follick Professor of Comparative Philology, University of Manchester, 1987–2011, now Professor Emeritus of General and Romance Linguistics; *b* 24 Sept. 1947; *s* of Denis George Vincent and Peggy Eliza Vincent; *m* 1st, 1971, Janet Elizabeth Hutchinson (marr. diss. 1999); two *d*; 2nd, 1999, Merethe Damsgård Sørensen; one *d*. *Educ:* Sexey's Sch., Bruton; Trinity Hall, Cambridge (BA 1st cl. hons Mod. and Medieval Langs 1970); Darwin Coll., Cambridge (Dip. Linguistics 1971). Lecturer: Birkbeck Coll., London, 1973–74; Univ. of Lancaster, 1974–76; Univ. of Hull, 1976–81; Univ. of Cambridge, 1981–87 (Fellow, Trinity Hall, 1983–87); University of Manchester: Res. and Graduate Dean of Arts, 1992–96; Associate Dean, Postgrad. Res. in Humanities, 2004–06; Associate Vice-Pres., Graduate Educn, 2006–11. British Acad. Res. Reader, 1996–98. Visiting Professor: Univ. of Pavia, 1983; Univ. of Rome, 1986; Ecole Pratique des Hautes Etudes, Paris, 1993; Australian Linguistic Inst., La Trobe Univ., 1994; Univ. of Copenhagen, 1997; Melbourne Univ., 2000; Erskine Fellow, Univ. of Canterbury, NZ, 2000. Member: Res. Grants Bd, ESRC, 1988–91; Council, Philological Soc., 1982–86, 1989–94, 1995–99 (Pres., 2000–03); Res. Gp Leader, EUROTYP Project, ESF, 1990–94; Humanities Res. Bd, 1994–96; Chm., Res. Assessment Panels, HEFCE, 1992, 1996, 2005–08; Vice-Pres. for Res. and Higher Educn Policy, British Acad., 2010–14; Pres., MHRA, 2013. Vice Pres., Società di Linguistica Italiana, 1990–92; President: Internat. Soc. of Historical Linguistics, 1993–95; Perm. Internat. Cttee of Linguists, 2013–14. Mem. Bd, British Inst. in Paris, 1999–2002. MAE 2013. Editor, Jl of Linguistics, 1984–93. *Publications:* (jtly) Studies in the Romance Verb, 1982; (jtly) The Romance Languages, 1988; (jtly) Parameters of Morphosyntactic Change, 1997; (jtly) Linguistic Areas, 2006; (jtly) Dialects and Diachrony, 2014; (jtly) Early and Late Latin: continuity or change?, 2016; articles in jls. *Recreations:* wine, all things Italian. *Address:* School of Arts, Languages and Cultures, University of Manchester, Manchester M13 9PL; 48–50 Lower Lane, Chinley, High Peak SK23 6BD. *T:* (01663) 750943. *E:* nigel.vincent@manchester.ac.uk.

VINCENT, Robert Warden, CBE 2010; Chief Executive, Doncaster Metropolitan Borough Council, 2010–11; *b* 27 Sept. 1951; *s* of Stanley and Joan Vincent; *m* 1974, Heather Hitchen; two *s* two *d*. *Educ:* King's Coll., Wimbledon; Univ. of Liverpool (BEng 1973; MCD 1975). MRTPI 1977. Town planning and policy posts, Dorset CC, 1973–78 and Tameside MBC, 1978–87; Kirklees Metropolitan Council: Asst Dir of Educn, 1987–90; Hd of Resources, 1990–94; Chief Educn Officer, 1994–98; Exec. Dir and Dep. Chief Exec., 1998–2004; Chief Exec., 2004–10. Non-executive Director: DCLG, 2008–10; Bradford Dist Care Trust, 2013– (Dep. Chair, 2014–); Adviser: to DoH, 2012–15; to Public Health England, 2013–15. Chair, Kirklees Theatre Trust, 2013–. *Recreation:* looking at buildings.

VINCENT, Simon Robert, OBE 2015; President, Europe, Middle East and Africa, Hilton Worldwide, since 2009; *b* Lymington, 28 May 1963; *s* of Leonard Roy Vincent and Mary Sheila Vincent; *m* 1994, Charlotte Helen; two *c*. *Educ:* Priestlanas Sch., Lymington; Brockenhurst Coll.; City Univ., London (BSc Banking and Internat. Finance 1985). With Midland Bank Internat., 1985–88; Thomas Cook, 1989–2002: Man. Dir, Tour Ops, 1997–99; Chief Operating Officer, UK Travel, 1999–2002; CEO, Opodo, 2004–06; Hilton Worldwide, 2007–. Mem., Pi Capital. *Recreations:* golf, tennis, sailing. *E:* vincentsr1@aol.com. *Club:* Wentworth Golf.

VINCENT, Sir William (Percy Maxwell), 3rd Bt *cr* 1936; Managing Director, Cambridge Associates Ltd, since 1995; *b* 1 Feb. 1945; *o s* of Sir Lacey Vincent, 2nd Bt, and Helen Millicent, *d* of Field Marshal Sir William Robert Robertson, 1st Bt, GCB, GCMG, GCVO, DSO; *S* father, 1963; *m* 1976, Christine Margaret, *d* of Rev. E. G. Walton; three *s*. *Educ:* Eton College. 2nd Lieutenant, Irish Guards, 1964–67. Director: Save and Prosper Investment Mgt, 1980–85; Touche Remnant & Co., 1985–92; M & G (N America) Ltd, 1992–95. *Recreations:* water ski-ing, sailing. *Heir:* *s* Edward Mark William Vincent, *b* 6 March 1978. *Address:* Battlegreen, Green Lane, Hambledon, Hants PO7 4TB.

VINE, Prof. Frederick John, FRS 1974; Emeritus Professor, School of Environmental Sciences, University of East Anglia, since 2004 (Professor, 1974–98; Professorial Fellow, 1998–2004); *b* 17 June 1939; *s* of Frederick Royston Vine and Ivy Grace Vine (*née* Bryant); *m* 1964, Susan Alice McCall; one *s* one *d*. *Educ:* Latymer Upper Sch., Hammersmith; St John's Coll., Cambridge (BA, PhD). Instructor, 1965–67, and Asst Professor, 1967–70, Dept of Geological and Geophysical Sciences, Princeton Univ., NJ, USA; Reader, 1970–74, Dean, 1977–80 and 1993–98, School of Environmental Sciences, UEA. Arthur L. Day Medal, Geol Soc. of America, 1968; Henry Bryant Bigelow Medal, Woods Hole Oceanographic Instn, 1970; J. J. Bigsby Medal, Geol Soc. of London, 1971; (jtly) S. Chapman Medal, RAS, 1973; (jtly) Arthur L. Day Prize, US NAS, 1975; (jtly) Charles Chree Medal, Inst. of Physics, 1977; (jtly) Balzan Foundn Prize for Geology and Geophysics, 1981; (jtly) Hughes Medal, Royal Soc., 1982; Prestwich Medal, Geol Soc. of London, 2007. *Publications:* (jtly) Global Tectonics, 1990, 3rd edn 2009; articles in Nature, Science, Phil. Trans Roy. Soc. London, etc. *Recreations:* walking, travel.

VINE, Jeremy; Presenter: Jeremy Vine Show, BBC Radio Two, since 2003; Eggheads, BBC2, since 2008; Points of View, BBC1, since 2008; *b* 17 May 1965; *s* of Dr Guy and Diana Vine; *m* 2002, Rachel Schofield; two *d*. *Educ:* Epsom Coll.; Durham Univ. (BA Hons English Lit. 1986). Coventry Evening Telegraph, 1986–87; joined BBC, 1987: News Trainee, 1987–89; Programme Reporter, Today, 1989–93; Political Corresp., 1993–97; Africa Corresp., 1997–99; Presenter: Newsnight, 1996–2002, full-time, 1999–2002; Politics Show, BBC TV, 2003–05; Panorama, BBC1, 2007–10. *Publications:* It's All News to Me, 2012. *Address:* c/o BBC Radio 2, Western House, W1A 1AA. *T:* (020) 7765 2129. *Clubs:* Reform, Soho House; Chelsea Football.

VINEALL, Sir Anthony (John Patrick), Kt 2002; Chairman, School Teachers' Review Body, 1996–2002; *b* 17 March 1932; *s* of George John Charles Vineall and Helen Fairley Vineall (*née* Bradshaw); *m* 1962, Dorothy Earnshaw; two *s*. *Educ:* Leeds Grammar Sch.; New Coll., Oxford (MA PPE). FCIPD (FIPD 1982). Nat. Service, commnd RA, 1951. Unilever: personnel posts in Animal Foods, Frozen Food, and in Ghana, 1955–67; Co. Personnel Manager, Walls Meat, 1967–70; Personnel Dir, SSC&B Lintas, 1970–75; Dir, Unilever UK Hldgs and Nat. Personnel Manager, 1975–81; Head of Corporate Mgt Develt, 1981–92. Chm., Tavistock and Portman NHS Trust, 1993–99. Member: Council, Foundn for Mgt Educn, 1976–92; Doctors' and Dentists' Pay Review Body, 1990–93; Review of Armed Forces Career and Rank Structure, 1994–95; Chairman: Exec. Cttee, Industrial Soc., 1982–85; Careers Res. Adv. Centre, 1991–96 (Mem. Council, 1981–); Vice Pres., Centre for Internat. Briefing, Farnham Castle, 1996– (Chm. Govs, 1987–96). Vice Chm. of Govs, Guildford Royal Grammar Sch., 2004–08 (Gov., 1994–). *Recreations:* gardening, travel, bridge. *Address:* Ways End, 34 Abbotswood, Guildford GU1 1UZ.

See also N. E. J. Vineall.

VINEALL, Nicholas Edward John; QC 2006; *b* 1 May 1963; *s* of Sir Anthony John Patrick Vineall, *qv*; *m* 1992, Kate Jenkins; two *s* one *d*. *Educ:* Royal Grammar Sch., Guildford; Christ's Coll., Cambridge (BA Natural Sci. 1985); Univ. of Pittsburgh (MA Hist. and Philosophy of Sci.); City Univ. (Dip. Law). Harkness Fellow, Univ. of Pittsburgh, 1985–86. Called to the Bar, Middle Temple, 1988, Bencher, 2015; in practice as barrister specialising in commercial and construction law. Mem., Council of Legal Educn, 1990–96. Member: Bar Council, 1990–96 (Chm., Young Bar, 1994); Exec. Cttee, Soc. of Cons. Lawyers, 1999–2007, 2009–12 (Chm., Res., 2003–05); Standards Cttee, Bar Standards Bd, 2010–14. Mem. (C) Southwark LBC, 2006–10 (Chm., Dulwich Community Council, 2006–10). Chm., Dulwich and W Norwood Cons. Assoc., 2000. Contested (C) Dulwich and W Norwood, 2001, Morley and Rothwell, 2005. Governor: Waverley Sch. and Harris Girls' Acad., E Dulwich, 1998–2008; Royal Grammar Sch., Guildford, 2011–. Chm., Free Representation Unit, 1988. Ed., Lloyd's Law Reports (Financial Crime), 2008–14. *Recreations:* music, microscopy, tennis, bridge. *Address:* 4 Pump Court, Temple, EC4Y 7AN. *T:* (020) 7842 5555.

VINEN, William Frank, (Joe), FRS 1973; Professor of Physics, 1962–74, Poynting Professor of Physics, 1974–97, University of Birmingham, now Emeritus Professor of Physics; *b* 15 Feb. 1930; *o s* of Gilbert Vinen and Olive Maud Vinen (*née* Roach); *m* 1960, Susan-Mary Audrey Master; one *s* one *d*. *Educ:* Watford Grammar Sch.; Clare College, Cambridge. Research Fellow, Clare College, 1955–58. Royal Air Force, 1948–49. Demonstrator in Physics, Univ. of Cambridge and Fellow of Pembroke Coll., 1958–62 (Hon. Fellow, 2014). Hon. Life Fellow, Coventry Univ. (formerly Poly.), 1989. Hon. FInstP, 2002. Hon. Dr Charles Univ., Prague, 2008. Simon Meml Prize, Inst. of Physics, 1963; Holweck Medal and Prize, Inst. of Physics and French Physical Soc., 1978; Rumford Medal, Royal Soc., 1980; Guthrie Medal and Prize, Inst. of Physics, 2005. *Recreation:* good food. *Address:* 52 Middle Park Road, Birmingham B29 4BJ. *T:* (0121) 475 1328. *E:* w.f.vinen@bham.ac.uk.

VINES, Prof. David Anthony, PhD; Professor of Economics, University of Oxford, since 2000; Fellow in Economics, Balliol College, Oxford, since 1992; Adjunct Professor of Economics, Research School of Economics, Australian National University, since 1991; *b* 8 May 1949; *s* of Robert Godfrey and Vera Frances Vines; *m* 1st, 1979, Susannah Lucy Robinson (marr. diss. 1992); three *s*; 2nd, 1995, Jane Elizabeth Bingham; two step *s*. *Educ:* Scotch Coll., Melbourne; Melbourne Univ. (BA 1971); Cambridge Univ. (BA 1974; MA 1977; PhD 1984). Cambridge University: Fellow, Pembroke Coll., 1976–85; Res. Officer and Sen. Res. Officer, Dept of Applied Econs, 1979–85; Adam Smith Prof. of Political Economy, Univ. of Glasgow, 1985–92; Reader in Econs, Oxford Univ., 1997–2000; Res. Fellow, Centre for Econ. Policy Res., London, 1985–. Board Member: Channel 4 Television, 1987–92; Glasgow Develt Agency, 1990–92. Economic Consultant to Sec. of State for Scotland, 1987–92; Consultant, IMF, 1988, 1989. Economic and Social Research Council: Member: Econ. Affairs Cttee, 1985–87; Res. Progs Bd, 1992–93; Dir, Res. Prog. on Global Econ. Instns, 1994–2000. Mem. Academic Panel, HM Treasury, 1986–95. Mem. Council, Royal Economic Soc., 1988–92. Bd Mem., Analysys, 1989–2002. Comr, BFI Enquiry into the Future of the BBC, 1992. Houblon Norman Fellow, Bank of England, 2002. Res. Dir, Politics and Econs of Global Governance Eur. Div. Res. Prog., Framework Seven, EU. Bd Mem., Scottish Early Music Consort, 1990–91. *Publications:* (with J. E. Meade and J. M. Maciejowski) Stagflation, Vol. II: Demand Management, 1983; (with D. A. Currie) Macroeconomic Interactions Between North and South, 1988; (jtly) Macroeconomic Policy: inflation, wealth and the exchange rate, 1989; (with G. Hughes) Deregulation and the Future of Commercial Television, 1989; (with A. Stevenson) Information, Strategy, and Public Policy, 1991; (with D. A. Currie) North South Interactions and International Macroeconomic Policy, 1995; (with Peter Drysdale) Europe, East Asia and APEC, 1998; (ed with Alan Montefiore) Integrity in the public and private domains, 1998; (jtly) The Asian Financial Crises, 1999; (with Chris Gilbert) The World Bank: structure and policies, 2000; (with Chris Gilbert) The IMF and its Critics: reform of global financial architecture, 2004; (with Peter Temin) The Leaderless Economy: why the world economic system fell apart and how to fix it, 2013; (with Peter Temin) Keynes: useful economics for the world economy, 2014; (with Nicholas Morris) Capital Failure: rebuilding trust in the financial system, 2014; papers on international macroeconomics, macro-economic policy, in professional jls. *Recreations:* hillwalking, music. *Address:* Balliol College, Oxford OX1 3BJ. *T:* (01865) 271067, *Fax:* (01865) 271094. *E:* david.vines@economics.ox.ac.uk.

VINET, Dr Luc; Aisenstadt Professor of Physics, and Director, Centre de Recherches Mathématiques, 1993–99 and since 2013, University of Montreal; *b* 16 April 1953; *m* Letitia Muresan; three *s* one *d*. *Educ:* Univ. of Montreal (BSc Hons Physics 1970; MSc Theoretical Physics 1974; PhD Theoretical Physics 1980); Dr in Theoretical Physics, Univ. Pierre & Marie Curie, 1979. Res. Associate, Center for Theoretical Physics, MIT, 1980–82; Department of Physics, University of Montreal: NSERC Res. Fellow, 1982–87; Asst Prof., 1987–88; Associate Prof., 1987–88; Prof., 1992–99; Associate Mem., Centre de recherches mathématiques, 1999–2002; Pres., Network for Computing and Mathematical Modelling (rcm2), 1996–99; Chief Exec., Bell Energis Univ. Lab., 1998; McGill University: Prof., Dept of Maths and Stats and Dept of Physics, 1999–2005; Vice-Principal (Acad.), 1999–2005; Provost, 2001–05; Rector, Univ. of Montreal, 2005–10. Chair: Panel of Experts, Canadian Foundn for Innovation; Conf. des Recteurs et des Principaux des Univs du Québec; Member: Groupe de travail sur les affaires médicales; Gen. Physics Steering Cttee; Inst. de finance mathématique de Montréal; Bd, Canadian Inst. for Telecommunications Res.; Comité Ministériel sur la pondération des activités; Bd, Maths of Information Technol. and Complex Systems; Bd, Ouranos; Bd, Industries de la science de la vie et biotechnologies. Member: Soc. for Industrial and Applied Maths; Canadian Assoc. Physicists; Canadian Mathematical Soc. Hon. Mem., Golden Key Nat. Honor Soc., 2000. Officier, Ordre des Palmes Académiques (France), 2009. *Address:* Mathematical Research Center, University of Montreal, PO Box 6128, Station Centre-Ville, Montreal, QC H3C 3J7, Canada.

VINEY, Anne Dorothy; Chief Executive, Cruse Bereavement Care, 2002–08; *b* 29 March 1948; *d* of Edward Walter Totman and Margaret Totman (*née* Fulljames); *m* 1970, Stephen John Viney. *Educ:* Bristol Univ. (BA Hons (French) 1969); King's Coll. London (PGCE 1970); Goldsmiths Coll., London (CQSW 1986); Open Univ. (MBA 2000). Teacher: London Borough of Sutton, 1970–71; Essex CC, 1971–75; London Borough of Barnet, 1975–76; Sec., NABC, 1976; Age Concern, Westminster: Sec., 1977; Welfare Worker, 1977–79; Dep. Organising Sec., 1979–85; Social Worker, Camden Social Services, at Gt Ormond St Hosp., 1986–87; Asst Dir, 1987–99, Hd of R&D, 1999–2001, Victim Support. FRSA. *Recreations:* music, films, theatre. *E:* anne.viney@runbox.com. *Club:* Royal Society of Medicine.

VINGT-TROIS, His Eminence Cardinal André Armand; *see* Paris, Archbishop of, (RC).

VINNEY, Prof. John Edward, PhD; CEng, FIMechE; FHEA; Professor and Vice-Chancellor, Bournemouth University, since 2010; *b* Croydon, 15 April 1965; *s* of Edward Vinney and Shirley Vinney (*née* Packer); *m* 1987, Maria Tiffany Rollason; three *d*. *Educ:* Dorset Inst. of Higher Educn (HND 1986); Bristol Poly. (BEng Hons 1990); Univ. of West of England (PhD 1998; PGCE 2001). FIMechE 2003. Projects Engr, Vickers Shipbuilding and Engrg Ltd, 1986–90; Design Engr, British Aerospace (Space Systems) Ltd, 1990–91; Lectr, Coventry Univ., 1991–92; University of the West of England: Sen. Lectr, 1992–99; Principal Lectr, 1999–2001; Hd of Sch., 2001–03; Associate Dean, 2003–05; Dean, 2005–06; Bournemouth University: Dean, 2006–08; Pro Vice-Chancellor, Resources, 2008–09, Educn and Professional Practice, 2009–10. FHEA 2004. *Publications:* articles in learned jls. *Recreations:* badminton, cycling, walking. *Address:* Bournemouth University, Talbot Campus, Fern Barrow, Poole, Dorset BH12 5BB. *T:* (01202) 965006, *Fax:* (01202) 965069. *E:* vice-chancellor@bournemouth.ac.uk.

VINSON, family name of **Baron Vinson**.

VINSON, Baron *cr* 1985 (Life Peer), of Roddam Dene in the County of Northumberland; **Nigel Vinson,** LVO 1979; DL; entrepreneur; Founder, 1952, Chairman, 1952–72, Plastic Coatings Ltd; Founder Director, Centre for Policy Studies, 1974–80; *b* Nettlestead Place, Kent, 27 Jan. 1931; *s* of late Ronald Vinson and Bettina Vinson (*née* Southwell-Sander); *m* 1972, Yvonne Ann Collin; three *d*. *Educ:* Pangbourne Naval Coll. Lieut, Queen's Royal Regt, 1949–51. Plastic Coatings Ltd: started in a Nissen hut, 1952, flotation, 1969; Queen's Award to Industry, 1971. Director: Fleming High Income Growth Trust (formerly Fleming Tech. Trust), 1972–2001; BAA, 1973–80; Electra Investment Trust, 1975–98 (Dep. Chm., 1990–98); Barclays Bank UK, 1982–88. Mem., H of L Select Cttee on Econ. Affairs, 2001–03. Member: Crafts Adv. Cttee, 1971–77; Design Council, 1973–80; Dep. Chm., CBI Smaller Firms Council, 1979–84; Chairman: CoSIRA, 1980–82; Rural Develt Commn, 1980–90 (Mem., 1978–90); Industry Year Steering Cttee, RSA, 1985–87; Pres., Industrial Participation Assoc., 1979–89 (Chm., 1971–78). Institute of Economic Affairs: Trustee, 1972–2004; Chm. of Trustees, 1989–95; Life Vice-Pres., 1998. Trustee, Civitas, 2005–. Hon. Dir, Queen's Silver Jubilee Appeal, 1976–78; Member: Northumbrian Nat. Parks Countryside Cttee, 1977–89; Regional Cttee, Nat. Trust, 1977–84. Chm., NE Region, PYBT, 1995–98; Pres., NE Civic Trust, 1999–2001. Council Mem., St George's House, Windsor Castle, 1990–96. Foundn Donor, Martinmere Wildfowl Reserve, 1972; gifted a village green to Holburn, Northumberland, 2006. Trustee, Chillingham Wild Cattle, 1989. FRSA. DL Northumberland, 1990. *Publications:* Personal and Portable Pensions for All, 1984; Owners All, 1985; Take upon Retiring, 1998. *Recreations:* fine art and craftsmanship, horses, farming. *Address:* 34 Kynance Mews, SW7 4QR. *T:* (01668) 217230. *Clubs:* Boodle's, Pratt's.

VINTER, Anne Elizabeth; *see* Baldock, A. E.

VINTON, Alfred Merton; Chairman, Electra Partners Ltd (formerly Electra Kingsway Managers, then Electra Fleming Ltd), 1995–2009; *b* 11 May 1938; *s* of Alfred Merton Vinton and Jean Rosalie Vinton (*née* Guiterman); *m* 1st, 1963, Mary Bedell Weber; two *s* one *d*; 2nd, 1983, Anna-Maria Hawser (*née* Dugan-Chapman); one *s* one *d*. *Educ:* Harvard College (AB Econs 1960). US Navy Lieut (JG), 1960–62. J. P. Morgan, 1962–88; Chief Operating Officer, N. M. Rothschild & Sons, 1988–92; Chief Exec. Officer, Entreprises Quilmes SA, 1992–94; Director: Sand Aire Investments plc, 1995–; Sagitta Investment Advrs Ltd, 1996–2001; Unipart Ltd, 1998– (Dep. Chm.); Amerindo Internet Fund plc, 2000–06; Lambert Howarth Gp plc, 2000–07; GP Investments Ltd, 2006–; Sen. Ind. Dir, European Goldfields Ltd, 2010–12. *Recreations:* golf, tennis, riding, music. *Address:* Stoke Albany House, Market Harborough, Leics LE16 8PT. *T:* (01858) 535227. *Clubs:* White's; Sunningdale Golf; Harvard (New York).

VIÑUALES, Prof. Jorge Enrique; Harold Samuel Professor of Law and Environmental Policy, since 2013, and Director, Cambridge Centre for Environment, Energy and Natural Resource Governance, since 2014, University of Cambridge; *b* Buenos Aires, 7 Jan. 1976; *s* of Ricardo Miguel Viñuales and Margit Viñuales (*née* Juhasz). *Educ:* Nat. Univ. of Central Buenos Aires (LLB); Univ. of Freiburg (LLB); Univ. of Geneva (BA; MA); Inst. Univ. de Hautes Études Internat. (BA, MA); Harvard Law sch. (LLM); Sciences Po Paris (Dr sciences politiques, 2008). Of Counsel, Lévy Kaufmann-Kohler, Switzerland, 2008–11; Pictet Chair of Internat. Envmtl Law, Grad. Inst., Geneva, 2009–13. Country Expert, Amnesty Internat., Swiss Section, 2003–05; Vis. Expert, Internat. Develt Law Orgn and UNESCO Chair (Burundi), 2007–08. Exec. Dir, Latin American Soc. of Internat. Law, 2006–12. *Publications:* (ed jtly) Diplomatic and Judicial Means of Dispute Settlement, 2012; Foreign Investment and the Environment in International Law, 2012; (ed jtly) Harnessing Foreign Investment to Promote Environmental Protection, 2013; (ed jtly) Unity and Diversity of International Law, 2014; (ed jtly) The Foundations of International Investment Law, 2014; (ed) The Rio Declaration on Environment and Development: a commentary, 2015; (with P. M. Dupuy) International Environmental Law, 2015. *Recreations:* Kung Fu (Baji style), travelling, cinema, art, cooking. *Address:* Cambridge Centre for Environment, Energy and Natural Resource Governance, University of Cambridge, 19 Silver Street, Cambridge CB3 9EP. *T:* (01223) 337147, *Fax:* (01223) 337130. *E:* jev32@cam.ac.uk.

VIRDEE, Sir Tejinder Singh, Kt 2014; PhD; FRS 2012; FInstP; Professor of Physics, Imperial College London, since 1996; *b* Nyeri, Kenya, 13 Oct. 1952; *s* of late Sardar Chain Singh and of Bibi Udham Kaur; *m* 1983, Vatsala Oza; one *s* one *d*. *Educ:* Kings Norton Boys Grammar Sch., Birmingham; Queen Mary Coll., Univ. of London (BSc 1974); Imperial Coll. London (PhD 1979). FInstP 2012. Joined CERN as Fellow, Experimental Physics Div., 1979; Co-founder, 1990, Dep. Spokesperson, 1993–2006, Spokesperson (Leader), 2007–10, Compact Muon Solenoid Collaboration, CERN Large Hadron Collider. High Energy Physics Prize, 2007, Chadwick Prize and Medal, 2009, Inst. of Physics; Fundamental Physics Prize, Fundamental Physics Prize Milner Foundn, 2012; High Energy and Particle Physics Prize, Eur. Physical Soc., 2013. Hon. DSc: QMUL, 2013; Univ. Claude Bernard, 2013. Sikh Award (Educn), 2010; India Internat. Award (Sci.), 2013; Person of the Year, GG2 Asian Leadership Awards, 2013; Outstanding Achievement in Sci. and Technol., Asian Awards, 2015. *Address:* Blackett Laboratory, Physics Department, Imperial College London, Prince Consort Road, SW7 2AZ; CERN, 1211 Geneva 23, Switzerland.

VIRLEY, Simon James, CB 2014; Chair, Energy and Natural Resources, KPMG UK, since 2015; *b* 7 June 1969; *s* of Brian Michael Virley and Jean Barbara (*née* Lofts); *m* 2005, Kate Jaggar; two *s*. *Educ:* Jesus Coll., Oxford (BA Hons PPE 1990, MA 1994); London Sch. of Econs (MSc Econs 1995). Econs tutor, Green Coll., Oxford, 1990–91; Economist, Dept of Transport, 1991–93; Policy Advr, 1993–99, Team Leader, 1999–2000, HM Treasury; Private Sec. (Econ. Affairs) to Prime Minister, 2000–03; Dir, Better Regulation Exec., Cabinet Office, 2003–05; Dir, Corporate Finance, KPMG (on secondment from Cabinet Office), 2005–07; Hd, Renewable Energy and Innovation Unit, later Chief Exec., Office for Renewable Energy Deployment, BERR, later DECC, 2008–09; Actg Dir Gen., Nat. Climate Change and Consumer Support, 2009, Dir Gen., Energy Markets and Infrastructure, 2009–15, DECC. Mem., ICA. *Publications:* contrib. to jls incl. Econ. Briefing, Treasury Occasional Papers, Transport Policy. *Recreations:* cricket, football, ski-ing, golf, tennis. *Address:* KPMG LLP, 15 Canada Square, E14 5GL.

VISCHER, Vivienne; *see* Cox, V.

VISSCHER, Stephen Hendrick, CBE 2013; Deputy Chief Executive and Chief Operating Officer, Biotechnology and Biological Sciences Research Council, since 2008; *b* Northampton, 12 Jan. 1955; *s* of Johannes Visscher and Marjorie Visscher; *m* 1979, Ann Patricia Bowles; two *s*. *Educ:* FCMA 1995. Biotechnology and Biological Sciences Research Council: Director: Finance and Estates, 1994–2000; Finance and Admin, 2000–05; Exec. Dir, 2005–07; Interim Chief Exec., 2007–08. Dir, Norwich Research Partners LLP, 2012–. Trustee, Med. Res. Foundn, 2012–. FIIA 1996; FRSB (FSB 2013); FRSA. *Recreations:* walking, ski-ing, gardening, tennis. *Address:* Biotechnology and Biological Sciences Research Council, Polaris House, North Star Avenue, Swindon, Wilts SN2 1UH. *T:* (01793) 413304. *E:* steve.visscher@bbsrc.ac.uk. *Club:* Farmers.

VISSER, John Bancroft; Associate Member and Governor, Powell's School, Cirencester, since 1992 (Chairman, 1999–2005); Governor, since 1998, and Trustee, Enrichment Fund, since 2011, Cirencester Deer Park School; Trustee, Powell's Educational Foundation, since 1991 (Vice-Chairman, since 2008); *b* 29 Jan. 1928; *o s* of late Gilbert and Ethel Visser; *m* 1955, Astrid Margareta Olson; two *s* one *d*. *Educ:* Mill Hill Sch.; New Coll., Oxford (Exhibnr). Entered Civil Service, Asst Principal, Min. of Supply, 1951; Principal, 1956; Min. of Aviation, 1959; Admin. Staff Coll., 1965; Asst Sec., 1965; Min. of Technology, 1967; Royal Coll. of Defence Studies, 1970; Civil Service Dept, 1971; Procurement Exec., MoD, 1971; Under-Sec., 1974; Sec. of Nat. Defence Industries Council, 1971–74; Dir of Admin, SRC, then SERC, 1974–88. *Recreations:* sport, music, gardening, art and antiques. *Address:* 79 Corinium Gate, Cirencester, Glos GL7 2PX. *T:* (01285) 652626. *Club:* Old Millhillians.

VITA-FINZI, Dr Claudio, FBA 2012; Scientific Associate, Department of Earth Sciences (formerly Mineralogy), Natural History Museum, since 2001; *b* Sydney, 21 Nov. 1936; *s* of Paolo Vita-Finzi and Nadia Vita-Finzi (*née* Touchmalova); *m* 1969, Penelope; one *s*. *Educ:* Quintin Sch.; St John's Coll., Cambridge (BA 1958; PhD 1962; ScD 1988). Res. Fellow, St John's Coll., Cambridge, 1961–64; University College London: Lectr in Geog., then Geology, 1964–87; Prof. of Neotectonics, 1987–2001, now Emeritus. Mem., Amer. Philosophical Soc., 1997–. G. K. Warren Prize, US NAS, 1994. *Publications:* The Mediterranean Valleys, 1969; Recent Earth History, 1973; Archaeological Sites, 1978; Recent Earth Movements, 1986; Monitoring the Earth, 2002; Planetary Geology, 2005; The Sun: a user's manual, 2008; Solar History, 2012; papers in scientific jls. *Recreation:* clarinet trios for two. *Address:* 22 South Hill Park, NW3 2SB. *T:* (020) 7794 4415, 07713 886687. *E:* cvitafinzi@aol.com.

VITMAYER, Janet, CBE 2011; Chief Executive, Horniman Museum and Gardens, since 1998; *b* 2 Sept. 1952; *d* of Arnost Vitmayer and Maria (*née* Pichler); one *s* one *d*. *Educ:* Univ. of Keele (BA Hons Hist. and American Studies 1976); City Univ. (MA Mus. and Gall. Mgt 1990). Imperial War Mus., 1976–83; Dir, Livesey Mus., 1983–93; Hd, Public Services, Horniman Mus. and Gardens, 1993–98. Visitor, Pitt Rivers Mus., Univ. of Oxford, 2000–. Chair, Medicine, History and Society Capital Awards Cttee, Wellcome Trust, 2008, 2009, 2011–13. Trustee: London Transport Mus., 2008–; Collections Trust, 2008–. *Recreations:* family pursuits, travel. *Address:* Horniman Museum, 100 London Road, Forest Hill, SE23 3PQ. *T:* (020) 8699 1872.

VITORIA, Dr Mary Christine; QC 1997; *m* Prof. Clive Ashwin. *Educ:* Bedford Coll., London (BSc, PhD Chemistry); LLB (ext.) London Univ. Called to the Bar, Lincoln's Inn, 1975, Bencher, 2004; Lectr in Law, QMC, 1977; in practice at the Bar, 1978–2008. Editor: Reports of Patent Cases, 1995–2011; Fleet Street Reports, 1995–2011. *Publications:* (jtly) Modern Law of Copyright and Designs, 1980, 4th edn 2011; (contrib.) Halsbury's Laws of England, 4th edn. *Recreations:* opera, bird watching. *Address:* 8 New Square, Lincoln's Inn, WC2A 3QP. *T:* (020) 7405 4321.

VITORINO, António; Member, European Commission, 1999–2004; Partner, Cuatrecascas, Gonçalves, Pereira & Associates, Lisbon, since 2005; *b* 12 Jan. 1957; *m*; two *c*. *Educ:* Lisbon Law Sch. (law degree 1981; Master in Law and Pol Sci. 1986). Lawyer, 1982; Asst Prof., Lisbon Law Sch., 1982; Prof., Lisbon Autonomous Univ., 1986; Judge, Constitutional Court of Portugal, 1989–94; Vice-Pres., Portugal Telecom Internacional, 1998–99; Prof., Internat. Univ., 1998–99. Deputy (Socialist Party) Portuguese Parlt, 1980–83, 1985–89; Sec. of State for Parly Affairs, 1984–85, for Admin and Justice, Macao govt, 1986–87; Dep. Prime Minister and Minister of Defence, 1995–97; Mem., European Parlt, 1994–96. Member: Jt EP and Portuguese Parlt Cttee on European Integration, 1980–84; Sino-Portuguese Jt Liaison Gp on Macao, 1987–89. Pres., Gen. Assembly, Santander Totta Bank, 2005–. Pres., Notre Europe. Former Chm., Eur. Policy Centre. *Publications:* books on European affairs, constitutional law and pol sci.

VIVIAN, family name of **Barons Swansea** and **Vivian**.

VIVIAN, 7th Baron *cr* 1841; **Charles Crespigny Hussey Vivian;** Bt 1828; *b* 20 Dec. 1966; *s* of 6th Baron Vivian and his 1st wife, Catherine Joyce (*née* Hope) (now Countess of Mexborough); *S* father, 2004. Dir, Pelham Bell Pottinger. *Recreations:* Rugby, water ski-ing. *Heir: uncle* Hon. Victor Anthony Ralph Brabazon Vivian [*b* 26 March 1940; *m* 1966, Inger Johanne Gulliksen; one *s* one *d*]. *Address:* 28 Walpole Street, SW3 4QS. *Club:* White's.

VIVIAN, James Antony, FRCO; Director of Music, St George's Chapel, Windsor, since 2013; *b* Worcester, 19 June 1974; *s* of Roy John Vivian and Pamela Ann Vivian (*née* Bromley); *m* 2004, Ann Elise Smoot; one *d*. *Educ:* Malvern Coll. (Music Scholar); King's Coll., Cambridge (BA 1996; MA 1999). FRCO 1994. Actg Asst Organist, Lincoln Cath., 1992–93; A. H. Mann Organ Scholar, King's Coll., Cambridge, 1993–97; Temple Church: Suborganist, 1997–2004; Organist, 2004–13; Dir of Music, 2006–13. Various broadcasts; recordings on EMI. Decca, Hyperion, Priory, Signum, Sony BMG. *Recreations:* American history, cooking, baseball.

VLESSING, Suzanna; *see* Taverne, S.

VLIEGHE, Dr Gertjan Willem; External Member, Monetary Policy Committee, Bank of England, since 2015; *b* Amsterdam, 1971; *m* 1996, Shakeh Harikian; one *s* one *d*. *Educ:* Vesalius Coll., Belgium (BA Business Econs 1993); Univ. of Sussex (DipEcon); London Sch. of Econs and Pol Sci. (MSc Econs 1998; PhD Econs 2005). Analyst and Associate, J P Morgan (Belgium), 1994–96; Bank of England: economist, 1998–2004; Econ. Asst to Gov., 2004–05; Dir, Deutsche Bank, 2005–07; Partner and Sen. Economist, Brevan Howard Asset Mgt, 2007–15. *Address:* c/o Bank of England, Threadneedle Street, EC2R 8AH.

VOAKE, Charlotte Elizabeth Mary; freelance author and illustrator; *b* 9 Jan. 1957; *d* of Colin and Margaret Voake; *m* 1983, Robert Atkins; one *s* one *d*. *Educ:* Birkenhead High Sch., GPDST; University Coll. London (BA Hons Hist. of Art). *Publications:* illustrator: The Best of Aesop's Fables by Margaret Clark, 1990; Elsie Piddock Skips in Her Sleep by Eleanor Farjeon, 2000; A Child's Guide to Wild Flowers by Kate Petty, 2004; Collected Poems by Allan Ahlberg, 2008; The Further Adventures of the Owl and the Pussycat by Julia Donaldson, 2013; The Owl and the Pussy-cat by Edward Lear, 2014; Say It by Charlotte Zolotow, 2015; Beatrix Potter and the Unfortunate Tale of a Borrowed Guinea Pig by Deborah Hopkinson, 2015; author and illustrator: Ginger, 1997 (Smarties Award, 1997); Pizza Kittens, 2002 (Smarties Award, 2002); Ginger Finds a Home, 2003; Hello Twins, 2006 (Best Illustrated Children's Bks Award, NY Times, 2006); Tweedle Dee Dee, 2008; A Little Guide to Trees, 2009; Ginger and the Mystery Visitor, 2010; Melissa's Octopus, 2014; *Recreations:* gardening, piano, violin.

VOBE, Helen Mary; *see* Jones, H. M.

VOGEL, Dr Dieter H.; Founder and Chairman, Lindsay Goldberg Vogel GmbH, since 1998; *b* 14 Nov. 1941; *m* 1970, Ursula Gross; two *c*. *Educ:* primary sch., Berchtesgaden; secondary sch., Frankfurt; Tech. Univ. of Darmstadt (Dip. Mech. Engrg); Tech. Univ. of Munich (Dr.Ing). Asst Prof., Thermic Turbo Engines, Tech. Univ. of Munich, 1967–69; Vice-Pres., Printing Div., Bertelsmann AG, 1970–74; Pegulan Ag, 1975–85 (Chm., 1978); Vice-Chm., Mgt Bd, Batig (BAT Industries), 1978–85; Thyssen Group, 1986–98: Chm., Thyssen Handelsunion AG, 1986–96; Mem., Exec. Bd, 1986–91, Dep. Chm., 1991–96, Chm., 1996–98, Thyssen AG; Chm., Deutsche Bahn AG, 1998–2001. Chairman, Supervisory Board: Mobilcom AG, 2003–07; Bertelsmann AG, 2004–07; Klöckner & Co., 2006–. Chm., Bd of Trustees, Bertelsmann Foundn, 2007–11. *Publications:* M & A—Ideal und Wirklichkeit, 2002. *Recreation:* ski-ing. *Address:* Lindsay Goldberg Vogel GmbH, Königsallee 60A, 40212 Düsseldorf, Germany.

VOGEL, Hans-Jochen, Hon. CBE; Dr jur; Chairman: Social Democratic Party (SPD), Federal Republic of Germany, 1987–91; Gegen Vergessen-Für Demokratie eV, 1993–2000; *b* 3 Feb. 1926; *s* of Dr Hermann Vogel and Caroline (*née* Brinz); *m* 1st, 1950, Ilse Leisnering (marr. diss. 1972); one *s* two *d*; 2nd, 1972, Liselotte Biersack. *Educ:* Göttingen and Giessen; Univs of Marburg and Munich (Dr jur 1950). Army service, 1943–45 (PoW). Admitted Bavarian Bar, 1951; Legal Asst, Bavarian Min. of Justice, 1952–54; District Court Counsel, Traunstein, 1954–55; staff of Bavarian State Chancellery, 1955–58; Munich City Council, 1958–60, Oberbürgermeister (Chief Executive), Munich, 1960–72 (re-elected, 1966); Vice-Pres., Org. Cttee, Olympic Games, 1972. Mayor of West Berlin, Jan.–June 1981, leader of opposition, 1981–83. Chm., Bavarian SPD, 1972–77; Mem. (SPD) Bundestag, 1972–81, 1983–94; Minister of regional planning, housing and urban develt, 1972–74; Minister of Justice, 1974–81; Leader of the Opposition, 1983–91. Bundesverdienstkreuz; Bavarian Verdienstorden. *Publications:* Städte im Wandel, 1971; Die Amtskette: Meine 12 Münchner Jahre, 1972; Reale Reformen, 1973; Nachsichten, 1996; Demokratie lebt auch vom Widerspruch, 2001; Politik und Anstand, 2005; Deutschland aus der Vogel Perspektive, 2007; Wie wollen wir leben?, 2011; Was zusammengehört: die SPD und die deutsche Einheit 1989/1990, 2014. *Recreations:* mountaineering, swimming, reading history. *Address:* Gegen Vergessen-Für Demokratie eV, Stauffenbergstrasse 13–14, 10785 Berlin, Germany.

VOGEL, Prof. Johannes Christian, PhD; Director General, Museum für Naturkunde, Berlin, and Professor of Biodiversity and Public Science, Humboldt University, Berlin, since 2012; *b* 15 May 1963; *s* of late Erich Vogel and Edith Vogel (*née* Froböse); *m* 2003, Dr Sarah Catherine Darwin; two *s*. *Educ:* Ratsgymnasium, Bielefeld; Bielefeld Univ. (Vordiplom Biol. 1986); Peterhouse, Cambridge (PhD 1996). Served Armed Forces, FRG, 1982–84. Researcher, Alpeninstitut, Munich, 1989–90; Natural History Museum: Researcher, Dept of Botany, 1995–2004; Hd, UK Biodiversity Prog., 1999–2004; Keeper of Botany, 2004–11; Dir, Angela Marmont Centre for Biodiversity, 2008–11. Chm., European Citizen Sci. Assoc., 2014–; Dep. Chm., German BioEconomy Council, 2012–. Member: UK Biodiversity Gp, 1999–2001; Biodiversity Res. Adv. Gp, 2001–07; DCMS Sustainable Develt Forum, 2001–05; Darwin Expert (formerly Initiative Adv.) Cttee, 2005–11; Interdisciplinary Panel on Plant Genomics, ESRC Genomic and Policy Forum, 2005–09; Scientific Adv. Cttee, Chelsea Physic Garden, 2008–12; Leopoldina AG Taxonomie, 2012–14; Expert Rev. Panel, Volkswagenstiftung, 2013–14. Member Board: Naturwissenschaftlicher Verein für Bielefeld und Umgegend e.V., 1985–90; Dachverband Naturwissenschaftlicher Vereine Deutschlands, 1995–2008; Landesverband der Museen zu Berlin, 2012–; Council Mem., Systematics Assoc., 1995–98. Trustee: Radio Bielefeld, 1988–2004; Nat. Biodiversity Network, 1999–2011. Expert Rev. Panel, Deutsche Forschungsgemeinschaft, 2000–08. Spokesperson, Leibnizverbund Biodiversity, 2012–. FLS 1994; FAAAS 2010. Strasburger Preis, Deutsche Botanische Gesellschaft, 1996. *Publications:* papers on role of natural history museums in science and society; scientific papers on plant evolution, genetics, biogeography, systematics and biodiversity conservation in range of learned scientific jls. *Recreations:* natural history, walking, photography, music. *Address:* Stiftung Museum für Naturkunde, Leibniz-Institut für Evolutions- und Biodiversitätsforschung an der Humboldt-Universität zu Berlin, Invalidenstraße 43, 10115 Berlin, Germany. *T:* (30) 20938424, *Fax:* (30) 20938561. *E:* generaldirektor@mfn-berlin.de.

VOGEL, Julian Andrew; Chief Creative Officer, Modus Publicity, since 1989; Communication Consultant, If You Knew, since 2011; *b* London, 6 May 1966; *s* of Peter and Juliet Vogel; *m* 1998, Sally Mackereth; one *s* one *d*. *Educ:* Mill Hill Sch.; Middlesex Univ. (BA Hons Business Studies); Inst. of Marketing (Dip. 1987). Associate Producer, Vidal Sassoon: The Movie, 2007–12; Producer, Out Takes: Vidal Sassoon exhibn, Somerset Hse, 2012. Member: Art Plus Cttee, Whitechapel Gall., 2006–13; Develt Cttee, Design Mus., 2007–12 (Trustee, 2012–); Develt Cttee, V&A Mus., 2011–. Co-Chair, Mending Broken Hearts, BHF, 2010–. Gov., St Christopher's Sch., Hampstead, 2009–15. Mem., Assoc. of Lighthouse Keepers, 2007–. *Recreations:* film, photography, art, family, architecture, travel, writing, running. *Clubs:* Soho House, Ivy, George, 5 Hertford Street.

VOGENAUER, Prof. Stefan; Director, Max Planck Institute for European Legal History, Frankfurt, since 2015; *b* 4 Aug. 1968; *s* of Gottfried Dieter Vogenauer and Brigitte Maria (*née* Franz); *m* 1997, Jutta Greive; two *s* one *d*. *Educ:* Johann-Heinrich-Voβ-Gymnasium, Eutin; Kiel Univ. (First State Exam. in Law 1994); Trinity Coll., Oxford (MJur 1995; Clifford Chance Prize; HLA Hart Prize); Regensburg Appeal Court (Second State Exam. in Law 2000). Res. Asst and Lectr (pt-time), Univ. of Regensburg, 1997–2002; Res. Fellow, Max-Planck-Inst. for Foreign Private Law and Private Internat. Law, Hamburg, 2002–03; Prof., later Linklaters Prof. of Comparative Law, 2003–15, Dir, Inst. of European and Comparative Law, 2004–15, Univ. of Oxford; Fellow, Brasenose Coll., Oxford, 2003–15. Scientific Mem., Max Planck Soc., 2014–. Lectr (pt-time), Bucerius Law Sch., Hamburg, 2002–04. Humboldt Res. Award, 2012. *Publications:* Die Auslegung von Gesetzen in England und auf dem Kontinent, 2001 (Max Weber Prize, Bavarian Acad. of Scis and Humanities, 2002; Otto Hahn Medal, Max Planck Soc., 2002; Prize of German Legal History Conf., 2008); Commentary on the UNIDROIT Principles of International Commercial Contracts, 2009; articles on comparative law, European legal hist., German, English and European private law and legal method. *Address:* Max Planck Institute for European Legal History, Hansaallee 41, 60323 Frankfurt/Main, Germany. *T:* (69) 789780, *Fax:* (69) 78978169. *E:* vogenauer@rg.mpg.de.

VOGTHERR, Dr Christoph Martin; Director, Wallace Collection, since 2011; *b* Uelzen, Germany, 17 Jan. 1965; *s* of Dr Hans-Jürgen Vogtherr and Susanne Vogtherr. *Educ:* Freie Universität, Berlin (MA 1992; PhD 1996); Ruprecht-Karls Universität, Heidelberg; Trinity Coll., Cambridge. Res. Asst, Preussische Akademie der Künste Berlin-Brandenburg, Berlin, 1995–96; Curatorial Asst, 1996–98, Curator, 1998–2007, Stiftung Preussische Schlösser und Gärten Berlin-Brandenburg, Potsdam; Curator, Wallace Collection, London, 2007–11. Trustee, Wigmore Hall, 2014–. *Address:* Wallace Collection, Manchester Square, W1U 3BN. *E:* christoph.vogtherr@wallacecollection.org.

VOLCKER, Paul A.; Frederick H. Schultz Professor of International Economic Policy, Princeton University, 1988–96, now Emeritus; Chairman: James D. Wolfensohn Incorporated, 1988–96; Volcker Alliance, since 2013; *b* Cape May, New Jersey, 5 Sept. 1927; *s* of Paul A. Volcker and Alma Louise Klippel; *m* 1st, 1954, Barbara Marie Bahnson (*d* 1998); one *s* one *d*; 2nd, 2010, Anke Maria Dening. *Educ:* Princeton Univ. (AB *summa cum laude*); Harvard Univ. (MA); LSE. Special Asst, Securities Dept, Fed. Reserve Bank, NY, 1953–57; Financial Economist, Chase Manhattan Bank, NYC, 1957–62; Vice-Pres. and Dir of Forward Planning, 1965–69; Dir, Office of Financial Analysis, US Treasury Dept, 1962–63; Dep. Under-Sec. for Monetary Affairs, 1963–65; Under-Sec. for Monetary Affairs, 1969–74; Senior Fellow, Woodrow Wilson Sch. of Public and Internat. Affairs, Princeton Univ., 1974–75; Pres. NY Federal Reserve Bank, 1975–79; Chairman: American Federal Reserve Board, 1979–87; J. Rothschild, Wolfensohn & Co., 1992–95. Chairman: Group of Thirty, 1989–2000; Trilateral Commn, 1992–2001; Internat. Accounting Standards Cttee, IASC Foundn, 2001–06; Independent Inquiry Cttee into UN Oil for Food Prog., 2004–06; President's Econ. Recovery Adv. Bd, 2009–11. *Address:* 151 E 79th Street, New York, NY 10075, USA; (office) 610 Fifth Avenue, Suite 420, New York, NY 10020, USA. *T:* (212) 2187878.

VOLFING, Prof. Annette Marianne, DPhil; FBA 2015; Professor of Medieval German Literature, University of Oxford, since 2008; Fellow in German, Oriel College, Oxford, since 1994; *b* Copenhagen, 5 Feb. 1965; *d* of Ole and Anne Volfing; *m* 1987, David Thomas. *Educ:* Internat. Sch. of Geneva; St Edmund Hall, Oxford (BA Philosophy and German 1985; DPhil Modern Langs (German) 1993). Lectr in Medieval German Lit., 1994–2006, Reader, 2006–08, Univ. of Oxford. Mem., Kommission für Deutsche Literatur des Mittelalters, Bavarian Acad. of Sci. and Humanities, 2014. *Publications:* Heinrich von Mügeln, Der Meide Kranz: a commentary, 1997; John the Evangelist and Medieval German Writing: imitating the inimitable, 2001; Medieval Literature and Intertextuality in Middle High German: reading and writing in Albrecht's Jüngerer Titurel, 2007. *Recreations:* running, writing poetry. *Address:* Oriel College, Oxford OX1 4EW. *T:* (01865) 276555. *E:* Annette.Volfing@oriel.ox.ac.uk.

VOLHARD, Christiane N.; *see* Nüsslein-Volhard.

VOLLRATH, Prof. Lutz Ernst Wolf; Professor of Histology and Embryology, University of Mainz, Germany, 1974–2004, now Emeritus; *b* 2 Sept. 1936; *s* of Pastor Richard Hermann Vollrath and Rita (*née* Brügmann); *m* 1963, Gisela (*née* Dialer); three *d*. *Educ:* Ulrich von Hutten-Schule, Berlin; Univs of Berlin, Kiel (Dr med 1961), and Tübingen. Wissenschaftlicher Assistent, Dept of Anatomy, Würzburg, Germany, 1963; Res. Fellow, Dept of Anatomy, Birmingham, 1964; Wissenschaftlicher Assistent, Dept of Anatomy, Würzburg, 1965–71 (Privatdozent, 1968; Oberassistent, 1969; Universitätsdozent, 1970); King's College London: Reader in Anatomy, 1971; Prof. of Anatomy, 1973–74. Hon. Mem., Romanian Soc. of Anatomists, 1996; Corresp. Mem., Saxonian Acad. of Scis in Leipzig, 1998; Hon. Mem., Anatomy Assoc., Costa Rica, 1999. Editor: Cell & Tissue Research, 1978–96; Annals of Anatomy, 1992–2010. Hon. DM Halle-Wittenberg, 2008. *Publications:* (co-editor) Neurosecretion: the final neuroendocrine pathway, 1974; The Pineal Organ, 1981; (ed) Handbook of Microscopic Anatomy (formerly Handbuch der mikr. Anat. des Menschen) (series), 1978–; research publications on histochemistry and ultrastructure of organogenesis and various aspects of neuroendocrinology, in Annals of Anatomy, Z Zellforsch., Histochemie, Phil. Trans Royal Society B, Erg. Anat. Entw.gesch. *Recreation:* gardening. *Address:* c/o Institut für Mikroanatomie und Neurobiologie, Universitaetsmedizin Mainz, Building 708, Langenbeckstr. 1, 55131 Mainz, Germany.

VOLPE, Michael; General Director, Opera Holland Park, since 1989; *b* London, 29 May 1965; *s* of Francesco Volpe and Lidia Volpe (*née* Perillo); *m* 2011, Sally Connew; one *s* two *d*. *Educ:* Woolverstone Hall Grammar Sch., Ipswich. Travel Features, London Newspaper Gp, 1983–86; Internat. Exhibns and Events Manager, Utell International, 1986–89. *Publications:* Noisy At The Wrong Times (memoir), 2015. *Recreations:* opera, jazz, sports, boxing, literature, film, ski-ing, art, cooking, Chelsea Football Club, whisky. *Address:* Opera Holland Park, 37 Pembroke Road, W8 6PW. *T:* (020) 7361 2507. *E:* volpe@operahollandpark.com.

von BERTELE, Maj. Gen. Michael James, CB 2012; OBE 1994; FRCP; Humanitarian Director, Save the Children, since 2013; *b* 23 Aug. 1956; *s* of Otto Bertele von Grenadenberg and Monica von Bertele (*née* Barrett); *m* 1985, Frances Mary Buist Loudon; one *s* two *d*. *Educ:* St Mary's, Darlington; Welsh Nat. Sch. of Medicine, Cardiff (MB BCh 1979); London Sch. of Hygiene and Tropical Medicine (DAvMed 1986; DIH 1989). MFOM 1991; FRCP 2013. Peripatetic drayman, Schwechat Brewery, Vienna, 1974–76; commnd RAMC, 1976; MO, Parachute Field Ambulance, 1980–83; Specialist in Aviation Medicine, 1983–91; Consultant in Occupational (Aviation) Medicine, 1991; Commanding Officer: 5 Armd Field Ambulance, 1992–94; British Med. Bn, UN Protection Force, 1993; Comdr, Med. 3 (UK) Div., 1996–98; rcds 2000; Col, Employment Policy (Army), 2001–03; Dir, Med. Operational Capability, MoD, 2004–06; Chief Exec., Defence Medical Educn and Trng Agency, 2006–08; Comdr, Jt Med. Comd, 2008–09; Dir Gen. Army Med. Services, 2009–12. Chief Exec., Picker Inst. Europe, 2012–13. QHS 2008–12. Chm., Toe in the Water, 2008. *Recreation:* walking with family and border terriers. *Address:* The Old Bakery, Old Coach Road, Bulford, Salisbury, Wilts SP4 9DA. *E:* michaelvonbertele@hotmail.com.

von DOHNÁNYI, Christoph; Principal Conductor, Philharmonia Orchestra, London, 1997–2008, now Honorary Conductor for Life; Chief Conductor, NDR Symphony Orchestra, Hamburg, 2004–10; *b* 8 Sept. 1929; *m* 1st, 1957, Renate Zillessen (marr. diss.); one *s* one *d*; 2nd, 1979, Anja Silja, *qv* (marr. diss.); one *s* two *d*. *Educ:* 2 years' law study; Musikhochschule, Munich; Florida State Univ.; with grandfather Ernst von Dohnányi in USA. Coach and asst conductor, Frankfurt Opera, 1953; Gen. Music Dir, Lübeck and Kassel, 1957–68; Chief Conductor, Radiosymphonie Orch., Cologne, 1964–70; London début with LPO, 1965; Gen. Music Dir, Frankfurt Opera, 1968–77; Dir, Städtische Bühnen, Frankfurt, 1972–77; Intendant and Chief Conductor, Hamburg Opera, 1977; Music Dir, Cleveland Orch., 1984–2002, Music Dir Laureate, 2002–. Guest Conductor of major orchestras and opera houses in Europe, Israel and USA; Artistic Advr, l'Orchestre de Paris, 1998–2000. Numerous recordings; honours, music prizes and hon. doctorates. *Address:* c/o HarrisonParrott, 5–6 Albion Court, Albion Place, W6 0QT.

von ETZDORF, Georgina Louise, RDI 1997; freelance designer of textiles, ceramics and life style; painter; Artistic Director, Georgina von Etzdorf, 1981–2006; Founder and Artistic Director, nice work if you can get it, since 2008; *b* 1 Jan. 1955; *d* of late Roderick Rudiger von Etzdorf and Audrey von Etzdorf (*née* Catterns). *Educ:* Downe House; St Martin's Sch. of Art; Camberwell Sch. of Art (BA Hons 1977). Freelance textile designer, 1978–79; freelance designer, developing designs from paper work and silk screens on to fabric, 1979–80; Founder, Georgina von Etzdorf Partnership, 1981; artistic dir of team producing biannual collections of clothing and accessories, 1992–. Lectures and teaching posts: Cooper Hewitt Mus., NYC; Nova Scotia Sch. of Art and Design; Glasgow Coll. of Art; St Martin's Sch. of Art; Royal Coll. of Art; Crafts Council. *Exhibitions:* Smithsonian Instn's Nat. Mus. of Design, Washington; Cooper Hewitt Mus., NY; V&A; Manchester City Art Gall. (25 yr retrospective), 2006. Gov., Univ. of the Arts, 2005. Hon. Fellow, London Inst., 2003. Hon. DDes Winchester Sch. of Art, Univ. of Southampton, 1996. Enterprise Award for Small Businesses, Radio 4, 1984; British Apparel Export Award, 1986; Manchester Prize for Art and Industry, British Gas Award, 1988. *Recreations:* singing, dancing, playing the ukelele. *Club:* Chelsea Arts.

von HASE, Bettina Ilse Friederike; Founder and Director, Nine AM Ltd, art advisory, since 1998; *b* Bonn, 24 Jan. 1957; *d* of Karl-Günther von Hase, *qv*. *Educ:* Francis Holland Sch., Clarence Gate; Marlborough Coll.; Lady Margaret Hall, Oxford (BA 1978). Graduate trainee scheme, Reuters, 1978–81; assistant producer: Enigma Productions Ltd, 1981–82; CBS News, London, 1982–83; producer, ARD German Television, 1983–86; Hubert Burda Media, 1987–88; Proj. Dir Arts, SRU Ltd, mgt consulting, 1988–93; Hd, Develt, Nat. Gall., London, 1993–94; Dir, New World Vision, Hubert Burda Media, 1994–97. *Recreations:* art, ocean, walking, reading, film.

von HASE, Karl-Günther, Hon. GCVO 1972; Hon. KCMG 1965; Hon. President, Deutsch-Englische Gesellschaft, Düsseldorf, since 1993 (Chairman, 1982–93); *b* 15 Dec. 1917; *m* 1945, Renate Stumpff; five *d*. *Educ:* German schools. Professional Soldier, 1936–45; War Academy, 1943–44; Training College for Diplomats, 1950–51; Georgetown Univ., Washington DC, 1952. German Foreign Service: German Embassy, Ottawa, 1953–56; Spokesman, Foreign Office Bonn, 1958–61; Head, West European Dept, 1961–62; Spokesman of German Federal Government, 1962–67; State Secretary, Min. of Defence, German Federal Govt, 1968–69; German Ambassador to the Court of St James's, 1970–77; Dir-Gen., Zweites Deutsches Fernsehen, 1977–82. Hon. LLD Manchester, 1987. Holds German and other foreign decorations. *Recreations:* shooting, music. *Address:* Am Stadtwald 60, 53177 Bonn, Germany.

See also B. I. F. von Hase.

von KLITZING, Prof. Klaus, PhD; Director, Max-Planck-Institut für Festkörperforschung, Stuttgart, since 1985; *b* 28 June 1943; *s* of Bogislav and Anny von Klitzing; *m* 1971, Renate Falkenberg; two *s* one *d*. *Educ:* Technische Univ., Braunschweig (Dipl Phys); Univ. of Würzburg (PhD; Habilitation (univ. teaching qual.). Prof., Technische Univ., München, 1980–84; Hon. Prof., Univ. of Stuttgart, 1985. Foreign Mem., Royal Soc., 2003. Hon. FInstP 2002. Nobel Prize for Physics, 1985. *Address:* Max-Planck-Institut für Festkörperforschung, Heisenbergstrasse 1, 70569 Stuttgart, Federal Republic of Germany. *T:* (711) 6891570.

von MALLINCKRODT, George Wilhelm, Hon. KBE 1997; President, Schroders plc, since 1995 (Chairman, 1984–95; Director, 1977–2008); Chairman, Schroders Incorporated, New York, since 1985; Chairman, J. Henry Schroder Bank AG, Zurich, 1984–2003; *b* 19 Aug. 1930; *s* of Arnold Wilhelm von Mallinckrodt and Valentine von Mallinckrodt (*née* von Joest); *m* 1958, Charmaine Schroder; two *s* two *d*. *Educ:* Salem, West Germany. Agfa AG Munich, 1948–51; Münchmeyer & Co., Hamburg, 1951–53; Kleinwort Sons & Co., London, 1953–54; J. Henry Schroder Banking Corp., New York, 1954–55; Union Bank of Switzerland, Geneva, 1956–57; J. Henry Schroder Banking Corp., NY, 1957–60; J. Henry Schroder & Co., subseq. J. Henry Schroder Wagg & Co., London, 1960–85, Director, 1967–; Schroders Incorp., NY, 1977–; Chm. and Chief Exec. Officer, J. Henry Schroder Bank & Trust Co., NY, 1984–86. Director: Schroder Asseily & Co., 1981–2000; Schroders Australia Hldgs Ltd, Sydney, 1984–2001; NM UK, 1986–90; Schroder Internat. Merchant Bankers, 1988–2000; Director: Allianz of America Inc. (NY), 1978–84; Banque Privée de Gestion Financière (Paris), 1980–83; Siemens plc, 1989–2000; Euris SA, Paris, 1989–98; Foreign & Colonial German Investment Trust PLC, 1992–98; British Invisibles, 1995–98. Vice-Pres., German-British Chamber of Industry and Commerce in UK, 1996– (Dir, 1971–91, Pres., 1992–95); Advr, McGraw Hill Inc., USA, 1986–89; Advr, Bain & Co., 1997–2005; Dir, Eur. Arts Foundn, 1987–2002. Member: British N American Cttee, 1988–2013; City Adv. Gp, CBI, 1990–; World Economic Forum (Chm. Council, 1995–97). Pres., German YMCA, London, 1961–; Member: Ct of Benefactors, Oxford Univ., 1990–; Nat. Art Collection Develt Fund, 1995–2005; BM Develt Trust, 1995–; INSEAD Circle of Patrons, 1995–; Finance Cttee, St George's Coll. Foundn, and Adv. Cttee on Finance to Dean and Canons, Windsor, 2003–; Council, John F. Kennedy Sch. of Govt, Harvard Univ., 2005–; Trustee: Prague Heritage Fund, 1992–2004; Christian Responsibility in Public Affairs, 1994–; Patron, Three Faiths Forum, 2005–. Freeman, City of London, 2004. FRSA 1986; CCMI (CBIM 1986). Hon. DCL: Bishop's Univ., Canada, 1994; Washington Univ., St Louis, Mo. Verdienstkreuz am Bande, 1986, Verdienstkreuz 1 Klasse, 1990, Grosse Verdienstkreuz, 2001, des Verdienstordens (Germany). Awarded Annual Sternberg Interfaith Award, 2005. KCSG 2012. *Recreations:* music, libraries.

von MOLTKE, Gebhardt; Chairman, Deutsch-Britische Gesellschaft, 2003–13; *b* 28 June 1938; *s* of late Hans-Adolf von Moltke and Davida, Gräfin Yorck von Wartenburg; *m* 1965, Dorothea Bräuer; one *s* one *d*. *Educ:* Univs of Grenoble, Berlin, Freiburg (Law); qualified as lawyer, 1967. German Trade Unions, 1967–68; Fed. Republic of Germany Diplomatic Service, 1968–2003: served Liverpool, Cabinet of Foreign Minister, Moscow, Jaoundé/Cameroon, and Foreign Office Personnel Dept; Washington Embassy, 1982–86; Head, US Desk, Foreign Office, 1986–91; Asst Sec.-Gen. for Political Affairs, NATO HQ, Brussels, 1991–97; Ambassador to UK, 1997–99; Perm. Rep. to NATO, 1999–2003. *Recreations:* music, art (Italian drawings), reading, tennis.

von OTTER, Anne Sofie; singer (mezzo-soprano); *b* Stockholm, 9 May 1955. *Educ:* Stockholm Acad. of Music; GSMD; vocal studies with Vera Rozsa, 1981–. With Basle Opera, 1983–85; freelance, 1985–; appearances at most major opera houses incl. Royal Opera, Covent Garden, 1985–; Metropolitan Opera, 1985–; La Scala, Milan, 1987–; Glyndebourne, Geneva, Aix-en-Provence, Paris, Vienna, Chicago, Berlin and Munich; has also given recitals worldwide. Rôles include: Mozart: Cherubino, Sextus, Idamante, Dorabella, Ramiro; Strauss: Octavian, Clairon, Componist; Bellini: Romeo; Rossini: Tancredi, Cenerentola; Bizet: Carmen; Gluck: Orfeo; Monteverdi: Nerone; Handel: Ariodante, Xerxes. Major recordings include: Così fan tutte; Orfeo ed Euridice; Hansel and Gretel; Der Rosenkavalier; Le Nozze di Figaro; Idomeneo; Ariodante; Werther; Les Contes d'Hoffmann; La Damnation de Faust; Nuits d'Eté, Mahler cycles, and lieder by Mahler, Brahms, Grieg, Wolf, etc. Hon. RAM 2002. *Address:* c/o HarrisonParrott Ltd, 5–6 Albion Court, Albion Place, W6 0QT.

von PLOETZ, Dr Hans-Friedrich; Ambassador of Germany to the Russian Federation, 2002–05; advisor to companies on strategy in Russian and other Commonwealth of Independent States markets, since 2005; *b* 12 July 1940; *m* 1971, Päivi Leinonen; two *s*. Diplomatic posts in: Morocco, 1967–68; Helsinki, 1968–73; Min. for Foreign Affairs, 1973–78; Washington, 1978–80; Min. for Foreign Affairs, 1980–88; Dep. Perm. Rep. of Germany, 1988–89, Ambassador and Perm. Rep. of Germany, 1989–93, on NATO Council; Dir-Gen. for Eur. Integration, Bonn, 1993–94; State Sec., Min. for Foreign Affairs, Bonn, 1994–99; Ambassador to UK, 1999–2002. Mem., Expert Gp on New Strategic Concept for NATO, 2009–10. Mem., Supervisory Bd, Robert Bosch GmbH, 2008–12; Sen. Advr, Wermuth Asset Mgt, Moscow and Frankfurt, 2009–. Chairman: Foundn on German-Russian Youth Exchange, 2006–11; Investment Adv. Council, Green Gateway Fund, 2011–; Adv. Bd, Center for Global Politics, Free Univ. Berlin. *Recreations:* music, golf, gardening. *Address:* Schloßstrasse 5, 14059 Berlin, Germany.

von PRONDZYNSKI, Prof. Ferdinand Victor René, PhD; Principal and Vice-Chancellor, Robert Gordon University, Aberdeen, since 2011; *b* Bevensen, Germany, 30 June 1954; *s* of Hans von Prondzynski and Irene von Prondzynski (*née* Countess Grote); *m* 1985, Heather Ingman; two *s*. *Educ:* Headfort Sch., Kells, Co. Meath; Schule Schloss Salem; Thomas Morus Gymnasium, Oelde; Trinity Coll. Dublin (BA; LLB 1978); Christ's Coll., Cambridge (PhD 1983). Bank official, Dresdner Bank AG, Germany, 1972–74; Lectr, TCD, 1980–90; Prof. of Law, Univ. of Hull, 1991–2000; Pres., Dublin City Univ., 2000–10. MRIA 2006; Mem., Royal Dublin Soc., 2011. KLJ 2010. *Publications:* Employment Law in Ireland (with C. McCarthy), 1984, 2nd edn 1987; Freedom of Association and Industrial Relations, 1986; contrib. articles and book chapters. *Recreations:* photography, English, Scottish and Irish literature, football. *Address:* Principal's Office, Garthdee House, Garthdee Road, Aberdeen AB10 7QB. *T:* (01224) 262002. *E:* f.von-prondzynski@rgu.ac.uk; Knockdrin Castle, Mullingar, Ireland.

von REITZENSTEIN, Hans-Joachim Freiherr; *see* Leech, John.

von RICHTHOFEN, Baron Hermann, Hon. GCVO 1992; Permanent Representative of the Federal Republic of Germany to NATO, 1993–98; *b* 20 Nov. 1933; *s* of Baron Herbert von Richthofen and Baroness Gisela von Richthofen (*née* Schoeller); *m* 1966, Christa, Countess von Schwerin; one *s* two *d*. *Educ:* Univs of Heidelberg, Munich and Bonn; Dr in law Cologne Univ. 1963. Joined Diplomatic Service of FRG, 1963; served Boston, Mass, 1963–64; FO, 1964–66; Saigon, 1966–68; Jakarta, 1968–70; FO, 1970–74; Dep. Hd, Sect. for Internat. Law, FO, 1974; Hd, Sect. for For. Policy, Perm. Mission to GDR, 1975–78; Hd of Dept for German and Berlin Affairs, FO, 1978–80; seconded to Fed. Chancellery as Hd of Intra-German Policy Unit, 1980–86; Dir Gen. of Legal Div., 1986, of Political Div., and Political Dir, 1986–88, FO; Ambassador to UK, 1988–93. Chm., British-German Assoc., Berlin, 1998–2003 (Hon. Mem.). Gov., Ditchley Foundn, 1988–93, 1996–. Trustee, 21st Century Trust, 1998–2009. Hon. Prof., Central Connecticut State Univ., 2001. Hon. LLD Birmingham, 2000. ER 1961, RR 1985, Johanniter Orden; Officer's Cross, Order of the Knights of Malta, 1967; Commander's Cross: Order of Merit (Italy), 1979; Legion of Honour (France), 1987; Grand Officer's Cross, Order of Infante D. Henrique (Portugal), 1988; Knight Commander's Cross, 2nd class (Austria), 1989; Grand Cross, Order of Merit (FRG), 1999; Grand Cross, Order of Merit (Luxembourg), 2000; Commander's Cross, Order of Merit (Poland), 2003; Order of Merit of Land Brandenburg (Germany), 2000. *Recreations:* reading history, arts. *Address:* Beckerstrasse 6a, 12157 Berlin, Germany.

von SCHIRNDING, Nicholas Kurt; Chief Executive Officer, Carajas Copper Company, since 2014; *b* 4 Aug. 1962; *s* of Kurt von Schirnding and Gisela von Schirnding; *m* 1993, Jessica Pudney; two *s* one *d*. *Educ:* Univ. of Cape Town (LLB 1985). Sub-Lieut, S African Navy, 1986–87; Treasury, Gold Finance, Anglo American Corp. SA, 1988–92; Indian Desk, De Beers, 1992–93; Finance Div., Minorco, 1994–98; Hd, Investor and Corporate Affairs, Anglo American plc, 1999–2011; Exec., 2011–12, CEO, 2013–14, Bumi, then Asia Resource Minerals plc. Vice Chm., PT Berau Coal Energy, 2014. *Recreations:* running, golf. *E:* von@vonschirnding.com. *Clubs:* Goodwood Kennels; Wimbledon Park Golf; Kelvin Grove (South Africa).

von STUMM, Johannes, FRBS 2004; PPRBS; sculptor; *b* Munich, 27 July 1959; *s* of Nikolaus and Ursula von Stumm; *m* 1992, Carolyn Wroughton; one *s* one *d*. *Educ:* Gymnasium Monastery Ettal; Oskar von Miller Gymnasium; Ludwig Maximilians Univ., Munich (Law and Politics); Acad. of Fine Arts, Munich. Self-employed sculptor, Munich, 1988–95: work with Peter Layton, London, Clifford Reney, London and at Exptl Glass Workshop, NY, 1989; teacher of sculpture, studio Keferloh, Munich, 1990–95; asst teacher, Bildwerk, Frauenau, 1993–95; opened studio, S Fawley, Wantage, Oxon, 1995. Guest Lecturer: Art Inst., Bournemouth, 2004; Christ Ch UC, Canterbury, 2005; Imperial Coll. London, 2006; Central St Martin's, London, 2006; Newbury Coll., 2010. Royal Society of British Sculptors: Mem., 1997–; Mem. Council, 2003–; Treas., 2004–09; Pres., 2009–12; Mem., Oxford Art Soc., 1999– (Pres., 2014–); Pres., Open Studios W Berks and N Hants; Founding Mem., Sculpture Network Europe, 2003; Mem., Deutscher Kuenstlerbund, 2005–. *Solo exhibitions* include: Turtle Key Gall., London, Film Hochschule, Munich, 1995; Mus. of Oxford, 1996; Watermill Th., Newbury, Galerie Neuendorf, Memmingen, Germany, 1997; Curwen Gall., London, 1998, 2000, 2002, 2004; Galerie Vromans, Amsterdam, 2001; Orangerie, Munich, 2003; *group exhibitions* include: James Colman Fine Art Gall., London, Art '97, London, 20th Century Art Fair, London, 1997; Hannah Peschar Gall., Surrey, 1997, 1999, Sussex, 2001; Galerie 410, Frankfurt, 1998; City of Munster, out of door sculpture, Germany, 1998, 2002; Open Studios, Newbury, 1998, 2000, 2002, 2004, 2014; Art '99, London, Kanazawa, Japan, Oxford Art Soc., Abingdon, 1999; Art 2000, London, Zürich Art Fair, Switzerland, Artfair, Brussels, 2000; RSBS, 2000, 2002, 2003, 2005, 2006; Mall Gall., London, 2001; Gall. Beaux Art, Bath, 2001, 2003; Goodwood Sculpture Park, 2001, 2003; Affordable Art Fair, NY, Haus der Deutschen Industrie, Berlin, Manchester Art Gall., Art 2002, London, 2002; Leicester Univ. Botanic Gdn, 2002, 2003; Cass Sculpture Foundn, 2004; Thompson's Gall., London, 2004, 2005, 2006, 2008, 2010, 2011; Royal Acad., London, Daniel Katz Gall., London, Sidney Cooper Gall., Canterbury, Wiseman Gall., Oxford, Art Fair, Chicago, 2005; Robert Bowman Gall., then Robert Bowman Contemp., later Modern, subseq. Bowman Sculpture, London, 2005, 2006, 2007, 2008, 2010, 2011, 2013; Curwen Gall., London, 2006, 2009; Jenny Granger Gall., Whitstable, Galerie Thiess, Munich, Fusion Gall., Altea, Spain, Abbey Hse Gdns, Malmesbury, Chichester Cathedral, 2007; Puthall Sculpture Park, 2008; Galerie Marschall, Bernried, Germany, Mus. für Konkrete Kunst, Freiburg, Fitzwilliam Mus., Cambridge, RWA, 2009; Aventurijn Galerie, Epe, Netherlands, Garden Gall., Broughton, 2010; Eton Coll., 2012; Patrick Heide Gall., London, Garden Gall., Broughton, OnForm, Asthall Manor, 2014; Jarfo Gall., Kyoto, Japan, 2014, 2015; Soul Gall., Winnipeg, Canada, Changsha Sculpture Park, 2015; *commissions* include: Prior's Court Sch., Newbury sculpture gdn, 2001; Prudential Corp. plc, Accel Venture Capital, 2002; public sculpture, Wantage, Oxon, 2003; public sculpture, Newbury, 2005; Slater Centre, New Greenham Common, 2009. *Address:* Wellhill House, South Fawley, Wantage, Oxon OX12 9NL. *T:* (01488) 638194, *Fax:* (01488) 638195. *E:* vonstumm@aol.com. *Club:* Chelsea Arts.

von WINTERFELDT, (Hans) Dominik; Partner, Boyden World Corporation, New York, since 1996; *b* 3 July 1937; *s* of late Curt von Winterfeldt and Anna Franziska Margaretha Luise (*née* Petersen); *m* 1966, Cornelia Waldthausen; one *s* one *d*. *Educ:* German schools; Stanford-INSEAD, Fontainebleau (Industriekaufmann). DipICC. Joined Hoechst AG, Frankfurt/Main, 1957; Asst Manager, Hoechst Colombiana Ltda, 1960; Commercial Manager, Pharmaceuticals, Hoechst Peruana SA, 1963; General Manager, Hoechst Dyechemie W. L. L., Iraq, 1965; Man. Dir, Hoechst Pakistan Ltd and Hoechst Pharmaceuticals Ltd, 1967; Hoechst UK Ltd: Dep. Man. Dir, 1972; Man. Dir and Chief Exec., 1975; Exec. Chm., 1984; Dir (Corporate PR and Communications), 1987–94; Dir, Cassella AG, 1994–95. Dir, GML Consulting Ltd, Hong Kong, 2006–. Mem., British Assoc. for Shooting and Conservation, 1979–. Mem., Rotary Club, Frankfurt, 1990–. KStJ 2008. *Recreations:* music, deer stalking, golf. *Address:* Viktoriastrasse 1, 61476 Kronberg, Germany. *T:* (6173) 601118.

VORDERMAN, Carol Jean, MBE 2000; broadcaster and author; *b* 24 Dec. 1960; *d* of Anton Joseph Maria Vorderman and Edwina Jean Vorderman; *m* 1st, 1985 (marr. diss. 1987); 2nd, 1990 (marr. diss. 2002); one *s* one *d*. *Educ:* Blessed Edward Jones High Sch., Rhyl; Sidney Sussex Coll., Cambridge (MA). Member: Action into Engrg Task Force, DTI, 1995; Home Office Internet Task Force, 2001–02. Founder Mem. and Trustee, NESTA, 1998–2001. Television programmes include: Countdown, 1982–2008; World Chess Championship (Kasparov *v* Short), 1993; Tomorrow's World, 1994–95; Computers Don't Bite, 1997; Mysteries with Carol Vorderman, 1997–98; Carol Vorderman's Better Homes, 1999–2003; Find a Fortune, 1999–2001; Star Lives (formerly Stars and Their Lives), 1999–2002; Tested to Destruction, 1999; Better Gardens, 2000; Pride of Britain Awards, 2000–; Britain's Brainiest Kids, 2001–02; Vorderman's Sudoku Live, 2005; Golden Lot, 2005; Loose Women, 2011–; Food Glorious Food, 2013. Columnist: Daily Telegraph, 1996–98; Mirror, 1998–2004. FRSA 1997. Hon. Fellow, Univ. of Wales, Bangor, 1999. Hon. MA Bath, 2000. *Publications:* Dirty, Loud and Brilliant, 1988; Dirty, Loud and Brilliant Too, 1989; How Mathematics Works, 1996; (with R. Young) Carol Vorderman's Guide to the Internet, 1998, 2nd edn 2001; Maths Made Easy, 1999; Science Made Easy, 2000; English Made Easy, 2000; Educating and Entertaining Your Children Online with Carol Vorderman, 2001; (with Ko Chohan) Detox for Life, 2001; Carol Vorderman's Summer Detox, 2003; Carol Vorderman's Detox Recipes, 2003; Carol Vorderman's 30 Day Cellulite Plan, 2004; Carol Vorderman's How to do Sudoku, 2005; Super Brain, 2007; It All Counts (autobiog.), 2009. *Address:* c/o John Miles Organisation, Cadbury Camp Lane, Clapton-in-Gordano, Bristol BS20 7SB. *T:* (01275) 854675.

VORHAUS, Jennifer; *see* Dixon, Jennifer.

VOS, Rt Hon. Sir Geoffrey (Charles), Kt 2009; PC 2013; **Rt Hon. Lord Justice Vos;** a Lord Justice of Appeal, since 2013; Chairman, Bar Council of England and Wales, 2007; *b* 22 April 1955; *s* of late Bernard Vos and Pamela Celeste Rose (*née* Heilbuth); *m* 1984, Vivien Mary Fieldhouse (*née* Dowdeswell); one *d* and one step *s* two step *d*. *Educ:* University College Sch., London; Gonville and Caius Coll., Cambridge (BA, MA). Called to the Bar, Inner Temple, 1977, Bencher, 2009; Bencher, Lincoln's Inn, 2000; QC 1993; Judge of Cts of Appeal of Jersey and Guernsey, 2005–09; Judge of Ct of Appeal of Cayman Islands, 2008–09; a Judge of the High Ct of Justice, Chancery Div., 2009–13. Chm., Chancery Bar Assoc., 1999–2001 (Hon. Sec., 1994–97; Vice-Chm., 1997–99). Bar Council: Chm., Fees Collection Cttee, 1995–2004; Vice Chm., 2001–03, Chm., 2004–05, Professional Standards Cttee; Mem., Gen. Mgt Cttee, 2004–07; Vice Chm., 2006. Mem., Panel on Fair Access to the Professions, 2009. Pres., Eur. Network of Councils for the Judiciary, 2015–June 2016. Trustee: Social Mobility Foundn, 2007–11 (Chm., 2008–11); Slynn Foundn, 2009–. *Recreations:* farming, wine, photography. *Address:* Royal Courts of Justice, Strand, WC2A 2LL. *Clubs:* Oxford and Cambridge; Worcestershire Golf.

VOS, His Honour Geoffrey Michael; a Circuit Judge, 1978–94; *b* 18 Feb. 1927; *s* of Louis and Rachel Eva Vos; *m* 1955, Marcia Joan Goldstone (marr. diss. 1977); two *s* two *d*; *m* 1981, Mrs Anne Wilson. *Educ:* St Joseph's College, Blackpool; Gonville and Caius College, Cambridge (MA, LLB). Called to the Bar, Gray's Inn, 1950. A Recorder of the Crown Court, 1976–78. *Recreations:* swimming, walking. *Address:* c/o The Crown Court, The Law Courts, Quayside, Newcastle upon Tyne NE1 3LA. *T:* (0191) 201 2000.

VOSPER, Christopher John; QC 2000; **His Honour Judge Vosper;** a Circuit Judge, since 2006; *b* 4 Oct. 1952; *s* of John Darvel Vosper and Hettie Vosper; *m* 1982, Ann Prosser Bowen; one *s* one *d*. *Educ:* Cowbridge Grammar Sch.; Pembroke Coll., Oxford (MA). Called to the Bar, Middle Temple, 1977; in practice as barrister, 1977–2006; a Recorder, 1998–2006. *Address:* Swansea Civil Justice Centre, Caravella House, Quay West, Quay Parade, Swansea SA1 1SP.

VOSS, Robert Andrew, CBE 2014; DL; Chairman: Amethyst (London) Ltd, since 2014; Voss International Ltd, 1987–2015; *b* London, 9 Feb. 1953; *s* of Richard Voss and Renate Voss; *m* 1975, Celia Gerard; two *s* one *d*. *Educ:* University College Sch., London; Univ. of Manchester (BSc Hons Mgt Sci.). Trading Manager, Brookside Metal Co. Ltd, 1975–80; Dir, Metramet Ltd, 1980–87; Chm., Advanced Steel Products Ltd, 1991–2011. Pres., Eurometrec, 1994–98 and 2006–14. Mem. Bd, 1986–2015, Chm., Internat. Trade Council, 2006–15, Bureau of Internat. Recycling, Brussels. Pres., British Secondary Metals Assoc., 1984–86. DL Herts, 2015. *Publications:* articles on internat. trade of metals and recycling. *Recreations:* golf, watching Rugby, soccer, cricket, music, travel, family, food, Europe, Young Entrepreneurs. *Address:* Greenway, Loudwater Drive, Loudwater, Herts WD3 4HJ. *T:* (01923) 710550, 07785 227933. *E:* robert@voss.uk.com. *Clubs:* MCC; Moor Park Golf; Middlesex CC; Lord's Taverners.

VOUSDEN, Prof. Karen Heather, (Mrs R. Ludwig), CBE 2010; PhD; FRS 2003; FMedSci; Director, Beatson Institute for Cancer Research, and Professor, University of Glasgow, since 2002; *b* 19 July 1957; *d* of William and Erna Vousden; *m* 1986, Robert Ludwig; one *d*. *Educ:* Queen Mary Coll., Univ. of London (BSc 1978; PhD 1982). Post-Doctoral Fellow, Inst. of Cancer Res., London, 1981–85, Nat. Cancer Inst., USA, 1985–87; Hd, Human Papillomavirus Gp, Ludwig Inst. for Cancer Res., 1987–95; Dir, Molecular Virology and Carcinogenesis Lab., Advanced Biosci. Lab. Basic Res. Prog., USA, 1995–99; Chief, Regulation of Cell Growth Lab., Nat. Cancer Inst., USA, 1999–2002. FMedSci 2006. *Publications:* contrib. numerous articles to learned jls. *Recreation:* hill-walking. *Address:* Beatson Institute for Cancer Research, Garscube Estate, Switchback Road, Bearsden, Glasgow G61 1BD. *T:* (0141) 330 2424, *Fax:* (0141) 943 0372. *E:* k.vousden@beatson.gla.ac.uk.

VRAALSEN, Tom; Commander, Royal Order of Saint Olav 1987; Ambassador and Special Advisor to Norwegian Ministry of Foreign Affairs, since 2004; *b* 26 Jan. 1936; *m* 1977, Viebecke Strøm; two *d*. *Educ:* Arhus Sch. of Econs and Business Admin, Denmark (MEcon). Entered Norwegian Foreign Service, 1960; served Peking, Cairo, Manila, 1960–71; Head of Div., Min. of Foreign Affairs, 1971–75; Minister-Counsellor, Perm. Mission of Norway to UN, NY, 1975–81; Dir-Gen., Min. of Foreign Affairs, 1981–82; Ambassador, Perm. Mission of Norway to UN, NY, 1982–89; Minister of Develt Assistance, 1989–90; Dir of Information, Saga Petroleum, 1991–92; Asst Sec. Gen., Min. of Foreign Affairs, 1992–94; Ambassador to: UK, 1994–96; USA, 1996–2001; to Finland, 2001–03. Special Envoy of UN Sec.-Gen. for humanitarian affairs, Sudan, 1998–2004. Chairman: Assessment and Evaluation Commn, Khartoum, 2005–08; Task Force for Internat. Cooperation on Holocaust Educn, Remembrance and Res., 2009–10. *Address:* Ministry of Foreign Affairs, 7 Juni plassen 1, 0032 Oslo, Norway.

VU QUANG MINH; Ambassador of Vietnam to the Court of St James's, 2011–14; *b* Hanoi; *m*; two *s*. *Educ:* Moscow International Relations Inst. (BA 1988); Princeton Univ. (MPA 1995). Joined Ministry of Foreign Affairs, 1990; worked in several depts incl. Dept for Soviet Union, UNESCO Nat. Secretariat, ASEAN Nat. Secretariat, Office of the Minister, and Multilateral Econ. Cooperation Dept, 1990–97; Personal Sec. to Dep. Prime Minister and Foreign Minister, Office of the Govt of Vietnam, 1997–2002; Counsellor, Hd of Econ. Section, USA, 2002–06; Director General: Multilateral Econ. Cooperation Dept, 2007–08; Econ. Affairs Dept, 2008–10; Asst Minister, 2011. *Recreations:* music, literature, movies, chess, table tennis, swimming. *Address:* c/o Embassy of Vietnam, 12–14 Victoria Road, W8 5RD.

VULLIAMY, Edward Sebastian; Senior Correspondent and writer, The Guardian and The Observer, since 1986; *b* 1 Aug. 1954; *s* of late John Sebastian Papendiek Vulliamy and of Shirley Hughes, *qv*; separated; two *d*. *Educ:* University Coll. Sch., London; Univ. di Firenze (Dip. Italian and Renaissance Studies 1973); Hertford Coll., Oxford (MA PPE 1976). Researcher, World in Action, Granada TV, 1979–85; The Guardian: gen. reporter, 1986–89; corresp. in Italy and Balkans, 1990–96; US corresp., Guardian and Observer, 1994–95 and 1997–2003. RTS Award, 1985; Internat. Reporter of Year, British Press Awards, 1992, 1997; Foreign Corresp. of Year, Granada/What the Papers Say Awards, 1992; Amnesty Internat. Award, 1992; James Cameron Meml Award, 1994. *Publications:* Seasons in Hell: understanding Bosnia's war, 1994; (with David Leigh) Sleaze: the corruption of Parliament, 1996; Amexica, 2010; The War is Dead, Long Live the War: Bosnia, the reckoning, 2012; contrib. chapters in books, incl. Crimes of War, ed Gutman and Reiff; contribs to jls incl. Internat. Affairs, Colombian Journalism Rev., Nat. Geographic. *Recreations:* opera, classical music, rock blues, jazz, history of painting, especially Italian Renaissance, Italy, football, politics, current affairs. *Address:* c/o The Guardian, Kings Place, 90 York Way, N1 9AG. *E:* ed.vulliamy@guardian.co.uk. *Club:* Frontline.

VULLIAMY, Shirley, (Mrs J. S. P. Vulliamy); *see* Hughes, S.

VULLO, Stephen; QC 2014; *b* London, 2 July 1967; *s* of Antonino Vullo and Jill Vullo; *m* 2004, Camilla Rosamund Hester Church; two *s* one *d*. *Educ:* St Gregory's High Sch., Kenton; City of London Poly. (LLB Hons Business). Called to the Bar, Middle Temple, 1996; in practice as a barrister, 2 Bedford Row, 2006–. *Recreations:* family, cooking, attempting to grow the perfect tomato in our mountain top house in Sicily. *Address:* 2 Bedford Row, WC1R 4BU. *T:* (020) 7440 8888. *E:* svullo@2bedfordrow.co.uk.

VUNAGI, Most Rev. David; *see* Melanesia, Archbishop of.

VUONG THUA PHONG; Ambassador of Vietnam to Belgium, since 2015; *b* 25 Oct. 1956; *m* Ngo Thi Phi Nga; two *s*. *Educ:* Soviet Union. Dep. Dir, Policy Planning Dept, Min. of Foreign Affairs, Vietnam; Private Sec. to Foreign Minister, 1994–98; Ambassador: to UK, 1998–2003; to Czech Republic, 2007–10; Dep. Dir, Commn for Ext. Affairs, Communist Party Central Cttee, Vietnam. Member: RIIA; London Diplomatic Assoc. *Recreation:* golf. *Address:* Embassy of Vietnam, General Jacqueslaan 1, 1050 Brussels, Belgium. *Club:* London Golf.

VYSE, Prof. Timothy James, PhD; FRCP; FMedSci; George Koukis Professor of Molecular Medicine, King's College London, since 2010; *b* Derby, 27 Jan. 1961; *s* of James and Teresa Vyse; *m* 1990, Varsha Jani; two *s*. *Educ:* Trinity Hall, Cambridge (BA 1982); Guy's Hosp. Med. Sch. (MB BS 1985); Royal Postgrad. Med. Sch., Univ. of London (PhD 1994). MRCP 1989, FRCP 2012. Fulbright Res. Fellow, Nat. Jewish Center for Immunol., Denver, Colo, 1994–98; Wellcome Trust Sen. Clin. Res. Fellow, 1998–2007, Prof. of Rheumatol., 2007–10, Imperial Coll. London. FMedSci 2013. *Address:* Department of Genetics, King's College London, Guy's Hospital, SE1 9RT. *T:* (020) 7188 8431. *E:* tim.vyse@kcl.ac.uk.

VYVYAN, Maj.-Gen. Charles Gerard Courtenay, CB 1998; CBE 1990 (MBE 1974); Gentleman Usher of the Scarlet Rod, Order of the Bath, since 2006; Defence Attaché and Head, British Defence Staff, Washington, 1997–2000; *b* 29 Sept. 1944; *er s* of John Michal Kenneth Vyvyan and Elizabeth Mary Lowder Vyvyan; *m* 1989, Elizabeth Frances (LVO 1998), 3rd *d* of Sir John Paget, 3rd Bt, Haygrass, Taunton. *Educ:* Winchester Coll.; Balliol Coll., Oxford (BA Mod. Hist. 1966; MA 1991); Nat. Defence Coll., Pakistan (MSc, Defence and Strategic Studies). Commnd, Royal Green Jackets (Rifle Bde), 1967; Sultan of Oman's Armed Forces, 1975–76; Staff Coll., 1978; CO 1st Bn RGJ, 1984–86; Col GS Mil. Ops, 1986–87; Comdr 3 Inf. Bde, 1988–90; student, Nat. Defence Coll., Pakistan, 1990–91; DCS, HQ UKLF, 1991–94; COS, HQ UKLF, later Land Command, 1994–97. Col Comdt, 1 RGJ, 1994–2000. Vis. Fellow, Eisenhower Inst., Washington, 2002–06. Gov., Cranleigh Sch., 2000–10. *Recreations:* mountains, gardens, travel, fishing, Alexander the Great. *Clubs:* Boodle's (Chm., 2007–10), Beefsteak.

VYVYAN, Sir (Ralph) Ferrers (Alexander), 13th Bt *cr* 1645, of Trelowarren, Cornwall; DL; *b* 21 Aug. 1960; *s* of Sir John Stanley Vyvyan, 12th Bt and of his 3rd wife, Jonet Noël, *e d* of Lt-Col Alexander Hubert Barclay, DSO, MC; *S* father, 1995, but his name does not appear on the Official Roll of the Baronetage; *m* 1986, Victoria Arabella, *y d* of M. B. Ogle; five *s*. *Educ:* Charterhouse; Sandhurst; Architectural Assoc. High Sheriff 2008, DL 2010, Cornwall. *Heir: s* Joshua Drummond Vyvyan, *b* 10 Oct. 1986. *Address:* Trelowarren, Mawgan, Helston, Cornwall TR12 6AF.

WABOSO, David Gogo, CBE 2014; CEng, FREng; FICE; Director of Capital Programmes, London Underground, since 2010; *b* London, 19 March 1956; *s* of Dr Marcus Feyi Waboso and Mrs Margaret Waboso (later Sheldrick); *m* 2009, Angela Bucknor; one *s* two *d*. *Educ:* Crypt Sch., Gloucester; Coventry Univ. (BSc 1978); Imperial Coll. London (MSc; DIC 1980); Templeton Coll., Oxford (AMP 1995). CEng 1985; FICE 1999; FREng 2009. Grad. engr, Ove Arup and Partners, 1982–84; Design Engr, Pell Frischmann Partners, 1984–86; Sen. Engr, Parkman Consulting Engrg, 1986–89; Nichols Gp Project Manager, DLR, 1990–95; Sen. Supervising Engr, Jubilee Line Extension, 1996–99; Sen. Vice Pres., Bechtel, 2000; Prog. Dir, Eur. Rail Traffic Mgt System, 2001–03; Tech. Dir, Strategic Rail Authy and non-exec. Dir, Rail Safety and Standards Bd, 2003–05; Dir of Engrg, London Underground, 2005–09. FIRSE 2002; FCGI 2010; FAPM 2011. Leader of the Year, Manufrg and Infrastructure, Black British Business Awards, 2014. *Publications:* contribs to tech. press incl. New Civil Engr, Infrastructure Intelligence. *Recreations:* jazz and guitar, football (West Ham), family, gardening, walking. *Address:* (office) Palestra, 197 Blackfriars Road, SE1 8NJ. *T:* (020) 3954 8228. *E:* David.Waboso@tube.tfl.gov.uk. *Clubs:* Old Cryptians; Woodford Wells.

WACE, Emma; *see* Chichester Clark, E.

WADDAMS, Prof. Catherine Mary, PhD; Professor, Norwich Business School, University of East Anglia, since 2000; *b* Lambeth, 12 July 1948; *d* of Herbert Waddams and Margaret Waddams (*née* Burgess); *m* 1st, 1970, F. Christopher Price (marr. diss. 1992); one *s* one *d*; 2nd, 1994, Morten Hviid. *Educ:* Simon Langton Grammar Sch. for Girls, Canterbury; Univ. of Nottingham (BSc Maths and Econs 1969; PhD Econs 1973). Lecturer in Economics: Lanchester Poly., 1972–73; Leicester Poly., 1974; Leicester Univ., 1979–95 (Dean, Social Scis, 1989–94); Prof., Warwick Business Sch. and Dir, Centre for Mgt Under Regulation, 1995–2000; Dir, Centre of Competition and Regulation, subseq. Centre for Competition Policy, 2000–11, UEA. Visiting Fellow: Dept of Applied Econs and Clare Hall, Cambridge, 1993; Univ. of Copenhagen, 1999; Univ. of Calif. Energy Inst., 2003, 2006. Mem., Competition Commn, 2001–09; non-exec. Dir, Ofwat, 2013–. Reader, Dio. Norwich, licensed to St George Colegate, 2014–. *Publications:* Welfare Economics in Theory and Practice, 1977; (ed jtly) Privatisation and Regulation: a review of the issues, 1994; (ed jtly) Utility Privatization and Regulation: a fair deal for consumers?, 2003; articles in acad. jls and policy contribs on privatisation, regulation, introduction of competition, consumer choice and distributional effect of reform, particularly in energy. *Recreations:* choral singing, canoeing, gardening. *Address:* ESRC Centre for Competition Policy, University of East Anglia, Norwich NR4 7TJ. *T:* (01603) 593715, *Fax:* (01603) 591622. *E:* c.waddams@uea.ac.uk.

WADDELL, Bruce; *b* 18 March 1959; *s* of Ken and Christina Ann Waddell; *m* 1994, Cathy Cullis; one *s*. Johnston Newspapers, 1977–87; Sub Ed., then Chief Sub Ed., Scottish Sun, 1987–90; Dep. Ed., Sunday Scot, 1990–91; Mktg and Sales Exec., Murray Internat., 1991–93; Dep. Ed., 1993–98, Ed., 1998–2003, Scottish Sun; Ed., Daily Record, 2003–09; Ed.-in-Chief, Scottish Daily Record and Sunday Mail Ltd, 2009–11; Dir of Media, BIG Partnership, 2012–13. *Recreations:* football, classic cars, cinema, golf.

WADDELL, Rear-Adm. William Angus, CB 1981; OBE 1966; *b* 5 Nov. 1924; *s* of late James Whitefield Waddell and Christina Waddell (*née* Maclean); *m* 1950, Thelma Evelyn Tomlins (*d* 2007); one *s* one *d*. *Educ:* Glasgow Univ. (BSc (Hons) Maths and Nat. Phil.; Cleland Gold Medal). CEng; FIET. Midshipman, Sub Lieut RNVR (Special Branch), HMS Ranee, HMS Collingwood, 1945–47; Instr Lieut, HMS Collingwood, HMS Glasgow, HMS Siskin, HMS Gambia, 1947–59 (RMCS 1956–57); Instr Comdr, HMS Albion, 1959–61; Staff of Dir, Naval Educn Service, 1961–63; Sen. British Naval Officer, Dam Neck, Virginia, 1963–66; Officer i/c RN Polaris Sch., 1966–68; Instr Captain, Staff of SACLANT (Dir, Inf. Systems Gp), 1969–72; Dean, RN Coll., Greenwich, 1973–75; Dir Naval Officer Appointments (Instr), 1975–78; Rear-Adm. 1979; Chief Naval Instructor Officer, 1978–81 and Flag Officer, Admiralty Interview Bd, 1979–81. ADC to HM the Queen, 1976–79. Assoc. Teacher, City Univ., 1973–75; Sec. and Chief Exec., RIPH&H, 1982–90. Hon. FRSPH (Hon. FRIPHH 1990). *Publications:* An Introduction to Servomechanisms (with F. L. Westwater), 1961, repr. 1968. *Address:* c/o National Westminster Bank, 80 Lewisham High Street, SE13 5JJ.

WADDINGTON, family name of **Baron Waddington**.

WADDINGTON, Baron *cr* 1990 (Life Peer), of Read in the County of Lancashire; **David Charles Waddington,** GCVO 1994; PC 1987; DL; QC 1971; Governor and Commander-in-Chief of Bermuda, 1992–97; a Recorder of the Crown Court, 1972–99; *b* 2 Aug. 1929; *o s* of late Charles Waddington and of Mrs Minnie Hughan Waddington; *m* 1958, Gillian Rosemary, *d* of late Alan Green, CBE; three *s* two *d*. *Educ:* Sedbergh; Hertford Coll., Oxford (Hon. Fellow, 1998). President, Oxford Univ. Conservative Assoc., 1950. 2nd Lieut, XII Royal Lancers, 1951–53. Called to Bar, Gray's Inn, 1951, Bencher, 1985. Contested (C): Farnworth Div., 1955; Nelson and Colne Div., 1964; Heywood and Royton Div., 1966; MP (C): Nelson and Colne, 1968–Sept. 1974; Clitheroe, March 1979–1983; Ribble Valley, 1983–90; a Lord Comr, HM Treasury, 1979–81; Parly Under-Sec. of State, Dept of Employment, 1981–83; Minister of State, Home Office, 1983–87; Parly Sec., HM Treasury and Govt Chief Whip, 1987–89; Sec. of State, Home Office, 1989–90; Mem., H of L, 1990–2015; Lord Privy Seal and Leader of H of L, 1990–92. DL Lancs 1991. *Address:* Old Bailiffs, South Cheriton, Templecombe, Somerset BA8 0BH.

See also Hon. J. C. Waddington.

WADDINGTON, Prof. David James; Professor of Chemical Education, University of York, 1978–2000, now Emeritus; *b* 27 May 1932; *s* of late Eric James and Marjorie Edith Waddington; *m* 1957, Isobel Hesketh; two *s* one *d*. *Educ:* Marlborough College; Imperial College, Univ. of London (BSc, ARCS, DIC, PhD). Head of Chemistry Dept, 1959, Head of Science Dept, 1961, Wellington College; York University: Sen. Lectr, 1965; Head Chemistry Dept, 1983–92; Pro-Vice-Chancellor, 1985–91. Hon. Prof., Mendeleev Univ. of Chem. Technol., Moscow, 1998–; Vis. Prof., Inst. für die Pädagogik der Naturwissenschaften, Univ. Kiel, 2000–. President: Educn Div., Royal Soc. of Chem., 1981–83; Inst. of Sci. Technol., 1995–2000; Sec., 1977, Chm., 1981–86, Cttee on Teaching of Chemistry, IUPAC; Sec., 1986–89, Chm., 1990–94, Cttee on Teaching of Science, ICSU. Liveryman, Salters' Co., 2001–; Freedom, City of London, 2001. Nyholm Medal, RSC, 1985; Brasted Award, ACS, 1988. Nat. Order of Scientific Merit (Brazil), 1997; ACS-CEI Award, 2012. *Publications:* Organic Chemistry, 1962, 4th edn 1969; (with H. S. Finlay) Organic Chemistry Through Experiment, 1965, 4th edn 1985; (with R. O. C. Norman) Modern Organic Chemistry, 1972, 4th edn 1987; (with A. Kornhauser and C. N. R. Rao) Chemical Education in the 70s, 1980; (ed) Teaching School Chemistry, 1985; (jtly) The Essential Chemistry Industry, 1985, 5th edn 2011; (ed) Education, Industry and Technology, 1987; (jtly) Introducing Chemistry: the Salters' approach, 1989; Chemistry: the Salters' approach, 1990; (jtly) Salters' Advanced Chemistry, 1994, 2nd edn 2000; (ed) Science for Understanding Tomorrow's World: global change, 1994, 2nd edn 2000; Global Environmental Change Science: education and training, 1995; (with J. N. Lazonby) Partners in Chemical Education, 1996; (jtly) Salters' Higher Chemistry, 1999; Evaluation as a Tool for improving Science Education, 2005; Context Based Learning of Science, 2005; Standards in Science Education, 2007. *Recreation:* gardening. *Address:* Department of Chemistry, University of York, York YO10 5DD.

WADDINGTON, Hon. James Charles; QC 2015; a Recorder, since 2004; *b* Preston, 12 Oct. 1960; *s* of Baron Waddington, *qv*; *m* 1990, Anne Miller (marr. diss. 2008); one *s* one *d*; partner, Anne Mannion. *Educ:* Aysgarth Prep. Sch.; Radley Coll.; Exeter Univ. (LLB). Called to the Bar, Gray's Inn, 1983; in practice as a barrister, specialising in criminal and civil law. Member: SE Circuit; Criminal Bar Assoc. *Recreations:* cricket, theatre, cinema, art, travel. *Address:* 9–12 Bell Yard, WC2A 2JR. *T:* (020) 7400 1800, *Fax:* (020) 7404 1405. *Club:* Travellers.

WADDINGTON, Leslie; Chairman, Waddington Custot Galleries (formerly Waddington Galleries), since 1966; *b* Dublin, 9 Feb. 1934; *s* of late Victor and Zelda Waddington; *m* 1st, 1967, Ferriel Lyle (marr. diss. 1983); two *d*; 2nd, 1985, Clodagh Frances Fanshawe. *Educ:* Portora Royal School; Ecole du Louvre (Diplômé). Formed Waddington Galleries with father, 1957. Chm., Modern Painting Sect., 1994–2004, Pictura Sect., 1996–2000, Maastricht Art Fair. Sen. Fellow, RCA, 1993. Feaga Award, Eur. Fedn of Art Gall. Assocs, 2013. *Recreation:* reading. *Address:* 11 Cork Street, W1S 3LT. *T:* (020) 7851 2200.

WADDINGTON, Susan Andrée; European Programme Director, National Institute of Adult Continuing Education, since 2000; *b* 23 Aug. 1944; *m* 1966, Ivan Waddington; one *s* one *d*. *Educ:* Blyth GS, Norwich; Leicester Univ. (BA; MEd). Assistant Director of Education: Derbys CC, 1988–90; Birmingham CC, 1990–94. Pres., European Assoc. for Educn of Adults, 2008. Mem. (Lab) Leics CC, 1973–91, 2003–07 and 2011–13. MEP (Lab) Leicester, 1994–99. Contested (Lab): Leics NW, 1987; E Midlands Reg., EP, 1999. *Address:* 5 Roundhill Road, Leicester LE5 5RJ. *E:* susan.waddington@ntlworld.com.

WADE, family name of **Baron Wade of Chorlton**.

WADE OF CHORLTON, Baron *cr* 1990 (Life Peer), of Chester in the County of Cheshire; **(William) Oulton Wade,** Kt 1982; farmer and cheese master; company director; consultant; Deputy Chairman, Miton Group plc (formerly Midas Capital, then MAM Funds) plc, since 2008 (Chairman, Midas Capital Partners Ltd, 2002–08); *b* 24 Dec. 1932; *s* of Samuel Norman Wade and Joan Ferris Wade (*née* Wild); *m* 1959 Gillian Margaret Leete, Buxton, Derbys; one *s* one *d*. *Educ:* Birkenhead Sch.; Queen's Univ., Belfast. Jt Treas., Cons. Party, 1982–90; Member: Refreshment Cttee, 2003–09, Sci. and Technol. Cttee, 2003–06 and 2010–, European Cttee G, 2007–10, H of L. Chairman: RisingStars Growth Fund Ltd, 2001–14; RockTron Ltd, 2003–14. Chairman: Cheshire Churches Preservation Trust, 1992–2012; Children's Safety Educn Foundn, 2004–13. Hon. DLaws Liverpool, 2006; Hon. DLit Chester, 2007. JP Cheshire 1967–82. Freeman, City of London, 1980; Liveryman, Farmers' Co., 1980–. *Publications:* contribs to Dairy Industries Internat., Jl of Soc. of Dairy Technol. *Recreations:* politics, reading, shooting, food, travel. *Address:* House of Lords, Westminster, SW1A 0PW. *Clubs:* Chester City (Chester); Portico Library (Manchester).

WADE, His Honour Charles; *see* Wade, His Honour R. C. B.

WADE, Gillian Anne; QC (Scot.) 2013; Sheriff of Tayside Central and Fife at Stirling, since 2015; *b* Glasgow, 26 April 1966; *d* of Kenneth William Eadie and Elizabeth Johnstone Eadie; *m* 1994, Paul Francis Joseph Wade (*d* 2011); partner, John Mauchline. *Educ:* Craigholme Sch.; Univ. of Glasgow (LLB Hons; DipLP). Solicitor: Scotland, 1989–98; England and Wales, 1992–98; Mem., Faculty of Advocates, 1998–; Mem., Mental Health Tribunal for Scotland, 2004–; Advocate Depute, 2008–; Sen. Advocate Depute, 2010–. Hd, Nat. Sexual Crimes Unit, 2011–13. Asst Ed., Tolley's Jl of Media Law, 1987–98. *Recreations:* reading, writing, walking, cooking. *Address:* Durnoch Mill, Crieff, Perthshire PH7 3QN. *T:* 07739 639319. *E:* gillian.a.wade@btinternet.com.

WADE, Ian; QC 2010; Assistant Coroner, East London, Mid-Kent and Medway, since 2014; *b* Chelmsford, 7 Sept. 1954; *s* of George Richard Wade and Alice Wade (*née* Lorentzen); *m* 1981, Paula Fernandes; two *d*. *Educ:* King Edward VI Sch., Norwich; Pembroke Coll., Cambridge (BA 1976). Called to the Bar, Gray's Inn, 1977; in practice as barrister specialising in criminal law; Asst Dep. Coroner, W London, 2012–14. Mem., Standards Cttee, Bar Standards Bd, 2012–. *Recreation:* good books. *Address:* 5 Paper Buildings, Temple, EC4Y 7HB. *T:* (020) 7583 6117. *E:* iw@5pb.co.uk. *Club:* Hurlingham.

WADE, Kathryn Jean, (Mrs H. P. Williams); freelance ballet teacher and adjudicator; Principal, Outreach Programme, Royal Ballet School, 2005–10; *b* 27 Dec. 1945; *d* of George Wade Brown and Sheila (*née* Gilbourne-Stenson); adopted surname Wade, 1965; *m* 1981, Hugh Patrick Williams, FRCS. *Educ:* Royal Ballet Sch., Jun. and Sen. With Royal Ballet Co., 1965–70; Sen. Soloist, London Fest. Ballet, 1970–72; Soloist, Royal Ballet Co., 1970–75; teacher, Royal Ballet Sen. Sch., 1975–88; Ballet Administrator, Jun. and Sen. Royal Ballet Schs, 1988–92; Dir, English Nat. Ballet Sch., 1992–2004. Internat. teacher and adjudicator at internat. ballet and dance comps. Mem., Exec. Cttee, Royal Acad. of Dance (formerly of Dancing), 1990–2005 (Trustee, 2009–). Trustee: Dance Teachers' Benevolent Fund, 1996–; Voices of British Ballet, 2002–; Ashton Trust, 2006–; Dancers' Continuing Develt, 2011–; Dame Margot Fonteyn Scholarship Fund, 2012–. Adeline Genée Gold

Medal, Royal Acad. of Dancing, 1965. *Publications:* (contrib.) The Ballet Goers' Guide, 1981; (tech. advr) My Ballet Book, 1988; contrib. to Dancing Times, Dance Now. *Recreations:* all performing arts, travelling, fly fishing. *E:* kathrynwadewilliams@yahoo.co.uk.

WADE, Laura Joanne; playwright; *b* Bedford, 16 Oct. 1977; *d* of Stuart Wade and Tina Wade (*née* Wingrove); partner, Samuel Alexander Joseph West, *qv*; one *d. Educ:* Univ. of Bristol (BA Hons Drama 1999). *Plays:* Limbo, Sheffield Crucible, 1996; 16 Winters, Bristol Old Vic Basement, 2000; Young Emma, Finborough Th., 2003; Colder Than Here, Soho Th., 2005; Breathing Corpses, Royal Court, 2005; Other Hands, Soho Th., 2006; Posh, Royal Court, 2010, Duke of York's Th., 2012, film adaptation as The Riot Club, 2014; Alice, Sheffield Crucible, 2010; Kreutzer *v* Kreutzer, Sydney Opera Hse and Australian tour, 2010; Tipping the Velvet, Lyric, 2015; *radio plays*: Otherkin, 2007; Coughs and Sneezes, 2009; Hum, 2009. *Publications:* Colder Than Here, 2005; Breathing Corpses, 2005; Other Hands, 2006; Posh, 2010; Alice, 2010; Plays One, 2012. *Recreation:* birdwatching. *Address:* c/o Knight Hall Agency Ltd, Lower Ground Floor, 7 Mallow Street, EC1Y 8RQ. *T:* (020) 3397 2901. *E:* office@knighthallagency.com.

WADE, Martyn John, OBE 2015; National Librarian, 2002–14, and Chief Executive, 2008–14, National Library of Scotland; *b* 24 March 1955; *s* of Albert R. Wade and Nancy Joan Wade; *m* 1978, Anne Patterson. *Educ:* Newcastle Poly. (BA); Univ. of Wales, Aberystwyth (MLib; Hon. Fellow 2010). MCLIP (ALA 1978). Trainee librarian, Northumberland CC, 1976–78; br. librarian, Sunderland MBC, 1978–81; br. librarian and librarian i/c, Sutton LBC, 1981–87; librarian, Northumberland CC, 1987–91; Area Librarian, Leics CC, 1991–93; Area Library Officer, Cambridgeshire CC, 1994–99; Hd, Libraries, Inf. and Learning, Glasgow CC, 1999–2002. Chair, Cttee on Freedom of Access to Inf. and Freedom of Expression, Internat. Fedn of Liby Assocs and Instns, 2013–; Trustee, 2013–, Chair of Council, 2014–, CLIP. Vice Chm., Edinburgh UNESCO City of Literature Trust, 2008. Hon. Prof., Dept of Information Mgt, Robert Gordon Univ., Aberdeen, 2011–. Chair, Govs, Mortification of Innerpeffray, 2014–. FRSA 2006. *Recreations:* motorcycling, reading, the arts, cooking. *Address:* 10 Beechwood, Linlithgow EH49 6SF. *E:* martynwade315@gmail.com. *Club:* Scottish Motorcycle.

WADE, Michael John; Crown Representative, Insurance, Cabinet Office, since 2013; *b* Woking, 22 May 1954; *s* of late Peter Wade and of Lorna Wade (*née* Harris); *m* 1997, Caroline Dashwood; one *s. Educ:* Royal Russell Sch.; N Staffs Coll. C. E. Heath Aviation Syndicate, Lloyd's, 1975; Hartley Cooper, Lloyd's, 1975–80; Founder and CEO, Holman Wade Ltd, Lloyd's Brokers, 1980–93, merged with Horace Clarkson, 1986; Founder and CEO, CLM Insce Fund plc, 1993–2000; Founder and CEO, Rostrum Gp, 2000–05; Founder and Chm., Optex Gp, 2006, merged into Besso, 2011, sold 2012. Member: Lloyd's Task Force, 1991; Council of Lloyd's, 1988–92. Chm., London Fest. Opera, 1991–. Made recording of Saint-Saëns Organ Symphony, as conductor, 2014. *Publications:* Lloyd's: a route forward, 1992. *Recreations:* music, architecture, economics, Trafalgar Park. *Address:* 87 Vincent Square, SW1P 2PQ. *T:* (020) 7821 0675. *E:* michaeljwade@hotmail.com. *Club:* Brooks's.

WADE, Rebekah; *see* Brooks, R.

WADE, Richard, PhD; CEng; FIET; CPhys, FInstP; Consultant, Richard Wade Associates Ltd, since 2013; *b* North Ferriby, 15 May 1954; *s* of Alan Wade and Kathleen Wade; *m* 1976, Elaine Rolfe; two *s. Educ:* Univ. of Essex (BSc Physics); Imperial Coll. London (PhD Physics 1979). CEng 1993; FIET 1997; FInstP 2010. Res. Scientist, Royal Observatory, Edinburgh, 1980–89; Associate Dir, Jt Astronomy Centre, Hawaii, 1989–92; Hd, Engrg, Rutherford Appleton Lab., 1992–2001; Dir, Progs, PPARC, 2001–07; Chief Operating Officer and Dep. Chief Exec., STFC, 2007–12. Pres., Council, Eur. Southern Observatory, 2005–08; Vice Pres., Council, CERN, 2011–12. Vis. Prof. in Physics, Univ. of Oxford, 2007–. *Publications:* over 50 papers in learned jls. *Recreations:* ski-ing, walking, keeping fit, running (completed London Marathon 2013). *Address:* 44 Henleys Lane, Drayton, Abingdon OX14 4HU. *T:* 07788 971048. *E:* richard.wade6@btinternet.com.

WADE, His Honour (Richard) Charles (Bathurst); a Circuit Judge, 2000–11; a Designated Family Judge, Swindon, 2006–11; *b* 16 Dec. 1946; *s* of David Ison Wade and Margaret Elizabeth Lucy Wade (*née* Wainwright); *m* 1972, Juliet Ann Jehring; one *s* three *d. Educ:* Malvern Coll. Admitted Solicitor, 1972; in private practice, 1972–89; County Court Registrar, 1989–91; Dist Judge, 1991–2000. Trustee: Gloucester Acad. of Music and Performing Arts, 1992–99; Harnhill Centre of Christian Healing, 2001–05; Community Foster Care and Community Family Care, 2014–. Mem. Council, Cheltenham and Gloucester Coll. of Higher Educn, 1999–2000. Pres., Foundn Fellows, Univ. of Gloucestershire, 2002–08, Hon. Vice-Pres., 2008–. *Recreations:* gardening, music, walking.

WADE, Richard Lawrence; writer, photographer, and campaigner for the modernisation of English orthography; *b* 5 July 1938; *s* of Wilfred George Wade and Frances Mary (*née* Smith); *m* 1st, 1962, Angela Lee Mikhelson (marr. diss. 1995); two *d*; 2nd, 1996, Angela Claire Mills (*née* Thomson). *Educ:* Bedford Sch.; New Coll., Oxford (MA Oriental Studies (Arabic and Persian); Pres., OU Gymnastics Club (Half Blue)). Management Trainee, Unilever Ltd, 1961–63; BBC TV, 1963–75: dir and producer, 1963–70; Editor, Tomorrow's World, 1970–75; Chief Asst, Radio 4 and Hd of Radio 4, 1975–83; Chief Asst to Man. Dir, BBC Radio, 1983–86; Dir, Foster Associates Ltd, 1986; Marketing Dir, BITC, 1986–88; Man. Dir, Business in the Cities, 1988–89; Dir Gen., Advertising Assoc., 1990–93; Fellow and Dir of Develt, St Edmund Hall, Oxford, 1993–96. Founder, Freespeling.com, 2001. Chm., Direct Marketing Assoc. (UK) Ltd, 1991–92. Mem., Calderdale Partnership, Halifax, 1987–89. Mem., BAFTA, 1968–. Freeman, City of London, 1988. *Recreations:* conversation, photography. *Address:* 49 Park Town, Oxford OX2 6SL. *T:* (01865) 511984. *Club:* Oxford and Cambridge.

WADE, (Sarah) Virginia, OBE 1986 (MBE 1969); tennis player; commentator: BBC Television, since 1980; British Eurosport; *b* 10 July 1945; *d* of late Eustace Holland Wade and of Joan Barbara Wade. *Educ:* Sussex Univ. (BSc). Won tennis championships: US Open, 1968; Italian, 1971; Australian, 1972; Wimbledon, 1977; played for GB in Wightman Cup and Federation Cup 20 times (record); Captain, GB team. Mem. Cttee, All England Lawn Tennis Club, 1983–91. Hon. LLD Sussex, 1985. Elected into Internat. Tennis Hall of Fame, 1989. *Publications:* Courting Triumph, 1978; Ladies of the Court, 1984. *Address:* c/o Once Upon A Time, Global House, 30 Great Pulteney Street, W1F 9NN.

WADE-GERY, Laura; Executive Director of multichannel and e-commerce, since 2011, and of UK Retail, since 2014, Marks and Spencer; *b* London, 26 Jan. 1965; *d* of Sir Robert Lucian Wade-Gery, KCMG, KCVO and of Sarah Wade-Gery (*née* Marris); *m* 2005, Simon Roberts. *Educ:* Magdalen Coll., Oxford (BA Modern Hist.); INSEAD, Fontainebleau (MBA). Kleinwort Benson Ltd, 1987–91; Gemini Consulting, 1993–97; Tesco: Targeted Mktg Dir, 1997–2000; Strategy Dir, 2000–03; CEO, Tesco.com and Tesco Direct, 2003–11. Non-exec. Dir, Trinity Mirror plc, 2006–12. Mem. Council, Aldeburgh Music; Mem., Bd of Trustees, Royal Opera House, 2012–. *Recreations:* gardening, running, opera. *Address:* Marks and Spencer plc, Waterside House, 35 North Wharf Road, W2 1NW.

WADHAM, John; solicitor and independent human rights consultant, since 2014; *b* 24 Jan. 1952; *s* of late Ernest George Wadham and Unity Winifred Wadham (*née* Errington). *Educ:* London School of Economics (BSc 1974); Surrey Univ. (CQSW 1978; MSc 1979). Legal Advr, Wandsworth Law Centres, 1978–86; articled clerk, Birnberg & Co., Solicitors, 1987–90; admitted Solicitor, 1989; Legal Officer, 1990–92, Dir of Law, 1992–95, Dir, 1995–2003, NCCL, later Liberty; Dep. Chm., Ind. Police Complaints Commn, 2003–07; Gen. Counsel (formerly Gp Dir, Legal), Equality and Human Rights Commn, 2007–13; Exec. Dir, INTERIGHTS (Centre for Legal Protection of Human Rights), 2013–15. Mem., Human Rights Act Task Force, 1999–2001; Chairman: Forum for Preventing Deaths in Custody, 2006–09; UK Human Rights Coalition, 2001–03; Internat. Network for Ind. Oversight of Policing, 2006–07. Hon. Fellow of Law, Univ. of Kent at Canterbury, 1992–2003; Hon. Lectr in Law, Univ. of Leicester, 2000–; Vis. Lectr in Law, Univ. of Auckland, 2012–; Visiting Fellow: Univ. of Bristol, 2014–; KCL. Series Editor, Blackstone's Human Rights Act series, 2000–04. *Publications:* (contrib.) The Penguin Guide to the Law, 3rd edn, 1992, 4th edn, 2001; (ed) Your Rights: the Liberty guide, 5th edn 1994 to 7th edn 2000; Blackstone's Guide to the Human Rights Act 1998, 1999, 7th edn 2015; Blackstone's Guide to the Freedom of Information Act 2000, 2001, 5th edn 2013; Blackstone's Guide to the Identity Cards Act 2006, 2006; Blackstone's Guide to the Equality Act 2010, 2010, 2nd edn 2012. *Recreation:* flying (private pilot). *Address:* 45 Cambridge Road, Stansted, Essex CM24 8BX.

WADHAMS, Prof. Peter, ScD; FRGS; Professor of Ocean Physics, Department of Applied Mathematics and Theoretical Physics, Cambridge University, since 2003 (Scott Polar Research Institute, 2001–02); Fellow, Clare Hall, Cambridge, since 2013; Professeur Associé Recherche, Université Pierre et Marie Curie, Paris, since 2007; *b* 14 May 1948; *s* of late Frank Cecil Wadhams and Winifred Grace Wadhams (*née* Smith); *m* 1980, Maria Pia Casarini. *Educ:* Palmer's Sch., Grays, Essex; Churchill Coll., Cambridge (BA Phys. 1969; MA 1972; ScD 1994); graduate res., Scott Polar Res. Inst. (PhD 1974). Res. Scientist, Bedford Inst. of Oceanography, Dartmouth, Canada, 1969–70 (asst to Sen. Scientist on Hudson '70 expedn, first circumnavigation of Americas); Fellow, NRC Canada, 1974–75 (Inst. Ocean Scis, Victoria, BC); Cambridge University: Scott Polar Research Institute, 1976–2002: leader, Sea Ice Gp, 1976; Asst Dir of Res., 1981; Dep. Dir, 1983–87; Dir, 1987–92; Sen. Res. Fellow, Churchill Coll., 1983–93; Reader in Polar Studies, 1992–2001. Leader, 43 field ops in Arctic, 5 in Antarctic; UK Deleg., Arctic Ocean Scis Bd, 1984–; Member: IAPSO Commn on Sea Ice, 1987– (Pres., 1999–); SCAR Gp of specialists in Antarctic Sea Ice, 1989–; IASC Wkg Gp on Global Change, 1992–; Co-ordinator, Internat. Prog. for Antarctic Buoys, World Climate Res. Prog., 1999–; Member: Scientific Cttee, EEA, Copenhagen, 2004–12; Scientific Commn for the Holy Shroud, Dio. of Turin, 2009–. Vis. Prof., Naval Postgrad. Sch., Monterey, 1980–81; Green Schol. Scripps Instn, 1987–88; Walker-Ames Vis. Prof., Univ. of Washington, WA, 1988; Visiting Professor: Nat. Inst. of Polar Res., Tokyo, 1995, 1996–97; Marine Sci. Inst., Università Politecnico delle Marche, Ancona, Italy, 2013–. Fellow, Scottish Assoc. of Marine Science, 2003–06; For. Mem., Finnish Acad. of Sci. and Letters, 2006. W. S. Bruce Prize, RSE 1977; Polar Medal, 1987; Italgas Prize for Envmtl Scis, 1990. *Publications:* (contrib.) The Nordic Seas, 1986; (contrib.) The Geophysics of Sea Ice, 1986; (ed) Ice Technology for Polar Operations, 1990; (contrib.) Microwave Remote Sensing of Sea Ice, 1992; (ed) Advances in Ice Technology, 1992; Marine, Offshore and Ice Technology, 1994; (ed) The Arctic and Environmental Change, 1996; Ice in the Ocean, 2000; Arctic Sea Ice Thickness: past, present and future, 2007; The Great Ocean of Truth, 2009; numerous sci. papers on glaciology and polar oceanography. *Recreations:* painting, music, sailing. *Address:* Centre for Mathematical Sciences, Wilberforce Road, Cambridge CB3 0WA.

WADHWANI, Sushil Baldev, CBE 2002; PhD; Chief Executive Officer, Wadhwani Asset Management LLP, since 2002; Partner, Caxton Associates, since 2012; *b* 7 Dec. 1959; *s* of Baldev and Meena Wadhwani; *m* 1st, 1991, Anjali Mirgh (marr. diss. 1994); 2nd, 1996, Renu Sakhrani; one *s* one *d. Educ:* London Sch. of Economics (BSc Econs; MSc Econs 1982; PhD 1986). Lectr, 1984–91, Reader, 1991–92, in Economics, LSE; Dir of Equity Strategy, Goldman Sachs Internat. Ltd, 1991–95; Dir of Res. and Partner, Tudor Gp, 1995–99; Mem., Monetary Policy Cttee, Bank of England, 1999–2002. Visiting Professor: Sir John Cass Business Sch., City of London (formerly City Univ. Business Sch.), 2000–; LSE, 2000–. Mem. Council, NIESR, 2000–. Asst Ed., Economic Policy, 1987–89; Mem. Editl Bd, New Economy, 1996–. *Publications:* articles in academic jls. *Address:* (office) 3rd Floor, 40 Berkeley Square, W1J 5AL. *T:* (020) 7663 3400.

WADIA, Jim, FCA; Chief Operating Officer, Linklaters, 2001–04; *b* 12 April 1948; *m* 1972, Joelle Garnier; one *s* one *d. Educ:* Le Rosey, Rolle, Switzerland; Inns of Court Sch. of Law. Called to the Bar, Inner Temple, 1969. Arthur Andersen: Partner, 1982–2000; Hd, London Tax, 1989–93; Man. Partner, UK, 1993–97; Worldwide Man. Partner, 1997–2000. FRSA 1993. *Recreations:* tennis, theatre. *Address:* 28 Eldon Road, W8 5PT. *T:* (020) 7937 7045.

WADKINS, Lanny; golfer; *b* 5 Dec. 1949; *s* of Jerry Lanston Wadkins and Frances Ann Wadkins (*née* Burnett); *m* 1971, Rachel Irene Strong (marr. diss.); one *d*; *m* 1978, Penelope Elizabeth Atwood; two *s. Educ:* Wake Forest Univ., USA. US Amateur Champion, 1970; tournament wins include: US World Series and US PGA, 1977; Tournament Players' Champion, 1979, 1982, 1983; Hawaiian Open, 1988, 1991; mem., US Ryder Cup Team, 1977, Captain, 1995. *Address:* c/o Professional Golfers' Association America/Senior Tour, 100 Avenue of the Champions, PO Box 109601, Palm Beach Gardens, FL 33410–9601, USA.

WADLEY, Veronica Judith Colleton; Chair, London Regional Council, and Member of Council, Arts Council England, since 2010; Senior Advisor to Mayor of London (Team London, Volunteering and Charities), since 2012; *b* 28 Feb. 1952; *d* of Neville John Wadley and late Anne Colleton Wadley (*née* Bowring); *m* 1985, Thomas Michael Bower, *qv*; one *s* one *d. Educ:* Francis Holland Sch., London; Benenden Sch., Kent. Condé Nast Pubns, 1971–74; Telegraph Mag., 1978–81; Mail on Sunday, 1982–86; Daily Telegraph: Features Ed., 1986–89; Asst Ed., 1989–94; Dep. Ed., 1994–95; Daily Mail: Associate Ed., 1995–98; Dep. Ed., 1998–2002; Ed., Evening Standard, 2002–09. Ind. Dir, Times Newspapers Hldgs, 2011–; non-exec. Dir, Berkeley Gp, 2012–. Member: Bd, Northern Ballet, 2009–14; Adv. Council, Arts & Business, 2009–11; GLA Music Educn Adv. Council, 2009–; Bd, Mayor of London's Fund for Young Musicians, 2011– (Chair, 2014); Dir, Yehudi Menuhin Sch., 2012–. Chair, London Music Awards, 2014–. FRSA. *Recreations:* visiting London's theatres, museums and concert halls, running, swimming and ski-ing, cooking for family and friends. *Address:* c/o City Hall, The Queen's Walk, SE1 2AA.

WADSWORTH, Antony Ronald, CBE 2011; Chairman, British Phonographic Industry, since 2007; *b* Bolton, Lancs, 21 Oct. 1956; *s* of Ronald and Margaret Wadsworth; *m* 1987, Susan Elizabeth Thornley; one *s* one *d. Educ:* Bolton Sch.; Univ. of Newcastle-upon-Tyne (BA Econs). Musician, 1978–79; Production Manager: Warwick Records, 1979–80; Transatlantic Records, then Logo Records, 1980–81; RCA Records, 1981–82; Production Manager, 1982–84, Gen. Manager, Strategic Mktg, 1984–87, EMI Records UK; Mktg Dir, 1987–92, Man. Dir, 1992–98, Parlophone Records; Chm. and CEO, EMI Music UK, 1998–2008. Vis. Prof., Univ. of Newcastle upon Tyne, 2007–. Chm., Brit Awards Ltd, 2007–. Chm., Julie's Bicycle, 2009–. Hon. DMus Gloucestershire, 2009. *Recreations:* music, theatre, art, walking, reading. *Address:* British Phonographic Industry, Riverside Building, County Hall, Westminster Bridge Road, SE1 7JA. *T:* (020) 7803 1300. *E:* tony.wadsworth@bpi.co.uk. *Club:* Soho House.

WADSWORTH, Brian; transport and public affairs consultant, since 2008; *b* 18 Jan. 1952; *s* of George David Brian Wadsworth and Betty (*née* Metcalfe); *m* 1987, Anne Jacqueline Beuselinck (OBE 2014). *Educ:* Univ. of British Columbia (BA Hons Eng. Lit. 1973). FILog 1998; FCILT 1999; FRIN 2010. Entered Department of Transport, 1974; Sec., Review of Main Line Rly Electrification, 1978–79; Sec. to Chief Exec., LB of Hounslow, 1981; Principal: Transport Policy Rev. Unit, 1981–83; London Transport Finance, 1984; Pvte Sec.

to Minister of State, 1985; Finance Transport Industries (BA, BAA, NBC privatisations), 1986–89; Sec. to BA plc, 1989–91; Asst Sec., Rlys Policy (BR privatisation), 1991–95; Sec. to British Oxygen plc, 1995; Under Sec., Dir of Finance, 1995–97; Dir, Freight Distribn and Logistics, DETR, 1997–99; Dir, Logistics and Maritime Transport, DETR, subseq. DTLR, then DfT, 1999–2007; Dir, Strategic Roads, Planning and Nat. Networks, DfT, 2007–08. Chm. Admin. Bd, European Maritime Safety Agency, 2003–09. Dir, Road Ahead Gp, 2011–. Freeman, City of London, 1997; Liveryman: Co. of Carmen, 1997– (Master, 2009–10); Co. of Plumbers, 2013–. *Publications:* Best Methods of Railway Restructuring and Privatisation, 1995. *Recreations:* travel, sailing, music. *Address:* 211 Ashley Gardens, Emery Hill Street, SW1P 1PA. *E:* wadsworth.brian@btinternet.com. *Clubs:* United Wards, Castle Baynard Ward; Phyllis Court (Henley).

WADSWORTH, His Honour James Patrick; QC 1981; a Circuit Judge, 2000–10; *b* 7 Sept. 1940; *s* of Francis Thomas Bernard Wadsworth, Newcastle, and Geraldine Rosa (*née* Brannan); *m* 1963, Judith Stuart Morrison, *e d* of Morrison Scott, Newport-on-Tay; one *s* one *d*. *Educ:* Stonyhurst; University Coll., Oxford (MA). Called to the Bar, Inner Temple, 1963, Bencher, 1988; a Recorder, 1980–2000. Member: Mental Health Rev. Tribunal, 1995–2012; Parole Bd, 2006–12. Member: Bar Council, 1992–95; Bar Professional Standards Cttee, 1993–95. *Recreations:* eating and idling. *Address:* 9½ Compton Avenue, N1 2XD.

WADSWORTH, Prof. Michael Edwin John, PhD; FFPH, FAcSS; Director, Medical Research Council National Survey of Health and Development, 1985–2006, now Hon. Senior Scientist, Lifelong Health and Ageing Unit, and Professor of Social and Health Life Course Research, Department of Epidemiology and Public Health Medicine, 2003–06, now Emeritus, Royal Free and University College Medical School, University College London (formerly University College London Medical School); *b* 20 Jan. 1942; *s* of Cecil and Amelia Wadsworth; *m* 1st, 1966, Jane Arnott (marr. diss. 1991); one *s* one *d*; 2nd, 2001, Kit Leighton-Kelly; one *d*. *Educ:* Leeds Univ. (BA, MPhil); London Sch. of Econs (PhD 1976). FFPH 2006 (Hon. MFPHM 1993); FAcSS 2014. Research Asst, Dept of Medicine, Guy's Hosp. Med. Sch., 1963–65; Res. Fellow, Dept of Gen. Practice, Univ. of Edinburgh Med. Sch., 1965–68; Res. Scientist, MRC Nat. Survey Health and Develt, 1968–2007. Vis. Prof., Royal Free and UC Med. Sch., UCL, 1992–2003. *Publications:* (jtly) Health and Sickness, 1971; Roots of Delinquency, 1976; (ed with D. Robinson) Studies in Everyday Medical Life, 1976; (ed with U. Gerhardt) Stress and Stigma, 1985; The Imprint of Time, 1991; (ed with M. G. Marmot) Fetal and Early Childhood Development, 1997; (ed jtly) Changing Britain, Changing Lives, 2003; (ed jtly) Epidemiological Methods in Life Course Research, 2007; (ed with J. Bynner) A Companion to Life Course Studies, 2011; numerous articles in learned jls in medicine and social scis. *Recreations:* music, living. *Address:* 12C Kingsdown Parade, Bristol BS6 5UD. *T:* (0117) 924 4906.

WADVANI, Sanjay Mark, OBE 2007; HM Diplomatic Service; Ambassador to Turkmenistan, since 2013; *b* Calcutta, 6 Dec. 1966; *s* of late Moti Shamdas Wadvani and of Jeanne Wadvani; *m* 2011, Rochelle Irene Selwyn. *Educ:* Taunton Sch.; Poly. of Central London. Entered FCO, 1987; Registry Officer: Hong Kong Dept, FCO, 1987–88; Beijing, 1989–91; Clearance Officer, then Mgt Officer, later Third Sec., Damascus, 1991–94; Resource Mgt Officer, Africa and Commonwealth Comd, FCO, 1995–98; Second Sec. (Commercial), Santiago, 1998–2002; Dep. Consul-Gen. and Hd, Trade and Investment, Guangzhou, 2002–05; Hd, China (Ext.) policy team, Far Eastern Dept, FCO, 2006–09; Dep. High Comr, Kolkata, 2009–13. *Recreations:* sport, theatre, reading, travel. *Address:* c/o Foreign and Commonwealth Office, King Charles Street, SW1A 2AH; British Embassy, Ashgabat, Turkmenistan. *T:* 12363462, *Fax:* 12363465. *E:* sanjay.wadvani@fco.gov.uk.

WAENA, Sir (Rahumaea) Nathaniel, GCMG 2005; CSI 2003; Governor General, Solomon Islands, 2004–09; *b* 1 Nov. 1945; *s* of Joseph Talo and Matilda Tahalata; *m* 1972, Alice Ole; three *s* three *d*. *Educ:* Alangaula, Pawa and Lae Tech. Trng Inst. Provincial Sec., 1978–82; Chief Admin. Officer, 1982–84; Perm. Sec., 1984–87. MP Solomon Is, 1987–2004; Minister: Provincial Govt and Rural Develt, 1989–90, 2000–01; Health and Medical Services, 1993–94; Nat. Unity, Reconciliation and Peace, 2001–04. Vice-Pres., Honiara Town Council, 1984–86. Chm. Council, Solomon Is Nat. Univ. (formerly Solomon Is Coll. of Higher Educn), 2011–. KStJ 2005. *Recreations:* gardening, reading, watching sports competitions. *Address:* c/o Government House, Honiara, Solomon Islands. *T:* 21777, *Fax:* 22533.

WAGERMAN, Josephine Miriam, OBE 1992; President, Board of Deputies of British Jews, 2000–03 (Senior Vice-President, 1997–2000); *b* 17 Sept. 1933; *d* of Emanuel and Jane Barbanel; *m* 1956, Peter Henry Wagerman; one *s* one *d*. *Educ:* John Howard Sch., London; Birkbeck Coll., London Univ. (BA Hons 1955); Inst. of Educn, London Univ. (PGCE 1956; Acad. Dipl. 1959; MA (Ed) 1970). Teacher, Battersea, Highgate, Hackney and Singapore, 1956–73; Jews' Free School: Head of Lower Sch., 1973–76; Dep. Head, 1976–85; Headteacher, 1985–93; Chief Exec., Lennox Lewis Coll., 1994–96. Ind. Assessor, NHS non-exec. Appts, 1996–. Former Pres., London Br., AMMA; former Member: Teachers' Pay and Conditions of Service Adv. Cttee, ILEA; London Standing Cttee Adv. Cttee on Religious Educn, ILEA; Council, Selly Oak Coll. Centre for Jewish-Christian Relns; Member: Acad. Panel, Stuart Young Awards, 1991–; Inner Cities Religious Council, DoE, 1994–2006; Adv. Bd, and Partnership 2000 Policy Cttee, United Jewish Israel Appeal, 1995–2013 (Chm., Legacy Div., 2009–13). Pres., European Jewish Congress, 2000–02. Trustee and Gov., Central Foundn Schs, London, 1995–2002. *Recreations:* gardening, cooking, entertaining friends, travel, Art Nouveau silver, Victorian painting. *Address:* 38 Crespigny Road, NW4 3DX.

WAGGOTT, Shuna Taylor; *see* Lindsay, S. T.

WAGNER, Erica Augusta; writer; Literary Editor, The Times, 1996–2013; *b* NYC, 24 Sept. 1967; *d* of Arthur Malcolm Wagner and Ellen Franklin Wagner; *m* 1993, Francis Jonathan Gilbert; one *s*. *Educ:* Brearley Sch., NYC; St Paul's Girls' Sch., London; Corpus Christi Coll., Cambridge (BA Hons 1989); UEA (MA Creative Writing 1991). Freelance editor/ researcher/journalist, 1992–95; The Times: Asst to Literary Editor, 1995; Dep. Literary Editor, 1996. A Judge, Man Booker Prize, 2002 and 2014. *Publications:* Gravity: stories, 1997; Ariel's Gift: Ted Hughes, Sylvia Plath and the story of Birthday Letters, 2000; Seizure, 2007. *Recreations:* bridges, cooking, fencing. *Address:* c/o Antony Harwood Ltd, 103 Walton Street, Oxford OX2 6EB. *T:* (01865) 559615.

WAGNER, Dame Gillian (Mary Millicent), (Lady Wagner), DBE 1994 (OBE 1977); Chairman: Carnegie UK Trust, 1995–2000 (Trustee, 1980–2002); Residential Forum, since 1994; *b* 25 Oct. 1927; *e d* of late Major Henry Archibald Roger Graham, and of Hon. Margaret Beatrix, *d* of 1st Baron Roborough; *m* 1953, Sir Anthony Wagner, KCB, KCVO; two *s* one *d*. *Educ:* Cheltenham Ladies' Coll.; Geneva Univ. (Licence ès Sciences Morales); London Sch. of Economics (Dip. Social Admin). PhD London 1977. Mem. Council, Barnardo's, 1969–97 (Chm., Exec./Finance Cttee, 1973–78; Chm. Council, 1978–84); Chairman: Nat. Centre for Volunteering (formerly Volunteer Centre), 1984–89 (Pres., 1990–2002); Review of Residential Care, 1986–88; Ct of Govs, Thomas Coram Foundn for Children, 1990–95; The Leche Trust, 1992–97; Chair, Community Care Inquiry for people with learning difficulties, Mental Health Foundn, 1995–96; President: Skill: Nat. Bureau for Students with Disabilities, 1978–91; IAPS, 1985–90; Abbeyfield UK, 2003–09; Patron, Abbeyfield Soc., 2010– (President, 1995–2002); Trustee, Princess Royal Trust for Carers, 1992–2002. Mem. Exec. Cttee, Georgian Gp, 1970–78. Chm. of Governors, Felixstowe Coll., 1980–87; Governor: Nat. Inst. for Social Work, 1988–96; LSE, 1991–96. FRSA 1995. Hon. DSc Bristol, 1989; Hon. LLD Liverpool, 1990. *Publications:* Barnardo, 1979; Children of the Empire, 1982; The Chocolate Conscience, 1987; Thomas Coram, Gent., 2004; various articles on residential care. *Recreations:* travelling, swimming. *Address:* Flat 31, 55 Ebury Street, SW1W 0PA. *T:* (020) 7730 0040; 46 Lee Road, Aldeburgh, Suffolk IP15 5HG. *T:* (01728) 454550. *E:* wagnerg934@aol.com. *Club:* Athenæum.

WAGNER, Prof. Leslie, CBE 2000; MA(Econ); Vice-Chancellor (formerly Principal and Chief Executive), and Professor, Leeds Metropolitan University, 1994–2003; *b* 21 Feb. 1943; *s* of Herman and Toby Wagner; *m* 1967, Jennifer Jean Fineberg; one *s* one *d*. *Educ:* Salford Grammar Sch.; Manchester Univ. (MA (Econ)). Economic Asst and Economic Advr, DEA, 1966–69; Economic Advr, Min. of Technology, 1969–70; Lectr in Econs, Open Univ., 1970–76; Hd of Social Sciences, 1976–82, Prof., 1980, Polytechnic of Central London; Asst Sec. (Academic), Nat. Adv. Body for Local Authy Higher Educn, 1982–85; Dep. Sec., Nat. Adv. Body for Public Sector Higher Educn, 1985–87; Dir, Poly. of N London, 1987–92, then Vice-Chancellor and Chief Exec., Univ. of N London, 1992–93. Member: Bd, Open Learning Foundn, 1990–96 (Chm., 1990–93); Bd, HEQC, 1992–97; Council for Industry and Higher Educn, 1992–2003; Leeds TEC, 1997–2001; DFEE Skills Task Gp, 1998–2000. Chairman: SRHE, 1994–96; Higher Educn for Capability, 1994–98; Yorks and Humberside Univs Assoc., 1996–99; UUK Wider Participation and Lifelong Learning Gp, 1998–2003; Leeds Common Purpose Adv. Gp, 2000–03; Univ. Vocational Awards Council, 2001–03; Higher Educn Acad., 2003–07; Foundn Degree Task Force, 2003–04; Educn Leeds, 2004–07. Councillor (Lab) London Bor. of Harrow, 1971–78, Chm., Educn Cttee, 1972–74. Contested (Lab) Harrow W, Feb. 1974. Dir, Leeds Business Services Ltd, 2001–03; Mem., Leeds Cares Leadership Gp, 2000–01. Vice-Pres., Utd Synagogue, 1992–93; Chairman: Jewish Community Allocations Bd, 1994–96; Commn on the Future of Jewish Schs, 2007–08; Vice-Chm., Inst. for Jewish Global Affairs, Jerusalem, 2010–; Mem. Bd, Jewish Chronicle Trust, 1999–2008. Trustee, Chief Rabbinate Trust, 2003–11. Chancellor, Univ. of Derby, 2003–08; Mem. Council, Open Univ., 2005–08. Fellow, Jerusalem Centre for Public Affairs, 2011–. Hon. Dr of Univ. Middlesex, 2003; DUniv: Leeds Metropolitan, 2003; Open, 2006; Derby, 2008; Hon. DCL Huddersfield, 2003. *Publications:* (ed) Readings in Applied Microeconomics, 1973, 2nd edn 1981; (ed) Agenda for Institutional Change in Higher Education, 1982; The Economics of Educational Media, 1982; (jtly) Choosing to Learn: a study of mature students, 1987. *E:* vcwagner@hotmail.com.

WAGONER, G. Richard; Chief Executive Officer, 2000–09, and Chairman, 2003–09, General Motors Corporation; *b* Wilmington, Delaware, 9 Feb. 1953. *Educ:* Duke Univ. (BS 1975); Harvard Univ. (MBA 1977). General Motors Corporation: analyst in treasurer's office, Manager, Latin American financing, Dir, Canadian and overseas borrowing, then Dir, capital analysis and investment, NY, 1977–81; Treas., 1981–84, Exec. Dir of Finance, 1984–87, São Paulo, Brazil; Vice-Pres. and Financial Manager, 1987–88, Gp Dir of strategic business planning, 1988–89, Canada; Vice-Pres. of Finance, Zurich, 1989–91; Pres. and Man. Dir, Brazil, 1991–93; Chief Financial Officer, 1992–94, and Head of Worldwide Purchasing Gp, 1993–94; Exec. Vice-Pres. and Pres. of N American ops, 1994–98; Chief Operating Officer, 1998–2000; Pres., 1998–2003; Mem., Bd of Dirs, 1998–2009; Dir, Graham Hldgs (formerly The Washington Post) Co., 2010–.

WAGSTAFF, Ven. Christopher John Harold; Archdeacon of Gloucester, 1982–2000, now Emeritus; *b* 25 June 1936; *s* of Harold Maurice Wagstaff and Kathleen Mary Wagstaff (*née* Bean); *m* 1964, Margaret Louise (*née* Macdonald); two *s* one *d*. *Educ:* Bishop's Stortford College, Herts; Essex Inst. of Agriculture, Chelmsford (Dipl. in Horticulture 1959); St David's Coll., Lampeter (BA 1962, Dipl. in Theol. 1963). Deacon 1963, priest 1964; Curate, All Saints, Queensbury, 1963–68; Vicar, St Michael's, Tokyngton, Wembley, 1968–73; Vicar of Coleford with Staunton, 1973–83; RD, South Forest, 1975–82. Diocese of Gloucester: Chairman: House of Clergy, 1983–95; Bd of Social Responsibility, 1983–96; Diocesan Trust, 1983–2000; Diocesan Assoc. for the Deaf, 1989–94; DAC, 1988–2000; Adv. Council for Ministry, 1996–2000. Mem., General Synod, 1988–98. Hon. Canon, St Andrew's Cathedral, Njombe, Tanzania, 1993–. Freeman, City of London; Liveryman, Co. of Armourers and Brasiers (Master, 2000–01). *Recreations:* gardening, entertaining, travel. *Address:* Karibuni, 1 Collafield, Littledean, Glos GL14 3LG. *T:* (01594) 825282.

WAGSTAFF, David St John Rivers; a Recorder of the Crown Court, 1974–94; barrister, retired; *b* 22 June 1930; *s* of late Prof. John Edward Pretty Wagstaff and Dorothy Margaret (*née* McRobie); *m* 1970, Dorothy Elizabeth Starkie; two *d*. *Educ:* Winchester Coll. (Schol.); Trinity Coll., Cambridge (Schol., MA, LLB). Called to Bar, Lincoln's Inn, 1954; practised on N Eastern Circuit. *Publications:* Man's Relationship with God, or Spiritual Adventure, 1996. *Recreations:* mountaineering, fencing. *Address:* 8 Breary Lane East, Bramhope, Leeds LS16 9BJ. *Clubs:* Alpine; Fell and Rock Climbing (Lake District).

WAGSTAFF, (Edward) Malise (Wynter); HM Diplomatic Service, retired; psychotherapist; *b* 27 June 1930; *s* of late Col Henry Wynter Wagstaff, CSI, MC, and Jean Mathieson, MB, BS; *m* 1st, 1957, Eva Margot (marr. diss. 1995), *d* of Erik Hedelius; one *s* two *d*; 2nd, 1995, Vivien Rosemary Manton, *d* of Winston and Marjorie Farrar. *Educ:* Wellington Coll.; RMA Sandhurst; Pembroke Coll., Cambridge (MA; Mech Scis Tripos); Staff Coll., Camberley; psc. Commissioned RE, 1949; served in UK, Germany and Gibraltar, 1950–62; seconded to Federal Regular Army, Fedn of S Arabia, 1963–65; Asst Mil. Attaché, Amman, 1967–69 (Major, 1962; GSM; South Arabia Radfan bar). Joined FCO, 1969; served Saigon, 1973, FCO, 1975, Oslo, 1976, Copenhagen, 1978, FCO, 1981; Counsellor, FCO, 1982–92; Advr, later Consultant FCO, 1992–95. Qualified as Psychosynthesis psychotherapist, 1993. Kt, First Degree, Order of Dannebrog, 1979. *Recreations:* God, concern for the bewildered, plumbing. *Address:* La Palmera, Calle Alta 7, 29788 Frigiliana, Málaga, Spain.

WAGSTAFF, Sheena Vanessa; Chairman, Modern and Contemporary Art, Metropolitan Museum of Art, New York, since 2012; *b* 30 Aug. 1956; *d* of Walton Wynter Wagstaff and Patricia (*née* Hugonin); *m* 1983, Mark Michael Peregrine Francis; one *s* one *d*. *Educ:* Univ. of East Anglia (BA Hons Hist. of Art and Arch. 1980). Postgraduate Fellow, Whitney Mus. of American Art, NY, 1982–83. Asst to Dir, MOMA, Oxford, 1976–77; Asst to Dir, Whitechapel Art Gall., 1980–82; Manager, Lisson Gall., 1983–84; freelance curator, 1984–93; curated exhibitions for: Whitney Mus. of American Art, NY; Kettle's Yard Gall., Cambridge; ICA, London; Centre Culturel de Courbevoie, Paris; Mattress Factory, Pittsburgh; Dir of Collection, Exhibns and Educn, Frick Art Mus., Pittsburgh, 1993–98; Hd of Exhibns and Displays, Tate Britain, 1998–2001; Chief Curator, Tate Modern, 2001–12. Member: Adv. Bd, Delfina Foundn, 2007–; Bd, Bidoun Mag., 2009–; Mayor's adv. Bd, Shubbak Fest., 2010–; Internat. Adv. Bd, Istanbul Modern, 2011–; Adv. Bd, Sch. of Visual Arts, 2013–; Nomination Bd, Praemium Imperiale, 2013–. Mem., Cranium. *Publications:* numerous exhibition catalogues. *Recreations:* historic and contemporary art, architecture, music, dance, literature, walking, gardening. *Address:* Metropolitan Museum of Art, 1000 Fifth Avenue, New York, NY 10028–0198, USA. *T:* (212) 3965192.

WAGSTAFFE, Christopher David; QC 2011; *b* Glossop, Derbys, 1967; *s* of David and Margaret Wagstaffe; *m* 1987, Vikki Ryder; two *s* two *d*. *Educ:* Glossop Sch., Derbys; Univ. of Essex (LLB Hons); Inns of Court Sch. of Law. Called to the Bar, Inner Temple, 1992. Mem., Derbys Police Authy, 1994–96. Member: Family Law Bar Assoc., 1995–; S Eastern Circuit, 2008–. Mem., Internat. Acad. Matrimonial Lawyers, 2012–. *Publications:* (ed jtly) Cohabitation and Trusts of Land, 2006, 2nd edn 2009; contrib. articles to Family Law, Trusts and Trustees. *Recreations:* sport, reading, theatre and cinema. *Address:* 29 Bedford Row, WC1R 4HE. *T:* (020) 7404 1044. *E:* cwagstaffe@29br.co.uk.

WAIKATO, Bishop of, since 2014; **Rt Rev. Dr Helen-Ann Macleod Hartley;** *b* Edinburgh, 28 May 1973; *d* of James Francis and Patricia Francis; *m* 2003, Myles Hartley. *Educ:* St Anthony's RC Girls Sch.; Univ. of St Andrews (MTheol Hons 1995); Princeton Theol Seminary (ThM 1996); Worcester Coll., Oxford (MPhil 2000; DPhil 2005; Hon. Fellow, 2015). Ordained deacon, 2005, priest, 2006; Curate, Wheatley Team, Oxford, 2005–09; Dir of Biblical Studies, Ripon Coll., Cuddesdon, 2009–12 (Hon. Fellow 2014); Dean for the New Zealand Dioceses, Coll. of St John the Evangelist, Auckland, 2012–14. *Publications:* Making Sense of the Bible, 2011. *Recreations:* walking, water-colour painting, astronomy. *Address:* Office of the Bishop, Charlotte Brown House, PO Box 21, Hamilton 3240, New Zealand. *T:* (7) 8570020. *E:* bishop@waikatoanglican.org.nz.

WAIN, Peter; a District Judge (Magistrates' Courts), 2004–11, a Deputy District Judge, 2011–14; *b* 3 Sept. 1947; *s* of late Frank and Margaret Wain; *m* 1972, Mary Carolyn Hilditch; two *s* one *d*. *Educ:* Bemrose Sch., Derby; Stamford Sch., Lincs; Univ. of Leeds (LLB Hons 1969). Called to the Bar, Gray's Inn, 1972; Clerk to the Felixstowe, Ipswich and Woodbridge Justices, 1978–87; practising barrister, 1987–2004. Pt-time Legal Mem., Mental Health Review Tribunal, 1995–2005. *Recreations:* bird watching, gardening, sculling on the River Deben, researching the lost medieval port of Goseford. *Clubs:* Bawdsey Bird; Felixstowe Ferry Sailing.

WAINE, Rt Rev. John, KCVO 1996; Bishop of Chelmsford, 1986–96; Clerk of the Closet to the Queen, 1989–96; an Honorary Assistant Bishop, Diocese of St Edmundsbury and Ipswich, since 2008; *b* June 1930; *s* of late William and Ellen Waine; *m* 1957, Patricia Zena Haikney; three *s*. *Educ:* Prescot Grammar Sch.; Manchester Univ. (BA); Ridley Hall, Cambridge. Deacon 1955, Priest 1956; Curate of St Mary, West Derby, 1955–58; Curate in Charge of All Saints, Sutton, 1958–60; Vicar of Ditton, 1960–64; Vicar of Holy Trinity, Southport, 1964–69; Rector of Kirkby, 1969–75; Bishop Suffragan of Stafford, 1975–78; Bishop of St Edmundsbury and Ipswich, 1978–86. Chm., Churches Main Cttee, 1991–96. Mem., Press Complaints Commn, 1997–2010. Chairman: Council, Univ. of Essex, 1995–2001; Foundn, Univ. of Essex, 2001–07. Master, Glass Sellers' Co., 1999–2000. Entered H of L, 1985. DUniv Essex, 2002. GCStJ 1999 (ChStJ 1983; Prelate, 1999–2007). *Recreations:* music, gardening. *Address:* Broadmere, Ipswich Road, Grundisburgh, Woodbridge, Suffolk IP13 6TJ. *T:* (01473) 738296. *Club:* Royal Air Force.

WAINE, Peter Edward; Chairman, Campaign to Protect Rural England, 2008–14; Co-founder, Hanson Green, since 1989; *b* Rugby, 27 June 1949; *s* of late Dr Theodore Edward Waine and Mary Florence Waine; *m* 1973, Stefanie Vuikaba Snow; one *d*. *Educ:* Bilton Grange; Worksop Coll.; Bradford Univ. (BSc 1970). Divisional Level Human Resources roles: GEC, 1970–74; Cape Industries, 1974–79; Coopers and Lybrand, 1979–83; Dir, CBI, 1983–88; CEO, Directorship Appointments Ltd, 1988–89. Chm., Core Care Ltd, 1990–92; non-executive Director: W. R. Royle & Sons Ltd, 1988–96; SSK Ltd, 1994–98; Wild Wiki Ltd, 2011–14; Sen. non-exec. Dir, Quarto Gp plc, 1998–2013. Non-executive Director: E Herts DHA, 1990–92; E Herts Trust, 1992–96. Mem., ICC, 1994–2005; Chairman: Tree Council, 1996–98 (Vice Pres., 1998–2000); Brogdale Horticl Trust, 2001–06; Trustee, ROH, 1999–2001. Visiting Professor: Warwick Business Sch., 2004–10; Cass Business Sch., 2004–10. Member Council: BIM, 1979–81; Eur. Business Sch., 1983–90. Vice Chm., Bow Gp, 1972 (Chm., Birmingham Gp, 1971). Mem., Rugby DC, 1973–77. Contested (C) Nottingham N, 1979. Mem., Judging Panel, Contrarian Prize, 2013–. Gov. and Chm. of Foundn, Bilton Grange Sch., Rugby, 2014–. Liveryman, Gardeners' Co., 2007 (Mem. Ct, 2013–). *Publications:* (with David Clutterbuck) The Independent Board Director, 1993; (with Mike Walker) Takeover, 2000 (trans. five langs); The Board Game, 2002; Under a Passing Sky: a poetry collection, 2011; various mags, newspapers incl. weekly columnist under pseudonym for London newspaper, 1984–87. *Recreation:* English countryside. *Club:* MCC.

WAINE, Very Rev. Stephen John; Dean of Chichester, since 2015; *b* 1959; one *s* one *d*; *m* 2015, Elizabeth Rowe. *Educ:* Univ. of E Anglia (BA Econ. and Social Studies); Westcott House, Cambridge. Ordained deacon 1984, priest 1985; Asst Curate, St Peter's, Wolverhampton, 1984–88; Minor Canon and Succentor, St Paul's Cathedral, 1988–93; Vicar, St Edward the Confessor's, Romford, 1993–2010; Priest-in-charge, St John's, Romford, 2002–10; Archdeacon of Dorset, 2010–15; Canon and Prebendary, Sarum Cathedral, 2010–15. *Recreations:* music (singing and listening), cooking, walking, DIY, golf, reading, sailing, armchair football and cricket. *Address:* The Deanery, Canon Lane, Chichester, W Sussex PO19 1PX. *E:* dean@chichestercathedral.org.uk.

WAINE, His Honour Stephen Phillip; a Circuit Judge, 2001–13; Designated Family Judge, Northampton, 2006–13; *b* 9 June 1947; *s* of late Dr Theodore Edward Waine and Mary Florence Waine; *m* 1st, 1976 (marr. diss.); 2nd, 1981, Clare (*née* Pryor); one *s* one *d*. *Educ:* Rugby Sch.; Southampton Univ. (LLB). Called to the Bar, Lincoln's Inn, 1969; a Recorder, Midland and Oxford Circuit, 1992–2001. Chm., Mental Health Tribunals, 2002–. Chm. and Trustee, Equata, 2013–; Trustee, Kidsaid Northampton, 2013–. FCIArb 1999–2015. *Recreations:* ski-ing, golf, gardening, watching sports, reading. *Address:* c/o Northampton Combined Court Centre, 85–87 Lady's Lane, Northampton NN1 3HQ. *Club:* MCC.
See also P. E. Waine.

WAINWRIGHT, Elizabeth-Anne; *see* Gumbel, E.-A.

WAINWRIGHT, (Elizabeth) Jane, MA; Co-Founder and Educational Consultant, Education Oxford, 2011; *b* 27 Sept. 1950; *d* of Eric Foster Wainwright and Marie Wainwright; civil partnership 2006, Kate Watkins. *Educ:* St Hugh's Coll., Oxford (MA; PGCE); Sch. of Oriental and African Studies, Univ. of London (MA); Open Univ. (Advanced Dip. Educnl Mgt 1987). Geography teacher: Sandford Sch., Addis Ababa, 1975–77; Peers Sch., Oxford, 1977–82; Hd of Geog., Plymouth High Sch., 1982–88; Dep. Hd, Lancaster Girls' GS, 1988–92; Headteacher: Aylesbury High Sch., 1992–2002; Wycombe High Sch., 2002–08. *Publications:* contrib. Jl of Res. on NE Africa. *Recreations:* travel, friends, photography, feminism, keeping up with information technology. *E:* jane_wainwright@btinternet.com.

WAINWRIGHT, Faith Helen, (Mrs K. J. Glynn), MBE 2012; FREng, FICE, FIStructE; Director, Ove Arup and Partners, since 1998; *b* Dunfermline, Fife, 25 May 1962; *d* of Comdr Brian Hebden Wainwright, RN and Anne Vera Wainwright (*née* Temple); *m* 1988, Kieran J. Glynn; one *s* two *d*. *Educ:* Queen Anne's Sch., Caversham; St Edmund Hall, Oxford (BA). MIStructE 1987, FIStructE 2003; FREng 2003; FICE 2003. Joined Arup, 1983; projects include: ITN London, 1990; Western Morning News, Plymouth, 1992; Lycée Albert Camus, Frejus, 1994; American Air Mus., Duxford, 1996; Tate Modern, London, 2000; Hongkong and Shanghai Banking Corp. HQ, Canary Wharf, 2002; London Bridge Tower, 2003; Dean, 2011–13, Hd of Tech. Skills, 2013–, Arup Univ. Non-exec. Dir, KTN Ltd, 2015–. Member: Standing Cttee on Structural Safety, 2001–07; Council, IStructE, 2003–06 (Vice Pres., 2013–); Adv. Council, BL, 2004–11; Council, RAEng, 2010–13; Vice Chairman: Cttee for Safety in Tall Buildings, 2001–03; Jt Bd of Moderators, 2004–10. Juror: BBC Design Awards, 1996; OASYS Design Awards, 2001. MInstD; MInstKT 2009. FRSA. Hon. DEng Bath 2014. *Publications:* (contrib. jtly) Fire Safety Engineering and the Case for Dynamic Robustness in the Design of Tall Buildings, 2002; (contrib. jtly) Extreme Event Mitigation in Buildings, 2006; (contrib.) Making Knowledge Management Work for your Organisation, 2012; contribs to learned jls on structural robustness and building projects, incl. Jl IStructE, Planning and Guidance, Ingenia. *Recreations:* family, sailing. *Address:* Arup, 13 Fitzroy Street, W1T 4BQ. *T:* (020) 7755 2061, *Fax:* (020) 7755 2150. *E:* faith.wainwright@arup.com.

WAINWRIGHT, Geoffrey John, MBE 1991; PhD; FSA, FLSW; archaeologist; *b* 19 Sept. 1937; *s* of Frederick and Dorothy Wainwright; *m* 1977, Judith; one *s* two *d*. *Educ:* Pembroke Docks Sch.; Univ. of Wales (BA); Univ. of London (PhD). FSA 1967; MIFA 1984, Hon. MIFA 1999. Prof. of Archaeology, Univ. of Baroda, India, 1961–63; Inspectorate of Ancient Monuments, English Heritage (formerly part of DoE), 1963–99; Principal Inspector, 1963–90; Chief Archaeologist, 1989–99; Founder, Bluestone Partnership, 1999. Chm., Wessex Archaeology, 2004–11. Mem., Royal Commn on Ancient and Historical Monuments in Wales, 1987–2000, Vice Chm., 2000–02; President: Cornwall Archaeological Soc., 1980–84; Prehistoric Soc., 1982–86; Cambrian Archaeol Assoc., 2002–03; Pembrokeshire Historical Soc., 2008–; Vice Pres., 1997–2001, Treasurer, 2001–07, Pres., 2007–10, Soc. of Antiquaries (Dir, 1984–90). Visiting Professor: Univ. of Southampton, 1991–; UCL, 1995–. Fellow, University Coll., Cardiff, 1985. FRSA 1991; FLSW 2011. Hon. Fellow, Univ. of Wales, Lampeter, 1996. Hon. Member: Europae Archaeologiae Consilium, 1999; German Archaeological Inst., 2009. Grahame Clark Medal, British Acad., 2006. *Publications:* Stone Age in North India, 1964; Coygan Camp, Carms, 1967; Durrington Walls, Wilts, 1971; Mount Pleasant, Dorset, 1979; Gussage All Saints, Dorset, 1979; The Henge Monuments, 1990; numerous articles in learned jls. *Recreations:* Rugby football, walking, food and drink. *Address:* March Pres, Pontfaen, Pembs SA65 9TT.

WAINWRIGHT, Jane; *see* Wainwright, E. J.

WAINWRIGHT, Prof. Mark Sebastian, AM 2004; PhD, DSc; FTSE, FIChemE, FIEAust, FRACI; Professor of Chemical Engineering, 1989–2009, now Emeritus, and Vice-Chancellor and President, 2004–06, University of New South Wales; Chairman: Smart Services CRC, since 2010 (Director, since 2009); Foundation for Australian Studies in China, since 2012; *b* 20 Oct. 1943; *s* of William Edward and Marjorie Wanda Wainwright; *m* Irene Eve Ruffio; two *d*. *Educ:* S Australia Inst. of Technol. (BAppSc Hons); Univ. of Adelaide (MAppSc); McMaster Univ. (PhD Chem. Engrg); Univ. of S Australia (DSc). University of New South Wales: School of Chemical Technology: Lectr in Industrial Chem., 1974–77; Sen. Lectr, 1978–80; School of Chemical Engineering and Industrial Chemistry: Associate Prof., and Hd, Dept of Industrial Chem., 1981–88; Hd, Dept of Chem. Engrg, 1989–91; Dean, Faculty of Engrg, 1991–2000; Actg Pro-Vice-Chancellor (Inf. Services), 1994; Pro-Vice-Chancellor (Res.), 1998–2000; Dep. Vice-Chancellor (Res. and Internat.), 2001–04. Chairman: Australia-China Council, 2006–11; Nat. Computational Infrastructure Steering Cttee, 2007–; INTERSECT Ltd, 2008–; Nat. Inst. for Promotion of ICT in Health. Mem. Bd, Engrg Aid Australia. Mem. Council, Univ. of Qld, 2009–. *Publications:* contrib. numerous papers; patents published. *Recreation:* golf. *Club:* Coast Golf.

WAINWRIGHT, Richard Barry; European Law consultant, FIPRA International, since 2008; Principal Legal Adviser, European Commission, 1992–2005; *b* 10 June 1940; *s* of Denys and Shelagh Wainwright; *m* 1966, Linda Sully; three *s* one *d*. *Educ:* Trinity Coll., Oxford (BA Hons); Inns of Court Sch. of Law. In practice as barrister, 1966–68; Solicitor's Office, Inland Revenue, 1968–69; Legal Advr, British Petroleum Co., 1969–73; with Legal Service, EC, 1973–2005. European Law consultant, Allen and Overy, London and Brussels, 2005–08. *Publications:* contribs to Common Market Law Rev., European Law Rev., Oxford Yearbook of European Law, Revue du Marché Commun. *Recreations:* music, reading, sailing, ski-ing, tennis, golf, walking. *Address:* 101 Swains Lane, N6 6PJ. *T:* (020) 8340 2131. *Club:* Château Ste Anne (Brussels).

WAINWRIGHT, Robert Mark; Director, Europol, since 2009; *b* Carmarthen, 17 Sept. 1967; *s* of Victor and Christine Wainwright; *m* 1994, Suzanne; one *s* two *d*. *Educ:* London Sch. of Econs and Pol Sci. (BSc (Econ) Internat. Relns 1989). Security Service: Desk Officer, 1989–94; Ops Team Leader, 1994–97; Dep. Hd, Serious Crime Section, 1997–2000; Chief, UK Liaison Bureau, Europol, 2000–03; International Director: Nat. Criminal Intelligence Service, 2003–06; SOCA, 2006–09. *Recreations:* sport, history, family. *Address:* Europol, Eisenhowerlaan 73, 2517 KK, The Hague, Netherlands. *T:* (70) 3025102. *E:* rob.wainwright@europol.europa.eu.

WAINWRIGHT, Sam, CBE 1982; Post Office Corporation: Member of Board, 1977–85; Deputy Chairman, 1981–85; Managing Director, National Girobank, 1977–85; Director, Postel Investment Ltd, 1982–85; *b* 2 Oct. 1924; *m* Ruth Strom; three *s* one *d*. *Educ:* Regent Street Polytechnic; LSE (MSc Econ). Financial journalist, Glasgow Herald, 1950; Deputy City Editor, 1952–55; Head of Research: Grieveson Grant, 1955–58; W. Greenwell, 1958–60; Director: Rea Brothers Ltd (Merchant Bankers), 1960–77 (Managing Dir, 1965–77); Furness Withy & Co. Ltd, 1971–77; Stothert & Pitt Ltd, 1970–77 (Chm., 1975–77); Dundee, Perth and London, 1974–76; Aeronautical & General Instruments Ltd, 1968–77; Manders (Hldgs), 1972–87 (Dep. Chm., 1985–86; Chm., 1986–87); BICC, 1985–90 (Chm., Audit Cttee, 1986–90); Lancashire & London Investment Trust Ltd, 1963–77; Scottish Cities Investment Trust Ltd, 1961–77; Scottish & Mercantile Investment Co. Ltd, 1964–77; AMDAHL (UK), 1987–93. Member: Post Office Audit Cttee, 1978–80; Monopolies and Mergers Commn, 1985–91. Chm., Jigsaw Day Nurseries, 1991–95. Mem. Council, Soc. of Investment Analysts, 1961–75, Fellow, 1980. Hon. Editor, The Investment Analyst, 1961–74. *Publications:* articles in various Bank Reviews. *Recreations:* reading, bridge, walking. *Address:* Flat 5, 29 Warrington Crescent, W9 1EJ. *T:* (020) 7286 8050. *Club:* Reform.

WAIT, John James; His Honour Judge Wait; a Circuit Judge, since 1997; *b* 19 Sept. 1949; *s* of Eric James Wait and Rachel Wait; *m* 1986, Patricia, (Tricia), Ann Hitchcock; two *s*. *Educ:* Queen Mary's Grammar Sch., Walsall; Nottingham Univ. (LLB 1971). Called to the Bar, Inner Temple, 1972, Bencher, 2011; Lectr in Law, UCW, Aberystwyth, 1972–74; in practice at the Bar, 1974–97; Asst Recorder, 1989–93; a Recorder, 1993–97; Midland and Oxford Circuit; Resident Judge, Derby Combined Court, 2000–08. Jt Dir, Criminal Induction Course, Judicial Studies Bd and Judicial Coll., 2008–13. *Address:* Wolverhampton Combined Court, Pipers Row, Wolverhampton WV1 3LQ.

WAITE, Rt Hon. Sir John (Douglas), Kt 1982; PC 1993; a Lord Justice of Appeal, 1993–97; *b* 3 July 1932; *s* of late Archibald Waite and Betty, *d* of late Ernest Bates; *m* 1966, Julia Mary, *er d* of late Joseph Tangye; three *s* two step *s*. *Educ:* Sherborne Sch.; Corpus Christi Coll., Cambridge (MA). President of Cambridge Union, 1955. Nat. Service, 2nd Lieut, RA, 1951–52. Called to Bar, Gray's Inn, 1956, Bencher, 1981; QC 1975; a Judge of the High Court of Justice, Family Div., 1982–93; Presiding Judge, North Eastern Circuit, 1990–93; Judge, Gibraltar Court of Appeal, 1997–2000. Pres., Employment Appeal Tribunal, 1983–85. Co-Chm., Ind. Asylum Commn, 2006–08. Chairman: UNICEF (UK), 1997–2004; Special Trustees, Middx and UC Hosps, 1997–2004; UCL Hosps Charitable Foundn, 1999–2004. *Recreations:* reading (haphazardly), sailing (uncertainly), gardening (optimistically). *Address:* 54 Church Street, Orford, Woodbridge, Suffolk IP12 2NT; Flat 19, Wentworth Mansions, Keats Grove, NW3 2RL. *Clubs:* Athenæum; Orford Sailing.

WAITE, Jonathan Gilbert Stokes; QC 2002; *b* 15 Feb. 1956; *s* of late Capt. David Waite, RN, and Joan Waite (*née* Paull). *Educ:* Sherborne Sch.; Trinity Coll., Cambridge (MA). Called to the Bar, Inner Temple, 1978; in practice, specialising in personal injury, industrial diseases and pharmaceutical product liability law, 1979–. *Recreations:* golf, ski-ing, bridge, wines of Bordeaux. *Address:* 76 Forthbridge Road, Battersea, SW11 5NY; Crown Office Chambers, 2 Crown Office Row, Temple, EC4Y 7HJ. *T:* (020) 7228 4488, *Fax:* (020) 7797 8100. *E:* waite@crownofficechambers.com. *Clubs:* Woking Golf, Aldeburgh Golf, Rye Golf, Royal St George's Golf.

WAITE, Judith Mary; *see* Rowe, J. M.

WAITE, Stephen, DPhil; Principal and Chief Executive Officer, Writtle College, since 2013; *b* Willesden, London, 25 Aug. 1954; *s* of Frederick John Waite and Gladys Violet Waite; *m* 1981, Alison Jean Mitchard; two *d*. *Educ:* Bishopsfield Secondary Modern Sch., Fareham; Fareham Technical Coll.; Univ. of Sussex (BSc Hons 1st Cl. Biol Scis; DPhil 1980); Open Univ. (BA Maths). MCIEEM (MIEEM 1992). Lectr in Ecol. and Plant Scis, Poly. of Central London, 1979–91; Brighton Polytechnic, later University of Brighton: Sen. Lectr in Ecol. and Envmtl Scis, 1991–95; Principal Lectr in Biol., 1995–2009; Dep. Hd, Sch. of Pharmacy and Molecular Scis, 2004–09; Vice Principal (HE) and Dean, Hartpury Coll., 2009–13. Course Dir, Cert. and Dip. in Field Biol., Birkbeck Coll., Univ. of London, 1991–98. *Publications:* Pollution: ecology and biotreatment, 1993; Statistical Ecology in Practice: a guide to analysing environmental and ecological field data, 2000; numerous articles on plant and landscape ecol. in learned jls. *Recreations:* science, reading, music, guitar, swimming, DIY. *Address:* Writtle College, Chelmsford, Essex CM1 3RR. *T:* (01245) 424200, *Fax:* (01245) 420456. *E:* stephen.waite@writtle.ac.uk. *Club:* Mid Sussex Marlins (Masters).

WAITE, Terence Hardy, CBE 1992 (MBE 1982); writer and lecturer; Adviser to Archbishop of Canterbury on Anglican Communion Affairs, 1980–92 (taken captive and held hostage in Lebanon, Jan. 1987–19 Nov. 1991); Fellow Commoner, Trinity Hall, Cambridge, 1992–93, now Emeritus; *b* 31 May 1939; *s* of Thomas William Waite and Lena (*née* Hardy); *m* 1964, Helen Frances Watters; one *s* three *d*. *Educ:* Wilmslow and Stockton Heath, Cheshire; Church Army Coll., London. Lay training adviser to Bishop and Diocese of Bristol, 1964–68; Adviser to Archbishop of Uganda, Rwanda and Burundi, 1968–71; Internat. Consultant working with Roman Catholic Church, 1972–79. Member, National Assembly, Church of England, 1966–68 (resigned on moving to Africa); Co-ordinator, Southern Sudan Relief Project, 1969–71. Vis. Fellow, Magdalen Coll., Oxford, 2006. Founder-Chairman: Y Care International, 1985–2000 (Pres., 2000–); Hostage UK, 2005–; Pres., Emmaus UK, 1998–. Chm., Prison Video Trust, 1998–. Pres., Llangollen Internat. Musical Eisteddfod, 2006–; Vice President: Suffolk Assoc. of Local Councils, 1999–; E Cheshire Hospice, Macclesfield, 2001–; English Music Fest., 2006–; Chester Music Soc., 2011–. Trustee, Butler Trust, 1986–2010 (Patron, 2010–). Patron: Bury St Edmunds Volunteer Centre, 1994–; Warrington Male Voice Choir, 1996–; Romany Soc., 1997–; W Suffolk Voluntary Assoc. for the Blind, 1998–; Suffolk Far East Prisoners of War (Pres.); Save our Parsonages, 1999–; Bridge Project, Sudbury, 1999–; Children (and Families) of Far Eastern Prisoners of War, 1999–; Friends of the Samaritans, Bury St Edmunds; One to One Children's Fund, 2001–; Under-Privileged Children's Charity, Bristol, 2003–; British Friends of Neve Shalom/Wahat al-Salam, 2003–; Habit for Humanity, 2004–; Children with Aids Charity, 2004–; Rapid UK, 2004–; Sunderland Counselling Services, 2004–; Tymes Trust, 2005–; Storybook Dads, 2007–; Henry Spink Foundation, 2009–; Escaping Victimhood, 2011–; Asylum Aid, 2012–. Ambassador for WWF, 2000–. Hon. DCL: Kent at Canterbury, 1986; City, 1992; Hon. LLD: Liverpool, 1992; Durham, 1992; Sussex, 1992; Yale, 1992; Robert Gordon, 2007; Hon. DHL Virginia Commonwealth Univ., 1996; Hon. LHD Wittenberg, 1992; Hon. DHumLit Southern Florida, 1992; Hon. DPhil Anglia Polytech. Univ., 2001; Hon. DLitt: Nottingham Trent, 2001; De Montfort, 2005; Chester, 2008; Open, 2009. Templeton UK Award, 1985; Franklin D. Roosevelt Four Freedom Award, 1992. *Publications:* Taken on Trust, 1993; Footfalls in Memory, 1995; Travels with a Primate, 2000; The Voyage of the Golden Handshake (novel), 2015. *Recreations:* music, travel (esp. in remote parts of the world), Jungian studies, international affairs. *Address:* Trinity Hall, Cambridge CB2 1TJ. *Clubs:* Travellers; Empire (Toronto).

WAJDA, Andrzej; Polish film and theatre director; Senator, Polish People's Republic, 1989–91 (one term); President, Andrzej Wajda Master School of Film Directing; *b* 6 March 1926; *s* of Jakub Wajda and Aniela Wajda; *m* 1st, 1967, Beata Tyszkiewicz (marr. diss.); one *d*; 2nd, 1975, Krystyna Zachwatowicz. *Educ:* Acad. Fine Arts, Cracow; Film Acad., Łódź. Asst Stage Manager, 1953; film dir, 1954–; Stage Manager, Teatr Stary, Cracow, 1973; Man. Dir, Teatr Powszechny, Warsaw, 1989–90. Pres., Polish Film Assoc., 1978–83. Chm. Bd, Kyoto-Kraków Foundn. Hon. Mem., Union of Polish Artists and Designers, 1977. Dr *hc*: American, Washington, 1981; Bologna, 1988; Jagiellonian, Cracow, 1989. British Acad. Award for Services to Film, 1982; BAFTA Fellowship, 1982; Hon. Academy Award for lifetime achievement, 2000. Order of Banner of Labour, 1975; Officer's Cross of Polonia Restituta; Officier, Légion d'Honneur (France), 1982; Order of Kirill and Methodius (Bulgaria). *Films:* Generation, 1954; I'm Going to the Sun, 1955; Kanal, 1956 (Silver Palm, Cannes, 1957); Ashes and Diamonds, 1957; Lotna, 1959; Innocent Sorcerers, 1959; Samson, 1960; Serbian Lady Macbeth, 1961; Love at Twenty, 1961; Ashes, 1965; Gates of Paradise, 1967; Everything For Sale, 1968; Jigsaw Puzzle (for TV), 1969; Hunting Flies, 1969; Macbeth (TV), 1969; Landscape After Battle, 1970; The Birch Wood, 1970; Pilatus (TV), 1971; Master and Margaret (TV), 1972; The Wedding, 1972 (Silver Prize, San Sebastian, 1973); The Promised Land, 1974 (Grand Prix, Moscow Film Festival, 1975); The Shadow Line, 1976; A Dead Class (TV), 1976; Man of Marble, 1977; Rough Treatment, 1978; The Orchestral Conductor, 1979; The Maids of Wilko, 1979 (Oscar nomination, 1980); Man of Iron, 1981 (Palme D'Or, Cannes, 1981); Danton, 1982; Love in Germany, 1985; Chronicle of Love Affairs, 1986; The Possessed, 1987; Korczak, 1990; The Ring with the Crowned Eagle, 1992; Nastasya, 1994; The Great Week, 1995; Miss Nobody, 1996; Pan Tadeusz, 2000; Katyn, 2009; *plays:* Hatful of Rain, 1959; Hamlet, 1960, 1980, 1989; Two on the Seesaw, 1960, 1990; The Wedding, 1962; The Possessed, 1963, 1971, 1975; Play Strindberg, 1969; Idiot, 1971, 1975; Sticks and Bones, Moscow, 1972; Der Mittmacher, 1973; November Night, 1974; The Danton Case, 1975, 1978; When Reason is Asleep, 1976; Emigrés, 1976; Nastasia Philipovna (improvisation based on Dostoyevsky's The Idiot), 1977; Conversation with the Executioner, 1977; Gone with the Years, Gone with the Days …, 1978; Antygone, 1984; Crime and Punishment, 1984, 1986, 1987; Miss Julia, 1988; Dybuk, 1988; Lesson of Polish Language, 1988; Nastasya (adapted from The Idiot), 1989, Osaka, 1993; Hamlet IV, 1989; Romeo and Juliet, 1990; The Wedding, 1991; Sonate of Spectres, 1994; Mishima, 1994; Wrocław's Improvisation, 1996. *Publications:* My Life in Film (autobiog.), 1989.

WAKE, Sir Hereward, 14th Bt *cr* 1621; MC 1942; Vice Lord-Lieutenant of Northamptonshire, 1984–91; Major (retired) King's Royal Rifle Corps; *b* 7 Oct. 1916; *e s* of Maj. Gen. Sir Hereward Wake, 13th Bt, CB, CMG, DSO, and Margaret W. (*d* 1976), *er d* of R. H. Benson; *S* father, 1963; *m* 1952, Julia Rosemary, JP, DL, *yr d* of late Capt. G. W. M. Lees, Falcutt House, near Brackley, Northants; one *s* three *d*. *Educ:* Eton; RMC, Sandhurst. Served War of 1939–45 (wounded, MC). Retired from 60th Rifles, 1947, and studied Estate Management and Agriculture. Fellow, University of Northampton (formerly Nene Coll., later UC, Northampton), 1997–. High Sheriff, 1955, DL 1969, Northants. *Heir: s* Hereward Charles Wake [*b* 22 Nov. 1952; *m* 1st, 1977, Lady Doune Ogilvy (marr. diss. 1995), *e d* of Earl of Airlie, *qv*; two *s* one *d* (and one *s* decd); 2nd, 1998, Mrs Joan Barrow]. *Address:* Old School House, Courteenhall, Northampton NN7 2QD. *Club:* Brooks's.

WAKEFIELD, Area Bishop of, since 2014; **Rt Rev. Anthony William Robinson;** *b* 25 April 1956; *m* 1981, Susan Boddy; two *s* one *d*. *Educ:* Bedford Modern Sch.; Salisbury and Wells Theol Coll. Ordained deacon, 1982, priest, 1983; Asst Curate, St Paul, Tottenham, 1982–85; Team Vicar, 1985–89, Team Rector, 1989–97, Resurrection, Leicester; Archdeacon of Pontefract, 1997–2003; Bishop Suffragan of Pontefract, 2002–14. Rural Dean, Christianity North, Leicester, 1992–97; Hon. Canon, Leicester Cathedral, 1994–97. *Address:* Pontefract House, 181a Manygates Lane, Wakefield WF2 7DR. *T:* (01924) 250781. *E:* bishop.tony@westyorkshiredales.anglican.org.

WAKEFIELD, Dean of; *see* Greener, Very Rev. J. D. F.

WAKEFIELD, Her Honour Anne Prudence; a Circuit Judge, 1999–2005; *b* 25 May 1943; *d* of John Arkell Wakefield and Stella Adelaide Wakefield; *m* 1974, James Robert Reid, *qv* (marr. diss. 2002); two *s* one *d*. *Educ:* London Sch. of Economics and Political Science (LLB); Newnham Coll., Cambridge (LLM 1969). Called to the Bar, Gray's Inn, 1968; in practice, 1970–75 and 1987–99; Asst Recorder, 1991–95; a Recorder, 1995–99. Lecturer in Law: LSE, 1969–70; pt-time, QMC, 1983–87. Pt-time Chm., Industrial Tribunals, 1992–99; a Judge of the Employment Appeal Tribunal, 2000–05. Associate, Newnham Coll., Cambridge, 2002–05.

WAKEFIELD, Sir (Edward) Humphry (Tyrrell), 2nd Bt *cr* 1962; *b* 11 July 1936; *s* of Sir Edward Birkbeck Wakefield, 1st Bt, CIE, and Constance Lalage, *e d* of Sir John Perronet Thompson, KCSI, KCIE, and *nephew* of 1st Baron Wakefield of Kendal; *S* father, 1969; *m* 1st, 1960, Priscilla (marr. diss. 1964), *e d* of O. R. Bagot; 2nd, 1966, Hon. Elizabeth Sophia (from whom he obt. a divorce, 1971), *e d* of 1st Viscount De L'Isle, VC, KG, PC, GCMG, GCVO, and former wife of G. S. O. A. Colthurst; one *s*; 3rd, 1974, Hon. Katharine Mary Alice Baring, *d* of 1st Baron Howick of Glendale, KG, GCMG, KCVO, and of Lady Mary Howick; one *s* one *d* (and one *s* decd). *Educ:* Gordonstoun; Trinity Coll., Cambridge (MA Hons). Formerly Captain, 10th Royal Hussars. Exec. Vice-Pres., Mallett, America Ltd, 1970–75; Chm., Tyrrell & Moore Ltd, 1978–92; Director: Mallett & Son (Antiques) Ltd, 1971–78; Tree of Life Foundn, 1976–. Dir, Spoleto Fest. of Two Worlds, USA and Italy, 1973–80. Chm., Wilderness Trust, 1999–2006 (Patron, 2011–); President: Northumberland Nat. Park Mountain Rescue (formerly Northumberland Nat. Park Search and Rescue) Team; Avison Trust; Tibetan Spaniel Assoc.; Patron: Action North East; Medicine and Chernobyl; Centre for Search Res. UK; Shadow Dance UK, etc; formerly Appeals Consultant, London Br., British Red Cross Soc. Mem., Standing Council of Baronetage. Mem., Soc. of Dilettante. Fellow, Pierpont Morgan Library. Joined NZ Everest Team, 1990, and also in their first ascent of Mount Wakefield; Mem., Norman Vaughan Antarctic Expedn, 1993. Life Mem., Scott-Polar Inst. FRGS. Order of Nat. Inst. (Greece), 1954. *Recreations:* riding, writing, music, shooting. *Heir: s* Capt. Maximilian Edward Vereker Wakefield [*b* 22 Feb. 1967; *m* 1994, Lucinda Katharine Elizabeth, *d* of Lt-Col and Mrs David Pipe; two *s*. *Educ:* Milton Abbey; RMA Sandhurst]. *Address:* Chillingham Castle, Chillingham, Northumberland NE66 5NJ. *Clubs:* Beefsteak, Cavalry and Guards, Turf; Harlequins Rugby Football (Twickenham) (Hon. Life Mem.).

See also G. H. C. Wakefield.

WAKEFIELD, Gerald Hugo Cropper, (Hady); Chairman, J & H Marsh & McLennan (Holdings) Ltd (formerly Bowring Group), 1996–99; *b* 15 Sept. 1938; *s* of Sir Edward Wakefield, 1st Bt, CIE, and (Constance) Lalage, *e d* of Sir John Perronet Thompson, KCSI, KCIE; *m* 1971, Victoria Rose Feilden; one *s*. *Educ:* Eton; Trinity Coll., Cambridge (MA). Started at Lloyd's, 1961; joined C. T. Bowring & Co., 1968, Dir 1983; Guy Carpenter & Co., NY: Dep. Chm., 1990; Pres., 1993; Chm., 1996. *Recreations:* fishing, shooting, ski-ing, opera. *Address:* Bramdean House, Alresford, Hants SO24 0JU. *T:* (01962) 771214. *Clubs:* White's, Cavalry and Guards, Beefsteak; The Brook (NY).

WAKEFIELD, Sir Humphry; *see* Wakefield, Sir E. H. T.

WAKEFIELD, Sir Norman (Edward), Kt 1988; Chairman, Y. J. Lovell (Holdings) plc, 1987–90; *b* 30 Dec. 1929; *s* of Edward and Muriel Wakefield; *m* 1953, Denise Mary Bayliss (*d* 1998); two *s* four *d*. *Educ:* Wallington County Sch.; Croydon and Brixton Technical Colls. Articled student, Wates Ltd, 1947; Man. Dir, Wates Construction Ltd, 1967; Pres., jt venture co., USA, between Wates and Rouse Co., 1970–73; Man. Dir, Holland, Hannen & Cubitts, 1973; Chief Exec., 1977–83, Chm. and Chief Exec., 1983–87, Y. J. Lovell (Holdings). Dep. Chm., Housing Corp., 1990–94. Director: Lloyds Abbey Life, 1986–93; English Estates, 1990–94. Pres., CIOB, 1985–86. Chm., 1995–2003, Dep. Chm., 2003–08, Nelson House Recovery Trust. Charity consultant, 1995–2010. *Recreations:* opera, walking, gardening. *Address:* 12 Rosemary Gate, Esher Park Avenue, Esher, Surrey KT10 9NZ. *Club:* Arts.

WAKEFIELD, His Honour Robert; a Circuit Judge, 1996–2011; *b* 14 Feb. 1946; *s* of Dudley James Wakefield and Violet Harriette Hart; *m* 1977, Anne Jennifer Gregory. *Educ:* Birmingham Univ. (LLB); Brasenose Coll., Oxford (BCL). Called to the Bar, Middle Temple, 1969; Recorder, 1993–96. *Address:* c/o Inner London Crown Court, Sessions House, Newington Causeway, SE1 6AZ.

WAKEFIELD, William Barry, CB 1990; Deputy Director (Research), National Commission on Education, 1991–95; *b* 6 June 1930; *s* of Stanley Arthur and Evelyn Grace Wakefield; *m* 1953, Elizabeth Violet (*née* Alexander); three *s* one *d*. *Educ:* Harrow County Grammar Sch.; University Coll., London. BSc; FSS. Statistician, NCB, 1953–62; DES, 1962–67; Chief Statistician, MoD, 1967–72, CSO, 1972–75; Asst Dir, CSO, Cabinet Office, 1975–79; Dir of Statistics, DES, 1979–90. Member, United Reformed Church. *Recreations:* horse racing, gardening, family history. *Address:* Egg Hall Cottage, 14 Birch Street, Nayland, Colchester CO6 4JA.

WAKEFORD, David Ewing, MBE 1992; External Trade Director, Africa Invest Fund Management Ltd, 2009–10; Managing Director, Global Trade Knowledge, 1999–2000 and 2006–11; *b* 30 Oct. 1944; *s* of Arthur Ewing Wakeford and late Gertrude Ada Wakeford (*née* Hall); *m* 1st, 1968 (marr. diss. 2006); three *s*; 2nd, 2007, SallyAnn Jackson. *Educ:* Hadham Hall Sch.; St Mary's Sch., Welwyn; Univ. of Manchester (MSc Polymer and Fibre Sci.). ICI, 1963–99: Res. Chemist, Plastics Div., 1963–78; Purchasing Manager, Petrochemicals and Plastics, 1978–85; Internat. Trade Manager, Head Office, 1985–99; Chief Exec., Simpler Trade Procedures Board, then SITPRO Ltd, 2000–05; Internat. Trade Dir, Commonwealth Business Council, 2006–09. Dir, Dorset Advocacy, 2014– (Vice Chm.). *Recreations:* sailing, bird-watching, country pursuits.

WAKEFORD, Sir (Geoffrey) Michael (Montgomery), Kt 2004; OBE 1995; Clerk to the Worshipful Company of Mercers, 1974–98; Barrister-at-Law; *b* 10 Dec. 1937; *o s* of late Geoffrey and Helen Wakeford; *m* 1966, Diana Margaret Loy Cooper, *y d* of late Comdr W. G. L. Cooper and of Patricia Cooper (*née* Fforde), Aislaby, N Yorks; two *s* two *d*. *Educ:* Downside; Clare Coll., Cambridge (Exhibnr; MA, LLB). Called to Bar, Gray's Inn and South Eastern Circuit, 1961; practised at Common Law Bar until 1971. Apptd Dep. Clerk to the Mercers Co., 1971. Director: Portman Settled Estates Ltd, 1998–2007; Alto Film Prodn LLP, 2004–. Clerk to Govs, St Paul's Schs, 1971–98; Governor: London Internat. Film Sch., 1981–85, 1990– (Vice Chm., 1997–2010; Hon. Associate, 2009); Molecule Theatre, 1986–; Unicorn Children's Theatre, 2005–11; Thomas Telford Sch., 1990–2001 (Chm., 1997–2001); Abingdon Sch., 2000–07; Guardian Angels RC Primary Sch., Tower Hamlets, 2000–07, 2011–15 (Chm., 2000–07; Associate, 2007–11); Walsall Acad., 2001–09 (Chm., 2001–09). *Address:* 15 Compton Terrace, N1 2UN. *Club:* Travellers.

WAKEFORD, Richard George; rural strategy consultant, since 2011; Director, Kazan Federal University Centre for Land Use and Sustainable Rural Development, since 2014; *b* 6 Oct. 1953; *s* of (Henry) Eric Wakeford and Mary Elisabeth Wakeford (*née* Parsons); *m* 1976, Susan Mary Beacham; three *s*. *Educ:* Chichester High Sch. for Boys; King's Coll., London (BSc Maths and Physics). Exec. Officer, 1975–80, Asst Private Sec. to Minister of State, 1979–80, DoE; HEO posts, DoE and Dept of Transport, 1980–83; Department of the Environment: Private Sec. to Permt Sec., 1983–85; Planning Inspectorate, 1985; Devlt Control, 1985–87; Bill Manager, Water Privatisation, 1988–89; Principal, Envmt White Paper Team, 1990; (last) Chief Exec., Crown Suppliers, 1991; Head of Devlt Plans and Policies, 1991–94; Asst Sec., Economic and Domestic Secretariat, Cabinet Office, 1994–96;

Chief Executive: Countryside Commn, 1996–99; Countryside Agency, 1999–2004; Hd, Scottish Exec. Envmt and Rural Affairs Dept, later Dir-Gen. Envmt, Scottish Govt, 2005–09; Dir-Gen. Rural Futures, Scottish Govt, 2009–10. UK Sustainable Develt Comr, 2000–04; Chm., UK Sustainable Develt Res. Network, 2011. Chm., Rural Wkg Party, OECD, 2007–12. Non-exec. Bd Mem., DEFRA, 2001–04. Mem., Cotswolds Area of Outstanding Natural Beauty, 2012–. Mem., Winchcombe Town Council, 2012–. Trustee, RICS Trust, 2013–. Mid Career Fellow, Princeton Univ., 1987–88; Vis. Prof., Birmingham City Univ., 2013–. Hon. MRTPI. Hon. Dr Glos. *Publications:* Speeding Planning Appeals, 1986; American Development Control: parallels and paradoxes from a British perspective, 1990. *Recreations:* gardening, photography, built and natural landscape, cycling. *Address:* Charingworth Court, Broadway Road, Winchcombe, Glos GL54 5JN. *T:* (01242) 603033.

WAKEHAM, family name of **Baron Wakeham**.

WAKEHAM, Baron *cr* 1992 (Life Peer), of Maldon in the County of Essex; **John Wakeham;** PC 1983; JP; DL; FCA; Chairman, Press Complaints Commission, 1995–2002; *b* 22 June 1932; *s* of late Major W. J. Wakeham and Mrs E. R. Wakeham; *m* 1st, 1965, Anne Roberta Bailey (*d* 1984); two *s*; 2nd, 1985, Alison Bridget Ward, MBE, DL, *d* of late Ven. E. J. G. Ward, LVO; one *s*. *Educ:* Charterhouse. Chartered Accountant. MP (C) Maldon, Feb. 1974–1983, Colchester South and Maldon, 1983–92; Asst Govt Whip, 1979–81; a Lord Comr of HM Treasury (Govt Whip), 1981; Parly Under-Sec. of State, DoI, 1981–82; Minister of State, HM Treasury, 1982–83; Parly Sec. to HM Treasury and Govt Chief Whip, 1983–87; Lord Privy Seal, 1987–88; Leader of the H of C, 1987–89; Lord Pres. of the Council, 1988–89; Sec. of State for Energy, 1989–92; Minister responsible for co-ordinating develt of presentation of govt policies, 1990–92; Lord Privy Seal and Leader of the H of L, 1992–94. Chm., Royal Commn on Reform of H of L, 1999. Chm., British Horseracing Bd, 1996–98 (Mem., 1995–98). Chancellor, Brunel Univ., 1998–2012, Chancellor Emeritus, 2013. Mem., Cttee of Mgt, RNLI, 1995–2005. JP Inner London, 1972; DL Hants, 1997. Hon. PhD Anglia Poly. Univ., 1992; DUniv Brunel, 1998. *Recreations:* sailing, racing, reading. *Address:* House of Lords, SW1A 0PW. *Clubs:* Carlton (Chm. 1992–98), Buck's, Garrick; Royal Yacht Squadron.

WAKEHAM, Sir William (Arnot), Kt 2009; FREng; Chairman: Exeter Science Park, since 2009; South East Physics Network, since 2009; *b* 25 Sept. 1944; *s* of Stanley William Wakeham; *m* 1st, 1969, Christina Marjorie Stone (marr. diss. 1974); one *s*; 2nd, 1978, Sylvia Frances Tolley; two *s*. *Educ:* Univ. of Exeter (BSc 1966; PhD 1969; DSc 1985). FREng (FEng 1997). Research Associate, Brown Univ., USA, 1969–71; Imperial College, London University: Lectr in Transport Processes, Dept of Chem. Engrg, 1971–78; Reader in Chemical Physics, 1978–85; Prof. in Chemical Physics, 1985–2001; Hd of Dept of Chem. Engrg and Chem. Technology, 1988–96; Pro Rector (Research), 1996–2001; Dep. Rector, 1997–2001; Vice-Chancellor, Univ. of Southampton, 2001–09. Chm., Commn of IUPAC, 1993–98. Mem., EPSRC, 2005–11. Treas., Euro-CASE, 2010–. Non-exec. Dir, Ilika plc, 2009–. Visiting Professor: Imperial Coll. London, 2002–; Univ. of Exeter, 2009–; Instituto Superior Técnico, Lisbon, 2009–. Sen. Vice-Pres., 2011–, and Hon. Sec. Internat. Affairs, 2009–, RAEng (Vice Pres., 2009); Pres., IChemE, 2011–12. FIC 2003. Hon. DSc: Lisbon, 1998; Exeter, 2007; Southampton Solent, 2007; Loughborough, 2010; Southampton 2011; Universidade Nova de Lisboa, 2012; Portsmouth, 2013. *Publications:* Intermolecular Forces: their origin and determination, 1981; Forces between Molecules, 1988; The Transport Properties of Fluids, 1987; International Thermodynamic Tables, vol. XI, 1989; Experimental Thermodynamics, vol. III, 1992; Commonly Asked Questions in Thermodynamics, 2011; numerous articles in learned jls. *Recreations:* power boats, cycling. *Address:* Beacon Down, Rewe, Exeter, Devon EX5 4DX.

WAKEHURST, 3rd Baron *cr* 1934, of Ardingly; **(John) Christopher Loder;** Chairman: Anglo & Overseas Trust PLC (formerly Anglo-American Securities Corporation), 1980–96 (Director, 1968–96); The Overseas Investment Trust PLC (formerly North Atlantic Securities Corporation), 1980–95; Morgan Grenfell Equity Income Trust PLC, 1991–95; *b* 23 Sept. 1925; *s* of 2nd Baron Wakehurst, KG, KCMG, and Dowager Lady Wakehurst, (Dame Margaret Wakehurst), DBE (*d* 1994); *S* father, 1970; *m* 1956, Ingeborg Krumbholz-Hess (*d* 1977); one *s* one *d*; *m* 1983, Brigid, *yr d* of William Noble, Cirencester. *Educ:* Eton; King's School, nr Sydney, NSW; Trinity College, Cambridge (BA 1948, LLB 1949, MA 1953). Served War as Sub Lieut RANVR and RNVR; South West Pacific, 1943–45. Barrister, Inner Temple, 1950. Chm., Morgan Grenfell Trust Managers Ltd, 1991–94; Director: Mayfair & City Properties plc, 1984–87; The Nineteen Twenty-Eight Investment Trust plc, 1984–86; Morgan Grenfell Latin American Cos Trust, 1994–96; Chm. and Dir, Hampton Gold Mining Areas, 1981–86; Chairman: Continental Illinois Ltd, 1973–84; Philadelphia National Ltd, 1985–90; Dep. Chm., London and Manchester Gp, 1981–95 (Dir, 1966–95). Trustee: The Photographers' Gallery Ltd, 1979–90; Photographers' Trust Fund, 1986–91. *Heir:* *s* Hon. Timothy Walter Loder, *b* 28 March 1958. *Address:* Trillinghurst Oast, Ranters Lane, Goudhurst, Kent TN17 1HL. *T:* (01580) 211502. *Club:* Chelsea Arts.

WAKELAM, Prof. Michael John Owen, PhD; Director and Chief Executive, BBSRC Babraham Institute, since 2007; Fellow, Downing College, Cambridge, since 2007; *b* 15 July 1955; *s* of John Wakelam and Sheila Wakelam; *m* 1980, Jane Catherine Fensome; two *s*. *Educ:* Univ. of Birmingham (BSc Med. Biochem. 1977; PhD Biochem. 1980). Res. Fellow, Univ. of Konstanz, 1981–83; Beit Meml Res. Fellow, Imperial Coll., London, 1983–85; Lectr, 1985–90, Sen. Lectr, 1991–92, Reader, 1992–93, in Biochemistry, Univ. of Glasgow; Prof. of Molecular Pharmacology, Univ. of Birmingham, 1993–2006. Hon. Prof., Sch. of Medicine, Univ. of Birmingham, 2007–; Hon. Prof. of Lipid Signalling, Faculty of Clinical Medicine, Univ. of Cambridge, 2011–; Vis. Prof., KCL, 2012–. Mem., MRC, 2004–08 (Chm., Molecular and Cellular Medicine Bd, 2004–08). *Publications:* contrib. to learned jls on cell signalling processes. *Recreations:* reading, music, walking. *Address:* Babraham Institute, Babraham Research Campus, Cambridge CB22 3AT.

WAKELEY, Amanda Jane, OBE 2010; fashion designer; Creative Director, Amanda Wakeley, since 1990; *b* 15 Sept. 1962; *d* of Sir John Cecil Nicholson Wakeley, 2nd Bt. *Educ:* Cheltenham Ladies' Coll. Worked, in fashion industry, NY, 1983–85, for private commns, 1987–90; Founder, Amanda Wakeley label, 1990; fashion and jewellery collections sold globally through over 100 outlets and online. Co-Chm., Fashion Targets Breast Cancer Appeal Cttee, 1996– (raised over £10 million). British Fashion Award for Glamour, 1992, 1993 and 1996. *Recreations:* music, travel, photography, ski touring, slalom water ski-ing, sailing. *Address:* 175–177 Fulham Road, SW3 6JW.

WAKELEY, (Sir) Nicholas Jeremy, (3rd Bt *cr* 1952, of Liss, Southampton); *b* 17 Oct. 1957; *er s* of Sir John Cecil Nicholson Wakeley, 2nd Bt, FRCS and of June (*née* Leney); *S* father, 2012, but his name does not appear on the Official Roll of the Baronetage; *m* 1991, Sarah Ann, *d* of Air Vice Marshal Brian Lewis Robinson, *qv*; four *s* one *d*. *Educ:* Uppingham. *Heir:* *s* Joshua Jeremy Wakeley, *b* 27 Sept. 1993.

WAKELIN, Prof. Daniel Leslie, PhD; Jeremy Griffiths Professor of Medieval English Palaeography, University of Oxford, since 2011; *b* Bury St Edmunds, 31 Jan. 1977; *s* of Roger and Jennifer Wakelin; civil partnership 2011, Dr Joel Harvey. *Educ:* Ixworth Middle Sch.; Thurston Upper Sch.; Trinity Hall, Cambridge (BA 1st Cl. Hons English 1998; MPhil Medieval and Renaissance Lit. 1999; PhD English 2003). Jun. Res. Fellow, St Catharine's Coll., Cambridge, 2002–04; Lectr and Fellow in English, Christ's Coll., Cambridge, 2004–11; Lectr in English, Univ. of Cambridge, 2006–11. Charles Owen Vis. Prof. of Medieval Studies, Univ. of Connecticut, 2009. Gov., N Oxfordshire Acad., 2011–15. *Publications:* Humanism, Reading and English Literature 1430–1530, 2007; (with Alexandra Gillespie) The Production of Books in England 1350–1500, 2011; Scribal Correction and Literary Craft: English manuscripts 1375–1510, 2014. *Recreations:* classic cinema, poetry, American history, travel, photography and the visual arts. *Address:* Faculty of English Language and Literature, University of Oxford, St Cross Buildings, Manor Road, Oxford OX1 3UL. *E:* daniel.wakelin@ell.ox.ac.uk.

WAKELIN, Michael Paul; Executive Associate in Public Education, Faculty of Divinity, University of Cambridge; Director, Cambridge Coexist Programme (formerly Abraham Project), since 2010; Executive Producer, TBI Media, since 2010; *b* 21 April 1961; *s* of Paul Oasland Wakelin and Rosemary Wakelin (*née* Sorrel); *m* 1997, Jacqueline Clare Jouannet; two *s* one *d*. *Educ:* Little Plumstead Primary Sch., Priors Court; Kingswood Sch., Bath; Birmingham Univ. (BA Hons Theol.). English teacher, Mokwon Univ., Taejon, S Korea, 1983–85; BBC Radio: researcher, 1986; producer, 1987; Exec. Producer, 1988–99; Series Producer, BBC TV, 1999–2006; Head of Religion and Ethics, BBC, 2006–09. Exec. Producer, Like for Like Productions, 2010–. Dir of Progs, Council of Christians and Jews, 2010–11; Consultant, Inter-faith Prog., Cambridge Univ., 2012. Co-Dir, Insight Film Fest., 2010 (Patron, 2013–). *Publications:* J. Arthur Rank: the man behind the gong, 1996. *Recreations:* bass guitarist for The Naked Covers, walking, cooking, supporting Norwich City. *E:* michael@michaelwakelin.co.uk. *W:* www.michaelwakelin.co.uk.

WAKELING, Richard Keith Arthur; Chairman, Polar Capital (formerly Henderson) Technology Trust PLC, 1996–2011; *b* 19 Nov. 1946; *s* of late Eric George Wakeling and Dorothy Ethel Wakeling; *m* 1971, Carmen; three *s*. *Educ:* Churchill Coll., Cambridge (MA). Called to the Bar, Inner Temple, 1971. Group Treasurer, BOC Group, 1977–83; Finance Dir, John Brown, 1983–86; Finance Dir, 1986–88, Acting Chief Exec., 1988–89, Charter Consolidated; Dep. Chief Exec., 1990, Chief Exec., 1991–94, Johnson Matthey. Dep. Chm., Celtic Group Holdings Ltd, 1994–97; Director: Costain, 1992–96; Laura Ashley Holdings, 1994–95; Logica, 1995–2002; Staveley Industries, 1995–99; Henderson Geared Income & Growth Trust (formerly HTR Income and Growth Split Trust), 1995–2003; Oxford Instruments plc, 1995–2001; MG plc, 1999–2000; Brunner Investment Trust plc, 2000–10. *Recreations:* mediaeval history and architecture, golf, music, gardening. *Address:* 46 The Bourne, Southgate, N14 6QS.

WAKEM, Dame Beverley (Anne), DNZM 2012; CBE 1990; Parliamentary Ombudsman, 2005–15, and Chief Ombudsman of New Zealand, 2008–15; *b* Wellington, NZ, 27 Jan. 1944; *d* of George Joseph Wakem and Sophie May Wakem; partner, Nicola Robyn Granville Chapman. *Educ:* St Mary's Coll., Wellington; Victoria Univ., Wellington (BA Hist. and Eng. 1968); Univ. of Kentucky (MA Communications 1973). FTCL 1967. Public Affairs Producer, Radio and TV, NZ Broadcasting Corp., 1963–72; Radio New Zealand: Exec. Producer, District Current Affairs, Wellington, 1974–75; Controller of Progs, 1975–84; Dir Gen., 1984–88; Chief Exec., 1988–91; Actg Chief Exec., NZ Broadcasting Corp., 1988; Wrightson Ltd: Commercial Dir, 1991; Gen. Manager, Human Resources and Corporate Affairs, 1992–96; Exec. Chm., Hill and Knowlton (NZ) Ltd, 1996–97; Dep. Chm., Remuneration Authy, 1997–2005. International Ombudsman Institute: Dir, 2008–14; Regl Vice-Pres., Aust. and Pacific, 2009–10; Pres., 2010–14. Dir, Pacific Ombudsman Alliance, 2008–14. Chm., Insce and Savings Ombudsman Commn, 2000–05; Member: Wkg Party on Teaching and Learning at a Distance, Educn Dept, 1975–76; Commn for the Future, 1975–82; Drug Adv. Cttee, 1980–82. Vice Pres., 1987, Pres., 1988–90, Asia Pacific Broadcasting Union. *Recreations:* theatre, opera. *Address:* PO Box 10 653, Wellington 6143, New Zealand. *T:* 274495798. *E:* bevwakem@actrix.co.nz. *Clubs:* Wellington, Rotary (Pres., 2004–05) (Wellington).

WAKSMAN, David Michael; QC 2002; **His Honour Judge Waksman;** a Senior Circuit Judge, since 2007; *b* 28 Aug. 1957. *Educ:* Royal Grammar Sch., Newcastle Upon Tyne; Manchester Univ. (LLB Hons); St Catherine's Coll., Oxford (BCL). Called to the Bar, Middle Temple, 1982; Bencher, Lincoln's Inn, 2009; Recorder of the Crown and County Courts, 2001–07. Hon. Lectr in Law, Manchester Univ.

WAKSMAN, Prof. Gabriel, PhD; FMedSci; FRS 2012; Courtauld Professor of Biochemistry, University College London, since 2007; Professor of Structural Molecular Biology and Director, Institute of Structural and Molecular Biology, University College London and Birkbeck, University of London, since 2003; *b* Corbeil Essonnes, France, 3 Sept. 1957; *s* of Roger Waksman and Rita Waksman (*née* Goldstein); *m* 1990, Susan Graham; two *s*. *Educ:* Univ. of Paris (BSc Genetics, BSc Physical Chem.; MSc Fundamental Biochem. 1980; PhD Fundamental Biochem. 1982). Washington University School of Medicine, Saint Louis: Asst Prof., 1993–98; Associate Prof., 1998–2000; Prof. of Biochem. and Molecular Biophysics, 2000; Alumni Endowed Prof. of Biochem. and Molecular Biophysics, 2000–02; P. Roy and Diana Vagelos Prof. of Biochem. and Molecular Biophysics, 2002–03; Hd, Dept of Biochem. and Molecular Biol., UCL and Hd, Dept of Biol Scis, Birkbeck, Univ. of London, 2006–. FMedSci 2008. Member: EMBO, 2007; German Acad. of Sci., 2013; MAE 2014. *Publications:* over 200 articles in scientific jls incl. Nature, Science and Cell. *Recreation:* long distance walking. *Address:* Anchor Cottage, Honor End Lane, Prestwood, Bucks HP16 9HG. *T:* (020) 7631 6833. *E:* g.waksman@ucl.ac.uk.

WALBY, Christine Mary, OBE 2005; Director of Social Services, Staffordshire County Council, 1991–96; independent consultant, 1997–2009; *b* 9 Feb. 1940; *d* of late Kathleen Walby (*née* Bradburn) and James Walby. *Educ:* University College of Wales, Aberystwyth (BA, DipEd); Manchester Univ. (Dip. Social Admin and Social Work); University College Cardiff (MSc Econ). Youth Leader Trainer, 1961–64; Social Worker, Children's Dept, Cheshire, 1964–70; Training Officer, Salford; Tutor, Manchester Univ.; Area Officer, Salford Social Services, 1970–74; Principal Officer, S Glam Social Services, 1974–81; Divl Dir, Berks Social Services, 1981–87; Dir, Social Services, Solihull MDC, 1987–91. Sen. Vis. Res. Fellow, Keele Univ., 1994–; Hon. Res. Fellow, Univ. of Wales Swansea, 1998–2006. Mem., Human Fertilization and Embryology Authy, 1991–93. Chm., Early Childhood Unit Adv. Gp, Nat. Children's Bureau, 1995–99; Trustee: Office for Children's Rights Comr, 1992–97; Children in Wales, 1998–2007 (Chm., 2002–); Bryn Melyn Gp Foundn, 2001–03; Triangle Trust 1949 Fund, 2004–06; Mem., Nat. Commn of Inquiry into Prevention of Child Abuse, 1994–96; Advr to Chair, Safeguarding Vulnerable Children Review, Welsh Assembly Govt, 2004–06; Chm., Bd of Dirs, Tros Gynnal, 2002–11 (Dir and Trustee, 2005–); Ind. Chm., Local Safeguarding Children Bd, Rhondda Cynon Taff, 2006–08. Mem. (Lab) Monmouthshire CC, 2008–12 (Chm., Children and Young People Select Cttee, 2010–12; Mem., Strong Communities Select Cttee, 2008–10). Hon. Life Mem. Council, NSPCC, 1993–. Chm., Homestart (Wales), 1999–2004. *Publications:* Who Am I?: identity, adoption and human fertilization (with Barbara Symons), 1990; contrib. professional jls. *Recreations:* walking, theatre, music, bird watching, holidays.

WALCOTT, Derek Alton; poet and playwright; *b* Castries, St Lucia, 23 Jan. 1930; twin *s* of late Warwick and Alix Walcott; *m* 1954, Fay Moston (marr. diss. 1959); one *s*; *m* 1962, Margaret Ruth Maillard (marr. diss.); two *d*; *m* Norline Metivier (marr. diss.). *Educ:* St Mary's Coll., St Lucia; Univ. of WI (BA 1953). Formerly teacher at schs in St Lucia and Grenada, and at Kingston Coll., Jamaica. Founded Trinidad Theatre Workshop, 1958. Lecturer: Rutgers Univ.; Yale Univ. Visiting Professor: Columbia Univ., 1981; Harvard Univ., 1982; Boston Univ., 1985–2008; Univ. of Essex, 2010; Dist. Schol. in Residence, Univ. of Alberta, 2009–11. Hon. DLitt Univ. of WI, 1972. Heinemann Award, RSL, 1966, 1983; Cholmondeley Award, 1969; Queen's Gold Medal for Poetry, 1989; Nobel Prize for

Literature, 1992. Order of the Hummingbird (Trinidad and Tobago), 1969. *Publications:* In a Green Night, 1962; Selected Poems, 1964; Castaway, 1965; Gulf and other poems, 1969; Another Life, 1973; Sea Grapes, 1976; Joker of Seville, 1979; Remembrance, and Pantomime, 1980; The Star-Apple Kingdom, 1980; The Fortunate Traveller, 1982; Midsummer, 1984; Collected Poems 1948–84, 1986; The Arkansas Testament, 1988; Three Plays: The Last Carnival, Beef No Chicken, A Branch of the Blue Nile, 1988; Collected Poems, 1990; Poems 1965–80, 1992; Omeros, 1990 (W. H. Smith Literary Award, 1991); Selected Poetry, 1993; Odyssey, 1993; The Bounty, 1997; (jtly) Homage to Robert Frost, 1998; What the Twilight Says (essays), 1998; Tiepolo's Hound, 2000; The Prodigal, 2005; Selected Poems, 2009; White Egrets, 2010 (T. S. Eliot Prize for Poetry, 2010); Moon-Child, 2012; The Poetry of Derek Walcott 1948–2013, 2014. *Address:* c/o Faber & Faber, Bloomsbury House, 74–77 Great Russell Street, WC1B 3DA; PO Box GM926, Becune Point, Castries, St Lucia, West Indies.

WALCOTT, Prof. Richard Irving, PhD; FRS 1991; FRSNZ; Professor of Geology, Victoria University, Wellington, New Zealand, 1985–99, now Emeritus; *b* 14 May 1933; *s* of James Farrar Walcott and Lilian Stewart (*née* Irving); *m* 1960, Genevieve Rae Lovatt; one *s* two *d*. *Educ:* Victoria Univ., Wellington (BSc Hons 1962; PhD 1965; DSc 1980). Meteorological Asst, Falkland Is Dependencies Survey, 1955–58; Post-doctoral Fellow, Geophysics Dept, Univ. of BC, 1966–67; Research Scientist: Earth Physics Br., Dept of Energy, Mines and Resources, Ottawa, 1967–74; Geophysics Div., Dept Sci. and Industrial Res., Wellington, NZ, 1975–84. FRSNZ 1982; Fellow, American Geophysical Union, 1993. Hector Medal, Royal Soc. NZ, 1994; Charles Whitten Medal, Amer. Geophysical Union, 1999. *Recreation:* gardening. *Address:* 24 Mahoe Street, Eastbourne, Wellington, New Zealand. *T:* (4) 5628040.

WALD, Sir Nicholas (John), Kt 2008; DSc; FRCP, FFPH, FRCOG, FMedSci; FRS 2004; CBiol, FRSB; Professor, since 1983, and Head (formerly Director), since 2003, Centre for Environmental and Preventive Medicine, and Chairman, Wolfson Institute of Preventive Medicine, 1991–95 and 1997–2003, Bart's and The London School of Medicine and Dentistry, Queen Mary (formerly St Bartholomew's Hospital Medical College, then St Bartholomew's and The Royal London School of Medicine and Dentistry, Queen Mary and Westfield College), University of London; Hon. Consultant, St Bartholomew's Hospital, since 1983; *b* 31 May 1944; *s* of Adolf Max Wald and Frieda (*née* Shatsow); *m* 1966, Nancy Evelyn Miller; three *s* one *d*. *Educ:* Owen's Sch., EC1; University Coll. London; University Coll. Hosp. Med. Sch. (MB BS); DSc (Med) London 1987. FRCP 1986 (MRCP 1971); FFPH (FFCM 1982; MFCM 1980); FRCOG 1992 (addendum); CBiol, FRSB (FIBiol 2000). VSO, India, 1966. Ho. appts, UCH and Barnet Gen. Hosp., 1968–69; Med. Registrar, UCH, 1970; Member: MRC Sci. Staff, MRC Epidemiology and Med. Care Unit, 1971; Sci. Staff, ICRF (formerly DHSS) Cancer Epidem. and Clin. Trials Unit, 1972–82, Dep. Dir, 1982–83. Wellcome Vis. Prof. in Basic Med. Scis, at Foundn for Blood Res., USA, 1980, then Hon. Sen. Res. Scientist; Hon. Prof., UCL, 2012–. Hon. Dir, Cancer Screening Gp, CRC, 1989–2000. Chairman: MRC Smoking Res. Rev. Cttee, 1986–89; MRC Study Monitoring Cttee of Randomised Trial of Colo-rectal Cancer Screening, 1986–2009; MRC Volatile Substance Abuse Wkg Party, 1985–87; NE Thames Reg. Breast Cancer Res. Cttee, 1988–96; Nat. Inst. of Child Health and Human Develt Wkg Gp on Quality Control of Alpha-fetoprotein Measurement, 1978; Steering Cttee for MRC Multicentre Aneurysm Screening Study, 1997–; Adv. Gp on Ionising Radiation, HPA, 2004–11; Member: MRC Neurosciences Bd, 1962–86; MRC Steering Cttee of Randomised Trial of Multivitamins and Neural Tube Defects, 1983–92; DHSS Cttee on Med. Aspects of Contamination of Air, Soil and Water, 1985–89; DHSS Cttee on Carcinogenicity of Chemicals in Food, Consumer Products and the Environment, 1984–89; DHSS Ind. Sci. Cttee on Smoking and Health, 1983–91; DoH (formerly DHSS) Adv. Cttee on Breast Cancer Screening, 1986–99; Central R&D Cttee, 1991–95; CMO's Health of the Nation Wkg Gp, 1991–97; DoH Population Screening Panel, 1992–98; CMO's Scientific Cttee on Tobacco and Health, 1993–2002; Folic Acid Sub-gp, DoH Cttee on Med. Aspects of Food and Nutrition Policy, 1996–2000; Antenatal Sub-gp, DoH Nat. Screening Cttee, 1997–2005; Nat. Screening Cttee, HPV/LBC Pilots Steering Gp, 2000–03; Adv. Gp for Evaluation of UK Colorectal Cancer Screening Pilot, 2000–03; ACOST Med. Res. and Health Cttee, 1991–92; RCP Cttee on Ethical Issues in Medicine, 1988–2010; RCP Computer Cttee, 1988–92; Physiol. and Pharmacol. Panel, Wellcome Trust, 1995–2000; MRC Scientific Adv. Cttee on Gulf War Syndrome, 1996–97; Adv. Gp on Nuclear Test Veterans, 2000–02; Council of Trustees, Foundn for Study of Infant Deaths, 2000–04; Cttee on Environmental Tobacco Smoke, Nat. Acad. of Sci., USA, 1985–86. 140th Cutter Lectr on Preventive Medicine, Harvard Sch. of Public Health, 2004; Rayner Lect., RCP, 2009; Feldman Lect., 2010; Jephcott Lect., RSocMed, 2011; Croonian Lect., RCP, 2015. Inaugural Ed., Jl of Medical Screening, 1994–. Pres., Med. Screening Soc., 2002–. William Julius Mickle Fellow, Univ. of London, 1990. Founder FMedSci 1998; Mem., Assoc. of Physicians of GB and Ire. Hon. DSc (Med) UCL, 2005. Joseph P. Kennedy Jr Foundn Award for Scientific Res., 2000; Hamdan Award for Med. Res. Excellence, Hamdan Awards Scientific Cttee, UAE Univ., 2012. *Publications:* (ed) Antenatal and Neonatal Screening, 1984, 2nd edn (ed with Ian Leck) 2000; (ed with Sir Richard Doll) Interpretation of Negative Epidemiological Evidence for Carcinogenicity, 1985; The Epidemiological Approach: an approach to epidemiology in medicine, 1985, 4th edn 2004; (ed jtly) UK Smoking Statistics, 1988; (ed with Sir Peter Froggatt) Nicotine, Smoking and the Low Tar Programme, 1989; (ed with J. Baron) Smoking and Hormone Related Disorders, 1990; (jtly) International Smoking Statistics, 1993, 2nd edn (ed jtly) 2000; articles in sci. jls on screening for neural tube defects, Down's Syndrome and other disorders, on health effects of tobacco, on the aetiology and prevention of cancer, cardiovascular disease and congenital malformations. *Recreations:* family, discussion, boating, economics. *Address:* Wolfson Institute of Preventive Medicine, Bart's and The London School of Medicine and Dentistry, Charterhouse Square, EC1M 6BQ. *T:* (020) 7882 6269; 9 Park Crescent Mews East, W1W 5AF. *T:* (020) 7636 2721. *Club:* Athenæum.

WALDECK, Pieter Willem, (Pim), Grand Cross of Honour, Order of House of Orange (Netherlands), 2006; Ambassador of the Netherlands to the Court of St James's, 2007–12; *b* 6 Nov. 1947; *s* of late Dr Karel Waldeck and of Elisabeth Waldeck (*née* Koster); *m* 1976, Jonkvrouw Cordula Catharina Agatha Quarles van Ufford; one *s* two *d*. *Educ:* Vrijzinnig Christelijk Lyceum, The Hague; Univ. of Leiden (Master of Law). Mem. Bd (Sales and Publicity), NBBS Student Travel, 1970–71; 2nd Lieutenant RNR, Naval Intelligence Service, 1973–75; entered Netherlands Foreign Service, 1975; Third Sec. (Political), Moscow, 1976–78; Second Sec., Develt Co-operation, ESCAP, Bangkok, 1978–81; First Sec., Hd of Econ. Section, Cairo, 1981–84; Private Sec. to HM Queen and HRH Prince Claus of Netherlands, 1984–88; Hd of Section, Dept of Eur. Integration, Min. of Foreign Affairs, 1988–92; Counsellor, Perm. Repn to EU, Brussels, 1992–97; Hd, Dept of Information, and Chief Spokesman, Min. of Foreign Affairs, 1997–2000; Principal Sec. to HM Queen of Netherlands, 2000–02; Grand Master of the House of HM Queen of Netherlands, 2002–06. Chair, Van den Berch van Heemstede Foundn; Member: Adv. Bd, Netherlands Dance Th., The Hague; Bd, Friends of Royal Picture Gall. Mauritshuis, The Hague; Bd, Nat. Archives Soc., The Hague. Grand Officer: Order of Isabella la Católica (Spain), 2001; Order of Three Stars (Latvia), 2006; Grand Cross: Order of Southern Cross (Brazil), 2003; Order of Merit (Chile), 2003; Order of White Elephant (Thailand), 2004; Order of Independence (Jordan), 2006; Order of the Crown (Belgium), 2006; Civil and Mil. Order of Merit, Adolf of Nassau (Luxembourg), 2006. *Publications:* articles in Nederlands Juristenblad, Mars Et Historia, Tijdschrift voor Zeegeschiedenis, Jaarboek Die Haghe. *Recreations:* drawing, bird watching, (naval) history, golf, sailing. *Address:* Groenhovenstraat 8, 2596 HT The Hague, Netherlands. *Clubs:* Haagsche (Plaats Royaal), Nieuwe Littéraire Sociëteit de Witte (The Hague); Broekpolder Golf.

WALDEGRAVE, family name of **Earl Waldegrave** and **Baron Waldegrave of North Hill**.

WALDEGRAVE, 13th Earl *cr* 1729; **James Sherbrooke Waldegrave;** Bt 1643; Baron Waldegrave 1685; Viscount Chewton 1729; *b* 8 Dec. 1940; *e s* of 12th Earl Waldegrave, KG, GCVO and Mary Hermione (*d* 1995), *d* of Lt-Col A. M. Grenfell, DSO; *S* father, 1995; *m* 1986, Mary Alison Anthea (marr. diss. 1996), *d* of late Sir Robert Furness, KBE, CMG, and Lady Furness; two *s*. *Educ:* Eton Coll.; Trinity Coll., Cambridge. *Heir: s* Viscount Chewton, *qv*. *Address:* Chewton House, Chewton Mendip, Radstock BA3 4LL. *Clubs:* Garrick; Leander.

WALDEGRAVE OF NORTH HILL, Baron *cr* 1999 (Life Peer), of Chewton Mendip in the county of Somerset; **William Arthur Waldegrave;** PC 1990; Provost of Eton College, since 2009 (Fellow, since 2007); *b* 15 Aug. 1946; *yr s* of 12th Earl Waldegrave, KG, GCVO and Mary Hermione (*née* Grenfell); *m* 1977, Caroline Burrows (*see* Caroline Waldegrave); one *s* three *d*. *Educ:* Eton Coll.; Corpus Christi Coll., Oxford (Hon. Fellow, 1991); Harvard Univ. (Kennedy Fellow). Fellow, All Souls Coll., Oxford, 1971–86 and 1999–. Central Policy Review Staff, Cabinet Office, 1971–73; Political Staff, 10 Downing Street, 1973–74; Head of Leader of Opposition's Office, 1974–75; GEC Ltd, 1975–81; a Man. Dir, Dresdner Kleinwort Wasserstein, 1998–2003; a Vice-Chm. and Man. Dir, 2003–08, Consultant, 2008–12, UBS. MP (C) Bristol West, 1979–97; contested (C) same seat, 1997. Parly Under-Sec. of State, DES, 1981–83, DoE, 1983–85. Minister of State for the Environment and Countryside, 1985–87, for Planning, 1986–88, and for Housing, 1987–88, DoE; Minister of State, FCO, 1988–90; Sec. of State for Health, 1990–92; Chancellor of the Duchy of Lancaster, 1992–94; Minister of Agric., Fisheries and Food, 1994–95; Chief Sec. to HM Treasury, 1995–97. Director: Waldegrave Farms Ltd, 1975–; Bristol and West plc (formerly Bristol and West Bldg Soc.), 1997–2006; Bank of Ireland Financial Services (UK) plc, 2002–06; Henry Sotheran Ltd, 1998– (Chm., 2007–15); Biotech. Growth Trust plc (formerly Finsbury Life Scis Investment Trust, then Finsbury Emerging Biotech Growth Trust), 1998– (Chm., 2012–); Fleming Family and Partners Ltd, 2008–12; Coutts and Co., 2012– (Chm., 2014–). Member: IBA Adv. Council, 1980–81; Internat. Adv. Bd, Teijin Ltd, 2006–08; Remuneration and Nomination Cttee, Bergesen Worldwide Gas ASA, 2006–08; Chm., Adv. Cttee, Royal Mint, 2011–. Chm., Nat. Mus. of Sci. and Industry, 2002–10; Mem., President's Adv. Cttee, Royal Soc., 2012–. Trustee: Rhodes Trust, 1992–2002 (Chm., 2002–11); Beit Meml Fellowships for Medical Res., 1998–2006; Mandela Rhodes Foundn, 2003–11; Dyson Sch. of Design Innovation, 2007–08; Strawberry Hill Trust, 2008–13; Cumberland Lodge, Windsor, 2009–. Mem. Bd, Lewis Walpole Liby, Yale Univ., 2008–. Founder Trustee and Chm., Bristol Cathedral Trust, 1989–2002. Pres., Royal Bath and West Soc., 2006. Hon. DCL Reading, 2015. JP Inner London Juvenile Court, 1975–79. *Publications:* The Binding of Leviathan, 1977; A Different Kind of Weather: a memoir, 2015. *Address:* 62 Hornton Street, W8 4NU; Provost's Lodge, Eton College, Windsor, Berks SL4 6DH. *Clubs:* White's, Beefsteak, Pratt's; Leander (Henley-on-Thames).

WALDEGRAVE, Caroline Linda Margaret, (Lady Waldegrave of North Hill), OBE 2000; Founding Principal, since 1975, and Director, since 2008, Leith's School of Food and Wine Ltd (Managing Director, 1977–2008); *b* 14 Aug. 1952; *y d* of late Major Philip Richard Miles Burrows and Molly Burrows (*née* Hollins); *m* 1977, Hon. William Waldegrave (*see* Baron Waldegrave of North Hill); one *s* three *d*. *Educ:* Convent of the Sacred Heart, Woldingham, Surrey; Postgrad. Dip. Psychodynamic Counselling. Mem., HEA, 1985–88. Chm., Guild of Food Writers, 1991–93; Pres., Hosp. Caterers Assoc., 2006–08. Advr, Nat. Life Story Collection, BL, 2014– (Trustee, 2005–14). Pres., Portobello Trust, 1987–2000. *Publications:* The Healthy Gourmet, 1986; Low Fat Gourmet, 1987; *jointly:* Leith's Cookery Course, 1980; Leith's Cookery School, 1985; Leith's Cookery Bible, 1991, 2nd edn 1996; Leith's Complete Christmas, 1992; Children's Cookery, 1993; Leith's Fish Bible, 1995; Leith's Easy Dinner Parties, 1995; Leith's Healthy Eating, 1996; Children's Fun to Cook Book, 1996; Sainsbury Book of Children's Cookery, 1997. *Recreations:* bridge, tennis. *Address:* Provost's Lodge, Eton College, Windsor, Berks SL4 6DH.

WALDEN, (Alastair) Brian; television and radio presenter and journalist; Chairman: Paragon, since 1996; Capital Fund, since 2006; *b* 8 July 1932; *s* of W. F. Walden; *m* Hazel Downes, *d* of William A. Downes; one *s* (and three *s* of former marriages). *Educ:* West Bromwich Grammar School; Queen's College and Nuffield College, Oxford; Pres., Oxford Union, 1957. University Lecturer. MP (Lab): Birmingham, All Saints, 1964–74; Birmingham, Ladywood, 1974–77. Mem., W Midland Bd, Central TV, 1981–84. Pres., Birmingham and Midland Inst., 2006. Columnist: London Standard, 1983–86; Thomson Regional Newspapers, 1983–86; Sunday Times, 1986–90. Presenter: Weekend World, LWT, 1977–86; The Walden Interview, ITV, 1988 and 1989; Walden, LWT, 1990–94; Walden on Labour Leaders, BBC, 1997; Walden on Heroes, BBC, 1998; Walden on Villains, BBC, 1999; A Point of View, BBC Radio 4, 2005–. Shell International Award, 1982; BAFTA Richard Dimbleby Award, 1985; Aims of Industry Special Free Enterprise Award, 1990; TV Times Favourite TV Current Affairs Personality, 1990; Television and Radio Industries Club ITV Personality of the Year, 1991. *Publications:* The Walden Interviews, 1990. *Recreations:* chess, reading. *Address:* Landfall, Fort Road, St Peter Port, Guernsey GY1 1ZU.

WALDEN, David Peter, CBE 2013; independent public policy consultant, since 2012; Director of Adult Services (formerly Adults and Regions), Social Care Institute for Excellence, 2009–12; *b* 23 Sept. 1954; *s* of Gerald Walden and Shirley Walden (*née* Rothfield); *m* 1981, Janet Day; one *s* one *d*. *Educ:* Newcastle upon Tyne Royal Grammar Sch.; St John's Coll., Oxford (BA Modern Hist. 1977). DHSS, subseq. DoH, 1977–2004: Principal, 1982; Management Side Secretary: Nurses' and Midwives' Whitley Council, 1982–85; NHS Consultants' Negotiating Body, 1985–86; Private Sec. to Dep. Chm., NHS Mgt Bd, 1986–87; Asst Sec., Doctors' Pay and Conditions, 1989–90; on secondment as Personnel Dir, Poole Hosp. NHS Trust, 1991–93; Head: Community Care Br., 1993–96; Health Promotion Div., 1996–99; Social Care Policy, 1999–2001; Dir, Health Services Develt, Anchor Trust, 2001–03 (on secondment); Dir, Office of Ind. Regulator for NHS Foundn Trusts, 2003–04; Dir of Strategy, Commn for Social Care Inspection, 2004–09. Dir, 2020health, 2012–; Bd Mem., Affinity Trust, 2011–. Trustee: Barchester Healthcare Foundn, 2013–; Elderly Accommodation Counsel, 2014–. *Address:* Glebe House, Trent, Sherborne, Dorset DT9 4SL. *T:* 07789 653522.

WALDEN, George Gordon Harvey, CMG 1981; writer; *b* 15 Sept. 1939; *s* of G. G. Walden; *m* 1970, Sarah Nicolette Hunt; two *s* one *d*. *Educ:* Latymer Upper Sch.; Jesus Coll., Cambridge; Moscow Univ. (post-graduate). Research Dept, Foreign Office, 1962–65; Chinese Language Student, Hong Kong Univ., 1965–67; Second Secretary, Office of HM Chargé d'Affaires, Peking, 1967–70; First Sec., FCO (Soviet Desk), 1970–73; Ecole Nationale d'Administration, Paris, 1973–74; First Sec., HM Embassy, Paris, 1974–78; Principal Private Sec. to Foreign and Commonwealth Sec., 1978–81; sabbatical year, Harvard, 1981; Head of Planning Staff, FCO, 1982–83; retired from HM Diplomatic Service, 1983. MP (C) Buckingham, 1983–97. PPS to Sec. of State for Educn and Science, 1984–85; Parly Under-Sec. of State, DES, 1985–87. Chm. of Judges, Booker Prize, 1995; Chm., Russian Booker Prize, 2003–10. Columnist: Evening Standard, 1991–2002; Times, 2009–; book reviewer, Bloomberg Muse, 2006–. *Publications:* Ethics and Foreign Policy, 1990; We Should Know Better: solving the education crisis, 1996; Lucky George (memoir), 1999; The New Elites:

making a career in the masses, 2000; Who is a Dandy?, 2002; God won't save America, 2006; Time to Emigrate?, 2006; China: a wolf in the world?, 2008.

See also P. S. Morgan.

WALDEN, Rt Rev. Graham Howard; Bishop of The Murray, 1989–2001; *b* 19 March 1931; *s* of Leonard Howard Walden and Mary Ellen Walden (*née* Cahalane); *m* 1964, Margaret Ann (*née* Brett); two *s* one *d*. *Educ:* Univ. of Queensland (BA 1952; MA 1954); Australian Coll. of Theol. (ThL 1954); Christ Church, Oxford (BLitt 1960; MLitt 1980). Ordained deacon 1954, priest 1955; Assistant Curate: West Hackney, 1954–56; St Saviour's, Poplar, 1957–58; permission to officiate, dio. of Oxford, 1955–59; Mem., Bush Brotherhood of the Good Shepherd, NSW, 1959–63; Vice Principal, Torres Strait Mission Theol Coll., 1963–65; Rector of Mudgee, NSW, 1965–70; Archdeacon of Barker, 1968–70; Archdeacon and Vicar-Gen. of Ballarat, 1970–89; Asst Bishop of Ballarat, 1981–89; Rector of Hamilton and Bishop in Hamilton, 1981–84. Nat. Chm., Anglican Men's Soc., 1983–93 (Vice-Pres., 1993–); Anglican Chm., Jt Anglican RC Diocesan Commn, 1977–89; Vice-Chm., Internat. Bishops' Conf., 1992–95; Member: Gen. Bd of Religious Educn, 1970–81; Anglican Lutheran Conversations constituted by Gen. Synod of Anglican Church of Australia, 1989–2001 (Co-Chm., 1993–2001); Gen. Synod Commn on Doctrine, 1989–98 (Chm., 1992–98); Council, Brotherhood of the Good Shepherd, 2003– (Episcopal Visitor to Company of the Good Shepherd, 2003–05). *Publications:* contrib. to jls and church papers. *Address:* Unit 61, Horizons Village, 57 Minore Road, Dubbo, NSW 2830, Australia.

WALDEN, Ian Mennie, MBE 1972; Independent Member, Hertfordshire Police Authority, 2007; *b* 23 Oct. 1940; *s* of Col Frank Walden, MBE, DL, and Mollie Walden (*née* Mennie); *m* 1st, 1965, Anne Frances Lacey (marr. diss.); three *s*; 2nd, 1995, Christine Anne Osbourn; one *d*, and two step *d*. *Educ:* Haileybury. Served Royal Marines, 1958–89, including: active service in ME, FE and NI; Temp. Equerry to Duke of Edinburgh, 1976; briefer to CDS, during Falklands War, 1980–82; CO, Commando Logistic Regt, 1983–85; Dep. COS, Trng and Reserve Forces, 1985–87; Dir, Jt Ops Centre, MoD, 1987–89. Campaign Manager, St John Ambulance, 1992–93; Dir, Internat. Spinal Res. Trust, 1993–97; Chief Executive: Br. Lung Foundn, 1997–2001; BLISS, the Premature Baby Charity, 2001–03; Watford & District Mencap, 2003–04. Former ind. consultant to the voluntary sector; Founder, Mosaic Consultancy Services, 2004. Chm., St Albans Dist CAB, 2008–09. Trustee, Counselling Foundn (formerly Herts and Beds Pastoral Foundn, then Herts and Beds Counselling Foundn), 2005–. Trustee, Over the Wall Gang Camp, 2000–09 (Chm., 2000–07). Mem., Lions Clubs Internat., 2000–. *Recreations:* woodwork, ski-ing, badminton, family life. *Address:* 50 Lyndhurst Drive, Harpenden, Herts AL5 5RJ. *T:* (01582) 462067.

WALDEN, William Michael; Director of Communications and Official Spokesman for Mayor of London, since 2012; *b* Guernsey, 8 June 1971; *s* of Michael and Kathleen Walden; *m* 2004, Daniela Relph; two *s* one *d*. *Educ:* Elizabeth Coll., Guernsey; Univ. of Durham (BA Modern Hist. 1993). Reporter: Channel TV (ITV), 1993–95; BBC Spotlight, 1995–97; reporter and producer, ITN News at Ten, 1997–99; Sen. Producer, Home and Foreign news desks, BBC News, 1999–2012: Sen. Political Producer, 2001–03; Dep. Bureau Chief, Washington, 2003–06; Westminster News Ed., 2006–12. Mem., Old Elizabethan Assoc. *Recreations:* family, golf, cricket. *Address:* City Hall, The Queen's Walk, More London, SE1 2AA. *T:* (020) 7983 4069. *E:* will.walden@london.gov.uk. *Club:* MCC.

WALDEN-SMITH, Karen Jane; Her Honour Judge Walden-Smith; a Circuit Judge, since 2010; Specialist Senior Chancery Circuit Judge, since 2013; Deputy High Court Judge, since 2013; *b* Crawley, W Sussex, 17 Dec. 1966; *d* of late Edward Walden-Smith and of Eileen Walden-Smith (*née* White); *m* 2000, Prof. James Russell Raven, *qv*; two *s*. *Educ:* Hazelwick Comprehensive Sch., Crawley; Clare Coll., Cambridge (BA 1989; MA 1993). Called to the Bar, Lincoln's Inn, 1990 (Hardwicke, Shelford and Wolfson Major Scholar; Inns of Court Studentship; Sir Louis Gluckstein advocacy prize), Bencher, 2013 (Mem. Bar Rep. Cttee, 2005–13); Recorder, 2004–10; a Judge, Upper Tribunal (Lands Chamber), 2011–; Diversity and Community Relations Judge, 2011–. Founder Mem., Property Bar Assoc. (Mem. Cttee, 2004–10; Sec., 2007–09); Barrister Mem., Bar Council/BSB Disciplinary Panels, 2004–10. Mem., Public Speaking Cttee, 2008–12, and Treas., local br., ESU, 2010–12. Parish Councillor, 2005–13; Gov., local primary sch., 2005–10. *Publications:* (contrib.) Butterworth's Forms and Precedents, vol. 33, 2008; contrib. articles to legal jls. *Recreations:* theatre, reading, art, having fun with sons. *Address:* Central London Civil Justice Centre, Thomas More Building, Royal Courts of Justice, WC2A 2LL. *E:* HHJudgekaren.walden-smith@judiciary.gsi.gov.uk.

WALDER, Edwin James, CMG 1971; NSW Civil Service, retired; *b* 5 Aug. 1921; *s* of Edwin James Walder and Dulcie Muriel Walder (*née* Griffiths); *m* 1944, Norma Cheslin; two *d*. *Educ:* North Newtown High Sch.; Univ. of Sydney (BEc). FRAIPA 1983. Apptd NSW Civil Service, 1938; NSW State Treasury: 1945; Asst Under-Sec. (Finance), 1959–61; Dep. Under-Sec., 1961–63; Under-Sec. and Comptroller of Accounts, 1963–65; Pres., Metrop. Water, Sewerage and Drainage Bd, Sydney, 1965–81. Member: State Pollution Control Commn, 1971–81; Metropolitan Waste Disposal Authority (Sydney), 1971–81; management consultant and co. dir, 1981–92. *Recreations:* genealogy, internet browsing. *Clubs:* Central Coast Leagues (Gosford); Avoca Beach Bowling; Probus (Avoca Beach, and Broadwater, Central Coast).

WALDMANN, Prof. Herman, FRS 1990; Professor, since 1994, and Head of Department of Pathology, 1994–2012, Oxford University; Fellow of Lincoln College, Oxford, since 1994; *b* 27 Feb. 1945; *s* of Leon and Rene Ryfka Waldmann; *m* 1971, Judith Ruth Young. *Educ:* Sir George Monoux Grammar Sch., Walthamstow; Sidney Sussex Coll., Cambridge (BA; Hon. Fellow, 2008); London Hosp. Med. Coll. (MB BChir); PhD Cantab. FRCPath, FRCP. Cambridge University: Dept of Pathology, 1971–94; Fellow, King's Coll., 1985–94; Kay Kendall Prof. of Therapeutic Immunology, 1989–93. Founder FMedSci 1998. Hon. Fellow: QMW, 1996; King's Coll., Cambridge, 2009. Dist. Prof. Lect., Univ. of Iowa, 2007. Hon. ScD Cambridge, 2008. Graham Bull Prize for Clinical Res., RCP, 1991; José Carreras Award, European Hematology Assoc., 2005; JDRF Excellence in Clinical Res. Award, 2005; Thomas E. Starzl Prize in Surgery and Immunol., 2007; Scrip Lifetime Achievement Award, 2007. *Publications:* Limiting Dilution Analysis (with Dr I. Lefkovits), 1977, 2nd edn 1998; The Immune System (with Dr I. McConnell and A. Munro), 1981; (ed) Monoclonal Antibodies, 1988; many scientific papers. *Recreations:* family, (less) food, friends, travel, music. *Address:* Sir William Dunn School of Pathology, South Parks Road, Oxford OX1 3RE. *E:* herman.waldmann@path.ox.ac.uk.

WALDNER, Benita Maria F.; *see* Ferrero-Waldner.

WALDRON, Prof. Jeremy James, DPhil; FBA 2011; Chichele Professor of Social and Political Theory, University of Oxford, 2010–14; Quondam Fellow, All Souls College, Oxford, since 2014 (Fellow, 2010–14); University Professor and Professor of Law, New York University, since 2006; *b* Invercargill, NZ, 13 Oct. 1953; *s* of Rev. Francis Herbert Waldron and Joyce Annette Waldron; *m* 1974, Helen Faye McGimpsey (marr. diss. 1987); one *s*; partner, Prof. Carol Sanger. *Educ:* Univ. of Otago (BA Hons 1974; LLB Hons 1978); University Coll., Oxford (DPhil Law 1986). Darby Fellow in Pol Theory, Lincoln Coll., Oxford, 1980–82; Lectr in Pols, Univ. of Edinburgh, 1983–87; Prof. of Law, Univ. of Calif, Berkeley, 1987–96; Univ. Prof. and Prof. of Law, Columbia Univ., 1997–2006. *Publications:* The Dignity of Legislation, 1999; Law and Disagreement, 1999; God, Locke and Equality, 2002; Torture, Terror and Trade-offs, 2010; The Harm in Hate Speech, 2012; Dignity, Rank and Rights, 2012; articles on legal and political philos. in learned jls. *Recreations:* travel, theatre, music. *Address:* All Souls College, Oxford OX1 4AL; 448 Riverside Drive, New York, NY 10027, USA. *E:* jeremy.waldron@nyu.edu.

WALDRON, William Francis; QC 2006; a Recorder, since 2000; *b* 27 Oct. 1957; *s* of William Henry Waldron, QC and Rosemary Waldron; *m* 2007, Julie Case; one *s*. *Educ:* St Edward's Coll., Liverpool; University Coll. of Wales, Cardiff (LLB 1979). Broadcaster, CBC Commercial Radio Station, Cardiff, 1980–85. Called to the Bar, Gray's Inn, 1986, Bencher, 2011; in practice specialising in catastrophic injury law. Judge, Mental Health Review Tribunal (Restricted Panel), 2012–. Dep. Chair (Circuits), Advocacy Trng Council, 2014. *Recreations:* Everton FC (lifelong, fanatical and ever-hopeful fan), acoustic guitar, flying (private pilot's licence/IMC), sailing. *Address:* Exchange Chambers, Derby Square, Liverpool L2 9XX. *T:* (0151) 236 7747. *E:* waldronqc@exchangechambers.co.uk. *Club:* Porthmadog Sailing.

WALDRON-RAMSEY, Waldo Emerson; QC (Barbados) 2009; Barrister and Attorney-at-Law; international consultant; *b* 1 Jan. 1930; *s* of Wyatt and Delcina Waldron-Ramsey; *m* 1954, Shiela Pamella Beresford, Georgetown, Guyana; one *s* three *d*. *Educ:* Barbados; Hague Academy; London Sch. of Economics; Yugoslavia. LLB Hons; BSc (Econ) Hons; PhD. Called to Bar, Middle Temple; practised London Bar and SW Circuit, 1957–60; Marketing Economist, Shell International, 1960–61; Tanzanian Foreign Service, 1961–70; High Comr for Barbados in UK, and Ambassador to France, Netherlands and Germany, 1970–71; Ambassador and Perm. Rep. for Barbados to UN, 1971–76. UN Legal Expert: in field of human rights, 1967–71; on Israel, 1968–71. Chairman: Sunny Investment & Finance Gp of Cos, 1994–; Edutech (Pty) Ltd, Windhoek, Cape Town, and Gaborone, 1994. Senator, Parlt of Barbados, 1983–85. Member: Amer. Acad. of Political and Social Sciences; Amer. Soc. of Internat. Law; Amer. Inst. of Petroleum (Marketing Div.). Hon. Fellow, Hebrew Univ. of Jerusalem, 1972. DSc (Pol. Econ.) Univ. of Phnom-Penh, 1973; Hon. LLD Chung-Ang Univ., Republic of Korea, 1975. Grand Officer (1st Class), Nat. Order of Honneur et Mérite, Republic of Haiti, 1968; Grand Officier, Ordre Nat. de l'Amitié et Mérite, Khymèr, 1973; Order of Distinguished Diplomatic Service Merit, Gwanghwa (1st Class), Republic of Korea, 1974. *Recreations:* cricket, tennis, bridge, travel. *Address:* (chambers) White Park Road, Bridgetown, Barbados. *T:* 4278280, 4242021; (chambers) 26 Court Street, Brooklyn, New York 11225, USA; The Monticello, 30 Park Avenue, Mount Vernon, New York 10550, USA. *T:* (London) (020) 7229 4870, *T:* (N Carolina) (336) 7650080. *Clubs:* Royal Automobile; Lincoln Lodge (Connecticut).

WALE, Kevin Ernest; President and Managing Director, General Motors China Group, 2005–12; Chief Country Operations Officer, China, India and ASEAN, General Motors, 2012; *b* 30 Oct. 1954; *m* 1976, Marilyn Joy Baensch; two *s*. *Educ:* Melbourne Univ. (BCom Hons); General Motors Inst., USA. General Motors: joined Finance Dept, Holden, Australia, 1975; Corp. Finance Dept, NY, 1983–85; various posts, Finance Div., subseq. Dir of Finance and Strategic Planning, Holden, Australia, 1985–93; Dir of Sales, Marketing and Aftersales, Holden, Australia, 1993–98; Exec. in Charge, General Motors Asia Pacific (Pte) Ltd, Singapore, 1998–2001; Chm. and Man. Dir, Vauxhall Motors Ltd, and Vice-Pres., General Motors Europe, 2001–05; Mem., European Strategy Bd, 2001. *Recreations:* golf, cricket, motor sports.

WALES, Archbishop of, since 2003; **Most Rev. Barry Cennydd Morgan,** PhD; Bishop of Llandaff, since 1999; *b* 31 Jan. 1947; *s* of Rees Haydn Morgan and Mary Gwyneth Morgan; *m* 1969, Hilary Patricia Lewis; one *s* one *d*. *Educ:* Ystalyfera Grammar Sch.; University Coll. London (BA Hons History 1969); Selwyn Coll., Cambridge (BA Hons Theol. 1971); Westcott House, Cambridge. MA Cantab 1974; PhD Wales 1986. Priest, Llandaff, 1973; Curate, St Andrew's Major, Dinas Powis, 1972–75; Chaplain, Bryn-y-Don Community Sch., 1972–75; Chaplain and Lectr, St Michael's Coll., Llandaff, 1975–77; Lectr, University Coll., Cardiff, 1975–77; Warden of Church Hostel, Bangor, Anglican Chap., UCNW and Lectr in Theology, UCNW, 1977–84; Rector of Wrexham, 1984–86; Archdeacon of Merioneth and Rector of Criccieth, 1986–92; Bishop of Bangor, 1993–99. Editor, Welsh Churchman, 1975–82. Exam. Chaplain to Abp of Wales, 1978–82, to Bp of Bangor, 1983; Diocese of Bangor: In-Service Trng Officer, 1979–84; Warden of Ordinands, 1982–84; Canon of Bangor Cathedral, 1983–84. Member: Archbishop's Doctrinal Commn, 1982–93 (Chm. 1989–93); Crown Nominations Commn, 2012–; Chm., Div. of Stewardship, Provincial Bd of Mission, 1988–95. Pres., Welsh Centre for Internat. Affairs, 2004–10. Vice-Chairman: Nat. Soc., 1999; Bible Soc., 1999. Fellow, Woodard Corp., 2001–. Pro-Chancellor, Univ. of Wales, 2006–. FLSW 2013. Hon. Fellow: Bangor Univ., 1994; UWIC, 2003; Lampeter Univ., 2004; Cardiff Univ., 2004; Swansea Univ., 2009; Trinity Univ. Coll., Carmarthen, 2009. *Publications:* O Ddydd i Ddydd, Pwyllgor Darlleniadau Beiblaidd Cyngor Eglwysi Cymru, 1980; History of the Church Hostel and Anglican Chaplaincy at University College of North Wales, Bangor, 1986; Concepts of Mission and Ministry in Anglican University Chaplaincy Work, 1988; Strangely Orthodox: R. S. Thomas and his poetry of faith, 2006. *Recreation:* golf. *Address:* Llys Esgob, The Cathedral Green, Llandaff, Cardiff CF5 2YE.

WALES, Andrew Nigel Malcolm; QC 2012; a Recorder, since 2010; *b* Edinburgh, 27 July 1970; *s* of David Wales and Wendy Wales; *m* 2002, Alice Irene Wrangham; one *s* one *d*. *Educ:* Dulwich Coll.; Trinity Coll., Cambridge (BA 1990); Univ. of Virginia Sch. of Law (LLM 1991). Called to the Bar, Gray's Inn, 1992; in practice as a barrister specialising in commercial law, 1993–. *Recreations:* family, reading. *Address:* 7 King's Bench Walk, Temple, EC4Y 7DS. *T:* (020) 7910 8300. *E:* clerks@7kbw.co.uk.

WALES, Jimmy; Founder, Wikipedia.org, 2001; Co-Founder and President, Wikia Inc., since 2004; *b* Huntsville, Ala, 7 Aug. 1966; *s* of Jimmy and Doris Wales; one *d*; *m* 2012, Kate Garvey; one *d*. *Educ:* Auburn Univ. (BA Finance); Univ. of Alabama (MA Finance). Res. Dir, Chicago Options Assoc., 1994–2000; Founder, Nupedia, 2000. Founder and Chm. Emeritus, Wikimedia Foundn, 2003. Board Member: iCommons, 2005; Creative Commons, 2006–. Co-Chairman: World Econ. Forum on Middle E, 2008; People's Operator, 2014–. Fellow, Berkman Center for Internet and Soc., Harvard Law Sch., 2005. Hon. LLD Knox Coll., Ill, 2006. Young Global Leader, World Econ. Forum, 2007. *Publications:* (contrib.) Advances in Futures and Options Research, 1994. *Recreations:* international travel, free speech supporter, free culture advocate, contributor and active editor on Wikipedia, commerce and technology. *Address:* Wikimedia Foundation, 149 New Montgomery Street, 3rd Floor, San Francisco, CA 94105, USA. *Fax:* (415) 8820495. *E:* jwales@wikia.com.

WALES, Prof. Kathleen Margaret; Special Professor in English, University of Nottingham, since 2008; *b* 8 Feb. 1946; *d* of Richard Derwent and Yvonne Derwent (*née* Atkins); *m* 1st, 1971, Brian Wales (marr. diss. 1988); one *s*; 2nd, 1993, David Bovey. *Educ:* Darlington High Sch. for Girls; Royal Holloway Coll., Univ. of London (BA 1st Cl. Hons English). Royal Holloway College, later Royal Holloway and Bedford New College, University of London: Lectr in English Lang., 1968–88; Sen. Lectr, 1988–94; Reader, 1994–95; Prof., 1995–96; Hd, English Dept, 1995–96; University of Leeds: Prof. of Modern English Lang., 1996–2005; Dean of Learning and Teaching, Faculty of Arts, 2000–03; Dir, Centre for Medieval Studies, 2002–03; Res. Prof. in English, Univ. of Sheffield, 2005–08. Sen. Res. Fellow, British Acad./Leverhulme Trust, 1992–93; Visiting Research Fellow: Lucy Cavendish Coll., Univ. of Cambridge, 1999–2000, 2004; Centre for Res. in Arts, Social Scis and Humanities, Univ. of Cambridge, 2004–05; Leverhulme Emeritus Res. Fellow, Inst. of English Studies, Univ. of London, 2005–06. Member: Exec. Cttee, Council for Coll. and Univ. English, 1998–2002; Adv. Bd, Inst. of English Studies, Univ. of London, 2000–05; Cttee of Mgt, British Inst. in

Paris, 2002–04; Peer Review Coll., AHRC, 2005–08 (Mem., PG Panel 5, 2006–07); Leverhulme Trust Adv. Panel, 2006–13; Internat. Adv. Bd, Aix-Marseille Univ., 2014–. Gov., Trinity and All Saints Coll., Leeds, 2001–04. FRSA 1996; FEA 2001. Ed., Jl Lang. and Lit., 1996–2005. *Publications:* Dictionary of Stylistics, 1989, 3rd edn 2011; The Language of James Joyce, 1992; (ed) Feminist Linguistics in Literary Criticism, 1994; Personal Pronouns in Present-Day English, 1996; (ed jtly) Shakespeare's Dramatic Language: a reader's guide, 2000; Northern English: a cultural and social history, 2006; numerous book chapters; contrib. articles to learned jls and children's joke books. *Recreations:* buying and selling at antique fairs and flea markets, keeping fit, collecting elephants, Fairport Convention. *Address:* 2 The Orchards, Great Shelford, Cambs CB22 5AB. *T:* (01223) 840506.

WALES, Sir Robert Andrew, (Sir Robin), Kt 2000; first elected Mayor of Newham, since 2002; two *c. Educ:* Glasgow Univ. (BSc). Formerly with BT, responsible for developing credit and fraud mgt systems. Newham Borough Council: Mem. (Lab), 1982–86 and 1992–; Leader of Council, 1996–2002. Chm., Assoc. of London Govt, 2000–06. Vice Chm., Culture, Tourism and Sport Bd, LGA, 2006–; Chm., LOCOG, 2006–13 (Mem. Bd, 2005–13; Chm., Remuneration Cttee, 2005–13); Mem. Bd, London Legacy Develt Corp., 2012–. Chm., Red Door Ventures Ltd, 2014–15. *Address:* c/o Newham Dockside, 1000 Dockside Road, E16 2QU.

WAŁĘSA, Lech, Hon. GCB 1991; Founder and Head of Lech Wałęsa Institute Foundation, since 1995; President of Poland, 1990–95; *b* Popowo, 29 Sept. 1943; *s* of late Bolesław Wałęsa and Feliksa Wałęsa; *m* 1969, Danuta; four *s* four *d. Educ:* Lipno primary and tech. schools; trained as electrician. Lenin Shipyard, Gdańsk, 1966–76, 1980–90 (Chm., Strike Cttees, 1970, 1980); founder Chm., Nat. Co-ordinating Commn of Ind. Autonomous Trade Union Solidarity (NSZZ Solidarność), 1981–82; in custody, 1981–82; returned to Gdańsk Shipyard, 1983; Leader, (outlawed) Solidarity, 1983–88, (re-instated) Solidarity, 1988–90. Founder and Pres., Christian Democratic Party of Third Republic, Poland, 1997–2001. Dr *hc*, including: Alliance Coll., Cambridge, Mass, 1981; Harvard, 1983; Gdańsk, 1990; Connecticut State, 1996. Nobel Peace Prize, 1983. Presidential Medal of Freedom (USA); Grand Cross, Legion of Honour (France); Order of Merit (Italian Republic); Order of Pius, 1st Cl. (Holy See); Grand Ribbon, Order of Leopold (Belgium). *Publications:* A Path of Hope: An Autobiography, 1987. *Address:* Lech Wałęsa Institute Foundation, Al. Jerozolimskie 11/19, 00508 Warsaw, Poland.

WALEY, Daniel Philip, PhD; FBA 1991; Keeper of Manuscripts, British Library, 1973–86 (Keeper of Manuscripts, British Museum, 1972–73); *b* 20 March 1921; *er s* of late Hubert David Waley and Margaret Hendelah Waley; *m* 1945, Pamela Joan Griffiths; one *s* one *d* (and one *d* decd). *Educ:* Dauntsey's Sch.; King's Coll., Cambridge (MA, PhD). Historical Tripos, Cambridge, 1939–40 and 1945–46 (cl. 1). Served War, 1940–45. Fellow of King's Coll., Cambridge, 1950–54. Asst Lectr in Medieval History, London School of Economics and Political Science, Univ. of London, 1949–51, Lectr, 1951–61, Reader in History, 1961–70, Prof. of History, 1970–72. Hon. Res. Fellow, Westfield Coll., London, 1986; Emer. Fellow, Leverhulme Trust, 1986–87. Lectures: British Acad. Italian, 1975; Emil Godfrey Meml, Lewes Priory Trust, 2002. Corresp. Fellow, Deputazione di Storia Patria per l'Umbria, 1991; FHA 2012. Prince Consort Award, Cambridge Univ., 1950; Serena Medal, British Acad., 1990. *Publications:* Mediaeval Orvieto, 1952; The Papal State in the 13th Century, 1961; Later Medieval Europe, 1964, 3rd edn (with P. Denley) 2001; The Italian City Republics, 1969, 4th edn (with T. Dean) 2009; British Public Opinion and the Abyssinian War, 1935–36, 1975; (ed) George Eliot's Blotter: A Commonplace-Book, 1980; (contrib.) Storia d'Italia, ed by G. Galasso, vol. 7, 1987; Siena and the Sienese in the Thirteenth Century, 1991; (ed) J. K. Hyde, Literacy and Its Uses: studies on late medieval Italy, 1993; (contrib.) Il Libro Bianco di San Gimignano, vol. 1, 1996; A Liberal Life: Sydney, Earl Buxton, 1853–1934, 1999; (introd.) N. Rubinstein, Studies in Italian History in the Middle Ages and the Renaissance, vol. 1, 2004; contributor to: Oxford DNB, Dizionario Biografico degli Italiani, English Hist. Review, Trans Royal Hist. Soc., Papers of British Sch. at Rome, Jl of Ecclesiastical Hist., Jl of the History of Ideas, Rivista Storica Italiana, Rivista di Storia della Chiesa in Italia, Procs Brit. Acad., British Library Jl, Bull. of John Rylands Liby, Sussex Archaeol Collections, Book Collector, Archives, etc. *Recreations:* scribble, squabble, Scrabble. *Address:* 33 Greyfriars Court, Court Road, Lewes, E Sussex BN7 2RF.

WALEY-COHEN, Sir Stephen (Harry), 2nd Bt *cr* 1961, of Honeymead, Co. Somerset; Managing Director, Mousetrap Productions, since 1994; *b* 22 June 1946; *s* of Sir Bernard Nathaniel Waley-Cohen, 1st Bt and Hon. Joyce Constance Ina Waley-Cohen (*d* 2013); *S* father, 1991; *m* 1st, 1972, Pamela Elizabeth (marr. diss.), *yr d* of J. E. Doniger; two *s* one *d*; 2nd, 1986, Josephine Burnett, *yr d* of late Duncan M. Spencer; two *d. Educ:* Wellesley House Sch.; Eton (Oppidan Scholar); Magdalene Coll., Cambridge (MA Hons). Financial journalist, Daily Mail, 1968–73; Publisher, Euromoney, 1969–83; Chief Exec., Maybox Theatres, 1984–89; Chairman: Thorndike Holdings, management training, 1989–98; Bridge Underwriting Agents (formerly Willis Faber & Dumas (Agencies)), 1992–99 (Dir, 1988–99); Policy Portfolio, 1993–97; Portsmouth & Sunderland Newspapers, 1998–99 (Dir, 1994–99); First Call Gp, 1996–98; Director: Badgworthy Land Co., 1982–; St Martin's Theatre, 1989–; Theatresoft, 1992–97; Theatre Investment Fund, 1992–; Exeter Selective Assets (formerly Preferred Capital) Investment Trust, 1992–2003; Usha Martin Education Systems (formerly Usha Martin Infotech), 2008–13; D & S Mgt Ltd, 2009–; Managing Director: Victoria Palace Th., 1989–2014; Vaudeville Th., 1996–2001; Savoy Th. Mgt, 1997–2005; Ambassadors Th., 2007–. Chm., Mousetrap Foundn for the Arts, 1996–; Mem., SOLT (formerly SWET), 1984– (Mem., Finance Cttee, 1989–2010; Chm., 1996–2002; Pres., 2002–05); Chm., Olivier Awards Cttee, 1995–2002. Pres. Council, JCA Charitable Foundn (formerly Jewish Colonisation Assoc.), 1995– (Mem. Council, 1985–); Chairman: Exec. Cttee, British American Project for Successor Generation, 1986–92; Mowbray Trust for Reproductive Immunology, 1996–. Chm., Combined Theatrical Charities, 2009–; Trustee: Theatres Trust, 1998–2004; Garrick Charitable Trust, 2004– (Chm., 2009–); Royal Theatrical Fund, 2009–. Member: Public Affairs Cttee, British Field Sports Soc., 1972–92; Cttee, Devon & Somerset Staghounds, 1974–2009. Member: UCL Finance Cttee, 1984–89; Council, RADA, 2003– (Chm., 2007–). Governor, Wellesley House Sch., 1974–97. Contested (C) Manchester, Gorton, Feb. and Oct. 1974. Hon. PhD Ben Gurion Univ. of the Negev, 2011. *Recreations:* family, theatre, hunting. *Heir: s* Lionel Robert Waley-Cohen [*b* 7 Aug. 1974; *m* 2007, Octavia Green; two *d*]. *Address:* 1 Wallingford Avenue, W10 6QA. *T:* (020) 8968 6268; Honeymead, Simonsbath, Somerset TA24 7JX. *T:* (01643) 831242. *Club:* Garrick.

WALFORD, Sir Christopher (Rupert), Kt 1995; TEM 1972; Lord Mayor of London, 1994–95; *b* 15 Oct. 1935; *s* of late John Rupert Charles Walford, MBE and Gladys Irene Walford (*née* Sperrin); *m* 1st, 1967, Anne Elizabeth Viggars (*d* 2004); two *s* (and one *s* decd); 2nd, 2009, Denise Anne Powlett (*née* Hudson). *Educ:* Charterhouse; Oriel College, Oxford (MA; Hon. Fellow, 1995). Solicitor (Hons). National Service, commissioned RA, 1954–56; HAC 1957–72 (to Warrant Officer). Allen & Overy, 1959–96 (Partner, 1970–96). Councillor, Kensington, 1962–65, Kensington & Chelsea, 1964–82, Dep. Mayor, 1974–75, Mayor, 1979–80; Alderman, Ward of Farringdon Within, 1982–2002; Sheriff, City of London, 1990–91. Member: Council, CGLI, 1984–98; Council, and Policy and Exec. Cttees, Inst. of Directors, 1986–94; Court of Assistants and Finance Cttee, Corp. of Sons of the Clergy, 1989–98; Trustee: St Paul's Cathedral Choir Sch. Foundn, 1985–97; Guildhall Sch., Music and Drama Foundn, 1989–97; Morden Coll., 1991–2014. Vice-Pres., Bridewell Royal Hosp., 1996–2002 (Gov., 1984–2002). Governor, Hon. Irish Soc., 1997–2000; Mem. Bd of Govs, London Guildhall Univ., 1997–2002. Freeman, City of London, 1964; Liveryman: Makers of Playing Cards Co., 1978 (Master, 1987; Hon. Liveryman, 2002); City of London Solicitors Co., 1983 (Master, 1993); Hon. Mem., Court of Assts, Builders Merchants' Co., 1992. FRSA. Hon. DCL City, 1994; Hon. LLD Ulster, 2000. *Recreations:* listening to music, watching Rugby football and cricket, horse racing. *Clubs:* Athenæum, East India, MCC.

WALFORD, Dr Diana Marion, CBE 2002; Principal, Mansfield College, Oxford, 2002–11; Pro-Chancellor and Chair, Board of Trustees, Regent's University London, since 2015; *b* 26 Feb. 1944; *d* of late Lt-Col Joseph Norton, LLM, and Thelma Norton (*née* Nurick); *m* 1970, Arthur David Walford, LLB; one *s* one *d. Educ:* Calder High Sch. for Girls, Liverpool; Liverpool Univ. (George Holt Medal, Physiol.; J. H. Abram Prize, Pharmacol.; BSc (1st Cl. Hons Physiol.) 1965; MB ChB 1968; MD 1976); London Univ. (MSc (Epidemiology) 1987); MA Oxon 2003. FRCP 1990 (MRCP 1972); FRCPath 1986 (MRCPath 1974); MFPHM 1989, FFPH (FFPHM 1994). Ho. Officer posts, Liverpool Royal Inf., 1968–69; Sen. Ho. Officer posts and Sen. Registrar, St Mary's Hosp., Paddington, and Northwick Park Hosp., Harrow, 1969–75; MRC Research (Training) Fellow, Clin. Res. Centre, 1975–76; Sen. MO 1976–79, PMO 1979–83, SPMO (Under Sec.), 1983–89, Dep. CMO, 1989–92, DHSS, subseq. Dept of Health; Dir, PHLS, 1993–2002. Hon. Consultant Haematologist, Central Middlesex Hosp., 1977–87. Non-executive Director: NHS Blood and Transplant Authy, 2005–09; UCLH NHS Foundn Trust, 2011–. Founder Member: British Blood Transfusion Soc., 1983–95; Faculty of Med. Leadership and Mgt, 2011–. Mem. Council, LSHTM, 2009– (Dep. Chm., 2010–); Gov., Ditchley Foundn, 2000–. Trustee, Sue Ryder (formerly Sue Ryder Care), 2008–. Mem., State Honours Cttee, 2010–. FRSocMed; FRSA. *Publications:* chapters on haematological side effects of drugs in: Meyler's Side Effects of Drugs, 9th edn 1980; Side Effects of Drugs Annual, 1980; Drug-Induced Emergencies, 1980; articles on alpha-thalassaemia. *Recreations:* theatre, painting, travel. *Address:* 290 West End Lane, West Hampstead, NW6 1LN.

WALFORD, Prof. Geoffrey, PhD; Professor of Education Policy, University of Oxford, 2000–09, now Emeritus; Fellow, Green Templeton College (formerly Green College), Oxford, 1995–2009, now Emeritus; *b* 30 April 1949. *Educ:* Univ. of Kent (BSc Physics 1971; PhD 1975); Open Univ. (BA Sociol. and Educn 1975; MSc 1985; MBA 1996); St John's Coll., Oxford (MPhil Sociol. 1978; MA 1995); Inst. of Educn, Univ. of London (MA Educnl Admin 1986). Aston University: Lectr in Sociol. of Educn, Dept of Educnl Enquiry, 1979–83; Lectr in Educn Policy and Mgt, 1983–90, Sen. Lectr in Sociol. and Educn Policy, 1990–94, Aston Business Sch.; University of Oxford: Lectr in Educnl Studies (Sociol.), 1995–97; Reader in Educn Policy, 1997–2000; Univ. Jun. Proctor, 2001–02. Jt Ed., Brit. Jl Educnl Studies, 1998–2002; Ed., Oxford Review of Educn, 2003–10. *Publications:* books include: Life in Public Schools, 1986; Restructuring Universities: politics and power in the management of change, 1987; Privatization and Privilege in Education, 1990; (with H. Miller) City Technology College, 1991; (ed) Doing Educational Research, 1991; Choice and Equity in Education, 1994; (ed) Researching the Powerful in Education, 1994; Educational Politics: pressure groups and faith-based schools, 1995; (ed with R. Pring) Affirming the Comprehensive Ideal, 1997; (ed) Doing Research about Education, 1998; (ed) Studies in Educational Ethnography, annually, 1998–; Policy, Politics and Education: sponsored grant-maintained schools and religious diversity, 2000; Doing Qualitative Educational Research, 2001; Private Education: tradition and diversity, 2005; Markets and Equity in Education, 2006; (ed) How to do Educational Ethnography, 2008; (ed jtly) The Sage Handbook of Measurement, 2010; (ed jtly) Education, Privatisation and Social Justice, 2014. *Recreations:* travel, walking. *Address:* Department of Education, University of Oxford, 15 Norham Gardens, Oxford OX2 6PY. *T:* (01865) 274141.

WALFORD, His Honour John de Guise; a Circuit Judge, 1993–2015; *b* 23 Feb. 1948; *s* of late Edward Wynn Walford and of Dorothy Ann Walford; *m* 1977, Pamela Elizabeth Russell; one *s* one *d. Educ:* Sedbergh Sch.; Queens' Coll., Cambridge (MA). Called to the Bar, Middle Temple, 1971; practice on NE Circuit, 1974; Asst Recorder, 1985–89; Recorder, 1989–93. Standing Counsel (Criminal) to DHSS, NE Circuit, 1991–93. Chancellor, Dio. of Bradford, 1999–2014. *Recreations:* cricket, tennis, opera, watching Middlesbrough FC. *Clubs:* Hawks (Cambridge); Free Foresters.

WALFORD, John Thomas, OBE 1985; a Vice President, Multiple Sclerosis Society of Great Britain and Northern Ireland, since 1995 (Deputy General Secretary, 1965–77; General Secretary, 1977–95); *b* 6 Feb. 1933; *s* of Frederick Thomas Walford and Rose Elizabeth Walford; *m* 1st, 1955, June Muriel Harding (marr. diss. 1970); two *s* one *d*; 2nd, 1996, Nansi Yvonne Long. *Educ:* Richmond and East Sheen County Grammar Sch. Served RAF, 1951–53. C. C. Wakefield & Co. Ltd, 1949–51 and 1953–55; Stanley Eades & Co., 1955–60; Moo Cow Milk Bars Ltd, 1960–64. Licensed Reader, Church in Wales, 2008–. DL Greater London, 1988–95. Editor, MS News (qly jl of Multiple Sclerosis Soc.), 1977–95. *Recreation:* collecting Victorian fairings. *Address:* Rhoslyn, Talley, Llandeilo, Carmarthenshire SA19 7AX. *T:* (01558) 685744. *Club:* Royal Society of Medicine.

WALFORD, Lionel Kingsley, PhD; FInstP; Assessor for Civil Service Fast Stream, since 1999; *b* 19 May 1939; *s* of late Edward Walford and Muriel (*née* Davies); *m* 1963, Linda Jones; one *d* (and one *d* decd). *Educ:* Whitchurch Grammar Sch., Cardiff; Univ. Coll. of South Wales and Monmouthshire (BSc 1st Cl. Hons Physics, Univ. of Wales, 1960); St Catharine's Coll., Cambridge (PhD 1963). FInstP 1972. Southern Illinois University, USA: Asst Prof., 1963–67; Associate Prof., 1967–72; Prof. of Physics, 1972–78; Research Consultant, McDonnell Douglas Corp., 1964–72; joined Welsh Office, 1978: Principal, 1978–84; Sen. Principal seconded to WDA, 1984–85; Dir, Manpower Services in Wales, 1985–88; Asst Sec., 1988–94, Under Sec. (Hd, then Dir), 1994–99, Welsh Office Agriculture Dept. Chm., Lantra Council for Wales, 2009–15; Ind. Mem., Agricl Wages Bd for England and Wales, 2007–13; Chm., Welsh Levy Bd, 2008–12. *Publications:* numerous articles in jls on applied physics; one US patent. *E:* lionel.walford@cantab.net.

WALKER, family name of **Barons Walker of Aldringham** and **Walker of Gestingthorpe**.

WALKER OF ALDRINGHAM, Baron *cr* 2006 (Life Peer), of Aldringham in the County of Suffolk; **Field Marshal Michael John Dawson Walker,** GCB 2000 (KCB 1995); CMG 1997; CBE 1990 (OBE 1982); DL; Chief of the Defence Staff, 2003–06; *b* 7 July 1944; *s* of William Hampden Dawson Walker and Dorothy Helena Walker (*née* Shiach); *m* 1973, Victoria Margaret Holme; two *s* one *d. Educ:* Milton Sch., Bulawayo; Woodhouse Grove Sch., Yorks; RMA Sandhurst. Commissioned Royal Anglian Regt, 1966; Regtl and Staff duties, 1966–82; Staff Coll., 1976–77; MA to CGS, 1982–85; CO 1 Royal Anglian Regt, 1985–87; Comdr, 20th Armoured Brigade, 1987–89; COS, 1 (Br) Corps, 1989–91; GOC NE District and Comdr, 2nd Inf. Div., 1991–92; GOC Eastern District, 1992; ACGS, MoD, 1992–94; Comdr, ACE Rapid Reaction Corps, 1994–97; Comdr, Land Component Peace Implementation Force, Bosnia, 1995–96; C-in-C, Land Comd, 1997–2000; ADC Gen. to the Queen, 1997–2006; CGS, 2000–03. Gov., Royal Hosp. Chelsea, 2006–11. Colonel Commandant: Queen's Div., 1991–2000; AAC, 1994–2004; Col, Royal Anglian Regt, 1997–2002 (Dep. Col, 1991–97). DL Gtr London, 2007. Hon. LLD UEA, 2002; Hon. DSc Cranfield, 2003. *Recreations:* ski-ing, sailing, shooting, golf, family. *Address:* House of Lords, SW1A 0PW.

WALKER OF GESTINGTHORPE, Baron *cr* 2002 (Life Peer), of Gestingthorpe in the County of Essex; **Robert Walker,** Kt 1994; PC 1997; a non-permanent Judge, Court of Final Appeal of Hong Kong, since 2009; *b* 17 March 1938; *s* of late Ronald Robert Antony Walker and Mary Helen Walker (*née* Welsh); *m* 1962, Suzanne Diana Leggi; one *s* three *d. Educ:* Downside Sch.; Trinity Coll., Cambridge (BA; Hon. Fellow, 2006). Called to Bar,

Lincoln's Inn, 1960, Bencher 1990, Treas., 2010; QC 1982; in practice at Chancery Bar, 1961–94; a Judge of the High Court of Justice, Chancery Div., 1994–97; a Lord Justice of Appeal, 1997–2002; a Lord of Appeal in Ordinary, 2002–09; a Justice of the Supreme Court of the UK, 2009–13. *Address:* House of Lords, SW1A 0PW.

WALKER, Prof. Alan Christopher, CBE 2014; DLitt; FBA 2011; Professor of Social Policy and Social Gerontology, University of Sheffield, since 1985 (Director, New Dynamics of Ageing Programme, 2005–15); Chair, Sheffield Health and Social Care NHS Trust, since 2008; *b* London, 20 April 1949; *s* of Alfred Charles and Joyce Margaret Walker; *m* 1972, Carol Anne Davey; one *s* one *d. Educ:* Smallberry Green Secondary Sch.; Spring Grove Grammar Sch.; Univ. of Essex (BA Hons Govt and Sociol. 1972; DLitt Sociol. 1990). Res. Asst, 1972–74, Res. Officer, 1974–75, Univ. of Essex; Sen. Res. Officer, Nat. Children's Bureau, 1975–77; Lectr in Social Policy, 1977–84, Sen. Lectr, 1983–84, Reader, 1984–85, Univ. of Sheffield. Non-exec. Dir, 1993–99, Chair, 1999–2003, Community Health Sheffield NHS Trust; Chair, Sheffield Care Trust, 2003–08. FAcSS (AcSS 1999). FRSA 1994. Hon. DSocSc Hong Kong Baptist 2006. *Publications:* (ed with P. Townsend) Disability in Britain, 1981; Unqualified and Underemployed: handicapped young people and the labour market, 1982; (ed) Public Expenditure and Social Policy: an examination of social spending and social priorities, 1982; (ed) Community Care: the family, the state and social policy, 1982; Social Planning, 1984 (Japanese edn 1995); (ed with C. Phillipson) Ageing and Social Policy: a critical assessment, 1986; (ed with C. Walker) The Growing Divide: a social audit 1979–1987, 1987 (Japanese edn 1994); (jtly) After Redundancy: the experience of economic insecurity, 1988; (with H. Qureshi) The Caring Relationship: family care of elderly people, 1989; (ed jtly) The Social Economy and the Democratic State, 1989; (jtly) Age and Employment: policies, attitudes and practices, 1993; (ed) The New Generational Contract: intergenerational relations, old age and welfare, 1996; (with L. Warren) Changing Services for Older People: the Neighbourhood Support Units innovation, 1996; (ed jtly) Sociology of Aging: international perspectives, 1996; (with T. Maltby) Ageing Europe, 1997; (ed with C. Walker) Britain Divided: the growth of social exclusion in the 1980s and 1990s, 1997; (ed jtly) The Social Quality of Europe, 1997; Ageing and Welfare Change in Europe: prospect and future, 1997; (ed) European Home and Community Care 1998/99, 1998; (ed jtly) Politische Beteiligung älter Menschen in Europa, 1997; (with P. Taylor) Combating Age Barriers in Employment: a European portfolio of good practice, 1998; (ed with G. Naegele) The Politics of Old Age in Europe, 1999; (ed jtly) Social Quality: a vision for Europe, 2001; (ed with C. Hagan Hennessy) Growing Older: quality of life in old age, 2004 (Japanese edn 2009); (ed) Growing Older in Europe, 2005; (ed with C. K. Wong) East Asian Welfare Regimes in Transition: from Confucianism to globalisation, 2005; (ed) Understanding Quality of Life in Old Age, 2005; (ed jtly) Aging, Globalisation and Inequality: the new critical gerontology, 2006; (ed with H. Mollenkopf) Quality of Life in Old Age: international and multidisciplinary perspectives, 2007; (ed with C. Aspalter) Securing the Future for Old Age in Europe, 2008; (ed with G. Naegele) Social Policy in Ageing Societies: Britain and Germany compared, 2009; (ed jtly) The Peter Townsend Reader, 2010; (ed jtly) Fighting Poverty, Inequality and Injustice, 2011 (ed with L. van der Maesen) Social Quality: from theory to indicators, 2012; The New Science of Ageing, 2014; (ed with L. Foster) The Political Economy of Ageing and Later Life: critical perspectives, 2014. *Recreations:* living with my amazing partner, gardening, reading, cooking, walking, ballet, theatre, Test cricket, cinema, art, music, trying not to support Arsenal FC. *Address:* Department of Sociological Studies, University of Sheffield, Elmfield, Northumberland Road, Sheffield S10 2TU. *T:* (0114) 222 6466/67. *E:* a.c.walker@sheffield.ac.uk.

WALKER, Prof. Alan Cyril, PhD; FRS 1999; Evan Pugh Professor of Anthropology and Biology, Pennsylvania State University, 2002–10, now Emeritus (Professor of Anthropology and Biology, 1995–96; Distinguished Professor of Anthropology and Biology, 1996–2002); *b* 23 Aug. 1938; *s* of Cyril Walker and Edith (*née* Tidd); *m* 1st, 1963, Patricia Dale Larwood (marr. diss.; she *d* 2012); one *s*; 2nd, 1976, Patty Lee Shipman. *Educ:* St John's Coll., Cambridge (BA 1962); Royal Free Hosp., London (PhD 1967). BM Scientific Associate, 1963–64; Asst Lectr in Anatomy, Royal Free Hosp. Sch. of Medicine, 1965; Lectr in Anatomy, Makerere UC, Kampala, 1965–69; Hon. Keeper of Paleontology, Uganda Mus., 1967–69; Sen. Lectr in Anatomy, Univ. of Nairobi, 1969–73; Harvard University: Vis. Lectr, Dept of Anatomy, 1973–74, Associate Prof. of Anatomy, 1974–78, Med. Sch.; Associate Prof. of Anthropol., 1974–78; Res. Associate, Peabody Mus., 1974–78; Mem., Cttee of Profs in Evolutionary and Organismic Biol., 1974–78; Prof. of Cell Biol. and Anatomy, Johns Hopkins Univ. Sch. of Medicine, 1978–95 (part-time, 1995–97). Associate Editor: Amer. Jl Physical Anthropol., 1974–79; Jl Human Evolution, 1994–98. John Simon Guggenheim Meml Foundn Fellow, 1986; John D. and Catherine T. MacArthur Foundn Fellow, 1988–93; Phi Beta Kappa Schol., 1995. Mem., American Acad. of Arts and Scis, 1996; Foreign Associate, NAS, USA, 2003. Hon. DSc Chicago, 2000. Internat. Fondation Fyssen Prize, 1998; Faculty Scholar's Medal, Pennsylvania State Univ., 1999. *Publications:* (ed jtly) Prosimian Biology, 1974; (jtly) Structure and Function of the Human Skeleton, 1985; (ed with R. Leakey) The Nariokotome Homo Erectus Skeleton, 1993; (with P. Shipman) The Wisdom of the Bones, 1996 (Rhône-Poulenc Prize, 1997); (with P. Shipman) The Ape in the Tree, 2005; contrib. numerous papers to jls and edited books. *Address:* 3140 Chatham Church Road, Moncure, NC 27559, USA. *T:* (919) 5425539.

WALKER, Surgeon Rear Adm. Alasdair James, OBE 2004; QHS 2010; Director Medical Policy and Operational Capability, Surgeon General HQ, Medical Director General (Naval), and Chief Naval Medical Officer, since 2014; *b* Glasgow, 22 June 1956; *s* of (William) Marshall Walker and Jean Isabell Walker (*née* Anderson); *m* 1st, 1986, Sheena Handley (marr. diss. 2005); two *s*; 2nd, 2006, Christine Parker; one step *s. Educ:* High Sch. of Glasgow; Univ. of Glasgow (MB ChB 1979). FRCSGlas 1985; FRCS ad eundem 2006. MO, HMS Plymouth, Falklands, 1982; Surgical Trainee, RN Hosps Haslar and Plymouth, Royal Infirmary Edinburgh, Basingstoke District Gen. Hosp., 1982–91; Consultant Gen. and Vascular Surgeon, 1991–95, Hd, Surgery, 1994–95, RN Hosp. Plymouth; Ministry of Defence Hospital Unit, Derriford, Plymouth: Consultant Gen. and Vascular Surgeon, 1995–2009; Clin. Dir of Surgery, 1999–2002; Divl Dir of Surgical Services, 2003–05; Asst Med. Dir, 2005–07; Mil. Clin. Dir, 2006–07; Defence Consultant Advr in Surgery, 2007–09; Med. Dir, Jt Med. Comd, 2009–13; rcds 2014. *Publications:* (contrib.) Essential Vascular Surgery, 1999; (contrib.) Rich's Vascular Trauma, 3rd edn 2015; articles in jls on surgery, vascular surgery, trauma mgt and mil. medicine. *Recreations:* genealogy, gardening, history, Rugby (spectator now), breeding Bergamasco dogs. *Address:* HQ Surgeon General, Coltman House, DMS Whittington, Whittington Barracks, Lichfield, Staffs WS14 9PY. *T:* (020) 7807 8126. *E:* alasdair.walker280@mod.uk. *Club:* Royal Naval Medical.

WALKER, Alexandra Margaret Jane; psychoanalytic psychotherapist; Director, Human Resources, Inland Revenue, 2000–03; *b* 31 Oct. 1945; *d* of late Frederic Douglas Walker and Hertha Julie (*née* Freiin Gemmingen von Massenbach); one *d. Educ:* Nikolaus Cusanus Gymnasium, Bonn; Lady Margaret Hall, Oxford (Schol.; BA Lit. Hum.); Univ. of Roehampton (MA Psychoanalytic Studies 2011). Joined MoD as admin. trainee, 1973; Principal, 1976; on secondment to: Plessey Co., 1979–81; LSE as Nancy Seear Fellow in Industrial Relns, 1981–82; Asst Sec. and Hd of Civilian Mgt (Industrial Relns), 1983–86; rcds 1987; Counsellor, British Embassy, Bonn, 1988–92; Asst Under-Sec. of State (Service Personnel), 1993–97; Dir Gen. Future Hd Office, 1997–2000. Chm., Foundn for Psychotherapy and Counselling, 2009–12. *Recreations:* walking, geology, amateur string quartets (cello), singing.

WALKER, Andrew Angus; Coroner, Greater London Northern District, since 2007; *b* Guildford, 8 Oct. 1964; *s* of Dr Andrew Allan Walker and Dr Janet Walker; *m* 1999, Rebecca Anne Byrne; one *s* one *d. Educ:* Westminster Univ. (LLB, BSc). Called to the Bar, Middle Temple, 1994; in private practice, 1994–2006; Door Tenant, 10 Kings Bench Walk, Temple, 2006–. *Recreation:* regulator and turret clock maker. *Address:* North London Coroner's Court, 29 Wood Street, High Barnet EN5 4BE.

WALKER, Prof. Andrew Charles, PhD; FRSE; Secretary and Treasurer, Carnegie Trust for the Universities of Scotland, since 2013; *b* Wembley, 24 June 1948; *s* of Maurice Frederick Walker and Margaret Florence Walker (*née* Rust); *m* 1972, Margaret Elizabeth Mortimer; one *s* one *d* (twins). *Educ:* Kingsbury Co. Grammar Sch.; Univ. of Essex (BA, MSc; PhD 1972). FInstP 1987. NRCC Postdoctoral Fellow, Ottawa, 1972–74; SRC Fellow, Univ. of Essex, 1974–75; SSO, UKAEA Culham Lab., 1975–83; Heriot-Watt University: Lectr in Physics, 1983; Reader, then Prof. of Modern Optics, 1985–2013, now Prof. Emeritus; Dir, Postgrad. Studies, 1998–2001; Dep. Principal (Resources), 2001–06; Vice-Principal, 2006–10; Sen. Dep. Principal, 2010–13; Dir, Heriot-Watt Malaysia Sdn Bhd, 2011–13 (CEO, 2011–12). Mem., SERC/DTI Advance Devices and Materials Cttee, 1992–94; Dir, Technol. Ventures Scotland, 2002–05. Institute of Physics: Mem. Cttee and Hon. Sec., Quantum Electronics Gp, 1979–85; Chm., Scottish Br., 1991–97 (Mem. Cttee, 1985–88). Royal Society of Edinburgh: FRSE 1994; Mem. Council and Sec. for Meetings, 1998–2001; Vice-Pres., 2001–04; Fellowship Sec., 2005–08. Non-exec. Dir and Chm., Terahertz Photonics Ltd, 1998–2000; non-exec. Dir, SeeByte Ltd, 2008–13. Trustee: RSE Scotland Foundn, 2002–05 (Chm., 2004–05); Scottish Building Fedn Edinburgh and Dist Charitable Trust, 2005–. Non-exec. Dir, Edinburgh Business Sch., 2001–. *Publications:* over 200 articles and letters in field of lasers and optoelectronics. *Recreations:* sailing (Cdre, Cramond Boat Club), music (piano). *Address:* Carnegie Trust for the Universities of Scotland, Andrew Carnegie House, Pittencrieff Street, Dunfermline KY12 8AW. *E:* a.c.walker@carnegie-trust.org; (home) 57 Cramond Glebe Road, Edinburgh EH4 6NT.

WALKER, Andrew Douglas; Senior Partner, Lovells, 2000–04; *b* 6 May 1945; *s* of Malcolm Douglas Walker and Jean Catherine Walker (*née* Ross-Scott); *m* 1973, Hilary Georgina Smith. *Educ:* Giggleswick Sch.; Exeter Coll., Oxford (MA 1966). Admitted Solicitor, England and Wales, 1970, Hong Kong, 1982; articled, 1968–70, Solicitor, 1970–71, Wilkinson Kimbers & Staddon; Lovell, White & King: Solicitor, 1971–75; Partner, 1975; Hong Kong office, 1982–87; Managing Partner, 1987–88; Lovell White Durrant (formed from merger with Durrant Piesse): Managing Partner, 1988–93; Sen. Partner, 1996–2000; Lovells formed 2000, from merger with Boesebeck Droste. *Recreations:* opera, classical music, ornithology. *Club:* Hong Kong.

WALKER, Andrew John; company director; Chairman, Mainstay Group Ltd, since 2013; *b* 27 Sept. 1951; *s* of late John Kenneth Walker, MD and Mary Magdaline (*née* Browne); *m* 1981, Pippa Robinson; two *s* one *d. Educ:* Ampleforth Coll., York; Gonville and Caius Coll., Cambridge (MA Engrg). FIMechE 2003. Chief Executive: SWALEC, 1993–96; McKechnie plc, 1997–2001; Chairman: Bioganix plc, 2004–09; Brintons Ltd, 2008–11 (Dir, 2006–11); Metalrax plc, 2010–13; Director: Ultra Electronics Hldgs plc, 1996–2009; Halma plc, 2003–07; API Gp plc, 2003–15; Manganese Bronze Hldgs plc, 2003–12; Delta plc, 2005–10; Porvair plc, 2005–14; Fountains plc, 2005–08; Plastics Capital plc, 2007–; May Gurney plc, 2009–13; Stemcor Hldgs Ltd, 2014–. Liveryman, Engineers' Co. *Address:* Mainstay Group Ltd, Whittington Hall, Whittington Road, Worcester WR5 2ZX. *Club:* Farmers.

WALKER, Andrew John; Director General of Human Resources and Change, House of Commons, since 2011; *b* 4 Jan. 1955; *s* of Edward Geoffrey Walker and Raymonde Dorothy Walker; *m* 1987, Alison Aitkenhead; two *s* one *d. Educ:* Newcastle-under-Lyme High Sch.; Univ. of Birmingham (BA Ancient Near Eastern Studies). CPFA 2008. Inland Revenue, 1976–89; Principal, Fiscal Policy Gp, HM Treasury, 1989–91; Asst Dir, Human Resources Strategy and Planning, Inland Revenue, 1992–96; House of Commons: Dir of Finance and Admin, 1997–2007; Dir Gen., Resources, 2008–11. Dir, Christadelphian Mag. and Publishing Assoc., 2014–. FCIPD 2012. *Address:* Department of Human Resources and Change, House of Commons, SW1A 0AA. *T:* (020) 7219 5460.

WALKER, Andrew Paul Dalton; QC 2011; *b* Chester, 22 Sept. 1968; *s* of Richard and Linda Walker; *m* 2003, Emma Bensted. *Educ:* King's Sch., Chester; Haberdashers' Aske's Sch., Elstree; Trinity Coll., Cambridge (BA 1990; MA). Called to the Bar, Lincoln's Inn, 1991. Mem., Bar Council, 2005–. Trustee, Industry and Parliament Trust, 2013–. *Recreations:* wine, walking, gun dogs, conservation, historic buildings. *Address:* Maitland Chambers, 7 Stone Buildings, Lincoln's Inn, WC2A 3SZ. *T:* (020) 7406 1200, *Fax:* (020) 7406 1300. *E:* awalker@maitlandchambers.com. *Club:* Oxford and Cambridge.

WALKER, Angus Henry; Senior Consultant, Europe Economics, 2006; *b* 30 Aug. 1935; *s* of late Frederick William Walker and of Esther Victoria (*née* Wrangle); *m* 1st, 1968, Beverly Phillpotts (*see* B. J. Anderson) (marr. diss. 1976); 2nd, 1979, Ann (*née* Griffiths), *widow* of Richard Snow; two *d* and two step *d. Educ:* Erith Grammar Sch., Kent; Balliol Coll., Oxford (Domus Scholar; 1st Cl. Hons BA Mod. Hist. 1959; Stanhope Prize, 1958; MA 1968). Nat. Service, 1954–56 (commnd RA). Senior Scholar, St Antony's Coll., Oxford, 1959–63; HM Diplomatic Service, 1963–68: FO, 1963–65; First Sec., Washington, 1965–68. Lectr, SSEES, London Univ., 1968–70; Univ. Lectr in Russian Social and Political Thought, Oxford, and Lectr, Balliol Coll., 1971–76; Fellow, Wolfson Coll., Oxford, 1971–76; Dir, SSEES, London Univ., 1976–79; British Petroleum Co. Plc, 1979–84; Dir, Corporate Strategy, British Telecom PLC, 1985–88; Managing Director: Strategic Planning Associates, 1988–91; A. T. Kearney, 1991–94; Partner, Mitchell Madison Gp, 1996–98. Co-opted Mem., Arts Sub-Cttee, UGC, for enquiry into Russian in British Univs, 1978–79; Governor, Centre for Economic Policy Res., 1986–89. Chairman: HemiHelp, 2004–11; Hampstead Garden Suburb Trust, 2007–13. FIET (FIEE 2002; CompIEE 1988). *Publications:* trans. from Polish: Political Economy, by Oskar Lange, vol. 1, 1963; Marx: His Theory in its Context, 1978, 2nd edn 1989. *Address:* Barclays Bank plc, 126 Station Road, Edgware HA8 7RY. *Club:* Reform.

WALKER, Hon. Anna Elizabeth Blackstock, (Hon. Mrs Walker), CB 2003; Chairman, Office of Rail and Road (formerly Office of Rail Regulation), since 2009; *b* 5 May 1951; *d* of Baron Butterworth, CBE; *m* 1983, Timothy Edward Hanson Walker, *qv*; three *d. Educ:* Benenden Sch., Kent; Bryn Mawr Coll., USA; Lady Margaret Hall, Oxford (MA History). British Council, 1972–73; CBI, 1973–74; joined Department of Trade, 1975: Commercial Relations and Exports Div. (ME), 1975; Post and Telecommunications Div., 1976; Private Sec. to Sec. of State for Industry, 1977–78; Shipping Policy Div. (Grade 7), 1979–82; Finance Div., 1983–84; Interdeptl Rev. of Budgetary Controls, 1985; Cabinet Office (on secondment), 1986; Personnel Div. (Grade 6), 1987–88; Competition Policy Div. (Grade 5), 1988–91; Dir, Competition, 1991–94, Dep. Dir Gen., 1994–98, Oftel; Dep. Dir Gen., 1998, Dir Gen., 1998–2001, Energy, DTI; Dir Gen., Land Use and Rural Affairs, DEFRA, 2001–03; Chief Exec., Healthcare Commn, 2004–09. Chm., Ind. Review of Charging for Household Water and Sewerage Services, 2008–09 (Report, 2009). Non-exec. Dir, Welsh Water, 2011–. Member, Council: Consumer Focus (formerly NCC), 2008–12; Which?, 2013–. Chm., Young Epilepsy (formerly Nat. Centre for Young People with Epilepsy), 2009–. Trustee, Operahouse Music Projects, 2004–. *Recreations:* family, travel, theatre, cycling. *Address:* Office of Rail and Road, One Kemble Street, WC2B 4AN. *T:* (020) 7282 3696. *E:* anna.walker@orr.gsi.gov.uk.

WALKER, Annabel; *see* Carr, E. A.

WALKER, Anthony Stanley L.; *see* Lau-Walker.

WALKER, Gen. Sir Antony (Kenneth Frederick), KCB 1987; Director-General, British Institute of Facilities Management, 1998–2001; *b* 16 May 1934; *o s* of late Kenneth Walker and Iris Walker; *m* 1961, Diana Merran Steward (marr. diss. 1983); one *s* one *d*; *m* 1991, Sqn Ldr Hannah Watts, WRAF. *Educ:* Merchant Taylors' School; RMA Sandhurst. Commissioned into Royal Tank Regt, 1954; served BAOR, Libya, Ghana, Northern Ireland, Hong Kong, Cyprus; Instructor, Staff Coll., 1971–73; CO 1st Royal Tank Regt, 1974–76 (despatches); Col GS HQ UK Land Forces, 1976–78; Comdr Task Force Golf (11 Armd Bde), 1978–80; Dep. Mil. Sec. (A), 1980–82; Comdr, 3rd Armoured Div., 1982–84; Chief of Staff, HQ UKLF, 1985–87; Dep. CDS (Commitments), MoD, 1987–89; Comdt, RCDS, 1990–92. Sec.-Gen., Opsis (Nat. Assoc. for Educn, Trng and Support of Blind and Partially Sighted People), 1992–96. Mil. Advr, Porton Internat. plc, 1992–94; Sen. Mil. Advr, Electronic Data Systems Ltd, 1994; Business Develt Dir, John Mowlem. Col Comdt, Royal Tank Regt, 1983–94 (Rep., 1985–91). Mem. Council, RUSI, 1982–85 and 1990–94. Governor, Centre for Internat. Briefing, Farnham Castle, 1987–91. Chairman: Army Bobsleigh Assoc., 1983–92; British Bobsleigh Assoc., 1992–98 (Mem. Council, 1989–); President: Services' Dry Fly Fishing Assoc., 1988–92; Combined Services' Winter Sports Assoc., 1990–92. Mem., Council of Management, Salisbury Festival, 1988–96 (Vice-Chm., 1990–93; Chm., 1994–96). Trustee, Tank Mus., 1994–. *Recreations:* bird watching, fly-fishing, music, practical study of wine. *Address:* c/o National Westminster Bank plc, PO Box 237, 72–74 High Street, Watford, Herts WD17 2GZ. *Club:* Royal Air Force (Associate).

WALKER, Bill; *see* Walker, W. C.

WALKER, (Brian) Stuart, RDI 1989; freelance film production designer, since 1990; *b* 5 March 1932; *s* of William and Annie Walker; *m* 1st, 1961, Adrienne Elizabeth Atkinson (marr. diss. 1997); two *d*; 2nd, 2000, Francesca Boyd; one *s*. *Educ:* Blackpool Sch. of Art (Intermediate Exam. in Arts and Crafts; Nat. Diploma in Painting (1st cl. Hons)); RA Schs (RA Dip.). BBC Television, 1958–90: Design Assistant, 1958; Designer, 1961; Sen. Designer, 1970. BAFTA Award for TV Design, 1983, 1990; RTS Award for Production Design, 1988. *Address:* c/o Casarotto Marsh Ltd, Waverley House, 7–12 Noel Street, W1F 8GQ. *T:* (020) 7287 4450.

WALKER, Brian Wilson; consultant in ecology and development, since 1996; Executive Director, Earthwatch Europe, 1989–95; *b* 31 Oct. 1930; *s* of Arthur Walker and Eleanor (*née* Wilson); *m* 1954, Nancy Margaret Gawith; one *s* five *d*. *Educ:* Heversham Sch., Westmorland; Leicester Coll. of Technol.; Faculty of Technol., Manchester Univ. Management Trainee, Sommerville Bros, Kendal, 1952–55; Personnel Manager, Pye Radio, Larne, 1956–61; Bridgeport Brass Ltd, Lisburn: Personnel Manager, 1961–66; Gen. Manager (Develt), 1966–69; Gen. Manager (Manufg), 1969–74; Dir Gen., Oxfam, 1974–83; Dir, Independent Commn on Internat. Humanitarian Issues, 1983–85; Pres., Internat. Inst. for Envmt and Develt, 1985–89. Chairman: Band Aid—Live Aid Projects Cttee, 1985–90; SOS Sahel, 1988–95. Founder Chm., New Ulster Movt, 1969–74; Founder Pres., New Ulster Movt Ltd, 1974. Member: Standing Adv. Commn on Human Rights for NI, 1975–77; World Commn on Food and Peace, 1989–95; Preparing for Peace, Westmorland Quakers, 2000–07. Mem., Editl Cttee, World Resources Report, 1985–95. Trustee: Cambodia Trust, 1989–95; Internat. Inst. for Environment and Develt, 1989–95; Artizan Trust, 1992–99; Nginn Karet Foundn, 1996–2002; Chm., Arnside Parish Plan Trust, 2003–07. Chm., Kent Estuary Labour Party, 2005–08. Chm. Govs, Dallam Sch., Cumbria, 1996–2003; Chm., Dallam Trust, 2003–11. Eponymous annual lecture inaugurated Oxford Univ., 1996. Hon. MA Oxon, 1983. Kt, Sov. Order of St Thomas of Acre; Kentucky Colonel, 1966. *Publications:* Authentic Development—Africa, 1986; various political/religious papers on Northern Ireland problem and Third World subjects. *Recreations:* gardening, Irish politics, classical music, active Quaker. *Club:* Athenæum.

WALKER, Carl, GC 1972; Police Inspector, 1976–82; *b* 31 March 1934; English; *m* 1955, Kathleen Barker; one *s*. *Educ:* Kendal Grammar Sch., Westmorland. RAF Police, 1952–54 (Corporal). Lancashire Police, Oct. 1954–March 1956, resigned; Blackpool Police, 1959–82 (amalgamated with Lancashire Constabulary, April 1968); Sergeant, 1971. Retired 1982, as a result of the injuries sustained from gunshot wounds on 23 Aug. 1971 during an armed raid by thieves on a jeweller's shop in Blackpool (GC). *Address:* 9 Lawnswood Avenue, Poulton-le-Fylde, Blackpool FY6 7ED.

WALKER, Caron Ann; Director, Collection and Production, Office for National Statistics, 2012–14; *b* Newport, S Wales, 4 June 1959; *d* of Michael Maguire and Gloria Maguire; *m* 1985, Graeme Walker; one *s* one *d*. *Educ:* Univ. of Southampton (BSc Maths with Actuarial Studies 1980). Business Statistics Office, then Central Statistical Office, later Office for National Statistics: Asst Statistician, 1981–86; Statistician, 1987–96; Sen. Statistician, 1996–2000; Dep. Dir, 2000–04; Temp. Dir, 2005–08; Dep. Dir, 2008–09; Dep. Dir, Nat. Statistician's Office, 2009–11; Temp. Dir, Sources, 2011–12. *Recreations:* judo black belt 4th dan, watching Manchester United, family, walking, theatre, music.

WALKER, Charles Ashley Rupert, OBE 2015; MP (C) Broxbourne, since 2005; *b* 11 Sept. 1967; *s* of late Timothy Walker and of Carola Walker (*née* Ashton) (she *m* 1976, Rt Hon. Sir Christopher John Chataway, PC); *m* 1995, Fiona Jane Newman; two *s* one *d*. *Educ:* American Sch. of London; Univ. of Oregon (BSc Pol Sci. 1990). Communications Dir, CSG plc, 1997–2001; Director: Blue Arrow Ltd, 1999–2001; LSM Processing Ltd, 2002–04. Mem., Wandsworth LBC, 2002–. Contested (C) Ealing North, 2001. *Recreations:* fishing, cricket. *Address:* House of Commons, SW1A 0AA. *T:* (020) 7219 3000. *E:* walkerc@parliament.uk. *Clubs:* Waltham Cross Conservative; Hoddesdon Conservative.

WALKER, Charls E., PhD; Consultant, Washington, DC, since 1973; *b* Graham, Texas, 24 Dec. 1923; *s* of Pinkney Clay and Sammye McCombs Walker; *m* 1949, Harmolyn Hart, Laurens, S Carolina; one *s* one *d*. *Educ:* Univ. of Texas (MBA); Wharton Sch. of Finance, Univ. of Pennsylvania (PhD). Instructor in Finance, 1947–48, and later Asst and Associate Prof., 1950–54, at Univ. of Texas, in the interim teaching at Wharton Sch. of Finance, Univ. of Pennsylvania; Associate Economist, Fed. Reserve Bank: of Philadelphia, 1953, of Dallas, 1954 (Vice-Pres. and Economic Advr, 1958–61); Economist and Special Asst to Pres. of Republic Nat. Bank of Dallas, 1955–56 (took leave to serve as Asst to Treasury Sec., Robert B. Anderson, April 1959–Jan. 1961); Exec. Vice-Pres., Amer. Bankers Assoc., 1961–69. Under-Sec. of the Treasury, 1969–72, Dep. Sec., 1972–73. Chm., American Council for Capital Formation; Co-founder, Cttee on the Present Danger; Mem. Council on Foreign Relations; Founder Chm., Bretton Woods Cttee. Adjunct Prof. of Finance and Public Affairs, Univ. of Texas at Austin, 1985–; Dist. Vis. Prof., Emory Univ., 2000–. Dist. Alumnus, Univ. of Texas, 1994. Hon. LLD Ashland Coll., 1970. Alexander Hamilton Award, US Treasury, 1973; Award for Outstanding Contribs to Minority Enterprise and Educn, Urban League, 1973; Baker Award, Nat. Council on Econ. Educn, 1991. Co-editor, The Banker's Handbook, 1988–. *Publications:* (ed) New Directions in Federal Tax Policy, 1983; (ed) The Consumption Tax, 1987; (ed) The US Savings Challenge, 1990; contribs to learned jls, periodicals. *Clubs:* Congressional Country, Burning Tree Golf (Bethesda, Md).

WALKER, Christopher Charles, FRCS; Consultant Plastic and Reconstructive Surgeon, 1983–2008; Medical Director, Mid Essex Hospitals NHS Trust, 2001–07; President, British Association of Plastic, Reconstructive and Aesthetic Surgeons, 2007; *b* 26 April 1945; *s* of Cyril and Evelyn Vera Walker; *m* 1981, Marlene Dawn Menner; one *d*. *Educ:* Univ. of Newcastle upon Tyne (MB BS 1968). FRCS 1974. SHO, Surgery Rotating, United Norwich Hosp., 1971–74; Registrar, Gen. Surgery, Leicester Royal Infirmary, 1974–75; MRC Res. Registrar, Burns Project, Mt Vernon Hosp., 1975–76; Registrar in Plastic Surgery, Mt Vernon Hosp. and UCH, 1976–80; Sen. Registrar in Plastic Surgery, Manchester Hosps, 1980–83; Consultant Plastic Surgeon: St Andrews Centre, Billericay, 1983–2008 (transf. to Broomfield Hosp., Chelmsford, 1998); Queen Elizabeth Children's Hosp. and Royal London Hosp., 1983–2001; Whipps Cross Hosp., 1983–2008. Founder and Chm., Broomfield Hosp. Arts Project, 1997–; Trustee, Changing Faces, 2008–. *Recreations:* jazz and classical music, wine and food, travel, art.

WALKER, Sir Christopher (Robert Baldwin), 5th Bt *cr* 1856, of Oakley House, Suffolk; *b* 25 Oct. 1969; *s* of Sir (Baldwin) Patrick Walker, 4th Bt and of Rosemary Ann Walker (*née* Hollingdrake); *S* father, 2005; *m* 2013, Keryn Barnes; one *d*. *Educ:* Diocesan Coll., Cape Town. Leading Seaman, South African Marine Corps, 1994–96; Sales Manager, 1996–2006; Dir, CSS Security and Technol. Centre, Ni9htwatcher Distribution, 2007–08; Sales Manager, Betafence SA, 2008–14. *Heir: cousin* Anthony Eric Charles Walker, *b* 1966. *Address:* 8 Waltham Way, Meadowridge, Cape Town 7806, South Africa.

WALKER, (Christopher) Roy, CB 1992; Chief Officer, Joint Nature Conservation Committee, 1993–96; *b* 5 Dec. 1934; *s* of late Christopher Harry Walker and Dorothy Jessica Walker; *m* 1961, Hilary Mary Biddiscombe; two *s*. *Educ:* Sir George Monoux Grammar Sch., E17; Sidney Sussex Coll., Cambridge (BA); Université Libre de Bruxelles. National Service, Essex Regt, 1952–54. BoT, 1958; CSD, 1968; Private Sec. to Lord Privy Seal, 1968–71; Treasury, 1973; DTI, 1973; Dept of Energy, 1974; Cabinet Office, 1974; Dept of Energy, 1975; Under Secretary: DES, 1977; Dept of Employment, 1986; seconded as Dir, Business in the Cities, 1989; Dep. Head of Sci. and Technol. Secretariat, Cabinet Office, 1989–92. Chm., Rockdale Housing Assoc., Sevenoaks, 2003–07. *Recreations:* hill walking, sailing. *Clubs:* Cruising Association; Chipstead Sailing (Sevenoaks).

WALKER, Sir David (Alan), Kt 1991; Chairman: Barclays Bank PLC, 2012–15; Winton Capital, since 2015; *b* 31 Dec. 1939; *m* 1963, Isobel Cooper; one *s* two *d*. *Educ:* Chesterfield Sch.; Queens' Coll., Cambridge (MA; Hon. Fellow, 1989). Joined HM Treasury, 1961; Private Sec. to Joint Permanent Secretary, 1964–66; seconded to Staff of International Monetary Fund, Washington, 1970–73; Asst Secretary, HM Treasury, 1973–77; joined Bank of England as Chief Adviser, then Chief of Economic Intelligence Dept, 1977; a Dir, 1981–93 (non-exec., 1988–93); Chairman: Johnson Matthey Bankers, later Minories Finance, 1985–88; SIB, 1988–92; Agricl Mortgage Corp., 1993–94; Dep. Chm., Lloyds Bank plc, 1992–94; Dir, Morgan Stanley Inc., 1994–97; Exec. Chm., Morgan Stanley Gp (Europe) plc, subseq. Morgan Stanley Dean Witter (Europe) Ltd, 1994–2000; Chm., Morgan Stanley Internat. Inc., 1995–2000; Mem., Mgt Bd, Morgan Stanley Dean Witter, 1997–2000; Sen. Advr, 2001–04, 2006–12, Exec. Chm., 2004–05, Morgan Stanley Internat. Ltd, later plc. Chairman: Steering Gp, Financial Markets Gp, LSE, 1986–93; Review of Disclosure and Transparency in Private Equity, 2007; Review of Corporate Governance in UK Banks and Other Financial Instns, 2009. Bd Mem., CEGB, 1987–89; Chm., RVC Greenhouse Fund, 1999–; non-executive Director: National Power, 1990, 1993–94; British Invisibles, 1993–97; Reuters Holdings, 1994–2000; Legal & General Assce Co., 2002–11 (Vice-Chm., 2004–11). Mem., 1993–, Treas., 1998–, and Trustee, 2007–, The Group of Thirty. Chairman: London Investment Bankers' Assoc., 2002–04; Moroccan British Business Council, 2000–07. Nominated Mem., Council of Lloyd's, 1988–92 (Chm., Inquiry into LMX Spiral, 1992). UK Co. Chm., Univ. of Cambridge 800th Anniversary Campaign, 2005–. Governor, Henley Management Coll., 1993–99. Chm., Community Links, East End charity, 1995–2011. Hon. FKC 2008. FRSA 1987; CCMI (CBIM 1986). Hon. LLD Exeter, 2002. *Recreations:* music, long-distance walking. *Address:* Winton Capital, Grove House, 27 Hammersmith Grove, W6 0NE. *Clubs:* Reform, Garrick.

WALKER, Air Marshal Sir David (Allan), KCVO 2011 (MVO 1992); OBE 1995; DL; Director, Strategic Difference Ltd, since 2014; non-executive Director, Alexander Mann Solutions, since 2015; an Extra Equerry to the Queen, since 2005; *b* 14 July 1956; *s* of late Allan Walker and Audrey Walker (*née* Brothwell); *m* 1983, Jane Alison Fraser Calder. *Educ:* City of London Sch.; Univ. of Bradford (BSc). RAF univ. cadet, 1974; RAF Coll., 1977–78; Equerry to the Queen, 1989–92; Loan Service, S Africa, 1994; Comd, RAF Halton, 1997–98; Director: Corporate Communication (RAF), 1998–2002; Personnel and Trng Policy (RAF), 2002–03; AOC RAF Trng Gp and Chief Exec., Trng Gp Defence Agency, 2003–04; retd in rank of Air Marshal, 2011. Senior Adviser: HSBC Gp Hldgs, 2013–14; Barclays Bank plc, 2014–15; PricewaterhouseCoopers, 2014–. Master of HM Household, 2005–13. Vice-Patron, Royal Internat. Air Tattoo, 2012– (Vice Pres., 2005–12). Hon. Pres., London Wing, ATC, 2012–; Hon. Air Cdre 603 (City of Edinburgh) Sqn, RAuxAF, 2015–. Trustee, Savoy Educnl Trust, 2015–. DL Glos, 2015. *Recreations:* walking dogs, keeping fit(ish), old cars, shooting, military history. *Address:* Alexander Mann Solutions, 7–11 Bishopsgate, EC2N 3AQ. *Clubs:* Brooks's, Royal Air Force.

WALKER, David Critchlow, CMG 1993; CVO 1988 (MVO 1976); HM Diplomatic Service, retired; Chairman, Impact UK, since 2003; *b* 9 Jan. 1940; *s* of John Walker and Mary Walker (*née* Cross); *m* 1965, Tineke van der Leek; three *s*. *Educ:* Manchester Grammar Sch.; St Catharine's Coll., Cambridge (BA, MA, DipEd). Assistant Lecturer, Dept of Geography, Manchester Univ., 1962; Commonwealth Relations Office, 1963; Third Secretary, British Embassy, Mexico City, 1965; Second Secretary, Brussels, 1968; First Secretary: FCO, 1970; Washington, 1973; First Sec., later Counsellor, FCO, 1978–83; Consul General, São Paulo, 1983–86; Minister, Madrid, 1986–89; Counsellor, FCO, 1989–92; High Comr, Ghana, and non-resident Ambassador, Togo, 1992–96; High Comr, Bangladesh, 1996–99. *Address:* 7 The Crescent, Thirsk YO7 1DE.

WALKER, David Frederick; Contributing Editor, Guardian Public, since 2010 (Founding Editor, 2004–08); Head of Policy, Academy of Social Sciences, since 2014; *b* Aberdeen, 8 Nov. 1950; *s* of John and Irene Walker; *m* 1974, Karen Irving (marr. diss. 1995); one *s*. *Educ:* Corby Grammar Sch.; St Catharine's Coll., Cambridge (BA); Univ. of Sussex (MA); Ecole Pratique des Hautes Etudes. Trainee, 1974–76, Chief Reporter, 1976, THES; Harkness Fellow, US Congress, Univ. of Calif, Berkeley, 1977; writer, Economist, 1979–81; Local Govt corresp., Leader Writer, then Whitehall corresp., The Times, 1981–87; Chief Leader Writer, London Daily News, 1987–88; presenter, Analysis prog., BBC Radio 4, 1988–93; Urban Affairs corresp., BBC, 1993–96; Chief Leader Writer, Independent, 1996–98; Analysis Ed. and Leader Writer, Guardian, 1998–2004; Man. Dir, Communications and Public Reporting, Audit Commn, 2008–10. Member: ESRC, 2007–13; Ethics and Governance Council, UK Biobank, 2014–. Non-exec. Dir, Places for People, 1999–2004. Trustee: Nat. Centre for Social Res., 2001–08; Nuffield Trust, 2005–08; Franco-British Council, 2008–. *Publications:* (with J. Tunstall) Media Made in California, 1981; Municipal Empire, 1983; (jtly) Sources Close to the Prime Minister, 1984; Public Relations in Local Government, 1998; (with Polly Toynbee): Did Things Get Better?, 2001; Better or Worse, 2005; Unjust Rewards, 2009; The Verdict, 2010; Cameron's Coup: how the Tories took Britain to the brink, 2015. *Recreations:* tennis, running, woodwind. *Address:* 2 Eton College Road, NW3 2BS. *E:* davidwlkr0@gmail.com. *Club:* Reform.

WALKER, David Ralph, FFPH; Deputy Chief Medical Officer for England, since 2013; *b* 28 Oct. 1962; *s* of David and Ada Walker; *m* 1995, Elisabeth Ann Martin; two *d*. *Educ:* Nottingham High Sch.; Univ. of Newcastle upon Tyne Med. Sch. (BMedSci 1986; MB BS 1987; MSc 1994). MRCP 1991; MFPHM 1995, FFPH 2006. Trng posts in medicine and public health, Newcastle upon Tyne, 1987–94; Vis. Scientist, Centers for Disease Control,

Atlanta, Ga, 1994–95; Consultant in Communicable Disease Control and Dep. Dir of Public Health, Co. Durham and Darlington HA, 1996–2001; Actg Dir of Public Health, Newcastle and N Tyneside HA, 2001–02; Dir of Public Health and Med. Dir, Co. Durham and Tees Valley Strategic HA, 2002–06; Actg Regl Dir of Public Health for NE of England, 2005–06; Regional Director of Public Health: E Midlands, 2006–11; NHS Midlands and East, 2011–13. Vis. Prof. of Public Health, Univ. of Lincoln, 2010–. *Publications:* articles in med. jls. *Recreations:* ski-ing, boogie-woogie piano playing. *Address:* Department of Health, Richmond House, 79 Whitehall, SW1A 2NS. *E:* David.walker@dh.gsi.gov.uk.

WALKER, Rt Rev. David Stuart; *see* Manchester, Bishop of.

WALKER, Maj.-Gen. Derek William Rothwell; Manager, CBI Overseas Scholarships, 1980–89, retired; *b* 12 Dec. 1924; *s* of Frederick and Eileen Walker; *m* 1950, Florence Margaret Panting; two *s* (and one *s* decd). *Educ:* Mitcham County Grammar Sch.; Battersea Polytechnic. FIMechE 1970–89; FIEE 1971–89. Commissioned REME, 1946; served: Middle East, 1947–50 (despatches 1949); BAOR, 1951–53; Far East, 1954–56 (despatches 1957); Near East, 1960–62; Far East, 1964–67; psc 1957. Lt-Col 1964, Col 1970, Brig. 1973. Appts include: Comdr, REME Support Group, 1976–77; Dir, Equipment Engineering, 1977–79. Mem. Council, IEE, 1975–79; Pres., SEE, 1979–81. *Recreations:* fishing, sailing, wine-making. *Address:* 20 Moor Lane, Strensall, York YO32 5UQ.

WALKER, Desmond; *see* Le Cheminant, Air Chief Marshal Sir P. de L.

WALKER, Rt Rev. Dominic Edward William Murray, OGS; DL; Bishop of Monmouth, 2003–13; an Hon. Assistant Bishop, Diocese of Swansea and Brecon, since 2013; *b* 28 June 1948; *s* of Horace John and Mary Louise Walker. *Educ:* Plymouth Coll.; King's Coll. London (AKC); Heythrop Coll., London (MA); Univ. of Wales (LLM). Ordained priest, 1972; Asst Curate, St Faith, Wandsworth, 1972–73; Domestic Chaplain to the Bishop of Southwark, 1973–76; Rector, Newington, 1976–85; Rural Dean, Southwark and Newington, 1980–85; Vicar, Team Rector, and Rural Dean of Brighton, 1985–97; Canon and Prebendary, Chichester Cathedral, 1985–97; Area Bishop of Reading, 1997–2003. Mem., CGA, 1967–83; Mem., OGS, 1983– (Superior, 1990–96). Vice-Pres., 2001–10, Hon. Vice-Pres., 2010–, RSPCA; Pres., Anglican Soc. for Welfare of Animals, 2008–. Governor: Univ. of Wales Newport, 2003–10; St Michael's Coll., Llandaff, 2003–13. DL Gwent, 2014. Hon. DLitt Brighton, 1998. *Publications:* The Ministry of Deliverance, 1997. *Address:* 2 St Vincent's Drive, Monmouth NP25 5DS.

WALKER, Prof. Donald, FRS 1985; Professor of Biogeography, Institute of Advanced Studies, Australian National University, Canberra, 1969–88; *b* 14 May 1928; *s* of Arthur Walker and Eva (*née* Risdon); *m* 1959, Patricia Mary Smith (*d* 2013); two *d*. *Educ:* Morecambe Grammar School; Sheffield Univ. (BSc); MA, PhD Cantab. Commission, RAF (Nat. Service), 1953–55. Research Scholar and Asst in Res., later Sen. Asst, Sub-Dept of Quaternary Res., Cambridge Univ., 1949–60; Fellow of Clare College, 1952–60 (Asst Tutor, 1955–60); Reader in Biogeography, ANU, 1960–68; Head of Dept of Biogeography and Geomorphology, ANU, 1969–88. Hon. Prof., Chinese Acad. of Science, 1986–. *Publications:* articles on plant ecology, palaeoecology and related topics in sci. jls. *Recreations:* pottery, architecture, prehistory. *Address:* Unit 67, The Grange, 67 Macgregor Street, Deakin, ACT 2600, Australia. *T:* (2) 62826751.

WALKER, Edward William F.; *see* Faure Walker.

WALKER, Prof. Frederick, MD, PhD; FRCPath; Regius Professor of Pathology, University of Aberdeen, 1984–2000, now Emeritus; Consultant Pathologist, Grampian Health Board, 1984–2000; *b* 21 Dec. 1934; *s* of Frederick James Walker and Helen Stitt Halliday; *m* 1st, 1963, Cathleen Anne Gordon, BSc (marr. diss.); two *d*; 2nd, 1998, Jean Winifred Keeling, FRCPath, FRCPE, FRCPCH. *Educ:* Kirkcudbright Academy; Univ. of Glasgow. MB ChB 1958; PhD 1964; MD (Hons and Bellahouston Medal) 1971. MRCPath 1966, FRCPath 1978. Lectr in Pathology, Univ. of Glasgow, 1962–67; Vis. Asst Prof., Univ. of Minnesota, 1964–65; Sen. Lectr in Pathology, Univ. of Aberdeen, 1968–73; Foundation Prof. of Pathology, Univ. of Leicester, 1973–84. Chm., Nat. Quality Assurance Adv. Panel (Histopathology and Cytology), 1991–96; Mem. Council, RCPath, 1990–93; Chm. and Gen. Sec., Pathol Soc. of GB and Ireland, 1992–2000 (Mem. Cttee, 1990–92). Editor, Jl of Pathology, 1983–93. *Publications:* papers in scientific and med. jls. *Recreations:* writing, walking. *Address:* 9 Forres Street, Edinburgh EH3 6BJ. *T:* (0131) 225 9673.

WALKER, George Robert, OBE 1992; Director-General, International Baccalaureate Organisation, 1999–2006; *b* 25 Jan. 1942; *s* of William Walker and Celia Walker (*née* Dean); *m* 1968, Jennifer Anne Hill; one *s* one *d*. *Educ:* Watford Boys' Grammar Sch.; Exeter Coll., Oxford (MA, MSc); Univ. of Cape Town (LRSM). Science teacher, Watford Grammar Sch., 1966–68; Salters' Inst. Schol., 1968–69; Lectr in Educn, Univ. of York, 1969–73; Dep. Headmaster, Carisbrooke High Sch., 1973–76; Headmaster: Heathcote Sch., Stevenage, 1977–81; Cavendish Sch., Hemel Hempstead, 1981–91; Dir-Gen., Internat. Sch. of Geneva, 1991–99. Chm., Centre for Study of Comprehensive Schs, 1980–85. Member: HMC, 1982–99; Nat. Curriculum Sci. Working Gp, 1987–88. Educn Advr to ICI plc, 1990–91. Hon. Sen. Vis. Fellow, Univ. of York, 1988–91; Vis. Prof., Univ. of Bath, 1997–2009. Mem. Council, Univ. of York, 2002–05. Hon. DEd Bath, 2003. *Publications:* (jtly) Modern Physical Chemistry, 1981, 3rd edn 1986; Comprehensive Themes, 1983; (ed jtly) International Education in Practice, 2002; To Educate the Nations, 2002; To Educate the Nations 2, 2004; International Education and the International Baccalaureate, 2004; Educating the Global Citizen, 2006; An A to Z of School Leadership, 2007; M. T. Maurette: pioneer of international education, 2009; Challenges from a New World, 2010; (ed) The Changing Face of International Education, 2011; Glimpses of Utopia, 2013. *Recreation:* piano-playing. *Address:* 4 Mayes Meadow, Moulton, Newmarket, Suffolk CB8 8SZ.

WALKER, Gordon; *see* Walker, T. G.

WALKER, Prof. Greg, PhD; Regius Professor of Rhetoric and English Literature, University of Edinburgh, since 2010; *b* Coventry, 8 Sept. 1959; *s* of Arthur Walker and Hilda Walker; *m* 1985, Sharon Joynt; two *s*. *Educ:* Horndean Sch.; Univ. of Southampton (BA English and Hist.; PhD 1986). British Acad. Postdoctoral Fellow, Univ. of Southampton, 1986–89; Lecturer: in English Lit., Univ. of Queensland, 1989–90; Univ. of Buckingham, 1991; University of Leicester: Lectr, 1991–95; Reader, 1995–98; Prof. of English, 1998–2007; Masson Prof. of English Lit., Univ. of Edinburgh, 2007–10. Mem., AHRC, 2011–. FRHS 1988; FEA 2002; FSA 2011. *Publications:* John Skelton and the Politics of the 1520s, 1988; Plays of Persuasion, 1991; Persuasive Fictions, 1996; The Politics of Performance in Early Renaissance Drama, 1998; (ed) Medieval Drama: an anthology, 2000; Alexander Korda's Private Life of Henry VIII, 2003; Writing under Tyranny, 2007; (with E. M. Treharne) The Oxford Handbook of Medieval Literature in English, 2010; (with Thomas Betteridge) The Oxford Handbook of Tudor Drama, 2012; Reading Literature Historically, 2013; (ed) The Oxford Anthology of Tudor Drama, 2014. *Recreations:* supporting Nottingham Forest FC; progressive rock music, dog walking, light irony. *Address:* English Department, University of Edinburgh, 50 George Square, Edinburgh EH8 9LH. *T:* (0131) 650 3049. *E:* greg.walker@ed.ac.uk.

WALKER, Sir Harold (Berners), KCMG 1991 (CMG 1979); HM Diplomatic Service, retired; *b* 19 Oct. 1932; *s* of late Admiral Sir Harold Walker, KCB, RN, and Lady Walker (*née* Berners); *m* 1st, 1960, Jane Bittleston (marr. diss.); one *s* two *d*; 2nd, 2004, Anne Savage (*née* Gourlay). *Educ:* Winchester; Worcester Coll., Oxford (BA 1955; MA). 2nd Lieut RE, 1951–52. Foreign Office, 1955; MECAS, 1957; Asst Political Agent, Dubai, 1958; Foreign Office, 1960; Principal Instructor, MECAS, 1963; First Sec., Cairo, 1964; Head of Chancery and Consul, Damascus, 1966; Foreign Office (later FCO), 1967; First Sec. (Commercial), Washington, 1970; Counsellor, Jedda, 1973; Dep. Head, Personnel Operations Dept, FCO, 1975–76, Head of Dept, 1976–78; Corpus Christi Coll., Cambridge, 1978; Ambassador to Bahrain, 1979–81, to United Arab Emirates, 1981–86, to Ethiopia, 1986–90, to Iraq, 1990–91; retd 1992. Member: Commonwealth War Graves Commn, 1992–97; Bd, CARE International UK, 1992–2001 (Chm., 1994–97); Pres., CARE Internat., 1997–2001; Chm., RSAA, 2001–08. President: Friends of Imperial War Mus., 1992–97; British Soc. for Middle Eastern Studies, 2006–10. Chm., Bahrain Soc., 1993–99. Mem. of Corp., Woking Sixth Form Coll., 1996–99. Trustee, Next Century Foundn, 2012–14. Chm., Blythe Sappers, 2013. Associate Fellow, RUSI, 1992–97. *Address:* 45 St Leonards Road, SW14 7LY. *E:* walker.turaco@btinternet.com. *Club:* Oxford and Cambridge.

WALKER, His Honour Judge Harry; *see* Walker, P. H. C.

WALKER, Iain; Director, Finance, Foreign and Commonwealth Office, since 2012; *b* Dundee, 6 Dec. 1976; *s* of Alfred Walker and Mabel Walker; *m* 2007, Claire; one *s* one *d*. *Educ:* Univ. of Dundee (LLB Hons). ACA 2003. Ernst & Young; GOAL, 2002–04; DEFRA, 2004–08; Cabinet Office, 2006–08; PricewaterhouseCoopers, 2008–10; Dep. Finance Dir, FCO, 2010–12. Trustee, GOAL, 2004–. *Recreations:* triathlon, golf, family. *Address:* Foreign and Commonwealth Office, King Charles Street, SW1A 2AH. *T:* (020) 7008 0927. *E:* iain.walker@fco.gov.uk.

WALKER, Rev. Dr James Bernard; Chaplain, 1993–2011, and Associate Director, Student Services, 2005–11 (Assistant Director, 1998–2005), St Andrews University; *s* of Rev. Dr Robert B. W. Walker and Grace B. Walker; *m* 1972, Sheila; three *s*. *Educ:* Hamilton Academy, Lanarkshire; Edinburgh Univ. (MA 1st cl. Hons Mental Philosophy 1968; BD 1st cl. Hons Systematic Theol. 1971); Merton Coll., Oxford (DPhil 1981). Church of Scotland minister, ordained 1975, Dundee; Associate Minister, Mid Craigie Parish Church linked with Wallacetown Parish Church, Dundee, 1975–78; Minister, Old and St Paul's Parish Church, Galashiels, 1978–87; Principal, Queen's Coll., Birmingham, 1987–93. *Publications:* Israel—Covenant and Land, 1986; (contrib.) Politique et Théologie chez Athanase d'Alexandrie (ed C. Kannengiesser), 1974; (contrib.) God, Family and Sexuality (ed D. W. Torrance), 1997. *Recreations:* golf, tennis, swimming, hill walking. *Address:* St Andrews.

WALKER, Prof. James Johnston, MD; FRCPSGlas, FRCPEd, FRCOG; Professor of Obstetrics and Gynaecology, University of Leeds, since 1994; *b* 17 March 1952; *s* of James and Catherine Walker; *m* 1976, Ann Mary Young; two *d*. *Educ:* High Sch. of Dundee; Univ. of Glasgow (MB ChB 1976; MD 1992). MRCOG 1981, FRCOG 1994; MRCP 1981; FRCPSGlas 1991; FRCPEd 1994. Jun. doctor, Obstetrics and Gynaecol., Glasgow, 1976–83; University of Glasgow: Res. Fellow in Obstetrics and Gynaecol., 1983–84; Lectr in Obstetrics and Gynaecol., 1984–87; Sen. Lectr, 1987–93; Reader, 1993. Clin. Advr (Obstetrics) to Nat. Patient Agency, 2003–11. Chm., Centre for Maternal and Child Enquiries, 2009–11. Sen. Vice Pres., RCOG, 2010–13. *Publications:* (with N. F. Gant) Hypertension in Pregnancy, 1997; (jtly) Problem-based Obstetrics and Gynaecology, 2003; (jtly) Pre-eclampsia, 2003; peer-reviewed articles in Obstetrics and Gynaecol. *Recreations:* travelling, cooking, swimming. *Address:* 12 Shire Oak Road, Headingley, Leeds LS6 2DE. *T:* (0113) 278 9599, *Fax:* (0113) 234 3450. *E:* j.j.walker@leeds.ac.uk. *Club:* Royal Society of Medicine.

WALKER, Jane Helen; *see* Darbyshire, J. H.

WALKER, Janet Sheila; Bursar, Eton College, since 2011; *b* Felton, 21 April 1953; *d* of David Walker and Sheila Walker (*née* Rapps); partner, Peter Corbett. *Educ:* Somerville Coll., Oxford (BA 1st Cl. PPE 1975); Institut des Hautes Études Internationales, Nice (Dip.). ACA 1979. Price Waterhouse, 1976–79; Chief Accountant, Handmade Films, 1980–81; Cost Controller, Channel 4, 1981–82; Hd, Programme Finance, Thames TV, 1982–84; London Films and Limehouse, 1984–87; Financial Dir, British Screen Finance, 1987–88; UK Rep., EURIMAGES Film Funding Orgn, 1987–88; Dep. Dir, Finance, Channel 4, 1988–94; Financial Controller for Regl Broadcasting, BBC, 1994–96; Financial Dir, Granada Media Gp, 1996–98; Dir, Finance and Business Affairs, Channel 4 Television, 1998–2003; Commercial and Finance Dir, Ascot Racecourse, 2003–10. Non-executive Director: Pizza Express plc, 1999–2003; Henderson High Income Trust plc, 2007–. Mem., Design Council, 2006–10. Mem. Bd, Young Vic Th., 1997–2005. Mem. Council, Royal Holloway, Univ. of London, 2009–10. Trustee, BAFTA, 2013–. *Recreations:* walking, gardening, modern fiction. *Address:* Eton College, Windsor SL4 6DJ.

WALKER, Janey Patricia Winifred, (Mrs H. F. Mykura); Member, Content Board, Ofcom, since 2011; Managing Director, Indie Training Fund; *b* 10 April 1958; *d* of Brig. Harry Walker and Patricia Walker; *m* 1997, Hamish Finlayson Mykura, *qv*; twin *d*. *Educ:* Brechin High Sch.; Benenden Sch.; York Univ. (BA Hist./Politics); Univ. of Chicago (Benton Fellow). BBC News and Current Affairs, 1983–89; The Late Show, BBC, 1990–94; Editor, Edge prog., WNET, and dir, BBC NY, 1994–95; Wall to Wall TV, London, 1995–96; Channel 4 Television: Commng Ed. Arts, 1996–99; Man. Ed. Commng, 1999–2010; Hd of Educn, 2006–10. Dir, Internat. Gateway for Gifted Youth, Univ. of Warwick, 2011–13. *Recreations:* walking, art, keeping chickens.

WALKER, Jeremy Colin Maclaren; Chair, Your Climate, since 2012; Member, North York Moors National Park Authority, since 2013; *b* 12 July 1949; *m* 1968, Patricia June Lockhart; two *s* one *d*. *Educ:* Brentwood Sch., Essex; Univ. of Birmingham (BA 1971). Dept of Employment, 1971–73; Pvte Sec. to Chm., MSC, 1974–75; HSE, 1975–76; Econ. Secretariat, Cabinet Office, 1976–78; MSC, 1978–82; Exchange Officer, Australian Dept of Employment and Industrial Relations, 1982–84; Manpower Services Commission: Regl Employment Manager, 1984–86; Hd, Community Prog. and New Job Trng Scheme, 1986–88; Regl Dir, Yorks and Humberside, Trng Agency and Dept of Employment, 1988–94; Regl Dir, Govt Office for Yorks and the Humber, 1994–99; Chief Exec., N Yorks CC, 1999–2005. Chairman: Yorks Regl Flood Defence Cttee, 2005–09; Adv. Cttee for Yorks and the Humber, Forestry Commn, 2007–13. Mem. Bd, Envmt Agency, 2009–15. Member: Bd, Yorks and Humberside Arts, 1994–99; N Yorks TEC, 1999–2001; Court, Univ. of York, 2001–; Court, Univ. of Leeds, 2002–11 (Mem. Council, 1992–2000); Nat. Employment Panel, 2002–05. Trustee: W Yorks Police Community Trust, 1996–99; York and N Yorks Community Trust, 2000–04. *Recreations:* walking, family, gardening.

WALKER, John; *see* Walker, N. J.

WALKER, His Honour John David; DL; a Circuit Judge, 1972–89; *b* 13 March 1924; *y s* of late L. C. Walker, MA, MB (Cantab), BCh, and late Mrs J. Walker, Malton; *m* 1953, Elizabeth Mary Emma (*née* Owbridge); one *s* two *d*. *Educ:* Oundle (1937–42); Christ's Coll., Cambridge (1947–50); BA 1950, MA 1953. War of 1939–45: commissioned Frontier Force Rifles, Indian Army, 1943; demob., Captain, 1947. Called to the Bar, Middle Temple, 1951; a Recorder, 1972. A Pres., Mental Health Review Tribunals, 1986–96. Mem., Parole Bd, 1992–95. Chm., Standards Cttee, ER of Yorks CC, 1999–. DL Humberside, subseq. ER of Yorks, 1985. *Recreations:* shooting, fishing. *Address:* 7 Waltham Lane, North Bar Within, Beverley, E Yorks HU17 8HB. *Club:* Lansdowne.

WALKER, John Eric Austin; *see* Austin, J. E.

WALKER, Sir John (Ernest), Kt 1999; DPhil; FRS 1995; Founding Director, 1998–2012, now Research Scientist, MRC Mitochondrial Biology (formerly MRC Dunn Human Nutrition) Unit, Cambridge; Fellow, Sidney Sussex College, since 1997, and Professor of Molecular Bioenergetics, since 2002, University of Cambridge; *b* Halifax, Yorks, 7 Jan. 1941; *s* of late Thomas Ernest Walker and Elsie (*née* Lawton); *m* 1963, Christina Jane Westcott; two *d. Educ:* Rastrick Grammar Sch., W Yorks; St Catherine's Coll., Oxford (BA Chem.; DPhil 1969; Hon. Fellow, 1998). Research Fellow, Univ. of Wisconsin, 1969–71; NATO Res. Fellow, CNRS, Gif-sur-Yvette, France, 1971–72; EMBO Res. Fellow, Pasteur Inst., Paris, 1972–74; Staff Scientist, MRC Lab. of Molecular Biol., Cambridge, 1974–98. Mem., EMBO, 1983. Smith-Kline Beecham Vis. Prof. to USA, Royal Soc. of Med. Foundn, 1995; Hon. Prof., Peking Union Med. Coll., Beijing, 2001–; Lee Kong Chian Dist. Prof., Nanyang Technol Univ., Singapore, 2010; Vis. Prof., Dept of Life Scis, Imperial Coll. London, 2013. Hon. Member: Biochem. Soc., 1998; British Biophysical Soc., 2000. Foreign Member: Royal Netherlands Acad. of Arts and Scis, 1999; l'Accademia Nazionale dei Lincei, Rome, 2003–; For. Associate, NAS, 2004–; Hon. Gentle Scientist, Mitochondrial Physiology Soc., Austria, 2012. Millennium Fellow, RSC 2000; Fellow, Science Mus., London, 2009. Hon. FRSB (FIBiol 2002); Hon. FMedSci 2013 (Founder FMedSci 1998); Hon. FRS NZ 2013. MAE 1998. Hon. DSc: Bradford, 1998; Buenos Aires, 1998; Huddersfield, 1998; UMIST, 1999; Oxon, 1999; Groningen, 1999; Leeds, 1999; London, 2002; Sussex, 2003; Liverpool, 2004; UEA, 2006; Moscow State, 2007; Toyo, Japan, 2007; Paul Sabatier, France, 2007. Johnson Foundn Prize, Univ. of Pennsylvania, 1994; Ciba Medal and Prize, Biochem. Soc., 1995; Peter Mitchell Medal, European Bioenergetics Conf., 1996; Gaetano Quagliariello Prize for Mitochondrial Res., Univ. of Bari, 1997; Nobel Prize for Chemistry, 1997; Messel Medal, SCI, 2000; RSC Award for Biomembrane Chemistry, 2003; Lifetime Achievement Award, GeneExpression Systems Inc., Massachusetts, 2008; Ahmed Zewail Medal, Wayne State Univ., Detroit, 2010; Skou Award, Aarhus Univ., 2011; Keilin Meml Medal (and Lect.), Biochem. Soc., 2011; Gold Seal, Univ. of Bari Aldo Moro, 2011; Copley Medal, Royal Soc., 2012. *Publications:* research papers and reviews in scientific jls. *Recreations:* cricket, opera music, walking. *Address:* MRC Mitochondrial Biology Unit, Wellcome Trust/MRC Building, Cambridge Biomedical Campus, Hills Road, Cambridge CB2 0XY. *T:* (01223) 252701, *Fax:* (01223) 252705.

WALKER, John Robert, CBE 2009; company director; *b* E Rainton, 3 Nov. 1946; *s* of John and Alice Walker; *m* 1990, Patricia Anne Henderson; one *d* and one *d* from previous marriage. *Educ:* Houghton Grammar Sch. CPFA 1969. Jun. Accountancy Asst, Hetton UDC, 1964–69; Accountancy Asst, Houghton UDC, 1969–70; Sen. Auditor, Sunderland CBC, 1970–73; Tyne and Wear County Council, 1973–85: Gp Auditor; Principal Audit/Technical Asst; Sen. Gp Accountant; Chief Accountant; Asst County Treas.; Chief Finance Officer, Northumbria Police, 1985–87; Finance Dir, Teesside Develt Corp., 1987–90; Mgt Consultant, Stoy Hayward, 1990–94; English Partnerships: Chief Accountant, 1994–96; Dir, Finance and Commercial Services, 1996–98; Finance and Admin Dir, 1998–2007; Regl Dir for NE, Yorks and E Midlands, 2003–04; Chief Operating Officer, 2004–07; Chief Exec., 2007–08. Comr for English Heritage, 2010–14. Non-executive Director: Esh Hldgs, 2009–; Wynyard Park Develts, 2009–; Gentoo Gp, 2009–. *Recreations:* walking, cycling. *Address:* Drift House, North Street, West Rainton, Houghton Le Spring, Tyne and Wear DH4 6NU. *T:* (0191) 584 5452. *E:* johnrwalker@yahoo.com.

WALKER, Julian Fortay, CMG 1981; MBE 1960; HM Diplomatic Service, retired; *b* 7 May 1929; *s* of Kenneth Macfarlane Walker, FRCS, and Eileen Marjorie Walker (*née* Wilson); *m* 1983, Virginia Anne Austin (*née* Stevens) (marr. diss. 1995); three step *d. Educ:* Harvey Sch., Hawthorne, New York; Stowe; Bryanston; Cambridge Univ. (MA). National Service, RN, 1947–49; Cambridge, 1949–52; London Univ. Sch. of African and Oriental Studies, 1952. Foreign Service: MECAS, 1953; Asst Political Agent, Trucial States, 1953–55; 3rd and 2nd Sec., Bahrain Residency, 1955–57; FCO and Frontier Settlement, Oman, 1957–60; 2nd and 1st Sec., Oslo, 1960–63; FCO News Dept Spokesman, 1963–67; 1st Sec., Baghdad, 1967; 1st Sec., Morocco (Rabat), 1967–69; FCO, 1969–71; Political Agent, Dubai, Trucial States, 1971, Consul-Gen. and Counsellor, British Embassy, Dubai, United Arab Emirates, 1971–72; Cambridge Univ. on sabbatical leave, 1972–73; Political Advr and Head of Chancery, British Mil. Govt, Berlin, 1973–76; NI Office, Stormont Castle, 1976–77; Dir, MECAS, 1977–78; Ambassador to Yemen Arab Republic and Republic of Jibuti, 1979–84; Ambassador to Qatar, 1984–87. Special Advr on Syria, 1987–93, and on Iraq, 1990–93, Res. and Analysis Dept, FCO. Manager, Kurdish Cultural Centre, 2001–05; Dir, British Develt Gp, Iraq and the Gulf, 2005–09; Consultant, Pell Frischmann; Mem., Iraq Research Gp, 2010–. *Publications:* (ed) The UAE Internal Boundaries and Boundaries with Oman, 8 vols, 1994; Tyro on the Trucial Coast, 1999. *Recreations:* music, cooking, gardening.

WALKER, Julian Guy Hudsmith, CB 1991; independent engineering consultant, since 1994; Director General, Policy and Special Projects, Ministry of Defence, 1992–94, retired; *b* 2 Oct. 1936; *s* of Nathaniel and Frieda Walker; *m* 1960, Margaret Burns (*née* Jamieson). *Educ:* Winchester College; Southampton Univ. (BSc Mech Eng). CEng, FIMechE. Hawker Aircraft Co., 1958–61; Logistic Vehicles, FVRDE, WO, subseq. MoD, 1961–69; Ministry of Defence: Special Projects, MVEE, 1970–80; Head, Vehicle Engrg Dept, 1980–84; Scientific Adviser (Land), 1984–87; Dir, Estabts and Research (B), 1987–89; Head, RARDE, Chertsey, 1989–92. *Recreations:* vintage cars, photography, wood-turning, Wombling, solving practical problems.

WALKER, Linda, (Mrs P. B. Walker); *see* Sutcliffe, Linda.

WALKER, Lorna Margaret S.; *see* Secker-Walker.

WALKER, Lorna Stuart, CChem, FCIWEM; Director, Lorna Walker Consulting Ltd, since 2004; *b* 2 Jan. 1952; *d* of Eric and Anne Walker; *m* 1992, Gareth James Young. *Educ:* Univ. of Cape Town (BSc Chem. and Maths; MSc Civil Engrg). MRSC; CChem 1978; FCIWEM 1978; MCIWM 1993; CWEM 2012. Dir, Ove Arup & Partners Ltd, 1977–2004. Vis. Prof. of Engrg Design for Sustainable Develt, Univ. of Sheffield, 2003–. Mem., CABE, 2006–11. Mem., UK Urban Taskforce, 1997–. Comr, Infrastructure Planning Commn, 2010–12; Examining Inspector, Nat. Infrastructure Directorate, Planning Inspectorate, 2012–. Academician, Acad. of Urbanism, 2011. FRSA. Hon. DEng Sheffield, 2007. *Publications:* (contrib.) London's Environment: prospects for a sustainable world city, 2001; (contrib.) Manufactured Sites, 2005. *Recreations:* gardening, reading, travelling. *Address:* Lorna Walker Consulting Ltd, 5 Heathfield Road, SW18 3HX. *T:* (020) 8874 3516. *E:* lwalker@lornawalker.co.uk.

WALKER, Malcolm Conrad, CBE 1995; Chairman, since 2012, and Chief Executive, since 2005, Iceland Foods Ltd; Chairman, Individual Restaurant Company; *b* 11 Feb. 1946; *s* of Willie Walker and Ethel Mary Walker; *m* 1969, Nest Rhianydd; one *s* two *d. Educ:* Mirfield Grammar Sch. Trainee Manager, F. W. Woolworth & Co., 1964–71; Jt Founder, Iceland Frozen Foods, 1970; Chief Exec., 1973–2000, Chm., 1973–2001, Iceland Frozen Foods plc, subseq. Iceland Gp plc; Founder and CEO, Cooltrader Ltd, 2001–06. Non-exec. Dir, DFS Furniture Co. plc, 1993–2004. *Recreations:* ski-ing, sailing, shooting, business, home and family.

WALKER, Martin John; a District Judge (Magistrates' Courts), since 2002; *b* 18 Sept. 1952; *s* of Eric and Olive Walker; *m* 1997, Rosalind Ann Jones; one *d*; one *s* one *d* from former marriage. *Educ:* Sheffield Univ. (LLB). Admitted solicitor, 1977; County Prosecutor; in practice as solicitor, Bakewell, 1981–2001. *Recreations:* boating, herbs. *Address:* Magistrates' Court, Teesside Law Courts, Victoria Square, Middlesbrough TS1 2AS. *T:* (01642) 240301.

WALKER, His Honour Michael; a Circuit Judge, 1978–2001; *b* 13 April 1931; *m* 1959, Elizabeth Mary Currie; two *s. Educ:* Chadderton Grammar Sch.; Sheffield Univ. (LLM). Called to the Bar, Gray's Inn, 1956; joined North Eastern Circuit, 1958; a Recorder of the Crown Court, 1972–78; Hon. Recorder of Sheffield, 1996–2001; authorised to sit in Ct of Appeal (Criminal Div.), 1997.

WALKER, Dr Michael John; Headmaster, Felsted School, 2008–15; *b* 24 Nov. 1955; *s* of Stephen Thomas Walker and Sheila Walker (*née* Ereaut); *m* 1st, 1977, Rita Bridget Carpenter (marr. diss. 2004); one *s* two *d*; 2nd, 2007, Corinne Anne Francis (marr. diss. 2014). *Educ:* Corpus Christi Coll., Cambridge (BA Hons Hist. 1977; CertEd 1979; MA 1980; PhD 1985). Asst Prof. of History, Birmingham-Southern Coll., Birmingham, Alabama, 1977–78; Asst Master, Dulwich Coll., 1982–86; Hd of History, Gresham's Sch., Norfolk, 1986–89; King Edward VI Grammar School, Chelmsford: Sen. Teacher, 1989–90; Dep. Head (Middle Sch.), 1990–92; Dep. Head (Sixth Form), 1992–99; Headmaster, 1999–2008. Member: Leading Edge Prog. Nat. Steering Gp, 2003–05; Forum for Learning and Res. Enquiry in Essex, 2003–05; Evaluation and Knowledge Transfer Wkg Gps, 2003–04; working with DfES Innovations Unit: leading Nat. Heads' Gp, 2004–07; leading Next Practice project on Higher Order Teaching Skills, 2005–06; Mem., Steering Gp, ARIA Project (UK-wide Assessment Reform Gp on evaluation of assessment develt projects), 2006–08. Mem., HMC, 2008–15. Dir, London Academies and Enterprise Trust, 2012–14. Vice-Pres., Helen Rollason Cancer Care Trust, 2001–. Dir, Eur. Reg., Round Square, 2013–15 (Mem., 2009–; Dep. Dir, 2012); Trustee: Friends of Round Square, 2012–; Sparkle Malawi Charity, 2015–; Greensward Charitable Trust, AET Sponsor, 2015–. Governor: Jack Petchey Acad., 2012–14; Sutton Valence Sch., 2012–. FRSA 2006. *Recreations:* painting, drawing, tennis, squash, horse-riding, walking, travel, reading, theatre. *Clubs:* East India; Essex.

WALKER, Michael John, CBE 2007; District Judge, since 1994, seconded to Office of the Senior Presiding Judge, Royal Courts of Justice, since 2007; *b* 8 July 1951; *s* of late Albert George Walker and of Joan Walker; *m* 1st, 1974, Jill Sandham (marr. diss. 1980); one *s*; 2nd, 1982, Elaine G. Robinson; two *d. Educ:* Sir John Deane's Grammar Sch., Northwich, Cheshire; Univ. of Kent (BA Hons Law 1972); Law Soc. Finals Hons 1973. Articled clerk, 1973–75, Solicitor, 1975–78, Norton Rose; Solicitor, then Partner, Carpenter & Co., (Solicitors), Wallington, 1979–94. Member: Judges' Council, 2002–; Bd, HM Courts Service, 2008–11; Bd, HM Courts and Tribunals Service, 2011–. Hon. Sec., Assoc. of HM District Judges (formerly Assoc. of Dist Judges), 2000–11. Hon. Bencher, Gray's Inn, 2014. Gov., Wallington High Sch. for Girls, 1988–2007. *Publications:* (contrib.) Jordan's Civil Court Service, 3rd edn 2000 to 35th edn 2015; Blackstone's Civil Practice, (contrib.) 5th edn 2004 to 10th edn 2010, (consultant ed.) 11th edn 2011 to 15th edn 2015. *Recreations:* sitting on committees, pottering around in the garden, listening to classical music and, in between times, enjoying food and wine and dreaming of Italy. *Address:* Room C16, Royal Courts of Justice, Strand, WC2A 2LL. *T:* (020) 7947 7752.

WALKER, Sir Michael Leolin F.; *see* Forestier-Walker.

WALKER, Hon. Sir Miles Rawstron, Kt 1997; CBE 1991; Chief Minister, Isle of Man, 1986–96; *b* 13 Nov. 1940; *s* of George Denis Walker and Alice (*née* Whittaker); *m* 1966, Mary Lilian Cowell; one *s* one *d. Educ:* Arbory Primary Sch.; Castle Rushen High Sch.; Shropshire Coll. of Agric. Company Dir, farming and retail dairy trade, 1960–. Mem. and Chm., Arbory Parish Comrs, 1970–76; Mem., House of Keys for Rushen, 1976–2001. Hon. LLD Liverpool, 1994. *Address:* Magher Feailley, Main Road, Colby, Isle of Man IM9 4AD. *T:* (01624) 833728.

WALKER, Prof. Neil Craig, PhD; FBA 2012; FRSE; Regius Professor of Public Law and the Law of Nature and Nations, University of Edinburgh, since 2008; *b* 5 July 1960; *s* of William Walker and Catherine Walker; *m* 1993, Gillian Couse; one *s* one *d*, and one *s* from former marriage. *Educ:* Univ. of Strathclyde (LLB 1st cl. 1981; PhD 1991). Lectr in Const. Law, 1986–92, Sen. Lectr, 1992–95, Univ. of Edinburgh; Prof. of Legal and Const. Theory, Univ. of Aberdeen, 1996–2000; Prof. of Eur. Law, European University Inst., Florence, 2000–08. FRSE 2011. Hon. LLD Uppsala, 2011. *Publications:* Managing the Police: law, organisation and democracy, 1986; The Scottish Community Charge, 1989; Policing the European Union, 1996; Policing in a Changing Constitutional Order, 2000; Civilizing Security, 2007; Intimation of Global Law, 2015; articles and collections on questions of constit. law and theory. *Recreations:* literature, sport, anything convivial. *Address:* School of Law, University of Edinburgh, Old College, South Bridge, Edinburgh EH8 9YL.

WALKER, (Noel) John; strategic development consultant; Managing Director, John Walker Consultants Ltd, since 1999; *b* 18 Dec. 1948; *s* of Robert and Nora Walker; *m* 1979, Pamela Gordon; two *s. Educ:* Liverpool Univ. (BSc 1970); Trent Polytechnic (DipTP 1972). Planning Officer, Hartlepool BC, 1972–74; Sen. Planner, Cleveland CC, 1974; travelled abroad, 1974–75; Milton Keynes Development Corporation: Employment Planner, 1975–76; Head of Policy Evaluation, 1976–78; Dep. Planning Manager, 1978–79; Planning Manager, 1979–80; Dir of Planning, 1980–87; Dep. Gen. Manager, 1987–92; Chief Exec., Commn for the New Towns, 1992–99; Dir, Competition for future use of Millennium Dome, 1999–2000; Chief Exec., BURA, 2000–02. Chairman: Bucks Manpower Cttee, 1982–83; Milton Keynes IT Exchange, 1983–86; Central Milton Keynes Project Bd, 2003–07; Milton Keynes and S Midlands Funding Gp, 2004–; Eco Towns Challenge Gp, 2008; Whitehill and Bordon Ecotown Delivery Board, 2010–13. Founder Mem., Nat. Energy Foundn, 1988– (Trustee, 1999–2005; Chm., 2012–). Dep. Chm., Milton Keynes Housing Assoc., 1986–89; Board Member: Milton Keynes Marketing, 1992–93; Telford Develt Agency, 1992; Peterborough Develt Agency, 1992–94; Ind. Bd Mem., Milton Keynes Develt Partnership, 2013–; Associate Dir, Garden City Develts CIC. Chm., Green Gauge Trust, 2009–; Trustee: Bletchley Park Trust, 2000–04; Milton Keynes Parks Trust, 2000–10; Milton Keynes Theatre and Gallery Co., 2002–08. Advr, ODPM, 2002–06; Develt Advr, TCPA, 2003–09. FRSA 1997. Hon. DArts De Montfort, 1998. *Recreations:* gardening, travelling, pottery, ski-ing. *Address:* Fullers Barn, The Green, Loughton, Milton Keynes MK5 8AW.

WALKER, Sir Patrick (Jeremy), KCB 1990; *b* 25 Feb. 1932; *s* of late Reginald Plumer Walker, sometime Chief Accountant, East African Railways, and Gladys Walker; *m* 1955, Susan Mary Hastings; two *s* one *d. Educ:* King's Sch., Canterbury; Trinity Coll., Oxford (MA). Uganda Admin, 1956–62; Security Service, 1963–92, Dir Gen., 1988–92. Chm., Bd, N Northants Together, 2005–06; Dep. Chm., Bd, N Northants Develt Co., 2007– (Co-Chm., 2006–07). Member: Iraq Commn, Foreign Policy Centre, 2007; Council, Overseas Service Pensioners' Assoc., 2010–. Trustee: Leonard Cheshire Foundn, 1994–2003 (Internat. Chm., 1995–2000; Vice Pres., 2003–); Northants Victoria County Records Trust, 2000–05. Gov., UC Northampton (formerly Nene Coll. of Higher Educn), 1997–2005 (Chm. Govs, 2000–05). Hon. Fellow, Univ. of Northampton, 2006. *Recreations:* music, African history, art. *Clubs:* Oxford and Cambridge, MCC.

WALKER, Paul Ashton; non-executive Chairman: Perform Group plc; Halma plc, since 2013, WANdisco, since 2014; *b* 17 May 1957. *Educ:* Univ. of York (BA). ACA. With Arthur Youngs, 1979–84; joined Sage, 1984; Chief Executive: Sage Gp plc, 1994–2010; Sage Software Ltd. Non-executive Director: Diageo plc, 2002; Experian plc, 2010–.

WALKER, Dr Paul Crawford; Regional Medical Officer, North East Thames Regional Health Authority, 1977–85; *b* 9 Dec. 1940; *s* of Joseph Viccars Walker, KHS, and Mary Tilley (*née* Crawford); *m* 1963, Barbara Georgina Bliss; three *d. Educ:* Queen Elizabeth Grammar Sch., Darlington; Downing Coll., Cambridge (MA); University College Hospital Med. Sch.

(MB, BChir); Edinburgh Univ. (DipSocMed); Harvard Bus. Sch. (Program for Health Systems Management, 1980). FFPH (FFCM 1980). Dep. Medical Officer of Health and Dep. Principal Sch. MO, Wolverhampton County Borough Council, 1972–74; District Community Physician, Staffordshire AHA, 1974–76; Area MO, Wakefield AHA, 1976–77; Dist Gen. Manager, Frenchay HA, 1985–88; Hon. Consultant in Community Medicine, Bristol and Weston HA, 1988–89; Dir of Public Health, Norwich HA, 1989–93; Sen. Lectr in Applied Epidemiology, Univ. of Wales Coll. of Medicine, 1993–94; Dir of Public Health, Powys and Ceredigion Health Bds, 2003–05. Hon. Sen. Lectr, Dept of Community Medicine, LSHTM, 1983–85; Co-Dir, Centre for Health Policy Res., UEA, 1990–93; Vis. Prof., QMC, London Univ., 1985; Visiting Fellow: UWE, 1999–2003; Univ. of Glamorgan, 2004–09. Governor, Moorfields Eye Hosp., 1981–82; Vice-Chm., Professional Adv. Gp, NHS Trng Authy, 1986–88; Member: Bd of Management, LSHTM, 1983–85; Adv. Council on Drug Misuse, 1983–87; Exec. Cttee, Greater London Alcohol Adv. Service, 1978–85; NHS Computer Policy Cttee, 1984–85; Editl Bd, Jl of Management in Medicine, 1985–88; Norwich HA, 1989–93; Frenchay Mental Handicap Trust, 1986–88; Frenchay Mental Health Trust, 1986–88; Norwich and Norfolk Care Trust, 1991–93; Frenchay Community Care Trust, 1994–97; Peckham Pioneer Health Centre Ltd, 1994–96; Powys Local Health Alliance, 1999–2002; Ceredigion Local Health Gp, 2001–03. Chm., Welsh Food Alliance, 1998–2002; Director: S Bristol Advice Services, 1998–2000; Bristol Health Co-op., 1999–2000; Dir/Trustee, Lles Cymru Wellbeing Wales, 2010–. Chairman: Socialist Health Assoc., 2003–08; Transform Drug Policy Foundn, 2007–11; Sec., Public Health Assoc. Cymru, 1998–2004 (Chm., 2004–). Trustee, UK Public Health Assoc., 2006–10. Mem. (Lab), Bristol CC, 1995–99; Member: Avon and Som Police Authy, 1998–99; Avon Probation Cttee, 1997–99. JP Epping and Ongar, 1980–85. Captain, RAMC (V). Jt Editor, Health Matters, 2008–10. *Publications:* Healthy Norfolk People, 1990; (ed) Helping People with Disabilities in East Anglia, 1991; From Public Health to Wellbeing: the new driver for policy and action, 2011; contribs to medical and health service jls. *Recreations:* music, natural history, railway history. *E:* paulcrawfordwalker@googlemail.com.

WALKER, Hon. Sir Paul (James), Kt 2004; **Hon. Mr Justice Walker;** a Judge of the High Court of Justice, Queen's Bench Division, since 2004; a President, Upper Tribunal (Administrative Appeals Chamber), 2009–12; *b* Wellington, NZ, 1954; *s* of James Edgar Walker and Dawne Walker (*née* McGowan); *m* 1988, Josephine Andrews; one *d*. *Educ:* St Peter's Coll., Adelaide; Magdalen Coll., Oxford (BA Law, BCL). Called to the Bar, Gray's Inn, 1979, Bencher, 2005; barrister in private practice, 1980–2004; QC 1999. Sen. Lectr in Law, Victoria Univ. of Wellington, 1994–96; Dir, NZ Inst. Public Law, 1996. Counsel to BSE Inquiry, 1998–2000. Mem. Adv. Bd, British Inst. of Internat. and Comparative Law, 2001–. Vis. Fellow, Victoria Univ. of Wellington, 2013. Fellow: Arbitrators and Mediators Inst., NZ, 1994. Mem. Adv. Bd, NZ Jl of Public and Internat. Law, 2003–. Mem., Sci. Cttee, Jl de Droit Comparé du Pacifique, 2012–. *Publications:* (ed with S. Rogers) Studies in Insurance Law, 1996; (ed jtly) Commercial Regulation and Judicial Review, 1998; (ed jtly) Judicial Review, 3rd edn 2005. *Address:* Royal Courts of Justice, Strand, WC2A 2LL.

WALKER, His Honour Philip Henry Conyers, (Harry); a Circuit Judge, 1979–99; *b* 22 Dec. 1926; *oc* of Philip Howard and Kathleen Walker; *m* 1953, Mary Elizabeth Ross (*d* 2012); two *s* two *d*; *m* 2014, Fiona Frances Rose Burra. *Educ:* Marlborough; Oriel Coll., Oxford. MA, BCL (Oxon); DipTh (London). Army (6 AB Sigs), 1944–48 (despatches, 1948). Solicitor in private practice, 1954–79; Dep. Coroner for Craven, 1965–74; a Recorder of the Crown Court, 1972–79. Mem., Church Assembly, Nat. Synod of C of E, 1960–80; Reader, C of E, 1965–. Chm., Agricultural Land Tribunal (Yorks & Lancs), 1977–79; Dep. Chm., Agricultural Land Tribunal (Western), 1989–99; Mem., Criminal Law Revision Cttee, 1981–. *Recreations:* fishing, shooting, sailing, walking. *Address:* Pond House, Askwith, Otley, West Yorks LS21 2JN. *T:* (01943) 463196.

WALKER, Dr Ranginui Joseph Isaac, DCNZM 2001; PhD; Professor of Maori Studies and Head of Department, Auckland University, 1993–97, now Professor Emeritus; Amorangi (Executive), Manukau Institute of Technology, 2000–03; *b* 1 March 1932; *s* of Isaac Walker and Wairata Walker; *m* 1953, Deirdre Patricia Dodson; two *s* one *d*. *Educ:* Univ. of Auckland (PhD Anthropol. 1970). Asst teacher (primary), 1953–62; Lectr, Auckland Teachers' Coll., 1962–66; Auckland University: Asst Lectr, 1967–69; Lectr (Contg Educn), 1970–85; Associate Prof., 1986–93; Pro Vice-Chancellor (Maori), 1996–97. Mem., Treaty of Waitangi Tribunal, 2004–. Elsdon Best Meml Medal, Jl of Polynesian Soc., 1997; NZ Prime Minister's Award for Literary Achievement, 2009. *Publications:* Years of Anger, 1987; Struggle Without End, 1990, rev. edn 2004; The Walker Papers, 1996; He Tipua: a biography of Sir Apirana Ngata, 2001; Opotiki-Mai Tawhiti, Capital of Whakatohea, 2007; Tohunga Whakairo: a biography of Pakaariki Harrison, 2008. *Recreations:* reading, boating, fishing, diving, ski-ing.

WALKER, His Honour Richard; a Circuit Judge, 1989–2006; *b* 9 March 1942; *s* of Edwin Roland Walker and Barbara Joan (*née* Swann); *m* 1969, Angela Joan Hodgkinson; two *d*. *Educ:* Epsom Coll.; Worcester Coll., Oxford (MA). Called to the Bar, Inner Temple, 1966; in practice at the Bar, 1966–89; Asst Boundary Comr, 1979–88; a Recorder, 1989. Judicial Mem., Mental Health Review Tribunal, 1991–2005. Commissary Gen., City and Dio. of Canterbury, 1995–2011. *Publications:* (ed jtly) Carter-Ruck on Libel and Slander, 3rd edn 1985, 4th edn 1992; The Treasure in a Field, 2012. *Address:* c/o 1 Brick Court, Temple, EC4Y 9BY. *T:* (020) 7353 8845.

WALKER, Richard John, OBE 1998; Director, EU Operations and Business Transformation, British Council, London, since 2013; *b* Reading, 1 Nov. 1952; *s* of George Lewis and Gwendolen Jayne Walker; *m* 1978, Lauren Michaela Barker, (writer, as Lauren O'Hara); one *s* one *d*. *Educ:* Woolverstone Hall; Guildford Coll.; St Peter's Coll., Oxford (BA Hons English Lang. and Lit.); Manchester Univ. (Dip. TEO, PGCE). English teacher, Internat. House, Spain and Kuwait, 1976–78; English Lectr, Manchester Univ. and Huddersfield Coll., 1979–83; Thai Govt English Advr, Bangkok, 1983–85; British Council: Dep. Dir, Literature Dept, London, 1985–87; Asst Dir, Lagos, 1987–89; on secondment to Internat. Educn Centre and Sen. Lectr, Coll. of St Mark and St John, Plymouth, 1989–92; Dir, Develt, 1992–94; First Sec. (Cultural), British High Commn, New Delhi, 1994–98; Dir, and Superintendent Gen., Cultura Inglesa, São Paulo, 1998–2000; Regl Dir, E Asia, London, 2000–05; Dir, Cyprus, 2005–07; Dir, Greece, 2007–11; Dir, EU Operations, Brussels, 2011–13. Writer of drama, monologues and short stories, BBC Radio 3 and Radio 4, 1985–95. FRSA. *Publications:* Language for Literature, 1983; A Curious Child, 1989; (ed) Penguin History of English Literature, 1990; contrib. reviews and articles to THES, Literary Rev. *Recreations:* tennis, walking, travel, history, visual arts, literature. *Address:* British Council, 10 Spring Gardens, SW1A 2BN. *E:* richard.walker@britishcouncil.org. *Club:* Manchester United.

WALKER, Robert M.; Chairman: Travis Perkins plc, since 2010; Enterprise Inns plc, since 2012; Eagle TopCo Ltd, since 2014; *b* 3 Feb. 1945; *s* of Arthur Norman Walker and Nancy (*née* Waugh); *m* 1970, Patricia Douglass; one *s* one *d*. *Educ:* Hampton Sch.; Magdalen Coll., Oxford (BA Hons Modern History 1966). Brand Manager, Procter & Gamble Ltd, 1966–70; Engagement Manager, McKinsey & Co. Inc., 1970–76; Div. Pres., PepsiCo Inc., 1976–99; Gp Chief Exec., Severn Trent plc, 2000–05 (non-exec. Dir, 1996–99). Chairman: Williams Lea Group Ltd, 2005–06; WH Smith plc, 2005–10; BCA Europe Ltd, 2007–09; Americana Internat. Hldgs, 2009–14. Non-executive Director: Thomson Travel Gp plc, 1998–2000; Wolseley plc, 1999–2007; Signet Gp plc, 2004–08; BAA plc, 2004–05; Williams Lea Hldgs Plc, 2006–09; Tate & Lyle, 2006– (Sen. Ind. Dir, 2010–). Advr, Cinven, 2005–07. Gov., Hampton Sch., 2007–. *Clubs:* Oxford and Cambridge, Brooks's.

WALKER, Robin Caspar; MP (C) Worcester, since 2010; *b* Worcs, 12 April 1978; *s* of Baron Walker of Worcester, PC, MBE and of Tessa (*née* Pout); *m* 2011, Charlotte Keenan. *Educ:* St Paul's Sch.; Balliol Coll., Oxford (Schol.; BA Ancient and Modern Hist. 2000). Chief Exec., Property Map Ltd, 2000–01; Res. Exec., i-Search Ltd, 2001–03; Finsbury Group: Exec., 2003–04; Sen. Exec., 2004–06; Associate Partner, 2006–09; Partner, 2009–10. Member: Welsh Affairs Select Cttee, 2011–12; BIS Select Cttee, 2012–15; PPS to Minister of State, NI, 2013–14, to Sec. of State, DEFRA, 2014–15. *Address:* House of Commons, SW1A 0AA.

WALKER, Sir Rodney (Myerscough), Kt 1996; Chairman: Myerscough Holdings Ltd, since 1976; Lightsong Media Ltd (formerly Lightsong Ltd), since 2009; Rom (formerly Sport) Pathways Ltd, since 2011; *b* 10 April 1943; *s* of Norman and Lucy Walker; *m* 1974, Anne Margaret Aspinall; two *s*. *Educ:* Thornes House Grammar Sch. CEng. Founder Chm., Myerscough Holdings, 1976; activities incl. civil engrg, motor retail, and develt. Chairman: W Yorks Broadcasting, 1986–2002; Brands Hatch Leisure plc, 1996–99; Leicester City plc, 1997–2002 (now Hon. Life Pres.); Spice Holdings plc, 2002–08; Goals Soccer Centres plc, 2002–13; World Snooker Ltd, 2003–09; Archial (formerly SMC) Gp, 2004–10; Brand Cellar Ltd, 2011–13. Chairman: Rugby Football League, 1993–2002; Sports Council of GB, 1994–96; English Sports Council, 1996–98; UK Sports Council, 1998–2003. Mem., Wakefield HA, 1982–90; Chairman: Bradford Hosps NHS Trust, 1990–96; NHS Trust Fedn, 1993–95 (Pres., 1995–97). Chm., Wakefield Theatre Trust, 1981–99, now Hon. Life Pres.; Vice Chm., Yorks Sculpture Park, 1984– (Trustee, 1995–). Trustee: Nat. Coal Mining (formerly Nat. Mining) Mus. of England, 1993–2014; English Nat. Stadium Trust, 1998–; London Marathon, 2005–; Chm., Wembley Nat. Stadium Ltd, 2000–02; Vice Chm., Wembley Nat. Stadium Trust, 2003–; Chair, TdF HUB 2014 Ltd, 2013–14; Chm., London Marathon Charitable Trust. Freeman, City of Wakefield, 2012. FInstD. Hon. Dr Huddersfield, 2014. KLJ 1997. *Recreations:* golf, theatre, travel. *Address:* Tower House, Bond Street, Wakefield WF1 2QP. *T:* (01924) 374349; Pine Lodge, Home Farm, Woolley, Wakefield WF4 2JS. *T:* (01226) 384089.

WALKER, Comdr Roger Antony Martineau-, LVO 1994; RN; Clerk to Trustees, and Chief Executive, United Westminster Almshouses Foundation, 1997–2007; *b* 15 Oct. 1940; *s* of Antony Philip Martineau-Walker and Sheila Hazeal Mayoh Wilson; *m* Inger Lene Brag-Nielsen; two *s*. *Educ:* Haileybury and Imperial Service College, Hertford; BRNC Dartmouth. Commissioned RN, 1962; served Malta, Singapore and Sarawak, 1962–65; Torpedo and Antisubmarine Course, HMS Vernon, 1968; HMS Galatea, 1973–76; NDC Latimer, 1977–78; Naval and Defence Staff, MoD, 1978–83; Naval Manpower Planning, with special responsibility for introd. of longer career for ratings (2nd Open Engagement), 1983–85; operational staff (UK commitments), 1985–87; Head, Naval Sec's Policy Staff, 1987–90; Pvte Sec. to Duke and Duchess of Kent, 1990–93. Trustee, St Giles-in-the-Fields United Charity, 2008–11. Bursar, Royal Sch. for Daughters of the Army, 1995–96. Foundn Gov., Burdett Coutts and Townshend C of E Primary Sch., 1998–2002 (Trustee, 2004–12). Churchwarden, St Hubert's, Idsworth, 2008–. *Recreations:* fly fishing, photographic conservation, music. *Address:* 13 The Peak, Rowlands Castle, Hants PO9 6AH. *Club:* Army and Navy.

WALKER, Ronald Jack; QC 1983; a Recorder, since 1986; *b* 24 June 1940; *s* of Jack Harris Walker and Ann Frances Walker; *m* 1st, 1964, Caroline Fox (marr. diss. 1997); two *s*; 2nd, 1999, Clare Oonagh Jane Devitt; one *s* one *d*. *Educ:* Owen's School, London; University College London. LLB (Hons). Called to the Bar, Gray's Inn, 1962, Bencher, 1993. Mem. Gen. Council of the Bar, 1993–96 (Chm. Professional Conduct Cttee, 1993–94). Mem., Mental Health Review Tribunal, 2000–12. *Publications:* (with M. G. Walker) English Legal System, 1967, 11th edn as Walker & Walker's English Legal System, 2011; contributing ed., Bullen & Leake & Jacob's Precedents of Pleadings, 13th edn 1990; (ed) Butterworths Professional Negligence Service, 1999. *Address:* 12 King's Bench Walk, Temple, EC4Y 7EL. *T:* (020) 7583 0811.

WALKER, Roy; *see* Walker, C. R.

WALKER, Sir Roy Edward, 6th Bt *cr* 1906, of Pembroke House, City of Dublin; *b* 10 Aug. 1977; *yr s* of Major Sir Hugh Ronald Walker, 4th Bt and of Norna Walker (*née* Baird); *S* brother, 2006.

WALKER, Sarah Elizabeth Royle, (Mrs R. G. Allum), CBE 1991; mezzo-soprano; *d* of Elizabeth Brownrigg and Alan Royle Walker; *m* 1972, Graham Allum. *Educ:* Pate's Grammar School for Girls, Cheltenham; Royal College of Music. FRCM 1987; LRAM. Prince Consort Prof. of Singing, RCM, 1993–; vocal performance consultant, GSMD, 1999–; joined vocal faculty, RAM, 2009–. Pres., Cheltenham Bach Choir, 1986–. Major appearances at concerts and in recital in Britain, America, Australia, New Zealand, Europe; operatic débuts include: Coronation of Poppea, Kent Opera, 1969, San Francisco Opera, 1981; La Calisto, Glyndebourne, 1970; Les Troyens, Scottish Opera, 1972, Wiener Staatsoper, 1980; Principal Mezzo Soprano, ENO, 1972–77; Die Meistersinger, Chicago Lyric Opera, 1977; Werther, Covent Garden, 1979; Giulio Cesare, Le Grand Théâtre, Genève, 1983; Capriccio, Brussels, 1983; Teseo, Sienna, 1985; Samson, NY Metropolitan Opera, 1986; numerous recordings and video recordings, incl. title rôle in Britten's Gloriana. FGS 2001 (FGSM 2000). *Recreations:* interior design, encouraging her husband with the gardening. *Address:* Cheffings, Witheridge, Devon EX16 8QD. *T:* (01884) 860132. *E:* megamezzo@sarahwalker.com. *Club:* University Women's.

WALKER, Simon Edward John; Director General, Institute of Directors, since 2011; *b* 28 May 1953; *s* of Louis Charles Vivian Walker and Joan Wallace Walker (*née* Keith); *m* 1980, Mary Virginia Strang; one *s* one *d*. *Educ:* South African Coll. Sch.; Balliol Coll., Oxford (BA PPE; Pres., Oxford Union, 1974; MA 1978). Personal Asst to Lord Sainsbury, 1974–75; reporter, TV NZ, Wellington, 1975–79; Knight Journalism Fellow, Stanford Univ., 1979–80; Communications Dir, NZ Labour Party, 1980–84; Director: Communicor Govt and PR, 1984–87; NZ Centre for Independent Studies, Auckland, 1987–89; Eur. Public Affairs, Hill & Knowlton PR, London, 1989–90; Man. Dir, Hill & Knowlton, Belgium, 1990–94; Partner, Brunswick PR, 1994–98 (on secondment to Policy Unit, 10 Downing St, 1996–97); Dir of Communications, British Airways, 1998–2000; Communications Sec. to the Queen, 2000–02; Dir of Corporate Mktg and Communications, Reuters, 2003–07; Chief Exec., British Private Equity and Venture Capital Assoc., 2007–11. Non-exec. Dir, Comair Ltd (SA), 2000–01. Member: Better Regulation Commn, 2006–08; H of C Speaker's Cttee on Public Engagement, 2009–. Trustee, NZ-UK Link Foundn, 2003–08; Gov., Hillary Summit (NZ), 2008–. *Publications:* Rogernomics: reshaping New Zealand's economy, 1989. *Recreations:* family, reading, music, travel. *Address:* Institute of Directors, 116 Pall Mall, SW1Y 5ED. *E:* simon.walker@iod.com. *Club:* Athenæum.

WALKER, Stuart; *see* Walker, B. S.

WALKER, Susannah Mary; a District Judge, Principal Registry, Family Division, 2006–14; Deputy District Judge, South Eastern and Western Circuits, since 2015; *b* 6 Aug. 1948; *d* of late Ronald Jack Marsh and Mary Marsh; *m* 1973, Robert Adrian Walker; one *s* one *d*. *Educ:* Univ. of Birmingham (BSocSc 1969; DipSW 1971); City Univ., London (Dip Law 1984). Social worker, 1971–80; called to the Bar, Inner Temple, 1985; an Immigration Judge, 2003–06. Mem., Mental Health Rev. Tribunal, 1996–2010.

WALKER, Terence William, (Terry Walker); *b* 26 Oct. 1935; *s* of William Edwin and Lilian Grace Walker; *m* 1959, Priscilla Dart (marr. diss. 1983); two *s* one *d*; *m* 1983, Rosalie Fripp. *Educ:* Grammar Sch. and Coll. of Further Educn, Bristol. Employed by Courage

(Western) Ltd at Bristol for 23 yrs, Mem. Chief Accountant's Dept. MP (Lab) Kingswood, Feb. 1974–1979; Second Church Estates Comr, 1974–79. Contested (Lab): Kingswood, 1983; Bristol NW, 1987. Member: Avon CC, 1981–96 (Vice-Chm., 1992–93; Chm., 1993–94), S Glos Unitary Council, 1996–2015 (Dep. Leader Labour Gp, 1996–2009); Cair, Avon Combined Fire Authy, 1996–2015. *Recreations:* cricket, football. *Address:* 43 The Furlong, Bristol BS6 7TF. *T:* (0117) 989 2694.

WALKER, Dr (Thomas) Gordon, OBE 2000; FInstP; Chief Executive, Council for the Central Laboratory of Research Councils, 2000–01; retired; *b* 4 Nov. 1936; *s* of James Smart Walker and Mary Margaret McIntosh Walker; *m* 1960, Una May Graham Stevenson; one *s* one *d*. *Educ:* Uddingston Grammar Sch.; Univ. of Glasgow (BSc, PhD). Rutherford High Energy Laboratory, National Institute for Research in Nuclear Science, later Rutherford Appleton Laboratory, Science and Engineering Research Council: Res. Physicist, 1960–71; Gp Leader, 1971–80; Head: Instrumentation Div., 1980–83; Technology Div., 1983–87; Dep. Dir, 1987–94; Head, 1994–96; Dir, R&D, CCLRC, 1996–2000. Mem., Renewable Energy Adv. Cttee, DTI, 1980–2000. Chief Sci. Advr (Civil Defence), Oxfordshire CC, 1983–93. Chm., Mgt Cttee, Didcot CAB, 1991–97; Pres., Didcot Rotary Club, 1977–78. Chm., Harwell Parish Council, 1988–91. *Publications:* papers in sci. jls on experimental particle physics. *Recreations:* golf, gardening. *Club:* Frilford Heath Golf.

WALKER, Ven. Thomas Overington; Archdeacon of Nottingham, 1991–96, now Emeritus; *b* 7 Dec. 1933; *m* 1957, Molly Anne Gilmour; one *s* one *d* (and one *d* decd). *Educ:* Keble Coll., Oxford (BA 1958; MA 1961); Oak Hill Theol Coll. Ordained 1960. Curate: St Paul, Woking, Dio. of Guildford, 1960–62; St Leon, St Leonards, Dio. of Chichester, 1962–64; Travelling Sec., Inter-Varsity Fellowship, 1964–67; Succentor, Birmingham Cathedral, 1967–70; Vicar, Harborne Heath, 1970–91; Priest-in-charge, St Germain, Edgbaston, 1983–91; Rural Dean, Edgbaston, 1989–91; Hon. Canon, Birmingham Cathedral, 1980–91. Proctor in Convocation, 1985–92. *Publications:* Renew Us By Your Spirit, 1982; The Occult Web, 1987, 3rd edn 1989; From Here to Heaven, 1987; Small Streams Big Rivers, 1991. *Recreations:* sport, music, reading, dry stone walling.

WALKER, Timothy; Lecturer in Plant Science, Somerville College, Oxford, since 1997; Stipendiary Lecturer in Botany, Pembroke College, Oxford, since 2014; *b* Chalfont St Giles, 10 July 1958; *s* of Gerald and Doreen Walker; *m* 1993, Jill Humphries; two *s* one *d*. *Educ:* Abingdon Sch.; University Coll., Oxford (BA Hons Botany 1980); Askham Bryan Coll., York (Nat. Cert. Horticulture 1983). MHort (RHS) 1985. Gen. foreman, 1986–88, Horti Praefectus, 1988–2014, Univ. of Oxford Botanic Gdn. *Publications:* Euphorbias, 2002; Plants, 2012; Plant Conservation, 2014. *Recreations:* walking, photography, gardening, natural history. *Address:* Somerville College, Oxford OX2 6HD.

WALKER, Hon. Sir Timothy (Edward), Kt 1996; a Judge of the High Court of Justice, Queen's Bench Division, and a Judge of the Commercial Court, 1996–2002; *b* 13 May 1946; *s* of George Edward Walker, solicitor, and Muriel Edith Walker; *m* 1968, Mary (*née* Tyndall); two *d*. *Educ:* Harrow Sch. (Totland Entrance Schol.; Clayton Leaving Schol.); University Coll., Oxford (Plumptre Schol., 1965; 1st Cl. Hons Jurisprudence, 1967; MA). Asst Lectr in Law, King's Coll., London, 1967–68; Profumo Schol., Inner Temple, 1968; Eldon Law schol., 1969; called to the Bar, Inner Temple, 1968, Bencher, 1996; QC 1985; a Recorder of the Crown Court, 1986–96. *Address:* c/o Royal Courts of Justice, Strand, WC2A 2LL.

WALKER, Timothy Edward Hanson, CB 1998; Third Church Estates Commissioner, 2006–12; *b* 27 July 1945; *s* of late Harris and Elizabeth Walker; *m* 1st, 1969, Judith Mann (*d* 1976); one *d*; 2nd, 1983, Hon. Anna Butterworth (*see* Hon. A. E. B. Walker); two *d*. *Educ:* Tonbridge Sch.; Brasenose Coll., Oxford (BA Chemistry, 1967; MA, DPhil 1969). Weir Jun. Res. Fellow, University Coll., Oxford, and Exhibnr of Royal Commn of 1851, Oxford and Paris, 1969; Harkness Fellow, Commonwealth Fund of New York, 1971, Univ. of Virginia, 1971 and Northwestern Univ., 1972; Strategic Planner, GLC, 1974; Principal, Dept of Trade, 1977; Sloan Fellow, London Business Sch., 1983; Department of Trade and Industry: Asst Sec., 1983; Dir (Admin), Alvey Programme, 1983; Head, Policy Planning Unit, 1985; Principal Private Sec. to successive Secs of State for Trade and Industry, 1986; Under Sec., 1987; Dir, Inf. Engrg Directorate, 1987; Head, Atomic Energy Div., Dept of Energy, then DTI, 1989–95; Dep. Sec., 1995, and Dir Gen., Immigration and Nationality Directorate, 1995–98, Home Office; Comr and Dep. Chm., HM Customs and Excise, 1998–2000; Dir-Gen., HSE, 2000–05. Non-exec. Dir, London Strategic Health Authy, 2006–09. UK Gov., IAEA, 1989–94; non-exec. Dir, Govt Div., UKAEA, 1994–95. Chm., Assembly of Donors, Nuclear Safety Account, EBRD, 1993–95; Mem., Sci. and Technol. Cttee, Internat. Risk Governance Council, 2004–12. Chm., Accountancy and Actuarial Discipline Bd, 2008–12; Exec. Dir, Financial Reporting Council, 2008–12. Non-exec. Dir, ICI Chemicals and Polymers Ltd, 1988–89. Mem., Audit Cttee, St John of Jerusalem Eye Hosp., 2013–. Governor, St Anne's Sch., Wandsworth, 1977–82; Council Member: Warwick Univ., 2000–06; Inst. of Employment Studies, 2001–05. Trustee: Prostate Cancer Charity, 2006–13; Lambeth Palace Library, 2007–12; De Morgan Foundation, 2007–12; Drinkaware, 2014–. CEng, FIET, FInstP 2003. FRSA 2000; CCMI 2002. Hon. Fellow, Warwick Manufacturing Gp, 2006–. Hon. DSc Cranfield, 2003. *Publications:* If You Can Read You Can Cook, 2009; Twixt the Commons, 2010; contribs to scientific jls. *Recreations:* cooking, travel, African tribal art.

WALKER, Sir Victor (Stewart Heron), 6th Bt *cr* 1868, of Sand Hutton, York and Beachampton, Bucks; *b* 8 Oct. 1942; *s* of Sir James Heron Walker, 5th Bt and Angela Margaret (*née* Beaufort); *S* father, 2003; *m* 1st, 1969, Caroline Louisa (marr. diss. 1982), *d* of Lt-Col F. E. B. Wignall; two *s* one *d*; 2nd, 1982, Svea (*d* 2013), *o d* of Captain Ernst Hugo Gothard Knutson Borg; 3rd, 2014, Mrs Sarah Gaunt, *e d* of Geoffrey Phillip Gillott. *Educ:* Eton. 2nd Lt Grenadier Guards, 1962–65; Lt Royal Wilts Yeo., 1965–73. Mem., RYS, 1972–. *Heir:* *s* James Frederick Heron Walker, *b* 14 Feb. 1970.

WALKER, Victoria Patricia Ann, (Mrs F. A. Woods Walker); *see* Woods, V. P. A.

WALKER, William Connoll, (Bill), OBE 1998; FIPM; Chairman, Walker Associates, since 1975; *b* 20 Feb. 1929; *s* of Charles and Williamina Walker; *m* 1956, Mavis Evelyn Lambert; three *d*. *Educ:* Logie Sch., Dundee; Trades Coll., Dundee; College for Distributive Trades. FIPM 1968. Message boy, 1943–44; office boy, 1944–46; commissioned RAF, 1946–49; Sqdn Leader, RAFVR, 1949–; salesman, public service vehicle driver, general manager, 1949–59; RAF, 1959–65; training and education officer, furnishing industry, 1965–67; company director, 1967–79; pt-time presenter, TV progs, 1969–75. MP (C) Perth and E Perthshire, 1979–83, Tayside N, 1983–97; contested (C) Tayside N, 1997. Director: Stagecoach Malaŵi, 1989–94; Stagecoach Internat. Services, 1989–94; Chm., Aerotech Marketing, 1995–2002. Dep. Chm., and Mem., UK Party Bd, Scottish Cons. Party, 2000–02. Chm., Scotland and NI Air Cadet Council, 1997–; Vice Pres., British Gliding Assoc., 1992–; Hon. Pres., Air Cadet Gliding, 1994–. FRSA 1970; FCMI. *Recreations:* RAFVR (T) (Gp Captain), gliding, caravanning, walking, youth work. *Club:* Royal Air Force.

WALKER, William George; Member for Dunfermline, Scottish Parliament, 2011–Sept. 2013 (SNP, 2011–12; Ind, 2012–13); *b* Edinburgh, 31 March 1942; *s* of George Stenhouse Walker and Mary Heriot Watt Walker. *Educ:* Univ. of Edinburgh (BSc 1st Cl. Electrical Engrg 1963; MBA Corporate Strategy and Finance 1982); Illinois Inst. of Technol., Chicago (Post Grad. Cert. Computer Programming 1968). CEng, FIET, FCMI. Technical R&D, then sales and marketing, business develt and gen. mgt in hi-tech engrg and electronics sector servicing healthcare, scientific, industrial and energy markets, USA and Europe, 1963–2007. Mem. (SNP) Fife Council, 2007–12. *Recreations:* gardening, walking, DIY, travel. *E:* williamgeorgewalker@gmail.com.

WALKER, William MacLelland; QC (Scot.) 1971; Social Security Commissioner, 1988–2003; a Child Support Commissioner, 1993–2003; *b* 19 May 1933; *s* of late Hon. Lord Walker; *m* 1957, Joan Margaret (*d* 2006), *d* of late Charles Hutchison Wood, headmaster, Dundee; one *d*. *Educ:* Edinburgh Academy; Edinburgh Univ. (MA, LLB). Advocate, 1957; Flying Officer, RAF, 1957–59; Standing Junior Counsel: Min. of Aviation, 1963–68; BoT (Aviation), 1968–71; Min. of Technology, 1968–70; Dept of Trade and Industry (Power), 1971; Min. of Aviation Supply, 1971. Hon. Sheriff, various Sheriffdoms, 1963–71. Chairman: Industrial Tribunals in Scotland, 1972–88; VAT Tribunals, 1985–88. *Recreations:* travel, photography. *Clubs:* Royal Air Force; New (Edinburgh).

WALKER-ARNOTT, Edward Ian; Consultant, Herbert Smith Freehills (formerly Herbert Smith), since 2000 (Senior Partner, 1992–2000); *b* 18 Sept. 1939; *s* of late Charles Douglas Walker-Arnott and Kathleen Margaret (*née* Brittain); *m* 1971, (Phyllis) Jane Ricketts; one *s* two *d*. *Educ:* Haileybury Coll.; London Univ. (LLB ext.); University Coll. London (LLM; Fellow, 1999; Vis. Prof., 2000–). Admitted solicitor, 1963; Partner, Herbert Smith, 1968–2000. Dir, Sturge Hldgs, 1989–95. Member: Cork Cttee on Review of Insolvency Law, 1977–82; Insolvency Practitioners Tribunal, 1987–. Mem. Council of Lloyds, 1983–88. Member: Regulation of Investigatory Powers, Guernsey Tribunal, 2006–; Takeover Appeal Bd, 2014–. Mem. Bd, RNT, 2000–08. Governor: S Bank Bd, 1999–2009; The Wellcome Trust, 2000–10. Member, Governing Body: Haileybury Coll., 1969–98; Benenden Sch., 1987–93. Author, report for Arts Council of England on relationship with Royal Opera House, Covent Garden (Walker-Arnott Report), 1997; Chm., ind. inquiry panel reporting to Univ. of Greenwich Court on Woolwich Incident, 2014. Hon. QC 2013. *Recreations:* reading, gardening, watching sport. *Address:* Manuden Hall, Manuden, near Bishop's Stortford, Herts CM23 1DY. *Club:* City of London.

WALKER-HAWORTH, John Leigh; Chairman, Black Rock (formerly Merrill Lynch) Greater Europe Investment Trust plc, 2004–13 (non-executive Director, Merrill Lynch European Investment Trust plc, 2000–04); *b* 25 Oct. 1944; *s* of William and Julia Walker-Haworth; *m* 1976, Caroline Mary Blair Purves; two *s*. *Educ:* Charterhouse; Pembroke College, Oxford. Called to the Bar, Inner Temple, 1967. Dir, 1981–93, Vice Chm., 1993–95, S. G. Warburg & Co.; Man. Dir, 1995–97, Advr, 1997–2000, UBS Warburg; Man. Dir, Integrated Finance Ltd, 2005–07. Chm. and Dir, GB Gp plc, 2002–10. Dep. Chm., Takeover Panel, 1997–2006 (Dir-Gen., City Panel on Takeovers and Mergers, 1985–87). Gov., Sutton's Hosp., Charterhouse, 1997–2003; Mem., Governing Body, Charterhouse, 2000–11 (Chm., 2004–11). *Address:* 7 Chancellor House, Hyde Park Gate, SW7 5DQ.

WALKER-OKEOVER, Sir Andrew Peter Monro, 5th Bt *cr* 1886, of Gateacre Grange, co. Lancaster and Osmaston Manor, co. Derby; *b* 22 May 1978; *s* of Sir Peter Ralph Leopold Walker-Okeover, 4th Bt and of Catherine Mary Maule (*née* Ramsay); *S* father, 2003; *m* 2007, Philippa Lucy Mettins, *yr d* of Lt-Col Charles Swabey; two *s*. *Heir:* *s* Peter Charles Monro Walker-Okeover, *b* 6 Feb. 2010. *Address:* Okeover Hall, Ashbourne, Derbyshire DE6 2DE.

WALKER-SMITH, Sir (John) Jonah, 2nd Bt *cr* 1960, of Broxbourne, Co. Herts; a Recorder of the Crown Court, 1980–2005; *b* 6 Sept. 1939; *s* of Baron Broxbourne (Life Peer), QC, TD and Dorothy (*d* 1999), *d* of late L. J. W. Etherton; *S* to baronetcy of father, 1992; *m* 1974, Aileen Marie Smith; one *s* one *d*. *Educ:* Westminster School; Christ Church, Oxford. Called to Bar, Middle Temple, 1963. Mem., Westminster CC, 1968–86 (Chm. of Social Services, Housing and Finance Cttees). *Heir:* *s* Daniel Derek Walker-Smith, *b* 26 March 1980. *Club:* Garrick.

WALL OF NEW BARNET, Baroness *cr* 2004 (Life Peer), of New Barnet in the London Borough of Barnet; **Margaret Mary Wall;** *b* 14 Nov. 1941; *d* of Thomas and Dorothy Mylott; *m* 1st, 1962, Peter Wall (marr. diss. 1990); one *s*; 2nd, 1992, Edwin Holdsworth. *Educ:* Notre Dame High Sch., Liverpool; Liverpool John Moores Univ. (Dip. Social Studies/Econs/Politics). Amicus (formerly MSF): Nat. Sec., 1995–98; Dir of Political Policy, 1999–2003. Fair Pay Champion, 1995–2003. Chair: Barnet and Chase Farm Hosps NHS Trust, 2005–14; Milton Keynes Hosp. NHS Foundn Trust, 2014–. Consultant, DES, 2004. Wainwright Trust Equalities Award, 2000. *Recreations:* walking, grandchildren, reading. *E:* margaret.wall@btconnect.com.

WALL, Alfreda, (Mrs D. R. Wall); *see* Thorogood, A.

WALL, (Alice) Anne, (Mrs Michael Wall), DCVO 1982 (CVO 1972; MVO 1964); Extra Lady in Waiting to HM the Queen (formerly Extra Woman of the Bedchamber), since 1981; *b* 1928; *d* of late Admiral Sir Geoffrey Hawkins, KBE, CB, MVO, DSC and late Lady Margaret Montagu-Douglas-Scott, *d* of 7th Duke of Buccleuch; *m* 1975, Commander Michael E. St Q. Wall, Royal Navy. *Educ:* Miss Faunce's PNEU School. Asst Press Sec. to the Queen, 1958–81. *Address:* Ivy House, Newbury Street, Lambourn, Hungerford, Berks RG17 8PB. *T:* (01488) 72348.

WALL, Brian Owen, CEng, FRINA; RCNC; Chief Naval Architect, Ministry of Defence, 1985–90; *b* 17 June 1933; *s* of Maurice Stanley Wall and Ruby Wall; *m* 1960, Patricia Thora Hughes; one *s*. *Educ:* Newport High School, Mon; Imperial Coll. of Science and Technology; RN Coll., Greenwich. BSc Eng. ACGI. MoD Bath: Ship Vulnerability, 1958–61; Submarine Design, 1961–66; Head of Propeller Design, Admiralty Experiment Works, Haslar, 1966–71; Staff of C-in-C Fleet, Portsmouth, 1971–73; Submarine Support and Modernisation Group, MoD Bath, 1973–77; RCDS 1977; MoD Bath: Ship Production Div., 1978–79; Project Director, Vanguard Class, 1979–84; Dir, Cost Estimating and Analysis, 1985. Gov., Imperial Coll., London, 1991–99. *Recreations:* photography, chess, music, walking. *Address:* Wychwood, 39 High Bannerdown, Batheaston, Bath BA1 7JZ.

WALL, Prof. Charles Terence Clegg, FRS 1969; Professor of Pure Mathematics, 1965–99, and Senior Fellow, 1999–2002, Liverpool University; *b* 14 Dec. 1936; *s* of late Charles Wall, schoolteacher; *m* 1959, Alexandra Joy, *d* of late Prof. Leslie Spencer Hearnshaw; two *s* two *d*. *Educ:* Marlborough Coll.; Trinity Coll., Cambridge. PhD Cantab 1960. Fellow, Trinity Coll., 1959–64; Harkness Fellow, Princeton, 1960–61; Univ. Lectr, Cambridge, 1961–64; Reader in Mathematics, and Fellow of St Catherine's Coll., Oxford, 1964–65. SERC Sen. Fellowship, 1983–88. Royal Soc. Leverhulme Vis. Prof., CIEA, Mexico, 1967. Pres., London Mathematical Soc., 1978–80 (Mem. Council, 1973–80 and 1992–96); Hon. Mem., Irish Math. Soc., 2001. Fellow: Royal Danish Academy, 1990; Amer. Maths Soc., 2012. Sylvester Medal, Royal Soc., 1988. *Publications:* Surgery on Compact Manifolds, 1970; A Geometric Introduction to Topology, 1972; (with A. A. du Plessis) The Geometry of Topological Stability, 1995; Singular Points of Plane Curves, 2004; papers on various problems in geometric topology, singularity theory, and related algebra. *Recreations:* reading, walking, gardening. *Address:* 5 Kirby Park, West Kirby, Wirral, Merseyside CH48 2HA. *T:* (0151) 625 5063.

WALL, James Francis, (Frank), CMG 1999; formerly Head of Shipping Policy 2 Division, Department for Transport; *b* 6 Jan. 1944; *s* of late James Wall, MA and Elizabeth Wall (*née* O'Sullivan); *m* 1970, Eileen Forrester McKerracher; two *d*. *Educ:* Belvedere Coll., SJ; University Coll., Dublin (BA 1966); Univ. of Liverpool (MCD 1968). MRTPI 1970. Asst to Prof. H. Myles Wright, Dublin Regl Planning Consultant, 1965–66; Planner then Sen. Planner, Antrim and Ballymena Develt Commn, 1968–71; Planning Officer, NI Min. of

Develt, 1971–72; Asst, S Hants Plan Technical Unit, 1972–74; Sen. Planning Officer, Hants CC, 1974; Planning Officer, then Principal Planning Officer, DoE, 1974–82; Principal, 1982, Asst Sec., 1993, Dept of Transport; Hd of Shipping Policy 3, later 2, Div., Dept of Transport, then DETR, subseq. DTLR, later DfT, 1993–2004. Chairman: UK Search and Rescue Strategy Cttee, 2000; Shipping Task Force, 2001. Internat. Maritime Prize, IMO, 2002; Dist. Public Service Award, US Coast Guard, 2002. *Publications:* contrib. conf. proc. and articles in maritime law jls. *Recreations:* Flower Class Corvettes, the Boeing 707–348C. *Address:* Collingwood, Elvetham Road, Fleet, Hants GU51 4HH.

WALL, Jasper V., PhD; Adjunct Professor, Department of Physics and Astronomy, University of British Columbia, since 2003; *b* 15 Jan. 1942; *s* of late Philip Errington Wall and Lilian Margaret (*née* Blackburn); *m* 1969, Jennifer Anne Lash; one *s* one *d. Educ:* Vankleek Hill Collegiate Inst.; Queen's Univ., Kingston (BSc 1963); Univ. of Toronto (MASc 1966); Australian Nat. Univ. (PhD 1970). Res. Scientist, Australian Nat. Radio Astronomy Observatory, Parkes, NSW, 1970–74; Leverhulme Fellow, RAS, 1974–75, Jaffé Donation Fellow, Royal Soc., 1975–79, Cavendish Lab.; Hd, Astrophysics and Astrometry Div., Royal Greenwich Observatory, 1979–87; Officer-in-Charge, Isaac Newton Gp of Telescopes, La Palma, Canary Is, 1987–90; Royal Greenwich Observatory: Hd, Technol. Div., 1990–91; Hd, Astronomy Div., 1991–95; Dep. Dir, 1991–93; Head, 1993–95; Dir, 1995–98. Vis. Reader, Univ. of Sussex, 1980–90; Vis. Prof., Univ. of Oxford, 1998–. FRAS 1975 (Mem. Council, 1992–96; Vice-Pres., 1996). Chm., Editl Bd, Astronomy & Geophysics, 1999–2002. *Publications:* (ed jtly) Modern Technology and its Influence on Astronomy, 1986; (ed jtly) Optics in Astronomy, 1993; (ed jtly) The Universe at High Redshifts, 1997; (with C. R. Jenkins) Practical Statistics for Astronomers, 2003, 2nd edn 2012; 180 papers in professional jls on observational cosmology and statistics for astronomers. *Recreations:* ski-ing, music. *Address:* Department of Physics and Astronomy, University of British Columbia, Vancouver, BC V6T 1Z1, Canada.

WALL, Sir (John) Stephen, GCMG 2004 (KCMG 1996; CMG 1990); LVO 1983; HM Diplomatic Service, retired; Official Government Historian, since 2007; *b* 10 Jan. 1947; *s* of John Derwent Wall and Maria Laetitia Wall (*née* Whitmarsh); *m* 1975, Catharine Jane Reddaway (marr. diss. 2015), *d* of late G. F. N. Reddaway, CBE and of Jean Reddaway, OBE; one *s. Educ:* Douai Sch.; Selwyn Coll., Cambridge (BA; Hon. Fellow, 2000). FCO 1968; Addis Ababa, 1969–72; Private Sec. to HM Ambassador, Paris, 1972–74; First Sec., FCO, 1974–76; Press Officer, No 10 Downing Street, 1976–77; Asst Private Sec. to Sec. of State for Foreign and Commonwealth Affairs, 1977–79; First Sec., Washington, 1979–83; Asst Head, later Head, European Community Dept, FCO, 1983–88; Private Secretary: to Foreign and Commonwealth Sec., 1988–90; to the Prime Minister, 1991–93; Ambassador to Portugal, 1993–95; Ambassador and UK Perm. Rep. to EU, Brussels, 1995–2000; Head of European Secretariat, Cabinet Office, and EU Advr to the Prime Minister, 2000–04; Principal Advr to Cardinal Archbp of Westminster, 2004–05; Vice Chm., Business for New Europe, 2005–. Official Govt historian, 2007–. Mem. Council, UCL, 2005–14 (Chm., 2008–14). Chairman: Federal Trust, 2008–; Cumberland Lodge, 2009–; Co-Chm., Belgo-British Conference, 2010–14. Trustee: Thomson Foundn, 2006–; Franco-British Council, 2009–; Kaleidoscope Trust, 2014–. Officer's Cross, Order of Merit (Germany), 2009; Chevalier, Légion d'Honneur (France), 2009. *Publications:* A Stranger in Europe: Britain and the European Union from Thatcher to Blair, 2008; The Official History of Britain and the European Community, 1963–75, 2012. *Recreations:* walking, photography, reading.

WALL, Jonathan; Controller, BBC Radio 5 Live and 5 Live Sports Extra, since 2013; *b* Manchester, 24 July 1972; *s* of Malcolm Wall and Noreen Wall; *m* 2004, Clare Condon; two *s. Educ:* Univ. of Central England (BA Hons Media and Communication 1993); Falmouth Coll. of Arts (Postgrad. Dip. Broadcast Journalism 1994). Sports Prod., Radio Humberside, 1994–96; BBC: Sports Researcher, BBC TV Sport, 1996–98; Sports Prod., BBC Radio Sport, 1998–2002; Editor, 5 Live Sport, 2002–08; Dep. Controller, Radio 5 Live, 2008–13. *Recreations:* political studies, sport, media studies. *Address:* BBC, Quay House, MediaCityUK, Salford Quays, Salford M50 2QH. *T:* (0161) 335 6723. *E:* jonathan.wall.01@bbc.co.uk.

WALL, Malcolm Robert; Chairman: dock10, since 2014; Audioboom plc; Disciple Media Ltd; Director, Malcolm Wall Media Ltd; *b* 24 July 1956; *s* of Maj. Gen. Robert Percival Walter Wall, CB, and of Patricia Kathleen Wall; *m* 1985, Elizabeth Craxford; three *d. Educ:* Allhallows Sch., Lyme Regis; Univ. of Kent (BA Hons). Sales Dir, Anglia TV, 1987; Sales and Mktg Dir, Granada TV, 1988–92; Dep. CEO, Meridian Broadcasting, 1992–94; Man. Dir, Anglia TV, 1994–96; Dep. CEO, 1996–99, CEO, 1999–2000, United Broadcasting and Entertainment; Chief Operating Officer, United Business Media plc, 2000–05; Chief Executive Officer: ntl:Telewest, 2006; Content, Virgin Media, 2006–09; Abu Dhabi Media, 2011; Advr to Abu Dhabi Media Zone Authy, 2013–15; Man. Dir, Song Lin, 2013–14. Former Dir, Redshift Strategy Consulting. Chm., Harlequin FC, 1997–2000 and 2009–11; non-executive Director: Five, 2000–05; ITE plc, 2006–11; Creston plc, 2007–11; Image Nation LLC, 2013–; Eagle Eye plc, 2014–. Member: RTS, 1995–; BAFTA, 2014–. *Recreations:* sport, reading, television. *Address:* The Close, 2 Longfield Drive, SW14 7AU. *Clubs:* Royal Automobile, MCC, Harlequin Football.

WALL, Mark Arthur; QC 2006; **His Honour Judge Wall;** a Circuit Judge, since 2014; *b* 4 March 1963; *s* of Arthur and Phyllis Wall; *m* 1987, Carmel Miriam (*née* Adler); one *s* one *d. Educ:* King Charles I Sch., Kidderminster; St John's Coll., Cambridge (BA 1984). Called to the Bar, Lincoln's Inn, 1985, Bencher, 2013; in practice, specialising in criminal law; a Recorder, 2002–14; Leader, Midland Circuit, 2011–14; a Dep. High Ct Judge (Admin. Ct), 2013–14. Mem., Bar Council, 2008–. *Recreations:* driving children around, occasionally escaping to the racecourse or holidaying abroad. *Address:* Birmingham Crown Court, 1 Newton Street, Birmingham B4 7NA. *E:* markandcarmel@wall132.fsnet.co.uk.

WALL, Mrs Michael; *see* Wall, A. A.

WALL, Rt Hon. Sir Nicholas (Peter Rathbone), Kt 1993; PC 2004; President of the Family Division, 2010–12; *b* 14 March 1945; *s* of late Frederick Stanley Wall and of Margaret Helen Wall; *m* 1973, Margaret Sydee, JP, MSc; four *c. Educ:* Dulwich College; Trinity Coll., Cambridge (Scholar; MA). Pres., Cambridge Union Soc., 1967; Mem., combined univs debating tour, USA, 1968. Called to the Bar, Gray's Inn, 1969, Bencher, 1993; QC 1988; Asst Recorder, 1988–90; a Recorder, 1990–93; a Judge of the High Ct of Justice, Family Div., 1993–2004; Family Div. Liaison Judge, Northern Circuit, 1996–2001 (Hon. Mem., Northern Circuit, 2001); a Judge of the Employment Appeal Tribunal, 2001–03; a Judge of the Administrative Ct, 2003–04; a Lord Justice of Appeal, 2004–10. Mem., Lord Chancellor's Adv. Bd on Family Law, 1997–2001 (Chm., Children Act Sub-Cttee, 1998–2001). Hershman/Levy Meml Lectr, Assoc. of Lawyers for Children, 2006. *Publications:* (ed jtly) Supplements to Rayden and Jackson on Divorce, 15th edn, 1988–91; (ed jtly) Rayden and Jackson on Divorce, 16th edn, 1991–97, 17th edn 1997; (ed and contrib.) Rooted Sorrows: psychoanalytic contributions to assessments and decisions in the family justice system, 1996; (contrib.) Divided Duties: care planning within the family justice system, 1998; A Handbook for Expert Witnesses in Children Act Cases, 2000, 2nd edn 2007; (contrib.) Delight and Dole: the Children Act ten years on, 2002; (contrib.) Durable Solutions: the collected papers of the 2005 Dartington Hall Conference, 2006; papers in med. and legal jls.

WALL, Gen. Sir Peter (Anthony), GCB 2013 (KCB 2009); CBE 2002 (OBE 1994); DL; Chief of the General Staff, 2010–14; Aide-de-Camp General to the Queen, 2009–14; *b* 10 July 1955; *s* of late John Ramsay Wall and of Dorothy Margaret (*née* Waltho); *m* 1980, Fiona Anne Simpson; two *s. Educ:* Whitgift Sch.; Selwyn Coll., Cambridge (BA 1978; MA 1980); psc; hcsc. Commnd RE, 1974; sc 1987; COS 5 AB Bde, 1988–89; OC 9 Para Sqn, RE, 1990–92; CO 32 Engr Regt, 1994–96; Commander: 24 Airmob Bde, 1999; 16 Air Assault Bde, 1999–2001; Chief of Jt Force Ops, 2001–03; GOC 1st (UK) Armoured Div., 2003–05; Dep. Chief of Jt Ops (Ops), 2005–07, DCDS (Commitments), 2007–09, MoD; C-in-C, Land Forces, 2009–10; Chief Royal Engr, 2009–13. Colonel Commandant: REME, 2002–09; RE, 2003–13; Bde of Gurkhas, 2012–. Pres., Combat Stress, 2014–. DL Som, 2015. Hon. FREng 2013; Hon. FICE 2013. *Recreation:* sport.

WALL, Sir Stephen; *see* Wall, Sir J. S.

WALLACE, family name of **Barons Dudley, Wallace of Saltaire** and **Wallace of Tankerness.**

WALLACE OF SALTAIRE, Baron *cr* 1995 (Life Peer), of Shipley in the County of West Yorkshire; **William John Lawrence Wallace;** PC 2012; Professor of International Relations, London School of Economics, 1999–2005, now Emeritus; *b* 12 March 1941; *s* of William E. Wallace and Mary A. Tricks; *m* 1968, Helen Sarah Rushworth (*see* Dame H. S. Wallace); one *s* one *d. Educ:* Westminster Abbey Choir School (Sen. Chorister, 1954); St Edward's Sch., Oxford; King's Coll., Cambridge (Exhibnr, 1959; BA Hist. 1962); Nuffield Coll., Oxford; Cornell Univ. (PhD Govt 1968). Lectr in Govt, Univ. of Manchester, 1967–77; Dep. Dir, RIIA, 1978–90; Sen. Res. Fellow in European Studies, St Antony's Coll., Oxford, 1990–95; Prof. of Internat. Studies, Central European Univ., Budapest, 1994–97; Reader in Internat. Relns, LSE, 1995–99. House of Lords: Mem., Select Cttee on EU, 1997–2001 (Chair, Sub-Cttee on justice and home affairs, 1997–2000); Lib Dem spokesman: on defence, 1998–2001; on foreign affairs, 2001–10; govt spokesman: on educn, foreign affairs, and on work and pensions, 2010–11; on Cabinet Office, foreign affairs and defence, 2011–12; on Cabinet Office and FCO, 2012–; a Lord in Waiting (Govt Whip), 2010–15; Dep. Leader, Lib Dem Gp, 2004–10. Contested (L): Huddersfield West, 1970; Manchester Moss Side, Feb. and Oct. 1974; Shipley, 1983 and 1987. Vice-Chm., Liberal Party Policy Cttee, 1977–87. Editor, Jl of Common Market Studies, 1974–78. Hon. Dr, Free Univ. of Brussels, 1992. Ordre pour la Mérite (France), 1995; Chevalier, Légion d'Honneur (France), 2005. *Publications:* Foreign Policy and the Political Process, 1972; The Foreign Policy Process in Britain, 1977; (ed with Helen Wallace, and contrib.) Policy-making in the European Union, 1977, 5th edn 2005; (with Christopher Tugendhat) Options for British Foreign Policy in the 1990s, 1988; The Transformation of Western Europe, 1990; Regional Integration: the West European experience, 1994; Why vote Liberal Democrat?, 1997. *Address:* House of Lords, SW1A 0PW.

WALLACE OF SALTAIRE, Lady; *see* Wallace, H. S.

WALLACE OF TANKERNESS, Baron *cr* 2007 (Life Peer), of Tankerness in Orkney; **James Robert Wallace;** PC 2000; QC (Scot.) 1997; Leader of Liberal Democrats, House of Lords, since 2013; *b* 25 Aug. 1954; *s* of John F. T. Wallace and Grace Hannah Wallace (*née* Maxwell); *m* 1983, Rosemary Janet Fraser; two *d. Educ:* Annan Academy; Downing College, Cambridge (BA 1975, MA 1979); Edinburgh University (LLB 1977). Called to the Scots Bar, 1979; practised as Advocate, 1979–83. Contested Dumfriesshire (L), 1979; contested South of Scotland (L), European Parlt election, 1979. Vice-Chm. (Policy), Scottish Liberal Party, 1982–85; Leader, Scottish Liberal Democrats, 1992–2005. MP Orkney and Shetland, 1983–2001 (L 1983–88, Lib Dem 1988–2001). Liberal spokesman on defence, 1985–87; Deputy Whip, 1985–87, Chief Whip, 1987–88; first Lib Dem Chief Whip, 1988–92; Alliance spokesman on Transport, 1987; Lib Dem spokesman on employment and training, 1988–92, on fisheries, 1988–97, on Scottish affairs, 1992–99, on maritime affairs, 1994–97. Mem. (Lib Dem) Orkney, Scottish Parlt, 1999–2007. Scottish Executive: Dep. First Minister, 1999–2005; Minister of Justice, 1999–2003; Minister for Enterprise and Lifelong Learning, 2003–05. Director: Northwind Associates Ltd, 2007–10; Jim Wallace Consultancy Ltd, 2007–10. Advocate Gen. for Scotland, 2010–15; Dep. Leader, H of L, 2013–15. Mem. Bd, St Magnus Internat. Fest. (formerly Fest.) Ltd, 2007–14. Hon. Prof., Inst. of Petroleum Engrg, Heriot-Watt Univ., 2007–10. Hon. Bencher, Lincoln's Inn, 2012. Hon. DLitt Heriot-Watt, 2007; DUniv Open, 2009; Dr *hc* Edinburgh, 2009. *Recreations:* golf, music, travel. *Address:* Northwood House, Tankerness, Orkney KW17 2QS. *T:* (01856) 861383; House of Lords, SW1A 0PW. *E:* wallacej@parliament.uk. *Clubs:* Caledonian; Scottish Liberal (Edinburgh).

WALLACE, Albert Frederick, CBE 1963 (OBE 1955); DFC 1943; Controller of Manpower, Greater London Council, 1978–82; *b* 22 Aug. 1921; *s* of Major Frederick Wallace and Ada Wallace; *m* 1940, Evelyn M. White (*d* 2005); one *s* one *d. Educ:* Roan School, Blackheath, SE3. MIPM, MCMI, MILGA. Regular Officer, Royal Air Force, 1939–69: served war of 1939–45, with 40 Sqn, 93 Sqn, 214 Sqn, 620 Sqn; overseas service in Egypt (Canal Zone), S Rhodesia, India, Cyprus; sc 1944–45; NDC 1959–60; sowc 1963; retired in rank of Group Captain. Regional Advisory Officer, Local Authorities Management Services and Computer Cttee, 1969–71; Asst Clerk of the Council, Warwickshire CC, 1971–73; County Personnel Officer, W Midlands CC, and Dir, W Midlands PTA, 1973–78. *Recreations:* golf, bridge. *Address:* Flat 14, Kepplestone, Staveley Road, Eastbourne BN20 7JY. *T:* (01323) 730668.

WALLACE, Angus; *see* Wallace, W. A.

WALLACE, Ben; *see* Wallace, R. B. L.

WALLACE, Lt-Gen. Sir Christopher (Brooke Quentin), KBE 1997 (OBE 1983; MBE 1978); DL; Commandant, Royal College of Defence Studies, 2001–04; *b* 3 Jan. 1943; *s* of late Major Robert Quentin Wallace, RA and Diana Pamela Quentin Wallace (*née* Galtrey); *m* 1969, Delicia Margaret Agnes Curtis; one *s* one *d. Educ:* Shrewsbury Sch.; RMA Sandhurst. Commissioned 1962; CO 3rd Bn Royal Green Jackets, 1983–85; Comdr, 7th Armd Brigade, 1986–88; Dir, Public Relations (Army), 1989–90; Comdr, 3rd Armd Div., 1990–93; Comdt, Staff Coll., Camberley, 1993–94; Perm. Jt HQ Implementation Team Leader, 1994–96; Chief of Jt Ops, Perm. Jt HQ (UK), Northwood, 1996–99. Rep. Col Comdt, Royal Green Jackets, 1995–98; Col Comdt, Light Div., 1998–99; Dep. Col Comdt, AGC, 1992–99. Pres., Army Golf Assoc., 1995–2000; Mem., RUSI Council, 1996–2000. Chm. Trustees, RGJ Mus., 1999–2015; Trustee, Imperial War Mus., 1999–2008 (Dep. Chm., 2006–08). DL Hants, 2004. *Publications:* A Brief History of The King's Royal Rifle Corps 1755–1965, 2005; Focus on Courage: the 59 Victoria Crosses of the Royal Green Jackets, 2006; Rifles and Kukris: Delhi, 1857, 2007. *Recreation:* military history. *Address:* c/o RHQ The Rifles, Peninsula Barracks, Winchester, Hants SO23 8TS. *Club:* Army and Navy.

WALLACE, Sir David (James), Kt 2004; CBE 1996; PhD; FRS 1986; FREng; FRSE; FInstP; Master, Churchill College, Cambridge, 2006–14; *b* 7 Oct. 1945; *s* of Robert Elder Wallace and Jane McConnell Wallace (*née* Elliot); *m* 1970, Elizabeth Anne Yeats; one *d. Educ:* Hawick High Sch.; Univ. of Edinburgh (BSc, PhD). FRSE 1982; FInstP 1991; FREng (FEng 1998). Harkness Fellow, Princeton Univ., 1970–72; Lecturer in Physics, 1972–78, Reader in Physics, 1978–79, Southampton Univ.; Tait Prof. of Mathematical Physics, 1979–93, Hd of Physics, 1984–87, Edinburgh Univ.; Vice-Chancellor, Loughborough Univ., 1994–2005; N. M. Rothschild & Sons Prof. of Mathematical Scis and Dir, Isaac Newton Inst. for Mathematical Scis, Univ. of Cambridge, 2006–11. Director: Edinburgh Concurrent Supercomputer, 1987–89; Edinburgh Parallel Computing Centre, 1990–93. Science and Engineering Research Council, subseq. Engineering and Physical Sciences Research Council: Chm., Physics Cttee, 1987–90; Chm., Science Bd, 1990–94; Mem. Council, 1990–98; Chm., Technical Opportunities Panel, 1994–98. European Commission: Physics Panel, Human

Capital and Mobility Prog., 1991–94; Large Scale Facilities Evaluation Panel, 1995–97; European Sci. and Technol. Assembly, 1997–98. Mem., Royal Commn for Exhibn of 1851, 2001–11. Chairman: CVCP/SCOP Task Force on sport in higher educn, 1995–97; Value for Money Steering Gp, HEFCE, 1997–2003; Member: Royal Soc. sci. and industl award Cttees, 1990–95; SHEFC, 1993–97; LINK Bd, OST, 1995–98; LINK/Teaching Co. Scheme Bd, 1999–2001; Chairman: e-Science Steering Cttee, OST, 2001–06; Teaching Co. Scheme Quinquennial Rev., 2001. Non-executive Director: Scottish Life Insurance Co., 1999–2001; Taylor & Francis Gp plc, 2000–04; UK eUnivs Worldwide Ltd, 2001–04. Chm., Council for Mathematical Scis, 2006–10. President: Physics Sect., BAAS, 1994; Inst. of Physics, 2002–04; Cambridge Soc. for Application of Res., 2014–; Vice-Pres. and Mem. Council, RSE, 2013–. Royal Society: Mem. Council, 2001–07; Treas. and Vice-Pres., 2002–07. Chm., RSE/IEEE James Clerk Maxwell Award, 2015. Mem. Court, St Andrews Univ., 2014–. Trustee, Royal Instn of GB, 2011–12. Gov., Harrow Sch., 2007–. DL Leics, 2001–06. Hon. FIMA, 2009. Hon. DEng Heriot-Watt, 2002; Hon. DSc: Edinburgh, 2003; Leicester, 2005; Loughborough, 2006; Southampton, 2006; East Anglia, 2009. Maxwell Medal of Inst. of Physics, 1980. *Publications:* in research and review jls, in a number of areas of theoretical physics and computing. *Recreations:* exercise, eating well, mycophagy. *E:* djw75@hermes.cam.ac.uk.

WALLACE, Fleming; *see* Wallace, J. F.

WALLACE, Graham Martyn, FCMA; Mentor, Merryck & Co., since 2006 (Chief Executive, 2006–08); *b* 26 May 1948; *s* of Ronald and May Wallace; *m* 1974, Denise Margaret Wallace (*née* Dyer); one *s* one *d*. *Educ:* Imperial College, London (BSc Eng; ACGI); Birkbeck Coll., London (MA London Studies 2005). Graduate trainee, Turner & Newall, 1969–72; Co. Accountant, Brandhurst Co. Ltd, 1972–74; various finance and mgt posts, Rank Xerox, 1974–83; Planning Manager, Imperial Gp, 1983–85; Finance Dir, Imperial Leisure and Retailing, 1985–86; Head of Finance and Planning, 1986–89, Finance Dir, 1989–92, Granada Gp plc; Chief Executive: Granada UK Rental, 1992–95; Granada Restaurants and Services, 1995–97; Cable & Wireless Communications plc, 1997–99; Cable and Wireless plc, 1999–2003. Non-executive Director: Barclays PLC, 2001–03; Barclays Bank PLC, 2001–03.

WALLACE, Helen Richenda, (Mrs D. Papp); Consultant Editor, BBC Music Magazine (Editor, 1999–2004); Editor-in-Chief, Kings Place Music Foundation; *b* 19 Nov. 1966; *d* of Dr Ian Wallace and Richenda Ponsonby; *m* 2000, David Papp; one *d*. *Educ:* St Peter's Coll., Oxford (MA English); Guildhall Sch. of Music and Drama (LGSM); London Coll. of Printing (Dip. Periodical Journalism). Features Ed., The Music Mag., 1991–92; Ed., The Strad, 1992–94; Dep. Ed., BBC Music Mag., 1994–99; Editor-in-Chief, South Bank mag., 2000. *Publications:* Fanfare (ed with D. Minshull), 1999; Spirit of the Orchestra, 2006; Boosey & Hawkes: the publishing story, 2007; The History and Future of Music, 2008. *Address:* c/o BBC Music Magazine, BBC Magazines Bristol, 9th Floor, Tower House, Fairfax Street, Bristol BS1 3BN.

WALLACE, Dame Helen Sarah, (Lady Wallace of Saltaire), DBE 2011; CMG 2000; PhD; FBA 2000; Centennial Professor, European Institute, London School of Economics and Political Science, 2007–10, Emeritus Professor, 2010–13; Foreign Secretary, British Academy, since 2011; *b* 25 June 1946; *d* of Edward Rushworth and Joyce Rushworth; *m* 1968, William John Lawrence Wallace (*see* Baron Wallace of Saltaire); one *s* one *d*. *Educ:* St Anne's Coll., Oxford (MA Classics); Coll. of Europe, Bruges (Dip. Eur. Studies 1968); Univ. of Manchester (PhD 1975). Lectr, UMIST, 1974–78; Lectr, then Sen. Lectr, CS Coll., 1978–85 (on secondment to FCO, 1979–80); Dir, Eur. Programme, RIIA, 1985–92; Dir, 1992–98, Co-Dir, 1998–2001, Sussex European Inst.; Dir, Robert Schuman Centre, European University Inst., 2001–06. Dir, One Europe or Several? Programme, ESRC, 1998–2001. Member: Better Regulation Commn, 2006–08; Bd, British Library, 2015–. Serves on various editl and adv. bds. Chevalier, Ordre Nationale du Mérite (France), 1996. *Publications:* (ed jtly) Policy Making in the European Union, 1977, 7th edn 2015; (jtly) The Council of Ministers of the European Union, 1997, 2nd edn 2006; (ed) Interlocking Dimensions of European Integration, 2001; contrib. numerous articles on European integration. *Recreations:* gardening, travelling.

WALLACE, Prof. Ian George, PhD; FRSC, FREng, FIExpE; Professor and Head of School, Cranfield Defence and Security, since 2009, and Pro Vice Chancellor, Defence and Security, since 2014, Cranfield University, Defence Academy of the United Kingdom; *b* Gourock, Renfrewshire, 21 Feb. 1948; *s* of John Wallace and Annie Wallace; *m* 1997, Maureen Clapton; two *s* two *d*. *Educ:* Heriot-Watt Univ., Edinburgh (BSc Hons Chem. 1973; PhD Chem. 1976). FRSC 2000. Ministry of Defence: Higher, then Sen. Scientific Officer, Explosives Res. and Devel Establishment, 1976–85; PSO, Procurement Exec., 1985–89; Dir Air Systems Controllerate Information Systems, 1989–92; Ordnance Scientific Advr to Chief Inspector of Naval Ordnance, 1992–97; Ministry of Defence: Dir Standardisation, Dir Safety Policy, Vice-Pres., Ordnance Bd, 1997–2000; Chief Inspector Explosives, Dir Ordnance Safety Gp, Defence Procurement Agency, 2000–01; Hd of Dept, Cranfield Univ., 2001–09. Member: Defence Nuclear Safety Cttee, 2005–15; Nuclear Res. Adv. Council, 2015–. FREng 2011; FIExpE 2012. *Publications:* 77 conf. papers and reports. *Recreations:* art, music, golf, tennis, sailing, football. *Address:* Cranfield Defence and Security, Cranfield University, Defence Academy of the United Kingdom, Shrivenham, Swindon SN6 8LA. *T:* (01793) 785436. *E:* i.g.wallace@cranfield.ac.uk. *Clubs:* Royal Over-Seas League; Defence Academy Golf; Highworth Tennis.

WALLACE, Ivan Harold Nutt, CB 1991; Senior Chief Inspector, Department of Education, Northern Ireland, 1979–95; *b* 20 Feb. 1935; *s* of late Harold Wallace and Annie McClure Wallace; *m* 1962, Winifred Ervine Armstrong; two *d*. *Educ:* Grosvenor High Sch., Belfast; QUB (BSc 1957). MRSC 1963. School Teacher: Leeds Central High Sch., 1957–60; Foyle Coll., Londonderry, 1960–69; Inspector of Schools, NI, 1969–75; Sen. Inspector, 1975–77; Staff Inspector, 1977–78; Chief Inspector, 1978–79. Hon. Prof., Sch. of Educn, QUB, 1996–2001. *Recreations:* music, walking.

WALLACE, (James) Fleming; QC (Scot) 1985; Counsel to Scottish Law Commission, 1979–93; *b* 19 March 1931; *s* of James F. B. Wallace, SSC and Margaret B. Gray, MA; *m* 1st, 1964, Valerie Mary (*d* 1986), *d* of Leslie Lawrence, solicitor, and Madge Lawrence, Ramsbury, Wilts; two *d*; 2nd, 1990, Linda Ann, solicitor, *d* of Robert Grant, civil engineer, and Alice Grant. *Educ:* Edinburgh Academy; Edinburgh University (MA 1951; LLB 1954). Served RA, 1954–56 (2nd Lieut); TA 1956–60. Admitted Faculty of Advocates, 1957; practised at Scottish Bar until 1960; Parly Draftsman and Legal Secretary, Lord Advocate's Dept, London, 1960–79. Part-time Chm., Industrial Tribunals, Scotland, 1993–2001. Volunteer, CAB, 2001–08. *Publications:* The Businessman's Lawyer (Scottish Section), 1965, 2nd edn 1973. *Recreations:* hill walking, choral singing, golf. *Address:* 17A Midmar Gardens, Edinburgh EH10 6DY.

WALLACE, Sir James (Hay), KNZM 2011 (ONZM 2001); Chairman and Managing Director, Wallace Corporation Ltd Group, since 1975; Director, James Wallace Arts Trust, since 1992; *b* Cambridge, NZ, 23 Nov. 1937; *s* of James Dunning Wallace and Frances Lindsay Hay Wallace (*née* Hay). *Educ:* King's Coll., Auckland; The Browne and Nichols Sch., Cambridge, Mass; Univs of Otago and Auckland (LLB). Admitted solicitor, 1960; called to the Bar, 1961; with Buddle Weir, Auckland, 1959–61, Ellis Piers and Young Jackson, London, 1962–64; Co. Sec. and Co. Solicitor, Kerridge Odeon Corp. Gp, incl. Rank Xerox NZ Ltd, 1965–70; Co. Solicitor and Exec., Fisher and Paykel Ltd, 1971–74. Dir, various cos. Chm., Trustee and Settlor, James Wallace Arts Trust, 1992–. Member: Tongariro Nat. Park Bd; NZ Film Commn Bd; Council, Meat Industry Assoc. Fellow, Knox Coll., Univ. of Otago, 2008. NZ Pres., AFS. Patron, Trustee and Bd Mem., charitable arts orgns. Founding Pres., Graduates' Ski Club; Treas., Ski Council, NZ Ski Assoc. *Recreations:* ski-ing, travel, opera and other performing and visual arts (sometime Member, Royal Choral Society and Dorian Singers NZ). *Address:* Rannoch, 77 Almorah Road, Epsom, Auckland 1023, New Zealand. *Club:* Northern (Auckland).

WALLACE, Prof. James Stuart, PhD; Senior Hydrologist, Centre for Tropical Water and Aquatic Ecosystem Research, since 2013; *b* 20 June 1952; *s* of Joseph Wallace and Anne Wallace (*née* Keenan); *m* 1974, Josephine Marie Richardson; one *s* three *d*. *Educ:* Lisburn Tech. Coll.; Queen's Univ., Belfast (BSc 1973); Univ. of Nottingham (PhD 1978). NERC Institute of Hydrology: Envmtl Physicist, 1978–2004; Head: Vegetation Water Use Section, 1989–93; Hydrological Processes Div., 1993–96; Dir, 1996–2000; Dep. Dir, and Dir of Hydrology, NERC Centre for Ecol. & Hydrol., 2000–04; Team Leader, Floodplain Hydrology Gp, Land and Water Div., CSIRO, 2004–12. Vis. Prof. in Hydrology, Univ. of Reading, 1997–2005. Consultant to UNDP Global Envmt Facility, 1995; Hydrological Advr to UK Perm. Rep. to WMO, 1999–2003. Chairman: Jt UNESCO/WMO Task Force for Hydrology for Envmt, Life and Policy initiative, 1999–2005; UK Inter-Deptl Cttee on Hydrology, 2000–03; Member: Dirs Mgt Bd, EurAqua, 2001–03; Steering Cttee, NERC Centres for Atmospheric Sci., 2002–03; Bd, British Oxygen Co. Foundn, 2003–07. Vice-Pres., Internat. Cttee on Atmosphere-Soil-Vegetation Relns, 1996. FRMetS 2003. *Publications:* (ed jtly) Soil Water Balance in the Sudano-Sahelian Zone, 1991; (ed jtly) Hydrology and Water Law - Bridging the Gap, 2006; papers on hydrological processes in Qly Jl RMetS, Proc. Royal Soc., Jl Hydrology, Agric. and Forest Meteorology, Marine Pollution Bulletin, etc. *Recreations:* gardening, golf, motorcycling with Gromit. *Address:* Centre for Tropical Water and Aquatic Ecosystem Research, Building No 145, James Cook University, Townsville, Qld 4811, Australia. *E:* jim.wallace@mail.com.

WALLACE, John Malcolm Agnew; JP; Vice Lord-Lieutenant, Dumfries and Galloway (District of Wigtown), 1990–2003; *b* 30 Jan. 1928; *s* of John Alexander Agnew Wallace and Marjory Murray Wallace; *m* 1955, Louise Haworth-Booth; one *s* two *d*. *Educ:* Brooks Sch., USA; Harrow; West of Scotland Agricultural College. Farmer. JP Stranraer, 1970; DL Dumfries and Galloway, 1971. *Address:* Lochryan, Stranraer DG9 8QY. *T:* (01581) 200284.

WALLACE, John Williamson, CBE 2011 (OBE 1995); Principal, Royal Conservatoire of Scotland (formerly Royal Scottish Academy of Music and Drama), 2002–14; freelance soloist, composer, conductor; *b* 14 April 1949; *s* of Christopher Kidd Wallace and Ann Drummond Allan; *m* 1971, Elizabeth Jane Hartwell; one *s* one *d*. *Educ:* Buckhaven High Sch.; King's Coll., Cambridge (MA); York Univ.; Royal Acad. of Music (ARAM 1983; FRAM 1990). ARCM 1968, Hon. RCM 1985, FRCM 2008; FRSAMD 1993; FRNCM 2008. Asst Principal Trumpet, LSO, 1974–76; Prin. Trumpet, Philharmonia Orch., 1976–94; founded The Wallace Collection (brass-interest music gp), 1986; Principal Trumpet, London Sinfonietta, 1987–2001; Artistic Dir of Brass, RAM, 1993–2001. Trumpet solo recordings. Hon. DMus Aberdeen, 2007; Hon. DLitt Strathclyde, 2007. Mercedes-Benz Prize, 1991; Assoc. of British Orchs Award, 2002. *Publications:* Five Easy Pieces, 1984; First Book of Trumpet Solos, 1985; Second Book of Trumpet Solos, 1985, 2nd edn 1987; Grieg's Seven Lyric Pieces, 1985; Kornukopia, 1986; Prime Number, 1990; Odd Number and Even Number, 1991; (jtly) Music Through Time, 1995; (ed jtly) Cambridge Companion to Brass Instruments, 1997; (jtly) The Trumpet, 2011. *Address:* 157B Camphill Avenue, Glasgow G41 3DR.

WALLACE, Major Malcolm Charles Robarts; Director of Regulation, British Horseracing Authority (formerly Jockey Club, then Horseracing Regulatory Authority), 1994–2008; Chairman: HPower Group, 2008–10; Martin Collins Group, since 2010; *b* 12 June 1947; *s* of Lionel John Wallace, MBE, TD and Maureen Winefride (*née* Robarts); *m* 1st, 1974, Caroline Anne Doyne-Ditmas (marr. diss. 1990); one *s* one *d*; 2nd, 1991, Mrs Jane Thelwall; two *s*. *Educ:* Blackrock College, Co. Dublin. Student pupil with Lt-Col J. Hume-Dudgeon at Burton Hall, Co. Dublin, 1965–67; Mons Officer Cadet Sch.; commissioned RA, 1967; gun line officer, 18 Light Regt, Hong Kong; 3rd Regt RHA, 1969; King's Troop RHA, 1970 (long equitation course, RAVC Melton Mowbray); Troop Comdr, 19 Field Regt, 1974; Adjutant 101 Northumbrian Field Artillery, 1976; Staff Officer, HQ UKLF, 1978–82; Comd King's Troop RHA, 1982–85, retired. Dir Gen., BEF, 1985–94. Chef d'Equipe to British Internat. and Olympic Three Day Event Teams, 1979–84; Chef de Mission, Equestrian Team, Olympic Games, Seoul, 1988 and Barcelona, 1992. Chm., Burghley Horse Trials, 2002–10. Freeman, Saddlers' Co., 1985. *Publications:* The King's Troop Royal Horse Artillery, 1984. *Recreations:* field and equestrian sports, training gun dogs, Leicester Tigers supporter! *Address:* Fishponds Farm, Stoke Albany, Market Harborough LE16 8PZ. *T:* (01858) 535250, *T:* 07785 390325. *Club:* Cavalry and Guards.

WALLACE, Margaret; Member (Lab) Kilmarnock and Loudoun, Scottish Parliament, 1999–2007; *b* 6 April 1953; *d* of late George and Margaret Wallace; *m* 1974, Russell Jamieson (marr. diss. 2002); one *d*. *Educ:* Grange Acad.; Ayr Coll. Official for UNISON (formerly NUPE), 1979–99. Mem. Bd, E Ayrshire Employment Initiative, 1998–. Scottish Parliament: Member: Audit Cttee, 1999–2007; Health and Community Care Cttees, 1999–2003. Convener, Scottish Commn for Public Audit, 2001–07.

WALLACE, Marjorie Shiona Douglas, CBE 2008 (MBE 1994); Founder, and Chief Executive, SANE, mental health charity, since 1989; broadcaster, author, journalist; *d* of William Wallace and Doris Tulloch; *m* 1974, Count Andrzej Skarbek (*d* 2011); three *s*; partner, Thomas Alan Margerison (*d* 2014); one *d*. *Educ:* Roedean; Johannesburg; Parsons' Mead, Ashtead; University College London (BA Hons Psych and Phil; Fellow, 2004). Television: The Frost Programme, 1966–68; ITV religious programmes, 1966–68; LWT current affairs, 1968–69; Dir/reporter, current affairs, BBC TV, 1969–72; Insight team (Thalidomide campaign), feature writer, Sunday Times, 1972–89, incl. Forgotten Illness, mental illness campaign, The Times, 1985–89; Guardian Res. Fellow, Nuffield Coll., Oxford, 1989–91. Founded SANE, and Prince of Wales Internat. Centre for SANE Res., Oxford (opened 2003). Institute of Psychiatry: Member: Cttee of Management, 1989–2002; Ethics Cttee (Res.), 1991–2002; Adv. Bd, Design for Patient Dignity, 2009–10. Trustee, UKCP, 2009–12. Chm., Friends of Open Air Theatre, 1991–2008. Patron, Hay Literary Festival, 2001–. Numerous internat. presentations and speeches, also broadcasts on TV and radio; TV documentaries: Whose Mind Is It?, 1988; Circles of Madness, 1994. Hon. FRCPsych 1997. Hon. DSc City, 2001. Campaigning Journalist of the Year, British Press Awards, 1982, 1986; John Pringle Meml Award, 1986; Book Trust Prize, 1987; Snowdon Special Award, 1988; Medical Journalist of the Year, 1988; Evian Health Award, 1991, and Best Use of Media award, 1995; Public Service award, British Neurosci. Assoc., 2002; Internat. Pioneer and Diversity Award, Muslim community, 2005; Healthcare Communications Advocate, Communiqué Awards, 2014. *Publications:* On Giant's Shoulders, 1976 (also original BBC TV screenplay (Internat. Emmy award), 1979); (jtly) Suffer the Children: the story of Thalidomide, 1978; (jtly) The Superpoison, The Dioxin Disaster, 1980; The Silent Twins, 1986 (also BBC TV screenplay; Best Docudrama, USA, HBO, 1989); Campaign and Be Damned, 1991. *Recreations:* poetry, piano, Victorian ballads, opera, musicals, dining out. *Address:* SANE, St Mark's Studios, 14 Chillingworth Road, Islington, N7 8QJ. *T:* (020) 7375 1002. *Clubs:* Athenæum, Groucho.

WALLACE, Rt Rev. Martin William; Bishop Suffragan of Selby, 2003–13; Assistant Bishop, Diocese of York, since 2013; *b* 16 Nov. 1948; *s* of Derek Philip William Wallace and Audrey Sybil Wallace (*née* Thomason); *m* 1971, Diana Christine Pratt; one *s* one *d*. *Educ:*

Varndean Grammar Sch., Brighton; Taunton's Sch., Southampton; King's Coll., London (BD Hons; AKC; Winchester Schol.); St Augustine's Theol Coll., Canterbury. Ordained deacon, 1971, priest, 1972; Assistant Curate: Attercliffe, Sheffield, 1971–74; New Malden, Surrey, 1974–77; Vicar, St Mark's, Forest Gate, 1977–93 and Priest-in-charge, Emmanuel, 1985–89, All Saints, 1991–93, Forest Gate; Chaplain, Forest Gate Hosp., 1977–80; Rural Dean, Newham, 1982–91; Chelmsford Diocesan Urban Officer, 1991–93; Priest-in-charge, Bradwell and St Lawrence, 1993–97; Industrial Chaplain, Maldon and Dengie, 1993–97; Archdeacon of Colchester, 1997–2003. Hon. Canon, Chelmsford Cathedral, 1989–97. *Publications:* Healing Encounters in the City, 1987; City Prayers, 1994; Pocket Celtic Prayers, 1996; Celtic Resource Book, 1998; (contrib.) Worship: window of the urban Church, 2007; In Good Company, 2009. *Recreation:* local history. *Address:* 28 Alexandra Court, Bridlington YO15 2LB. *T:* (01262) 670265. *E:* mdw28@btinternet.com.

WALLACE, Moira Paul, OBE 1997; Provost, Oriel College, Oxford, since 2013; *b* 15 Aug. 1961; *d* of Prof. and Mrs W. V. Wallace; *m* 2009, David Archer. *Educ:* Coleraine High Sch.; Emmanuel Coll., Cambridge (MA Mod. Langs 1983; Hon. Fellow 2014); Harvard Univ. (Kennedy Schol.; AM Comparative Lit. 1985). Joined HM Treasury, 1985; Private Sec. to Chancellor of Exchequer, 1987–90; Econ. Affairs Private Sec. to Prime Minister, 1995–97; Dir, Social Exclusion Unit, Cabinet Office, 1997–2002; Dir Gen., Criminal Justice Gp, Home Office, 2002–04; Chief Exec., Office for Criminal Justice Reform, 2004–05; Dir Gen., Crime, Policing and Counter Terrorism, then Crime Reduction and Community Safety Gp, Home Office, 2005–08; Permanent Sec., DECC, 2008–12. Vis. Fellow, Nuffield Coll., Oxford, 1999–2007. Hon Fellow, TCD, 2014. *Address:* Oriel College, Oxford OX1 4EW.

WALLACE, Pauline; Head, UK Public Policy and Regulatory Affairs, PricewaterhouseCoopers LLP, 2009–13; *b* London, 19 March 1954; *d* of Sidney Robert Wallace and Hilda Mary Wallace; *m* 1983, Ron Alpe; one *s*. *Educ:* Harrow Co. Grammar Sch. for Girls; Univ. of Nottingham (BA French and German). ACA 1979. Trainee accountant, Spicer & Pegler, 1976–80; Under Sec., Accounting Standards Cttee, 1981–83; Technical Dir, Hong Kong Soc. of Accountants, 1983–86; Arthur Andersen: Sen. Manager, Hong Kong, 1986–89, 1991–95; Partner, 1995–2002; Partner, PricewaterhouseCoopers, 2002–13. Affiliate, FTI Consulting, 2015–. Member: Accounting Standards Bd, 2010–; Regulatory Decisions Cttee, Financial Conduct Authy, 2014–. Dir and Chm., Audit Cttee, Paradigm Trust, 2013–. Gov., Middleton Sch., 2013–. *Publications:* Company Law in Hong Kong, 1986, 2nd edn 1990. *Recreations:* walking my dogs, cooking, reading novels.

WALLACE, Richard Alexander; Principal Finance Officer, Welsh Office, 1990–97; *b* 24 Nov. 1946; *s* of late Lawrence Mervyn and Norah Wallace; *m* 1970, Teresa Caroline Harington Smith (*d* 2006); three *c* (and one *c* decd). *Educ:* Bembridge and Sandown C of E Primary Schools; Clifton Coll. Prep. Sch.; Clifton Coll.; King's Coll., Cambridge (MA). Asst Master, Woking County GS for Boys, 1967; Min. of Social Security, 1968; Principal, DHSS, 1972, Asst Sec., 1981; transf. to Welsh Office, 1986; Under Sec., 1988.

WALLACE, Richard David; Executive Producer, Syco Entertainment, since 2012; *b* 11 June 1961; *s* of Bill and Maureen Wallace. *Educ:* Ratcliffe Coll., Leics. Leicester Mercury, 1979–83; EMI Records, 1983–84; Oxon Bucks News Agency, 1984–86; Daily Mail, 1986–88; The Sun, 1988–90; Daily Mirror: show business reporter, then show business ed., 1999–2000; Hd of News, 2000–02; US Ed., 2002–03; Dep. Ed., Sunday Mirror, 2003–04; Ed., Daily Mirror, 2004–12. Mem., Editors' Code of Practice Cttee, 2010–12. *Recreations:* travel, contemporary American literature. *Club:* Savile.

WALLACE, (Robert) Ben (Lobban); MP (C) Wyre and Preston North, since 2010 (Lancaster and Wyre, 2005–10); Parliamentary Under-Secretary of State, NI Office, since 2015; *b* 15 May 1970; *m* 2001, Liza Cooke; two *s* one *d*. *Educ:* Millfield Sch., Somerset; RMA Sandhurst. Ski Instructor, Austrian Nat. Ski Sch., 1987–89; advertising, RGSH Boston, USA; commissioned, Scots Guards, 1991; Platoon Comdr, 1991–93 (despatches, 1992); Ops Officer, 1993, Intelligence, 1994–97; Co. Comdr, 1997; served Windsor, London, N Ireland, Central America, BAOR, Egypt, Cyprus; retired 1998. EU Dir, QinetiQ, 2003–05. MSP (C) NE Scotland, 1999–2003; Mem., EU Cttee, health spokesman, Scottish Parlt. Shadow Minister of State for Scotland, 2006–10; PPS to Lord Chancellor and Sec. of State for Justice, 2010–12, to Minister without Portfolio, 2012–14; an Asst Govt Whip, 2014–15. Mem., Scottish Select Cttee, 2005–10, NI Grand Cttee, H of C, 2005–10; Chm., All Party Parly Gp on Iran, 2006–14. Mem., Queen's Body Guard for Scotland (Royal Co. of Archers), 2006–. *Recreations:* ski-ing, sailing, Rugby, horse racing. *Address:* House of Commons, SW1A 0AA; c/o Village Centre, Great Eccleston Village Centre, 59 High Street, Great Eccleston PR3 0YB. *Club:* Third Guards.

WALLACE, Sharmila; *see* Nebhrajani, S.

WALLACE, Stephanie Vera; *see* Hilborne, S. V.

WALLACE, Victoria Louise; Director General and Secretary, Commonwealth War Graves Commission, since 2014; *b* Pembury, Kent, 12 March 1966; *d* of Michael John Stickland and Janet Catherine Stickland (*née* Allen); *m* 1997, Seán Michael Wallace; two *d*. *Educ:* Cranbrook Sch., Kent; Univ. of Exeter (LLB Hons). HM Diplomatic Service, 1987–99: Asst Desk Officer, Sci. Space and Telecoms, FCO, 1987; Thai lang. trng, SOAS, 1988; Vice Consul, Bangkok, 1989–92; Desk Officer, Security Policy Dept, FCO, 1992–94; Second Sec. (Pol), Dar es Salaam, 1994–97; Asst Dir, British Council, Dar es Salaam (on secondment), 1997–98; Hd, Wider Europe Resource Mgt Unit, FCO, 1998–99; Justices' Chief Exec., Sussex Magistrates' Courts, 1999–2004; Chief Exec., Leeds Castle Foundn, 2004–14. Non-exec. Dir, Kent Tourism Alliance, 2004–08. Mem. Council, Assoc. of Ind. Museums, 2012–. Ambassador, Kent Co. Agricl Soc., 2010–14. Trustee, Army Museums Ogilby Trust, 2014–. *Recreations:* travel, curating a cabinet of curiosities, historic buildings, shopping with my daughters. *Address:* Commonwealth War Graves Commission, 2 Marlow Road, Maidenhead, Berks SL6 7DX. *T:* (01628) 507152. *E:* victoria.wallace@cwgc.org.

WALLACE, (Wellesley) Theodore (Octavius); a Judge of the Tax and Chancery Chamber of the Upper Tribunal, 2009–12; *b* 10 April 1938; *s* of late Dr Caleb Paul Wallace and Dr Lucy Elizabeth Rainsford (*née* Pigott); *m* 1988, Maria Amelia Abercromby, *d* of Sir Ian Abercromby, 10th Bt; one *s* one *d*. *Educ:* Charterhouse; Christ Church, Oxford. 2nd Lt, RA, 1958; Lt, Surrey Yeomanry, TA, 1959–62. Called to the Bar, Inner Temple, 1963 (Duke of Edinburgh Schol.). Mem., Lincoln's Inn (*ad eundem*), 1973. Chm., VAT and Duties (formerly VAT) Tribunal, 1989–2009 (pt-time, 1989–92); Special Comr of Income Tax, 1992–2009. Hon. Sec., Taxation of Sub-cttee, Soc. of Cons. Lawyers, 1974–92. Contested (C): Pontypool, Feb. 1974; S Battersea, Oct. 1974, 1979. *Publications:* (jtly with John Wakeham) The Case Against Wealth Tax, 1968. *Recreations:* bridge, lawn tennis, ski-ing, golf. *Address:* 46 Belleville Road, SW11 6QT. *T:* (020) 7228 7740; Whitecroft, W Clandon, Surrey GU4 7TD. *T:* (01483) 222574.

WALLACE, Prof. (William) Angus, FRCS, FRCSE, FFSEM; Professor of Orthopaedic and Accident Surgery, School of Clinical (formerly Medical and Surgical) Sciences, University of Nottingham, 1985–2015, now Emeritus; *b* 31 Oct. 1948; *s* of late Dr William Bethune Wallace and Dr Frances Barret Wallace (*née* Early), Dundee; *m* 1971, Jacqueline Vera Studley; two *s* one *d*. *Educ:* Dundee High Sch.; Univ. of St Andrews (MB ChB 1972); FRCSE 1977; Cert. of Orthopaedic Higher Specialist Trng 1984; FRCSE (Orth) 1985; FRCS 1997; FFSEM 2006. Jun. House Officer, Dundee Royal Infirmary and Maryfield Hosp., 1972–73; Sen. House Officer, Derby, 1974–75; Registrar (Basic Surg. Trng), Newcastle and Gateshead Hosps, 1975–77; Orthopaedic Registrar, Nottingham Hosps, 1978–81; MRC Res. Fellow, 1979; Lectr (Hon. Sen. Registrar) in Orthopaedic Surgery, Univ. of Nottingham, 1981–84; Vis. Res. Fellow, Toronto Western Hosp., Canada, 1983; Med. Dir, North Western Orthotic Unit, and Med. Advr, Dept of Orthopaedic Mechanics, Univ. of Salford, 1984–85. Advr, Rail Accident Investigation Bd, 2007. Mem., ABC Club, 1988–. Member: RSocMed 1988; Council, RCSE, 1990–2000, 2004–07 (Vice-Pres., 1997–2000); Council, Faculty of Sport and Exercise Medicine, 2005–10, 2015–; Internat. Bd for Shoulder Surgery, 1992–; Council, British Orthopaedic Assoc., 2008–10; Council, Inst. of Advanced Motorists, 2011–; Dean, Faculty of Medical Informatics, RSCE, 2000–05; Dir for Professional Affairs for E Midlands, RCS, 2014–. Chairman: Nat. Sports Medicine Inst. of UK, 1999–2003; Inter-Collegiate Bd in Trauma and Orthopaedic Surgery, 2002–05; Specialist Adv. Cttee for Trauma and Orthopaedic Surgery, 2008–10; Nat. Nottingham Repository, 2011–. President: British Elbow and Shoulder Soc., 2001–03; Internat. Congress for Shoulder and Elbow Surgery, 2010. Inventor/co-inventor of surgical and medical devices; (jtly) developer, The Orthopaedic eLogbook, Faculty of Health Informatics, RCSE, 2002–. Consultant: LockDown Medical Ltd, 2008–14; JRI Orthopaedics Ltd, 2010–; Xiros Ltd, 2015–. Foundn Fellow, Faculty of Sports and Exercise Medicine (UK), 2005–14. Hon. Fellow: Hong Kong Coll. of Orthopaedic Surgeons, 2011; Hungarian Orthopaedic Assoc., 2011. Sir Walter Mercer Gold Medal, 1985, Sir Walter Mercer Medal, 2015, RCSE; Weigelt-Wallace Award for exceptional med. care, Univ. of Texas, 1995; Great Scot Sci. and Medicine Award, Sunday Mail, Scotland, 1995; People of the Year Award, RADAR, 1995. *Publications:* Shoulder Arthroscopy, 1992; Management of Disasters and their Aftermath, 1994; Joint Replacement of the Shoulder and Elbow, 1998; A Handbook of Sports Medicine, 1999; over 350 articles in learned jls on osteoporosis, shoulder surgery, sports medicine and med. informatics. *Recreations:* narrow boating, information technology, DIY. *Address:* High Trees, Foxwood Lane, Woodborough, Nottingham NG14 6ED. *T:* (0115) 965 2372, *Fax:* (0115) 965 4638. *E:* Angus.Wallace@rcsed.ac.uk.

WALLACE-HADRILL, Prof. Andrew Frederic, OBE 2004; DPhil; FBA 2010; Director of Research, Faculty of Classics, University of Cambridge, since 2012; Scientific Director, Herculaneum Conservation Project, since 2013 (Director, 2001–13); *b* 29 July 1951; *s* of John Michael Wallace-Hadrill and Anne (*née* Wakefield); *m* 1976, Josephine Claire Braddock; one *s* one *d*. *Educ:* Rugby Sch.; Corpus Christi Coll., Oxford (MA; Hon. Fellow 2009); St John's Coll., Oxford (DPhil; Hon. Fellow 2009). Fellow and Dir of Studies in Classics, Magdalene Coll., Cambridge, 1976–83; Lectr in Ancient History, Univ. of Leicester, 1983–87; Prof. of Classics, Reading Univ., 1987–2009; Dir, British Sch. at Rome, 1995–2009; Master, Sidney Sussex Coll., Cambridge, 2009–13; Dep. Vice-Chancellor, Univ. of Cambridge, 2010–12. Editor, Jl of Roman Studies, 1991–95. Hon. DLitt Reading, 2014. *Publications:* Suetonius: the scholar and his Caesars, 1983, 2nd edn 1995; (ed) Patronage in Ancient Society, 1989; (ed with J. W. Rich) City and Country in the Ancient World, 1991; Augustan Rome, 1993; Houses and Society in Pompeii and Herculaneum, 1994; (ed with R. Laurence) Domestic Space in the Roman World: Pompeii and beyond, 1997; The British School at Rome: one hundred years, 2001; Rome's Cultural Revolution, 2008; Herculaneum: past and future, 2011.

WALLARD, Prof. Andrew John, CBE 2011; PhD; Director, International Bureau of Weights and Measures, 2004–10, now Emeritus Director (Director Designate, 2002–03); *b* 11 Oct. 1945; *s* of late William John Wallard and of Marjorie Meredith Wallard (*née* Briggs); *m* 1969, Barbara Jean Pritchard; two *s*. *Educ:* Liverpool Inst. High Sch. for Boys; Univ. of St Andrews (BSc Hons 1968; PhD 1971). CPhys 1990; CEng 2000; FInstP 2000. Laser physicist, NPL, 1968–78; Chief Scientist's Unit, DTI, 1978–80; Mktg Unit, NPL, 1980–81; Department of Trade and Industry, 1981–90: Res. and Technol. Policy Div.; Sec. of State's Policy Unit; Electronics Applications Div.; Alvey/Information Engrg Directorate; ESPRIT prog.; Dep. Dir and Chief Metrologist, NPL, 1990–2002. Member: Central Policy Review Staff, 1980–82; Panel, CSSB, 1985–95; Steering Cttee, Ilkley R&D Conf., 1988–2002; Internat. Cttee for Weights and Measures, 1995–2002 (President Consultative Committee: for Photometry and Radiometry, 1995–2002; for Acoustics, Ultrasound and Vibration, 1999–2003); Bd Mem., Nat. Conf. of Standards Labs Internat., 2002–10. Council Mem., 1998–2001, Chm., 2001–03, Res. and Develt Soc.; Vice Pres., Inst. of Physics, 2001–04 (Council Mem., 1996–2001); Member, Science Council: Istituto di Metrologia "Gustavo Colonnetti", 2002–10; Istituto Elettrotecnico "Galileo Ferraris", 2002–10. Mem., Ext. Panel, Physics Dept, Univ. of Wales, Aberystwyth, subseq. Aberystwyth Univ., 1997–2010 (Hon. Vis. Prof., 2001–). Hon. Ed., Kaye and Laby (a table of physical and chem. constants), 2014–. Chm., Alice Ruston Housing Assoc., 1986–95; Mem., Send PCC, 1988–95; Gov., Send First Sch., 1995–99. FRSA. Fellow: Acad. of Scis of Turin, 2003; Russian Acad. of Metrology, 2007. Hon. DSc Huddersfield, 1999. Lifetime Achievement Award, Co. of Scientific Instrument Makers, 2000; Gold Medal, NPL, 2002; Wildhack Award, Nat. Conf. of Standards Laboratories Internat., 2009. *Publications:* contribs to various books and over 40 contribs to learned jls. *Recreations:* reading the newspapers, the garden, choosing wines, choral evensong. *Address:* Bureau International des Poids et Mesures, Pavillon de Breteuil, 92312, Sèvres Cedex, France. *T:* (1) 4507 7070, *Fax:* (1) 4534 8670. *E:* andrew.wallard@gmail.com; Mas Vacquier - La Bergerie, St André d'Olérargues, Gard 30330, France. *Club:* Athenæum.

WALLENBERG, Jacob; Chairman of the Board, Investor AB, since 2005; *b* 13 Jan. 1956; *s* of late Peter Wallenberg, Hon. KBE and Suzanne Fleming; one *s* two *d*. *Educ:* Wharton Sch., Univ. of Pennsylvania (BSc Econ 1980; MBA 1981). Officer, Swedish Naval Reserve. Joined J. P. Morgan, NY, 1981; Hambros Bank, London, 1983; Enskilda Securities, London, 1984, then with Skandinaviska Enskilda Banken, Sweden, 1985; Exec. Vice Pres., Investor AB, 1990–92; rejoined Skandinaviska Enskilda Bank Gp, 1993: Dep. Chief Operating Officer, 1994, Chief Operating Officer, 1995–97, Enskilda Div.; Pres. and CEO, 1997–98; Chm. of Bd, 1998–2005; Vice-Chm., 2005–. Vice Chairman: Atlas Copco, 1998–; SAS, 2001–; Scandinavian Airlines, 2001–; Board Member: ABB Ltd, 1999–; Coca-Cola Co., 2007–14; Ericsson, 2011–. Mem. Bd, Knut and Alice Wallenberg Foundn, 1985–. *Recreations:* golf, sailing, ski-ing. *Address:* Investor AB, 10332 Stockholm, Sweden. *T:* (8) 6142000.

WALLENBERG, Marcus; Chairman: Skandinaviska Enskilda Banken, since 2005 (a Deputy Chairman, 2002–05); Saab AB, since 2006 (Vice Chairman, 1993–2006); Luossavaara-Kiirunavaara AB, since 2011; *b* 2 Sept. 1956; *s* of Marc and Olga Wallenberg; *m* Fanny Sachs; four *c*. *Educ:* Georgetown Univ., Washington (BSc Foreign Service). Lieut, Royal Swedish Naval Acad., 1977. Citibank NA, New York, 1980–82; Deutsche Bank AG, Frankfurt and Hamburg, 1983; S. G. Warburg Co. Ltd, London, 1983; Citicorp, Hong Kong, 1984; Skandinaviska Enskilda Banken, Stockholm and London, 1985–90; Dir, Stora Feldmuhle AG, Dusseldorf, 1990–93; Investor AB: Exec. Vice Pres., 1993–99; Pres. and Chief Exec., 1999–2005. Chm., Electrolux, 2007–14 (Dir, 2005–07); Vice Chm., L. M. Ericsson. Holds numerous directorships. *Recreations:* sports, tennis, sailing, ski-ing, hunting. *Address:* Skandinaviska Enskilda Banken, Kungsträdgårdsgatan 8, 10640 Stockholm, Sweden.

WALLER, Gary Peter Anthony; business analyst; *b* 24 June 1945; *s* of late John Waller and Elizabeth Waller. *Educ:* Rugby Sch.; Lancaster Univ. (BA Hons 1967); Open Univ. Business Sch. (MBA 2001). Chairman: Lancaster Univ. Conservative Assoc., 1965; Spen Valley Civic Soc., 1978–80; Vice-Chm., Nat. Assoc. of Cons. Graduates, 1970–73 and 1976–77. Exec. Sec., Wider Share Ownership Council, 1973–76. Contested (C): Kensington, Bor. Council elecns, 1971, 1974; Leyton, GLC elecn, 1973; Rother Valley, parly elecn, Feb. and Oct. 1974. MP (C) Brighouse and Spenborough, 1979–83, Keighley, 1983–97; contested (C) Keighley, 1997. PPS to Sec. of State for Transport, 1982–83. Chm., Select Cttee on Information,

1992–97 (Mem., 1991–97); Member: H of C Select Cttee on Transport, 1979–82; Jt Cttee on Consolidation Bills, 1982–92; Select Cttee on Finance and Services, 1992–97; Chm., All Party Wool Textile Gp, 1984–89 (Sec., 1979–83); Vice-Chairman: Parly Food and Health Forum, 1985–97; Parly IT Cttee, 1987–97 (Treas., 1981–87); Cons. Parly Transport Cttee, 1992–94, 1996–97 (Sec., 1985–87, 1988–92); Secretary: Cons. Parly Sport and Recreation Cttee, 1979–81; Yorkshire Cons. Members, 1979–83; All-Party Rugby League Gp, 1989–97; Chm., Cons. Technology Forum, 2000–04; Hon. Secretary: Parly and Scientific Cttee, 1988–91; Parly Univs Gp, 1995–97. Lay Mem., Dental Complaints Service Adv. Bd, GDC, 2006–14. President: Brighouse Citizens Advice Bureau, 1979–83; Harlow Cons. Assoc., 2008–; Vice-President: Newham S Cons. Assoc., 1979–95 (Chm., 1971–74); Keighley Cons. Assoc., 1998–. Vice-President: Trading Standards Inst. (formerly Inst. of Trading Standards Admin), 1988–; Keighley Sea Cadets, 1984–97; Friends of the Settle-Carlisle Railway, 1987–; AMA, 1992–97. Council Mem., Consumers' Assoc., 1995–2011; Dir, Which? Ltd, 2002–04, 2006–11. Chm., Gustav Mahler Soc. UK, 2012–. Member: Hatfield Heath Parish Council, 2008–; (C) Epping Forest DC, 2011– (Safer, Greener and Transport Portfolio Holder, 2012–). Chm., Epping Forest Dist Community Safety Partnership, 2012–; Mem., Essex Police and Crime Panel, 2012–. Chm., Southern Gp, Yorks CCC, 2004–06. FRSA 2005. *Recreations:* music, photography, sport, classic cars, 19th and 20th century decorative arts. *Address:* Monksfield, Sawbridgeworth Road, Hatfield Heath, Bishop's Stortford, Herts CM22 7DR. *T:* (01279) 739345. *E:* gary.waller@which.net. *Club:* Carlton.

WALLER, Rt Hon. Sir (George) Mark, Kt 1989; PC 1996; Lord Justice of Appeal, 1996–2010; Vice-President, Court of Appeal (Civil Division), 2006–10; Intelligence Services Commissioner, since 2011; *b* 13 Oct. 1940; *s* of Rt Hon. Sir George Waller, OBE; *m* 1967, Rachel Elizabeth, *d* of His Honour Christopher Beaumont, MBE; two *s* (and one *s* decd). *Educ:* Oundle Sch.; Durham Univ. (LLB). Called to the Bar, Gray's Inn, 1964, Bencher, 1988 (Vice-Treas., 2008; Treas. 2009); QC 1979; a Recorder, 1986–89; a Judge of the High Court of Justice, QBD, 1989–96; Presiding Judge, NE Circuit, 1992–95; Judge i/c Commercial List, 1995–96. Chm., Judicial Studies Bd, 1999–2003. Pres., Council of Inns of Court, 2003–06. *Recreations:* tennis, golf. *Address:* Serle Court, 6 New Square, Lincoln's Inn, WC2A 3QS. *Clubs:* Garrick, MCC; Huntercombe Golf.
See also R. B. Waller.

WALLER, Guy de Warrenne, MA, MSc; Headmaster, Cranleigh School, 1997–2014; *b* 10 Feb. 1950; *s* of late Col Desmond de Warrenne Waller and of Angela Mary Waller (*née* Wright); *m* 1980, Hilary Ann Farmbrough; four *d*. *Educ:* Hurstpierpoint Coll.; Worcester Coll., Oxford (MA; Hon. Sec., OUCC; cricket blue, 1974; hockey blue, 1974, 1979); Wolfson Coll., Oxford (MSc). Head of Chemistry and Housemaster, Radley Coll., 1974–93; Headmaster, Lord Wandsworth Coll., 1993–97. *Publications:* Thinking Chemistry, 1980; Advancing Chemistry, 1982; Condensed Chemistry, 1985. *Recreations:* sports, keeping up with family and friends, chess, music. *Clubs:* MCC; Vincent's (Oxford); Oxford University Tennis.

WALLER, Sir (John) Michael, 10th Bt *cr* 1780, of Newport, Co. Tipperary; PhD; Provost, National Security Enterprise, since 2014; *b* 14 May 1962; *s* of Sir Robert William Waller, 9th Bt and Carol Anne Waller (*née* Hines); *S* father, 2000; *m* 1986, Maria Renee Gonzalez (marr. diss. 2012); four *s* three *d*. *Educ:* George Washington Univ. (BA 1985); Boston Univ. (MA 1989; PhD 1993). Vice Pres., Center for Security Policy, Washington, DC, 2000–; Walter and Leonore Annenberg Prof. of Internat. Communication, Inst. of World Politics, Washington, DC, 2001–13. *Publications:* The Third Current of Revolution, 1991; Secret Empire: the KGB in Russia today, 1994; The Public Diplomacy Reader, 2007; Strategic Influence, 2007. *Heir: s* John Michael Waller, *b* 18 Feb. 1990.

WALLER, Rt Hon. Sir Mark; *see* Waller, Rt Hon. Sir G. M.

WALLER, Sir Michael; *see* Waller, Sir J. M.

WALLER, Peter Graham; political researcher and voluntary worker, since 2008; Director, Energy Group, Department for Business, Enterprise and Regulatory Reform (formerly Department of Trade and Industry), 2004–08; *b* 3 Jan. 1954; *s* of Raymond and Phyllis Waller; *m* 1991, Erica Zimmer. *Educ:* King's Sch., Macclesfield; Mansfield Coll., Oxford (BA Jurisp. 1976). Dept of Prices and Consumer Protection, subseq. Departments of Industry and of Trade, then Department of Trade and Industry, 1976–2001: various posts incl. Private Sec. to Minister of Consumer Affairs, 1981–83; privatisation of Rolls Royce, British Steel and water industry, 1987–91; Dir, Mkt Intelligence Unit, 1990–91; policy on future of PO, 1991–95; Dir, Business Links Services, 1995–97, Business Links, 1997–99; Dep. Chief Exec., Small Business Service, 2000–01; Dep. Dir Gen., Oftel, 2002–03. *Recreations:* watching lower league football, gardening, Shakespeare, walking in London. *Address:* 22 Grove Park, Wanstead, E11 2DL. *E:* petergwaller@btinternet.com.

WALLER, Philip Anthony, CBE 2011; **His Honour Judge Philip Waller;** a Circuit Judge, since 2013; *b* 12 Oct. 1952; *s* of late Robert Waller and of Olive (*née* Deakin); *m* 1978, Linda Andrews; two *d*. *Educ:* Whitgift Sch.; Univ. of Exeter (LLB Hons 1974); Inns of Court Sch. of Law. Called to the Bar, Inner Temple, 1975, Bencher, 2011; with Reed, Smith, Shaw & McClay, Attorneys, Pittsburgh, USA, 1976; practised London, 1977–93; a District Judge, 1994–2004; Sen. District Judge of the Family Div., 2004–13; a Recorder, 2009–13. Adv. editor, Atkin's Court Forms, 2010–. *Publications:* (co-ed) Rayden and Jackson's Law and Practice in Divorce and Family Matters, 17th edn 1997, 18th edn 2005. *Recreations:* choral singing, early music, historic houses and gardens, wine, France. *Address:* Watford County Court, 3rd Floor, Cassiobury House, 11–19 Station Road, Watford WD17 1EZ.

WALLER, Rev. Dr Ralph; Principal, and Tutor in Theology, Harris Manchester (formerly Manchester) College, since 1988, and Pro-Vice-Chancellor, since 2010, University of Oxford; Director, Farmington Institute for Christian Studies, since 2001; *b* 11 Dec. 1945; *s* of Christopher Waller and Ivy (*née* Miller); *m* 1968, Carol Roberts; one *d*. *Educ:* John Leggott Grammar Sch., Scunthorpe; Richmond Coll. Divinity Sch., Univ. of London (BD); Univ. of Nottingham (MTh); King's Coll. London (PhD 1986); MA Oxon. VSO in India, teaching maths and PE, and House Master, Shri Shivajh Mil. Sch., Poona, 1967–68; Maths Master, Riddings Comprehensive Sch., Scunthorpe, 1968–69; Methodist Minister, Melton Mowbray, 1972–75; ordained, 1975; Minister, Elvet Methodist Ch, Durham City, and Methodist Chaplain, Univ. of Durham, 1975–81; Chaplain, St Mary's Coll. and St Aidan's Coll., Univ. of Durham, 1979–81; Chaplain, Tutor in Theol. and Resident Tutor, Westminster Coll., Oxford, 1981–88; University of Oxford: Chm., Faculty of Theol., 1995–97; Chm., Envmtl Cttee, 1997–2000; Mem., Hebdomadal Council, 1997–2000; Chm., Curators of the Univ. Parks, 2010–. Gov., Cumberland Lodge, 2007–. Hon. Fellow, Homerton Coll., Cambridge, 2011–. Hon. DLitt Menlo Coll., Calif, 1994; Hon. DHum: Ball State Univ., Indiana, 1998; St Olaf, 2001; Indianapolis, 2006; Hon. DTheol Uppsala, 1999; Hon. DHL Christopher Newport, 2005; Hon. DD Hartwick, 2003. UK Templeton Prize, 1993. *Publications:* (contrib.) Truth, Liberty and Religion, 1986; (ed with Benedicta Ward) Christian Spirituality, 1999; John Wesley: a personal portrait, 2003; (ed with Benedicta Ward) Joy of Heaven, 2003. *Recreations:* swimming, walking, browsing round second-hand bookshops. *Address:* Harris Manchester College, Mansfield Road, Oxford OX1 3TD. *T:* (01865) 271006. *Club:* Oxford and Cambridge.

WALLER, Richard Beaumont; QC 2012; *b* London, 5 Dec. 1969; *s* of Rt Hon. Sir (George) Mark Waller, *qv*; *m* 1997, Katharine; three *s* one *d*. *Educ:* Radley Coll.; Trinity Coll., Cambridge (BA 1992). Called to the Bar, Gray's Inn, 1994. *Recreations:* cricket, golf, pub walks. *Address:* 35 Chalcot Crescent, NW1 8YE. *T:* (020) 7722 1529, 07971 414469. *E:* rwaller@7kbw.co.uk. *Club:* Brooks's.

WALLER, Stephen Philip; His Honour Judge Stephen Waller; a Circuit Judge, since 1996; *b* 2 Jan. 1950; *s* of Ronald Waller and Susannah Waller; *m* 1st, 1974, Anne Brooksbank (marr. diss.); one *s* one *d*; 2nd, 1986, Jennifer Welch; one *d*. *Educ:* Mill Hill Sch.; University College London (LLB Hons). Called to the Bar, Inner Temple, 1972.

WALLERSTEINER, Dr Anthony Kurt; Headmaster, Stowe School, since 2003; *b* 7 Aug. 1963; *m* 1994, Valerie Anne Macdougall-Jones; one *s* two *d*. *Educ:* King's Sch., Canterbury (Sen. Schol.); Trinity Coll., Cambridge (Open Schol.; BA Hist. Tripos 1985; MA 1993); Univ. of Kent at Canterbury (PhD Hist. and Theory of Art 2001). Crawford Travelling Schol., 1984; Assistant Master: Bancroft's Sch., Woodford Green, 1986; Sherborne, 1986–89; St Paul's Sch., 1989–92; Hd of Hist., 1993–2000, Housemaster, 1999–2003, Tonbridge Sch. Council Mem., Tate St Ives, 2006–09. Governor: Ashfold Prep. Sch., 2004–; Winchester House Prep. Sch., 2004–; Summer Fields Prep. Sch., 2006–; Maidwell Sch., 2009–; Buckingham Sch., 2009–10. *Publications:* (contrib.) The Head Speaks, 2008; (contrib.) Cradles of Success: Britain's traditional public schools, 2008; contrib. reviews to Burlington Mag. *Recreations:* galleries, music, travel, family and friends. *Address:* Kinloss, Stowe, Buckingham MK18 5EH.

WALLEY, Joan Lorraine; Chairman, Aldersgate Group, since 2015; *b* 23 Jan. 1949; *d* of late Arthur Walley and Mary Walley; *m* 1980, Jan Ostrowski; two *s*. *Educ:* Biddulph Grammar School; Hull Univ. (BA); University Coll. Swansea (Dip. Community Work). Alcoholics Recovery Project, 1970–73; Swansea City Council, 1974–78; Wandsworth Borough Council, 1978–79; NACRO, 1979–82. Mem., Lambeth Borough Council, 1982–86 (Chair: Health and Consumer Services Cttee, 1982–86; Assoc. of London Authorities Public Protection Cttee, 1982–86). MP (Lab) Stoke-on-Trent N, 1987–2015. Opposition front-bench spokesman on envmtl protection, 1988–90, on transport, 1990–95; Chm., Envmtl Audit Select Cttee, 2010–15 (Mem., 1997–2010); Mem., Liaison Select Cttee, 2010–15; Vice-Chairman: All Party Football Gp, 1997–2000 and 2005–15; All Party Eur. Gp, 2001–12; Chairman: All Party Lighting Gp, 2000–15; All Party Regeneration Gp, 2000–10; Associate Envmt Gp, 2002–05; Mem., Speaker's Panel, 2007–11. Vice-President: Inst. of Environmental Health Officers, 1987 (Life Mem.); Socialist Envmt and Resources Assoc. Member: UNISON; Globe Internat. Hon. Pres., 235 (1st Stoke-on-Trent) Sqn, ATC. Freeman, Kidsgrove Town Council. Patron, Haywood Acad. VI Form. Hon. Fellow, Keele Univ., 2015. Hon. Dr Staffs. *Clubs:* Fegg Hayes Sports and Social; Port Vale Supporters (Hon. Pres.).

WALLEY, Prof. Thomas Joseph, MD; CBE 2008; FRCP, FRCPI; FMedSci; Professor of Clinical Pharmacology, University of Liverpool, since 1994; *b* Dublin, 28 Aug. 1956; *s* of Thomas Walley and Margaret Walley. *Educ:* Belvedere Coll., Dublin; Nat. Univ. of Ireland (MB BCh BAO 1980; MD 1990). FRCPI 1993; FRCP 1995. Sen. Lectr in Clin. Pharmacol., Univ. of Liverpool, 1991–94. Consultant Physician, Royal Liverpool and Broadgreen Univ. Hosps Trust, 1991–. Director: NIHR Health Technol. Assessment Prog., 2004–15; NIHR Evaluation, Trials and Studies Prog., 2008–. FMedSci 2013. *Publications:* Medical Pharmacology, 1996, 3rd edn 2007; Regulation of Pharmaceuticals in Europe, 2004; Pharmacoeconomics, 2004; over 200 articles in learned jls. *Recreations:* sailing, Irish literature, military history. *Address:* University of Liverpool, 70 Pembroke Place, Liverpool L69 3GT. *T:* (0151) 794 8123, *Fax:* (0151) 794 8126. *E:* twalley@liv.ac.uk.

WALLFISCH, Raphael; 'cellist; *b* 15 June 1953; *s* of Peter Wallfisch, pianist and Anita Lasker-Wallfisch, 'cellist; *m* Elizabeth; two *s* one *d*. *Educ:* Univ. of Southern California; Royal Acad. of Music; studies with Amaryllis Fleming, Amadeo Baldovino, Derek Simpson and Gregor Piatigorsky. FRAM; FGS. London début, QEH, 1974. Professor: Zürcher Hochschule für Musik; RNCM. 1st recordings of compositions by Bax, Strauss and others; numerous other recordings. Won Gaspar Cassadó Internat. Cello competition, 1977.

WALLIAMS, David; *see* Williams, D. E.

WALLINGER, Mark; artist; *b* Chigwell, 1959. *Educ:* Loughton Coll.; Chelsea Sch. of Art; Goldsmiths' Coll., London (MA 1985). Contemporary artist; work includes painting, sculpture, photography, video and installations. Henry Moore Fellow, British Sch. at Rome, 1998; Artist-in-residence for Year of the Artist, Oxford Univ., 2000–01; represented GB at Venice Biennale, 2001; Artist-in-residence, Edinburgh Coll. of Art, 2008. Work in *group exhibitions* includes: Manchester City Art Galls, 1996; ICA, 1996; Royal Acad., 1997; Century City, Tate Modern, 2001; Sanctuary, Gall. of Modern Art, Glasgow, 2003; The End, Whitney Mus. of Amer. Art, NY, 2007; On Time, Courtauld Inst., 2008; Blink!, Denver Art Mus., 2011; Metamorphosis, Nat. Gall., 2012; *solo exhibitions* include: Serpentine Gall., London, Ikon Gall., Birmingham, 1995; Anthony Reynolds Gall., London, 1997, 2003, 2004, 2010, 2013; Canary Wharf Window Gall., 1997; Palais des Beaux Arts, Brussels, Portikus, Frankfurt, 1999; Ecce Homo, The Fourth Plinth, Trafalgar Sq., 1999; British Sch. at Rome, Tate Liverpool, 2000; Milton Keynes Gall., Southampton City Art Gall., Univ. Mus. of Natural Hist., Oxford, Whitechapel Art Gall., 2001; Christmas Tree, Tate Britain, 2003; Carlier Gebauer, Berlin, 2003, 2004, 2007, 2010; Laing Gall., Newcastle, Neue Nat. Gall., Berlin, 2004; Galerie Krinzinger, Vienna, 2005; Donald Young Gall., Chicago, 2007; State Britain, Tate Britain, 2007; Kunstnernes Hus, Oslo, 2010; Mus. De Pont, Tilburg, 2011; SITE, Baltic, Gateshead, 2012; Carlier Gebauer, Berlin, 2014. *Film:* The Lark Ascending, 2004. Designed set, Undance, Sadler's Wells, 2011. Hon. Fellow, London Inst., 2002. Hon. Dr UCE, 2003. Turner Prize, 2007. *Publications:* (with M. Warnock) Art for All?: their policies and our culture; (ed jtly) On the Border: contemporary artists in Essex and Suffolk. *Address:* c/o Hauser & Wirth, 23 Savile Row, W1S 2ET.

WALLINGTON, Peter Thomas; QC 2008; barrister; *b* Maidstone, Kent, 25 March 1947; *s* of Thomas Edwin and Doris Evelyn Wallington; *m* 1972, Barbara Alice Rowland. *Educ:* Hemel Hempstead Grammar Sch.; Trinity Hall, Cambridge (BA 1968; LLM 1969); Inns of Court Sch. of Law (Cert. of Hon. and CLE Scholar 1987). Lecturer in Law: Univ. of Edinburgh, 1969–72; Univ. of Liverpool, 1972–73; Asst Lectr, then Lectr in Law, Univ. of Cambridge, and Fellow, Trinity Hall, Cambridge, 1973–79; Prof. of Law, 1979–88, Hd, Dept of Law, 1979–86, Univ. of Lancaster; Prof. of Law and Hd, Dept of Law, Brunel Univ., 1988–91. Called to the Bar, Gray's Inn, 1987; in practice as barrister specialising in employment law; pt-time Employment Judge, London E Reg., 2003–09, Scotland, 2009–. Mem. editl team, Harvey on Industrial Relations and Employment Law, 2000–. *Publications:* Civil Liberties and a Bill of Rights (with Jeremy McBride), 1976; (ed) Butterworths Employment Law Handbook, 1979, 23rd edn 2015; (jtly) Labour Law Cases and Materials, 1980; (ed and contrib.) Civil Liberties 1984, 1984; (jtly) The Police, Public Order and Civil Liberties: legacies of the miners strike, 1988; (with R. G. Lee) Blackstone's Public Law Statutes, 1988, 18th edn 2008; (contrib.) Supperstone and Goudie on Judicial Review, 1992, 3rd edn 2005; (contrib.) Tolley's Employment Law Handbook, 9th edn 1995 to 29th edn 2015. *Recreations:* music, walking, reading. *Address:* c/o 11 KBW Chambers, 11 King's Bench Walk, Temple, EC4Y 7EQ. *T:* (020) 7632 8500. *E:* peter.wallington@11kbw.com.

WALLINGTON, Susan Margaret; *see* Bullock, S. M.

WALLIS, (Diana) Lynn, OBE 2015; Artistic Director, Royal Academy of Dance (formerly of Dancing), since 1994; *b* 11 Dec. 1946; *d* of Dennis Blackwell Wallis and Joan Wallis. *Educ:* Tonbridge Grammar Sch. for Girls; Royal Ballet Upper Sch. FISTD. Royal Ballet Touring Co., 1965–68; Royal Ballet School: Ballet Mistress, 1969–81; Dep. Principal, 1981–84; National Ballet of Canada: Artistic Co-ordinator, 1984–86; Associate Artistic Dir, 1986–87; Co-Artistic Dir, 1987–89; Dep. Artistic Dir, English National Ballet, 1990–94. *Recreations:* music, theatre, cinema.

WALLIS, Diana Paulette; Member (Lib Dem) Yorkshire and the Humber, 1999–Jan. 2012, and Vice President, 2007–12, European Parliament; President, European Law Institute, since 2013; *b* 28 June 1954; *d* of John Frederick Wallis and Jean Elizabeth Wallis (*née* Jones); *m* 1989, Stewart David Arnold. *Educ:* N London Poly. (BA Hist.); Univ. of Kent at Canterbury (MA Local Govt); Coll. of Law, Chester. Admitted Solicitor, 1983. Mem. (Lib Dem) Humberside CC, subseq. E Riding of Yorks UA, 1994–99 (Dep. Leader, 1995–99). European Parliament: Member: Legal Affairs Cttee, 1999–2012; Petitions Cttee, 2004–12; Vice-Pres., delegn to Switzerland, Iceland and Norway, 1999–2004; Pres., delegn to Switzerland, Iceland, Norway and Eur. Econ. Area, 2004–07; Leader, Lib Dem European Parly Party, 2002–04, 2006–07. Accredited Mediator, 2012; MCIArb 2012. Hon. Sen. Fellow, Univ. of Hull Law Sch., 2013–. Mem. Bd, Internat. Mediation Inst., 2012–. Pres., Inst. of Translation and Interpreting, 2002–10. *Club:* National Liberal.

WALLIS, Edmund Arthur, CBE 2015; FREng; Chairman, Natural Environment Research Council, 2007–14; *b* 3 July 1939; *s* of late Reuben Wallis and of Iris Mary Cliff; *m* 1964, Gillian Joan Mitchell; two *s*. CEng 1978; MIET (MIEE 1971); MIMechE 1972; FREng (FEng 1995). Central Electricity Generating Board: Stn Manager, Oldbury Nuclear Power Stn, 1977–79; Dir of System Op., 1981–86; Divl Dir of Ops, 1986–88; PowerGen, subseq. Powergen: Chief Exec., 1988–2001 and 2002–03; Chm., 1996–2002; Dep. Chm., 2002–03. Chm., WS Atkins, 2005–10 (Dir, 2004–10); non-executive Director: BSI, 1992–97; LucasVarity plc, 1995–99 (Chm., 1998–99); London Transport, 1999–2003 (Chm., 2001–03); Ind. non-exec. Dir, Mercury European Privatisation Trust plc, 1994–2004; Mem. Adv. Bd, RWE, Germany, 1994–98. Lay Mem. Council, Aston Univ., 1992–98. Chm., Birmingham Royal Ballet Sch., 1996–2004; Mem. Bd, Birmingham Royal Ballet, 2005–; Gov., Royal Ballet Sch., 2006–. CCMI (CBIM 1991; AMBIM 1973).

WALLIS, Eithne Victoria, CB 2004; Managing Director, Government Business (formerly Central Government Business Unit), Fujitsu Services UK, 2005–11; *b* 14 Dec. 1952; *d* of Ewing Walsh and late Marion Walsh; *m* 1st, 1977, Phillip Wallis (marr. diss. 2001); one *s* two *d*; 2nd, 2006, Baron Birt, *qv*. *Educ:* High Sch. for Girls, Dungannon, NI; Manchester Univ. (BA Econ 1973; MA Social Studies 1979). Probation Officer, 1979–87, mgt, 1987–94, Manchester; Asst Chief Probation Officer, Cambs, 1991–94; Dep. Chief Probation Officer, Inner London, 1994–97; Chief Probation Officer, Oxon and Bucks, 1997–2000; on secondment to Home Office, 2000; led team which created Nat. Probation Service for England and Wales, Dir Gen., 2001–04; Sen. Partner, Fujitsu Services UK, 2005. *Recreations:* reading, walking, gardening.

WALLIS, Frederick Alfred John E.; *see* Emery-Wallis.

WALLIS, (George James) Stewart, OBE 2002; Executive Director, new economics foundation, since 2003; *b* 29 Aug. 1948; *s* of George and Jean Wallis; *m* 1987, Mary Jane Wallis; four *d* and one step *s*. *Educ:* Fitzwilliam Coll., Cambridge (MA Natural Sci. Tripos); London Business School (MSc Business and Econs 1976). Geologist and Financial Analyst, Rio Tinto Zinc Corp. Ltd, 1970–74; Industrial and Finance Economist, E Asia and Adminr Young Professional Prog., World Bank, Washington, DC, 1976–83; Dir and Gen. Manager, Special Products, 1983–86, Man. Dir, 1987–92, Robinson Packaging; Dep. Dir and Internat. Dir, Oxfam, 1992–2002; Livelihoods Dir, Oxfam GB and Livelihoods Lead, Oxfam Internat., 2002–03. Trustee: Overseas Develt Inst.; New Econs Inst. *Publications:* (contrib.) Democracy and Capitalism, 2006; (contrib.) Surviving the Century, 2007; (with S. Spratt) From old economics to new economics: radical reform and a sustainable future, 2007. *Recreations:* landscape photography, walking, reading, cinema. *Address:* new economics foundation, 3 Jonathan Street, SE11 5NH. *T:* (020) 7820 6321. *E:* Stewart.wallis@neweconomics.org.

WALLIS, Prof. Kenneth Frank, FBA 1994; Professor of Econometrics, University of Warwick, 1977–2001, now Emeritus; *b* 26 March 1938; *s* of late Leslie Wallis and Vera Daisy Wallis (*née* Stone); *m* 1963, Margaret Sheila Campbell; one *d* by previous partner. *Educ:* Wath-on-Dearne GS; Manchester Univ. (BSc, MScTech); Stanford Univ. (PhD). Mem. Exec., NUS, 1961–63. Lectr, then Reader, in Stats, LSE, 1966–77; Dir, ESRC Macroeconomic Modelling Bureau, 1983–99. Member: HM Treasury Academic Panel, 1980–2001 (Chm., 1987–91); Nat. Statistics Methodology Adv. Cttee, 2001–11. Member Council: Royal Stat. Soc., 1972–76; Royal Econ. Soc., 1989–94; Econometric Soc., 1995–97 (Fellow, 1975); British Acad., 2002–05. Fellow, Internat. Inst. of Forecasters, 2003. Hon. Dr Groningen, 1999. *Publications:* Introductory Econometrics, 1972; Topics in Applied Econometrics, 1973; (ed with D. F. Hendry) Econometrics and Quantitative Economics, 1984; Models of the UK Economy 1–4, 1984–87; (ed) Macroeconometric Modelling, 1994; Time Series Analysis and Macroeconometric Modelling, 1995; (ed with D. M. Kreps) Advances in Economics and Econometrics: theory and applications, 1997; articles in learned jls. *Recreations:* travel, music, gardening, swimming. *Address:* Department of Economics, University of Warwick, Coventry CV4 7AL. *T:* (024) 7652 3055. *E:* K.F.Wallis@warwick.ac.uk; 4 Walkers Orchard, Stoneleigh, Warwicks CV8 3JG. *T:* (024) 7641 4271.

WALLIS, Lynn; *see* Wallis, D. L.

WALLIS, Maria Assumpta, QPM 2002; Chief Constable, Devon and Cornwall Constabulary, 2002–06; *b* 13 Aug. 1955; *d* of late Philip and Margaret O'Donnell; *m* 1983, Michael Wallis. *Educ:* Bristol Univ. (BSc Jt Hons Sociol. and Social Admin). Metropolitan Police, 1976–94; Asst, then Dep. Chief Constable, Sussex Police, 1994–2002. *Recreations:* gardening, walking, reading. *Address:* c/o Devon and Cornwall Constabulary, Police HQ, Middlemoor, Exeter EX2 7HQ.

WALLIS, Sir Peter (Gordon), KCVO 1992; CMG 1990; HM Diplomatic Service, retired; High Commissioner to Malta, 1991–94; *b* 2 Aug. 1935; *s* of late Arthur Gordon Wallis, DFC, BScEcon, and Winifred Florence Maud Wallis (*née* Dingle); *m* 1965, Delysia Elizabeth (*née* Leonard); three *s* one *d*. *Educ:* Taunton and Whitgift Schools; Pembroke Coll., Oxford (MA). Ministry of Labour and National Service, 1958; HM Customs and Excise, 1959 (Private Sec., 1961–64); HM Diplomatic Service, 1968; Tel Aviv, 1970; Nairobi, 1974; Counsellor (Econ. and Comm.), Ankara, 1977; RCDS, 1981; Cabinet Office, 1982; Hd, Perm. Under-Sec.'s Dept, FCO, 1983; Minister, Pretoria, 1987; Minister, British Liaison Office, 1989, and subseq. Acting High Comr, 1990, Windhoek, Namibia; Political Advr to Jt Comdr, British Forces in the Gulf, Jan.–April 1991, to Comdr, British Forces, SE Turkey and N Iraq, May–July 1991. Advr to Learmont Enquiry into Prison Security, 1995. Head, UK delegn to EC monitor mission, Balkans, 1996, 1997, 1998, 1999. Member: Regl Adv. Council, subseq. Regl Audience Council, BBC West, 2005–09; Readers' Panel, Economist, 2010–. Chm., 2004–07, Pres., 2009–, Taunton and Dist Br., ESU. Mem., Taunton Area Cttee, Somerset CCC, 2005–11 (Vice-Chm., 2006–09; Actg Chm., 2009). Trustee: Friends of Somerset Churches, 2007–14; Somerset Cricket Mus., 2009– (Chm., 2014–). *Recreations:* reading, music, walking. *Address:* Parsonage Farm, Curry Rivel, Somerset TA10 0HG.

WALLIS, Peter Ralph; Deputy Controller, Aircraft Weapons and Electronics, Ministry of Defence, 1980–84; *b* 17 Aug. 1924; *s* of Leonard Francis Wallis and Molly McCulloch Wallis (*née* Jones); *m* 1949, Frances Jean Patricia Cowie; three *s* one *d*. *Educ:* University College Sch., Hampstead; Imperial Coll. of Science and Technology, London (BScEng). CEng 1967; FIET (FIEE 1967); FIMA 1968. Henrici and Siemens Medals of the College, 1944. Joined Royal Naval Scientific Service 1944; work at Admty Signal and Radar Estab. till 1959, Admty Underwater Weapons Estab. till 1968; Asst Chief Scientific Advr (Research), MoD, 1968–71, Dir Gen. Research Weapons, 1971–75, Dir Gen. Guided Weapons and Electronics, 1975–78, Dir Gen. Research A (Electronics) and Dep. Chief Scientist (Navy), 1978–80. Vice Pres., Hampstead Scientific Soc., 1992– (Hon. Sec., 1974–90; Hon. Treas., 1988–2009). FCGI. Marconi Award, IERE, 1964. *Publications:* articles in Jl of IEE, IERE and Op. Res. Quarterly. *Recreations:* ski-ing, mountain walking, archæology, sailing, egyptology, geology, travel. *Address:* 22 Flask Walk, Hampstead, NW3 1HE. *Clubs:* Alpine Ski, Eagle Ski.

WALLIS, Peter Spencer; a District Judge (Magistrates' Courts) (formerly Metropolitan Stipendiary Magistrate), 1993–2010; a Recorder, 2000–15; a Deputy Judge Advocate, 2008–15; *b* 31 March 1945; *s* of Philip Wallis and Winifred Wallis; *m* 1970, Ann Margaret Bentham; one *s* one *d*. *Educ:* Maidstone Grammar Sch.; Lincoln Coll., Oxford (MA). Pilot, RAF, 1967–72. Admitted solicitor, 1976. Clerk to: Tonbridge and Malling Justices, 1977–88; Dover and Ashford Justices, 1988–93; Folkestone and Hythe Justices, 1990–93. An Asst Recorder, 1997–2000. Mem. Council, Justices' Clerks' Soc., 1983–93 (Pres., 1993). *Publications:* The Transport Acts 1981 and 1982, 1982, 2nd edn 1985; Road Traffic: guide to Part I of the 1991 Act, 1991; General Editor, Wilkinson's Road Traffic Offences, 13th edn 1987 to 23rd edn 2007, Consultant Editor, 24th edn 2009 to 26th edn 2013. *Recreations:* flying, watching cricket, choral singing. *Club:* Royal Air Force.

WALLIS, Robert; Chief Executive, Transport Research Foundation and TRL Ltd, since 2013; *b* Bishop's Stortford, Herts, 11 July 1964; *s* of George and Catherine Ann Wallis; *m* 2009, Dr Julie Mullan. *Educ:* Leventhorpe Secondary Sch.; Cass Business Sch. (Strategic Thought Leadership and Innovation Prog. (Corporate) 2006). Shift Leader, ICT Data Centre and Ops, CAA, 1980–88; Internat. Sales and Prog. Delivery, EDS Inc., 1988–97; EDS Systems Engr Graduating Prog., 1989; Man. Dir, Transport Logistics and Commercial, CMG, 1997–2002; Dir, UK Business Develt, LogicaCMG, 2002–05; Man. Dir, Transport, EDS Inc., 2005–07; Hd of Transport, Hedra plc, 2007–08; Man. Dir, BSI, 2008–12. FInstD 2001; FCIHT 2013. *Address:* TRL Ltd, Crowthorne House, Nine Mile Ride, Wokingham, Berks RG40 3GA. *T:* (01344) 770001. *E:* rob.wallis@trl.co.uk.

WALLIS, Dame Sheila (Ann), DBE 2002; Director and Education Consultant, Wallis Partnership Ltd, since 2002; *b* 13 Feb. 1940; *d* of John and Lilian Pearson; *m* 1964, Brian Wallis; two *s*. *Educ:* Chelsea Sch. of Human Movt; Univ. of London (BEd); Univ. of Brighton (MEd). Physical education teacher: Kings Manor Sch., Shoreham, 1962–64; Bognor Regis Grammar Sch., 1964–66; Davison High School for Girls: physical educn teacher, 1971–81; Dep. Headteacher, 1981–88; Headteacher, 1988–2002. Comr, NCC Commn into Public Services, 2003–. FRSA 1998. Hon. MEd Brighton, 2003. *Publications:* contribs to educn jls and govt papers. *Recreations:* jogging, swimming, travelling, cooking. *Address:* Drake House, River Road, Arundel, W Sussex BN18 9EY. *T:* and *Fax:* (01903) 882171.

WALLIS, Simon Philip Zbigniew, OBE 2015; Director, The Hepworth Wakefield, since 2008; *b* London, 7 Jan. 1967; *s* of Andrew Wallis and Malgosia Chelminska; *m* 2001, Deborah Marks; one *s* one *d*. *Educ:* Falmer Comp. Sch., Brighton; Varndean Sixth Form Coll., Brighton; Brighton Poly.; Chelsea Sch. of Art (BA Hons Fine Art); Univ. of Manchester (MA Art Gall. and Museum Studies). Curator: Kettle's Yard, Univ. of Cambridge, 1994–99; Tate Liverpool, 1999–2002; Sen. Exhibn Organiser, ICA, 2002–03; Dir, Chisenhale Gall., 2004–08. *Publications:* Hybrids, 2001; Remix, 2002; Folkert de Jong, 2004; Clare Woods, 2006; Philip Guston, 2006; Eva Rothschild, 2011. *Recreations:* photography, walking, jazz, chamber music, football, tennis, museums. *Address:* The Hepworth Wakefield, Gallery Walk, Wakefield, West Yorks WF1 5AW. *E:* simonwallis@hepworthwakefield.org.

WALLIS, Stewart; *see* Wallis, G. J. S.

WALLIS, Stuart Michael; Chairman: H. H. Associates, since 2010; Synseal Ltd, since 2011; Edif Ltd, since 2011; Ashridge Automobiles, since 2006; BCS Global Networks Ltd, since 2005; *b* 8 Oct. 1945; *s* of Stanley Oswald Wallis and Margaret Ethel Wallis; *m* 1971, Eileen; one *s*. *Educ:* Hawesdown Sch., West Wickham, Kent. FCA, CTA. Roland Goodman & Co., 1962–68; Chrysler, 1968–71; Shipton Automation, 1971–73; Star Computer Services, 1973–74; Hestair Gp, 1974–85 (Main Board, 1977); Exec. Dir, Octopus, 1985–87; Main Board Dir, Bowater plc, 1988–94; Chief Exec., Fisons plc, 1994–95; Chairman: Sheffield Forgemasters Ltd, 1996–98; LLP Gp, 1996–98; Yorkshire Gp, 1996–2000; SSL Internat., 1996–2001; John Mansfield Gp, then Communisis plc, 1997–2003; Euramax Internat., 1997–2005; Hay Hall Gp Ltd, 1997–2004; Protherics plc, 1999–2008; Trident Components Gp, 1999–2005; Tetley Group Ltd, 1999–2000; Eleksen Ltd (formerly ElektroTextiles), 2000–03; Worldmark Internat., 2000–02; Simply Smart Gp Ltd, 2004–08; Plethora Solutions Hldgs plc, 2005–10; TSL Education Ltd, 2005–07; LGC Hldgs Ltd, 2007–10; Egan Property Asset Mgt, 2011–13. *Recreations:* golf, swimming, ski-ing, fishing. *Club:* Ashridge Golf.

WALLIS, Sir Timothy (William), Kt 1994; Managing Director, Alpine Deer Group; *b* 9 Sept. 1938; *s* of Arthur Wallis and Janice Blunden; *m* 1974, Prudence Ann Hazledine; four *s*. *Educ:* Christ's Coll., Christchurch. Founding Dir, Tourism Holdings Ltd. Mem. Council, NZ Deer Farmers' Assoc., 1977–84 (Hon. Life Mem.); founding Chm. and Hon. Life Mem., NZ Wapiti Soc. DCom (*hc*) Lincoln Univ., 2000. E. A. Gibson Award, 1980, for contribs to NZ aviation; Sir Arthur Ward Award, 1985, for contribs to agric.; Commem. Medal for services to deer industry, 1990; Sir Jack Newman Award, 1999, for outstanding contrib. to NZ tourism industry; Speights Southern Man Award, 2001; Laureate, NZ Business Hall of Fame, 2002; World Wide Gold Medal, RAeS, 2005. *Relevant publications:* Hurricane Tim: the story of Sir Tim Wallis, by Neville Peat, 2005; (for children) Winging It: the adventures of Tim Wallis, by Neville Peat, 2006. *Recreations:* scuba diving, hunting, fly fishing; represented West Coast-Buller 1958, S Canterbury 1959, at Rugby. *Address:* Benfiddich, Mount Barker, Wanaka 9192, New Zealand.

WALLOP, family name of **Earl of Portsmouth**.

WALLS, Geoffrey Nowell; Executive Director, Pearls of the Orient (Wholesale) (formerly International) Ltd, since 2006; *b* 17 Feb. 1945; *s* of Andrew Nowell Walls and Hilda Margaret Thompson; *m* 1975, Vanessa Bodger; one *s* three *d*. *Educ:* Trinity Grammar Sch., Melbourne; Univ. of Melbourne (BComm 1965). Australian Regular Army, 2nd Lieut RAAOC, 1966–69; Australian Trade Comr Service, 1970–79; served Jakarta, Singapore, Cairo, Beirut, Bahrain, Manila, Baghdad; Regional Dir, Adelaide, Commonwealth Dept of Trade, 1980–83; Gen. Manager, ATCO Industries (Aust) Pty Ltd, 1983–86; Agent Gen. for S Australia in London, 1986–98. CIH Ltd (formerly Clipsal Industries (Holdings) Ltd): Regl Manager, Sharjah, 1998–2000; Regl Dir, 2000–02; Exec. Dir, 2002–05; non-exec. Dir, 2005–07. Mem., S Australian Cricket Assoc. *Recreations:* golf, tennis, gardening. *Address:* Bollards, Ropes Lane, Fernhurst, Surrey GU27 3JD.

WALLS, Stephen Roderick; Partner, Next Wave Partners LLP, since 2007; *b* 8 Aug. 1947; *s* of late R. W. Walls and of D. M. Walls; *m*; two *s*. Accountant. Senior Auditor, Deloitte & Co., 1969; Group Chief Accountant, Lindustries, 1971; Financial Planning Exec., Vernons, 1974; Chesebrough Ponds: Finance Dir, UK and Geneva, 1975; Internat. Finance Dir,

Geneva, 1981; Vice-Pres., Finance, 1981–87; Dir of Finance, 1987, Man. Dir, 1988–89, Plessey Co.; Chm., 1990–91, Chief Exec., 1990–92, Wiggins Teape Appleton, later Arjo Wiggins Appleton; Chm., The Albert Fisher Gp, 1992–97; Partner: Compass Partners Internat., 1998–2001; Bridley Capital Partners Ltd, 2001–05. Chairman: VPS Hldgs Ltd, 2003–10; Pourshins plc, 2004–07; Petainer, 2009–. Chm., CHASE Children's Hospice, 2004–09. Mem., Financial Reporting Council, 1990–95. *Recreations:* running, flying, horseriding, shooting. *Address:* c/o Next Wave Partners LLP, 42 Wigmore Street, W1U 2RY. *Club:* Royal Automobile.

WALLSTRÖM, Margot; Minister for Foreign Affairs, Sweden, since 2014; *b* 28 Sept. 1954; *m* 1984, Håkan Wallström; two *s*. *Educ:* Nordanå Upper Secondary Sch., Skellefteå. Adminr, Swedish Social Democratic Youth League, 1974–77; Accountant, 1977–79, Sen. Accountant, 1986–87, Alfa Savings Bank, Karlstad; MP (SDP), Sweden, 1979–85; Minister for: Civil Affairs, 1988–91; Culture, 1994–96; Health and Social Affairs, 1996–98; CEO, TV Värmland, 1993–94; Exec. Vice-Pres., Worldview Global Media, Sri Lanka, 1998–99. Mem., 1999–2010, a Vice-Pres., 2004–10, Eur. Commn; UN Special Rep. on Sexual Violence in Conflict, 2010–12. Mem. Exec. Cttee, Swedish SDP, 1993–99. Chm. Bd, Lund Univ., Sweden, 2012–14. Hon. Dr: Chalmers Univ., Sweden, 2001; Mälardalen Univ., Sweden, 2004. Comdr, Légion d'Honneur (France), 2014. *Publications:* (jtly) The People's Europe, or Why is it so Hard to Love the EU?, 2004. *Address:* Ministry for Foreign Affairs, Gustav Adolfs torg 1, 103 39 Stockholm, Sweden.

WALLWORK, John, CBE 2012; DL; FRCSE; Consultant Cardiothoracic Surgeon, Papworth Hospital, 1981–2011 (Director of Transplantation, 1989–2006; Medical Director, 1997–2002); Chairman, Papworth Hospital NHS Foundation Trust, since 2014; *b* 8 July 1946; *s* of Thomas and Vera Wallwork; *m* 1973, Elizabeth Ann Medley; one *s* two *d*. *Educ:* Accrington Grammar Sch.; Edinburgh Univ. (BSc Hons Pharm. 1966; MB ChB 1970); MA Cantab 1986. FRCSE 1974; FRCS 1992 *ad eundem*, FRCPE 1999, FRCP 2001. Surgical Registrar, Royal Infirmary, Edinburgh, 1975–76; Senior Registrar: Adelaide Hosp., SA, 1977–78; Royal Infirmary, Glasgow, 1978–79; St Bartholomew's Hosp., 1979–81; Chief Resident in Cardiovascular and Cardiac Transplant Surgery, Stanford Univ. Med. Sch., 1980–81. Hon. Prof. of Cardiothoracic Surgery, Cambridge Univ., 2002–11. Lister Prof., RCSE, 1985–86. FMedSci 2002. DL Cambs, 2007. *Publications:* (with R. Stepney) Heart Disease: what it is and how it is treated, 1987; (ed) Heart and Heart-Lung Transplantation, 1989; numerous papers on cardiothoracic and cardiopulmonary topics. *Recreations:* tennis, conversation, making phone calls from the bath. *Address:* 3 Latham Road, Cambridge CB2 7EG. *T:* (01223) 352827. *Club:* Sloane.

WALMSLEY, Baroness *cr* 2000 (Life Peer), of West Derby in the co. of Merseyside; **Joan Margaret Walmsley;** Director, Walmsley Jones Communications, 1999–2003; *b* 12 April 1943; *d* of Leo Watson and Monica Watson (*née* Nolan); *m* 1st, 1966, John Newan Caro Richardson (marr. diss. 1979); one *s* one *d*; 2nd, 1986, Christopher Roberts Walmsley (*d* 1995); one step *s* two step *d*; 3rd, 2005, Baron Thomas of Gresford, *qv*. *Educ:* Notre Dame High Sch., Liverpool; Univ. of Liverpool (BSc Hons Biology); Manchester Poly. (PGCE). Cytologist, Christie Hosp., Manchester, 1966–67; teacher, Buxton Coll., 1979–87; Mkting Officer, Ocean Youth Club, 1987–88; PR Consultant: Intercommunication, Manchester, 1988–89; Hill & Knowlton UK Ltd, 1989–97; Joan Walmsley Public Relations, 1997–99. Co-Chair, Lib Dem Parly Cttee on Educn, Young People and Families (formerly Lib Dem spokesman on educn and children), H of L, 2004–12; Conveyor of Lib Dem Papers, 2014–. *Recreations:* music, theatre, keeping fit, good company, gardening. *Address:* House of Lords, SW1A 0PW. *T:* (020) 7219 6047.

WALMSLEY, Brian; Under Secretary, Social Security Policy Group, Department of Social Security, 1990–94; *b* 22 April 1936; *s* of late Albert Edward Walmsley and Ivy Doreen Walmsley (*née* Black); *m* 1st, 1956, Sheila Maybury (marr. diss. 1993); two *d*; 2nd, 1994, Margaret Wilson. *Educ:* Prescot Grammar School. National Service, RAF, 1955–57. Joined Min. of Pensions and Nat. Insurance, 1957, later Min. of Social Security and DHSS; Sec. to Industrial Injuries Adv. Council, 1978–79; Asst Sec., 1979; Under Sec., 1985; Civil Service Comr, OMCS, Cabinet Office (on secondment), 1988–90. *Recreations:* following cricket, playing golf, reading, gardening. *Clubs:* MCC; Chester Golf.

WALMSLEY, Rt Rev. Francis Joseph, CBE 1979; Roman Catholic Bishop of the Forces, 1979–2002, now Bishop Emeritus; *b* 9 Nov. 1926; *s* of Edwin Walmsley and Mary Walmsley (*née* Hall). *Educ:* St Joseph's Coll., Mark Cross, Tunbridge Wells; St John's Seminary, Wonersh, Guildford. Ordained, 1953; Asst Priest, Woolwich, 1953; Shoreham-by-Sea, Sussex, 1958; Chaplain, Royal Navy, 1960; Principal RC Chaplain, RN, 1975; retired from RN, 1979. Prelate of Honour to HH Pope Paul VI, 1975; ordained Bishop, 1979. *Recreations:* photography, gardening. *Address:* St John's Convent, Kiln Green, Reading, Berks RG10 9XP.

WALMSLEY, Prof. Ian Alexander, PhD; FRS 2012; Hooke Professor of Physics, since 2005, and Pro-Vice-Chancellor (Research, Academic Services and University Collections), since 2011, University of Oxford; Fellow of St Hugh's College, Oxford, since 2001; *b* 13 Jan. 1960; *s* of Richard M. and Hazel F. Walmsley; *m* 1986, Katherine Frances Pardee; two *s* one *d*. *Educ:* Imperial Coll., Univ. of London (BSc 1980); Univ. of Rochester, NY (PhD 1986). Res. Associate, Cornell Univ., NY, 1986–88; Institute of Optics, University of Rochester, New York: Asst Prof., 1988–94, Associate Prof., 1994–98, Prof., 1998–2000, of Optics; Dir, 2000; Oxford University: Prof. of Exptl Physics, 2001–05; Head, Subdept of Atomic and Laser Physics, 2002–09; Pro-Vice-Chancellor (Res.), 2009–11. Vis. Prof. of Physics, Ulm Univ., 1995; Sen. Vis. Fellow, Princeton Univ., 2002–05. FInstP 2004; Fellow: Optical Soc. of America, 1997; APS, 2000. Dr *hc* Libre de Bruxelles, 2008. Leibinger Innovationspreis, Berthold Leibinger Stiftung, 2006; Wolfson Res. Merit Award, Royal Soc., 2007; Joseph Keithley Award, APS, 2011; Thomas Young Medal, Inst. of Physics, 2011. *Publications:* contrib. to books and professional jls. *Recreations:* Tae Kwon Do (4th dan, World Assoc.), cycling, choral music. *Address:* Department of Physics, University of Oxford, Clarendon Laboratory, Parks Road, Oxford OX1 3PU. *T:* (01865) 272205; University Offices, University of Oxford, Wellington Square, Oxford OX1 2JD.

WALMSLEY, Nigel Norman; Chairman, Broadcasters' Audience Research Board Ltd, 2002–13; Deputy Chairman, Authority for Television on Demand (formerly Association for Video on Demand), since 2010; *b* 26 Jan. 1942; *s* of late Norman and Ida Walmsley; *m* 1969, Jane Walmsley, broadcaster, author and producer; one *d*. *Educ:* William Hulme's Sch.; Brasenose Coll., Oxford (BA English). Joined the Post Office, 1964; Asst Private Secretary to Postmaster General, 1967; Asst Director of Marketing, Post Office, 1973–75; Asst Sec., Industrial Planning Division of Dept of Industry, 1975–76; Director of Marketing, Post Office, 1977–81, Board Mem. for Marketing, 1981–82; Man. Dir, Capital Radio, 1982–91; Chief Exec., 1991–94, Chm., 1994–2001, Carlton TV; Exec. Dir, 1992–2001, Dep. Chief Exec., 2000–01, Carlton Communications plc; Chm., GMTV, 1994–96, 2000–01. Chm., Tourism SE, 2003–09. Board Member: Ind. Radio News, 1983–91; South Bank Centre, 1985–92 and 1997–2002; Director: The Builder Gp, 1986–92; General Cable plc, 1994–97; non-exec. Chm., Central Television, 1996–2001; non-executive Director: Energis plc, 1997–2002; ONdigital, subseq. ITV Digital, plc, 1997–2001; ITN, 2000–01; Ambassador Theatre Gp, 2001–04; de Vere plc, 2001–06; Eagle Rock, 2007–14 (Chm., 2002–07). Member Council: ASA, 2004–11; Postwatch, 2006–08; Mem., Rail Passengers' Council (Passenger Focus), 2005–13; Member Board: Assoc. for Television On-Demand, 2010–; London Ambulance Service PCT, 2010–11. Chm., GLAA, 1985–86; Vice Chm., Advertising Assoc., 1992–2003. *Recreation:* intensive inactivity. *Address:* Authority for Television on Demand, 27 Sheen Street, Windsor, Berks SL4 1BN.

WALMSLEY, Peter James, MBE 1975; Director-General (formerly Director) of Petroleum Engineering Division, Department of Energy, 1981–89; *b* 29 April 1929; *s* of George Stanley and Elizabeth Martin Walmsley; *m* 1970, Edna Fisher; three *s* one *d*. *Educ:* Caterham Sch., Surrey; Imperial Coll., London (BSc; ARSM). Geologist: Iraq Petroleum Co., 1951–59; BP Trinidad, 1959–65; BP London, 1965–72; Exploration Manager, BP Aberdeen, 1972–78; Dep. Chief Geologist, BP London, 1978–79; Regional Exploration Manager, BP London, 1979–81. Chairman, Petroleum Exploration Soc. of Gt Britain, 1971–72; Pres., RSM Assoc., 1995–96. *Publications:* contribs to various learned jls on North Sea geology. *Recreation:* home and garden. *Address:* Elm Tree Cottage, 10 Great Austins, Farnham, Surrey GU9 8JG.

WALMSLEY, Sir Robert, KCB 1995; FREng, FIET; Chief of Defence Procurement, Ministry of Defence, 1996–2003; Chief Executive, Defence Procurement Agency, 1999–2003; *b* Aberdeen, 1 Feb. 1941; *s* of late Prof. Robert Walmsley, TD, FRCPE, FRCSE and Dr Isabel Mary Walmsley; *m* 1st, 1967 (marr. diss. 2009); one *s* two *d*; 2nd, 2010, Alexandra Ashbourne. *Educ:* Fettes Coll.; RN Coll., Dartmouth; Queens' Coll., Cambridge (MA MechScis); RN Coll., Greenwich (MSc Nuclear Sci.). FIET (FIEE 1994); FREng (FEng 1998). HMS Ark Royal, 1962–63; HMS Otus, 1964–66; HMS Churchill, 1968–72; Ship Dept, MoD, 1973–74; HM Dockyard, Chatham, 1975–78; MoD, PE, 1979–80; Chm., Naval Nuclear Technical Safety Panel, 1981–83; Naval Staff, 1984; MoD, PE, 1985–86; Dir Operational Requirements (Sea), 1987–89; ACDS (Communications, Command, Control and Information Systems), 1990–93; Dir Gen. Submarines, Chief Naval Engr Officer and Sen. Naval Rep. in Bath, 1993–94; Controller of the Navy, in rank of Vice-Adm., 1994–96. Non-exec. Chm., Universal Credit, DWP, 2013–; non-executive Director: British Energy, 2003–09; Cohort plc, 2006–; Ultra Electronic Hldgs plc, 2009–; Independent Director: Gen. Dynamics, USA, 2004–15; EDO Corp., USA, 2004–08; Stratos Global, Canada, 2006–08; Chm., Major Projects Assoc., 2004–13; Sen. Advr, Morgan Stanley, 2004–12. Crown Rep., Crown Commercial Service, 2014–. Hon. Col, 71st (Yeomanry) Signal Regt, 2001–07. Freeman, City of London, 1996; Liveryman, Co. of Engrs, 1999; Hon. Freeman, Co. of Shipwrights, 2001. FRSA 1997. Hon. FCIPS 2002. Hon. DSc Cranfield, 2002. *Recreations:* fly fishing, West Ham United FC, Scotland. *Address:* c/o Lloyds Bank, 110 Putney High Street, SW15 1RG. *Clubs:* Reform, Army and Navy; Hawks; Woking Golf.

WALPOLE, family name of **Baron Walpole**.

WALPOLE, 10th Baron *cr* 1723, of Walpole; **Robert Horatio Walpole;** Baron Walpole of Wolterton, 1756; *b* 8 Dec. 1938; *s* of 9th Baron Walpole, TD and Nancy Louisa, OBE, *y d* of late Frank Harding Jones; *S* father, 1989; *m* 1st, 1962, S. Judith Schofield (later S. J. Chaplin, OBE, MP; marr. diss. 1979; she *d* 1993); two *s* two *d*; 2nd, 1980, Laurel Celia, *o d* of S. T. Ball; two *s* one *d*. *Educ:* Eton; King's College, Cambridge (MA, Dip Agric). Member, Norfolk CC, 1970–81 (Chm. of various cttees). Elected Mem., H of L, 1999. Chairman: Area Museums Service for South East England, 1976–79; Norwich School of Art, 1977–87; Textile Conservation Centre, 1981–88 (Pres. 1988); East Anglian Tourist Board, 1982–88. Hon. Fellow, St Mary's UC, Strawberry Hill, 1997. JP Norfolk, 1972. *Heir:* *s* Hon. Jonathan Robert Hugh Walpole [*b* 16 Nov. 1967; *m* 2006, Eileen Margaret Sean, *d* of Edward James Quinn]. *Address:* Mannington Hall, Norwich NR11 7BB. *T:* (01263) 587763.

See also Hon. A. L. Walpole.

WALPOLE, Hon. Alice Louise; HM Diplomatic Service; Ambassador to Luxembourg, since 2011; *b* Norwich, 1 Sept. 1963; *d* of Baron Walpole, *qv* and (Sybil) Judith Walpole (later Judith Chaplin, OBE, MP); *m* 1990, Dr Angel Carro Castrillo (marr. diss. 2010); three *s* three *d*. *Educ:* Norwich High Sch., GDST; New Hall, Cambridge (MA). Entered FCO, 1985; Desk Officer, Eastern Eur. Dept, FCO, 1985–86; Conf. Support Officer, UK Mission to UN, NY, 1986–87; Desk Officer, Information Dept, FCO, 1987; Third Sec., Develt, UK Rep. to EC, 1987–90; Swahili lang. trng, 1990; Second Sec. (Pol), Dar es Salaam, 1991–94; Desk Officer, Policy Planning Staff, FCO, 1994–96; Hd, Peacekeeping Unit, UN Dept, FCO, 1996–98; First Secretary: Eur. Defence, UK Delegn to NATO, 1998–2000; UK Rep. to EU, Brussels, 2000–01; Envmt, UK Mission to UN, NY, 2001–06; Deputy Head: Stabilisation Unit, 2006–08; Corporate Communication Gp, FCO, 2008–09; Consul Gen., Basra, 2009–11. *Recreations:* travelling, cinema, gardening, sewing. *Address:* British Embassy, 5 Boulevard Joseph II, 1840, Luxembourg. *T:* 225450. *E:* alice.walpole@fco.gov.uk.

WALPORT, Sir Mark (Jeremy), Kt 2009; PhD; FRCP, FRCPath, FMedSci; FRS 2011; Chief Scientific Adviser to the Government and Head, Government Office for Science, Department for Business, Innovation and Skills, since 2013; Director, Wellcome Trust, 2003–13; *b* 25 Jan. 1953; *s* of Samuel Walport and Doreen Walport (*née* Music); *m* 1986, Julia Elizabeth Neild; one *s* three *d*. *Educ:* St Paul's Sch., London; Clare Coll., Cambridge (Hon. Fellow, 2012); Middlesex Hosp. Med. Sch., London (MA, MB BChir; PhD 1986). FRCP 1990; FRCPath 1997. House Officer, Middlesex Hosp. and Queen Elizabeth II Hosp., Welwyn, 1977–78; SHO, 1978–80; Hon. Registrar, Brompton Hosp., 1980; Registrar, Hammersmith Hosp., 1980–82; MRC Trng Fellow, MRC Mechanisms in Tumour Immunity Unit, Cambridge, 1982–85; Harrison-Watson Student, Clare Coll., Cambridge, 1982–85; Royal Postgraduate Medical School, subseq. Imperial College Faculty of Medicine: Sen. Lectr in Rheumatology, 1985–90; Reader in Rheumatological Medicine, 1990–91; Prof. of Medicine, 1991–2003; Vice Dean for Res., 1994–97; Hd, Div. of Medicine, 1997–2003; Hon. Cons. Physician, Hammersmith Hosp., 1985–2003; Dir, R&D, Hammersmith Hosps Trust, 1994–98. Member: Scientific Adv. Bd, Cantab Pharmaceuticals, Cambridge, 1989–; R&D Adv. Bd, SmithKline Beecham, 1998–. Member: Council, British Soc. for Rheumatology, 1989–95 (Chm., Heberden Cttee, 1993–95); Wkg Cttee on Ethics of Xenotransplantation, Nuffield Bioethics Council, 1995–96; Council, British Soc. for Immunology, 1998–2000; Council for Sci. and Technol., 2004–; Chairman: Ethics Cttee, Hammersmith and Queen Charlotte's SHA, 1990–94; Molecular and Cell Panel, Wellcome Trust, 1998–2000. Gov., Wellcome Trust, 2000–03; Trustee, Kennedy Meml Trust, 2015–. Philip Ellman Lecture, RCP, 1995 (Graham Bull Prize in Clin. Sci., 1996). Founder FMedSci 1998 (Registrar, 1998–2003); Fellow, ICSTM, 2006; FIC 2006. Asst Ed., British Jl of Rheumatology, 1990–97; Series Ed., 1998–2001, Chm., Editl Bd, 2001–03, British Med. Bulletin; Ed., Clin. and Exptl Immunology, 1998–2000. Hon. DSc: Sheffield, 2006; KCL, 2007; Aberdeen, 2009; Leicester, 2012; Glasgow, 2013; Keele, 2013; Cranfield, 2013; DUniv York, 2011; Hon. DCL Newcastle upon Tyne, 2013. Roche Prize for Rheumatology, 1991. *Publications:* (ed jtly) Clinical Aspects of Immunology, 5th edn 1993; (jtly) Immunobiology, 3rd edn 1997 to 7th edn 2007; papers in sci. jls on immunology and genetics of rheumatic diseases. *Recreations:* natural history, food. *Address:* Government Office for Science, Department for Business, Innovation and Skills, 1 Victoria Street, SW1H 0ET.

WALSALL, Archdeacon of; *see* Weller, Ven. S. K.

WALSBY, Prof. Anthony Edward, PhD; FRS 1993; Melville Wills Professor of Botany, 1980–2006, now Professor Emeritus, and Senior Research Fellow, since 2006, University of Bristol. *Educ:* Birmingham Univ. (BSc); PhD London. Asst Lectr, then Lectr in Botany, Westfield Coll., London Univ., 1965–71; Miller Fellow, Univ. of Calif at Berkeley, 1971–73; Lectr, then Reader, Department of Marine Science-Marine Biology, UCNW, Bangor, 1973–80. *Address:* School of Biological Sciences, University of Bristol, Woodland Road, Bristol BS8 1UG. *T:* (0117) 928 7490. *E:* a.e.walsby@bristol.ac.uk.

WALSH, Arthur Stephen, CBE 1979; FREng, FIET; Chairman, Simoco International Ltd, 1997–2000; *b* 16 Aug. 1926; *s* of Wilfred and Doris Walsh; *m* 2nd, 1985, Judith Martha Westenborg. *Educ:* Selwyn Coll., Cambridge (MA). FIET (FIEE 1974); FREng (FEng 1980). GEC Group, 1952–79: various sen. appts within the Group; Managing Director: Marconi Space and Defence Systems, 1969–86; Marconi Co., 1982–85; Dir, GEC, 1983; Chief Exec., 1985–91, Chm., 1989–91, STC. Chairman: Telemetrix plc, 1991–97; Nat. Transcommunications Ltd, 1991–96; Dir, FKI plc, 1991–99. Hon. DSc: Ulster, 1988; Southampton, 1993. *Recreations:* ski-ing, golf. *Address:* Aiglemont, Trout Rise, Loudwater, Rickmansworth, Herts WD3 4JS. *T:* (01923) 770883.

WALSH, Colin Stephen; Organist Laureate, Lincoln Cathedral, since 2002 (Organist and Master of the Choristers, 1988–2002); *b* 26 Jan. 1955. *Educ:* Portsmouth Grammar Sch.; St George's Chapel, Windsor Castle (Organ Scholar); Christ Church, Oxford (Organ Scholar; MA 1980; PGCE 1978). ARCM 1973; FRCO 1976. Asst Organist, Salisbury Cathedral, 1978–85; Master of the Music, St Alban's Cathedral, 1985–88. Recitals in UK (incl. Royal Festival Hall) and many other countries. Recordings incl. French organ music, esp. by Vierne. Hon. DMus Lincoln, 2013. *Recreations:* walking, dining out, theatre, travel. *Address:* 12 Minster Yard, Lincoln LN2 1PJ. *T:* (01522) 561646.

WALSH, Dominic Gerard; Chief Executive, Hospital Services Ltd, since 2015; *b* Belfast, 20 Oct. 1961; *s* of George Walsh and Philomena Walsh; *m* 1987, Carmel; one *s* one *d*. *Educ:* Belfast Royal Acad.; Queen's Univ. Belfast (BSc Hons, MBA). CEng; MIMechE. Chief. Exec., MSO Gp Ltd, 2002–14. Pres., BPIF, 2005–07. Chm., Sport NI, 2008–12; Mem. Bd, UK Sport, 2008–12. Trustee, Mary Peters Trust, 2009–. *Recreations:* Rugby, golf, soccer, being optimistic and cheerful as at worst it confuses people and at best is infectious. *Clubs:* Academy Rugby Football, Fortwilliam Golf.

WALSH, Fergus; Medical Correspondent, BBC, since 2005; *b* Leicester, 16 Sept. 1961; *s* of Michael Walsh and Ita Walsh (*née* Cogavin); *m* 2005, Véronique Maguin; one *s* two *d*. *Educ:* Royal Grammar Sch., High Wycombe; Univ. of Leeds (BA Hons Eng. Lit. 1983); Falmouth Coll. (Dip. Radio Journalism 1984). Freelance radio reporter, 1984–86; sub-editor, 1986–87, reporter, 1987–88, BBC Radio News; Home and Legal Affairs Corresp., BBC, 1988–90; reporter, BBC TV News, 1990–93; BBC News: Health Corresp., 1993–2000; Sci. Corresp., 2000–05. Hon. DCL Newcastle, 2009. *Recreations:* photography, road cycling, theatre, making espresso, gardening with my wife, playing croquet with my children. *Address:* BBC, Room 02D, New Broadcasting House, Portland Place, W1A 1AA. *E:* fergus.walsh@bbc.co.uk.

WALSH, Rt Rev. (Geoffrey David) Jeremy; Bishop Suffragan of Tewkesbury, 1986–95; an Honorary Assistant Bishop, Diocese of St Edmundsbury and Ipswich, since 2008; *b* 7 Dec. 1929; *s* of late Howard Wilton Walsh, OBE and Helen Maud Walsh (*née* Lovell); *m* 1961, Cynthia Helen, *d* of late F. P. Knight, FLS, VMH, and H. I. C. Knight, BEM; two *s* one *d*. *Educ:* Felsted Sch., Essex; Pembroke Coll., Cambridge (MA Econ.); Lincoln Theological Coll. Curate, Christ Church, Southgate, London, 1955–58; Staff Sec., SCM, and Curate, St Mary the Great, Cambridge, 1958–61; Vicar, St Matthew, Moorfields, Bristol, 1961–66; Rector of Marlborough, Wilts, 1966–76; Rector of Elmsett with Aldham, 1976–80; Archdeacon of Ipswich, 1976–86. Hon. Canon, Salisbury Cathedral, 1973–76. *Recreations:* gardening, golf, bird-watching. *Address:* 6 Warren Lane, Martlesham Heath, Ipswich IP5 3SH. *T:* (01473) 620797.

WALSH, Graham Robert, FCA; Deputy Chairman, Moss Bros Group plc, 1999–2001 (Director, 1988–2001); *b* 30 July 1939; *s* of Robert Arthur Walsh and Ella Marian (*née* Jacks); *m* 1967, Margaret Ann Alexander; one *s* one *d*. *Educ:* Hurstpierpoint Coll., Sussex. Qualified as chartered accountant, 1962; joined Philip Hill Higginson Erlangers (now Hill Samuel & Co. Ltd), 1964; Director, Hill Samuel, 1970, resigned 1973; Dir, 1973–87, Head of Corporate Finance Div., and Mem. Management Cttee, 1981–87, Morgan Grenfell & Co. Ltd; Man. Dir, Bankers Trust Co., 1988–91; Director: Morgan Grenfell Group plc (formerly Morgan Grenfell (Holdings)), 1985–87; Armitage Shanks Group Ltd, 1973–80; Phoenix Opera Ltd, 1970–87; Ward White Group plc, 1981–89; Rush & Tompkins Gp plc, 1988–90; Haslemere Estates, 1989–92; Rodamco UK BV, 1992–98. Dir Gen., Panel on Takeovers and Mergers, 1979–81; Chm., Issuing Houses Assoc., 1985–87 (Dep. Chm., 1979 and 1983–85). Gov., Dulwich Coll. Prep. Sch., 1995–97. *Recreations:* opera, theatre, music, gardening.

WALSH, Henry George; Deputy Chairman, Building Societies Commission, 1991–95; *b* 28 Sept. 1939; *s* of James Isidore Walsh and Sybil Bertha Bazeley; *m* 1999, Elizabeth Long; one *d*; two *d* by previous *m*. *Educ:* West Hill High Sch., Montreal; McGill Univ.; Churchill Coll., Cambridge. HM Treasury, 1966–74; Private Secretary to Chancellor of the Duchy of Lancaster, 1974–76; HM Treasury, 1976–78; Cabinet Office Secretariat, 1978–80; Counsellor (Economic), Washington, 1980–85; HM Treasury: Hd of Monetary Policy Div., 1985–86; Hd of IMF and Debt Div., 1986–89; Hd of Financial Instns and Markets Gp, 1989–91. *Recreations:* golf, model railways, being taken for walks by Labrador retrievers. *Address:* 60 Roxburgh Road, SE27 0LD. *Clubs:* Model Railway; Dulwich and Sydenham Hill Golf.

WALSH, Rt Rev. Jeremy; *see* Walsh, Rt Rev. G. D. J.

WALSH, Jill P.; *see* Paton Walsh.

WALSH, John; Director, J. Paul Getty Museum, 1983–2000, now Director Emeritus; Vice-President, J. Paul Getty Trust, 1998–2000; *b* 9 Dec. 1937; *s* of John J. Walsh and Eleanor Walsh (*née* Wilson); *m* 1961, Virginia Alys Galston; two *s* one *d*. *Educ:* Yale Univ. (BA 1961); Univ. of Leyden, Netherlands; Columbia Univ. (MA 1965; PhD 1971). Lectr, Research Asst, Frick Collection, NY, 1966–68; Metropolitan Museum of Art, NY: Associate for Higher Educn, 1968–71; Associate Curator and Curator, 1970–75, Vice-Chm., 1974–75, Dept of European Paintings; Columbia University: Adjunct Associate Prof., 1972–75; Prof. of Art History, Barnard Coll., 1975–77; Mrs Russell W. Baker Curator of Paintings, Museum of Fine Arts, Boston, 1977–83. Visiting Professor: of Fine Arts, Harvard, 1979; of History of Art, Yale Univ., 2003, 2011, 2015; Mem., Inst. for Advanced Study, Princeton Univ., 2001–02. Member: Governing Bd, Yale Univ. Art Gallery, 1975–; Bd of Fellows, Claremont Grad. Sch. and Univ. Center, 1988–2000; Bd of Dirs, Hammer Mus., 2008–. Member: Assoc. of Art Museum Dirs, 1983–2001 (Trustee, 1986–90; Pres., 1989); Amer. Antiquarian Soc., 1984–. Mem., Amer. Acad. of Arts and Scis, 1997. Trustee, Burlington Mag. Foundn, 1995–. Hon. LHD Wheaton Coll., 2000. *Publications:* Things in Place: landscapes and still lifes by Sheridan Lord, 1995; Jan Steen, The Drawing Lesson, 1996; (with D. Gribbon) The J. Paul Getty Museum and its Collections: a museum for the new century, 1997; numerous contribs to learned jls. *Address:* c/o J. Paul Getty Museum, 1200 Getty Center Drive, Ste 1000, Los Angeles, CA 90049–1679, USA. *Club:* Century Association (NY).

WALSH, John Henry Martin; Assistant Editor, Independent, since 1998; *b* 24 Oct. 1953; *s* of Martin Walsh and Anne Walsh (*née* Durkin); one *s* two *d*; *m* Angie O'Rourke. *Educ:* Wimbledon Coll.; Exeter Coll., Oxford (BA Hons); University Coll., Dublin (MA). Advertisement Dept, Tablet Magazine, 1977; Publicity Dept, Victor Gollancz, 1978–79; Associate Editor, The Director, 1979–83; freelance writer, 1983–87; Literary Editor, 1987, Features and Literary Editor, 1988, Evening Standard; Literary Editor, Sunday Times, 1988–92; Editor, Independent Magazine, 1993–95; Literary Editor, Independent, 1995–96. Presenter, Books and Company, BBC Radio 4, 1995–97. Artistic Dir, Cheltenham Festival of Literature, 1997–98. Chm. Judges, Forward Poetry Prize, 2000. *Publications:* Growing Up Catholic, 1989; The Falling Angels, 1999; Are You Talking to Me?, 2003; Sunday at the Cross Bones, 2007. *Recreations:* drinking, talking, music. *Address:* 4 Westbourne Park Villas, W2 5EA. *T:* 07881 625609. *Club:* Groucho.

WALSH, Rev. Mgr John Michael; Principal Roman Catholic Chaplain to the Royal Air Force, 2007–10; Parish Priest, St Jerome's Roman Catholic Church, Formby, since 2012; *b* London, 22 June 1959; *s* of Vincent John and Elizabeth Philomena Walsh. *Educ:* St Raphael's RC Prim. Sch., Manchester; St George's RC Sec. Mod. Sch., Manchester; St Joseph's Coll., Upholland; St Cuthbert's Coll., Ushaw, Durham (CTh 1982); Pontifical Univ. of St Thomas Aquinas, Rome (STL 2012). Ordained priest, 1983; Assistant Priest: Metropolitan Cath. of Christ the King, 1983–89; St Mary's, Blackbrook, 1989–91; St Joseph's Penketh, 1991–92; Parish Priest, St Elizabeth's, Litherland, 1992–95; Community of St Laurence, Ampleforth, 1995–98; Parish Priest, St Michael's, Ditton, 1999–2003; Commnd as Chaplain, RAF, 2003; RAF Coll. Cranwell, 2003; RAF Brize Norton, 2003–04; RAF Halton, 2004–05; RAF Marham, 2005–07; RAF Coll. Cranwell, 2007; Vicar General, 2007. Papal Prelate of Honour, 2007. *Recreations:* aviation, reading, classical music.

WALSH, John P.; *see* Pakenham-Walsh.

WALSH, (Mary) Noëlle; Editor, The Good Deal Directory, since 1992; Director, The Value for Money Company Ltd, since 1992; *b* 26 Dec. 1954; *d* of late Thomas Walsh and of Mary Kate Ferguson; *m* 1988, David Heslam; one *s* one *d*. *Educ:* Univ. of East Anglia (BA Hons European Studies (History and German)). Editorial Asst, PR Dept, St Dunstan's Orgn for the War-Blinded, 1977–79; News Editor, Cosmopolitan, 1979–85; Editor, London Week newspaper, 1985–86; freelance writer, 1986; Dep. Editor, 1986–87, Editor, 1987–91, Good Housekeeping; Dep. Editor, You and Your Family, Daily Telegraph, 1992; Editor, The Good Deal Directory monthly newsletter, 1992–97; Founder: gooddealdirectory website, 2000; gooddealhouse website, 2004. Member: Network; 300 Group; Forum UK. FRSA. *Publications:* Hot Lips, the Ultimate Kiss and Tell Guide, 1985; (co-ed) Ragtime to Wartime: the best of Good Housekeeping 1922–39, 1986; (co-ed) The Home Front: the best of Good Housekeeping 1939–1945, 1987; (co-ed) The Christmas Book: the best of Good Housekeeping at Christmas 1922–1962, 1988; (ed jtly) Food Glorious Food: eating and drinking with Good Housekeeping 1922–1942, 1990; Things my Mother Should Have Told Me, 1991; Childhood Memories, 1991; (ed) The Good Deal Directory, annually, 1994–; (ed) The Good Deal Directory Food Guide, 1993; (ed) The Home Shopping Handbook, 1994; Baby on a Budget, 1995; Wonderful Weddings that won't cost a fortune, 1995; The Factory Shopping and Sightseeing Guide to the UK, 1996; The Good Mail Order Guide, 1996; contrib. to Sunday Times annual Good Deal Guide. *Recreation:* medieval Irish history. *Address:* Cottage by the Church, Filkins, Lechlade, Glos GL7 3JG.

WALSH, Michael Jeffrey; Senior Vice President, Business Development, Europe, Velti, 2011–13 (Vice President, 2009–11); *b* 1 Oct. 1949; *s* of Kenneth Francis Walsh and Edith Walsh; *m* 1983, Sally Elizabeth Hudson; one *s* one *d*. *Educ:* Hulme Grammar Sch., Oldham; Durham Univ. (BA Hons Geog.). Joined Young and Rubicam as grad. trainee, 1972; Dir, 1980–83; New Business Dir, 1981–83; Mem., Exec. Cttee, 1982–83; Ogilvy & Mather, 1983–2005: Man. Dir, 1986–89, Chm., 1989–90, UK; Chm., UK Gp, 1990–99 and 2002–05; CEO, Europe, Africa and Middle East, 1994–2005; non-exec. Dir, Ogilvy & Mather SA, 1985–. Exec. Dir, Brand Union, 2013–. Non-exec. Dir, Archant, 2010–. Chm., UK Disasters Emergency Cttee, 2005–11. Bd Mem., MLA, 2006. Hon. Vice-Chm. and Trustee, BRCS, 1994–2004; Worldwide Trustee, WWF, 1996–99. *Recreations:* collecting children's books, antiques, golf, sailing. *Clubs:* Royal Automobile, Mark's; Royal West Norfolk Golf, Archerfield Golf.

WALSH, Maj.-Gen. Michael John Hatley, CB 1980; CBE 1996; DSO 1968; Director of Overseas Relations, St John's Ambulance, 1989–95; *b* 10 June 1927; *s* of Captain Victor Michael Walsh, late Royal Sussex, and Audrey Walsh; *m* 1952, Angela, *d* of Col Leonard Beswick; two *d*. *Educ:* Sedbergh Sch. Commnd, KRRC, 1946; served in Italy, Malaya, Germany, Cyprus, Suez, Aden, Australia and Singapore; Bde Maj. 44 Parachute Bde, 1960–61; GSO1 Defence Planning Staff, 1966; CO 1 Para Bn, 1967–69; Col AQ 1 Div., 1969–71; Comdr, 28 Commonwealth Bde, 1971–73; BGS HQ BAOR, 1973–76; GOC 3rd Armoured Div., 1976–79; Dir of Army Training, MoD, 1979–81. Hon. Col, 1st Bn Wessex Regt, TA, 1981–89. Chief Scout of the UK and Dependent Territories, 1982–88; Vice Pres., Scout Assoc., 1988–. Council Mem., Operation Raleigh, 1984; Royal National Life-boat Institution: Member: Cttee of Management, 1988–2003; Search and Rescue Sub-cttee, 1989–99; Fund Raising Sub-cttee, 1991–2001; Vice Pres., 1998–. Kt Pres., Hon. Soc. of Knights of the Round Table, 1988–95 (Kt 1986–); Mem., St John Council, Wilts, 1989–99, London, 1995–2000. Pres., 1525 Soc., 2004–09; Vice Pres., Old Sedberghian Club, 2005–11. DL Greater London, 1986–99. Freeman, City of London, 1987. KStJ 1993 (Mem., Chapter Gen., 1989–99). Surgeon-Gen. John White Medal for Services to Health and Internat. Relns, 2008. *Publications:* One Man in his Time, 2007. *Recreations:* athletics, boxing (Life Pres., Army Boxing Assoc., 1986), parachuting (Pres., Army Parachute Assoc., 1979–81), sailing, Australian Rules football, photography (LRPS). *Address:* c/o Barclays Bank, James Street, Harrogate HG1 1QX.

WALSH, Michael Thomas; Head of Research, Community (formerly Iron and Steel Trades Confederation), 1999–2008; *b* 22 Oct. 1943; *s* of late Michael Walsh and Bridget (*née* O'Sullivan); *m* 1972, Margaret Patricia Blaxhall; two *s* two *d*. *Educ:* Gunnersbury Grammar Sch.; Exeter Coll., Oxford (Hons degree PPE). Internat. Dept, TUC, 1966; Deputy Overseas Labour Adviser, FCO, 1977–79; Head, Internat. Dept, TUC, 1980–99. Economic and Social Committee of the European Community: Mem., 1976–77 and 1979–80; Alternate Mem., Consultative Commn on Industrial Change, 2003; Mem., World of Work Cttee, Catholic Bishops' Conf. of England and Wales, 1992–2001; Dep. Mem., Exec. Cttee, Eur. Metalworkers' Fedn, 2003. Member: Wilton Park Academic Council, 1994–2003; Governing Body, Plater Coll., Oxford, 1995–2001; Grant-Making Body, Charles Plater Trust, 2007–. *Publications:* (ed) Report of International Confederation of Free Trade Unions, 1994–99; (ed) ISTC reports; contrib. professional and Catholic jls. *Recreations:* cricket, moral philosophy, historical research, music. *Address:* 77 Uvedale Road, Enfield EN2 6HD.

WALSH, Noëlle; *see* Walsh, M. N.

WALSH, Patrick Edward; Co-Founder and Chairman, Conville & Walsh, literary agency, since 2000; *b* Zeist, Holland, 2 April 1965; *s* of Peter Walsh and Tina Walsh (*née* Posthuma-Jorna). *Educ:* Gonville and Caius Coll., Cambridge (Exhibnr; BA Law 1987). Jun. post, Watson Little, 1988–92; Christopher Little Agency, 1992–2000. Mem. Bd, WildlifeDirect, 2013–. *Recreations:* fishing, scuba diving, reading, conservation, adventure. *Address:* 19 Little Russell Street, WC1A 2HL. *E:* patrick@convilleandwalsh.com. *Clubs:* Ivy, Academy.

WALSH, Most Rev. Patrick Joseph; Bishop of Down and Connor, (RC), 1991–2008; *b* 9 April 1931; *s* of Michael and Nora Walsh. *Educ:* Queen's Univ. Belfast (MA); Christ's Coll., Cambridge (MA); Pontifical Lateran Univ., Rome (STL). Ordained 1956; Teacher, St MacNissi's Coll., Garron Tower, 1958–64; Chaplain, Queen's Univ., Belfast, 1964–70; Pres., St Malachy's Coll., Belfast, 1970–83; Auxiliary Bishop of Down and Connor, 1983–91. *Recreations:* walking, music, theatre. *Address:* 6 Waterloo Park North, Belfast BT15 5HW. *T:* (028) 9077 8182.

WALSH, Paul S.; Chairman, Compass Group, since 2014; *b* Manchester, 1 May 1955; *s* of Arthur and Anne Walsh; *m* (marr. diss.); one *s*; *m* 2013, Julie Lewis. *Educ:* Manchester Poly. (accounting qualifications). GrandMet, subseq. Diageo plc: joined Brewing Div., 1982; Finance Dir, Intercontinental Hotels, 1986–90; Div. Chief Exec., Pillsbury, 1990–92; CEO, Pillsbury Co., 1992–2000; Mem. Bd, 1995–2013; Chief Operating Officer, 2000; CEO, 2000–13; Advr, 2013–14. Non-executive Director: Fedex Corp.; Centrica plc, 2005–09; Unilever, 2009–15; Avanti Communications plc, 2012– (Chm., 2013–); RM2 Internat., 2014–; Mem. Bd, United Spirits Ltd, 2013–14. Mem., Prime Minister's Business Adv. Gp, 2010–12; Lead non-exec. Dir, DECC, 2011–. Business Ambassador for food and drink industries, BIS, 2012–. Chm., Scotch Whisky Assoc., 2008–11. Gov., Henley Mgt Coll., 2003. *Recreations:* outdoor activities, sailing. *Address:* Compass Group, Compass House, Guildford Street, Chertsey KT16 9BQ.

WALSH, Robin; Controller, BBC Northern Ireland, 1991–94; *b* 6 Feb. 1940; *s* of Charles and Ellen Walsh; *m* 1964, Dorothy Beattie; two *d*. *Educ:* Foyle College, Londonderry; Royal Belfast Academical Instn. Reporter, Belfast Telegraph, 1958–65; Reporter/News Editor, Ulster TV, 1965–74; BBC: News Editor, NI, 1974–81; Dep. Editor, TV News, 1982–85; Managing Editor, News and Current Affairs—TV, 1985–88; Asst Controller, News and Current Affairs, Regions, 1988–90. *Recreations:* cricket, walking. *Address:* Holly Lodge, 3A Ballymullan Road, Crawfordsburn, Co. Down NI BT19 1JG. *T:* (028) 9185 2709.

WALSH, Samuel Maurice Cossart, AO 2010; Chief Executive Officer, Rio Tinto plc, since 2013; *b* Brighton, Vic, 27 Dec. 1949; *s* of Maurice John Walsh and Winifred Margaret Lois Walsh; *m* 2002, Leanne Joy Roki; two *s* one *d*. *Educ:* Brighton Grammar Sch.; Taylor's Coll.; Univ. of Melbourne (BCom); Kettering Univ. FAIM 2005; FAICD 2005; FCIPSA 2011. Buyer, 1972–74, Purchasing Agent, 1974–76, Coordinator Purchasing Admin, 1976–78, Sen. Purchasing Agent, 1978–83, Purchasing Manager, 1983–86, Materials Manager, 1986–87, Holden; Dir, Product Develt and Supply, 1987–89, Exec. Dir Ops, 1989–91, Nissan; Rio Tinto: Managing Director: Comalco Foundry Products, 1991–93; Sales and Mktg, 1994–97; Ops, 1997–2000; Hamersley Iron, 2000–01; Chief Executive: Comalco Ltd, 2001–04; Rio Tinto Iron Ore, 2004–13. Dir, Seven West Media Ltd, 2008–12. Co-Chm., Australia-India CEO Forum, 2015–. Chm., Chamber of Arts and Culture, WA, 2010–13; Chm., Black Swan State Th. Co., 2009–13; Patron: Baden Powell Soc., 2009–; Univ. of WA Hackett Foundn, 2010–13; Blackswan State Th., WA, 2013–; Australian Purchasing Managers' Index, 2013–. Trustee, Royal Opera Hse Covent Gdn Foundn, 2014–. Fellow: Australasian Inst. Mining and Metallurgy, 2005; Australian Acad. Technol Scis and Engrg, 2012. Hon. DCom: Edith Cowan, 2010; WA, 2014. *Recreations:* antiques, fine arts, opera, theatre, ballet, orchestra. *Address:* c/o Rio Tinto plc, 6 St James's Square, SW1Y 4JU. *T:* (020) 7781 2000. *Clubs:* Weld (Perth); Melbourne Cricket; Royal Freshwater Bay Yacht.

WALSH, Simon; JP; barrister in private practice, since 1988; *b* 7 Jan. 1962; *s* of Thomas Walsh and Jean Walsh (*née* Morris). *Educ:* Manchester Grammar Sch.; Balliol Coll., Oxford (BA 1984, MA 1987); City Univ., London (Dip. Law 1986). MCIArb 1999. Called to the Bar, Middle Temple, 1987, Inner Temple, Lincoln's Inn, *ad eundem*. Chm., Valuation Tribunals, 1998–2008. City of London Corporation: Common Councilman, 1989–2000; Alderman, Ward of Farringdon Without, 2000–13; Chairman: Housing Cttee, 1995–98; Police Authy, 2002–05; Licensing Authy, 2007–10. Mem., London Fire and Emergency Planning Authy, 2008–11. Freeman, City of London, 1987–; Liveryman: Glovers' Co., 1989–; Fletchers' Co., 2001–; Court Assistant: Parish Clerks' Co., 2004–12 (Under Warden, 2008–09); Guild of Freemen, 2004–06. Parish Clerk, St Augustine Old Change, 1993–; Churchwarden, St Dunstan-in-the-West, 2002–. Chm., City Br., Royal Soc. of St George, 2004–05. Governor: City of London Sch., 1992–2000, City of London Sch. for Girls, 2005–06; (ex officio): Christ's Hosp., 2000–13; Bridewell Royal Hosp., 2000–13. Pres., Alumni Assoc., City Univ., 2001–05. JP City of London, 2000–10, Haringey, 2010. CLJ 1999. *Recreations:* the Commonwealth, civic responsibility, 19th century French novels, municipal tramways, promoting the survival of real ale. *Address:* 5 Essex Court, Temple, EC4Y 9AH. *Clubs:* City Livery, Farringdon Ward; Golden Lane Community Association Social.

WALSH, His Honour Terence Michael; a Circuit Judge, North East Circuit, 2001–12; *b* 10 March 1945; *s* of late Gerrard Walsh and Freda Alice Walsh (now Kay); *m* 1969, Pauline Totham; two *s* one *d*. *Educ:* Belle Vue Boys' Grammar Sch., Bradford. Admitted as solicitor, 1974; Sen. Partner, Chivers Walsh Smith, Solicitors, Bradford, 1991–2001. Dep. Registrar, later Dep. Dist Judge, 1984–94; Asst Recorder, 1989–94; Recorder, 1994–2001. Pres., Bradford Law Soc., 1990–91; Mem., Children's Panel, Law Soc., 1994–2001. Consulting Ed., Practitioner's Guides, 1991–2011. *Publications:* Child Care and the Courts, 1988; Child Protection Handbook, 1995. *Recreations:* history, cricket, music, walking.

WALSH, Most Rev. William; Bishop of Killaloe, (RC), 1994–2010; *b* 16 Jan. 1935; *s* of Bill Walsh and Ellen Maher. *Educ:* St Flannan's Coll., Ennis; St Patrick's Coll., Maynooth (BSc); Irish Coll., Rome; Lateran Univ., Rome (LTh, DCL); Univ. Coll., Galway (HDipEd). Ordained priest, 1959; postgrad. studies, 1959–63; Teacher of mathematics and physics, St Flannan's Coll., Ennis, 1963–88; Curate at Ennis Cathedral, 1988–94; Priest Dir, 1969–94, Pres., Nat. Exec., 1995–2010, ACCORD (formerly Catholic Marriage Adv. Council); Mem., Episcopal, R&D and Pastoral Commns, 2003–10. *Publications:* contribs to books, Furrow Magazine and other theol jls. *Recreations:* hurling (sometime coach/selector of many teams), golf, walking, choral singing. *Clubs:* Eire Og Hurling (Ennis); Ennis, Lahinch and Woodstock Golf.

WALSH, Willie; Chief Executive, International Airlines Group (formerly British Airways), since 2005; *b* 1961; *m* Caragh; one *d*. *Educ:* Ardscoil Rís Sch., Dublin; Trinity Coll., Dublin (MSc 1992). Joined Aer Lingus as cadet pilot, 1979, Captain, 1990; Chief Exec., Futura, 1998–2000; COO, 2000–01, CEO, 2001–05, Aer Lingus. Non-exec. Dir, Fyffes plc, 2004–07. Chm., Nat. Treasury Mgt Agency, Ireland, 2013– (Chm. Adv. Cttee, 2013–). *Address:* International Airlines Group, 2 World Business Centre Heathrow, Newall Road, London Heathrow Airport, Hounslow TW6 2SF.

WALSHAM, Prof. Alexandra Marie, PhD; FBA 2009; FRHistS, FAHA; Professor of Modern History, University of Cambridge, since 2010; Fellow, Trinity College, Cambridge, since 2010; *b* Hayle, Cornwall, 4 Jan. 1966; *d* of Bruce and Ann Walsham. *Educ:* Presbyterian Ladies' Coll., Melbourne; Univ. of Melbourne (BA 1987; MA 1990); Univ. of Cambridge (PhD 1995). Res. Fellow, Emmanuel Coll., Cambridge, 1993–96; University of Exeter: Lectr in Hist., 1996–2000; Sen. Lectr in Hist., 2000–05; Prof. of Reformation Hist. (Personal Chair), 2005–10. FRHistS 1999; FAHA 2013. *Publications:* Church Papists: Catholicism, conformity and confessional polemic in early modern England, 1993; Providence in Early Modern England, 1999 (Longman History Today Prize; Morris D. Forkosch Prize, Amer. Histl Assoc., 2000); (ed with J. Crick) The Uses of Script and Print 1300–1700, 2004; (ed jtly) Richard Carew, The Survey of Cornwall (1602), facsimile edn, 2004; Charitable Hatred: tolerance and intolerance in England 1500–1700, 2006; (ed with P. Marshall) Angels in the Early Modern World, 2006; (ed with E. Jones) Syon Abbey and its Books 1400–1700, 2010; (ed) Relics and Remains, 2010; The Reformation of the Landscape: religion, identity and memory in Early Modern Britain, 2011 (Leo Gershoy Award, Amer. Histl Assoc., Wolfson Hist. Prize (jtly), Roland H. Bainton Prize, Sixteenth Century Studies Conf., 2011); Catholic Reformation in Protestant Britain, 2014; (ed jtly) Religion and the Household, 2014; contrib. articles to learned jls, incl. Past and Present, English Histl Rev., Histl Jl, Jl Ecclesiastical Hist., Jl British Studies, Histl Res. *Address:* Trinity College, Cambridge CB2 1TQ.

WALSHAM, Prof. Geoffrey, LittD; Professor of Management Studies, University of Cambridge, 2001–10, now Emeritus; *b* 10 June 1946; *s* of Harry Walsham and Charlotte Gladys Walsham; *m* 1970, Alison Jane Evans; three *s* one *d*. *Educ:* St Catherine's Coll., Oxford (BA Maths 1966; MA 1971); Warwick Univ. (MSc Maths 1968); Univ. of Cambridge (LittD 2010). Lectr in Maths, Mindanao State Univ., Philippines, 1966–67; OR Analyst, BP Chemicals, 1968–72; Lectr in OR, Univ. of Nairobi, Kenya, 1972–75; Cambridge University: Lectr in Mgt Studies, 1975–94; Fellow, Fitzwilliam Coll., 1979–94; Prof. of Information Mgt, Lancaster Univ., 1994–96; University of Cambridge: Dir, MBA course, 1997–98; Res. Prof. of Mgt Studies, 1998–2001. *Publications:* Interpreting Information Systems in Organizations, 1993; Making a World of Difference: information technology in a global context, 2001; jl articles in information systems, organisational studies, operational res. *Recreations:* mountain walking, travel. *Address:* Judge Business School, University of Cambridge, Cambridge CB2 1AG. *T:* (01223) 339606, *Fax:* (01223) 339701. *E:* g.walsham@jbs.cam.ac.uk.

WALSHAM, Sir Gerald (Percy Robert), 6th Bt *cr* 1831, of Knill Court, Herefordshire; *b* 7 Feb. 1939; *s* of Percy Robert Stewart Walsham, *g s* of 2nd Bt and Tamara (*née* Ellis); *S* cousin, 2011, but his name does not appear on the Official Roll of the Baronetage; *m* 1984, Evelyn Niebes. RAF (Flt Lt) retired. *Heir:* none.

WALSINGHAM, 9th Baron *cr* 1780; **John de Grey,** MC 1952; Lieut-Colonel, Royal Artillery, retired, 1968; *b* 21 Feb. 1925; *s* of 8th Baron Walsingham, DSO, OBE, and Hyacinth (*d* 1968), *o d* of late Lt-Col Lambart Henry Bouwens, RHA; *S* father, 1965; *m* 1963, Wendy, *er d* of E. Hoare, Southwick, Sussex; one *s* two *d*. *Educ:* Wellington Coll.; Aberdeen Univ.; Magdalen Coll., Oxford; RMCS. BA Oxon, 1950; MA 1959. Army in India, 1945–47; Palestine, 1947; Oxford Univ., 1947–50; Foreign Office, 1950; Army in Korea, 1951–52; Hong Kong, 1952–54; Malaya, 1954–56; Cyprus, Suez, 1956; Aden, 1957–58; Royal Military Coll. of Science, 1958–60; Aden, 1961–63; Malaysia, 1963–65. Co. Dir, 1968–96. FInstD 1978. *Publications:* On the Origins of Speaking, 2006; Lithic Language, 2013; One More Onion Peeled (memoirs), 2016. *Heir:* *s* Hon. Robert de Grey [*b* 21 June 1969; *m* 1995, Josephine Elizabeth, *d* of Richard Haryott; one *s* two *d*]. *Address:* The Hassocks, Merton, Thetford, Norfolk IP25 6QP. *T:* (01953) 885385, *Fax:* (01953) 881431; 19B Calle Palmera, PO Box 202, Los Gigantes, Santiago Del Teide 38683, Tenerife, Canary Islands, Spain. *T:* 922862486. *E:* hassocks@lineone.net.

WALTER, Dame Harriet (Mary), DBE 2011 (CBE 2000); actress; *b* 24 Sept. 1950; *d* of late Roderick Walter and Xandra Carandini de Trafford (*née* Lee). *Educ:* Cranborne Chase Sch.; LAMDA. Associate Artist, RSC, 1987, now Hon. Associate Artist. Hon. DLitt Birmingham, 2001. Pragnell Shakespeare Award, 2007. *Theatre:* Ragged Trousered Philanthropists, Joint Stock Co., 1978; Hamlet, Cloud Nine, Royal Court, 1980; Nicholas Nickleby, RSC, 1980; Seagull, Royal Court, 1981; RSC seasons, 1981–83: Midsummer Night's Dream; All's Well That Ends Well (also on Broadway, 1983); The Castle, RSC, 1985; Merchant of Venice, Royal Exchange, Manchester, 1987; RSC seasons, 1987–89: Cymbeline; Twelfth Night; Three Sisters; Question of Geography (Best Actress, Olivier Awards, 1988); Duchess of Malfi, RSC, 1989–90; Three Birds Alighting on a Field, Royal Court, 1991–92, NY, 1994; Arcadia, 1993, The Children's Hour, 1994, National; Old Times, Wyndham's, 1995; Hedda Gabler, Chichester, 1996; Ivanov, Almeida, 1997; The Late Middle Classes, Watford and UK tour, 1999; Macbeth, RSC, 1999; Life x 3, RNT, 2000, transf. Old Vic, 2001; The Royal Family, Th. Royal, Haymarket, 2001; Much Ado About Nothing, RSC, 2002; Dinner, RNT, 2002, transf. Wyndham's, 2003; Us & Them, Hampstead, 2003; The Deep Blue Sea, Th. Royal, Bath and UK tour, 2003; Mary Stuart, Donmar Warehouse, transf. Apollo, 2005 (Best Actress, Evening Standard Th. Awards, 2005), NY 2009; Antony and Cleopatra, RSC, 2006; Fallujah, Old Truman Brewery, London, 2007; Women Beware Women, RNT, 2010; Julius Caesar, Donmar, 2012; Henry IV, Donmar, 2014; Boa, Trafalgar Studios, 2015; Death of a Salesman, RSC, 2015; *television:* The Imitation Game, 1980; Cherry Orchard, 1981; The Price, 1985; Lord Peter Wimsey, 1987; Benefactors, 1989; The Men's Room, 1991; Ashenden, 1991; A Dance to the Music of Time, 1997; Unfinished Business, 1998; Macbeth, 1999; George Eliot, 2002; Ballet Shoes, 2007; Little Dorrit, 2008; A Short Stay in Switzerland, 2009; Law and Order: UK, 2009–13; Downton Abbey, 2013–15; many radio performances (Sony Award, Best Actress, 1988 and 1992); *films:* Turtle Diary, 1985; The Good Father, 1986; Milou en Mai, 1990; Sense and Sensibility, 1996; The Governess, Bedrooms and Hallways, 1998; Onegin, 1999; Villa des Roses, 2002; Bright Young Things, 2003; Chromophobia, 2004; Babel, 2005; Atonement, 2007; Abraham's Point, 2008; Morris: A Life with Bells on, The Young Victoria, From Time to Time, 2009; A Royal Affair, The Wedding Video, 2012; Suite Française, Man Up, 2015. *Publications:* Other People's Shoes, 1999; Actors on Shakespeare: Macbeth, 2002; Facing It: reflections on images of older women, 2011; contribs to: Clamorous Voices, 1988; Players of Shakespeare, Vol. III, 1993; Mothers by Daughters, 1995; Renaissance Drama in Action, 1999; Living with Shakespeare, 2013. *Address:* c/o Tavistock Wood Management Ltd, 45 Conduit Street, W1S 2YN.

WALTER, Natasha; author and campaigner; Director, Women for Refugee Women, since 2007; *b* London, 20 Jan. 1967; *d* of Nicolas Walter and Ruth Walter; partner, Mark Lattimer; one *s* one *d*. *Educ:* North London Collegiate Sch.; St John's Coll., Cambridge (BA 1st Cl. English Lit. 1988); Harvard Univ. (Frank Knox Fellow, 1988). Dep. Literary Ed., Independent, 1993–94; feature writer and columnist, Guardian, Independent and Observer, 1995–2007. Humanitas Vis. Prof. in Women's Rights, Univ. of Cambridge, 2015. *Publications:* The New Feminism, 1998; Living Dolls: the return of sexism, 2010. *Address:* c/o Anna Webber, United Agents, 12–26 Lexington Street, W1F 0LE. *E:* awebber@unitedagents.co.uk.

WALTER, Neil Douglas, CNZM 2002; Chair, NZ on Air, 2006–12; *b* 11 Dec. 1942; *s* of Ernest Edward Walter and Anita Walter (*née* Frethey); *m* 1966, Berys Anne (*née* Robertson); one *s* two *d*. *Educ:* New Plymouth Boys' High School; Auckland University (MA). Second Sec., Bangkok, 1966–70; First Sec., NZ Mission to UN, NY, 1972–76; Official Sec., Tokelau Public Service, Apia, 1976–78; Minister, Paris and NZ Permt Deleg. to Unesco, 1981–85; Dep. High Comr for NZ in London, 1985–87; Asst Sec., Ministry of External Relations, NZ, 1987–90; NZ Ambassador to Indonesia, 1990–94; Dep. Sec., Ministry of Foreign Affairs and Trade, NZ, 1994–98; NZ Ambassador to Japan, 1998–99; NZ Sec. of Foreign Affairs and Trade, 1999–2002; Chair: Envmtl Risk Mgt Authy of NZ, 2003–08; NZ Broadcasting Commn, 2007–12. *Recreations:* sport, reading.

WALTER, Robert John; *b* 30 May 1948; *s* of late Richard and of Irene Walter; *m* 1970, Sally Middleton (*d* 1995); two *s* one *d*; *m* 2011, Feride Alp. *Educ:* Lord Weymouth Sch., Warminster; Aston Univ. (BSc 1971). Formerly farmer, S Devon; Mem., Stock Exchange, 1983–; internat. banker. Dir and Vice Pres., Aubrey G. Lanston & Co., Inc., 1986–97. Vice Pres., Cons. Gp for Europe, 1995–97 (Vice Chm., 1984–86; Dep. Chm., 1989–92; Chm., 1992–95). Contested (C) Bedwellty, 1979. MP (C) N Dorset, 1997–2015. Opposition spokesman on constitutional affairs and Wales, 1999–2001. Member: Health Select Cttee, 1997–99; Eur. Scrutiny Select Cttee, 1998–99; Internat. Develt Select Cttee, 2001–03; Treasury Select Cttee, 2003–05; Vice-Chm., Cons. Agric. Cttee, 1997–99; Sec., Cons. Eur. Affairs Cttee, 1997–99; Treasurer: All Party British-Japanese Parly Gp, 1997–2015; All Party Gp on Charities and Vol. Sector, 1997–2015; British-Caribbean Parly Gp, 1997–2015; Vice Chairman: All Party Gp on Lupus, 2000–15; All Party Human Rights Gp; Mem., British-Irish Parly Assembly (formerly Body), 1997–2015 (Chm., Eur. Affairs Cttee, 2001–15); Member: Parly Assembly of Council of Europe, 2001–15 (Leader, UK Delegn, 2010; Vice-Pres., 2011–15; Chm., Eur. Democrat Gp, 2011–15); Assembly of WEU, 2001–11 (Chm., Defence

Cttee, 2006–08; Leader, Federated Gp of Christian Democrats and European Democrats, 2006–15; Pres., Eur. Security and Defence Assembly, 2008–11); Chm., British Gp, IPU, 2011–15. Hon. Sec., 1999–2015, Rear Cdre, 2001–15, H of C Yacht Club. Chm. Bd of Governors, Tachbrook Sch., 1980–2000. Freeman, City of London, 1983; Liveryman, Needlemakers' Co., 1983. *Club:* Constitutional (Blandford).

WALTERS, Sir Dennis, Kt 1988; MBE 1960; *b* 28 Nov. 1928; *s* of late Douglas L. Walters and Clara Walters (*née* Pomello); *m* 1st, 1955, Vanora McIndoe (marr. diss. 1969); one *s* one *d*; 2nd, 1970, Hon. Celia (*née* Sandys) (marr. diss. 1979); one *s*; 3rd, 1981, Bridgett (marr. diss. 2004), *d* of late J. Francis Shearer; one *s* one *d*. *Educ:* Downside; St Catharine's College (Exhibitioner), Cambridge (MA). War of 1939–45: interned in Italy; served with Italian Resistance Movement behind German lines after Armistice, 1943–44; repatriated and continued normal educn, 1944. Chm., Fedn of Univ. Conservative and Unionist Assocs, 1950; Personal Asst to Lord Hailsham throughout his Chairmanship of Conservative Party, 1957–59; Chm., Coningsby Club, 1959. Contested (C) Blyth, 1959 and Nov. 1960; MP (C) Westbury Div. of Wilts, 1964–92. Jt Hon. Sec., Conservative Parly Foreign Affairs Cttee, 1965–71, Jt Vice-Chm., 1974–78; Jt Chm., Euro-Arab Parly Assoc., 1978–81; Mem., UK Parly Delegn to UN, 1966; UK Deleg. to Council of Europe and Assembly of WEU, 1970–73. Introduced Children and Young Persons (Amendment) Bill, 1985 (Royal Assent, 1986). Founder/Patron, Cons. ME Council, 2007– (Chm., 1980–92; Pres., 1992–2007). Director: The Spectator, 1983–84; Middle East Internat., 1971–90 (Chm., 1990–2006). Chm., Asthma Research Council, 1968–88; Vice Pres., Nat. Asthma Campaign, 1989–2001. Joint Chairman: Council for Advancement of Arab British Understanding, 1970–82 (Jt Vice-Chm., 1967–70); UK/Saudi Cultural Cttee, 1988–2007; Kuwait British Friendship Soc., 1996–2007 (Hon. Pres., 2007–); Mem., Kuwait Investment Adv. Cttee, 1969–; ME Consultant, JCB, 2005–. Governor, British Inst. of Florence, 1965–95. Comdr, Order of Cedar of Lebanon, 1969. *Publications:* Not Always with the Pack (autobiographical memoirs), 1989 (trans. Italian, rev. edn, as Benedetti Inglesi Benedetti Italiani, 1991). *Address:* Flat 43, 5 Sloane Court East, SW3 4TQ. *Clubs:* Boodle's, Hurlingham, Queen's.

WALTERS, Sir Donald, Kt 1983; Chairman, Llandough Hospital NHS Trust, 1992–98; *b* 5 Oct. 1925; *s* of Percival Donald and Irene Walters; *m* 1950, Adelaide Jean McQuistin; one *s*. *Educ:* Howardian High Sch., Cardiff; London School of Economics and Political Science (LLB). Called to Bar, Inner Temple, 1946; practised at Bar, Wales and Chester circuit, 1948–59. Dir, 1959–85, Dep. Man. Dir, 1975–85, Chartered Trust plc. Member: Welsh Develt Agency, 1980–93 (Dep. Chm., 1984–92); Develt Bd for Rural Wales, 1984–99; Dir, WNO, 1985–2000 (Vice-Chm., 1990); Chm., Wales Council for Voluntary Action, 1987–93; Mem. Council, Cardiff Univ. (formerly UWCC), 1988–2010 (Chm., 1988–98), Vice Pres., 2010–. High Sheriff, S Glamorgan, 1987–88. Treas., Friends of Llandaff Cathedral, 1998–; Clerk to Dean and Chapter, Llandaff Cathedral, 2001–. Hon. LLD Wales, 1990; Hon. Dr Glamorgan, 1997. *Recreations:* gardening, walking. *Address:* 120 Cyncoed Road, Cardiff CF23 6BL. *T:* (029) 2075 3166.

WALTERS, Ian, FIMechE; Chief Executive, Action Mental Health, 2002–10; *b* 20 March 1943; *s* of John and Olive Walters; *m* 1968, Carol Ann Flanders; two *s* one *d*. *Educ:* Moseley Hall Grammar Sch., Cheadle; Univ. of Manchester (BSc; DipTechSc 1966). MIET (MIEE 1970); MIGEM (MIGasE 1972); FIMechE 1997. With Parkinson Cowan Measurement, rising to Factory Manager, Manchester, then Belfast, 1966–72; Dep. Principal, then Principal, Dept of Commerce, NI, 1972–80; Industrial Development Board for Northern Ireland: Dir, then Sen. Dir, IDB N America, NY, 1980–84; Executive Director: Food Div., 1985–89; Internat. Mktg Div., 1989–91; Internat. Repn Div., 1991–92; Corporate Services Group: Actg Dep. Chief Exec., 1992–93; Sen. Exec. Dir, Jan.–Oct. 1993; Dir, Business Support Div., 1993–95, Chief Exec., 1995–2001, Trng and Employment Agency, NI. Dir, Open Coll. Network, NI. FCMI (MCMI; MBIM 1980); FRSA 2000. Mem., Governing Body, Belfast Metropolitan Coll., 2007– (Vice Chm., 2007–). Hon. Treas., Arthritis Care, NI, 2011–. Chm., Bd of Govs, Belvoir Park Primary Sch., 2011–14. Hon. Dr Rocky Mountain Coll., Montana, 1999. *Recreations:* photography, swimming, gardening.

WALTERS, John Latimer; QC 1997; Judge of the First-Tier Tribunal and Deputy Judge of the Upper Tribunal, since 2009; *b* 15 Sept. 1948; *o s* of late John Paton Walters and Charlotte Alison Walters (*née* Cunningham); *m* 1st, 1970, Victoria Anne Chambers (marr. diss. 1987; she *d* 1996); 2nd, 1990, Caroline Elizabeth, *d* of late John Vipond Byles and of Doreen Violet Byles, Norwich; two *d*, and one step *s*. *Educ:* Rugby Sch.; Balliol Coll., Oxford (MA; Wylie Prize, 1970). Called to the Bar, Middle Temple, 1977 (Astbury Scholar); practice at Revenue Bar, 1978–. Special Comr and Chm. (part-time), VAT and Duties Tribunals, 2002–09. Local Preacher in the Methodist Church (Waveney Ecumenical Partnership). *Recreations:* gardening, painting, design and work embroidery, genealogy, singing, esp. hymns, formerly Lieder. *Address:* Gray's Inn Tax Chambers, 36 Queen Street, EC4R 1BN. *T:* (020) 7242 2642.

WALTERS, Joyce Dora; Headmistress, Clifton High School, Bristol, 1985–95; *m* 1st, 1979, Lt-Col Howard C. Walters (*d* 1983); one *s*; 2nd, 2004, Prof. Richard Lynn, *qv*. *Educ:* St Anne's College, Oxford (BA Lit.Hum.). Headmistress, St Mary's, Calne, 1972–85. *Recreations:* travelling, reading, cooking, bridge. *Address:* 4 Longwood House, Failand, Bristol BS8 3TL. *T:* (01275) 392092.

WALTERS, Julie, CBE 2008 (OBE 1999); actress; *b* 22 Feb. 1950; *d* of late Thomas and Mary Walters; *m* 1997, Grant Roffey; one *d*. *Educ:* Holly Lodge Grammar Sch., Smethwick; Manchester Polytechnic (Teaching Certificate). *Theatre:* Educating Rita, 1980 (Drama Critics' Most Promising Newcomer Award; Variety Club Best Newcomer); Having a Ball, Lyric, Hammersmith, 1981; Fool for Love, NT, 1984; Macbeth, Leicester Haymarket, 1985; When I was a Girl I used to Scream and Shout, Whitehall, 1986; Frankie and Johnny in the Clair de Lune, Comedy, 1989; The Rose Tattoo, Playhouse, 1991; All My Sons, RNT, 2000 (Best Actress, Laurence Olivier Awards, 2001); Acorn Antiques the Musical, Th. Royal, Haymarket, 2005; The Last of the Haussmans, NT, 2012. *Films:* Educating Rita, 1983 (Variety Club of GB's Award for best film actress; BAFTA Award for best actress; Hollywood Golden Globe Award); She'll be Wearing Pink Pyjamas, 1985; Car Trouble, 1986; Personal Services, 1987 (British Video Award, Best Actress); Prick Up Your Ears, 1987; Buster, 1988; Killing Dad, 1989; Stepping Out (Variety Club Best Film Actress), 1991; Just Like a Woman, 1992; Sister My Sister, 1995; Intimate Relations, 1996; Girls' Night, 1998; Titanic Town, 1999; Billy Elliot (Evening Standard Award, Best Actress; BAFTA Award, Best Supporting Actress), 2000; Harry Potter and the Philosopher's Stone, 2001; Before You Go, Harry Potter and the Chamber of Secrets, 2002; Calendar Girls, 2003; Harry Potter and the Prisoner of Azkaban, 2004; Wah-Wah, Driving Lessons, 2006; Becoming Jane, Harry Potter and the Order of the Phoenix, 2007; Mamma Mia!, 2008; Harry Potter and the Half-Blood Prince, 2009; Harry Potter and the Deathly Hallows, Pt 1, 2010, Pt 2, 2011; One Chance, 2013; Effie Gray, Paddington, 2014; *television:* My Beautiful Son, 2001 (Best Actress, BAFTA, 2002); The Return, 2003; Canterbury Tales: The Wife of Bath, 2003 (Best Actress, BAFTA, 2004); Ahead of the Class, 2005; Ruby in the Smoke, 2006; series include: Wood and Walters, 1981–82; Victoria Wood as Seen on TV, 1985–87; The Secret Diary of Adrian Mole, 1985; Victoria Wood Series, 1989; GBH, 1991; Jake's Progress, 1995; Melissa, 1997; dinnerladies, 1998–99; films: Clothes in the Wardrobe, Wide Eyed and Legless, 1993; Bambino Mio, Pat and Margaret, 1994; Little Red Riding Hood, 1995; Brazen Hussies, 1996; Filth: The Mary Whitehouse Story, 2008; A Short Stay in Switzerland, 2009; Mo (Best Actress, BAFTA and Broadcasting Press Guild Awards), 2010; Henry IV, 2012; Henry V, 2012; serials: Oliver Twist, 1999; Murder, 2002 (BAFTA Award, Best Actress, RTS Best Actress, 2003); The Jury, 2011; Indian Summers, 2015; also television plays, incl. monologues in series, Talking Heads, 1988, 1998. Show Business Personality of the Year, Variety Club of GB, 2001; Lifetime Achievement Award, South Bank Sky Arts Awards, 2013; Fellow, BAFTA, 2014. *Publications:* Baby Talk, 1990; Maggie's Tree (novel), 2006; That's Another Story (autobiog.), 2008. *Recreations:* reading, television, travel, walking. *Address:* c/o Independent Talent Agency Ltd, 40 Whitfield Street, W1T 2RH.

WALTERS, Prof. Kenneth, PhD, DSc; FRS 1991; Professor of Applied Mathematics, 1973–94, now Distinguished Research Professor, Institute of Mathematics, Physics and Computer Science (formerly of Mathematics and Physics), Aberystwyth University (formerly University of Wales, Aberystwyth); *b* 14 Sept. 1934; *s* of late Trevor Walters and Lilian (*née* Price); *m* 1963, Mary Ross Eccles; two *s* one *d*. *Educ:* University Coll. of Swansea (BSc 1956; MSc 1957; PhD 1959; DSc 1984; Hon. Fellow, 1992). Dept of Mathematics, University Coll. of Wales, Aberystwyth: Lectr, 1960–65; Sen. Lectr, 1965–70; Reader, 1970–73. Vis. Fellow, Peterhouse, Cambridge, 1996. Mem., Sci. Adv. Council for Wales, 2010–. Pres., European Soc. of Rheology, 1996–2000; Chm., Internat. Cttee on Rheology, 2000–04. Church Warden, St Michael's, Aberystwyth, 1993–99, 2001–07. Founding FLSW 2010. For. Mem., NAE, USA, 1995; Mem., Internat. Acad. of Engrg, 2014. Dr *hc* Joseph Fourier, Grenoble, 1998; Hon. DSc Strathclyde, 2011. Gold Medal, British Soc. of Rheology, 1984; Weissenberg Award, European Soc. of Rheology, 2002. *Publications:* Rheometry, 1975; (ed) Rheometry: industrial applications, 1980; (with M. J. Crochet and A. R. Davies) Numerical Simulation of non-Newtonian Flow, 1984; (with H. A. Barnes and J. F. Hutton) An Introduction to Rheology, 1989; (with D. V. Boger) Rheological Phenomena in Focus, 1993; (with R. I. Tanner) Rheology: an historical perspective, 1998; The Way it Was, 2003; More Personal Stories from New Testament Times, 2012. *Address:* Institute of Mathematics and Physics and Computer Science, Aberystwyth University, Penglais, Aberystwyth, Ceredigion SY23 3BZ. *T:* (01970) 622750; 8 Pen y Graig, Aberystwyth, Ceredigion SY23 2JA. *T:* (01970) 615276.

WALTERS, Lucy Mary Elizabeth; *see* Crowe, L. M. E.

WALTERS, Minette Caroline Mary; crime writer, since 1992; *b* 26 Sept. 1949; *d* of Capt. Samuel Henry Desmond Jebb and Minette Colleen Helen Jebb (*née* Paul); *m* 1978, Alex Hamilton Walters; two *s*. *Educ:* Godolphin Sch.; Durham Univ. (BA). Magazine journalist, 1972–77; freelance journalist and writer, 1977–82. Hon. DLitt: Bournemouth, 2005; Southampton Solent, 2006. John Creasey Award, 1992, Gold Dagger Award, 1994, 2002, CWA; Edgar Allen Poe Award, 1994. *Publications:* The Ice House, 1992; The Sculptress, 1993; The Scold's Bridle, 1994; The Dark Room, 1995; The Echo, 1997; The Breaker, 1998; The Shape of Snakes, 2000 (Palle Rosenkrantz Prize, Danish Acad. of Crime, 2001); Acid Row, 2001; Fox Evil, 2002; Disordered Minds, 2003; The Tinder Box, 2004; The Devil's Feather, 2005; Chickenfeed, 2006 (Quick Reads Award, 2006); The Chameleon's Shadow, 2007; A Dreadful Murder, 2013; The Cellar, 2015. *Recreations:* crosswords, jigsaw puzzles, DIY, cinema, TV, Radio 4, sailing, reading, wine. *Address:* c/o Gregory & Co., Authors' Agents, 3 Barb Mews, W6 7PA. *T:* (020) 7610 4676.

WALTERS, Sir Peter (Ingram), Kt 1984; non-executive Director, Nomura International plc, 2004–10 (Senior Adviser, 2002–04); *b* 11 March 1931; *s* of late Stephen Walters and of Edna Walters (*née* Redgate); *m* 1st, 1960, Patricia Anne (*née* Tulloch) (marr. diss. 1991); two *s* one *d*; 2nd, 1992, Meryl Marshall. *Educ:* King Edward's Sch., Birmingham; Birmingham Univ. (BCom). NS Commn; RASC, 1952–54; British Petroleum Co., 1954–90: Man. Dir, 1973–90; Chm., 1981–90; Vice-Pres., BP North America, 1965–67; Chairman: BP Chemicals, 1976–81; BP Chemicals Internat., 1981; Blue Circle Industries PLC, 1990–96; SmithKline Beecham, subseq. Glaxo SmithKline: Dir, 1989–2000; Chm., 1994–2000; Jt Dep. Chm., 2000–02; Dep. Chm., Thorn EMI, later EMI, 1990–99 (Dir, 1989–99). Dir, 1981–89, Dep. Chm., 1988–89, Nat. Westminster Bank; Chm., Midland Bank, 1991–94; Dep. Chm., HSBC Hldgs, 1992–2001. Member: Indust. Soc. Council, 1975–90; Post Office Bd, 1978–79; Coal Industry Adv. Bd, 1981–85; Inst. of Manpower Studies, 1986–88 (Vice-Pres., 1977–80; Pres., 1980–86); Gen. Cttee, Lloyds Register of Shipping, 1976–90; President's Cttee, CBI, 1982–90; President: Soc. of Chem. Industry, 1978–80; Gen. Council of British Shipping, 1977–78; Inst. of Directors, 1986–92; Inst. Business Ethics, 2001–10. Chm. Governors, London Business Sch., 1987–91 (Governor, 1981–91); Governor Nat. Inst. of Economic and Social Affairs, 1981–90; Mem. Foundn Bd, 1982–83, Chm., 1984–86, Internat. Management Inst.; Trustee: Nat. Maritime Museum, 1983–90; E Malling Res. Station, 1983–2010; Inst. of Economic Affairs, 1986–2007. Pres., Police Foundn, 2001–10 (Chm., Trustees, 1985–2001). Hon. DSocSc Birmingham, 1986; DUniv Stirling, 1987. Comdr, Order of Leopold (Belgium), 1984. *Recreations:* golf, gardening, sailing. *Address:* 1 St James's Square, SW1Y 4PD. *Clubs:* Athenæum; West Sussex Golf.

WALTERS, Rhodri Havard, CB 2014; DPhil; Reading Clerk and Head of Corporate Services, House of Lords, 2007–14; *b* Merthyr Tydfil, 28 Feb. 1950; *s* of Havard Walters and Veigan Walters (*née* Hughes). *Educ:* Cyfarthfa Castle Grammar Sch., Merthyr Tydfil; Jesus Coll., Oxford (Meyricke Exhibnr; BA 1971; DPhil 1975). Clerk, Parliament Office, House of Lords, 1975–2014: on secondment to Cabinet Office as Private Sec. to Leader of the House and Govt Chief Whip, 1986–89; Civil Service Nuffield and Leverhulme Travelling Fellow, attached to US Congress, 1989–90; Clerk to Select Cttee on Sci. and Technol., H of L, 1990–93; Establishment Officer, 1993–2000; Clerk of Public Bills, 2000–02; Sec. to Ecclesiastical Cttee, 2000–03; Clerk: of Cttees, 2002–07; of the Overseas Office, 2002–14; of Jt Cttee on Draft H of L Reform Bill, 2011–12. *Publications:* How Parliament Works (with Robert Rogers), 1987, 7th edn 2015; (contrib.) The British Constitution in the Twentieth Century, 2003; Law in Politics, Politics in Law, 2013; articles in Econ. Hist. Rev., Welsh Hist. Rev., The Table. *Recreations:* rowing, gardening, ski-ing, church music. *Address:* 40 Cleveland Gardens, SW13 0AG. *T:* (020) 8878 7494. *E:* rhwalters@blueyonder.co.uk.

WALTERS, Sam Robert, MBE 1999; Artistic Director, Orange Tree Theatre, 1971–2014 (Founder, 1971); *b* 11 Oct. 1939; *s* of Denbigh Robert Walters and Elizabeth Walters (*née* Curry); *m* 1964, Auriol Smith; two *d*. *Educ:* Felsted Sch., Essex; Merton Coll., Oxford (MA PPE); LAMDA. Actor, 1963–67; Resident Dir, Worcester Repertory Co., Swan Theatre, 1967–69; Dir, Jamaica Theatre Co. and Jamaica Theatre Sch., 1970–71; freelance dir, West End, regl theatres, and in Israel and Holland, 1970–; at Orange Tree Theatre has dir. premières of plays by Alan Ayckbourn, Rodney Ackland, Harley Granville Barker, Vaclav Havel and James Saunders, amongst many others. Hon. Freeman, Richmond upon Thames, 2014. Hon. DLitt Kingston, 2009. Special Achievement Awards: Off West End Th. Awards, 2012; Peter Brook Empty Space Awards, 2013. *Recreations:* no time, alas, but now he has retired from the Orange Tree Theatre he may discover some!

WALTHER, Robert Philippe, FIA; Deputy Chairman, Nationwide Building Society, 2006–12 (Director, 2002–12); *b* 31 July 1943; *s* of Prof. D. P. Walther and Barbara (*née* Brook); *m* 1969, Anne Wigglesworth. *Educ:* Charterhouse; Christ Church, Oxford (MA). FIA 1970. Clerical Medical Investment Group: Investment Manager, 1974–85; Investment Dir, 1985–94; Dep. Man. Dir, 1994–95; Gp Chief Exec., 1995–2001; Chairman: JP Morgan Fleming (formerly Fleming Claverhouse Investment Trust), 1999–2005 (Dir, 1993–99); Fidelity European Values, 1999–2010 (Dir, 1993–2010). Dir, BUPA, 2004–09. *Recreations:* golf, sailing, bridge, fishing. *Address:* Ashwells Barn, Chesham Lane, Chalfont St Giles, Bucks HP8 4AS. *T:* (01494) 875575.

WALTHO, Lynda Ellen; Head of Public Affairs, Green Bus Company, since 2010; Managing Director, Clearvu Communications, since 2012; *b* 22 May 1960; *d* of Charles and Eunice Abbott; *m* Stephen J. Waltho (marr. diss. 2014); two *s*. *Educ:* Keele Univ.; Univ. of Central England (PGCE). School teacher, Birmingham, Sandwell and Dudley LEAs, 1981–94;

Assistant to: Simon Murphy, MEP, 1995–97; Sylvia Heal, MP, 1997–2001; Agent, W Midlands Regional Labour Party, 2001–04; Principal Advr to Neena Gill, MEP, 2004–05. MP (Lab) Stourbridge, 2005–10; contested (Lab) same seat, 2010. PPS to Minister of State, NI Office, 2005–07, MoJ, 2007–10, to Prisons Minister, 2007–08; Dep. Minister for W Midlands, 2008–10.

WALTON, family name of **Baron Walton of Detchant**.

WALTON OF DETCHANT, Baron *cr* 1989 (Life Peer), of Detchant in the County of Northumberland; **John Nicholas Walton,** Kt 1979; TD 1962; FRCP; Warden, Green College, University of Oxford, 1983–89; *b* 16 Sept. 1922; *s* of Herbert Walton and Eleanor Watson Walton; *m* 1946, Mary Elizabeth Harrison (*d* 2003); one *s* two *d*. *Educ:* Alderman Wraith Grammar Sch., Spennymoor, Co. Durham; Med. Sch., King's Coll., Univ. of Durham. MB, BS (1st Cl. Hons) 1945; MD (Durham) 1952; DSc (Newcastle) 1972; MA(Oxon) 1983; FRCP 1963 (MRCP 1950). Ho. Phys., Royal Victoria Inf., Newcastle, 1946–47; service in RAMC, 1947–49; Med. Registrar, Royal Vic. Inf., 1949–51; Research Asst, Univ. of Durham, 1951–56; Nuffield Foundn Fellow, Mass. Gen. Hosp. and Harvard Univ., 1953–54; King's Coll. Fellow, Neurological Res. Unit, Nat. Hosp., Queen Square, 1954–55; First Asst in Neurology, Newcastle upon Tyne, 1956–58; Cons. Neurologist, Newcastle Univ. Hosps, 1958–83; Prof. of Neurology, 1968–83, and Dean of Medicine, 1971–81, Univ. of Newcastle upon Tyne. Numerous named lectureships and overseas visiting professorships. Member: MRC, 1974–78; GMC, 1971–89 (Chm. Educn Cttee, 1975–82; Pres., 1982–89); President: BMA, 1980–82; Royal Soc. of Medicine, 1984–86 (Hon. Fellow, 1988); ASME 1982–94; Assoc. of British Neurologists, 1987–88; World Fedn Neurol., 1989–97 (First Vice-Pres., 1981–89; Chm., Res. Cttee); Chm., Hamlyn Nat. Commn on Educn, 1991–95; UK Rep., EEC Adv. Cttee, Med. Educn, 1975–83; Editor-in-Chief, Jl of Neurological Sciences, 1966–77; Chm., Muscular Dystrophy Gp of GB, 1970–95 (Hon. Life Pres., Muscular Dystrophy UK, 2011). Chm., H of L Select Cttee on Med. Ethics, 1993–94; Mem., H of L Select Cttee on Sci. and Technol., 1992–97, 1999–2001 (Chm., Sub-Cttee 1, 1994–96 and 1999–2001). Col (late RAMC) and OC 1 (N) Gen. Hosp. (TA), 1963–66; Hon. Col 201(N) Gen. Hosp. (T&AVR), 1971–77. Freeman, City of London, 1978. Founder FMedSci 1998. Foreign Member: Norwegian Acad. of Sci. and Letters, 1987; Venezuelan Acad. of Medicine, 1992; Russian Acad. of Med. Scis, 1993; Hon. Mem., Osler Club of London; Hon. Foreign Member: Amer. Neurological Assoc., Amer. Acad. of Neurology, Assoc. Amer. Phys., Amer. Osler Soc., Japan Osler Soc., and of Canadian, French, German, Australian, Austrian, Belgian, Spanish, Polish, Venezuelan, Thai, Japanese, Russian and Brazilian Neurological Assocs. Hon. FACP 1980; Hon. FRCPE 1981; Hon. FRCP (Can) 1984; Hon. FRCPath 1993; Hon. FRCPsych 1993; Hon. FRCPCH 1996; Hon. Fellow, Inst. of Educn, Univ. of London, 1994. Dr de l'Univ. (Hon.) Aix-Marseille, 1975; Hon. DSc: Leeds, 1979; Leicester, 1980; Hull, 1988; Oxford Brookes, 1994; Durham, 2002; Hon. MD: Sheffield, 1987; Mahidol, Thailand, 1998; Hon. DCL: Newcastle, 1988; Northumbria, 2013; Laurea *hc* Genoa, 1992. Hon. Freeman: Newcastle upon Tyne, 1980; Soc. of Apothecaries, 2013. Hewitt Award, RSM Foundn Inc., 2006; Gold Medal, RSocMed, 2014. *Publications:* Subarachnoid Haemorrhage, 1956; (with R. D. Adams) Polymyositis, 1958; Essentials of Neurology, 1961, 6th edn 1989; Disorders of Voluntary Muscle, 1964, 6th edn (ed jtly) 1994; Brain's Diseases of the Nervous System, 7th edn 1969, 10th edn 1993; (with F. L. Mastaglia) Skeletal Muscle Pathology, 1982, 2nd edn 1991, etc; (ed jtly) The Oxford Companion to Medicine, 1986; The Spice of Life (autobiog.), 1993; (ed jtly) The Oxford Medical Companion, 1994; numerous chapters in books and papers in sci. jls. *Recreations:* cricket, golf and other sports, reading, music. *Address:* 15 Croft Way, Belford, Northumberland NE70 7ET. *T:* (01668) 219009. *E:* waldetch@aol.com. *Clubs:* Athenæum, Oxford and Cambridge, MCC; Bamburgh Castle Golf (Pres., 1998–).

WALTON, His Honour Christopher Thomas; a Circuit Judge, 1997–2014; *b* 20 March 1949; *s* of George Edward Taylor Walton and Margaret Walton; *m* 1992, Brenda Margaret Laws. *Educ:* St Cuthbert's GS, Newcastle upon Tyne; Downing Coll., Cambridge (MA). Called to the Bar, Middle Temple, 1973; a Recorder, 1992–97; North Eastern Circuit. *Publications:* (gen. ed.) Charlesworth & Percy on Negligence, 9th edn 1996, 13th edn 2014. *Recreations:* tennis, golf, suffering with Newcastle United FC, history, music, Scottish art.
See also S. E. Wood.

WALTON, Ven. Geoffrey Elmer; Archdeacon of Dorset, 1982–2000, now Archdeacon Emeritus; *b* 19 Feb. 1934; *s* of Harold and Edith Margaret Walton; *m* 1961, Edith Mollie O'Connor; one *s*. *Educ:* St John's Coll., Univ. of Durham (BA); Queen's Coll., Birmingham (DipTh). Asst Curate, Warsop with Sookholme, 1961–65; Vicar of Norwell, Notts, 1965–69; Recruitment and Selection Sec., ACCM, 1969–75; Vicar of Holy Trinity, Weymouth, 1975–82; RD of Weymouth, 1980–82; Non-Residentiary Canon of Salisbury, 1981–2000. Chairman: E Dorset Housing Assoc., 1991–2003; Dorset County Scout Council, 1995–2013; Synergy Housing Gp, 2003–05. *Recreations:* conjuring, religious drama. *Address:* Priory Cottage, 6 Hibberds Field, Cranborne, Dorset BH21 5QL. *T:* (01725) 517167.

WALTON, John William Scott; Director of Statistics, Board of Inland Revenue, 1977–85; *b* 25 Sept. 1925; *s* of late Sir John Charles Walton, KCIE, CB, MC, and late Nelly Margaret, Lady Walton, *d* of late Prof. W. R. Scott. *Educ:* Marlborough; Brasenose Coll., Oxford. Army (RA), 1943–47. Mutual Security Agency, Paris, 1952; Inland Revenue, 1954; Central Statistical Office, 1958, Chief Statistician, 1967, Asst Dir, 1972. *Publications:* (contrib. jtly) M. Perlman, The Organization and Retrieval of Economic Knowledge, 1977; (contrib.) ECB Workshop on Pensions, 2009; articles in The Review of Income and Wealth, Economic Trends, Business Economist, Statistical News. *Club:* Oxford and Cambridge.

WALTON, Margaret Anita; *see* Clark, M. A.

WALTON, Peter David; Director, Human Resources and Workplace Services, Department for Communities and Local Government (formerly Office of the Deputy Prime Minister), 2005–06; *b* 24 Feb. 1954; *s* of Kenneth Walton and Sheila Walton; *m* 1998, Margaret Anita Clark, *qv*. *Educ:* Robert Gordon's Coll., Aberdeen; Univ. of Durham (BA Hons (Geog.) 1975). Joined DoE, administrative trainee, 1975; various policy posts; Grade 7, 1980; various policy and finance posts, incl. secondment to RDA; sen. Civil Service posts in housing, finance, central policy planning and agency sponsorship, 1991–2001; Exec. Dir, Change Mgt, then Human Resources and Business Change, subseq. Orgnl Devclt and Resources, ONS, 2001–05. Mem., Puddletown Parish Council, 2013–. Chm., Tolpuddle Village Hall, 2012–. *Recreations:* watching sport, music and opera, DIY, collecting and entertaining eccentric friends.

WALTON, Richard Arthur, CB 2003; PhD; FIMA, FIET; information assurance consultant, 2003–13; *b* 22 Sept. 1947; *s* of Lt Col Gordon Walton and Audrey Mary Walton (*née* Varah); *m* 1st, 1968, Jacqueline Elisabeth Roberts (*d* 1990); one *d*; 2nd, 1992, Mary Elizabeth Mackenzie. *Educ:* Shene Grammar Sch.; Univ. of Nottingham (BSc Hons Maths 1968; PhD 1971); Open Univ. (BA Hons 1987). FIMA 1999; CMath 1999; MBCS 2004; FIET 2005; CEng 2005. Lectr in Maths, N Staffordshire Poly., 1971–73; GCHQ: various posts, 1973–98; Dir, CESG (Nat. Technical Authy for Inf. Assurance), 1999–2002; Office of the e-Envoy, Cabinet Office, 2002–03. Vis. Prof., Royal Holloway, Univ. of London, 2002–. Mem., Elmley Castle Parish Council, 2004–15. Honorary Treasurer: Elmley Castle Cricket Club, 1984–2004; Elmley Castle PCC, 2001–15. Mem., Inst. of Information Security Professionals, 2008–. *Recreations:* supporting cricket and Rugby, concerts, theatre. *E:* richard@walton-mackenzie.com. *Clubs:* Civil Service; New (Cheltenham).

WALTON, Sarah Louise; *see* Rowland-Jones, S. L.

WALTON, Dr Suzy, CDir, CSci, CPsychol; *b* Nottingham, 8 Dec. 1963; *d* of Michael Brett and Greta Brett (*née* Lowe); five *s* one *d*; partner, Andrew James Griffin. *Educ:* Nottingham Girls' High Sch.; Univ. of Herts (BSc 1st Cl. Hons 1994); Cranfield Univ. (MSc 1995; PhD Mil. Suicide 1999). CPsychol 1997; CSci 2007. Actress, Children of a Lesser God, 1983–85; producer, presenter and ed., Time Off (weekly travel prog.), LBC Radio, 1986–90; News Producer, Sky News, 1990–91; mil. psychologist, MoD, 1995–2000; Sen. Civil Servant, DTI, 2000; Cabinet Office: Prime Minister's Strategy Unit, 2000–04; Prime Minister's Delivery Unit, 2005–07. Member: Nat. Specialist Commng Gp, DoH, 2007–13; Ethics Gp, Nat. DNA Database, Home Office, 2007–14; Sci. Adv. Council, DEFRA, 2009–11; Bd, HEFCE, 2012–; State Hons Cttee, Cabinet Office, 2012–. Deputy Chairman of Board: Univ. of Westminster, 2005–14; Internet Watch Foundn, 2008–14; Director: Combat Stress, 2008– (Chm., Med. Services Cttee); Birmingham Children's Hosp., 2008–11. Member, Board: RSA, 2008– (Dep. Chm.); IoD, 2013– (Dep. Chm., Chartered Dir Cttee, 2010–); ACCA, 2014–. CDir 2008. FRSocMed; FRSA. *Publications:* Suicide in the British Army, Parts 1–5, 1996–99. *E:* suzy.walton1@ntlworld.com.

WALTON, William Stephen; Chief Education Officer, Sheffield, 1985–90; *b* 28 March 1933; *s* of Thomas Leslie Walton and Ena Walton (*née* Naylor); adopted French nationality, 2008; *m* 1964, Lois Elicia Petts; three *d* (incl. twins). *Educ:* King's School, Pontefract; Univ. of Birmingham (BA). RAF, gen. duties (flying), 1951–55. Production Management, Dunlop Rubber Co., 1958–61; Derbyshire Local Educn Authy School Teacher, 1961–67; Educational Administration: Hull, 1967–70; Newcastle upon Tyne, 1970–79; Sheffield 1979–90. Visiting Professor: Univ. of Simon Fraser, BC, 1990–91; Univ. of Portland, Oregon, 1990–91. Pres., Soc. of Educn Officers, 1989–90; Chm., Sch. Curriculum Industry Partnership/Mini Enterprise Schs Project, 1990–95. Dir, Outward Bound, 1989–95. Registered Inspector of Schools, 1993–2003. Hon. Fellow, Sheffield City Polytechnic, 1990. *Recreation:* travel. *Club:* Royal Air Force.

WALWYN, Peter Tyndall, MBE 2012; racehorse trainer, 1960–99; *b* 1 July 1933; *s* of late Lt-Col Charles Lawrence Tyndall Walwyn, DSO, OBE, MC, Moreton in Marsh, Glos; *m* 1960, Virginia Gaselee (*d* 2014), *d* of A. S. Gaselee, MFH; one *s* one *d*. *Educ:* Amesbury Sch., Hindhead, Surrey; Charterhouse. Leading trainer on the flat, 1974, 1975; leading trainer, Ireland, 1974, 1975; a new record in earnings (£373,563), 1975. Major races won include: One Thousand Guineas, 1970, Humble Duty; Oaks Stakes, 1974, Polygamy; Irish Derby, 1974, English Prince, and 1975, Grundy; King George VI and Queen Elizabeth Stakes, Ascot, 1975, Grundy; Epsom Derby, 1975, Grundy. Chm., Lambourn Trainers' Assoc., 1989–; Member: Jockey Club, 1999–; Council of Mgt, Animal Health Trust, 1998–. Trustee, Lambourn Valley Housing Trust, 1996–. President: Vine and Craven Foxhounds, 1975–; British Racing Sch., Newmarket, 2006–; Berks Br., CLA, 2010–. Freeman, City of London, 2005; Yeoman, Saddlers' Co., 2005. *Publications:* Handy All the Way: a trainer's life, 2000. *Recreations:* foxhunting, shooting, watercolours, mole catching. *Address:* Rockfel, Wantage Road, Lambourn, Berks RG17 8UF. *Clubs:* Turf, Jockey.

WAN, Joseph Sai Cheong, FCA; FCIArb; Chief Executive Officer, Harvey Nichols Group Ltd, 1992–2014; *b* Hong Kong, 27 Feb. 1954; *s* of Yuk Lin Wan and Lai Bing Ho; *m* 1986, Flora Mei Yee; two *d*. *Educ:* St Louis Sch., Hong Kong. FCA 1984; FCIArb 2000. Qualified Asst, then Associate, Hong Kong Office, KPMG, 1978–87 (incl. one year in London office); Gp Finance Dir, Dickson Concepts Internat. Ltd, 1987–92. Chartered Arbitrator 2002. Fellow, Hong Kong Inst. Certified Public Accountants, 1986; FInstD 1989. FRSA. *Recreations:* reading (legal and finance), swimming, table tennis, travelling.

WANAMAKER, Zoë, CBE 2001; actor; *b* 13 May; *d* of late Sam Wanamaker, Hon. CBE, and Charlotte (*née* Holland); acquired British passport, 2001; *m* 1994, Gawn Grainger. *Stage includes:* A Midsummer Night's Dream, 69 Theatre Co., 1970; repertory at Royal Lyceum, 1971–72, Oxford Playhouse, 1974–75 and Nottingham, 1975–76; Royal Shakespeare Company: The Devil's Disciple, Ivanov, Wild Oats, 1976; Captain Swing, The Taming of the Shrew, Piaf, 1978 (NY, 1980); Once in a Lifetime, 1979 (Olivier Award/SWET Award); Comedy of Errors, Twelfth Night, The Time of your Life, 1983; Mother Courage (Drama magazine award), 1984; Othello, 1989; National Theatre: The Importance of Being Earnest, 1982; The Bay at Nice, Wrecked Eggs, 1986; Mrs Klein, 1988, transf. Apollo, 1989; The Crucible, 1990; Battle Royal, 1999; His Girl Friday, 2003; The Rose Tattoo, Much Ado About Nothing, 2007; The Cherry Orchard, 2011; West End: The Last Yankee, Young Vic, 1993; Dead Funny, Hampstead, transf. Vaudeville, 1994; The Glass Menagerie, Donmar, transf. Comedy, 1995; Sylvia, Apollo, 1996; The Old Neighbourhood, Duke of York's, 1998; Boston Marriage, Donmar, transf. New Ambassadors, 2001; All My Sons, Apollo, 2010 (whatsonstage.com Award); Passion Play, Duke of York's, 2013; Chichester: Electra, 1997 (Olivier Award, Variety Club Award, and Callaway Award, US Equity, 1998), transf. Princeton and NY, 1998–99; Stevie, Minerva, Chichester, 2014, transf. Hampstead, 2015; Loot, NY, 1986; Awake and Sing!, NY, 2006; Zorba, NY, 2015; *films include:* Inside the Third Reich, The Hunger, 1982; The Raggedy Rawney, 1987; Amy Foster, 1996; Wilde, 1996; Harry Potter and the Philosopher's Stone, 2001; Five Children and It, 2004; It's a Wonderful Afterlife, 2010; My Week with Marilyn, 2011; *television includes:* Strike, 1981; Richard III, 1982; Enemies of the State, 1982; The Edge of Darkness, 1984; Paradise Postponed, 1985; Once in a Lifetime, 1987; The Dog it was that Died, 1988; Prime Suspect, 1990; Love Hurts, 1991, 1992, 1993; The Blackheath Poisonings, 1991; Memento Mori, 1991; The Countess Alice, 1991; The Widowing of Mrs Holroyd, 1995; A Dance to the Music of Time, 1997; Leprechauns, 1999; David Copperfield, 1999; Gormenghast, 1999; My Family, 2000–11 (Best Sitcom Actress Rose d'Or, 2005); Adrian Mole: the Cappuccino Years, 2000; Miss Marple: A Murder is Announced, 2004; A Waste of Shame, 2005; Dr Who, 2005, 2006; Poirot: Cards on the Table, 2005, Mrs McGinty's Dead, 2008, The Third Girl, 2008, Halloween Party, 2010, Dead Man's Folly, Elephants Can Remember, 2013; Johnny and the Bomb, 2006; The Old Curiosity Shop, 2007; The Man, 2012; Wodehouse in Exile, 2013; Mr Selfridge, 2015; has also appeared in radio plays. Patron, Prisoners of Conscience, 2003–; Vice Patron, The Actors' Centre, 2005–; Hon. Pres., Shakespeare's Globe, 2005–; Hon. Vice-Pres., Dignity in Dying (formerly Voluntary Euthanasia Soc.), 1994. Hon. DLitt: S Bank, 1993; Amer. Internat. Univ., London, 1999; UEA, 2012. BPG TV Award for Best Actress, 1992; Theatre Sch., DePaul Univ., Chicago, Award for Excellence in the Arts. 2004. *Address:* c/o Peggy Thompson, 1st & 2nd Floor Offices, 296 Sandycombe Road, Kew, Richmond, Surrey TW9 3NG.

WANDSWORTH, Archdeacon of; *see* Kiddle, Ven. J.

WANG Gungwu, Prof., CBE 1991; FAHA; University Professor, National University of Singapore, since 2007; Director, East Asian institute, Singapore, 1997–2007 (Chairman, since 2007); Vice-Chancellor, University of Hong Kong, 1986–95; *b* 9 Oct. 1930; *s* of Wang Fo Wen and Ting Yien; *m* 1955, Margaret Lim Ping-Ting; one *s* two *d*. *Educ:* Anderson Sch., Ipoh, Malaya; Nat. Central Univ., Nanking, China; Univ. of Malaya, Singapore (BA Hons, MA); Univ. of London (PhD 1957). University of Malaya, Singapore: Asst Lectr, 1957–59; Lectr, 1959; University of Malaya, Kuala Lumpur: Lectr, 1959–61; Sen. Lectr, 1961–63; Dean of Arts, 1962–63; Prof. of History, 1963–68; Australian National University: Prof. of Far Eastern History, 1968–86, Emeritus Prof., 1988; Dir, Res. Sch. of Pacific Studies, 1975–80; Univ. Fellow, 1996–97. Rockefeller Fellow, 1961–62, Sen. Vis. Fellow, 1972, Univ. of London; Vis. Fellow, All Souls Coll., Oxford, 1974–75; John A. Burns Distinguished Vis. Prof. of History, Univ. of Hawaii, 1979; Rose Morgan Vis. Prof. of History, Univ. of Kansas,

1983; Dist. Professorial Fellow, Inst. of SE Asian Studies, 1999–2002; Dist. Fellow, Hong Kong Inst. for the Humanities and Social Scis, Univ. of Hong Kong, 2009; Rector, Cinnamon Coll., NUS, 2010–. Dir, East Asian History of Science Foundation Ltd, 1987–95. MEC, Hong Kong, 1990–92. Co-Patron, Asia-Link, Melbourne, 1994–. Chairman: Australia-China Council, 1984–86; Envmt Pollution Cttee, HK, 1988–93; Adv. Council on the Envmt, 1993–95; Council for the Performing Arts, HK, 1989–94; Asia-Pacific Council, Griffith Univ., 1997–2001; Asia Scholarship Foundn, 2002–07; Internat. Adv. Council, Universiti Tunku Abdul Rahman, Malaysia, 2002–; Bd of Trustees, Inst. SE Asian Studies, 2002–; Singapore Higher Educn Accreditation Council, 2004–06; Bd, Lee Kuan Yew Sch. for Public Policy, 2005–. Member: Commn of Inquiry on Singapore Riots, 1964–65; Internat. Adv. Panel, E-W Center, Honolulu, 1979–91; Cttee on Aust.-Japan Relations, 1980–81; Regional Council, Inst. of SE Asian Studies, Singapore, 1982–2002; Admin. Bd, Assoc. of SE Asian Instns of Higher Learning, 1986–92; Council, Chinese Univ. of Hong Kong, 1986–95; Exec. Council, WWF, HK, 1987–95; Council, Asia-Aust. Inst., Sydney, 1991–95, 1999–; Council, Asia Soc., HK, 1991–95; Council, IISS, 1992–2001; Nat. Arts Council, Singapore, 1996–2000; Nat. Heritage Bd, Singapore, 1997–2002; Nat. Library Bd, 1997–2003; Bd, Social Sci. Council, NY, 2000–; Council, Nat. Univ. of Singapore, 2000–04; Bd, Inst. of Policy Studies, 2002–09; Vice-Chm., Chinese Heritage Centre, Singapore, 2000–. President: Internat. Assoc. of Historians of Asia, 1964–68, 1988–91; Asian Studies Assoc. of Aust., 1979–80; Australian Acad. of the Humanities, 1980–83 (Fellow 1970); Hon. Corresp. Mem. for Hong Kong, RSA, 1987 (Fellow 1987; Chm., Hong Kong Chapter, 1992–95). Mem., Academia Sinica, 1992. For. Hon. Mem., Amer. Acad. of Arts and Scis, 1995; Hon. Mem., Chinese Acad. of Social Scis, 1996. Editor: (also Councillor), Jl of Nanyang Hsueh-hui, Singapore, 1958–68; (also Vice-Pres.), Jl of RAS, Malaysian Br., 1962–68; China, an internat. jl, 2002–07; Gen. Editor, East Asian Historical Monographs series for OUP, 1968–95. Hon. Fellow: SOAS, London Univ., 1996; Wolfson Coll., Cambridge, 2009. Hon. DLitt: Sydney, 1992; Hull, 1998; Hong Kong, 2002; Cambridge, 2009; Hon. LLD: Monash, 1992; ANU, 1996; Melbourne, 1997; DUniv: Soka, 1993; Griffith, 1995. Darjah Dato' Paduka Makhota Perak, 2011. *Publications:* The Nanhai Trade: a study of the early history of Chinese trade in the South China Sea, 1958, 2nd edn 1998; A Short History of the Nanyang Chinese, 1959; Latar Belakang Kebudayaan Pendudok di-Tanah Melayu: Bahagian Kebudayaan China (The Cultural Background of the Peoples of Malaysia: Chinese culture), 1962; The Structure of Power in North China during the Five Dynasties, 1963; (ed) Malaysia: a survey, 1964; (ed jtly) Essays on the Sources for Chinese History, 1974; (ed) Self and Biography: essays on the individual and society in Asia, 1975; China and the World since 1949: the impact of independence, modernity and revolution, 1977; (ed jtly) Hong Kong: dilemmas of growth, 1980; Community and Nation: essays on Southeast Asia and the Chinese, 1981; (ed jtly) Society and the Writer: essays on literature in modern Asia, 1981; Dongnanya yu Huaren (Southeast Asia and the Chinese), 1987; Nanhai Maoyi yu Nanyang Huaren (Chinese Trade and Southeast Asia), 1988; (ed with J. Cushman) Changing Identities of Southeast Asian Chinese since World War II, 1988; Lishi di Gongneng (The Functions of History), 1990; China and the Chinese Overseas, 1991 (Zhongguo yu Haiwai Huaren, 1994); The Chineseness of China: selected essays, 1991; Community and Nation: China, Australia and Southeast Asia, 1992; The Chinese Way: China's position in international relations, 1995; (ed with S. L. Wong) Hong Kong's Transition, 1995; (ed) Global History and Migrations, 1997; (ed) Xianggang shi Xinbian (Hong Kong History: new perspectives), 2 vols, 1997; (ed with S. L. Wong) Hong Kong in the Asia-Pacific Region, 1997; (ed with S. L. Wong) Dynamic Hong Kong: business and culture, 1997; (ed with L. C. Wang) The Chinese Diaspora, 2 vols, 1998; China and Southeast Asia, 1999; (ed with J. Wong) Hong Kong in China, 1999; (ed with J. Wong) China: two decades of reform and change, 1999; The Chinese Overseas: from earthbound China to the quest for autonomy, 2000; Joining the Modern World: inside and outside China, 2000; (ed with Y. Zheng) Reform, Legitimacy and Dilemmas: China's politics and society, 2000; Don't Leave Home: migration and the Chinese, 2001; Sino-Malay Encounters, 2001; (ed) Wang Fo-wen Jinianji (Wang Fo-wen, 1903–1972: a memorial collection of poems, essays and calligraphy), 2002; To Act Is To Know: Chinese dilemmas, 2002; Wang Gengwu zixuanji: selected works, 2002; Bind Us In Time: nation and civilisation in Asia, 2002; Haiwai Huaren Yanjiu di Dashiye yu Xinfangxiang (Overseas Chinese Research: new directions), 2002; (ed with Y. Zheng) Damage Control: the Chinese Communist Party and the era of Jiang Zemin, 2003; (ed with I. Abrahms) The Iraq War and its Consequences, 2003; (ed jtly) Sino-Asiatica, 2003; Anglo-Chinese Encounters since 1800: war, trade, science and governance, 2003; Ideas Won't Keep: the struggle for China's future, 2003; Diasporic Chinese Ventures, 2004; (ed with C. K. Ng) Maritime China in Transition, 2004; (ed) Nation-building: five Southeast Asian histories, 2005; Yimin yu xingqi de Zhongguo, 2005; Divided China: preparing for reunification, 883–947, 2006; Lixiang bietu: jingwai kanzhonghua (China and its Cultures: from the periphery), 2007; Chuka Bunmei to Chugoku no yukue (Chinese Civilization and China's Position), 2007; (ed with Y. Zheng) China and the New International Order, 2008; (ed with Y. Zheng) Zhongguo de 'zhuyi' zhi zheng (China's Ideological Battles since the May Fourth Movement), 2009; (ed with W. Ong) Voice of Malayan Revolution: the CPM radio war against Singapore and Malaysia, 1960–81, 2009; Wang Gungwu: In Conversation with Asad-ul Iqbal Latif, 2010; Renewal: the Chinese State and the new global history, 2013; Huaren yu Zhongguo, 2013; Another China Cycle: committing to reform, 2014; Wudai Shiqi Beifang Zhongguo di Quanli Jiegou, 2014; The Eurasian Core and its Edges: dialogue with Wang Gungwu on the history of the world, 2015; contribs to collected vols on Asian history; articles on Chinese and Southeast Asian history in internat. jls. *Recreations:* music, reading, walking. *Address:* East Asian Institute, Bukit Timah Campus, National University of Singapore, Singapore 259770. *T:* 67752033, *Fax:* 67756607. *E:* eaiwgw@nus.edu.sg.

WANGARATTA, Bishop of, since 2008; **Rt Rev. (Anthony) John Parkes,** AM 2011; *b* Leamington Spa, Warwicks, 6 Aug. 1950; *s* of Dennis Arthur Parkes and Eleanor Margaret Parkes (*née* Burrill); *m* 1984, Margaret Anne O'Meara; one *s* one *d*. *Educ:* Warwick Sch.; Univ. of Sheffield (LLB Hons); St Mark's Nat. Theol Centre, Canberra (BTh Hons; Laurence Murchison Prize for Academic Excellence); Melbourne Coll. of Divinity (MTh 1995). Formerly in legal practice; ordained deacon, 1989; Asst Curate, All Saints, Ainslie, 1990; Asst Priest, Holy Trinity, Orange, NSW, 1991–93; Rector, Wellington, Dio. of Bathurst, 1993–96; Acting Archdeacon, 1996, Archdeacon, 1997, Young, NSW; Rector and Team Rector, Young District Anglican Ministry, 1996–98; Rector, All Saints, Ainslie, 1998–2003; Archdeacon: S Canberra, 1998–2001; Dio. of Canberra and Goulburn, 2001–03; Dean, St John's Cathedral, Brisbane, 2004–08; Asst Bishop, Dio. of Brisbane, 2007–08. Dir, Aust. Centre of Christianity and Culture, 2001–02. Mem., Gen. Synod of Anglican Church, 2001–. Mem., Appellate Tribunal, Anglican Ch of Australia, 2014–. Inaugural Chair, Careforce (Anglicare), Bathurst, 1992–. Mem. Bd, Trinity Coll., Univ. of Melbourne, 2012– (Chm., Theol Sch. Cttee, 2012–). *Recreations:* reading, singing, fly fishing. *Address:* Bishop's Lodge, PO Box 457, Wangaratta, Vic 3676, Australia. *Clubs:* Melbourne (Melbourne); Albury (NSW).

WANLESS, Peter Thomas, CB 2007; Chief Executive, National Society for the Prevention of Cruelty to Children, since 2013; *b* 25 Sept. 1964; *s* of Thomas and Pam Wanless; *m* 1999, Beccy King; one *s*. *Educ:* Sheldon Sch., Chippenham; Univ. of Leeds (BA Hons Internat. History and Politics). HM Treasury, 1986–94; Private Sec. to Treasury Chief Sec., 1992–94; Head of Information, Dept of Employment, 1994–95; Head of Private Finance Policy, HM Treasury, 1996–98; Dir of Strategy and Communications, DfEE, subseq. DfES, 1998–2003; Dir of Secondary Educn, DfES, 2003–06; Dir of School Perf. and Reform, Sch. Standards Gp, DfES, subseq. DCSF, 2006–07; Dir, Families Gp, DCSF, 2007–08; Chief Exec., Big Lottery Fund, 2008–13. Chm., UK Lottery Forum, 2010–13. Non-exec. Mem. Cttee, Som CCC, 2014–. CCMI 2012. FRSA. *Recreations:* Somerset County Cricket, Twitter. *Address:* National Society for the Prevention of Cruelty to Children, 42 Curtain Road, EC2A 3NH. *Club:* MCC.

WANSBROUGH, Rev. Dom (Joseph) Henry, OSB; Master, St Benet's Hall, Oxford, 1990–2004; Alexander Jones Professor of Biblical Studies, Liverpool Hope University, since 2011; *b* 9 Oct. 1934; *s* of George Wansbrough and Elizabeth Wansbrough (*née* Lewis). *Educ:* Ampleforth Coll.; St Benet's Hall, Oxford (MA 1963); Univ. of Fribourg (STL 1964); Ecole Biblique Française, Jerusalem; Pontifical Biblical Commn, Rome (LSS 1965). Asst Master, 1965–90 and 2011–, Housemaster, 1969–90, Ampleforth Coll.; Chm., Oxford Fac. of Theology, 2001–03; Magister Scholarum of English Benedictines, 2002–09. Chairman: Catholic Biblical Assoc. of GB, 1985–91; Mgt Bd, Keston Inst., 1993–2001; Member: Pontifical Biblical Commn, 1996–2007; ARCIC III, 2011. Exec. Sec., Internat. Commn for Preparing an English Language Lectionary, 2006–. Cathedral Prior: of Norwich, 2004–10; of Durham, 2010–. *Publications:* The Sunday Word, 1979; New Jerusalem Bible, 1985; The Lion and the Bull, 1996; The Passion and Death of Jesus, 2003; The Story of the Bible, 2006; The Use and Abuse of the Bible, 2010; The Sunday Word, 2012; The Psalms, 2014; Introducing the New Testament, 2015; numerous articles and reviews in The Times, The Tablet, Priests & People and TLS. *Recreations:* music, running. *Address:* Ampleforth Abbey YO62 4EN.

WAPSHOTT, Nicholas Henry; author and journalist; Opinion Editor, Newsweek, since 2014 (International Editor, 2013–14); *b* 13 Jan. 1952; *s* of Raymond Gibson Wapshott, DFC and Olivia Beryl Darch; *m* 1980, Louise Nicholson; two *s*. *Educ:* Dursley County Primary Sch.; Rendcomb Coll., Cirencester; Univ. of York (BA Hons). The Scotsman, 1973–76; The Times, 1976–84; The Observer, 1984–92, Political Editor, 1988–92; Editor: The Times Magazine, 1992–97; The Saturday Times, 1997–2001; North America Correspondent, The Times, 2001–04; Nat. and Foreign Ed., 2006–08, Contrib. Ed. and columnist, 2008–09, New York Sun; Sen. Ed., The Daily Beast, 2008–09; editl consultant, oprah.com, 2009–10. Columnist, Reuters, The New Statesman, 2011–14. *Publications:* Peter O'Toole, 1982; (with George Brock) Thatcher, 1983; The Man Between: a biography of Carol Reed, 1990; Rex Harrison, 1991; (with Tim Wapshott) Older: a biography of George Michael, 1998; Ronald Reagan and Margaret Thatcher: a political marriage, 2007; Keynes Hayek: the clash that defined modern economics, 2011; The Sphinx: Franklin Roosevelt, the isolationists and the road to World War II, 2014. *Recreations:* cinema, music, elephants. *Address:* c/o Raphael Sagalyn, The Sagalyn Agency, 4922 Fairmont Avenue, Suite 200, Bethesda, MD 20814, USA. *Clubs:* Garrick; Century Association (New York).

WARBECK, Stephen; freelance film and theatre composer, since 1977; Associate Artist, Royal Shakespeare Co., since 1999; *b* 21 Oct. 1953; *s* of Harold Robert Wood and Olive Patricia Wood; name changed to Warbeck, 1977. *Educ:* Lewes Priory Sch.; Bristol Univ. (BA Hons). Scores composed include: *theatre:* An Inspector Calls, NT, 1992; RSC prodns incl. Alice in Wonderland; Pericles, Globe, 2005; *films:* Mrs Brown, 1997; Shakespeare in Love, 1999 (Oscar for Best Soundtrack); Billy Elliot, Quills, 2000; Captain Corelli's Mandolin, Charlotte Gray, 2001; Deséo, 2002; Blackball, Love's Brother, 2003; Two Brothers, Proof, Mickybo and Me, Oyster Farmer, 2004; On a Clear Day, 2005; Balcon Sur la Mer, 2010; Polisse, 2011; Doomsday, 2012; Papadopoulos & Sons, Jadoo, Day of the Flowers, 2013; Seve the Movie, The Tempest, 2014; *television:* Indian Summers, 2015. *Recreation:* the hKippers (*sic*). *Address:* c/o Lynda Mamy, United Agents, 12–26 Lexington Street, W1F 0LE.

WARBOYS, Prof. Brian Charles, CEng, FBCS, CITP; Professor of Software Engineering, University of Manchester, 1985–2007, now Emeritus; *b* 30 April 1942; *s* of Charles Bernard and Vera Beatrice Warboys; *m* 1965, Gillian Whitaker; one *s* one *d*. *Educ:* Univ. of Southampton (BSc Maths). CEng 1990; FBCS 1996; CITP 1998. English Electric, subseq. ICL: Software Engr, 1963–71; Chief Designer, ICL mainframe computer VME operating system, 1971–79; Manager, Systems Strategy, Mainframes Div., 1979–85; first ICL Fellow, 1984–89; Sen. ICL Fellow (pt-time), 1989–96. Visiting Professor: of Information Technol., Stirling Univ., 1984–87 (Hon. Prof., 1987–92); of Computer Sci., Univ. de Bretagne-Sud, 2005. *Publications:* Business Information Systems: a process approach, 1999. *Recreations:* playing golf badly, supporting Millwall Football Club and Sale Rugby Club, reading, spending time with my family and my four grandchildren. *Address:* School of Computer Science, University of Manchester, Manchester M13 9PL. *T:* (0161) 275 6182, *Fax:* (0161) 275 6204. *E:* brian@cs.man.ac.uk.

WARBRICK, Prof. Colin John; Professor of Law, 2006–08, Barber Professor of Jurisprudence, 2007–08, Hon. Professor, 2008–12, now Emeritus Professor, University of Birmingham; *b* 7 Aug. 1943; *s* of George and Nancy Warbrick; *m* 1974, Rosemary Goodwin (*d* 2013); one *s* one *d*. *Educ:* Barrow-in-Furness Grammar Sch.; Corpus Christi Coll., Cambridge (LLB 1966; MA 1969); Michigan (LLM 1969; Fulbright Schol. and Ford Foundn Fellow). Law Department, University of Durham: Lectr, then Sen. Lectr, 1970–96; Prof. of Law, 1996–2006; Chm., 1998–2001. Vis. Prof., Coll. of Law, Univ. of Iowa, 1981–82, 1985; Sen. Associate, St Antony's Coll., Oxford, 2001. Consultant on Human Rights, Council of Europe, 1991–2002; Specialist Advr, Constitution Cttee, H of L, 2005–06. *Publications:* (ed with Vaughan Lowe) The United Nations and the Principles of International Law, 1993; (with David Harris and Michael O'Boyle) Law of the European Convention on Human Rights, 1995; (ed with S. Tierney) Towards an International Legal Community, 2006; (contrib.) Halsbury's Laws of England, vol. 61, 5th edn 2010; articles on internat. law and human rights. *Recreations:* Rugby, allotment. *Address:* 19 Nevilledale Terrace, Durham DH1 4QG. *T:* (0191) 384 7531. *E:* c.warbrick@bham.ac.uk.

WARBURTON, David; Senior National Officer: GMB (formerly General, Municipal, Boilermakers and Allied Trades Union), 1973–95; APEX (white collar section of GMB), since 1990; *b* 10 Jan. 1942; *s* of Harold and Ada Warburton; *m* 1966, Carole Anne Susan Tomney; two *d*. *Educ:* Cottingley Manor Sch., Bingley, Yorks; Coleg Harlech, Merioneth, N Wales. Campaign Officer, Labour Party, 1964; Educn Officer, GMWU, 1965–66, Reg. Officer, 1966–73. Co-Chm., Crazy Horse Investment Trust, 2001–. Secretary: Chemical Unions Council; Rubber Industry Jt Unions, 1980–86; Chm., Paper and Packaging Industry Unions, 1988–92. Mem., Eur. Co-ord. Cttee, Chem., Rubber and Glass Unions, 1975–81. Chm., Chem. and Allied Industries Jt Indust. Council, 1973–86; Mem., Govt Industrial Workers Jt Consultative Cttee, 1988–92; Sec., Home Office Jt Indust. Council, 1989–; Treas., Electricity Supply Nat. Jt Council, 1990–; Member: Industrial Tribunal, 1995–99; Employment Tribunal, 1999–. Vice-Pres., Internat. Fedn of Chemical, Energy and Gen. Workers, 1986–94. Member: NEDC, 1973–86; Commonwealth Develt Corp., 1979–87; TUC Energy Cttee, 1978–92; Nat. Jt Council for Civil Air Transport, 1992–95; Chm., TUC Gen. Purposes Cttee, 1984–95; Dir, Union Liaison Services, 1995–. Nat. Sec., UK Friends of Palestine, 1983–. Campaign Dir, Friends of The Speaker, 1996–2000. *Publications:* Pharmaceuticals for the People, 1973; Drug Industry: which way to control, 1975; UK Chemicals: The Way Forward, 1977; Economic Detente, 1980; The Case for Voters Tax Credits, 1983; Forward Labour, 1985; Facts, Figures and Damned Statistics, 1987. *Recreations:* music, American politics, flicking through reference books, films of the thirties and forties.

WARBURTON, David John; MP (C) Somerton and Frome, since 2015; *b* Burnham, Bucks, 28 Oct. 1965; *s* of John and Erica Warburton; *m* 2002, Harriet Katharine Baker-Bates; one *s* one *d*. *Educ:* Reading Sch.; Waingels Coll.; Royal Coll. of Music (Dip. RCM); King's Coll. London (MMus). Professional composer, 1992–95; Teacher of Music, Hurlingham and Chelsea Sch., and RCM Jun. Dept, 1995–99; Man. Dir, Music Solution Ltd, 1999–2002;

Chief Exec., 2002–05, Chm., 2005–08, Pitch Entertainment Gp; Man. Partner, Oflang Partners LLP, 2008–15; Chm., MyHigh Ltd, 2012–15. Chm., Wells Cathedral Sch. Parents' Assoc., 2010–14; Mem., Capital Exec. Cttee, Shakespeare's Globe Th., 2008–10. Trustee, Ups and Downs Southwest, 2013–. Patron, Royal Bath and West Soc., 2013–. Member: MENSA, 1994–; ESU, 2008–. FRSA. *Recreations:* playing the piano and thinking out loud, both of which to the annoyance of friends and family. *Address:* House of Commons, SW1A 0AA.

WARBURTON, Ivor William; Vice President and General Manager Operations, Tangula Railtours, Shanghai, 2006–09; *b* 13 Aug. 1946; *s* of late Dennis and Edna Margaret Warburton; *m* 1969, Carole-Ann Ashton (marr. diss. 1982); three *d*. *Educ:* Dulwich Coll.; Queens' Coll., Cambridge (MA); Univ. of Warwick (MSc). FCILT (FCIT 1989); FCIM 1994. British Railways, 1968–97: graduate trainee, 1968–70; local ops posts, London Midland Region, 1970–73; Divl Passenger Manager, Bristol, 1974–78; Overseas Tourist Manager, 1978–82; Regional Passenger Manager, York, 1982–83; Dir, Passenger Marketing Services, 1984–85; Asst Gen. Manager, London Midland Region, 1985–87; Employee Relations Manager, 1987–88; Dir of Operations, 1988–90; Gen. Manager, London Midland Region, 1990–92; Dir, 1992–95, Man. Dir, 1995–97, InterCity West Coast; Dir, Business Develt and Industry Affairs, Virgin Rail Gp, 1997–99. Chm., Assoc. of Train Operating Cos, 1997–99. President: Railway Study Assoc., 1993–94; Retired Railway Officers' Soc., 2003–04; Alleyn Club, 2014–15. *Recreations:* Chinese language and culture, music, opera, handicapped scouting. *Address:* 34 St Clair's Road, Croydon CR0 5NE. *T:* (020) 8681 6421.

WARBURTON, John Kenneth, CBE 1983; Director General, Birmingham Chamber of Commerce and Industry, 1994 (Chief Executive, 1978–94); *b* 7 May 1932; *s* of Frederick and Eva Warburton; *m* 1960, Patricia Gordon (*d* 2009); one *d*. *Educ:* Newcastle-under-Lyme High Sch.; Keble Coll., Oxford (MA Jurisprudence). Called to Bar, Gray's Inn, 1977. London Chamber of Commerce, 1956–59; Birmingham Chamber of Commerce and Industry, 1959–94. President, British Chambers of Commerce Executives, 1979–81; Member: Steering Cttee, Internat. Bureau of Chambers of Commerce, 1976–94; Nat. Council, Assoc. of British Chambers of Commerce, 1978–94; European Trade Cttee and Business Link Gp, BOTB, 1979–87; E European Trade Council, BOTB, 1984–93; Review Body on Doctors' and Dentists' Remuneration, 1982–92; MSC Task Gp on Employment Trng, 1987; Lord Chancellor's Birmingham Adv. Cttee, 1993–99; Ind. Remuneration Panel, Birmingham CC, 2001–07; Chm., Adv. Council, W Midlands Industrial Develt Assoc., 1983–86. Mediator, Centre for Dispute Resolution, 1994–. Director: National Garden Festival 1986 Ltd, 1983–87; National Exhibition Centre Ltd, 1989–95. Chm., Birmingham Macmillan Nurses Appeal, 1994–97; Dep. Chm., Birmingham Children's Hosp. Appeal, 1996–98. Vol. advr, BESO, Slovakia, 1994, and Mongolia, 1995. Companion, BITC, 1992–. Trustee, Holy Child Sch., Edgbaston, 1992–96; Gov., Newman Coll., 1993–2002 (Exec. Chm., 1999–2002; Hon. Life Fellow, 2003); Life Mem., Court, Birmingham Univ., 1981 (Gov., 1982–99). Hon. DUniv UCE, 1999. *Address:* 35 Hampshire Drive, Edgbaston, Birmingham B15 3NY. *T:* (0121) 454 6764.

WARBURTON, Jonathan; Company Chairman, Warburtons Ltd, since 2001; *b* Bolton, Lancs, 1 June 1957; *s* of Derrick Warburton and Joyce Warburton; *m* 1990, Kim Latisevs; three *s* (incl. twins) one *d*. *Educ:* Millfield Sch. Sales Rep., Unilever, 1979–81; Warburtons Ltd: Sales Rep., 1981–84; Mktg and Sales Dir, 1984–92; Jt Man. Dir, 1992–2001. Non-exec. Dir, Samworth Bros Ltd, 1997–. Hon. DBA Manchester Metropolitan, 2002. *Recreations:* enthusiastic amateur sportsman, golfer, shooter, skier and traveller. *Address:* c/o Warburtons Ltd, Back O' Th' Bank House, Hereford Street, Bolton BL1 8HJ. *T:* (01204) 531004. *E:* jw@warburtons.co.uk, jw1876@gmail.com. *Clubs:* Royal and Ancient Golf (St Andrews), Trevose Golf.

WARBURTON, Richard Maurice, OBE 1987; Director General, Royal Society for the Prevention of Accidents, 1979–90; *b* 14 June 1928; *s* of Richard and Phylis Agnes Warburton; *m* 1952, Lois May Green; two *s*. *Educ:* Wigan Grammar Sch.; Birmingham Univ. (BA 1st Cl. Hons). Flying Officer, RAF, 1950–52. HM Inspector of Factories, 1952–79; Head of Accident Prevention Advisory Unit, Health and Safety Executive, 1972–79. *Recreations:* golf, gardening, fell walking. *Address:* Cornaa, Wyfordby Avenue, Blackburn, Lancs BB2 7AR. *T:* (01254) 56824.

WARBY, Hon. Sir Mark (David John), Kt 2014; **Hon. Mr Justice Warby;** a Judge of the High Court of Justice, Queen's Bench Division, since 2014; *b* 10 Oct. 1958; *s* of David James Warby, FIMechE, and Clare Warby; *m* 1985, Ann Kenrick, OBE; one *s* two *d*. *Educ:* Bristol Grammar Sch.; St John's Coll., Oxford (Schol.; MA Jurisprudence). Called to the Bar, Gray's Inn, 1981, Bencher, 2007; QC 2002; a Recorder, 2009–14; a Dep. Judge, QBD (Admin. Court), 2013–14. Jt Hd of Chambers, 2011–14. *Publications:* (jtly) The Law of Privacy and the Media, 2002, (ed jtly and contrib.) 3rd edn 2015; (contrib.) Blackstone's Guide to the Defamation Act 2013, 2013; (contrib.) Sport: law and practice, 3rd edn 2013. *Recreations:* surfing, guitar, tennis, cycling, architecture. *Address:* Royal Courts of Justice, Strand, WC2A 2LL. *Clubs:* Union; Butterfly Tennis; Crackington Haven Tennis; Crackington Haven Surf.

WARCHUS, Matthew; theatre and film director; Artistic Director, Old Vic, since 2015; *b* 24 Oct. 1966; *s* of Michael Warchus and Rosemary Warchus. *Educ:* Bristol Univ. (BA 1st Cl. Hons Music and Drama). Associate Dir, W Yorkshire Playhouse, 1992–94. Plays directed include: Sejanus: his fall, Edinburgh, 1988; The Suicide, 1989, Coriolanus, 1990–91, NYT; Master Harold and the Boys, Bristol Old Vic, 1990; West Yorkshire Playhouse, 1992–94: Life is a Dream, 1992; Who's Afraid of Virginia Woolf, 1992; Fiddler on the Roof, 1992; The Plough and the Stars, 1993; Death of a Salesman, 1994; Betrayal, 1994; True West, 1994; Much Ado About Nothing, Queen's, 1993; The Life of Stuff, Donmar Warehouse, 1993; Henry V, 1994, The Devil is an Ass, 1995, RSC; Troilus and Cressida, Opera North, 1995; Volpone, RNT, 1995; Peter Pan, W Yorks Playhouse, 1995; The Rake's Progress, WNO, 1996; Art, Wyndham's, 1996, NY, 1998; Falstaff, Opera North and ENO, 1997; Hamlet, 1997, The Unexpected Man, Duchess, 1998, NY 2000, RSC; Life x 3, RNT, transf. Old Vic, 2000, NY, 2003; Follies, NY, 2001; The Winter's Tale, RSC, 2002; Cosi fan tutte, ENO, 2002; Our House (musical), Cambridge, 2002; Tell me on a Sunday, Gielgud, 2003; Buried Child, NT, 2004; Endgame, Albery, 2004; The Lord of the Rings, Th. Royal, 2007; Boeing Boeing, Comedy, 2007, NY, 2008; I Am Shakespeare, Chichester, 2007; Speed-the-Plow, Old Vic, 2008; The Norman Conquests, Old Vic, 2008, NY, 2009; God of Carnage, Gielgud, 2008, NY, 2009; La Bête, Comedy, transf. NY, 2010; Deathtrap, Noël Coward Th., 2010; Matilda, RSC, 2010, Cambridge Th., 2011, NY, 2013 (Olivier Award for Best Dir, 2012); Ghost The Musical, Piccadilly Th., 2011; Future Conditional, Old Vic, 2015. Films: Simpatico (also screenplay), 1999; Pride, 2014. Hon. DLitt Bristol, 2010. *Address:* c/o Old Vic, The Cut, Waterloo, SE1 8NB.

WARD, family name of **Earl of Dudley** and of **Viscount Bangor**.

WARD, Rt Hon. Sir Alan Hylton, Kt 1988; PC 1995; a Lord Justice of Appeal, 1995–2013; *b* 15 Feb. 1938; *s* of late Stanley Victor Ward and of Mary Ward; *m* 1st, 1963 (marr. diss. 1982); one *s* two *d*; 2nd, 1983, Helen Madeleine Gilbert (*see* H. M. Ward); one *d* (and one twin *d* decd). *Educ:* Christian Brothers Coll., Pretoria; Univ. of Pretoria (BA, LLB); Pembroke Coll., Cambridge (MA, LLB; Hon. Fellow, 1998). Called to the Bar, Gray's Inn, 1964, Bencher, 1988, Treas., 2006 (Vice-Treas., 2005); QC 1984; a Recorder, 1985–88; a Judge of the High Court, Family Div., 1988–95; Family Div. Liaison Judge, Midland and Oxford Circuit, 1990–95. Formerly an Attorney of Supreme Court of South Africa. Mem., Matrimonial Causes Procedure Cttee, 1982–85. Consulting Editor, Children Law and Practice, 1991–2013. Hon. LLD: East Anglia, 2001; BPP University Coll., 2012. *Recreations:* as gamekeeper turned poacher, preaching the gospel, 'Mediate, don't Litigate'. *E:* alanward@civilmediation.org. *Clubs:* Garrick, MCC.

WARD, Mrs Ann Sarita; non-executive Director, Lambeth, Southwark, Lewisham Family Health Services Authority, 1991–96; *b* 4 Aug. 1923; *d* of Denis Godfrey and Marion Phyllis Godfrey; *m* Frank Ward (*d* 1991); two *s*. *Educ:* St Paul's Girls' Sch., Hammersmith. Professional photographer; photo journalist, Daily Mail, 1962–67, Daily Mirror, 1967–70; award winner, British Press Photographs of Year, 1967. Councillor, London Bor. of Southwark, 1971–86 (Dep. Leader, 1978–83); Chm., ILEA, 1981–82. Pol Advr to Barbara Follett, MP, 1996–2001. Contested (Lab) Streatham, 1970. Associate Mem., Camberwell HA, 1990–93 (Mem., 1982–90). Special Trustee, KCH, 1983–88. Mem., Exec. Cttee, Stevenage, Abbeyfield Soc., 2002–. Bd Mem., Internat. Shakespeare Globe Centre, 1988–92; Hon. Vice Pres., Friends of Shakespeare's Globe, 1992– (Chm., 1987–92). Co-ordinator, Emily's List UK, 1992–96. *Recreations:* theatre, gardening. *Address:* Tadworth Grove Residential and Nursing Home, The Avenue, Tadworth, near Epsom, Surrey KT20 5AT.

WARD, Anthony Richard Bangor; Co-Founder, Armajaro Holdings Ltd, since 1998; *b* Aldershot, 5 May 1960; *s* of Gen. Sir Richard Erskine Ward, GBE, KCB, DSO and Bar, MC and of (Stella) Elizabeth Ward; two *s* by Carolyn Ward. *Educ:* Marlborough Coll. Sime Derby Ltd, 1979–80; E. F. Hutton, 1980–82; V. Berg & Sons Ltd, 1982–89; J H Rayner (Cocoa) Ltd, 1989–94; Dir and Global Business Manager, Cocoa and Coffee, Phibro GmbH, 1994–98. Principal Portfolio Manager, CC+ Fund, 2007–; Chm., Financial Express (Hldgs) Ltd, 1998–. Formerly Chairman: Eur. Cocoa Assoc.; Fedn of Cocoa Commerce Ltd. Formerly Director: LIFFE (Hldgs) ltd; LIFFE Admin and Mgt Ltd; London Commodity Exchange Ltd; Cocoa Assoc. of London. Chevalier, Ordre du Mérite Agricole (France), 2011. *Recreations:* sailing, ski-ing, shooting. *Clubs:* Queens; Royal Thames Yacht, Sea View Yacht.

WARD, Hon. Sir Austin; *see* Ward, Hon. Sir L. A.

WARD, Caroline Jane; *see* Drummond, C. J.

WARD, Cecil, CBE 1989; JP; Town Clerk, Belfast City Council, 1979–89; *b* 26 Oct. 1929; *s* of William and Mary Caroline Ward. *Educ:* Technical High Sch., Belfast; College of Technology, Belfast. Employed by Belfast City Council (formerly Belfast County Borough Council), 1947–89; Asst Town Clerk (Administration), 1977–79. Mem., Local Govt Staff Commn, 1983–89. Member: Arts Council NI, 1980–85, 1987–89; Bd, Ulster Mus., 1989–95; Dir, Ulster Orchestra Soc., 1980–94 (Chm., 1990–94). Mem., Senate, QUB, 1990–2001. Mem., Bd, Mater Hosp., 1994–2002. JP Belfast, 1988. Hon. MA QUB, 1988. *Recreations:* music, reading, hill walking. *Address:* 24 Thornhill, Malone, Belfast, Northern Ireland BT9 6SS. *T:* (028) 9066 8950; Hatter's Field, Drumawier, Greencastle, Co. Donegal, Ireland.

WARD, (Charles John) Nicholas; company chairman; *b* 1 Aug. 1941; *s* of late John Newman Ward and Vivienne Grainger Ward; *m* 1967, Deirdre Veronica Shaw; two *d*. *Educ:* Charterhouse; INSEAD (MBA 1968). FCA 1964. Early career spanned several cos engaged in textiles, venture capital, overseas trading, retailing, distribution, healthcare, leisure and property, subseq. Chairman or non-exec. dir of numerous cos in retail, textiles, healthcare, transport, stockbroking and fund mgt, coal mining, student accommodation, bio-fuels and agriculture and envmt sectors. Chairman: NHS Supplies Authy, 1995–98; Ryan Group Ltd, 1995–2004; ADAS Hldgs, 1998–2007; UPP Projects Ltd, 2006–07; Interactive Prospect Targeting Hldgs plc, 2008–10; Dep. Chm., Albert E. Sharp Hldgs, 1996–98; non-executive Director: Anglia and Oxford RHA, 1990–96; D1 Oils plc, 2010. Consultant to: Deutsche Bank, 1995–2014; Bank of Austria, 1995–2014; 3i, 1998–2007; Swiss Re, 2008–09. Ind. Mem., Steering Bd, Insolvency Service, DTI, 2004–06; Public Mem., Network Rail Ltd, 2011–13. Chairman: Make a Difference Team, 1994–96; The Volunteering Partnership, 1995–96; British Liver Trust, 1999–2004; CORGI Trust, 2005; Sulgrave Manor Trust, 2011–13; Co-Chm., The Volunteering Partnership Forum for England, 1996–97; Pres., Ind. Custody Visiting Assoc. (formerly Nat. Assoc. for Lay Visiting), 1996–2006 (Chm., 1992–96); Chm., Lay Visiting Charitable Trust, 1995–. Fellow, Inst. for Turnaround (formerly Soc. of Turnaround Professionals), 2001–11. Liveryman, Tylers' and Bricklayers' Co., 1963– (Master, 1991–92). Dist. Fellow, INSEAD, 2014. *Address:* Bacon House, Greatworth, Banbury, Oxon OX17 2DX. *T:* (01295) 712732, 07774 184762. *E:* nicholasward@variouscompanies.co.uk; Flat 12, 77 Warwick Square, SW1V 2AR. *T:* (020) 7834 9175. *Club:* Royal Society of Medicine.

WARD, Christopher Gordon; an Upper Tribunal Judge (Administrative Appeals Chamber) (formerly a Social Security and Child Support Commissioner), since 2008; *b* Bromley, 18 Sept. 1957; *s* of late Rev. Stanley Ward and of Mary Ward (*née* Lance); *m* 1990, Katharine Alyson Klopper; one *s* two *d*. *Educ:* Nottingham High Sch.; Jesus Coll., Cambridge (BA Hons 1979); Coll. of Law. Admitted solicitor, 1982; Solicitor, Clifford-Turner, 1982–84; legal posts in local govt and voluntary sector, 1984–89; Solicitor, Nabarro Nathanson, 1989–98; Partner, Beachcroft Stanleys, later Beachcroft Wansbroughs, 1998–2005; London Bor. of Waltham Forest, 2006–08. Chm. (pt-time), Appeal Tribunals, 2002–08. *Publications:* contrib., principally on local govt and administrative law, to books and jls. *Recreations:* performing and listening to classical and traditional music, languages, racket sports. *Address:* c/o Upper Tribunal (Administrative Appeals Chamber), 5th Floor, Rolls Building, 7 Rolls Buildings, Fetter Lane, EC4A 1NL.

WARD, Christopher John; Joint Founder, 1983, and Chairman, since 2006, Redwood Publishing (Editorial Director, 1983–2002; Vice-Chairman, 2002–06); *b* 25 Aug. 1942; *s* of John Stanley Ward and Jacqueline Lane-Hume Costin; *m* 1st, 1971 (marr. diss.); one *s* two *d*; 2nd, 1990, Nonie Niesewand (*née* Fogarty). *Educ:* King's Coll. Sch., Wimbledon. Successively on staff of Driffield Times, 1959, and Newcastle Evening Chronicle, 1960–63; reporter, sub-editor, then feature writer and columnist, 1963–76, Daily Mirror; Assistant Editor: Sunday Mirror, 1976–79; Daily Mirror, 1979–81; Editor, Daily Express, 1981–83. Director: Acorn Computer plc, 1983–99; College Valley Estates, 2008–. Chm., Redwood Custom Communications, Toronto, 2007–08. Mem., Eur. Adv. Cttee to Chm., All Nippon Airways, 2003–10. Co-Chair, PPA, 2010–14. WWF: Trustee, 1994–2000; Chm., UK, 2002–08. Mem., Farne Is Cttee, 2004–. Mark Boxer award, British Soc. of Magazine Eds, 1995. *Publications:* How to Complain, 1974; Our Cheque is in the Post, 1980; And the Band Played On, 2011. *Recreations:* walking in the Scottish Borders, shooting, photography, breeding bantams, meteorology. *Address:* Glenburn Hall, Jedburgh TD8 6QB. *T:* (01835) 865801. *E:* cj.ward@btinternet.com. *Club:* Garrick.

WARD, Christopher John Ferguson; solicitor; *b* 26 Dec. 1942; *m* Janet Ward, JP, LLB; one *s* one *d* and two *s* one *d* by former marr. *Educ:* Magdalen College Sch.; Law Society Sch. of Law. MP (C) Swindon, Oct. 1969–June 1970; contested (C) Eton and Slough, 1979. Mem., Berks CC, 1965–81 (Leader of the Council and Chm., Policy Cttee, 1979–81). Gov., Chiltern Nursery Trng Coll., 1975–97 (Chm., 1988–91). Treas., United & Cecil Club, 1993 (Hon. Sec., 1982–87). *Address:* Ramblings, Maidenhead Thicket, Berks SL6 3QE.

WARD, (Christopher) John (William); Development Advisor, Welsh National Opera, since 2003; *b* 21 June 1942; *s* of late Thomas Maxfield and Peggy Ward; *m* 1st, 1970, Diane Lelliott (marr. diss. 1988); 2nd, 2008, Susan Corby. *Educ:* Oundle Sch.; Corpus Christi Coll., Oxford (BA LitHum); Univ. of East Anglia (Graduate DipEcon). Overseas and Economic Intelligence Depts, Bank of England, 1965; General Secretary, Bank of England Staff Organisation, 1973; Gen. Sec., Assoc. of First Div. Civil Servants, 1980; Head of

Development, Opera North, 1988–94; Dir of Corporate Affairs, W Yorks Playhouse, 1994–97; Develt Dir, ENO, 1997–2002; Dir of Fundraising, Crafts Council, 2003–04. *Recreations:* opera, theatre, football. *Address:* c/o Welsh National Opera, Wales Millennium Centre, Bute Place, Cardiff CF10 5AL. *Club:* Swindon Town Supporters.

WARD, Claire Margaret; Director, Capewells Ltd Consultancy; *b* 9 May 1972; *d* of Frank and Catherine Ward; *m* 2003, John Simpson; one *s* one *d*. *Educ:* Loreto Coll., St Albans; Univ. of Hertfordshire (LLB Hons); Brunel Univ. (MA). Trainee Solicitor, Pattinson & Brewer, 1995–97; qualif. Solicitor, 1998–. Mem. (Lab) Elstree and Borehamwood Town Council, 1994–98 (Mayor, 1996–97). MP (Lab) Watford, 1997–2010; contested (Lab) same seat, 2010. PPS to Minister of State for Health, 2001–05; an Asst Govt Whip, 2005–06; a Lord Comr of HM Treasury (Govt Whip), 2006–08; Vice-Chamberlain of HM Household, 2008–09; Parly Under-Sec. of State, MoJ, 2009–10. Mem., NEC, Lab. Party, 1991–95. Mem., Select Cttee on Culture, Media and Sports, 1997–2001. Jt Sec., All Party Film Industry Gp, 1997–2005. Chief Exec., Ind. Pharmacy Fedn, 2011–15. Non-exec. Dir, Sherwood Forest Hosps NHS Foundn Trust, 2013–. Chm., Pharmacy Voice, 2015–. Patron, Young European Movement, 1999. *Recreations:* films, Association Football (Watford FC), eating out.

WARD, Colin; Associate, Capgemini, 2003–09; *b* 23 June 1947; *s* of Simon Myles Ward and Ella May McConnell; *m* 1969, Marjory Hall Milne. *Educ:* Daniel Stewart's Coll., Edinburgh; Heriot-Watt Univ. (BA 1970). CA 1974. Ernst & Young, Edinburgh, 1970–74; Price Waterhouse, Glasgow, 1974–75; BSC, 1975–77; SDA, latterly Chief Accountant, 1977–90; Student Loans Co., 1990–2003: Loans Dir, 1990–92; Asst Man. Dir, 1992–96; Main Board, 1994–2003; Chief Exec., 1996–2003. Loans Scheme consultant to Hungarian Govt, 1999–2000. CCMI 2003. *Recreations:* sailing, gardening, classical music. *Address:* 108 Sinclair Street, Helensburgh, Argyll G84 9QE. *T:* (01436) 676048.

WARD, David; Partner, 1964–98, Consultant, 1998–2009, Atkinson Ritson (formerly Atkinson & North), Solicitors, Carlisle; President, The Law Society, 1989–90; *b* 23 Feb. 1937; *s* of Rev. Frank Ward, Darfield, Yorks, and Elizabeth Ward (*née* Pattinson), Appleby, Westmorland; *m* 1978, Antoinette, *d* of Maj.-Gen. D. A. B. Clarke, CB, CBE; two *s* one *d*. *Educ:* Dame Allan's Sch., Newcastle upon Tyne; Queen Elizabeth Grammar Sch., Penrith; St Edmund Hall, Oxford (BA). Admitted solicitor, 1962. Articled Clerk, 1959, Assistant, 1962, Atkinson & North. Mem., Lord Chancellor's Adv. Cttee on Legal Educn and Conduct, 1991–97. Mem. Council, 1972–91, Vice-Pres., 1988–89, Law Soc.; Pres., Carlisle and District Law Soc., 1985–86. Pres., Carlisle Mountaineering Club, 1985–88. Methodist local preacher, 1955–. *Recreations:* mountaineering, choral and church music. *Address:* Mardale, Upton, Caldbeck, Wigton, Cumbria CA7 8EU. *T:* (01697) 478220.

WARD, David; *b* 24 June 1953; *m* 1974, Jacqueline Ann Dodd; two *s*. *Educ:* Boston Grammar Sch.; N Kesteven Grammar Sch.; Trent Poly. (CIPFA 1977); Univ. of Bradford (MBA 1981; MPhil 1984); Univ. of Leicester (MSc 1996). Accountant, Lincs CC, 1971–79; Leeds Polytechnic, later Leeds Metropolitan University: Prin. Lectr, 1985–2004; on secondment as Manager, Bradford Sports Partnership, 2004–10. Dir, Bantams Community Prog., 2005–. Mem. (Lib Dem) Bradford MDC, 1984–2010. Contested (Lib Dem) Bradford N, Nov. 1990, 1992, 2001, 2005. MP (Lib Dem) Bradford E, 2010–15; contested (Lib Dem) same seat, 2015. Member: Business, Innovation and Skills Select Cttee, 2010–12; Educn Select Cttee, 2012–15.

WARD, David; HM Diplomatic Service; Ambassador to Eritrea, since 2014; *b* 11 June 1968; *s* of Robert Norton Ward and Elizabeth Pestell Ward (*née* Byfield). *Educ:* Dame Allan's Boys' Sch., Newcastle upon Tyne; Magdalene Coll., Cambridge (BA 1989). Joined FCO, 1992; Tokyo, 1994–98, Second Sec. (Pol), 1995–98; FCO, 1998–2002; Dep. Hd of Mission, Kathmandu, 2002–05; Dep. Counsellor (Pol), Beijing, 2006–09; FCO, 2010–11; Dep. Hd of Mission, Tripoli, 2011–12; Dep. Hd, Provincial Reconstruction Team, Lashkar Gah, 2013–14. Mem., Japan Soc. *Recreations:* amateur piano, winter sports. *Address:* c/o Foreign and Commonwealth Office, King Charles Street, SW1A 2AH.

WARD, David Gordon; HM Diplomatic Service, retired; *b* 25 July 1942; *s* of late Major Gordon Alec Ward, MBE and Irene Ward; *m* 1st, 1966, Rosemary Anne Silvester (marr. diss. 1979); two *s* one *d*; 2nd, 1980, Margaret (*née* Martin); one *s* one *d*, and one step *s*. *Educ:* Rutlish Sch., Merton. With CRO, 1961–65; entered FCO, 1965; Montevideo, 1967–70; Dakar (also accredited to Nouakchott, Bamako and Conakry), 1970–74; FCO, 1974–76; Victoria, 1977–80; Libreville, 1980; Luxembourg, 1981–83; Consul, Oporto, 1983–87; FCO, 1988–90; Harare, 1990–95; FCO, 1995–98; Ambassador to Dominican Rep., 1998–2002 and (non-resident) to Haiti, 1999–2002; British Consul, Tenerife, 2002–07. Hon. Cavaleiro da Confraria do Vinho do Porto, 1986. Grand Silver Cross, Order of Merit of Duarte Sanchez and Mella (Dominican Republic), 2002. *Recreations:* theatre, visual arts, tennis. *E:* david_warduk@yahoo.co.uk.

WARD, (Elizabeth) Alison; *see* Platt, E. A.

WARD, Emma Marion, (Mrs R. H. Billey); Director, Strategy and Growth, Department for Business, Innovation and Skills, since 2015; *b* Harlow, 21 Aug. 1973; *d* of Malcolm G. Ward and Marion Ward; *m* 2004, Ray Hamilton Billey; one *s*. *Educ:* Chelmer Valley High Sch.; Middlesex Univ. (BA Hons); Fachhochschule für Technik un Wirtschaft, Reutlingen (Diplom Betriebswirt); Univ. of Manchester Inst. for Sci. and Technol. (MSc Internat. Business). Various posts, DTI, later BERR, then BIS, 2000–10; Exec. Dir, Shareholder Exec., 2010–11; Dir, Local Growth, BIS, 2012–14. *Recreations:* music (pianist), pottery. *Address:* Department for Business, Innovation and Skills, 1 Victoria Street, SW1H 0ET. *T:* (020) 7215 4152. *E:* emma.m.ward@bis.gsi.gov.uk.

WARD, Very Rev. Frances Elizabeth Fearn, PhD; Dean of St Edmundsbury, since 2010; *b* Geelong, Vic, 16 Sept. 1959; *d* of Hubert Ward, *qv*; *m* 1986, Peter Powell; three *s* one *d*. *Educ:* King's Sch., Ely; Univ. of St Andrews (MTheol 1983); Univ. of Manchester (PhD 2000). Ordained deacon, 1989, priest, 1994; Tutor, Northern Coll. (URC and Congregational), 1993–98; Vicar, St Peter's, Bury, 1999–2005; Residentiary Canon, Bradford Cathedral, 2006–10. *Publications:* Lifelong Learning, 2005; (ed jtly) Studying Local Churches, 2005; (ed jtly) Theological Reflection Methods, 2005; (ed jtly) Theological Reflection Sources, 2007; Why Rousseau was Wrong: Christianity and the secular soul, 2013. *Recreations:* walking, sailing, reading, the Arts. *Address:* The Deanery, The Great Church Yard, Bury St Edmunds, Suffolk IP33 1RS. *T:* (cathedral office) (01284) 748720. *E:* fefward@gmail.com.

See also V. J. Ward.

WARD, Prof. Geoffrey Christopher, PhD; Principal, Homerton College, Cambridge, since 2013; *b* Oldham, 18 Feb. 1954; *s* of Clifford Ward and Marjorie Ward; *m* 1992, Prof. Marion Wynne-Davies; two *s*. *Educ:* Manchester Grammar Sch. (Foundn Scholar); Clare Coll., Cambridge (BA 1st Cl. Hons Eng. 1975; PhD 2006). Lectr, 1978–93, Sen. Lectr, 1993–95, in Eng., Univ. of Liverpool; Prof. of Eng., 1995–2006, Dep. Principal, 2002–06, Univ. of Dundee; Royal Holloway, University of London: Prof. of Eng. and Creative Writing, 2006–13; Dean, Faculty of Arts, 2006–08; Vice Principal, 2008–13. Chm., Fitzwilliam Mus. Cambridge, 2014–. Occasional writer and presenter, broadcasts on Amer. writers, BBC Radio 3. Mem., Editl Bd, Cambridge Qly, 1992–. FRSA 2002 (Life Mem.). Hon. Fellow, Harris Manchester Coll., Oxford, 2013. *Publications:* Comeuppance (poetry), 1980; Statutes of Liberty: the New York School of Poets, 1993, 2nd edn 2001; Language Poetry and the American Avant-Garde, 1993; (ed) The Bloomsbury Guide to Romantic Literature, 1993; (ed jtly) Re: Joyce, 1998; The Writing of America: literature and cultural identity from the Puritans to the present, 2002; Worry Dream (poetry), 2013. *Recreation:* beachcombing. *Address:* c/o Homerton College, Hills Road, Cambridge CB2 8PH. *T:* (01223) 747131. *E:* gw355@cam.ac.uk. *Club:* Oxford and Cambridge.

WARD, Rev. Canon Prof. Graham John; Regius Professor of Divinity, University of Oxford, since 2012; Fellow and Canon of Christ Church, Oxford, since 2012; *b* Salford, 25 Oct. 1955; *s* of John Herbert Ward and Mary Margaret Ward (*née* Hardman); *m* 1988, Mary Janet Jackson; one *s* one *d*. *Educ:* Salford Grammar Sch.; Fitzwilliam Coll., Cambridge (BA Hons 1979; MA; PGCE (Dist.) 1981; PhD 1994); Westcott Hse and Selwyn Coll., Cambridge. MA Oxon 1992. English master, John Lyon Sch., Harrow, 1981–84; Hd of Drama and Oral English, Latymer Sch., Edmonton, 1984–87; ordained deacon, 1990, priest, 1991; Chaplain Fellow and Tutor in Theol. and Philos., Exeter Coll., Oxford, 1992–95; Mem., Theol. Faculty Bd, Univ. of Oxford, 1993; Lectr (pt-time), Religious Studies Dept, Birmingham Univ., 1993–95; University of Cambridge: Dean and Dir of Studies for Theol. and Religious Studies, Peterhouse, 1995–97; Mem., Faculty of Divinity and Faculty of English, 1995–97; Manchester University: Sen. Fellow in Religion and Gender, 1997–98; Prof. of Contextual Theol. and Ethics, 1998–2010; Samuel Fergusson Prof. of Philosophical Theol. and Ethics, 2010–12; Director: Centre for Religion, Culture and Gender, 1998–2003; Centre for Religion and Political Culture, 2003–12; Hd, Sch. of Arts, Histories and Cultures, 2005–11; Res. Dir, Manchester Inst. for Res. in Religion and Civil Society, 2006–10. Ed., Lit. and Theol., 1990–2005. Vice-Pres., 2008–09, Pres., 2009–11, Soc. for Study of Theol.; Dir, Internat. Soc. of Religion and Lit., 2000–; Mem., Amer. Acad. of Religion, 1997–. Hon. Fellow, Exeter Coll., Oxford, 2012. *Publications:* Karl Barth, Jacques Derrida and the Language of Theology, 1995; Theology and Contemporary Critical Theory, 1996 (trans. Greek, 2001); (contrib.) Oxford Companion to Christian Thought, 1999; Cities of God, 2000; True Religion, 2002; (jtly) God and Beauty, 2003; Christ and Culture, 2005; (trans. and ed with M. Hoelzl) Carl Schmitt's Political Theology II, 2008; The Politics of Discipleship, 2010 (trans. Chinese); Unbelievable: why we believe and why we don't, 2014; *edited:* The Postmodern God: a reader in contemporary philosophy of religion, 1997; (jtly) Radical Orthodoxy, 1998 (trans. Swedish); Michel de Certeau: The Reader, 1999 (trans. Chinese, 2001); The Blackwell Companion to Postmodern Theology, 2001 (trans. Portuguese, 2004); (with M. Hoelzl) Religion and Political Theory: a critical reader, 2006 (trans. Rumanian); (with M. Hoelzl) The New Visibility of Religion, 2008; (trans. and ed with M. Hoelzl) Carl Schmitt's Dictatorship, 2014; contrib. chapters in books; contribs to jls incl. Lit. and Theol., Theol., Modern Theol., New Blackfriars, THES. *Recreations:* swimming, growing vegetables, cooking. *Address:* Christ Church, Oxford OX1 1DP.

WARD, Graham Norman Charles, CBE 2004; FCA; FEI; Chief Commissioner, Independent Commission for Aid Impact, 2010–15; non-executive Director, Civil Aviation Authority, since 2013; Vice-Chairman, World Energy Council, 2008–14 (Hon. Officer, 2014); *b* 9 May 1952; *s* of late Ronald Charles Edward Ward and Hazel Winifred Ward (*née* Ellis); *m* 1975, Ingrid Imogen Sylvia Baden-Powell (marr. diss. 1981); two *s*; *m* 1993, Ann Mistri; one *s*. *Educ:* Dulwich Coll.; Jesus Coll., Oxford (Boxing Blue; MA). ACA 1977, FCA 1983; CIGEM (CIGasE 1997); FEI (FInstE 1999). Price Waterhouse, subseq. PricewaterhouseCoopers: articled clerk, 1974–77; Personal Technical Asst to Chm., Accounting Standards Cttee, 1978–79; on secondment to HM Treasury, 1985; Partner, 1986; Dir, Electricity Services Europe, 1990–94; Direct Business Develt, 1993–94; Chm., World Utilities Gp, 1994–96; Dep. Chm., World Energy Gp, 1996–98; World Utilities Leader, 1998–2000; Sen. Partner, World Energy and Utilities Gp, 2000–10. Member: Panel on Takeovers and Mergers, 2000–01; Financial Reporting Council, 2001–07 (Dep. Chm., 2000–01); Bd, UK India Business Council (formerly Indo British Partnership Network), 2005–13 (Vice-Chm., 2008–13); Financial Services Sector Adv. Bd, UK Trade & Investment, 2006–09. Chairman: Consultative Cttee of Accountancy Bodies, 2000–01; Power Sector Adv. Gp, UK Trade & Investment (formerly Trade Partners UK), 2001–04; Mem. Council, Soc. of Pension Consultants, 1988–90; Mem., Auditing Practices Bd, 2001–04 (Vice-Chm., 2003–04); Member: Cttee, British Energy Assoc., 1997–2004 (Vice-Chm., 1998–2001; Chm., 2001–04); Exec. Council, Parly Gp for Energy Studies, 1998–. Chairman: Young Chartered Accountants' Gp, 1980–81; London Soc. of Chartered Accountants, 1989–90 (Mem. Cttee, 1983–91); Chartered Accountants in the Community, 1996–2002; Member: Council, ICAEW, 1991–2003 (Vice-Pres., 1998–99; Dep. Pres., 1999–2000; Pres., 2000–01); Bd, Internat. Fedn of Accountants, 2000–06 (Pres., 2004–06). Vice Pres., Epilepsy Res. UK (formerly Epilepsy Res. Foundn), 1997–. Vice President: Univ. of Oxford Amateur Boxing Club, 1990–; Soc. of Conservative Accountants, 1992–2001; President: Jesus Coll. Assoc., 1990–91; Chartered Accountant Students' Soc. of London, 1992–96 (Vice-Pres., 1987–92). Governor: Goodenough Coll., 2004–; Dulwich Coll., 2008–. Hon. Financial Advr, St Paul's Cathedral, 2008–; Auditor, Duchy of Cornwall, 2001–10. FRSA 1996. Freeman: City of London, 1994; Co. of Chartered Accountants in England and Wales, 1994 (Mem., Ct of Assts, 1997–; Master, 2009–10). *Publications:* The Work of a Pension Scheme Actuary, 1987; Pensions: your way through the maze, 1988; (consultant ed) A Practitioner's Guide to Audit Regulation in the UK, 2004; (contrib.) The Handbook of International Corporate Governance, 2009. *Recreations:* boxing, Rugby, opera, ballet. *Address:* Civil Aviation Authority, 45–59 Kingsway, WC2B 6TE. *T:* (020) 7453 6757. *Clubs:* Carlton; Vincent's (Oxford).

WARD, Prof. Harriet, CBE 2012; PhD; Professor of Child and Family Research, Loughborough University, since 2004 (Founding Director, Centre for Child and Family Research, 2002–14); *b* Sheffield, 22 Sept. 1948; *d* of late Stephen Blaxland and Elizabeth Alice Blaxland (*née* Brierly); *m* 1974, Christopher David Ward; three *s*. *Educ:* Princess Helena Coll.; St Andrews Univ. (MA French Lang. and Lit.); Linacre Coll., Oxford (Dip. Social and Admin. Studies; CQSW 1973); Univ. of Bristol (PhD 1990). Social worker: London Bor. of Wandsworth, 1973–74; Exeter CC, 1974–75; Caithness CC, 1975–76; S Yorks CC, 1976–77; Res. Associate, 1989–91, Res. Fellow, 1991–96, Univ. of Bristol; Sen. Lectr, Dept of Social Work, Univ. of Leicester, 1996–99; Sen. Res. Fellow, Loughborough Univ., 1999–2004. Founder Mem., Internat. Res. Network on Transitions to Adulthood from Care, 2003–; Acad. Advr, DoH/DFE Res. Initiative on Safeguarding Children, 2005–12; Co-Dir, Childhood Wellbeing Res. Centre, 2010–14. Mem. Bd, Eur. Scientific Assoc. for Residential and Foster Care, 2007–. *Publications:* (ed jtly) Looking After Children: assessing outcomes in child care, 1991; (ed) Looking After Children: research into practice, 1995; (ed with W. Rose) Approaches to Needs Assessment in Children's Services, 2002; Outcomes for Vulnerable Children, vol. 1 (ed with J. Scott), Promoting the Wellbeing of Children, Families and Communities, 2005, vol. 2 (jtly), Babies and Young Children in Care: life pathways, decision-making and practice, vol. 3 (jtly), Costs and Consequences of Placing Children in Care, 2008; (with C. Davies) Safeguarding Children Across Services: messages from research, 2012; (jtly) Safeguarding Babies and Very Young Children from Abuse and Neglect, 2012. *Recreations:* family and friends, English and French literature, theatre, films. *Address:* Centre for Child and Family Research, Department of Social Sciences, Loughborough University, Loughborough, Leics LE11 3TU. *T:* (01509) 223672, *Fax:* (01509) 223943. *E:* h.ward@lboro.ac.uk.

WARD, Helen Madeleine, (Lady Ward); Partner, Stewarts Law LLP, since 2012; a Deputy District Judge, since 1992; a Recorder, since 1997; *b* 28 May 1951; *d* of Kenneth and Ruth Gilbert; *m* 1983, Rt Hon. Sir Alan Hylton Ward, *qv*; one *d* (and one twin *d* decd). *Educ:* King Alfred Sch., Hampstead; Birmingham Univ. (LLB). Admitted Solicitor of the Supreme Court, 1978; Partner: Ward Bowie/Penningtons, 1978–94; Manches LLP, 1994–2012. *Recreations:* family, friends, music, theatre, gardening. *Address:* Stewarts Law LLP, 5 New Street Square, EC4A 3BF. *T:* (020) 7936 8187. *E:* hward@stewartslaw.com.

WARD, Hubert, OBE 1996; MA; Headmaster (formerly Principal), English College, Prague, 1992–96; *b* 26 Sept. 1931; *s* of Allan Miles Ward and Joan Mary Ward; *m* 1st, 1958, Elizabeth Cynthia Fearn Bechervaise (*d* 2005); one *s* two *d*; 2nd, 2007, Judith Marion Hart (*née* Gay). *Educ:* Westminster Sch.; Trinity Coll., Cambridge. Asst Master (Maths), Geelong C of E Grammar Sch., Victoria, 1955–66; Asst Master (Maths), Westminster Sch., London, 1966–69; Headmaster, King's Sch., Ely, 1970–92. Mem. (L) Cambs CC, 1985–89. JP Cambs, 1976–92. *Publications:* (with K. Lewis) Starting Statistics, 1969. *Recreations:* rowing, sailing, bird-watching. *Address:* 1 The Green, Mistley, Manningtree, Essex CO11 1EU.
See also Very Rev. F. E. F. Ward, V. J. Ward.

WARD, Prof. Ian Macmillan, FRS 1983; FInstP, FIMMM; Research Professor, University of Leeds, since 1994 (Professor of Physics, 1970–94, and Cavendish Professor, 1987–94); *b* 9 April 1928; *s* of Harry Ward and Joan Ward; *m* 1960, Margaret (*née* Linley); two *s* one *d*. *Educ:* Royal Grammar Sch., Newcastle upon Tyne; Magdalen Coll., Oxford (MA, DPhil). FInstP 1965; FIMMM (FPRI 1974). Technical Officer, ICI Fibres, 1954–61; seconded to Division of Applied Mathematics, Brown Univ., USA, 1961–62; Head of Basic Physics Section, ICI Fibres, 1962–65, ICI Research Associate, 1964; Sen. Lectr in Physics of Materials, Univ. of Bristol, 1965–69; Chm., Dept of Physics, Univ. of Leeds, 1975–78, 1987–89; Dir, Interdisciplinary Res. Centre in Polymer Sci. and Technol., Univs of Leeds, Bradford and Durham, 1989–94. Vis. Prof., Univ. of Bradford, 2008–. Secretary, Polymer Physics Gp, Inst. of Physics, 1964–71, Chm. 1971–75; Chairman, Macromolecular Physics Gp, European Physical Soc., 1976–81; Pres., British Soc. of Rheology, 1984–86. Hon. DSc Bradford, 1993. A. A. Griffith Medal, Plastics and Rubber Inst., 1982; S. G. Smith Meml Medal, Textile Inst., 1984; Swinburne Medal, Plastics and Rubber Inst., 1988; Charles Vernon Boys Medal, 1993, Glazebrook Medal, 2004, Inst. of Physics; Netlon Medal, IOM^3, 2004; Staudinger-Durrer Prize, ETH, 2013. Ed., Polymer, 1974–2002. *Publications:* Mechanical Properties of Solid Polymers, 1971, 3rd edn (with J. Sweeney) 2013; (ed) Structure and Properties of Oriented Polymers, 1975, 2nd edn 1997; (ed jtly) Ultra High Modulus Polymers, 1979; (with D. Hadley) An Introduction to the Mechanical Properties of Solid Polymers, 1993, 2nd edn (with J. Sweeney) 2004; (ed jtly) Solid Phase Processing of Polymers, 2000; contribs to Polymer, Jl of Polymer Science, Jl of Materials Science, Proc. Royal Soc., etc. *Recreations:* music, walking. *Address:* Kirskill, 2 Creskeld Drive, Bramhope, Leeds LS16 9EL. *T:* (0113) 267 3637.

WARD, Janice Elizabeth, CBE 2015; Founder and Chief Executive Officer, Corrotherm International Ltd, since 1992; *b* Southampton, 25 Sept. 1957; *d* of Owen George and Elizabeth Louise Ward; *m* 2005, Jonathan Charles Holmes; one *s* (and one *s* decd). *Educ:* BSc Mech. Engrg. Non-exec. Chair, AnTech Ltd, 2016–; non-executive Director: UKTI, 2012–15; Hardide plc, 2015–. Business Dir, Solent LEP, 2012–. Pres., Southampton Chamber of Commerce and Industry, 2010–13; non-exec. Dir, Hants Chamber of Commerce, 1993–. Member: Saudi British Jt Business Council, 2008–; UAE UK Business Council, 2015–. Judge: Queen's Awards for Enterprise, 2013–; Manufacturer of Year Awards, The Manufacturer, 2013–. Founding Trustee, Ben Voller G4 Fund, 2005–; Trustee, Southampton Cultural Develt Trust, 2009–. MIEx. FInstD. *Recreations:* motor cycling, ski-ing, sailing, walking, collecting books, trying to make a change for the good if I can. *Address:* 1 Bramblebank Cottages, Calshot, Southampton SO45 1BR. *T:* (023) 8024 3424. *E:* jan.ward@corrotherm.co.uk.

WARD, John; *see* Ward, C. J. W.

WARD, Sir John (MacQueen), Kt 2003; CBE 1995; FRSE; FIET; Chairman, Scottish Enterprise, 2004–09; *b* 1 Aug. 1940; *m* Barbara MacIntosh; one *s* three *d*. *Educ:* Edinburgh Acad.; Fettes Coll. CA. FRSE 2005; FIET 2007. IBM UK Ltd: Plant Controller, 1966–75; Dir, Inf. Systems for Europe, 1975–79; Manufacturing Controller, 1979–81; Dir, Havant Plant, 1982–90 (numerous quality awards); Dir, UK Public Service Business, 1991–95; Res. Dir, Scotland and N England, 1991–96; Chairman: Scottish Homes, 1996–2002; Scottish Post Office Bd, 1997–2001; Macfarlane Gp (Clansman), subseq. Macfarlane Gp plc, 1998–2003. Chm., European Assets Trust, 1995–2015; non-exec. Chm., Dunfermline Building Soc., 1995–2007. Chairman: Scottish CBI, 1993–95; Scottish Qualifications Authy, 2000–04. Chm. or former Chm., advisory bodies and councils in Scotland. Trustee, Nat. Mus Scotland (formerly Nat. Mus of Scotland), 2005–12. FRSA 1999. *Recreations:* walking, DIY, reading. *Clubs:* New (Edinburgh); Bruntsfield Links Golf.

WARD, Rev. Prof. (John Stephen) Keith, FBA 2001; Regius Professor of Divinity, University of Oxford, 1991–2003; Canon of Christ Church, Oxford, 1991–2003; Professorial Research Fellow, Heythrop College, London, since 2010; *b* 22 Aug. 1938; *s* of John George Ward and Evelyn (*née* Simpson); *m* 1963, Marian Trotman; one *s* one *d*. *Educ:* UCW, Cardiff (BA 1962); Linacre Coll., Oxford (BLitt 1968); Trinity Hall, Cambridge (MA 1972); Westcott House, Cambridge. DD Oxon, 1998; DD Cantab, 1999. Ordained priest of Church of England, 1972. Lecturer in Logic, Univ. of Glasgow, 1964–69; Lectr in Philosophy, Univ. of St Andrews, 1969–71; Lectr in Philosophy of Religion, Univ. of London, 1971–75; Dean of Trinity Hall, Cambridge, 1975–82; F. D. Maurice Prof. of Moral and Social Theology, Univ. of London, 1982–85; Prof. of History and Phil. of Religion, King's Coll. London, 1985–91. Gresham Prof. of Divinity, 2004–08. Jt Editor, Religious Studies, 1990–98. Jt Pres., World Congress of Faiths, 1992–2001. *Publications:* Ethics and Christianity, 1970; Kant's View of Ethics, 1972; The Divine Image, 1976; The Concept of God, 1977; The Promise, 1981; Rational Theology and the Creativity of God, 1982; Holding Fast to God, 1982; The Living God, 1984; Battle for the Soul, 1985; Images of Eternity, 1987; The Rule of Love, 1989; Divine Action, 1990; A Vision to Pursue, 1991; Religion and Revelation, 1994; Religion and Creation, 1996; God, Chance and Necessity, 1996; God, Faith and the New Millennium, 1998; Religion and Human Nature, 1998; Religion and Community, 2000; God: a guide for the perplexed, 2002; The Case for Religion, 2004; What the Bible Really Teaches, 2004; Pascal's Fire, 2006; Is Religion Dangerous?, 2006, new edn 2011; Christianity: a guide for the perplexed, 2007; Re-thinking Christianity, 2007; The Big Questions in Science and Religion, 2008; Religion and Human Fulfilment, 2008; Why There Almost Certainly Is a God: doubting Dawkins, 2008; The God Conclusion, 2009; The Word of God: the Bible after modern scholarship, 2010; More than Matter, 2010; Is Religion Irrational?, 2011; The Philosopher and the Gospels, 2011; Morality, Autonomy and God, 2013; The Evidence for God, 2014. *Recreations:* music, walking. *Address:* 39 Coopers Lane, Abingdon, Oxon OX14 5GU. *T:* (01235) 539799.

WARD, Joseph Haggitt; *b* 7 July 1926; *s* of Joseph G. and Gladys Ward; *m* 1961, Anthea Clemo (*d* 2010); one *s* one *d*. *Educ:* St Olave's Grammar School; Sidney Sussex College, Cambridge. Asst Principal, Min. of National Insurance, 1951; Private Sec. to Minister of Social Security, 1966–68; Asst Sec., 1968; Min. of Housing, later DoE, 1969–72; DHSS, 1972; Under-Sec. (pensions and nat. insce contributions), DHSS, 1976–86. *Recreations:* music, history of music, sequence dancing. *Address:* 34 Uffington Road, SE27 0ND. *T:* (020) 8670 1732.

WARD, Sir Joseph James Laffey, 4th Bt *cr* 1911; *b* 11 Nov. 1946; *s* of Sir Joseph George Davidson Ward, 3rd Bt, and Joan Mary Haden (*d* 1993), *d* of Major Thomas J. Laffey, NZSC; *S* father, 1970; *m* 1968, Robyn Allison, *d* of William Maitland Martin, Rotorua, NZ; one *s* one *d*. *Heir:* *s* Joseph James Martin Ward, *b* 20 Feb. 1971.

WARD, Julian Anthony; Headmaster, St Michael's Catholic Grammar School, Barnet, since 2012; *b* Whalley, Lancs, 19 Jan. 1954; *m* 1979, Bernadette Crossin; one *s* two *d*. *Educ:* Pilgrim Grammar Sch., Bedford; Univ. of Manchester (BA Hons 1975); Bradford Univ. Business Sch. (DipBA 1976); Christ's Coll., Liverpool (PGCE 1977). Teacher of Economics: John Griffiths RC Boys' Sch., Wandsworth, 1977–81; Bishop Challoner RC Girls' Sch., Tower Hamlets, 1981–84; Sir John Cass Foundn and Redcoat Sch., Tower Hamlets, 1984–88; St Michael's Catholic GS, Barnet, 1988–. *Recreations:* walking, gardening, badminton. *Address:* c/o St Michael's Catholic Grammar School, Nether Street, North Finchley, N12 7NJ. *E:* jward@st-michaels.barnet.sch.uk. *Club:* Romford Golf.

WARD, Julie Carolyn; Member (Lab) North West Region, European Parliament, since 2014; *b* Ripon, 7 March 1957; *d* of Frederick and Sheila Ward; two *s*. *Educ:* RAF Seletar Secondary Sch.; Pilton Comprehensive Sch., Barnstaple; N Devon Coll.; Univ. of Newcastle upon Tyne (MEd 2012). Community Drama Worker, Mid-Pennine Arts, 1977–78; Community Drama Worker, Contact Theatre, Manchester, 1979–83; Asst Dir, Coventry Fest., 1984; Dir, Northern SHAPE, 1984–86; Founder and Dir, Jack Drum Arts, 1986–; Mem., Theatre for Young Audiences, 1999–2011; NE Regl Co-ordinator, ARROW and INDRA, 2009–11. Member, Board: Culture NE, 2004–08; Nat. Drama, 2011–; Regl Council Mem., Arts Council England, 2009–11; Mem., Co. Durham Cultural Partnership, 2011–13. Patron: Dance Syndrome; Performing Arts Network and Develt Agency. Churchill Fellow, 1995. Mem., RSA, 2015. *Publications:* Secret Lives, 1989; You're Not a Kid Anymore, 1989; I Can Fly, 1993; The Likes of Us, 1993; Stitches in Time, 1994; Parents Know It All, 1996; Wild Words for Wild Places, 2000; Stepping Up, 2000; Visions and Voices, 2002; Water Borne, Seed Blown, 2003; From Cuna Dun to Coundon Now, 2005; History of a Village: Sunniside, 2007. *Recreations:* theatre, music, arts and galleries, reading, writing poetry, swimming, Oxfam volunteer. *Address:* European Parliament, 60 Rue Wiertz, 1047 Brussels, Belgium; (office) Workington Town Hall, Oxford Street, Workington CA14 2RS. *E:* julie.ward@europarl.europa.eu.

WARD, Keith; *see* Ward, Rev. J. S. K.

WARD, Keith David; Chief Executive, British Medical Association, since 2013; *b* London, 7 April 1960; *s* of Ronald and Rosalyn Ward; *m* 1990, Joanna Mary Martin; one *s* one *d*. *Educ:* St George's Sch., Harpenden; Hatfield Poly. (BA Hons Business). ACMA 1986; CGMA 2012. Project Accountant, British Aerospace, 1983–84; Financial Planning Manager, Dunn & Bradstreet, 1985–88; Finance Director: Datastream Internat., 1989–95; Primark Corp., 1996–2001; self-employed consultant, 2001–04; Finance Dir, 2004–06, Chief Operating Officer, 2007–10, C&G; Finance Dir, BMA, 2011–13. Trustee and Hon. Treas., London Youth, 2011–. Hon. MCGI 2011. *Recreations:* family, music, golf and (now spectating) other sport. *Address:* c/o British Medical Association, BMA House, WC1H 9JP. *T:* (020) 7383 6004. *E:* kward@bma.org.uk. *Club:* Berkhamsted Golf.

WARD, Lawrence George; Serjeant at Arms, House of Commons, since 2012; *b* London, 20 June 1968; *s* of Theresa Ward; *m* 1996, Jayne Moreton; two *s*. *Educ:* Tring Sch.; Open Univ. (Dip. Mgt Studies 1996). Post Office: postal cadet, 1984–86; Operational Mgt, 1986–95; Area Ops Manager, Royal Mail, 1995–97; House of Commons: Postmaster, 1997–2002; Mail Security Consultant, 2002–06; Security Contract Manager, 2006–08; Asst Serjeant at Arms, 2008–12. *Recreations:* music, DIY, sailing, travel. *Address:* Serjeant at Arms, House of Commons, SW1A 0AA. *T:* (020) 7219 3030, *Fax:* (020) 7799 2178. *E:* saaenquiries@parliament.uk.

WARD, Hon. Sir (Lisle) Austin, Kt 2006; Justice of Appeal, Bermuda, 2004; *b* 14 Nov. 1935; *s* of Sir Erskine Rueul La Tourette Ward, KA; *m* 1961, Francisca Sorhaindo; two *d*. *Educ:* Harrison Coll., Barbados. Called to the Bar, Middle Temple, 1962; Solicitor Gen., Bermuda, 1981–85; QC Bermuda 1983; Puisne Judge, Bermuda, 1985–93; Chief Justice, 1993–2004. *Publications:* Digest of Judgements of the Court of Appeal, 1985. *Address:* PO Box WK1, Warwick WKBX, Bermuda.

WARD, His Honour Malcolm Beverley; a Circuit Judge, Midland and Oxford Circuit, 1979–97; *b* 3 May 1931; *s* of Edgar and Dora Mary Ward; *m* 1958, Muriel Winifred, *d* of Dr E. D. M. Wallace, Perth; two *s* two *d*. *Educ:* Wolverhampton Grammar Sch.; St John's Coll., Cambridge (Open Mathematical Schol.; MA, LLM). Called to the Bar, Inner Temple, 1956; practised Oxford (later Midland and Oxford) Circuit; a Recorder of the Crown Court, 1974–79. Gov., Wolverhampton Grammar Sch., 1972–2012 (Chm., 1981–2001). *Recreations:* golf, music, (in theory) horticulture.

WARD, Malcolm Stanley; Founder and Managing Director, M60 Strategic Communications, since 2011; *b* 24 Sept. 1951; *s* of Hugh Ward and Rebecca Ward (*née* Rogerson). *Educ:* Gilberd School, Colchester. Dep. Editor, Gulf News, Dubai, 1978–79; Editor, Woodham and Wickford Chronicle, Essex, 1979–81; Dep. Editor, Gulf Times, Qatar, 1981–84; Dep. Editor, 1984–86, Dir and Editor, 1986–91, Daily News, Birmingham; Editor, Metro News, Birmingham, 1991–92; Ed., Evening News, Worcester, 1992–95; Man. Ed., The Peninsula, Qatar, 1995–98; News Ed., Gulf News, Dubai, 1998–2001; Account Dir, MCS Action, Dubai, 2001–06; Gp Account Dir, 2006–09, Dep. Man. Dir, 2009–11, JiWin, Dubai. *Recreations:* writing, travel, soccer, driving, tennis. *Address:* PO Box 440173, Dubai, UAE.

WARD, Mary Angela, MBE 1996; Co-Founder, and Artistic Director, 1974–2015, Chickenshed (formerly Chicken Shed Theatre Co.); *b* 2 Dec. 1944; *d* of Patrick O'Dwyer and Dot O'Dwyer (*née* Johnson); *m* 1971, Manus Ward; two *s*. *Educ:* Ilford Ursuline High Sch.; Digby Stuart Coll. Teacher, 1966–85; with Jo Collins, MBE, founded Chicken Shed Th. Co., 1974, with aim of producing pieces of theatrical and musical excellence to open the performing arts to all, incl. those denied access elsewhere. DUniv Middx, 1998. *Recreation:* Chickenshed!! *Address:* c/o Chickenshed, 290 Chase Side, Southgate, N14 4PE. *T:* (020) 8351 6161, ext. 204.

WARD, Michael; researcher and consultant in local economic development and regeneration; Chief Executive, British Urban Regeneration Association, 2008–09; *b* 15 Oct. 1949; *s* of late Donald Albert Ward; *m* Hilary Knight; one *s* one *d*. *Educ:* Wimbledon Coll., London; University Coll., Oxford (BA PPE 1972); Birkbeck Coll., London (MA Social and Econ. Hist. 1980). Mem. (Lab), GLC, 1981–86 (Chm., Industry and Employment Cttee, 1981–86; Dep. Leader, 1985–86). Dir, Centre for Local Econ. Strategies, Manchester, 1987–2000 (Chm., 2009–). Chm., Manchester City Labour Party, 1995–2000; Chief Executive: London Develt Agency, 2000–04; QMW Public Policy Seminars, Univ. of London, 2004–05; Kent Thameside Delivery Bd, 2005–08. Member: Poverty and Disadvantage Cttee, Joseph Rowntree Foundn, 2002–06; Bd, London Pensions Fund Authy, 2004–08 (Dep. Chm., 2005–08). Res. Fellow, Smith Inst., 2010–; Associate, Centre for London, 2013–. Chm., Twin and Twin Trading Ltd, 2011–. *Publications:* reports for Smith Inst. *W:* www.michaelwardconsulting.co.uk.

WARD, Michael Jackson, CBE 1980; British Council Director, Germany, 1990–91, retired; *b* 16 Sept. 1931; *s* of late Harry Ward, CBE, and Dorothy Julia Ward (*née* Clutterbuck); *m* 1955, Eileen Patricia Foster; one *s* one *d*. *Educ:* Drayton Manor Grammar Sch.; University Coll. London (BA); Univ. of Freiburg; Corpus Christi Coll., Oxford. HM Forces, 1953–55; 2nd Lieut Royal Signals. Admin. Officer, HMOCS, serving as Dist Comr and Asst Sec. to Govt, Gilbert and Ellice Is; British Council, 1961–91: Schs Recruitment Dept, 1961–64; Regional Rep., Sarawak, 1964–68; Dep. Rep., Pakistan, 1968–70; Dir, Appointments Services Dept, 1970–72; Dir, Personnel Dept, 1972–75; Controller, Personnel and Appts Div., 1975–77; Representative, Italy, 1977–81; Controller, Home Div., 1981–85; Asst Dir-Gen., 1985–90. Hon. Mem., British Council, 1991. *Recreations:* music, golf. *Address:* 1 Knapp Rise, Haslingfield, Cambridge CB23 1LQ. *E:* mjward@spanner.org. *Club:* Gog Magog Golf.

WARD, Neil David; independent business consultant, 2008–14; Director, Quality Transformation Ltd, 2008–11; *b* 14 March 1953; *s* of Tom Ward and Vera Ward (*née* Dowd); *m* 1979, Jane Gray; one *s* one *d*. *Educ:* St Francis Xavier's Coll., Liverpool; Wallasey Grammar Sch. HM Treasury, 1972–73; NI Office, 1973–87; DoH, 1987–89; Sen. Civil Service, 1989–91, 1994–; DSS, 1989–90; Chief Exec., Pegasus Retirement Homes (SE) Ltd, 1991–93; DWP (formerly DSS), 1994–99; Chief Exec., Appeals Service, 1999–2003; Department for Constitutional Affairs, subseq. Ministry of Justice: Dir, Judicial Appts, 2003–04; Dir, Criminal Justice, 2004–05; Dir, Crime, HM Courts Service, 2005–06; Chief Operating Officer, HM Courts Service, 2006–07; Interim Chief Exec., HM Courts Service, 2007–08. Asst Comr, Boundary Commn for England, 2011–12. *Recreations:* sport (golf, ski-ing and swimming and as a spectator of all sports), quizzes.

WARD, Nicholas; *see* Ward, C. J. N.

WARD, Peter Simms; a District Judge (Magistrates' Courts), Lancashire, 2006–13; *b* 20 June 1943; *s* of Norman and Marie Ward; *m* 1974, Monica Stalker; three *s*. *Educ:* Bolton Sch.; Bristol Univ. (LLB). Articled to J. J. Rothwell, Solicitor, Salford; admitted Solicitor, 1969; Partner, Rothwell & Evans, Solicitors, Salford, Gtr Manchester, 1969–94; Provincial Stipendiary Magistrate, subseq. Dist Judge (Magistrates' Courts), Merseyside, 1994–2001; Dist Judge (Magistrates' Courts), Manchester, 2001–06. *Recreations:* reading, walking, gardening. *E:* mstalkerward@fastmail.fm.

WARD, Phillip David; Chairman, Resource Futures Ltd, since 2011; *b* 1 Sept. 1950; *s* of Frederick William Ward and Phyllis Mavis Ward; *m* 1974, Barbara Patricia, (Pip), Taylor; two *d*. *Educ:* Sir John Talbot's GS, Whitchurch; Sheffield Univ. (BJur 1973). Department of the Environment, later Department of the Environment, Transport and the Regions: Admin. Trainee, 1973–78; Hackney/Islington Inner City Partnership, 1978–80; Principal, Local Govt Finance Directorate, 1980–85; Asst Sec., Local Govt Finance Review, 1985–90; Principal Private Sec. to Sec. of State for the Envmt, 1990–92; Dir (Under Sec.), Construction Sponsorship, 1992–97; Dir, Energy, Envmt and Waste, 1997–2001; Dir of Finance, then Prin. Finance Officer, DETR, subseq. DTLR, then ODPM, 2001–02; Dir, Local Govt Performance Unit, OPDM, 2002–04; Dir, Waste and Resources Action Prog. Ltd, 2004–11. Dir, OPRL Ltd, 2014–. *Recreations:* sailing, Rugby, cinema.

WARD, Rear-Adm. Rees Graham John, CB 2002; FIET; Managing Director, Eversfield Advisors Ltd, since 2013; *b* 1 Oct. 1949; *s* of John Walter Ward and Helen Burt Ward (*née* Foggo); *m* 1st, 1973, Christina Glen Robertson (marr. diss.); two *s*; 2nd, 1980, Phyllis Gentry Pennington; two *d*. *Educ:* Queens' Coll., Cambridge (MA); Cranfield Univ. (MSc 1981; MSc (Corp. Mgt) 2001). FIET (FIEE 1998). Joined RN, 1967; served: HMS Russel, 1972–73; HMS Brighton, 1977–79; MoD PE, 1981–83; jsdc 1984; HMS Ark Royal, 1984–87; Naval Asst to Controller of Navy, 1988–89; Asst DOR (Sea), 1990–92; NA to Chief of Defence Procurement, 1992–94; DOR (Sea), 1995–97; rcds 1998; hcsc 1999; ACDS, Operational Requirements (Sea Systems), 1999; Capability Manager (Strategic Deployment), MoD, 1999–2002; Chief Exec., Defence Communications Services Agency, 2002–07; Dir Gen. Inf. Systems and Services, Defence Equipment and Support, 2007. Dir Gen., Defence Manufrs Assoc., 2007–09; Chief Exec., ADS, 2009–11, ADS Gp, 2011–12. Rep. GB and Scotland at athletics cross country running, 1972–77. CRAeS 2008. *Recreations:* reading, running marathons, mountain biking. *Clubs:* Army and Navy; Hawks (Cambridge).

WARD, Reginald George; Director, Analysis and Research (formerly Statistics and Economic Office), Inland Revenue, 1994–2001; *b* 6 July 1942; *s* of Thomas George and Ada May Ward; *m* 1964, Chandan Mistry; two *s* one *d*. *Educ:* Leicester, Aberdeen and Oxford Universities; London Business Sch. Lectr in Economics, St Andrews Univ., 1965; Analyst, National Cash Register, 1969; Economist, ICL, 1970; DTI, 1971; Chief Statistician: HM Treasury, 1978; Cabinet Office, 1982; Dir, Business Statistics Office, DTI, 1986; Asst Dir, CSO, 1989–94. *Recreation:* sailing.

WARD, Richard Churchill, PhD; Chairman: Brit plc, since 2014; Cunningham Lindsey Group, since 2014; *b* 6 March 1957; *s* of Alan and Margaret Ward; *m* 1990, Carol Cole; two *s*. *Educ:* Wellington Coll.; Univ. of Exeter (BSc 1979; PhD 1982). Scientist, SERC, 1982–88; Sen. Manager, BP Research, 1988–91; Hd of Business Develt, BP Oil Trading Internat., 1991–94; Hd of Mktg, Tradition Financial Services, 1994–95; International Petroleum Exchange, subseq. ICE Futures: Dir, Product Develt and Res., 1995–96; Exec. Vice Pres., 1996–99; Chief Exec., 1999–2005; Vice Chm., 2005–06; Chief Exec., Lloyd's of London, 2006–13. Non-exec. Dir, Partnership Assce Gp, 2013–. *Publications:* scientific res. papers in Chem. Soc. Rev., Jl of Applied Crystallography, Europhysics Letters, Molecular Physics, Nature, etc. *Recreations:* sailing, road cycling, hockey, ski-ing. *Address:* Brit Insurance, 55 Bishopsgate, EC2N 3AS.

WARD, Prof. Richard Samuel, DPhil; FRS 2005; Professor of Mathematics, since 1991, Head, Department of Mathematical Sciences, 2004–07, University of Durham; *b* 6 Sept. 1951; *s* of late Walter Ward and Eileen Ward (*née* Phillips); *m* 1991, Rebecca Nora, *d* of Horace Basil Barlow, *qv*; one *s* one *d*. *Educ:* Rhodes Univ. (BSc Hons 1973, MSc 1974); St John's Coll., Oxford (DPhil 1977). Jun. Res. Fellow, Merton Coll., Oxford, 1977–79; Lectr and Fellow, TCD, 1979–82; Mem., Inst. for Theoretical Physics, Stony Brook, NY, 1982; Lectr, Sen. Lectr, then Reader, Univ. of Durham, 1983–91. Life Mem., Clare Hall, Cambridge. Jun. Whitehead Prize, LMS, 1989. *Publications:* (with R. O. Wells, Jr) Twistor Geometry and Field Theory, 1990; articles on mathematical physics in learned jls. *Recreations:* family, music, reading. *Address:* Department of Mathematical Sciences, University of Durham, Durham DH1 3LE. *T:* (0191) 334 3118. *E:* richard.ward@durham.ac.uk.

WARD, Maj.-Gen. Robert William, CB 1989; MBE 1972; DL; plantsman, landscape and garden design consultant, since 1992; *b* 17 Oct. 1935; *s* of late Lt-Col William Denby Ward and Monica Thérèse Ward (*née* Collett-White); *m* 1966, Lavinia Dorothy Cramsie; two *s* one *d*. *Educ:* Rugby School; RMA Sandhurst. Commissioned Queen's Bays (later 1st Queen's Dragoon Guards), 1955; served Jordan, Libya, BAOR, Borneo, NI, and Persian Gulf; MA to C-in-C BAOR, 1973–75; CO 1st Queen's Dragoon Guards, 1975–77; Col GS Staff Coll., 1977–79; Comdr 22 Armd Brigade, 1979–82; RCDS Canada, 1982–83; Asst Chief of Staff, Northern Army Group, 1983–86; GOC Western Dist, 1986–89, retd. Col, 1st Queen's Dragoon Guards, 1991–97; Hon. Col, Royal Mercian and Lancastrian Yeomanry, 1995–2001. Sec., Game Conservancy, Shropshire, 1993–2000; Chairman: Nat. Meml Arboretum, 1996–98; Shropshire Parks and Gardens Trust, 1996–2002. Pres., SSAFA, Shropshire, 1994–. DL Shropshire, 2000. *Recreations:* gardening, outdoor sports, country pursuits, travel, food, wine. *Clubs:* MCC, I Zingari.

WARD, Rev. Robin, PhD; Principal, St Stephen's House, Oxford, since 2006; *b* 24 Jan. 1966; *s* of late Peter Herbert Ward and of Maureen Ann Ward; *m* 1997, Ruth Suzanne (*née* Sheard); two *s*. *Educ:* Hassenbrook Sch.; City of London Sch.; Magdalen Coll., Oxford (BA 1987, MA 1991); St Stephen's House, Oxford; King's Coll. London (PhD 2003). Ordained deacon, 1991, priest, 1992; Assistant Curate: St Andrew Romford, 1991–94; St Andrew and St Francis, Willesden Green, 1994–96; Vicar, St John the Baptist, Sevenoaks, 1996–2006. Hon. Canon, and Hon. Canon Theologian, Rochester Cathedral, 2004–06, Canon Emeritus, 2006–. Proctor in Convocation, 2000–05. *Publications:* On Christian Priesthood, 2011; reviews in Jl of Theol Studies and Jl of Ecclesiastical Hist. *Recreation:* cultivation of rhododendrons. *Address:* St Stephen's House, 16 Marston Street, Oxford OX4 1JX. *T:* (01865) 247874. *Club:* Travellers.

WARD, Robin William; Director-General, West Yorkshire Passenger Transport Executive, 1976–82; *b* 14 Jan. 1931; *s* of William Frederick and Elsie Gertrude Ward; *m* 1974, Jean Catherine Laird; three *s*. *Educ:* Colston's Sch., Bristol; University Coll. London. BScEcon, 1st Cl. Hons. Pilot Officer/Flying Officer, RAF Educn Br., 1954–55. Various posts, London Transport Exec., 1955–67; seconded to Brit. Transport Staff Coll. as mem. staff and latterly Asst Principal (incl. course at Harvard Business Sch.), 1967–70; Industrial Relations Officer, London Transport Exec., 1970–74; Dir of Personnel, W Yorks Passenger Transport Exec., 1974–76. *Recreation:* trying to learn the piano and organ. *Address:* 13 Turnbury Street, Little Mountain, Qld 4551, Australia.

WARD, Rt Rev. Simon B.; *see* Barrington-Ward.

WARD, Simon Howe B.; *see* Brooks-Ward.

WARD, Thomas; Sheriff of North Strathclyde at Dunoon, since 2010; *b* Glasgow, 3 April 1953; *s* of Thomas and Mary Ward; *m* 1980, Ruth Zegleman; three *s*. *Educ:* St Mary's Coll., Blairs; St Aloysius Coll., Glasgow; Univ. of Dundee (LLB Hons). Partner, Blair & Bryden, Greenock, 1979–2000; Immigration Judge (pt-time), 2001–10; Mem. (pt-time), PMETB, 2005–10; Sheriff (pt-time), 2005–10. Legal Assessor, GMC and NMC, 2002–10. Mem., CICAP, 2001–10. *Recreations:* golf, watching cricket, walking, visiting France. *Address:* 107 Finnart Street, Greenock PA16 8HN. *T:* (01475) 723055. *E:* sheriffward@scotcourts.gov.uk.

WARD, Timothy Justin; QC 2011; *b* Macclesfield, 16 Oct. 1966; *s* of Anthony and Sally Ward; *m* 1994, Catherine Temma Davidson; one *s* one *d*. *Educ:* Cheadle Hulme Sch.; University Coll. London (BA); Univ. of Southern Calif (MA); Trinity Coll., Cambridge. Called to the Bar, Gray's Inn, 1994; in practice as barrister, specialising in EU, competition and public law. Chm., Bar Eur. Gp, 2013–15. Ed. in Chief, Human Rights Law Reports: UK cases, 2000–. Barrister of Year, The Lawyer, 2013. *Publications:* (ed) Judicial Review and the Human Rights Act, 2000; (jtly) The Strasbourg Case Law: leading cases from the European Human Rights Law Reports, 2001; (jtly) Competition Litigation in the UK, 2005. *Recreations:* family, music, the outdoors. *Address:* Monckton Chambers, 1–2 Raymond Buildings, Gray's Inn, WC1R 5NR. *T:* (020) 7405 7211.

WARD, Tony, OBE 1998; Group Services Director, BAA plc, 1999–2007 (Group Human Resources Director, 1997–99); non-executive Director: SThree, since 2006; OCS Group Ltd, since 2007; *b* 20 Feb. 1950; *s* of Kenneth H. Ward and Elsie M. Ward; *m* 1972, Margaret Harrison; one *d*. *Educ:* Univ. of Leeds (BSc 1st Class Hons 1972). Personnel Manager, Stone Platt Industries, 1972–81; Personnel Director (Divisional), GrandMet, 1981–91; Dir of Human Resources, Kingfisher plc, 1992–97. Mem., 1990–95, Dep. Chm., 1993–95, CRE. Chm., Equal Opportunities Panel, CBI; Mem. Council, Consumers' Assoc., 2011– (Dep. Chm., 2015–); Mem. Bd, Which? Ltd, 2011–. FCIPD 1991; FRSA 2000. *Recreations:* golf, yoga, art, cycling. *Clubs:* Lambourne, Home House.

WARD, Vanessa Jane; HM Inspector (Education), Ofsted, since 2015; *b* Guildford, 20 Oct. 1964; *d* of Hubert Ward, *qv*; *m* 1989, Michael Petley; two *s*. *Educ:* King's Sch., Ely; Univ. of Edinburgh (MA Hons Eng. Lit. 1988); College of Law (CPE 1989; Law Soc. Finals 1991); Roehampton Inst., Univ. of Surrey (PGCE 1998); Nat. Coll. of Sch. Leadership (NPQH 2009). Admitted Solicitor, 1993. Trainee solicitor, 1991–93, Solicitor, 1993–96, Simkins Partnership; in-house Legal Advr, Judy Daish Associates, 1996; English Teacher, Nonsuch High Sch. for Girls, 1998–2001; Second i/c, English Dept, Wilson's Sch., 2001–02; Hd, English Dept, 2003–05, Asst Headteacher, 2005–08, Dep. Headteacher, 2008–10, St Philomena's Catholic High Sch. for Girls; Headteacher, Tiffin Girls' Sch., 2010–15. Vice Chair, Royal Bor. of Kingston upon Thames Schs Forum, 2013–15. Gov., Tiffin Sch., 2007–10. Trustee: Thames Youth Orch., 2010–; Beat (Beating Eating Disorders), 2014–. *Recreations:* theatre, walking, reading, current affairs, DIY, camping. *Club:* Lansdowne.
See also Very Rev. F. E. F. Ward.

WARD, William Alec; HM Diplomatic Service, retired; *b* 27 Nov. 1928; *s* of William Leslie Ward and Gladys Ward; *m* 1955, Sheila Joan Hawking; two *s* two *d*. *Educ:* King's Coll. Sch., Wimbledon; Christ Church, Oxford. HM Forces, 1947–49. Colonial Office, 1952; Private Sec. to Permanent Under-Sec., 1955–57; Singapore, 1960–64; seconded to CRO, 1963; Karachi, 1964–66; Islamabad, 1966–68; joined HM Diplomatic Service, 1968; FCO, 1968–71; Salisbury, 1971–72; Dep. High Comr, Colombo, 1973–76; High Comr, Mauritius, 1977–81. *Recreations:* music, walking. *Address:* 19 Beech Court, South Walks Road, Dorchester DT1 1DX.

WARD-THOMAS, Evelyn, (Mrs Michael Ward-Thomas); *see* Anthony, Evelyn.

WARD THOMAS, Gwyn Edward; *see* Thomas, Gwyn E. W.

WARDALE, Sir Geoffrey (Charles), KCB 1979 (CB 1974); Second Permanent Secretary, Department of the Environment, 1978–80; *b* 29 Nov. 1919; *m* 1944, Rosemary Octavia Dyer (*d* 2013); one *s* one *d*. *Educ:* Altrincham Grammar Sch.; Queens' Coll., Cambridge (Schol.). Army Service, 1940–41. Joined Ministry of War Transport as Temp. Asst Princ., 1942; Private Sec. to Perm. Sec., 1946; Princ., 1948; Asst Sec., 1957; Under-Sec., Min. of Transport, later DoE, 1966; Dep. Sec., 1972. Led inquiry: into the Open Structure in the Civil Service (The Wardale Report), 1981; into cases of fraud and corruption in PSA, 1982–83. Mem. Council, Univ. of Sussex, 1986–92; Chm., Brighton Coll. Council, 1985–90. President: Friends of Lewes Soc., 1992–97; Lewes Area CABx, 1989–99. *Recreations:* transport history, painting, listening to music. *Address:* 89 Paddock Lane, Lewes, East Sussex BN7 1TW. *T:* (01273) 473468.

WARDELL, Gareth Lodwig; environmental and planning consent consultant, since 2007; *b* 29 Nov. 1944; *s* of John Thomas Wardell and Jenny Ceridwen Wardell; *m* 1967, Jennifer Dawn Evans; one *s*. *Educ:* London Sch. of Econs and Pol Science (BScEcon, MSc). Geography Master, Chislehurst and Sidcup Technical High Sch., 1967–68; Head of Econs Dept, St Clement Danes Grammar Sch., 1968–70; Sixth Form Econs Master, Haberdashers' Aske's Sch., Elstree, 1970–72; Educn Lectr, Bedford Coll. of Physical Educn, 1972–73; Sen. Lectr in Geography, Trinity Coll., Carmarthen, 1973–82. MP (Lab) Gower, Sept. 1982–1997. A Forestry Comr, 1999–2007. Mem. Bd, Envmt Agency, 1997–2004. Lay Mem., GMC, 1995–2008. *Publications:* articles on regional issues in British Econ. Survey. *Recreations:* cycling, cross-country running.

WARDELL, Susan Toni, CBE 2010; Vice President, Corporate Services, African Development Bank Group, since 2012; *b* London, 12 Feb. 1954; *d* of Thomas Alfred Wardell and Joyce Ann Wardell (*née* Canter). *Educ:* Roehampton Inst. of Higher Educn, Univ. of London (BA 1st Cl. Hons Educn); Inst. of Educn, Univ. of London (MA Sociol. of Educn Double Dist.). Lectr in Sociol. and Psychol., Church Teacher's Coll., Jamaica, 1978–81; Principal Econ. and Employment Officer, London Bor. of Hackney, 1982–87; Field Dir, VSO Pacific Prog., 1987–91; Hd of Estimates and Resources Section, 1991–93, Prog. Manager, S Africa, 1993–99, ODA; Regl Dir, W and Southern Africa, Save the Children UK, 1996–99; Department for International Development: Head, Nepal, 1999–2001, Perf. and Effectiveness Dept, 2001–04, Southern Africa, 2004–06; Capability Rev. Manager, 2006–07; Dir, ME, Caribbean, Asia (N, Central, E) and Overseas Territories, 2007–10; Dir, Conflict, Humanitarian, Security, ME and N Africa, 2010–12; Chief Exec., Queen Elizabeth Diamond Jubilee Trust (on secondment), 2012. *Recreations:* listening to music, particularly African jazz, sailing, cricket, walking, cycling, theatre and arts. *Address:* African Development Bank, BP 323, 1002 Tunis Belvedere, Tunisia. *E:* s.wardell@afdb.org.

WARDINGTON, 3rd Baron *cr* 1936, of Alnmouth in the county of Northumberland; **William Simon Pease;** *b* 15 Oct. 1925; *s* of 1st Baron Wardington and Hon. Dorothy Charlotte, *er d* of 1st Baron Forster and *widow* of Hon. Harold Lubbock; *S* brother, 2005; *m* 1962, Hon. Elizabeth Jane Ormsby-Gore (*d* 2004), *d* of 4th Baron Harlech, KG, GCMG, PC. *Educ:* Eton; New Coll., Oxford (MA 1956); St Thomas's Hosp. Med. Sch. (MB BS Lond. 1956). FRCS 1961. Captain, Grenadier Guards, 1947. Consultant ENT Surgeon, Central Middlesex and Northwick Park Hosps, 1967–85. *Recreations:* golf, sailing, gardening. *Heir:* none. *Address:* Lepe House, Exbury, Southampton SO45 1AD. *T:* (023) 8089 3724; Flat 45, Elizabeth Court, 47 Milmans Street, SW10 0DA. *T:* (020) 7351 0954. *Clubs:* Royal Yacht Squadron, Island Sailing (Cowes).

WARDLAW, Sir (Henry) Justin, 22nd Bt *cr* 1631, of Pitreavie; *b* 10 Aug. 1963; *s* of Sir Henry John Wardlaw, 21st Bt, and of Julie-Ann, *d* of late Edward Patrick Kirwan; *S* father, 2005, but his name does not appear on the Official Roll of the Baronetage; *m* 1988, Rachel Jane, *y d* of James Kennedy Pitney; two *s* one *d*. *Heir: s* Henry James Wardlaw, *b* 8 Dec. 1999.

WARDLE, Charles Frederick; immigration policy adviser and international consultant; *b* 23 Aug. 1939; *s* of late Frederick Maclean Wardle and Constance Wardle (*née* Roach); *m* 1964, Lesley Ann, *d* of Sidney Wells; one *d*. *Educ:* Tonbridge Sch.; Lincoln Coll., Oxford; Harvard Business Sch. MA Oxon 1968; MBA Harvard. Asst to Pres., American Express Co., NY, 1966–69; Merchant Banking, London, 1969–72; Chairman: Benjamin Priest Gp plc, 1977–84 (Dir, 1972–74, Man. Dir, 1974–77); Warne, Wright and Rowland, 1978–84. Mem. Council, CBI, 1980–84. MP (C) Bexhill and Battle, 1983–2001. PPS: to Sec. of State for Social Services, 1984–87; to Sec. of State for Scotland, 1990–92; Parly Under-Sec. of State, and Immigration Minister, Home Office, 1992–94, DTI, 1994–95. Member Select Committee: on Trade and Industry, 1983–84; on Treasury and Civil Service, 1990; on Public Accounts, 1995–2000. Public Affairs Dir, Harrods Ltd, 2000–02; claims settlement for Equitas Ltd with Libya, Iraq and UN Compensation Commn, 2003–06. Chm., Cons. One Nation Forum, 1989–90. Member: Commercial and Econ. Cttee, EEF, 1981–83; Midlands Cttee, IoD, 1981–83. FRGS 1977. *Recreations:* books, sport, travel. *Address:* Shepherds, Cranbrook, Kent TN17 3EN. *Clubs:* Farmers, Travellers.

WARDLE, Prof. (Frances) Jane, PhD; FBPsS; FMedSci; FBA 2013; Professor of Clinical Psychology, since 1996 and Director, Cancer Research UK Health Behaviour Research Centre, since 1997, University College London; *b* Oxford, 30 Oct. 1950; *d* of Peter Brian Wardle and Marcella Frances Wardle; *m* 1st, 1976, Nicholas Stirling (marr. diss. 1986); one *d*; 2nd, 1991, Prof. Andrew Patrick Arthur Steptoe, *qv*; one *s*. *Educ:* St Anne's Coll., Oxford (BA 1973); Inst. of Psychiatry, Univ. of London (MPhil 1975; PhD 1986). FBPsS 1989. Institute of Psychiatry, University of London: Lectr in Clin. Psychol., 1976–86; Sen. Lectr in Clin. Psychol., 1987–91; Reader in Health Psychol. and Sen. Scientist, ICRF Health Behaviour Unit, 1991–95; Clin. Psychologist, Maudsley Hosp., London, 1976–96. Founder and Res. Dir, Weight Concern, 1990–. Associate Ed., British Jl Clin. Psychol., 1992–95; Ed., British Jl Health Psychol., 1995–2001. Chm., Health Psychol. Div., BPsS, 2000–01. Fellow: Soc. of Behavioral Medicine, 2003; Amer. Psychol Soc., 2011; FMedSci 2012. MAE 2007. *Publications:* Psychosocial Processes and Health: a reader, 1994; contrib. articles to scientific jls on health psychol., cancer screening, obesity. *Recreations:* reading, theatre, friends, family. *Address:* Department of Epidemiology and Public Health, University College London, 1–19 Torrington Place, WC1E 6BT. *T:* (020) 7679 1734, *Fax:* (020) 7679 8354. *E:* j.wardle@ucl.ac.uk.

WARDLE, John; *see* Wardle, R. J. S.

WARDLE, (John) Irving; Drama Critic, The Independent on Sunday, 1990–95; *b* 20 July 1929; *s* of John Wardle and Nellie Partington; *m* 1958, Joan Notkin (marr. diss.); *m* 1963, Fay Crowder (marr. diss.); two *s*; *m* 1975, Elizabeth Grist; one *s* one *d*. *Educ:* Bolton Sch.; Wadham Coll., Oxford (BA); Royal Coll. of Music (ARCM). Joined Times Educational Supplement as sub-editor, 1956; Dep. Theatre Critic, The Observer, 1960; Drama Critic, The Times, 1963–89. Editor, Gambit, 1973–75. Plays: The Houseboy, prod Open Space Theatre, 1974, ITV, 1982; devised A Kurt Tucholsky Cabaret, Arcola Th., 2010. *Publications:* The Theatres of George Devine (biog.), 1978; Theatre Criticism, 1992. *Recreation:* piano playing. *Address:* 51 Richmond Road, New Barnet, Herts EN5 1SF. *T:* (020) 8440 3671.

WARDLE, Peter; Chief Executive, Electoral Commission, 2004–15; *b* 3 July 1962; *s* of late Alec Peter Wardle and of Rev. Patricia Wardle (*née* Haker); *m* 2005, Jo Gray. *Educ:* Emanuel Sch.; Merton Coll., Oxford (BA Hons 1985). Inland Revenue, 1985–87; Private Sec. to Minister for Higher Educn and Sci., 1987–89; Inland Revenue: Principal, 1989–94; Asst Dir, 1994–98; Dir, Strategy and Planning, 1998–2000; Dir, Corporate Services, Cabinet Office, 2000–04. Non-exec. Dir, Basildon and Thurrock Univ. Hosp. NHS Foundn Trust (formerly Basildon and Thurrock Univ. Hosp. NHS Trust), 2004–12 (Vice Chm., 2007–10); Mem. Gp Audit and Risk Cttee, Circle (formerly Circle Anglia) Gp, 2008–. *Recreations:* fell-walking, cycling, music. *Club:* Essex Roads Cycling.

WARDLE, Robert James; Consultant, DLA Piper, 2008–13; *b* 23 Dec. 1951; *s* of late William James Wardle and Peggy Mary Wardle. *Educ:* Stamford Sch.; Univ. of Hull (LLB Hons). Admitted solicitor, 1976; articled clerk, 1974–76, asst solicitor, 1976–78, Greenwoods; Prosecuting Solicitor, Essex CC, 1978–80; Cambridgeshire County Council: Prosecuting Solicitor, 1980–86; Sen. Crown Prosecutor, 1986–88; Serious Fraud Office: Case Controller, 1988–92; Asst Dir, 1992–2003; Dir, 2003–08. *Recreations:* walking, shooting. *T:* (01733) 554929. *E:* wardle522@btinternet.com.

WARDLE, Brig. (Robin) John (Stuart), OBE 1987; DL; Chairman, NHS Staff College Council, since 2010; Vice Lord-Lieutenant, North Yorkshire, 2014–15; *b* Loxwood, 7 Nov. 1944; *s* of Norman Henry Russell Wardle, TD and Joan Deirdrie Wardle (*née* Hadden); *m* 1970, Sarah Jane Ingham; one *s* one *d*. *Educ:* Cheltenham Coll.; Queen's Univ., Kingston, Canada (Draper's Schol.); Mons Officer Cadet Sch. (Sen. Under Officer and Stick of Honour). Commnd Coldstream Guards, 1964; psc 1977; Acad. Adjt, RMA, 1980–83; CO, 1st Bn, Coldstream Guards, 1985–87; Comdr, 52 Lowland Bde, 1993–95. Chairman: Northallerton Health Services NHS Trust, 1996–2002; Craven and Harrogate PCT, 2002–06; NHS N Yorks and York, 2006–09. Freeman, Co. of Merchants to the Staple of England. DL N Yorks, 2004. *Recreation:* yachting. *Address:* Bellwood Hall, Ripon, N Yorks HG4 3AA. *T:* (01765) 602005. *E:* john_wardle@talk21.com. *Clubs:* Royal Yacht Squadron; Household Division Yacht (Cdre, 2010–).

WARE, Anna, (Mrs T. D. O. Ware); *see* Pavord, A.

WARE, Howard Elliott, FRCS; Consultant Orthopaedic Surgeon, since 1994, and Director, Wellington Knee Surgery Unit, since 2010, Wellington Hospital; Consultant Orthopaedic Surgeon, and Head, Lower Limb Arthroplasty, Royal Free London NHS Foundation Trust, since 2014; *b* 2 Nov. 1955; *s* of David Frederick Ware and Ann Julia Ware; *m* 1979, Carol Frances Davis; one *s* two *d*. *Educ:* Lady Owen's Sch.; St Bartholomew's Med. Sch. (MB BS 1980). FRCS 1985; FRCS(Orth) 1992. Consultant Orthopaedic Surgeon: St Bartholomew's Hosp., 1992–94; Chase Farm Hosp., Enfield, 1994–2014. Med. Advr, Worldwide Healthcare Associates, 2014–. Hon. Sen. Lectr, Univ. of Dundee, 2001–. *Publications:* contribs to BMJ, Jl Bone and Joint Surgery. *Recreations:* travel, films, reading, gardening. *Address:* Wellington Knee Surgery Unit, Wellington Hospital South, Wellington Place, NW8 9LE. *T:* (020) 7586 5959.

WARE, Joni; *see* Lovenduski, J.

WARE, Michael John, CB 1985; QC 1988; barrister-at-law; Solicitor and Legal Adviser, Department of the Environment, 1982–92; *b* 7 May 1932; *s* of Kenneth George Ware and Phyllis Matilda (*née* Joynes); *m* 1966, Susan Ann Maitland; three *d*. *Educ:* Cheltenham Grammar Sch.; Trinity Hall, Cambridge (BA (Law), LLB). Called to Bar, Middle Temple. Nat. Service, 2/Lieut RASC, 1954–56. Board of Trade (later Dept of Trade and Industry): Legal Asst, 1957–64; Sen. Legal Asst, 1964–72; Asst Solicitor, 1972–73; Dir, Legal Dept, Office of Fair Trading, 1973–77; Under Secretary: Dept of Trade, 1977–81; DoE, 1982. Chm., Meat Hygiene Appeals Tribunals for England and Wales, 1993–2002.

WAREHAM, Prof. Nicholas John, PhD; FRCP, FFPH; Director, Medical Research Council Epidemiology Unit, since 2003; Professor, University of Cambridge, since 2013; *b* Gravesend, 1 March 1962; *s* of Michael Wareham and Christine Wareham; *m* 1985, Alison Butts; one *s* one *d*. *Educ:* Trinity Sch., Croydon; St Thomas's Hosp. Med. Sch., London (MB BS 1986); London Sch. of Hygiene and Tropical Medicine, Univ. of London (MSc 1991); Univ. of Cambridge (PhD 1997). FRCP 2003; FFPH (FFPHM 2003). MRC Clinician Scientist, 1997–2001; Wellcome Trust Sen. Clin. Fellow, Univ. of Cambridge, 2001–03. Hon. Consultant, Addenbrooke's Hosp., Cambridge, 1997–; Hon. Prof., Univ. of Cambridge, 2006–13. *Recreations:* cricket, hockey, watching Arsenal FC, musical theatre, opera. *Address:* MRC Epidemiology Unit, University of Cambridge, Box 285, Institute of Metabolic Science, Addenbrooke's Hospital, Cambridge CB2 0QQ. *T:* (01223) 330315, *Fax:* (01223) 330316. *E:* nick.wareham@mrc-epid.cam.ac.uk.

WAREING, Michael Peter, CMG 2010; FCA, FCCA; Senior Independent Director: Cobham plc, since 2010; Intertek plc, since 2011; *b* Birmingham, 9 Feb. 1954; *s* of Anthony Peter and Margaret Florence Wareing; *m* 1998, Isabella Janusz; two *s* three *d* (and one *s* decd). *Educ:* Belmont Abbey Sch. FCA 1977; FCCA 1984; MCSI (MSI 1986). Partner, KPMG, 1985–2009: Chief Exec., Europe, ME and Asia, 2002–05; Internat. Chief Exec., 2005–09. Dir, Wolseley plc, 2009–; Chm., Iraq Adv. Bd, G4S plc, 2011–12. Prime Minister's Envoy for Reconstruction of Southern Iraq, 2007–09; Chm., Basra Develt Commn, 2007–09; Internat. Investment Advr to Min. of Mines, Afghan Govt, 2011–. Dir, BITC, 2008; Chm., BITC Internat., 2009. *Recreations:* horse riding (ex-amateur jockey), ski-ing, scuba diving, tennis. *Address:* Intertek plc, 25 Savile Row, W1S 2ES.

WARHAM, Mark Francis; Executive Vice Chairman, Rothschild, since 2014; *b* 2 Jan. 1962; *s* of Joseph Warham and Eileen Warham (*née* Northover); *m* 2000, Olivia Dagtoglou; three *d*. *Educ:* St Thomas Aquinas Grammar Sch., Leeds; St Catherine's Coll., Oxford (BA PPE 1982). 3i plc, 1982–86; J. Henry Schroder Wagg & Co. Ltd, 1986–2000, Dir, 1995–2000; Morgan Stanley: Man. Dir, 2000–09; Chm., UK Investment Banking, 2007–09; Vice Chm., 2008–09; Dir Gen., The Takeover Panel, 2005–07 (on secondment); Barclays (formerly Barclays Capital): Man. Dir, and Co-Hd, EMEA (formerly European) M&A, 2009–13; Vice Chm., Investment Banking, and Hd, EMEA M&A, 2013–14. *Recreations:* mountaineering, photography, ornithology. *Clubs:* Alpine, Brooks's.

WARHURST, Alan, CBE 1990; Director, Manchester Museum, 1977–93; *b* 6 Feb. 1927; *s* of W. Warhurst; *m* 1953, Sheila Lilian Bradbury; one *s* two *d*. *Educ:* Canon Slade Sch., Bolton; Manchester Univ. (BA Hons History 1950). FSA 1958; FMA 1958. Commnd Lancashire Fusiliers, 1947. Asst, Grosvenor Museum, Chester, 1950–51; Asst Curator, Maidstone Museum and Art Gallery, 1951–55; Curator, Northampton Museum and Art Gallery, 1955–60; Director: City Museum, Bristol, 1960–70; Ulster Museum, 1970–77. Vice-Pres., NW Museum and Art Gallery Service, subseq. NW Museums Service, 1997–2002 (Dep. Chm., 1987–92; Chm., 1992–97). Mem., Museums and Galls Commn, 1994–99. Chm., Irish Nat. Cttee, ICOM, 1973–75; President: S Western Fedn Museums and Galls, 1966–68; Museums Assoc., 1975–76; N Western Fedn of Museums and Art Galls, 1979–80; Hon. Sec., Univ. Museums Gp, 1987–93. Trustee, Boat Mus., Ellesmere Port, 1990–92. Chm., Hulme Hall Cttee, Univ. of Manchester, 1986–93; Gov., Hulme Hall Trust Foundn, 1994–2000. Hon. MA Belfast, 1982. *Publications:* various archaeological and museum contribs to learned jls. *Address:* Calabar Cottage, Woodville Road, Altrincham, Cheshire WA14 2AL.

WARHURST, Pamela Janice, CBE 2005; Chair: Pennine Prospects Rural Regeneration Co., since 2006; Incredible Edible Ltd, since 2009; Incredible Edible Todmorden Ltd, since 2013; *b* 12 Sept. 1950; *d* of Fred and Kathleen Short; marr. diss.; one *d*. *Educ:* Manchester Univ. (BA Hons Econ; MA Econs). Chm., Bear Healthfood Co-operative, 1985–. Mem. (Lab), Calderdale MBC, 1991–99 (Council Leader, 1995–99); Dep. Chair, Regl Assembly for Yorks and Humber, 1997–99; Yorks Rep., Cttee of the Regions in Europe, 1997–99; Dep. Chair, Countryside Agency, 1999–2006; Chair, Forestry Commn, 2010–12. Member Board: Yorks Forward RDA, 1996–99; Natural England, 2006–10; Handmade Parade Ltd, 2014–; Chm., Outta Place Ltd, 2012–14. Chair: Calderdale NHS Trust, 1998–2000; Yorks Reg., RSA, 2011–. Hon. Fellow: Landscape Inst. 2012; Leeds Sustainability Inst. 2012. *Recreations:* cooking, travelling, dog walking. *Address:* 21 Mons Road, Todmorden, Lancs OL14 8EF. *T:* (01706) 819803. *E:* pam@bearco-op.com.

WARING, Sir (Alfred) Holburt, 3rd Bt *cr* 1935; *b* 2 Aug. 1933; *s* of Sir Alfred Harold Waring, 2nd Bt, and Winifred (*d* 1992), *d* of late Albert Boston, Stockton-on-Tees; *S* father, 1981; *m* 1958, Ana, (Anita), *d* of late Valentin Medinilla, Madrid; one *s* two *d*. *Educ:* Rossall School; Leeds College of Commerce. Director: SRM Plastics Ltd; Waring Investments Ltd; Property Realisation Co. Ltd. *Recreations:* golf, squash, swimming. *Heir: s* Michael Holburt Waring, *b* 3 Jan. 1964. *Club:* Moor Park Golf (Rickmansworth).

WARK, Prof. David Lee, PhD; FRS 2007; FInstP; Professor in Experimental Particle Physics, University of Oxford; Director, Particle Physics Department, STFC Rutherford Appleton Laboratory; Fellow, Balliol College, Oxford; *b* 8 June 1958; *s* of William L. Wark and Maxine V. Wark; *m* 1988, Sally Annette Martinez; one *s* one *d*. *Educ:* Indiana Univ. (BSc Physics 1980); California Inst. of Technol. (MS Physics 1982; PhD 1987). FInstP 2003. Postdoctoral Fellow, Los Alamos Nat. Lab., 1987–89; Res. Officer, 1990–92, Lectr in Phys, 1992–99, Oxford Univ.; Fellow, Balliol Coll., Oxford, 1992–99; Prof. of Phys, Univ. of Sussex and Rutherford Appleton Lab., 1999–2003; Prof. of Phys, Imperial Coll. London and Rutherford Appleton Lab., 2004. PPARC Lectr-Fellow, 1996–99. Chm., High Energy and Particle Phys Div., Eur. Phys. Soc., 2005–07. Rutherford Prize, Inst. of Phys, 2003. *Publications:* over 100 articles in learned jls. *Recreations:* reading, cooking, juggling, ski-ing, playing guitar (badly) and blues harp (worse). *Address:* Department of Physics, University of Oxford, Denys Wilkinson Building, Keble Road, Oxford OX1 3RH.

WARK, Kirsty Anne; journalist and television presenter, since 1976; *b* 3 Feb. 1955; *d* of James Allan Wark and Roberta Eason Forrest; *m* 1990, Alan Clements; one *s* one *d*. *Educ:* Wellington Sch., Ayr; Edinburgh Univ. (BA 1976). Joined BBC, 1976: radio then TV producer, politics and current affairs progs, 1977–90; formed independent prodn co., Wark Clements & Co. Ltd, with husband, 1990; Presenter: The Late Show, and Edinburgh Nights, 1990–93; Newsnight, Review Show (formerly Newsnight Rev.) and Newsnight Specials, 1993–; One Foot In The Past, 1993–2000; Words With Wark, 1995–99; Building a Nation, 1998; Gen. Elections, Scottish Gen. Elections and Referendum, and Rough Justice, 1998–; The Kirsty Wark Show, 1999–2001; Tales from Europe, 2004; Tales from Spain, 2005; The Book Quiz, 2008–09; A Question of Genius, 2009, 2010; The Review Show, 2010–; The Home Movie Road Show, 2010; A Question of Taste, 2012; The Man Who Collected the World: William Burrell, 2013; Kirsty Wark Meets Donna Tartt, 2013; Blurred Lines: the new battle of the sexes, 2014; The Summer Exhibition: BBC Arts at the Royal Academy, 2014; Scotland's Art Revolution: The Maverick Generation, 2014; Our World: kidnapped for a decade, 2015; series of interviews for BBC2 and BBC4, 2002–; finalist, Celebrity MasterChef,

2011. Patron: Scottish Blind Golf Soc., 2000–; Maggie's Centre, 2001–; Cambodia Trust, 2001–; Crichton Foundn, 2001–; RIAS, 2001–; Ambassador: Nat. AIDS Trust, 2000–; The Prince's Trust, 2004– (Mem. Council, 2000–04). Hon. FRIAS 2000; Hon. FRIBA 2001. Hon. DLitt Abertay, 1995; Dr *hc* Edinburgh, 2000; Hon. LLD Aberdeen, 2001. Scotland Journalist of Year, 1993, Scotland Presenter of Year, 1997, Outstanding Contribn to Broadcasting, 2013, BAFTA Scotland; Scot of the Year, Scotland on Sunday, 1998; Richard Dimbleby Award for Best Presenter, Factual, Features and News, BAFTA, 2000. *Publications:* Restless Nation, 1997; The Legacy of Elizabeth Pringle (novel), 2014. *Recreations:* reading, tennis, beachcombing, architecture, cooking, film, music. *Address:* c/o Black Pepper Media Ltd, PO Box 26323, Ayr KA7 9AY. *T:* (0141) 404 6355. *E:* info@blackpeppermedia.com.

WARKE, Rt Rev. Robert Alexander; Bishop of Cork, Cloyne and Ross, 1988–98; *b* 10 July 1930; *s* of Alexander and Annie Warke; *m* 1964, Eileen Charlotte Janet Minna Skillen; two *d. Educ:* Mountmellick National School; The King's Hospital; Trinity Coll., Dublin (BA 1952, BD 1960); Union Theol Seminary, New York (Dip. in Ecumenical Studies). Ordained, 1953; Curate: St Mark's, Newtownards, 1953–55; St Catherine's, Dublin, 1956–59; Rathfarnham, Dublin, 1959–64; Rector: Dunlavin, Hollywood and Ballymore-Eustace, 1964–67; Drumcondra, North Strand and St Barnabas, 1967–71; Zion, Dublin, 1971–88; Archdeacon of Dublin, 1980–88. *Publications:* St Nicholas Church and Parish, 1967; Light at Evening Time, 1986; The Passion according to St Matthew, 1990; Ripples in the Pool, 1993; In Search of the Living God, 2000; On Being a Bishop, 2004. *Recreations:* following sport, theatre, reading. *Address:* 6 Kerdiff Park, Naas, Co. Kildare, Ireland.

WARKENTIN, Juliet; Director, Brand and Creative, Amazon Fashion EU, since 2014; *b* 10 May 1961; *d* of John and Germaine Warkentin; *m* 1991, Andrew Lamb (separated). *Educ:* Univ. of Toronto (BA History). Editor: Toronto Life Fashion Magazine, 1989–91; Drapers Record Magazine, 1993–96; Marie Claire, 1996–98; Man. Dir, Mktg and Internet Develt, Arcadia Gp plc, 1998–2000; Partner, The Fourth Room, 2000–02; Editl Dir, Redwood, 2002–07; Content Dir, WGSN, 2007–11; Co-founder and Chief Creative Officer, StylistPick.com, 2011–13. FRSA 2004. National Magazine Award, Canada, 1990; PPA Business Editor of the Year, 1995. *Address:* 71A Regents Park Road, NW1 8UY.

WARLOW, Prof. Charles Picton, MD; FRCP, FRCPE, FRCPGlas, FMedSci; FRSE; Professor of Medical Neurology, 1987–2008, now Emeritus, and Hon. Consultant Neurologist, University of Edinburgh, since 1987; *b* 29 Sept. 1943; *s* of Charles Edward Picton Warlow and Nancy Mary McLennan (*née* Hine); *m* (marr. diss.); two *s* one *d*; partner, Cathie Sudlow; one *s* one *d. Educ:* Haileybury and Imperial Service Coll.; Sidney Sussex Coll., Cambridge (BA 1st Cl. Hons 1965; MB BChir with Dist. in Medicine 1968; MD 1975); St George's Hosp. Med. Sch. FRCP 1983; FRCPE 1987; FRCPGlas 1993; FRSE 2006. Clinical Reader in Neurology and Hon. Consultant Neurologist, Univ. of Oxford, 1977–86; Fellow, Green Coll., Oxford, 1979–86; Head, Dept of Clinical Neuroscis, Univ. of Edinburgh, 1990–93 and 1995–98. Pres., Assoc. of British Neurologists, 2001–03. Ed., Practical Neurology, 2001. Founder FMedSci 1998. *Publications:* Handbook of Clinical Neurology, 1991; (with G. J. Hankey) Transient Ischaemic Attacks of the Brain and Eye, 1994; (jtly) Stroke: a practical guide to management, 1996, 3rd edn 2008; (ed) Lancet Handbook of Treatment in Neurology, 2006. *Recreations:* sailing, photography, mountains, theatre. *Address:* Department of Clinical Neurosciences, Western General Hospital, Crewe Road South, Edinburgh EH4 2XU. *T:* (0131) 537 2081.

WARMAN, Matthew; MP (C) Boston and Skegness, since 2015; *b* Enfield, London, 1 Sept. 1981; *m* Dr Rachel Weaver. *Educ:* Haberdashers' Aske's Boys' Sch.; Univ. of Durham (BA Hons English Lit. 2004). The Telegraph: writer, 1999–2009; Consumer Technol. Ed., 2008–13; Technol. Ed. (Hd of Technol.), 2013–15. *Recreation:* eating and consequential exercise. *Address:* House of Commons, SW1A 0AA. *T:* (020) 7219 8643. *E:* matt.warman.mp@parliament.uk.

WARMAN, Oliver Byrne, RBA 1984; ROI 1989; Partner: Normandy Battlefield Tours, since 1989; War History 1944, since 1989; Chief Executive, Federation of British Artists, 1984–96; *b* 10 June 1932. *Educ:* Stowe; Exeter Univ.; Balliol Coll., Oxford. Commissioned Welsh Guards, 1952; GSO3 Cabinet Office and Prime Minister; Instructor, Intelligence Centre; Staff College; RMCS; retired 1989. Dir, Exports and Public Relations, 1987–90, Dir, Public Relations, 1990–94, Ship and Boat Builders Fedn. Vis. Lectr on Conflicts in Europe, 1869–1945, US Naval Coll., Annapolis and 3 US Corps, Atlanta, 1991–. First exhibited RA, 1980; exhib. at RBA, RWA, NEAC, RSMA, ROI; work in public collections, incl. US Embassy, Sultanate of Oman, Crown Commn, clearing banks, Warburgs Bank, Co-operative Gp, Shell UK and Emir of Kuwait. Officer, ROI, 1998–. Gold Medal, 1997, Gourlay Prize, 1998, ROI. *Publications:* Arnhem 1944, 1970; Omaha Beach 1944, 2002; France and Flanders 1940, 2011; articles on wine and military history, 1968–; articles in RUSI Jl and Army Qly. *Recreations:* France, food, wine, sailing, painting, small mongrel dogs, walking in Welsh Mountains, S German uplands and the SW Coast Path. *E:* objwarman@aol.com. *Clubs:* Cavalry and Guards, Chelsea Arts, Special Forces; Royal Cornwall Yacht.

WARMINGTON, Sir Rupert (Marshall), 6th Bt *cr* 1908, of Pembridge Square, Royal Borough of Kensington; Director, Tradeweb, since 2004; *b* 17 June 1969; *s* of Sir David Marshall Warmington, 5th Bt and Susan Mary Warmington; *S* father, 2005; *m* 2002, Joanne Emma Mewse; two *s. Educ:* Charterhouse; Exeter Univ. (BA Hons). Dir, Fixed Income Dept, ABN AMRO, 1999–2004; Dir, Credit Markets, TradWeb, 2004–10. *Recreations:* golf, tennis, riding. *Heir:* *s* Oliver Charles Warmington, *b* 23 Oct. 2004.

WARNE, (Ernest) John (David), CB 1982; Secretary, Institute of Chartered Accountants in England and Wales, 1982–90; *b* 4 Dec. 1926; *m* 1st, 1953, Rena Wolfe (*d* 1995); three *s*; 2nd, 1997, Irena Zajac. *Educ:* Univ. of London (BA(Hons)). Civil Service Commission, 1953; Asst Comr and Principal, Civil Service Commn, 1958; BoT, later DTI and Dept of Industry: Principal, 1962; Asst Sec., 1967; Under-Sec., 1972; Dir for Scotland, 1972–75; Under-Secretary: Personnel Div., 1975–77; Industrial and Commercial Policy Div., 1977–79; Dep. Sec., Dep. Dir-Gen., OFT, 1979–82. *Recreations:* reading, collecting prints, languages. *Address:* 4 Priest Row, Wells, Somerset BA5 2PY. *T:* (01749) 674271.

WARNE, (Frederick) John (Alford), CB 2000; Staff Counsellor, Serious Organised Crime Agency, 2007–13; *b* 7 March 1944; *m* 1st, 1967 (marr. diss. 1979); two *s*; 2nd, 2002, Elaine Carol Smith. *Educ:* Liskeard Grammar Sch., Cornwall. Home Office: Pvte Sec. to Minister of State, 1966–69; Principal, 1974–83; Asst Sec., 1984–93; Under-Sec., Police Dept, 1993–95; Dir, Organised Crime, 1996–98; Dir Gen., Organised Crime, Drugs and Internat. Gp, 1998–2002; Actg Perm. Sec., 2001–02, retd. Staff Counsellor, Security and Intelligence Agencies, 2004–09. Trustee, East Looe Town Trust, 2009–11 (Chm., 2011–). *Recreations:* sport, gardening, walking, spending time with grandchildren, exploring Cornwall. *Address:* Glendower, Dawes Lane, Looe, Cornwall PL13 1JE.

WARNER, family name of **Baron Warner**.

WARNER, Baron *cr* 1998 (Life Peer), of Brockley in the London Borough of Lewisham; **Norman Reginald Warner;** PC 2006; *b* 8 Sept. 1940; *s* of Albert Henry Edwin Warner and Laura Warner; *m* 1961, Anne Lesley Lawrence (marr. diss. 1981); one *s* one *d*; *m* 1990, Suzanne Elizabeth Reeve (*see* S. E. Warner); one *s. Educ:* Dulwich College; University of California, Berkeley (MPH). Min. of Health, 1959; Asst Private Sec. to Minister of Health, 1967–68, to Sec. of State for Social Services, 1968–69; Executive Councils Div., DHSS, 1969–71; Harkness Fellowship, USA, 1971–73; NHS Reorganisation, DHSS, 1973–74; Principal Private Sec. to Sec. of State for Social Services, 1974–76; Supplementary Benefits Div., 1976–78; Management Services, DHSS, 1979–81; Regional Controller, Wales and S Western Region, DHSS, 1981–83; Gwilym Gibbon Fellow, Nuffield Coll., Oxford, 1983–84; Under Sec., Supplementary Benefits Div., DHSS, 1984–85; Dir of Social Services, Kent CC, 1985–91; Man. Dir, Warner Consultancy and Trng Services Ltd, 1991–97. Children's Social Care Comr, Birmingham CC, 2014–15. Advr to Govt on family policy and related matters, 1998–2001. Parly Under-Sec. of State, 2003–05, Minister of State, 2005–06, DoH. Mem., H of L Select Cttee on Sci. and Technol., 2007–12, on Adoption Legislation, 2012–13; Member, Joint Select Committee: on Draft Care and Support Bill, 2012–13; on Draft Modern Slavery Bill, 2013–14. Mem., Ind. Commn on Funding of Care and Support, 2010–11. Sen. Fellow in European Social Welfare and Chm., European Inst. of Social Services, Univ. of Kent, 1991–97. Chairman: City and E London FHSA, 1991–94; London Sports Bd, Sport England, 2003. Mem., Local Govt Commn, 1995–96. Chm., Expert Panel for UK Harkness Fellowships, 1994–97. Chairman: Nat. Inquiry into Selection, Develt and Management of Staff in Children's Homes, 1991–92 (report, Choosing with Care, 1992); Govt Task Force on Youth Justice, 1997–98; Youth Justice Bd for Eng. and Wales, 1998–2003; Provider Develt Agency, NHS London, 2007–09. Mem. Nat. Mgt Cttee, Carers Nat. Assoc., 1991–94. Trustee: Leonard Cheshire Foundn, 1994–96; MacIntyre Care, 1994–97; Royal Philanthropic Soc., 1992–99 (Chm., 1993–98); Chairman: Residential Forum, 1994–97; Include, 2000–01; NCVO, 2001–03. *Publications:* (ed) Commissioning Community Alternatives in European Social and Health Care, 1993; A Suitable Case for Treatment: the NHS and reform, 2011; articles in Jl of Public Admin, Community Care, The Guardian, Local Govt Chronicle, etc. *Recreations:* reading, cinema, theatre, exercise, travel. *Address:* House of Lords, SW1A 0PW.

WARNER, Lady; *see* Warner, S. E.

WARNER, Prof. David Allan, CBE 2009; FLSW; Senior Provost, University of Wales Trinity St David, 2012–14, now Emeritus Professor; Deputy Director, Oxford Centre for Higher Education Policy Studies, since 2001; Senior Research Fellow, Harris Manchester College, Oxford, 2013–14; *b* Coventry, 19 Sept. 1947; *s* of Raymond and Cecily Warner; partner, Prof. Ann Edworthy; one *d. Educ:* King Henry VIII Sch., Coventry; Warwick Univ. (BA 1970; MA 1971). Trainee quantity surveyor, 1965–66, sch. teacher, 1967, Coventry CC; Admin. Asst and Tutor, Univ. of Warwick, 1971–74; Sen. Admin. Asst, UEA, 1974–75; Asst Registrar, then Sen. Asst Registrar and Tutor, subseq. Sen. Lectr, Univ. of Warwick, 1975–85; Pro-Vice-Chancellor, UCE, 1985–98; Vice-Chancellor, Swansea Inst. Higher Educn, then Swansea Metropolitan Univ., 1998–2012. Commng Ed., Managing Univs and Colls book series, 1997–. FLSW 2013. *Publications:* An Educational Market Survey of Taiwan, 1988; (jtly) The Income Generation Handbook, 1992, 2nd edn 1997; How to Manage a Merger… or Avoid One, 1998; co-editor: Visual and Corporate Identity, 1989; Managing Educational Property, 1993; Human Resource Management in Higher and Further Education, 1995; Higher Education Management: the key elements, 1996; Higher Education and the Law: a guide for managers, 1998; The State of UK Higher Education: managing change and diversity, 2001; Higher Education Law, 2002; Managing Crisis, 2003. *Recreations:* reading, particularly ancient history, my family. *E:* davidwarner1909@gmail.com.

WARNER, Deborah, CBE 2006; free-lance theatre and opera director, since 1980; *b* 12 May 1959; *d* of Ruth and Roger Warner. *Educ:* Sidcot Sch., Avon; St Clare's Coll., Oxford; Central Sch. of Speech and Drama. Founder, 1980, and Artistic Dir, 1980–86, Kick Theatre Co.; Resident Dir, RSC, 1987–89; Associate Dir, Royal Nat. Theatre, 1989–98. *Productions:* Kick Theatre Co.: The Good Person of Szechwan, 1980; Woyzeck, 1981, 1982; The Tempest, 1983; Measure for Measure, 1984; King Lear, 1985; Coriolanus, 1986; Royal Shakespeare Co.: Titus Andronicus, 1987 (Laurence Olivier and Evening Standard Awards for Best Dir); King John, Electra, 1988; Electra (also in Paris), 1991; The School for Scandal, 2011; Royal National Theatre: The Good Person of Sichuan, 1989; King Lear, 1990; Richard II, 1995 (filmed, 1997); The Diary of One Who Vanished (also ENO), 1999; The PowerBook, 2002–03; Happy Days, European and USA tour, 2007–08; Mother Courage and Her Children, 2009; other productions: Wozzeck, Opera North, 1993 and 1996; Coriolan, Salzburg Fest., 1993 and 1994; Hedda Gabler, Abbey Theatre, Dublin, and Playhouse, 1991 (Laurence Olivier Award for Best Dir and Best Prodn); Don Giovanni, Glyndebourne Festival Opera, 1994 and 1995 (also Channel 4); Footfalls, Garrick, 1994; The Waste Land, Brussels, Dublin, Paris, Toronto, Montreal, NY, Cork, London, Adelaide, Brighton, Bergen, Perth, 1995–99 (televised, 1995); Une Maison de Poupée, Paris, 1996; The Turn of the Screw, Royal Opera, 1997; Bobigny (S Bank Arts Award; Evening Standard Award), 1998; Tower Project (London Internat. Fest. of Theatre), 1999; St John Passion, ENO, 2000; Medea, Abbey Th., Dublin, 2000, Queen's, 2001, USA tour and NY, 2002–03; The Angel Project, Perth Internat. Arts Festival, 2000 and NY, 2003; Fidelio, Glyndebourne, 2001, Châtelet, Paris, 2002, revived Glyndebourne, 2006; The Rape of Lucrece, Munich, 2004; Julius Caesar, Barbican, 2005; Dido and Aeneas, Vienna, 2006; La Voix Humaine, Opera North, 2006; Death in Venice, ENO, 2007, La Monnaie, Brussels, 2009, ENO, 2013; Messiah, ENO, 2009; The Waste Land, Wilton's Music Hall, 2009, Madrid Fest., 2010; Eugene Onegin, ENO, 2011; The Testament of Mary, NY 2013, Barbican, 2014; Between Worlds, Barbican, 2015. *Film:* The Last September, 2000. Officier de l'Ordre des Arts et des Lettres (France), 2000 (Chevalier, 1992). *Recreation:* travelling. *Address:* c/o Askonas Holt, Lincoln House, 300 High Holborn, WC1V 7JH. *T:* (020) 7400 1700; c/o The Agency, 24 Pottery Lane, Holland Park, W11 4LZ. *T:* (020) 7727 1346.

WARNER, Edmond William, OBE 2012; Chairman, UK Athletics, since 2007; *b* Farnborough, Kent, 17 Aug. 1963; *s* of William John Warner and Kathleen Elizabeth Warner (*née* Rooke-Matthews); *m* 1988, Katharine Louise Wright; two *d. Educ:* St Olave's Grammar Sch., Orpington; Worcester Coll., Oxford (BA Hons PPE). Fund Manager, GT Management, 1985–87; Strategy Unit, UBS Phillips & Drew, 1987–89; Sen. Investment Dir, Thornton Management, 1989–91; Hd, Pan European Res., Baring Securities, 1991–93; Hd, Strategy and Econs, and Hd, Global Res., Dresdner Kleinwort Benson, 1993–97; Man. Dir, Natwest Markets, then BT Alex.Brown, 1997–99; Chief Executive: Old Mutual Securities, 1999–2001; Old Mutual Financial Services, 2001–03; IFX Gp, 2003–06; Chairman: Cantos Communications, 2007–10; LMAX, 2009–; Panmure Gordon, 2010– (non-exec. Dir, 2009–); Standard Life Eur. Private Equity Trust, 2013– (non-exec. Dir, 2008–). Non-executive Director: Clarkson plc, 2008–; Grant Thornton UK LLP, 2010–; SafeCharge Internat. Gp, 2014–. *Recreation:* running with the Fittleworth Flyers. *Address:* c/o UK Athletics, Athletics House, Alexander Stadium, Walsall Road, Perry Barr, Birmingham B42 2BE.

WARNER, Francis (Robert Le Plastrier), DLitt; poet and dramatist; Emeritus Fellow, St Peter's College, Oxford, since 1999; Hon. Fellow, St Catharine's College, Cambridge, since 1999; *b* Bishopthorpe, Yorks, 21 Oct. 1937; *s* of Rev. Hugh Compton Warner and Nancy Le Plastrier (*née* Owen); *m* 1st, 1958, Mary Hall (marr. diss. 1972); two *d*; 2nd, 1983, Penelope Anne Davis; one *s* one *d. Educ:* Christ's Hosp.; London Coll. of Music; St Catharine's Coll., Cambridge (Choral Exhibitioner; BA, MA); DLitt Oxon 2002. Supervisor in English, St Catharine's Coll., Cambridge, 1959–65; Staff Tutor in English, Cambridge Univ. Bd of Extra-Mural Studies, 1963–65; Oxford University: Fellow and Tutor, 1965–99, Fellow Librarian, 1966–76, Dean of Degrees, 1984–2006, and Vice-Master, 1987–89, St Peter's Coll.; University Lectr (CUF), 1966–99; Pro-Proctor, 1989–90, 1996–97, 1999–2000; Chm., Examiners, English Hon. Mods, 1993. Founder, Elgar Centenary Choir and Orch., 1957; cond. Honegger's King David, King's Coll. Chapel, 1958. Blitz Requiem perf. by Bach Choir and RPO (music by D. Goode), St Paul's Cath., 2013. Co-curator, Bacon/Moore: Flesh and Bone, Ashmolean Mus., 2013, Art Gall. of Ont, 2014. Foreign Academician, Acad. de Letras e Artes, Portugal, 1993. Hon. DMus William Jewell Coll., USA, 2012. Messing Internat. Award for distinguished contribs to Literature, 1972. Benemeriti Silver Medal, Kts of St George, Constantinian Order (Italy), 1990. *Publications: poetry:* Perennia, 1962; Early Poems, 1964; Experimental Sonnets, 1965; Madrigals, 1967; The Poetry of Francis Warner, USA 1970; Lucca Quartet, 1975; Morning Vespers, 1980; Spring Harvest, 1981; Epithalamium, 1983; Collected Poems 1960–84, 1985; Nightingales: poems 1985–96, 1997; Cambridge: a poem, 2001; Oxford: a poem, 2002; By the Cam and the Isis, 2005; (with D. Goode) Blitz Requiem, 2013; (with D. Goode) Six Anthems and Other Compositions, 2014; *prose:* Beauty for Ashes: selected prose, 2012, 2nd edn 2013; *plays:* Maquettes, a trilogy of one-act plays, 1972; Requiem: Pt 1, Lying Figures, 1972, Pt 2, Killing Time, 1976, Pt 3, Meeting Ends, 1974; A Conception of Love, 1978; Light Shadows, 1980; Moving Reflections, 1983; Living Creation, 1985; Healing Nature: the Athens of Pericles, 1988; Byzantium, 1990; Virgil and Caesar, 1993; Agora: an epic, 1994; King Francis 1st, 1995; Goethe's Weimar, 1997; Rembrandt's Mirror, 2000; *edited:* Eleven Poems by Edmund Blunden, 1965; Garland, 1968; Studies in the Arts, 1968; *relevant publications:* by G. Pursglove: Francis Warner and Tradition, 1981; Francis Warner's Poetry: a critical assessment, 1988. *Recreations:* grandchildren, cathedral music, travel. *Address:* St Peter's College, Oxford OX1 2DL. *T:* (01865) 278900; St Catharine's College, Cambridge CB2 1RL. *T:* (01223) 338300. *Club:* Athenæum.

WARNER, Sir Gerald (Chierici), KCMG 1995 (CMG 1984); HM Diplomatic Service, retired; Intelligence Co-ordinator, Cabinet Office, 1991–96; *b* 27 Sept. 1931; *s* of Howard Warner and Elizabeth (*née* Chierici); *m* 1st, 1956, Mary Wynne Davies (*d* 1998), DMath, Prof., City Univ.; one *s* two *d*; 2nd, 2000, Catherine Mary Humphrey. *Educ:* Univ. of Oxford (BA). 2 Lieut, Green Howards, 1949–50; Flight Lt, RAFVR, 1950–56. Joined HM Diplomatic Service, 1954; 3rd Sec., Peking, 1956–58; 2nd Sec., Rangoon, 1960–61; 1st Sec., Warsaw, 1964–66, Geneva, 1966–68; Counsellor, Kuala Lumpur, 1974–76; FCO, 1976–90, retd. Mem., Police Complaints Authy, 1990–91. Mem., Adv. Bd, Tavistock Inst., 1998–; Chairman: Glos Council for Drugs and Alcohol, 1997–2009; Independence Trust, 2009–. *Address:* c/o Coutts & Co., 440 Strand, WC2R 0QS.

WARNER, Graeme Christopher; Sheriff of Grampian, Highland and Islands, 1992–98; Part-time Sheriff, since 2001 (Temporary Sheriff, 1985–91); *b* 20 Oct. 1948; *s* of Richard James Lewis Warner and Jean McDonald McIntyre or Warner; *m* 1st, 1976, Rachel Kidd Gear (marr. diss. 1994); one *s* one *d*; 2nd, 1996, Jean Raeburn. *Educ:* Belmont House, Glasgow; Strathallan, by Perth; Edinburgh Univ. (LLB). NP, WS. Law Apprentice, 1969–71; Law Assistant, 1971–72; Partner: Boyd, Janson & Young, WS, Leith, 1972–76; Ross Harper & Murphy, WS, Edinburgh, 1976–88; Macbeth, Currie & Co., WS, Edinburgh, 1989–91, Consultant, 1999–2000. Member: Parole Bd for Scotland, 2003–04; Mental Health Tribunal for Scotland, 2013–. Mem., Lothian Health Bd, 2012–. *Recreation:* staying alive! *Address:* 6 Mortonhall Road, Edinburgh EH9 2HW. *T:* (0131) 668 2437.

WARNER, Jeremy; Columnist, since 2009 and Associate Editor, since 2013, The Daily Telegraph (Assistant Editor, 2009–13); *b* 23 Sept. 1955; *s* of Jonathan and Marigold Warner; *m* 1988, Henrietta Jane Franklin; one *s* two *d*. *Educ:* Magdalen Coll. Sch., Oxford; University Coll. London (BA 1st cl. Hons Hist. 1977). Reporter, The Scotsman, 1979–83; Business Correspondent: The Times, 1983–86; The Independent, 1986–91; City Editor, The Independent on Sunday, 1991–94; Business and City Editor, The Independent, 1994–2009. Specialist Writer of the Year, British Press Awards, 1990; Financial Journalist of the Year, Wincott Foundn, 1992; Special Award for outstanding contribn in defence of freedom of the press, Assoc. of British Editors, 1997. *Address:* The Daily Telegraph, 111 Buckingham Palace Road, SW1W 0DT. *T:* (020) 7931 2000.

WARNER, Jocelyn; textile designer, since 1986; *b* 16 April 1963; *d* of Brian and Jackie Warner; *m* 1993, Simon Bore; one *s*. *Educ:* Lewes Priory Sch.; Brighton Poly. (Foundn in Art); Camberwell Sch. of Arts and Crafts (BA Hons Textile Design); Central St Martin's Sch. of Art (MA Textile Design). Established: Jocelyn Warner Studio for printed textile design, 1986; Jocelyn Warner Ltd (contemporary wallpaper products and consultancy in surface design), 1999. Elle Decoration Award for Best in Wall Coverings, 2003. *Recreations:* looking at things, collecting bits and pieces from nature, taking photographs and scanning plants, walking, being with friends and family. *Address:* 4 The Old Dairy, Glynde, Lewes, E Sussex BN8 6SH. *W:* www.jocelynwarner.com.

WARNER, His Honour John Charles; a Circuit Judge, 1996–2015; Resident Judge, Wolverhampton Crown Court, 2007–15; *b* 30 Aug. 1945; *s* of late Frank Charles Warner and Kathleen Moyra Warner; *m* 1975, Kathleen Marion Robinson; one *s* one *d*. *Educ:* King Edward's Sch., Birmingham. Solicitor, 1969; Partner, Adie Evans & Warner, 1971–96; Asst Recorder, 1988–92; Recorder, 1992–96.

WARNER, Prof. John Oliver, OBE 2013; MD; FRCP, FRCPCH; FMedSci; Professor of Paediatrics, Imperial College London, since 2006; *b* 19 July 1945; *s* of Henry Paul Warner and Ursula Mina Warner; *m* 1st, 1968, Wendy Margaret Cole (marr. diss. 1989); one *s* two *d*; 2nd, 1990, Jill Amanda Price; two *d*. *Educ:* Sheffield Univ. Med. Sch. (MB ChB 1968; DCH 1970; MD 1979). FRCP 1986 (MRCP 1972); FRCPCH 1997. Gen. prof. trng, Children's Hosp. and Royal Hosp., Sheffield, 1968–72; Great Ormond Street Children's Hospital: Registrar, 1972–74; research, 1974–77; Sen. Registrar, 1977–79; Consultant, 1979–90, Sen. Lectr, 1979–88, Reader, 1988–90, London Cardiothoracic Inst., Brompton Hosp.; Prof. of Child Health, Univ. of Southampton, 1990–2006. NIHR Sen. Investigator, 2010–14. Pepys Lectr, 2011, Harry Morrow-Brown Lectr, 2014, British Soc. Allergy and Clin. Immunol. Pres., Academic Paediatric Assoc. of GB and Ireland, 2010–14. FMedSci 1999; Foundn Fellow, Eur. Respiratory Soc., 2014. Lifetime Achievement Award, Eur. Respiratory Soc., 2009. *Publications:* A Colour Atlas of Paediatric Allergy, 1994; The Bronchoscope - Flexible and Rigid - in Children, 1995; (ed jtly) Textbook of Pediatric Asthma: an international perspective, 2001; over 400 papers in med jls. *Recreations:* cricket, horse riding. *Address:* Navaho, Hurdle Way, Compton Down, Winchester SO21 2AN. *Club:* MCC.

WARNER, Keith Reginald; freelance opera and theatre director, since 1989; *b* 6 Dec. 1956; *s* of Gordon Lawrence Warner and Sheila Mary Ann (*née* Collinson); *m* 1984, Emma Belinda Judith Besly. *Educ:* Bristol Univ. (BA Jt Hons English and Drama). Asst Dir, ENO, 1981–84; Associate Director: Scottish Opera, 1984–85; ENO, 1985–89; Associate Artistic Director, Opera Omaha, USA, 1991–94; Artistic Dir, Royal Opera, Copenhagen, 2011–12. *Recreations:* movie-going, reading, modern/contemporary art. *E:* KeithRWarner@aol.com.

WARNER, Dame Marina (Sarah), DBE 2015 (CBE 2008); FBA 2005; FRSL; writer and critic; Professor of English and Creative Writing, Birkbeck, University of London, since 2014; Professor, School of Arts and Humanities, University of London, since 2014; Professorial Research Fellow, School of Oriental and African Studies, University of London, since 2014; *b* 9 Nov. 1946; *d* of Esmond Pelham Warner and Emilia (*née* Terzulli); *m* 1st, 1971, Hon. William Shawcross, *qv*; one *s*; 2nd, 1981, John Dewe Mathews (marr. diss. 1999); partner, Graeme Bryce Segal, *qv*. *Educ:* Lady Margaret Hall, Oxford (MA Mod. Langs, French and Italian; Hon. Fellow, 2000). FRSL 1985. Getty Schol., Getty Centre for Hist. of Art and Humanities, Calif, 1987–88; Vis. Fellow, BFI, 1992; Whitney J. Oakes Fellow, Princeton Univ., 1996; Tinbergen Prof., Erasmus Univ., Rotterdam, 1991; Mellon Prof., Univ. of Pittsburgh, 1997; Visiting Professor: Univ. of Ulster, 1995; QMW, 1995–2008; Paris XIII, 2003; RCA, 2008–12; NYU Abu Dhabi, 2012; Distinguished Visiting Professor: Stanford Univ., 2000; NYU Abu Dhabi, 2014; Visiting Fellow: Trinity Coll., Cambridge, 1998; Humanities Res. Centre, Warwick Univ., 1999; All Souls Coll., Oxford, 2001; Hon. Res. Fellow, Birkbeck Coll., Univ. of London, 1999–2005; Prof., Dept of Lit., Drama and Visual Studies, subseq. Lit., Film and Theatre Studies, Univ. of Essex, 2004–14; Sen. Fellow, Erich Remarque Inst., NY Univ., 2006; Dist. Vis. Fellow, QMUL, 2009–12; Fellow, All Souls Coll., Oxford, 2013–15, now Quondam Fellow; Sen. Fellow, Italian Acad., Columbia Univ., 2013–; Vis. Schol., Center for Ballet and Arts, NY Univ., 2015; Hon. Res. Fellow, Archive of Greek and Roman Performance, 2015; Weidenfeld Prof., Univ. of Oxford, May 2016–. Contributing Ed., London Rev. of Books, 2013–. Lectures: Reith, 1994; Tanner, Yale Univ., 1999; Clarendon, Oxford Univ., 2001; Robb, Auckland Univ., 2004; Beatrice Blackwood, Oxford, 2005; Sebald, UEA, 2007; Presidential, Stanford Univ., 2008; Jane Harrison, Cambridge Univ., 2008; Hussey, Oxford Univ., 2008; Graham Storey, Cambridge Univ., 2009; BIRTHA, Bristol Univ., 2009; Edward Saïd Meml, BM, 2010; Hughes, Birmingham, 2012; Freud Mus., 2012; Leconfield, Italian Inst., 2012. Mem. Adv. Bd, Royal Mint, 1986–93. Member: Council, Charter 88, 1990–98; Cttee of Management, NCOPF, 1990–99 (Vice-Pres., 2000–); Adv. Council, British Liby, 1992–98; Cttee, London Liby, 1997–2000; Literature Panel, Arts Council, 1992–98; Council, Inst. of Historical Res., Univ. of London, 1999–2000; Cttee, PEN, 2001–04; Bd, NPG, 2008–; Council, British Sch. at Rome, 2008– (Vice-Pres., 2013–16). Chair, Man Booker Internat. Prize, 2015. Jt Curator, Metamorphing, Wellcome Trust exhibn at Sci. Mus., 2002–03; Curator, Only Make Believe: Ways of Playing, Compton Verney, 2004; Adv. Curator, Eyes, Lies and Illusions, Hayward Gall., 2006. Trustee: Artangel, 1997–2004; Orwell Foundn, 2004–09. Pres., Virgil Soc., 2004–05; Pres., British Comparative Literature Assoc., 2010–. Patron: Med. Foundn for Victims of Torture, 2000–; Soc. for Story-telling, 2003–; Longford Trust, 2003–; Hosking Houses Trust, 2006–; Reprieve, 2008–; J-News, 2010–; Bloodaxe Poetry Books, 2014–. Hon. DLitt: Exeter, 1995; York, 1997; St Andrews, 1998; Kent, 2005; Oxford, 2006; Leicester, 2006; KCL, 2009; Hon. Dr: Sheffield Hallam, 1995; North London, 1997; East London, 1999; RCA, 2004; Kent, 2005. Chevalier de l'Ordre des Arts et des Lettres (France), 2000; Stella dell'Ordine della Solidarietà (Italy), 2005. Libretti: The Legs of the Queen of Sheba, 1991; In the House of Crossed Desires, 1996. *Publications:* The Dragon Empress, 1972; Alone of All Her Sex: the myth and the cult of the Virgin Mary, 1976, new edn 2013; Queen Victoria's Sketchbook, 1980; Joan of Arc: the image of female heroism, 1981, new edn 2013; Monuments and Maidens: the allegory of the female form, 1985; L'Atalante, 1993, repr. 2015; Managing Monsters: six myths of our time (Reith Lectures), 1994; From the Beast to the Blonde: on fairy tales and their tellers, 1994; The Inner Eye: art beyond the visible, 1996 (touring exhibn catalogue); No Go the Bogeyman: scaring, lulling and making mock, 1998; Fantastic Metamorphoses, Other Worlds (Clarendon Lectures), 2002; Signs and Wonders: essays on literature and culture, 2003; Phantasmagoria: spirit visions, metaphors, and media into the twenty-first century, 2006; Stranger Magic: charmed states after the Arabian Nights, 2012 (Nat. Book Critics' Circle Award, 2012; Truman Capote Award for Literary Criticism, Truman Capote Foundn, Sheykh Zayed Award, Cultural Foundn of Abu Dhabi, 2013); (ed with P. Kennedy) Scheherazade's Children: global encounters and The Arabian Nights, 2013; Once Upon a Time: a short history of fairy tale, 2014; *fiction:* In a Dark Wood, 1977; The Skating Party, 1983; The Lost Father, 1988; Indigo, 1992; The Mermaids in the Basement, 1993; (ed) Wonder Tales, 1994; The Leto Bundle, 2001; Murderers I Have Known (short stories), 2002; Fly Away Home (short stories), 2015; *children's books:* The Impossible Day, 1981; The Impossible Night, 1981; The Impossible Bath, 1982; The Impossible Rocket, 1982; The Wobbly Tooth, 1984; *juvenile:* The Crack in the Teacup, 1979; pamphlet in Counterblasts series; short stories, arts criticism, radio and television broadcasting. *Recreations:* friends, travels, reading. *Address:* c/o Rogers, Coleridge & White, 20 Powis Mews, W11 1NJ.
See also C. Shawcross.

WARNER, Prof. Mark, PhD; FRS 2012; Professor of Theoretical Physics, University of Cambridge, since 2001; Fellow, Corpus Christi College, Cambridge, since 1986; *b* New Zealand. *Educ:* Auckland Grammar Sch., NZ; Corpus Christi Coll., Cambridge (BA 1974); Univ. of London (PhD). Stanford Univ.; IBM Corp. EPSRC Sen. Res. Fellow, 2008–13. Hon. Fellow, Royal Soc. NZ, 2002. Maxwell Medal and Prize, Inst. of Physics, 1989; Alexander von Humboldt Res. Prize, 2000; EuroPhysics Prize, Eur. Physical Soc., 2003; Hopkins Prize, Cambridge Philosophical Soc., 2009; Colwyn Medal, IMMM, 2013; G. W. Gray Medal, British Liquid Crystal Soc., 2014. *Publications:* (ed jtly) Self Order and Form in Polymers, 1995; (ed with E. M. Terentjev) Liquid Crystal Elastomers, 2003, rev. edn 2007; (with A. Cheung) A Cavendish Quantum Mechanics Primer, 2012; articles in jls. *Address:* Department of Physics, University of Cambridge, Mott Building, Cavendish Laboratory, JJ Thomson Avenue, Cambridge CB3 0HE. *E:* mw141@cam.ac.uk.

WARNER, Rt Rev. Martin Clive; *see* Chichester, Bishop of.

WARNER, Sir Philip (Courtenay Thomas), 4th Bt *cr* 1910, of Brettenham, Suffolk; *b* 3 April 1951; *e s* of Sir (Edward Courtenay) Henry Warner, 3rd Bt and of Jocelyn Mary, *d* of Sir Thomas Lubbock Beevor, 6th Bt; *S* father, 2011; *m* 1982, Penelope Anne Elmer; one *s* four *d*. *Educ:* Eton. Called to the Bar, Inner Temple. Dir, 1979–2013, Chm., 1993–2013, Warner Estate Hldgs PLC. *Heir:* *s* Charles Thomas Courtenay Warner, *b* 30 Sept. 1989.

WARNER, Stephen Clifford; His Honour Judge Stephen Warner; a Circuit Judge, since 2006; *b* 5 Aug. 1954; *s* of Jack and Marion; *m* 1979, Dr Amanda Craig; two *s*. *Educ:* Carmel Coll., Wallingford; St Catherine's Coll., Oxford (MA Hons). Called to the Bar, Lincoln's Inn, 1976; in practice as barrister, 1976–2006; Asst Recorder, 1999–2000; Recorder, 2000–06. Legal Mem., First-tier Tribunal (Mental Health, Restricted Panel) (formerly Mental Health Review Tribunals (Restricted Panel)), 2009–. Trustee, Finchley Youth Music Centre, 2008–. *Recreations:* cricket, music, walking, foreign travel. *Address:* c/o St Albans Crown Court, Bricket Road, St Albans, Herts AL1 3JW.

WARNER, Suzanne Elizabeth, (Lady Warner), OBE 2006; Chairman, Botanic Gardens Conservation International, 1999–2005; *b* 12 Aug. 1942; *d* of Charles Clifford Reeder and Elizabeth Joan Armstrong Reeder; *m* 1st, 1967, Jonathan Reeve (marr. diss. 1980); one *s*; 2nd, 1990, Norman Reginald Warner (*see* Baron Warner); one *s*. *Educ:* Badminton Sch., Bristol; Univ. of Sussex (BA Hons History); Univ. of Cambridge (Dip. Criminology). Home Office Res. Unit, 1966–67; Personal Assistant to Sec. of State for Social Services, DHSS, 1968–70; Principal, DHSS, 1970–73; Central Policy Review Staff, 1973–74; Asst Sec., DHSS, 1979–85; Sec., 1985–88, Actg Chm., 1987–88, ESRC; Exec. Dir, Food from Britain, 1988–90; Chief Exec., Foundn for Educn Business Partnerships, 1990–91; Personal Advr to Dep. Chm., BT plc, 1991–93; Hd of Gp Govt Relations, 1993–96, Gp Dir of Govt Relations, 1996–97, Cable and Wireless plc; Dep. Chm., Broadcasting Standards Commn, 1998–2003. Member: Management Bd, Sci. Policy Support Unit, Royal Soc., 1991–93; Technology Foresight Steering Gp, OST, 1994–97; Council, Industry and Parlt Trust, 1994–97; Acad. Council, Wilton Park, 1995–2004 (Chm., 1999–2004); Bd, Envmt Agency, 2006–12 (Chm., Audit and Risk Cttee, 2009–12). University of Sussex: Mem. Adv. Bd, Sci. Policy Res. Unit, 1998–2007; Mem., Court, 2000–07; Vice-Chm. of Council, 2001–07. Non-executive Director: SE Thames RHA, 1993–94; S Thames RHA, 1994–96; Broadmoor Hosp. Authy, 1996–98. *Recreations:* family life, cooking, gardening, reading, films.

WARNOCK, family name of **Baroness Warnock**.

WARNOCK, Baroness *cr* 1985 (Life Peer), of Weeke in the City of Winchester; **(Helen) Mary Warnock,** DBE 1984; Mistress of Girton College, Cambridge, 1985–91; *b* 14 April 1924; *d* of late Archibald Edward Wilson, Winchester and Ethel Mary Wilson (*née* Schuster); *m* 1949, Sir Geoffrey Warnock (*d* 1995); two *s* two *d* (and one *d* decd). *Educ:* St Swithun's,

Winchester; Lady Margaret Hall, Oxford (Hon. Fellow 1984). Fellow and Tutor in Philosophy, St Hugh's Coll., Oxford, 1949–66; Headmistress, Oxford High Sch., GPDST, 1966–72; Talbot Res. Fellow, Lady Margaret Hall, Oxford, 1972–76; Sen. Res. Fellow, St Hugh's Coll., Oxford, 1976–84 (Hon. Fellow, 1985). Member: IBA, 1973–81; Cttee of Inquiry into Special Educn, 1974–78 (Chm.); Royal Commn on Environmental Pollution, 1979–84; Adv. Cttee on Animal Experiments, 1979–85 (Chm.); SSRC, 1981–85; UK Nat. Commn for Unesco, 1981–84; Cttee of Inquiry into Human Fertilization, 1982–84 (Chm.); Cttee of Inquiry into Validation of Public Sector Higher Educn, 1984; Cttee on Teaching Quality, PCFC, 1990 (Chm.); European Adv. Gp on Bioethics, 1992–94; Archbishop of Canterbury's Adv. Gp on Medical Ethics, 1992–2005; Adv. Gp on Nazi Spoliation, 2003–; Chm., Educn Cttee, GDST (formerly GPDST), 1994–2001. Mem., H of L, 1985–2015. Visitor, RHBNC, 1997–2001. Gifford Lectr, Univ. of Glasgow, 1991–92; Reed Tuckwell Lectr, Univ. of Bristol, 1992. Leverhulme Emeritus Fellow, 1992–94. FRCP 1979; FRSocMed 1989; Hon. FIC 1986; Hon. FBA 2000. Hon. Fellow, Hertford Coll., Oxford, 1997. Hon. degrees: Open, Essex, Melbourne, Manchester, Bath, Exeter, Glasgow, York, Nottingham, Warwick, Liverpool, London, St Andrews and Ulster Univs; Leeds Poly.; Leicester Poly.; King Alfred's Coll., Winchester; Brighton. Albert Medal, RSA, 1999. *Publications:* Ethics since 1900, 1960, 3rd edn 1978; J.-P. Sartre, 1963; Existentialist Ethics, 1966; Existentialism, 1970; Imagination, 1976; Schools of Thought, 1977; (with T. Devlin) What Must We Teach?, 1977; Education: a way forward, 1979; A Question of Life, 1985; Teacher Teach Thyself (Dimbleby Lect.), 1985; Memory, 1987; A Common Policy for Education, 1988; Universities: knowing our minds, 1989; The Uses of Philosophy, 1992; Imagination and Time, 1994; (ed) Women Philosophers, 1996; An Intelligent Person's Guide to Ethics, 1998; A Memoir, 2000; Making Babies, 2002; Nature and Morality: recollections of a philosopher in public life, 2003; (with E. Macdonald) Easeful Death: is there a case for assisted suicide?, 2008; Dishonest to God: how to keep religion out of politics, 2010; A Critical Reflection on Ownership, 2015. *Recreations:* music, gardening. *Address:* 101 Moremead Road, SE6 3LS. *T:* (020) 3659 0779.

WARNOCK, (Alastair) Robert (Lyon); His Honour Judge Warnock; a Circuit Judge, since 2003; Senior Judge of the Sovereign Base Areas (Cyprus), since 2012; *b* 23 July 1953; *s* of Alexander Nelson Lyon Warnock and Annabel Forest Lyon Warnock; *m* 1993, Sally Mary Tomkinson. *Educ:* Sedbergh Sch.; Univ. of East Anglia (BA History); Coll. of Law. Called to the Bar, Lincoln's Inn, 1977; Jun., Northern Circuit, 1980–81; Asst Recorder, 1996–2000, Recorder, 2000–03. Mem. Bd, Merseyside Probation Trust, 2013–15. Pres., SW Lancs Magistrates' Assoc., 2006–12. Pres., Royal Liverpool Village Play, 2000–14; Vice-Pres., Artisan Golfers' Assoc., 2002–. *Recreations:* golf, travel, food and wine, cricket. *Address:* c/o Queen Elizabeth II Combined Court Centre, Derby Square, Liverpool L2 1XA. *T:* (court) (0151) 473 7373. *E:* HHJudge.Warnock@judiciary.gsi.gov.uk. *Clubs:* Artists' (Liverpool); Royal Liverpool Golf.

WARNOCK, Andrew Ronald; QC 2012; *b* Magherafelt, Co. Londonderry, 31 Aug. 1970; *s* of Ronald John Warnock and Eleanor Heather Warnock (*née* Crooks); *m* 2003, Linda Clare Robb; two *s* one *d*. *Educ:* Cookstown High Sch.; Sidney Sussex Coll., Cambridge (BA 1992); Inns of Court Sch. of Law. Called to the Bar, Inner Temple, 1993. Ind. Funding Adjudicator, 2006–, Mem., Special Controls Rev. Panel, 2008–, Legal Services Commn. Chm. Res., Soc. of Cons. Lawyers, 2013–. *Publications:* (contributing ed.) Local Authority Liability, 1998, 6th edn 2012. *Recreations:* North Antrim coast, travel, scuba diving. *Address:* c/o 1 Chancery Lane, WC2A 1LF. *T:* 0845 634 6666, *Fax:* 0845 634 6667. *E:* awarnock@1chancerylane.com.

WARNOCK, Robert; *see* Warnock, A. R. L.

WARNOCK-SMITH, Shân; QC 2002; *b* 13 Sept. 1948; *d* of Thomas John Davies and Denise Dorothy Davies; one *s* one *d*; partner, Andrew De La Rosa. *Educ:* King's Coll., London (LLB Hons 1970, LLM 1972). Called to the Bar, Gray's Inn, 1971; Lectr, Inns of Court Sch. of Law, 1970–72; Sen. Lectr, City of London Poly., 1972–80; in practice as barrister, specialising in trusts, estates and internat. wealth structuring, 1979–. Regular speaker and chm. at trust confs. *Publications:* contrib. articles to private client jls. *Recreations:* interior design, travel. *Address:* 5 Stone Buildings, Lincoln's Inn, WC2A 3XT. *T:* (020) 7242 6201, *Fax:* (020) 7831 8102. *E:* swarnocksmith@5sblaw.com; ICT Chambers, Grand Cayman. *T:* 9265211. *E:* sws@ictchambers.com.

WARR, John James; Deputy Chairman, Clive Discount Co. Ltd, 1973–87, retired; President of the MCC, 1987–88; *b* 16 July 1927; *s* of late George and Florence May Warr; *m* 1957, Valerie Powell (*née* Peter) (*d* 2000); two *d*. *Educ:* Ealing County Grammar Sch.; Emmanuel Coll., Cambridge (BA Hons 1952). Served RN, 1945–48. Man. Dir, Union Discount Co., 1952–73. Chm., Racecourse Assoc., 1989–93. Mem., Jockey Club, 1977–. Pres., Berks CCC, 1990. *Recreations:* racing, cricket, golf, good music. *Address:* Orchard Farm, Touchen End, Maidenhead, Berks SL6 3TA. *T:* (01628) 622994. *Clubs:* Saints and Sinners (Chm., 1991–92), MCC, XL, I Zingari; Temple Golf, Berkshire Golf.

WARRELL, Prof. David Alan, DM, DSc; FRCP, FRCPE, FMedSci; Professor of Tropical Medicine and Infectious Diseases, 1987–2006, now Emeritus, and Head, Nuffield Department of Clinical Medicine, 2002–04 (Deputy Head, 2004–06), University of Oxford; Fellow, St Cross College, Oxford, 1977–2006, Hon. Fellow, since 2007; International Director (Hans Sloane Fellow), Royal College of Physicians, since 2012; *b* 6 Oct. 1939; *s* of late Alan and Mildred Warrell; *m* 1975, Dr Mary Jean Prentice; two *d*. *Educ:* Portsmouth Grammar Sch.; Christ Church, Oxford (MA, BCh 1964; DM 1970; DSc 1990). MRCS 1965; FRCP 1977; FRCPE 1999. Oxford Univ. Radcliffe Travelling Fellow, Univ. of Calif at San Diego, 1969–70; Sen. Lectr, Ahmadu Bello Univ., Zaria, Nigeria, 1970–74; Lectr, RPMS, London, 1974–75; Consultant Physician, Radcliffe Infirmary, Oxford, 1975–79; Founding Dir, Wellcome-Mahidol Univ. Oxford Tropical Medicine Research Programme in Bangkok, 1979–86; Founding Dir, Centre for Tropical Medicine, Univ. of Oxford, 1991–2001, now Emeritus. Hon. Clin. Dir, Alistair Reid Venom Res. Unit, Liverpool Sch. of Tropical Med., 1983–2009; Vis. Prof., Mahidol Univ., 1997–2006; Hon. Prof., Univ. Nacional Mayor de San Marcos, Lima, 2005–; Adjunct Prof., Dept of Infectious Diseases, Xi'an Med. Coll., China, 2009–; Principal Fellow, Dept of Pharmacol., Univ. of Melbourne, 1997–. WHO Consultant on malaria, rabies and snake bite, 1979–. Chm., MRC's AIDS Therapeutic Trials Cttee, 1987–93; MRC's China-UK Res. Ethics Cttee, 2007–; Mem., MRC's Tropical Medicine Res. Bd, 1986–89; Advr to MRC on tropical medicine, 2001–; Mem., FCO Pro Bono Medical Panel, 2002–. Hon. Consultant Malariologist to the Army, 1989–; Hon. Medical Adviser: RGS, 1993–; Earthwatch Internat., 2008–. Pres., Internat. Fedn of Tropical Medicine, 1996–2000; Pres., RSTM&H, 1997–99. Delegate, OUP, 1999–2006. RCP Lectures: Marc Daniels, 1977; Bradshaw, 1989; Croonian, 1996; College, 1999; Harveian Oration, 2001; Lloyd-Roberts Lectr, RSocMed, 2004. FRGS 1989. Founder FMedSci 1998. Hon. Member: Assoc. Physicians of GB & Ireland, 2003; Amer. Soc. of Tropical Medicine and Hygiene, 2003; Instituto de Medicina Tropical Alexander von Humboldt, Universidad Peruana Cayetano Heredia, Lima, 2010. Hon. Fellow, Ceylon Coll. of Physicians, 1985; Hon. Fellow (Conservation), Zool Soc., 2009. Chalmers Medal, RSTM&H, 1981; Ambuj Nath Bose Prize, RCP, 1994; Busk Medal, RGS, 2003; Guthrie Medal, RAMC, 2004; Mary Kingsley Centenary Medal, Liverpool Sch. of Tropical Medicine, 2005; Osler Meml Medal, Univ. of Oxford, 2010; Redi Award, Internat. Soc. of Toxinology, 2012. Companion, Order of White Elephant (Thailand), 2004. *Publications:* Rabies—the Facts, 1977, 2nd edn 1986; (ed) Oxford Textbook of Medicine, 1983, 5th edn 2010; (ed) Essential Malariology, 3rd edn 1993 to 5th edn 2009; Expedition Medicine, 1998, 2nd edn 2002; Oxford Handbook of Expedition and Wilderness Medicine, 2008, 2nd edn 2015; (ed) Oxford Textbook of Medicine: infection, 2012; chapters in textbooks of medicine and herpetology; papers in learned jls (Lancet, New England Jl of Medicine, etc) on respiratory physiology, malaria, rabies, infectious diseases and snake bite. *Recreations:* book collecting, music, bird watching, hill walking. *Address:* University of Oxford, Nuffield Department of Clinical Medicine, John Radcliffe Hospital, Headington, Oxford OX3 9DU. *T:* (01865) 234664, *Fax:* (01865) 760683. *E:* david.warrell@ndm.ox.ac.uk.

WARRELL, David Watson, MD; FRCOG; urological gynaecologist, 1969–94; Chairman, Mid-Cheshire Hospitals NHS Trust, 1994–97; *b* 20 June 1929; *s* of late Charles Warrell and Sarah (*née* Gill); *m* 1955, Valerie Jean Fairclough; one *s* one *d*. *Educ:* Sheffield Univ. MB ChB 1953; MD 1964; FRCOG 1970. Sen. Lectr and Hon. Consultant Obstetrician and Gynaecologist, Jessop Hosp. for Women, 1965–69; St Mary's Hosp., Manchester, 1969–94: established Dept of Urological Gynaecology; Med. Dir, 1991–92, Chief Exec., 1992–94, Central Manchester Health Care Trust. Blair Bell Travelling Fellowship, 1967. *Publications:* chapters and papers on urinary control in women. *Address:* Beudy y Chain, Llanfaglan, Caernarfon, Gwynedd LL54 5RA.

WARREN, Very Rev. Alan Christopher; Provost of Leicester, 1978–92, now Provost Emeritus; *b* 27 June 1932; *s* of Arthur Henry and Gwendoline Catherine Warren; *m* 1957, Sylvia Mary (*née* Matthews); three *d*. *Educ:* Dulwich College; Corpus Christi Coll., Cambridge (Exhibnr, MA); Ridley Hall, Cambridge. Curate, St Paul's, Margate, 1957–59; Curate, St Andrew, Plymouth, 1959–62; Chaplain of Kelly College, Tavistock, 1962–64; Vicar of Holy Apostles, Leicester, 1964–72; Coventry Diocesan Missioner, 1972–78; Hon. Canon, Coventry Cathedral, 1972–78; Proctor in Convocation, 1977–78, 1980–85. Mem., Cathedral Statutes Commn, 1981–85. Trustee, St Martin's, Birmingham, 1981–2011. Chm., Leicester Council of Christians and Jews, 1985–92; President: Leicester Council of Churches, 1985–92; Leicester Civic Soc., 1983–92. Tutor, Adult Educn, Norfolk, 1993–99; Dir of Music, W Norfolk Choral Soc., 1993–2000. Chm., Hunstanton Arts Fest. Cttee, 1994–99; Founder and Mem., Brancaster Music Fest., 2001–14. Mem., MCC, 1960–76. Pres., Alleyn Club, 1991–92 (Vice-Pres., 1990–91). *Publications:* Putting it Across, 1975; The Miserable Warren, 1991; articles on church music, evangelism and sport in Church Times and other journals; *compositions:* Incarnatus for Organ, 1960; Piano Sonata, 1996. *Recreations:* music, golf, steam trains. *Address:* 9 Queens Drive, Hunstanton, Norfolk PE36 6EY. *T:* (01485) 534533. *Clubs:* Free Foresters; Hunstanton Golf.

See also Ven. N. L. Warren, R. H. C. Warren.

WARREN, Prof. Alan John, PhD; FRCP, FRCPath; FMedSci; Professor of Haematology, University of Cambridge, since 2003; Honorary Consultant Haematologist, Cambridge University Hospitals NHS Foundation Trust (formerly Addenbrooke's NHS Trust), since 1997; *b* 22 Nov. 1961; *s* of John Rundle Warren and Marion Wallace Warren; *m* 1989, Nina Louise Johnman; one *s* one *d*. *Educ:* Univ. of Glasgow (BSc Hons (Biochem.) 1983; MB ChB 1986); Gonville and Caius Coll., Cambridge (PhD (Molecular Biol.) 1995). MRCP 1989, FRCP 2002; MRCPath (Haematol.) 1997, FRCPath (Haematol.) 2005. House officer posts, medicine and surgery, Royal Infirmary, Glasgow, 1986–87; Sen. House Officer, Western Infirmary Med. Rotation, Glasgow, 1987–89; Registrar in Haematol., Hammersmith and Ealing Hosps, London, 1989–91; MRC Laboratory of Molecular Biology, Cambridge: MRC Trng Fellow, 1991–94; MRC Clinician Scientist and Hon. Sen. Registrar, 1994–95; MRC Clinician Scientist, 1997–2000, and Hon. Consultant Haematologist, 1997–2003; MRC Sen. Clinical Fellow, 2000–03; Sen. Registrar in Haematol., Addenbrooke's Hosp., Cambridge, 1995–97. FMedSci 2005. *Publications:* articles of research in peer-reviewed primary scientific jls. *Recreations:* avid camellia collector, cycling. *Address:* Cambridge Institute for Medical Research, University of Cambridge, Cambridge Biomedical Campus, Wellcome Trust/MRC Building, Hills Road, Cambridge CB2 0XY. *T:* (01223) 267281, *Fax:* (01223) 213556. *E:* ajw1000@cam.ac.uk.

WARREN, Catherine; *see* Graham-Harrison, C.

WARREN, Rt Rev. Cecil Allan; Rector, Old Brampton and Loundsley Green, 1983–88; Assistant Bishop, Diocese of Derby, 1983–88; *b* 25 Feb. 1924; *s* of Charles Henry and Eliza Warren; *m* 1947, Doreen Muriel Burrows. *Educ:* Sydney Univ. (BA 1950); Queen's Coll., Oxford (MA 1959). Deacon 1950, priest 1951, Dio. of Canberra and Goulburn; appointments in Diocese of Oxford, 1953–57; Canberra, 1957–63; Organising Sec. Church Society, and Director of Forward in Faith Movement, Dio. of Canberra and Goulburn, 1963–65; Asst Bishop of Canberra and Goulburn, 1965–72; Bishop of Canberra and Goulburn, 1972–83. *Publications:* A Little Foolishness: an autobiographical history, 1993. *Address:* Symesthorpe, 69 Stenner Street, Toowoomba, Qld 4350, Australia.

WARREN, Sir David (Alexander), KCMG 2012 (CMG 2007); HM Diplomatic Service, retired; Ambassador to Japan, 2008–12; Chairman, Japan Society, since 2013; Associate Fellow, Asia Programme, Royal Institute of International Affairs, since 2014; *b* 11 Aug. 1952; *s* of late Alister Charles Warren and Celia Warren (*née* Golding); *m* 1992, Pamela, *d* of late Benjamin Ivan Pritchard and Violet Pritchard (*née* Sherman). *Educ:* Epsom Coll.; Exeter Coll., Oxford (MA English; Hon. Fellow, 2012; Pres., Oxford Union Soc., 1973). Entered HM Diplomatic Service, 1975; FCO, 1975–77; Third, later Second, then First Sec., Tokyo, 1977–81; FCO, 1981–87; First Sec. and Hd of Chancery, Nairobi, 1987–90; FCO, 1990–91; on secondment as Hd, Internat. Div., Sci. and Technol. Secretariat, later OST, then OPSS, Cabinet Office, 1991–93; Counsellor (Commercial), Tokyo, 1993–98; Hd, Hong Kong Dept, later China Hong Kong Dept, FCO, 1998–2000; Dir, Trade Partners UK, British Trade Internat., subseq. UK Trade and Investment, 2000–04; Dir, HR, FCO, 2004–07. Sen. Advr, Montrose Associates, 2014–. Visiting Professor: Sheffield Univ., 2013–; De Montfort Univ., 2013–. Member: UK/Japan 21st Century Gp, 2013–; Bd, Sainsbury Inst. for Study of Japanese Arts and Cultures, 2013–. Mem., 2013–, Chair, 2014–, Council, Univ. of Kent at Canterbury. Member, Advisory Council: LSO, 2013–; Migration Matters Trust, 2013–. Trustee, Oxford Literary and Debating Union Trust, 2014–. Hon. DLitt: Sheffield, 2011; De Montfort, 2013. *Recreations:* books, history of theatre and music hall. *Address:* c/o Japan Society, 13/14 Cornwall Terrace, NW1 4QP. *E:* David.Warren@japansociety.org.uk. *Club:* Oxford and Cambridge.

WARREN, Frank John; Chief Executive Officer, Sports Network Europe, since 1996; *b* London, 28 Feb. 1952; *s* of Frank and Iris Warren; *m* 1983, Susan Margaret Cox; four *s* two *d*. *Educ:* Highbury Co. Grammar Sch. Sport and boxing promoter and manager, 1978–; clients have included Nigel Benn, Frank Bruno, Chris Eubank, Mike Tyson, Ricky Hatton, Naseem Hamed, Joe Calzaghe and Amir Khan. Promoter, Frank Sinatra in London. Chm., Bedford RFC, 1996–99. Former Chm., London Arena. Founder and Dir, BoxNation TV, 2011–. *Recreations:* music, reading, art, sport. *Address:* Sports Network Europe, Ground Floor, Turnford Place, Turnford, Herts EN10 6NH. *T:* (01992) 505550, *Fax:* (01992) 505552. *E:* emmahedley@frankwarren.com. *Club:* Royal Automobile.

WARREN, Sir (Frederick) Miles, ONZ 1995; KBE 1985 (CBE 1974); FNZIA; ARIBA; Senior Partner, Warren & Mahoney, Architects Ltd, 1958–94; *b* Christchurch, 10 May 1929. *Educ:* Christ's Coll., Christchurch; Auckland Univ. DipArch; ARIBA 1952; FNZIA 1965. Founded Warren & Mahoney, 1958. Award-winning designs include: Christchurch Town Hall and Civic Centre; NZ Chancery, Washington; Canterbury Public Library; Michael Fowler Centre, Wellington; St Patrick's Church, Napier; Ohinetahi, Governors Bay; Rotorua Dist Council Civic Offices; Mulholland Hse, Wanganui; Parkroyal Hotel, Christchurch. Pres., Canterbury Soc. of Arts, 1972–76. Gold Medal, NZIA, 1960, 1964, 1969, 1973; Nat.

Awards, NZIA, 1980, 1981, 1983–86, 1988, 1989, 1990, 1991. *Publications:* Warren & Mahoney Architects, 1990; Miles Warren: an autobiography, 2008; Ohinetahi, 2014. *Recreation:* making a garden.

WARREN, Prof. Graham Barry, PhD; FRS 1999; Scientific Director, Max F. Perutz Laboratories, Vienna, since 2007; *b* 25 Feb. 1948; *s* of late Joyce Thelma and Charles Graham Thomas Warren; *m* 1966, Philippa Mary Adeline (*née* Temple-Cole); four *d*. *Educ:* Willesden County Grammar Sch.; Pembroke Coll., Cambridge (MA, PhD). MRC Fellow, Nat. Inst. for Med. Research, 1972–75; Royal Soc. Stothert Research Fellow, Dept of Biochemistry, Cambridge, 1975–77; Research Fellow, Gonville & Caius Coll., Cambridge, 1975–77; Group Leader then Senior Scientist, European Molecular Biology Lab., Heidelberg, 1977–85; Prof. and Hd of Dept of Biochemistry, Dundee Univ., 1985–88; Prin. Scientist, ICRF, 1989–99; Prof. of Cell Biology, Yale Univ. Med. Sch., 1999–2007. Mem., EMBO, 1986. Mem., Austrian Acad. Scis, 2011. *Publications:* papers in learned jls on cell biology. *Recreation:* woodworking. *Address:* Max. F. Perutz Laboratories, Dr Bohr-Gasse 9, 1030 Vienna, Austria. *T:* (1) 4277 24011, *Fax:* (1) 4277 9240. *E:* graham.warren@mfpl.ac.at.

WARREN, Joëlle Susan; Executive Chairman, Warren Partners Ltd, since 2010 (Managing Director, 1998–2010); Vice Lord-Lieutenant, Cheshire, since 2010; *b* Liverpool, 1 Nov. 1962; *d* of Rod and Tessa Howgate; *m* 1986, Andrew Mark Warren; two *s*. *Educ:* Withington Girls' Sch., Manchester; Univ. of Durham (BA Hons Econs 1984). ACIB 1987. Lloyds Bank plc: grad. trainee posts, 1984–86; Asst Manager, Corporate Banking Div., 1986–88; Manager: Stock Exchange Br., 1988–90; Portman Sq. Br., 1990–92; Trng, 1992–94; Partner, Howgate Sable, 1994–97. Bishops' Selection Advr, C of E, 2006–. Gov. and Vice Chair, Manchester Metropolitan Univ., 2001–10. Chair, Cheshire Community Foundn, 2010–. Church Warden and Leadership Team, Christ Church Alsager, 2000–. DL Cheshire, 2010. *Recreations:* living life in all its fullness, Church, family, entertaining, ski-ing, walking, cycling. *Address:* Warren House, Rudheath Way, Gadbrook Park, Northwich, Cheshire CW9 7LT. *T:* (01606) 812781, 07973 897536, *Fax:* (0845) 261 0606. *E:* jwarren@warrenpartners.co.uk.

WARREN, John; QC 1994; a Recorder, Midland and Oxford Circuit, 1993–2004; *b* 25 Aug. 1945; *s* of Frank Warren and Dora Warren (*née* Thomas); *m* 1968, Anne Marlor; one *s* one *d* (twins). *Educ:* Chadderton Grammar Sch., near Oldham; Univ. of Nottingham (LLB). Called to the Bar, Gray's Inn, 1968. *Recreations:* opera and classical music, supporting Nottingham Forest FC, doing The Times crossword with my wife, playing the classical guitar. *Address:* 11 Parc yr Eglwys, Dinas Cross, Newport, Pembrokeshire SA42 0SH. *T:* (01348) 811214. *Club:* Newport Boat.

WARREN, John; Regional Employment Judge (formerly Regional Chairman, Employment Tribunals), London South, 2003–08, fee-paid Judge, 2008–13; *b* 26 Sept. 1943; *s* of William John Warren and Phyllis Eliza Warren; one *s* one *d*. Solicitor. Fee-paid Chm., Employment Tribunals, 2008–. Pool Mem., Review Panel, Catholic Safeguarding Commn, 2009–. *Recreations:* walking, photography, gardening, touring by car.

WARREN, (John) Robin, AC 2007; MD; FAA; FRCPA; Pathologist, Royal Perth Hospital, 1968–99, now Emeritus Consultant Pathologist; Emeritus Professor, University of Western Australia, since 2005; *b* Adelaide, 11 June 1937; *s* of John Roger Hogarth Warren and Helen Josephine Warren (*née* Verco); *m* 1962, Winifred Teresa Williams (*d* 1998); four *s* two *d*. *Educ:* St Peter's Coll.; Univ. of Adelaide Sch. of Medicine (MB BS 1961; MD 2000). FRCPA 1967; FAA 2006. Jun. RMO, Queen Elizabeth Hosp., Woodville, 1961; Registrar in Haematology and Clinical Pathology, Inst. of Med. and Vet. Sci., Adelaide, 1962; Temp. Lectr in Pathology, Univ. of Adelaide, and Hon. Clinical Asst in Pathology, Royal Adelaide Hosp., 1963; Registrar in Clinical Pathology, 1964–66, in Pathology, 1966–68, Royal Melbourne Hosp. Member: AMA 1960; BMA 1960; Australian Soc. of Cytology, 1975; Internat. Acad. of Pathology, 1975. Honorary Member: Polish Soc. of Gastroenterology, 2006; German Soc. of Pathology, 2007. Hon. FRACP 2006. Hon. MD: Western Aust., 1997; Romana Studiorum, 2008; Sydney, 2012; DUniv Adelaide, 2006; Dr *hc* Toyama, 2007; Otto-von-Guericke Universität, 2007. (Jtly) Warren Alpert Foundn Prize, Harvard Med. Sch., 1994; Western Aust. Br. Award, AMA, 1995; Dist. Fellows Award, RCPA, 1995; Medal, Univ. of Hiroshima, 1996; Paul Ehrlich and Ludwig Darmstaedter Award, Paul Ehrlich Foundn, 1997; Faulding Florey Medal, 1998; (jtly) Nobel Prize in Physiology or Medicine, 2005; Gold Medal, AMA, 2006; Western Australian of the Year, 2007; Medal of Hirosaki Univ. Sch. of Med., 2007; Distinguished Pathologist Medal, Internat. Acad. of Pathol. (Australia), 2008. *Publications:* contrib. numerous letters and articles in learned jls. *Recreations:* photography, philately, computer processing, music, sports (not active at present), rifle shooting and cycling. *Address:* 178 Lake Street, Perth, WA 6000, Australia. *T:* (8) 93289248, *Fax:* (8) 93289248. *E:* jrwarren@aapt.net.au.

WARREN, Sir Kenneth (Robin), Kt 1994; Eur Ing, CEng, FRAeS; FCILT; consultant in engineering and management; *b* 15 Aug. 1926; *s* of Edward Charles Warren and Ella Mary Warren (*née* Adams); *m* 1962, Elizabeth Anne Chamberlain (*d* 2013), MA Cantab and MA Lond; one *s* two *d*. *Educ:* Midsomer Norton; Aldenham; London Univ.; De Havilland Aeronautical Technical Sch.; Univ. of Buckingham (MA 2012). Fulbright Scholar, USA, 1949; Research Engineer, BOAC, 1951–57; Personal Asst to Gen. Manager, Smiths Aircraft Instruments Ltd, 1957–60; Elliott Automation Ltd, 1960–69; Military Flight Systems: Manager, 1960–63; Divisional Manager, 1963–66; Marketing Manager, 1966–69. MP (C) Hastings, 1970–83, Hastings and Rye, 1983–92. Mem., Select Cttee on Science and Technology, 1970–79 (Chm., Offshore Engrg Sub-Cttee, 1975–76); Mem., Council of Europe, 1973–81; Chm., WEU, Science, Technology and Aerospace Cttee, 1976–79; Chm., Cons. Parly Aviation Cttee, 1975–77; PPS to Sec. of State for Industry, 1979–81, to Sec. of State for Educn and Sci., 1981–83; Chairman: Select Cttee on Trade and Industry, 1983–92; British Soviet Parly Gp, 1986–92. Former branch officer, GMWU. Chairman: Computer Security Adv. Bd, LSE, 1991–2001; Anglo-Japanese Adv. Bd on Financial Regulation, 1999–. President: British Resorts Assoc., 1987–92; Inst. of Travel Mgt, 1999–2002. Pres., Winkle Club charity, Hastings, 2010–. Liveryman, Hon. Co. of Air Pilots (formerly GAPAN); Freeman, City of London. Hon. Fellow, Exeter Univ., 1994. *Publications:* various papers on aeronautical engineering, hi-tech mgt, inf. technol. and econ. crime in UK, USA, France, Hungary, Malaysia, Netherlands and Japan. *Recreations:* mountaineering, flying, gardening. *Address:* The Garden House, High Street, Cranbrook, Kent TN17 3EN. *T:* (01580) 714464. *E:* Kenneth.Warren647@btinternet.com. *Clubs:* Athenæum, Garrick, Special Forces.

WARREN, Prof. Lynda May, PhD; FRSB; Professor of Environmental Law, Aberystwyth University (formerly University of Wales, Aberystwyth), 1996–2003, now Emeritus; Member, Royal Commission on Environmental Pollution, 2005–11; *b* Croydon, 26 April 1950; *d* of Leonard Warren and Peggy Warren (*née* Tatnell); *m* 1986, Barry Archie Thomas; one *s*. *Educ:* Bedford Coll., Univ. of London (BSc 1971; PhD 1975); Univ. of London (LLB 1986 ext.); Univ. of Wales, Cardiff (MSc). FRSB (FIBiol 1991). Senior Lecturer: in Marine Biol., Poly. of Central London, 1981–84; in Zool., Goldsmiths' Coll., London, 1984–89; Lectr, then Sen. Lectr in Law, Cardiff Law Sch., Univ. of Wales, Cardiff, 1989–95. Hon. Prof., Bangor Univ., 2015–. Chairman: Salmon and Freshwater Fisheries Rev., 1998–2000; Wales Coastal and Maritime Partnership, 2007–12; Wildlife Trust of S and W Wales, 2009–15; Dep. Chm., JNCC, 2008–12; Member: Countryside Council for Wales, 1993–2003; Bd, EA, 2000–06; Cttee on Radioactive Waste Mgt, 2003–; Bd , British Geol Survey, 2004–11; Sci. Adv. Council, DEFRA, 2011–; Natural Resources Wales, 2012–; Ind. Envmtl Advr, Dŵr Cymru Welsh Water, 2012–13. Hon. Prof., Birmingham City Univ., 2010–13. Founding Editor: Law, Science and Policy (formerly Internat. Jl of Bioscience and the Law), 1996–2010; Envmtl Law Rev., 1999–2013. *Publications:* over 100 articles on law and science. *Recreations:* travel, reading, cinema, fashion. *Address:* Ynys Einion, Eglwys Fach, Machynlleth SY20 8SX. *T:* (01654) 781344, 07764 848230. *E:* lm.warren@btopenworld.com.

WARREN, Marta Zofia; *see* Kwiatkowska, M. Z.

WARREN, Sir Miles; *see* Warren, Sir F. M.

WARREN, Nicholas John; a Judge of the Upper Tribunal, 2010–15; *b* 24 June 1951; *s* of late Stanley and of Barbara Warren; *m* 1976, Catherine Mackie; two *s* three *d*. *Educ:* Blessed John Rigby Grammar Sch., Wigan; St Catherine's Coll., Oxford (MA Juris.). Admitted solicitor, 1975; Solicitor: Arthur Smiths, Wigan, 1973–77; Child Poverty Action Gp, 1977–80; Family Rights Gp, 1980–81; Birkenhead Resource Unit, 1981–92; a Recorder, 1992–2010; full-time Chm., Social Security Tribunals, 1992–98, Regl Chm., 1998–2008. Pres., Gambling Appeals Tribunal, 2007–10; a Regl Tribunal Judge (Social Security), 2008–10; Pres., Gen. Regulatory Chamber of the First-tier Tribunal, 2011–15. Member: Lord Chancellor's Adv. Cttee on Legal Aid, 1992–95; Tribunal Procedure Cttee, 2008–11. Mem. Bd, Judicial Coll., 2011–15. Trustee, Cafod, 1993–2009. *Publications:* articles on social security and family law. *Recreations:* watching National Hunt racing and Tranmere Rovers FC, listening to Leonard Cohen. *Address:* 29 Grafton Street, Birkenhead CH43 4UJ. *T:* (0151) 652 2192.

WARREN, Hon. Sir Nicholas Roger, Kt 2005; **Hon. Mr Justice Warren;** a Judge of the High Court of Justice, Chancery Division, since 2005; *b* 20 May 1949; *s* of Roger Warren and Muriel (*née* Reeves); *m* 1st, 1978 (marr. diss. 1989); two *s* one *d*; 2nd, 1994, Catherine Graham-Harrison, *qv*. *Educ:* Bryanston Sch.; University Coll., Oxford. Called to the Bar, Middle Temple, 1972, Bencher, 2001; QC 1993; a Recorder, 1999–2005; a Pres., Upper Tribunal (Tax and Chancery (formerly Finance and Tax) Chamber), 2009–15. *Recreations:* music, sailing. *Address:* c/o Royal Courts of Justice, 7 Rolls Building, Fetter Lane, EC4A 1NL.

WARREN, Ven. Norman Leonard; Archdeacon of Rochester, 1989–2000; *b* 19 July 1934; *s* of Arthur Henry Warren and Gwendoline Catherine Warren; *m* 1961, Yvonne Sheather; three *s* two *d*. *Educ:* Dulwich College; Corpus Christi Coll., Cambridge (MA). Asst Curate, Bedworth, 1960–63; Vicar, St Paul's, Leamington Priors, 1963–77; Rector of Morden, 1977–89; RD of Merton, 1984–88. Musical Editor: Hymns for Today's Church, 1982; Jesus Praise, 1982; Sing Glory, 1999. *Publications:* Journey into Life, 1964; The Way Ahead, 1965; Directions, 1969; What's the Point?, 1986; The Path of Peace, 1988; A Certain Faith, 1988; Is God there?, 1990; Why Believe?, 1993; (ed) Responsorial Psalms of the Alternative Services Book, 1994; Psalms for the People, 2001. *Recreations:* cricket, soccer and Rugby, walking, music. *Address:* 6 Hillview, Stratford-upon-Avon CV37 9AY. *T:* (01789) 414255.

See also Very Rev. A. C. Warren, R. H. C. Warren.

WARREN, Peter Francis; Chairman, Hammond Communications, 1994; non-executive Chairman, Radio Advertising Bureau, 1995–2001; *b* 2 Dec. 1940; *s* of Francis Joseph Warren and Freda Ruth Hunter; *m* 1962, Susan Poole; two *s* one *d*. *Educ:* Finchley Grammar School. Deputy Managing Dir, Ogilvy Benson & Mather Ltd, 1977; Dir, Ogilvy & Mather International Inc., 1978; Managing Dir, Ogilvy Benson & Mather Ltd, 1978; Chairman: Ogilvy & Mather (Hldgs), subseq. The Ogilvy Gp (Hldgs) Ltd, 1981–90; Ogilvy & Mather Europe, 1988–90; Consultant, Ogilvy & Mather Worldwide, 1991 (Dir, 1985–90). Dir, Abbott Mead Vickers, 1992–99.

WARREN, Prof. Peter Michael, PhD; FSA; FBA 1997; Professor of Ancient History and Classical Archaeology, 1977–2001, now Emeritus, and Senior Research Fellow, since 2001, University of Bristol; *b* 23 June 1938; *s* of Arthur George Warren and Alison Joan Warren (*née* White); *m* 1966, Elizabeth Margaret Halliday; one *s* one *d*. *Educ:* Sandbach Sch.; Llandovery Coll.; University College of N Wales, Bangor (Ellen Thomas Stanford Schol.; BA 1st Cl. Hons Greek and Latin); Corpus Christi Coll., Cambridge (Exhibnr; BA Classical Tripos Pt II 1962; MA 1966; PhD 1966; Fellow, 1965–68); student, British Sch. at Athens, 1963–65. FSA 1973. Research Fellow in Arts, Univ. of Durham, 1968–70; Asst Director, British Sch. at Athens, 1970–72; University of Birmingham: Lectr in Aegean Archaeol., 1972–74; Sen. Lectr, 1974–76; Reader, 1976; Bristol University: Dean, Faculty of Arts, 1988–90; Pro-Vice-Chancellor, 1991–95; Fellow, 1995–96. Vis. Prof., Univ. of Minnesota, 1981; Geddes-Harrower Prof. of Greek Art and Archaeol., Univ. of Aberdeen, 1986–87; Neubergh Lectr, Univ. of Göteborg, 1986. Dir of excavations, Myrtos, Crete, 1967–68; Debla, Crete, 1971; Knossos, 1971–73, 1978–82, 1997. Mem., Rev. Panel, Italian Nat. Res. Council, 2009. Member: Managing Cttee, British Sch. at Athens, 1973–77, 1978–79, 1986–90, 1994–98, 1999–2004, 2006–10 (Chm., 1979–83, 2003–04; Vice-Pres., 2005–); Council, Soc. for Promotion of Hellenic Studies, 1978–81; President: Bristol Anglo-Hellenic Cultural Soc., 1987–97; Birmingham and Midlands Br., Classical Assoc., 1996–97. Bristol and Gloucestershire Archaeological Society: Vice-Chm. Council, 1980–81; Chm., 1981–84; Vice-Pres., 1989–93; Pres., 2000–01. Hon. Sec., Friends of British Sch. at Athens (UK), 2011–. Hon. Fellow, Archaeol Soc. of Athens, 1987; Corresp. Fellow, Soc. for Cretan Historical Studies, 1992; Corresp. Mem., Österreichische Akad. der Wissenschaften, 1997; For. Fellow, Onassis Public Benefit Foundn, 2007. Hon. Dr Univ. of Athens, 2000. *Publications:* Minoan Stone Vases, 1969, repr. 2010; Myrtos, an Early Bronze Age Settlement in Crete, 1972; The Aegean Civilizations, 1975, 2nd edn 1989; Minoan Religion as Ritual Action, 1988; (with V. Hankey) Aegean Bronze Age Chronology, 1989; (with S. Alexiou) The Early Minoan Tombs of Lebena, Southern Crete, 2004; Ardtornish House: the architectural and decorative marbles and granite, 2012; (with G. Rethemiotakis) Knossos: a Middle Minoan III building in Bougadha Metochi, 2014; articles on Aegean Bronze Age, particularly Minoan archaeology, in archaeol, science and classical jls. *Recreations:* growing *Cistaceae* (Nat. Collection), Manchester United, history of Greek botany. *Address:* Claremont House, 5 Merlin Haven, Wotton-under-Edge, Glos GL12 7BA. *T:* (01453) 842290.

WARREN, Peter Tolman, CBE 1998; PhD; Executive Secretary, Royal Society, 1985–97; *b* 20 Dec. 1937; *s* of late Hugh Alan Warren and Florence Christine Warren (*née* Tolman); *m* 1961, Angela Mary (*née* Curtis); two *s* one *d*. *Educ:* Whitgift Sch., Croydon; Queens' Coll., Cambridge (MA, PhD); CGeol. Geological Survey of GB, 1962; Chief Scientific Adviser's Staff, Cabinet Office, 1972; Private Sec. to Lord Zuckerman, 1973–76; Science and Technology Secretariat, Cabinet Office, 1974–76; Safety Adviser, NERC, 1976–77; Dep. Exec. Sec., Royal Soc., 1977–85; Dir, World Humanity Action Trust, 1997–99, then Consultant, 1999–2001, Trustee, 2001–03 and Mem., Exec. Cttee, 2001–05, Stakeholder Forum for our Common Future; Adminr, Livery Schs Link, 2004–06. Founder and Chm., Funding Exchange, 2013–15. Advr, Schs Funding Network, 2013–. Mem. Council, Parly and Scientific Cttee, 1992–2011 (Vice-Pres., 1995–97, 2001–04). Member: Council, GDST (formerly GPDST), 1989–2004; Ct of Governors and Council, Amgueddfa Cymru, Nat. Mus. of Wales (formerly Nat. Mus and Galls of Wales), 2000–06. Vice-President: Geol Soc., 1992–96; BAAS, 1997–2002; Chm., 2000–05, Vice-Pres., 2005–10, Pres., 2010–, Cambridge Soc. (Surrey Br.), later Cambridge Soc. of Surrey. Pres., Old Whitgiftian Assoc., 2008–09. Chm., Wingate Scholarships Cttee, 2005–12. Ct Asst, Co. (formerly Guild) of Educators, 2002– (Middle Warden, 2005–06; Upper Warden, 2006–07; Master, 2007–08). Editor, Monographs of Palaeontographical Soc., 1968–77. *Publications:* (ed) Geological Aspects of Development and Planning in Northern England, 1970; (co-author) Geology of the Country around Rhyl and Denbigh, 1984; papers on geology in learned jls. *Recreations:* geology, gardening. *Address:* 34 Plough Lane, Purley, Surrey CR8 3QA. *T:* (020) 8660 4087. *Club:* Athenæum.

WARREN, Prof. Raymond Henry Charles, MusD; Stanley Hugh Badock Professor of Music, University of Bristol, 1972–94; *b* 7 Nov. 1928; *s* of Arthur Henry Warren and Gwendoline Catherine Warren; *m* 1953, Roberta Lydia Alice Smith; three *s* one *d*. *Educ:* Bancroft's Sch.; Corpus Christi Coll., Cambridge (MA, MusD). Music Master, Woolverstone Hall Sch., 1952–55; Queen's University Belfast: Lectr in Music, 1955–66; Prof. of Composition, 1966–72; Resident Composer, Ulster Orchestra, 1967–72. Compositions incl. 3 symphonies, 3 string quartets, 6 operas and 4 song cycles. *Publications: compositions:* The Passion, 1963; String Quartet No 1, 1967; Violin Concerto, 1967; Songs of Old Age, 1971; Continuing Cities (oratorio), 1989; The Death of Orpheus (choral cantata), 2009; *book:* Opera Workshop, 1995. *Recreation:* walking. *Address:* 4 Contemporis, Merchants Road, Bristol BS8 4HB. *T:* (0117) 923 7687.

See also Very Rev. A. C. Warren, Ven. N. L. Warren.

WARREN, Rebecca, RA 2014; sculptor, since 1993; *b* Pinhoe, Exeter, 21 March 1965; *d* of William David Warren and Encarnación Brigida Warren (*née* Zarzalejo). *Educ:* Tunbridge Wells Girls' Grammar Sch.; West Kent Coll.; Paddington Tech. Coll.; Goldsmiths' Coll., Univ. of London (BA Hons Fine Art 1992); Chelsea Coll. of Art (MA Fine Art 1993). Artist in Residence, Ruskin Sch. of Art, Oxford Univ., 1993–94; Prof. of Painting and Sculpture, Kunstakademie, Dusseldorf, 2014–. Solo exhibitions include: Dark Passage, Kunsthalle Zurich, Zurich, 2004; Serpentine Gall., 2009; Renaissance Soc., Univ. of Chicago, 2010; Mus. Dhondt-Dhaenens, Ghent, 2012; The Living, Kunstverein München, Munich, 2013. *Publications:* Every Aspect of Bitch Magic, 2012. *Address:* c/o Maureen Paley, 21 Herald Street, E2 6JT.

WARREN, Robin; *see* Warren, J. R.

WARREN, Rupert Miles; QC 2012; *b* London, 13 Sept. 1969; *s* of George Warren and Diane Warren; *m* 2007, Emma Cawley; one *s*. *Educ:* Whitgift Sch.; Christ Church, Oxford (BA Lit.Hum. 1st). Called to the Bar, Gray's Inn, 1994; in practice as a barrister, specialising in planning law, Landmark Chambers, 1994–. *Publications:* (contrib. ed.) Encyclopedia of Planning Law and Practice, 2008–. *Recreations:* opera, theatre, writing, Chelsea FC. *Address:* Landmark Chambers, 180 Fleet Street, EC4A 2HG. *T:* (020) 7430 1221. *E:* rwarren@landmarkchambers.co.uk. *Club:* Travellers.

WARREN EVANS, (John) Roger; consultant, as lawyer and administrator, since 1995; *b* 11 Dec. 1935; *s* of Thomas and Mary Warren Evans; *m* 1966, Elizabeth M. James; one *s* one *d*. *Educ:* Leighton Park Sch., Reading; Trinity Coll., Cambridge (BA History, 1st Cl.); London Sch. of Economics. Called to Bar, Gray's Inn, 1962. Television Interviewer, Anglia Television, 1960–61; Research Officer, Centre for Urban Studies, London, 1961; practice at Bar, 1962–69; Legal Correspondent, New Society, 1964–68; general management functions with Bovis Gp, in construction and develt, 1969–74, incl. Man. Dir, Bovis Homes Southern Ltd, 1971–74; Under-Secretary, DoE, 1975; Industrial Advr on Construction, DoE, 1975–76; Man. Dir, Barratt Develts (London), Ltd, 1977–79; Dir, Swansea Centre for Trade and Industry, 1979–85; Man. Dir, Demos Ltd, 1985–87; SavaCentre Property Develt Manager, 1987–88; Regl Property Dir, J. Sainsbury plc, 1988–94. Dir, Estates & Agency Hldgs plc, 1995–2004. Partner, Steele Evans Questors, 2014. Member: Welsh Consumer Council, 1992–95; Cttee, Community Selfbuild Agency, 1995–99. Mem. Bd, Assoc. of Self Employed, 1995–96. Immigration Advr, Office of Immigration Services Comr, 2005–14. Gov., Gillespie Primary Sch., Islington, 1993–96. Trustee: Inst. of Community Studies, 1975–2001; Mutual Aid Centre, 1975–2005 (Chm., 2003–05); Aquaterra Leisure, 1999–2005; Hygeia Trust, 1999–2005; Croeso Trust, 2000–05; Libri Trust, 2000–04; Mumbles Community Leisure Trust, 2003–05; Asylum Justice Trust, 2005–11, 2012–14 (Chm., 2005–11, 2012–14; Patron, 2014–). Sec., 2003, Chair, 2014–, Coll. of Questors. Member: Hackney BC, 1971–73; Mumbles Community Council, Swansea, 1999–2004. Sec., RBL, Mumbles, 2004–06. Convenor, Fabian Soc., Wales, 1999–2004. FCIOB 1976. Hon. Fellow, Coll. of Estate Mgt, 1982. *Recreations:* painting, writing, talking. *Address:* 23 St Peter's Road, Newton, Swansea SA3 4SB. *E:* roger@warrenevans.net.

WARREN-GASH, Haydon Boyd; HM Diplomatic Service, retired; Director: FORO Consulting, since 2010; Chairman, Veventis, since 2013; *b* 8 Aug. 1949; *s* of late Alexis Patrick and Cynthia Warren-Gash; *m* 1973, Caroline Emma Bowring Leather; one *s* one *d*. *Educ:* Sidney Sussex Coll., Cambridge (MA Econs). Joined Foreign and Commonwealth Office, 1971; language training, SOAS, London Univ., 1972 (on secondment); Third Sec., Ankara, 1973–76; Second, subseq. First, Sec., Madrid, 1977–80; First Sec., FCO, 1980–82; Private Sec. to Minister of State, 1982–85; First Sec. (Commercial), Paris, 1985–89; Asst Head, Southern European Dept, FCO, 1989–91; Dep. High Comr, Nairobi, 1991–94; Hd, Southern European Dept, FCO, 1994–97; Ambassador to Côte d'Ivoire, to Niger, Burkina Faso and Liberia, 1997–2001; FCO, 2001–02; Ambassador: to Morocco and Mauritania, 2002–05; to Columbia, 2005–08. Dir, British and Columbian Chamber of Commerce, 2009– (Chm., 2013–). *Recreations:* travel, opera and the arts, food and wine, nature and wildlife. *Club:* Muthaiga (Nairobi).

WARRENDER, family name of **Baron Bruntisfield**.

WARRINGTON, Bishop Suffragan of, since 2009; **Rt Rev. Richard Finn Blackburn;** *b* 22 Jan. 1952; *s* of William Brow Blackburn and Ingeborg Blackburn (*née* Lerche-Thomsen); *m* 1980, Helen Claire Davies; one *s* three *d*. *Educ:* Aysgarth Sch.; Eastbourne Coll.; St John's Coll., Durham Univ. (BA); Hull Univ. (MA); Westcott House, Cambridge. National Westminster Bank, 1976–81; deacon 1983, priest 1984; Curate, St Dunstan and All Saints, Stepney, 1983–87; Priest-in-charge, St John the Baptist, Isleworth, 1987–92; Vicar of Mosborough, 1992–99; RD of Attercliffe, 1996–99; Hon. Canon, 1998–99, Residentiary Canon, 1999–2005, Sheffield Cathedral; Archdeacon of Sheffield and Rotherham (formerly Archdeacon of Sheffield), 1999–2009. Dignitary in Convocation, 2000–05. Mem., C of E Pensions Bd, 2003–09 (Vice Chm., 2006–09); Chair, Churches Regl Commn for Yorks and the Humber, 2005–08. Member, School Council: Worksop Coll., 2000–09; Ranby House Sch., 2000–09. *Recreations:* rowing, walking, gardening, music. *Address:* (office) St James' House, 20 St James Road, Liverpool L1 7BY. *T:* (0151) 705 2140. *E:* bishopofwarrington@liverpool.anglican.org.

WARRINGTON, Archdeacon of; *no new appointment at time of going to press.*

WARRINGTON, Prof. Elizabeth Kerr, FRS 1986; Professor of Clinical Neuropsychology, 1982–96, now Emeritus, and Hon. Consultant, since 1996, National Hospital for Neurology and Neurosurgery; *d* of late Prof. John Alfred Valentine Butler, FRS and Margaret Lois Butler; one *d*. *Educ:* University College London (BSc 1954; PhD 1960; DSc 1975; Fellow 1994). Research Fellow, Inst. of Neurology, 1956; National Hospital: Senior Clinical Psychologist, 1960; Principal Psychologist, 1962; Top Grade Clinical Psychologist, 1972–82. Dr *hc* Psicologia, Bologna, 1998; Univ. Louis Pasteur, Strasbourg, 2006; DUniv York, 1999. *Publications:* (with R. A. McCarthy) Cognitive Neuropsychology, 1990; numerous papers in neurological and psychological jls. *Recreations:* entertaining granddaughters, cruising. *Address:* Dementia Research Centre, Institute of Neurology, Queen Square, WC1N 3BG. *T:* (020) 3448 3291.

WARRY, Peter Thomas, PhD; CEng, FREng, FIET, FIMechE; FCMA; FSA; Chairman: Royal Mint, since 2012; Cobalt Health, since 2014; *b* 31 Aug. 1949; *s* of late William Vivian Warry and Pamela Warry; *m* 1981, Rosemary Furbank; one *d*. *Educ:* Clifton Coll., Bristol; Merton Coll., Oxford (MA; Hon. Fellow, 2007); LLB London Univ.; Reading Univ. (PhD 2005). CEng 1979; FIET (FIEE 1995); FIMechE 1995; FCMA 1983; FREng 2006; CGMA 2012. Man. Dir, Self-Changing Gears Ltd, 1979–82; Gp Man. Dir, Aerospace Engineering plc, 1982–84; Director: Plessey Telecoms, 1986–87; Norcros plc, 1988–94; Nuclear Electric plc, 1995–96; British Energy plc, 1996–98; Chief Exec., Nuclear Electric Ltd, 1996–98. Non-executive Director: Heatherwood & Wexham Park Hosps NHS Trust, 1992–95; PTS Gp plc, 1995–98; Kier Gp plc, 1998–2004 (Chm., 2004–07); Office of the Rail Regulator, 1999–2004; Thames Water Utilities, 2001–05; River and Mercantile Gp plc, 2014–. Chairman: Victrex plc, 1999–2008; BSS Gp plc, 2004–10 (non-exec. Dir, 1999–2003); Morrison Utility Services Gp Ltd, 2008–13; Mutual Energy (formerly Northern Ireland Energy Hldgs) Ltd, 2008–13; Keepmoat Gp (formerly Apollo Gp Hldgs Ltd), 2009–14. Chairman: PPARC, 2001–07; STFC, 2007–09. Special Advr, Prime Minister's Policy Unit, 1984–86; Mem., Deregulation Task Force, DTI, 1993–94; Chm., Econ. Impact Gp (Warry Report), Office of Sci. and Innovation, 2006. Indust. Prof., Warwick Univ., 1993–. Reading University: Mem. Council, 2006–11; Treas., 2009–11; Vis. Res. Fellow in Archaeology, 2011–. Mem. Council, Royal Acad. of Engrg, 2007–10. Trustee, Oxford Archaeology, 2009–. FRSA 2008; FSA 2013. *Publications:* A New Direction for the Post Office, 1991; Tegulae: manufacture, typology and use in Roman Britain, 2006; contribs to Archaeology, Economics and Engineering Jl. *Recreations:* tennis, walking, archeology, history. *E:* peter.warry@merton.oxon.org.

WARSHAW, Justin Alexander Edward; QC 2015; *b* Paddington, 7 Oct. 1970; *s* of Clive Warshaw and Michele Warshaw (*née* Steiner); *m* 2001, Stephanie Marshall; two *d*. *Educ:* Christ Church, Oxford (BA 1992). Called to the Bar, Gray's Inn, 1995; in practice as a barrister, specialising in divorce, 1995–. *Address:* 1 Hare Court, Temple, EC4Y 7BE. *T:* (020) 7797 7070. *Clubs:* MCC; North Hatley (Quebec).

WARSI, Baroness *cr* 2007 (Life Peer), of Dewsbury in the County of West Yorkshire; **Sayeeda Hussain Warsi;** PC 2010; *b* 1971; *m* 1st (marr. diss.); one *d*; 2nd, 2009, Iftikhar Azam. *Educ:* Birkdale High Sch.; Dewsbury Coll.; Leeds Univ. (LLB). Admitted Solicitor, 1996. Chm., Savayra Foundn UK, 2002–. Comr, Joseph Rowntree Charitable Trust Destitution Inquiry, 2007. Vice Chm., 2005–07, Chm., 2010–12, Cons. Party. Contested (C) Dewsbury, 2005. Shadow Minister for Community Cohesion and Social Action, 2007–10; Shadow Minister for Sheffield, 2007–10; Minister of State (Minister without Portfolio), 2010–12; Sen. Minister of State, FCO and DCLG (Minister for Faith and Communities), 2012–14. *Address:* House of Lords, SW1A 0PW.

WARSI, Perween, CBE 2002 (MBE 1997); Managing Director, S&A Foods Ltd, since 1987; *b* 10 Aug. 1956; *m* 1972, Dr Talib Warsi; two *s*. Started S&A Foods from own kitchen, 1986; founded business, 1987; entered partnership with Hughes Foods Gp, 1988; with husband, completed mgt buy-out, 1991; S&A Foods began exporting, 1995; company created 1300 jobs in inner-city Derby, achieved annual growth rate of 40–50%, and has recd 31 awards, 1995– (incl. Gold and Silver Awards, Grocer Food and Drink Awards). Member: Govt Adv. Cttee on Competitiveness, 1997–; Nat. Cttee, CBI, 2004–. Everywoman Ambassador, 2008–. Member: Derby Renaissance Bd, 2010–; Derby Culture Bd, 2011–. Mem., Key Supporter Gp, Women's Aid. Patron, Leics Asian Business Assoc., 2011–. Hon. MBA Derby, 1997; Hon. DBA: Internat. Mgt Centres, 1999; Coventry, 2005; Hon. LLD Nottingham, 2006. Midlands Business Woman of Year Award, 1994; RADAR People of Year Award, 1995; Woman Entrepreneur of World Award, 1996; First Woman Lifetime Achievement Award, 2005. *Address:* S&A Foods Ltd, Sir Francis Ley Industrial Park, 37 Shaftesbury Street South, Derby DE23 8YH. *T:* (01332) 270670, *Fax:* (01332) 270523.

WARTNABY, Dr John; Keeper, Department of Earth and Space Sciences, Science Museum, South Kensington, 1969–82; *b* 6 Jan. 1926; *o s* of Ernest John and Beatrice Hilda Wartnaby; *m* 1962, Kathleen Mary Barber, MD, MRCP, DPM; one *s* one *d*. *Educ:* Chiswick Grammar Sch.; Chelsea Coll. (BSc 1946); Imperial Coll. of Science and Technology (DIC 1950); University Coll., London (MSc 1967; PhD 1972). FInstP 1971; FRAS 2004. Asst Keeper, Dept of Astronomy and Geophysics, Science Museum, 1951; Deputy Keeper, 1960. *Publications:* Seismology, 1957; The International Geophysical Year, 1957; Surveying, 1968; papers in learned jls. *Recreations:* country walking, Zen. *Address:* c/o 22 Priory Road, Cambridge CB5 8HT.

WARWICK; *see* Turner-Warwick.

WARWICK, 9th Earl of, *cr* 1759; **Guy David Greville;** Baron Brooke 1621; Earl Brooke 1746; *b* 30 Jan. 1957; *s* of 8th Earl of Warwick and of Sarah Anne Chester Greville (*née* Beatty; now Mrs Harry Thomson Jones); *S* father, 1996; *m* 1st, 1981, Susan McKinlay Cobbold (marr. diss. 1992); one *s*; 2nd, 1996, Louisa Heenan; one *s*. *Educ:* Summerfields; Eton; Ecole des Roches. *Recreation:* golf. *Heir:* *s* Lord Brooke, *qv*. *Address:* 19 Walter Street, Claremont, WA 6010, Australia. *Club:* White's.

WARWICK OF UNDERCLIFFE, Baroness *cr* 1999 (Life Peer), of Undercliffe in the county of West Yorkshire; **Diana Warwick;** Chairman, Human Tissue Authority, 2010–14; *b* 16 July 1945; *d* of Jack and Olive Warwick; *m* 1969. *Educ:* St Joseph's Coll., Bradford; Bedford Coll., Univ. of London (BA Hons). Technical Asst to the Gen. Sec., NUT, 1969–72; Asst Sec., CPSA, 1972–83; Gen. Sec., AUT, 1983–92; Chief Executive: Westminster Foundn for Democracy, 1992–95; Universities UK (formerly Cttee of Vice Chancellors and Principals), 1995–2009. Member: Bd, Lattice plc, 2000–02; Mgt Bd, USS, 2001–09; Pension Protection Fund, 2011–. Mem., Cttee on Standards in Public Life, 1994–2000. Member: Bd, British Council, 1985–95; Employment Appeal Tribunal, 1987–99; Exec. and Council, Industrial Soc., 1987–2001; TUC Gen. Council, 1989–92; Council, Duke of Edinburgh's Seventh Commonwealth Study Conf., 1991; Chm., VSO, 1994–2003. Gov., Commonwealth Inst., 1988–95. Trustee: Royal Anniversary Trust, 1991–93; St Catharine Foundn, Windsor, 1996–2008. FRSA 1984. Hon. DLitt Bradford, 1993; DUniv Open, 1998; Hon. DSSc Royal Holloway, London, 2006; Hon. DPhil London Metropolitan, 2009; Hon. DEd Brunel, 2010. *Recreations:* theatre, opera, looking at pictures. *Address:* House of Lords, SW1A 0PW.

WARWICK, Bishop Suffragan of, since 2005; **Rt Rev. John Ronald Angus Stroyan;** *b* 5 May 1955; *s* of His Honour Ronald Angus Ropner Stroyan, *qv*; *m* 1990, Mary (*née* Ferguson); two *d*. *Educ:* St Andrews Univ. (MTh 1976); Queen's Coll., Birmingham; Ecumenical Inst., Geneva; MA (Dist.) Univ. of Wales, 2007. Ordained deacon, 1983, priest, 1984; Curate, Coventry E Team, St Peter's, Hillfields, 1983–87; Vicar: St Matthew with St Chad, Smethwick, 1987–94; Bloxham with Milcombe and S Newington, 1994–2005; Area Dean, Deddington, 2002–05. Chm., Coventry Council of Churches, 1986–87. Mem., Rural Bishops' Panel, 2009. Pres., Community of Cross of Nails (UK), 2007–. Mem., Internat. Commn for Anglican Orthodox Theol Dialogue, 2009–. Co-Moderator, Coventry and Warwickshire Churches Together, 2009–12; Co-Chair, Reuilly Contact Gp, 2013–. *Publications:* contribs to Credo in The Times; contribs to jls incl. The Way, Meditation Jl. *Recreations:* theatre, cinema, travel, walking. *Address:* Warwick House, 139 Kenilworth Road, Coventry CV4 7AP. *T:* (024) 7641 2627, *Fax:* (024) 7641 5254. *E:* Bishop.Warwick@CovCofE.org.

WARWICK, Archdeacon of; *see* Rodham, Ven. M.

WARWICK, Dawn Lesley; Director, Education and Social Services, Wandsworth Borough Council; *b* Leeds; *d* of Geoffrey Warwick and June Warwick; *m* 1991, Colin Livingstone; one *s* one *d*. *Educ:* Univ. of Nottingham (BA Hons 1981; MA 1983; CQSW 1983); Kingston Business Sch. (DMS 1991). Social Worker, 1983–86, Sen. Social Worker, 1986–88,

Leicestershire CC; Principal Officer (Mental Health), 1988–91, Sen. Manager, 1991–94, Hounslow LBC; Asst Dir, 1994–97, Dep. Dir, Social Services, Hillingdon LBC, 1997–2001; Dir, Social Services, 2001–07, Dep. Chief Exec., 2005–07, Slough BC; Dir, Adult Social Services, Wandsworth LBC, 2007. Asst Hon. Sec. and Trustee, ADSS, 2003–07; Asst Hon. Sec. and Trustee, 2007–, Co-Chm., Older People's Network, 2008–, ADASS. *Recreations:* gym, theatre, running, horse riding. *Address:* Wandsworth Borough Council, Bridas House, 90 Putney Bridge Road, SW18 1HR. *E:* dwarwick@wandsworth.gov.uk.

WARWICK, Hannah Cambell Grant; *see* Gordon, H. C. G.

WARWICK, Kenneth Scott; economics consultant; Director of Analysis, Department for Business, Innovation and Skills, 2009–11; *b* 23 April 1955; *s* of John Warwick and Mary Orr Warwick (*née* Osborne); *m* 1978, Susan Eileen Finch; one *s* one *d. Educ:* Christ's Coll., Cambridge (BA Hons 1976); Yale Univ. (MPhil 1982). Economist, MAFF, 1976–84; Econ. Advr, FCO, 1984–89; Economist, IMF, 1989–92; Senior Economic Adviser: FCO, 1992–96; DTI, 1996–2003; Dep. Chief Econ. Advr, DTI, then BERR, later BIS, 2003–09; Actg Dir Gen. Econs, BIS, 2010. Mem., Regulatory Policy Cttee, 2012–. *Recreations:* golf, music, family history. *T:* 07823 535316. *E:* kenwarwick@btinternet.com. *Club:* West Byfleet Golf.

WARWICK, Prof. Kevin, PhD; FIET; Deputy Vice-Chancellor (Research), Coventry University, since 2014; *b* 9 Feb. 1954; *s* of Stanley and Jessie Allcock; *née* Kevin Warwick Allcock; adopted Warwick as surname by Deed Poll, 1974; *m* 1st, 1974, Sylvia Margaret Walsh (marr. diss. 1991); one *s* one *d*; 2nd, 1991, Irena Vorackova. *Educ:* Lawrence Sheriff Sch., Rugby; Aston Univ. (BSc); Imperial Coll., London (PhD 1982; DIC 1982); DSc (Eng) London 1993. FIET (FIEE 1987). British Telecom Apprentice, 1970–76; Res. Asst, Imperial Coll., London, 1982; Lectr, Newcastle upon Tyne Univ., 1982–85; Res. Lectr, Oxford Univ., 1985–87; Sen Lectr, Warwick Univ., 1987–88; Prof. of Cybernetics, Univ. of Reading, 1988–2014. FCGI 1992. Presenter, Royal Instn Christmas Lectures, 2000. Hon. Mem., Acad. of Scis, St Petersburg, 1999. DSc Czech Acad. of Scis, 1994; Hon. DSc: Aston, 2008; Coventry, 2008; Bradford, 2010; Bedfordshire, 2012; Portsmouth, 2012; Kingston, 2014; Skopje, 2015; Hon. DTech: Robert Gordon, 2011; Edinburgh Napier, 2015. Future of Health Technol. Award, MIT, 2000; Achievement Award, IEE, 2004; Mountbatten Medal, IET, 2008; Ellison-Cliffe Medal, RSocMed, 2011. *Publications:* (ed jtly) Neural Nets for Control and Systems, 1992; March of the Machines, 1997; In the Mind of the Machine, 1998; QI: The Quest for Intelligence, 2000; I, Cyborg, 2002; Artificial Intelligence: the basics, 2011; contribs to books and jls on control, robotics, machine intelligence and cyborgs. *Recreations:* soccer (Viktoria Zizkov FC supporter), travel, theatre. *Address:* Vice-Chancellor's Office, Coventry University, Priory Street, Coventry CV1 5FB. *T:* (024) 7765 9893.

WARWICK, Mark Granville; QC 2013; *b* London, 11 Dec. 1951; *s* of Roy John Warwick and Marjorie Sylvia Warwick; *m* (marr. diss.); two *d. Educ:* Bexley Grammar Sch.; Univ. of Leeds (LLB Hons). Called to the Bar, Inner Temple, 1974; in private practice as a barrister, specialising in real property, 1975–. *Publications:* (jtly) Warwick and Trompeter on Break Clauses, 2011; contrib. to various legal jls. *Recreations:* foreign travel, running, walking. *Address:* Selborne Chambers, 10 Essex Street, WC2R 3AA. *T:* (020) 7420 9500, *Fax:* (020) 7420 9555. *E:* mark.warwick@selbornechambers.co.uk.

WARWICK THOMPSON, Paul; Rector and Vice-Provost, Royal College of Art, since 2009; *b* 9 Aug. 1959; *s* of Sir Michael Thompson, *qv*; *m* 1984, Adline Finlay; one *s* one *d. Educ:* Bryanston Sch.; Univ. of Bristol (BA Jt Hons); Univ. of East Anglia (MA, PhD). Design Council, 1987–88; Design Museum, 1988–2001, Dir, 1992–2001; Dir, Smithsonian Cooper-Hewitt Nat. Design Mus., NY, 2001–09. Adjunct Prof., Imperial Coll. London, 2014–. Chm., Adv. Bd, Fabrica, Italy, 2012–15. Trustee, V&A Mus., 2009–. Visitor, Ashmolean Mus., 2010–. *Recreations:* theatre, cinema, gardening. *Address:* Royal College of Art, Kensington Gore, SW7 2EU.

WASHINGTON, Denzel; actor; *b* Mt Vernon, NY, 28 Dec. 1954; *s* of late Denzel Washington and of Lennis Washington; *m* 1983, Pauletta Pearson; two *s* two *d* (incl. twin *s* and *d*). *Educ:* Oakland Acad., New Windsor, NY; Fordham Univ. (BA 1977). American Conservatory Theater, San Francisco. *Theatre includes:* Coriolanus, 1979; Spell No 7; The Mighty Gents; One Tiger to a Hill; Ceremonies in Dark Old Men; When the Chickens Come Home to Roost, 1981; A Soldier's Play, 1981; Checkmates, 1988; Split Second; Richard III, 1990; Fences (Tony Award), 2010; A Raisin in the Sun, 2014; *films include:* Carbon Copy, 1981; A Soldier's Story, 1984; Power, 1986; Cry Freedom, 1987; For Queen and Country, The Mighty Quinn, Glory (Best Supporting Actor, Acad. Awards, 1990), 1989; Heart Condition, Love Supreme, Mo' Better Blues, 1990; Ricochet, 1991; Mississippi Masala, Malcolm X, 1992; Much Ado About Nothing, 1993; The Pelican Brief, Philadelphia, 1994; Crimson Tide, Virtuosity, Devil in a Blue Dress, 1995; Courage Under Fire, 1996; The Preacher's Wife, 1997; Fallen, He Got Game, 1998; The Siege, 1999; The Bone Collector, The Hurricane (Best Actor, Golden Globe Awards), 2000; Remember the Titans, 2001; Training Day (Best Actor, Acad. Awards), 2002; The Manchurian Candidate, Man on Fire, 2004; Inside Man, Déjà Vu, 2006; American Gangster, 2007; The Taking of Pelham 123, 2009; The Book of Eli, Unstoppable, 2010; Safe House, 2012; Flight, 2 Guns, 2013; The Equalizer, 2014; *director:* Antwone Fisher, 2002; *television includes:* Wilma, 1977; Flesh and Blood, 1979; St Elsewhere (series), 1982–88; License to Kill, 1984; The George McKenna Story, 1986.

WASHINGTON, Neville James Cameron, OBE 1992; Founder and Director, Washington Consulting, since 2010; *b* 8 May 1948; *s* of Peter Washington and Sybil Joan Washington (*née* Cameron); *m* 1980, Jennifer Anne Frideswide Kekewich; two *s* one *d. Educ:* Marlborough Coll.; Trinity Hall, Cambridge (MA). Research on chimpanzee behaviour, Gombe, Tanzania, 1969–70. Joined Queen's Own Highlanders (Seaforth & Camerons), 1971; Army Staff Coll., Camberley, 1982; jsdc 1987; comd 3rd Bn, UDR, 1987–89 (despatches); left Army in rank of Lieut-Col, 1992. Dir of Human Resources, Victoria Infirmary, Glasgow, 1992–94; Chief Exec., Coal Authy, 1994–97; Partner, Odgers Ray & Berndtson, 1998–2006; Dir, Harvey Nash Scotland, 2006–10. *Recreations:* sheep, sailing. *Address:* Rottenrow, Crosshands, by Mauchline, Ayrshire KA5 5TN.

WASINONDH, Kitti; Ambassador of Thailand to the Court of St James's, 2007–12; *b* 23 Nov. 1951; *m* Nutchanart; one *d. Educ:* Chulalongkorn Univ., Bangkok (Bachelor Pol Sci. 1974); Nat. Inst. Develt Admin, Bangkok (Master Develt Admin 1976); Univ. of Oxford (Cert. Diplomatic Studies 1981). Consul-Gen. of Thailand in Sydney, 2000–02; Director-General: Dept of ASEAN Affairs, 2003–06; Dept of Information, and Spokesman of Min. of Foreign Affairs, 2006–07. *Recreation:* golf.

WASS, Sir Douglas (William Gretton), GCB 1980 (KCB 1975; CB 1971); Senior Adviser, Nomura International plc, 1998–2002 (Chairman, 1986–98); Permanent Secretary to HM Treasury, 1974–83, and Joint Head of the Home Civil Service, 1981–83; *b* 15 April 1923; *s* of late Arthur W. and late Elsie W. Wass; *m* 1954, Dr Milica Pavičić; one *s* one *d. Educ:* Nottingham High Sch.; St John's Coll., Cambridge (MA; Hon. Fellow, 1982). Served War, 1943–46: Scientific Research with Admiralty, at home and in Far East. Entered HM Treasury as Asst Principal, 1946; Principal, 1951; Commonwealth Fund Fellow in USA, 1958–59; Vis. Fellow, Brookings Instn, Washington, DC, 1959; Private Sec.: to Chancellor of the Exchequer, 1959–61; to Chief Sec. to Treasury, 1961–62; Asst Sec., 1962; Alternate Exec. Dir, Internat. Monetary Fund, and Financial Counsellor, British Embassy, Washington, DC, 1965–67; HM Treasury: Under-Sec., 1968; Dep. Sec., 1970–73; Second Permanent Sec., 1973–74. Chairman: Equity & Law, subseq. Axa Equity & Law, Life Assurance Soc., 1986–95 (Dir, 1984–95); NCM (Credit Insce), 1991–95; Director: Barclays Bank, 1984–87; De La Rue Company plc, 1984–93; Equitable Cos Inc., 1992–95; Equitable Life Assurance Soc., USA, 1992–93; NCM (NV), Amsterdam, 1992–95; Soho Theatre Co., 1996–2000. Administrateur, Axa SA (formerly Cie du Midi), 1987–95; Consultant to Coopers & Lybrand, 1984–86. Chairman: British Selection Cttee of Harkness Fellowships, 1981–84; UN Adv. Gp on Financial Flows for Africa, 1987–88; SIB Adv. Cttee on Pension Transfers, 1993–94; Syndicate on the Government of Univ. of Cambridge, 1988–89. Pres., Market Res. Soc., 1987–91. Dep. Chm., Council of Policy Studies Inst., 1981–85; Vice-Pres., 1984–91, and Mem. Adv. Bd, Constitutional Reform Centre; Vice Chm., Africa Capacity Building Foundn, 1991–98; Governor, Ditchley Foundn, 1981–2000; Member, Council: Centre for Econ. Policy Res., 1983–90; Employment Inst., 1985–92; Univ. of Bath, 1985–91; British Heart Foundn, 1990–96; ODI, 1991–98. Lectures: Reith, BBC, 1983; Shell, St Andrews Univ., 1985; Harry Street Meml, Univ. of Manchester, 1987. Hon. DLitt Bath, 1985. *Publications:* Government and the Governed, 1984; Decline to Fall: the making of British macro-economic policy and the 1976 IMF crisis, 2008; articles in newspapers and jls. *Address:* 6 Dora Road, SW19 7HH. *Club:* Reform.

See also S. Wass.

WASS, Prof. John Andrew Hall, MD; FRCP; Professor of Endocrinology, University of Oxford, since 1998; Fellow of Green Templeton College (formerly Green College), Oxford, 1995–2011, now Emeritus; Consultant Physician, Department of Endocrinology, Churchill Hospital, Oxford, since 1995; *b* 14 Aug. 1947; *s* of Samuel Hall Wass and June Mary Vaudine Wass (*née* Blaikie); *m* 1st, 1970, Valerie Vincent (marr. diss. 1997); one *s* one *d*; 2nd, 1998, Sally Smith. *Educ:* Rugby; Guy's Hosp. Med. Sch., Univ. of London (MB BS 1971; MD 1980). FRCP 1986. Sub-Dean, Med. Coll. and Prof. of Clin. Endocrinol., St Bartholomew's Hosp., London, 1989–95. Admissions Tutor, Green Coll., Oxford, 2001–03. Advr, Cancer Bacup, 1985–. Ed., Clin. Endocrinol. Jl, 1991–94. Linacre Fellow, 1994–98, Academic Vice-Pres., 2012–15, RCP. Chm., Soc. for Endocrinol., 2005–09; President: Eur. Fedn of Endocrine Socs, 2001–03; Pituitary Soc. (NY), 2006–07. Co-founder, Pituitary Foundn, 1994. Gov., Purcell Sch., 2000–12. Chm., Bart's Choral Soc., 1992–95. Dist. Physician Award, Amer. Endocrine Soc., 2012. *Publications:* (jtly) Clinical Endocrine Oncology, 1997, 2nd edn 2008; Oxford Textbook of Endocrinology, 2002, 2nd edn 2011; Oxford Handbook of Endocrinology, 2002, 3rd edn 2014; articles and chapters on acromegaly, pituitary tumours and osteoporosis. *Recreations:* music, theatre, wine, Scotland. *Address:* Department of Endocrinology, Churchill Hospital, Oxford OX3 7LJ. *T:* (01844) 358031. *E:* john.wass@nhs.net. *Club:* Garrick.

WASS, Sasha, (Mrs N. R. A. Hall); QC 2000; a Recorder, since 2000; *b* 19 Feb. 1958; *d* of Sir Douglas William Gretton Wass, *qv*; *m* 1986, Nigel R. A. Hall; one *s* one *d. Educ:* Wimbledon High Sch.; Liverpool Univ. (LLB Hons). Called to the Bar: Gray's Inn, 1981, Bencher, 2003; Gibraltar, 2008; Cayman Is, 2012; Asst Recorder, 1997–2000. Criminal Bar Association: Mem. Cttee, 1992–; Treas., 1997–99; Dir of Educn, 2002. *Address:* 21 College Hill, EC4R 2RP. *T:* (020) 3301 0910.

WASSALL, Philip Hugh; His Honour Judge Wassall; a Circuit Judge, since 2004; *b* 11 March 1950; *s* of late Derek William Wassall and Avril Mary Holden Wassall; *m* 1991, Julia Lesley; two *d. Educ:* Aldridge Grammar Sch.; Chelmsford Coll. (LLB Hons ext. London). Criminal Law Clerk, 1969–75; Articled Clerk, 1976–78; Solicitor, 1979–94; a District Judge (Magistrates' Courts) (formerly Provincial Stipendiary Magistrate, Devonshire), 1994–2004; a Recorder, 2000–04. *Recreations:* golf, music, fishing, food technology, managing teenagers, keeping fit. *Address:* Exeter Combined Court, Southerhay Gardens, Exeter EX1 1UH. *T:* (01392) 415300.

WASSERMAN, family name of **Baron Wasserman.**

WASSERMAN, Baron *cr* 2011 (Life Peer), of Pimlico in the City of Westminster; **Gordon Joshua Wasserman;** consultant, since 1995; Joint Founder and Chairman, Yes Please Foods GmbH, since 2006; Founding Chairman, Cahoot Justice Systems Ltd, since 2014; *b* Montreal, 26 July 1938; *s* of late John J. Wasserman, QC, and Prof. Rachael Chait Wasserman, Montreal; *m* 1964, Cressida Frances (separated 2006), *yr d* of late Rt Hon. Hugh Gaitskell, PC, CBE, MP, and Baroness Gaitskell; two *d. Educ:* Westmount High Sch., Montreal; McGill Univ. (BA); New Coll., Oxford (MA). Rhodes Scholar (Quebec and New Coll.), 1959; Sen. Research Scholar, St Antony's Coll., Oxford, 1961–64; Lectr in Economics, Merton Coll., Oxford, 1963–64; Research Fellow, New Coll., Oxford, 1964–67; joined Home Office as Economic Adviser, 1967, Sen. Econ. Adviser, 1972, Asst Sec., 1977–81; Head, Urban Deprivation Unit, 1973–77; Civil Service Travelling Fellowship in USA, 1977–78; Under Sec., Central Policy Review Staff, Cabinet Office, 1981–83; Asst Under Sec. of State, Home Office (Head, Police Science and Technology Gp), 1983–95; Special Advr (Sci. and Technol.) to Police Comr, NY Police Dept, 1996–98; COS, 1998–2002, Special Advr to Police Comr, Philadelphia Police Dept, 1998–2003; Advr to HM Govt on Policing and Criminal Justice, 2010–12. Founder and Chm., Public Safety Forum, 2013–. Mem., US Justice Dept Adv. Panel on Sci. and Technol., 1996–2003; Chm., Rev., US Justice Dept Rev. of R&D post-11/11, 2005. Mem. Bd, Centre for Justice Innovation, 2013–. Chm., Ion Track Inc., 2000–02; Chm. and CEO, Gordon Wasserman Gp LLC, 2003–. Vice Chm., All Party Parly Gp on Basketball, 2014–. Member: Exec., ELITE Gp, 1993–96; Bd, SEARCH Gp Inc., USA, 1994–2000, 2004–07; Bd, Orchid Cellmark Inc., 2004–06. Trustee, McGill Univ. (Canada) Trust, 1995–96. Fellow, Koret Inst., USA, 1996–98. Vice-Pres., English Basket Ball Assoc., 1983–86; Pres., Inst. for Public Safety, Crime and Justice, Univ. of Northampton, 2014–. *Recreations:* listening to music, reading. *Address:* House of Lords, SW1A 0PW. *Clubs:* Reform, Beefsteak.

WATANABE-O'KELLY, Prof. Helen, FBA 2012; Professor of German, University of Oxford, since 1989; Fellow, Exeter College, Oxford, 1989–2013, now Emeritus; *b* Cork, Ireland, 2 June 1948; *d* of Michael J. O'Kelly and Claire O'Kelly (*née* O'Donovan); *m* 1st, 1975, Toshio Watanabe (marr. diss. 2003); two *d*; 2nd, 2004, Ekkehard Henschke. *Educ:* Ursuline Convent, Blackrock, Cork; University Coll., Cork (BA 1969, MA 1971, Nat. Univ. of Ireland); Univ. of Basel (Dr phil 1976). Lectr in German, Univ. of Reading, 1974–89. Founder and first Chair, Women in German Studies, 1988; Chair, RAE panel for German, Scandinavian and Dutch, 2005–08; Mem., Specialist Panel, German Excellence Initiative, 2007–13. Mem., Scientific Commn, Einstein Foundn, Berlin, 2009–. *Publications:* Melancholie und die melancholische Landschaft: Ein Beitrag zur Geistesgeschichte des 17. Jahrhunderts, 1978; Triumphal Shews: tournaments at German-speaking courts in their European context 1560–1730, 1992; The Cambridge History of German Literature, 1997; (ed with Pierre Béhar) Spectaculum Europaeum: theatre and spectacle in Europe, Histoire du Spectacle en Europe, 1580–1750, 1999; (with Anne Simon) Festivals and Ceremonies: a bibliography of works relating to court, civic and religious festivals in Europe 1500–1800, 2000; Court Culture in Dresden from Renaissance to Baroque, 2002; (jtly) Europa Triumphans: court and civic festivals in early modern Europe, 2004; (with Sarah Colvin) Women and Death: warlike women in the German literary and cultural imagination since 1500, 2009; Beauty or Beast?: the woman warrior in the German imagination from the Renaissance to the present, 2010. *Recreations:* theatre, opera, cinema, music, walking the streets of Berlin. *Address:* Faculty of Modern Languages, 47 Wellington Square, Oxford OX1 2JF. *E:* helen.watanabe@mod-langs.ox.ac.uk.

WATERFALL, Air Vice-Marshal Gary Martin, CBE 2012 (OBE 2008); Air Officer Commanding Number 1 Group, Royal Air Force, since 2014; *b* RAF Wegberg, Germany, 7 Jan. 1967; *s* of Eric Sydney Waterfall and Elizabeth Pamela Waterfall (*née* Rogers); *m* 1992, Yvonne Elisabeth Appleby; one *s* one *d*. *Educ:* King's Sch., Grantham. Harrier pilot, 3 (Fighter) Sqdn, 1990–94; Instructor and display pilot, Harrier OCU, 1994–96; pilot, RAF Aerobatic Team (Red Arrows), 1997–99; Harrier pilot, 1 (Fighter) Sqdn, 2000–01; OC 41 Operational Evaluation Sqdn, 2004–07; delegated release to Service Authy, 2007–09; Stn Comdr, RAF Cottesmore, 2009–11; Comdr, UK Air Component, Op. Ellamy, 2011; Air Officer, Combat, ISTAR Gp, 2012; Typhoon Force Comdr, 2013–14. *Recreations:* cycling, private flying, travel. *Address:* Headquarters No 1 Group, Hurricane Block, RAF High Wycombe, Bucks HP14 4UE. *T:* (01494) 496902. *E:* H2ofal@hotmail.co.uk. *Club:* Royal Air Force.

WATERFALL, Simon, RDI 2008; Vice President and Creative Director, OnCue, since 2014; *b* Portsmouth, 1971; *s* of John and Jenny Waterfall. *Educ:* Brunel Univ. (BSc Hons); Royal Coll. of Art (MA). Co-Founder, Deepend Design, 1995–2001; Creative Director: Poke, London, 2001–09; Fray, 2010–12; Vice Pres. and Creative Dir, Intel Media, USA, 2012–14. Pres., D&AD, 2007–08. Award for Interactive Design, BAFTA, 2006. *Club:* Shoreditch House.

WATERFIELD, Giles Adrian, FSA, FRHistS; writer and curator; *b* 24 July 1949; *s* of late Anthony and Honor Waterfield. *Educ:* Eton College; Magdalen College, Oxford (BA); Courtauld Institute (MA). FSA 1991; FRHistS 2013. Education Officer, Royal Pavilion, Art Gallery and Museums, Brighton, 1976–79; Dir, Dulwich Picture Gall., 1979–96; Jt Dir, Attingham Summer Sch., 1995–2003; Dir, Royal Collection Studies, 1995–. Consultant Curator, Compton Verney, 1996–98. Heritage Advr, Esmée Fairbairn Foundn, 2002–07; Associate Lectr, Courtauld Inst. of Art, 2002–; Schol., Getty Res. Inst., 2011, 2012. Mem., Museums Expert Panel, 1996–2000, Trustee, 2000–06, Heritage Lottery Fund. Mem. Exec. Cttee, London Library, 1997–2001; Mem. Adv. Cttee, Paul Mellon Centre for British Art; Mem., Arts Panel, Nat. Trust, 2006–14. Vice-Pres., NADFAS, 1998–2006. Judge, Mus. of the Year Awards, Nat. Heritage, 1999–2003; Chm. Judges, Art Book Prize, 2008–14. Trustee: Holburne Mus., Bath, 1999–2003; Edward James Foundn, 1999–2003; Charleston Trust, 2005–13 (Chm., 2006–10); Garden Mus., London, 2012–; Emery Walker Trust, 2014–. Paul Mellon Lectr, London and Yale, 2007. *Publications:* Faces, 1983; (ed) Collection for a King (catalogue), 1985; Soane and After, 1987; Rich Summer of Art, 1988; (ed) Palaces of Art, 1991; (ed) Art for the People, 1994; (ed) Soane and Death, 1996; (contrib.) Art Treasures of England (catalogue), 1998; (contrib.) In Celebration: the art of the country house (catalogue), 1998; (ed jtly) Below Stairs (catalogue), 2003; (ed) Opening Doors: learning and the historic environment, 2004; The Artist's Studio (catalogue), 2009; The People's Galleries: art museums and exhibitions in Britain 1800–1914, 2015; *novels:* The Long Afternoon, 2000 (McKittrick Prize, 2001); Hound in the Left Hand Corner, 2002; Markham Thorpe, 2006; The Iron Necklace, 2015; articles in Apollo, Art Newspaper, Burlington Magazine, Connoisseur, Country Life, London Review, TLS. *Recreations:* sightseeing, theatre. *Address:* 48 Claylands Road, SW8 1NZ.

WATERFIELD, Prof. Michael Derek, PhD; FRCPath, FMedSci; FRS 1991; Courtauld Professor of Biochemistry, 1991–2006, now Emeritus Professor of Biochemistry and Molecular Biology, and Director of Proteomics Unit, Ludwig Institute for Cancer Research, 2004–07, University College London; *b* 14 May 1941; *s* of Leslie N. Waterfield and Kathleen A. (*née* Marshall); *m* 1982, Sally E. James, MB BS, PhD; two *d*. *Educ:* Brunel Univ. (BSc 1963); Univ. of London (PhD 1967). FRCPath 1994. Res. Fellow, Harvard Univ. Med. Sch., 1967–70; Sen. Res. Fellow, CIT, 1970–72; Hd, Protein Chem. Lab., ICRF Labs, 1972–86; Dir of Research, Ludwig Inst. for Cancer Res., UCL, 1986–2007; Head, Dept of Biochem. and Molecular Biology, UCL, 1991–2001. Founder and Dir, Piramed, 2003–08. Founder FMedSci 1998. Hon. MD Ferrara, Italy, 1991. *Publications:* numerous articles in scientific jls on biochem. and molecular biol. as applied to cancer research. *Recreations:* pottering about the garden and kitchen, and walking hills and dales. *Address:* Chantemerle, Speen Lane, Newbury, Berks RG14 1RJ.

WATERFORD, 9th Marquess of, *cr* 1789; **Henry Nicholas de la Poer Beresford;** Baron La Poer, 1375; Bt, 1668; Viscount Tyrone, Baron Beresford, 1720; Earl of Tyrone, 1746; Baron Tyrone (Great Britain), 1786; *b* 23 March 1958; *e s* of 8th Marquess of Waterford and Lady Caroline Wyndham-Quin, *yr d* of 6th Earl of Dunraven and Mount-Earl, CB, CBE, MC; *S* father, 2015; *m* 1986, Amanda, *d* of Norman Thompson; two *s* one *d*. *Educ:* Harrow School. *Heir: s* Earl of Tyrone, *qv*.

WATERHOUSE, David Martin; Regional Director for South Asia and Pacific, British Council, 1994–97; *b* 23 July 1937; *s* of Rev. John W. Waterhouse and Dr Esther Waterhouse; *m* 1966, Verena Johnson; one *s* two *d*. *Educ:* Kingswood Sch., Bath; Merton Coll., Oxford (MA). Joined British Council, 1961; Enugu, Nigeria, 1962–65; Glasgow, 1965–68; Ndola, Zambia, 1968–71; Inst. of Educn, London Univ., 1971–72; Representative: Nepal, 1972–77; Thailand, 1977–80; Dir, Personnel Management Dept, 1980–85; Rep., Nigeria, 1985–89; Controller, Home Div., subseq. Dir, Exchanges and Training Div., British Council, 1989–91; Dir, Germany, 1991–93. Chairman: Hoffman de Visme Foundn, 1998–2002; Charles Wallace Pakistan Trust, 2007–12; Friends of Shrewsbury Mus. and Art Gall., 2007–. Vice-Pres., Royal Asiatic Soc., 2003–06. *Publications:* The Origins of Himalayan Studies: Brian Houghton Hodgson in Kathmandu and Darjeeling 1820–1858, 2004. *Recreations:* walking, music. *Address:* Courtyard Cottage, Council House Court, Shrewsbury SY1 2AU.

WATERHOUSE, Frederick Harry; systems consultant and advisor, since 1995; *b* 3 June 1932; *m* 1954, Olive Carter; two *d*. *Educ:* King Edward's, Aston, Birmingham; London Univ. (BScEcon). Associate Mem., CIMA. Chief Accountant, Copper Div., Imperial Metal Industries, 1967–70; Asst Chief Accountant, Agricl Div., ICI, 1970–72; Chief Accountant, Plant Protection Div., ICI, 1972–78; Dir, Société pour la Protection d'Agriculture (SOPRA), France, 1976–78; Dir, Solplant SA, Italy, 1976–78; Bd Member, Finance and Corporate Planning, The Post Office, 1978–79; Treasurer's Dept, ICI Ltd, Millbank, 1980–82. Partner, Bognor Antiques, 1984–87; Chief Accountant, Jelkeep Ltd, Deerhyde Ltd and Thawscroft Ltd, Selsey, 1988–94. *Recreations:* reading, gardening. *Address:* Pendennis, Fishers, St Lawrence, Ventnor, Isle of Wight PO38 1UU.

WATERHOUSE, Dame Rachel (Elizabeth), DBE 1990 (CBE 1980); PhD; Chairman, Consumers' Association, 1982–90 (Member Council, 1966–96, Deputy Chairman, 1979–82); *b* 2 Jan. 1923; *d* of Percival John Franklin and Ruby Susanna Franklin; *m* 1947, John A. H. Waterhouse; two *s* two *d*. *Educ:* King Edward's High Sch., Birmingham; St Hugh's Coll., Oxford (BA 1944, MA 1948); Univ. of Birmingham (PhD 1950). WEA and Extra-mural tutor, 1944–47. Birmingham Consumer Group: Sec., 1964–65, Chm., 1966–68, Mem. Cttee, 1968–2005; Member: Nat. Consumer Council, 1975–86; Consumers' Consultative Cttee of EEC Commn, 1977–84; Price Commn, 1977–79; Council, Advertising Standards Authority, 1980–85; NEDC, 1981–91; BBC Consultative Gp on Industrial and Business Affairs, 1984–89; Richmond Cttee on Microbiol Safety of Food, 1989–90; HSC, 1990–95; Adv. Cttee on Microbiological Safety of Food, 1991–95. Ministerial nominee to Potato Marketing Bd, 1969–81; Chm., Council for Licensed Conveyancers, 1986–89; Member: Home Office Working Party on Internal Shop Security, 1971–73; Adv. Cttee on Asbestos, 1976–79; Council for the Securities Industry, 1983–85; Securities and Investments Board, 1985–92; Organising Cttee, Marketing of Investments Bd, 1985–86; Council, Office of the Banking Ombudsman, 1985–95; Duke of Edinburgh's Inquiry into British Housing, 1984–85; Adv. Bd, Inst. of Food Res., 1988–93. Pres., Inst. of Consumer Ergonomics, Univ. of Loughborough, 1980–90 (Chm., 1970–80); Vice-President: Nat. Fedn of Consumer Gps, 1980–96; Birmingham Centre for Business Ethics, 1999–2005; Member: Council, Birmingham and Midland Inst., 1993 (Pres., 1992); Court of Govs, Univ. of Birmingham, 1992–2012; Provost, Selly Oak Colls, 1997–2000. Chm., Birmingham Gp, Victorian Soc., 1966–67, 1972–74; Vice-Chm., Lunar Soc., 1996–98 (Chm., 1990–96). Trustee: Joseph Rowntree Foundn, 1990–98; Affirming Catholicism, 1991–2001; Gov., Foundn of Lady Katherine Leveson, 2001–04. Hon. FGIA (Hon. CGIA 1988). Hon. DLitt Univ. of Technology, Loughborough, 1978; Hon. DSocSc Birmingham, 1990; Hon. DSc Aston, 1998. *Publications:* The Birmingham and Midland Institute 1854–1954, 1954; A Hundred Years of Engineering Craftsmanship, 1957; Children in Hospital: a hundred years of child care in Birmingham, 1962; (with John Whybrow) How Birmingham became a Great City, 1976; King Edward VI High School for Girls 1883–1983, 1983. *Address:* 8 Prestbury Court, Castle Rise, Prestbury, Macclesfield SK10 4UR.

WATERHOUSE, Roger William; Vice-Chancellor, University of Derby, 1992–2004; *b* 29 April 1940; *s* of Ronald Waterhouse and Dorthy May Waterhouse (*née* Holmes); *m* 1st, 1962, Mania Jevinsky (marr. diss.); one *s* two *d*; 2nd, 1979, Jacqueline Mary Dymond; one *s* one *d*. *Educ:* Corpus Christi Coll., Oxford (BA, MA Phil. & Psychol.). Lectr, Shoreditch Coll., 1961–62; Teacher, Kibbutz Ma'abarot, Israel, 1962–64; Hd of Econs, Myers Grove Comprehensive Sch., Sheffield, 1966–68; Asst Lectr, Lectr, Sen. Lectr and Principal Lectr, Hendon Coll. of Technol., 1968–73; Hd, Dept of Humanities and Dean of Humanities, Middx Poly., 1973–86; Dep. Dir (Acad. Planning), Wolverhampton Poly., 1986–89; Dir, Derbys Coll. of Higher Educn, 1989–92. Chairman: Derbyshire Careers Service Ltd, 1995–2001; High Peak Rural Action Zone, 2003–05. Mem., Peak Dist Artisans, 2014–. FRSA 1993. DUniv: Middlesex, 1998; Derby 2006. Name inscribed in Keren Hakayemet (Jewish Nat. Fund) Golden Book, 2004. *Publications:* A Heidegger Critique, 1981; jl articles on modern European philosophy, higher educn, credit accumulation and transfer. *Recreation:* wood-turning.

WATERLOW, Sir Christopher Rupert, 5th Bt *cr* 1873; Camera Supervisor, QVC, since 2014 (Senior Lighting Cameraman, 2000–14); *b* 12 Aug. 1959; *s* of (Peter) Rupert Waterlow (*d* 1969) and Jill Elizabeth (*d* 1961), *e d* of E. T. Gourlay; *S* grandfather, 1973; *m* 2009, Shirley Patricia, *o d* of late Robert Anderson and of Irene Anderson, Crawley. *Educ:* Stonyhurst Coll., Lancs; Ravensbourne Coll. (HND Broadcast Technical Ops, 1999). Fellow, Inst. of Videography, 2001; Mem., Guild of Television Cameramen, 2005. Mem., Standing Council of the Baronetage. *Publications:* VideoSkills: the core competencies of videography, 2008, 3rd edn 2011; The House of Waterlow: a printer's tale, 2013. *Recreations:* playing and listening to music, supporting Wasps RFC and San Francisco 49ers. *Address:* 59 Sissinghurst Close, Pound Hill, Crawley, W Sussex RH10 7FY. *Club:* Stonyhurst Association.

WATERLOW, Sir (Thomas) James, 5th Bt *cr* 1930, of Harrow Weald, Middlesex; *b* 20 March 1970; *o s* of Sir (James) Gerard Waterlow, 4th Bt and of Diana Suzanne Waterlow (*née* Skyrme); *S* father 2013; *m* 1999, Theresa Walsh; two *d*. *Heir: uncle* John William Waterlow [*b* 14 Nov. 1945; *m* 1972, Camilla Dudley Farmer; two *s*].

WATERMAN, Adrian Mark; QC 2006; a Recorder, since 2003; *b* 24 March 1964; *s* of Brian and Pamela Waterman; *m* 1992, Dr Amanda Jones; one *s* one *d*. *Educ:* King Edward VI Sch., Stourbridge; QMC, Univ. of London (LLB Hons). Called to the Bar, Inner Temple, 1988. *Recreations:* music, movies, reading, cycling. *Address:* c/o KBW Chambers, The Engine House, 1 Foundry Square, Leeds LS11 5DL.

WATERMAN, Dame Fanny, DBE 2005 (CBE 2000; OBE 1971); FRCM; Chairman, Leeds International Pianoforte Competition, since 1963, also Chairman of Jury, since 1981; *b* 22 March 1920; *d* of Myer Waterman and Mary Waterman (*née* Behrmann); *m* 1944, Dr Geoffrey Michael de Keyser (*d* 2001); two *s*. *Educ:* Allerton High Sch., Leeds; Tobias Matthay, Cyril Smith, Royal College of Music, London (FRCM 1972). Concert pianist, teacher of international reputation. Vice-President: European Piano-Teachers Assoc., 1975–; World Fedn of Internat. Music Competitions, 1992–2000; Trustee, Edward Boyle Meml Trust, 1981–96. Governor, Harrogate Fest., 1983–99; Vice-Pres., Harrogate Internat. Fest., 1999–. Founded (with Marion Harewood) Leeds International Pianoforte Competition, 1961. Member of International Juries: Beethoven, Vienna, 1977, 1993; Casagrande, Terni, 1978, 1994; Munich, 1979, 1986; Bach, Leipzig, 1980, 1984, 1988; Calgary, 1982; Gina Bachauer, Salt Lake City, 1982, 1984; Viña del Mar (Chm.), 1982, 1987, 1992; Maryland, 1983; Cologne, 1983, 1986, 1989, 1996; Pretoria, 1984, 1992; Santander, 1984; Rubinstein, Israel (Vice-Pres.), 1986, 1989; Tchaikowsky, Moscow, 1986; Vladigerov, Bulgaria, 1986; Lisbon, 1987, 1991; Canadian Broadcasting Corp., Toronto, 1989; first Internat. Pianoforte Competitions, China, 1994, and Korea, 1995; Casagrande, Italy, 2002; Hong Kong (Asia) Piano Open Comp., 2005 (Chm.); Clara Haskil Comp., 2005; International Piano Competitions: Horowitz, 2005; Chopin, 2005; Dublin, 2006; Hamamatsu, 2006. Piano Progress series on ITV Channel 4. Hon. MA 1966, Hon. DMus 1992, Leeds; DUniv York, 1995. Hon. Freeman, City of Leeds, 2004. Dist. Musician Award, ISM, 2000; World Fedn of Internat. Comps Lifetime Achievement Award, 2002; Yorks Soc. Lifetime Achievement Award, 2003. *Publications:* (with Marion Harewood): series of Piano Tutors, 1967–: 1st Year Piano lessons: 1st Year Repertoire; 2nd Year Piano lessons: 2nd Year Repertoire; 3rd Year Piano lessons: 3rd Year Repertoire; Duets and Piano Playtime, 1978; Recital Book for pianists, Book 1, 1981; Sonatina and Sonata Book, 1982; Four Study Books for Piano (Playtime Studies and Progress Studies), 1986; (with Paul de Keyser) Young Violinists Repertoire books, 1–4; Fanny Waterman on Piano Playing and Performing, 1983; Music Lovers Diary, 1984–86; Merry Christmas Carols, 1986; Christmas Carol Time, 1986; Nursery Rhyme Time, 1987; Piano for Pleasure, Bks 1 and 2, 1988; Me and my Piano series, Book 1, 1988, Book 2, 1989, repertoire and duets, Books 1 and 2, 1992, superscales for the young pianist, 1995; Animal Magic, 1989; Monkey Puzzles, Books 1 and 2, 1990; (with Wendy Thompson) Piano Competition: the story of the Leeds, 1990; Young Pianist's Dictionary, 1992. *Recreations:* travel, reading, voluntary work, cooking. *Address:* Woodgarth, Oakwood Grove, Leeds LS8 2PA. *T:* (0113) 265 5771.

WATERMAN, Peter Alan, OBE 2005; DL; record producer; Chairman, Peter Waterman Entertainment Ltd (formerly PWL Empire), since 1983; *b* 15 Jan. 1947; *s* of John Waterman and Stella Waterman; *m* 1st, 1970, Elizabeth Reynolds (marr. diss. 1974; she *d* 2010); (one *s* decd); 2nd, 1980, Julie Reeves (marr. diss. 1984); one *s*; 3rd, 1991, Denise Gyngell (marr. diss. 2000); two *d*. *Educ:* Frederick Bird Secondary Sch. Disc jockey at local pubs and Mecca dance hall, 1961–83; arts and repertoire man for various record cos, 1973–; formed Loose Ends Prodns with Peter Collins, 1977–83; Founder Partner with M. Stock and M. Aitken, Stock Aitken Waterman, 1984–93. Judge, TV series, Pop Idol, 2000, 2003. Has produced numerous charity records. Waterman Railway Trust formed 1994. DL Cheshire, 2010. Hon. DBA Coventry, 2001; Hon. DMus Liverpool, 2004. Awards for songwriting and for records produced include: BPI Best British Producer Award, 1988; Music Week Top Producers Award, 1987, 1988 and 1989; Ivor Novello Award, 1987, 1988 and 1989. *Publications:* I Wish I Was Me: Pete Waterman (autobiog.), 2000; A Train is for Life, 2008; Just Like the Real Thing: modelling railways, 2009; Fame Factor, 2009. *Recreation:* railways: models and the real thing. *Address:* (office) Suite 5, 6 The Vineyard, SE1 1QL.

WATEROUS, Johanna Elizabeth Martin, CBE 2013; Senior Independent Director: RSA plc, since 2014 (Independent Director, since 2009); Rexam plc, since 2012; Chairman, Sandpiper CI, since 2010; *b* Brantford, Ont, 12 Sept. 1957; *d* of Richard Norman Haan

Waterous and Joan Martin Waterous; *m* 1990, Roger George Parry, *qv*; one *s*. *Educ:* Brantford Collegiate Inst.; Univ. of Western Ontario (BSc Hons Chem. and Maths 1979); Harvard Business Sch. (MBA 1985). Intelligence analyst, Royal Canadian Signal Corps, 1977–79; Res. Chemist, Dow Chemical Canada, 1979–83; Dir, Retail and Consumer Mktg Practice, McKinsey and Co., 1985–2008. Operating Partner, Duke Street LLP, 2009–; non-exec. Dir, Wm Morrison Supermarkets plc, 2010–. Trustee, Royal Botanic Garden Kew, 2008–; Mem., Commercial Bd, RHS, 2011–. *Recreations:* extreme gardening, reckless ski-ing, theatre, tennis. *E:* jwaterous@gmail.com. *Club:* Ocean (Bahamas).

WATERPARK, 8th Baron *cr* 1792 (Ire.); **Roderick, (Rory) Alexander Cavendish;** Bt 1755; airline pilot, British Airways, since 1991; *b* 10 Oct. 1959; *o s* of 7th Baron Waterpark and of Danièle Alice Cavendish (*née* Guirche); *S* father 2013; *m* 1989, Anne, *d* of late Hon. Luke Asquith; two *s*. *Educ:* Harrow; Vassar. *Heir: s* Hon. Luke Frederick Cavendish, *b* 17 Sept. 1990. *Address:* London, SW6.

WATERS, Alan Victor; HM Diplomatic Service, retired; High Commissioner, Solomon Islands, 1998–2001; *b* 10 April 1942; *s* of late George and Ruth Waters; *m* 1977, Elizabeth Ann Newman; one *s* one *d*. *Educ:* Judd Sch., Tonbridge. Joined CO, 1958, CRO, 1961; Freetown, 1963–66; UKDEL to ECSC, Luxembourg, 1967–68; Prague, 1968–70; Anguilla, 1970–71; Peking, 1971–73; FCO, 1973–76; Second Secretary: Kinshasa, 1976–80; Bombay, 1980–83; FCO, 1984–86; First Secretary: FCO, 1986–87; Copenhagen, 1987–91; FCO, 1991–95; acting Adminr, Tristan da Cunha, 1995–96; First Sec., Islamabad, 1996–98. *Recreations:* walking, watching cricket, golf.

WATERS, Caroline Ann, OBE 2010; Deputy Chair, Equality and Human Rights Commission, since 2013; Vice President, Carers UK, since 2013; *b* Birmingham, 21 July 1961; *d* of Thomas and Teresa Murphy; *m* 1989, Keith Waters. *Educ:* Swanshurst Sch., Birmingham; Birmingham Poly. (HNC Business Studies 1985). Joined BT, 1979, HR Dir, People & Policy, 1999–2013. Founding Dir, CW Consulting Box Ltd, 2012–; Associate, Marylebone Exec. Search, 2013–. Member, Board: UK Resource Centre for Women, 2007–12; Whole Educn, 2009–; Roffey Park Inst., 2010–; Incredibull Ltd, 2013–. Founder and Chair: Employers Forum on Belief, 2003–13; Employers for Fathers, 2005–11; Chm., Employers for Carers, 2003–13. Trustee, Employers Forum on Age, 2001–13. HR Dir of the Year, HR Excellence Awards, 2009. *Recreations:* walking, dog training, gardening, art. *Address:* CW Consulting Box Ltd, Meadow Bank, Church Road, Stevington, Bedford MK43 7QB.

WATERS, Gen. Sir (Charles) John, GCB 1995 (KCB 1988); CBE 1981 (OBE 1977); DL; Deputy Supreme Allied Commander, Europe, 1993–94; Aide-de-Camp General to the Queen, 1992–95; *b* 2 Sept. 1935; *s* of Patrick George Waters and Margaret Ronaldson Waters (*née* Clark); *m* 1962, Hilary Doyle Nettleton; three *s*. *Educ:* Oundle; Royal Military Academy, Sandhurst. Commissioned, The Gloucestershire Regt, 1955; GSO2, MO1 (MoD), 1970–72; Instructor, GSO1 (DS), Staff Coll., Camberley, 1973–74; Commanding Officer, 1st Bn, Gloucestershire Regt, 1975–77; Colonel General Staff, 1st Armoured Div., 1977–79; Comdr 3 Infantry Bde, 1979–81; RCDS 1982; Dep. Comdr, Land Forces, Falkland Islands, May–July 1982; Comdr 4th Armoured Div., 1983–85; Comdt, Staff Coll., Camberley, 1986–88; GOC and Dir of Ops, NI, 1988–90; C-in-C, UKLF, 1990–93. Col, The Gloucestershire Regt, 1985–91; Col Comdt, POW Div., 1988–91; Hon. Colonel: Royal Wessex Yeomanry, 1991–97; Royal Devonshire Yeomanry, 1991–97. President: (Army) Officers' Assoc., 1997–2006; Devon RBL, 1998–2002. Mem. Adv. Council, Victory Meml Mus., Arlon, Belgium, 1989–97; Mem. Council, Cheltenham Coll., 1991–2002; Chm. Council, Nat. Army Mus., 1997–2005; Gov., Colyton Primary Sch., 1997–2003. Pres., Honiton and Dist Agricl Assoc., 2004–05; Patron, Royal Albert Meml Mus., Exeter, 2006–. Admiral: Army Sailing Assoc., 1990–93; Infantry Sailing Assoc., 1990–93. Kermit Roosevelt Lectr, USA, 1992. FRSA 1993. JP: Axminster and Honiton, 1998; Central Devon, 1998–2006; DL Devon, 2001. *Recreations:* sailing, ski-ing, painting, gardening. *Address:* c/o Lloyds Bank, Colyton, Devon EX24 6JS. *Clubs:* Army and Navy; British Kiel Yacht.

WATERS, David Ebsworth Benjamin; QC 1999; *b* 24 April 1945; *s* of William Thomas Ebsworth Waters and Esther Jane Waters; *m* 1996, Sonia Jayne Bound. *Educ:* Greenhill Grammar Sch., Tenby. Admitted Solicitor, 1969; called to the Bar, Middle Temple, 1973; Junior Treasury Counsel, 1989–94, Sen. Treasury Counsel, 1994–99, CCC. *Recreations:* golf, fishing. *Address:* 2 Hare Court, Temple, EC4Y 7BH. *T:* (020) 7353 3982. *Clubs:* MCC; Royal Wimbledon Golf, Woking Golf.

WATERS, Donald Henry, OBE 1994; CA; Chief Executive, 1987–97, and Deputy Chairman, 1993–97, Grampian Television PLC; *b* 17 Dec. 1937; *s* of late Henry Lethbridge Waters, WS, and Jean Manson Baxter; *m* 1962, June Leslie, *d* of late Andrew Hutchison; one *s* two *d*. *Educ:* George Watson's, Edinburgh; Inverness Royal Acad. Mem. ICA(Scot.) 1961; CA 1961. Dir, John M. Henderson and Co. Ltd, 1972–75; Grampian Television: Company Sec., 1975; Dir of Finance, 1979. Chairman: Glenburnie Properties, 1993–97 (Dir, 1976–93); Central Scotland Radio Ltd, 1994–96; Director: Scottish TV and Grampian Sales Ltd, 1980–98; Blenheim Travel, 1981–91; Moray Firth Radio, 1982–97; Independent Television Publications Ltd, 1987–90; Cablevision (Scotland) PLC, 1987–91; FirstBus (formerly GRT Bus Group), 1994–96; British Linen Bank, 1995–99; British Linen Bank Gp, 1995–99; Aberdeen Royal Hosp. NHS Trust, 1996–99; Scottish Post Office Bd, 1996–2003; Digital 3 and 4 Ltd, 1997–98; Scottish Media Group plc, 1997–2005; James Johnston of Elgin Ltd, 1999–; North Bd, Bank of Scotland, 1999–2001; Aberdeen Asset Mgt plc, 2000–11. Vis. Prof. of Film and Media Studies, Stirling Univ., 1991–. Mem., BAFTA, 1980– (Scottish Vice Chm., 1992–); Chm., Celtic Film and Television Assoc., 1994–96 (Trustee for Scotland, 1990–96); Dir, ITVA, 1994–97. Mem. Council, CBI Scotland, 1994–2001. Chairman: Police Dependent Trust, Aberdeen, 1991–96; Project Steering Gp, New Royal Aberdeen Children's Hosp., 1999–2002; Jt Chm., Grampian Cancer MacMillan Appeal, 1999–2003; Member: Council, Cinema and Television Benevolent Fund, 1986–99; Grampian & Islands Family Trust, 1986–2005. Gov., Univ. of Aberdeen, 1998–99. Burgess of Guild, Aberdeen, 1979– (Assessor, 1998–2001). FRTS 1998 (Mem., 1988); FRSA 1990. *Recreations:* gardening, travel, hill-walking. *Address:* Balquhidder, Milltimber, Aberdeen AB13 0JS. *T:* (01224) 867131. *E:* donaldwaters@btinternet.com. *Club:* Royal Northern and University (Aberdeen) (Chm., 1987–88).

WATERS, Emily; *see* Watson, Emily.

WATERS, Gen. Sir John; *see* Waters, Gen. Sir C. J.

WATERS, Keith Stuart, FCA; Clerk, Fishmongers' Company, 1994–2009 (Assistant Clerk, 1987–93); *b* 18 March 1951; *s* of late Thomas Charles Waters and of Elsie Lillian (*née* Addison); *m* 1976, Elizabeth Jane Weeks; one *s* two *d*. *Educ:* Leigh GS; Wigan Tech. Coll.; Univ. of Newcastle upon Tyne (BA 1973). FCA 1976. Deloitte Haskins & Sells, Manchester, 1973–77; audit senior, Peat Marwick Mitchell, Kingston, Jamaica, 1978; with Price Waterhouse: audit senior, Miami, Fla, 1979–80; Manager, Melbourne, Aust., 1980–82; Sen. Manager, London, 1982–85; Gp Financial Accountant, Guinness plc, 1985–87. Chm., Livery Cos Mutual Ltd, 1999–. Sec., Bd of Trustees, City and Guilds of London Art Sch., 1993–2008. Gresham's School, Holt: Clerk to Govs, 1993–2008; Dep. Chm., 2009–; Chm., Gresham's Sch. Foundn, 2009–14. *Recreations:* theatre, concerts, ballet, tennis, watersports, running, food and wine. *Address:* The Cow Shed, Bard Hill, Salthouse, Norfolk NR25 7XB. *T:* (01263) 740227.

WATERS, Malcolm Ian; QC 1997; *b* 11 Oct. 1953; *s* of late Ian Power Waters and Yvonne Waters (*née* Mosley); *m* 2002, Setsuko Sato. *Educ:* Whitgift Sch.; St Catherine's Coll., Oxford (MA, BCL). Called to the Bar, Lincoln's Inn, 1977; in practice, 1978–. *Publications:* (jtly) The Building Societies Act 1986, 1987; (ed jtly) Wurtzburg & Mills, Building Society Law, 15th edn, 1989 (with annual updates); (ed jtly) The Law of Investor Protection, 2nd edn, 2003; (Cons. Ed.) Friendly Societies, 2007, Mutual Societies, 2008, Halsbury's Laws of England; (jtly) Retail Mortgages: law regulation and procedure, 2013. *Recreations:* music, opera. *Address:* Radcliffe Chambers, 11 New Square, Lincoln's Inn, WC2A 3QB. *T:* (020) 7831 0081.

WATERS, Sir Neil; *see* Waters, Sir T. N. M.

WATERS, Sarah, PhD; author, since 1995; *b* 21 July 1966; *d* of Ron and Mary Waters. *Educ:* Univ. of Kent (BA Hons English and American Lit. 1987); Univ. of Lancaster (MA Contemp. Literary Studies 1988); Queen Mary and Westfield Coll., London (PhD 1995). Tutor, Open Univ., 1996–2000. *Publications:* Tipping the Velvet, 1998 (televised 2002); Affinity, 1999 (televised 2008); Fingersmith, 2002 (televised 2005); The Night Watch, 2006 (televised, 2011); The Little Stranger, 2009; The Paying Guests, 2014. *Recreations:* cinema, theatre. *Address:* c/o Greene & Heaton (Authors' Agents) Ltd, 37 Goldhawk Road, W12 8QQ. *T:* (020) 8749 0315.

WATERS, Sir (Thomas) Neil (Morris), Kt 1995; PhD; DSc; FRSNZ; Vice-Chancellor, Massey University, 1983–95, now Emeritus Professor; *b* New Plymouth, 10 April 1931; *s* of Edwin Benjamin Waters and Kathleen Emily (*née* Morris); *m* 1959, Joyce Mary (ONZM 2006), *d* of Ven. T. H. C. Partridge. *Educ:* Auckland Univ. (BSc 1953; MSc 1954; PhD 1958; DSc 1969); FNZIC 1977; FRSNZ 1982. Sen. Res. Fellow, UKAEA, 1958–60; Auckland University: Lectr in Chemistry, 1961–62; Sen. Lectr, 1963–65; Associate Prof., 1966–69; Prof., 1970–83, Emeritus Prof., 1984–; Asst Vice-Chancellor, 1979–81; Acting Vice-Chancellor, 1980. Visiting Scientist: Univ. of Oxford, 1964, 1971; Northwestern Univ., Illinois, 1976. Chm., NZ Vice-Chancellors' Cttee, 1985–86, 1994 (Mem., 1983–95). Hon. DSc East Asia, Macao, 1988; Hon. DLitt Massey, 1995. *Address:* Box 25–463, St Heliers, Auckland 1740, New Zealand.

WATERSON, Prof. Michael John, PhD; Professor of Economics, University of Warwick, since 1991; *b* 29 July 1950; *s* of Geoffrey and Christine Mary Waterson; *m* 1972, Sally Ann Davis; one *s* one *d*. *Educ:* Bude Grammar Sch.; Univ. of Warwick (BA 1971; PhD 1977); London Sch. of Econs (MSc Econ 1972). Lectr in Econs, 1974–86, Reader in Econs, 1986–88, Univ. of Newcastle upon Tyne; Prof. of Econs, Univ. of Reading, 1988–91. Gen. Ed., Jl Industrial Econs, 1994–99. Associate Fellow, ZEW Univ. of Mannheim, 2013–15. Member: Competition Commn, 2005–14; Econs Reference Gp, Cooperation and Competition Panel, 2010–. Specialist Advr, H of L Subcttee B, 2005, 2006; Expert Advr, Eur. Res. Council, 2015–16; Ad hoc Advr on energy matters, Nat. Audit Office. Chm., Utilities Appeals Panel, States of Guernsey, 2002–07. Pres., Eur. Assoc. for Res. in Industrial Econs, 1999–2001. Mem., Scientific Adv. Bd, DIW Berlin, 2009–. FRSA 1989. *Publications:* Economic Theory of the Industry, 1984; Regulation of the Firm and Natural Monopoly, 1988; (jtly) Buyer Power and Competition in European Food Retailing, 2002; (ed jtly) Empirical Industrial Organization, 2004; contrib. jls incl. Amer. Econ. Rev., Qly Jl Econs, Econ. Jl, Eur. Econ. Rev. *Recreations:* walking, playing musical instruments, travel. *Address:* Department of Economics, University of Warwick, Coventry CV4 7AL. *T:* (024) 7652 3427, *Fax:* (024) 7652 3032. *E:* michael.waterson@warwick.ac.uk.

WATERSON, Nigel Christopher; Chairman: Equity Release Council, since 2012; Abbeyfield (East Sussex), since 2011; *b* 12 Oct. 1950; *s* of James Waterson and Katherine (*née* Mahon); *m* 1999, Dr Barbara Judge; one *s* one *d*. *Educ:* Leeds Grammar Sch.; Queen's Coll., Oxford (MA Jurisprudence); College of Law. Called to the Bar, Gray's Inn, 1973; admitted solicitor, 1979. Pres., Oxford Univ. Cons. Assoc., 1970. Res. Asst to Sally Oppenheim, MP, 1972–73. Cllr, London Borough of Hammersmith, 1974–78. Chairman: Bow Gp, 1986–87 (Hon. Patron, 1993–95); Hammersmith Cons. Assoc., 1987–90; Hammersmith and Fulham Jt Management Cttee, 1988–90; Member: Cons. Gtr London Area Exec. Cttee, 1990–91; Soc. of Cons. Lawyers Exec. Cttee, 1993–97; Conservative Political Centre: Mem., Adv. Cttee, 1986–90; Mem., Gtr London Gen. Purposes Cttee, 1990–91. MP (C) Eastbourne, 1992–2010; contested (C) same seat, 2010. PPS to Minister of State, DoH, 1995, to Dep. Prime Minister, 1996–97; an Opposition Whip, 1997–99; Opposition spokesman on local govt and housing, 1999–2001, on trade and industry, 2001–02, on pensions, 2003–10. Mem., Select Cttee on Nat. Heritage, 1995–96; Vice Chairman: Cons. Backbench Tourism Cttee, 1992–97; Cons. Backbench Transport Cttee, 1992–97; Sec., Cons. Backbench Shipping and Shipbuilding Cttee, 1992–97; Vice Chairman: All-Party Daylight Extra Gp, 1993–97; All-Party British Greek Gp, 1993–2010; Sec., British Cyprus Gp, CPA, 1992–2010. Member: London West European Constituency Council, 1987–91; Management Cttee, Stonham Housing Assoc. Hostel for Ex-Offenders, 1988–90. Trustee: Internat. Longevity Council, 2010–; Age and Employment Network, 2011–; Chm., Trustee Bd, NOW: Pensions, 2011–. Gov., Pension Policy Inst., 2012–. *Publications:* papers on an Alternative Manifesto, 1973, the future of Hong Kong, and on shipping. *Recreations:* walking on Downs, reading, music, visiting France. *E:* nigel@nigelwaterson.com. *Clubs:* Coningsby, 1900.

WATERSTON, Dr Charles Dewar, FRSE; formerly Keeper of Geology, Royal Scottish Museum; *b* 15 Feb. 1925; *s* of Allan Waterston and Martha Dewar (*née* Robertson); *m* 1965, Marjory Home Douglas (*d* 2008). *Educ:* Highgate Sch., London; Univ. of Edinburgh (BSc 1st Cl. Hons 1947; Vans Dunlop Scholar, PhD 1949; DSc 1980). FRSE 1958. Asst Keeper, Royal Scottish Museum, 1950–63, Keeper, 1963–85. Member: Scottish Cttee, Nature Conservancy, 1969–73; Adv. Cttee for Scotland, Nature Conservancy Council, 1974–82; Chairman's Cttee, 1978–80, Exec. Cttee, 1980–82, Council for Museums and Galleries in Scotland; Adv. Cttee on Sites of Special Scientific Interest, 1992–95; Gen. Sec., RSE, 1986–91 (Mem. Council, 1967–70; Vice-Pres., 1980–83; Sec., 1985–86); Hon. Sec., Edinburgh Geol Soc., 1953–58 (Pres., 1969–71). Chm., Judges Panel, Scottish Mus. of Year Award, 1999–2000. Keith Prize, 1969–71, Bicentenary Medal, 1992, RSE; Clough Medal, Edinburgh Geol Soc., 1984–85; (first) A. G. Brighton Medal, Geol Curators' Gp, 1992. *Publications:* (with G. Y. Craig and D. B. McIntyre) James Hutton's Theory of the Earth: the lost drawings, 1978; (with H. E. Stace and C. W. A. Pettitt) Natural Science Collections in Scotland, 1987; Collections in Context, 1997; (with D. Guthrie) The Royal Society Club of Edinburgh 1820–2000, 1999; (with A. Macmillan Shearer) Biographical Index of Former Fellows of the Royal Society of Edinburgh 1783–2002, 2 vols, 2006; Perth Entrepreneurs: the Sandemans of Springland, 2008; technical papers in jls, chiefly relating to extinct arthropods, the history of geology, genealogy and local history. *Address:* 51 Homescott House, 6 Goldenacre Terrace, Edinburgh EH3 5RE.

WATERSTONE, Timothy John Stuart; Founder, Waterstone's Booksellers, 1982; *b* 30 May 1939; *s* of Malcolm Waterstone and Sylvia Sawday; *m* 1st, Patricia Harcourt-Poole (marr. diss.); two *s* one *d*; 2nd, Claire Perkins (marr. diss.); one *s* two *d*; 3rd, Mary Rose, (Rosie), *d* of Rt Hon. Michael Alison, PC and of Sylvia Mary (*née* Haigh); two *d*. *Educ:* Tonbridge; St Catharine's College, Cambridge (MA). Carritt Moran, Calcutta, 1962–64; Allied Breweries, 1964–73; W. H. Smith, 1973–81; Founder, Chm. and Chief Exec., Waterstone's Booksellers Ltd, 1982–93; Dep. Chm., Sinclair-Stevenson Ltd, 1989–92; Chairman: Priory Investments Ltd, 1990–95; Golden Rose Radio (London Jazz FM), 1992–93; Founder and Exec. Chm., Chelsea Stores Ltd (Daisy & Tom), 1996–2007 (acquired Early Learning Centre Hldgs, 2004); Founder Chm., HMV Media Gp plc (merged businesses of Waterstone's and HMV), 1998–2001; Member of Board: Yale Univ. Press, 1992–; Future Start, 1992–2009; Virago

Press., 1995–96; Hill Samuel UK Emerging Cos Investment Trust PLC, 1996–2000; National Gallery Co. Ltd, 1996–2003; Downing Classic VCT, 1998–2003. Chm., DTI Working Gp on Smaller Quoted Cos and Private Investors, 1999. Chm., Shelter 25th Anniversary Appeal Cttee, 1991–92. Member: Bd of Trustees, English International (Internat. House), 1987–92; Bd, London Philharmonic Orch., 1990–97 (Trustee, 1995–98); Portman House Trust, 1994–96; Chairman: Acad. of Ancient Music, 1990–95; London Internat. Festival of Theatre, 1991–92; Elgar Foundn, 1992–98; Library Bd, KCL, 2000–02; Vis. Cttee, Cambridge Univ. Library, 2007–. Co-Founder: BOOKAID, 1992–93; Moscow booksellers Bookberry, 2003. Adv. Mem., Booker Prize Management Cttee, 1986–93; Chm. of Judges, Prince's Youth Business Trust Awards, 1990. Chancellor, Edinburgh Napier (formerly Napier) Univ., 2007–. Bishop's nominee to Southwark Cathedral Council, 2012–. *Publications: novels:* Lilley & Chase, 1994; An Imperfect Marriage, 1995; A Passage of Lives, 1996; In For a Penny, In For a Pound, 2010; *non-fiction:* Swimming Against the Stream, 2006. *Recreation:* talking with Rosie Alison. *Address:* 64 Portland Road, W11 4LQ. *Club:* Garrick.

WATERWORTH, Sir Alan (William), KCVO 2007; JP; Lord-Lieutenant of Merseyside, 1993–2006 (Vice Lord-Lieutenant, 1989–93); *b* 22 Sept. 1931; *s* of late James and Alice Waterworth, Liverpool; *m* 1955, Myriam, *d* of late Edouard Baete and Magdelaine Baete, formerly of Brussels; three *s* one *d. Educ:* Uppingham Sch.; Trinity Coll., Cambridge (MA). National Service, commnd King's Regt, 1950. Waterworth Bros Ltd: progressively, Dir, Man. Dir, Chm., 1954–69. Gen. Comr, Inland Revenue, 1965–72. Dir, NHS Hosp. Trust, Liverpool, 1992–93. Member: Skelmersdale Develt Corp., 1971–85 (Dep. Chm., 1979–85); Merseyside Police Authority, 1984–92; Cttee, Merseyside Br., Inst. of Dirs, 1965–77 (Chm., 1974–77). Chm., IBA Adv. Cttee for Radio on Merseyside, 1975–78. Chairman: Liverpool Boys' Assoc., 1967–75; Merseyside Youth Assoc., 1971–75; Everton FC, 1973–76 (Dir, 1970–93). Mem. Council, Liverpool Univ., 1993–2004. Trustee, Nat. Museums and Galls on Merseyside, 1994–2004. Mem. Council, Liverpool Cathedral, 2004–09. JP Liverpool 1961 (Chm., Juvenile Panel, 1974–83; Chm. of Bench, 1985–89); DL Co. Merseyside 1986, High Sheriff, Co. Merseyside, 1992. Hon. Col, Merseyside Cadet Force, 1994–2007; Pres., RFCA, NW England and I of M, 2004–07. Hon. Fellow, Liverpool John Moores, 1995. Hon. LLD Liverpool, 2001. KStJ 1994. *Recreations:* local history, bibliomania. *Address:* Crewood Hall, Kingsley, Cheshire WA6 8HR. *T:* (01928) 788316. *Clubs:* Army and Navy; Athenæum, Artists' (Liverpool).

WATERWORTH, Peter Andrew; HM Diplomatic Service, retired; Chief Administrative Officer, Municipality of Jasper, Alberta, Canada, 2012–14; *b* 15 April 1957; *s* of Bobby and Betty Waterworth; *m* 1994, Catherine Margaret. *Educ:* Univ. of Durham (BA Hons); Downing Coll., Cambridge (LLB Hons 1982); Inns of Court Sch. of Law. Standing Adv. Commn on Human Rights, NI, 1979–81; called to the Bar; barrister, 1983–87; joined FCO, 1987; Asst Legal Advr, FCO, 1987–90; Legal Advr, Bonn, 1990–94; Middle Eastern Dept, FCO, 1994–96; First Sec., Rome, 1996–2000; NI Office, 2000–03; Pol Counsellor, Islamabad, 2003–05, Iraq, 2005; Dep. High Comr and Consul-Gen., Lagos, 2005–07; Governor of Montserrat, 2007–11. *Recreations:* ski-ing, football, cooking, golf, reading.

WATES, Andrew Trace Allan, OBE 2013; Vice Lord-Lieutenant of Surrey, since 2013; Chairman: Wates Group (formerly Wates Ltd), 2000–06; Wates Family Holdings, 2000–08; *b* 16 Nov. 1940; 4th *s* of Sir Ronald Wallace Wates and Phyllis Mary Wates (*née* Trace); *m* 1965, Sarah Mary de Burgh Macartney; four *s* (and one *s* decd). *Educ:* Oundle Sch.; Emmanuel Coll., Cambridge (BA Estate Mgt 1960). Joined Wates, 1964; Dir, Wates Construction, 1972–2000; Chairman: Wates Leisure Gp, later Pinnacle Leisure Gp, 1972–99; Wates Estate Agency Services, 1976–2000; Director: Wates Ltd, 1973–2000; Wates Hldgs, 1973–. Chairman: United Racecourses Ltd, 1996–; Leisure and Media plc, 2001–; Director: Racecourse Hldgs Trust, 1996; Fontwell Park plc, 1991–2001. Chm., Inst. for Family Business, 2007–. Vice-Chm., Bd of Mgt, Royal Albert and Alexandra Sch., 2000–. Mem., Jockey Club, 1977–. High Sheriff, Surrey, 2003–04; DL Surrey, 2006. *Recreations:* horse-racing, shooting, fishing, golf. *Address:* Henfold House, Beare Green, Dorking, Surrey RH5 4RW. *T:* (01306) 631324. *Clubs:* White's, Turf.

See also M. E. Wates, P. C. R. Wates.

WATES, Sir Christopher (Stephen), Kt 1989; BA; FCA; Chairman, Wates Holdings, 2000–05; Chief Executive, Wates Group (formerly Wates Building Group), 1984–2000; *b* 25 Dec. 1939; *s* of Norman Edward Wates and Margot Irene Sidwell; *m* 1965, Sandra Mouroutsos (marr. diss. 1975); three *d*; *m* 1992, Georgina Ferris McCallum. *Educ:* Stowe School; Brasenose College, Oxford (BA 1962; Rugby blue, 1961; Hon. Fellow, 1993). FCA 1975 (ACA 1965). Financial Director, Wates Ltd, 1970–76. Chm., Criterion Hldgs, 1981–96. Director: Electra Investment Trust, 1980–93; Equitable Life Assurance Society, 1983–94; Scottish Ontario Investment Co. Ltd, 1978–83; 3i Smaller Quoted Cos Trust (formerly North British Canadian Investment Co., then NB Smaller Cos Trust), 1983–98 (Chm., 1996–98); Wates City of London Properties plc, 1984–2000; Mem., 1980–89, Chm., 1983–89, English Industrial Estates Corp.; Chm., Keymer Brick & Tile Co. Ltd, 1985–89. A Church Comr, 1992–96. Gov. of Council, 1984–2006, Chm., 1997–2010, Goodenough Coll. (formerly London House for Overseas Graduates, then London Goodenough Trust) (Dep. Chm., 1989–96); Gov., Frewen Coll., 2004–06. Trustee: Chatham Historic Dockyard Trust, 1984–87; Science Museum, 1987–2002; Lambeth Palace Library, 1990–2005. Chm., Industrial Soc., 1998. FRSA 1988. Hon. Mem., RICS, 1990. *Address:* Tufton Place, Northiam, Rye, East Sussex TN31 6HL. *T:* (01797) 252125.

WATES, James Garwood Michael, CBE 2012; Chairman, Wates Group, since 2013 (Director, since 1997; Deputy Chairman, 2006–13); *b* London, 9 April 1960; *s* of Michael Edward Wates, *qv*; *m* 1991, Laurie Lindsey; two *s. Educ:* Downside Sch.; Poly. of Central London; Harvard Business Sch. With Wates Gp, 1983–: Line Manager, Wates Construction Ltd, 1983–89; Man. Dir, Wates Integra Ltd, 1989–92; Gp Sales and Marketing Manager, Wates Construction Ltd, 1992–94; Chm., Nominations Cttee and Mem., Remuneration Cttee, Wates Gp, 1997–; Chm., Charles Barratt Interiors, 1999–2000; Exec. Chm., Wates Interiors Ltd, 2000–01. Non-Exec. Dir, Argent Gp LLP, 2015–. Mem., UK Commn for Employment Skills, 2009–15. Chairman: Construction Confedn, 2006–09; UK Contractors Gp, 2009–; Construction Skills, CITB, 2010–. Pres., British Council for Offices, 2012– (Vice Pres., 2010–12). Pres., Chartered Inst. of Building, 2010–11. Mem., Court of Govs, Univ. of Westminster, 2013–. Trustee: Queen Elizabeth's Foundn, 2004–; BRE Trust, 2010–15 (Chm., 2015–). *Recreations:* golf, sailing, shooting, family. *Address:* Field Place, Hookhouse Lane, Dunsfold, Surrey GU8 4LR. *T:* (01483) 201125; Wates House, Station Approach, Leatherhead, Surrey KT22 7SW. *T:* (01372) 861262. *E:* james.wates@wates.co.uk. *Clubs:* Cavalry and Guards; Royal London Yacht; Walton Heath Golf.

WATES, Michael Edward, CBE 1998; Chairman, Wates Group (formerly Wates Ltd), 1974–2000; *b* 19 June 1935; 2nd *s* of Sir Ronald Wallace Wates and Phyllis Mary Wates (*née* Trace); *m* 1959, Caroline Josephine Connolly; four *s* one *d. Educ:* Oundle School; Emmanuel College, Cambridge (MA); Harvard Business Sch. (PMD 1963). Served RM, 1953–55. Joined Wates 1959; Director: Wates Construction, 1963; Wates Built Homes, 1966. Mem., Nat. Housebuilding Council, 1974–80. Chm., British Bloodstock Agency plc, 1986–92; Member: Council, Thoroughbred Breeders Assoc., 1978–82 (Chm., 1980–82); Horserace Betting Levy Bd, 1987–90. King's College Hospital: Deleg., Sch. of Medicine and Dentistry, 1983–2004; Chm., Equipment Cttee, 1983–91; Special Trustee, 1985 (Chm., Trustees, 1985). Hon. FRIBA. *Address:* Manor House, Langton Long, Blandford Forum, Dorset DT11 9HS. *T:* (01258) 455241.

See also A. T. A. Wates, J. G. M. Wates, P. C. R. Wates.

WATES, Paul Christopher Ronald, FRICS; Managing Director, 1984–94, Chairman, 1994–2001, Wates City of London Properties plc; *b* 6 March 1938; 3rd *s* of Sir Ronald Wallace Wates and Phyllis Mary Wates (*née* Trace); *m* 1965, Annette Beatrice Therese Randag; three *s* three *d.* Chesterton & Sons, 1958–59; Nat. Service, 14th/20th King's Hussars, 1959–61; joined Wates Ltd, 1962; Director: Wates Gp, 1969–2006; Wates Holdings (formerly Wates Family Holdings), 1973–. Chm., C&G, 1991–99 (Vice Pres., 2006–; Hon. FCGI). Mem. Court, Clothworkers' Co. (Master, 2003). *Address:* Bellasis House, Mickleham, Dorking, Surrey RH5 6DH. *Clubs:* White's, Turf, Cavalry and Guards, MCC.

See also A. T. A. Wates, M. E. Wates.

WATHEN, Julian Philip Gerard; Chairman: Hall School Charitable Trust, 1972–97; City of London Endowment Trust for St Paul's Cathedral, 1983–2002; *b* 21 May 1923; *s* of late Gerard Anstruther Wathen, CIE, and Melicent Louis (*née* Buxton); *m* 1948 Priscilla Florence Wilson; one *s* two *d. Educ:* Harrow. Served War, 60th Rifles, 1942–46. Third Secretary, HBM Embassy, Athens, 1946–47. Barclays Bank DCO, 1948; Ghana Director, 1961–65; General Manager, 1966; Sen. Gen. Manager, Barclays Bank International, 1974; Vice Chm., 1976; Vice Chairman: Barclays Bank, 1979–84; Banque du Caire, Barclays International, 1976–83; Dep. Chm., Allied Arab Bank, 1977–84; Director: Barclays Australia International, 1973–84; Barclays Bank of Kenya, 1975–84; Mercantile & General Reinsurance Co., 1977–91. Pres., Royal African Soc., 1984–89 (Chm., 1978–84). Member Council: Goodenough Coll. (formerly London House for Overseas Graduates, then London Goodenough Trust), 1971–2001 (Vice-Chm., 1984–89); Book Aid Internat., 1988–2008; Governor: St Paul's Sch., 1981–99 (Chm., 1995–99); St Paul's Girls' Sch., 1981–2003; SOAS, 1983–92; Overseas Develt Inst., 1984–96; Dauntsey's Sch., 1985–2005; Abingdon Sch., 1985–95; Dep. Chm., Thomas Telford Sch., 1990–97. Mem. Cttee, GBA, 1986–94. Master, Mercers' Co., 1984–85. *Address:* 10 The Chipping, Wotton-under-Edge, Glos GL12 7AD. *T:* (01453) 844568. *Club:* Travellers.

WATHERSTON, John Anthony Charles, CBE 2005; Registrar of the Privy Council, 1998–2005; *b* 29 April 1944; *yr s* of Sir David Watherston, KBE, CMG and Lady Watherston; *m* 1976, Jane (*née* Chaytor), *widow* of John Atkinson; one *s*, and one step *s* one step *d. Educ:* Winchester Coll.; Christ Church, Oxford (BA Jurisp. 1966; MA 1970); Heythrop Coll., Univ. of London (Postgrad. Cert. Christian Ethics 2010). Called to the Bar, Inner Temple, 1967; Lord Chancellor's Department: Legal Asst, 1970–74; Sec., Phillimore Cttee on Law of Contempt of Court, 1971–74; Sen. Legal Asst, 1974–80; Private Sec. to Lord Chancellor, 1975–77; Asst Solicitor (Grade 5), 1980–85, 1988–98; Sen. Crown Counsel, Attorney Gen.'s Chambers, Hong Kong, 1985–88. Consultant Registrar, Dubai Internat. Financial Centre Courts, 2005–06. Lay Reader, Chelsea Old Church, Dio. of London, 1995–; Mem., London Diocesan Synod, 2000–09. *Publications:* (contrib.) Halsbury's Laws of England, vol. 10, 4th edn, 2002; (ed and contrib.) Jowitt's Dictionary of English Law, 3rd edn, 2010. *Club:* Reform.

See also Baron Freyberg.

WATHEY, Prof. Andrew, DPhil; FRHistS, FSA; Vice-Chancellor and Chief Executive, Northumbria University, since 2008; *b* Plymouth, 19 July 1958; *m* 1995, Charlotte. *Educ:* St Edmund Hall, Oxford (BA Hons 1st Cl. Music 1979; MA 1983; DPhil 1987). FRHistS 1986; FSA 1989. Jun. Res. Fellow, Merton Coll., Oxford, 1982–85; Res. Fellow, Downing Coll., Cambridge, 1985–88; Lectr in Music, Univ. of Lancaster, 1988–89; Royal Holloway, University of London: Lectr in Music, 1989–94; Sen. Lectr in Music, 1995; Reader in Music, 1995–99; Dean, Graduate Sch., 1996–98; Prof. of Music Hist., 1999–2008; Hd, Music Dept, 2000–02; Dean of Arts, 2002; Vice-Principal (Planning and Resources), 2003–06; Sen. Vice-Principal, 2006–08. Vis. Prof., Keio Univ., Tokyo, 1987; Vis. Res. Fellow, All Souls Coll., Oxford, 1998. Dep. Chm., Univ. Alliance, 2009–12. Chm., Student Loans Co. Stakeholder Forum, 2010–. FRSA 2005. *Publications:* Music in the Royal and Noble Households in Late Medieval England: studies of sources and patronage, 1989; Manuscripts of Polyphonic Music: the British Isles 1100–1400, 1993; (ed with M. Bent) Fauvel Studies: allegory, chronicle, music and image in Paris, Bibliothèque Nationale de France, MS Français 146, 1998. *Address:* Vice-Chancellor's Office, Northumbria University, Ellison Building, Ellison Place, Newcastle upon Tyne NE1 8ST. *T:* (0191) 227 4002, *Fax:* (0191) 227 4417. *E:* andrew.wathey@northumbria.ac.uk. *Club:* Reform.

WATKIN, Prof. David John, LittD; FSA; Fellow of Peterhouse, Cambridge, 1970–2008, now Emeritus; Professor of History of Architecture, 2001–08, University of Cambridge, now Emeritus; *b* 7 April 1941; *o s* of late Thomas Charles and Vera Mary Watkin. *Educ:* Farnham Grammar Sch.; Trinity Hall, Cambridge (Exhibnr; BA (1st Cl. Hons Fine Arts Tripos); PhD; LittD 1994). University of Cambridge: Librarian, Fine Arts Faculty, 1967–72; University Lectr in History of Art, 1972–93; Head, Dept of History of Art, 1989–92, 2006–07; Reader in Hist. of Architecture, 1993–2001. Mem., Historic Bldgs Council for England, then Historic Bldgs Adv. Cttee, Historic Bldgs and Monuments Commn for England, 1980–95. Hon. FRIBA 2001. Hon. DArts De Montfort Univ., 1996. Henry Hope Reed Award, Sch. of Architecture, Univ. of Notre Dame, 2013. *Publications:* Thomas Hope (1769–1831) and the Neo-Classical Idea, 1968; (ed) Sale Catalogues of Libraries of Eminent Persons, vol. 4, Architects, 1970; The Life and Work of C. R. Cockerell, RA, 1974 (Alice Davis Hitchcock medallion, 1975); The Triumph of the Classical, Cambridge Architecture 1804–34, 1977; Morality and Architecture, 1977 (trans. French, Italian, Japanese and Spanish); English Architecture, a Concise History, 1979, 2nd edn 2001; The Rise of Architectural History, 1980; (with Hugh Montgomery-Massingberd) The London Ritz, a Social and Architectural History, 1980; (with Robin Middleton) Neo-Classical and Nineteenth-century Architecture, 1980 (trans. French, German and Italian); (jtly) Burke's and Savills Guide to Country Houses, vol. 3, East Anglia, 1981; The Buildings of Britain, Regency: a Guide and Gazetteer, 1982; Athenian Stuart, Pioneer of the Greek Revival, 1982; The English Vision: The Picturesque in Architecture, Landscape and Garden Design, 1982; (contrib.) John Soane, 1983; The Royal Interiors of Regency England, 1984; Peterhouse: an architectural record 1284–1984, 1984; A History of Western Architecture, 1986 (trans. German, Italian, Dutch, Greek, Polish, Spanish and Russian), 5th edn 2011; (with Tilman Mellinghoff) German Architecture and the Classical Ideal: 1740–1840, 1987 (trans. Italian); (contrib.) The Legacy of Rome: a new appraisal, 1992; (contrib.) Public and Private Doctrine: essays in English history presented to Maurice Cowling, 1993; (contrib.) The Golden City: essays on the architecture and imagination of Beresford Pite, 1993; Creations and Recreations: Alec Cobbe, thirty years of design and painting, 1996; Sir John Soane: enlightenment thought and the Royal Academy lectures, 1996 (Sir Banister Fletcher Award, 1997); Sir John Soane: the Royal Academy lectures, 2000; The Age of Wilkins: the architecture of improvement, 2000; Morality and Architecture Revisited, 2001; (ed) Alfred Gilbey: a memoir by some friends, 2001; (contrib.) New Offerings, Ancient Treasures: studies in medieval art for George Henderson, 2001; (contrib.) William Beckford, 1760–1844: an eye for the magnificent, 2001; (with Richard John) John Simpson: The Queen's Gallery, Buckingham Palace, and other works, 2002; (contrib.) Royal Treasures: a golden jubilee celebration, 2002; The Architect King: George III and the culture of the enlightenment, 2004; Radical Classicism: the architecture of Quinlan Terry, 2006; (contrib.) James "Athenian" Stuart: the rediscovery of antiquity, 2007; (contrib.) A History of St Mary le Bow, 2007; (contrib.) Carl Laubin: paintings, 2007; (ed and contrib.) Thomas Hope: Regency designer, 2008; The Roman Forum, 2009; The Classical Country House: from the archives of Country Life, 2010; (contrib.) Moggerhanger Park, Bedfordshire: an architectural and social history, 2012; (contrib.) John Nash: architect of the picturesque, 2013; (contrib.) Classical Interiors: historical and contemporary, 2013; (contrib.) The Art of Classical Details: theory, design, and craftsmanship, 2013; (contrib.) William Kent: designing Georgian Britain, 2013; (contrib.) The Architectural Capriccio: memory, fantasy, and invention, 2013; The

Practice of Classical Architecture: the architecture of Quinlan and Francis Terry 2005–15, 2015; The Architecture of John Simpson: a classical renaissance, 2016. *Address:* St Margaret's Place, King's Lynn, Norfolk PE30 5DL; Peterhouse, Cambridge CB2 1RD. *Clubs:* Beefsteak, Brooks's; University Pitt (Cambridge).

WATKIN, (Richard) Owen, OBE 2006; DL; Chairman, Local Democracy and Boundary Commission for Wales (formerly Local Government Boundary Commission for Wales), since 2012; *b* Aberystwyth, 12 Jan. 1947; *s* of T. Ll. Watkin and A. M. Watkin; *m* 1972, G. M. Watkin; two *c. Educ:* Cathays High Sch., Cardiff; University Coll. of Wales, Aberystwyth (LLB 1968); Univ. of London (DPA); Univ. of Wales Trinity St David (MA 2014). Solicitor, 1971–2005. Asst Solicitor, Cardiganshire CC, 1972–74; Sen. Solicitor, Dyfed CC, 1974; Ceredigion District Council, 1974–95: Asst Solicitor; Asst Dir, Admin; Dep. Dir, Admin; Dir, Admin; Chief Exec., Ceredigion CC, 1995–2006. DL Dyfed, 2009. *Recreation:* various. *Address:* Llanfihangel Genau'r Glyn, Bow Street, Ceredigion SY24 5DD.

WATKINS, Dr Alan Keith; Chairman, Senior plc (formerly Senior Engineering Group), 1996–2001 (Director, 1994–2001; Deputy Chairman, 1995–96); *b* 9 Oct. 1938; *s* of late Wilfred Victor Watkins and Dorothy Hilda Watkins; *m* 1963, Diana Edith Wynne (*née* Hughes); two *s. Educ:* Moseley Grammar School, Birmingham; Univ. of Birmingham (BSc Hons, PhD). FIMMM (Mem. Council, 1990–95); CEng; FIMfgE (Vice-Pres., 1991). Lucas Research Centre, 1962; Lucas Batteries, 1969, subseq. Manufacturing Dir; Lucas Aerospace, 1975; Man. Dir, Aerospace Lucas Industries, 1987–89; Man. Dir and Chief Exec., Hawker Siddeley Gp, 1989–91; London Transport: Chief Exec., 1992–94; Vice-Chm., 1992–93; Dep. Chm., 1993–94. Director: Dobson Park Industries plc, 1992–95; Hepworth plc, 1995–98; Chm., High Duty Alloys Ltd, 1997–2000. Member: DTI Aviation Cttee, 1985–89; Review Bd for Govt Contracts, 1993–2002. Member Council: SBAC, 1982–89 (Vice-Pres., 1988–89); CBI, 1992–94. Vice-Pres., EEF, 1989–91, 1997–2001. *Recreations:* tennis, veteran and vintage cars, hot-air ballooning, photography.

WATKINS, Barbara Janet; *see* Fontaine, B. J.

WATKINS, Brian, CMG 1993; HM Diplomatic Service, retired; Immigration Judge, 1993–2007; *b* 26 July 1933; *s* of late James Edward Watkins and late Gladys Anne Watkins (*née* Fletcher); *m* 1st, 1957 (marr. diss. 1978); one *s*; 2nd, 1982, Elisabeth Arfon-Jones, *qv*; one *d. Educ:* London School of Economics (BSc Econ); Worcester College, Oxford. Solicitor. Flying Officer, RAF, 1955–58. HMOCS, Sierra Leone, 1959–63; Local Govt, 1963–66; Administrator, Tristan da Cunha, 1966–69; Lectr, Univ. of Manchester, 1969–71; HM Diplomatic Service, 1971; FCO, 1971–73; New York, 1973–75; seconded to N Ireland Office, 1976–78; FCO, 1978–81; Counsellor, 1981; Dep. Governor, Bermuda, 1981–83; Consul General and Counsellor (Economic, Commercial, Aid), Islamabad, 1983–86; Consul Gen., Vancouver, 1986–90; High Comr to Swaziland, 1990–93. First Pres., Council of Immigration Judges, 1997–2000, now Emeritus. Swazi Rep., 1993–2002, Royal Canadian Legion, Rep., 2002–, on Council, Royal Commonwealth Ex-Services League (Mem. Exec. Cttee, 1996–; Hon. Legal Advr, 2001–); Patron, Friends of Swaziland Hospice (UK), 1997–; Chm., Swaziland Soc., 1998–2002; Trustee, S Asian Assoc. for Regl Co-operation Foundn (UK), 2001–07. Patron, Vancouver Welshmen's Choir, 1987–92; Trustee, Gwent Shrievalty Police Trust, 2003–09; Pres., Chepstow Rifle Club, 2006–15. Mem., Livery Co. of Wales (formerly Welsh Livery Guild), 2010–. High Sheriff Gwent, 2004–05. OStJ 1994 (Chm., Monmouthshire Council, 1996–2002; Mem., Welsh Chapter, 1996–2002). *Publications:* Feathers on the Brain!: a memoir, 2011. *Recreations:* reading history and spy stories, watching theatre, dancing. *Address:* c/o Royal Bank of Scotland, Drummonds Branch, Charing Cross, SW1A 2DX. *Clubs:* Athenæum, Royal Over-Seas League.

WATKINS, David James, CB 2002; Director, DJW Consulting (Northern Ireland) Ltd, 2004–13; *b* 3 Aug. 1948; *s* of John Walter Watkins and Elizabeth Watkins (*née* Buckley); *m* 1974, Valerie Elizabeth Graham; one *s* one *d. Educ:* Royal Belfast Academical Instn; Trinity Coll., Dublin (BA Hons Modern Langs). Public Expenditure Control Div., NI Dept of Finance and Personnel, 1972–77; State Aids Directorate, DGIV, Eur. Commn, 1978–79; NI Dept of Econ. Develt, 1979–86; Private Sec. to Sec. of State for NI, 1986–88; Dep. Chief Exec., IDB, 1989–92; Dir, Central Secretariat, 1992–98; Sen. Dir, and Dir of Policing and Security, NI Office, 1998–2004. *Recreations:* reading, gardening, holidays in France.

WATKINS, Prof. David John; Research Professor of Jewellery, Department of Goldsmithing, Silversmithing, Metalwork and Jewellery, Royal College of Art, since 2006 (Professor of Metalwork and Jewellery, 1984–2006); sculptor and jewellery designer; *b* 14 Nov. 1940; *s* of Jack Watkins and Dorothy May Watkins (*née* Burgwin); *m* 1962, Wendy Anne Jopling Ramshaw, *qv*; one *s* one *d. Educ:* Wolverhampton Grammar Sch.; Reading Univ. (BA Fine Art 1963). Sculptor, musician, special effects model maker (incl. 2001: A Space Odyssey) and jewellery designer, 1963–71; own studios for jewellery and sculpture, 1971–; designer, Olympic medals, London 2012. Artist in Residence, Western Australian Inst. for Technol., 1978. Vis. Lectr, Berks Coll. of Art and Guildford Sch. of Art, 1964–66; Vis. Prof., Bezalel Acad., Jerusalem, 1984. *Solo exhibitions* include: American Inst. of Architects, Philadelphia, 1973; Goldsmiths' Hall, Electrum Gall., London, 1973; Arnolfini Gall., Bristol, 1977; Nat. Gall. of Victoria, Melbourne, 1978; Gall. Am Graben, Vienna, 1980; City Art Gall., Leeds, 1985; Stedelijk Mus., Amsterdam, 1986; Contemporary Applied Art, London, 1989; City Art Gall., Birmingham, 1990; Mikimoto Hall, Tokyo, 1993; Handwerksmesse, Munich, 1999; Galerie Louise Smit, Amsterdam, 2000; *group exhibitions* include: V&A Mus., 1976; Künstlerhaus, Vienna, 1980; Crafts Council, London, 1982 and 1996; NMOMA, Tokyo, 1983; Barcelona, 1987; Nat. Mus of Scotland, 1998; American Crafts Mus., NY, 2001; *work in major collections* including: American Craft Mus.; Australian Nat. Gall.; Birmingham City Mus. and Art Gall.; Crafts Council, London; Kunstgewerbe Mus., Berlin; Musée des Arts Décoratifs, Paris; Nat. Gall. of Victoria; Nat. Mus. of Modern Art, Tokyo; Nat. Mus of Scotland; Science Mus., London; V&A Mus. Crafts Council: Member: Membership Cttee, 1976–78; Collection Cttee, 1983–84. Mem., Bd of Trustees, Haystack Mt Sch. of Crafts, Maine, 1999–. FCSD 1984; FRSA 1991. Freeman, 1988, Liveryman, 1989, Co. of Goldsmiths. Diamonds Today Award, De Beers, 1974; Art for Architecture Award, RSA, 1995. *Publications:* The Best in Contemporary Jewellery, 1994; A Design Sourcebook: Jewellery, 1999; The Paper Jewelry Collection, 2000. *Recreations:* being in my studio, listening to jazz and classical music. *Address:* Royal College of Art, Kensington Gore, SW7 2EU. *T:* (020) 7590 4261. *E:* david.watkins@rca.ac.uk.

WATKINS, (Edward) Maurice, CBE 2011; Senior Partner, Brabners LLP (formerly Brabners Chaffe Street LLP), solicitors, since 2006; *b* Manchester, 30 Nov. 1941. *Educ:* Manchester Grammar Sch.; University Coll. London (LLB, LLM; Hon. Fellow 2011). Admitted solicitor, 1966; Solicitor; Partner, 1968–2006, Sen. Partner, 1999–2006, James Chapman & Co., Solicitors. Director: Manchester United FC Ltd, 1984–2012; Manchester United plc, 1991–2004; Regl Chm., Coutts Bank, 2002–13. Chairman: Greyhound Bd of GB, 2008–14; Rugby League Eur. Fedn, 2012–; Barnsley FC, 2013–; Dir, Rugby Football League, 2002–14 (report, Watkins Review of Rugby League Governance, 2012; Actg Chm., 2012). Dir, British Assoc. for Sport and Law, 1992– (Chm., 1992–2000; Pres., 2000–06, 2015–). Mem., Legal Cttee, Fédération Internationale de Natation, 2013–. Chm. Govs, Manchester Grammar Sch., 2008–; Chairman: Central Manchester Univ. Hosps NHS Foundn Trust Charity, 2009– (Chm., New Children's Hosp. Appeal, 2005–09); Breakthrough Breast Cancer NW Appeal, 2010–14; British Swimming, 2012–; New Islington Free Sch. Proj., 2013–; Trustee, Professional Footballers Pension Scheme, 2014–. *Recreations:* most sports, raising money for charity (particularly in education and health). *Address:* Brabners LLP, 55 King Street, Manchester M2 4LQ. *T:* (0161) 836 8818, *Fax:* (0161) 836 8801. *E:* maurice.watkins@brabners.com. *Club:* Lancashire CC (Dir, 2012–).

WATKINS, Elisabeth; *see* Arfon-Jones, E.

WATKINS, Dr George Edward, CBE 2000; Chairman and Managing Director, Conoco (UK) Ltd, 1993–2002; Chairman, Petro Matad Ltd, 2012–15; *b* 19 Aug. 1943; *s* of George Robert Leonard Watkins and Laura Watkins; *m* 1966, Elizabeth Mary Bestwick; two *s. Educ:* Leeds Univ. (BSc Mining, MSc Geophysics; PhD Geophysics 1968); Stanford Univ., Calif (MS Mgt 1985). Geophysicist, Shell Internat. Petroleum Co., 1968–73; Conoco (UK) Ltd: Geophysicist, 1973–80; Dir, Exploration, 1980–84; Dir, Prodn, 1985–90; Vice Pres., Exploration Prodn, Conoco Inc., Houston, 1990–93. Non-executive Director: Abbot Gp plc, 2002–08; Paladin Resources plc, 2003–05; ITI Scotland Ltd, 2003–09; Defence Procurement Agency, 2005–07; Petroleum Services Network Ltd, 2006–11; Bridge Resources Corp., 2006–12; Panoro Energy ASA, 2012–14. Sloan Fellow, Stanford Univ., 1984–85. Chm., Scottish Enterprise Grampian, 2002–04. Chm., UK Oil & Gas Step Change in Safety, 1997–2000. Pres., UKOOA, 1996. Gov., Robert Gordon Univ., Aberdeen, 2005–12. Hon. DEng Heriot-Watt, 2001. Van Weelden Award, Eur. Assoc. Exploration Geophysicists, 1967. *Recreations:* cinema, gardening, walking, fishing. *Address:* Springfield House, Sway Road, Brockenhurst, Hants SO42 7SG. *T:* (01590) 623308.

WATKINS, Gerwyn Rhidian; a District Judge (Magistrates' Courts) (formerly Stipendiary Magistrate), South Glamorgan, 1993–2009; *b* 22 Jan. 1943; *s* of late William Watkins and Margaret Watkins (*née* Evans); *m* 1966, Eleanor Margaret Hemingway; two *s. Educ:* Ardwyn Grammar Sch., Aberystwyth; University Coll. of Wales, Aberystwyth (LLB). Articled to Thomas Andrews, Bracknell, 1966–68; Court Clerk, Cardiff Magistrates' Court, 1968–71; Justices' Clerk: Bromsgrove and Redditch, 1971–74; Vale of Glamorgan, 1974–93. Pres., Barry Rotary Club, 1990–91.

WATKINS, Maj.-Gen. Guy Hansard, CB 1986; OBE 1974; Chief Executive, Royal Hong Kong Jockey Club, 1986–96; *b* 30 Nov. 1933; *s* of Col A. N. M. Watkins and Mrs S. C. Watkins; *m* 1958, Sylvia Margaret Grant; two *s* two *d. Educ:* The King's Sch., Canterbury; Royal Military Academy, Sandhurst. Commissioned into Royal Artillery, 1953; CO 39 Medium Regt RA, 1973; Comd Task Force 'B'/Dep. Comd 1 Armd Div., 1977; Director, Public Relations (Army), 1980; Maj. Gen. RA and GOC Artillery Div., 1982; Dir Gen., Army Manning and Recruiting, 1985; retd 1986. Hon. Col, The Royal Hong Kong Regt (The Volunteers), 1993–95. Director: British Bloodstock Agency, 1996–2001; Racecourse Holdings Trust, 1996–2003. *Recreations:* racing, golf, fishing, ski-ing. *Address:* The Mill House, Fittleworth, near Pulborough, West Sussex RH20 1EP. *T:* (01798) 865717, *Fax:* (01798) 865684. *Clubs:* Hong Kong Jockey, Shek O (Hong Kong); W Sussex Golf.

WATKINS, Prof. Hugh Christian, MD, PhD; FRCP, FMedSci; Field Marshal Alexander Professor of Cardiovascular Medicine, 1996–2013, and Head, Radcliffe Department of Medicine, since 2012, University of Oxford; Fellow, Exeter College, Oxford, since 1996; *b* 7 June 1959; *s* of David Watkins, MB, BCh, and late Gillian Mary Watkins; *m* 1987, Elizabeth Bridget Hewett; one *s* one *d. Educ:* Gresham's Sch., Norfolk; St Bartholomew's Hosp. Med. Sch., London (BSc 1st Cl. Hons; MB, BS; Brackenbury & Bourne Prize in Gen. Medicine, 1984); PhD 1995, MD 1995, London. MRCP 1987, FRCP 1997. House Physician, Professorial Med. Unit, St Bartholomew's Hosp., 1984–85; Senior House Officer: in Medicine, John Radcliffe Hosp., Oxford, 1985–87; in Neurology, St Bartholomew's, 1987; Registrar, Medicine and Cardiology, St Thomas' Hosp., London, 1987–89; Lectr in Cardiological Scis, St George's, London, 1990–94, Hon. Sen. Lectr, 1995; Res. Fellow in Medicine, Harvard Med. Sch. and Brigham & Women's Hosp., Boston, 1990–94; Asst Prof. of Medicine, Harvard Med. Sch. and Associate Physician, Brigham & Women's Hosp., 1995. BHF Clinical Scientist Fellow, 1990; Sen. Investigator, NIHR, 2009. Goulstonian Lectr, RCP, 1998; Lectures: Thomas Lewis, British Cardiac Soc., 2004; Ransom, Nottingham, 2005; Lord Rayner Meml, RCP, 2010; Paul Dudley White, Amer. Heart Assoc., 2011. FMedSci 1999. Young Res. Worker Prize, British Cardiac Soc., 1992; Graham Bull Prize, RCP, 2003. *Publications:* papers in scientific jls incl. New England Jl Medicine, Jl Clinical Investigation, Cell, Nature Genetics. *Recreations:* photography, Chinese and Japanese porcelain. *Address:* Radcliffe Department of Medicine, John Radcliffe Hospital, Oxford OX3 9DU. *T:* (01865) 234657, *Fax:* (01865) 234658.

WATKINS, Prof. Jeffrey Clifton, PhD; FMedSci; FRS 1988; FRSB; Hon. Professor of Pharmacology, 1989–99, and Leader of Excitatory Amino Acid Group, Department of Pharmacology, 1973–99, School of Medical Sciences (formerly The Medical School), Bristol (Hon. Senior Research Fellow, 1983–89), now Professor Emeritus; *b* 20 Dec. 1929; *s* of Colin Hereward and Amelia Miriam Watkins; *m* 1973, Beatrice Joan Thacher; one *s* one *d. Educ:* Univ. of Western Australia (MSc 1954); Univ. of Cambridge (PhD 1954). Research Fellow, Chemistry Department: Univ. of Cambridge, 1954–55; Univ. of Yale, 1955–57; Res. Fellow, 1958–61, Fellow, 1961–65, Physiology Dept, ANU; Scientific Officer, ARC Inst. of Animal Physiology, Babraham, Cambridge, 1965–67; Res. Scientist, MRC Neuropsychiatry Unit, Carshalton, Surrey, 1967–73; Senior Research Fellow, Depts of Pharmacology and Physiology, The Med. Sch., Bristol, 1973–83. MAE 1989; FRSB (FIBiol 1998); FMedSci 1999. Hon. FBPhS (Hon. FBPharmacolS 1996); Hon. Fellow, Univ. of Bristol, 2015. Wakeman Foundn Award for Dist. Res. in Neuroscis, 1992; Dana Foundn Award for Pioneering Achievement in Health, 1994; Bristol-Myers Squibb Award for Dist. Achievements in Neuroscience Res., 1995; Thudichum Medal, British Biochemical Soc., 2000; Wellcome Gold Medal, British Pharmacol Soc., 2001. *Publications:* The NMDA Receptor, 1989, 2nd edn 1994; approx. 250 pubns in learned jls, e.g. Jl of Physiol., Brit. Jl of Pharmacol., Nature, Brain Res., Exptl Brain Res., Eur. Jl of Pharmacol., Neuroscience, Neuroscience Letters, Jl of Neuroscience, Neuropharmacology. *Address:* 8 Lower Court Road, Lower Almondsbury, Bristol BS32 4DX. *T:* (01454) 613829.

WATKINS, Maurice; *see* Watkins, E. M.

WATKINS, Paul Rhys; 'cellist and conductor; Music Director and Principal Conductor, English Chamber Orchestra, since 2009; Artistic Director, Great Lakes Chamber Music Festival, since 2015; Member, Emerson String Quartet, since 2013; *b* 4 Jan. 1970; *s* of John Watkins and Esther Elizabeth Picton Watkins; *m* 1993, Jennifer Laredo; two *d. Educ:* Yehudi Menuhin Sch.; St Catharine's Coll., Cambridge. Finalist, BBC Young Musician of Year, 1988; Principal 'Cellist, BBC SO, 1990–98; Mem. ('cellist), Nash Ensemble, 1998–2013. Principal Guest Conductor, Ulster Orch., 2009–12. Prof., RAM, 1996–2002. Featured soloist, Masterworks, BBC TV, 1999. Solo and conducting appearances with LSO, LPO, Philharmonia and English Chamber Orch., 2005–06; soloist, First Night of the Proms, 2007; solo début, Carnegie Hall, 2010; conducting début, BBC Proms, 2010. Recordings: 14 solo recordings, 2001–12; début recording as conductor, BBC SO, 2004. Winner, Leeds Conducting Competition, 2002. *Recreations:* wine, sleep, Lego. *Address:* c/o Thomas Walton, IMG Artists, The Light Box, 111 Power Road, W4 5PY. *T:* (020) 7957 5800. *E:* twalton@imgartists.com.

WATKINS, Penelope Jill, (Mrs M. J. Bowman); a District Judge (Magistrates' Courts) (formerly Stipendiary Magistrate), Mid-Glamorgan, 1995–2014, and South Wales, 1996–2014; a Recorder, 2000–14; *b* 19 April 1953; *d* of Laurence Gordon Watkins and Dorothy Ernestine Watkins; *m* 1977, Michael James Bowman. *Educ:* Howell's Sch., Llandaff; Henbury Sch., Bristol; Somerville Coll., Oxford (BA Jurisp. 1974; MA). Called to the Bar,

Lincoln's Inn, 1975; Inner London Magistrates' Courts Service: Dep. Chief Clerk, serving at London Courts, 1976–90; Dep. Training Officer, 1983–86; Justices' Clerk: Wells Street, 1990–91; Camberwell Green, 1991–95. An Asst Recorder, 1998–2000. *Recreations:* reading, music, travel. *Address:* Pontypridd Magistrates' Court, Union Street, Pontypridd CF37 1SD. *T:* (01443) 480750.

WATKINS, Peter Derek, CBE 2004; FRAeS; Director General Security Policy, Ministry of Defence, since 2014; *b* 8 Feb. 1959; *s* of Vivian Derek Watkins and Eunice Mary Watkins (*née* Wilkinson). *Educ:* Strode's Sch., Egham; Peterhouse, Cambridge (BA Hist. 1980). FRAeS 2008. Joined MoD, 1980; various posts, 1980–90; Private Sec. to Minister for Defence Procurement, 1990–93; Dir (Finance and Secretariat) Air, 1994–96; Counsellor (Defence Supply and Aerospace), Bonn/Berlin, 1996–2000; Team Leader, Smart Acquisition, 2000–01; Private Sec. to Defence Sec., 2001–03; Comd Sec., RAF Strike Comd, 2004–06; Fellow, Weatherhead Center for Internat. Affairs, Harvard Univ., 2006–07; Dir Gen. Typhoon, 2007–08, Dir Operational Policy, 2008–11, MoD; Dir Gen., Defence Acad., 2011–14. MInstD 2012. Liveryman, Coachmakers' Co., 2008–. *Recreations:* overseas travel, historic buildings. *Address:* Ministry of Defence, Main Building, Whitehall, SW1A 2HB. *E:* peter.watkins262@mod.uk.

WATKINS, Peter Rodney; Office for Standards in Education Inspector, 1993–98; *b* 8 Oct. 1931; *s* of late Frank Arthur Watkins and Mary Gwyneth Watkins (*née* Price); *m* 1971, Jillian Ann Burge (marr. diss. 1998); two *d. Educ:* Solihull Sch.; Emmanuel Coll., Cambridge (Exhibnr; Hist. Tripos Pts I and II 1952, 1953; Cert. in Educn 1954; MA 1957). Flying Officer, RAF, 1954–56; History Master, East Ham Grammar Sch., 1956–59; Sixth Form Hist. Master, Brentwood Sch., 1959–64; Sen. Hist. Master, Bristol Grammar Sch., 1964–69; Headmaster, King Edward's Five Ways Sch., Birmingham, 1969–74; Headmaster, Chichester High Sch. for Boys, 1974–79; Principal, Price's Sixth Form Coll., Fareham, 1980–84; Dep. Chief Exec., Sch. Curriculum Develt Cttee, 1984–88, Nat. Curriculum Council, 1988–91. Exec., SHA, 1980–84. Chm., Christian Educn Movement, 1980–87. Reader, St Peter's, Bishop's Waltham, dio. of Portsmouth, 1989–2010. Gov., St Luke's C of E Aided Sch., Portsmouth, 1992–2003 (Chm., 1998–2003). *Publications:* The Sixth Form College in Practice, 1982; Modular Approaches to the Secondary Curriculum, 1986; St Barnabas' Church, Swanmore 1845–1995, 1995; Swanmore since 1840, 2001; Jerusalem or Athens?, 2005; Not Like Uncle Tom: an autobiography, 2006; Bishop's Waltham: parish, town and church, 2007; The Villages of the Meon Valley: aspects of their history, 2010. *Recreations:* travel, walking, writing, local history, theology. *Address:* 1 Greenways, Spring Lane, Swanmore, Southampton SO32 2RL. *T:* (01489) 894789. *E:* p.watkins31@btinternet.com.

WATKINS, Wendy Anne Jopling; *see* Ramshaw, W. A. J.

WATKINSON, Dame Angela (Eileen), DBE 2013; MP (C) Hornchurch and Upminster, since 2010 (Upminster, 2001–10); *b* 18 Nov. 1941; *m* 1961, Roy Michael Watkinson (marr. diss.); one *s* two *d. Educ:* Wanstead County High Sch.; Anglia Poly. (HNC 1989). Bank of NSW, 1958–64; Special Sch. Sec., Essex CC, 1976–88; Cttee Clerk, Barking and Dagenham BC, 1988–89; Cttee Manager, Basildon DC, 1989–94. Member (C): Havering BC, 1994–98; Essex CC, 1997–2001. An Opposition Whip, 2002–04 and 2006–10; Shadow Minister: for Health and Educn in London, 2004–05; for Local Govt and Communities, 2005; a Lord Comr of HM Treasury (Govt Whip), 2010–12. Mem., Work and Pensions Select Cttee, 2013–15. Member: Parly Assembly, Council of Europe, 2012–; Cttee on Standards in Public Life, 2013–. Freeman, City of London, 2004. *Address:* (office) 23 Butts Green Road, Hornchurch, Essex RM11 2JS; c/o House of Commons, SW1A 0AA.

WATLING, His Honour Rev. (David) Brian; QC 1979; a Circuit Judge, 1981–2001; Resident Judge, Chelmsford Crown Court, 1997–2001; *b* 18 June 1935; *o s* of late Russell and Stella Watling; *m* 1964, Noelle Louise Bugden. *Educ:* Charterhouse; King's Coll., London (LLB). Sub-Lieut RNR. Called to Bar, Middle Temple, 1957, Lincoln's Inn, 1998; Advocate, Gibraltar, 1980. Various Crown appts, 1969–72; Treasury Counsel, Central Criminal Court, 1972–79; a Recorder of the Crown Court, 1979–81. Vis. Lectr, 1978–80, Vis. Prof. in Criminal Law, 1980–84, University Coll. at Buckingham (now Univ. of Buckingham). Judicial Mem., Parole Bd, 2002–07; Legal Assessor, GMC, 2002–07. Reader, dio. of St Edmundsbury and Ipswich, 1985; ordained deacon 1987, priest 1988; Hon. Curate: Lavenham, 1987–90; Nayland with Wissington, 1990–2002; Boxford with Groton etc., 2002–03 (retd); permission to officiate, 2003–. Pres., Dedham Vale Soc., 1994–2002. *Publications:* (contrib.) Serving Two Masters, 1988. *Recreations:* theatre and ballet, fireside reading, the company of old friends. *Address:* 7 Lady Street, Lavenham, Suffolk CO10 9RA.

WATMORE, Ian Charles; Governor, Church Commissioners, since 2014; *b* 5 July 1958; *s* of late Dr Kenneth Watmore and Kathleen Watmore; *m* 1987, Rev. Georgina; four *s. Educ:* Trinity Sch. of John Whitgift, Croydon; Trinity Coll., Cambridge (BA 1980). UK Man. Dir, Accenture, 2000–04; Govt CIO and Hd, e-Govt Unit, Cabinet Office, 2004–05; Chief Advr to Prime Minister on Delivery and Hd, Prime Minister's Delivery Unit, 2005–07; Permanent Sec., DIUS, 2007–09; Chief Exec., FA, 2009–10; Chief Operating Officer, 2010–11, Permanent Sec., 2011–12, Cabinet Office. Board Member: e-skills uk, 2000–06; English Inst. for Sport, 2002–; England Rugby 2015, 2011–; Inf. Comr's Office, 2012–. Non-exec. Chair, Quantum Sports, 2014–. Mem., Adv. Bd, Westminster Business Sch., 2010–13. Pres., Mgt Consultants Assoc., 2003–04. Chm., Migraine Trust, 2010– (Trustee, 2008–). Hon. DLitt Westminster, 2009. *Recreations:* golf, new technology, rock music, football.

WATSON, family name of **Barons Manton** and **Watson of Richmond**.

WATSON OF INVERGOWRIE, Baron *cr* 1997 (Life Peer), of Invergowrie in Perth and Kinross; **Michael Goodall Watson;** *b* 1 May 1949; *s* of late Clarke Watson and Senga (*née* Goodall); *m* 2004, Clare Thomas; one *s. Educ:* Invergowrie Primary Sch., Dundee; Dundee High Sch.; Heriot-Watt Univ., Edinburgh (BA 2nd Cl. Hons Econs and Industrial Relns). Development Officer, WEA, E Midlands Dist, 1974–77; full-time official, ASTMS, then MSF, 1977–89. Director: PS Communications Consultants Ltd, Edinburgh, 1997–99; Dundee United FC, 2003–05; Caledonia Consulting, Edinburgh, 2007–12. MP (Lab) Glasgow Central, 1989–97. Mem., Public Accounts Cttee, 1995–97. Mem., Scottish Exec. Cttee, Labour Party, 1987–90; Chm., PLP Overseas Develt Aid Cttee, 1991–97. Mem. (Lab) Glasgow Cathcart, Scottish Parlt, 1999–2005; Minister for Tourism, Culture and Sport, 2001–03. *Publications:* Rags to Riches: the official history of Dundee United Football Club, 1985; Year Zero: an inside view of the Scottish Parliament, 2001. *Recreations:* Dundee United FC, cycling, running. *Address:* House of Lords, SW1A 0PW.

WATSON OF RICHMOND, Baron *cr* 1999 (Life Peer), of Richmond in the London Borough of Richmond-upon-Thames; **Alan John Watson,** CBE 1985; Chairman: Corporate Television Networks (CTN), since 1992; Burson-Marsteller UK, 1994–2004; Burson-Marsteller Europe, 1996–2007; Raisin Social, since 2005; Director, Burson-Marsteller Worldwide, 1992–2004; *b* 3 Feb. 1941; *s* of Rev. John William Watson and Edna Mary (*née* Peters); *m* 1965, Karen Lederer; two *s. Educ:* Diocesan Coll., Cape Town, SA; Kingswood Sch., Bath, Somerset; Jesus Coll., Cambridge (Open Schol. in History 1959, State Schol. 1959; MA Hons; Hon. Fellow 2004). Vice-Pres., Cambridge Union; Pres., Cambridge Univ. Liberal Club. Research Asst to Cambridge Prof. of Modern History on post-war history of Unilever, 1962–64. General trainee, BBC, 1965–66; Reporter, BBC TV, The Money Programme, 1966–68; Chief Public Affairs Commentator, London Weekend Television, 1969–70; Reporter, Panorama, BBC TV, 1971–74; Presenter, The Money Programme, 1974–75; Head of TV, Radio, Audio-Visual Div., EEC, 1975–79; Dir, Charles Barker City Ltd, 1980–85 (Chief Exec., 1980–83); Dep. Chm., Sterling PR, 1985–86; Chairman: City and Corporate Counsel Ltd, 1987–94; Threadneedle Publishing Gp, 1987–94; Corporate Vision Ltd, 1989–98. Mem. Bd, Y & R Partnership, 1999–2002; Chm., Coca-Cola European Adv. Bd, 2003–06; Exec. Chm., Havas Media Gp UK, 2013–. Mem., Exec. Bd, Unicef, 1985–92; Mem. Bd, POW Business Leaders Forum, 1996–; non-exec. Dir, Community and Charities Cttee, BT Bd, 1996–2004. Pres., Liberal Party, 1984–85. Vice Chm., European Movt, 1995–2001. Chm., Jt Commonwealth Socs Council, 2003–13. Chairman: UK Koenigswinter Steering Cttee, 2003–10; British Accreditation Council, 2007–12. Presenter: You and 1992, BBC 1 series, 1990; The Germans, Channel 4, 1992; Key Witness, Radio 4, 1996. Vis. Prof. in English Culture and European Studies, Louvain Univ., 1990–; Vis. Fellow, Oriel Coll., Oxford, 2003–; Hon. Professor: German Studies, Birmingham Univ., 1997–; Political Studies, St Petersburg State Univ., 2003–; Business Studies, Korea Univ., 2004–. Chairman: RTS, 1992–94 (Mem. Council, 1989–95; FRTS 1992); CBI Media Industries Gp, 1995–98. President: British-German Assoc., 2000– (Chm., 1992–2000); Franco-British Soc., 2012–. Pres., Heathrow Assoc. for Control of Aircraft Noise, 1992–95. Co-Chair, British Jamestown Cttee, 2006–08. Chairman: Chemistry Adv. Bd, Cambridge Univ., 1999–; Cambridge Foundn, 2005–; High Steward (Dep. Chancellor), Cambridge Univ., 2010–. Mem. Adv. Council: John Smith Meml Trust, 1998–2002; Univ. of Virginia Center for Politics, 2011–. Chm. of Govs, Westminster Coll., Oxford, 1988–94; Governor: Kingswood Sch., 1984–90; ESU, 1993– (Internat. Dep. Chm., 1995–99; Chm., 2000–05, now Emeritus; Churchill Medal, 2005; Vice Pres., Worldwide, 2012–); Trustee, British Studies Centre, Humboldt Univ., Berlin, 1998–; Patron: Richmond Soc., 2001–; Mus. of Richmond, 2002–. Fellow, Internat. Visual Communications Assoc., 1997. Hon. FCIPR (Hon. FIPR 1998). Hon. DHL: St Lawrence Univ., 1992; Richmond American Internat. Univ., 2007; Hon Dr: Moldova Univ., 2007; Richmond American Internat. Univ., 2008; Tirana Univ., 2010; Hon. LLD: Bucharest, 2011; Birmingham, 2012. Grand Prix Eurodiaporama of EC for European TV Coverage, 1974. Order of Merit (Germany), 1995, Grand Cross, 2001, Knight's Grand Cross, 2007; Order of Merit, Grand Cross (Romania), 2004; Commonwealth of Virginia Cert. of Public Recognition, 2007; George Kastrioti Skanderberg Medal (Albania), 2012; Knight of Habsburg-Lothringen Order of St Georg, 2015. *Publications:* Europe at Risk, 1972; The Germans: who are they now?, 1992 (German, US, Japanese, Polish and Chinese edns); Thatcher and Kohl: old rivalries renewed, 1996; Jamestown: the voyage of English, 2007; The Queen and the USA, 2012. *Recreations:* historical biography, wine, the Thames. *Address:* Cholmondeley House, 3 Cholmondeley Walk, Richmond upon Thames, Surrey TW9 1NS; Somerset Lodge, Nunney, Somerset BA11 4NP. *Clubs:* Brooks's, Royal Automobile, Kennel, Beefsteak, Oxford and Cambridge.

See also Hon. S. H. W. Watson.

WATSON, Alan; *see* Watson, W. A. J.

WATSON, Alan, CBE 2001; Deputy Parliamentary Commissioner for Administration, 2000–03; Deputy Scottish Parliamentary Commissioner for Administration, 2000–02; Deputy Welsh Administration Ombudsman, 2000–03; *b* 23 Nov. 1942; *s* of late Dennis Watson and of Dorothy Watson; *m* 1st, 1966, Marjorie Eleanor Main (marr. diss.); one *s* one *d*; 2nd, 1991, Susan Elizabeth Beare (*née* Dwyer); one step *s. Educ:* King Edward VI Grammar Sch., Morpeth. Min. of Pensions and Nat. Insce, later Min. of Social Security, then DHSS, 1962–76; Staff Inspection, CSD, 1976–80; Mgt Trng, DSS, 1980–84; Investigations Manager with Parly Comr for Admin, 1984–89; Personnel, DSS, 1989–92; Dir, Field Ops, with Contributions Agency, 1992–94; Dir of Investigations, with Parly Comr for Admin, 1994–2000. Dep. Ind. Football Ombudsman, 2008– (Dir, 2002–08, Dep. Chm., 2004–08, Ind. Football Commn). *Recreations:* cricket, football, football referee, walking, books.

WATSON, Prof. Alan Andrew, FRS 2000; FRAS, FInstP; Professor of Physics, 1984–2003, now Emeritus, Research Professor, 2003–10, Visiting Professor, since 2010, University of Leeds; *b* 26 Sept. 1938; *s* of William John Watson and Elsie Robinson; *m* 1973, Susan Lorraine Cartman; one *s* one *d. Educ:* Daniel Stewart's College, Edinburgh; Edinburgh Univ. (BSc 1st cl. hons Physics 1960; PhD 1964). FInstP 1998. Asst Lectr, Univ. of Edinburgh, 1962–64; University of Leeds: Lectr, 1964–76; Reader in Particle Cosmic Physics, 1976–84; Chm., Physics Dept, 1989–93; Pro Vice-Chancellor, 1994–97; Hd, Dept of Physics and Astronomy, 1997–2000. Mem., Cosmic Ray Commn, IUPAP, 1991–95. Spokesman, Pierre Auger Observatory, Argentina, 2001–07, now Emeritus. Hon. Prof., Univ. of Edinburgh, 2009–; Vis. Prof., Univ. of Durham, 2014–Dec. 2016. Leverhulme Emeritus Fellow, 2011–12. Dr *hc* Santiago de Compostela, 2009. O'Ceallaigh Medal, Cosmic Ray Commn, IUPAP, 2011; Faraday Medal, InstP, 2011. *Publications:* contribs to Physical Review Letters, Astrophysical Jl, Jl of Physics, Nuclear Instruments and Methods, Astroparticle Physics, Nature, Physical Review D. *Recreations:* malt whisky tasting, golf, watching Scotland win Calcutta Cup games, theatre. *Address:* School of Physics and Astronomy, University of Leeds, Leeds LS2 9JT. *T:* (0113) 343 3888. *E:* a.a.watson@leeds.ac.uk. *Club:* Crail Golfing Society.

WATSON, Alistair Gordon; Sheriff of North Strathclyde at Kilmarnock, since 2005; *b* Dundee, 1 July 1959; *s* of Robert and Isobel Watson; *m* 1985, Susan Gibson; one *s* two *d. Educ:* High Sch. of Dundee; Univ. of Dundee (LLB 1980; DipLP 1981). NP 1982. Solicitor, 1981–2005; Dir, Public Defence Solicitors' Office, 1998–2005. *Recreations:* family, photography, walking, gardening. *Address:* Kilmarnock Sheriff Court, St Marnock Street, Kilmarnock, Ayrshire KA1 1ED.

WATSON, Sir Andrew; *see* Watson, Sir J. A.

WATSON, Prof. Andrew James, PhD; FRS 2003; Royal Society Research Professor, College of Life and Environmental Sciences, University of Exeter, since 2013; *b* 30 Nov. 1952; *s* of Leslie John Watson and Ena Florence Watson (*née* Bence); *m* 1978, Jacqueline Elizabeth Pughe; two *s. Educ:* Steyning Grammar Sch.; Imperial Coll., London (BSc Physics 1975); Univ. of Reading (PhD 1978). Research Scientist: Dept of Atmospheric and Oceanic Sci., Univ. of Michigan, Ann Arbor, 1978–81; Marine Biological Assoc., Plymouth, 1981–88; Res. Scientist and Project Leader, Plymouth Marine Lab., 1988–95; Prof. of Envmtl Sci., 1996–2009, Royal Soc. Res. Prof., Sch. of Envmtl Sci., 2009–13, UEA. Visiting Scientist: Lamont-Doherty Geol Observatory, Columbia Univ., 1985, 1987; Woods Hole Oceanographic Inst., 2000. *Publications:* numerous articles and papers in scientific jls. *Recreations:* acoustic and electric guitar, cycling, walking. *Address:* Laver Building, College of Life and Environmental Sciences, University of Exeter, North Park Road, Exeter EX4 4QE. *T:* (01392) 723792.

WATSON, Rt Rev. Andrew John; *see* Guildford, Bishop of.

WATSON, Maj.-Gen. Andrew Linton, CB 1981; Lieutenant Governor and Secretary, Royal Hospital, Chelsea, 1984–92; *b* 9 April 1927; *s* of Col W. L. Watson, OBE, and Mrs D. E. Watson (*née* Lea); *m* 1952, Mary Elizabeth, *d* of Mr and Mrs A. S. Rigby, Warrenpoint, Co. Down; two *s* one *d. Educ:* Wellington Coll., Berks. psc, jssc, rcds. Commnd The Black Watch, 1946; served, 1946–66: with 1st and 2nd Bns, Black Watch, in UK, Germany, Cyprus and British Guiana; with UN Force, Cyprus; as GSO 2 and 3 on Staff, UK and Germany; GSO 1 HQ 17 Div./Malaya Dist, 1966–68; CO 1st Bn The Black Watch, UK, Gibraltar and NI, 1969–71; Comdr 19 Airportable Bde, Colchester, 1972–73; RCDS, 1974; Comdr British Army Staff, and Military Attaché, Washington, DC, 1975–77; GOC Eastern District, 1977–80; COS, Allied Forces, Northern Europe, 1980–82. Col, The Black Watch, 1981–92. Chm., Inner London Br., Army Benevolent Fund, 1983–2000; Trustee, Royal Cambridge

Home for Soldiers' Widows, 1992–2001. *Recreations:* golf, walking, classical music. *Address:* c/o Royal Bank of Scotland, 12 Dunkeld Road, Perth PH1 5RB. *T:* (01738) 21777. *Club:* Pitt.

See also T. D. H. Davies.

WATSON, Sir Andrew Michael M.; *see* Milne-Watson.

WATSON, (Angus) Gavin; freelance writer and editor; Secretary, Pevsner (formerly Buildings) Books Trust, 1997–2014; *b* 14 April 1944; *s* of late H. E. and M. Watson; *m* 1967, Susan Naomi Beal (marr. diss. 1991); two *s* (and one *d* decd). *Educ:* Carlisle Grammar School; Merton College, Oxford; Peterhouse, Cambridge. Joined Dept of the Environment, 1971; Private Office, Secretary of State, 1975–77; Asst Sec., 1980–86; Under Secretary, 1986–97; Head: Directorate of Public Housing Mgt and Resources, 1986–91; Water Directorate, June–July 1991; Directorate of Envmtl Policy and Analysis, 1991–94; Cities, Countryside and Private Finance Directorate, 1994–95; Govt Offices Central Unit, 1995–97; Chm., Fortunegate Community Housing, 1998–2004. Adjudicator, Nat. Rlwy Heritage Awards, 2003–. *Publications:* contribs to Pevsner Architectural Guides. *Recreations:* looking at buildings, industrial archaeology, fell walking. *Address:* 19 Castle Street, Bishop's Castle, Shropshire SY9 5BU. *T:* (01588) 630444.

WATSON, Anthony, CBE 2009; Chairman, Marks & Spencer Pension Trust Ltd, 2006–11; *b* 2 April 1945; *s* of Lt Comdr Andrew Patrick Watson and Harriet Watson; *m* 1972, Heather Jane Dye; two *s* one *d*. *Educ:* Campbell Coll., Belfast; Queen's Univ., Belfast (BSc Hons Econ). ASIP (AIIMR 1972). Called to the Bar, Lincoln's Inn, 1976, Bencher, 2002. Dir, Touche, Remnant & Co., 1980–85; Chief Investment Officer, Citibank NA, 1985–91; Dir Internat. Investments, 1991–95, Man. Dir, 1995–98, AMP Asset Management plc; Chief Investment Officer, 1998–2001, Chief Exec., 2002–06, Hermes Pensions Mgt Ltd. Chm., Asian Infrastructure Fund Ltd, 1998–2010; Director: Virgin Direct Ltd, 1995–98; Innisfree plc, 1996–98; MEPC, 2000–06 (Chm., 2003–06); Securities Inst., 2000–06; Edinburgh Fund Managers plc, 2001–02; Investment Mgt Assoc. Ltd, 2002–05; Vodafone Gp PLC, 2006–14; Hammerson Gp PLC, 2006–09 (Sen. Ind. Dir, 2009–); Witan Investment Trust PLC, 2006– (Sen. Ind. Dir, 2009–); Lloyds Banking Gp, 2009–12 (Sen. Ind. Dir, 2012–); Mem. Adv. Bd, Norges Bank Investment Mgt, 2006–; Mem. Adv. Gp, 2008–09, Dir, 2009–14, Shareholder Exec., BERR, later BIS. Chm., Strategic Investment Bd (NI), 2002–09. Mem., Financial Reporting Council, 2004–07. Dir, Queen's Univ. Foundn Bd, 2003–15. Trustee: Women Caring Trust, 1996–2006; Lincoln's Inn Pension Fund, 2002–; Investment Property Educnl Trust, 2004–06. Hon. FCSI (Hon. FSI 2006). Freeman, City of London, 2007; Liveryman, Leathersellers' Co., 2007 (Master, 2014–15). Hon. DSc Econs QUB, 2012. *Recreations:* golf, ski-ing, history, tennis, Rugby. *E:* tonywatson11@btinternet.com. *Clubs:* Royal Automobile, MCC; Royal St Davids Golf (Harlech).

WATSON, Anthony David F.; *see* Forbes Watson.

WATSON, (Anthony) Dennis; QC 2009; **His Honour Judge Dennis Watson;** a Circuit Judge, since 2012; *b* Crosby, June 1963; *s* of Keith Watson and Margaret Watson; *m* 1994, Nicola Jane Hunt; one *s* one *d*. *Educ:* Uppingham Sch.; Leeds Poly. (BA Hons Law 1984); Inns of Court Sch. of Law. Called to the Bar, Inner Temple, 1985; in practice on N Circuit, 1985–2012; Recorder, 2003–12. *Recreations:* golf, ski-ing, family. *Address:* Liverpool Crown Court, The Queen Elizabeth II Law Courts, Derby Square, Liverpool, Merseyside L2 1XA. *Clubs:* Royal Birkdale Golf (Capt., 2008), Royal & Ancient Golf, Royal Cinque Ports Golf.

WATSON, Anthony Gerard; Managing Director, Press Association, since 2008; *b* 28 May 1955; *s* of George Maurice Watson and Ann (*née* McDonnell); *m* 1st, 1982, Susan Ann Gutteridge (marr. diss. 1994); two *s* one *d*; 2nd, 1994, Sylvie Helen Pask; one *s* one *d*. *Educ:* St John Fisher Sch., Peterborough; N Staffs Polytechnic (BA Pol. and Internat. Relns). Journalist with E Midlands Allied Press, Peterborough, 1977–79; joined Westminster Press—Evening Despatch, Darlington, 1979, News Editor, 1983–84; Yorkshire Post, 1984–86; Researcher, World in Action, Granada TV, 1986–88; Dep. Editor, 1988–89, Editor, 1989–2002, Yorkshire Post; Head of Business Develt, 2003–04, Editl Dir, 2004–06, Ed.-in-Chief, 2007–08, Press Assoc. Provincial Journalist of the Year, British Press Awards, 1987. *Address:* The Press Association, 292 Vauxhall Bridge Road, SW1V 1AE.

WATSON, Antony Edward Douglas; QC 1986; *b* 6 March 1945; *s* of William Edward Watson and Margaret Watson (*née* Douglas); *m* 1972, Gillian Mary Bevan-Arthur; two *d*. *Educ:* Sedbergh School; Sidney Sussex College, Cambridge (MA). Called to the Bar, Inner Temple, 1968. Dep. Chm., Copyright Tribunal, 1994–97. *Publications:* (jtly) Terrell on Patents (1884), 13th edn 1982, 14th edn 1994. *Recreations:* wine, opera, country pursuits. *Address:* The Old Rectory, Milden, Suffolk IP7 7AF. *T:* (01449) 740227. *Club:* Boodle's.

WATSON, Arthur James, RSA 2005 (ARSA 1986); artist; Senior Lecturer, Fine Art, Duncan of Jordanstone College of Art and Design, University of Dundee, since 1995; President, Royal Scottish Academy, since 2012 (Secretary, 2007–12); *b* Aberdeen, 24 June 1951; *s* of David Lyall Watson and Nance Harding Nicol; *m* 1st, 1972, Jennifer Moncrieff Sutherland Murray (marr. diss.); 2nd, 1981, Joyce Winifred Cairns, RSA (marr. diss.). *Educ:* Aberdeen Grammar Sch.; Gray's Sch. of Art, Aberdeen (Dip. Art 1973; Postgrad. Dip. 1974). Founder Artistic Dir, Peacock Printmakers (Aberdeen) Ltd, 1974–95. Mem., Awards to Artists Panel, 1982–84, Exhibns Panel, 1984–85, Combined Arts Cttee, 1985–89, Scottish Arts Council. Chair, Royal Scottish Acad. Foundn, 2013–. Member, Board: Scottish Sculpture Workshop, 1980–99; 369 Gall., Edinburgh, 1985–87; Richard Demarco Gall., 1987–92 (Chm., 1990–92); Workshop and Studio Provision, Scotland, 1999–2013; Friends of Royal Scottish Acad., 2007–; Trustee: Demarco Eur. Art Foundn, 1992–2006; Pier Arts Centre, Orkney, 2010; Perth Contemporary Art Trust, 2012–. Patron: Grampian Hosps Art Trust, 2012–; Perthshire Art Assoc., 2013–. Exhibited widely in UK, Poland, Hungary, Romania, Italy, USA and Japan; (jtly) represented Scotland at Venice Biennale, 1990; Singing for Dead Singers, five venues in Aberdeen, 2000; (with Doug Cocker) Leaving Jericho, 2003; 10 Dialogues: Richard Demarco, Scotland and the European Avant Garde, Royal Scottish Acad., 2010; Towards Double Diablerie exhibn and performance, Nagoya, 2010. Hon. Mem., Aberdeen Artists Soc., 2004; HRHA 2012. *Recreations:* filing stuff, Scottish Traditional Song (particularly if sung by elderly ladies). *Address:* 5B Melville Street, Perth PH1 5PY. *T:* 07837 672337. *E:* a.j.watson@dundee.ac.uk; Royal Scottish Academy, The Mound, Edinburgh EH2 2EL. *T:* (0131) 225 6671. *E:* info@royalscottishacademy.org.

WATSON, Her Honour Barbara Joan; a Circuit Judge, 2000–13; *b* 13 Oct. 1950; *d* of Gordon Smith Watson and Joan Watson; *m* 1975, James David Heyworth (marr. diss. 1982); one *s*. *Educ:* Nelson Grammar Sch., Lancs; Southampton Univ. (LLB Hons 1972). Called to the Bar, Gray's Inn, 1973; in practice as barrister, Northern Circuit, 1973–75 and 1981–2000; Lectr in Law, Manchester Poly., 1973–80; Asst Recorder, 1992–97; Recorder, 1997–2000; Hon. Recorder, Bor. of Burnley, 2004–13; Designated Family Judge for Lancs, 2007–11. Mem., Council of Circuit Judges, 2008–11. *Recreations:* opera, travel, watching Rugby Union.

WATSON, Charles; Chairman, Teneo International, since 2015; *b* Dartmouth, 5 March 1962; *s* of Basil Watson and Heather Howard; *m* 1989, Fiona; one *s* one *d*. *Educ:* Sherborne Sch.; King's Coll. London (BA Hist.). Good Relations Ltd, 1984–87; Valin Pollen Ltd, 1987–89; Financial Dynamics, 1990–2011, Gp Chief Exec., 2001–11; Chm., Strategic Communications, Financial Dynamics, later FTI Consulting, 2011–12; Chairman: Karma Commns Gp Ltd, 2011–14; Atlas 90 Hldgs, 2012–14. Chairman: Bedales Schs Develt Trust; New Coll. of the Humanities, 2011–14. *Recreations:* ski-ing, mountain climbing, fishing, sailing. *Address:* D5I Montevetro, 100 Battersea Church Road, SW11 3YL. *T:* 07887 787508. *Club:* Royal Cruising.

WATSON, Dr David, FREng; Director, Emerging Technology Services, IBM UK Ltd, since 2007; *b* Consett, Co. Durham, 5 May 1960; *s* of Gordon Watson and Mary Elizabeth Watson; *m* 1985, Julia Margaret Moriarty. *Educ:* Loughborough Univ. (BSc Hons Geog. 1981); Univ. of Southampton (PhD Geog. 1986). CEng 2012; FREng 2013. IBM UK Ltd: Res. Scientist and Programmer, 1984–97; Software Tech. Manager, 1997–2000; Software Develt Prog. Dir, 2000–01; Services and Technol. Prog. Dir, 2001–06. Mem., EPSRC, 2009–. *Publications:* (ed with R. A. Earnshaw) Animation and Scientific Visualization, 1993. *Recreations:* swimming, photography, cabinet making, walking, travel. *Address:* IBM UK Ltd, Hursley Park, Hursley, Winchester SO21 2JN. *T:* (01962) 815379. *E:* dwatson@uk.ibm.com.

WATSON, David James P.; *see* Pitt-Watson.

WATSON, Dennis; *see* Watson, A. D.

WATSON, Very Rev. Derek Richard; Dean of Salisbury, 1996–2002; *b* 18 Feb. 1938; *s* of Richard Goodman and Honor Joan Watson; *m* 1985, Sheila Anne Atkinson (*see* Ven. S. A. Watson). *Educ:* Uppingham Sch.; Selwyn Coll., Cambridge (MA 1965); Cuddesdon Coll., Oxford. Ordained deacon, 1964, priest, 1965; Asst Curate, All Saints, New Eltham, 1964–66; Chaplain, Christ's Coll., Cambridge, 1966–70; Domestic Chaplain to Bishop of Southwark, 1970–73; Vicar, St Andrews and St Mark's, Surbiton, 1973–78; Canon Treasurer, Southwark Cathedral and Diocesan Dir of Ordinands and Post Ordination Training, 1978–82; Rector, St Luke and Christchurch, Chelsea, 1982–96. Preacher of Lincoln's Inn, 2007–. Chm., Chelsea Festival, 1993–96. *Recreations:* cycling, croquet. *Address:* 29 The Precincts, Canterbury, Kent CT1 2EP. *Club:* Hurlingham.

WATSON, Edward, MBE 2015; Principal Dancer, Royal Ballet, since 2005; *b* Bromley, 21 May 1976. *Educ:* Royal Ballet Sch., White Lodge; Royal Ballet Upper Sch. Joined Royal Ballet, 1994; First Artist, 1998–2001; Soloist, 2001–02; First Soloist, 2002–05. *Address:* Royal Ballet, Royal Opera House, Covent Garden, WC2E 9DD. *T:* (020) 7212 9165. *Club:* Hospital.

WATSON, Prof. Elaine Denise, PhD, DSc; FRCVS; FRSB; Dean, Ross University School of Veterinary Medicine, St Kitts, West Indies, since 2012; Vice President, DeVry Medical International, since 2013; *b* Ayrshire, 8 Sept. 1955; *d* of Alexander and Isabel Watson; *m* 1989, Dr Christopher Clarke; one *s*. *Educ:* Univ. of Glasgow (BVMS 1978; MVM 1979); Univ. of Bristol (PhD 1987); Univ. of Edinburgh (DSc 2002). FRCVS 1990; FRSB (FSB 2014). Res. Officer, MAFF Cattle Breeding Centre, Shinfield, 1979–82; Veterinary Res. Officer, AFRC Inst. for Res. on Animal Diseases, Compton, 1982–84; Res. Asst, Univ. of Bristol Sch. of Veterinary Sci., 1984–87; Asst Prof. of Equine Reproduction, Univ. of Pennsylvania, 1987–91; Royal (Dick) School of Veterinary Studies, University of Edinburgh: Sen. Lectr and Hd of Reproduction, 1991–95; Reader, 1995–99; Prof. of Veterinary Reproduction, 1999–2011; Hon. Prof., 2011–; Dean, 2003–11. ARAgS 2013. *Publications:* (ed jtly) Equine Medicine, Surgery and Reproduction, 1997; contrib. scientific papers and abstracts. *Recreations:* cycling, walking, travel, cinema, books, good food and wine. *Address:* Ross University School of Veterinary Medicine, Basseterre, St Kitts, West Indies. *T:* 4654161, ext. 1100. *E:* RUSVMDean@rossvet.edu.kn.

WATSON, (Elizabeth) Joyce; Member (Lab) Wales Mid and West, National Assembly for Wales, since 2007; *b* 2 May 1955; *d* of late William Roberts and Jean Roberts (*née* Rennie); *m* 1986; three *c*. *Educ:* Manorbier Sch.; Cosheston Sch.; Cardigan Comprehensive Sch.; Pembroke Coll.; Univ. of Wales, Swansea (BScEcon Politics). Self-employed, retail and hospitality trade, 1980–2002; Manager, Women's Voice, 2002–07. *Publications:* Not Bad for a Woman, 2002; Knowing No Boundaries—Local Solutions to an International Crime: trafficking of women and children in Wales, 2010. *Recreations:* coastal path walking with dog, reading, bird watching, family meals. *Address:* National Assembly for Wales, Cardiff CF99 1NA. *T:* 0300 200 7093. *Club:* Soroptimist.

WATSON, Emily Margaret, (Mrs J. Waters), OBE 2015; actress; *b* 14 Jan. 1967; *m* 1995, Jack Waters; one *s* one *d*. *Educ:* Bristol Univ. (BA Hons English). *Films:* Breaking the Waves, 1997 (Best Actress, Variety Club, Eur. Film Award, LA Film Critics Assoc. Award, Evening Standard Film Award; Most Promising Newcomer, London Film Critics' Circle Awards); Metroland, The Boxer, Hilary and Jackie (Best Actress, British Ind. Film Awards, London Film Critics' Circle Awards), 1998; Cradle Will Rock, 1999; Angela's Ashes (London Film Critics' Circle Award), The Luzhin Defense, Trixie, 2000; Equilibrium, 2001; Punch-Drunk Love, Gosford Park, Red Dragon (Best Supporting Actress, London Film Critics' Circle Awards, 2003), 2002; The Life and Death of Peter Sellers, 2004; Separate Lies, 2005; Wah Wah, The Proposition, Corpse Bride, Miss Potter, 2006; The Water Horse: Legend of the Deep, 2007; Synecdoche, New York, 2008; Within the Whirlwind, Cold Souls, Fireflies in the Garden, 2009; Cemetery Junction, 2010; Oranges and Sunshine, 2011; War Horse, Anna Karenina, 2012; The Book Thief, Belle, 2014; Testament of Youth, 2014; Theory of Everything, A Royal Night Out, Everest, 2015; *television:* Mill on the Floss, 1997; The Memory Keeper's Daughter, 2008; Appropriate Adult, 2011 (Best Leading Actress, BAFTA, 2012); The Politician's Husband, 2013; A Song for Jenny, 2015; *theatre:* Uncle Vanya, Twelfth Night, Donmar Warehouse, 2002, Brooklyn Acad. of Music, NY, 2003. *Address:* c/o Independent Talent Group Ltd, 40 Whitfield Street, W1T 2RH.

WATSON, (Francis) Paul; QC 2002; **His Honour Judge Paul Watson;** a Circuit Judge, since 2012; *b* 10 Sept. 1953; *s* of Ray and Hilda Watson; *m* 1980, Sally; one *s*. *Educ:* Churcher's Coll., Petersfield; Leeds Poly. (BA Hons). Called to the Bar, Gray's Inn, 1978; Magistrate's Clerk, 1978–80; Army Officer, Army Legal Corps, 1980–85, retd in rank of Major; in practice as barrister, 1986–2012; a Recorder, 1998–2012. *Recreations:* sailing, avid supporter of Middlesbrough FC. *Address:* Sheffield Combined Court Centre, The Law Courts, 50 West Bar, Sheffield S3 8PH.

WATSON, Gavin; *see* Watson, A. G.

WATSON, George William P.; *see* Pascoe-Watson.

WATSON, Gerald Walter; Treasurer, Hempnall Group of Parishes, since 2005; *b* 13 Dec. 1934; *s* of Reginald Harold Watson and Gertrude Hilda Watson (*née* Ruffell); *m* 1961, Janet Rosemary (*née* Hovey); one *s* two *d*. *Educ:* King Edward VI Sch., Norwich; Corpus Christi Coll., Cambridge (MA). National Service, RAF Regt, 1953–55. War Office, 1958–64; MoD, 1964–69; Civil Service Dept, 1969–73; Northern Ireland Office, 1973–75; CSD, 1975–81; HM Treasury, 1981–86; Dir, Central Computer and Telecommunications Agency, 1978–82; Dep. Chm., Building Socs Commn, 1986–88; Partner, Banking Gp, Ernst & Young (formerly Arthur Young), 1989–98. Chm., Centaur Trust, 1999–2013. *Recreations:* opera and theatre going, equestrian sports.

WATSON, Gillian Anne McGregor; Senior Managing Director, ES Noble & Company Ltd, since 2013; *b* Ayr, 27 Nov. 1964; *d* of James Gray Watson and Patricia Anne McGregor Watson; *m* 1990, Peter Julian Boyle; two *s* one *d*. *Educ:* Wellington Sch., Ayr; Hutchesons' Grammar Sch., Glasgow; Univ. of Edinburgh (BSc Hons Maths); INSEAD (MBA). Sen. Analyst, Morgan Stanley Internat., 1986–90; Sen. Manager, Standard Chartered Asia Ltd, 1990–93; Hd, Gp Strategy, 1995–99, Vice Pres., Iberia, 1999–2000, Eastern Gp, subseq. TXU Europe; Dir, Corporate Strategy, Endesa SA, 2000–05; consultant, 2006–07;

CEO, Giltech Ltd, 2008–13. Non-executive Director: Martin Currie Global Investment Fund, 2013–; Meallmore Ltd. Mem. Bd, Scottish Enterprise, 2013–; non-exec. Dir, Royal Edinburgh Mil. Tattoo Ltd, 2013–; Trustee: Royal Edinburgh Mil. Tattoo (Charities) Ltd, 2013–; Boswell Book Fest. *Recreations:* family, keeping fit, reading, travel. *E:* gillianamwatson@btinternet.com.

WATSON, Sir Graham (Robert), Kt 2011; Member (Lib Dem) South West Region, England, 1999–2014, also Gibraltar, 2004–14, European Parliament (Somerset and North Devon, 1994–99); *b* 23 March 1956; *s* of late Gordon Graham Watson and of Stephanie Revill-Johnson; *m* 1987, Rita Giannini; one *s* one *d. Educ:* City of Bath Boys' Sch.; Heriot-Watt Univ. (BA Hons Mod. Langs). Freelance interpreter and translator, 1979–80; Administrator, Paisley Coll. of Tech., 1980–83; Head, Private Office of Rt Hon. David Steel, MP, 1983–87; Sen. Press Officer, TSB Group, 1987–88; HSBC Holdings: Public Affairs Manager, 1988–91; Govt Affairs Manager, 1992–94. European Parliament: Chm., Justice and Home Affairs Cttee, 1999–2002; Mem., Foreign Affairs Cttee, 2009–14; Member, delegations: to China, 2009–14; to India, 2009–14 (Chm.). Contested (Lib Dem) SW England, EP, 2014. Pres., Alliance of Liberals and Democrats for Europe (formerly Eur. Lib Dem and Reform Party), 2011– (Leader of Parly Gp, 2002–09). Chm., e-Parliament, 2009–14. *Publications:* (ed) The Liberals in the North-South Dialogue, 1980; (ed) To the Power of Ten, 2000; (ed) Liberalism and Globalisation, 2001; Liberal Language, 2003; EU've Got Mail, 2004; Liberal Democracy and Globalisation, 2006; The Power of Speech, 2006; Building a Liberal Europe: the ALDE Project, 2010; Letters from Europe, 2012; Continental Drift, 2014; pamphlets; articles on politics in magazines and nat. newspapers. *Recreations:* sailing, walking. *Address:* Bagehot's Foundry, Beard's Yard, Langport, Somerset TA10 9PS.

WATSON, Maj.-Gen. (Henry) Stuart (Ramsay), CBE 1973 (MBE 1954); *b* 9 July 1922; *yr s* of Major H. A. Watson, CBE, MVO and Mrs Dorothy Bannerman Watson, OBE; *m* 1965, Susan (*d* 2012), *o d* of Col W. H. Jackson, CBE, DL; two *s* one *d. Educ:* Winchester College. Commnd 2nd Lieut 13th/18th Royal Hussars, 1942; Lieut 1943; Captain 1945; Adjt 13/18 H, 1945–46 and 1948–50; psc 1951; GSO2, HQ 1st Corps, 1952–53; Instr RMA Sandhurst, 1955–57; Instr Staff Coll. Camberley, 1960–62; CO 13/18 H, 1962–64; GSO1, MoD, 1964–65; Col GS, SHAPE, 1965–68; Col, Defence Policy Staff. MoD, 1968; idc 1969; BGS HQ BAOR, 1970–73; Dir Defence Policy, MoD, 1973–74; Sen. Army Directing Staff, RCDS, 1974–76. Col, 13th/18th Royal Hussars, 1979–90. Exec. Dir, 1977–85, Dep. Dir Gen., 1985–88, Inst. of Dirs; Dir, Treasurers' Dept, Cons. Central Office, 1992–94. *Recreation:* golf. *Address:* 18 Abbey Mews, Amesbury, Wilts SP4 7EX. *Clubs:* Cavalry and Guards; Huntercombe Golf; St Enodoc Golf.

WATSON, Dr Iain Arthur; Technical Director, Thales UK, 2007–10; *b* 21 Nov. 1947; *s* of Alastair Cameron Watson and Lilian Ellen Watson (*née* Smith); *m* 1st, 1968, Janet Marshall (marr. diss. 1995); one *s* one *d*; 2nd, 1998, Pamela Chambers (*née* Low). *Educ:* Stratford Grammar Sch.; Dundee Univ. (BSc Pure Maths 1970; MSc Maths 1972; PhD 1976). Ministry of Defence: Underwater Research, Portland, 1974–89; Director: IT Systems, 1989–91; IT Strategy, 1991–92; Fleet Support (Communications and Inf. Systems), 1992–97; Dir Gen., Command Inf. Systems, 1997–99; Integrated Project Team Leader, BOWMAN and Land Digitization, 1999–2002; Dep. Tech. Dir, Thales Underwater Systems, 2002–03; Exec. Dir, 2003–04, Dir, Information Superiority, 2004–06, Defence Procurement Agency. *Recreations:* dinghy sailing, basketball, car restoration, history.

WATSON, Ven. Ian Leslie Stewart; Archdeacon of Coventry, 2007–12, now Archdeacon Emeritus; *b* Carlton, Nottingham, 17 Sept. 1950; *s* of Leslie Arthur Watson and Joan Harrison Watson (*née* Bramley); *m* 1972, Denise Macpherson; one *s* one *d. Educ:* Nottingham High Sch.; Britannia Royal Naval Coll. (French Interpreter); Army Staff Coll.; Wycliffe Hall, Oxford. Officer, RM, 1969–79; ordained deacon, 1981, priest, 1982; Curate, St Andrew's, Plymouth, with St Paul's, Stonehouse, 1981–85; Vicar (and Methodist Minister), Matchborough, 1985–89; Vicar, 1989–92, Team Rector, 1992–95, Woodley; Anglican Chaplain, Amsterdam and Noord Holland, 1995–2001; Chief Exec., Intercontinental Church Soc., 2001–07. Canon, Gibraltar Cathedral, 2002–07, now Canon Emeritus. Chm., All Netherlands Anglican Council, 1997–2001; Diocesan Dir of Ordinands, Benelux, 1998–2001; Mem., Archbishop's Bd of Mission and Partnership in World Mission, 2001–07. Officiating Chaplain, RN, 1981–85; Chaplain: Actors' Christian Union, 1981–85; Freedom Fields Gen. Hosp., Plymouth, 1981–85; City of Coventry Freeman's Guild, 2008–09; Warwickshire Fire and Rescue Service, 2009–12. Asst Mechanic, RNLI Plymouth Lifeboat, 1983–85; Retained Firefighter, Royal Berks Fire and Rescue Service, 1991–93. Chm., Soc. for Relief of Poor Clergy, 2010–. Pres., RBL, Welton Br., 2015–. Bishop Kirkby's Meml Lect., Australia, 2003. GSM (NI) 1973; Silver Jubilee Medal, 1977; Vellum Service Cert., RNLI, 1985. *Recreations:* sport (Rugby, cricket, golf, rock climbing and potholing, now sedentary due to disability), music (singing, cellist), fishing, boating (Mem., Derby Motor Boat Club), wheelchair sports (Mem., Steelers Wheelers Sports Club, Scunthorpe). *Address:* Church View Barn, Atterby, Market Rasen, Lincs LN8 2BJ. *T:* (01673) 818121. *E:* i.watson440@btinternet.com. *Clubs:* Nottinghamshire CC; Rotary International (Brigg).

WATSON, Sir (James) Andrew, 5th Bt *cr* 1866; *b* 30 Dec. 1937; *s* of Sir Thomas Aubrey Watson, 4th Bt and Ella Marguerite, *y d* of late Sir George Farrar, 1st Bt, DSO; *S* father, 1941; *m* 1965, Christabel Mary, *e d* of K. R. M. Carlisle and Hon. Mrs Carlisle; two *s* one *d. Educ:* Eton. Called to the Bar, Inner Temple, 1966; a Recorder, 1985–2003. Gov., RSC, 1990–2003. Chm., Warwicks Br., CPRE. *Heir: s* Roland Victor Watson, *b* 4 March 1966. *Address:* Talton Wing, Newbold-on-Stour, Stratford-upon-Avon, Warwickshire CV37 8UB.

WATSON, Prof. James Dewey, Hon. KBE 2002; Chancellor, Cold Spring Harbor Laboratory, 2003–07, now Emeritus (Director, 1968–94; President, 1994–2003); *b* 6 April 1928; *s* of James D. and Jean Mitchell Watson; *m* 1968, Elizabeth Lewis; two *s. Educ:* Univ. of Chicago (BS); Indiana Univ. (PhD); Clare Coll., Cambridge (Hon. Fellow, 1967). Senior Res. Fellow in Biology, California Inst. of Technology, 1953–55; Harvard University: Asst Prof. of Biology, 1956–58; Associate Prof., 1958–61; Prof. of Molecular Biology, 1961–76. Dir, Nat. Center for Human Genome Res., NIH, 1989–92. Newton-Abraham Vis. Prof., Oxford, 1994. Member: US National Acad. Sciences, 1962–; Amer. Acad. of Arts and Sciences, 1958; Royal Danish Acad. 1962; Amer. Philosophical Soc., 1977; Foreign Member: Royal Soc., 1981; Acad. of Scis, Russia (formerly USSR), 1989; NAS, Ukraine, 1995; Hon. Member: Nat. Acad. of Scis, India, 2001; Internat. Acad. of Humanism, 2004 (Humanist Laureate 2005); RIA, 2005. Hon. FIBiol 1995; Hon. Fellow, Tata Inst. of Fundamental Res., Bombay, 1996. Hon. degrees include: Hon. DSc: Chicago, 1961; Indiana, 1963; Long Island, 1970; Adelphi, 1972; Brandeis, 1973; Albert Einstein Coll. of Medicine, 1974; Hofstra, 1976; Harvard, 1978; Rockefeller, 1980; Clarkson Coll., 1981; SUNY, 1983; Rutgers, 1988; Bard Coll., 1991; Univ. of Stellenbosch, S Africa, 1993; Fairfield Univ., Conn, 1993; Cambridge, 1993; Oxford, 1995; Melbourne, 1996; Univ. of Judaism, LA, 1999; London, Illinois Wesleyan, 2000; Widener, Dartmouth, TCD, 2001; Barcelona, 2005; Hon. MD: Buenos Aires, 1986; Charles Univ., Prague, 1998; Hon. LLD Notre Dame, 1965; Dhc: Barcelona, 2005; Moscow State, 2009; Patras, Greece, 2011. Awards include: Nobel Prize for Physiology or Medicine (jointly), 1962; Carty Medal, US NAS, 1971; Kaul Foundn Award for Excellence, 1992; Copley Medal, Royal Soc., 1993; Nat. Biotechnol. Venture Award, 1993; Nat. Medal of Science, USA, 1997; Mendel Medal, Czechoslovakia, 1998; Univ. of Chicago Medal, 1998; Heald Award, Illinois Inst. of Technol., 1999; NY Acad. of Medicine Award, 1999; Univ. Medal, SUNY, 2000; UCL Prize, 2000; (jtly) Benjamin Franklin Medal, APS, 2001; Gairdner Award, 2002; Lotos Club Medal of Merit, 2004; Othmer Medal, Chemical Heritage Foundn, 2005. Liberty Medal, City of Philadelphia, 2000. US Presidential Medal of Freedom, 1977. *Publications:* (jtly) Molecular Biology of the Gene, 1965, 4th edn 1986; The Double Helix, 1968; (with John Tooze) The DNA Story, 1981; (with others) The Molecular Biology of the Cell, 1983, 3rd edn 1994; (with John Tooze and David T. Kurtz) Recombinant DNA: a short course, 1984, 2nd edn (with others) 1992; A Passion for DNA, 2000; Genes, Girls and Gamow (autobiog.), 2001; DNA: the secret of life, 2003; (ed and commentary) Darwin: the indelible stamp, 2005; Avoid Boring People: and other lessons from a life in science (autobiog.), 2007; scientific papers on the mechanism of heredity. *Recreation:* tennis. *Clubs:* Century, Piping Rock, Lotos, Brook (New York).

WATSON, James Kay Graham, PhD; FRS 1987; FRSC 1990; Principal Research Officer, National Research Council of Canada, 1987–2007, now Researcher Emeritus (Senior Research Officer, 1982–87); *b* Denny, Stirlingshire, 20 April 1936; *s* of Thomas Watson and Mary Catherine (*née* Miller); *m* 1981, Carolyn Margaret Landon Kerr, *e d* of late Robert Reid Kerr. *Educ:* Denny High Sch.; High School of Stirling; Univ. of Glasgow (BScChem, PhD). Postdoctoral Fellow: UCL, 1961–63; Nat. Res. Council, Ottawa, 1963–65; Univ. of Reading, 1965–66; Lectr in Chem. Physics, Univ. of Reading, 1966–71; Vis. Associate Prof. of Physics, Ohio State Univ., Columbus, 1971–75; SRC Sen. Res. Fellow in Chemistry, Univ. of Southampton, 1975–82. Fellow, American Physical Soc., 1990. Award for Theoretical Chemistry and Spectroscopy, Chemical Soc., 1974; Plyler Prize, Amer. Phys. Soc., 1986; Joannes Marcus Marci Medal, Czech and Slovak Spectroscopic Soc., 1996; H. M. Tory Medal, Royal Soc. of Can., 1999; E. Bright Wilson Award in Spectroscopy, Amer. Chem. Soc., 2004. *Publications:* 165 articles on molecular physics and spectroscopy in learned jls. *Recreations:* music, golf, tree-watching. *Address:* 183 Stanley Avenue, Ottawa, ON K1M 1P2, Canada. *T:* (613) 7457928; (business) Steacie Institute for Molecular Sciences, National Research Council of Canada, Ottawa, ON K1A OR6, Canada. *T:* (613) 9900739. *E:* james.watson@nrc-cnrc.gc.ca.

WATSON, James Kenneth, FCA; Chairman: Alldays (formerly Watson & Philip) plc, 1994–99; NFC plc (formerly National Freight Consortium), 1991–94 (Finance Director, 1982–84; Deputy Chairman, 1985–90); *b* 16 Jan. 1935; *s* of James and Helen Watson; *m* 1st, 1959, Eileen Fay Waller (marr. diss. 1998); two *s* one *d*; 2nd, 2001, Sylvia Grace Bailey. *Educ:* Watford Grammar Sch.; Stanford Univ., California, USA. Baker Sutton & Co., Chartered Accountants, 1964; Financial Controller, Times Group, 1968; Finance Director: British Road Services Ltd, 1970–76; Nat. Freight Corp., later Nat. Freight Co., 1977–82. Non-executive Director: Gartmore, 1993–96; Henlys Group, 1994–2000; National Express, 1994–2001. Chm., Chairmen's Forum Ltd, 2001–09, now Chm. Emeritus. Chm., Inst. of Management, 1993–96. *Publications:* contribs to transport, management and financial press. *Recreations:* cricket, theatre, history. *Address:* Benton Potts, Hawridge Common, near Chesham, Bucks HP5 2UH. *Clubs:* Royal Automobile, MCC.

WATSON, Prof. James Patrick; Professor of Psychiatry, Guy's, King's and St Thomas' School of Medicine of King's College London (formerly UMDS), 1974–2000, now Emeritus; *b* 14 May 1936; *e s* of Hubert Timothy Watson and Grace Emily (*née* Mizen); *m* 1962, Dr Christine Mary Colley; four *s. Educ:* Roan Sch. for Boys, Greenwich; Trinity Coll., Cambridge; King's Coll. Hosp. Med. Sch., London. MA, MD; FRCP, FRCPsych, DPM, DCH. Qualified, 1960. Hosp. appts in Medicine, Paediatrics, Pathology, Neurosurgery, at King's Coll. Hosp. and elsewhere, 1960–64; Registrar and Sen. Registrar, Bethlem Royal and Maudsley Hosps, 1964–71; Sen. Lectr in Psychiatry, St George's Hosp. Med. Sch., and Hon. Consultant Psychiatrist, St George's Hosp., 1971–74. *Publications:* (ed jtly) Personal Meanings, 1982; papers on gp, family, marital and behavioural psychotherapy, treatment of phobias, hospital ward environmental effects on patients, postnatal depression, community psychiatry, in BMJ, Lancet, British Jl of Psychiatry, British Jl of Med. Psychology, British Jl of Clin. Psychology, Behaviour Research and Therapy. *Recreations:* mountains; music, especially opera, especially Mozart.

WATSON, Prof. Janet Constance Elizabeth, PhD; FBA 2013; Leadership Chair for Language@Leeds, University of Leeds, since 2013; *b* Pudsey, Leeds, 31 May 1959; *d* of Peter Charles Ernest Watson and Constance Lucia Watson (*née* Coidan); *m* 1989, James Dickins; one *s* one *d. Educ:* Wyndham Sch., Egremont, Cumbria; Univ. of Exeter (BA Arabic and Islamic Studies 1984); Sch. of Oriental and African Studies, Univ. of London (Dip. Linguistics 1985; PhD Linguistics 1989). Temp. Lectr in Arabic, Univ. of Edinburgh, 1987–88; British Acad. Post-doctoral Fellow, Univ. of Durham, 1990–92; Temp. Lectr in Arabic, Univ. of Salford, 1992–94; Lectr, 1994–98, Sen. Lectr in Arabic, 1998–2005, Univ. of Durham; Prof. of Arabic Linguistics, Univ. of Salford, 2005–13. Vis. Prof. of Semitic Studies, Univ. of Heidelberg, 2003–04; Vis. Associate Prof. of Arabic, Univ. of Oslo, 2004–05. *Publications:* A Syntax of San'ani Arabic, 1993; Lexicon of Arabic Horse Terminology, 1996; Sbahtu! A Course in San'ani Arabic, 1996; (with J. Dickins) Standard Arabic: an advanced course, 1999; Wasf San'a: texts in San'ani Arabic, 2000; Phonology and Morphology of Arabic, 2002, 2nd edn 2007; (with Abd al-Rahman Mutahhar) Social Issues in Popular Yemeni Culture, 2002; (ed with L. Edzard) Grammar as a Window onto Arabic Humanism: a collection of articles in honour of Michael G. Carter, 2006; (ed jtly) Arabic in the City, 2007; (ed with J. Retsö) Relative Clauses and Genitive Constructions in Semitic, 2009; (ed) A. Sima, Mehri-Texte aus der jemenitischen Sharqīyah: Transkribiert unter Mitwirkung von Askari Hugayran Saad, 2009; (ed jtly) The Semitic Languages: an international handbook, 2011; The Structure of Mehri, 2012; contrib. articles to Linguistic Inquiry, Phonology, Morphology, Zeitschrift für Arabische Linguistik, Jl Semitic Studies, Folia Orientalia, Lang. and Linguistics. *Recreations:* cycling, horse riding, guinea pigs, walking, swimming, ski-ing, novels, learning new languages. *Address:* School of Modern Languages and Cultures, University of Leeds, Leeds LS2 9JT. *T:* (0113) 343 7069. *E:* j.c.e.watson@leeds.ac.uk.

WATSON, Ven. Jeffrey John Seagrief; Archdeacon of Ely, 1993–2004, now Archdeacon Emeritus; *b* 29 April 1939; *s* of late John Cole Watson and Marguerite Freda Rose Watson; *m* 1969, Rosemary Grace Lea; one *s* one *d. Educ:* University College Sch., Hampstead; Emmanuel Coll., Cambridge (MA Hons Classics); Clifton Theol Coll., Bristol. Curate: Christ Church, Beckenham, 1965–69; St Jude, Southsea, 1969–71; Vicar: Christ Church, Winchester, 1971–81; Holy Saviour, Bitterne, 1981–93; Examining Chaplain to Bishop of Winchester, 1976–93; RD of Southampton, 1983–93; Hon. Canon: Winchester Cathedral, 1991–93; Ely Cathedral, 1993–2004. Mem., Gen. Synod, 1985–95; Chm., C of E Vocations Adv. Sub-Cttee, 1991–99; Chm., Ministry Div. Candidates' Panel, 1999–2009. *Recreations:* photography, barbershop singing, walking, travel. *Address:* 7 Ferry Road, Hythe, Southampton SO45 5GB. *T:* (023) 8084 1189.

WATSON, Jennifer, (Jenny); Chairman, Electoral Commission, since 2009; *b* 25 Jan. 1964; *d* of Ronald Watson and Phyllis Watson (*née* Avery). *Educ:* Coopers' Co. and Coborn Sch., Upminster; Sheffield Hallam Univ. (BA Communications Studies); Univ. of Westminster (MA 20th Century British Hist.). Promotions Manager, Liberty (NCCL), 1993–95; Campaign and Communications Manager, Charter 88, 1996–98; Media and PR Manager, Victim Support, 1999; Devclt Dir, Human Rights Act Res. Unit, KCL, 2000–01; Dir and Co-Founder, 2004–05, Associate, 2007–08, Global Partners and Associates. Equal Opportunities Commission: Comr, 1999–2000; Dep. Chair, 2000–05; Chair, 2005–07. Member: Banking Code Standards Bd, 2001–06 (Dep. Chair, 2005–06); Cttee on Radioactive Waste Mgt, 2003–06; Audit Commn, 2007–10; Chair: Ind. Transparency Rev. Panel, Nirex UK, 2001–03; Ind. Complaints Panel, Portman Gp, 2013–. Dir, WRAP, 2007–14. Mem. Bd, Money Advice Trust, 2008–; Trustee, Charities Aid Foundn, 2009–12. Chm., Fawcett Soc., 1997–2001. Mem., Mgt Cttee, Liby of Women, London Guildhall

Univ., 2001–08. *Publications:* (jtly) Human Rights Act Toolkit, 2003. *Recreations:* gardening, singing (Mem., London Philharmonic Choir), reading, walking. *Address:* Electoral Commission, 3 Bunhill Row, EC1Y 8YZ.

WATSON, Prof. Jeremy Daniel McKendrick, CBE 2013; DPhil; CEng, FREng; Chief Scientist and Engineer, BRE, since 2014; Professor of Engineering Systems, and Vice Dean, Engineering Sciences, University College London, since 2013; *b* Worthing, 5 May 1952; *s* of Stanley Albert and Alice Rose Watson; *m* 1980, Penny Noel Rannard; two *s*. *Educ:* Worthing Boys' High Sch.; Univ. of London (BSc, MSc); Univ. of Sussex (DPhil). Technol. Dir, BOC Edwards, 1996–2006; Dir, Global Res., Arup, 2006–14; Chief Scientific Advr, DCLG, 2009–12. Member: Governing Bd, Technol. Strategy Bd, 2006–10; Council, EPSRC, 2011–15. Hon. Prof., Faculty of the Built Envmt, UCL, 2011–. Dep. Pres., 2014–Oct. 2016, Pres., Oct. 2016–, IET. FIET; FICE; FREng 2010. *Publications:* (with N. B. Jones) Digital Signal Processing Principles, Devices and Applications, 1990. *Recreations:* hill walking, choral singing. *Address:* UCL Science, Technology, Engineering and Public Policy, Boston House, 36–38 Fitzroy Square, W1T 6EY.

WATSON, John Grenville Bernard, OBE 1998; Member (C), North Yorkshire County Council, 2005–13; *b* 21 Feb. 1943; *s* of Norman V. Watson and Ruby E. Watson; *m* 1965, Deanna Wood (*d* 2009); one *s* two *d*. *Educ:* Moorlands Sch., Leeds; Bootham Sch., York; College of Law, Guildford. Articled, 1962, qualified as solicitor, 1967; joined John Waddington Ltd as managerial trainee, 1968; Export Director, Plastona John Waddington Ltd, 1972; Marketing Dir, 1975, Man. Dir, 1977, Waddington Games Ltd, responsible for Security Printing Div., 1984–89, for Johnsen & Jorgensen, 1988–89; Director: John Waddington PLC, 1979–89; Goddard Kay Rogers (Northern) Ltd, 1989–92; Yorkshire Bldg Soc., 1995–2004; Chief Exec., Bradford City Challenge Ltd, 1992–97. Chairman: NYnet Ltd, 2010–; PIF Ltd, 2010–; EAL Ltd, 2010–15. Chm., Bradford Community NHS Trust, 1996–2002. Mem., Leeds Develt Corp., 1988–92; Chairman: Heritage Lottery Fund, Yorks and Humber, 2005–11; Morley and Outwood Business Assoc., 2015–. Joined Young Conservatives, 1965; Chairman, Yorkshire YC, 1969; Personal Asst to Rt Hon. Edward Heath, 1970; Chm., Nat. YC, 1971; contested (C) York, general elections, Feb. and Oct. 1974. MP (C): Skipton, 1979–83; Skipton and Ripon, 1983–87. Chm., Conservative Candidates Assoc., 1975–79. Mem., Parly Select Cttee on Energy, 1980–82; PPS, NI Office, 1982–83; PPS, Dept of Energy, 1983–85. Chm., British Atlantic Gp of Young Political Leaders, 1982–84; Nat. Vice Pres., Young Conservative Orgn, 1984–86. Pres., British Youth Council, 1980–83. *Recreations:* travel, property renovation. *Address:* Evergreen Cottage, Main Street, Kirk Deighton, Leeds LS22 4DZ. *T:* (01937) 588273.

WATSON, Joyce; *see* Watson, E. J.

WATSON, Julian Howard R.; *see* Richmond-Watson.

WATSON, (Leslie) Michael (Macdonald) S.; *see* Saunders Watson.

WATSON, Lynn Deborah; *see* Roberts, L. D.

WATSON, Marc; Chief Executive, Television Group, BT, 2009–14; Executive, Premier Boxing Champions; *b* Dunstable, 1 Nov. 1969; *s* of Christopher Watson and Susan Watson; *m* 2006, Rosina Ladd; three *s*. *Educ:* Deer Park Sch., Cirencester; Univ. of Hull (LLB); Inns of Court Sch. of Law. Called to the Bar, Inner Temple, 2003; lawyer, subseq. gen. counsel, Northern and Shell, 1996–99; Dir, Reel Enterprises, 1999–2007; Commercial Dir, BT Vision, 2007–09. Non-executive Director: Shed Media, 2009–11; Youview, 2011–13; Chm., Industrious Recruitment Ltd, 2012–. Dir, Cotswold Barn Conversions Ltd, 2012–. *E:* mc100watson@gmail.com.

WATSON, Prof. Oliver James, PhD; Ieoh Ming Pei Professor of Islamic Art and Architecture, University of Oxford, since 2011; *b* London, 4 Aug. 1949; *s* of William and Katherine Watson; *m* 1992, Susan McCormack; three *d*. *Educ:* University Coll. Sch., London; Univ. of Durham (BA Hons 1971); Sch. of Oriental and African Studies, Univ. of London (PhD 1977). V&A Museum: Asst Keeper, 1979–91, Chief Curator, 1991–2001, Dept of Ceramics; Chief Curator, Islamic Section, Asian Dept, 2001–05; Keeper, Eastern Art, Ashmolean Mus., Univ. of Oxford, 2005–08; Dir, Mus. of Islamic Art, Doha, Qatar, 2008–11. *Publications:* Persian Lustre Ware, 1985; British Studio Ceramics, 1990; Ceramics from Islamic Lands, 2004; contrib. articles to specialist jls. *Recreation:* music. *Address:* Khalili Research Centre, University of Oxford, 3 John Street, Oxford OX1 2LG.

WATSON, Paul; *see* Watson, F. P.

WATSON, Dr Paul Stephen; Regional Director, Midlands and East, NHS England, since 2012; *b* Liverpool, 7 April 1964; *s* of Ronald Watson and Sylvia Watson; *m* 1989, Mary Eileen Campbell Hogg; two *s*. *Educ:* Birkenhead Sch.; Gonville and Caius Coll., Cambridge (BA 1985; MB BChir 1988); Univ. of Leeds (MPH 1992). DCH 1990; FFPH 1996 (MFPHM 1992). Consultant in Public Health Medicine, Wakefield HA, 1993–96; Dir of Acute Services, Cambridge & Huntingdon HA, 1996–99; Dir, Public Health, N Essex HA, 1999–2002; Med. Dir and Dep. Chief Exec., Essex Strategic HA, 2002–06; Dir, Commissioning, and Dep. Chief Exec., East of England Strategic HA, 2006–10; Chief Exec., Suffolk PCT, 2010–12. *Publications:* articles and book chapters on public health and health service mgt. *Recreations:* dark comedy, historical narrative, all things Italian, The Smiths. *Address:* (office) Victoria House, Capital Park, Fulbourn, Cambridge CB21 5XB. *T:* (01223) 730001. *E:* paul.watson12@nhs.net.

WATSON, Dr Peter, OBE 1988; FREng; Executive Chairman, AEA Technology, 2002–05 (Chief Executive, 1994–2001); *b* 9 Jan. 1944; *m* 1966, Elizabeth Buttery; two *s*. *Educ:* Univ. of Leeds (BSc 1966); Univ. of Waterloo, Canada (MSc 1968; PhD 1971). FIMechE; FREng (FEng 1998); FCIPS. PSO, British Railways Res., 1971–76; GKN Technology Ltd, 1976–89 (Chm., 1982–89); Chm., GKN Axles Ltd, 1986–91; Technical Dir, British Railways, 1991–94. Chairman: Lontra Ltd, 2006–; Sorption Energy Ltd, 2009–; non-executive Director: Spectris (formerly Fairey) Plc, 1997–2003; Martin Currie Enhanced Income Trust, 2000–; HSL Ltd, 2006–; SVL Ltd, 2007–. Vis. Prof., Imperial Coll., London, 2005–. Pres., Engrg Integrity Soc., 1988–. Mem. Bd, Univ. of Wolverhampton, 1993–2004. Chm., S Staffs Golf Club Ltd, 2010–. Hon. FAPM. FRSA 1988. *Publications:* numerous articles on metal fatigue and management. *Address:* 49 Suckling Green Lane, Codsall, Wolverhampton, W Midlands WV8 2BT. *T:* (01902) 845252.

WATSON, Rt Rev. Peter Robert; Archbishop of Melbourne and Metropolitan of the Province of Victoria, 2000–05; *b* 1 Jan. 1936; *s* of Noel Frederick and Helen Elizabeth Watson; *m* 1962, Margo Eleanor Deans; three *d*. *Educ:* Canterbury Boys' High Sch., Sydney; Sydney Univ. (BEc); Moore Theological Coll., Sydney (ThL). Asst Priest, St Paul's, Chatswood, 1961–63; Curate-in-Charge, Lalor Park and Seven Hills, 1963–73; Rector, Lalor Park and Seven Hills, 1973–74; RD of Prospect, 1968–74; Canon, Prov. Cathedral of St John, Parramatta, 1969–74; Rector: St Luke's, Miranda, 1974–84; St Thomas, North Sydney, 1984–89; Area Dean, North Sydney, 1986–89; Bishop of Parramatta, 1989–93, of South Sydney, 1993–2000; an Asst Bp of Sydney, 1989–2000. *Recreations:* caravanning, walking, travel, swimming. *Address:* 8/41 Rocklands Road, Wollstonecraft, NSW 2065, Australia. *T:* (2) 89040330. *E:* prmewatson@iinet.net.au.

WATSON, Philip Stuart, CBE 2006; RIBA; FCIH; public sector consultant; Chief Executive, Blackburn with Darwen Unitary Authority, 1996–2006; *b* Blackburn, 22 Feb. 1946; *s* of late Herbert and Aimée Watson; *m* 1973, Shirley Clark; one *s* two *d*. *Educ:* Wensley Fold Primary Sch., Blackburn; Queen Elizabeth's Grammar Sch., Blackburn; Sheffield Univ. (BArch Hons 1968). Chartered Architect 1970; RIBA 1970; FCIH 1976. Blackburn Borough Council: various posts from architect to Dep. Borough Architect, 1968–85; Asst Chief Exec., 1985–96; Dep. Chief Exec., 1994–96. Non-exec. Dir, NHS Blackburn with Darwen, 2008–10; Independent Chairman: Blackburn with Darwen and Bolton Building Schs for Future Local Educn Partnership, 2010–13; Gtr Manchester Healthier Together Shared Cttees in Common, 2013–. Associate, Centre for Public Service Partnerships, 2008–. Gov., Blackburn Coll., 2005– (Hon. Fellow 2011; Vice Chair, 2011–). *Recreations:* Blackburn Rovers, running, crown green bowling, golf. *Address:* Westleigh, Lawley Road, Blackburn BB2 6SG. *Clubs:* Blackburn Golf; Alexandra Bowling; Railway Bowling.

WATSON, Sir Robert (Tony), Kt 2012; CMG 2003; PhD; FRS 2011; Professor of Environmental Sciences, and Director of Strategic Development, Tyndall Centre for Climate Change Research, University of East Anglia, since 2007; Sir Louis Matheson Distinguished Visiting Professor, Monash Sustainability Institute, Monash University, since 2012; Chief Scientific Adviser, Department for Environment, Food and Rural Affairs, 2007–12. *Educ:* Queen Mary Coll., Univ. of London (BSc 1st Cl. Chem. 1969; PhD 1973). Dir and Chief Scientist, Science Div., Office of Mission to Planet Earth, NASA; Associate Dir for Envmt, Office of Sci. and Technol. Policy, Exec. Office of the Pres. of USA; World Bank: Sen. Scientific Advr, then Dir, Envmt Dept; Hd, Envmt Sector Bd, 1997; Chief Scientist and Sen. Advr for Environmentally and Socially Sustainable Develt. Dir and Co-Chair, Internat. Assessment of Agricl Sci. and Technol. for Develt; Co-Chair: Internat. Scientific Assessment of Stratospheric Ozone, 1980–; Bd, Internat. Millennium Ecosystem Assessment, 2000–05; Chm., UNEP/WMO Intergovtl Panel on Climate Change, 1997–2002. Member: BBSRC, 2007–09; NERC, 2007–12. *Publications:* (ed jtly) Land Use, Land Use Change and Forestry, 2001; (ed) Climate Change 2001, 2002; contribs to Jl Envmtl Monitoring, Environmentally Sustainable Develt Proc., Phil Trans. Royal Soc. B, Ambio. *Address:* Tyndall Centre, School of Environmental Sciences, University of East Anglia, Norwich NR4 7TJ.

WATSON, Sir Ronald (Mathew), Kt 1997; CBE 1989; Member, Sefton Metropolitan Borough Council, 1974–91 and 1992–2014 (C, 1974–91 and 1992–2011, Ind, 2011–14); Chairman, Southport and Ormskirk NHS Trust, 2007–14; *b* 24 May 1945; *s* of Ralph and Rheta Mary Watson; *m* 1966, Lesley Ann McLean; one *s* one *d*. *Educ:* South Shields GS; Waterloo GS. General Manager: Laycock Travel Services, 1972–79; Morrisons Travel Agents, 1979–92. Mem. (C), Southport CBC, 1969–74; Leader, Sefton MBC, 1983–87. Leader, Cons. Gp, AMA, 1992–97. Director: Southport Mktg and Enterprise Bureau, 1983–97; Liverpool Airport plc, 1993–97; non-exec. Dir, Southport & Formby, subseq. Sefton, HA, 1991–2001; Dep. Chairman: Cheshire and Merseyside Strategic HA, 2002–06; Cheshire W PCT, 2006–07. Mem. Bd, Merseyside Develt Corp., 1993–97; Trustee, NW Trng Council, 1996–. Local Government Association: Dep. Leader, Cons. Gp, 1996–2000; Vice-Chm., 1997–2000; Chm., Tourism Exec., 1998–2003; Chm., Envmt and Regeneration Exec., 2003–04; Dep. Chm., Regeneration Bd, 2005–06; Vice Chm., Urban Commn, 2006–10. Mem., EU Cttee of the Regions, 1998–2009. Consultant, Eur. Advice Unit, Barnetts, Solicitors, Southport, 1994–2007. Member: Audit Commn, 1995–2001; Mental Health Tribunal, 2002–May 2016; Standards for England (formerly Standards Bd for England), 2006–12; Bd, Solicitors Regulation Authy, 2010–12; Cttee, Merseyside Br., Benenden Health Care. Vice-Pres., British Resorts Assoc., 1998–. Founder Mem. and Fellow, Tourism Soc., 1978; Fellow, Inst. of Travel and Tourism, 1989. Mem., Sherlock Holmes Soc. of London, 2012–. *Recreation:* writer on jazz and blues. *Address:* 7 Carnoustie Close, Oxford Road, Birkdale, Southport PR8 2FB. *Club:* Athenæum (Liverpool).

WATSON, Ven. Sheila Anne; Archdeacon of Canterbury, since 2007; *b* 20 May 1953; *d* of William Calderhead Atkinson and Margaret Atkinson (*née* Gray); *m* 1985, Derek Richard Watson, *qv*. *Educ:* Ayr Acad.; St Andrews Univ. (MA 1975, MPhil 1980); Corpus Christi Coll., Oxford; Edinburgh Theol Coll. Ordained deaconess, 1979, deacon, 1987, priest, 1994; Deaconess: St Saviour, Bridge of Allan and St John's, Alloa, 1979–80; St Mary, Monkseaton, 1980–84; Adult Educn Officer, Kensington Episcopal Area, 1984–87; Hon. Curate, St Luke and Christchurch, Chelsea, 1987–96; Selection Sec., 1992–93, Sen. Selection Sec., 1993–96, ABM; Advr, CME, 1997–2002, Dir of Ministry, 1998–2002, dio. Salisbury; Hon. Canon, Salisbury Cathedral, 2000–02; Archdeacon of Buckingham, 2002–07. *Recreations:* theatre, cycling. *Address:* 29 The Precincts, Canterbury, Kent CT1 2EP. *T:* (01227) 865238, *Fax:* (01227) 785209. *E:* archdeacon@canterbury-cathedral.org.

WATSON, Sir Simon (Conran Hamilton), 6th Bt *cr* 1895, of Earnock, co. Lanarks; *b* 11 Aug. 1939; *s* of Leslie Dundas Watson, *g s* of 1st Bt, and Enid Margaret Watson (*née* Conran); *S* cousin, Lt-Col Sir John Inglefield-Watson, 5th Bt, 2007; *m* 1st, 1971, Madeleine Stiles (*d* 1998), *d* of W. Mahlon Dickerson; 2nd, 2007, Patricia Wheatley Burt, *d* of Dennis Anthony Wheatley. *Educ:* Harrow Sch. Balfour Williamson Co. Ltd, 1958–62; Bank of London & S America and Lloyds Bank International, 1962–83; Managing Director: Gulf Trust & Credit Ltd, 1984; Yelverton Investments plc, 1984–88; Chairman: Southend Stadium plc, 1985–87; Director: Steaua Romana plc, 1985–88; Clabir Internat. Corp., 1985–87; Imperial Waterproofing Systems Ltd, 1995–97; Bloxham Gp Ltd, 1996–2002; Internet Research Co. Ltd, 1997–2002; Netpoll Ltd, 1997–02; Ardohr Ltd (formerly Independent Telecommunications Mgt Co.), 1997–2012. Member, Executive Committee: Royal Acad. of Culinary Arts Chefs Adopt a School Trust, 1999–; Standing Council of the Baronetage, 2010– (Chm., 2014–). Trustee, British Friends of Ballet Nacional de Cuba, 2008–; Patron, New Roots-Neilsland and Earnock Heritage Gp, 2012–. *Recreations:* travel, theatre, wine, cooking, eating. *Heir: cousin* Julian Frank Somerled Watson, *b* 12 Nov. 1931. *Address:* 133 Elborough Street, SW18 5DS. *T:* (020) 8265 7595. *E:* sirsimonwatson@gmail.com.

WATSON, Hon. Stephen Hartwig Willoughby; Chief Executive, CTN Communications, since 2000; *b* Dorking, Surrey, 21 Sept. 1966; *s* of Baron Watson of Richmond, *qv*; *m* 2004, Emma Grace Winsor-Cundell; one *s* one *d*. *Educ:* European Sch., Brussels; Kingswood Sch., Bath; Royal Holloway Coll., Univ. of London (BA Hons Hist. and Politics 1987). Asst producer, BBC, 1987; Gen. Manager, Corporate Vision Ltd, 1988–90; Managing Director: Burson-Marsteller, 1990–92; Corporate Television Networks Ltd, 1992–2000. Chm., Internat. Visual Communications Assoc., 1996–98. Chm., British-German Assoc., 2007–. Contested (C) Caerphilly, 2005. Hon. Comdr, 2013–15, Hon. Capt., 2015, RNR. Trustee: Tusk Trust, 1995–2013 (Chm., 2013–); RN and RM Charity, 2013–. Order of Merit (Germany), 2015. *Recreations:* military history, wine, countryside. *Address:* 10 Kensington Place, W8 7PT. *T:* (020) 7395 4460. *E:* stephen.watson@ctn.co.uk. *Clubs:* Brooks's, Royal Automobile.

WATSON, Prof. Stephen Roger; Principal, Henley Management College, 2001–05; Fellow of Emmanuel College, Cambridge, since 1968; *b* 29 Aug. 1943; *s* of John C. Watson and Marguerite F. R. Watson; *m* 1969, Rosemary Victoria Tucker; one *s* one *d*. *Educ:* University College Sch., Hampstead; Emmanuel Coll., Cambridge (BA 1964; MA 1968; PhD 1969; MMath 2011). Research Fellow, Emmanuel Coll., Cambridge, 1968–70; Shell International, 1970–71; Cambridge University: Univ. Lectr in Operational Research, Engineering Dept, 1971–86; Tutor, Emmanuel Coll., 1973–85; Peat, Marwick Prof. of Management Studies, 1986–94; Dir, Judge Inst. of Management Studies, 1990–94; Dean, Lancaster Univ. Mgt Sch., 1994–2001. Director: Cambridge Decision Analysts Ltd, 1984–95; Environmental Resources Management, 1989–95. Assoc. Dean, Reims Mgt Sch., Reims, 2005–09. Special Advr to Pres., Assoc. to Advance Collegiate Schs of Business, Tampa, Florida, 2005–12. Chm.,

Practical Action, 2006–13. *Publications:* Decision Synthesis (with D. M. Buede), 1987; papers in learned jls. *Recreations:* singing, development issues. *Address:* 33 De Freville Avenue, Cambridge CB4 1HW.

WATSON, Maj.-Gen. Stuart; *see* Watson, Maj.-Gen. H. S. R.

WATSON, Thomas; MP (Lab) West Bromwich East, since 2001; *b* 8 Jan. 1967; *s* of Tony and Linda Watson; *m* 2000, Siobhan Corby. *Educ:* Hull Univ. Fundraiser, Save the Children, 1988–89; Chair, Nat. Orgn of Labour Students, 1992–93; Dep. Gen. Election Co-ordinator, Labour Party, 1993–97; Nat. Political Organiser, AEEU, 1997–2001. An Asst Govt Whip, 2004–05 and 2007–08; a Lord Comr of HM Treasury (Govt Whip), 2005–06; Parly Under-Sec. of State, MoD, 2006; a Parly Sec., Cabinet Office, 2008–09. Dep. Chm., Labour Party and Campaign Co-ordinator, 2011–13; Dep. Leader, Labour Party, 2015–. *Recreation:* gardening. *Address:* House of Commons, SW1A 0AA. *Club:* Friar Park and West Bromwich Labour.

WATSON, Thomas Sturges; professional golfer, since 1971 (Champions tour, since 1999); *b* 4 Sept. 1949; *s* of Raymond Etheridge Watson and Sarah Elizabeth Watson (*née* Ridge); *m* 1973, Linda Tova Rubin (marr. diss. 1998); one *s* one *d*. *Educ:* Stanford Univ. (BS 1971). Championships include: Open, 1975, 1977, 1980, 1982, 1983; US Open, 1982; Masters, 1977, 1981; Mem., Ryder Cup team, 1977, 1981, 1983, 1989, Captain, 1993 and 2014. *Address:* 1901 W 47th Place, Suite 200, Shawnee Mission, KS 66205, USA.

WATSON, William Albert, CB 1989; PhD; FRCVS; international veterinary consultant, 1990–2009; *b* 8 March 1930; *s* of Henry Watson and Mary Emily Watson; *m* 1956, Wilma, *d* of Rev. Theodorus Johannas Henricus Steenbeck; one *s* one *d*. *Educ:* Preston Grammar School; University of Bristol (PhD, BVSc). Private practice, Garstang, Lancs, 1954–55; Asst Vet. Investigation Officer, Weybridge, 1954–56, Leeds, 1956–66; Animal Health Expert, FAO, Turkey, 1966–67; Vet. Investigation Officer, Penrith, 1967–71; Dep. Regional Vet. Officer, Nottingham, 1971–75; Regional Vet. Officer, Edinburgh, 1975–77; Asst Chief Vet. Officer, Tolworth, 1977–84; Dep. Dir, 1984–86, Dir, 1986–90, Vet. Labs, MAFF, Weybridge. External Examr, London, Liverpool, Dublin and Edinburgh Univs. *Publications:* contribs to vet. jls and textbooks. *Recreations:* gardening, farming.

WATSON, Prof. William Alexander Jardine, (Alan); Ernest P. Rogers Professor of Law, since 1989, and Distinguished Research Professor, since 1996, University of Georgia; *b* 27 Oct. 1933; *s* of James W. and Janet J. Watson; *m* 1st, 1958, Cynthia Betty Balls, MA, MLitt (marr. diss.); one *s* one *d*; 2nd, 1986, Harriett Camilla Emanuel, BA, MS, JD, LLM; one *d*. *Educ:* Univ. of Glasgow (MA 1954, LLB 1957); Univ. of Oxford (BA (by decree) 1957, MA 1958, DPhil 1960, DCL 1973). Lectr, Wadham Coll., Oxford, 1957–59; Lectr, 1959–60, Fellow, 1960–65, Oriel Coll., Oxford; Pro-Proctor, Oxford Univ., 1962–63; Douglas Prof. of Civil Law, Univ. of Glasgow, 1965–68; Prof. of Civil Law, Univ. of Edinburgh, 1968–79; University of Pennsylvania: Prof. of Law and Classical Studies, 1979–84; Dir, Center for Advanced Studies in Legal Hist., 1980–89; Nicholas F. Gallichio Prof. of Law, 1984–86; Univ. Prof. of Law, 1986–89. Visiting Professor of Law: Tulane Univ., 1967; Univ. of Virginia, 1970 and 1974; Univ. of Cape Town, 1974 and 1975; Univ. of Michigan, 1977. Mem. Council, Stair Soc., 1970–; Hon. Mem., Speculative Soc., 1975. Corresp. FRSE 2004. Hon. LLD: Glasgow, 1993; Pretoria, 2002; Edinburgh, 2002; Palermo, 2003; Belgrade, 2004; Stockholm, 2005. *Publications:* (as Alan Watson): Contract of Mandate in Roman Law, 1961; Law of Obligations in Later Roman Republic, 1965; Law of Persons in Later Roman Republic, 1967; Law of Property in Later Roman Republic, 1968; Law of the Ancient Romans, 1970; Roman Private Law Around 200 BC, 1971; Law of Succession in Later Roman Republic, 1971; Law Making in Later Roman Republic, 1974; Legal Transplants, An Approach to Comparative Law, 1974, 2nd edn 1993; (ed) Daube Noster, 1974; Rome of the Twelve Tables, 1975; Society and Legal Change, 1977; The Nature of Law, 1977; The Making of the Civil Law, 1981; Sources of Law, Legal Change, and Ambiguity, 1984; The Evolution of Law, 1985, enlarged edn as The Evolution of Western Private Law, 2000; (ed) The Digest of Justinian (4 vols), 1986; Failures of the Legal Imagination, 1988; Slave Law of the Americas, 1989; Roman Law and Comparative Law, 1991; The State, Law and Religion: pagan Rome, 1991; Studies in Roman Private Law, 1991; Legal Origins and Legal Change, 1991; The State, Law and Religion: archaic Rome, 1992; Joseph Story and the Comity of Errors, 1993; International Law in Archaic Rome, 1993; The Spirit of Roman Law, 1995; Jesus and the Jews, 1995; The Trial of Jesus, 1995; Jesus and the Law, 1996; The Trial of Stephen, 1996; Jesus: a profile, 1998; Ancient Law and Modern Understanding, 1989; Law Out of Context, 2000; Legal History and a Common Law for Europe, 2002; Authority of Law and Law, 2003; Shame of American Legal Education, 2005; Comparative Law: law, reality and society, 2007, 2nd edn 2008; various articles. *Recreations:* Roman numismatics, shooting. *Address:* School of Law, University of Georgia, Herty Drive, Athens, GA 30602–6012, USA.

WATT, Alison Jane, OBE 2008; RSA; artist; *b* 11 Dec. 1966; *d* of James Watt and Annie Watt (*née* Sinclair); *m* 2000, Ruaridh Nicoll. *Educ:* Glasgow Sch. of Art (BA Fine Art 1987, MA Fine Art 1989). Associate Artist, Nat. Gall., 2006–08. *Solo exhibitions:* Contemporary Art Season, Glasgow Art Gall. and Mus., 1990; New Paintings, 1993, Paintings, 1995, Monotypes, 1997, Flowers East, London; New Paintings, Charles Belloc Lowndes, Chicago, 1996; Fold, Fruitmarket Gall., Edinburgh, 1997, Aberdeen Art Gall. and Mus. and Leeds Metropolitan Gall., 1998; Shift, Scottish Nat. Gall. of Modern Art, 2000; New Paintings, Dulwich Picture Gall., 2002; Still (installation), Old St Paul's Ch, Edinburgh, 2004; Dark Light, Pier Arts Centre, Orkney, 2007; Phantom, Nat. Gall., London, 2008; Ingleby Gall., Edinburgh, 2011; Generation, Scottish Nat. Gall. of Modern Art, 2014; (retrospective) Perth Mus. and Art Gall., 2014. First Prize for Painting, RA, 1986; BP Portrait Award, 1987; City of Glasgow Lord Provost Prize, 1993; Scottish Arts Council Award, 1996; Creative Scotland Award, 2004; ACE Award for Art in a Religious Space, 2005. *Publications:* catalogues for exhibitions and monographs. *Recreations:* visiting the Highlands, eating in great restaurants, cooking, walking. *Address:* c/o Ingleby Gallery, 15 Calton Road, Edinburgh EH8 8DL. *T:* (0131) 556 4441, *Fax:* (0131) 556 4454. *E:* mail@inglebygallery.com.

WATT, Prof. David Anthony, PhD; Professor of Computing Science, University of Glasgow, since 1995; *b* 5 Nov. 1946; *s* of Francis Watt and Mary Watt (*née* Stuart); *m* 1974, Helen Dorothy Day; one *s* one *d*; *m* 2000, Carol Ann Laing. *Educ:* Univ. of Glasgow (BSc (Eng) 1st Cl. Hons; Dip. Comp. Sci. (Dist.); PhD 1974). University of Glasgow: programmer, Computing Service, 1969–72 and 1974; Department of Computing Science: Lectr, 1974–85; Sen. Lectr, 1985–90; Reader, 1990–95; Head of Dept, 1993–96; Vice-Dean, Faculty of Sci., 1996–. Vis. Associate Prof., Univ. of Calif, Santa Cruz, 1981–82; Vis. Res. Associate, Univ. of Calif, Berkeley, 1985; Vis. Prof., Univ. of Queensland. *Publications:* (with W. Findlay) Pascal: an introduction to methodical programming, 1978, 3rd edn 1985; (jtly) Ada: language and methodology, 1987; Programming Language Concepts and Paradigms, 1990; Programming Language Syntax and Semantics, 1991; Programming Language Processors: compilers and interpreters, 1993; (with D. Brown) Programming Language Processors in Java, 2000; (with D. Brown) Java Collections, 2001; Programming Language Design Concepts, 2004. *Recreations:* chess, running, science, history. *Address:* School of Computing Science, University of Glasgow, Glasgow G12 8QQ. *T:* (0141) 330 4470.

WATT, Prof. Fiona Mary, FRS 2003; Director, Centre for Stem Cells and Regenerative Medicine, King's College London, since 2012; *b* 28 March 1956; *d* of David Mackie Watt and Janet Elizabeth Watt (*née* MacDougall); *m* 1979, James Cuthbert Smith, *qv*; two *s* one *d*. *Educ:* New Hall, Cambridge (BA Hons); Univ. of Oxford (DPhil 1979). Postdoctoral Associate, MIT, 1979–81; Head: Molecular Cell Biol. Lab., Kennedy Inst. of Rheumatology, 1981–86; Keratinocyte Lab., ICRF, then CRUK London Res. Inst., 1987–2006; Herchel Smith Prof. of Molecular Genetics, and Dep. Dir, Wellcome Trust Centre for Stem Cell Res., Univ. of Cambridge, 2006–12; Dep. Dir, Cancer Res. UK Cambridge Res. Inst., 2005–12. *Publications:* numerous contribs to learned jls. *Recreations:* fishing, reading novels, playing flute, modern art. *Address:* Centre for Stem Cells and Regenerative Medicine, Floor 28, Tower Wing, Guy's Hospital, Great Maze Pond, SE1 9RT. *E:* fiona.watt@kcl.ac.uk.

WATT, Iain Alasdair; non-executive Director, Edinburgh Dragon Trust plc, 1988–2012; *b* Edinburgh, 30 March 1945; *s* of Andrew Watt and Margaret Fawns Watt; *m* 1982, Lynne Neilson. *Educ:* Edinburgh Acad.; Univ. of Hull (BSc Econs). FCIBS. Bank of Scotland, 1969–86: bank clerk in branches, 1976–84; Manager, Investment Services; Pensions Funds Investment Manager; Dir, British Linen Bank, 1984; Edinburgh Fund Managers Group plc: Dir, 1986–2002; Chief Investment Officer, 1989–90, 2001–02; Man. Dir, 1989–90; Chief Exec., 1996–2002. Trustee, Nat. Mus of Scotland, 2007–14. *Recreations:* golf, tennis, bridge. *Address:* Sycamore Bank, North Queensferry, Fife KY11 1HE. *T:* (01383) 413645. *E:* iain.watt@sycamorebank.co.uk.

WATT, Sir James H.; *see* Harvie-Watt.

WATT, James Wilfrid, CVO 1997; HM Diplomatic Service, retired; Ambassador to Egypt, 2011–14; *b* 5 Nov. 1951; *s* of late Anthony James MacDonald Watt and Sona Elvey (*née* White); *m* 1st, 1980, Elizabeth Ghislaine Villeneuve (*d* 1998), *d* of late Marcel Villeneuve and Lorna Oliver Tudsbery; one *s* one *d*; 2nd, 2004, Amal Saad, *d* of Ibrahim and Alice Saad. *Educ:* Ampleforth Coll., York; Queen's Coll., Oxford (MA Mod. Langs 1974). Kleinwort Benson, 1974–75; freelance broadcaster and interpreter, Madrid, 1975–77; entered HM Diplomatic Service, 1977; MECAS, 1978; FCO, 1979–80; Abu Dhabi, 1980–83; FCO, 1983–85; UK Permanent Mission to UN, NY, 1985–89; Dep. Hd, UN Dept and Hd, Human Rights Unit, FCO, 1989–92; Dep. Hd of Mission and Consul Gen., Amman, 1992–96; Dep. High Comr, Islamabad, 1996–98; Res. Studentship, SOAS, 1999–2000; Head, Consular Div., then Dir for Consular Services, FCO, 2000–03; Ambassador: to Lebanon, 2003–06; to Jordan, 2006–11. *Club:* Athenæum.

WATT, John Gillies McArthur; QC (Scot.) 1992; *b* 14 Oct. 1949; *s* of Peter Julius Watt and Nancy (*née* McArthur); *m* 1st, 1972, Catherine (marr. diss. 1988), *d* of Robert Russell, Toronto, Canada; two *d*; 2nd, 1988, Susan, *d* of Dr Tom C. Sparks, Ardmore, Oklahoma, and Breckenridge, Colorado, USA. *Educ:* Clydebank High Sch.; Glasgow Univ.; Edinburgh Univ. (LLB 1971). Solicitor, 1974–78; Advocate at Scottish Bar, 1979; Advocate Depute *ad hoc*, 1990; Temporary Sheriff, 1991; called to the Bar, Middle Temple, 1992. *Recreations:* shooting, ski-ing, sailing, opera, golf. *Address:* 301 Country Club Road, Ardmore, OK 73401–1125, USA. *T:* (580) 798 4595, *Fax:* (580) 798 4595. *E:* jgmwatt1@eagleranch.com. *Clubs:* Lansdowne; Royal Western Yacht (Glasgow); Dornick Hills Country (Oklahoma).

WATT, Maureen, (Mrs Bruce Donaldson); Member (SNP) Aberdeen South and Kincardine North, Scottish Parliament, since 2011 (North East Scotland, April 2006–2011); Minister for Public Health, since 2014; *b* 23 June 1951; *d* of late Hamish Watt; *m* 1987, Bruce Donaldson; one *s* one *d*. *Educ:* Univ. of Strathclyde (BA Hons Politics 1972); Univ. of Birmingham (PGCE 1973). Teacher, Bulmershe Sch., Woodley, Reading, 1974–76; Personnel Asst, then Personnel Mgr, Deutag Drilling, Aberdeen, 1977–91; Assessor for Office of Comr for Public Appts in Scotland, 1999–2006. Scottish Parliament: Minister for Schs and Skills, 2007–09; Convener: Rural Affairs and Envmtl Cttee, 2009–11; Infrastructure and Capital Investment Cttee, 2011–14. *Recreations:* gardening, yoga, swimming. *Address:* (office) 51 Victoria Road, Torry, Aberdeen AB11 9LS. *T:* (01224) 876743. *E:* maureen.watt.msp@scottish.parliament.uk.

See also S. B. Donaldson.

WATT, Miranda Lucy Mary C.; *see* Carruthers-Watt.

WATT, Peter Martin; Director, National Services, National Society for the Prevention of Cruelty to Children, since 2014 (Director, Child Protection Advice and Support, 2011–14); political commentator and blogger; *b* 20 July 1969; *s* of David Watt and Sandra Watt; *m* 2003, Vilma Bermudez; one *s* four *d*, and one step *d*. *Educ:* Inst. of Health, Bournemouth Univ. (RGN 1992); Open Univ. Business Sch. (Professional Cert. in Mgt 2004). Student nurse, Inst. of Health, Bournemouth Univ., 1989–92; Staff Nurse, then Sen. Staff Nurse, Poole Hosp. NHS Trust, 1992–96; Labour Party: Local Organiser, Battersea/Wandsworth, 1996–98; Nat. Elections Delivery and Local Recruitment Officer, 1998–2001; Membership Taskforce Leader, 2000–01; Regl Dir, Labour East, 2001–02; Taskforce Leader, Financial and Legal Compliance, 2003–05; Dir of Finance and Compliance, 2005; Gen. Sec., 2006–07; Chief Executive: The Campaign Co., 2008–10; Counsel and Care, 2011. Chm., Kingston Foster Carers Assoc., 2008–. Foster carer (with wife), Kingston-upon-Thames BC. Jt author, Giving Victims a Voice, report into allegations of sexual abuse made against Jimmy Savile, 2013. *Publications:* Inside Out, 2010; (contrib.) What next for Labour?: ideas for a new generation, 2011. *Recreations:* watching sport (cricket and Liverpool Football Club in particular), reading crime novels.

WATT, Thorhilda Mary Vivia A.; *see* Abbott-Watt.

WATT-PRINGLE, Jonathan Helier; QC 2008; barrister; *b* 8 June 1958; *s* of Louis Roy Watt-Pringle and late Molly Alleyne Watt-Pringle (*née* Payn). *Educ:* Queen's Coll., Queenstown; Univ. of Stellenbosch (BA 1978; LLB 1980); Keble Coll., Oxford (Rhodes Scholar; BA 1983; BCL 1984; MA 1987). Advocate, Supreme Court of South Africa, 1984–86; called to the Bar, Middle Temple, 1987; in practice at London Bar, 1988–. Chm., Appeal Cttee, HFEA, 2009–15. *Recreations:* bridge, theatre, travel, cycling. *Address:* Temple Garden Chambers, 1 Harcourt Buildings, Temple, EC4Y 9DA. *E:* jwpringle@tgchambers.com. *Club:* Reform.

WATTERS, David George; Strategic Consultant, International Patient Organisation for Primary Immunodeficiencies, 2011–13 (Executive Director, 2005–11); *b* 14 Jan. 1945. *Educ:* Stromness Acad., Orkney Is. Church of Scotland lay worker, 1964–68; Social Worker, St Martin-in-the-Fields, 1968–73; Director: Threshold Centre, 1973–78; Alone In London Service, 1978–81; Gen. Sec., Haemophilia Soc., 1981–93; Gen. Sec., subseq. Chief Exec., Primary Immunodeficiency Assoc., 1994–2005. Chair: Downderry and Seaton Assoc., 2009–; Quay Lane Surgery Patient Participation Gp, St Germans, 2012–. Clerk, Sir Walter Moyle's Almshouses, St Germans, 2009–. Trustee, St Germans Priory Trust, 2012–14. Churchwarden: All Saints, Tooting, 1978–84 and 1994–98; St Germans Gp Parish, 2015–. Licensed Reader, Truro Dio., 2008–. JP Inner London, 1980–2000. *Recreations:* music, photography, birdwatching, travel, Cornwall, Orkney, theology, reading, cooking, community affairs. *Address:* Firside, Main Road, Downderry, Cornwall PL11 3LE.

WATTLEY, Graham Richard; Director, Driver and Vehicle Licensing Directorate, Department of Transport, 1985–90, retired; *b* 12 March 1930; *s* of R. C. H. Wattley and Sylvia Joyce Wattley (*née* Orman); *m* 1st, 1953, Yvonne Heale (*d* 1990); one *s* two *d*; 2nd, 1997, M. Rose Daniel (*née* Dawson). *Educ:* Devonport High School. Pilot Officer, RAF, 1949–50. Min. of Works, 1950–71; Dept of the Environment, 1971–73; Department of Transport, 1973–90: Asst Sec., DVLC Computer Div., 1978–85; Dir, DVLC, 1985; Under Sec., 1986. Treas., Dewi Sant Housing Assoc., 1991–95. Mem., Governing Body, Church in Wales, 1992–94. Warden, St Paul's Church, Sketty, 1991–96. Walk Leader, HF Holidays, 1994–2004. *Recreations:* walking, reading, bird-watching. *Address:* 36 The Ridge, Derwen Fawr, Swansea SA2 8AG. *T:* (01792) 290408. *Club:* Civil Service.

WATTS, Prof. Anthony, PhD; DSc; FRSC; FInstP; FRSB; Professor of Biochemistry, since 1996, and Associate Head, Department of Biochemistry, since 2011, University of Oxford; C. W. Maplethorpe Fellow in Biological Sciences, since 1983, and Vice Principal, since 2015, St Hugh's College, Oxford; *b* 7 Jan. 1950; *s* of late Wilfred Thomas Watts and of Ingrid Hiltraud Watts; *m* 1972, Valerie Maud Lewis; one *s* two *d*. *Educ:* Ludlow Grammar Sch.; Leeds Univ. (BSc; PhD 1976); DSc Oxon 1995. FRSC 2011; FInstP 2011; FRSB (FSB 2011). Max Planck Res. Fellow, Göttingen, 1976–80; University of Oxford: Deptl Demonstrator, 1980–83; New Blood Lectr, 1983–88; BBSRC Sen. Res. Fellow, 1997–2002; Rutherford Appleton Laboratory, Didcot: Sen. Scientist, ISCis (formerly ISIS) Facility, 1996–; Dir, Nat. Biol Solid State NMR Facility, 1997–. Fulbright Fellow and Vis. Prof., Harvard Univ., 1987; Fellow, IACR, 1998; Willsmore Fellow, Melbourne Univ., 2000. Lectr, Aust. and NZ Magnetic Resonance Soc., 1998. Moses Gomberg Lectr, Univ. Michigan, 2001. Chm., ESF Network on Molecular Dynamics of Biomembranes, 1990–92; UK rep., Membrane Commn, IUPAB, 1994–; Mem. Cttee, then Chm., BBSRC Biol Neutron Adv. Panel and Mem., ISIS Scheduling Panels, 1995–99. Member: Cttee, Biochem. Soc. of GB, 1989–98; Cttee, Biophysical Soc., 1998– (Chm., 2002–07, 2010–; Fellow). Principal Ed., Biophysical Chem., 1994–2000; Managing Ed., European Biophysics Jl, 2000–. Fellow, Amer. Biophysical Soc., 2011. 350th Commemorative Medal, Helsinki Univ., 1990; SERC-CNRS Maxime Hanss Prize for Biophysics, 1992; Morton Medal, British Biochem. Soc., 1999; Award for Biomembrane Chem., 2001, Interdisciplinary Award, 2015, Royal Soc. Chem.; Anatrace Award, Biophysical Soc., 2015. *Publications:* (with J. J. H. H. M. de Pont) Progress in Protein-Lipid Interactions, Vol. 1 1985, Vol. 2 1986; Protein-Lipid Interactions, 1993; over 320 peer reviewed scientific papers and numerous contribs to learned jls. *Address:* Biomembrane Structure Unit, Department of Biochemistry, South Parks Road, Oxford OX1 3QU. *T:* (01865) 613219. *E:* anthony.watts@bioch.ox.ac.uk.

WATTS, Prof. Anthony Brian, PhD, DSc; FRS 2014; Professor of Marine Geology and Geophysics, University of Oxford, since 1990; *b* 23 July 1945; *s* of Dennis Granville Watts and of late Vera Mabel (*née* Fisher); *m* 1970, Mary Tarbit; two *d*. *Educ:* University Coll. London (BSc); Univ. of Durham (PhD); DSc Oxon 2003. Post-Doctoral Fellow, Nat. Res. Council of Canada, 1970–71; Res. Scientist, Lamont-Doherty Geol Observatory, Palisades, NY, 1971–81; Arthur D. Storke Meml Prof. of Geol Scis, Columbia Univ., NY, 1981–90. Fellow: Amer. Geophysical Union, 1986; Geol Soc. of Amer., 2006; Eur. Geoscis Union, 2008 (Arthur Holmes Medal, 2008); MAE 1999. A. I. Levorsen Meml Award, Amer. Assoc. Petroleum Geologists, 1981; Rosenstiel Award, Univ. of Miami, 1982; Murchison Medal, Geol Soc., 1993; George P. Woollard Award, Geol Soc. of America, 2005. *Publications:* Isostasy and flexure of the lithosphere, 2001; numerous articles in scientific jls. *Recreations:* cricket, carpentry. *Address:* Department of Earth Sciences, University of Oxford, South Parks Road, Oxford OX1 3AN. *T:* (01865) 272032. *Club:* Geological Society.

WATTS, Prof. Colin, DPhil; FRS 2005; FRSE; FMedSci; Professor of Immunobiology, University of Dundee, since 1998; *b* 28 April 1953; *s* of George Watts and Kathleen Mary Watts (*née* Downing); *m* 1979, Susan Mary Light; one *s* two *d*. *Educ:* The Friends Sch., Saffron Walden; Univ. of Bristol (BSc Hons 1975); Univ. of Sussex (DPhil 1980). EMBO Fellow, UCLA, 1980–82; Beit Meml Fellow, MRC Lab. of Molecular Biol., Cambridge, 1982–85; Lectr, 1986–92, Reader, 1992–98, Univ. of Dundee. Mem., Basel Inst. for Immunology, 1991; E. de Rothschild & Y. Mayent Fellow, Institut Curie, 1999. Mem., EMBO, 1996. FRSE 1999; FMedSci 2009. Margaret Maclellan Prize, Tenovus Scotland, 2000; (jtly) Descartes Prize, EU, 2002. *Publications:* res. papers, reviews and commentaries in scientific jls. *Recreations:* music, cities, armchair sport. *Address:* Wellcome Trust Biocentre, College of Life Sciences, University of Dundee, Dundee DD1 5EH. *T:* (01382) 384233, *Fax:* (01382) 345783. *E:* c.watts@dundee.ac.uk.

WATTS, David Leonard; *b* 26 Aug. 1951; *s* of Leonard and Sarah Watts; *m* 1972, Avril Davies; two *s*. *Educ:* Huyton Hey Secondary Sch. Labour Party Orgnr, until 1992; Researcher for John Evans, MP, 1992–97. MP (Lab) St Helens N, 1997–2015. PPS to Minister of State, MoD, 2000–01, to Minister of State (Minister of Transport), DfT (formerly DTLR), 2001–03, to Dep. Prime Minister, 2003–05; a Lord Comr of HM Treasury (Govt Whip), 2005–10; an Opposition Whip, 2010–15. Mem., Foreign Affairs Select Cttee, 2010–15. Chm., Parly Labour Party, 2012–15. *Recreations:* reading, football, travel.

[Created a Baron (Life Peer) 2015 but title not yet gazetted at time of going to press.]

WATTS, Diana; *see* Ellis, D.

WATTS, Donald Walter, AM 1998; PhD; FTSE; FRACI; FACE; Emeritus Professor, 1995, and Dean, Research and Postgraduate Studies, 1995–2003, University of Notre Dame Australia (Senior Policy Adviser to the Vice Chancellor, 2004–05); *b* 1 April 1934; *s* of late Horace Frederick Watts and Esme Anne Watts; *m* 1960, Michelle Rose Yeomans; two *s*. *Educ:* Hale Sch., Perth; University of Western Australia (BSc Hons, PhD); University College London. FRACI 1967. Post-Doctoral Fellow, UCL, 1959–61; University of Western Australia: Sen. Lectr, 1962; Reader, 1969; Associate Prof., 1971; Personal Chair in Physical and Inorganic Chemistry, 1977–79; Dir, W Australian Inst. of Tech., 1980–86, renamed Vice-Chancellor, Curtin Univ. of Tech., Jan.–June 1987; Pres. and Vice-Chancellor, Bond Univ., Australia, 1987–90, now Emeritus. Vis. Scientist, Univ. of S California, 1967; Visiting Professor: Australian National Univ., 1973; Univ. of Toronto, 1974; Japan Foundn Vis. Fellow, 1984. Chairman: Aust. Cttee of Dirs and Principals in Advanced Education Ltd, 1986–87; NT Employment and Trng Authy, 1991–93; NT Trade Develt Zone Authy, 1993–95. Member: Aust. Science and Technol. Council, 1984–90; Technology Develt Authority of WA, 1984–87; Chm., Australian Space Council, Canberra, 1993–95. Chairman: Advanced Energy Systems Ltd, 1997–2003 (Dir, 1995–2003); Technical Trng Inst. Pty Ltd, 2001–03; Woodside Valley Foundn, 2003–10. Hon. Fellow, Marketing Inst. of Singapore, 1987–95. Hon. DTech Curtin, 1987; Hon. DEd WA, 2001; DUniv Bond, 2009. *Publications:* Chemical Properties and Reactions (jtly) (Univ. of W Aust.), 1978 (trans. Japanese, 1987); (jtly) Chemistry for Australian Secondary School Students (Aust. Acad. of Sci.), 1979; (jtly) The School Chemistry Project—a secondary school chemistry syllabus for comment, 1984; Earth, Air, Fire and Water, and associated manuals (Aust. Acad. of Sci. Sch. Chem. Project), 1984; numerous papers on phys. and inorganic chemistry in internat. jls; several papers presented at nat. and internat. confs. *Recreations:* tennis (Mem. Interstate Tennis Team, 1952–53), squash (Mem. Interstate Squash Team, 1957–66), golf. *Address:* University of Notre Dame Australia, 19 Mouat Street, Fremantle, WA 6160, Australia. *Clubs:* Royal Kings Park Tennis (Perth); Nedlands Tennis (Nedlands); Lake Karrinyup Golf (Karrinyup); Vines Resort (Swan Valley).

WATTS, Edward, (Ted), FRICS; property advisor; Director, Cedar Rydal Ltd, since 2006; *b* 19 March 1940; *s* of Edward Samuel Window Watts and Louise Coffey; *m* 1960, Iris Josephine Frost; two *s* (one *d* decd). *Educ:* SW Essex Technical Coll. FRICS 1971 (ARICS 1962). Established own practice, Watts & Partners, 1967 (surveyors, architects and engineers), Chm., 1967–99. Founder Chm., Hyde Housing Assoc., 1967–70 (Mem., 1967–85; Hon. Life Pres., 2007). Director: People Need Homes, 1991–97; Avilla Develts Ltd, 1999–2013; non-executive Director: WSP Gp, 1993–2002; Thamesmead Town, 1994–2000; Mem. Adv. Bd, Property Hldgs, 1992–96. Chairman: Empty Homes Agency, 1997–2002; Tilfen Ltd, 1999–2001; Blackheath Preservation Trust Ltd, 2001–09. Member: ARCUK, 1991–97; Urban Villages Gp, 1992–96; Ministerial Adv. Bd, Property Advrs to the Civil Estate. Royal Institution of Chartered Surveyors: Pres., 1991–92; Mem., Gen. Council, 1982–95; Dir, RICS Journals Ltd, 1982–88 (Chm., 1986–88). Freeman, City of London, 1985. Hon. DSc London South Bank, 1992. *Recreations:* sailing, cruising. *Address:* Flexford Farm, South Sway Lane, Sway, Lymington, Hants SO41 6DP. *T:* (01590) 681053. *E:* ted.watts@flexfordfarm.co.uk. *Clubs:* Royal Cruising; Lymington Town Sailing, Royal Lymington Yacht.

WATTS, Elizabeth Anne; soprano; *b* Norwich, 16 Feb. 1979; *d* of Peter Frederick Watts and Rosemary Jane Watts; *m* 2012, Guy Charles Kemp Robinson. *Educ:* Norwich High Sch.; Univ. of Sheffield (BA 1st Cl. Hons Archaeol. and Prehistory); Royal Coll. of Music (Postgrad. Dip. Advanced Opera). Début at Royal Opera, Covent Garden, 2011; Artist in Residence, Southbank Centre, 2011; performed at Last Night of the Proms, 2014; recitals incl. Wigmore Hall, Concertgebouw, Amsterdam, Tonhalle, Zürich. Has made numerous recordings. Hon. DMus Sheffield, 2013. Kathleen Ferrier Award, 2006; BBC Cardiff Singer of World Rosenblatt Recital Song Prize, 2007; Borletti-Buitoni Trust Award, 2011. *Recreations:* green issues, gardening, renovation of truculent old house, Norwich City FC. *Address:* c/o Maxine Robertson Management, 14 Forge Drive, Claygate, Kent KT10 0HR. *T:* (020) 7993 2917. *E:* sk@maxinerobertson.com. *W:* www.elizabethwattssoprano.com.

WATTS, Garry, MBE 2009; FCA; Chairman: Spire Healthcare Group, since 2011; BTG plc, since 2012; Foxtons, since 2013; *b* London, 1956; *s* of late Jack Watts and of Patricia May Watts; one *s* two *d*. *Educ:* Hounslow Coll. FCA 1987. Trainee Accountant, 1975–81, Qualified Accountant, 1981–84, Thomson McLintock; Manager, Thomson McLintock, later KPMG, 1984–90; Partner, KPMG, 1990–95; Director: Medeva plc, 1996–2000; Celltech Gp plc, 1999–2000; Financial Dir, 2001–04, CEO, 2004–10, SSL Internat. plc. Non-executive Director: Protherics plc, 2004–08; Stagecoach plc, 2007–; Coca-Cola Enterprises, 2010–. Mem., Supervisory Bd, Medicines and Healthcare Products Regulatory (formerly Medicines Control) Agency, 1991–2008. *Recreations:* fishing, shooting, ski-ing, horseracing, gardening, opera. *Address:* Spire Healthcare Ltd, 3 Dorset Rise, EC4Y 8EN. *T:* (020) 7427 9007. *E:* garry.watts@spirehealthcare.com. *Clubs:* Naval; New (Edinburgh).

WATTS, Graham Clive, OBE 2008; Chief Executive, Construction Industry Council, since 1991 (Director, since 1989); dance writer and critic; *b* 5 Aug. 1956; *s* of Clifford Bertie Watts and late Monica Kathleen Watts; *m* 1981, Tamara Jemima Ingrid Esposito; two *d*. *Educ:* Bedford Modern Sch.; Westfield Coll., London (BA Hons Hist. 1979); University Coll., Chichester (MA module, dance, writing and criticism, 2005). Society of Architectural and Associated Technicians: Sec. for Educn and Membership, 1979–82; Chief Exec., 1983–86; Chief Exec., British Inst. of Architectural Technicians, 1986–91. Director: Nat. Centre for Construction, 1996–; Considerate Constructors Scheme, 2001–; Construction Umbrella Body (Hldgs) Ltd, 2003–. Chm., Construction Skills Standards and Qualifications Strategic Cttee, 2007–13; Sec., Strategic Forum for Construction, 2002–10; Member: Council and Strategic Partnership Panel, Sector Skills Council for Construction, 2006–15; Construction Leadership Council Delivery Gp, 2013–; Governing Body, BRE Global, 2010–14; Trustee: Interbuild Fund, 1997–2003; Sir Ian Dixon Meml Trust, 2001–12; Happold Trust, 2002–15. Vis. Prof., Univ. of Northumbria, 2000–12. Manager, British Fencing Team, 1995–2010; Performance Dir, British Fencing, 2000–10; Olympic Team Manager for Fencing, 2001–10, Team Manager, 2004 and 2008 Olympic Games; Commonwealth Bronze Medal, 1990; British Sabre Capt., 1992 Olympic Games and 7 World Championships; Chm., Sabre Club, 1988–2008; Internat. Fencing Referee, 1991–2010. Consultant Editor, PSA and Local Government Rev., 1993; columnist: Atrium, 1987–90; New Civil Engineer, 1996–99; dance writer and critic, writing for specialist dance magazines in the UK, Europe, North America, Japan and on internet. Member: Soc. of Dance Research, 2005–; Chichester Gp of Dance Writers, 2005–; Critics' Circle, 2009– (Sec., 2010–11, Chm., 2011–, Dance Section; Mem. Council, 2010–); UNESCO Internat. Dance Council, 2011–. Sec., 2010, Chm., 2011–, Nat. Dance Awards. MCMI 1983; FRSA 1983. Hon. Member: Chartered Inst. of Architectural Technologists, 1991; RICS, 2001 (Chm., Nat. Procurement Framework Wkg Gp, 2015–; Mem., Construction and Infrastructure Forum, 2015–); Hon. Fellow: RIBA, 2000 (Mem., Fellowship Assessment Panel, 2015–); Assoc. of Building Engrs, 2000; Inst. of Building Control, 2000–01; Faculty of Building, 2003; CIBSE, 2006; Inst. of Clerks of Works and Construction Inspectors, 2010; British Inst. of Interior Design, 2012. Hon. Fellow, Chartered Inst. of Civil Engrg Surveyors, 2014. Peter Stone Award, Assoc. of Building Engrs, 1996; President's Medal, Chartered Inst. of Building, 2000; Silver Medal, British Fencing Assoc., 2005. *Publications:* (jtly) Architectural Technology: the constructive link, 1984; (with D. Klimentová) Agony and Ecstasy: my life in dance, 2013; Irina Kolesnikova, Prima Ballerina of St Petersburg Ballet Theatre, 2015; regular contrib. to Dancing Times, Dance Tabs, LondonDance, Dance Europe, Shinshokan Dance Mag. and others; contrib. articles in Building and many other jls and mags associated with built envmt. *Recreations:* ballet and all forms of contemporary dance, dance writing, reading (especially modern literature and biographies), my dogs, being in N Norfolk, voice and life of Maria Callas, British Spanish Society, Friends of the Lake District, lifelong fan of Wolverhampton Wanderers FC, member of Penya Blaugrana London (supporter of FC Barcelona). *Address:* c/o Construction Industry Council, The Building Centre, 26 Store Street, WC1E 7BT. *T:* (020) 7399 7402, *Fax:* (020) 7399 7425. *E:* gwatts@cic.org.uk.

WATTS, Jane Angharad, (Mrs C. D. G. Ross), FRCO; concert organist, since 1980; *b* 7 Oct. 1959; *d* of J. Maldwyn Watts and J. Leonora Watts; *m* 1985, Callum David George Ross; one *s*. *Educ:* Royal Coll. of Music (ARCM 1978, LRAM 1979); postgrad. studies with Mme Marie-Claire Alain, Paris. FRCO 1980; GRSM 1981. Mem. Council, RCO, 1994–2000. Débuts: BBC Radio, 1980; BBC TV, 1981; RFH, with LPO, 1983; recital, 1986; BBC Prom. Concerts, 1988; New York recital, 2008; Organist and accompanist, Bach Choir, 1991–. Numerous engagements throughout UK, 1980–, with orchestras incl. BBC Nat. Orch. of Wales, LPO, Ulster Orch., London Mozart Players, etc; recital series incl. complete cycle of Widor Organ Symphonies, Brangwyn Hall, Swansea, 1999 and 2000 and St John's Smith Square, 2001; Duruflé series, Brangwyn Hall, 2002; has performed in USA, Europe, Hong Kong, Barbados, Australia and NZ, 1991–. Jury Mem., St Albans Internat. Organ Festival, 2005. Numerous recordings incl. recitals in Westminster Abbey, Salisbury Cathedral, Chartres Cathedral, Orleans Cathedral, Belfast, Glasgow, Sydney, Brisbane and Wellington; Handel and Popplewell organ concertos. First Performer of Year, RCO, 1986. *Recreations:* cookery, maintaining links with Wales and Welsh-speaking community. *Address:* c/o Callum Ross, Yr Ysgubor, 10 Bury Farm Close, Horton Road, Slapton, Bucks LU7 9DS. *T:* (01525) 222729. *Club:* London Welsh.

WATTS, John Arthur, FCA; *b* 19 April 1947; *s* of late Arthur and Ivy Watts; *m* 1974, Susan Jennifer Swan; one *s* three *d*. *Educ:* Bishopshalt Grammar Sch., Hillingdon; Gonville and Caius Coll., Cambridge (MA). Qual. as chartered accountant, 1972; FCA 1979. Chairman: Cambridge Univ. Cons. Assoc., 1968; Uxbridge Cons. Assoc., 1973–76; Mem., Hillingdon Bor. Council, 1973–86 (Leader, 1978–84). MP (C) Slough, 1983–97; contested (C) Reading E, 1997. PPS: to Minister for Housing and Construction, 1984–85; to Minister of State, Treasury, 1985; Minister of State, Dept of Transport, 1994–97. Chm., Treasury and CS Select Cttee, 1992–94 (Mem., 1986–94). *Recreation:* reading. *Address:* The Hustings, 34 West Lane Close, Keeston, Haverfordwest, Pembs SA62 6EW.

WATTS, Sir John (Augustus Fitzroy), KCMG 2000; CBE 1988; President of the Senate, Grenada, 1967, 1985–90 and 1995–2003; *b* 31 May 1923; *s* of Cecil and Pearl Watts; *m* 1963, Dorothy Paterson. *Educ:* Michigan State Univ. (BSc); New York Univ. (DDS 1952). Founder and Leader, Grenada Nat. Party, 1955; Mem. and Dep. Speaker, Grenada Legislative Council, 1962–67; Leader of Opposition, Senate, 1968–72. Director: Caribbean Hotel Assoc., 1965–67; Grenada Airports Authy, 1985–90; Chairman: Grenada Tourist Bd, 1959–67, 1980–90; Carnival Develt Cttee, 1960–65; Pres., Caribbean Tourist Assoc., 1965–67. Pres.,

Granada Dental Assoc., 1998–2000. Charter Pres., Rotary Club of Grenada, 1968–69; Gov., Dist 404, Rotary Internat., 1974–79. Dist. Service Award, Rotary Internat. *Recreations:* music, golf, politics. *Address:* Church Street, St George's, Grenada, West Indies. *T:* 4402606. *Clubs:* Rotary of Grenada, Grenada Golf and Country (St George's) (Pres., 1966).

WATTS, Mark Francis; Director and co-owner, Luther Pendragon, Brussels, since 2010; *b* 11 June 1964; *s* of Albert Charles Watts and Carole Emmah Watts (*née* Fleischman); *m* 1st, 1988, Kim McEachan (marr. diss. 2003); two *s*; 2nd, 2003, Jessica D'Souza; one *d*. *Educ:* Maidstone Grammar Sch.; LSE (BSc Econ; MSc Econ). Planning Officer, Royal Borough of Kingston-upon-Thames, 1988–94. Associate Dir, Waterfront Partnership, 2004–09. MEP (Lab) Kent E, 1994–99, SE Region, 1999–2004; Spokesman on transport, EP, 1995–2004. Co-Chm., Eur. Transport Safety Council, 1996–2004; Sec., Labour Transport Gp, 2010–. Maidstone Borough Council: Councillor, 1986–96; Leader, Lab. Gp, 1990–94. Co-founder, Labour Finance and Industry Gp, Brussels, 2015–. Pres., E Kent Eur. Movt, 1999–. Mem. Court, Univ. of Kent at Canterbury, 2012– (Mem. Council, 2006–12). Pres., Old Maidstonians Soc., 1996–97. FRSA 2009. *Recreations:* history, walking, cycling, spending time with my family. *Address:* Luther Pendragon Brussels, Rue d'Arlon 40, Brussels 1000, Belgium. *T:* and *Fax:* (2) 2350530. *E:* markwatts@lpbrussels.com.

WATTS, Mela Lesley Jane, CBE 2008; Director of Free Schools, University Technical Colleges and Studio Schools, Department for Education, since 2010; *b* Chalfont St Peter, 12 Sept. 1963; *d* of late Edward Watts and of Pamela Watts (*née* Burke). *Educ:* Dr Challoner's High Sch., Bucks; Portsmouth Poly. (BSc Hons Biol.). Joined DES (later DFE, then DFEE, subseq. DFES, then DCSF), 1986; estabd Funding Agency for Schs; Private Sec. to Minister of Sport; estabd Nursery Educn Voucher Scheme; Bill Manager, Special Educnl Needs and Disability Act 2002; Curriculum Div.; Principal Private Sec to Sec. of State for Children, Schs and Families, 2004–08; Dir, Sch. Performance and Reform, 2008–10. *Recreations:* wine tasting, walking, travelling. *Address:* Department for Education, Sanctuary Buildings, Great Smith Street, SW1P 3BT. *T:* (020) 7783 8421. *E:* Mela.Watts@education.gsi.gov.uk.

WATTS, Neil Robert; Member, Board: Architects Registration Board, since 2009; Office of Qualifications and Examinations Regulation, since 2010; *b* Middleton, near Manchester, 8 Dec. 1951; *s* of late Kenneth Leach Watts and of Joan Watts (*née* Morgan); *m* 1983, Sadie Wood; one *s* one *d*. *Educ:* Chadderton Grammar Sch.; Magdalene Coll., Cambridge (BA 1973; MA 1976); Univ. of Leicester (PGCE Econs). Teacher of Econs, King Henry VIII Sch., Coventry, 1974–78; Hd of Econs and Business Studies, Hedingham Comp. Sch., Halstead, 1978–81; Hd of Sixth Form, Stowupland High Sch., Stowmarket, 1981–84; Dep. Headteacher, Northgate High Sch., Ipswich, 1985–88; Headteacher: Sudbury County Upper Sch., 1988–92; Northgate High Sch., Ipswich, 1992–2009; Consultant Headteacher, Suffolk CC, 2009–13. Mem. Council, 2004–11, Dep. Chm., 2009–11, Advertising Standards Authy; Public Mem., Press Complaints Commn, 2011–14; Mem., IPSO, 2014–. *Publications:* Competition, Monopoly and Public Policy, 1982; Selected Topics in Applied Economics, 1987. *Recreations:* remaining optimistic whilst supporting Rochdale AFC, theatre, wining and dining. *T:* 07850 117831. *E:* neilwattsoc@gmail.com. *Club:* Rochdale Exiles.

WATTS, Rev. Sir Philip (Beverley), KCMG 2003; FInstP, FEI, FRGS, FGS; Group Managing Director, 1997–2004, and Chairman, Committee of Managing Directors, 2001–04, Royal Dutch/Shell Group; Managing Director, 1997–2004, and Chairman, 2001–04, Shell Transport and Trading plc; Priest-in-charge, Waltham St Lawrence, Berks, since 2013; *b* 25 June 1945; *s* of Samuel Watts and Phillippa (*née* Wale); *m* 1966, Janet Lockwood; one *s* one *d*. *Educ:* Wyggeston Grammar Sch., Leicester; Univ. of Leeds (BSc Hons Physics, MSc Geophysics); Open Univ. (DipRS); Oxford Brookes (BA Hons Religion and Theol. 2011). FInstP 1980; FEI (FInstPet 1990); FRGS 1998; FGS 1998. Sci. teacher, Methodist Boys High Sch., Freetown, Sierra Leone, 1966–68; joined Shell International, 1969: seismologist, Indonesia, 1970–74; geophysicist, UK/Europe, 1974–77; Exploration Manager, Norway, 1978–81; Div. Head, Malaysia, Brunei, Singapore, London, 1981–83; Exploration Dir, UK, 1983–85; Head, Exploration & Production Liaison—Europe, The Hague, 1986–88; Head, Exploration & Production Econs and Planning, The Hague, 1989–91; Man. Dir, Nigeria, 1991–94; Regl Co-ordinator—Europe, The Hague, 1994–95; Dir, Planning, Envmt and Ext. Affairs, London, 1996–97. Member: Exec. Cttee, World Business Council for Sustainable Develt, 1998–2003 (Chm., 2002–03); Governing Body, ICC UK, 1997–2004 (Chm., 1998–2004); ICC Exec. Bd (Worldwide), 1997–2000; CfBT Educn Trust, 2009–13. Ordained deacon, 2011, priest, 2012; Curate, Binfield, Berks, 2011–13. *Recreations:* travel, gardening, reading. *Club:* Travellers.

WATTS, Rolande Jane Rita; *see* Anderson, R. J. R.

WATTS, Susan Janet; science and technology journalist; Head of Public Engagement and Communications, MRC Clinical Sciences Centre, since 2015; *b* Crystal Palace, 13 July 1962; *d* of Derek Watts and Judith Ann Mary Watts (*née* Collett); *m*; two *s* two *d*. *Educ:* Haberdashers' Aske's Hatcham Girls' Sch.; Imperial Coll., London (BSc Physics); City Univ. (Dip. Journalism). Computer Weekly, 1985–89; New Scientist, 1989–91; Independent, 1991–95; BBC Newsnight, 1995–2013 (Sci. Ed., 2000–13). *T:* 07982 142327. *E:* susan.watts@susanwatts.org.

WATTS, Vincent Challacombe, OBE 1998; Founding Chairman, East of England Development Agency, 1998–2003; Vice-Chancellor, University of East Anglia, 1997–2002; *b* 11 Aug. 1940; *s* of Geoffrey Watts and Lilian Watts (*née* Pye); *m* 1st, 1967, Rachel Rosser (*d* 1998), Prof. of Psychiatry, UCL Med. Sch.; one *s* one *d*; 2nd, 2009, Hilary (*née* Miles). *Educ:* Sidcot Sch.; Peterhouse, Cambridge (MA 1966); Birmingham Univ. (MSc 1967). FCA 1976. Joined Andersen Consulting, 1963, Partner, 1976–97; seconded to: Dept of Health as Founder Mem., Operational Res. Unit, 1970–71; HM Treasury, 1974; Financial Management Unit, Cabinet Office/HM Treasury, 1982–85. Mem. Council, John Innes Centre, 1997–2010; Mem. Council and Chair, Audit Cttee, LSC, 2002–03. CMC 1986; FIC (FIMC 1986); CCMI 2001. FRSA 2001. Hon. LittD East Anglia, 2002. *Publications:* papers on performance evaluation in health services. *Recreations:* sailing, gardening, exploring. *Clubs:* Oxford and Cambridge; Jesters.

WAUCHOPE, Sir Roger Hamilton D.; *see* Don-Wauchope.

WAUGH, Andrew Peter; QC 1998; *b* 6 Nov. 1959; *m* 1980, Catrin Prys Davies; four *s*. *Educ:* City Univ. (BSc 1st Cl. Hons 1980; DipLaw 1981). Called to the Bar, Gray's Inn, 1982; in practice as barrister, 1982–; specialist in Intellectual Property Law. *Address:* 3 New Square, Lincoln's Inn, WC2A 3RS. *T:* (020) 7405 1111.

WAUGH, Rev. Eric Alexander; Consultant on Christian Education, Theology and Worldviews, Every Nation Leadership Institute, Cape Town, South Africa, 2003–06 (Dean, 1996–98, Vice-Chancellor, 1998–2003, His People Institute); *b* 9 May 1933; *s* of Hugh Waugh and Marion Waugh (*née* McLay); *m* 1955, Agnes-Jean (Sheena) Saunders; two *s*. *Educ:* Glasgow Univ.; Edinburgh Univ. (LTh). Local government officer, 1948–64. Assistant Minister, High Church, Bathgate, 1969–70; Missionary, Kenya Highlands, 1970–73; Minister, Mowbray Presbyterian Church, Cape Town, 1973–78; Missioner, Presbyterian Church of Southern Africa, 1978–85; Minister, City Temple, URC, 1986–91; Missioner, Kingdom Communications Trust, S Africa, 1992–95. *Recreations:* walking, fly fishing, acrylic painting. *Address:* 20 Queens Lane, Bridge of Allan, Stirling FK9 4NY. *T:* (01786) 834044. *E:* eandswaugh@btinternet.com.

WAUGH, Stephen Rodger, AO 2003; cricketer; Captain, Australian Test Cricket Team, 1999–2004; *b* Sydney, NSW, 2 June 1965; *s* of Rodger and Beverley Waugh; *m* Lynette; one *s* two *d*. *Educ:* East Hills High Sch. Cricketer: with NSW, 1984–2004; with Somerset CCC, 1987–88; Mem., Australian Cricket Team, 1985–2004; Captain, One Day Internats team, 1997–2002; Mem. of winning team, World Cup, 1987; Captain of winning team, World Cup, 1999. Passed 10,000 Test runs, 2003. Life Member: BCCI, India; Bankstown Canterbury CC, NSW; Hon. Member: SCG; MCG. Allan Border Medal, 2001; Steve Waugh Medal, 2003. *Publications:* South African Tour Diary, 1995; Steve Waugh's West Indies Tour Diary, 1996; Steve Waugh's World Cup Diary, 1997; Steve Waugh's 1997 Ashes Diary, 1997; (with Nasser Hussain) Ashes Summer, 1997; Images of Waugh, 1998; Steve Waugh: no regrets—a captain's diary, 2000; Never Satisfied, 2000; Ashes Diary, 2001; Steve Waugh—Captain's Diary, 2002; Out Of My Comfort Zone (autobiog.), 2006. *Address:* c/o The Steve Waugh Foundation, GPO Box 3331, Sydney, Australia. *W:* www.stevewaughfoundation.com.au.

WAUMSLEY, Lance Vincent; a Judge of the Upper Tribunal (Immigration and Asylum Chamber) (formerly a Vice President, Immigration Appeal Tribunal, later a Senior Immigration Judge, Asylum and Immigration Tribunal), 2003–12; *b* 30 July 1947; *s* of Leslie Vincent Waumsley and Cecilia Daisy Waumsley (*née* Burden); *m* 2006, Sherrie Lee (*née* McCargar); two step *s* one step *d*. *Educ:* Wycliffe Coll., Glos; Selwyn Coll., Cambridge (MA, LLM). Admitted solicitor, 1972; with Collyer-Bristow and Co., 1970–76; Partner: Halsey Lightly and Hemsley, 1976–84; Macdonald Stacey, subseq. incorporated in Kidd Rapinet, 1984–97; Adjudicator of Immigration Appeals, 1997–2003. Mem., Special Immigration Appeals Commn, 2005–12. Hon. Treas., Council of Immigration Judges, 2001–03. Sec., Yapp Welfare Trust and Yapp Educn and Res. Trust, 1987–97; Trustee and Founder Mem., Arts and Entertainment (formerly Comic Heritage) Charitable Trust, 1993–2001; Mem., Soc. of Trust and Estate Practitioners, 1994–. *Recreations:* genealogy, music, reading, crosswords. *Address:* 656 Lamplighter Circle SE, Salem, OR 97302, USA.

WAVERLEY, 3rd Viscount *cr* 1952, of Westdean; **John Desmond Forbes Anderson;** *b* 31 Oct. 1949; *s* of 2nd Viscount Waverley and Myrtle Ledgerwood (*d* 2013); *S* father, 1990; *m* 1994; one *s*. *Educ:* Malvern. Elected Mem., H of L, 1999. Chm., Parly Gps on Kazakhstan, Kyrgyzstan, Tajikistan, Turkmenistan and Uzbekistan; Co-Chm., Mongolia Parly Gp. Chm., League of Gentlemen Consultants; Vice-Chm., British Azerbaijan Business Council; Hon. Co-Chm., Internat. Tax and Investment Centre, Washington, DC. Advr, CCC Gp of Cos. Mem., RIIA. Jubilee Medal, Kazakhstan, 2002. Grand Cross, Order of San Carlos (Colombia), 1998. *Recreations:* golf, walking. *Heir:* *s* Hon. Forbes Alastair Rupert Anderson, *b* 15 Feb. 1996. *Address:* c/o House of Lords, SW1A 0PW.

WAVERLEY, Viscountess; *see* Barrow, U. H.

WAWRZYNSKI, Dame Dana R.; *see* Ross-Wawrzynski.

WAX, Kenneth Howard; theatre producer; Chief Executive Officer, Kenneth H. Wax Ltd, since 1995; *b* Cheshire, 23 June 1967; *s* of Robert and Valerie Wax; *m* 2000, Daniella; three *c*. *Educ:* Carmel Coll.; Poly. of Central London (BA Hons). King's Head Th., 1991–93; Imagination, 1993–95. *Recreations:* tennis, golf, keeping wife and children happy. *Address:* Kenny Wax Ltd, 3rd Floor, 62 Shaftesbury Avenue, W1D 6LT. *T:* (020) 7437 1736.

WAX, Ruby, Hon. OBE 2015; actor, comedian and writer; *b* 19 April 1953; *d* of Edward Wax and Berta Wax (*née* Goldmann); *m* 1988, Edward Richard Morison Bye; one *s* two *d*. *Educ:* Evanston High Sch.; Berkeley Univ.; RSAMD. *Theatre:* Crucible, 1976; Royal Shakespeare Co., 1978–82; Stressed (one-woman show), UK, Australia and NZ tour, 2000; The Witches, Wyndhams Th., 2005; Ruby Wax: Losing It, Corn Exchange, Newbury, 2010, Menier Chocolate Factory, 2011, Duchess Th., 2011; Ruby Wax: Sane New World, UK tour, 2014; *television:* Not the Nine O'Clock News, 1982–83; Girls on Top, 1983–85; Don't Miss Wax, 1985–87; Hit and Run, 1988; Full Wax, 1987–92; Ruby Wax Meets…, 1996, 1997, 1998; Ruby, 1997, 1998, 1999, 2000; Ruby's American Pie, 1999, 2000; Hot Wax, 2001; The Waiting Game (quiz show), 2001, 2002; Life with Ruby (chat show), 2002; Commercial Breakdown, 2002; Ruby Wax With…, 2003; Ruby Does the Business, 2004; Ruby Wax's Mad Confessions, 2012; *films:* Miami Memoirs, 1987; East Meets Wax, 1988; Class of '69; Ruby Takes a Trip, 1992. *Publications:* How Do You Want Me?, 2002; Sane New World, 2013. *Address:* c/o The Rights House, 34–43 Russell Street, WC2B 5HA.

WAXMAN, Prof. Jonathan Hugh, MD; FRCP; Professor of Oncology, Imperial College, University of London, since 1999; *b* 31 Oct. 1951; *s* of David Waxman and Shirley Waxman (*née* Friedman); one *s* one *d*; *m* Naomi Heaton. *Educ:* Haberdashers' Aske's Sch., Elstree; University Coll. London (BSc); University Coll. Hosp. (MB BS 1975; MD 1986). MRCP 1978, FRCP 1988. House Officer, UCH and Addenbrooke's Hosp., Cambridge, 1975–76; SHO, UCH, London Chest Hosp. and St Mary's Hosp., London, 1976–78; Registrar, St Mary's Hosp., 1979–81; ICRF Res. Fellow, St Bartholomew's Hosp., 1981–86; Consultant Physician, Hammersmith Hosp., 1986–99. Founder Mem., All Party Gp on Cancer, 1998–. Founder and Life Pres., Prostate Cancer Charity, 1996–. *Publications:* The New Endocrinology of Cancer, 1987; The Molecular Biology of Cancer, 1989; Urological Oncology, 1992; Interleukin 2, 1992; Molecular Endocrinology of Cancer, 1996; The Fifth Gospel, 1997; Cancer Chemotherapy Treatment Protocols, 1998; Cancer and the Law, 1999; Treatment Options in Urological Oncology, 2002; The Prostate Cancer Book, 2002; Lecture Notes in Oncology, 2006, 3rd edn 2015; The Elephant in the Room, 2011; The Sweetest Pill, MacLeod's Introduction to Medicine, 2013; Big Prick, 2014; contrib. various scientific papers on cancer res. *Recreation:* family and friends. *Address:* Department of Oncology, Hammersmith Hospital, Du Cane Road, W12 0NN. *T:* (020) 8383 4651.

WAY, Andrew Mark; Chief Executive, Alfred Health, Melbourne, Vic, since 2009; *b* 27 Feb. 1959; *s* of Maxwell Andrew Way and Jane Kathleen Way (*née* Palliser). *Educ:* Bournemouth Sch.; Bristol Sch. of Nursing (RN); City Univ. (BSc Hons 1990); Keele Univ. (MBA 1994). Gen. Manager, St George's Hosp., London, 1993–95; Gen. Manager, 1995–2000, Chief Operating Officer, 2000–02, Hammersmith Hosps NHS Trust; Chief Executive: Heatherwood & Wexham Park Hosps NHS Trust, 2002–05; Royal Free Hampstead NHS Trust, 2005–09. *Recreations:* swimming, ski-ing, bridge. *Address:* The Alfred, PO Box 315, Prahran, Vic 3181, Australia. *T:* (3) 90766000, *Fax:* (3) 90766434. *E:* andrew-way@bigpond.com.

WAY, David Edward, CBE 2011; Visiting Professor, University of Winchester, since 2014; adviser on skills and business development; *b* Bridgwater, Somerset, 8 Jan. 1953; *s* of Edward Way and Dorothy Way; *m* 2003, Margaret Egan; one *s* one *d*. *Educ:* Doctor Morgan's Grammar Sch., Bridgwater; City Univ., London (BSc Econ 1974); London Sch. of Econs and Pol Sci. (MSc 1975). Mgt trainee, Dept of Employment, 1975–78; mgt posts, Jobcentre, 1978–85; Hd, Strategy, Employment Service, 1985–90; Ops Dir, Employment Service, Wales, 1990–92; Dir, Strategy and Corp. Develt, Govt Office for SW, 1992–97; Dir, Business and Learning, Govt Office for West Midlands, 1997–2001; Exec. Dir, Black Country Learning and Skills Council, 2001–04; Nat. Dir, Skills, Learning and Skills Council, 2004–08; Chief Operating Officer and Dep. Chief Exec., 2008–12, Chief Exec., 2012–14, Nat. Apprenticeship Service. Warden, St Mary Magdalene, Tanworth-in-Arden, 2011–; Mem., Deanery Synod, 2014–. *Recreations:* watching Somerset play cricket, walking, visiting National Trust houses and gardens, entertaining two granddaughters. *Address:* Tanworth-in-Arden, Warwickshire. *E:* way744@btinternet.com.

WAY of Plean, George Alexander; Baron of Plean in the County of Stirlingshire; Sheriff of Tayside Central and Fife, since 2009; *b* Edinburgh, 22 May 1956; *s* of Robert Blair Way and Annie Sanderson Way (*née* Gauld); *m* 1st, 1979, Rosemary Calder (marr. diss. 2009); one *s*; 2nd, 2012, Lynn Louisa Harrison, SSC. *Educ:* Boroughmuir Sch.; Univ. of Edinburgh (LLB Hons 1978); Pembroke Coll., Oxford (Masters Dip. Orgnl Leadership 2014). Solicitor, then Sen. Partner, Beveridge & Kellas SSC, Leith, 1978–2008; Solicitor Advocate, 2003; Procurator Fiscal to Court of the Lord Lyon King of Arms, 2003–09. Member: Lord Coulsfield's Rev. of Civil Justice, 2005; Sheriff Court Rules Council, 2006–09; Scottish Govt Debt Action Forum, 2009. Pres., Soc. of Solicitors to Supreme Courts of Scotland, 2002–05; Mem. Council, Law Soc. of Scotland, 2009. Scottish Law Agent, Shipwrecked Fishermen and Mariners' Royal Benevolent Soc., 1986–2009. Lt-Col, JAG, California State Mil. Reserve, 1986; Privy Counsellor to Royal House of Portugal, 2000. Sec., Standing Council of Scottish Clan Chiefs, 1985–2003. FSAScot 1985; FRSA 1986. Calif State Mil. Service Medal, 2000; Queen's Golden Jubilee Medal, 2002. MStJ 1999. Comendador, Order of Our Lady of Vila Viçosa (Portugal), 1988; Knight, Order of Rose of Lippe (Germany), 1989; Cavaliere, Order of St Maurice and St Lazarus (Italy), 2002; Companion, SMO of Malta, 2004. *Publications:* Scottish Clans and Tartans, 1998; Homelands of the Clans, 1999; Collins Clan and Family Encyclopaedia, 1998, 3rd edn 2009; Collins Everyday Scots Law, 2000. *Recreations:* Scots heraldry and peerage, collecting, haunting auction rooms. *Address:* Sheriff Court House, 6 West Bell Street, Dundee DD1 9AD. *E:* sheriffgaway@scotcourts.gov.uk. *Clubs:* New (Edinburgh); Confederate Yacht (California).

WAY, Nicholas John; Director General, Historic Houses Association, since 2005; *b* 28 Aug. 1955; *s* of John Francis Way and Margaret Helen Laura Way (*née* Ewins); *m* 1987, Susan Clark; two *s* one *d*. *Educ:* Clare Coll., Cambridge (BA Econs 1978; MA). MAFF, 1978–89; CLA, 1989–2005, Dir of Policy, 2001–05. Mem. Bd, English Rural Housing Assoc., 1999–2005, 2010–; Trustee, Heritage Alliance (formerly Heritage Link), 2005–; Mem. Council, Attingham Trust, 2005–; Sec., Heritage Conservation Trust, 2005–. Mem., Adv. Council, Sch. of Rural Economy and Land Mgt, RAC, 2002–05. *Recreations:* family, countryside, history and historic houses, football (spectator). *Address:* Historic Houses Association, 2 Chester Street, SW1X 7BB. *T:* (020) 7259 5688, *Fax:* (020) 7259 5590. *E:* nick.way@hha.org.uk.

See also P. E. Way.

WAY, Patrick Edward; QC 2013; *b* Solihull, 6 Feb. 1954; *s* of John Francis Way and Margaret Helen Laura Way (*née* Ewins); *m* 1978, Judith Anne, *d* of late Peter Orchard Williams, CBE; three *s*. *Educ:* Solihull Sch.; Univ. of Leeds (BA Hons). Admitted solicitor, 1979; Solicitor, Lawrence Graham, 1979–82; Asst Solicitor, 1982–85, Tax Partner, 1985–87, Nabarro Nathanson; Partner and Hd, Corporate Tax, Gouldens, 1987–94; called to the Bar, Lincoln's Inn, 1994; Member: 8 Gray's Inn Sq., 1994–2001; Gray's Inn Tax Chambers, 2001–14; Co-Founder, Field Ct Tax Chambers, 2014–. Mem., Attorney Gen.'s B Panel to the Crown, 2010–13. Dir, Richmond (Rugby) Football Club Ltd, 2010–. Founder Ed., Trusts and Estates, 1985–86; Tax Ed., BES Mag., 1986–94. *Publications:* Death and Taxes, 1985; (contrib.) Tolley's Tax Planning, 1985–2012; Maximising Opportunities under the BES, 1986; The BES and Assured Tenancies: the new rules, 1988; Tax Advice for Company Transactions, 1992; The Enterprise Investment Scheme, 1994; (ed and contrib.) Joint Ventures, 1994. *Recreations:* watching Richmond Rugby Club, contemporary art. *Address:* Field Court Tax Chambers, Gray's Inn, WC1R 5EP. *T:* (020) 3693 3700. *E:* pw@fieldtax.com. *Club:* Travellers.

See also N. J. Way.

WAYMAN, Caroline; Chief Ombudsman and Chief Executive, Financial Ombudsman Service, since 2014; *b* Sunderland, 23 June 1975; *d* of Eric Wayman and Wendy Wayman; partner, Simon Horner. *Educ:* Weald of Kent Grammar Sch.; Nottingham Law Sch. (LLB Hons Law); Inns of Court Sch. of Law (BVC). Called to the Bar, Middle Temple, 1998; Adjudicator, Insurance Ombudsman Bureau, 1999; Financial Ombudsman Service: Service and Ops Manager, 2000–07; Lead Ombudsman, 2007–11; Principal Ombudsman and Legal Dir, 2011–14. Non-exec. Mem. Bd, Claims Mgt Regulator, 2014–. *Recreations:* playing football, running, watching Rugby. *E:* caroline.wayman@financial-ombudsman.org.uk.

WAYNE, Philip Brian; Headmaster, Royal Grammar School, High Wycombe, since 2015; *b* Great Barr, Birmingham, 22 Dec. 1966; *s* of Brian and Lorna Wayne; *m* 1997, Elen Môn Jones; one *s* one *d*. *Educ:* Dartmouth High Sch.; Univ. of Manchester (MusB 1988); Univ. of Birmingham (PGCE); Nat. Coll. of Sch. Leadership (NPQH). ARCO 1985; LGSM 1992. Freelance musician, 1988–92; Dartmouth High School: Music Teacher, 1992–94; Dir of Music, 1994–99; Asst Head, 1999–2004; Dep. Headmaster, John Hampden GS, 2004–07; Headmaster, Chesham GS, 2007–15. Gov., Pipers Corner Sch. *Recreations:* family, food, cooking, organ and piano playing, sport. *Address:* Royal Grammar School, Amersham Road, High Wycombe, Bucks HP13 6QT. *T:* (01494) 524955. *E:* headmaster@rgshw.com. *Club:* Lansdowne.

WAYWELL, Prof. Geoffrey Bryan, FSA 1979; Professor of Classical Archaeology, King's College, University of London, 1987–2004; Director, Institute of Classical Studies, University of London, 1996–2004; *b* 16 Jan. 1944; *s* of Francis Marsh Waywell and Jenny Waywell; *m* 1970, Elisabeth Ramsden; two *s*. *Educ:* Eltham Coll.; St John's Coll., Cambridge (BA, MA, PhD). Walston Student, Cambridge Univ., 1965–67; School Student, British Sch. at Athens, 1966–67; King's College, London: Asst Lectr in Classics, 1968; Lectr in Classics, 1970; Reader in Classical Archaeology, 1982; Hon. Curator, Ashmole Archive, 1985; FKC 2004. Dir of excavations at ancient Sparta, 1989–98. *Publications:* The Free-Standing Sculptures of the Mausoleum at Halicarnassus in the British Museum, 1978; The Lever and Hope Sculptures, 1986; Sculptors and Sculpture of Caria and the Dodecanese, 1997; (ed) Pheidias: the sculptures and ancient sources, by C. Cullen Davison, 3 vols, 2009; *relevant publication:* Exploring Ancient Sculpture: essays in honour of Geoffrey Waywell, ed by Fiona Macfarlane and Catherine Morgan, 2010; numerous articles and reviews in archaeol and classical jls. *Recreations:* music, excavating. *Address:* 47 Bird-in-Hand Lane, Bickley, Bromley, Kent BR1 2NA.

WEAIRE, Prof. Denis Lawrence, PhD; FRS 1999; Erasmus Smith's Professor of Natural and Experimental Philosophy, 1984–2007, now Emeritus, and Fellow, 1987, now Emeritus, Trinity College, Dublin; *b* 17 Oct. 1942; *s* of Allen Maunder Weaire and Janet Eileen (*née* Rea); *m* 1969, Colette Rosa O'Regan; one *s*. *Educ:* Belfast Royal Acad.; Clare Coll., Cambridge (MA Maths; PhD 1968). Harkness Fellow, Calif and Chicago, 1964–66; researcher, Cavendish Lab., Univ. of Cambridge, 1966–69; Fellow, Clare Coll., Cambridge, 1967–69; Res. Fellow, Harvard Univ., 1969–70; Yale University: Instructor, 1970–72; Asst Prof., 1972–73; Heriot-Watt University: Associate Prof., 1973–74; Sen. Lectr, 1974–77; Reader, 1977–79; Prof. of Exptl Physics, UC Dublin, 1980–84 (Hd of Dept, 1983–84); Trinity College, Dublin: Hd of Dept, 1984–89, 2003–05; Dean of Science, 1989–92. Vis. Prof., Univ. of Auckland, 2012; Gledden Fellow, Univ. of Western Australia Perth, 2014. Ed., Jl Physics: Condensed Matter, 1994–97. Pres., Eur. Physical Soc., 1997–99 (Vice Pres., 1996–97 and 1999–2000). MRIA 1987; MAE 1998 (Vice Pres., 2005–08). Dr *hc* Tech. Univ., Lisbon, 2001. Cecil Powell Medal, Eur. Phys. Soc., 2001; Cunningham Medal, RIA, 2005; Holwech Medal, Inst. of Physics and French Phys. Soc., 2008. *Publications:* (ed jtly) Tetrahedrally Bonded Amorphous Semiconductors, 1974; (ed with D. Pettifor) The Recursion Method, 1985; (with P. G. Harper) Introduction to Physical Mathematics, 1985; (ed with C. Windsor) Solid State Science, 1987; (ed jtly) Tradition and Reform, 1988; (ed jtly) Epioptics, 1995; (ed) The Kelvin Problem, 1997; (ed with J. Banhart) Foams and Films, 1999; (ed jtly) Richard Helsham's Course of Lectures on Natural Philosophy, 1999; (with S. Hutzler) The Physics of Foams, 1999; (with T. Aste) The Pursuit of Perfect Packing, 2000, 2nd edn 2008; (ed jtly) George Francis Fitzgerald, 2009; (ed jtly) Hutchie, 2012; contrib. numerous scientific papers. *Recreations:* theatre, humorous writing. *Address:* 26 Greenmount Road, Terenure, Dublin, Republic of Ireland. *T:* (1) 4902063.

WEALE, Prof. Albert Peter, CBE 2013; PhD; FBA 1998; Professor of Political Theory and Public Policy, University College London, since 2010; *b* 30 May 1950; *s* of Albert Cecil and Margaret Elizabeth Weale; *m* 1st, 1976, Jane Leresche (marr. diss. 1987); 2nd, 1994, Janet Felicity Harris. *Educ:* St Luke's Primary Sch., Brighton; Varndean Grammar Sch., Brighton; Clare Coll., Cambridge (BA Theol.; PhD Social and Political Scis 1977). Sir James Knott Fellow, Dept of Politics, Univ. of Newcastle upon Tyne, 1974–76; University of York: Lectr, Dept of Politics, 1976–85; Asst Dir, Inst. for Res. in Social Scis, 1982–85; Prof. of Politics, UEA, 1985–92; Prof. of Govt, Univ. of Essex, 1992–2009. Chairman: Nuffield Council on Bioethics, 2008–12 (Mem., 1998–2004); Cttee on Ethical Issues in Medicine, RCP, 2014–. Chm. Grants Cttee, 1997–2001, Mem. Mgt Cttee, 1997–2001, King's Fund. FRSA 1993. *Publications:* Equality and Social Policy, 1978; Political Theory and Social Policy, 1983; The New Politics of Pollution, 1992; Democracy, 1999, 2nd edn 2007; Democratic Citizenship and the European Union, 2005; Democratic Justice and the Social Contract, 2013; *jointly:* Lone Mothers, Paid Work and Social Security, 1984; Controlling Pollution in the Round, 1991; The Theory of Choice, 1992; Environmental Governance in Europe, 2000; *edited:* Cost and Choice in Health Care, 1988; (with L. Roberts) Innovation and Environmental Risk, 1991; (jtly) Environmental Standards in the European Community in an Interdisciplinary Framework, 1994; (with P. Lehning) Citizenship, Democracy and Justice in the New Europe, 1997; (with Michael Nentwich) Political Theory and the European Union, 1998; Risk, Democratic Citizenship and Public Policy, 2002; articles in learned jls. *Recreations:* walking, music, the company of friends. *Address:* Department of Political Science, School of Public Policy, University College London, 29/30 Tavistock Square, WC1H 9QU.

WEALE, Anthony Philip; Secretary of Faculties, 1984–2005 and Academic Registrar, 1999–2005, University of Oxford; Fellow of Worcester College, Oxford, 1982–2005, now Emeritus; *b* 4 Dec. 1945; *s* of Geoffrey Arthur Weale and Jocelyn Mary Weale (*née* Weeks); *m* 1975, Katharine O'Connell; two *d*. *Educ:* Kimbolton Sch.; University Coll., Oxford (Scholar; BA 1st Cl. Jurisprudence (Martin Wronker Prize for Law), 1967; MA 1971). GKN Ltd, 1967–71; Admin. Service, Oxford Univ., 1971–2005 (Sec., Medical Sch., 1977–84). Treas., Historic Towns Trust, 1975–. Governor: Pusey House, Oxford, 1977–85; Kimbolton Sch., 2001–14; Bishop Wordsworth's Sch., 2008–. Trustee: St Bartholomew's Sch. Foundn, Newbury, 2006–10; Sarum Coll., 2010– (Sec. to Trustees, 2007–10). *Recreations:* family, dabbling in military and political history, gardening, travel, talking to neighbours. *Address:* 40 Harnwood Road, Salisbury, Wilts SP2 8DB.

WEALE, Rear Adm. John Stuart, OBE 2009; Flag Officer Scotland and Northern Ireland and Assistant Chief Naval Staff Submarines, since 2015; *b* Glasgow, 14 July 1962; *s* of Victor and Maureen Weale; *m* 1986, Julie; one *s* three *d*. *Educ:* St Augustine's Coll.; Westminster Univ. (BSc Hons Life Scis); Cranfield Univ. (MDA). Joined RN, 1985; qualified Submarine CO Course, 1995; i/c HMS Trafalgar, nuclear submarine, 1999; Lead Planning Officer, UK Maritime Battle Staff, 2006–07; COS Maritime Coalition Combined Task Force 158 Iraq, 2007–08; Dir Submarine Sea and Shore Trng, 2008–10; Team Leader, Submarine Trng and Educn Prog., 2010–12; Dep. Flag Officer Sea Trng, 2012–15. Mem., Assoc. of RN Officers. *Recreations:* family, fishing, small holding, reading, walking. *Address:* Catchfrench East Lodge, Saltash, Cornwall PL12 5BY. *E:* johnweale898@btinternet.com.

WEALE, Martin Robert, CBE 1999; Member, Monetary Policy Committee, Bank of England, since 2010; *b* 4 Dec. 1955; *s* of late Prof. R. A. Weale and M. E. Weale. *Educ:* Clare Coll., Cambridge (BA 1977; ScD 2006). ODI Fellow, Nat. Statistical Office, Malawi, 1977–79; University of Cambridge: Research Officer, Dept of Applied Econs, 1979–87; Lectr, Faculty of Econs and Politics, 1987–95; Fellow, Clare Coll., 1981–95; Dir, NIESR, 1995–2010 (Sen. Res. Fellow, 2011–). Prof. of Econs, QMUL, 2011–. Houblon-Norman Fellow, Bank of England, 1986–87. Member: Stats Commn, 2000–08; Bd for Actuarial Standards, 2006–10. Hon. Treasurer, Alzheimer's Trust, 1992–2008. Hon. FIA 2001. Hon. DSc City, 2007. *Publications:* (with J. Grady) British Banking, 1986; (jtly) Macroeconomic Policy: inflation, wealth and the exchange rate, 1989; (with J. Sefton) Reconciliation of National Income and Expenditure, 1995; articles in learned jls. *Recreations:* bridge, music, travel. *Address:* 63 Noel Road, N1 8HE. *T:* (020) 7359 8210. *Club:* Athenæum.

WEARE, Trevor John, OBE 1990; PhD; Chairman, 1999–2007, Member of Board, 2007–09, HR Wallingford Group, Ltd; *b* 31 Dec. 1943; *s* of Trevor Leslie Weare and Edna Margaret (*née* Roberts); *m* 1964, Margaret Ann Wright; two *s*. *Educ:* Aston Technical Coll.; Imperial College of Science and Technology (BSc Physics, PhD). Post-doctoral Research Fellow: Dept of Mathematical Physics, McGill Univ., Montreal, 1968–70; Dept of Theoretical Physics, Univ. of Oxford, 1970–72; Sen. Scientific Officer, Hydraulics Res. Station, 1972; Principal Scientific Officer, 1975; Sen. Principal Scientific Officer, Head of Estuaries Div., 1978; Chief Scientific Officer, DoE, 1981; Chief Exec., Hydraulics Res. Ltd, then HR Wallingford Gp Ltd, 1984–99. *Publications:* numerous contribs to scientific jls on theoretical High Energy Nuclear Physics, and on computational modelling in Civil Engineering Hydraulics; archaeological paper in Oxoniensia. *Recreations:* music, walking, archaeology, golf, sailing. *Address:* 14 Trenithick Meadow, Mount Hawke, Truro, Cornwall TR4 8GN. *T:* (01209) 890082.

WEARING, Gillian, OBE 2011; RA 2007; artist; *b* 1963. *Educ:* Goldsmiths' Coll., Univ. of London (BA Hons Fine Art 1990). *Solo exhibitions:* Maureen Paley/Interim Art, London, 1994, 1996–97, 1999; Hayward Gall., 1995; Le Consortium, Dijon, 1996; Jay Gorney Modern Art, NY, Chisenhale Gall., London, Kunsthaus Zürich, 1997; Centre d'Art Contemporain, Geneva, 1998; De Vleeshal, Middleburg, The Netherlands, 1999; Serpentine Gall., Regen Projects, LA, Contemp. Art Center, Cincinnati, 2000; Bluecoat Gall., Liverpool, la Caixa, Madrid, Musée d'Art Moderne, Paris, Museo do Chiado, Lisbon, Kunstverein München, Angel Row Gall., Nottingham, 2001; Trilogy, Vancouver, 2002; Mass Observation, MCA Chicago, Kunsthaus Glarus, and tour, 2002; Regen Projects, LA, 2004, 2008; Snapshot, Bloomberg Space, London, 2005; Aust. Center for Contemp. Art, 2006; Family History, Ikon, Birmingham, 2006; Family Monument, Galleria Civica di Arte Contemporanea, Trento, 2007; Confessions: Portraits, Vidéos, Musée Rodin, Paris, 2009; Real Birmingham Families, Ikon, Birmingham, 2012; Whitechapel Gall. (retrospective), 2012; K20 Kunstsammlung Nordrhein-Westfalen, Düsseldorf, 2012; Museum Brandhorst, Munich, 2013; *group exhibitions* include: BT Young Contemporaries, UK tour, 1993; Brilliant! New Art from London, Walker Art Center, Minneapolis, 1995; Life/Live, Musée d'Art Moderne, Paris, 1996; Pandaemonium, London Fest. of Moving Images, ICA, 1996; Sensation, RA, and Mus. für Gegenwart, Berlin, 1998; Real/Life: new British art, Japanese Mus. tour, 1998; Let's Entertain, Walker Art Centre, Minneapolis, 2000; New British Art, Tate Britain, London, 2000; Century City, Tate Modern, London, 2001; ABBILD recent portraiture and depiction, Graz, Birmingham, 2001; I Promise it's Political, Cologne, 2002; Remix: Contemporary Art and Pop, Tate Liverpool, São Paulo, 2002; Of Mice and Men, Berlin Biennial for Contemp. Art, A Short History of Performance Part IV, Whitechapel Art Gall., 2006; Local Stories, Modern Art Oxford, 2006; Aftershock, Contemporary British Art 1990–2006, Guangdong Mus. of Art, Guangzhou, Capital Mus., Beijing, 2006; Global Feminisms, Brooklyn Mus., NY, 2007; The Turner Prize: a retrospective, Tate Britain, 2007; exhibns in Europe. Trustee, Tate Gall., 1999–2005. Turner Prize, 1997. *Address:* c/o Maureen Paley, 21 Herald Street, E2 6JT. *T:* (020) 7729 4112.

WEATHERALL, Sir David (John), Kt 1987; DL; MD, FRCP; FRCPE 1983; FRS 1977; Chancellor, University of Keele, 2002–11; Regius Professor of Medicine, University of Oxford, 1992–2000; Student of Christ Church, Oxford, 1992–2000; Hon. Director: Molecular Haematology Unit, Medical Research Council, 1980–2000; Institute for Molecular Medicine, University of Oxford, 1988–2000 (renamed Weatherall Institute of Molecular Medicine, 2000); *b* 9 March 1933; *s* of late Harry and Gwendoline Weatherall; *m* 1962, Stella Mayorga Nestler; one *s*. *Educ:* Calday Grange Grammar Sch.; Univ. of Liverpool (MB, ChB 1956; MD 1962); MA Oxon 1974. FRCP 1967; FRCPath 1969. Ho. Officer in Med. and Surg., United Liverpool Hosps, 1956–58; Captain, RAMC, Jun. Med. Specialist, BMH, Singapore, and BMH, Kamunting, Malaya, 1958–60; Research Fellow in Genetics, Johns Hopkins Hosp., Baltimore, USA, 1960–62; Sen. Med. Registrar, Liverpool Royal Infirmary, 1962–63; Research Fellow in Haematology, Johns Hopkins Hosp., 1963–65; Consultant, WHO, 1966–70; Univ. of Liverpool: Lectr in Med., 1965–66; Sen. Lectr in Med., 1966–69; Reader in Med., 1969–71; Prof. of Haematology, 1971–74; Consultant Physician, United Liverpool Hosps, 1966–74; Nuffield Prof. of Clinical Medicine, Univ. of Oxford, 1974–92; Fellow, Magdalen Coll., Oxford, 1974–92, Emeritus 1992–. Mem. Soc. of Scholars, and Centennial Schol., Johns Hopkins Univ., 1976; Physician-in-Chief *pro tem.*, Peter Bent Brigham Hosp., Harvard Med. Sch., 1980. RSocMed Foundn Vis. Prof., 1981; Sims Commonwealth Vis. Prof., 1982; Phillip K. Bondy Prof., Yale, 1982. K. Diamond Prof., Univ. of Calif in San Francisco, 1986; HM Queen Elizabeth the Queen Mother Fellow, Nuffield Prov. Hosps Trust, 1982; Fogarty Scholar, NIH, USA, 2003. Lectures: Watson Smith, RCP, 1974; Foundn, RCPath, 1979; Darwin, Eugenics Soc., 1979; Croonian, RCP, 1984; Fink Meml, Yale, 1984; Sir Francis Frazer, Univ. of London, 1985; Roy Cameron, RCPath, 1986; Hamm Meml, Amer. Soc. of Haematology, 1986; Still Meml, BPA, 1987; Harveian, RCP, 1992. President: British Soc. for Haematology, 1980; Internat. Soc. of Haematology, 1992; BAAS, 1992–93; Chm., Med. and Scientific Adv. Panel, Leukaemia Res. Fund, 1985–89; Mem. Council, Royal Soc., 1989– (Vice Pres., 1990–91); Mem., MRC, 1994–96; Trustee: Wellcome Trust, 1990–2000; Wolfson Foundn, 2001–. Founder FMedSci 1998. DL Oxfordshire, 2000. Foreign Member: Nat. Acad. of Scis, USA, 1990; Inst. of Medicine, Nat. Acad. of Scis, USA, 1991; Internat. Mem. (formerly Foreign Mem.), Amer. Philosophical Soc., 2005; Hon. Member: Assoc. of Physicians of GB and Ireland, 1968 (Pres., 1989); Assoc. of Amer. Physicians, 1976; Amer. Soc. of Haematology, 1982; Eur. Molecular Biology Orgn, 1983; Amer. Acad. of Arts and Scis, 1988; Alpha Omega Alpha Honor Med. Soc., USA, 1988; British Soc. of Immunology, 2014; Hon. Fellow, Royal Coll. Physicians, Thailand, 1988; Hon. FRACP 1986; Hon. FRCOG 1988; Hon. FIC 1989; Hon. FACP 1991; Hon. FRSocMed 1998. Hon. Fellow, Green Coll., Oxford, 1993. Hon. DSc: Manchester, 1988; Edinburgh, 1989; Leicester, 1991; Aberdeen, 1991; London, 1993; Keele, 1993; Oxford Brookes, 1995; South Bank, 1995; Exeter, 1998; Cambridge, 2004; Hon. MD: Leeds, 1988; Sheffield, 1989; Nottingham, 1993; Kelaniya (Sri Lanka), 2008; Hon. DHL Johns Hopkins, 1990; Hon. LLD: Liverpool, 1992; Bristol, 1994; Dundee, 2009. Ambuj Nath Bose Prize, RCP, 1980; Ballantyne Prize, RCPE, 1982; Stratton Prize, Internat. Soc. Haematology, 1982; Feldberg Prize, 1984; Royal Medal, Royal Soc., 1989; Gold Medal, RSM, 1992; Conway Evans Prize, RCP and Royal Soc., 1992; Buchanan Medal, Royal Soc., 1994; (jtly) Helmut Horten Res. Award, 1995; Manson Medal, 1998; Prince Mahidol Award, Thailand, 2002; Gold Medal, BMA, 2002; Allen Award, Amer. Soc. of Human Genetics, 2003; Mendel Medal, Genetics Soc., 2006; Lasker-Koshland Award, 2010; (jtly) Karl Landsteiner Meml Prize, AABB, 2011; Wallace H. Coulter Award, Amer. Soc. of Haematology, 2013; Anthony Cerami Award in Translational Medicine, 2014. Commandeur de l'Ordre de la Couronne (Belgium), 1994. *Publications:* (with J. B. Clegg) The Thalassaemia Syndromes, 1965, 4th edn 2001; (with R. M. Hardisty) Blood and its Disorders, 1973, 2nd edn 1981; The New Genetics and Clinical Practice, 1982, 3rd edn 1991; (ed, with J. G. G. Ledingham and D. A. Warrell) Oxford Textbook of Medicine, 1983, 3rd edn 1995; Science and the Quiet Art, 1995; many papers on Abnormal Haemoglobin Synthesis and related disorders. *Recreations:* music, oriental food. *Address:* 8 Cumnor Rise Road, Cumnor Hill, Oxford OX2 9HD. *T:* (01865) 222398.

WEATHERALL, Vice-Adm. Sir James (Lamb), KCVO 2001; KBE 1989; DL; an Extra Equerry to the Queen, since 2001; HM Marshal of the Diplomatic Corps, 1992–2001; *b* 28 Feb. 1936; *s* of Alwyn Thomas Hirst Weatherall and Olive Catherine Joan Weatherall (*née* Cuthbert); *m* 1962, Hon. Jean Stewart Macpherson, *d* of 1st Baron Drumalbyn, KBE, PC; two *s* three *d*. *Educ:* Glasgow Academy; Gordonstoun School. Joined RN 1954; commanded HM Ships: Soberton, 1966–67; Ulster, 1970–72; Tartar, 1975–76; Andromeda, 1982–84 (incl. Falklands conflict); Ark Royal, 1985–87; with SACEUR, 1987–89; Dep. Supreme Allied Comdr Atlantic, 1989–91. Chairman: Sea Cadet Council, 1992–98; Sea Cadet Assoc., 1992–98 (Sea Cadet Medal, 1998). Pres., Internat. Social Service (UK), 1996–2001. Patron, Marwell Wildlife (formerly Preservation Trust), 2007– (Trustee, 1992–2007; Chm., 1999–2007). Chm., Lord Mayor of London's Appeal, 1997–98. Chairman, Board of Governors: Box Hill Sch., 1993–2003 (Trustee, 1992–; Warden, 2003–); Gordonstoun Schs, 1996–2003 (Gov., 1994–; Warden, 2004–11). Member: Ct of Assts, Shipwrights' Co., 1989– (Prime Warden, 2001–02); Incorp. of Hammermen of Glasgow, 1998–; HM Lieut, City of London, 2001–. Younger Brother, Corp. of Trinity House, 1986–. Fellow, WWF (UK), 2008– (Trustee, 2001–07). DL Hampshire, 2004. *Recreations:* stamp collecting, fishing. *Address:* Craig House, Street End, Bishop's Waltham, Hampshire SO32 1FS. *Club:* Royal Navy of 1765 and 1785.

WEATHERBY, Jonathan Roger; Chairman, Weatherbys Bank Ltd and Weatherbys Ltd (formerly Weatherbys Group Ltd), since 1993; *b* 30 Nov. 1959; *s* of late Christopher Nicholas Weatherby and of Alison Beatrix (*née* Pease); *m* 1993, Sophie Frances Cliffe-Jones; two *s* two *d*. *Educ:* Eton Coll. Joined Weatherbys, 1979; Dir, 1988–. Chairman: Gazelle Investments Ltd, 1992–; Wild Boar Inns Ltd, 1994–2001. Mem., Jockey Club, 1997–. Trustee, Ascot Authority, 1998–. *Recreations:* horse-racing, soccer, hunting. *Address:* Weatherbys, Sanders Road, Wellingborough, Northants NN8 4BX. *T:* (01933) 304728. *Clubs:* White's, Turf.

See also Baron Daresbury, R. N. Weatherby.

WEATHERBY, Roger Nicholas; Chief Executive, Weatherbys Bank Ltd, since 2000; *b* Oxford, 6 Aug. 1962; *s* of late Christopher Nicholas Weatherby and of Alison Beatrix Weatherby (*née* Pease); *m* 1998, Semantha Horne; two *s* two *d*. *Educ:* Eton Coll.; RMA Sandhurst; London Business Sch. (MSc Finance). Commnd 15/19 King's Royal Hussars, 1982. Internat. Sales, Cazenove and Co., 1985–96; Finance Dir, Weatherbys Gp Ltd, 1997–. Chairman: Racing Welfare, 2008–12 (Trustee, 2001–12); Racing Foundn, 2012–. Mem., 2007–, Steward, 2013–14, Sen. Steward, 2014–, Jockey Club. *Recreations:* country sports, family, exploration, horseracing, gardening. *Address:* Weatherbys Bank Ltd, Sanders Road, Wellingborough, Northants NN8 4BX. *T:* (01933) 304777. *E:* rweatherby@weatherbys.co.uk. *Clubs:* White's, Turf, Hertford Street.

See also Baron Daresbury, J. R. Weatherby.

WEATHERHEAD, Alexander Stewart, (Sandy), OBE 1985; TD 1964 (clasp 1973); Partner, 1960–97 and Senior Partner, 1992–97, Tindal Oatts & Rodger, then Tindal Oatts Buchanan and McIlwraith, subsequently Tindal Oatts, and Brechin Tindal Oatts, Solicitors, Glasgow (Consultant, 1997–98); *b* Edinburgh, 3 Aug. 1931; *er s* of Kenneth Kilpatrick Weatherhead and Katharine Weatherhead (*née* Stewart); *m* 1972, Harriett Foye, *d* of Rev. Dr Arthur Organ, Toronto, Canada; two *d*. *Educ:* George Watson's, Edinburgh; Larchfield Sch., Helensburgh; Glasgow Acad.; Glasgow Univ. MA 1955, LLB 1958. Served in RA, 1950–52, 2nd Lieut, 1950. Solicitor, 1958; Temp. Sheriff, 1985–92. Hon. Vice-Pres., Law Society of Scotland, 1983–84 (Mem. Council, 1971–84); Member: Royal Faculty of Procurators in Glasgow, 1960– (Mem. Council, 1992–2001; Dean, 1992–95; Hon. Mem., 1997); Council, Soc. for Computers and Law, 1973–86 (Vice-Chm., 1973–82; Chm., 1982–84; Hon. Mem., 1986); Mem., Royal Commn on Legal Services in Scotland, 1976–80. Trustee, Nat. Technol. and Law Trust (formerly Nat. Law Library Trust), 1979–86; Examr in Conveyancing, Univ. of Aberdeen, 1984–86. Dir, Glasgow Chamber of Commerce, 1992–95. Member: Local Res. Ethics Cttee, Royal Infirmary, Glasgow, 1999–06; Multi Centre Res. Ethics Cttee for Scotland (B), 2005–06. Mem. Business Cttee, Gen. Council, Univ. of Glasgow, 2001–05 and 2007–11. Joined TA, 1952; Lt-Col Comdg 277 (A&SH) Field Regt, RA (TA), 1965–67; The Lowland Regt (RA(T)), 1967 and Glasgow & Strathclyde Univs OTC, 1971–73; Col 1974; TAVR Col Lowlands (West), 1974–76; ADC (TAVR) to the Queen, 1977–81; Member: TAVR Assoc. Lowlands, 1967–2000 (Vice-Chm., 1987–90; Chm., 1990–93); RFCA Lowlands, 2000–; RA Council for Scotland, 1972– (Vice Chm., 1997–2001; Patron, 2001–). Hon. Col, Glasgow and Strathclyde Univs OTC, 1982–98. Commodore, Royal Western Yacht Club, 1995–98 (Vice Cdre, 1991–95; Hon. Sec., 1981–84). *Recreations:* reading, music, tennis, sailing. *Address:* 52 Partickhill Road, Glasgow G11 5AB. *T:* (0141) 334 6277. *E:* sandywd@aol.com. *Clubs:* New (Edinburgh); Royal Highland Yacht (Oban); Royal Western Yacht, Clyde Cruising (Glasgow).

WEATHERHEAD, Very Rev. James Leslie, CBE 1997; Principal Clerk of the General Assembly of the Church of Scotland, 1985–93 and 1994–96 (Moderator, 1993–94); Chaplain to the Queen in Scotland, 1991–2001, Extra Chaplain, since 2001; *b* 29 March 1931; *s* of Leslie Binnie Weatherhead, MBE, MM and Janet Hood Arnot Smith or Weatherhead; *m* 1962, Dr Anne Elizabeth Shepherd; two *s*. *Educ:* High Sch., Dundee; Univ. of Edinburgh (MA, LLB; Senior Pres., Students' Repr. Council, 1953–54); New Coll., Univ. of Edinburgh (Pres., Univ. Union, 1959–60). Temp. Acting Sub-Lieut RNVR (Nat. Service), 1955–56. Licensed by Presb. of Dundee, 1960; ordained by Presb. of Ayr, 1960; Asst Minister, Auld Kirk of Ayr, 1960–62; Minister, Trinity Church, Rothesay, 1962–69; Minister, Old Church, Montrose, 1969–85. Convener, Business Cttee of Gen. Assembly, 1981–84. Mem., Broadcasting Council for Scotland, BBC, 1978–82. Gov., Fettes Coll., Edinburgh, 1994–99. Hon. DD Edinburgh, 1993. *Publications:* (ed) The Constitution and Laws of the Church of Scotland, 1997. *Recreation:* music. *Clubs:* Victory Services; RNVR Yacht.

WEATHERHEAD, Sandy; *see* Weatherhead, A. S.

WEATHERILL, Barry Nicholas Aubrey, CBE 2005; Consultant, Wedlake Bell, solicitors, since 2003; Chairman, IC Philanthropy, since 2012; *b* 17 July 1938; *s* of Percival Aubrey and Flora Evelyn Weatherill; *m* 1965, Wouterina Johanna Cornelia van den Bovenkamp; one *s* two *d*. *Educ:* Caldicott Sch.; Felsted Sch.; Clare Coll., Cambridge (BA 1962). Admitted solicitor, 1966; Wedlake Bell: Partner, 1966–2003; Finance Partner, 1975–81; Sen. Partner, 1984–94. Trustee, 1975–2007, Chm., 2000–07, Guide Dogs for the Blind Assoc. All England Lawn Tennis Club: Mem., Cttee of Mgt, 1981–2002; Vice Pres., 2002–; Trustee, 2003–; Chm., Council of Internat. Lawn Tennis Clubs, 1991–2012 (Vice-Pres., 2014–); Pres., Internat. Lawn Tennis Club of GB, 2008–. *Recreations:* tennis, golf, gardening, music, investment. *Clubs:* Jesters; Hawks (Cambridge); All England Lawn Tennis and Croquet; International Lawn Tennis Club of GB, (and those of France, USA and the Netherlands); Berkshire Golf.

WEATHERILL, Hon. Bernard Richard; QC 1996; a Recorder, since 2000; *b* 20 May 1951; *er s* of Baron Weatherill, PC and of Lyn Weatherill; *m* 1st, 1977, Sally Maxwell Fisher (marr. diss. 2001); one *s* one *d*; 2nd, 2005, Diana Clare Forsyth. *Educ:* Malvern Coll.; Principia Coll., Illinois, USA; Kent Univ. (BA Hons). Called to the Bar, Middle Temple, 1974, Bencher, 2002; an Asst Recorder, 1998–2000. Non-exec. Dir, A. Cohen & Co. plc, 1989–2000. Member: General Council of the Bar, 1990–95 (Mem., Professional Conduct Cttee, 1998–99); Council, Justice, 2010–; Chm., Bar Services Co. Ltd, 2000–08; non-exec. Dir, Croydon Business Venture Ltd, 2009–. Mem. Council, Tennis and Rackets Assoc., 2010–. FCIArb 1999. *Recreations:* lawn tennis, Real tennis, golf, wine, avoiding gardening, cultivating friendships. *Address:* Enterprise Chambers, 9 Old Square, Lincoln's Inn, WC2A 3SR. *Clubs:* Hurlingham; All England Lawn Tennis, Royal Tennis Court, Bar Lawn Tennis Society, Jesters; Royal Wimbledon Golf, Lucifer Golfing Society; Holyport Real Tennis.

WEATHERILL, Rt Rev. Garry John; *see* Ballarat, Bishop of.

WEATHERILL, Prof. Nigel Peter, PhD, DSc; CEng, FREng; FRAeS; FIMA; CSci; CMath; Vice-Chancellor, Liverpool John Moores University, since 2011; *b* 1 Nov. 1954; *s* of Ernest and Barbara Weatherill; *m* 1976, Dr Barbara Ann Hopkins; one *s* one *d*. *Educ:* Whitcliffe Mount Grammar Sch., Cleckheaton, Yorks; Southampton Univ. (BSc 1st Cl. Hons Maths; PhD Maths 1979; DSc 1994). CEng 1996, FREng 2003; FIMA 1987; CMath 1991; FRAeS 1996; CSci 2005. Asst Team Leader, Regl Res. Team, Anglian Water Authy, Cambridge, 1979–81; Sen. Project Supervisor, Aircraft Res. Assoc., Bedford, 1981–87; Swansea University (formerly University of Wales, Swansea): Department of Civil Engineering: Lectr, 1987–90; Sen. Lectr, 1990–92; Reader, 1992–95; Prof. of Civil Engineering, 1995–2008; Hd of Dept, 1996–2001; Dir, Centre of Excellence in Computation and Simulation, 2000–08; Hd, Sch. of Engineering, 2001–07; Pro-Vice-Chancellor (Research), 2002–08; Hon. Fellow, 2009; Pro-Vice-Chancellor and Hd, Coll. of Engineering and Physical Scis, Univ. of Birmingham, 2008–11. Vis. Res. Fellow, Dept of Mechanical and Aerospace Engrg, Princeton Univ., 1985; Res. Consultant, Nat. Grid Generation Project, USA, NSF Engrg Res. Center, Mississippi State Univ., 1991–92, Adjunct Prof., 1992–98; Vis. Scientist-in-Residence, Inst. of High Performance Computing, A*Singapore, 2006–11. Ed., Internat. Jl Numerical Methods in Fluids, 1999–2011. FRSA 2012. *Publications:* (jtly) Multiblock Grid Generation, 1993; (jtly) Handbook of Grid Generation, 1999; (jtly) Probabilistic Methods in Fluids, 2003. *Recreations:* fly fishing, gardening, travelling. *Address:* Office of the Vice-Chancellor, Liverpool John Moores University, Egerton Court, 2 Rodney Street, Liverpool L1 2UA. *E:* vc@ljmu.ac.uk.

WEATHERILL, Prof. Stephen Robson; Jacques Delors Professor of European Law, University of Oxford, since 1998; Fellow, Somerville College, Oxford, since 1998; *b* 21 March 1961. *Educ:* Queens' Coll., Cambridge (MA); Univ. of Edinburgh (MSc). Brunel Univ., 1985; Reading Univ., 1986–87; Manchester Univ., 1987–90; Nottingham Univ., 1990–97, Jean Monnet Prof. of European Law, 1995–97. *Publications:* Cases and Materials on EC Law, 1992, 10th edn as Cases and Materials on EU Law, 2012; (with P. Beaumont) EC Law, 1993, 3rd edn 1999; Law and Integration in the European Union, 1995; (with G. Howells) Consumer Protection Law, 1995, 2nd edn 2004; EC Consumer Law and Policy, 1997, 2nd edn 2005; (with H. Micklitz) European Economic Law, 1997. *Address:* Somerville College, Oxford OX2 6HD. *T:* (01865) 270600.

WEATHERLEY, Christopher Roy, MD; FRCS, FRCSE, FRCSE (Orth); Consultant Spinal Surgeon, Royal Devon & Exeter Hospital, since 1987; *b* 26 Sept. 1943; *s* of Dudley Graham Weatherley and Hilda Ada Weatherley (*née* Wilson). *Educ:* Queen Elizabeth's Sch., Crediton; Liverpool Univ. Med. Sch. (MB ChB; MD 1968). FRCSE 1973; FRCS 1974; FRCSE (Orth) 1984. Sen. Res. Associate, MRC Decompression Sickness Unit, Newcastle upon Tyne, 1973–76; Sen. Registrar in Orthopaedics, Robert Jones and Agnes Hunt Orthopaedic Hosp., 1979–87. Eur. Res. Fellow, Inst. Calôt, Berck-Plage, France, 1981–82; Consultant Spinal Surgeon, St Vincent's Hosp., Melbourne, 1985–86. Hon. Civilian Consultant, RN, 1991. Fellow, Brit. Orthopaedic Assoc., 1983; FRSocMed 1991. Member: Exec. Cttee, Brit. Scoliosis Soc., 1993– (Sec. and Treas., 1996–99; Pres., 2006–07); Council, Brit. Scoliosis Res. Foundn, 1998–; Eur. Cervical Spine Soc., 1984. Gold Medal Lectr, Old Oswestrians Annual Meeting, 2000. *Publications:* (reviewer) Gray's Anatomy, 40th edn 2008;

contrib. chapters in books, editorials and papers on: decompression sickness and dysbaric osteonecrosis; spinal tumours; scoliosis; back pain; surgical approaches to the spine; spinal fusion; ankylosing spondylitis; stress fractures in fast bowlers. *Recreations:* the fine line, the creation of myths. *Address:* 1 The Quadrant, Wonford Road, Exeter, Devon EX2 4LE. *T:* (01392) 272951. *Club:* Royal Society of Medicine.

WEATHERLEY, Mike; *b* Clevedon, Som, 2 July 1957; *s* of Derrick and Kirsten Weatherley; two *s* one *d*. *Educ:* South Bank Univ. (BA Hons Business Studies). Finance Dir and Jt Owner, Cash Bases GB Ltd, 1994–2000; Financial Controller, Pete Waterman Ltd, 2000–05; Vice-Pres., Motion Picture Licensing Co. Ltd, 2007–10 (non-exec. Dir, 2010–13). Mem. (C) Crawley BC, 2006–07. Contested (C) Barking, 2001; Brighton Pavilion, 2005. MP (C) Hove, 2010–15. Former Intellectual Property Advr to the Prime Minister. FCMA. *Recreations:* rock music, football (former amateur referee), motorbikes.

WEATHERSTON, (William) Alastair (Paterson), CB 1993; Under Secretary, Scottish Office Education Department, 1989–95; *b* 20 Nov. 1935; *s* of William Robert Weatherston and Isabella (*née* Paterson); *m* 1961, Margaret Jardine (*d* 2004); two *s* one *d*. *Educ:* Peebles High Sch.; Edinburgh Univ. (MA Hons History). Asst Principal, Dept of Health for Scotland and Scottish Educn Dept, 1959–63; Private Sec. to Permanent Under Sec. of State, Scottish Office, 1963–64; Principal, Scottish Educn Dept, 1964–72, Cabinet Office, 1972–74; Assistant Secretary: SHHD, 1974–77; Scottish Educn Dept, 1977–79; Central Services, Scottish Office, 1979–82; Dir, Scottish Courts Admin, 1982–86; Fisheries Sec., Dept of Agric. and Fisheries for Scotland, 1986–89. Sec., Gen. Council, Univ. of Edinburgh, 1997–2001. Mem., Murrayfield Community Council, 2005–11. *Recreations:* reading, music. *Address:* 1 Coltbridge Terrace, Edinburgh EH12 6AB. *T:* (0131) 337 3339.

WEATHERUP, Rt Hon. Sir Ronald Eccles, Kt 2001; PC 2015; **Rt Hon. Mr Justice Weatherup;** a Lord Justice of Appeal, Northern Ireland, since 2015. *Educ:* Methodist Coll.; Queen's Univ., Belfast. Called to the Bar, NI, 1971; QC (NI) 1993; Judge of the High Court of Justice, NI, 2001–15. Jun. Crown Counsel, 1989–93, Sen. Crown Counsel, 1997–2001, for NI. Mem., NI Judicial Appts Commn, 2005. *Address:* Royal Courts of Justice, Chichester Street, Belfast BT1 3JF.

WEAVER, (Christopher) Giles (Herron), FCA; Chairman: Charter European Trust, 2003–12; Helical Bar plc, 2005–12 (non-executive Director, 1993–2012); Tamar (formerly Kenmore) European Property Fund, 2006–14; *b* 4 April 1946; *s* of Lt Col John Weaver and Ursula (*née* Horlick); *m* 1975, Rosamund Betty Mayhew; two *s* two *d*. *Educ:* Eton Coll.; London Business Sch. (MSc 1973). FCA 1978. Dir, UK and Pensions Investment, Ivory & Sime, 1976–86; Man. Dir, Pension Mgt, Prudential Corp., 1986–90; Murray Johnstone Ltd, 1990: Chief Investment Officer, 1990–93; Man. Dir, 1993–99; Chm., 1999–2000. Chm., Murray Emerging Growth & Income Trust plc, 2001–05; non-executive Director: James Finlay, 1996–; Aberdeen Asset Management plc, 2000–13; IRP Property Investments Ltd (formerly ISIS Property Trust II Ltd), 2004–13; EP Global Opportunities Trust plc, 2011–. Trustee and Dep. Chm., Nat. Galls of Scotland, 1998–2005; Chm., HHA in Scotland, 1999–2004. Trustee: Lutyens Trust, 1986–; Flemings Wyfold Art Foundn, 2011–. *Recreations:* ski-ing, golf, tennis, bridge. *Address:* Hill Fort House, Drem, E Lothian EH39 5AZ. *T:* (01620) 880573. *Clubs:* Boodle's, Hurlingham, Queen's; New (Edinburgh); Hon. Company of Edinburgh Golfers (Muirfield).

WEAVER, Susan Alexandra, (Sigourney); actress; *b* New York, 8 Oct. 1949; *d* of late Sylvester Laflin, (Pat), Weaver and Elizabeth Weaver (*née* Inglis); *m* 1984, James Simpson; one *d*. *Educ:* Stanford Univ. (BA); Sch. of Drama, Yale Univ. (MFA). Founder, Goat Cay Productions. *Theatre includes:* Gemini, 1976, Crazy Mary, 2007, Playwrights Horizons, NY; Beyond Therapy, Marymount Manhattan Th., NY, 1981; Hurlyburly, Ethel Barrymore Th., NY, 1984; The Merchant of Venice, Classic Stage Co., NY, 1986; The Guys, 2002, Mrs Farnsworth, 2004, Flea Th., NY; The Mercy Seat, Acorn Th., NY, 2002. *Films include:* Annie Hall, 1977; Madman, 1978; Alien, 1979; Eyewitness, 1981; The Year of Living Dangerously, 1982; Deal of the Century, 1983; Ghostbusters, 1984; Walls of Glass, Une Femme ou Deux, 1985; Half Moon Street, Aliens, 1986; Gorillas in the Mist (Best Actress, Golden Globe Awards, 1989), Working Girl (Best Supporting Actress, Golden Globe Awards, 1989), 1988; Ghostbusters II, 1989; Alien^3 (also co-prod.), 1492: Conquest of Paradise, 1992; Dave, 1993; Death and the Maiden, 1995; Jeffrey, Copycat, 1996; Snow White: a Tale of Terror, Alien: Resurrection (also co-prod.), 1997; Ice Storm, 1998; A Map of the World, Galaxy Quest, 1999; Company Man, 2000; Heartbreakers, 2001; The Guys, 2002; Tadpole, Holes, 2003; The Village, 2004; Imaginary Heroes, 2005; Snow Cake, The TV Set, Infamous, 2006; Vantage Point, The Girl in the Park, 2008; Avatar, 2009; You Again, 2010; Paul, Cedar Rapids, 2011; Red Lights, The Cabin in the Woods, The Cold Light of Day, 2012; Exodus: Gods and Kings, 2014; Chappie, 2015. *Address:* c/o United Talent Agency, 9336 Civic Center Drive, Beverly Hills, CA 90210–3604, USA; Goat Cay Productions, PO Box 38, New York, NY 10150, USA.

WEBB, Sir Adrian (Leonard), Kt 2000; DLitt; FLSW; Chairman, Big Lottery Fund Wales, since 2011 (non-executive Director, Big Lottery Fund, since 2011); Chair, Review of Higher Education in North East Wales, since 2012; Vice-Chancellor, University of Glamorgan, 1993–2004; *b* 19 July 1943; *s* of Leonard and Rosina Webb; *m* 1st, 1966, Caroline Williams (marr. diss. 1995); two *s*; 2nd, 1996, Monjulee Dass. *Educ:* Birmingham Univ. (1st cl. Hons BSocSci 1965); LSE (MSc (Econ) 1966); DLitt Loughborough 1993. Lectr, LSE, 1966–74; Res. Dir, Personal Social Services Council, 1974–76; Loughborough University: Prof. of Social Policy, 1976–93; Dir, Centre for Res. in Social Policy, 1983–90; Dean, then Pro Vice-Chancellor, subseq. Sen. Pro Vice-Chancellor, 1986–93. Member: Nat. Cttee of Inquiry into Higher Educn (Dearing Cttee), 1996–97; BBC Broadcasting Council for Wales, 1998–2001; HM Treasury Public Sector Productivity Panel, 2000–06; Nat. Council, Educn and Learning in Wales, 2001–06; Beecham Review of Public Services in Wales, 2005–06; Administrative Justice and Tribunals Council, 2008–12 (Chair, Wales Cttee, 2013–); Wales Comr, UK Commn for Employment and Skills, 2008–12; Chairman: Welsh Review Group (Nursing, Midwifery and Health Workers), 1999–2002; Higher Educn Wales, 2000–02; Rev. of Further and Post-14 Educn in Wales, 2006–07; Welsh Employment and Skills Bd, 2008–12. Non-executive Director: E Glamorgan NHS Trust, 1997–99; Exec. Bd, Nat. Assembly for Wales, 2003–08; Wales Govt Bd, 2013–. Chm., Pontypridd & Rhondda NHS Trust, 2005–08. Founder Mem., Bevan Foundn, 2002–07. Gov., Thames Valley Univ., 2006–08. FCGI; FRSA; FLSW 2011. *Publications:* Change, Choice and Conflict in Social Policy, 1975; Planning Need and Scarcity: essays on the personal social services, 1986; The Economic Approach to Social Policy, 1986; Social Work, Social Care and Social Planning, 1987; Joint Approaches to Social Policy: rationality and practice, 1988; contribs on social policy and public admin to scholarly and professional periodicals. *Recreations:* walking, painting (water colour), ornithology.

See also G. T. Webb.

WEBB, Prof. Colin, PhD; CEng, FIChemE; Professor of Chemical Engineering, University of Manchester, since 1994; *b* Hereford, 11 Oct. 1954; *s* of late Sidney Webb and Stella Webb; *m* 1984, Ann Elizabeth Kelly; one *s* one *d*. *Educ:* Leominster Grammar Sch.; Aston Univ. (BSc Chem. Engrg 1976; PhD 1980). CEng 1992; MIChemE 1992, FIChemE 1995; CSci 2003. University of Manchester Institute of Science and Technology, later University of Manchester: Res. Associate, 1979–83; Lectr, 1983–91, Sen. Lectr, 1991–94, in Chem. Engrg; Dir, Satake Centre for Grain Process Engrg, 1994–2004; Hd, Dept of Chem. Engrg, 2000–04; Associate Dean (Estates), 2004–05; Hd, Sch. of Chemical Engrg and Analytical Sci., 2005–07. Vis. Academic, Monash Univ., 1988. Process Technol. Examnr, Inst. of Brewing, 1998–2002; Vice-Pres. (Qualifications), IChemE, 2012–. Fellow, Internat. Acad. of Food Sci. and Technol., 1999. Ed.-in-Chief, Biochemical Engineering Jl, 1998–. *Publications:* Process Engineering Aspects of Immobilised Cell Systems, 1986; Plant and Animal Cells: process possibilities, 1987; Studies in Viable Cell Immobilisation, 1996; Cereals: novel uses and processes, 1997; Comprehensive Biotechnology, vol. 2, Engineering Fundamentals, 2nd edn 2011; Food Industry Wastes: assessment and recuperation of commodities, 2013; over 250 articles in learned jls on biochem. engrg. *Recreations:* cycling, walking, watching football, checking e-mails, meeting friends I haven't seen for 25 years. *Address:* School of Chemical Engineering and Analytical Science, University of Manchester, C77, The Mill, Oxford Road, Manchester M13 9PL. *T:* (0161) 306 4379. *E:* colin.webb@manchester.ac.uk.

WEBB, Prof. Colin Edward, MBE 2000; DPhil; FRS 1991; FInstP; Professor, Department of Physics, University of Oxford, 1992–2002, now Emeritus; Senior Research Fellow, Jesus College, Oxford, 1988–2005, now Emeritus; Founder and Chairman, Oxford Lasers Ltd, 1977–2014, now non-executive Director; *b* 9 Dec. 1937; *s* of Alfred Edward Webb and Doris (*née* Collins); *m* 1st, 1964, Pamela Mabel Cooper White (*d* 1992); two *d*; 2nd, 1995, Margaret Helen (*née* Dewar); two step *d*. *Educ:* Univ. of Nottingham (BSc 1960); Oriel Coll., Oxford (DPhil 1964). FInstP 1985. Mem., Technical Staff, Bell Labs, Murray Hill, NJ, 1964–68; University of Oxford: AEI Res. Fellow in Physics, Clarendon Lab., 1968–71; Univ. Lectr, 1971–90; Tutorial Fellow, Jesus Coll., 1973–88; Reader, 1990–92, Prof., 1992, Dept of Physics; Hd of Atomic and Laser Physics, 1995–99. Visiting Professor: Dept of Pure and Applied Physics, Univ. of Salford, 1987–2002; Dept of Mechanical Engrg, Cranfield Univ., 1999–2002. Fellow, Optical Soc. of America, 1988. Gov., Launceston Coll., 2012–. Hon. DSc Salford, 1996. Duddell Medal and Prize, 1985, Glazebrook Medal and Prize, 2001, Inst. of Physics; Clifford Paterson Lect. and Medal, Royal Soc., 1999. *Publications:* (Ed-in-Chief) Handbook of Laser Technology and Applications, 2003; (with S. M. Hooker) Laser Physics, 2010; contribs on lasers, laser mechanisms and applications to learned jls. *Recreations:* travel, photography, music, reading. *Address:* Clarendon Laboratory, Parks Road, Oxford OX1 3PU. *T:* (01865) 272254.

WEBB, Prof. David Charles, PhD; Professor of Finance, London School of Economics and Political Science, since 1991; *b* 13 July 1953; *s* of Charles Ronald Webb and Margaret Jane Webb (*née* Oldham). *Educ:* Hurworth Secondary Sch., Darlington; Grangefield Grammar Sch., Stockton-on-Tees; Univ. of Manchester (BA Econs 1974; MA Econs 1975); London School of Economics and Pol Sci. (PhD 1979). Lectr, Univ. of Bristol, 1978–84; London School of Economics and Political Science: Lectr, 1984–90; Reader in Econs, 1991; Director: Financial Mkts Gp Res. Centre, 1991–2008; UBS Pensions Res. Prog., 2001–06; Hd, Dept of Finance, 2009. Vis. Associate Prof., Queen's Univ., Canada, 1982–84; Vis. Prof. of Economics, Univ. of Iowa, 1991. Consultant, Asian Develt Bank, 1998–; Mem., Adv. Bd, Centro de Estudios Monetarios y Financieros, Madrid, 1998–. Mem. Council, Royal Economic Soc., 2008–. Editor, Economica, 1989–97. *Publications:* articles in Econs and Finance, Qly Jl of Econs, Rand Jl of Econs, Internat. Econ. Review, Econ. Jl and Jl of Public Econs. *Recreation:* ski-ing. *Address:* Department of Finance, London School of Economics and Political Science, Houghton Street, WC2A 2AE. *T:* (020) 7955 6301.

WEBB, Prof. David John, MD, DSc; FRCPE, FRCP, FFPM, FMedSci, FBPhS; FRSE; Christison Professor of Therapeutics and Clinical Pharmacology, since 1995, and Director, Education Programme, Wellcome Trust Clinical Research Facility, since 1998, University of Edinburgh; Director, Wellcome Trust Scottish Translational Medicine and Therapeutics Initiative, since 2009; Consultant Physician, Lothian University Hospitals NHS Trust, since 1990; *b* 1 Sept. 1953; *s* of Alfred William Owen Webb and Edna May Webb (*née* Parish); *m* 1st, 1984, Margaret Jane Cullen (marr. diss. 2007); three *s*; 2nd, 2009, Dr Louise Eleanor Bath. *Educ:* Dulwich Coll. (Kent Schol.); Royal London Hosp.; MB BS 1977, MD 1990, London; DSc Edinburgh 2000. MRCP 1980, FRCP 1994; FRCPE 1992; FFPM (FFPHM 1993); FBPhS (FBPharmacolS 2004). House Officer posts, Royal London Hosp. scheme, 1977–78; Senior House Officer: Chelmsford Hosps, 1978–79; Stoke Mandeville Hosp., 1979–80; Registrar: Royal London Hosp., 1980–82; in Medicine, and MRC Clin. Scientist, MRC BP Unit, Western Infirmary, Glasgow, 1982–85; Lectr in Clin. Pharmacol., St George's Med. Sch., London, 1985–89; Sen. Registrar in Medicine, St George's Hosp., London, 1985–89; University of Edinburgh: Sen. Lectr in Medicine, 1990–95; Dir, Clin. Res. Centre, 1990–96; Head: Dept of Medicine, 1997–98; Dept of Med. Scis, 1998–2001; Wellcome Trust Res. Leave Fellow, and Leader, Wellcome Trust Cardiovascular Res. Initiative, 1998–2001; Convenor, Cardiovascular Interdisciplinary Gp, 1999–2000; Hd, Centre for Cardiovascular Sci., 2000–04. Chm., Scottish Medicines Consortium, 2005–08 (Chm., New Drugs Cttee, 2001–05); Chair, Scientific Adv. Cttee, Nat. Inst. for Biol Standards and Control, 2014–; Jt Chair, Prescribing Safety Assessment Exec. Cttee, 2014–; Dir, Wellcome Trust Scottish Translational Medicine and Therapeutics Initiative, 2008–; non-exec. Dir, Medicines and Healthcare products Regulatory Agency, 2013–; Dep. Dir, Scottish Clinical Pharmacol. and Pathol. Prog., 2010–. Vice-Pres., Clin. Div., Internat. Union for Pharmacol., 2004–. Res. Dir, High Blood Pressure Foundn, 1993– (Trustee, 1991–). President: Eur. Assoc. for Clin. Pharmacol. and Therapeutics, 2009–; Scottish Soc. of Physicians, 2010; Vice-Pres., RCPE, 2007–09; Mem., Exec. Cttee, British Hypertension Soc., 1991–94; British Pharmacological Society: Mem., Exec. Cttee, 1994–98; Clin. Vice-Pres., 1995–98; Dir and Trustee, 1996–99 and 2004–; Chm., Cttee of Profs and Hds of Clin. Pharmacol. & Therapeutics, 2004–; Vice Pres., Meetings, 2012–13; Pres., Jan. 2016–; Mem., Sectional Cttee 1, Acad. Med. Scis, 2000–02. Dir, Court, Edinburgh Acad., 2008–. Internat. Fellow, Amer. Heart Assoc., 1998; FMedSci 1999; FESC 2001; FRSE 2004; FAHA. *Publications:* (with G. A. Gray) The Molecular Biology and Pharmacology of the Endothelins, 1995; (ed with P. J. T. Vallance) The Endothelium in Hypertension, 1996; (ed with P. J. T. Vallance) Vascular Endothelium in Human Physiology and Pathophysiology, 1999; (jtly) The Year in Therapeutics, Vol. 1, 2005. *Recreations:* summer and winter mountaineering, scuba diving, reading late at night. *Address:* Queen's Medical Research Institute, Centre for Cardiovascular Science, University of Edinburgh, E3.22, 47 Little France Crescent, Edinburgh EH16 4TJ. *T:* (0131) 242 9215, *Fax:* 0870 134 0897. *E:* d.j.webb@ed.ac.uk; 75 Great King Street, Edinburgh EH3 6RN. *T:* (0131) 556 7145, 07770 966786. *Club:* Scottish Mountaineering.

WEBB, Geraint Timothy; QC 2013; *b* London, 17 July 1971; *s* of Sir Adrian Leonard Webb, *qv*; *m* 1999, Ilfa Charlotte, *d* of Sir David Paul Brandes Goldberg, *qv*; two *s* two *d*. *Educ:* Loughborough Grammar Sch.; Christ Church, Oxford (BA Mod. Hist. 1st Cl. 1992). Called to the Bar, Inner Temple, 1995; in practice as a barrister, specialising in commercial law, product liability, mass tort/group action claims and insurance law, Henderson Chambers, 2 Harcourt Bldgs, 1995–. *Recreations:* family, walking, photography, goldsmithing. *Address:* Henderson Chambers, 2 Harcourt Buildings, Temple, EC4Y 9DB. *T:* (020) 7583 9020. *E:* gwebb@hendersonchambers.co.uk.

WEBB, Justin Oliver; Presenter, Today Programme, BBC Radio 4, since 2009; *b* 3 Jan. 1961; *s* of late Peter Woods and Gloria Webb (*née* Crocombe); *m* 1996, Sarah Gordon; one *s* two *d* (of whom one *s* one *d* are twins). *Educ:* London Sch. of Econs (BSc Econ 1983). BBC: Reporter: Radio Ulster, 1985–87; Today Prog., 1987–89; Foreign Affairs Corresp., TV News, 1989–94; Presenter: Breakfast TV News, 1994–98; One O'Clock TV News, 1998–99; Chief Europe Corresp., 1999–2002; Chief Washington Corresp., 2002–07; North America Ed., 2007–09. *Publications:* Have a Nice Day: a history of anti-Americanism, 2009; Notes on

Them and US: reflections on relations between the UK and US, 2011. *Recreations:* watching Bath Rugby, reading. *Address:* BBC Broadcasting House, Portland Place, W1A 1AA. *E:* justin.webb@bbc.co.uk.

WEBB, Prof. (Leslie) Roy, AO 2003; Vice-Chancellor, Griffith University, 1985–2001, Emeritus Professor, 2002; *b* 18 July 1935; *s* of Leslie Hugh Charles Webb and Alice Myra Webb; *m* 1966, Heather, *d* of late H. Brown; one *s* one *d. Educ:* Wesley College, Univ. of Melbourne (BCom 1957); Univ. of London (PhD 1962). FASSA 1986; FAIM 1989; FACE 1997. Sen. Lectr in Economics, Univ. of Melbourne, 1964–68; Reader in Economics, La Trobe Univ., 1968–72; University of Melbourne: Truby Williams Prof. of Economics, 1973–84, Prof. Emeritus, 1984; Pro-Vice-Chancellor, 1982–84; Chm., Academic Bd, 1983–84. Vis. Prof., Cornell, 1967–68. Chairman: Bd, Qld Tertiary Admissions Centre, 1986, 1991, 1992 (Mem., 1985–2001); Australian-Amer. Educnl Foundn (Fulbright Program), 1986–90 (Mem., 1985–89); Qld Non-State Schs Accreditation Bd, 2001–09; Library Bd of Qld, 2002–08; Member: Bd of Dirs, Australian Vice-Chancellors' Cttee, 1991–94; Cttee, Sir Robert Menzies Australian Studies Centre, Univ. of London, 1990–92; Bd of Govs, Foundn for Develt Co-operation, 1990–2007. Consultant, UN Conf. on Trade and Develt, 1974–75; Chm., Cttee of Inquiry into S Australian Dairy Industry, 1977; Mem., Council of Advice, Bureau of Industry Economics, 1982–84; Pres., Victoria Branch, Econ. Soc. of Aust. and NZ, 1976. DUniv: Qld Univ. of Technol., 2002; Griffith, 2002; Hon. DLitt Southern Qld, 2002. Award for outstanding achievement, US Inf. Agency, 1987. Joint Editor, The Economic Record, 1973–77. Cavaliere dell'Ordine al Merito (Italy), 1995. *Publications:* (ed jtly) Industrial Economics: Australian studies, 1982. *Recreations:* music, art. *Address:* 3 Davrod Street, Robertson, Qld 4109, Australia.

WEBB, Lynn Margaret; *see* Tayton, L. M.

WEBB, Margaret Elizabeth Barbieri; *see* Barbieri, M. E.

WEBB, Nicholas John David; His Honour Judge Webb; a Circuit Judge, since 2003; *b* 13 Oct. 1949; *s* of late David Frederick and of Joyce Mary Webb; *m* 1973, Jane Elizabeth; two *s. Educ:* Nottingham High Sch.; Downing Coll., Cambridge (BA 1971). Called to the Bar, Middle Temple, 1972; barrister, Midland and Oxford, later Midland Circuit, 1972–2003, specialising in crime and personal injury; Asst Recorder, 1996–2001, Recorder, 2001–03. Mem., Parole Bd, 2010–. Chairman: Cambridge Univ. Conservative Assoc., 1971; Edgbaston Constituency Conservative Assoc., 1989–93; Dep. Chm., West Midlands Area Conservative Assoc., 1992–94. Contested (C) Birmingham Sparkbrook, 1979. *Recreations:* jazz (New Orleans to be-bop), cricket, medieval and modern history. *Address:* Wolverhampton Crown Court Centre, Pipers Row, Wolverhampton WV1 3LQ.

WEBB, Dame Patricia M.; *see* Morgan-Webb.

WEBB, Pauline Mary, FKC; retired; author and broadcaster; *b* 28 June 1927; *d* of Rev. Leonard F. Webb. *Educ:* King's Coll., London Univ. (BA English Hons 1948; AKC, FKC 1985); Teacher's Diploma, London Inst. of Educn, 1949; Union Theological Seminary, New York (STM). Asst Mistress, Thames Valley Grammar Sch., 1949–52; Editor, Methodist Missionary Soc., 1955–66; Vice-Pres., Methodist Conf., 1965–66; Dir, Lay Training, Methodist Church, 1967–73; Area Sec., Methodist Missionary Soc., 1973–79; Chm., Community and Race Relns Unit, BCC, 1976–79; Organiser, Religious Broadcasting, BBC World Service, 1979–87. Vice-Chm., Central Cttee, WCC, 1968–75; Jt Chm., World Conf. on Religion and Peace, 1989–93. Pres., Feed the Minds, 1998–2003. Hon. Life Mem., World Assoc. of Christian Communication, 1998. Hon. Dr in Protestant Theology, Univ. of Brussels, 1984; Hon. DSL Victoria Univ., Toronto, 1985; Hon. DHL Mt St Vincent Univ., Nova Scotia, 1987; Hon. DD Birmingham, 1997. *Publications:* Women of Our Company, 1958; Women of Our Time, 1960; Operation-Healing, 1964; All God's Children, 1964; Are We Yet Alive?, 1966; Agenda for the Churches, 1968; Salvation Today, 1974; Eventful Worship, 1975; Where are the Women?, 1979; Faith and Faithfulness, 1985; Celebrating Friendship, 1986; Evidence for the Power of Prayer, 1987; Candles for Advent, 1989; (ed jtly) Dictionary of the Ecumenical Movement, 1991; She Flies Beyond, 1993; (ed) The Long Struggle: the World Council of Churches' involvement with South Africa, 1994; (ed) All Loves Excelling, 1997; Worship in Every Event, 1998; (compiler) Living by Grace (anthol.), 2001; World-Wide Webb, 2006; Now Think On, 2010. *Address:* 21 Padfield Court, 4 Forty Avenue, Wembley HA9 8JS. *Club:* BBC.

WEBB, Richard John; Corporate Director, Health and Adult Services, North Yorkshire County Council, since 2014; *b* Portsmouth, 13 Feb. 1971; *s* of Harry and Joan Webb; *m* 2003, Stephanie, *d* of Eric and Bea Lare. *Educ:* Court Lane Sch., Portsmouth; Springfield Sch., Portsmouth; Portsmouth Sixth Form Coll.; Univ. of Durham (BA Hons Politics 1992). NHS nat. mgt trainee, Newcastle upon Tyne and N Tyneside, 1992–94; Operational Manager, Gateshead Healthcare NHS Trust, 1994–95; Service Manager, Learning Disabilities, 1995–97, Actg Divl Manager, Mental Health, 1997–98, N Tees Health NHS Trust; Gen. Manager, Learning Disabilities, Stockton on Tees BC and NHS, 1998–2000; Asst Dir (Adults), Social Services, Stockton on Tees BC, 2000–02; Dir, Service Develt, Stockton on Tees BC and N Tees PCT, 2002–05; Corporate Dir, Adult and Consumer Care, Telford and Wrekin Council, 2005–09; Exec. Dir, Communities, Sheffield City Council, 2009–14. LGA Peer Reviewer, 2013. Nat. Co-Chair, Mental Health, Drugs and Alcohol Policy Network, 2008–11, Hon. Sec., 2011–, ADASS. *Recreations:* family, walking, reading, theatre, music, good food. *Address:* c/o North Yorkshire County Council, County Hall, Northallerton, North Yorks DL7 8AD. *T:* (01609) 532217. *E:* richard.webb@northyorks.gov.uk.

WEBB, Richard Murton Lumley; Chairman, Morgan Grenfell & Co. Ltd, 1989–96; *b* 7 March 1939; *s* of Richard Henry Lumley Webb and Elizabeth Martin (*née* Munro Kerr); *m* 1966, Juliet Wendy English Devenish; one *s* one *d. Educ:* Winchester Coll.; New Coll., Oxford (BA Modern Hist.). Mem., Inst. Chartered Accountants of Scotland, 1965. Brown Fleming & Murray, 1961–68; Director: Morgan Grenfell & Co. Ltd, 1973–96; Morgan Grenfell Gp PLC, 1988–96. Chairman: Medway Housing Society Ltd, 1996–2004; Wax Lyrical Ltd, 1997–99; Dir, Scottish Provident Instn, 1997–2001. *Address:* 12 Gwendolen Avenue, Putney, SW15 6EH. *Club:* Hurlingham.

WEBB, Prof. Robert, PhD, DSc; FRSE; Principal and Chief Executive Officer, Scotland's Rural College, 2012–13; Professor of Agriculture, University of Glasgow, 2012–13; *b* Nottingham, 18 June 1950; *s* of Gordon David and Audrey Irene Webb; *m* 1976, Jeanette Mary Caddick; two *s* one *d. Educ:* Arnold Co. High Sch., Nottingham; Notts Agricl Coll. (C&G Pig, Beef and Milk Prodn 1969); Univ. of Nottingham (BSc; PhD 1977); Univ. of Edinburgh (DSc 2012). Farmworker, 1968–70; Ford Foundn Fellow, Univ. of Michigan, 1977–79; Sen. Scientist, Dept of Obstetrics and Gynaecol., Univ. of Oxford, 1979–81; Principal Res. Scientist, Roslin Inst., Edinburgh, BBSRC, 1981–97; University of Nottingham: Prof. of Animal Scis, 1997–2012; Hd, Sch. of Bioscis, 2003–06; Dean, Faculty of Sci., 2007–08; Pro-Vice Chancellor (Res.), 2008–12; Hon. Prof., 2012–. Mem., AgriTech Leadership Council, 2013–. FRSE 2013. Marshall Medal, Soc. for Reproduction and Fertility, 2011. *Publications:* contrib. papers to jls, books and conf. procs. *Recreations:* music, walking, trekking, sport.

WEBB, Robert Stopford; QC 1988; General Counsel, Rolls-Royce plc, since 2012; *b* 4 Oct. 1948; *s* of late Robert Victor Bertram Webb, MC and Isabella Raine Webb (*née* Hinks); *m* 1975, Angela Mary Freshwater; two *s. Educ:* Wycliffe Coll.; Exeter Univ. (LLB 1970). Called to the Bar, Inner Temple, 1971 (Bencher, 1997), and Lincoln's Inn, 1996; Head of Chambers, 5 Bell Yard, 1988–98; a Recorder, 1993–98; Door Tenant, Brick Court Chambers, 2009–12. Gen. Counsel, British Airways, 1998–2009. Chairman: Autonomy plc, 2009–12; BBC Worldwide, 2009–12; Sciemus Ltd, 2010–11; Darktrace Ltd, 2014–; non-executive Director: Air Mauritius, 1998–2005; London Stock Exchange, 2001–15; London First, 2002–09; Holdingham Gp (formerly Hakluyt and Co.) Ltd, 2005–; Emerging Health Threats Forum CIC (formerly Forum for Global Health Protection), 2006–12; BBC, 2007–12; Argent Gp plc, 2009–12. Chm., Air Law Gp, RAeS, 1988–93 (FRAeS 1992); English Bar Rep., Internat. Bar Assoc., 1994–99; Chm., Internat. Relations Cttee, Bar Council, 1997–98. Vis. Prof., Bournemouth Univ., 2009–11. Trustee: Migratory Salmon Fund, 1997–; Comic Relief, 2011–. Fellow, Internat. Acad. of Trial Lawyers, 1990. Hon. Fellow, UNICEF, 2006. *Recreations:* golf, conservation. *Clubs:* Brooks's, Royal Automobile, Reform, Soho House, Flyfishers'; Royal Wimbledon Golf, Royal Lytham St Anne's Golf, Hampstead Golf, Prestbury Golf.

WEBB, Roy; *see* Webb, L. R.

WEBB, Simon, CBE 1991; Executive Director, The Nichols Group, since 2010; *b* 21 Oct. 1951; *s* of Rev. Canon Bertie Webb and Jane Webb (*née* Braley); *m* 1975, Alexandra Jane Culme-Seymour; one *s* one *d. Educ:* King's Sch., Worcester (Schol.); Hertford Coll., Oxford (Meeke Schol.; MA). FICE 2014. Entered MoD, 1972: Asst Private Sec. to Minister of State, 1975; Principal, 1977; Public Enterprises, HM Treasury, 1982–85; Dir of Resources and Progs (Warships), MoD, 1985–88; Rand Corp., Santa Monica, Calif, 1988–89; Head, Agency Team, MoD, 1989; Private Sec. to Sec. of State for Defence, 1989–92; Minister (Defence Materiel), Washington, 1992–96; Dir Gen. Resources, PE, MoD, 1996–98; Team Leader, Smart Procurement, 1998–99; Asst Under Sec. of State (Home & Overseas), subseq. Dir Gen., Operational Policy, MoD, 1999–2001; Policy Dir, MoD, 2001–04; Dir Gen., Delivery and Security, 2004–07, Internat. Networks and Envmt, 2007–09, DfT. Dir, Major Projects Assoc., 2010–. Gov., Ditchley Foundn, 2008–. Edgell Sheppee Prize for Engrg and Econs. *Publications:* Defense Acquisition and Free Markets, 1990. *Recreations:* cycling, gardens, church music. *Club:* Reform.

WEBB, Rt Hon. Steven (John); PC 2014; Director of Policy and External Communications, Royal London, since 2015; *b* 18 July 1965; *s* of Brian and Patricia Webb; *m* 1993, Rev. Helen Edwards; one *s* one *d. Educ:* Hertford Coll., Oxford (1st Cl. BA Hons PPE). Economist, Inst. for Fiscal Studies, 1986–95; Prof. of Social Policy, Bath Univ., 1995–97. MP (Lib Dem) Northavon, 1997–2010, Thornbury and Yate, 2010–15; contested (Lib Dem) same seat, 2015. Lib Dem spokesman on health, 2005–07, on envmt, energy, food and rural affairs, 2008, on energy and climate change, 2008–09, on work and pensions, 2009–10; Minister of State for Pensions, DWP, 2010–15. Lib Dem Manifesto Chair, 2007. *Publications:* (with Alissa Goodman and Paul Johnson) Inequality in the UK, 1997. *Recreations:* internet issues, church organ, oboe.

WEBB, Prof. William Timothy, PhD; FREng, FIET, FIEEE; Chief Executive Officer, Weightless SIG, since 2012; Consultant, Webb Search Ltd, since 2013; *b* Hersham, Surrey, 4 May 1967; *s* of Christopher and Genebeth Webb; *m* 1995, Alison Porter; two *d. Educ:* Southampton Univ. (BEng 1st Cl. Electronic Engrg 1989; PhD 1992); Southampton Univ. (MBA 1997). FIET 1995; FREng 2005; FIEEE 2008. Tech. Dir, Multiple Access Communications Ltd, 1989–93; Principal Consultant, Smith System Engrg Ltd, 1993–97; Hd, wireless local loop div., Netcom Consultants, 1997–98; Dir, Corporate Strategy, Motorola, 1998–2001; Managing Consultant, Wireless Practice, PA Consulting, 2001–03; Dir, Technol. Resources, Ofcom, 2003–11; Chief Tech. Officer, Neul, 2011–13. Visiting Professor: Centre for Communication Systems Res., Surrey Univ., 2003–; De Montfort Univ., 2007–12; Southampton Univ., 2014–; TCD, 2014–. Mem. Bd, Cambridge Wireless, 2009–. Vice Pres., 2004–07 and 2009–12, Dep. Pres., 2013–14, Pres., 2014–, IET; Royal Academy of Engineering: Mem., editl panel, Ingenia, 2007–; Mem., Ext. Engagement Cttee, 2010–13. Judge, Wall St Jl Innovation Awards, 2002–12. Hon. DSc Southampton, 2015; Hon. DTech Anglia Ruskin, 2015. *Publications:* (with L. Hanzo) Quadrature Amplitude Modulation, 1994, 2004; Introduction to Wireless Local Loop, 1998, 2000; Understanding Cellular Radio, 1998; The Complete Wireless Communications Professional, 1999; The Future of Wireless Communications, 2001; Wireless Communications: the future, 2007; (jtly) Essentials of Modern Spectrum Management, 2007; Being Mobile: future wireless technologies and applications, 2010; Understanding Weightless, 2012; Dynamic White Space Spectrum Access, 2013; Using Spectrum, 2015. *Recreations:* cycling, including some of the world's toughest sportives, such as the Cent Cols Challenge and the route of Tour de France. *E:* wwebb@theiet.org.

WEBB-CARTER, Maj. Gen. Sir Evelyn (John), KCVO 2000; OBE 1989; DL; Chief Executive, ABF The Soldiers' Charity (formerly Controller, Army Benevolent Fund), 2003–12; *b* 30 Jan. 1946; *s* of Brig. Brian Webb-Carter, DSO, OBE and Rosemary Webb-Carter (*née* Hood); *m* 1973, Hon. Anne Celia Wigram, *yr d* of Baron Wigram, *qv*; one *s* two *d. Educ:* Wellington Coll.; RMA Sandhurst. Commissioned Grenadier Guards, 1966; Commanded: 1st Bn Grenadier Guards, 1985–88; 19 Mechanised Bde, 1991–93; Multi National Div. (SW) in Bosnia, 1996–97; GOC London Dist and Maj. Gen. Comdg Household Div., 1997–2000. Special Advr to CRE, 2001–03. Regtl Lt-Col, Grenadier Guards, 1995–2000; Col, Duke of Wellington's Regt, 1999–2006; Hon. Regtl Col, King's Troop, RHA, 2001–11; Hon. Col, Glos ACF, 2011–. Chairman: Mounted Infantry Club, 1993–; Waterloo Assoc. (formerly Assoc. of Friends of Waterloo Cttee), 2002–; Adv. Council, First Aid Nursing Yeomanry, 2003–12 (Vice Pres., 2012–); Commemoration Cttee, 200th Anniversary of Battle of Waterloo, 2007–15; Waterloo 200 Ltd, 2007–; Trustees, Brooke Hosp. for Animals, 2013–. Patron, Burnaby Blue Foundn, 2001–. Mem. Ct of Assts, Farriers' Co., 2004– (Liveryman, 2003–; Master, 2012–13). DL Glos, 2009. *Recreations:* hunting, military history, riding in foreign parts. *Address:* Horcott House, Fairford, Glos GL7 4BY. *Clubs:* Boodle's; Banja Luka Hunt (Bosnia).

WEBBER; *see* Lloyd Webber.

WEBBER, Prof. Bryan Ronald, PhD; FRS 2001; FInstP; Professor of Theoretical Physics, University of Cambridge, 1999–2010, now Emeritus; Fellow, Emmanuel College, Cambridge, since 1973; *b* 25 July 1943; *s* of Frederick Ronald Webber and Iris Evelyn Webber (*née* Hutchings); *m* 1968, Akemi Horie. *Educ:* Colston's Sch., Bristol; Queen's Coll., Oxford (MA); Univ. of Calif, Berkeley (PhD 1969). FInstP 1987. Physicist, Lawrence Berkeley Nat. Lab., Calif, 1969–71; Department of Physics, University of Cambridge: Res. Asst, 1971–73; Demonstrator, 1973–78; Lectr, 1978–94; Reader, 1994–99. Hon. PhD Lund, 2012. Dirac Medal for Theoretical Physics, Inst. of Physics, 2008; J. J. Sakurai Prize for Theoretical Physics, Amer. Physical Soc., 2012. *Publications:* (jtly) QCD and Collider Physics, 1996; contrib. articles on high energy physics. *Address:* Cavendish Laboratory, J. J. Thomson Avenue, Cambridge CB3 0HE. *T:* (01223) 337200.

WEBBER, Howard Simon; Chief Executive, Postwatch, 2006–08; *b* 25 Jan. 1955; *s* of Manny and Josie Webber; *m* 1978, Sandra Wagman; one *s. Educ:* Univ. of Birmingham (LLB 1976); Harvard Univ. (MPA 1987); King's Coll. London (MA 2011). Joined Home Office, 1976; seconded to Royal Commn on Criminal Procedure, 1979–80 and Cabinet Office, 1986; Harkness Fellow, USA, 1986–87; Prison Bldg Budget Manager, Home Office, 1987–88; Dir, Incentive Funding, 1988–91, Hd, Policy and Planning, 1991–94, Arts Council; Manager, Public Sector MBA, Cabinet Office, 1994; Hd, Voluntary Services Unit/Active Community Unit, Home Office, 1995–99; Chief Exec., Criminal Injuries Compensation Authy, 1999–2006. Advr, Business and Enterprise Cttee, H of C, 2009; Board Member:

Metropolitan Housing Partnership, 2008–13; Kingston Liberal Synagogue, 2008–; PhonepayPlus, 2010–. Chair, Lambeth and Southwark Housing Assoc., 2015–. Mem., Standards Cttee, SRA, 2014–. *Publications:* (jtly) A Creative Future: a national strategy for the arts and media, 1993. *Recreations:* travel, the arts. *E:* howardwebber@gmail.com.

WEBBER, Rev. Lionel Frank; Chaplain to the Queen, 1994–2001; Hon. Curate, St Mary, Burnham-on-Crouch, since 2005; *b* 12 July 1935; *s* of Nellie and Sydney Webber; *m* 1961, Jean Thomas; one *d*. *Educ:* Danetree Road Co. Secondary Sch., Ewell; Kelham Theol Coll.; St Michael's Theol Coll., Llandaff. Ordained deacon, 1960, priest, 1961; Curate: The Saviour, Bolton, 1960–63; Holy Trinity, Aberavon, 1963–65; Rector, Stowell Meml Parish Ch, Salford, 1965–69; Vicar, Holy Trinity, Aberavon, 1969–74; Team Vicar, Stantonbury, Milton Keynes, 1974–76; Rector of Basildon, 1976–2001. Hon. Canon, Chelmsford Cathedral, 1984–2001. Chaplain, Vintage Sports Car Club. Life Vice Cdre, Royal Naval Sailing Assoc., 2008. *Recreations:* motor racing, sailing. *Address:* 12 Ramblers Way, Burnham-on-Crouch, Essex CM0 8LR.

WEBBER, Roy Seymour, FCCA; Town Clerk and Chief Executive, Royal Borough of Kensington and Chelsea, 1979–90; *b* 8 April 1933; *s* of A. E. and A. M. Webber; *m* 1960, Barbara Ann (*née* Harries); one *s* three *d*. *Educ:* Ipswich School. Ipswich CBC, 1949–55; Coventry CBC, 1955–58; St Pancras BC, 1958–61; IBM (UK) Ltd, 1961–62; Woolwich BC, 1962–65; Greenwich LBC, 1965–68; Royal Borough of Kensington and Chelsea: Dep. Borough Treasurer, 1968–73; Director of Finance, 1973–79. *Recreation:* walking. *Address:* 11 River Park, Marlborough, Wilts SN8 1NH. *T:* (01672) 511426.

WEBBER, Timothy John; visual effects supervisor and film director, and Chief Creative Officer, since 1998, Framestore Ltd; *b* Cardiff, 4 Dec. 1964; *s* of Thomas John Webber and Margaret Denise Webber; *m* 2001, Fiona Jane Walkinshaw; two *s* one *d*. *Educ:* Summer Fields, Oxford; Marlborough Coll.; St Catherine's Coll., Oxford (BA). Joined Framestore Ltd, 1988, Partner, 1992–; visual effects supervisor of films: Harry Potter and the Goblet of Fire, 2005; Children of Men, 2006; The Dark Knight, 2008; Where the Wild Things Are, 2009; Avatar, 2009; Gravity, 2013 (Oscar for Best Visual Effects (jtly), 2014; BAFTA for Best Special Visual Effects (jtly), 2014). Hon. FRPS 2014. Emmy Award, 1996, (jtly) 1998, 2000, (jtly) 2002; Progress Medal, RPS, 2014. *Recreations:* art, photography, cinema, croquet, family. *E:* timjwebber@gmail.com.

WEBBON, Peter Michael, PhD; Chief Executive, Animal Health Trust, 2007–13; *b* Leicester, 9 Jan. 1948; *s* of late Robert Ernest Webbon and Grace Webbon (*née* Salt); *m* 1st, 1970, Phyllis Mary Christine (marr. diss. 2008), *d* of late Major John Frederick Langdon, MC; one *s* three *d*; 2nd, 2012, Lynn Louise Hillyer, *d* of Roger Walkey; two *d*. *Educ:* Wyggeston Boys' Grammar Sch.; Royal Veterinary Coll., London (BVetMed Hons 1971; DVR 1975; PhD 1989). MRCVS. Res. Trng Scholar, Horserace Betting Levy Bd, 1971–74; Lectr, 1974–83, Sen. Lectr, 1983–96, RVC, London; Chief Vet. Advr, 1996–2001, Vet. Dir, 2002–06, Jockey Club; Chief Exec., HRA, 2006. Hon. Prof., RVC, 2007. Official veterinarian, FEI; Veterinary Advr, Internat. Stud Book Cttee. Chm., Equine Sector Council; Ind. Dir, Greyhound Bd of GB. *Publications:* (ed and contrib.) A Guide to Diagnostic Radiography in Small Animal Practice, 1981; chapters in books on diagnostic imaging and equine medicine; articles in scientific and gen. jls; contrib. professional and lay societies. *Recreations:* keeping Ryeland sheep, gardening, ski-ing, golf. *E:* pwebbon@hotmail.co.uk.

WEBER, Prof. Axel Alfred; Chairman, UBS AG, since 2012; *b* Kusel, 8 March 1957; *m*; two *c*. *Educ:* Univ. of Constance (degree Econs and Mgt 1982); Univ. of Siegen (Doctorate 1987; Habilitation Econs 1994). Prof. of Econ. Theory, Rheinische Friedrich Wilhelms Univ., Bonn, 1994–98; Prof. of Applied Monetary Econs, Johann Wolfgang Goethe Univ., Frankfurt am Main, 1998–2001; Dir, Center for Financial Studies, Frankfurt am Main, 1998–2002; Prof. of Internat. Econs, Univ. of Cologne, 2001–04; Pres., Deutsche Bundesbank and Mem., Governing Council, European Central Bank, 2004–11. Mem., German Council of Economic Experts, 2002–04. *Address:* c/o UBS AG, Bahnhofstr. 45, PO Box, 8098 Zurich, Switzerland.

WEBER, Catherine Elisabeth Dorcas; *see* Bell, C. E. D.

WEBER, Prof. Jonathan Norden, PhD; FRCP, FRCPath, FMedSci; Jefferiss Professor of Genito-Urinary Medicine and Communicable Diseases, Imperial College and St Mary's Hospital, since 1991; Director of Research, Imperial College Healthcare NHS Trust, since 2007; Director of Research, since 2008, and Vice Dean, since 2009, Faculty of Medicine, Imperial College London; Director: Imperial NIHR Biomedical Research Centre, since 2009; Imperial Academic Health Science Centre, since 2014; *b* 29 Dec. 1954; *s* of Dr Geoffrey Norden Weber and Rosalie Weber; *m* 1996, Prof. Sophie Elisabeth Day; three *s*. *Educ:* Gonville and Caius Coll., Cambridge (BA 1976; PhD 2003); St Bartholomew's Med. Sch. (MB BChir 1979). FRCP 1993; FRCPath 1997. Wellcome Trust Res. Fellow, St Mary's Hosp. Med. Sch., 1982–85; Wellcome Trust Lectr in Cell and Molecular Biol., Inst. Cancer Res., 1985–88; Sen. Lectr, Dept of Medicine, RPMS, 1988–91; Chm., Wright-Fleming Inst., 2000–04, Dean, St Mary's Campus, 2001–04, Hd, Div. of Medicine, 2004–09, Imperial Coll. London. Chm. Governors, William Tyndale Primary Sch., 2007–12. FMedSci 2000. *Publications:* The Management of AIDS Patients, 1986; contribs to The Lancet, etc. *Recreations:* motor-bikes, boats. *E:* j.weber@imperial.ac.uk.

WEBER, Jürgen; Hon. Chairman, Supervisory Board, Deutsche Lufthansa AG, since 2013 (Chairman: Executive Board, 1991–2003; Supervisory Board, 2003–13); *b* 17 Oct. 1941; *m* 1965, Sabine Rossberg; one *s* one *d*. *Educ:* Stuttgart Tech. Univ. (Dipl. Ing. Aeronautical Engrg 1965); MIT (Sen. Mgt Trng 1980). Joined Lufthansa, 1967: Engrg Div., 1967–74; Director: Line Maintenance Dept, 1974–78; Aircraft Engrg Sub-div., 1978–87; Chief Operating Officer (Tech.), 1987–89; Dep. Mem., Exec. Bd, 1989–90; Chief Exec., Tech., 1990–91. Chm., Supervisory Bd, Bogner Sport GmbH; Member, Supervisory Board: Deutsche Post AG, 2003–08 (Chm., 2006–08); Bayer AG. *Recreations:* jogging, ski-ing. *Address:* c/o Deutsche Lufthansa AG, Von-Gablenz-Strasse 2–6, 50679 Cologne, Germany.

WEBER, Prof. Richard Robert, Jr, PhD; Churchill Professor of Mathematics for Operational Research, Cambridge University, since 1994; Fellow, Queens' College, Cambridge, since 1978; *b* 25 Feb. 1953; *s* of Richard Robert Weber and Elizabeth Bray. *Educ:* Walnut Hills High Sch., USA; Solihull Sch.; Downing Coll., Cambridge (BA 1974; MA 1978; PhD 1980). Cambridge University: Asst Lectr and Lectr in Engrg, 1978–92; Reader in Management Sci., Engrg, 1992–94; Dir, Statistical Lab., 1999–2009; Queens' College, Cambridge: Res. Fellow, 1977–78; Tutor, 1979–92; Dir of Studies (Maths), 1985–94; Vice Pres., 1996–2007. *Publications:* (with C. Courcoubetis) Pricing Communication Networks, 2003; (jtly) Multi-armed Bandit Allocation Indices, 2011; numerous articles on stochastic systems, scheduling and queueing theory. *Recreations:* hiking, travel. *Address:* Queens' College, Cambridge CB3 9ET; Statistical Laboratory, Centre for Mathematical Sciences, Wilberforce Road, Cambridge CB3 0WB. *T:* (01223) 335570, 337944.

WEBLEY, Prof. Paul, CBE 2015; PhD; FAcSS; Director, School of Oriental and African Studies, 2006–15, and Deputy Vice-Chancellor, 2010–15, University of London; *b* Hayes, Middx, 19 Nov. 1953; *s* of Reginald Sidney Webley and Sylvia Mary Webley; *m* 1976, Julie Dawick; two *s* one *d*. *Educ:* London Sch. of Econs (BSc Soc. Psychol. 1976; PhD 1981). Lectr in Soc. Psychol., Univ. of Southampton, 1979–80; University of Exeter: Lectr, 1980–91, Sen. Lectr, 1991–95, in Psychol.; Reader in Econ. Psychol., 1995–98; Prof. of Econ. Psychol., 1998–2006; Hd, Sch. of Psychol., 1998–2003; Dep. Vice-Chancellor, 2003–06. Visiting Professor: of Sociol. of Law, Erasmus Univ., Rotterdam, 1988; Agder University Coll., Kristiansand, 2002–06; Visiting Research Fellow: Univ. of Tilburg, 1994, 1998; Internat. Centre for Econ. Res., Turin, 1999; Agder Univ., Kristiansand, Norway, 2011. FAcSS (AcSS 2010). *Publications:* (jtly) The Individual in the Economy, 1987; (jtly) Tax Evasion: an experimental approach, 1991; (ed jtly) New Directions in Economic Psychology: theory, experiment and application, 1992; (with Edmund Sonuga-Barke) Children's Saving, 1993; (jtly) The New Economic Mind, 1995; (ed with Catherine Walker) Handbook for the Teaching of Economic and Consumer Psychology, 1999; (jtly) The Economic Psychology of Everyday Life, 2001; (jtly) Psicologia economica della vita quotidiana, 2004. *Recreations:* fell-walking, eating, conversation.

WEBLIN, Harold; Chairman, Liberty's, 1984–95 (Chief Executive, 1984–93); *b* 10 April 1930; *s* of E. W. Weblin and B. Weblin; *m* 1954, June Weblin (decd); two *s*. *Educ:* Walpole Grammar School, London. General Manager, Way-In, Harrods, 1948–71; General Manager, Liberty's, 1971–84. *Recreation:* gardening. *Address:* 2 Roman Close, Avenue Gardens, Acton, W3 8HE.

WEBSTER, Alistair Stevenson; QC 1995; a Recorder, since 1996 (an Assistant Recorder, 1992–96); *b* 28 April 1953; *s* of His Honour Ian Stevenson Webster; *m* 1977, Barbara Anne Longbottom; two *d*. *Educ:* Hulme Grammar Sch., Oldham; Brasenose Coll., Oxford (BA Hons Jurisp.). Called to the Bar, Middle Temple, 1976; practice on Northern Circuit, 1976–. Hon. Sec., Northern Circuit, 1988–93; Mem., Bar Council, 1995–96. *Recreations:* cricket, tennis, ski-ing, football. *Address:* Lincoln House Chambers, Tower 12, The Avenue North, Spinningfields, 18–22 Bridge Street, Manchester M3 3BZ. *T:* (0161) 832 5701; 33 Chancery Lane, WC2A 1EN. *T:* (020) 7440 9950. *Clubs:* Rochdale Racquets; Gentlemen Gardeners Cricket.

WEBSTER, Maj.-Gen. Bryan Courtney, CB 1986; CBE 1981; Director of Army Quartering, 1982–86; *b* 2 Feb. 1931; *s* of Captain H. J. Webster, Royal Fusiliers (killed in action, 1940) and late M. J. Webster; *m* 1957, Elizabeth Rowland Waldron Smithers, *d* of Prof. Sir David Smithers; two *s* one *d*. *Educ:* Haileybury College; RMA Sandhurst. Commissioned Royal Fusiliers, 1951; ADC to GOC, 16 Airborne Div., 1953–55; served BAOR, Korea, Egypt, Malta, Gibraltar, Hong Kong; Directing Staff, Staff Coll., 1969–70; Comd 1st Bn Royal Regt of Fusiliers, 1971–73; Comd 8th Inf. Brigade, 1975–77 (despatches); Dep. Col, Royal Regt of Fusiliers (City of London), 1976–89; Nat. Defence Coll., India, 1979; Staff appts, Far East, MoD, incl. Dir of Admin. Planning (Army), 1980–82. Chm., Army Benevolent Fund, Surrey, 1986–2000. Mem. Council, Wine Guild of UK, 1995–2001. Pres., CPRE Hants, 2001–08. FCMI. Freeman, City of London, 1984. *Recreations:* ornithology, shooting, wine. *Address:* c/o HSBC, 69 High Street, Sevenoaks, Kent TN13 1LB.

WEBSTER, Charles, DSc; Senior Research Fellow, All Souls College, Oxford, 1988–2004, now Emeritus Fellow. Reader in the History of Medicine, University of Oxford, 1972–88; Director, Wellcome Unit for the History of Medicine, 1972–88; Fellow of Corpus Christi College, Oxford, 1972–88. FBA 1982–99. *Publications:* (ed) Samuel Hartlib and the Advancement of Learning, 1970; The Great Instauration, 1975; From Paracelsus to Newton, 1982; Problems of Health Care: the National Health Service before 1957, 1988; (ed) Aneurin Bevan on the National Health Service, 1991; (ed) Caring for Health, History and Diversity, 1993; Government and Health Care: the British National Health Service 1958–1979, 1996; The National Health Service: a political history, 1998. *Address:* All Souls College, Oxford OX1 4AL. *T:* (01865) 279379.

WEBSTER, David Gordon Comyn; Director, Temple Bar Investment Trust, since 2009; *b* 11 Feb. 1945; *s* of Alfred Edward Comyn Webster and Meryl Mary Clutterbuck; *m* 1972, Pamela Gail Runnicles; three *s*. *Educ:* Glasgow Acad.; Glasgow Univ. (LLB). Lieut, RNR, retd 1970. Admitted Solicitor, 1968; Corporate Finance Manager, Samuel Montagu & Co., 1969–72; Finance Dir, Oriel Foods Ltd, 1973–76; Co-Founder and Finance Dir, 1977–89, Dep. Chm., 1989–97, Chm., 1997–2004, Argyll Gp, subseq. Safeway plc; Chairman: InterContinental Hotels Gp, 2004–12 (Dir, 2003–12); Makinson Cowell, 2004–13. Non-executive Director: Reed International plc, 1992–2002; Reed Elsevier, 1993–2002; Elsevier NV, 1999–2002; Amadeus IT Holding, SA, 2010–. Member: Nat. Employers Liaison Cttee, 1992–2002; Appeals Cttee, Panel on Takeovers and Mergers, 2007–. Pres., Inst. of Grocery Distribn, 2001–02. Trustee, Nat. Life Story Collection, 2005–15. KStJ 2004. *Recreations:* military history, ski-ing, sailing, gardening, walking. *E:* dgcwebster@gmail.com.

WEBSTER, His Honour David MacLaren; QC 1980; a Circuit Judge, 1987–2003 (Resident Judge, Salisbury); Hon. Recorder of Salisbury, 2002–05; *b* 21 Dec. 1937; *s* of late John MacLaren Webster and Winning McGregor Webster (*née* Rough); *m* 1964, Frances Sally McLaren, RE, *o d* of late Lt-Col J. A. McLaren and of Mrs H. S. Scammell; three *s*. *Educ:* Hutchesons', Glasgow; Christ Church, Oxford (MA (Eng. Lang. and Lit.)); Conservatoire d'Art Dramatique and Sorbonne (French Govt Schol. 1960–61). Radio and television work in drama and current affairs, Scotland, incl. Dixon of Dock Green, A Nest of Singing Birds, and Muir of Huntershill, 1949–64; called to the Bar, Gray's Inn, 1964; Western Circuit; a Dep. Circuit Judge, 1976–79; a Recorder, 1979–87. Chairman: Salisbury & Dist Family Mediation Service, 1987–2001; Area Criminal Justice Liaison Cttee for Hants, Dorset and IoW, 1994–99; Area Criminal Justice Strategy Cttee, Hants and IoW, 2000–01. Member: Bar Council, 1972–74; Senate of Inns of Court and Bar, 1974–79, 1982–85 (Senate Representative, Commonwealth Law Conf., Edinburgh, 1977). Chm., Salisbury Safety Partnership, 1998–2004; Member: Salisbury Playhouse Develt Cttee, 2006–11; Standards Cttee for Wilts, 2009–12. Gold Medal, LAMDA, 1954; LRAM 1955. President, Oxford Univ. Experimental Theatre Club, 1958–59; Secretary, Mermaid's, 1958; Chm., Bar Theatrical Soc., 1976–86. Governor, Port Regis Sch., 1983–94. *Recreations:* theatre, sailing, cricket, reading, still training Juno and Jazzmine. *Clubs:* Garrick, MCC; Bar Yacht.

WEBSTER, Edward; *see* Webster, K. E.

WEBSTER, Evelyn Ann; Executive Vice President, Time Inc., since 2011; *b* Wakefield, W Yorks, 12 May 1969. *Educ:* Univ. of Greenwich (BA Hons Business Studies with Mktg). IPC Media Ltd: Graduate Trainee, 1992; Client Services Exec., Marketforce, 1993; Mktg Manager, New Scientist, 1994; Asst Publisher, Sci. and Special Interest Gp, 1995–97; Publisher, Specialist Gp, 1997; Gp Publisher (Special Projects), 1998; Publishing Dir, Country and Equestrian titles, 1999–2003; Managing Director: IPC Country and Leisure Media, 2003–04; IPC Connect, 2004–08; Chief Exec., IPC Media Ltd, 2009–10 (Dir, 2003–10). *Recreations:* running, yoga. *Address:* Time Inc., Time and Life Building, 1271 Avenue of the Americas, NY 10020, USA. *T:* (212) 5225471. *E:* evelyn.webster@timeinc.com.

WEBSTER, Rt Rev. Glyn Hamilton; *see* Beverley, Bishop Suffragan of.

WEBSTER, Janice Helen, WS; Judge, First-tier Tribunal, Social Entitlement Tribunal (formerly part-time Chairman, Appeals Service), 1996–2015; legal expert to Council of Europe, 1993–97; *b* 2 April 1944; *d* of James Bell Reid and Janet (*née* Johnston); *m* 1968, R. M. Webster; two *d*. *Educ:* Edinburgh Univ. (LLB 1964). Solicitor and Notary Public. Legal Asst, then Sen. Solicitor, Falkirk Town Council, 1967–71; in private practice, Alston Nairn & Hogg, Edinburgh, 1971–74; Dep. Sec., Law Soc. of Scotland, 1974–80; Crown Counsel, then Magistrate, Govt of Seychelles, 1980–82; Law Society of Scotland, 1982–90 (Dep. Sec., Dir, European Affairs and Sec., Scottish Lawyers' European Gp); Dir Gen., CCBE, 1991–93; Consultant, Bell & Scott, WS, Edinburgh, 1994–96. Sec., Scottish Law Agents Soc., 1998–2004. Mem., Scottish Records Adv. Council, 1995–2000. Director: Scottish Archive

Network, 1998–2002; Franco-British Lawyers' Soc. Ltd, 1998–2000; Chm., Scottish Soc. for Computers and Law, 2001–04. Member: Council, WS Soc., 1998–2000; Governing Council, Erskine Stewart's Melville, 1998–2002. Ed., Human Rights and UK Practice, 1999–2009. *Publications:* (with R. M. Webster) Professional Ethics and Practice for Scottish Solicitors, 3rd edn 1996, 4th edn 2004. *Recreations:* singing, walking, gardening. *Club:* New (Edinburgh).

WEBSTER, Rev. Prof. John Bainbridge, PhD; Professor of Divinity, St Mary's College, University of St Andrews, since 2013; *b* 20 June 1955; *s* of Gordon and Ruth Webster; *m* 1978, Jane Goodden; two *s*. *Educ:* Clare Coll., Cambridge (MA, PhD 1982). Stephenson Fellow, Dept of Biblical Studies, Univ. of Sheffield, 1981–82; ordained deacon, 1983, priest, 1984; Dep. Sen. Tutor, Tutor in Systematic Theology, and Chaplain, St John's Coll., Univ. of Durham, 1982–86; Wycliffe College, University of Toronto: Associate Prof. of Systematic Theology, 1986–93; Professor, 1993–95; Ramsay Armitage Prof., 1995–96; Lady Margaret Prof. of Divinity, Univ. of Oxford, and Canon of Christ Church, Oxford, 1996–2003; Prof. of Systematic Theol., Univ. of Aberdeen, 2003–13. FRSE 2005. Hon. DD Aberdeen, 2003. *Publications:* Eberhard Jüngel: an introduction to his theology, 1986; (ed) The Possibilities of Theology, 1994; Barth's Ethics of Reconciliation, 1995; Barth's Moral Theology, 1998; (ed) Theology after Liberalism, 2000; (ed) The Cambridge Companion to Karl Barth, 2000; Karl Barth, 2000; Word and Church, 2001; Holiness, 2002; Holy Scripture, 2003; Confessing God, 2005; Barth's Earlier Theology, 2005; (ed) Oxford Handbook of Systematic Theology, 2007; The Grace of Truth, 2011; The Domain of the Word, 2012; God Without Measure, 2015. *Address:* St Mary's College, School of Divinity, University of St Andrews, South Street, St Andrews KY16 9JU.

WEBSTER, Vice-Adm. Sir John (Morrison), KCB 1986; RSMA; painter; President, Royal Naval Benevolent Trust, 1991–98; *b* 3 Nov. 1932; *s* of late Frank Martin Webster and Kathleen Mary (*née* Morrison); *m* 1962, Valerie Anne Villiers (*d* 2005); two *d* (one *s* decd). *Educ:* Pangbourne College. Joined RN, 1951; specialised navigation, 1959; RAN, 1959–61; HMS Lowestoft, 1961–63; BRNC Dartmouth, 1963–65; HMS Dido, 1965–67; RN Tactical Sch., 1967–69; in command HMS Argonaut, 1969–71; MoD Navy, 1971–73; RNLO Ottawa, 1974–76; in command HMS Cleopatra and 4th Frigate Sqdn, 1976–78; MoD, Director Naval Warfare, 1980–82; Flag Officer Sea Trng, 1982–84; C of S to C-in-C Fleet, 1984–86; Flag Officer Plymouth, Naval Base Comdr Devonport, Comdr Central Sub Area Eastern Atlantic and Comdr Plymouth Sub Area Channel, 1987–90; retired. Lt-Comdr 1963, Comdr 1967, Captain 1973, Rear-Adm. 1982, Vice-Adm. 1985. Younger Brother of Trinity House, 1970–. Life Mem., Armed Forces Art Soc., 2008 (Mem., 1967–2008; Chm., 1990–96). One-man exhibitions of paintings: Canada, 1976; Winchester, 1980; London, 1982, 1984, 1986, 1988, 1991, 1993, 1996, 1999, 2002, 2004, 2007, 2009, 2011; Jersey, 2006. Governor: Canford Sch., 1984–2003; Pangbourne College, 1990–2000 (Chm., 1992–2000); FBA, 2002–08. Associate, RSMA, 1998, RSMA 2001. *Recreations:* painting, travel. *Address:* Old School House, Soberton, Hants SO32 3PF. *Clubs:* Royal Cruising, Royal Naval Sailing Association.

WEBSTER, Prof. (John) Paul (Garrett); Emeritus Professor of Agricultural Business Management, Imperial College London, since 2005; *b* 16 July 1942; *s* of Leonard Garrett Webster and Dorothy Agnes Webster (*née* White); *m* 1972, Dr Amanda Jane Hetigin; one *s* one *d*. *Educ:* Leys Sch., Cambridge; Reading Univ. (BSc); Wye Coll., London Univ. (PhD). FIAgrM 1995; FRAgS 2003. Wye College (merged with Imperial College of Science, Technology and Medicine, 2000): Department of Agricultural Economics, 1965–2005: Asst Lectr, 1965–67; Lectr in Agricl Econs, 1967–76; Sen. Lectr, 1976–81; Reader, 1981–91; Prof. of Agricl Business Mgt, 1991–2005. Visiting appointments: Makerere Univ., Uganda, 1970–71; Drapers Lectr, Univ. of New England, Australia, 1974–75; Economist, Internat. Rice Res. Inst., Philippines, 1980–81; Prof., Lincoln Univ., NZ, 1999–2000. Ind. Mem., Adv. Cttee on Pesticides, MAFF, 1992–99. Pres., Agricl Econs Soc., 1999–2000. President: City of Canterbury Swimming Club, 2004–06; E Invicta Amateur Swimming Assoc., 2007–08. FCMI (FBIM 1985); FRSA 1987. Hon. Freeman, Farmers' Co., 2000. *Publications:* articles in Jl Agricl Econs, Amer. Jl Agricl Econs, Farm Mgt, etc. *Recreation:* masters swimming (UK rankings; 100m French Open Champion 2012 (70+ age group)). *Address:* 25 Chequers Park, Wye, Kent TN25 5BB. *Club:* Farmers.

WEBSTER, Prof. (Keith) Edward, PhD; Professor of Anatomy and Human Biology (formerly Professor of Anatomy), King's College, University of London, 1975–2000; *b* 18 June 1935; *e s* of Thomas Brotherwick Webster and Edna Pyzer; 1st marr. diss. 1983; two *s*; 2nd marr. diss. 1990. *Educ:* UCL (BSc 1957, PhD 1960); UCH Med. Sch. (MB, BS 1962). University Coll. London: Lectr in Anatomy, 1962–66; Sen. Lectr in Anat., 1966–74; Reader in Anat., 1974–75. Symington Prize, British Anatomical Soc., 1966. *Publications:* A Manual of Human Anatomy, Vol. 5: The Central Nervous System (with J. T. Aitken and J. Z. Young), 1967; papers on the nervous system in Brain Res., Jl of Comp. Neurol., Neuroscience and Neurocytology. *Recreations:* Mozart, Wagner and language: the deification of the unspeakable.

WEBSTER, Leslie Elizabeth, FSA; Keeper, Department of Prehistory and Europe, British Museum, 2003–07; *b* 8 Nov. 1943; *d* of James Lancelot Dobson and Elizabeth Marjorie Dobson (*née* Dickenson); *m* 1966, William Ian Webster; one *s* two *d*. *Educ:* Central Newcastle High Sch.; Westfield Coll., Univ. of London (Open Exhibnr; BA 1st Cl. Hons 1964). British Museum: Asst Keeper, Dept of British and Medieval Antiquities, 1964–69; Asst Keeper, 1969–85, Dep. Keeper, 1985–2002, Dept of Medieval and Later Antiquities, subseq. Dept of Medieval and Modern Europe; Actg Keeper, Dept of Medieval and Modern Europe, 2002–03. Hon. Vis. Prof. (formerly Vis. Prof.), Inst. of Archaeol., UCL, 2002–. Chair, Res. Adv. Panel, Staffs Hoard, 2011–14; Member: Adv. Panel, NHMF, 2012–; Reviewing Cttee for the Export of Works of Art, 2013–. Pres., Soc. for Medieval Archaeol., 2007–10; Vice-Pres., Royal Archaeol Inst., 2007–12. UK rep., Koordinierend Ausschuss der Internationalen Arbeitsgemeinschaft für Sachsenforschung, 1986–99. FSA 1973. *Publications:* (ed) Aspects of Production and Style in Dark Age Metalwork, 1982; (jtly) The Golden Age of Anglo-Saxon Art 966–1066, 1984; (with J. Backhouse) The Making of England: Anglo-Saxon art and culture AD 700–900, 1991; (ed with M. Brown) The Transformation of the Roman World, 1997; (ed jtly) Form and Order in the Anglo-Saxon World AD 600–1100, 2009; (ed with J. Roberts) Anglo-Saxon Traces, 2011; Anglo-Saxon Art: a new history, 2012; The Franks Casket, 2012; (ed with A. Reynolds) Early Medieval Art and Archaeology in the Northern World, 2013; contrib. numerous articles to learned jls and chapters in monographs, on Anglo-Saxon material culture. *Recreations:* books, music, walking, cooking, France, whistling. *Address:* c/o Department of Prehistory and Europe, British Museum, Great Russell Street, WC1B 3DG.

WEBSTER, Ven. Martin Duncan; Archdeacon of Harlow, since 2009; *b* Hornchurch, 1952; *m* Vicky; three *s*. *Educ:* Nottingham Univ. (BSc 1974); Lincoln Theol Coll. Ordained deacon, 1978, priest, 1979; Asst Curate, St Peter and St Michael's, Thundersley, 1978–81; Asst Curate, 1981–82, Team Vicar, 1982–86, Canvey Island Team Ministry; Vicar, All Saints, Nazeing, 1986–99; Rural Dean, Harlow, 1988–99; Team Rector, Holy Cross, Waltham Abbey, 1999–2009. Hon. Canon, Chelmsford Cathedral, 2000–09. *Recreations:* oil and acrylic landscape painting, coarse fishing, walking. *Address:* Glebe House, Church Lane, Sheering, Bishop's Stortford CM22 7NR. *T:* (01279) 734524. *E:* a.harlow@chelmsford.anglican.org.

WEBSTER, Maj. Michael; *see* Webster, R. M. O.

WEBSTER, Patrick; a Chairman, Industrial, then Employment, Tribunals, Cardiff Region, 1965–2000 (full-time Chairman, 1976–93); a Recorder, 1972–93; *b* 6 Jan. 1928; *s* of late Francis Glyn Webster and Ann Webster; *m* 1955, Elizabeth Knight; two *s* four *d*. *Educ:* Swansea Grammar Sch.; Rockwell Coll., Eire; St Edmund's Coll., Ware; Downing Coll., Cambridge (BA). Called to Bar, Gray's Inn, 1950. Practised at Bar, in Swansea, 1950–75; Chm., Medical Appeals Tribunal (part-time), 1971–75. *Recreations:* listening to music, watching rowing and sailing. *Address:* Langland, 24 Maillard's Haven, Penarth, South Glam CF64 5RF. *T:* (029) 2070 4758. *Clubs:* Penarth Yacht; Beechwood (Swansea).

WEBSTER, Paul; film producer; Director, Shoebox Films, since 2011; *b* 19 Sept. 1952. Co-Dir, Osiris Film, London, 1979–81; Founder, Palace Pictures, 1982–88; launched Working Title Films, LA, 1990–92; Head of Prodn, Miramax Films, 1995–97 (films incl. The English Patient, Welcome to Sarajevo, Wings of the Dove); Head of Film Div., Channel 4, subseq. Chief Exec., FilmFour Ltd, 1998–2002; Film Producer, Kudos Pictures, 2004–11. Producer: The Tall Guy, 1988; Drop Dead Fred, 1990; Bob Roberts, 1992; Romeo is Bleeding, 1993; Little Odessa, 1994; The Pallbearer, 1995; Gridlock'd, 1996; The Yards, 1998; Pride and Prejudice, 2005; Atonement, 2007; Eastern Promises, 2008; Crimson Wing, 2009; Brighton Rock, 2010; Salmon Fishing in the Yemen, Anna Karenina, 2012; Hummingbird, 2013; Locke, 2014; Executive Producer: The Motorcycle Diaries, 2004; Miss Pettigrew Lives for a Day, 2008. Member: UK Film Council, 2000–03; BAFTA; Acad. of Motion Picture Arts and Scis; Producers Guild of America.

WEBSTER, Paul; *see* Webster, J. P. G.

WEBSTER, Philip George; Editor, The Times digital editions, since 2010; *b* 2 June 1949; *s* of Bertie and Eva Webster. *Educ:* Rockland St Mary Primary Sch.; County GS; Wymondham Coll.; Harlow Coll. (NCTJ Cert.). Eastern Counties Newspapers, 1967–73; The Times: Parly Reporter, 1973–81; Pol Reporter, 1981–86; Chief Pol Correspondent, 1986–93; Pol Ed., 1993–2010. *Recreations:* golf, ski-ing, cricket, squash, football. *Address:* 4 St Georges Square, Narrow Street, E14 8DL. *T:* 07774 617815. *Clubs:* Richmond Golf, Rookery Park Golf.

WEBSTER, Maj. (Richard) Michael (Otley); Secretary, The Royal Hampshire Regiment Trust, 2004–06; one of HM Body Guard, Honourable Corps of Gentlemen-at-Arms, 1993–2012 (Standard Bearer, 2010–12); *b* 11 Aug. 1942; *s* of late Brig. Frederick Richard Webster and Beryl Helena Sellars (*née* Otley); *m* 1971, Joanna Gay Enid Simpson, *d* of Lt-Col R. H. O. Simpson, DSO; two *s*. *Educ:* Charterhouse; RMA, Sandhurst. Commnd RA, 1962; 1 RHA, Germany and Aden, 1963–66; Army Staff Coll., 1975; CO, King's Troop, RHA, 1976–78. United Racecourses, 1979–96; Clerk of the Course: Kempton Park, 1980–96; Lingfield Park, 1986–87; Epsom, 1988–95; Chester, 2001–03; Clerk of the Course and Manager, Bangor-on-Dee, 1996–2003. Member: Horseracing Adv. Council, 1987–90; Nat. Jt Pitch Council, 2000–03. *Recreations:* cricket, racing, shooting, Soay sheep. *Address:* Coopers Farm, Hartley Wespall, Hook, Hants RG27 0BQ. *Club:* Army and Navy.

WEBSTER, Robert; Chief Executive, NHS Confederation, since 2014; *b* Barrow-in-Furness, 26 Sept. 1968; *s* of Robert and Beryl Webster; *m* 2000, Jane Grace; one *s* one *d*. *Educ:* Newcastle Univ. (BSc Hons Stats 1987). Department of Health: Asst Statistician, NHS Dentistry, 1990–92; Asst Statistician and Section Hd, Medical Workforce Planning, 1992–93; Statistician and Section Hd, Corporate Analysis Team, 1994–96, Waiting, Patient's Charter and League Tables, 1996–97; Section Hd, Acute Services, 1998, Public Expenditure Team, 1998–2000; Nat. Dep. Dir, Gen. Medical Services, 2000–02; Nat. Dir, Primary Care Services, 2002–03; Prog. Dir, Primary Care Contracts, 2003–04; Nat. Dir, Workforce Capacity, 2004–06; Dir, Prime Minister's Delivery Unit, Cabinet Office, 2006–07; Chief Executive: NHS Calderdale, 2007–11; Leeds Community Healthcare NHS Trust, 2011–14. Vis. Prof., Leeds Beckett Univ., 2014–. Hon. Fellow, Queen's Nursing Inst. Trustee, Leeds Mencap, 2000–10. *Recreations:* music, literature, gigs, food, travel, running, record shops, being a servant to my two children. *Address:* c/o NHS Confederation, Floor 4, 50 Broadway, SW1H 0DB. *Club:* Royal Society of Medicine.

WEBSTER, Prof. Robert Gordon, FRS 1989; Professor of Virology and Molecular Biology, St Jude Children's Research Hospital, Memphis, USA; *b* 5 July 1932; *s* of Robert Duncan Webster and Mollie Sherriffs; *m* 1957, Marjorie Freegard; two *s* one *d*. *Educ:* Otago Univ., NZ (BSc, MSc); Australian Nat. Univ., Canberra (PhD). Virologist, NZ Dept of Agric., 1958–59; Postdoctoral Fellow, Sch. of Public Health, Univ. of Michigan, Ann Arbor (Fulbright Schol.), 1962–63; Res. Fellow, then Fellow, Dept of Microbiology, John Curtin Med. Sch., ANU, 1964–67; Associate Mem., then Mem., Dept of Virology and Molecular Biol., 1968–88, apptd Head of Dept and Rose Marie Thomas Prof., 1988, St Jude Children's Res. Hosp. Fogarty Internat. Sen. Fellow, Nat. Inst. for Med. Res., MRC, London, 1978–79. Mem., Nat. Acad. of Sci., USA, 1998. *Publications:* contribs on influenza viruses etc to learned jls, incl. Virology, Nature, and Cell. *Recreations:* gardening, sea-fishing, walking. *Address:* Department of Infectious Diseases, St Jude Children's Research Hospital, 262 Danny Thomas Place, Memphis, TN 38105–3678, USA. *T:* (901) 5953400. *Club:* Royal Society of Medicine.

WEBSTER, Prof. Robin Gordon MacLennan, OBE 1999; RSA 2008 (ARSA 1995); RIBA; FRIAS; Partner, cameronwebster architects, since 2005; Professor of Architecture, Scott Sutherland School of Architecture, Robert Gordon University, Aberdeen, 1984–2004; *b* 24 Dec. 1939; *s* of Gordon Webster and Sheila Webster; *m* 1st, 1967, Katherine Crichton (*d* 2003); one *s* two *d*; 2nd, 2011, Pauline Lawrence. *Educ:* Glasgow Acad.; Rugby Sch.; St John's Coll., Cambridge (MA); University Coll., London (MA Arch). ARIBA 1967; FRIAS 1996. Partner, Spence & Webster, 1972–84; Principal, Robin Webster Associates, 1984–2004. Comr, Royal Fine Art Commn for Scotland, 1990–98. Chm., Alexander Thomson Soc., 2007–13; Trustee, Glasgow City Heritage Trust, 2006–13. *Publications:* Stonecleaning, and the nature, soiling and decay mechanisms of stone, 1992. *Recreations:* looking at buildings, drawing. *Address:* 7 Walmer Crescent, Glasgow G51 1AT. *T:* (0141) 427 4494. *E:* robin.webster@mac.com.

WEBSTER, Stephen, MBE 2013; designer of fine and silver jewellery; Founder and Creative Director, Stephen Webster Ltd, since 1989; Director, Garrard, since 2007; *b* Gravesend, 13 Aug. 1959; *m* 1998, Anastasia Vatnitsky; two *d*. *Educ:* Medway Coll. of Design. Established and ran jewellery studio and retail venture for Silverhorn Jeweller, Santa Barbara, Calif, 1986–89. Hon. MA Univ. of Creative Arts, 2007. Hon. Liveryman, City of London, 2009. British Luxury Jeweller of Year, 2000, 2001, 2003, 2005, Jewellery Designer of Year, 1997, 1999, 2006, Retail Jeweller. *Address:* 24 Albemarle Street, W1S 4HT. *T:* 0845 539 1800, 0845 539 1849. *E:* info@stephenwebster.com.

WEBSTER, Toby Crawford Gordon; Founding Director, The Modern Institute, since 1998; *b* Glasgow, 4 Dec. 1968; *s* of Martyn and Shery Webster; *m* 2007, April; one *s* two *d*. *Educ:* Glasgow Sch. of Art (BA 1st Cl. Hons 1993). Mem. Cttee, Transmission Gall., 1995–97; Gall. Manager and Curator, Centre for Contemporary Arts, Glasgow, 1996–98. Board Member: Grizedale Arts, 2004–08; Common Guild, 2006–08. *Publications:* My Head is on Fire but My Heart is Full of Love, 2002; Strange I've Seen that Face Before, 2006. *Recreations:* walking, sailing, ski-ing, reading, raising children, talking to varied people, collecting art and looking at it. *Address:* The Modern Institute, 14–20 Osborne Street, Glasgow G1 5QN. *T:* (0141) 248 3711, *Fax:* (0141) 552 5988. *E:* mail@themoderninstitute.com.

WECHSLER, David Keith; Chief Executive, London Borough of Croydon, 1993–2007; *b* 17 June 1946; *s* of late Bernard James Victor Wechsler and Kathleen Nora Wechsler (*née* Ramm); *m* 1968, Muriel-Anne (Polly) Stuart; one *s* one *d*. *Educ:* Sloane Sch., Chelsea; Leicester Univ. (BA Social Sci.). London Borough of Croydon: grad. trainee, 1970–72; Corporate Planner, 1972–79; Hd, Exec. Office, 1979–87; Dep. Chief Exec., 1987–91; Dir, Econ. and Strategic Devolt, 1991–93. Director: S London TEC, 1993–99; Croydon Business

Venture, 1993–2007. Chm., Emergency Planning Sub-cttee, London Local Authorities, 2002–07. Dep. Regl Returning Officer, EP elections, 2004. Dir, London Mozart Players, 2007–. *Publications:* articles on corporate planning and local govt mgt in specialist jls. *Recreations:* sailing, music, swimming, making ice cream.

WEDD, George Morton, CB 1989; South-West Regional Director, Departments of the Environment and Transport, Bristol, 1983–90; *b* 30 March 1930; *s* of Albert Wedd and Dora Wedd; *m* 1953, Kate Pullin; two *s* one *d*. *Educ:* various schs in Derbyshire; St John's Coll., Cambridge (BA 1951). Joined Min. of Housing and Local Govt, later DoE, 1951; Principal, 1957; Asst Sec., 1966; Under Sec., 1976. *Address:* The Lodge, Church Hill, High Littleton, Somerset BS39 6HG.

WEDDERBURN, Sir Andrew John Alexander O.; *see* Ogilvy-Wedderburn.

WEDELL, Prof. (Eberhard Arthur Otto) George; Professor of Communications Policy, University of Manchester, 1983–92, Professor Emeritus since 1992; Vice President, European Institute for the Media, 1993–97 (Director, then Director-General, 1983–93); *b* 4 April 1927; *er s* of late Rev. Dr H. Wedell and Gertrude (*née* Bonhoeffer); *m* 1948, Rosemarie (*née* Winckler) (*d* 2010); three *s* one *d*. *Educ:* Cranbrook; London School of Economics (BSc Econ., 1947). Ministry of Education, 1950–58; Sec., Bd for Social Responsibility, Nat. Assembly of Church of England, 1958–60; Dep. Sec., ITA, 1960–61, Secretary, 1961–64; Prof. of Adult Educn and Dir of Extra-Mural Studies, Manchester Univ., 1964–75; Vis. Prof. of Employment Policy, Manchester Business Sch., 1975–83; Head, Employment Policy Div., European Commn, 1973–82. Emeritus Fellow, Leverhulme Trust, 1994–96. Contested (L) Greater Manchester West, 1979, (L-SDP Alliance) Greater Manchester Central, 1984, European Parly elections; Chm., British Liberals in EEC, 1980–82; Vice-President: Greater Manchester Liberal Party, 1984–88; EC-ACP Cultural Foundn, 1992–94. Chairman: Wyndham Place Trust, 1983–2001; Beatrice Hankey Foundn, 1984–2001; Christians and the Future of Europe, 1997–99. Director, Royal Exchange Theatre Company, 1968–89, Hon. Mem., 1989. Patron, Mosscare Housing Assoc., 1998–. FRSA; FRTS. Hon. MEd Manchester, 1968; Dr *hc* Internat. Journalistics Inst., Kazakhstan, 1994. Lord of the Manor of Clotton Hoofield in the County Palatine of Chester. Letters Patent of Armorial Ensigns, 1997. Chevalier de l'Ordre des Arts et des Lettres (France), 1989; Verdienstkreuz (1 Klasse) des Verdienstordens (Germany), 1991; Comdr, Order of Merit (Portugal), 1993. *Publications:* The Use of Television in Education, 1963; Broadcasting and Public Policy, 1968; (with H. D. Perraton) Teaching at a Distance, 1968; (ed) Structures of Broadcasting, 1970; (with R. Glatter) Study by Correspondence, 1971; Correspondence Education in Europe, 1971; Teachers and Educational Development in Cyprus, 1971; (ed) Education and the Development of Malawi, 1973; (with E. Katz) Broadcasting in the Third World, 1977 (Nat. Assoc. of Educational Broadcasters of USA Book of the Year Award, 1978); (with G. M. Luyken and R. Leonard) Mass Communications in Western Europe, 1985; (ed) Making Broadcasting Useful, 1986; (with G. M. Luyken) Media in Competition, 1986; (ed and contrib.) Europe 2000: what kind of television?, 1988; (with P. Crookes) Radio 2000, 1991; (with R. Rocholl) Vom Segen des Glaubens, 1995 (trans. as A Memoir of Troubled Times, 2008); (ed and contrib.) No Discouragement, 1997; (with B. Luckham) Television at the Crossroads, 2001; A Post-War Half Century, 2012; contrib. Oxford DNB; general editor, Media Monographs, 1985–93. *Recreations:* gardening, theatre, reading. *Address:* 18 Cranmer Road, Manchester M20 6AW. *T:* (0161) 445 5106; Vigneau, Lachapelle, 47350 Seyches, France. *T:* (5) 53838871. *Club:* Athenæum.

WEDGWOOD, family name of **Baron Wedgwood**.

WEDGWOOD, 5th Baron *cr* 1942, of Barlaston; **Antony John Wedgwood;** *b* London, 31 Jan. 1944; *s* of late Dr John Wedgwood, CBE, FRCP and Margaret Webb Wedgwood (*née* Mason); *S* cousin, 2014; *m* 1970, Angela Margaret Mary, *d* of Dr Ernest Donald Page; one *s* two *d*. *Educ:* Marlborough Coll.; Trinity Coll., Cambridge (BA 1965; MA 1970). FCA (ACA 1969). With Peat, Marwick, Mitchell & Co., later KPMG, 1966–2001 (Partner, 1981–2001). Member: Financial Reporting Review Panel, 2001–07; various professional cttees of Auditing Practices Bd, ICAEW. Trustee, Historic Churches Preservation Trust and Nat. Churches Trust, 2002–12. *Publications:* (jtly) A Guide to the Financial Services Act 1986, 1986. *Recreations:* reading, travel, old cars and wirelesses. *Heir:* *s* Captain the Hon. Josiah Thomas Antony Wedgwood, RAMC, *b* 20 April 1978. *Address:* 10 Milner Place, N1 1TN. *Club:* Athenæum.

WEDGWOOD, Pamela, Lady, (Pamela Tudor-Craig), PhD; FSA; Medieval art historian; *b* 26 June 1928; *d* of Herbert Wynn Reeves and Madeline Marion Wynn Reeves (*née* Brows); *m* 1st, 1956, Algernon James Riccarton Tudor-Craig (*d* 1969); one *d*; 2nd, 1982, Sir John Hamilton Wedgwood, 2nd Bt (*d* 1989). *Educ:* Courtauld Inst. Fine Art (BA 1st Cl. Hons Hist. of Art London 1949; PhD 1952). FSA 1958. Lectr at American Colls in UK, 1969–96. Mem., Cathedrals Adv. Commn, 1973–88; Chm., Wall Paintings Cttee, and Vice-Chm., Panel Paintings Cttee, 1975–92, Vice Chm., Paintings Cttee, 1992–96, Council for Care of Churches; Mem., Wells Cathedral West Front Cttee, 1973–86; Member, Architectural Advisory Panel: Westminster Abbey, 1979–98; Exeter Cathedral, 1985–90; Member, Fabric Committee: Lincoln Cathedral, 1986–92; Peterborough Cathedral, 1987–96; Southwell Minster, 1984–2001. Founder, Cambs Historic Churches Trust, 1982; Chm. Friends, Sussex Historic Churches Trust, 2002–10. Founder, Annual Harlaxton Symposium of English Medieval Studies, 1984. Hon. Member: SPAB; Richard III Soc. TV broadcasts, incl. series, The Secret Life of Paintings, 1986–87; contribs to numerous radio programmes. Hon. DHum William Jewell Coll., USA, 1983. Medal, Soc. of Antiquaries, 2014. *Publications:* Richard III (exhibn catalogue), 1973; (with R. Foster) The Secret Life of Paintings, 1986; 'Old St Paul's': the Society of Antiquaries' Diptych, 1616, 2004; The Catalogue of Paintings in the Society of Antiquaries of London, 2015; contrib. numerous chapters and articles in books and exhibn catalogues; contrib. to History Today, Church Times and other scholarly jls. *Address:* 9 St Anne's Crescent, Lewes, E Sussex BN7 1SB. *T:* (01273) 479564.

WEDGWOOD, Sir Ralph (Nicholas), 4th Bt *cr* 1942, of Etruria, Co. Stafford; PhD; Professor of Philosophy, University of Southern California, since 2012; *b* Vancouver, 10 Dec. 1964; *o s* of Sir (Hugo) Martin Wedgwood, 3rd Bt and of Alexandra Mary, *er d* of late Judge Alfred Gordon Clark; *S* father, 2010. *Educ:* Westminster Sch.; Magdalen Coll., Oxford (BA); King's Coll. London (MPhil); Cornell Univ. (PhD 1994). Asst Prof. of Philos., 1995–99, Associate Prof. of Philos., 1999–2002, MIT; Lectr in Philos., 2002–07, Prof. of Philos., 2007–11, Univ. of Oxford; Fellow, Merton Coll., Oxford, 2002–11. Visiting Research Fellow: Princeton Univ., 2005; Hebrew Univ. of Jerusalem, 2008; ANU, 2010; Dist. Res. Prof., Univ. of Birmingham, 2013–. *Publications:* The Nature of Normativity, 2007; articles in learned philosophical jls. *Recreations:* hill-walking, music. *Heir:* *uncle* (John) Julian Wedgwood [*b* 17 June 1936; *m* 1961, Sheila Mary, *d* of late George Robert Meade; three *s*]. *Address:* School of Philosophy, University of Southern California, 3709 Trousdale Parkway, Los Angeles, CA 90089–0451, USA. *E:* wedgwood@usc.edu.

WEDZICHA, Prof. Jadwiga Anna, (Wisia), MD; FRCP, FMedSci; Professor of Respiratory Medicine, National Heart and Lung Institute, Imperial College London, since 2014; Honorary Consultant Physician, Royal Brompton Hospital, since 2014; *b* 17 Sept. 1953; *d* of Karol and Irena Wedzicha. *Educ:* Somerville Coll., Oxford (BA 1975); St Bartholomew's Hosp. Med. Coll., London Univ. (MB BS 1978; MD 1985). FRCP 1994. Consultant Physician, London Chest Hosp., 1988–96; Reader in Respiratory Medicine, 1996–2000, Prof. of Respiratory Medicine, 2000–05, Bart's and The London, Queen Mary's Sch. of Medicine and Dentistry; Prof. of Respiratory Medicine, UCL, 2005–14. Hon. Consultant Physician, Royal Free Hospital NHS Trust, 2005–14. Sen. Investigator, NIHR, 2011–. European Respiratory Society: Guidelines Dir, 2009–12; Chair, Pubns Cttee, 2010–14. Clinical Lead, Home Oxygen Services, England, 2009–13. Ed. in Chief, Thorax, 2002–10; Ed., American Jl of Respiratory and Critical Care Medicine, 2015–. FMedSci 2013; FERS 2014. *Publications:* (ed with M. Pearson) Chronic Obstructive Pulmonary Disease: critical debates, 2003; (ed with F. J. Martinez) Chronic Obstructive Pulmonary Disease Exacerbations, 2008; papers in New England Jl of Medicine, BMJ, American Jl of Respiratory and Critical Care Medicine, Thorax, Chest. *Recreations:* gardening, tennis, music. *Address:* National Heart and Lung Institute, Imperial College London, Guy Scadding Building, Dovehouse Street, SW3 6LY. *T:* (020) 7594 7947. *E:* j.wedzicha@imperial.ac.uk.

WEEDEN, John, CB 2003; a Recorder, 2012–14; *b* 21 June 1949; *s* of Denis Claude Weeden and Winifred Marion Weeden; *m* 1971, Marjanne Dita De Boer; three *s* two *d*. *Educ:* Brighton Coll.; Univ. of Bristol (LLB Hons). SSC 1973. Articled to Griffith Smith, Brighton, 1971–73, Asst Solicitor, 1973–74; joined RAF Legal Br. as Flight Lieut, 1974; worked in UK and Europe, undertaking court martial prosecutions and gen. legal work involving administrative, internat. and operational law; Deputy Director: Cyprus, 1984–87; Germany, 1991–92; Legal Services (RAF), MoD, 1992–97; Dir of Legal Services (RAF) and RAF Prosecuting Authy, MoD, 1997–2002; retd in rank of Air Vice Marshal. Comr, Criminal Cases Rev. Commn, 2002–12; Adjudicator, Solicitors Regulation Authy, 2008–13; Panel Chair, Conduct Cttees, Nursing and Midwifery Council, 2012–. Trustee, RAF Benevolent Fund, 2004–08. *Recreations:* golf, photography, cars.

WEEDS, John Ian; Head Teacher, Cranbrook School, since 2012; *b* Horsham, W Sussex, 21 Oct. 1962; *s* of Mike and Barbara Weeds; *m* 1990, Sarah Louise Turner; three *s*. *Educ:* Collyer's Sch., Horsham; Pembroke Coll., Cambridge (BA 1986); Durham Univ. (PGCE); Nottingham Univ. (MPhil); Roehampton Univ. (EdD 2014). Teacher of Classics: Hampton Sch., 1987–90; Bolton Sch., 1990–93; Hd of Classics and Housemaster, Bedford Sch., 1993–2000; Dep. Hd, Slough GS, 2000–06; Principal, Reading Sch., 2006–12. Mem., Friends of Mt Athos. *Recreations:* travel writing, banjo or guitar according to mood, children's literature, philosophy. *Address:* School House, Cranbrook School, Waterloo Road, Cranbrook, Kent TN17 3JD. *T:* (01580) 715638. *E:* the_weeds@btinternet.com. *Club:* Lansdowne.

WEEDY, Maj.-Gen. Michael Anthony C.; *see* Charlton-Weedy.

WEEKES, Anesta Glendora; QC 1999; a Recorder, since 2000; *b* 10 June 1955; *d* of late Joseph Weekes and of Sarah Weekes. *Educ:* Keele Univ. (BA Hons). Called to the Bar, Gray's Inn, 1981, Bencher, 2003; in practice at the Bar, specialising in criminal law and public inquiries; Counsel to Stephen Lawrence Inquiry, 1999; Asst Recorder, 1999–2000. Arbitrator (part-time), Commonwealth Secretariat Arbitral Tribunal, 2000–. Dir, ENO, 2001–09. *Recreations:* music, opera, dance, travel books. *Address:* 23 Essex Street, WC2R 3AA. *T:* (020) 7413 0353.

WEEKES, Sir Everton (de Courcy), KCMG 1995; GCM; OBE; international bridge player; former international cricketer; *b* Bridgetown, Barbados, 26 Feb. 1925. *Educ:* St Leonard's Sch., Bridgetown. First class début, 1944, for Barbados; played for Barbados, 1944–64 (Captain), for West Indies, 1947–58 (48 Test matches; 15 centuries, incl. 5 double centuries in England, 1950); on retirement from Test cricket, held world record for five consecutive centuries (*v* England and India), 1948–49, and for seven consecutive half-centuries. *Publications:* (with Hilary McD. Beckles) Mastering the Craft, 2007. *Address:* c/o West Indies Cricket Board of Control, Letchworth Complex, The Garrison, St Michael, Barbados, West Indies.

WEEKS, Gillian Margaret, (Mrs Tony Dean), OBE 2011; Owner and Director, Dean Weeks Consultants Ltd, since 2013; *b* Hull, 29 July 1955; *d* of Fred and Mavis Weeks; *m* 2002, Tony Dean; one step *s* one step *d*. *Educ:* St Hilda's Sch., Whitby; Hull Coll. of Technol. (OND Scis 1973); Hull Coll. of Higher Educn (HNC Biol. 1980); John Moores Univ., Liverpool (LLB Hons 1996). CEnv 2006. Waste Regulation Site Inspector, Tyne and Wear CC, 1980–83; Waste Regulation Licensing Officer, Humberside CC, 1983–85; Regulation and Envmt Dir, Cleanaway Ltd, 1985–2006; Regulatory Affairs Dir, Veolia Envmtl Services, 2006–13; Interim Policy Dir, Envmtl Services Assoc., 2010–11. Mem. Bd, Envmt Agency, 2014–. Mem., UK Envmtl Law Assoc., 1997–. Fellow, Industry Parliament Trust, 2000; FCIWM 2007. *Recreations:* travel, ski-ing, walking, flying. *Address:* 8 Trevone Close, Knutsford, Cheshire WA16 9EJ. *T:* 07740 958358. *E:* gill@deanweeks.co.uk.

WEEKS, His Honour John Henry; QC 1983; a Circuit Judge, 1991–2006; *b* 11 May 1938; *s* of Henry James and Ada Weeks; *m* 1970, Caroline Mary, *d* of Lt Col J. F. Ross; one *s* two *d*. *Educ:* Cheltenham Coll.; Worcester Coll., Oxford (MA). Called to Bar, Inner Temple, 1963, Bencher, 1996; in practice in Chancery, 1963–91. *Publications:* Limitation of Actions, 1989. *Recreation:* walking the dog. *Address:* 18 Centrepoint House, 15A St Giles High Street, WC2H 8LW. *T:* (020) 7497 9560.

WEEKS, Wilfred John Thomas, OBE 2006; Chairman, European Public Affairs, Weber Shandwick, 2002–11; *b* 8 Feb. 1948; *s* of late William Weeks and Kathleen Weeks (*née* Penhale); *m* 1981, Anne Veronica Harrison; three *s*. *Educ:* Shebbear Coll.; KCL (BD Hons). Private Sec. to Rt Hon. Edward Heath, 1976–80; Jt Founder, GJW Govt Relns, 1980–2000; Chm., BSMG UK, 2000–02. Non-exec. Dir, Helical Bar, 2005–12. Chm., Friends of the Tate, 1990–99, Mem. Council, Tate Britain, 2000–03; Chairman: Dulwich Picture Gall., 2000–06 (Trustee, 1994–2006); Heritage Educn Trust, 2005–08; Spitalfields Fest., 2006–08; British Future, 2012–; Edward Heath Charitable Foundn, 2013–; Develt Bd, Charterhouse, 2013–; Trustee: LAMDA, 2000–10 (Chm. Develt Bd, 2002–06); Trust for London (formerly City Parochial Foundn and Trust for London), 2007–; Buccleuch Living Heritage Trust, 2011–; Prison Advice and Care Trust, 2011–; Resource for London, 2011–; Gainsborough's House, 2014–. Hon. Treas., Hansard Soc., 1996–2007. Goodman Award, Arts and Business, 2004. *Recreations:* gardening, collecting. *Address:* 25 Gauden Road, SW4 6LR. *T:* (020) 7622 0532. *Club:* Garrick.

WEEPLE, Edward John, CB 2004; Chairman, Board of Management, Edinburgh's Telford College, 2007–10; Head of Lifelong Learning Group, Scottish Executive Enterprise, Transport and Lifelong Learning (formerly Enterprise and Lifelong Learning) Department, 1999–2003; *b* 15 May 1945; *s* of Edward Weeple and Mary Catherine (*née* McGrath); *m* 1970, Joan (*née* Shaw); three *s* one *d*. *Educ:* St Aloysius' Coll., Glasgow; Glasgow Univ. (MA). Asst Principal, Min. of Health, 1968–71; Private Sec. to Minister of Health, 1971–73; Principal: DHSS, 1973–78; Scottish Econ. Planning Dept, 1978–80; Assistant Secretary: SHHD, 1980–85; Dept of Agriculture and Fisheries for Scotland, 1985–90; Under Sec., Scottish Office Industry Dept, 1990–95; Hd of Further and Higher Educn, Trng and Sci., then Lifelong Learning, Gp, Scottish Office Educn and Industry Dept, 1995–99. First Minister's Assessor, Carnegie Trust for Univs of Scotland, 2005–; non-exec. Dir, Interactive Univ., 2005–07. Mem., Court, Heriot-Watt Univ., 2005–10 (Chm., Audit Cttee, 2009–10); Mem., Bd of Mgt, Garvald Edinburgh, 2009–10; Special Advr, Paisley Univ., 2005–07. Sec., Goodison Gp in Scotland, 2003–05. *Address:* 19 Lauder Road, Edinburgh EH9 2JG. *T:* (0131) 668 1150.

WEERERATNE, (Rufina) Aswini; QC 2015; *b* Colombo, Sri Lanka, 6 June 1963; *d* of Rienzie and Elaine Weereratne; *m* 1997, David Pallister; one *s*. *Educ:* Ursuline Convent Sch., Wimbledon; Sussex Univ. (BSc Exptl Psychol.); City Univ. (DipLaw); Inns of Court Sch. of

Law; Sch. of Oriental and African Studies, Univ. of London (LLM Internat. Human Rights Law). Called to the Bar, Gray's Inn, 1986; in practice as a barrister, specialising in mental health law, human rights, and cases relating to vulnerable and mentally disabled people, including historic child abuse. Judge (pt-time) of First-Tier Tribunal (Health, Educn and Social Care Chamber), 2001–. Dep. Chm., Investigative Cttee, Gen. Pharmaceutical Council, 2014–. *Publications:* (jtly) Butterworth's New Law Guide to the Mental Capacity Act 2005, 2008; (Consultant Ed.) Halsbury's Laws of England, Mental Health Vol., 2004, 2012; contrib. articles to jls and the press. *Recreations:* baking bread, singing, playing tennis, a fluffy labradoodle. *Address:* 54 Doughty Street, WC1N 2LS. *T:* (020) 7404 1313, *Fax:* (020) 7404 2283. *E:* a.weereratne@doughtystreet.co.uk.

WEETCH, Kenneth Thomas; *b* 17 Sept. 1933; *s* of Kenneth George and Charlotte Irene Weetch; *m* 1961, Audrey Wilson (decd); two *d*. *Educ:* Newbridge Grammar Sch., Mon; London School of Economics (MSc(Econ)), London Inst. of Educn (DipEd). National Service: Sgt, RAEC, Hong Kong, 1955–57; Walthamstow and Ilford Educn Authorities and Research at LSE, 1957–64; Head of History Dept, Hockerill Coll. of Educn, Bishop's Stortford, 1964–74. Contested (Lab): Saffron Walden, 1970; Ipswich, 1987. MP (Lab) Ipswich, Oct. 1974–1987. PPS to Sec. of State for Transport, 1976–79. Member: Lab Select Cttee on Home Affairs, 1981–83; Select Cttee on Parly Comr for Administration, 1983–87. *Recreations:* walking, reading, watching Association football, playing the piano in pubs, eating junk food. *Club:* Silent Street Labour (Ipswich).

WEETMAN, Prof. Anthony Peter, MD, DSc; FRCP, FRCPE; FMedSci; Sir Arthur Hall Professor of Medicine, since 1991, and Pro-Vice-Chancellor for Medicine, since 2008, University of Sheffield; *b* 29 April 1953; *s* of Kenneth Weetman and Evelyn Weetman (*née* Healer); *m* 1982, Sheila Thompson; one *s* one *d*. *Educ:* Univ. of Newcastle upon Tyne (BMedSci 1974; MB BS 1977; MD 1983; DSc 1991). FRCP 1990; FRCPE 2004. MRC Trng Fellow, Welsh Nat. Sch. of Medicine, 1980–84; MRC Travelling Fellow, NIH, Bethesda, USA, 1984–85; Wellcome Trust Sen. Res. Fellow in Clin. Sci., RPMS and Univ. of Cambridge, 1985–89; Lectr in Medicine, Univ. of Cambridge, 1989–91; Dean, Medical Sch., Univ. of Sheffield, 1999–2008. Hon. Consultant Physician: Hammersmith Hosp., 1986–87; Addenbrooke's Hosp., 1987–91; Northern Gen. Hosp., Sheffield, 1991–2001; Sheffield Teaching Hosps NHS Trust, 2001–. Chm., UK Healthcare Educn Adv. Cttee, 2011–. President: British Thyroid Assoc., 2005–08; Assoc. of Physicians, 2015–16; Chm., Medical Schs Council, 2009–13. FMedSci 1998. H. C. Jacobæus Prize, Nordisk Foundn, 2012; Paul Starr Award, American Thyroid Assoc., 2013. *Publications:* Autoimmune Endocrine Disease, 1991; papers on endocrine autoimmunity and disease, esp. concerning the thyroid. *Recreations:* fell walking (Munroist number 2342), squash, ski-ing. *Address:* Faculty of Medicine, Dentistry and Health, Barber House, 387 Glossop Road, Sheffield S10 2HQ. *T:* (0114) 222 8712, *Fax:* (0114) 222 8756. *E:* a.p.weetman@sheffield.ac.uk.

WEGG-PROSSER, Benjamin Charles; Managing Partner, Global Counsel, since 2011; *b* Paddington, 11 June 1974; *s* of Stephen and Victoria Wegg-Prosser; *m* 2004, Yulia Khabibullina; two *s* one *d*. *Educ:* Southbank Sch.; Sheffield Univ. (BA Politics 1995). Res. asst, Office of Peter Mandelson, MP, 1995–97; political advr, Cabinet Office, 1997–98; Special Advr, DTI, 1998–99; Communications Manager, Pearson PLC, 1999–2000; Publisher: Slate UK, 2000; Guardian newspaper, 2000–05; Dir, Strategic Communications Unit, Office of the Prime Minister, 2005–07; Dir, Corporate Develt, SUP Media, 2007–10. *Recreations:* cooking, politics, football, travel, running. *Address:* Global Counsel, 5 Welbeck Street, W1G 9YQ. *T:* (020) 3667 6500. *Club:* Soho House.

WEI, Baron *cr* 2010 (Life Peer), of Shoreditch in the London Borough of Hackney; **Nathanael Ming-Yan Wei;** Government Adviser on Big Society, Cabinet Office, 2010–11; Founding Partner, The Shaftesbury Partnership, 2006–10, now Honorary Founding Partner; founding non-executive Director, Manchester China Forum, since 2013; *b* 19 Jan. 1977; *m* Cynthia; two *c*. *Educ:* Jesus Coll., Oxford. Consultant, McKinsey & Co.; Founder: Teach First, 2002; Future Leaders; Co-founder, Challenge Network; Hd, New Prog. Develt (Ventures), Absolute Return for Kids; Advr, Community Foundn Network, 2011–. Trustee, Asia House, 2011–. Fellow, Young Foundn. *Address:* House of Lords, SW1A 0PW.

WEIDENFELD, family name of **Baron Weidenfeld**.

WEIDENFELD, Baron *cr* 1976 (Life Peer), of Chelsea; **Arthur George Weidenfeld,** GBE 2011; Kt 1969; Chairman, Weidenfeld & Nicolson Ltd, since 1948; *b* 13 Sept. 1919; *o s* of late Max and Rosa Weidenfeld; *m* 1st, 1952, Jane Sieff; one *d*; 2nd, 1956, Barbara Connolly (*née* Skelton) (marr. diss. 1961; she *d* 1996); 3rd, 1966, Sandra Payson Meyer (marr. diss. 1976); 4th, 1992, Annabelle Whitestone. *Educ:* Piaristen Gymnasium, Vienna; University of Vienna (Law); Konsular Akademie (Diplomatic College). BBC Monitoring Service, 1939–42; BBC News Commentator on European Affairs on BBC Empire & North American service, 1942–46. Wrote weekly foreign affairs column, News Chronicle, 1943–44; Founder: Contact Magazine and Books, 1945; Weidenfeld & Nicolson Ltd, 1948. One year's leave as Political Adviser and Chief of Cabinet of President Weizmann of Israel. Consultant, Bertelsmann Foundn, 1992–; Mem. Bd, Herbert-Quandt-Foundn, Bad Homburg, 1999–2008; Dir, Cheyne Capital, 2000–09; Trustee, Alfred Herrhausen Ges. (Deutsche Bank), 2004–. Consultant, Burda Medien, 1983–; Dir, Encyclopædia Britannica, 2011–. Columnist: Die Welt and Die Welt am Sonntag, 1999–; Bild am Sonntag, 2002–; Huffington Post, 2010–. Vice Chm., EU-Israel Forum, 2002–08. Jt Vice-Pres., Campaign for Oxford, 1992–95; Vice-Chm., Oxford Develt Prog., 1995–. Chm., Trialogue Educnl Trust, 1999–. Chm., Bd of Governors, Ben Gurion Univ. of the Negev, Beer-Sheva, 1996–2004 (Vice-Chm., 1976–96; Hon. Chm., 2004–); Governor: Weizmann Inst. of Science, 1964–; Univ. of Tel Aviv, 1980–; Hon. Senator, Univ. of Bonn, 1997; Hon. Gov., Diplomatic Acad., Vienna, 1998. Member: South Bank Bd, 1986–99; ENO Bd, 1988–98; Trustee, Nat. Portrait Gall., 1988–95. Founder and Pres., Weidenfeld Inst. for Strategic Dialogue, 2006–; Hon. Vice Pres., World Jewish Congress, 2014. FKC 2005. Hon. Fellow: St Peter's Coll., Oxford, 1992; St Anne's Coll., Oxford, 1994. Hon. PhD Ben Gurion Univ. of the Negev, 1984; Hon. MA Oxon, 1992; Hon. DLitt: Exeter, 2001; Oxford, 2010. Charlemagne Medal for European Media, Aachen, Germany, 2000; Lifetime Achievement Award, London Book Fair/Trilogy, 2007; Golden Book of City of Potsdam, 2008; Teddy Kollek Life Achievement Award, Jerusalem, 2009; M100 Sanssouci Media Award, Potsdam, 2011; Tolerance Rings Award, Eur. Acad. of Scis and Arts, Frankfurt, 2012. Golden Kt's Cross with Star, Order of Merit (Austria), 1989; Chevalier, Légion d'Honneur (France), 1990; Kt Comdr, Cross, Badge and Star, Order of Merit (Germany), 1991; Cross of Merit for Arts and Science (Austria), 2002; Decoration of Honour in Gold for services to Vienna (Austria), 2003; Grande Ufficiale, Ordine del Merito (Italy), 2005; Order of Merit, Baden-Wuerttemberg (Germany), 2008; Bene Merito Dist. Award (Poland), 2011. *Publications:* The Goebbels Experiment, 1943 (also publ. USA); Remembering My Good Friends (autobiog.), 1994. *Recreations:* travel, opera. *Address:* 9 Chelsea Embankment, SW3 4LE. *Club:* Garrick.

See also C. A. Barnett.

WEIDMANN, Dr Jens; President, Deutsche Bundesbank, since 2011; Member, Governing Council, European Central Bank, since 2011; *b* Solingen, Germany, 20 April 1968; *m* Dr Anja; one *s* one *d*. *Educ:* Univ. de Droit, d'Economie et des Sciences, Aix-Marseilles III and Rheinische Friedrich-Wilhelms Univ., Bonn (BA Econs 1993); Bonn Univ. (PhD 1997). Res. asst, Inst. for Internat. Econ. Policy, Univ. of Bonn, 1994–97; IMF, Washington, 1997–99; Sec. Gen., German Council of Econ. Experts, 1999–2003; Hd, Monetary Policy and Analysis Div. and Dep. Hd, Econs Dept, Deutsche Bundesbank, 2003–06; Hd, Dept for Econ. and Financial Policy, Federal Chancellor's Office, 2006–11; personal rep. of Federal Chancellor preparing for world econ. summits of G8 and G20 countries. Gov., IMF. Member: Bd of Dirs, Bank for Internat. Settlements; Steering Cttee, Financial Stability Bd; Bd of Dirs and Steering Cttee, European Systemic Risk Bd. *Address:* Deutsche Bundesbank, Wilhelm-Epstein-Strasse 14, 60431 Frankfurt am Main, Germany. *T:* (69) 95663511, *Fax:* (69) 95663077. *E:* info@bundesbank.de.

WEIGHILL, Maj. Gen. Robert Peter Mark, CBE 2012; Deputy Chief of Staff (Plans), Joint Force Command Naples, NATO, 2012–15; *b* London, 5 June 1961; *s* of late Peter Weighill and Rosemary Weighill; *m* 1989, Caroline Louise Payne; one *s* two *d*. *Educ:* St Neot's Prep. Sch.; Dauntsey's Sch.; RMA Sandhurst; King's Coll. London (MA Internat. Relns (Dist.) 2006); Manchester Business Sch. (Advanced Mgt Achievement Course 2015). FCMI 2015. Commnd RA, 1981; 2 Field Regt RA, 1983–86; 7th Regt RHA, 1987–89; Platoon Instructor, RMA Sandhurst, 1989–91; acsc 1992–93; SO2 J3 Jt Ops HQ British Forces HK, 1994–95; Batt. Comdr 22 Regt RA, 1996–97; SO1 Chief G3 Ops HQ ARRC, 1998–2000; CO 47th Regt RA, 2000–03; Asst Dir Concept Develt, MoD, 2003–05; RCDS 2006; Dep. Commanding Gen., Min. of Interior Transition Team, Iraq, 2007; Comdr RA 1 (UK) Armoured Div., 2008–09; Hd Jt Plans, Jt Force Comd Naples, NATO, 2010–12; Dir Ops, Operation Unified Protector, Libya, 2011. Hon. Regtl Col, 47th Regt RA, 2013–. Vice Pres. (Alpine), Army Winter Sports Assoc., 2014–. NATO Meritorious Service Medal, 2012. *Publications:* contrib. articles in RUSI Defence. *Recreations:* ski-ing, running, military history.

WEIGHTMAN, Michael William, CB 2013; DPhil; FREng; HM Chief Inspector of Nuclear Installations, and Director, Health and Safety Executive, 2005–13; Chief Executive, Office for Nuclear Regulation, 2011–13; *b* 6 Feb. 1949; *s* of William Henry Weightman and Hilda Weightman; *m* 1974, Elizabeth Anne; two *s*. *Educ:* Lutterworth Grammar Sch.; Univ. of Sussex; Univ. of Bristol. BSc, MSc; DPhil. CEng; MInstP. HM Principal Inspector of Nuclear Installations, 1988; Hd, Nuclear Policy, HSE, 1995; HM Dep. Chief Inspector of Nuclear Installations, 2000–05. Chm., Potters Bar Rail Crash Investigation Bd, 2002; Hd, IAEA Internat. Fact Finding Mission to Japan on Fukushima Dai-ichi nuclear accident, 2011. MIOM. FREng 2010. *Recreations:* family, Rugby Union, village community, arts. *Club:* Chester Rugby Union Football.

WEIGHTMAN, Prof. Peter, PhD; Professor of Physics, University of Liverpool, since 1989; *b* Alfreton, Derbys, 21 Oct. 1944; *s* of Arthur and Gertrude Edith Weightman; *m* 1st, 1974, Anne Susan Kirby (marr. diss. 1993); two *s*; 2nd, 2001, Susan Clare Nobay. *Educ:* Univ. of Keele (BA 1st Cl. Hons Phys and Maths 1967; PhD 1970). Res. Fellow, Phys Dept, Univ. of Essex, 1970–71; University of Liverpool: Lectr, 1971–81, Sen. Lectr, 1981–85, Reader, 1985–89, Dept of Phys; Dep. Dir, 1988–98, Dir, 1998–2001, Interdisciplinary Res. Centre in Surface Sci.; Dir, Grad. Sch. in Engrg and Physical Sci., 1994–98. Fulbright Sen. Res. Scholar, Chem. Dept, Oregon State Univ., 1980–81. Mem. of numerous cttees of UK res. councils, SERC, EPSRC, CCLRC, STFC and MRC; UK Mem., High Technol. Panel, 1993–98, Physical and Engrg Sci. and Technol. Panel, 1999–2000, NATO; European Synchrotron Radiation Facility: Mem., Sci. Adv. Cttee, 1995–97, 1997–99; Mem. Council, 2000–03; Chm., Scientific Steering Cttee, UK Fourth Generation Light Source, 2000–08. Chm., Condensed Matter Physics Div., Inst. of Physics, 2008–. Mem. Council, European Physical Soc., 2007–10. Mott Medal and Prize, Inst. of Physics, 2006; Sen. Prize and John Yarwood Meml Medal, British Vacuum Council, 2011. *Publications:* 300 res. papers in learned jls. *Recreations:* reading history books, listening to music. *Address:* Physics Department, University of Liverpool, Oxford Street, Liverpool L69 3BX. *T:* (0151) 794 3871, *Fax:* (0151) 794 3441. *E:* peterw@liverpool.ac.uk.

WEILL, Michel Alexandre D.; *see* David-Weill.

WEINBERG, Prof. Anton; solo clarinettist; teacher of music; woodwind consultant; writer; *b* 25 Nov. 1944; *s* of Louis and Gladys Weinberg; *m* 1987, Brenda Teresa Douglas; three *s* one *d*. *Educ:* Royal Acad. of Music (Associated Bd, Royal Schs of Music Schol.; 1st clarinettist to hold both Hawkes and Solomon prizes; LRAM); 5 yrs study with the late Hans Keller (Arts Council of GB Award). ARCM; ARAM 1987. Prof., GSMD, 1979–86, Prof. of Performance and Communication Skills course, 1983–85; Prof. of Music, Indiana Univ., 1984–90. Artistic Dir, Capitol Prodns Ltd, 1984–87; Music Dir, New Music Prodns, 1984–87; Founding Prof., Nat. Youth Orch. of Spain, 1984–86; Consultant: Jumping Sideways Ltd, 2002–; in woodwind and mouthpiece design, Dawkes Music Ltd, 2002–. Visiting Professor: Nat. Centre of Orchestral Studies, NY; Dartington Internat. Summer Sch. Various lecture progs, BBC Radio 3, 1970–84, incl. writer/presenter, Contrasting Styles of Playing, 1974; writer/presenter, The Keller Instinct, Channel 4; In Short (series), BBC; Brahms Muhlfeld and the Clarinet, BBC; BBC broadcast on develt of stylistic personality in music students. Dir, Mozart and Salieri by Pushkin (theatre production). Solo clarinettist, Wallfisch/Weinberg Trio, 1974–86. Distinguished Teacher, White House Commn on Presidential Scholars, USA, 1989. Represented UK in first Anglo-American cultural visits to China in 1970s. Cert. of Excellence, White House Commn of Educn, Washington, 1989. *Publications:* Unfinished Sentences, 1987; Clarinet and Saxophone Mouthpieces: what you need to know, 2008; Reshaping Thoughts, 2013; numerous articles in the Listener, Classical Music Mag. and Musical Times, 1970–84. *Recreations:* supporting my wife who is Founder and Chair of United Families and Friends Campaign (Deaths in Custody), art, furniture restoration techniques, travel, cooking, writing, my family. *Address:* 78 Smallwood Road, SW17 0TW. *T:* (020) 8672 5903, 07951 706687. *E:* anton@antonweinberg.com.

WEINBERG, Prof. Julius Rolf, DM; FRCP, FFPH; Vice-Chancellor, Kingston University, since 2011; *b* 27 Dec. 1954; *s* of Willy Wolfgang Weinberg and Jose Letitia Weinberg; two *s* one *d*. *Educ:* Queen's Coll., Oxford (BM BCh 1979; MA 1979; DM 1992); MSc London; Open Univ. (MEd 2011). FRCP 2001; FFPH (FFPHM 2002). Lectr and Sen. Registrar, Charing Cross Hosp. Sch. of Medicine, 1984–89; Lectr and Hon. Consultant, Univ. of Zimbabwe Sch. of Medicine, 1989–93; Consultant, WHO Mission to Bosnia, 1993–94; Consultant Epidemiologist, PHLS, 1994–99; City University: Pro Vice-Chancellor (Res.), 1999–2006; Dir, Inst. of Health Scis, 2002–06; Dep. Vice Chancellor, 2006–11; Actg Vice Chancellor, 2009–10. Vis. Prof., of Health Policy, City Univ., 1996–99. Mem. Bd, Ofqual, 2012– (Dep. Chm., 2012–); Trustee, London Higher, 2012– (Chm., Access HE, 2012–). Principal FHEA, 2014. *Publications:* (jtly) Communicable Disease Control Handbook, 2001, 2nd edn 2005; contrib. peer-reviewed jls on physiol. of shock, internat. outbreak control, modelling hosp. services and health informatics. *Recreations:* pottery, cycling, ski-ing. *Address:* Kingston University, River House, 53–57 High Street, Kingston-upon-Thames KT1 1LQ.

WEINBERG, Sir Mark (Aubrey), Kt 1987; Chairman: St James's Place Group (formerly J Rothschild Assurance), 1991–2004 (President, since 2004); Pension Insurance Corporation Holdings, since 2006; *b* 9 Aug. 1931; *s* of Philip and Eva Weinberg; *m* 1st, 1961, Sandra Le Roith (*d* 1978); three *d*; 2nd, 1980, Anouska Hempel; one *s*. *Educ:* King Edward VII Sch., Johannesburg; Univ. of the Witwatersrand (BCom, LLB); London Sch. of Econs (LLM). Called to the Bar, South Africa, 1955. Barrister, S Africa, 1955–61; Man. Dir, Abbey Life Assurance Co., 1961–70; Hambro Life Assurance, subseq. Allied Dunbar Assurance: Man. Dir, 1971–83; Chm., 1984–90; Chm., Life Assce Hldg Corp., 1994–2003. Chm., Organizing Cttee, Marketing of Investments Bd, 1985–86; Dep. Chm., Securities and Investment Bd, 1986–90 (Mem., 1985–90). Sen. Advr, Stamford Associates Ltd, 2011–. Trustee, Tate Gall., 1985–92. Hon. Treas., NSPCC, 1983–91. *Publications:* Take-overs and Mergers, 1962, 5th edn 1989. *Recreation:* bridge. *Address:* Spencer House, 27 St James's Place, SW1A 1NR. *T:* (020) 7514 1960. *Clubs:* Army and Navy, Portland, Royal Automobile.

WEINBERG, Prof. Steven, PhD; Josey Regental Professor of Science, University of Texas, since 1982; *b* 3 May 1933; *s* of Fred and Eva Weinberg; *m* 1954, Louise Goldwasser; one *d*. *Educ:* Cornell Univ. (AB); Copenhagen Institute for Theoretical Physics; Princeton Univ. (PhD). Instructor, Columbia Univ., 1957–59; Research Associate, Lawrence Berkeley Laboratory, 1959–60; Faculty, Univ. of California at Berkeley, 1960–69; full prof., 1964; on leave: Imperial Coll., London, 1961–62; Loeb Lectr, Harvard, 1966–67; Vis. Prof., MIT, 1967–69; Prof., MIT, 1969–73; Higgins Prof. of Physics, Harvard Univ., and concurrently Senior Scientist, Smithsonian Astrophysical Observatory, 1973–83 (Sen. Consultant, 1983–). Morris Loeb Vis. Prof., Harvard Univ., 1983–; Dir, Jerusalem Winter Sch. of Theoretical Physics, 1983–94. Lectures: Richtmeyer, Amer. Assoc. of Physics Teachers, 1974; Scott, Cavendish Lab., 1975; Silliman, Yale Univ., 1977; Lauritsen, Calif Inst. of Technol., 1979; Bethe, Cornell, 1979; Schild, Texas, 1979; de Shalit, Weizmann Inst., 1979; Henry, Princeton, 1981; Harris, Northwestern, 1981; Cherwell-Simon, Oxford, 1983; Bampton, Columbia, 1983; Einstein, Israel Acad. of Arts and Sciences, 1984; Hilldale, Wisconsin, 1985; Dirac, Cambridge, 1986; Klein, Stockholm, 1989; Brittin, Colorado, 1992; Gibbs, Amer. Math. Soc., 1996; Bochner, Rice, 1997; Witherspoon, Washington, 2001; Messenger, Cornell, 2007; Phi Beta Kappa Oration, Harvard, 2008; Sackler, Niels Bohr Inst., Copenhagen, 2009; Clark, Univ. of Texas at Dallas, 2010. Mem., Science Policy Cttee, Superconducting Supercollider Lab., 1989–93. Mem., Bd of Dirs, Daedalus, 1990–. Fellow, Amer. Acad. of Arts and Scis; Member: US Nat. Acad. of Scis; Amer. Philosophical Soc.; Phil Soc. of Texas (Pres., 1994); IAU; Texas Inst. of Letters; For. Mem., Royal Soc.; Hon. MRIA. Hon. ScD: Knox Coll. 1978; Chicago, 1978; Rochester, 1979; Yale, 1979; City Univ. of New York, 1980; Clark, 1982; Dartmouth Coll., 1984; Columbia, 1990; Salamanca, 1992; Padua, 1992; Barcelona, 1996; Bates Coll., 2002; McGill, 2003; Hon. PhD Weizmann Inst., 1985; Hon. DLitt, Washington Coll., 1985. J. R. Oppenheimer Prize, 1973; Heinemann Prize in Mathematical Physics, 1977; Amer. Inst. of Physics—US Steel Foundn Science Writing Award, 1977; Elliott Cresson Medal of Franklin Inst., 1979; (jtly) Nobel Prize in Physics, 1979; Madison Medal, Princeton, 1991; US Nat. Medal of Sci., 1991; Gemant Prize, Amer. Inst. of Physics, 1997; Piazz Prize, govts of Sicily and Palermo, 1998; Lewis Thomas Prize, Rockefeller Univ., 1999; Humanist of the Year Award, Amer. Humanist Assoc., 2002; Benjamin Franklin Medal, Amer. Philosophical Soc., 2004; Trotter Prize, Texas A & M Univ., 2008; James Joyce Award, University Coll., Dublin, 2009. Hon. Citizen, Padua, 2007. *Publications:* Gravitation and Cosmology: principles and applications of the general theory of relativity, 1972; The First Three Minutes: a modern view of the origin of the universe, 1977; The Discovery of the Subatomic Particles, 1982; (jtly) Elementary Particles and the Laws of Physics, 1988; Dreams of a Final Theory, 1993; The Quantum Theory of Fields, vol. I, 1995, vol. II, 1996, vol. III, 2000; Facing Up, 2001; Glory & Terror, 2004; Cosmology, 2008; Lake Views, 2009; Lectures on Quantum Mechanics, 2012; To Explain the World: the discovery of modern science, 2015; numerous articles in learned jls. *Recreation:* reading history. *Address:* Physics Department, University of Texas, Austin, TX 78712, USA. *T:* (512) 4714394. *Clubs:* Saturday (Boston, Mass); Cambridge Scientific (Cambridge, Mass); Headliners, Tuesday (Austin, Texas).

WEINER, Edmund Simon Christopher; Deputy Chief Editor, Oxford English Dictionary, 1993–98 and since 2001 (Co-Editor, 1984–93; Principal Philologist, 1998–2001); Supernumerary Fellow, Kellogg College (formerly Rewley House), Oxford, since 1991; *b* 27 Aug. 1950; *s* of late Prof. Joseph Sidney Weiner and Marjorie Winifred (*née* Daw); *m* 1973, Christine Mary Wheeler (changed name by deed poll to Clare Mariella Howard, 2014); two *s* one *d*. *Educ:* Westminster; Christ Church, Oxford (BA Eng. Lang. and Lit.; MA). Lectr, Christ Church, Oxford, 1974–77; Mem. Staff, A Supplement to The Oxford English Dictionary, 1977–84. *Publications:* Oxford Guide to English Usage, 1983, 2nd edn (with A. Delahunty) 1993; (ed with John Simpson) The Oxford English Dictionary, 2nd edn, 1989; (with Sylvia Chalker) The Oxford Dictionary of English Grammar, 1994; (with Sidney Greenbaum) The Oxford Reference Grammar, 2000; (with Peter Gilliver and Jeremy Marshall) The Ring of Words: J. R. R. Tolkien and the Oxford English Dictionary, 2006. *Recreations:* language, music, family life, the Church, history, cooking, gardening, elementary carpentry. *Address:* Oxford University Press, Great Clarendon Street, Oxford OX2 6DP. *T:* (01865) 556767.

WEINIGER, Matthew Gideon; QC 2014; Partner, International Arbitration, Herbert Smith Freehills LLP, since 2003; *b* Hull, E Yorks, 3 Oct. 1970; *s* of Noah Weiniger and Elaine Finestein (*née* March); *m* 1994, Suzanne Cohen; four *s* one *d*. *Educ:* Hymers Coll., Hull; Downing Coll., Cambridge (BA Law 1993). Admitted solicitor, 1996. Herbert Smith Freehills, 1994–: Mem., Internat. Arbitration Gp. Vis. Professorial Fellow, QMUL (formerly QMW), 2005–. *Publications:* (contrib.) Blackstone's Civil Practice, 1999–2014; (jtly) International Investment Arbitration: substantive principles, 2007, 2nd edn 2014. *Recreation:* sports. *Address:* Herbert Smith Freehills LLP, Exchange House, Primrose Street, EC2A 2EG. *T:* (020) 7374 8000, *Fax:* (020) 7098 5364.

WEINSTEIN, Harvey, Hon. CBE 2004; film producer; Co-Chairman, The Weinstein Company, since 2005; *b* 19 March 1952; *s* of late Max Weinstein and of Miriam Weinstein; *m* 1986, Eve (marr. diss. 2004); three *d*; *m* 2007, Georgina Chapman; one *d*. Co-Chm., Miramax Films Corp., 1979–2005. Films produced include: Playing for Keeps, 1986; Scandal, 1989; Strike it Rich, Hardware, 1990; A Rage in Harlem, 1991; The Crying Game, 1992; The Night We Never Met, Benefit of the Doubt, True Romance, 1993; Mother's Boys, Like Water for Chocolate, Pulp Fiction, Pret-a-Porter, 1994; Smoke, A Month by the Lake, The Crossing Guard, The Journey of August King, Things To Do In Denver When You're Dead, The Englishman Who Went Up A Hill But Came Down A Mountain, Blue in the Face, Restoration, 1995; Scream, The Pallbearer, The Last of the High Kings, Jane Eyre, Flirting with Disaster, The English Patient, Emma, The Crow: City of Angels, Beautiful Girls, 1996; Addicted to Love, Air Bud, Cop Land, Good Will Hunting, Scream 2, Jackie Brown, 1997; Velvet Goldmine, Shakespeare in Love, Rounders, The Prophecy II, A Price Above Rubies, Playing by Heart, The Mighty, Little Voice, Heaven, Halloween H20: Twenty Years Later, The Faculty, B. Monkey, Phantoms, Senseless, Ride, Wide Awake, Night Watch, 54, Talk of Angels, 1998; Guinevere, Allied Forces, Wasteland, She's All That, My Life So Far, The Yards, 1999; Scary Movie, Boys and Girls, The Crow: Salvation, Reindeer Games, Love's Labour's Lost, Scream 3, About Adam, Highlander: Endgame, Chocolat, Dracula, 2000; Bounce, Spy Kids, Texas, Scary Movie 2, The Others, The Fellowship of the Ring, 2001; Iris, Shipping News, Spy Kids 2, Equilibrium, Waking up in Reno, The Two Towers, Gangs of New York, Chicago, 2002; Human Stain, Kill Bill: Vol. 1, Confessions of a Dangerous Mind, Spy Kids 3-D, Scary Movie 3, The Return of the King, Cold Mountain, 2003; Kill Bill: Vol. 2, Fahrenheit 9/11, Shall We Dance, 2004; The Aviator, The Brothers Grimm, 2005; An Unfinished Life, Proof, Derailed, Scary Movie 4, 2006; Miss Potter, 2007; The Reader, 2008; The No 1 Ladies' Detective Agency (TV), Crossing Over, Inglourious Basterds, Halloween II, 2009; Piranha, 2010; The King's Speech, The Fighter, Scream 4, I Don't Know How She Does It, The Artist, 2011; Untouchable, Silver Linings Playbook, Django Unchained, 2012; Scary Movie 5, One Chance, 2013; Mandela: Long Walk to Freedom, August: Osage County, Paddington, 2014. *Publications:* (with Robert Weinstein) The Art of Miramax: the inside story. *Address:* The Weinstein Company, 345 Hudson Street, 13th Floor, New York, NY 10014, USA.

WEINSTOCK, Anne Josephine, CBE 1993; Executive Chair, Sheffield Futures, 2011–12; *b* 28 Dec. 1950; *d* of late Dr Kevin Maher and Brenda Maher; *m* 1976, Dr Harold Weinstock; one *s* two *d*. *Educ:* Manchester Victoria Univ. (BA Hons Econs). Manager: Stopover hostel for homeless girls, 1972–73; Lance Project for Single Homeless, 1973–75; Regl Manager, then Principal Organiser, NACRO, 1975–79; Mem., Home Office Parole Bd, 1979–84; Chief Exec., Rathbone Soc., later Community Industry, then Rathbone CI, 1985–99; Dir, Millennium Volunteers, 1999–2000 (on secondment); Chief Exec., Connexions Service, DfES, 2000–03; Dir, Supporting Children and Young People Gp, DfES, subseq. DCSF, 2003–08; Hd, Youth Task Force, DCSF, subseq. DFE, 2008–10. Director: Manchester TEC, 1989–98; Manchester Careers Partnership, 1995–98; Member: NW FEFC, 1995–98; Govt Skills Task Force, 1998–2000. Fellow, Univ. of Central Lancs, 2001. *Publications:* contrib. articles on raising standards in educn and trng, impact of league tables, alternative educn for disaffected youth, and encouraging young people to become volunteers. *Recreations:* running, walking, swimming, friends and family, reading. *Address:* 12 Warwick Drive, Hale, Cheshire WA15 9DY. *T:* (0161) 980 5070.

WEIR, family name of **Baron Inverforth** and **Viscount Weir**.

WEIR, 3rd Viscount *cr* 1938; **William Kenneth James Weir;** Chairman: The Weir Group PLC, 1983–99; Balfour Beatty (formerly BICC) plc, 1996–2003; CP Ships Ltd, 2001–03; Director: St James's Place Capital (formerly J. Rothschild Holdings) plc, 1985–2004 (Vice-Chairman, 1985–95); Canadian Pacific Railway Co., 1989–2004; *b* 9 Nov. 1933; *e s* of 2nd Viscount Weir, CBE, and Lucy (*d* 1972), *d* of late James F. Crowdy, MVO; *S* father, 1975; *m* 1st, 1964, Diana (marr. diss.), *o d* of Peter L. MacDougall; one *s* one *d*; 2nd, 1976, Mrs Jacqueline Mary Marr (marr. diss.), *er d* of late Baron Louis de Chollet; 3rd, 1989, Marina, *d* of late Marc Sevastopoulo; one *s*. *Educ:* Eton; Trinity Coll., Cambridge (BA). Dir, BSC, 1972–76; Dir, 1977–91, Dep. Chm., 1991–96, BICC Ltd. Dir, 1970, Chm., 1975–82, Great Northern Investment Trust Ltd; Co-Chm., RIT and Northern plc, 1982–83; Chairman: Major British Exporters, 1992–2003; British Water, 1998–2000. Member: London Adv. Cttee, Hongkong & Shanghai Banking Corp., 1980–92; Court, Bank of England, 1972–84; Export Guarantees Adv. Council, 1992–98. Chm., Engrg Design Res. Centre, 1989–91; Pres., BEAMA, 1988–89, 1994–95; Vice Pres., China-Britain Business Council, 1994–2003. Chm., Patrons of Nat. Galls of Scotland, 1985–95. Mem., Queen's Body Guard for Scotland (Royal Co. of Archers). FRSA. Hon. FREng (Hon. FEng 1993). Hon. DEng Glasgow, 1993. *Recreations:* shooting, golf, fishing. *Heir: s* Hon. James William Hartland Weir [*b* 6 June 1965; *m* 2001, Benedicte Marie Françoise, *d* of Louis Virard]. *Address:* Rodinghead, Mauchline, Ayrshire KA5 5TR. *T:* (01563) 884233. *Club:* White's.

WEIR, Hon. Lord; David Bruce Weir; a Senator of the College of Justice in Scotland, 1985–97; *b* 19 Dec. 1931; *yr s* of late James Douglas Weir and Kathleen Maxwell Weir (*née* Auld); *m* 1964, Katharine Lindsay, *yr d* of Hon. Lord Cameron, KT, DSC; three *s*. *Educ:* Kelvinside Academy; Glasgow Academy; The Leys Sch., Cambridge; Glasgow Univ. (MA, LLB). Royal Naval Reserve, 1955–64, Lieut RNR. Admitted to Faculty of Advocates, 1959; Advocate Depute for Sheriff Court, 1964; Standing Junior Counsel: to MPBW, 1969; to DoE, 1970; QC (Scot.) 1971; Advocate Depute, 1979–82; Justice of Ct of Appeal, Botswana, 1999–2002; Hon. Sheriff, N Strathclyde at Campbeltown, 2004–. Chairman: Medical Appeal Tribunal, 1972–77; Pensions Appeal Tribunal for Scotland, 1978–84 (Pres., 1984–85); NHS Tribunal, Scotland, 1983–85; Member: Criminal Injuries Compensation Bd, 1974–79 and 1984–85; Transport Tribunal, 1979–85; Parole Bd, Scotland, 1989–92. Mem., Law Adv. Cttee, 1988–95, Chm., Scottish Law Cttee, 1994–95, British Council. Governor, Fettes Coll., 1986–95 (Chm., 1989–95). Mem. Bd, Scottish Internat. Piano Competition, 1997–2007. Vice-Chm., S Knapdale Community Council, 1998–2004. Mem. Council, RYA, 2005–08. *Publications:* (contrib.) The Laws of Scotland: Stair Memorial Encyclopaedia, 1990; (contrib.) The Baltic Sea Pilot, 3rd edn, 2010. *Recreations:* sailing, music. *Clubs:* New (Edinburgh); Royal Cruising; Royal Highland Yacht.

WEIR, Alison; historian and novelist; *d* of Ronald James Matthews and Doreen Ethel (*née* Marston, now Cullen); *m* 1972, Rankin Alexander Lorimer Weir; one *s* one *d*. *Educ:* City of London Sch. for Girls; N Western Poly., London. Civil Service, 1974–83; Principal and Proprietor, Henry Tudor Sch. for Children with Special Needs, 1991–97. Chief Exec., Alison Weir Tours Ltd, 2010–. Hon. Life Patron, Historic Royal Palaces, 2011. FRSA 2003. *Publications:* Britain's Royal Families, 1989; The Six Wives of Henry VIII, 1991; The Princes in the Tower, 1992; Lancaster and York, 1995; Children of England: the heirs of Henry VIII, 1996; Elizabeth the Queen, 1998; Eleanor of Aquitaine, 1999; Henry VIII: King and Court, 2001; Mary, Queen of Scots and Murder of Lord Darnley, 2003; Isabella, She Wolf of France, Queen of England, 2005; Innocent Traitor, 2006; Katherine Swynford: the story of John of Gaunt and his scandalous Duchess, 2007; The Lady Elizabeth, 2008; The Lady in the Tower, 2009; The Captive Queen, 2010; Traitors of the Tower, 2010; (jtly) The Ring and the Crown: a history of royal weddings 1066–2011, 2011; Mary Boleyn: 'the great and infamous whore', 2011; A Dangerous Inheritance, 2012; Elizabeth of York, 2013; The Marriage Game, 2014. *Recreations:* royal and aristocratic genealogy, reading, music, foreign travel, art, poetry.

WEIR, David Bruce; *see* Weir, Hon. Lord.

WEIR, Prof. David Thomas Henderson; Chairman: Fourth Paradigm Consulting, since 2014; Editorial Advisory Board, Cambridge Scholars, since 2013; *b* 10 April 1939; *s* of late Johnstone Mather Weir and Irene Florence Brooks; *m* 1st, 1959, Janeen Elizabeth Whitson Fletcher; one *s* one *d*; 2nd, 1967, Mary Willows; one *s*. *Educ:* Ilkley Grammar Sch.; Bradford Grammar Sch.; Queen's Coll., Oxford (Hastings Scholar, Sir William Akroyd's Scholar, MA, Dip PSA). Research and lecturing, Univs of Aberdeen, Leeds, Hull, Manchester, 1961–72; Sen. Lectr, Manchester Business Sch., 1972–74; University of Glasgow: Prof. of Organizational Behaviour, 1974–89; Head, Dept of Management Studies, 1981–89; Dean, Scottish Business Sch., 1977–79; Chm., Glasgow Business Sch., 1985–89; Dir and Prof. of Mgt, Univ. of Bradford Sch. of Mgt, 1989–97; Dean and Dir, Newcastle Business Sch., and Prof. of Mgt, Univ. of Northumbria at Newcastle, 1998–2000, now Prof. Emeritus; Prof. of Mgt, Centre for Educn and Res. Applied to Mgt, France, 2001–07; Prof. of Intercultural Mgt, Liverpool Hope Univ., 2007–11; Prof. of Business and Enterprise, and Hd, Sch. of Business, Leadership and Enterprise, Univ. Campus Suffolk, 2011–14. Visiting Professor: Bolton Inst., 1993; Southampton Inst., 1994; (in Mgt Develt) Lancaster Sch. of Mgt, 2000–; Bristol Business Sch., 2002–; Lincoln Univ., 2011–; Edgehill Univ., 2014–; York St John; Hull Univ. Dist. Vis. Prof., eTQM Coll., Dubai, 2007; Affiliate Prof. of Mgt, Ecole Supérieure de Commerce, Rennes, 2007–13; Sen. Enterprise Fellow, Essex Univ., 2005–; Barrie Turner Meml Lectr, Middlesex Univ., 1998. Keynote address, Gulf Economic Summit, 2002. Dir, Gulliver Foods, 1980–81; Arbitrator, Dairy Industry, Scotland, 1985–89; Chm., Forever Broadcasting, Yorks, 2000–01. Consultant, World Bank, Unesco, SDA, Arthur Andersen and many companies; Strategic Advr, Emerald Gp, 2000–. Member: Sociology and Social Admin Cttee, SSRC, 1976–78; Cttee of Inquiry, Engrg Profession (Finniston Cttee), 1977–79; Teaching Co. Cttee, SERC, 1983–87 (Chm., 1986–87); CNAA, 1986–89; Incorp. of Gardeners of Glasgow, 1985; Conseil Scient. de l'Univ. des eaux de vie, Segonzac, 1989; Strategic Audit Panel for Review of Dutch Business Educn, Eur. Foundn for Mgt Educn, 1994–95. Chm., Assoc. of Business Schs, 1994–96; Mem. Council, Nat. Forum for Management Educn and Develt, 1994–96. Member Council: Prague Internat. Business Sch., 1992–99; Cyprus Internat. Business Sch., 1990–99. Pres., Emerald Acad. for Online Action and Learning, 2006–. Fellow, Leadership Trust Foundn. CCMI (FBIM 1984); FRSA. Burgess, City of Glasgow, 1985; Ambassador for Bradford, 1996–. Halloran Prize, Acad. of Mgt, USA, 2012. *Publications:* with Eric Butterworth: Sociology of Modern Britain, 1970, 3rd edn 1980; Social Problems of Modern Britain, 1972; New Sociology of Modern Britain, 1984; Men and Work in Modern Britain, 1973; (with Camilla Lambert) Cities in Modern Britain, 1974; (jtly) Computer Programs for Social Scientists, 1972; (with Gerald Mars) Risk Management: theories and models, 2000; (with Gerald Mars) Risk Management: practice and prevention, 2000; (jtly) Critical Management into Critical Practice, 2009; (contrib.) Bards in the Bog (poetry), 2009; (with Nabil Sultan) From Critique to Action: the practical ethics of the organizational world, 2011; (ed jtly) The New Post-Oil Arab Gulf, 2011; (with Deborah Regal) Islam and Africa, 2013; (ed jtly) Ethnography Friendship, 2013; (with Paresh Wankhade) Modern Policing. *Recreations:* playing cricket, supporting Leeds United FC, listening to music, fell walking, wine appreciation, writing poetry, performing poetry. *Address:* Hadleigh House, Main Street, Skirpenbeck, York YO41 1HF. *E:* dweir@runbox.com. *Clubs:* Athenæum, Groucho; Riviera Cricket.

WEIR, Fiona; Chief Executive, Gingerbread (formerly One Parent Families | Gingerbread), since 2008; *b* Bellshill, N Lanarks, 20 Oct. 1959; *d* of John Morrison Weir and Wendy Elisabeth Christine Weir; partner, 1986, Toby Peter Shelley; two *s*. *Educ:* Lady Margaret Hall, Oxford (BA Hons PPE). Nat. organiser, Eur. Nuclear Disarmament, 1984–87; Sen. Climate Change and Air Pollution Campaigner, Friends of the Earth, 1988–95; Dir of Campaigns, Amnesty Internat. UK, 1995–2000; Hd, Public Affairs, Consumers' Assoc., 2000–02; Dir, Policy and Communications, Save the Children, 2002–07; freelance consultant to charities on strategy, communications and campaigning, 2007. Mem., BBC Appeals Adv. Cttee, 2007–11. Mem. RSA. *Recreations:* family, food, films, travel, football (Arsenal). *Address:* Gingerbread, 520 Highgate Studios, 53–79 Highgate Road, NW5 1TL. *T:* (020) 7428 5400.

WEIR, Dame Gillian (Constance), DBE 1996 (CBE 1989); concert organist; Prince Consort Professor, Royal College of Music, since 1999; *b* Martinborough, NZ, 17 Jan. 1941; *d* of Cecil Alexander Weir and Clarice M. Foy Weir (*née* Bignell); *m* 1st, 1967, Clive Rowland Webster (marr. diss. 1971); 2nd, 1972, Lawrence Irving Phelps (*d* 1999). *Educ:* Royal College of Music, London. LRSM, LRAM, LTCL; Hon. FRCO. Winner of St Albans Internat. Organ Competition, 1964; Début, 1965: Royal Festival Hall, solo recital; Royal Albert Hall, concerto soloist, opening night of Promenade Concerts; since then, internat. career as touring concert organist and harpsichordist; concerto appearances with all major British orchestras, also with Boston Symphony, Seattle Symphony, Württemberg Chamber Orch., and others; solo appearances at leading internat. Festivals, incl. Bath, Aldeburgh, Edinburgh, English Bach, Europalia, Europe and USA (AGO Nat. Conventions, RCCO Diamond Jubilee Nat. Convention, etc). Frequent radio and television appearances: BBC Third Prog., USA, Australasia, Europe, Far East; TV film, Toccata: two weeks in the life of Gillian Weir, 1981 (shown NZ TV 1982); presenter and performer, The King of Instruments, 6 part TV series BBC2 and Europe, Australia etc, 1989; many first performances, incl. major works by Fricker, Connolly, Camilleri, Messiaen. Dist. Vis. Artist, Peabody Conservatory of Music, Baltimore, 2004–12; retired from public performance, 2012; master-classes, adjudicator internat. competitions, UK, Europe, N America, Japan; exponent of and authority on Messiaen. President: Incorp. Assoc. of Organists, 1981–83; ISM, 1992–93; RCO, 1994–96 (Hon. Fellow and Mem. Council, 1977–); Hon. RAM 1989; Hon. FRCM 2000. Hon. Fellow: Royal Canadian Coll. of Organists, 1983; Hatfield Coll., Durham, 2014. Hon. Bencher, Middle Temple, 2012. Hon. DMus: Victoria Univ. of Wellington, NZ, 1983; Hull, 1999; Exeter, 2001; Leicester, 2003; Aberdeen, 2004; London, 2009; Durham, 2013; Hon. DLitt Huddersfield, 1997; DUniv UCE, 2001. Internat. Performer of the Year Award, NY Amer. Guild of Organists, 1981; Internat. Music Guide's Musician of the Year Award, 1982; Turnovsky Prize for outstanding achievement in the arts, Turnovsky Foundn for the Arts, NZ, 1985; Silver Medal, Albert Schweitzer Assoc., Sweden, 1998; Evening Standard Award for outstanding performance, 1999; award-winning recordings include complete organ works of Messiaen, 1994, and of Franck, 1997. *Publications:* contributor to: Grove's Internat. Dictionary of Music and Musicians, 1980; The Messiaen Companion; musical jls and periodicals. *Recreation:* theatre. *W:* www.gillianweir.com.

See also Sir R. B. Weir.

WEIR, Col James Mathieson Knight, OBE (mil.) 1988; TD 1971 (clasp 1977); FRICS; DL; Vice Lord-Lieutenant of Rutland, 1997–2006; Chairman, Rutland County Council, 1997–99; *b* 3 March 1931; *s* of James Weir and Elspet Mathieson Weir (*née* Knight); *m* 1961, Mary, *d* of Thomas Maden; two *s*. *Educ:* George Heriot's Sch., Edinburgh; Heriot-Watt Coll. FRICS 1954. Nat. Service, 1954–57; RSME; commnd RE; served UK, Germany, Belgium and Holland. Territorial Army: RE in Scotland, 1958–74; attached 4 Armd Div., 1974–81; Territorial, Auxiliary & Volunteer Reserve Association: Mem., Council, 1996–2000; Mem. for E Midlands, 1983–2000; Chm., Leics and Rutland Cttee, 1996–2000; Chm., ACF Cttee, E Midlands, 1998–2000; Co. Comdt, Leics and Northants ACF, 1982–92 (Hon. Col, Leics, Northants and Rutland ACF, 1995–2002); Mem., ACFA Council, 1998–2002. Director: Mitchell Construction Kinnear Moodie Gp, 1966–73; Jeakins Weir Ltd, 1973–. Mem. Bd, Anglian Water Authy, 1981–87. Mem. (C), Leics CC, 1981–93 (Chm., Public Protection Cttee, 1989–93); Mem., Leics Police Authy, 1986–93; Chm., Rutland & Melton Police/Community Consultative Cttee, 1990–93; Mem. (C), Rutland DC, 1991–97 (Vice Chm., 1996–97). DL: Leics, 1984–97; Rutland, 1997. Chm., Leics and Rutland Campaign Army Benevolent Fund, 1989–99. Constituency Conservative Association: Chm., Rutland & Stamford, 1982–83; Rutland & Melton, 1983–85 and 1991–94. Trustee: Peterborough Cathedral Preservation Trust, 1988–2014; Oakham Sch., 1989–2011; Rutland Trust, 2006–. Governor: C of E Co. Primary Sch., Oakham, 1984–92; Rutland Sixth Form Coll., 1985–93; Vale of Catmose Coll., 1986–95. *Recreations:* golf, visual arts, Rugby Union. *Address:* Swooning House, Oakham, Rutland LE15 6JD. *T:* (01572) 724273. *Club:* Army and Navy.

WEIR, Judith, CBE 1995; composer; Master of the Queen's Music, since 2014; *b* 11 May 1954; *d* of Jack and Ishbel Weir. *Educ:* King's Coll., Cambridge (MA). Cramb Fellow, Glasgow Univ., 1979–82; Fellow-Commoner, Trinity Coll., Cambridge, 1983–85; Composer-in-Residence, RSAMD, Glasgow, 1988–91; Fairbairn Composer in assoc. with CBSO, 1995–98; Artistic Dir, Spitalfields Fest., 1998–2000 (Jt Artistic Dir, 1994–97). Hambro Vis. Prof. of Opera Studies, Oxford Univ., 1999; Vis. Prof. of Composition, Princeton Univ., 2001; Fromm Foundn Vis. Prof., Harvard Univ., 2004; Vis. Res. Prof., Cardiff Univ., 2006–13. Critics' Circle Award, 1994; Lincoln Center Stoeger Award, 1996; South Bank Show Award, 2000; Queen's Medal for Music, 2007; Distinguished Musician Award, ISM, 2010. *Publications: compositions:* King Harald's Saga, 1979; The Consolations of Scholarship, 1985; Missa Del Cid, 1988; Heaven Ablaze In His Breast, 1989; Music Untangled, 1991–92; Heroic Strokes of the Bow, 1992; Moon and Star, 1995; Forest, 1995; Piano Concerto, 1997; Storm, 1997; We are Shadows, 2000; The Welcome Arrival of Rain, 2002; Tiger under the Table, 2003; Piano Trio Two, 2004; Vertue, 2005; Winter Song, 2007; Concrete, 2008; Blue-Green Hill, 2012; I give you the end of a golden string, 2013; Day Break Shadows Flee, 2014; Good Morning, Midnight, 2015; *operas:* A Night at the Chinese Opera, 1987; The Vanishing Bridegroom, 1990; Blond Eckbert, 1994; Armida, 2005; Miss Fortune, 2011. *Address:* c/o Chester Novello, 14–15 Berners Street, W1T 3LJ. *T:* (020) 7612 7400.

WEIR, Michael; MP (SNP) Angus, since 2001; *b* 24 March 1957; *s* of James and Elizabeth Weir; *m* 1985, Anne Jack; two *d*. *Educ:* Arbroath High Sch.; Aberdeen Univ. (LLB). Solicitor: Charles Wood and Son, Kirkcaldy, 1981–83; Myers and Wills, Montrose, 1983–84; J. & D. G. Shiell, Brechin, 1984–2001. Dean, Faculty of Procurators and Solicitors in Angus, 2001. Mem. (SNP), Angus DC, 1984–88. Contested (SNP) Aberdeen S, 1987. Pres., Aberdeen Univ. Student Nationalist Assoc., 1979; Mem., Nat. Exec., Young Scottish Nationalists, 1982. *Address:* House of Commons, SW1A 0AA; (office) 16 Brothock Bridge, Arbroath, Angus DD11 1NG. *T:* (01241) 874522.

WEIR, Peter James; barrister; Member, North Down, Northern Ireland Assembly, since 1998 (UU, 1998–2001, DemU, since 2002); *b* 21 Nov. 1968; *s* of late James Weir and of Margaret Lovell Weir. *Educ:* Ballyholme Primary Sch.; Bangor Grammar Sch.; Queen's Univ., Belfast (LLB Law and Accountancy; MSSc; Cert. Professional Legal Studies). Called to the Bar, NI, 1992; Lectr in Constitutional and Admin. Law, Univ. of Ulster, 1993. Mem., NI Forum, 1996–98. Northern Ireland Assembly: Member: Finance Cttee, 2007–; Envmt Cttee, 2007–; Assembly Commn, 2010–; Justice Cttee, 2011–13; Vice Chm., Employment and Learning Cttee, 2010–11. Chief Whip, DUP, 2010–. Chm., Ulster Young Unionist Council, 1993–95. Mem., North Down BC, 2005–. Pres., NI LGA, 2005–06; Member: S Eastern Educn and Liby Bd, 2005–11; NI Police Bd, 2006–10. Mem., Senate, QUB, 1997–2005. *Publications:* (jtly) The Anglo-Irish Agreement: three years after, 1988; (jtly) Unionism, National Parties and Ulster, 1991. *Recreations:* sport, history, reading. *Address:* 6 Vernon Park, Bangor, Co. Down BT20 4PH; (office) 94 Abbey Street, Bangor, Co. Down BT20 4JB. *T:* and *Fax:* (028) 9145 4500.

WEIR, Peter Lindsay, AM 1982; film director, since 1969; *b* 21 Aug. 1944; *s* of Lindsay Weir and Peggy Barnsley Weir; *m* 1966, Wendy Stites; one *s* one *d*. *Educ:* Scots Coll., Sydney; Vaucluse High Sch.; Sydney Univ. Short Film: Homesdale, 1971; Feature Films: The Cars That Ate Paris, 1973; Picnic at Hanging Rock, 1975; Last Wave, 1977; The Plumber (for TV), 1979; Gallipoli, 1980; The Year of Living Dangerously, 1982; Witness, 1985; The Mosquito Coast, 1986; Dead Poets Society, 1989; Green Card, 1991; Fearless, 1994; The Truman Show, 1998; Master and Commander, 2003; The Way Back, 2010. Chevalier, Ordre des Arts et des Lettres (France), 2010; Commander's Cross (Poland), 2011.

WEIR, Robert Thomas Macdonald; QC 2010; *b* London, 19 May 1969; *s* of Neil and Sue Weir; *m* 1995, Rachel Robert-Blunn; two *s* one *d*. *Educ:* Downside Sch.; Christ's Coll., Cambridge (BA 1st Cl. Law 1991); King's Coll. London (MA Med. Law and Ethics). Called to the Bar, Middle Temple, 1992; in practice as barrister, specialising in personal injuries. *Recreation:* outdoor activities with family and friends. *Address:* Devereux Chambers, Ground Floor South, Queen Elizabeth Building, EC4Y 9BS. *T:* (020) 7353 7534. *E:* weir@devchambers.co.uk.

WEIR, Sir Roderick (Bignell), Kt 1984; JP; Chairman, Rod Weir Co. Ltd; Director, New Zealand Enterprise Trust; *b* 14 July 1927; *s* of Cecil Alexander Weir and Clarice Mildred Foy; *m* 1952, Loys Agnes Wilson (*d* 1984); one *d*; *m* 1986, Anna Jane Mcfarlane. *Educ:* Wanganui Boys' Coll., NZ. Various positions to regional manager, Dalgety NZ Ltd, Wanganui, 1943–63; formed stock and station co., Rod Weir & Co. Ltd, 1963; formed Crown Consolidated Ltd, 1976; Dir, 1980–98, Chm., 1988–98, McKechnie Pacific Ltd; Chm., Danaflex Packaging Corp. Ltd, 1990–98; former Chm., Rangatira Ltd; former Dir, NZ SO. Former Patron, Massey Coll. Business & Property Trust. Past President: NZ Stock and Station Agents' Assoc.; ASEAN Business Council. Former Mem., NZ Inst. of Econ. Res. Inc.; former Board Member and Patron: Massey Univ. Foundn; Medic Alert; Wellington Sch. of Medicine; Wellington Med. Res. Foundn. Former Trustee: Link Foundn; Wanganui Old Boys' Assoc. Almoner, Wellington Cathedral of St Paul, 2000–. Hon. Consul-Gen., Austria, 1982–87. Dist. Fellow, Inst. of Dirs in NZ, 2003; FNZIM 1982. JP NZ 1972. Hon. DSc Massey, 1993. NZ Business Hall of Fame, 2010. *Recreations:* fishing, shooting, boxing. *Address:* The Grove, 189 Main Road, Waikanae, New Zealand. *T:* and *Fax:* (4) 2936373. *Clubs:* Wellington (Wellington); Levin (Levin).

See also Dame G. C. Weir.

WEIR, Stuart Peter; Senior Research Fellow, Human Rights Centre, Essex University, since 1991 (Director, 1991–2009, Associate Director, 2009–12, Democratic Audit); Visiting Professor, Essex University, since 1999; *b* 13 Oct. 1938; *e s* of Robert Hendry Weir, CB and Edna Frances (*née* Lewis); *m* 1st, 1963, Doffy Burnham; two *s*; 2nd, 1987, Elizabeth Ellen Bisset; one *s* two *d*. *Educ:* Peter Symonds Sch., Winchester; Brasenose Coll., Oxford (BA Hons Modern History). Feature writer, Oxford Mail, 1964–67; diarist, The Times, 1967–71; Dir, Citizens Rights Office, CPAG, 1971–75; Founding Editor, Roof magazine, 1975–77; Dep. Editor, New Society, 1977–84; Editor: New Socialist, 1984–87; New Statesman, 1987–88, New Statesman and Society, 1988–90. WEA and Adult Educn lectr, 1969–73. Founder Chair, Family Rights Gp, 1975; Founder, Charter 88, 1988, Exec. Mem., 1988–95 and 1997–; Chm., Charter 88 Trust, 1991–92. Associate Consultant, British Council, 1997–2001; Consultant, State of Democracy Project, Inst. for Democracy and Electoral Assistance, Stockholm, 1998–2002. Policy Vice Chair, Unlock Democracy, 2007–. Member: Exec., CPAG and Finer Jt Action Cttee, 1970–84; (Founding), Labour Co-ordinating Cttee, 1979. Active in anti-racist and community groups, Oxford and Hackney, 1964–72; Mem. (Lab), London Bor. of Hackney Council, 1972–76. Mem., Human Rights Commn, Helsinki Citizens Assembly, 1990–92; Sen. Internat. Facilitator, EU Democracy and Governance Project, Namibia, 1994–95; Facilitator, Parly Reform Project, Zimbabwe, 1996–98; Head, UNDP Parly Assessment, Zimbabwe, 2002–03; consultant on Parly reform, Malawi, 2004–06. Special Advr, Public Admin Select Cttee, H of C, 2000–01, 2002–03. Trustee: Civil Liberties Trust, 1990–97; The Scarman Trust, 1997–99. Columnist: Community Care, 1973–75; London Daily News, 1987; script consultant: Spongers, BBC TV, 1977; United Kingdom, BBC TV, 1980–81; editorial consultant: The People's Parliament, 1994–96; C4 Dispatches, Behind Closed Doors, 1995. *Publications:* (contrib.) Towards Better Social Services, 1973; Social Insecurity, 1974; Supplementary Benefits: a social worker's guide, 1975; (ed and contrib.) Manifesto, 1981; (contrib.) The Other Britain, 1982; (contrib.) Consuming Secrets, 1982; (with W. Hall) EGO-TRIP, 1994; (with W. Hall) Behind Closed Doors, 1995; Consolidating Parliamentary Democracy in Namibia, 1995; (with F. Klug and K. Starmer) The Three Pillars of Liberty: political rights and freedoms in the UK, 1996; (jtly) Making Votes Count, 1997; (with D. Beetham) Political Power and Democratic Control in Britain, 1998; (jtly) Voices of the People, 2001, 2nd edn 2005; (jtly) The IDEA Handbook on Democracy Assessment, 2001; (jtly) The State of Democracy, 2002; (jtly) Democracy Under Blair, 2003; (jtly) Not in Our Name, 2005; Unequal Britain: the human rights route to social justice, 2006; (jtly) The Rules of the Game: terrorism, community and human rights, 2007; (jtly) Power and Participation in Modern Britain, 2008; (jtly) Assessing the Quality of Democracy: a practical guide, 2008; The Unspoken Constitution, 2009; (jtly) Fairness Review of Cambridge, 2015. *Recreations:* active in community politics, in Cambridge, and with Unlock Democracy; cooking, football, family.

WEISKRANTZ, Lawrence, FRS 1980; Professor of Psychology, Oxford University, 1967–93, now Emeritus; Fellow, Magdalen College, Oxford, 1967–93, now Emeritus; *b* 28 March 1926; *s* of Dr Benjamin Weiskrantz and Rose (*née* Rifkin); *m* 1954, Barbara Collins; one *s* one *d*. *Educ:* Girard College; Swarthmore; Univs of Oxford and Harvard. Part-time Lectr, Tufts University, 1952; Research Assoc., Inst. of Living, 1952–55; Sen. Postdoctoral Fellow, US Nat. Res. Council, 1955–56; Research Assoc., Cambridge Univ., 1956–61; Asst Dir of Research, Cambridge Univ., 1961–66; Reader in Physiological Psychology, Cambridge Univ., 1966–67. Dep. Editor, Brain, 1981–89; Co-Editor, Oxford Psychology Series, 1979–. Member: US Nat. Acad. of Scis, 1987; Council, Royal Soc., 1988–89. Ferrier Lectr, Royal Soc., 1989; Hughlings Jackson Lectr/Medallist, RSM, 1990; Camp Lectr, Stanford Univ., 1997; Heisenberg Lectr, Bavarian Acad. of Sci., 1998. Kenneth Craik Research Award, St John's Coll., Cambridge, 1975–76; Williams James Award, Amer. Psychol Soc., 1992; McGovern Prize Lecture, AAAS, 2002. *Publications:* (jtly) Analysis of Behavioural Change, 1967; The Neuropsychology of Cognitive Function, 1982; Animal Intelligence, 1985; Blindsight, 1986; Thought Without Language, 1988; Consciousness Lost and Found, 1997; articles in Science, Nature, Quarterly Jl of Experimental Psychology, Jl of

Comparative and Physiological Psychology, Animal Behaviour, Brain. *Recreations:* music, walking. *Address:* Department of Experimental Psychology, Tinbergen Building, 9 South Parks Road, Oxford OX1 3UD.

WEISMAN, Malcolm, OBE 1997; Barrister-at-law; a Recorder of the Crown Court, since 1980; *s* of David and Jeanie Pearl Weisman; *m* 1958, Rosalie, *d* of Dr and Mrs A. Spiro; two *s*. *Educ:* Harrogate Grammar Sch.; Parmiter's Sch.; London School of Economics; St Catherine's Coll., Oxford (MA). Blackstone Pupillage Prize. Chaplain (Sqdn Ldr), Royal Air Force, 1956; called to Bar, Middle Temple, 1961; Head of Chambers, 1982–90. Asst Comr of Parly Boundaries, 1976–85; Special Adjudicator, Immigration Appeals, 1998–. Mem., Bar Disciplinary Cttee, Inner Temple, 1990–. Senior Jewish Chaplain, HM Forces, 1972; Religious advisor to small congregations, and Hon. Chaplain, Oxford, Cambridge and new universities, 1963–; Chm. and Sec.-Gen., 1981–92, Pres., 1993–, Allied Air Forces in Europe Chief of Chaplains Cttee; Sec., Former Chiefs of Chaplains Assoc., 1994; Mem. Exec., USA Jewish Chaplains Assoc., 1992–; Member: MoD Adv. Cttee on Chaplaincy, 1972–; Exec. Council, CCJ, 1998–; Exec. Council, Three Faiths Forum, 1998–. Mem., Cabinet of the Chief Rabbi, 1967–; Hon. Chaplain to: Lord Mayor of Westminster, 1992–93; Mayor of Barnet, 1994–95; Assoc. of Jewish Ex-Servicemen and Women, 1999–; Chaplain to Mayor: of Redbridge, 2005–06; of Montgomery, 2006–07; Officiating Chaplain to the Military, 2009; Chaplain to: HM Prisons, 1960s–; US Forces in UK, 2010–. Hon. Vice-Pres., Monash Br., RBL, 1992–. Mem., Senior Common Room, Essex, Kent and Lancaster Univs, 1964–; Fellow, Centre for Theol. and Soc. (formerly Inst. of Theology), Univ. of Essex, 1992– (Mem. Council, 2000–). Member of Court: Univ. of Lancaster, 1970–; Univ. of Kent, 1970–; Warwick Univ., 1983–; Univ. of East Anglia, 1985–; Essex Univ., 1990–; Sussex Univ., 1992–; Mem. Council, Selly Oak Coll., Birmingham, 1992–; Gov., 1980–, Trustee, 1994–, Parmiter's Sch.; Gov., Carmel Coll., 1995–98. Trustee: B'nai B'rith Music Fest., 1995–; Internat. Multi-faith Chaplaincy, Univ. of Derby, 2000. Patron, Jewish Nat. Fund (formerly Holy Land Trust), 1993–. Hon. Fellow, Univ. of Lancaster, 2006. B'nai B'rith Award for Outstanding Communal Service, 1980; Chief Rabbi's Award for Excellence, 1993; US Jewish Military Special Chaplains' Chaplain Award, 1998; Inter-faith Gold Medallion, Internat. CCJ, 2001; Outstanding Leadership Award, United Synagogue Rabbinic Conf., 2005; Special Award, Canadian Military Chaplains, 2008; Peterborough Inter-faith Award, 2009, 2011, 2013, 2015. Editor, Menorah Jl, 1972–. *Recreations:* travelling, reading, doing nothing. *Address:* 1 Gray's Inn Square, WC1R 5AA. *T:* and *Fax:* (020) 7405 0001.

WEISS, Althea McNish; *see* McNish, A. M.

WEISS, John Roger, CB 2004; Deputy Chief Executive and Member of Management Board, Export Credits Guarantee Department, 2004–05; *b* 27 Dec. 1944; *s* of Ernst Weiss, Basel, and Betsy Weiss (*née* Hallam); *m* 1967, Hazel Kay Lang. *Educ:* St Helen's Coll., Thames Ditton. Tax Officer, Inland Revenue, 1961–64; ECGD, 1964–2005: Dir, Asset Management Gp, 1990–95; Gp Dir, Underwriting, 1995–2001; Dir, Business Gp, 2001–04. *Recreations:* music, walking. *Address:* 17 Portland Square, E1W 2QR.

WEISS, Julian; *see* Huck, S.

WEISS, Prof. Nigel Oscar, FRS 1992; Professor of Mathematical Astrophysics, Cambridge University, 1987–2004, now Emeritus; Fellow of Clare College, Cambridge, since 1965; *b* 16 Dec. 1936; *s* of Oscar and Molly Weiss; *m* 1968, Judith Elizabeth Martin; one *s* two *d*. *Educ:* Hilton College, Natal; Rugby School; Clare College, Cambridge (BA 1957; PhD 1962; ScD 1993). Research Associate, UKAEA Culham Lab., 1962–65; Cambridge University: Lectr, Dept of Applied Maths and Theoretical Physics, 1965–79; Reader in Astrophysics, 1979–87; Sen. Fellow, SERC, 1987–92; Chm., Sch. of Physical Scis, 1993–98. Visiting Professor: Sch. of Math. Scis, QMC, then QMW, London, 1986–96; Dept of Applied Maths, Univ. of Leeds, 2001–07; temporary appointments: MIT; Max Planck Inst. für Astrophysik, Munich; Nat. Solar Observatory, New Mexico; Harvard-Smithsonian Center for Astrophysics; Sci. Univ. of Tokyo; Ecole Normale Supérieure, Paris. Pres., Royal Astronomical Soc., 2000–02. Gold Medal, RAS, 2007. *Publications:* (with J. H. Thomas) Sunspots and Starspots, 2008; (with M. R. E. Proctor) Magneto Convection, 2014; papers on solar and stellar magnetic fields, astrophysical and geophysical fluid dynamics and nonlinear systems. *Recreation:* travel. *Address:* Department of Applied Mathematics and Theoretical Physics, Centre for Mathematical Sciences, Wilberforce Road, Cambridge CB3 0WA. *T:* (01223) 337910; 10 Lansdowne Road, Cambridge CB3 0EU. *T:* (01223) 355032.

WEISS, Prof. Robert Anthony, (Robin), PhD; FRCPath; FRS 1997; Professor of Viral Oncology, University College London, 1999–2012, now Professor Emeritus; *b* 20 Feb. 1940; *s* of Hans Weiss and Stefanie Löwinsohn; *m* 1964, Margaret Rose D'Costa; two *d*. *Educ:* University College London (BSc, PhD; Fellow, 2006). Lecturer in Embryology, University Coll. London, 1963–70; Eleanor Roosevelt Internat. Cancer Research Fellow, Univ. of Washington, Seattle, 1970–71; Visiting Associate Prof., Microbiology, Univ. of Southern California, 1971–72; Staff Scientist, Imperial Cancer Research Fund Laboratories, 1972–80, Gustav Stern Award in Virology, 1973; Institute of Cancer Research: Dir, 1980–89; Prof. of Viral Oncology, 1984–98; Dir of Res., 1990–96; Hon. Fellow, 1999. Researching into viruses causing cancer and AIDS. Chm., Governing Body, Inst. of Animal Health, 2003–06. Pres., Soc. for Gen. Microbiol., 2006–09. For. Associate, US Nat. Acad. of Scis, 2013. Founder FMedSci 1998. Hon. Fellow, LSHTM, 2003. Hon. FRCP 1998. Hon. MD Uppsala, 2003. *Publications:* RNA Tumour Viruses, 1982, 2nd edn (2 vols) 1985; various articles on cell biology, virology and genetics. *Recreations:* music, natural history. *Address:* Division of Infection and Immunity, Cruciform Building 1.3, University College London, Gower Street, WC1E 6BT. *T:* (020) 3108 2137. *E:* r.weiss@ucl.ac.uk.

WEISSBERG, Prof. Peter Leslie, MD; FRCP, FMedSci; Medical Director, British Heart Foundation, since 2004; Fellow of Wolfson College, Cambridge University, since 1993; *b* 4 Oct. 1951; *s* of Edmund and Dorcas Alfreda Weissberg; *m* 1976, Alison (*née* Prowse), MB ChB; two *s*. *Educ:* Warwick Sch.; Univ. of Birmingham (MB ChB Hons 1976; MD 1985); MA Cantab 2009. MRCP 1978, FRCP 1992; FRCPE 1996. Lectr in Cardiovascular Medicine, Univ. of Birmingham, 1983–88; MRC Res. Fellow, Baker Inst., Melbourne, Australia, 1985–87; University of Cambridge: BHF Sen. Res. Fellow, 1988–92; Lectr in Medicine, 1993–94; BHF Prof. of Cardiovascular Medicine, 1994–2004. FESC 1994; FMedSci 1999. Hon. DSc Birmingham, 2013. *Publications:* numerous contribs to sci. jls. *Address:* British Heart Foundation, Greater London House, 180 Hampstead Road, NW1 7AW. *T:* (020) 7554 0340.

WEISSELBERG, Tom; QC 2014; *b* London, 3 Feb. 1971; *s* of Kiffer and Alison Weisselberg; *m* 1998, Kate Douglas; one *s* one *d*. *Educ:* Westminster Sch.; Merton Coll., Oxford (MA 1st Cl. 1993); City Univ. (CPE 1994). Called to the Bar, Inner Temple, 1995; in practice as barrister, 1996–, specialising in commercial and public law. *Recreations:* walking, theatre, opera, family. *Address:* Blackstone Chambers, Blackstone House, Temple, EC4Y 9BW. *T:* (020) 7583 1770. *E:* clerks@blackstonechambers.com.

WEITZENHOFFER, (Aaron) Max; producer; President: Weitzenhoffer Productions, New York and London, since 1965; Weitzenhoffer Theatres Ltd, since 2001; Chairman, Nimax Theatres Ltd, since 2005; *b* 30 Oct. 1939; *s* of Aaron and Clara Weitzenhoffer; *m* 1st, Frances (*d* 1991); 2nd, 2000, Ayako Takanashi; one *s* one *d*. *Educ:* Univ. of Oklahoma (BFA Drama 1962). Productions include: Dracula, NY (Tony Award), 1978; Song and Dance, NY, 1985; The Will Rogers Follies (Tony Award), NY, 1991; Defending the Caveman, Apollo (Olivier Award), 2000; Feel Good, Garrick, 2001; One Flew over the Cuckoo's Nest, Gielgud, 2004; Who's Afraid of Virginia Woolf, Apollo, 2006; A Moon for the Misbegotten, NY, 2007; A Little Night Music, NY, 2010; Long Day's Journey into Night, Apollo (Olivier Award), 2012. Member: Amer. League of Theatres and Producers, 1977–; SOLT, 2001–. Regent, Univ. of Oklahoma, 2003–. Hon. DHL Oklahoma, 2000. *Recreation:* trying to keep up with my children. *Address:* Nimax Theatres Ltd, 11 Maiden Lane, WC2E 7NA. *T:* (020) 7395 0780, *Fax:* (020) 7240 4540. *E:* mweitzenhoffer@cox.net. *Clubs:* Friars, Century Association, Players (New York).

WEITZMAN, Peter; QC 1973; a Recorder of the Crown Court, 1974–98; *b* 20 June 1926; *s* of late David Weitzman, QC, and Fanny Weitzman (*née* Galinski); *m* 1954, Anne Mary Larkam; two *s* two *d*. *Educ:* Cheltenham Coll.; Christ Church, Oxford (Gibbs Schol. in Mod. Hist., Newdigate Prize, 1949; BA 1950). Lt RA, 1945–48. Called to Bar, Gray's Inn, 1952; Bencher, 1981; Leader, Midland and Oxford Circuit, 1988–92 (Dep. Leader, 1985–88). Mem., Senate of Inns of Court, 1980–81, 1984–92. Member: Mental Health Review Tribunal, 1986–98; Criminal Injuries Compensation Bd, 1986–2000; Criminal Injuries Compensation Appeals Panel, 2000–02. *Recreation:* hedging and ditching. *Address:* 21 St James's Gardens, W11 4RE; Little Leigh, Kingsbridge, Devon TQ7 4AG.

See also T. E. B. Weitzman.

WEITZMAN, Thomas Edward Benjamin; QC 2003; a Recorder, since 2009; *b* 11 Sept. 1959; *s* of Peter Weitzman, *qv*; *m* 1995, Maria Villegas; one *s* one *d*. *Educ:* St Paul's Sch.; New Coll., Oxford (BA Hons). Called to the Bar, Gray's Inn, 1984, Bencher, 2008; in practice, specialising in commercial, insurance and reinsurance and professional negligence law. *Recreations:* looking, reading, walking. *Address:* 3 Verulam Buildings, Gray's Inn, WC1R 5NT. *T:* (020) 7831 8441.

WELANDER, Rev. Canon David Charles St Vincent; Canon Residentiary and Librarian, Gloucester Cathedral, 1975–91, now Emeritus; *b* 22 Jan. 1925; *s* of late Ernest Sven Alexis Welander, Orebro and Uppsala, Sweden, and Louisa Georgina Downes Welander (*née* Panter); *m* 1952, Nancy O'Rorke Stanley; two *s* three *d*. *Educ:* Unthank Coll., Norwich; London Univ. (BD 1947, Rubie Hebrew Prize 1947); ALCD (1st Cl.) 1947; Toronto Univ., 1947–48 (Hon. Mem. Alumni, Wycliffe Coll., 1948). FSA 1981. Deacon 1948, Priest 1949; Asst Curate, Holy Trinity, Norwich, 1948–51; Chaplain and Tutor, London Coll. of Divinity, 1952–56; Vicar: of Iver, Bucks, 1956–62; of Christ Church, Cheltenham, 1963–75; Rural Dean of Cheltenham, 1973–75. Member: Council, St Paul's and St Mary's Colls of Educn, Cheltenham, 1963–78; Council, Malvern Girls' Coll., 1982–91; Bishops' Cttee on Inspections of Theol Colls, 1967–81; Sen. Inspector of Theol Colls, 1970–84; Mem., Gen. Synod of C of E, 1970–85. Mem., Cathedrals Cttee, English Heritage, 1990–94. Trustee: Church Patronage Trust, 1969–78; Stained Glass Mus., 1986–95. *Publications:* History of Iver, 1954; Gloucester Cathedral, 1979; The Stained Glass of Gloucester Cathedral, 1984; Gloucester Cathedral: its history, art and architecture, 1990; Gloucester Cathedral, A Visitor's Handbook, 2001; contrib. Expository Times, etc. *Recreations:* walking, church architecture, music. *Address:* 1 Sandpits Lane, Sherston Magna, near Malmesbury, Wilts SN16 0NN. *T:* (01666) 840180.

WELBANK, (John) Michael, MBE 2014; RIBA; architect and planner, retired; *b* London, 2 Aug. 1930; *s* of William Stephenson Welbank and Alice Mary Welbank (*née* Robson); *m* 1952, Alison Mary Hopkins; two *s* one *d*. *Educ:* Highgate Sch.; University Coll., London (BA; DipTP). RIBA 1957; MRTPI 1959. Planning Officer, LCC, 1957–59; Architect, Min. of Educn, 1959–64; Associate, Shankland Cox Associates, 1965–71; Partner, Shankland Cox Partnership, 1972–89; Dir, EntecUK, 1990–97. Vis. Prof., Oxford Brookes Univ., 1992–97. Churchill Travelling Fellow, 1989. Mem., Envmtl Audit Bd, Northumbrian Water Gp, 1990–95. Chm. Council, British Consultants Bureau, 1985. Pres., RTPI, 1992. Governor: Mus. of London, 2008–; GSMD, 2008–. Common Councilman, City of London Corp., 2005– (Chm., Planning and Transportation Cttee, 2014–). Master, Chartered Architects' Co., 1994. FRSA. *Recreations:* hill walking, watercolour painting. *Address:* 1 The Porticos, 53–55 Belsize Avenue, NW3 4BN. *T:* (020) 7431 6789. *Club:* Reform.

WELBY, Sir Bruno; *see* Welby, Sir R. B. G.

WELBY, Most Rev. and Rt Hon. Justin Portal; *see* Canterbury, Archbishop of.

WELBY, Sir (Richard) Bruno (Gregory), 7th Bt *cr* 1801; *b* 11 March 1928; *s* of Sir Oliver Charles Earle Welby, 6th Bt, TD, and Barbara Angela Mary Lind (*d* 1983), *d* of late John Duncan Gregory, CB, CMG; *S* father, 1977; *m* 1952, Jane Biddulph, *y d* of late Ralph Wilfred Hodder-Williams, MC; three *s* one *d*. *Educ:* Eton; Christ Church, Oxford (BA 1950). *Heir: s* Charles William Hodder Welby [*b* 6 May 1953; *m* 1978, Suzanna, *o d* of Major Ian Stuart-Routledge, Harston Hall, Grantham; three *d*]. *Address:* Denton Manor, Grantham, Lincs NG32 1JX.

WELCH, Andrew Richard; theatre producer; Managing Director, Andrew Welch Ltd, since 2005; *b* 5 Feb. 1949; *s* of Richard Joseph Welch and Ruth Jordan Welch; *m* 1980, Louisa Mary Emerson; two *s*. *Educ:* Bedford Sch., Bedford; UC of Swansea, Univ. of Wales (BA). Dir, Arts Centre, Univ. of Warwick, 1977–81; General Manager: Hong Kong Arts Centre, 1981–84; Theatre Royal, Plymouth, 1984–90; Producer, Carnival Films and Theatre Ltd, 1990–95; Chief Exec., Theatre of Comedy Ltd, 1996–98; Fest., subseq. Theatre, Dir, Chichester Fest. Th., 1998–2002; Gen. Dir, Dance Umbrella, 2002–04 (Mem. Bd, 1985–88). Chm., Michael Clark Dance Co., 2003–09. FRSA 2004. Hon. MA UC Chichester, 2002. *Recreations:* music, walking. *Address:* 12 Westwood Road, SW13 0LA. *T:* (020) 8876 9292. *Club:* Garrick.

WELCH, Prof. Graham Frederick, PhD; Professor of Music Education, Institute of Education, University College London (formerly Institute of Education, University of London), since 2001; *b* London, 25 Nov. 1947; *s* of George and Joyce Welch; *m* 1st Ann Whitwell (marr. diss.); two *s*; 2nd, 2001, Sally Thompson; one *s*. *Educ:* Froebel Inst., London (BEd, Cert Ed); Inst. of Educn, Univ. of London (MA; PhD 1983). Teacher: St Mary's Primary Sch., 1971–73; Smallwood Junior Sch., 1973–76; Dep. Headteacher, Beatrix Potter Primary Sch., 1976–84; Principal Lectr in Educn, Bristol Poly., 1985–89; Dean and Dir of Educnl Res., Roehampton Inst., later Univ. of Surrey, Roehampton, 1989–2001. Chair, Soc. for Educn, Music and Psychol. Res., 2000–. Mem., Rev. Coll. for Music, AHRC, 2007–. Pres., ISME, 2010–12. Consultant to govt agencies in UK, Italy, UAE, Ukraine, Argentina and S Africa. Arts and Health Award (jtly), RSPH, 2011. *Publications:* The Misunderstanding of Music, 2001 (Greek edn 2008); (ed with L. Thurman) Bodymind and Voice: foundations of voice education, 2000; (ed with G. McPherson) The Oxford Handbook of Music Education, 2012; over 300 academic pubns. *Recreations:* walking, gardening. *Address:* 2 Backfields, Rectory Lane, Winchelsea, E Sussex TN36 4AB. *T:* (01797) 227750, 07785 535440. *E:* g.welch@ioe.ac.uk.

WELCH, Sir John K.; *see* Kemp-Welch.

WELCH, Sir John (Reader), 2nd Bt *cr* 1957; Partner, Wedlake Bell, 1972–96; Chairman, John Fairfax (UK) Ltd, 1977–90; *b* 26 July 1933; *s* of Sir (George James) Cullum Welch, 1st Bt, OBE, MC, and Gertrude Evelyn Sladin Welch (*d* 1966); *S* father, 1980; *m* 1962, Margaret Kerry, *o d* of late K. Douglass, Killara, NSW; one *s* twin *d*. *Educ:* Marlborough College; Hertford Coll., Oxford (MA). National service in Royal Signals, 1952–54 (2nd Lt; GSM with Canal Zone Clasp); TA, 1954–62 (Capt., Middlesex Yeomanry). Admitted a solicitor, 1960. Partner, Bell Brodrick & Gray, 1961–71. Ward Clerk of Walbrook Ward, City of London, 1961–74, Common Councilman, 1975–86 (Chm., Planning and Communications Cttee,

1981, 1982); Chm., Walbrook Ward Club, 1978–79; Hon. Solicitor, 1983–90, Pres., 1986–87, City Livery Club; Registrar of Archdeaconry of London, 1964–99. Governor: City of London Sch. for Girls, 1977–82; Haberdashers' Aske's Schs, Elstree, 1981–85 and 1990–91. FRSA. Liveryman, Haberdashers' Co., 1955 (Court of Assistants, 1973; Master, 1990–91, now Past Master Emeritus); Freeman, Parish Clerks' Co. (Master, 1967, now Past Master Emeritus); Clerk, Furniture Makers' Co., 1963–66. Chm., Cttee of Management, London Homes for the Elderly, 1980–90; Pres., Freemasons' Grand Charity, 1985–95; Sen. Grand Warden, United Grand Lodge of England, 1998–2000. CStJ 1981. *Recreations:* piano, walking. *Heir: s* James Douglass Cullum Welch, *b* 10 Nov. 1973. *Address:* 28 Rivermead Court, Ranelagh Gardens, SW6 3RU. *Club:* Hurlingham.

WELCH, Ven. Stephan John; Archdeacon of Middlesex, since 2006; *b* 16 Oct. 1950; *s* of Ernest Ian Welch and Regina Welch; *m* 1990, Jennifer Clare (*née* Gallop); three *s*. *Educ:* Hull Univ. (BA French Lang. and Lit. 1974); Birmingham Univ. (Postgrad. Dip. in Theol. 1976); London Univ. (MTh 1998). Ordained deacon, 1977, priest, 1978; Curate, Christ Church, Waltham Cross, 1977–80; Priest-in-charge: Reculver, 1980–86; St Bartholomew, Herne Bay, 1982–86; Vicar: Reculver and St Bartholomew, Herne Bay, 1986–92; Hurley and Stubbings, 1992–2000; Priest-in-charge, St Peter, Hammersmith, 2000–06. Area Dean, Hammersmith and Fulham, 2001–06. *Recreations:* French language and literature, French wine, sailing, patristic theology. *Address:* 98 Dukes Avenue, W4 2AF. *T:* (020) 8742 8308. *E:* archdeacon.middlesex@london.anglican.org.

WELCHMAN, His Honour Charles Stuart; a Circuit Judge, 1998–2013; *b* 7 April 1943; *s* of late Edward James Welchman and Marjorie (*née* Williams, later Parsons); *m* 1972, Rosemary Ann Fison, *d* of late Dr Thomas Notley Fison and of Nancy Jean Laird Fison; one *s* one *d*. *Educ:* W Buckland Sch.; Exeter Tech. Coll.; University Coll. London (LLB Hons 1965). Called to the Bar, Gray's Inn, 1966 (Mould Scholar 1966), Bencher, 2011; an Asst Recorder, 1990–94; a Recorder, 1994–98. Mem., Restricted Patients Panel, Mental Health Review Tribunal, 2002–13. Mem., Exec. Cttee, Professional Negligence Bar Assoc., 1996–98. Contested (L): Esher, Oct. 1974, 1979; Putney, 1982. Best Individual Speaker, Observer Mace Nat. Debating Competition, 1965. *Recreations:* inland waterways, theatre, jazz. *Address:* 21 Winsham Grove, SW11 6NB. *Clubs:* National Liberal; Surrey County Cricket.

WELCHMAN, Zoe; *see* Kourtzi, Z.

WELD FORESTER, family name of **Baron Forester**.

WELDON, Sir Anthony (William), 9th Bt *cr* 1723; *b* 11 May 1947; *s* of Sir Thomas Brian Weldon, 8th Bt, and Marie Isobel (who *m* 1984, 6th Earl Cathcart, CB, DSO, MC), *d* of Hon. William Joseph French; *S* father, 1979; *m* 1980, Mrs Amanda Wigan (marr. diss. 2006), *d* of Major Geoffrey and Hon. Mrs North; two *d*. *Educ:* Sherborne. Formerly Lieutenant, Irish Guards. Dir, Bene Factum Publishing Ltd, 1983–; Asst Dir and Gen. Manager, ViRSA Educnl Trust, 2003–05. *Publications:* (ed) Breakthrough: handling career opportunities and changes, 1994; (jtly) Numeroids: any number of things you didn't know, 2008; Words of War: speeches that inspired heroic deeds, 2012. *Recreations:* country sports, cricket, books, champagne. *Heir: cousin* Kevin Nicholas Weldon [*b* 19 April 1951; *m* 1973, Catherine Main; one *s*]. *Clubs:* White's, Pratt's, Stranded Whales.

WELDON, Duncan Clark; theatrical producer; Chairman and Managing Director, Duncan C. Weldon Productions Ltd, since 1964; *b* 19 March 1941; *s* of Clarence Weldon and Margaret Mary Andrew; *m* 1967, Helen Shapiro; *m* 1974, Janet Mahoney; one *d*; *m* 2005, Ann Sidney. *Educ:* King George V School, Southport. Formerly a photographer; first stage production, A Funny Kind of Evening, with David Kossoff, Theatre Royal, Bath, 1965; co-founder, Triumph Entertainment Ltd, 2000; Director: Triumph Proscenium Productions Ltd, 1994–; Malvern Festival Theatre Trust Ltd, 1997–; Artistic Dir, Chichester Festival Theatre, 1995–97. First London production, Tons of Money, Mayfair Theatre, 1968; productions in the West End include: When We are Married, 1970 (also 1996); The Chalk Garden, Big Bad Mouse, The Wizard of Oz, 1971; Lord Arthur Savile's Crime, Bunny, The Wizard of Oz, 1972; Mother Adam, Grease, The King and I, 1973; Dead Easy, 1974; The Case in Question, Hedda Gabler (RSC), Dad's Army, Betzi, On Approval, 1975; 13 Rue de l'Amour, A Bedful of Foreigners, Three Sisters, The Seagull, Fringe Benefits, The Circle, 1976; Separate Tables, Stevie, Hedda Gabler, On Approval, The Good Woman of Setzuan, Rosmersholm, Laburnum Grove, The Apple Cart, 1977; Waters of the Moon, Kings and Clowns, The Travelling Music Show, A Family, Look After Lulu, The Millionairess, 1978; The Crucifer of Blood, 1979; Reflections, Rattle of a Simple Man, The Last of Mrs Cheyney, Early Days, 1980; Virginia, Overheard, Dave Allen, Worzel Gummidge, 1981; Murder In Mind, Hobson's Choice (also 1995), A Coat of Varnish, Captain Brassbound's Conversion, Design for Living, Uncle Vanya (also 1996), Key for Two, The Rules of the Game, Man and Superman, 1982; The School for Scandal, DASH, Heartbreak House (also 1992), Call Me Madam, Romantic Comedy, Liza Minnelli, Beethoven's Tenth, Edmund Kean, Fiddler on the Roof, A Patriot for Me, Cowardice, Great and Small, The Cherry Orchard, Dial 'M' for Murder, Dear Anyone, The Sleeping Prince, Hi-De-Hi!, 1983; Hello, Dolly!, The Aspern Papers, Strange Interlude, Serjeant Musgrave's Dance, Aren't We All?, American Buffalo, The Way of the World, Extremities, 1984; The Wind in the Willows, The Lonely Road, The Caine Mutiny Court-Martial, Other Places, Old Times (also 1995), The Corn is Green, Waste, Strippers, Guys and Dolls, Sweet Bird of Youth, Interpreters, Fatal Attraction, The Scarlet Pimpernel, 1985; The Apple Cart, Across From the Garden of Allah, Antony and Cleopatra, The Taming of the Shrew, Circe & Bravo, Annie Get Your Gun, Long Day's Journey Into Night, Rookery Nook, Breaking the Code, Mr and Mrs Nobody, 1986; A Piece of My Mind, Court in the Act!, Canaries Sometimes Sing, Kiss Me Kate (RSC), Melon, Portraits, Groucho: a Life In Review, A Man for All Seasons, You Never Can Tell, Babes in the Wood, 1987; A Touch of the Poet, The Deep Blue Sea, The Admirable Crichton, The Secret of Sherlock Holmes, A Walk in the Woods, Richard II, Orpheus Descending, 1988; Richard III (also RSC, 1999), The Royal Baccarat Scandal, Ivanov, Much Ado About Nothing, The Merchant of Venice, Frankie & Johnny, Veterans Day, Another Time, The Baker's Wife, London Assurance, 1989; Salome (RNT), Bent (RNT), An Evening with Peter Ustinov (also 1994), The Wild Duck, Henry IV, Kean, Love Letters (also 1999), Time and the Conways, 1990; The Homecoming, The Philanthropist, The Caretaker, Becket, Tovarich, The Cabinet Minister, 1991; Talking Heads (also 1996), A Woman of No Importance (RSC), Lost in Yonkers, Trelawny of the "Wells", Cyrano de Bergerac, Hamlet, 1992; Relative Values, Two Gentlemen of Verona, Macbeth, 1993; Travesties (RSC), A Month in the Country, Rope, Arcadia (RNT), Home, Saint Joan, Lady Windermere's Fan, The Rivals, The Clandestine Marriage, Peer Gynt, 1994; Dangerous Corner, Cell Mates, The Duchess of Malfi, Taking Sides, Communicating Doors, The Hothouse, 1995; The Cherry Orchard (RSC), 1996; Live and Kidding, The Herbal Bed (RSC), Life Support, A Letter of Resignation, The Magistrate, Electra, 1997; New Edna—The Spectacle, Rent, 1998; The Prisoner of Second Avenue, Hay Fever, The Importance of Being Earnest (also 2001), Collected Stories, 1999; Enigmatic Variations, Napoleon, God Only Knows, 2000; Peggy Sue Got Married, Private Lives, My One and Only, 2002; The Tempest, Coriolanus (RSC), The Merry Wives of Windsor (RSC), The Master Builder, Thoroughly Modern Millie, 2003; Rattle of a Simple Man, Suddenly Last Summer, 2004; The Birthday Party, The Philadelphia Story, As You Desire Me, 2005; Stones in his Pockets, 2006; The Last Confession, Macbeth, Nicholas Nickleby, 2007; Waiting for Godot, Taking Sides, Collaboration, 2009; Private Lives, When We Are Married, 2010; Blithe Spirit, Pygmalion, Rosencrantz and Guildenstern are Dead, The Tempest, 2011; presented on Broadway: Brief Lives, 1974; Edmund Kean, Heartbreak House, 1983; Beethoven's Tenth, 1984; Strange Interlude, Aren't We All?, 1985; Wild Honey, 1986; Blithe Spirit, Pygmalion, Breaking the Code, 1987; Orpheus Descending, The Merchant of Venice, 1989; Taking Sides, 1996; Electra, 1999; Stones in his Pockets, 2001; Private Lives, 2002; Macbeth, 2008; has also presented in Europe, Australia, Canada and Hong Kong. *Television:* Co-producer, Into the Blue, 1997. *Address:* Triumph Entertainment, 16 Westbourne Park Road, W2 5PH.

WELDON, Fay, CBE 2001; writer; Professor of Creative Writing, Bath Spa University, since 2012; *b* 22 Sept. 1931; *d* of Frank Birkinshaw and Margaret Jepson; *m* 1962, Ron Weldon (*d* 1994); four *s*; *m* 1994, Nicolas Fox. *Educ:* Hampstead Girls' High Sch.; St Andrews Univ. (MA 1952). Has written or adapted numerous television and radio plays, dramatizations, and series, and ten stage plays. Prof. of Creative Writing, Brunel Univ., 2007–12. Chm. of Judges, Booker McConnell Prize, 1983. Hon. DLitt St Andrews, 1990; Hon. Dr: Birmingham; Worcester; Bath; Connecticut. *Libretto:* A Small Green Space, 1989. *Publications:* The Fat Woman's Joke, 1967; Down Among the Women, 1972; Female Friends, 1975; Remember Me, 1976; Little Sisters, 1977 (as Words of Advice, NY, 1977); Praxis, 1978 (Booker Prize Nomination); Puffball, 1980; Watching Me, Watching You (short stories), 1981; The President's Child, 1982; The Life and Loves of a She-Devil, 1984 (televised, 1986; filmed as She-Devil, 1990); Letters to Alice—on First Reading Jane Austen, 1984; Polaris and other Stories, 1985; Rebecca West, 1985; The Shrapnel Academy, 1986; Heart of the Country, 1987 (televised, 1987); The Hearts and Lives of Men, 1987; The Rules of Life, 1987; Leader of the Band, 1988; (for children) Wolf the Mechanical Dog, 1989; The Cloning of Joanna May, 1989 (televised, 1992); (for children) Party Puddle, 1989; Darcy's Utopia, 1990; (contrib.) Storia 4: Green, 1990; Moon over Minneapolis or Why She Couldn't Stay (short stories), 1991; Life Force, 1992; Growing Rich, 1992; Affliction, 1994; Splitting, 1995; (with David Bailey) The Lady is a Tramp: portraits of Catherine Bailey, 1995; Wicked Women (short stories), 1995; Worst Fears, 1996; (for children) Nobody Likes Me!, 1997; Big Women, 1998 (televised, 1998); A Hard Time to Be a Father (short stories), 1998; Godless in Eden: a book of essays, 1999; Rhode Island Blues, 2000; The Bulgari Connection, 2001; Auto Da Fay (autobiog.), 2002; Nothing to Wear & Nowhere to Hide (short stories), 2003; Mantrapped, 2004; She May Not Leave, 2005; What Makes Women Happy, 2006; The Spa Decameron, 2007; The Stepmother's Diary, 2008; Chalcot Crescent, 2009; Kehua!, 2010; Habits of the House, 2012; Long Live the King, 2013; The New Countess, 2013; Mischief (short stories), 2015. *Address:* c/o Georgina Capel Associates Ltd, 29 Wardour Street, W1D 6PS.

WELDON, Thomas Daryl; Chief Executive, Penguin Random House UK, since 2013 (Chief Executive Officer, Penguin UK, 2011–13); *b* London, 9 Aug. 1963; *s* of Patrick Weldon and Pamela Weldon (*née* Grant); civil partnership 2006, Colquitto A. McDonnell. *Educ:* Westminster Sch.; St John's Coll., Oxford (BA Modern Hist.). Ed., Macmillan Publishers, 1985–88; Edtl Dir, William Heinemann, 1989–96; Penguin UK: Publishing Dir, 1997–2001; Man. Dir, Gen. Div., 2001–09; Dep. Chief Exec., 2009–11. *Recreations:* horse racing, walking, travel, movies, exhibitions, restaurants. *Address:* 10 Chesterton Road, W10 5LX.

WELEMINSKY, Judith Ruth; Chair, Jewish Resource Centre, University of Roehampton, since 2012; Founder, 2014, and Chair, since 2015, Pro Israel, Pro Palestinian, Pro Peace; *b* 25 Oct. 1950; *d* of Dr Anton Weleminsky and Gerda Weleminsky (*née* Loewenstamm); *m* 2003, Robert James Armstrong Smith; two *d*. *Educ:* Birmingham Univ. (BSc Hons Psych); Lancaster Univ. (MA Organisational Psych). Personnel and Training Officer, Lowfield (Storage and Distribn), 1973–75; Community Relations Officer, Lambeth, 1975–78; Equal Opportunities Officer, Wandsworth, 1978–80; Employment Development Officer, NACRO, 1980–82; Dir, Nat. Fedn of Community Orgns, 1982–85; Dir, Nat. Schizophrenia Fellowship, 1985–90; Dir, NCVO, 1991–94; Associate, Centre for Voluntary Sector and Not for Profit Mgt, City Univ. Bus. Sch., 1994–97; Sen. Consultant, Compass Partnership, 1994–2005; Chief Executive: Mental Health Providers Forum, 2005–11; Three Wings Trust, 2012. Partner, Mentoring Dirs, 1995–97. Member: Bd, Children and Family Court Adv. Support Service, 2001–04; Gen. Social Care Council, 2001–04. Trustee: Makaton Vocabulary Develt Project, 1998–2010; Makaton Charity, 2007–12; Renaissance Publishing, 2015–. Mem., S London Israel Forum, 2014–. Council Mem., Wimbledon and Dist Synagogue, 2005–06, 2011–14 (Co. Sec., 2011–13); Chair, Israel Cttee, Wimbledon Synagogue, 2013–. FRSA. *Recreations:* family, friends, food. *E:* judywele@blueyonder.co.uk.

WELFARE, Jonathan William; Chief Executive, Elizabeth Finn Care (formerly Distressed Gentlefolk's Aid Association, then Elizabeth Finn Trust), 1998–2010; *b* 21 Oct. 1944; *s* of late Kenneth William Welfare and Dorothy Patience Athol Welfare (*née* Ross); *m* 1969, Deborah Louise Nesbitt; one *s* three *d*. *Educ:* Bradfield Coll., Berks; Emmanuel Coll., Cambridge (MA Econs and Land Economy 1969; boxing blue). Economist, Drivers Jonas & Co., 1966–68; Consultant, Sir Colin Buchanan and Partners, 1968–70; Economist and Corporate Planning Manager, Milton Keynes Develt Corp., 1970–74; Economist, then Dep. Chief Exec., S Yorks CC, 1974–84; Director: Landmark Trust, 1984–86; Oxford Ventures Gp, 1986–90; Man. Dir, Venture Link Investors, 1990–95; Chief Exec., Bristol 2000, 1995–96; mgt consultant, 1995–98. Director: Oxford Innovation, 1987–96; Granite TV, 1988–2003; Interconnect Ltd, 1990–94; Calidair Ltd, 1990–95; Meridian Software, 1990–95; English Community Care Assoc., 1999–2010; Elizabeth Finn Homes Ltd, 2005–10. Trustee: Oxford Trust, 1985–2001, 2011– (Chm., 1985–95); Northmoor Trust, 1986–99 (Chm., 1986–95); Turn2Us, 2007–10; Nominet Trust, 2009–12 (Chm., 2009–12); Gingerbread, 2014– (Chair, 2014–). FRSA 1992. Freeman: City of London, 1991; Co. of Information Technologists, 1991. *Recreations:* family, cricket, architecture, gardening. *Address:* The Garden House, R/O 34 Street, Hungerford, Berks RG17 0NF. *T:* (01488) 684228. *Club:* Hawks (Cambridge).

WELLAND, Colin, (Colin Williams); actor, playwright; *b* 4 July 1934; *s* of John Arthur Williams and Norah Williams; *m* 1962, Patricia Sweeney; one *s* three *d*. *Educ:* Newton-le-Willows Grammar Sch.; Bretton Hall Coll.; Goldsmiths' Coll., London (Teacher's Dip. in Art and Drama; Hon. Fellow, 2000). Art teacher, 1958–62; entered theatre, 1962; Library Theatre, Manchester, 1962–64; television, films, theatre, 1962–. Freelance sports writer: The Observer; The Independent. Films (actor): Kes; Villain; Straw Dogs; Sweeney; Dancing through the Dark; (original screenplay): Yanks, 1978; Chariots of Fire, 1980 (won Oscar, Evening Standard and Broadcasting Press Guild Awards, 1982); Twice in a Lifetime, 1986; A Dry White Season, 1989; War of the Buttons, 1994; television (actor): Blue Remembered Hills; The Fix; Bramwell, 1998. Plays (author): Say Goodnight to Grandma, St Martin's, 1973; Roll on Four O'clock, Palace, 1981. Award winning TV plays include: Roll on Four O'clock, Kisses at 50, Leeds United, Jack Point, Your Man from Six Counties, Bambino Mio. Best TV Playwright, Writers Guild, 1970, 1973 and 1974; Best TV Writer, and Best Supporting Film Actor, BAFTA Awards, 1970; Broadcasting Press Guild Award (for writing), 1973. *Publications:* Northern Humour, 1982; plays: Roomful of Holes, 1972; Say Goodnight to Grandma, 1973. *Recreations:* sport, theatre, cinema, politics, dining out. *Address:* c/o United Agents, 12–26 Lexington Street, W1F 0LE.

WELLAND, Sir Mark (Edward), Kt 2011; PhD; FRS 2002; FREng, FIET, FInstP; Professor of Nanotechnology, University of Cambridge, since 1999; Fellow, St John's College, Cambridge, since 1986; *b* 18 Oct. 1955; *s* of John Michael Welland and Pamela June Welland (*née* Davey); *m* 1981, Dr Esme Lynora Otun; two *s* two *d*. *Educ:* Univ. of Leeds (BSc Physics 1979); Univ. of Bristol (PhD Physics 1984); MA Cambridge 1988. FInstP 2001; FREng 2002; FIET (FIEE 2002). Lectr in Electrical Engrg, 1986–95, Reader in Nanoscale Sci., 1995–99, Univ. of Cambridge. Chief Scientific Advr, MoD, 2008–12. World Trade Vis. Scientist, IBM Res. Div., Yorktown Heights, USA, 1985–86. Turing Lect., IEE and BCS, 2002; Sterling Lectr, Russell Gp Univs, 2003; Materials Res. Soc. of India Lect., 2004; Max-

Planck Soc. Lect., 2007. Foreign Mem., Danish Acad. of Scis, 2010. Foreign Fellow, Nat. Acad. of Scis, India, 2008. Gold Medal, Nat. Nuclear Security Admin, Dept of Energy, USA, 2011; Office of Sec. of Defense Medal for Exceptional Public Service, Dept of Defense, USA, 2011. *Publications:* numerous contribs to learned jls, Trans Royal Soc. and NATO pubns. *Recreations:* bee-keeping, squash, ski-ing. *Address:* 32 Wingate Way, Trumpington, Cambridge CB2 9HD. *T:* (01223) 760305, *Fax:* (01223) 760306. *E:* mew10@cam.ac.uk.

WELLER, Sir Ian Vincent Derrick, Kt 2015; MD; FRCP; Professor, Centre for Sexual Health and HIV Research, Department of Infection and Population Health, University College London (formerly at University College London Medical School, later Royal Free and University College Medical School of University College London), 1991–2011, now Emeritus Professor; *b* 27 March 1950; *s* of Derrick Charles William Weller and Eileen Weller; *m* 1972, Darryl McKenna; two *d. Educ:* Westlain Grammar Sch., Brighton; St Bartholomew's Hosp. Med. Sch. (BSc 1st Cl. Hons 1971; MB BS 1974; MD 1983). MRCP 1977, FRCP 1990. House physician, Med. Unit, St Bartholomew's Hosp. and house surgeon, Hackney Hosp., 1975; SHO rotation, Northwick Park Hosp., 1976–77; Med. Registrar rotation, St Mary's Hosp., London, 1977–79; Ingram Res. Fellow, then Hon. Lectr and MRC Trng Fellow, Acad. Dept of Medicine, Royal Free Hosp., 1979–82; Lectr and Hon. Sen. Registrar, Acad. Dept of Genito-Urinary Medicine, 1982–84, Wellcome Trust Sen. Lectr in Infectious Diseases, 1984–88, Middx Hosp. Med. Sch.; Reader in Genito-Urinary Medicine, UCL Med. Sch., 1988–91; Hd, Dept of Sexually Transmitted Diseases, UCL Med. Sch., subseq. Royal Free and University Coll. Med. Sch. of UCL, 1994–2003. Dir, Camden PCT, 2002–10 (Mem. and Dep. Chm., Ethics Cttee, 1995–2010). Member: UK Adv. Panel for Health Care Workers Infected with Blood Borne Viruses, DoH, 1993–2005 (Chair, tripartite wkg gp, 2007–); Genito-Urinary Specialist Cttee, RCP, 1994–2005; Adv. Gp to HEA, 1994–97; Jt Med. Adv. Cttee to HEFC, 2000–06; MRC Committees: AIDS Res. Co-ordinating Cttee, 1994–; AIDS Therapeutics Cttee, 1987–2000 (Dep. Chm.; Chm., Anti-viral Sub-gp); Data and Safety Monitoring Bd of two internat. breast cancer trials (IBISII and DCIS), and nat. trial in HIV infection; Vice Chair, Commn on Human Medicines (formerly Cttee on Safety of Medicines), 1999–2014; Chairman: Steering Gp, N Thames Regl AIDS/HIV Educn Prog., 1994–2001; internat. study steering cttees of six internat. trials in HIV/AIDS funded by MRC, DFID and Eur. and Developing Countries Clinical Trials Partnership in Uganda, Zimbabwe, Malawi, Zambia and Kenya, 2003–; HIV/Viral Diseases Scientific Adv. Gp, Cttee for Human Medicinal Products, EMEA, 2005–; Collaboration of Observational HIV Epidemiology Res. Europe, 2005–; Specialist Adv. Gp on HIV and Viral Diseases, EMEA, 2006–; Chm. of Scientific Cttee and organiser, Internat. Congress on Drug Therapy in HIV Infection, 1992–2012. Member: Eur./Australian Internat. Co-ordinating Cttee for trials in HIV infection and AIDS, 1989–2000; Internat. Sci. Adv. Gp, Agence Nationale de Recherches sur le SIDA, 2000–; Bd, Internat. AIDS Soc., 2001–08 (Treas.); Ind. Expert Mem., Strategic Working Gp, Div. of AIDS, NIH, 2007–. Mem. and Chm. of Bd, Terrence Higgins Trust, 1998–2001; Trustee, HIV Trust, 2011–. Hon. FRCPGlas 2012. *Publications:* over 200 pubns in peer reviewed jls and numerous book chapters and review articles. *Recreations:* golf, walking, farming, soccer and horseball supporter. *Address:* c/o Ms Sandy Gale, Centre for Sexual Health and HIV Research, University College London, Mortimer Market Centre, Mortimer Market, off Capper Street, WC1E 6JP.

WELLER, Prof. Marc, Dr jur, Dr phil, PhD; Professor of International Law and International Constitutional Studies, and Director, Lauterpacht Centre for International Law, University of Cambridge, since 2010; Fellow of Hughes Hall, Cambridge, since 1997; barrister; *b* Hamburg, 1960; *s* of Wulf P. G. and Antye Weller; *m* 2006, Leonora Visoka; one *s* one *d. Educ:* Univ. of Frankfurt (Dr jur); Univ. of Hamburg (Dr phil); Univ. of Cambridge (MA; PhD); Fletcher Sch. of Law and Diplomacy, Tufts Univ. (MALD). FCIArb; Accredited Mediator. Called to the Bar, Middle Temple; University of Cambridge: Mem., Faculty of Law, 1990–; Fellow, Lauterpacht Centre (formerly Res. Centre) for Internat. Law, 1990–; Dep. Dir, Centre for Internat. Studies, 1997–2000; Dir, Grad. Educn, Dept of Politics and Internat. Studies, 2008–. Dir, Europ. Centre for Minority Issues, 2000–09; Sen. Mediation Expert, Dept of Pol Affairs, UN Secretariat, NY, 2011–12. Former Dir of Studies, Hague Acad. for Internat. Law; former Vis. Prof., Univ. of Paris. *Publications:* (jtly) The Kuwait Crisis: basic documents, 1991; Democracy and Politics in Burma, 1993; Iraq and Kuwait: the hostilities and their aftermath, 1993; Regional Peace-keeping and International Enforcement: the Liberian crisis, 1994; (with Daniel Bethlehem) The Yugoslav Crisis in International Law: general issues, 1997; The Crisis in Kosovo 1989–99, 1999, 2nd edn 2001; The Kosovo Conflict: the conduct and termination of hostilities and the renewed search for a settlement, 2001; (ed with Jorn Kuehl) Minority Governance in Action, 2005; (ed with Stefan Wolff) Autonomy, Self-Governance and Conflict Resolution, 2005; (ed with Alexander H. E. Morawa) Mechanisms for the Implementation of Minority Rights, 2005; (ed) The Rights of Minorities: commentary on the European Framework Convention for the Protection of National Minorities, 2005; (ed with Stefan Wolff) Internationalized State-building after Violent Conflict: Dayton after ten years, 2007; (ed) Universal Minority Rights: a commentary on the jurisprudence of international court and treaty bodies, 2007; (ed with Barbara Metzger) Settling Self-determination Conflicts, 2008; Peace Lost: missed opportunities for conflict prevention in Kosovo, 2008; (ed with Stefan Wolff) Institutions for the Management of Ethnopolitical conflict in Eastern and Central Europe, 2008; (ed jtly) The Protection of Minorities in the Wider Europe, 2008; Escaping the Self-determination Trap, 2008; Contested Statehood: Kosovo's struggle for independence (Shtetesia e kuntestuar), 2009; (ed with Katherine Nobbs) Asymmetrical State Design as a Tool of Ethnopolitical Conflict Settlement, 2010; Iraq and the Use of Force in International Law, 2010; (ed with Katherine Nobbs) Political Participation of Minorities, 2010. *Recreations:* sailing, fencing, drums. *E:* mw148@cam.ac.uk.

WELLER, Ven. Dr Susan Karen; Archdeacon of Walsall, since 2015; *b* Beverley, 20 Aug. 1965; *s* of Brian and June Spence; *m* 1997, David Weller; one *d. Educ:* Wolfreton Sch.; Univ. of Leeds (BSc Botany and Zool. 1986); Univ. of Liverpool (PhD Marine Pollution 1989); Univ. of Oxford (BA Theol. 1995). Higher Scientific Officer, 1989–93; ordained deacon, 1996, priest, 1997; Curate, Caverswall, Weston Coyney and Dilhorne, 1996–99; Associate Minister: Wilnecote, 2000–05; Christ Church, Rio de Janeiro, 2005–11; Interim Minister: Wednesfield, 2012–14; Darlaston and Moxley, 2014. *Recreation:* travel. *Address:* Small Street Centre, 1A Small Street, Walsall WS1 3PR. *T:* (01922) 707861. *E:* archdeacon.walsall@lichfield.anglican.org.

WELLESLEY, family name of **Duke of Wellington** and of **Earl Cowley**.

WELLESLEY, Viscount; Arthur Darcy Wellesley; *b* 4 Jan. 2010; *s* and *heir* of Earl of Mornington, *qv*.

WELLINGS, Prof. Paul William, CBE 2012; PhD; Vice Chancellor and Professor of Population Ecology, University of Wollongong, New South Wales, since 2012; *b* 1 Nov. 1953; s of late William and Beryl Wellings; *m* 1990, Annette Frances Schmidt. *Educ:* Royal Grammar Sch., Lancaster; King's Coll. London (BSc Hons); Durham Univ. (MSc); Univ. of E Anglia (PhD 1980). NERC Res. Fellow, 1980–81; Res. Scientist, 1981–95, Chief of Div. of Entomol., 1995–97, CSIRO; First Asst Sec., Dept of Industry, Sci. and Resources, Australia, 1997–99; Dep. Chief Exec., CSIRO, Australia, 1999–2002; Vice Chancellor and Prof. of Population Ecology, Lancaster Univ., 2002–11. Chm., 1994 Gp, 2009–11. Board Member: Australian Nuclear Sci. and Technol. Orgn, 1996–99; Australian Centre for Internat. Agricl Res., 2000–02; HEFCE, 2006–11; UUK, 2006–11. Member, Board of Trustees: Guangdong Univ. of Foreign Studies, 2011; Univ. of Wollongong in Dubai, 2012. Member, Board: Cumbria Rural Regeneration Co., 2003–06; Bundanon Trust, 2015–; Member: New Colombo Plan Adv. Cttee, Canberra, 2013–; Res. Infra Rev. Wkg Gp, Canberra, 2014–. Higher Educn Policy Inst. Lect., 2014. FAICD 2001; CCMI 2005; FRSA 2005. Hon. DSc Lancaster, 2014. DL Lancs, 2009. *Publications:* numerous contribs in fields of insect ecology and pest mgt. *Recreations:* cricket, fell-walking, visual arts. *Address:* University of Wollongong, Northfields Avenue, Wollongong, NSW 2522, Australia. *T:* (2) 42213932. *E:* wellings@wollongong.edu.au.

WELLINGTON, 9th Duke of, *cr* 1814; **Arthur Charles Valerian Wellesley,** OBE 1999; DL; Baron Mornington, 1746; Earl of Mornington, Viscount Wellesley, 1760; Viscount Wellington of Talavera and Wellington, Somersetshire, Baron Douro, 1809; Earl of Wellington, Feb. 1812; Marquess of Wellington, Oct. 1812; Marquess of Douro, 1814; Prince of Waterloo, 1815, Netherlands (now Belgium); Count of Vimeiro, Marquess of Torres Vedras and Duke of Victoria in Portugal; Duke of Cuidad Rodrigo in Spain, 1812 and a Grandee of Spain 1st class; Chairman, Richemont Holdings UK Ltd (formerly Vendôme Luxury Group Ltd), since 1993; Director: Compagnie Financière Richemont, since 1999; RIT Capital Partners plc, since 2010; *b* 19 Aug. 1945; *e s* of 8th Duke of Wellington, KG, LVO, OBE, MC and Diana Ruth Wellesley (*née* McConnel), MBE; *S* father, 2014; *m* 1977, Antonia von Preussen (*see* Duchess of Wellington); two *s* three *d. Educ:* Eton; Christ Church, Oxford. Deputy Chairman: Thames Valley Broadcasting, 1975–84; Deltec Panamerica SA, 1985–89; Guinness Mahon Hldgs, 1988–91; Director: Antofagasta and Bolivia Railway Co., 1977–80; Eucalyptus Pulp Mills, 1979–88; Transatlantic Hldgs, 1983–95; Global Asset Mgt Worldwide Inc., 1984–2013; Continental and Industrial Trust plc, 1987–90; Sanofi (formerly Sanofi-Synthélabo, then Sanofi-aventis) SA, 2002–; Pernod Ricard SA, 2003–11; Chairman: Deltec Securities (UK) Ltd, 1985–89; Dunhill Holdings, 1991–93; Sun Life Corp., subseq. Sun Life and Provincial Hldgs plc, 1995–2000; Framlington Gp plc, 1994–2005. Comr, English Heritage, 2003–07. Chm. Council, King's Coll. London, 2007–Aug. 2016. MEP (C): Surrey, 1979–84, Surrey West, 1984–89; contested (C) Islington N, Oct. 1974; Mem., Basingstoke Borough Council, 1978–79. Elected Mem., H of L, 2015–. High Steward, Winchester Cathedral, 2013–. DL Hants, 1999. Grand Officer, Order of Merit (Portugal), 1987; Grand Cross, Order of Isabel the Catholic (Spain), 2000. *Heir: s* Earl of Mornington, *qv. Address:* Apsley House, Piccadilly, W1J 7NT; Stratfield Saye House, Hants RG7 2BZ.

WELLINGTON, Duchess of; Antonia Elisabeth Brigid Luise Wellesley, OBE 2008; President, Guinness Partnership (formerly Guinness Trust), since 2007 (Trustee, 1976–2007; Chairman, 1984–2007); Chairman, Royal Ballet School, since 2009; *b* 28 April 1955; *d* of late Prince Friedrich of Prussia and Lady Brigid (*née* Guinness; she *m* 2nd, Maj. A. P. Ness); *m* 1977, Marquess of Douro (*see* Duke of Wellington); two *s* three *d. Educ:* Cobham Hall, Kent; King's Coll., London (BA). Director: Thames Valley Broadcasting, 1984–87; English Nat. Ballet, 1987–90; Scenarist, Frankenstein (ballet), Covent Garden, 1987. Mem. Cttee, London Library, 1981–86; Trustee: Getty Endowment Fund for Nat. Gall., 1985–92; Hermitage Develt Trust, Somerset House, 2000–05; NPG, 2004–12. Pres., Royal Hosp. for Neuro-disability, 1991–2001. Patron, Loddon Sch., 1996–. Fellow, Eton Coll., 2008–. *Address:* Stratfield Saye House, Hants RG7 2BZ; Apsley House, Piccadilly, W1J 7NT.

WELLINGTON (NZ), Archbishop of, (RC), since 2005; **Most Rev. John Atcherley Dew;** Metropolitan, and Military Ordinary, for New Zealand, since 2005; *b* 5 May 1948; *s* of Alfred George Dew and Joan Theresa Dew (*née* McCarthy). *Educ:* St Joseph's Coll., Masterton; Holy Name Seminary, Christchurch; Holy Cross Coll., Mosgiel (BTh 1975). Ordained deacon, 1975, priest, 1976; Asst Priest, St Joseph's Parish, Upper Hutt, 1976–79; Parish Priest, St Joseph's Cathedral Parish, Dio. Rarotonga, Cook Is, 1980–82; Leader, Archdiocesan Youth Ministry Team and Chaplain to Cook Is Maori Community, 1983–87; Dir, First Year Formation, Holy Cross Coll., Mosgiel, 1988–91; study leave, St Anselm, Kent, England, 1991–92; Parish Priest, St Anne's, Newtown, 1993–95; Auxiliary Bishop, Archdio. Wellington, 1995–2004; Co-adjutor Archbishop of Wellington, 2004. *Address:* Archdiocese of Wellington, PO Box 1937, Wellington 6140, New Zealand. *T:* (4) 4961766, *Fax:* (4) 4961330. *E:* j.dew@wn.catholic.org.nz.

WELLINGTON (NZ), Bishop of, since 2012; **Rt Rev. Justin Charles Hopkins Duckworth;** *b* Lower Hutt, NZ, 25 Nov. 1967; *s* of Leslie Duckworth and Alison Claire Duckworth; *m* 1991, Jennifer Boland; one *s* two *d. Educ:* Victoria Univ. (BSc 1989; BA Hons 1995); Massey Univ. (MPhil 1999); Melbourne Coll. of Divinity (BDiv 1999). Ordained deacon, 2005, priest, 2006; Asst Priest, Waikanae, 2006–12. *Publications:* (with Jenny Duckworth) Against the Tide, Towards the Kingdom, 2011. *Recreations:* running, tramping. *Address:* c/o Diocese of Wellington, PO Box 12046, Wellington 6144, New Zealand. *T:* (4) 4718597, *Fax:* (4) 4991360. *E:* justin@wn.ang.org.nz.

WELLINK, Arnout Henricus Elisabeth Maria; Executive Director, 1982–2011, and President, 1997–2011, De Nederlandsche Bank; *b* 27 Aug. 1943; *m* 1989, Monica Victoria Volmer; three *s* two *d. Educ:* Gymnasium B; Leyden Univ. (law degree 1968); Univ. of Rotterdam (PhD Econs 1975). Teaching asst in econs, and staff mem., Leyden Univ., 1965–70; Ministry of Finance: staff mem., 1970–75; Hd, Directorate Gen. for Financial and Econ. Policy, 1975–77; Treas. Gen., 1977–81. Mem. Bd of Dirs, 1997–2011, Pres., 2002–04, BIS, Basle (Mem., Banking and Risk Cttee, 2007–11); Chm., Basel Cttee on Banking Supervision, 2006–11; Member: Council, Eur. Monetary Inst., 1997–98; Gp of Ten Governors, Basel, 1997–2011; Governing Council and Gen. Council, 1999–2011, Audit Cttee, 2007–11, European Central Bank; Financial Stability Bd, 1999–2011; Trilateral Commn, 2000–11; Gov., IMF, 1997–2011. Ind. non-exec. Dir, Bank of China, 2012–. Mem. Bd of Govs, Nat. Acad. for Finance and Economy, 2003. Chairman: Bd of Trustees, Mus. of Mauritius; King William I Foundn, 1997; Supervisory Bd (formerly Bd of Trustees), Nederlands Openlucht Mus., 2003; Supervisory Bd, Leiden Univ., 2008–May 2016; Member: Bd, Foundn for Orthopaedic Patients' Interests, 1995; Foundn for Postgrad. Med. Trng in Indonesia, 1997; N. G. Pierson Fund Foundn, 1997–. Kt, Order of Lion (Netherlands), 1981; Comdr, Order of Orange-Nassau (Netherlands), 2011.

WELLINS, Robert Coull; freelance improvising saxophonist and composer; *b* 24 Jan. 1936; *s* of Maximillian and Catherine Wellins; *m* 1966, Isabella Brotherston Teer; two *d. Educ:* Carnwadric Primary Sch., Glasgow; Shawlands Acad.; RAF Sch. of Music, Uxbridge. Teacher, Chichester Coll. of Further Educn. Big bands, 1950s; joined, 1960s: Buddy Featherstonhaugh's Quintet; Tony Crombie Jazz Inc.; Stan Tracey Quartet; toured with Charlie Watts Orch., E Coast USA, 1986, W Coast USA, 1987. Best tenor sax, British Jazz Awards, 1994, 1998, 2000. *Recreation:* walking. *Address:* 30 Frith Road, Bognor Regis, W Sussex PO21 5LL. *T:* (01243) 863882. *W:* www.bobbywellins.co.uk.

WELLS, Dean of; *see* Clarke, Very Rev. J. M.

WELLS, Archdeacon of; *see* Sullivan, Ven. N. A.

WELLS, Andrew Mark; Director: Moat Homes Ltd, since 2010; Temple Wells Ltd, since 2011; Marine Management Organisation, since 2013; *b* 22 Feb. 1955; *s* of Richard Frederick Wells and Eunice Mary Wells (*née* Williams); partner, Pam Temple; one *d. Educ:* Bristol Grammar Sch.; St John's Coll., Cambridge (MA Maths 1976). Grad. trainee, 1976–83, Principal, Local Govt Finance, 1983–87, DoE; on loan as Principal, Econ. Secretariat, Cabinet Office, 1987–90; Department of the Environment: Divl Manager, Local Govt Rev. Team, 1990–92; Hd, London Policy Unit, 1992–93; Divisional Manager: Local Authy Housing, 1993–96; Water Supply and Regulation, 1996–99; on loan as Dir, Modernising Govt, Cabinet Office, 1999–2000; Dir, Regl Co-ordination Unit, Cabinet Office, then ODPM, 2000–03;

Dir, New Homes and Sustainable Communities, ODPM, then DCLG, 2003–08; Dir, Planning, DCLG, 2009–11. Advr, London Legacy Develt Corp., 2011–12. *Recreations:* walking, cycling.

WELLS, Bowen; international development specialist, since 2001; *b* 4 Aug. 1935; *s* of late Reginald Laird Wells and of Agnes Mary Wells (*née* Hunter); *m* 1975, Rennie Heyde; two *s*. *Educ:* St Paul's School; Univ. of Exeter (BA Hons); Regent St Polytechnic School of Management (Dip. Business Management). National Service, RN (promoted to Sub Lt), 1954–56. Schoolmaster, Colet Court, 1956–57; sales trainee, British Aluminium, 1957–58; Univ. of Exeter, 1958–61; Commonwealth Development Corporation, 1961–73; Owner Manager, Substation Group Services Ltd, 1973–79. Board Member: CARE UK, 2001–07; AMREF UK, 2001–07. MP (C) Hertford and Stevenage, 1979–83, Hertford and Stortford, 1983–2001. Parliamentary Private Secretary: to Minister of State for Employment, 1982–83; to Minister of State at Dept of Transport, 1992–94; an Asst Govt Whip, 1994–95; a Lord Comr of HM Treasury (Govt Whip), 1994–97. Member: For. Affairs Select Cttee, 1981–92; European Legislation Select Cttee, 1983–92; Chairman: Select Cttee on Internat. Develt, 1997–2001; UN Parly Gp, 1983–92; British-Caribbean Gp, 1983–95; Jt Hon. Sec., Parly Cons. Trade and Industry Gp, 1984–91 (Vice-Chm., 1983–84); Sec., All Party Overseas Develt Gp, 1984–94; Sec., Cons. Envmt Cttee, 1991–92; Mem., 1922 Exec.; Mem., British-American Gp, 1985. Mem. Exec. Bd, 2004–, Treas., 2010–15, Assoc. of Former MPs. Member: UK Br. Exec., CPA, 1984–2001 (Treas., 1997–2001); Exec. Cttee, Internat. CPA, 1994–98 (Treas., 1998–2001). Trustee, Industry and Parlt Trust, 1985–2001. Gov., Inst. of Development Studies, 1980–94; Mem. Bd, ODI, 1997–2008. Rep. of BVI, 2002–03. *Publications:* (jtly) Bridging the Gap, 2011. *Recreations:* music, walking, gardening, cooking, sailing. *Address:* Saltings, Harbour Road, Bosham, Chichester, W Sussex PO18 8JE. *Club:* Bosham Sailing.

WELLS, Brigid; *see* Wells, J. B. E.

WELLS, Christopher; *see* Wells, J. C. D.

WELLS, Sir Christopher (Charles), 3rd Bt *cr* 1944, of Felmersham, co. Bedford; *b* 12 Aug. 1936; *s* of Sir Charles Maltby Wells, 2nd Bt and of Katharine Boulton Wells; *S* father, 1996; *m* 1st, 1960, Elizabeth Florence Vaughan (marr. diss. 1983), *d* of I. F. Griffiths; two *s* two *d*; 2nd, 1985, Lynda Ann Cormack; one *s*. *Educ:* McGill Univ., Montreal (BSc); Univ. of Toronto (MD). MD in family practice, retired 1995. Assoc. Prof., Faculty of Medicine, Univ. of Toronto, 1975–95. *Heir: s* Michael Christopher Gruffydd Wells, *b* 24 Oct. 1966. *Address:* 1268 Seaforth Crescent, RR#3, Lakefield, ON K0L 2H0, Canada.

WELLS, Hon. Clyde (Kirby); Chief Justice of Newfoundland, 1999–2009; Counsel, Cox and Palmer, St John's, Newfoundland; *b* 9 Nov. 1937; *s* of Ralph Pennell Wells and Maude Wells (*née* Kirby); *m* 1962, Eleanor, *d* of Arthur and Daisy Bishop; two *s* one *d*. *Educ:* All Saints Sch., Stephenville Crossing; Memorial Univ., Newfoundland (BA 1959); Dalhousie Univ. Law Sch. (LLB 1962). Served with Canadian Army, JAG's Office, 1962–64; called to the Bar, Nova Scotia, 1963, Newfoundland, 1964; Partner, Barry and Wells, and successor law firms, 1964–81; Senior Partner, Wells & Co., 1981–87; QC (Newfoundland) 1977; Counsel, O'Reilly, Noseworthy, 1996–98; Justice, Court of Appeal, Newfoundland, 1998–99. Dir, 1978–87, and Chm., 1985–87, Newfoundland Light & Power Co. Ltd. MHA (L): Humber East, 1966–71; Windsor-Buchans, Dec. 1987–1989; Bay of Islands, 1989–96; Minister of Labour, 1966–68; Leader of Liberal Party, 1987; Premier of Newfoundland and Labrador, 1989–96. Hon. LLD Memorial, Newfoundland, 1996. *Address:* Cox and Palmer, Suite 1000, Scotia Centre, 235 Water Street, St John's, NL A1C 1B6, Canada; 305–25 Bonaventure Avenue, St John's, NL A1C 6N8, Canada. *E:* ckwells@coxandpalmer.com.

WELLS, Prof. David Arthur; Professor of German, Birkbeck College, University of London, 1987–2006, now Emeritus; *b* 26 April 1941; *s* of Arthur William Wells and Rosina Elizabeth (*née* Jones). *Educ:* Christ's Hosp., Horsham; Gonville and Caius Coll., Cambridge; Univs of Strasbourg, Vienna and Münster. Mod. and Med. Langs Tripos, BA 1963, Tiarks Studentship 1963–64, MA, PhD Cantab 1967. Asst Lectr 1966–67, Lectr 1967–69, in German, Univ. of Southampton; Lectr in German, Bedford Coll., Univ. of London, 1969–74; Sec., London Univ. Bd of Staff Examiners in German, 1973–74; Tutor, Nat. Extension Coll., Cambridge, 1966–74; Prof. of German, QUB, 1974–87. Lecture tour of NZ univs, 1975. Mem., Managing Body, Oakington Manor Jun. Mixed and Infant Sch., London Bor. of Brent, 1972–74. Hon. Treasurer: Assoc. for Literary and Linguistic Computing, 1973–78; MHRA, 2001–09 (Hon. Sec., 1969–2001); Pres., Internat. Fedn for Modern Langs and Lits, 2005–08 (Sec.-Gen., 1981–2005). Jt Editor, The Year's Work in Modern Language Studies, 1976–2004 (Editor, 1982). FRSA 1983. *Publications:* The Vorau Moses and Balaam: a study of their relationship to exegetical tradition, 1970; The Wild Man from the Epic of Gilgamesh to Hartmann von Aue's Iwein, 1975; A Complete Concordance to the Vorauer Bücher Moses (Concordances to the Early Middle High German Biblical Epic), 1976; (contrib.) MHRA Style Guide: a handbook for authors, 2002; The Central Franconian Rhyming Bible, 2004; articles, monographs and reviews in learned jls. *Recreations:* travel, theatre, music. *Address:* School of Languages, Linguistics and Culture, Birkbeck College, 43 Gordon Square, WC1H 0PD. *T:* (020) 7631 6103.

WELLS, David George; Managing Director, Service, British Gas plc, 1993–96; *b* 6 Aug. 1941; *s* of George Henry Wells and Marian (*née* Trolley); *m* 1967, Patricia Ann Fenwick; two *s*. *Educ:* Market Harborough Grammar Sch.; Reading Univ. (BA). FCA 1966. Hancock, Gilbert & Morris, 1962–67; Esso Chemical Ltd, 1967–69; joined Gas Council, 1969; Investment Accountant (Investment Appraisal), 1970–73; British Gas Corporation: Chief Accountant, Admin, 1973–76; Chief Investment Accountant, 1976; Dir of Finance, SE Reg., 1976–83; Dep. Chm., W Midlands Reg., 1983–88; Regl Chm., S Eastern, 1988–93; Man. Dir, Regl Services, 1993. Director: Metrogas Bldg Soc., 1978–86 (Dep. Chm., 1979–83); Port Greenwich Ltd, 1989–. Chm., S London Trng and Enterprise Council, 1989–93. CIGEM (CIGasE 1988); CCMI (CBIM 1990); FRSA 1991. *Recreations:* world travel, walking, reading, photography, bridge, U3A activities, gardening. *Address:* 11 Parklands, Oxted, Surrey RH8 9DP.

WELLS, Dominic Richard Alexander; screenwriter and freelance journalist, since 2007; *b* 7 March 1963; *s* of late Prof. Colin M. Wells and of Catherine Wells; two *s*. *Educ:* Winchester Coll.; New Coll., Oxford (BA Hons Modern History). Gofer, Muller, Blond & White Publishing Ltd, 1985–86; Sub-Editor, London's Alternative Magazine, 1986–87; Time Out magazine: Sub-Editor, then Chief Sub-Editor, subseq. Dep. Editor, 1987–92; Editor, 1992–98; Editorial Dir, AOL Bertelsmann Online, 1999–2001; Editor in Chief, AOL UK, 2001–02; Ed., Play mag., 2002–03, The Eye, later The Knowledge mag., 2003–07, Saturday Times. Editor of the Year, BSME, 1992, 1994, 1995, 1998. *Recreation:* Texas Hold 'Em poker. *Address:* 3 Chantrey Road, SW9 9TD. *T:* (020) 3133 2060. *E:* DominicRAWells@aol.com.

WELLS, Doreen Patricia, (Doreen, Marchioness of Londonderry); dancer and actress; Ballerina of the Royal Ballet, 1955–74; Founder, Doreen Wells Summer Ballet School, East Bridgford Hill, since 2013; *m* 9th Marquess of Londonderry, (marr. diss. 1989; he *d* 2012); two *s*. *Educ:* Walthamstow; Bush Davies School; Royal Ballet School. Engaged in Pantomime, 1952 and 1953. Joined Royal Ballet, 1955; became Principal Dancer, 1960; has danced leading roles in Noctambules, Harlequin in April, Dance Concertante, Sleeping Beauty, Coppelia, Swan Lake, Sylvia, La Fille mal Gardée, Two Pigeons, Giselle, Invitation, Rendezvous, Blood Wedding, Raymonda, Concerto, Nutcracker, Romeo and Juliet, Concerto No 2 (Ballet Imperial); has created leading roles in Toccata, La Création du Monde, Sinfonietta, Prometheus, Grand Tour; also starred in musical shows. Choreographer and Co-Dir, Canterbury Pilgrims for the Canterbury Fest., 2000; Reader, 600th anniv. of Geoffrey Chaucer, Southwark Cathedral and Westminster Abbey, 2000; Consultant, Images of Dance performing gp, London Studio Centre, 2005–. Founder Mem., Foundn of Purcell Sch., 2004–. Patron: British Ballet Orgn; ISTD Ballet; Chelmsford Ballet Co.; Liverpool Proscenium Youth Ballet Co.; Liverpool Th. Sch. and Coll. Ltd; Tiffany Sch. of Dancing; Sussex Internat. Piano Competition; GB Fest. of Music and Dance; Casa dei Mezzo Music Fest., Crete; Hon. Chm., London Children's Ballet, 2003–04; Hon. Patron, London ArtFest. Pres., Radionic Assoc., 2004–. Hon. Prof. of Classical Ballet, Dublin Metropolitan Univ., 2011. Hon. MA, 2011, Hon. DLit, 2011, Dublin Metropolitan Univ. Adeline Genée Gold Medal, 1954. *Recreations:* music, theatre-going, charity fundraising.

See also Marquess of Londonderry.

WELLS, Prof. George Albert, MA, BSc, PhD; Professor of German, Birkbeck College, University of London, 1968–88, now Emeritus; *b* 22 May 1926; *s* of George John and Lilian Maud Wells; *m* 1969, Elisabeth Delhey. *Educ:* University College London (BA, MA German; PhD Philosophy; BSc Geology). Lecturer in German, 1949–64, Reader in German, 1964–68, University Coll. London. Hon. Associate, Rationalist Press Assoc., 1989–2002 (Dir, 1974–89). Mem., Acad. of Humanism, 1983– (Humanist Laureate, 1983). *Publications:* Herder and After, 1959; The Plays of Grillparzer, 1969; The Jesus of the Early Christians, 1971; Did Jesus Exist?, 1975, 2nd edn 1986; Goethe and the Development of Science 1750–1900, 1978; The Historical Evidence for Jesus, 1982; The Origin of Language: aspects of the discussion from Condillac to Wundt, 1987; (ed and contrib.) J. M. Robertson (1856–1933), Liberal, Rationalist and Scholar, 1987; Religious Postures, 1988; Who Was Jesus? a critique of the New Testament record, 1989; Belief and Make Believe: critical reflections on the sources of credulity, 1991; What's in a Name?: reflections on language, magic and religion, 1993; The Jesus Legend, 1996; The Jesus Myth, 1998; The Origin of Language, 1999; Can We Trust the New Testament?: reflections on the reliability of Early Christian Testimony, 2004; Cutting Jesus Down to Size: what higher criticism has achieved and where it leaves Christianity, 2009; articles in Jl of History of Ideas, Jl of English and Germanic Philology, German Life and Letters, Question, Trivium, Wirkendes Wort, Think, Free Inquiry. *Recreation:* walking. *Address:* 35 St Stephen's Avenue, St Albans, Herts AL3 4AA. *T:* (01727) 851347.

WELLS, Howard James Cowen, OBE 2013; Chairman, Memorial Walls Ltd (County Cemetery Services Ltd), 2013–14; Chief Executive, Sport Pathways Ltd, 2013–14; *b* 9 Jan. 1947; *s* of late Harold Arthur James Wells and Joan Wells (*née* Cowen, later Moore); *m* 1971, Linda Baines; one *s* one *d*. *Educ:* Leeds Univ. (BEd, Cert Ed); Carnegie Coll. (Dip. in Phys. Educn). Head of Boys' Phys. Educn, Brooklands Sch., Leighton Buzzard, 1970–72; Lectr-in-Charge of Phys. Recreation, Hitchin Coll., 1972–74; Dep. Dir, Bisham Abbey Nat. Sports Centre, 1975–81; Operations Manager, 1981–84, Chief Exec., 1984–89, Jubilee Sports Centre, Hong Kong; Chief Executive: Hong Kong Sports Develt Bd, 1989–96; UK Sports Council, 1996–98; Watford Assoc. FC, 1998–99; Ipswich Town FC, 1999–2000; Chm., CCPR, 2001–05; CEO, Irish Football Assoc., 2005–08. Director: Premier Sport & Media Ltd, 2000–05; Sportsgate Ltd, 2002–05; Chm., Rebben Ltd, 2007–. Dep. Chm., Sport and Recreation Alliance, 2011–13 (Dir, 2000–). Mem., Saudi Arabian-UK Memorandum of Understanding Gp in Sport, 1996–2010. Governor: Shatin Coll., Hong Kong, 1984–96; Ashlyns Sch., Berkhamsted, 1996–2003. *Publications:* Start Living Now, 1979. *Recreations:* Football Association (full qualifying coaching licence, 1973), theatre, travel. *Address:* Sport and Recreation Alliance, Burwood House, Caxton Street, SW1W 0QT. *Clubs:* Oriental, Scribes.

WELLS, Jack Dennis; Vice President, Aircraft Owners and Pilots Association, since 2011 (Executive Director, 1991–2010; Vice-Chairman, 1996–98); Assistant Director, Central Statistical Office, 1979–88; *b* 8 April 1928; *s* of late C. W. Wells and H. M. Wells (*née* Clark); *m* 1st, 1953, Jean Allison; one *s* one *d*; 2nd, 1987, Cynthia Palmer. *Educ:* Hampton Grammar Sch.; Polytechnic of Central London. AIS 1955. Ministry of Fuel and Power, 1947; Royal Air Force, 1947–49; Min. of (Fuel and) Power, 1949–69; Private Secretary to Paymaster General, 1957–59; Chief Statistician, Dept of Economic Affairs, 1969; Min. of Technology, 1969; HM Treasury, 1970; Dept of (Trade and) Industry, 1971–79. Pres., CS Aviation Assoc., 1988–2009. Sec. and Dir, 1997–2002, Vice Pres., 2003–, Gen. Aviation Awareness Council. Vice Pres., Old Hamptonians Assoc., 2011– (Past Chm.). *Publications:* contribs to Long Range Planning, Economic Trends, Statistical News, Review of Income and Wealth, Jl of Banking and Finance, BIEC Yearbook. *Recreations:* watching cricket, jazz, travel. *Clubs:* Civil Service, United Services, MCC, Probus.

WELLS, James Henry; Member (DemU) South Down, Northern Ireland Assembly, since 1998; *b* 27 April 1957; *s* of Samuel Henry Wells and Doreen Wells; *m* 1983, Violet Grace Wallace; one *s* two *d*. *Educ:* Lurgan Coll.; Queen's Univ., Belfast (BA Hons Geog. 1979; DipTP 1981). Mem. (DemU) S Down, NI Assembly, 1982–86; research asst, RSPB, 1987–88; Asst Regl Public Affairs Manager, NI Reg., NT, 1989–98. Minister for Health, Social Services and Public Safety, NI, 2014–15. Contested (DUP) S Down, 2010, 2015. *Recreations:* birdwatching, hill-walking. *Address:* 12 Bridge Street, Kilkeel, Newry BT34 4AD.

WELLS, James Nicholas M.; *see* Murray Wells.

WELLS, (Jennifer) Brigid (Ellen), (Mrs Ian Wells); Chairman Assessor, Civil Service Selection Board, 1989–95; *b* 18 Feb. 1928; *d* of Dr Leonard John Haydon, TD, MA Cantab, MB BCh and Susan Eleanor Haydon (*née* Richmond), actress; *m* 1962, Ian Vane Wells; three *d*. *Educ:* schools in UK, USA, Canada; Edinburgh Univ.; Lady Margaret Hall, Oxford (scholar; BA Mod. Hist.; MA); PG Dip. Couns., Univ. of Brighton, 1995. Commonwealth Relations Office, 1949; UK High Commn, NZ, 1952–54; Private Sec. to Parly Under-Sec. of State, CRO, 1954–56; MAFF, 1956–62; teaching: LCC, 1962–63; Haringey, 1967; Camden Sch. for Girls, 1969–75 (to Head of Dept); Head of Dept, St David's and St Katharine's, Hornsey, 1975–77; Headmistress, Brighton and Hove High Sch., GPDST, 1978–88. Qualified team inspector: OFSTED, 1994; ISI (formerly ARCS), 1995–2003. Chm. designate, W Sussex Ambulance NHS Trust, 1992–93. Member: Local Radio Council, 1980–82; Broadcasting Complaints Commn, 1986–93 (Chm., Jan.–June 1992); Chairman: Educn Cttee, GSA, 1987–88; SE Region, GSA, 1984–86. Project Manager (USA), GAP, 1989–91; Mem., British Atlantic Council, 1988–93; Governor, Woldingham Sch., 1989–97; Comr, Duke of York's Royal Mil. Sch., Dover, 1993–2004. Chm., Friends of GPDST (now GDST), 1991–2003. JP Inner London, 1972–77, Brighton and Hove, 1980–98. *Publications:* (ed jtly) The First Crossing, 2007; articles in learned jls. *Recreations:* gardening, travel. *Address:* Cherry Trees, Bradford Road, Lewes, E Sussex BN7 1RD. *T:* (01273) 477491.

WELLS, Sir John, KNZM 2009 (DCNZM 2009); Founder, 1986, and non-executive Chairman, since 2005, Bancorp Group (Executive Chairman, 1986–2005); *b* Wanganui, NZ, 21 July 1943; *s* of Charles and Mary Wells; *m* 1969, Sheryl Gavin; two *s*. *Educ:* Auckland Grammar Sch.; Auckland Univ. (ACA 1973). FCIS 1986. NZI Financial Corporation: Ops Manager, 1973–76; Co. Sec. and Asst Gen. Manager, 1976–80; Chief Gen. Manager and Dir, 1973–86. Chairman: Greenpark Hldgs Ltd, 1993–; Sheffield Gp Ltd, 2006–10; Auckland City Property Enterprise, 2006–10; Fisher Funds Mgt Ltd, 2008–; Sheffield N Island Ltd, 2010–; Auckland Council Property Ltd, 2010–; CBL Insurance Ltd, 2012–; CBL Corp. Ltd, 2013–; Dir, Martin Jenkins & Associates Ltd, 2011–; Member: Adv. Bd, Marsh Ltd, 2005–; Karapiro 2010 Ltd (World Rowing Championships), 2007–11. Chairman: NZ Finance Houses Assoc., 1980–84; Hillary Commn, 2001. Chairman: Sport and Recreation NZ, 2001–09; Auckland Stopover Local Organising Cttee, Volvo Ocean Race, 2010–12; Triathlon World Championships 2012 Ltd, 2010–13; World Masters Games 2017 Ltd, 2013–; Member: Rugby

World Cup 2011 Bid Cttee, 2005; RWC 2011 Estabt Bd, 2005–06; Rugby NZ 2011 Ltd, 2006–12. Chm., NZ Sports Foundn Charitable Trust, 2001–09; Trustee, Auckland Grammar Sch. Foundn Trust, 2011–; former Trustee, Life Educn Trust - Northern. *Recreations:* all sports, cycling, walking. *Address:* PO Box 3710, Shortland Street, Auckland 1140, New Zealand. *T:* 93028522, *Fax:* 93072733. *E:* jwells@bancorp.co.nz.

WELLS, Prof. John Christopher, PhD; FBA 1996; FCIL; Professor of Phonetics, University College London, 1988–2006, now Emeritus; *b* 11 March 1939; *s* of Rev. Philip Cuthbert Wells and Winifred May (*née* Peaker); civil partnership 2006, Gabriel Parsons. *Educ:* St John's Sch., Leatherhead; Trinity Coll., Cambridge (BA 1960; MA 1964); University Coll., London (MA 1962; PhD 1971). FCIL (FIL 1982). University College London: Asst Lectr in Phonetics, 1962–65; Lectr, 1965–82; Reader, 1982–88; Head, Dept of Phonetics and Linguistics, 1990–2000. Sec., Internat. Phonetic Assoc., 1973–86 (Pres., 2003–); President: World Esperanto Assoc., 1989–95; Simplified Spelling Soc., 2003–. Mem., Esperanto Acad., 1971–. Editor, Jl Internat. Phonetic Assoc., 1971–87. Contribs to radio and TV programmes. *Publications:* Concise Esperanto and English Dictionary, 1969; (with G. Colson) Practical Phonetics, 1971; Jamaican Pronunciation in London, 1973; (jtly) Jen Nia Mondo 1, 1974 (trans. Italian, Icelandic, Swedish, Finnish); (jtly) Jen Nia Mondo 2, 1977; Lingvistikaj aspektoj de Esperanto, 1978, 2nd edn 1989 (trans. Danish, Korean, German); Accents of English (three vols and cassette), 1982; Geiriadur Esperanto/Kimra vortaro, 1985; (pronunciation editor) Universal Dictionary, 1987; (pronunciation editor) Hutchinson Encyclopedia, 8th edn 1988, and subsequent editions; Longman Pronunciation Dictionary, 1990, 3rd edn 2008; English Intonation: an introduction, 2006; Sounds Interesting: observations on English and general phonetics, 2014; articles in learned jls and collective works. *Recreations:* reading, walking, playing the melodeon. *Address:* 5 Poplar Road, SW19 3JR. *T:* (020) 8542 0302. *E:* j.wells@ucl.ac.uk.

WELLS, (John) Christopher (Durant), FRCA; Consultant in Pain Relief, since 1982; President, European Federation of IASP Chapters, since 2014; *b* 5 Oct. 1947; *s* of late Colin Durant Wells and of Barbara Gwynneth Wells; *m* 1st, 1971, Sheila Frances Murphy (marr. diss. 2000); two *d*; 2nd, 2004, Susan Lynn Corness. *Educ:* Manchester Grammar Sch.; Liverpool Univ. (MB ChB 1970). LRCP 1970; MRCS 1970; LMCC 1974; FRCA (FFARCS 1978). Consultant in Pain Relief: Spire (formerly BUPA N) Cheshire Hosp., Stretton, 2000–; Spire Liverpool Hosp.; BMI Beaumont Hosp., Bolton. Hon. Consultant, Pain Res. Inst., Liverpool, 1995–. Dir, Pain Relief Res. Foundn, 1984–95. Director: Pain Matters Ltd, 2000–; Pain Management Co., 2006–. Trustee, World Inst. of Pain Foundn. Hon. Member: British Pain Soc., 2008–; Neuropathic Pain Special Interest Gp, 2010–. Hon. Fellow of Interventional Pain Practice, 2001. *Publications:* (with C. Woolf) Pain Mechanisms and Management, 1991; (with G. Nown) In Pain?, 1993, 2nd edn as The Pain Relief Handbook, 1996; (with D. Jankowicz) Regional Blockade, 2001; contrib. to British Med. Bull. *Recreations:* curling (for Wales), ski-ing, boating. *Address:* (office) 25 Rodney Street, Liverpool L1 9EH. *T:* (0151) 708 9344, *Fax:* (0151) 707 0609. *E:* cxwells@aol.com.

WELLS, Sir John (Julius), Kt 1984; DL; *b* 30 March 1925; *s* of A. Reginald K. Wells, Marlands, Sampford Arundel, Som; *m* 1948, Lucinda Meath-Baker; two *s* two *d*. *Educ:* Eton; Corpus Christi College, Oxford (MA). War of 1939–45: joined RN as ordinary seaman, 1942; commissioned, 1943, served in submarines until 1946. Contested (C) Smethwick Division, General Election, 1955. MP (C) Maidstone, 1959–87. Chairman: Cons. Party Horticulture Cttee, 1965–71, 1973–87; Horticultural sub-Cttee, Select Cttee on Agriculture, 1968; Parly Waterways Group, 1974–80; Vice-Chm., Cons. Party Agriculture Cttee, 1970; Mem., Mr Speaker's Panel of Chairmen, 1974. Hon. Freeman, Borough of Maidstone, 1979. DL Kent, 1992. Kt Comdr, Order of Civil Merit (Spain), 1972; Comdr, Order of Lion of Finland, 1984. *Recreation:* country pursuits. *Address:* Mere House Barn, Mereworth, Kent ME18 5NB. *E:* john@merehousebarn.plus.com.

WELLS, Prof. Michael, MD; FRCPath, FRCOG; Professor of Gynaecological Pathology, University of Sheffield, 1997–2014, now Emeritus; Consultant Histopathologist, Leeds Teaching Hospitals, since 2015; *b* Wolverhampton, 7 Aug. 1952; *s* of John Thomas Wells and Lily Wells (*née* Ellis); *m* 1994, Lynne Margaret Walker; one *s* one *d*, and two step *s*. *Educ:* Univ. of Manchester (BSc Hons 1974; MB ChB 1976; MD 1986). FRCPath 1995; FRCOG (*ad eundem*) 2004. Hon. Consultant, United Leeds Teaching Hosps NHS Trust, 1983–93; Prof. of Gynaecol Pathol., Univ. of Leeds, St James's Univ. Hosp., 1994–96; Dir of Internat. Affairs, Faculty of Medicine, Dentistry and Health, Univ. of Sheffield, 2013–14; Hon. Consultant Histopathologist, Sheffield Teaching Hosps, 1997–2014. President: British Gynaecol Cancer Soc., 1994–97; Internat. Soc. of Gynecol Pathologists, 2003–05; Eur. Soc. of Pathol., 2009–11. Royal College of Pathologists: Mem. Council, 1998–2001, 2008–11; Mem., Exec. Cttee, 2008–11; Chm., Specialty Adv. Cttee on Histopathology, 2008–11; Vice Pres., 2011–14; Pres., British Div., Internat. Acad. of Pathol., 2012–14. Ed.-in-Chief, Histopathology, 2003–11. *Publications:* Haines and Taylor Obstetrical and Gynaecological Pathology, (Asst Ed.) 4th edn 1995, (Co-Ed.) 5th edn 2003; over 230 original papers, review articles and book chapters. *Recreations:* singing, ski-ing, gardening, reading for pleasure. *Address:* Woodend, 57 Ranmoor Crescent, Sheffield S10 3GW. *T:* (0114) 230 8260. *E:* m.wells@sheffield.ac.uk. *Club:* Athenæum.

WELLS, Michael Andrew; Group Chief Executive, Prudential plc, since 2015 (Executive Director, 2011–15); *b* Ontario, Canada, 9 April 1960; *s* of Garnet and Constance Wells; *m* 1992, Lindsay; two *s*. *Educ:* San Diego State Univ. (BSc Econs). FINRA Principal. Pres., Jackson Nat. Life Distributors Inc., 1995–2001; Vice Chm., 2001–02, Chief Operating Officer, 2002–11, Pres. and CEO, 2011–15, Jackson Nat. Life Insce Co. Mem. Bd of Managers, Curian Capital LLC. *Recreations:* outdoors, music. *Address:* Prudential plc, 12 Arthur Street, EC4R 9AQ.

WELLS, Nicholas Mark; Chief Executive Officer, Whistl (formerly TNT Post UK), since 2003; *b* Wellingborough, 1959; *s* of Raymond Wells and Gwendoline Wells; *m* 1988, Ruth; one *s* two *d*. *Educ:* Univ. of Warwick (BA Hons 1980). Circular Distributors Ltd: Sales and Mktg Dir, 1987–94; Man. Dir, 1994–2003. Non-exec. Chm., Lifecycle Mktg, 2012–. *Recreations:* golf, ski-ing, family, travel, wine. *Address:* Whistl, One Globeside, Fieldhouse Lane, Marlow, Bucks SL7 1HY. *T:* (01628) 816757.

WELLS, Prof. Peter Neil Temple, CBE 2009; FRS 2003; FREng; FMedSci; FLSW; Distinguished Research Professor, School of Engineering, Cardiff University, since 2004; Professor of Physics and Engineering in Medicine, Bristol University, 2000–01, now Emeritus; *b* 19 May 1936; *s* of Sydney Parker Temple Wells and Elizabeth Beryl Wells; *m* 1960, Valerie Elizabeth Johnson; three *s* one *d*. *Educ:* Clifton Coll., Bristol; Aston Univ., Birmingham (BSc 1958); Bristol Univ. (MSc 1963; PhD 1966; DSc 1978). FInstP 1970; FIET (FIEE 1978); FREng (FEng 1983). Res. Asst, United Bristol Hosps, 1960–71; Prof. of Medical Physics, Welsh Nat. Sch. of Medicine, 1972–74; Area Physicist, Avon AHA, 1975–82; Chief Physicist, Bristol and Weston HA, subseq. United Bristol Healthcare NHS Trust, 1982–2000. Hon. Prof. in Clinical Radiology, Bristol Univ., 1986–2000. Visiting Professor: Imperial Coll. London, 2002–; UCL, 2011–. Hon. DSc Aston, 2010; Hon. DTech Lund, 1997; Hon. MD Erasmus, 1998. FMedSci 2005; FLSW 2010. MAE 2014. Royal Medal, Royal Soc., 2013; Sir Frank Whittle Medal, RAEng, 2014. *Publications:* Physical Principles of Ultrasonic Diagnosis, 1969; (ed) Ultrasonics in Clinical Diagnosis, 1972, 3rd edn (jtly) 1983; Biomedical Ultrasonics, 1977; (with J. P. Woodcock) Computers in Ultrasonic Diagnostics, 1977; (ed jtly) New Techniques and Instrumentation in Ultrasonography, 1980; (ed) Scientific Basis of Medical Imaging, 1982; (ed jtly) Emerging Technologies in Surgery, 1984; (ed jtly) Clinical Applications of Doppler Ultrasound, 1988, 2nd edn 1995; (ed) Advances in Ultrasound Imaging and Instrumentation, 1993; (ed jtly) The Perception of Visual Information, 1993, 2nd edn 1997; (ed jtly) The Invisible Light: one hundred years of medical radiology, 1995; (ed jtly) Acoustical Imaging, vol. 25, 2000; numerous papers, mainly on medical applications of ultrasonics. *Recreation:* cooking. *Address:* The Old Meeting House, Silver Street, Weston in Gordano, N Somerset BS20 8QA. *T:* (01275) 848348. *E:* WellsPNT@aol.com.

WELLS, Petrie Bowen; *see* Wells, Bowen.

WELLS, Richard Burton, QPM 1987; Chief Constable of South Yorkshire, 1990–98; Director, E-Quality Leadership, 1998–2007; *b* 10 Aug. 1940; *s* of Walter Percival Wells and Daphne Joan Wells (*née* Harris); *m* 1970, Patricia Ann Smith; one *s* one *d*. *Educ:* Sir Roger Manwood's Grammar Sch., Sandwich; Priory Sch. for Boys, Shrewsbury; St Peter's Coll., Oxford (Open Exhibnr 1959; BA 1962; MA 1965); principal educn, 36 yrs with the police service. Constable, Bow Street, 1962–66; Sergeant, Notting Hill, 1966–68; Special Course, Police Staff Coll., 1966–67; Inspector, Leman St, and Hendon Police Trng Sch., 1968–73; Chief Inspector, Notting Hill, 1973–76; Supt, Hampstead, 1976–79; Chief Supt, Hammersmith and New Scotland Yard, 1979–82; Sen. Command Course, Police Staff Coll., 1981; Comdt, Hendon Training Sch., 1982–83; Dep. Asst Comr, Dir of Public Affairs, New Scotland Yard, 1983–86; Dep. Asst Commissioner, OC NW London, 1986–90. Chairman: Media Adv. Gp, ACPO, 1992–98; Nat. Conf. of Police Press and PROs, 1994–98; Personnel and Trng Cttee, ACPO, 1996–98 (Sec., 1993–96). Sec., Provincial Police Award Selection Cttee, 1990–98. Member: Rathbone Corporate Partnership Gp, 1993–98; Selection Cttee, Fulbright Fellowship in Police Studies, 1991–98; Forensic Psychotherapy Course Adv. Gp, 1990–98; Barnsley City Challenge Bd, 1992–98; Sheffield Common Purpose Adv. Gp and Council, 1993–98. President: Young Enterprise Bd for S Yorks and S Humberside, 1993–98; Deepcar Brass Band, 1992–98; Patron: S Yorks Br., RLSS, 1990–98; Weston Park Hosp. Cancer Care Appeal, 1993–98. President: St Peter's Soc., Oxford Univ., 1989–96; Police Athletics Assoc. Men's Hockey, 1996–98 (Vice Pres., 1989–96). Mem., St John Council for S and W Yorks, 1990–98. Freeman, City of London, 1992. CCMI (CBIM 1991; Pres., Exeter & Torbay Br., 2004). Chm. Editl Bd, Policing Today, 1994–98. *Publications:* (contrib.) Leaders on Leadership, 1996; (contrib.) Learning Organisations in the Public Sector, 1997; (contrib.) On Work and Leadership, 1999. *Recreations:* T'ai Chi, cooking and jam-making, philately, genealogy, local history, scanning the medical horizon for new prostheses. *Address:* Bidwell Farm, Upottery, Devon EX14 9PP. *T:* (01404) 861122. *E:* rbwells@rbwells.demon.co.uk.

WELLS, Ven. Roderick John; Archdeacon of Stow, 1989–2001, and of Lindsey, 1994–2001, now Archdeacon Emeritus; *b* 17 Nov. 1936; *s* of Leonard Arthur and Dorothy Alice Wells; *m* 1969, Alice Louise Scholl; one *s* two *d*. *Educ:* Durham Univ. (BA Hons Theol.); Hull Univ. (MA). Insurance clerk, 1953–55 and 1957–58. RAF, 1955–57 (Radar Mechanic). Asst Master, Chester Choir School, 1958–59; Asst Curate, St Mary at Lambeth, 1965–68, Priest-in-Charge 1968–71; Rector of Skegness, 1971–78; Team Rector, West Grimsby Team Ministry (Parish of Great and Little Coates with Bradley), 1978–89; Area Dean of Grimsby and Cleethorpes, 1983–89. *Recreations:* music (pianist and organist), walking, geology, golf. *Address:* 17 Ruddle Way, Langham, Oakham, Rutland LE15 7NZ.

WELLS, Rosemary; writer and illustrator of children's books, since 1968; *b* 29 Jan. 1943; *m* Thomas M. Wells; two *d*. Mem., Soc. of Illustrators, NY. Best Illustrated Book of the Year, New York Times (twice); Horn Best Book of the Year; Notable Book, American Library Assoc. (40 times); numerous other awards. *Publications* include: Noisy Nora, 1973; Benjamin and Tulip, 1973; Timothy Goes to School, 1981; Voyage to the Bunny Planet, 1992; Edward Unready for School, 1995; My Very First Mother Goose, 1996; Bunny Cakes, 1997; Bunny Money, 1997; The Bear Went Over the Mountain, 1998; The Itsy-Bitsy Spider, 1998; Max's Toys, 1998; Max's Bath, 1998; Yoko, 1998; Morris's Disappearing Bag, 1999; Max Cleans Up, 2000; Emily's First 100 Days of School, 2000; Timothy Goes to School, 2000; Mama, Don't Go!, 2001; The School Play, 2001; The Halloween Parade, 2001; Bunny Party, 2001; Ruby's Beauty Shop, 2003; Max Drives Away, 2003; Ruby's Tea for Two, 2003; My Kindergarten, 2004; Bunny Mail, 2004; The Gulps 2007; Red Moon at Sharpsburg, 2007; Otto Runs for President, 2008; Yoko Writes her Name, 2008; My Havana: memories of a Cuban boyhood, 2010; Max & Ruby's Bedtime Book, 2010; On the Blue Comet, 2010; Yoko's Show-and-Tell, 2011; Hands Off, Harry!, 2011; Max & Ruby's Treasure Hunt, 2012; Time Out for Sophie, 2013; Ivy Takes Care, 2013; Yoko Finds her Way, 2014.

WELLS, Rev. Canon Dr Samuel Martin Bailey; Vicar, St Martin-in-the-Fields, London, since 2012; Visiting Professor of Christian Ethics, King's College, London, since 2012; *b* Chatham, Ont, 24 April 1965; *s* of late Stephen Wells and Ruth Wells (*née* Moran); *m* 1994, Rev. Dr Joanne Bailey; one *s* one *d*. *Educ:* Bristol Grammar Sch.; Merton Coll., Oxford (BA Modern Hist. 1987; MA 1995); Univ. of Edinburgh (BD Systematic Theol. 1991); Univ. of Durham (PhD Christian Ethics 1996). Ordained deacon, 1991, priest, 1992; Assistant Curate: St Luke's, Wallsend, 1991–95; St Andrew's, Cherry Hinton with All Saints, Teversham, 1995–97; Priest-in-charge, Earlham St Elizabeth, Norwich, 1997–2003; Rural Dean, Norwich South, 1999–2003; Priest-in-charge, Newnham St Mark, Cambridge, 2003–05; Dean of the Chapel, and Res. Prof. of Christian Ethics, Duke Univ., N Carolina, 2005–12. Theological Canon, Chichester Cathedral, 2004–. Sen. Mem. and Hon. Chaplain, Wolfson Coll., Cambridge, 2003–05. *Publications:* Transforming Fate into Destiny: the theological ethics of Stanley Hauerwas, 1998; (ed jtly) Faithfulness and Fortitude: in conversation with the theological ethics of Stanley Hauerwas, 2000; Community-Led Estate Regeneration and the Local Church, 2003; Improvisation: the drama of Christian ethics, 2004; (ed jtly) The Blackwell Companion to Christian Ethics, 2004, 2nd edn 2011; God's Companions: reimagining Christian ethics, 2006; Power and Passion: six characters in search of resurrection, 2007; Speaking the Truth: preaching in a pluralistic culture, 2008; (ed jtly) Praying for England: priestly presence in contemporary culture, 2008; (jtly) Living Out Loud, 2010; Liturgy Comes to Life, 2010; (jtly) Introducing Christian Ethics, 2010; Christian Ethics: an introductory reader, 2010; (jtly) Living Without Enemies: being present in the midst of violence, 2011; What Episcopalians Believe: an introduction, 2011; What Anglicans Believe: an introduction, 2011; Be Not Afraid, 2011; Crafting Prayers for Public Worship: the art of intercession, 2013; Learning to Dream Again: rediscovering the heart of God, 2013. *Recreations:* tennis, cricket, watching sports, reading, hill-walking. *Address:* 6 St Martin's Place, WC2N 4JJ. *T:* (020) 7766 1107. *E:* sam.wells@smitf.org.

WELLS, Prof. Stanley William, CBE 2007; Professor of Shakespeare Studies, and Director of the Shakespeare Institute, University of Birmingham, 1988–97, now Emeritus Professor and Hon. Fellow; General Editor of the Oxford Shakespeare since 1978; Chairman, Shakespeare Birthplace Trust, 1991–2011, now Hon. President; *b* 21 May 1930; *s* of Stanley Cecil Wells, MBE, and Doris Wells; *m* 1975, Susan Elizabeth Hill, *qv*; two *d* (and one *d* decd). *Educ:* Kingston High Sch., Hull; University Coll., London (BA; Fellow, 1995); Shakespeare Inst., Univ. of Birmingham (PhD). FRSL 2014. Fellow, Shakespeare Inst., 1962–77: Lectr, 1962; Sen. Lectr, 1971; Reader, 1973–77; Hon. Fellow, 1979–88; Head of Shakespeare Dept, OUP, 1978–88. Sen. Res. Fellow, Balliol Coll., Oxford, 1980–88 (Hon. Fellow, 2014); Vis. Fellow, UCL, 2006–07. Consultant in English, Wroxton Coll., 1964–80. Chm., Membership Cttee, 1991–99, Collections Cttee, 1992–99, RSC; Mem., Exec. Council, 1976–, Exec. (formerly F and GP) Cttee, 1991–, Educn Cttee, Royal Shakespeare Theatre (Gov., 1974–, Vice Chm. of Govs, 1991–2003, Hon. Gov. Emeritus, 2004–); Dir, Royal Shakespeare Theatre Summer Sch., 1971–98. Pres., Shakespeare Club of Stratford-upon-Avon, 1972–73, 2011–12; Chm., Internat. Shakespeare Assoc., 1996–2001, Mem. Exec., 2001– (Vice-Chm.,

1991–96); Member: Council, Malone Soc., 1967–90; Exec. Cttee, Shakespeare Birthplace Trust, 1976–78, 1988– (Trustee, 1975–81, 1984–2004; Life Trustee, 2003–); Trustee, Rose Theatre, 1991–; Dir, Globe Theatre, 1992– (Trustee, 1998–2004); President: Wolverhampton Shakespeare Soc., 1992–93; Birmingham and Midland Inst., 2008–09. Governor, King Edward VI Grammar Sch. for Boys, Stratford-upon-Avon, 1973–77. Guest lectr, British and overseas univs; Lectures: British Acad. Annual Shakespeare, 1987; Hilda Hulme Meml, 1987; first annual Globe, 1990; Melchiori, Rome, 1991; Walter Clyde Curry Annual Shakespeare, Vanderbilt Univ., 1998. Hon. DLitt: Furman Univ., SC, 1978; Hull, 2005; Durham, 2005; Craiova, 2008; Warwick, 2008; Marburg, 2010; Hon. DPhil Munich, 1999. Walcott Award, LA, 1995. Associate Editor: New Penguin Shakespeare, 1967–; Oxford DNB, 1998–; Editor, Shakespeare Survey, 1980–99; Gen. Editor, Penguin Shakespeare, 2005–. Sam Wanamaker Award, Globe Th., 2010; Internat. Shakespeare Prize, Craiova Internat. Shakespeare Fest., 2014. *Publications:* (ed) Thomas Nashe, Selected Writings, 1964; (ed, New Penguin Shakespeare): A Midsummer Night's Dream, 1967, Richard II, 1969, The Comedy of Errors, 1972; Shakespeare, A Reading Guide, 1969, 2nd edn 1970; Literature and Drama, 1970; (ed, Select Bibliographical Guides): Shakespeare, 1973 (new edn 1990), English Drama excluding Shakespeare, 1975; Royal Shakespeare, 1977, 2nd edn 1978; (compiled) Nineteenth-Century Shakespeare Burlesques (5 vols), 1977; Shakespeare: an illustrated dictionary, 1978, 2nd edn 1985, revised as Oxford Dictionary of Shakespeare, 1998; Shakespeare: the writer and his work, 1978; (ed with R. L. Smallwood) Thomas Dekker, The Shoemaker's Holiday, 1979; (with Gary Taylor) Modernizing Shakespeare's Spelling, with three studies in the text of Henry V, 1979; Re-Editing Shakespeare for the Modern Reader, 1984; (ed) Shakespeare's Sonnets, 1985; (ed with Gary Taylor *et al*) The Complete Oxford Shakespeare, 1986; (ed) The Cambridge Companion to Shakespeare Studies, 1986; (with Gary Taylor *et al*) William Shakespeare: a textual companion, 1987; An Oxford Anthology of Shakespeare, 1987; Shakespeare: a dramatic life, 1994, rev. edn as Shakespeare: the poet and his plays, 1997; (ed with E. A. Davies) Shakespeare and the Moving Image, 1994; (ed with R. Warren) Twelfth Night, 1994; (ed) Shakespeare in the Theatre: an anthology of criticism, 1997; (ed) Summerfolk, 1997; William Shakespeare: the quiz book, 1998; (ed) King Lear, 2000; (ed with C. M. S. Alexander) Shakespeare and Race, 2001; (ed with M. de Grazia) The Cambridge Companion to Shakespeare, 2001; (ed with Michael Dobson) The Oxford Companion to Shakespeare, 2001; (ed with C. M. S. Alexander) Shakespeare and Sexuality, 2001; Shakespeare For All Time, 2002; (ed with Lena Orlin) A Shakespeare Study Guide, 2002; Looking for Sex in Shakespeare, 2004; (with Paul Edmondson) Shakespeare's Sonnets, 2004; Shakespeare and Co., 2006; Is It True What They Say About Shakespeare?, 2007; (with P. Edmondson) Coffee with Shakespeare, 2008; Shakespeare Found!, 2009; (ed with Margreta de Grazia) New Cambridge Companion to Shakespeare, 2010; Shakespeare, Sex, and Love, 2010; (with P. Edmondson) Shakespeare Beyond Doubt, 2013; Great Shakespeare Actors, 2015; William Shakespeare: a very short introduction, 2015; (with P. Edmondson) The Shakespeare Circle, 2016; contrib. Shak. Survey, Shak. Qly, Shak. Jahrbuch, Theatre Notebook, Stratford-upon-Avon Studies, TLS, The Stage, NY Rev. of Books, etc. *Recreations:* music, theatre, the countryside. *Address:* 9 New Street, Stratford-upon-Avon, Warwicks CV37 6BX. *T:* 07769 336533. *E:* Stanley.Wells@shakespeare.org.uk.

WELLS, Susan Elizabeth, (Mrs Stanley Wells); *see* Hill, S. E.

WELLS, Timothy Nigel Carl, PhD, ScD; Chief Scientific Officer, Medicines for Malaria Venture, Geneva, since 2007; *b* Derby, 30 March 1962; *s* of Carl Allan Walter Wells and Joan Hazel Wells (*née* Hughes); partner, Susan Jane Self; two *s* two *d. Educ:* Churchill Coll., Cambridge (BA Natural Scis 1984); Imperial Coll. London (PhD Chem. 1987); Univ. of Cambridge (ScD Biol. 2009). Dept Hd, Glaxo Inst. for Molecular Biol., Geneva, 1990–97; Hd, Res., Serono Internat., 1998–2007. FMedSci 2012. *Publications:* (with Michael J. Palmer) Neglected Diseases and Drug Discovery, 2012. *Address:* Medicines for Malaria Venture, 20 route de Pré-Bois, 1215 Geneva, Switzerland. *E:* tim.wells@bluewin.ch.

WELLS, Sir William (Henry Weston), Kt 1997; FRICS; Chairman: Pure Sports Medicine plc, since 2007; Restore (formerly Mavinwood) plc, since 2009; *b* 3 May 1940; *s* of Sir Henry Wells, CBE, and Lady Wells; *m* 1966, Penelope Jean Broadbent; two *s* (and one *s* decd). *Educ:* Radley Coll.; Magdalene Coll., Cambridge (BA). Joined Chesterton, 1959, Partner, 1965–92; Chairman: Land and House Property Gp, 1977 (Dir, 1972–76); Frincon Holdings Ltd, 1977–87; Chesterton plc, 1992–97; Pres., Chesterton Internat. plc, London, 1998–2004. Chairman: Covenant Healthcare, 2005–10; ADL plc, 2006–; CMG plc, 2007–; Ashley House plc, 2007–13; St Wenceslas Property Adv. Bd, 2007–; SUSD (formerly CAM) plc, 2008–13; Transform plc, 2010–14; Libra Holdco, 2011–; The Practice plc, 2013–; Director: London Life Assoc., 1984–89; AMP (UK) plc, 1994–2002; Pearl Gp Ltd (formerly Pearl Assurance), 1994–2005; Norwich and Peterborough Bldg Soc., 1994–2003; NFC plc, 1996–2000; AMP (UK) Holdings, 1997–2005; NPI Ltd, 1999–2005; Nat. Provident Life Ltd, 1999–2005; Exel plc, 2000–05; Hillgate (220) Ltd, 2002–; HHG plc, 2003–05; ARC Fund Mgt, 2006–08; SQW Ltd, 2007–14; Dods plc, 2010–; HCOne plc, 2011–; Skyfall Ltd, 2014–. Advisor: Healthcare at Home, 2008–; Dr Foster, 2008–10; ipp, 2009–; Mem. Council, NHS Trust Fedn, 1991–93 (Vice Chm., 1992–93). Chairman: Hampstead HA, 1982–90; Royal Free Hampstead NHS Trust, 1990–94; S Thames RHA, 1994–96; S Thames Region, NHS Exec., DoH, 1996–99; NHS Appointments Commn, 2001–07; Commercial Adv. Bd, DoH, 2003–07; Regl Chm., SE, NHS Exec., 1999–2001. Member: Board of Governors, Royal Free Hosp., 1968–74; Camden and Islington AHA, 1974–82; Chm., Special Trustees of Royal Free Hosp., 1979–2001; Member, Council: Royal Free Hosp. Sch. of Medicine, 1977–91; UMDS, Guy's and St Thomas' Hosps, 1994–98; St George's Hosp. Med. Sch., 1994–98; Univ. of Surrey, 1998– (Vice Chm., 1999–2000, Chm., 2001–06); KCL, 1998–2001; City Univ., 1999–2001; Member: Delegacy, King's Coll. Sch. of Medicine and Dentistry, 1994–98; Council and Mgt Cttee, King's Fund, 1995–2010; Chm., Guy's and St Thomas' Charity, 2010–. Pro-Chancellor, Univ. of Surrey, 2007–. Trustee: Nat. Mus. of Science and Industry, 2003–11; Action Med. Res., 2005–07. Pres., Royal Free Hosp. Retirement Fellowship, 1994–; Vice President: RCN, 2006– (Hon. Treas., 1988–2005); Attend (formerly Nat. Assoc. of Leagues of Hosp. Friends), 2004– (Hon. Treas., 1992–2004). Mem. Council, Priory of England and the Is, 2000–02. Hon. FRCP 2002. *Recreations:* family, gardening. *Club:* Boodle's.

WELSBY, John Kay, CBE 1990; Chief Executive, 1990–98, and Chairman, 1995–99, British Railways Board; *b* 26 May 1938; *s* of late Samuel and Sarah Ellen Welsby; *m* 1964, Jill Carole Richards; one *s* one *d. Educ:* Heywood Grammar Sch.; Univ. of Exeter (BA); Univ. of London (MSc). FCILT (FCIT 1990). Govt Economic Service, 1966–81; British Railways Board: Dir, Provincial Services, 1982–84; Managing Dir, Procurement, 1985–87; Mem. Bd, 1987–99; Director: London & Continental Rlys Ltd, 1999–2007; LCR Finance plc, 1999–2007. Chm., CIT, 1998–99. Pres., Inst. of Logistics and Transport, 1999–2002. Member: Business Adv. Council, Transport Dept, Northwestern Univ., Evanston, Ill., 1995–2000. CCMI (CIMgt 1991). Freeman, City of London, 1992; Liveryman, Carmen's Co., 1992. *Publications:* articles on economic and transport matters. *Recreations:* walking, music, swimming. *Address:* Stone Barn, Bow, Crediton, Devon EX17 6LB.

WELSER-MÖST, Franz; Music Director, Cleveland Orchestra, since 2002; General Music Director, Vienna State Opera, 2010–14; *b* 16 Aug. 1960. Music Dir, LPO, 1990–96; Chief Conductor, 1995–2002, Principal Conductor, 2002–05, Gen. Music Dir, 2005–08, Zürich Opera; conducts Bayerischer Rundfunk, Vienna Philharmonic, Salzburg Fest., Berlin Philharmonic and all major US orchestras; numerous recordings. Awards from USA and UK. *Address:* c/o IMG Artists, The Light Box, 111 Power Road, W4 5PY.

WELSH, Andrew Paton; DL; Member (SNP) Angus, Scottish Parliament, 1999–2011; *b* 19 April 1944; *s* of William and Agnes Welsh; *m* 1971, Sheena Margaret Cannon; one *d. Educ:* Univ. of Glasgow (MA (Hons) History and Politics; DipEd, 1980); Open Univ. (Dip. French 2005). Teacher of History, 1972–74; Lectr in Public Admin and Economics, Dundee Coll. of Commerce, 1979–83; Sen. Lectr in Business and Admin. Studies, Angus Technical Coll., 1983–87. MP (SNP) South Angus, Oct. 1974–1979; contested (SNP) Angus E, 1983; MP (SNP) Angus E, 1987–97, Angus, 1997–2001. SNP Parly Chief Whip, 1978–79, 1987–97; SNP spokesman on: housing, 1974–78; self employed affairs and small businesses, 1975–79, 1987–2001; agriculture, 1976–79, 1987–2001; local govt, 1987–97; local govt, housing and educn, 1997–2001. Member: Scottish Affairs Select Cttee, 1992–2001; Speaker's Panel of Chairmen, 1997–2001. Scottish Parliament: Member: Corporate Body, 1999–2006; Commn of Accounts, 2000–07; Audit Cttee, 2007–09 (Convener, 1999–2003; Dep. Convener, 2004–07); Dep. Convener, Local Govt and Transport Cttee, 2003–04; Convener, Finance Cttee, 2007–11. SNP Exec. Vice Chm. for Admin, 1979–87; SNP Vice-Pres., 1987–2004. Mem., Angus District Council, 1984–87; Provost of Angus, 1984–87. Freeman of Angus, 2013. DL Angus, 2013. *Recreations:* music, horse riding, languages. *Address:* Montquhir Farm House, Carmyllie, Arbroath, Angus DD11 2QS. *Club:* Glasgow University Union.

WELSH, Prof. Dominic; *see* Welsh, J. A. D.

WELSH, Frank Reeson, FRHistS; writer; Director, Grindlays Bank, 1971–85; *b* 16 Aug. 1931; *s* of F. C. Welsh and D. M. Welsh; *m* 1954, Agnes Cowley; two *s* two *d. Educ:* Gateshead and Blaydon Grammar Schools; Magdalene Coll., Cambridge (schol.; MA). With John Lewis Partnership, 1954–58; CAS Group, 1958–64; Man. Dir, William Brandt's Sons & Co. Ltd, 1965–72; Chairman: Hadfields Ltd, 1967–79; Jensen Motors Ltd, 1968–72; Cox & Kings, 1972–76; Dir, Henry Ansbacher & Co., 1976–82. Member: British Waterways Board, 1975–81; Gen. Adv. Council, IBA, 1976–80; Royal Commn on Nat. Health Service, 1976–79; Health Educn Council, 1978–80. Dir, Trireme Trust, 1983–. Vis. Lectr and Alcoa Schol., Graduate Sch. of Business Studies, Univ. of Tennessee, Knoxville, 1979–85. CCMI. *Publications:* The Profit of the State, 1982; (contrib.) Judging People, 1982; The Afflicted State, 1983; First Blood, 1985; (with George Ridley) Bend'Or, Duke of Westminster, 1985; Uneasy City, 1986; Building the Trireme, 1988; Companion Guide to the Lake District, 1989, 2nd edn 1997; Hong Kong: a history (US edn as A Borrowed Place), 1993, 2nd edn 1997 (Chinese edn 2001, 2014); A History of South Africa, 1998; Dangerous Deceits, 1999; The Four Nations, 2002; Great Southern Land: a new history of Australia, 2004; (jtly) Victoria's Empire, 2007; The Battle for Christendom, 2008; A History of the World, 2011, 2nd edn 2013. *Recreations:* sailing, correcting Radio 4's pronunciation and grammar. *Address:* 33 rue St Bartélémy, 16500 Confolens, France. *Club:* Oxford and Cambridge.

WELSH, Ian, OBE 2015; Chief Executive, Health and Social Care (formerly Long Term Conditions) Alliance Scotland, since 2010; *b* 23 Nov. 1953; *m* 1977, Elizabeth McAndrew; two *s. Educ:* Prestwick Acad.; Ayr Acad.; Glasgow Univ. (MA Hons Eng. Lit. and Hist.); Jordanhill Coll. (Dip. in Educnl Mgt); Open Univ. (MA). Former professional football player, Kilmarnock FC; English teacher: James Hamilton Acad., Kilmarnock, 1977–80; Auchinleck Acad., 1980–97 (Dep. Head Teacher, 1992–97); Dir of Human Resources and Public Affairs, Prestwick Internat. Airport, 1997; Chief Executive: Kilmarnock FC, 1997–99 and 2000–01; Momentum Scotland, 2001–07; Dir, UK Services, Rehab Gp, 2007–10. Member (Lab): Kyle and Carrick Council, 1984–95 (Leader, 1990–92); S Ayrshire Council, 1995–99 (Leader); MSP (Lab) Ayr, 1999. Chairman: Scottish Adv. Cttee to Voluntary Sector NTO, 2002–05; Ayrshire Business in the Community, 2007–09; Ayr United Football Acad., 2007–; E Ayrshire Jt Integration Bd, 2015–; Member of Board: Scottish Enterprise, Ayrshire, 2002–07; Irvine Bay Regeneration Co., 2007–10; Ayrshire and Arran NHS, 2011–. Director: Borderline Theatre Co., 1990– (Chm., 2002–07); Prestwick Internat. Airport, 1992–97; Chm., Ayr Gaiety Partnership, 2010–. Mem. Ct, Univ. of W Scotland, 2007– (Chm., 2013–). FRSA. *Address:* Health and Social Care Alliance Scotland, Venlaw Building, 349 Bath Street, Glasgow G2 4AA; 35 Ayr Road, Prestwick, Ayrshire KA9 1SY.

WELSH, Prof. (James Anthony) Dominic, DPhil; Professor of Mathematics, 1992–2005, and Chairman of Mathematics, 1996–2001, Oxford University; Fellow of Merton College, Oxford, 1966–2005, now Emeritus; *b* 29 Aug. 1938; *s* of late James Welsh and Teresa Welsh (*née* O'Callaghan); *m* 1966, Bridget Elizabeth Pratt; two *s* (and one *s* decd). *Educ:* Bishop Gore Grammar Sch., Swansea; Merton Coll., Oxford (MA DPhil); Carnegie Mellon Univ. (Fulbright Scholar). Bell Telephone Labs, Murray Hill, 1961; Oxford University: Jun. Lectr, Mathematical Inst., 1963–66; Tutor in Maths, Merton Coll., 1966–90; Reader in Maths, 1990–92. Vis. appts, Univs of Michigan, Waterloo, Calgary, Stockholm, North Carolina; John von Neumann Prof., Univ. of Bonn, 1990–91; Vis. Oxford Fellow, Univ. of Canterbury, NZ, 2005; Res. Visitor, Centre de Recerca Matemàtica, Barcelona, 2006–07. Chm., British Combinatorial Cttee, 1983–87. Hon. Dr Math. Waterloo, 2006. *Publications:* (ed) Combinatorial Mathematics and its Applications, 1971; (ed jtly) Combinatorics, 1973; Matroid Theory, 1976; (with G. R. Grimmett) Probability: an introduction, 1986, 2nd edn 2014; Codes and Cryptography, 1988, German edn 1991, Japanese edn 2004; (ed jtly) Disorder in Physical Systems, 1990; Complexity: knots, colourings and counting, 1993; (with J. Talbot) Complexity and Cryptography: an introduction, 2006; articles in math. jls. *Recreations:* most sports, walking. *Address:* Merton College, Oxford OX1 4JD. *T:* (01865) 276310.

WELSH, Jolyon Rimmer; HM Diplomatic Service; Senior Director, Consulum Strategic Communications Counsel, since 2014; *b* Manchester, 22 Dec. 1967; *s* of Frank Welsh and Imelda Welsh; *m* 1999, Susan Lynley Kelly; one *s* one *d. Educ:* Trinity Coll., Cambridge (BA Hons Hist. 1990; MA). Entered HM Diplomatic Service, 1990; G7 Unit, 1991; Far Eastern Dept, 1991–92; Second Sec., Colombo, 1992–95; W Eur. Dept, 1996; Human Rights Policy Dept, 1997–98; First Sec., UK Mission to the UN, NY, 1998–2002; Sanctions Unit, 2003; Middle E and N Africa Directorate, 2003–06; Hd, Public Diplomacy, 2006–08; Dep. High Comr, Canberra, 2008–12; Hd of Govt to Govt Contracting, FCO, 2012–14. Chevalier de la Légion d'honneur (France), 1996. *Publications:* (ed with D. Fearn) Engagement: public diplomacy in a globalised world, 2008. *Address:* c/o Foreign and Commonwealth Office, King Charles Street, SW1A 2AH.

WELSH, Michael John, MBE 2014; non-executive Director, Lancashire Teaching Hospitals Trust, since 2013; *b* 22 May 1942; *s* of Comdr David Welsh, RN, and Una Mary (*née* Willmore); *m* 1963, Jennifer Caroline Pollitt; one *s* one *d. Educ:* Dover Coll.; Lincoln Coll., Oxford (BA (Hons) Jurisprudence). Proprietors of Hays Wharf Ltd, 1963–69; Levi Strauss & Co. Europe Ltd, 1969–79 (Dir of Market Development, 1976). Chm., Chorley and S Ribble NHS Trust, 1994–98. MEP (C) Lancashire Central, 1979–94; contested (C) Lancashire Central, Eur. Parly elecns, 1994; Chm., Cttee for Social Affairs and Employment, Eur. Parlt, 1984–87. Mem. (C) Lancs CC, 1997–2013 (Leader, Cons. Gp, 2003–08). Chm., Positive Europe Gp, 1988–94; Chief Exec., Action Centre for Europe Ltd, 1995–2004. Chm., Lancs County Develts Ltd, 2009–13. Mem., Local Adv. Bd, Cuadrilla Resources Ltd, 2013–. *Recreations:* sailing, rough walking. *Address:* Watercrook, 181 Town Lane, Whittle le Woods, Chorley, Lancs PR6 8AG. *T:* (01257) 276992. *Club:* Carlton.

WELSH, Peter, OBE 2001; CEng, FIET; Executive Director, United Kingdom Atomic Energy Authority (Dounreay Division), 1998–2003; *b* 25 March 1941; *s* of late Robert Welsh and Florence Welsh (*née* Gollege; later Armory); *m* 1964, Margaret Philips; two *s. Educ:* Sunderland Poly. (BSc 1st Cl. Hons Electrical Engrg 1966). CEng 1966; FIET (FIEE 2000). Manager: Dungeness A Power Station, CEGB, 1987–91; Hinkley Point A and B Power

Station, Nuclear Electric Plc, 1991–95; Dir, Business Improvement, Magnox Electric Plc, 1995–98. Chm., Somerset TEC, 1994–96; Dir, Somerset Careers Bd, 1994–96; non-exec. Director: Trng Standards Council, 1998–2001; Sector Skills Develt Agency, 2002–06. Mem. Council, SW Reg., CBI, 1998–2001. Gov., Somerset Coll. of Art and Technol., 1995–98. *Recreations:* walking, ski-ing, golf, travel.

WELTEKE, Ernst; President, Deutsche Bundesbank, 1999–2004; *b* Korbach, 21 Aug. 1942. *Educ:* Univ. of Marburg; Univ. of Frankfurt am Main (grad. in econs). Apprentice agricl machine mechanic, 1959–62; Office of Prime Minister of Hesse, 1972–74; MP (SDP) Hesse, 1974–95; Minister of Econs, Transport and Technol., 1991–94; Minister of Finance, 1994–95; Pres., Land Central Bank, Hesse, and Mem., Central Bank Council, Deutsche Bundesbank, 1995–99. Chm., Parly Gp, SDP, 1984–Apr. 1987 and Feb. 1988–1991. Mem. Governing Council, European Central Bank, 1999–2004.

WEMYSS, 13th Earl of, *cr* 1633, **AND MARCH**, 9th Earl of, *cr* 1697; **James Donald Charteris;** DL; Lord Wemyss of Elcho, 1628; Lord Elcho and Methil, 1633; Viscount Peebles, Baron Douglas of Neidpath, Lyne and Munard, 1697; Baron Wemyss of Wemyss (UK), 1821; *b* 22 June 1948; *s* of 12th Earl of Wemyss and March, KT and Mavis Lynette Gordon (*née* Murray); *S* father, 2008; *m* 1st, 1983, Catherine Ingrid (marr. diss. 1988), *d* of Baron Moyne, *qv*, and Mrs Paul Channon; one *s* one *d*; 2nd, 1995, Amanda Claire, *y d* of late Basil Feilding. *Educ:* Eton; University College, Oxford (BA 1969, MA 1974); St Antony's Coll., Oxford (DPhil 1975); Royal Agricultural Coll., Cirencester (Diploma, 1978); MRICS (ARICS 1983). Page of Honour to HM Queen Elizabeth the Queen Mother, 1962–64. Mem., Royal Co. of Archers (Queen's Body Guard for Scotland), 1978–. Mem. Council, Nat. Trust for Scotland, 1987–92; Chm., Heart of England Reg., Hist. Houses Assoc., 1991–96. DL Glos, 2005. *Publications:* The Singapore Naval Base and the Defence of Britain's Eastern Empire 1919–42, 1981. *Heir: s* Lord Elcho, *qv*. *Address:* Stanway, Cheltenham, Glos GL54 5PQ. *T:* (01386) 584469. *Clubs:* Brooks's, Pratt's, Ognisko Polskie; Puffin's, New (Edinburgh).

WEMYSS, Rear-Adm. Martin La Touche, CB 1981; *b* 5 Dec. 1927; *s* of late Comdr David Edward Gillespie Wemyss, DSO, DSC, RN, and Edith Mary Digges La Touche; *m* 1st, 1951, Ann Hall (marr. diss. 1973); one *s* one *d*; 2nd, 1973, Elizabeth Loveday Alexander; one *s* one *d*. *Educ:* Shrewsbury School. CO HMS Sentinel, 1956–57; Naval Intell. Div., 1957–59; CO HMS Alliance, 1959–60; CO Commanding Officers' Qualifying Course, 1961–63; Naval Staff, 1963–65; CO HMS Cleopatra, 1965–67; Naval Asst to First Sea Lord, 1967–70; CO 3rd Submarine Sqdn, 1970–73; CO HMS Norfolk, 1973–74; Dir of Naval Warfare, 1974–76; Rear-Adm., 1977; Flag Officer, Second Flotilla, 1977–78; Asst Chief of Naval Staff (Ops), 1979–81. Clerk to Brewers' Co., 1981–91. *Recreation:* gardening. *Address:* The Old Post House, Emberton, near Olney, Bucks MK46 5BX. *T:* (01234) 713838. *Club:* Army and Navy.

WEN, Prof. Eric Lewis; freelance writer and music producer; Professor of Music Theory, Juilliard School of Music, New York, since 2014 (Lecturer, 2013–14); Lecturer, Graduate Center, City University of New York, since 2013; *b* 18 May 1953; *s* of Adam and Mimi Wen; *m* 1st, 1989, Louise Barder (marr. diss. 1998); two *d*; 2nd, 1999, Rachel Stadlen; one *s*. *Educ:* Columbia Univ. (BA); Yale Univ. (MPhil); Cambridge Univ. Lecturer: Guildhall Sch. of Music, 1978–84; Goldsmiths' Coll., Univ. of London, 1980–84; Mannes Coll. of Music, NY, 1984–86; Editor: The Strad, 1986–89; The Musical Times, 1988–90; Man. Dir, Biddulph Recordings, 1990–99; Lectr, 1999–2002 and 2008–, Chm. of Musical Studies, 2002–08, Curtis Inst. of Music; Edward Aldwell Prof. of Music, Mannes Coll. of Music, NY, 2008–13. *Publications:* (contrib.) Schenker Studies, 1989; (contrib.) Trends in Schenkerian Research, 1990; (ed) The Fritz Kreisler Collection, 1990; (contrib.) Cambridge Companion to the Violin, 1992; (ed) The Heifetz Collection, 1995; (contrib.) Schenker Studies 2, 1999; (ed) The Joseph Szigeti Collection, 2000; (ed) Hebrew Melodies, 2001; (ed) Masterpieces for Violin, 2005; (contrib.) Structure and Meaning in Tonal Music, 2006; (contrib.) Essays from the Third Schenker Symposium, 2006; (ed) Masterworks for Violin, 2006; (ed) Solos for Violin, 2006; (contrib.) Essays from the Fourth Schenker Symposium, 2008; (contrib.) Bach to Brahms, 2015; (contrib.) Schubert's Late Music: history, theory, style, 2015; contrib. various music jls. *Recreations:* music, chess, cooking, legerdemain.

WENBAN, Sarah Ann; *see* Thane, S. A.

WENBAN-SMITH, (William) Nigel, CMG 1991; HM Diplomatic Service, retired; Secretary General, Commonwealth Magistrates' and Judges' Association, 1993–94; *b* 1 Sept. 1936; *s* of William Wenban-Smith, CMG, CBE; *m* 1st, 1961, Charlotte Chapman-Andrews (marr. diss 1975; she *m* 2nd, Sir Peter Evelyn Leslie); two *s* two *d*; 2nd, 1976, Charlotte Susanna Rycroft (*d* 1990); two *s*; 3rd, 1993, Frances Catharine Barlow; two step *d*. *Educ:* King's Sch., Canterbury; King's Coll., Cambridge (BA); MA Buckingham 2000. National Service, RN. Plebiscite Supervisory Officer, Southern Cameroons, 1960–61; Asst Principal, CRO, 1961–65 (Private Sec. to Parly Under Sec., 1963–64); Second Sec., Leopoldville, 1965–67; First Sec. and (1968) Head of Chancery, Kampala, 1967–70; FCO, 1970–74; Dublin, 1975; Commercial Sec., 1976–78, Commercial Counsellor, 1978–80, Brussels; on loan to Cabinet Office, 1980–82; Hd of E Africa Dept and Comr, British Indian Ocean Territory, FCO, 1982–85; National Defence Coll. of Canada, 1985–86; Deputy High Comr, Ottawa, 1986–89; High Comr, Malaŵi, 1990–93. Chm., Friends of the Chagos Assoc., 1996–2002. *Recreations:* walking, gardening, history of Chagos archipelago. *Address:* Highbank, The Quarry, Brockhampton, Cheltenham GL54 5XL.

WEND, Prof. Petra, PhD; FRSE; Principal and Vice-Chancellor, Queen Margaret University, Edinburgh, since 2009; *b* Gütersloh, Germany, 21 Jan. 1959; *d* of Peter and Thekla Wend; partner, Prof. Philip James; one *d*. *Educ:* Münster Univ. (Staatsexamen in Italian and French lang. and lit., and educn); Univ. of Leeds (PhD Italian Lang. and Lit. 1990). Middlesex Polytechnic, later Middlesex University: Lectr, Sen. Lectr, then Principal Lectr, 1989–97; Dep. Hd, Sch. of Langs, 1996–97 (Acting Hd, 1995); Dir of Curriculum, Learning and Quality, 1997–99; Dean, Faculty of Humanities and Educn, 1999–2002, Pro Vice-Chancellor (Learning and Teaching), 2000–02, Univ. of N London; Dir of Learning, Teaching and Student Affairs, London Metropolitan Univ., 2002–05; Dep. Vice-Chancellor and Dep. Chief Exec., Oxford Brookes Univ., 2005–09. Convener, Learning and Teaching Cttee, 2010–12, Vice-Convener, 2012–, Universities Scotland; Chair, Nat. Implementation Bd, Teaching Scotland's Future, 2012–. Member: QAA, 2010– (Mem., Scotland Cttee, 2011–); Skills Cttee, Jt Govt and Scottish Funding Council, 2010–13; Scotland Cttee, British Council, 2011–; Commn for Widening Access, 2015–. Member: Edinburgh Business Forum, 2010– (Chair, Productivity and Skills Sub-Gp, 2010–12); Goodison Gp Forum, 2012–; Edinburgh Partnership Bd, 2013–. Mem., Soc. of Renaissance Studies, 1991. FRSA 2009; FRSE 2015. *Publications:* The Female Voice: lyrical expression in the writings of the five Italian Renaissance poets, 1994; German Interlanguage, 1996, 2nd edn 1998; Geschäftsbriefe schnell und sicher formulieren, 2004; contrib. articles to learned jls on linguistics and on instnl strategies. *Recreations:* painting, sport, Arsenal FC (season ticket holder). *Address:* Queen Margaret University, Edinburgh, Queen Margaret University Drive, Musselburgh, Edinburgh EH21 6UU. *T:* (0131) 474 0483, *Fax:* (0131) 474 0001. *E:* pwend@qmu.ac.uk.

WENDT, Henry, Hon. CBE 1995; Chairman: SmithKline Beecham, 1989–94; Global Health Care Partners, DLJ Merchant Banking, 1997–2002; Arrail Dental (China) Ltd, 1999–2012; *b* 19 July 1933; *s* of Henry Wendt and Rachel L. (*née* Wood); *m* 1956, Holly Peterson; one *s* one *d*. *Educ:* Princeton Univ. (AB 1955). Joined SmithKline & French Labs, 1955: various positions in Internat. Div.; Pres., 1976–82; Chief Exec. Officer, 1982–87; Chm., 1987–89 (merger of SmithKline Beckman and Beecham, 1989). Director: Arjo Wiggins Appleton plc, 1990–92; Cambridge Labs plc, 1996–; West Marine Inc., 1997–2001; Wilson Greatbatch Ltd, 1997–2003; Computerised Med. Systems, 1997–; Charles River Labs, 2000–01; Prometheus Labs, 2000–03; Focus Technologies Inc., 2000–03. Chairman: Healdsburg Performing Arts Theatre, 2000–03; Sonoma County Community Foundn, 2001–04. Trustee: Philadelphia Museum of Art, 1979–94; Amer. Enterprises Inst., 1987–96. Order of the Rising Sun with Gold and Silver Star (Japan), 1994. *Publications:* Global Embrace, 1993. *Recreations:* sailing, flyfishing, tennis, viticulture. *Address:* 560 Warbass Way, Friday Harbor, WA 98250, USA. *Clubs:* Flyfishers'; New York Yacht (New York).

WENDT, Robin Glover, CBE 1996; DL; community activist; Vice-Chairman, Action for Children (formerly NCH), 2000–08; *b* 7 Jan. 1941; *er s* of late William Romilly Wendt and Doris May (*née* Glover), Preston, Lancs; *m* 1965, Prudence Ann Dalby; two *d*. *Educ:* Hutton GS, Preston; Wadham Coll., Oxford Univ. (BA 1962; MA 1992). Asst Principal 1962, Principal 1966, Min. of Pensions and Nat. Insurance; Principal Private Sec. to Sec. of State for Social Services, 1970; Asst Sec., DHSS, 1972; Dep. Sec., 1975, Chief Exec., 1979–89, Cheshire CC; Clerk of Cheshire Lieutenancy, 1979–90; Sec., ACC, 1989–97; Chief Exec., Nat. Assoc. of Local Councils, 1997–99. Sec., Manchester Airport Consultative Cttee, 1979–89. Member: Cheshire Area Manpower Bd, 1982–89; Social Security Adv. Cttee, 1982–2002; PCFC, 1989–93; Council, RIPA, 1989–92; Council for Charitable Support, 1991–97; DoH Wider Health Working Gp, 1991–97; Carnegie Third Age Enquiry, 1992–96; Adv. Bd, Fire Service Coll., 1992–96; Citizenship Foundn Adv. Council, 1993–97; Joseph Rowntree Foundn Income and Wealth Inquiry, 1993–95; Royal Commn on Long-Term Care of the Elderly, 1997–99; Bd, FAS, 1997–99; Council, Action for Children (formerly NCH Action for Children, then NCH), 1997–2008; Bd, YMCA Chester, 1997–2008; Benefits Agency Standards Cttee, 1999–2002; Joseph Rowntree Foundn Adv. Gp on Long-Term Care of the Elderly, 2003–06; NCH/Nat. Family and Parenting Inst./Joseph Rowntree Foundn Family Commn, 2005–06. Non-exec. Dir, NIMTECH, 2000–13. Mem., S Cheshire HA, 2001–02; Vice-Chm., Cheshire and Merseyside Strategic HA, 2002–04. Chairman: Cheshire Rural Forum, 2000–04; Chester in Partnership, 2001–06. Mem. Exec., Chester Music Soc., 1999–2008 and 2011–; Chairman: Chester Summer Music Fest., 2001–08; Chester Fests, 2003–06; Dir, Chester Performing Arts Centre Ltd, 2006–08. Pres., Cheshire Assoc. of Town and Parish Councils, 1997–2004. Sec., NW Says No Campaign, 2003–04. Trustee: Ind. Living Funds, 1993–2001; Vision Homes Assoc., 2011–; Cheshire W Citizens Advice, 2012–. DL Cheshire, 1990. Contributor (as Ted Browning), Tribune, 1999–2004. *Publications:* various letters, articles and reviews on public service issues; occasional music reviews. *Recreations:* music, following sport, travel. *Address:* 25 Bowling Green Court, 2 Brook Street, Chester CH1 3DP. *T:* (01244) 340455. *E:* robin.wendt@icloud.com. *Club:* Chester FC.

WENGER, Arsène, Hon. OBE 2003; Chevalier, Légion d'Honneur, 2002; Manager, Arsenal Football Club, since 1996; *b* 22 Oct. 1949. *Educ:* Strasbourg Univ. (BEc 1974). Amateur football player, Mutzig, then Mulhouse, 1969–78; professional football player, Strasbourg, 1978–83 (Coach, Youth team, 1981–83); Player/Coach, Cannes, 1983; Manager: AS Nancy, 1984–87; AS Monaco, 1987–94; Nagoya Grampus Eight, Japan, 1995–96. Arsenal won Premier League and FA Cup, 1998, 2002, FA Cup, 2003, 2005, 2014, Premier League, 2004; Champions League finalists, 2006. *Address:* Arsenal Football Club, Highbury House, 75 Drayton Park, N5 1BU.

WENGER, (John) Patrick; Chairman, Stoke Further Education College, 2005–10; *b* 23 Nov. 1943; *s* of Richard John Wenger and Hilda Wenger (*née* Hardy); *m* 1969, Sheila Ann Baddeley; one *s* one *d*. *Educ:* Repton; N Staffs Tech. Coll. (Pottery Managers Dip.; Ceramic Technicians Dip.); Harvard (AMP); Cranfield Univ. Allied English Potteries: Mgt trainee, 1960–65; works manager, 1966; PA to Man. Dir, 1967–68; Gen. Works Manager, 1969–70; Asst Chief Exec., Paragon Div., 1971; Exec. i/c Paragon, following merger with Royal Doulton, 1972–84; Chief Executive: Hotel and Airlines Div., 1985–86; Ext. Sales Div., 1986–89; Internat. Sales Dir, 1989–93; Chief Operating Officer (following demerger from Pearson PLC), 1993–97; Chief Exec., Royal Doulton plc, 1997–99. Retired due to serious car accident whilst in Australia in business. Dir, North Staffs Risk Capital Fund plc, 2004–. Chm., Newcastle Sch., 2004–11 (Gov., 2003–). Mem., Ancient Corp. of Hanley, 1985–. *Recreations:* sailing, golf, tennis, hockey, cricket, travel. *Address:* Foxley, Mill Lane, Standon, near Eccleshall, Staffs ST21 6RP. *Club:* Potters' (Stoke-on-Trent).

WENNER, Michael Alfred; HM Diplomatic Service, retired; President, Wenner Communications (formerly Wenner Trading Co.), 1982–2002; *b* 17 March 1921; *s* of Alfred E. Wenner and of Simone Roussel; *m* 1st, 1950, Gunilla Cecilia Ståhle (*d* 1986), *d* of Envoyé Nils K. Ståhle, CBE, and Birgit Olsson; four *s*; 2nd, 1990, Holly (Raven) Adrianne Johnson, *d* of Adrian W. Johnson and Ophelia A. Matley. *Educ:* Stonyhurst; Oriel College, Oxford (Scholar). Served E Yorks Regt, 1940; Lancs Fusiliers and 151 Parachute Bn, India, 1941–42; 156 Bn, N Africa, 1943; No 9 Commando, Italy and Greece, 1944–45. Entered HM Foreign Service, 1947; 3rd Sec., Stockholm, 1948–51; 2nd Sec., Washington, 1951–53; Foreign Office, 1953–55; 1st Sec., Tel Aviv, 1956–59; Head of Chancery, La Paz, 1959–61, and at Vienna, 1961–63; Inspector of Diplomatic Establishments, 1964–67; Ambassador to El Salvador, 1967–70. Commercial Advr, Consulate-Gen. of Switzerland in Houston, Texas, 1974–91. Founder, Academia Británica Cuzcatlea, El Salvador, 1970. Hon. Mem., Consular Corps of Houston, Texas, 1992–2008. *Publications:* Advances in Controlled Droplet Application, Agrichemical Age, 1979; So It Was (memoirs), 1993; (translated) Kidnapped by Brigands, by Isaac Friedli, 1995; Telephone Tales, 1996. *Recreations:* fly-fishing, old maps, choral singing, volunteer teaching, elocution. *Address:* The Old Coach House, Broadbottom, Hyde, Cheshire SK14 6AH; Laythams Farm, Slaidburn, Clitheroe, Lancs BB7 3AJ. *T:* (01200) 446677.

WENSLEY, Prof. (John) Robin (Clifton), PhD; Professor of Policy and Marketing, University of Warwick, 1986–2012, now Professor Emeritus; Professor of Strategic Marketing, Open University, since 2013; *b* 26 Oct. 1944; *s* of George Leonard Wensley and Jeannette Marion Wensley; *m* 1970, Susan Patricia Horner; one *s* two *d*. *Educ:* Perse Sch., Cambridge; Queens' Coll., Cambridge (BA 1966); London Business Sch. (MSc; PhD). Lectr, then Sen. Lectr, London Business Sch., 1974–85; University of Warwick: Chm., Warwick Business Sch., 1989–94; Chair, Faculty of Soc. Studies, 1996–99; Dep. Dean, Warwick Business Sch., 2001–04; Dir, Advanced Inst. of Mgt Res., 2004–12. Chm. Council, Tavistock Inst. of Human Relns, 1998–2003; Council Mem., ESRC, 2001–04; Mem., Adv. Council, Warburg Inst., 2012–; Mem., Bd of Advrs, Faculty of Business and Law, Southampton Univ., 2013–. Member: Warwickshire Wildlife Trust, 1997–; Sustrans, 1997–. *Publications:* Strategic Marketing: planning, implementation and control, 1983; Interface of Marketing and Strategy, 1990; Rethinking Marketing, 1994; Handbook of Marketing, 2002; Effective Management in Practice: analytical insights and critical questions, 2013. *Recreations:* walking, DIY, reading, cycling. *Address:* 147 Leam Terrace, Leamington Spa CV31 1DF. *T:* (01926) 425022. *E:* robin.wensley@warwick.ac.uk.

WENSLEY, Penelope Anne, AC 2011 (AO 2001); Governor of Queensland, 2008–14; *b* Toowoomba, Qld, 18 Oct. 1946; *d* of Neil Wensley and Doris McCulloch; *m* 1974, Stuart McCosker; two *d*. *Educ:* Penrith High Sch.; Rosa Bassett Grammar Sch., London; Univ. of Queensland (BA 1st Cl. Hons 1967; Alumnus of Yr 1994). Joined Dept of Foreign Affairs, Australia, 1968; Third Sec., later Second Sec., then First Sec., Paris, 1969–73; Gen. Assembly, Aust. Mission to UN, NY, 1974–75; Dep. Hd of Mission, Mexico, 1975–77; Dep. High Comr, Wellington, 1982–85; Consul-Gen., Hong Kong and Macau, 1986–88; Department of Foreign Affairs and Trade: Asst Sec., E Asia Br., 1989–90; Principal Advr, 1991–92; First Asst Sec., Internat. Orgns and Legal Div., 1992; Ambassador for the Environment, 1992–95; Ambassador and Perm. Rep. to UN, Geneva, 1993–95; Actg Dep. Sec., 1996; First Asst Sec., N Asia Div., 1996–97; Ambassador and Perm. Rep. to UN, NY, 1997–2001; High Comr to India, 2001–04, and Ambassador (non-resident) to Bhutan, 2003–04; Ambassador to France, 2005–08, and (non-resident) to Algeria, Mauritania and Morocco, 2005–08 and Monaco, 2007–08; First Asst Sec., Eur. Div., 2008. Chm., UN Fifth Cttee (Budget and Finance), 1999–2000; Co-Chm., UN Gen. Assembly Special Session on HIV/AIDS, 2001. Hon. DPhil: Queensland, 1994; Griffith, 2008; Queensland Univ. of Technol., 2011; James Cook Univ., 2013. Peace Medal, UN Assoc. of Australia, 1998. Grand Officer, Order of Merit (France), 2009. *Recreations:* reading, music. *Clubs:* National Press (Canberra); Moreton, United Service (Brisbane).

WENSLEY, Robin; *see* Wensley, J. R. C.

WENT, David; Chairman, Irish Times Ltd, 2007–13; *b* 25 March 1947; *s* of Arthur Edward James Went and Phyllis (*née* Howell); *m* 1972, Mary Christine Milligan; one *s* one *d*. *Educ:* High Sch., Dublin; Trinity Coll., Dublin (BA Mod; LLB). Called to the Bar, King's Inns, Dublin, 1970. Graduate Trainee, Citibank, Dublin, 1970; Gen. Manager, Citibank, Jeddah, 1975–76; Dir 1976, Chief Exec. 1982, Ulster Investment Bank; Ulster Bank: Dep. Chief Exec., 1987; Chief Exec., 1988–94; Chief Exec., Coutts Gp, 1994–97; Man. Dir, Irish Life, 1998, Gp Chief Exec., 1999–2007, Irish Life & Permanent PLC. Non-executive Director: Vhi Healthcare, 2007–10; Goldman Sachs Bank (Europe) Ltd, 2007–13; Covestone Asset Mgt Ltd, 2012–. Chm., NI Bankers' Assoc., 1988–89; President: Irish Bankers' Fedn, 1991–92; Inst. of Bankers in Ireland, 1993–94. Chm., Trinity Foundn, 2002–12. Hon. LLD Trinity Coll., Dublin, 2013. *Recreations:* tennis, reading. *Address:* Twyzel Lodge, Lordello Road, Rathmichael, Co. Dublin, Ireland. *Clubs:* Kildare Street and University (Dublin); Fitzwilliam Lawn Tennis; Killiney Golf.

WENT, Rt Rev. John Stewart; Bishop Suffragan of Tewkesbury, 1996–2013; House-for-duty Assistant Chaplain, Chenies with Little Chalfont, Latimer and Flaunden, since 2013; an Honorary Assistant Bishop, Diocese of Oxford, since 2013; *b* 11 March 1944; *s* of Douglas and Barbara Went; *m* 1968, Rosemary Evelyn Amy (*née* Dunn); three *s*. *Educ:* Corpus Christi Coll., Cambridge (1st Cl Classics Pt I, starred 1st Theology Pt II; MA). Curate, Emmanuel, Northwood, Middx, 1969–75; Vicar, Holy Trinity, Margate, 1975–83; Vice-Principal, Wycliffe Hall, Oxford, 1983–89; Archdeacon of Surrey, 1989–95. Warden of Readers, Gloucester dio., 1996–2000. Chairman: Diocesan Council for Unity and Mission, Guildford, 1990–95; Vocation, Recruitment and Selection Cttee, C of E Ministry Div., 2002–08. Member Council: Bible Reading Fellowship, 1989–2015; World Vision, 1996–2006; Interserve, 2009–; Chm., British Tantur Trust, 2009–. *Publications:* (contrib.) Changing Rural Life: a Christian response to key rural issues (ed J. Martineau, L. J. Francis and P. Francis), 2004; contrib. to One in Christ and Rural Theology Jl. *Recreations:* music, photography, crosswords. *Address:* The Rectory, Latimer, Chesham HP5 1UA.

WENTWORTH, Stephen, CB 2003; Fisheries Director, Department for Environment, Food and Rural Affairs (formerly Fisheries Secretary, Ministry of Agriculture, Fisheries and Food), 1993–2003; *b* 23 Aug. 1943; *s* of Ronald Wentworth, OBE and Elizabeth Mary Wentworth (*née* Collins); *m* 1970, Katharine Laura Hopkinson; three *d*. *Educ:* King's College Sch., Wimbledon; Merton Coll., Oxford (MA 1970; MSc 1970); Open Univ. (Dip. Lit. 2005); Birkbeck, Univ. of London (MA Japanese Cultural Studies 2008; MA World History 2014). Joined Ministry of Agriculture, Fisheries and Food, 1967; seconded to CSSB, 1974, and to FCO, as First Sec., UK Perm. Repn to EEC, Brussels, 1976; Head of Beef Div., 1978; seconded to Cabinet Office, 1980; Head of: Milk Div., 1982; European Communities Div., 1985; Under-Sec. and Head of Meat Gp, 1986; Head of Livestock Products Gp, 1989; Head of EC and External Trade Policy Gp, 1991.

WERNER, Ronald Louis, AM 1980; MSc, PhD; President, New South Wales Institute of Technology, 1974–86; Emeritus Professor, University of Technology Sydney, since 1988; *b* 12 Sept. 1924; *s* of Frank Werner and Olive Maude Werner; *m* 1948, Valerie Irene (*née* Bean) (*d* 2002); two *s* one *d*. *Educ:* Univ. of New South Wales (BSc (1st Cl. Hons; Univ. Medal); MSc, PhD). FRACI. Sen. Lectr, 1954–60, Associate Prof., 1961–67, Head of Dept of Phys. Chemistry, 1964–67, Univ. of New South Wales; Dep. Dir, 1967–68, Director, 1968–73, NSW Inst. of Technology. Chm., NSW Advanced Educn Bd, 1969–71; Trustee, Mus. of Applied Arts and Scis, 1973–86 (Pres., Bd of Trustees, 1976–84); Chairman: Conf. of Dirs of Central Insts of Technology, 1975; ACDP, 1982–83; Member: Science and Industry Forum, Aust. Acad. of Science, 1971–76; Council for Tech. and Further Educn, 1970–85; Hong Kong UPGC, 1972–90; NSW Bicentennial Exhibition Cttee, 1985–88; Adv. Council, Univ. of Western Sydney, 1986–88; Governor, College of Law, 1972–76. Director: NRMA Ltd, 1977–95; NRMA Life Ltd, 1985–95; NRMA Travel Ltd, 1986–95; Open Road Publishing Co., 1986–95; NRMA Sales & Service, 1986–95; NRMA Finance Ltd, 1992–95. Councillor, Nat. Roads and Motorists Assoc., 1977–95. DUniv Univ. of Tech. Sydney, 1988. *Publications:* numerous papers in scientific jls. *Recreation:* Mesopotamian writing origins. *Address:* 13 Capri Close, Clareville, NSW 2107, Australia.

WERNICK, Jane Melville, CBE 2015; CEng, FREng, FIStructE, FICE; Director, Jane Wernick Associates Ltd, since 1998; *b* 21 April 1954; *d* of Doreen and Irving Wernick. *Educ:* Christchurch Primary Sch., Hampstead; Haberdashers' Aske's Sch., Acton; Southampton Univ. (BSc Civil Engrg). CEng 1985; MStructE 1985, FIStructE 1993; MICE 1989, FICE 2008; FREng 2009. Grad. engr, Ove Arup & Partners, 1976–80; project engr, Birdair Structures Inc., 1980–81; Ove Arup & Partners, 1981–98: Associate, 1984; Principal i/c LA Office, 1986–89; Associate Dir, London Office, 1989–98. Visiting Professor: Harvard Univ. Grad. Sch. of Design, 1995; Architecture Dept, Oxford Brookes Univ., 1999–2008; Bedford Vis. Prof., Rensselaer Poly. Inst., 1998; RAEng Vis. Prof. of Design, Civil Engrg Dept, Univ. of Southampton, 2001–14. Diploma Unit Master, AA, 1998–2003. Mem., Design Rev. Panel, 2001–06, Schools Design Rev. Panel, 2009–11, CABE; Mem., Nat. Design Rev. Panel, Design Council CABE, 2011–. Liveryman, Co. of Engrs, 2000. FRSA. Hon. FRIBA 2006. *Publications:* (contrib.) Lunar Bases and Space Activities of the 21st Century, Vol. 2, 1988; (contrib.) Arups on Engineering, 1996; (ed) Building Happiness: architecture to make you smile, 2008; contribs to Structural Engr, Architectural Research Qly. *Recreations:* making music, making art, making things, gardening, reading, socializing, travelling, snorkelling. *Address:* c/o Jane Wernick Associates Ltd, Unit 10D, Printing House Yard, Hackney Road, E2 7PR. *T:* (020) 7749 1066.

WERRETT, Dr David John; Chief Executive, Forensic Science Service, 2001–07; Managing Director, Cedere Ltd, since 2007; *b* 24 Oct. 1949; *s* of Kenneth John Werrett and Heather Victoria Werrett; *m* 2004, Rebecca Lesley; one *s* one *d*, and one step *s* one step *d*. *Educ:* Univ. of Birmingham (BSc; PhD 1974). With Forensic Sci. Service, 1974–2007 (Mem. Bd, 1986–2007). MInstD 2002. *Publications:* contrib. numerous scientific papers to jls, incl. Nature. *Recreations:* good food, good wine, good company, preferably on a sail boat. *Club:* Lyme Regis Sailing.

WESKER, Sir Arnold, Kt 2006; FRSL 1985; playwright; director; Founder Director of Centre Fortytwo, 1961 (dissolved 1970); Chairman, British Centre of International Theatre Institute, 1978–82; President, International Playwrights' Committee, 1979–83; *b* 24 May 1932; *s* of Joseph Wesker and Leah Perlmutter; *m* 1958, Dusty Bicker; two *s* (one *d* decd); one *d* by Disa Hastad. *Educ:* Upton House School, Hackney. Furniture Maker's Apprentice, Carpenter's Mate, 1948; Bookseller's Asst, 1949 and 1952; Royal Air Force, 1950–52; Plumber's Mate, 1952; Farm Labourer, Seed Sorter, 1953; Kitchen Porter, 1953–54; Pastry Cook, 1954–58. Former Mem., Youth Service Council. Hon. Fellow, QMW, 1995. Hon. LittD UEA, 1989; Hon. DHL Denison, Ohio, 1997. Author of plays: The Kitchen, produced at Royal Court Theatre, 1959, 1961, 1994, at NT, 2011 (filmed, 1961; adapted for film, 2005); Trilogy of plays (Chicken Soup with Barley, Roots, I'm Talking about Jerusalem) produced Belgrade Theatre (Coventry), 1958–60, Royal Court Theatre, 1960, Roots perf. Donmar Warehouse, 2013; Chips with Everything, Royal Court, 1962, Vaudeville, 1962 and Plymouth Theatre, Broadway, 1963; The Four Seasons, Belgrade Theatre (Coventry) and Saville, 1965; Their Very Own and Golden City, Brussels and Royal Court, 1966 (Marzotto Drama Prize, 1964); The Friends, Stockholm and London, 1970 (also dir); The Old Ones, Royal Court, 1972; The Wedding Feast, Stockholm, 1974, Leeds 1977; The Journalists, Coventry (amateur), 1977, Yugoslav TV, 1978, Germany, 1981; The Merchant, subseq. entitled Shylock, Stockholm and Aarhus, 1976, Broadway, 1977, Birmingham, 1978 (adapted for radio, 2005); Love Letters on Blue Paper, Nat. Theatre, 1978 (also dir); Fatlips (for young people), 1978; Caritas (Scandinavian Project commission), 1980, Nat. Theatre, 1981, adapted as opera libretto (music by Robert Saxton), 1991; Sullied Hand, 1981, Edinburgh Festival and Finnish TV, 1984; Four Portraits (Japanese commn), Tokyo, 1982, Edinburgh Festival, 1984; Annie Wobbler, Süddeutscher Rundfunk, Germany, Birmingham and New End Theatre, 1983, Fortune Theatre, 1984, New York, 1986; One More Ride on the Merry-Go-Round, Leicester, 1985; Yardsale, Edinburgh Fest. and Stratford-on-Avon (RSC Actors' Fest.), 1985 (also dir); When God Wanted A Son, 1986; Whatever Happened to Betty Lemon (double-bill with Yardsale), Lyric Studio, 1987 (also dir); Little Old Lady (for young people), Sigtuna, Sweden, 1988; The Mistress, 1988, Rome (also dir); Beorhtel's Hill, Towngate, Basildon, 1989; Three Women Talking (later entitled Men Die Women Survive), 1990, Chicago, 1992; Letter to a Daughter, 1990; Blood Libel, 1991; Wild Spring, 1992, Tokyo, 1994; Denial, Bristol Old Vic, 2000; Groupie, Fest. di Todi, Italy, 2001; Longitude, 2002, Greenwich Th., 2005; Letter To Myself, Studio Th., Univ. of Aberystwyth, 2004; GRIEF (libretto for one-woman opera), 2004, Suntory Hall, Tokyo, 2008; abridged version of Much Ado About Nothing and Henry V, NYT, Hackney Empire, 2005; Deliverance, Tricycle Th., Kilburn, 2011. *Film scripts:* Lady Othello, 1980; Homage to Catalonia, 1990; Maudie, 1995 (adapted from Diary of Jane Somers, by Doris Lessing). *Television:* (first play) Menace, 1963; Breakfast, 1981; (adapted) Thieves in the Night, by A. Koestler, 1984; (adapted) Diary of Jane Somers, by Doris Lessing, 1989; Barabbas, 2000. *Radio:* Yardsale, 1984; Bluey (Eur. Radio Commn), Cologne Radio 1984, BBC Radio 3, 1985 (adapted as stage play, 1993); Groupie, 2001; Amazed and Surprised, BBC Radio 3, 2006; The Rocking Horse, 2007 (commnd for 75th Anniv. of BBC World Service; adapted as stage play, titled The Rocking Horse Kid, 2009). *Publications:* Chicken Soup with Barley, 1959; Roots, 1959; I'm Talking about Jerusalem, 1960; The Wesker Trilogy, 1960; The Kitchen, 1961; Chips with Everything, 1962; The Four Seasons, 1966; Their Very Own and Golden City, 1966; The Friends, 1970; Fears of Fragmentation (essays), 1971; Six Sundays in January, 1971; The Old Ones, 1972; The Journalists, 1974 (in Dialog; repr. 1975); Love Letters on Blue Paper (stories), 1974, 2nd edn 1990; (with John Allin) Say Goodbye! You May Never See Them Again, 1974; Words—as definitions of experience, 1976; The Wedding Feast, 1977; Journey Into Journalism, 1977; Said the Old Man to the Young Man (stories), 1978; The Merchant, 1978; Fatlips (for young people), 1978; The Journalists, a triptych (with Journey into Journalism and A Diary of the Writing of The Journalists), 1979; Caritas, 1981; Distinctions, 1985; Yardsale, 1987; Whatever Happened to Betty Lemon, 1987; Little Old Lady, 1988; Shoeshine, 1989; Collected Plays: vols 1 and 5, 1989, vols 2, 3, 4 and 6, 1990, vol. 7, 1994; As Much As I Dare (autobiog.), 1994; Circles of Perception, 1996; Break, My Heart, 1997; Denial, 1997; The Birth of Shylock and the Death of Zero Mostel (journals), 1997; The King's Daughters (stories), 1998; Honey (novel), 2005; Longitude, 2006; All Things Tire of Themselves (poetry), 2008; Wesker's Love Plays, 2008; Wesker's Monologues, 2008; Wesker's Social Plays, 2009; Wesker's Political Plays, 2010; Wesker's Essays on Theatre, 2010; Joy and Tyranny, 2011; Ambivalences: a portrait of Arnold Wesker from A to W, 2011; Groupie, 2011; The Kitchen, 2011; Wesker's Historical Plays, 2012; Wesker's Domestic Plays, 2012; Wesker's Comedies, 2012. *Address:* 14 Champions Row, Wilbury Avenue, Hove BN3 6AZ. *T:* (01273) 734013.

WESSELY, Clare; *see* Gerada, C.

WESSELY, Sir Simon (Charles), Kt 2013; MD; FRCP, FRCPsych, FMedSci; Professor of Psychological Medicine (formerly Professor of Epidemiological and Liaison Psychiatry), since 1996, Head, Department of Psychological Medicine, since 2005, and Vice Dean, Academic Psychiatry, Institute of Psychiatry, since 2010, King's College London; President, Royal College of Psychiatrists, since 2014; *b* 23 Dec. 1956; *s* of Rudi and Wendy Wessely; *m* 1988, Dr Clare Gerada, *qv*; two *s*. *Educ:* King Edward VII Sch., Sheffield; Trinity Hall, Cambridge (BA 1978); University Coll., Oxford (BM BCh 1981); London Sch. of Hygiene and Tropical Medicine (MSc 1989); MD London 1993. MRCP 1984, FRCP 1997; MRCPsych 1986, FRCPsych 2000. SHO in Gen. Medicine, Freeman Hosp., Newcastle upon Tyne, 1982–84; SHO, then Registrar, Maudsley Hosp., 1984–87; Sen. Registrar, Nat. Hosp. for Neurol., 1987–88; Wellcome Res. Trng Fellow in Epidemiol., 1988–91; Sen. Lectr, Dept of Psychol Medicine, GKT, 1991–96; Director: Chronic Fatigue Syndrome Res. Unit, KCL, 1994–; Gulf War Illness Res. Unit, later King's Centre for Mil. Health Res., KCL, 1996–. Civilian Consultant Advr in Psychiatry, British Army, 2001–; Sen. Investigator, NIHR, 2008–; Mem., Defence Scientific Adv. Council, 2008–. FMedSci 1999. *Publications:* (jtly) Psychosis in the Inner City, 1998; Chronic Fatigue and its Syndromes, 1998; Clinical Trials in Psychiatry, 2003; From Shellshock to PTSD: a history of military psychiatry, 2005; Psychological Reactions to the New Terrorism: a NATO Russia dialogue, 2005; numerous contribs to learned jls on epidemiol., schizophrenia, chronic fatigue syndrome, unexplained symptoms and syndromes, somatisation, deliberate self-harm, Gulf War illness, military health, psychol aspects of terrorism, risk communication and med. history. *Recreations:* modern history, skiing, cycling to Paris, wasting time in Viennese cafes. *Address:* Department of Psychological Medicine, Weston Education Centre, Cutcombe Road, Camberwell, SE5 9RJ. *T:* (020) 7848 5411, *Fax:* (020) 7848 5408. *E:* simon.wessely@kcl.ac.uk.

WESSON, Jane Louise; Independent Public Appointments Assessor, 2001–12; Chairman, Council for Healthcare Regulatory Excellence (formerly Council for the Regulation of Healthcare Professionals), 2003–07; executive coach, since 2010; *b* 26 Feb. 1953. *Educ:* Univ. of Kent (BA Hons Law). Solicitor of the Supreme Court; Solicitor, Hepworth & Chadwick, 1978–89; Consultant, Ashworth Tetlow & Co., 1995–2005. Chairman: Ind. Tribunal Service, 1992–99; Nat. Clinical Assessment Authy, 2000–02. Chm., Harrogate Healthcare NHS Trust, 1993–2000; Board Member: Northern Counties Housing Assoc., 1993–96; Anchor Housing, 2003–09; Nuffield Health (formerly Nuffield Hosps), 2005–14; Age UK (formerly Help the Aged and Age Concern), 2009–12. *Club:* Royal Automobile.

WEST; *see* Sackville-West, family name of Baron Sackville.

WEST, family name of **Baron West of Spithead**.

WEST OF SPITHEAD, Baron *cr* 2007 (Life Peer), of Seaview in the County of Isle of Wight; **Adm. Alan William John West,** GCB 2004 (KCB 2000); DSC 1982; PC 2010; *b* 21 April 1948; *m* 1973, Rosemary Anne Linington Childs; two *s* one *d*. *Educ:* Windsor Grammar Sch.; Clydebank High Sch. Joined RN 1965; BRNC Dartmouth; seagoing appts, 1966–73; CO HMS Yarnton, 1973; qualified Principal Warfare Officer, 1975; HMS Juno, 1976; HMS Ambuscade, 1977; RN Staff Course, 1978; qualified Advanced Warfare Officer, 1978; HMS Norfolk, 1979; CO HMS Ardent, 1980; Naval Staff, 1982; CO HMS Bristol, 1987; Defence Intell. Staff, 1989; RCDS 1992; Higher Comd and Staff Course, Camberley, 1993; Dir, Naval

Staff Duties, 1993; Naval Sec., 1994–96; Comdr UK Task Gp, and Comdr Anti Submarine Warfare Striking Force, 1996–97; Chief of Defence Intelligence, 1997–2001; C-in-C Fleet, C-in-C E Atlantic and Comdr Allied Naval Forces N, 2001–02; Chief of Naval Staff and First Sea Lord, 2002–06; First and Principal Naval ADC to the Queen, 2002–06. Parly Under-Sec. of State for Security and Counter Terrorism, Home Office, 2007–10; Minister for Cyber Security, 2009–10. Chairman: Defence Adv. Bd, QinetiQ, 2006–07; Nat. Security Forum, 2008–10; Mem., Internat. Adv. Bd, HSBC, 2010–11. Trustee, Imperial War Mus., 2006–14. Chm., Cadet Vocational Qualification Orgn, 2006–12. Chancellor, Southampton Solent Univ., 2006–. Yr Brother, Trinity House. President: Bollington Sea Cadet Corps; Ardent Assoc.; Ship Recognition Corps. Pres., Britannia Assoc., 2006–14; Knight Pres., Knights of the Round Table, 2009–. Member: RUSI, 1977–; St Barbara Assoc., 1978–; Royal Naval Sailing Assoc., 1984–; Anchorites, 1992–; Royal Naval Assoc., 2000–; Pepys Club, 2002–; Destroyer Club, 2002–; Pilgrims, 2003–. Patron: Care for St Anne's Limehouse, 2008–; Dockland Sinfonia, 2008–; Merchant Navy Medal Fund. Member: Master Mariners' Co.; Soc. of Merchants Trading to the Continent; Freeman, Watermen and Lightermen's Co., 2005. *Recreations:* sailing, military and local history, member of Parliament Choir. *Address:* House of Lords, SW1A 0PW. *Clubs:* Naval, Royal Navy of 1765 and 1785; Royal Yacht Squadron.

WEST, Anthony; *see* West, J. A. H.

WEST, Brian John; media consultant; Director and Chief Executive, Association of Independent Radio Companies, 1983–95; *b* 4 Aug. 1935; *s* of Herbert Frank West and Nellie (*née* Painter); *m* 1st, 1960, Patricia Ivy White (marr. diss. 1986); 2nd, 1987, Gillian Bond. *Educ:* Tiffin Sch., Kingston upon Thames. Sub-Lt (O), Fleet Air Arm, RN, 1956–58. Journalist, Richmond Herald, Surrey Comet and Western Morning News, 1952–60; Surrey Comet: Asst Editor, 1960–64; Editor, 1964–70; Editor, Leicester Mercury, 1970–74; Head of Advertising and PR, Littlewoods Orgn Plc, 1974–83. Founder Pres., Assoc. of European Radios, 1992–93; Council Mem., Advertising Assoc., 1987–95; Dir, Radio Jt Audience Res. Ltd, 1992–94. Churchill Fellow, 1995; Beaverbrook Foundn Fellow, 1995; Fellow, Radio Acad., 1995. *Publications:* Radio Training in the United States, 1996. *Recreations:* voluntary work for the blind and partially-sighted, computers, music, horses and dogs, walking, gardening, photography, cherishing my wife. *Address:* Melrose, 33 Cwm Road, Dyserth, Denbighshire LL18 6BA. *T:* and *Fax:* (01745) 570568. *E:* brigil9@tiscali.co.uk.

WEST, Catherine Elizabeth; MP (Lab) Hornsey and Wood Green, since 2015; *b* Mansfield, Vic, Australia; *m* 1996, Dr Colin Sutherland; one *s* one *d*. *Educ:* Univ. of Sydney (BA, BSW); Sch. of Oriental and African Studies, Univ. of London (MA Chinese Politics). Social worker, Australia; caseworker for David Lammy, MP, 2000. Mem., Islington LBC, 2000–14 (Leader of Opposition, 2004–10; Leader of Council, 2010–13). Chm., Transport and Envmt Cttee, London Councils, 2010–14. *Recreations:* swimming, cricket. *Address:* House of Commons, SW1A 0AA. *T:* (020) 7219 6141. *E:* catherine.west.mp@parliament.uk.

WEST, Prof. Christopher David; Chief Executive, Royal Zoological Society of Scotland, since 2012; *b* 16 Aug. 1959; *s* of Donald Frank Hartley West and Delia Handford West; *m* 1993, Diane Linda Keetch; two *s* three *d*. *Educ:* Poole Grammar Sch.; Purbeck Sch.; Royal Veterinary Coll., London (BVetMed 1983; Cert. Lab. Animal Sci. 1986). CBiol, MRSB (MIBiol 1985). Houseman, 1983, Registrar, 1985, Surgery Dept, RVC; Vet. Surgeon and Res. Scientist, Clinical Res. Centre, MRC, 1985–87; Gp Manager, ICI Pharmaceuticals, 1987–91; Named Vet. Surgeon, Zeneca-CTL, 1991–97; Chief Curator, Chester Zoo, 1997–2001; Zool Dir, Zool Soc. of London, 2001–05; Chief Exec., Royal Zool Soc. of Australia, 2006–12. Prof. of Zoology, Univ. of Adelaide, 2006–12; Prof. of Biodiversity Conservation, Flinders Univ., 2007–12. Vis. Prof. in Conservation Medicine, Vet. Faculty, Univ. of Liverpool, 2001; Vis. Lectr, Univ. of Gothenburg, 2002. Chm. Trustees, Wildlife Vets Internat., 2005–06. Chm., Jane Goodall Inst., Australia, 2007–11. *Publications:* papers in Animal Behaviour, Animal Welfare, etc. *Recreations:* organic gardening, visiting deserts, tree planting (to offset international travel), cooking curries, worrying about climate change, working for Chinese species conservation. *Address:* Royal Zoological Society of Scotland, Edinburgh Zoo, 134 Corstorphine Road, Edinburgh EH12 6TS.

WEST, David Arthur James; Assistant Under Secretary of State (Naval Personnel), Ministry of Defence, 1981–84, retired; *b* 10 Dec. 1927; *s* of Wilfred West and Edith West (*née* Jones). *Educ:* Cotham Grammar Sch., Bristol. Executive Officer, Air Ministry, 1946; Higher Executive Officer, 1955; Principal, 1961; Assistant Secretary, 1972; Asst Under Sec. of State, 1979. *Address:* 66 Denton Road, East Twickenham TW1 2HQ. *T:* (020) 8409 0274.

WEST, Dominic Gerard Francis Eagleton; actor; *b* Sheffield, 15 Oct. 1969; *s* of George West and Moya West; one *d* by Polly Astor; *m* 2010, Catherine FitzGerald; two *s* two *d*. *Educ:* Eton Coll.; Trinity Coll., Dublin (BA Hons); Guildhall Sch. of Music and Drama (BA Hons; Hon. Fellow 2012). *Films* include: 3 Joes, 1991; Richard III, 1995; 28 Days, 2000; Rock Star, 2001; Chicago, 2002; Mona Lisa Smile, 2003; The Forgotten, 2004; 300, 2007; Centurion, 2010; The Awakening, 2011; John Carter, 2012; Pride, 2014; *television* series include: The Wire, 2002–08; The Hour, 2011–12; Appropriate Adult, 2011 (Best Actor, BAFTA, 2012); The Affair, 2014–15; TV film, Burton and Taylor, 2013. *Theatre* includes: The Seagull, Old Vic, 1996 (Ian Charleson Award); De La Guarda, Roundhouse, 1999; The Voysey Inheritance, NT, 2006; Rock 'n' Roll, Duke of York's, 2007; Life is a Dream, Donmar, 2009; Butley, Duchess, 2011; Othello, Sheffield Crucible, 2011; The River, Royal Ct, 2012; My Fair Lady, Sheffield Crucible, 2012. Hon. Dr Sheffield Hallam, 2011. *Recreation:* boomerang. *Address:* c/o Tavistock Wood, 45 Conduit Street, W1S 2YN. *T:* (020) 7494 4767. *E:* wood@tavistockwood.com.

WEST, Prof. Donald James; Professor of Clinical Criminology 1979–84, now Emeritus, and Director 1981–84, University of Cambridge Institute of Criminology; Fellow of Darwin College, Cambridge, 1967–91, now Emeritus; Hon. Consultant Psychiatrist, National Health Service, 1961–86, retired; *b* 9 June 1924; *s* of John Charles and Jessie Mercedes West. *Educ:* Merchant Taylors' Sch., Crosby; Liverpool Univ. (MD). LittD Cambridge. FRCPsych. Research Officer, Soc. for Psychical Research, London, and pt-time graduate student in psychiatry, 1947–50; in hospital practice in psychiatry, 1951–59; Sen. Registrar, Forensic Psychiatry Unit, Maudsley Hosp., 1957–59; Inst. of Criminology, Cambridge, 1960–84. Leverhulme Emeritus Fellow, 1988–89. Mental Health Act Comr, 1989–97. Vice Pres., 1981–, and former Pres., British Soc. of Criminology; Pres., Soc. for Psychical Research, 1963–65, 1984–87, 1998–2000; Chm., Forensic Section, World Psychiatric Assoc., 1983–89; Chm., Streetwise Youth, 1986–92. *Publications:* Psychical Research Today, 1954, rev. edn 1962; Eleven Lourdes Miracles (med. inquiry under Parapsych. Foundn Grant), 1957; The Habitual Prisoner (for Inst. of Criminology), 1963; Murder followed by Suicide (for Inst. of Criminology), 1965; The Young Offender, 1967; Homosexuality, 1968; Present Conduct and Future Delinquency, 1969; (ed) The Future of Parole, 1972; (jtly) Who Becomes Delinquent?, 1973; (jtly) The Delinquent Way of Life, 1977; Homosexuality Re-examined, 1977; (ed, jtly) Daniel McNaughton: his trial and the aftermath, 1977; (jtly) Understanding Sexual Attacks, 1978; Delinquency: its roots, careers and prospects, 1982; Sexual Victimisation, 1985; Sexual Crimes and Confrontations, 1987; (jtly) Children's Sexual Encounters with Adults, 1990; Male Prostitution, 1992; (ed) Sex Crimes, 1994; (ed with R. Green) Sociolegal Controls on Homosexuality: a multi-nation comparison, 1997; Gay Life, Straight Work, 2012; various contribs to British Jl of Criminology, Criminal Behaviour and Mental Health, Jl Forensic Psychiatry and Jl Soc. for Psychical Res. *Recreations:* travel, parapsychology. *Address:* Flat 1, 11 Queen's Gate Gardens, SW7 5LY. *T:* (020) 2581 2875. *E:* donjwest@hotmail.com.

WEST, Edward Mark, CMG 1987; Deputy Director-General, Food and Agriculture Organization of the United Nations, 1982–86; *b* 11 March 1923; *m* 1948, Lydia Hollander; three *s*. *Educ:* Hendon County Sch.; University Coll., Oxford (MA). Served RA (W/Lieut), 1943; ICU BAOR (A/Captain), 1945. Asst Principal, Colonial Office, 1947; Private Sec., PUS, Colonial Office, 1950–51, Principal, 1951–58; Head of Chancery, UK Commn, Singapore, 1958–61; Private Secretary to Secretary of State, Colonial Affairs, 1961–62; Private Secretary to Secretary of State for Commonwealth and Colonial Affairs, 1963; Asst Sec., ODM, 1964–70; Food and Agriculture Organization: Director, Programme and Budget Formulation, 1970; Asst Dir-Gen., Administration and Finance Dept, 1974; Asst Dir-Gen., Programme and Budget Formulation, 1976; Special Rep., Internat. Conf. on Nutrition, 1992. *Address:* 10 Warwick Mansions, Cromwell Crescent, SW5 9QR.

WEST, Emma Louise; *see* Johnson, E. L.

WEST, Lt-Col George Arthur Alston-Roberts-, CVO 1988; Comptroller, Lord Chamberlain's Office, 1987–90 (Assistant Comptroller, 1981–87); an Extra Equerry to the Queen, since 1982; *b* 1937; *s* of Major W. R. J. Alston-Roberts-West, Grenadier Guards (killed in action 1940) and late Mrs W. R. J. Alston-Roberts-West; *m* 1970, Hazel, *d* of late Sir Thomas and Lady Cook. *Educ:* Eton Coll.; RMA, Sandhurst. Commissioned into Grenadier Guards, Dec. 1957; served in England, Northern Ireland, Germany and Cyprus; retired, 1980. Dir, Care Ltd, 1991–95. DL Warwicks, 1988. *Address:* Atherstone Hill Farm, Stratford-on-Avon, Warwicks CV37 8NF. *Club:* Boodle's.

WEST, Rev. Jeffrey James, OBE 2006; FSA; Associate Minister, St Mary's, Banbury, since 2011 (Curate, 2007–11); Area Dean of Deddington, since 2012; *b* 15 Oct. 1950; *s* of late Walter Edward West and (Frances) Margaret West (*née* Tatam); *m* 1987, Juliet Elizabeth Allan. *Educ:* Bedford Modern Sch.; Worcester Coll., Oxford (BA PPE 1972; BPhil Politics 1974; MA 1976; DipTh 2006); Oxford Brookes Univ. (PGDipMin 2007); Ripon Coll., Cuddesdon. FSA 2011. Joined Ancient Monuments Inspectorate, Department of Environment, 1974: Asst Inspector, 1974–79; Inspector, 1979–81; seconded as Principal, Local Govt Finance, DoE, 1981–83; Principal Inspector of Historic Buildings, DoE, later English Heritage, 1983–86; English Heritage: Regl Dir of Historic Properties (Midlands and E Anglia), 1986–97; Actg Dir of Historic Properties, 1997–98; Dep. Dir of Conservation, and Dir, Conservation Mgt, 1998–2002; Policy Dir, 2002–05. Ordained deacon, 2007, priest, 2008. Member: Oxford Diocesan Synod, 2008–; Oxford Diocesan Adv. Cttee for the Care of Churches, 2009–. Member: Council, Royal Archaeol Inst., 1980–83; Home Office Burials and Cemeteries Adv. Gp, 2001–05; Rural Affairs Forum for England, 2002–04; Exec. Cttee, ICOMOS (UK), 2006–12 (Mem., Res. and Recording Cttee, 1997–2004; Chm., Develt Cttee, 2009–12). Dir, BURA, 2004–07; Chm., Cotswolds Conservation Bd, 2009–14 (Vice-Chm., 2005–09). FRSA 2001. *Publications:* (with Nicholas Palmer) Haughmond Abbey, Shropshire: excavation of a 12th-century cloister in its historical and landscape context, 2014; contrib. articles, notes and reviews on individual historic bldgs and theory and practice of conservation in learned jls. *Recreation:* architectural and landscape history. *Address:* c/o St Mary's Centre, Horsefair, Banbury, Oxon OX16 0AA.

WEST, (John) Anthony (Hawthorne); Vice Lord Lieutenant of Berkshire, since 2015; *b* Reading, 1 Aug. 1941; *s* of John Lewis West and Camilla Hawthorne West (*née* Lydall); *m* 1966, Sarah Hamilton Mays-Smith; three *s*. *Educ:* Radley Coll.; Sch. of Law. Admitted as solicitor, 1964; in private practice as solicitor with Darley Cumberland, subseq. Cumberland Ellis Peirs, London, 1964–99; Solicitor to Carpenters' Co., 1978–99 (Liveryman, 1999). Member: Bd, Royal Alfred Seafarers' Soc., 1970–2000 (Vice Pres., 2000–); Council, Shipwrecked Mariners' Soc., 1995–2011 (Chm., 2002–08; Vice Pres., 2011–). Trustee: Radley Coll. War Meml Funds, 1968–2010 (Chm., 1989–2010); Royal Merchant Navy Sch. Foundn/Bearwood Coll., 1985–97; Upper Thames Rowing Club, 1998–; Serth and Gates Charity, 2008–; former Trustee, Docklands Settlements; Founding Trustee, Charlie Waller Meml Trust, 1998–2005 (Treas., 1998–2004; Patron, 2005–). Governor: Clothworkers' Foundn, 1995–2012; Mary Hare Sch. for Deaf, 1995–2007 (Vice Chm., 2008; Vice Pres., 2009–). Liveryman, Clothworkers' Co., 1980– (Mem. Ct, 1997–; Master, 2008–09). High Sheriff, 2004–05, DL, 2007, Berks. *Recreations:* sailing, golf (occasional), horseracing, Freemasonry, philately. *Address:* Remenham Manor, Henley-on-Thames, Oxon RG9 3DD. *T:* (01491) 574750; The Old Rectory, Gerrans, Truro, Cornwall TR2 5ES. *T:* (01872) 580102. *E:* jahwest@aol.com. *Clubs:* St Mawes Sailing, Huntercombe Golf.

WEST, Prof. John Clifford, CBE 1977; PhD, DSc; FREng; Vice-Chancellor and Principal, University of Bradford, 1979–89; *b* 4 June 1922; *s* of J. H. West and Mrs West (*née* Ascroft); *m* 1946, Winefride Mary Turner; three *d*. *Educ:* Hindley and Abram Grammar School; Victoria Univ., Manchester (PhD 1953; DSc 1957). Matthew Kirtley Entrance Schol., Manchester Univ., 1940. Electrical Lieutenant, RNVR, 1943–46. Lecturer, University of Manchester, 1946–57; Professor of Electrical Engineering, The Queen's University of Belfast, 1958–65; University of Sussex: Prof. of Electrical and Control Engineering, 1965–78; Founder Dean, Sch. of Applied Scis, 1965–73, Pro-Vice-Chancellor, 1967–71; Dir, Phillips' Philatelic Unit, 1970–78. Director, A. C. E. Machinery Ltd, 1966–79. Member: UGC, 1973–78 (Chm., Technology Sub-Cttee, 1973–78); Science Res. Council Cttee on Systems and Electrical Engineering, 1963–67; Science Res. Council Engrg Bd, 1976–79; Vis. Cttee, Dept of Educn and Science, Cranfield; Civil Service Commn Special Merit Promotions Panel, 1966–72; Naval Educn Adv. Cttee, 1965–72; Crawford Cttee on Broadcasting Coverage, 1973–74; Inter-Univ. Inst. of Engrg Control, 1967–83 (Dir, 1967–70); Chairman: Council for Educnl Technology, 1980–85; Educn Task Gp, IStructE, 1988–89. Pres., IEE, 1984–85 (Dep. Pres. 1982–84); Chm., Automation and Control Div., IEE, 1970–71. Vice-Chm., Yorkshire Cancer Res. Campaign, 1989– (Treas., 1989–97). Chm., Internat. Commn on Higher Educn, Botswana, 1990; UK deleg., Conf. on Higher Educn, Madagascar, 1992. Member: Royal Philatelic Soc., 1960–; Sociedad Filatélica de Chile, 1970–2001; Chm., British Philatelic Council, 1980–81; Trustee, Nat. Philatelic Trust, 1989–2002; Keeper of the Roll of Distinguished Philatelists, 1992–2004, Signatory, 2000. FRPSL 1970; Fellow, Inst. of Paper Conservation, 1980; FREng (FEng 1983). Hon. FInstMC 1984; Hon. FIET (Hon. FIEE 1992). Hon. DSc Sussex, 1988; DUniv Bradford, 1990. Hartley Medal, Inst. Measurement and Control, 1979; International Philatelic Gold Medal: Seoul, 1994; Seville, 1996. *Publications:* Textbook of Servomechanisms, 1953; Analytical Techniques for Non-Linear Control Systems, 1960; The Postmarks of Valparaiso, 1997; The Postal History of Chile, 2002; Tierra del Fuego, 2004; papers in Proc. IEE, Trans Amer. IEE, Brit. Jl of Applied Physics, Jl of Scientific Instruments, Proc. Inst. Measurement and Control. *Recreations:* philately, postal history. *Address:* North End House, 19 The Street, Stedham, West Sussex GU29 0NQ. *T:* (01730) 810833, *Fax:* (01730) 810834. *E:* j.west422@btinternet.com. *Club:* Athenæum.

WEST, Kenneth, CChem, FRSC; Deputy Chairman, ICI Fibres Division, 1980–84 (Technical Director, 1977–80); *b* 1 Sept. 1930; *s* of Albert West and Ethel Kirby (*née* Kendall); *m* 1980, Elizabeth Ann Borland (*née* Campbell); one step *s*, and three *d* by a previous marriage. *Educ:* Archbishop Holgate's Grammar Sch., York; University Coll., Oxford (BA). Customer Service Manager, ICI Fibres, 1960; Res. and Engrg Manager, FII, 1967; Director: South African Nylon Spinners, Cape Town, 1970; Fibre Industries Inc., N Carolina, 1974; Man. Dir, TWA, 1984–85; Dir, Water Res. Council, 1984–85. Dir, Seahorse Internat. Ltd,

1987–89. Mem., British Assoc. of the Var, 2000–. FRSA. *Recreations:* sailing, flying, music, wine, amateur dramatics. *Address:* La Salamandre, Route de Repenti, 83340 Le Luc, France. *Clubs:* Don Mills Variety; Oxford and Cambridge (Var Br.); Yacht International (Bormes les Mimosas).

WEST, Lawrence Joseph; QC 2003; a Recorder, since 2000; *b* 6 July 1946; *s* of Lionel Chaffey West and Catherine Agnes (*née* Daly); *m* 1972, Cathryn Hudson; two *s*. *Educ:* De La Salle Oaklands Sch., Toronto; Univ. of Toronto (BA 1967; LLB 1970); London Sch. of Econs (LLM 1971). MCIArb 2003. Called: to Law Soc. of Upper Canada, 1973; to the Bar, Gray's Inn, 1979. *Recreations:* chess, fencing and other arts of controlled violence. *Address:* Henderson Chambers, 2 Harcourt Buildings, Temple, EC4Y 9DB. *T:* (020) 7583 9020, *Fax:* (020) 7583 2686. *E:* lwest@hendersonchambers.co.uk.

WEST, Mary Cecilia; *see* Kenny, M. C.

WEST, Prof. Michael Alun, PhD; FBPsS; FCIPD; Professor of Organisational Psychology, and Chair, Centre for Performance-Led HR, University of Lancaster, since 2011; *b* Loughborough, 6 March 1951; *m* 2006, Gillian Hardy; one *s* two *d*; one *s* from previous marriage. *Educ:* Univ. of Wales Inst. of Sci. and Technol. (BSc Econ Hons 1973; PhD 1977). FBPsS 1992; FCIPD 2006. Aston Business School, Aston University: Res. Dir, 2001–06; Prof. of Organisational Psychol., 2001–11; Exec. Dean, 2007–11. Dir, Aston Organisational Development Ltd, 2004–. FBAM 1999; FHEA 2007; FRSA. Fellow: Amer. Psychol Assoc., 1998; Internat. Assoc. of Applied Psychol., 2006. *Publications:* (jtly) The Transition from School to Work, 1983; (ed) The Psychology of Meditation, 1987; (jtly) Managerial Job Change: men and women in transition, 1988; (ed jtly) Innovation and Creativity at Work, 1990; (ed jtly) Women at Work: psychological and organizational perspectives, 1990; Effective Teamwork: practical lessons from organisational research, 1994, 2nd edn 2004; (ed) Handbook of Work Group Psychology, 1996; Developing Creativity in Organizations, 1997; (jtly) Effective Top Management Teams, 2001; (ed jtly) International Handbook of Organizational Teamwork and Cooperative Working, 2003; (with L. Markiewicz) Building Team-based Working: a practical guide to organizational transformation, 2004; The Secrets of Successful Team Management, 2004; (ed jtly) The Essentials of Teamworking: international perspectives, 2005; (jtly) Teamwork, teamdiagnose, teamentwicklung, 2005; (jtly) Aston Team Performance Inventory: management set, 2006. *Address:* Centre for Performance-Led HR, Charles Carter Building, University of Lancaster, Bailrigg, Lancaster LA1 4YX.

WEST, Nigel; *see* Allason, R. W. S.

WEST, Paul, QPM 2004; Managing Director, Policing First Ltd, since 2011; *b* 29 March 1958; *s* of Derrick and Constance West; *m* 1993, Rosemary Helen Goundry; three *s* three *d*. *Educ:* Durham Johnston Sch.; Pembroke Coll., Oxford (BA (Physics) 1979, MA 1983); Michigan State Univ. (MSc (Criminal Justice) 1987); Durham Univ. (MA (Human Resource Mgt and Develt) 1998). Joined Durham Constabulary, 1979: Constable, 1979–83; Sergeant, 1983–85; Insp., 1985–90; Harkness Fellow, 1986; Chief Insp., 1990–92; Supt, 1992–98; Thames Valley Police: Asst Chief Constable, 1998–2000; Dep. Chief Constable, 2000–03; Chief Constable, W Mercia Police, 2003–11. Bishop's Advr on Penal Affairs, Dio. of Worcester, 2013–. *Recreations:* classical music, sports (partic. football), gardening, poultry and small animal rearing, family.

WEST, Peter Bernard, CMG 2015; HM Diplomatic Service; High Commissioner to Sierra Leone, since 2013; *b* 29 June 1958; *s* of late Bernard West and Alice West (*née* Bowen); *m* 1980, Julia Anne Chandler; two *s* (twins) one *d*. Joined FCO, 1977; Third Secretary: Buenos Aires, 1980–83; Auckland, 1984–85; Second, then First, Sec., FCO, 1986–91; First Sec. (Political/EU), Copenhagen, 1992–97; Dep. Hd, S Asian Dept, FCO, 1997–99; Counsellor and Dep. Hd of Mission, Bangkok, 2000–04; Consul-Gen., Melbourne, 2004–08; Dep. High Comr, Abuja, 2008–11; Dep. High Comr, Lagos, 2011–12. *Recreations:* family, sport, travel. *Address:* c/o Foreign and Commonwealth Office, King Charles Street, SW1A 2AH. *Club:* Melbourne Football (Melbourne).

WEST, Prof. Peter Christopher, PhD; FRS 2006; FInstP; Professor, Department of Mathematics, King's College, London, since 1986; *b* 4 Dec. 1951; *s* of Ronald West and Martha West (now Williams); *m* 1980, Susan Amanda Back; one *s* one *d*. *Educ:* Imperial Coll., London (BSc 1973; PhD 1976). FInstP 2007. Postdoctoral Fellow: Ecole Normale Supérieure, Paris, 1976–77; Imperial Coll., London, 1977–78; Lectr, 1978–85, Reader, 1985–86, KCL. Visiting appointments: CIT, 1984; CERN, 1986–89, 2000; Chalmers 150th Anniv. Prof., Sweden, 1992. FKC 2007. *Publications:* Introduction to Supersymmetry and Supergravity, 1983, 2nd edn 1990; Introduction to Strings and Branes, 2012; more than 200 scientific pubns. *Recreations:* classical music, cycling, travelling in remote regions, gardening. *Address:* Department of Mathematics, King's College London, Strand, WC2R 2LS. *T:* (020) 7848 2224, *Fax:* (020) 7848 2017. *E:* peter.west@kcl.ac.uk.

WEST, Prunella Margaret Rumney, (Mrs T. L. West); *see* Scales, Prunella.

WEST, Prof. Richard Gilbert, FRS 1968; FSA; FGS; Fellow of Clare College, Cambridge, since 1954; Professor of Botany, University of Cambridge, 1977–91; *b* 31 May 1926; *m* 1st, 1958; one *s*; 2nd, 1973, Hazel Gristwood (*d* 1997); two *d*. *Educ:* King's School, Canterbury; Univ. of Cambridge. Cambridge University: Demonstrator in Botany, 1957–60; Lecturer in Botany, 1960–67; Dir, Subdept of Quaternary Research, 1966–87; Reader in Quaternary Research, 1967–75; Prof. of Palaeoecology, 1975–77. Member: Council for Scientific Policy, 1971–73; NERC, 1973–76; Ancient Monuments Bd for England, 1980–84. Darwin Lecturer to the British Association, 1959; Lyell Fund, 1961, Bigsby Medal, 1969, Lyell Medal, 1988, Geological Society of London. Hon. MRIA. *Publications:* Pleistocene Geology and Biology, 1968, 2nd edn 1977; (jtly) The Ice Age in Britain, 1972, 2nd edn 1981; The Pre-glacial Pleistocene of the Norfolk and Suffolk coasts, 1980; Pleistocene Palaeoecology of Central Norfolk, 1991; Plant Life in the Quaternary Cold Stages, 2000; From Brandon to Bungay, 2009; Quaternary Research in Britain and Ireland, 2014; Evolution of a Breckland Landscape, 2015. *Address:* 3A Woollards Lane, Great Shelford, Cambs CB22 5LZ. *T:* (01223) 842578; Clare College, Cambridge CB2 1TL.

WEST, Samuel Alexander Joseph; actor and director; Artistic Director, Sheffield Theatres, 2005–07; Associate Artist, Royal Shakespeare Company; *b* 19 June 1966; *s* of Timothy Lancaster West, *qv* and Prunella Margaret Rumney West (*see* Prunella Scales); partner, Laura Joanne Wade, *qv*; one *d*. *Educ:* Alleyn's Sch., Dulwich; Lady Margaret Hall, Oxford (BA Hons Eng. Lit.). First professional stage appearance, The Browning Version, Birmingham Rep., 1985; London début, Les Parents Terribles, Orange Tree, Richmond, 1988; West End début, A Life in the Theatre, Haymarket, 1989; *theatre* includes: Hidden Laughter, Vaudeville, 1990; Royal National Theatre: The Sea, 1991; Arcadia, 1993; Antony and Cleopatra, 1998; Cain (Byron), Chichester, 1992; The Importance of Being Earnest, Manchester, 1993; Henry IV parts I & II, English Touring Th., 1996; Richard II, 2000, Hamlet, 2001, RSC; Dr Faustus, The Master and Margarita, Chichester, 2004; Much Ado About Nothing, Crucible Th., Sheffield, 2005; Betrayal, Donmar Warehouse, 2007; Drunk Enough To Say I Love You?, NY, 2008; The Family Reunion, Donmar Warehouse, 2008; Enron, Chichester, transf. Royal Court, 2009, then Noël Coward, 2010; A Number, Menier, 2010; Uncle Vanya, Vaudeville, 2012; director: The Lady's Not For Burning, Chichester, 2002; Les Liaisons Dangereuses, Bristol Old Vic, 2003; Cosi fan tutte, ENO, 2003; Three Women and a Piano Tuner, Chichester, 2004, Hampstead, 2005; Insignificance, Lyceum, Sheffield, 2005; The Romans in Britain, The Clean House, 2006, As You Like It, 2007, Crucible Th., Sheffield; Dealer's Choice, Menier, 2007; Waste, Almeida, 2008; Close the Coalhouse Door, Northern Stage, Newcastle, 2012; After Electra, Tricycle Th., 2015; *television* includes: serials: Stanley and the Women, 1990; Over Here, 1995; Out of the Past, 1998; Hornblower, 1998; Waking the Dead, 2002; Cambridge Spies, 2003; Foyle's War, 2004; E=mc^2, 2005; The Inspector Lynley Mysteries, 2006; The Long Walk to Finchley, 2008; Desperate Romantics, 2009; New Tricks, 2009; Garrow's Law, 2010; Any Human Heart, 2010; Poirot: Murder on the Orient Express, 2010; Law and Order, 2011; Eternal Law, 2012; Mr Selfridge, 2012, 2013, 2014; Fleming, 2014; W1A, 2015; Jonathan Strange and Mr Norrell, 2015; films: Frankie and Johnny, 1985; Voices in the Garden, 1991; A Breed of Heroes, 1995; Persuasion, 1995; Longitude, 2000; Random Quest, 2006; *films* include: Reunion, 1989; Howards End, 1991; Archipel (in French), 1992; Carrington, 1994; A Feast at Midnight, 1995; Jane Eyre, 1995; Stiff Upper Lips, 1996; The Ripper, 1997; Rupert's Land, 1997; Notting Hill, 1998; Pandæmonium, 1999; Iris, 2001; Van Helsing, 2003; Schweitzer, 2009; Hyde Park on Hudson, 2012; The Riot Club, 2014; *radio* includes: more than forty plays; regular reader for Words and Music. Reciter and reader for concerts with orchs incl. LSO, BBC SO and CBSO. Member: Council, Equity, 1996–2000, 2008–14; Bd, Nat. Campaign for the Arts, 2006– (Chair, 2012–); Bd, Belarus Free Th., 2013–. *Recreations:* birding, travelling, poker, growing chillies, supporting AFC Wimbledon. *Address:* c/o United Agents, 12–26 Lexington Street, W1F 0LE. *T:* (020) 3214 0800. *Clubs:* Century, Groucho.

WEST, Shani; *see* Rhys-James, S.

WEST, Prof. Shearer Carroll, PhD; FRHistS; Deputy Vice-Chancellor, University of Sheffield, since 2015; *b* Rocky Mount, Va, 18 Jan. 1960; *d* of Edgar Allen West and Natalie Carroll West; *m* 1992, Nicholas Sinclair Davidson; one *d*. *Educ:* Coll. of William and Mary, Va (BA Art Hist. (major), English (minor) 1981); St Andrews Univ. (PhD Art Hist. 1986). FRHistS 1995. Sub-editor, Macmillan's Dictionary of Art, 1986–87; Lectr, 1987–96, Sen. Lectr, 1996, in Hist. of Art, Univ. of Leicester; University of Birmingham: Sen. Lectr and Hd, Dept of Fine Art, 1996–2000; Prof. of Art Hist., 2000–11; Hd, Sch. of Historical Studies, 2004–07; Actg Hd, Coll. of Arts and Law, 2008; Dir, Res., AHRC, 2008–11; Hd of Humanities Div., Univ. of Oxford, 2011–15; Fellow of Magdalen Coll., Oxford, 2011–15. FHEA 2000; FRSA 2002. Hon. Fellow, Mansfield Coll., Oxford, 2010. *Publications:* Chagall, 1990 (trans. French 1991); The Image of the Actor: verbal and visual representation in the age of Garrick and Kemble, 1991; Fin de Siècle: art and society in the age of uncertainty, 1993; (ed with Marsha Meskimmon) Visions of the 'neue Frau': women and the visual arts in Weimar Germany, 1995; (ed) The Bloomsbury Guide to Art, 1996; (ed) The Victorians and Race, 1996; (ed) Italian Culture in Northern Europe in the Eighteenth Century, 1999; The Visual Arts in Germany, 1890–1937: utopia and despair, 2000; Portraiture, 2004; articles in learned jls incl. Art History, Eighteenth-Century Studies, Eighteenth-Century Life, Brit. Jl for Eighteenth-century Studies, Victorian Studies, Nineteenth-Century Theatre, Theatre Notebook, Jl of Victorian Culture. *Recreations:* running, swimming, classical music, theatre, opera, ballet. *Address:* Office of the Deputy Vice-Chancellor, University of Sheffield, Firth Court, Western Bank, Sheffield S10 2TN. *T:* (0114) 222 1101. *E:* shearer.west@sheffield.ac.uk. *Club:* Priory (Edgbaston, Birmingham).

WEST, Dr Stephanie Roberta, FBA 1990; Senior Research Fellow in Classics and Fellow Librarian, Hertford College, Oxford, 1990–2005, now Emeritus Fellow; *b* 1 Dec. 1937; *d* of Robert Enoch Pickard and Ruth (*née* Batters); *m* 1960, Martin Litchfield West, OM, FBA (*d* 2015); one *s* one *d*. *Educ:* Nottingham High Sch. for Girls; Somerville Coll., Oxford (1st cl. Classics Mods 1958, 1st cl. Lit. Hum. 1960; Gaisford Prize for Greek Verse Composition 1959; Ireland Scholar 1959, Derby Scholar 1960); MA 1963, DPhil 1964, Oxon. Oxford University: Mary Ewart Res. Fellow, Somerville Coll., 1965–67; Lecturer: in Classics, Hertford Coll., 1966–90; in Greek, Keble Coll., 1981–2005. Foreign Mem., Polish Acad. of Arts and Scis, 2012. Mem. Council, GPDST, 1974–87. *Publications:* The Ptolemaic Papyri of Homer, 1967; Omero, Odissea 1 (libri I–IV), 1981; (with A. Heubeck and J. B. Hainsworth) A commentary on Homer's Odyssey 1, 1988; Demythologisation in Herodotus, 2002; articles and reviews in learned jls. *Recreations:* opera, curious information. *Address:* 42 Portland Road, Oxford OX2 7EY. *T:* (01865) 556060.

WEST, Dr Stephen Craig, FMedSci; FRS 1995; Senior Group Leader, Francis Crick Institute, since 2015; *b* 11 April 1952; *s* of Joseph and Louise West; *m* 1985, Phyllis Fraenza. *Educ:* Univ. of Newcastle upon Tyne (BSc 1974; PhD 1977). Post-doctoral Research Associate: Univ. of Newcastle upon Tyne, 1977–78; Dept of Molecular Biophysics and Biochemistry, and Therapeutic Radiology, Yale Univ., 1978–83 (Res. Scientist, Dept of Therapeutic Radiology, 1983–85); Sen. Scientist, 1985–89, Principal Scientist, 1989–2015, ICRF, then Cancer Res. UK. Mem., EMBO, 1994; FMedSci 2000. Hon. Prof., UCL, 1997–. Swiss Bridge Prize for Cancer Research, 2001, 2009; Louis-Jeantet Prize for Medicine, 2007; Novartis Lect and Prize, Biochem. Soc., 2008; GlaxoSmithKline Prize, Royal Soc., 2010; Medal, Genetics Soc., 2012. *Publications:* over 200 res. articles in biochem. and molecular biol. *Recreations:* squash, ski-ing, music. *Address:* Francis Crick Institute, Clare Hall Laboratories, South Mimms, Potters Bar, Herts EN6 3LD.

WEST, Prof. Steven George, FChS, FCPodMed, FRSocMed; DL; Professor, since 1995, and Vice-Chancellor and Chief Executive Officer, since 2008, University of the West of England, Bristol; *b* Luton, 27 March 1961; *s* of Paul West and Jean West; *m* 1999, Samantha Watson; two *s* three *d*. *Educ:* Denbigh High Sch., Luton; Luton Sixth Form Coll.; Chelsea Sch. of Chiropody, Paddington Tech. Coll. (Grad. Dip. Chiropody 1982), Poly. of Central London (BSc 1st Cl. Hons Podiatry 1986); King's Coll. London. FChS 1990; MPodA 1992; FCPodMed 2009; MIPEM 1986. Sen. Chiropodist, Chiropody and Res. Unit, City and Hackney HA, 1982–84; Chelsea School of Chiropody, Paddington Technical College, later Paddington College: vis. clinical teacher, 1982–83; Lectr, 1984–87; Sen. Lectr, 1987–90; University of Huddersfield: Head of Podiatry and Associate Dean, 1990–95; Dean, Sch. of Human and Health Scis, 1992–95; University of the West of England, Bristol: Dean of Faculty, 1995–2005; Dean and Asst Vice-Chancellor, 1998–2001; Pro Vice-Chancellor (Resources and Planning), 2005–06; Dep. Vice-Chancellor, 2006–07. Chairman: Univs South West, 2010–12; Univ. Alliance Mission Gp, 2012–15; West of England Academic Health Sci. Network, 2013– (Interim Chm., 2012–13); SW Region CBI, 2014–Sept. 2016; Member, Board: Higher Educn Leadership Foundn, 2010–; UUK, 2011– (Chm., Health and Res. Cttee, 2011–); Health Educn England SW, 2012–. Dir, Bristol UWE Healthcare Training Ltd, 2002–. Non-executive Director: Avon, Gloucester and Wilts Strategic HA, 2003–06; South West Strategic HA, 2006– (Vice-Chair, 2009–); South Strategic HA, 2011– (Chm., Patient and Care Standards Cttee, 2011–); Chm., NHS Regl Trng Bd, 2006–. Trustee, Bristol Urological Inst., 2007–; Regl Trustee, Prince's Trust, 2008–. Pres., Business West and Bristol Chamber of Commerce and Initiative, 2013–March 2016. Mem., Biol Engrg Soc., 1989. Fellow, Leadership Foundn, 2005. FRSocMed 2006. FRSA 2012. Mem., Soc. of Merchant Venturers, Bristol, 2014–. DL Glos 2012. Hon. DLaws Bristol, 2014. *Publications:* articles in podiatric and learned jls. *Recreations:* scuba diving, driving nice cars, swimming. *Address:* Vice-Chancellor's Office, University of the West of England, Bristol BS16 1QY. *T:* (0117) 328 2201. *E:* steven.west@uwe.ac.uk.

WEST, Susan Fiona Dorinthea; *see* Michie, S. F. D.

WEST, Timothy Lancaster, CBE 1984; actor and director; *b* 20 Oct. 1934; *s* of late Harry Lockwood West and Olive Carleton-Crowe; *m* 1st, 1956, Jacqueline Boyer (marr. diss.); one *d*; 2nd, 1963, Prunella Scales, *qv*; two *s*. *Educ:* John Lyon Sch., Harrow; Regent Street

Polytechnic. Entered profession as asst stage manager, Wimbledon, 1956; first London appearance, Caught Napping, Piccadilly, 1959; Mem., RSC, 1964–66; Prospect Theatre Co., 1966–72: Dr Samuel Johnson, Prospero, Bolingbroke, young Mortimer in Edward II, King Lear, Emerson in A Room with a View, Alderman Smuggler in The Constant Couple, and Holofernes in Love's Labour's Lost; Otto in The Italian Girl, 1968; Gilles in Abelard and Heloise, 1970; Robert Hand in Exiles, 1970; Gilbert in The Critic as Artist, 1971; Sir William Gower in Trelawny (musical), Bristol, 1972; Falstaff in Henry IV Pts I and II, Bristol, 1973; Shpigelsky in A Month in the Country, Chichester, 1974 (London, 1975); Brack in Hedda Gabler, RSC, 1975; Iago in Othello, Nottingham, 1976; with Prospect Co.: Harry in Staircase, 1976, Claudius in Hamlet, storyteller in War Music, and Enobarbus in Antony and Cleopatra, 1977; Ivan and Gottlieb in Laughter, and Max in The Homecoming, 1978; with Old Vic Co.: Narrator in Lancelot and Guinevere, Shylock in The Merchant of Venice, 1980; Beecham, Apollo, 1980, NZ, 1983, Dublin, 1986; Uncle Vanya, Australia, 1982; Stalin in Master Class, Leicester, 1983, Old Vic, 1984; Charlie Mucklebrass in Big in Brazil, 1984; The War at Home, Hampstead, 1984; When We Are Married, Whitehall, 1986; The Sneeze, Aldwych, 1988; Bristol Old Vic: The Master Builder, 1989; The Clandestine Marriage, Uncle Vanya, 1990; James Tyrone, in Long Day's Journey into Night, 1991, also at NT; Andrew in It's Ralph, Comedy, 1991; King Lear, Dublin, 1992; Willie Loman in Death of a Salesman, Theatr Clwyd, 1993; Christopher Cameron in Himself, Southampton, 1993; Sir Anthony Absolute in The Rivals, Chichester, 1994; Macbeth, Theatr Clwyd, 1994; Mail Order Bride, 1994, Getting On, 1995, W Yorks Playhouse; Twelve Angry Men, Comedy, 1996; Falstaff, in Henry IV Pts 1 and 2, Old Vic, 1997; Gloucester, in King Lear, RNT, 1997; The Birthday Party, Piccadilly, 1999; The Master Builder, tour, 1999; The External, tour, 2001; Luther, RNT, 2001; Lear in King Lear, tour, 2002, Old Vic, 2003; National Hero, Edinburgh and tour, 2005; The Life of Galileo, Birmingham Rep, 2005; The Old Country, Trafalgar Studio, 2006; Menenius in Coriolanus, RSC, 2007; The Collection, Comedy, 2008; The Winslow Boy, tour, 2009; Quartet, tour, 2010; A Number, Menier Chocolate Factory, 2010; Uncle Vanya, Chichester Festival Th., 2012; The Handyman, tour, 2012; The Vote, Donmar, 2015. *Directed:* plays for Prospect Co., Open Space, Gardner Centre, Brighton, and rep. at Salisbury, Bristol, Northampton and Cheltenham; HMS Pinafore, Carl Rosa Co., 2003; own season, The Forum, Billingham, 1973; Artistic Dir, Old Vic Co., 1980–81. *Television includes:* Edward VII, 1973; Hard Times, 1977; Crime and Punishment, 1979; Brass, 1982–84, 1990; The Last Bastion, 1984; The Nightingale Saga, Tender is the Night, 1985; The Monocled Mutineer, 1986; The Train, 1987; A Shadow on the Sun, 1988; The Gospels, Framed, 1992; Bramwell, 1998; Midsomer Murders, 1999; Murder in Mind, 2000; Bedtime, 2001, 2002, 2003; Going Postal, 2010; Coronation Street, 2013; Last Tango in Halifax, 2013; Great Canal Journeys, 2014–15; Eastenders, 2014–15; The Vote, 2015; *plays:* Richard II, 1969; Edward II, The Boswell and Johnson Show, 1970; Horatio Bottomley, 1972; Churchill and the Generals, 1979 (RTS Award); The Good Doctor Bodkin Adams, 1986; What the Butler Saw, Harry's Kingdom, When We Are Married, Breakthrough at Reykjavik, 1987; Strife, The Contractor, 1988; Blore, MP, Beecham, 1989; Survival of the Fittest, 1990; Bye Bye Columbus, 1991; Reith to the Nation, Smokescreen, 1993; Hiroshima, Eleven Men Against Eleven, Cuts, 1995; The Place of the Dead, 1996; King Lear, 1997; Bleak House, 2005; A Room with a View, 2007; Exile, 2010. *Films:* The Looking-Glass War, 1968; Nicholas and Alexandra, 1970; The Day of the Jackal, 1972; Hedda, 1975; Joseph Andrews, and The Devil's Advocate, 1976; William Morris, 1977; Agatha, and The 39 Steps, 1978; The Antagonists, 1980; Murder is Easy, and Oliver Twist, 1981; Cry Freedom, 1986; Consuming Passions, 1987; Ever After, 1997; Joan of Arc, 1998; Iris, 2001; Beyond Borders, 2002; Villa des Roses, 2002; The Endgame, 2008. Compiles and dir. recital progs; sound broadcaster. Dir, All Change Arts Ltd, 1986–2006; Dir and Trustee, Nat. Student Drama Fest., 1990–2007; Pres., LAMDA, 2003– (Gov., 1992–). Pres., Soc. for Theatre Res., 1999–. FRSA 1992. DUniv Bradford, 1993; Hon. DLitt: West of England, 1994; East Anglia, 1996; Westminster, 1999; London, 2004; Hull, 2004. Hon. Dr Drama, RSAMD, 2004. *Publications:* I'm Here, I Think, Where are You? (collected letters), 1994; A Moment Towards the End of the Play, 2001; (with Prunella Scales) So You Want to be an Actor?, 2005. *Recreations:* theatre history, travel, music, old railways, inland waterways. *Address:* c/o Gavin Barker Associates Ltd, 2D Wimpole Street, W1G 0EB. *Clubs:* Garrick, Groucho.

See also S. A. J. West.

WEST CUMBERLAND, Archdeacon of; *see* Pratt, Ven. Dr R. D.

WEST HAM, Archdeacon of; *see* Cockett, Ven. E. W.

WEST INDIES, Archbishop of the, since 2009; **Most Rev. Dr John Walder Dunlop Holder,** CBE 2011; Bishop of Barbados, since 2000; *b* Barbados, 1948; *m* 1988, Betty Lucas-Holder; one *s*. *Educ:* Modern High Sch., Barbados; Codrington Coll. (DTh); Univ. of West Indies (BA Theol.); Univ. of the South (STM); Univ. of London (PhD); Cert. in HIV/AIDS Educn and Counselling. Ordained deacon, 1974, priest, 1975; Curate, St George Cathedral, St Vincent, 1975–77; Lectr in Old Testament, Codrington Coll., Barbados, 1977–2000. Member: Adv. Gp, Anglican Observer at UN, 2003–06, 2010–; Metropolitan Council of Cuba, 2010–; Alternate Deleg., Standing Cttee and Finance Cttee, Anglican Communion, 2011–; Church in the Province of the West Indies: Chm., Provincial Social Justice and Human Rights Commn, 2003–; Chm., Provincial Commn on Doctrine, 2009–; Chair, Provincial Synod, 2009–. Chairman: Joe Forte Trust, 2000–; Aubrey Collymore Scholarship Cttee, 2000–; Barbados Christian Council, 2007–11; Member: Privy Council, Barbados, 2001–; Adv. Cttee, Chronic Disease Task Res. Centre, Barbados, 2010–. Chm., Codrington Coll. Trust, 2011– (Mem., Bd of Mgt, 2003–). *Publications:* A Layman's Guide to the Bible, Part 1: an examination of the Bible in its Socio-Political, Historical and Literary Context, Part 2: outlines of the books in the Bible, 1989; Religion and Theology: a journey into the experiential, 1990; The Issue of Race: a search for a biblical perspective, 1993; The Intertestamental Period, 1994; The Ten Commandments, 1995; Is This the Word of the Lord?: in search of biblical theology and hermeneutics, 2000; (contrib.) The Anglican Communion and Homosexuality, 2008; (contrib.) The Africana Bible, 2010. *Recreations:* walking, swimming, reading, listening to music. *Address:* Mandeville House, Henry's Lane, Collymore Rock, St Michael, Barbados.

WEST-KNIGHTS, Laurence James; QC 2000; a Recorder, since 1999; *b* 30 July 1954; *o s* of late Major Jan James West-Knights and Amy Winifred West-Knights (*née* Gott); *m* 1st, 1979 (marr. diss. 1983); 2nd, 1992, Joanne Anita Florence Ecob (marr. diss. 2013); one *s* two *d*. *Educ:* Perse Sch., Cambridge; Hampton Sch.; Emmanuel Coll., Cambridge (MA 1976). FCIArb 1993. RNR, 1979–94 (Lt Comdr 1993, retd). Called to the Bar, Gray's Inn, 1977, Bencher, 2004; W Circuit; in practice at the Bar, 1977–; Asst Recorder, 1994–99. Chm., Steering Cttee, IT Industry Enquiry into Govt IT Contracts, 2000; Member: IT Cttees, Bar Council, 1996–2001; Incorporated Council of Law Reporting, 1997–2005; IT and the Courts, 1998–2006 (Mem., Civil Litigation Wkg Party, 1997–2005); Founding Trustee and Exec. Dir, British and Irish Legal Information Inst. Jt Chm., Soc. for Computers and Law, 2001–02 (Mem. Council, 1995–2001; Vice-Chm., 1996–2001). Lay Chm., PCC, Christ Church, Turnham Green, 1998–2001. Mem. Editl Bd, Jl of Judicial Studies Bd, 1997–2003. Writer, www.LawOnLine.cc, legal web site, 1997–. Winner, Kennett Shoot Trophy, 2003. *Publications:* (contrib.) Researching the Legal Web, 1997; (contrib.) Jordan's Civil Court Service, 1999–; numerous papers and articles on free access to the law via the Internet and on civil procedure. *Recreations:* motorcycling, sailing, scuba diving, ski-ing, watching and listening to cricket, shooting, New Zealand, his children. *Address:* Hailsham Chambers, 4 Paper Buildings, Temple, EC4Y 7EX. *T:* (020) 7643 5000, *Fax:* (020) 7353 5778. *E:* laurie.west-knightsqc@hailshamchambers.com. *Clubs:* MCC; Royal Naval Volunteer Reserve Yacht; Bar Yacht; Cambridge University Motorcycle.

WESTABY, Prof. Stephen, FRCS; Senior Cardiac Surgeon, John Radcliffe Hospital, since 1986; Professor of Biomedical Sciences, University of Wales, since 2006; *b* 27 July 1948; *s* of Kenneth and Doreen Westaby; *m*; one *s* one *d*. *Educ:* Charing Cross Hosp. Med. Sch., Univ. of London (BSc Biochemistry 1969; MB BS 1972; MS 1986); PhD (Bioeng). FRCS 1986; FESC, FETCS, FICA. Surgical training: Addenbrooke's Hosp., Hammersmith Hosp., RPMS, Hosp. for Sick Children, Great Ormond Street, Harefield Hosp., Middlesex Hosp., Univ. of Alabama. Dist. Ralph Cicerone Prof., Univ. of California, 2006; adult and paediatric surgeon; specialist surgeon in congenital heart disease, thoracic aortic surgery, valvular and coronary heart disease; designated a pioneer in artificial heart technology by Jl of Amer. Heart Assoc.; developed first artificial heart res. prog., UK; established Oxford Heart Centre, John Radcliffe Hosp., internat. teaching centre for valve and aortic surgery; has performed over 10,000 open heart ops on adults and children. Member: Soc. for Thoracic Surgery, USA, 1995; Amer. Assoc. for Thoracic Surgery, 1998; European Assoc. for Cardiothoracic Surgery, 1998. Editor, Jl of Heart Failure Clinics of N Amer., surgical edn. *Publications:* editor/joint author: Wound Care, 1985; Stentless Bioprosthesis, 1995, 2nd edn 1999; Landmarks in Cardiac Surgery, 1997; Surgery of Acquired Aortic Valve Disease, 1997; Principles and Practice of Critical Care, 1997; Trauma Pathogenesis and Treatment, 1998; Ischemic Heart Disease: surgical management, 1998; Cardiothoracic Trauma, 1999; more than 50 chapters in books, and over 260 scientific papers. *Recreations:* writing, shooting. *Address:* Oxford Heart Centre, John Radcliffe Hospital, Headley Way, Headington, Oxford OX3 9DU. *T:* (01865) 220269. *E:* swestaby@ahf.org.uk.

WESTAD, Prof. Odd Arne, PhD; FBA 2011; S. T. Lee Professor in US-Asia Relations, Kennedy School of Government, Harvard University, since 2015; *b* Alesund, Norway, 5 Jan. 1960; *s* of Arne and Oddbjorg Westad; *m* 1985, Dr Ingunn Bjornson; one *s* one *d*. *Educ:* Univ. of Oslo (BA Hist., Phil. and Mod. Langs); Univ. of North Carolina (PhD Hist. 1990). Dir, Res., Nobel Inst., 1990–98; Prof. of Internat. History, 1998–2015, Hd, Internat. History Dept, 2004–07, Co-Dir, LSE IDEAS, 2008–15, LSE. Visiting Professor: Hong Kong Univ., 1994; Univ. of Cambridge, 1998; New York Univ., 2002; Ca' Foscari Univ., Venice, 2012. *Publications:* Cold War and Revolution, 1993; (jtly) Beyond the Cold War: future dimensions in international relations, 1993; (jtly) The Soviet Union in Eastern Europe, 1994; The Fall of Détente, 1997; Brothers in Arms, 1998; Reviewing the Cold War: approaches, interpretations, theory, 2000; Decisive Encounters: the Chinese Civil War, 2003; (jtly) The Cold War: a history in documents and eyewitness accounts, 2003; The Global Cold War, 2005; (ed with M. Leffler) The Cambridge History of the Cold War, 3 vols, 2010; Restless Empire: China and the world since 1750, 2012. *Recreations:* hill walking, travel. *Address:* Kennedy School of Government, Harvard University, 79 John F. Kennedy Street, Cambridge, MA 02138, USA. *E:* oaw@oaw.cn.

WESTBROOK, Rear Adm. Jonathan Simon, CBE 2013 (MBE 1990); Director, Jon Westbrook Ltd, since 2013; Member, Armed Forces Pay Review Body, since 2014; *b* Chatham, Kent, 29 Aug. 1958; *s* of Derrick and Pam Westbrook; *m* 1980, Alison, (Jill), Finney; one *s* two *d*. *Educ:* Chester City Grammar Sch.; BRNC Dartmouth; NATO Defence Coll. Joined RN, as jun. seaman, 1975; HMS Bristol, 1978–79; HMS Soberton, 1981–82; HMS Sheffield, 1982; HMS Otter, 1983–85; HMS Superb, 1985–87; HMS Sovereign, 1987–88; HMS Torbay, 1988–90; Submarine Comd Course, 1990; XO, HMS Trenchant, 1991–93; Exchange USA, 1993–95; CO, HMS Talent, 1995–97; Comdr, UK Task Gp, 1997–98; MoD, 1998–2001; HMS Raleigh, 2001–02; Capt., FOST, 2002–04; MoD, 2004–07; Cdre, PJHQ, 2007–09; Comdr, Devonport Flotilla and Faslane Flotilla, 2009–11; Dep. Rear Adm., Submarines, 2010–11; COS Allied Maritime Comd, 2011–13. Sen. Bd Advr, Torchlight Solutions, 2013–; Bd Advr, Autonomous Surface Vehicles Ltd, 2013–. Member: British Assoc. for Shooting and Conservation, 1996–; Royal Naval Assoc., 2013–; Pres., Liskeard RBL, 2013–; Chm., Friends of Royal Navy Submarine Mus., 2014–. CCMI 2011. *Recreations:* shooting, fishing, the countryside, Blues music. *Address:* Caradon Town, Liskeard, Cornwall.

WESTBROOK, Michael John David, OBE 1988; composer, pianist and band-leader; *b* 21 March 1936; *s* of Philip Beckford Westbrook and Vera Agnes (*née* Butler); *m* 1976, Katherine Jane (*née* Duckham), singer, songwriter and painter; one *s* one *d* of previous marriage. *Educ:* Kelly Coll., Tavistock; Plymouth Coll. of Art (NDD); Hornsey Coll. of Art (ATD). Formed first band at Plymouth Art Sch., 1958; moved to London, 1962, and has since led a succession of groups incl. The Mike Westbrook Brass Band, formed with Phil Minton in 1973, The Mike Westbrook Orch., 1974–, Westbrook Trio (with Kate Westbrook and Chris Biscoe), formed in 1982, Kate Westbrook Mike Westbrook Duo, 1995–, Westbrook & Company, 1998–, The New Westbrook Orchestra, 2001–, and The Village Band, 2004–. Has toured extensively in Britain and Europe, and performed in Australia, Canada, NY, Singapore and Hong Kong. Has written commissioned works for fests in Britain, France and other European countries, composed music for theatre, radio, TV and films, and made numerous LPs. Principal compositions/recordings include: Marching Song, 1967; Metropolis, 1969; Tyger: a celebration of William Blake (with Adrian Mitchell), 1971, also The Westbrook Blake, 1980 and Glad Day, 1999; Citadel/Room 315, 1974; On Duke's Birthday (dedicated to the memory of Duke Ellington), 1984; Off Abbey Road, 1988; Bean Rows and Blues Shots (saxophone concerto), 1991; Coming Through Slaughter (opera), 1994; Bar Utopia (lyrics by Helen Simpson), 1995; Blues for Terenzi, 1995; Cable Street Blues, 1997; The Orchestra of Smith's Academy, 1998; Classical Blues, 2001; Glad Day Live, 2014; TV scores incl. Caught on a Train, 1983; film scores: Moulin Rouge, 1990; Camera Makes Whoopee, 1996; with Kate Westbrook: concert works incorporating European poetry and folk song, notably The Cortège, for voices and jazz orch., 1979, London Bridge is Broken Down, for voice, jazz orch. and chamber orch., 1987, and Chanson Irresponsable, 2001; Turner in Uri, 2003; also a succession of music-theatre pieces and recordings, with Kate Westbrook, including: Mama Chicago, 1978; Westbrook-Rossini, 1984; The Ass (based on poem by D. H. Lawrence), 1985; Pier Rides, 1986; Quichotte (opera), 1989; Goodbye Peter Lorre, 1991; Measure for Measure, 1992; Good Friday 1663 (TV opera; libretto by Helen Simpson), 1994; Stage Set, 1996; Love Or Infatuation, 1997; Platterback, 1998; Jago (opera), 2000; L'Ascenseur/The Lift, 2002; Art Wolf, 2003; The Nijinska Chamber, 2005; Waxeywork Show, 2006; Cape Gloss (opera), 2007; English Soup or the Battle of the Classic Trifle, 2008; Fine 'n Yellow, 2009; allsorts, 2009; The Serpent Hit, 2010; Three into Wonderfull, 2012; Five Voyages, 2012; Rossini Re-Loaded, 2013; A Bigger Show, 2013. Hon. DMus Plymouth, 2004. *Recreation:* walking by the sea. *Address:* PO Box 92, Dawlish, Devon EX7 9WN. *E:* admin@westbrookjazz.co.uk.

WESTBROOK, Roger, CMG 1990; HM Diplomatic Service, retired; Chief Hon. Steward, Westminster Abbey, 2006–14; *b* 26 May 1941; *e s* of Edward George Westbrook and Beatrice Minnie Westbrook (*née* Marshall). *Educ:* Dulwich Coll.; Hertford Coll., Oxford (MA Modern History). Foreign Office, 1964; Asst Private Sec. to Chancellor of Duchy of Lancaster and Minister of State, FO, 1965; Yaoundé, 1967; Rio de Janeiro, 1971; Brasilia, 1972; Private Sec. to Minister of State, FCO, 1975; Head of Chancery, Lisbon, 1977; Dep. Head, News Dept, FCO, 1980; Dep. Head, Falkland Is Dept, FCO, 1982; Overseas Inspectorate, FCO, 1984; High Comr, Negara Brunei Darussalam, 1986–91; Ambassador to Zaire, 1991–92; High Comr, Tanzania, 1992–95; Ambassador to Portugal, 1995–99. UK Comr, EXPO 98, Lisbon. Chm., Spencer House, 2000–06. Chairman: Anglo-Portuguese Soc., 2000–04; FCO Assoc.,

2003–09. Mem. Council, Book Aid Internat., 2002–. Pres., Hertford Soc., 2009–15. Freeman, City of London, 2002; Liveryman, Tylers' and Bricklayers' Co., 2002– (Master, 2014–15). *Recreations:* doodling, sightseeing, theatre, reading, dining. *Address:* 33 Marsham Court, Marsham Street, SW1P 4JY. *Club:* Travellers.

WESTBURY, 6th Baron *cr* 1861, of Westbury, co. Wilts; **Richard Nicholas Bethell,** MBE 1979; *b* 29 May 1950; *e s* of 5th Baron Westbury, CBE, MC and of Ursula Mary Rose (*née* James); *S* father, 2001; *m* 1st, 1975, Caroline Mary Palmer (marr. diss. 1991); one *s* two *d*; 2nd, 1993, Charlotte Sara Jane (marr. diss. 2004), *d* of John Temple Gore; 3rd, 2009, Hilary Luise Kindersley. *Educ:* Harrow; RMA Sandhurst. Major, Scots Guards, retd. *Heir: s* Hon. (Richard) Alexander (David) Bethell, *b* 21 Dec. 1986.

WESTCOTT, David Guy; QC 2003; *s* of Walter Dennis Westcott and Eileen Patricia Westcott; *m* Sara Paterson-Brown; one *s* one *d*. *Educ:* Cranleigh Sch.; Brasenose Coll., Oxford (BA Juris; BCL). Called to the Bar, Middle Temple, 1982. Jt Hd, Outer Temple Chambers, 2012–. Captain, GB Men's Hockey team (winners of Bronze Medal), LA Olympics, 1984. Mem., 1988–2009, Vice-Chm., 2006–09, Governing Body, Cranleigh Sch. *Recreations:* outdoor sports, theatre.

WESTCOTT, Dr Nicholas James, CMG 1999; HM Diplomatic Service; Managing Director for Middle East and North Africa, European External Action Service (on secondment), since 2015 (Managing Director for Africa, 2011–15); *b* 20 July 1956; *s* of Prof. John Hugh Westcott, FRS and Helen Fay Westcott (*née* Morgan); *m* 1989, Miriam Pearson; one *s* one *d*. *Educ:* Epsom Coll.; Sidney Sussex Coll., Cambridge (MA; PhD History 1982). Entered Foreign and Commonwealth Office, 1982; on secondment to EC, 1984–85; UK Perm. Rep. to EC, Brussels, 1985–89; FCO, 1989–93; Head of Common Foreign and Security Policy Unit, 1992–93; Dep. High Comr, Dar es Salaam, 1993–96; Head of Economic Relations Dept, FCO, 1996–98; Minister-Counsellor (Trade and Transport), Washington, 1999–2002; Head of IT Strategy, subseq. Chief Information Officer, FCO, 2002–07; High Comr to Ghana, and (non-resident) Ambassador to Côte d'Ivoire, Togo, Niger and Burkina Faso, 2008–11. *Publications:* (contrib.) Africa and the Second World War, 1986; (with P. Kingston and R. G. Tiedemann) Managed Economies in World War II, 1991; articles in jls. *Recreations:* swimming, writing, music, travelling. *Address:* European External Action Service, 1046 Brussels, Belgium.

WESTENRA, family name of **Baron Rossmore**.

WESTERMAN, Gillian Barbara, (Jill), (Mrs Martin Rapier), CBE 2010; Principal and Chief Executive, Northern College for Residential Adult Education, since 2007; *b* Wakefield, W Yorks, 30 Nov. 1955; *d* of Albert and Sheila Westerman; *m* 1999, Martin Rapier; two *d*. *Educ:* Wakefield Girls' High Sch.; Durham Univ. (BA English Lit. 1978); Birkbeck Coll., London Univ. (MA English Lit. 1984); Garnett Coll. (Cert Ed 1985). Tutor, W Midlands Travellers' Sch., 1975; TEFL tutor, Internat. Hse, Spain, 1978–79; refuge worker, Hackney Women's Aid, 1979–82; community worker, Springfield Project, 1982–84; Tutor: Bede Educn Centre, 1984–87; Camden Adult Educn Inst., 1987–91; Sen. Lectr, Kingsway Coll., 1992–93; Tutor, Rotherham Coll. of Art and Technol., 1993–94; Northern College for Residential Adult Education: Tutor, 1994–2000; Sen. Tutor, 2000–02; Prog. Dir, 2002–07. *Publications:* contrib. res. articles on leadership in adult and further educn. *Recreations:* finding the fun in things, reading, family, hill walking, cycling. *Address:* Northern College for Residential Adult Education, Wentworth Castle, Stainborough, Barnsley S75 3ET. *T:* (01226) 776000, *Fax:* (01226) 776035. *E:* j.westerman@northern.ac.uk.

WESTERN AUSTRALIA, Metropolitan of; *see* Perth, Archbishop of.

WESTGARTH, Peter Allen; Chief Executive, Duke of Edinburgh's Award, since 2005; *b* 17 May 1953; *s* of Allen and Elizabeth Westgarth; *m* 2007, Rachael Molsom; one *s* one *d* (twins); three *d* from previous marriage. *Educ:* City of Birmingham Sch. of Educn (Cert Ed). Secondary sch. teacher, Walbottle High Sch., 1974–75; advertising sales exec., Newcastle Chronicle, 1976; Exec. Manager, Help the Aged, 1976–80; Fundraising Manager, MIND, 1980–83; PR Officer, NE Co-op., 1983–86; UK Dir, Livewire, 1986–90; Chief Exec., Young Enterprise UK, 1990–2005. Hon. Pres., Young Enterprise Europe, 1991–98. Bata Lifetime Achievement Award for Young Enterprise Achievement, 2004; Queen's Award for Enterprise Promotion, 2006. *Recreations:* playing guitar, hill-walking, travel, BBQ, red wine, reading, and work. *Address:* Duke of Edinburgh's Award, Gulliver House, Madeira Walk, Windsor SL4 1EU. *T:* (01753) 727400. *E:* peter.westgarth@dofe.org.

WESTHAVER, Rev. Dr George Derrick; Principal, Pusey House, Oxford, since 2013; Fellow, St Cross College, Oxford, since 2013; *b* Halifax, NS, 5 May 1968; *s* of Reid Westhaver and Judy Gates; *m* 1994, Karen Conrod; two *d*. *Educ:* McGill Univ., Montreal; St Mary's Univ., Halifax, NS (BA 2002); Wycliffe Coll., Univ. of Toronto (MDiv 2008); Univ. of Durham (PhD 2013); MA Oxon 2013. Ordained deacon, 1997, priest, 1998; Asst Curate, St Andrew, Cherry Hinton and All Saints, Teversham, 1997–2000; Team Vicar, The Ramseys and Upwood Team Ministry, Dio. of Ely, 2000–03; Asst Minister, St Michael at the North Gate, Oxford, 2003–06; Chaplain, Lincoln Coll., Oxford, 2003–06; Rector, Parish of St George, Halifax, NS, 2007–13. *Recreations:* sport, travel, reading, walking, exploring the artistic expression of Christian doctrine in art and music, church crawling. *Address:* Pusey House, Oxford OX1 3LZ. *E:* gwesthaver@gmail.com.

WESTHEIMER, Prof. Gerald, AM 2009; FRS 1985; Professor of Neurobiology, University of California, Berkeley, since 1989 (Professor of Physiology, 1967–89; Head of Division of Neurobiology, 1989–92); *b* Berlin, 13 May 1924; *s* of late Isaac Westheimer and Ilse Westheimer (*née* Cohn); Australian citizen, 1945. *Educ:* Sydney Tech. Coll. (Optometry dip. 1943, Fellowship dip. 1949); Univ. of Sydney (BSc 1947); Ohio State Univ. (PhD 1953); postdoctoral training at Marine Biol. Lab., Woods Hole, 1957 and at Physiolog. Lab., Cambridge, 1958–59. Practising optometrist, Sydney, 1945–51; faculties of Optometry Schools: Univ. of Houston, 1953–54; Ohio State Univ., 1954–60; Univ. of California, Berkeley, 1960–67. Associate: Bosch Vision Res. Center, Salk Inst., 1984–92; Neurosciences Res. Program, NY, 1985–95; Chairman: Visual Scis Study Sect., NIH, 1977–79; Bd of Scientific Counsellors, Nat. Eye Inst., 1981–83; Bd of Editors, Vision Research, 1986–91; service on numerous professional cttees. Adjunct Prof., Rockefeller Univ., NY, 1992–. Fellow or Member, scientific socs, UK and overseas; Fellow, Amer. Acad. of Arts and Scis. Lectures: Sackler, in Med. Sci., Tel Aviv Univ., 1989; Perception, Eur. Conf. on Visual Perception, 1989; D. O. Hebb, McGill Univ., Canada, 1991; Ferrier, Royal Soc., 1992; Wertheimer, Frankfurt Univ., 1998. Hon. Prof., Univ. of Electronic Sci. and Technol., China, 2010. Hon. DSc: New South Wales, 1988; SUNY, 1990; Hon. MD Tübingen, 2005. Tillyer Medal, Optical Soc. of America, 1978; Proctor Medal, Assoc. for Res. in Vision and Ophthalmology, 1979; von Sallmann Prize, Coll. of Physicians and Surgeons, Columbia Univ., 1986; Prentice Medal, Amer. Acad. of Optometry, 1986; Bicentennial Medal, Aust. Optometric Assoc., 1988; Collin Res. Medal, Optometrists Assoc. of Australia, 2009; Fry Medal in Physiol Optics, Ohio State Univ., 2014. *Publications:* research articles in sci. and professional optometric and ophth. jls; editl work for sci. jls. *Recreations:* chamber music (violin), foundation and history of sensory physiology. *Address:* 582 Santa Barbara Road, Berkeley, CA 94707, USA. *E:* gwestheimer@berkeley.edu. *Club:* Cosmos (Washington).

WESTLEY, Stuart Alker, MA; General Secretary, Association of Governing Bodies of Independent Schools, since 2009; *b* 21 March 1947; *s* of Arthur Bancroft Westley and Gladys Westley; *m* 1979, Mary Louise Weston; one *d*. *Educ:* Lancaster Royal GS; Corpus Christi Coll., Oxford (BA 1969; MA 1972). Professional cricketer, 1969–71; Mathematics Teacher, King Edward VII Sch., Lytham, 1969–72; Housemaster and Dir of Studies, Framlingham Coll., 1973–84; Dep. Headmaster, Bristol Cathedral Sch., 1984–89; Principal, King William's Coll., IOM, 1989–96; Master of Haileybury, 1996–2009. *Recreations:* golf, fly fishing, gardening, architecture, choral and classical music, computers. *E:* gensec@agbis.org.uk. *Club:* East India, Devonshire, Sports and Public Schools.

WESTMACOTT, Sir Peter John, KCMG 2003 (CMG 2000); LVO 1993; HM Diplomatic Service, retired; Ambassador to United States of America, 2012–15; *b* 23 Dec. 1950; *s* of late Rev. Prebendary Ian Field Westmacott and of Rosemary Patricia Spencer Westmacott; *m* 1st, 1972, Angela Margaret Lugg (marr. diss. 1999); two *s* one *d*; 2nd, 2001, Susan Nemazee. *Educ:* Taunton Sch.; New Coll., Oxford (MA). Entered FCO 1972; served Tehran 1974, Brussels, 1978; First Sec., Paris, 1980; Private Sec. to Minister of State, FCO, 1984; Head of Chancery, Ankara, 1987; Dep. Private Sec. to Prince of Wales, 1990; Counsellor, Washington, 1993; Dir, Americas, FCO, 1997; Dep. Under-Sec. of State, FCO, 2000–01; Ambassador to: Turkey, 2002–06; France, 2007–11. *Recreations:* tennis, ski-ing.

WESTMACOTT, Richard Kelso; Chairman, Hoare Govett Ltd, 1975–90; *b* 20 Feb. 1934; *s* of Comdr John Rowe Westmacott, RN and Ruth Pharazyn; *m* 1965, Karen Husbands; one *s* one *d*. *Educ:* Eton College. Royal Navy, 1952–54. Hoare & Co., 1955; Mem., Stock Exchange, 1960; Chm., Security Pacific Hoare Govett (Holdings) Ltd, 1985–90; Dep. Chm., Maritime Trust, 1992–99. Dir, Prudential-Bache Internat. Bank Ltd, 1996–2002; Chm., Country Gardens plc, 1998–2001. Master, Mercers' Co., 1998–99; Younger Brother, Trinity House, 2000–. *Recreations:* sailing, shooting. *Clubs:* White's; Royal Yacht Squadron.

WESTMEATH, 13th Earl of, *cr* 1621; **William Anthony Nugent;** Baron Delvin, by tenure temp. Henry II; by summons, 1486; Senior Master, St Andrew's School, Pangbourne, 1980–88; *b* 21 Nov. 1928; *s* of 12th Earl of Westmeath and Doris (*d* 1968), 2nd *d* of C. Imlach, Liverpool; *S* father, 1971; *m* 1963, Susanna Margaret, *o d* of His Honour James Leonard; two *s*. *Educ:* Marlborough Coll. Captain, RA, retired. Staff of St Andrew's Sch., Pangbourne, 1961–88. *Heir: s* Hon. Sean Charles Weston Nugent, *b* 16 Feb. 1965. *Address:* Farthings, Rotten Row Hill, Bradfield, Berks RG7 6LL. *T:* (0118) 974 4426.

WESTMINSTER, 6th Duke of, *cr* 1874; **Gerald Cavendish Grosvenor,** KG 2003; CB 2008; CVO 2012; OBE 1995; TD 1994; CD 2008; DL; Bt 1622; Baron Grosvenor, 1761; Earl Grosvenor and Viscount Belgrave, 1784; Marquess of Westminster, 1831; *b* 22 Dec. 1951; *s* of 5th Duke of Westminster, TD, and Viola Maud (*d* 1987), *d* of 9th Viscount Cobham, KCB, TD; *S* father, 1979; *m* 1978, Natalia, *d* of Lt-Col H. P. J. Phillips; one *s* three *d*. *Educ:* Harrow. Commnd Queen's Own Yeomanry, RAC, TA, 1973; Captain, 1979; Major, 1985; Lt-Col, 1992; Comd, 1993–95; Col, 1995–97; Dep. Comdr, 143 W Midlands Bde, 1997–99; Brig., TA HQ Adjt Gen., 2000–02; Dir, Reserve Forces and Cadets, 2002–04; Maj. Gen., ACDS (Reserves and Cadets), 2004–07; on unposted list 2007–11; Deputy Commander: Army Reserves, 2011–13; Land Forces, 2011–12. Chairman: Grosvenor, 1979–2007; Grosvenor Gp (formerly Grosvenor Gp Hldgs) Ltd, 1999–2007; Chm. of Trustees, Grosvenor Estate, 1974–; Director: Internat. Students Trust, 1976–93; Suttonridge Pty (Aust.), 1979–2000; Claridge's Hotel Ltd, 1981–93; Marcher Sound Ltd, 1982–97; Westminster Christmas Appeal Trust Ltd, 1989–94; NW Business Leadership Team Ltd, 1990–97; BITC, 1991–95; Manchester Olympic Games Co-ordinating Cttee Ltd, 1991–94. Life Gov., RASE; Pro-Chancellor, Univ. of Keele, 1986–93; Chancellor, Manchester Metropolitan Univ., 1992–2002; first Chancellor, Univ. of Chester, 2005–. President: NW Industrialists' Council, 1979–93; London Fedn of Boys' Clubs, later of Clubs for Young People, 1979–2000; SCOPE (formerly Spastics Soc.), 1982–2005; Nat. Kidney Res. Fund, 1985–97; RNIB, 1986–2012; N of England Zool Soc., 1987–; Drug and Alcohol Foundn, 1987–97; Holstein UK & Ireland (formerly British Holstein Soc.), 1988–; Country Trust, 1989–; Abbeyfield Soc., 1989–95; Inst. of Envmtl Scis, 1989–2013; BLESMA, 1992–; British Assoc. for Shooting and Conservation, 1992–2000; Youth Sports Trust, 1996–2004; Manchester Commonwealth Games, 1998–2002; Life Educn Centres (Drug Prevention), 2000–12; Tank Mus., 2002–; Atlantic Salmon Trust, 2004–; Yeomanry Benevolent Fund, 2005–; Vice-President: Fountain Soc., 1985–2012; Freshwater Biol Assoc., 1985–; Royal Soc. of St George, 1987–; Royal Engrs Mus. Foundn, 1990–94; RUSI, 1993–2012; RBL, 1993–; Royal Assoc. of British Dairy Farmers, 1995–; Reserve Forces, Ulysses Trust, 1995–; CLA, 1999–; Game and Wildlife Conservation Trust (formerly Game Conservancy Trust), 2000– (Pres., 1987–2000); Youth Fedn, 2000–; Royal Soc. of Friends of St George's and Descendants of the Knights of the Garter, 2003–; Not Forgotten Soc., 2004–; Royal Smithfield Club, 2004–; Community Network Foundn UK, 2005–; Life Vice-Pres., NSPCC, 1988–. Member, Committee: Nat. Army Mus., 1988–97; Prince's Trust NW Region, 1989–; Rural Target Team, 1992; N Amer. Adv. Gp, BOTB, 1994; Nuffield Hosps, 1995–; Supporters of Nuclear Energy, 1998–; Special Appeal, St George's House, Windsor Castle, 2000–; Nat. Army Mus., 2013–; Mem., Prince's Council, Duchy of Cornwall, 2001–11; Chm., RICS Foundn, 2000–02. Patron: Worcs CCC (Pres., 1984–86); British Kidney Patients Assoc., 1979–84 (Mem. Council, 1984–2007); MIND, 1984–2012; Royal Fine Art Commn, 1988–; Dyslexia Inst., 1989–98; Inst. for Rural Health, 1989–; Rural Stress Inf. Network, 1996–2012; Royal Ulster Agricl Soc., 1997–2003; The Prince's Trust in the NW, 2001–; Emeka Anyaoku Chair in Commonwealth Studies, 2001–; Changing Faces, 2001–12; Blue Cross Animal Hosp., 2001–; Barrowmore, 2002–; Arthritis Care, 2003– (Pres., 1987–2003); Emmaus, 2003–12; Soil Assoc., 2004–; London's Air Ambulance, 2012–; Vice-Patron, Animals in War Meml Fund, 2002–04. Chm. Trustees, Nuffield Trust for Forces of the Crown, 1992–; Trustee: TSB Foundn for England and Wales, 1986–97; Westminster Abbey Trust, 1988–97; Westminster Foundn; Westminster Housing Trust. Freeman: Chester, 1973; England, 1979; City of London, 1980. Liveryman: Gunmakers' Co.; Weavers' Co.; Armourers' and Brasiers' Co.; Marketors' Co.; Goldsmiths' Co.; Fishmongers' Co. DL Cheshire, 1982. FIStructE 1997; FRSA; FRAS; FCIM; FCIOB; Fellow, Liverpool John Moores Univ., 1990. Hon. MRICS; Hon. Fellow: Liverpool Poly., 1990; Univ. of Central Lancs, 2001. Hon. LLD: Keele, 1990; Liverpool, 2000; Hon. DLitt: Manchester Metropolitan, 1993; Salford, 2000. Hon. Colonel: 7 Regt AAC, 1993–2009; Northumbrian Univs OTC, 1995–2003; Northumberland OTC; Royal Mercian and Lancastrian Yeomanry, 2001–08; Col in Chief, Royal Westminster Regt, 1991; Col Comdt, Yeomanry Assoc., 2005–11; Dep. Col Comdt, AAC, 2009–14. KStJ 1991. Knight Grand Cross, Royal Order of Francis I, 2005. *Recreations:* shooting, fishing. *Heir: s* Earl Grosvenor, *qv*. *Address:* Eaton Hall, Chester, Cheshire CH4 9JF. *Clubs:* Cavalry, MCC; Royal Yacht Squadron.

See also Lady J. M. Dawnay.

WESTMINSTER, Archbishop of, (RC), since 2009; **His Eminence Cardinal Vincent Gerard Nichols;** *b* 8 Nov. 1945; *s* of Henry Joseph Nichols and Mary Nichols (*née* Russell). *Educ:* St Mary's College, Crosby; Gregorian Univ., Rome (STL PhL); Manchester Univ. (MA Theol); Loyola Univ., Chicago (MEd). Chaplain, St John Rigby VI Form College, Wigan, 1972–77; Priest, inner city of Liverpool, 1978–81; Director, Upholland Northern Inst., with responsibility for in service training of clergy and for adult Christian educn, 1981–84; Gen. Sec., RC Bishops' Conf. of England and Wales, 1984–91; Auxiliary Bishop of Westminster (Bishop in N London), 1992–2000; Titular Bishop of Othona, 1992–2000; Archbishop of Birmingham, (RC), 2000–09. Cardinal, 2014. Chm., Catholic Educn Service, 1998–; Chm., Dept of Catholic Educn and Formation, 1998–, Pres., 2009–, RC Bishops' Conf. of Eng. and Wales. Advr to Cardinal Hume and Archbishop Worlock, Internat. Synods of Bishops, 1980, 1983, 1985, 1987. Deleg. of Bishops' Conf. to Synod of Bishops, 1994; Mem., Synod of Bishops for Oceania, 1998, for Europe, 1999. *Publications:* Promise of Future Glory, 1997;

Missioners, 2007; St John Fisher: bishop and theologian in Reformation and controversy, 2011; articles in Priests and People, Business Economist. *Address:* Archbishop's House, Ambrosden Avenue, Westminster, SW1P 1QJ.

WESTMINSTER, Auxiliary Bishops of, (RC); *see* Arnold, Rt Rev. J. S. K.; Hudson, Rt Rev. N.; Sherrington, Rt Rev. J. F.

WESTMINSTER, Dean of; *see* Hall, Very Rev. J. R.

WESTMORLAND, 16th Earl of, *cr* 1624; **Anthony David Francis Henry Fane;** Baron Burghersh, 1624; independent art adviser; Director: Phillips Auctioneers, 1994–2001; Bonhams Auctioneers, 2001–04; Watson Westmorland Ltd, since 2003; *b* 1 Aug. 1951; *s* of 15th Earl of Westmorland, GCVO and Jane, *d* of Lt-Col Sir Roland Lewis Findlay, 3rd Bt; *S* father, 1993; *m* 1985, Caroline Eldred, *d* of Keon Hughes; one *d*. *Educ:* Eton. Mem., Orbitex North Pole Expedn, 1990. FRGS. *Heir:* *b* Hon. Harry St Clair Fane [*b* 19 March 1953; *m* 1984, Tessa, *d* of Captain Michael Philip Forsyth-Forrest; one *s* one *d*]. *Address:* London, SW7. *Club:* Turf.

WESTMORLAND AND FURNESS, Archdeacon of; *see* Driver, Ven. P. M.

WESTON, Prof. Arthur Henry, PhD, DSc; FMedSci; Leech Professor of Pharmacology, University of Manchester, 1990–2011, now Emeritus; *b* 31 May 1944; *s* of Arthur Edward Weston and Betty Nutt Weston (*née* Wetherell); *m* 1967, Kathleen Margaret Goodison; one *s* one *d*. *Educ:* Hymers Coll., Hull; Univ. of Manchester (BSc 1st Cl. Hons 1966, MSc 1968; PhD 1970; DSc 1994). Lectr in Pharmacol., 1970–75, Sen. Lectr, 1975–88, Reader, 1988–90, Univ. of Manchester. Alexander von Humboldt Fellow, Univ. of Marburg, 1974, Univ. of Heidelberg, 1985; Vis. Prof., Univ. of Kyushu, 1987; Vis. Fellow, Magdalen Coll., Oxford, 2011–12. Trustee and Hon. Treas., British Pharmacol Soc., 2000–07; Pres., Fedn of Eur. Pharmacol Socs, 2006–08; Hon. Mem., Finnish Pharmacol Soc., 2008. FMedSci 2001; FBPharmacolS 2004–12, Hon. FBPhS (Hon. FBPharmacolS 2012). Gaddum Memorial Award, British Pharmacol Soc., 2008; Rodolfo Paoletti Medal, Fedn of Eur. Pharmacol Socs, 2014. *Publications:* (jtly) Pharmacology of the Hypothalamus, 1978; (with T. C. Hamilton) Potassium Channel Modulators, 1992; contrib. original papers to British Jl Pharmacol., Jl Pharmacol. and Exptl Therapeutics, Nature, Naunyn Schmiedeberg's Archives of Pharmacol. *Recreations:* gardening, mechanical watches, visiting Germany, early British postage stamps. *Address:* Faculty of Life Sciences, University of Manchester, 3rd Floor, CTF Building, 46 Grafton Street, Manchester M13 9NT. *T:* (0161) 275 5490, *Fax:* (0161) 275 5600. *E:* arthur.weston@manchester.ac.uk.

WESTON, Christopher John; Life President, Phillips Son & Neale (Chairman and Chief Executive, 1972–98); Chairman and Chief Executive Officer, Plaxbury Group, since 1998; *b* 3 March 1937; *s* of Eric Tudor Weston and Evelyn Nellie Weston; *m* 1969, Josephine Annabel Moir; one *d*. *Educ:* Lancing Coll. FIA (Scot.). Director: Phillips, 1964–98; Foreign and Colonial Pacific Investment Trust, 1984–99; Hodder Headline Plc (formerly Headline Book Publishing PLC), 1986–99 (Chm., 1997–99); Foreign & Colonial Enterprise Trust plc, 1987–99. Vice-Pres., Quit - Soc. of Non Smokers, 1993–. FRSA (Mem. Council, 1985). *Recreations:* theatre, music. *Address:* 5 Hillside Close, Carlton Hill, NW8 0EF. *T:* (020) 7372 5042. *E:* plaxbury@gmail.com. *Club:* Oriental.

WESTON, Rev. Canon David Wilfrid Valentine, PhD; Residentiary Canon of Carlisle Cathedral, 1994–2006; Canon Librarian, 1995–2006; *b* 8 Dec. 1937; *s* of Rev. William Valentine Weston and Mrs Gertrude Hamilton Weston; *m* 1984, Helen Strachan Macdonald, *d* of James and Barbara Macdonald; two *s*. *Educ:* St Edmund's Sch., Canterbury; Lancaster Univ. (PhD 1993). Entered Nashdom Abbey, 1960; deacon, 1967, priest, 1968; Novice Master, 1969–74; Prior, 1971–74; Abbot, 1974–84; Curate, St Peter's, Chorley, 1984–85; Vicar, St John the Baptist, Pilling, 1985–89; Domestic Chaplain to Bishop of Carlisle, 1989–94; Actg Dean, Carlisle, 2003–04. Chm., Carlisle Tourism Forum, 1996–98. Freeman, City of London; Liveryman, Salters' Co. *Publications:* Carlisle Cathedral History, 2000; (ed jtly) Carlisle and Cumbria, 2004; Rose Castle and the Bishops of Carlisle 1133–2012, 2013. *Address:* The Pond House, Ratten Row, Dalston, Carlisle CA5 7AY.

WESTON, Galen; *see* Weston, W. G.

WESTON, George Garfield; Chief Executive, Associated British Foods plc, since 2005; *b* 4 March 1964; *s* of late Garfield Howard Weston and Mary Ruth Weston (*née* Kippenberger); *m* 1996, Katharine Mary Acland; three *s* one *d*. *Educ:* Westminster Sch.; New Coll., Oxford (MA PPE); Harvard Business Sch. (MBA). N. B. Love Mills, 1988–92; Managing Director: Westmill Foods, 1992–98; Allied Bakeries, 1999–2003; Chief Exec., George Weston Foods Ltd (Australia), 2003–05. *Recreations:* tennis, gardening. *Address:* Associated British Foods plc, 10 Grosvenor Street, W1K 4QY. *T:* (020) 7399 6500.

See also A. C. Hobhouse, G. H. Weston.

WESTON, Guy Howard; Chairman, Garfield Weston Foundation, since 2000; *b* Sydney, NSW, 3 July 1960; *s* of late Garfield Howard Weston and Mary Ruth Weston; *m* 1986, Charlotte Emily Brunet; three *s* one *d*. *Educ:* Westminster Sch.; Merton Coll., Oxford (BA 1981; Hon. Fellow 2007); INSEAD (MBA 1988). Morgan Grenfell & Co. Ltd, 1984–87; Managing Director: Jacksons of Piccadilly Ltd, 1990–93; Ryvita Co. Ltd, 1993–2000. Chairman: Heals plc, 2001–12; Wittington Investments Ltd, 2002–. Trustee, Thrombosis Res. Inst., 2002–; Chairman: Garfield Weston Fund for Westminster Abbey, 2007–; Bodleian Liby Appeal Cttee, 2010–. Hon. LLD Buckingham, 2005; Hon. DSc Imperial Coll. London, 2008. *Recreations:* theatre, travel, history, sailing, ski-ing. *Address:* Garfield Weston Foundation, 10 Grosvenor Street, W1K 4QY. *Club:* Reial Club Nàutic Port de Pollença.

See also A. C. Hobhouse, G. G. Weston.

WESTON, Hon. Hilary Mary, CVO 2015; CM 2003; OOnt 2001; Lieutenant Governor of Ontario, 1997–2002; *b* 12 Jan. 1942; *d* of Michael Frayne and Noel Elizabeth Guerrini; *m* 1966, W(illard) Galen Weston, *qv*; one *s* one *d*. *Educ:* Loretto Abbey, Dalkey. Dep. Chm., Holt, Renfrew & Co., 1986–96; Design Dir, Windsor, Florida, 1988–96. Founder, Ireland Fund of Canada, 1979. Chm., Royal Ontario Mus. Renaissance Campaign, Toronto, 2002–09. Trustee, Foundn of Coll. of St George, Windsor Castle. Hon. Col, 437 Transport Sqdn, CFB Trenton & The Princess of Wales' Own Regt, Kingston, 1998–2002. Hon. DLittS Univ. of St Michael's Coll., Toronto, 1997; Hon. LLD: Western Ontario, 1997; UC of Cape Breton, 1999; Toronto, 2000; Niagara, York, 2002; Dublin, 2004; Queen's, Kingston, 2008; Concordia, Montreal, 2008; Hon. DLitt UCD, 2009. Woodrow Wilson Award for Public Service, 2005; Women of Distinction President's Award, YWCA, 2009. DStJ 1997. *Publications:* (jtly) In a Canadian Garden, 1989; (jtly) At Home in Canada, 1995; No Ordinary Time, 2006. *Recreations:* tennis, riding. *Address:* 22 St Clair Avenue East, Toronto, ON M4T 2S3, Canada. *T:* (416) 9354050; Fort Belvedere, Ascot, Berks SL5 7SD. *Club:* National (Toronto).

See also A. E. Weston Cochrane.

WESTON, Jeremy Paul; QC 2011; *b* Dorchester, 3 Sept. 1969; *s* of David and Ann Weston; *m* 2001, Kate Stilgoe; one *s* two *s*. *Educ:* Reading Blue Coat Sch.; Staffordshire Univ. (LLB Hons). Called to the Bar, Inner Temple, 1991; in practice as barrister, specialising in family law; 8 Fountain Court, 1992–96, St Ives Chambers, 1996–. *Recreations:* family, gardening, cooking, golf. *Address:* St Ives Chambers, Whittall Street, Birmingham B4 6DH. *T:* (0121) 236 0863, *Fax:* (0121) 236 6961. *E:* jeremy.weston@stiveschambers.co.uk.

WESTON, Sir John; *see* Weston, Sir P. J.

WESTON, John Pix, CBE 1994; FRAeS; FREng; Chairman: MB Aerospace, since 2007; Accesso plc (formerly Lo-Q), since 2011; Fibercore, since 2012; Windar Photonics, since 2015; *b* 16 Aug. 1951; *s* of late John Pix Weston and Ivy (*née* Glover); *m* 1974, Susan West; one *s* one *d*. *Educ:* King's Sch., Worcester; Trinity Hall, Cambridge (MA Eng.). CEng 1992; FRAeS 1992. British Aerospace, subseq. BAE SYSTEMS: undergrad. apprenticeship, 1970–74; sales appts on Jaguar and Tornado projects, 1974–82; on secondment to MoD Sales Orgn, 1982–85; Military Aircraft Division, Warton: ME Sales Manager, Project Manager, Al Yamamah Project and Exec. Dir, Saudi Ops, 1985–89; Dir, 1989–92; Man. Dir, 1990–92; Chm. and Man. Dir, British Aerospace Defence Ltd, 1992–96; Dir, 1994–2002; Gp Man. Dir, 1996–98; Chief Exec., 1998–2002. Chairman: Spirent plc, 2002–06; Acra Controls, 2003–11; INBIS plc, 2004–05; Ufi learn-direct Ltd, 2004–11; i-SOFT, 2005–07; AWS Ltd, 2008–12; Torotrak plc, 2011–15. Vice-Pres., RUSI, 2000–. FREng 2000; FRSA. Commander, Order of the Pole Star (Sweden), 2000. *Recreations:* ski-ing, photography, hill-walking. *E:* johnpweston@btinternet.com.

WESTON, Dame Margaret (Kate), DBE 1979; BScEng (London); CEng, FIET, FNucl; FMA; Director of the Science Museum, 1973–86; *b* 7 March 1926; *oc* of late Charles Edward and Margaret Weston. *Educ:* Stroud High School; College of Technology, Birmingham (now Univ. of Aston). Engineering apprenticeship, General Electric Co. Ltd, 1945–49; development work, very largely on high voltage insulation problems. Science Museum: Assistant Keeper, Dept of Electrical Engineering and Communications, 1955–61; Deputy Keeper, 1962; Keeper, Dept of Museum Services, 1967–72. Member: Ancient Monuments Bd for England, 1977–84; 1851 Commission, 1987–96; Museums and Galleries Commission, 1988–96; Steering Gp, Museum in Docklands, 1986–90. Member: SE Elec. Bd, 1981–90; BBC Sci. Consultative Gp, 1986–89. Chairman: Brunel Goods Shed Cttee, Stroud, 2004–07; Heritage Network (formerly Heritage Forum), Stroud, 2005–; Mem. Hunterian Bd, RCS, 1981–2012; Trustee: Brooklands, 1987–2002; Fleet Air Arm Mus., 1992–2000; British Empire and Commonwealth Mus., Bristol, 1999–2002 (Chm., 1999–2002); Museum in the Park, Stroud, 2004– (Chm. Trustees, 2004–05). Horniman Public Museum and Public Park: Chm. Trust, 1990–96; Mem. Develt Cttee, 1996–2002; Pres., Friends, 1996–2003; Chm. Trustees, Horniman Mus., Trust, 1997–2002. Patron, Stroudwater Textile Trust, 2002–. Governor: Imperial Coll., 1974–90 (FIC 1975); Ditchley Foundn, 1984–2008 (Mem., Mgt Council, 1984–2003). Pres., 1985–2011, Patron, 2011–, Heritage Railways Assoc. (formerly Assoc. of Railway Preservation Socs, then Assoc. of Independent Railways and Preservation Socs); Mem., Adv. Panel, Railway Heritage Trust, 1987–2011. FMA 1976; Sen. Fellow, RCA, 1986; FRSA (Mem. Council, 1985–90); CCMI. Hon. Fellow, Newnham Coll., Cambridge, 1986. Hon. DEng Bradford, 1984; Hon. DSc: Aston, 1974; Salford, 1984; Leeds, 1987; Loughborough, 1988; DUniv Open, 1987. *Address:* Ryland Lodge, Ashlane, Randwick, nr Stroud, Glos GL6 6EX. *T:* (01453) 766694.

WESTON, Sir Michael (Charles Swift), KCMG 1991; CVO 1979; JP; HM Diplomatic Service, retired; UK Permanent Representative to Conference on Disarmament, Geneva (with personal rank of Ambassador), 1992–97; *b* 4 Aug. 1937; *s* of late Edward Charles Swift Weston and Kathleen Mary Weston (*née* Mockett); *m* 1st, 1959, Veronica Anne Tickner (marr. diss. 1990); two *s* one *d*; 2nd, 1990, Christine Julia Ferguson; one *s* one *d*. *Educ:* Dover Coll.; St Catharine's Coll., Cambridge (Exhibitioner; BA, MA). Joined HM Diplomatic Service, 1961; 3rd Sec., Kuwait, 1962; 2nd Sec., FCO, 1965; 1st Secretary: Tehran, 1968; UK Mission, New York, 1970; FCO, 1974; Counsellor, Jedda, 1977; RCDS, 1980; Counsellor (Information), Paris, 1981; Counsellor, Cairo, 1984; Head of Southern European Dept, FCO, 1987; Ambassador to Kuwait, 1990–92. Member: UN Sec.-Gen.'s Gp of Experts on Small Arms, 1998–99; Special Immigration Appeals Commn, 1999–2007. Chm. Adv. Gp, Comprehensive Nuclear-Test-Ban Treaty Orgn, 2009–. JP West Kent, 2002. *Recreations:* tennis, squash, walking. *Address:* Beech Farm House, Beech Lane, Matfield, Kent TN12 7HG. *T:* (01892) 824666. *Club:* Oxford and Cambridge.

WESTON, Sir (Philip) John, KCMG 1992 (CMG 1985); HM Diplomatic Service, retired; British Permanent Representative to the United Nations, 1995–98; *b* 13 April 1938; *s* of Philip George Weston and Edith Alice Bray (*née* Ansell); *m* 1967, Margaret Sally Ehlers; two *s* one *d*. *Educ:* Sherborne; Worcester Coll., Oxford (1st Cl. Hons, Honour Mods Classics and Lit. Hum.; Hon. Fellow, 2003). Served with 42 Commando, Royal Marines, 1956–58. Entered Diplomatic Service, 1962; FO, 1962–63; Treasury Centre for Admin. Studies, 1964; Chinese Language student, Hong Kong, 1964–66; Peking, 1967–68; FO, 1969–71; Office of UK Permanent Representative to EEC, 1972–74; Asst Private Sec. to Sec. of State for Foreign and Commonwealth Affairs (Rt Hon. James Callaghan, Rt Hon. Anthony Crosland), 1974–76; Counsellor, Head of EEC Presidency Secretariat, FCO, 1976–77; Vis. Fellow, All Souls Coll., Oxford, 1977–78; Counsellor, Washington, 1978–81; Hd Defence Dept, FCO, 1981–84; Asst Under-Sec. of State, FCO, 1984–85; Minister, Paris, 1985–88; Dep. Sec. to Cabinet, Cabinet Office, 1988–89 (on secondment); Dep. Under-Sec. of State (Defence), FCO, 1989–90; Political Dir, FCO, 1990–91; Ambassador and UK Perm. Rep. to N Atlantic Council (NATO), 1992–95, to Perm. Council of WEU, 1992–95. Non-executive Director: BT Gp, 1998–2002; Rolls Royce Gp, 1998–2004; Hakluyt and Co. Ltd, 2001–07. Trustee: NPG, 1999–2008; Poetry Soc., 2005–08; Chm. Trustees, The Poetry Sch., 2005–08. Council Mem., IISS, 2001–05. Governor: Sherborne Sch., 1995–2007 (Chm., 2002–07); Ditchley Foundn, 1999–2011. Trustee, Amer. Associates of the Royal Acad. Trust, 1998–2004. Pres., Worcester Coll. Soc., 2003–12. Hon. Pres., Community Foundn Network (UK), 1999–2008. *Publications:* (contrib.) Take Five 04 (anthol. poems), 2004; Chasing The Hoopoe (poems), 2005; Echo Soundings (poems), 2012; poems in many magazines (various prizes). *Recreations:* poetry, bee-keeping, fly-fishing, running, birds. *Address:* 139 Queen's Road, Richmond, Surrey TW10 6HF. *Club:* Garrick.

WESTON, Simon, OBE 1992; motivational speaker, writer and performer, since 1985; *b* 8 Aug. 1961; *s* of Harold Hatfield and Pauline Hatfield; *m* 1990, Lucy Veronica (*née* Titherington); two *s* one *d*. *Educ:* Lewis Boys' Sch., Pengam, Mid Glam. Joined Welsh Guards, 1978; served Berlin, NI, Kenya and Falklands; Co-Founder and Vice Pres., Weston Spirit, 1988–2009. Documentaries: Simon's War, Simon's Peace, Simon's Triumph, Simon's Return, Simon's Journey, Simon's Heroes, BBC TV; Saving Simon, ITV. Vice Pres. and advocate, Royal Star and Garter Home, 1991. Pres., Fleming Fulton Special Needs Sch. Poultry Club, 1990. Freedom, City of Liverpool, 2002. Fellow, Univ. of Wales Sch. of Midwifery, 2001. Hon. Fellow: John Moores Univ., Liverpool, 2003; Open Univ., 2003; Cardiff Univ., 2005. Hon. degree in humanities, 1994, Hon. DHum, 2002, Glamorgan; Hon. Dr Heriot-Watt, 2008. *Publications:* *autobiography:* Walking Tall, 1989; Going Back, 1992; Moving On, 2003; *novels:* Cause of Death, 1995; Phoenix, 1996; *for children:* A Nod from Nelson, 2008; Nelson to the Rescue, 2010; Nelson at Sea, 2011; Get Fit With Nelson, 2013. *Recreations:* reading, keeping fit, music, watching sport, jogging. *Address:* Abingdon Management Company, Rosedale House, Rosedale Road, Richmond, Surrey TW9 2SZ. *T:* (020) 8939 9019, *Fax:* (020) 8939 9080.

WESTON, Susan Elizabeth; *see* Murray, S. E.

WESTON, W(illard) Galen, OC 1990; OOnt 2004; Chairman, George Weston Ltd, Toronto, since 1978 (former President); former Executive Chairman, Loblaw Companies Ltd; *b* England, 29 Oct. 1940; *s* of W. Garfield Weston and Reta Lila (*née* Howard); *m* 1966, Hon. Hilary Mary Frayne (*see* Hon. H. M. Weston); one *s* one *d*. Chairman: Selfridges & Co.; Holt Renfrew & Co. Ltd; Brown Thomas; Wittington Investments Ltd; Vice-Chm., Fortnum & Mason plc (UK); Director: Associated British Foods plc (UK); Brown Thomas Group Ltd (Eire). Pres. and Trustee, W. Garfield Weston Foundation, Canada. Hon. LLD Univ. of

Western Ont. *Recreations:* outdoor sports, contemporary arts. *Address:* George Weston Ltd, 22 St Clair Avenue East, Toronto, ON M4T 2S7, Canada. *T:* (416) 9222500, *Fax:* (416) 9224394. *Clubs:* Guards' Polo; Toronto, York (Toronto); Windsor (Florida); Deep Dale (NY).

See also A. E. Weston Cochrane.

WESTON, William John, MVO 2002; independent management consultant to cultural, heritage and leisure sectors; *b* 4 July 1949; *s* of Eric Gordon and Pauline Violet Weston; *m* 1978, Patricia April (decd); two *d*; *m* 1995, Jane Henriques; one step *s* one step *d*. *Educ:* Wymondham Coll., Norfolk; Royal Manchester Coll. of Music; Poly. of Central London. Concerts Manager, Bournemouth SO, 1971–73; City Arts Administrator, Southampton CC, 1973–77; Administrator, Irish Th. Co., Dublin, 1977–80; Exec. Dir and Creator, W Yorks Playhouse, Leeds, 1980–93; freelance TV producer, 1993–95; Gen. Manager, RSC, 1995–2000; Chief Exec., Royal Parks Agency, 2000–05. Non-exec. Dir, England Nat. Cttee, Forestry Commn, 2008–14. Chm., Heart of Teesdale Landscape Partnership, 2010–14; Member: Yorks Dales Nat. Park Authy, 2006–14; Barnard Castle Regeneration Partnership, 2011–14. Associate Dir, Georgian Th., Richmond, 2012–14. *Recreations:* the arts, walking, gardening, open spaces, jazz, sailing. *Address:* 93 Seacon Tower, 5 Hutchings Street, E14 8JX.

WESTON COCHRANE, Alannah Elizabeth; Deputy Chairman, Selfridges Group, since 2014 (Creative Director, Selfridges & Co., 2004); *b* Dublin, 8 Jan. 1972; *d* of W(illard) Galen Weston, *qv* and Hon. Hilary Mary Weston, *qv*; *m* 2007, Alexander Desmond Sursock Cochrane, *s* and *heir* of Sir (Henry) Marc (Sursock) Cochrane, *qv*; two *d*. *Educ:* Havergal Coll., Toronto; Merton Coll., Oxford (MA English). Contrib. Ed., Telegraph mag., 1994–98; Press Officer, Burberry, 1998–2000; Creative Dir, Windsor art gall., Florida, 2001–04. Dir, Zephyr Projects, 2003–04. Trustee: Reta Lila Howard Foundn and Reta Lila Weston Trust, 1998– (Chm. Trustees, 2011–14); Blue Marine Foundn, 2012–. *Publications:* The Beach, 2001; Christo and Jeanne-Claude: the Weston Collection, 2002; Ed Ruscha, 2003; Heel to Heal: the collection of paintings, drawings and photographs of Bruce Weber and Nan Bush, 2003; The Family, 2004; Peter Doig: works on paper, 2004; (jtly) A Book of Wonder, 2007. *Recreations:* travel, reading, riding, cycling, canoeing. *Address:* Selfridges & Co., 400 Oxford Street, W1A 1AB. *Clubs:* Soho House, Hertford Street; Windsor (Florida); Ojibway (Pointe au Baril, Ont).

WESTWELL, Alan Reynolds, OBE 1996; PhD, MSc; CEng, MIMechE, MIET; FCILT; Managing Director and Chief Executive, Dublin Buses Ltd, 1997–2005; *b* 11 April 1940; *s* of Stanley Westwell and Margaret (*née* Reynolds); *m* 1967, Elizabeth Aileen Birrell; two *s* one *d*. *Educ:* Old Swan Coll.; Liverpool Polytechnic (ACT Hons); Salford Univ. (MSc 1983); Keele Univ. (PhD 1991). Liverpool City Transport Dept: progressively, student apprentice, Technical Asst, Asst Works Manager, 1956–67; Chief Engineer: Southport Corporation Transport Dept, 1967–69; Coventry Corp. Transport Dept, 1969–72; Glasgow Corp. Transport Dept, 1972–74; Director of Public Transport (responsible for bus/rail, airport, harbours), Tayside Regional Council, 1974–79; Dir Gen., Strathclyde PTE, 1979–86; Chm., Man. Dir and Chief Exec., Strathclyde Buses Ltd, 1987–90; Man. Dir and Chief Exec., Greater Manchester Buses Ltd, 1990–93, Greater Manchester Buses North Ltd, 1993–97. Professional Advr, COSLA, 1976–86. President: Scottish Council of Confedn of British Road Passenger Transport, 1982–83 (Vice-Pres., 1981–82); Bus and Coach Council, UK, 1989–90 (Vice Pres., 1985–88; Sen. Vice-Pres., 1988–89). Mem., Parly Road Transport Cttee, 1986–97. Chm., IMechE, Automobile Div., Scottish Centre, 1982–84; Mem. Council, CIT, UK, 1986–89 (Chm. Scottish Centre, 1983–84). International Union of Public Transport: Vice Pres., 1997; Member: Management Cttee, 1991–; Internat. Metropolitan Railway Cttee, 1979–86; Internat. Gen. Commn on Transport and Urban Life (formerly Internat. Commn, Traffic and Urban Planning), 1986–; UITP-EU (formerly European Action) Cttee, 1988–; Chm., UK Members, 1993–97. Hon. Vice Pres., UITP, 2003. Chm., Altrincham Probus Club, 2012–13. *Publications:* various papers. *Recreations:* swimming, music, reading. *Address:* 6 Amberley Drive, Hale Barns, Altrincham, Cheshire WA15 0DT. *T:* (0161) 980 3551.

WESTWOOD, family name of **Baron Westwood**.

WESTWOOD, 3rd Baron *cr* 1944, of Gosforth; **William Gavin Westwood;** *b* 30 Jan. 1944; *s* of 2nd Baron Westwood and of Marjorie, *o c* of Arthur Bonwick; *S* father, 1991; *m* 1969, Penelope, *e d* of Dr C. E. Shafto; two *s*. *Educ:* Fettes. *Recreations:* music, reading, golf. *Heir: s* Hon. (William) Fergus Westwood, *b* 24 Nov. 1972. *Address:* 9 Princes Close, Brunton Park, Newcastle upon Tyne NE3 5AS. *E:* lordwestwood@hotmail.com.

WESTWOOD, Dr Albert Ronald Clifton, FREng; consultant in research and technology management, since 2000; Vice President, Research and Exploratory Technology, Sandia National Laboratories, 1993–96, now Emeritus; *b* 9 June 1932; *s* of Albert Sydney Westwood and Ena Emily (*née* Clifton); *m* 1956, Jean Mavis Bullock; two *d*. *Educ:* King Edward's Sch., Birmingham; Univ. of Birmingham (BSc Hons 1953; PhD 1956; DSc 1968). FInstP 1967; FIMMM (FIM 1998). Joined Research Institute for Advanced Studies, subseq. Martin Marietta Labs, Baltimore, 1958, Dir, 1974–84; Martin Marietta Corporation: Corporate Dir, R&D, 1984–87; Vice Pres., R&D, 1987–90; Corporate Vice Pres., Res. and Technol., 1990–93. Chm. and Chief Exec., CCLRC, UK, 1998–2000. Chairman: Commn on Engrg and Technical Systems, Nat. Res. Council, 1992–97; Cttee on Global Aspects of Intellectual Properties Rights in Sci. and Technol., Nat. Res. Council, 1992–93; and numerous govt, academic, civic, music and humanities councils and adv. bds. Mem. Bd, US Civilian R&D Foundn, 1995–. President: Industrial Res. Inst., US, 1989–90; Minerals, Metals and Materials Soc., 1990 (Fellow, 1990). Mem., Bd of Sci. and Technol., Univ. of New Mexico, 1995– (Interim Pres., 2007). Fellow, Amer. Soc. for Materials Internat., 1974; FAAAS 1986; FREng (FEng 1996). Member: US NAE, 1980; Royal Swedish Acad. Engrg Scis, 1989; Russian Acad. Engrg, 1995; Georgia Acad. of Engrg, 2007. Pianist and arranger accompanying wife in concerts and recitals in US and around world. Has received numerous awards, prizes and lectureships in recognition of scientific and managerial contribs. *Publications:* (ed) Environment Sensitive Mechanical Behavior, 1966; (ed) Mechanisms of Environment Sensitive Cracking of Materials, 1977; about 125 scientific papers. *Recreations:* music, theatre, arts, travel. *Address:* 13539 Canada Del Oso, High Desert, Albuquerque, NM 87111, USA. *E:* arwestwood@aol.com.

WESTWOOD, Dr David, QPM 2001; Chief Constable, Humberside Police, 1999–2005; Owner, Just Things, Fairtrade shop, Ilminster, since 2012; *b* 1 April 1948; *s* of late Sqdn Ldr William Westwood and Judith Westwood (*née* Green); *m* 1969, Wendy Stevenson; three *s* one *d*. *Educ:* Collyer's Sch., Horsham; Lady Margaret Hall, Oxford (MA Juris.); Bristol Poly. (PhD 1991). Constable, Sussex Police, 1963–73; Constable to Supt, Avon and Somerset Police, 1973–92; Chief Supt, Humberside Police, 1992–95; Asst Chief Constable, Merseyside Police, 1995–97; Dep. Chief Constable, Humberside Police, 1997–99. Hd, Business Area for Race and Community Relns, ACPO, 2000–03. Commn Officer, United Reformed Church of England and Wales, 2011–. *Recreations:* theatre, organic gardening, Fairtrade. *Address:* Park View, Long Close, Ilminster, Somerset TA19 0EP. *E:* enquiries@just-things.co.uk.

WESTWOOD, Nicola Ann; *see* Sullivan, N. A.

WESTWOOD, Dame Vivienne (Isabel), DBE 2006 (OBE 1992); RDI 2001; fashion designer; *b* 8 April 1941; *née* Vivienne Isabel Swire; two *s*. In partnership with Malcolm McLaren, designed a series of influential avant-garde collections showcased at World's End (formerly named Let It Rock, Too Fast to Live Too Young to Die, Sex, Seditionaries), 430 King's Rd, Chelsea, 1971–82; opened Vivienne Westwood shop, 6 Davies St, W1, 1990, flagship shop, 44 Conduit St, W1, 1992, head office, Milan, 1998, shop, Los Angeles, 2011, and stores worldwide; collections include: Anglomania, 1993–; Vivienne Westwood Man (Milan), 1996–; Red Label, London, 1997–, Paris, 1998–, New York, 2000–; Gold Label, 1999–. Launched fragrances: Boudoir, 1998; Libertine, 2000; Boudoir Sin City, 2007; Let It Rock, 2007. Exhibitions at V & A Museum: (contrib.) Radical Fashion, 2001; (contrib.) Men in Skirts, 2002; (contrib.) Tiaras, 2002; Vivienne Westwood 36 Years in Fashion, 2004 and subseq. world tour; launched manifesto at Wallace Collection, 2007. Professor of Fashion: Acad. of Applied Arts, Vienna, 1989–91; Hochschule der Künste, Berlin, 1993–. Launched Climate Revolution, 2012. Trustee, Civil Liberties Trust, 2007–. Hon. Sen. FRCA 1992; Hon. FKC 2008; Dr *hc*: Heriot-Watt, 2008; RCA, 2008. British Designer of the Year, 1990, 1991, Outstanding Achievement in Fashion, 2007, British Fashion Council; Queen's Award for Export, 1998; Moët & Chandon Red Carpet Dresser, 2006; André Leon Talley Lifetime Achievement Award, SCAD Mus. of Art, 2015. *Publications:* (with Ian Kelly) Vivienne Westwood, 2014. *Address:* Vivienne Westwood Ltd, Westwood Studios, 9–15 Elcho Street, Battersea, SW11 4AU. *T:* (020) 7924 4747.

WETHERED, Julian Frank Baldwin; Director, International Division, United States Banknote Corporation, 1992–94; *b* 9 Nov. 1929; *s* of late Comdr Owen Francis McTier Wethered, RN retd and Betty (*née* Baldwin); *m* 1st, 1952, Britt Eva Hindmarsh (marr. diss. 1971); one *s* one *d*; 2nd, 1973, Antonia Mary Ettrick Roberts; two *s*. *Educ:* Eton Coll.; Jesus Coll., Cambridge (BA Hons Hist. 1952; MA); BA Hons Open Univ. 2002. National Service, RM, HMS Diadem, 1948–49. Trainee, Expandite Ltd, 1952–54; Sales Rep., Remington Rand, 1955–56; Thomas De La Rue and Co.: trainee, 1956; Mem., PA Study Team, 1957; Printing Preliminaries Manager, Currency Div., 1958–62; Special Rep., Africa, 1963–67; Manager, Banknote Printing Co., 1968–69; Regl Manager, FE, 1970–75; Associate Dir of Sales, Africa and FE, 1976–83; Regl Dir, FE, De La Rue Co. plc, 1984–88; Associate Dir of Sales, Thomas De La Rue & Co., 1989. Dir Gen., RoSPA, 1990–91. Dir, Whatman Far East Pte Ltd, 1987–88. Chm., Riding for the Disabled Assoc. of Singapore, 1987–88. Pres., British Business Assoc. of Singapore, 1988. FInstD; FRSA. *Recreations:* sailing, riding, the arts. *Address:* Brunton Barn, Collingbourne Kingston, Marlborough, Wilts SN8 3SE. *Club:* Travellers.

WETHERELL, Gordon Geoffrey, CMG 2011; HM Diplomatic Service, retired; Governor, Turks and Caicos Islands, 2008–11; *b* 11 Nov. 1948; *s* of late Geoffrey and Georgette Maria Wetherell; *m* 1981, Rosemary Anne Myles; four *d*. *Educ:* Bradfield Coll., Berks; New Coll., Oxford (BA 1969; MA 1975); Univ. of Chicago (MA 1971). Joined HM Diplomatic Service, 1973; FCO (concurrently British Embassy, Chad), 1973–74; E Berlin, 1974–77; First Sec., FCO, 1977; UK Delegn to Comprehensive Test Ban Negotiations, Geneva, 1977–80; New Delhi, 1980–83; FCO, 1983–85; on secondment to HM Treasury, 1986–87; Asst Head, European Communities Dept (External), FCO, 1987–88; Counsellor and Dep. Head of Mission, Warsaw, 1988–92; Counsellor (Politico-Military), Bonn, 1992–94; Hd, Personnel Services Dept, FCO, 1994–97; Ambassador: to Ethiopia and (non-resident) to Eritrea and Djibouti, 1997–2000; to Luxembourg, 2000–04; High Comr to Ghana, and (non-resident) Ambassador to Togo, Niger, Burkina Faso and Côte d'Ivoire, 2004–07. *Recreations:* tennis, reading, travel, Manchester United Football Club. *Clubs:* Oxford and Cambridge; Cercle Munster (Luxembourg).

WETTON, Hilary John D.; *see* Davan Wetton.

WETTON, Philip Henry Davan, CMG 1993; HM Diplomatic Service, retired; Consul-General, Milan, 1990–96; *b* 21 Sept. 1937; *s* of late Eric Davan Wetton, CBE and Kathleen Valerie Davan Wetton; *m* 1983, Roswitha Kortner. *Educ:* Westminster; Christ Church, Oxford (MA). Unilever Ltd, 1958–65; FCO, 1965–68; served Tokyo, Osaka and FCO, 1968–73; Head of Division, later Director, Secretariat of Council of Ministers of European Communities, 1973–83; Counsellor, Seoul, 1983–87; FCO, 1987–90. Founded Philip Wetton Chair of Astrophysics, Oxford Univ., 2000; endowed Grad. Scholarship in Astrophysics, Christ Church, Oxford, 2005. *Recreations:* rowing, music, astronomy. *Address:* Aller's End, East Kennett, Marlborough, Wilts SN8 4EY.

See also H. J. Davan Wetton.

WETZEL, Dave; Chief Executive Officer and International Speaker on Transport and Land Value Capture, Transforming Communities Consultancy, since 2008; *b* 9 Oct. 1942; *s* of Fred Wetzel and Ivy Donaldson; *m* 1973, Heather Allman; two *d*. *Educ:* Spring Grove Grammar Sch.; Southall Technical Coll., Ealing Coll., and the Henry George Sch. of Social Sciences (part-time courses). Student apprentice, Wilkinson Sword/Graviner, 1959–62; Bus Conductor/Driver, 1962–65, Bus Official, 1965–69, London Transport; Br. Manager, Initial Services, 1969–70; Pilot Roster Officer, British Airways, 1970–74 (ASTMS Shop Steward); Political Organiser, London Co-op., 1974–81; Proprietor, Granny's Attic Antique Shop, Mevagissey, 1994–99; Partner, Yun Kim's family restaurant, 1997–2015. Member (Lab): for Hammersmith N, GLC, 1981–86 (Transport Cttee Chair, 1981–86); Hounslow Borough Council, 1964–68, 1986–94 (Dep. Leader and Chair, Environmental Planning, 1986–87; Leader, 1987–91). Vice-Chair, Transport for London, 2000–08 (Chair, Safety, Health and Envmt Cttee, 2004–08); Chair: London Buses, 2000–01; Transport Trading Ltd, 2000–01. Contested (Lab): Richmond upon Thames, Twickenham, 1979; Mevagissey, Restormel DC, 1995; St Austell West, Cornwall CC, 1997. Vice-Chm., Public Transport Cttee, AMA, 1993–94; Mem. Management Cttee, Hounslow Community Transport and Central London Dial-a-Ride, 1991–94; Mem. Bd, Capital Transport Campaign, London, 1991–94. Exec. Dir, DaRT (Dial-a-Ride and Taxicard Users), 1989–94. Pres., W London Peace Council, 1982–94; Pres., Labour Land Campaign, 1982–2016; Chair, Professional Land Reform Gp, 2004–; Hon. Gen. Sec., Internat. Union for Land Value Taxation and Free Trade, 2010–12 (Pres., 2013–15). Mem. Bd, Riverside Studios, Hammersmith, 1983–86. Founder and co-ordinator, Trade Union and Co-op Esperanto Gp, 1976–80. Pres., Thames Valley Esperanto Soc., 1982–94; Vice-Pres., Transport Studies Soc., London Univ., 1992–99 (Pres., 1991–92). Vice Chm., Mevagissey Chamber of Commerce, 1996–98. Member: Cttee, Mevagissey Folk Mus., 1995–99; Bd, London Transport Mus., 2007–08. Mem. Bd, Socialist Envmtl Resources Assoc., 2006–08. Mem. Editl Bd, Voice of the Unions, 1975–79; Editor, Civil Aviation News, 1978–81. FRSA 2001–08; FILT, then FCILT, 2002–12. *Recreations:* politics (Labour, 1960–69, 1971–2014; Green Party, 2014–), Esperanto, land reform. *Address:* 40 Adelaide Terrace, Great West Road, Brentford, Middlesex TW8 9PQ. *T:* (020) 8568 9004, 07715 322926. *E:* Dave.C.Wetzel@gmail.com.

WEYLAND, Joseph; Ambassador of Luxembourg to United States of America, 2005–08; *b* 24 April 1943; *s* of Adolphe Weyland and Marie Kox; *m* 1st, 1969, France Munhowen; two *s*; 2nd, 1993, Bénédicte Boucqueau. *Educ:* LLD, and Dip. of Inst. d'Etudes Politiques, Univ. of Paris. Foreign Ministry, Luxembourg, 1968; served Bonn and EEC, Brussels; Ambassador to UN, NY, 1982; Perm. Rep. to EEC, Brussels, 1985 (Mem., Intergovt Conf. leading to Single European Act, 1985, later Chm., Intergovt Conf. on Political Union leading to Treaty of Maastricht, 1991; Sec.-Gen., Foreign Ministry, Luxembourg, 1992; Ambassador to UK, 1993–2002; Ambassador to NATO and to Belgium, 2003–05. Mem., Reflection Gp, IGC, 1995. *Publications:* (jtly) Le Traité de Maastricht, 1993. *Recreations:* art, sports, music. *Club:* Rotary.

WEYMAN, Anne Judith, OBE 2000; FCA; mentor and adviser to chief executives and senior managers, since 2008; Vice Chair and Chair of Audit, Islington Clinical Commissioning Group, 2012–15; *b* 1 Feb. 1943; *d* of Stanley Weyman and Rose Weyman; *m* 1977, Christopher Leonard Bulford; one *d*. *Educ:* Tollington GS; Bristol Univ. (BSc Physics);

London Sch. of Econs (BScSoc). FCA 1973. Articled Clerk and Audit Manager, Finnie, Ross, Welch & Co., Chartered Accts, 1964–68; Audit Manager, Foster Weyman & Co., Chartered Accts, 1968–69; Research Officer: LSE, 1972–74; Queen Mary's Hosp., Roehampton, 1974–77; Hd of Finance and Admin, Internat. Secretariat, Amnesty Internat., 1977–86; Dir of Inf. and Public Affairs and Co. Sec., Nat. Children's Bureau, 1986–96; Chief Exec., fpa (Family Planning Assoc.), 1996–2008. Chm., Pinter Publishers Ltd, 1989–95. Mem. (Lab), Westminster CC, 1978–82. Mem., NW Thames RHA, 1978–80; non-executive Director: Islington PCT, 2002–13 (Vice Chm., 2011–13); Haringey PCT, 2011–13. Vice-Chair: Sexual Health Strategy Reference Gp, 1999–2000; Ind. Adv. Gp on Sexual Health and HIV, 2003–10; Member: Ind. Adv. Gp on Teenage Pregnancy, 2000–07; Women's Nat. Commn, 1999–2003; Bd, Forum UK, 2008–10; GMC, 2009–12; Chm., Programme Develt Gp in Personal Social and Health Educn, 2007–10, and Programme Develt Gp on Contraception, 2008–10, NICE. Chair, Islington U3A, 2013–. Trustee: Family & Parenting Inst., 2006–12 (Vice-Chair, 2011–12); Galapagos Conservation Trust, 2009–14 (Vice-Chair, 2013–14). Hon. Pres., Sex Educn Forum (Founder, 1987). Hon. LLD Bristol, 2005. *Publications:* (with J. Westergaard and P. Wiles) Modern British Society: a bibliography, 1977; (with J. Unell) Finding and Running Premises, 1985; (with S. Capper and J. Unell) Starting and Running a Voluntary Group, 1989; (jtly) RCGP Handbook of Sexual Health in Primary Care, 1998, 2nd edn 2006; (with M. Duggan) Individual Choices, Collective Responsibility: sexual health, a public health issue, 1999; (jtly) Sexual and Reproductive Health and Rights in the UK: 5 years on from Cairo, 1999; articles on health, mental health and sex educn. *Recreations:* travel, theatre, cinema, walking.

WEYMES, John Barnard, OBE 1975; HM Diplomatic Service, retired; Managing Director, Cayman Islands News Bureau, Grand Cayman, 1981–83; *b* 18 Oct. 1927; *s* of William Stanley Weymes and Irene Innes Weymes; *m* 1978, Beverley Pauline Gliddon; three *c* by a previous marr. *Educ:* Dame Allan's Sch., Newcastle upon Tyne; King's Coll., Durham Univ., Newcastle upon Tyne. Served HM Forces, 1945–48. Foreign Office, 1949–52; 3rd Sec., Panama City, 1952–56; 2nd Sec., Bogotá, 1957–60; Vice-Consul, Berlin, 1960–63; Dep. Consul, Tamsui, Taiwan, 1963–65; 1st Sec., FCO, 1965–68; Prime Minister's Office, 1968–70; Consul, Guatemala City, 1970–74; 1st Sec., FCO, 1974–77; Consul-Gen., Vancouver, 1977–78; Ambassador to Honduras, 1978–81. *Recreations:* outdoor sport, partic. cricket; chess, reading. *Address:* Holmesdale, Lower Lane, Dalwood, Axminster, Devon EX13 7EG. *T:* (01404) 881114. *Club:* MCC.

WEYMOUTH, Viscount; Ceawlin Henry Laszlo Thynn; Director: Longleat Enterprises, since 2010; Cheddar Caves, since 2010; *b* 6 June 1974; *s* and *heir* of Marquess of Bath, *qv*; *m* 2013, Emma Clare McQuistan; one *s*. *Heir:* *s* Hon. John Alexander Ladi Thynn, *b* 26 Oct. 2014.

WHALEN, Sir Geoffrey (Henry), Kt 1995; CBE 1989; FIMI, FIPD; Director (formerly Chairman), Camden Ventures (formerly Camden Motors) Ltd, since 1996; *b* 8 Jan. 1936; *s* of Henry and Mabel Whalen; *m* 1961, Elizabeth Charlotte; two *s* three *d*. *Educ:* Magdalen College, Oxford (MA Hons Modern History). National Coal Board, Scotland (industrial relations), 1959–66; Divl Personnel Manager, A. C. Delco Div., General Motors, Dunstable, 1966–70; British Leyland, 1970–78; Personnel Dir, Leyland Cars, 1975–78; Personnel Dir, Rank Hovis McDougall Bakeries Div., 1978–80; Personnel and Indust. Rel. Dir, 1980–81, Asst Man. Dir, 1981–84, Talbot Motor Co.; Man. Dir, 1984–95, Dep. Chm., 1990–2003, Peugeot Motor Co. plc. Director: Coventry Bldg Soc., 1992–2006 (Chm., 1999–2005); Novar (formerly Caradon) plc, 1996–2005; Chm., Hills Precision Components Ltd, 1990–2001. Pres., SMMT, 1988–90 and 1993; Chm., Coventry and Warwicks TEC, 1990–94. FIMI 1986; FCGI 1989; CCMI (CBIM 1987). Hon. DBA Coventry Univ., 1995. Midlander of the Year Award, Bass Mitchells & Butlers Ltd, 1988; Midlands Businessman of the Year, 1992. Chevalier de la Légion d'Honneur (France), 1990. *Address:* Victoria Lodge, 8 Park Crescent, Abingdon, Oxon OX14 1DF. *Club:* Oxford and Cambridge.

WHALEY, Prof. Joachim, PhD, LittD; FBA 2015; FRHistS; Professor of German History and Thought, University of Cambridge, since 2013; Fellow, Gonville and Caius College, Cambridge, since 1987; *b* Dulwich, London, 25 Aug. 1954; *s* of John Whaley and Elselore Whaley; *m* 2000, Alice Castle. *Educ:* St Joseph's Acad., Blackheath, London; Christ's Coll., Cambridge (BA Hons Hist. 1975); PhD 1983, LittD 2013, Cantab. FRHistS 1984. University of Cambridge: Fellow and Lectr in Hist., Christ's Coll., 1976–78; Fellow and Lectr in Hist., Robinson Coll., 1978–86; Department of German: Asst Lectr, 1980–84; Lectr, 1984–2000; Sen. Lectr, 2000–13; Hd of Dept, 2001–05; Lectr in Mod. Langs, 1987–, Sen. Tutor, 1989–98, Gonville and Caius Coll. FHEA 2001. Pilkington Teaching Prize, Univ. of Cambridge, 2010. *Publications:* (ed) Mirrors of Mortality: studies in the social history of death, 1981, reissued 2011; Religious Toleration and Social Change in Hamburg 1529–1819, 1985 (trans. German, 1992); Germany and the Holy Roman Empire, 2 vols, 2012 (trans. German 2014); articles in learned jls. *Recreation:* visiting historic houses and museums. *Address:* Gonville and Caius College, Cambridge CB2 1TA. *T:* (01223) 332454. *E:* jw10005@cam.ac.uk. *Clubs:* Athenæum, Lansdowne.

WHALLEY, Jeffrey; Chairman and Chief Executive, Gartland Whalley & Barker plc, 2005–08 (Director, 1995–2008); Chairman: Tangent (formerly Ofquest) Office Furniture Ltd, since 2009; Whalley Jones Holdings Ltd, since 2009; *b* 20 Nov. 1942; *s* of William Henry and Elsie Whalley; *m* 1st, 1965; three *s*; 2nd, 1996, Karn Jane Jamieson. *Educ:* Grammar School and Polytechnic. Managing Director: Dynamo Electrical Services, 1970–75; Whipp & Bourne Switchgear, 1975–80; FKI Electricals, 1980–87; Man. Dir and Dep. Chm., FKI Babcock, 1987–89; Jt Dep. Chm., Babcock International, 1989–95; Man. Dir, Gartland & Whalley Securities, later Gartland Whalley & Barker Ltd, 1989–95; Chairman: FKI, 1991–99; British Aluminium plc, 1996–2006. Non-exec. Dir, Towcester Racecourse Ltd, 1998–2006. FRSA; FInstD. *Recreations:* tennis, fishing, football.

WHALLEY, John Mayson, FRTPI; FRIBA; PPLI; Principal, JMW International, since 1994; *b* 14 Sept. 1932; *s* of George Mayson Whalley and Ada Florence Cairns; *m* 1966, Elizabeth Gillian Hide; one *s* two *d*. *Educ:* Grammar Sch., Preston; Univ. of Liverpool (BArch, 1st Cl. Hons; Sir Charles Reilly Medal and Prize for thesis design, 1956; MCivic Des.); Univ. of Pennsylvania (MLandscape Arch). FLI 1970. Leverhulme and Italian Govt Fellowships for study in Scandinavia and Univ. of Rome, 1957; Fulbright Schol., 1958; Manchester Soc. of Architects Winstanley Fellowship, 1965. Asst architect to Sir Frederick Gibberd, Harlow, 1956; architect/landscape architect: Oskar Stonorov, Philadelphia, 1958–60; Grenfell Baines and Hargreaves Building Design Partnership, Preston, 1960–62; Associate, 1963–68, Sen. Partner, 1968–93, Derek Lovejoy & Partners. Design Co-ordinator, Kishiwada Port Develt Corp., Osaka, Japan, 1997–2001; Special Advr, Takemoto Foods Co. Ltd, 2013–. Chm., NW Region, RIBA, 1984–85; President: Manchester Soc. of Architects, 1980–81; Landscape Inst., 1985–87; Mem. Council, National Trust, 1989–94; Trustee and Dir, Rural Heritage (formerly Rural Bldgs Preservation) Trust, 1996–2002; Chm., Rivington Heritage Trust, 1997–2004; Pres., Preston Grammar Sch. Assoc., 2009–14. Civic Trust awards: W Burton Power Stn, 1968; Cheshire Constabulary HQ, 1969; Rochdale Canal, 1973; Royal Life Offices, Peterborough, 1992; design competitions 1st prizes: Cergy-Pontoise Urban Park, 1970; La Courneuve Regional Park, Paris, 1972; Liverpool Anglican Cathedral precinct, 1982; Urban Park, Vitoria-Gasteiz, 1991; Regional Park, Mito City, Japan, 1992; Garden Festivals: Liverpool, 1982; Stoke-on-Trent, 1983; Glasgow, 1985. Civic Trust awards assessor, 1970–94; UN Tech. Expert, Riyadh, 1975. Mem., Ordre des Architectes de France; FRSA. Contribs to radio and TV. *Publications:* Selected Architects Details, 1958; articles in professional jls. *Recreations:* using imagination - to play jazz piano, opening for Lancashire and England, playing twenty pounds salmon and owning French vineyard! *Address:* Dilworth House, Longridge, Preston, Lancs PR3 3ST. *T:* and *Fax:* (01772) 783262. *E:* johnmwhalley@aol.com. *Clubs:* Ronnie Scott's; St James's (Manchester).

WHALLEY, Robert Michael, CB 2005; Independent Reviewer, Justice and Security (Northern Ireland) Act 2007, 2008–14; *b* 17 Feb. 1947; *s* of William Lambert Whalley and Edith Mary Whalley; *m* 1981, Teresa Jane, *yr d* of Dr D. W. Hall; three *d*. *Educ:* King Edward's Sch., Birmingham; Pembroke Coll., Cambridge (MA). Home Office, 1970–72; Private Sec. to Sec. of State for NI, 1972–73; Principal, 1975, Private Sec. to Perm. Sec., 1978–80, Home Office; Cabinet Office, 1980–82; Private Sec. to Lord President of the Council, 1983; Home Office: Asst Sec., Prison Dept, 1984–87; Emergency Planning Div., 1987–89; Sec., Hillsborough Stadium Disaster Inquiry, 1989–90; Personnel Dept, 1990–93; Dir, Immigration and Nationality Policy, 1993–2000; Hd of Unit, Organised and Internat. Crime Directorate, 2000–03; Dir, Crime Reduction and Community Safety Gp, 2003–05. Consulting Sen. Fellow, IISS, 2006–11; Vis. Fellow, Cranfield Univ., 2008–11. *Recreations:* gardens, music. *Address:* c/o Home Office, 2 Marsham Street, SW1P 4DF.

WHALLEY, Maj.-Gen. William Leonard, CB 1985; *b* 19 March 1930; *m* 1955, Honor Mary (*née* Golden); one *d*. *Educ:* Sir William Turner's Sch., Coatham. Joined Army (Nat. Service), 1948; sc 1962; Commander, RAOC, 1st Div., 1968–71; Dir of Ordnance Services, BAOR, 1980–83; Dir Gen. of Ordnance Services, MoD, 1983–85. Colonel Commandant: RAOC, 1986–93; RLC, 1993. Life Vice-Pres., Army Boxing Assoc. (Chm., 1983–85). Pres., Little Aston Br., Conservative Assoc., 1996– (Chm., 1987–96, 1998–2005). Chm. of Govs, Brooke Weston (formerly Corby) City Technol. Coll., 1991–96 (Project Dir, 1989–91). Pres., RAOC Charitable Trust, 1996–2000. *Recreations:* bridge, computers, cabinet making. *Address:* HSBC, 67 The Parade, Sutton Coldfield, West Midlands B72 1PU.

WHARFE, Dr James Richard; independent environment consultant; Senior Scientific Advisor, Environment Agency, 2010–14 (Head of Science Programmes, 2004–10); *b* Hertford, 7 Dec. 1947; *s* of late Harry Wharfe and Constance Wharfe (*née* Brown); partner, Caroline Budd; three *s* one *d*. *Educ:* Hertford Grammar Sch.; Sir John Cass Coll., Univ. of London (BSc 1st Cl. Hons Applied Biol.; PhD Envmtl Pollution 1976). Posts with DoE, MAFF and Welsh Water Authy; Regl Biologist, Southern Water Authy, 1981–87; Regl Scientist, NRA, 1988–96; Hd, Nat. Centre for Hazardous Substances, EA, 1997–2004. Chair, Sci. Adv. Gp, Resource Recovery from Waste prog., NERC, 2013–; Member: Ministerial Marine Sci. Coordinating Cttee, 2009–14; Sci. and Innovation Strategy Bd, 2010–13, Valuing Nature Prog. Adv. Gp, 2015–, NERC; Res. and Innovation Steering Cttee, UK Water, 2013–15; Res. and Innovation Steering Gp, UK Water Partnership, 2015–. NERC Advr, UK Energy Res. Centre Funders Gp, 2014–. *Publications:* (ed jtly) Toxic Waste Impact on the Aquatic Environment, 1996; contrib. scientific papers to jls. *Recreation:* fitness fanatic. *Address:* 2 Cedar Chase, Cross Lane, Findon, W Sussex BN14 0US. *T:* (01903) 872696.

WHARMBY, Debbie; *see* Wiseman, D.

WHARNCLIFFE, 5th Earl of, *cr* 1876; **Richard Alan Montagu Stuart Wortley;** Baron Wharncliffe 1826; Viscount Carlton 1876; President, Royal Construction Services, Maine, USA; *b* 26 May 1953; *s* of Alan Ralph Montagu-Stuart-Wortley (*d* 1986) and Virginia Anne (*d* 1993), *d* of W. Martin Claybaugh; *S* cousin, 1987; *m* 1st, 1979, Mary Elizabeth Reed (*d* 2005); three *s*; 2nd, 2013, Jessica Caroline Rathbun. *Heir:* *s* Viscount Carlton, *qv*.

WHARTON, 12th Baron *cr* 1544–45; **Myles Christopher David Robertson;** *b* 1 Oct. 1964; *e s* of Baroness Wharton (11th in line) and Henry McLeod Robertson; *S* mother, 2000; *m* 2003, Barbara Kay, *d* of Colin Paul Marshall; one *d*. *Educ:* King's Coll., Wimbledon. *Heir:* *d* Hon. Meghan Ziki Mary Robertson, *b* 8 March 2006.

WHARTON, James Stephen; MP (C) Stockton South, since 2010; Parliamentary Under-Secretary of State, Department for Communities and Local Government, since 2015; *b* Stockton-on-Tees, 16 Feb. 1984; *s* of Stephen Wharton and Karen Wharton. *Educ:* Yarm Sch., Yarm; St Peter's Sch., York; Durham Univ. (LLB Hons); Coll. of Law, York. Admitted solicitor, 2008; Solicitor, BHP Law, Darlington and Stockton. *Recreation:* walking, usually whilst delivering leaflets. *Address:* House of Commons, SW1A 0AA.

WHARTON, Rt Rev. (John) Martin, CBE 2011; Bishop of Newcastle, 1997–2014; *b* 6 Aug. 1944; *s* of John and Marjorie Wharton; *m* 1970, Marlene Olive Duckett; two *s* one *d*. *Educ:* Van Mildert Coll., Durham (BA 1969); Linacre Coll., Oxford (BA 1971; MA 1976); Ripon Hall, Oxford, 1969. Ordained: deacon, 1972, priest, 1973; Assistant Curate: St Peter, Birmingham, 1972–75; St John the Baptist, Croydon, 1975–77; Dir of Pastoral Studies, Ripon Coll., Cuddesdon, 1977–83; Asst Curate, Cuddesdon, 1979–83; Exec. Sec., Bd of Ministry and Training, dio. of Bradford, 1983–91; Hon. Canon, Bradford Cathedral, 1984; Bishop's Officer for Ministry and Training, 1992; Residentiary Canon, Bradford Cathedral, 1992; Area Bishop of Kingston-upon-Thames, 1992–97. *Recreation:* sport. *Address:* 20 Thamespoint, Fairways, Teddington TW11 9PP.

WHARTON, Malcolm, CBE 2012; education business consultant, since 2012; Principal, Hartpury College, Gloucester, 1990–2012; *b* Penrith, 19 Nov. 1948; *s* of Robinson Wharton and Mary Wharton; *m* 1990, Sarah Newham; one *s* four *d*. *Educ:* Kirkby Stephen Grammar Sch.; Royal Agricultural Coll. (NDA Agric.); Univ. of Birmingham (PGCE); Coll. of St Mark and St John (BEd Hons). Lectr, Bicton Coll., 1973–84; Vice Principal, Duchy Coll., Cornwall, 1984–90. Rugby Football Union: Mem., Council, 2011–; Chm., Community Game Bd, and Mem., Bd, 2013–; Chm., Rugby Football Foundn, 2015–. Dir, Sidmouth Rugby Club Ltd, 2015–. Trustee, British Eventing Charitable Trust, 2014–. *Recreations:* Rugby, fly fishing, sea fishing, eventing, dog walking. *Address:* Pendragon, Lodge Lane, Axminster, Devon EX13 5RT. *T:* (01297) 32020. *E:* malcolmwharton@hotmail.com.

WHATELY, Helen Olivia Bicknell; MP (C) Faversham and Mid Kent, since 2015; *b* Surrey, 23 June 1976; *m* Marcus Whately; one *s* two *d*. *Educ:* Lady Margaret Hall, Oxford (BA PPE 1998). Consultant, PricewaterhouseCoopers, 1998–2001; Manager, Strategic Alliances Gp, AOL Europe, 2003–05; Sen. Manager, AOL UK, 2005–06; Advr to Shadow Sec. of State for Culture, Media and Sport, 2006–07; Engagement Manager, and Associate, McKinsey & Co., 2007–15. Mem., Health Select Cttee, 2015–; Co-Chair, All Pty Parly Gp on Healthcare, 2015–; Vice-Chair, All Pty Parly Gp on Mental Health, 2015–. Contested (C) Kingston and Surbiton, 2010. *Address:* House of Commons, SW1A 0AA.

WHATELY, Kevin; actor; *b* 6 Feb. 1951; *s* of late Richard Whately and Mary Whately (*née* Pickering); *m* 1984, Madelaine Newton; one *s* one *d*. *Educ:* Barnard Castle Sch.; Central Sch. of Speech and Drama. Rep. theatre, incl. Old Vic Co., 1975–82; Gypsy, Chichester, 2014; *television:* rôles include: Neville in Auf Wiedersehen Pet, 1992–2002; Sgt Lewis in Inspector Morse, 1986–2001; Jack Kerruish in Peak Practice, 1992–95; Inspector Lewis in Lewis, 2005–14; Joe in Joe Maddison's War, 2010; *films:* rôles include: Hardy in The English Patient, 1996. Ambassador for: Prince's Trust, 1992–; Alzheimer's Soc., 2007–; Vice-Pres., Action for Children (formerly NCH), 2003–; Patron, Sparks, 1993–. Ambassador for: Newcastle and Gateshead, 2002–; City of Sunderland, 2005–. Hon. Fellow, Royal Central Sch. of Speech and Drama, 2013. Hon. DCL Northumbria, 2000; Hon. DArts Bedfordshire, 2013. *Recreation:* charity golf (Captain, Variety Club of GB Golf Soc., 2013). *Address:* c/o Caroline Dawson Associates, 4th Floor, 167–169 Kensington High Street, W8 6SH. *T:* (020) 7937 2749, *Fax:* (020) 7937 5120. *Club:* Bamburgh Castle Golf.

WHATLEY, Prof. Frederick Robert, FRS 1975; Sherardian Professor of Botany, Oxford University, 1971–91; Fellow of Magdalen College, Oxford, since 1971; *b* 26 Jan. 1924; *s* of Frederick Norman Whatley and Maud Louise (*née* Hare); *m* 1951, Jean Margaret Smith Bowie; two *d*. *Educ:* Bishop Wordsworth's Sch., Salisbury; (Scholar) Selwyn Coll., Cambridge University (BA, PhD). Benn W. Levy Student, Cambridge, 1947. Sen. Lectr in Biochemistry, Univ. of Sydney, 1950–53; Asst Biochemist, Univ. of California at Berkeley, 1954–58; Associate Biochemist, 1959–64; Guggenheim Fellowship (Oxford and Stockholm), 1960; Prof. of Botany, King's Coll., London, 1964–71. Vis. Fellow, ANU, 1979. *Publications:* articles and reviews in scientific jls. *Address:* 12 The Swallows, Patron's Way West, Denham Garden Village, Denham UB9 5PB.

WHATMORE, Prof. Sarah Jane, PhD, DSc; FBA 2014; Professor of Environment and Public Policy, University of Oxford, since 2004 (Head, School of Geography and the Environment, 2012–15); Fellow, Keble College, Oxford, since 2012; *b* 25 Sept. 1959; *d* of late Col Denys Edwin Whatmore and of (Freda) Pauline Whatmore. *Educ:* University Coll. London (BA Hons 1st cl. (Geog.) 1981; MPhil Town Planning 1983; PhD (Geog.) 1988); Univ. of Bristol (DSc 2000); MA Oxon 2004. Policy Res. Officer, GLC, 1983–84; Res. Associate, Dept of Geog., UCL, 1984–87; Lectr, Dept of Geog., Univ. of Leeds, 1988–89; University of Bristol: Lectr, 1989–93, Reader, 1993–99, in Human Geog.; Prof. of Human Geog., 1999–2001; Prof. of Envmtl Geog., OU, 2001–04. Member: Social Sci. Expert Panel, DEFRA and DECC, 2012–March 2016; Sci. Adv. Council, DEFRA, 2015–. FRGS 1994 (Mem. Council, 2004–07; Vice Pres., 2014–May 2016; Chm., RGS/IBG Annual Conf., 2015); FAcSS (AcSS 2002). Cuthbert Peek Award, RGS, 2003. *Publications:* Farming Women: gender, work and family enterprise, 1991; Hybrid Geographies: natures, cultures, spaces, 2002; (ed jtly) Using Social Theory: thinking through research, 2003; (with Thrift) Cultural Geography: critical concepts, 2004; (ed jtly) Dictionary of Human Geography, 5th edn 2009; (with Braun) Political Matter: technoscience, democracy and public life, 2010; numerous other ed vols, book chapters, papers in learned jls and policy reports. *Recreations:* gardening, antiquarian books, reading, modern art and architecture. *Address:* School of Geography and the Environment, University of Oxford, South Parks Road, Oxford OX1 3QY.

WHATMOUGH, Rev. Michael Anthony, (Tony); Priest-in-charge, St Michael and All Angels, Headingley, Leeds, since 2012; Team Rector, Headingley Team Ministry, since 2014; *b* 14 Oct. 1950; *s* of Derrick and Molly Whatmough; *m* 1st, 1975, Jean Macdonald Watt (marr. diss. 2004); two *s* two *d*; 2nd, 2006, Catherine, *d* of Richard and Margaret Ainley. *Educ:* Exeter Univ. (BA 1972); Edinburgh Univ. (BD 1981). ARCO 1972. Teacher of music, Forrester High Sch., Edinburgh, 1973–74; Sub-Organist, Old St Paul's Church, Edinburgh, 1973–78; Music Master, George Watson's Coll., Edinburgh, 1974–78; ordained deacon, 1981, priest, 1982; Curate, St Hilda and St Fillan, Edinburgh, 1981–84; Vis. Lectr in Music, Faculty of Divinity, Edinburgh Univ., 1981–84; Curate and Rector, Salisbury St Thomas, 1984–93; Rural Dean, Salisbury, 1990–93; Vicar, St Mary Redcliffe, Bristol, 1993–2005; Teacher of RE, Fair Oaks Business and Enterprise Coll., Rugeley, 2005–12; non-stipendiary priest, parishes of Coven and Bilbrook, Dio. Lichfield, 2008; Associate Minister, St Luke and St Barnabas, Cannock, with St Thomas, Huntingdon, 2010–12. *Recreations:* playing clavichord and organ, cooking, hill walking, singing. *Address:* Headingley Vicarage, 16 Shire Oak Road, Leeds LS6 2DE. *T:* (0113) 274 3238. *E:* tony@whatmough.org.uk.

WHEADON, Richard Anthony; Principal, Elizabeth College, Guernsey, 1972–88, retired; *b* 31 Aug. 1933; *s* of Ivor Cecil Newman Wheadon and Margarita Augusta (*née* Cash); *m* 1961, Ann Mary (*née* Richardson); three *s*. *Educ:* Cranleigh Sch.; Balliol Coll., Oxford (MA (Physics)). Commissioned RAF, 1955 (Sword of Honour); Air Radar Officer, 1955–57; Asst Master, Eton Coll., 1957–66; Dep. Head Master and Head of Science Dept, Dauntsey's Sch., 1966–71. Mem., HMC, 1972–88. Mem., Wilts Educn Cttee's Science Adv. Panel, 1967–71. Rowed bow for Oxford, 1954, for GB in European Championships and Olympic Games, 1956; Captain RAF VIII, 1956 and 1957; Olympic Selector and Nat. Coach, 1964–66. Contingent Comdr, Dauntsey's Sch. CCF, 1969–70; Sqdn Leader, RAFRO, 1970–. Reader, C of E, dio. of Winchester, 1995–2013, now Emeritus Reader; Member: Guernsey Standing Adv. Council for Religious Educn, 1997–2003; Diocesan Readers' Selection Bd, 1998–2013; Admin. Sec., 2001–03, Hon. Sec., 2003–05, Guernsey Readers' Centre. *Publications:* The Principles of Light and Optics, 1968. *Recreations:* French horn, photography, electronics, singing, sailing, words. *Address:* L'Enclos Gallienne, Rue du Court Laurent, Torteval, Guernsey, Channel Islands GY8 0LH. *T:* (01481) 264988.

WHEARE, Thomas David, MA; Headmaster of Bryanston School, 1983–2005; *b* 11 Oct. 1944; *s* of late Sir Kenneth Wheare, CMG, FBA, and Lady (Joan) Wheare; *m* 1977, Rosalind Clare Spice; two *d*. *Educ:* Dragon Sch.; Magdalen College Sch., Oxford; King's Coll., Cambridge (BA, MA); Christ Church, Oxford (DipEd). Assistant Master, Eton College, 1967–76; Housemaster of School House, Shrewsbury School, 1976–83. Chm., HMC, 2000 (Hon. Treas., 1993–98). Ed., Conference & Common Room, 2005–. FRSA 1989. *Recreations:* music, supporting Arsenal FC. *Address:* 63 Chapel Lane, Zeals, Warminster, Wilts BA12 6NP.

WHEAT, Rev. Fr (Charles Donald) Edmund, SSM; Assistant Curate (Non-Stipendiary Minister), St John, South Bank, diocese of York, 2003–07; *b* 17 May 1937; *s* of Charles and Alice Wheat. *Educ:* Kelham Theol Coll.; Nottingham Univ. (BA); Sheffield Univ. (MA). Curate, St Paul's, Arbourthorne, Sheffield, 1962–67; licensed, Dio. Southwell, 1967–70; Mem., SSM, 1969–; Chaplain, St Martin's Coll., Lancaster, 1970–73; Prior, SSM Priory, Sheffield, 1973–75; Curate, St John, Ranmoor and Asst Chaplain, Sheffield Univ., 1975–77, Chaplain 1977–80; Provincial, English Province, 1981–91, Dir, 1982–89, Provincial Bursar, 1992–98, Provincial of European Province, 1999–2001, SSM; Vicar, All Saints', Middlesbrough, 1988–95; Prior, St Antony's Priory, Durham, 1998–2001; Vicar, St Thomas', Middlesbrough, 2001–03; licensed, dio. of Oxford, 2011. Chaplain: Whitelands Coll., 1996–97; Order of the Holy Paraclete, Whitby, 1997–98, 2008–10. Mem., Gen. Synod, 1975–80. *Recreations:* reading, watching soap operas. *Address:* SSM Priory, The Well, Willen, Milton Keynes MK15 9AA.

WHEATCROFT, Baroness *cr* 2010 (Life Peer), of Blackheath in the London Borough of Greenwich; **Patience Jane Wheatcroft;** Editor-in-Chief, The Wall Street Journal Europe, 2009–11; *b* 28 Sept. 1951; *d* of Anthony Wheatcroft and Ruth Wheatcroft (*née* Frith); *m* 1976, Anthony Salter; two *s* one *d*. *Educ:* Univ. of Birmingham (LLB). Dep. City Ed., The Times, 1984–86; Asst City Ed., Daily Mail, 1986–88; Ed., Retail Week, 1988–93; Dep. City Ed., Mail on Sunday, 1994–97; Business and City Ed., The Times, 1997–2006; Ed., The Sunday Telegraph, 2006–07. Non-executive Director: Barclays plc, 2008–09; Shaftesbury plc, 2008–09; FCA Automobiles NV (formerly Fiat SpA), 2012–; St James's Place plc, 2012–; Mem., Adv. Bd, Huawei, 2011. Chm., Appointments and Oversight Cttee, FT, 2014–. Mem., Bd of Trustees, British Museum, 2010– (Dep. Chm.). *Recreations:* ski-ing, opera, theatre.

WHEATCROFT, Geoffrey Albert; author; freelance journalist, since 1997; *b* 23 Dec. 1945; *s* of Stephen Frederick Wheatcroft, *qv* and late Joy Wheatcroft (*née* Reed); *m* 1990, Sally, *d* of late Frank Muir, CBE and Polly Muir; one *s* one *d*. *Educ:* University Coll. Sch.; New Coll., Oxford (Schol.; MA Modern Hist.); London Coll. of Printing. In publishing, 1968–75: prodn asst, then publicity manager, Hamish Hamilton, 1968–70; editor: Michael Joseph, 1971–73; Cassell & Co., 1974–75; asst ed., 1975–77, Literary Ed., 1977–81, Spectator; reporting and researching in S Africa, 1981–84; Ed., Londoner's Diary, Evening Standard, 1985–86; columnist, Sunday Telegraph, 1987–91; feature writer, Daily Express, 1996–97; contributing editor, The New Republic, 2013–14. *Publications:* The Randlords, 1985; Absent Friends, 1989; The Controversy of Zion, 1996 (Amer. Nat. Jewish Book Award); Le Tour: a history of the Tour de France, 2003, 3rd edn 2013; The Strange Death of Tory England, 2005; Yo, Blair!, 2007. *Recreations:* bibliophily and hypochondria. *Address:* 11 Southstoke Road, Combe Down, Bath BA2 5SJ. *T:* (01225) 835540. *E:* wheaty@compuserve.com. *Clubs:* Garrick, Beefsteak, Colony Room, MCC.

WHEATCROFT, Stephen Frederick, OBE 1974; Director, Aviation and Tourism International Ltd, 1983–2000; *b* 11 Sept. 1921; *s* of late Percy and Fanny Wheatcroft; *m* 1st, 1943, Joy (*d* 1974), *d* of late Cecil Reed; two *s* one *d*; 2nd, 1974, Alison, *d* of late Arnold Dessau; two *s*. *Educ:* Latymer Sch., N9; London Sch. of Economics (BScEcon 1942; Hon. Fellow, 1998). Served War, Pilot in Fleet Air Arm, 1942–45. Commercial Planning Manager, BEA, 1946–53; Simon Research Fellow, Manchester Univ., 1953–55; private practice as Aviation Consultant, 1956–72; retained as Economic Adviser to BEA. Commns for Govts of: Canada, India, W Indies, E African Community, Afghanistan; Consultant to World Bank; Assessor to Edwards Cttee on British Air Transport in the Seventies; Mem. Bd, British Airways (Dir of Economic Develt), 1972–82. Governor, London Sch. of Economics, 1970–2003, (first) Emeritus Governor, 2003. FRAeS, FCILT (Pres., CIT, 1978–79); FAIAA. *Publications:* Economics of European Air Transport, 1956; Airline Competition in Canada, 1958; Air Transport Policy, 1966; Air Transport in a Competitive European Market, 1986; European Liberalisation and World Air Transport, 1990; Europe's Senior Travel Market, 1993; Aviation and Tourism Policies, 1994; Europe's Youth Travel Market, 1995; articles in professional jls. *Recreation:* travel. *Address:* 49 Dovehouse Street, SW3 6JY. *T:* (020) 7351 1511. *Club:* Reform.

See also G. A. Wheatcroft.

WHEATER, Prof. Howard Simon, PhD; FREng; FICE; CEng; Professor of Hydrology, 1993–2010, now Emeritus, and Distinguished Research Fellow, since 2010, Department of Civil and Environmental Engineering, Imperial College London; Canada Excellence Research Chair in Water Security, since 2010, and Director, Global Institute for Water Security, since 2011, University of Saskatchewan, Canada; *b* 24 June 1949; *s* of late Claude and Marjorie Wheater; *m* 1st, 1970 (marr. diss. 2004); two *s*; 2nd, 2007, Prof. Valerie Susan Isham (marr. diss. 2010); 3rd, 2010, Prof. Patricia Ann Gober. *Educ:* Nottingham High Sch.; Queens' Coll., Cambridge (BA 1971, MA Engrg Scis); Univ. of Bristol (PhD 1977). CEng 1978; FICE 1999. Grad. apprentice, Aero Engine Div., Rolls-Royce Ltd, 1967–72; Res. Asst, Dept of Civil Engrg, Univ. of Bristol, 1972–78; Department of Civil and Environmental Engineering, Imperial College London: Lectr, 1978–87; Sen. Lectr, 1987–90; Reader, 1990–93; Hd, Envmtl and Water Resource Engrg, 1995–; Chm., Centre for Envmtl Control and Waste Mgt, 1995–; Dir, Envmt Forum, 2008–09. Mem. and Chair, nat. and internat. adv. panels and cttees, incl. MAFF, DEFRA, Envmt Agency, NERC, UNESCO. Consultant: Northern Oman Flood Study, 1981; to State of Nevada concerning proposed Yucca Mt nuclear waste repository, 2003–; Counsel and Advocate for Republic of Hungary at Internat. Court of Justice concerning GNBS Danube barrage system, 1993–97, for Republic of Argentina, Internat. Court of Justice concerning River Uruguay, 2006–10. Chairman: UNESCO Global Network for Water and Develt Inf. for Arid Lands prog., 2003–; Council of Canadian Academies Expert Panel on Sustainable Mgt of Water in Agricl Landscapes of Canada, 2011–13; Vice-Chm., Scientific Steering Gp, World Climate Prog., Global Energy and Water Experiment, 2010–13; Member: Internat. Ct of Arbitration, Indus Waters Treaty, 2010–13; Alberta Provincial Envmtl Monitoring Panel, 2011. Pres., British Hydrological Soc., 1999–2001. Fellow, Amer. Geophysical Union, 2010. Life Mem., Internat. Water Acad., Oslo. FREng 2003. Prince Sultan bin Abdulaziz Internat. Water Prize, 2006. *Publications:* (ed jtly) Hydrology in a Changing Environment, 3 vols, 1998; (jtly) Rainfall-Runoff Modelling in Gauged and Ungauged Catchments, 2004; (jtly) Biosphere Implications of Deep Disposal of Nuclear Waste: the upwards migration of radionuclides in vegetated soils, 2007; (jtly) Hydrological Modelling in Arid and Semi-Arid Areas, 2008; (jtly) Groundwater Modelling in Arid and Semi-Arid Areas, 2010; 200 refereed papers. *Recreations:* sailing (dinghy racing and yacht cruising), music (orchestral trumpet player). *Address:* University of Saskatchewan, National Hydrology Research Centre, 11 Innovation Boulevard, Saskatoon, SK S7N 3H5, Canada. *E:* howard.wheater@usask.ca.

WHEATER, Roger John, OBE 1991; CBiol, FRSB; FRSE; Chairman, National Trust for Scotland, 2000–05; *b* 24 Nov. 1933; *m* 1963, Jean Ord Troup; one *s* one *d*. *Educ:* Brighton, Hove and Sussex Grammar Sch.; Brighton Tech. Coll. Commnd Royal Sussex Regt, 1953; served Gold Coast Regt, 1953–54; 4/5th Bn, Royal Sussex Regt (TA), 1954–56. Served Colonial Police, Uganda, 1956–61; Chief Warden, Murchison Falls Nat. Park, 1961–70; Director: Uganda Nat. Parks, 1970–72; RZSScot, 1972–98. Hon. Prof., Univ. of Edinburgh, 1993–. Mem. Editl Bd, Internat. Zoo Year Book, 1987–99. Consultant, World Tourist Orgn, UN, 1980–. Mem., Sec. of State for Scotland's Wkg Gp on Envmtl Educn, 1990–94. Mem., Co-ordinating Cttee, Nuffield Unit of Tropical Animal Ecol.; Chm., Beaver-Salmonid Wkg Gp, Nat. Species Reintroduction Forum, 2009–15; Member: Council, NT for Scotland, 1973–78 and 2000– (Mem., Exec. Cttee, 1982–87); Bd, Scottish Natural Heritage, 1995–99 (Dep. Chm., 1997–99); Strategic Develt Fund Panel, Royal Soc. of Wildlife Trusts, 2008–12; Assessor, Council, Scottish Wildlife Trust, 1973–92 (Pres., 2007–09). Chm., Wkg Party on Zoo Licensing Act, 1981–84. Pres., Assoc. of British Wild Animal Keepers, 1984–99 (Chm., Membership and Licensing Cttee, 1984–91); Chairman, Advisory Committee: Whipsnade Wild Animal Park, 1999–2002; London Zoo, 2002–03. Chm., Fedn of Zool Gardens of GB and Ireland, 1993–96. Dep. Chm., Zoo Forum, 1999–2002; Chairman: Access Forum, 1996–2000; Tourism and Envmt Forum, 1999–2003. Chm., Eur. Assoc. of Zoos and Aquaria, 1994–97; Mem. Council, 1980, Pres., 1988–91, Internat. Union of Dirs of Zool Gdns. Vice-President: Eur. Network of Nat. Heritage Orgns, 2000–05; Scottish Heritage USA, 2001–05. Chm., Cammo Estate Adv. Cttee, 1980–95; Dir, Nat. Park Lodges Ltd; Mem., Uganda Nat. Res. Council; Vice-Chm., Uganda Tourist Assoc. Chm., Anthropoid Ape Adv. Panel, 1977–91. Mem. Council, 1991–92, 1995–99, 2000–03, Vice Pres., 1999, Zool Soc. of London; Mem. Bd, Royal Zool Soc. of Scotland, 2011–. Vice-Pres., World Pheasant Assoc., 1994–. Vice Chm., Edinburgh Br., ESU, 1977–81. Trustee: The Gorilla Orgn (formerly Dian Fossey Gorilla Fund), 1995–2010 (Chm., 2008–10); Thyne Scholarship, 1997– (ESU William Thyne Schol., 1975); and Founder Patron, Dynamic Earth, 1999–2012; Tweed Foundn, 2007–; Chm., Heather Trust, 1999–2002. Pres., Tweedale Soc., 2007–; Pres., Probus Club, Innerleithen, Walkerburn and Traquair, 2010–11 (Vice Pres., 2009–10). Gov., Mweka Coll. of Wildlife Mgt, Tanzania, 1970–72. FRSE 1985; FRSB (FIBiol 1987); FRSA 1995. Hon. FRSGS 1995; Hon. FRZSScot 1999. DUniv Open, 2004. *Publications:* numerous papers on wildlife mgt and conservation to professional jls. *Recreations:* country pursuits, painting, gardening. *Address:* 17 Kirklands, Innerleithen, Peeblesshire EH44 6NA. *T:* (01896) 830403. *E:* roger.wheater@btinternet.com. *Clubs:* Edinburgh Special Mobile Angling (Pres., 1982–86), Cockburn Trout Angling (Pres., 1997–).

WHEATLEY, Rt Hon. Lord; John Francis Wheatley; PC 2007; a Senator of the College of Justice in Scotland, 2000–10; *b* 9 May 1941; *s* of John Thomas Wheatley (Baron Wheatley, PC) and late Agnes Nichol; *m* 1970, Bronwen Catherine Fraser; two *s*. *Educ:* Mount St Mary's Coll., Derbyshire; Edinburgh Univ. (BL). Called to the Scottish Bar, 1966; Standing Counsel to Scottish Develt Dept, 1971; Advocate Depute, 1975; Sheriff of Tayside Central and Fife, at Dunfermline, 1979–80, at Perth, 1980–2000; Temp. High Ct Judge, 1992; QC (Scot.) 1993. Chm., Judicial Studies Cttee, 2002–06. *Recreations:* gardening, music. *Address:* Braefoot Farmhouse, Crook of Devon, Fossoway, Kinross-shire KY13 7UL. *T:* (01577) 840212.

WHEATLEY, Alan Edward, FCA; Chairman: Sasial Technologies Ltd, since 2007; Burlington Chase Ltd, since 2008; *b* 23 May 1938; *s* of late Edward and of Margaret Wheatley (*née* Turner); *m* 1962, Marion Frances (*née* Wilson); two *s* one *d*. *Educ:* Ilford Grammar School. Chartered Accountant. Norton Slade, 1954–60, qualified 1960; joined Price Waterhouse, 1960; admitted to partnership, 1970; Mem., Policy Cttee, 1981–92; Sen. Partner (London Office), 1985–92; Chm., 3i Gp, 1992–93; Dep. Chm., Ashtead Gp, 1994–2003; Chm., Foreign and Colonial Special Utilities, subseq. Special Utilities, Investment Trust plc, 1993–2003. Non-executive Director: EBS Investments (Bank of England sub.), 1977–90; British Steel plc (formerly BSC), 1984–94; Babcock International Gp, 1993–2002; Legal & General Gp, 1993–2002; Forte, 1993–96; N M Rothschild & Sons, 1993–99; Chairman: New Court Financial Services Ltd, 1996–99; Utilico Investment Trust plc, 2003–07; Isis Solar Ltd, 2011–13; Govt Dir, Cable & Wireless, 1981–84, non-exec. Dep. Chm., 1984–85. Mem., Ind. Develt Adv. Bd, 1985–92. Trustee, V&A Mus., 1996–99. Governor, Solefield School, 1985–95. *Recreations:* golf, bridge. *Club:* Wildernesse (Seal, Kent).

WHEATLEY, Rear-Adm. Anthony, CB 1988; General Manager, National Hospital for Neurology and Neurosurgery, Queen Square, 1988–96; *b* 3 Oct. 1933; *yr s* of late Edgar C. Wheatley and Audrey G. Barton Hall; *m* 1962, Iona Sheila Haig; one *d*. *Educ:* Berkhamsted School. Entered RN Coll., Dartmouth, 1950; RNEC, Manadon, 1953–57; HMS Ceylon, 1958–60; HMS Ganges, 1960–61; HMS Cambrian, 1962–64; Staff of RNEC, Manadon, 1964–67; Staff of Comdr British Navy Staff, Washington, 1967–69; HMS Diomede, 1970–72; Staff of C-in-C Fleet, 1972–74; Exec. Officer, RNEC Manadon, 1975–76; MoD Procurement Exec., 1977–79; British Naval Attaché, Brasilia, 1979–81; RCDS course 1982; HMS Collingwood (in Command), 1982–85; Flag Officer, Portsmouth, Naval Base Comdr and Head of Establishment of Fleet Maintenance and Repair Orgn, Portsmouth, 1985–87. Non-exec. Dir, Queen Square Enterprises Ltd, 1988–2011. Vice-President: Nat. Soc. for Epilepsy, 2004– (Trustee, 1996–2003, Chm., 1998–2003); Friends of the Elderly, 2008– (Trustee, 1997–2008). *Recreations:* cricket, golf, music. *Address:* The Gate House, Castle Reach, 63 New Road, Framlingham, Suffolk IP13 9EH. *T:* (01728) 727446. *Clubs:* Army and Navy (Chm., 2006–09; Trustee, 2010–12); Free Foresters, Incogniti, Royal Navy Cricket (Vice-Pres., 1988–).

WHEATLEY, Bruce David; Chief Information Officer and Director of Information Management and Technology, Central London Community Health NHS Trust, 2014–15; *b* Brighton; *s* of Captain Walter Wheatley and Ana Wheatley; *m* 1978, Julia Fletcher; two *d*. *Educ:* Brighton, Hove and Sussex Grammar Sch. Practitioner in Prog., Project and Risk Mgt, Office of Govt Commerce; Financial Planning Cert., Chartered Insce Inst.; Cert. of Competence in Occupational Testing, BPsS. Waitrose Ltd: Mgt Trainee, 1976–77; Section Manager, 1977–83; Trng Manager, 1983–88; Proj. Manager, 1988–90; Prudential Assurance: HR Manager, 1990–92; Br. Manager, 1993–97; Sen. Proj. Manager, 1997–2000; HR Dir, Eurolink Consulting, 2000–01; Prog. Dir and IT Dir, Wynnwith Engrg, 2002–04; Prog. Manager, Enterprise Develt Prog., WS Atkins plc and BAA, 2004–05; Prog. Implementation Manager, Phoenix Prog., EDS plc and MoJ, 2006–07; Dir, Shared Services Prog., DIUS, later Dir, Finance Systems, BIS, 2008–09; Hd of Business Solutions, Res. Councils UK Shared Service Centre, 2010–11; Transition Dir, Sussex Health Informatics Service, NHS Sussex, 2012; Dep. Dir, Police ICT Directorate, Home Office, 2013–14. *Recreations:* wine tasting, food tasting and extensive research into both, theme parks and roller coasters (but only in the front row), especially in Florida. *Address:* 18 Woodland Avenue, Hove, E Sussex BN3 6BL. *T:* 07979 590864. *E:* brucewheatley@tiscali.co.uk.

WHEATLEY, Catherine; *see* Wood, C.

WHEATLEY, Prof. David John, MD; British Heart Foundation Professor of Cardiac Surgery, University of Glasgow, 1979–2006; Hon. Consultant Cardiac Surgeon, Glasgow Royal Infirmary, 1979–2006; *b* 2 Aug. 1941; *s* of John Henry Wheatley and Dorothy Wheatley (*née* Price); *m* 1964, Ann Marie Lamberth; two *d*. *Educ:* South African Coll., Cape Town; Univ. of Cape Town Med. Sch. (MB ChB 1964; ChM 1976; MD 1979). FRCSE 1969; FRCSGlas 1979; FRCPE 1997; FRCS 1998. Senior Registrar: Nat. Heart Hosp., London, 1972–73; Mearnskirk Hosp., Glasgow, 1974–76; Sen. Lectr, Royal Infirmary, Edinburgh, 1976–79. Special Prof., Dept of Cardiothoracic Surgery, Univ. of the Free State, SA, 2005–. Director: SA Cardiosynthetics (Pty) Ltd, 2012–; Wheatley Res. Ltd, 2015–; Wheatley Cardiosynthetics Ltd, 2015–. Mem. Council, RCSE, 1986–90, 1992–97, 1997–2002; President: Soc. of Cardiothoracic Surgeons of GB and Ireland, 1996–98; European Assoc. for Cardiothoracic Surgery, 1998–99. Founder FMedSci 1998; FECTS 2002. *Publications:* Surgery of Coronary Artery Disease, 1986, 2nd edn 2003; author or jt author of 175 articles on cardiac surgery. *Recreations:* piano, classical music, opera. *Address:* 13 Lochend Drive, Bearsden, Glasgow G61 1ED. *T:* (0141) 942 1381.

WHEATLEY, Derek Peter Francis; QC 1981; Barrister-at-Law; Member, Joint Law Society/Bar Council Working Party on Banking Law, 1976–94; 3rd *s* of late Edward Pearse Wheatley, company director, and Gladys Wheatley; *m* 1955, Elizabeth Pamela (*d* 2015), *d* of John and Gertrude Reynolds; two *s* one *d*. *Educ:* The Leys Sch., Cambridge; University Coll., Oxford (MA). Served War of 1939–45, Army, 1944–47: (short univ. course, Oxford, 1944); commissioned into 8th King's Royal Irish Hussars, 1945, Lieut. University Coll., Oxford, 1947–49; called to the Bar, Middle Temple, 1951; Deputy Coroner: to the Royal Household, 1959–64; for London, 1959–64; Recorder of the Crown Court, 1972–74. Chief Legal Advr to Lloyds Bank, 1974–89. Member: Commercial Court Cttee, 1976–90; Senate of Inns of Court and the Bar, 1975–78, 1982–85; Exec. Cttee, Bar Council, 1982–85; Bar Council, 1986–90, 1995–96, 1999–2000 (Member: Professional Standards Cttee, 1986–88; F and GP Cttee, 1988–); Chm., Bar Assoc. for Commerce, Finance and Industry, 1982–83 and 1999–2000 (Vice-Pres., 1986–). Chm., Legal Cttee, Cttee of London and Scottish Bankers, 1985–87. FRSA 1994. *Publications:* The Silent Lady (novel), 2008; articles in legal jls and The Times, etc. *Recreation:* sailing. *Address:* Three The Wardrobe, Old Palace Yard, Richmond, Surrey TW9 1PA. *T:* (020) 8940 6242, *Fax:* (020) 8332 0948. *E:* derek.wheatley3@btinternet.com. *Clubs:* Roehampton, Sloane; Bar Yacht.

WHEATLEY, John Derek, CBE 1993; Member, National Rivers Authority, 1989–96 (Chief Executive, 1991–92); *b* 24 July 1927; *s* of Leslie Sydney and Lydia Florence Wheatley; *m* 1956, Marie Gowers; one *s* one *d*. *Educ:* Sir Thomas Rich's Sch., Gloucester; Loughborough Coll., 1944–46 (Teacher's Cert.); Carnegie College of Physical Educn, 1952–53 (DipPE). Served RAF, 1946–52; Surrey Education Authority, 1953–54; Central Council of Physical Recreation: London and SE, 1954–58; Secretary, Northern Ireland, 1959–69; Principal Regional Officer, SW, 1970–72; Sports Council: Regional Director, SW, 1972–80; Director of Administrative Services, Headquarters, 1980–83; Dir Gen., 1983–88. Chm., Nat. Small-Bore Rifle Assoc., 1989–95. *Recreations:* gardening, music.

WHEATLEY, Rt Hon. John Francis; *see* Wheatley, Rt Hon. Lord.

WHEATLEY, Oswald Stephen, (Ossie), CBE 1997; Chairman, Sports Council for Wales, 1990–99; company director; *b* 28 May 1935; *s* of late Harold Wheatley and Laura Wheatley (*née* Owens); *m* 1st, 1964, Christine Mary Godwin (*d* 2000); one *s* (two *d* decd); 2nd, 2011, Janet Mary Parry-Jones. *Educ:* King Edward's Sch., Birmingham; Caius Coll., Cambridge (MA Econs and Law). 2nd Lieut, RA, 1954. Cambridge Cricket Blue, 1957–58; played for Warwicks CCC, 1957–60; Glamorgan CCC, 1961–69 (Captain, 1961–66); Chm., Glamorgan CCC, 1977–84. Test and County Cricket Board: Test Selector, 1972–74; Chairman: Discipline Cttee, 1978–83; Cricket Cttee, 1987–95; Mem., England Cttee, 1989–93; Chm., Cricket Foundn, 1996–2008. Member: Sports Council of GB, 1984–88 and 1990–96; UK Sports Council, 1997–99; Broadcasting Council for Wales, 1990–95; Sch. Exam and Assessment Council, 1992–93. Chm., Nat. Sports Medicine Inst., St Bartholomew's Hosp., 1991–96. Hon. Fellow, Cardiff Metropolitan Univ. (Hon. Fellow, Univ. of Wales Inst., 1995). Freeman, City of Newcastle-upon-Tyne, 1976. *Recreations:* sport, art. *Address:* 78 Adventurers Quay, Cardiff Bay, Cardiff CF10 4NQ. *Clubs:* MCC, Free Foresters; Cardiff and County; Glamorgan CC.

WHEATLEY, Ven. Paul Charles; Archdeacon of Sherborne and Priest in Charge of West Stafford with Frome Billet, 1991–2003, now Archdeacon Emeritus; *b* 27 May 1938; *s* of Charles Lewis and Doris Amy Wheatley; *m* 1963, Iris Mary Lacey; two *s* one *d*. *Educ:* Wycliffe Coll.; St John's Coll., Durham (BA 1961); Lincoln Theol Coll. Ordained deacon 1963, priest 1964; Curate, Bishopston, Bristol, 1963–68; Youth Chaplain, dio. of Bristol, 1968–73; Team Rector, Dorcan, Swindon, 1973–79; Rector, Ross, Hereford, 1979–81; Team Rector, Ross with Brampton Abbots, Bridstow, Peterstow, 1979–91; Prebendary, Hereford Cathedral, 1987–91; Ecumenical Officer, Hereford, 1987–91; Hon. Canon, Salisbury Cathedral, 1991–2003, now Hon. Canon Emeritus. *Recreations:* travel, gardening, opera. *Address:* The Farthings, Bridstow, Herefordshire HR9 6QF.

WHEATLEY, Rt Rev. Peter William; Area Bishop of Edmonton, 1999–2014; an Honorary Assistant Bishop: Diocese of Southwark, since 2013; Diocese of London, since 2015; Diocese of Chichester; *b* 7 Sept. 1947; *er s* of late William Nobes Wheatley and Muriel (*née* Ounsted). *Educ:* Ipswich Sch. (Queen's and Foundn Schol.); Queen's Coll., Oxford (Styring Schol., MA); Pembroke Coll., Cambridge (MA); Coll. of the Resurrection, Mirfield; Ripon Hall, Oxford. Deacon 1973, priest 1974; Asst Curate, All Saints, Fulham, 1973–78; Vicar: Holy Cross with St Jude and St Peter, St Pancras, 1978–82; St James, W Hampstead, 1982–95; Priest-in-charge: St Mary, Kilburn, 1982–90; St Mary with All Souls, Kilburn, 1990–95; Curate-in-charge, All Souls, S Hampstead, 1982–90; Archdeacon of Hampstead, 1995–99. Proctor in Convocation and Mem. Gen. Synod, C of E, 1975–95. *Recreation:* music. *Address:* 47 Sedlescombe Road South, St Leonards-on-Sea, E Sussex TN38 0TB. *E:* peter.wheatley@btconnect.com.

WHEATLEY, Philip Martin, CB 2004; Director, Wheatley & Roy Associates Ltd, management consultancy, since 2012; *b* 4 July 1948; *s* of Alan Osborne Wheatley and Ida Mary Wheatley; *m* 1st, 1969, Merryll Angela Francis (marr. diss. 1989); one *s* one *d*; 2nd, 1990, Anne Eleanor Roy. *Educ:* Leeds Grammar Sch.; Sheffield Univ. (LLB Hons). HM Prison Service: Prison Officer, 1969–70; Asst Gov., 1970; Hull Prison, 1971–74; Prison Service Coll., 1974–78; Leeds Prison, 1978–82; Dep. Gov., Gartree Prison, 1982–86; Governor, Hull Prison, 1986–90; Prison Service Area Manager for E Midlands, 1990–92; Asst Dir, Custody Gp, Prison Service HQ, 1992–95; Dir of Dispersals, i/c 6 highest security prisons, 1995–99; Dep. Dir Gen., 1999–2003; Dir Gen., 2003–08; Chief Exec., then Dir Gen., Nat. Offender Mgt Service, MoJ, 2008–10. Non-exec. Dir, NI Prisons Bd, 2010 and 2011–; Mem., NI Prison Review Team, 2010–11. Associate consultant, G4S, 2011–. Trustee: St Giles Trust, 2010–; Feltham Community Chaplaincy Trust, 2013–. CCMI. FRSA. *Recreations:* good wine, good food and holidays to enjoy them, history, current affairs, politics, criminology. *E:* pmwheatley@hotmail.co.uk. *Club:* Reform.

WHEATON, Rev. Canon David Harry; Vicar of Christ Church, Ware, 1986–96; Chaplain to the Queen, 1990–2000; *b* 2 June 1930; *s* of Harry Wheaton, MBE, and Kathleen Mary (*née* Frost); *m* 1956, Helen Joy Forrer (*d* 2014); one *s* two *d*. *Educ:* Abingdon Sch.; St John's Coll., Oxford (Exhibnr; MA); London Univ. (BD (London Bible Coll.)); Oak Hill Theol Coll. NCO, Wiltshire Regt, 1948–49. Deacon, 1959; priest, 1960; Tutor, Oak Hill Coll., 1954–62; Rector of Ludgershall, Bucks, 1962–66; Vicar of St Paul, Onslow Square, S Kensington, 1966–71; Chaplain, Brompton Chest Hosp., 1969–71; Principal Oak Hill Theol Coll., 1971–86; RD of Hertford, 1988–91. Hon. Canon, Cathedral and Abbey Church of St Alban, 1976–96, now Canon Emeritus. *Publications:* (jtly) Witness to the Word, 2002; *contributed to:* Baker's Dictionary of Theology, 1960; New Bible Dictionary, 1962; New Bible Commentary (rev.), 1970, 21st century edn 1994; Lion Handbook to the Bible, 1973, 4th edn 2009; Evangelical Dictionary of Theology, 1984; Here We Stand, 1986; Restoring the Vision, 1990. *Recreations:* walking, carpentry and do-it-yourself, preserved railways. *Address:* 17 Riverside Road, Blandford Forum, Dorset DT11 7ES. *T:* (01258) 489996.

WHEELDON, David John; Headmaster, King Edward VI Five Ways School, Birmingham, 2003–12; *b* Newcastle-under-Lyme, 28 Oct. 1949; *s* of John Wheeldon and Edna Wheeldon; *m* 1975, Janet Alexander (*d* 2014); two *s*. *Educ:* Alleyne's Grammar Sch., Staffs; Worcester Coll. of Educn (Cert Ed 1971); Univ. of Birmingham (BEd 1972); Birmingham Poly. (BA 1979); Open Univ. (AdvDip Educn Mgt 1987); Coventry Univ. (MSc 1996). Asst teacher, Oswestry High Sch. for Boys, 1972–74; King Edward VI Five Ways School: Hd of Dept of Social Scis and Gen. Studies, 1974–86; Hd of Sixth Form, 1986–89; Dep. Head, 1989–97; Head Master, Altrincham Grammar Sch. for Boys, 1997–2003. Associate Dir, CJHutt Associates, 2012–; Advr/Consultant to Foundation of King Edward VI schs, Birmingham, 2012–. Mem. Exec., Grammar Schs Heads Assoc., 2008–12 (Associate Mem., 2012–). Governor: Bishop Vesey's Grammar Sch., 2012–; King Edward VI Camp Hill Sch. for Boys, Birmingham, 2014–. Mem., Birmingham Lunar Soc., 2011–. FRSA. *Recreations:* local history, antiques, travel, a lapsed bee keeper… and lapsed Rotarian. *Address:* 59 Hill Grove Crescent, Kidderminster, Worcs DY10 3AR. *T:* (01562) 741695. *E:* djwheeldon@btinternet.com. *Club:* Lansdowne.

WHEELDON, Nusrat; *see* Ghani, N.

WHEELER, Baroness *cr* 2010 (Life Peer), of Blackfriars in the City of London; **Margaret Eileen Joyce Wheeler,** MBE 2005; Director of Organisation and Staff Development, UNISON, 1993–2010; *b* 25 March 1949. With COHSE, later UNISON, 1973–2010. Former Mem., Commn on Social Justice. Former Mem., Enquiry Panel into productivity and high performance, DTI/Work Foundn; seconded to Nat. Care Strategy Team, DoH, 2009–11; Mem., Investors in People Adv. Bd, UK Commn for Employment and Skills, 2010–13. House of Lords: Opposition frontbench spokesperson on health and social care, 2010–; an Opposition Whip, 2010–. Member, All-Party Parliamentary Group: on Stroke, 2010–; on Carers, 2010–. Mem., Specialist Health Care Alliance, 2013–. Trustee: Blackfriars Settlement, 2003–; Carer Support, Elmbridge, 2011–. *Address:* House of Lords, SW1A 0PW.

WHEELER, Rev. Canon Dr Andrew Charles; Mission Pastor and Director of Mission Education, St Saviour's Church, Guildford, since 2002; World Mission Advisor, Guildford Diocese, since 2006; *b* 14 April 1948; *s* of Charles Hildred Wheeler and Ruth Goss Wheeler (*née* Rhymes); *m* 1979, Susan Jane Snook; one *s* one *d*. *Educ:* Corpus Christi Coll., Cambridge (MA); Makerere Univ., Kampala (MA); Leeds Univ. (PGCE); Trinity Coll., Bristol (BA Theol.). Asst Master in Hist., Harrogate Granby High Sch., 1972–75; theol teacher, for CMS, Bishop Gwynne Coll., Mundri, Sudan, 1977–86; ordained deacon, 1988, priest, 1988; Asst Curate, Aldbourne, Salisbury dio., 1988–89; Hon. Curate, with resp. for care of Sudanese refugees, 1989–92, Hon. Canon, 2005, All Saints Cathedral, Cairo; Theol Trng Co-ordinator, New Sudan Council of Churches, 1992–96; Sudan Church Res. Project Dir, 1996–2000; Archbishop's Sec. for the Anglican Communion, 2000–01. DD Lambeth, 2008. *Publications:* (Gen. Ed.) Faith in Sudan series, 13 vols, 1997–2000 (ed and contrib. to vols 1, 5 and 6); (jtly) Day of Devastation, Day of Contentment: the history of the Sudanese Church across 2000 years, 2000; (ed) Voices from Africa, 2002; Bombs, Ruins and Honey: journeys of the spirit with Sudanese Christians, 2006. *Recreations:* music, walking, squash.

WHEELER, Anthony Ian, AO 2014; Co-founder, 1973, and Joint Director, 1973–2007, Lonely Planet Publications; Co-Founder and Director, Planet Wheeler Foundation, since 2007; *b* 20 Dec. 1946; *s* of late Ian James Wheeler and of Hilary Audrey Wheeler; *m* 1971, Maureen Dixon; one *s* one *d*. *Educ:* Warwick Univ. (BSc); London Business Sch. (MSc). *Publications:* Across Asia on the Cheap, 1973; South-East Asia on a Shoestring, 1975; Australia, 1977; New Zealand, 1977; West Asia on a Shoestring, 1978; Papua New Guinea, 1978; Burma, 1979; Sri Lanka, 1979; India, 1981; Malaysia, Singapore and Brunei, 1981; Bali and Lombok, 1984; Rarotonga and the Cook Islands, 1986; Islands of Australia's Great Barrier Reef, 1990; Nepal, 1990; Japan, 1991; Dublin, 1993; Britain, 1995; San Francisco, 1996; Tahiti and French Polynesia, 1996; Chasing Rickshaws, 1998; Tahiti and French Polynesia: diving and snorkeling, 2001; Time and Tide: the Islands of Tuvalu, 2001; Rice Trails, 2004; East Timor, 2004; Falkland Islands and South Georgia, 2004; Once While Travelling: the Lonely Planet story, 2005; Bad Lands: a tourist on the axis of evil, 2007; Dark Lands, 2013. *Recreations:* walking, trekking, scuba diving, running, cycling, travel (as much as possible). *E:* tony@tonywheeler.com.au.

WHEELER, Captain Arthur Walter; RN retd; CEng; Keeper, HMS Belfast, 1983–88; *b* 18 Oct. 1927; *s* of Walter Sidney Wheeler and Annie Ethel Marsh; *m* 1st, 1957, Elizabeth Jane Glendinning Bowman (marr. diss. 1968); two *s*; 2nd, 1968, Mary Elvis Findon; one *s*. *Educ:* Woodhouse Sch., Finchley; HMS Fisgard, Torpoint; RN Engineering Coll., Manadon. FIMechE, MIMarE. Joined Royal Navy as artificer apprentice, 1943; served in cruiser Birmingham, 1947–50. Progressively, Sub Lieut 1950 to Captain 1974. Served in frigate Palliser and aircraft carriers Bulwark, Hermes and Ark Royal 1954–74; Sea Trng Staff at Portland, 1961–63; MoD, Ship Dept, 1966–70 and 1975–78; CSO(Engrg) to Flag Officer Third Flotilla, 1979–80; HMS Daedalus in comd, 1980–82, retired. Received into RC Church, 1987; returned to C of E, 2008. *Recreations:* music, reading, painting, walking.

WHEELER, (Belinda) Christian; *see* Rucker, B. C.

WHEELER, David Arthur; Founder and Editor, Hortus, since 1987; *b* Thrupp, Glos, 2 Oct. 1945; *s* of Arthur Wheeler and Lily Wheeler (*née* Eckford). *Educ:* none. Advertising Executive: Southern Evening Echo, Southampton, 1963–70; Observer, 1970–75; Advertising Manager, Spectator, 1975–79; Campaigns Dir, RSPCA, 1979–82; jobbing gardener, 1982–87. Founder, Convivium: the journal of good eating, 1993. Gold Veitch Meml Medal, RHS, 2009. *Publications:* (ed) By Pen and By Spade, 1990; (ed) The Generous Garden, 1991; Panorama of English Gardens, 1991; Over the Hills from Broadway: images of Cotswold gardens, 1991; (ed) The Penguin Book of Garden Writing, 1996. *Recreations:* gardening, travel, gastronomy, orchestral, chamber and instrumental music, opera, chasing moonbeams and the ghosts of Ottoman gardeners. *Address:* Hortus, Bryan's Ground, Presteigne, Herefordshire LD8 2LP. *E:* d.a.wheeler@hotmail.com.

WHEELER, Frank Basil, CMG 1990; HM Diplomatic Service, retired; *b* 24 April 1937; *s* of late Harold Gifford Wheeler and Winifred Lucy Wheeler (*née* Childs); *m* 1st, 1959, Catherine Saunders Campbell (*d* 1979); one *s*; 2nd, 1984, Alyson Ruth Lund (*née* Powell) (marr. diss. 1989); 3rd, 1991, Susana Plaza Larrea. *Educ:* Mill Hill Sch. HM Forces, 1956–58. HM Foreign Service, 1958–: Foreign Office, 1958–61; Third Sec., Moscow, 1961–63; Asst Private Sec. to Minister of State, FO, 1963–65; Second Sec., Berne, 1965–67; First Sec., FO (later FCO), 1967–72; Wellington, 1972–75; FCO, 1975–77; Counsellor and Head of Chancery, Prague, 1977–79; Inspector, 1979–82; Head of Personnel Policy Dept, FCO, 1982–84; Counsellor and Head of Chancery, UK Delegn to NATO, Brussels, 1984–86; Counsellor, on loan to DTI, 1986–89; Ambassador: to Ecuador, 1989–93; to Chile, 1993–97; Chm., British-Chilean Chamber of Commerce, 1997–2003. Dir, Vicor Inc., Florida, 2011–13. Internat. Advr, FA, 1997–2000. Grand Cross, Order of Merit (Chile), 1998. *Recreations:* music, tennis. *Address:* 28–30 Theobalds Road, WC1X 8NX; Costa Rica.

WHEELER, Fraser William; HM Diplomatic Service, retired; consultant in low carbon international development; Consultant: Forbury Investment Network; Commonwealth Environmental investment Platform; Sensitivity Reviewer, Foreign and Commonwealth Office; *b* 23 March 1957; *s* of Albert, (Bill), and Janet Wheeler; *m* 1988, Sarah Humphreys; one *s* one *d*. *Educ:* Univ. of Warwick (BA Hons Politics). Trainee, Deloitte, 1979–80; entered FCO, 1980; Finance Dept, FCO, 1980–82; Third Secretary: Accra, 1982–85; UK Mission to UN, Geneva, 1986–89; Desk Officer, Soviet Dept, 1990–91; Dep. Hd, Trade Section, Moscow, 1991–94; Dep. Consul Gen., Vancouver, 1995–2000; PR Consultant, Vancouver, 2000–01 (on special leave); Policy Planning Staff, 2001–03, Hd, Partnerships and Networks Gp, 2003–05, FCO; Hd, British Embassy Office, Basra, Iraq, 2005–06; High Comr to Guyana, and concurrently Ambassador to Suriname and CARICOM, 2006–10. *Recreations:* the fruitless pursuit of the life of old Reilly, travel with a point to it, playing with a Harley Davidson, country walking in bad weather, smoky and cramped jazz bars, sport for fun, banter with the best of them over fine wine or good coffee.

WHEELER, Heather; MP (C) South Derbyshire, since 2010; *b* Norwich, 14 May 1959; *d* of Charles Peter Clough Wilkinson and Freda Mary Wilkinson; *m* 1986, Robert James Wheeler; one *d*. *Educ:* Grey Coat Hosp., Westminster. ACII 1985. Placing Manager, RICS Insce Services Ltd, 1977–87. Member (C): Wandsworth BC, 1982–86; S Derbys DC, 1995–2011 (Leader, 2007–10). Contested (C) Coventry S, 2001, 2005. Member, Select Committee: on Standards and Privileges, 2010–13; on Communities and Local Govt, 2011–15. Chm., All Party Parly Local Govt Gp, 2010–. Mem. Exec., 1922 Cttee, 2011–. *Recreations:* watching sport, DIY, listening to The Archers. *Address:* House of Commons, SW1A 0AA.

WHEELER, Joanne Elizabeth; Partner (communications, satellite and space law), Bird & Bird LLP, since 2014; *b* Edinburgh, 4 Feb. 1971; *d* of Joseph Duff Wheeler and Elizabeth Anne Wheeler; *m* 2005, Alexander James Monk; three *d*. *Educ:* George Watson's Coll., Edinburgh; Univ. of Aberdeen (LLB Hons 1993; DipLP 1995); Rotterdam Univ. (LLM Law and Econs (with distinction) 1994); Univ. of Oxford (MSt Law and Econs 1996); BPP Law Sch. (Qualified Lawyers Transfer Test 1998); Queen Mary, Univ. of London (Dip. Telecommunications Law 2002). Admitted solicitor, Scotland, 1996, England and Wales, 1998; NP 1996. Trainee solicitor, McGrigor Donald, 1995–97; Assistant Solicitor: Slaughter and May, 1997–99; Baker & McKenzie, 1999–2001; Sen. Associate, Allen & Overy, 2001–03; Lawyer: ESA, Paris, 2003–06; OFCOM, 2006–07; Sen. Associate, Milbank Tweed Hadley & McCloy, 2007–09; Partner (communications, satellite and space law), CMS Cameron McKenna LLP, 2009–14. Rep. of UK Govt to UN Cttee on the Peaceful Uses of Outer Space, 2011–. Co-Chm., Satellite Finance Network, 2012–; Chm., Space Cttee, Internat. Bar Assoc., 2014–; Dep. Chm., Space Law (UK) Cttee, Internat. Law Assoc., 2007–; Sec. for UK Nat. Point of Contact, Eur. Centre of Space Law, 2001–. FRAS 2010. Mem., Internat. Inst. of Space Law, 2001–. Columnist: Satellite Finance, 2011–; Via Satellite, 2013–. *Publications:* (contrib.) The International Space Station: commercial utilisation from a European perspective, 2006; (contrib.) Yearbook on Space Policy 2010/2011, 2013; contrib. articles in Scots Law Times, Jl of Aerospace Engrg, Harvard Internat. Rev., Satellite Finance, Via Satellite. *Recreations:* family, space law and policy, hiking, art, ballet, wildlife. *Address:* Bird & Bird LLP, 15 Fetter Lane, EC4A 1JP. *T:* (020) 3017 6847, *Fax:* (020) 7415 6111. *E:* joanne.wheeler@twobirds.com.

WHEELER, Rt Hon. Sir John (Daniel), Kt 1990; PC 1993; JP; DL; Chairman, Service Authorities for National Criminal Intelligence Service and National Crime Squad, 1997–2002; *b* 1 May 1940; *s* of late Frederick Harry Wheeler and of Constance Elsie (*née* Foreman); *m* 1967, Laura Margaret Langley; one *s* one *d*. *Educ:* county sch., Suffolk; Staff Coll., Wakefield. Home Office: Asst Prison Governor, 1967–74; Res. Officer (looking into causes of crime and delinquency and treatment of offenders), 1974–76; Dir-Gen., BSIA, 1976–88 (Hon. Mem., 1990). Dir, National Supervisory Council for Intruder Alarms, 1977–88. Chairman: Nat. Inspectorate of Security Guard Patrol and Transport Services, 1982–92; Security Systems Inspectorate, 1987–90; Inspectorate of the Security Industry, 1992–93; govt review of airport security, 2002; Airport Security and Policing Review, Fed. Govt of Aust., 2005; Dep. Chm., UK Border Security Adv. Cttee, 2007–08. Chm. and non-exec. dir, various cos, 1976–93. Chairman: Capital Link, 1997–2002; Adv. Bd, Avarae Global Coins plc, 2006–. MP (C) City of Westminster, Paddington Div., 1979–83, Westminster N, 1983–97. Minister of State, NI Office, 1993–97. Member: Home Office Crime Prevention Cttee, 1976–92; Cons. Party National Adv. CPC Cttee, 1978–80; Home Affairs Select Cttee, 1979–92 (Chm., 1987–92); Chairman: Home Affairs Sub-Cttee, Race Relations and Immigration, 1980–87; All Party Penal Affairs Gp, 1986–93 (Vice-Chm., 1979–86); Vice-Chairman: Cons. Home Affairs Cttee, 1987–92 (Jt Sec., 1980–87); British Pakistan Parly Gp, 1987–93; Chm., Cons. Greater London Area Members' Cttee, 1983–90 (Jt Sec., 1980–83). Mem., Lloyd's, 1986–97. Pres., Paddington Div., St John Ambulance, 1998–99 (Vice Pres., 1990–98). Trustee, Police Foundn, 2004– (Vice Chm., 2010–). Freeman, City of London, 1987. JP Inner London, 1978; DL Greater London, 1989; Rep. DL, LB of Merton, 1997–2015. James Smart Lecture, SHHD, 1991 (Silver Medal). KStJ 1997 (Mem. Council, Order of St John for London, 1990–; Mem., Chapter Gen., 1993–99; Registrar, 1997–99, Sub-Chancellor, 1999–2002, Order of St John; Trustee and Mem., 1999–2008, Chancellor, 2002–08, Priory Chapter of England and the Islands). Hilal-i-Quaid-i-Azam (Pakistan), 1991. *Publications:* Who Prevents Crime?, 1980; (jtly) The Standard Catalogue of the Coins of the British Commonwealth, 1642 to present day, 1986. *Recreation:* enjoying life. *Club:* Travellers (Chm., 2014–).

WHEELER, Sir John (Frederick), (Jim), 4th Bt *cr* 1920, of Woodhouse Eaves, co. Leicester; *b* 3 May 1933; *s* of Sir John Hieron Wheeler, 3rd Bt and Gwendolen Alice Wheeler (*née* Oram); *S* father, 2005; *m* 1963, Barbara Mary, *d* of Raymond Flint; two *s* one *d*. *Educ:* Bedales; London Sch. of Printing. *Heir:* *s* Lt-Col John Radford Wheeler [*b* 27 Dec. 1965; *m* 1991, Sarah, *d* of Comdr Tim Howard-Jones; two *s* two *d*]. *Address:* Round Hill, Aldeburgh, Suffolk IP15 5PG.

WHEELER, (John) Stuart; Founder, Chief Executive, 1974–2002, and Chairman, 1985–2003, IG Group (formerly IG Index); Treasurer, UK Independence Party, 2011–14; *b* 30 Jan. 1935; adopted by late Capt. Alexander Hamilton Wheeler and Betty Lydia Wheeler; *m* 1979, Teresa Anne Codrington; three *d*. *Educ:* Eton Coll.; Christ Church, Oxford (LLB Hons). Nat Service, 2nd Lieut, Welsh Guards, 1953–55. Called to the Bar, Inner Temple, 1959, in practice as barrister, 1959–62; Asst Manager, Investment Dept, Hill Samuel, 1962–68; Manager, Investment Dept, J. H. Vavasseur, 1968–73; First Nat. Finance Corp., 1973. Contested (Trust) Bexhill and Battle, 2010. Coronation Me dal, 1953. *Publications:* A Crisis of Trust, 2010. *Recreations:* tennis, bridge, poker. *Address:* Chilham Castle, Canterbury, Kent CT4 8DB. *T:* (01227) 733100. *Clubs:* White's, Portland.

WHEELER, Karen Stephanie, CBE 2007; National Director, Transformation and Corporate Operations, NHS England, since 2014; *b* Isleworth, London, 30 Nov. 1956; *d* of Reginald William Wheeler and June Heather Wheeler; *m* 2009, Stuart Lynas. *Educ:* Reigate Co. Sch. for Girls; Durham Univ. (BSc Physics). Intelligence Officer, Security Service, 1978–88; Change Mgt Manager, Andersen Consulting, 1988–95; Change Mgt Consultant, Practick Ltd, 1995–99; Sen. Manager, Penna Consulting, 1999–2003; Change Prog. Manager, DCA, 2003–06; Change Dir, 2006–08, Delivery Dir, 2008–09, MoJ; Digital Delivery Dir, Cabinet Office, 2009–10; Transition Dir, 2010–12, Dir Gen., Gp Ops and Assurance, 2012–14, DoH. *Recreations:* opera, jazz, choral singing, walking. *Address:* NHS England, 80 London Road, SE1 6LH.

WHEELER, Air Vice-Marshal Leslie William Frederick; Independent Inspector for Public Inquiries and Chairman of Appointments Boards for Civil Service Commissioners and Ministry of Defence, 1984–94; *b* 4 July 1930; *s* of late George Douglas and Susan Wheeler; *m* 1961, Joan, *d* of late Harry and Evelyn Carpenter; two *d*. *Educ:* Creighton School, Carlisle. Commnd, 1952; Egypt and Cyprus, 1954–56; Specialist in Signals, 1958; Aden, 1958–60; V-force (Valiants), 1961–65; India (Staff Coll.), 1965–66; Headquarters Signals Command, 1966–69; OC 360 Sqdn, 1970–72; Dir, RAF Staff Coll., 1972–74; Electronic Warfare and Recce Operations, MoD, 1975–77; Stn Comdr, RAF Finningley, 1977–79; Air Cdre Policy & Plans, Headquarters RAF Support Comd, 1979–83; Dir-Gen., Personal Services (RAF), MoD, 1983–84, retired. *Recreations:* walking, philately, genealogy. *Address:* c/o HSBC, English Street, Carlisle CA3 8JW.

WHEELER, Dame Margaret Anne; *see* Brain, Dame M. A.

WHEELER, Michael Antony; a District Judge (Magistrates' Courts), since 2009; a Recorder, since 2012; *b* Coventry, 23 May 1959; *s* of Alan James Wheeler and Doris Joan Wheeler; *m* 1986, Kim Lorna Osborne; one *s* one *d*. *Educ:* Bablake Sch., Coventry; Liverpool Poly. (BA Hons Law 1980). Admitted as solicitor, 1983; sole practitioner, Michael Wheeler, Solicitor (criminal defence practice), 1995–2009; a Dep. Dist Judge (Magistrates' Courts), 2003–09. *Recreations:* clay pigeon shooting, running, golf, squash, crosswords. *Address:* Wolverhampton Magistrates' Court, North Street, Wolverhampton WV1 1RA. *T:* (01902) 773151, *Fax:* 0870 739 4167. *E:* districtjudgemichael.wheeler@judiciary.gsi.gov.uk.

WHEELER, Nicholas Charles Tyrwhitt; Chairman, Charles Tyrwhitt, since 1986; *b* 20 Jan. 1965; *s* of John Vashon Tyrwhitt Wheeler and late Geraldine Noel Wheeler; *m* 1995, (Belinda) Christian Rucker, *qv*; one *s* three *d*. *Educ:* Eton Coll.; Univ. of Bristol (BSc 1987). Charles Tyrwhitt, 1986–; Bain & Co., 1987–89. *Recreations:* tennis, ski-ing, photography. *E:* nickw@ctshirts.co.uk. *Club:* Hurlingham.

WHEELER, Prof. Nicholas John, PhD; Professor of International Relations, and Director, Institute for Conflict, Cooperation and Security, University of Birmingham, since 2012; *b* Hereford, 7 April 1962; *s* of John and Lola Wheeler; one *d*. *Educ:* Staffordshire Poly. (BA Hons Modern Studies (Internat. Relns and Econs) 1983); Southampton Univ. (MSc (Econ) Internat. Studies; PhD 1988). Tutor, Dept of Internat. Politics, University Coll. of Wales, Aberystwyth, 1985–86; Res. Fellow, Dept of War Studies, KCL, 1987–88; Res. Associate, Internat. Inst. for Strategic Studies, 1988–89; Lectr, Dept of Politics, Univ. of Hull, 1989–93; Department of International Politics, University of Wales, Aberystwyth, later Aberystwyth University: Lectr, 1993–97; Sen. Lectr, 1997–2002; Reader, 2002–04; Prof. of Internat. Politics, 2004–12, Dir, 2005–10, David Davies Meml Inst. of Internat. Studies. ESRC/AHRC Fellow, Global Uncertainties Prog., Res. Councils UK, 2009–13. *Publications:* (with I. Clark) The British Origins of Nuclear Strategy, 1945–55, 1989; (ed with T. Dunne) Human Rights in Global Politics, 1999; Saving Strangers: humanitarian intervention in international society, 2000; (ed with C. McInnes) Dimensions of Military Intervention, 2002; (ed with Jean-Marc Coicaud) National Interest Versus Solidarity: particular and universal ethics in international life, 2008; (with K. Booth) The Security Dilemma: fear, cooperation and trust in world politics, 2008; (jtly) Special Responsibilities: global problems and American power, 2012. *Recreations:* swimming, walking, cycling. *Address:* College of Social Sciences, School of Government and Society, Muirhead Tower, University of Birmingham, Edgbaston, Birmingham B15 2TT.

WHEELER, Prof. Quentin D., PhD; President, College of Environmental Science and Forestry, State University of New York, since 2014; *b* 31 Jan. 1954; *s* of Quentin Wheeler and Hattie (*née* Philips); *m* 2004, Darlene Marie Platt; one *s* four *d*. *Educ:* Ohio State Univ.,

Columbus (BS 1976, MS 1977; PhD 1980). Cornell University: Prof., 1980–2004; Chm., Entomology, 1989–93; Dir, L. H. Bailey Hortorium, 1988–89. US National Science Foundation: Prog. Officer, 2001; Dir, Div. of Envmtl Biology, 2001–04; Keeper and Hd of Entomol., Natural History Mus., 2004–06; Arizona State University: Prof. of Natural History and the Envmt, Sch. of Life Scis, 2006–14; Vice Pres. and Dean, Coll. of Liberal Arts and Scis, 2006–11; Dir, Internat. Inst. for Species Exploration, 2007–14. Mem., Willi Hennig Soc. FAAAS 2003; FLS 2003; FRES 2004. *Publications:* Fungus/Insect Relationships: perspectives in ecology and evolution, 1984; Extinction and Phylogeny, 1992; Species Concepts and Phylogenetic Theory: a debate, 2000; more than 100 articles in scientific jls. *Recreations:* furniture making, insect collecting, hiking, photography, wines and coffees. *Address:* College of Environmental Science and Forestry, State University of New York, 1 Forestry Drive, Syracuse, NY 13210, USA.

WHEELER, Raymond Leslie, RDI 1995; FRAeS; FRINA; *b* 25 Oct. 1927; *s* of Edmund Francis Wheeler and Ivy Geraldine Wheeler; *m* 1950, Jean McInnes; one *s* two *d.* *Educ:* Southampton Univ. (BSc (Eng) 1948); Imperial Coll., London (MSc (Eng) 1953; DIC). FRAeS 1974; FRINA 1975. Apprentice, 1945–48, Aircraft stressman, 1953–62, Chief Stressman, 1962–65, Saunders Roe Ltd, then Saunders Roe Div. of Westland Aircraft Ltd; Chief Structural Designer and Project Engr, SRN4 (world's largest hovercraft), 1965; British Hovercraft Corp. Ltd, subseq. Westland Aerospace Ltd: Chief Designer, 1966–85; Technical Dir, 1972–85; Dir, 1985–91. President: IoW Hockey Club; IoW Br., RAeS; IoW Young Enterprise; E Cowes Br., RNLI. *Publications:* (with A. E. Tagg) From Sea to Air: the heritage of Sam Saunders, 1989; From River to Sea: the marine heritage of Sam Saunders, 1993; Saunders Roe, 1998; (with J. B. Chaplin) In the Beginning: the SRNI hovercraft, 2007; A 20th Century Engineer, 2011. *Recreations:* gardening, photography, pottery, painting, archaeology, sport. *Address:* Brovacum, 106 Old Road, East Cowes, Isle of Wight PO32 6AX.

WHEELER, Gen. Sir Roger (Neil), GCB 1997 (KCB 1993); CBE 1983; Constable, HM Tower of London, 2001–09; Chief of the General Staff, 1997–2000; Aide-de-camp General to the Queen, 1996–2000; *b* 16 Dec. 1941; *s* of Maj.-Gen. T. N. S. Wheeler, CB, CBE; *m* 1980, Felicity Hares; three *s* one *d* by former marriage. *Educ:* All Hallows Sch., Devon; Hertford Coll., Oxford (BA Hons 1964; MA 1974; Hon. Fellow 2002). Early Army service in Borneo and ME, 1964–70; Bde Major, Cyprus Emergency, 1974; Mem., Lord Carver's Staff, Rhodesia talks, 1977; Bn Comd, Belize, Gibraltar, Berlin and Canada, 1979–82; COS, Falkland Is, June–Dec. 1982; Bde Comd, BAOR, 1985–86; Dir, Army Plans, 1987–89; Comdr, 1st Armoured Div., BAOR, 1989–90; ACGS, MoD, 1990–92; GOC and Dir of Military Ops, NI, 1993–96; C-in-C, Land Comd, 1996–97. Col, Royal Irish Regt, 1996–2001; Col Comdt, Intell. Corps, 1996–2000. Hon. Colonel: QUB OTC, 2000–08; Oxford Univ. OTC, 2000–06. President: Army RFU, 1995–99; Army Rifle Assoc., 1995–2000; Mem. Council, NRA, 2000–02. Non-executive Director: Thales plc, 2001–11; Aegis Defence, 2003–11; Serious Organised Crime Agency, 2005–09. President: Ex Services Mental Welfare Soc., Combat Stress, 2001–09; Forces Pension Soc., 2006–13. Patron, Police Foundn, 2001–. Pres. and Patron, Lady Grover's Fund, 2003–. Chm. Trustees, Tank Mus., Bovington, 2002–10. Trustee, Salmon and Trout Assoc., 2012–. FRGS 2000. Liveryman, Painter-Stainers' Co. (Master, 2010–11). *Recreations:* fly-fishing, cricket, shooting, ornithology. *Clubs:* Army and Navy, Beefsteak.

WHEELER, Sara Diane, FRSL; writer; *b* 20 March 1961; *d* of John Wilfred Wheeler and Diane Pauline Wheeler (*née* Vernon, now Price); partner, Peter Graham; two *s.* *Educ:* Redland High Sch., Bristol; Brasenose Coll., Oxford (BA Hons). Hawthornden Fellow, 2010; Vis. Tutor, RHUL, 2014–15. Writer and presenter, BBC Radio 4 series, Captain Scott's Men, 2012. FRSL 1999 (Mem. Council, 2000–05). Trustee: London Liby, 2006–09 and 2014–; Sibs, 2010–. Contributing Ed., Literary Rev., 2009–. *Publications:* An Island Apart: travels in Evia, 1992; Travels in a Thin Country: a journey through Chile, 1994; Terra Incognita: travels in Antarctica, 1996; (ed jtly) Amazonian: the Penguin Book of women's new travel writing, 1998; Cherry: a biography of Apsley Cherry-Garrard, 2001; Too Close to the Sun: a biography of Denys Finch Hatton, 2006; The Magnetic North: notes from the Arctic Circle, 2009 (Best Adventure Travel Book, Banff Mountain Fest., 2011); Access All Areas: selected writings 1990–2010, 2011; O My America!: second acts in a new world, 2013. *Address:* c/o Aitken Alexander Associates, 291 Gray's Inn Road, WC1X 8EB. *E:* reception@aitkenalexander.co.uk. *Club:* Academy.

WHEELER, Stuart; *see* Wheeler, J. S.

WHEELER, Prof. Timothy Jerome; DL; PhD; CPsychol; Principal and Vice-Chancellor, University of Chester, since 2005; *b* 22 Oct. 1950; *s* of George Edward Wheeler and Mary Wheeler (*née* Carter); *m* 1975, Marilyn Sutton Jones; three *d.* *Educ:* Colwyn Bay Grammar Sch.; University Coll. of N Wales, Bangor (BA 1972; PhD 1977); Llandrillo Coll. (FE Teacher's Cert.). CPsychol 1988. Lectr, then Sen. Lectr, Sheffield Poly., 1974–80; Hd of Sch. and Dean of Faculty, Dublin City Univ., 1980–85; Hd, Sch. of Social Scis, Robert Gordon's Inst. of Technol., Aberdeen, 1985; Hd, Communication and Media, Dorset Inst., subseq. Bournemouth Poly., 1986–91; Southampton Institute: Dir, Envmt Sch., 1991–96; Dep. Dir, 1996–97; Dir, 1997–98; Principal, Chester Coll., subseq. UC Chester, 1998–2005. Vis. Prof., Communication Studies, Calif State Univ., Sacramento, 1982; Sen. Schol., St John's Coll., Oxford, 1988; Visiting Professor: Xiamen Univ. of Sci. and Technol., 2014–; Beijing Foreign Studies Univ., 2015–; Shanghai Jiao Tong Univ., 2015–. Dep. Chm., UCAS, 1999–2005. Chair: NW Universities Assoc., 2007–10; Univ. of Chester Academies Trust, 2011–. Chair, Cathedrals Gp (formerly Church Univs and Colls Gp), 2009–11. Member: LLSC Cheshire and Warrington, 2001–08; Cheshire & Warrington Econ. Alliance, 2001–11; Warrington Collegiate, 2002–10; Diocesan Bd of Educn, 2002–; NW Regl Assembly and Exec., 2006–08; NW Leaders' Forum, 2008–11; NW Skills and Employment Bd, 2008–10; Jt Econ. Commn for the NW, 2008–10; Cheshire and Warrington Local Enterprise Partnership, 2011–; Daresbury Educn Action Zone, 2011–; C of E Bd of Educn, 2011–; Pres., Warrington Chamber of Commerce, 2007–10, 2011–12. Governor: S Cheshire Coll., 2002–14; Priestley Coll., 2011–14; Univ. C of E Acad., Ellesmere Port, 2009–12. Lay Canon, 2003–, Mem. Chapter, 2004–14, Chester Cathedral. DL Cheshire, 2003. Member Editorial Boards: Dyslexia: an Internat. Jl of Res. and Practice, 1996–; Internat. Jl of Corporate Communications, 1997–. *Publications:* Handbook of Safety Management, 1989; contribs to scientific jls, chapters in books, reviews. *Recreations:* collector of antique oriental ceramics, keen interest in contemporary film, catholic tastes in music, active in a number of charities. *Address:* Senate House, University of Chester, Parkgate Road, Chester, Cheshire CH1 4BJ. *T:* (01244) 511000, *Fax:* (01244) 511308. *E:* t.wheeler@chester.ac.uk. *Clubs:* Chester Business; Chester City; Cheshire Pitt.

WHEELER, Prof. Timothy Robert, PhD; Professor of Crop Science, University of Reading, since 2008; Deputy Chief Scientific Adviser, Department for International Development, since 2010; *b* Overton, 8 Aug. 1963; *s* of Robert and Margaret Wheeler; partner, Ruth Smith; two *s* three *d.* *Educ:* Queen Mary's Coll., Basingstoke; Keele Univ. (BSc Biol. 1986); Reading Univ. (MSc Crop Physiol. 1987; PhD Agric. 1991). University of Reading: Res. Fellow, 1991–96; Lectr, 1996–2004; Reader, 2004–08. Specialist Advr, H of L, 2009–10. Mem. Council, BBSRC, 2012–. *Publications:* contribs to scientific pubns. *Recreations:* reading, running, surfing, vegetable growing, beekeeping. *Address:* Department of Agriculture, University of Reading, Reading RG6 6AR. *T:* (0118) 378 8495. *E:* t.r.wheeler@reading.ac.uk.

WHEELER-BOOTH, Sir Michael (Addison John), KCB 1994; Special Lecturer in Politics, Magdalen College, Oxford, 1998–2009; Clerk of the Parliaments, 1991–97; *b* 25 Feb. 1934; *s* of Addison James Wheeler and Mary Angela Wheeler-Booth (*née* Blakeney-Booth); *m* 1982, Emily Frances Smith; one *s* two *d.* *Educ:* Leighton Park Sch.; Magdalen Coll., Oxford (Exhibnr; MA; Hon. Fellow, 2003). Nat. Service, Midshipman (Sp.) RNVR, 1952–54. A Clerk, House of Lords, 1960–97; seconded to HM Treasury as Private Secretary to Leader of House and Government Chief Whip, 1965; seconded as Jt Sec., Inter-Party Conference on House of Lords Reform, 1967–69; Clerk of the Journals, 1970–74, 1983–90; Chief Clerk, Overseas and European Office, 1972, Principal Clerk, 1978; Reading Clerk, 1983; Clerk Asst, 1988. Treas. and Co-Ed. Jl, Soc. of Clerks at the Table in Commonwealth Parlts, 1962–65. Comr, Welsh Nat. Assembly Standing Orders, 1998–99. Chm., 1984–87, Pres., 2004–09, Study of Parliament Gp; Member: Royal Commn on H of L reform, 1999–2000; Fabian Commn on the Monarchy, 2002–03; Commn on Powers and Electoral Arrangements of Nat. Assembly for Wales, (Richard Commn), 2002–04; Chm., Ind. Review Panel on Salaries, Pensions and Allowances for Welsh Assembly Mems, 2007–08. Waynflete Lectr, 1998, Vis. Fellow, 1997–98, Magdalen Coll., Oxford. Trustee: History of Parliament Trust, 1991–97; Industry and Parliament Trust, 1994–97. Gov., Magdalen Coll. Sch., 2001–10 (Chm., F and GP Cttee, 2004–09). *Publications:* (contrib.) Griffith and Ryle, Parliament, 1989, 2nd edn 2003; (ed jtly) Halsbury's Laws of England on Parliament, 4th edn 1997; contribs to parly jls. *Recreations:* reading, ruins, pictures, opera, the countryside. *Address:* Northfields, Sandford St Martin, Chipping Norton, Oxon OX7 7AG. *T:* (01608) 683632. *E:* wbsmith@btinternet.com. *Clubs:* Brooks's, Garrick.

WHEELHOUSE, Keith Oliver B.; *see* Butler-Wheelhouse.

WHEELHOUSE, Paul; Member (SNP) Scotland South, Scottish Parliament, since 2011; Minister for Community Safety and Legal Affairs, since 2014; *b* Dundonald, NI, 22 June 1970; *m* 2002, Lorna; one *s.* *Educ:* Stewart's Melville Coll., Edinburgh; Univ. of Aberdeen (MA Econ. Sci. 1992); Univ. of Edinburgh (MBA 1999). Asst Economist, then Econ. Consultant, Pieda plc, 1992–98; Econ. Consultant, then Sen. Econ. Consultant, DTZ Pieda Consulting/DTZ Consulting & Research, 1998–2009; Sen. Consultant, BiGGAR Economics Ltd, 2009–10; Dir, Paul Wheelhouse Consultancy Ltd. Scottish Parliament: Minister for Envmt and Climate Change, 2012–14; Member: Finance Cttee, 2011–12; Standards, Procedures and Public Appts Cttee, 2011–12. *Address:* Scottish Parliament, Edinburgh EH99 1SP.

WHEEN, Francis James Baird; author and journalist; *b* 22 Jan. 1957; *s* of James Francis Thorneycroft Wheen and Patricia Winifred Wheen (*née* Ward); *m* 1985, Joan Alison Smith, *qv* (marr. diss. 1993); partner, Julia Jones; two *s.* *Educ:* Copthorne Sch.; Harrow; Royal Holloway Coll., London (BA 1978; Hon. Fellow, 2008). Office boy, The Guardian, 1974–75; reporter: New Statesman, 1978–84; Private Eye, 1987–; columnist: Independent, 1986–87; Independent on Sunday, 1990–91; Observer, 1993–95; Esquire, 1993–98; Guardian, 1994–2001; Evening Standard, 2006–07. Panellist, News Quiz, BBC Radio, 1989–. Columnist of Year, Granada/What the Papers Say awards, 1997. *Publications:* The Sixties, 1982; World View, 1982; The Battle for London, 1985; Television: a history, 1985; Tom Driberg: his life and indiscretions, 1990; (ed) The Chatto Book of Cats, 1993; (ed) Lord Gnome's Literary Companion, 1994; Karl Marx, 1999 (Isaac Deutscher Prize); Hoo-Hahs and Passing Frenzies, 2002 (George Orwell Prize); Who Was Dr Charlotte Bach?, 2002; How Mumbo-Jumbo Conquered the World, 2004; Marx's Das Kapital: a biography, 2006; Strange Days Indeed: the golden age of paranoia, 2009. *Recreation:* cricket. *Address:* Sokens, Green Street, Pleshey, Chelmsford, Essex CM3 1HT. *T:* (01245) 231566. *Clubs:* MCC; Essex CC, High Roding Cricket.

WHEEN, Natalie Kathleen; broadcaster, writer and lecturer on olive oil; Partner, AVLAKI Superb Organic Olive Oils, since 2007; *b* Shanghai, China, 29 July 1947; *d* of late Edward Leslie Lee Wheen and Galina (*née* Yourieff). *Educ:* Downe House, Newbury; London Univ. (BMus 1967); Royal Coll. of Music (ARCM). BBC, 1968–80: radio studio manager; attachments as Asst Producer, BBC TV Music and Arts, 1970; Radio 3 Music Producer, Manchester and London, 1971–72; Asst Producer, Music Now, Radio 3, 1972–73; Producer, Music Now, Talking About Music and various documentaries, 1973–80 (Best Music Documentary, Imperial Tobacco Soc. Authors Awards for Radio, 1978); London Arts Corresp., Canadian Broadcasting; freelance broadcaster, 1980–; Presenter: Kaleidoscope, Radio 4, 1980–95; Mainly for Pleasure, subseq. In Tune, Radio 3, 1980–97; Music Review, World Service; Cardiff Singer of the World, BBC2, 1993, 1995 and 1997; presenter, Classic FM: Week-end Afternoons, 1999–2008; Access All Areas, 2000–01; Tonight at 11, 2001–03; Natalie Wheen's Full Works Concert, week-ends, 2008–10; special programme series, 2010–; contributor: The Food Programme, R4; The Influence of Effluent, R4, 1998; Compère, Gramophone Awards, 1995 and 1996; interviews, Third Ear, etc; interviewer and co-producer: Tippett's Time, C4, 1995; Visions of Paradise Intervals, R3, 1995; documentaries on arts subjects; performance, Talking Dirty (one woman show), 2007–. Partner: Worsley Wheen prodns, 1983–88; ind. media prodn with Natalie Wheen & Associates. Contributing Editor, 3 mag., 1983–86. Jury Member: Sony Awards for Radio, 1994, 2003; Prudential Awards for the Arts, 1996; Masterprize, 2003; Kathleen Ferrier Scholarship, 2003; David Parkhouse Award, 2005. Director/Trustee: Hackney Music Develt Trust, 1995–2002; Creative Dance Artists Trust, 1995–96; Matthew Hawkins and the Fresh Dances Gp, 1995–97. Lectr and Workshop Leader in presentation and communication skills; Consultant, GSMD, 1991–92; Presenter, British Airways In-flight Light Classics Channel, 1991–95. Mem. Council, ENO Works, 1996–98. Governor, Downe House Sch., 1986–98. Contributor: www.theartsdesk.com, 2010–; Dancing Times. *Publications:* (jtly) A Life on the Fiddle: Max Jaffa's Autobiography, 1991; publications on trng and employment for Careers and Occupational Information Centre, and Dept of Employment; contribs to Spectator, Independent (Travel), Classic FM mag., Opera Now. *Recreations:* olives, fishing, laughter, anarchy. *Address:* c/o Arlington Enterprises Ltd, 1–3 Charlotte Street, W1T 1RD.

WHELAN, Michael George; Director, Whelan Associates Ltd, 2006–11; *b* 13 Oct. 1947; *s* of George Henry Whelan and Vera Frances Whelan (*née* Davies); *m* 1st, 1968, Veronica Gemma Merron (marr. diss. 1986); one *s* one *d*; 2nd, 1987, Anne Vivien Williams, JP; one *s.* *Educ:* Univ. of London (BSc(Econ) Hons, MSc(Econ)). Operational Manager, Walton Hosp., Liverpool, then Good Hope Hosp., Sutton Coldfield, and Hope Hosp., Salford, 1964–72; Tutor in Management, and Principal Trng Officer, N Western RHA, 1972–74; Deputy Chief Officer: Tameside and Glossop HA, 1974–78; Surrey AHA, 1978–80; Chief Officer, SW Surrey HA, 1980–85; Gp Manager, Healthcare, KPMG Management Consultants, 1985–90; Partner, Pannell Kerr Forster, 1990–92; Chief Exec., Parkinson's Disease Soc., 1992–94; healthcare business consultant, 1994–97; Principal, Watson Wyatt Actuaries and Consultants, 1997–98; Chief Exec., Thomson, Snell & Passmore, Solicitors, 1998–2000; Practice Dir, T. V. Edwards (Solicitors), 2000–02; healthcare mgt consultant, 2002–03; Project Dir, Surrey and Sussex SHA, 2003–05; Registrar, Faculty of Dental Surgery, RCS, 2005; Chief Exec., Inst. of Optometry, 2007; Operational Manager (Medicine), Portsmouth NHS Trust, 2007–08. AIPM 1975; FHSM 1980. *Recreations:* music, entertaining, family, gardening, literature. *Address:* Chambord, 46 Pewley Way, Guildford, Surrey GU1 3QA.

WHELAN, Prof. Michael John, MA, PhD, DPhil; FRS 1976; FInstP; Professor of Microscopy of Materials, Department of Materials, University of Oxford, 1992–97, now Emeritus Professor; Fellow of Linacre College, Oxford, since 1967; *b* 2 Nov. 1931; *s* of William Whelan and Ellen Whelan (*née* Pound). *Educ:* Farnborough Grammar Sch.; Gonville and Caius Coll., Cambridge. FInstP 1976. Fellow of Gonville and Caius Coll., 1958–66; Demonstrator in Physics, Univ. of Cambridge, 1961–65; Asst Dir of Research in Physics,

Univ. of Cambridge, 1965–66; Reader, Dept of Materials, Univ. of Oxford, 1966–92. Hon. Prof., Univ. of Sci. and Technol. Beijing, China, 1995. Hon. FRMS 2001; Hon. Fellow: Japanese Soc. of Microscopy, 2003; Microscopy Soc. of Amer., 2009. C. V. Boys Prize, Inst. of Physics, 1965; Hughes Medal, Royal Soc., 1988; Distinguished Scientist Award, Microscopy Soc. of Amer., 1998; Gjønnes Medal, Internat. Union of Crystallography, 2012. *Publications:* (jtly) Electron Microscopy of Thin Crystals, 1965; Worked Examples in Dislocations, 1990; (jtly) High-Energy Electron Diffraction and Microscopy, 2004; numerous papers in learned jls. *Recreation:* gardening. *Address:* 18 Salford Road, Old Marston, Oxford OX3 0RX. *T:* (01865) 244556.

WHELAN, Prof. William Joseph, PhD, DSc; FRS 1992; Professor of Biochemistry and Molecular Biology, University of Miami Miller School of Medicine (formerly University of Miami School of Medicine), since 1967 (Chairman of Department, 1967–91); *b* 14 Nov. 1924; *s* of William Joseph Whelan and Jane Antoinette Whelan (*née* Bertram); *m* 1st, 1951, Margaret Miller Birnie (*d* 1993); 2nd, 2009, Alina Akin. *Educ:* Univ. of Birmingham, England (BSc Hons 1944; PhD 1948; DSc 1955). Asst Lectr, Univ. of Birmingham, 1947–48; Asst Lectr, Lectr and Sen. Lectr, UCNW, Bangor, 1948–55; Sen. Mem., Lister Inst. of Preventive Medicine, Univ. of London, 1956–64; Prof. and Head, Dept of Biochemistry, Royal Free Hosp. Sch. of Medicine, Univ. of London, 1964–67. Sec. Gen., FEBS, 1965–67. Co-Dir, Miami Winter Symposia, 1968–. Dir, Enterprise Florida Technol. Develt Bd (formerly Enterprise Florida Innovation Partnership), 1993–98. President: Portland Press Inc., 1994–98; Frontiers of Knowledge Inc., 1999–2003. Gen. Sec., 1978–83, Pres., 1997–2000, Internat. Union of Biochemistry and Molecular Biol. (formerly Internat. Union of Biochemistry). FAAAS 1989. Hon. MRCP 1985; Hon. Mem., Biochemical Soc., 1993. Hon. DSc La Trobe, 1997. Alsberg Medal, 1967; Ciba Medal, 1968; Saare Medal, 1979; FEBS Millennium Medal, 2000. Editor-in-Chief: Trends in Biochemical Sciences, 1975–78; BioEssays, 1984–89; Fedn Procs, 1986–87; FASEB Jl, 1987–96; IUBMB Life, 2000–. *Recreations:* publishing, travel. *Address:* Department of Biochemistry and Molecular Biology, University of Miami Miller School of Medicine, PO Box 016129, Miami, FL 33101–6129, USA. *T:* (305) 3738039. *E:* wwhelan@miami.edu. *Club:* Athenæum.

WHELER, Sir Trevor (Woodford), 15th Bt *cr* 1660, of City of Westminster; *b* 11 April 1946; *s* of Sir Edward Woodford Wheler, 14th Bt, and Molly Ashworth, *e d* of Thomas Lever, Devon; *S* father, 2008; *m* 1974, Rosalie Margaret, *d* of late Ronald Thomas Stunt; two *s*. *Educ:* St Edmund's Sch., Canterbury; St Mary's Sch., Nairobi. Air Traffic Control, RAF, 1966–71, CAA, 1971–2006. *Heir:* *s* Edward William Wheler [*b* 14 June 1976; *m* 2004, Monika Polešáková; one *s* one *d*]. *Address:* 83 Middle Park, Inverurie, Aberdeenshire AB51 4QW. *T:* (01467) 622642. *E:* trevor.wheler@sky.com.

WHELON, (Charles) Patrick (Clavell); a Recorder of the Crown Court, 1978–97; *b* 18 Jan. 1930; *s* of Charles Eric Whelon and Margaret Whelon; *m* 1968, Prudence Mary (*née* Potter); one *s* one *d*. *Educ:* Wellington Coll.; Pembroke Coll., Cambridge (MA Hons). Called to Bar, Middle Temple, 1954. Liveryman of Vintners' Co., 1952–. *Recreations:* gardening, cartooning. *Address:* Russets, Pyott's Hill, Old Basing, Hants RG24 8AP. *T:* (01256) 469964.

WHELTON, David William, OBE 2015; pianist, organist, music administrator; Managing Director, Philharmonia Orchestra, since 1988; *b* 16 June 1954; *s* of William and Nora Whelton; *m* 1977, Caroline Rachel Gardner; one *s*. Mem. of Staff, GSMD, 1978–83; Dir of Music, Royal GS, Guildford, 1979–83; Music Officer, Yorks Arts Assoc., 1983–85; Principal Arts Officer, Leeds CC, 1985–86; Music Officer, Arts Council of GB, 1986–88. Director: Assoc. of British Orchestras, 1997–; Internat. Musicians Seminar, Prussia Cove, 1998–. Chm., Leeds Conductors' Comp., 2005, 2009; Member Jury: Besançon Conductors Comp., 2001; Windsor Fest. Internat. String Comp., 2008, 2009, 2012, 2013, 2014, 2015; Sheepdrove Piano Comp., 2009, 2011, 2012, 2013, 2014; Svetlanov Internat. Conductors Comp., 2014. Mem., Adv. Bd, Chateauville Foundn, 2012–. Trustee: Mayfield Valley Arts Trust, 1986–; Philharmonia Trust, 1988–. Pres., Amer. Friends of Philharmonia Orch., 2008–. Hon. Vice Pres., Ernst Bloch Soc., 2008–. Trustee: Richard Hickox Foundn, 2009–14; Hattori Foundn, 2011–. Hon. RCM 2013; FRSA. Freeman, City of London, 2005; Mem., Musicians' Co. *Recreations:* gardening, architecture, history. *Address:* Philharmonia Orchestra, 6 Chancel Street, SE1 0UX. *T:* (020) 7921 3916. *Club:* Garrick.

WHETNALL, Andrew Donard, CB 1996; Director for Local Government, Office of the Deputy Prime Minister (formerly Department of the Environment, Transport and the Regions, then Department for Transport, Local Government and the Regions), 1996–2003; *b* 18 May 1948; *s* of late Donard and of Joan Whetnall (*née* Mummery); *m* 1972, Jane Lepel Glass; two *s* two *d*. *Educ:* King's Norton Grammar Sch.; Univ. of Sussex (MA). Joined DoE, 1975; Principal, Dept of Transport, 1980–83; Department of the Environment: Principal, 1983–87, Asst Sec., 1987–88, Inner Cities; Water Legislation, 1988–89; Head, Machinery of Govt Div., Cabinet Office, 1989–96 (Under Sec., 1993). Lay Mem., Information Rights Tribunal, 2005–. *Recreations:* reading, music.

WHETSTONE, Rear-Adm. Anthony John, CB 1982; Chairman, Bridgeworks Trust, 1999–2004; *b* 12 June 1927; *s* of Albert and Anne Whetstone; *m* 1951, Elizabeth Stewart Georgeson; one *s* two *d*. *Educ:* King Henry VIII School, Coventry. Joined RN, 1945; specialised in submarines, 1949; Commanded: HMS Sea Scout, 1956–57; HMS Artful, 1959–61; HMS Repulse, 1968–70; HMS Juno, 1972–73; HMS Norfolk, 1977–78; Flag Officer Sea Training, 1978–80; Asst Chief of Naval Staff (Operations), 1981–83. Director-General: Cable TV Assoc., 1983–86; Nat. Television Rental Assoc., 1983–87. Dep. Sec., Defence Press and Broadcasting Cttee, 1987–92. Dir, DESC Ltd, 1991–96. Mem., Adv. Cttee on Historic Wreck Sites, 1996–2002. Nat. Pres., Submariners Assoc., 1988–2002. Chm. Trustees, Royal Navy Submarine Mus., 1990–98. FCMI (FBIM 1979). *Recreations:* fishing, gardening, theatre (Chm., Civil Service Drama Fedn, 1985–92), music. *Address:* 17 Alverstoke Court, Alverstoke, Hants PO12 2LX. *Club:* Civil Service.

WHETSTONE, Rachel Marjorie Joan; Senior Vice President, Policy and Strategy, Uber, since 2015; *b* London, 22 Feb. 1968; *d* of Francis Whetstone and Linda Whetstone; *m* 2008, Steve Hilton; two *s*. *Educ:* Benenden Sch.; Univ. of Bristol (BA Hist.). Conservative Res. Dept, Conservative Central Office, 1990–94; One2one, Public Affairs, 1994–96; Special Advr to the Home Sec., 1994–97; Carlton Communications plc, 1996–2001; Political Sec. to Leader of the Opposition, 2003–05; Google Inc.: Dir, Communications, EMEA, 2005–08; Vice Pres., Global Communications, 2008–09; Vice Pres., 2009–11, Sen. Vice Pres., 2011–15, Global Communications and Policy. *Recreations:* gardening, riding, family, travel. *Address:* Tuscaloosa Avenue, Atherton, CA 94027, USA.

WHEWAY, (Jonathan) Scott; Independent non-executive Director, Aviva plc, since 2007 (Chairman, Aviva Insurance Ltd, since 2015); Senior Independent Director, Santander UK plc, since 2013; *b* Sheffield, 26 Aug. 1966; *s* of Barry and Cynthia Wheway; *m* 2000, Amanda Smith; one *s* one *d*. *Educ:* Rowlinson Sch., Sheffield. With Tesco plc, 1984–2003: Stores Dir, 1995–2000; Ops Dir, 2000–03; CEO, Japan, 2003; Man. Dir and Retail Dir, Boots the Chemist, 2003–07; CEO, Best Buy Europe, 2009–11. Dir, British Retail Consortium, 2006–07. *Recreations:* mountains, cricket, technology, growing fruit, mending tractors. *Club:* Lansdowne.

WHINNEY, Rt Rev. Michael Humphrey Dickens; an Hon. Assistant Bishop, Diocese of Birmingham, since 1996 (Assistant Bishop, 1988–95); Canon Residentiary, Birmingham Cathedral, 1992–95; *b* 8 July 1930; *s* of late Humphrey Charles Dickens Whinney and Evelyn Lawrence Revell Whinney (*née* Low); great-great-grandson of Charles Dickens; *m* 1958, Veronica (*née* Webster); two *s* one *d*. *Educ:* Charterhouse; Pembroke Coll., Cambridge (BA 1955, MA 1958); Ridley Hall, Cambridge; General Theological Seminary, NY (STM 1990). National Service commission, RA, 1949 (served in 5th Regt, RHA and Surrey Yeo. Queen Mary's Regt). Articled clerk to Chartered Accountants, Whinney Smith & Whinney (now Ernst Young), 1950–52. Curate, Rainham Parish Church, Essex, 1957–60; Head, Cambridge University Mission Settlement, Bermondsey, 1960–67, Chaplain, 1967–72; Vicar, St James' with Christ Church, Bermondsey, 1967–73; Archdeacon and Borough Dean of Southwark, 1973–82; Bishop Suffragan of Aston, 1982–85; Bishop of Southwell, 1985–88. Archbishop's Episcopal Commissary for Birmingham, 2005–06. Pres., Birmingham and Midland Inst., 2012–13; Vice President: Dickens Fellowship, 1986–; Lee Abbey Fellowship, 2001–. *Publications:* Episcope Today and Tomorrow, 1989; Type in the Churches, 2004; Who are the Anglican Bishops?, 2011; Green Shoots through the Concrete, 2011; Rainbows through the Rain, 2014. *Address:* Moorcroft, 3 Moor Green Lane, Moseley, Birmingham B13 8NE.

WHIPPLE, Hon. Dame Philippa Jane Edwards, DBE 2015; **Hon. Mrs Justice Whipple;** a Judge of the High Court of Justice, Queen's Bench Division, since 2015; *b* 7 May 1966; *d* of John Braham Scott Edwards and Veronica Mary Edwards; *m* 1992, Sam Whipple; three *s*. *Educ:* St Mary's Sch., Ascot; Merton Coll., Oxford (MA). Admitted solicitor, 1991; Solicitor, Freshfields, 1989–93; called to the Bar, Middle Temple, 1994, Bencher, 2012; in practice as barrister, specialising in tax, medical and admin. law, 1994–2015; a Recorder, 2007–15; QC 2010. *Address:* Royal Courts of Justice, Strand, WC2A 2LL.

WHISH, Prof. Richard Peter; Professor of Law, King's College London, 1991–2013, now Emeritus; *b* 23 March 1953; *s* of Thomas Stanton Whish and Avis Mary Whish (*née* Sullivan). *Educ:* Clifton Coll., Bristol; Worcester Coll., Oxford (BA 1st Cl. Hons 1974; BCL 1st Cl. Hons 1978). Qualified as solicitor, 1977; University of Bristol: Lectr in Law, 1978–88; Reader in Commercial Law, 1988–90; Partner, Watson, Farley and Williams (Solicitors), London, 1989–98. Mem., Exec. Council, Centre for European Law, KCL, 1991–. Chm., Adv. Body to Dir Gen. of Gas and Electricity Mgt, 2000–01. Member: Adv. Cttee, Centre for Study of Regulated Industries, 1991–2009; Adv. Panel, Dir Gen. of Fair Trading, 2001–03; non-executive Director: OFT, 2003–09; Energy Mkts Authy of Singapore, 2005–11. Member: Editl Bd, European Business Law Review, 1994–; Adv. Bd, Competition Law Jl, 2002–. FRSA 1995. Hon. QC 2014. *Publications:* (jtly) Conveyancing Solutions, 1987; (Gen. Ed.) Butterworth's Competition Law, 1991; Competition Law, 3rd edn 1993 to 7th edn 2012; (jtly) Merger Cases in the Real World: a study of merger control procedures, 1994; (ed) Halsbury's Laws of England, Vol. 47, 4th edn 1994; The Competition Act, 1998; numerous articles, case-notes and book reviews in legal periodicals and books. *Recreations:* opera and music, travelling (in particular in the sub-continent), gardening, conservation, Bristol Rovers FC. *Address:* 14 Glebe House, 15 Fitzroy Mews, W1T 6DP. *E:* richard.whish@kcl.ac.uk. *Club:* Groucho.

WHISHAW, Anthony Popham Law, RA 1989 (ARA 1980); RWA; *b* 22 May 1930; *s* of Robert Whishaw and Joyce (*née* Wheeler); *m* 1957, Jean Gibson; two *d*. *Educ:* Tonbridge Sch. (Higher Cert.); Chelsea Sch. of Art; Royal College of Art (ARCA 1955). Travelling Schol., RCA; Abbey Minor Schol.; Spanish Govt Schol.; Abbey Premier Schol., 1982; Lorne Schol., 1982–83. RWA 1992, Hon. RWA 2003. John Moores Minor Painting Prize, 1982; (jtly) 1st Prize, Hunting Group Art Awards, 1986. *One-man exhibitions:* Librería Abril, Madrid, 1956; Rowland Browse and Delbranco, London, 1960, 1961, 1963, 1965, 1968; ICA, 1971; New Art Centre, 1972; Folkestone Arts Centre, 1973; Hoya Gall., London, 1974; Oxford Gall., Oxford, 1974; ACME, London, 1978, 2010; Newcastle upon Tyne Polytech. Gall., 1979; (with Martin Froy) New Ashgate Gall., Farnham, 1979; Nicola Jacobs Gall., London 1981; From Landscape, Kettle's Yard, Cambridge, Ferens Gall., Hull, Bede Gall., Jarrow, 1982–84; Works on Paper, Nicola Jacobs Gall., 1983; Paintings, Nicola Jacobs Gall., 1984; Mappin Art Gall., Sheffield, 1985; Large Paintings, RA 1986; Reflections after Las Meninas (touring): Royal Acad., and Hatton Gall., Newcastle upon Tyne, 1987; Mead Gall., Warwick Univ., John Hansard Gall., Southampton Univ., and Spacex Gall., Exeter, 1988; Infaust Gall., Shanghai and Hamburg, 1989; Blason Gall., London, 1991; artspace, London, 1992, 1994 and 1995; RWA Bristol, 1993; Barbican, 1994 and tour, Mappin Gall., Sheffield, Royal Albert Meml Mus., Exeter, 1994, Newport Mus. and Art Gall., Bolton Metropolitan Mus. and Art Gall., 1995; Maclaurin Gall., Ayr, Huddersfield Gall., Royal Hibernian Acad. of Arts, Gallagher Gall., Dublin, Hatton Gall., Newcastle, 1994; Art First, London, 1997; Friends' Room, Royal Acad., 2000; Stephen Lacey Gall., London, 2000; Osborne Samuel Gall., London, 2007; Tate Britain, 2010; Kings Place Gall., London, 2010; Fine Art Soc., London, 2010. *Group exhibitions:* Gimpel Fils, AIA Gall., Café Royal Centen., Towards Art (RCA), Camden Arts Centre, London, Ashmolean Mus., Oxford, 1957–72; Brit. Drawing Biennale, Teesside, 1973; British Landscape, Graves Art Gall., Sheffield, Chichester Nat. Art, 1975; Summer Exhibn, RA, 1974–2014; British Painting, 1952–77, RA, 1977; London Group, Whitechapel Open, 1978, A Free Hand, Arts Council (touring show), 1978; The British Art Show, Arts Council (touring), Recent Arts Council Purchases and Awards, Serpentine Gall., First Exhibition, Nicola Jacobs Gall., Tolly Cobbold (touring), 55 Wapping Artists, London, 1979; Four Artists, Nicola Jacobs Gall., Sculpture and Works on Paper, Nicola Jacobs, Wapping Open Studios, Hayward Annual, Hayward Gall., Whitechapel Open, Whitechapel Gall., John Moore's Liverpool Exhibn 12, 1980, Exhibn 13, 1982, Walker Art Gall., Liverpool; London Gp, S London Art Gall., Wapping Artists, 1981; Images for Today, Graves Art Gall., Sheffield, 1982; Nine Artists (touring), Helsinki, 1983; Tolly Cobbold/Eastern Arts Fourth (touring), 1983; Three Decades 1953–83, RA, 1983; Romantic Tradition in Contemporary British Painting (touring), Murcia and Madrid, Spain, and Ikon Gall., Birmingham, 1988; Cello Factory, London, 2010; RWA, Bristol, 2010; Richmond Hill Gall., London, 2010; St Paul's Crypt, London, 2010; Visual Centre for Contemporary Art, Carlow, Ireland, 2010. *Works in collections:* Arts Council of GB, Tate Gall., Coventry Art Gall., Leicester Art Gall., Nat. Gall. of Wales, Sheffield City Art Galls, Financial Times, Shell-BP, Museo de Bahia, Brazil, Nat. Gall. of Victoria, Melb., Seattle Mus. of Art, Bank of Boston, Chantrey Bequest, W Australia Art Gall., Bayer Pharmaceuticals, DoE, Nat. Westminster Bank, Power Art Gall., Aust. European Parlt, Ferens Art Gall., Museum, Murcia, Spain, Alliance & Leicester, Rosehaven PLC, Royal Academy, Linklater and Paines, Mus. of Contemp. Art, Helsinki, Christchurch, Kensington, Long Term Credit Bank of Japan, Andersen Consulting, Ashikaga Bank of Tokyo, Tetrapak, Zeneca, RWA, Deutsche Morgan-Grenfell, Mercury Asset Mgt, Ladbrokes, Crown Commodities, Stanhope, Baring Asset Mgt, St Anne's Coll., Oxford. *Recreations:* chess, badminton. *Address:* 7a Albert Place, Victoria Road, W8 5PD. *T:* (020) 7937 5197. *W:* www.anthonywhishaw.com.

WHISTON, John Joseph; Managing Director, Continuing Drama (formerly Creative Director, Soaps), ITV Studios, since 2011; *b* 10 Oct. 1958; *s* of Peter Rice Whiston and Kathleen Whiston (*née* Parker); partner, Nickie Lister; one *s* two *d*. *Educ:* Edinburgh Acad.; Balliol Coll., Oxford (BA Eng.). Follow spot operator, for Rowan Atkinson, 1982; joined BBC, 1982: gen. trainee, 1983–85; Producer, Music and Arts, 1985–94; Head: Youth and Entertainment Features, 1994–96; Entertainment and Features, 1996–98; Director of Programmes: Yorkshire Tyne Tees Prodns, 1998–2001; Granada Content (North), 2001–02; Dir, Drama, Children's, Arts and Features, Granada Content, subseq. Drama, Kids and Arts, Granada, 2002–05; Dir, ITV Prodns, 2005–09; Dir, ITV Studios, 2009–11. Motoring corresp., Vogue, 1991–93. *Recreations:* power tools, sailing dinghies. *Address:* Ashcliffe, Tighnabruaich, Argyll PA21 2EJ. *T:* (01700) 811799.

WHITAKER, family name of **Baroness Whitaker**.

WHITAKER, Baroness *cr* 1999 (Life Peer), of Beeston in the county of Nottinghamshire; **Janet Alison Whitaker;** Deputy Chair, Independent Television Commission, 2001–03; *b* 20 Feb. 1936; *d* of late Alan Harrison Stewart and Ella Stewart (*née* Saunders); *m* 1964, Benjamin Charles George Whitaker, CBE (*d* 2014); two *s* one *d*. *Educ:* Nottingham High Sch. for Girls; Girton Coll., Cambridge (Major Scholar); Bryn Mawr Coll., USA (Farley Graduate Fellow); Harvard Univ. (Radcliffe Fellow). Teacher, Lycée Français de Londres, 1958–59; Editor, André Deutsch Ltd, 1961–66; Health and Safety Executive, 1974–88: Hd of Gas Safety, 1983–86; Hd of Nuclear Safety Admin, 1986–88; Department of Employment: Hd of Health and Safety Br., 1988–92; Hd of Sex Equality Div., 1992–96; Leader, UK delegn to Fourth UN Conf. on Women, 1995. Chair, Working Men's Coll. for Men and Women Corp., 1998–2001 (Fellow, 2010). Member: Sub Cttee on Social Affairs, Educn and Home Affairs, EU Select Cttee, H of L, 1999–2002; Jt Parly Cttee on Human Rights, 2000–03; Jt Parly Cttee on Corruption Bill, 2003; Jt Parly Cttee on Draft Bribery Bill, 2009; Vice-Chair, All-Party Groups: on Ethiopia, 2003–09; on Overseas Develt, 2005–; on Landmine Eradication, 2005–07; on Gypsy and Traveller Law Reform, 2006–; Vice-Chair: PLP Civil Rights Cttee, 2002–05; PLP Internat. Develt Cttee, 2003–10. Co-Chair, Design in Public Procurement Inquiry, 2009; Vice Chair, Associate Parly Gp on Design and Innovation, 2011–. Member: OECD Wkg Pty on Rôle of Women in the Economy, 1992–96; Employment Tribunals, 1996–2000; ACORD Gender Cttee, 1996–2002; SOS Sahel Mgt Cttee, 1997–2004 (Council, 2004–); Immigration Audit Complaints Cttee, 1998–99; Bd and Trustee, Overseas Develt Inst., 2003–09; Chm., DFE Stakeholder Gp for Gypsy, Traveller and Roma Educn, 2013–; Pres., Friends, Families and Travellers, 2013–. Chair, Camden Racial Equality Council, 1999. Assessor, Citizen's Charter Chartermark Unit, 1996. Dir, Tavistock & Portman NHS Trust, 1997–2001. Member: Friends Provident Cttee of Reference, 2000–08; Adv. Council, Transparency Internat. (UK), 2001–10; Adv. Council, British Inst. of Human Rights, 2005–; Council, African and W Eur. Parly Assoc., 2005–08; UNA-UK Adv. Panel, 2006–; Design Commn, 2011–. Patron: Runnymede Trust, 1997–; British Stammering Assoc., 2003–; Student Partnerships Worldwide, 2005–; Hillcrest Community Centre, Newhaven, 2015–. Trustee: One World Trust, 2000–04 (Vice-Pres., 2004–); UNICEF UK, 2003–09. President: S Downs Soc., 2012–; Adv. Council for Educn of Romany and other Travellers, 2014–. Member: Fabian Soc., 1970; British Humanist Assoc., 1970 (Vice-Pres., then Patron, 2004–). FRSA 1993–2014. Hon. FRIBA 2013. *Recreation:* travelling hopefully. *Address:* House of Lords, SW1A 0PW. *Club:* Reform.

WHITAKER, Claire Lois, OBE 2015; Director: Serious, international music producers, since 1996; London International Jazz Festival, since 1996; Arts Programme Advisor, Paul Hamlyn Foundation, 2009–15; *b* Heswall, Cheshire, 1 Dec. 1963; *d* of Raymond Spinks and Anne Flight; *m* 1989, Simon Whitaker; one *s* one *d*. *Educ:* City Univ. (MA Cultural Leadership 2009). Lending Officer, Natwest Corp. Banking Unit, 1982–89; Business Affairs Exec., Decca Records, 1989–90; Develt Dir, Southbank Centre, 1990–92; Dir, Africa 95, 1992–96. Advr, African Odyssey, Kennedy Center, 1997–2001; Representative: DCMS Live Music Forum, 2004–07; DCMS Music Export Gp, 2008–; Mem. Adv. Bd, Sing Up, 2007–. Chair, Steering Gp, ArtWorks, 2010–15. Trustee, Caine Prize for African Writing, 1999–; Founder Judge, Young Marketeer of the Year, 1999, Fellow, 2010, Marketing Soc. Chm., Royal Commonwealth Soc., 2014– (Dep. Chm., 2007–13). *Recreations:* playing piano and flute, singing, ski-ing, reading. *Address:* Serious, 51 Kingsway Place, Sans Walk, Clerkenwell, EC1R 0LU. *T:* (020) 7324 1880, *Fax:* (020) 7324 1881. *E:* claire@serious.org.uk.

WHITAKER, David Haddon, OBE 1991; Chairman, J. Whitaker & Sons, Ltd, 1982–97 (Director, 1966–97; Editorial Director, 1980–91); *b* 6 March 1931; *s* of late Edgar Haddon Whitaker, OBE and of Mollie Marian, *y d* of George and Louisa Seely; *m* 1st, 1959, Veronica Wallace (decd); two *s* two *d*; 2nd, 1976, Audrey Miller (marr. diss. 1979); 3rd, 1994, Marguerite van Reenen. *Educ:* Boscastle Infants' Sch.; Marlborough Coll.; St John's Coll., Cambridge. Joined family firm of publishers, J. Whitaker & Sons, Ltd, 1955; Dir, 1966; Editor, The Bookseller, 1977–79. Member: Adv. Panel, Internat. Standard Book Numbering Agency (Berlin), 1979–97 (Chm., 1990–97); Adv. Panel, Registrar for Public Lending Right, 1983–93 (Chm., 1989–93); Standing Cttee on Technology, Booksellers' Assoc., 1984–89; Library and Information Services Council, 1985–89; Chairman: Information and Library Services Lead Body for Nat. Vocational Qualifications, 1992–95; British Nat. Bibliography Res. Fund, 1992–2001. Chairman: Soc. of Bookmen, 1984–86; Book Trade Electronic Data Interchange Standards Cttee, 1987–90. Trustee, 2002–07, Chm., 2005–07, Laser Foundn. Hon. Vice-Pres., LA, 1990. Hon. Fellow, Amer. Nat. Inst. of Standards Orgns, 1997. *Recreations:* reading, walking. *Address:* 4 Ufton Grove, N1 4HG. *T:* (020) 7241 3501. *Clubs:* Beefsteak, Garrick, Thames Rowing; Leander (Henley-on-Thames); Boscastle and Crackington Haven Gig.

WHITAKER, (Edwin) John, MBE 1991; show-jumper; *b* 5 Aug. 1955; *er s* of Donald Whitaker and Enid (*née* Lockwood); *m* 1979, Claire Barr; one *s* two *d*. British champion, 1992, 1993; other European championship wins: team and individual silver medals, 1983 (Ryan's Son); team gold and individual bronze, 1985 (Hopscotch); team gold and individual silver, 1987 (Milton); individual and team gold, 1989 (Milton); team bronze, 2007 (Peppermill), 2011 (Peppermill). World Cup gold medals, 1990, 1991 (Milton); Olympic individual and team silver medals, 1980, and team silver medal, 1984 (Ryan's Son); jumping Derby, 1983 (Ryan's Son), 1998 (Gammon), 2000 (Virtual Village Welham); King George V Gold Cup, 1986 (Ryan's Son), 1990 (Milton), 1997 (Virtual Village Welham); Aachen Grand Prix, 1997 (Virtual Village Welham); Rome Grand Prix, 2007 (Peppermill); Alltech Grand Prix, 2010 (Uniek). Leading Jumper of the Year, Horse of the Year Show, 1993, 1998; numerous other wins and awards. Dir, John Whitaker Internat. Ltd, 1998–. *Address:* c/o British Show Jumping Association, Stoneleigh, Warwicks CV8 2LR.

See also M. Whitaker.

WHITAKER, Sir John James Ingham, (Sir Jack), 4th Bt *cr* 1936, of Babworth, Nottinghamshire; farmer; *b* 23 Oct. 1952; *o s* of Sir James Herbert Ingham Whitaker, 3rd Bt, OBE and Mary Elisabeth Lander Whitaker (*née* Johnston); *S* father, 1999; *m* 1981, Elizabeth Jane Ravenscroft Starke; one *s* three *d*. *Educ:* Eton; Bristol Univ. (BSc). FCA; MIET. Pres., Royal Forestry Soc., 2013–15 (Treas., 1993–2008). High Sheriff, Notts, 2001. *Heir: s* Harry James Ingham Whitaker, *b* 16 March 1984. *Address:* Babworth Hall, Retford, Notts DN22 8EP.

WHITAKER, Michael; show-jumper; *b* 17 March 1960; *yr s* of Donald Whitaker and Enid (*née* Lockwood); *m* 1980, Veronique Dalems, *d* of Dino Vastapane (marr. diss.); *m* 2013, Melissa Braybrooke; one *s* two *d*. British champion, 1984, 1989; other European championship wins: Junior, 1978; team gold medal, 1985 (Warren Point); team gold, 1987 (Amanda); team gold and individual silver, 1989 (Monsanta); team silver and individual silver, 1995; team bronze, 1997; team gold (Viking), 2013; Olympic silver medal, 1984 (Amanda); Jumping Derby: 1980 (Owen Gregory); 1991 and 1992 (Monsanta); 1993 (My Messieur); King George V Gold Cup: 1982 (Disney Way); 1989 (Didi); 1992, 1994 (Midnight Madness); bareback high jump record, Dublin, 1980. *Address:* c/o British Show Jumping Association, Stoneleigh, Warwicks CV8 2LR.

See also E. J. Whitaker.

WHITAKER, Steven Dixon; Senior Master of the Senior Courts (formerly Supreme Court), Queen's Bench Division, and Queen's Remembrancer, 2007–14; *b* 28 Jan. 1950; *s* of George and Elsie Whitaker; *m* Tereska Anita Christiana Stawarz; one *s* one *d*. *Educ:* Burnley Grammar Sch.; Churchill Coll., Cambridge (MA). Called to the Bar, Middle Temple, 1973, Bencher, 2010–14; in practice as a barrister, specialising in property and professional negligence law, 1973–2002; Dep. Dist Judge, 1998–2002; Master of Supreme Court, QBD, 2002–07. Mem., Civil Procedure Rules Cttee, 2002–08. Liveryman, Glaziers' and Painters of Glass Co., 2008. Chief Consultant Editor, Atkin's Court Forms, 2008–14; Jt Gen. Editor, Civil Procedure (the White Book), 2011–14. *Recreations:* horses, music, poetry.

WHITAKER, Thomas Kenneth; Chancellor, National University of Ireland, 1976–96; Member, Council of State, Ireland, 1991–97; Chairman, Constitution Review Group, 1995–96; President, Royal Irish Academy, 1985–87; *b* 8 Dec. 1916; *s* of Edward Whitaker and Jane O'Connor; *m* 1st, 1941, Nora Fogarty (*d* 1994); five *s* one *d*; 2nd, 2005, Mary Moore. *Educ:* Christian Brothers' Sch., Drogheda; London Univ. (External Student; BScEcon, MScEcon). Irish CS, 1934–69 (Sec., Dept of Finance, 1956–69); Governor, Central Bank of Ireland, 1969–76; Dir, Bank of Ireland, 1976–85. Dir, Arthur Guinness Son & Co. Ltd, 1976–84. Chairman: Bord na Gaeilge, 1975–78; Agency for Personal Service Overseas, 1973–78; Mem., Seanad Éireann, 1977–82. Jt Chm., Anglo-Irish Encounter, 1983–89. Former Pres., Econ. and Social Res. Inst.; Chm. Council, Dublin Inst. for Advanced Studies. Freeman of Drogheda, 1999. Hon. DEconSc National Univ. of Ireland, 1962; Hon. LLD: Univ. of Dublin, 1976; Queen's Univ. of Belfast, 1980; Hon. DSc NUU, 1984; Hon. PhD Dublin City Univ., 1995. Commandeur de la Légion d'Honneur, France, 1976. *Publications:* Financing by Credit Creation, 1947; Economic Development, 1958; Interests, 1983. *Recreations:* fishing, golf, music. *Address:* 148 Stillorgan Road, Donnybrook, Dublin 4, Ireland. *T:* (1) 2693474.

WHITBREAD, Jasmine; Chief Executive Officer, Save the Children International, since 2010; *b* 1 Sept. 1963; *d* of Gerald and Ursula Whitbread; *m* 1994, Howard Exton-Smith; one *s* one *d*. *Educ:* Bristol Univ. (BA Hons English); Stanford Univ. (Exec. Prog.). Dir, Global Mktg, Cortex Corp., 1986–90; Mgt Trainer, Nat. Union of Disabled Persons of Uganda/VSO, 1990–92; Man. Dir, Thomson Financial, 1994–99; Regl Dir, W Africa, 1999–2002, Internat. Dir, 2002–05, Oxfam GB; Chief Exec., Save the Children UK, 2005–10. Non-executive Director: BT plc, 2011–; Standard Chartered plc, 2015–. Hon. LLD Bristol, 2014. *Recreation:* competing with City of Oxford Rowing Club. *Address:* Save the Children International, St Vincent House, 30 Orange Street, WC2H 7HH. *T:* (020) 3272 0300. *E:* jasmine.whitbread@savethechildren.org.

WHITBREAD, Sir Samuel (Charles), KCVO 2010; Director: Whitbread plc, 1972–2001 (Chairman, 1984–92); Whitbread Farms Ltd (formerly S. C. Whitbread Farms), since 1985; Lord-Lieutenant of Bedfordshire, 1991–2012; *b* 22 Feb. 1937; *s* of late Major Simon Whitbread and Helen Beatrice Margaret (*née* Trefusis); *m* 1961, Jane Mary Hayter; three *s* one *d*. *Educ:* Eton College. Beds and Herts Regt, 1955–57. Joined Board, Whitbread & Co., 1972, Dep. Chm., Jan. 1984. Director: Whitbread Investment Co., 1977–93; Sun Alliance Gp, 1989–92; Chm., Hertfordshire Timber Supplies, 2000–. Chm., Mid-Beds Conservative Assoc., 1969–72 (Pres., 1986–91). President: Shire Horse Soc., 1990–92; E of England Agricl Soc., 1991–92; St John Council for Beds, 1991–2012; Beds RFCA (formerly Beds TA&VRA), 1991–2012; Vice-Pres., E Anglia RFCA (formerly E Anglia TA&VRA), 1991–2000, 2005– (Pres., 2000–05). Bedfordshire: JP, 1969–83, 1991; High Sheriff, 1973–74; DL, 1974; County Councillor, 1974–82. FRSA 1986; FLS 1994; FSA 2007. Hon. LLD: De Montfort, 2002; Bedfordshire, 2007. Bledisloe Gold Medal, RASE, 1989. KStJ 1992. *Publications:* Straws in the Wind, 1997; Plain Mr Whitbread: seven centuries of a Bedfordshire family, 2007; February: birthday celebrations around the world, 2014. *Recreations:* shooting, painting, music. *Address:* Glebe House, Southill, Biggleswade, Beds SG18 9LL. *T:* (01462) 813272. *Club:* Brooks's.

WHITBURN, Vanessa Victoria, OBE 2014; Editor, The Archers, BBC Radio, 1991–2013; additional responsibility for Radio Drama in the Midlands, BBC, 1995–2013; freelance radio drama consultant, and drama producer and director, since 2013; *b* 12 Dec. 1951; *d* of late Victor D. Whitburn and Eileen Whitburn. *Educ:* Mount St Mary's Convent, Exeter; Univ. of Hull (BA Hons). Studio Manager, BBC, 1974–76; Asst Floor Manager, BBC TV, 1976–77; Producer and Sen. Producer, Radio Drama, Pebble Mill, 1977–88; Producer, Brookside, Channel 4, 1988–90; Producer and Director, BBC TV, Pebble Mill, 1990–91; additional responsibility: for Silver Street, 2004–09; for drama, Asian Network, 2010–13; Ed., Ambridge Extra, 2011–13. Consultant: Midwest Radio Theater Workshop, Missouri, 1985–; to ODA, on Ndiga Nacio (Kenyan radio soap opera), 1987–; to S African Broadcasting Corp. on radio soap drama, 2006–; Mem., Adv. Bd, Nat. Audio Th. Festivals, USA, 2005–. Hon. DLitt Hull, 2012. *Publications:* The Archers: the official inside story, 1996. *Recreations:* opera, theatre, spending time with friends, travel. *Address:* 19 West Street, Stratford Upon Avon, Warwicks CV37 6DW.

WHITBY, Baron *cr* 2013 (Life Peer), of Harborne in the City of Birmingham; **Michael John Whitby;** Chairman and Managing Director, Skeldings Ltd, Smethwick (Director, 1992); *b* 6 Feb. 1948; *m* 1987, Gaynor Baldwin. Non exec. Dir, Marketing Birmingham Ltd, 2002–14. Mem. (C) Birmingham CC, 1997–2014 (Leader, 2004–12). Contested (C): Midlands W, European Parlt, 1989; Delyn, 1992.

WHITBY, Bishop Suffragan of, since 2014; **Rt Rev. Paul John Ferguson;** *b* 13 July 1955; *s* of Thomas and Joyce Ferguson; *m* 1982, Penelope Hewitt-Jones; two *s* one *d*. *Educ:* Birkenhead Sch.; New Coll., Oxford (BA 1976, MA 1980); Westminster Coll., Oxford (PGCE); King's Coll., Cambridge (BA 1984, MA 1988); Westcott Hse, Cambridge. FRCO 1975. Ordained deacon, 1985, priest 1986; Curate, St Mary's Chester, 1985–88; Chaplain and Sacrist, 1988–92, Precentor, 1992–95, Westminster Abbey; Precentor and Residentiary Canon, York Minster, 1995–2001; Archdeacon of Cleveland, 2001–14. *Publications:* (jtly) Sing His Glory, 1997; Great is the Mystery of Faith: exploring faith through the words of worship, 2011; reviews, articles on music and liturgy. *Address:* 21 Thornton Road, Stainton, Middlesbrough TS8 9DS. *T:* (01642) 593273.

WHITBY, Mrs Joy; Managing Director, Grasshopper Productions Ltd, since 1986; *b* 27 July 1930; *d* of James and Esther Field; *m* 1954, Anthony Charles Whitby (*d* 1975); three *s*. *Educ:* St Anne's Coll., Oxford. Schools Producer, BBC Radio, 1956–62; Children's Producer, BBC Television, 1962–67; Executive Producer, Children's Programmes, London Weekend Television, 1967–70; freelance producer and writer, 1970–76; Head of Children's Programmes, Yorkshire TV, 1976–85. Dir, Bd of Channel 4, 1980–84; Member: Adv. Panel for Youth, Nat. Trust, 1985–89; Bd, Unicorn Theatre, 1987–92. Trustee, Internat. Childcare Trust, 1995–97. Devised for television: Play School, 1964; Jackanory, 1965; The Book Tower, 1979; Under the Same Sky (EBU Drama Exchange), 1984. Key productions include: The Growing Summer, 1968; Catweazle, 1970. Independent film productions: Grasshopper Island, 1971; A Pattern of Roses, 1983; Emma and Grandpa, 1984; East of the Moon, 1988; The Angel and the Soldier Boy, 1989 (ACE Award, 1991); On Christmas Eve, 1992; The Mousehole Cat, 1993; The Story of Arion and the Dolphin, 1996; (with Alan Bennett and Richard Briers) Mouse and Mole (five-minute series), 1995–99; A Small Miracle, 2002; (stage prodn) Grasshopper Rhymes from Other Times, 2004; (with Alan Bennett, Richard Briers and Imelda Staunton) Mouse and Mole at Christmas Time, 2013. BAFTA Award and Prix Jeunesse: for Play School, 1965; for The Book Tower, 1980 (also BAFTA Award, 1983); Eleanor Farjeon Award for Services to Children's Books, 1979. *Publications:* Grasshopper Island, 1971; Emma and Grandpa (4 vols), 1984. *E:* whitby165@btinternet.com.

WHITBY, Mark, FICE, FREng; Director, Davies Maguire + Whitby, since 2010; Co-founder and Chairman, Whitby & Mohajer Engineers, since 2010; *b* 29 Jan. 1950; *s* of George Whitby, MBE, FRIBA and Rhona Charmian Whitby (*née* Butler); one *s* by Alison Scott; *m* 1991, Janet Taylor; two *s* two *d*. *Educ:* Ealing Grammar Sch. for Boys; King's Coll., London

(BSc). FICE 1992; FREng 1996. Founding Partner and Dir, Whitby Bird & Partners, then whitbybird, later Ramboll Whitbybird, subseq. Ramboll UK, 1984–2009. Major projects include: York and Lancaster Millennium Bridges, 2000; British Embassies in Dublin, 1995, Berlin, 2000, and Sana, 2006. Special Prof. of Sustainable Construction, Nottingham Univ., 2005–. Founder, The Engineering Club, 1990; Founder and Trustee, Engineering Timelines, 1996–. Chairman: Urban Design Alliance, 2001–02; Sustainability and Urban Renaissance Sector Gp, SEEDA, 2002–06; EVO Energy, 2010–12. Pres., ICE, 2001–02. Mem., Nat. House Building Council, 2009–. Trustee, Construction and Develt Partnership, 2007–. Gov., Building Centre Trust, 1997–. Hon. FRIBA 1999. *Recreations:* canoeing (Mem., Olympic Team, 1968), running (London Marathon 2001), 20th Century engineering history, the children.

WHITCHURCH, Sir Graeme (Ian), Kt 2006; OBE 1984; Senior Advisor, Leaders Benefits, National Parliament of Papua New Guinea, since 1970; Officer of the Parliamentary Service, Papua New Guinea, since 1970; *b* 8 Dec. 1945; *s* of late Roy Frederick Whitchurch and Alpha Aimee Whitchurch; *m* 1967, Kaia Edith Heni; three *s* three *d*. *Educ:* Punchbowl State Sch., Launceston, Tasmania; Launceston State High Sch. Civil Servant: PMG's Dept, Australia, 1961–64; Public Service of PNG, 1964–70. Mem., Rotary Club of Boroko, PNG, 1990–2007 (Pres., 1995–96). *Recreation:* Australian Rules Football (Life Mem., Koboni FC, Port Moresby). *Address:* PO Box 413, Konedobu, Papua New Guinea. *T:* (home) 6753211255, (office) 6753277789, *Fax:* 6753254346. *E:* gwhit@daltron.com.pg. *Clubs:* Papua (1912) (Mem. Cttee, 2002–07; Pres., 2009–), Aviat Social and Sporting (Life Mem., 1994, Pres., 1984–98), Royal Papua Yacht (Port Moresby).

WHITE, family name of **Baron Annaly**.

WHITE, Sir Adrian (Edwin), Kt 2015; CBE 1993; DL; CSci; Founder Chairman, Biwater Holdings Ltd (formerly Biwater plc), since 1968; Governor of the BBC, 1995–2000; *b* 25 July 1942; *s* of Raymond Gerard White and Lucy Mildred White (*née* Best); *m* 1971, Gillian Denise Evans; four *s* one *d*. *Educ:* Cray Valley Technical High; City of London Coll. Chartered Water Engineer; FCIWEM; CSci 2005. Biwater Holdings Ltd (formerly Biwater plc) (holding co. for Biwater International and other cos), 1968–. Gp Chm., British Water Industries Gp, 1992–93; Founder Chm., British Water, 1993–98; Chm., Cascal NV, 2009–10. Vice-Pres., Small Business Bureau, 1980–90; Governor, Engineering, World Economic Forum, 1989–2006; Mem., Overseas Projects Bd, DTI, 1993–95. Chm., Epsom Healthcare NHS Trust, 1990–94, 1997–99. President: Epsom Medical Equipment Fund, 1999–; Surrey Care Trust, 2007–. Founder: Denbies and St Kilda Charitable Trusts; Surrey Jobmatch, 2007; Chm., The Children's Trust, Tadworth, 2008–12. Founder, Denbies Wine Estate, 1985–. President: Dorking Swimming Club, 1988–; Dorking Scouts and Guides, 1988–; Surrey Performing Arts, 1996–; Friends of Dorking Hospital, 1999–; Dorking & District Preservation Soc., 2006–. Mem., Surrey Scout Council, 2000–. Governor: Stanway Sch., 1984–94; Queen Elizabeth's Foundn (formerly Queen Elizabeth's Foundn for Disabled People), 1989–; Parkside Sch., 1994–96; Chm. Bd of Governors, Millfield Schs, 1997–2009. DL, 2002, High Sheriff, 2006–07, Surrey. Hon. Fellow, Regent's Park Coll., Oxford, 2005. DUniv Surrey, 2010. Winner, Free Enterprise Award, 1985. *Recreations:* family, golf, theatre. *Address:* Biwater Holdings Ltd, Biwater House, Station Approach, Dorking, Surrey RH4 1TZ. *T:* (01306) 740740; Denbies, Ranmore Common, Dorking, Surrey RH5 6SP. *T:* (01306) 886640.

See also Rev. B. R. White.

WHITE, Aidan Patrick; Director, Ethical Journalism Network, since 2011; General Secretary, International Federation of Journalists, 1987–2011; *b* Derry, N Ireland, 2 March 1951; *s* of Thomas White and Kathleen Ann McLaughlin. *Educ:* King's Sch., Peterborough. Journalist, reporter and sub-ed., Peterborough, Lincoln and Birmingham, 1968–74; sub-ed., London Evening News, 1974; chief sub-ed., Stratford Express Gp, 1975–77; Dep. Gp Ed., Stratford Express, 1977–79; journalist, The Guardian, 1980–87. Mem., Press Council, 1978–80. National Union of Journalists: Mem. Exec. Council, 1974, 1976, 1977; Treasurer, 1984–86; Chm., National Newspapers Council, 1981. Chm., EC Inf. Soc. Forum Wkg Gp, 1996–98. Mem., Exec. Council, Global Union Council (formerly ICFTU), 1989; Steering Cttee, ETUC, 1997–2000. Founder and Mem. Bd, Internat. News Safety Inst., 2003–12; Chm., Council of Global Unions, 2010–12. Trustee, Statewatch, 2011–; Chm., Internews Europe, 2013–. *Publications:* Making a World of Difference, 2006; Journalism, Civil Liberties and the War on Terror, 2006; To Tell You the Truth: ethical journalists initiative, 2008; Journalism as a Public Good, 2011; reports on ethics of journalism for UNESCO, UNICEF and Council of Europe. *Address:* 11 Vicarage Road, E15 4HD. *T:* 07946 291511. *E:* aidanpatrickwhite@gmail.com.

WHITE, Aileen Elizabeth; *see* Campbell, A. E.

WHITE, Alan, CMG 1985; OBE 1973; HM Diplomatic Service, retired; Ambassador to Chile, 1987–90; *b* 13 Aug. 1930; *s* of William White and Ida (*née* Hall); *m* 1st, 1954, Cynthia Maidwell (*d* 2004); two *s* one *d*; 2nd, 1980, Clare Corley Smith. SSC Army 1954 (Capt.); Hong Kong, 1959–63; MoD (Central), 1965; First Sec., FO (later FCO), 1966; Mexico City, 1969; First Sec., UK Disarmament Delegn, Geneva, 1974; Counsellor (Commercial), Madrid, 1976; Counsellor and Head of Chancery, Kuala Lumpur, 1980–83; Hd, Trade Relns and Exports Dept, FCO, 1983–85; Ambassador to Bolivia, 1985–87. *Recreations:* reading, travel. *Address:* c/o Foreign and Commonwealth Office, SW1A 2AH.

WHITE, Alan, FCA; Chairman, Hotter Ltd, since 2014; *b* 15 April 1955; *s* of Ronald and Margaret White; *m* 2009, Gillian Mills; one *s* one *d* by a previous marriage. *Educ:* Warwick Univ. (LLB). FCA 1979. Audit Senior, Arthur Andersen, 1976–79; Gen. Manager, Finance, Sharp Electronics, 1979–85; Finance Dir, N Brown Gp, 1985–99; Gp Finance Dir, Littlewoods plc, 1999–2002; Chief Exec., N Brown Gp plc, 2002–13. Non-executive Director: Topps Tiles plc, 2008–; Direct Wines Ltd, 2013–. *Recreations:* tennis, squash, ski-ing, waterski-ing, Manchester United.

WHITE, Rt Rev. Alison Mary; *see* Hull, Bishop Suffragan of.

WHITE, Andrew; QC 1997; *b* 25 Jan. 1958; *s* of Peter White and late Sandra Jeanette White (*née* Lovelace); *m* 1987, Elizabeth Denise Rooney; two *s*. *Educ:* University Coll. Cardiff (LLB Hons). Called to the Bar, Lincoln's Inn (Hardwick Schol., Megarry Schol.), 1980, Bencher, 2003; in practice at the Bar, 1981–; Hd of Chambers, 2011–. *Publications:* (contrib.) Encyclopaedia of Forms and Precedents, vol. 5: Building and Engineering Contracts, 5th edn (1986). *Recreations:* farming, sailing, music. *Address:* 1 Atkin Building, Gray's Inn, WC1R 5AT. *T:* (020) 7404 0102; Afflington Manor, Corfe Castle, Wareham, Dorset BH20 5HT.

WHITE, Air Vice-Marshal Andrew David, CB 2003; Chief Executive, National Security Inspectorate, 2006–10; *b* 2 Jan. 1952; *s* of Edward and Margaret White; *m* 1975, Christine Ann Spratt; two *s*. *Educ:* Loughborough Univ. (BTech Hons Aeronautical Engrg); RAF Cranwell. Joined RAF, 1970; served Nos 17, 151, 20 Sqdns, 1977–84; Flt Comdr, No 14 Sqdn, 1984–85; NATO staff, 1985–88; jsdc 1988; MoD staff, 1988–91; Sqdn Comdr, Nos 15 and 9 Sqdns, 1991–94; PSO to CAS, 1994–96; Station Comdr, RAF Cottesmore, 1996–99; Staff Officer, HQ Strike Comd, 1999–2003; AOC No 3 Gp, 2003–06. Non-exec. Dir, NATS, 2006–13. Chm. Govs, Cottesmore Co. Primary Sch., 1996–99. *Recreations:* golf, aviation, ski-ing, walking. *Club:* Royal Air Force.

WHITE, Rev. Canon Andrew Paul Bartholomew; President and Chief Executive Officer, Foundation for Relief and Reconciliation in the Middle East (formerly Foundation for Reconciliation in the Middle East), since 2005; Anglican Chaplain to St George's, Baghdad, since 2003; Director, US Department of Defense and Iraqi Government Religious Sectarianism Programme, since 2007; *b* 29 June 1964; *s* of Maurice and Pauline White; *m* 1991, Caroline Spreckley; two *s*. *Educ:* Picardy Sch.; St Thomas' Hosp., London; Ridley Hall, Cambridge; Hebrew Univ., Jerusalem. Student Operating Dept Practitioner, St Thomas' Hosp., London, 1981–84; Operating Department Practitioner: Obstetrics, Derby City Hosp., 1984; St Thomas' Hosp., 1985–86 (Hon. Operating Dept Practitioner, 1990–97); ordained deacon, 1990, priest, 1991; Asst Curate, St Mark's Ch, Battersea Rise, London, 1990–93; Vicar, Ch of the Ascension, Balham Hill, London, 1993–98; Canon, Coventry Cathedral, and Dir, Internat. Centre for Reconciliation, 1998–2005. Archbishop of Canterbury's Special Representative: to Middle East, 2002–04; to Alexandria Process, 2004–09; Internat. Dir, Iraqi Inst. of Peace, 2003–. Sen. Inter-religious Advr to Iraqi Prime Minister, 2006. Vis. Lectr, Wheaton Coll., Illinois, 1999–; Vis. Fellow, Harvard Univ., 2008. Chm., Young Leadership Section, Internat. CCJ, 1990–95 (Prize for Intellectual Contribn to Jewish Christian Relns, 1993). Mem. for Balham, Wandsworth BC, 1998 (Dep. Chm., Social Services, 1998). Eric Lane Fellow, Clare Coll., Cambridge, 2003. Hon. PhD Gloucester, 2010. Anglo Israel Assoc. Prize, 1998; Sternberg Inter Faith Prize, Three Faith Forum, 2003; Tannenbaum Peace Prize, 2005; Cambridge Centre for Jewish Christian Relations Peacemaker Award, 2007; Prize for Peace, Woolf Inst., Cambridge, 2007; Iraq Peace Prize, Baghdad Shia Leaders; Civil Courage Prize, Train Foundn, 2010; Internat. First Freedom Award, First Freedom Center, 2011; Colson Center William Wilberforce Award, 2014. Grand Comdr and Companion of Honour, OSMTH, 2003; Cross of Valour, American OSMTH, 2005; GCStG, 2011. *Publications:* Iraq: people of hope, land of despair, 2003; Iraq: searching for hope, 2005 (Christian Book Award, 2006), rev. edn 2007; (with Hope Jones) By the Rivers of Babylon, 2008; The Vicar of Baghdad: fighting for peace in the Middle East, 2009 (Best Christian Book in Britain, Christian Resources Together, 2010); Suffer the Children, 2010; Faith Under Fire, 2010 (Ultimate Christian Liby Bk Award, 2012); Father Forgive, 2013; Jews and Christians, 2013; Suffering and Glory, 2014; The Older and Younger Brother: the tragic treatment of the Jews by the Christians, 2014; various newspaper articles and chapters in books on conflict resolution, Jewish Christian relns, interfaith issues, Israel/Palestine and the Middle East. *Recreations:* angora goats, cleaning, cooking, collecting crosses from around the world, collecting sebaha beads, fountain pens and books. *Address:* Foundation for Relief and Reconciliation in the Middle East, PO Box 229, Petersfield, Hants GU32 9DL. *T:* (01730) 267673. *E:* office@frrme.org, apbw2@cam.ac.uk. *Clubs:* Carlton, Royal Over-Seas League; Alwyah (Baghdad).

WHITE, Dr Anthony Alfred Leigh, MBE 2004; Chairman, BW Energy Ltd, since 2009; a Commissioner, Crown Estate, since 2011; *b* London, 15 March 1953; *s* of Joseph and Patricia White; *m* 1984, Anne Brewis; one *s* two *d*. *Educ:* Alleyn's Sch., Dulwich; Keble Coll., Oxford (BA 1st Cl. Physics; Johnson Meml Prize); Wolfson Coll., Oxford (DPhil 1977); City Univ. (MBA). Res. scientist, CEGB, 1979; Harkness Fellow, Los Alamos Lab., Electric Power Inst., Brown Univ., 1980–82; Strategy, Safety and Finance Depts, CEGB, 1982–88; Sen. Analyst, James Capel, Electricity Privatisation, 1989–92; National Grid: Hd, Transmission Develt, 1992–93; Mem., Exec., 1992–96; Hd, Corporate Strategy, 1994–96; Man. Dir, Kleinwort Benson and Citigroup, 1996–2002; Dir and Founder, Climate Change Capital, 2002–08. Mem., Adv. Panel, UK Energy, 1993–2003. Non-exec. Dir, Nat. Renewable Energy Centre, 2004–12. *Publications:* contribs to scientific jls, incl. Nature. *Recreations:* hiking, cooking, travelling. *Address:* The Old Vicarage, West Street, Long Buckby, Northants NN6 7QF. *T:* (01327) 843560. *E:* thewhitefamily@clara.co.uk. *Club:* Travellers.

WHITE, Antony Dennis Lowndes; QC 2001; *b* 22 Jan. 1959; *s* of Albert Dennis White and Marion Seymour White; partner, Kate Ursula Macfarlane; one *s* two *d*. *Educ:* Huish's Grammar Sch., Taunton; Clare Coll., Cambridge (MA). Called to the Bar, Middle Temple, 1983; called to the Gibraltar Bar, 1998. *Publications:* (with S. Greer) Abolishing the Diplock Courts, 1986; *contributed to:* Justice Under Fire, 1988; The Jury Under Attack, 1988; Bullen & Leake & Jacob's Precedents of Pleadings, 14th edn, 2001 to 17th edn, 2012; Privacy and the Media: the developing law, 2002; Civil Appeals, 2002, 2nd edn 2013; Enforcing Contracts in Transition Economies, 2005; Freedom of Information Handbook, 2006, 2nd edn 2008; Information Rights, 4th edn 2014. *Recreations:* classic cars and motorcycles, walking, swimming, cooking, wine, modern literature, contemporary art. *Address:* Matrix Chambers, Griffin Building, Gray's Inn, WC1R 5LN. *T:* (020) 7404 3447.

WHITE, Rev. Barrington Raymond; Principal, Regent's Park College, Oxford, 1972–89, now Principal Emeritus (Senior Research Fellow and Tutor in Ecclesiastical History, 1989–99); *b* 28 Jan. 1934; *s* of Raymond Gerard and Lucy Mildred White; *m* 1957, Margaret Muriel Hooper; two *d*. *Educ:* Chislehurst and Sidcup Grammar Sch.; Queens' Coll., Cambridge (BA Theol, MA); Regent's Park Coll., Oxford (DPhil). Ordained, 1959; Minister, Andover Baptist Church, 1959–63; Tutor in Ecclesiastical History, Regent's Park Coll., Oxford, 1963–72. First Breman Prof. of Social Relations, Univ. of N Carolina at Asheville, 1976. FRHistS 1973. *Publications:* The English Separatist Tradition, 1971; Association Records of the Particular Baptists to 1660, Part I, 1971, Part II, 1973, Part III, 1974; Authority: a Baptist view, 1976; Hanserd Knollys and Radical Dissent, 1977; contrib. Reformation, Conformity and Dissent, ed R. Buick Knox, 1977; The English Puritan Tradition, 1980; contrib. Biographical Dictionary of British Radicals in the Seventeenth Century, ed Greaves and Zaller, 1982–84; The English Baptists of the Seventeenth Century, 1983; (contrib.) A Transcription of the Glasshouse Yard Church Book 1832 to 1857, 2000; contribs to Baptist Qly, Jl of Theological Studies, Jl of Ecclesiastical History, Welsh Baptist Studies. *Recreation:* recorded music. *Address:* Regent's Park College, Oxford OX1 2LB.

See also Sir A. E. White.

WHITE, Brian Arthur Robert; consultant on technology, energy and regulatory issues; Chairman of Trustees, National Energy Foundation, 2007–12 (Trustee, 2004–13, now Member, Advisory Council); *b* 5 May 1957; *s* of Edward and Jean White; *m* 1984, Leena Lindholm; two step *s*. *Educ:* Methodist Coll., Belfast. Systems analyst: HM Customs, 1977–83 (consultant, 1983–84); Canada Life Assurance, 1984–86; Abbey National, 1986–97. MP (Lab) Milton Keynes NE, 1997–2005. Contested (Lab) Milton Keynes NE, 2005. Mem. (Lab), Milton Keynes BC, until 1997 and 2006–. *E:* brian@brianwhite.org.uk.

WHITE, Bryan Oliver; HM Diplomatic Service, retired; *b* 3 Oct. 1929; *s* of Thomas Frederick White and Olive May Turvey; *m* 1958, Helen McLeod Jenkins; one *s* two *d*. *Educ:* The Perse Sch.; Wadham Coll., Oxford (Lit.Hum.). HM Forces, 1948–49; FO, 1953; Kabul, Vienna, Conakry, Rio de Janeiro, the Cabinet Office, and Havana, 1953–79; Counsellor, Paris, 1980–82; Head of Mexico and Central America Dept, FCO, 1982–84; Ambassador to Honduras and (non-resident) to El Salvador, 1984–87; Consul-Gen., Lyon, 1987–89. *Recreation:* the Romance languages. *Address:* 14 Stonebridge Lane, Fulbourn, Cambridge CB21 5BW.

WHITE, (Charles) John (Branford); HM Diplomatic Service, retired; Director for Development, Aquaculture Stewardship Council, since 2011; *b* 24 Sept. 1946; *s* of Frederick Bernard White and Violet Phyllis White (*née* Palmer); *m* 1975, Judith Margaret Lewis. *Educ:* Taunton Sch.; Brentwood Sch.; Pembroke Coll., Cambridge (Trevelyan Schol., MA); University Coll. London (MSc 1983). ODI Fellow, Govt of Botswana, 1968–71; ODA, 1971–77; Economic Advr, E Africa Develt Div., ODM, 1977–82; ODA, 1983–86; Asst Head, Economic Relations Dept, FCO, 1986–90; First Sec., Lagos, 1990–93; Dep. Hd of

Mission, Consul Gen. and Counsellor, Tel Aviv, 1993–97; Hd, S Atlantic and Antarctic, subseq. UK Overseas Territories, Dept, FCO, and Comr (non-resident), British Antarctic Territory and British Indian Ocean Territory, 1997–2001; High Comr, Barbados and the Eastern Caribbean States, 2001–05. Dir for Develt, Marine Stewardship Council, 2006–10. Gov., Atlantic Coll., 2012. *Recreations:* walking, golfing, opera going. *Address:* 26 Turner House, Clevedon Road, Twickenham, Middx TW1 2TE. *Club:* Royal Mid-Surrey Golf.

WHITE, Christopher; MP (C) Warwick and Leamington, since 2010; *b* 28 April 1967. *Educ:* Univ. of Manchester (BE); Univ. of Bath (MBA). Work at Longbridge with MG Rover; freelance PR consultant. Mem. (C) Warwick DC, 2007–10. Contested (C): Birmingham Hall Green, 2001; Warwick and Leamington, 2005. PPS to Minister of State for Policing Crime and Criminal Justice, 2015–, for Security, 2015–. Member: Internat. Develt Select Cttee, 2010–15; Business, Innovation and Skills Select Cttee, 2015–. Co-Chair, All Party Parly Gp on Manufg, 2010–; Chair, All Party Parliamentary Group on: Video Games, 2014–; Nat. Citizen Service, 2014–; Vice Chair, All Party Parly Gp on Poverty, 2010–15. Introd. Private Mem.'s Bill, resulting in Public Services (Social Value) Act, 2012. Mem. Bd and Vice Chm., Policy Connect. Trustee: Warwicks Assoc. of Youth Clubs; Webb Meml Trust, 2011–; Motionhouse Dance Charity, 2011–. *Address:* House of Commons, SW1A 0AA.

WHITE, Prof. Sir Christopher (John), Kt 2001; CVO 1995; PhD; FBA 1989; Director, Ashmolean Museum, Oxford, 1985–97; Fellow of Worcester College, 1985–97, and Professor of the Art of the Netherlands, 1992–97, now Professor Emeritus, Oxford University; *b* 19 Sept. 1930; *s* of late Gabriel Ernest Edward Francis White, CBE and Elizabeth Grace Ardizzone; *m* 1957, Rosemary Katharine Desages; one *s* two *d*. *Educ:* Downside Sch.; Courtauld Institute of Art, London Univ. BA (Hons) 1954, PhD 1970. Served Army, 1949–50; commnd, RA, 1949. Asst Keeper, Dept of Prints and Drawings, British Museum, 1954–65; Director, P. and D. Colnaghi, 1965–71; Curator of Graphic Arts, Nat. Gall. of Art, Washington, 1971–73; Dir of Studies, Paul Mellon Centre for Studies in British Art, 1973–85; Adjunct Prof. of History of Art, Yale Univ., 1976–85; Associate Dir, Yale Center for British Art, 1976–85. Dutch Govt Schol., 1956; Hermione Lectr, Alexandra Coll., Dublin, 1959; Adjunct Prof., Inst. of Fine Arts, New York Univ., 1973 and 1976; Conference Dir, European-Amer. Assembly on Art Museums, Ditchley Park, 1975; Visiting Prof., Dept of History of Art, Yale Univ., 1976; Vis. Curator, Courtauld Gall., 2011. Trustee: V & A Mus., 1997–2004; NACF, 1998–2005; Mauritshuis, The Hague, 1999–2008. Gov., British Inst. of Florence, 1994–2002. Dir, Burlington Magazine, 1981– (Chm., 1996–2002). Reviews Editor, Master Drawings, 1967–80. *Publications:* Rembrandt and his World, 1964; The Flower Drawings of Jan van Huysum, 1965; Rubens and his World, 1968; Rembrandt as an Etcher, 1969, 2nd edn 1999; (jtly) Rembrandt's Etchings: a catalogue raisonné, 1970; Dürer: the artist and his drawings, 1972; English Landscape 1630–1850, 1977; The Dutch Paintings in the Collection of HM The Queen, 1982; (ed) Rembrandt in Eighteenth Century England, 1983; Rembrandt, 1984; Peter Paul Rubens: man and artist, 1987 (Eugène Baie Prize, 1983–87); (jtly) Drawing in England from Hilliard to Hogarth, 1987; (jtly) Rubens in Oxford, 1988; (jtly) One Hundred Old Master Drawings from the Ashmolean Museum, 1991; (jtly) The Dutch and Flemish Drawings at Windsor Castle, 1994; Anthony van Dyck: Thomas Howard, the Earl of Arundel, 1995; Dutch, Flemish and German Paintings in the Ashmolean Museum, 1999; (ed jtly) Rembrandt by Himself, 1999; The Later Flemish Pictures in the Collection of HM The Queen, 2007; (jtly) The Dutch and Flemish Drawings in the Victoria and Albert Museum, 2014; film (script and commentary), Rembrandt's Three Crosses, 1969; various exhibn catalogues; contribs to Burlington Mag., Master Drawings, etc. *Address:* 34 Kelly Street, NW1 8PH. *T:* (020) 7485 9148; Shingle House, St Cross, Harleston, Norfolk IP20 0NT. *T:* (01986) 782264.

WHITE, Sir Christopher (Robert Meadows), 3rd Bt *cr* 1937, of Boulge Hall, Suffolk; *b* 26 Aug. 1940; *s* of Sir (Eric) Richard Meadows White, 2nd Bt, and Lady Elizabeth Mary Gladys (*d* 1950), *o d* of 6th Marquess Townshend; *S* father, 1972, but his name does not appear on the Official Roll of the Baronetage; *m* 1st, 1962, Anne Marie Ghislaine (marr. diss. 1968), *yr d* of Major Tom Brown, OBE; 2nd, 1968, Dinah Mary Sutton (marr. diss. 1972), Orange House, Heacham, Norfolk; 3rd, 1976, Ingrid Carolyn Jowett, *e d* of Eric Jowett, Great Baddow; two step *s*. *Educ:* Bradfield Coll., Berks. Imperial Russian Ballet School, Cannes, France, 1961; schoolmaster, 1961–72; Professore, Istituto Shenker, Rome, and Scuola Specialisti Aeronauta, Macerata, 1962–63; Housemaster, St Michael's Sch., Ingoldisthorpe, Norfolk, 1963–69. Hon. Pres., Warnborough House, Oxford, 1973–. Lieutenant, TA, Norfolk, 1969. *Recreations:* dogs, vintage cars, antiques. *Address:* c/o Mrs Edwin Steinschaden-Silver, Pinkney Court, Malmesbury, Wilts SN16 0PD.

WHITE, Prof. David Clifford Stephen, CBE 2009; DPhil; documentary, portrait and natural environment photographer, since 2009; Director, Institute of Food Research, 2004–09; *b* 8 March 1941; *s* of late Clifford George White and of Joyce Beatrice White (*née* Lawley); *m* 1st, 1965, Ailsa Pippin (marr. diss.); one *s* one *d*; one *s*; 2nd, 1987, Patricia Spallone. *Educ:* Berkhamsted Sch.; New Coll., Oxford (BA 1962; MA 1967; DPhil 1967). Deptl Demonstrator, Dept of Zool., Univ. of Oxford, 1967–71; Department of Biology, University of York: Lectr, 1971–86; Sen. Lectr, 1986–90; Reader, 1990–95; Prof., 1995–97; Head of Dept, 1990–97; Dir of Sci. and Technol., BBSRC, 1997–2004. Photographic exhibition: The Living Medieval Parish Churches of Norwich, Hostry of Norwich Cath., 2011; The Restoration and Renewal of St Stephen's Church, Norwich, St Stephen's Church, 2013; Life, Light and Insight, Blickling Hall, 2014. *Publications:* Biological Physics, 1973; The Kinetics of Muscle Contraction, 1973; The Living Mediaeval Parish Churches of Norwich, 2012. *Recreations:* walking, photography. *Address:* 16 The Crescent, Chapelfield Road, Norwich NR2 1SA. *T:* (01603) 630489. *E:* whitedcs@onetel.com. *W:* www.davidwhitephotography.co.uk.
See also A. F. Moore-Gwyn.

WHITE, Sir David Harry, Kt 1992; DL; Chairman, Mansfield Brewing, 1993–2000; Director, 1970–88, a Deputy Chairman, 1988–90, Chairman of Trustees, 1986–2000, National Freight Consortium; *b* 12 Oct. 1929; *s* of late Harry White, OBE, FCA, and Kathleen White; *m* 1971, Valerie Jeanne White; one *s* three *d* (and one *d* decd). *Educ:* Nottingham High Sch.; HMS Conway. Master Mariner's F. G. Certificate. Sea career, apprentice to Master Mariner, 1944–56; Terminal Manager, Texaco (UK) Ltd, 1956–64; Operations Manager, Gulf Oil (GB) Ltd, 1964–68; Asst Man. Dir, Samuel Williams Dagenham, 1968–70; Trainee to Gp Managing Director, British Road Services Ltd, 1970–76; Group Managing Director: British Road Services, 1976–82; Pickfords, 1982–84; NFC Property Gp, 1984–87; Chm., Nottingham HA, 1986–98; Director (non-executive): BR Property Bd, 1985–87; Y. J. Lovell Ltd, 1987–94; Hilda Hanson Ltd, 1996–2010; James Bell (Nottingham) Ltd, 1997–2010; Nottingham Forest FC, 1999–2004; Alkane Energy plc, 2000–04; non-exec. Chm., EPS Ltd, 1997–2000. Mem., British Coal Corp., 1993–94; Chm., Coal Authy, 1994–99. Mem. Editorial Bd, Nottingham Evening Post, 2003–10. Chairman: Nottingham Develt Enterprise, 1987–93; Bd of Governors, Nottingham Trent Univ. (formerly Nottingham Poly.), 1989–99. Trustee, Djanogly City Technology Coll., 1989–99. Hon. Pres., Notts County Branch, RSPCA, 1987–2010. Governor, Nottingham High Sch., 1987–99. DL Notts, 1989. Hon. DBA Nottingham Trent, 1999; Hon. DLaw Nottingham, 2011. *Recreations:* football supporter (Nottingham Forest), walking. *Address:* Whitehaven, 6 Croft Road, Edwalton, Nottingham NG12 4BW.

WHITE, David Thomas, (Tom), CBE 1990; Principal and Chief Executive, NCH Action for Children (formerly National Children's Home), 1990–96; *b* 10 Oct. 1931; *s* of Walter Henry White and Annie White; *m* 1956, Eileen May Moore; two *d* (and one *s* decd). *Educ:* Council Primary and Maesydderwen Grammar Sch., Ystradgynlais, Swansea Valley; University Coll., Swansea (Social Sci.); London School of Economics (Social Work). Clerical Officer, CS, 1947–54; National Service, RAF, 1951–53. Social work and management posts, Devon CC, 1957–61; Dep. Children's Officer, Monmouthshire, 1961–65; Dep. County Children's Officer, Lancs, 1965–70; Dir of Social Services, Coventry, 1970–85; Dir of Social Work, Nat. Children's Home, 1985–90. Past President: Assoc. of Child Care Officers; Assoc. of Directors of Social Services; Gov., Nat. Inst. of Social Work, 1973–96 (Hon. Fellow, 1996); Chm., Nat. Foster Care Assoc., 1996–99. Mem. (Lab), Coventry CC, 1996–2004. Hon. DBA Coventry, 1998. Coventry Award of Merit, Coventry CC, 2002. *Publications:* (contrib.) Social Work, the Media and Public Relations, 1991. *Recreations:* gardening, golf, walking. *Address:* Heathcote House, Little Tew, Chipping Norton, Oxon OX7 4JE. *T:* (01608) 683873.

WHITE, David Vines; Somerset Herald of Arms, since 2004; Registrar, College of Arms, since 2014; *b* 27 Oct. 1961; *s* of late Peter Vines White and Sheila White (*née* Chatterton, *widow* of Lt Comdr (E.) John William Windley Baker, RN). *Educ:* Kelvinside Acad.; Marlborough Coll.; Pembroke Coll., Cambridge (MA); Courtauld Inst. (MA). Res. Asst, College of Arms, 1988–95; Rouge Croix Pursuivant, 1995–2004. Member, Council: British Record Soc., 1998–; Heraldry Soc., 2000–12 (Chm., 2006–09; Hon. Vice Pres., 2013–). Hon. Vice Pres., Cambridge Univ. Heraldic and Genealogical Soc., 2002–; Hon. Genealogist, Royal Victorian Order, 2010–. Trustee, Marc Fitch Fund, 2008–. *Address:* College of Arms, Queen Victoria Street, EC4V 4BT. *T:* and *Fax:* (020) 7248 1766. *E:* somerset@college-of-arms.gov.uk. *Club:* Travellers.

WHITE, Rt Rev. Francis, (Frank); Assistant Bishop of Newcastle, since 2010; *b* 26 May 1949; *s* of John Edward White and Mary Ellen White; *m* 1982, Alison Mary Dumbell (*see* Bishop Suffragan of Hull). *Educ:* St Cuthbert's GS, Newcastle upon Tyne; Consett Tech. Coll.; UWIST, Cardiff (BScEcon); UC Cardiff (DipSocSci); St John's Coll., Nottingham (Dip. Pastoral Studies); Nottingham Univ. (DipTh). Dir, Youth Action York, 1971–73; Detached Youth Worker, Manchester, 1973–77; Asst Curate, St Nicholas, Durham, 1980–84; Sen. Curate, St Mary and St Cuthbert, Chester-le-Street, 1984–87; Chaplain, Durham HA Hosps, 1987–89; Vicar, St John the Evangelist, Birtley, 1989–97; RD of Chester-le-Street, 1993–97; Archdeacon of Sunderland, 1997–2002; Bishop Suffragan of Brixworth, 2002–10. Proctor in Convocation, Gen. Synod of C of E, 1987–2000. Hon. Canon: Durham Cathedral, 1997–2002; Peterborough Cathedral, 2002–10; St Nicholas Cathedral, Newcastle, 2010–. *Recreations:* birdwatching, walking, motor cars, theatre, soccer. *Address:* Bishop's House, 29 Moor Road South, Newcastle upon Tyne NE3 1PA. *T:* (0191) 285 2220.

WHITE, Frank Richard; JP; former executive director and industrial relations adviser; Director, National Training College, GMB (formerly General, Municipal, Boilermakers and Allied Trades Union), 1988–2000; *b* 11 Nov. 1939; *m*; two *s* one *d*. *Educ:* Bolton Tech. Coll. Member: Bolton CC, 1963–74; Greater Manchester CC, 1973–75; Bolton MBC (formerly DC), 1986–2012 (Cabinet Mem. for HR, Perf. Mgt and Community Cohesion, 2001–12; Mayor, 2005–06). Member: GMB; IPM; Inst. of Management Services. Contested (Lab): Bury and Radcliffe, Feb. 1974; Bury North, 1983; Bolton NE, 1987. MP (Lab) Bury and Radcliffe, Oct. 1974–1983; PPS to Minister of State, Dept of Industry, 1975–76; Asst Govt Whip, 1976–78; Opposition Whip, 1980–82; opposition spokesman on church affairs, 1980–83. Chairman: All Party Paper Industry Gp, 1979–83; NW Lab Gp, 1979–83; Mem., NW Regional Exec., Labour Party, 1986–88. Director: Lancs Co-op. Develt Agency, 1984–; Bolton/Bury TEC, 1995–2004; Mem., Greater Manchester Police Authy, 1997–2004; Mem. Area Bd, United Norwest Co-op., 1994–2004. Chairman: Bolton FM Community Radio, 2005–12; Age Concern, Bolton, 2008–13. President: Bolton United Services Veterans' Assoc., 1988–2012; Bolton Male Voice Choir, 1992–2004; Vice-Pres., E Lancs Railway Preservation Soc., 1983–2005. Hon. Alderman, Bolton MBC, 2013. JP Bolton, 1968–2010 (Chm. Bench, 1993–95). Hon. Fellow, Bolton Inst., 1993. DUniv Bolton, 2010. *Address:* 23 Dovedale Road, Bolton, Lancs BL2 5HT.

WHITE, Sir George (Stanley James), 4th Bt *cr* 1904, of Cotham House, Bristol; FSA; Keeper of the Collection of the Worshipful Company of Clockmakers, since 1988; *b* 4 Nov. 1948; *s* of Sir George Stanley Midelton White, 3rd Bt, and Diane Eleanor, *d* of late Bernard Abdy Collins, CIE; *S* father, 1983; *m* 1st, 1974; one *d*; 2nd, 1979; one *s* one *d*; 3rd, 2006, Joanna, *d* of Kazimierz Migdal. *Educ:* Harrow School. Pres., Gloucestershire Soc., 1993; Member: Gloucester DAC for Care of Churches, 1985– (Clocks Advr, 1986–); Council, Bristol and Glos Archaeological Soc., 1987–2000 (Chm., 1992–95); Council, Nat. Trust, 1998–2004. Pres., British Horological Inst., 2001. Chm. Adv. Bd, Bristol Cars, 2011–14. Liveryman, Co. of Clockmakers, 1986– (Asst, 1994–; Master, 2001); Brother, Parish Clerks' Co., 2009. High Sheriff, Avon, 1989; JP Bristol, 1991–95. Parish Clerk, St Mary the Virgin, Aldermanbury, 2009–. FSA 1988. *Publications:* English Lantern Clocks, 1989; Tramlines to the Stars, 1995; The Clockmakers of London, 1998; contrib. Antiquaries' Jl, Antiquarian Horology, etc. *Heir: s* George Philip James White, *b* 19 Dec. 1987.

WHITE, His Honour Graham Brian Newton; a Circuit Judge, 2007–12; Judicial Member, Parole Board, since 2010; *b* London, 6 Dec. 1942; *s* of Pat and Molly White; *m* 1971, Lesley Williams; five *s* two *d*. *Educ:* Uxendon Manor Co. Prim. Sch., Wembley; Haberdashers' Aske's Hampstead Sch.; College of Law; Univ. of London (LLB by private study 1966). Admitted solicitor, 1965; Dep. District Judge, 1979–2007; Asst Recorder, 1992–96; Recorder, 1996–2007. Mem. Council, Law Soc., 1989–2007; Pres., Herts Law Soc., 1995. *Recreation:* rock 'n' roll drummer. *E:* gwhitesol@btinternet.com.

WHITE, Graham John; Chairman, Marine Aviation and General (London) Ltd, since 2014 (Director, since 2011); *b* 4 June 1946; *s* of William Kenneth White and Evelyn White (*née* Marshall); *m* 1989, Rosemary Maude Hadow; four *d* (and one *d* decd). *Educ:* University Coll. Sch., Hampstead; Gonville and Caius Coll., Cambridge (BA 1968); Cranfield Sch. of Mgt (MBA 1973). Willis Faber Gp, 1968–83 (Gp Co. Sec., 1980); Man. Dir, Richard Beckett Underwriting Agencies Ltd, 1983–86; NY Rep., Merrett Syndicates Ltd, 1987–88; Dir, Jardine Thompson Graham Ltd, 1989–96; Chairman: Bankside Members' Agency Ltd, 1996–97; Murray Lawrence Members' Agency, 1997–98; Chief Exec., Amlin Pvte Capital Ltd, 1998–2000; Chairman: CBS Pvte Capital Ltd, 2000–06; Argenta Private Capital Ltd, 2011– (Dir, 2006–; Man. Dir, 2008–11); Director: CBS Insce Hldgs Ltd, 2000–07; Argenta Holdings plc, 2008–; Newton Follis Partnership Ltd, 2011–. Mem. Council, Lloyd's of London, 2006– (Dep. Chm., 2007–14); Vice Pres., Insurance Inst. of London, 2011– (Mem. Exec. Cttee, 2014–). Director: Music Platform Company Ltd, 2007–11 (Director: English Pocket Opera Ltd, 2002–07; Children's Music Workshop Ltd, 2006–07); City of London Fest., 2009–. Chm., Lloyd's Charities Trust, 2008–09; Trustee, Lloyd's Patriotic Fund, 2010–. *Recreations:* snow-shoeing, golf, tennis, theatre, opera, watching Tottenham Hotspur. *Address:* Marine Aviation and General (London) Ltd, 10 Eastcheap, EC3M 1AJ. *T:* (020) 7398 4010, *Fax:* (020) 7398 4011. *E:* gwhite@maglondon.com. *Clubs:* Travellers, City of London; Kandahar Ski (Mürren).

WHITE, Harvey, DM; FRCS; Consulting Surgeon: Royal Marsden Hospital, since 1976; King Edward VII Hospital for Officers, since 1983; *b* 10 March 1936; *s* of Arthur White and Doris (*née* Dunstan); *m* 1965, Diana Mary Bannister; one *s* one *d*. *Educ:* Winchester Coll.; Magdalen Coll., Oxford (DM, MCh); St Bartholomew's Hosp. FRCS 1970. St Bartholomew's Hospital: Lectr in Physiol., 1966–71; Sen. Surgical Registrar, 1971–76; Chm., Div. of Surgery, Royal Marsden Hosp., 1987–89. Editor: Oxford Med. Gazette, 1956–57; St Bartholomew's Hosp. Jl, 1960–61; Clinical Oncology, 1983–84; European Jl of Surgical Oncology, 1985–87; Chm., Royal Society of Medicine Press Ltd, 1997–. Hunterian Prof.,

RCS, 1988; Hunterian Oration, 1993. Vice-President: Brit. Assoc. of Surgical Oncology, 1984; RSocMed, 2008–10; President: Med. Soc. of London, 1995–96; Hunterian Soc., 2004–05. Mem. Council, Cancer Relief Macmillan Fund, 1991–95. Lead Vice-Patron, Brendoncare Foundn of Elderly, 2014– (Chm., 1986–2003); Trustee, Duchess of Somerset's Almshouses, 1992. Ernest Miles Medal, Brit. Assoc. of Surgical Oncology, 1989; Royal Soc. of Medicine Medal, 2012. *Publications:* (jtly) The Greater Omentum, 1983, Russian edn 1989; (jtly) The Omentum and Malignant Diseases, 1984; An Atlas of Omental Transposition, 1987; contrib. to: History of Surgery, 1974; Royal Hospital St Bartholomew, 1974; Surgical Oncology for Nurses, 1978; The Laser in General Surgery, 1979; Oxford Companion to Medicine, 1986; European Handbook of Oncology, 1989; Aird's Companion to Surgery, 1992; ed. and contrib. various learned books, surgical and cancer jls. *Recreations:* dog-walking, rackets and Real tennis, sailing, fishing. *Address:* Carley Cottage, Bapton, Wylye, Wilts BA12 0SD. *T:* 07860 330444. *Clubs:* Garrick, Royal Society of Medicine, Flyfishers'.

WHITE, Ian; Member (Lab) Bristol, European Parliament, 1989–99; former Partner, McCarthy and White, solicitors. Contested (Lab) SW Reg., EP elecn, 1999.

WHITE, Prof. Ian Hugh, PhD; CEng, FREng, FIET; Van Eck Professor of Engineering, University of Cambridge, since 2001 (Pro-Vice-Chancellor, 2010–11); Fellow, since 2001, and Master, since 2011, Jesus College, Cambridge; *b* 6 Oct. 1959; *s* of Oliver Morrow White and Emily Greenaway White; *m* 1983, Margaret Rosemary Hunt; one *s* one *d*. *Educ:* Belfast Royal Acad.; Jesus Coll., Cambridge (BA 1980, MA 1984; PhD 1984). FREng 2006. Res. Fellow, 1983–84, Asst Lectr, 1984–90, Univ. of Cambridge; Prof. of Physics, Univ. of Bath, 1990–96; University of Bristol: Prof. of Optical Communication Systems, 1996–2001; Hd, Dept of Electrical and Electronic Engrg, 1998–2001. Royal Soc. Leverhulme Res. Fellow, Univ. of Bath, then Bristol, 1995–96. *Publications:* numerous contribs on semiconductor optoelectronic components, optical communications and sensors to learned jls. *Recreations:* church, music. *Address:* Electrical Engineering Division, Department of Engineering, Cambridge University, 9 J. J. Thomson Avenue, Cambridge CB3 0FA. *T:* (01223) 748340, *Fax:* (01223) 748342. *E:* ihw3@cam.ac.uk; Master's Lodge, Jesus College, Cambridge CB5 8BL.

WHITE, Rev. Ian Thomas; President of the Methodist Conference, 2002–03; *b* 6 July 1939; *s* of Sydney White and Annie (*née* Heathcote); *m* 1967, Diana (*née* Casson); two *d*. *Educ:* Hartley Victoria Theol Coll., Manchester. Methodist Minister: Hull Trinity Circuit, 1965–69; Retford Circuit, 1969–72; Bristol South Circuit, 1972–78; Bristol Kingswood Circuit, 1978–87 (Supt Minister, 1981–87); Sec., Bristol Dist Synod, 1978–87; Chairman: Bristol Dist, 1987–98; Channel Is Dist, 1998–2004; Supt Minister, Jersey Circuit, 1998–2004. Moderator, Bristol Free Ch Council, 1989–93. Chm., Methodist Ministers' Housing Soc., 2009–12. *Recreations:* reading, jigsaws, current affairs, theatre, music. *Address:* 26 Aln Crescent, Newcastle upon Tyne NE3 2LU. *T:* (0191) 285 5975.

WHITE, James Ashton V.; *see* Vallance White.

WHITE, Sir Jan Hew D.; *see* Dalrymple-White.

WHITE, Jeremy Nigel; President, White Foundation, since 2001; Chairman, White Capital Partners, since 2009; *b* 20 Jan. 1955; *s* of Colin Lawrence White and Drusilla Marie Goodman; *m* 1989, Kim-Marie Klinger; one *s* three *d*. *Educ:* Leeds Grammar Sch.; Leeds Polytechnic (Dip. Management, Accounting and Finance, Marketing); City Univ. (MBA); Pepperdine Univ. (MA Educn and Psychology; Dist Alumni 1995). Man. Dir, RSS Gp, 1975–79; Chm., White Gp Electronics, 1979–85; Britannia Group: Jt Man. Dir, 1985–86; Pres., 1986–88; Chm., Data Safe Inc., 1988–94; Chief Exec. and Dep. Chm., Prince's Youth Business Trust, 1994–95; Dep. Chm., Youthnet UK, 1995–2000; Chm., Nettec plc, 1995–2001, 2003–06; Dir, Vizual Business Tools Ltd, subseq. OneclickHR plc, 1997–2003; Chm., Newfound International Resorts NV, 2006–08. Mem., Bd, British-Amer. Chamber of Commerce, S Calif, 1993–94, and other LA orgns, 1992–94. Member: Council, Industry and Parlt Trust, 1984–88 and 1995–2000; Young Enterprise Nat. Council, 1986–98; Adv. Council Educn and Trng, Inst. of Econ. Affairs, 1996–2000; DoI Business Links Accreditation Adv. Bd, 1996–98; Small and Medium Size Enterprises Task Gp and Basic Skills Gp, Univ. for Industry, 1999–2000; Economic Wkg Gp, Acad. for Develt of a Democratic Envmt, Malta, 2012–13; Business Start-up Council, Malta Enterprise, 2013–14; Mem., Strategy Bd, Cass Business Sch., 2012–. Trustee: Prince of Wales Award for Innovation, 1995–2014; Technology Coll. Trust, 1998–2000. Gov., Pepperdine Univ., 1993–; Mem. Council, City Univ. Business Sch., 1995–99; Mem. Ct Govs, Univ. of Westminster, 1999–2002. Founder and Judge, World Sax Competition, Montreux, 2002–06. Produced film, Virtuosic Saxophones, 2002. Mem., BSES exp. to W Himalayas, 1989; flying records: Lisbon to LA, 1990; LA to Albuquerque, 1990; Buenos Aires to LA, 1991; La Paz to LA, 1991. FRGS; FLS. *Publications:* The Retail Financial Services Sector, 1985; 21st Century Schools—Educating for the Information Age, 1997. *Recreations:* private flying, collecting, jazz music, photography. *E:* info@whitefoundation.com. *Clubs:* Brooks's, Pilgrims, Royal Geographical; Royal Malta Yacht.

WHITE, Jeremy Richard, (Jerry); Visiting Professor in Modern London History, Birkbeck, University of London, since 2009 (Visiting Professor in London History, 2004–09); Commissioner for Local Administration in England (Local Government Ombudsman), 1995–2009; *b* 23 March 1949; *s* of John Robert White and Molly Loiseau; *m* 1st, 1981, Sandra Margaret Smith (marr. diss. 1995); two *s* one *d*; 2nd, 1995, Rosie Cooper; one *d*. *Educ:* Swanage Grammar Sch.; Cosham and Hackney Technical Colls. Sen. Public Health Inspector, Islington, 1970–81; Asst Borough Housing Officer, Haringey, 1981–84; London Borough of Hackney: Head, Environmental Health, 1984–87; Dir, Environmental Health and Consumer Protection, 1987–89; Chief Exec. and Town Clerk, 1989–95. Vis. Prof., Sch. of Arts, Middlesex Univ., 1996–. Associate Fellow, Centre for Social History, Univ. of Warwick, 1997–. FRHistS 2008. Hon. DLitt London, 2005. *Publications:* Rothschild Buildings: life in an East End tenement block 1887–1920, 1980; The Worst Street in North London: Campbell Road, Islington, between the wars, 1986; Fear of Voting: local democracy and its enemies 1894–1994, 1994; (with Michael Young) Governing London, 1996; London in the Twentieth Century: a city and its people (Wolfson History Prize), 2001; London in the Nineteenth Century: a human awful wonder of God, 2007; London in the Eighteenth Century: a great and monstrous thing, 2012; (ed with Andrew Whitehead) London Fictions, 2013; Zeppelin Nights: London in the First World War, 2014 (Social History Book of the Year, Spear's Book Awards, 2014). *Recreations:* reading, music, London. *Address:* Birkbeck, University of London, Malet Street, WC1E 7HX. *T:* 0845 6010174. *Club:* Reform.

WHITE, John; *see* White, C. J. B.

WHITE, Rev. Canon John Austin, CVO 2012 (LVO 2004); Canon, 1982–2012, and Vice-Dean, 2004–12, Windsor; *b* 27 June 1942; *s* of Charles White and Alice Emily (*née* Precious). *Educ:* The Grammar Sch., Batley, W Yorkshire; Univ. of Hull (BA Hons); College of the Resurrection, Mirfield. Assistant Curate, St Aidan's Church, Leeds, 1966–69; Asst Chaplain, Univ. of Leeds, 1969–73; Asst Dir, post ordination training, Dio. of Ripon, 1970–73; Chaplain, Northern Ordination Course, 1973–82. Dir of Clergy Courses, 1998–2012, Warden, 2000–03, St George's House, Windsor Castle; European Dep. for Dio. Mexico, Anglican Ch of Mexico, 2003–; Hon. Canon, Anglican Cathedral of N Mexico, 2012–. Liveryman, Masons' Co., 2009–. *Publications:* (with Julia Neuberger) A Necessary End: attitudes to death, 1991; (with L. R. Muir) Nicholas Ferrar: materials for a life, 1997; Phoenix in Flight, 1999; (with Mark Stenning) Spoken Light, 2007; poems and various articles. *Recreations:* medieval iconography, drama, Italy, cooking, poetry, Mexico. *Address:* 24 Camm Avenue, Windsor, Berks SL4 4NW.

WHITE, Prof. John Edward Clement Twarowski, CBE 1983; FSA; Durning-Lawrence Professor of the History of Art, University College London, 1971–90 (Vice-Provost, 1984–88; Pro Provost, 1990–95); *b* 4 Oct. 1924; *s* of Brigadier A. E. White and Suzanne Twarowska; *m* 1950, Xenia Joannides (*d* 1991). *Educ:* Ampleforth College; Trinity College, Oxford; Courtauld Institute of Art, University of London. Served in RAF, 1943–47. BA London 1950; Junior Research Fellow, Warburg Inst., 1950–52; PhD Lond. 1952; MA Manchester 1963. Lectr in History of Art, Courtauld Inst., 1952–58; Alexander White Vis. Prof., Univ. of Chicago, 1958; Reader in History of Art, Courtauld Inst., 1958–59; Pilkington Prof. of the History of Art and Dir of The Whitworth Art Gallery, Univ. of Manchester, 1959–66; Vis. Ferens Prof. of Fine Art, Univ. of Hull, 1961–62; Prof. of the History of Art and Chm., Dept of History of Art, Johns Hopkins Univ., USA, 1966–71. Member: Adv. Council of V&A, 1973–76; Exec. Cttee, Assoc. of Art Historians, 1974–81 (Chm., 1976–80); Art Panel, Arts Council, 1974–78; Vis. Cttee of RCA, 1977–86; Armed Forces Pay Review Body, 1986–92; Chm., Reviewing Cttee on Export of Works of Art, 1976–82 (Mem., 1975–82). Trustee, Whitechapel Art Gall., 1976–93 (Vice-Chm., 1985–93); Trustee and Hon. Sec., London Shogyoji Trust, 1997–. Mem., Cttee, Burma Campaign Soc., 2003–09. Membre Titulaire, 1983–95, Membre du Bureau, 1986–92, Comité International d'Histoire de l'Art. *Publications:* Perspective in Ancient Drawing and Painting, 1956; The Birth and Rebirth of Pictorial Space, 1957, 3rd edn 1987 (trans. Italian 1971; trans. French 1992; trans. Spanish 1994); Art and Architecture in Italy, 1250–1400, 1966, 3rd edn 1993 (trans. Spanish 1989); Duccio: Tuscan Art and the Medieval Workshop, 1979; Studies in Renaissance Art, 1983; Studies in Late Medieval Italian Art, 1984; Poems Poèmes Poesie, 1992; Quartet Quartett Quartetto Quatuor, 1993; Trinity Trinita Trinité, 1994; You that I love, 1998; The Breath in the Flute, 2001 (English/Japanese bilingual text); On the Razor's Edge, 2004; New Moon, Old Moon, 2006; Enlightenment, 2010; Postscript, 2011; Pondskaters, 2014; articles in Art History, Art Bulletin, Burlington Magazine, Jl of Warburg and Courtauld Institutes. *Address:* Flat 16, 27 Onslow Square, SW7 3NH. *Club:* Athenæum.

WHITE, John William, CMG 1981; DPhil; FRS 1993; FRSC; FAA; Professor of Physical and Theoretical Chemistry, Australian National University, Canberra, since 1985 (Pro Vice-Chancellor and Chairman, Board of Institute of Advanced Studies, 1992–94; Dean, Research School of Chemistry, 1995–98); *b* Newcastle, Australia, 25 April 1937; *s* of late George John White and Jean Florence White; *m* 1966, Ailsa Barbara, *d* of A. A. and S. Vise, Southport, Qld; one *s* three *d*. *Educ:* Newcastle High Sch.; Sydney Univ. (MSc); Lincoln Coll., Oxford (1851 Schol., 1959; MA, DPhil). ICI Fellow, Oxford Univ.; Research Fellow, Lincoln Coll., 1962; University Lectr, Oxford, 1963–85, Assessor, 1981–82; Fellow, St John's Coll., Oxford, 1963–85 (Vice-Pres. 1973; Hon. Fellow, 1995). Neutron Beam Coordinator, AERE, Harwell, 1974; Asst Director, 1975, Director 1977–80, Institut Laue-Langevin, Grenoble. Argonne Fellow, Argonne Nat. Lab. and Univ. of Chicago, 1985; Christensen Fellow, St Catherine's Coll., Oxford, 1991; Distinguished Vis. Fellow, Victorian Inst. of Chemical Scis, 2007; Distinguished Vis. Prof., CSIRO, 2012. President: Soc. of Crystallographers, Aust., 1989–92; Royal Aust. Chemical Inst., 2000–02; Aust. Inst. of Nuclear Sci. and Engrg, 2004–07 (Vice Pres., 2002–04); Asia-Oceania Neutron Scattering Assoc., 2010–12 (Mem., Exec. Cttee, 2008–); Chairman: Nat. Cttee for Crystallography, Aust., 1992–2001; Neutron Scattering Commn, Internat. Union of Crystallography, 1994–99; Internat. Adv. Cttee on Japanese Atomic Energy Inst./High Energy Physics Lab. Jt Project, J-PARC (formerly Internat. Adv. Cttee, J-PARC project, Japan), 2001–10; Internat. Steering Cttee, Review of Australia's Antarctic Res., 2002; Ext. Review, 2004, 3rd Year Review, 2008, Australian Co-operative Res. Centre for Polymers; Review Cttee, NZ's Antarctic Sci. Report, 2005; Internat. Adv. Cttee, Bragg Inst., 2006–10; Member: Internat. Review Panel, 1998, Internat. Adv. Panel, 2001, Faculty of Science, Nat. Univ. of Singapore; Internat. Review Cttee, Jt Proposal of Japan Hadron Facility and Neutron Sci. Project, 1999; Internat. Cttee on Future of Neutron Sources, IUPAP, 2000; Internat. Adv. Panel, RAE, HEFC, 2001–02; Internat. Adv. Cttee, Central Lab. of the Res. Councils, 2002–; Chemicals and Plastics Sector Adv. Cttee, 2000–03, Emerging Sci. Oversight Cttee, 2004–06, CSIRO; Internat. Review Panel of Chemistry, Argonne Nat. Lab., 2004; Working Gp on Nuclear Physics, OECD, 2005–08; Foresight Cttee, KEK Tsukuba, Japan, 2008. Sec. for Sci. Policy, and Mem. Council, Aust. Acad. of Sci., 1997–2001. Chm., Dirs' Adv. Council, Intense Pulsed Neutron Source, Argonne Nat. Lab., and Univ. of Chicago, 1989–92. Pres., ISCAST Australia, 1991–2006. Chm., James Fairfax-Oxford Australia Scholarship Cttee, 1997–. Hon. Chm., Internat. Adv. Cttee, J-PARC, Tokai, Japan, 2013. Lectures: Tilden, Chemical Soc., 1975; Liversidge, Sydney Univ., 1985; Hinshelwood, Oxford Univ., 1991; Foundn, Assoc. of Asian Chemical Socs, 1991; H. G. Smith, RACI, 1997–98; T. G. H. Jones Meml, Univ. of Qld, 1998; Hudnall-Cars Distinguished, Univ. of Chicago, 1998; 50th Anniversary, Internat. Union of Crystallography, 1998; Founder's, St John's Coll., Oxford, 2007; Liversidge, Royal Soc. NSW, 2010; Kashiwa Public, Univ. of Tokyo, 2011. Member of Council: Epsom Coll., 1981–85; Wycliffe Hall, Oxford, 1983–85; St Mark's Nat. Theol Centre, Canberra, 1997–. Dist. Friend, Oxford Univ., 2008. FRSC 1982; FRACI 1985; FAIP 1986; FAA 1991. Marlow Medal, Faraday Soc., 1969; H. G. Smith Medal and Prize, 1997, Leighton Medal, 2005, RACI; Craig Medal, Aust. Acad. of Sci., 2005. *Publications:* over 300 pubns in scientific jls. *Recreations:* family, squash, ski-ing. *Address:* 2 Spencer Street, Turner, ACT 2612, Australia. *T:* (2) 62486836.

WHITE, Sir John (Woolmer), 4th Bt *cr* 1922; *b* 4 Feb. 1947; *s* of Sir Headley Dymoke White, 3rd Bt and Elizabeth Victoria Mary (*d* 1996), *er d* of late Wilfrid Ingram Wrightson; *S* father, 1971; *m* 1987, Joan Borland; one *s*. *Educ:* Hurst Court, Hastings; Cheltenham College; RAC, Cirencester. *Heir:* *s* Kyle Dymoke Wilfrid White, *b* 16 March 1988. *Address:* Salle Park, Reepham, Norwich, Norfolk NR10 4SG. *Clubs:* Athenæum, MCC.

WHITE, Keith George, CBE 2009; consultant, since 2011; Senior Advisor, ES-KO Group, since 2015 (Chairman, ES-KO (UK) Ltd, 2009–15); Chief Executive, Crown Agents for Oversea Governments and Administrations Ltd, 2005–11; *b* 12 Oct. 1948; *s* of Arthur and Rose White; *m* 1971, Philomena Smith; one *s* one *d*. *Educ:* Bec Sch.; Kingston Poly. (BA London ext.); City of London Poly. (MA Business Law). Crown Agents: Corporate Sec., 1980–98; Dir, 1997–2011; Chief Operating Officer, 1997–2005. Vice Pres., HF Holidays Ltd, 2014– (Pres., 1987–2014); Chm., St Helena Line Ltd, 1992–2005; Dir, SITPRO Ltd, 2000–05. CO, Engr and Logistic Staff Corps, RE (V), 2007–. FCILT 2005; FInstRE 2008. FRSA. *Recreations:* family, walking, browsing in walking kit shops, playing guitar. *Address:* c/o Board Services, ES-KO Group, St Nicholas House, Sutton, Surrey SM1 1EL. *T:* 07714 238454. *Clubs:* Victory Services, Oriental.

WHITE, Kenneth James, MBE 2011; District Judge, Principal Registry of Family Division, 1991–2013; *b* 24 March 1948; *s* of Kenneth William John White and Pamela Blanche Emily White (*née* Seth); *m* 1971, Anne Christine Butcher; one *s* one *d*. *Educ:* Gosport County Grammar Sch., Hants; QMC, Univ. of London (LLB Hons 1969). Qualified as Solicitor, 1972; Partner, R. V. Stokes & Co., Solicitors, Portsmouth, 1974, Sen. Partner, 1991. Mem., Family Cttee, Judicial Studies Bd, 1999–2004. Mem., Portsmouth & Southsea Voluntary Lifeguards, 1968– (Pres. 1985–); Royal Life Saving Society UK: Vice-Pres., 1994–98; Pres., 1998–2004; Chm., Nat. Lifeguard Cttee, 1992–98; Mem., Commonwealth Council, 1998–2004; Pres., Wessex Br., 1981; Dir, Internat. Life Saving Fedn, 2000–09; Hon. Legal Advr, Internat. Life Saving of Europe, 2009–. Knight, Order of Lifesaving, Internat.

Lifesaving Fedn, 2011. *Publications:* (consulting editor) Family Court Reporter, 1992; (contrib.) Atkin's Court Forms, 1994–2013. *Recreations:* swimming, reading, travel, lifesaving, grandchildren.

WHITE, Kevin Charles Gordon, CB 2003; Director General, Human Resources, Home Office, since 2007; *b* 20 July 1950; *s* of John Gordon White and Dorothy Marion White; *m* 1977, Louise Sarah Watt (marr. diss. 2011); three *s. Educ:* Haberdashers' Aske's, Elstree; Univ. of E Anglia (BA Hons); Univ. of Warwick (MA). Senior CS posts in Dept for Employment, 1977–95; Human Resources Dir, Employment Service, 1995–2001; Gp Dir of Human Resources, DWP, 2001–07. FCIPD 1996. FRSA 2002. *Recreations:* music, cooking, theatre. *Address:* Home Office, 2 Marsham Street, SW1P 4DF. *Club:* Druidstone (Broadhaven, Pembrokeshire).

WHITE, Lindsey Anne; *see* Clay, L. A.

WHITE, Malcolm D.; *see* Davis-White.

WHITE, Marco Pierre; chef and restaurateur; *b* 11 Dec. 1961; *s* of late Frank and Maria Rosa White; *m* 1st, 1988, Alexandra McCarthy (marr. diss.); one *d*; 2nd, 1992, Lisa Butcher (marr. diss.); 3rd, 2000, Matilda Conejero-Caldera; two *s* one *d. Educ:* Firtree Primary Sch.; Allerton High Sch., Leeds. Commis: Hotel St George, Harrogate, 1978; Box Tree, Ilkley, 1979; Chef de Partie: Le Gavroche, 1981; Tante Claire, 1983; Sous Chef, Manoir aux Quat' Saisons, 1984–85; Proprietor and Chef: Harveys, 1986–93; The Canteen Restaurant, Chelsea Harbour, 1992–96; Restaurant Marco Pierre White, 1993; Marco Pierre White's Criterion, 1995–2009; Quo Vadis, 1996–2001; Oak Room, Le Meridien, 1997–99; MPW Canary Wharf, 1997; Café Royal Grill Room, 1997; Mirabelle Restaurant, Curzon St, 1998; Belvedere, 1999–; Wheeler's of St James's, 2002; Luciano, 2005; Proprietor, L'Escargot, 1995–2000; Jt Proprietor, Frankie's, 2004–. Michelin Stars 1988, 1990, 1995 (youngest and first GB winner of 3 Michelin stars). Television series: Hell's Kitchen, 2007, 2009; Marco's Great British Feast, 2008; The Chopping Block, USA, 2009; Marco's Kitchen Burnout, 2010. *Publications:* White Heat, 1990; Wild Food from Land and Sea, 1994; Canteen Cuisine, 1995; Glorious Puddings, 1998; The Mirabelle Cookbook, 1999; White Slave: the autobiography, 2006; Marco Pierre White's Great British Feast, 2008. *Recreations:* shooting, fishing, bird watching.

WHITE, Martin Andrew C.; *see* Campbell-White.

WHITE, Maj.-Gen. Martin Spencer, CB 1998; CBE 1991; Lord-Lieutenant of the Isle of Wight, since 2006 (Vice Lord-Lieutenant, 1999–2006); *b* 25 March 1944; *s* of Harold Spencer White and Mary Elizabeth White; *m* 1966, Fiona Margaret MacFarlane; three *s* one *d. Educ:* Sandown GS, IoW; Welbeck Coll.; RMA Sandhurst. FCIT 1992; FILog 1993. Commnd, RASC/RCT, 1966; Staff Coll., Camberley, 1977–78; Comd 4 Div., Transport Regt, 1983–85; Directing Staff, Army Staff Coll., 1985–87; Command: Logistic Support Gp, 1987–89; Force Maintenance Area (Gulf), 1990–91; Transport 1(BR) Corps, 1991–92; RCDS, 1993; Dir of Support, HQ Allied Land Forces Central Europe, 1993–95; Dir-Gen., Logistic Support (Army), 1995–98. Senior Military Adviser: Ernst & Young, subseq. Cap Gemini Ernst & Young, 1999–2003; Deloittes, 2003–08. Col Comdt, RLC, 1998–2009. Hon. Colonel: Southampton Univ. OTC, 1999–2004; 165 Regt RLC, 2001–09. Governor, Ryde Sch., 1997–2006. Liveryman, Co. of Carmen, 1996–2007. DL Isle of Wight, 1998. CStJ 2010. *Publications:* Gulf Logistics: Black Adder's war, 1995. *Recreations:* cricket, sailing. *Address:* Oak Lodge, Seagrove Farm Road, Seaview, Isle of Wight PO34 5HU. *Clubs:* Victory Services; Royal Yacht Squadron; Sea View Yacht.

WHITE, Mary Catherine; *see* Restieaux, M. C.

WHITE, Matthew Graham; Partner, since 2005 and Head of Planning, London, since 2013, Herbert Smith Freehills LLP (formerly Herbert Smith LLP); *b* W Sussex, 30 March 1972; *s* of Graham White and Margaret White (*née* Leighs, later Broad); *m* 2001, Claire Cosgrave; one *s* two *d. Educ:* Imberhorne Comp. Sch., East Grinstead; Clare Coll., Cambridge (BA Hons Econs and Law 1994); Coll. of Law, York (DipLP 1995). Admitted as solicitor, 1997. Herbert Smith: trainee solicitor, 1995–97; Associate, 1997–2005. Trustee, Architecture Foundn, 2013–. LMRTPI 2015. *Recreations:* cycling, triathlon, photography, The Archers. *Address:* Herbert Smith Freehills LLP, Exchange House, Primrose Street, EC2A 2EG. *T:* (020) 7466 2461. *E:* matthew.white@hsf.com.

WHITE, Michael Charles; Associate Editor, since 1989, and Assistant Editor (Politics), since 2006, The Guardian; *b* 21 Oct. 1945; *y s* of Henry Wallis White, master mariner of St Just in Penwith, Cornwall and of Kay (*née* Wood); *m* 1973, Patricia Vivienne Gaudin; three *s. Educ:* Bodmin Grammar Sch.; University Coll. London (BA Hist. 1966; Fellow, 2002). Reporter: Reading Evening Post, 1966–70; London Evening Standard, 1970–71; The Guardian, 1971–: Parly Sketchwriter, 1977–84; Washington Corresp., 1984–88; Political Ed., 1990–2006. Columnist, Health Service Jl, 1977–84, 1992–. Vis. Fellow, Woodrow Wilson Foundn, Princeton, NJ, 1990–. Hon. Fellow, UC Falmouth, 2006. What the Papers Say Sketchwriter of the Year Award, 1982; Political Writer Award, House Magazine, 2003. *Address:* Press Gallery, House of Commons, SW1A 0AA. *T:* (020) 7219 4700; 56 Digby Mansions, Hammersmith Bridge Road, W6 9DF. *Club:* Garrick.

WHITE, Michael John; critic, broadcaster and author; *b* 4 April 1955; *s* of Albert E. White and Doris M. White (*née* Harvey). *Educ:* Langdon Sch., London; Mansfield Coll., Oxford (MA Jurisp.). Called to the Bar, Middle Temple, 1978 (non-practising) (Harmsworth Scholar and Middle Temple Advocacy Prize). Contribs to Observer and Guardian; joined Independent, 1986; Music Critic, The Independent on Sunday, 1990–2000. Columnist: Catholic Herald, 2008–; (online) Daily Telegraph, 2009–; Opera Now, 2012–. Broadcasts for BBC Radio and TV, Channel 4, Classic FM (voted Britain's least boring music critic); presenter: Best of 3, R3, 1998–2000; Opera in Action, R3, 2000–02; Sound Barrier series, R4, 1999; opera libretti writer; awards judge. Lectr, Wigmore Hall and internat. fests. Member, Board of Directors: Spitalfields Fest., 1992–2000; London Internat. Piano Comp., 2002–. Created biographical website for soprano Jennifer Vyvyan, 2010. *Publications:* Wagner for Beginners, 1995; Opera and Operetta, 1997; Introducing Wagner: a graphic guide, 2013. *Recreations:* other people's dogs, researching English singers of the 50s and 60s, church on Sunday. *Address:* 16 Willow Road, Hampstead, NW3 1TJ.

WHITE, Michael Simon; theatre and film producer; *b* 16 Jan. 1936; *s* of Victor R. and Doris G. White; *m* 1965, Sarah Hillsdon (marr. diss. 1973); two *s* one *d*; 2nd, 1985, Louise M. Moores, *d* of late Nigel Moores; one *s. Educ:* Lyceum Alpinum, Zuoz, Switzerland; Pisa University; Sorbonne, Paris. Asst to Sir Peter Daubeny, 1956–61; *stage:* London productions include: The Connection, 1961; Blood Knot, 1966; American Hurrah, 1967; Oh, Calcutta!, 1970; Joseph and the Technicolor Dreamcoat, 1972; Rocky Horror Show, 1973; Loot, 1975; A Chorus Line, 1976; Sleuth, 1978; Deathtrap, 1978; Annie, 1978; Pirates of Penzance, 1982; On Your Toes, 1984; Metropolis, 1989; Bus Stop, 1990; Crazy for You, 1993; Me and Mamie O'Rourke, 1994; She Loves Me, 1994; Fame, 1995; Voyeurz, 1996; Boys in the Band, 1997; Disney's Beauty and the Beast, 1997; Black Goes with Everything, 2000; Notre-Dame de Paris, 2000; Contact, 2002; The Harder They Come, 2008; *films:* include: Monty Python and the Holy Grail, 1974; Rocky Horror Picture Show, 1975; The Comic Strip Presents…, 1983; My Dinner with André, 1984; Ploughman's Lunch, 1984; Moonlighting, 1984; Stranger's Kiss, 1985; The Supergrass, 1985; High Season, 1986; Eat the Rich, 1987; White Mischief, 1987; The Deceivers, 1988; Nuns on the Run, 1989; The Pope Must Die, 1991; Robert's Movie, 1993; Widow's Peak, 1994; Enigma, 2000. Contrib. film, The Last Impressario, 2014. Special Award, Olivier Awards, 2014. *Publications:* Empty Seats, 1984. *Recreations:* art, ski-ing, racing. *Address:* 13 Duke Street, St James's, SW1Y 6DB.

See also S. N. White.

WHITE, Neville Helme; Stipendiary Magistrate for Humberside, 1985–99; *b* 12 April 1931; *s* of Noel Walter White and Irene Helme White; *m* 1958, Margaret Jennifer Catlin (*d* 2013); two *s* one *d. Educ:* Newcastle-under-Lyme High School. RAF, 1949–51. Partner, Grindey & Co., Solicitors, Stoke-on-Trent, 1960–85. Pres., N Staffs Law Soc., 1980–81. Pres., Hull Boys' Club, 1985–99. *Recreations:* music, walking, gardening, reading, all sports, paintings. *Address:* 6 Whybrow Gardens, Castle Village, Berkhamsted HP4 2GU.

WHITE, Prof. Nicholas John, OBE 1999; MD, DSc; FRCP, FMedSci; FRS 2006; Chairman, Wellcome Trust Southeast Asian Tropical Medicine Research Programmes, since 2001; Professor of Tropical Medicine, Mahidol University, Bangkok, since 1995, and University of Oxford, since 1996; *b* 13 March 1951; *s* of John Carlisle White and Eileen Margaret White (*née* Millard); *m* 1997, Jitda; three *d. Educ:* Guy's Hosp. Med. Sch., London (BSc Pharmacol. 1971; MB BS 1st Cl. Hons 1974); MD 1984, DSc 1995, London Univ. Dir, Wellcome Trust Mahidol Univ.-Oxford Tropical Medicine Res. Prog., 1986–2001. Hon. Consultant Physician, John Radcliffe Hosp., Oxford, 1986–. Chm., WHO Antimalarial Treatment Guidelines Cttee, 2004. FMedSci 2001. Gairdner Global Health Award, Gairdner Foundn, Canada, 2010; Prince Mahidol Award, Prince Mahidol Award Foundn, 2010. *Publications:* over 800 scientific articles in jls. *Recreations:* cricket, squash, guitar, gardening. *Address:* Faculty of Tropical Medicine, Mahidol University, 420/6 Rajvithi Road, Bangkok 10400, Thailand. *T:* (2) 2036301, *Fax:* (2) 3549169. *E:* nickw@tropmedres.ac. *Clubs:* British (Bangkok); Royal Bangkok Sports.

WHITE, Sir Nicholas (Peter Archibald), 6th Bt *cr* 1802, of Wallingwells, Nottinghamshire; *b* 2 March 1939; *s* of Captain Richard Taylor White, DSO (2 bars), RN (*d* 1995) and Gabrielle Ursula White (*née* Style) (*d* 1996); *S* uncle, 1996; *m* 1st, 1970, Susan Irene (*d* 2002), *d* of G. W. B. Pollock; two *s* one *d*; 2nd, 2007, Elaine Jeanne Hume, *d* of R. J. Dickson. *Educ:* Eton. Nat. Service, 2nd Lt 2/10th PMO Gurkha Rifles, 1957–59. Courage Ltd, 1959–84; wine trade, 1984–94; Gulf Eternit Industries, Dubai, UAE, 1994–2000; Future Pipe Industries Gp, 2001–06. *Recreations:* tennis, travelling, music. *Heir: s* Christopher David Nicholas White [*b* 20 July 1972; *m* 1st, 2004, Nathalie Hester (marr. diss. 2009); 2nd, 2010, Philippa Sarah Tayler]. *Address:* Little Westlands, Lingfield, Surrey RH7 6DE.

WHITE, Prof. Nigel David, PhD; Professor of Public International Law, since 2009, and Head, School of Law, since 2014, University of Nottingham; *b* Sheffield, 9 April 1961; *s* of David White and Barbara White; *m* 1987, Gillian Ann Hickey; two *s. Educ:* Carlton-le-Willows Comp. Sch., Nottingham; Pembroke Coll., Oxford (BA Hons Juris. 1982); Univ. of Nottingham (PhD 1988). University of Nottingham: Lectr in Law, 1987–95; Sen. Lectr in Law, 1995–99; Prof. of Internat. Orgns, 2000–05; Prof. of Internat. Law, Univ. of Sheffield, 2005–09. *Publications:* The United Nations and the Maintenance of International Peace and Security, 1990; Keeping the Peace, 1997; The United Nations System: toward international justice, 2002; The Law of International Organisations, 2005; Democracy Goes to War, 2009; Advanced Introduction to International Conflict and Security Law, 2014; The Cuban Embargo under International Law, 2014. *Recreations:* gardening, guitars, vinyl. *Address:* School of Law, University of Nottingham, University Park, Nottingham NG7 2RD. *T:* (0115) 846 8238, *Fax:* (0115) 951 5696. *E:* nigel.white@nottingham.ac.uk.

WHITE, Patrick Rockliff; Director, Local Government Policy and Productivity, Department for Communities and Local Government, since 2011; *b* Reading, 5 Oct. 1976; *s* of Ian White and Mary White; *m* 2008, Louise Dunkerley; one *s. Educ:* Thomas Adams Sch., Wem; Manchester Univ. (BA Hons Eng. Lit.); Vienna Univ. Cabinet Office, 1996–2003: various posts, incl. Defence and Overseas Secretariat and Civil Contingencies Secretariat; Exec. Dir, Policy, North West RDA, 2003–09; Cabinet Office: Principal Private Sec. to Minister for the Cabinet Office, 2009–10; Econ. and Domestic Secretariat, 2010–11. *Recreations:* cycling, gardening, electronic music, English literature. *Address:* Department for Communities and Local Government, 2 Marsham Street, SW1P 4DF. *T:* 0303 444 4644. *E:* patrick.white@communities.gsi.gov.uk. *Club:* Reform.

WHITE, Rt Rev. Paul Raymond; an Assistant Bishop, Diocese of Melbourne (Bishop of the Southern Region), since 2007 (Bishop of the Western Region, 2002–07); *b* Sydney, 31 March 1949; *s* of Ronald White and Betty White (*née* Stephenson); *m* 1970, Robyn Jamieson, *d* of Robert Jamieson and Maxine Jamieson (*née* Lang); one *s* one *d. Educ:* Cronulla High Sch.; Bathurst Teachers' Coll.; St Mark's Coll., Canberra (BTh 1985, Dip. Min., 1986, ACT); Heythrop Coll., Univ. of London (MTh 1989). Teacher, NSW Dept of Educn, 1968–71; voluntary work in community-based progs made poss. by periods of paid work in business, industry and educn, 1971–82. Ordained deacon, 1985, priest, 1986; Asst Curate, N Goulburn, NSW, 1985–87; Lucas-Tooth Schol. and Acting Priest i/c, Reigate, UK, 1987–89; Rector, Queanbeyan, NSW, 1989–92; Vicar: Redhill, UK, 1992–96; E Ivanhoe, Vic, 1996–2000. Dir, Theol Educn, dio. Melbourne, 2000–07. *Address:* The Anglican Centre, 209 Flinders Lane, Melbourne, Vic 3000, Australia.

WHITE, Peter Richard; non-executive Director, Reckitt Benckiser (formerly Reckitt & Colman), 1997–2008 (Chairman, Audit Committee, 1998–2006, and Member, Nomination Committee, 1999–2008); *b* 11 Feb. 1942; *m* 1968, Mary Angela Bowyer; one *s* one *d. Educ:* St Paul's School. FCA; FCIB, FCT. Price Waterhouse, 1965–69; Management Accountant, Chief Internal Auditor, Financial Controller, Treasurer, Abbey National Building Soc., 1970–82; Gen. Manager (Finance and Management Services), Alliance Building Soc., 1982–85; Alliance & Leicester Building Society: Gen. Manager (Admin. and Treasury), 1985–87; Dir and Gen. Manager (Develt and Treasury), 1987–89; Dep. Group Chief Exec. and Man. Dir, 1989–91; Gp Chief Exec., Alliance & Leicester Bldg Soc., subseq. Alliance & Leicester plc, 1991–99. Dir, 1990–99, Chm., 1996–99, Girobank plc; Dir, Alliance & Leicester Pensions Investments Ltd, 1989–99. Chairman: Metropolitan Assoc. of Buildings Socs, 1994–95; Council of Mortgage Lenders, 1995–98; Dep. Chm., BSA, 1995–96; Mem. Council, BBA, 1996–99. Trustee: Crimestoppers Trust, 1997–98; Develt Trust (for the Mentally Handicapped), 1997–99. Freeman, City of London, 1996. MInstD; CCMI. *Recreations:* golf, opera, arts. *Address:* 4 Osten Mews, SW7 4HW.

WHITE, Peter Robert, OBE 2006; FSA; Secretary, Royal Commission on the Ancient and Historical Monuments of Wales, 1991–2005; *b* 28 Nov. 1944; *y s* of late John Edward White and Lily Agnes Lois White (*née* Powell); *m* 1973, Christine Margaret Joyce Robertson; two *d. Educ:* Eastbourne Grammar Sch.; Univ. of Leeds (BA History); Univ. of Southampton. FSA 1988; IHBC 1998. Asst Insp. of Ancient Monuments, MPBW, 1966–71; Insp., 1971–82, Prin. Insp., 1982–89, DoE; Head, Historic Buildings Listing, English Heritage, 1989–91. Member: Res. Cttee on Industrial Archaeol., Council of British Archaeol., 1969–91; Wkg Party on Industrial Archaeol., Council of Europe, 1984–89; Exec. Cttee, Soc. of Antiquaries of London, 1994–2002 (Mem. Council, 1992–94); Editl Bd, Cardiganshire County History, 1997–2005; Nat. Adv. Panel, Eur. Assoc. of Archaeologists, 1998–99; Chm., Industrial Archaeol. Panel, English Heritage, 2011–14 (Mem., 1991–2011). Hon. Res. Fellow, Univ. of Wales Lampeter, 2007–10. Vice-Pres., Royal Archaeol Inst., 1994–99 (Mem. Council, 1975–78, 1991–94). Chairman: Hafod Adv. Panel, Natural Resources (formerly Forestry Commn) Wales, 2006–; Wales Cttee, Assoc. of Preservation Trusts, 2007–09; Chm., Ethical Standards Cttee, Dyfed-Powys Police Authy, 2009–12 (Vice-Chm., 2007–09). Chm., Ironbridge Heritage Foundn Ltd, 2013– (Trustee/Dir, 2005–13). FRSA 1999. Hon. Fellow, UC, Northampton, 1999. *Publications:* (with Alan Cook) Sherborne Old Castle, Dorset:

archaeological investigations 1930–1990, 2015; Stott Park Bobbin Mill, 2015; contribs to books and learned jls, particularly on industrial archaeol. *Recreations:* walking, orchestral music. *E:* peterrw@lineone.net.

WHITE, Richard Michael, MBE 1983; HM Diplomatic Service, retired; Head, Foreign and Commonwealth Office Outplacement Service (Prosper), since 2007; *b* 12 July 1950; *s* of late Geoffrey Richard White and of Frances Kathleen (*née* Kendrick); *m* 1979, Deborah Anne Lewis, *d* of Kenneth H. Lewis, OBE and Jean Lewis (*née* Tearle); one *s* one *d*. *Educ:* King's Sch., Pontefract; Richmond Sch., Yorkshire. VSO, Senegal, 1968–69; entered HM Diplomatic Service, 1969: Attaché, UK Delegn to EEC, Brussels, 1971–74; Persian lang. studies, SOAS, and Yazd, Iran, 1974–75; Third Sec. (Commercial), Tehran, 1975–77; Second Sec. and Asst Private Sec. to Minister of State, Lord Privy Seal, FCO, 1978–79; FCO, 1979–80; Second Sec. (Commercial/Admin) and Consul, Dakar, 1980–84; First Secretary: (Technol.), Paris, 1984–88; FCO, 1988–92; Dep. High Comr, Valletta, 1992–95; FCO, 1996–2002, Hd, Migration and Visa Div., 1997–2000, Asst Dir, Personnel Services, 2000–02; Counsellor (Mgt), Paris, 2003–07. *Recreations:* family history, French cuisine, walking. *Address:* c/o Foreign and Commonwealth Office, King Charles Street, SW1A 2AH. *E:* richard.white@fco.gov.uk.

WHITE, Prof. Robert George, PhD, DSc; FREng; Professor of Vibration Studies, University of Southampton, 1983–98, now Emeritus; *b* 11 Dec. 1939; *s* of N. A. J. White and G. M. White; *m* 1988, Patricia Margaret (*née* Sidley); one step *s* one step *d*. *Educ:* Farnborough Coll. of Technology; Southampton Univ. (PhD 1970; DSc 1992). FInstP 1981; FIOA 1985; FRAeS 1986; FREng (FEng 1995). RAE, Farnborough, 1957–67; Dir, Inst. of Sound and Vibration Res., 1982–89, Inst. of Transducer Technol., 1989–93, Hd of Dept of Aeronautics and Astronautics, 1995–98, Southampton Univ. Hon. FIOA 2003. (Jtly) Simms Prize, RAeS, 1982; Tyndall Medal, 1984, Engrg Medal, 2008, Inst. of Acoustics. *Publications:* (ed jtly) Noise and Vibration, 1982; 210 conf. papers and contribs to jls. *Recreations:* flying, walking. *Address:* 41 Lower Bere Wood, Waterlooville, Hants PO7 7NQ.

WHITE, Prof. Robert Stephen, FRS 1994; FGS; Professor of Geophysics, Cambridge University, since 1989; Fellow, since 1988, Founding Director, 2006, and Director, since 2012, Faraday Institute for Science and Religion, St Edmund's College, Cambridge; *b* 12 Dec. 1952; 2nd *s* of James Henry White and Ethel Gladys (*née* Cornick); *m* 1976, Helen Elizabeth (*née* Pearce); one *s* one *d*. *Educ:* Market Harborough and West Bridgford Comprehensive Schs; Emmanuel Coll., Cambridge (Sen. Schol., 1972–74; Bachelor Schol., 1974–77; BA, MA, PhD). FRAS 1979; FGS 1989. Research Assistant: Berkeley Nuclear Labs, CEGB, 1970–71; Dept of Geodesy and Geophysics, Cambridge, 1978; postdoctoral schol., Woods Hole Oceanographic Instn, USA, 1978–79; Res. Fellow, Emmanuel Coll., Cambridge, 1979–82; Sen. Asst in Res., 1981–85, Asst Dir of Res., 1985–89, Dept of Earth Scis, Cambridge Univ. Cecil and Ida H. Green Schol., Scripps Instn of Oceanography, UCSD, USA, 1987; Guest Investigator, Woods Hole Oceanographic Instn, 1988. Adjunct Prof., Univ. of Iceland, 2009–; Harold Jeffreys Lectr, RAS, 2013. Bigsby Medal, Geol Soc., 1991; George P. Woollard Award, Geol Soc. Amer., 1997. *Publications:* (with D. Alexander) Beyond Belief: science, faith and ethical challenges, 2004; (with N. Spencer) Christianity, Climate Change and Sustainable Living, 2007; Creation in Crisis: Christian perspectives on sustainability, 2009; (with J. A. Moo) Hope in an Age of Despair, 2013; Who is to Blame?: disasters, nature and acts of God, 2014; papers in many internat. jls. *Recreations:* reading, walking, messing around in the garden and house. *Address:* Bullard Laboratories, Madingley Road, Cambridge CB3 0EZ. *T:* (01223) 337187, *Fax:* (01223) 360779.

WHITE, Robin Bernard G.; *see* Grove-White.

WHITE, Roger, FSA 1986; Executive Secretary, Garden History Society, 1992–96; *b* 1 Sept. 1950; *s* of Geoffrey and Zoë White. *Educ:* Ifield Grammar School; Christ's College, Cambridge (1st class Hons, Hist. of Art Tripos); Wadham College, Oxford. GLC Historic Buildings Div., 1979–83; Sec., Georgian Gp, 1984–91; Mem., Chiswick House Adv. Panel, 1991–2007. Trustee, Pell Wall Preservation Trust, 1994–98. Curator: John Piper: Georgian Arcadia, Marlborough Fine Art, 1987; Nicholas Hawksmoor and the Replanning of Oxford, RIBA, 1997, Ashmolean Mus., 1998; Europe and the English Baroque, V&A Mus., 2009. Chichele Lectr, All Souls Coll., Oxford, 1999; Hugh Shirreff Lect., Historic Houses Assoc., 2011. Contributing Ed., House and Garden, 1994–. *Publications:* John Vardy, 1985; Georgian Arcadia: architecture for the park and garden, 1987; The Architectural Evolution of Magdalen College, Oxford, 1993; Chiswick House and Gardens, 2001; The Architectural Drawings of Magdalen College, Oxford, 2001; Witley Court and Gardens, 2003, 2nd edn 2008; Belsay Hall, Castle and Gardens, 2005; (with Graham Byfield) Oxford Sketchbook, 2005; (ed) A Life of Frederick, Prince of Wales 1707–1751, 2007; Holkham Hall, 2010; (contrib.) William Kent: designing Georgian Britain, 2013; contribs to Architectural Hist., Jl of Garden Hist., Country Life, World of Interiors. *Recreation:* visiting and writing about historic buildings. *Address:* 142 Weir Road, SW12 0ND.

WHITE, Sandra; Member (SNP) Glasgow Kelvin, Scottish Parliament, since 2011 (Glasgow, 1999–2011); *b* 17 Aug. 1951; *d* of Henry Harley and Elizabeth Rodgers; *m* 1971, David White; two *s* one *d*. *Educ:* Garthamlock Sen. Sec. Sch.; Cardonald Coll. of Further Educn; Glasgow Coll. (Social Science degree). Clerkess, Gray Dunn, 1966–68; Timothy Whites, then Boots Chemist, 1968–73; Littlewoods Pools, 1973–88. Member (SNP): Renfrew DC, 1989; Renfrewshire CC, 1995–99. *Recreations:* walking, reading, gardening. *Address:* Scottish Parliament, Edinburgh EH99 1SP. *T:* (0131) 348 5000.

WHITE, Sasha Nicolas; QC 2013; *b* London, 8 Aug. 1967; *s* of Michael Simon White, *qv* and Sarah White; *m* 1997, Clare Heather Banks Skinner; two *s* one *d*. *Educ:* Bedales Sch.; Trinity Coll., Cambridge (BA Law 1990). Called to the Bar, Inner Temple, 1991; in practice as a barrister, specialising in planning law, Chambers of Lionel Read, QC, 1993–2002, Landmark Chambers, 2002–. Liveryman, Cordwainers' Co., 2000– (Renter Warden, 2012–13). *Publications:* Planning Appeals, 1997. *Recreations:* cricket, golf, tennis, football, Rugby, Northumberland, Scotland. *Address:* Landmark Chambers, 180 Fleet Street, EC4A 2HG. *T:* (020) 7430 1221, *Fax:* (020) 7421 6060. *E:* sashawhite@landmarkchambers.co.uk. *Clubs:* Royal Automobile, MCC; Kent County Cricket, Primrose Hill Cricket, Aston Rowant Cricket (Life Vice Pres., 2010–; Vice Chm., 2014–); Alnmouth Golf, Huntercombe Golf; Arsenal Football, Rangers Football; Western Province Cricket (Cape Town).

WHITE, Sharon Michele, (Mrs R. W. Chote); Chief Executive, Ofcom, since 2015; *b* 21 April 1967; *d* of Curtis Gustavus White and Bernice White; *m* 1997, Robert William Chote, *qv*; two *s*. *Educ:* Fitzwilliam Coll., Cambridge (BA Hons Econs 1988); University Coll. London (MSc Econs 1993). HM Treasury, 1990–95; First Sec., Econ., Washington, 1995–97; Advr on Welfare Reform to the Prime Minister, 1997–99; Sen. Economist, World Bank, 1999–2002; Dir of Policy, DFID, 2003–06; Dir of Welfare to Work, DWP, 2006–09; Ministry of Justice: Chief Exec., Office for Criminal Justice Reform, 2009–10; Dir Gen., Strategy, 2010; Dir Gen., Law, Rights and Internat., 2010–11; Acting Dir Gen., Middle E and N Africa, DFID, 2011; Dir Gen., Public Spending, 2012–13, Second Permanent Sec., 2013–15, HM Treasury. *Recreation:* childcare. *Address:* Ofcom, Riverside House, 2A Southwark Bridge Road, SE1 9HA.

WHITE, Prof. Simon David Manton, PhD; FRS 1997; Director, Max Planck Institute for Astrophysics, since 1994; *b* 30 Sept. 1951; *s* of David and Gwynneth White; *m* 1st, 1984, Judith Dianne Jennings (marr. diss. 1990); 2nd, 1994, Guinevere Alice Mei-Ing Kauffmann; one *s*. *Educ:* Christ's Hosp.; Jesus Coll., Cambridge (BA 1973; MA 1976; PhD 1977); Univ. of Toronto (MSc 1974). Lindemann Fellow, 1977–78, Sen. Res. Fellow, 1980–83, Univ. of Calif at Berkeley; Res. Fellow, Churchill Coll., Cambridge, 1978–80; Associate Prof., 1983–87, Prof., 1987–90, Univ. of Arizona; Sheepshanks Reader, Univ. of Cambridge, 1990–94. Scientific Mem., Max Planck Soc., 1994–. *Publications:* Morphology and Dynamics of Galaxies, 1983. *Recreations:* ski-ing, singing, violin, Morris Dancing. *Address:* Max Planck Institut für Astrophysik, Karl Schwarzschild Strasse 1, 85748 Garching bei München, Germany. *T:* (89) 300002211.

WHITE, Stephen Fraser; consulting engineer; *b* 13 May 1922; *s* of Robert and Iola White; *m* 1953, Judith Hamilton Cox; two *s* one *d*. *Educ:* Friars, Bangor; Nottingham Univ. BSc; FICE, MIWEM. War Service in Indian Electrical and Mechanical Engineers, discharged 1947. G. H. Hill and Sons, Consulting Civil Engineers, 1947–59; Cardiff Corporation, 1959–62; Engineering Inspector, Min. of Housing and Local Govt, 1962–70; Dir of Water Engineering, Dept of the Environment, 1970–77; Sen. Technical Advr to Nat. Water Council, 1977–83. *Recreations:* golf, bridge. *Address:* Rosehill, 4 Goodens Lane, Great Doddington, Northants NN29 7TY.

WHITE, Prof. Stephen Leonard, PhD, DPhil, LittD; FBA 2010; James Bryce Professor of Politics, University of Glasgow, since 1991; *b* Dublin, 1 July 1945; *s* of William John White and Edna White (*née* McGuckin); *m* 1973, Ishbel MacPhie; one *s*. *Educ:* Trinity Coll., Dublin (BA 1st Cl. Hons Pols and Mod. Hist. 1967; Exhibnr, Foundn Scholar; LittD 2001); Univ. of Glasgow (PhD Soviet Studies 1973); Wolfson Coll., Oxford (MA, DPhil Pols 1987). University of Glasgow: Lectr in Politics, 1971–85; Reader in Politics, 1985–91; Sen. Associate Mem., Sch. of Central and E Eur. Studies, 1993–. Vis. Prof., Inst. of Applied Pols, Moscow, 1992–; Adjunct Prof. of Eur. Studies, Bologna Center, Johns Hopkins Univ., 2008–11. Pres., British Assoc. for Slavonic and E Eur. Studies, 1994–97. Founder AcSS 1999; FRSE 2002. Gen. Ed., Cambridge Russian, Soviet and Post-Soviet Monographs, 1990–2000; Ed., Jl of Communist Studies and Transition Politics, 1994–2011; Member, Editorial Board: Europe-Asia Studies, 1980–; Slavonica (formerly Scottish Slavonic Review), 1989–; Pol Sci. Qly, 1998–2004; Perspectives on Eur. Politics and Soc., 2000–; Comparative Eur. Politics, 2003–; Internat. Politics, 2004–; Politics, 2006–; Post-Soviet Affairs, 2011–; Mem., Editl Cttee, BASEES/Routledge Series on Russian and E Eur. Studies, 2001–. *Publications:* The USSR: portrait of a superpower, 1978; Political Culture and Soviet Politics, 1979; Britain and the Bolshevik Revolution: a study in the politics of diplomacy 1920–24, 1980; (ed with Dan Nelson) Communist Legislatures in Comparative Perspective, 1982; (jtly) Communist Political Systems: an introduction, 1982, 2nd edn 1987; (ed with W. B. Simons) The Party Statutes of the Communist World, 1984; The Origins of Detente: the Genoa conference and Soviet-Western relations, 1921–1922, 1986; (ed with Dan Nelson) Communist Politics: a reader, 1986; (ed with A. Pravda) Ideology and Soviet Politics, 1988; The Bolshevik Poster, 1988; Soviet Communism: programme and rules, 1989; (ed jtly) Gorbachev and Gorbachevism, 1989; (jtly) Communist and Postcommunist Political Systems, 3rd edn, 1990; (ed jtly) Developments in Soviet Politics, 1990, 3rd edn as Developments in Soviet and Post-Soviet Politics, 1994; Gorbachev in Power, 1990; (ed and contrib.) Handbook of Reconstruction in Eastern Europe and the USSR, 1991; Gorbachev and After, 1991, 4th edn 1993; (ed) New Directions in Soviet History, 1991; Developments in Central and East European Politics, 1993; (jtly) The Politics of Transition: shaping a post-Soviet future, 1993; (ed jtly) The Soviet Transition: from Gorbachev to Yeltsin, 1993; Russia Goes Dry: alcohol, state and society, 1996; (ed jtly) Developments in Russian Politics 4, 1997; (jtly) How Russia Votes, 1997; (jtly) Elections and Voters in Post-Communist Russia, 1998; Developments in Central and East European Politics 2, 1998; Russia's New Politics, 2000; (with Evan Mawdsley) The Soviet Elite from Lenin to Gorbachev: the CPSU Central Committee and its members 1917–1991, 2000; Communism and its Collapse, 2001; (ed with Dan Nelson) The Politics of the Postcommunist World, 2001; (ed with Rick Fawn) Russia After Communism, 2002; (ed jtly) Postcommunist Belarus, 2005; (jtly) Putin's Russia and the Enlarged Europe, 2006; (ed with Paul Webb) Party Politics in New Democracies, 2007; (jtly) Politics in Europe, 3rd edn 2003 to 6th edn 2015; (ed jtly) Developments in Central and East European Politics 4, 2007, 5, 2013; (ed) Media, Culture and Society in Putin's Russia, 2008; (ed) Politics and the Ruling Group in Putin's Russia, 2008; (ed jtly) Developments in Russian Politics 7, 2010; Understanding Russian Politics, 2011; (ed with Lena Jonson) Waiting for Reform under Putin and Medvedev, 2012; (ed jtly) Developments in Russian Politics 8, 2014; (with Valentina Feklyunina) Identities and Foreign Policies in Russia, Ukraine and Belarus, 2014. *Recreations:* film, theatre, travel. *Address:* (home) 11 Hamilton Drive, Glasgow G12 8DN; Department of Politics, Adam Smith Building, 40 Bute Gardens, University of Glasgow, Glasgow G12 8RT. *T:* (0141) 330 5352. *E:* s.white@socsci.gla.ac.uk.

WHITE, Air Vice-Marshal Terence Philip, CB 1987; DL; CEng, FIET; at leisure; *b* 1 May 1932; *s* of Horace Arthur White and Evelyn Annie White (*née* Simpson); *m* 1956, Sheila Mary (*née* Taylor) (*d* 2015); three *d*. *Educ:* Wellingborough Technical Inst.; Rugby Coll. of Technology and Arts; RAF Engineering College. Electrical engineering apprentice, BTH Co., 1948–53; Junior Design Engineer, BTH Co., 1953; commissioned RAF Signals Officer, 1954–56; RAF Permt commn, Elect. Engr, 1957; attached RAAF, 1958–60; RAF weapons, communications and radar appts, 1963–67; OC Wing, RAF, Fylingdales, 1967–70; RAF Staff Coll., 1971; commanded RAF N Luffenham, 1972–74; Mem., RCDS, 1975; Senior Elect. Engr, HQ RAF Strike Command, 1976–77; Dir, Engineering Policy MoD (Air), 1978–80; Air Officer, Engrg and Supply, HQ RAF Germany, 1981–82; AOC Maintenance Units and AO Maintenance, RAF Support Comd, 1983–87. Vice Chm. (Air), E Midlands TAVRA, 1988–98. Hon. Air Cdre, County of Lincoln RAuxAF Sqn, 1992–2005; Hon. County Rep., Lincs, RAF Benevolent Fund, 1995–2003. DL Lincoln, 1994. *Publications:* contribs to RAF and professional jls. *Recreations:* antiques, travel. *Address:* Eccleston, 45 Lansdown Road, Cheltenham, Glos GL51 6PT. *Club:* Royal Air Force.

WHITE, Tom; *see* White, D. T.

WHITE, Rev. Canon Prof. Vernon Philip; Canon Theologian of Westminster Abbey, since 2011; Visiting Professor of Theology, King's College London, since 2011; *b* London, 16 March 1953; *s* of Raymond and Yvonne White; *m* 1977, Joy Valerie Hillyer; one *s*. *Educ:* Eltham Coll.; Clare Coll., Cambridge (BA 1975; MA 1979); Oriel Coll., Oxford (MLitt). Ordained deacon, 1977, priest, 1978; Tutor, Wycliffe Hall, Oxford, 1977–83; Lazenby Chaplain and Lectr, Exeter Univ., 1983–87; Dir of Ordinands, Dio. of Guildford, and Rector, Wotton and Holmbury St Mary, 1987–93; Chancellor of Lincoln Cathedral, 1993–2001; Special Lectr, Nottingham Univ., 1993–2001; Principal, Southern Theol Educn and Trng Scheme, 2001–11. Hon. Canon Theologian, Winchester Cath., 2006–11. *Publications:* The Fall of a Sparrow, 1985; Atonement and Incarnation, 1991; Paying Attention to People, 1996; Identity, 2002; Counterpoints, 2005; Life Beyond Death, 2006; Purpose and Providence: taking soundings in Western thought, literature and theology, 2015; articles in Theology. *Recreations:* mountain walking, 19th and 20th Century English literature, cricket. *Address:* 3 Little Cloister, Westminster Abbey, SW1P 3PL. *E:* vernon.white@westminster-abbey.org.

WHITE, Sir Willard Wentworth, OM (Jamaica) 2000; Kt 2004; CBE 1995; singer, actor; President, Royal Northern College of Music, since 2008; *b* 10 Oct. 1946; *s* of Egbert and Gertrude White; *m* 1972, Gillian Jackson; three *s* one *d*. *Educ:* Excelsior High Sch., Kingston, Jamaica; Juilliard Sch. of Music (BM). Guest singer, recitalist and recording artist, UK and overseas; singing rôles include Sarastro, Osmin, Sprecher, Leporello, Banquo, King Philip, Grand Inquisitor, Ferrando, Wotan, Klingsor, Hunding, Fafner, King Henry, Orestes, Porgy, Golaud, Pizarro, Prince Khovansky, Mephistopheles (Gounod's Faust and Berlioz's

Damnation of Faust); Nekrotzar, Moses, four villains in Tales of Hoffman, Wanderer, Don Fernando; *stage:* title rôle, Othello, RSC, 1989. Prime Minister of Jamaica's Medal of Appreciation, 1987.

WHITE, William Kelvin Kennedy, CMG 1983; HM Diplomatic Service, retired; *b* 10 July 1930; *y s* of late Kennedy White, JP, Caldy, Cheshire, and Violet White; *m* 1957, Susan Margaret, *y d* of late R. T. Colthurst, JP, Malvern, Worcs; three *s. Educ:* Birkenhead Sch.; Merton Coll., Oxford. 2nd Lieut Manchester Regt, 1949–50; Lieut 13th (Lancs) Bn, Parachute Regt, TA, 1950–54. Entered HM Foreign (later Diplomatic) Service, 1954; Foreign Office, 1954–56, attending UN Gen. Assemblies, 1954 and 1955; 3rd Sec., Helsinki, 1956–57; 2nd Sec., Commissioner-General's Office, Singapore, 1957–61; 2nd Sec., then 1st Sec., FO, 1961–66; 1st Sec. (Commercial), Stockholm, 1966–69; 1st Sec., then Counsellor and Head of Republic of Ireland Dept, FCO, 1969–74; Counsellor, New Delhi, 1974–77; Head of South Asian Dept, FCO, 1978–80; Minister, Canberra, 1980–81; Dep. Chief Clerk and Chief Inspector, FCO, 1982–84; High Comr to Zambia, 1984–87; Ambassador to Indonesia, 1988–90. Mem. Council, Univ. of Surrey, 1991–97. *Address:* Church Farm House, North Moreton, near Didcot, Oxon OX11 9BA. *Club:* Moreton CC.

WHITE, Ven. William Robert S.; *see* Stuart-White.

WHITE-COOPER, (William) Robert (Patrick), FCII; Director, Marsh & McLennan Companies, 1998–2000; *b* 17 March 1943; *s* of William Ronald White-Cooper and Alison Mary White-Cooper; *m* 1965, Jennifer Margaret Hayward; one *s* three *d. Educ:* Diocesan Coll., Cape Town. FCII 1970. Various exec. posts, Price Forbes Gp, S Africa, 1962–83; Chairman: Sedgwick UK Ltd, 1986–89; Sedgwick Europe Ltd, 1989–93; Sedgwick Noble Lowndes Gp, 1993–96; Chief Exec., Sedgwick Gp plc, 1997–98. Chm., Adv. Bd, Sapiens, 2004–07. Past President: Insce Inst. of London; Insce Inst. of Cape of Good Hope. Dep. Chm., Addaction, 2001–13. *Recreations:* tennis, golf, spectating cricket and Rugby, biographies, antiques. *Clubs:* MCC; Swinley Forest Golf, Wentworth; Kelvin Grove, Steenberg Golf, Western Province Cricket (Cape Town).

WHITE-SPUNNER, Lt Gen. Sir Barnabas William Benjamin, (Sir Barney), KCB 2011; CBE 2002; Executive Chairman, Countryside Alliance, since 2012; *b* 31 Jan. 1957; *s* of late Benjamin Nicholson, (Tommy), White-Spunner and Elizabeth, (Biddy), White-Spunner; *m* 1989, Amanda Faulkner; one *s* two *d. Educ:* Eton; Univ. of St Andrews (MA 1978). Commnd Blues and Royals, 1979; Dep. Leader, British-Chinese Taklamakan Expedn, 1993; MA to CDS, 1994–96; CO Household Cavalry Regt, 1996–98; Dep. Dir Defence Policy, 1998–2000; Commander: 16 Air Assault Bde, 2000–02; NATO Op. Harvest Macedonia, 2001; Kabul Multi-Nat. Bde, 2002; Chief of Jt Force Ops UK, 2003–05; COS HQ Land Comd, 2005–07; GOC 3rd (UK) Div., 2007–09; GOC Multi Nat. Div., SE Iraq, 2008; Comdr Field Army, 2009–12. Chairman: From Poverty to Opportunity, CAFOD, 2013–; Sandpit Investments, 2013–. Trustee, Nat. Army Mus., 2012–. Corresp., The Field, 1992–2000; Ed., Baily's Hunting Directory, 1996–2009. Hon. Colonel: Kent and Sharpshooter Yeo., 2008–10; Tayforth Univs OTC, 2009–13; Colonel Commandant: HAC, 2010–13; Royal Yeo., 2010–. Hon. Legionnaire 1st Cl., French Foreign Legion; Legion of Merit (USA), 2009. *Publications:* Baily's Hunting Companion, 1994; Our Countryside, 1996; Great Days, 1997; Horse Guards, 2006; Of Living Valour: the story of the soldiers of Waterloo, 2015. *Recreations:* Central Asia, hunting, fishing. *Address:* Countryside Alliance, Old Town Hall, 367 Kennington Road, SE11 4PT. *Clubs:* Turf, Pratts.

WHITEFIELD, Gavin, CBE 2011; Chief Executive, North Lanarkshire Council, since 2000; *b* 7 Feb. 1956; *s* of late Gavin Whitefield and Annie Whitefield; *m* 1981, Grace Tait; two *d. Educ:* DPA 1990; CPFA 1996. Audit Asst, Exchequer and Audit Dept, 1974–76; Clydesdale District Council: Asst Auditor, 1976–84; Computer Develt Officer, 1984–86; Principal Housing Officer (Finance and Admin), 1986–89; Asst Dir of Housing (Finance and Admin), Motherwell DC, 1989–95; Dir, Housing and Property Services, N Lanarks Council, 1995–2000. Chm., Solace Scotland, 2007–08. *Recreations:* hill walking, football. *Address:* North Lanarkshire Council, Civic Centre, Windmillhill Street, Motherwell ML1 1AB. *T:* (01698) 302252, *Fax:* (01698) 230265. *E:* chief.executive@northlan.gov.uk.

WHITEFIELD, Karen; Member (Lab) Airdrie and Shotts, Scottish Parliament, 1999–2011; *b* 8 Jan. 1970; *d* of William and Helen Whitefield. *Educ:* Calderhead High Sch.; Glasgow Poly. (BA Hons Public Admin and Mgt). Civil Servant, Benefits Agency, 1992; Personal Asst to Rachel Squire, MP, 1992–99. Contested (Lab) Falkirk, 2015. Mem., Girls' Bde, Scotland. *Recreations:* reading, travel, swimming.

WHITEFORD, Eilidh, PhD; MP (SNP) Banff and Buchan, since 2010; *b* Aberdeen, 24 April 1969; *d* of Douglas Dodson Whiteford and Kathleen Whiteford (*née* MacLeod); *m* 2010, Stephen Smith. *Educ:* Banff Acad.; Univ. of Glasgow (MA Hons 1991; PhD 1998); Univ. of Guelph (MA 1994). Lectr in Scottish Literature and Academic Develt Officer, Univ. of Glasgow, 1999; Co-ordinator, Scottish Carers' Alliance, 2001–03; Campaigns Manager, Scotland, Oxfam, 2003–09. *Recreation:* music. *Address:* House of Commons, SW1A 0AA. *T:* (020) 7219 7005. *E:* eilidh.whiteford.mp@parliament.uk.

WHITEHEAD, Dr Alan Patrick Vincent; MP (Lab) Southampton Test, since 1997; *b* 15 Sept. 1950; *m*; one *s* one *d. Educ:* Southampton Univ. (BA 1973; PhD 1976). Dep. Dir, 1976–79, Dir, 1979–83, Outset; Dir, British Inst. of Industrial Therapy, 1983–92; Prof. of Public Policy, Southampton Inst., 1992–97. Mem. (Lab), Southampton CC, 1980–92 (Leader, 1984–92). Parly Under-Sec. of State, DTLR, 2001–02. Member: Select Cttee on Envmt, Transport and Regions, 1997–99, on constitutional affairs, 2003–10, on Energy and Climate Change, 2008–; Envmtl Audit Select Cttee, 2010–15; Standards and Privileges Cttee, 2005–13; Chairman: All Party Ports Gp, 1998–2001; Parly Renewable and Sustainable Energy Gp, 2003–; Parly Sustainable Resource (formerly Waste) Gp, 2003–; British-Polish Parly Gp, 2008–. *Address:* House of Commons, SW1A 0AA. *T:* (020) 7219 3000.

WHITEHEAD, Hon. Dame Annabel Alice Hoyer, DCVO 2014 (CVO 2002; LVO 1987); Lady in Waiting to the Queen, since 2002; *b* Washington, DC, 1943; *d* of 1st Baron Inchyra, GCMG, CVO; *m* 1973, Christopher Whitehead; one *s* one *d.* Lady in Waiting to Princess Margaret, 1971–2002. *Address:* Seend Lodge, Seend, Wilts SN12 6NU.

WHITEHEAD, Edward Anthony, (Ted); playwright; *b* 3 April 1933; *s* of Edward Whitehead and Catherine Curran; *m* 1st, 1958, Kathleen Horton (marr. diss. 1976); two *d*; 2nd, 1976, Gwenda Bagshaw. *Educ:* Christ's Coll., Cambridge (MA). Military Service, King's Regt (Infantry), 1955–57. *TV plays:* Under the Age; The Peddler; The Proofing Session; The Blonde Bombshell; *TV adaptations:* The Detective; Jumping the Queue; The Life and Loves of a She-Devil; Firstborn; The Free Frenchman; The Cloning of Joanna May; A Question of Guilt; Tess of the D'Urbervilles; The Mayor of Casterbridge; *stage adaptation:* The Dance of Death; *radio play:* Features Like Mine, 2005. Evening Standard Award, and George Devine Award, 1971; BAFTA Award, 1986. *Publications:* The Foursome, 1972; Alpha Beta, 1972; The Sea Anchor, 1975; Old Flames, 1976; The Punishment, 1976; Mecca, 1977; World's End, 1981; The Man Who Fell in Love with his Wife, 1984; Collected Plays, 2005. *Recreations:* soccer, obituaries, cats. *Address:* c/o Mark Casarotto, Waverley House, 7–12 Noel Street, W1F 8GQ. *T:* (020) 7287 4450.

WHITEHEAD, Frank Ernest; Deputy Director (Statistics), Office of Population Censuses and Surveys, 1987–89; *b* 21 Jan. 1930; *s* of Ernest Edward Whitehead and Isabel Leslie; *m* 1961, Anne Gillian Marston; three *s. Educ:* Leyton County High School; London School of Economics. BSc (Econ). National Service, RAF, 1948–49. Rio Tinto Co. Ltd, 1952–54; Professional Officer, Central Statistical Office, Fedn of Rhodesia and Nyasaland, 1955–64; Statistician, General Register Office, 1964–68; Chief Statistician, Min. of Social Security, later DHSS, 1968–77; Head of Social Survey Div., Office of Population Censuses and Surveys, 1977–82; Under Secretary, 1982; Dep. Dir, OPCS, 1982–87. Vice-Pres., Royal Statistical Soc., 1988–89 (Council, 1987–92). *Publications:* Social Security Statistics: reviews of United Kingdom statistical sources, vol. II (ed W. F. Maunder), 1974; contribs to Statistical News, Population Trends. *Recreations:* family history, gardening.

WHITEHEAD, (Godfrey) Oliver, CBE 1987; FICE; President, Smeatonian Society of Civil Engineers, 2012; *b* 9 Aug. 1941; *s* of late Clarence Whitehead and Mary Whitehead (*née* Gartside); *m* 1965, Stephanie McAllister; three *s* one *d. Educ:* Hulme Grammar Sch., Oldham; Univ. of Bradford (BSc Civil Engrg). FICE 1992. John Laing Plc, 1963–86: Man. Dir, John Laing Construction Ltd, 1982–86; Exec. Dir, John Laing Plc 1983–86; Chm., Jt Venture (Laing-Mowlem-ARC) which built Mt Pleasant Airport, Falkland Is, 1983–86; Chm., John Laing Internat., 1986; Exec. Dir, AMEC Plc, 1986–89; Gp Chief Exec., Babcock Internat. Gp PLC, 1989–93; Chief Exec., 1993–2003, Chm., 2002–07 (non-exec. Chm., 2003–07), Alfred McAlpine plc; Chairman: Minerva plc, 2007–11; Norland Managed Services Ltd, 2008–11. Non-exec. Dir, PSA, 1989–91. Manchester Ringway Developments PLC: Chm., 1987–89; Pres., 1989–2002. Col, 1996, CO, 2001, Engr and Logistics Staff Corps, TA (Major, 1984; Chm., Liaison Cttee, 1991–2000). Liveryman, Paviors' Co., 1986– (Master, 2007–08). *Recreations:* gardening, shooting, opera.

WHITEHEAD, Graham Wright, CBE 1977; President, Jaguar Cars Inc., 1983–90; Chairman, Jaguar Canada Inc., Ontario, 1983–90; Director: Jaguar Cars Ltd, 1982–90; Jaguar plc, 1984–90; *m* Gabrielle Whitehead, OBE; one *s* one *d.* Joined Wolseley Motors, 1945; moved to US, 1959; Pres., BL Motors Inc., later Jaguar Rover Triumph Inc., NJ, 1968–83; Chm., Jaguar Rover Triumph Canada Inc., Ont, 1977–83. President: British-American Chamber of Commerce, NY, 1976–78; British Automobile Manufacturers Assoc., NY; St George's Soc. of NY; Governor, Nat. Assoc. of Securities Dealers, 1987–90. *Address:* 20 Meadow Place, Old Greenwich, CT 06870–2123, USA. *Club:* Riverside Yacht (Conn).

WHITEHEAD, Joanne; *see* Wicks, J.

WHITEHEAD, Oliver; *see* Whitehead, G. O.

WHITEHEAD, Sir Philip Henry Rathbone, 6th Bt *cr* 1889, of Highfield House, Catford Bridge, Kent; security specialist; *b* 13 Oct. 1957; *s* of Sir Rowland John Rathbone Whitehead, 5th Bt and of Marie-Louise (*née* Gausel); *S* father, 2007; *m* 1987, Emma Charlotte Milne Home (marr. diss. 2002); two *s. Educ:* Eton; Bristol Univ. (BSc Hons); RMA, Sandhurst. 1st Bn Welsh Guards, 1977; 22 SAS (R), 1982; Credit Suisse First, Boston, 1987; private security companies, 1994–. Mem., RGS. Gen. Service Medal, NI, 1980; Long Service and Good Conduct Medal, 1992. *Recreations:* travel, photography, flying (Mem., British Microlight Aircraft Assoc.), motorcycling. *Heir: s* Orlando James Rathbone Whitehead, *b* 8 Oct. 1994. *Address:* 15 Russell Close, W4 2NU. *Club:* Special Forces.

WHITEHEAD, Dr Roger George, CBE 1992; nutrition consultant; Director, Dunn Nutrition Centre, Medical Research Council, Cambridge and Keneba, The Gambia, 1973–98; Fellow of Darwin College, Cambridge, 1973–2001, now Emeritus Fellow; *b* 7 Oct. 1933; *s* of late Arthur Charles Sanders Whitehead and Eleanor Jane Whitehead (*née* Farrer); *m* 1958, Jennifer Mary Lees; two *s* one *d. Educ:* Ulverston Grammar Sch.; Univ. of Leeds (BSc 1956; PhD 1959); MA Cantab 1973. FRSB (FIBiol 1973); Hon. MRCP 1986, Hon. FRCP 1993; Hon. FRCPCH 1997; Hon. FAfN 2012. Scientific Staff, MRC, 1959–98; Dir, Child Nutrition Unit, Kampala, 1968–73; Vice Master, Darwin Coll., Cambridge, 1989–97. Visiting Professor: KCL, 1992–; Oxford Brookes Univ., 2002–; Hon. Professor: Shenyang Univ., China, 1995–; Chinese Acad. of Preventive Medicine, 1995–; Fellow, Internat. Union of Nutritional Scis, 1997; Mem. Internat. Staff, Makerere Univ., Uganda, 2003. Committee on Medical Aspects of Food Policy: Mem., 1975–91; Chm., Dietary Reference Panel, 1987–91; Mem., MAFF Food Adv. Cttee, 1988–95. Hon. Sen. Scientist, Human Nutrition Res., MRC, Cambridge, 1999–. FAO consultant, 2004–06. Pres., Nutrition Soc., 1989–92 (Hon. Mem., 2000); Chm., British Nutrition Foundn, 1994–96 (Vice-Chm., 1993–94; Gov. Emeritus, 2005). Hon. DSc Ulster, 2000. Drummond Prize, Nutrition Soc., 1968; Unesco Science Prize, 1983; British Nutrition Foundn Prize, 1990; Nutricia Internat. Award for Nutritional Sci., 1994. *Publications:* (jtly) Protein-Energy Malnutrition, 1977; (ed) Maternal Nutrition during Pregnancy and Lactation, 1980; (ed) New Techniques in Nutritional Research, 1991; contribs to learned jls. *Recreations:* photography, licensed amateur radio operator, G3ZUK, 5X5NA, C53U. *Address:* Church End, Weston Colville, Cambridge CB21 5PE. *T:* (01223) 290524. *E:* rogergwhitehead@aol.com.

WHITEHEAD, Simon Christopher, PhD; Founding Partner, Joseph Hage Aaronson LLP (formerly Hage Aaronson), since 2013; *b* Castle Donnington, 31 Jan. 1963; *s* of late John Whitehead and Patricia Helena Whitehead; *m* 1991, Frances Mary Somers; two *d. Educ:* Cranbrook Sch.; Univ. of Sydney (BA 1st cl. Hons 1985; LLB 1987; PhD 1993). St Paul's Coll. Council Scholar, 1985; Australian and Commonwealth Postgrad. Res. Award, 1987–91. Admitted solicitor, England and Wales, 1991, NSW, 1987, High Court of Australia, 1998; Partner and Hd of Civil Litigation, Saunders & Co., 1994–98; solicitor, NSW, 1998–2000; returned to practice in England, 2000; Partner and Hd of Litigation, PricewaterhouseCoopers Legal, 2002–03; Partner and Co-Hd of Trial (Europe), 2003–13, Partner in Charge, Internat., 2010–13, Dorsey & Whitney LLP. *Publications:* (contrib.) Roman Crossings: theory and practice in the Roman Republic, 2005; (ed) The Tax Disputes and Litigation Review, 2013, 3rd edn 2015; articles in EC Tax Rev., Tax Jl, Solicitors' Jl, Taxation, Internat. Tax Rev., Tax Notes Internat., New Law Jl. *Recreations:* curing meat, homebrewing, engineering projects with Patrick Somers. *Address:* Joseph Hage Aaronson LLP, 280 High Holborn, WC1V 7EE. *T:* (020) 7851 8800. *E:* swhitehead@jha.com.

WHITEHEAD, Stephen; Chief Executive Officer, Association of the British Pharmaceutical Industry, since 2011; *b* Steeton, W Yorks, 12 Nov. 1963; *s* of Colin Whitehead and Shirley Whitehead. *Educ:* Ilkley Grammar Sch.; Univ. of Manchester (BA Hons American Hist. and Society). Hd, Communications, GlaxoWellcome, 1991–95; Gp Alcohol Policy Dir, Diageo plc, 1995–98; Corporate Affairs Dir, Eli Lilly & Co. Europe, 1998–2003; Group Corporate Affairs Director: Allied Domecq plc, 2003–05; Barclays plc, 2005–07; Gp Communications Dir, Prudential plc, 2007–11. *Recreations:* theatre, cinema, walking, dogs, family. *Address:* Association of the British Pharmaceutical Industry, 7th Floor, Southside, 105 Victoria Street, SW1E 6QT. *T:* (020) 7747 1424. *E:* swhitehead@abpi.org.uk. *Clubs:* Soho House, Home House.

WHITEHEAD, Ted; *see* Whitehead, E. A.

WHITEHEAD, (Victoria) Jane; *see* Bruton, V. J.

WHITEHORN, Katharine Elizabeth, (Mrs Gavin Lyall), CBE 2014; Columnist: The Observer, 1960–96 (Associate Editor, 1980–88); Observer Magazine, since 2015; Agony Aunt, Saga Magazine, since 1997; *b* London; *d* of late A. D. and E. M. Whitehorn; *m* 1958, Gavin Tudor Lyall (*d* 2003); two *s. Educ:* Blunt House; Roedean; Glasgow High School for Girls, and others; Newnham Coll., Cambridge. Publisher's Reader, 1950–53; Teacher-Secretary in Finland, 1953–54; Grad. Asst, Cornell Univ., USA, 1954–55; Picture Post, 1956–57; Woman's Own, 1958; Spectator, 1959–61. Member: Latey Cttee on Age of Majority, 1965–67; BBC Adv. Gp on Social Effects of Television, 1971–72; Board, British Airports Authority, 1972–77; Council, Open Section, RSocMed, 1982–85. Director:

Nationwide Building Soc., 1983–91; Nationwide Anglia Estate Agents, 1987–90. Vice-Pres., Patients Assoc., 1983–96. Rector, St Andrews Univ., 1982–85. Advr, Inst. for Global Ethics, 1993–2011. Mem., ESU. Hon. LLD St Andrews, 1985; Hon. DLitt London Guildhall, 2000. Woman That Makes A Difference Award, Internat. Women's Forum, 1992. *Publications:* Cooking in a Bedsitter, 1960; Roundabout, 1961; Only on Sundays, 1966; Whitehorn's Social Survival, 1968; Observations, 1970; How to Survive in Hospital, 1972; How to Survive Children, 1975; Sunday Best, 1976; How to Survive in the Kitchen, 1979; View from a Column, 1981; How to Survive your Money Problems, 1983; Selective Memory (autobiog.), 2007. *Address:* 14 Provost Road, NW3 4ST. *Clubs:* University Women's (Hon. Mem.), Royal Society of Medicine, English-Speaking Union; Forum UK.

WHITEHORN, William Elliott; Chairman, Speed Communications, since 2011; *b* Edinburgh, 22 Feb. 1960; *s* of Donald Punyer Whitehorn and Marjorie Elliott Whitehorn; *m* 1987, Louise Mary Farquhar (marr. diss. 2014); one *s* one *d*. *Educ:* Edinburgh Acad.; Univ. of Aberdeen (MA Hons Hist. with Econs 1981). Pres., Aberdeen Univ. Student Union, 1981–82. Helicopter crewman, British Airways, 1982–84; grad. trainee, Thomas Cook, 1984–85; Mkt Intelligence Manager, TSB Bank plc, 1985; Account Dir, Lombard Communications, 1985–86; Investor Relns Manager, Virgin Gp, 1987–91; Special Projects Dir, Virgin Atlantic, 1990–2007; Brand Develt and Corporate Affairs Dir, Virgin Mgt, 1993–2007; Pres., Virgin Galactic, 2004–10; various non-exec. directorships, Virgin Gp, 1987–2007; Chm., Loewy Gp, 2010–12. Mem., Adv. Bd, Writtle Hldgs Ltd, 2012–; non-executive Director: SECC, Glasgow, 2010– (Chm., 2014–); Stagecoach Gp plc, 2011–. Mem., Sci. and Technol. Facilities Council, 2010–13; Chm. Bd, Transport Systems Catapult, 2013–. FRAeS 2012; FCILT 2013; Fellow, Mktg Soc., 2015. Mem., Forresters' Assoc., Bisley. Space Medal (Geoffrey Pardoe Space Award), RAeS, 2010. *Recreations:* shooting, farming, hill-walking. *Address:* Speed Communications, Ground Floor, 30 Park Street, SE1 9EQ. *T:* 07941 228844. *Club:* Caledonian.

WHITEHOUSE, Prof. Colin Ralph, PhD; CPhys, FInstP; FIMMM; FREng; independent consultant and adviser on science, technology and innovation, since 2012; *b* 21 Aug. 1949; *s* of Clifford William Whitehouse and Edith Elizabeth Whitehouse (*née* Pearson); *m* 1973, Mary Elizabeth Wilks; two *d*. *Educ:* Queen Elizabeth Coll., London (BSc Physics 1970); Univ. of Birmingham (MSc Physics 1971); Univ. of Brighton/GEC Hirst Res. Centre (PhD Semiconductor Growth 1978). CPhys 1994; FInstP 1994; FREng 2002; FIMMM 2002. Res. Scientist, GEC Hirst Res. Centre, Wembley, 1974–77; Sen. Res. Associate, Univ. of Newcastle upon Tyne, 1977–80; Higher SO, 1980–83, SSO, 1983–87, PSO, 1987–93, RSRE Malvern; University of Sheffield: Prof. of Electronic Materials, 1993–2003; Dir, EPSRC Nat. Centre for III–V Semiconductor Technologies, 1993–2003; Hd, Electronic and Electrical Engrg Dept, 1994–2000; Dir of Res., Engrg and Physical Scis Res. Div., 1996–99; Pro-Vice-Chancellor: for Res. and Internat. Affairs, 1999–2001; for Res. and Res. Exploitation, 2001–03; Council for the Central Laboratory of the Research Councils: Dir of Engrg, 2003–04; Dir, Daresbury Lab., 2004–06; Chief Technologist, 2005–06; Dep. Chief Exec., 2006–07; Science and Technology Facilities Council: Hd of Daresbury Lab., 2007–12; Mem., 2007–09; Dep. Chief Exec., 2007–12; Dir of Knowledge Exchange, 2007–08; Dir of Campus Strategy, 2008–12. Dep. Dir, UK IRC for Semiconductor Materials, 1993–98. Sci. Advr to Nu-Instruments Ltd, Wrexham, 2012–14. Visiting Professor: in Materials Sci., Univ. of Oxford, 2003–08; Sch. of Engrg, Univ. of Birmingham, 2005–. Member: UK North West Sci. Council, 2004–11; UK Yorks and Humberside Innovation Council, 2005–11; Knowledge Transfer and Economic Impact Gp, Res. Councils UK, 2006–08; Technology Strategy Bd, Res. Councils UK Strategy Gp, 2007–10; Northern Way Innovation Strategy Gp, 2008–11; Hercules Foundn Sci. Bd, Brussels, 2009–. Member Board: Sheffield Univ. Enterprises Ltd, 1999–2003; White Rose Univs Res. Ltd, 1999–2003; Malvern Girls' Coll., 2000–06; CLIK, 2004–07; Microvisk, 2004–06; Halton Borough Chamber of Commerce and Enterprise, 2005–07; Daresbury Sci. and Innovation Campus, 2006–12; Didcot First, 2007–10; Quadrant, 2007–10; Oxford Economic Partnership, 2007–10; STFC Innovations, 2007–11; Spectrum, 2008–10; Res. and Develt Soc., 2008–; STEMNET, 2008–14; Science Vale UK, 2009–12; Aalto Univ., Helsinki, 2012–; Member: Oxfordshire Local Enterprise Bd, 2010–12; Liverpool Knowledge Economy Gp, 2010–12; Adv. Council, Liverpool City Region Local Enterprise Partnership, 2012–; Welsh Govt Innovation Task and Finish Gp, 2012–13; Sci. and Innovation Commn, Inst. of Physics, 2015–. *Publications:* numerous contribs to learned jl and prestigious conf. papers, relating to semiconductor materials, semiconductor processing, nanotechnology and nanoscience, next-generation devices and sensors, the knowledge economy, innovation and open innovation. *Recreations:* classical music, theatre, sports, walking, cycling, gardening. *Address:* 3 Christchurch Road, Malvern, Worcs WR14 3BH. *T:* (01684) 572120. *E:* WhitehouseCR@aol.com.

WHITEHOUSE, David Rae Beckwith; QC 1990; *b* 5 Sept. 1945; *s* of late (David) Barry Beckwith Whitehouse, MA, MD, FRCS, FRCOG and Mary Beckwith Whitehouse, JP; *m* 1971, Linda Jane, *d* of Eric Vickers, CB and Barbara Mary Vickers; (one *s* decd). *Educ:* Ellesmere College; Choate Sch., Wallingford, Conn., USA; Trinity College, Cambridge (MA). English-Speaking Union Scholarship, 1964. Called to the Bar, Gray's Inn, 1969; in practice as a barrister specialising in criminal law and fraud cases, 1969–2011; Asst Recorder, 1983–87, Recorder, 1987–2010. Criminal cases include: Last Tango in Paris (obscene pubns); George Davis (five robbery trials and three appeals); Handless Corpse Murder; Cyprus Spy trial; murder trial of Lennie The Guv'nor McLean; Colombian Cartel and Mafia drug trials; Thomas ap Rhys Pryce murder trial; Christopher Langham case; defence of Adams, Arif, McAvoy, Richardson, Tibbs and Tobin families. Fraud cases include: Barlow Clowes (investment and co. takeover fraud); Norton plc (rights issue fraud); Abbey National plc (corruption); local authy frauds involving W Wilts and Brent Councils; John (Goldfinger) Palmer (timeshare fraud); read The Sun for defamation and contempt, 1969–76. Member: Criminal Bar Assoc., 1969–2011; Central Criminal Court Bar Mess, 1970–2011. *Recreations:* the arts, esp. architecture, music and cinema; walking, wild gardening. *E:* dw@dwhitehouse.com. *Club:* Reform.

WHITEHOUSE, Elly; *see* Jansen, E.

WHITEHOUSE, Prof. (Julian) Michael (Arthur), MD; FRCP, FRCR, FRCPEd, FMedSci; Professor Emeritus, Imperial College School of Medicine, London, 2000; Vice Principal for Undergraduate Medicine, Imperial College School of Medicine and Professor of Medical Oncology, University of London, 1997–2000; *b* 2 June 1940; *s* of Arthur Arnold Keer Whitehouse and Kathleen Ida Elizabeth (*née* Elliston); *m* 1965, Diane France de Saussure; one *s* two *d*. *Educ:* Queens' Coll., Cambridge (BA 1963; MB, BChir 1966; MA 1967; MD 1975); St Bartholomew's Hosp. Med. Coll., London. FRCP 1979; FRCR 1992; FRCPEd 1994. Sen. Lectr and Actg Dir, ICRF Dept of Med. Oncology, and Hon. Consultant Physician, St Bartholomew's Hosp., London, 1975–76; Prof. of Med. Oncology and Dir, CRC Wessex Regl Med. Oncology Unit, Univ. of Southampton, and Hon. Consultant Physician, Southampton Gen. Hosp., 1976–97; Dean, Charing Cross and Westminster Med. Sch., 1997. Chm., Educn Trng Bd, Eur. Orgn for Res. and Treatment of Cancer, 1997–2001. Chm. Council, Paterson Inst., Christie Hosp., Manchester, 1997–2002; Member: Council, CRC, 1997–2002; GMC Fitness to Practise panel, 2000–. Governor: Canford Sch., Dorset, 1986–2010; (and Mem. Council) St Swithun's Sch., Winchester, 1996–; City of London Sch., 2000–. FMedSci 2000. *Publications:* CNS Complications of Malignant Disease, 1979; Recent Advances in Clinical Oncology, 1982, 2nd edn 1986; A Pocket Consultant in Clinical Oncology, 1983; Cancer Investigation and Management, 1984; Cancer: the facts, 1996; contrib. numerous papers in various jls on res. and treatment of cancer. *Recreations:* devising projects, ski-ing, sailing, travelling, genealogy. *E:* m.whitehouse@imperial.ac.uk. *Club:* Athenæum.

WHITEHOUSE, Michael; Chief Operating Officer, National Audit Office, since 2009; *b* 14 Nov. 1957; *s* of late Bernard Joseph Whitehouse and Margaret Whitehouse (*née* Hutchings). *Educ:* King Edward VI Grammar Sch., Birmingham; Univ. of Exeter (BA Hons). Joined Exchequer and Audit Dept, 1979; Dir, 1990–92; Min. of Finance, Zambia, 1992–94; Office of Auditor Gen., NZ, 1994–95; Dir, Value for Money Develt and Modernising Govt, 1996–2002; Asst Auditor Gen., Nat. Audit Office, 2002–09. *Recreations:* sport, travel, reading, theatre, history. *Address:* National Audit Office, 157–197 Buckingham Palace Road, SW1W 9SP. *T:* (020) 7798 7078. *E:* michael.whitehouse@nao.gsi.gov.uk.

WHITEHOUSE, Paul; writer, actor and producer; *m* Fiona (separated); two *d*. *Educ:* Univ. of E Anglia. Formerly plasterer. Dir, Tomboy Films Ltd. *Television includes:* writer (with Charlie Higson) and actor: Harry Enfield's Television Programme, 1990, 1992; Harry Enfield and Chums, 1994, 1997; The Fast Show, 1994–97 (also co-producer; Best Light Entertainment Perf., BAFTA Awards, 1998); Randall and Hopkirk, 1999; Happiness (also co-producer), 2001, 2003; writer (with Chris Langham) and actor, Help, 2005; writer and actor: Ruddy Hell! It's Harry and Paul, 2007; Harry and Paul, 2008, 2010, 2012 (Best Comedy Prog., BAFTA Awards, 2009); Bellamy's People (also co-dir), 2010; Nurse (also co-producer and co-dir), 2015; An Evening with Harry Enfield and Paul Whitehouse, 2015; actor, David Copperfield, 1999. *Films include:* Love's Labour's Lost, 2000; Kevin and Perry Go Large, 2000; Alice in Wonderland, 2010; Burke and Hare, 2010. *Theatre:* The Fast Show Live, Apollo, Hammersmith, 2002; The Fast Show Live: shamelessly plugging the DVD, Dominion, 2007. Writers' Guild of GB Award, British Comedy Awards, 2013. *Address:* c/o Curtis Brown Group Ltd, Haymarket House, 28–29 Haymarket, SW1Y 4SP.

WHITEHOUSE, Paul Chapple, QPM 1993; Chairman, Gangmasters Licensing Authority, 2005–11; Chief Constable, Sussex Police, 1993–2001; *b* 26 Sept. 1944; *s* of Beatrice and Jack Whitehouse, Cambs; *m* 1970, Elizabeth Dinsmore; one *s* one *d*. *Educ:* Ipswich Sch.; Emmanuel Coll., Cambridge (BA 1967; MA 1969). VSO, Starehe Boys' Centre, Nairobi, 1963–64; Durham Constabulary, 1967–74; Northumbria Police, 1974–83; Asst Chief Constable, Greater Manchester Police, 1983–87; Dep. Chief Constable, W Yorkshire Police, 1987–93. Association of Chief Police Officers: Chairman: Communications Gp, 1995–2001; Personnel Mgt (formerly Personnel and Trng) Cttee, 1998–2001; Vice Chm., Media Adv. Group, 1994–2001; Member: Finance and Resources Cttee, 1994–2001; Inf. Mgt Cttee, 1995–2001. Chm., Brighton and Hove Common Purpose Adv. Gp, 1994–2001; Member Council: IAM, 1993–2002; NACRO, 1994–2007 (Vice-Chm., 2003–07); Centre for Crime and Justice Studies, 1997–2002. Chairman: Starehe UK (formerly Starehe Endowment Fund (UK)), 1994–2013, now Trustee; Anti-Slavery Internat., 2011–14; Finding Rhythms, 2015–. Treasurer: Ludlow Assembly Rooms, 2002–07; Dutch Barge Assoc., 2002–12; Quakers and Business Gp, 2006–. Trustee, Friends Trusts Ltd, 2013–. Chm. of Govs, Sidcot Sch., 2007–. *Recreations:* collecting people, IT, steam, disputation, keeping the peace. *Address:* 1 Slate Cottages, Manor Lane, Abbots Leigh, Bristol BS8 3RX. *T:* 07813 802783. *E:* paul@dunstanburgh.net. *Club:* Oxford and Cambridge.

WHITEHOUSE, Sarah Alice; QC 2014; *b* Kampala, Uganda, 13 Jan. 1961; *d* of Rev. Canon William Beadon Norman and Beryl Norman; *m* 1988, Andrew Timothy Brian Whitehouse (marr. diss. 2008); one *s* one *d*. *Educ:* Felixstowe Coll., Suffolk; St Andrews Univ. (MA Hons); Westminster Univ. (Postgrad. DipLaw). Asst Dir, Barclays de Zoete Wedd, 1989–91; called to the Bar, Lincoln's Inn, 1993; Sen. Treasury Counsel (Criminal), 2014–. *Publications:* (contrib.) Fraud (looseleaf), 2008; (contrib.) Millington & Sutherland Williams on The Proceeds of Crime, 2013; (contrib.) EU Law in Criminal Practice, 2013. *Recreation:* theatre. *Address:* 6KBW College Hill, 21 College Hill, EC4R 2RP. *T:* (020) 3301 0910. *E:* sarah.whitehouse@6kbw.com. *Club:* Carlton.

WHITEHOUSE-JANSEN, Elly; *see* Jansen, E.

WHITELEY, family name of **Baron Marchamley**.

WHITELEY, Dame Jane (Elizabeth), DBE 1990; *b* 14 July 1944; *d* of Major Charles Packe (killed in action, July 1944) and Hon. Margaret (*née* Lane Fox); *m* 1st, 1966, Ian Gow, TD, MP (*d* 1990); two *s*; 2nd, 1994, Lt-Col Michael Whiteley. *Educ:* St Mary's School, Wantage. Governor: three special schs in S London, 1968–72; Hankham CP Sch., 1976–85; St Bede's Sch., Eastbourne, 1980–87; Park Coll., Eastbourne, 1985–88; Grenville Coll., Bideford, 1997–2005; Mem. Council, Cheltenham Coll., 1996–98. Trustee: Ian Gow Meml Fund, 1990–2003; Exeter Cathedral Music Foundn Trust, 2005–14; Visitor: Henry Smith Charity, 2001–07; Trusthouse Charitable Foundn, 2005–07. Freeman, Bor. of Eastbourne, 1992. *Recreations:* playing organ and piano, reading. *Address:* Hornbeams, Tenterden Road, Biddenden, Kent TN27 8BJ.

WHITELEY, Sir (John) Miles H.; *see* Huntington-Whiteley.

WHITELEY, Prof. Paul Frederick, PhD; FBA 2012; FAcSS; Professor of Government, University of Essex, since 2001; *b* Batley, Yorks, 6 Feb. 1946; *s* of Frederick Whiteley and Constance Whiteley; *m* 1968, Susan Alison Everest; one *s* two *d*. *Educ:* Bournemouth Grammar Sch.; Univ. of Sheffield (BA Econ); Univ. of Essex (PhD 1984). Lecturer: Kingston Poly., 1971–78; Univ. of Bristol, 1978–88; Prof., Univ. of Arizona, 1988–90; Pamela Harriman Prof. of Govt, Coll. of William and Mary, Va, 1990–94; Prof. of Politics, Univ. of Sheffield, 1994–2001. FAcSS (AcSS 2011). *Publications:* Labour's Grassroots: the politics of party membership, 1992; True Blues: the politics of Conservative Party membership, 1994; Political Choice in Britain, 2004; Affluence, Austerity and Electoral Change in Britain, 2013. *Recreations:* jogging, walking, film, popular science. *Address:* Department of Government, University of Essex, Wivenhoe Park, Colchester CO4 3SQ. *T:* (01206) 872641. *E:* whiteley@essex.ac.uk.

WHITELEY, Gen. Sir Peter (John Frederick), GCB 1979 (KCB 1976); OBE 1960; DL; Lieutenant-Governor and Commander-in-Chief, Jersey, 1979–84; *b* 13 Dec. 1920; *s* of late John George Whiteley; *m* 1948, Nancy Vivian, *d* of late W. Carter Clayden; two *s* two *d*. *Educ:* Bishop's Stortford Coll.; Bembridge Sch.; Ecole des Roches. Joined Royal Marines, 1940; 101 Bde, 1941; HMS: Resolution, 1941; Renown, 1942; HMNZS Gambia, 1942; seconded to Fleet Air Arm, 1946–50; Adjt 40 Commando, 1951; Staff Coll., Camberley, 1954; Bde Major 3rd Commando Bde, 1957; Instructor, Staff Coll., Camberley, 1960–63; CO 42 Commando, 1965–66 (despatches, Malaysia, 1966); Col GS Dept of CGRM, 1966–68; Nato Defence Coll., 1968; Comdr 3rd Commando Bde, 1968–70; Maj.-Gen. Commando Forces, 1970–72; C of S, HQ Allied Forces Northern Europe, 1972–75; Commandant General, Royal Marines, 1975–77; C-in-C Allied Forces Northern Europe, 1977–79. Col Comdt, RM, 1985–87; Hon. Col, 211 (Wessex) Field Hosp. RAMC (Volunteers), TA, 1985–90. Mem., Council, Union Jack Club, 1985–91; Vice Chm., Theatre Royal, Plymouth, 1991–97; Pres., W Devon Area, 1985–87, Pres., Devon, 1987–96, St John's Ambulance Bde; Vice-Pres., Devon Care Trust, 1995–2003. Life Trustee, Durrell Wildlife Conservation Trust. Governor: Bembridge Sch., 1981–95; Kelly Coll., 1985–94; St Michael's Sch., Tavistock, 1985–89. Member: Royal Commonwealth Soc., 1981–; Anglo Norse Soc., 1980–; Anglo Danish Soc., 1980–; Jersey Soc. in London, 1984–. Liveryman, Fletchers' Co., 1982 (Hon. Life Liveryman, 1999); Guild of Freemen of City of London: Mem. Ct of Assistants, 1980–; Master, 1987–88. DL Devon, 1987. CCMI. KStJ 1980;

Chevalier, Ordre de la Pléiade, Assoc. of French Speaking Parliaments, 1984. *Publications:* contribs to Jane's Annual, NATO's Fifteen Nations, RUSI Jl, Nauticus. *Recreations:* music, painting, wood carving. *Club:* Royal Naval Sailing Assoc.

WHITEMAN, Hon. Burchell Anthony, OJ 2006; Senior Adviser, Office of the Prime Minister of Jamaica, since 2012; High Commissioner of Jamaica in the United Kingdom, 2007–10; *b* May Pen, Jamaica, 21 Feb. 1938; *s* of Edgar James Whiteman and Merab Wilhelmina Whiteman (*née* Morgan); *m* 1970, Joline Ann Davis; two *d.* *Educ:* Munro Coll., Jamaica; University Coll. of the West Indies (BA Hons); Univ. of London; Univ. of Birmingham (MEd 1965; Dip. Educnl Admin 1974). Principal, York Castle High Sch., Jamaica, 1959–75; Principal, Brown's Town Community Coll., Jamaica, 1975–89; Minister of State, Jamaican Govt, 1989–91; Minister of Educn, 1992–2002; Minister of Information, 2002–06; Sen. Advr to the Gov. Gen. of Jamaica, 2006. Mem., Electoral Adv. Cttee, Jamaica, 2002–06. Chm., University Council of Jamaica, 2012–. Chm. Bd of Govs, Commonwealth of Learning, Vancouver, 2008– (Actg Chm., 2007–08; Mem., 2001–08). Hon. Mem., Order of the Southern Cross (Brazil), 1998. *Recreation:* occasional writing. *E:* burchell.whiteman@gmail.com.

WHITEMAN, Prof. John Robert, PhD; CMath, FIMA; Professor of Numerical Analysis, since 1981, and Distinguished Professor, since 2004, Brunel University; Director, Brunel Institute of Computational Mathematics, since 1976; *b* 7 Dec. 1938; *s* of Robert Whiteman and Rita (*née* Neale); *m* 1964, Caroline Mary Leigh; two *s* (one *d* decd). *Educ:* Bromsgrove Sch.; Univ. of St Andrews (BSc); Worcester Coll., Oxford (DipEd); Univ. of London (PhD). FIMA 1970. Sen. Lectr, RMCS, Shrivenham, 1963–67; Assistant Professor: Univ. of Wisconsin, 1967–68; Univ. of Texas, Austin, 1968–70; Reader in Numerical Analysis, Brunel Univ., 1970–76; Richard Merton Gastprofessor, Univ. of Münster, 1975–76; Brunel University: Hd of Dept of Maths and Statistics, 1982–90; Vice Principal, 1991–96; Public Orator, 1999–2004. Visiting Professor: Univ. of Pisa, 1975; Univ. of Kuwait, 1986; Texas A & M Univ., 1986, 1988, 1989, 1990, 1992; Univ. of Stuttgart, 1989, 1992; Vis. Prof., 1996, Dist. Res. Fellow, 1997–2015, Univ. of Texas at Austin. Lectures: Geary, City Univ., 1986; Robert Todd Gregory, Univ. of Texas, Austin, 1990; Collatz Gedenkkolloquium, Hamburg Univ., 1991; Univ. of Stuttgart, 1995; Brunel, Brunel Univ., 2004; Ravenscroft, Co. of Glass Sellers, 2004; Maths Master Class, Royal Instn, 2008. Vice Pres., UK Inst. of Maths and Its Applications, 2004–05. Member: SERC Maths Cttee, 1981–86 and Science Bd, 1989–91; Bd of Dirs, Eur. Scientific Assoc. for Forming Processes, 1997–. Renter Warden, 2002, Prime Warden, 2003, Master, 2004, Co. of Glass Sellers (Chm., Charity Fund Trustees, 2008–). FRSA. Hon. DSc West Bohemia Univ., 1995. Editor, Numerical Methods for Partial Differential Equations, 1985–; Member, Editorial Board: Computer Methods in Applied Mechanics and Engrg; Communications in Applied Numerical Methods; Internat. Jl for Numerical Methods in Fluids; Jl of Mathematical Engrg in Industry; Jl of Engrg Analysis; Computational Mechanics Advances. *Publications:* (ed) The Mathematics of Finite Elements and Applications, vols 1–10, 1973, 1976, 1979, 1982, 1985, 1988, 1991, 1994, 1997, 2000, 2003; Finite Elements: an introduction to the method and error estimation, 2010; numerous works on numerical solution of partial differential equations, particularly finite element methods for singularities in elliptic problems and for problems of linear and non linear solid mechanics, incl. viscoelasticity and applications to problems of thermoforming. *Recreations:* walking, swimming, golf, orchestral and choral music. *Address:* Brunel Institute of Computational Mathematics, Brunel University, Uxbridge, Middx UB8 3PH. *T:* (01895) 265185. *E:* john.whiteman@brunel.ac.uk.

WHITEMAN, Joslyn Raphael; High Commissioner for Grenada in the United Kingdom, since 2013; *b* Grenada, 19 Oct. 1939; *s* of late Francis Ignatius and Veronica Whiteman; *m* 1964, Lydia Theodora Purcell; two *s* two *d.* *Educ:* Presentation Brothers Coll., Grenada. Manager, insce office, London, 1969–87; self-employed, 1987–94; Minister of Agriculture, 1995–96, of Tourism, 1996–2000, of Information, 2000–01, of Implementation, 2001–03, Govt of Grenada; High Comr for Grenada in UK, 2004–05; Ambassador to China, 2005–08; proprietor, own business, 2008–13. Black Businessman of Year, Afro Caribbean Chamber of Industry and Commerce, 1988. *Recreations:* gardening, reading. *Address:* High Commission of Grenada, The Chapel, Archel Road, W14 9QH. *E:* millhavenhouse@hotmail.com.

WHITEMAN, Peter George; QC 1977; barrister-at-law; a Recorder, since 1989; a Deputy High Court Judge, since 1994; Attorney and Counselor at Law, State of New York; *b* 8 Aug. 1942; *s* of David Whiteman and Betsy Bessie Coster; *m* 1971, Katherine Ruth (*née* Ellenbogen) (*d* 2009); two *d.* *Educ:* Warwick Secondary Modern Sch.; Leyton County High Sch.; LSE (LLB, LLM with Distinction). Called to the Bar, Lincoln's Inn, 1967, Bencher, 1985; *ad eundem* Middle Temple, 1977. Lectr, London Univ., 1966–70; Prof. of Law, Univ. of Virginia, 1980. Mem., Faculty of Laws, Florida Univ., 1977; Visiting Professor: Virginia Univ., 1978; Univ. of California at Berkeley, 1980. Mem. Cttee, Unitary Tax Campaign (UK), 1982–. Pres., Dulwich Village Preservation Soc., 1987–97; Chm., Dulwich Jt Residents' Cttee, 1991–97. Member: Cttee, Dulwich Picture Gall., 1989–97 (Pres., Community Cttee, 2010); Adv. Cttee, Dulwich Estate Govs' Scheme of Management, 1988–97; Focus Gp, Patrons Cttee and Benjamin West Patrons Cttee, RA, 2010–. FRSA 1973. Mem. Bd, Univ. of Virginia Jl of Internat. Law, 1981–. *Publications:* Whiteman on Capital Gains Tax, 1967, 5th edn 2009; Whiteman on Income Tax, 1971, 4th edn 2009; contrib. British Tax Encyc. *Recreations:* opera, long distance travelling, tennis, mountain-walking, jogging, croquet. *Address:* QEB Hollis Whiteman Chambers, 1–2 Laurence Pountney Hill, EC4R 0EU. *T:* (020) 7933 8855, (020) 7283 7273.

WHITEMAN, Robert Arthur; Chief Executive, Chartered Institute of Public Finance and Accountancy, since 2013; *b* 4 Dec. 1961; *s* of late William Whiteman and of Joan Whiteman (*née* Elliott); *m* 1988, Hilary Barbara Cannon; two *s* one *d.* *Educ:* Univ. of Essex (BA Hons). IRRV 1988; CPFA 1995. W. H. Smith plc, 1983–86; London Borough of Newham, 1986–88; Corp. of London, 1988; Head of Revenues, London Borough of Camden, 1988–96; London Borough of Lewisham: Asst Dir of Finance, 1996–99; Exec. Dir for Resources, 1999–2005; Dep. Chief Exec., 2001–05; Chief Exec., London Bor. of Barking and Dagenham, 2005–10; Man. Dir, Improvement and Develt Agency, later Local Govt Improvement and Develt, 2010–11; Chief Exec., UK Border Agency, 2011–13; Dir Gen., Operational Systems Mgt, Home Office, 2013. Mem., non-exec. Bd, and Chm., Audit Cttee, DECC, 2009–13. Mem. Council, CIPFA, 2004–06. JP Newham, 1996–2005. *Publications:* regular contribs to local authy jls. *Recreations:* DIY, music, gardening. *Address:* Chartered Institute of Public Finance and Accountancy, 77 Mansell Street, E1 8AN.

WHITEMAN, Ven. Rodney David Carter; Archdeacon of Cornwall, 2000–05, now Archdeacon Emeritus; *b* Par, Cornwall, 6 Oct. 1940; *s* of Leonard Archibald Whiteman and Sybil Mary (*née* Morshead); *m* 1969, Christine Anne Chelton; one *s* one *d.* *Educ:* St Austell Grammar School; Pershore Coll. of Horticulture; Ely Theological Coll. Deacon 1964, priest 1965; Curate of Kings Heath, Birmingham, 1964–70; Vicar: St Stephen, Rednal, Birmingham, 1970–79; St Barnabas, Erdington, 1979–89; RD of Aston, 1981–89; Hon. Canon of Birmingham Cathedral, 1985–89; Priest-in-charge of Cardinham with Helland, 1989–94; Hon. Canon of Truro Cathedral, 1989–2005, now Canon Emeritus; Archdeacon of Bodmin, 1989–99. Trustee, Corp. of the Sons and Friends of the Clergy, 1996–2015. *Recreations:* gardening, music, historic buildings and monuments, walking. *Address:* 22 Treverbyn Gardens, Sandy Hill, St Austell, Cornwall PL25 3AW.

WHITEMORE, Hugh John; dramatist; *b* 16 June 1936; *s* of late Samuel George Whitemore and Kathleen Alma Whitemore (*née* Fletcher); *m* 1st, Jill Brooke (marr. diss.); 2nd, 1976, Sheila Lemon (marr. diss.); one *s*; 3rd, 1998, Rohan McCullough. *Educ:* King Edward VI School, Southampton; RADA. FRSL 1999. Vis. Prof. in Broadcasting Media, Oxford Univ., 2003–04. Hon. Fellow, KCL, 2006. *Stage:* Stevie, Vaudeville, 1977; Pack of Lies, Lyric, 1983; Breaking the Code, Haymarket, 1986, transf. Comedy, 1987 (Amer. Math. Soc. Communications Award, 1990); The Best of Friends, Apollo, 1988, Hampstead, 2006; It's Ralph, Comedy, 1991; A Letter of Resignation, Comedy, 1997, transf. Savoy, 1998; Disposing of the Body, Hampstead, 1999; God Only Knows, Vaudeville, 2000; (adaptation) As You Desire Me, Playhouse, 2005; (with Simon Gray) The Last Cigarette, Minerva, Chichester, 2009; A Marvellous Year for Plums, Chichester, 2012; *television:* plays and dramatisations include: Elizabeth R (Emmy award, 1970); Cider with Rosie (Writer's Guild award, 1971); Country Matters (Writer's Guild award, 1972); Dummy (RAI Prize, Prix Italia, 1979); Concealed Enemies (Emmy award, Neil Simon Jury award, 1984); The Final Days, 1989; A Dance to the Music of Time, 1997 (Script Prize, Monte Carlo Fest., 1998); The Gathering Storm, 2002 (Emmy award, Golden Globe, Writers' Guild of America Award, Peabody Award, 2002); Into the Storm, 2009; *films:* Stevie, 1980; The Return of the Soldier, 1982; 84 Charing Cross Road, 1986 (Scriptor Award, Los Angeles, 1988); Utz, 1992; Jane Eyre, 1996. *Publications:* (contrib.) Elizabeth R, 1972; Stevie, 1977, new edn 1984; (contrib.) My Drama School, 1978; (contrib.) Ah, Mischief!, 1982; Pack of Lies, 1983; Breaking the Code, 1986; The Best of Friends, 1988; It's Ralph, 1991; A Letter of Resignation, 1997; Disposing of the Body, 1999; God Only Knows, 2001; As You Desire Me (from Pirandello), 2005. *Recreations:* music, movies, reading. *Address:* 67 Peel Street, W8 7PB.

WHITEN, Prof. (David) Andrew, PhD; FBA 2000; FRSE; FBPsS; Professor of Evolutionary and Developmental Psychology, since 1997, and Wardlaw Professor, since 2000, University of St Andrews; *b* 20 April 1948; *s* of Bernard Wray Whiten and Maisie (*née* Gathercole); *m* 1973, Dr Susie Challoner; two *d.* *Educ:* Sheffield Univ. (BSc 1st Cl. Hons Zool. 1969); Bristol Univ. (PhD 1973). FBPsS 1991. SSRC Conversion Fellow, Queen's Coll., Oxford, 1972–75; St Andrew's University: Lectr in Psychol., 1975–90; Reader, 1991–97; Leverhulme Res. Fellow, 1997, 2003–06; Royal Soc. Leverhulme Trust Sen. Res. Fellow, 2006–07. Vis. Prof., Zurich Univ., 1992; F. M. Bird Prof., Emory Univ., 1995–96; British Acad. Res. Reader, 1999–2001. FRSE 2001; Fellow, Cognitive Sci. Soc., 2013. Hon. DSc Heriot-Watt, 2015. Jean-Marie Delwart Internat. Scientific Prize, Acad. Royale des Scis de Belgique, 2001; Rivers Meml Medal, RAI, 2007; Osman Hill Meml Medal, Primate Soc. of GB, 2010; Sir James Black Prize and Medal, 2013, Sen. Prize for Public Engagement, 2014, RSE. *Publications:* (ed) Natural Theories of Mind: evolution, development and simulation of everyday mindreading, 1991; (ed with E. Widdowson) Natural Diet and Foraging Strategy of Monkeys, Apes and Humans, 1992; (ed with R. Byrne) Machiavellian Intelligence: social expertise and the evolution of intellect, 1988; Machiavellian Intelligence II: extensions and evaluations, 1997 (trans. Japanese 2000); (ed jtly) Culture Evolves, 2012; contrib. many articles on evolution and develt of social intelligence and cultural transmission to learned jls. *Recreations:* friends, family, art, painting, film, music, garden. *Address:* School of Psychology & Neuroscience, University of St Andrews, St Andrews, Fife KY16 9JP.

WHITEOAK, John Edward Harrison, MA, CPFA; Managing Director (formerly Managing Partner), Whiteoak Associates Ltd (Public Sector Consultancy), since 1998; *b* 5 July 1947. *Educ:* Sheffield Univ. (MA). CPFA 1971. Cheshire County Council: Dep. County Treas., 1979–81; County Treas., 1981–94; Gp Dir, Resources, 1994–98; Treas., Cheshire Police Authy, 1995–98. Non-exec. Director: VALPAK Ltd, 1998–2004; Industrial Properties Ltd, 1997–. Lead negotiator on local govt finance for local authorities in England, 1994–97; lead finance advr to English County Councils, 1994–98. Member: Soc. of County Treasurers, 1981–98 (Pres., 1997–98); Accounting Standards Cttee, 1984–87. Chartered Institute of Public Finance and Accountancy: Mem., Technical Cttee, 1986–87 and 1991–2010; Mem., Accounting Panel, 1984–87 (Chm., 1987); Chm., Financial Reporting Panel, 1991–94; Chm., Corporate Governance Panel, 1994–2013; Pres., NW Region, 1994–95. *Publications:* (jtly) Public Sector Accounting and Financial Control, 1992; contrib. various professional and management journals. *Recreations:* social golf, tennis. *Clubs:* Royal Automobile; City (Chester); Chester Lawn Tennis.

WHITEREAD, Rachel, CBE 2006; artist, sculptor; *b* 20 April 1963. *Educ:* Brighton Poly. (BA 1st Cl. Hons); Slade Sch. of Art (DipHE). *Solo exhibitions* include: Ghost, Chisenhale Gall., London, 1990; Stedelijk Van-Abbemuseum, Eindhoven, 1992; Mus. of Contemporary Art, Chicago, 1993; Kunsthalle, Basel, ICA, Philadelphia, ICA, Boston, 1994–95; retrospective, Tate Gall., Liverpool, 1996–97; Reina Sofia, Madrid, 1997; Venice Biennale (Award for Best Young Artist), 1997; Anthony d'Offay Gall., 1998; Serpentine Gall. and Scottish Nat. Gall. of Modern Art, 2001; Deutsche Guggenheim, Berlin, and Solomon Guggenheim Mus., NY, 2001–02; Room 101, V&A Mus., 2003–04; Mus. de Arte Moderna, Rio de Janeiro and São Paulo, 2004; Kunsthaus Bregenz, Austria, Gagosian Gall., London, Embankment for Turbine Hall, Tate Modern, 2005; Luhring Augustine Gall., NY, 2006; Donnaregina Mus. of Contemp. Art, Naples, 2007; Galleria Lorcan O'Neill, Rome, 2007; Centro Arte Contemporáneo, Málaga, 2007; Gagosian Gall., London, 2010; Drawings, Hammer Mus., LA, Nasher Sculpture Center, Dallas and Tate Britain, 2010; Galerie Nelson-Freeman, Paris, 2010; Long Eyes, Luhring Augustine Gall., NY, 2011; Looking On, Galleria Lorcan O'Neill, Rome, 2011; Detached, Gagosian Gall., London, 2013. *Public sculptures:* Water Tower Project, NY, 1998; Holocaust Meml, Judenplatz, Vienna, 2000; Monument, Fourth Plinth, Trafalgar Sq., 2001; Tree of Life, Whitechapel Gall., 2012. Deutscher Akademischer Austauschdienst, Berlin, 1992; Turner Prize, 1993; Herbert von Karajan Prize, Salzburg, 1996; Nord LB Art Prize, 2004. *Address:* c/o Lawrence Luhring, Luhring Augustine Gallery, 531 West 24th Street, New York, NY 10011, USA. *T:* (212) 206 9100, *Fax:* (212) 206 9055. *E:* info@luhringaugustine.com; c/o Gagosian Gallery, 6–24 Britannia Street, WC1X 9JD. *T:* (020) 7841 9960, *Fax:* (020) 7841 9961. *E:* london@gagosian.com.

WHITESIDE, Bernard Gerrard, MBE 1994; HM Diplomatic Service, retired; Ambassador to Ecuador, 2007–08; *b* 3 Oct. 1954; *s* of late Joseph Whiteside and Phoebe Anna (*née* Cummings). *Educ:* St Michael's Coll., Kirkby Lonsdale; Westfield Coll., Univ. of London (BA Hons French and Latin 1977); Univ. of London (Dip. Mediaeval Hist. 2006). Entered HM Diplomatic Service, 1979; Moscow, 1983–86; UK Disarmament Delegn, Geneva, 1986–89; News Dept, FCO, 1989–91; Bogotá, 1991–95; FCO, 1995–99; Russia Prog. Manager, DFID, 1999–2001; Ambassador to Moldova, 2002–06. Trustee, All We Can (formerly Methodist Relief and Develt Fund), 2010–14. *Recreations:* modern music, mediaeval history, the Lake District. *E:* bernardwhiteside@hotmail.com.

WHITEWAY, Paul Robin; HM Diplomatic Service, retired; Director, London, Independent Diplomat, since 2011 (Director, External Relations, 2010–11); *b* 1 Dec. 1954; *s* of Frank Whiteway and Patricia (*née* Callaway); *m* 1st, 1980, Melanie Jane Blew (marr. diss.); one *d*; 2nd, 1996, Maha Georges Yannieh; one *s.* *Educ:* Henley Grammar Sch.; Merton Coll., Oxford (BA Hons Mod. History; MA). Joined FCO, 1977; Far Eastern Dept, 1977–79; Third, later Second Sec., Dublin, 1980–83; First Secretary: Nuclear Energy Dept, 1984–86; Port Stanley, 1986–87; Mexico and Central America Dept, 1987–88; seconded to MoD (Navy), 1988–90; Dep. High Comr, Uganda, 1990–93; Asst Head, Southern Africa Dept, 1993–96; Counsellor and Deputy Head of Mission: Syria, 1996–99; Chile, 2000–03; Dir Internat., Inward Investment Gp, 2003–06, Dir Internat. Sales, Business Gp, 2006–08, UK Trade and

Investment; consultant in Foreign Direct Investment promotion, 2008–10. *Recreations:* history, travel, fishing. *Address:* c/o Independent Diplomat, Hamilton House, 1 Temple Avenue, EC4Y 0HA.

WHITFIELD, family name of **Baron Kenswood**.

WHITFIELD, Adrian; QC 1983; a Recorder of the Crown Court, 1981–2000; *b* 10 July 1937; *s* of Peter Henry Whitfield and Margaret Mary Burns; *m* 1st, 1962, Lucy Caroline Beckett (marr. diss.); two *d*; 2nd, 1971, Niamh O'Kelly; one *s* one *d*. *Educ:* Ampleforth Coll.; Magdalen Coll., Oxford (Demy; MA). 2nd Lieut, KOYLI (Nat. Service), 1956–58. Called to the Bar, Middle Temple, 1964, Bencher 1990, Treasurer 2005. *Publications:* contribs on legal matters in legal and medical pubns. *Recreations:* reading, visual arts, travel. *Address:* 47 Faroe Road, W14 0EL. *T:* (020) 7603 8982.

WHITFIELD, Alan; transport consultant, 1998–2014; *b* 19 April 1939; *s* of John J. Whitfield and Annie Fothergill-Rawe; *m* 1964, Sheila Carr; two *s*. *Educ:* Consett Grammar Sch., Durham; Sunderland and Newcastle Colls of Advanced Technology. MICE 1968; MIMunE 1969; FCIHT (FIHT 1984). Surveyor/Engr, NCB, 1956–62; Engrg Asst, Northumberland CC, 1962–70; Department of Transport: Main Grade Engr, 1970–73; Prin. Professional, 1973–76; Suptg Engr, 1976–80; Dep. Dir, Midlands Road Construction Unit, 1980–83; Dir (Transport), W Midlands Reg. Office, 1983–89; Regl Dir (Under Sec.), Eastern Region, DoE and Dept of Transport, 1989; Road Prog. Dir, Dept of Transport, 1989–94, Highways Agency, 1994–95 (acting Dep. Sec.). Director: Ove Arup & Partners, 1995–98; Ove Arup & Partners Internat., 1995–98; Chm., Arup Transport, 1996–98. Associate Consultant, Waterfront Partnership, 1998–2002. *Publications:* papers on cost benefit analysis, centrifugal testing soils, road design and construction, etc to IHT, ICE, Inst. Geo. Sci., etc. *Recreations:* restoration of old property, golf, choral singing, travel.

WHITFIELD, Prof. Charles Richard, MD; FRCOG; FRCPGlas; Regius Professor of Midwifery in the University of Glasgow, 1976–92, now Emeritus; *b* 21 Oct. 1927; *s* of Charles Alexander and Aileen Muriel Whitfield; *m* 1953, Marion Douglas McKinney (*d* 2011); one *s* two *d*. *Educ:* Campbell Coll., Belfast; Queen's Univ., Belfast (MD). House Surg. and Ho. Phys. appts in Belfast teaching hospitals, 1951–53; Specialist in Obstetrics and Gynaecology, RAMC (Lt-Col retd), 1953–64; Sen. Lectr/Hon. Reader in Dept of Midwifery and Gynaecology, Queen's Univ., Belfast, 1964–74; Consultant to Belfast teaching hosps, 1964–74; Prof. of Obstetrics and Gynaecology, Univ. of Manchester, 1974–76. Mem. Council, RCOG, 1985–91 (Chairman: Subspecialty Bd, 1984–89; Scottish Exec. Cttee, 1985–91; Higher Trng Cttee, 1989–92). *Publications:* (ed) Dewhurst's Obstetrics and Gynaecology for Postgraduates, 4th edn 1985, 5th edn 1995; papers on perinatal medicine, pregnancy anaemia and other obstetric and gynaec. topics in med. and scientific jls. *Recreations:* food, travel, sun-worship.

WHITFIELD, Clovis; Director, Whitfield Fine Art Ltd, since 1979; *b* 21 Oct. 1940; *s* of late Prof. John Humphreys Whitfield; *m* 1st, 1964, Sarah Oppenheim (marr. diss. 1986); two *d*; 2nd, 1986, Dr Irene Cioffi; one *s* one *d*. *Educ:* Corpus Christi Coll., Cambridge (MA 1962); Courtauld Inst. of Art, London. Vis. Prof., Indiana Univ., 1967–68; Associate Dir, Thomas Agnew & Sons Ltd, London, 1970–77; Director: Colnaghi, London, 1978–81, NY, 1983–84; Walpole Gall., London, 1987–91. Cavaliere al Merito (Italy), 1978. Exhibitions: (co-ordinator and joint editor): Painting in Naples: Caravaggio to Giordano, RA and Nat. Gall., Washington, 1982; Classicismo e Natura: la lezione di Domenichino, Capitoline Gall., (joint editor) Rome, 1996; Caravaggio's Friends and Foes, Whitfield Fine Art, 2010. *Publications:* Caravaggio's Eye, 2011 (trans. Italian, 2011); contrib. Burlington mag. *Recreation:* bee-keeping. *Address:* Whitfield Fine Art Ltd, 23 Dering Street, W1S 1AW. *T:* (020) 7355 0040. *E:* fineart@whitfieldfineart.com. *Club:* Brooks's.

WHITFIELD, Hugh Newbold, FRCS; Consultant Urological Surgeon: London Clinic, since 1979; King Edward VII Hospital, since 1988; *b* 15 June 1944; *s* of George Joshua Newbold Whitfield and Audrey Priscilla Whitfield; *m* 1969, Penelope Joy Craig; two *s*. *Educ:* Gonville and Caius Coll., Cambridge (BA 1965, MA 1969; MB BChir 1968); St Bartholomew's Med. Coll., London (MA 1969, MChir 1978). FRCS 1972. Short service commn, RAMC, 1969–74; Res. Registrar, Inst. of Urology, London, 1974–76; Sen. Registrar, St Bartholomew's Hosp., 1976–79; Consultant Urological Surgeon: St Bartholomew's Hosp., 1979–93; Central Middlesex Hosp., 1993–2000; Reader in Urol., Inst. of Urol. and Nephrol., UCL, 1993–2001; Consultant Urol Surgeon, Royal Berks Hosp., 2001–06. Hon. Consultant: in Urol. to the Army, 1997–; in Paediatric Urol., Hosp. for Sick Children, Gt Ormond St, 1999–2006. Ed., British Jl Urol. Internat., 1994–2002. *Publications:* Urology Pocket Consultant, 1985; Textbook of Genito-Urinary Surgery, 1985, 2nd edn 1998; Rob & Smith's Operative Surgery: Genito-Urinary Surgery, 1992; ABC in Urology, 1996, 2nd edn 2006; articles in urological jls. *Recreations:* music, golf, country pursuits, veteran rowing. *Address:* King Edward VII Consulting Rooms, Emmanuel Kaye House, 37a Devonshire Street, W1G 6QA. *T:* (020) 7935 3095, *Fax:* (020) 7467 4375. *E:* urology@whitfield.uk.net. *Clubs:* Garrick; Leander (Henley).

WHITFIELD, John; Consultant Solicitor, Ramsdens Whitfield Hallam, of Batley, Dewsbury and Mirfield, 2010–12 (Senior Partner, Whitfield Hallam Goodall, 1997–2010); *b* 31 Oct. 1941; *s* of Sydney Richard Whitfield and Mary Rishworth Whitfield; *m*; three *s*; *m* 1999, Janet Gissing (*née* Oldroyd). *Educ:* Sedbergh Sch.; Leeds Univ. (LLB). Solicitor: Bird & Bird, 1966–67; Whitfield Son and Hallam, then Whitfield Hallam Goodall, 1967–2010. MP (C) Dewsbury, 1983–87. Contested (C): Hemsworth, 1979; Dewsbury, 1987 and 1992. *Recreations:* fishing, shooting, walking with dogs, supporting Yorkshire Carnegie (Rugby Union). *Address:* Haugh Top Farm, Krumlin, Barkisland, Halifax HX4 0EL. *T:* (01422) 822994. *Clubs:* Tanfield Angling (Hon. Sec.); Octave (Elland).

WHITFIELD, Jonathan; QC 2010; *b* 3 Sept. 1961; *s* of Ronald John Whitfield and Pamela Whitfield; *m* 1991, Joanna. *Educ:* St Mary's Coll., Southampton; London Metropolitan Univ. (BA Hons). Called to the Bar, Middle Temple, 1985; a Tribunal Judge, First-tier Tribunal (Mental Health), 2005–. Legal Assessor to GMC, 2007. *Recreations:* sailing, photography, music (banjo, flute, tabla), walking. *Address:* 54 Doughty Street, WC1N 2LS. *T:* (020) 7404 1313. *E:* j.whitfield@doughtystreet.co.uk.

WHITFIELD, June Rosemary, (Mrs T. J. Aitchison), CBE 1998 (OBE 1985); actress; *b* 11 Nov. 1925; *d* of John Herbert Whitfield and Bertha Georgina Whitfield; *m* 1955, Timothy John Aitchison (*d* 2001); one *d*. *Educ:* Streatham Hill High School; RADA (Diploma 1944). Revue, musicals, pantomime, TV and radio; worked with Arthur Askey, Benny Hill, Frankie Howerd, Dick Emery, Bob Monkhouse, Leslie Crowther, Ronnie Barker; first worked with Terry Scott in 1969; *radio:* JW at the BBC, 1997; June Whitfield at the Beeb, 1999; A Month of June, 2012; series include: Take It From Here (with Dick Bentley and Jimmy Edwards, 1953–60; The News Huddlines (with Roy Hudd and Chris Emmett), 1984–2000; JW Radio Special, 1992; Like They've Never Been Gone (with Roy Hudd), 1998–; Not Talking, 2007; serials (as Miss Marple): Murder at the Vicarage, 1993; A Pocketful of Rye, 1994; At Bertram's Hotel, 1995; The 4.50 from Paddington, 1996; The Caribbean Mystery, 1997; Nemesis, The Mirror Cracked, 1998; The Body in the Library, 1999; A Murder is Announced, 1999; The Moving Finger, 2001; They Do It With Mirrors, 2001; musical, Gigi, 1997; *films:* Carry on Nurse, 1959; Carry on Abroad, 1972; Bless This House, 1972; Carry on Girls, 1973; Carry On Columbus, 1992; Jude the Obscure, 1996; The Last of the Blonde Bombshells, 2000; *television:* This Is Your Life, 1976 and 1995; South Bank Show, 2007; Dr Who, 2009; The Many Faces of June Whitfield, 2009; guest appearance, Amer. TV series, Friends, 1998; series include: Fast and Loose (with Bob Monkhouse), 1954; Faces of Jim (with Jimmy Edwards), 1962, 1963; Beggar My Neighbour, 1966, 1967; Scott On… (with Terry Scott), 1969–73; Happy Ever After, 1974–78; Terry and June, 1979–87; Cluedo, 1990; Absolutely Fabulous, 1993–96, 2001, 2003, 2011; What's My Line?, 1994, 1995; Common As Muck, 1996; Family Money, 1997; The Secret, 2000; Last of the Summer Wine, 2005, 2006, 2007, 2008; Green Green Grass, 2007, 2008; Kingdom, Harley Street, 2008; Coronation St, 2010; Boomers, 2014–15; East Enders, 2015; Cider with Rosie, 2015; *stage:* An Ideal Husband, Chichester, 1987; Ring Round the Moon, Chichester, 1988; Over My Dead Body, Savoy, 1989; Babes in the Wood, Croydon, 1990, Plymouth, 1991, Cardiff, 1992; Cinderella, Wimbledon, 1994; Bedroom Farce, Aldwych, 2002; On the Town, ENO, 2007; We'll Meet Again (tour), 2009, 2010. Freeman, City of London, 1982. Lifetime Achievement Award, British Comedy Awards, 1994; RTS Hall of Fame, 1999; TRIC Special Award, 2012. *Publications:* And June Whitfield (autobiog.), 2000; June Whitfield: at a glance (photographic autobiog.), 2009. *Address:* c/o Maureen Vincent, United Agents, 12–26 Lexington Street, W1F 0LE.

WHITFIELD, Dr Michael, CChem, FRSC; FGS; Vice President, Marine Biological Association, since 2000 (Director and Secretary, 1987–99); Director, Plymouth Marine Laboratory, 1994–96 (Deputy Director, 1988–94); *b* 15 June 1940; *s* of Arthur and Ethel Whitfield; *m* 1961, Jean Ann Rowe (*d* 1984); one *s* three *d*. *Educ:* Univ. of Leeds (BSc 1st cl. Hons Chem.; PhD Chem.). FRSC 1980; FRSB (FIBiol 1994); FGS 2001. Research Scientist, CSIRO Div. of Fisheries and Oceanography, Cronulla, NSW, 1964–69; Vis. Res. Fellow, KTH Stockholm, 1969, Univ. of Liverpool, 1970; Res. Scientist, Marine Biol. Assoc., 1970–87. Vice Pres., Sir Alister Hardy Foundn for Ocean Science, 1991–99; Pres., Challenger Soc. for Marine Science, 1996–98. FRSA 1992. Dr (*hc*): Göteborg, 1991; Plymouth, 2000. *Publications:* Ion-selective electrodes for the analysis of natural waters, 1970; Marine Electrochemistry, 1981; Tracers in the Ocean, 1988; Light and Life in the Sea, 1990; Aquatic Life Cycle Strategies, 1999; numerous papers in professional jls. *Recreations:* hill walking, bird watching, photography. *Address:* The Laboratory, Citadel Hill, Plymouth PL1 2PB. *T:* (01752) 633331.

WHITFIELD, Prof. Roderick; Percival David Professor of Chinese and East Asian Art, University of London, 1993–2002, now Professor Emeritus (Professor of Chinese and East Asian Art, and Head of Percival David Foundation of Chinese Art, 1984–93); *b* 20 July 1937; *s* of late Prof. John Humphreys Whitfield and Joan Herrin, ARCA; *m* 1st, 1963, Frances Elizabeth Oldfield, PhD (marr. diss 1983), *e d* of late Prof. R. C. Oldfield and Lady Kathleen Oldfield; one *s* two *d*; 2nd, 1983, Prof. Youngsook Pak, PhD, art historian, *e d* of late Pak Sang-Jon, Seoul. *Educ:* Woodbourne Acad.; King Edward's Sch., Birmingham; Sch. of Oriental and African Studies (Civil Service Interpreter, 2nd cl.); St John's Coll., Cambridge (BA Hons 1960, Oriental Studies Tripos; MA 1966); Princeton Univ. (MFA 1963, PhD 1965). Research Associate and Lectr, Princeton, 1965–66; Research Fellow, St John's Coll., Cambridge, 1966–68; Asst Keeper I, Dept of Oriental Antiquities, British Museum, 1968–84. Visiting Professor: Univ. of Heidelberg, 1996; Univ. of Helsinki, 1997; Univ. of Barcelona, 1998; Univ. of Oslo, 2002; City Univ. of Hong Kong, 2003; Univ. of Hong Kong, 2004; Yale Univ., 2007; ELTE Univ., Budapest, 2013; MaMa Charitable Foundn Vis. Prof. in Buddhist Studies, Hong Kong Univ., 2015. Teetzel Lectr, Univ. of Toronto, 1995; Keynote Lecturer: Freie Universitaet Berlin, 2013; Inaugural Conf. of Eur. Assoc. of Asian Art and Archaeology, 2014. Pres., Circle of Inner Asian Art, 1996–. Trustee, Inst. of Buddhist Studies, 1987–. Corresp. Fellow, Dunhuang Res. Acad., 1999–; Fellow, Palace Mus., Beijing, 2003–. Mem. Editl Bd, Artibus Asiae, 1992–; Sen. Ed., Internat. Jl of Korean Art, 2008–12. *Publications:* In Pursuit of Antiquity: Chinese paintings of Ming and Ch'ing dynasties in collection of Mr and Mrs Earl Morse, 1969; The Art of Central Asia: the Stein collection at the British Museum, 3 vols, 1983–85 (vol. I trans. Chinese, 2014); (ed) Treasures from Korea, 1984; (ed) Korean Art Treasures, 1986; (ed) Early Chinese Glass, 1988; Caves of the Thousand Buddhas, 1990; (ed) Problems in Meaning in Early Chinese Ritual Bronzes, 1993; Fascination of Nature: plants and insects in Chinese paintings and ceramics of the Yuan dynasty, 1993; Dunhuang, Caves of the Singing Sands: Buddhist Art from the Silk Road, 2 vols, 1995; (trans. jtly) The Arts of Central Asia: the Pelliot Collection in the Musée Guimet, 1996; (ed jtly) Exploring China's Past: new researches and discoveries in Chinese archaeology, 2000; (jtly) The Mogao Caves, 2000; (jtly) Handbooks of Korean Art: pottery and celadon, 2002; (jtly) Buddhist Sculpture, 2002; (ed) Folk Painting, 2002; (contrib.) New Perspectives on China's Past: Chinese archaeology in the twentieth century, 2004; (trans. jtly) Korean Art from the Gompertz and other Collections in the Fitzwilliam Museum, 2004; (trans. and ed jtly) Korean True-View Landscape: paintings by Chŏng Sŏn (1676–1759), 2005; (contrib.) China at the Court of the Emperors, 2008; (contrib.) Il Celeste Impero, 2008; (contrib.) The Printed Image in China from the 8th to the 21st Centuries, 2010; (contrib.) What Makes a Masterpiece?: encounters with great works of art, 2010; (jtly) Catalogue of the Wou Lien-Pai Museum of Chinese Antiquities, 2011; (contrib.) Studies on Sino-Tibetan Buddhist Art, 2011; (contrib.) Bridges to Heaven: essays on East Asian art in honor of Professor Wen C. Fong, 2011; (contrib.) New Perspectives on Qingming shanghe tu, 2012; (ed and trans. jtly) Collected Works of Korean Buddhism, vol. IX: collection of Chinese poetry of the Great Monks of Korea, 2012; (contrib.) Glanz der Kaiser von China: Kunst und Leben in der Verbotenen Stadt, 2012; (ed jtly) A Lost Generation: Luo Zhenyu, Qing loyalists and the formation of modern Chinese culture, 2013; (contrib.) Qingming shanghe tu de gushi, 2013; (contrib.) Masterpieces of Chinese Painting, 8th to 12th centuries, 2013; articles in Asiatische Studien, Artibus Asiae, Buddhica Britannica, Orientations, Burlington Magazine, British Liby Jl, Bukkyo Geijutsu (Ars Buddhica), Zijincheng, Dunhuang yanjiu, TLS, Arts of Asia and other jls. *Address:* 7 St Paul's Crescent, NW1 9XN. *T:* (020) 7267 2888.

WHITFIELD, Sir William, Kt 1993; CBE 1976; RIBA; Partner, Whitfield Lockwood Architects, since 2003; Senior Partner, Whitfield Partners, architects, 1991–2003. DipArch; DipTP. Prof. of Architecture, Victoria Univ. of Manchester, 1981. Surveyor to the Fabric, St Paul's Cathedral, 1985–90. Formerly: Mem., Royal Fine Art Commn; Trustee, British Museum.

WHITFORD, Dr Philippa; MP (SNP) Central Ayrshire, since 2015; *b* Belfast, 24 Dec. 1958; *d* of Philip Whitford and Elizabeth Whitford; *m* 1987, Hans Josef Pieper; one *s*. *Educ:* Douglas Acad., Milngavie; Univ. of Glasgow (MB ChB 1982; MD 1991). FRCSGlas 1986. Surgical training: Royal Victoria Hosp., Belfast, 1983–84; Belfast City Hosp., 1984; Glasgow Royal Infirmary, 1984–85; Registrar: Monklands Dist Gen. Hosp., Airdrie, 1985–86; Royal Hosp. for Sick Children, Glasgow, 1986–87; Canniesburn Hosp., Glasgow, 1987; Glasgow Royal Infirmary, 1987; Res. Fellow, Depts of Surgery and Biochem., Univ. of Glasgow, 1987–89; Registrar (Gen. Surgery), Inverclyde Royal Hosp., 1989–91; Volunteer Consultant Surgeon in Gen. Surgery and Urology, Ali Ahli Hosp., Gaza, 1991–92; Volunteer Health Care Planning and Gen. Surgery, Al Hamshary Hosp., Sidon, Lebanon Balsam Hosp., 1993; Sen. Registrar (Gen. Surgery and Breast Surgery), Aberdeen Royal Infirmary, 1994–96; Consultant Breast Cancer Surgeon, Crosshouse Hosp., Kilmarnock, 1996–2014. Lead clinician in breast cancer, Ayshire and Arran Health Bd, 1996–2010. Mem., Health Select Cttee, 2015–. *Publications:* articles on breast cancer and surgery in British Jl of Surgery, British Jl of Cancer, Eur. Jl of Cancer. *Recreations:* singing, playing cello, painting. *Address:* (office) 14 Eglinton Street, Irvine KA12 8AS. *T:* (01294) 311160. *E:* philippa.whitford.mp@parliament.uk.

WHITING, Prof. Brian, MD; FRCPGlas, FRCPE, FMedSci; Professor of Clinical Pharmacology, 1986–2001, Dean, Faculty of Medicine, and Head of Clinical Medicine Planning Unit, 1992–2000, University of Glasgow; *b* 6 Jan. 1939; *s* of late Leslie George Whiting and Evelyn Irene Edith Whiting (*née* Goss); *m* 1st, 1967, Jennifer Mary Tait (marr.

diss. 1983); two *d*; 2nd, 1990, Marlene Shields (*née* Watson); two step *s*. *Educ:* Univ. of Glasgow (MB ChB 1964; MD 1970). FRCPGlas 1979; FRCPE 1996. House Officer, Western Infirmary and Stobhill Gen. Hosp., Glasgow, 1964; University of Glasgow: Department of Materia Medica: Hutchison Res. Schol., 1965; Registrar in Medicine, 1966–68; Lectr and Sen. Registrar in Clinical Pharmacol., 1969–77; Sen. Lectr and Consultant Physician, 1977–82; Reader in Clinical Pharmacol., 1982–86; Hd, Div. of Clinical Pharmacol., Dept of Medicine and Therapeutics, 1989–91. Dir, Clinical Pharmacokinetics Lab., Stobhill Gen. Hosp., Glasgow, 1980–90. Vis. Scientist, Div. of Clinical Pharmacol., Univ. of Calif, San Francisco, 1978–79; Internat. Union of Pharmacol. Vis. Consultant, India and Nepal, 1985; Visiting Professor of Clinical Pharmacology: Univ. of Auckland, 1987; (British Council) Japan, 1988; British Council and Internat. Union of Pharmacol., India and Nepal, 1990. Non-exec. Mem., Gtr Glasgow Health Bd, 1994–2000. Member: Assoc. of Physicians of GB and Ireland, 1985–; GMC, 1991–96. Founder FFPM (by Dist.) 1990; Founder FMedSci 1998. *Publications:* (ed jtly) Lecture Notes on Clinical Pharmacology, 1982, 6th edn 2001; contrib. numerous articles or book chapters, principally in field of clinical pharmacology. *Recreations:* painting, music (listening and composition), mountaineering. *Address:* 2 Milner Road, Glasgow G13 1QL. *T:* (0141) 959 2324.

WHITING, Clifford Hamilton, ONZ 1999; artist; Kaihautu (Leader), Te Papa Tongarewa Museum of New Zealand, 1993–2000; *b* 6 May 1936; *s* of Frank Whiting and Huriana Herewini (Whanau A-Apanui Tribal Gp); *m* 1957, Heather Leckie; three *s*. *Educ:* Wellington Teachers' Coll.; Dunedin Teachers' Coll. (Trained Teachers' Cert.). Art Advr, Dept of Educn, 1958–71; Lectr in Art, Palmerston North Teachers' Coll., 1972–81; freelance artist, multi media murals, illustrations, photography, print-making, carving, engraving and painting, 1981–. Mem. and Chm., Maori and S Pacific Arts Council and TeWakaToi, 1980–94; Vice-Chm., QEII Arts Council, 1990–93. Hon. DLitt Massey, 1996. *Publications:* Mataora, 1996. *Recreations:* fishing, yachting, diving. *Address:* 24 Gould Street, Russell 0202, Bay of Islands, New Zealand. *T:* (9) 4037726.

WHITING, (David) John, OBE 2008; Tax Director, Office of Tax Simplification, since 2010; *b* Hull, Yorks, 20 March 1951; *s* of (Charles) Peter Whiting and Isabel Norah Whiting; *m* 1977, Susan Barbara Jones; three *d*. *Educ:* Hymers Coll., Hull; Univ. of Manchester (BSc Hons Maths 1972). FCA 1975; CTA 1978. Price Waterhouse, later PricewaterhouseCoopers, 1972–2009, Tax Partner, 1984–2009; Tax Policy Dir, Chartered Inst. of Taxation, 2009–13. Mem., First-tier Tribunal (Tax), 2009–13. Pres., Chartered Inst. of Taxation, 2001–02. Non-exec. Dir, HMRC, 2013–; Mem. Bd, Revenue Scotland, 2015–. *Publications:* (contrib.) Dimensions of Tax Design: the Mirrlees Review, 2011; contrib. articles in taxation jls incl. British Tax Review. *Recreations:* family life, history, watching cricket, music (especially Fairport Convention), DIY. *Address:* Office of Tax Simplification, 1 Horse Guards Road, SW1A 2HQ. *T:* (020) 7270 1169. *E:* john.whiting@ots.gsi.gov.uk. *Club:* MCC.

WHITING, Maj.-Gen. Graham Gerald M.; *see* Messervy-Whiting.

WHITING, John; *see* Whiting, D. J.

WHITING, Rev. Peter Graham, CBE 1984; Minister, Beechen Grove Baptist Church, 1985–95; *b* 7 Nov. 1930; *s* of late Rev. Arthur Whiting and Olive Whiting; *m* 1960, Lorena Inns; two *s* three *d*. *Educ:* Yeovil Grammar Sch.; Irish Baptist Theol Coll., Dublin. Ordained into Baptist Ministry, 1956. Minister, King's Heath, Northampton, 1956–62; commnd RAChD, 1962; Regtl Chaplain, 1962–69 (Chaplain to 1st Bn The Parachute Regt, 1964–66); Sen. Chaplain, 20 Armd Bde and Lippe Garrison, BAOR, 1969–72; Staff Chaplain, HQ BAOR, 1973–74; Sen. Chaplain, 24 Airportable Bde, 1974–75; Dep. Asst Chaplain Gen., W Midland Dist, Shrewsbury, 1975–78 (Sen. Chaplain, Young Entry Units, 1976–78); Asst Chaplain Gen., 1st British Corps, BAOR, 1978–81; Dep. Chaplain Gen. to the Forces (Army), 1981–84. QHC 1981–85. *Address:* 5 Pook Lane, Warblington, Havant, Hants PO9 2TH. *T:* (023) 9247 2291.

WHITLAM, Michael Richard, CBE 2000; charity consultant; Director and Owner, Mike Whitlam - Solutions for Charity, consultancy, since 2001; *b* 25 March 1947; *s* of late Richard William Whitlam and Mary Elizabeth Whitlam (*née* Land); *m* 1968, Anne Jane McCurley; two *d*. *Educ:* Morley Grammar Sch.; Tadcaster Grammar Sch.; Coventry Coll. of Educn, Univ. of Warwick (Cert. of Educn); Home Office Prison Dept Staff Coll. (Qual. Asst Governor Prison Dept); Cranfield Coll. of Technology (MPhil 1988). Biology teacher, Ripon, 1968–69; Asst Governor, HM Borstal, Hollesley Bay and HM Prison, Brixton, 1969–74; Dir, Hammersmith Teenage Project, NACRO, 1974–78; Dep. Dir/Dir, UK ops, Save the Children Fund, 1978–86; Chief Exec., RNID, 1986–90; Dir-Gen., BRCS, 1991–99; Chief Exec., Mentor Foundn (Internat.), 1999–2001; Chief Executive Officer: Internat. Agency for the Prevention of Blindness, 2002–05; Vision 2020 the Right to Sight, 2002–05. Special Charity Advr to Russam GMS, 2005–. Board Member: Britcross Ltd, 1991–99; British Red Cross Events Ltd, 1991–99; British Red Cross Trading, 1991–99; REACH, 1997–; Chm., Sound Advantage plc, 1988–90. Chm., Ofcom Adv. Cttee for Older and Disabled People, 2004–10. Non-exec. Dir, Hillingdon PCT, 2004–11. Member: Exec. Council, Howard League, 1974–84; Community Alternative Young Offenders Cttee, NACRO, 1979–82; Exec. Council, Nat. Children's Bureau, 1980–86; Bd, City Literary Inst., 1989–90; Bd, Charity Appointments Ltd, 1990–99; Dir, Watford FC Community Educn Trust, 2007– (Vice Chm., 2010–); Chairman: London Intermediate Treatment Assoc., 1980–83; and Founder, ACEVO (formerly ACENVO), 1988– (Mem. Policy and Res. Gp, 1994–99); Prisoners Abroad, 1999–2003; Chalker Foundn for Africa, 2007–; Chm., CLICK Rukiga (link between Ickenham and Rukiga, Uganda), 2008–; Chair, Ickenham Police Ward Panel, 2011–. Trustee, CMS, 2012–. FRSA 1995; CCMI (CIMgt 1997). Mem., St Giles Church, Ickenham. *Publications:* numerous papers on juvenile delinquency and charity management. *Recreations:* painting, walking, family activities, voluntary organisations, politics, visiting France, cooking, motorcaravanning. *Address:* 40 Pepys Close, Ickenham, Middx UB10 8NY. *T:* (01895) 678169. *E:* m.whitlam@btinternet.com.

WHITLAM, Nicholas Richard; company director; Chairman, Port Authority of New South Wales, since 2014 (Chairman, since 2005, and Chief Executive Officer, 2013–14, Port Kembla Port Corporation; Chairman: Sydney Ports Corporation, since 2013; Newcastle Port Corporation, 2013–14); *b* 6 Dec. 1945; *s* of Hon. (Edward) Gough Whitlam, AC, QC and Margaret Elaine Whitlam, AO; *m* 1973, Sandra Judith Frye; two *s* one *d*. *Educ:* Sydney High Sch.; Harvard Coll. (AB cum laude); London Business Sch. (MSc). Morgan Guaranty Trust Co., 1969–75; American Express Co., 1975–78; Banque Paribas, 1978–80; Comr, Rural Bank of New South Wales, 1980–81, then Man. Dir, State Bank of New South Wales, 1981–87; Man. Dir, Whitlam Turnbull & Co. Ltd, 1987–90; Chm., Whitlam & Co., 1990–2002 and 2003–; Dep. Chm., Export Finance and Insurance Corp., 1991–94; Advr, Asian Capital Partners, 1993–96. Director: GreenCell Ltd, 2011–; Crescent Wealth, 2015–. Proprietor, Mt Kembla Hotel, 2004–07. Board Member: Aust. Trade Commn, 1985–91; Integral Energy Aust., 1996–99. Pres., NRMA, 1996–2002 (Dep. Pres., 1995–96); Chm., NRMA Insce Ltd, 1996–2001. Chm., Lifetime Care and Support Authy, 2009–12 (Dir, 2006–12); Deputy Chairman: Workers' Compensation Insce Fund Investment Bd (formerly WorkCover Insce Investment Bd), 2005–12; WorkCover Authy, 2010–12. Board Member: Aust. Graduate Sch. of Management, 1982–97 (Chm., 1988–97); Aust. Sports Foundn, 1986–95; Chm., Sydney Symphony Orch., 1991–96; Mem. Symphony Council, 1996–2005; Trustee, Sydney Cricket and Sports Ground, 1984–88. DUniv NSW, 1996. *Publications:* Nest of Traitors (with John Stubbs), 1974; Still Standing, 2004. *Recreations:* swimming, cycling, reading. *Address:* PO Box 3072, Austinmer, NSW 2515, Australia. *Fax:* (2) 42682566. *Clubs:* Hong Kong; Tattersall's (Sydney) (Chm., 1993–96).

WHITLEY, Edward John, OBE 2013; Founder and Director, Whitley Asset Management, since 2001; *b* Shrewsbury, 6 June 1961; *s* of Edward and Penelope Whitley; *m* 1986, Araminta Ramsay; one *s* three *d*. *Educ:* Shrewsbury Sch.; St Anne's Coll., Oxford (Exhibnr; BA Hons English; Blue in Modern Pentathlon 1980). Manager, N M Rothschild & Sons Ltd, 1983–90; author, 1990–2000. Founder and Trustee, Whitley Fund for Nature, 1992– (Chm., 1992–); Trustee: Sheila Whitley Trust, 1988–; Whitley Animal Protection Trust, 1988–; Tavistock Trust for Aphasia, 2014–. Mem., George Eliot Fellowship, 2015–. *Publications:* The Graduates, 1986; Gerald Durrell's Army, 1992; Rogue Trader, 1996. *Recreations:* Shakespeare, fishing, tennis, exploration. *Address:* Whitley Asset Management, 116 Princedale Road, W11 4NH. *T:* (020) 7221 2145. *Clubs:* Vincent's; Plowden Fishing; University College Boat.

WHITLEY, Edward Thomas; Chairman, St Julian's Estate Ltd, since 2009; *b* 6 May 1954; *s* of John Caswell Whitley and Shirley Frances Whitley (*née* Trollope); *m* 1984, Hon. Tara Olivia Chichester-Clark, *d* of Baron Moyola, PC (NI); one *s*. *Educ:* Harrow Sch.; Univ. of Bristol (BSc). Chartered accountant; Price Waterhouse, 1976–81; Cazenove & Co., 1981–2001, Partner, 1988–2001; CEO, Internat. Financial Services, London, 2001–07. Dir, Henderson Strata Investments plc, 1990–2005. Chm., Sofas & Stuff Ltd, 2012–. Chm., Financial Services Sector Adv. Gp, 2005–06. Mem., Council of Mgt, Restoration of Appearance and Function Trust, 1999–2011; Trustee, World Trade Center Disaster Fund, 2001–06. Hon. Pres., S Derry Wildfowl and Game Preservation Soc., 2002–. FCSI 2010.

WHITLEY, Susan Alison; *see* Bradbury, S. A.

WHITMARSH, Martin Richard; Chief Executive, Ben Ainslie Racing, since 2015; *b* Lyndhurst, Hants, 29 April 1958; *s* of Kenneth Whitmarsh and Betty Whitmarsh; *m* 1996, Deborah Ann Kirby; one *s* one *d*. *Educ:* Portsmouth Poly. (BSc 1980). CEng, MRAeS 1995. Joined British Aerospace plc, 1980, Manuf. Dir, 1988–89; McLaren Racing Ltd: Hd of Ops, 1989–97; Man. Dir, 1997–2004; CEO, Formula 1 Team, 2004; Chief Operating Officer, 2005–10, Chief Exec., 2010–14, McLaren Gp; Dep. Chm., McLaren Automotive, 2010–14; Team Principal, Vodafone McLaren Mercedes Formula 1 Team, 2009–14. Chm., Formula One Teams Assoc., 2010–14. Hon. LLD Portsmouth, 2009; Hon. DTech Southampton Solent, 2009. *Club:* British Racing Drivers'.

WHITMARSH, Prof. Timothy John Guy, PhD; A. G. Leventis Professor of Greek Culture, University of Cambridge, since 2014; Fellow, St John's College, Cambridge, since 2014; *b* Chelmsford, 23 Jan. 1970; *s* of Guy Whitmarsh and Judy Whitmarsh; partner, Emily Kneebone; one *s* one *d*. *Educ:* Ashford Carbonell Primary Sch.; Moor Park Sch.; Malvern Coll.; King's Coll., Cambridge (BA Classics 1992; MPhil Classics 1994); St John's Coll., Cambridge (PhD Classics 1998). Jun. Res. Fellow, 1997–99, Fellow and Coll. Lectr, 1999–2001, St John's Coll., Cambridge; Newton Trust Lectr, Univ. of Cambridge, 1999–2001; University of Exeter: Lectr in Classics, 2001–03; Reader in Greek Lit., 2003–06; Prof. of Ancient Literatures, 2006–07; University of Oxford: Lectr in Greek Lang. and Lit., 2007–11; Prof. of Ancient Literatures, 2011–14; Fellow, Tutor and E. P. Warren Praelector, Corpus Christi Coll., 2007–14. *Publications:* Greek Literature and the Roman Empire: the politics of imitation, 2001; (trans.) Achilles Tatius, Leucippe and Clitophon, 2001; Ancient Greek Literature, 2004; The Second Sophistic, 2005; (ed with Jason König) Ordering Knowledge in the Roman Empire, 2007; (ed) The Cambridge Companion to the Greek and Roman Novel, 2008; (ed jtly) Galen and the World of Knowledge, 2009; (ed) Local Knowledge and Microidentities in the Roman Greek World, 2010; Narrative and Identity in the Ancient Greek Novel: returning romance, 2011; Beyond the Second Sophistic: adventures in Greek postclassicism, 2013; (ed with Stuart Thomson) The Romance between Greece and the East, 2013; Battling the Gods: atheism in the ancient world, 2015. *Recreations:* football, music, guitar. *Address:* Faculty of Classics, Sidgwick Avenue, Cambridge CB3 9DA. *T:* (01223) 335166.

WHITMORE, Sir Clive (Anthony), GCB 1988 (KCB 1983); CVO 1983; Director, N. M. Rothschild & Sons Ltd, 1994–2010; *b* 18 Jan. 1935; *s* of Charles Arthur Whitmore and Louisa Lilian Whitmore; *m* 1961, Jennifer Mary Thorpe; one *s* two *d*. *Educ:* Sutton Grammar Sch., Surrey; Christ's Coll., Cambridge (BA). Asst Principal, WO, 1959; Private Sec. to Permanent Under-Sec. of State, WO, 1961; Asst Private Sec. to Sec. of State for War, 1962; Principal, 1964; Private Sec. to Permanent Under-Sec. of State, MoD, 1969; Asst Sec., 1971; Asst Under-Sec. of State (Defence Staff), MoD, 1975; Under Sec., Cabinet Office, 1977; Principal Private Sec. to the Prime Minister, 1979–82; Dep. Sec., 1981; Permanent Under-Secretary of State: MoD, 1983–88; Home Office, 1988–94. Director: Racal Electronics, 1994–2000; Boots Co., 1994–2001; Morgan Crucible Co. PLC, 1994–2004. Mem., Security Commn, 1998–2007. Chancellor, De Montfort Univ., 1995–97; Chm. Council, Inst. of Educn, Univ. of London, 1995–2000. *Recreations:* gardening, listening to music.

WHITMORE, David John Ludlow, FCA; Vice Chairman, 2011–14, and President, Americas, 2012–14, Information Services Group, Inc.; *b* 20 July 1959; *s* of Dr John L. Whitmore and Joan C. Whitmore (*née* Hale); *m* 1984, Monica Mary Boyd; two *s* one *d*. *Educ:* Carisbrooke High Sch., IoW; Univ. of Warwick (BSc Hons Accounting and Financial Analysis). ACA 1984, FCA 1989; CPA(US) 1988. Joined Arthur Andersen, 1980; worked in: London, 1980–84; LA, 1984–86; World HQ, Chicago, 1986–87; LA, 1987–89; London, 1989–2002; Partner, 1991; Head, Commercial Assurance and Business Adv. Practice, 1995–97; Managing Partner: UK Assurance and Business Adv. Practice, 1997–2001; Global Assurance and Business Adv. Markets, 2001–02; Pres., Europe, Proudfoot Consulting, 2004; Chief Executive: 4 Future Gp, 2005–06; Compass Mgt Consulting Gp, 2007–11. Non-exec. Dir, Bevan Brittan LLP, 2009–. Mem. Adv. Bd, Warwick Business Sch., 2001–12. *Recreations:* golf, tennis, reading. *Clubs:* Royal Automobile; Liphook Golf.

WHITMORE, Sir John (Henry Douglas), 2nd Bt *cr* 1954; Chairman, Performance Consultants International, since 1998; *b* 16 Oct. 1937; *s* of Col Sir Francis Henry Douglas Charlton Whitmore, 1st Bt, KCB, CMG, DSO, TD, and Lady Whitmore (*née* Ellis Johnsen); *S* father, 1961; *m* 1st, 1962, Gunilla (marr. diss. 1969), *e d* of Sven A. Hansson, OV, KLH, Danderyd, and *o d* of Mrs Ella Hansson, Stockholm, Sweden; one *d*; 2nd, 1977, Diana Elaine (marr. diss. 2007), *e d* of Fred A. Becchetti, California, USA; one *s*. *Educ:* Stone House, Kent; Eton; Sandhurst; Cirencester. Active in personal development and social change; retired professional racing driver; business trainer and sports psychologist. *Publications:* The Winning Mind, 1987; Superdriver, 1988; Coaching for Performance, 1992; Need, Greed or Freedom, 1997; Mind Games, 1998. *Recreations:* ski-ing, squash. *Heir:* *s* Jason Whitmore, *b* 26 Jan. 1983. *Address:* Unit 6, Park Lane, Crowborough, E Sussex TN6 2QN. *E:* Johnwhitmore@performanceconsultants.com. *Club:* British Racing Drivers'.

WHITMORE, Mark Graham; Director of Collections and Research, Imperial War Museum, 2010 (Director of Collections, 2003–10); *b* 8 July 1952; *s* of late Prof. Raymond L. Whitmore, AM and of Ruth H. Whitmore; *m* 1975, Laura Diane Vincent; one *s* three *d*. *Educ:* Univ. of Queensland (BRTP Hons 1975); Univ. of Melbourne (MEnvS 1986). Urban and Envmtl Planner, Gutteridge, Haskins and Davey, 1983–87; Sen. Curator, Hist. of Technol., Qld Mus., 1987–90; Australian War Memorial: Sen. Curator, Military Technol., 1990–95; Asst Dir (Nat. Collection), 1995–2003. Museums Australia: Pres., ACT Br., 2000–03; Mem.,

Nat. Council, 2000–03. Trustee: Sir Winston Churchill Archive, 2006–; Tank Mus., 2008–. *Publications:* 'Mephisto' A7V Sturmpanzerwagen 506, 1989. *Recreations:* music, photography, art, travel, operating antique steam machinery, restoring classic cars.

WHITNEY, Prof. David John; Director, Clinical Management Unit, Keele University, 2001–06; *b* 1 Sept. 1950; *s* of Leonard and Joyce Susannah Whitney; *m* 1979, Pauline Jane; one *s* two *d. Educ:* Exeter Univ. (BA Hons); London Univ. (MA). Dep. House Governor, Moorfields Eye Hosp., 1982–85; Regl Dir of Planning, Trent RHA, 1985–90; Chief Exec., Central Sheffield Univ. Hosps NHS Trust, 1991–2001. Prof. Associate, Sheffield Sch. of Health and Related Res., Univ. of Sheffield, 1995–2012 (Hon. Prof., 2012–). Chm., Derby Health United, 2015–. Lay Trustee, RCS, 2014–. Chm., Weston Park Hosp. Cancer Care and Res. Fund, 2012–. *Recreations:* soccer, tennis, squash, art, music.

WHITNEY, John Norton Braithwaite, CBE 2008; Chairman: Friends Provident Charitable Foundation, 2002–06; Council, Royal Academy of Dramatic Art, 2003–07; *b* 20 Dec. 1930; *s* of Dr Willis Bevan Whitney and Dorothy Anne Whitney; *m* 1956, Roma Elizabeth Hodgson; one *s* one *d. Educ:* Leighton Park Friends' Sch. Radio producer, 1951–64; formed Ross Radio Productions, 1951, and Autocue, 1955; founded Radio Antilles, 1963; Founder Dir, Sagitta Prodns, 1968–82; Man. Dir, Capital Radio, 1973–82; Dir Gen., IBA, 1982–89; Dir, The Really Useful Group Ltd, 1990–97 (Man. Dir, 1989–90; Chm., 1990–95); Chm., Trans World Communications plc, 1992–94. Dir, Duke of York's Theatre, 1979–82. Chm., Friends' Provident Ethical Investment Trust plc, 1992–; Dir, Friends' Provident Life Office, 1982–2002 (Chm., Friends' Provident Stewardship Cttee of Reference, 1985–2000); Chairman: Radio Joint Audience Research Ltd, 1992–2002; Sony Music Pace Partnership (National Bowl), 1992–95; Enterprise Radio Hldgs Ltd, 1994–96; Radio Partnership, 1996–99; Caspian Publishing Ltd, 1996–2002; Director: VCI plc, 1995–98; Galaxy Media Corp. plc, 1997–2000; Far Pavilions Ltd, 1997–; Bird & Co. International, 1999–2001 (Chm.). Chm., Assoc. of Ind. Local Radio Contractors, 1973, 1974, 1975 and 1980. Wrote, edited and devised numerous television series, 1956–82. Chm., Sony Radio Awards Cttee, 1991–97; Vice Pres., Japan Festival 1991, 1991–92 (Chm., Festival Media Cttee, 1991); Trustee, Japan Educn Trust, 1993–; Member: Bd, NT, later RNT, 1982–94 (Trustee, Pension and Life Assce, RNT, 1994–2003); Films, TV and Video Adv. Cttee, British Council, 1983–89; RCM Centenary Develt Fund (formerly Appeals Cttee), 1982– (Chm., Media and Events Cttee, 1982–94); Bd, Open Coll., 1987–89; Council for Charitable Support, 1989–92; Bd, City of London Sinfonia, 1994–2001; Exec. Cttee, Musicians Benevolent Fund, 1995–2001; Council: Royal London Aid Society, 1966–90; TRIC, 1979–89 (Pres., 1985–86; Companion, 1989–); Fairbridge (formerly Drake Fellowship, then Fairbridge Drake Soc.), 1981–96 (Vice Pres., 1996–); RSA, 1994–99; Chm., British Amer. Arts Assoc., 1992–95. Pres., London Marriage Guidance Council, 1983–90; Vice President: Commonwealth Youth Exchange Council, 1982–83; RNID, 1988–; Chm., Trustees, Soundaround (National Sound Magazine for the Blind), 1981–2000 (Life Pres., 2000); Chm., Artsline, 1983–2000 (Life Pres., 2001); Trustee: Venture Trust, 1982–86; Hosp. Broadcasting Assoc. Patron, MusicSpace Trust, 1990–; Governor: English Nat. Ballet (formerly London Festival Ballet), 1989–91; Bd, Performing Arts and Technol. Sch., 1992–2001; Chm., Theatre Investment Fund, 1990–2001. Fellow and Vice Pres., RTS, 1986–89; Fellow, Radio Acad., 1996. FRSA; Hon. RCM. *Recreations:* chess, photography, sculpture. *Address:* 5 Church Close, Todber, Dorset DT10 1JH. *E:* john@johnwhitney.co.uk. *Clubs:* Garrick, Whitefriars.

WHITROW, Benjamin John; actor; *b* 17 Feb. 1937; *s* of Philip and Mary Whitrow; *m* 1972, Catherine Cook; one *s* one *d*; one *s* by Celia Imrie. *Educ:* RADA (Leverhulme Schol.). *Stage:* Nat. Theatre, 1967–74; West End productions: Otherwise Engaged, Queen's, 1975; Dirty Linen, Arts, 1976; Ten Times Table, Globe, 1978; Passion Play, Aldwych, 1980; Uncle Vanya, Vaudeville, 1986; Noises Off, Savoy, 1983; Man for All Seasons, Savoy, 1987; Falstaff, Merry Wives of Windsor, RSC, 1992; Wild Oats, RNT, 1996; The Invention of Love, RNT, 1998; The Rivals, RSC, 2000; Henry IV Part II, 2001; Tom and Viv, Almeida, 2006; Entertaining Angels, Chichester, 2006 and tour, 2009; Richard II, Bristol Tobacco Factory, 2011; *films:* Quadrophenia, 1979; Clockwise; Personal Services, 1987; Scenes of a Sexual Nature, 2007; Bomber, 2008; *television* includes: Pride and Prejudice, 1995; Tom Jones, 1997; Henry VIII, 2003; Island at War, 2004; Midsummer Murders, 2009; Little Crackers, 2011; Casualty, 2012; Wolf Hall, 2015. *Recreations:* golf, reading, bridge. *Address:* c/o Lou Coulson, 37 Berwick Street, W1F 8RS. *T:* (020) 7734 9633.

WHITSON, Sir Keith (Roderick), Kt 2002; Group Chief Executive, HSBC Holdings plc, 1998–2003 (Director, 1994–2003); *b* 25 March 1943; *s* of William Cleghorn Whitson and Ellen (*née* Wade); *m* 1968, Sabine Marita, *d* of Ulrich Wiechert; one *s* two *d. Educ:* Alleyn's Sch., Dulwich. FCIB. Joined Hong Kong and Shanghai Banking Corporation Ltd, 1961; Manager, Frankfurt, 1978–80; Manager, Indonesia, 1981–84; Asst Gen. Manager, Finance, Hong Kong, 1985–87; Chief Exec. Officer, UK, 1987, Exec. Dir, Marine Midland Bank, NY, 1990–92; Midland Bank: Dep. Chief Exec., 1992–94; Chief Exec., 1994–98; Dep. Chm., 1998–2003. Chairman: Merrill Lynch HSBC, 2000–02; HSBC Bank AS, 2001–03; Vice-Chm., HSBC Bank North America Inc., 2002–03; Director: HSBC Bank Argentina, 1997–2003; HSBC Bank USA, 1998–2003; HSBC Bank Canada, 1998–2003; Dep. Chm. Supervisory Bd, HSBC Trinkaus und Burkhardt Dusseldorf, 1993–2003. Non-executive Director: FSA, 1998–2003; Tetra Laval, 2005–14.

WHITTAKER, Andrew Mark; Group General Counsel, Lloyds Banking Group, 2013–15; *b* Rawtenstall, Lancs, 1956; *s* of Edmund and Margaret Whittaker; *m* 1993, Clare Margaret Potter; two *d. Educ:* Torquay Boys' Grammar Sch.; Balliol Coll., Oxford (BA 1977; MA 1980). Admitted as solicitor, 1980; in private practice as solicitor, 1977–82; Legal Asst, 1982–84, Sen. Legal Asst, 1984–85, DTI; Securities and Investments Board: Asst Dir, 1985–87; Dep. Dir, 1987–92; Hd, Internat. and Mkts Policy, 1993–95; Hd, Securities Mkt Supervision, 1995–97; Jt Actg Mkts Dir, 1997; Dep. Gen. Counsel, 1997–2000, Gen. Counsel, 2000–13, FSA. Mem., Legal Services Bd, 2008–14. Trustee, British Inst. of Internat. and Comparative Law, 2014–. Gen. Ed., Financial Services: Law and Practice, 1987–97; Cons. Ed., Butterworth's Financial Regulation Service, 1997–2006. *Publications:* (with G. Morse) The Financial Services Act 1986: a guide to the new law, 1987; contributor: Current Legal Problems, 1990; The Future for the Global Securities Market: legal and regulatory aspects, 1996; European Securities Markets: the Investment Services Directive and beyond, 1998; Commercial Law and Commercial Practice, 2003; Conflicts of Interest, 2005; Crisis and Recovery: ethics, economics and justice, 2010. *Recreations:* family, photography, travel. *Club:* Athenæum.

See also S. J. Whittaker.

WHITTAKER, Craig; MP (C) Calder Valley, since 2010; *b* Radcliffe, Lancs, 30 Aug. 1962; *s* of Frank Whittaker and Marjorie Whittaker; *m* 2011, Elaine Wilkinson; one *s* two *d* by a previous marriage. *Educ:* Belmont State High Sch., NSW. Restaurant Manager: Pizza Hut (Australia) Pty Ltd, 1980–84; Pizza Hut (UK) Ltd, 1984–85; Licensee: Liberty Taverns Ltd, 1985–86; J. W. Lees (Brewers) Ltd, 1986–88; Dir, Food Retail (Australia), Kezdem Pty Ltd, 1988–92; Retail Branch Manager, Wilkinson Home and Garden Stores, 1992–98; Retail Gen. Manager, PC World, DSG Internat. plc, 1998–2009. Mem. (C) Calderdale MBC, 2003–04, 2007–11 (Lead Mem., Children and Young People, 2007–10). Mem., Educn Select Cttee, 2010–15; Jt Chm., All Party Parly Gp on Street Children, 2011–; Chm., All Party Parly Gp on Looked After Children and Care Leavers, 2012–, on Adoption and Fostering, 2012–. Chm., Together for Looked-after Children charity, 2011–. *Recreations:* scuba diving, travel. *Address:* House of Commons, SW1A 0AA. *T:* (020) 7219 7031, *Fax:* (020) 7219 1054. *E:* craig.whittaker.mp@parliament.uk.

WHITTAKER, Air Vice-Marshal David, CB 1988; MBE 1967; Air Officer Administration and Air Officer Commanding Directly Administered Units, RAF Support Command, 1986–89, retired; *b* 25 June 1933; *s* of Lawson and Irene Whittaker; *m* 1956, Joyce Ann Noble (*d* 2006); two *s. Educ:* Hutton Grammar School. Joined RAF, 1951; commissioned 1952; served No 222, No 3, No 26 and No 1 Squadrons, 1953–62; HQ 38 Group, 1962–63; HQ 24 Bde, 1963–65; Comd Metropolitan Comms Sqdn, 1966–68; RAF Staff Coll., 1968; Asst Air Adviser, New Delhi, 1969–70; RAF Leeming, 1971–73; Coll. of Air Warfare, 1973; Directing Staff, RNSC Greenwich, 1973–75; Staff of CDS, 1975–76; DACOS (Ops), AFCENT, 1977–80; RCDS 1980; Defence and Air Adviser, Ottawa, 1983–86. *Recreations:* fishing, gardening, travel. *Address:* Seronera, Copgrove, Harrogate, North Yorks HG3 3SZ. *T:* (01423) 340459. *Club:* Royal Air Force.

WHITTAKER, John, PhD; Member (UK Ind) North West Region, European Parliament, 2004–09; *b* 7 June 1945; *m*; four *s. Educ:* Queen Mary Coll., Univ. of London (BSc Physics 1966); Univ. of Cape Town (PhD Physics 1980; BA Econs 1982). Industrial Engr, Magnesium Elektron Ltd, Manchester, 1966–68; Sales Engr, 1968–72, Manager Controls Div., 1972–75, Bestobell Engrg Ltd, Cape Town; University of Cape Town: Lectr in Physics, 1978–85, in Econs, 1984–90; Associate Prof., Econs, 1990–93; Prin. Lectr, Econs, Staffs Univ., 1994–96; Sen. Lectr, Econs, 1996–2004, Vis. Fellow, 2004–, Univ. of Lancaster. Contested (UK Ind): Littleborough and Saddleworth, July 1995; Lancaster and Wyre, 1997; Wigan, Sept. 1999, 2005; NW Reg., EP, 1999. *Publications:* articles in jls.

WHITTAKER, Prof. John Brian, PhD, DSc; FRES; Professor of Ecology, University of Lancaster, 1987–2004, now Emeritus; *b* 26 July 1939; *s* of Roland Whittaker and Freda (*née* Lord); *m* 1st, 1964, Helen May Thorley (*d* 1998); two *s*; 2nd, 2007, Kathleen Wendy Cann. *Educ:* Bacup and Rawtenstall Grammar Sch.; Univ. of Durham (BSc, PhD, DSc). FRES 1979, Hon. FRES 2008. Res. Officer, Univ. of Oxford, 1963–66; University of Lancaster: Lectr, then Sen. Lectr, 1966–87; Hd, Dept of Biol Scis, 1983–86 and 1991–94. Mem., Adv. Cttee on Sci., NCC, 1978–81; Chm., Terrestrial Life Scis Cttee, NERC, 1991–95. Pres., British Ecol Soc., 2000–01 (Vice-Pres., 1987–89; Mem. Council, 1970–75, 1984–86); Member: Council, Freshwater Biol Assoc., 1988–91; Exec. and Council, UK Bioscis Fedn, 2002–06; Council, Royal Entomol Soc., 2005– (Vice-Pres., 2007–08). Hon. Fellow, Lancaster Univ., 2006. British Ecol Soc. Award, 2004. *Publications:* Practical Demonstration of Ecological Concepts, 1988; (ed jtly) Toward a More Exact Ecology, 1989; (with D. T. Salt) Insects on dock plants, 1998; (ed jtly) 100 Influential Papers: published in 100 years of the British Ecological Society journals, 2013; contribs to books and jls in insect ecology. *Recreations:* Gillow furniture, fell-walking, family. *Address:* Department of Biological Sciences, Lancaster University, Lancaster LA1 4YQ. *T:* (01524) 65201.

WHITTAKER, Sandra Melanie; *see* Smith, Sandra M.

WHITTAKER, Prof. Simon John, DPhil, DCL; Professor of European Comparative Law, University of Oxford, since 2006; Fellow and Tutor in Law, St John's College, Oxford, since 1987; barrister; *b* Widnes, 5 Oct. 1958; *s* of Edmund Harry and Margaret Whittaker; *m* 1990, Judith Finch; two *s* one *d. Educ:* Torquay Boys' Grammar Sch.; St John's Coll., Oxford (BCL, MA; DPhil 1987; DCL 2008). Called to the Bar, Lincoln's Inn, 1987. Lectr in Laws, KCL, 1982–87; Lectr, 1987–2001, Reader in European Comparative Law, 2001–06, Univ. of Oxford. *Publications:* Liability for Products: English law, French law and European harmonization, 2005; (jtly) Principles of French Law, 1998, 2nd edn 2008; (contributing ed.) Chitty on Contracts, 26th edn 1989 to 31st edn 2012; contrib. articles to acad. jls. *Recreations:* gardens, architecture. *Address:* St John's College, Oxford OX1 3JP. *T:* (01865) 277300.

See also A. M. Whittaker.

WHITTAKER, Stanley Henry, FCA, CGMA; Director of Finance and Planning, British Railways Board, 1988–91; *b* 14 Sept. 1935; *s* of Frederick Whittaker and Gladys Margaret (*née* Thatcher); *m* 1959, Freda Smith; two *s. Educ:* Bec School. ACA 1958, FCA 1969; ACMA 1971; CGMA 2012. Articled clerk, G. H. Attenborough & Co., Chartered Accountants, 1953–57; Sen. Assistant, Slater, Chapman & Cooke, 1960–62; Partner, Tiplady, Brailsford & Co., 1962–65; Finance Manager, NCB, 1965–68; British Railways: Finance Manager, 1968–74; Corporate Budgets Manager, 1974–78; Sen. Finance Manager, 1978–80; Chief Finance Officer, Western Reg., 1980–82; Director: Budgetary Control, 1982–86; Finance Develt, 1986–87; Group Finance, 1987–88. *Recreations:* flying, ski-ing, industrial archaeology, travel. *Address:* 12 Kennylands Road, Sonning Common, Reading, Berks RG4 9JT. *T:* (0118) 972 2951.

WHITTAM, Richard; *see* Whittam, W. R. L.

WHITTAM, Prof. Ronald, FRS 1973; Emeritus Professor, Leicester University, since 1983 (Professor of Physiology, 1966–83); *b* 21 March 1925; *e s* of Edward Whittam and May Whittam (*née* Butterworth), Oldham, Lancs; *m* 1957, Christine Patricia Margaret, 2nd *d* of Canon J. W. Lamb; one *s* one *d. Educ:* Council and Technical Schools, Oldham; Univs of Manchester and Sheffield and King's College, Cambridge. BSc 1st Class Hons (Manchester); PhD (Sheffield and Cambridge); MA (Oxon). Served RAF, 1943–47. John Stokes Fellow, Dept of Biochem., Univ. of Sheffield, 1953–55; Beit Memorial Fellow, Physiological Lab., Cambridge, 1955–58; Mem. Scientific Staff, MRC Cell Metabolism Research Unit, Oxford, 1958–60; Univ. Lectr in Biochemistry, Oxford, 1960–66; Bruno Mendel Fellow of Royal Society, 1965–66; Dean of Fac. of Science, Leicester Univ., 1979–82. Mem. Editorial Bd of Biochem. Jl, 1963–67; Hon. Sec., 1969–74, Hon. Mem., 1986, Physiological Soc.; Mem. Biological Research Bd of MRC, 1971–74, Co-Chm., 1973–74; Member: Biological Sciences Cttee, UGC, 1974–82; Educn Cttee, Royal Soc., 1979–83; Chm., Biological Educn Cttee, Royal Soc. and Inst. Biol., 1974–77. *Publications:* Transport and Diffusion in Red Blood Cells, 1964; scientific papers dealing with cell membranes. *Recreation:* walking. *Address:* 9 Guilford Road, Leicester LE2 2RD.

WHITTAM, (William) Richard (Lamont); QC 2008; First Senior Treasury Counsel, Central Criminal Court, since 2013; a Recorder, since 2009; *b* 23 Nov. 1959; *s* of late William Wright Whittam and of Elizabeth Mary Whittam (*née* Lamont); *m* 1987, Carol Rosemary van Herwaarden; one *s* one *d. Educ:* Marple Hall Sch.; University Coll. London (LLB Hons); Inns of Court Sch. of Law. Called to the Bar, Gray's Inn, 1983, Bencher, 2013; Jun. Treasury Counsel, 1998–2002, First Jun. Treasury Counsel, 2002–06, Sen. Treasury Counsel, 2006–13, Central Criminal Court. Member: S Eastern Circuit Cttee, 1991–93; CPS Bar Standards Cttee, 2000–05. *Recreations:* pyrotechnics, waterski-ing, men's lacrosse, Rugby, golf. *Address:* 2 Bedford Row, WC1R 4BU. *Clubs:* Garrick; Denham Waterski.

WHITTAM SMITH, Sir Andreas, Kt 2015; CBE 2003; First Church Estates Commissioner, since 2002; *b* 13 June 1937; *s* of Canon J. E. Smith and Mrs Smith (*née* Barlow); *m* 1964, Valerie Catherine, *d* of late Wing Comdr J. A. Sherry and of Mrs N. W. H. Wyllys; two *s. Educ:* Birkenhead Sch., Cheshire; Keble Coll., Oxford (MA; Hon. Fellow, 1990). With N. M. Rothschild, 1960–62; Stock Exchange Gazette, 1962–63; Financial Times, 1963–64; The Times, 1964–66; Dep. City Editor, Daily Telegraph, 1966–69; City Editor, The Guardian, 1969–70; Editor, Investors Chronicle and Stock Exchange Gazette, and Dir, Throgmorton Publications, 1970–77; City Editor, Daily Telegraph, 1977–85; Founder and Editor, The Independent, 1986–94; Editor-in-Chief, Independent on Sunday, 1991–94. Dir, 1986–98, Chief Exec., 1987–93, Chm., 1994–95, Newspaper Publishing plc; Director: Ind. News & Media (UK), 1998–2010; Independent Print Ltd, 2010– (Chm., 2014–). Pres., BBFC, 1998–2002; Chairman: Financial Ombudsman Service Ltd, 1999–2003; With Profits Cttee, Prudential Assurance, 2005–14; Children's Mutual, 2006–10. Vice Pres., Nat. Council for

One Parent Families, 1991– (Hon. Treas., 1982–86). Chm., Sir Winston Churchill Archive Trust, 1995–2000. Trustee, Architecture Foundn, 1994–2000. Hon. Fellow: UMIST, 1989; Liverpool John Moores, 2001. Hon. DLitt: St Andrews; Salford; City; Liverpool, 1992; Hon. LLD Bath. Wincott award, 1975; Marketing Man of the Year, Inst. of Marketing, 1987; Journalist of the Year, British Press Awards, 1987; Hemingway Europa Prize, 1988; Editor of the Year, Granada TV What the Papers Say award, 1989. *Recreations:* music, history, walking. *Address:* 154 Campden Hill Road, W8 7AS. *Club:* Garrick.

WHITTELL, James Michael Scott, CMG 1998; OBE 1984; Chief Executive, Interstate Programmes (2000) Ltd, since 2004 (Founder and Chief Executive, Interstate Programmes Ltd, 1999–2004); Founder and Director, The Physics Factory, since 2008; *b* 17 Feb. 1939; *s* of late Edward Arthur Whittell and Helen Elizabeth Whittell (*née* Scott); *m* 1962, Eleanor Jane Carling; three *s*. *Educ:* Gresham's School, Holt; Magdalen College, Oxford (MA, BSc); Manchester Univ. Teaching, Sherborne School, 1962–68, Nairobi School, 1968–72; British Council: Ibadan, Nigeria, 1973–76; Enugu, Nigeria, 1976–78; Director General's Dept, 1978–81; Rep., Algiers, 1981–85; Sec. to the British Council and Head, Director General's Dept, 1985–88; seconded to PM's Efficiency Unit, 1988; Rep., subseq. Dir, Nigeria, 1989–92; Dir, Africa and ME Div., 1992; Regl Dir, EC, later EU, 1993–96; Dir, British Council in Europe, 1996–99. *Recreations:* walking, mountaineering, books, music. *Address:* 15 Stratford Grove, SW15 1NU. *Club:* Alpine.

WHITTEMORE, Prof. Colin Trengove; Professor of Agriculture and Rural Economy, University of Edinburgh, 1990–2007, now Emeritus (Postgraduate Dean, College of Science and Engineering, 2002–07); *b* 16 July 1942; *s* of Hugh Ashcroft Whittemore and Dorothea Whittemore (*née* Nance); *m* 1966, Mary Christine Fenwick; one *s* three *d*. *Educ:* Rydal Sch.; Harper Adams Agricl Coll. (NDA); Univ. of Newcastle upon Tyne (BSc, PhD, DSc). FRSB (FIBiol 1989); FRSE 1994. Lectr, Univ. of Edinburgh, 1970–79; Head, Animal Production Adv. and Devélt, E of Scotland Coll. of Agric., 1979–84; University of Edinburgh: Prof. of Animal Prodn, 1984–90; Head, Dept of Agric., 1989–90; Head, Inst. of Ecology and Resource Mgt, 1990–2000. Pres., British Soc. of Animal Sci., 1998–99. Sir John Hammond Award, British Soc. of Animal Prodn, 1983; Res. Gold Medal, RASE, 1984; Oscar della Suinicoltura, Assoc. Mignini, 1987; David Black Award, Meat and Livestock Commn, 1990. *Publications:* Practical Pig Nutrition (with F. W. H. Elsley), 1976; Lactation, 1980; Pig Production, 1980; Elements of Pig Science, 1987; The Science and Practice of Pig Production, 1993, 3rd edn 2006; Newlands, 2014; Curling, 2014. *Recreations:* ski-ing, horses. *Address:* Rowancroft, 17 Fergusson View, West Linton, Peeblesshire EH46 7DJ. *Club:* Farmers.

WHITTING, Ian Robert, OBE 2011; HM Diplomatic Service; Ambassador to Montenegro, since 2013; *b* 2 April 1953; *s* of Robert Stanley Whitting, ARIBA, and Mary Elizabeth (*née* Tindall); *m* 1986, Tracy Gallagher; two *d*. *Educ:* Chichester High Sch. for Boys. Joined FCO, 1972; Attaché, Moscow, 1975–76; Third Sec., Tunis, 1976–79; Press Attaché, Athens, 1980–83; FCO, 1983–85; Second Sec., Moscow, 1985–88; FCO, 1988–90; First Sec., Dublin, 1990–94; Dep. Hd of Mission, Abidjan, 1994–97; Dep. Hd, Africa Dept (Equatorial), and Sec. of State's Special Rep. for Great Lakes, 1998–2002; Hd, EU Dept (Bilateral), FCO, 2002–03; Dir, EU and Econ. Affairs, Athens, 2003–04; Counsellor, Dep. Hd of Mission and HM Consul-Gen., Athens, 2005–08; Ambassador to Iceland, 2008–12. *Recreations:* tennis, sailing, walking. *Address:* c/o Foreign and Commonwealth Office, King Charles Street, SW1A 2AH.

WHITTING, John Justin; QC 2011; *b* Claverdon, 15 Nov. 1966; *s* of Leonard and Barbara Whitting; *m* 1995, Emma Elizabeth Fallon; one *s* two *d*. *Educ:* King Edward VI Grammar Sch., Stratford on Avon; Oriel Coll., Oxford (BA Hons Juris.); King's Coll. London (LLM Commercial Law). Called to the Bar, Middle Temple, 1991; in practice as barrister, specialising in professional negligence, 1992–. *Recreations:* running, golf, my family. *Address:* The Old Rectory, Wimpstone, Warwicks CV37 8NS; 1 Crown Office Row, Temple, EC4Y 7HH. *E:* john.whitting@1cor.com. *Clubs:* Oxford and Cambridge; Leander (Henley-on-Thames).

WHITTINGDALE, Rt Hon. John (Flasby Lawrance), OBE 1990; PC 2015; MP (C) Maldon, since 2010 (Colchester South and Maldon, 1992–97; Maldon and East Chelmsford, 1997–2010); Secretary of State for Culture, Media and Sport, since 2015; *b* 16 Oct. 1959; *s* of late John Whittingdale and of Margaret Esmé Scott Napier; *m* 1990, Ancilla Campbell Murfitt (marr. diss. 2008); one *s* one *d*. *Educ:* Sandroyd Sch.; Winchester Coll.; University Coll. London (BScEcon). Head of Political Section, Conservative Research Dept, 1982–84; Special Adviser to Sec. of State for Trade and Industry, 1984–87; Manager, N. M. Rothschild & Sons, 1987; Political Sec. to the Prime Minister, 1988–90; Private Sec. to Rt Hon. Margaret Thatcher, 1990–92. PPS to Minister of State for Educn, 1994–95, for Educn and Employment, 1995–96; an Opposition Whip, 1997–98; Opposition Treasury spokesman, 1998–99; PPS to Leader of the Opposition, 1999–2001; Shadow Sec. of State for Trade and Industry, 2001–02, for Culture, Media and Sport, 2002–03 and 2004–05, for Agriculture, Fisheries and Food, 2003–04. Member, Select Committee: on Health, 1993–97; on Trade and Industry, 2001; Chairman: Select Cttee on Culture, Media and Sport, 2005–15; Jt Cttee on Privacy and Injunctions, 2011–12. Sec., Conservative Parly Home Affairs Cttee, 1992–94; Mem. Exec., Cons. 1922 Cttee, 2005–15 (Vice Chm., 2006–15). Parly Mem., Cons. Party Bd, 2006–09. FRSA 2008. *Recreations:* cinema, music. *Address:* c/o House of Commons, SW1A 0AA. *Club:* Essex.

WHITTINGSTALL, Hugh Christopher Edmund F.; *see* Fearnley-Whittingstall.

WHITTINGTON, Prof. Dorothy Allan, CPsychol; Professor of Health Psychology, University of Ulster, 1999–2003, Professor Emeritus, 2005; *b* 14 Dec. 1941; *d* of Eric George Whittington and Margaret Cowan Whittington (*née* Allan). *Educ:* Hutchesons' Girls' Grammar Sch., Glasgow; Univ. of Glasgow (MA, MEd, Teaching Cert.). AFBPsS 1970; CPsychol 1988. Infant teacher, Glasgow primary schs, 1962–67; Lectr in Psychol., Callendar Park Coll. of Educn, Falkirk, 1967–72; Sen. Lectr in Educn, 1972–73, Principal Lectr in Psychol., 1973–84, Ulster Poly.; University of Ulster: Sen. Lectr in Psychol., 1984–94; Dir, Centre for Health and Social Res., 1990–95; Hd, Sch. of Health Scis, 1994–96; Dir, Health Care Distance Learning, 1997–2003. Mem., Nat. Council, Assoc. for Quality in Health Care, 1989–92; Dir, Trustee and Mem. Academic Council, Higher Educn Acad., 2008–10; Partner, Postgrad. Med. Educnl Trng Bd, 2008–10. Chairman, Advisory Group: Centre for Health Scis and Practice, Learning and Teaching Support Network, 2002–05; Centre for Medicine, Dentistry, Vet. Medicine and Health Scis, Higher Educn Acad., 2005–10. Dir of Educn, R&D, N Bristol NHS Trust, 2003–07; non-exec. Dir, Northern Health and Social Care Trust, NI, 2007–. Co-founder, NI Parents' Advice Centre, 1978. Mem., Accreditation Panel, Pharmaceutical Soc. of NI, 2010–12; Mem., Accreditation Panel, and Associate, Gen. Pharmaceutical Council, 2012–. Associate, GMC, 2010–12. *Publications:* (jtly) Quality Assurance: a workbook for health professionals, 1992 (trans. Italian and Portuguese); with R. Ellis: A Guide to Social Skill Training, 1981; New Directions in Social Skill Training, 1983; Quality Assurance in Health Care, 1993; Quality Assurance in Social Care: an introductory workbook, 1998; contrib. papers and book chapters on social skill, communication in professional contexts, quality and governance in health and social care, needs assessment and prog. evaluation in primary and community care, patient and public involvement in health and social care planning, professional regulation and higher education. *Recreations:* sailing, music.

WHITTINGTON, Prof. Geoffrey, CBE 2001; Price Waterhouse Professor of Financial Accounting, Cambridge University, 1988–2001, now Emeritus; Fellow of Fitzwilliam College, Cambridge, 1966–72 and 1988–2001, now Life Fellow; Senior Research Fellow, Centre for Financial Analysis and Policy, Judge Business School, Cambridge, since 2006; Honorary Professor, University of Sussex, since 2014; *b* 21 Sept. 1938; *s* of late Bruce Whittington and Dorothy Gwendoline Whittington (*née* Gent); *m* 1963, Joyce Enid Smith; two *s*. *Educ:* Dudley Grammar Sch.; LSE (Leverhulme Schol.; BSc Econ); Fitzwilliam Coll., Cambridge (MA; PhD 1972; ScD 2009). FCA. Chartered Accountancy training, 1959–62; research posts, Dept of Applied Econ., Cambridge, 1962–72; Dir of Studies in Econs, Fitzwilliam Coll., Cambridge, 1967–72; Prof. of Accountancy and Finance, Edinburgh Univ., 1972–75; University of Bristol: Prof. of Accounting and Finance, 1975–88; Head of Dept of Econs, 1981–84; Dean, Faculty of Social Scis, 1985–87. Professorial Res. Fellow, Inst. of Chartered Accountants of Scotland, 1996–2001. Hon. Prof., Univ. of Sussex, 2014–. Part-time Econ. Adviser, OFT, 1977–83; part-time Mem., Monopolies and Mergers Commn, 1987–96; Accounting Standards Board: Acad. Advr, 1990–94; Mem., 1994–2001 and 2006–09; Member: Adv. Body on Fair Trading in Telecommunications, 1997–98; Internat. Accounting Standards Bd, 2001–06; Academic Adv. Panel, CMA (formerly Competition Commn), 2014–. Hon. DSc (SocSci) Edinburgh, 1998; DUniv Sussex, 2014. Dist. Academic of Year Award, British Accounting Assoc. and Chartered Assoc. of Certified Accountants, 1994; Chartered Accountants Founding Societies Centenary Award, 2003. *Publications:* Growth, Profitability and Valuation (with A. Singh), 1968; The Prediction of Profitability, 1971; Inflation Accounting, 1983; (with D. P. Tweedie) The Debate on Inflation Accounting, 1984; (ed jtly) Readings in the Concept and Measurement of Income, 1986; The Elements of Accounting, 1992; Profitability, Accounting Theory and Methodology, 2007; contribs to jls and books in accounting, economics and finance. *Recreations:* music, walking, usual academic pursuits of reading my own books and laughing at my own jokes, visual arts. *Address:* Fitzwilliam College, Cambridge CB3 0DG. *Club:* Athenæum.

WHITTINGTON, Prof. Richard C., PhD; Professor of Strategic Management, University of Oxford, since 2002; Fellow of New College, Oxford, since 1996. *Educ:* Aston Univ. (MBA); Univ. of Manchester (PhD); MA Oxon. Lectr in Industrial Sociology, Imperial Coll., Univ. of London; Lectr, Sen. Lectr, then Reader in Marketing and Strategic Mgt, Warwick Business Sch., Univ. of Warwick; Reader in Mgt Studies, Univ. of Oxford, 1996–2002. Pierre de Fermat Distinguished Prof., Univ. of Toulouse, 2007–10. *Publications:* Corporate Strategies in Recession and Recovery, 1989; (jtly) Rethinking Marketing, 1999; What is Strategy - and Does it Matter?, 2nd edn 2000; (jtly) The European Corporation: strategy, structure, and social science, 2000; (jtly) The Handbook of Strategy and Management, 2001; (jtly) Innovative Forms of Organising, 2003; (jtly) Exploring Corporate Strategy, 8th edn 2007; (jtly) Strategy as Practice: research directions and resources, 2007; articles in learned jls. *Address:* Saïd Business School, University of Oxford, Park End Street, Oxford OX1 1HP.

WHITTINGTON-SMITH, Marianne Christine, (Mrs C. A. Whittington-Smith); *see* Lutz, M. C.

WHITTLE, Prof. Alasdair William Richardson, DPhil; FBA 1998; Distinguished Research Professor of Archaeology, Cardiff University (formerly University of Wales College of Cardiff), since 1997; *b* 7 May 1949; *s* of late Charles and Grizel Whittle; *m* 1971, Elisabeth Sampson; three *d*. *Educ:* Christ Church, Oxford (BA; DPhil 1976). Lectr, UC Cardiff, then Univ. of Wales Coll. of Cardiff, 1978–97. Jt Ed., Proc. Prehistoric Soc., 1988–94. Leader: Avebury Area Excavation Project, 1987–93; The Times of Their Lives Project, 2012–. Member: Panel for Archaeol., RAEs, 1996, 2001; Ancient Monuments Adv. Bd for Wales, 2000–10. *Publications:* Neolithic Europe, 1985; Scord of Brouster, 1986; Problems in Neolithic Archaeology, 1988; Europe in the Neolithic, 1996; Sacred Mound, Holy Rings, 1997; The Harmony of Symbols, 1999; The Archaeology of People, 2003; (jtly) Places of Special Virtue, 2004; (jtly) Histories of the Dead, 2007; (jtly) Building Memories, 2007; Neolithic on the Great Hungarian Plain, 2007; (jtly) Gathering Time, 2011; (ed jtly) The First Farmers of Central Europe, 2013; (ed jtly) Early Farmers, 2014. *Recreations:* golf, fishing, travel. *Address:* Department of Archaeology and Conservation, Cardiff University, John Percival Building, Colum Drive, Cardiff CF10 3EU.

WHITTLE, Eve; *see* Salomon, E.

WHITTLE, Kenneth Francis, CBE 1987; Chairman, South Western Electricity Board, 1977–87; *b* 28 April 1922; *s* of Thomas Whittle and May Whittle; *m* 1945, Dorothy Inskip; one *s* one *d*. *Educ:* Kingswood Sch., Bath; Faculty of Technol., Manchester Univ. (BScTech). Served War, Electrical Lieut, RNVR, 1943–46. Metropolitan Vickers Elec. Co. Ltd, 1946–48; NW Div., CEGB, 1948–55; North West Electricity Board: various posts, 1955–64; Area Commercial Officer, Blackburn, 1964–69; Manager, Peak Area, 1969–71; Manager, Manchester Area, 1971–74; Chief Commercial Officer, 1974–75; Dep. Chm., Yorks Elec. Bd, 1975–77. Chairman: British Electrotechnical Approvals Bd, 1985–96; British Approvals Bd for Telecommunications, 1985–96. *Recreation:* golf.

WHITTLE, Lindsay Geoffrey; Member (Plaid Cymru) South Wales East, National Assembly for Wales, since 2011; *b* Caerffili, 24 March 1953; *s* of Thomas Ivor Whittle and Margaret May Whittle; one *d* by Adele Roberts. *Educ:* Cwm Ifor Primary Sch.; Caerffili Boys Grammar Tech. Sch.; Cardiff Univ. (Postgrad. Dip. Housing 1995). Archaeological excavator, 1970; aluminium foundry worker, 1971–82; Housing Manager, Hafod Housing Assoc., 1981–2006. Member: Rhymney Valley DC, 1976–95; Caerffili CBC, 1976– (Leader of Opposition, 1995–99 and 2004–08; Leader, 1999–2004 and 2008–11). *Recreations:* regular attendee at Edinburgh Fringe Festival, gardening, antique collecting, and of course Rugby. *Address:* National Assembly for Wales, Cardiff Bay, Cardiff CF99 1NA. *T:* 0300 200 7188. *E:* lindsay.whittle@assembly.wales.

WHITTLE, Prof. Martin John, MD; FRCPGlas, FRCOG; Professor of Fetal Medicine, 1991–2006, and Associate Dean for Education, 2004–06, University of Birmingham (Head, Division of Reproductive and Child Health, 1998–2003), now Professor Emeritus; *b* 6 July 1944; *s* of Bruce and Eveline Whittle. *Educ:* William Grimshaw Secondary Modern Sch., London; Univ. of Manchester Med. Sch. (MB ChB 1972; MD 1980). FRCOG 1988; FRCPGlas 1988. House Physician and Surgeon, Manchester Royal Infirmary, 1972–73; Res. Fellow, LAC-USC Med. Center, Los Angeles, 1978–79; Lectr, Queen Mother's Hosp., Glasgow, 1979–82; Consultant Obstetrician and Gynaecologist, Queen Mother's Hosp. and Royal Samaritan Hosp., Glasgow, 1982–91; Consultant, Birmingham Women's Hosp., 1991–2006; Clinical Co-Dir, Nat. Collaborating Centre for Women and Children's Health, Nat. Inst. for Health and Clinical Excellence, 2006–09. Hon. MO, Jubilee Sailing Trust, 2010–. *Publications:* (with J. M. Connor) Prenatal Diagnosis in Obstetric Practice, 1989, 2nd edn 1995; (with C. H. Rodeck) Fetal Medicine: Basic Science and Clinical Practice, 1999, 2nd edn 2009; contrib. articles on fetal medicine and high-risk obstetric practice. *Recreations:* sailing, flying, diving, art. *E:* mwhittle@doctors.net.uk.

WHITTLE, Prof. Peter, FRS 1978; Churchill Professor of Mathematics for Operational Research, University of Cambridge, 1967–94, now Professor Emeritus; Fellow of Churchill College, Cambridge, since 1967; *b* 27 Feb. 1927; *s* of Percy and Elsie Whittle; *m* 1951, Käthe Hildegard Blomquist; three *s* three *d*. *Educ:* Wellington Coll., New Zealand. Docent, Uppsala Univ., 1951–53; employed New Zealand DSIR, 1953–59, rising to Senior Principal Scientific Officer; Lectr, Univ. of Cambridge, 1959–61; Prof. of Mathematical Statistics, Univ. of Manchester, 1961–67. Sen. Fellow, SERC, 1988–91. Mem., Royal Soc. of NZ, 1981–. Hon. DSc Victoria Univ. of Wellington, NZ, 1987. *Publications:* Hypothesis Testing in Time Series

Analysis, 1951; Prediction and Regulation, 1963; Probability, 1970; Optimisation under Constraints, 1971; Optimisation over Time, 1982; Systems in Stochastic Equilibrium, 1986; Risk-sensitive Optimal Control, 1990; Probability via Expectation, 1992; Optimal Control: basics and beyond, 1996; Neural Nets and Chaotic Carriers, 1998; Networks: optimisation and evolution, 2007; contribs to Jl Roy. Statistical Soc., Proc. Roy. Soc., Jl Stat. Phys, Systems and Control Letters. *Recreation:* variable. *Address:* 268 Queen Edith's Way, Cambridge CB1 8NL; Statistical Laboratory, University of Cambridge CB3 0WB.

WHITTLE, Stephen Charles, OBE 2006; Chairman, Broadcast Training and Skills Regulator, 2007–11; Controller of Editorial Policy, BBC, 2001–05; *b* 26 July 1945; *s* of Charles William Whittle and Vera Lillian Whittle (*née* Moss); *m* 1988, Claire Walmsley (marr. diss. 1999); *m* 2004, Eve Coulter Salomon, *qv*. *Educ:* St Ignatius College, Stamford Hill; University College London (LLB Hons). Asst Editor, New Christian, 1968–70; Communications Officer, World Council of Churches, Geneva, 1970–73; Editor, One World, WCC, 1973–77; Asst Head, Communications Dept, WCC, 1975–77; BBC: Sen. Producer, Religious Programmes, Manchester, 1977–82; Producer, Newsnight, 1982; Editor, Songs of Praise and Worship, 1983–89; Hd of Religious Progs, 1989–93; Chief Advr, Editl Policy, Policy and Planning Directorate, 1993–96; Director: Broadcasting Standards Council, 1996–97; Broadcasting Standards Commn, 1997–2001. Member: Regulation Bd, Law Soc., subseq. SRA, 2005–11; GMC, 2009–13; Council, Public Concern at Work, 2010–. Gov., Eur. Inst. for the Media, 1997–2004. Trustee: Sandford St Martin Trust, 2002–11; Fifth Trust, 2010–. Vis. Fellow, Reuters Inst. for Study of Journalism, Oxford Univ., 2007–. FRSA. Freeman, City of London, 1990. Sandford St Martin Award for contrib. to religious broadcasting, 1993. *Publications:* Tickling Mrs Smith, 1970; Privacy, Probity and Public Interest, 2009; contribs to Media Guardian and The Tablet. *Recreations:* cinema, theatre, music, reading, walking. *Address:* 4 Carmarthen Place, SE1 3TS.

WHITTON, David Forbes; Member (Lab) Strathkelvin and Bearsden, Scottish Parliament, 2007–11; *b* 22 April 1952; *s* of David Whitton and May Whitton (*née* Hoy); *m* 1971, Marilyn MacDonald; one *s* one *d*. *Educ:* Morgan Acad., Dundee. Journalist on Scottish weekly and daily and nat. newspapers, 1970–86; various posts at Scottish Television, 1986–96, incl. Hd of Public Affairs, 1994–96; Dir, Media House, PR firm, 1996–98; Special Advr to Scottish Sec. and First Minister of Scotland, 1998–2000; Man. Dir, Whitton pr Ltd, 2000–07. Contested (Lab) Strathkelvin and Bearsden, Scottish Parlt, 2011. *Recreations:* golf, music (listening and playing my electric drum kit), playing with my grandchildren. *Club:* Crail Golfing Society.

WHITTON, Prof. Peter William; Deputy Vice-Chancellor, University of Melbourne, 1979–84, retired; *b* 2 Sept. 1925; *s* of William Whitton and Rosa Bungay; *m* 1950, Mary Katharine White; two *s* three *d*. *Educ:* Latymer Upper Sch., London; Southampton Univ. (BScEng); Imperial College of Science and Technology, London (DIC, PhD); ME Melbourne 1965. Engineering Cadet, English Electric Co., Preston, 1942–46; Wireless Officer, Royal Signals, Catterick and Singapore, 1946–48; Sen. Lectr in Mech. Engrg, Univ. of Melbourne, 1953–56; Head, Engrg Sect., ICI Metals Div. Research Dept, Birmingham, 1956–60; Foundation Prof. and Dean, Faculty of Engrg, Univ. of the West Indies, 1960–64; University of Melbourne: Prof. of Mech. Engrg, 1965–77, Emeritus Prof., 1977–; Dean, Faculty of Engrg, 1966; Principal, Royal Melbourne Inst. of Technology, 1977–78. *Publications:* various papers on metal forming, in Proc. IMechE, London, and Jl of Inst. of Metals, London. *Recreation:* reading. *Address:* 7/16 Small Street, Hampton, Vic 3188, Australia.

WHITTOW, Hugh John; Editor, Daily Express, since 2011; *b* Haverfordwest, 20 March 1951; *s* of Jack Whittow and Marion Whittow; *m* 1984, Lesley Grant; two *d*. *Educ:* Haverfordwest Grammar Sch. Reporter: Western Telegraph, Haverfordwest, 1968–71; Western Daily Press, Bristol, 1971; South Wales Echo, Cardiff, 1971–73; London Evening News, 1973–78; Daily Star, 1978–82; The Sun, 1982–87; Dep. Ed., Daily Star, 1987–2001; Launch Ed., Daily Star Sunday, 2002–03; Dep. Ed., Daily Express, 2003–11. Freeman of Haverfordwest, 1998. *Recreations:* family, ski-ing, Rugby, golf, walking our dog 'Darcey' on Newgale Beach. *Address:* Daily Express, Northern and Shell Building, No 10 Lower Thames Street, EC3R 6EN. *T:* (020) 8612 7468, *Fax:* (020) 7098 2704.

WHITTY, family name of **Baron Whitty**.

WHITTY, Baron *cr* 1996 (Life Peer), of Camberwell in the London Borough of Southwark; **John Lawrence Whitty, (Larry);** PC 2005; Chairman, Consumer Focus (formerly National Consumer Council), 2006–10; *b* 15 June 1943; *s* of Frederick James and Kathleen May Whitty; *m* 1969, Tanya Margaret (marr. diss. 1986); two *s*; *m* 1993, Angela Forrester. *Educ:* Latymer Upper School; St John's College, Cambridge (BA Hons Economics). Hawker Siddeley Aviation, 1960–62; Min. of Aviation Technology, 1965–70; Trades Union Congress, 1970–73; General, Municipal, Boilermakers and Allied Trade Union (formerly GMWU), 1973–85; Gen. Sec., 1985–94, European Co-ordinator, 1994–97, Labour Party. A Lord in Waiting (Govt Whip), 1997–98; Parly Under-Sec. of State, DETR, subseq. DEFRA, 1998–2005. Member: Nat. Water Services Regulation Authy, 2006; Bd, Envmt Agency, 2006–12. *Recreations:* theatre, cinema, swimming. *Address:* 61 Bimport, Shaftesbury, Dorset SP7 8AZ. *T:* (01747) 854619, (0171) 834 8890.

See also G. J. Whitty.

WHITTY, Prof. Christopher John MacRae, CB 2015; FRCP; FMedSci; Professor of Public and International Health, London School of Hygiene and Tropical Medicine, University of London, since 2005; Consultant Physician, Hospital for Tropical Diseases and University College London Hospital, since 2001; *b* Gloucester, 21 April 1966; *s* of Kenneth Whitty and Susannah Whitty. *Educ:* Pembroke Coll., Oxford (BA 1988; DSc 2011); Wolfson Coll., Oxford (BM BCh 1991); London Sch. of Hygiene and Tropical Medicine, Univ. of London (DTM&H 1996; MSc 1996); Open Univ. (DipEcon); Northumbria Univ. (LLM 2005); Heriot-Watt Univ. (MBA 2010). FRCP 2004; FFPH 2009. Clinical and res. posts, UK, Africa and Asia, 1991–2001; Sen. Registrar, London, 1996–2001; Lectr, Univ. of Malawi, 1998–2000; Sen. Lectr, LSHTM, 2001–05; Chief Scientific Advr and Dir, Res. and Evidence, DFID, 2009–15. Vis. Prof. of Public Health, Gresham Coll., 2014–. FMedSci 2011. *Address:* Clinical Research Department, London School of Hygiene and Tropical Medicine, Keppel Street, WC1B 7HT.

WHITTY, Prof. Geoffrey James, CBE 2011; DLit; Director, Institute of Education, University of London, 2000–10, now Emeritus; Research Professor, Bath Spa University, since 2014; Global Innovation Chair, University of Newcastle, Australia, since 2014; *b* 31 Dec. 1946; *s* of Frederick James Whitty and Kathleen May Whitty; *m* 1st, 1969, Gillian Patterson (marr. diss. 1989); one *s* one *d*; 2nd, 1989, Marilyn Toft; one *d*. *Educ:* Latymer Upper Sch.; St John's Coll., Cambridge (BA, MA); Inst. of Educn, London Univ. (PGCE, MA, DLit). Teacher: Lampton Sch., Hounslow, 1969–70; Thomas Bennett Sch., Crawley, 1970–73; Lecturer: Univ. of Bath, 1973–80; KCL, 1981–84; Prof. of Educn, Bristol Poly., 1985–89; Goldsmiths' Prof. of Policy and Mgt, Goldsmiths Coll., Univ. of London, 1990–92; Karl Mannheim Prof. of Sociol. of Educn, Inst. of Educn, Univ. of London, 1992–2000. Prof. of Public Sector Mgt, Univ. of Bath, 2011–13. Vis. Prof., Univ. of Wisconsin-Madison, 1979–80. Chairman: Bristol Educn Partnership Bd, 2001–03; Educn Adv. Cttee, British Council, 2002–07. President: Coll. of Teachers, 2005–09; British Educnl Res. Assoc., 2005–07. FAcSS (AcSS 2002). FRSA 1998. Hon. FCT 2001. Hon. DEd: UWE, 2001; Hong Kong Inst. of Educn, 2012. *Publications:* (jtly) Society, State and Schooling, 1977; Sociology and School Knowledge, 1985; (jtly) The State and Private Education, 1989; (jtly) Specialisation and Choice in Urban Education, 1993; (jtly) Devolution and Choice in Education, 1998; (jtly) Teacher Education in Transition, 2000; Making Sense of Education Policy, 2002; (jtly) Education and the Middle Class, 2003. *Recreations:* travel, football, reading, politics. *Address:* c/o Institute of Education, 20 Bedford Way, WC1H 0AL. *T:* (020) 7612 6004. *Club:* Athenæum.

See also Baron Whitty.

WHITTY, Niall Richard, FRSE; Member, Scottish Law Commission, 1995–2000; *b* 28 Oct. 1937; *s* of Richard Hazleton Whitty and Muriel Helen Margaret Scott or Whitty; *m* 1977, Elke Mechthild Maria Gillis; three *s* one *d*. *Educ:* John Watson's Sch., Edinburgh; Morrison's Acad., Crieff; St Andrews Univ. (MA Hons 1960); Edinburgh Univ. (LLB 1963). Admitted solicitor, 1965. Legal Officer, 1967–70, Sen. Legal Officer, 1970–77, Asst Solicitor, 1977–94, Scottish Office; seconded to legal staff, Scottish Law Commn, 1971–94. Vis. Prof., Sch. of Law, Univ. of Edinburgh, 2000–. Gen. Editor, The Laws of Scotland, Stair Memorial Encyclopaedia, 2000–14. FRSE 2003. *Publications:* (ed with Reinhard Zimmermann) Rights of Personality in Scots Law: a comparative perspective, 2009; contrib. Stair Memorial Encyclopaedia, and legal jls. *Address:* St Martins, Victoria Road, Haddington, East Lothian EH41 4DJ. *T:* (01620) 822234.

WHITWAM, Derek Firth, CEng, FRINA; RCNC; Director of Quality Assurance, Ministry of Defence, 1985–88; *b* 7 Dec. 1932; *s* of Hilton and Marion Whitwam; *m* 1954, Pamela May (*née* Lander); one *s* one *d*. *Educ:* Royds Hall Sch., Huddersfield; Royal Naval Coll., Dartmouth; Royal Naval Engineering Coll., Manadon; Royal Naval Coll., Greenwich. Work on ship design, MoD (N) Bath, 1957–65; Rosyth Dockyard, 1965–68; Singapore Dockyard, 1968–70; DG Ships Bath, 1970–77; RCDS 1978; Production Manager, Rosyth Dockyard, 1979–80; Gen. Manager, Portsmouth Dockyard, 1981–84; Principal Dir of Planning and Policy, Chief Exec. Royal Dockyards, 1984–85. *Publications:* papers for Trans Royal Inst. of Naval Architects. *Recreations:* golf, music, walking. *Club:* Bath Golf.

WHITWORTH, Diana Storey; non-executive Consultant, The Young Foundation, 2008–09; *b* 5 April 1949; *d* of Barrington Allen Whitworth and Rosemary Whitworth (*née* Braithwaite); one *d* by Anthony Beauchamp; *m* 2008, Guy Dehn. *Educ:* Badminton Sch.; King's High Sch., Warwick; South Bank Poly. (MA Applied Eur. Studies). Consumer Advr, London Borough of Hillingdon, 1973–77; Sen. R&D Officer, NACAB, 1980–88; Sen. Policy and Develt Officer, then Hd, Public Affairs, NCC, 1988–99; Chief Exec., Carers Nat. Assoc., subseq. Carers UK, 1999–2003; Jt Chief Exec., Grandparents plus, 2004–08. Chair, Consumer Congress, 1983–85; Member: Adv. Cttee on Work Life Balance, DFEE, 2000–02; Commng Bd, NHS Service Delivery and Orgn R&D, 2000–09; NHS Mental Health Task Force, 2000–02; NHS Older People's Task Force, 2002–03; Appeals Adv. Cttee, BBC, 2002–07; Strategic Res. Bd, ESRC, 2003–06; Council, ASA, 2005–11; Social Security Adv. Cttee, 2013–; Chair, External Ref. Gp, Nat. Service Framework for Long term Conditions, 2002–05. Mem., Ind. Complaints Panel, Portman Gp, 1998–2003; Bd Mem., Big Lottery Fund, 2004–12. Trustee: Cranstoun Drug Services (formerly Odyssey Trust), 2000–13; John Ellerman Foundn, 2008–; Headway E London, 2011–. Gov., Stoke Newington Sch., 1996–2001. *Recreations:* reading, gardening, cycling, allotment. *E:* dianawhitworth@me.com.

WHITWORTH, Francis John, OBE 1994; Member, Economic and Social Committee of the European Communities, 1986–98; *b* 1 May 1925; *s* of late Captain Herbert Francis Whitworth, OBE, RNVR, and Helen Marguerite Whitworth (*née* Tait); *m* 1956, Auriol Myfanwy Medwyn Hughes; one *s* one *d*. *Educ:* Charterhouse (Jun. Schol.); Pembroke Coll., Oxford (Holford Schol.; MA Jurisprudence 1949). Served War, Royal Marines, 1943–46. Called to Bar, Middle Temple, 1950. Joined Cunard Steam-Ship Co., 1950; Personnel Director, 1965, Managing Dir Cunard Line, 1968, Group Admin. Dir, 1969; joined British Shipping Fedn as Dir, Industrial Relations, 1972; Dep. Dir-Gen., Gen. Council of British Shipping, 1980–87; Dir, Internat. Shipping Fedn, 1980–88; Mem., Nat. Maritime Bd, 1962–87. Chairman: Internat. Cttee of Passenger Lines, 1968–71; Atlantic Passenger Steamship Conf., 1970–71; Employers' Gp, Jt Maritime Commn of ILO, 1980–88; Employers' Gp, Internat. Maritime (Labour) Conf. of ILO, 1986–87; Social Affairs Cttee, Comité des Assocs d'Armateurs des Communautés Européennes, 1983–88; Nat. Sea Training Schs, 1980–87; Merchant Navy Officers' Pension Fund Trustees, 1987–93; Member: Industrial Tribunals for England and Wales, 1978–94; Council, Mission to Seafarers (formerly Missions to Seamen), 1985–2010; Vice-Pres., Marine Soc. and Sea Cadets, 2004–. FCMI (FBIM 1980; MBIM 1967). Freeman, City of London, 1999; Liveryman, Shipwrights' Co., 1999–. *Recreations:* racing, opera, music, cricket. *Address:* 5 Beaumond Green, Winchester SO23 8GF. *Club:* Oxford and Cambridge.

WHITWORTH, Prof. Judith Ann, AC 2001; DSc, MD, PhD; FRACP; FTSE; Director, John Curtin School of Medical Research, Australian National University, 1999–2008, Emeritus Professor and Visiting Fellow, since 2010; Director, Therapeutic Innovation Australia, since 2011; *b* 1 April 1944; *d* of Arthur Howard Whitworth and Margaret Edith Wilson Whitworth (*née* Dobbs); *m* 1981, John Ludbrook (marr. diss. 1992); partner, Colin Nicholson Chesterman. *Educ:* St Michael's C of E Girls' Grammar Sch.; Univ. of Melbourne (BS; MD 1974; PhD 1978; DSc 1992). FRACP 1975. RMO/Registrar, Royal Melbourne Hosp., 1968–71; Sen. Registrar, Queen Elizabeth Hosp., Adelaide, 1972; Winthrop Travelling Fellow, RACP, 1973; Vis. Registrar, Guy's Hosp., London, 1974–75; NHMRC Schol., Howard Florey Inst., 1975–77; Physician, 1978–81; Chm. Bd, Postgrad. Educn, 1983–91, Dep. Dir, Dept of Nephrology, 1990–91, Royal Melbourne Hosp.; Professorial Associate, Univ. of Melbourne, 1987–91; Prof. of Medicine, Univ. of NSW, 1991–99; CMO, Dept of Health and Family Services, 1997–99. Vis. Scientist, MRC Blood Pressure Unit, Glasgow, 1985; Naturalia et Biologia Fellow, Hosp. Tenon, Paris, 1985. Mem., NH&MRC Med. Res. Cttee, 1991–94 (Chm., 1994–97); Pres., High Blood Pressure Res. Council of Australia, 1998–2001; Co-Chair, NSW Health Care Adv. Council, 2006–11. Mem. Council, RACP, 1984–93; Pres., Australian Soc. for Med. Res., 1984. Member: WHO Global Adv. Cttee on Health Res., 2000–11 (Chm., 2004–11); Nominating Cttee, Internat. Soc. for Nephrology, 1990–93; Foundn Council, Global Forum for Health Res., 2004–11. Councillor, Internat. Soc. of Hypertension, 1992–2000. Member: Council, Charles Darwin Univ., 2003–06; Bd, Menzies Sch. of Health Res., 2004–06; Bd, Menzies Res. Inst., Tasmania, 2005–. FTSE 2009. MD *hc* Sydney, 2004; NSW, 2005; Hon. DSc Glasgow, 2008; Hon. DLitt Charles Darwin, 2011; Hon. LLD Melbourne, 2012. Smith Kline and French Award, Internat. Soc. for Hypertension, 1984; Howard Florey Inst. Medal, 1990; RACP Medal, 1994; ACT Australian of the Year, 2004; Kincaid-Smith Medal, Australian Kidney Foundn, 2010. Centenary Medal, Australia, 2003; John Curtin Medal, ANU, 2011. *Publications:* Dictionary of Medical Eponyms, 1987, 2nd edn 1996; The Kidney, 2nd edn 1987; Textbook of Renal Disease, 1987, 2nd edn 1994; Hypertension Management, 1990; Clinical Nephrology in Medical Practice, 1992; numerous contribs to med. and scientific pubns. *Recreations:* books, cricket, film, French. *Address:* PO Box 967, Edgecliff, NSW 2027, Australia. *T:* and *Fax:* (2) 93261963. *Clubs:* Melbourne Cricket, Lord's Taverners.

WHITWORTH-JONES, Anthony; General Director, Garsington Opera, 2005–12; *b* 1 Sept. 1945; *s* of Henry Whitworth-Jones and Patience Martin; *m* 1974, Camilla (*née* Barlow); one *d*. *Educ:* Wellington College. Mem., Inst. of Chartered Accountants of Scotland. Thomson McLintock & Co., 1970–72; Administrative Dir, London Sinfonietta, 1972–81; Administrator, Glyndebourne Touring Opera and Opera Manager, Glyndebourne Fest. Opera, 1981–89; Gen. Adminr, then Gen. Dir, Glyndebourne Fest. Opera, 1989–98; Gen. Dir, The Dallas Opera, 2000–02; Artistic Dir, Casa da Musica, Porto, Portugal, 2004–05. Dir, SE Arts Bd, 1993–96. Chm., Michael Tippett Musical Foundn, 1998–. Member: Adv. Bd, Voices of Change, Dallas, 2001–02; Exec. Bd, Meadows Sch. of the Arts, Southern Methodist

Univ., Dallas, 2001–02; Council, Spitalfields Fest., 2003–06 (Hon. Advr, 2006–). Trustee: Leonard Ingrams Foundn, 2006–; Young Classical Artists Trust (formerly Young Concert Artists Trust), 2007–14; ENO, 2012–. *Recreations:* enjoying the spirit and countryside of Wales, Portugal and Greece, arts in general, architecture, jazz. *Address:* 81 St Augustine's Road, NW1 9RR. *T:* (020) 7267 3154, *Fax:* (020) 7482 7017. *E:* antwjones@gmail.com.

WHOMERSLEY, Christopher Adrian, CMG 2014; HM Diplomatic Service; Deputy Legal Adviser, 2002–14, and Head, Maritime Policy Unit (formerly Law of Sea Section), 2008–14, Foreign and Commonwealth Office; consultant on international law, particularly law of the sea and deep sea mining; *b* 18 April 1953; *s* of Harry and Doreen Whomersley; *m* 1977, Jeanette Diana Szostak; one *s* two *d. Educ:* London Sch. of Economics (LLB); Christ's Coll., Cambridge (LLM). Called to the Bar, Middle Temple, 1981; Asst Legal Advr, 1977–91, Legal Counsellor, 1991–94, FCO; Legal Secretariat to Law Officers, 1994–97; Legal Counsellor, FCO, 1997–2002. Mem., UK Delegn to Channel Tunnel Intergovtl Commn, 1986–94, 1997–2014; Leader of UK Delegn and Mem., Finance Cttee, Internat. Sea-Bed Authy, 2007–14; Legal Advr to UK Delegn to Bermuda II Negotiations, 1991–94, 1997–2004; Govt Agent before the European Court of Human Rights, 2000–04; Leader, UK Delegn to Assembly of States Parties, Internat. Criminal Court, 2003–10; Chm., UK Internat. Humanitarian Law Cttee, 2003–07. *Recreations:* reading modern literature and history, philately, following Coventry City FC and Warwickshire CCC. *Address:* 26 The Avenue, Bedford Park, W4 1HT. *Club:* MCC.

WHYBREW, Edward Graham, (Ted), CBE 2002; employment arbitrator, since 2000; Partner, Museum Replicas, 1997–2004; Certification Officer for Trade Unions and Employers' Associations, 1992–2001; *b* 25 Sept. 1938; *s* of Ernest Whybrew and Winifred (*née* Castle); *m* 1967, Julia Helen Baird (OBE 2001); one *s* two *d. Educ:* Hertford Grammar Sch.; Balliol Coll., Oxford (BA 1961); Nuffield Coll., Oxford. Economist: NEDO, 1963; DEA, 1964–69; Dept of Employment, subseq. EDG, 1969–92; Asst Sec., Employment, Trng and Industrial Relations, 1977–85; Under Sec., Industrial Relations Div., 1985–89; Dir, Personnel and Staff Develt, 1989–92. ACAS Arbitrator. Associate Partner, Jamieson Scott (Exec. Search), 1993–98. Advr to Inter Party talks on Funding Political Parties, 2007; Ind. Adjudicator on compensation payments to former Icelandic water trawlermen, 2000–12. *Publications:* Overtime Working in Great Britain, 1968; (contrib.) The Rise and Fall of the Dock Labour Scheme, 2010. *Recreations:* watching cricket, ceramic restoration, gardening. *Address:* Grangelea, Grange Park, Steeple Aston, Bicester, Oxon OX25 4SR.

WHYBROW, Christopher John; QC 1992; *b* 7 Aug. 1942; *s* of Herbert William Whybrow, OBE and Ruby Kathleen Whybrow (*née* Watson); *m* 1st, 1969, Marian Janet Macaulay (marr. diss. 1976); 2nd, 1979, Susan Younge (marr. diss. 1990). *Educ:* Colchester Royal Grammar Sch.; King's Coll., London (LLB). Called to the Bar, Inner Temple, 1965; in practice at the Bar, 1966–2009. A Dep. Upper Tribunal Judge (formerly a Dep. Social Security Comr), 1996–2011. *Publications:* (contrib.) Atkins Court Forms; contribs to Jl of Planning and Environment Law. *Recreations:* history, cricket, tennis, walking, gardening, country life, reading, conversation. *E:* C.whybrow180@btinternet.com. *Clubs:* Lansdowne, MCC; Leavenheath Cricket.

WHYBROW, John William; Chairman, AZ Electronic Materials, 2010–14; *b* 11 March 1947; *s* of Charles Ernest James Whybrow and Doris Beatrice Whybrow (*née* Abbott); *m* 1968, Paula Miriam Hobart; one *s* one *d. Educ:* Hatfield Tech. GS; Imperial Coll., London (BSc Hons Mech. Engrg); Manchester Business Sch. (MBA); ACGI. English Electric, Rugby, 1968–70; Philips Electronics: Northern Operational Res. Gp, 1970–78; Ind. Engrg Head, Mullard Simonstone, 1979–82; Div. Manager, 1982–83, Plant Dir, 1983–87, Mullard Blackburn; Plant Dir, Hazel Grove, 1987–88; Man. Dir, TDS Circuits plc, 1988–90; Tech. Dir, Philips Components, 1990–91; Industrial Dir, 1991–93, Chm. and Man. Dir, 1993–95, Philips Electronics UK; Pres. and CEO, Philips Lighting Holding BV, 1995–2001; Exec. Vice-Pres., Main Bd, Royal Philips Electronics, 1998–2002. Chairman: Lumileds Lighting BV, 1997–2000; CSR plc, 2004–07 (Dir, 2003–07); Wolseley PLC, 2002–11 (Dir, 1997–2011); non-executive Director: Teletext Hldgs, 1993–95; DSG Internat. (formerly Dixons) PLC, 2003–10. Chm., Petworth Cottage Nursing Home, 2002–13. Mem. Council, RNLI, 2012–. MInstD 1993. Order of Merit (Poland), 2002. *Recreations:* sailing, shooting. *Address:* Wild Harrys, Hayes Lane, Slinfold, Horsham RH13 0SL. *E:* john@thewhybrows.com. *Clubs:* East India, City Livery Yacht; Royal Solent Yacht.

WHYTE, Anne Lynne; QC 2010; *b* Wegberg, 19 June 1969; *d* of Peter Whyte and Carol Whyte (*née* Jones); *m* 2002, Simon Gorton. *Educ:* Luckley Oakfield Sch., Wokingham; Worcester Coll., Oxford (BA Hons Hist.; DipLaw). Called to the Bar, Lincoln's Inn, 1993; in practice as a barrister, 1994–. *Address:* Atlantic Chambers, 4–6 Cook Street, Liverpool L2 9QU. *T:* (0151) 236 4421. *E:* annewhyte@atlanticchambers.co.uk.

WHYTE, Duncan; consultant; Chairman, Wales and West Utilities Ltd, 2005–12; *b* 27 July 1946; *s* of Andrew Montgomery Whyte and Margaret Steedman Whyte; *m* 1971, Marion McDonald McCready; one *s. Educ:* Kilsyth Acad. CA 1968; ATII 1968. Trainee Chartered Accountant, Paterson and Benzies, 1963–69; Arthur Andersen & Co., 1969–83 (Man. Partner, Edinburgh office, 1980–83); Financial Dir, Kwikfit Hldgs plc, 1983–88; Scottish Power: Exec. Dir, 1988–99; Finance Dir, 1988–93; Chief Operating Officer, 1993–95; Exec. Dir, Multi Utility, 1995–99; Chief Exec., Weir Gp plc, 1999–2000. Non-exec. Dir, Motherwell Bridge Hldgs Ltd, 1997–2003. *Recreations:* golf, badminton, reading history.

WHYTE, Hugh Francis D.; *see* Durrant-Whyte.

WHYTE, Prof. Iain Boyd, PhD; FRSE; Professor of Architectural History, University of Edinburgh, 1996–2014, now Emeritus, and Honorary Professorial Fellow, since 2014; *b* 6 March 1947; *s* of Thomas Boyd Whyte and Mary Whyte (*née* Macpherson); *m* 1973, Deborah Smart; one *s* one *d. Educ:* Nottingham Univ. (BA 1969; MPhil 1971); Cornell Univ.; Jesus Coll., Cambridge (PhD 1979); Leeds Univ. (MA 1987). FRSE 1998. British Acad./Wolfson Fellow, 1976–77; Alexander von Humboldt-Stiftung Fellow, 1979–82; Leverhulme Trust Res. Fellow, 1985–87; University of Edinburgh: Lectr in Architectl Hist., 1988–93; Reader, 1993–95. Getty Schol., 1989–90; Getty Sen. Schol., 1998–2000; Sen. Prog. Officer, Getty Grant Prog., LA, 2002–04. Samuel H. Kress Prof., Center for Advanced Studies in Visual Arts, Nat. Gall. of Art, Washington, DC, 2015–16. Trustee, Nat. Galls of Scotland, 1998–2002. Co-Curator: Council of Europe Exhibn, Art and Power - Europe under the Dictators 1930–46, Hayward Gall., London, Centre de Cultura Contemporània, Barcelona, Deutsches Historisches Mus., Berlin, 1995–96; Darwin's Edinburgh exhibn, Talbot Rice Gall., Univ. of Edinburgh, 2009. Chm., Internat. Assoc. of Res. Centres in Hist. of Art, 2010–; Internat. Advr, Slovenian Res. Agency, 2014–. FRSA. Founder Editor, Art in Translation, 2009–. *Publications:* Bruno Taut and the Architecture of Activism, 1982 (German edn 1981); (ed) The Crystal Chain Letters, 1985 (trans. German 1986); Emil Hoppe, Marcel Kammerer, Otto Schönthal, 1989; (introd and co-trans.) Hendrik Petrus Berlage on Style 1886–1909, 1996; (jtly) John Fowler, Benjamin Baker: The Forth Bridge, 1997; Modernism and the Spirit of the City, 2003; Man-made Future: planning, education and design in mid-twentieth-century Britain, 2007; (jtly) Das Erhabene in Wissenschaft und Kunst: über Vernunft und Einbildungskraft, 2010; (jtly) Beyond the Finite: the sublime in art and science, 2011; (jtly) Metropolis Berlin: 1880–1940, 2013. *Recreations:* violin playing, sculling. *Address:* 3 West Silvermills Lane, Edinburgh EH3 5BD. *T:* (0131) 556 4008. *Clubs:* Leander (Henley-on-Thames); New (Edinburgh); Akademischer Ruderclub zu Berlin (Berlin).

WHYTE, (John) Stuart Scott, CB 1986; Under Secretary, Department of Health and Social Security, 1978–86; *b* 1 April 1926; *er s* of late Thomas and Mysie Scott Whyte, Sandycove, Co. Dublin; *m* 1950, Jocelyn Margaret, *o d* of late George Hawley, CBE, Edinburgh; two *s* one *d. Educ:* St Andrew's Coll., Dublin; Trinity Coll., Univ. of Dublin. BA 1947; LLB 1948. Asst Principal, Dept of Health for Scotland, 1948; Principal, 1955; Principal Private Sec. to Sec. of State for Scotland, 1959; Asst Sec., Scottish Develt Dept, 1962; Asst Sec., Cabinet Office, 1969; Asst Under-Sec. of State, Scottish Office, 1969–74; Under Sec., Cabinet Office, 1974–78. *Address:* La Bâtisse, Bonin, 47120 Duras, France. *T:* 553837031.

WHYTE, Prof. Moira Katherine Brigid, (Mrs D. C. Crossman), OBE 2014; PhD; FRCP, FMedSci; Professor of Respiratory Medicine, and Director, MRC Centre for Inflammation Research, University of Edinburgh, since 2014; *b* 25 Sept. 1959; *d* of Maurice and Anne Whyte; *m* 1988, David Christopher Crossman, *qv*; two *s. Educ:* Convent of Notre Dame, Plymouth; Plymouth Coll.; St Bartholomew's Hosp. Med. Coll., London (BSc 1st cl. Hons Anatomy 1981; MB BS 1984); Royal Postgraduate Med. Sch., London (PhD 1993). MRCP 1987, FRCP 1997. Jun. med. posts, London, 1984–87; Registrar in Respiratory Medicine, Dept of Medicine, Hammersmith Hosp., 1987–89; MRC Trng Fellow, RPMS, 1989–92; Sen. Registrar in Respiratory Medicine, Hammersmith Hosp., 1992–94; Wellcome Advanced Fellow and Hon. Consultant Physician, Univ. of Nottingham and ICRF, London, 1994–95; University of Sheffield: Prof. of Respiratory Medicine, 1996–2014; Sir George Franklin Prof. of Medicine, 2013–14; Hd, Section of Infection, Inflammation and Immunity, 2006–09; Hd, Dept of Infection and Immunity, 2009–14. Member: Wellcome Trust Clinical Interest Gp, 1997–2002; Wellcome Trust Physiol Scis Panel, 2002–05; Population and Systems Medicine Bd, MRC, 2010–. Chm., Scientific Cttee, British Lung Foundn, 2003–06. Mem., Dorothy Hodgkin Grants Panel, Royal Soc., 2006–. Registrar, Acad. of Med. Scis, 2012–. FMedSci 2005. *Publications:* papers on cell death in inflammation and inflammatory lung disease. *Recreations:* reading, my children's current hobbies. *Address:* MRC Centre for Inflammation Research, University of Edinburgh, Queen's Medical Research Institute, 47 Little France Crescent, Edinburgh EH16 4TJ. *T:* (0131) 242 6656, *Fax:* (0131) 242 6578. *E:* moira.whyte@ed.ac.uk.

WHYTE, Stuart Scott; *see* Whyte, J. S. S.

WIBBERLEY, Dr (Edward) John, FRAgS; Principal, Rural Extension Agriculture Land Management, since 1989; *b* Quarndon, Derbys, 10 May 1947; *s* of Edward and Beatrice Enid Wibberley; *m* 1969, Jane. E. R. Weeks; two *s. Educ:* Ecclesbourne Grammar Sch., Duffield, Derbys; Univ. of Reading (BSc Hons Agric.; MSc Soil Microbiol.; MA Comparative Educn; PhD Agricl Extension 1992; Nuffield Scholar, 1988); London Sch. of Theol. (MTh Brunel Univ.); Univ. of Exeter (Cert. Theol.); Coll. of Preceptors, London (DipEd). FRAgS 1987; FRGS 2010. Lectr and Asst Warden, Askham Bryan Coll., York, 1969–70; Hd, Applied Sci., Berks Coll. of Agric., 1970–75; Hd of Agric., Gindiri, N Nigeria, 1975–76; Royal Agricultural College, Cirencester: Lectr, Sen. Lectr, Principal Lectr and Hd of Agric., 1976–89; Coordinator, Cirencester Cereal Study Gp, 1977–89. Vis. Prof., Comparative Agric. and Rural Extension, RAU (formerly RAC), Cirencester, 1999– (Vis. Fellow, 1989–99); Adjunct Prof., Rural Extension Studies, Univ. of Guelph, Canada, 1995–98; Vis. Fellow, Agricl Extension and Rural Develt, Univ. of Reading, 1994–2004. British Council Diamond Jubilee Public Lect., Freetown, Sierra Leone, 2004; Ralph Melville Meml Lect., Tropical Agric. Assoc., 2010. Presenter, W Country Farming, HTV, 1989–92. Christian Stewardship Advr, Anglican Dio. Exeter and Dio. Portsmouth, 1993–2003. Mem., Area Gp, IoW, Envmt Agency, 1996–99. Coordinator, Steering Gp on Exploration of Professionalism in UK Agric., 2006–08. Sec. of State Appointee, Exmoor Nat. Park Authy, 2008–; Chm., Exmoor Hill Farm Project, 2009–13; Deputy Chairman: Exmoor Parish and Consultative Forum, 2010–; Planning Cttee, Exmoor Nat. Park, 2013–15. Member: Council, RASE, 2005–; Adv. Council, Sch. of Agric., Royal Agricl Univ. (formerly RAC), 2005–; Faculty, Prince of Wales's Summer Sch. on Food and Farming, 2007–. UK Chm., Farm Crisis Network, 1998–2003; Chairman: Rural Issues Gp, IoW, 1999–2003; Devon Farming Community Network, 2014–; UK Agricl Christian Fellowship, 1977–79; Agriculturalist, UK Overseas Develt Cttee and Vice-Chm., Tearfund, 1977–89. Mem. Bd, African Enterprise, 1995–; Coordinator (CEO), Communications Unit for Africa, Rural Develt Counsellors through Christian Churches in Africa, 1996–2013 (Hon. Associate, 2013); UK Coordinator (CEO), Council for Awards of Royal Agricl Socs, 1999–. Chm., SW Br., Tropical Agric. Assoc., 2014–. Chm., Carisbrooke Priory Trust, 1997–2000; Mem. Council, NT, 2014–; Trustee, Bicton Overseas Agricl Trust, 2004–11 (Hon. Associate, 2012). Governor: Long Ashton Res. Stn, Univ. of Bristol, 1986–89; Redcliffe Coll., Gloucester, 1997–2009. Trehane Award, Nuffield Farming Scholarships Trust, 1988. *Publications:* (with D. C. Joy) A Tropical Agriculture Handbook, 1979; Spring Wheat, 1984; Cereal Husbandry, 1989; (ed) Farming Fun and Wisdom: notes, quotes and anecdotes, 2001; Cereals, 2006; contrib. chapters in books; contrib. papers to jls incl. Internat. Jl Agricl Mgt. *Recreations:* family, walking, boating, gardening, the arts. *E:* ejwibberley@btinternet.com. *Club:* Farmers.

WIBLIN, Derek John, CB 1992; Under Secretary, Principal Establishment and Finance Officer, Crown Prosecution Service, 1988–93; *b* 18 March 1933; *s* of late Cyril G. H. Wiblin and of Winifred F. Wiblin; *m* 1960, Pamela Jeanne Hamshere; one *s* one *d. Educ:* Birmingham University (BSc Hons Chem. 1954). RAF, 1954–57. Courtaulds Ltd, 1957–58; joined DSIR Building Research Station, 1958; Civil Service Commission, 1967–71; Asst Sec., Local Govt Div., DoE, 1971–79; Ports Div., Dept of Transport, 1979–81; Estabs Div., DoE, 1981–83; Under Sec., Principal Estabt and Finance Officer, Lord Chancellor's Dept, 1984–88. Chm., First Division Pensioners' Gp, 1993–98. *Recreations:* making violins, collecting books. *Address:* 19 Woodwaye, Oxhey, Watford, Herts WD19 4NN. *T:* (01923) 228615. *Clubs:* Athenæum, Royal Air Force.

WICKENS, Prof. Alan Herbert, OBE 1980; FREng, FIMechE; Director of Engineering Research and Development, British Rail, 1984–89; *b* 29 March 1929; *s* of late Herbert Leslie Wickens and of Sylvia Wickens; *m* 1st, 1953, Eleanor Joyce Waggott (*d* 1984); one *d*; 2nd, 1987, Patricia Anne McNeil. *Educ:* Ashville Coll., Harrogate; Loughborough Univ. of Technol. (DLC Eng, BScEng London, 1951; DSc Loughborough, 1978). CEng, FIMechE 1971; MRAeS. Res. Engr, Sir W. G. Armstrong Whitworth Aircraft Ltd, Coventry, 1951–55; Gp Leader, Dynamics Analysis, Canadair Ltd, Montreal, 1955–59; Head of Aeroelastics Section, Weapons Res. Div., A. V. Roe & Co., Ltd, Woodford, 1959–62; British Rail: Supt, Res. Dept, 1962–67; Advanced Projs Engr, 1967–68; Dir of Advanced Projs, 1968–71; Dir of Labs, 1971–78; Dir of Research, 1978–84. Loughborough University of Technology: Industrial Prof. of Transport Technol., 1972–76; Prof. of Dynamics, Dept of Mechanical Engrg, 1989–92; Vis. Industrial Prof., Dept of Mech. Engrg, later Wolfson Sch. of Mech. and Manufg Engrg, 1993–2012. Vis. Prof., Dept of Mech. Engrg, Design and Manufacture, Manchester Metropolitan Univ., 1998–2001. Pres., Internat. Assoc. of Vehicle System Dynamics, 1981–86 (Hon. Mem., 2001); Chm., Office of Res. and Experiments, Union Internationale de Chemins de fer, 1988–90. Mem., Amer. Inst. Aeronautics and Astronautics, 1958. FBIS; FRSA. Hon. Fellow, Derbyshire Coll. of Higher Educn, 1984. Hon. DTech: CNAA, 1978; Loughborough, 2006; Hon. Dr Open Univ., 1980. George Stephenson Res. Prize, IMechE, 1966; (jtly) MacRobert Award, 1975. *Publications:* Fundamentals of Rail Vehicle Dynamics, 2003; papers on dynamics of railway vehicles, high speed trains and future railway technology, publ. by IMechE, Amer. Soc. of Mech. Engrs, Internat. Jl of Solids and Structures, and Jl of Vehicle System Dynamics. *Recreations:* gardening, travel, music. *Address:* Ecclesbourne Farmhouse, Ecclesbourne Lane, Idridgehay, Derbys DE56 2SB. *T:* (01773) 550368. *Club:* Royal Air Force.

WICKER-MIURIN, Fields, OBE 2007; Partner, Leaders' Quest Ltd, since 2002; *b* 30 July 1958; *d* of Warren Jake Wicker and Marie Peachee Wicker; *m* 1994, Dr Paolo Miurin. *Educ:* Univ. of Virginia (BA *cum laude* Foreign Affairs and French); Institut d'Etudes Politiques, Paris (Cert. d'Etudes Politiques); Johns Hopkins Sch. of Advanced Internat. Studies (MA Econs and Pol Affairs). Vice Pres., Philadelphia Nat. Bank, 1982–89; Partner and Hd Financial Services Practice, Europe, Strategic Planning Associates, 1989–94; Finance Dir and Dir of Strategy, London Stock Exchange, 1994–97; Partner and Vice Pres., Hd Global Financial Markets, AT Kearney, 1998–2000; Chief Operating Officer and Partner, Vesta Capital Advisors Ltd, 2000–02. Non-exec. Dir, 2002–08, Chm. Investment Cttee, 2002–06, BERR (formerly DTI); Member: Technol. Adv. Council, NASDAQ, 2000–04; Panel of Experts, Econ. and Monetary Affairs Cttee, EP, 2002–06; Internat. Adv. Council, Batten Sch. of Leadership, Univ. of Virginia, 2011–. Non-executive Director: Utd Business Media plc, 1998–2004; Savills plc, 2002–10 (Chm., Audit Cttee, 2003–10); Royal London Gp, 2003–06 (Chm., Investment Cttee, 2003–06); Carnegie & Co. AB, 2003–07; CDC Gp plc, 2004–14 (Chm., Impact Cttee, 2010–14); BNP Paribas, 2011–; Ballarpur Internat. Graphic Paper Hldgs, 2011– (Sen. Ind. Dir, 2014–; Chairman: Corp. Social Responsibility Cttee, 2014–; Remuneration and Nominations Cttee, 2014–); SCOR, 2013–; MoJ, 2013–. Trustee: London Internat. Fest. of Theatre, 1997–2004; Arts & Business UK, 1998–2001; London Musici, 2000–03; Council, Tate Members, 2000–06; Brogdale Horticultural Trust, 2002–04. Frequent speaker on leadership. Governor, KCL, 2002–11. FKC 2010. FRSA 1997. Global Leader for Tomorrow, World Econ. Forum, 1997. *Publications:* numerous articles about leadership and financial innovation. *Recreations:* the open countryside, dressage and training horses, opera, exploring new ideas and ways of seeing the world. *Address:* Leaders' Quest Ltd, 11–13 Worple Way, Richmond, Surrey TW10 6DG. *T:* (020) 8948 5200, *Fax:* (020) 8332 6423.

WICKERSON, Sir John (Michael), Kt 1987; Partner, 1962–98, Consultant, 1998–2011, Ormerods (previously Ormerod, Morris & Dumont, later Ormerod Wilkinson Marshall, then Ormerod Heap & Marshall); President, Law Society, 1986–87; *b* 22 Sept. 1937; *s* of Walter and Ruth Wickerson; *m* 1963, Shirley Maud Best; one *s*. *Educ:* Christ's Hospital; London University (LLB). Admitted solicitor, 1960; Mem. Council, Law Society, 1969 (Chm., Contentious Business Cttee; Vice-Pres., 1985–86). Member: Matrimonial Causes Rules Cttee, 1982–86; Royal Commn on Criminal Justice, 1991–93. Pres., London Criminal Courts Solicitors Assoc., 1980–81. Chairman: Mansell plc (formerly R. Mansell Ltd), 1994–2002; Investors' Compensation Scheme Ltd, 1996–2001; United Healthcare (Farnborough Hospital) Ltd, 2000–; Hospital Co. (Darenth) Ltd, 2001–; Hospital Co. (Swindon and Marlborough) Ltd, 2002–11. Chm., Croydon Community NHS Trust, 1991–98. Hon. Member: Amer. Bar Assoc., 1986; Canadian Bar Assoc., 1986; NZ Law Soc., 1987. *Publications:* Motorist and the Law, 1975, 2nd edn 1982. *Recreation:* golf. *Address:* 26 Eglise Road, Warlingham, Surrey CR6 9SE. *T:* (01883) 622126.

WICKES, Charles G.; *see* Goodson-Wickes.

WICKHAM, Prof. Christopher John, DPhil; FBA 1998; Chichele Professor of Medieval History, University of Oxford, since 2005 (Chair, Faculty of History, 2009–12); Fellow of All Souls College, Oxford, since 2005; *b* 18 May 1950; *s* of Cyril George Wickham and Katharine Brenda Warington Wickham (*née* Moss); *m* 1990, Prof. Leslie Brubaker. *Educ:* Millfield Sch.; Keble Coll., Oxford (BA 1971; DPhil 1975). University of Birmingham: Lectr, 1977–87; Sen. Lectr, 1987–89; Reader, 1989–93; Prof. of Early Medieval History, 1993–2005. Jt Ed., Past & Present, 1994–2009. *Publications:* Early Medieval Italy, 1981; The mountains and the city, 1988; (with J. Fentress) Social memory, 1992; Land and power, 1994; Community and Clientele, 1998 (Italian edn 1995); Courts and Conflict, 2003 (Italian edn 2000); Framing the Early Middle Ages, 2005; The Inheritance of Rome: a history of Europe from 400 to 1000, 2009; Medieval Rome, 2014 (Italian edn 2013). *Recreations:* politics, travel. *Address:* All Souls College, Oxford OX1 4AL.

WICKHAM, Daphne Elizabeth, (Mrs J. K. A. Alderson); a District Judge (Magistrates' Courts) (formerly Metropolitan Stipendiary Magistrate), 1989–2012; a Recorder, 1997–2012; Deputy Chief Magistrate and Deputy Senior District Judge (Magistrates' Courts), 2003–12; *b* 31 Aug. 1946; *d* of late Major Harry Temple Wickham and Phyllis Wickham (*née* Roycroft); *m* 1983, John Keith Ameers Alderson. *Educ:* Sydenham High Sch.; Chislehurst and Sidcup Girls' Grammar School. Called to the Bar, Inner Temple, 1967. *Recreation:* laughter. *Address:* Chief Magistrate's Office, Westminster Magistrates' Court, 181 Marylebone Road, NW1 5BR. *Club:* Reform.

WICKHAM, David Ian; Director, Singlehurst Consulting Ltd, since 2003; Chairman, Mhub Ltd, since 2011; *b* 23 Oct. 1957; *s* of Edwin and Betty Wickham; *m* 1982, Joanne Frances Carter; two *s*. *Educ:* St Olave's Grammar Sch., Orpington; S London Coll. (HND Business Studies). Various develt roles in UK, Europe and S Pacific to 1985; Mktg Dir, C&W Systems Ltd, Hong Kong, 1985–87; Mercury Communications Ltd: Gen. Manager, Residential and Operator Services, 1987–91; Mktg Dir, Business and Consumer Services, 1991–94; Man. Dir, Partner Services, 1994–96; Ops Dir, 1996–97; Man. Dir, Internat. and Partner Services, Cable & Wireless Communications Ltd, 1997–98; Chief Exec., Global Network, Cable and Wireless plc, 1998–99; Energis plc: Chief Operating Officer, 1999–2001; Chief Exec., 2001–02; Dep. Chief Exec., 2002; CEO, Vtesse Networks Ltd, 2012–14. Chairman: Telecom Direct Ltd, 2003–08; 3c plc, 2004–06; YAC Ltd, 2005–06 (non-exec. Dir, 2003–04, 2006–07); Synchronica plc, 2006–08. *Recreations:* golf, theatre, family, travel. *Club:* London Golf.

WICKHAM, Janie; *see* Dee, J.

WICKHAM, John Ewart Alfred, FRCS; specialist in minimally invasive surgery and urology; Surgeon and Senior Research Fellow, Guy's Hospital, 1993–98; Director, Academic Unit, Institute of Urology, University of London, 1979–98; Surgeon: St Peter's Hospital, 1967–95; King Edward VII Hospital, 1972–98; Middlesex Hospital, 1973–95; *b* 10 Dec. 1927; *s* of Alfred James Wickham and Hilda May Wickham (*née* Cummins); *m* 1961, (Gwendoline) Ann Loney; three *d*. *Educ:* Chichester Grammar Sch.; London Univ.; St Bartholomew's Hosp. Med. Coll. (BSc Hons 1953; MB BS 1955; MS 1966). FRCS 1959. Nat. Service, RAF, 1947–49. St Bartholomew's Hosp. and RPMS, 1955–66; Sen. Consultant Urological Surgeon, St Bart's, 1966–85; Sen. Lectr, 1967–92, and Sub Dean, 1967–79, Inst. of Urology, Univ. of London; Civilian Consultant Urologist, RAF, 1973–98. Director: Lithotripter Units of London Clinic, 1984–98, and of NE Thames Region, 1987–95; Minimally Invasive Therapy, London Clinic, 1989–99. First Pres., Internat. Soc. of Urological Endoscopy, 1982; President: Urological Sect., RSM, 1984–85; Internat. Soc. of Minimally Invasive Therapy, 1989–2000; Founder Mem., Eur. Soc. of Urology, 1969; Member: Internat. Soc. of Urology, 1970; Italian-Belgian Soc. of Urology, 1980; Irish Soc. of Urology, 1984; American Soc. of Urology, 1990; Japanese Soc. of Urology, 1993. Hon. FRCP 1993; Hon. FRCR 1993; Hon. FRSocMed 2008. Freeman, City of London; Liveryman, Barber Surgeon's Co., 1971. Hon. MD Gothenburg, 1994. Hunterian Prof. and Medal, RCS, 1967; Cutlers Prize and Medal, Assoc. of Surgeons, 1984; James Berry Medal, RCS, 1985; St Peter's Medal, British Assoc. of Urological Surgeons, 1985; J. K. Latimer Medal, Amer. Urological Assoc., 1990; Cecil Joll Prize, RCS, 1993; Rovsing Medal, Danish Soc. of Surgery, 1993; Cook Medal, RCR, 1998; Galen Medal, Soc. of Apothecaries, 1998; Award for Innovations in Urology, Eur. Assoc. of Urology, 2012; Cheselden Medal, RCS, 2014. Editor, Jl of Minimally Invasive Therapy, 1990–2000. *Publications:* Urinary Calculus Disease, 1979; Percutaneous Renal Surgery, 1983; Intrarenal Surgery, 1984; Lithotripsy II, 1987; Urinary Stone Metabolic Basis and Clinical Practice, 1989; An Open and Shut Case, 2015; over 150 papers on urology and minimally invasive surgery. *Recreations:* mechanical engineering, tennis. *Address:* The Cottage, 18 Rose Hill, Dorking, Surrey RH4 2EA. *T:* (01306) 882451. *Club:* Athenæum.

WICKHAM, Rt Rev. Robert James; *see* Edmonton, Area Bishop of.

WICKHAM, His Honour William Rayley; a Circuit Judge, 1975–97; Hon. Recorder of Liverpool and Senior Circuit Judge, Liverpool, 1992–97; *b* 22 Sept. 1926; *s* of late Rayley Esmond Wickham and Mary Joyce Wickham; *m* 1957, Elizabeth Mary (*née* Thompson); one *s* two *d*. *Educ:* Sedbergh Sch.; Brasenose Coll., Oxford (MA, BCL). Served War of 1939–45, Army, 1944–48. Called to Bar, Inner Temple, 1951. Magistrate, Aden, 1953; Chief Magistrate, Aden, 1958; Crown Counsel, Tanganyika, 1959; Asst to Law Officers, Tanganyika, 1961–63; practised on Northern Circuit, 1963–75; a Recorder of the Crown Court, 1972–75. *Recreations:* fell walking, music, amateur dramatics. *Address:* 115 Vyner Road South, Prenton, Merseyside CH43 7PP.

WICKRAMASINGHE, Prof. (Nalin) Chandra, PhD, ScD; Professor, 2000–10 and 2011–14, and Emeritus Professor of Applied Mathematics and Astronomy, since 2006, Cardiff University; Director, Buckingham Centre for Astrobiology, and Hon. Professor, University of Buckingham, since 2011 (Director, Cardiff Centre for Astrobiology, 2000–10); Visiting Fellow, Churchill College, Cambridge, since 2015; *b* 20 Jan. 1939; *s* of Percival Herbert Wickramasinghe and Theresa Elizabeth Wickramasinghe; *m* 1966, Nelum Priyadarshini Pereira; one *s* two *d*. *Educ:* Royal Coll., Colombo, Sri Lanka; Univ. of Ceylon (BSc); Univ. of Cambridge (MA, PhD, ScD). Commonwealth Scholar, Trinity Coll., Cambridge, 1960; Powell Prize for English Verse, 1961; Jesus College, Cambridge: Research Fellow, 1963–66; Fellow, 1967–73; Tutor, 1970–73; Staff Mem., Inst. of Theoretical Astronomy, Univ. of Cambridge, 1968–73; Prof. and Hd of Dept of Applied Maths and Astronomy, UC, Cardiff, 1973–88; Prof., Sch. of Maths, UWCC, subseq. Cardiff Univ., 1988–2000. Visiting Professor: Vidyodaya Univ. of Ceylon, Univ. of Maryland, USA, Univ. of Arizona, USA, Univ. of Kyoto, Japan, 1966–70; Univ. of W Ontario, 1974, 1976; Inst. of Space and Astronautical Studies, Japan, 1993; Univ. of WI, Kingston, Jamaica, 1994; Peradeniya Univ., Sri Lanka; UNDP Cons. and Scientific Advisor to President of Sri Lanka, 1970–81; Dir, Inst. of Fundamental Studies, Sri Lanka, 1982–83 (Vis. Prof., 1997–). Collaborator with Prof. Sir Fred Hoyle, and propounder with Hoyle of the theory of the space origin of life and of microorganisms. Hon. Prof., Glamorgan Univ., 2007. Hon. DSc: Soka Univ., Japan, 1996; Ruhana Univ., Sri Lanka, 2004. Dag Hammarskjöld Gold Medal in science, Académie Diplomatique de la Paix, 1986; Scholarly Achievement Award, Inst. of Oriental Philosophy, Japan, 1989; Internat. Peace and Culture Award, Soka Gakkai, 1993; Sahabdeen Internat. Award for Science, A. M. M. Sahabdeen Trust Foundn, 1996; John Snow Lecture Medal, Assoc. of Anaesthetists of GB and Ire., 2004. Vidya Jyothi (Sri Lanka), 1992. *Publications:* Interstellar Grains, 1967; (with F. D. Kahn and P. G. Mezger) Interstellar Matter, 1972; Light Scattering Functions for Small Particles with Applications in Astronomy, 1973; The Cosmic Laboratory, 1975; (with D. J. Morgan) Solid State Astrophysics, 1976; Fundamental Studies and the Future of Science, 1984; (with F. Hoyle and J. Watkins) Viruses from Space, 1986; (with Daisaku Ikeda) Emergent Perspectives for 2000 AD, 1992; (with D. Ikeda) The Wonders of Life and the Universe, 1993; Glimpses of Life, Time and Space: an anthology of poetry, 1994; Cosmic Dragons: life and death of our planet, 2001; A Journey with Fred Hoyle, 2005, 2nd edn 2013; Quest for the Origins of Life, 2014; A Destiny of Cosmic Life: chapters in the life of an astrobiologist, 2014; (with F. Hoyle): Lifecloud: the origin of life in the universe, 1978; Diseases From Space, 1979; The Origin of Life, 1980; Evolution From Space, 1981; Space Travellers, the Bringers of Life, 1981; From Grains to Bacteria, 1984; Living Comets, 1985; Archaeopteryx, the Primordial Bird: a case of fossil forgery, 1986; Cosmic Life Force, 1987; Theory of Cosmic Grains, 1991; Our Place in the Cosmos: the unfinished revolution, 1993; Life on Mars?: the case for a cosmic heritage, 1997; (with F. Hoyle) Astronomical Origins of Life: steps towards panspermia, 2000; (with J. T. Wickramasinghe and W. M. Napier) Comets and the Origin of Life, 2010; The Search for Our Cosmic Ancestry, 2015; Where Did We Come From? Life of an astrobiologist, 2015; Vindication of Cosmic Biology, 2015; over 300 articles and papers in astronomical and scientific jls; contributor to anthologies of Commonwealth Poetry, incl. Young Commonwealth Poets '65, ed P. L. Brent, 1965. *Recreations:* photography, poetry—both writing and reading, history and philosophy of science. *Address:* 24 Llwyn Y Pia Road, Lisvane, Cardiff CF14 0SY. *E:* ncwick@gmail.com.

WICKREMESINGHE, Sarath Kusum; Chairman, 2008–09, Adviser to the Board, since 2012, Senkadagala Finance Company Ltd, Colombo; *b* 26 Jan. 1928; *m* 1953, Damayantha Hulugalle (*d* 2011). *Educ:* St Thomas' Coll., Mt Lavinia; Univ. of Ceylon (BSc Hons Physics). Exec. in ICI (Export) Ltd, Colombo, 1951–66; Chief Exec., 1966–80, Chm., 1966–94, ICI associate co. in Sri Lanka; Chm., subsid. and associate cos, Coates Internat., 1982–84, BAT, 1985–91, and Standard Chartered Bank, 1989–94; High Comr for Sri Lanka in London, 1995–99; Chairman: Sri Lankan Airlines Ltd, 1999–2002; National Development Bank Ltd, Colombo, 1999–2008. *Address:* 8 Claessen Place, Colombo 5, Sri Lanka. *Club:* Sri Lanka Turf.

WICKS, Geoffrey Leonard; a District Judge (Magistrates' Courts) (formerly Metropolitan Stipendiary Magistrate), 1987–2002 (a Deputy District Judge (Magistrates' Courts), 2002–09); Immigration Adjudicator (part-time), 1996–2003; *b* 23 July 1934; *s* of late Leonard James Wicks and Winifred Ellen Wicks; *m* 1st, 1959, Catherine Margaret Shanks (marr. diss. 1977); one *s* one *d*; 2nd, 1978, Maureen Evelyn Neville (*d* 2012). *Educ:* Tollington Sch., N10; Law Society's Sch. of Law, London. Admitted Solicitor, 1957. National Service, 1957–59. Asst Solicitor, LCC, 1959–60; Asst Solicitor, 1960–61, Partner, 1961–79 (Abu Dhabi office, 1978), Oswald Hickson, Collier & Co., Solicitors, London, Chesham, Amersham, Slough; Principal, Geoffrey Wicks & Co., Solicitors, Chesham, Hemel Hempstead, 1979–82; Partner, Iliffes, Solicitors, London, Chesham, 1982–87. Chairman: Family Courts, 1991–97; Youth Courts, 1991–2002; Mem., Inner London Magistrates' Courts Cttee, 1995–99, 2000–01. Mem., Home Sec.'s Task Force for Youth Justice, 1997–98. Ind. Adjudicator (pt time), HM Prisons, 2002–09. Member: Chesham Round Table, 1962–75 (Chm. 1968–69, Area Chm. Area 42, 1972–73); Chesham Rotary Club, 1974–77. *Recreations:* walking, opera, ballet. *Address:* c/o Chief Magistrate's Office, Westminster Magistrates' Court, 181 Marylebone Road, NW1 5BR.

WICKS, Joanne; QC 2010; *b* Thornbury, 25 April 1967; *d* of David James Wicks and Sheila Esther Wicks; *m* 1997, John Whitehead; two *s*. *Educ:* Cotham Grammar Sch., Bristol; W Bridgford Comprehensive Sch., Nottingham; Hertford Coll., Oxford (BA 1st Cl. Hons Juris.; BCL). Called to the Bar, Lincoln's Inn, 1990; in practice as barrister (self-employed), specialising in chancery commercial work, esp. property litigation and professional negligence, 17 Old Bldgs, Lincoln's Inn, 1990–97, Wilberforce Chambers, Lincoln's Inn, 1997–. *Publications:* (ed) Butterworth's Property Law Handbook, 7th edn 2007, 9th edn 2011. *Recreation:* chatting. *Address:* Wilberforce Chambers, 8 New Square, Lincoln's Inn, WC2A 3QP. *T:* (020) 7306 0102, *Fax:* (020) 7306 0095. *E:* jwicks@wilberforce.co.uk.

WICKS, Sir Nigel (Leonard), GCB 1999 (KCB 1992); CVO 1989; CBE 1979; Chairman, BBA, 2012–15; non-executive Director, Edinburgh Investment Trust plc, since 2005; *b* 16 June 1940; *s* of late Leonard Charles and Beatrice Irene Wicks; *m* 1969, Jennifer Mary (*née* Coveney) three *s*. *Educ:* Beckenham and Penge Grammar Sch.; Portsmouth Coll. of Technology; Univ. of Cambridge (MA); Univ. of London (MA). The British Petroleum Co. Ltd, 1958–68; HM Treasury, 1968–75; Private Sec. to the Prime Minister, 1975–78; HM Treasury, 1978–83; Economic Minister, British Embassy, Washington, and UK Exec. Dir,

IMF and IBRD, 1983–85; Principal Private Sec. to the Prime Minister, 1985–88; Second Perm. Sec. (Finance), HM Treasury, 1989–2000. Chm., CRESTCo, 2001–02; Dep. Chm., 2002–06, Chm., 2006–12, Euroclear plc; Mem. Bd, BNOC, 1980–82; non-exec. Dir, Morgan Stanley Bank Internat. Ltd, 2004–06. Comr, Jersey Financial Services Commn, 2007–12. Chairman: Cttee on Standards in Public Life, 2001–04; Scrutiny Cttee, Actuarial Profession, 2004–06; Selection Panel for Appts, Judicial Appts Commn, 2005–06. Gov., King's Coll. Sch., Wimbledon, 1993–2005. Hon. LLD: Bath, 1999; Portsmouth, 2002.

WICKSTEAD, Myles Antony, CBE 2006; Visiting Professor of International Relations: Open University, since 2005; King's College London, since 2015; Senior Advisor: Hand in Hand International; Development Initiatives; *b* 7 Feb. 1951; *s* of John Horace Wickstead and Eva Mary Wickstead (*née* Fouracre); *m* 1990, Shelagh Paterson; one *s* one *d*. *Educ:* Blundell's Sch.; St Andrews Univ. (MA 1st Cl. Hons Eng. Lang. and Lit. 1974); New Coll., Oxford (MLitt). Joined ODM, 1976; Asst Private Sec. to Lord Privy Seal, FCO, 1979–80; Asst to UK Exec. Dir, IMF/IBRD, 1980–84; Principal, ODA, 1984–88; Private Sec. to Minister for Overseas Develt, 1988–90; Head: EC and Food Aid Dept, ODA, 1990–93; British Develt Div. in Eastern Africa, 1993–97; UK Alternate Exec. Dir, World Bank, and Counsellor (Develt), Washington, 1997–2000; Ambassador to Ethiopia and (non-res.) to Djibouti, 2000–04; Hd of Secretariat, Commn for Africa, 2004–05. Specialist Advr, Internat. Develt Select Cttee, 2010–13. Chm. Bd, One World Media, 2009–14; Member: Adv. Council, Wilton Park, 2006–; Council, Baring Foundn, 2007–; Comic Relief Internat. Grants Cttee, 2008–13; Bd, Internat. Inspiration, 2009–; Bd, Enterprise for Develt, 2014–; Gov., Westminster Foundn for Democracy, 2006–12. Hon. DEd Leeds Metropolitan, 2009; DUniv Open, 2011; Hon. DLitt Ulster, 2011. *Address:* The Manor House, Great Street, Norton sub Hamdon, Som TA14 6SJ. *T:* (01935) 881385. *Club:* Muthaiga (Nairobi).

WICKSTEED, Elisabeth Helen; Clerk to City Livery Club, since 2014; *b* 24 June 1964; *d* of Andrew and Monica Hutchinson; *m* 2001, Michael Wicksteed. *Educ:* Univ. of York (BA Hons). Lord Chancellor's Dept, 1987–98; Private Sec. to Lord Chancellor, 1997–98; Dep. Sec., Sierra Leone Arms Investigation, June–July 1998; Econ. and Domestic Secretariat, 1998–2002, Legislative Prog. Manager, 2000–02, Cabinet Office; Home Office: Hd, Crime Reduction Progs and Partnership Unit, subseq. Asst Dir, Crime Reduction Delivery Team, 2002–04; Hd, Violent Crime Unit, 2004–06; Hd, HR Strategy and Policy, 2006–07; Institute of Cancer Research: Registry Officer, 2008–09; Quality, Governance and Events Manager, subseq. Quality and Governance Manager, 2009–11; Asst Dir, Academic Services (Quality and Governance), 2011–13; Asst Dir and Hd of Registry, 2013–14. Volunteer performer, Opening Ceremony, Olympic Games, London, 2012. *Publications:* (ed) Private Ire, 2007; (ed) The Brithdays Book, 2009. *Address:* City Livery Club, Bell Wharf lane, EC4R 3TB.

WIDDECOMBE, Rt Hon. Ann (Noreen); PC 1997; *b* 4 Oct. 1947; *d* of late James Murray Widdecombe, CB, OBE and Rita Noreen (*née* Plummer). *Educ:* La Sainte Union Convent, Bath; Univ. of Birmingham; Lady Margaret Hall, Oxford (BA Hons, MA). Marketing, Unilever, 1973–75; Senior Administrator, Univ. of London, 1975–87. Contested (C): Burnley, 1979; Plymouth, Devonport, 1983. MP (C) Maidstone, 1987–97, Maidstone and The Weald, 1997–2010. PPS to Tristan Garel-Jones, MP, Nov. 1990; Parly Under-Sec. of State, DSS, 1990–93, Dept of Employment, 1993–94; Minister of State: Dept of Employment, 1994–95; Home Office, 1995–97; Shadow Sec. of State for Health, 1998–99; Shadow Home Sec., 1999–2001. *Publications:* Layman's Guide to Defence, 1984; Strictly Ann (memoir), 2013; novels: The Clematis Tree, 2000; An Act of Treachery, 2002; Father Figure, 2005; An Act of Peace, 2005; Sackcloth and Ashes, 2013. *Recreations:* reading, researching Charles II's escape, walking. *Address:* Widdecombe's Rest, Haytor, Newton Abbot, Devon TQ13 9XT. *T:* (01364) 661154.

WIDDICOMBE, David Graham; QC 1965; a Recorder, 1985–96; a Deputy High Court Judge, 1983–96; *b* 7 Jan. 1924; *s* of Aubrey Guy Widdicombe and Margaret (*née* Puddy); *m* 1961, Anastasia Cecilia (*née* Leech) (marr. diss. 1983); two *s* one *d*. *Educ:* St Albans Sch.; Queens' Coll., Cambridge (BA 1st cl. Hons; LLB 1st cl. Hons; MA). Called to the Bar, Inner Temple, 1950, Bencher, 1973; Attorney at Law, State Bar of California, 1986; retired from legal practice, 2004. Mem., Cttee on Local Govt Rules of Conduct, 1973–74; Chairman: Oxfordshire Structure Plan Examination in Public, 1977; Cttee of Inquiry into Conduct of Local Authority Business, 1985–86. *Publications:* (ed) Ryde on Rating, 1968–83. *Address:* 5 Albert Terrace, NW1 7SU. *T:* (020) 7586 5209. *Club:* Athenæum.

WIDDOWSON, Prof. Henry George; Professor of English Linguistics, University of Vienna, 1998–2001, now Hon. Professor; *b* 28 May 1935; *s* of George Percival Widdowson and Edna Widdowson; *m* 1st, 1966, Dominique Dixmier (marr. diss.); two *s*; 2nd, 1997, Barbara Seidlhofer. *Educ:* Alderman Newton's Sch., Leicester; King's Coll., Cambridge (MA); Univ. of Edinburgh (PhD). Lectr, Univ. of Indonesia, 1958–61; British Council Educn Officer, Sri Lanka, 1962–63; British Council English Language Officer, Bangladesh, 1963–64, 1965–68; Lectr, Dept of Linguistics, Univ. of Edinburgh, 1968–77; Prof. of Educn, Univ. of London, at Inst. of Educn, 1977–2000, now Prof. Emeritus; Prof. of Applied Linguistics, Univ. of Essex, 1993–98. Chm., English Teaching Adv. Cttee, British Council, 1982–91; Mem., Kingman Cttee of Inquiry into Teaching of English Language, 1986–88. Advr for Applied Linguistics, OUP, 1978–2008. Editor, Jl of Applied Linguistics, 1980–85. Dr *hc*: Oulu, 1994; Lorraine, 2012. *Publications:* Stylistics and the Teaching of Literature, 1975 (Japanese edn 1989); Teaching Language as Communication, 1978 (French edn 1981, Ital. edn 1982, Japanese edn 1991); Explorations in Applied Linguistics I, 1979; Learning Purpose and Language Use, 1983 (Italian edn 1986); Explorations in Applied Linguistics II, 1984; (with Randolph Quirk) English in the World, 1985; Aspects of Language Teaching, 1990; Practical Stylistics, 1992 (Japanese edn 2004); Linguistics, 1996 (Korean edn 2000); Defining Issues in English Language Teaching, 2003; Text, Context, Pretext, 2004; Discourse Analysis, 2007; Selected Works on Applied Linguistics, 2009; editor of series: English in Focus; Communicative Grammar; Language Teaching: a scheme for teacher education; Oxford Introductions to Language Study; papers in various jls. *Recreations:* poetry, bird-watching, walking. *Address:* Institut für Anglistik, Universität Wien, Universitätcampus AAKH/Hof 8, Spitalgasse 2–4, 1090 Vienna, Austria. *T:* (1) 427742441.

WIDE, Charles Thomas; QC 1995; **His Honour Judge Wide;** a Circuit Judge, since 2001; a Senior Circuit Judge, since 2011; *b* 16 April 1951; *s* of late Nicholas Scott Wide, MC, and of Ruth Mildred Norton Wide; *m* 1979, Hon. Ursula Margaret Bridget Buchan, *qv*; one *s* one *d*. *Educ:* The Leys Sch., Cambridge; Exeter Univ. (LLB). Called to the Bar, Inner Temple, 1974, Bencher, 2010; Midland and Oxford Circuit Junior, 1983; Standing Counsel to: HM Customs and Excise (Crime), 1989–95; Inland Revenue (Crime), 1991–95; Asst Recorder, 1991–95; Recorder, 1995–2001; Resident Judge, Northampton, 2003–11. Mem., Criminal Procedure Rule Cttee, 2004–12. Reader, Dio. of Peterborough, 2007–. *Recreations:* fell walking, bee keeping. *Address:* Central Criminal Court, Old Bailey, EC4M 7EH. *Club:* Travellers.

WIDE, Hon. Ursula Margaret Bridget; *see* Buchan, Hon. U. M. B.

WIEMAN, Prof. Carl Edwin, PhD; Professor of Physics, Stanford University, since 2013; *b* Oregon, 26 March 1951; *s* of N. Orr Wieman and Alison Wieman; *m* 1984, Sarah Gilbert. *Educ:* MIT (BS 1973); Stanford Univ. (PhD 1977). Asst Res. Scientist, Dept of Physics, 1977–79, Asst Prof. of Physics, 1979–84, Univ. of Michigan; University of Colorado, Boulder: Associate Prof., 1984–87, Prof., 1987–97, Distinguished Prof., 1997–2013, of Physics; Dir, Sci. Educn Initiative, 2006–13; Fellow, Jt Inst. for Lab. Astrophysics, Boulder, 1985 (Chm., 1993–95); Prof. of Physics and Dir, Carl Wieman Sci. Educn Initiative, UBC, 2007–13. Associate Dir for Sci., Office of Sci. and Technol. Policy, Exec. Office of Pres. of USA, 2010–12. (Jtly) Nobel Prize for Physics, 2001. *Address:* Department of Physics, 382 Via Pueblo Mall, Stanford University, Stanford, CA 94305–4060, USA.

WIENER, Elizabeth Anne, (Libby); Political Correspondent, ITN, since 2003; *b* Stockton-on-Tees, 2 March 1959; *d* of late Hans Wiener and of Irene Wiener; *m* 1995, Dr Bruce Kirkham; one *s* two *d*, and one step *s*. *Educ:* Hendon Sch.; Univ. of Leeds (BA Hons Hist. 1981); Centre for Journalism Studies, Cardiff (Postgrad. Dip. Journalism 1982). Reporter, Southern Evening Echo, Southampton, 1982–85; producer, BBC TV South, 1985–87; ITN: producer, 1987–88; Home Affairs Corresp., 1988–91; Europe Corresp., 1991–94; Australia Corresp., 1995–2000; Royal Corresp., 2000–02. *Recreations:* reading, art, theatre, swimming, ski-ing, travelling to the antipodes. *Address:* ITN, Press Gallery, House of Commons, SW1A 0AA. *T:* (020) 7430 4990. *E:* libby.wiener@itn.co.uk.

WIESCHAUS, Prof. Eric Francis, PhD; Professor of Molecular Biology, since 1987, and Squibb Professor, since 1993, Princeton University; *b* 8 June 1947; *s* of Leroy Wieschaus and Marcella Wieschaus (*née* Carner); *m* 1983, Trudi Schüpbach; three *d*. *Educ:* Univ. of Notre Dame, Indiana (BS 1969); Yale Univ. (PhD 1974); Univ. of Zürich. Postdoctoral Fellow, Zool. Inst., Univ. of Zürich, 1975–78; EMBO Fellowship, France, 1976; Vis. Researcher, Center of Pathology, Univ. of California, Irvine, 1977; Group Leader, EMBL, Heidelberg, 1978–81; Asst Prof., 1981–83, and Associate Prof., 1983–87, Princeton Univ. Fellow, Amer. Acad. of Arts and Scis; Mem., Nat. Acad. of Scis. Awards include: John Spangler Niclaus Prize, Yale, 1974; NIHHD Merit Award, 1989; Nobel Prize in Physiology or Medicine (jtly), 1995. *Publications:* From Molecular Patterns to Morphogenesis: the lessons from Drosophila, in the Nobel Prize 1995 (ed T. Fransmyr), 1996; numerous contribs to Jl of Cell Biology and other sci. jls. *Address:* Department of Molecular Biology, Princeton University, Washington Road, Princeton, NJ 08544, USA.

WIESEL, Prof. Elie, Hon. KBE 2006; Andrew W. Mellon Professor in the Humanities and University Professor, since 1976, and Professor of Philosophy and Religion, College of Arts and Sciences, since 1988, Boston University; *b* 30 Sept. 1928; naturalised US citizen, 1963; *m* 1969, Marion Erster; one *s*, one step *d*. *Educ:* The Sorbonne, Univ. of Paris. Distinguished Prof. of Judaic Studies, City Coll., City Univ. of New York, 1972–76; Dist. Vis. Prof. of Literature and Philosophy, Florida Internat. Univ., 1982; Henry Luce Vis. Scholar in the Humanities and Social Thought, Whitney Humanities Center, Yale Univ., 1982–83. Founder and Pres., Elie Wiesel Foundn for Humanity, 1987. Chairman: US Holocaust Meml Council, 1980–86; US President's Commn on the Holocaust, 1979–80; Adv. Bd, World Union of Jewish Students, 1985–; Member, Board of Directors: Nat. Cttee on Amer. Foreign Policy, 1983– (Special Award, 1987); Internat. Rescue Cttee, 1985– (Internat. Vice Pres.); HUMANITAS; Member, Board of Trustees: Yeshiva Univ., 1977–; Elaine Kaufman Cultural Center (formerly Hebrew Arts Sch.), 1980–; Amer. Jewish World Service, 1985–; Member, Board of Governors: Tel-Aviv Univ., 1976–98 (Hon. Mem., 1998); Haifa Univ., 1977–. Fellow: Jewish Acad. of Arts and Sciences; Amer. Acad. of Arts and Sciences, 1986; Member: Amnesty Internat.; Writers Guild of America (East); Authors' Guild; Writers and Artists for Peace in ME; Royal Norwegian Soc. of Sciences and Letters, 1987; Hon. Life Mem., Foreign Press Assoc., 1960. Holds over 100 hon. degrees from univs and colls. Elie Wiesel Chair in Judaic Studies endowed at Connecticut Coll., 1990. Nobel Peace Prize, 1986; other awards include: Anatoly Shcharansky Humanitarian Award, 1983; US Congressional Gold Medal, 1985; US Medal of Liberty Award, 1986; Achievement Award, Israel, 1987; Ellis Island Medal of Honor, 1992; Presidential Medal of Freedom (USA), 1992; Nat. Humanities Medal, USA, 2010. Grand Cross: Légion d'Honneur (France), 2001 (Commandeur, 1984; Grand Officier, 1990); Order of the Southern Cross (Brazil), 1987; Order of Rio Branco (Brazil), 2001; Grand Officer, Nat. Order of the Star (Romania), 2002; Comdr's Cross, Order of Merit (Hungary), 2004; King Hussein Award (Jordan), 2005. *Publications:* Night (memoir), 1960; The Jews of Silence (personal testimony), 1966; Legends of Our Time (essays and stories), 1968; One Generation After (essays and stories), 1970; Souls on Fire: portraits and legends of the Hasidic masters, 1972; Messengers of God: portraits and legends of Biblical heroes, 1976; (with Harry James Cargas) In Conversation with Elie Wiesel, 1976, expanded edn 1992; A Jew Today (essays, stories and dialogues), 1978; Four Hasidic Masters and their Struggle Against Melancholy, 1978; Images from the Bible, 1980; The Testament, 1981 (Prix Livre-Inter, and Bourse Goncourt, France, 1980; Prix des Bibliothécaires, France, 1981); Five Biblical Portraits, 1981; Paroles d'étranger (essays, stories and dialogues), 1982; Somewhere a Master: further Hasidic portraits and legends, 1982; The Golem, 1983; Signes d'Exode (essays, stories and dialogues), 1985; Against Silence: the voice and vision of Elie Wiesel (collected shorter writings, ed Irving Abrahamson), 3 vols, 1985; Job ou Dieu dans la Tempête (dialogue and commentary with Josy Eisenberg), 1986; The Nobel Address, 1987; (with Albert Friedlander) The Six Days of Destruction, 1988; Silences et Mémoire d'hommes (essays), 1989; From the Kingdom of Memory (reminiscences), 1990; Evil and Exile (dialogues with Philippe-Michaël de Saint-Cheron), 1990; (with John Cardinal O'Connor) A Journey of Faith, 1990; Sages and Dreamers: portraits and legends from the Bible, the Talmud, and the Hasidic tradition, 1991; Célébration talmudique: portraits et légendes, 1991; A Passover Haggadah (commentaries), 1993; (with Shlomo Malka) Monsieur Chouchani: l'énigme d'un maître du XXe siècle, 1994; Tout les Fleuves vont à la Mer (memoirs), vol. I, 1994, English trans., as All Rivers Run to the Sea, 1995; (with Jorge Semprun) Se taire est impossible, 1995; Et la mer n'est pas remplie (memoirs) vol. II, 1996, English trans., as And the Sea is Never Full, 1999; Memoir in Two Voices (with François Mitterrand), 1996; Célébration Prophétique, Portraits et légendes, 1998; King Solomon and His Magic Ring (for children), 1999; Le Mal et L'Exil, Dix ans après (dialogues with Philippe-Michaël de Saint-Cheron), 1999; D'où viens-tu? (essays), 2001; (with Richard Heffner) Conversations with Elie Wiesel, 2001; After the Darkness: reflections on the Holocaust, 2002; (ed Robert Franciosi) Elie Wiesel: conversations, 2002; Wise Men and Their Tales, 2003; Et où vas-tu? (essays), 2004; (with Kofi A. Annan) Confronting Anti-Semitism (essays), 2006; Rashi, 2009; Coeur ouvert, récit, 2011; *novels:* Dawn, 1961; The Accident, 1962; The Town beyond the Wall, 1964; The Gates of the Forest, 1966; A Beggar in Jerusalem, 1970; The Oath, 1973; The Testament, 1981; The Fifth Son, 1985 (Grand Prix de la Littérature, Paris); A Song for Hope, 1987; Twilight, 1988; L'Oublié, 1989 (The Forgotten, 1992); The Judges, 2002; Le Temps des Déracinés, 2003 (The Time of the Uprooted, 2005); Un désir fou de danser, 2006 (A Mad Desire to Dance, 2009); Le cas Sonderberg, 2008 (The Sonderberg Case, 2010); Otage, 2010; (cantata) Ani Maamin, 1973; *plays:* Zalmen, or the Madness of God, 1974; The Trial of God, 1979. *Address:* Elie Wiesel Center for Judaic Studies, Boston University, 147 Bay State Road, Boston, MA 02215, USA. *Clubs:* PEN, Lotos.

WIESEL, Prof. Torsten Nils, MD; Secretary-General, Human Frontier Science Program, 2000–09; Vincent & Brooke Astor Professor and Head of Laboratory of Neurobiology, 1983–98, and President, 1992–98, now Emeritus, Rockefeller University; *b* 3 June 1924; *s* of Fritz S. Wiesel and Anna-Lisa Wiesel (*née* Bentzer); *m* 1st, 1956, Teeri Stenhammar (marr. diss. 1970); 2nd, 1973, Ann Yee (marr. diss. 1981); one *d*; 3rd, 1995, Jean Stein; *m* 2008, Lizette Mususa Reyes. *Educ:* Karolinska Inst., Stockholm (MD 1954). Instructor, Dept of Physiol., Karolinska Inst., 1954–55; Asst, Dept of Child Psychiatry, Karolinska Hosp., Stockholm, 1954–55; Fellow in Ophthalmol., 1955–58, Asst Prof. of Ophthalmic Physiol., 1958–59, Johns Hopkins Univ. Med. Sch., Baltimore; Harvard Medical School: Associate in Neurophysiol. and Neuropharmacol., 1959–60; Asst Prof., 1960–67; Prof. of Physiol., 1967–68; Prof. of Neurobiol., 1968–74; Chm., Dept of Neurobiol., 1973–82; Robert Winthrop Prof. of Neurobiol., 1974–83. Dir, Leon Levy and Shelby White Center for Mind, Brain & Behavior, Rockefeller Univ., 1999–. Scientific Advr, Bristol Myers-Squibb Corp.

Lectures: Ferrier, Royal Soc., 1972; Grass, Soc. for Neurosci., 1976. Co-Chm., Bd of Govs, Okinawa Inst. of Sci. and Technol., 2002–. Member: Amer. Physiol Soc.; AAAS; Amer. Acad. of Arts and Scis; Amer. Philosophical Soc.; Soc. for Neurosci. (Pres. 1978–79); Nat. Acad. of Scis; Swedish Physiol Soc.; Harvard Bd of Overseers; Foreign Mem., Royal Soc., 1982; Hon. Mem., Physiolog. Soc., 1982. Has received hon. degrees from univs in Sweden, Norway, Italy and USA. Awards and Prizes: Dr Jules C. Stein, Trustees for Research to Prevent Blindness, 1971; Lewis S. Rosenstiel, Brandeis Univ., 1972; Friedenwald, Assoc. for Res. in Vision and Ophthalmology, 1975; Karl Spencer Lashley, Amer. Phil. Soc., 1977; Louisa Gross Horwitz, Columbia Univ., 1978; Dickson, Pittsburgh Univ., 1979; Ledlie, Harvard Univ., 1980; Soc. for Scholars, Johns Hopkins Univ., 1980; Nobel Prize in Physiology or Medicine, 1981. *Publications:* (contrib.) Physiological and Biochemical Aspects of Nervous Integration, 1968; (contrib.) The Organization of the Cerebral Cortex, 1981; (with David Hubel) Brain and Visual Perception: the story of a 25 year collaboration, 2004; contribs to professional jls, symposia and trans of learned socs. *Address:* Rockefeller University, 1230 York Avenue, New York, NY 10065, USA. *T:* (212) 3277093. *Club:* Harvard (Boston).

WIGAN, (Desmond Patrick) Neil; HM Diplomatic Service; Ambassador (non-resident) to Somalia, 2013–15; *m* Yael Banaji; one *s* one *d*. *Educ:* Univ. of Oxford (BA Hist.); Univ. of London (MSc Econs); Sch. of Advanced Internat. Studies, Johns Hopkins Univ. (Postgrad. Dip.). Entered FCO, 2000; Desk Officer, EU Econ. Policy, EU Dept (Internal), FCO, 2000–02; Head: Political Section, Tel Aviv, 2002–06; Arab Israel and N Africa Gp, FCO, 2006–08; Dep. Dir for Wider World, Foreign and Defence Policy Secretariat, Cabinet Office, 2008–09; Ambassador to Democratic Rep. of Congo and Rep. of Congo, 2010–13. *Address:* c/o Foreign and Commonwealth Office, King Charles Street, SW1A 2AH.

WIGAN, Sir Michael (Iain), 6th Bt *cr* 1898, of Clare Lawn, Mortlake, Surrey and Purland Chase, Ross, Herefordshire; journalist and author; *b* 3 Oct. 1951; *s* of Sir Alan Lewis Wigan, 5th Bt, and of Robina, 2nd *d* of Sir Iain Colquhoun of Luss, 7th Bt, KT, DSO; *S* father, 1996; one *s* by Lady Alexandra Hay; *m* 1989, Julia Teresa, *d* of late John de Courcy Ling, CBE; three *s* one *d*. *Educ:* Eton; Exeter Coll., Oxford. *Publications:* The Scottish Highland Estate: preserving an environment, 1991; Stag at Bay, 1993; The Last of the Hunter Gatherers, 1998; Grimersta: the story of a great fishery, 2001; The Salmon: the extraordinary story of the king of fish, 2013. *Recreations:* deer stalking, fishing, literature. *Heir: s* Fergus Adam Wigan, *b* 30 April 1990. *Address:* Borrobol, Kinbrace, Sutherland KW11 6UB. *T:* (01431) 831264.

WIGAN, Neil; *see* Wigan, D. P. N.

WIGDORTZ, Brett Harris, OBE 2013; Founder and Chief Executive Officer, Teach First, since 2002; *b* New Jersey, USA, 9 Oct. 1973; *s* of Larry Wigdortz and Judith Wigdortz; *m* 2005, Nicole Jacobs; one *s* two *d*. *Educ:* Univ. of Richmond (BA Econs); Univ. of Hawaii (MA Econs). Researcher, East-West Center, Honolulu, 1995–97; freelance journalist, 1998–99; Mgt Consultant, McKinsey & Co., Indonesia, Singapore and the Philippines, 2000–02. Co-Founder, Teach for All, 2007. *Publications:* Success Against the Odds, 2012. *Recreations:* family and friends, sailing, travelling. *Address:* Teach First, 4 More London Riverside, SE1 2AU.

WIGFIELD, Timothy B.; *see* Byram-Wigfield.

WIGGHAM, Hon. (Edward) Barrie, CBE 1991; JP; Hong Kong Commissioner, USA, 1993–97; *b* 1 March 1937; *s* of Edward and Agnes Wiggham; *m* 1961, Mavis Mitson (*d* 2003); two *d* (one *s* decd). *Educ:* Woking Grammar Sch.; Queen's Coll., Oxford (MA Mod. Langs). Hong Kong Government: Admin. Officer, 1961–63; Dist Officer, New Territories, 1963–71; postings in finance, econ., security and information branches, 1971–79; Comr for Recreation and Culture, 1979–83; Regl Sec., 1983–86; seconded to British Embassy, Peking, 1986; Sec., General Duties, 1986–90; Mem. Gov's Exec. Council, 1989–92; Sec. for CS, 1990–93. JP Hong Kong, 1973. *Recreations:* music, people. *Address:* Cefn Mably Lodge, Old St Mellons, Cardiff CF3 6LP. *Clubs:* Hong Kong, Foreign Correspondents', United Services (Hong Kong); George Town, National Press (Washington).

WIGGIN, Sir Richard Edward John, 6th Bt *cr* 1892, of Metchley Grange, Harborne, Staffs; *b* Guildford, 1 July 1980; *o s* of Sir Charles Rupert John Wiggin, 5th Bt and Mary Burnett-Hitchcock (*née* Chambers); *S* father, 2012; *m* 2013, Phillipa Helen Bean; one *d*. *Educ:* Harrow Sch. *Heir: uncle* Benjamin Henry Edward Wiggin, *b* 23 Aug. 1951. *Address:* Honington Hall, Shipston-on-Stour, Warwickshire CV36 5AA.

WIGGIN, William David; MP (C) North Herefordshire, since 2010 (Leominster, 2001–10); *b* 4 June 1966; *s* of Sir Alfred William, (Jerry), Wiggin, TD and of Rosemary Janet (*née* Orr, now Dale Harris); *m* 1999, Camilla Chilvers; two *s* one *d*. *Educ:* Eton; UCNW, Bangor (BA Hons Pure Econs). Trader: Rayner Coffee Internat., 1988–90; Mitsubishi Corp., 1990–91; Union Bank of Switzerland, 1991–94; Associate Dir, Dresdner Kleinwort Benson, 1994–98; Manager, Commerzbank, 1998–2001. Opposition spokesman on envmt, 2003, on agric. and fisheries, 2005–09; Shadow Sec. of State for Wales, 2003–05; Opposition Whip, 2009–10; an Asst Govt Whip, 2010–12. *Recreations:* motor bikes, Hereford cattle, country sports. *Address:* House of Commons, SW1A 0AA. *Clubs:* Hurlingham, Annabel's.

WIGGINS, (Anthony) John, CMG 2002; consultant on public financial management, control and audit, since 2002; *b* 8 July 1938; *s* of late Rev. Arthur Wiggins and of Mavis Wiggins (*née* Brown); *m* 1962, Jennifer Anne Walkden; one *s* one *d*. *Educ:* Highgate Sch.; The Hotchkiss Sch., Lakeville, Conn, USA; Oriel Coll., Oxford (MA). Assistant Principal, HM Treasury, 1961; Private Sec. to Permanent Under Sec., Dept of Economic Affairs, 1964–66; Principal: Dept of Economic Affairs, 1966–67; HM Treasury, 1967–69; Harkness Fellow, Harvard Univ., 1969–71 (MPA 1970); Asst Sec., HM Treasury 1972–79; Principal Private Sec. to Chancellor of the Exchequer, 1980–81; Under Sec., Dept of Energy, 1981–84 (Mem. of BNOC, 1982–84); Under Sec., Cabinet Office, 1985–87; Under Sec., 1987–88, Dep. Sec., 1988–92, DES, subseq. DFE, on secondment to HM Treasury, 1992; Mem., Ct of Auditors of European Communities, 1993–2001. Sec. to Royal Opera House Develt Bd, 1987–93 (Sec. to cttees, 1982–87). *Recreations:* mountaineering, ski-ing, opera. *Address:* Clayhanger Farm, Wadeford, Chard, Somerset TA20 3BD. *T:* (01460) 61610.

WIGGINS, Bernard; *see* Cornwell, B.

WIGGINS, Sir Bradley (Mark), Kt 2013; CBE 2009 (OBE 2005); professional cyclist, Team WIGGINS, since 2015; *b* Ghent, Belgium, 28 April 1980; *s* of Garry and Linda Wiggins; *m* 2004, Catherine; one *s* one *d*. Professional cyclist: La Française des Jeux team, 2002–04; Credit Agricole team, 2004–05; Confidis team, 2006–07; Team High Road, 2008; Team Garmin-Slipstream, 2009; Team Sky, 2010–15. Bronze Medal, Team Pursuit, Sydney Olympics, 2000; Gold Medal, Individual Pursuit, Silver Medal, Team Pursuit, Bronze Medal, Madison, Athens Olympics, 2004; Gold Medal, Individual Pursuit, Gold Medal, Team Pursuit, Beijing Olympics, 2008; Gold Medal, Individual Time Trial, London Olympics, 2012; Gold Medal, Individual Pursuit, 2003, 2007, 2008, Team Pursuit, 2007, 2008, 2011, Madison, 2008, Track World Championships; Silver Medal, Individual Time Trial, Road World Championships, 2011; 4th place, Tour de France, 2009; 3rd place, Vuelta a España, 2011; winner, Tour de France, 2012; winner, Tour of Britain, 2013; Silver Medal, Individual Time Trial, Road World Championships, 2013; winner, Tour of Calif, 2014; Silver Medal, Team Pursuit, Commonwealth Games, Glasgow, 2014; 3rd place, Tour of Britain, 2014; Gold Medal, Individual Time Trial, Road World Championships, 2014. BBC Sports Personality of the Year Award, 2012. *Publications:* In Pursuit of Glory, 2008; My Time (autobiog.), 2012. *Address:* c/o XIX Entertainment, 33 Ransomes Dock, 35–37 Parkgate Road, SW11 4NP.

WIGGINS, Prof. David, FBA 1978; Wykeham Professor of Logic, and Fellow of New College, Oxford University, 1994–2000, now Emeritus Fellow; *b* 8 March 1933; *s* of late Norman Wiggins and Diana Wiggins (*née* Priestley); *m* 1969, Hideko Ishiguro (marr. diss); *m* 1979, Jennifer Hornsby (marr. diss.); one *s*; *m* 2010, Phillida Gili. *Educ:* St Paul's Sch.; Brasenose Coll., Oxford (BA 1955; MA 1958; Hon. Fellow 2010). Asst Principal, Colonial Office, London 1957–58. Jane Eliza Procter Vis. Fellow, Princeton Univ., 1958–59; Lectr, 1959, then Fellow and Lecturer, 1960–67, New College, Oxford; Prof. of Philosophy, Bedford Coll., Univ. of London, 1967–80; Fellow and Praelector in Philosophy, University Coll., Oxford, 1981–89; Prof. of Philosophy, Birkbeck Coll., Univ. of London, 1989–94. Visiting appointments: Stanford, 1964 and 1965; Harvard, 1968 and 1972; All Souls College, 1973; Princeton, 1980; New York Univ., 1988; Boston Univ., 2001; Fellow, Center for Advanced Study in the Behavioral Sciences, Stanford, 1985–86. Mem., Ind. Commn on Transport, 1973–74; Chm., Transport Users' Consultative Cttee for the South East, 1977–79. Pres., Aristotelian Soc., 1999–2000. Mem., Institut International de Philosophie. For. Hon. Mem., Amer. Acad. of Arts and Scis, 1992. DUniv York, 2005. *Publications:* Identity and Spatio-Temporal Continuity, 1967; Truth, Invention and the Meaning of Life, 1978; Sameness and Substance, 1980; Needs, Values, Truth, 1987, 3rd edn 1998, rev. 2002; Sameness and Substance Renewed, 2001; Ethics: twelve lectures on the philosophy of morality, 2006; Solidarity and the Root of the Ethical, 2008; Identity Substance and Existence: selected essays, 2016; philosophical articles in Philosophical Review, Analysis, Philosophy, Synthèse, Phil Qly, Ratio, Proc. Aristotelian Soc., Mind, Eur. Jl of Philosophy; articles on environmental and transport subjects in Spectator, Times, Tribune, and ed collections.

WIGGINS, John; *see* Wiggins, A. J.

WIGGLESWORTH, Jack; Chairman, London International Financial Futures Exchange, 1995–98; Deputy Chairman, Durlacher Corp. plc, 2002–05; *b* 9 Oct. 1941; *s* of Jack Wigglesworth and Gladys Maud Wigglesworth; *m* 1970, Carlota Josefina Paéz; one *s* one *d*. *Educ:* Jesus Coll., Oxford (MA). Gilt Desk Economist and Bond Salesman, Phillips & Drew, 1963–71; Gilt Desk Bond Salesman, 1971–86, Partner, 1973–86, W. Greenwell & Co.; London International Financial Futures and Options Exchange: Founder Mem., Wkg Party, 1980–81; Mem., Steering Cttee, 1981–82; Dir, 1982–98; Designed Gilt Contract, 1982; Chm., Membership and Rules Cttee, 1988–92; Dep. Chm., 1992–95. Dir of Marketing, Citifutures Ltd, 1993–97; Chairman: ABN Amro Futures Ltd, 1997–99; CableNet Internat., 2001–03; LitComp plc, 2002–03; London Asia Capital plc, 2003–09; LOPPEX, 2010–. Director: Stace Barr Angerstein plc, 1997–2001; Clivia Ltd, 1998–2002; Capital Value Brokers Ltd, 1998–2005. Mem., London Stock Exchange, 1968–91; Director: Securities Inst., 1992–2003; Futures and Options Assoc., 1995–2000; Financial Services NTO, 2001–06. Member: Financial Services Adv. Gp, QCA, 1999–2001; Adv. Bd, OMFIF, 2012–. Chm., Hackney Educn Action Zone, 1999–2004; Member: Business Sch. Council, London Guildhall Univ., 1998–2002; Council, Gresham Coll., 1999–2011. Master, World Traders' Co., 2006–07. Hon. DSc City, 1998. *Recreations:* music, films, computers, gardening. *Address:* 3 Deacons Heights, Elstree, Herts WD6 3QY. *T:* (020) 8953 8524. *Clubs:* Athenæum, City of London.

WIGGLESWORTH, Mark Harmon; orchestral conductor; Music Director, English National Opera, since 2015; *b* 19 July 1964; *s* of Martin Wigglesworth and Angela (*née* Field). *Educ:* Bryanston Sch.; Manchester Univ. (BMus); Royal Acad. of Music. Winner, Kondrashin Comp., 1989. Founder and Music Dir, Première Ensemble, 1989–; Associate Conductor, BBC SO, 1991–93; Music Director: Opera Factory, 1991–94; BBC Nat. Orch. of Wales, 1996–2000; Prin. Guest Conductor, Swedish Radio SO, 1998–2001. Débuts: Glyndebourne Fest. Opera, 2000; ENO, 2001; Royal Opera House, Covent Gdn, 2002; Metropolitan Opera, NY, 2005; Bayerische Staatsoper, Munich, 2011; has conducted many orchestras incl. Berlin Philharmonic, Royal Concertgebouw, NY, LA Philharmonic, Boston, Cleveland, Philadelphia, Chicago, San Francisco, Montreal Symphony, Minnesota Orch., Sydney Symphony, Melbourne Symphony, Tokyo Symphony, Hong Kong Philharmonic, London Philharmonic, London Symphony, La Scala, Santa Cecilia; also at BBC Proms and Hollywood Bowl; recordings include complete Shostakovich Symphony cycle with Netherlands Radio Philharmonic. *Address:* c/o Intermusica Artists' Management, Crystal Wharf, 36 Graham Street, N1 8GJ; English National Opera, London Coliseum, St Martin's Lane, WC2N 4ES.

WIGGLESWORTH, Raymond; QC 1999; a Recorder, since 1990; *b* 24 Dec. 1947; *s* of Kenneth Holt Wigglesworth and Marguerite (*née* Lonsdale); *m* 1982, Amanda Jane Littler; two *s* one *d*. *Educ:* Manchester Univ. (LLB). Called to the Bar, Gray's Inn, 1974; in practice on Northern Circuit, 1974–; Asst Recorder, 1987–90; Standing Counsel to HM Customs and Excise, 1995–99. *Recreations:* mountaineering, ski-ing, golf, sailing. *Address:* 18 St John Street, Manchester M3 4EA. *T:* (0161) 278 1800. *Club:* Wilmslow Golf.

WIGGLESWORTH, Prof. Sarah Heath, MBE 2003; RIBA; RDI 2012; architect; Founder and Director, Sarah Wigglesworth Architects, since 1994; Professor of Architecture, University of Sheffield, since 1997; *b* London, 16 May 1957; *d* of Gordon Hardy Wigglesworth and Cherry Diana Heath Wigglesworth; partner, Prof. Jeremy William Till, *qv*. *Educ:* Camden Sch. for Girls; Newnham Coll., Cambridge (BA 1979; MA; DipArch 1983). RIBA 1984; ARB 1985. Studio Tutor, Univ. of Cambridge, 1985–87; Lectr, 1989–92, Sen. Lectr, 1992–98, Kingston Univ. *Publications:* (ed jtly) Desiring Practices: architecture, gender and the interdisciplinary, 1996; (ed with J. Till) The Everyday and Architecture, 1998; (ed) Around and About Stock Orchard Street, 2011. *Recreations:* making things, food (growing, cooking, eating), cycling. *Address:* Sarah Wigglesworth Architects, 10 Stock Orchard Street, N7 9RW. *T:* (020) 7607 9200, *Fax:* (020) 7607 5800. *E:* sarah@swarch.co.uk.

WIGGLESWORTH, William Robert Brian; Director, Reedheath Ltd, 1994–2012; Joint Director, International Institute for Regulations in Telecommunications, Westminster University, 1998–2006 (City University, 1994–98); *b* 8 Aug. 1937; *s* of Sir Vincent Wigglesworth, CBE, FRS; *m* 1969, Susan Mary (MBE 2015), *d* of late Arthur Baker, JP, Lavenham; one *s* one *d*. *Educ:* Marlborough; Magdalen College, Oxford (BA). Nat. Service, 2nd Lieut, Royal Signals, 1956–58. Ranks, Hovis McDougall Ltd, 1961–70: trainee; Gen. Manager, Mother's Pride Bakery, Cheltenham; PA to Group Chief Exec.; Gen. Manager, Baughans of Colchester; Board of Trade, 1970; Fair Trading Div., Dept of Prices and Consumer Protection, 1975; Posts and Telecommunications Div., 1978, Inf. Tech. Div., 1982, Dept of Industry; Dep. Dir Gen. of Telecommunications, 1984–94, Actg Dir, 1992–93. Prin. Advr, Telecoms Forum, Internat. Inst. of Communications, 1994–97; Mem. Bd, UKERNA, 1994–98. *Recreations:* fishing, gardening, history. *Address:* Millfield House, Heath Road, Polstead, Colchester CO6 5AN. *T:* (01787) 210029.

WIGGS, His Honour (John) Samuel; a Circuit Judge, Western Circuit, 1995–2014; *b* 23 Nov. 1946; *s* of late Kenneth Ingram Wiggs and of Marjorie Ruth Wiggs (*née* Newton); *m* Elizabeth Jones (decd); *m* Kerry Martley; two *d*, and two step *d*. *Educ:* Chigwell Sch.; Southampton Univ. (LLB). Called to the Bar, Middle Temple, 1970; in practice, London, 1971–95; Recorder, 1991; Resident Judge, Bournemouth, 1999–2007, Bournemouth and Dorchester, 2007–13; pt-time Judge, Mental Health Tribunals, 2014–. Chancellor, Dio. of Salisbury, 1997–. *Recreations:* playing the bassoon and saxophone, church choir singing, gardening, hill walking. *Address:* Courts of Justice, Deansleigh Road, Bournemouth, Dorset BH7 7DS. *T:* (01202) 502800, *Fax:* (01202) 502801.

WIGGS, Roger Sydney William Hale; Group Chief Executive, Securicor plc, 1996–2001, non-executive Director, 2001–03; *b* 10 June 1939; *s* of Sydney Thomas Wiggs and Elizabeth Alice Wiggs (*née* Coomber); *m* 1st, 1963, Rosalind Anne Francis (*d* 2004); four *s*; 2nd, 2008, Sally Elizabeth Mote (*née* Buzzard). *Educ:* Tiffin Sch., Kingston upon Thames. Admitted Solicitor, 1962; Partner, Hextall, Erskine & Co., 1963–74; Overseas Dir, Securicor Ltd, 1974–80; Man. Dir, Securicor Internat. Ltd, 1980–89; Dir, 1977, Dep. Gp Chief Exec., 1985–88, Gp Chief Exec., 1988–96, Securicor Gp plc, and Security Services plc. Non-exec. Dir, Crown Agents for Oversea Govts and Admins Ltd, 1997–2005. *Recreations:* sport, particularly soccer, Rugby, motor racing.

WIGGS, Samuel; *see* Wiggs, J. S.

WIGHT, Ven. Dennis Marley; Archdeacon of St Davids, since 2013; *b* 1953. *Educ:* Southern Univ. (BTh 1987); Sarum and Wells Theol Coll. Ordained deacon, 1985, priest, 1986; Curate, Gillingham, 1985–87; Vicar, Christ Church, Coseley, 1990–94; Rector, Stoke Prior, Wychbold and Upton Warren, 1994–2002; Rural Dean, Droitwich, 1996–99; Vicar, Dale and St Brides with Marloes, 2002–10; Area Dean, Roose, 2005–10; Diocese of St Davids: Warden of Ordinands, 2009–11, 2012–13; Bishop's Chaplain, 2010–14; Dir of Ministry, 2010–. Hon. Canon, St Davids Cath., 2009–. *Address:* The Vicarage, Water Street, Ferryside SA17 5RT. *T:* (01267) 267192.

WIGHT, Robin, CVO 2000; President, WCRS and Engine Group, since 2008 (Chairman, WCRS, 1983–2008); Founder and Chairman, The Ideas Foundation, since 2002; *b* 6 July 1944; *s* of late Brig. I. L. Wight and of C. P. Wight; *m* 1st (marr. diss.); two *s* one *d*; 2nd (marr. diss.); one *s* one *d*; 3rd (marr. diss.); two step *c*; 4th, 2013, Countess Paola von Csaky. *Educ:* Wellington Coll.; St Catharine's Coll., Cambridge. Copywriter: Robert Sharp and Partners, 1966; CDP and Partners, 1967; Creative Director: Richard Cope and Partners, 1968; Euro Advertising, 1968; Creative Partner, Wight, Collins, Rutherford, Scott, 1979. Marketing Adviser to Rt Hon. Peter Walker, 1982–84. Chm., Duke of Edinburgh Award Charter for Business, 1992–2000. Mem. Council, Arts & Business (formerly ABSA), 1994–97 (Chm., 1997–2005). Contested (C) Bishop Auckland, 1987. *Publications:* The Day the Pigs Refused to be Driven to Market, 1972; The Peacock's Tail and the Reputation Reflex, 2008. *Address:* Engine, 60 Great Portland Street, W1W 7RT.

WIGHTMAN, (Andrew Norman) Scott, CMG 2009; HM Diplomatic Service; High Commissioner to Singapore, since 2015; *b* 17 July 1961; *s* of Andrew James Scott Wightman and Joan MacDonald Wightman (*née* Campbell); *m* 1988, Anne Margaret Roberts; two *d*. *Educ:* George Heriot's Sch., Edinburgh; Edinburgh Univ. (MA Hons French and Contemp. European Instns). FCO, 1983; Second Sec., Peking, 1986; Cabinet Office, 1989; FCO, 1991; First Sec., Paris, 1994; Asst Dir, Personnel Policy, FCO, 1998; Minister and Dep. Hd of Mission, Rome, 2002–06; Dir for Global and Econ. Issues, FCO, 2006–08; Dir, Asia Pacific, FCO, 2008–10; Ambassador to Republic of Korea, 2011–15. *Address:* British High Commission, 100 Tanglin Road, Singapore 247919.

WIGHTMAN, Very Rev. David; *see* Wightman, Very Rev. W. D.

WIGHTMAN, John Watt, CVO 1998; CBE 1986; RD; WS; Chairman, Craig & Rose plc, 1994–2000; Solicitor to the Queen in Scotland, 1983–99; *b* 20 Nov. 1933; *s* of Robert Johnson Wightman and Edith Wilkinson (*née* Laing); *m* 1962, Isla Fraser MacLeod; one *s* two *d*. *Educ:* Daniel Stewart's Coll.; Univ. of St Andrews (MA); Univ. of Edinburgh (LLB). Partner, Morton Fraser, WS, 1961–99. Cdre, RNR, 1982–85; Chairman: Lowland TAVRA, 1992–95; Regl Adv. Cttee for S Scotland, Forestry Commn, 1998–2004. Dir, Douglas Haig Memorial Homes, then Trustee, Haig Housing Trust, 1998–2013; Dir, Earl Haig Fund Scotland, 2000–04. *Recreations:* sailing, fishing, ornithology. *Address:* 58 Trinity Road, Edinburgh EH5 3HT. *T:* (0131) 551 6128. *Clubs:* Naval; Royal Scots (Edinburgh).

WIGHTMAN, Scott; *see* Wightman, A. N. S.

WIGHTMAN, Very Rev. (William) David; Provost of St Andrew's Cathedral, Aberdeen, 1991–2002; Priest in charge of St Ninian, Aberdeen, 1991–2002; *b* 29 Jan. 1939; *s* of William Osborne Wightman and Madge Wightman; *m* 1963, Karen Elizabeth Harker; two *s* two *d*. *Educ:* Alderman Newton's GS, Leicester; George Dixon GS, Birmingham; Univ. of Birmingham (BA Hons Theol.); Wells Theol Coll. Ordained deacon, 1963; priest, 1964; Curate: St Mary and All Saints, Rotherham, 1963–67; St Mary, Castlechurch, Stafford, 1967–70; Vicar: St Aidan, Buttershaw, Bradford, 1970–76; St John the Evangelist, Cullingworth, Bradford, 1976–83; Rector: St Peter, Peterhead, 1983–91; St John Longside, St Drostan, Old Deer and All Saints, Strichen, 1990–91; Chaplain, HM Prison, Peterhead, 1989–91; Dir, Training for Ministry, Dio. of Aberdeen and Orkney, 1989–94. Hon. Canon, Christ Church Cathedral, Hartford, Conn, USA, 1991. *Recreations:* fishing, choral music, swimming, gardening. *Address:* 66 Wold Road, Pocklington, E Yorks YO42 2QG. *T:* (01759) 301369.

WIGLEY, family name of **Baron Wigley**.

WIGLEY, Baron *cr* 2011 (Life Peer), of Caernarfon in the County of Gwynedd; **Dafydd Wigley;** PC 1997; industrial economist; President, National Library of Wales, 2007–11; Hon. President, Plaid Cymru, since 2006; *b* 1 April 1943; *s* of late Elfyn Edward Wigley, sometime County Treasurer, Caernarfonshire CC; *m* 1967, Elinor Bennett (*née* Owen), *d* of late Emrys Bennett Owen, Dolgellau; one *s* one *d* (and two *s* decd). *Educ:* Caernarfon Grammar Sch.; Rydal Sch., Colwyn Bay; Manchester Univ. Ford Motor Co., 1964–67; Chief Cost Accountant and Financial Planning Manager, Mars Ltd, 1967–71; Financial Controller, Hoover Ltd, Merthyr Tydfil, 1971–74. Chm., ADC Ltd, 1981–91. Mem., Merthyr Tydfil Borough Council, 1972–74. MP (Plaid Cymru) Caernarfon, Feb. 1974–2001. Mem., Select Cttee on Welsh Affairs, 1983–87. Vice-Chairman: Parly Social Services Gp, 1985–88; All-Party Disablement Gp, 1992–2001; British-Slovene Parly Gp, 1993–2001; Mem., Standing Cttee on Eur. Legislation, 1991–96. Sponsor, Disabled Persons Act, 1981. Pres., Plaid Cymru, 1981–84 and 1991–2000. National Assembly for Wales: Mem. (Plaid Cymru) Caernarfon, 1999–2003; Leader, Plaid Cymru, 1999–2000; Chm., Audit Cttee, 2002–03. Contested (Plaid Cymru), N Wales, Eur. Parly elecns, 1994. Vice-Pres., Nat. Fedn of Industrial Develt Authorities, 1981–2001. Chairman: Ymddiriedolaeth Hybu Gwyddoniaeth Cyf, 2002–06; Una Cyf, 2004–08; non-exec. Dir, Gwernafalau Cyf, 2001–; Member: Adv. Bd for Wales, BT, 2003–07; S4C Authority, 2003–06. Pres., CAB, Gwynedd, 2003–09; Chm., N Wales Crimebeat, 2003–09. Pro-Chancellor, Univ. of Wales, 2003–06; Chm., Adv. Bd, Sch. of Business (formerly Sch. of Business and Regl Develt), Bangor Univ. (formerly Univ. of Wales, Bangor), 2003–. Pres., Spastic Soc. of Wales, 1985–90; Jt Pres., Mencap Wales, 1997–; Trustee, Hope House, 2003–10. Pres. (unpaid), S Caernarfonshire Creamery, 1988–2003. Mem., Writers' Guild, 2000–. Fellow, UCNW, Bangor, 1994. Hon. LLD: Wales, 2002; Glamorgan, 2003. *Publications:* An Economic Plan for Wales, 1970; O Ddifri, 1992; Dal Ati, 1993; A Democratic Wales in a United Europe, 1995; A Real Choice for Wales, 1996; Maen i'r Wal, 2001. *Address:* Hen Efail, Bontnewydd, Caernarfon, Gwynedd LL54 7YH. *E:* dafydd_wigley@hotmail.com.

WIGLEY, Prof. Dale Brian, PhD; FRS 2004; Professor of Structural Biology, Imperial College London; *b* 10 May 1961; *s* of Brian Wigley and Joan Wigley. *Educ:* Univ. of York (BSc Hons (Biochem.) 1985); Univ. of Bristol (PhD (Biochem.) 1988). Post-doctoral Fellow: Univ. of Leicester, 1988–90; Univ. of York, 1990–92; Lectr, 1993–97, Reader, 1997–2000, Univ. of Oxford; Principal Scientist, CRUK, Clare Hall Labs, 2000–10; Prof. of Protein Crystallography, Inst. of Cancer Res., 2010–14. Mem., EMBO, 2002. *Recreation:* fly-fishing. *Address:* Section of Structural Biology, Department of Medicine, Imperial College London, South Kensington Campus, SW7 2AZ. *E:* dale.wigley@imperial.ac.uk.

WIGLEY, Robert Charles Michael; Chairman: NetOTC Holdings, SARL, since 2012; Llamabrook plc (First Global Trust Bank), since 2013; Captive Minds Group Communications Ltd, since 2013; Justinvesting Ltd, since 2014; *b* 4 Feb. 1961; *s* of Harold and Elizabeth Margaret Wigley; *m* 1996, Sarah Joan Molony; three *s*. *Educ:* Sch. of Mgt, Univ. of Bath (BSc Business Admin 1983). FCA 1986. Dir, Morgan Grenfell plc, until 1996; Man. Dir, Merrill Lynch Internat., 1996–2004; Chm., EMEA, Merrill Lynch, 2004–09; Chm., Merrill Lynch Internat. Bank Ltd, 2005–09; Operating Partner, Advent Internat., 2009–11. Non-executive Director: Royal Mail Gp plc, 2003–06 (Chm., Audit Cttee, 2003–06); Court, 2006–09, Risk Policy Cttee, 2006–09, Bank of England; LCH Clearnet Gp Ltd, 2005–09; Euroclear plc, 2007–09; Orca Exploration Inc., 2010–12; Altitude Med. Systems Inc., 2011–14; Qatar Financial Centre Authy, 2012– (Chm., Audit Cttee, 2012–); Member: Internat. Business Adv. Bd, British Airways plc, 2012–14; Adv. Bd, Tetronics Internat. Ltd, 2012–; Loyalty Angels, 2015–; Symphony Environmental, 2015–; Chairman: Sovereign Reversions plc, 2009–10; hibu (formerly Yell Gp) plc, 2009–14; Stonehaven Search LLP, 2010–; Expansys, 2010–14; Skrill Hldgs Inc., 2011; Telemetry plc, 2014–15. Dep. Chm., BITC, 2005–10 (Chm., Educn Leadership Team, 2005–09); Member: Sen. Practitioner Cttee, FSA, 2005–10; Panel on Takeovers and Mergers, 2007–09 (Mem., Remuneration Cttee); Adv. Bd, London Corp., 2005–10; Adv. Council, Business for New Europe, 2006–12; Chancellor's High Level Gp of Key London Financial Stakeholders, 2006–09; Nat. Council for Educnl Excellence, 2007–10; Mayor of London's Panel of Economic Advrs, 2008–14; Ministerial Wkg Gp on Sch. Governance for Sec. of State, DCSF, 2008–09; Chairman: Nat. Educn Employer Taskforce, 2009–11; Green Investment Bank Commn, 2010; Adv. Bd, Green Investment Bank, 2011–12; Prime Minister's Ambassador for UK Business, 2011–12. Author of commissioned reports: (for Mayor of London) London, Winning in a Changing World, 2008; (for Nat. Council of Educn Excellence) Governing Our Schools, 2008. Vis. Fellow, Saïd Business Sch., 2008–, Chm., Global Adv. Gp, Centre for Corporate Reputation, 2007–, Univ. of Oxford; Mem., Adv. Bd, Doughty Centre for Corp. Responsibility, Cranfield Sch. of Mgt, 2008–. Member: Court, Internat. Bankers' Co., 2006– (Master, 2009–10); Council, RCM, 2012–. Trustee: Whizz Kidz Ltd, 2000–06; Peter Jones Foundn, 2011–. Hon. DBA Bath, 2008. *Recreations:* tennis, golf, vintage cars, fine wine, entertaining. *Address:* (office) 1 Babmaes Street, SW1Y 6HD. *Clubs:* Royal Automobile, Queen's (Chm., Estates Cttee, 2014–), Annabel's; Aston Martin Owners.

WIGNALL, Michael Thomas; Head Chef, Michael Wignall at The Latymer, Pennyhill Park Hotel, since 2007; Creative Director, Football Café, since 2013; *b* Preston, Lancs, 23 May 1967; *s* of Alan Wignall and Catherine Wignall (*née* Dunn); partner, Johanna Bethan Cole; one *s*. *Educ:* St Cuthbert Mayne High Sch., Preston; Preston Coll. Jun. sous chef, Heathcotes, Longridge, 1987–89; Head Chef: The Old Beams, Waterhouses, 1993–95 (Michelin Star); Waldo's, Cliveden, 1996–98 (Michelin Star); Michael's Nook, Grasmere, 1998–2002 (Michelin Star); Exec. Head Chef, The Devonshire Arms, N Yorks, 2002–07 (Michelin Star). Pop-up restaurants: Stockholm, 2013; Selfridges, London, 2014. Charity event, India, Creative Services Support Gp, 2013; Bobby Moore Fund, 2014, 2015. A judge, BBC MasterChef: The Professionals, 2013, 2014. Best dessert under 21s and best overall entrant, Salon Culinaire, 1986; winner, Northwest Chefs Circle, 1987; Best Restaurant Newcomer of the Yr, Good Food Guide, 2009; winner, SW, Britain's Best Dish, ITV, 2010; Michael Wignall at The Latymer awarded 2 Michelin Stars, 2012, 5 AA Rosettes, 2012. *Recreations:* wakeboarding, snowboarding, heliboarding, downhill mountain biking, Lotus sport, photography, surfing. *Address:* 1 Homestead Cottages, London Road, Windlesham, Surrey GU20 6LG. *E:* Michael.Wignall@outlook.com.

WIGODER, Hon. Charles; Executive Chairman, Telecom Plus plc, since 2009; *b* London, 2 March 1960; *s* of Baron Wigoder, QC; *m* 1988, Elizabeth; one *s* three *d*. *Educ:* Westminster Sch.; Univ. of Kent (BA 1981). Chartered Accountant. Chartered Accountant, KPMG, 1981–84; Investment Analyst, Grieveson Grant, 1984–85; Head, Corporate Finance and Development: Carlton Communications plc, 1985–87; Quadrant Gp plc, 1987–88; Founder and Chief Exec., Peoples Phone, 1988–95; Chief Exec., Telecom Plus plc, 1996–2009. Hon. Dr of Laws Kent, 2010. *Recreations:* bridge, theatre, ballet, opera, philanthropy. *Address:* Utility Warehouse, Network HQ, 508 Edgware Road, NW9 5AB. *T:* (020) 8955 5002. *E:* charles@wigoder.com. *Clubs:* Annabel's, TGRs; Cercle de l'Union Interalliée (Paris).

WIGRAM, family name of **Baron Wigram**.

WIGRAM, 2nd Baron *cr* 1935, of Clewer; **George Neville Clive Wigram,** MC 1945; JP; DL; *b* 2 Aug. 1915; *s* of Clive, 1st Baron Wigram, PC, GCB, GCVO, CSI, and Nora Mary (*d* 1956), *d* of Sir Neville Chamberlain, KCB, KCVO; *S* father, 1960; *m* 1941, Margaret Helen (*d* 1986), *yr d* of late General Sir Andrew Thorne, KCB, CMG, DSO; one *s* two *d*. *Educ:* Winchester and Magdalen College, Oxford. Page of Honour to HM King George V, 1925–32; served in Grenadier Guards, 1937–57: Military Secretary and Comptroller to Governor-General of New Zealand, 1946–49; commanded 1st Bn Grenadier Guards, 1955–56. Governor of Westminster Hospital, 1967–74. JP Gloucestershire, 1959, DL 1969. *Heir: s* Major Hon. Andrew (Francis Clive) Wigram, MVO, late Grenadier Guards [*b* 18 March 1949; *m* 1st, 1974, Gabrielle Diana (marr. diss. 2010), *y d* of late R. D. Moore; three *s* one *d*; 2nd, 2011, Mrs Henrietta Charrington]. *Address:* 20 Courtbrook, Fairford, Gloucestershire GL7 4BE. *T:* (01285) 711356, *Fax:* (01285) 711596. *Club:* Cavalry and Guards.

See also Sir E. J. Webb-Carter.

WIGRAM, Sir John (Woolmore), 9th Bt *cr* 1805, of Walthamstow, Essex; Director, JW Consultancy Ltd, since 2013; *b* 25 May 1957; *s* of late Peter Woolmore Wigram and of Sylvia Mary Wigram; *S* cousin, 2003; *m* 1996, Sally Jane Winnington; three *s*. *Educ:* Bedford Coll., London Univ. (BA Hons Hist.); Insead, Fontainebleau (MBA). Davidson Pearce, 1981–84; Leo Burnett, 1984–87; Davis Wilkins, 1987–91; CLK, 1993–96; Doner Cardwell Hawkins, 1996–98; ARC, 1998–2003; Dir, Rise Communications, 2003–06; Worldwide Planning Dir, Publicis, 2006–09; Dir, BPRI, 2010–13. *Heir: s* James Woolmore Wigram, *b* 10 Feb. 1997.

WIGSTON, Air Vice-Marshal Michael, CBE 2013; Administrator, Sovereign Base Areas, and Commander, British Forces Cyprus, since 2015; *b* Portsmouth, 25 Feb. 1968; *s* of Michael Vernon Wigston and Pamela Florence Wigston (*née* Workman); *m* 1994, Kate Louise Nielson; one *s* one *d*. *Educ:* Friars Sch., Bangor; Oriel Coll., Oxford (MA Engrg Sci. 1992); King's Coll. London (MA Defence Studies 2004). Commnd RAF, 1986; Tornado GR1/4 pilot: II(AC) sqdn, 1992; 14 Sqdn, 1995; 31 Sqdn, 1998; II(AC) Sqdn, 1999; Officer Commanding: 12(B) Sqdn, 2005; 903 Expeditionary Air Wing, Basra, 2007; Ops Directorate, MoD, 2008; Targeting and Information Ops, MoD, 2010; Dir Air Ops, ISAF Jt Comd, Kabul, 2011; Tornado Force Comdr, 2013; PSO to CDS, 2013–15. *Recreation:* sailing. *Address:* Command Group, HQ British Forces Cyprus, Episkopi, BFPO 53.

WIKELEY, Nicholas John; an Upper Tribunal Judge (Administrative Appeals Chamber) (formerly a Social Security and Child Support Commissioner), since 2008; *b* Farnborough, Kent, 27 Sept. 1957; *s* of Nigel Derek Telford Wikeley and Olga Mary Wilson Wikeley (*née* Naylor); *m* 1983, Clare Elaine Phillips; two *s* one *d*. *Educ:* Sevenoaks Sch.; Trinity Hall, Cambridge (Exhibnr; BA 1980). Called to the Bar, Gray's Inn, 1981; Lectr, 1984–92, Sen. Lectr, 1992–94, Faculty of Law, Univ. of Birmingham; Prof. of Law, 1994–2008, now Emeritus, Dean of Faculty, 1996–99, Univ. of Southampton. Pt-time Chm., Social Security

Appeal Tribunals, 1992–2008; Dep. Social Security and Child Support Comr, 2000–08. Society of Legal Scholars: Hon. Sec., 2001–06; Vice-Pres., 2008–09; Pres., 2009–10. *Publications:* (jtly) Judging Social Security, 1992; Compensation for Industrial Disease, 1993; (jtly) Child Support in Action, 1998; (with A. Ogus) The Law of Social Security, 4th edn 1995, 5th edn 2002; Child Support Law and Policy, 2006; (jtly) Social Security Legislation, vol. 2, Income Support, Jobseeker's Allowance, State Pension Credit and the Social Fund, annually 2000–13; (with D. Williams) Social Security Legislation, vol. 4, Tax Credits, Child Trust Funds and HMRC-Administered Social Security Benefits, annually 2003–13; contrib. articles to learned jls. *Recreations:* ferries, Danish islands, Swedish crime novels. *Address:* Upper Tribunal, Administrative Appeals Chamber, 5th Floor, Rolls Building, 7 Rolls Buildings, Fetter Lane, EC4A 1NL. *Club:* Tottenham Hotspur Football.

WIKSTRÖM, Prof. Per-Olof Helge, PhD; FBA 2011; Professor of Ecological and Developmental Criminology, University of Cambridge, since 2001; Fellow, Girton College, Cambridge, since 1997; *b* Uppsala, Sweden, 30 July 1955; *s* of late William Wikström and Signe Wikström (*née* Lindeberg); *m* 1991, Suzanna Maxe; four *d*. *Educ:* Stora Brynässkolan; Stenebergsskolan; Vasaskolans Gymnasium; Univ. of Stockholm (BA 1976; PhD 1985; Docent 1988). Various res. associate and lectr posts, Dept of Criminol., Univ. of Stockholm, 1979–90 (Dep. Hd of Dept, 1987–90); Sen. Res. Officer, 1985–90, Dir, Res. Dept, 1990–94, Nat. Council for Crime Prevention, Sweden; Principal Res. Fellow, Res. Unit, Nat. Police Coll., Sweden, 1995–96; Adjunct Prof. of Sociol. of Crime, Univ. of Stockholm, 1993–96; Univ. Lectr, 1997–99, Reader, 1999–2001, Inst. of Criminol., Univ. of Cambridge. Visiting Professor: Univ. of Malmö, 2007–12; Univ. of Münster, 2008. Member: Bd, Scandinavian Res. Council for Criminol., 1992–97; Scientific Commn of Internat. Soc. for Criminol., 1995–99; Bd, Eur. Soc. Criminol., 2000–01 and 2004–05. Fellow: Center for Advanced Study in Behavioral Scis, Stanford Univ., 2002; Amer. Soc. Criminol., 2010. Northern Schol. Award, Univ. of Edinburgh, 1991; Sellin-Glueck Award, Amer. Soc. Criminol., 1994. *Publications:* Everyday Violence in Contemporary Sweden: ecological and situational aspects, 1985; Crime and Measures against Crime in the City, 1990; Urban Crime, Criminals and Victims, 1991; Integrating Individual and Ecological Aspects of Crime, 1993; Integrating Crime Prevention Strategies: propensity and opportunity, 1995; Criminal Deterrence and Sentence Severity, 1998; The Explanation of Crime: context, mechanisms and development, 2006; Adolescent Crime: individual differences and life styles, 2006; Breaking Rules: the social and situational dynamics of young people's urban crime, 2012; contrib. chapters in books and papers to jls incl. Criminol., Eur. Jl of Criminol., Jl of Quantitative Criminol. *Recreations:* news, coffee, golf. *Address:* Institute of Criminology, University of Cambridge, Sidgwick Avenue, Cambridge CB3 9DA. *T:* (01223) 335378. *E:* pow20@cam.ac.uk. *Club:* Gog MaGog Golf.

WILBOURNE, Rt Rev. David Jeffrey; Assistant Bishop of Llandaff, since 2009; *b* Chesterfield, 15 Sept. 1955; *s* of Geoffrey Wilbourne and Eileen Wilbourne; *m* 1983, Rachel Margaret Powell; three *d*. *Educ:* Jesus Coll., Cambridge (MA 1981); Westcott House, Cambridge. Ordained deacon, 1981, priest, 1982; Asst Curate, Stainton-in-Cleveland, 1981–85; Rector, Monk Fryston and S Milford, 1985–91; Domestic Chaplain to Archbishop of York, and Dir of Ordinands, Dio. of York, 1991–97; Vicar, Helmsley, York, 1997–2009; Priest-in-charge, Upper Ryedale, 2009. *Publications:* Archbishop's Diary, 1995; A Vicar's Diary, 1998, 3rd edn 2002; A Virgin's Diary, 1999; A Summer's Diary, 2001, 2nd edn, 2002; You Were Made for Me, 2001; The Helmsley Chronicles, 2012; Expecting Christ, 2013; The Voice of Jesus, 2014. *Recreations:* cycling, hill-walking, writing, New Testament textual criticism. *Address:* Llys Esgob, The Cathedral Green, Llandaff, Cardiff CF5 2YF. *T:* (029) 2056 2400. *E:* asstbishop@churchinwales.org.uk.

WILBRAHAM; *see* Bootle-Wilbraham, family name of Baron Skelmersdale.

WILBRAHAM, Sir Richard B.; *see* Baker Wilbraham.

WILBY, David Christopher; QC 1998; a Recorder, since 2000; a Deputy High Court Judge, since 2008; *b* 14 June 1952; *s* of Alan Wilby and late June Wilby; *m* 1976, Susan Arding; one *s* three *d*. *Educ:* Roundhay Sch., Leeds; Downing Coll., Cambridge (MA). Called to the Bar, Inner Temple, 1974, Bencher, 2002; Mem., North Eastern Circuit. Member: Judicial Studies Bd, 2005–09; Criminal Injuries Compensation Tribunal (formerly Appeals Panel), 2007–. Member: Exec. Cttee, Professional Negligence Bar Assoc., 1995–2009; Bar Council, 1996–99; Chm., Bar Conf., 2000. Member: Commonwealth Lawyers Assoc., 1995; Internat. Assoc. of Defense Counsel, 1998; Associate Mem., American Bar Assoc., 1996; Chm., Northern Administrative Law Assoc., 2008–. Editor: Professional Negligence and Liability Law Reports, 1995–; Professional Negligence Key Cases, 1999–; HSE sect., Atkin's Court Forms, 2002, 2006 and 2010. *Publications:* The Law of Damages, 2003, 2nd edn 2010; (contrib.) Munkman, Employers Liability, 14th edn 2006 to 16th edn 2013. *Recreations:* being in France, golf, Rugby, Association Football. *Address:* Old Square Chambers, 10–11 Bedford Row, WC1R 4BU. *T:* (020) 7269 0300; Park Lane Plowden Chambers, 19 Westgate, Leeds LS1 2RD. *T:* (0113) 228 5000. *Clubs:* Royal Over-Seas League; Moortown Golf, Pannal Golf, Royal Cinque Ports Golf.

WILBY, Peter John; Editor, New Statesman, 1998–2005; *b* 7 Nov. 1944; *s* of Lawrence Edward Wilby and Emily Lavinia Wilby; *m* 1967, Sandra James; two *s*. *Educ:* Kibworth Beauchamp Grammar Sch., Leics; Univ. of Sussex (BA Hons). Reporter, Observer, 1968–72; Education Correspondent: Observer, 1972–75; New Statesman, 1975–77; Sunday Times, 1977–86; Educn Editor, Independent, 1986–89; Independent on Sunday: Home Editor, 1990–91; Dep. Editor, 1991–95; Editor, 1995–96; Books Editor, New Statesman, 1997–98. Columnist, Guardian and New Statesman, 2005–. *Publications:* Parents' Rights, 1983; Sunday Times Good University Guide, 1984; Sunday Times Good Careers Guide, 1985; Eden, 2006; (ed with Henry Pluckrose): The Condition of English Schooling, 1981; Education 2000, 1982. *Recreations:* reading, cooking, lunching. *Address:* 51 Queens Road, Loughton, Essex IG10 1RR.

WILCE, Penelope Jane; *see* Reed, P. J.

WILCOCK, Christopher Camplin, CB 1997; Director, Financial Advisory Services, PricewaterhouseCoopers (formerly Price Waterhouse), 1997–99; *b* 13 Sept. 1939; *s* of late Arthur Camplin Wilcock and Dorothy (*née* Haigh); *m* 1965, Evelyn Clare Gollin; two *d*. *Educ:* Berkhamsted and Ipswich Schs; Trinity Hall, Cambridge (BA 1st Cl. Hons; MA). FO, 1962–63; MECAS, 1963–64; 3rd Sec., Khartoum, 1964–66; FO, 1966–68; 2nd Sec., UK Delegn to NATO, 1968–70; FO, 1970–72; Hosp. Bldg Div., DHSS, 1972–74; Petroleum Prodn, subseq. Continental Shelf Policy Div., Dept of Energy, 1974–78, Asst Sec. 1976; Electricity Div., 1978–81; on secondment to Shell UK Ltd, 1982–83; Department of Energy, subseq. of Trade and Industry: Hd of Finance Br., 1984–86; Dir of Resource Management (Grade 4), 1986–88; Grade 3, 1988; Hd of Electricity Div. A, 1988–91; Hd of Electricity Div., 1991–94; Hd of Electricity and Nuclear Fuels Div., 1994–95; Hd of Nuclear Power Privatization Team, 1995–96. Order of the Two Niles, Fifth Cl. (Sudan), 1965. *Recreations:* reading, riding.

WILCOCK, Prof. Gordon Keith, DM; FRCP; Professor of Geratology (formerly Clinical Geratology), 2006–12, now Emeritus, Director, Clinical Dementia Research Programme, until 2012, and Director, Oxford Project to Investigate Memory and Ageing, since 2008, University of Oxford; Emeritus Consultant in Clinical Geratology, Oxford University Hospitals NHS Trust, 2013; *b* 5 Sept. 1945; *m* 1969, Louise Molden; three *s* two *d*. *Educ:* St Catherine's Coll., Oxford; London Hosp. Med. Coll. (BSc 1st cl. Hons 1967); Oxford Univ. Med. Sch. (BM BCh 1970; DM 1977). FRCP 1984. MRC Clinical Res. Fellow, Dept of Regius Prof. of Medicine, Oxford, 1973–75; Sen. Registrar in Geriatric Medicine, Cambridge, 1976; Consultant Physician to Depts of Geriatric and Gen. Medicine, Oxfordshire HA (Teaching), 1976–84; Clinical Lectr in Geriatric and Gen. Medicine, Univ. of Oxford, 1978–84; Prof. of Care of the Elderly, Univ. of Bristol, and Hon. Consultant Physician, N Bristol NHS Trust, at Frenchay Hosp., 1984–2006. Invited Public Lectr, Royal Instn, 2001–04. Visiting Professor in Geriatric Medicine: Univ. of Hong Kong, 2000, 2009; UWE; Beijing Univ. of Chinese Medicine (Academic Master, 111 Project, 2008–12). Founder Chm., Alzheimer's Soc., 1979–86 (Vice Pres., 1987–); Vice Pres. for Academic Affairs, British Geriatrics Soc. 2012–15. Chm., Med. Adv. Cttee, Sir Halley Stuart Trust, 2003–. Gov., BUPA Foundn, 2004–09. Hon. DSc UWE, 2006. Dhole-Eddlestone Meml Prize, BGS, 2006. *Publications:* (with J. M. Gray) Our Elders, 1981; (with A. Middleton) Geriatric Medicine, 1980, 2nd edn 1989; (jtly) Geriatric Problems in General Practice, 1982, 2nd edn 1991; Living with Alzheimer's Disease, 1990, 2nd edn 1999 (Italian edn 1992); (ed jtly) Oxford Textbook of Geriatric Medicine, 2000; contrib. over 300 articles on Alzheimer's disease and dementia in med. and scientific jls. *Recreations:* ornithology, photography, beekeeping. *Address:* Nuffield Department of Clinical Neuroscience, Level 6, John Radcliffe Hospital, Oxford OX3 9DU. *E:* gordon.wilcock@ndcn.ox.ac.uk.

WILCOCKS, Rear-Adm. Philip Lawrence, CB 2007; DSC 1991; DL; Owner and Director, CEMPA (Leadership) Ltd, since 2009; *b* 14 April 1953; *s* of Lt Comdr Arthur Wilcocks, RN and Marjorie Wilcocks; *m* 1976, Kym; two *s*. *Educ:* Oakham Sch.; Wallington County Grammar Sch.; Univ. of Wales (BSc). Navigation Officer, HMS Torquay, 1977–78; CO, HMS Stubbington, 1978–80; Warfare Officer, HMS Ambuscade (incl. Falklands Campaign), 1980–84; HMS Newcastle/York, 1984–89; CO, HMS Gloucester (incl. Gulf War), 1990–92; MoD, 1992–98; Capt., 3rd Destroyer Sqdn, HMS Liverpool, 1998–99; Dir Naval Ops, MoD, 1999–2001; Cdre, Maritime Warfare Sch., 2001–04; Dep. Chief of Jt Ops (Operational Support), PJHQ, 2004–06; FO Scotland, Northern England and NI, and FO Reserves, 2006; COS (Capability) to C-in-C Fleet and Rear Adm. Surface Ships, 2007–08. President: HMS Hood Assoc., 2009–; Type 42 Destroyer Assoc., 2013–. Churchwarden, Dore Abbey, 2010–. DL Herefordshire, 2013. *Recreations:* walking, cycling, hill climbing. *Clubs:* Royal Navy of 1765 and 1785, Destroyer.

WILCOCKSON, Ven. Stephen Anthony; Archdeacon of Doncaster, since 2012; *b* Connahs Quay, N Wales, 15 May 1951; *s* of Stephen Donald Wilcockson and Edna Wilcockson; *m* 1986, Heather Mitchell; one *s* one *d*. *Educ:* Park High Sch., Birkenhead; Nottingham Univ. (BA Hons French); Oxford Univ. (MA Theol.). Ordained deacon, 1976, priest, 1977; Curate, Pudsey Parish Church, 1976–78; Sen. Curate, All Saints, Wandsworth, 1978–81; Vicar: St Peter, Rock Ferry, 1981–86; St Mark, Lache-cum-Saltney, Chester, 1986–95; St Paul, Howell Hill, Surrey, 1995–2009; Rural Dean, Epsom, 2000–07; Parish Devclt Officer, Dio. of Chester, 2009–12. *Recreations:* sport, music, walking, reading. *Address:* 14 Armthorpe Lane, Doncaster DN2 5LZ. *T:* (01302) 325787. *E:* steve.wilcockson@sheffield.anglican.org.

WILCOX, Baroness *cr* 1995 (Life Peer), of Plymouth in the County of Devon; **Judith Ann Wilcox;** *d* of John and Elsie Freeman; *m* 1st, 1961, Keith Davenport; one *s*; 2nd, 1986, Sir Malcolm George Wilcox, CBE (*d* 1986). *Educ:* St Dunstan's Abbey, Devon; St Mary's Convent, Wantage; Plymouth Polytechnic. Management of family business, Devon, 1969–79; Financial Dir, Capstan Foods, Devon, 1979–84; Chm., Channel Foods, Cornwall, 1984–89; Pres. Dir Gen., Pecheries de la Morinie, France, 1989–91; Chm., Morinie et Cie, France, 1991–94. Chm., Nat. Consumer Council, 1990–96; Comr, Local Govt Commn, 1992–95; Mem., Prime Minister's Adv. Panel to Citizen's Charter Unit, 1992–97; Chm., Citizen's Charter Complaints Task Force, 1993–95. Board Member: AA, 1991–; Inland Revenue, 1991–96; PLA, 1993– (Vice-Chm., 2000–); non-executive Director: Carpetright plc, 1997–; Cadbury Schweppes plc, 1997–2007; Johnson Services PLC, 2004–. Shadow Spokesman on Energy and Climate Change, H of L, 2008–10; Parly Under-Sec. of State, BIS, 2010–12; Chm., H of L Sci. Select Cttee Enquiry into Aircraft Cabin Envmt, 2000–01; Member: Tax Law Review Cttee, 1989–; H of L European Select Cttee, Envmt, Public Health and Consumer Affairs, 1996; Lord Chancellor's Review of Court of Appeal, 1996. Parly Deleg. to Council of Europe, 2012–. President: NFCG; Inst. of Trading Standards Admin; Mem., Governing Body, Inst. of Food Res. Vice-Pres., Guide Assoc. Gov., Imperial Coll. London, 2006–10; Chm. of Govs, Falconwood Acad., 2008–10. Chairman: Trustees, Community of St Mary Virgin, 2012–; Diocesan Adv. Cttee for London, 2012. FRSA. *Recreations:* sailing, walking, calligraphy. *Address:* House of Lords, SW1A 0PW. *Clubs:* Athenæum; St Mawes Sailing.

See also Hon. S. N. Davenport.

WILCOX, Claire, (Mrs J. F. Stair); Senior Curator, Furniture, Textiles and Fashion (formerly Fashion), Victoria and Albert Museum, since 2009; *b* London, 7 Oct. 1954; *d* of Sydney William and Margaret Jean Wilcox; *m* 1992, Julian Francis Stair, *qv*; two *d* (one *s* decd). *Educ:* Godolphin and Latymer Sch.; Exeter Univ. (BA Hons English Lit. 1977); Gerrit Rietveld Acad. of Art, Amsterdam; Camberwell Sch. of Art (BA Hons 1987); Univ. of East Anglia (Mus. Leadership Prog. 2010). Curatorial Asst, V&A Mus., 1979–83; Curator, Brixton Artists' Collective, 1987; freelance writer and curator, 1987–99; Curator, 1999–2004, Sen. Curator, Modern Fashion, 2004–08, Acting Hd of Contemporary Progs, 2008–09, V&A Mus.; Prof. in Fashion Curation, London Coll. of Fashion, Univ. of the Arts London (on secondment), 2013–15. Member: Mgt Council, British Fashion Council, 2006–10; Peer Review Coll., AHRC, 2010–14. Trustee, Council, Royal Sch. of Needlework, 2010–14. *Publications:* (with V. Mendes) Modern Fashion in Detail, 1991, 5th edn 2009; A Century of Style: bags, 1997; Handbags, 1999, 2nd edn 2008; (ed jtly) The Ambassador: fashion and trade in post-war Britain, 2012; exhibition catalogues. *Recreations:* reading, planting. *Address:* c/o Victoria and Albert Museum, SW7 2RL. *T:* (020) 7942 2000. *E:* c.wilcox@vam.ac.uk.

WILCOX, His Honour David John Reed; a Judge of the Technology and Construction Court of the High Court, 1998–2012; a Judge of the Employment Appeal Tribunal, 1999–2012; *b* 8 March 1939; *s* of Leslie Leonard Kennedy Wilcox and Margaret Ada Reed Wilcox (*née* Rapson); *m* 1st, 1962, Wendy Feay Christine Whiteley (*d* 2003); one *s* one *d*; 2nd, 2005, Roberta Piera Prosio de Pardo. *Educ:* Wednesbury Boys' High Sch.; King's Coll., London (LLB Hons). Called to the Bar, Gray's Inn, 1962. Directorate, Army Legal Services (Captain): Legal Staff, 1962–63; Legal Aid, Far East Land Forces, Singapore, 1963–65. Crown Counsel, Hong Kong, 1965–68; Lectr in Law, Univ. of Hong Kong, 1966–68; Member, Hong Kong Bar, 1968; in practice, Midland and Midland and Oxford Circuits, 1968–85; Hd of Chambers, College St, Nottingham, 1973–85; a Recorder of the Crown Court, 1979–85; a Circuit Judge, 1985–98; an Official Referee, 1996–98. Resident Judge, Great Grimsby Combined Court Centre, 1989–94; County Court Judge: Lincs and S Humberside, 1989–94; Birmingham, 1994–96; Care Judge, Birmingham, 1994–96. Appeal Judge, Special Chamber Privatisation related matters EU Rule of Law Mission, Supreme Court, Kosovo, 2013–14. Lord Chancellor's Rep., Humberside Probation Cttee, 1989–94. Chm., Nottingham Friendship Housing Assoc., 1970–75. Trustee and Vice-Pres., Pug Dog Welfare and Rescue Assoc., 2013– (Treas., 2012–13); Dir, John Townsend Trust, 2015–. *Recreations:* pugs, gardening, travel. *E:* wilcoxdjr@hotmail.com.

WILCOX, Rt Rev. David Peter; an Honorary Assistant Bishop, Diocese of Chichester, since 1995; *b* 29 June 1930; *s* of John Wilcox and Stella Wilcox (*née* Bower); *m* 1956, Pamela Ann Hedges; two *s* two *d*. *Educ:* Northampton Grammar School; St John's Coll., Oxford (MA); Lincoln Theological Coll. Deacon 1954, priest 1955; Asst Curate, St Peter's, St Helier,

Morden, Surrey, 1954–56; Asst Curate, University Church, Oxford and SCM Staff Secretary in Oxford, 1956–59; on staff of Lincoln Theological Coll., 1959–64; USPG Missionary on staff of United Theological Coll., Bangalore, and Presbyter in Church of S India, 1964–70; Vicar of Great Gransden with Little Gransden, dio. Ely, 1970–72; Canon Residentiary, Derby Cathedral and Warden, E Midlands Joint Ordination Training Scheme, 1972–77; Principal of Ripon College, Cuddesdon and Vicar of All Saints', Cuddesdon, 1977–85; Bishop Suffragan of Dorking, dio. Guildford, 1986–95. Assisting in parish of St Mary's, Willingdon, Eastbourne, 1995–. *Recreations:* walking, music, art, painting. *Address:* 4 The Court, Hoo Gardens, Willingdon, Eastbourne BN20 9AX. *T:* (01323) 506108.

WILCOX, Dame Esther Louise; *see* Rantzen, Dame E. L.

WILCOX, Very Rev. Dr Peter Jonathan; Dean of Liverpool, since 2012; *b* 1961; *m* 1984, Catherine Fox; two *s*. *Educ:* St John's Coll., Durham (BA 1984); Ridley Hall, Cambridge; St John's Coll., Oxford (DPhil 1993). Ordained deacon, 1987, priest, 1988; Curate, Preston on Tees, 1987–90; Non-stipendiary Minister, St Margaret with St Philip and St James with St Giles, Oxford, 1990–93; Team Vicar, St Edmund's Chapel, Gateshead, 1993–98; Dir, Urban Mission Centre, Cranmer Hall, 1993–98; Priest-in-charge, St Paul's at the Crossing, Walsall, 1998–2006; Canon Residentiary, Lichfield Cath., 2006–12. *Publications:* Living the Dream: Joseph for today, 2007; Walking the Walk: the rise of King David for today, 2009; Talking the Talk: the fall of King David for today, 2011. *Address:* Liverpool Cathedral, St James' Mount, Liverpool L1 7AZ. *T:* (0151) 702 7220.

WILCZEK, Prof. Frank Anthony, PhD; Herman Feshbach Professor of Physics, Massachusetts Institute of Technology, since 2000; *b* 15 May 1951; *s* of Frank John Wilczek and Mary Rose Wilczek (*née* Cona); *m* 1973, Elizabeth Jordan Devine; two *d*. *Educ:* Univ. of Chicago (BS 1970); Princeton Univ. (MA 1972; PhD 1974). Princeton University: Asst Prof., 1974–76; Vis. Fellow, Inst. for Advanced Study, 1976–77; Asst Prof., 1977–78; Associate Prof., 1978–80; Prof., 1980–81, 1989–2000; Prof., Univ. of Calif, Santa Barbara, 1980–88. (Jtly) Nobel Prize in Physics, 2004. *Publications:* A Beautiful Question, 2015; articles in learned jls. *Address:* Center for Theoretical Physics, Massachusetts Institute of Technology, 77 Massachusetts Avenue, Cambridge, MA 02139–4307, USA; (home) 4 Wyman Road, Cambridge, MA 02138–2218, USA.

WILD, Dr David; Director of Public Health, South West Thames Regional Health Authority, 1989–90, retired; *b* 27 Jan. 1930; *s* of Frederick and Lena Wild; *m* 1954, Dr Sheila Wightman; one *s* one *d*. *Educ:* Manchester Grammar Sch.; Univ. of Manchester (MB, ChB); Univ. of Liverpool (DPH; FFCM, DMA). Deputy County Medical Officer, 1962, Area Medical Officer, 1974, West Sussex; Regional MO, 1982–86, Dir of Prof. Services, 1986–89, SW Thames RHA. Non-exec. Dir, Worthing DHA, 1990–95. Dir, Inf. Unit for Conf. of Med. Royal Colls and their Faculties in UK, 1991–93. Editor (with Dr Brian Williams), Community Medicine, 1978–84. *Publications:* contribs Jl Central Council of Health Educn, Medical Officer, Archives of Disease in Childhood. *Recreation:* conversation. *Address:* 16 Brandy Hole Lane, Chichester, Sussex PO19 5RY. *T:* (01243) 527125. *E:* davidwild9238@yahoo.com.

WILD, (John) Robin; Chief Dental Officer, Department of Health, 1997–2000; Consultant in Dental Public Health, Dumfries and Galloway Health Board, 2005–07; *b* 12 Sept. 1941; *s* of John Edward Brooke Wild and Teresa (*née* Ballance); *m* 1965, Eleanor Daphne Kerr; two *d* (one *s* decd). *Educ:* Sedbergh Sch., Cumbria; Edinburgh Univ. (BDS); Dundee Univ. (DPD). DGDP RCS; FDS RCSE. Dental practice, 1965–71; Dental Officer, E Lothian CC, 1971–74; Chief Admin. Dental Officer, Borders Health Bd, 1974–87; Regl Dental Postgrad. Advr, SE Scotland, 1982–87; Dep. Chief Dental Officer, Scottish Office, 1987–93; Chief Dental Officer and Dir of Dental Services, NHS, Scottish Office, 1993–97. Pres., Council of European Chief Dental Officers, 1999–2000; Vice Pres., Commonwealth Dental Assoc., 1997–2003. JP Scottish Borders, 1982–2011; Chairman: Scottish Borders Justices Cttee, 2000–05; Dist Courts Assoc., 2002–04; Member: Disciplinary Panel, Inst. and Faculty of Actuaries, 2001–; Judicial Council for Scotland, 2007–09. Life FRSocMed; Fellow, BDA; Founding Fellow, Inst. of Contemp. Scotland. *Publications:* contribs to Scottish Office Health Bulletin. *Address:* Braehead House, St Boswells, Roxburghshire TD6 0AZ. *T:* (01835) 823203. *Clubs:* Royal Society of Medicine, Frontline.

WILD, Prof. Raymond, DSc, PhD; consultant, since 2001; Principal, Henley Management College, 1990–2001; *b* 24 Dec. 1940; *s* of Alice Wild and Frank Wild; *m* 1965, Carol Ann Mellor; one *s* one *d*. *Educ:* Stockport College; Bradford University (PhD (Mgt), MSc (Eng), MSc (Mgt)); DSc Brunel, 1988; WhF. Engineering apprentice, Crossley Bros, 1957–62, design engineer, 1962–63, research engineer, 1963–65; postgrad. student, Bradford Univ., 1965–66; production engineer, English Electric, 1966–67; Res. Fellow then Senior Res. Fellow, Bradford Univ., 1967–73; Dir of Grad. Studies, Admin. Staff Coll., Henley, 1973–77, Mem., Senior Staff, Henley Management Coll., 1973–2001; Brunel University: Dir, Special Engineering Programme, 1977–84; Hd, Dept of Engrg and Management Systems, 1977–86; Hd, Dept of Prodn Technology, 1984–86; Hd, Dept of Manufacturing and Engrg Systems, 1986–89; Pro-Vice-Chancellor, 1988–89. DUniv Brunel, 2001. Editor-in-Chief, Internat. Jl of Computer Integrated Manufacturing Systems, 1988–91. *Publications:* The Techniques of Production Management, 1971; Management and Production, 1972, trans. Greek 1984; (with A. B. Hill and C. C. Ridgeway) Women in the Factory, 1972; Mass Production Management, 1972; (with B. Lowes) Principles of Modern Management, 1972; Work Organization, 1975; Concepts for Operations Management, 1977; Production and Operations Management, 1979, 5th edn 1994; Operations Management: a policy framework, 1980; Essentials of Production and Operations Management, 1980, 5th edn 2002; (ed) Management and Production Readings, 1981; Read and Explain (4 children's books on technology), 1982 and 1983, trans. French, Swedish, German, Danish; How to Manage, 1983, 2nd edn 1995; (ed) International Handbook of Production and Operations Management, 1989; (ed) Technology and Management, 1990; Operations Management, 2001; Essentials of Operations Management, 2001; papers in learned jls. *Recreations:* writing, restoring houses, travel, painting. *Address:* Broomfield, New Road, Shiplake, Henley on Thames, Oxon RG9 3LA. *T:* (0118) 940 4102.

WILD, Robert; Director, Project Underwriting Group, Export Credits Guarantee Department, 1989–92; *b* 19 April 1932; *s* of Thomas Egan Wild and Janet Wild; *m* 1955, Irene Whitton Martin; two *d*. *Educ:* King Edward VII Sch., Lytham. Board of Trade, 1950; Export Credits Guarantee Dept, 1959. *Recreations:* bird watching, archaeology, reading.

WILD, Robin; *see* Wild, J. R.

WILDASH, Richard James, LVO 1997; HM Diplomatic Service; Deputy Head of Mission, Riyadh, since 2014; *b* 24 Dec. 1955; *s* of Arthur Ernest Wildash and Sheila Howard Wildash; *m* 1981, Elizabeth Jane Walmsley; two *d*. *Educ:* Corpus Christi Coll., Cambridge (MA). Joined HM Diplomatic Service, 1977; FCO, 1977–79: Third Secretary: E Berlin, 1979–81; Abidjan, 1981–84; Second Sec., FCO, 1984–88; First Secretary: Harare, 1988–92; FCO, 1992–94; New Delhi, 1994–98; Dep. High Comr, Kuala Lumpur, 1998–2002; High Comr, Cameroon and Ambassador (non-res.), Equatorial Guinea, Gabon, Central African Republic and Chad, 2002–06; High Comr, Malaŵi, 2006–09; Ambassador to Angola and concurrently to São Tomé and Príncipe, 2010–14. AIL 1977, MCIL (MIL 1990). FRGS 1991; FLS 2013. *Recreations:* the arts, travel. *Address:* Flat 5, 26 Medway Street, SW1P 2BD. *E:* wildash@tusker.co.uk.

WILDBLOOD, Stephen Roger; QC 1999; **His Honour Judge Wildblood;** a Circuit Judge, since 2007; Designated Family Judge, Avon, North Somerset and Gloucestershire, since 2013; *b* 18 Aug. 1958; *s* of F. R. J. Wildblood and late P. A. M. Wildblood; *m*; one *s* one *d*; *m* 2003, Emma Jane Bassett; two *s* two *d*. *Educ:* Sheffield Univ. (LLB). Called to the Bar, Inner Temple, 1980; Asst Recorder, 1997–2000; Recorder, 2000–07; Dep. High Court Judge, 2004–07. Legal Mem., Mental Health Review Tribunal, 2003–09. *Publications:* (ed jtly) Encyclopedia of Financial Provision in Family Matters, 1998. *Recreations:* sport, reading, languages. *Address:* Bristol Civil and Family Justice Centre, Redcliff Street, Bristol BS1 6GR.

WILDE, Imogen; Director, British and Foreign School Society, since 2009; Associate, Education Practice, Harvey Nash plc, since 2011 (Director, 2007–11); *b* 22 Jan. 1949; *d* of late John William Luxton and Eva Luxton; *m* 1978, Patrick John Wilde (*d* 1999); two *d*. *Educ:* Colston's Girls' Sch., Bristol; Durham Univ. (BA Hons Hist. 1969). Postgrad. res., Inst. of Historical Research, 1969–71; joined Department of Education and Science, 1971; Sec. to Warnock Cttee on Educn of Children with Special Educnl Needs, 1975–78; Principal Private Sec. to Sec. of State for Educn and Sci., 1982–83; DES, subseq. DFE, 1983–91; Asst Sec., UGC (on secondment), 1986–88; British Petroleum plc (on secondment), 1988–91; various posts DFE, subseq. DfEE, 1991–99, incl. Divl Manager, HE Funding and Orgn, 1997–99; Dir, Curriculum and Communications, subseq. Assessment, Curriculum and e Learning in Schools, DfEE, subseq. DfES, 1999–2002; Dir, Norman Broadbent, 2003–07. *Address:* British and Foreign School Society, Maybrook House, Godstone Road, Caterham CR3 6RE. *T:* (01883) 331177. *E:* director@bfss.org.uk.

WILDE, John; HM Diplomatic Service, retired; High Commissioner to Botswana, 1998–2001; *b* 6 Oct. 1941; *s* of John William and Clara Wilde; *m* 1965, Jeanette Grace Reed; one *s* one *d*. *Educ:* Malet Lambert Sch., Hull. Foreign Office, 1959; served Conakry, Pretoria, Kuwait, Tripoli, FCO and Zagreb, to 1976; Singapore, 1976–79; FCO, 1979–82; Asst to Dep. Governor, Gibraltar, 1982–85; jsdc, 1985; First Sec., FCO, 1985–87; Dep. High Comr, Lilongwe, 1987–91; FCO, 1991–95 (Mem., EC Monitor to former Yugoslavia, 1991; ECMM Service Medal, 1994); High Comr, The Gambia, 1995–98. *Recreations:* golf, music, reading. *Address:* 115 Main Street, Willerby, E Yorks HU10 6DA.

WILDEN, Jonathan James; Headmaster, Wallington County Grammar School, since 2013 (Deputy Headteacher, 2010–13); Executive Headteacher, WCGS Academy Trust, since 2015; *b* Ipswich, Suffolk, 8 Jan. 1976; *s* of John Edward and Margaret Patricia Wilden; *m* 2005, Joann Marie Croudace; two *s* one *d*. *Educ:* St Joseph's Coll., Ipswich; Univ. of Wales, Lampeter (BA Hons Geog.); Univ. of Bath (PGCE); Univ. of Sussex (DipEd); Inst. of Educn (NPQH). Teacher of Geography: St Andrew's Sch., Leatherhead, 1998–99; Riddlesdown High Sch., Croydon, 1999–2003; Subject Leader for Geog., Wimbledon Coll., 2003–09; Dep Headteacher, Evelyn Grace Acad., Brixton, 2009–10. *Recreations:* triathlon and adventure racing, climbing Munros, open water swimming, family. *Address:* Wallington County Grammar School, Croydon Road, Wallington, Surrey SM6 7PH. *Clubs:* Lansdowne; Tri Surrey Triathlon (Co-Founder and Chm., 2012–) (Sanderstead, Surrey), Walcountians Sports (Surrey).

WILDGOOSE, James Richmond, DPhil; Head, Scotland Office, 2005–07; *b* 17 April 1949; *s* of Thomas Wildgoose and Annie Wildgoose; *m* 1982, (Charlotte) Dorothy Campbell; one *s* one *d*. *Educ:* Melville Coll., Edinburgh; Univ. of Edinburgh (BSc 1971); DPhil Oxon 1978. Economist and policy postings, MAFF, 1975–90; Chief Economist, Agric. and Fisheries Dept, Scottish Office, 1990–96, Hd of Profession, 1994–95; Rural Affairs Department, Scottish Office, then Scottish Executive: Hd, Food Safety Animal Health and Welfare Div., 1996–2000; Hd, CAP Mgt Div., 2000–02; Hd, Agricl Policy and Food Div., 2002–05. Member: Scottish Food Adv. Cttee, 2009– (Chm., 2012–); Bd, Food Standards Agency, 2011–15. *Recreations:* bridge, piano, travel.

WILDING, Alison, RA 1999; sculptor; *b* Blackburn, Lancs, 7 July 1948; *m*. *Educ:* Nottingham Coll. of Art; Ravensbourne Coll. of Art and Design, Bromley, Kent; Royal Coll. of Art. Solo exhibitions include: Serpentine Gall., London, 1985; MOMA, NY, 1987; retrospective, Tate Gall., Liverpool, 1991; New Art Centre, Roche Court, Wilts, 1997, 2000; Northern Gall. for Contemp. Art, Sunderland, 1998; Henry Moore Foundn Studio, Dean Clough Galls, Halifax, 2000; group exhibitions in UK, Ireland and Canada. Sculpture in public places incl. Ambit, Sunderland, 1999. *Address:* c/o Karsten Schubert, 5–8 Lower John Street, Golden Square, W1F 9DR.

WILDING, Barbara, CBE 2006; QPM 2000; Chief Constable, South Wales Police Authority, 2004–09; *m* Jeffrey E. Rees, QPM; two *d*. *Educ:* London Sch. of Econs (Dip. Criminology, 1980). WPC, States of Jersey Police; Detective, Metropolitan Police; Asst Chief Constable, Personnel, 1994–96, Crime, 1996–98, Kent Constabulary; Dep. Asst Comr, Corporate Strategic Resourcing, 1998–2000, Security and Protection Comd, 2000–03, Metropolitan Police. Member: RIIA, 2001–; RCDS, 2003–; Nat. Exec. Inst., FBI, 2005–; Adv. Bd, BITC Wales, 2006–09; Council, Prince's Trust Cymru, 2006–09; Bd, Big Lottery Cymru, 2006–14; Internat. Adv. Gp, Cardiff Business Sch., 2008–11; Adv. Bd, Out of Trouble Prison Reform Trust, 2009–12; Council, High Sheriff Assoc., 2012. Founder, Univ. Police Sci. Inst., Univ. of S Wales (formerly Glamorgan Univ.) and Cardiff Univ., 2007–. Gov., Cardiff Metropolitan Univ. (formerly UWIC), 2010– (Chm., 2011–). Trustee: S Wales Police Youth Trust, 2009–12; Nat. Crimebeat, 2010– (Chm., 2013–); Butler Trust, 2014–. Life Member: ACPO, 2010; British Assoc. of Women Police, 2010. Vice President: Age Cymru, 2010; Cardiff Business Club, 2011. Liveryman, Livery Co. of Wales (formerly Mem., Welsh Livery Guild), 2006. CCMI 2005. FRSA 2006. High Sheriff, Mid Glamorgan, 2011–12. Hon. Fellow: Cardiff Univ., 2007; Swansea Univ., 2009. DUniv Glamorgan, 2008. *E:* rt.associates@live.co.uk.

WILDING, Christine Mary; Director, British Institute of Florence, 1998–2003; *b* 7 Oct. 1941; *d* of Lionel Walter Haines and Marjorie Gibson Haines (*née* Hall); *m* 1964, Malcolm David Wilding (marr. diss. 1999); two *s* one *d*. *Educ:* Univ. of Leeds (BA Italian 1962). Various teaching posts, 1963–78; Res. Asst, Univ. of Aston, 1979–82; Sec., Jt Council of Lang. Assocs, 1982–89; Dir, Assoc. for Lang. Learning, 1989–97. Vis. Lectr, Univs of Warwick and Aston in Birmingham, 1977–79. Co-ordinator, Fest. of Langs and Young Linguists Awards, 1982–92. Mem., Bd of Trustees, Studio Art Centers Internat. Florence, 2015– (Mem., President's Adv. Council, 2009–15). Chevalier, Ordre des Palmes Académiques (France), 1988. *Publications:* research papers and articles to promote use of foreign langs in business, and to motivate language learning. *Recreations:* family, cooking, walking, art history, Italy, meeting people, travel. *Address:* Les Cèdres, 1 rue des Tilleuls, 74500 Amphion-les-Bains, Haute Savoie, France. *T:* (04) 50810868. *E:* cwilding04@gmail.com.
See also Prof. R. D. Wilding.

WILDING, Keith; His Honour Judge Wilding; a Circuit Judge, since 2013; *b* London, 9 Feb. 1953; *s* of Sidney and Lilian Wilding; *m* 1973, Jane Catherine Flanagan; two *d*. *Educ:* London Nautical Sch.; Coll. of Law, London. Admitted as solicitor, 1977; a Dep. Dist Judge, 1991–2002; a Dist Judge, 2002–13. *Recreations:* family, Rugby, golf, theatre, cinema. *Address:* Watford Family and County Court, Cassiobury House, 11–19 Station Road, Watford WD17 1EZ. *Club:* Old Albanian Rugby Football.

WILDING, Prof. Richard David, OBE 2013; PhD; FIET; FCILT; Professor and Chair of Supply Chain Strategy (formerly Professor and Chair of Supply Chain Risk Management), Cranfield School of Management, Cranfield University, since 2010; *b* Sheffield, 8 May 1965; *s* of Dr Malcolm David Wilding and Christine Mary Wilding, *qv*; *m* 1990, Janice Caroline

Lowe; one *s* one *d*. *Educ:* Princethorpe Coll., Princethorpe, Rugby; Univ. of Sheffield (BSc Tech. Hons); Univ. of Warwick (PhD Engrg 1998). Prodn Manager, Steetley Brick and Concrete Products Ltd, Newcastle-under-Lyme, 1987–89; systems engr, IMI Refiners Ltd, Walsall, 1989–91; Fellow, 1991–93, Sen. Fellow, 1993–97, and Principal Fellow in Logistics and Supply Chain Mgt, 1997–98, Warwick Mfg Gp, Univ. of Warwick; Cranfield School of Management, Centre for Logistics and Supply Chain Management, Cranfield University: Lectr, 1998–2000; Sen. Lectr, 2000–02; Director: In-company Progs, 2002–04; Customised Progs, 2004–06; Prof. and Chair of Supply Chain Risk Mgt, 2006–10. Vis. Prof., RMIT, 2008–10. Institute of Logistics and Transportation Research Network, CILT: Mem., Dirs' Forum, 1991–2010, Exec. Cttee, Leaders in Supply Chain, UK, 2010– (Co-Chm., 2012–); Founding Mem., Steering Cttee, 1994; Tech. Advr, careers video, 1998–99; Bd Dir and Trustee, 2011–. Advr on ops mgt and supply chain texts to Internat. Thompson Publishing and Wiley Publishing, 1999–. Vice Patron, Beds Garden Carers, 2012–. Freeman: City of London, 2013; Carmen's Co., 2012 (Liveryman, 2013). FHEA (Fellow, Inst. for Learning and Teaching in HE 2001); FCILT 2006; FIET 2007. Dist. Service Award, Eur. Supply Chain Distinction Awards, 2008; Individual Contribution Award, Eur. Supply Chain Excellence Awards, 2010; Viscount Nuffield Silver Medal for Achievement in Design and Production, IET, 2013. *Publications:* contributor: Idol-Lottery (poetry), 1997; The Gower Handbook of Purchasing Management, 3rd edn 2002; World Market Series Business Briefings: global purchasing and supply chain strategies 2004, 2004; (jtly) The Financial Times Handbook of Management, 3rd edn 2004; (jtly) Managing Business Risk: a practical guide to protecting your business, 3rd edn 2006; articles in British Jl Mgt, Internat. Jl Physical Distribn and Logistics Mgt, Eur. Jl Mktg, Jl Mktg Mgt, Supply Chain Mgt, FT. *Recreations:* walking, pinball and jukebox, cleaning cars (car detailing), very amateur magician, BBQs, supporting local Church. *Address:* Cranfield School of Management, Cranfield, Bedford MK43 0AL. *T:* (01234) 751122. *W:* www.richardwilding.info.

WILDING, Richard William Longworth, CB 1979; Head of Office of Arts and Libraries, Cabinet Office, 1984–88; *b* 22 April 1929; *er s* of late L. A. Wilding; *m* 1954, Mary Rosamund de Villiers (*d* 2014); one *s* two *d*. *Educ:* Dragon Sch., Oxford; Winchester Coll.; New Coll., Oxford (MA). HM Foreign Service, 1953–59; transf. to Home Civil Service, 1959; Principal, HM Treasury, 1959–67; Sec., Fulton Cttee on Civil Service, 1966–68; Asst Sec., Civil Service Dept, 1968–70; Asst Sec., Supplementary Benefits Commn, DHSS, 1970–72; Under-Sec., Management Services, 1972–76, Pay, 1976, CSD; Deputy Secretary: CSD, 1976–81; HM Treasury, 1981–83. Review of Structure of Arts Funding in England, 1989; Review of Redundant Churches Fund, 1990. Trustee, Nat. Museums and Galleries on Merseyside, 1989–97. *Publications:* (with L. A. Wilding) A Classical Anthology, 1954; Key to Latin Course for Schools, 1966; The Care of Redundant Churches, 1990; Civil Servant - a memoir, 2006; The Odyssey of Homer - a new translation, 2011; articles in Jl Public Administration, Social Work Today, Studies. *Address:* 22 Deanery Walk, Avonpark Village, Limpley Stoke, Bath BA2 7JQ. *Club:* Athenæum.

WILDISH, Vice-Adm. Denis Bryan Harvey, CB 1968; *b* 24 Dec. 1914; *s* of late Engr Rear-Adm. Sir Henry William Wildish, KBE, CB; *m* 1941, Leslie Henrietta Jacob; two *d*. *Educ:* RNC Dartmouth; RNEC. Entered Royal Navy, 1932; sea service HM Ships Ramillies, Revenge, Nelson, 1932–39; War service, Atlantic, Mediterranean, FE, HM Ships Prince of Wales, Kedah and Isis (despatches); subseq. various Admiralty appts; HMS Implacable, 1946–48; Planning Staff, Exercise Trident, 1948–49; Asst Naval Attaché, Rome, Berne, 1951–53; HMS Eagle, 1953–56; Asst Dir, then Dir, Fleet Maintenance, 1960–64; Commodore Naval Drafting and i/c HMS Centurion, 1964–66; Adm. Supt, HM Dockyard, Devonport, 1966–70; Dir Gen. of Personal Services and Trng (Navy) and Dep. Second Sea Lord, 1970–72; retired. Rep. RN at cricket, also RN, Combined Services, Devon, and W of England (Divisional Trials), at hockey. *Recreations:* walking, cricket, painting (Mem., Armed Forces Art Soc.). *Address:* Flat 4 Armstrong House, Front Street, Bamburgh, Northumberland NE69 7BJ. *Clubs:* Army and Navy, MCC; I Zingari, XL, Incogniti, Devon Dumplings, Royal Navy Cricket.

WILDMAN, Maj. Gen. Murray Leslie, CBE 2001; business consultant, 2001–12; Director General, Whole Fleet Management, Ministry of Defence, 1999–2001; *b* 10 Feb. 1947; *s* of late Peter Wildman and Margery Wildman (*née* Littlechild) and step *s* of Elizabeth Susan Wildman (*née* White); *m* 1974, Lindsay Anne Johnson. *Educ:* Reading Sch.; Royal Military Coll. of Sci. (BSc (Eng) 1969). CEng 1987; Eur Ing 1991; FIET (FIEE 1991). Army service, 1968–2001, mainly in engrg and equipt support field; rcds 1993; Dir, Equipt Support, MoD, 1993–96; Defence Advr, Pretoria, S Africa, 1996–99. Dir, Defence Business Solutions Ltd, 2001–12. Non-exec. Dir, G3 Systems Ltd, 2003–08. Chm., CCF Assoc., 2004–11. Chm., ABF Fundraising Cttee, Wilts, 2001–12. President: TA Rifle Assoc., 2006–14; Old Redingensians Assoc., 2010. *Recreations:* ski-ing, classic cars. *Clubs:* Victory Services; Alpbach Visitors Ski.

WILDOR, Sarah; ballet dancer; *b* 1972; *m* Adam Cooper, *qv*; one *d*. *Educ:* Royal Ballet Sch. Royal Ballet, 1991–2001: soloist, 1994; Principal, 1999; main rôles include: Juliet, in Romeo and Juliet; Giselle; Ondine; Manon; Anastasia; Cinderella; Titania, in The Dream; Lise, in La Fille Mal Gardée; with Adventures in Motion Pictures, Cinderella, 1998; The Two Pigeons, Scottish Ballet, 2002; (and acted) Contact, Queen's, 2002; On Your Toes, RFH, 2003; Les Liaisons Dangereuses, Japan, then Sadler's Wells, 2005; You Can't Take It With You, Southwark Playhouse, 2007; Shall We Dance, Sadler's Wells, 2009.

WILDS, Ven. Anthony Ronald; Archdeacon of Plymouth, 2001–10; *b* 4 Oct. 1943; *s* of Ernest and Eva Wilds; *m* 1967, Elizabeth Mary Prince; three *d*. *Educ:* Univ. of Durham (BA 1964); Bishops' Coll., Cheshunt. Ordained deacon, 1966, priest, 1967, Asst Curate, Newport Pagnell, 1966–72; Priest in charge, Chipili, Zambia, 1972–75; Vicar: Chandlers Ford, Hants, 1975–85; Andover, Hants, 1985–97; Rector, Solihull, W Midlands, 1997–2001. *Recreations:* travel, walking, gardening, Rugby Union. *Address:* 9 Rue du Commerce, Meigne le Vicomte 49490, France. *T:* (2) 41822452.

WILDSMITH, Brian Lawrence; artist and maker of picture books for young children; *b* 22 Jan. 1930; *s* of Paul Wildsmith and Annie Elizabeth Oxley; *m* 1955, Aurelie Janet Craigie Ithurbide; one *s* three *d*. *Educ:* de la Salle Coll.; Barnsley Sch. of Art; Slade Sch. of Fine Arts. Art Master, Selhurst Grammar School for Boys, 1954–57; freelance artist, 1975–. Exhibitions include: World of Seven English Picture Book Artists, tour of Japan, 1998–99; one-man shows: Hong Kong, Kobe, Yokohama, Mihara, Imabari, 1992; Nakano, Sumida (both Tokyo), Fukuoka, Sendai, Kuwana, Yamaguchi, 1993; World of Brian Wildsmith, Tokyo and tour of Japan, 1995; New World of Brian Wildsmith, Tokyo and tour of Japan, 1997; World of Nursery Tales, Fukui, 1997; Brian Wildsmith Mus. of Art, Kohoku Tokyu, 1998; Kyoto Mus., 2000; Okazaki Mus. for Children, 2001; Taiwan Mus. of Fine Art and tour of Japan, 2004; retrospective exhibn, Fantasia from a Fairy Land, Tokyo Fuji Art Mus., and tour of Japan, 2003; lecture tours in USA, Canada, S Africa, Japan, Australia and NZ. Production design, illustrations, titles and graphics for first USA-USSR Leningrad film co-production of the Blue Bird, 1974. Brian Wildsmith Museum opened Izukogen, Japan, 1994. Mem. Bd of Visitors, Mazza Galleria, Univ. of Findlay, USA, 1999–. Kate Greenaway Medal, 1962; Soka Gakkai Japan Educn Medal, 1988; USHIO Publication Culture Award, 1991; Gold Medal, Tokyo Fuji Mus., 2003. *Publications:* ABC, 1962 (Kate Greenaway Award, 1962); The Lion and the Rat, 1963; The North Wind and the Sun, 1964; Mother Goose, 1964; 1; 2; 3;, 1965; The Rich Man and the Shoemaker, 1965; A Child's Garden of Verses (Lewis Carroll Shelf Award, 1966); The Hare and the Tortoise, 1966; Birds, 1967; Animals, 1967; Fish, 1968; The Miller, the Boy and the Donkey, 1969; The Circus, 1970; Puzzles, 1970; The Owl and the Woodpecker, 1971; The Twelve Days of Christmas, 1972; The Little Wood Duck, 1972; The Lazy Bear, 1973; Squirrels, 1974; Pythons Party, 1974; The Blue Bird, 1976; The True Cross, 1977; What the Moon Saw, 1978; Hunter and his Dog, 1979; Animal Shapes, 1980; Animal Homes, 1980; Animal Games, 1980; Animal Tricks, 1980; The Seasons, 1980; Professor Noah's Spaceship, 1980; Bears Adventure, 1981; The Trunk, 1982; Cat on the Mat, 1982; Pelican, 1982; The Apple Bird, 1983; The Island, 1983; All Fall Down, 1983; The Nest, 1983; Daisy, 1984; Who's Shoes, 1984; Toot Toot, 1984; Give a Dog a Bone, 1985; Goats Trail, 1986; My Dream, 1986; What a Tail, 1986; If I Were You, 1987; Giddy Up…, 1987; Carousel, 1988; The Christmas Story, 1989; The Snow Country Prince, 1990; The Cherry Tree, 1991; The Princess and the Moon, 1991; Over the Deep Blue Sea, 1992; The Easter Story, 1993; Noah's Ark Pop Up, 1994; Saint Francis, 1995; The Creation (pop up), 1995; Brian Wildsmith's Amazing World of Words, 1996; (with HIH Princess Hisako Takamodo) Katie and the Dream Eater, 1996; Joseph, 1997; Exodus, 1998; The Bremen Town Band, 1999; The Seven Ravens, 2000; My Flower, 2000; If Only, 2000; Knock Knock, 2000; Not Here, 2000; Can You Do This?, 2000; How Many, 2000; Jesus, 2000; Mary, 2002; The Road to Bethlehem, 2003; with Rebecca Wildsmith: Wake Up Wake Up, 1993; Whose Hat Was That?, 1993; Look Closer, 1993; What Did I Find?, 1993; Jack and the Meanstalk, 1995; Footprints in the Snow, 1996; Tug, Tug, 1996; Christmas Crib: a nativity pop up and story, 2003. *Recreation:* music (piano). *Address:* 11 Castellaras Le-Vieux, 333 Allee Du Domaine, 06370 Mouans-Sartoux, France. *T:* 0493752411.

WILDSMITH, Prof. John Anthony Winston, (Tony), MD; FRCA, FRCPE, FRCSE, FDSRCS; Foundation Professor and Head of Department of Anaesthesia, University of Dundee, 1995–2007; Hon. Consultant Anaesthetist, Tayside University (formerly Dundee Teaching) Hospitals NHS Trust, 1995–2007; *b* 22 Feb. 1946; *s* of Winston Wildsmith and Phyllis Wildsmith (*née* Jones); *m* 1969, Angela Fay Smith; three *d*. *Educ:* King's Sch., Gloucester; Edinburgh Univ. Med. Sch. (MB ChB 1969; MD 1982). FRCA (FFARCS 1973); FRCPE 1996; FRCSE 2005; FDSRCS 2008. Grad. Res. Fellow, Dept of Physiology and Anaesthetics, Univ. of Edinburgh, 1971–72; Rotating Registrar in Anaesthesia, Edinburgh Trng Scheme, 1972–75; Lectr in Anaesthesia, Univ. of Edinburgh, 1975–77; Royal Infirmary of Edinburgh: Consultant Anaesthetist, 1977–95; part-time Sen. Lectr, 1977–95; Clin. Dir of Anaesthesia, Theatres and Intensive Care, 1992–95. Vis. Lectr in Anaesthesia, Harvard Med. Sch., 1983–84. President: Scottish Soc. of Anaesthetists, 2003–04; History of Anaesthesia Soc., 2008–10; Dundee Med. Club, 2008–09. Mem. Council, RCAnaes, 1997–2007 (Hon. Archivist, 2012–15). *Publications:* edited jointly: Principles and Practice of Regional Anaesthesia, 1987 (trans. German 1991), 4th edn 2013; Induced Hypotension, 1991; Conduction Blockade for Postoperative Analgesia, 1991; Anaesthesia for Vascular Surgery, 2000; chapters and papers on aspects of regional anaesthesia, acute pain relief, induced hypotension and history of anaesthesia. *Recreations:* golf, travel, wine, model railways. *Address:* 6 Castleroy Road, Broughty Ferry, Dundee DD5 2LQ. *T:* (01382) 732451. *Clubs:* Royal Automobile; Royal Burgess Golfing Soc.

WILES, Sir Andrew (John), KBE 2000; PhD; FRS 1989; Professor of Mathematics, 1982–88 and since 1990, and James S. McDonnell Professor of Mathematics, since 2009, Princeton University (Eugene Higgins Professor, 1994); Royal Society 2010 Anniversary Research Professor, Mathematical Institute, University of Oxford, since 2011; Fellow, Merton College, Oxford, since 2011; *b* 11 April 1953; *s* of Rev. Prof. Maurice Frank Wiles, FBA; *m*; two *d*. *Educ:* Merton Coll., Oxford (BA 1974; MA 1988; Hon. Fellow); Clare Coll., Cambridge (MA 1977; PhD 1980). Jun. Res. Fellow, Clare Coll., Cambridge, 1977–80; IAS, Princeton Univ., 1981; Guggenheim Fellow, Paris, 1985–86; Royal Society Res. Prof. in Maths and Professorial Fellow of Merton Coll., Oxford Univ., 1988–90. Solved and proved Fermat's Last Theorem, 1994. For. Mem., US NAS, 1996; Hon. Mem., LMS, 2001. Hon. DSc: Oxon, 1999; Cambridge, 2010. (Jtly) Jun. Whitehead Prize, LMS, 1988; Royal Medal, Royal Soc., 1996; IMU Silver Plaque, 1998. *Publications:* Modular elliptic curves and Fermat's Last Theorem, in Annals of Mathematics, 1995; contrib. to learned jls. *Address:* Department of Mathematics, Princeton University, 602 Fine Hall, Washington Road, Princeton, NJ 08544, USA; Mathematical Institute, University of Oxford, Andrew Wiles Building, Radcliffe Observatory Quarter, Woodstock Road, Oxford OX2 6GG.

WILES, Clive Spencer; a District Judge (Magistrates' Courts) (formerly Stipendiary Magistrate), Middlesex, 1996–2013; *b* 1 Dec. 1942; *s* of late Ernest George Wiles and of Emily Louise Wiles (*née* Cummings); *m* 1966, Marie Susan Glasgow; two *s*. *Educ:* Leggatts Sch., Watford. Articled clerk to Clerk to Justices, Watford, 1962–67; admitted Solicitor, 1968; Solicitor, subseq. Partner, Ellis Hancock, Watford, later Hancock Quins, 1968–96. *Recreations:* golf, walking, gardening, reading, photography.

WILES, Harry; HM Diplomatic Service, retired; Ambassador to Nicaragua, 2000–02; *b* 17 June 1944; *s* of John Horace Wiles and Margaret, (Peggy), Wiles; *m* 1966, Margaret Bloom; two *d*. *Educ:* Hull Grammar Sch. Joined Foreign Office, 1964: Ankara, 1966–68; Paris, 1969–72; Algiers, 1972–75; FCO, 1975–78; Vice Consul, Bilbao, 1978–81; Third Sec. (Admin), Jedda, 1981–83; Second Secretary: (Admin), Riyadh, 1983–84; (Commercial), Abu Dhabi, 1984–88; Second, later First, Sec., on loan to ECGD, 1988–90; Consul (Commercial) and Dep. Consul Gen., Barcelona, 1990–94; First Sec. (Commercial), Buenos Aires, 1994–98; Dep. Hd of Security Comd, FCO, 1998–2000. *Recreations:* golf, Rugby League (spectating), music, reading.

WILES, Air Vice-Marshal Matthew John Gethin, CB 2013; CBE 2008; FCILT; FCIPS; FCIPD; Strategic Partnership Director, Serco Strategic Partnerships, since 2014; Operations Director and Managing Director, Serco Defence, since 2014; *b* 9 Feb. 1961; *s* of Wallace and Elizabeth Anne Wiles; *m* 1989, Rebecca White; one *d*. *Educ:* Fakenham Grammar Sch.; Open Univ. (MBA 2000). Jun. logistics roles, 1982–90; PSO to DG Support Mgt (RAF), 1990–92; OC Supply and Movts Sqn, RAF Odiham, 1992–94; RAF Advanced Staff Course, 1995; Wing Comdr Resources, HQ Strike Comd, 1995–96; Head of Tri Star/Royal Sqn Support Authy, 1996–98; Prog. Dir, Defence Logistics Orgn, 1998–2001; RCDS, 2002; Asst Dir Internat., MoD (Air Staff), 2002–04; Dir Supply Chain Support, Defence Logistics Orgn, 2004–06; HCSC 2005; ACOS Personnel and Logistics, UK Perm. Jt HQ, 2006–07; Hd, RAF Logistics (formerly Supply) Branch, 2007–11; Dir Gen. Jt Supply Chain, later Dir Jt Support Chain, Defence Equipment and Support, 2008–10; Comd Exec. Officer, HQ Air Comd, 2010–11; Air Sec. and COS Personnel, HQ Air Comd, 2011–13. FCILT 1998; FCIPS 2009; FCIPD 2013. *Recreations:* collecting (and sampling) fine wine, horse riding, travel, keeping up with my family. *E:* matt.wiles@serco.com. *Club:* Royal Air Force (Chm., Bd of Trustees, 2008–10, 2012–14; Vice-Pres., 2014–).

WILES, Paul Noel Porritt, CB 2005; Chief Scientific Adviser, and Director of Research, Development and Statistics, Home Office, 2002–10 (Director of Research, 1999–2002); Government Chief Social Scientist, 2007–10; *b* 24 Dec. 1944; *m* 1989, Merlyn Alice Greenhalgh (*née* Morton); one *s* one *d*, and three step *s*. *Educ:* London Sch. of Economics (BSc Econ. 1967); Trinity Hall, Cambridge (Dip Criminol. 1968). Lectr in Sociology, LSE, 1969–70; Res. Fellow, Inst. of Criminology, Univ. of Cambridge, 1970–72; University of Sheffield: Lectr in Criminology, 1972–76, Sen. Lectr, 1976–88; Dir, Centre for Criminological and Socio-legal Studies, 1985–89; Prof. of Criminology, 1988–99; Dean, Faculty of Law, 1990–96. Vis. Prof. of Criminology, Univ. of Oxford, 2006–09; Fellow, Wolfson Coll., Oxford, 2006–09. Member: Local Govt Boundary Commn for England, 2010–; Bd, Food Standards Agency, 2012–. Mem., Mechanics Inst., Eyam, 1979–. *Publications:* monographs, contribs to books, and papers in learned jls on criminology and socio-legal studies. *Recreation:* fell walking.

WILEY, Francesca; QC 2015; *b* London, 1971; *d* of Stewart and Catherine Wiley; *m* 1993, Carl Slater; two *c*. *Educ:* Trinity Coll., Oxford (BA). Called to the Bar, Gray's Inn, 1996; in practice as barrister, 1996–, specialising in family and criminal law. *Recreations:* ski-ing, sailing, cinema, music. *Address:* 1 Garden Court, Temple, EC4Y 9BJ. *T:* (020) 7797 7900. *E:* wiley@1gc.com.

WILFORD, Daisy Georgia; *see* Goodwin, D. G.

WILFORD, (Jacqueline Lee) Penelope; *see* Woods-Wilford, J. L. P.

WILFORD, Michael James, CBE 2001; RIBA; architect; Senior Partner, Michael Wilford Architects, since 2000; *b* 9 Sept. 1938; *s* of James Wilford and Kathleen Wilford; *m* 1960, Angela Spearman; two *s* three *d*. *Educ:* Kingston Tech. Sch.; Northern Poly. Sch. of Architecture; Regent St Poly Planning Sch. (Hons DipArch with Dist.). Sen. Asst to James Stirling and James Gowan, 1960–63; Associate Partner, with James Stirling, 1964–71; Partner, James Stirling, Michael Wilford and Associates, 1971–92; Senior Partner: Michael Wilford and Partners, 1993–2000; Wilford Schupp Architekten, 2002–13. Major projects include: Staatsgalerie, Stuttgart, 1983; Clore Gall., Tate Gall., 1986; Tate Gall., Liverpool, 1988; No 1 Poultry, 1996; The Lowry, Salford, 2000; British Embassy, Berlin, 2000; Esplanade, Theatres on the Bay, Singapore, 2001; History Mus., Stuttgart, 2002; Carnegie Liby and Acad., Peace Palace, The Hague, 2007; British Embassy, Tbilisi, 2010; Carnegie Visitor Centre, Peace Palace, The Hague, 2012. Hon. Mem., Bund Deutscher Architekten, 1997. Hon. FAIA 2006. Hon. DLitt: Sheffield, 1987; Salford, 2002; Hon. DSc: Newcastle, Australia, 1993; Leicester, 2011. *Publications:* Recent Work of James Stirling, Michael Wilford and Associates, 1990; James Stirling, Michael Wilford and Associates Design Philosophy and Recent Projects, 1990; The Museums of James Stirling and Michael Wilford, 1990; James Stirling and Michael Wilford Architectural Monograph, 1993; James Stirling, Michael Wilford and Associates Buildings and Projects 1975–1992, 1994; Wilford-Stirling-Wilford, 1996; Michael Wilford and Partners, 1999; Michael Wilford - Selected Buildings and Projects 1992–2012, 2014; Stirling + Wilford: American buildings, 2014. *Recreation:* earth moving and landscaping. *Address:* Lone Oak Hall, Chuck Hatch, Hartfield, E Sussex TN7 4EX. *T:* (01892) 770980. *E:* michaelwilford@michaelwilford.com.

WILIAM, Eurwyn, PhD; FSA; Chairman, Royal Commission on Ancient and Historical Monuments in Wales, since 2009 (Vice-Chairman, 2003–06; Member, 1993–2006); *b* 26 Feb. 1949; *s* of Griffith Owen Williams and Morfudd (*née* Griffith); surname changed to Wiliam, 1970; *m* 1974, Mary Middleton; one *s* one *d*. *Educ:* Botwnnog Grammar Sch.; Univ. of Wales Cardiff (BA Hons Archaeol. 1970); Univ. of Manchester (MA 1972; PhD 1980). FSA 1993. Welsh Folk Museum, National Museum of Wales: Asst Keeper, 1971–76, Asst Keeper in charge, 1976–80, Keeper, 1980–84, Dept of Buildings; Keeper, Dept of Buildings and Domestic Life, 1984–91; Curator, 1991–94; Amgueddfa Cymru - Nat. Mus. Wales (formerly Nat. Mus and Galls of Wales): Assistant Director: Museums Develt, 1994–96; Collections and Res., 1996–99; Dir of Collections and Res. and Dep. Dir-Gen., 1999–2009, now Emeritus Keeper; Acting Dir-Gen., 2002–03. Mem., Historic Buildings Council for Wales, 1994–2004; non-exec. Dir, Council of Museums in Wales, 2003–04; Vice-Pres., ICOMOS UK, 2007–10. Pres., Welsh Mills Soc., 1990–; Trustee, Nantgarw China Clay Works Trust, 2007–. Chm., Ethnology and Folk Life Section, Guild of Grads, Univ. of Wales, 1993–2005 (Pres., 2005–). Hon. Prof., Sch. of Hist. and Archaeol., Univ. of Wales Cardiff, 1993–2005. *Publications:* Traditional Farm Buildings in North-East Wales 1550–1900, 1982; The Historical Farm Buildings of Wales, 1986; Home-made Homes, 1988; Hen Adeiladau Fferm, 1992; Welsh Long-houses, 1992; Welsh Cruck Barns, 1994; The Welsh Cottage, 2010; Y Bwthyn Cymreig, 2010; numerous articles in learned jls. *Recreations:* books, antiques, art, travel. *Address:* 42 St Fagans Drive, St Fagans, Cardiff CF5 6EF.

WILK, Christopher David; Keeper, Furniture, Textiles and Fashion Department, Victoria & Albert Museum, since 2001; *b* 28 Dec. 1954; *s* of Maurice Wilk and Norma Wilk (*née* Bloomberg); *m* 1st, 1980, Susan Harris (marr. diss. 1983); 2nd, 1984, Ann Curtis (marr. diss. 1997); two *d*; 3rd, 2002, Carolyn Sargentson; one *s*. *Educ:* Vassar Coll. (AB 1976); Columbia Univ. (MA 1979). Researcher, 1976–78, Curatorial Asst, 1978–79, NY Mus. of Modern Art; freelance curator and writer, 1979–82; Asst Curator, 1982–87, Associate Curator, 1987–88, Brooklyn Mus.; Victoria and Albert Museum: Asst Keeper, 1988–90; Curator and Head of Dept, 1990–96; Chief Curator, Furniture and Woodwork Dept, and British Galls Project, 1996–2001. Member: Adv. Council, The Art Fund (formerly NACF), 1992–; Adv. Bd, American Mus. in Bath, 2005–; Member Council: Attingham Trust, 1989–2003; 20th Century Soc., 1990–97; Furniture History Soc., 1992–2002 (Chm., Ingram Fund, 1995–2002, Reviews Ed., 1995–2006); Trustee: Emery Walker Trust, 2007–; Isokon Trust, 2005–11. Editl Advr, Studies in the Decorative Arts, 1993–2009. *Publications:* Thonet: 150 years of furniture, 1980; Marcel Breuer: furniture and interiors, 1981; Frank Lloyd Wright: the Kaufmann Office, 1993; (ed) Western Furniture, 1996; (ed) Creating the British Galleries at the V&A: a study in museology, 2004; (ed) Modernism: designing a new world, 2006; contribs to learned jls. *Recreations:* cycling, soccer (Brentford FC), music. *Address:* Furniture, Textiles and Fashion Department, Victoria and Albert Museum, SW7 2RL. *T:* (020) 7942 2286.

WILKEN, Sean David Henry; QC 2010; barrister; *b* Bromley, 20 Aug. 1967; *s* of J. H. F. Wilken and E. W. Wilken; *m* 1999, Theresa Anne Villiers (marr. diss.); partner, Julia Smith; one *s*. *Educ:* Hulme Grammar Sch., Oldham; Brasenose Coll., Oxford (BA Hons 1989); City Univ., London (DipLaw 1990). Called to the Bar, Middle Temple, 1991; in practice as a barrister, 1993–; Counsel, Attorney Gen.'s A Panel, 2003–10. UK Legal Rep., Fedn Internat. du Ski, 2010. *Publications:* Waiver, Variation and Estoppel (jtly), 1998, 3rd edn as The Law of Waiver, Variation and Estoppel, 2012. *Recreations:* ski-ing, climbing, hiking, fencing, diving, photography. *Address:* 39 Essex Street, WC2R 3AT. *T:* (020) 7832 1111, *Fax:* (020) 7353 3978. *E:* sean.wilken@39essex.com. *Clubs:* Lansdowne, Ivy.

WILKES, Rev. David Edward, CB 2008; OBE 1995; Chaplain-General to the Land Forces, 2004–08; *b* 7 June 1947; *s* of Edward and Mary Wilkes; *m* 1967, Dianne Butters; one *s* two *d*. *Educ:* Sandbach Sch., Cheshire; Hartley Victoria Coll. (Methodist Ch Theol Coll.), Manchester. Ordained Methodist minister, 1976; Worsley, 1973–78, Kettering and Corby, 1978–80, Methodist Circuit; Chaplain, HM Forces, 1980–: Sen. Chaplain, NI, 1993–95; Dep. Chaplain-Gen., 2000–04. Ecumenical Canon, Ripon Cathedral, 2005–08, now Canon Emeritus. QHC, 2000–08. Regtl Chaplain, Yorks Regt Assoc., 2011–. *Recreations:* fly-fishing, walking, reading, travelling, Rugby Union supporter. *Address:* 18 Terrys Mews, Bishopthorpe Road, York YO23 1PG. *T:* (01904) 633811.

WILKES, Prof. John Joseph, FSA; FBA 1986; Yates Professor of Greek and Roman Archaeology, University College London, 1992–2001, Professor Emeritus, since 2001; *b* 12 July 1936; *s* of Arthur Cyril Wilkes and Enid Cecilia Eustance; *m* 1980, Dr Susan Walker; (one *s* decd). *Educ:* King Henry VIII Grammar Sch., Coventry; Harrow County Grammar Sch.; University Coll. London (BA); Univ. of Durham (St Cuthbert's Society) (PhD). FSA 1969. Research Fellow, Univ. of Birmingham, 1961–63; Asst Lectr in History and Archaeology, Univ. of Manchester, 1963–64; Lectr in Roman History, 1964–71, Sen. Lectr 1971–74, Univ. of Birmingham; Prof. of Archaeology of the Roman Provinces, Univ. of London, 1974–92. Chm., Faculty of Archaeology, Hist. and Letters, British Sch. at Rome, 1979–83. Vis. Fellow, Inst. of Humanistic Studies, Pennsylvania State Univ., 1971. Mem., Ancient Monuments Bd for Scotland, 1981–91. Hon. Vice-Pres., Soc. for Promotion of Roman Studies, 1978; President: London and Middx Archaeological Soc., 1982–85; Assoc. for Roman Archaeology, 2010–. Corresp. Mem., German Archaeol Inst., 1976. Governor, Mus. of London, 1981–95. Member: Council, British Sch. at Rome, 1988–96; Mgt Cttee, British Sch. at Athens, 1990–97. Editor, Britannia, 1980–84. *Publications:* Dalmatia (Provinces of Roman Empire series), 1969; (jtly) Diocletian's Palace: joint excavations in the southeast quarter, Pt 1, Split, 1972; (ed jtly) Victoria County History of Cambridgeshire, vol. VII, Roman Cambridgeshire, 1978; Rhind Lectures (Edinburgh), 1984; Diocletian's Palace, Split (2nd Ian Saunders Meml Lecture, expanded), 1986; (jtly) Strageath: excavations within the Roman Fort 1973–1986, 1989; The Illyrians, 1992; (jtly) Excavations at Sparta 1988–95, reports 1994–98; (ed jtly) Epigraphy and the Historical Sciences, 2012; papers, excavation reports and reviews in learned jls of Britain, Amer., and Europe. *Recreations:* listening to music, watching Association football.

WILKES, Ven. Michael Jocelyn James P.; *see* Paget-Wilkes.

WILKES, Richard Geoffrey, CBE 1990 (OBE (mil.) 1969); TD 1959; DL; FCA; company director; Director, Cassidy, Davis Insurance Group, 1989–99 (Chairman, 1998–99); Partner, Price Waterhouse, Chartered Accountants, 1969–90; *b* 12 June 1928; *s* of Geoffrey W. Wilkes and Kathleen (*née* Quinn); *m* 1953, Wendy Elaine, *d* of Rev. C. Ward; one *s* three *d*. *Educ:* Repton (Exhibnr). ACA 1952; FCA 1957. Partner, Bolton Bullivant, Chartered Accountants, Leicester, 1953–69. Pres., Leics and Northants Soc. of Chartered Accountants, 1967–68; Mem. Council, Inst. of Chartered Accountants in England and Wales, 1969–90 (Dep. Pres., 1979–80; Pres., 1980–81); Chairman: UK Auditing Practices Cttee, 1976–78; CA Compensation Scheme, 1990–98; International Federation of Accountants: UK Rep; Mem. Council, 1983–87; Dep. Pres., 1985–87; Pres., 1987–90; Mem., Internat. Auditing Practices Cttee, 1978–79; Adviser on self-regulation, Lloyd's of London, 1983–85. Governor, CARE for the Mentally Handicapped, 1972–98 (Chm., 1995–98). Commnd RHA, 1947; served TA, RA and Royal Leics Regt, 1948–69; CO 4/5th Bn Royal Leics Regt (TA), 1966–69; Col TAVR E Midlands Dist, 1969–73; ADC (TAVR) to the Queen, 1972–77. Dep. Hon. Col, Royal Anglian Regt (Leics), 1981–88; Vice Chm., E Midlands TA&VRA, 1980–89 (Chm., Leics Co. Cttee, 1980–89); Chm., E Midlands TAVRA Employers Liaison Cttee, 1990–98. Comdt, Leics Special Constab., 1972–79. Chm., Leics SSAFA, 1991–98 (Treas., 1969–91). Mem., Court, Worshipful Co. of Chartered Accountants in England and Wales, 1977–98 (Master, 1991–92). DL Leics, 1967. Internat. Award, ICA, 1990. *Recreations:* shooting, sailing, gardening. *Club:* Army and Navy.

WILKES, Very Rev. Robert Anthony; Vicar, St Michael at the North Gate with St Martin and All Saints, Oxford, since 2013 (Priest-in-charge, 2009–13); City Rector, Oxford, since 2009; *b* 2 Sept. 1948; *s* of Leslie Robert Wilkes and Diana Napier Wilkes; *m* 1974, Sheila Katherine Hare; one *s* three *d*. *Educ:* Pocklington Sch., York; Trinity Coll., Oxford (MA Lit.Hum.); Wycliffe Hall, Oxford. Ordained deacon, 1974, priest, 1975; Curate, 1974–77, Vicar, 1977–81, St Oswald, Netherton, Bootle; Chaplain and Press Officer to Rt Rev. David Sheppard, Bp of Liverpool, 1981–85; Mission Partner, then Regl Sec., CMS, ME and Pakistan, 1985–98; Priest-in-charge, then Team Rector, Mossley Hill, Liverpool, 1998–2006; Dean of Birmingham, 2006–09. Chm., Ch of Pakistan Partners Forum, 1987–97; Focal person, ME Forum, CTBI, 1993–97; Pres., Internat. Assistance Mission, Afghanistan, 1992–97. Chairman: Lifelong Learning, Liverpool Dio., 2000–03; Merseyside Council of Faiths, 2005–06; Asylum Welcome, Oxford, 2014–; Trustee, Restore, Oxford, 2013–. *Recreations:* singing, fell walking, swimming.

WILKIE, Hon. Sir Alan (Fraser), Kt 2004; **Hon. Mr Justice Wilkie;** a Judge of the High Court, Queen's Bench Division, since 2004; Presiding Judge North Eastern Circuit, 2007–10; *b* 26 Dec. 1947; *s* of late James and Helen Wilkie; *m* 1972, Susan Elizabeth Musgrave; one *s* one *d*. *Educ:* Hutchesons' Grammar Sch., Glasgow; Manchester Grammar Sch.; Balliol Coll., Oxford (BA, BCL). Lecturer in Law: Exeter Coll., Oxford, 1971–72; Southampton Univ., 1972–74; called to the Bar, Inner Temple, 1974, Bencher, 2001; QC 1992; an Asst Recorder, 1992–95; a Recorder, 1995–97; a Circuit Judge, 1997–2004; a Law Comr, 2000–04. Mem., Judicial Appts Commn, 2012–. *Recreations:* music, films, watching football, playing 5 a side, cycling. *Address:* Royal Courts of Justice, Strand, WC2A 2LL.

WILKIE, Prof. Alex James, FRS 2001; PhD; Fielden Professor of Pure Mathematics, University of Manchester, since 2007; *b* 1 Aug. 1948; *s* of late Alan George Wilkie and Hilda Grace Wilkie (*née* Mitchell); *m* 1987, Catrin Roberts; one *s* one *d*. *Educ:* University Coll. London (BSc); Bedford Coll., London (MSc, PhD 1972). Lectr in Maths, Univ. of Leicester, 1972–73; Res. Fellow in Maths, Open Univ., 1973–78; Jun. Lectr in Maths, Oxford Univ., 1978–80 and 1981–82; Res. Fellow in Maths, Univ. Paris VII, 1982–83; SERC Advanced Res. Fellow, 1983–84, Lectr in Maths, 1984–86, Univ. of Manchester; Reader in Math. Logic, 1986–2007, and titular Prof., 1996–2007, Univ. of Oxford; Fellow, Wolfson Coll., Oxford, 1986–2007, now Emeritus. Vis. Asst Prof. in Maths, Yale Univ., 1980–81. Carol Karp Prize, Assoc. for Symbolic Logic, 1993, 2013. *Publications:* contrib. numerous papers in maths and mathematical logic jls. *Address:* School of Mathematics, Alan Turing Building, University of Manchester, Manchester M13 9PL. *T:* (0161) 275 5800.

WILKIE, Prof. Andrew Oliver Mungo, FRCP; FMedSci; FRS 2013; FRSB; Nuffield Professor of Pathology, University of Oxford, since 2003; *b* 14 Sept. 1959; *s* of late Douglas Robert Wilkie, FRS and June Rosalind Wilkie (*née* Hill); *m* 1989, Jane Elizabeth Martin; two *s*. *Educ:* Arnold House Sch.; Westminster Sch.; Trinity Coll., Cambridge (BA 1980, MA 1984); Merton Coll., Oxford (BM BCh 1983; DM 1992). MRCP 1986, FRCP 1998; DCH 1987; FRSB (FSB 2013). MRC Trng Fellow, Univ. of Oxford, 1987–90; Clinical Res. Fellow, Inst. of Child Health, London, 1990–91; Sen. Registrar, Inst. of Medical Genetics, Cardiff, 1992–93; Wellcome Trust Advanced Trng Fellow, 1993–95, then Sen. Res. Fellow in Clinical Sci., 1995–2003, Univ. of Oxford. Hon. Consultant in Clinical Genetics, Oxford Univ. Hosps (formerly Oxford Radcliffe Hosps) NHS Trust, 1993–. Galton Lectr, Galton Inst., 2014. Mem., EMBO, 2006. FMedSci 2002. Oon Internat. Award, Downing Coll., Cambridge, 2015. *Publications:* articles on genetics mechanisms of skull and limb malformations, and on mutations associated with paternal age effect in learned jls, inc. Nature, Cell, Nature Genetics, Science. *Recreations:* ornithology, Munros (mainly in winter), wild camping, visual arts, Test Match Special. *Address:* Weatherall Institute of Molecular Medicine, John Radcliffe Hospital, Headington, Oxford OX3 9DS. *T:* (01865) 222619, *Fax:* (01865) 222500. *E:* andrew.wilkie@imm.ox.ac.uk.

WILKIE, Kim Edward Kelvin, RDI 2009; landscape architect, since 1984; *b* 30 Oct. 1955. *Educ:* Winchester Coll.; New Coll., Oxford (MA); Univ. of California, Berkeley (MLA). MLI (ALI 1987). Marketing Manager, Unilever, 1978–81; Associate, Land Use Consultants, 1984–89; Principal, Kim Wilkie (formerly Kim Wilkie Associates), 1989–. Awards: Amer. Soc. of Landscape Architects, 1984; Francis Tibbalds, RTPI, 1994; Landscape Inst., 1995; RTPI, 1996; Centenary, Country Life, 1997; for Place Design, Envmtl Design Res. Assoc., US, 1999. Hon. FRIBA 2002. *Publications:* Thames Landscape Strategy: Hampton to Kew, 1994; Indignation!, 2000; Led by the Land, 2012. *Address:* Franklin Farm, Dean Lane, Bishop's Waltham SO32 1FX.

WILKIN, Richard Cecil, LVO 1979; MBE (mil.) 1976; DL; Secretary, Estates Business Group, since 2005; *b* 17 Sept. 1944; *s* of late Comdr Henry Egbert Peter Wilkin, RN, and Frances Anne Wilkin (*née* Chichester; she *m* 1984, Vice Adm. Sir (Robert) Alastair Ewing, KBE, CB, DSC); *m* 1st, 1983, Jane Susan Elliott (marr. diss. 1989), *d* of Sir Roger James Elliott, *qv*; 2nd, 2002, Sally Ashley Brown, *d* of Col Ashley Brown, OBE, RM. *Educ:* Eton; RMA Sandhurst. Commnd HM Armed Forces 17th/21st Lancers, 1964; served Rhine Army, Berlin, Libya, British Forces Gulf, Cyprus; Captain 1968; GSO III HQ NI, 1973 (despatches 1974); retired 1975. Joined HM Diplomatic Service, 1975; UK Delegn to Rhodesia Constitutional Conf., Geneva, 1976; First Sec. (Political and Press), Lusaka, 1978; E

Caribbean, 1988; attached MoD, 1990; Counsellor, FCO, 1992; retired 1996. Dir Gen., HHA, 1996–2005. Member: Country Land and Business Assoc. Tax Cttee, 1998–; Council, Attingham Trust, 1999–2005; British Tourism Develt Cttee, 2000–05; Exec. Cttee, Historic Envmt Review, 2001–05; NT Wessex Cttee, 2003–10 (Chm., 2006–10). Trustee: Heritage Link, 2002–05; Nat. Heritage Meml Fund, 2006–12 (Chm., Finance Cttee, 2009–12). DL Dorset, 2012. *Recreations:* fishing, painting, fine art and architecture, restoring historic buildings, motor cars, National Hunt racing. *Address:* c/o Messrs C. Hoare & Co., 37 Fleet Street, EC4P 4DQ. *Clubs:* Farmers; New (Edinburgh).

WILKIN, Rev. Rose Josephine H.; *see* Hudson-Wilkin.

WILKINS, Baroness *cr* 1999 (Life Peer), of Chesham Bois in the county of Buckinghamshire; **Rosalie Catherine Wilkins;** *b* 6 May 1946; *d* of late Eric Frederick Wilkins and Marjorie Phyllis Elizabeth Wilkins. *Educ:* Univ. of Manchester (BA). PA to Dir, Central Council for the Disabled, 1971–74; Information Officer, MIND (Nat. Assoc. for Mental Health), 1974–78; presenter/researcher, Link magazine programme and documentaries, ATV Network and Central Television, 1975–88; freelance video and documentary producer/presenter on disability issues, 1988–96; Information Officer, Nat. Centre for Independent Living, 1997–99. Mem., H of L, 1999–2015. Vice-Chairman: All Party Parly Gp on Disability, 2004–15; All Party Parly Gp on Deafness, 2005–15. Pres., Coll. of Occupational Therapists, 2003–08. Snowdon Award (for outstanding work for the benefit of disabled people), Action Research, 1983. *Recreations:* friends, gardening, theatre, cinema.

WILKINS, John Anthony Francis, MBE 1998; Editor of The Tablet, 1982–2003; *b* 20 Dec. 1936; *s* of Edward Manwaring Wilkins and Ena Gwendolen Francis. *Educ:* Clifton Coll., Bristol (Scholar); Clare Coll., Cambridge (State Scholar, 1954; Major Scholar and Foundn Scholar; Classical Tripos 1959, Theol Tripos 1961; BA 1961; MA 2004). Served 1st Bn Glos Regt, 1955–57 (2nd Lieut). Planning Div., Marine Dept, Head Office of Esso Petroleum, London, 1962–63; Asst Editor: Frontier, 1964–67; The Tablet, 1967–72; features writer, BBC External Services, 1972–81; Producer, Radio 4, 1978. Vis. Fellow, Clare Coll., Cambridge, 1996. MA Lambeth, 2004. Ondas Radio Prize, 1973; John Harriott Meml Prize, ITC, 1996; Christian Culture Gold Medal, Assumption Univ., Windsor, Canada, 2001. *Publications:* (ed) How I Pray, 1993; (ed) Understanding Veritatis Splendor, 1994; (ed jtly) Spiritual Stars of the Millennium, 2001. *Recreation:* ornithology.

WILKINS, Prof. Malcolm Barrett, FRSE 1972; Regius Professor of Botany, University of Glasgow, 1970–2000, now Emeritus; *b* 27 Feb. 1933; *s* of Barrett Charles Wilkins and Eleanor Mary Wilkins (*née* Jenkins); *m* 1959, Mary Patricia Maltby; one *s* (one *d* decd). *Educ:* Monkton House Sch., Cardiff; King's Coll., London. BSc 1954, 1955; PhD London 1958; AKC 1958; DSc 1972. Lectr in Botany, King's Coll., London, 1958–64; Rockefeller Foundn Fellow, Yale Univ., 1961–62; Research Fellow, Harvard Univ., 1962–63; Lectr in Biology, Univ. of East Anglia, 1964–65; Prof. of Biology, Univ. of East Anglia, 1965–67; Prof. of Plant Physiology, Univ. of Nottingham, 1967–70; Glasgow University: Dean, Faculty of Science, 1984–87; Chm., Sch. of Biol Scis, 1988–92. Darwin Lectr, British Assoc. for Advancement of Science, 1967. Member: Biol. Sci. Cttee of SRC, 1971–74; Governing Body: Hill Farming Res. Orgn, 1971–80; Scottish Crops Research Inst., 1974–89; Glasshouse Crops Res. Inst., 1979–88; W of Scotland Agricl Coll., 1983–92; Exec. Cttee, Scottish Field Studies Assoc.; British Nat. Cttee for Biology, 1977–82; Life Science Working Gp, ESA, 1983–89 (Chm., 1987–89); Microgravity Adv. Cttee, ESA, 1985–89; NASA Lifesat Science Cttee, 1986–91; Court, Glasgow Univ., 1993–97. Vice-Pres., RSE, 1994–97 (Mem. Council, 1989–92). Trustee, Royal Botanic Gdn, Edinburgh, 1990–99 (Chm., 1994–99; Hon. Fellow, 1999); Adv. Council, Scottish Agricl Coll. Corresp. Mem., Amer. Soc. of Plant Physiologists, 1985. Dir, West of Scotland Sch. Co.; Chm., Laurel Bank Sch. Co. Ltd. Cons. Editor in Plant Biology, McGraw-Hill Publishing Co., 1968–80; Managing Editor, Planta, 1977–2001. *Publications:* (ed) The Physiology of Plant Growth and Development, 1969; (ed) Advanced Plant Physiology, 1984; Plantwatching, 1988; papers in Jl of Experimental Botany, Plant Physiology, Planta, Nature, Proc. Royal Soc. *Recreations:* fishing, model engineering. *Address:* 5 Hughenden Drive, Glasgow G12 9XS. *T:* (0141) 334 8079. *E:* Profmwilkins@hotmail.com. *Clubs:* Caledonian; New (Edinburgh).

WILKINS, Nancy; barrister-at-law; *b* 16 June 1932; three *s* one *d*. *Educ:* School of St Helen and St Katharine, Abingdon, Berkshire. Called to the Bar, Gray's Inn, Nov. 1962; in practice, Midland Circuit, 1962–85; Dep. Circuit Judge, 1974–78; a Recorder, 1978–85; practised in solicitors' office, 1986–90; retired. *Publications:* An Outline of the Law of Evidence (with late Prof. Sir Rupert Cross), 1964, 5th edn 1980; Thomas of Moulton, 2002; Ayscoughfee: a great place in Spalding, 2007; A Little Book of Spalding, 2010; All About Ivo Taillbois, 2010. *Recreation:* failing to grow old gracefully.

WILKINS, Prof. Raphael Ashley; President, College of Teachers, since 2011; *b* Eltham, London, 14 Aug. 1951; *s* of Anthony Wilkins and Nina Wilkins; *m* 1975, Mary Harvey; one *d*. *Educ:* Goldsmiths' Coll., London (BSc 1973; PGCE 1974); Inst. of Educn, Univ. of London (DipEd 1976; MA 1979); Open Univ. (MSc 1985); Durham Univ. (MBA 1992); Lincoln Univ. (EdD 2002). ACP 1977, FCOT 2003; ACIS 1982, FCIS 2010. Teacher, Langley Park Sch. for Boys, 1974–78; Professional Asst, London Bor. of Sutton, 1978–79; Proj. Develt Officer, London Bor. of Newham, 1980–83; Principal Educn Officer, Royal Bor. of Kingston upon Thames, 1983–85; Select Cttee Specialist Asst, H of C, 1985–87; Educn Officer, Assoc. of London Authorities, 1987–88; Asst Dir of Educn, London Bor. of Sutton, 1988–97; Dir of Educn, Thurrock Council, 1997–2000; Dir, Raphael Wilkins Educnl Ltd, 2001–06; Hd, Consultancy and Knowledge Transfer, London Centre for Leadership in Learning, 2006–08; Asst Dir, Inst. of Educn, Univ. of London, 2008–14. *Publications:* Research Engagement for School Development, 2011; Education in the Balance: mapping the global dynamics of school leadership, 2014; articles in learned jls. *Recreations:* watercolour painting, clay pigeon shooting. *Address:* College of Teachers, Institute of Education, University of London, 20 Bedford Way, WC1H 0AL. *T:* (020) 7911 5536, *Fax:* (020) 7612 6618. *E:* rwilkins@collegeofteachers.ac.uk.

WILKINSON; *see* Browne-Wilkinson.

WILKINSON, Rev. Canon Alan Bassindale, PhD, DD; lecturer and writer; honorary priest, Portsmouth Cathedral, 1988–2014 (Cathedral Chaplain, 1994–2001; diocesan theologian, 1993–2001); *b* 26 Jan. 1931; *s* of late Rev. J. T. Wilkinson, DD; *m* 1975, Fenella Holland; two *s* one *d* of first marriage. *Educ:* William Hulme's Grammar Sch., Manchester; St Catharine's Coll., Cambridge; College of the Resurrection, Mirfield. MA 1958, PhD 1959, DD 1997 Cambridge. Deacon, 1959; priest, 1960; Asst Curate, St Augustine's, Kilburn, 1959–61; Chaplain, St Catharine's Coll., Cambridge, 1961–67; Vicar of Barrow Gurney and Lecturer in Theology, College of St Matthias, Bristol, 1967–70; Principal, Chichester Theol Coll., 1970–74; Canon and Prebendary of Thorney, 1970–74, Canon Emeritus, 1975; Warden of Verulam House, Dir of Training for Auxiliary Ministry, dio. of St Albans, 1974–75; Lectr in Theology and Ethics, Crewe and Alsager Coll. of Higher Educn, 1975–78; Dir of Training, Diocese of Ripon, 1978–84; Hon. Canon, Ripon Cathedral, 1984; Priest-in-Charge, Darley with Thruscross and Thornthwaite, 1984–88; Tutor, Open Univ., 1988–96. Vis. Fellow, Chichester Inst. of Higher Educn, 1995–97; Fellow, George Bell Inst., Chichester, 1996–; Vis. Lectr, Portsmouth Univ., 1998–2005. Hulsean Preacher, 1967–68; Select Preacher, Oxford Univ., 1982. Mem., Bd of Educn, Gen. Synod, 1981–85; Vice-Chm., Leeds Marriage and Personal Counselling Service, 1981–83. Governor: SPCK, 1982–91; Coll. of Ripon and York St John, 1985–88. Scott Holland Trustee, 1993–95, 1998–2015 (Scott Holland Lectr, 1998). *Publications:* The Church of England and the First World War, 1978, 3rd edn 2014; Would You Believe It?, 1983; More Ready to Hear, 1983; Christian Choices, 1983; Dissent or Conform?, 1986, 2nd edn 2010; The Community of the Resurrection: a centenary history, 1992; (jtly) An Anglican Companion: words from the heart of faith, 1996, 3rd edn 2014; Christian Socialism: Scott Holland to Tony Blair, 1998; One Foot in Eden, 2011; contributor to: Cambridge Sermons on Christian Unity, 1966; Catholic Anglicans Today, 1968; A Work Book in Popular Religion, 1986; Chesterton and the Modernist Crisis, 1990; Britain and the Threat to Stability in Europe, 1993; Forever Building, 1995; The Changing Face of Death, 1997; The Impact of New Labour, 1999; Piety and Learning: the Principals of Pusey House 1884–2002, 2002; Walter Frere, 2011; also to: Faith and Unity, Sobornost, Preacher's Quarterly, London Quarterly Holborn Review, Theology, Clergy Review, New Fire, Church Times, Chesterton Review, Internat. Christian Digest, Modern Hist. Rev., Oxford DNB, Expository Times, Humanitas. *Recreations:* gardening, walking, cinema, Victorian architecture. *Address:* 39 Henty Gardens, Chichester, W Sussex PO19 3DL. *T:* (01243) 839578.

WILKINSON, Alexander Birrell; QC (Scot.) 1993; Sheriff of Lothian and Borders at Edinburgh, 1996–2001; *b* 2 Feb. 1932; *o s* of late Captain Alexander Wilkinson, MBE, The Black Watch and Isabella Bell Birrell; *m* 1965, Wendy Imogen, *d* of late Ernest Albert Barrett and R. V. H. Barrett; one *s* one *d*. *Educ:* Perth Academy; Univs of St Andrews and Edinburgh. Walker Trust Scholar 1950, Grieve Prizeman in Moral Philosophy 1952, MA (Hons Classics) 1954, Univ. of St Andrews. National Service, RAEC, 1954–56. Balfour Keith Prizeman in Constitutional Law 1957, LLB (with distinction) 1959, Univ. of Edinburgh. Admitted to Faculty of Advocates, 1959; in practice at Scottish bar, 1959–69; Lecturer in Scots Law, Univ. of Edinburgh, 1965–69; Sheriff of Stirling, Dunbarton and Clackmannan at Stirling and Alloa, 1969–72; Prof. of Private Law, 1972–86, and Dean of Faculty of Law, 1974–76 and 1986, Univ. of Dundee; Sheriff of: Tayside, Central and Fife at Falkirk, 1986–91; Glasgow and Strathkelvin, 1991–96; Temp. Judge of Court of Session and High Court of Justiciary, 1993–2003. Chancellor: Dio. of Brechin, 1982–98; Dio. of Argyll and the Isles, 1985–98. Chairman: Central Scotland Marriage Guidance Council, 1970–72; Scottish Marriage Guidance Council, 1974–77; Legal Services Gp, Scottish Assoc. of CAB, 1979–83. Pres., Sheriffs' Assoc., 1997–2000 (Vice-Pres., 1995–97). Trustee, Gen. Synod of Scottish Episcopal Ch, 2005–. *Publications:* (ed jtly) Gloag and Henderson's Introduction to the Law of Scotland, 8th edn 1980, 9th edn 1987; The Scottish Law of Evidence, 1986; (jtly) The Law of Parent and Child in Scotland, 1993; (contrib.) Macphail's Sheriff Court Practice, 2nd edn 1998; (contrib.) Legal Systems of Scottish Churches, 2009; articles in legal periodicals. *Recreations:* collecting books and pictures, reading, travel. *Address:* 1 Weston Gardens, Haddington, East Lothian EH41 3DD. *T:* (01620) 822891. *Club:* New (Edinburgh).

See also W. P. Saunders.

WILKINSON, Prof. Andrew Robert, FRCP; Professor of Paediatrics, University of Oxford, 1997–2011, now Emeritus; Fellow, All Souls College, Oxford, 1992–2011, now Emeritus; Director of Neonatal Medicine, John Radcliffe Hospital, Oxford, 1981–2011; *b* 30 Oct. 1943; *s* of late Rev. Thomas Richard Wilkinson and (Winifred) Frances Wilkinson (*née* Steel). *Educ:* Heath Grammar Sch., Halifax; Univ. of Birmingham Med. Sch. (MB ChB 1968); Univ. of Calif, San Francisco; DCH (Eng) 1972; MA Oxon 1992. MRCP 1972, FRCP 1986; FRCPCH 1997, Hon. FRCPCH 2010. House officer: in medicine and surgery, Dudley Rd Hosp., Birmingham, 1968–69; in paediatrics, Warwick Hosp., 1969–70; SHO in medicine, Dudley Rd Hosp., Birmingham, 1970–71; Registrar in medicine, Stratford-on-Avon, 1971–72; Hse Officer in paediatrics, Gt Ormond St Hosp., 1972–73; SHO in neonatal medicine, Oxford, 1973–74; Registrar, Southampton, 1973–74; Nuffield Med. Res. Fellow, Univ. of Oxford, 1974–75; Fellow, Cardiovascular Res. Inst., Univ. of Calif, San Francisco, 1975–77; Clin. Lectr in Paediatrics, Univ. of Oxford, 1978–81; Consultant Paediatrician, Oxfordshire HA, 1981–92; Clin. Reader in Paediatrics, Univ. of Oxford, 1992–97. Vis. Prof. of Paediatrics, Univ. of Southampton, 2011–. Member: Nat. Adv. Bd for Confidential Enquiry into Stillbirths and Deaths in Infancy, 1995–2000 (Interim Chm., 2000–03); Board: Nat. Neonatal Audit Prog., 2006–; Neonatal Data Analysis Unit, 2007–; Medicines for Neonates, 2008–. Chairman: Children and Young People's Specialised Services Project, Welsh Assembly Govt, 2004–06; Mem., All Wales Standards for Neonatal Services, 2004–06. President: British Assoc. of Perinatal Medicine, 1999–2002; Neonatal Soc., 2003–06. Royal College of Paediatrics and Child Health: Chm., Acad. Bd, 1997–98; Chm., Acad. Regl Advrs, 2006–11; Sir James Spence Medal, 2011; Council Trustee for Sen. Members, 2012–. Trustee: Helen and Douglas Hse Hospice, 2004–; Oxford Radcliffe Hosps Charitable Trust, 2005–15. Dir, Friends of Warneford Meadow, Town Green, 2012–. Mem. Cttee, Oxford Univ. RFC, 2014–. Knight 1st Cl., Order of the White Rose (Finland), 2003. *Publications:* over 190 papers, articles and chapters in textbooks on care of sick children and specifically in neonatal medicine. *Recreations:* sailing, hill walking, lawn maintenance. *Address:* All Souls College, Oxford OX1 4AL.

See also C. R. Wilkinson.

WILKINSON, Brian; *see* Wilkinson, W. B.

WILKINSON, Christopher John, OBE 2000; RA 2006; Principal (formerly Chairman), Wilkinson Eyre (formerly Chris Wilkinson) Architects Ltd, since 1989; Partner, Wilkinson Design Studios LLP, since 2012; *b* 1 July 1945; *s* of Edward Anthony Wilkinson and Norma Doreen Wilkinson; *m* 1976, Diana Mary Edmunds; one *s* one *d*. *Educ:* St Albans Sch.; Regent Street Poly. (DipArch). RIBA; FCSD. Architect: Foster Associates, 1973–74; Michael Hopkins Architects, 1975–79; Richard Rogers Partnership, 1979–83; founded Chris Wilkinson Architects, 1983; partnership with James Eyre, 1986–; formed Wilkinson Eyre Architects, 1999. *Projects include:* Stratford Market Depot, 1997 (FT Architecture Award, British Construction Industry Building Award, RIBA Commercial Architecture Award, Structural Steel Design Awards, Industrial Buildings Award, 1997; Civic Trust Design Award, 1998) and Stratford Station, for Jubilee Line Extension, 1998 (RIBA Category Award, 1999; Civic Trust Award, 2000); South Quay Footbridge, 1997 (AIA Excellence in Design Award, 1997; Civic Trust Design Award, 1998); Hulme Arch, 1997; Challenge of Materials Gall., Science Mus., 1997; HQ for Dyson Appliances Ltd, 1999; Explore at Bristol, 2000 (RIBA Award, 2001); Gateshead Millennium Bridge, 2002 (RA/Bovis Grand Award, 1997; RIBA Stirling Prize, 2002); Magna Millennium Project, Rotherham (RIBA Stirling Prize, 2001); Liverpool Arena and Conf. Centre, King's Dock (RIBA Award); Nat. Waterfront Mus., Swansea (RIBA Award); Anglia Poly. Univ. Campus and Business Sch., Chelmsford; City & Islington Coll.; Audi Regl HQ, Hammersmith; Empress State Bldg, Earls Court; John Madejski Acad., Reading, 2007; Bristol Brunel Acad., 2007; Bath Bus Station, 2009; Bridge Learning Campus, 2009; Earth Scis Dept, Oxford Univ., 2010; Hauser Forum, Cambridge Univ., 2010; Guangzhou Internat. Finance Centre, 2010 (Best Tall Bldg in Asia and Australasia, Council on Tall Bldgs and Urban Habitat, 2011; Lubetkin Award, 2012); Humanities Dept and Maths Dept, QMUL, 2012; Basketball Arena, London Olympic Games, 2012; From Landscape to Portrait, RA Courtyard, 2012; Brislington Enterprise Coll.; *current projects:* Mary Rose Final Voyage Mus., Portsmouth (RIBA Award, 2014; Civic Trust Award, 2014); Gardens by the bay, Singapore (World Building of Year Award, 2012; Lubetkin Award, 2013; Internat. Architect Award, 2013); Univ. of Exeter Forum Project; Worthing New Pools; Siemens Urban Sustainability Centre, London; The Polygon, West Town, Cairo; Swinburne Univ. Advanced Manufg Centre, Melbourne; Maggie's Centre, Oxford; Royal Docks Cable Car; Landscape to Portrait sculpture, RA Courtyard, 2012. Mem. Council, Steel Construction Inst., 1998–2001; Comr, English Heritage, 2007–11 (Mem. Urban Panel, 2000–09); Founding Cttee, London Fest. of Architecture, 2004–; Mem., RA Architecture Cttee, 2006–; Chm., RA Client Cttee (formerly Works Cttee), 2012–. Patron, Nat. Trust

Design Awards, 2011–. RIBA Lectr, 1996, 2001; Vis. Prof., 1997–98, Mies van der Rohe Lectr, 2003, Illinois Inst. of Technol., Chicago; Vis. Prof., Harvard Grad. Sch. of Design, 2004. Work exhibited: Union of Architects, St Petersburg, 2008; British Design Innovation in the Modern Age, V&A, 2012; IX Venice Biennale; Royal Acad.; Science Mus.; RIBA; Architecture Foundn; Design Council Millennium Products touring exhibn; Love Architecture Fest., Turner Contemporary Mus., Margate, 2013; Lookout. Architecture with a View, Swiss Architecture Mus., Basel, 2013–14; Practical Utopias, AIA Centre, NY, 2013–14; The Brits Who Built the Modern World, RIBA, 2014. External Examiner: Univ. of Westminster, 1996–99; Mackintosh Sch. of Art, 2000–04; Bartlett Sch. of Architecture, 2012–. Hon FAIA 2007. Hon. DLit Westminster, 2002; Hon. Dr Oxford Brookes, 2007. Designer of the Year, CSD, 1996; FX Designer of the Year, 2001; over 150 design awards. *Publications:* Supersheds, 1991, 2nd edn 1995 (trans. Japanese 1995); (with James Eyre) Bridging Art and Science, 2001; Exploring Boundaries, 2007; Tectonics: a building for earth sciences, 2011; Wilkinson Eyre Architects: works, 2014 contribs World Architecture, Architects Jl. *Recreations:* golf, painting, travel, olive farm in Tuscany. *Address:* 52 Park Hall Road, SE21 8BW. *T:* (020) 8761 7021. *Clubs:* Chelsea Arts; FABS; Dulwich and Sydenham Golf.

WILKINSON, Christopher Richard; Adviser, Internet Governance, Directorate General, Information Society and the Media (formerly Telecommunications Information Market and Exploitation of Research) (DG XIII), Commission of the European Communities, 1993–2005, now Hon. Director, European Commission; Head of Secretariat, Governmental Advisory Committee, Internet Corporation for Assigned Names and Numbers, 2002–05 (EU Representative, 1999–2002; Vice-Chairman, 2001–02); *b* 3 July 1941; *s* of late Rev. Thomas Richard Wilkinson and Winifred Frances Wilkinson (*née* Steel). *Educ:* Hymers Coll., Kingston upon Hull; Heath Grammar Sch., Halifax; Selwyn Coll., Cambridge (MA). Commonwealth Economic Cttee, 1963–65; OECD, Paris and Madrid, 1965–66; World Bank, Washington DC and Lagos, 1966–73; EEC: Head of Division: Directorate Gen. for Regional Policy, 1973–78; Directorate Gen. for Internal Market and Industrial Affairs, 1978–82; Directorate Gen. for Telecommunications, Information Industries and Innovation, 1983–93. Mem., Internet Policy Oversight Cttee, 1997–2000; Dir, Bd, EURid, 2010– (Mem., Strategic Cttee, 2010–); Chm., Internet Soc. European Co-ordinating Council, 2007–12. Vis. Fellow, Center for Internat. Affairs, Harvard Univ., 1982–83. Vice-Pres., European School Parents Assoc., Brussels, 1974, 1976–77, Alicante, 2005–06; Pres., Interparents, Assoc. of the Parents' Assocs of European Schs, 2008–09. *Recreations:* mountain walking, gardening, cooking.
See also A. R. Wilkinson.

WILKINSON, Clive Victor; Chairman, John Taylor Hospice, since 2011; *b* 26 May 1938; *s* of Mrs Winifred Jobson; *m* 1961, Elizabeth Ann Pugh; two *d*. *Educ:* Four Dwellings Secondary Sch., Quinton; Birmingham Modern Sch. Birmingham City Council: Member, 1970–84; Leader, 1973–76 and 1980–82; Leader of Opposition, 1976–80, 1982–84. Dir, Nat. Exhibn Centre, 1973–84; Financial and Commercial Dir, Birmingham Rep. Theatre, 1983–87. Chm., CoSIRA, 1977–80; Dep. Chairman: AMA, 1974–76; Redditch Develt Corp., 1977–81. Chairman: Sandwell DHA, 1986–94; Wolverhampton Health Care NHS Trust, 1995–97; W Midlands Region, NHS Exec., DoH, 1997–2001; Birmingham Heartlands and Solihull NHS Trust, subseq. Heart of England NHS Foundn Trust, 2001–11. Member: Develt Commn, 1977–86; Electricity Consumers Council, 1977–80; Audit Commn, 1987–96; Black Country Develt Corp., 1989–92; Local Govt Commn, 1992–95; Midlands Industrial Assoc., 1978– (Chm., 1980–88). Non-exec. Dir, FSA, 2001–13. Chairman: Birmingham Civil Housing Assoc., 1979–2011; Customer Services Cttee, Severn Trent Region, Office of Water Services, 1990–2001. Mem. Council, Univ. of Birmingham, 1974–84. Trustee, Bournville Village Trust, 1982–. Hon. Alderman, City of Birmingham, 1984. *Recreations:* watching Birmingham City Football Club, playing squash. *Address:* 53 Middle Park Road, Birmingham B29 4BH.

WILKINSON, Rev. Prof. David Adam, PhD; Principal, St John's College, since 2006, Professor, since 2011, University of Durham; *b* 16 May 1963; *s* of late Adam and Margaret Wilkinson; *m* 1992, Alison Mary Russell; one *s* one *d*. *Educ:* Greencroft Comprehensive Sch., Co. Durham; Univ. of Durham (BSc 1984, PhD 1987 and 2004); Fitzwilliam Coll., Cambridge (MA 1989); Wesley House, Cambridge. FRAS 1989. Methodist Minister, Letchworth, 1990–91; Methodist Minister and Univ. Chaplain, Liverpool, 1991–99; University of Durham: Fellow in Christian Apologetics, St John's Coll., 1999–2004; Wesley Res. Lectr in Theol. and Science, Dept of Theol. and Religion, 2004–06. *Publications:* God, the Big Bang and Stephen Hawking, 1993, 2nd edn 1996; Thinking Clearly About God and Science, 1996, 2nd edn 1997; Alone in the Universe: the X-Files, aliens and God, 1997; A New Start: hopes and dreams for the millennium, 1999; The Power of the Force: the spirituality of the Star Wars films, 2000; Holiness of the Heart, 2000; God, Time and Stephen Hawking, 2001; Creation, 2002; The Case Against Christ, 2006; The Call and the Commission, 2009; Reading Genesis After Darwin, 2009; Christian Eschatology and the Physical Universe, 2010; Science, Religion and the Search for Extraterrestrial Intelligence, 2013; When I Pray, What Does God Do?, 2015. *Recreations:* Star Wars, the Simpsons, Newcastle United. *Address:* St John's College, 3 South Bailey, Durham DH1 3RJ. *T:* (0191) 334 3500, *Fax:* (0191) 334 3501. *E:* david.wilkinson@durham.ac.uk.

WILKINSON, David Anthony, CB 1994; Lay Member, Information Tribunal, since 2005; *b* 27 Nov. 1947; *s* of Ambrose Wilkinson and Doreen (*née* Durden); *m* 1973, Meryl, *d* of Edison and Margaret Pugh; three *d*. *Educ:* Boteler Grammar Sch., Warrington; Wigan and District Mining and Technical Coll.; Bedford Coll., Univ. of London (BA History); London School of Economics; Moscow State Univ. Department of Education and Science, 1974–92: Under Sec., and Hd of Sci. Br., 1989–92; Under Sec., OST, then OPSS, Cabinet Office, 1992–94; RCDS, 1995; Dir, Machinery of Govt and Standards Gp, OPS, 1996–98, Hd of Central Secretariat, 1998–2000, Cabinet Office; Dir of Regl Policy, DETR, 2000–01; Business Co-ordinator, Civil Contingencies Secretariat, Cabinet Office, 2001–02; Sec., Govt Communication Review Gp, Cabinet Office, 2002–03. *Address:* 15 Rayleigh Road, Wimbledon, SW19 3RE. *Clubs:* Wimbledon Squash and Badminton, AFC Wimbledon.

WILKINSON, Dr David George; Group Leader, Francis Crick Institute, since 2015; *b* 8 March 1958; *s* of George Arthur Wilkinson and Barbara May Wilkinson (*née* Hayton); *m* 1991, Qiling Xu. *Educ:* Aylesbury Grammar Sch.; Hymers Coll., Hull; Univ. of Leeds (BSc Hons 1979, PhD 1983). Postdoctoral Fellow, Fox Chase Cancer Center, Philadelphia, 1983–86; MRC National Institute for Medical Research: Postdoctoral Fellow, 1986–88; scientific staff, 1988–2015; Hd, Div. of Develtl Neurobiol., and Genetics and Develt (formerly Genes and Cellular Controls) Gp, 2000–15. Mem., EMBO, 2000. Editor in Chief: Mechanisms of Develt, 2010–; Gene Expression Patterns, 2010–. FMedSci 2000. *Publications:* (ed) In Situ Hybridisation, 1992, 2nd edn 1998; (ed jtly) Extracellular Regulators of Differentiation and Development, 1996; contrib. numerous scientific articles to various jls. *Recreations:* natural history, music, poetry. *Address:* Francis Crick Institute, Mill Hill Laboratory, The Ridgeway, Mill Hill, NW7 1AA. *T:* (020) 8959 3666.

WILKINSON, Sir David Graham Brook; *see* Wilkinson, Sir Graham.

WILKINSON, Prof. David Gregor, (Greg), FRCPEd; FRCPsych; consultant psychiatrist in independent and medico-legal practice, since 2005; Professor of Liaison Psychiatry, Liverpool University, 1994–2005; *b* 17 May 1951; *s* of David Pryde Wilkinson and Joan (*née* McCabe); *m* 1984, Christine Mary Lewis; three *s* one *d*. *Educ:* Lawside Acad., Dundee; Edinburgh Univ. (BSc, MB ChB); MPhil London. FRCPEd 1989; FRCPsych 1991. House Physician and Surgeon, Royal Infirmary, Edinburgh, 1975–76; Sen. House Physician, Leith Hosp., 1976–78; Registrar, Maudsley Hosp., 1978–81; Sen. Registrar, Maudsley Hosp. and KCH, 1981–83; Res. Worker and Lectr, then Sen. Lectr, Inst. of Psychiatry, Univ. of London, 1983–89; Sen. Lectr and Reader, Academic Sub-dept of Psychol Medicine in N Wales, 1989–91; Prof. of Psychiatry, London Hosp. Med. Coll., London Univ., 1992–94. Editor, Brit. Jl of Psychiatry, 1993–2003. *Publications:* Mental Health Practices in Primary Care Settings, 1985; (jtly) Mental Illness in Primary Care Settings, 1986; (jtly) The Provision of Mental Health Services in Britain, 1986; Coping with Stress, 1987, 2nd edn as Understanding Stress, 1993; Depression, 1989; Recognising and Treating Depression in General Practice, 1989; (jtly) The Scope of Epidemiological Psychiatry, 1989; Recognising and Treating Anxiety in General Practice, 1992; Talking About Psychiatry, 1993; (jtly) Psychiatry and General Practice Today, 1994; (jtly) A Carers Guide to Schizophrenia, 1996, 2nd edn 2000; (ed jtly) Textbook of General Psychiatry, 1998, 2nd edn 2007; (jtly) Critical Reviews in Psychiatry, 1998, 2nd edn 2000; (jtly) Seminars in Psychosexual Disorders, 1998; (jtly) Treating People with Depression, 1999; Treating People with Anxiety and Stress, 1999; articles in general and specialist med. jls. *Recreations:* family, rural pursuits. *Address:* Craig y Castell, Bryniau, Dyserth, Denbighshire LL18 6DE. *T:* (01745) 571858. *Club:* Athenæum.

WILKINSON, Sir Denys (Haigh), Kt 1974; FRS 1956; Vice-Chancellor, University of Sussex, 1976–87 (Emeritus Professor of Physics, 1987); *b* Leeds, Yorks, 5 Sept. 1922; *o s* of late Charles Wilkinson and Hilda Wilkinson (*née* Haigh); *m* 1st, 1947, Christiane Andrée Clavier (marr. diss. 1967); three *d*; 2nd, 1967, Helen Sellschop; two step *d*. *Educ:* Loughborough Gram. Sch.; Jesus Coll. Cambridge (Fellow, 1944–59, Hon. Fellow 1961). BA 1943, MA, PhD 1947, ScD 1961. British and Canadian Atomic Energy Projects, 1943–46; Univ. Demonstrator, Cambridge, 1947–51; Univ. Lecturer, 1951–56; Reader in Nuclear Physics, Univ. of Cambridge, 1956–57; Professor of Nuclear Physics, Univ. of Oxford, 1957–59; Prof. of Experimental Physics, Univ. of Oxford, 1959–76, Head of Dept of Nuclear Physics, 1962–76; Student, Christ Church, Oxford, 1957–76, Emeritus Student, 1976, Hon. Student, 1979. Dir, Internat. Sch. of Nuclear Physics, Erice, Sicily, 1975–83. Mem. Governing Board of National Institute for Research in Nuclear Science, 1957–63 and 1964–65; Member: SRC, 1967–70; Wilton Park Acad. Council, 1979–83; Council, ACU, 1980–87; Royal Commn for the Exhibn of 1851, 1983–90 (Chm., Science Scholarships Cttee, 1983–90); British Council, 1987– (Chm., Sci. Adv. Panel and Cttee, 1977–86); Chairman: Nuclear Physics Board of SRC, 1968–70; Physics III Cttee, CERN, Geneva, 1971–75; Radioactive Waste Management Adv. Cttee, 1978–83; Pres., Inst. of Physics, 1980–82; Vice-Pres., IUPAP, 1985–93. Lectures: Welch, Houston, 1957; Scott, Cambridge Univ., 1961; Rutherford Meml, Brit. Physical Soc., 1962; Graham Young, Glasgow Univ., 1964; Queen's, Berlin, 1966; Silliman, Yale Univ., 1966; Cherwell-Simon, Oxford Univ., 1970; Distinguished, Utah State Univ., 1971, 1983, 1988; Goodspeed-Richard, Pennsylvania Univ., 1973 and 1986; Welsh, Toronto Univ., 1975; Tizard Meml, Westminster Sch., 1975; Lauritsen Meml, Cal. Tech., 1976; Herbert Spencer, Oxford Univ., 1976; Schiff Meml, Stanford Univ., 1977; Racah Meml, Hebrew Univ. Jerusalem, 1977; Cecil Green, Univ. of BC, 1978; Distinguished, Univ. of Alberta, 1979; Wolfson, Oxford Univ., 1980; Waterloo-Guelph Distinguished, Guelph Univ., 1981; Herzberg, Ottawa, 1984; Solly Cohen Meml, Hebrew Univ., Jerusalem, 1985; Peter Axel Meml, Univ. of Illinois, 1985; Breit Meml, Yale Univ., 1987; Moon, Birmingham Univ., 1987; Rochester, Durham Univ., 1988; Pegram, Brookhaven Nat. Lab., 1989; W. B. Lewis Meml, Chalk River, Ont, 1989; Humphry Davy, Académie des Sciences, Paris, 1990; Rutherford Meml, Royal Soc., 1991; W. V. Houston Meml, Rice Univ., 1994; Hudspeth, Univ. of Texas at Austin, 1994; Anna McPherson, McGill Univ., 1995; Pickavance Meml, Rutherford Lab., 1997; B. W. Sargent, Queen's Univ., Canada, 1998; Director's Distinguished, Livermore Nat. Lab., 1999; Meghnad Saha Meml, Calcutta, 2001; Glenn Knoll, Univ. of Michigan, 2002. Walker Ames Prof., Univ. of Washington, 1968; Battelle Distinguished Prof., Univ. of Washington, 1970–71; Vis. Prof., Tokyo Univ., 1995; Visiting Scientist: Brookhaven Nat. Lab., 1954–80; TRIUMF, Vancouver, 1987–; Los Alamos Nat. Lab., 1990–93. For. Mem., Royal Swedish Acad. of Scis, 1980; Mem. Acad. Europaea, 1990. Holweck Medal, British and French Physical Socs, 1957; Rutherford Prize, British Physical Soc., 1962; Hughes Medal, Royal Society, 1965; Bruce-Preller Prize, RSE, 1969; Bonner Prize, American Physical Soc., 1974; Royal Medal, Royal Soc., 1980; Guthrie Medal and Prize, Inst. of Physics, 1986; Gold Medal, Centro Cultura Scientifica Ettore Majorana, Sicily, 1988. Hon. Mem., Mark Twain Soc., 1978. Hon. DSc: Saskatchewan, 1964; Utah State, 1975; Guelph, 1981; Queen's, Kingston, 1987; William and Mary, Va, 1989; Hon. FilDr Uppsala, 1980; Hon. LLD Sussex, 1987. Comdr Bontemps Médoc et Graves, 1973. *Publications:* Ionization Chambers and Counters, 1951; (ed) Isospin in Nuclear Physics, 1969; (ed) Progress in Particle and Nuclear Physics, 1978–84; (ed jtly) Mesons in Nuclei, 1979; Our Universes, 1991; papers on nuclear physics and bird navigation. *Recreations:* mediæval church architecture, watching birds. *Address:* Gayles Orchard, Friston, Eastbourne, East Sussex BN20 0BA. *T:* (01323) 423333.
See also J. P. Curry.

WILKINSON, Endymion Porter, PhD; independent scholar, since 2014; Visiting Professor, Peking University, 2001–04 and 2007–14; *b* 15 May 1941; *s* of late George Curwen Wilkinson and Pamela Algernon Wilkinson (*née* Black). *Educ:* King's Coll., Cambridge (BA 1964; MA 1967); Princeton Univ. (PhD 1970). Teacher, Peking Inst. of Languages, 1964–66; Lectr in History of Far East, SOAS, London Univ., 1970–74; joined European Commn, 1974: Head of Economic and Commercial Section, Tokyo, 1974–79; China Desk, Brussels, 1979–82; Dep. Head, SE Asia Repn, Bangkok, 1982–88; Head, Asia Div., Brussels, 1988–94; Ambassador and Hd of Delegn to China, EC, 1994–2001. Sen. Fellow, Asia Center, 2001–07, Associate, Fairbank Center for E Asian Res., 2007–12, Harvard Univ. Vis. Prof., Tsinghua Univ., 2005. *Publications:* The History of Imperial China: a research guide, 1973; Studies in Chinese Price History, 1980; Japan versus Europe: a history of misunderstanding, 1982 (trans. Japanese, Chinese, French, German and Italian); Japan versus the West, 1991; Chinese History: a manual, 1998, 2nd edn 2000; Chinese History: a new manual, 2013, 4th edn 2015; *translations:* The People's Comic Book, 1973; Landlord and Labour in Late Imperial China, by Jing Su and Luo Lun, 1978. *Recreations:* Chinese history, swimming. *E:* epw2012@gmail.com.

WILKINSON, Sir Graham, 3rd Bt *cr* 1941; Managing Director, S.E.I.C. Services (UK) Ltd, 1985–89; *b* 18 May 1947; *s* of Sir David Wilkinson, 2nd Bt, DSC, and of Sylvia Anne, *d* of late Professor Bosley Alan Rex Gater; *S* father, 1972; *m* 1977, Sandra Caroline Rossdale (marr. diss. 1996); two *d*; *m* 1998, Hilary Jane Griggs, *d* of late W. H. C. Bailey, CBE. *Educ:* Millfield; Christ Church, Oxford. Orion Royal Bank Ltd, 1971–85 (Dir, 1979–85); non-executive Director: Galveston-Houston Co., USA, 1986–89; Sovereign Management Corp., USA, 1987–94; Lamport Gilbert Ltd, 1992–97. Pres., Surrey County Agricultural Soc., 2006–08; Mem. Council, RASE, 2005–10. Gov., Queen's Gate Sch. Trust, 1989–2005. Master, Farmers' Co., 2006–07. KStJ 2003. *Clubs:* Vincent's (Oxford); Royal Ocean Racing; Royal Yacht Squadron.

WILKINSON, Graham Paul; a District Judge (Magistrates' Courts), since 2009; *b* Barking, Essex, 1 Nov. 1968; *s* of Trevor and Pamela Wilkinson; *m* 2008, Adelle; one step *d*. *Educ:* Judd Sch., Tonbridge; Trent Poly. (LLB Hons); Coll. of Law, York. Articled clerk, 1991–93, Solicitor, 1993–99, Russell-Cooke, Potter & Chapman, Putney; Solicitor, then Partner, EBR Attridge, 1999–2009. *Recreations:* walking, natural history, film, supporting West Ham United. *Address:* c/o Wolverhampton Magistrates' Court, The Law Courts, North Street, Wolverhampton WV1 1RA. *T:* (01902) 329003.

WILKINSON, Greg; *see* Wilkinson, David Gregor.

WILKINSON, Rev. Canon Guy Alexander, CBE 2012; Vicar, St Andrew's, Fulham Fields, since 2012; *b* 13 Jan. 1948; *m* 1971, Tessa Osbourn; two *s*. *Educ:* Magdalene Coll., Cambridge (BA 1969); Ripon Coll., Cuddesdon. Commn of Eur. Communities, 1973–80; Dir, 1980–85, non-exec. Dir, 1985–87, Express Foods Gp; ordained deacon 1987, priest 1988; Curate, Caludon, Coventry, 1987–90; Priest i/c, 1990–91, Rector, 1991–94, Ockham with Hatchford; Domestic Chaplain to Bishop of Guildford, 1990–94; Vicar, Small Heath, Birmingham, 1994–99; Archdeacon of Bradford, 1999–2004; Archbishop of Canterbury's Sec. for Inter Religious Relns, 2005–10; C of E Nat. Advr, 2005–10; Area Dean, Hammersmith and Fulham, 2012–15. Co. Sec., Near Neighbours, 2008–14; Chair, Faiths Forum for London, 2010–13; Trustee, St Ethelburga Centre for Reconciliation and Peace, 2013.

WILKINSON, Rt Hon. Dame Heather; *see* Hallett, Rt Hon. Dame H. C.

WILKINSON, James Hugh; freelance journalist and broadcaster; *b* 19 Sept. 1941; *s* of Hugh Davy Wilkinson and Marjorie Wilkinson (*née* Prout); *m* 1978, Rev. Elisabeth Ann Morse; two *s*. *Educ:* Westminster Abbey Choir Sch.; King's Coll., London (BSc Hons); Inst. of Educn., Univ. of Cambridge (CertEd). Health and Sci. Corresp., Daily Express, 1964–74; Sci. and Air Corresp., BBC Radio News, 1974–83; Sci. Corresp., BBC News and Current Affairs, 1983–99. Vis. Fellow, Inst. of Food Res., 1992–96. Mem., Educn Cttee, CRC, 1977–82; Mem., Adv. Bd, CIBA Foundn Media Resource Service, 1994–99 (Mem., Steering Cttee, 1985–94). Hon. Steward, Westminster Abbey, 1999– (Sec., Brotherhood of St Edward, 1984–99). Mem., Editl Cttee, Sci. and Public Affairs Jl, 1989–99. Founder Mem., Med. Journalists' Assoc. (Chm., 1972–74). FSA 2010. Glaxo Wellcome Sci. Writers' Award, 1996. *Publications:* The Conquest of Cancer, 1973; Tobacco: the truth behind the smokescreen, 1986; Green or Bust, 1990; Westminster Abbey: 1000 years of music and pageant, 2003; The Royal Wedding: Westminster Abbey official souvenir, 2011; The Queen's Coronation: the inside story, 2011; To Drink, to Sing: a short history of the Noblemen and Gentlemen's Catch Club, 2014; booklets about aspects of Westminster Abbey incl. Poet's Corner and the Coronation Chair. *Recreations:* music, bookbinding, editing The Westminster Abbey Chorister. *Club:* Oxford and Cambridge.

WILKINSON, Jeffrey Vernon; management consultant; Consultant, Apax Partners & Co. (formerly Alan Patricof Associates), 2000–07 (Director, 1986–2000; Partner, 1988–2000); Chairman of several private companies, 1985–2007; *b* 21 Aug. 1930; *s* of late Arthur Wilkinson and Winifred May Allison; *m* 1955, Jean Vera Nurse; two *d*. *Educ:* Matthew Humberstone Foundation Sch.; King's Coll., Cambridge (BA Hons, MA; Fellow Commoner, 2001–); Sorbonne. FBCS. Joined Joseph Lucas as graduate apprentice, 1954; Director, CAV, 1963; Director and General Manager, Diesel Equipment, CAV, 1967; Director: Simon Engineering, 1968; Joseph Lucas, 1974; Dir and Gen. Manager, Lucas Electrical, 1974; Divisional Man. Dir, Joseph Lucas Ltd, 1978; Jt Gp Man. Dir, Lucas Industries plc, 1979–84; Chm. and CEO, Spear & Jackson plc, 1992–2000. Chairman: Automotive Components Manufacturers, 1979–84; Plastics Processing EDC, 1985–87; Mem. Council and Exec., SMMT, 1979–84. CCMI. Liveryman, Wheelwrights Company, 1971–2006. Mem., 2002–, Chm., 2004–07, Develt Cttee, King's Coll., Cambridge. *Recreations:* reading, theatre, art. *Address:* Hillcroft, 15 Mearse Lane, Barnt Green, Birmingham B45 8HG. *T:* (0121) 447 7750.

WILKINSON, John Francis; Director of Public Affairs, BBC, 1980–85; *b* 2 Oct. 1926; *s* of late Col W. T. Wilkinson, DSO, and Evelyn S. Wilkinson (*née* Ward); *m* 1951, Alison (*d* 2015), *d* of late Hugh and Marian Malcolm; two *s* one *d*. *Educ:* Wellington Coll.; Edinburgh Univ. Naval Short Course, 1944–45; Cambridge and London Univs Colonial Course, 1947–48. Served Royal Navy (Fleet Air Arm trainee pilot, 1945), 1945–47; HM Colonial Service, N Nigeria, 1949; Asst District Officer, Bida, 1949; Asst Sec., Lands and Mines, Kaduna, 1950; Private Sec. to Chief Comr, N Nigeria, 1951; transf. to Nigerian Broadcasting Corp., 1952; Controller: Northern Region, 1952–56; National Programme, Lagos, 1956–58; joined BBC African Service as African Programme Organiser, 1958; East and Central African Programme Organiser, 1961; BBC TV Production Trng Course and attachment to Panorama, 1963; Asst Head, 1964, Head, 1969, BBC African Service; attachment to Horizon, 1972; Head of Production and Planning, BBC World Service, 1976; Secretary of the BBC, 1977–80. Dir, 1986–90, Trustee, 1990–99, The One World Broadcasting Trust. Chm. of Governors, Centre for Internat. Briefing, Farnham Castle, 1977–87, Vice-Pres., 1987–2004. Vice-Pres., Royal African Soc., 1978–82. MUniv Open, 1989. *Publications:* Broadcasting in Africa, in African Affairs (Jl of Royal African Soc.), 1972; (contrib.) Broadcasting in Africa, a continental survey of radio and television, 1974; (contrib.) Was it Only Yesterday, Northern Nigerian Administration Service anthology, 2002. *Address:* Compass Cottage, Box, Minchinhampton, near Stroud, Glos GL6 9HD. *T:* (01453) 833072.

WILKINSON, John Nicholas Ralph; Partner, Cooley LLP, since 2015; *b* Nottingham, 7 Oct. 1964; *s* of Ronald James Wilkinson and June Christine Wilkinson; *m* 1998, Barbara Radha; one *s* two *d*. *Educ:* Bilborough Sixth Form Coll.; Imperial Coll. London (BSc Chem.); Coll. of Law (CPE 1993). Development Chemist: Laporte Industries, 1986–89; AstraZeneca, 1989–91; trainee solicitor, 1993–95, solicitor, 1995–98, Lovells; Legal Counsel, Cancer Res. Technol., 1998–2000; Partner: Bird & Bird LLP, 2000–03; Reed Smith LLP, 2005–15. *Recreations:* family, fishing, windsurfing, making things. *Address:* Cooley LLP, Dashwood House, 69 Old Broad Street, EC2M 1QS. *T:* (020) 7556 4387, *Fax:* (020) 7900 3819. *E:* jwilkinson@cooley.com.

WILKINSON, Jonathan Peter, CBE 2015 (OBE 2004; MBE 2003); Rugby Union football player; Managing Director, Fineside Ltd, since 2009; Rugby pundit, Sky Sports, since 2014; *b* 25 May 1979; *s* of Philip Wilkinson and Philippa Wilkinson; *m* 2013, Shelley Jenkins. *Educ:* Lord Wandsworth Coll., Hants. Player (fly half): Newcastle Falcons RFU Club, 1997–2009; Toulon Rugby Club, 2009–14 (Captain, 2011–12, 2013–14; Jt Captain, 2012–13; winners, Heineken Cup, 2013, 2014); Member, England Rugby Team, 1998–2011 (91 caps); member, winning team: Five Nations Championship, 1999; Six Nations Championship, 2000, 2001, 2003; World Cup, 2003; played World Cup, 2011. Member, British Lions tour, Australia, 2001, NZ, 2005. World record internat. points scorer (1246 points). Freedom: City of Newcastle Upon Tyne, 2004; Town of Bandol, France, 2013; City of Toulon, France, 2014. Hon. DCL Northumbria, 2004; DUniv Surrey, 2009. Player of the Year, Internat. Rugby Players Assoc., 2002, 2003; Player of the Year, Internat. Rugby Bd, 2003; BBC Sports Personality of the Year, 2003; European Player of the Year, Eur. Rugby Cup, 2013. *Publications:* Lions and Falcons: my diary of a remarkable year, 2001; My World (autobiog.), 2004; How to Play Rugby My Way, 2005; (with Steve Black) Tackling Life, 2008; (with Owen Slot) Jonny: my autobiography, 2011. *W:* www.jonnywilkinson.com.

WILKINSON, Rev. Canon Keith Howard; Conduct, Eton College, since 2008; *b* 25 June 1948; *s* of Kenneth John Wilkinson and Grace Winifred (*née* Bowler); *m* 1972, Carolyn Gilbert; two *d*. *Educ:* Beaumont Leys Sch.; Gateway Sch., Leicester; Univ. of Hull (BA Hons); Emmanuel Coll., Cambridge (Lady Romney Exhibnr, MA status); Westcott House, Cambridge. Hd of Religious Studies, Bricknell High Sch., 1970–72; Hd of Faculty (Humanities), Kelvin Hall Comprehensive Sch., Kingston upon Hull, 1972–74; Deacon 1976; Priest 1977; Asst Priest, St Jude, Westwood, Peterborough, 1977; Asst Master and Chaplain, Eton Coll., Windsor, 1979–84; Sen. Chaplain and Hd of Religious Studies, Malvern Coll., 1984–89; Sen. Tutor, Malvern Coll., 1988–89; Headmaster: Berkhamsted Sch., 1989–96; King's Sch., Canterbury, 1996–2007. Hon. Canon, Canterbury Cathedral, 1996–. *Publications:* various articles and reviews. *Recreations:* films, theatre, music, walking, buildings and building, ecology. *Address:* Eton College, Windsor SL4 6DW. *Clubs:* East India, Lansdowne.

WILKINSON, His Honour Kenneth Henry Pinder; a Circuit Judge, 1996–2005; Designated Family Judge, Merseyside, 2002–05; *b* 5 Aug. 1939; *s* of late Henry Wilkinson and Alice Wilkinson; *m* 1966, Margaret Adams; two *s* one *d*. *Educ:* Wigan GS; Univ. of Manchester (LLB Hons). Admitted solicitor, 1965; in private practice, 1965–80; Dep. Dist Registrar, 1977–80; Dist Judge, 1980–96; Asst Recorder, 1990–93; Recorder, 1993–96. Chm. (part-time), Industrial Tribunal, 1977–80; Member: Matrimonial Causes Rule Cttee, 1978–80; County Court Rule Cttee, 1988–92. Mem., Family Law Cttee, Law Soc., 1976–80. *Publications:* (jtly) A Better Way Out, 1979; (contrib.) Personal Injury Litigation Service, 1984; (with I. S. Goldrein) Commercial Litigation: pre-emptive remedies, 1987, 3rd edn 1996; (with M. De Haas) Property Distribution on Divorce, 1989; (Consult. Ed.) County Court Litigation, 1993. *Recreations:* gardening, music, walking, watching sport, birdwatching. *Address:* School House, Chorley Road, Bispham, Ormskirk, Lancs L40 3SL.

WILKINSON, Leon Guy, FCIB; a General Commissioner of Income Tax, City of London, 1989–2003; part-time Member, VAT Tribunal, 1989–2004; *b* 6 Nov. 1928; *s* of Thomas Guy and Olive May Wilkinson; *m* 1953, Joan Margaret; one *s* one *d*. *Educ:* Bude Grammar Sch. CMS Oxon. Lloyds Bank: Regional Gen. Man., N and E Midlands, 1976–79; Asst Gen. Man., 1979–83; Gen. Man. (Finance), 1984–86; Chief Financial Officer, 1986–88. *Recreation:* sports. *Clubs:* MCC, Royal Over-Seas League; Nevill Golf (Tunbridge Wells).

WILKINSON, Rear-Adm. Nicholas John, CB 1994; Press Complaints Commissioner, 2005–08; Cabinet Office Historian, 2005–10; freelance lecturer on modern history, 2010–; *b* 14 April 1941; *s* of late Lt-Col Michael Douglas Wilkinson, RE and Joan Mary Wilkinson (*née* Cosens); *m* 1st, 1969, Penelope Ann Stephenson (marr. diss. 1996; she *d* 2003); three *s* one *d*; 2nd, 1998, Juliet Rayner (*née* Hockin). *Educ:* English School, Cairo; Cheltenham College; BRNC Dartmouth. Served HM Ships Venus, Vidal and Hermes, 1960–64; RN Air Station, Arbroath, 1964–65; HMS Fife, 1965–67; Asst Sec. to Vice-Chief of Naval Staff, 1968–70; HMS Endurance, 1970–72; Army Staff Course, 1973 (Mitchell Prizewinner); Clyde Submarine Base, 1974–75; Sec. to ACNS (Policy), 1975–77; HMS London, 1977–78; Asst Dir, Naval Officer Appts (SW), 1978–80; Trng Comdr, HMS Pembroke, 1980–82; NATO Defence Coll., Rome, 1982–83; MA to Dir, NATO Internat. Mil. Staff, 1983–85; RCDS, 1986; Dir, Defence Logistics, 1986; Sec. to First Sea Lord, 1989–90; Sen. Mil. Mem., Defence Organisation Study and Project Team, 1991–92; Dir Gen. of Naval Manpower and Trng, 1992–94; Chief Naval Supply and Secretariat Officer, 1993–97; Comdt, JSDC, 1994–97; mgt consultant, 1998–99; Maj.-Gen., RCDS, 1999; Sec., Defence, Press and Broadcasting Adv. Cttee (DA Notice Sec.), 1999–2004. Chm., Assoc. RN Officers, 1998–2004; Member Council: Forces Pension Soc., 1994–2005; Victory Services Assoc., 1998–2008 (Chm., 2001–08). Trustee, Greenwich Foundn, 2003–10. Mem., Develt Council, Trinity Coll. of Music, 2001–05; Ambassador, Trinity Laban Conservatoire of Music and Dance, 2005–. Chm., Adv. Cttee, Maritime Inst., Univ. of Greenwich, 2003–14. Gov., Princess Helena Coll., 1994–2004. President: Royal Naval Assoc. (Swindon), 1999–; Swindon Sea Cadets, 1999–; Great Bedwyn Cricket Club, 2010–. *Publications:* Secrecy and the Media, 2009; (contrib.) Spinning Intelligence, 2009; articles in The Naval Review and media publications. *Recreations:* cricket, opera. *Address:* 37 Burns Road, SW11 5GX. *Clubs:* Savile (Chm., 2008–14), Victory Services (Vice Pres., 2008–), MCC (Mem., Memship Cttee, 2000–03, 2005–14).

WILKINSON, Nigel Vivian Marshall; QC 1990; a Recorder, since 1992; a Deputy High Court Judge, since 1997; *b* 18 Nov. 1949; *s* of late John Marshall Wilkinson and Vivien Wilkinson; *m* 1974, Heather Carol Hallett (*see* Rt Hon. Dame Heather Hallett); two *s*. *Educ:* Charterhouse; Christ Church, Oxford (Holford exhibnr; MA). Called to the Bar, Middle Temple, 1972, Bencher, 1997; Astbury Scholar, 1972; Midland and Oxford Circuit, 1972–; an Asst Recorder, 1988–92; Hd of Chambers, 2008–12. Dep. Chm., Appeals Cttee, Cricket Council, 1991–97. Gov., Brambletye Sch., 1992–98. *Recreations:* cricket, golf, theatre. *Address:* Mint House, The Mint, Rye, E Sussex TN31 7EW. *Clubs:* Garrick, MCC; Vincent's (Oxford); I Zingari, Butterflies CC, Invalids CC, Armadillos CC, Rye Golf (Captain, 2012–13), Hon. Co. of Edinburgh Golfers.

WILKINSON, Vice Adm. Peter John, CB 2010; CVO 2007; Deputy Chief of Defence Staff (Personnel), 2007–10; *b* 28 May 1956; *s* of Sir Philip (William) Wilkinson and Eileen Patricia Wilkinson (*née* Malkin); *m* 1981, Tracey Kim Ward; two *d*. *Educ:* Royal Grammar Sch., High Wycombe; St David's Coll., Lampeter, Univ. of Wales (BA 1978). FCIPD 2003. Joined RN, 1975; trng, 1975–80; qualified submarines, 1980; Torpedo Officer, HMS Onslaught, 1981; Staff, C-in-C Fleet, 1982; trng courses, 1983; Tactics and Sonar Officer, HMS Resolution, 1984–86; Navigating Officer, HMS Churchill, 1986–87; submarine comd course, 1987; CO, HMS Otter, 1988–89; Staff of Captain (SM) Sea Trng, 1989–90; CO, HMS Superb, 1991–92; Comdr (SM), Maritime Tactical Sch., 1992–94; CO, HMS Vanguard, 1994–96; Asst Dir, Nuclear Policy, MOD, 1996–99; Capt., 2nd Submarine Sqn, 1999–2001; Director: RN Service Conditions, 2001–03; RN Life Mgt, 2003–04; Naval Sec., and Dir Gen., Human Resources (Navy), 2004–05; Defence Services Sec., 2005–07. Dir, Hook Park Consulting Ltd, 2011–13. Member: RNSA, 2011–; Council, Forces Pension Soc., 2011– (Chm., 2014–). Pres., RN Football Assoc., 2004–10; Hon. Vice Pres., FA, 2004–10; Nat. Pres., RBL, 2012–. Patron, Loch Class Frigates Assoc., 2012–. Chm., Seafarers UK, 2010–. Clerk, Cooks' Co., 2011–. Hon. Fellow, Univ. of Wales Trinity St David, 2013. *Recreations:* genealogy, gardening, watching all sports. *Address:* c/o Naval Secretary, Leach Building, Whale Island, Portsmouth, Hants PO2 8ER. *Club:* Army and Navy.

WILKINSON, Rhiannon Jane; Headmistress, Wycombe Abbey School, since 2013; *b* Ashton under Lyne, Lancs, 8 March 1962; *d* of David Fell and Letty Fell; *m* 2000, Donald Wilkinson; two *s*, and one step *d*. *Educ:* Fairfield High Sch. for Girls, Droylsden; St Hugh's Coll., Oxford (BA Hist.); Univ. of Bath (PGCE 1984); Manchester Univ. (MEd 2004). Teacher of History: King Edward VI Coll., Totnes, 1984–87; Bramhall High Sch., Stockport, 1987–91; Head of Hist., 1991–93, Head of Sixth Form, 1993–97, Shatin Coll., Hong Kong; Deputy Head: Cheadle Hulme, 1998–99; Jerudong Internat. Sch., Brunei, 2000–04; Dir of Studies, 2004–09, Housemistress, 2007–09, Haileybury; Principal, Harrogate Ladies' Coll., 2009–13. *Recreations:* travel, theatre, reading, food. *Address:* Wycombe Abbey School, High Wycombe, Bucks HP11 1PE. *T:* (01494) 520381. *E:* wilkinsonr@wycombeabbey.com.

WILKINSON, Richard Denys, CVO 1992; HM Diplomatic Service, retired; Ambassador to Chile, 2003–05; *b* 11 May 1946; *y s* of late Denys and Gillian Wilkinson; *m* 1982, Maria Angela Morris; two *s* one *d*. *Educ:* Eton Coll. (King's Schol.); Trinity Coll., Cambridge (MA, MLitt, Wace Medallist); Ecole Nat. des Langues Orientales Vivantes, Univ. de Paris; Ecole des Langues Orientales Anciennes, Inst. Catholique de Paris. Hayter Postdoctoral Fellow in Soviet Studies, SSEES, London, 1971; joined Diplomatic Service, 1972: Madrid, 1973; FCO, 1977; Vis. Prof., Univ. of Michigan, Ann Arbor, 1980; FCO, 1980; Ankara, 1983; Mexico City, 1985; Counsellor (Information), Paris, 1988; Head of Policy Planning Staff, FCO, 1993–94; Head of Eastern Dept, FCO, 1994–96; Ambassador to Venezuela, 1997–2000; Dir, Americas and Overseas Territories, FCO, 2000–03. Hd of Spanish, Winchester Coll., 2007–11. Chm. Govs, Univ. of Winchester, 2011–. *Publications:* articles and reviews in learned jls. *Recreations:* sightseeing, oriental studies. *Address:* 1 Westley Close, Winchester, Hants SO22 5LA. *Club:* Oxford and Cambridge.

WILKINSON, Dr Robert Edward; Principal, Hills Road Sixth Form College, Cambridge, 2002–08; *b* 23 Jan. 1950; *s* of Sydney Arthur Wilkinson and Winifred Wilkinson (*née* Hawker); *m* 1974, Diana Viader; one *s* two *d*. *Educ:* Bexley-Erith Tech. High Sch. for Boys, Bexley; University Coll., Swansea (BA 1971; PhD 1982); PGCE Oxford. Teacher of Hist., Scarborough Sixth Form Coll., 1975–82; Hd of Hist., John Leggott Coll., Scunthorpe, 1982–89; Vice Principal, Hills Rd Sixth Form Coll., Cambridge, 1989–94; Principal, Wyggeston & Queen Elizabeth I Coll., Leicester, 1994–2002. Registered Inspector, FEFC, 1995–2001; Addnl Inspector, Ofsted, 2001–04. Gov., Beaminster Sch., Dorset, 2010–. *Recreations:* bird-watching, walking, music, opera and ballet, theatre, history.

WILKINSON, Robert Purdy, OBE 1990; *b* 23 Aug. 1933; *s* of Robert Purdy and Lily Ingham Wilkinson; *m* 1957, June (*née* Palmer); two *d*. *Educ:* Univ. of Durham (BA; DipEd 1957). Kleinwort Sons & Co., 1958–62; Estabrook & Co., 1962–64; Partner, W. I. Carr Sons & Co., 1966–81. Stock Exchange: Mem. Council, 1978–81; Cttee Chm., 1980–81; Stock Exchange Inspector, 1981–84; Dir of Surveillance, Stock Exchange, 1984–90; Dir of Enforcement and Dep. Chief Exec., Securities Assoc., 1987–90. Dir, Tradepoint, 1994–2001; Chm., Bovill Ltd, 2003–05. Consultant: Morgan Grenfell Internat., 1991; S Africa Financial Markets Bd, 1991; Johannesburg Stock Exchange, 1991; DTI Inspector, 1987, 1989, 1991; Invesco Gp, 1997–2003 (Dir, 1994–97). Mem., Financial Services Tribunal, 1991–94; Special Advisor: Assoc. of Swiss Stock Exchanges, 1991; Czech Ministry of Finance, 1995; Bulgarian Ministry of Finance, 1997–99; Romanian Securities Commn, 1997–99; Tallinn Stock Exchange, 1999; Jordan Securities Commn, 1999–2002. Testified US Congress Cttee, 1988. Chm. of Govs, Sevenoaks Sch., 1992–2002; Chairman: Sevenoaks Sch. Foundn, 2003–12; Chevening C of E Sch., 2009–10. *Publications:* various articles on securities regulation and insider dealing. *Recreations:* schools' sport, education, church affairs.

WILKINSON, Dr Toby Alexander Howard; Egyptologist and author; Director, International Strategy, University of Cambridge, since 2015 (Head, International Strategy Office, 2011–15); Fellow, Clare College, Cambridge, since 2003; *b* Fareham, 25 March 1969; *s* of William Frederick Howard Wilkinson and Ann Elizabeth Wilkinson (*née* Rathbone); civil partnership 2006, Michael Timothy Eric Bailey. *Educ:* Portsmouth Grammar Sch.; Downing Coll., Cambridge (BA 1st cl. Hons 1990; Thomas Mulvey Prize 1990; MA 1994); Christ's Coll., Cambridge (PhD 1994). Lady Wallis Budge Jun. Res. Fellow, Christ's Coll., Cambridge, 1993–97; Leverhulme Trust Special Res. Fellow, Univ. of Durham, 1997–99; Develt Dir, and Fellow, Christ's Coll., Cambridge, 1999–2003; Develt Dir, Clare Coll., Cambridge, 2003–11; Chm., Cambridge Colls Develt Gp, 2007–11. *Publications:* State Formation in Egypt, 1996; Early Dynastic Egypt, 1999; Royal Annals of Ancient Egypt, 2000; Genesis of the Pharaohs, 2003; The Thames and Hudson Dictionary of Ancient Egypt, 2005; Lives of the Ancient Egyptians, 2007; (ed) The Egyptian World, 2007; The Rise and Fall of Ancient Egypt, 2010 (Hessell-Tiltman Prize); The Nile: downriver through Egypt's past and present, 2014; numerous articles in learned jls. *Recreations:* writing, gardening, travel, history. *Address:* Clare College, Cambridge CB2 1TL; c/o Rogers, Coleridge and White Ltd, 20 Powis Mews, W11 1JN.

WILKINSON, Tom, OBE 2005; actor; *b* 5 Feb. 1948; *m* 1998, Diana Hardcastle; two *d*. *Educ:* Univ. of Kent (BA); Royal Acad. of Dramatic Art. *Theatre includes:* The Cherry Orchard (tour); Peer Gynt; Brand; Three Sisters; Uncle Vanya; Henry IV; Henry V; Julius Caesar; The Merchant of Venice; As You Like It; Hamlet, RSC, 1981; King Lear, Tom and Viv, 1983, My Zinc Bed, 2000, Royal Court; Ghosts, 1986 (Critics' Circle Award, 1986), An Enemy of the People, 1988 (Critics' Circle Award, 1988), Young Vic; The Crucible, White Chameleon, 1991, RNT. *Films include:* Sylvia, Wetherby, 1985; Sharma and Beyond, 1986; Paper Mask, 1990; In the Name of the Father, 1993; Priest, A Business Affair, 1994; Sense and Sensibility, 1995; The Ghost and the Darkness, 1996; Jilting Joe, Oscar and Lucinda, Smilla's Sense of Snow, Wilde, The Full Monty, 1997; The Governess, Shakespeare in Love, Rush Hour, 1998; Molokai: The Story of Father Damien, Ride with the Devil, 1999; The Patriot, Essex Boys, Chain of Fools, 2000; In the Bedroom, Another Life, Black Knight, 2001; The Importance of Being Earnest, Before You Go, 2002; Girl with a Pearl Earring, 2003; If Only, Eternal Sunshine of the Spotless Mind, Stage Beauty, Piccadilly Jim, A Good Woman, 2004; Ripley Under Ground, Batman Begins, The Exorcism of Emily Rose, A Good Woman, Separate Lies, 2005; The Night of the White Pants, The Last Kiss, 2006; Dedication, Michael Clayton, 2007; Cassandra's Dream, RocknRolla, 2008; Valkyrie, Duplicity, 2009; The Best Exotic Marigold Hotel, The Samaritan, 2012; The Lone Ranger, 2013; The Grand Budapest Hotel, Belle, 2014; Selma, Unfinished Business, Good People, 2015. *Television includes:* Prime Suspect, 1991; All Things Bright and Beautiful, 1994; Martin Chuzzlewit, 1994; The Gathering Storm, 2002. *Address:* c/o Lou Coulson Associates Ltd, 1st Floor, 37 Berwick Street, W1F 8RS.

WILKINSON, Prof. (William) Brian, PhD; FGS; FICE; FCIWEM; Senior Consultant, Solutions to Environmental Problems, since 1999; *b* 20 Jan. 1938; *s* of James Edmund Wilkinson and Gladys (*née* Forster); *m* 1962, Gillian Warren; two *s* one *d*. *Educ:* Univ. of Durham (BSc Hons Civil Engrg, BSc Hons Geol.); Univ. of Manchester (PhD 1968). FGS 1974; FCIWEM (FIWEM 1984); FICE 1989. Asst engr, Babtie Shaw and Morton, Consulting Engrs, 1961–63; Lectr, Dept of Civil Engrg, Univ. of Manchester, 1963–69; Sen. Engr, Water Resources Bd, 1969–74; Sen. Principal Hydrologist, Severn Trent Water Authy, 1974–75; Hd, Water Resources Div., Water Res. Centre, 1975–83; Prof. of Civil Engrg, RMCS, Cranfield Univ., 1983–88; Dir, Inst. of Hydrology, 1988–94, Dir, Centre for Ecology and Hydrology, 1995–99, NERC. Visiting Professor: in Hydrol., Univ. of Reading, 1989–; in Dept of Civil Engrg, Univ. of Newcastle upon Tyne, 2000–. Dir, Oxford Vacs, 1997–99. Mem. and Project Co-ordinator, Ind. Rev. Gp for Decommissioning Brent N Sea Platforms, 2007–; Advr, Safety Health and Envmt Cttee, Transport for London, 2007–10. Fellow, Russian Acad. of Nat. Sci., 1997. *Publications:* (ed) Groundwater Quality, Measurement, Prediction and Protection, 1976; (ed jtly) Applied Groundwater Hydrology, 1991; (ed) Groundwater Problems in Urban Areas, 1994; numerous articles covering geotechnics and envmtl sci. *Recreations:* classical music, French wines, water colour painting, choral singing, archaeology, Shukokai karate. *Address:* Millfield House, High Street, Leintwardine, Craven Arms, Shropshire SY7 0LB. *T:* (01547) 540356. *E:* gb.wilk@dsl.pipex.com.

WILKINSON, Dr William Lionel, CBE 1987; FRS 1990; FREng; a Director, British Nuclear Fuels plc, 1984–94; *b* 16 Feb. 1931; *s* of Lionel and Dorothy Wilkinson; *m* 1955, Josephine Anne Pilgrim; five *s*. *Educ:* Christ's Coll., Cambridge (MA, PhD, ScD). Salters' Res. Schol., Christ's Coll., Cambridge, 1953–56; Lectr in Chem. Engrg, UC Swansea, 1956–59; UKAEA Production Gp, 1959–67; Prof. of Chem. Engrg, Univ. of Bradford, 1967–79; British Nuclear Fuels Ltd: Dep. Dir, 1982–84; Technical Dir, 1984–86; Dep. Chief Exec., 1986–92; non-exec. Dir, 1992–94; Dep. Chm., Allied Colloids plc, 1992–98 (non-exec. Dir, 1989–98). Vis. Prof. of Chemical Engrg, Imperial Coll., London, 1980–2004. Chm., British Nuclear Industry Forum, 1992–97; Pres., Eur. Atomic Forum, 1994–96. Member: SRC, 1981–85; ACOST, 1990–95. FIChemE (Pres., 1980); FREng (FEng 1980). Liveryman, Salters' Co., 1985. Hon. DEng Bradford, 1989. *Publications:* Non-Newtonian Flow, 1960; contribs to sci. and engrg jls on heat transfer, fluid mechanics, polymer processing, process dynamics and nuclear fuel processing. *Recreations:* bridge, gardening. *Address:* Tree Tops, Legh Road, Knutsford, Cheshire WA16 8LP. *T:* (01565) 653344. *Club:* Athenæum.

WILKS, Ann; *see* Wilks, M. A.

WILKS, Maj. Gen. Carew Lovell, CB 2014; CBE 2007; CEng, FIET; Chief Operating Officer, NIMR LLC, since 2013; *b* Cuckfield, Sussex, 10 May 1960; *s* of Richard Lovell Wilks and Sheila Gillian Jean Wilks (*née* Bowack, now Olford); *m* 1983, Janey Prior-Willeard; two *s*. *Educ:* Malvern Coll.; Lincoln Coll., Oxford (MA Engrg Sci.); RMA Sandhurst; RSME. CEng 1992; FIET 2007. Commnd RE, 1978; Troop Comdr, 1983–86; on secondment to industry, 1987–88; Adjt, 28 Amphibious Engr Regt, 1989–90; Berlin Works Office, 1991–93; OC 5 Field Sqdn, 1994–96; Project Manager, MoD Procurement Exec., 1996–98; OC 529 Specialist Team RE (Air Support), 1998–99; Directing Staff, RMCS, 1999–2000; CO, 25 Engr Regt, NI, 2000–02; Team Leader, Combat Support Vehicles, 2002–04; Director: Army Infrastructure Orgn, 2004–07; Energy Ops, Iraq, 2007–08; Hd, Individual Capability, MoD, 2008–11; Dir Land Equipment, MoD, 2011–13. Pres., Instn of RE, 2012–. *Recreations:* overland travel, dinghy sailing, shooting, deer management. *E:* carew.wilks@btinternet.com. *Club:* Naval and Military.

WILKS, (David) Michael (Worsley); President, Standing Committee of European Doctors, 2008–09; Chairman, eHealth Users' Stakeholder Group; *b* 26 May 1949; *s* of Dennis Worsley Wilks and Bridget Wilks (*née* Chetwynd-Stapylton, later Sewter); *m* 1972, Patricia Hackforth (marr. diss. 1992); one *s* two *d*. *Educ:* St John's Sch., Leatherhead; St Mary's Hosp. Med. Sch., London (MB BS 1972). DObstRCOG 1975. House officer posts at St Mary's Hosp., Paddington and Wembley Hosp., 1972–74; GP trng, London, 1974; Principal in gen. practice, Kensington and Richmond, 1975–92; Metropolitan Police: Sen. Police Surgeon, 1992–97; Principal Forensic Med. Examr, 1997–2010. Vis. Lectr, Kingston Univ., 1997–. Asst Med. Advr, Richmond Council Housing Dept, 1991–; Med. Referee and Trustee, Sick Doctors' Trust, 1997–; Chm. of Trustees, Rehabilitation of Addicted Prisoners Trust, 2006–; Trustee, Drinkaware Trust, 2009–. British Medical Association: Member: Trainees Sub-Cttee, 1974–75; Gen. Med. Services Cttee, 1977–89; New Charter Wkg Gp, 1982; Council, 1997–; Mem., 1979–86, 1995, Chm., 1997–2006, Med. Ethics Cttee; Chm., Representative Body, 2004–07 (Dep. Chm., 2001–04). Observer, Standards Cttee, GMC, 1997–; Mem., Ethics in Medicine Cttee, 1998–, Euthanasia wkg party (jtly with RCGP), 1999–, RCP. *Publications:* contribs to med. jls on ethical issues, addiction medicine, forensic medicine. *Recreations:* photography, theatre, art, literature, cinema, walking, Mozart. *Address:* c/o Standing Committee of European Doctors, Rue Grimard 15, 1040 Brussels, Belgium. *E:* mwilks@bma.org.uk. *Club:* Royal Society of Medicine.

WILKS, Jonathan Paul, (Jon), CMG 2012; HM Diplomatic Service; Ambassador to Oman, since 2014; *b* Callow End, Worcs, 30 Sept. 1967; *s* of Douglas Edwin Ian Wilks and Veronica Kaye Wilks (*née* Mills); *m* 2015, Hon. Patricia Marie Haslach. *Educ:* Chase High Sch., Malvern; Durham Univ. (BSc Hons Natural Scis 1989; MA Dist. Middle East Politics 2000); St Antony's Coll., Oxford (MPhil Internat. Relns 2002). FRGS 1996. Entered FCO, 1989; Asst Desk Officer, Iran Desk, 1990–91; Arabic lang. trng, London, 1991–92, Cairo, 1992–93; Second Sec., Khartoum, 1993–96; First Sec., Riyadh, 1996–99; on secondment to Cabinet Office Assessments Staff, 2002–03; Deputy Head: British Office, Baghdad, 2003; Iraq Policy Unit, FCO, 2004; Security Policy Gp, FCO, 2005–07; Regl Arabic Spokesman, Dubai, 2007–09; Dep. Hd of Mission, Baghdad, 2009–10; Ambassador to Yemen, 2010–11; HCSC 2012; UK Special Rep. to the Syrian Opposition, 2012–13; UK Special Rep. for Syria, 2014. Iraq Reconstruction Medal, 2004. *Recreations:* horse racing, music. *Address:* c/o Foreign and Commonwealth Office, King Charles Street, SW1A 2AH. *Clubs:* Travellers, National Liberal.

WILKS, (Margaret) Ann, CBE 2004; Secretary, Financial Reporting Council, and Financial Reporting Review Panel, 1998–2004; *b* 11 May 1943; *d* of Herbert Robson and Margaret Robson (*née* Culbert); *m* 1977, Victor Wilks; two *d*. *Educ:* Putney High Sch., GPDST; Lady Margaret Hall, Oxford (BA Modern Hist., BPhil American Hist.); Univ. of Pennsylvania (Thouron Schol.). Asst Principal, Min. of Power and DTI, 1968–71; Department of Trade and Industry: Private Sec. to Perm. Sec. (Trade) and Parly Sec., 1971–72; Principal, 1972–73; journalist, Economist, 1973–74; Principal: DTI, 1974–76; Cabinet Office, 1976–78; (pt-time) DTI, 1982–84; (pt-time) Asst Sec., DTI, 1984–96 (Hd, Industrial Develt Unit, and Sec., Industrial Develt Adv. Bd, 1991–96); Dir, Metals, Minerals and Shipbuilding, DTI, 1996–98. Mem., Tribunal Panel, Financial Reporting Council Disciplinary Scheme (formerly Accountancy Investigation and Discipline Bd, then Accountancy and Actuarial Discipline Bd), 2004–13. Chm., Hornsey Town Hall Community Partnership Bd and Creative Trust, 2008–11. Trustee, 2002–11, and Chm. of Govs, 2004–11, Nat. Centre for Young People with Epilepsy, Lingfield. Mem. Cttee, Thouron Scholarship, 1974–80. *Recreations:* tennis, cookery, theatre, walking, sightseeing. *Address:* 28 Berkeley Road, N8 8RU.

WILKS, Michael; *see* Wilks, D. M. W.

WILKS, Prof. Stephen Robert Mark, PhD; Professor of Politics, 1990–2013, now Emeritus, and Deputy Vice Chancellor, 1999–2002 and 2004–05, University of Exeter; *b* 2 Jan. 1949; *s* of late Ernest Gordon Fawcett Wilks and Florence Wilks (*née* Wilson); *m* 1976, Philippa Mary Hughes; three *d*. *Educ:* Buckhurst Hill Co. High Sch.; City of Westminster Coll.; Univ. of Lancaster (BA); Univ. of Manchester (PhD 1980). FCA 1978. Chartered Accountant, Fryer Whitehill and Co., London, 1968–72; University of Liverpool, Department of Political Theory and Institutions: Lectr, 1978–86; Sen. Lectr, 1986–89; Reader, 1989–90. Vis. Prof., Faculty of Law, Kyoto Univ., 1989. Member: ESRC, 2001–05 (Chm., Res. Priorities Bd, 2001–05); Competition Commn, 2001–09; Competition Appeal Tribunal, 2011–. *Publications:* Industrial Crisis (ed with K. Dyson), 1983; Industrial Policy and the Motor Industry, 1984, 2nd edn 1988; (ed with M. Wright) Comparative Government-Industry Relations, 1987; (ed with B. Doern) Comparative Competition Policy, 1996; (ed with B. Doern) Regulatory Institutions in Britain and North America, 1998; In the Public Interest: competition policy and the Monopolies and Mergers Commission, 1999; (ed jtly) Reforming Public and Corporate Governance, 2002; The Political Power of the Business Corporation, 2013. *Recreations:* walking, wine, gardening, tea. *Address:* Department of Politics, University of Exeter, Amory Building, Rennes Drive, Exeter EX4 4RJ. *T:* (01392) 263168. *E:* s.r.m.wilks@exeter.ac.uk.

WILL, Prof. Robert George, CBE 2000; MD; FRCP; Professor of Clinical Neurology, University of Edinburgh, since 1998; Consultant Neurologist, Western General Hospital, Edinburgh, since 1987; Co-ordinator, European Creutzfeldt-Jakob Disease Surveillance, since 2002; *b* 30 July 1950; *s* of George and Margaret Will; *m* 1976, Jayne; one *s* one *d*. *Educ:* Glenalmond Coll.; St John's Coll., Cambridge (MB BChir 1974; MA, MD 1985); London Hosp. Med. Coll. FRCP 1994. London Hosp., Nat. Hosp., Queen Sq. and N Middx Hosp., 1974–79; res. at Univ. of Oxford, 1979–82; Registrar, St Thomas' Hosp., 1982–84; Sen. Registrar, Nat. Hosp., Queen Sq. and Guy's Hosp., 1994–97. Dir, Nat. CJD Surveillance Unit, 1990–2002. FMedSci 2001. FRSA 1998. *Publications:* contrib. articles on Creutzfeldt-Jakob Disease. *Address:* 4 St Catherine's Place, Edinburgh EH9 1NU. *T:* (0131) 667 3667.

WILLACY, Michael James Ormerod, CBE 1989; Managing Director (formerly Managing Partner), Michael Willacy Associates Ltd, 1990–2010; *b* 7 June 1933; *s* of James and Marjorie Willacy (*née* Sanders); *m* 1st, 1961, Merle Louise de Lange; two *s* one *d*; 2nd, 1985, Victoria Stuart John; three *s* one *d*. *Educ:* Taunton Sch., Somerset. FCIPS. Purchasing Agent, Shell Venezuela, 1964–73; Procurement Advr, Shell Internat., The Hague, 1974–77; Supt, Shell Stanlow, 1978–80; Manager, Shell Wilmslow, 1981–83; Gen. Man., Shell Materials Services, 1983–85; Dir, Central Unit on Purchasing, 1985–90, Procurement Advr, 1991–92, HM Treasury. Chairman: Macclesfield Chamber of Commerce, 1981–83; Macclesfield Business Ventures, 1982–83. Old Tauntonian Association: Gen. Sec., 1978–91; Pres., 1988–89; Vice-Pres., 1990–; Gov., Taunton Sch., 1993–2008; Chm., St Dunstan's Abbey Sch., Plymouth,

1997–2004; Hon. Vice-Pres., Plymouth Coll., 2005–. *Recreations:* golf, travel, gardening. *Address:* 2 Erme Park, Ermington, Ivybridge, Devon PL21 9LY. *Clubs:* Old Tauntonian Association (Taunton); Bigbury Golf (Chm., 2007–10).

WILLASEY-WILSEY, Timothy Andrew, CMG 2007; HM Diplomatic Service, retired; International Advisor: Royal Bank of Scotland, since 2008; Coutts, since 2011; *b* 12 Sept. 1953; *s* of Maj.-Gen. Anthony Patrick Willasey-Wilsey, CB, MBE, MC, and of Dorothy Willasey-Wilsey (*née* Yates); *m* 1983, Alison Middleton Mackie; three *s*. *Educ:* Shrewsbury Sch.; Univ. of St Andrews (MA 1st Cl. Hons Mod. Hist. 1976). Teacher, English Sch., Addis Ababa, 1971–72; Metal Box Ltd, 1976–81: Export Sales Manager, 1977–79; Factory Mgt, 1979–81; joined HM Diplomatic Service, 1981; FCO, 1981–83; First Sec., Luanda, 1983–86; Hd of Chancery, later Dep. Hd of Mission, San Jose, Costa Rica, 1986–89; also Consul, San Jose and Managua, Nicaragua, 1986–89; FCO, 1989–93; Counsellor (Political), Islamabad, 1993–96; FCO, 1996–99; Counsellor, UK Mission to UN, Geneva, 1999–2002; Dir, FCO, 2002–08. Vis. Sen. Res. Fellow, Dept of War Studies, KCL, 2012–. Ext. Expert, Indian Council on Global Relns, 2013–. Asst Ed., The Victorian Web, 2014–. *Recreations:* history, travel, reading, cricket. *Address:* c/o Royal Bank of Scotland, 280 Bishopsgate, EC2M 4RB. *Clubs:* Royal Over-Seas League, MCC.

WILLBY, Christopher Roy, CEng; Director, Hazardous Installations Directorate, Health and Safety Executive, 2003–05; *b* 11 March 1945; *s* of Brian George Willby and Jean Marjorie Willby; *m* 1967, Sheila Burton (marr. diss. 1991); two *d*. *Educ:* Temple Moor Grammar Sch., Leeds; Univ. of Manchester Inst. of Sci. and Technol. (BSc Hons); Leeds Poly. (DMS). CEng, MInstE 1983. Asst Engr, Southern Project Gp, CEGB, 1966–70; Section Hd, UKAEA Risley, later NNC, 1970–78; Engrg Manager for subsid. co., Hickson Gp, 1978–82; Health and Safety Executive: Principal Inspector, 1982–87, Superintendent Inspector, 1987–91, NII; Dep. Chief Inspector, Nuclear and Radioactive Waste Policy, 1991–98; Regl Dir, Yorks and NE, 1998–2002. Chm., Potters Bar Rail Inquiry Bd, 2007–09. Co. Sec., Welsh Highland Rly Ltd, 2006–. *Recreations:* gardening, walking, theatre, renovating old motorcycles. *E:* chriswillby@tiscali.co.uk.

WILLCOCKS, Sir David (Valentine), Kt 1977; CBE 1971; MC 1944; conductor; Musical Director of the Bach Choir, 1960–98, Conductor Laureate, since 1998; General Editor, OUP Church Music, since 1961; *b* 30 Dec. 1919; *s* of late T. H. Willcocks; *m* 1947, Rachel Gordon, *d* of late Rev. A. C. Blyth, Fellow of Selwyn Coll., Cambridge; one *s* two *d* (and one *s* decd). *Educ:* Clifton Coll.; King's Coll., Cambridge (MA; MusB). Chorister, Westminster Abbey, 1929–33; Scholar, Clifton Coll., 1934–38; FRCO, 1938; Scholar at College of St Nicolas (RSCM), 1938–39; Organ Scholar, King's Coll., Cambridge, 1939–40; Open Foundation Scholarship, King's Coll., Cambridge, 1940; Stewart of Rannoch Scholarship, 1940. Served War of 1939–45, 5th Bn DCLI, 1940–45. Organ Scholar, King's Coll., Cambridge, 1945–47; Fellow of King's Coll., Cambridge, 1947–51, Hon. Fellow, 1979–; Organist of Salisbury Cathedral, 1947–50; Master of the Choristers and Organist, Worcester Cathedral, 1950–57; Fellow and Organist, King's Coll., Cambridge, 1957–73; Univ. Lectr in Music, Cambridge Univ., 1957–74; Univ. Organist, Cambridge Univ., 1958–74; Dir, RCM, 1974–84. Conductor: Cambridge Philharmonic Soc., 1947; City of Birmingham Choir, 1950–57; Bradford Festival Choral Soc., 1957–74; Cambridge Univ. Musical Soc., 1958–73. President: RCO, 1966–68; ISM, 1978–79; Old Cliftonian Soc., 1979–81; Nat. Fedn of Music Socs, 1980–89; Assoc. of British Choral Dirs, 1993–. Mem. Council, Winston Churchill Trust, 1980–90. Freeman, City of London, 1981. FRSCM 1965; FRCM 1971; FRNCM 1977; FRSAMD 1982; Hon. RAM 1965; Hon. FTCL 1976; Hon. GSM 1980; Hon. FRCCO 1967. Hon. MA Bradford, 1973; Hon. DMus: Exeter, 1976; Leicester, 1977; Westminster Choir Coll., Princeton, 1980; Bristol, 1981; St Olaf Coll., Minnesota, 1991; RCM, 1998; Victoria, BC, 1999; Rowan, 2007; Hon. DLitt: Sussex, 1982; Newfoundland, 2003; Hon. Dr of Sacred Letters, Trinity Coll., Toronto, 1985; Hon. Dr of Fine Arts, Luther Coll., Iowa, 1998; Hon. LLD Toronto, 2001. *Publications:* miscellaneous choral and instrumental works; *relevant publication:* A Life in Music: conversations with Sir David Willcocks and friends (ed by William Owen), 2008. *Address:* 13 Grange Road, Cambridge CB3 9AS. *T:* (01223) 359559. *Club:* Athenæum.

See also J. P. Willcocks.

WILLCOCKS, Prof. Dianne Marie, CBE 2008; DL; Leadership Consultant and Emeritus Professor, York St John University, since 2010; *b* 5 May 1945; *d* of late Jack and Georgina Kitson; *m* 1965, Peter Willcocks (marr. diss. 1984); two *d*. *Educ:* Ealing Coll. of Higher Educn (DipM 1966); Univ. of Surrey (BSc Hons Human Scis 1976). Dir of Res., then Dean, Envmtl and Social Scis, Poly., then Univ., of N London, 1980–93; Prof. of Social Gerontology, Univ. of N London, 1992–93; Asst Principal, Sheffield Hallam Univ., 1993–99; Principal, York St John Coll., later York St John Univ. Coll., then Vice-Chancellor, York St John Univ., 1999–2010; Dir, Governor Develt Progs, Leadership Foundn for HE, 2011–14. Mem. Bd, HEFCE, 2006–09. Vice-Chairman: York Teaching Hosp. Foundn Trust, 2010–; Joseph Rowntree Foundn, 2011–; Chm. Bd, York Th. Royal, 2003–13. Gov., London Metropolitan Univ., 2010–; Vice-Chm., Rose Bruford Coll., 2010–. DL N Yorks, 2010. Hon. Dr Sheffield Hallam, 2012. *Publications:* (jtly) Private Lives in Public Places, 1987; (jtly) Residential Care Revisited, 1997. *Recreations:* family, friends, fitness. *Address:* 61 Rowntree Wharf, York YO1 9XA. *T:* (01904) 670884. *E:* D.Willcocks@sircles.net.

WILLCOCKS, Jonathan Peter; freelance conductor and composer, since 1975; *b* Worcester, 9 Jan. 1953; *s* of Sir David Valentine Willcocks, *qv*; *m* 1999, Dr Alice Emerson; three *s* two *d*. *Educ:* Clifton Coll.; Trinity Coll., Cambridge (BA 1974; PGCE). Director of Music: Portsmouth Grammar Sch., 1975–78; Bedales Sch., 1978–89; Dir, Jun. Acad., RAM, 1989–2008. Musical Director: Portsmouth Choral Union, 1975–2012; Chichester Singers, 1979–; Southern Pro Musica, 1990–; Guildford Choral Soc., 2012–. Hon. RAM 1996. Compositions include major choral works, works for children's choir, shorter pieces and instrumental works. *Recreations:* golf, theatre, eating and drinking. *Address:* 3 The Square, Compton, Chichester, W Sussex PO18 9HA. *T:* (023) 9263 1369. *E:* jonathan@jonathanwillcocks.com. *Clubs:* Liphook Golf, St Enodoc Golf.

WILLCOCKS, Lt-Gen. Sir Michael (Alan), KCB 2000 (CB 1997); CVO 2009; Independent Reviewer (formerly Chartered Commissioner), Press Complaints Commission, 2009–12; Gentleman Usher of the Black Rod and Serjeant-at-Arms, House of Lords, and Secretary to the Lord Great Chamberlain, 2001–09; Director, IKOS CIF, since 2010; *b* 27 July 1944; *s* of late Henry Willcocks and Georgina Willcocks (*née* Lawton); *m* 1966, Jean Paton Weir; one *s* two *d*. *Educ:* St John's Coll.; RMA Sandhurst; London Univ. (BSc Hons). Commnd RA, 1964; served Malaya, Borneo, NI, Germany, 1965–72; Instructor, RMA Sandhurst, 1972–74; MoD, 1977–79; Comd M Battery, RHA, 1979–80; Directing Staff, Staff Coll., 1981–83; CO, 1st Regt, RHA, 1983–85; Dep. ACOS, HQ UKLF, 1985–87; ACOS, Intelligence/Ops, HQ UKLF, 1988; CRA, 4th Armd Div., 1989–90; rcds 1991; ACOS, Land Ops, Joint War HQ, Gulf War, 1991; Dir Army Plans and Programme, 1991–93; Dir Gen. Land Warfare, 1993–94; COS Allied Command Europe Rapid Reaction Corps, 1994–96; COS Land Component Implementation Force, Bosnia-Herzegovina, 1995–96; ACGS, MoD, 1996–99; Dep. Comdr (Ops), Stabilisation Force, Bosnia-Herzegovina, 1999–2000; UK Mil. Rep. to NATO and the EU, 2000–01. Comr, Royal Hosp., Chelsea, 1996–99. Col Comdt, RA, 2000–05; Representative Col Comdt, RA, 2004–05. Hon. Col, 1 RHA, 1999–2006. Mem., European-Atlantic Gp, 1994–. Mem., Pilgrims, 2002–. Trustee, Lifeline Energy (formerly Freeplay Foundn), 2006–13. MSM (USA), 1996, 2000. Hon. DLitt Hull, 2008. Kt Comdr, Sacred Military Order of St George, 2006; PJK 2006. *Publications:* Airmobility and the Armoured Experience, 1989. *Recreations:* books, music, fishing, sailing, shooting. *Clubs:* Beefsteak, National Liberal, Pitt, Saints and Sinners.

WILLEMS, Julia Ann; *see* Cheetham, J. A.

WILLEMS, Lodewijk; Chief Executive Officer, Edwards & Willems, since 2013; Advisor to Chief Executive Officer and Chief Operating Officer, BNP Paribas Fortis, since 2013; *b* 6 April 1948; *s* of Frans and Leona Willems-Hendrickx; *m* 1976, Lindsay Edwards; three *s* one *d*. *Educ:* Univ. of Brussels (Licentiate Pol Science and Internat. Relns 1971); Yale Univ. (MA Pol Science 1975). Entered Belgian Diplomatic Service, 1976; Dep. Perm. Rep., IAEA, Vienna, 1977; Advr to Dep. Prime Minister and Minister for Econ. Affairs, 1977–81; Dep. Sec. Gen., Benelux Econ. Union, 1981–85; Political Counsellor, Kinshasa, 1985–88; Chef de Cabinet to Minister for Econ. Affairs, 1988–91; Dep. Perm. Rep. to EU, 1991–92; Chef de Cabinet to Minister of Foreign Affairs, 1992–94; Perm. Rep. (Ambassador rank), UN, Geneva, 1994–97; Ambassador: to UK, 1997–2002; to Germany, 2002–06. Dir of External Affairs, then Dir of Ext. and Govtl Affairs, Fortis Bank, later BNP Paribas Fortis, 2006–13. Chm., Internat. Relns Commn, Fédération des Entreprises de Belgique/Verbond van Belgische Ondernemingen, 2008–14; Board Member: BASF Antwerp, 2006–15; Flanders Festival, 2008–. Commn for Relief of Belgium Fellow, Belgian-American Educnl Foundn, 1973. Grand Officier, Order of Leopold II (Belgium), 2005. *Recreations:* theatre, classical music. *Address:* (office) Rue Royale 20, 1000 Brussels, Belgium.

WILLEMS, Marc Paul Bernard Albert; QC 2015; a Recorder, since 2005; *b* Manchester, 6 May 1966; *s* of Bernard and Berthe Willems; *m* 1991, Julia Ann Cheetham, *qv*; two *s* one *d*. *Educ:* St Bede's Coll., Manchester; Nottingham Univ. (BA Law 1989); Inns of Court Sch. of Law. Called to the Bar, 1990. *Recreations:* cycling, running, family, France, music concerts. *Address:* Cobden House Chambers, 19 Quay Street, Manchester M3 3HN. *T:* (0161) 833 6000, *Fax:* (0161) 833 6001. *E:* marc.willems@cobden.co.uk. *Club:* Pyrenean Cycling.

WILLERS, Marc Lawrence George; QC 2014; *b* Newton, Cambs, 28 Nov. 1964; *s* of Peter Willers and Diane Waters (*née* Dobrashian); *m* 1999, Zoe Uney; one *d*. *Educ:* Haydon Sch., Middx; Chelmer Coll. of Higher Educn (LLB). Called to the Bar, Lincoln's Inn, 1987; in practice as a barrister, specialising in human rights law, 1987–. *Publications:* (ed jtly) Gypsy and Traveller Law, 2004, 2nd edn 2007; Ensuring Access to Rights for Roma and Travellers, 2009. *Recreations:* sport, theatre, travelling, cooking, Gypsy music. *Address:* Garden Court Chambers, 57–60 Lincoln's Inn Fields, WC2A 3LJ. *T:* (020) 7993 7600, *Fax:* (020) 7993 7700. *E:* marcw@gclaw.co.uk.

WILLESDEN, Area Bishop of, since 2001; **Rt Rev. Peter Alan Broadbent;** *b* 31 July 1952; *s* of Philip and Patricia Broadbent; *m* 1974, Sarah Enderby; one *s*. *Educ:* Merchant Taylors' Sch., Northwood, Middx; Jesus Coll., Cambridge (MA 1978); St John's Coll., Nottingham (DipTh 1975). Ordained deacon, 1977, priest 1978; Assistant Curate: St Nicholas, Durham City, 1977–80; Emmanuel, Holloway, 1980–83; Chaplain, Poly. of N London, 1983–89; Vicar, Trinity St Michael, Harrow, 1989–94; Archdeacon of Northolt, 1995–2001; Acting Bishop of Edmonton, 2015. Proctor in Convocation, London, 1985–2001. Member: Archbishops' Council, C of E, 1999–2000; Central Governing Body, City Parochial Foundn, 1999–2003; Gen. Synod, 2004–. Chm. Council, St John's Coll., Nottingham, 2002–10. Trustee, Church Urban Fund, 2002–11. Mem. (Lab) Islington BC, 1982–89. *Publications:* contrib. to theol books and jls. *Recreations:* football, theatre and film, railways. *Address:* 173 Willesden Lane, NW6 7YN. *T:* (020) 8451 0189, *Fax:* (020) 8451 4606. *E:* bishop.willesden@btinternet.com.

WILLETT, Prof. Keith Malcolm, FRCS; Professor of Orthopaedic Trauma Surgery, University of Oxford, since 2004; Fellow, Wolfson College, Oxford, since 2004; National Director for Acute Episodes of Care, NHS England, since 2012; *b* 9 Sept. 1957; *s* of Aubrey and Ruth Willett; *m* 1980, Lesley Kiernan; three *s* two *d*. *Educ:* Charing Cross Hosp. Med. Sch., Univ. of London (MB BS 1981). LRCP, MRCS 1981, FRCS 1985. Fellow in Trauma, Sunnybrook Health Sci. Center, Toronto, 1991–92; Consultant, Nuffield Orthopaedic Centre, Oxford, 1992–95; Consultant Orthopaedic and Trauma Surgeon, John Radcliffe Hospital, 1992–2004, Hon. Consultant, 2004–; Nat. Clinical Dir for Trauma Care, NHS, 2009–12. *Publications:* research papers on child accident prevention, functional outcomes after injury and surgical trng. *Recreation:* football. *Address:* Kadoorie Centre for Critical Care Research and Education, John Radcliffe Hospital, Oxford OX3 9DU. *T:* (01865) 851021, *Fax:* (01865) 857611.

WILLETT, Michael John, FRAeS; Board Member, Civil Aviation Authority and Group Director, Safety Regulation, 1992–97; *b* 2 Oct. 1944; *s* of Reginald John Willett and Nora Else Willett; *m* 1st, 1967, Gillian Margaret Pope (marr. diss. 1998); two *s* one *d*; 2nd, 1998, Paulene Ann Parkinson. *Educ:* Grammar Sch., Tottenham; Open Univ. (BA Hons); Open Business Sch. (MBA). RAF, 1963–71; Airline Captain, Laker Airways, 1973–82; Flight Ops Inspectorate, CAA, 1982–92. Member (C): W Sussex CC, 1999–2001; Horsham DC, 2015–. Liveryman, Hon. Co. of Air Pilots (formerly GAPAN), 1991– (Master, 2003–04). *Recreations:* horse riding, guitar playing. *Club:* Royal Air Force.

WILLETT, Prof. Peter, PhD, DSc; Professor of Information Science, University of Sheffield, since 1991; *b* 20 April 1953; *s* of David and Patricia Willett; *m* 1978, Marie-Therese Gannon; one *d*. *Educ:* Exeter Coll., Oxford (MA); Univ. of Sheffield (MSc 1976; PhD 1979; DSc 1997). Lectr, 1979–86, Sen. Lectr, 1986–88, Reader, 1988–91, Univ. of Sheffield. Pres., Chemical Structure Assoc., 1998–2002. Chm., Bd of Govs, Cambridge Crystallographic Data Centre, 2001–03. *Publications:* Similarity and Clustering in Chemical Information Systems, 1987; (with J. Ashford) Text Retrieval and Document Databases, 1988; (with E. M. Rasmussen) Parallel Database Processing, 1990; Three-Dimensional Chemical Structure Handling, 1991; (jtly) Readings in Information Retrieval, 1997; (with Y. C. Martin) Designing Bioactive Molecules, 1998; over 550 articles, reports, and book chapters. *Recreations:* classical music, current affairs, military history. *Address:* Information School, University of Sheffield, 211 Portobello Street, Sheffield S1 4DP. *T:* (0114) 222 2633, *Fax:* (0114) 278 0300. *E:* p.willett@sheffield.ac.uk.

WILLETTS, Rt Hon. David (Lindsay); PC 2010; Chair, British Science Association, since 2015; Executive Chair, Resolution Foundation, since 2015; *b* 9 March 1956; *s* of late John Roland Willetts and of Hilary Sheila Willetts; *m* 1986, Hon. Sarah Harriet Ann, *d* of Lord Butterfield; one *s* one *d*. *Educ:* King Edward's Sch., Birmingham; Christ Church, Oxford (BA 1st cl. Hons PPE). Res. Asst to Nigel Lawson, MP, 1978; HM Treasury, 1978–84: Pvte Sec. to Financial Sec., 1981–82; Principal Monetary Policy Div., 1982–84; Prime Minister's Downing Street Policy Unit, 1984–86; Dir of Studies, Centre for Policy Studies, 1987–92. MP (C) Havant, 1992–2015. PPS to Chm. of Cons. Party, 1993–94; an Asst Govt Whip, 1994–95; a Lord Comr of HM Treasury (Govt Whip), 1995; Parly Sec., Office of Public Service, Cabinet Office, 1995–96; HM Paymaster General, 1996; Opposition front bench spokesman on employment, 1997–98; Shadow Secretary of State: for educn and employment, 1998–99; for social security, 1999–2001; for work and pensions, 2001–05; DTI, 2005; for Educn and Skills, 2005–07; for Univs and Skills (formerly Innovation, Univs and Skills), 2007–10; Minister of State (Minister for Univs and Sci.), BIS, 2010–14. Consultant Dir, 1987–92, Chm., 1997, Cons. Res. Dept; Hd of Policy Co-ordination, Cons. Party, 2003–04. Director: Retirement Security Ltd, 1988–94; Electra Corporate Ventures Ltd, 1988–94; Economic Advr, Dresdner Kleinwort Benson, 1997–2007; Sen. Advr, Punter Southall, 2005–09. Mem. Adv. Bd, British Council, 2001–05. Vis. Fellow, Nuffield Coll., Oxford,

1999–2007; Visiting Professor: Pensions Inst., Cass Business Sch., 2005–09; Policy Inst., KCL, 2014–. Non-exec. Dir, Nat. Centre for Univs and Business, 2015–. Member: Social Security Adv. Cttee, 1989–92; Global Commn on Ageing, 2000–09. Trustee, Sci. Mus. Gp, 2015–. Member: Parkside HA, 1988–90; Lambeth, Lewisham and Southwark FPC, 1987–90. Mem., Prog. Cttee, 1998–2010, Gov., 2004–, Ditchley Foundn. Mem. Council, Inst. for Fiscal Studies, 2003–. Mem., Sen. Common Room, Christ Church, Oxford, 2007–. *Publications:* Modern Conservatism, 1992; Civic Conservatism, 1994; Blair's Gurus, 1996; Why Vote Conservative?, 1997; (jtly) Is Conservatism Dead?, 1997; Welfare to Work, 1998; After the Landslide, 1999; Tax Credits: do they add up?, 2002; Old Europe? demographic change and pension reform, 2003; Conservatives in Birmingham, 2008; The Pinch: how baby-boomers took their children's future - and why they should give it back, 2010; paper, The Role of the Prime Minister's Policy Unit, 1987 (Haldane Medal, RIPA); various pamphlets. *Recreations:* swimming, reading.

[Created a Baron (Life Peer) 2015 but title not yet gazetted at time of going to press.]

WILLI, Prof. Andreas Jonathan, DPhil; Diebold Professor of Comparative Philology, University of Oxford, since 2005; Fellow of Worcester College, Oxford, since 2005; *b* Altstätten, Switzerland, 17 Dec. 1972; *s* of Thomas Willi and Ina Willi-Plein; *m* 2005, Helen Kaufmann; one *s* two *d*. *Educ:* Primarschule Peters, Basel; Humanistisches Gymnasium, Basel; Universität Basel (lic.phil. Classics, Slavonic Langs/Lits 1997); Université de Lausanne; Univ. of Michigan; Univ. de Fribourg (lic.phil. Comparative Philology 1998); Corpus Christi Coll., Oxford (DPhil Classics 2001). Oberassistent, Classics, 2001–04, Privatdozent für Klassische Philologie, 2007–, Univ. of Basel. *Publications:* (ed) The Language of Greek Comedy, 2002; The Languages of Aristophanes, 2003; Sikelismos: Sprache, Literatur und Gesellschaft im griechischen Sizilien, 2008. *Address:* Worcester College, Oxford OX1 2HB.

WILLIAMS; *see* Rees-Williams.

WILLIAMS; *see* Sims-Williams.

WILLIAMS, family name of **Barons Williams of Baglan**, **Williams of Elvel** and **Williams of Oystermouth**, and **Baronesses Williams of Crosby** and **Williams of Trafford**.

WILLIAMS OF BAGLAN, Baron *cr* 2010 (Life Peer), of Neath Port Talbot in Glamorgan; **Michael Charles Williams,** PhD; United Nations Special Co-ordinator for Lebanon, 2008–11; Distinguished Visiting Fellow, Chatham House, since 2011; *b* 11 June 1949; *s* of Emlyn Glyndwr Williams and Mildred May Williams (*née* Morgan); *m* 1st, 1974, Margaret Rigby (marr. diss. 1984); one *d*; 2nd, 1992, Isobelle Jaques; one *s*. *Educ:* UCL (BSc (Internat. Relns) 1971); SOAS, London (MSc (Politics) 1973; PhD (Politics) 1984). Researcher, Amnesty Internat., 1977–78; Lectr in Politics, UEA, 1978–80; Hd, Asia Res., Amnesty Internat., 1980–84; Sen. Commentator/Ed., E Asia, BBC World Service, 1984–92; Director: of Human Rights, UN Mission to Cambodia, 1992–93; of Inf., UN Mission to Former Yugoslavia, 1993–95; Sen. Fellow, IISS, 1996–98; Dir, Office for Children and Armed Conflict, UN, NY, 1998–99; Special Advr to Sec. of State for Foreign Affairs, 2000–05; Dir, ME and Asia, 2005–06, and Asst Sec.-Gen. and Special Advr on the Middle East, 2006–07, UN, NY; UK Special Rep. on Middle East and Special Projects, FCO, 2007–08. Consultant, UNHCR, 1998–. Chm., Mines Adv. Gp, 2014–. Trustee, BBC Trust, 2011–. Sen. Fellow, 21st Century Trust, 2000–. Member: RIIA, 1978–; IISS, 1990–; Bd, BBC World Service Trust, 2000–05; Exec. Cttee and Council, Chatham House, 2000–06. Gov., SOAS, Univ. of London, 2012–; Mem. Council, Swansea Univ., 2012–. *Publications:* Communism, Religion and Revolt in Banten, West Java, 1990; Vietnam at the Crossroads, 1992; Civil Military Relations and Peacekeeping, 1998. *Recreations:* reading, travel, history and politics of Southeast Asia, the Middle East and Europe, military history, food and wine. *Address:* House of Lords, SW1A 0PW. *E:* drmcwilliams@gmail.com.

WILLIAMS OF CROSBY, Baroness *cr* 1993 (Life Peer), of Stevenage in the County of Hertfordshire; **Shirley Vivian Teresa Brittain Williams;** PC 1974; Co-founder, Social Democratic Party, 1981, President, 1982–88; Leader, Liberal Democrats, House of Lords, 2001–04; Public Service Professor of Elective Politics, John F. Kennedy School of Government, Harvard University, 1988–2000, now Emeritus; *b* 27 July 1930; *d* of late Prof. Sir George Catlin, and late Mrs Catlin, (Vera Brittain); *m* 1st, 1955, Prof. Bernard Arthur Owen Williams, FBA (marr. diss. 1974; he *d* 2003); one *d*; 2nd, 1987, Prof. Richard Elliott Neustadt (*d* 2003). *Educ:* eight schools in UK and USA; Somerville Coll., Oxford (scholar; MA, Hon. Fellow, 1970); Columbia Univ., New York (Smith-Mundt Scholar, 1952). General Secretary, Fabian Soc., 1960–64 (Chm., 1980–81). Contested: (Lab) Harwich, Essex, 1954 and 1955, and Southampton Test, 1959; (SDP) Crosby, 1983; (SDP/Alliance) Cambridge, 1987. MP: (Lab) Hitchin, 1964–74; (Lab) Hertford and Stevenage, 1974–79; (first-elected SDP MP) Crosby, Nov. 1981–1983; PPS, Minister of Health, 1964–66; Parly Sec., Min. of Labour, 1966–67; Minister of State: Education and Science, 1967–69; Home Office, 1969–70; Opposition spokesman on: Social Services, 1970–71, on Home Affairs, 1971–73; Prices and Consumer Protection, 1973–74; Sec. of State for Prices and Consumer Protection, 1974–76; Sec. of State for Educn and Science, 1976–79; Paymaster General, 1976–79. Bd Mem., Rand Corp., Europe, 1993–2001. Chm., OECD study on youth employment, 1979; Member: Council of Advrs to Praesidium, Ukraine, 1991–97; Adv. Council to UN Sec.-Gen. for Fourth World Women's Conf., Beijing, 1995; EC Comité des Sages, 1995–96; Council, Internat. Crisis Gp, 1998–2004; Internat. Adv. Cttee, Council on Foreign Relns, NY; Comr, Internat. Commn on Nuclear Non-proliferation and Disarmament, 2008–10. Advr on Nuclear Non-proliferation to Rt Hon. Gordon Brown, 2007–10. Mem., Labour Party Nat. Exec. Cttee, 1970–81. Dep. Leader, Liberal Democrat Party, H of L, 1999–2001. Visiting Fellow, Nuffield College, Oxford, 1967–75; Res. Fellow, PSI, 1979–85; Visiting Faculty, Internat. Management Inst., Geneva, 1979–88; Fellow, Inst. of Politics, Harvard, 1979–80 (Mem., Sen. Adv. Council, 1986–99; Acting Dir, 1989–90); Director: Turing Inst., Glasgow, 1985–90; Learning by Experience Trust, 1986–94; Educn Devel Centre, Newton, Mass, 1991–98; Internat. Mgt Inst., Kiev, 1990–2000; Project Liberty, 1990–98; Bd Mem., Moscow Sch. of Political Studies, 1993–2007. Co-Pres., RIIA, 2002–06. Chm. of Judges, Nat. Teaching Awards, 2007–10. Trustee: The Century Foundn (formerly Twentieth Century Fund), NY, 1978–; IPPR, 2001–10. Lectures: Godkin, Harvard, 1980; Rede, Cambridge, 1980; Janeway, Princeton, 1981; Regents', Univ. of Calif., Berkeley, 1991; Erasmus, Notre Dame, 2001–02. Hon. Fellow, Newnham Coll., Cambridge, 1977. Hon. DEd CNAA, 1969; Hon. Dr Pol Econ.: Univ. of Leuven, 1976; Radcliffe Coll., Harvard, 1978; Leeds, 1980; Bath, 1980; Hon. LLD: Sheffield, 1980; Southampton, 1981; Liverpool, 2008; Cambridge, 2009; Hon. DLitt Heriot-Watt, 1980; Hon. DSc Aston, 1981; Hon. Dr Monterey Inst., Calif, 2006. *Publications:* Politics is for People, 1981; Jobs for the 1980s; Youth Without Work, 1981; (jtly) Unemployment and Growth in the Western Economies, 1984; A Job to Live, 1985; Snakes and Ladders: a diary of a political life, 1996; (contrib.) Realizing Human Rights, ed Power and Alison, 2000; (contrib.) Making Globalization Good, 2003; God and Caesar, 2003; Climbing the Bookshelves, 2009. *Recreations:* music, poetry, hill walking.

WILLIAMS OF ELVEL, Baron *cr* 1985 (Life Peer), of Llansantffraed in Elvel in the County of Powys; **Charles Cuthbert Powell Williams,** CBE 1980; PC 2013; *b* 9 Feb. 1933; *s* of late Dr Norman Powell Williams, DD, and Mrs Muriel de Lérisson Williams (*née* Cazenove); *m* 1975, Jane Gillian (*née* Portal), DL; one step *s*. *Educ:* Westminster Sch.; Christ Church, Oxford (MA); LSE. Nat. Service, KRRC, 1955–57 (2nd Lieut, 1956–57). British Petroleum Co. Ltd, 1958–64; Bank of London and Montreal, 1964–66; Eurofinance SA, Paris, 1966–70; Baring Brothers and Co. Ltd, 1970–77 (Man. Dir, 1971–77); Chm., Price Commn, 1977–79; Man. Dir 1980–82, Chm. 1982–85, Henry Ansbacher & Co. Ltd; Chief Exec., Henry Ansbacher Holdings PLC, 1982–85. Parly Candidate (Lab), Colchester, 1964. House of Lords: Dep. Leader of Opposition, 1989–92; Opposition spokesman on trade and industry, 1986–92, on energy, 1988–90, on defence, 1990–97, on the envmt, 1992–97. Founder Mem., Labour Econ. Finance and Taxation Assoc. (Vice-Chm., 1975–77, 1979–83). Director: Pergamon Holdings Ltd, 1985–91; Mirror Group Newspapers Ltd, 1985–91, Mirror Group Newspapers PLC, 1991–92. Pres., Campaign for Protection of Rural Wales, 1989–95 (Vice-Pres., 1995–2009; Pres., Radnor Branch, 1995–2014). Chm., Mid Wales Chamber Orch., 2009–13; Trustee, Cambrian Music Trust, 2009–14. Patron, Llandrindod Wells Spa Town Trust, 1995–. *Publications:* The Last Great Frenchman: a life of General de Gaulle, 1993; Bradman: an Australian hero, 1996; Adenauer, the Father of the new Germany, 2000; Pétain, 2005 (Elizabeth Longford Prize for Histl Biog., 2006); Harold Macmillan, 2009; Gentlemen and Players: the death of amateurism in cricket, 2012. *Recreations:* cricket (Oxford Univ. CC, 1953–55, Captain 1955; Essex CCC, 1953–59), music. *Address:* House of Lords, SW1A 0PW. *T:* (020) 7219 6054. *Clubs:* Beefsteak, Reform, MCC.

See also Archbishop of Canterbury.

WILLIAMS OF OYSTERMOUTH, Baron *cr* 2013 (Life Peer), of Oystermouth in the City and County of Swansea; **Rt Rev. and Rt Hon. Rowan Douglas Williams;** Royal Victorian Chain, 2012; PC 2002; DPhil, DD; FBA 1990; Master, Magdalene College, Cambridge, since 2013; an Assistant Bishop, Diocese of Ely, since 2013; *b* 14 June 1950; *s* of Aneurin Williams and Nancy Delphine Williams; *m* 1981, Hilary Jane Paul; one *s* one *d*. *Educ:* Dynevor School, Swansea; Christ's College, Cambridge (BA 1971, MA 1975); Christ Church and Wadham College, Oxford (DPhil 1975; DD 1989). Lectr, College of the Resurrection, Mirfield, 1975–77; ordained deacon, 1977, priest, 1978; Chaplain, Tutor and Director of Studies, Westcott House, Cambridge, 1977–80; Cambridge University: Univ. Lectr in Divinity, 1980–86; Fellow and Dean of Clare Coll., 1984–86; Lady Margaret Prof. of Divinity, and Canon of Christ Church, Oxford, 1986–92; Bishop of Monmouth, 1992–2002; Archbishop of Wales, 2000–02; Archbishop of Canterbury, 2002–12. Hon. Asst Priest, St George's, Cambridge, 1980–83; Canon Theologian, Leicester Cathedral, 1981–92; Hon. Canon, Ely Cathedral, 2014–. Examining Chaplain to Bishop of Manchester, 1987–92. Chm., Bd of Trustees, Christian Aid, 2013–. Chancellor, Univ. of S Wales, 2013–. Lectures: Gifford, Edinburgh Univ., 2013; Tanner, Harvard Univ., 2014. FRSL 2004. Hon. Fellow: UC, Swansea, 1993; Clare Coll., Cambridge, 1994; Univ. of Wales Coll., Newport, 2000; UC, Cardiff, 2002; UC, Aberystwyth, 2005. Hon. DTheol Erlangen, 1999; Hon. DD: Nashotah Hse, USA, 2000; Exeter, 2001; Aberdeen, 2002; Kent, 2003; Wales, 2003; Bonn, 2004; Cambridge, 2006; DUniv Open, 2004; Hon. DCL Oxford, 2005; Hon. Dr: St Vladimir's Orthodox Seminary, NY, 2010; Athens, 2010; Catholic Univ., Leuven, 2011; Hon. Dr Pastoral Theology Anglia Ruskin, 2013; Hon. DTh Nijmegen, 2014; Hon. DHL Fordham, NY, 2014. Presidential Decree, Order of Friendship (Russia), 2009; Star of Pakistan, 2012. *Publications:* The Wound of Knowledge, 1979; Resurrection, 1982; The Truce of God, 1983; (with Mark Collier) Beginning Now; peacemaking theology, 1984; Arius: heresy and tradition, 1987; (ed) The Making of Orthodoxy, 1989; Teresa of Avila, 1991; Open to Judgement, 1994; After Silent Centuries (poems), 1994; Sergii Bulgakov: towards a Russian political theology, 1999; On Christian Theology, 1999; Lost Icons, 2000; Christ on Trial, 2000; (ed jtly) Love's Redeeming Work: the Anglican quest for holiness, 2001; Remembering Jerusalem (poems), 2001; (ed jtly) The New Dictionary of Pastoral Studies, 2002; Ponder These Things: praying with icons of the Virgin, 2002; The Poems of Rowan Williams, 2002; The Dwelling of the Light, 2003; Silence and Honey Cakes, 2003; Anglican Identities, 2004; Why Study the Past?, 2005; Grace and Necessity, 2005; Tokens of Trust: an introduction to Christian belief, 2007; Wrestling with Angels: conversations in modern theology, 2007; Dostoevsky: language, fiction and faith, 2008; Headwaters (poems), 2008; A Margin of Silence: the Holy Spirit in Russian Orthodox theology, 2008; (ed jtly) Crisis and Recovery, 2010; A Silent Action, 2011; Faith in the Public Square, 2012; The Lion's World, 2012; Choose Life, 2013; Being Christian, 2014; The Poems of Rowan Williams, 2014; The Edge of Words: God and the habits of language, 2014; Meeting God in Mark, 2014; The Other Mountain (poems), 2014; contribs to Theologische Realencyklopädie, Jl of Theological Studies, Downside Review, Eastern Churches Review, Sobornost, New Blackfriars, New Statesman, Prospect. *Recreations:* music, fiction, languages. *Address:* The Master's Lodge, Magdalene College, Cambridge CB3 0AG.

WILLIAMS OF TRAFFORD, Baroness *cr* 2013 (Life Peer), of Hale in the County of Greater Manchester; **Susan Frances Maria Williams;** Parliamentary Under-Secretary of State, Department for Communities and Local Government, since 2015; *b* Cork, Ireland, 16 May 1967; *d* of John Henry McElroy and Mary McElroy; *m* 2005, Alexander Williams; one *s* two *d*. *Educ:* La Sagesse High Sch., Jesmond, Newcastle upon Tyne; Huddersfield Poly. (BSc Hons Applied Nutrition). Nutritionist, Multiple Sclerosis charity, 1992–2002. Mem. (C) Trafford MBC, 1998–2011 (Leader, 2004–09). NW Chm., Heritage Lottery Fund, 2011–12; CEO, Atlantic Gateway, 2012–14; Dir, NW Rail Campaign, 2011–14. A Baroness in Waiting (Govt Whip), 2014–15. Contested (C) Bolton West, 2010. *Recreations:* hill walking in Scotland, backgammon, pub quizzes. *Address:* House of Lords, SW1A 0PW.

WILLIAMS, Adèle; *see* Williams, J. A.

WILLIAMS, Adrian Spencer Vaughan, CBE 2003; Headteacher, Bury St Edmunds County Upper School, 1985–2005; *b* 23 May 1945; *s* of Bill and Eileen Williams; *m* 1972, Janet Daniels; one *s* two *d*. *Educ:* Colston's Sch., Bristol; St Catharine's Coll., Cambridge (BA 1967, MA 1971; DipEd). Asst teacher, King's Coll. Sch., Wimbledon, 1968–74; Hd, History Dept, Frome Coll., Som., 1974–79; Dep. Headteacher, Eggbuckland Sch., Plymouth, 1979–84. Lay Canon, St Edmundsbury Cathedral, 2005–10 (Lay Canon Emeritus, 2011–). Chairman: Suffolk Educn Business Partnership, 2007–; William and Ellen Vinten Trust, 2009–15; Trustee: Guildhall Feoffment Trust, 1988–2015; St Nicholas' Hospice, 1998– (Chm., 2012–); Lund Trust, 2005–. *Recreations:* (nearly) all things French, relentless pursuit of the misuse of the apostrophe, watching cricket and Ipswich Town Football Club. *Address:* Gatehouse, 1 Byfield Way, Bury St Edmunds, Suffolk IP33 2SN. *T:* (01284) 763339. *E:* williams@byfieldway.plus.com.

WILLIAMS, Rt Rev. Alan; *see* Brentwood, Bishop of, (RC).

WILLIAMS, Alan Lee, OBE 1973; Director, Atlantic Council, 1993–2007 (Director, 1972–74 and 1992–93, Chairman, 1980–83, British Atlantic Committee); *b* 29 Nov. 1930; *m* 1st, 1954, Molly Steer (marr. diss. 1958); 2nd, 1963, Karen Holloway (marr. diss. 1971); two *s*; 3rd, 1974, Jennifer Ford (*née* Bunnett); two step *d*. *Educ:* Roan Sch., Greenwich; Ruskin Coll., Oxford. National Service, RAF, 1951–53; National Youth Officer, Labour Party, 1956–62. Dir-Gen., E-SU, 1979–86; Warden and Chief Exec., Toynbee Hall, 1987–92. MP (Lab) Hornchurch, 1966–70, Havering, Hornchurch, Feb. 1974–1979; PPS to Sec. of State for Defence, 1969–70, 1976; PPS to Sec. of State for NI, 1976–78; Chm., Parly Lab. Party Defence Cttee, 1976–79. Member: Parly Assembly, Council of Europe and WEU, 1967–70; N Atlantic Parly Assembly, 1974–79; FO Adv. Cttee on Disarmament and Arms Control, 1975–79; Council, RUSI, 1975–78; Adv. Council on Public Records, 1977–84; Chm., Delegn to 4th Cttee of UN, NY, 1969; Chm., Transport on Water Assoc.; Deputy Director, European Movement, 1970–71; Vice Pres., European-Atlantic Gp, 1983–; Pres., Atlantic Treaty Assoc., 2000–03; Chm., European Working Gp of Internat. Centre for Strategic and Internat. Studies, Washington, 1987–99 (Mem., 1974–); Member: Council, RUSI, 1968–79; Trilateral Commn, 1976–2002. Chm., Beveridge Foundn, 2006–14. Vis. Prof., Queen Mary Univ. of London, 2003–. Chairman: Cedar Centre, Isle of Dogs, 1991–2008; Toynbee

Housing Assoc., 1993–99. Chm. of Govs, City Coll., 1990–. Freeman: City of London, 1969; Co. of Watermen and Lightermen, 1952–. Fellow, QMW, 1993. FRSA 1987. DLitt (*hc*) Schiller Internat. Univ., 1987. Golden Laurel Branch (Bulgaria), 2002. *Publications:* Radical Essays, 1966; Europe or the Open Sea?, 1971; Crisis in European Defence, 1973; The European Defence Initiative: Europe's bid for equality, 1985; The Decline of Labour and the Fall of the SDP, 1989; Islamic Resurgence, 1991; Prospects for a Common European Foreign and Security Policy, 1995; NATO's Future in the Balance: time for a rethink, 1995; NATO and European Defence: a new era of partnership, 1997; NATO's Strategy for Securing the Future, 1999; (with Geoffrey Lee Williams) A Couple of Duffers Go to War, 2011. *Recreations:* reading, history, walking. *Address:* 6 North Several, Blackheath, SE3 0QR. *Clubs:* Reform, Pilgrims, Mid-Atlantic (Chm., 2006–), English-Speaking Union.

WILLIAMS, Dr Alan Wynne; freelance solar energy research; *b* 21 Dec. 1945; *s* of late Tom and Mary Hannah Williams; *m* 1973, Marian Williams. *Educ:* Carmarthen Grammar School; Jesus College, Oxford (BA Chem. 1st cl. hons; DPhil). Senior Lecturer in Environmental Science, Trinity College, Carmarthen, 1971–87. MP (Lab) Carmarthen, 1987–97, Carmarthen E and Dinefwr, 1997–2001; contested Carmarthen E and Dinefwr, 2001. *Recreations:* reading, watching sport. *Address:* 79 Parklands Road, Ammanford, Carmarthenshire SA18 3TD.

WILLIAMS, Sir Alastair Edgcumbe James D.; *see* Dudley-Williams.

WILLIAMS, (Albert) Trevor; management scientist; *b* 7 April 1938; *s* of Ben and Minnie Williams; *m* 1st, 1970, Mary Lynn Lyster; three *s*; 2nd, 1978, Deborah Sarah Fraser Duncan (*née* Milne); one *s*, and one step *s* two step *d*. *Educ:* King George V Sch., Southport; Queens' Coll., Cambridge (Open Exhibnr; MA); Univ. of Ghana (Rotary Foundn Fellow); Cranfield Institute of Technology (MSc). Commnd RA, 1957. Director: Business Operations Research Ltd, 1965–68; Novy Eddison and Partners, 1971–74; Dep.-Dir for Futures Research, Univ. of Stellenbosch, 1974–78; Dep. Chief Scientific Officer, Price Commission, 1978–79; Advisor on Technology Projects, Scottish Development Agency, 1979; Dir, Henley Centre for Forecasting, 1980–81. Consultant and Sen. Industrial Advr, Monopolies and Mergers Commn, 1982–90; advr to cos in UK, continental Europe, S Africa and USA, 1989–2005, 2012–. Various academic appointments, 1968–95, 2012–, incl. visiting and hon. professorships: Graduate Sch. of Business, Cape Town Univ.; Sussex Univ.; INSEAD; Wisconsin Univ.; Hong Kong Univ.; LSE. Mem., Editl Adv. Bd, Futures, 1984–98. FInstD; AMRI. *Publications:* A Guide to Futures Studies, 1976; (contrib.) Futures, 1985–98; (contrib.) Foresight. *Recreation:* reviewing the last fifty years. *Club:* Athenæum.

WILLIAMS, Aled Tudno; President, Eurojust, 2010–12; *b* Newton Abbot, Devon, 11 Aug. 1947; *s* of Llew and Sian Williams; *m* 1975, Mercedes Morillo; two *d*. *Educ:* King Edward VI Grammar Sch., Chelmsford; Gonville and Caius Coll., Cambridge (BA 1968; MA 1972). Admitted as solicitor, 1984; Crown Prosecutor, 1986–2012; UK Liaison Magistrate to Spain, 2002–06; Dep. UK Nat. Mem., 2006–08, UK Nat. Mem., 2008–12, Eurojust. Order of San Raimundo de Peñafort (Spain), 2006. *Recreations:* theatre, reading, walking. *Club:* Oxford and Cambridge.

WILLIAMS, Alexander, CB 1991; FInstP; Government Chemist, 1987–91; *b* 30 March 1931; *s* of Henry and Dorothy Williams; *m* 1957, Beryl Wynne Williams (*née* Williams); one *s*. *Educ:* Grove Park Grammar Sch., Wrexham; University College of North Wales, Bangor (BSc). National Service, REME, 1953–55; Monsanto Chemicals, 1955–56; Southern Instruments, Camberley, 1956–59; National Physical Laboratory: Div. of Radiation Science, 1959–78; Head, Div. of Mechanical and Optical Metrology, 1978–81; Under Sec., Res. and Technology Policy Div., DTI, 1981–87. Dir, Assoc. of Official Analytical Chemists, 1989–93. Pres., British Measurement and Testing Assoc., 1995–2001. Freeman, City of London, 1997; Liveryman, Co. of Scientific Instrument Makers, 1997–. *Publications:* (with P. J. Campion and J. E. Burns) A Code of Practice for the Detailed Statement of Accuracy, 1973; (ed with H. Günzler) Handbook of Analytical Techniques, 2001; numerous papers on measurements of radio-activity etc and quality assce in analytical chem., to Internat. Jl of Applied Radiation and Isotopes, Nucl. Instruments and Methods, Accreditation and Quality Assurance, etc. *Recreations:* bell-ringing, music, opera, walking.

WILLIAMS, (Alun) Craig; MP (C) Cardiff North, since 2015; *b* Welshpool, 7 June 1985; *s* of David Williams and Andrea Williams; *m* 2013, Clare Bath; one *s* one *d*. Mem. (C), Cardiff CC, 2008–15 (Chm., Economy Cttee, 2012–15). Dir, Cardiff Bus, 2011–15. *Recreations:* Rugby, real ale, walking, Welsh springer spaniels, school governor (primary). *Address:* House of Commons, SW1A 0AA. *T:* (020) 7219 8245. *E:* craig.williams.mp@parliament.uk. *Clubs:* Carlton; Cardiff and County.

WILLIAMS, Prof. Alun Edward, PhD; Professor of Veterinary Diagnostic Pathology, University of Cambridge, since 2009; Fellow, Wolfson College, Cambridge, since 2009; *b* York, 6 Nov. 1960; *s* of Arthur and Margaret Williams; *m* 1995, Marianna Fletcher; one *s* one *d*. *Educ:* Univ. of Glasgow (BVMS 1985; MRCVS 1985); Wolfson Coll., Cambridge (PhD 1989). Diplomate, Eur. Coll. of Vet. Pathologists, 1998. AFRC Vet. Schs Fellow, Univ. of Cambridge, 1985–89; MRC Univ. Res. Fellow, Univ. of Oxford, 1989–90; Principal Res. Scientist and Named Vet. Surgeon, Inst. for Animal Health, Edinburgh, 1990–97; Sen. Lectr, 1997–2001, Reader, 2001–03, Dept of Veterinary Pathol., Univ. of Glasgow; Prof. of Pathol. and Infectious Diseases, RVC, Univ. of London, 2003–09 (Hd of Dept, 2003–07). FHEA 2009. *Recreations:* music (performing in orchestras and choirs), growing vegetables. *Address:* Department of Veterinary Medicine, University of Cambridge, Madingley Road, Cambridge CB3 0ES. *T:* (01223) 337640. *E:* aw510@cam.ac.uk.

WILLIAMS, Angela Joy, CMG 2005; Director, Relief and Social Services, United Nations Relief and Works Agency Affairs for Palestine Refugees in the Near East, 1988–98; *b* 24 Sept. 1944; *d* of Douglas Granville Needham and Annie Needham (*née* Balshaw); *m* 1984, Edward Hunter Williams; two step *s* one step *d*. *Educ:* Girls' Div., Bolton Sch.; Univ. of Birmingham (BSocSci Hons 1966); American Univ. of Beirut (Middle Eastern studies). VSO, Ghana, 1966–68; Asst Educn Officer, Community Relns Commn, 1969–71; UN Relief and Works Agency for Palestine Refugees in the Near East, 1971–2004: Chief of Secretariat, 1980–83; Chief of External Relns, 1984–85; Dep. Dir of Ops, Gaza, 1985–88; Dir of UNRWA Affairs, Syrian Arab Republic, 1998–2004. Music in Me: Dir, Prog. Implementation, 2005–08; Consultant, 2008–09. Trustee, Damask Rose Trust, 2008–11. *Recreations:* exploring cultural diversity and cross-cultural communication through reading, writing, music, photography and travel. *Address:* Grafenegg 1, Wallhaus Süd-Ost, 3485 Haitzendorf, Austria. *T:* (2735) 36219; 3–111 Echo Drive, Ottawa, ON K1S 5K8, Canada. *T:* (613) 2308610. *E:* ajwilliams_241@hotmail.com.

WILLIAMS, Anna Maureen, (Mrs G. H. G. Williams); *see* Worrall, A. M.

WILLIAMS, Sir Anthony Geraint, 3rd Bt *cr* 1953, of Cilgeraint, co. Caernarvon; *b* 22 Dec. 1958; *s* of Sir Robin Philip Williams, 2nd Bt, and of Wendy Adèle Marguerite, *o d* of late Felix Joseph Alexander; *S* father, 2013; *m* 1990, Rachel Jane, *e d* of Norman Jennings; three *s* one *d*. *Heir: s* Thomas Alexander Philip Williams, *b* 30 Aug. 1992.

WILLIAMS, Anthony Neville; Managing Partner (formerly Managing Director), Jomati Consultants LLP (formerly Jomati Ltd), since 2002; *b* 8 July 1956; *s* of late David Leslie Williams and Rose Williams (*née* Mingay); *m* 1979, Johannah McDonnell; one *s* one *d*. *Educ:* Southampton Univ. (LLB 1978). Admitted Solicitor, England, 1981, Hong Kong, 1985; Solicitor and Barrister, Victoria, Australia, 1986. Solicitor: Turner Garrett & Co., 1981; Coward Chance, 1981–87, Clifford Chance (following merger), 1987–2000: Hong Kong office, 1984–90; Partner, 1988–2000; Man. Partner, Moscow office, 1995–97; Firmwide Man. Partner, 1998–2000; Man. Partner Worldwide, Andersen Legal, 2000–02. Vis. Prof., Univ. of Law, 2015–. *Publications:* (jtly) Intellectual Property in the People's Republic of China, 1986; (jtly) The Hong Kong Banking Ordinance, 1987; (contrib.) Butterworths Guide to the Legal Services Act 2007, 2009; numerous articles on law firm mgt strategy. *Recreations:* horse racing, cricket, wine. *Address:* Jomati Consultants LLP, 3 Amen Lodge, Warwick Lane, EC4M 7BY. *E:* tony.williams@jomati.com.

WILLIAMS, Dr Anthony Peter; HM Inspector of Constabulary (non-police), 1993–96; *b* 18 June 1936; *s* of late Dr Emlyn Williams, OBE, Principal, Hendon Coll. of Technology, and Gwyneth Mair Williams (*née* Williams); *m* 1964, Vera Georgiadou; one *s* one *d*. *Educ:* St Paul's Sch., London; Keble Coll., Oxford (BA 1961; MA 1965); Birkbeck Coll., London (PhD 1971). Research and teaching, 1961–67; Principal Psychologist, CSSB, 1967–71; Consultant, Hay-MSL Ltd, 1971–76; Head of Personnel, BOC Gases, 1976–78; Consultant and Manager, Hay Associates, NY, 1979–84; Dir of Personnel, World Bank, 1984–88; Worldwide Partner and Dir, Hay Management Consultants, 1989–93. Vis. Sen. Fellow, 1997–2003, Vis. Prof., 2003–, Sir John Cass Business Sch., City of London (formerly City Univ. Business Sch.). Mem., Corporate Governance Wkg Party, Assoc. of Investment Trust Cos, 1999–2000. *Publications:* Just Reward?: the truth about top executive pay, 1994; Who Will Guard the Guardians?: corporate governance in the Millennium, 1999; (with Bill Pitkeathley) Executive Express: a swift and practical route to tomorrow's top jobs, 2006; numerous articles in professional and management jls. *Recreations:* international affairs, use of language, travel, cultural diversity, opera, good food and wine, intelligent conversation, asking difficult questions. *Address:* 49 Talbot Road, W2 5JJ. *Clubs:* Athenæum, Oxford and Cambridge.

WILLIAMS, (Arthur) Ronald, OBE 1991; Chief Executive, Publishers Association, 1998–2007; *b* 29 Oct. 1942; *s* of late Alfred Arthur Williams, OBE and Marjory Williams (*née* Heenan); *m* 1st, 1968, Lynne Diana Merrin; two *d*; 2nd, 1993, Antoinette Catherine Naldrett. *Educ:* Rossall Sch., Lancs; Selwyn Coll., Cambridge (Exhibnr, Trevelyan Scholar; MA). HM Diplomatic Service, 1964–79, served Jakarta, Singapore, Budapest and Nairobi (First Sec.); Chief Exec., Timber Growers UK, 1981–87; Exec. Dir, Forestry Industry Council of GB, 1987–97. Mem., Exec. Cttee, Fedn of European Publishers, 1998–2007; Dir, Digital Content Forum (UK), 2003–07. Ambassador, Highlands and Islands Enterprise, 1994–98. FRSA. *Publications:* Montrose: cavalier in mourning, 1975; The Lords of the Isles, 1985; The Heather and the Gale, 1997; Sons of the Wolf, 1998; The Portrait of Montrose in Warwick Castle, 2014. *Recreations:* fly-fishing, walking, writing, portrait miniatures, Heritage sites. *Address:* Sea Villa, The Promenade, Laxey, Isle of Man IM4 7DF. *T:* (01624) 860059.

WILLIAMS, Betty; *see* Williams, Elizabeth.

WILLIAMS, Betty Helena; *b* 31 July 1944. *Educ:* Ysgol Dyffryn Nantlle; Coleg y Normal, Bangor (BA (Hons) Wales, 1995). Member (Lab): Llanllyfni Parish Council, 1967–83; Gwyrfai Rural DC, 1970–74; Arfon BC, 1970–91 (Mayor, 1990–91); Gwynedd CC, 1976–93. Contested (Lab) Caernarfon, 1983, Conwy, 1987 and 1992. MP (Lab) Conwy, 1997–2010. Mem., Welsh Affairs Select Cttee, 1997–2005. Vice Pres., Univ. of Wales, Bangor, 2001–06 (Hon. Fellow, 2000). Ordained deacon, 1996; Deacon, Seion Chapel, Talysarn, 1996–. Pres., Gwynedd and De Ynys Môn CAB, 2010–; Mem. Bd, Mantell Gwynedd, 2010–. Pres., Lleisiau Traeth Lafan, 2007–. Member: Gorsedd (White Robe), 2006–; Llandudno and Dist Soroptimist Internat., 2010–15.

WILLIAMS, Brian Owen, CBE 2011; MD; FRCP, FRCPE, FRCPGlas; President, Royal College of Physicians and Surgeons of Glasgow, 2006–09; Interim Postgraduate Dean, West of Scotland, NHS Education for Scotland, 2012–13; *b* 27 Feb. 1947; *s* of William and Joan Williams; *m* 1970, Martha Carmichael; two *d*. *Educ:* Kings Park Sch., Glasgow; Univ. of Glasgow (MD 1984). FRCPGlas 1983; FRCP 1989; FRCPE 1991; FCPS 1996; FRCSLT 1996; FRCPI 1999; FRACP 2007. Consultant Geriatrician, 1977–; Consultant Geriatrician, Gartnavel Gen. Hosp., Glasgow, 1982–. President: British Geriatric Soc., 1998–2000; EU Geriatric Medicine Soc., 2000–02. Hon. Prof., Univ. of Glasgow, 2007–. Chairman: Bd of Govs, Hutchesons' Grammar Sch., Glasgow, 2013–; Abbeyfield Societies in Scotland, 2013–. Hon. DSc Glasgow Caledonian, 2007. *Recreations:* music, literature, gardening, Rotarian. *Address:* 15 Thorn Drive, High Burnside, Glasgow G73 4RH. *T:* (0141) 634 4480. *E:* brianwilliams@gmx.com.

WILLIAMS, Rear Adm. Bruce Nicholas Bromley, CBE 2008 (OBE 2002); Deputy Director General European Union Military Staff, 2011–14; *b* Liverpool, 3 Nov. 1957; *s* of Dr Cecil William Llewellyn Williams and Judith Elizabeth Williams; *m* 1985, Julia Anne Quick; one *s* two *d*. *Educ:* Kingswood Sch., Bath; Lancaster Univ. (BSc Hons Ecol.). Commnd RN, 1980; served HMSs Kingfisher, Argonaut, Galatea, Danae, Brilliant, 1981–92; RNSC, 1992; Asst Defence Advr, RN Liaison Officer and CO, Naval Party 1022 Singapore, 1993–96; COS Co-ordinator, UK PJHQ, Northwood, 1996–98; CO, HMS Norfolk, 1998–2000; Desk Officer, Directorate Policy Planning, 2000–01; Asst Dir, Directorate Naval Ops, 2001–03; CO, HMS Campbeltown, 2003–04; Dep. Flag Officer, Sea Trng, 2005; Commander: Coalition Task Force 58 (Iraq-N Gulf), 2005–06; UK Task Gp and Dep. Comdr, UK Maritime Force, 2006–07; Coalition Task Force 150 (Indian Ocean), 2006–07; Dep. Comdt, JSCSC, 2007–09; ADC to the Queen, 2008–09; COS and Sen. UK Rep., Allied Maritime HQ, Naples, 2009–11. Non-exec. Dir, The Military Mutual, 2014–. Dir, Ubique Ltd, 2015–. Younger Brother, Trinity House, 2006. CCMI 2008. QCVS 1999; General Service Medals: NI, 1982; NATO Article 5, 2003; Afghanistan Campaign, 2004; Iraq Campaign, 2006. *Recreations:* sailing, walking. *E:* bruce.williams@live.co.uk.

WILLIAMS, Sir Charles (Othniel), Kt 2000; Executive Chairman, C. O. Williams Construction and group of companies, since 1969; *b* 24 Nov. 1932; *s* of Elliot Williams and Lillian Williams; *m* 1st, 1956, Diane Walcott (marr. diss. 1999); two *s* one *d*; 2nd, 2000, Mary-Ann Gemmell (*née* Stewart-Richardson). *Educ:* Lodge Secondary Sch., Barbados. Overseer, Brighton Plantation, St George, 1951–54; Under Manager: Hothersall Plantation, St John, 1954–56; Guinea Sugar Factory, St John, 1956; Manager, Foster Hall Plantation, St Joseph, 1956–60; leased Foster Hall, 1960–75; founded: C. O. Williams, 1960; C. O. Williams Construction Co. Ltd, 1969; Co-Founder, Ready Mix/Ready Block Ltd, 1969; Director: Ready Mix Ltd, 1970–; Williams Industries Inc., 1973–; Fairway Developments, 1990–; Exec. Chm. and major shareholder, Dixie Farms Ltd, 1995; Co-Developer and Director: Port St Charles, residential marina, 1996; Apes Hill Golf and Polo Club, 2005. Champion breeder of thoroughbred horses in Barbados, 2005, 2009, 2010, 2011, 2012. Master Entrepreneur of the Year, Ernst & Young Awards, 1997. *Recreations:* polo, deep-sea fishing, horse-racing. *Address:* Bromefield Plantation House, St Lucy, Barbados. *Clubs:* Sloane; Port St Charles Yacht (Barbados); Barbados Polo (Capt., 1969–2004), Barbados Turf, Barbados Yacht, Carlton Cricket (Barbados), Wanderers Cricket (Barbados).

WILLIAMS, Chris Morgan; Chief Executive, Buckinghamshire County Council and Clerk to the Lieutenancy, since 2000; Chief Executive, South East England Councils, since 2009; *b* Rhayader, Powys, Wales, 26 Nov. 1948; *s* of Harold and May Williams; *m* 1973, Julie Gleave; two *d*; *m* 2013, Clare Hedger; two step *s*. *Educ:* Lanchester Poly., Coventry (BA Hons); Univ. of Sussex (MA). MRTPI 1976. Co. Planning Officer, E Sussex, 1989–96; Dir, Envmtl Services, Bucks CC, 1996–2000. Vis. Res. Fellow, Univ. of Sussex, 1992–. Pres., Co.

Planning Officers' Soc., 1993–94. MCMI. *Recreations:* travel, wine, Rugby. *Address:* Buckinghamshire County Council, County Hall, Walton Street, Aylesbury, Bucks HP20 1UA.

WILLIAMS, Rt Rev. Christopher; *see* Williams, Rt Rev. J. C. R.

WILLIAMS, Christopher Beverley, FRCP, FRCS; Consultant Physician in Gastrointestinal Endoscopy: Endoscopy Unit, London Clinic, 1975–2013; Wolfson Unit for Endoscopy, St Mark's Hospital for Colorectal and Intestinal Disorders, 1975–2003, then Hon. Consultant; *b* 8 June 1938; *s* of late Denis John Williams, CBE, MD, FRCP and Dr Joyce Beverley Williams (*née* Jewson); *m* 1970, Christina Janet Seymour, MB, FRCP, *d* of Reginald S. Lawrie, MD, MS, FRCS, FRCP, and Jean E. Lawrie, CBE, MB; one *s* one *d*. *Educ:* Dragon Sch.; Winchester Coll.; Trinity Coll., Oxford (BA Hons Physiol., BM BCh, MA); UCH. MRCS 1965, FRCS 1999; LRCP 1965, MRCP 1968, FRCP 1983. House appointments: UCH, 1965; Whittington and Brompton Hosps, 1966; SHO, Nat. Hosp. for Nervous Diseases, and Hammersmith Hosp., 1966–67; Registrar, UCH, 1968–70; Registrar, 1970–72, Res. Fellow and Hon. Sen. Registrar, 1972–74, St Mark's Hosp.; Consultant Physician, St Bartholomew's Hosp., 1975. Hon. Consultant Physician (Endoscopy): Royal Free Hosp.; Great Ormond Street Hosp. for Sick Children; King Edward VII Hosp. for Officers; St Luke's Hosp. for the Clergy. Vis. Prof., Sydney Univ., 1973; demonstrations, teaching courses and invited lectures world-wide on colonoscopy and colorectal cancer prevention; Foundn Lectr, British Soc. of Gastroenterology, 1976, 1995 (Vice-Pres., Endoscopy, 1987). Member: Soc. of Apothecaries, 1956–; Medical Soc. of London, 1983–; FRSocMed 1970. Mem., several internat. editl bds. *Publications:* (ed jtly) Colorectal Disease, 1981; (jtly) Practical Gastrointestinal Endoscopy, 1983, 7th edn as Cotton and Williams' Practical Gastrointestinal Endoscopy, 2014 (trans. Italian 1980, German 1985, French 1986, Spanish 1992, Portuguese, 1998, Korean, 2003, Turkish 2010); (jtly) Annual of Gastrointestinal Endoscopy, annually 1988–97; (ed jtly) Colonoscopy: principles and practice, 2003, 2nd edn 2009 (trans. Portuguese 2010); numerous articles and chapters on colonoscopy, colorectal disease and teaching methodology. *Recreations:* travel, fine wine, good food, the arts. *Address:* 11 Frognal Way, Hampstead, NW3 6XE. *T:* (020) 7435 4030, *Fax:* (020) 7435 5636. *E:* christopher@candcwilliams.co.uk.

WILLIAMS, Christopher Guy; Partner, Perella Weinberg Partners, since 2015; *b* Carshalton, 24 May 1965; *s* of John Monro Williams and Sheila Marion Williams; *m* 1993, Amanda Jane Waggott; three *s*. *Educ:* Christ's Hosp. Sch.; Birmingham Univ. (BSc Hons Chem. Engrg). Hill Samuel & Co. Ltd, 1987–89; Vice Pres., Bankers Trust Internat., 1989–92; Man. Dir and Co-Head, European Banks Advisory, Goldman Sachs, 1992–2005; Co-Head, Global Financial Instns, Citicorp, 2005–09; Vice Chm., Investment Banking EMEA, Credit Suisse, 2009–14; Exec. Vice Chm., Global Financial Instns, Credit Suisee, 2014–15. Donation Gov., Christ's Hosp., 2008–. Mem., Amicable Soc. of Blues, 2012–. *Recreations:* daydreaming, rock music, harvesting apples. *Address:* Perella Weinberg Partners, 20 Grafton Street, W1S 4DZ. *T:* (020) 7268 2800.

WILLIAMS, Dr Christopher John Hacon, FRCP; Consultant Medical Oncologist, Bristol Haematology and Oncology Centre, 2003–11 (Clinical Director, 2003–07); *b* 3 Aug. 1946; *s* of Owen Henry Williams and Joyce May Hacon Deavin; *m* 1970, Susan Tennant (marr. diss. 1995); two *d*; *m* 1999, Mary Quirk. *Educ:* Reed's Sch., Surrey; London Univ., St Mary's Hosp. (MBBS); DM Southampton 1980; Metanoia Inst. and Middlesex Univ. (MSc Creative Writing for Therapeutic Purposes). Jun. posts, London Hosps, 1971–74; Jun. Registrar, Med. Oncology, St Bartholomew's, 1974–75; Postdoctoral Res. Fellow, Stanford Univ., 1975–77; Res. Fellow, 1977–80, Sen. Lectr and Hon. Consultant Physician in Medical Oncology, 1980–96, Southampton Univ.; Dir, Cochrane Cancer Network, Inst. of Health Scis, Oxford, 1996–2003. Chairman: MRC Gynaecol Cancer Working Party, 1989–93; MRC Cancer Therapy Cttee, 1994–97; steering cttees and ind. data monitoring cttees for large-scale trials in breast and ovarian cancer; Member: Protocol Rev. Cttee, EORTC, 1993–2003; Oncology Trials Adv. Cttee, MRC, 1997–2003; Steering Gp, Cochrane Collaboration, 1998–2002; Co-ordinator, ICON trials for ovarian carcinoma, 1991–96. Mem., Council, Inst. of Health Scis, Oxford, 1997. Mem. Bd of Editors, Annals of Oncology, 1996; Co-ordinating Ed., Cochrane Gynaecol Cancer Collaborative Rev. Gp, 1997–2011. *Publications:* Recent Advances in Clinical Oncology, 1982; All About Cancer, 1983; Lung Cancer: the facts, 1984, 3rd edn (with S. Falk) 2009; Cancer Investigations and Management, 1985; Cancer: a guide for patients and family, 1986; (with R. B. Buchanan) Medical Management of Breast Cancer, 1987; Textbook of Uncommon Cancer, 1988; Cancer Biology and Management, 1989; (with J. S. Tobias) Cancer: a colour atlas, 1991; Introducing New Treatments for Cancer, 1992 (Medical Textbook of the Year, 1993); Supportive Care of the Cancer Patient, 1997; (jtly) Cancer: a comprehensive guide, 1998; Evidence-based Oncology, 2003; One Day in the Life of an Executioner, 2012; papers on new therapies for cancer, esp. clinical trials and systematic reviews. *Recreations:* active participation in painting and sculpture, writing, gentle walking, wildlife and landscape photography; passive participation in theatre, music, films, books; gathering art objects, creative writing. *Address:* Spring Vale, Mill Hill, Brockweir, Chepstow NP16 7NW. *T:* (01291) 680060. *E:* chrisjhwilliams@btinternet.com.

WILLIAMS, Prof. Christopher Mark, PhD; Professor of History, and Head, School of History, Archaeology and Religion, Cardiff University, since 2013; *b* Griffithstown, Monmouthshire, 9 March 1963; *s* of Peter Hale Williams and Josephine Anne Williams; *m* 1st, 1985, Siobhan Elizabeth McClelland (marr. diss. 1993); one *s*; 2nd, 2003, Sara Louise Spalding; two *s*. *Educ:* Churchfields Comp. Sch., Swindon; Balliol Coll., Oxford (BA Mod. Hist. 1985); University Coll., Cardiff (PhD 1991). Lectr in Hist., University Coll., Cardiff, then Cardiff Univ., 1988–2001; Prof. of Mod. and Contemp. Wales, Univ. of Glamorgan, 2001–04; Prof. of Welsh Hist., 2005–13, Dir, Res. Inst. for Arts and Humanities, 2010–13, Swansea Univ. Mem., Royal Commn on Ancient and Historical Monuments of Wales, 2008–. *Publications:* Democratic Rhondda: politics and society, 1885–1951, 1996; Capitalism, Community and Conflict: the South Wales Coalfield, 1898–1947, 1998; With Dust Still in His Throat: A. B. L. Coombes anthology, 1999, 2nd edn 2014; B. L. Coombes, 1999; The Labour Party in Wales, 1900–2000, 2000; These Poor Hands: the autobiography of a miner working in South Wales, 2002, 2nd edn 2011; A Companion to Nineteenth-Century Britain, 2004; Postcolonial Wales, 2005; Debating Nationhood and Government in Britain, 1885–1945, 2006; Wales and War: society, politics and religion in the nineteenth and twentieth centuries, 2007; Gwent County History: Vol. 4, Industrial Monmouthshire, 1780–1914, 2011, Vol. 5, The Twentieth Century, 2013; Robert Owen and his Legacy, 2011; The Richard Burton Diaries, 2012 (Richard Burton: Die Tagebucher, 2013); The Art of the Possible: politics and governance in modern British history: essays in memory of Duncan Tanner (1958–2010), 2015. *Recreations:* hillwalking, cycling. *Address:* 59 Tyfica Road, Graigwen, Pontypridd CF37 2DB. *T:* (01443) 402593. *E:* williamsc92@cardiff.ac.uk.

WILLIAMS, Prof. Clyde, OBE 2009; PhD; Professor of Sports Science, Loughborough University, 1986–2008, now Emeritus; *b* Maesteg, Glamorgan, 11 Aug. 1940; *s* of Thomas John Williams and Elsie May Williams; *m* 1964, Joan Bryant; three *d*. *Educ:* Bridgend Tech. Coll.; Univ. Coll. of Wales, Aberystwyth (BSc Chem. 1964; DipEd 1965); Washington State Univ. (MSc Exercise Physiol. 1969); Univ. of Aberdeen (PhD Physiol. 1978). Chemistry Master, Devizes Grammar Sch., 1965–67; Lectr, Dept of Physiol., Univ. of Aberdeen, 1970–78; Loughborough University: Sen. Res. Fellow, 1978–83; Sen. Lectr, 1983–86; Pro-Vice-Chancellor, 1995–98. Founder Chm., 1984–87, Chm., 2002–04, non-exec. Dir, 2014–, British Assoc. of Sports Scis, subseq. British Assoc. of Sport and Exercise Scis; Founder Chm., Bd for Registration of Professionals in Sport and Exercise Nutrition, British Dietetic Assoc., 2005; Dep. Chm., Bd of Dirs, Nat. Inst. of Sports Medicine, 1999; Chm., sub-panel for sport-related subjects, HEFCE RAE 2008. Internat. Vis. Prof., Vrije Univ., Brussels, 2011; E. W. Barker Vis. Prof., Inst. of Educn, Nanyang Tech. Univ., Singapore, 2013; Vice Chancellor's Fellow and Adjunct Prof., Victoria Univ., Melbourne, 2013–. Hon. Fellow, Fac. of Sport and Exercise Medicine, RCP and RCPE, 2011. Hon. Fellow, Aberystwyth Univ., 2009. Hon. DSc Loughborough, 2015. *Publications:* (ed jtly) Foods, Nutrition and Sports Performance, 1992; (ed jtly) Oxford Textbook of Sports Medicine, 1994, 2nd edn 1998; (ed jtly) ABC of Sport and Exercise Medicine, 1995, 3rd edn 2005; approx. 250 articles mainly on nutritional influences on exercise performance in jls incl. Medicine and Sci. in Sport and Exercise, Jl of Applied Physiol., Nature, Eur. Jl of Sports Medicine, Eur. Jl of Applied Physiol., Scandinavian Jl of Sport and Exercise Medicine, Amer. Jl of Clin. Nutrition, Brit. Jl of Nutrition, Jl of Sports Sci., Brit. Jl of Sport and Exercise Medicine. *Recreations:* tennis, cycling for charity, hillwalking, theatre, travel, family. *Address:* 2 Tynedale Road, Loughborough, Leics LE11 3TA. *T:* (01509) 214151. *E:* c.williams@lboro.ac.uk. *Club:* Charnwood Lawn Tennis (Chm, 2015–).

WILLIAMS, Colin; *see* Welland, C.

WILLIAMS, Ven. Colin Henry; Archdeacon in Europe, since 2015; *b* 12 Aug. 1952; *s* of William Henry Williams and Blanche Williams. *Educ:* King George V Grammar Sch. for Boys, Southport; Pembroke Coll., Oxford (BA 1973; MA 1977); Coll. of Law, Chester; St Stephen's House, Oxford (BA Oxon 1981). Asst Solicitor, Gibson, Russell & Adler, solicitors, Wigan, 1974–78; ordained deacon 1981, priest 1982; Asst Curate, St Paul Stoneycroft, Liverpool, 1981–84; Team Vicar, St Aidan, Walton, 1984–89; Domestic Chaplain to Bishop of Blackburn, and Chaplain, Whalley Abbey Retreat and Conf. Centre, 1989–94; Vicar, St Chad, Poulton-le-Fylde, 1994–99; Archdeacon of Lancaster, 1999–2005, now Archdeacon Emeritus; Gen. Sec., Conf. of European Churches, 2005–10; Team Rector, Ludlow Team Ministry, 2010–15. Mem., Gen. Synod of C of E, 1995–2005. Mem., Meissen Commn, 1996–2005. Mem., Council for Christian Unity, 2003–05. Hon. Canon and Preb., Hereford Cathedral, 2014–15. *Recreations:* walking, singing, developing knowledge of all things German.

WILLIAMS, Coram; Chief Financial Officer, Pearson plc, since 2015; *b* Aberystwyth, 8 Jan. 1974; *s* of Karel and Gwenda Williams; *m* 2001, Juliane Fürst; two *d*. *Educ:* Penglais Sch., Aberystwyth; Christ Church, Oxford (BA PPE); London Business Sch. (MBA). Road tester, Autocar, 1997–98; Consultant, Arthur Andersen, 1998–2002; Finance Dir, ELT, Pearson Educn, 2002–05; Hd, Financial Planning, Pearson plc, 2005–08; Chief Financial Officer: Penguin Gp, 2008–13; Penguin Random House, 2013–15. Trustee, NESTA, 2009–12. *Recreations:* opera, literature, cycling, fast cars. *Address:* Pearson plc, 80 Strand, WC2R 0RL. *E:* coram.williams@pearson.com.

WILLIAMS, Craig; *see* Williams, A. C.

WILLIAMS, Craig H.; *see* Howell Williams.

WILLIAMS, Sir Daniel (Charles), GCMG 1996; QC 1996; Governor-General of Grenada, 1996–2008; international legal consultant; Founder and Head, Danny Williams and Co.; *b* 4 Nov. 1935; *s* of Adolphus D. Williams and Clare Stanislaus; *m* 1960, Cecilia Patricia Gloria Modeste; one *s* three *d*. *Educ:* Primary and comprehensive schs, Grenada; LLB London Univ.; Council of Legal Educn, London. Called to the Bar, Lincoln's Inn, 1968; Barrister, 1969–70, 1974–84, 1990–96; Magistrate, St Lucia, 1970–74; MP (New Nat. Party) St David's, Grenada, 1984–89; Minister of Health, Housing and Envmt, 1984–89; Minister of Legal Affairs, and Attorney Gen., 1988–89; Acting Prime Minister, July 1988. Sec., Grenada Bar Assoc., 1977–81. Held several lay positions in RC Ch, incl. Chm., Dio. Pastoral Council. Was active Scout, incl. Dist Comr and Dep. Chief Comr; Chief Scout, 1996–2009. Founder and Mem., Grenada Foundn for Needy Students, 1996–. Sponsor, Danny Williams annual cricket tournament for primary schs in St David's, Grenada, 1985–. *Publications:* Index of Laws of Grenada 1959–79; (contrib.) Modern Legal Systems Cyclopedia: Central America and the Caribbean, vol. 7, 1985; The Office and Duties of the Governor-General of Grenada, 1998; A Synoptic View of the Public Service of Grenada, 1999; Prescriptions for a Model Grenada, 2000; God Speaks, 2001; The Layman's Lawbook, 2002; The Love of God, 2004; Government of the Global Village, 2007. *Recreations:* lawn tennis, gardening. *Clubs:* St George's Lions (Pres.) (St George's); Vieux Fort Lions (Pres.) (St Lucia).

WILLIAMS, Darius James; *see* James, Darius.

WILLIAMS, Prof. David, FRS 1984; Emeritus Honorary Professor, Wales Institute of Mathematical and Computational Sciences, since 2009; Professor of Mathematical Sciences, Bath University, 1992–99, now Emeritus; *b* 9 April 1938; *s* of Gwyn Williams and Margaret Elizabeth Williams; *m* 1966, Sheila Margaret Harrison; two *d*. *Educ:* Jesus College, Oxford (DPhil; Hon. Fellow, 2008); Grey College, Durham. Instructor, Stanford Univ., 1962; Lectr, Durham Univ., 1963; Shell Research Lectr, Statistical Lab., and Res. Fellow, Clare Coll., Cambridge, 1966; Lectr, 1969, Prof. of Maths, 1972, University Coll., Swansea; Prof. of Mathematical Stats and Professorial Fellow, Clare Coll., Cambridge Univ., 1985–92; (part-time) Res. Prof. of Maths, Univ. of Wales Swansea, later Swansea Univ., 1999–2008. Vis. Fellow, Bath Univ., 1991–92. Hon. Fellow, UC, Swansea, 1991–. *Publications:* Diffusions, Markov processes, and martingales, vol. 1, Foundations, 1979, 2nd edn (with L. C. G. Rogers) 1994, vol. 2 (with L. C. G. Rogers), Itô calculus, 1987; Probability with martingales, 1991; Weighing the odds, 2001; papers in Séminaire de probabilités and other jls. *Recreations:* music, cycling, walking.

WILLIAMS, David; Chairman, Horbury Group, since 2009; Senior Adviser, Premira, since 2009; Deputy Chairman, Sheffield Children's Hospital Foundation Trust, since 2012 (non-executive Director, since 2007); *b* 22 Nov. 1950; *s* of Stanley and Ethel Williams; *m* 1972, Joan Elizabeth Martin; three *s*. *Educ:* Sheffield Coll. of Further Educn (HNC Business Studies 1972). Joined Sheffield Insulations Ltd, 1983, Sales and Mktg Dir, 1988; Dir, Main Bd, 1993, Dep. Chief Exec., 2001, Gp Chief Exec., 2002–08, Sheffield Insulations Gp plc, subseq. SIG plc. Mem. Adv. Bd, Sheffield Univ. Business Sch., 2006–. Member: Northern, RSPB; I of M Marshalls Assoc. *Recreations:* motorcycling, bird watching, shooting, walking, travel, gardening, golf, music of Bob Dylan, control of grey squirrels and magpies. *Club:* Rotherham Golf.

WILLIAMS, Prof. David Arnold, OBE 2000; PhD, DSc; CPhys, FInstP; FRAS; Perren Professor of Astronomy, University College London, 1994–2002; *b* 9 Sept. 1937; *s* of James Arnold Williams and Frances Barbara Williams (*née* Begg); *m* 1964, Doreen Jane Bell; two *s*. *Educ:* Larne Grammar Sch.; Queen's Univ., Belfast (BSc, PhD); Manchester (DSc). CPhys 1968; FInstP 1994; FRAS 1967. Maths Dept, Manchester Coll. of Sci. and Technol., 1963–65; NASA Goddard Space Flight Centre, Md, USA, 1965–67; Lectr, Sen. Lectr, Reader, Maths Dept, 1967–84, Prof. of Theoretical Astrophysics, 1984–94, UMIST. Pres., RAS, 1998–2000. *Publications:* (with J. E. Dyson) The Physics of the Interstellar Medium, 1980, 2nd edn 1997; (with W. W. Duley) Interstellar Chemistry, 1984; (with T. W. Hartquist) The Chemically Controlled Cosmos, 1995; (with T. W. Hartquist) The Molecular Astrophysics of Stars and Galaxies, 1998; (with T. W. Hartquist) The Cosmic-Chemical Bond, 2013; (with S. Viti) Observational Molecular Astronomy, 2013; contrib. numerous articles in learned jls. *Recreations:* hill-walking, choral singing, beer and wine. *Address:* Department of Physics and Astronomy, University College London, Gower Street, WC1E 6BT.

WILLIAMS, David Basil; QC 2013; *b* Bedford, 18 June 1964; *s* of John Williams and Barbara Williams; *m* 2000, Siobhan Hoy; two *s* one *d*. *Educ:* Cedars Upper Sch., Leighton Buzzard; Univ. of Leicester (LLB); Inns of Court Sch. of Law (BVC). Exec. Officer, Legal Aid Bd, 1986–89; called to the Bar, Inner Temple, 1990; in practice as a barrister: 3 Dr Johnson's Bldgs, 1990–2000; 4 Paper Bldgs, 2000– (mediator, 2007–). Contested (Lab) Wycombe, 2015. Member: Labour Party, 1987–; Soc. of Labour Lawyers, 1990–. Contrib. Ed., Butterworths Family Law Service, 2012–; Mem., Editl Bd, Internat. Family Law Jl, 2013–; Ed., Rayden and Jackson, 2015–. *Publications:* articles in Family Law Jl and Internat. Family Law. *Recreations:* motorcycles, cycling, football (Arsenal), modern European history. *Address:* 4PB, 4 Paper Buildings, Temple, EC4Y 7EX. *T:* (020) 7427 5200, *Fax:* (020) 7353 4979. *E:* dw@4pb.com.

WILLIAMS, David Edward, (David Walliams); actor and writer, since 1992; *b* London, 20 Aug. 1971; *s* of Peter and Kathleen Williams; *m* 2010, Lara Stone; one *s*. *Educ:* Reigate Grammar Sch.; Bristol Univ. (BA Hons Drama). *Television* appearances include: Rock Profile, 1999–2000; Little Britain, 3 series, 2003–06 (Best Comedy Perf., RTS, 2003; Best TV Comedy, British Comedy Awards, 2004; Best Comedy Prog., 2003, 2004, Best Comedy Perf., 2004, BAFTA); Little Britain Abroad, 2005–06; Little Britain USA, 2008; Capturing Mary, 2007; Frankie Howerd: Rather You Than Me, 2008; Come Fly with Me, 2010; Mr Stink, 2012; Big School, 2013, 2014; Gangsta Granny, 2013; The Boy in the Dress, 2014; Partners in Crime (series), 2015; Judge, TV series, Britain's Got Talent, 2012, 2013, 2014, 2015; Presenter, Perspectives on Roald Dahl, 2012; *film* includes: Stardust, 2007; Dinner for Schmucks, 2010; Great Expectations, 2012; The Look of Love, 2013; *theatre*: Little Britain Live, UK and Australian tour, 2005–07; No Man's Land, Duke of York's, 2008; A Midsummer Night's Dream, Noel Coward Th., 2013. *Publications:* The Boy in the Dress, 2008; Mr Stink, 2009; Billionaire Boy, 2010; Gangsta Granny, 2011; Ratburger, 2012; Camp David (autobiog.), 2012; Demon Dentist, 2013; The Slightly Annoying Elephant, 2013; Awful Auntie, 2014; The First Hippo on the Moon, 2014; The Queen's Orang-Utan (for Comic Relief), 2015. *Recreation:* swimming (swam the Channel, 2006, in 10.5 hours, raising over £1million for Sport Relief; swam 140 mile stretch of River Thames, 2011, raising £2.5million for Sport Relief). *Address:* Troika Talent Agency, 10a Christina Street, EC2A 4PA.

WILLIAMS, Prof. David Edward, PhD; FRSC; FRSNZ; FNZIC; Professor of Chemistry, University of Auckland, since 2006; *b* 6 Feb. 1949; *s* of William and Gertrude Williams; *m* 1972, Lindsay Mary Sutherland; one *s* one *d*. *Educ:* Lynfield Coll., Auckland; Univ. of Auckland (BSc; MSc Hons; PhD 1974). CChem 1977, FRSC 1986; FRSNZ 2009; FNZIC 2007. Gp Leader, Solid State Chemistry, Harwell Lab., UKAEA, 1980–90; Chief Scientist in Applied Electrochemistry, AEA Technol., 1990–91; University College London: Thomas Graham Prof. of Chemistry, 1991–2002; Hd, Dept of Chemistry, 1999–2002; Vis. Prof. of Chemistry, 2002–; Chief Scientist, Unipath Ltd, 2002–06. Hon. Prof., Royal Instn of GB, 2002–. *Publications:* (ed jtly) Techniques and Mechanisms in Gas Sensing, 1991; approx. 200 papers in jls of chemistry and materials sci. *Recreations:* ski-ing, yachting. *Address:* Department of Chemistry, University of Auckland, Private Bag 92019, Auckland, New Zealand. *E:* david.williams@auckland.ac.nz.

WILLIAMS, Prof. David Franklyn, PhD, DSc; FREng; Professor, and Director of International Affairs, Wake Forest Institute of Regenerative Medicine, North Carolina, since 2008; *b* 18 Dec. 1944; *s* of late Henry Sidney and Margaret Williams; *m* 2001, Margaret Mary O'Donnell; three *s*. *Educ:* Thornbury Grammar Sch.; Univ. of Birmingham (BSc 1965; PhD 1969; DSc 1982). CEng, FIPEM 1982; FIMMM (FIM 1982). University of Liverpool: Department of Clinical Engineering: Lectr, 1968–78; Sen. Lectr, 1978–84; Prof., 1984–2001; Hd of Clinical Engrg, 1984–2007; Prof. of Tissue Engrg, 2001–07, now Emeritus; Dir, UK Centre for Tissue Engrg, 2004–07; Pro-Vice-Chancellor, 1997–2001. Hon. Consultant Scientist, Royal Liverpool Univ. Hosp., 1990–2007. Visiting Professor: Shanghai Jiao Tong Med. Univ., 2008–; Christiaan Barnard Dept of Cardiothoracic Surgery, Cape Town, 2008–; Grad. Sch. of Biomedical Engrg, Univ. of NSW, 2008–; Guest Prof., Tsinghua Univ., Beijing, 2007–. Mem., CCLRC, 2001–04. Chm., Strait Access Technologies Pty Ltd, S Africa, 2012–. Pres., Tissue Engrg and Regenerative Medicine Internat. Soc., 2013–15. FREng 1999; MAE 1999; Fellow, American Inst. for Med. and Biol Engrg 2000; Foreign Fellow, Indian NAE, 2014. Ed.-in-Chief, Biomaterials, 1996–2014. *Publications:* include: Implants in Surgery, 1973; Biocompatibility of Implant Materials, 1976; Materials in Clinical Dentistry, 1979; Biocompatibility, 14 vols, 1981–86; Definitions in Biomaterials, 1987; Concise Encyclopaedia of Medical and Dental Materials, 1990; The Williams Dictionary of Biomaterials, 1999; Essential Biomaterials Science, 2014; over 400 papers in learned jls. *Recreations:* painting, photography, travel, writing poetry. *Address:* One Sheffield Place, Winston-Salem, NC 27104, USA. *T:* (336) 6718895. *E:* dfwillia@wfubmc.edu. *Club:* Athenæum.

WILLIAMS, David Frederick, PhD; Executive Director, National Facilities and Collections, Commonwealth Scientific and Industrial Research Organisation, since 2014; Director: Pawsey Supercomputing Centre, since 2014; National Computational Infrastructure, since 2014; International Centre for Radio Astronomy Research, since 2015; *b* 21 Sept. 1951; *s* of Frederick Sefton Williams and Dorothy Williams (*née* Banks); *m* 1985, Jeannie Elizabeth Rickards; one *s* two *d*. *Educ:* Hutton Grammar Sch., Preston; Univ. of Reading (BSc 1974; PhD 1978). Lectr, Dept of Geography, Reading Univ., 1977–78; Clyde Surveys, 1978–82; NERC, 1982–89; BNSC, DTI, 1989–96; Hd, Strategy and Internat. Relns, Eur. Orgn for the Exploitation of Meteorol Satellites, Darmstadt, 1996–2006; United Kingdom Space Agency: Dir Gen., British Nat. Space Centre, 2006–10; Acting Chief Exec., 2010–11; Chief Exec., 2011–12; Gp Exec., Inf. Services Gp, CSIRO, 2012–14. Chm., European Space Agency, 2010–12; Dir, AARNet Pty Ltd, 2014–. Member: Steering Cttee, Global Climate Observing System, 2000–11; Internat. Acad. of Astronautics, 2012–. Trustee, Nat. Space Centre, Leicester, 2006–12. *Publications:* various articles in jls. *Recreations:* football, gardening, renovation. *Address:* CSIRO North Ryde, Riverside Corporate Park, 11 Julius Avenue, North Ryde, NSW 2113, Australia. *T:* (2) 9490 5620.

WILLIAMS, Rt Rev. David Grant; *see* Basingstoke, Bishop Suffragan of.

WILLIAMS, David Huw Anthony; QC 2008; *b* Neath, W Glamorgan, 26 Feb. 1964; *s* of late Thomas Brinley Williams and Mair E. Williams (*née* Anthony); *m* 1994, Denise Dolan; two *s*. *Educ:* Gnoll Prim. Sch., Neath; Cefn Saeson Sch., Neath; Univ. of Wales, Swansea (BSc Hons 1983). Called to the Bar, Inner Temple, 1988; in practice as barrister specialising in crime and fraud. *Publications:* (contrib.) Fraud: law, practice and procedure, 2004; Smith's Law of Theft (with David Ormerod), 9th edn 2007. *Recreations:* tennis, Welsh Rugby, film, reading, theatre (particularly the work of Stephen Sondheim). *Address:* Fulcrum Chambers LLP, 11 Old Square, Lincoln's Inn, WC2A 3TS.

WILLIAMS, David John, QPM 1992; Chief Constable, British Transport Police, 1997–2001; Associate Director, Reliance Security Services Ltd, 2001–02; *b* 7 April 1941; *s* of late John Isaac Williams and Edith (*née* Stoneham); *m* 1962, Johanna Murphy; two *s*. *Educ:* Ystalyfera Grammar Sch.; University Coll. London (LLB Hons). Called to the Bar, Middle Temple, 1977. Metropolitan Police, 1960–84; FBI Nat. Acad., 1982; on secondment to Home Office Inspectorate, 1983; Herts Constabulary, 1984–89; Dep. Chief Constable, 1989–91, Chief Constable, 1991–97, Surrey Police; Nat. Exec. Inst., USA, 1994. Chm., Traffic Cttee, ACPO, 1995–97. Mem. Council, St John Ambulance, Herts, 2004–11; Dir and Trustee, Relate, N London, 2004–07; Chm., Child Accident Prevention Trust, 2007–09; Gov./Trustee, Corps of Commissionaires Trust, 2008–09; Patron, Isabel Hospice, 2006–. Chm. and Trustee, Three Valleys Male Voice Choir, 2011–13. OStJ 1995. Queen's Commendation for Bravery, 1976; Police Long Service and Good Conduct Medal, 1982. *Recreations:* music, Rugby football, walking, golf, choir singing. *Club:* Royal Over-Seas League.

WILLIAMS, David John, FRCP, FRCPE, FRCS, FRCSE, FRCA, FRCEM; JP; Clinical Director, Accident & Emergency Services, Guy's and St Thomas' Hospitals NHS Trust, 1993–2000; *b* 23 April 1938; *s* of Frank Williams, CBE and Kathleen Williams; *m* 1977, Ann Andrews (*née* Walker-Watson); one *s* one *d*, and one step *s* one step *d*. *Educ:* Highgate Sch.; Hotchkiss Sch., USA; Trinity Coll., Cambridge (MA, MB, BChir); St Thomas' Hosp. Med. Sch. MRCP 1970, FRCP 1982; MRCGP 1972; FRCEM (FFAEM 1993); FRCS 1997; FRCPE 1998; FRCSE 1999; FRCA 2000. Jun. med. posts, St Thomas' Hosp., Kingston Hosp., Guy's-Maudsley Neurosurgical Unit, 1964–65; RMO, Nat. Heart Hosp., 1966, Middlesex Hosp., 1967–70; Registrar, Maudsley Hosp., 1970–71; GP, 1971–72; Consultant, Accident and Emergency Medicine: Middlesex Hosp., 1973–84; St Thomas' Hosp., 1984–2000. Clin. Advr, Health Service Comr, 2000–05; Mem., Criminal Injuries Compensation Tribunal (formerly Appeals Panel), 2000–12; Sen. Medical Mem., Tribunal Service (formerly Appeals Tribunals), 2006–13. Sec., Casualty Surgeons Assoc., 1978–84; President: British Assoc. for A&E Medicine, 1987–90; Intercollegiate Faculty of A&E Medicine, 1993–97; Eur. Soc. for Emergency Medicine, 2004–07 (Vice-Pres., 2000–04); Chairman: UEMS Cttee on Emergency Medicine, 2005–12; Eur. Bd of Emergency Medicine, 2010–; Pres., UEMS Section on Emergency Medicine, 2012–. Invited Member Council: RCP, 1994–2000; RCS, 1994–2000; Royal Coll. of Anaesthetists, 1994–2000. JP Sutton, 2004–08. Fellow, Internat. Fedn of Emergency Medicine, 2000; Hon. Member: Amer. Coll. Emergency Physicians, 1990; Amer. Acad. of Emergency Medicine, 2005; German Assoc. for Emergency Medicine, 2010; Czech Soc. for Emergency and Disaster Medicine, 2013; Hon. Life Mem., British Assoc. for A&E Medicine, 1998–2008; Hon. FRSocMed 2001. *Recreations:* reading, collecting books, theatre, travel. *Address:* 154 Durham Road, West Wimbledon, SW20 0DG. *T:* (020) 8946 3785.

WILLIAMS, (David John) Delwyn; company director; *b* 1 Nov. 1938; *s* of David Lewis Williams and Irena Violet Gwendoline Williams; *m* 1963, Olive Elizabeth Jerman; one *s* one *d*. *Educ:* Welshpool High School; University College of Wales, Aberystwyth. LLB. Sometime Solicitor and company director. MP (C) Montgomery, 1979–83; former Member: Select Cttee on Wales; Statutory Instruments Cttee; Jt Sec., All-Party Leisure and Recreation Industry Cttee. Contested (C) Montgomery, 1983. Former Mem., British Field Sports Soc. *Recreations:* race horse owner; cricket, golf, small bore shooting.

WILLIAMS, David Lincoln; Chairman and Managing Director, Costa Rica Coffee Co. Ltd, 1988–2002; *b* 10 Feb. 1937; *s* of Lewis Bernard Williams and Eileen Elizabeth Cadogan; *m* 1959, Gillian Elisabeth, *d* of Dr William Phillips; one *s* one *d*. *Educ:* Cheltenham College. Served RA Gibraltar, 1955–57. Chairman: Allied Windows (S Wales) Ltd, 1971–85; Cardiff Broadcasting PLC, 1979–84; Allied Profiles Ltd, 1981–96; Chm. and Man. Dir, John Williams of Cardiff PLC, 1983–88 (Dir, 1968–88). Chm., Cox (Penarth), 1987–94. President, Aluminium Window Assoc., 1971–72. Member: CBI Welsh Council, 1986–89; Welsh Arts Council, 1987–94 (Chm., Music Cttee, 1988–94). Pres., Vale of Glamorgan Festival, 1995– (Chm., 1978–95); Director: Cardiff Bay Opera House Trust, 1994–97; WNO, 1994–2001 (Nat. Chm., 1980–2000, Vice-Pres., 2005–, Friends of WNO). Freeman, City of London, 1986; Liveryman, Founders' Co., 1986. *Recreations:* opera, gardening, fine weather sailing. *Address:* Rose Revived, Llantrithyd, Cowbridge, Vale of Glamorgan CF71 7UB. *T:* (01446) 781357. *Club:* Cardiff and County (Cardiff).

WILLIAMS, Prof. David Michael, PhD; FRCPath, FDSRCS; Professor of Global Oral Health, Bart's and the London School of Medicine and Dentistry, Queen Mary University of London, since 2011; Professor of Pathology, University of Southampton, 2004–11, now Emeritus (Dean, Faculty of Medicine, Health and Life Sciences, 2004–10; Vice Provost, 2010–11); *b* 4 Nov. 1946; *s* of late Reginald Albert Williams and Mary Williams (*née* Holland); *m* 1970, Gillian Elizabeth Regester; one *s* one *d*. *Educ:* Plymouth Coll.; London Hosp. Med. Coll., Univ. of London (BDS Hons 1969; MSc 1972; PhD 1976). FRCPath 1991; FDSRCS 1994. London Hospital Medical College: Sen. Lectr in Oral Pathology, 1982–89; Reader in Oral Pathology, 1989–93; Prof. of Oral Pathology, 1994–2004, Dean of Clinical Dentistry, 1994–98, Dep. Warden, 1998–2001, St Bartholomew's and Royal London Sch. of Medicine and Dentistry, QMW, Univ. of London, subseq. Bart's and The London, Queen Mary's Sch. of Medicine and Dentistry; Vice-Principal, Queen Mary, Univ. of London, 2001–04; Hon. Consultant: Bart's and the London NHS Trust (formerly Royal London Hosp., then Royal Hosps NHS Trust), 1982–2004; Southampton Univ. Hosps NHS Trust, 2004–11 (non-exec. Dir, 2005–); non-exec. Dir, S Central Ambulance Service NHS Foundn Trust, 2012–. Chm., Dentistry Sub-panel 2008 RAE. Mem., GDC, 1998–2003 (Chm., Registration Sub-Cttee, 1999–2003). Pres., British Soc. for Dental Res., 2002–04; International Association for Dental Research: Pres., Pan-European Fedn, 2004–05; Vice-Pres., 2007–08; Pres.-elect, 2008–09; Pres., 2009–10. Mem., several editl bds. *Publications:* (jtly) Pathology of Periodontal Disease, 1992; (ed jtly) The Challenge of Oral Disease: a call for global action, 2nd edn, 2015; numerous articles in learned jls. *Recreations:* golf, scuba diving, hill walking, sailing. *Address:* Bart's and the London School of Medicine and Dentistry, Turner Street, Whitechapel, E1 2AD. *E:* d.m.williams@qmul.ac.uk. *Club:* Athenæum.

WILLIAMS, Rev. David Michael; JP; Vicar, Benefice of St Giles, Great Coxwell, with St Mary the Virgin, Buscot, All Saints, Coleshill, and St Michael and All Angels, Eaton Hastings, since 2014 (Priest-in-Charge, 2011–14); Tutor in Foundations for Denominational Ministry, Department of External Studies, St. John's College Nottingham; *b* 6 April 1950; *s* of David Woodget Williams and Edith Olive Williams (*née* Hance); *m* (marr. diss.). *Educ:* Exeter Univ. (BA Hons 1971); UCL (Dip. Liby and Inf. Studies 1974); London Univ. (MA 1977); Univ. of Kent (Dip. Applied Christian Theology 2008). On staff, Council for the Care of Churches, 1972–73, 1974–87; Church of England: on staff, 1987–94, Sec., 1994–99, Central Bd of Finance; Clerk to the Gen. Synod, 1999–2011; Dir, Central Services, 1999–2002, Hd, Central Secretariat, 2002–11, Archbishops' Council. Ordained deacon 2008, priest 2009. FSA 1981; FRSA 1982. JP: SE Surrey, 1986; Oxon, 2012. *Publications:* articles in jls on hist. of English parochial libraries. *Recreations:* numismatics, ecclesiology, art and architecture, horticulture, cycling, walking. *Address:* The Vicarage, Great Coxwell, Faringdon, Oxon SN7 7NG. *T:* (01367) 240665.

WILLIAMS, David Oliver; General Secretary, Confederation of Health Service Employees, 1983–87; *b* 12 March 1926; *m* 1949, Kathleen Eleanor Jones, Dinorwic; two *s* five *d* (and one *s* decd). *Educ:* Brynrefail Grammar Sch.; North Wales Hospital, Denbigh (RMN 1951). COHSE: full-time officer, Regional Secretary, Yorkshire Region, 1955; National Officer, Head Office, 1962; Sen. National Officer, 1969; Asst General Secretary, 1974. Chairman: Nurses and Midwives Whitley Council Staff Side, 1977–87; General Whitley Council Staff Side, 1974–87. Member: NEC, Labour Party, 1981–83; TUC Gen. Council, 1983–87. Occasional Tech. Advr to WHO. Jubilee Medal, 1977. *Recreations:* walking, birdwatching, swimming, music. *Address:* 1 King's Court, Beddington Gardens, Wallington, Surrey SM6 0HR. *T:* (020) 8647 6412.

WILLIAMS, Air Vice-Marshal David Owen C.; *see* Crwys-Williams.

WILLIAMS, Sir David (Reeve), Kt 1999; CBE 1990; Member (Lib Dem), Richmond upon Thames Borough Council, 1974–2014 (Leader, 1983–2001; Cabinet Member, 2001–02, 2006–10); *b* 8 June 1939; *s* of Edmund George Williams and May Williams (*née* Partridge); *m*

1964, Christine Margaret Rayson. *Educ:* St Cuthbert's Soc.; Univ. of Durham (BA Hons Politics and Econs). Computer systems analyst, 1961–95: IBM UK Ltd, 1961–70; Insurance Systems and Services, 1970–78; David Williams and Associates, 1978–91; Teleglobe Insce Systems Ltd, 1991–95. Dep. Chm., and Leader, Lib Dem Gp, LGA, 1996–2001. *Recreations:* collecting books, particularly about Lloyd George, listening to jazz, particularly Charlie Parker. *Address:* 8 Arlington Road, Petersham, Richmond, Surrey TW10 7BY. *T:* (020) 8940 9421.

WILLIAMS, David Whittow; Chief Executive, Amari Plastics plc, since 2004; *b* 18 Aug. 1957; *s* of David Whittow Williams and Eileen Williams; *m* 1992, Helle Nordensgaard. *Educ:* Birkenhead Sch.; Mansfield Coll., Oxford (MA). Exec. Vice Pres., Melwire Inc., 1982–86; Mkting Dir, Vickers Healthcare, 1986–88; Eur. Business Develt Manager, Blue Circle Cement, 1988–90; Business Develt Dir, Blue Circle Home Products plc, 1991–94; Man. Dir, Potterton/Myson, 1994–96; Chief Executive: Magnet, 1996–99; Berisford, subseq. Enodis plc, 1999–2001. *Recreations:* Rugby, tennis, cricket.

WILLIAMS, Dr David William; a Judge of the Upper Tribunal (Administrative Appeals Chamber), 2009–15; a Judge of the First-tier Tribunal (Tax Chamber), 2009–14 (a Social Security and Child Support Commissioner, 1998–2009; Deputy Special Commissioner of Income Tax, and part-time Chairman, VAT and Duties Tribunal, 2003–09); *b* 13 Feb. 1946; *s* of J. W. (Bill) Williams, DFC, and Joan Adair (*née* Wallis); *m* 1968, Elisabeth Jones Pierce; three *s*. *Educ:* Queen Elizabeth's Grammar Sch., Faversham; Univ. of Bristol (LLB; LLM; PhD 1979). ATII 1970. Admitted Solicitor, 1970; Lectr, Faculty of Law, Univ. of Bristol, 1969–76; Faculty of Law, University of Manchester: Lectr, then Sen. Lectr, 1976–86; Reader, 1986–87; Dean of Faculty, 1984–86; Queen Mary and Westfield College, University of London: Prof. of Tax Law, 1987–98; Vis. Prof., 1998–2010; Dean, Faculty of Laws, 1991–93. Vis. Lectr, Univ. of Liverpool, 1978–80; Visiting Professor: Univ. of Buckingham, 1992–93; Univ. of Sydney, 1997; Tech. Univ. of Vienna, 1997–2001; Sorbonne, Paris, 1998–99. Consultant, OECD Fiscal Affairs Dept, 1993–97. Pt-time Chairman: Medical Appeal Tribunals, 1990–98; Social Security Appeal Tribunals, 1984–96; Dep. Social Security Comr, 1996–98. Member: Educn Cttee, Chartered Inst. Taxation, 1988–92; Revenue Law Cttee, Law Soc., 1992–97; Perm. Scientific Cttee, Internat. Fiscal Assoc., 1996–98; Tax Law Rewrite Consultative Cttee, 1997–2010. Mem. Bd, Centre for Juridico-Economic Investigation, Univ. of Porto, 1997–. *Publications:* Maladministration: remedies for injustice, 1979; (with G. K. Morse) Profit Sharing, 1979; Running Your Own Business, 1979; Tax for the Self-Employed, 1980; Social Security Taxation, 1982; National Insurance Contributions Handbook, 1987; Trends in International Taxation, 1991; Taxation Principles and Practice, 1993; EC Tax Law, 1998; editor: (with G. K. Morse) Introduction to Revenue Law, 1985; Tax on International Transfers of Information, 1991; Principles of Tax Law, 1996, 7th edn 2012; Practical Application of Double Tax Conventions, 1998; (with N. Wikeley) Social Security Legislation, vol. iv, Tax Credits, 2003–, vol. i, Retirement Pensions, 2014–; consulting editor: Reader's Digest Guide to the Law, 8th–10th edn, 1986–92; Reader's Digest Know Your Rights, 1997; contrib. articles to legal jls. *Address:* The Old Rectory, Rhiw, Pwllheli, Gwynedd LL53 8AD.

WILLIAMS, Dr (David) Wynford, CB 2007; Chairman, Public Weather Customer Service Group, since 2013; *b* 19 July 1946; *s* of late Thomas Elwyn Williams and of Nancy Williams; *m* 1969, Dilys Arthur; one *s* one *d*. *Educ:* Amman Valley Grammar Sch., Ammanford; University Coll., Swansea (BSc 1967, PhD 1971). CPhys 1987, CEng 1987; FInstP 1981; FRAeS 1981; FIMarEST 2006. Scientist: ASWE, MoD, 1971–81; British Naval Staff, Washington, 1981–84; Ministry of Defence: ACOS (Operational Analysis), C-in-C Fleet, 1984–87; Supt, RAE Ranges, 1987–91; Dir, A&AEE Boscombe Down, 1991–95; rcds 1996; Dir, Sea Systems Sector, DERA, 1997–2000; Chief Exec., UK Hydrographic Office, and UK Nat. Hydrographer, 2001–06. Chm., Pelydryn Ltd, 2008–13. Pres., Inst. of Marine Engrg, Sci. and Technol., 2007–08. Non-exec. Dir, S Wales Probation Trust, 2007–. Chm., Bath and Wells Diocesan Bd of Finance, 2006–10. *Recreations:* Rugby, golf, music (orchestral and choral). *Address:* Rhos Colwyn, Welsh St Donats, Vale of Glamorgan CF71 7SS. *T:* (01446) 771243. *E:* wyn.dil@talktalk.net.

WILLIAMS, Delwyn; *see* Williams, D. J. D.

WILLIAMS, Derrick; *see* Williams, R. D.

WILLIAMS, Sir Dillwyn; *see* Williams, Sir E. D.

WILLIAMS, Rev. Doiran George; Non-Stipendiary Minister, Greater Whitbourne, since 1993; *b* 27 June 1926; *s* of Rev. Dr Robert Richard Williams and Dilys Rachel Williams; *m* 1st, 1949, Flora Samitz (decd); one *s* one *d*; 2nd, 1977, Maureen Dorothy Baker; one *d*. *Educ:* Hereford Cathedral Sch.; Colwyn Bay Grammar Sch.; Liverpool Coll.; John F. Hughes Sch., Utica, NY. Served Army (Infantry), 1944–47. Called to the Bar, Gray's Inn, 1952; practised in Liverpool, 1952–58; Dept of Dir of Public Prosecutions, 1959, Asst Dir, 1977–82, Principal Asst Dir of Public Prosecutions, 1982–86; Chm., Med. Appeal Tribunals, 1987–98. Sec., Liverpool Fabian Soc., 1956–58. Reader: Liverpool Dio., 1953–58; London Dio., 1959–63; Southwark Dio., 1963–88; Hereford Dio., 1988–93; Mem., Southwark Readers' Bd, 1977–88. Ordained deacon, 1993, priest, 1994. *Recreations:* arts, mountains, sport, wine. *Address:* Howberry, Whitbourne, Worcester WR6 5RZ.

WILLIAMS, Sir Donald Mark, 10th Bt *cr* 1866; *b* 7 Nov. 1954; *s* of Sir Robert Ernest Williams, 9th Bt, and of Ruth Margaret, *d* of Charles Edwin Butcher, Hudson Bay, Saskatchewan, Canada; *S* father, 1976; *m* 1982, Denise, *o d* of Royston H. Cory; three *d* (one *s* decd). *Educ:* West Buckland School, Devon. *Heir:* *b* Barton Matthew Williams [*b* 21 Nov. 1956; *m* 1st, 1980, Karen Robinson (marr. diss.); one *s* one *d*; 2nd, 1985, Sarah (marr. diss.); one *d*]. *Address:* Upcott House, Barnstaple, N Devon EX31 4DR.

WILLIAMS, Dr Dyfri John Roderick, FSA; Research Keeper, Department of Greek and Roman Antiquities, British Museum, 2008–12; *b* 8 Feb. 1952; *s* of Roderick Trevor Williams and Eira Williams (*née* Evans); *m* 1980, Korinna Pilafidis; one *s* one *d*. *Educ:* Repton Sch.; University Coll. London (BA); Lincoln Coll., Oxford (DPhil). FSA 1987. Shuffrey Jun. Res. Fellow, Lincoln Coll., Oxford, 1976–79; Department of Greek and Roman Antiquities, British Museum, 1979–: Res. Asst, 1979–83; Asst Keeper, 1983–93; Keeper, 1993–2008. Corresp. Mem., German Archaeol Inst., 1984. *Publications:* Greek Vases, 1985, rev. and enlarged edn 1999; Corpus Vasorum Antiquorum, BM fasc. 9, 1993; Greek Gold: jewellery of the classical world, 1994; (ed) The Art of the Greek Goldsmith, 1998; Warren Cup, 2006; Masterpieces: classical art, 2009. *Recreations:* family, reading, music.

WILLIAMS, Prof. Sir (Edward) Dillwyn, Kt 1990; FRCP, FRCPath, FMedSci, FLSW; Professor of Histopathology, 1992–96, now Emeritus, and Hon. Senior Visiting Fellow, Department of Public Health, since 2010, University of Cambridge; *b* 1 April 1929; *s* of Edward Williams and Ceinwen Williams (*née* James); *m* 1st, 1954, Ruth Hill (marr. diss. 1973); one *s* two *d* (and one *s* decd); 2nd, 1976, Olwen Williams (marr. diss. 2000); one *s* one *d*. *Educ:* Christ's Coll., Cambridge (MA, MD; Hon. Fellow, 1991); London Hospital Med. Coll. Jun. appts, London Hosp. and RPMS; successively Lectr, Sen. Lectr, Reader, in Morbid Anatomy, RPMS; Prof. of Pathology, 1969–92, Vice-Provost, 1982–84, Univ. of Wales Coll. of Medicine. Consultant Pathologist, Cardiff, 1969–92. Res. Fellowship, Harvard Univ., 1962–63. President: RCPath, 1987–90; BMA, 1998–99; Hd and Prin. Investigator of WHO's Internat. Reference Centre for Endocrine Tumours, 1972–; Chm., Welsh Sci. Adv. Cttee, 1985–92; Mem., GMC, 1987–90. Chairman: Scientific Project Panel of Chernobyl Tissue Bank, 1998–2004; Agenda for Res. on Chernobyl Health, 2010–. Mem., Sci. Scholarships Cttee, Royal Commn for Exhibn of 1851, 2000–12. Corresp. Mem., Amer. Thyroid Assoc.; President: Thyroid Club of GB, 1987–90; European Thyroid Assoc., 1993–96. Founder FMedSci 1998; Founder FLSW 2010. *Publications:* International Histological Classification of Tumours: histological typing of endocrine tumours, 1980; Pathology and Management of Thyroid Disease, 1981; Current Endocrine Concepts, 1982; numerous contribs to learned jls in field of endocrine pathology and carcinogenesis, identifying cell of origin, humoral and genetic associations of medullary carcinoma of thyroid, clonality studies of thyroid and colon, radiation and thyroid cancer, in particular recently on thyroid carcinoma following Chernobyl nuclear accident. *Recreations:* natural history in general, birdwatching in particular, mountain walking. *Address:* 9 Cow Lane, Fulbourn, Cambs CB21 5HB. *T:* (01223) 880738.

WILLIAMS, Elizabeth, (Betty); working for peace, since 1976; Founder and President, World Centers of Compassion for Children International, since 1997; *b* 22 May 1943; *m* 1st, 1961, Ralph Williams (marr. diss.); one *s* one *d*; 2nd, 1982, James T. Perkins. *Educ:* St Dominic's Grammar School. Office Receptionist. Co-founder and Leader, NI Peace Movement, 1976–78; Chm., Inst. for Asian Democracy, Washington, DC; Patron, Internat. Peace Foundn, Vienna. Hon. LLD, Yale Univ., 1977; Hon. HLD, Coll. of Sienna Heights, Michigan, 1977. Nobel Peace Prize (jtly), 1976; Carl-von-Ossietzky Medal for Courage, 1976; Eleanor Roosevelt Award; Frank Foundn Child Assistance Internat. Oliver Award; Peace Building Award, Together for Peace Foundn, 1995. Paul Harris Fellow, Rotary Internat., 1995. *Publications:* Madness in My Country, 2009. *Recreation:* gardening.

WILLIAMS, Felicity Ann; Senior Regional Official, National Association of Schoolmasters/Union of Women Teachers, since 2008; General Secretary, Wales Trade Union Congress, 2004–08 (Assistant General Secretary, 2000–04); *b* 29 Oct. 1960; *d* of Ivan and Doris Parker; *m* 1981, David Williams. *Educ:* Univ. of Bristol. FIBMS 1988. Biomed. scientist, then Dep. Hd of Microbiology 1988–97, Welsh Blood Service. *Recreations:* travel, reading, good food and wine, theatre.

WILLIAMS, Francis Julian, CBE 1986; JP; Vice Lord-Lieutenant, Cornwall, 1998–2002; Member of Prince of Wales' Council, Duchy of Cornwall, 1969–85; *b* 16 April 1927; 2nd *s* of late Alfred Martyn Williams, CBE, DSC; *m* Delia Fearne Marshall (*d* 2013), *e d* of Captain and Mrs Campbell Marshall, St Mawes; two *s*. *Educ:* Eton; Trinity Coll., Cambridge (BA). RAF, 1945–48. Chm., Cambridge Univ. Conservative Assoc., 1950; Pres., Cambridge Union, 1951. Contested (C) All Saints Div. of Birmingham, 1955. Chm., Royal Instn of Cornwall, 1998–2005. Succeeded to Caerhays, 1955. Pres., Cornwall Cricket Club. Mem., Cornwall CC, 1967–89 (Vice-Chm., 1974; Chm., 1980–89). JP 1970, DL 1977, Cornwall. *Recreation:* gardening. *Address:* Caerhays Castle, Gorran, St Austell, Cornwall PL26 6LY. *T:* (01872) 501310. *Clubs:* Brooks's, White's.

WILLIAMS, Sir Francis Owen Garbett, (Sir Frank), Kt 1999; CBE 1987; Managing Director, 1992–2012, Team Principal, since 2012, Williams F1 (formerly Williams Grand Prix Engineering Ltd); *b* 16 April 1942; *s* of Owen Garbett Williams; *m* 1974, Virginia Jane, *d* of Raymond Berry; three *c*. *Educ:* St Joseph's Coll., Dumfries. Racing driver to 1966, competing first in Austin A40; grand prix team management, 1969–; Formula One with Brabham BT 26A; founded Frank Williams Racing Cars, 1975; first Grand Prix race, with FW07, Silverstone, 1979; won Constructors' Cup, 1980, 1981, 1986, 1987, 1992, 1993, 1994, 1996, 1997; introduced active ride system, 1988, semi-automatic 6-speed gear box, 1991. Helen Rollason Award, BBC Sports Personality of the Year, 2010. *Address:* Williams F1, Grove, Wantage, Oxon OX12 0DQ.

WILLIAMS, Frank John; actor and playwright; *b* 2 July 1931; *s* of William Williams and Alice (*née* Myles). *Educ:* Ardingly Coll.; Hendon County Sch. *Theatre* includes: Stage Manager and actor, Gateway Theatre, London, 1951; *writer:* No Traveller, 1952; The TV Murders, 1960; The Substitute, 1961; Murder by Appointment, 1985; Alibi for Murder, 1989; Murder Weekend, 1993; Mask for Murder, 1993; The Playing Fields, 2003; *actor:* The Cresta Run, Royal Court, 1965; The Waiters, Watford, 1967; Dad's Army, Shaftesbury, and tour, 1975–76; The Editor Regrets, tour, 1978; Stage Struck, 1980, The Winslow Boy, 1982, Vienna; Lloyd George Knew My Father, tour, Middle East and Far East, 1993; A Midsummer Night's Dream, Almeida, and tour, 1996–97; *television* includes: The Call Up, 1952; The Queen came by, 1955; The Army Game, 1958–61; Anna Karenina, 1961; Diary of a Young Man, 1964; After Many a Summer, 1967; Dad's Army, 1969–77; How Many Miles to Babylon, 1981; Grey Granite, 1982; Love's Labour Lost, 1984; You Rang M'Lord, 1989–92; *films* include: Shield of Faith, 1954; The Extra Day, 1955; The Square Peg, 1958; The Bulldog Breed, 1960; Dad's Army, 1970; Jabberwocky, 1976; The Human Factor, 1979. Member: Gen. Synod, 1985–2000; Crown Appts Commn, 1992–97; Trustee, Annunciation Trust, 1995–2006. Mem., Equity Council, 1984–88, 1990–94, 1998–2010; Dir, Equity Charitable Trust (formerly Equity Trust Fund), 1992–2013. *Publications:* Vicar to Dad's Army, 2002. *Recreations:* theatre, cinema, collecting boys' school books. *Address:* 31 Manor Park Crescent, Edgware, Middx HA8 7NE. *T:* (020) 8952 4871.

WILLIAMS, Prof. Gareth, MD, ScD; FRCP, FRCPE; Professor of Medicine, University of Bristol, 2003–13, now Emeritus Professor and Senior Research Fellow in Philosophy (Dean, Faculty of Medicine and Dentistry, 2003–08); *b* 17 March 1952; *s* of Sir Alwyn Williams, FRS, and Joan Williams (*née* Bevan); *m* 1983, Caroline Anne Evans; one *s* one *d*. *Educ:* Royal Belfast Academical Instn (Sir Hans Sloane Medal 1970); Clare Coll., Cambridge (Open and Foundn Scholar); Middlesex Hosp. Med. Sch. (MB BChir Hons Medicine and Pharmacol. 1977); Univ. of Cambridge (MD 1986; ScD 2003). FRCP 1991; FRCPE 1999. Jun. hosp. posts, Middlesex, Hammersmith and Brompton Hosps, London, and Hôpital Cantonal, Geneva, 1977–79; Res. Registrar, Guy's Hosp., London, 1980–83; Med. Registrar, Ealing and Hammersmith Hosps, 1983–85; R. D. Lawrence Res. Fellow, British Diabetic Assoc., 1986–88; University of Liverpool: Sen. Lectr, 1988–92, Reader, 1992, in Medicine; Prof. of Medicine, 1995–2003; Hon. Consultant Physician, Royal Liverpool Univ. Hosp., 1988–92; Foundn Prof. of Medicine and Hon. Consultant Physician, Univ. Hosp. Aintree, Liverpool, 1995–2003. Lectures: Henry Cohen Hist. of Medicine, Liverpool Med. Inst., 2011; Gresham Coll., London, 2011, 2013; Milroy, RCP, 2012. Non-exec. Dir, United Bristol Healthcare Trust, 2005–07. Member: Obesity Leadership Gp, Coalition for Better Health, 2009–10; Expert Rev. Gp, History of Medicine and Med. Humanities, Wellcome Trust, 2011–14. Vis. Prof., Fac. of Medicine, Univ. of Alberta, 1988–89. UK Pres., Anglo-French Med. Soc., 1993–2000; Mem. Council, Eur. Soc. for Clinical Investment, 1996–2000 (Vice-Pres., 2000); Chm., MEDINE (Med. Educn in Europe), 2004–07. Trustee, Jenner Trust and Dr Jenner's House (formerly Jenner Mus.), 2009–11 (Chm., 2010–11). Editl Bd, Peptides, 1994–2003. Mem. Cttee, Med. Writers' Gp, Soc. of Authors, 2001– (Chm., 2007). Ambassador, British Polio Fellowship, 2013–. Dr *hc* Angers, 2007. Novartis UK Award for Achievement in Diabetes, 1999. *Publications:* (ed jtly) Textbook of Diabetes, 1990, 2nd edn 1995 (BMA Medicine Book of the Yr; Soc. of Authors prize), 3rd edn 2004; (ed jtly) Handbook of Diabetes, 1992, 3rd edn 2004; (contrib.) Oxford Textbook of Medicine, 4th edn 2004 to 5th edn 2010; (ed jtly) Obesity: science to practice, 2009; The Angel of Death: the story of smallpox, 2010; Paralysed with Fear: the story of polio, 2013; A Monstrous Commotion: the mysteries of Loch Ness, 2015; papers on diabetes and obesity in sci. and med. jls, and articles of gen. medicine interest. *Recreations:* playing music (reputable and disreputable), exploring Gloucestershire by bike, bird-watching, French, dabbling in fiction. *Address:* Vellow, Rockhampton, Berkeley, Glos GL13 9DY. *T:* (0117) 331 1690, *Fax:* (0117) 331 1687. *E:* Gareth.Williams@bris.ac.uk. *Clubs:* Bristol Savages; Twenty (Liverpool); Flying Shack (Cheltenham).

WILLIAMS, Gareth Charlton; Director of Strategy, since 2014, and Company Secretary, since 2011, Eurostar International Ltd (Regulatory Affairs Director, 2011–14); *b* Crawley, Sussex, 25 March 1968; *s* of Vivian Graham Williams and Margaret Aileen Williams. *Educ:* Ipswich Sch.; Webb Sch. of Calif; Nottingham Univ. (BA Hons Hist. 1990). Various posts, Govt Office for London, Office of Passenger Rail Franchising and DfT, 1991–2000; Hd, Envmt Agency Sponsorship, DEFRA, 2000–02; Divl Manager, Disability and Work, DWP, 2002–04; Department for Transport: Divisional Manager: Rail Finance, 2004–05; Rail Strategy, 2005–07; London and Continental Railways Restructuring and Sale, 2007–11. *Recreations:* writing trashy screenplays, cooking pretentious dinners, eating the Michelin Guide, ski-ing, scuba diving. *Address:* Eurostar International Ltd, Times House, Bravingtons Walk, N1 9AW. *Club:* National Liberal.

WILLIAMS, Prof. Gareth Lloyd; Professor of Educational Administration, Institute of Education, University of London, 1984–2001, now Emeritus; *b* 19 Oct. 1935; *s* of Lloyd and Katherine Enid Williams; *m* 1960, Elizabeth Ann Peck; two *s* one *d*. *Educ:* Creeting St Mary; Framlingham; Cambridge Univ. (MA). Res. Officer, Agricl Econs Res. Inst., Oxford Univ., 1959–62; Res. Fellow, OECD, Athens, 1962–64; Principal Administrator, OECD, Paris, 1964–68; Associate Dir, Higher Educn Res. Unit, LSE, 1968–73; Prof. of Educnl Planning, Univ. of Lancaster, 1973–84. Visiting Professor: Melbourne Univ., 1981–82; Coll. of Europe, 1994–. Specialist Adviser to Arts and Educn Sub-Cttee to House of Commons Cttee on Expenditure, 1972–76; Consultant to OECD, ILO, UNESCO, and World Bank. Member: Council, Policy Studies Inst., 1979–85; Governing Council for Soc. for Res. into Higher Educn, 1970– (Chm., 1978–80, 1986–88). Mem. Bd, Red Rose Radio PLC, 1981–92. FRSA 1982. *Publications:* (with Greenaway) Patterns of Change in Graduate Employment, 1973; (with Blackstone and Metcalf) The Academic Labour Market in Britain, 1974; Towards Lifelong Learning, 1978; (with Zabalza and Turnbull) The Economics of Teacher Supply, 1979; (with Woodhall) Independent Further Education, 1979; (with Blackstone) Response to Adversity, 1983; Higher Education in Ireland, 1985; (with Woodhall and O'Brien) Overseas Students and their Place of Study, 1986; Changing Patterns of Finance in Higher Education, 1992; The Enterprising University, 2004. *Address:* 2 Kempton Road, Lancaster LA1 4LS. *T:* (01524) 66002.

WILLIAMS, Sir Gareth R.; *see* Rhys Williams, Sir A. G. L. E.

WILLIAMS, Geoffrey; QC 2003; barrister; *b* 29 April 1954; *s* of Trevor and Eunice Williams; partner, Kathy Wiley; two *s*. *Educ:* Jones' W Monmouth Grammar Sch., Pontypool; Trent Polytech., Nottingham (BA Hons Law); Coll. of Law, Chester (2nd cl. Hons Solicitors' Finals). Admitted solicitor, 1978; Partner, specialising in regulatory and disciplinary law, solicitors' firm, 1980–98; Sen. Partner, Geoffrey Williams & Christopher Green, Solicitor Advocates, 1998–2013; called to the Bar, Gray's Inn, 2013. Higher Rights of Audience (Civil), 1997. *Recreations:* sport (particularly racing, cricket and Rugby), current affairs. *Address:* Farrar's Building, Temple, EC47 7BD. *T:* (020) 7583 9241. *E:* law@gwcg.globalnet.co.uk. *Club:* Royal Automobile.

WILLIAMS, Prof. Geraint Trefor, OBE 2011; MD; FRCP, FRCPath, FMedSci; FLSW; Professor of Pathology, Cardiff University (formerly University of Wales College of Medicine), since 1991; *b* 10 Sept. 1949; *s* of late Rev. William Trefor Williams and of Eleanor Doris Williams (*née* Evans), Cefngorwydd; *m* 1974, Vivienne Elizabeth Jones; two *d*. *Educ:* Builth Wells Grammar Sch.; Univ. of Wales, Cardiff, and Welsh National Sch. of Medicine (BSc 1st cl. Hons Physiol. 1970; MB BCh Hons 1973; MD 1981). MRCP 1975, FRCP 1991; FRCPath 1991. Jun. med. appts, Univ. Hosp. of Wales, Cardiff, and Hammersmith and Brompton Hosps, London, 1973–76; Lectr in Pathology, St Bartholomew's Hosp. and St Mark's Hosp., London, 1976–79; Sen. Lectr, 1980–88, Reader, 1988–91, Univ. of Wales Coll. of Medicine; Admissions Sub-Dean, Cardiff Univ. Medical Sch., 2004–10. Hon. Consultant Histopathologist, Cardiff and Vale Univ. Health Bd (formerly Cardiff and Vale NHS Trust), 1980–2011. Mem., Cttee on Carcinogenicity of Chemicals in Food, Consumer Products and the Envmt, DoH, 1993–2003; Chm., Welsh Scientific Adv. Cttee, Welsh Assembly Govt, 2000–04. Mem. Council, RCPath, 2004–07; Mem. Council, 1985–88, Vice Pres., 1999–2002, Assoc. of Clinical Pathologists; Chm., Pathology Sect., British Soc. of Gastroenterology, 1996–99; Member, Executive Committee: Pathological Soc. of GB and Ire., 1996–99; Eur. Soc. of Pathology, 1991–95; Councillor, 2004–06, Pres. elect, 2006–08, Pres., 2008–10, British Div., Internat. Acad. of Pathology. FMedSci 2002; FLSW 2011. Hon. Mem. RCR, 2003. *Publications:* (jtly) Morson and Dawson's Gastrointestinal Pathology, 3rd edn 1990 to 5th edn 2013; (ed) Current Topics in Pathology: Gastrointestinal Pathology, 1990; (jtly) Tumors of the Intestines, 2003; numerous contribs to learned jls on gut pathology and carcinogenesis. *Recreations:* ornithology, photography, music, cat watching. *Address:* 11 Cyncoed Crescent, Cardiff CF23 6SW. *E:* GTWilliams@doctors.org.uk.

WILLIAMS, Rev. Gethin A.; *see* Abraham-Williams.

WILLIAMS, Prof. Glynn Anthony, FRBS, FRCA; sculptor; Professor of Sculpture, Royal College of Art, 1990–2009, now Emeritus (Head, School of Fine Art, 1995–2009); *b* 30 March 1939; *s* of Idris Merion Williams and Muriel Elizabeth Purslow; *m* 1963 (marr. diss. 2001); two *d*. *Educ:* Wolverhampton Grammar Sch.; Wolverhampton Coll. of Art (NDD Sculpture Special Level); British Sch. in Rome (Rome Scholar). Head of Sculpture Departments: Leeds Coll. of Art, later Leeds Polytechnic, 1968–75; Wimbledon Sch. of Art, 1976–90. 24 one-man exhibns incl. retrospective, Margam Park, S Wales, 1992; numerous group exhibns incl. British Sculpture of 20th Century, Whitechapel Gall., 1981; rep. GB, Kotara Takamura Grand Prize Exhibn, Japan, 1984; work in collections: Arts Council of GB; Bottisham Village Coll., Cambridge; Bradford City Art Gall.; British Sch. in Rome; Grisedale Theatre in the Forest, Cumbria; Hakone Open Air Mus., Japan; Hampshire Sculpture Trust; Haroldwood Hosp., Essex; Hemel Hempstead Arts Trust; Henry Moore Centre for Sculpture, Leeds; Hove Mus. and Art Gall.; Hull City Art Gall.; Leeds City Council; Lincoln City Council; London Borough of Hounslow; Middlesbrough Council; Milton Keynes Develt Corp.; Nat. Portrait Gall.; Newport (Gwent) Educn Cttee; Northern Arts Assoc.; Peterborough Develt Corp.; Southern Arts Assoc.; Tate Gall.; V & A; Welsh Arts Council; Welsh Sculpture Trust; Wolverhampton Educn Cttee; Yorkshire Arts Assoc. Commissions: 14′ bronze meml to Henry Purcell, Flowering of the English Baroque, City of Westminster, 1995; Lloyd George Meml, Parliament Sq., 2007. Trustee, Forest of Dean Sculpture Trail, 2012. FRCA 1991; FRBS 1992. FRSA 1996. Hon. Fellow, Wolverhampton Polytechnic, 1989. *Publications:* contribs to arts magazines, jls, TLS. *Recreations:* cooking, crosswords, music. *Address:* c/o Bernard Jacobson Gallery, 6 Cork Street, W1S 3EE. *Club:* Chelsea Arts.

WILLIAMS, Gordon; *see* Williams, James G.

WILLIAMS, Prof. Gordon, OBE 2011; FRCS; Consultant Urologist, Bethel Hospital and Medical School, Addis Ababa, Ethiopia, since 2012; Advisor in Medical Education, Ministry of Health, Ethiopia, since 2015; *b* 27 June 1945; *s* of Charles and Marjorie Williams; *m* 1st, 1968, Susan Gubbins (marr. diss. 1989); two *d*; 2nd, 1989, Clare Forbes (marr. diss. 2005). *Educ:* Bishop Vesey's Grammar Sch., Sutton Coldfield; University Coll. London (MB BS 1968). FRCS 1973; FRCSEd *ad eundem* 2001; Hon. FRCSGlas 2004. Consultant Urologist and the surgery of renal failure, Hammersmith Hosp., 1978–2007. Chairman: Specialist Adv. Cttee Urology, 2000–04; Jt Cttee of Higher Surgical Trng, 2003–07; Prof. of Surgery, and Dean, St Paul's Millennium Med. Sch., Addis Ababa, 2007–08; Med. Dir, Addis Ababa Fistula Hosp., 2008–12. Mem. numerous editl bds. King James IV Professor of Surgery, RCSE, 2005. Albert Schweitzer Internat. Teaching Award, Internat. Soc. of Urology, 2006; St Peter's Medal, British Assoc. of Urological Surgeons, 2008; Sir James Young Simpson Medal, RCSE, 2011; Frederick Salmon Medal, RSM, 2013. *Publications:* Urological Oncology (with J. Waxman), 1991; contrib. 32 chapters in books and over 200 articles. *Recreations:* playing tennis badly, eating Indian food, helping the developing world provide surgical care to rural areas and with such poverty and deprivation trying to understand how there could possibly be a God. *Address:* PO Box 420, Code 1056, Addis Ababa, Ethiopia.

WILLIAMS, Air Vice-Marshal Graham Charles, AFC 1970 and Bar 1975; FRAeS; Director, Lockheed Martin UK (formerly Loral International Inc., then Lockheed Martin International), 1993–2004; Commandant General, RAF Regiment and Director General of Security (RAF), 1990–91; *b* 4 June 1937; *s* of Charles Francis Williams and Molly (*née* Chapman); *m* 1962, Judith Teresa Ann Walker; one *s* one *d*. *Educ:* Marlborough College; RAF College, Cranwell. FRAeS 1984. 54 Sqn, 229 OCU, 8 Sqn, Empire Test Pilots' School, A Sqn, A&AEE, 1958–70; RAF Staff Coll., 1971; OC 3 Sqn, Wildenrath, 1972–74; Junior Directing Staff (Air), RCDS, 1975–77; OC RAF Brüggen, 1978–79; Group Captain Ops, HQ RAF Germany, 1980–82; CO Experimental Flying Dept, RAE, 1983; Comdt, Aeroplane and Armament Exptl Estabt, 1983–85; Dir, Operational Requirements, MoD, 1986; ACDS, Operational Requirements (Air), 1986–89. Harmon Internat. Trophy for Aviators, USA, 1970. *Recreations:* old cars, golf. *Address:* Vine House, 5 High Street, Hallaton, Market Harborough, Leics LE16 8UD. *Club:* Royal Air Force.

WILLIAMS, Gwyneth; Controller, BBC Radio 4 and BBC Radio 4 Extra (formerly BBC Radio 7), since 2010; *b* 14 July 1953; *d* of Prof. Owen Williams and Beryl Williams (*née* Harrett); *m* 1982, David Nissan; one *s* one *d*. *Educ:* St John's High Sch., Pietermaritzburg, Natal; St Hugh's Coll., Oxford (BA Hons PPE 1975; Dip. Soc. Anth. 1976; Hon. Fellow, 2011). Current affairs talks writer, BBC Bush House, 1976; Res. Asst, ODI, 1977; BBC: Prod., The World Tonight, 1979; career break to be with children, 1984–89; Prod. and Ed., various progs on Radio 4 and Radio Five Live, 1989–94; Editor: Foreign Affairs Radio, 1994; Home Current Affairs, Bi-media, 1996; Reith Lectures, 1999–2007; various special series and progs on Radio 4 and World Service; Hd, Radio Current Affairs, BBC News, 2004; Dir, BBC World Service English, 2007–10. Mem. Editl Bd, Political Qly, 1996–2004. *Publications:* Third World Political Organizations, 1981, 2nd edn 1987; (with Brian Hackland) The Contemporary Political Dictionary of Southern Africa, 1988. *Recreations:* reading, music, dog walking. *Address:* (home) 13 King Henry's Road, NW3 3QP. *T:* (020) 7586 2748; (office) BBC Radio 4, Broadcasting House, Portland Place, W1A 1AA. *T:* (020) 7580 4468. *E:* gwyneth.williams@bbc.co.uk.

WILLIAMS, Heather Jean; QC 2006; barrister; *b* 1963; *d* of Leonard Archibald Williams and Dorothy Jean Williams; *m* 1997, Trevor William Bragg; one *s* one *d*. *Educ:* King's Coll. London (LLB 1st cl. Hons 1984). Called to the Bar, Gray's Inn, 1985 (Scarman Scholarship 1985), Bencher, 2012; in practice as a barrister, 1987–. Pt-time Judge (formerly Chm.), Employment Tribunals, 2005–. *Publications:* (jtly) Police Misconduct: legal remedies, 4th edn 2005. *Recreations:* listening to music, attending concerts and festivals, spending time with my children, yoga, reading. *Address:* Doughty Street Chambers, 53–54 Doughty Street, WC1N 2LS. *T:* (020) 7404 1313, *Fax:* (020) 7404 2283/4. *E:* h.williams@doughtystreet.co.uk.

WILLIAMS, Helen Elizabeth Webber, MA; Principal, RNIB New College, Worcester, 1995–2000; *b* 28 April 1938; *o d* of Alwyn and Eleanor Thomas; *m* 1962, Dr Peter Williams (marr. diss. 1974); one *s* one *d*. *Educ:* Redland High Sch., Bristol; Girton Coll., Cambridge (MA; DipEd). Assistant English Mistress: St Paul's Girls' Sch., 1962–63; St George's Sch., Edinburgh, 1963–64; Edinburgh University: Asst Lectr, Dept of English, 1964–67; Lectr in English and Dir of Studies, Faculty of Arts, 1967–78; Headmistress, Blackheath High Sch., 1978–89; High Mistress, St Paul's Girls' Sch., 1989–92; Trevelyan Fellow, Trevelyan Coll., Univ. of Durham, 1993; English teacher, The Brearley Sch., NY, 1993–94. Member: HMC, 1994–2000; Governing Body, SOAS, 1988–96; Council, City Univ., 1990–92; Governing Body, Stowe Sch., 1992. *Publications:* (ed) T. S. Eliot: The Wasteland, 1968. *Recreations:* music, drama, cookery, gardening. *Address:* 4/2 Advocates Close, The Royal Mile, Edinburgh EH1 1PS.

WILLIAMS, Helen Mary, (Mrs D. M. Forrester), CB 2006; Director, School Curriculum and Pupil Well-Being, Department for Education (formerly Department for Education and Skills, then Department for Children, Schools and Families), 2006–11; *b* 30 June 1950; *d* of late Graham Myatt and of Mary (*née* Harrison); *m* 1st, 1975, Ian Vaughan Williams (marr. diss. 1982); 2nd, 1993, David Michael Forrester, *qv*; one *s* one *d*. *Educ:* Allerton High Sch., Leeds; St Hilda's Coll., Oxford (MA Hons Mod. Hist.). Joined DES, 1972; Private Sec. to Joan Lester and to Margaret Jackson, 1975–76; Asst Sec., DES, subseq. DFE, 1984–93; Under-Sec., then Dir, OST, Cabinet Office, subseq. DTI, 1993–98; Dir, Sch. Orgn and Funding, DFEE, subseq. DFES, 1999–2002; Department for Education and Skills: Dir, Primary Educn and e Learning, 2002–04; Co-Dir, Sch. Standards, 2004–06. Trustee, Girls Day Sch. Trust, 2013–. Governor: Greig City Acad., Haringey, 2011–; Prior Weston Primary Sch., Islington, 2012–; mentor of care system leavers, 2012–; Mem., St Mary Magdalene Educnl Trust, 2013–. *Recreations:* bell-ringing, badminton, playing the piano, hill-walking, family history. *E:* helen.mary.forrester@gmail.com.

WILLIAMS, (Henry) Nigel, FRSL; author and broadcaster; *b* 20 Jan. 1948; *s* of late David Ffrancon Williams and Sylvia Margaret Williams (*née* Hartley); *m* 1973, Suzan Elizabeth Harrison; three *s*. *Educ:* Highgate Sch.; Oriel Coll., Oxford (MA Hist.). BBC: gen. trainee, 1969–73; Producer/Dir, Arts Dept, 1973–85; Editor: Bookmark, 1985–92; Omnibus, 1992–96; writer/presenter, 1997–2000. *Plays:* Class Enemy, Royal Court, 1978 (Most Promising Playwright Award, Plays and Players mag.); Sugar and Spice, Royal Court, 1980; Line 'Em, NT, 1980; Trial Run, Oxford Playhouse, 1980; My Brother's Keeper, Greenwich, 1985; Country Dancing, RSC, 1987; Lord of the Flies (adapted), RSC, 1996; My Face, NT, 2008; *television plays* include: Charlie, 1980; Breaking Up, 1986; The Last Romantics, 1990; Skallagrig, 1994 (BAFTA Award); Dirty Tricks, 2000 (Internat. Emmy Award); Bertie and Elizabeth, 2002; Uncle Adolf, 2005; Elizabeth I, 2005 (Emmy Award for outstanding mini-series, 2006; Golden Globe Award for best mini-series, 2007); Footprints in the Snow, 2005; HR, 2006; Wodehouse in Exile, 2013; *radio:* HR (series), 2009; HR2 (series), 2010; HR3 (series), 2011; HR4 (series), 2013; HR5 (series), 2014; *films:* Seawolf, 2009; BP Centenary Film, 2009; Moby Dick (adapted screenplay), 2011. FRSL 1994. *Publications:* (novels): My Life Closed Twice, 1978 (Somerset Maugham Award); Jack Be Nimble, 1980; Star Turn, 1985; Witchcraft, 1987; Black Magic, 1988; The Wimbledon Poisoner, 1990; They Came from SW19, 1992; East of Wimbledon, 1993; 2½ Men in a Boat, 1993; Scenes from a Poisoner's Life, 1994 (televised); From Wimbledon to Waco, 1995; Stalking Fiona, 1997; Fortysomething, 1999 (adapted for television, 2003); Hatchett and Lycett, 2002; Unfaithfully Yours, 2013; R.I.P., 2015. *Recreations:* swimming, drinking, walking, talking, family, dogs, Harry. *Address:* 18 Holmbush Road, Putney, SW15 3LE.

WILLIAMS, Hugh Richard Bonneville, (Hugh Bonneville); actor, producer and writer; *b* London, 10 Nov. 1963; *s* of John Pritchard Williams, FRCS and late Patricia Williams; *m* 1998, Lulu Evans (*née* Conner); one *s*. *Educ:* Sherborne Sch.; Corpus Christi Coll., Cambridge (BA Theol. 1985). Actor: *theatre:* Midsummer Night's Dream, Romeo and Juliet, Arms and The Man, Open Air Th., Regent's Park, 1986; French Without Tears, Leicester Haymarket, 1987; Taking Steps, The Circle, Taming of the Shrew, Look Back in Anger, Dick Whittington, Siege, Colchester Mercury, 1987–88; Yerma, School for Wives, Entertaining Strangers, Juno and the Paycock, School for Scandal, The Devil's Disciple, NT, 1987–94; Two Gentlemen of Verona, The Virtuoso, 'Tis Pity She's a Whore, The Alchemist, Amphibians, Hamlet, RSC, 1991–93; Habeas Corpus, Donmar Warehouse, 1995; My Night with Reg, Criterion/Playhouse, 1996; The Handyman, Chichester Fest. Th. and tour, 1998; Us and Them, Hampstead, 2003; Cloaca, Old Vic, 2004; numerous TV and film appearances, 1990–; *television* includes: Mosley, 1998; Take a Girl Like You, 2000; The Cazalets, 2001; The Gathering Storm, 2002; Tipping the Velvet, 2002; Daniel Deronda, 2002; Love Again, 2003; The Robinsons, 2005; Tsunami: The Aftermath, 2006; The Diary of a Nobody, 2007; DSI Iain Barclay in Five Days, 2007 and Hunter, 2009; Freezing, 2007–08; Filth: The Mary Whitehouse Story, 2008; Bonekickers, 2008; Lost in Austen, 2009; Miss Austen Regrets, 2009; Ben Hur, 2010; The Silence, 2010; Downton Abbey, 2010, 2011, 2012, 2013, 2014, 2015; Twenty Twelve, 2011, 2012; Rev, 2011, 2012, 2014; Mr Stink, 2012; W1A, 2014, 2015; Galavant, 2015; *films* include: Frankenstein, 1994; Notting Hill, 1999; Mansfield Park, 1999; Iris, 2002; Stage Beauty, 2004; Asylum, 2005; Scenes of a Sexual Nature, 2006; French Film, 2008 (Best Actor, Monte Carlo Comedy Film Fest., 2008); Glorious 39, 2009; Burke & Hare, 2010; From Time to Time, 2010; Third Star, 2011; The Monuments Men, Paddington, 2014. Co-producer, Beautiful Thing, Duke of York's Th., 1994; co-writer and producer (with Christopher Luscombe): Half Time, Donmar Warehouse and tour, 1994. Patron: Scene and Heard, 2008–; Centre Stage Acad., 2008–; Giant Olive Theatre Co., 2009–; Nat. Youth Th. of GB, 2013–. *Recreation:* enjoys getting cross about health and safety. *Address:* c/o Gordon & French Ltd, 12–13 Poland Street, W1F 8QB. *E:* mail@gordonandfrench.net. *W:* www.hughbonneville.uk. *Clubs:* Garrick, Soho House.

WILLIAMS, Hugo Mordaunt; writer; *b* 20 Feb. 1942; *s* of late Hugh Williams, actor and playwright, and Margaret Vyner; *m* 1965, Hermine Demoriane; one *d*. *Educ:* Eton College. Asst Editor, London Magazine, 1961–70; Arts Editor, New Review, 1973–74; television critic, 1983–88, and poetry editor, 1984–93, New Statesman; theatre critic, The Sunday Correspondent, 1989–91; columnist, TLS, 1988–; film critic, Harpers & Queen, 1993–98. Henfield Writer's Fellowship, Univ. of East Anglia, 1981. Awards (for poetry): Eric Gregory, 1965; Cholmondeley, 1970; Geoffrey Faber Memorial Prize, 1979; Queen's Gold Medal for Poetry, 2004. *Publications: poems:* Symptoms of Loss, 1965; Sugar Daddy, 1970; Some Sweet Day, 1975; Love-Life, 1979; Writing Home, 1985; Selected Poems, 1989; Self-Portrait With A Slide, 1990; Dock Leaves, 1994; Billy's Rain (T. S. Eliot Prize), 1999; Collected Poems, 2002; Dear Room, 2006; West End Final, 2009; I Knew the Bride, 2014; *travel:* All the Time in the World, 1966; No Particular Place to Go, 1981; *journalism:* Freelancing, 1995; *edited:* Curtain Call, 101 Portraits in Verse, 2001; John Betjeman, Selected Poems, 2006. *Address:* 3 Raleigh Street, N1 8NW. *T:* (020) 7226 1655.

WILLIAMS, Hywel; MP (Plaid Cymru) Arfon, since 2010 (Caernarfon, 2001–10); *b* 14 May 1953; *s* of late Robert Williams and of Jennie Page Williams; *m* 1st, 1977, Sian Davies (marr. diss. 1998); three *d*; 2nd, 2010, Dr Myfanwy Davies. *Educ:* Ysgol Glan y Mor, Pwllheli, Gwynedd; UC Cardiff (BSc Hons Psychol. 1974); UCNW, Bangor (CQSW 1980). Approved Social Worker (Mental Health), 1984. Social Worker: Child Care and Long Term Team, Social Services Dept, Mid Glam CC, 1974–76; Mental Health Team, Social Services Dept, Gwynedd CC, 1976–78 and 1980–84; Welsh Office funded project worker, 1985–91, Hd of Centre, 1991–93, N and W Wales Practice Centre, UCNW, Bangor; freelance lectr, consultant and author in social work and social policy, 1994–2001. CCETSW Cymru: Mem. Welsh Cttee and Chm., Welsh Lang. Sub-cttee, 1989–92; Mem., Welsh Lang. Pubns Adv. Panel, 1992–93. *Publications:* (contrib.) Social Work in Action in the 1980s, 1985; (compiled and ed) A Social Work Vocabulary, 1988; (gen. ed.) Child Care Terms, 1993; (contrib. and gen ed.) Social Work and the Welsh Language, 1994; (compiled and ed) An Index of Trainers and Training, 1994; (contrib. and ed jtly) Gofal: a training and resource pack for community care in Wales, 1998; Speaking the Invisible, 2002. *Recreations:* walking, cinema, reading. *Address:* House of Commons, SW1A 0AA. *T:* (020) 7219 5021; 8 Stryd Y Castell, Caernarfon, Gwynedd LL15 1SE. *T:* (01286) 672076.

WILLIAMS, Prof. Hywel Charles, PhD, DSc; FRCP, FMedSci; Professor of Dermato-Epidemiology, University of Nottingham, since 1998; Director, NIHR Health Technology Assessment Programme, from Jan. 2016 (Director-designate, 2015); *b* Swansea, 15 July 1958; *s* of Elwyn Williams and Mair Lloyd Williams; *m* 1984, Molly Chan; one *d*. *Educ:* Cymmer Afan Comp. Sch.; Glanafan Comp. Sch.; Charing Cross Hosp. Med. Sch., Univ. of London (BSc Anatomy 1979; MB BS (Dist.) 1982); London Sch. of Hygiene and Tropical Medicine (MSc 1990); St Thomas' Hosp. (PhD 1994); Univ. of Nottingham (DSc 2013). FRCP 1995. Jun. doctor trng at Charing Cross Hosp., Kingston Hosp., Hammersmith Hosp., King's Coll. Hosp. and St Thomas' Hosp., 1982–93; University of Nottingham: Sen. Lectr in Dermato-Epidemiol., 1994–98; Co-Dir, Centre of Evidence Based Dermatol., 2002–; Hon. Consultant Dermatologist, Nottingham Univ. Hosps NHS Trust, 1994–. NIHR Sen. Investigator, 2008; Chm., NIHR Health Technol. Assessment Commng Bd, 2010–15; Dep. Dir, NIHR Health Technol. Assessment Prog., 2010–15. FMedSci 2014. Gold Distinction Award, NHS, 2013. *Publications:* The Challenge of Dermato-Epidemiology, 1997; Atopic Dermatitis: the epidemiology, causes and prevention of atopic eczema, 2000; Evidence-Based Dermatology, 2004, 3rd edn 2014; over 400 articles in learned jls. *Recreations:* gardening (especially delphiniums, cacti, orchids), classic cars (Member, Midland Lotus Owners Club), jazz (trombone and keyboards), marine tropical fish. *Address:* Department of Dermatology, C Floor South Block, Queen's Medical Centre, Nottingham University Hospitals NHS Trust, Nottingham NG7 2UH. *T:* (0115) 823 1048, *Fax:* (0115) 823 1046. *E:* hywel.williams@nottingham.ac.uk.

WILLIAMS, Prof. (James) Gordon, FRS 1994; FREng; Professor of Mechanical Engineering, Imperial College, London, 1990–2003, now Emeritus (Head, Department of Mechanical Engineering, 1990–2000); *b* 13 June 1938; *s* of John William and Eira Williams; *m* 1960, Ann Marie Joscelyne; two *s* one *d*. *Educ:* Imperial Coll. (BScEng, PhD, DScEng); FCGI; FREng (FEng 1982). RAE, Farnborough, 1956–61; Imperial College: Asst Lectr, 1962–64; Lectr, 1964–70; Reader, 1970–75; Prof. of Polymer Engrg, 1975–90. *Publications:* Stress Analysis of Polymers, 1973, 2nd edn 1981; Fracture Mechanics of Polymers, 1984. *Recreations:* gardening, mountains (walking and ski-ing), golf. *Address:* Mechanical Engineering Department, Imperial College London, Exhibition Road, South Kensington, SW7 2BX. *T:* (020) 7594 7200.

WILLIAMS, Jane; independent adviser to further education; Executive Director for Further Education and 14 to 19 (formerly Skills and Regeneration, later Further Education, Regeneration and Delivery), Becta (formerly British Education Communications Technology Agency), 2007–11; *b* 13 April 1953; *d* of John and Gwenllian Williams; *m* 1993, Robert Walker; one *s* one *d*. *Educ:* Univ. of Bristol (BA Hons); Univ. of Birmingham (Cert Ed). Teacher, Swanshurst Sch., 1975–78; Lectr, Bournville Coll., 1979–81; Sen. Lectr, Telford Coll., 1981–84; Principal Lectr, Accredited Training Centre, Telford, 1984–89; Asst Principal, Solihull Coll., 1989–92; Vice Principal, North Warwickshire Coll., Nuneaton, 1992–96; Principal: Wulfrun Coll., Wolverhampton, 1996–99; City of Wolverhampton Coll., 1999–2002; Dir, Teaching and Learning, and Head, Standards Unit, subseq. Dir, Improvement Gp, DFES, 2003–07. Chairman: Focus Housing Assoc., 2000–02; Wolverhampton Strategic Partnership, 2002; Ind. Quality Bd, Energy and Utility Skills, 2013–. Mem. Bd, Ufi Ltd, 2008–12. Mem., Corporation, Birmingham Metropolitan Coll., 2010–14 (Vice Chair, 2010–14). FRSA 1999. Hon. DEd Wolverhampton, 2003. *Recreations:* music, travel, painting. *E:* jw@jane-williams.co.uk.

WILLIAMS, (Jean) Adèle, (Mrs A. Patience); Her Honour Judge Williams; a Circuit Judge, since 2000; *b* 28 July 1950; *d* of David James Williams and Dorothy Williams; *m* 1975, Andrew Patience, *qv*; one *s* one *d*. *Educ:* Llanelli Girls' Grammar Sch.; University Coll. London (LLB). Called to the Bar, Gray's Inn, 1972; in practice on S Eastern Circuit, 1972–2000; a Recorder, 1995–2000; Resident Judge, Canterbury Crown Court, 2008–. Sen., Kent Bar Mess, 1997–2000. *Recreations:* cinema, theatre, holidays, conversation. *Address:* Canterbury Crown Court, Chaucer Road, Canterbury, Kent CT1 1ZA. *T:* (01227) 819200.

WILLIAMS, Jennifer Mary, (Jenny); Commissioner and Chief Executive, Gambling Commission (formerly Gaming Board for Great Britain), 2004–15; *b* 26 Sept. 1948; *d* of Baron Donaldson of Lymington, PC, and Dame (Dorothy) Mary Donaldson, GBE; *m* 1970, Michael Lodwig Williams, *qv*; three *s*. *Educ:* New Hall, Cambridge (BA 1970). Joined Home Office, 1973; Dir, PSA Privatisation and Strategy, DoE, 1990–93; Dir, Railways Privatisation and Regulation Directorate, Dept of Transport, 1993–97; Dir, Local Govt Finance Policy, DoE, later DETR, 1997–98; Dir, Company, later Business, Tax Div., Bd of Inland Revenue, 1998–2000; Dir Gen., Judicial Gp, and Sec. of Commns, LCD, 2001–03. Non-exec. Dir, Northumbrian Water Gp PLC, 2006–10. Board Member: The Connection at St Martin's, 2004– (Vice-Chm., 2012–); Nat. Campaign for the Arts, 2004–07. Trustee, Internat. Assoc. of Gaming Regulators, 2011–14. Non-exec. Dir, Morley Coll., 1993–2000. *Address:* 46 Durand Gardens, SW9 0PP.

WILLIAMS, John, AO 1987; OBE 1980; guitarist; *b* Melbourne, 24 April 1941. Studied with father, Segovia and at the Accademia Musicale Chigiana, Siena and RCM, London; since when has given recitals, concerts, and made TV and radio appearances worldwide. Mem., Sky, 1979–84. Artistic Dir, South Bank Summer Music, 1984 and 1985; Artistic Dir, Melbourne Arts Fest., 1987. Wide range of recordings with other musicians including Julian Bream, John Dankworth and Cleo Laine, NYJO, Itzhak Perlman, Inti Illimani, etc, and many orchestras. Hon. FRCM; Hon. FRNCM. *Recreations:* people, living, chess, table-tennis, music. *Address:* c/o Askonas Holt Ltd, Lincoln House, 300 High Holborn, WC1V 7JH.

WILLIAMS, John; Director, West One Communications, since 2006; *b* 20 Feb. 1954; *s* of Roy and Barbara Williams; *m* 1976, Pamela Blackburn; two *s* one *d*. *Educ:* Sir Roger Manwood's Sch., Sandwich. Reporter: Chatham News, 1973–77; Birmingham Evening Mail, 1977–80; Industrial Corresp., 1980–85, Political Corresp., 1985–93, London Evening Standard; political columnist, Daily Mirror, 1993–98; Dep. Hd, News Dept, FCO, 1998–2000; Press Sec., FCO, 2000–04; Dir, Communications, FCO, 2004–06. *Publications:* Victory, 1997. *Recreations:* gardening, guitar, books, family, walking. *Address:* Cherry Trees, Fore Street, Weston, Hitchin, Herts SG4 7AS. *T:* (01462) 790536.

WILLIAMS, John, FRICS; Director, Aston Rose Chartered Surveyors, since 2000; *b* 18 March 1968; *s* of David and Chantal Williams. *Educ:* Epsom Coll.; Univ. of Reading (BSc Hons Est. Mgt 1990). ARICS 1992, FRICS 1998. Dir, Ernest Owers & Williams, 1986–2000. Royal Institution of Chartered Surveyors: Nat. Jun. Org. Cttee, 1988–2003, Chm., Nat. Jun. Org., 2000–01; Member: Gen. Council, 1999–2001; Internat. Governing Council, 2001–06; Sen. Vice Pres., 2004–05. Lionheart: Steward, 1988–2000; Fundraising Cttee, 1989–2001; Trustee, 2000–07. Liveryman, Chartered Surveyors' Co., 2002– (Property, Advertising, Mktg and Design Awards Cttee (PAMADA), 2002–07). *Recreations:* ski-ing, reading, film. *Address:* Aston Rose, St Albans House, 57/59 Haymarket, SW1Y 4QX. *T:* (020) 7629 1533, *Fax:* (020) 7925 2492. *E:* johnwilliams@astonrose.co.uk.

WILLIAMS, (John Bucknall) Kingsley; solicitor, retired; *b* 28 July 1927; *s* of Charles Kingsley Williams and Margaret Elizabeth (*née* Bucknall); *m* 1st, 1961, Brenda (*née* Baldwin) (marr. diss. 2001); two *s*; 2nd, 2001, Eleanor Marion Yates. *Educ:* Kingswood Sch., Bath; Trinity Hall, Cambridge (MA, LLB). Partner, Dutton Gregory & Williams, Solicitors, Winchester, 1956–91. Chm., Wessex RHA, 1975–82. Member: Winchester City Council, 1966–73; Hampshire CC, 1973–75; Assoc. of County Councils, 1973–75. Chairman: Exec. Cttee, NHS Supply Council, 1980–82; Adv. Cttee, Wessex Inst. of Public Health Medicine, 1991–96. Chm. Council, Southampton Univ., 1987–98 (Mem., 1977–98); Chm. of Governors, Winchester Sch. of Art, 1986–96. DUniv Southampton, 1999. *Address:* Danesacre, Worthy Road, Winchester, Hants SO23 7AD. *T:* (01962) 852594.

WILLIAMS, John Charles, OBE 1997; PhD; FREng; Secretary and Chief Executive, Institution of Electrical Engineers, 1989–99; *b* 17 July 1938; *s* of Frank and Miriam Williams; *m* 1968, Susan Winifred Ellis; two *s* one *d*. *Educ:* High Wycombe Royal GS; Queen Mary Coll. (BScEng (1st Cl. Hons), 1960; PhD 1964; Fellow, 1995). Philips Research Labs, 1964–78; GEC Marconi Space and Defence Systems, Stanmore, 1978–80; GEC Central Res. Labs, Wembley, 1980–82; GEC Marconi Res. Centre, Gt Baddow, 1982–88. Freeman, City of London, 1996. FREng (FEng 1990). Hon. FIEE 2000. *Recreations:* traditional jazz, contract bridge, walking, gardening, tennis, listening to his family play music, enjoying company of his grandson Arturo. *Address:* Beightons, Bassetts Lane, Little Baddow, Chelmsford, Essex CM3 4DA. *T:* (01245) 225092. *E:* johnchaswilliams@btinternet.com.

WILLIAMS, Rt Rev. (John) Christopher (Richard); Bishop of The Arctic, 1991–2002; *b* 22 May 1936; *s* of Frank Harold and Ceridwen Roberts Williams; *m* 1964, Rona Macrae (*née* Aitken); one *s* one *d*. *Educ:* Manchester Grammar Sch.; Univ. of Manchester (BA Comm); Univ. of Durham, Cranmer Hall (DipTh). Ordained: deacon, Stretford, England, 1960; priest, Sugluk, PQ, 1962; Missionary, Diocese of The Arctic: Sugluk, PQ, 1961–72; Cape Dorset, NWT, 1972–75; Baker Lake, NWT, 1975–78; Archdeacon of The Keewatin, 1975–87; Rector, Yellowknife, NWT, 1978–87; Bp Suffragan, 1987–90, Coadjutor Bp, 1990, Dio. of The Arctic. Hon. DD: Emmanuel and St Chad Coll., Saskatoon, 1997; Wycliffe Coll., Toronto Univ., 2000. Queen's Diamond Jubilee Medal, 2013. *Recreation:* stage and piano. *Address:* 4916–44th Street, Yellowknife, NT X1A 1J8, Canada.

WILLIAMS, John Eirwyn F.; *see* Ffowcs Williams.

WILLIAMS, Hon. Sir John G.; *see* Griffith Williams.

WILLIAMS, John Leighton; QC 1986; a Recorder of the Crown Court, 1985–2014; a Deputy High Court Judge, 1995–2014; *b* 15 Aug. 1941; *s* of Reginald John Williams and Beatrice Beynon; *m* 1969, Sally Elizabeth Williams; two *s*. *Educ:* Neath Boys' Grammar School; King's College London (LLB); Trinity Hall, Cambridge (MA). Called to the Bar, Gray's Inn, 1964, Bencher, 1994 (Vice-Treas., 2009; Treas. 2010). Mem., Criminal Injuries Compensation Bd, 1987–2002. Mem. Council, Med. Protection Soc., 1998–2007. *Address:* Farrar's Building, Temple, EC4Y 7BD. *T:* (020) 7583 9241.

WILLIAMS, John Llewellyn, CBE 1999; FRCS, FRCSE, FDSRCS, FDSRCSE, FRCA; Consultant Oral and Maxillofacial Surgeon, St Richard's Hospital, Chichester, Worthing and Southlands Hospitals, Worthing and St Luke's Hospital, Guildford, 1973–2003, now Hon. Consultant Emeritus; Vice-President, Royal College of Surgeons of England, 1997–99; *b* 24 Jan. 1938; *s* of David John Williams and Anne Rosamund Williams (*née* White); *m* 1960, Gillian Joy Morgan; three *d*. *Educ:* Christ's Hosp.; Guy's Hosp. Med. Sch. (MB BS, BDS). FDSRCS 1966; FRCSE 1991; FRCS 1996; FRCA 2000; FDSRCSE *ad hominem* 2000. Registrar in Oral and Maxillofacial Surgery, Plymouth, 1970; Sen. Registrar, Westminster Hosp., UCH and Queen Mary's, Roehampton, 1970–73; Postgrad. Tutor, BMPF, 1973–95; Hon. Consultant: Queen Mary's, Roehampton, 1974–2003; King Edward VII Hosp., Midhurst, 1974–2006; Hon. Clinical Tutor, Guy's and St Thomas', subseq. Guy's, King's and St Thomas' Hosps' Med. and Dental Sch. of KCL, 1976–2003. Hon. Consultant to Army, Cambridge Hosp., 1992–. Chairman: Nat. Cttee of Enquiry into Perio-operative Deaths, 1998–2003; Cttee on Safety of Devices, Med. Devices Agency, DoH, 2001–09; non-exec. Dir, Medicines and Healthcare Products Regulatory Agency Bd, 2009–. Dean, Faculty of Dental Surgery, RCS, 1996–99; Vice Chm., Acad. of Med. Royal Colls, 1998–2000; President: Eur. Assoc. for Cranio-Maxillofacial Surgery, 1998–2000; BAOMS, 2000; Internat.

Assoc. of Oral and Maxillofacial Surgeons, 2005–07 (Pres.-elect, 2003–05); Chm., Oral and Maxillofacial Surgery Foundn, 2007–. Mem. Ct of Patrons, RCS, 2004–. Hon. Fellow: Amer. Assoc. Oral and Maxillofacial Surgeons, 1998; Aust. and NZ Assoc. of Oral and Maxillofacial Surgeons; Hon. Life Mem., BDA, 2010. Evelyn Sprawson Prize, RCS, 1961; Down Surgical Prize, BAOMS, 1996; John Tomes Medallist, BDA, 1998; Colyer Gold Medallist, RCS, 2000. *Publications:* (with N. L. Rowe) Maxillofacial Injuries, Vols I and II, 1985, 2nd edn 1994; (with P. Stoelinga) 50 Years of the IAOMS: the development of the specialty, 2012; contribs to Brit. Dental Jl, RCS Annals. *Recreations:* gardening (garden open under Nat. Gardens Scheme), sailing (RYA Race Training Instructor). *Address:* Cookscroft, Bookers Lane, Earnley, Chichester, W Sussex PO20 7JG. *T:* (01243) 513671. *Clubs:* Oral Surgery of Great Britain; Hayling Island Sailing.

WILLIAMS, Prof. (John) Mark (Gruffydd), DSc; FBPsS; FBA 2008; FMedSci; Professor of Clinical Psychology, University of Oxford, 2004–13, now Emeritus, and Honorary Research Fellow, since 2014; Fellow of Linacre College, Oxford, 2004–13, now Emeritus; Director, Oxford Mindfulness Centre, 2008–13; *b* 23 July 1952; *s* of John Howard Williams and Anna Barbara Mary Williams (*née* Wright); *m* 1973, Phyllis Patricia Simpson; one *s* two *d*. *Educ:* Stockton-on-Tees Grammar Sch.; St Peter's Coll., Oxford (BA 1973; MSc 1976; MA 1977; DPhil 1979; DSc 1998); E Anglian Ministerial Trng Course. FBPsS 1984. Lecturer in: Psychology, Magdalen Coll., Oxford, 1977–79; Applied Psychology, Univ. of Newcastle upon Tyne, 1979–82; Scientist, then Sen. Scientist, MRC Applied Psychol. Unit, Cambridge, 1983–91; University College of North Wales (Bangor) subseq. University of Wales, Bangor: Prof. of Clinical Psychology, 1991–97; Dir, Centre for Medical and Health Scis, subseq. Inst. for Med. and Social Care Res., 1997–2002; Pro Vice-Chancellor, 1997–2001; Wellcome Principal Res. Fellow, Dept of Psychiatry, Univ. of Oxford, 2003–12. Member: Grants Cttee, Neuroscis Bd, MRC, 1992–96; Neuroscis & Mental Health Panel, Wellcome Trust, 1997–2001; Panel Mem. for Psychology, RAE 2001. Ordained deacon, Ely, 1989, priest 1990; Asst Curate (NSM), Girton, 1989–91; permission to officiate, dio. of Bangor, 1991–2003; Asst Curate, 2003–08, Associate Priest (NSM), 2008–10, Wheatley. Hon. Canon, Christchurch Cathedral, Oxford, 2011. Gov., NE Wales Inst. of Higher Educn, 1999–2001. FMedSci 2004. *Publications:* Psychological Treatment of Depression, 1983, 2nd edn 1992; (jtly) Cognitive Psychology and Emotional Disorders, 1988, 2nd edn 1997; (with F. Watts) The Psychology of Religious Knowing, 1988; (jtly) Cognitive Therapy and Clinical Practice, 1989; Cry of Pain: understanding suicide and self-harm, 1997; (with Z. Segal and J. D. Teasdale) Mindfulness-based Cognitive Therapy for Depression: a new approach to preventing relapse, 2002; Suicide and Attempted Suicide, 2002; (jtly) The Mindful Way Through Depression: freeing yourself from chronic unhappiness, 2007; (with D. Penman) Mindfulness: a practical guide to finding peace in a frantic world, 2011; (with J. Kabat-Zinn) Mindfulness: diverse perspectives on its meanings, origins and applications, 2013; (jtly) The Mindful Way Workbook, 2013; Cry of Pain: understanding suicide and the suicidal mind, 2014; (jtly) Mindfulness and the Transformation of Despair: working with people at risk of suicide, 2015; papers in scientific jls on psychological models and treatment of depression and suicidal behaviour. *Recreation:* piano and organ playing. *Address:* Oxford Mindfulness Centre, Department of Psychiatry, University of Oxford, Warneford Hospital, Oxford OX3 7JX. *T:* (01865) 613151.

WILLIAMS, John Peter Rhys, MBE 1977; FRCSEd; Consultant in Trauma and Orthopaedic Surgery, Princess of Wales Hospital, Bridgend, 1986–2004; *b* 2 March 1949; *s* of Peter Williams, MB, BCh and Margaret Williams, MB, BCh; *m* 1973, Priscilla Parkin, MB, BS, DObst, RCOG, DA; one *s* three *d*. *Educ:* Bridgend Grammar School; Millfield; St Mary's Hosp. Med. School. MB, BS London 1973; LRCP, MRCS, 1973; Primary FRCS 1976; FRCSEd 1980. University Hosp., Cardiff, Battle Hosp., Reading, St Mary's Hosp., London, 1973–78; Surgical Registrar, 1978–80, Orthopaedic Registrar, 1980–82, Cardiff Gp of Hosps; Sen. Orthopaedic Registrar, St Mary's Hosp., London, 1982–86. Played Rugby for Bridgend, 1967–68, 1976–79 (Captain, 1978–79), 1980–81, for London Welsh, 1968–76; 1st cap for Wales, 1969 (Captain, 1978); British Lions tours, 1971, 1974; a record 55 caps for Wales, to 1981; won Wimbledon Lawn Tennis Junior Championship, 1966. *Publications:* JPR (autobiog.), 1979; JPR: Given the Breaks - My Life in Rugby (autobiog.), 2006. *Recreation:* sport and music. *Address:* Llansannor Lodge, Llansannor, near Cowbridge, South Glamorgan CF71 7RX. *Club:* Lord's Taverners.

WILLIAMS, John Towner; composer of film scores; *b* 8 Feb. 1932. *Educ:* Juilliard Sch., NY. Conductor, Boston Pops Orchestra, 1980–93, then Laureate. Hon. DMus: Berklee Coll. of Music, Boston, 1980; St Anselm Coll., Manchester, NH, 1981; Boston Conservatory of Music, 1982; Hon. DHL S Carolina, 1981; Hon. Dr of Fine Arts Northeastern Univ. (Boston), 1981; Hon. DMus: William Woods Coll., USA, 1982; Juilliard Sch., 2004. 40 Acad. Award nominations and five Awards for: Fiddler on the Roof (filmscore arrangement), 1971; Jaws, 1976; Star Wars, 1978; E. T., 1983; Schindler's List, 1994; 18 Grammies, 2 Emmys, 14 Golden Globes and many other awards. Kennedy Center Honor, 2004. *Composer of film scores* including: The Secret Ways, 1961; Diamond Head, 1962; None but the Brave, 1965; How to Steal a Million, 1966; Valley of the Dolls, 1967; The Cowboys, 1972; The Poseidon Adventure, 1972; Tom Sawyer, 1973; Earthquake, 1974; The Towering Inferno, 1974; Jaws, 1975; Jaws 2, 1976; The Eiger Sanction, 1975; Family Plot, 1976; Midway, 1976; The Missouri Breaks, 1976; Black Sunday, 1977; Star Wars, 1977; Close Encounters of the 3rd Kind, 1977; The Fury, 1978; Superman, 1978; Dracula, 1979; The Empire Strikes Back, 1980; Raiders of the Lost Ark, 1981; E. T. (The Extra Terrestrial), 1982; Return of the Jedi, 1983; Indiana Jones and the Temple of Doom, 1984; Empire of the Sun, 1988; Indiana Jones and the Last Crusade, Born on the Fourth of July, 1989; Home Alone, 1990; Hook, JFK, 1991; Home Alone 2, Far and Away, 1992; Jurassic Park, 1993; Schindler's List, 1994; The Lost World, Seven Years in Tibet, 1997; Amistad, Saving Private Ryan, 1998; Star Wars, Episode I: The Phantom Menace, Angela's Ashes, 1999; The Patriot, 2000; AI, Harry Potter and the Philosopher's Stone, 2001; Star Wars, Episode II: Attack of the Clones, Minority Report, Harry Potter and the Chamber of Secrets, 2002; Catch Me if You Can, 2003; The Terminal, Harry Potter and the Prisoner of Azkaban, 2004; Star Wars, Episode III: Revenge of the Sith, War of the Worlds, 2005; Munich, 2005; Memoirs of a Geisha, 2006; Indiana Jones and the Kingdom of the Crystal Skull, 2008; Harry Potter and the Half-Blood Prince, 2009; War Horse, 2012; Lincoln, 2013; The Book Thief, 2014; many TV films. *Address:* c/o Gorfaine/Schwartz Agency Inc., 4111 W Alameda Avenue, Suite 509, Burbank, CA 91505, USA.

WILLIAMS, Rev. Prof. John Tudno, PhD; FLSW; Professor of Biblical Studies, 1973–2003, Principal, 1998–2003, United Theological College, Aberystwyth; Moderator of the General Assembly, Presbyterian Church of Wales, 2006–07 (Moderator of the Association in the South, 2002–03); *b* 31 Dec. 1938; *s* of late Rev. Arthur Tudno Williams and Primrose (*née* Hughes Parry); *m* 1964, Ina Lloyd-Evans; one *s* one *d*. *Educ:* Liverpool Inst. High School; Colfe's GS, Lewisham; Jesus Coll., Oxford (MA); UCW, Aberystwyth (PhD); United Theol Coll., Aberystwyth. Ordained as Welsh Presbyterian Minister, 1963; Minister in Borth, Cards, 1963–73; Part-time Lecturer: United Theol Coll., 1966–73; UCW (Religious Studies), 1976–87; Tutor responsible for Religious Studies, external degree through medium of Welsh, UCW, 1984–2003; Dean, Aberystwyth and Lampeter Sch. of Theology, 1985–87, 1994–97. Vis. Prof., Acadia Divinity Coll., Nova Scotia, 1997. Margaret and Ann Eilian Owen Fellow, Nat. Liby of Wales, 2001–; Hon. Res. Fellow, Univ. of Wales Trinity St David (formerly Univ. of Wales Lampeter), 2003–. Moderator, Free Church Federal Council, 1990–91. Secretary: Theology Section, Univ. of Wales Guild of Graduates, 1967–2003; Educn Cttee, Gen. Assembly of Presbyterian Church of Wales, 1979–2000; Bd of Trustees, Davies Lecture, 1983– (Lectr, 1993). External examr, QUB, Sheffield Univ., Univ. of Glos and Univ. of Wales, Bangor; examiner in religious studies and member of various educn cttees. Mem., Aberystwyth Town Council, 1979–87. FLSW 2012. Hon. DD Wales, 2006. *Publications:* Cewri'r Ffydd (Heroes of the Faith), 1974, 2nd edn 1979; Problem Dioddefaint a Llyfr Job (The Problem of Suffering and the Book of Job), 1980; Yr Epistol Cyntaf at y Corinthiaid (Commentary on I Corinthians), 1991; Y Llythyrau at y Galatiaid a'r Philipiaid (Commentary on the Letters to the Galatians and to the Philippians), 2001; contrib. to: Studia Biblica, 1978, Vol. ii 1980; C. H. Dodd, The Centenary Lectures, 1985; You Shall Be My Witnesses: festschrift for A. A. Trites, 2003; Protestant Nonconformity in the Twentieth Century, 2003; Ecumenical and Eclectic: festschrift for Alan Sell, 2007; The Reception of the Hebrew Bible in the Septuagint and the New Testament, 2013; Dictionary of Welsh Biography; contrib. T. & T. Clark Companion to Nonconformity, 2013; articles in Welsh jls, Expository Times; *festschrift*: The Bible in Church, Academy and Culture: essays in honour of the Reverend Dr John Tudno Williams (ed Alan P. Sell), 2011. *Recreations:* music (singing), Welsh language and culture. *Address:* Brynawel, Capel Seion, Aberystwyth SY23 4EF. *T:* (01970) 880489. *Club:* Penn.

WILLIAMS, Dr Jonathan Hugh Creer, FSA, FRHistS, FLSW; Deputy Director, British Museum, since 2013; *b* 19 Aug. 1967; *s* of Hugh Williams and Ann Williams (*née* Creer); *m* 2001, Konstanze Scharring; one *s* one *d*. *Educ:* Birkenhead Sch.; University Coll., Oxford (MA Classics); St Hugh's Coll., Oxford (DPhil Ancient Hist. 1994). Lectr in Ancient Hist., St Anne's Coll., Oxford, 1992–93; British Museum: Curator, Iron Age and Roman Coins, 1993–2005; Internat. Policy Manager, 2006–07; Keeper, Dept of Prehistory and Europe, 2007–12; Dir of Collections, 2012–13. Member, Board: British Mus. Co., 2009–; Fulham Palace Trust, 2011–14; Mem., UNESCO UK Culture Cttee, 2009–11. Sec., Royal Numismatic Soc., 2001–05. FRHistS 2005; FSA 2007; FLSW 2015. *Publications:* (ed jtly) Money, A History, 1997, 2nd edn 2007; (with C. Cheesman) Rebels, Pretenders and Imposters, 2000; Beyond the Rubicon: Gauls and Romans in Republican Italy, 2001; articles on ancient hist. and coins in learned jls. *Address:* Directorate, British Museum, Great Russell Street, WC1B 3DG. *E:* jwilliams@britishmuseum.org.

WILLIAMS, Jonathan R.; *see* Rees-Williams.

WILLIAMS, Dame Josephine, DBE 2007 (CBE 2000); DL; Commissioner, 2008–12, and Chair, 2010–13, Care Quality Commission; Chief Executive, Royal Mencap Society, 2002–08; *b* 8 July 1948; *d* of Frank Heald and Catherine Heald; *m* 1980, Robert Williams; two step *s*. *Educ:* Univ. of Keele (BA Hons Sociol. and Soc. Studies 1970; Dip. Applied Soc. Work 1971). Social Services in North West, for 20 yrs; Director Social Services: Wigan MBC, 1992–97; Cheshire CC, 1997–2002. Chair, Prison Reform Trust, 2009–11. Pres., Assoc. of Dirs of Social Services, 1999–2000. Trustee: EveryChild, 2004– (Vice Chair, 2011–); Dartington Hall Trust, 2010–. FCGI 2009. DL Cheshire, 2009. *Recreations:* running, tennis, ballet, travel, cooking for family and friends.

WILLIAMS, Dame Judi; *see* Dench, Dame J. O.

WILLIAMS, Prof. Julie, CBE 2012; PhD; Professor of Neuropsychological Genetics, Cardiff University, since 2001; Chief Scientific Adviser for Wales, since 2013; *b* Merthyr Tydfil, 11 Sept. 1957; *d* of Eric Valentine Baker and Jean Terry Baker; *m* 1976, John Glenville Williams; two *d*. *Educ:* Cardiff Univ. (BSc Occupational Psychol.; PhD). Cardiff University: Hd, Neurodegeneration Section, MRC Centre for Neuropsychiatric Genetics and Genomics; Dean of Res., Med. Sch. Former Mem., MRC Neurosci. and Mental Health Bd. Chief Scientific Advr, Alzheimer's Research UK, 2008. *Publications:* over 140 articles in jls incl. Lancet, Nature Genetics, New England Jl of Medicine. *Address:* Haydn Ellis Building, Cardiff University, Maindy Road, Cathays, Cardiff CF24 4HQ. *E:* WilliamsJ@cf.ac.uk.

WILLIAMS, Juliet Susan Durrant, CBE 2009; Founder Director, Strategic Management Resources Ltd, since 1991; *b* 17 April 1943; *d* of Robert Noel Williams and Frances Alice Williams (*née* Durrant). *Educ:* Cheltenham Ladies' Coll.; Bedford Coll., Univ. of London (BSc Hons Geog. with Econs); Hughes Hall, Cambridge (PGCE (Dist.)). Commng Ed., Macmillan, 1966–68; Ed., Geographical Mag., 1968–73; Marketing Dir and Gen. Manager, Readers' Union, 1973–78; CEO, Marshall Cavendish Mail Order, 1978–82; Man. Dir, Brann Direct Marketing, 1983–89; CEO, Marketing Communications Div., BIS Gp, 1985–91; Chairman: Alden Gp Ltd, 1993–2007; Waddie & Co., Edinburgh, 1996–99. Chairman: SW RDA, 2002–09; SW Regl Employment and Skills Partnership, 2005–09; Dir, VisitBritain, 2005–09. Non-exec. Dir, Oxfam, 1984–90. Mem., Industrial Develt Adv. Bd, DTI, 2003–09. Chm. of Govs, Univ. (formerly Univ. Coll.) of St Mark and St John, Plymouth, 2012–. FRGS 1968. DUniv Oxford Brookes, 2005; Hon. PhD Gloucestershire, 2010. *Publications:* papers and articles in jls, magazines and newspapers. *Recreations:* writing, sport (esp. sailing, motorsport, Welsh Rugby), the sea, the countryside, walking, gundogs. *Address:* PO Box 54, Newton Abbot, Devon TQ12 5AP. *T:* (01626) 361655, 07831 097946. *E:* juliet@strategic-management-resources.co.uk.

WILLIAMS, Katherine Frances Maria D.; *see* Dienes-Williams.

WILLIAMS, Katherine Lyndsay; *see* Mavor, K. L.

WILLIAMS, Katherine Ruth, (Kate), DPhil; historian and writer. *Educ:* Edgbaston High Sch., Birmingham; Somerville Coll., Oxford (BA Hons; DPhil); Queen Mary, Univ. of London (MA); Royal Holloway, Univ. of London (MA). Lectr in Creative Writing, Royal Holloway, Univ. of London. *Publications:* England's Mistress: the infamous life of Emma Hamilton, 2006; Becoming Queen: Princess Charlotte and Queen Victoria, 2008; The Pleasures of Men (novel), 2012; Young Elizabeth: the making of our Queen, 2012; The Extraordinary Life of Josephine Bonaparte, 2013; The Storms of War: 1914–1918, 2014. *Recreations:* dry and dusty documents, family trees, parish registers, living in the past, drinking hot water. *Address:* Royal Holloway, University of London, 11 Bedford Square, WC1B 3RF.

WILLIAMS, Kathryn Jean; *see* Wade, K. J.

WILLIAMS, Katrina Jane; Director General, International, Science and Resilience, Department of Energy and Climate Change, since 2013; *b* 30 July 1962; *d* of Ian Clive Williams and June Elizabeth Williams (*née* Dedman); *m* 2005, Paul Allen Green. *Educ:* Cheadle Hulme Sch.; Lady Margaret Hall, Oxford (BA Hons English Lang. and Lit.). MAFF, London, 1983–93; First Sec. (Agriculture), UK Perm. Representation to EU, 1993–96; Hd of Br., EU Div., MAFF, 1996–98; Principal Private Sec. to Minister of Agriculture, Fisheries and Food, 1998–99; Counsellor (Agric., Fisheries and Food), UK Perm. Repn to EU, Brussels, 1999–2003; Dep. Hd, Eur. Secretariat, Cabinet Office, 2003–06; Department for Environment, Food and Rural Affairs: Dir, Transmissible Spongiform Encephalopathies, later Food and Farming, 2006–08; Dir Gen., Food and Farming, 2008–12; Dir Gen., Strategy, Evidence and Customers, 2012–13. Hon. Nat. Chm., Civil Service Retirement Fellowship, 2004–09. *Address:* Department of Energy and Climate Change, 3 Whitehall Place, SW1A 2AW.

WILLIAMS, Keith Ronald, RIBA; architect; Design Director and Founder, Keith Williams Architects, since 2001; *b* 21 April 1958; *s* of Ronald Albert Williams and Sheila Lillian Grace Williams (*née* Dobson); *m* 2002, Vanessa Lillian Shrimpton. *Educ:* Kingston Grammar Sch.; Kingston Sch. of Architecture (BA Hons 1979); Greenwich Sch. of Architecture (DipArch Hons 1982). RIBA 1983; MRIAI 2004. Sheppard Robson, 1984–85; Terry Farrell & Partners, 1985–87; Partner, Pawson Williams Architects, 1987–2000. Major works include:

Earth Galls Masterplan, Natural Hist. Mus., London, 1995–96; remodelling of Birmingham Repertory Th., 1996–99; Athlone Civic Centre, Co. Westmeath, Ire., 2001–04; Unicorn Th., London, 2001–05; The Long House, St John's Wood, London, 2001–06; Clones Liby and County HQ, Co. Westmeath, 2004–08; new Wexford Opera House, 2005–08; Luan Art Gall., Athlone, Ireland, 2005–12; new Marlowe Th., Canterbury, 2007–11; Novium Mus., Chichester, 2007–12. Mem., Design Council CABE (formerly Nat. Design Review Panel, CABE), 2008–. Ext. Examr, Dept of Architecture, Univ. of Strathclyde, 2010–13; Mem., Nat. Panel Jury, Civic Trust Awards, 2011–; Chm., Lewisham Design Rev. Panel, 2013–. Hon. Prof. of Arch., Zhengzhou Univ., China, 2010. FRSA 2005. Richmond Soc. Award, 2004; RIAI Awards, 2005, 2006, 2007, 2009; RIBA Awards, 2005, 2006, 2008, 2009; OPUS Arch. and Construction Award, Bank of Ireland, 2005, 2008; Irish Concrete Soc. Award, 2005; Public Bldg Architect of the Yr, BD, 2006, 2008; AIA Award, 2006, 2010; Chicago Athenaeum Prize, 2006, 2008; Merit Award, US Inst. for Th. Technol., 2007; Copper in Arch. Award, Copper Develt Assoc., 2008; Quadrennial Award for Practical Design Excellence, Soc. of Theatre Consultants, 2010; Civic Trust Award, 2010; LAMA Nat. Impact Award, 2010; RIBA Downland Award, 2012; two Civic Trust Awards and Civic Trust Michael Middleton Special Award, 2013; RIAI Best Cultural Bldg Award, 2013; Civic Trust Award, 2014; RIBA Regl Award, 2014; RIBA Nat. Award, 2014. *Publications:* Keith Williams: architecture of the specific, 2009; numerous internat. and nat. articles, etc. *Recreations:* cricket, running, ski-ing, sailing, opera, travel, art, food. *Address:* Keith Williams Architects, 130–124 Pentonville Road, N1 9JE. *T:* (020) 7843 0070. *E:* studio@keithwilliamsarchitects.com.

WILLIAMS, Kenneth Robert, CVO 2003; CBE 2002; QPM 1992; HM Inspector of Constabulary, North of England and Northern Ireland, 2002–09; *b* 28 April 1944; *s* of Sydney Williams and Margaret Elizabeth Williams (*née* Howell); *m* 1969, Jean Margaret Ballantyne; two *d*. *Educ:* Wellacre Sch., Flixton; BA Soc. Scis Open Univ. Greater Manchester Police: Constable, Salford S Div., Salford City Police, 1963–68; Sergeant, N Manchester Div., 1968–72; Patrol Inspector, Salford Div., 1973–74; Inspector, then Chief Inspector, HQ, 1974–76; Sub-Divl Comd, Bolton Div., 1976–78; N Manchester Div., 1978–79; directing staff, Police Staff Coll., Bramshill, 1979–81; Greater Manchester Police: Sub-Divisional Command: Manchester Central Div., 1981; Manchester Internat. Airport, 1981–84; Departmental Command: Computer Project Branch HQ, 1984–85; Ops Support Branch HQ, 1985–86; Divl Comd, N Manchester, 1986–87; Sen. Comd course, Police Staff Coll., Bramshill, 1987; Asst Chief Constable, Greater Manchester Police, 1987–90; Dep. Chief Constable, Durham Constabulary, 1990–93; Chief Constable, Norfolk Constabulary, 1993–2002. *Recreations:* swimming, walking, reading, music. *Address:* Walton Lodge, Surlingham, Norwich NR14 7AN.

WILLIAMS, Kingsley; *see* Williams, J. B. K.

WILLIAMS, Kirsty; *see* Williams, V. K.

WILLIAMS, Prof. Laurence Glynn, CEng, FREng, FIMechE, FNucI; Professor of Nuclear Safety and Regulation, University of Central Lancashire, 2010–14, now Emeritus; Chair: Committee on Radioactive Waste Management, Department of Energy and Climate Change, since 2012; Defence Nuclear Safety Committee, Ministry of Defence, since 2013; Senior Research Fellow, Imperial College London, since 2014; *b* 14 March 1946; *s* of Hugh Williams and Ruby Williams (*née* Lawrence); *m* 1976, Lorna Susan Rance (marr. diss. 1997); one *s* one *d*. *Educ:* Liverpool Poly. (BSc Hons Mech. Engrg); Univ. of Aston in Birmingham (MSc Nuclear Reactor Technol. 1972). CEng 1976; FIMechE 1991; FNucI (FINucE) 1998; FREng 2004. Design engr, Nuclear Power Gp, 1970–71; nuclear engr, CEGB, 1973–76; Health and Safety Executive: Nuclear Installations Inspectorate: Inspector, 1976–78; Principal Inspector, 1978–86; Superintending Inspector, 1986–91; Dep. Chief Inspector, 1991–96; Div. Head, Safety Policy Directorate, 1996–98; HM Chief Inspector of Nuclear Installations and Dir, Nuclear Safety Directorate, 1998–2005; Dir, Nuclear Safety, Security and Envmt (formerly Nuclear Safety and Security), 2005–08, Chief Engr, 2007–08, Nuclear Decommissioning Authy. Nuclear safety and security consultant, 2008–10. Member: Defence Nuclear Safety Cttee, 2006–13; Civil Nuclear Police Authy, 2007–08; UK Mem., Higher Scientific Council, European Nuclear Soc., 2011–. Chm., UN/IAEA Commn on Safety Standards, 2000–05; Pres., UN Jt Convention on Safety of Spent Fuel and Radioactive Waste Mgt, 2003–06; Chm., EC High Level Panel for EURATOM FP7 ex-post evaluation, 2015–; Advr on Nuclear Safety, EBRD, 1996–; Member: Safety Review Gp, 1996–; Internat. Adv. Gp on Chernobyl, 1996–; Chm., Expert Adv. Gp on NW Russia, 2005–12. Chm., Internat. Nuclear Regulators' Assoc., 2000–02. Vis. Prof., KCL, 2012–; Vis. Sen. Fellow, Nat. Nuclear Lab., 2012–. Chm., Editl Cttee, Nuclear Inst., 2012–. *Recreations:* cycling, keeping fit, walking, music, theatre, supporting Liverpool Football Club. *Address:* Centre for Nuclear Engineering, Department of Materials, Imperial College London, South Kensington Campus, SW7 2AZ. *E:* laurence.williams@imperial.ac.uk.

WILLIAMS, Sir Lawrence (Hugh), 9th Bt *cr* 1798, of Bodelwyddan, Flintshire; farmer; *b* 25 Aug. 1929; *s* of Col Lawrence Williams, OBE, DL (*d* 1958) (*gs* of 1st Bt), and his 2nd wife, Elinor Henrietta (*d* 1980), *d* of Sir William Williams, 4th Bt of Bodelwyddan; *S* half-brother, 1995; *m* 1952, Sara Margaret Helen, 3rd *d* of Sir Harry Platt, 1st Bt; two *d*. *Educ:* Royal Naval Coll., Dartmouth. Commnd Royal Marines, 1947; served Korea 1951, Cyprus 1955, Near East 1956; Captain, 1959, retired 1964. Chm., Parciau Caravans Ltd, 1964–. Underwriting Mem., Lloyds, 1977–96. Lieut Comdr, RNXS, 1965–87. High Sheriff, Anglesey, 1970. *Recreations:* enjoying all aspects of country life, gentle sailing. *Heir:* none. *Address:* Old Parciau, Marianglas, Anglesey LL73 8PH. *Club:* Royal Naval Sailing Association.

See also Baron Suffield.

WILLIAMS, Manon Bonner; *see* Antoniazzi, M. B.

WILLIAMS, Marjorie Eileen, CB 2005; Tax Expert, International Monetary Fund, since 2006; *b* 18 Dec. 1946; *d* of Leslie Vernon Cuttle and Mary Fleming Cuttle (*née* Howie); *m* 1970, Graham Terence Williams. *Educ:* Reading Univ. (BSc Hons Geog. with Geol. 1968); Centre for W African Studies, Birmingham Univ. (postgrad. studies). Joined Inland Revenue, 1972; Regl Dir, SW Reg., 1994–96; Dir, Large Business Office, 1996–2000, Capital and Savings Tax Policy, 2000–03; Dir, Local Services, Bd of Inland Revenue, subseq. HM Revenue and Customs, 2003–06. *Publications:* Birdwatching in Lesbos, 1992. *Recreations:* birdwatching, gardening, Romanian needlework. *E:* maggiewcb@btinternet.com.

WILLIAMS, Mark; *see* Williams, J. M. G.

WILLIAMS, Mark Fraser; MP (Lib Dem) Ceredigion, since 2005; *b* 24 March 1966; *s* of Ronald and Pauline Williams; *m* 1997, Helen Refna Wyatt; one *s* three *d* (of whom one *s* one *d* are twins). *Educ:* University Coll. of Wales, Aberystwyth (BSc Econ 1987); Rolle Faculty of Educn, Univ. of Plymouth (PGCE 1993). Res. Asst to Lib, then Lib Dem, Peers and Constituency Asst to Geraint Howells, MP, 1987–92; Primary School Teacher: Madron Daniel Sch., Penzance, 1993–96; Forches Cross Sch., Barnstaple, 1997–2000; Dep. Hd, Llangors Church in Wales Sch., nr Brecon, 2000–05. Lib Dem spokesman on schools, 2005–06, on Wales, 2005–; Dep. Leader, Welsh Lib Dems, 2015–. Mem., Welsh Affairs Select Cttee, 2005–. Co-Chm., Lib Dem Backbench Cttee for political and constitutional reform, 2010–12, for Welsh Affairs, 2012–. Contested (Lib Dem): Monmouth, 1997; Ceredigion, Feb. 2000, 2001. Pres., Ceredigion Lib Dems, 1999–2000. *Recreations:* gardening, reading, biographies, walking. *Address:* 32 North Parade, Aberystwyth, Ceredigion SY23 2NF. *T:* (01970) 627721. *E:* williamsmf@parliament.uk.

WILLIAMS, Ven. Martin Clifford L.; *see* Lloyd Williams.

WILLIAMS, Martin John, CVO 1983; OBE 1979; HM Diplomatic Service, retired; High Commissioner, New Zealand, Governor (non-resident) of Pitcairn, Henderson, Ducie and Oeno Islands, and High Commissioner (non-resident), Samoa, 1998–2001; *b* 3 Nov. 1941; *s* of John Henry Stroud Williams and Barbara (*née* Benington); *m* 1964, Susan Dent; two *s*. *Educ:* Manchester Grammar Sch.; Corpus Christi Coll., Oxford (BA). Joined Commonwealth Relations Office, 1963; Private Sec. to Permanent Under Secretary, 1964; Manila, 1966; Milan, 1970; Civil Service College, 1972; FCO, 1973; Tehran, 1977; FCO, 1980; New Delhi, 1982; Rome, 1986; Hd of S Asian Dept, FCO, 1990; on secondment to NI Office as Asst Under-Sec. of State (Political), Belfast, 1993; High Comr, Zimbabwe, 1995–98. UK Consultant to NZ Antarctic Heritage Trust, 2002–12; Chm., NZ-UK Link Foundn, 2004–08. *Recreations:* music, gardening, woodworking. *Address:* Russet House, Lughorse Lane, Yalding, Kent ME18 6EG. *Club:* Royal Over-Seas League.

WILLIAMS, Martin Lloyd, PhD; FIEnvSc; Professor, Environmental Research Group, King's College London, since 2010; *b* Mountain Ash, Wales, 22 Nov. 1947; *s* of Chester Lloyd Williams and Muriel Williams; *m* 1982, Rosemary Anne Hudlestone; two *s*. *Educ:* Mountain Ash Grammar Sch.; University Coll., Cardiff (BSc 1st Cl. Hons Chem. 1968); Univ. of Bristol (PhD Chem. 1971). FIEnvSc 2008. Res. Fellow, Univs of British Columbia and Bradford, 1971–75; Hd, Air Pollution Modelling, Warren Spring Lab., 1975–81; Tech. Asst to Chief Scientist, DTI, 1981–82; Hd, Air Pollution Div., Warren Spring Lab., 1982–93; Hd, Air Quality Sci. Unit, DoE, 1993–2002; Hd, Atmospheric Quality and Industrial Pollution, DEFRA, 2002–10. Visiting Professor: Univ. of Southampton, 2007–. Chm., Exec. Body, UNECE Convention on Long Range Transboundary Air Pollution, 2005–. Burntwood Lect. and John Rose Award for Envmtl Sci., Instn of Envmtl Sci., 2007. *Publications:* numerous scientific papers in specialist jls. *Recreations:* drawing, painting, cycling, walking, guitar, ukelele. *Address:* Environmental Research Group, King's College London, Franklin Wilkins Building, 150 Stamford Street, SE1 9NH. *T:* (020) 7848 3844. *E:* martin.williams@kcl.ac.uk. *Club:* Verulam Cycling.

WILLIAMS, Martin Wykeham; Director, Office of Manpower Economics, since 2014; *b* Manchester, 15 May 1959; *s* of David John Wykeham Williams and Marjorie Williams (*née* Turnbull); *m* 1990, Eve Samson; one *s* one *d*. *Educ:* Winchester Coll.; Trinity Hall, Cambridge (BA Hist. 1980); École Nat. d'Admin, Paris (Dip. Internat. Public Admin 1990). Department of Employment, later Employment Department Group, then Department for Education and Employment, subseq. Department for Education and Skills: MSC and HSC, 1982–97; Hd of Strategy, 1997–2000; Grade 5, Sch. Workforce, 2000–03; Higher Educn (HE Act), 2003–06; Parents Policy, 2006–07; Dir, Higher Educn Strategy, DIUS, then Dir, Higher Educn, BIS, 2007–12; Dir, Educn and Procurement Industrial Strategies, and Office of Life Scis, BIS, 2012–14. Chair: The Brix at St Matthews, 1994–2005 (Trustee, 2005–); St Jude's Primary Sch., Lambeth, 2005–10. Trustee: Working With Men, 2009–; Fulbright Commn, 2009–14. *Recreations:* trombone, English concertina, fell-walking. *Address:* Office of Manpower Economics, Fleetbank House, 2–6 Salisbury Square, EC4Y 8JX. *T:* (020) 7211 8109. *E:* martin.williams@bis.gsi.gov.uk.

WILLIAMS, Sir Max; *see* Williams, Sir W. M. H.

WILLIAMS, Major Michael Ingouville, MBE 2001; Lord Lieutenant, East Lothian, since 2014 (Vice Lord Lieutenant, 2010–14); *b* Winchester, 15 March 1946; *s* of Roger Williams and Norah Williams; *m* 1971, Barbara Mary Campbell Williams; two *s* one *d*. *Educ:* Bradfield Coll.; RMA, Sandhurst. Commnd RTR, 1966; retd as Major, 1985. Farmer, E Lothian, 1986–2014. DL E Lothian, 1997. *Recreations:* farm conservation, forestry, golf, shooting, walking, countryside management. *Address:* Duncastle, Eaglescairnie Mains, Gifford, Haddington E Lothian EH41 4HN. *T:* (01620) 810491. *E:* mw.eagles@btinternet.com.

WILLIAMS, Michael John; Editor, New Musical Express, since 2012; *b* Wrexham, 4 Feb. 1979; *s* of Peter Williams and Sandra Williams; *m* Eleanor Stevenson. *Educ:* Univ. of Wales, Aberystwyth (Film and TV Studies 2000). Editor, Kruger Mag., 2003–10; New Musical Express: Features Editor, 2010–11; Dep. Editor, 2011–12. *Recreations:* watching football, chopping vegetables, debating with myself and others the greatest albums, films and crisp flavours of all time, distracting others. *Address:* New Musical Express, 110 Southwark Street, SE1 0SU. *T:* (020) 3148 6832. *E:* mike.williams@timeinc.com.

WILLIAMS, Rev. Canon Michael Joseph; Vicar of Bolton, 1999–2007, and Priest-in-charge, St Philip, Bolton le Moors, 2004–07; *b* 26 Feb. 1942; *s* of James and Edith Williams; *m* 1971, Mary Miranda Bayley; one *s* one *d*. *Educ:* St John's College, Durham (BA in Philosophy 1968). Apprentice Mechanical Engineer, then Engineer, with W & T Avery, Birmingham, 1958–63 (HNC in Mech. Eng 1962). Deacon 1970, priest 1971; Curate, then Team Vicar, St Philemon, Toxteth, 1970–78; Director of Pastoral Studies, St John's Coll., Durham, 1978–88; Principal, Northern Ordination Course, 1989–99; Area Dean, Bolton, 2001–05. Hon. Tutor in Pastoral Theology, Univ. of Manchester, 1990–2000. Hon. Canon: Liverpool Cathedral, 1992–99; Manchester Cathedral, 2000–07, now Canon Emeritus. Reviewer, Clergy Rev. Panel, Dio. of Manchester, 2014–. Mem., EU Energy Transparency Task Gp, 2013–15. Part-time Lectr, Liverpool Hope Univ., 2007–09; Tutor, Southern Theol Educn and Trng Scheme, 2013–. Chaplain, Bolton Normandy Veterans Assoc., 2004–10; Advr, Bolton Chaplaincy Training Course, 2010–13. Hon. Mem., Bolton Royal Artillery Assoc., 2008–11. Pres., Northern Fedn for Trng in Ministry, 1991–93. Chm. Trustees, Hands Around The World, 2014– (volunteer, 2009–13); volunteer, Bolton Steam Mus., 2012–. *Publications:* The Power and the Kingdom, 1989. *Address:* 51 Cotswold Drive, Horwich, Bolton BL6 7DE.

WILLIAMS, Michael Lodwig, CB 2003; consultant on government debt and cash management, since 2003; Chief Executive, UK Debt Management Office, 1998–2003; *b* 22 Jan. 1948; *s* of John and Eileen Williams; *m* 1970, Jennifer Mary Donaldson (*see* J. M. Williams); three *s*. *Educ:* Wycliffe Coll., Stonehouse, Glos; Trinity Hall, Cambridge (BA 1969; MA); Nuffield Coll., Oxford. Min. of Finance, Lusaka, Zambia, 1969–71; HM Treasury, 1973–2003: on secondment to Price Waterhouse, 1980–81; Under Sec., then Dep. Dir, Industry, 1992–98. Non-exec. Dir, Euroclear UK and Ireland Ltd (formerly CRESTCo Ltd), 1998–2002, 2004–13. *T:* (020) 7735 8694. *E:* mike.williams@mj-w.net.

WILLIAMS, Prof. Michael Maurice Rudolph; consultant engineer; Professor of Nuclear Engineering, University of Michigan, 1987–89; Professor of Nuclear Engineering, 1970–86, now Emeritus, and Head of Department, 1980–86, Queen Mary College, London University; *b* 1 Dec. 1935; *s* of late M. F. Williams, RAFVR and G. M. A. Williams (*née* Redington); *m* 1958, Ann Doreen Betty; one *s* one *d*. *Educ:* Ewell Castle Sch.; Croydon Polytechnic; King's Coll., London; Queen Mary Coll., London. BSc, PhD, DSc; CEng; FNucI; CPhys, FInstP. Asst Experimental Officer, AWRE, Fort Halstead, 1954–55; Engr with Central Electricity Generating Board, 1962; Research Associate at Brookhaven Nat. Lab., USA, 1962–63; Lectr, Dept of Physics, Univ. of Birmingham, 1963–65; Reader in Nuclear Engrg, 1965–70, Dir, Nuclear Reactor, 1980–83, QMC, London Univ.; Prin. Scientist, Electrowatt Engrg Services (UK) Ltd, 1989–95. Vis. Prof., Imperial Coll., London, 2002–. Augustin-Frigon Lecture, École Polytechnique de Montréal, 2001. Mem., Adv. Cttee on Safety of Nuclear Installations, 1983–86. UN Advr on Engrg Educn in Argentina, 1979–89. Vice-Pres., Instn of Nuclear Engrs, 1971–73. Mem., Electrical Engrg Coll., EPSRC, 1995–97. Chm. of Governors, Ewell Castle Sch., 1976–79; Mem., Academic Bd, RNC, Greenwich, 1975–86. Foreign Mem., Royal Soc. of Arts and Scis, Goteborg, Sweden, 2008–. Exec. Editor, Annals of Nuclear

Energy, 1973–2013. Fellow, American Nuclear Soc. (Arthur Holly Compton Award, 1994; Eugene P. Wigner Award, 2000; G. C. Pomraning Award, 2011). *Publications:* The Slowing Down and Thermalization of Neutrons, 1966; Mathematical Methods in Particle Transport Theory, 1971; Random Processes in Nuclear Reactors, 1974; Aerosol Science, 1991; contribs to Proc. Camb. Phil. Soc., Nucl. Science and Engrg, Jl Nuclear Energy, Jl Physics. *Address:* 6 Lincoln Close, Eastbourne, E Sussex BN20 7TZ.

WILLIAMS, Michael Roger; Director, Business and International Tax (formerly Business and Indirect Tax), HM Treasury, since 2010; *b* 2 July 1957; *s* of Roger Williams and Margaret Laura Williams (*née* Dawes). *Educ:* Bradford Grammar Sch.; Balliol Coll., Oxford (MA Physics 1978). Entered Inland Revenue, 1978: various tax inspector posts, 1978–93; Principal Inspector, Large Business Office, 1993–97; Asst Dir, Company Tax, then Personal Tax, 1997–99; Hd, Social Security Team, HM Treasury, 1999–2001; Dep. Dir, Internat., IR, 2001–04; Dir, Internat. Tax, 2004–07, Personal Tax and Welfare Reform, 2008–10, HM Treasury. *Recreations:* visiting France, reading, ice skating, going to the gym. *Address:* HM Treasury, 1 Horse Guards Road, SW1A 2HQ. *T:* (020) 7270 5000. *E:* mike.williams@hmtreasury.gsi.gov.uk.

WILLIAMS, Nicholas Michael Heathcote; QC 2006; **His Honour Judge Heathcote Williams;** a Circuit Judge, since 2014; *b* 5 Nov. 1954; *s* of Sir Edgar Trevor Williams, CB, CBE, DSO, and Gillian Williams (*née* Gambier-Parry); *m* 1987, Corinna Mary Mitchell; two *s* one *d*. *Educ:* St Catharine's Coll., Cambridge (Briggs Scholar; BA 1975); RMA Sandhurst. Commnd and served Royal Green Jackets, 1977–80. Called to the Bar, Inner Temple, 1976; in practice at the Bar, 1980–2014; a Recorder, 2000–14. *Recreations:* reading, art, film, sport (particularly cricket). *Address:* Woolwich Crown Court, 2 Belmarsh Road, SE28 0EY. *Clubs:* Royal Green Jackets, MCC.

WILLIAMS, Sir Nicholas Stephen, (Sir Nick), Kt 2013; Principal, BRIT School for the Performing Arts and Technology, 2002–12; Chief Executive Officer, Future Schools Trust, since 2014; *b* Solihull, 29 Dec. 1953; *s* of John Williams and Jane Williams; *m* 1990, Joanna Arkwright; one *s* three *d*. *Educ:* Univ. of Kent (BA Hons Amer. Lit.); King's Coll., London (PGCE). Teacher of English and Media, Battersea County Sch., Wandsworth, 1977–85; Hd of English, Dunraven Sch., Lambeth, 1985–89; Educn Advr, ILEA, 1989–90; Schs Inspector, London Bor. of Southwark and Ofsted, 1990–95; Dep. Headteacher, Pimlico Sch., Westminster, 1995–96; Headteacher, Thomas Tallis Sch., Greenwich, 1996–2001. DFE (formerly DCSF) Academies Educn Advr, 2008–. Consultant Leader, London Leadership Centre, 2004–10. Trustee: Centre for Learning in Primary Educn, 1993–96; Imperial War Mus., 2008–; E London Acad. of Music, 2014–. Chm. Govs, Crescent Primary Sch., 2011–; Founder and Gov., Birmingham Ormiston Acad., 2011–. FRSA 1998. *Publications:* various educnl articles. *Recreations:* arts, education, family.

WILLIAMS, Nicola; Service Complaints Commissioner for the Armed Forces, 2015–Jan. 2016; Service Complaints Ombudsman for the UK Armed Forces, from Jan. 2016; *b* London; *b* 24 Oct.; *d* of Andrew Matthew Sylvester Williams and Waveney Leonie Williams. *Educ:* Poly. of the South Bank (BA Hons Law 1984); Inns of Court Sch. of Law. Called to the Bar, Lincoln's Inn, 1985; barrister in private practice, 1985–2001; Complaints Comr, Cayman Is, 2009–15; a Recorder, 2009–. Member: Bd, Police Complaints Authy, 2001–04; Ind. Police Complaints Commn, 2004–09. *Publications:* Without Prejudice (novel), 1997. *Recreations:* dancing, film, music, travel. *Address:* Office of the Service Complaints Commissioner for the Armed Forces, PO Box 72252, SW1P 9ZZ. *T:* (020) 7877 3444. *E:* externalrelations2@oscc.gsi.gov.uk.

WILLIAMS, Nigel; *see* Williams, H. N.

WILLIAMS, Nigel Christopher Ransome, CMG 1985; HM Diplomatic Service, retired; UK Permanent Representative to the Office of the United Nations and other international organisations, Geneva, 1993–97; *b* 29 April 1937; *s* of late Cecil Gwynne Ransome Williams and Corinne Belden (*née* Rudd). *Educ:* Merchant Taylors' Sch.; St John's Coll., Oxford. Joined Foreign Service and posted to Tokyo, 1961; FO, 1966; Private Secretary: to Minister of State, 1968; to Chancellor of Duchy of Lancaster, 1969; UK Mission to UN, New York, 1970; FCO, 1973; Counsellor (Economic), Tokyo, 1976; Cabinet Office, 1980; Hd of UN Dept, FCO, 1980–84; Minister, Bonn, 1985–88; Ambassador to Denmark, 1989–93. *Address:* Frederiksberg Allé 45, 1.th, 1820 Frederiksberg C, Denmark.

WILLIAMS, Very Rev. Nigel Howard; Dean of St Asaph, since 2011; *b* St Asaph; *m* Nia; two *d*. *Educ:* Llysfasi Agricultural Coll.; St Michael's Coll., Llandaff; Univ. of Wales, Cardiff. Depot Manager, Wynnstay Farmers, Llanrwst; ordained deacon, 1995, priest, 1996; Asst Curate, St Mary's, Denbigh, 1995–97; Rector, Llanrwst and Llanddoget, 1998–2004; Vicar, St Paul's, Colwyn Bay, 2004–08; Area Dean, Rhos, 2004–09; Vicar, Colwyn Bay with Bryn y Maen, 2008–11. Archbishop's Advr on Rural Ministry. *Address:* Cathedral Office, High Street, St Asaph LL17 0RD. *T:* (01745) 582245.

WILLIAMS, Nigel L.; *see* Leader-Williams.

WILLIAMS, Nigel Lamplough, CEng; FIMarEST; Secretary, Royal Commission for the Exhibition of 1851, since 2010; *b* Yeovil, 15 July 1953; *s* of late Rear Adm. David Apthorp Williams, CB, DSC and Susan Eastlake Williams (*née* Lamplough); *m* 1986, Sarah Joanna Christie; one *s* one *d*. *Educ:* Cheltenham Coll.; BRNC Dartmouth; RNEC Manadon (BSc). MIMarE 1980; CEng, 1980; FIMarEST 2005. Served Royal Navy: HM Ships Torquay, Apollo, Bristol, Intrepid, 1976–82; Asst Naval Attaché, Bonn, 1983–85; HMS Aurora, 1985–87; on staff: FO Scotland and NI, 1987–89; Second Sea Lord, 1989–92; Capt. in Charge, Hong Kong, 1992–94; Cdre (E), HM Yacht Britannia, 1994–96; Dir Trng, HMS Sultan, 1996–99; Captain 1999; staff of Second Sea Lord, 1999–2002; Superintendent Fleet Maintenance, Portsmouth, 2002–04; Dir, Naval Officer Appts (E), 2004–06; Job Evaluation Judge (Navy), 2006–08. Freeman, City of London, 2011; Liveryman, Shipwrights' Co., 2012 (Clerk, 2008–10; Freeman, 2011). Member: RNSA, 1970–; Anchorites, 2006–. *Recreations:* sailing, ski-ing, music. *Address:* c/o Royal Commission for the Exhibition of 1851, Sherfield Building, Imperial College London, SW7 2AZ. *Clubs:* Royal Yacht Squadron, Royal London Yacht.

WILLIAMS, Prof. Sir Norman Stanley, Kt 2015; FRCS, FRCP, FRCPE, FMedSci, FRCA; Professor of Surgery, since 1986 and Director of Surgical Innovation, since 2011, Academic Surgical Unit, and Director, National Centre for Bowel Research and Surgical Innovation, since 2011, Barts and The London School of Medicine and Dentistry, Queen Mary University of London (formerly London Hospital Medical College, London University), since 1986 (Head, Academic Surgical Unit, 1986–2011); President, Royal College of Surgeons of England, 2011–14; *b* 15 March 1947; *s* of Jules Williams and Mabel Sundle; *m* 1977, Linda Feldman; one *s* one *d*. *Educ:* Roundhay Sch., Leeds; London Hosp. Med. Coll., Univ. of London (MB BS, MS). LRCP; MRCS; FRCP 2013; FRCPE 2014; FRCA 2014. House and Registrar appts, London Hosp., 1970–76; Registrar, Bristol Royal Infirmary, 1976–78; Res. Fellow and Lectr, Leeds Gen. Infirmary, 1978–80; Res. Fellow, UCLA, 1980–82; Sen. Lectr, Leeds Gen. Infirmary, 1982–86. Fulbright Scholar, UCLA, 1980; Ethicon Foundn Fellow, RCS, 1980; Moynihan Fellow, Assoc. of Surgeons of GB and Ireland, 1985. President: Ileostomy and Internal Pouch Support Group, 1992–2008; European Digestive Surgery, 1997–98; Chm., UK Co-ordinating Cttee of Cancer Res. Sub-Cttee on Colorectal Cancer, 1996–2001. Mem., Steering Gp, Nat. Cancer Res. Network, 2001–03. Mem. Council, 2005–, Chm., Acad. and Res. Bd, 2006–11, RCS. Pres., Soc. of Academic and Res. Surgery, 2009–11. Vice-Chm., British Jl of Surgery, 1995–2001. FMedSci 2004. Hon. Fellow, Amer. Surgical Assoc., 2008; Hon. FACS 2013; Hon. FDS 2014; Hon. FRCSI 2014. Patey Prize, Surgical Res. Soc., 1978; Nessim Habif Prize, Univ. of Geneva, 1995; Galen Medal in Therapeutics, Soc. of Apothecaries, 2002; (jtly) Cutler's Surgical Prize, 2011. *Publications:* (jtly) Surgery of the Anus, Rectum and Colon, 1993 (BUPA and Soc. of Authors Med. Writer's Gp Prize), 3rd edn 2008; (ed jtly) Bailey and Love's Short Practice of Surgery, 22nd edn 1995 to 26th edn 2013; (ed) Colorectal Cancer, 1996; scientific papers. *Recreations:* long distance swimming, Rugby football, cinema, reading about crime, fact and fiction. *Address:* Blizard Institute, Barts and London School of Medicine and Dentistry, National Centre for Bowel Research and Surgical Innovation, 1st Floor, Abernethy Building, 2 Newark Street, E1 2AT. *T:* (020) 78828755.

WILLIAMS, Dr Paul David; Chief Executive, Seafish Industry Authority, 2010–15; *b* Urmston, Manchester, 29 Jan. 1958; *s* of Stanley and June Williams; *m* 1993, Christine Kendall. *Educ:* William Hulme Grammar Sch., Manchester; Hatfield Poly. (BSc); Univ. of Manchester (PhD 1983). Res. Fellow, Univ. of Manchester, 1984–88; Manager, Plant Biotech Ltd, 1988–92; Project Manager, Proteus, Macclesfield, 1992–95; Manager, Ewos Tech. Centre, Scotland, 1995–2000; Man. Dir, Ewos Innovation, Norway, 2000–03; Res. Dir, Seafish Industry Authy, 2003–10. Non-exec. Mem. Bd, Gangmasters Licensing Authy, 2015–. *Publications:* contrib. res. papers on aquaculture and fisheries issues. *Recreations:* fly fishing, reading, walking.

WILLIAMS, Rt Rev. Paul Gavin; *see* Southwell and Nottingham, Bishop of.

WILLIAMS, Paul Maurice, OBE 2014; RDI 2005; RIBA; Director, Stanton Williams Architects, since 1985; *b* 8 Oct. 1949; *s* of Maurice Williams and Joan Williams (*née* Neighbour); *m* 1984, Beth Stockley; one *s* one *d*. *Educ:* Birmingham Coll. of Art (BA Hons; HDipAD). RIBA 2002. V&A Museum, 1975–80, Hd of Design, 1978–80: exhibns incl. Fabergé, Biedermeier, Renaissance Jewels and Tudor Miniatures; Design Consultant, Royal Liby, Windsor, 1978–87 (worldwide touring exhibns, Leonardo da Vinci Anatomical and Nature Study Drawings); private practice, 1980–85: exhibns incl. Romanesque, Matisse, Renoir, Hayward Gall.; Japanese Gall., V&A; formed partnership Stanton Williams Architects with Alan Stanton, 1985. *Award-winning projects* include: Design Mus. Galls, London, 1989; Issey Miyake Retail Shops, London, 1990–99; Triforium Mus., Winchester Cath., 1992; Leo Burnett Office Bldg, 60 Sloane Ave, London, 1994; Four Brindley Place, Birmingham, 1999; Wellcome Trust Millennium Seed Bank, Sussex, 2000; Whitby Abbey Visitor Centre, Yorks, 2002; Compton Verney Art Gall., 2004; Tower Hill Environs Scheme, London, 2004; Casa Fontana, Switzerland, 2004; Belgrade Th. Extension, 2008; Cadbury Offices, Bournville, 2009; Sainsbury Lab., Cambridge, 2011; Central Saint Martins, Univ. of Arts, London, 2012; Eton Manor, London, 2012. Exhibitions include: Art of Ancient Mexico, Yves Klein, Jasper Johns, Leonardo da Vinci, Romanesque Art, Hayward Gall.; Gothic Exhibn, RA; Bridget Riley, Tate Britain; Gerhard Richter, NPG, 2009. Architectural Advr, Heritage Lottery Fund, 1998–2002; Advr/Enabler, CABE, 2002–11; Member: Architectural Adv. Panel, Kensington and Chelsea, 2008–; St Paul's Cathedral, 2009–. External Examiner, Schools of Architecture: Westminster Univ., 1993–96; Plymouth Univ., 2000–04; Dundee Univ., 2005–07; Birmingham Univ., 2009–; lectured and taught in Europe and USA. Trustee: Whitechapel Art Gall., 1994–99; SPACE, 2011–. FRSA. Hon. Dr Univ. of Arts, London, 2012. *Publications:* work published and exhibited widely in architectural books and jls. *Recreations:* the arts, all sports. *Address:* Stanton Williams, 36 Graham Street, Islington, N1 8GJ. *T:* (020) 7880 6400, *Fax:* (020) 7880 6401. *E:* p.williams@stantonwilliams.com.

WILLIAMS, Sir Paul Michael, Kt 2011; OBE 2000; DL; Bailiff of St David's, St John Cymru—Wales, since 2014 (Chancellor, 2011–12, Registrar, 2012–14, Order of St John, Priory for Wales, 2011); *b* Cardiff, 25 June 1948; *s* of Leonard and Marion Williams; *m* 1982, Glenys Williams, JP. *Educ:* St Illtyd's Coll., Cardiff; Glamorgan Poly. (DMS). Joined NHS as clerk, Welsh Hosp. Bd, 1966; Asst Dist Gen. Manager, Mid Glamorgan HA; CEO, Bridgend and Dist NHS Health Trust, 1993–99; Chief Executive: Bro Morgannwg NHS Trust; Abertawe Bro Morgannwg Univ. NHS Trust; Dir Gen., Health and Social Services, and Chief Exec., NHS Wales, Welsh Govt, 2008–11. Non-exec. Dir, Natural Resources Wales, 2012–. Trustee: St John Cymru—Wales, 2008–; RVS, 2011–; Royal Masonic Benevolent Instn, 2011–. Fellow, UWIC, 2010. High Sheriff, 2007–08, DL 2010, S Glamorgan. CCMI; CIHM. KStJ 2015 (CStJ 2011). Hon. Dr S Wales, 2013. *Recreations:* fly fishing, walking, music. *Address:* 191 Cyncoed Road, Cyncoed, Cardiff CF23 6AJ. *Club:* Cardiff County.

WILLIAMS, Dr Paul Randall, CBE 1996; DL; FInstP; Chairman and Chief Executive, Council for Central Laboratory of Research Councils, 1995–98; *b* 21 March 1934; *s* of Fred and Eileen Westbrook Williams; *m* 1957, Marion Frances Lewis; one *s* one *d*. *Educ:* Baines Grammar School; Loughborough College (BSc London external; DLC); Liverpool Univ. (PhD). ICI Research Fellow, Liverpool Univ., 1957; Research Physicist, British Nat. Bubble Chamber, 1958–62; Rutherford Lab., SRC, 1962–79 (Dep. Div. Head, Laser Div., 1976–79); Science and Engineering Research Council: Head, Astronomy, Space and Radio Div., 1979–81; Head, Engineering Div., 1981–83; Dep. Dir, 1983–87, Dir, 1987–94, Rutherford Appleton Lab.; Dir, Daresbury and Rutherford Appleton Lab., EPSRC, 1994–95. Chm., Abingdon Coll. Corp., 1993–95. Local Preacher, Methodist Church. DL Oxfordshire, 1998. Hon. DSc Keele, 1996. Glazebrook Medal, Inst. of Physics, 1994. *Recreations:* listening to music, choral singing, travel. *Address:* 5 Tatham Road, Abingdon, Oxon OX14 1QB. *T:* (01235) 524654.

WILLIAMS, Maj. Gen. Peter Gage, CMG 2005; OBE 1994 (MBE 1984); Head of NATO Military Liaison Mission, Moscow, 2002–05; Editor, The Guards Magazine, 2009–13; *b* 25 June 1951; *s* of Col G. T. G. Williams; *m* 1982, Anne Rankine; one *s* two *d*. *Educ:* Eton; Magdalene Coll., Cambridge (BA 1972). Commnd Coldstream Guards, 1969; Sultan of Oman's Forces, 1976–78; served NI and Berlin; psc; MA to SACEUR, 1990–92; CO 1st Bn Coldstream Guards, 1992–94; served NI (despatches), Bosnia, with MoD Intelligence; ocds (Aust.), 1999 (Fellow, 1999); Dep. Mil. Rep., EU Mil. Cttee, 2001–02. Patron, British Ex-Servicemen's Assoc., Western Australia, 2009–; Chm., BRIXMIS Assoc., 2010. Mem., Chartered Inst. of Linguists, 1996 (Associate Mem., 1981). Gov., Rendcomb Coll., 2011. Legion of Merit (USA), 2005. *Recreations:* tourism, military history. *Address:* Northcot House, Highworth, Wiltshire SN6 7BW.

WILLIAMS, Sir Peter (Michael), Kt 1998; CBE 1992; PhD; FRS 1999; FREng; Chairman, Daiwa Anglo-Japanese Foundation, since 2012 (Trustee, since 2009); *b* 22 March 1945; *s* of Cyril Lewis and Gladys Williams; *m* 1970, Jennifer Margaret Cox; one *s*. *Educ:* Hymers College, Hull; Trinity College, Cambridge (MA, PhD). Mullard Research Fellow, Selwyn College, Cambridge, 1969–70; Lectr, Dept of Chemical Engineering and Chemical Technology, Imperial College, 1970–75; VG Instruments Group, 1975–82 (Dep. Man. Dir, 1979–82); Oxford Instruments Group plc, 1982–99: Man. Dir, 1983–85; Chief Exec., 1985–98; Chm., 1991–99; Master, St Catherine's Coll., Oxford, 2000–02. Chairman: Isis Innovation Ltd, Oxford Univ., 1997–2001; Kromek, 2015–; non-executive Director: GKN plc, 2001–10; WS Atkins plc, 2004–11. Chairman: PPARC, 1994–99; Trustees, Science Museum, 1996–2002; Engrg and Technol. Bd, 2002–06; NPL, 2002–14. Mem., Council for Sci. and Technology, 1993–98; President: Inst. of Physics, 2000–02; BAAS, 2002–03. Supernumerary Fellow, St John's Coll., Oxford, 1988–2000. Chancellor, Univ. of Leicester, 2005–10. FREng (FEng 1996). FIC 1997; FCGI 2002. Hon. FIChemE 2003; Hon. FIET (Hon. FIEE 2004); Hon. FCMI 2007; Hon. FIMechE 2008. Hon. Fellow: Selwyn Coll., Cambridge, 1997; UCL, 1997; St Catherine's Coll., Oxford, 2002. Hon. DSc: Leicester,

1995; Nottingham Trent, 1995; Loughborough, 1996; Brunel, 1997; Wales, 1999; Sheffield, 1999; Salford, 2003; Staffordshire, 2004; City, 2007; Hull, 2010; Bedfordshire, 2010. Guardian Young Business Man of the Year, 1986. *Publications:* numerous contribs to jls relating to solid state physics. *Recreations:* ski-ing, walking. *Address:* Kews, Oxford Road, Frilford Heath, Oxon OX13 5NN.

WILLIAMS, Peter Richard Michael; Joint Founder and Chief Executive Officer, Jack Wills, clothing and homeware, 1999–2013 and since 2015; *b* Bolton, 12 July 1974; *s* of Michael and Diana Williams; *m* 2003, Laura; two *s* one *d*. *Educ:* King Edward's Sch., Birmingham; University Coll. London (BSc). Launched Aubin & Wills, 2008. Mem., Young President's Orgn. *Recreation:* family and sport. *Address:* 94 Lansdowne Road, W11 2LS. *E:* peter@jackwills.com.

WILLIAMS, Peter Robert, CBE 2009; international consultant on quality assurance in higher education; Chief Executive, Quality Assurance Agency for Higher Education, 2002–09 (Acting Chief Executive, 2001–02); *b* 20 April 1948; *s* of Gilbert David Williams and Phyllis Williams, Oxford; *m* 1st, 1979, Katherine Pickles (marr. diss.); 2nd, 1987, Fiona Pollock-Gore; two *s*. *Educ:* City of Oxford High Sch.; Univ. of Exeter (BA Hons English 1969). Mgt trainee, Hazell, Watson and Viney Ltd, 1969–70; Admin. Asst, Univ. of Surrey, 1970–74; University of Leicester: Sen. Admin. Asst, 1974–79; Asst Registrar, 1979–82, Sec., 1982–84, Medical Sch.; Dep. Sec., British Acad., 1984–90; Director: CVCP Academic Audit Unit, 1990–92; of Quality Audit, 1992–94, of Quality Assurance, 1994–97, HEQC; of Institutional Review, QAA, 1997–2001. British Accreditation Council for Independent Further and Higher Education: Member: Council, 1998–; Exec. Cttee, 2000–; Chm., 2012–; European Association (formerly European Network) for Quality Assurance in Higher Education: Mem., Steering Cttee, 2000–04; Mem. Bd, 2004–08; Vice-Pres., 2004–05, Pres., 2005–08. Mem., Burgess Scoping Gp, 2003–04, Steering Gp, 2005–07, Implementation Gp, 2008–12, Universities UK/GuildHE. Mem., Educn Honours Cttee, 2010–. Chm., Accreditation Rev. Cttee, Nat. Commn for Academic Accreditation and Assessment, Saudi Arabia, 2011–. Mem. Cttee, 1981–84, Chm., Leicester Gp, 1981–84, Victorian Soc. Gov., Cardiff Metropolitan Univ. (formerly UWIC), 2009– (Vice Chm., Bd of Govs, 2012–14; Chm., Audit Cttee, 2012–); Trustee, Richmond, American Internat. Univ. in London, 2012– (Mem. 2010–12, Chm., 2012–14, Bd of Academic Advrs (formerly Bd of Academic Govs); Chm., Academic Cttee, 2014–). Mem. Bd, Improving Dispute Resolution Adv. Service, 2010– (Dep. Chm., 2011–12). Lord Upjohn Lect., Assoc. of Law Teachers, 2009. Hon. Treas., Little Malvern Priory, 2010–. Fellow, Univ. of Worcester, 2009. FRSA 2002. Hon. Fellow, Coll. of Teachers, 2011. Hon. LLD: Higher Educn Trng and Awards Council, Ireland, 2008; Leicester, 2010; Hon. PhD Gloucestershire, 2010. Freeman, City of London, 2012; Freeman, then Liveryman, Co. (formerly Guild) of Educators, 2002 (Ct Asst, 2002–; Master, 2014–15). *Publications:* articles in books and jls on quality assurance and higher educn. *Recreations:* music, books, pictures, English topography, la comédie humaine, pedantry. *Address:* 66 St Andrews Road, Malvern, Worcs WR14 3PP. *E:* prw101@gmail.com. *Club:* City Livery.

WILLIAMS, Peter Wodehouse; Chairman, boohoo.com plc, since 2014; *b* 18 Dec. 1953; *s* of John and Claire Williams; *m* 1981, Gwen Knight; two *s*. *Educ:* Univ. of Bristol (BSc Maths). ACA 1978. Audit Senior, Arthur Andersen, 1975–78; Consultant, Accenture, 1978–82; Financial Controller, Aiwa (UK) Ltd, 1982–84; Finance Dir, Bandive Ltd, 1984–87; Finance Divl Manager, Freemans plc, 1987–91; Finance Dir, 1991–2003, Chief Exec., 2003–04, Selfridges plc; Chief Exec., Alpha Gp (formerly Alpha Airports), 2006–08; Director: JJB Sports plc, 2009; Maltby Investments Ltd, 2010. Non-executive Director: Capital Radio plc, 2003–05; GCap Media plc, 2005–08; Asos plc, 2006–13; Cineworld Gp plc, 2006–15; Silverstone Hldgs Ltd, 2009–14; Sportech plc, 2011–; London Transport Mus., 2012–; non-executive Chairman: Blacks Leisure, 2011–12; Erno Lazlo, 2011–13; Without Prejudice, 2012–14; Brissi, 2013–; Mister Spex, 2013–; OfficeTeam, 2013–14; Jaeger, 2014–15. Member: Bd of Mgt, British Retail Consortium, 2003–04; Design Council, 2006–. Member: Business Adv. Bd, Comic Relief, 2002–14; Finance Cttee, British Red Cross, 2002–08. Trustee: GCap Charities (formerly Capital Charities), 2003–10. *Recreations:* film, tennis, ski-ing, Southampton Football Club, shopping. *Address:* 3 Rayners Road, SW15 2AY. *T:* (020) 8788 5346. *E:* Williams5000@hotmail.com. *Clubs:* Home House; Bank of England Sports.

WILLIAMS, Sir Philip; *see* Williams, Sir R. P. N.

WILLIAMS, Rhodri John; QC 2010; *b* Cardiff, 3 Jan. 1963; *s* of David Barry Williams, QC and Angela Joy Williams; *m* 1991, Rachel Margaret Williams; one *s* two *d*. *Educ:* Cardiff High Sch.; Exeter Coll., Oxford (BA Hons Mod. Langs 1985; MA 2002); Poly. of Central London (Dip. Law 1986). Called to the Bar, Gray's Inn, 1987; in practice as barrister, specialising in EU law, and public and admin. law, 1987–. Fonctionnaire, Commn of EC, 1992–97. Mem., Editl Bd, Public Procurement Law Rev., 2000–. *Recreations:* Rugby, fencing, walking. *Address:* Henderson Chambers, 2 Harcourt Buildings, Temple, EC4Y 9DB. *T:* (020) 7583 9020, *Fax:* (020) 7583 2686. *E:* clerks@hendersonchambers.co.uk. *Club:* Cardiff and County.

WILLIAMS, Richard Charles John; Founder Director, Williams Murray Hamm Ltd, since 1997; *b* 19 Oct. 1949; *s* of Herbert Charles Lionel Williams and Barbara Dorothy Williams; *m* 1973, Agnieszka Wanda Skrobanska; one *s* one *d*. *Educ:* Highgate Sch.; London College of Printing (DipAD 1973). Founder Dir, Design Bridge, 1986–95. Director: Design Business Assoc., 1989 and 2005; Writtle Hldgs; Mem., Design Council, 2005–10. *Publications:* (with Richard Murray and Garrick Hamm) The Little Book of Don'ts in Brand Design, 2002; (jtly) Seemed Like a Good Idea at the Time, 2009. *Recreations:* motor sport, sailing. *Address:* Williams Murray Hamm Ltd, 10 Dallington Street, EC1V 0DB. *T:* (020) 3217 0000, *Fax:* (020) 3217 0002. *E:* richardw@creatingdifference.com.

WILLIAMS, (Richard) Derrick, MA; Principal, Gloucestershire College of Arts and Technology, 1981–89; *b* 30 March 1926; *s* of Richard Leslie Williams and Lizzie Paddington; *m* 1949, Beryl Newbury Stonebanks; four *s*. *Educ:* St John's Coll., Cambridge (MA). Asst Master, Lawrence Sheriff Sch., Rugby, 1950–51; Lectr, University Coll., Ibadan, Nigeria, 1951–52; Adult Tutor, Ashby-de-la-Zouch Community Coll., Leicestershire, 1952–54; Further Educn Organising Tutor, Oxfordshire, 1954–60; Asst Educn Officer: West Suffolk, 1960–65; Bristol, 1965–67; Dep. Chief Educn Officer, Bristol, 1967–73; Chief Educn Officer, County of Avon, 1973–76; Dir, Glos Inst. of Higher Educn, 1977–80. *Recreations:* cricket, music. *Address:* Glan y Nant, Bryniau, Brithdir, Dolgellau, Gwynedd LL40 2TY.

WILLIAMS, Richard Evan Huw; a District Judge (Magistrates' Courts), Gwent (formerly South Wales), since 2004; a Recorder, since 2012; *b* 17 Feb. 1959; *s* of Evan Howell Williams, FIChemE and Muriel Maynard Williams (*née* Cooke); *m* 1991, Lindsey Ann Duckworth; two *d*. *Educ:* Ysgol Gyfun Rhydfelen, Pontypridd; Univ. of Bristol (LLB Hons 1991). Metropolitan Police, 1978–88; called to the Bar, Lincoln's Inn, 1992; a barrister, 1992–2004; a Dep. Dist Judge (Magistrates' Courts), 2000–04. Mem., Sentencing Council for England and Wales, 2014–. *Recreations:* family, music, cycling. *Address:* Gwent Magistrates' Court, The Law Courts, Faulkner Road, Newport NP20 4PR. *E:* districtjudgerichard.williams@judiciary.gsi.gov.uk.

WILLIAMS, Prof. Richard James Willson, OBE 2010; TD 1995; FRCPsych (Hon.), FRCPCH; Professor of Mental Health Strategy, Welsh Institute for Health and Social Care, University of South Wales (formerly University of Glamorgan), 1998–2014, now Emeritus; Honorary Consultant Disaster Psychiatrist and Public Mental Health Physician, Extreme Events and Health Protection Section, Public Health England (formerly Health Protection Agency), since 2012; *b* 5 Feb. 1949; *s* of Ernest James Williams and Eleanor Mary Willson Williams; *m* 1971, Janet May Simons; one *s* two *d*. *Educ:* Bristol Grammar Sch.; Univ. of Birmingham (MB ChB 1972); DPM 1976. MRCPsych 1976, FRCPsych 1990, Hon. FRCPsych 2014; MRCPCH 1996, FRCPCH 1997; DMCC 2009. House Physician, Selly Oak Hosp., Birmingham, 1972–73; House Surgeon, Worcester Royal Infirmary, 1973; Sen. House Officer in Psychiatry, Whitchurch Hospital Mgt Cttee, Cardiff, 1973–74; Registrar in Psychiatry, S Glamorgan AHA (T), 1974–77; Sen. Registrar in Child and Adolescent Psychiatry, S Glamorgan AHA (T) and Welsh Nat. Sch. of Medicine, 1977–80; Consultant Child and Adolescent Psychiatrist: Bristol Royal Hosp. for Sick Children, 1980–98; Aneurin Bevan Health Bd (formerly Gwent Healthcare NHS Trust), 1998–2014; Advanced Trauma Life Support Instructor, RCS, 1996–; Lead Officer for Disaster Mgt, RCPsych, 2008. Director: NHS Health Adv. Service, 1992–96; Drugs Adv. Service, 1992–96; Vice Chm., Mental Health Act Commn, 1997–2001. Special Advr on Child and Adolescent Mental Health to Welsh Assembly Govt, 1999–2010; Mem., Adv. Bd for Healthcare Standards in Wales, 2004–08 (Chm., Ethics Cttee, 2005–); Chm., Wales Collaboration in Mental Health, 2003–09; Vice Chm., Wales Cttee, Adv. Cttee on Clin. Excellence Awards, 2009–12; Member: Emergency Planning Clinical Leadership Adv. Gp, DoH, 2005–; Cttee on the Ethical Aspects of Pandemic Influenza, UK Govt, 2006–; Pandemic Influenza Clin. and Operational Adv. Gp to UK's Chief Med. Officers, 2008–; Scientific Adviser on Psychosocial and Mental Healthcare: to Dir of Emergency Preparedness, DoH, 2006–13; to Jt Med. Cttee, NATO, 2007–09. Chm., Assoc. for Psychiatric Study of Adolescents, 1989–92. Gov. and Mem. Exec. Cttee, Inst. of Child Health, Univ. of Bristol, 1988–94 (Treas., 1989–91); Sen. Fellow, Health Services Mgt Centre, Univ. of Birmingham, 1996–99. Society of Apothecaries: Mem., Bd of Examrs, Dip. in Med. Care of Catastrophes, 1997–; Mem., Exec. Cttee, Faculty of Conflict and Catastrophe Medicine, 2006–. Hon. Professor: of Child and Adolescent Mental Health, Sch. of Public Health and Clinical Scis, Univ. of Central Lancs, 2006–11; of Disaster Healthcare, Robert Gordon Univ., 2009–13; Humanitarian and Conflict Response Inst., Univ. of Manchester, 2012–. Dir of Confs, 2001–07, Presidential Lead Officer for Disaster Mgt, 2008–14, RCPsych. Chm., 2004–06, Vice Chm., 2002–03, 2006–08, Acad. of Med. Royal Colls in Wales; Mem., Acad. of Med. Royal Colls, 2002–08. MIHM 1994; MInstD 1995. Ed., child and adolescent psychiatry, Current Opinion in Psychiatry, 1993–; Asst Ed., 1992–97, Mem. Editl Bd, 1997–, Jl of Adolescence. Served TA, 1967–2009 (Mem., Birmingham Univ. OTC, 1967–70; Commnd Officer, UK TA, 1970–2009; OC Basic Wing Bristol Univ. OTC, 1984–97; jsc 1997; CO Ambulance Train Gp RAMC (V), 1997–2001). Freeman, City of London, 2000; Liveryman, Soc. of Apothecaries, 2004– (Convener, DMCC, 2012–). Queen's Golden Jubilee Medal, 2002; VRSM, 2005. *Publications:* (ed jtly) A Concise Guide to the Children Act 1989, 1992; (ed and contrib.) Comprehensive Mental Health Services, 1994; (ed and contrib.) Clinicians in Management, 1994; (ed jtly) Suicide Prevention, 1994; (ed and contrib.) Comprehensive Health Services for Elderly People, 1994; (ed and contrib.) Drugs and Alcohol, 1994; (ed jtly and contrib.) Together We Stand, 1995; (ed jtly and contrib.) A Place in Mind, 1995; (ed jtly and contrib.) The Substance of Young Needs, 1996; (ed jtly) Safeguards for Young Minds, 1996, 2nd edn 2004; (ed jtly and contrib.) Heading for Better Care, 1996; (ed jtly and contrib.) Addressing the Balance, 1997; (ed jtly) Voices in Partnership, 1997; (ed jtly and contrib.) Forging New Channels, 1998; (jtly) Promoting Mental Health in a Civil Society, 2001; (jtly) Deaths of Detained Patients in England and Wales, 2001; (ed jtly) Child and Adolescent Mental Health Services, 2005; contrib. many chapters in books, major reports to govts and other authorities, and leading articles, editorials and papers in learned jls. *Recreations:* walking on Bodmin Moor, licensed radio amateur, preserved steam railways, military history, coastal powerboating. *Address:* Welsh Institute for Health and Social Care, Faculty of Life Sciences and Education, University of South Wales CF37 1DL. *T:* (01433) 483070. *E:* richard.williams@southwales.ac.uk. *Club:* Athenæum.

WILLIAMS, Dr Richard Wynne; Chief Executive Officer, Rathbone, 2004–12; *b* 28 March 1954; *m* 1981, Sandra Hauxwell; one *s*. *Educ:* Thames Poly. (BA Hons 1972); Univ. of London (PGCE 1979); DMan Univ. of Herts 2005. Lectr, City & E London Coll., 1979–84; Sen. Lectr, Paddington Coll., 1984–87; Head of Faculty, 1987–91, Dep. Principal, 1987–96, Hendon Coll.; Principal: Kingsway Coll., 1996–2000; Westminster Kingsway Coll., 2000–04. *Publications:* contributor: A Complexity Perspective on Researching Organizations, 2005; Complexity and the Experience of Leading Organisations, 2005; Experiencing Emergence in Organizations, 2005; Complexity and the Experience of Managing in Public Sector Organizations, 2005. *Recreations:* theatre, modern jazz, walking.

WILLIAMS, Prof. Robert Hughes, (Robin), CBE 2004; FRS 1990; CPhys, FInstP; FLSW; Vice-Chancellor, University of Wales, Swansea, 1994–2003, now Emeritus Professor; *b* 22 Dec. 1941; *s* of Emrys and Catherine Williams; *m* 1967, Gillian Mary Harrison; one *s* one *d*. *Educ:* Bala Boys' Grammar Sch.; University College of North Wales, Bangor (BSc, PhD, DSc). Res. Fellow, Univ. of Wales, 1966–68; Lectr, then Reader and Prof., New University of Ulster, 1968–83; Prof. and Hd of Dept of Physics, later Physics and Astronomy, 1984–94, Dep. Principal, 1993–94, Univ. of Wales Coll. of Cardiff. Visiting Professor: Max Planck Inst., Stuttgart, 1975; Xerox Res. Labs, Palo Alto, USA, 1979; IBM Res. Labs, Yorktown Heights, USA, 1982; Distinguished Res. Fellow, La Trobe Univ., Melbourne, 2003. Mott Lectr, Inst. of Physics, 1992. Member: Council, HEFCW, 2009–15; Sci. Adv. Council for Wales, 2010–13; Council, Learned Soc. of Wales, 2010– (Founding Fellow, 2010). Hon. DSc Ulster, 2003; Hon. DLaws Wales, 2005. Silver Medal, British Vacuum Council, 1988; Max Born Medal and Prize, German Physics Soc. and Inst. of Physics, 1989. *Publications:* Metal-Semiconductor Contacts (with E. H. Rhoderick), 1988; over 300 pubns in field of solid state physics and semiconductor devices. *Recreations:* walking, fishing, soccer. *Address:* Dolwerdd, Trerhyngyll, Cowbridge, Vale of Glamorgan CF71 7TN. *T:* (01446) 773402.

WILLIAMS, Sir (Robert) Philip (Nathaniel), 4th Bt *cr* 1915; JP, DL; landowner; *b* 3 May 1950; *s* of Sir David Philip Williams, 3rd Bt and Elizabeth Mary Garneys, *d* of late William Ralph Garneys Bond; *S* father, 1970; *m* 1979, Catherine Margaret Godwin, *d* of Canon Cosmo Pouncey, Tewkesbury; one *s* three *d*. *Educ:* Marlborough; St Andrews Univ. MA Hons. Mem., Ind. Monitoring Bd, HM YOI, Portland, 2000– (Chm., 2007–09). Lay Canon, Salisbury Cathedral, 2010–. JP W Dorset PSA (formerly Dorchester), 1992; DL 1995, High Sheriff, 2016–, Dorset. *Heir: s* David Robert Mark Williams, *b* 31 Oct. 1980. *Address:* Bridehead, Littlebredy, Dorchester, Dorset DT2 9JA. *T:* (01308) 482232. *Club:* MCC.

WILLIAMS, Robin; *see* Williams, Robert H.

WILLIAMS, Maj.-Gen. Robin Guy, CB 1983; MBE 1969; retired; Chief Executive Officer, Auckland Regional Trust Board, Order of St John, 1993–98; *b* 14 Aug. 1930; *s* of Dr John Upham and Dr Margaret Joan Williams; *m* 1953, Jill Rollo Tyrie; one *s* two *d*. *Educ:* Nelson Coll., New Zealand. psc(UK) 1963, jssc(AS) 1972, rcds(UK) 1976. Commissioned RMC, Duntroon, 1952; 1 Fiji Inf. Regt Malaya, 1953–54; Adjt/Coy Comd 2 NZ Regt Malaya, 1959–61 Chief Instructor Sch. of Inf. (NZ), 1964–65; BM 28 Comwel Inf. Bde, Malaysia, 1965–68; CO 1 Bn Depot (NZ), 1969; CO 1 RNZIR (Singapore), 1969–71; GSO1 Field Force Comd (NZ), 1972–73; C of S Field Force Comd (NZ), 1973–74; Col SD, Army GS, 1974–75; Comd Field Force, 1977–79; ACDS (Ops/Plans), 1979–81; DCGS 1981; CGS, 1981–84. Hon. Col 1 RNZIR, 1986–88; Col, RNZIR, 1988–90. Chm., Bell Helicopter (BH) Pacific, 1988–90. Vice-Chm., 1985–86, Chm., 1986–88, Operation Raleigh, NZ; Chief Executive: Order of St John (NZ), 1986–87; Auckland Div., Cancer Soc. of NZ,

1988–93. *Recreations:* golf, swimming, walking. *Address:* Apt 1A, 463 Remuera Road, Remuera, Auckland 1050, New Zealand. *T:* (9) 5201547. *Clubs:* Northern (Auckland); Royal Auckland Golf (Middlemore, NZ).

WILLIAMS, Roderick Gregory Coleman; baritone, since 1992; *b* Barnet, Herts, 19 Nov. 1965; *s* of Adrian John and Norma-Rose Alesia Williams; *m* 1988, Miranda Jane Clasen; one *s* two *d*. *Educ:* Haberdashers' Aske's Sch., Elstree; Magdalen Coll., Oxford (BA); Inst. of Educn, Univ. of London (PGCE); Guildhall Sch. of Music and Drama. Hd, Choral Studies, Tiffin Boys' Sch., 1989–92. Has sung concert repertoire with BBC Orchestras and ensembles, incl. Royal Scottish Nat. Orch., Philharmonia, London Sinfonietta, Manchester Camerata, Royal Liverpool Philharmonic Orch., Hallé Orch., Britten Sinfonia, Bournemouth SO, Scottish Chamber Orch., Deutsches Symphonie-Orch. Berlin, Russian Nat. Orch., Orch. Philharmonique de Radio France, Ensemble Orchestral de Paris, Acad. Ancient Music, The Sixteen, Le Concert Spirituel, Rias Kammerchor, Bach Collegium Japan. Composer of works performed at Wigmore Hall, Barbican Hall, Purcell Room, including: O Adonai, 1998; Soundbites, 2000; Jazz Choral Evensong, 2006; O Brother Man - A New England Symphony, 2015. Artistic Dir, Leeds Lieder, 2016. *Recreations:* walking, composing. *Address:* c/o Ingpen & Williams Ltd, 7 St George's Court, 131 Putney Bridge Road, SW15 2PA. *T:* (020) 8874 3222.

WILLIAMS, Sir Rodney (Errey Lawrence), GCMG 2014; KGN 2014; Governor-General of Antigua and Barbuda, since 2014; *b* Antigua and Barbuda, 2 Nov. 1947; *s* of Hon. Ernest Emanuel Williams and Irene B. Williams; *m* 2005, Sandra; three *s*. *Educ:* Antigua Grammar Sch.; Univ. of W Indies (Jamaica) (MB BS 1976); RAF Inst. of Aviation Medicine (Cert. Aviation Medicine 1978); Cert. Sports Medicine. Intern, Queen Elizabeth Hosp., Barbados, 1976–78; in private med. practice, Antigua and Barbuda, 1978–84. MP Antigua and Barbuda, 1984; Dep. Speaker, House of Reps, 1984–86; Minister: of Econ. Develt, Industry and Tourism, 1986–89; of Educn, Sports, Youth and Community Develt, 1989–94; of Tourism, Culture and Envmt, 1994–99; of Educn, Culture and Technol., 1999–2004. Member: Sports Medicine Assoc.; Airline Med. Dirs' Assoc.; Civil Aviation Med. Assoc. (Mem., Bd of Trustees, 2006–; Mem., Exec. Bd, 2010–); Amer. Aerospace Assoc. (Exec. Fellow, 2011). FRSocMed 1986; Fellow, US Civil Aviation Med. Assoc., 2007. KStJ 2014; Kt Grand Cross, Royal Order of Francis I, 2014. *Recreation:* tennis. *Address:* Government House, Independence Drive, St John's, Antigua, West Indies. *T:* 4620002/3/4. *E:* govgenab@gmail.com.

WILLIAMS, Prof. Sir Roger, Kt 2006; Vice-Chancellor of The University of Reading, 1993–2002; Chairman, Higher Education Funding Council for Wales, 2002–08 (Member, 1995–2008; Acting Chairman, 2000–02); *b* 21 March 1942; *s* of late M. O. Williams, MBE and W. Williams; *m* 1967, Rae Kirkbright; two *d*. *Educ:* Tredegar Grammar Sch.; Worcester Coll., Oxford (BA Nat. Scis (Physics), MA; Hon. Fellow, 1999); Univ. of Manchester (MA). Operational Res. Br., Nat. Coal Bd, 1963–64; Department of Government, University of Manchester: Res. Student, 1964–66; Asst Lectr, Lectr, Sen. Lectr, 1966–78; Prof. of Govt and Sci. Policy, 1979–93; Founding Dir, Policy Res. in Engrg, Sci. and Technol., 1979–93; Hd of Dept, 1984–88; Dean of Economic and Social Studies, 1989–92. NATO Envmtl Fellowship, 1977–79; Aust. Univs Fellowship, 1984; Vis. Prof., Univ. of Montreal, 1981. Sci. Advr, Sci. Council of Canada (on secondment), 1974–75; Advr, OECD, 1980–81; Specialist Advr, H of L Select Cttees on Sci. and Technology, 1986–92, on European Communities, 1990; Member: Adv. Bd, Sci. Policy Res. Unit, 1987–97; Cabinet Office Wkg Gp on internat. collaboration in sci. and technol., 1989–91. Chm., Jt SERC-ESRC Cttee, 1991–93; Member: ESRC, EPSRC and NERC Cttees; Quality Assurance Agency for Higher Educn, 1997–2002. Mem. Editl Bd, Government and Opposition, 1994–. Associate, Technical Change Centre, 1981–85. British Council Delegn to China, 1985. FLSW 2011. Hon. Fellow, Cardiff Univ., 2008. Hon. DCL Reading, 2002; Hon. DSc Glamorgan, 2008. *Publications:* Politics and Technology, 1972; European Technology, 1973; The Nuclear Power Decisions, 1980; Public Acceptability of New Technology, 1986; contrib. to approx. 22 books and more than 20 acad. articles. *Club:* Athenæum.

WILLIAMS, Roger Hugh, CBE 2013; farmer, since 1969; *b* 22 Jan. 1948; *s* of Morgan Glyn Williams and Eirlys Williams; *m* 1973, Penelope James; one *s* one *d*. *Educ:* Llanfilo Co. Primary Sch.; Christ Coll., Brecon; Selwyn Coll., Cambridge (BA). Mem. (Lib Dem) Powys CC, 1981–2001. MP (Lib Dem) Brecon Radnorshire, 2001–15; contested (Lib Dem) same seat, 2015. Dir, Develt Bd for Rural Wales, 1989–97. Chm., Brecon Beacons Nat. Park, 1991–96. *Recreations:* sport, walking. *Address:* Tredomen Court, Llanfilo, Brecon, Powys LD3 0RL.

WILLIAMS, Prof. Roger Stanley, CBE 1993; MD; FRCP, FRCS, FMedSci; Professor of Hepatology, University of London, 1994–2010; Director, Institute of Hepatology, Foundation for Liver Research, since 1996; *b* 28 Aug. 1931; *s* of Stanley George Williams and Doris Dagmar Clatworthy; *m* 1st, 1954, Lindsay Mary Elliott (marr. diss. 1977); two *s* three *d*; 2nd, 1978, Stephanie Gay de Laszlo; one *s* two *d*. *Educ:* St Mary's Coll., Southampton; London Hosp. Med. Coll., Univ. of London. MB, BS (Hons), MD; LRCP, MRCP, FRCP 1966; MRCS, FRCS 1988; FRCPE 1990; FRACP 1991. House appointments and Pathology Asst, London Hospital, 1953–56; Jun. Med. Specialist, Queen Alexandra Hospital, Millbank, 1956–58; Medical Registrar and Tutor, Royal Postgrad. Med. Sch., 1958–59; Lectr in Medicine, Royal Free Hospital, 1959–65; Consultant Physician, Royal South Hants and Southampton General Hospital, 1965–66; Consultant Physician, KCH, 1966–96; Dir, Liver Res. Unit, then Inst. of Liver Studies, KCH and Med. Sch., then King's Coll. Sch. of Medicine and Dentistry, 1966–96; Hon. Consultant Physician, UC Hosps NHS Trust, 1996–2011. Hon. Consultant: Foundn for Liver Res., 1974–; in medicine to the Army, 1988–. Member: Clinical Standards Adv. Gp, 1994–; Adv. Gp on Hepatitis, DHSS, 1980–; Transplant Adv. Panel, DHSS, 1974–83; WHO Scientific Gp on Viral Hepatitis, Geneva, 1972. Rockefeller Travelling Fellowship in Medicine, 1962; Legg Award, Royal Free Hosp. Med. Sch., 1964; Sir Ernest Finch Vis. Prof., Sheffield, 1974; Hans Sloane Fellow, RCP, 2004–; Hon. Prof., Birkbeck, Univ. of London, 2011–. Lectures: Melrose Meml, Glasgow, 1970; Goulstonian, RCP, 1970; Searle, Amer. Assoc. for the Study of Liver Diseases, 1972; Fleming, Glasgow Coll. of Physicians and Surgeons, 1975; Sir Arthur Hurst Meml, British Soc. of Gastroenterology, 1975; Skinner, Royal Coll. of Radiologists, 1978; Albert M. Snell Meml, Palo Alto Med. Foundn, 1981; Milford Rouse, Baylor Med. Center, Dallas, 1989; Norman Tanner Meml, St George's Hosp., 1992; Searle Special, St Bartholomew's Hosp., 1992; Datta Meml Oration, India, 1984; Quadrennial Review, World Congress of Gastroenterol., Sydney, 1990; Sir Jules Thorn, RCP, 1994. Vice-Pres., RCP, 1991–93; President: Internat. Med. Club, 1989–99; British Liver Trust, 2002–; Member: European Assoc. for the Study of the Liver, 1966– (Cttee Mem., 1966–70; Pres., 1983; Hon. Pres., 2008); Harveian Soc. of London (Sec., Councillor and Vice-Pres., 1963–70, Pres., 1974–75); British Assoc. for Study of Liver (formerly Liver Club) (Sec. and Treasurer, 1968–71; Pres., 1984–86); Royal Soc. of Medicine (Sec. of Section, 1969–71); British Soc. of Gastroenterology (Pres., 1989). Chm., Cons. Health, 2012–. FKC 1992; FMedSci 1999. Hon. FACP 1992; Hon. FRCPI 2001. Hon. Fellow, UCL, 2008. Gold Medal, Canadian Liver Foundn, 1992; Lifetime Achievement Award, British Assoc. for the Study of the Liver, 2003; Wyeth Senior Achievement Award for Clinical Transplantation, Amer. Soc. of Transplantation, 2004; Hans Popper Life Achievement Award, Internat. Liver Congress, Hong Kong, 2008; Distinguished Service Award, Internat. Liver Transplantation Soc., 2011; Distinguished Achievement Award, Amer. Assoc. for Study of Liver Disease, 2013. *Publications:* (ed) Fifth Symposium on Advanced Medicine, 1969; edited jointly: Immunology of the Liver, 1971; Artificial Liver Support, 1975; Immune Reactions in Liver Disease, 1978; Drug Reactions and the Liver, 1981; Variceal Bleeding, 1982; Antiviral Agents in Chronic Hepatitis B Virus Infection, 1985; The Practice of Liver Transplantation, 1995; International Developments in Health Care, 1995; Acute Liver Failure, 1996; Fulminant Hepatic Failure: seminars in liver disease, 2003; Clinical Dilemmas in Primary Liver Cancer, 2011; author of over 2000 scientific papers, review articles and book chapters. *Recreations:* tennis, sailing, opera. *Address:* Brickworth House, Whiteparish, Wilts SP5 2QE; 30 Devonshire Close, W1G 7BE; Institute of Hepatology, Foundation for Liver Research, 69–75 Chenies Mews, WC1E 6HX. *Clubs:* Athenæum, Saints and Sinners, Royal Ocean Racing; Royal Yacht Squadron (Cowes).

WILLIAMS, Ronald; *see* Williams, A. R.

WILLIAMS, Rt Rev. Ronald John Chantler; Bishop of the Southern Region, and an Assistant Bishop, Diocese of Brisbane, 1993–2007; *b* 19 July 1938; *s* of Walter Chantler Williams and Constance Bertha Williams (*née* Pool); *m* 1963, Kathryn Rohrsheim; two *s* one *d*. *Educ:* Prince Alfred Coll., Adelaide; St John's Coll., Morpeth (ThL); St Mark's Coll., Adelaide Univ. (BA); Bristol Univ. (MSc 1974); Australian Management Coll., Mt Eliza (AMP). Ordained deacon, 1963, priest, 1964; Curate, Toorak Gardens, 1963–64; Australian Bd of Missions, Sydney, 1965; Domestic Chaplain, Bishop of Polynesia, 1966–67; Priest, Labasa, Fiji, 1967–71; Hon. Priest, Bedminster, Bristol, 1972–74; Dean of Suva, Fiji, 1974–79; Rector, Campbelltown, Adelaide, 1979–84; Priest to City of Adelaide and founding Dir, St Paul's Centre, 1984–93; Hon. Canon, St Peter's Cathedral, Adelaide, 1986–93. *Recreation:* jazz musician—double bass. *Address:* 42 Princess Street, Bulimba, Qld 4171, Australia. *T:* (7) 33999818. *E:* rk.will@bigpond.com.

WILLIAMS, Ronald Millward, CBE 1990; DL; Member, Essex County Council, 1970–93 and 1997–2005 (Chairman, 1983–86); *b* 9 Dec. 1922; *s* of George and Gladys Williams; *m* 1943, Joyce; one *s* two *d*. *Educ:* Leeds College of Technology. Electrical Engineer, then Industrial Eng Superintendent, Mobil Oil Co. Ltd, 1954–82. Member: Benfleet Urban Dist Council, 1960–74 (Chm. 1963–66, 1972–74); Castle Point Dist Council, 1974–87 (Chm. 1980–81; Leader, 1981–87); Essex County Council: Leader Cons. Gp, 1977–83, 1986–87; Chairman: County Planning Cttee, 1981–83; County Highways Cttee, 1989–93; Envmtl Services Bd, 1998–2000; Exec. Mem., with strategic planning and transportation portfolio, 2000–01; Cabinet Mem., Highways and Transportation, 2001–03; Hon. Alderman, 2005. Chm., Southend Health Authority, 1982–90, Southend Health Care Services, NHS Trust, 1990–96. Chm., SE Essex Abbeyfield Soc., 1983–88. DL Essex, 1983. Hon. Freeman, Borough of Castle Point, 2006. *Recreations:* supporter, football, cricket, bowls, tennis; video filming of countryside.

WILLIAMS, Roy, CB 1989; Deputy Secretary, Department of Trade and Industry, 1984–94; *b* 31 Dec. 1934; *s* of Eric Williams and Ellen Williams; *m* 1959, Shirley, *d* of Captain and Mrs O. Warwick; one *s* one *d*. *Educ:* Liverpool Univ. (1st Cl. BA Econs). Asst Principal, Min. of Power, 1956; Principal, 1961; Harkness Commonwealth Fellow, Univs of Chicago and Berkeley, 1963–64; Principal Private Sec., Minister of Power and subseq. Paymaster Gen., 1969; Asst Sec., DTI, 1971; Principal Private Sec., Sec. of State for Industry, 1974; Under-Sec., DoI, later DTI, 1976–84. Dir, EIB, 1991–94. Chm., EU High Level Gp on Eureka prog., 1995–96; Mem., Design Council, 1995–2001. Chm. Trustees, Nat. Centre for Young People with Epilepsy, St Pier's, Lingfield, 1995–2009; Trustee, Victorian Soc., 2005–. *Address:* Darl Oast, The Street, Ightham, Sevenoaks, Kent TN15 9HH. *T:* (01732) 883944.

WILLIAMS, Rev. Samuel Lewis; Minister, St Columba's United Reformed Church, Gosport, 1991–96; *b* 8 Jan. 1934; *s* of Thomas John Williams and Miriam Mary Williams (*née* West); *m* 1958, Mary Sansom (*née* Benjamin); one *s* one *d*. *Educ:* Pagefield College Public Day School, Newport, Gwent; Memorial Coll. (Congregational), Brecon. Local government officer, 1950–52; RAF, 1952–55; theol. training, 1955–58. Ordained Congregational (URC) Minister, 1958; Mill Street Congregational Church, Newport, Gwent, 1958–63; Bettws Congregational Church, 1963–68; Llanvaches Congregational Church, 1966–68; Free Churches Chaplain, St Woolas Hosp., Newport, 1964–68. Entered RN as Chaplain, 1968; served HMS: Seahawk, 1968–69; Hermes, 1969–70; Raleigh, 1970–71; Seahawk, 1971–73; Daedalus, 1973–74; served Malta, 1974–76; C-in-C Naval Home Comd staff, 1977–81; HMS Sultan, 1981–84; Flag Officer Scotland and NI staff, 1984–86; HMS Heron, 1986; Prin. Chaplain (Navy), Ch of Scotland and Free Churches, 1986–91; RN retired, 1991. QHC, 1986–91. *Recreations:* oil painting, golf, hill walking, music, gardening, Rugby. *Address:* 18 Brodrick Avenue, Gosport, Hants PO12 2EN. *T:* (023) 9258 1114.

WILLIAMS, Sara Ann, (Sally); *see* Muggeridge, S. A.

WILLIAMS, Sarah Rosalind; *see* Palmer, S. R.

WILLIAMS, Sean Mountford Graham; Group Director, Strategy, Policy and Portfolio, BT Group plc, since 2011 (Managing Director, Strategy, Portfolio, Legal and Regulatory Services, 2008–11); *b* London, 1 June 1963; *s* of Tony Williams and Sheelagh Williams; *m*; three *s* one *d*. *Educ:* Charterhouse; Worcester Coll., Oxford (BA 1986); Kennedy Sch. of Govt, Harvard Univ. (MPA 1990). Man. Dir, Williams Lea & Co., 1990–92; Gp Finance Dir, Williams Lea Gp, 1993–95; Special Advr, Prime Minister's Policy Unit, 1995–97; Partner, LEK Consulting LLP, 1997–2003; Exec. Dir, OFCOM, 2003–07; Exec. Dir, Markets and Projects, OFT, 2007–08. Non-exec. Dir, Williams Lea Hldgs plc, 1995–2008. Trustee, Gaia Hse Trust, 2010–. *Recreations:* cycling, meditation, singing, family. *Address:* 6 Coates Castle, Fittleworth, W Sussex RH20 1EU. *T:* (01798) 865164; 62 Warwick Square, SW1V 2AL. *E:* smgwilliams@btinternet.com.

WILLIAMS, Serena Jameka; tennis player; *b* Mich, USA, 26 Sept. 1981; *d* of Richard and Oracene Williams. *Educ:* Fort Lauderdale Art Inst. (degree in fashion design). Professional tennis player, 1995–: Grand Slam wins: (singles): US Open, 1999, 2002, 2008, 2012, 2013, 2014; French Open, 2002, 2013, 2015; Wimbledon, 2002, 2003, 2009, 2010, 2012, 2015; Australian Open, 2003, 2005, 2007, 2009, 2010, 2015; (doubles, with Venus Williams): French Open, 1999; US Open, 1999, 2012, 2013; Wimbledon, 2000, 2002, 2008, 2009, 2012; Australian Open, 2001, 2003, 2010; (mixed doubles, with Max Mirnyi) Wimbledon, US Open, 1998. Winner, Women's Tennis Assoc. Championships, 2001, 2009, 2012, 2013, 2014. Member: US Fedn Cup Team, 1999, 2003, 2007, 2012, 2013; US Olympic Team, Sydney, 2000 (Gold Medallist, doubles, with Venus Williams), Beijing, 2008 (Gold Medallist, doubles, with Venus Williams); London, 2012 (Gold Medallist singles and doubles, with Venus Williams); ranked world No 1, 2002, 2009, 2013, 2014. Player of the Year, Women's Tennis Assoc., 2002, 2008, 2009, 2012, 2013. Founder and designer, fashion label, Aneres, 2004–; launched Serena Williams Collection by Nike, apparel and footwear collection, 2005; numerous appearances as actress on TV progs. *Publications:* (with Venus Williams and Hilary Beard) Venus & Serena - Serving from the Hip: 10 rules for living, loving and winning, 2005; Queen of the Court (autobiog.), 2009. *Address:* c/o William Morris Endeavor Entertainment, 9601 Wilshire Boulevard, Beverly Hills, CA 90210, USA; c/o US Tennis Association, 70 West Red Oak Lane, White Plains, NY 10604, USA.

See also V. E. S. Williams.

WILLIAMS, Sian Mary; journalist and broadcaster; BBC1 News presenter, since 1999; BBC Events commentator, since 2013; Presenter, BBC1 Sunday Morning Live, since 2014; *b* London, 28 Nov. 1964; *d* of John Price Williams and late Katherine Elizabeth Rees; *m* Paul Woolwich; one *s* one *d*; two *s* from previous marriage. *Educ:* Oxford Brookes Univ. (BA Hons English and History); Univ. of Westminster (MSc Psychol. (Dist.)). BBC Radio trng scheme,

1987–88; reporter, BBC Radio Merseyside, 1988–90; Sen. Producer, BBC Radio 4 World at One/PM, 1990–97; Editor, 1997, Sen. Presenter, 1997–99, BBC News 24; Special Corresp., BBC 6 O'Clock News, 1999–2001; Presenter, 2001–05, Main Presenter, 2005–12, BBC1 Breakfast; Co-host, Saturday Live, BBC Radio 4, 2012–13; occasional presenter, BBC1 and BBC Radio 4 progs. Pres., Television and Radio Industries Club, 2007–08, 2009–10. Patron: Sparks; Hearing Link. *Recreations:* cinema, wine, walking. *Address:* c/o Sue Ayton, Knight Ayton Management, 35 Great James Street, WC1N 3HB. *T:* (020) 7831 4400. *E:* info@knightayton.co.uk.

WILLIAMS, Rear Adm. Simon Paul, CVO 2015; Naval Secretary and Flag Officer Reserves, since 2015; *b* Bristol, 13 July 1960; *s* of Philip Williams and June Williams; *m* 1986, Charlotte Jane Anderson; one *s* one *d*. *Educ:* Salisbury Cathedral Sch.; Kingsbridge Sch.; City Univ. (BSc (Hons) Systems and Mgt). PWO(CEW) 1990. Gunnery Officer, HMS Pollington, 1983–85; Navigating Officer, HMS Minerva, 1986–87; Exec. Officer, HMS Orkney, 1987–89; Principal Warfare Officer, HMS Sheffield, 1990–92; Amphibious Warfare Staff, 1992–94; Sea Trng Staff, 1995–96; CO HMS Brecon, 1997; Navy Plans, 1997–99; Equipment Plans, 1999–2000; CO HMS Sheffield, 2001–02; Asst Dir Strategy Naval Staff, 2002–04; CO HMS Cornwall, 2005–06; Dep. Dir Operational Capability, 2006–08; Dir Naval Personnel Strategy, 2008–11; Cdre Naval Core Trng and CO, BRNC, 2011–12; Defence Services Sec. and ACDS (Personnel and Trng), 2012–15. CCMI 2012. *Recreations:* amateur artisan dabbling in cars, decrepit houses and sundry equipments, driving cars and boats, experimenting in canal transits, cycling, camping. *Address:* Navy Command Headquarters MP3.1, Whale Island, Portsmouth PO2 8BY. *E:* simon.williams286@mod.uk. *Club:* Royal Navy of 1765 and 1785.

WILLIAMS, Rear Adm. Simon Thomas, OBE 2004; Chairman, Clarion Defence and Security Ltd, since 2012; Director, RedDrig Ltd, since 2012; *b* Swansea, 22 March 1957; *s* of Derek and Catherine Williams; *m* 1984, Catherine White; two *s* one *d*. *Educ:* Reigate Grammar Sch.; City Univ., London (BSc Hons); King's Coll. London (MA). Joined RN, 1976; HM Submarines, 1981–88; Submarine Command Course, 1988; XO, HMS Turbulent, 1988–90; on exchange in USA, 1990–92; Commanding Officer: HMS Superb, 1992–94; Submarine Command Course, 1994–96; Staff, Flag Officer Submarines, 1996–98; Desk Officer, Navy Plans, MoD, 1998–2000; Asst Dir (ME), MoD, 2000–03; DACOS Fleet (Ops), 2003–05; UK Maritime Component Comdr, Bahrain, 2005–06; Dir, Strategic Plans, MoD, 2006–09; Sen. Directing Staff (Navy), RCDS, 2009–11. Non-executive Director: 3CN Ltd, 2012–; Corp. Governance Gp, Welsh Govt, 2012–. *Recreations:* reading, walking.

WILLIAMS, Stephen Geoffrey; Chief Legal Officer and Group Secretary, Unilever plc and Unilever NV, 1986–2010; *b* Ilford, 31 Jan. 1948; *s* of Alfred Earnest Williams and Edith Betty Williams (*née* Harding); *m* 1972, Susan Jennifer Cottam; one *s*. *Educ:* Brentwood Sch., Essex; King's Coll., London (LLB Hons). Admitted as solicitor, 1972; solicitor, Slaughter and May, 1970–75; Attorney, ICI, 1975–86. Director: Bunzl plc, 1995–2004; Arriva plc, 2004–10; Whitbread plc, 2009–; Croda International PLC, 2010–; Eversheds LLP, 2011–. Sen. Advr, Spencer Stuart LLP, 2011–. Mem., Companies Cttee, CBI, 1998–. Chm., De La Warr Pavilion, 2008–. Member, Board: Leverhulme Trust, 2011–; Moorfields Hosp. Trust, 2012–. FRSA. *Recreations:* contemporary fiction, vulgar automobiles, modern art and architecture. *Address:* 15 Queens Gate Gardens, SW7 5LY. *E:* stevewilliams247@gmail.com. *Clubs:* Royal Automobile, 2 Brydges Place.

WILLIAMS, Stephen Michael; Director of European Affairs, Channel Islands Brussels Office, since 2011; *b* 20 July 1959; *s* of Very Rev. H. C. N. Williams and of Pamela Williams; *m* 1983, Fiona Michele Hume; one *s* two *d*. *Educ:* Sidney Sussex Coll., Cambridge (BA 1980, MA). Entered Foreign and Commonwealth Office, 1981; Third, later Second, Sec., Sofia, 1984–87; EU Dept (Ext.), FCO, 1987–90; on secondment to Barclays Bank, 1990–91; Hd, Econ. and Commercial Sect., Oslo, 1991–95; First Sec. (Ext. Relns), UK Perm. Repn to EU, Brussels, 1995–98; Dep. Hd, EU Dept (Int.), FCO, 1998–2000; Minister and Dep. Hd of Mission, Buenos Aires, 2001–03; Hd, Latin America & Caribbean Dept, FCO, 2003–05; Dir, Americas, FCO, 2005–07; Ambassador to Bulgaria, 2007–11. *Recreations:* walking, sport, music. *Address:* Channel Islands Brussels Office, Rond Point Schuman 6/8, 1040 Brussels, Belgium. *T:* (2) 26391440. *E:* info@channelislands.eu.

WILLIAMS, Stephen Roy; *b* 11 Oct. 1966. *Educ:* Mountain Ash Comprehensive Sch., Glamorgan; Univ. of Bristol (BA 1988). Coopers and Lybrand, Bristol, 1988–95; Tax Manager: Kraft Jacobs Suchard Ltd, 1995; Grant Thornton, Cheltenham, 1996–98, Bristol, 1998–2001; Tax Accountant for Orange plc, Wincanton plc and RAC plc, 2001–05. Member (Lib Dem): Avon CC, 1993–96; Bristol CC, 1995–99. Contested (Lib Dem): Bristol S, 1997; Bristol W, 2001. MP (Lib Dem) Bristol W, 2005–15. Shadow Minister: for Public Health, 2005–06; for Further and Higher Education, 2006–07; for Schools, 2007; Shadow Sec. of State for Innovation, Univs and Skills, 2007–10; Parly Under-Sec. of State, DCLG, 2013–15. Member: Educn Select Cttee, 2005–07; Public Accounts Cttee, 2005–06; Children, Schs and Families Select Cttee, 2007–08; Political and Constitutional Reform Select Cttee, 2010–13; Chair: All Party Parly Gp on Smoking and Health, 2010–13; Lib Dem Backbench Treasury Cttee, 2010–13.

WILLIAMS, Stuart John; Regional Employment Judge, Wales, 2009–15; *b* Caerleon, 8 April 1949; *s* of Arthur Williams and Ann Williams; *m* 1980, Lindsey Keatley; one *s* one *d*. *Educ:* Jones' West Monmouth Sch., Pontypool; Magdalen Coll., Oxford (BA Hons Mod. Langs); Sch. of Oriental and African Studies, Univ. of London (MA African Studies). VSO, 1970–72; Lector, British Council, Slovakia, 1972–73; Technical Translator, 1975–81; called to the Bar, Gray's Inn, 1981; pt-time Chm., Employment Tribunals, 1992–95; full-time Chm., Employment Tribunals, later Employment Judge, 1995–2009. *Recreations:* Rugby (passive only), cricket (still slightly active), singing (active and passive), gardening.

WILLIAMS, Susan Elizabeth, OBE 2000; Director of Nursing, Lanarkshire Primary Care NHS Trust, 2001–03; *b* 30 Oct. 1942; *d* of late Ernest George Fost and of Kathleen Beatrice Maud Fost; *m* 1st, 1964, Dennis Norman Carnevale (decd); one *s* one *d*; 2nd, 1977, Keith Edward Williams (marr. diss. 1996). *Educ:* Grammar School for Girls, Weston-super-Mare; Wolverhampton Polytechnic (Post-grad. DipPsych); Bristol Royal Hosps (RSCN, RGN, RNT); BEd (Hons), DipN London. Ward Sister, Royal Hosp. for Sick Children, Bristol, 1972–76; Nurse Tutor, Salop Area Sch. of Nursing, 1976–80; Sen. Tutor, Dudley AHA, 1980–83; Reg. Nurse (Educn and Res.), W Midlands RHA, 1983–87; Chief Nurse Advr/Dir of Nurse Educn, Bromsgrove and Redditch HA, 1987–88; Regl Dir of Nursing and Quality Assurance, W Midlands RHA, 1988–93; Dep. Dir of Nursing Management Exec., DoH, 1993–94; Dir of Nursing, Greater Glasgow Community and Mental Health NHS Trust, 1994–98; Nurse Advr to Greater Glasgow Health Bd, 1998–2001. Board Member: Erskine Hospital, 2001; Prince and Princess of Wales Hospice, 2003–05. *Recreations:* hill walking, photography, reading, listening to music, foreign travel.

WILLIAMS, Susan Frances; a District Judge, Magistrates' Courts, West London, since 2002; a Recorder, since 2006; *b* 27 Nov. 1955; *d* of Major John Trelawny Williams and Joyce Williams. *Educ:* Kent Coll.; Bristol Univ. (LLB Hons). Called to the Bar, Middle Temple, 1978; barrister in private practice specialising in criminal law, 1978–2002. Mem., Criminal Bar Assoc., 1987–2002. Member: Hall Cttee, Middle Temple, 1984–94; N London Bar Mess, 1994–2002 (Jun. for Wood Green Crown Court). *Recreations:* gardening (Mem., RHS), malt whisky tasting (Mem., Scotch Malt Whisky Soc.). *Address:* Hammersmith Magistrates' Court, 181 Talgarth Road, W6 8DN. *T:* (020) 8700 9303.

WILLIAMS, Rt Rev. Thomas Anthony; Auxiliary Bishop of Liverpool, (RC), Vicar General, and Titular Bishop of Mageo, since 2003; Apostolic Administrator, Archdiocese of Liverpool, 2013–14; *b* Liverpool, 10 Feb. 1948; *s* of late Richard and Margaret Williams. *Educ:* Christleton Hall, Chester; English Coll., Lisbon; St Joseph's Coll., Upholland. Ordained priest, 1972; Curate: St Francis of Assisi, Garston, 1972–75; Sacred Heart, Liverpool, 1975–83 (Chaplain to Royal Liverpool Hosp.); Our Lady of Walsingham, Netherton, 1983–84; Parish Priest, Liverpool: Our Lady Immaculate, 1984–89 and 1999–2003; St Anthony's, 1989–2003. Mem., Catholic Bishops' Conf. of England and Wales, 2003– (Bishop responsible for Hosp. Chaplaincy, 2003–). Member: Archdiocesan Finance Adv. Cttee, 1977–2013; George Andrew Fund Cttee, 1994–; Liverpool City Centre Ecumenical Team, 1996–; Trustee: Archdiocese of Liverpool, 2003–; Nugent Care Soc., 2003–. Mem., Archdiocese of Liverpool Chapter of Canons, 2001. KC*HS 2008. *Recreations:* music, golf. *Address:* (office) 14 Hope Place, Liverpool L1 9BG.

WILLIAMS, His Eminence Cardinal Thomas Stafford, ONZ 2000; DD; Archbishop of Wellington, (RC), and Metropolitan of New Zealand, 1979–2005, now Emeritus Archbishop; *b* 20 March 1930; *s* of Thomas Stafford Williams and Lillian Maude Kelly. *Educ:* Holy Cross Primary School, Miramar; SS Peter and Paul Primary School, Lower Hutt; St Patrick's Coll., Wellington; Victoria University Coll., Wellington; St Kevin's Coll., Oamaru; Holy Cross Coll., Mosgiel; Collegio Urbano de Propaganda Fide, Rome (STL); University Coll., Dublin (BSocSc); Hon. DD. Assistant Priest, St Patrick's Parish, Palmerston North, 1963–64; Director of Studies, Catholic Enquiry Centre, Wellington, 1965–70; Parish Priest: St Anne's Parish, Leulumoega, W Samoa, 1971–75; Holy Family Parish, Porirua, NZ, 1976–79. Cardinal, 1983. *Address:* 40 Walton Avenue, Waikanae 5036, New Zealand. *T:* (4) 2934684.

WILLIAMS, Prof. Timothy John, PhD; FMedSci; FRS 2012; Asthma UK Professor of Applied Pharmacology and Head of Leukocyte Biology Section, National Heart and Lung Institute, Faculty of Medicine, Imperial College London, 1988–2010, now Professor Emeritus; *b* Gloucester, 31 March 1945; *s* of Francis Edward and Joyce Edith Williams; *m* 1st, 1968, Susan Jean Condie (marr. diss. 1983); one *s* one *d*; 2nd, 1988, Helen Mary Carey; two *d*. *Educ:* Sir Thomas Rich's Grammar Sch., Gloucester; University Coll. London (BSc Hons Physiol. 1968); Kennedy Inst. of Rheumatol. and University Coll. London (PhD Pharmacol. 1978). Lectr, Dept of Pharmacol., Inst. of Basic Med. Scis, RCS, 1979–84; MRC Sen. Career Scientist, Clin. Res. Centre, Northwick Park, Harrow, 1984–88; Jt Dir, KCL/Imperial Coll. London MRC and Asthma UK Centre in Allergic Mechanisms of Asthma, 2005–10; Campus Dean, Faculty of Medicine, S Kensington Campus, Imperial Coll. London, 2006–10. Exec. Dir and Hd of Asthma and Allergy, Novartis Insts for BioMed. Res., Horsham, 2010–11. For. Mem., Brazilian Acad. of Scis, 2007. FMedSci 2000. Pfizer Academic Prize, 1984; Gaddum Meml Prize, British Pharmacol Soc., 2000; Jack Pepys Lectureship Award, British Soc. for Allergy and Clin. Immunol., 2003; Ulf von Euler Meml Lectureship Award, Karolinska Inst., Stockholm, 2010; Derek Willoughby Lectureship Award, William Harvey Inst., 2011; Paul Ehrlich Lectureship Award, Internat. Eosinophil Soc., Quebec City, 2011. *Publications:* contrib. chapters in books and 255 peer-reviewed papers, editorials and articles in scientific press; patents covering discovery of Eotaxin molecule. *Recreations:* photography, collecting optical instruments. *Address:* National Heart and Lung Institute, Faculty of Medicine, Sir Alexander Fleming Building, Imperial College London, S Kensington, SW7 2AZ. *T:* (020) 7594 3159, *Fax:* (020) 7594 3119. *E:* tim.williams@imperial.ac.uk.

WILLIAMS, Trevor; *see* Williams, A. T.

WILLIAMS, Rt Rev. Trevor Russell; Bishop of Limerick and Killaloe, 2008–14; Chairman, Christian Aid Ireland, since 2010; *b* Dublin, 29 June 1948; *s* of James Williams and Ada Clare Williams; *m* 1972, Joyce Milne; three *s*. *Educ:* Trinity Coll. Dublin (BA Natural Scis 1971); St John's Theol Coll., Nottingham (BA Theol. 1973; Dip. in Pastoral Theol. 1974). Ordained deacon, 1974, priest, 1975; Curate, St Mary's, Maidenhead, 1974–77; Asst Chaplain, QUB, 1977–80; Religious Broadcasting Producer, BBC Ulster, 1980–88; Rector, St John's Parish, Newcastle, Dio. of Down and Dromore, 1988–93; Leader, Corrymeela Community, 1993–2003; Rector, Holy Trinity and St Silas Joanmount with Immanuel Ardoyne, Dio. of Connor, 2003–08. Canon, St Patrick's Cathedral, Dublin, 2001–08. *Recreations:* sailing, computing, music. *Address:* 50 Murlough View, Dundrum, Co. Down BT33 0WE. *T:* (028) 4375 1838. *E:* bishoptrevor.williams@gmail.com.

WILLIAMS, Venetia Mary; racehorse trainer, since 1996; *b* 10 May 1960; *d* of late John Williams and Patricia Williams. *Educ:* Downe House Sch., Newbury. Trained winners of: King George VI Gold Cup, Kempton Park; Hennessy Gold Cup, Newbury; Welsh Grand Nat., Chepstow (twice); Scottish Champion Hurdle, Ayr; Grand Annual Chase, Cleeve Hurdle (3 times), Coral Cup, Racing Post Plate, Pertemps Final Hurdle and Festival Plate Chase (twice), Cheltenham; Ascot Chase; Grand National (Mon Mome, 2009). *Recreations:* ski-ing (snow and water), travel. *Address:* Aramstone, Kings Caple, Hereford HR1 4TU. *T:* (01432) 840646, 07770 627108. *E:* venetia.williams@virgin.net.

WILLIAMS, Venus Ebony Starr; tennis player; *b* Calif, USA, 17 June 1980; *d* of Richard and Oracene Williams. Professional tennis player, 1994–: Grand Slam wins: (singles): Wimbledon, 2000, 2001, 2005, 2007, 2008; US Open, 2000, 2001; (doubles, with Serena Williams): French Open, 1999; US Open, 1999; Wimbledon, 2000, 2002, 2008, 2009, 2012; Australian Open, 2001, 2003, 2010; (mixed doubles, with Justin Gimelstob) Australian Open, French Open, 1998. Member: US Fedn Cup Team, 1995, 1999, 2003; US Olympic Team, Sydney, 2000 (Gold Medallist, singles and doubles), Athens, 2004, Beijing, 2008 (Gold Medallist, doubles, with Serena Williams); London, 2012 (Gold Medallist, doubles, with Serena Williams); ranked world No 1, 2002. Pres. and CEO, V Starr Interiors, 2002–. *Publications:* (with Serena Williams and Hilary Beard) Venus & Serena - Serving from the Hip: 10 rules for living, loving and winning, 2005; Come to Win, 2010. *Address:* V Starr Interiors, 4191 Main Street, Jupiter, FL 33458, USA; c/o US Tennis Association, 70 West Red Oak Lane, White Plains, NY 10604, USA.

See also S. J. Williams.

WILLIAMS, Victoria Helen; *see* McCloud, V. H.

WILLIAMS, Victoria Kirstyn, (Kirsty), CBE 2013; Member (Lib Dem) Brecon and Radnorshire, since 1999, and Leader, Welsh Liberal Democrats, since 2008, National Assembly for Wales; *b* 19 March 1971; *d* of Edward G. Williams and Pamela M. Williams (*née* Hall); *m* 2000, Richard John Rees; three *d*. *Educ:* St Michael's Sch., Llanelli; Univ. of Manchester (BA Hons Amer. Studies 1993); Univ. of Missouri. Marketing and PR Exec., 1994–97. National Assembly for Wales: Chm., Health and Social Services Cttee, 1999–2003, Standards Cttee, 2003–08 (Mem., 2011–), Sustainability Cttee, 2010–11; Mem., Health and Social Services Cttee, 2003–05, 2011–, Local Govt and Public Services Cttee, 2003–04, Economic Develt and Transport Cttee, 2005–08, Proposed Learner Travel Measure and Learning and Skills Measure Cttees, 2008, Finance Cttee, 2008–. Lib Dem Business Manager, 2000–08. Dep. Pres., Welsh Liberal Democrats, 1997–99. *Recreations:* horse riding, sport, farming. *Address:* National Assembly for Wales, Crickhowell House, Cardiff CF99 1NA. *T:* 0300 200 7277.

WILLIAMS, Sir (William) Max (Harries), Kt 1983; solicitor; Senior Partner, Clifford Chance, 1989–91 (Joint Senior Partner, 1987–89); *b* 18 Feb. 1926; *s* of Llwyd and Hilary Williams; *m* 1951, Jenifer (*d* 1999), *d* of late Rt Hon. E. L. Burgin, LLD, and Mrs Burgin, JP; two *d*. *Educ:* Nautical Coll., Pangbourne. Served 178 Assault Field Regt RA, Far East

(Captain), 1943–47. Admitted Solicitor, 1950. Sen. Partner, Clifford Turner, 1984–87. Mem. Council, 1962–85, Pres., 1982–83, Law Society. Mem., Crown Agents for Oversea Govts and Administration, 1982–86; Lay Mem., Stock Exchange Council, 1984–93; Mem., Stock Exchange Appeals Cttee, 1989–2000. Director: Royal Insurance plc, 1985–95 (Dep. Chm., 1992–95); 3i Group plc, 1988–96 (Dep. Chm., 1993–96; Chm. Audit Cttee, 1991–96); Garden Pension Trustees Ltd, 1990–96; Royal Insurance Co. of Canada, 1991–95. Chairman: Review Bd for Govt Contracts, 1986–93; Police Appeals Tribunal, 1993–99. Member: Royal Commission on Legal Services, 1976–79; Cttee of Management of Inst. of Advanced Legal Studies, 1980–86; Council, Wildfowl Trust (Hon. Treasurer, 1974–80). Pres., City of London Law Soc., 1986–87. Mem., Amer. Law Inst., 1985–; Hon. Member: Amer. Bar Assoc.; Canadian Bar Assoc. Master, Solicitors' Co., 1986–87. Hon. LLD Birmingham, 1983. *Recreations:* golf, fishing, ornithology. *Address:* Orinda, Holly Lane, Harpenden, Herts AL5 5DY. *Clubs:* Garrick; Brocket Hall Golf.

WILLIAMS, Hon. Sir Wyn (Lewis), Kt 2007; FLSW; **Hon. Mr Justice Wyn Williams;** a Judge of the High Court of Justice, Queen's Bench Division, since 2007; a Presiding Judge, Wales Circuit, 2012–15; *b* 31 March 1951; *s* of Ronald and Nellie Williams; *m* 1973, Carol Ann Bosley; one *s* one *d*. *Educ:* Rhondda County Grammar Sch.; Corpus Christi Coll., Oxford (MA). Called to the Bar, Inner Temple, 1974, Bencher, 2007; in practice at the Bar, Cardiff, 1974–88, and London, 1998–2004; QC 1992; a Recorder, 1992–2004; a Circuit Judge (specialist Chancery Circuit Judge for Wales and Chester Circuit), 2004–07. Dep. Chm., Boundary Commn for Wales, 2012–; Chairman: Lord Chancellor's Standing Cttee on Welsh Lang., 2012; Wales Trng Cttee, Judicial Coll., 2013. Mem., Disciplinary Panel, Internat. Rugby Bd, 1999–; Chm., Professional Rugby Game Bd for Wales, 2013. Pres., Pendyrus Male Choir, 2008–. FLSW 2013. Hon. LLD Glamorgan, 2012. *Recreations:* sport, particularly Rugby, music, reading. *Address:* Royal Courts of Justice, Strand, WC2A 2LL. *Clubs:* Cardiff and County; Tylorstown Rugby Football.

WILLIAMS, Wynford; *see* Williams, D. W.

WILLIAMS-BULKELEY, Sir Richard (Thomas), 14th Bt *cr* 1661 of Penrhyn, Caernarvonshire; Vice Lord-Lieutenant of Gwynedd, 2006–14; *b* 25 May 1939; *s* of Sir Richard Harry David Williams-Bulkeley, 13th Bt, TD and Renée Arundell (*d* 1994), *yr d* of Sir Thomas Neave, 5th Bt; *S* father, 1992; *m* 1964, Sarah Susan, *er d* of Rt Hon. Sir Henry Josceline Phillimore, OBE; twin *s* one *d*. *Educ:* Eton. FRICS 1989. Captain, Welsh Guards, 1964. High Sheriff, 1993, DL 1998, Gwynedd. *Recreation:* astronomy. *Heir: s* Major Richard Hugh Williams-Bulkeley, Welsh Guards [*b* 8 July 1968; *m* 1995, Jacqueline, *er d* of David Edwards; two *s* one *d*].

WILLIAMS-WYNN, Sir (David) Watkin, 11th Bt *cr* 1688, of Gray's Inn; DL; *b* 18 Feb. 1940; *s* of Sir Owen Watkin Williams-Wynn, 10th Bt, CBE and Margaret Jean (*d* 1961), *d* of late Col William Alleyne Macbean, RA; *S* father, 1988; *m* 1st, 1967, Harriet Veryan Elspeth (marr. diss. 1981), *d* of Gen. Sir Norman Tailyour, KCB, DSO; two *s* twin *d*; 2nd, 1983, Victoria Jane Dillon (marr. diss. 1998), *d* of late Lt-Col Ian Dudley De-Ath, DSO, MBE; twin *s*. *Educ:* Eton. Lt Royal Dragoons, 1958–63; Major Queen's Own Yeomanry, 1970–77. DL 1970, High Sheriff, 1990, Clwyd. *Recreation:* foxhunting and other field sports. *Heir: s* Charles Edward Watkin Williams-Wynn, *b* 17 Sept. 1970. *Address:* Plas-yn-Cefn, St Asaph, N Wales LL17 0EY. *T:* (01745) 585515. *Clubs:* Pratt's, Cavalry and Guards.

WILLIAMSON, family name of **Baron Forres**.

WILLIAMSON, Adrian John Gerard Hughes; QC 2002; a Recorder, since 2004; *b* 25 Nov. 1959; *s* of late Dennis Walter Williamson and of Margaret Teresa Williamson; *m* 1983, Gillian Herrod; two *s* one *d*. *Educ:* Highgate Sch.; Trinity Hall, Cambridge (BA 1st Cl. Hons Law 1982, MA 1985). Called to the Bar, Middle Temple, 1983; in private practice as barrister, specialising in construction law, 1985–. Pt-time Supervisor in Law, Churchill Coll., Cambridge, 1982–84. Gov., St Thomas More Primary Sch., Saffron Walden, 1996–2003. *Publications:* (contrib.) Keating on Building Contracts, 5th edn 1991 to 8th edn 2005; (ed jtly) Halsbury's Laws of England, vol. 4(3): Building Contracts, Building Societies, 2002; (gen. ed.) Keating on JCT Contracts, 2006. *Recreations:* family, Arsenal FC, squash. *Address:* Keating Chambers, 15 Essex Street, WC2R 3AA. *T:* (020) 7544 2600, *Fax:* (020) 7240 7722. *E:* awilliamson@keatingchambers.com.

WILLIAMSON, Aldon Thompson; Head, Dame Alice Owen's School, 1994–2005; *b* 19 June 1944; *d* of Gordon Anderson Baxter and Margaret Sophia Baxter; *m* 1966, Prof. James Williamson; one *s* one *d*. *Educ:* Aberdeen Univ. (MA Hons); Inst. of Educn, Univ. of London (PGCE). Maths teacher, S Hampstead High Sch. (GPDST), 1967–69, Head of Maths, 1969–71; Dep. Head, Dame Alice Owen's Sch., 1983–89; Head, Leventhorpe Sch., Herts, 1989–94. FRSA 1997. *Recreations:* opera, art, reading.

WILLIAMSON, Andrew George, CBE 1999; Chairman: Cornwall and Isles of Scilly Primary Care Trust, 2006–13; Coastal West Sussex Clinical Commissioning Group; Exeter Primary Care; *b* 29 Feb. 1948; *s* of Albert and Jocelyn Williamson; *m* 1972, Mary Eleanor White; one *s* one *d*. *Educ:* Southern Grammar Sch., Portsmouth; Oxford Poly. (Dip. in Social Work; CQSW); Birmingham Univ. (Advanced Management Develt Prog., 1982). Residential Child Care, Portsmouth, 1967; Child Care Officer, Hants, 1969; social work management positions in Northumberland and Wandsworth; Asst Dir of Social Services, East Sussex, 1983; Dep. Dir, West Sussex, 1986; Dir of Social Services, Devon CC, 1990–99. Chm., N and E Devon HA, 2000–02; non-exec. Dir, SW Peninsular Strategic HA, 2002–06 (Vice-Chm., 2006). Member: Top Mgt Programme, 1992–; Criminal Justice Consultative Council, 1992–95; Sec. of State for the Home Dept's Youth Justice Task Force, 1997–; Co-Chm., MoJ/DCFS Inquiry into use of restraint in secure accommodation, 2008–10. Chm., Devon and Cornwall Workforce Confedn, 2001–04. Adviser: Nat. Authy for Child Protection, Govt of Rumania, 2000–; to Minister, HSS, States of Jersey, on services for children and young people, 2011–14. Hon. Sec., Assoc. of Dirs of Social Services, 1996–99. FRSA 1995. *Recreations:* reading, cricket, music, theatre. *Address:* Victoria House, Clyst St George, Exeter EX3 0RE. *T:* (01392) 879725.

WILLIAMSON, Sir Brian; *see* Williamson, Sir R. B.

WILLIAMSON, Christopher; *b* Derby, 16 Sept. 1956; *s* of George Williamson and Eileen Williamson; *m* 1997, Lonny Wilsoncroft (*d* 2004); one *s* one *d*; partner, Maggie Amsbury. *Educ:* St John Fisher Primary Sch.; Castle Donington High Sch.; St Thomas More Sch., Derby; Leicester Poly. (CQSW 1985). Mechanical engr apprentice, 1972–73; bricklayer, 1973–78; market trader, 1978–79; social work asst, 1979–83, social worker, 1983–86, Derby; Welfare Rights Officer, Derbys, 1986–2000. Mem. (Lab) Derby CC, 1991–2011 (Dep. Leader, 2000–02; Leader, 2002–03, 2005–08). MP (Lab) Derby N, 2010–15; contested (Lab) same seat, 2015. Mem., Select Cttee on Communities and Local Govt, 2013–15. *Recreations:* watching Derby County, walking, rambling.

WILLIAMSON, Prof. Edwin Henry, PhD; King Alfonso XIII Professor of Spanish Studies, University of Oxford, since 2003; Fellow, Exeter College, Oxford, since 2003; *b* 2 Oct. 1949; *s* of Henry Alfred Williamson and Renée Williamson (*née* Clarembaux); *m* 1976, Susan Jane Fitchie; two *d*. *Educ:* Edinburgh Univ. (MA; PhD 1980). Jun. Lectr in Spanish, TCD, 1974–77; Lectr in Spanish, Birkbeck Coll., Univ. of London, 1977–90; Forbes Prof. of Hispanic Studies, Univ. of Edinburgh, 1990–2003. Leverhulme Res. Fellow, 1995–96; British Acad. Res. Leave Award, 1996–97; Leverhulme Major Res. Fellow, 2015–; Visiting Professor: Univ. of São Paulo, Brazil, 1997; Stanford Univ., Calif, 1999; Brettschneider Vis. Scholar, Cornell Univ., 2006; Univ. of Colorado, Denver, 2010; Dist. Vis. Scholar, UCLA, 2011. Comdr, Orden de Isabel la Católica (Spain). *Publications:* The Half-way House of Fiction: Don Quixote and Arthurian romance, 1984, 2nd edn 1986; El Quijote y los libros de caballerías, 1991; The Penguin History of Latin America, 1992, rev. edn 2009 (trans. Portuguese, 2012, Spanish 2014); Cervantes and the Modernists, 1994; Borges: a life, 2004 (trans. Spanish and Dutch, 2006, Romanian, 2007, Hungarian, 2010, Brazilian, 2011, Chinese, 2013); (ed jtly) Autoridad y poder en el Siglo de Oro, 2009; (ed) The Cambridge Companion to Jorge Luis Borges, 2013; (ed jtly) La autoridad política y el poder de las letras en el Siglo de Oro, 2013; articles in learned jls. *Recreations:* hill-walking, cinema, theatre, visual arts, exploring cities, going abroad. *Address:* Exeter College, Turl Street, Oxford OX1 3DP. *T:* (01865) 270476, *Fax:* (01865) 270757. *E:* edwin.williamson@exeter.ox.ac.uk.

WILLIAMSON, Elizabeth Ann; Executive Editor, Victoria History of the Counties of England, 2010–13 (Architectural Editor, 1997–2010); Reader in Architectural History, University of London; Senior Research Fellow, Institute of Historical Research, University of London, since 2013; *b* 10 May 1950; *d* of late Walter Felce Williamson and Elizabeth Joan (*née* Ford); *m* 1995, Malcolm Slade Higgs. *Educ:* High Sch., Stamford; Courtauld Inst. of Art, London (BA Hons (Hist. of European Art) 1973). Asst, then Dep. Ed., Buildings of England, Ireland, Scotland and Wales, Penguin Books, 1976–97. Historic England (formerly English Heritage): Comr, 2003–11; Mem., Adv. Cttee, 2003–, London Adv. Cttee, 2003–07; Chm., Historic Parks and Gardens Panel, 2007–14; Mem., Designation Review Cttee, 2013–. FSA 1998. *Publications:* The Buildings of England: revisions of 5 vols in series, 1978, 1979, 1983, 1984, 1994, London Docklands, 1998; (with Anne Riches and Malcolm Higgs) The Buildings of Scotland: Glasgow, 1990; contribs to 25 vols in Victoria History of the Counties of England, 1998–2013, and to England's Past for Everyone, 2007–10. *Recreation:* places and buildings in fact and fiction. *Address:* Institute of Historical Research, University of London, Senate House, WC1E 7HU.

WILLIAMSON, Rt Hon. Gavin (Alexander); PC 2015; MP (C) South Staffordshire, since 2010; *b* Scarborough, 25 June 1976; *s* of Ray and Beverley Williamson; *m* 2001, Joanne Elizabeth Eland; two *d*. *Educ:* Raincliffe Secondary Sch.; Scarborough Sixth Form Coll.; Univ. of Bradford (BSc Hons Social Scis). Glynwed Gp, 1998–2004; Gen. Manager, Aynsley China, 2004–08; Divl Man. Dir and Gp Dir, NPS Gp, 2008–10. Mem. (C) N Yorks CC, 2001–05. Contested (C) Blackpool N and Fleetwood, 2005. PPS to Minister of State for NI, 2011–12, to Sec. of State for Transport, 2012–13, to Prime Minister, 2013–. Mem., NI Affairs Select Cttee, 2010–11; Chm., All Party Parly Gp on Motor Neurone Disease, 2010–14; Co-Chm., Associate Parly Design and Innovation Gp, 2010–14. Mem., Exec. Cttee, UK Br., CPA, 2010–12. *Address:* House of Commons, SW1A 0AA.

WILLIAMSON, Sir (George) Malcolm, Kt 2007; FCIB; Chairman: Friends Life Group Ltd (formerly Friends Provident Holdings (UK) plc, then Friends Life Group plc), 2010–15 (Independent Director, 2009–15); Senior Independent Director, Aviva plc, since 2015; *b* 27 Feb. 1939; *s* of George and Margery Williamson; *m* Hang Thi Ngo; one *s* one *d*, and one *s* one *d* by a previous marriage. *Educ:* Bolton School. FIB. Barclays Bank: various posts, 1957–80; Local Director, 1980–81; Asst Gen. Manager, 1981–83; Regional Gen. Manager, 1983–85; Bd Mem., Post Office, and Man. Dir, Girobank plc, 1985–89; Gp Exec. Dir, Standard Chartered Bank, 1989–91; Gp Man. Dir, 1991–93, Gp Chief Exec., 1993–98, Standard Chartered PLC; Pres. and CEO, Visa Internat., San Francisco, 1998–2004. Chairman: Nat. Australia Gp Europe Ltd, 2004–12; Clydesdale Bank PLC, 2004–12; Britannic Gp plc, 2004–05 (Dep. Chm., 2002); CDC Gp plc, 2004–09; SAV Credit Ltd, 2010–11; NewDay Ltd (formerly Progressive Credit Ltd), 2010–; NewDay Gp (formerly Invicta Card Services Ltd), 2010–; Resolution Ltd, 2013–14; non-executive Director: National Grid Group, 1995–99; British Invisibles, 1996–98; Gp 4 Securicor, subseq. G4S, plc, 2004–08; Nat. Australia Bank, 2004–12; JP Morgan Cazenove Hldgs, 2005–10; Resolution plc, 2005–08 (Dep. Chm., 2005–08); Signet Jewelers Ltd (formerly Signet Gp plc), 2006–12 (Chm., 2006–08); Internat. Business Leaders Forum, 2006–10. Chairman: The Prince's Youth Business International (formerly Youth Business Internat. Adv. Bd), 2005–; Youth Business America, 2009–11 (non-exec. Dir, 2009–13). Mem. Council, Industrial Soc., 1996–98. Chairman: Strategy and Develt Bd, Cass Business Sch., 2008–; Governing Council, Centre for the Study of Financial Innovation, 2012–. Hon. DSc: City, 2010; ifs Sch. of Finance, 2013. *Recreations:* mountaineering, golf, chess. *Address:* Aviva plc, St Helens, 1 Undershaft,, EC3P 3DQ. *Clubs:* Rucksack, Pedestrian (Manchester).

WILLIAMSON, Hazel Eleanor; *see* Marshall, H. E.

WILLIAMSON, Helen Sheppard, (Sarah); *see* Kay, H. S.

WILLIAMSON, Prof. Hugh Godfrey Maturin, OBE 2015; FBA 1993; Regius Professor of Hebrew, and Student of Christ Church, Oxford University, 1992–2014; *b* 15 July 1947; *s* of Thomas Broadwood Williamson and Margaret Frances (*née* Davy); *m* 1971, Julia Eiluned Morris; one *s* two *d*. *Educ:* Rugby Sch.; Trinity Coll., Cambridge (BA 1st cl. Hons Theol., 1969; MA); St John's Coll., Cambridge; PhD 1975, DD 1986, Cantab. Cambridge University: Asst Lectr in Hebrew and Aramaic, 1975–79; Lectr, 1979–89; Reader, 1989–92; Fellow of Clare Hall, 1985–92. Chm., Anglo-Israel Archaeol Soc., 1990–2010. Pres., SOTS, 2004. Vice-Pres., British Acad., 2010–11. Corresp. Mem., Göttingen Akademie der Wissenschaften, 2008. *Publications:* Israel in the Books of Chronicles, 1977; 1 and 2 Chronicles, 1982; Ezra, Nehemiah, 1985; Ezra and Nehemiah, 1987; Annotated Key to Lambdin's Introduction to Biblical Hebrew, 1987; (ed jtly) The Future of Biblical Studies, 1987; (ed jtly) It is Written: essays in honour of Barnabas Lindars, 1988; Jesus is Lord, 1993; The Book Called Isaiah, 1994; (ed jtly) Wisdom in Ancient Israel: essays in honour of J. A. Emerton, 1995; Variations on a Theme: King, Messiah and Servant in the Book of Isaiah, 1998; (ed jtly) Reading from Right to Left: essays in honour of David J. A. Clines, 2003; (ed jtly) Prophetie in Israel, 2003; Studies in Persian Period History and Historiography, 2004; Confirmation or Contradiction?: archaeology and Biblical history, 2004; (ed jtly) Dictionary of the Old Testament Historical Books, 2005; Isaiah 1–5: a critical and exegetical commentary, 2006; (ed) Understanding the History of Ancient Israel, 2007; Holy, Holy, Holy: the story of a liturgical formula, 2008; (ed jtly) Interpreting Isaiah: issues and approaches, 2009; He Has Shown You What is Good: Old Testament justice then and now, 2012; contrib. to learned jls incl. Vetus Testamentum, Jl of Theol Studies, Jl of Biblical Lit., Jl of Semitic Studies, Jl for Study of OT, Palestine Exploration Qly, Zeitschrift für die alttestamentliche Wissenschaft, Oudtestamentische Studiën. *Recreations:* allotment tending, model yacht sailing. *Address:* 7 Chester Road, Southwold, Suffolk IP18 6LN. *T:* (01502) 722319.

WILLIAMSON, James Hunter; Sheriff, Tayside Central and Fife at Kirkcaldy, since 2009; *b* Edinburgh, 9 Feb. 1961; *s* of James Hunter Williamson and Elizabeth Williamson (*née* Brown); *m* 1992, Christine Margaret Gillan; two *d*. *Educ:* Broughton High Sch., Edinburgh; Univ. of Dundee (LLB). Partner, Lawson, Coull & Duncan Solicitors, Dundee, 1990–2009; pt-time Sheriff, 2003–09. Tutor in Criminal Advocacy, 1990–2003, Lectr in Criminal Procedure, 2000–03, Univ. of Dundee. *Recreations:* golf, architecture, football, backgammon, American pulp fiction circa 1930–1950. *Address:* 344 Blackness Road, Dundee DD2 1SD. *T:* (01382) 669603. *Clubs:* Downfield Golf; El Club De Golf Rosa de Sombrero (Champion, 2004, 2015).

WILLIAMSON, Marshal of the Royal Air Force Sir Keith (Alec), GCB 1982 (KCB 1979); AFC 1968; Chief of the Air Staff, 1982–85; Air ADC to the Queen, 1982–85; *b* 25 Feb. 1928; *s* of Percy and Gertrude Williamson; *m* 1953, Patricia Anne, *d* of W/Cdr F. M. N. Watts; two *s* twin *d*. *Educ:* Bancroft's Sch., Woodford Green; Market Harborough Grammar

Sch.; RAF Coll., Cranwell. Commissioned, 1950; flew with Royal Australian Air Force in Korea, 1953; OC 23 Sqdn, 1966–68; Command, RAF Gütersloh, 1968–70; RCDS 1971; Dir, Air Staff Plans, 1972–75; Comdt, RAF Staff Coll., 1975–77; ACOS (Plans and Policy), SHAPE, 1977–78; AOC-in-C, RAF Support Comd, 1978–80; AOC-in-C, RAF Strike Command and C-in-C, UK Air Forces, 1980–82. *Recreation:* golf.

WILLIAMSON, Lucy Maria; *see* Powell, L. M.

WILLIAMSON, Sir Malcolm; *see* Williamson, Sir G. M.

WILLIAMSON, Martin Charles; HM Diplomatic Service, retired; Head, Research Analysts, Foreign and Commonwealth Office, 2007–10; *b* 28 Jan. 1953; *s* of Charles Frederick Williamson and Marie Williamson; *m* 1978, Elizabeth Michelle Darvill; two *s*. *Educ:* Univ. of Keele (BA Hons 1975); London Sch. of Econs (MSc 1977). Entered FCO, 1977; FCO, 1977–84; Res. Dept, IMF, 1984–87; Econ. Advr, FCO, 1987–89; Cabinet Office, 1989–91; OECD, 1991–94; Foreign and Commonwealth Office: Sen. Econ. Advr, 1994–99; Dep. Hd, Econ. Policy Dept, 1999; Hd, Resource Budgeting Dept, 1999–2003; Prism Team, 2003–04; Dep. High Comr, Wellington, 2004–06. Research student: Univ. of Kent, 2010–13; Univ. of Exeter, 2013–. *Publications:* Acquisition of Foreign Assets by Developing Countries, 1986. *Recreations:* walking, gym, reading, music. *Address:* c/o Department of Politics, University of Exeter, Amory Building, Rennes Drive, Exeter, Devon EX4 4RJ. *E:* martin@martinwilliamson.plus.com.

WILLIAMSON, Matthew; designer; Founder and President, Matthew Williamson Ltd, since 1997; *b* Manchester, 23 Oct. 1971; *s* of Maureen and David Williamson. *Educ:* Central St Martins Coll. (BA Design and Printed Textiles 1994). First store opened, London, 2004, NY and Dubai, 2009; Creative Dir, Emilio Pucci, 2005–08. Retrospective exhibn, Matthew Williamson: 10 Years in Fashion, Design Mus., 2007. Elle Designer of Year, 2004; Red Carpet Designer of Year Award, British Fashion Awards, 2008. *Relevant publication:* Matthew Williamson, by Colin McDowell, 2010. *Address:* 46 Hertford Street, W1J 7DP. *T:* (020) 7491 6220, *Fax:* (020) 7491 6252. *E:* estella@matthewwilliamson.co.uk.

WILLIAMSON, Nigel; writer; *b* 4 July 1954; *s* of Neville Albert and Anne Maureen Williamson; *m* 1976, Magali Patricia Wild; two *s*. *Educ:* Chislehurst and Sidcup Grammar School; University College London. Tribune: Journalist, 1982–84; Literary Editor, 1984; Editor, 1984–87; Editor: Labour Party News, 1987–89; New Socialist, 1987–89; The Times: political reporter, 1989–90; Diary Editor, 1990–92; Home News Editor, 1992–95; Whitehall correspondent, 1995–96; freelance interviewer and music writer, 1996–; contrib. ed., Uncut mag., 1997–; weekly columnist and contrib. ed., Billboard, 1999–; specialist music advr, British Council, 2002–. A Judge, Mercury Music Prize, 1999–2004. *Publications:* The SDP (ed), 1982; The New Right, 1984; (contrib.) The Rough Guide to World Music, 2000; Journey Through the Past: the stories behind the songs of Neil Young, 2002; The Rough Guide to Bob Dylan, 2004; (ed and contrib.) The Rough Guide Book of Playlists, 2005; The Rough Guide to the Blues, 2007; The Rough Guide to Led Zeppelin, 2007; The Rough Guide to the Best Music You've Never Heard, 2008; The Straight Ahead Guide to Bob Dylan, 2014; The Straight Ahead Guide to Led Zeppelin, 2014. *Recreations:* world music, cricket, gardening, opera. *Address:* Long Tilings, Hever Lane, Hever, Kent TN8 7ET. *T:* (01342) 851472.

WILLIAMSON, Prof. Oliver E., PhD; Professor of Economics and Law, Graduate School, 1988–2004, now Emeritus, and Edgar F. Kaiser Professor of Business, Haas School of Business, 1998–2004, now Emeritus, University of California, Berkeley; *b* Superior, Wisconsin, 27 Sept. 1932; *s* of Scott and Lucille Williamson; *m* 1957, Dolores Celeni; three *s* two *d*. *Educ:* Massachusetts Inst. Technol. (SB 1955); Stanford Univ. (MBA 1960); Carnegie-Mellon Univ. (PhD 1963). Asst Prof. of Econs, Univ. of Calif, Berkeley, 1963–65; University of Pennsylvania: Associate Prof., 1965–68; Prof., 1968–83; Chair, Dept of Econs, 1971–72 and 1976–77; Dir, Centre for Study of Organizational Innovation, 1976–83; Charles and William L. Day Prof. of Econs and Social Sci., 1977–83; Gordon B. Tweedy Prof. of Econs of Law and Orgn, Yale Univ., 1983–88; Prof., Haas Sch. of Business, Univ. of Calif, Berkeley, 1988–98. Visiting Professor: Univ. of Warwick, 1973; Indiana Univ., 1987; of Econs and Transamerica Prof. of Business Admin, Univ. of Calif, Berkeley, 1988; Saarbrücken Univ., 1991; Paris 1 (Sorbonne), 1994; Dist. Vis. Prof., Univ. of Kyoto, 1983; Taussig Res. Prof. of Econs, Harvard Univ., 1987; Pritzker Dist. Vis. Prof., Northwestern Univ. Law Sch., 1993; Vis. Fellow, Res. Sch. of Social Scis, ANU, 1996. Distinguished Fellow: Industrial Orgn Soc., 2005; Amer. Econ. Assoc., 2007; Fellow: Econometrics Soc., 1977; Amer. Acad. Arts and Scis, 1983; Amer. Acad. Pol and Social Scis, 1997. Mem., NAS, 1994. (Jtly) Nobel Prize in Econs, 2009. *Publications:* The Economics of Discretionary Behaviour, 1964 (trans. Japanese); Corporate Control and Business Behaviour, 1970 (trans. Japanese); Markets and Hierarchies, 1975 (trans. Japanese); The Economic Institutions of Capitalism, 1985 (trans. Spanish, Italian, German, Russian, French, Polish); The Mechanisms of Governance, 1996 (trans. Italian); contribs to Amer. Econ. Rev., Jl Econ. Perspectives. *Address:* Walter A. Haas School of Business, University of California, Berkeley, CA 94720–1900, USA.

WILLIAMSON, Dr Paul, FSA; FRHistS; Keeper of Sculpture, Metalwork, Ceramics and Glass, Victoria and Albert Museum, since 2001; *b* 4 Aug. 1954; *s* of late Peter Williamson and Mary Teresa Williamson (*née* Meagher); *m* 1984, Emmeline Mary Clare Mandley, MBE; one *s*. *Educ:* Wimbledon Coll.; Univ. of East Anglia (BA Hons; MPhil; LittD). Res., British Sch. at Rome, 1978; Major State Student, DES, 1978–79; Department of Sculpture, Victoria and Albert Museum: Asst Keeper, 1979–89; acting Keeper, 1989; Chief Curator, 1989–2001; Sen. Chief Curator, 1995–98; Dir of Collections, 2004–07; Acting Dep. Dir, 2013. Member: Wells Cathedral West Front Specialist Cttee, 1981–83; Wall Paintings Sub-Cttee, Council for the Care of Churches, 1987–90; Cttee, British Acad. Corpus of Romanesque Sculpture in Britain and Ireland, 1990–97; Lincoln Cathedral Fabric Adv. Council, 1990–2001; Internat. Adv. Bd, Courtauld Inst. of Art (Wall Paintings Conservation), 2005–; Expert Advr on Sculpture, Reviewing Cttee on Export of Works of Art, 1989–. Member, Consultative Committee: Sculpture Jl, 1997–; Burlington Mag., 2003– (Dir and Trustee, 2008–); Walpole Soc., 2004–. Lansdowne Vis. Prof., Univ. of Victoria, BC, 2001; Diskant Lectr, Philadelphia Mus. of Art, 2001. FSA 1983 (Mem. Council, 1997–2003; Vice-Pres., 1999–2003); FRHistS 2011. Trustee, Stained Glass Mus., Ely, 2005–09. *Publications:* An Introduction to Medieval Ivory Carvings, 1982 (trans. German); Catalogue of Romanesque Sculpture in the Victoria and Albert Museum, 1983; (ed) The Medieval Treasury: the art of the Middle Ages in the Victoria and Albert Museum, 1986, 3rd edn 1998; The Thyssen-Bornemisza Collection: medieval sculpture and works of art, 1987; Northern Gothic Sculpture 1200–1450, 1988; (ed jtly) Early Medieval Wall Painting and Painted Sculpture in England, 1990; Gothic Sculpture 1140–1300, 1995 (trans. Spanish 1997, trans. Portuguese, 1998); (ed) European Sculpture at the Victoria and Albert Museum, 1996; Netherlandish Sculpture 1450–1550, 2002; (ed jtly) Wonder: painted sculpture from medieval England, 2002; Medieval and Renaissance Stained Glass in the Victoria and Albert Museum, 2003; (ed jtly) Gothic: art for England 1400–1547, 2003; Medieval and Later Treasures from a Private Collection, 2005; (ed jtly) Medieval and Renaissance Treasures from the V&A, 2007; Medieval Ivory Carvings: early Christian to Romanesque, 2010; (ed) Object of Devotion: medieval English alabaster sculpture from the Victoria and Albert Museum, 2010; (with Glyn Davies) Medieval Ivory Carvings 1200–1550, 2014; contribs to numerous exhibn catalogues; articles and book reviews in learned jls. *Recreation:* travel. *Address:* Victoria and Albert Museum, SW7 2RL. *T:* (020) 7942 2611. *E:* p.williamson@vam.ac.uk.

WILLIAMSON, Peter John; Chairman of the Board, Solicitors Regulation Authority (formerly Regulation Board, Law Society of England and Wales), 2005–09; President, Law Society of England and Wales, 2003–04; Chairman, Independent Schools Inspectorate, since 2012; *b* 20 Aug. 1947; *s* of late John Reginald Williamson and Margaret Audrey Williamson (*née* Morrison); *m* 1974, Patricia Anne Mitchell Miller; one *s* one *d*. *Educ:* Berkhamsted Sch. Admitted as solicitor, 1972; Partner: Kenneth Brown Baker Baker, subseq. Turner Kenneth Brown, 1974–91 (Man. Partner, 1986–90); Dawson & Co., subseq. Dawsons, 1991–98 (Consultant, 1998–2007). Dep. Dist Judge, 1995–2001; Asst Recorder, 1997–2000; Recorder, 2000–08. Law Society: Chm., Associate Mems Gp, 1970; Mem. Council, 1992–2005; Dep. Vice-Pres., 2001–02; Vice-Pres., 2002–03. Dir, Solicitors Indemnity Fund Ltd, 1995–2002 (Chm., 1997–2002). Pres., Holborn Law Soc., 1989–90. Trustee, Slynn Foundn, 2010– (Chm., 2012–). Berkhamsted School (formerly Berkhamsted Collegiate School): Pres., Old Berkhamstedians Assoc., 1979–81; Gov., 1991–2012 (Chm. Govs, 1995–2012); Gov., Coll. of Law, 2002–05. *Recreations:* watching and reading about sport, particularly cricket, listening to classical music, travel. *E:* peter.williamson47@btinternet.com. *Clubs:* Lansdowne, MCC.

WILLIAMSON, Peter Roger; HM Diplomatic Service, retired; Chairman, Risk Resolution Group; *b* 20 April 1942; *s* of Frederick W. and Dulcie R. Williamson; *m* 1977, Greta Helen Clare Richards; one *s* one *d*. *Educ:* Bristol Grammar Sch.; St John's Coll., Oxford (MA). Journalist and teacher, Far East, 1965–66; joined FCO, 1966; Kuala Lumpur, 1970; 1st Sec., FCO, 1973; Hong Kong, 1975; FCO, 1979; Counsellor: Kuala Lumpur, 1985–88; FCO, 1988–92; on loan to Cabinet Office, 1992–94; Counsellor, Nairobi, 1994–97. *Recreations:* tennis, travel, theatre, cinema, forest and farmland management.

WILLIAMSON, Philip Frederick, CBE 2008; Chief Executive, Nationwide Building Society, 2002–07; Chairman, Investors in People UK, 2006–11; *b* 11 Dec. 1947; *s* of late Philip Gordon Williamson and of Elsie May Williamson; *m* 1993, Theresa Taylor; two *d*. *Educ:* Calday Grange Grammar Sch.; Newcastle Univ. (BA Hons Econ); Harvard Business Sch. FCIB 2002. Joined Lloyds Bank as grad. trainee, 1970; Dir, UK Land plc, 1988–91; Nationwide Building Society, 1991–2007: Divisional Director: Business Planning, 1994–95; Corporate Develt, 1996; Marketing and Commercial Dir, 1996–99; Retail Ops Dir, 1999–2001; Chm., Nationwide Life, 1999–2001. Chm., Acenden Ltd, 2011–; non-executive Director: Visa Europe, 2006–; In-Deed Online plc, 2011–. Chairman: Council of Mortgage Lenders, 2000–01; Corporate Forum for Internat. Service, 2004–; BSA, 2005–06; Founder Dir, Regulatory and Retail Faculty Bd, Inst. of Financial Services; UK Vice-Pres., Eur. Mortgage Fedn, 2004–. *Recreations:* hockey, proficient golfer (7 handicap), stamp collecting. *Address:* Gable House, Sandridge Lane, Lindfield, Haywards Heath, West Sussex RH16 1XY.

WILLIAMSON, Richard Arthur; Director, Midland Region, Crown Prosecution Service, 1987–89; *b* 9 Jan. 1932; *s* of George Arthur and Winifred Mary Williamson; *m* 1957, Christina Elizabeth, *d* of Harry Godley Saxton, Worksop, Notts, and Helena Saxton; two *s*. *Educ:* King Edward VI Grammar Sch., East Retford; Sheffield Univ. (statutory year). Solicitor, 1956. National Service, RN (Sub-Lieut), 1956–58. Asst Solicitor, Lancs CC, 1958–61; Sen. Asst Solicitor, Lincs (Lindsey) CC, 1961–65; private practice, Partner in Hetts, Solicitors, Scunthorpe, 1965–76; Prin. Prosecuting Solicitor, Greater Manchester, 1976–83; Chief Prosecuting Solicitor, Lincs, 1983–85; Asst Hd of Field Management, Crown Prosecution Service, 1985–87. Prosecuting Solicitors Soc. of England and Wales: Mem. Exec. Council, 1978–85; Treas., 1978–85; Chm., Hds of Office, 1984–85. Mem., York and the Humber War Pensions Cttee, 1997–2010. *Recreations:* family, theatre, gardening. *Address:* The Lookout, Back Street, Alkborough, near Scunthorpe, North Lincolnshire DN15 9JN. *T:* (01724) 720843.

WILLIAMSON, Prof. Robert, AO 2004; FRCP, FRCPath; FRS 1999; Director, Murdoch Childrens Research Institute (formerly Murdoch Research Institute), Royal Children's Hospital, Melbourne, 1995–2006, now Honorary Senior Research Fellow; Research Professor of Medical Genetics, University of Melbourne School of Medicine, 1995–2005; *b* 14 May 1938; *s* of John and Mae Williamson; *m* 1st, 1962, Patricia Anne Sutherland (marr. diss. 1994); one *s* one *d*; 2nd, 1994, Robyn Elizabeth O'Hehir; one *s* one *d*. *Educ:* Bronx High School of Science, NY; Wandsworth Comprehensive School; University College London (BSc, MSc, PhD). FRCP 1990; FAA 2001. Lectr, Univ. of Glasgow, 1963–67; Sen. Scientist (Molecular Biol.), Beatson Inst. for Cancer Research, Glasgow, 1967–76; Prof. of Biochem., St Mary's Hosp. Med. Sch., London Univ., 1976–95. Sen. Fellow, Carnegie Instn of Washington, Baltimore, 1972–73. External Examr, Malaysia, Saudi Arabia. Member: UK Genetic Manipulation Adv. Cttee, 1976–91; Grants Cttees, MRC Cancer Research Campaign, 1976–95; Action Research for Crippled Child; Cystic Fibrosis Research Trust. Francqui Hon. Prof., Belgian Univs, 1995. Hon. MRCP 1986. Hon. MD Turku, 1987. Wellcome Award, Biochem. Soc., 1983; King Faisal Internat. Prize for Medicine, 1994. *Publications:* (ed) Genetic Engineering, vol. 1, 1981, vol. 2, 1982, vol. 3, 1982, vol. 4, 1983; articles in Nature, Cell, Procs of US Nat. Acad. of Scis, Biochemistry, Nucleic Acids Research. *Recreations:* reading, sport. *Address:* The Dean's Ganglion, Faculty of Medicine, University of Melbourne, 4/766 Elizabeth Street, Melbourne, Vic 3010, Australia. *T:* (3) 83444181. *E:* r.williamson@unimelb.edu.au.

WILLIAMSON, Sir (Robert) Brian, Kt 2001; CBE 1989; Chairman: London International Financial Futures and Options Exchange, 1985–88 and 1998–2003 (Director, 1982–89); Electra Private Equity PLC (formerly Electra Investment Trust plc), 2000–10 (Director, 1994–2010); Resolution PLC (formerly Resolution Life Group), 2004–05 (Director, 2004–08); *b* 16 Feb. 1945; *m* 1986, Diane Marie Christine de Jacquier de Rosée. *Educ:* Truro Sch.; Trinity College, Dublin (MA). Personal Asst to Rt Hon. Maurice Macmillan (later Viscount Macmillan), 1967–71; Editor, International Currency Review, 1971; Man. Dir, Gerrard & National Hldgs, 1978–89; Chairman: GNI Ltd, 1985–89; Gerrard & Nat. Hldgs, later Gerrard Gp PLC, 1989–98; Fleming Worldwide Investment Trust, 1998 (Dep. Chm., 1996–98); MT Fund Management Ltd, 2004–. Director: Fleming Internat. High Income Investment Trust plc, 1990–96; Court, Bank of Ireland, 1990–98; Barlows plc, 1997–98; HSBC Hldgs plc, 2002–12; Templeton Emerging Markets Investment Fund plc, 2002–03; Liv-Ex Ltd, 2005–; Open Europe, 2005–08; Waverton (formerly J. O. Hambro) Investment Mgt Ltd, 2010–15; Climate Exchange plc, 2007–10; Aggregated Micro Power Hldgs plc, 2012–. Member: Bd, Bank of Ireland Britain Hldgs, 1986–90; Council, 1985–88, Council, Eur. Cttee, 1988–90, British Invisible Exports Council; FSA (formerly SIB), 1986–98; Supervisory Bd, NYSE Euronext (formerly Euronext NV), 2002–13. Sen. Advr, Fleming Family and Partners, 2003–09. Dir, Politeia, 1999–. Chm., Adv. Bd, Armed Forces (formerly Army) Common Investment Fund, 2002–09. Gov. at Large, Nat. Assoc. of Securities Dealers, USA, 1995–98; Mem., Internat. Markets Adv. Bd, NASDAQ Stock Market, 1993–98 (Chm., 1996–98). Mem. Governing Council, Centre for Study of Financial Innovation, 2000–. Mem., City of London Lord Mayor's Appraisal Panel, 2009–. Mem. HAC, commissioned 1975. Dir, Rowing Mus., Henley Foundn, 1992–94. Mem., Royal Opera House Develt Cttee, 2004–09; Mem., Adv. Circle, Royal Opera House Foundn, 2009–12; Member, Council: St George's House, 1996–2002, St George's Chapel, 2002–; Dir, St George's House Trust (Windsor Castle), 1998–2002; Trustee: St Paul's Cathedral Foundn, 1999–2005; Winston Churchill Meml Trust, 2009–; Edenbeg Trust Corporation Ltd (formerly Fallon Family Bd), 2012–. Freeman, 1994, HM Lieut, 2003, City of London. Contested (C) Sheffield Hillsborough, Feb. and Oct. 1974; prosp. parly cand., Truro, 1976–77. FRSA 1991. Hon. Bencher, Inner Temple, 2006. *Clubs:* Pratt's, White's; Kildare Street and University (Dublin); Brook (New York); St Moritz Tobogganing (Pres., 2009–14).

WILLIAMSON, Rt Rev. Robert Kerr, (Roy); Bishop of Southwark, 1991–98; Honorary Assistant Bishop, Diocese of Southwell and Nottingham, since 1998; *b* 18 Dec. 1932; *s* of James and Elizabeth Williamson; *m* 1956, Anne Boyd Smith (*d* 2004); three *s* two *d*. *Educ:* Elmgrove School, Belfast; Oak Hill College, London. London City Missionary, 1955–61; Oak Hill Coll., 1961–63; Asst Curate, Crowborough Parish Church, 1963–66; Vicar: St Paul, Hyson Green, Nottingham, 1966–71; St Ann w. Emmanuel, Nottingham, 1971–76; St Michael and All Angels, Bramcote, 1976–79; Archdeacon of Nottingham, 1978–84; Bishop of Bradford, 1984–91. Chm., Central Religious Adv. Cttee to BBC and ITC, 1993–97; Co-Chm., Inter-Faith Network for the UK, 1994–99. *Publications:* Can You Spare a Minute?, 1991; Funny You Should Say That, 1992; For Such a Time as This, 1996; Joyful Uncertainty, 1999; Open Return, 2000; Not Least in the Kingdom, 2001; Wholly Alive, 2002; Loved By Love, 2004. *Recreations:* walking, bird watching, reading, music.

WILLIAMSON, Prof. Robin Charles Noel, FRCS; Professor of Surgery, Imperial College School of Medicine (formerly Professor and Head of Department of Surgery, Royal Postgraduate Medical School), University of London, 1987–2009, now Honorary; Chairman, London Clinic, since 2012 (Member, Board of Trustees, since 2010); *b* 19 Dec. 1942; *s* of James Charles Frederick Lloyd Williamson and Helena Frances Williamson (*née* Madden); *m* 1967, Judith Marjorie (*née* Bull); three *s*. *Educ:* Rugby School; Emmanuel College, Cambridge; St Bartholomew's Hosp. Med. Coll. MA, MD, MChir (Cantab). Surgical Registrar, Reading, 1971–73; Sen. Surgical Registrar, Bristol, 1973–75; Clin. and Res. Fellow, Mass Gen. Hosp. Boston and Harvard Med. Sch., 1975–76; Consultant Sen. Lectr, Bristol, 1977–79; Prof. of Surgery, Univ. of Bristol, 1979–87. Consultant Surgeon, Hammersmith Hosp., 1987–2009; Deanery Tutor in Surgery, Imperial Coll. Med. Sch., 2008–12; Foundn Trng Prog. Dir, Imperial Coll. Healthcare NHS Trust, 2009–12. Mem., Cell Biology and Disorders Bd, MRC, 1987–91. Fulbright-Hays Sen. Res. Scholar, USA, 1975; Sen. Penman Vis. Fellow, South Africa, 1985; Paul Grange Vis. Fellow, Univ. of Monash, 1986; Hunterian Prof., RCS, 1981–82; Raine Vis. Prof., Univ. of Western Australia, 1983; Richardson Prof., Mass Gen. Hosp., 1985; Visiting Professor: Univ. of Lund, Sweden, 1985; Univ. of Hong Kong, 1987; Univ. of Hamburg, 1999; Johnson and Johnson Vis. Prof., Univ. of Calif, San Francisco, 1989; Edwin Tooth Guest Prof., Royal Brisbane Hosp., Qld, 1989; Totalisator Bd Vis. Prof., Nat. Univ. of Singapore, 1994. Lectures: Arris and Gale, RCS, 1977–78; Finlayson Meml, RCPSG, 1985; Sir Gordon Bell Meml, RACS, NZ, 1988; Stuart, RSocMed and RCSE, 2007; Farndon Meml, Soc. of Acad. and Res. Surgery, 2008; Stevens, RSocMed, 2011; Hunterian Soc., 2011; Med. Soc. of London, 2013. Association of Surgeons of GB and Ireland: Moynihan Fellow, 1979; Mem. Council, 1993–99; Chm., Scientific Cttee, 1995–97; Vice Pres., 1997–98; Pres., 1998–99. Royal Society of Medicine: Associate Dean, 2001–02; Dean, 2002–06; Emeritus Dean, 2006–08; Pres., 2008–10. President: Pancreatic Soc. of GB and Ireland, 1984–85; Internat. Hepato-Pancreato-Biliary Assoc., 1996–98 (Sec. Gen., 1994–96); Assoc. of Upper Gastrointestinal Surgeons, 1996–98; European Soc. of Surgery, 1998; James IV Assoc. of Surgeons, 2002–06; Chm., Educn Cttee, British Soc. of Gastroenterology, 1981–87; Member: Med. Adv. Cttee, British Council, 1988–94; Clin. Res and Trng and Career Panel, MRC, 1997–2003; Internat. Adv. Bd, Nat. Univ. of Singapore, 1998–2000; Res. Cttee, Mason Med. Res. Foundn, 1999–2010 (Chm., 2004–10); Sec. Gen., World Assoc. of Hepato-Pancreato-Biliary Surgery, 1990–94 (Treas., 1986–90); Jt Adv. Bd, Weill Cornell Medical Coll., Qatar, 2014–. Examiner: Primary FRCS, 1981–87; Intercollegiate Bd in General Surgery, 1994–2002 (Mem., Intercollegiate Examng Bd in Gen. Surg., 1998–2002). Chm., Retired Fellows Soc., RSocMed, 2013–. FRSocMed 2000. FRCSE (*ad hominem*) 2009; Hon. FRCS Thailand, 1992. Hon. DSc Med. Mahidol Univ., Thailand, 1994. Hallett Prize, RCS, 1970; Research Medal, British Soc. of Gastroenterology, 1982; Bengt Ihre Medal, Swedish Soc. of Gastroenterology, 1998; Gold Medal, IHPBA, 2004. Sen. Ed., British Jl of Surgery, 1991–96 (Co. Sec., 1983–91); Ed., HPB, 1999–2003; Ed.-in-Chief, HPB Surgery, 2006–11. *Publications:* edited jointly: Colonic Carcinogenesis, 1982; General Surgical Operations, 2nd edn 1987; Emergency Abdominal Surgery, 1990; Surgical Management, 2nd edn 1991; Clinical Gastroenterology: gastrointestinal emergencies, 1991; Scott, An Aid to Clinical Surgery, 6th edn 1998; Hepatobiliary and Pancreatic Tumours, 1994; Upper Digestive Surgery: oesophagus, stomach and small intestine, 1999; Surgery, 2000; Surgery: core principles and international practice, 2015; numerous papers in surgical and med. jls. *Recreations:* travel, military uniforms and history. *Address:* The Barn, 88 Lower Road, Gerrards Cross, Bucks SL9 8LB. *T:* (01753) 889816. *E:* r.williamson@imperial.ac.uk, robin.williamson@btinternet.com. *Club:* Oxford and Cambridge.

WILLIAMSON, Rt Rev. Roy; *see* Williamson, Rt Rev. Robert K.

WILLIAMSON, Prof. Stephen, FREng; Deputy Vice-Chancellor (Research and Innovation), University of Surrey, 2009–13; *b* 15 Dec. 1948; *s* of Donald Williamson and Patricia K. M. Williamson (*née* Leyland); *m* 1970, Zita Mellor; one *s* two *d*. *Educ:* Burnage Grammar Sch., Manchester; Imperial Coll. of Science and Technology (scholarship, 1968; Sylvanus P. Thompson Prize, 1969; BScEng, ACGI, PhD, DIC; DScEng 1989). FIEEE 1995; FREng (FEng 1995). Lectr in Engrg, Univ. of Aberdeen, 1973–81; Sen. Lectr, 1981–85, Reader, 1985–89, Dept of Electrical Engrg, Imperial College; Prof. of Engrg, 1989–97, and Fellow, St John's Coll., 1990–97, Cambridge Univ.; Technical Dir, Brook Hansen, later Invensys Brook Crompton, 1997–2000; Prof. of Electrical Engrg, 2000–09, Hd, Sch. of Electrical Engrg and Electronics, 2003–09, UMIST, later Univ. of Manchester. Non-exec. Dir, Tesla Engrg, 2009–. Chm., Electrical, Controls, and System Electronics Adv. Bd, Rolls Royce, 2002–; Member: Scientific Adv. Council, MoD, 2005–11; Bd of Trustees, IET, 2009–12; Res. and Knowledge Exchange Strategic Adv. Cttee (formerly Res. and Innovation Scientific Adv. Council), HEFCE, 2011–. FCGI 1989. Institution of Electrical Engineers: John Hopkinson Premium, 1981; Crompton Premium, 1987, 1996, 1998; Swan Premium, 1989; Science, Educn and Technol. Div. Premium, 1991; Power Div. Premium, 1995; Achievement Medal, 2000; Nikola Tesla Award, IEEE, 2001. *Publications:* papers relating to induction machines. *Recreations:* reading, walking, gardening.

WILLIAMSON, Prof. Timothy, FRSE; FBA 1997; Wykeham Professor of Logic, and Fellow of New College, Oxford University, since 2000; *b* 6 Aug. 1955; *er s* of late Colin Fletcher Williamson and of Karina Williamson (*née* Side; she *m* 2nd, Prof. Angus McIntosh, FBA, FRSE); *m* 1st, 1984, Elisabetta Perosino (marr. diss. 2003); one *s* one *d*; 2nd, 2004, Ana Mladenović; one *s*. *Educ:* Henley Grammar Sch.; Balliol Coll., Oxford (Hon. Fellow 2014); Christ Church, Oxford (MA 1981; DPhil 1981); MA *aeg* Dublin 1986. FRSE 1997. Sen. Scholar, Christ Church, Oxford, 1976–80; Lectr in Philosophy, TCD, 1980–88; Fellow and Praelector in Philosophy, University Coll., and CUF Lectr in Philosophy, Univ. of Oxford, 1988–94; Prof. of Logic and Metaphysics, Edinburgh Univ., 1995–2000. Visiting Professor: MIT, 1994; Princeton, 1998–99; Visiting Fellow: ANU, 1990, 1995; Centre for Advanced Study, Oslo, 2004; Vis. Erskine Fellow, Univ. of Canterbury, NZ, 1995; Nelson Dist. Prof., 2003, Nelson Vis. Prof., 2013–15, Univ. of Michigan; Vis. Prof., Yale Univ., 2016–; Townsend Visitor in Philos., Berkeley, 2006; Tang Chun-I Vis. Prof., Chinese Univ. of Hong Kong, 2007; Leverhulme Trust Major Res. Fellowship, 2009–12. Lectures: Henriette Herz, British Acad., 1996; Weatherhead, Tulane Univ., 1998; Jacobsen, UCL, 2001; Skolem, Oslo Univ., 2004; Jack Smart, ANU, 2005; Wedberg, Stockholm Univ., 2006; Gaos, Nat. Autonomous Univ. of Mexico, 2006; Hempel, Princeton, 2006; Amherst, Amherst Coll., 2009; Zeno, Utrecht Univ., 2009; Mesthene, Rutgers, 2010; Ortlieb, Claremont, 2012; Petrus Hispanus, Lisbon, 2012; Hägerström, Uppsala Univ., 2013; Kim Young-Jung, Seoul Nat. Univ., 2013; Nanqiang, Xiamen Univ., 2014; Ruth Manor, Tel-Aviv Univ., 2015; Bergmann, Univ. of Iowa, 2015. President: Aristotelian Soc., 2004–05; Mind Assoc., 2006–07 (Vice-Pres., 2005–06); Vice-Pres., British Logic Colloquium, 2007–12. FRSA 2011. MAE 2014. For. Mem., Norwegian Acad. of Sci. and Letters, 2004; For. Hon. Mem., Amer. Acad. of Arts and Scis, 2007; Hon. Mem., RIA, 2014. Dr *hc* Bucharest. *Publications:* Identity and Discrimination, 1990; Vagueness, 1994; Knowledge and its Limits, 2000; The Philosophy of Philosophy, 2007; Modal Logic as Metaphysics, 2013; Tetralogue: I'm right, you're wrong, 2015; articles in Jl of Phil., Phil Rev., Mind, Jl of Symbolic Logic, Jl of Phil Logic, Studia Logica, etc; *relevant publication:* Williamson on Knowledge, ed P. Greenough and D. Pritchard, 2009. *Address:* New College, Oxford OX1 3BN. *T:* (01865) 279555.

WILLING, Dame Paula; *see* Rego, Dame M. P. F.

WILLINGHAM, Anne Julie; *see* Desmet, A. J.

WILLINK, Sir Edward (Daniel), 3rd Bt *cr* 1957, of Dingle Bank, City of Liverpool; PhD; Chief Technical Consultant, Thales Research and Technology, 2000–12; *b* Windsor, 18 Feb. 1957; *o s* of Sir Charles William Willink, 2nd Bt and of Elizabeth, *d* of Humfrey Andrewes; *S* father, 2009; *m* 2004, Sally Margaret Hooker. *Educ:* Eton; Magdalene Coll., Cambridge (BA 1978; MA); Surrey Univ. (PhD 2002). CEng, MIEE 1993. Committer, Eclipse Foundn. *Publications:* various digital signal processing and software modelling workshop and conf. procs. *Recreation:* open source software. *Heir: cousin* Henry Augustine Willink [*b* 12 May 1971; *m* 2011, Aisha Mary Ellen Jung; three *s*].

See also S. J. L. Linnett.

WILLIS, family name of **Baron Willis of Knaresborough**.

WILLIS OF KNARESBOROUGH, Baron *cr* 2010 (Life Peer), of Harrogate in the County of North Yorkshire; **George Philip Willis;** *b* 30 Nov. 1941; *s* of George Willis and Hannah (*née* Gillespie); *m* 1974, Heather Elizabeth Sellars; one *s* one *d*. *Educ:* City of Leeds and Carnegie Coll.; Univ. of Leeds (Cert Ed 1963); Univ. of Birmingham (BPhil 1978). Asst teacher, Middleton Co. Secondary Boys' Sch., 1963–65; Head of History, Moor Grange Co. Secondary Boys' Sch., 1965–67; Sen. Master, Primrose Hill High Sch., Leeds, 1967–74; Dep. Hd, W Leeds Boys' GS, 1974–78; Head Teacher: Ormsby Sch., Cleveland, 1978–82; John Smeaton Community Sch., 1983–97. MP (Lib Dem) Harrogate and Knaresborough, 1997–2010. Front bench spokesman on further and higher educn, 1997–99, on educn and employment, 1999–2001, on educn and skills, 2001–05. Mem., Educn and Employment Select Cttee, 1999–2001; Chm., Innovation, Universities, Science and Skills (formerly Sci. and Technol.) Select Cttee, 2005–10. Treas., All-Party Gp on medical res., 2005–10. Chairman: AMRC, 2010–; Yorks and Humber Collab. for Leadership in Applied Health Res. and Care, NIHR, 2014–; Mem., NERC, 2010–. Chm., eLearning Foundn, 2010–. Hon. DSc Salford, 2013. *Recreations:* Leeds United season ticket holder, dance (ballet), current affairs, fishing. *Address:* House of Lords, SW1A 0PW. *Club:* National Liberal.

WILLIS, Prof. Anne Elizabeth, PhD; Director, Medical Research Council Toxicology Unit, since 2010; *b* London; *d* of Edward Willis and Winifred Willis; *m* 1996, Kenneth Siddle, *qv*; one *s*. *Educ:* Henrietta Barnett Sch., London; Univ. of Kent (BSc Biochem. 1984); Imperial Coll. London (PhD 1987). Res. Associate, Biochem., Univ. of Cambridge, 1988–92; Jun. Res. Fellow, 1988–92, Lectr, 1991–92, Churchill Coll., Cambridge; Lectr, 1992–2002, Reader, 2002–04, Prof., 2004, Univ. of Leicester; Prof. of Cancer Cell Biol., Univ. of Nottingham, 2004–10. *Recreation:* running. *Address:* MRC Toxicology Unit, Lancaster Road, Leicester LE1 9HN. *T:* (0116) 252 5611. *E:* aew5@le.ac.uk.

WILLIS, Air Vice-Marshal Gerald Edward; Director, Projects Defence Estates, 2003–04; *b* 25 Oct. 1949; *s* of John Morris Willis and Dorothy Maud Willis; *m* 1st, 1973, Janet Seaman (marr. diss. 1995); one *s* one *d*; 2nd, 1996, Angela Suter. *Educ:* Cardiff High Sch. for Boys; Univ. of Bristol (BSc Hons 1971). Asst Prodn Manager, GKN, 1971–73; commnd Engr Br., RAF, 1973; Dir, Corporate Develt, RAF Trng Gp Defence Agency, 1999–2000; Asst Comdt, Jt Services Comd and Staff Coll., 2000–01; Dir, Project Alexander Implementation Team, 2001–03. *Recreations:* choral singing, badminton, squash, amateur dramatics. *Address:* Fairford, Glos. *E:* gerrywillis@mail.com.

WILLIS, Jane; Director, Cross-cutting Interventions, Health and Safety Executive, 2009–15; *b* 26 Aug. 1955; *d* of Ernest and Lena England; *m* 1974, Howard Willis; one *s* one *d*. *Educ:* Watford Grammar Sch. for Girls; Open Univ. (BA Hons 1987). Joined Civil Service, 1973; Health and Safety Executive, 1988–2015: Head: Safety Policy Div., 1998–2002; Planning Efficiency and Finance Div., 2002–03; Strategic Policy, subseq. Strategic Prog., Dir, 2003–09. Gov., Watford Grammar Sch. for Girls, 2009–. *Recreations:* going to the ballet and theatre, gardening.

WILLIS, John Edward; Chief Executive, Mentorn and Creative Director, Tinopolis Group, since 2006 (Director, Tinopolis plc, since 2006); *b* 4 April 1946; *s* of Baron Willis and of Lady (Audrey Mary) Willis (*née* Hale); *m* 1972, Janet Ann Sperrin; one *s* one *d*. *Educ:* Eltham Coll.; Fitzwilliam Coll., Cambridge (MA); Bristol Univ. (PG Cert. in Film and TV). Yorkshire Television: journalist, 1970–75; Documentary Dir, 1975–82; Controller of Documentaries and Current Affairs, 1982–88; Channel Four Television: Controller of Factual Progs, 1988–89; Dep. Dir of Progs, 1990–92; Dir of Progs, 1993–97; Man. Dir, 1997–98, Chief Exec., 1998–2000, United (formerly United Film and Television) Productions; Man. Dir, LWT and United Prodns, 2000–01; Vice-Pres. for Nat. Programming, WGBH, 2002–03; Dir, Factual and Learning, BBC, 2003–06. Member, Board: Channel 5 Broadcasting, 1998–2000; ITN, 1999–2000. Chairman: Broadcasting Support Services, 1997–2002; Edinburgh Internat. Television Fest., 1998–2002; Internat. Television Enterprises Ltd Distributors, 1999–2000; Granada Wild (formerly United Wildlife), 1999–2001; Cosgrove Hall Ltd, 1999–2001; Dir, Sheffield Internat. Documentary Fest., 2007–. Vis. Industrial Prof. in Television, Univ. of Bristol, 1999–; Hon. Prof., Univ. of Stirling, 1997–. Ombudsman, 1998–2002, External Ombudsman, 2006–, The Guardian. Mem., Ind. Football Commn, 2002. Advr, Convergence Think Tank, DCMS and BIS (formerly BERR), 2007–. Trustee: Future Lab, 2006–12; BAFTA, 2007– (Dep. Chm., 2011–12, 2014–15; Chm., 2012–14); Disasters Emergency Cttee, 2008–14; One World Media, 2014– (Chm., 2014–). FRTS 1993; FRSA 1997. Numerous prizes and awards. *Publications:* Johnny Go Home, 1976; Churchill's Few: the Battle of Britain remembered, 1985. *Recreations:* cycling, soccer, cinema, theatre. *Address:* Mentorn Productions, Elsinore House, 77 Fulham Palace Road, W6 8JA.

WILLIS, Prof. John Raymond, PhD; FRS 1992; FIMA; Professor of Theoretical Solid Mechanics, University of Cambridge, 1994–2000 and 2001–07, now Emeritus; Fellow of Fitzwilliam College, Cambridge, 1966–72, 1994–2000 and 2001–07; *b* 27 March 1940; *s* of John V. G. and L. Gwendoline Willis; *m* 1964, Juliette Louise Ireland; three *d*. *Educ:* Imperial Coll., London (BSc, PhD); MA Cantab 1966. ARCS, DIC; FIMA 1966. Asst Lectr, Imperial Coll., 1962–64; Res. Associate, NY Univ., 1964–65; Cambridge University: Sen. Asst in Research, 1965–67; Asst Dir of Research, 1968–72; Dir of Studies in Maths, Fitzwilliam Coll., 1966–72; Bath University: Prof. of Applied Maths, 1972–94; Prof. of Maths, 2000–01. Editor-in-Chief, 1982–92, Jt Editor, 1992–, Jl Mechanics and Physics of Solids. Foreign Associate: NAE, 2004; French Acad. of Scis, 2009. Hon. DSc Bath, 2007. Timoshenko Medal, ASME, 1997; Prager Medal, Soc. of Engrg Sci., 1998; Solid Mechanics Prize, EUROMECH, 2012. *Publications:* papers on mechanics of solids in learned jls. *Recreations:* swimming, hiking, music. *Address:* Department of Applied Mathematics and Theoretical Physics, Centre for Mathematical Sciences, Wilberforce Road, Cambridge CB3 0WA. *T:* (01223) 339251.

WILLIS, Hon. Ralph, AO 2011; Treasurer of Australia, Dec. 1990 and 1993–96; Chairman, Western Health, since 2004; *b* 14 April 1938; *s* of S. Willis; *m* 1970, Carol Dawson; one *s* two *d*. *Educ:* Footscray Central Sch.; University High Sch.; Melbourne Univ. (BCom). Australian Council of Trade Unions: Research Officer, 1960–70; Industrial Advocate, 1970–72. MP (ALP) Gellibrand, Vic, 1972–98; instrumental in developing econ., finance and ind. relns policies for Opposition, 1976–83; Opposition spokesperson on: Ind. Relns, 1976–77; Econ. Affairs, 1977–83; Econ. Develt, Jan.–March 1983; Minister for Employment and Ind. Relns and Minister Assisting the Prime Minister for Public Service Matters, 1983–88; Minister for Transport and Communications, 1988–90; Minister of Finance, 1990–93. Chm., C+BUS Industry Superannuation Fund, 2000–09. *Recreations:* tennis, reading, football. *Address:* 24a Gellibrand Street, Williamstown, Vic 3016, Australia.

WILLIS, Rebecca; environmental consultant, since 2004; *b* 20 Feb. 1972; *d* of Dave and Jane Willis; *m* (marr. diss.); two *s*. *Educ:* King's Coll., Cambridge (BA Hons Social and Pol Scis 1994); Univ. of Sussex (MA Envmt, Develt and Policy 1996). Policy Advr, EP, Brussels, 1997–98; Green Alliance: Hd of Policy, 1998–2001; Dir, 2001–04; Associate, 2004–. Vice Chm., Sustainable Develt Commn, 2004–11. Member: NERC, 2011–; Scientific Adv. Cttee, RCUK Energy Prog. Freelance writer and policy consultant. Associate, Futerra. *Publications:* See-through Science: why public engagement needs to move upstream (with James Wilsdon), 2004; Grid 2.0: the next generation, 2006; (with Nick Eyre) Demanding Less: why we need a new politics of energy, 2011. *Recreations:* fell-walking, running, wild swimming. *Address:* 5 Bankfield, Kendal, Cumbria LA9 5DR. *W:* www.rebeccawillis.co.uk.

WILLIS, Very Rev. Robert Andrew; DL; Dean of Canterbury, since 2001; *b* 17 May 1947; *s* of Thomas Willis and Vera Rosina Willis (*née* Britton). *Educ:* Kingswood Grammar Sch.; Warwick Univ. (BA); Worcester Coll., Oxford (DipTheol); Cuddesdon Coll., Oxford. Ordained deacon, 1972, priest, 1973; Curate, St Chad's, Shrewsbury, 1972–75; Vicar Choral, Salisbury Cathedral and Chaplain to Cathedral Sch., 1975–78; Team Rector, Tisbury, Wilts, 1978–87; Chaplain, Cranborne Chase Sch. and RAF Chilmark, 1978–87; RD, Chalke, 1982–87; Vicar, Sherborne with Castleton and Lillington, 1987–92; Chaplain, Sherborne Sch. for Girls, 1987–92; RD, Sherborne, 1991–92; Dean of Hereford, 1992–2001; Priest-in-charge, St John the Baptist, Hereford, 1992–2001. Canon and Prebendary of Salisbury Cathedral, 1988–92; Proctor in Convocation, 1985–92, 1994–. Member: Council, Partnership for World Mission, 1990–2002; Cathedrals' Fabric Commn for England, 1994–; C of E Liturgical Commn, 1994–98; Chm., Deans' (formerly Deans' and Provosts') Conf., 1999–. Governor: Cranborne Chase Sch., 1985–87; Sherborne Sch., 1987–92; Chairman of Governors: Hereford Cathedral Sch., 1993–2001; King's Sch., Canterbury, 2001–. Mem. Council, Univ. of Kent, 2003–. FRSA 1993. DL Kent 2011. Freeman, City of Canterbury, 2008. Hon. Fellow, Canterbury Christ Ch Univ., 2004; Hon. FGCM 2006. Hon. DD Yale, 2009; Hon. DCL Kent, 2011. KStJ 2009 (CStJ 2001; Sub ChStJ 1991; Sub Dean, 1999). Cross of St Augustine, 2012. *Publications:* (contrib.) Hymns Ancient and Modern, New Standard edn, 1983; (jtly) The Chorister's Companion, 1989; (contrib.) Common Praise, 2000; (contrib.) New English Praise, 2006; (contrib.) Sing Praise, 2011. *Recreations:* music, literature, travel. *Address:* The Deanery, 20 The Precincts, Canterbury, Kent CT1 2EP. *T:* (01227) 762862, *Fax:* (01227) 865222. *Club:* Oxford and Cambridge.

WILLISON, Ian Roy, CBE 2005; Senior Research Fellow, Institute of English Studies, School of Advanced Study, University of London, since 1999; *b* 17 Aug. 1926; *s* of Charles Walter Willison and Daisy Willison (*née* Farmer). *Educ:* Colfe's Grammar Sch.; Peterhouse, Cambridge (BA 1948, MA 1953); Sch. of Librarianship and Archive Admin, UCL (Postgrad. Dip. 1953). Asst Keeper, Dept of Printed Books, BM, 1953–74; Dep. Keeper and Hd, Rare Books Br., then Hd, English Lang. Br., BL, 1974–87. Vis. Prof. of Histl Bibliography, Grad. Liby Sch., Univ. of Chicago, 1959; Cline Vis. Prof., Univ. of Texas at Austin, 1989. Sec., then Chm., Rare and Precious Books and Documents Section, Internat. Fedn of Liby Assocs, 1978–86; Chm., UK Book Trade Hist. Gp, 1985–98; Mem., Colloque d'Histoire Mondiale du Livre et de l'Edition, 2001–05. Jt Gen. Ed., Cambridge History of the Book in Britain, 1999–. Hon. FCLIP (Hon. FLA 1988). *Publications:* (ed jtly) The New Cambridge Bibliography of English Literature, vol. 4 1900–1950, 1972; (ed jtly) Modernist Writers and the Marketplace, 1996; (ed jtly) Literary Cultures and the Material Book, 2007. *Recreation:* classical music. *Address:* Institute of English Studies, School of Advanced Study, University of London, Senate House, Malet Street, WC1E 7HU. *T:* (020) 7862 8707, *Fax:* (020) 7862 8720. *E:* ian.willison@sas.ac.uk.

WILLISON, Prof. Keith Robert, PhD; molecular biologist; Professor of Chemical Biology, Imperial College London, since 2012; *b* 12 Oct. 1953; *s* of late Dr Robin Gow Willison and of Gillian Margaret Willison (*née* Caven-Irving); *m* 1979, Jennifer Anne Bardsley; two *s*. *Educ:* New College Sch., Oxford; St Edward's Sch., Oxford (Schol.); Univ. of Sussex (BSc Hons 1975); St John's Coll., Cambridge (PhD 1979). MRC Schol., MRC Lab. of Molecular Biol., Cambridge, 1975–78; Postdoctoral Fellow, Cold Spring Harbor Labs, NY, 1979–81; Institute of Cancer Research: Res. Scientist, 1981–2011; Hd, Chester Beatty Labs, 1996–2005; Hd, Haddow Labs, 2002–05; Personal Chair in Molecular Cell Biol., at BPMF, subseq. Inst. of Cancer Res., Univ. of London, 1995–2011. Vis. Prof., Osaka Univ., 1990–91; Weston Vis. Prof., Weizmann Inst. of Sci., Rehovot, 2011–12; JSPS Vis. Prof., Hyogo Univ., 2013. Institute of Cancer Research: Member: Exec. Cttee, 1994–2000; Bd of Mgt, 1997–2000; Corp. Mgt Gp, 2000–05; Mem., Jt Res. Cttee, Royal Marsden NHS, subseq. NHS Foundn, Trust and Inst. Cancer Res., 2000–09. Mem. Council, Royal Marsden NHS, subseq. NHS Foundn, Trust, 2003–11. Mem., Governing Body, Charterhouse, 2004–. FRSC 2013. *Publications:* contrib. papers to scientific jls on topics in genetics and protein biochem. *Recreations:* cricket (Mem., Presidents XI CC, Wimbledon, 1983–99), football. *Address:* Institute of Chemical Biology, Department of Chemistry, Imperial College London, South Kensington Campus, SW7 2AZ. *T:* (020) 7594 5807. *Club:* Athenæum.

WILLMAN, John; editorial consultant, since 2009; *b* 27 May 1949; *s* of late John Willman and Kate Willman (*née* Thornton); *m* 1978, Margaret Shanahan; one *s* two *d*. *Educ:* Bolton Sch.; Jesus Coll., Cambridge (MA); Westminster Coll., Oxford (CertEd). Teacher, Brentford Sch. for Girls, Brentford, Middx, 1972–76; Financial Researcher, Money Which?, 1976–79; Editor, Taxes and Assessment (Inland Revenue Staff Fedn pubn), 1979–83; Pubns Manager, Peat, Marwick, Mitchell & Co., 1983–85; Gen. Sec., Fabian Soc., 1985–89; Jt Editor, New Socialist, 1989; Editor, Consumer Policy Review, 1990–91; Financial Times: Public Policy Editor, 1991–94; Features Editor, 1994–97; Consumer Industries Editor, 1997–2000; Banking Editor, 2000–01; Chief Leader Writer, 2002–06; Associate Editor, 2002–09; UK Business Editor, 2006–09. Visiting Research Fellow: IPPR, 1990–91; Social Market Foundn, 1997; Sen. Res. Fellow, Policy Exchange, 2009–. Specialist Advisor: Treasury Cttee, H of C, 2011–15; Parly Commn on Banking Standards, 2012–13. Journalist of the Year, Financing Healthcare, Norwich Union, 1998; Financial Journalist of the Year, British Press Awards, 2001; Business Journalist of the Year, Best Banking Submission, 2002. *Publications:* Lloyds Bank Tax Guide, annually, 1987–2000; Make Your Will, 1989; Labour's Electoral Challenge, 1989; Sorting Out Someone's Will, 1990; The Which? Guide to Planning and Conservation, 1990; Work for Yourself, 1991; A Better State of Health, 1998. *T:* 07767 301225. *E:* johnwillman@btinternet.com.

WILLMAN, Prof. Paul William, DPhil; Professor of Management, London School of Economics, since 2006; *b* 24 Aug. 1953; *s* of late William Willman and Marjorie Willman; *m* 1997, Kathleen Pickett. *Educ:* St Catharine's Coll., Cambridge (BA, MA); Trinity Coll., Oxford (DPhil 1979). Lectr in Industrial Sociol., Imperial Coll., London, 1979–83; Lectr, Sch. of Mgt, Cranfield Inst. of Technol., 1983–84; London Business School: Asst, 1984–88; Associate Prof., 1988–91; Prof. of Organisational Behaviour, 1991–2000; Ernest Butten Prof. of Mgt Studies, Saïd Business Sch., Univ. of Oxford, 2000–06; Fellow, Balliol Coll., Oxford, 2000–06. Mem. Council, ACAS, 2014–. *Publications:* Fairness, Collective Bargaining and Incomes Policy, 1982; (jtly) Power Efficiency and Institutions, 1983; (ed jtly and contrib.) The Organisational Failures Framework and Industrial Sociology, 1983; (jtly) Innovation and Management Control, 1985; (jtly) The Car Industry: labour relations and industrial adjustment, 1985; Technological Change, Collective Bargaining and Industrial Efficiency, 1986; (jtly) The Limits to Self-Regulation, 1988; Union Business, Trade Union Organisation and Financial Reform in the Thatcher Years, 1993; (jtly) Union Organisation and Activity, 2004; (jtly) Traders: managing risks and decisions in financial markets, 2004; Understanding Management, 2014; contrib. books and learned jls on industrial relations etc. *Recreations:* opera, parish churches, dogs. *Address:* Department of Management, London School of Economics and Political Science, Houghton Street, WC2A 2AE. *T:* (020) 7955 6739.

WILLMER, John Franklin; QC 1967; Lloyd's Appeal Arbitrator in Salvage Cases, 1991–2000; *b* 30 May 1930; *s* of Rt Hon. Sir (Henry) Gordon Willmer, OBE, TD and Barbara, *d* of Sir Archibald Hurd; *m* 1st, 1958, Nicola Ann Dickinson (marr. diss. 1979); one *s* three *d*; 2nd, 1979, Margaret Lilian, *d* of Chester B. Berryman. *Educ:* Winchester; Corpus Christi Coll., Oxford. National Service, 2nd Lieut, Cheshire Regt, 1949–50; TA Cheshire Regt, 1950–51; Middlesex Regt, 1951–57 (Captain). Called to Bar, Inner Temple, 1955, Bencher, 1975. A Gen. Comr of Income Tax for Inner Temple, 1982–2005. Member: panel of Lloyd's Arbitrators in Salvage Cases, 1967–91; panel from which Wreck Commissioners appointed, 1967–79, reapptd 1987–2000; Admiralty Court Cttee, 1980–95. Leader, Admiralty Bar, 1992–95. Retired from practice at Bar, 1995, from practice as Arbitrator, 2003. Freeman, Arbitrators' Co., 1992. St Mellitus Medal, Dio. London, 2012. *Recreations:* walking, visiting ancient sites and buildings, amateur dramatics. *Address:* Flat 4, 23 Lymington Road, NW6 1HZ. *T:* (020) 7435 9245. *Club:* Oxford and Cambridge.

WILLMORE, Prof. (Albert) Peter, FRAS; Professor of Space Research, University of Birmingham, 1972–97, now Emeritus; *b* 28 April 1930; *s* of Albert Mervyn Willmore and Kathleen Helen Willmore; *m* 1st, 1963, Geraldine Anne Smith; two *s*; 2nd, 1972, Stephanie Ruth Alden; one *s* one *d*. *Educ:* Holloway Sch.; University Coll. London (BSc, PhD). Research interests: fusion res., AERE, 1954–57; upper atmosphere, using sounding rockets and satellites, esp. Ariel I (launched 1962), UCL, 1957–70; X-ray astronomy, using sounding rockets and satellites, UCL, 1970–72, Univ. of Birmingham, 1972–. Academician, Internat. Acad. of Astronautics, 1996. Tsiolkovsky Medal, USSR, 1987; Vikram Sarabhai Medal, COSPAR, 2004; Distinguished Service Medal, COSPAR, 2012. *Publications:* approx. 150 papers in learned jls, together with many other articles and reviews. *Recreations:* music, playing the violin (though this may not be music), literature, Bronze Age history, travel, sailing. *Address:* 38 Grove Avenue, Moseley, Birmingham B13 9RY. *T:* (0121) 449 2616.

WILLMOT, Prof. Derrick Robert, PhD; FDSRCPSGlas, FDSRCS; Specialist Orthodontist, Ferndale House Dental Practice, Chesterfield, since 2011; Dean, Faculty of Dental Surgery, Royal College of Surgeons of England, 2008–11; *b* Chesterfield, Derbys; *s* of Jack and Olive Willmot; *m* 1971, Patricia, *d* of Robert Creighton, San Luis, Minorca; two *s*. *Educ:* Chesterfield Boys Grammar Sch.; University Coll. London and UCH Dental Sch. (BDS 1970); PhD Sheffield 2000. LDS RCS 1969, FDS RCS 2007; FDSRCPSGlas 1978; DOrthRCS 1980, MOrthRCS 1988; DDO Glasgow 1980. Resident Dental Hse Surgeon, Royal Portsmouth Hosp., 1970; Partner, gen. dental practice, Ashbourne, Derbys, 1970–77; Registrar, then Sen. Registrar, UCH Dental Sch., 1977–84; Consultant Orthodontist: Chesterfield Royal Hosp., 1984–92; Sheffield Teaching Hosps NHS Trust, 1992–2010; Hon. Prof. of Orthodontics, Sheffield Univ., 2005–10, now Emeritus. Pres., S Yorks Br., BDA, 1992–93. Vice Chm. Govs, Chesterfield Grammar Sch., 1988–92. Mem., Round Table, Ashbourne, St Albans, Chesterfield, 1972–87. Chm., Chesterfield 41 Club, 2013–14. Pres., Old Cestrefeldians, 2015–16. FHEA 2002. John Tomes Medal, BDA, 2001; Distinction Award, British Orthodontic Soc., 2011. *Publications:* contrib. peer reviewed scientific papers, abstracts, letters and book chapters. *Recreations:* fishing, shooting, gardening, Member of Chesterfield Scarsdale Rotary Club (Pres., 2000–01). *Address:* Ashcroft, Matlock Road, Walton, Chesterfield S42 7LD. *E:* d.willmot@sheffield.ac.uk. *Clubs:* Flyfishers'; Royal Society of Medicine.

WILLMOTT, Prof. Andrew John, PhD; Professor of Physical Oceanography and Head, School of Marine and Science Technology, Newcastle University, since 2014; *b* 1 Aug. 1954; *s* of David Edward Willmott and Margaret Ethel Willmott (*née* Punt); *m* 1979, Sasithorn Aranuvachapun; two *d*. *Educ:* Bristol Univ. (BSc 1st Cl. Hons Maths); Univ. of E Anglia (MSc; PhD Applied Maths 1978). Res. Fellow, Univ. of BC, 1978–81; Asst Prof., Naval Postgrad. Sch., Monterey, 1981–83; Lectr in Applied Maths, 1983–96, Reader in Geophysical Fluid Dynamics, 1991–96, Univ. of Exeter; Prof. of Applied Maths and Hd, Sch. of Computing and Maths, Keele Univ., 1996–2005; Dir, NERC Proudman Oceanographic Lab., 2005–10; Dir of Sci. and Technol., NERC Nat. Oceanography Centre, 2010–13. Visiting Professor: Dept of Earth and Ocean Scis, Univ. of Liverpool, 2005–May 2016; in Applied Maths, 2005, in Ocean and Climate Dynamics, 2013–Feb. 2016, Keele Univ. *Publications:* numerous contribs to refereed jls, and book chapters, on ocean dynamics and sea ice processes relating to polynya modelling. *Recreations:* racquet sports, hiking, gardening, wine tasting. *Address:* School of Marine Science and Technology, Armstrong Building, Newcastle University, Newcastle upon Tyne NE1 7RU. *E:* andrew.willmott@ncl.ac.uk. *Club:* Oceanography.

WILLMOTT, Dennis James, CBE 1988; QFSM 1981; Group Contingency Manager, 1988–93, and Fire Safety Consultant, 1993–98, Avon Rubber plc; *b* 10 July 1932; *s* of James Arthur Willmott and Esther Winifred Maude Willmott (*née* Styles); *m* 1958, Mary Patricia Currey; three *s*. *Educ:* St Albans County Grammar School. MIFireE. Regular Army Service, East Surrey Regt, 1950–51, Royal Norfolk Regt, 1951–57. London, Bucks, Hants and Isle of Wight Fire Brigades, 1957–74; Dep. Chief Officer, Wilts Fire Brigade, 1974–76; Chief Staff Officer, 1976–81, Dep. Chief Officer, 1981–83, London Fire Brigade; Chief Fire Officer, Merseyside Fire Brigade, 1983–88. Member: Kennet DC, 1991–2009 (Leader, 1999–2003; Chm., 2008–09); (C) Wilts CC, 1993–2009 (Chm., 2003–04). Chairman: Devizes Constituency Cons. Assoc., 1999–2002 (Vice Pres., 2002–); Wilts and Swindon Combined Fire Authy, 2000–09; SW Regl Mgt Bd, 2004–05; Chm. Bd of Dirs, SW Local Authy Controlled Co., 2007–09; Mem., Veteran's Adv. and Pensions Cttee for the SW, 2010–. *Recreation:* walking. *Address:* 27 Highlands, Potterne, Devizes, Wilts SN10 5NS. *T:* (01380) 730115. *E:* djwillmott@btinternet.com. *Clubs:* Victory Services, Union Jack; Conservative (Devizes); Royal British Legion (Potterne).

WILLMOTT, Maj.-Gen. Edward George, CB 1990; OBE 1979; CEng, FICE; Chairman, Hereford Futures Ltd, since 2009; *b* 18 Feb. 1936; *s* of late T. E. Willmott and E. R. Willmott (*née* Murphy); *m* 1960, Sally Penelope (*née* Banyard); two *s* one *d*. *Educ:* Gonville and Caius Coll., Cambridge (MA). FICE 1989; CEng 1990. Commissioned RE 1956; psc 1968; active service, N Borneo 1963, N Ireland 1969, 1970, 1971, 1972, 1977; comd 8 Field Sqdn, 1971–73; 23 Engr Regt, 1976; 2 Armd Div. Engr Regt, 1977–78; 30 Engr Bde, 1981–82; RCDS 1983; Dep. Comdt RMCS, 1984–85; Vice-Pres. (Army), Ordnance Bd, 1985–86; Pres., Ordnance Bd, 1986–88; Dir Gen., Weapons (Army), 1988–90. Chief Exec., CITB, 1991–98. Col Comdt, RE, 1987–97. Hon. Col 101 (London) Engr Regt (V), 1990–97. Chm., Herefordshire Primary Care Trust, 2000–06; non-executive Director: Healthcare Purchasing Consortium, 2006–09; ESG Ltd, 2006–09. Pres., Instn of Royal Engrs, 1987–90.

Master, Engineers' Co., 2004–05 (Warden, 2001–04). Mem. Council, Roedean Sch., 1994–2004. Gov., Hereford Cathedral Trust, 2015. *Recreations:* gardening, fishing. *Club:* Oriental.

WILLMOTT, Dame Glenis, DBE 2015; Member (Lab) East Midlands Region, European Parliament, since 2006; Leader, European Parliamentary Labour Party, since 2009; *b* 4 March 1951; *d* of Cyril Montgomery Barden and Lily Barden; *m* 1999, Edward Charles Willmott; one *d*, and one step *s* one step *d*. *Educ:* Trent Poly. (HNC Med. Scis, Clin. Chem.; HNC Med. Scis, Haematol.). Med. scientist, King's Mill and Mansfield Hosps, 1968–87; Parly Asst, 1987–90; Pol Officer, 1990–2006, Organiser, 1992–95, Sen. Organiser, 1995–2006, GMB. Mem. (Lab), Notts CC, 1989–93. Sec., E Midlands Regl Trade Union and Labour Party Orgn, 1990–2006. *Recreations:* reading, pilates, cooking, crosswords and sudoku. *Address:* (office) Harold Wilson House, 23 Barratt Lane, Attenborough, Nottingham NG9 6AD. *T:* (0115) 922 9717, *Fax:* (0115) 922 4439. *E:* office@gleniswillmott.org.uk.

WILLMOTT, Prof. Hugh Christopher, PhD; FBA 2015; Research Professor of Organization Studies, Cardiff University, since 2005; Professor of Management, Cass Business School, City University London, since 2014; *b* 17 Sept. 1950; *s* of David P. T. Willmott and Mary Elizabeth Willmott (*née* Kitchen); *m* 1977, Irena Niezgoda; three *d*. *Educ:* Univ. of Manchester (BSc 1st Cl. 1972; PhD 1977). Univ. of Aston, 1977–85; Prof. of Organizational Analysis, Manchester Sch. of Mgt, UMIST, 1995–2001; Diageo Prof. of Mgt Studies, Judge Inst. of Mgt, Cambridge Univ., 2001–05. Visiting Professor: Copenhagen Business Sch., 1989; Uppsala Business Sch., 1990; Univ. of Lund, Sweden, 1999–2004; Cranfield Univ., 2000–03. Hon. PhD Lund, 2011. *Publications:* (with M. Alvesson) Making Sense of Management, 1996; (with D. Knights) Management Lives, 1999; (ed jtly) Managing Knowledge, 2000; contrib. numerous articles to acad. jls. *Recreations:* cycling, walking, gardening, swimming. *Address:* Cass Business School, City University London, 106 Bunhill Row, EC1Y 8TZ.

WILLMOTT, Rt Rev. Trevor; *see* Dover, Bishop Suffragan of.

WILLOCHRA, Bishop of, since 2012; **Rt Rev. John Stead;** *b* Bexleyheath, 11 March 1956; *s* of James Joseph Stead and Evelyn May Stead; *m* 1979, Janet Ellen, (Jan); two *s*. *Educ:* Deakin High Sch.; Univ. of Canberra (BEd); Sydney Coll. of Divinity (BTh). Archdeacon, Dio. of Canberra and Goulburn, 2004–09; Asst Bishop of Bathurst, 2009–12. Liaison Bishop, Mission to Seafarers, Australia, 2013–; Bishop Protector, First Order Soc. of St Francis, Province of the Divine Compassion, 2014–. Nat. Clerical Chair, Anglican Men's Soc., 2012–. Mem., Alban Inst. *Recreations:* cooking, walking, watching movies. *Address:* PO Box 88, Gladstone, SA 5473, Australia.

WILLOTT, Brian; *see* Willott, W. B.

WILLOTT, Rt Hon. Jennifer Nancy; PC 2014; *b* 29 May 1974; *d* of (William) Brian Willott, *qv*; *m* 2009, Andrew Poole; two *s*. *Educ:* Univ. of Durham (BA Hons Classics 1996); London Sch. of Econs (MSc Develt Studies 1997). Consultant, Adithi NGO, Bihar, 1995; Hd of Office, Lembit Öpik, MP, 1997–2000; Researcher, Nat. Assembly for Wales, 2000–01; Project Adminr, Derwen Fostering and Adoption Project, Barnardo's, 2001; Hd of Advocacy, UNICEF UK, 2001–03; Chief Exec., Victim Support S Wales, 2003–05. Mem., Merton BC, 1998–2000. Contested (Lib Dem) Cardiff Central, 2001. MP (Lib Dem) Cardiff Central, 2005–15; contested (Lib Dem) same seat, 2015. PPS to Sec. of State for Energy and Climate Change, 2010; an Asst Govt Whip, 2012–14; Parliamentary Under Secretary of State: Employment Relations and Consumer Affairs, 2013–14; Women and Equality, 2013–14. Member: Work and Pensions Select Cttee, 2005–10; Public Admin Select Cttee, 2005–10. *Recreations:* travelling, music, singing, reading.

WILLOTT, (William) Brian, CB 1996; PhD; Chair, Gwent Healthcare NHS Trust, 2003–08; *b* 14 May 1940; *s* of late Dr William Harford Willott and Dr Beryl P. M. Willott; *m* 1970, Alison Leyland Pyke-Lees; two *s* two *d*. *Educ:* Trinity Coll., Cambridge (MA, PhD). Research Associate, Univ. of Maryland, USA, 1965–67; Asst Principal, Board of Trade, 1967–69; Principal: BoT, 1969–73; HM Treasury, 1973–75; Asst Sec., Dept of Industry, 1975–78; Secretary: Industrial Development Unit, DoI, 1978–80; NEB, 1980–81; Chief Exec., British Technology Gp (NEB and NRDC), 1981–84; Head of IT Div., DTI, 1984–87; Hd of Financial Services Div., DTI, 1987–92; Chief Exec., ECGD, 1992–97; Chief Exec., WDA, 1997–2000. Dir, Dragon Internat. Studios Ltd, 2002–. Dir, Wales Mgt Council, 2000–03. Mem. Council, Nat. Museums and Galls of Wales, subseq. Trustee, Nat. Museum Wales, 2001–10. Mem., Church of Wales Governing Body, 2012–15. *Recreations:* music, reading, gardening. *Address:* Coed Cefn, Tregare, Monmouth NP25 4DT.
See also Rt Hon. J. N. Willott.

WILLOUGHBY, family name of **Baron Middleton**.

WILLOUGHBY DE BROKE, 21st Baron *cr* 1491; **Leopold David Verney;** DL; *b* 14 Sept. 1938; *s* of 20th Baron Willoughby de Broke, MC, AFC, AE and Rachel (*d* 1991), *d* of Sir Bourchier Wrey, 11th Bt; *S* father, 1986; *m* 1st, 1965, Petra (marr. diss. 1989), 2nd *d* of Sir John Aird, 3rd Bt, MVO, MC; three *s*; 2nd, 2003, Alexandra, Comtesse du Luart. *Educ:* Le Rosey; New College, Oxford. Chairman: S. M. Theatre Co. Ltd, 1992–; Compton Verney Opera and Ballet Project, 1992–2002; St Martins Magazines plc, 1992–2008. President: Heart of England Tourist Bd, 1996–2005; CPRE Warwicks, 2005–; Patron, Warwicks Assoc. of Boys' Clubs, 1991–2004; Chm., Warwicks Hunt Ltd, 2005–12. Hon. Gov., RSC. Mem. Council, Anglo-Hong Kong Trust, 1989–2006. Mem., H of L Select Cttee on EC, 1996–2001; elected Mem., H of L, 1999. DL Warwickshire, 1999. *Heir: s* Hon. Rupert Greville Verney, *b* 4 March 1966. *Address:* Ditchford Farm, Moreton-in-Marsh, Glos GL56 9RD.

WILLOUGHBY DE ERESBY, Baroness (27th in line), *cr* 1313 (by some reckonings 28th in line); **Nancy Jane Marie Heathcote-Drummond-Willoughby;** *b* 1 Dec. 1934; *d* of 3rd Earl of Ancaster, KCVO, TD, and Hon. Nancy Phyllis Louise Astor (*d* 1975), *d* of 2nd Viscount Astor; *S* to Barony of father, 1983. Trustee, Nat. Portrait Gall., 1994–2004. Mem. (Ind.), South Kesteven DC, 1969–82. DL Lincs, 1993–2009. OStJ 2000. *Heir: co-heirs:* Lt-Col Sebastian St Maur Miller [*b* 7 Feb. 1965; *m* 1991, Emma Caroline Harries; one *s* one *d*]; Sir John Aird, Bt, *qv*. *Address:* Grimsthorpe, Bourne, Lincs PE10 0LZ.

WILLS, family name of **Barons Dulverton** and **Wills**.

WILLS, Baron *cr* 2010 (Life Peer), of North Swindon in the County of Wiltshire and of Woodside Park in the London Borough of Barnet; **Michael David Wills;** PC 2008; *b* 20 May 1952; *s* of Stephen Wills and Elizabeth Wills (*née* McKeowen); *m* 1984, Jill Freeman; three *s* two *d*. *Educ:* Haberdashers' Aske's Sch., Elstree; Clare Coll., Cambridge (BA 1st cl. Hons Hist.). HM Diplomatic Service, 1976–80; Researcher, 1980–82, Producer, 1982–84, LWT; Dir, Juniper Productions, 1985–97. MP (Lab) N Swindon, 1997–2010. Parliamentary Under-Secretary of State: DTI, 1999; DFEE, 1999–2001; Parly Sec., LCD, 2001–02; Parly Under-Sec. of State, Home Office, 2002–03; Minister of State, MoJ, 2007–10. *Publications:* as David McKeowen: Grip, 2005; Trapped, 2007. *Address:* House of Lords, SW1A 0PW.

WILLS, Arthur William, OBE 1990; DMus (Dunelm), FRCO (CHM), ADCM; composer; Organist and Director of Music, Ely Cathedral, 1958–90; Professor, Royal Academy of Music, 1964–92; *b* 19 Sept. 1926; *s* of Violet Elizabeth and Archibald Wills; *m* 1953, Mary Elizabeth Titterton; one *s* one *d*. *Educ:* St John's Sch., Coventry. Sub-Organist, Ely Cathedral, 1949; Director of Music, King's School, Ely, 1953–64. Mem. Council, RCO, 1966–95; Examr to Royal Schs of Music, 1966–2002. Recital tours in Canada, Europe, USA, Australia and New Zealand; recording artist. Composer, opera, Winston and Julia '1984' (unpublished). Hon. RAM, Hon. FLCM, FRSCM. *Publications:* (contrib.) English Church Music, 1978; Organ, 1984, 2nd edn 1993; Full with Wills (memoir), 2006; numerous musical *compositions* include: *organ:* Sonata, Trio Sonata, Christmas Meditations, Prelude and Fugue (Alkmaar), Tongues of Fire, Variations on Amazing Grace, Symphonia Eliensis, Concerto (organ, strings and timpani), The Fenlands (symphonic suite: for brass band and organ; for orchestral brass and organ), Etheldreda Rag (organ or piano); Wondrous Machine! A Young Person's Guide to the Organ; *brass band:* Overture: A Muse of Fire; *guitar:* Sonata, Pavane and Galliard, Hommage à Ravel, Four Elizabethan Love Songs (alto and guitar), Moods and Diversions, The Year of the Tiger, Suite Africana, Concerto Lirico for Guitar Quartet; Concerto for guitar and organ; *chamber:* Sacrae Symphoniae: Veni Creator Spiritus; A Toccata of Galuppi's (counter-tenor and string quartet); *piano:* Sonata; *choral:* Missa Eliensis, The Child for Today (carol sequence), The Light Invisible (double choir, organ and percussion), Missa in Memoriam Benjamin Britten, An English Requiem, Jerusalem Luminosa (choir and organ), Ely (part-song for treble voices), Caedmon: a children's cantata, The Gods of Music (choral concerto), Missa Sancti Stephani; Missa Incarnationis; That Wondrous Birthday: three carols and a coda; Crossing the Bar; Remembrance: the world of light; Love bade me welcome (communion motet); *vocal:* When the Spirit Comes (four poems of Emily Brontë), The Dark Lady (eight Shakespeare Sonnets); Eternity's Sunrise (three poems of William Blake); *orchestra:* Symphony No 1 in A minor. *Recreations:* travel, antique collecting, Eastern philosophy. *Address:* Paradise House, 26 New Barns Road, Ely, Cambs CB7 4PN. *T:* (01353) 662084.

WILLS, Sir David James Vernon, 5th Bt *cr* 1923 of Blagdon, co. Somerset; *b* 2 Jan. 1955; *s* of Sir John Vernon Wills, 4th Bt, KCVO, TD and of Diana Veronica Cecil, (Jane), (*née* Baker); *S* father, 1998; *m* 1999, Mrs Paula Burke. Master, Soc. of Merchant Venturers, 2005. *Heir: b* Anthony John Vernon Wills [*b* 10 Dec. 1956; *m* 1983, Katherine Wilks; three *s*]. *Address:* Langford Court, Langford, Bristol BS40 5DA.

WILLS, Sir (David) Seton, 5th Bt *cr* 1904, of Hazelwood and Clapton-in-Gordano; FRICS; *b* 29 Dec. 1939; *s* of Major George Seton Wills (*d* 1979) (*yr s* of 3rd Bt) and Lilah Mary, *y d* of Captain Percy Richard Hare; *S* uncle, 1983; *m* 1968, Gillian, twin *d* of A. P. Eastoe; one *s* three *d*. *Educ:* Eton. FRICS 1976. *Heir: s* James Seton Wills [*b* 24 Nov. 1970; *m* 2003, Katy Gascoigne-Pees; two *s* one *d* (of whom one *s* one *d* are twins)]. *Address:* Tower House, Hollington Lane, Woolton Hill, Newbury, Berks RG20 9XX.

WILLS, Dean Robert, AO 1994 (AM 1986); Chairman: Transfield Services Ltd, 2001–05; John Fairfax Holdings Ltd, 2002–05 (Director, 1994–2005); *b* 10 July 1933; *s* of Walter William Wills and Violet Wills (*née* Kent); *m* 1955, Margaret Florence Williams, *d* of E. G. Williams; one *s* two *d*. *Educ:* Sacred Heart Coll., S Aust.; SA Inst. of Technology. AASA. Dir, 1974, Man. Dir, 1977–83, Chm., 1983–86, W. D. & H. O. Wills (Australia) Ltd; Amatil Ltd, later Coca-Cola Amatil Ltd: Dir, 1975–99; Dep. Chm., 1983–84; Man. Dir, 1984–94; Chm., 1984–99; Chm., Australian Eagle Insurance Co., 1986–89. Chairman: Nat. Mutual Life Assoc., 1997–2000 (Dir, 1991; Vice Chm., 1992–97); Nat. Mutual Hldgs Ltd, 1997–2000 (Dep. Chm., 1995–97); Coca-Cola Australia Foundn Ltd, 2002–05; Director: Australian Grand Prix Corp., 1994–2002 (Dep. Chm., 1994–2002); Westfield Hldgs/Westfield America Trust, 1994–2008. Member: Business Council of Aust., 1984–94 (Vice Pres., 1987–88, Pres., 1988–90); Bd of Aust. Graduate Sch. of Management, Univ. of NSW, 1985–92. Pres., 1991, Gov., 1992–94, Med. Foundn. Trustee, Mus. of Applied Arts and Sciences (Powerhouse Mus.), NSW, 1986–90. *Recreations:* tennis, performance cars. *Address:* 175 Forest Way, Belrose, NSW 2085, Australia.

WILLS, Kathryn Ann; *see* Matthews, K. A.

WILLS, Nicholas Kenneth Spencer; international consultant and company director; *b* 18 May 1941; *s* of Sir John Spencer Wills and Elizabeth Drusilla Alice Clare Garcke; *m* 1st, 1973, Hilary Ann Flood (marr. diss. 1983); two *s* two *d*; 2nd, 1985, Philippa Trench Casson, *d* of Rev. Donald and Marion Casson; one *d*. *Educ:* Rugby Sch.; Queens' Coll., Cambridge (MA; Hon. Fellow, 1990). ACA 1967, FCA 1977–2013. Binder Hamlyn & Co., 1963–67; Morgan Grenfell, 1967–70; BET plc, 1970–92 (Director, 1975–92; Man. Dir, 1982–91; Chief Exec., 1985–91; Chm., 1991–92). Managing Director: Birmingham & Dist Investment Trust, 1970–91; Electrical & Industrial Investment, 1970–91; National Electric Construction, 1971–91; Chairman: Argus Press Hldgs, 1974–83; Electrical Press, 1974–83; Boulton & Paul plc, 1979–84; Initial plc, 1979–87; BET Building Services Ltd, 1984–87; Dep. Chm., Nat. Mutual Home Loans, 1994–96; Director: Bradbury, Agnew & Co. Ltd, 1974–83; National Mutual Life Assce Soc., 1974–85, 1991–2002 (Dep. Chm., 1992–99; Chm., 1999–2002; Chm. Supervisory Bd, 2002–08); St George Assce Co. Ltd, 1974–81; Colonial Securities Trust Co. Ltd, 1976–82; Cable Trust Ltd, 1976–77; Globe Investment Trust plc, 1977–90; Drayton Consolidated, 1982–92; Tribune (formerly Barings Tribune) Investment Trust, 1992–2004; Hitchin Priory Ltd, 1992–2002 (Dep. Chm., 1994–99; Chm., 1999–2002); Onslow Trading and Commercial, 1994–99; Manchester Trading and Commercial, 1995–2000; Toye & Co., 1996–2013; SMC Gp plc, 1999–2009; American Chamber of Commerce (UK), 1985–2000 (Vice-Pres., 1988–2000); United World Colls (Internat.) Ltd, 1987–95; IQ-Ludorum plc, 2000–05; Solid Terrain Modeling Inc., 2000–11; Archial Gp plc, 2009–10; Member, Advisory Board: City and West End, National Westminster Bank, 1982–91; Charterhouse Buy-Out Funds, 1990–98. Member: Council, CBI, 1987–92 (Member: Overseas Cttee, 1987–90; Public Expenditure Task Force, 1988; Economic Affairs Cttee, 1991–96); Council, Business in the Community, 1987–92; Advisory Board: Fishman-Davidson Center for Study of Service Sector, Wharton Sch., Univ. of Pennsylvania, 1988–92; Centre of Internat. Studies, Cambridge Univ., 1999–2006 (Hon. Fellow, 2000). Mem. Adv. Council, Prince's Youth Business Trust, 1988–2004 (Hon. Treas., 1989–92; Mem., Investment Cttee, 1992–98); Chm., Internat. Trustees, Internat. Fedn of Keystone Youth Orgns, 1990–2002. Chm., Involvement & Participation Assoc., 1991–96. Chm., Mgt Cttee, Cambridge Rev. of Internat. Affairs, 1998–2003. Treasurer and Churchwarden, Church of St Bride, Fleet Street, 1978–2001; Asst, Co. of Haberdashers, 1981– (Master, 1997–98); Gov., Haberdashers' Aske's Schs, Elstree, 1989–98 (Chm., Girls' Sch. Cttee, 1994–97). Hon. Mem., Clan McEwan. CCMI; FCIM; FCT; FRSA. *Recreations:* ski-ing on blue runs, trying to farm in the Highlands. *Address:* The Great House, Great Milton, Oxon OX44 7PD. *Clubs:* White's, Royal Automobile; Beaver Creek, Arrowhead Alpine (Colorado, USA).

WILLS, Sir Seton; *see* Wills, Sir D. S.

WILLS-GOLDINGHAM, Claire Louise Margaret; QC 2012; *b* Glos, 12 Nov. 1965. *Educ:* Birmingham Univ. (LLB Hons). Called to the Bar, Inner Temple, 1988. Legal Mem., Mental Health Rev. Tribunal, 2006–. Panel Judge, Side Saddle Assoc. Dep. Ed., Family Law Weekly. Website Ed., Court of Protection Hub, 2015–. *Publications:* (jtly) Atkin's Court Forms (Family), 2002, 2006, 2011; (jtly) Encyclopaedia of Forms and Precedents, 2001–; (contrib.) Essential Family Practice, 2000, 2001, 2002; (contrib.) Jackson's Matrimonial Finance and Taxation, 2010; (jtly) Family Finance in Practice, 2006, 3rd edn 2011; Family Law Case Library (Finance), 2008, 2012; Court of Protection Made Easy, 2015. *Recreations:* horses, side saddle panel judge, HGV licence. *Address:* Colleton Chambers, Colleton Crescent, Exeter EX2 4DG. *T:* (01392) 274898. *E:* CWGQC@colletonchambers.co.uk.

WILMERS, Mary-Kay; Editor, London Review of Books, since 1992; *b* 19 July 1938; *d* of Charles Wilmers and Cesia (*née* Eitingon); *m* 1968, Stephen Arthur Frears, *qv* (marr. diss. 1975); two *s*. *Educ:* Athénée Royal d'Uccle, Brussels; Badminton Sch., Bristol; St Hugh's Coll., Oxford (BA; Hon. Fellow 2002). Editor, Faber & Faber, 1961–68; Dep. Ed., The

Listener, 1968–73; Fiction Ed., TLS, 1974–79; Dep. Ed., then Co-Ed., London Rev. of Books, 1979–92. *Publications:* The Eitingons: a twentieth century story, 2009. *Address:* c/o London Review of Books, 28 Little Russell Street, WC1A 2HN. *T:* (020) 7209 1101.

WILMOT, Sir Benjamin John E.; *see* Eardley-Wilmot.

WILMOT, Sir David, Kt 2002; QPM 1989; DL; Chief Constable, Greater Manchester Police, 1991–2002; *b* 12 March 1943; *m* Ann Marilyn (*née* Doyle). *Educ:* Southampton Univ. (BSc). Lancashire Constabulary, 1962; Merseyside Police, 1974; W Yorkshire Police, 1983; Deputy Chief Constable, Greater Manchester Police, 1987. Trustee, Broughton House, home for disabled ex-servicemen, 2005–13. Pres., Greater Manchester Fedn of Clubs for Young People, 2006–13. Hon. RNCM 2001. Greater Manchester: DL 1996; High Sheriff, 2005–06. Hon. DSc Salford, 2000. *Recreations:* wine, travel. *Club:* Army and Navy.

WILMOT, Sir Henry Robert, 9th Bt *cr* 1759; *b* 10 April 1967; *s* of Sir Robert Arthur Wilmot, 8th Bt, and of Juliet Elvira, *e d* of Captain M. N. Tufnell, RN; *S* father, 1974; *m* 1995, Susan Clare, *er d* of John Malvern, *qv*; two *s* one *d* (of whom one *s* one *d* are twins). *Recreation:* Trebuchet. *Heir: s* Oliver Charles Wilmot, *b* 12 July 1999. *Club:* Bucks.

WILMOT-SITWELL, Peter Sacheverell; Joint Chairman, 1986–90, Chairman, 1990–94, Consultant, 1995–98, S. G. Warburg (formerly S. G. Warburg, Akroyd, Rowe & Pitman, Mullens) Securities Ltd; *b* 28 March 1935; *s* of late Robert Bradshaw Wilmot-Sitwell and Barbara Elizabeth Fisher; *m* 1960, Clare Veronica Cobbold (LVO 1991); two *s* one *d*. *Educ:* Eton Coll.; Oxford Univ., 1955–58 (BA, MA). Commnd Coldstream Guards, 1953–55. Trainee, Hambros Bank Ltd, 1958–59; Partner 1959–82, Sen. Partner 1982–86, Rowe & Pitman; Vice-Chm., S. G. Warburg Gp, 1987–94. Chm., Merrill Lynch (formerly Mercury) World Mining Trust, 1993–2006; non-executive Director: W. H. Smith Ltd, 1987–96; Stock Exchange Bd, 1991–94; Minorco, 1993–99; Foreign & Colonial Income Growth Investment Trust, 1994–; Close Bros, 1995–2004; Southern Africa Investors, 1996–98; Anglo American plc, 1999–2002. *Recreations:* shooting, golf, tennis. *Address:* Portman House, Dummer, near Basingstoke, Hants RG25 2AD. *Clubs:* White's; Swinley Forest (Ascot).

WILMOT-SMITH, Richard James Crosbie; QC 1994; a Recorder, 2000–14; *b* 12 May 1952; *s* of late John Patrick Wilmot-Smith and Rosalys Wilmot-Smith (*née* Massy); *m* 1978, Jenny (marr. diss. 2005), *d* of late R. W. Castle and L. M. Castle; one *s* two *d*. *Educ:* Charterhouse; Univ. of N Carolina (Morehead Schol.; AB 1975). Called to the Bar, Middle Temple, 1978 (Benefactors Law Schol.; Bencher, 2003); Asst Recorder, 1995–2000. Trustee, Free Representation Unit, 1997–2007. *Publications:* Encyclopedia of Forms and Precedents, 5th edn: (contrib. and ed) Vol. 5, Building and Engineering Contracts, 1986; (contrib.) Vol. 12, Contracts for Services, 1994; (ed jtly) Human Rights in the United Kingdom, 1996; Construction Contracts: law and practice, 2006, 3rd edn 2014. *Recreations:* music, theatre, cinema, horse racing and breeding, cricket. *Address:* 39 Essex Street, WC2R 3AT. *T:* (020) 7832 1111. *Club:* Kent CC.

WILMOTT, Anthony Raymond, FSA; Senior Archaeologist, Historic England (formerly English Heritage), since 2002; *b* Derby, 24 Feb. 1956; *s* of Raymond Arthur Wilmott and Margaret Eileen Wilmott; partner, 2011, Varenna Othen. *Educ:* High Storrs Grammar Sch., Sheffield; Univ. of Newcastle upon Tyne (BA Combined Studies (Hist. and Archaeol.)); Univ. of Birmingham (MA Medieval Archaeol.). MCIfA (MIFA 1982); FSA 2000. Archaeologist: Hereford and Worcester CC, 1977, 1978–79; Birmingham City Mus., 1977; Mus. of London, 1979–85; West Yorks CC, 1985–87; English Heritage, 1987–2002. Director of Excavations: Kenchester, Herefords, 1977–79; London Wall, 1983; Pontefract, W Yorks, 1985–86; Birdoswald Roman Fort, Cumbria, 1987–92, 1997–98, 2009; Whitby Abbey, N Yorks, 1993–95, 2002, 2007, 2014; Richborough, Kent, 2001, 2008; Maryport, Cumbria, 2011–14; small sites on Hadrian's Wall, 1996, 1999–2000. Seconded (seasonally) to Indiana Univ. excavations at Castle Copse, Wilts, 1983–86. Hon. Editor, Trans of London and Middx Archaeol Soc., 1982–87. Archaeologist of the Year, Current Archaeology awards, 2012. *Publications:* Excavations in the Middle Walbrook Valley, City of London 1929–60, 1991; Birdoswald: excavations of a Roman fort on Hadrian's Wall and its successor settlements 1987–92, 1997; (ed with P. Wilson) The Late Roman Transition in the North, 2000; Birdoswald Roman Fort: 800 years on Hadrian's Wall, 2001; The Roman Amphitheatre in Britain, 2008; (ed) Roman Amphitheatres and Spectacula: a 21st century perspective, 2009; (ed) Hadrian's Wall: archaeological research by English Heritage, 1976–2000, 2009; English Heritage guidebooks: Birdoswald Roman Fort, 1995, 2005; Richborough and Reculver, 2012; articles in archaeol jls and mags. *Recreations:* gardening, travel, English Civil War re-enactment, sailing tall ships, archaeology. *Address:* Three Gables, 21 Castle Street, Portchester, Fareham, Hants PO16 9PY. *T:* 07808 461261. *E:* t.wilmott@mail.com.

WILMOTT, Peter Graham, CMG 1996; business consultant; *b* 6 Jan. 1947; *s* of John Joseph Wilmott and Violet Ena Wilmott; *m* 1969, Jennifer Carolyn Plummer; two *d*. *Educ:* Hove Grammar Sch.; Trinity Coll., Cambridge (MA). Asst Principal, Customs and Excise, 1968; Second Sec., UK Delegn to EEC, Brussels, 1971; Principal, Customs and Excise, 1973; First Sec., UK Perm. Rep.'s Office to EEC, Brussels, 1977; Asst to UK Mem., European Ct of Auditors, Luxembourg, 1980; Asst Sec., Customs and Excise, 1983; a Comr of Customs and Excise, 1988; Dir-Gen. (Customs and Indirect Taxation), Commn of the EC, 1990–96; Partner, Prisma Consulting Gp SA, 1996–2000; First Vice-Prés., Office de Dévelt par l'Automatisation et la Simplification du Commerce Extérieur, Paris, 2004–08 (Prés., 2000–04). Director: Ad Valorem Internat. Ltd, 2000–08; SITPRO Ltd, 2001–07; GlobalLink Border Solutions Ltd, 2006–13. Chairman: Internat. VAT Assoc., 1998–2000; Europro, 2010–12. *Recreations:* travelling, building and mending things, languages, spending time in SW France. *Address:* 1 Tunsgate, Jarvis Lane, Steyning, W Sussex BN44 3EZ.

WILMSHURST, Elizabeth Susan, CMG 1999; Distinguished Fellow, International Law (formerly Head of International Law Programme, then Senior Fellow, International Law), Royal Institute of International Affairs (Chatham House), since 2004; *b* 28 Aug. 1948; *d* of Owen David Wilmshurst and Constance Hope Wilmshurst (*née* Brand). *Educ:* Clarendon Sch., N Wales; King's Coll., London (LLB 1969, AKC 1969). Admitted Solicitor, 1972. Asst Lectr, Bristol Univ., 1973–74; HM Diplomatic Service, 1974–2003: Asst Legal Advr, FCO, 1974–86; Legal Counsellor: Attorney-Gen.'s Chambers, 1986–91; FCO, 1991–94, 1997–99; Legal Advr, UKMIS to UN, NY, 1994–97; Dep. Legal Advr, FCO, 1999–2003. Vis. Prof., UCL, 2004–12.

WILMUT, Sir Ian, Kt 2008; OBE 1999; PhD; FRS 2002; Chair, Scottish Centre for Regenerative Medicine and Professor Emeritus, since 2012, and Senior Honorary Professorial Fellow, since 2011, University of Edinburgh (Director, Scottish Centre for Regenerative Medicine, 2006–08; Director, MRC Centre for Regenerative Medicine, 2008–11); *b* 7 July 1944; *s* of Leonard (Jack) and Eileen Mary Wilmut; *m* 1967, Vivienne Mary Craven; two *d*, one adopted *s*. *Educ:* Nottingham Univ. (BSc 1967); Darwin Coll., Cambridge (PhD 1971). Post-doctoral Fellow, Unit of Reproductive Physiol. and Biochem., Cambridge, 1971–73; Animal Breeding Research Organisation, ARC, subseq. BBSRC Roslin Institute: res. posts, 1973–81; Principal Investigator, 1981–2000; Hd, Dept of Gene Expression and Develt, 2000–05; Prof. of Reproductive Sci., Univ. of Edinburgh, 2005. Hon. Prof., Edinburgh Univ., 1998. Hon. DSc Nottingham, 1998. FRSE 2000. *Publications:* (with Colin Tudge) The Second Creation, 2000; (with Roger Highfield) After Dolly: the uses and misuses of human cloning, 2006; contrib. papers to Nature and Science on cloning of Dolly the sheep, first animal produced from an adult cell, using procedure developed at Roslin Inst. and use of this procedure to introduce genetic changes in sheep. *Recreations:* walking in countryside, photography, music, gardening, reading. *Address:* MRC Centre for Regenerative Medicine, SCRM Building, University of Edinburgh, Edinburgh BioQuarter, 5 Little France Drive, Edinburgh EH16 4UU. *T:* (0131) 651 9500.

WILSEY, Gen. Sir John (Finlay Willasey), GCB 1996 (KCB 1991); CBE 1985 (OBE 1982); DL; Chairman, Western Provident Association, 1996–2009; *b* 18 Feb. 1939; *s* of Maj.-Gen. John Harold Owen Wilsey, CB, CBE, DSO and Beatrice Sarah Finlay Wilsey; *m* 1975, Elizabeth Patricia Nottingham; one *s* one *d*. *Educ:* Sherborne Sch.; RMA Sandhurst. Commissioned, Devonshire and Dorset Regt, 1959; regtl service in Cyprus, Libya, British Guyana, Germany, Malta, UK; Instructor, RMA, 1967–68; Great Abbai (Blue Nile) Expedition, 1968; Staff Coll., 1973, Defence Policy Staff, MoD, 1974–75; Co. Comdr, 1976–77, BAOR and NI (despatches 1976); Directing Staff, Staff Coll., 1978–79; Comd 1st Bn Devonshire and Dorset Regt, 1979–82 (despatches 1981); COS, HQ NI, 1982–84; Comdr 1st Inf. Brigade, 1984–86; RCDS 1987; COS, HQ UKLF, 1988–90; GOC NI, 1990–93; C-in-C, UK Land Forces then Land Comd, 1993–96; Jt Comdr, British Forces in Former Republic of Yugoslavia, 1993–96; ADC Gen. to the Queen, 1994–96. Col, Devonshire and Dorset Regt, 1990–97; Col Comdt, POW Div., 1991–94. Hon. Col, Royal Jersey Militia Sqdn, RE, 1993–2006. Mem., Commonwealth War Graves Commn, 1998–2005 (Vice Chm., 2001–05). President: Army Winter Sports Assoc., 1993–97; Army Catering Corps Assoc., 1996–; Wilts ACF, 2006–09. Governor: Sherborne Sch., 1994–2001 (Vice-Chm., 1996–2001); Sherborne Sch. for Girls, 1996–2001; Sutton's Hosp., Charterhouse, 1996–2001; Comr, Royal Hosp. Chelsea, 1996–2002. Chm., Salisbury Cathedral Council, 2001–10. Patron, Hope and Home for Children, 1996–2006. Mem., Scientific Exploration Soc. DL Wilts, 1996. *Publications:* Service for the Nation: Seaford papers, 1987; H. Jones, VC, the Life and Death of an Unusual Hero, 2002; The Ulster Tales, 2011. *Recreations:* sailing, ski-ing, fishing, breeding alpacas. *Address:* c/o Lloyds Bank, 9 Broad Street, St Helier, Jersey, CI. *Clubs:* Army and Navy; Royal Yacht Squadron, Royal Channel Islands Yacht.

WILSEY, Timothy Andrew W.; *see* Willasey-Wilsey.

WILSHAW, Sir Michael (Norman), Kt 2000; Her Majesty's Chief Inspector of Education, Children's Services and Skills, since 2012; *b* 3 Aug. 1946; *s* of Norman and Verna Wilshaw; *m*; one *s* two *d*. *Educ:* Birkbeck Coll., London Univ. (BA Hons). Teacher, later Head of Department, Inner London comprehensive schools, 1968–81: St Michael's, Bermondsey; Edith Cavell, Hackney; St Thomas the Apostle, Peckham; Dep. Headteacher, Trinity High Sch., Redbridge, 1981–85; Headteacher, St Bonaventure's RC Comp. Sch., 1985–2004; Principal, Mossbourne Community Acad., 2004–11; Dir of Educn, ARK Schs, 2007–11. *Recreations:* sport of all kinds, reading, theatre and cinema. *Address:* Ofsted, Aviation House, 125 Kingsway, WC2B 6SE.

WILSHIRE, David; *b* 16 Sept. 1943; *m* 1967, Margaret Weeks (separated 2000); one *s* (one *d* decd). *Educ:* Kingswood School, Bath; Fitzwilliam College, Cambridge. Partner, Western Political Research Services, 1979–2000; Co-Director, Political Management Programme, Brunel Univ., 1986–91; Partner, Moorlands Res. Services, 2000–07. Mem., Avon CC, 1977–81; Leader, Wansdyke DC, 1981–87. MP (C) Spelthorne, 1987–2010. Parliamentary Private Secretary: to Minister for Defence Procurement, 1991–92; to Minister of State, Home Office, 1992–94; an Opposition Whip, 2001–05. Leader, Cons. Parly Delegn, 2005–10, Chm., Eur. Democrat Gp, 2009–10, Parly Assembly of Council of Europe. *Recreations:* gardening, cider making.

WILSON; *see* Marslen-Wilson.

WILSON, family name of **Barons Moran, Nunburnholme, Wilson of Dinton** and **Wilson of Tillyorn.**

WILSON OF DINTON, Baron *cr* 2002 (Life Peer), of Dinton in the County of Buckinghamshire; **Richard Thomas James Wilson,** GCB 2001 (KCB 1997; CB 1991); Master, Emmanuel College, Cambridge, 2002–12, now Life Fellow; *b* 11 Oct. 1942; *s* of late Richard Ridley Wilson and Frieda Bell Wilson (*née* Finlay); *m* 1972, Caroline Margaret, *y d* of Rt Hon. Sir Frank Lee, GCMG, KCB and Lady Lee; one *s* one *d*. *Educ:* Radley Coll.; Clare Coll., Cambridge (Exhibnr; BA 1964, LLB 1965; MA 2002). Called to the Bar, Middle Temple, 1965. Joined BoT as Asst Principal, 1966; Private Sec. to Minister of State, BoT, 1969–71; Principal: Cabinet Office, 1971–73; Dept of Energy, 1974; Asst Sec., 1977–82; Under Sec., 1982; Prin. Estabt and Finance Officer, Dept of Energy, 1982–86; on loan to Cabinet Office (MPO), 1986–87; Dep. Sec., Cabinet Office, 1987–90; Dep. Sec. (Industry), HM Treasury, 1990–92; Perm. Sec., DoE, 1992–94; Perm. Under-Sec. of State, Home Office, 1994–97; Sec. of the Cabinet and Head, Home Civil Service, 1998–2002. Chm., C. Hoare & Co., Bankers, 2006–. Non-executive Director: BSkyB, 2003–13; Xansa plc, 2003–07. Mem. Council, Cambridge Univ., 2005–08. Syndic, Fitzwilliam Mus., 2005–11. Trustee: Ewing Foundn, 1994–2015; Leeds Castle Foundn, 2002–06; Royal Anniversary Trust, 2003–06; Cicely Saunders Foundn, 2004–15; Dir, Cambridge Arts Th. Trust, 2008–12; Trustee, Cambridge Film Trust, 2014–. Chm., Prince's Teaching Inst., 2006–09. Pres., CIPD, 2004–06. Mem. Council, Radley Coll., 1995–2010 (Chm., 2004–10). Chm. of Friends, 2013–, Trustee, 2014–, Kettle's Yard. Chm., Cambridge Univ. Boat Club Foundn, 2014–. Hon. Fellow: Univ. of Cardiff, 1999; LSE, 2000; Univ. of Wales Coll., Newport, 2002. Hon. LLD: Birmingham, 2000; City, 2001; Exeter, 2003. *Recreations:* movies, small gardens, Cambridge rowing. *Address:* Emmanuel College, Cambridge CB2 3AP. *Club:* Brooks's.

WILSON OF TILLYORN, Baron *cr* 1992 (Life Peer), of Finzean in the District of Kincardine and Deeside and of Fanling in Hong Kong; **David Clive Wilson,** KT 2000; GCMG 1991 (KCMG 1987 CMG 1985); PhD; FRSE; Master of Peterhouse, Cambridge, 2002–08 (Hon. Fellow, 2008); Deputy Vice-Chancellor, University of Cambridge, 2005–08; President, Royal Society of Edinburgh, 2008–11; Registrar, Order of Saint Michael and Saint George, 2001–10; Lord High Commissioner, General Assembly, Church of Scotland, 2010–11; *b* 14 Feb. 1935; *s* of Rev. William Skinner Wilson and Enid Wilson; *m* 1967, Natasha Helen Mary Alexander; two *s*. *Educ:* Trinity Coll., Glenalmond; Keble Coll., Oxford (schol., MA; Hon. Fellow, 1987); PhD London 1973. FRSE 2000. National Service, The Black Watch, 1953–55; entered Foreign Service, 1958; Third Secretary, Vientiane, 1959–60; Language Student, Hong Kong, 1960–62; Second, later First Secretary, Peking, 1963–65; FCO, 1965–68; resigned, 1968; Editor, China Quarterly, 1968–74; Vis. Scholar, Columbia Univ., New York, 1972; rejoined Diplomatic Service, 1974; Cabinet Office, 1974–77; Political Adviser, Hong Kong, 1977–81; Hd, S European Dept, FCO, 1981–84; Asst Under-Sec. of State, FCO, 1984–87; Governor and C-in-C, Hong Kong, 1987–92. Chm., Scottish Hydro-Electric, then Scottish and Southern Energy, 1993–2000; Dir, Martin Currie Pacific Trust plc, 1993–2003. Mem. Board, British Council, 1993–2002 (Chm., Scottish Cttee, 1993–2002). Chm., Scottish Peers Assoc., 2000–02 (Vice Chm., 1998–2000). Chm. Trustees, Nat. Museums of Scotland, 2002–06 (Trustee, 1999–2006); Vice-Pres., Scotland's Churches Trust (formerly Scotland's Churches Scheme), 2015– (Trustee, 1999–2002, 2008–15); Trustee, Carnegie Trust for the Univs of Scotland, 2000–. Member: Council, CBI Scotland, 1993–2000; Adv. Cttee on Business Appts, 2000–09 (Chm., 2008–09). Chancellor's Assessor, Court, Univ. of Aberdeen, 1993–97; Chancellor, Univ. of Aberdeen, 1997–2013; Member: Governing Body, SOAS, 1992–97; Council, Glenalmond Coll., 1994–2005 (Chm. Council, 2000–05). Oxford Univ. Somaliland Expedn, 1957; British Mt Kongur Expedn (NW China), 1981. President: Bhutan Soc. of UK, 1993–2008; Hong Kong Assoc., 1994–2015; Hong Kong Soc., 1994–2012; Vice Pres., RSGS, 1996–. Chm., Adv. Cttee, St Paul's Cathedral,

2009–15. Burgess, Guild of City of Aberdeen, 2004. Hon. LLD: Aberdeen, 1990; Chinese Univ. of Hong Kong, 1996. Hon. DLitt: Sydney, 1991; Abertay Dundee, 1994; Hong Kong, 2006; Dhc Edinburgh, 2011. KStJ 1987. *Recreations:* hill-walking, theatre, reading. *Address:* c/o House of Lords, SW1A 0PW. *Clubs:* Alpine; New (Edinburgh); Royal Northern and University (Aberdeen).

See also Hon. P. M. A. Wilson.

WILSON OF CULWORTH, Rt Hon. Lord; Nicholas Allan Roy Wilson, Kt 1993; PC 2005; a Justice of the Supreme Court of the United Kingdom, since 2011; *b* 9 May 1945; *s* of late Roderick Peter Garratt Wilson and Dorothy Anne Wilson (*née* Chenevix-Trench); *m* 1974, Margaret (*née* Higgins); one *s* one *d*. *Educ:* Bryanston School; Worcester College, Oxford (BA 1st cl. hons Jurisp. 1966; Hon. Fellow, 2008). Eldon Scholar, 1967. Called to the Bar, Inner Temple, 1967, Bencher, 1993; QC 1987; a Recorder, 1987–93; a Judge of the High Court, Family Div., 1993–2005; a Lord Justice of Appeal, 2005–11. Pres., Family Mediators Assoc., 1998–2013. Hon. Dr Staffordshire, 2004. Editor-in-Chief, Family Court Practice, 2008–. *Recreation:* grandson. *Address:* Supreme Court of the United Kingdom, Parliament Square, SW1P 3BD.

WILSON, Sir Alan (Geoffrey), Kt 2001; FRS 2006; FBA 1994; Professor of Urban and Regional Systems, University College London, since 2007; *b* 8 Jan. 1939; *s* of Harry Wilson and Gladys (*née* Naylor); *m* 1987, Sarah Caroline Fildes. *Educ:* Corpus Christi Coll., Cambridge (MA; Hon. Fellow, 2004). Scientific Officer, Rutherford High Energy Lab., 1961–64; Res. Officer, Inst. of Econs and Statistics, Univ. of Oxford, 1964–66; Math. Adviser, MoT, 1966–68; Asst Dir, Centre for Environmental Studies, London, 1968–70; University of Leeds: Prof. of Urban and Regl Geog., 1970–2004; Pro-Vice-Chancellor, 1989–91; Vice-Chancellor, 1991–2004; Dir-Gen., Higher Educn, DfES, 2004–06; Master of Corpus Christi Coll., Cambridge, 2006–07. Hon. Prof., Urban and Regl Geog., Univ. of Cambridge, 2006–07. Mem., Kirklees AHA, 1979–82; Vice-Chm., Dewsbury HA, 1982–85; non-exec. Mem., Northern and Yorks RHA, 1994–96. Chm., AHRC, 2007–13; Mem., ESRC, 2000–04 (Vice-Chm. Environment and Planning Cttee, 1986–88). Chm., Sci. Adv. Council, Home Office, 2013–; Chm., Lead Expert Gp, Govt Office for Sci. Foresight Project, Future of Cities, 2013–. Dir, GMAP Ltd, 1991–2001. MAE 1991; FAcSS (AcSS 2000). FCGI 1997. Honorary Fellow: UCL, 2003; Regional Sci. Assoc. Internat., 2007. Hon. DSc Pennsylvania State, 2002; DUniv Bradford, 2004; Hon. DEd Leeds Metropolitan, 2004; Hon. LLD: Leeds, 2004; Teesside, 2006; Hon. DSocSci, KCL, 2010. Gill Meml Award, RGS, 1978; Honours Award, Assoc. of Amer. Geographers, 1987; Founder's Medal, RGS, 1992; Lauréat d'Honneur, IGU, 2004; European Prize, Regl Sci. Assoc., 2004. *Publications:* Entropy in Urban and Regional Modelling, 1970; Papers in Urban and Regional Analysis, 1972; Urban and Regional Models in Geography and Planning, 1974; (with M. J. Kirkby) Mathematics for Geographers and Planners, 1975, 2nd edn 1980; (with P. H. Rees) Spatial Population Analysis, 1977; (ed with P. H. Rees and C. M. Leigh) Models of Cities and Regions, 1977; Catastrophe Theory and Bifurcation: applications to urban and regional systems, 1981; (jtly) Optimization in Locational and Transport Analysis, 1981; Geography and the Environment: Systems Analytical Methods, 1981; (with R. J. Bennett) Mathematical Methods in Geography and Planning, 1985; (ed jtly) Urban Systems, 1987; (ed jtly) Urban Dynamics, 1990; (ed jtly) Modelling the City, 1994; (jtly) Intelligent Geographical Information Systems, 1996; Complex Spatial Systems, 2000; Knowledge Power, 2010; The Science of Cities and Regions, 2012; (ed) Urban Modelling, 5 vols, 2013; (with J. Dearden) Explorations in Urban and Regional Dynamics, 2015. *Recreation:* writing. *Address:* Centre for Advanced Spatial Analysis, University College London, 90 Tottenham Court Road, W1T 4TG. *T:* (020) 3108 3901. *Club:* Athenæum.

WILSON, (Alan) Martin; QC 1982; a Recorder of the Crown Court, 1979–2005; *b* 12 Feb. 1940; *s* of late Joseph Norris Wilson and Kate Wilson; *m* 1st, 1966, Pauline Frances Kibart (marr. diss. 1975); two *d*; 2nd, 1976, Julia Mary Carter; one *d*. *Educ:* Kilburn Grammar Sch.; Nottingham Univ. (LLB Hons). Called to the Bar, Gray's Inn, 1963; in practice as a barrister, until 2010; door tenant, 7 Bedford Row, 2010–. Occasional Mem., Hong Kong Bar, 1988–; admitted to Malaysian Bar, 1995; Temp. Advocate, IOM Bar, 2004. Trustee, Broadway Arts Fest., 2010–. *Publications:* The Little Book of Anger, 2012; Unbidden Guests, 2013. *Address:* 7 Bedford Row, WC1R 4BS.

WILSON, Rt Rev. Alan Thomas Lawrence; *see* Buckingham, Area Bishop of.

WILSON, Alastair James Drysdale; QC 1987; a Recorder, since 1996; *b* 26 May 1946; *s* of late A. Robin Wilson and of Mary Damaris Wilson; *m*; one *s* two *d*. *Educ:* Wellington College; Pembroke College, Cambridge. Called to the Bar, Middle Temple, 1968. *Recreations:* gardening, restoring old buildings, shopping at boot fairs, mending things. *Address:* Hogarth Chambers, 5 New Square, Lincoln's Inn, WC2A 3RJ. *T:* (020) 7404 0404, *Fax:* (020) 7404 0505. *E:* alastairwilson@hogarthchambers.com; Rainthorpe Hall, Tasburgh, Norfolk NR15 1RQ.

WILSON, Alastair John; Chief Executive, School for Social Entrepreneurs, since 2004; *b* Edinburgh, 22 Nov. 1968; *s* of Iain and Shirley Wilson. *Educ:* Milburn Acad., Inverness; Napier Univ. (BA Hons Business Studies); Sch. for Social Entrepreneurs (Fellow, 1998). Business Develt Manager, ICL, 1993–97; Founder and Manager, Homeless Direct, 1999–2003; Develt Dir, Sch. for Social Entrepreneurs, 2003–04. Dir, Tonic Housing CIC, 2015–. Trustee: Sheila McKechnie Foundn, 2007–; Access Foundn, 2015. *Recreations:* theatre, politics, travel, ski-ing. *Address:* School for Social Entrepreneurs, 2nd Floor, The Fire Station, 139 Tooley Street, SE1 2HZ. *E:* alastair.wilson@sse.org.uk.

WILSON, Allan; Member (Lab) Cunninghame North, Scottish Parliament, 1999–2007; *b* 5 Aug. 1954; *s* of Andrew Wilson and Elizabeth (*née* Lauchlan); *m* 1981, Alison Isabel Melville Liddell; two *s*. *Educ:* Spiers Sch., Beith. Trainee Officer, 1972–75, Area Officer, 1975–93, NUPE; Sen. Regl Officer, UNISON, 1993–94; Head of Higher Educn, UNISON (Scotland), 1994–99. Contested (Lab) Cunninghame N, Scottish Parlt, 2007 and 2011. Dep. Minister for Sport, the Arts and Culture, 2001, for Envmt and Rural Develt, 2001–04, for Enterprise and Lifelong Learning, 2004–07, Scottish Exec. *Recreations:* football, reading, golf. *Address:* 44 Stoneyholm Road, Kilbirnie, Ayrshire KA25 7JS. *Clubs:* Garnock Labour, Place Golf (Kilbirnie).

WILSON, Air Chief Marshal Sir Andrew; *see* Wilson, Air Chief Marshal Sir R. A. F.

WILSON, Andrew; *see* Wilson, R. A.

WILSON, Prof. Andrew Ian, DPhil; Professor of the Archaeology of the Roman Empire, University of Oxford, and Fellow of All Souls College, Oxford, since 2004; *b* 29 Feb. 1968; *s* of Anthony Keith Wilson, *qv*; *m* 1994, Heather Mary Claire Grabbe, *qv* (marr. diss. 2009); two *d*. *Educ:* Corpus Christi Coll., Oxford (BA (Lit.Hum.) 1991; MA 1996); Magdalen Coll., Oxford (DPhil 1998). Fellow by Exam., Magdalen Coll., Oxford, 1996–2000; Univ. Lectr in Roman Archaeol., Univ. of Oxford, and Fellow, Wolfson Coll., Oxford, 2000–04. Hon. Sec., 2001–08, Chm., 2008–11, Soc. for Libyan Studies; Foreign Corresp. Mem., Soc. Nat. des Antiquaires de France, 2004. Ed., Libyan Studies, 1998–2002. *Publications:* ed books, and numerous articles in archaeol jls. *Recreation:* moderate hedonism. *Address:* Institute of Archaeology, 36 Beaumont Street, Oxford OX1 2PG.

WILSON, Andrew John; Managing Partner, Charlotte Street Partners, since 2014; *b* Lanark, 27 Dec. 1970; *s* of Harry Arthur Wilson and Dorothy Wilson (*née* Bunting); *m* 2004, Karen Isabella Doyle (marr. diss. 2014); two *s* one *d*. *Educ:* Coltness High Sch., Wishaw; Univ. of St Andrews; Univ. of Strathclyde (BA Hons Econs and Politics). Economist, Government Economic Service: Forestry Commn, 1993–95; Scottish Office, 1995–96; Dir of Business for Scotland, 1996–97; Economist and Sen. Researcher, SNP, 1996–97; Economist, Royal Bank of Scotland, 1997–98; Royal Bank of Scotland Group: Hd of Gp Media Relns, 2003–05; Dep. Chief Economist, 2005–08; Hd of Gp Corporate Affairs, 2008–10; Hd of Gp Communications, 2010–12; Client Team Leader, WPP Gp, 2012–13. MSP (SNP) Central Scotland, 1999–2003; Scottish Parliament: Shadow Minister: Finance, 1999–2001; Economy and Transport, 2001; Economy, Enterprise and Lifelong Learning, 2001–03; contested (SNP) Cumbernauld and Kilsyth, 2003. Columnist: Sunday Mail, 1999–2003; Scots Independent, 2001–03; Scotland on Sunday, 2012–. Member: Inst. of Fiscal Studies, 2002–; David Hume Inst., 2012–. Member: Develt Bd, Barnardo's (Scotland), 2008–10; Bd of Govs, Scottish Crop Res. Inst., 2009–11; Public Policy Adv. Bd, Univ. of Glasgow, 2013–. Trustee, John Smith Meml Trust, 2005–. Dir, Motherwell FC, 2010–. FCIBS 2004; MInstD 2012. *Publications:* contribs to various jl and conf. papers. *Recreations:* family, football, current affairs, travel, golf. *Address:* (office) 15 Rathbone Street, W1T 1LY; 16 Alva Street, Edinburgh EH2 4GG; (home) 2 Johnsburn Green, Balerno, Edinburgh EH14 7NB. *Clubs:* Travellers, Ivy.

WILSON, Andrew Morley; Chief Executive, North York Moors National Park Authority, since 2000; *b* Leamington Spa, 20 Feb. 1958; *s* of David and Elizabeth Wilson; *m* 1995, Helen Jayne Ashworth; two *d*. *Educ:* St Benedict's Sch.; Univ. of Southampton (BSc 1980). Mem. Exec., NUS, 1982; agric. officer, RSPB, 1982–85; researcher, Nat. Campaign for the Arts, 1986; Parly agric. advr, 1987; Sen. Policy Officer, CPRE, 1987–92; Hd, Park Mgt, Northumberland Nat. Park, 1992–2000. Mem. Bd, Natural England, 2009–14. *Recreations:* birdwatching, growing hostas, reading history, skimming stones, my family. *Address:* North York Moors National Park Authority, The Old Vicarage, Bondgate, Helmsley, York YO62 5BP. *T:* (01439) 770657. *E:* a.wilson@northyorkmoors.org.uk.

WILSON, Andrew Norman; author; *b* 27 Oct. 1950; *s* of late Norman Wilson, Lt-Col RA, potter and industrialist, and Jean Dorothy Wilson (*née* Crowder); *m* Katherine Duncan-Jones, *qv*; two *d*; *m* 1991, Dr Ruth Alexandra Guilding; one *d*. *Educ:* Rugby; New College, Oxford (MA). Chancellor's Essay Prize, 1971, and Ellerton Theological Prize, 1975. Asst Master, Merchant Taylors' Sch., 1975–76; Lectr, St Hugh's Coll. and New Coll., Oxford, 1976–81; Literary Editor: Spectator, 1981–83; Evening Standard, 1990–97. Television work incl. (as presenter): Eminent Victorians, 1988; Jesus Before Christ, 1991; The Genius of Josiah Wedgwood, 2013; C. S. Lewis, 2014; Betjeman land, 2014; frequent contribs to radio. Mem., AAIL, 1988. FRSL 1981. *Publications: novels:* The Sweets of Pimlico, 1977 (John Llewellyn Rhys Memorial Prize, 1978); Unguarded Hours, 1978; Kindly Light, 1979; The Healing Art, 1980 (Somerset Maugham Award, 1981; Arts Council National Book Award, 1981; Southern Arts Prize, 1981); Who was Oswald Fish?, 1981; Wise Virgin, 1982 (W. H. Smith Literary Award, 1983); Scandal, 1983; Gentlemen in England, 1985; Love Unknown, 1986; Incline Our Hearts, 1988; A Bottle in the Smoke, 1990; Daughters of Albion, 1991; The Vicar of Sorrows, 1993; Hearing Voices, 1995; A Watch in the Night, 1996; Dream Children, 1998; My Name is Legion, 2004; A Jealous Ghost, 2005; Winnie and Wolf, 2007; The Potter's Hand, 2012; *for children:* Stray, 1987; Hazel the Guinea-pig, 1997; Furball and the Mokes, 2011; *non fiction:* The Laird of Abbotsford, 1980 (John Llewellyn Rhys Memorial Prize, 1981); A Life of John Milton, 1983; Hilaire Belloc, 1984; How Can We Know?, 1985; (jtly) The Church in Crisis, 1986; The Lion and the Honeycomb, 1987; Penfriends from Porlock, 1988; Tolstoy, 1988 (Whitbread Biography Award); Eminent Victorians, 1989; C. S. Lewis, a biography, 1990; Against Religion, 1991; Jesus, 1992; (ed) The Faber Book of Church and Clergy, 1992; The Rise and Fall of the House of Windsor, 1993; (ed) The Faber Book of London, 1993; Paul: the mind of the apostle, 1997; God's Funeral, 1999; The Victorians, 2002; Iris Murdoch as I Knew Her, 2003; London: a short history, 2004; After the Victorians, 2005; Betjeman, 2006; Our Times, 2008; Dante in Love, 2011; The Elizabethans, 2011; Hitler, 2012; Victoria, 2014; The Book of the People: how to read the Bible, 2015. *Address:* 5 Regent's Park Terrace, NW1 7EE. *Clubs:* Travellers, Beefsteak.

See also Viscount Runciman of Doxford.

WILSON, Angela Christine; *see* Smith, Angela C.

WILSON, Anthony Joseph, (Joe); Member (Lab) North Wales, European Parliament, 1989–99; *b* 6 July 1937; *s* of Joseph Samuel Wilson and Eleanor Annie (*née* Jones); *m* 1st, 1959, June Mary Sockett (marr. diss. 1987); one *s* two *d*; 2nd, 1998, Sue Bentley (*d* 2012). *Educ:* Birkenhead Sch.; Loughborough Coll. (DLC); Univ. of Wales (BEd Hons). National Service, RAPC, 1955–57. Teacher: Vauvert Sec. Mod. Sch., Guernsey, 1960–64; Les Beaucamps Sec. Mod. Sch., Guernsey, 1964–66; Man., St Mary's Bay Sch. Journey Centre, Kent, 1966–69; Lectr in PE, Wrexham Tech. Coll., subseq. NE Wales Inst. of Higher Educn, 1969–89. Contested (Lab) Wales, EP elecn, 1999. *Recreations:* basketball, camping, boules, tennis. *Address:* 79 Ruabon Road, Wrexham, North Wales LL13 7PU. *T:* (01978) 352808. *E:* joewilson7779@gmail.com.

WILSON, Anthony Keith; Chief Executive of the Press, University Printer and Secretary, Press Syndicate, Cambridge University Press, 1992–99; Fellow of Wolfson College, Cambridge, 1994–2006, now Emeritus; *b* 28 Sept. 1939; *s* of late Sidney Walter Wilson and Doris Jessie Wilson (*née* Garlick), Streatham; *m* 1963, Christina Helen, *d* of late Ivor Gray Nixon and Margaret Joan Nixon (*née* Smith); two *s* one *d*. *Educ:* Lexden House Sch.; Dulwich Coll.; Corpus Christi Coll., Cambridge (Maj. Scholar; BA Hons Modern and Medieval Langs 1961; MA 1966). Longmans Green & Co. Ltd, 1961–64; Thomas Nelson & Sons Ltd, 1964–68; George Allen & Unwin Ltd, 1968–72; Cambridge University Press, 1972–99: Sen. Editor, R&D, 1972–73; Publishing Ops Dir, 1973–82; Dep. Sec., Press Syndicate, 1979–92; Actg Man. Dir, 1982–83, Man. Dir, 1983–92, Publishing Div.; Dep. Chief Exec., 1991–92. Royal Shakespeare Company: Gov., 1983–2008; Mem. Council, 1991–2000; Mem., Exec. Cttee, 1991–2000; Mem. Bd, 2001–06; Chm., Budget Cttee, 1991–96; Chm., Budget and Audit Cttee, 1996–2000; Chm., Audit Cttee, 2000–06. Gov., Perse Sch. for Girls, Cambridge, 1979–99 (Chm. Govs, 1988–99); Hon. Treas., Westcott House, Cambridge, 2000–09. FInstD 1978 (Life-Mem.). *Recreations:* walking, talking, walking and talking. *Address:* Wolfson College, Cambridge CB3 9BB.

See also A. I. Wilson.

WILSON, Arthur Andrew; Director of Planning and Finance, Bristol South & West Primary Care Trust, 2002–06; *b* 23 July 1946; *s* of late Arthur James Wilson and Hilda Mellor Wilson (*née* Kennedy); *m* 1968, Susan Ann Faulkner; one *s* one *d*. *Educ:* Moulton Sch., Northampton; Bath Spa Univ. (MA 2007). CIPFA; IHSM. W. H. Grigg & Co., 1963; Calne and Chippenham RDC, 1963–66; Berkshire CC, 1966–67; Bath City Council, 1967–73; Chief Accountant, Avon CC, 1973–76; Principal Asst Regl Treasurer, SW RHA, 1976–82; Dist Treasurer, Plymouth HA, 1982–84; South Western RHA: Regl Treasurer, 1984–91; Dep. Regl Gen. Manager, 1991–93; Chief Exec., Plymouth Hosps NHS Trust, 1993–2000; Prog. Dir, Avon, Glos and Wilts HA, 2000–02. Mem. Mgt Council, 1997–2000, Chm. Exec. Cttee, 1998–2000, UC of St Mark and St John, Plymouth. *Recreations:* golf, reading, listening to music, musical theatre, first editions of modern novels. *Address:* 38 Cambridge Road, Clevedon, N Som BS21 7DW. *T:* (01275) 342238.

WILSON, Barbara Ann, OBE 1998; PhD; Director of Research, Oliver Zangwill Centre, Princess of Wales Hospital, Ely, 1996–2007, now Visiting Scientist; Clinical Neuropsychologist, Raphael Medical Centre, since 2009; *b* 23 Oct. 1941; *d* of William David Forester and Miriam Clara Forester; *m* 1962, Michael John Wilson; one *s* one *d* (and one *d* decd). *Educ:* Univ. of Reading (BA 1st Cl. Hons 1975); MPhil 1977, PhD 1985, London.

CPsychol 1977; FBPsS 1987; FMedSci 2001; FAcSS (AcSS 2002). Sen. Clinical Psychologist, Rivermead Rehab. Centre, Oxford, 1979–85; Principal Clinical Psychologist, Charing Cross Hosp., London, 1985–87; Reader in Rehabilitation Studies, 1987–90, Hon. Prof. of Rehabilitation Studies, 1995–, Univ. of Southampton; Sen. Scientist and Clinical Psychologist, MRC Cognition and Brain Sci. Unit, 1990–2007, now Vis. Scientist. Hon. ScD UEA, 2005. May Davidson Award for Clin. Psychol., 1984; Dist. Scientist Award, British Psychol Soc., 2000; Professional of the Yr, Encephalitis Soc., 2002; Robert L. Moody Prize for Services to Rehabilitation, Univ. of Texas, 2006; Ramon Y Cahal Award for dist. contribs to neuropsychiatry, Internat. Neuropsychiatric Assoc., 2011. *Publications:* (jtly) Families in Other Places, 1974; Rehabilitation of Memory, 1987; (jtly) Selecting, Administering and Interpreting Cognitive Tests, 1996; (jtly) Coping with Memory Problems, 1997; Case Studies in Neuropsychological Rehabilitation, 1999 (Book of the Yr Award, British Psychol Soc., 2003); (jtly) The Handbook of Memory Disorders, 2002; (ed) Neuropsychological Rehabilitation: theory and practice, 2003; (jtly) Behavioural Approaches in Neuropsychological Rehabilitation, 2003; (jtly) The Essential Handbook of Memory Disorders for Clinicians, 2004; First Year: Worst Year: coping with the unexpected death of our grown up daughter, 2004; *edited jointly:* Clinical Management of Memory Problems, 1984, 2nd edn 1992; Self-Injurious Behaviour, 1985; Everyday Cognition in Adulthood and Late Life, 1989; Developments in the Assessment and Rehabilitation of Brain-damaged Patients, 1993; Handbook of Memory Disorders, 1995; Rehabilitation Studies Handbook, 1997; 8 neuropsychological tests; over 250 book chapters and articles in jls. *Recreation:* travel. *Address:* Oliver Zangwill Centre, Princess of Wales Hospital, Lynn Road, Ely, Cambs CB6 1DN. *E:* barbara.wilson00@gmail.com.

WILSON, Barbara Jolanta Maria, PhD; Director of Organisational Development and Personnel, Catholic Agency for Overseas Development, 2005–10; *b* 26 June 1947; *d* of late Edward Szczepanik and Anne Szczepanik (*née* Janikowska); *m* 1971, Peter Brian Wilson (*d* 1996); one *s* one *d. Educ:* King George V Sch., Hong Kong; Convent of the Sacred Heart, Tunbridge Wells; St Anne's Coll., Oxford (MA Maths); Keele Univ. (PhD 1975); Heythrop Coll., Univ. of London (MA Christian Spirituality 2011). Statistical Res. Unit in Sociol., Keele Univ., 1969–73; Welsh Office, 1974–99: Sen. Asst Statistician, 1974–76; Statistician, 1976–84; Principal, Local Govt Finance, 1984–86; Educn Dept, 1986–89; Head of: Resource and Quality Mgt Div., 1989–92; Community Care Div., 1992–96; Personnel, 1996–99; Principal Estabts Officer, April–Aug. 1999; Dep. Clerk, Nat. Assembly for Wales, 1999–2000; Dir of Res. and Develt, 2000–03, Dir for Public Service Develt, 2003–05, Welsh Assembly Govt. Founder Trustee and Treas., WAY (Widowed and Young) Foundn, 1997–2002. *Recreations:* walking, music, cooking.

WILSON, Vice-Adm. Sir Barry (Nigel), KCB 1990; Deputy Chief of Defence Staff (Programmes and Personnel), 1989–92; *b* 5 June 1936; *s* of Rear-Adm. G. A. M. Wilson, CB, and of Dorothy Wilson; *m* 1961, Elizabeth Ann (*née* Hardy) (*d* 2014); one *s* one *d. Educ:* St Edward's Sch., Oxford; Britannia Royal Naval Coll. Commanded: HMS Mohawk, 1973–74; HMS Cardiff, 1978–80; RCDS 1982; Dir Navy Plans, 1983–85; Flag Officer Sea Training, 1986–87; ACDS (Progs), 1987–89. Chairman: Council, SSAFA Forces Help (formerly SSAFA), 1994–2000; Trustees, Royal Naval Mus., Portsmouth, 1994–2003. Chm. Bd of Visitors, Guys Marsh HMP/YOI, 1997–99; Chm., Friends of Guys Marsh, 2004–08. *Recreations:* walking, gardening. *Address:* 6 Hays Park, Sedgehill, Shaftesbury, Dorset SP7 9JR.

WILSON, Brian Alfred Samuel; Member (Green) North Down, Northern Ireland Assembly, 2007–11; *b* 15 May 1943; *s* of Alfred and Sheila Wilson; *m* 1979, Anne Campbell; three *s* one *d. Educ:* Bangor Grammar Sch.; Open Univ. (BA Hons); Univ. of Strathclyde (MSc). Lectr, Belfast Inst. of Further and Higher Educn, 1976–2003. Mem., N Down BC, 1981– (Alliance 1981–96, Ind. 1996–2004, 2011–, Green 2004–11) (Alderman, 2001–11). *Recreations:* sports, walking. *Address:* 1 Innisfayle Drive, Bangor BT19 1DN. *T:* (028) 9145 5189. *E:* brian.wilson@northdown.gov.uk.

WILSON, Rt Hon. Brian David Henderson; PC 2003; UK Business Ambassador, since 2012; Chairman, Harris Tweed Hebrides, since 2007; *b* 13 Dec. 1948; *s* of late John Forrest Wilson and Marion MacIntyre; *m* 1981, Joni Buchanan; two *s* one *d. Educ:* Dunoon Grammar School; Dundee Univ. (MA Hons); University College Cardiff (Dip. Journalism Studies). Publisher and founding editor, West Highland Free Press, 1972–97. MP (Lab) Cunninghame N, 1987–2005. Opposition front bench spokesman on Scottish affairs, 1988–92, on transport, 1992–94 and 1995–96, on trade and industry, 1994–95, on election planning, 1996–97; Minister of State: Scottish Office, 1997–98 and 1999–2001; (Minister for Trade), DTI, 1998–99; FCO, Jan.–June 2001; (Minister for Industry and Energy, then for Energy and Construction), DTI, 2001–03; Prime Minister's Special Rep. on Overseas Trade, 2003–06. Director: West Highland Publishing Co., 1972–97 and 2005–10; Amec Nuclear, 2005–14; Celtic plc, 2005–; Chairman: Airtricity UK, 2005–08; Mangersta Ltd, 2005–; Britain's Energy Coast, West Cumbria (formerly West Cumbria Vision), 2009–14; Havana Energy, 2010–. Vis. Prof. in Govt and Media, Glasgow Caledonian Univ., 2007–. Member, Board: UK Energy Excellence, 2008–; Community Land Scotland, 2010–. Hon. Pres., Industrial Power Assoc., 2005–. Led review of Support for Scottish Exporting, 2014. Hon. Fellow, Univ. of the Highlands and Islands, 2009. Hon. Keeper of the Quaich, Scotch Whisky Industry, 2014. First winner, Nicholas Tomalin Meml Award, 1975; UK Global Dir of the Year, IoD, 2011. *Publications:* Celtic: a century with honour, 1988; The Official History of Celtic Football Club, 2014; contribs to various newspapers and periodicals. *Address:* Cnoc na Meinn, 7A Mangersta, Isle of Lewis HS2 9EY. *E:* brianwilson@mangersta.net. *Clubs:* Soho House; Stoke Park; Archerfield.

WILSON, Prof. Brian Graham, AO 1995; Vice-Chancellor, University of Queensland, 1979–95; *b* 9 April 1930; *s* of Charles Wesley Wilson and Isobel (*née* Ferguson); *m* 1st, 1959, Barbara Elizabeth Wilkie; two *s* one *d*; 2nd, 1978, Margaret Jeanne Henry; 3rd, 1988, Joan Patricia Opdebeeck; three *s* (incl. twins). *Educ:* Queen's Univ., Belfast (BSc Hons); National Univ. of Ireland (PhD Cosmic Radiation). Post-doctoral Fellow, National Research Council, Canada, 1955–57; Officer in Charge, Sulphur Mt Lab., Banff, 1957–60, Associate Res. Officer, 1959–60; Associate Prof. of Physics, Univ. of Calgary, 1960–65, Prof., 1965–70, Dean of Arts and Science, 1967–70; Prof. of Astronomy and Academic Vice-Pres., Simon Fraser Univ., 1970–78. Pres., Internat. Develt Program of Australian Univs and Colls, 1991–93; Chairman: Australian Vice-Chancellors' Cttee, 1989–90 (Dep. Chm., 1987–88); Quality Assurance in Higher Educn, 1993–95. Founder and Chm., Uniquest Ltd, 1983–88. Member: Council, Northern Territory Univ., 1988–93; Council, Univ. of South Pacific, 1991–95. FTS 1990. Hon. LLD Calgary, 1984; DUniv Queensland Univ. Tech., 1995; Hon. DSc Queensland, 1995. *Publications:* numerous, on astrophysics and on higher educn issues, in learned jls. *Recreations:* golf, swimming. *Address:* Les Grezes, 11410 Montauriol, France. *E:* opdebeeck.wilson@orange.fr.

WILSON, Brian William John Gregg, MA; Headmaster, Campbell College, Belfast, 1977–87; *b* 16 June 1937; *s* of late Cecil S. and Margaret D. Wilson; *m* 1969, Sara Remington (*née* Hollins); two *d. Educ:* Sedbergh Sch., Yorks; Christ's Coll., Cambridge (MA; Otway Exhibnr and Scholar). Sec. and Capt., Cambridge Univ. Rugby Fives Club, 1959–60. NI short service commn, RIrF, 1955–57; Flt Lt, RAFVR (T), 1964–71. Asst Master, Radley Coll., 1960–65; Housemaster, King's Sch., Canterbury, 1965–73; Dir of Studies, Eastbourne Coll., 1973–76; Dep. Hd, St Mary's Sch., Wantage, 1989–97. Project Manager, Navan Fort Initiative Gp, 1987–88. Chief Examiner, Latin A Level, NI Schs Examinations Council, 1987–88. Mem., and Chm. Planning Cttee, Wantage Town Council, 1999–2000. Member, Management Committee: NISTRO, 1980–87; Adv. Council on Schs Industry Liaison, 1981–87; Central Religious Adv. Cttee, BBC/ITV, 1982–86; Researcher and Cttee Mem., Progressive Christianity Network, 2007–09. Hon. Sec., Ancient History Cttee, JACT, 1967–77; Treas., JACT Ancient History Bureau, 1998–2000. Guest Speaker, Swan Hellenic Cruises, 1998–2003. Secretary: Wantage PCC, 1999–2000; Cleeve PCC, 2001–04; Mem., Cleeve Parish Council, 2002–03; Chm., N Som Neighbourhood Watch Assoc., 2004–05. *Publications:* (with W. K. Lacey) Res Publica, 1970; (with D. J. Miller) Stories from Herodotus, 1973; (jtly) The Age of Augustus, 2003; A Faith Unfaithful, 2004; Experience is an Arch, 2007; (jtly) Tiberius to Nero, 2011; Hannibal's Invasion and Defeat, 2011; Lost Certainties, 2012; (jtly) Translation of The Sarum Missal, 2014. *Recreations:* fives, squash, golf, cricket, hockey, etc; translating, theology, stock market, drama, walking, birds, trees, letter-writing, rambling. *Address:* 30 Warner Close, Cleeve, Bristol BS49 4TA.

WILSON, Rt Rev. Bruce Winston; Bishop of Bathurst (NSW), 1989–2000; *b* 23 Aug. 1942; *s* of Alick Bruce Wilson and Maisie Catherine (*née* Pye); *m* 1966, Zandra Robyn Parkes; one *s* one *d. Educ:* Canterbury Boys' High School; Univ. of Sydney (MA); London Univ. (BD); Univ. of NSW (BA); Australian Coll. of Theology (ThL). Curacies, Darling Point and Beverly Hills, Sydney, 1966–69; Anglican Chaplain, Univ. of NSW, 1970–75; Rector of St George's, Paddington, Sydney, 1975–83; Director, St Mark's Theol Coll., Canberra, 1984–89; Asst Bishop, Diocese of Canberra and Goulburn, 1984–89. Exec., Nat. Council of Churches in Australia, 1994–2000. Co-editor, Market Place, 2005–08. *Publications:* The Human Journey: Christianity and Modern Consciousness, 1981; Can God Survive in Australia?, 1983; Reasons of the Heart, 1998. *Recreations:* jogging, motor car restoration, reading, cooking. *Address:* 84–88 Mount Street, Leura, NSW 2780, Australia.

WILSON, Caroline Elizabeth; HM Diplomatic Service; Consul General to Hong Kong and (non-resident) to Macao, since 2012; *b* Wimbledon, 12 Aug. 1970; *d* of Peter Wilson and Elizabeth Wilson. *Educ:* Sevenoaks Sch.; Downing Coll., Cambridge (BA 1992); Inst. for Eur. Studies, Université Libre de Bruxelles (Licence Spéciale en droit européen 1994). Called to the Bar, Middle Temple, 1993, Bencher 2013. Entered FCO, 1995; First Secretary: Beijing, 1997–2000; UK Perm. Repn to EU, 2001–04; Private Sec. to Sec. of State for Foreign and Commonwealth Affairs, 2004–06; Dep. Dir, Eur. Secretariat, Cabinet Office, 2006–07; Minister Counsellor (Econ.), Moscow, 2008–12. *Recreations:* classical music, ice skating, foreign languages (Cantonese less 'recreational' than Italian). *Address:* British Consulate-General, 1 Supreme Court Road, Hong Kong. *T:* 29013021, *Fax:* 29013040. *E:* c.wilson@fco.gov.uk. *Club:* Athenæum.

WILSON, Catherine Mary, (Mrs P. J. Wilson), OBE 1996; FMA, FSA; Director, Norfolk Museums Service, 1991–98; *b* 10 April 1945; *d* of Arthur Thomas Bowyer and Kathleen May (*née* Hawes); *m* 1968, Peter John Wilson. *Educ:* Windsor County Grammar Sch. FMA 1984 (AMA 1972); FSA 1990. Museum Asst, Lincoln City Museums, 1964; Curator, Museum of Lincolnshire Life, 1972; Asst Dir (Museums), Lincs CC, 1983. Member: Museums and Galleries Commn, 1996–2000; Railway Heritage Cttee, 2000–10; E Midlands Regl Cttee, Heritage Lottery Fund, 2002–08. President: Soc. for Folklife Studies, 2000–02; Soc. for Lincs History and Archaeol., 2005–10. FRGS 1998. *Publications:* Lincolnshire's Farm Animals, 2012. *Recreations:* industrial archaeology, vernacular architecture, all local history.

WILSON, Prof. Catherine Warren, PhD; FRSC; Anniversary Professor of Philosophy, University of York, since 2012; *b* New York, 28 March 1951; *d* of Robert F. Warren and Martha Helson; one *s* one *d. Educ:* Westtown Sch., Penn; Yale Univ. (BA Phil. 1972); Lady Margaret Hall, Oxford (BPhil Phil. 1974); Princeton Univ. (PhD Phil. 1977). FRSC 2003. University of Oregon: Asst Prof., 1978–84; Associate Prof., 1984–90; Prof., 1990–92; Professor: Univ. of Alberta, 1992–99; Univ. of BC, 1999–2005; Grad. Center, City Univ. of NY, 2005–09; Regius Prof. of Philosophy, Univ. of Aberdeen, 2009–12. Visiting Professor: Univ. of Notre Dame, 1990–91; Princeton Univ., 2008–09; Vis. Fellow Commoner, Trinity Coll., Cambridge, 2004–05. *Publications:* Leibniz's Metaphysics, 1989; The Invisible World, 1995, 2nd edn 2009; Descartes's Meditations, 2003; Moral Animals, 2004; Epicureanism at Origins of Modernity, 2008. *Address:* Department of Philosophy, University of York, Heslington, York YO10 5DD.

WILSON, Cedric Gordon; Member, Strangford, Northern Ireland Assembly, 1998–2003 (UKU 1998–99, NIU 1999–2003); Leader, Northern Ireland Unionist Party, 1999–2003; *b* 6 June 1948; *s* of Samuel Wilson and Elizabeth Wilson; *m* 1975, Eva Kverneland; one *s* two *d. Educ:* Hillcrest Prep. Sch.; Belmont Primary Sch.; Orangefield High Sch. Dir, Hollymount Develts Ltd, 1988. Mem., 1981–89, Dep. Mayor, 1982–83, Mayor, 1983–84, Castlereagh BC. *Recreations:* art, music, photography. *Address:* 12 Sandylands, Ballyhalbert, Newtownards, Co. Down BT22 1BT.

WILSON, Prof. Charles Crichton, (Chick), PhD, DSc; FInstP, FRSC; Professor of Physical Chemistry, since 2010, and Director of Research, since 2013, University of Bath; *b* 11 Oct. 1961; *s* of David Cherrie Wilson and Isabella Kennedy Wilson; *m* 2002, Victoria Marie Nield, DPhil. *Educ:* Craigbank Secondary Sch., Glasgow; Univ. of Glasgow (BSc Hons Chem. Physics 1982; DSc Chemistry 2004); PhD Physics Dundee 1985. FInstP 2002; FRSC 2002. Council for the Central Laboratory of the Research Councils: Sen. Scientist and Hd, ISIS Crystallography Gp, 1992–2004; Associate Scientist, 2003–06; Regius Prof. of Chemistry, 2003–10, Hd of Dept, 2009–10, Hon. Sen. Res. Associate, 2010–12, Univ. of Glasgow. Vis. Lectr, J. J. Thomson Physical Lab., Univ. of Reading, 1993–96; Vis. Prof. in Chemistry, Univ. of Durham, 2001–06; Adjunct Prof. of Chemistry, Univ. of Tennessee, Knoxville, 2006–. Dir, WestCHEM, 2008–10 (Dep. Dir, 2006–08). Pres., British Crystallographic Assoc., 2003–06. Thomas Graham Medal, Royal Philosophical Soc. of Glasgow, 2011. *Publications:* Single Crystal Neutron Diffraction from Molecular Materials, 2000; over 300 articles in learned scientific jls. *Recreations:* walking, running, reading, music (listening, not making), gardens, enthusing people about science. *Address:* Department of Chemistry, University of Bath, Bath BA2 7AY. *T:* (01225) 386143. *E:* C.C.Wilson@bath.ac.uk.

WILSON, Charles Martin; Managing Director, Mirror Group (formerly Mirror Group Newspapers) plc, 1992–98 (Editorial Director, 1991–92); Managing Director and Editor-in-chief, The Sporting Life, 1990–98; *b* 18 Aug. 1935; *s* of Adam and Ruth Wilson; *m* 1st, 1968, Anne Robinson, *qv* (marr. diss. 1973); one *d*; 2nd, 1980, Sally Angela O'Sullivan, *qv* (marr. diss. 2001); one *s* one *d*; 3rd, 2001, Rachel, *d* of Baroness Pitkeathley, *qv. Educ:* Eastbank Academy, Glasgow. News Chronicle, 1959–60; Daily Mail, 1960–71; Dep. Northern Editor, Daily Mail, 1971–74; Asst Editor, London Evening News, 1974–76; Editor, Glasgow Evening Times, Glasgow Herald, Scottish Sunday Standard, 1976–82; The Times: Exec. Editor, 1982; Dep. Editor, 1983; Editor, 1985–90; Internat. Develts Dir, News Internat. plc, 1990. Non-exec. Dir, Chelsea and Westminster NHS Trust, 2000–11. Mem., Newspaper Panel, Competition Commn, 1999–2006; Board Member: Youth Justice, 1998–2004; Countryside Alliance, 1998–2005, 2008–; IPSO, 2014–. Mem., Jockey Club, 1993–. Trustee: WWF-UK, 1996–2002; Addaction, 1998–; Royal Naval Mus., 1999–2009; Nat. Mus. of Royal Navy, 2011–. *Recreations:* reading, riding, horse racing, countryside. *Address:* 23 Campden Hill Square, W8 7JY. *T:* (020) 7727 3366.

WILSON, Ven. Christine Louise; Archdeacon of Chesterfield, since 2010; *b* Brighton, 26 March 1958; *d* of Ronald and late Dinah Bravery; *m* 1976, Alan Ronald Wilson; two *d* (and one *d* decd). *Educ:* Margaret Hardy Secondary Modern; Southern Theol Educn and Trng Scheme 1994; DipTh. Ordained deacon, 1997, priest, 1998; Curate, Henfield with Shermanbury and Woodmancote, 1997–2002; Team Vicar, Hove, 2002–08; Vicar, Goring-by-the-Sea, 2008–10. Mem., Gen. Synod. 2011–; Regl Rep., House of Bishops,

2013–. Chair: Cornerstone Community Centre, Hove, 2002–08; Brunswick Community Develt Project, Brighton and Hove, 2002–08; Peak Centre, 2010–. Non-executive Director: Ecclesiastical Insurance Group plc, 2012–; Ecclesiastical Insurance Office plc, 2012–. *Recreations:* gardening, travel, entertaining. *Address:* The Old Vicarage, Church Street, Baslow, Bakewell, Derbyshire DE45 1RY. *T:* (01246) 583023. *E:* archchesterfield@derby.anglican.org.

WILSON, Maj. Gen. Christopher Colin, CB 2009; CBE 2004; Strategy Director, Thales Land and Air Systems, since 2011; *b* 14 Sept. 1953; *s* of Brig. Colin David Hastings Wilson and Eileen Edna Wilson (*née* Fort); *m* 1988, Marguerite Rose Laurraine Stewart; two *d. Educ:* Sedbergh Sch.; RMA, Sandhurst. Commnd RA, 1973; Staff Coll., 1986; CO 47 Regt RA, 1993–95; CRA Land and Comdr 1st Artillery Bde, 1998–2000; Dir Capability Integration (Army), 2001–03; Dir RA, 2004; ADC, 2004; Sen. Directing Staff, RCDS, 2005–06; Dep. Comdr, Coalition Forces Comd (Afghanistan), 2006; Capability Manager (Battlespace Manoeuvre), 2006–10; Master Gen. of the Ordnance, 2006–10. Col Comdt, RA, 2005–12. Trustee, Services Sound and Vision Corp., 2010–. CGIA Mil. Technol. Officer, Legion of Merit (USA), 2009. *Recreations:* sailing, gardening. *Address:* c/o Army and Navy Club, 36–39 Pall Mall, SW1Y 5JN. *Clubs:* Army and Navy; Royal Artillery Yacht (Rear Cdre, 1993–95).

WILSON, Christopher G.; *see* Grey-Wilson.

WILSON, Clive Hebden; Chairman, Shared Lives South West (formerly South West Adult Placement Scheme), 2004–13; *b* 1 Feb. 1940; *s* of Joseph and Irene Wilson; *m* 1976, Jill Garland Evans; two *d. Educ:* Leeds Grammar Sch.; Corpus Christi Coll., Oxford. Joined Civil Service, 1962; Ministry of Health: Asst Principal, 1962–67; Asst Private Sec. to Minister of Health, 1965–66; Principal, 1967–73; Assistant Secretary: DHSS, 1973–77; Cabinet Office, 1977–79; DHSS, 1979–82; Under Sec., DHSS, later DoH, 1982–98: Dir of Estabs (HQ), 1982–84; Child Care Div., 1984–86; Children, Maternity, Prevention Div., 1986–87; Medicines Div., 1987–90; Priority Health Services Div., subseq. Health Care (A) Div., 1990–92; on secondment from Department of Health: Hd of Health and Community Care Gp, NCVO, 1992–95; Dir, Office of Health Service Comr, 1995–96; Dep. Health Service Comr, 1996–98; Clerk Advr, H of C, 1998–2001; Independent Complaints Reviewer: Nat. Lottery Charities Bd, subseq. Community Fund, 1998–2004; New Opportunities Fund, 2000–04; Awards for All Scheme, 2000–05; Arts Council England, 2003–05; Big Lottery Fund, 2004–05; Lottery Forum, 2005–10. *Recreations:* walking, gardening.

WILSON, Colin; *see* Wilson, D. C. E.

WILSON, Colin Alexander Megaw; First Scottish Parliamentary Counsel, 2006–12; *b* 4 Jan. 1952; *s* of James Thompson Wilson and Sarah Elizabeth Howard Wilson (*née* Megaw); *m* 1987, Mandy Esca Clay (marr. diss. 2012); one *s* one *d. Educ:* Glasgow High Sch.; Edinburgh Univ. (LLB Hons 1973). Admitted solicitor, Scotland, 1975; Asst Solicitor, then Partner, Archibald Campbell & Harley, WS, Edinburgh, 1975–79; Asst, later Depute, Parly Draftsman for Scotland, 1979–93; Asst Legal Sec. to Lord Advocate, 1979–99; Scottish Parly Counsel, 1993–2006. *Recreations:* choral singing, hill walking, reading.

WILSON, Prof. Colin James Ness, PhD; FRS 2015; FRSNZ; Professor of Volcanology, Victoria University of Wellington, since 2009; *b* Wantage, 19 July 1956; *s* of Donald Wilson and Joyce Wilson; *m* 1989, Katharine Horton; one *s* two *d. Educ:* Imperial Coll. London (BSc Hons 1977; PhD 1981). Post-doctoral Res. Fellow, Univ. of Auckland, 1981–87; Royal Soc. Univ. Res. Fellow, Univs of Cambridge and Bristol, 1987–93; Volcanologist, Inst. of Geol and Nuclear Sci, Taupo and Lower Hutt, 1993–2005; Prof. of Volcanol., Univ. of Auckland, 2005–09. FRSNZ 2001; Fellow, Amer. Geophysical Union, 2006. *Publications:* articles in scientific jls. *Recreation:* sleeping. *Address:* School of Geography, Environment and Earth Sciences, Victoria University of Wellington, PO Box 600, Wellington 6140, New Zealand. *T:* (4) 4639510, *Fax:* (4) 4635168. *E:* colin.wilson@vuw.ac.nz.

WILSON, Corri; MP (SNP) Ayr, Carrick and Cumnock, since 2015; *b* Ayr, 1963; *d* of John and Mary Wilson; one *s* one *d. Educ:* West of Scotland Univ. New Deal Advr, DSS subseq. DWP, 1982–2003; project worker, Barnardo's, 2005–09; Police Custody Welfare Officer, Strathclyde Jt Police Bd, 2007–08; Dir, Caledonii Resources Ltd, 2012–. Mem. (SNP) S Ayrshire Council, 2012–. *Address:* House of Commons, SW1A 0AA. *E:* corri.wilson.mp@parliament.uk.

WILSON, Prof. David, PhD; Professor of Criminology, Birmingham City University (formerly University of Central England, Birmingham), since 1997; *b* 23 April 1957; *s* of late William and Margaret Wilson; *m* 1990, Anne Maguire; one *s* one *d. Educ:* Univ. of Glasgow (MA Hons 1979); Selwyn Coll., Cambridge (PhD 1984). Prison Governor, various prisons incl. HM Prisons Wormwood Scrubs, Grendon and Woodhill, 1983–97. Nat. Teaching Fellowship, England and Wales, Higher Educn Acad., 2012. Vice Chm., Howard League for Penal Reform, 1999–14. Presenter, BBC Television series: Crime Squad, 1999–2001; Leave No Trace, 2006; Who Killed Ivan the Terrible?, 2007; Identity, 2008; presenter: Channel 5: Banged Up, 2009; Killers Behind Bars, 2012; First Kill, Last Kill, 2013; Bring Back Borstal, ITV1. Editor, Howard Jl, 1999–2015. *Publications:* (jtly) The Prison Governor: theory and practice, 1998; The Longest Injustice: the strange story of Alex Alexandrowicz, 1999; Prison(er) Education: stories of change and transformation, 2000; (jtly) What Everyone in Britain Should Know about Crime and Punishment, 2001; (jtly) What Everyone in Britain Should Know about the Police, 2001; (jtly) Innocence Betrayed, 2002; (jtly) Images of Incarceration, 2004; (jtly) Student Handbook of Criminal Justice and Criminology, 2004; Death at the Hands of the State, 2005; Serial Killers: hunting Britons and their victims 1960–2006, 2007; (with P. Harrison) Hunting Evil, 2008; A History of British Serial Killing, 1888–2008, 2009; (with P. Harrison) The Last British Serial Killer, 2010; Looking for Laura: public criminology and hot news, 2011; Mary Ann Cotton: Britain's first female serial killer, 2013; Pain and Retribution: a short history of British prisons, 1066 to the present, 2014; (with E. Yardley and A. Lynes) Serial Killers and the Phenomenon of Serial Murder, 2015. *Recreations:* Rugby, tennis. *Address:* c/o Curtis Brown, 28–29 Haymarket, SW1Y 4SP. *T:* (020) 7393 4460. *E:* profw@globalnet.co.uk.

WILSON, Dr David; Principal and Director, David Wilson Fine Art Ltd, since 2012. *Educ:* Colchester Inst. of Higher Educn; Anglia Ruskin Univ. (BA Hons); Univ. of West of England; London Sch. of Econs and Pol Sci. (LLM); Univ. of Warwick (PhD 2011). Chartered Sec. 1996; FCIS 1996. Solicitor's clerk and articled clerk, Farrer & Co., 1983–86; admitted solicitor, Supreme Court, 1986; Solicitor: Holman, Fenwick & Willan, 1987–88; Gouldens, 1988–90; BAT Industries plc: Asst Solicitor, 1990–93; Gp Co. Sec., 1993–97; Dir, subsidiary cos; Co. Sec. and Gen. Counsel, Debenhams plc and Dir, Debenhams Retail plc, 1998–99; Co. Sec., PIA and IMRO, 2000–01; Registrar, Stock Exchange Quotations Cttee, 2000–01; self-employed contractor to Cazenove and Co., 2001; Gp Co. Sec. and Legal Dir, Safeway plc, and Dir and Sec., Safeway Stores plc, 2001–04; Trustee, 2005, Robert Woof Dir and Chief Exec., 2006–08, Wordsworth Trust; Dir of Policy and Strategy, 2008–09, Chief Exec., 2009–11, ICSA. Trustee, Henry Moore Foundn, 2010–. Antiquary, art historian and writer. FSA 2007. *Publications:* Guide to Best Practice for Annual General Meetings, 1996; A Portrait of Raja Rammohun Roy: a masterpiece in ivory, 2013; Johan Zoffany RA and The Sayer Family of Richmond: a masterpiece of conversation, 2014; articles on legal issues and corporate governance; articles on history and art of 18th and 19th centuries in acad. jls. *Recreations:* music, sport, art, history, literature. *Address:* David Wilson Fine Art Ltd, 328 Linen Hall, 162–168 Regent Street, W1B 5TD. *T:* (020) 7528 4786. *E:* info@davidwilsonfineart.com.

WILSON, David Geoffrey, OBE 1986; DL; Chairman, East Manchester Partnership, 1996–2006; Vice Lord-Lieutenant, Greater Manchester, 2003–08; *b* 30 April 1933; *s* of late Cyril Wilson and Winifred Wilson (*née* Sutton); *m* 1980, Dianne Elizabeth Morgan. *Educ:* Leeds Grammar Sch.; Oldham Hulme Grammar Sch. Williams Deacon's Bank, 1953–70 (Co. Sec., 1965–70); Co. Sec., 1970–72, Sen. Manager, 1973–81, Williams & Glyn's Bank; Regl Dir (NW), NEB, 1981–85; Dir of Banking (NW), British Linen Bank, 1986–91. Non-executive Director: Lancastrian Building Soc., 1991–92; Healthsure Gp Ltd, 1998–2003. Chm., Manchester Business Link Ltd, 1993–2000; Dir, 1998–2001, and Chm., 1999–2001, Business Link Network Co. Chairman: N Manchester HA, 1991–93; N Manchester Healthcare NHS Trust, 1993–97; Dir, Manchester Chamber of Commerce and Industry, 1974–2001 (Pres., 1978–80); non-exec. Dir, Manchester TEC, 1998–2001. Non-executive Director: Halle Concerts Soc., 1980–97 (Treas., 1986–92; Dep. Chm., 1992–97); NW Arts Bd, 1991–96. Pres., Manchester Literary and Philosophical Soc., 1981–83. Chairman: Manchester Settlement, 1999–2009; Manchester Outward Bound Assoc., 2002–; Pres., Gtr Manchester Victim Support and Witness Service, 2001–; Vice-Pres., St Ann's Hospice, 1991– (Sec., 1968–72; Treas., 1975–91). Mem. Court, Manchester Univ., 1980–99; Mem. Council, Salford Univ., 1996–2005; Governor: Salford Coll. of Technol., 1988–96; Manchester Coll. of Arts and Technol., 1999–2008. Hon. Consul for Iceland, 1981–. High Sheriff, 1991–92, DL 1985, Gtr Manchester. Hon. MA: Manchester, 1983; Salford, 1995. *Recreations:* gardening, music. *Address:* 28 Macclesfield Road, Wilmslow, Cheshire SK9 2AF. *T:* (01625) 524133, *Fax:* (01625) 520605. *E:* wilsondg@talk21.com. *Clubs:* Army and Navy; Lancashire County Cricket.

WILSON, Sir David (Mackenzie), Kt 1984; FBA 1981; Director of the British Museum, 1977–92; *b* 30 Oct. 1931; *e s* of Rev. Joseph Wilson; *m* 1955, Eva, *o d* of Dr Gunnar Sjögren, Stockholm; one *s* one *d. Educ:* Kingswood Sch.; St John's Coll., Cambridge (LittD; Hon. Fellow, 1985); Lund Univ., Sweden. Research Asst, Cambridge Univ., 1954; Asst Keeper, British Museum, 1954–64; Reader in Archaeology of Anglo-Saxon Period, London Univ., 1964–71; Prof. of Medieval Archaeology, Univ. of London, 1971–76; Jt Head of Dept of Scandinavian Studies, UCL, 1973–76 (Hon. Fellow, 1988). Slade Prof., Cambridge, 1985–86. Member: Ancient Monuments Bd for England, 1976–84; Historic Bldgs and Monuments Commn, 1990–97. Governor, Museum of London, 1976–81; Trustee: Nat. Museums of Scotland, 1985–87; Nat. Museums of Merseyside, 1986–2001. Crabtree Orator 1966. Member: Royal Swedish Acad. of Sci.; Royal Acad. of Letters, History and Antiquities, Sweden; Norwegian Acad. of Science and Letters; German Archaeological Inst.; Royal Gustav Adolf's Acad. of Sweden; Royal Soc. of Letters of Lund; Vetenskapssocieteten, Lund; Royal Soc. of Sci. and Letters, Gothenburg; Royal Soc. of Sci., Uppsala; Royal Norwegian Soc. of Sci. and Letters; FSA; MAE; Hon. MRIA; Hon. Mem., Polish Archaeological and Numismatic Soc.; Hon. FMA. Sec., Soc. for Medieval Archaeology, 1957–77; Pres., Viking Soc., 1968–70; Pres., Brit. Archaeological Assoc., 1962–68. Mem. Council, Nottingham Univ., 1988–94. Foundn Fellow, Birmingham Univ., 2008. Hon. FilDr Stockholm; Hon. Dr Phil: Aarhus; Oslo; Hon. DLitt: Liverpool; Birmingham; Nottingham; Leicester; Hon LLD Pennsylvania. Félix Neubergh Prize, Gothenburg Univ., 1978; Gold Medal, Royal Gustav Adolf's Acad. of Sweden, 1994; Gold Medal, Soc. of Antiquaries, 1995. Order of Polar Star, 1st cl. (Sweden), 1977. *Publications:* The Anglo-Saxons, 1960, 3rd edn 1981; Anglo-Saxon Metalwork 700–1100 in British Museum, 1964; (with O. Klindt-Jensen) Viking Art, 1966; (with G. Bersu) Three Viking Graves in the Isle of Man, 1969; The Vikings and their Origins, 1970, 2nd edn 1980; (with P. G. Foote) The Viking Achievement, 1970; (with A. Small and C. Thomas) St Ninian's Isle and its Treasure, 1973; The Viking Age in the Isle of Man, 1974; (ed) Anglo-Saxon Archaeology, 1976; (ed) The Northern World, 1980; The Forgotten Collector, 1984; Anglo-Saxon Art, 1984; The Bayeux Tapestry, 1985, 2nd edn 2004; The British Museum: purpose and politics, 1989; Awful Ends, 1992; Showing the Flag, 1992; Vikingatidens Konst, 1995; Vikings and Gods in European Art, 1997; The British Museum: a history, 2002; (ed jtly) The Hoen Hoard, 2006; The Vikings in the Isle of Man, 2008; (ed jtly) Aggersborg: the viking-age settlement and fortress, 2014. *Address:* The Lifeboat House, Castletown, Isle of Man IM9 1LD. *T:* (01624) 822800. *Club:* Athenæum.

WILSON, David William, CBE 2011; DL; FCIOB; Chairman: Wilson Bowden PLC, 1987–2007; Beacon Hill Group (formerly Eastern Range Ltd) and subsidiaries, Go Plant Ltd and Davidsons Ltd, since 2004; Founder, David Wilson Foundation, since 1995; *b* 5 Dec. 1941; *s* of Albert Henry Wilson and Kathleen May Wilson; *m* 1st, 1964, Ann Taberner; one *s* one *d*; 2nd, 1985, Laura Isobel Knifton; two *s. Educ:* Ashby Boys' Grammar Sch.; Leicester Polytechnic. Created from scratch what is now Wilson Bowden PLC. Pres., Leics CCC, 2003–. DL Leics, 2008. Hon. Canon, Leicester Cathedral, 2009. FCIOB 2004. Hon. LLD: Leicester, 2004; De Montfort, 2010. *Recreation:* farming. *Address:* Lowesby Hall, Lowesby, Leics LE7 9DD. *T:* (0116) 259 5321.

WILSON, Prof. Deirdre Susan Moir, PhD; FBA 1990; Professor of Linguistics, University College London, 1991–2007, now Emeritus; *b* 1941; *m* 1975, Dr Theodore Zeldin, *qv. Educ:* Somerville Coll., Oxford (BA 1964); Nuffield Coll., Oxford (BPhil 1967); Massachusetts Inst. of Technol. (PhD 1974). Lectr in Philosophy, Somerville Coll., Oxford, 1967–68; Harkness Fellow, MIT, 1968–70; University College London: Lectr in Linguistics, 1970–85; Reader, 1985–91; British Acad. Res. Reader, 1988. Hon. DLitt: Geneva, 2007; Oslo, 2014. *Publications:* Presuppositions and Non-truth Conditional Semantics, 1975; (with Neil Smith) Modern Linguistics: the results of Chomsky's Revolution, 1979; (novel) Slave of the Passions, 1991; (with Dan Sperber) Relevance: communication and cognition, 1995; (with Dan Sperber) Meaning and Relevance, 2012; contrib. to learned jls. *Address:* UCL Linguistics, Chandler House, 2 Wakefield Street, WC1N 1PF.

WILSON, Derek Robert; Chief Executive, Slough Estates, 1996–2002; *b* 10 Oct. 1944; *m* 1972, Maureen Thorpe; one *s* one *d. Educ:* Bristol Univ. (BA Econs and Accounting). FCA 1970. Deloitte Haskins & Sells, London and Geneva, 1966–72; Cavenham, 1973–78; Wilkinson Match, 1978–83; Dir of Finance, Cadbury Schweppes, 1983–86; Finance Dir, 1986, Gp Man. Dir, 1992–96, Slough Estates. Director: Candover Investments, 1994–2005; Westbury, 1996–2005. Trustee, Nat. Soc. for Epilepsy, 2003–14. Gov., St Mary's Sch., Gerrards Cross, 1996– (Chm. Govs, 2007–). *Recreation:* golf.

WILSON, Des; author; public affairs adviser; *b* 5 March 1941; *s* of Albert H. Wilson, Oamaru, New Zealand; *m* 1985, Jane Dunmore; one *s* one *d* by a previous marriage. *Educ:* Waitaki Boys' High Sch., New Zealand. Journalist-Broadcaster, 1957–67; Director, Shelter, Nat. Campaign for the Homeless, 1967–71; Head of Public Affairs, RSC, 1974–76; Editor, Social Work Today, 1976–79; Dep. Editor, Illustrated London News, 1979–81; Chm., 1981–85, Project Advr, 1985–89, CLEAR (Campaign for Lead-Free Air); Dir of Public Affairs, 1993–94, World Wide Vice Chm., Public Affairs, 1994, Burson-Marsteller; Dir of Corporate and Public Affairs, BAA plc, 1994–2000. Non-executive Director: Carphone Warehouse plc, 2000–03; Earls Court and Olympia Holdings, 2001–04. Chairman: Friends of the Earth (UK), 1982–86; Campaign for Freedom of Information, 1984–91; Citizen Action, 1983–91; Parents Against Tobacco, 1990. Member: Nat. Exec., Nat. Council for Civil Liberties, 1971–73; Cttee for City Poverty, 1972–73; Bd, Shelter, 1982–86 (Trustee, 1982–86); Council, Nat. Trust, 2001–02; Trustee, Internat. Year of Shelter for the Homeless (UK), 1985–87. Member: Bd, BTA, 1997–2004; UK Sports Council, 2000–02; Mgt Bd, ECB, 2003–04; Sen. Vice Chm., Sport England, 1999–2002 (Chm., Lottery Panel, 1999–2002). Columnist: The Guardian, 1968–70; The Observer, 1971–75; New Statesman, 1997–; regular contributor, Illustrated London News, 1972–85. Contested (L) Hove, 1973, 1974; Liberal Party: Mem. Council, 1973–74 and 1984–85; Mem., Nat. Exec., 1984–85; Pres., 1986–87; Pres., NLYL,

1984–85; Mem. Federal Exec., SLD, 1988; Gen. Election Campaign Dir, Lib Dems, 1990–92. ITN Environmentalist of the Decade, 1989; PR Week Outstanding Individual Award, 1992; Sheila McKechnie Foundn Lifetime Achievement Award, 2015. *Publications:* I Know It Was the Place's Fault, 1970; Des Wilson's Minority Report (a diary of protest), 1973; So you want to be Prime Minister: a personal view of British politics, 1979; The Lead Scandal, 1982; Pressure, the A to Z of Campaigning in Britain, 1984; (ed) The Environmental Crisis, 1984; (ed) The Secrets File, 1984; The Citizen Action Handbook, 1986; Battle for Power - Inside the Alliance General Election Campaign, 1987; Costa Del Sol (novel), 1990; Campaign (novel), 1992; Campaigning, 1993; (with Sir John Egan) Private Business, Public Battleground, 2002; Swimming with the Devilfish: under the surface of professional poker, 2006; Ghosts at the Table: a history of poker, 2007; Memoirs of a Minor Public Figure (autobiog.), 2011; Growing Old: the last campaign, 2014. *Address:* Pryors Cottage, Nancegollan, Helston, Cornwall TR13 0AZ.

WILSON, Donald; Lord Lieutenant and Lord Provost of Edinburgh, since 2012; *b* Selkirk, 4 Dec. 1959; *s* of George Wilson and May Wilson; partner, Elaine Brand; one step *s* one step *d*. *Educ:* Galashiels Acad.; Univ. of Stirling (BA Hons); City Univ., London (MSc Information Sci.); Moray House Coll. of Educn (TQ Secondary). Teacher of Computing, 1984–2012; Adult Educn Tutor, 1984–2012; Actg Sen. Teacher, 1997–99, Curriculum Develt Officer, 1999–2001, ICT. Mem. (Lab) Edinburgh CC, 1999– (Bailie, 2007–12). Chm., 1999–2007, Pres., 2012–, Edinburgh Internat. Sci. Fest.; Chairman: Edinburgh Sci. Foundn, 1999–2007; Edinburgh Convention Bureau, 2003–05; Edinburgh and Lothians Tourist Bd, 2003–05; Convener, Edinburgh SW Neighbourhood Partnership, 2007–12; Chairman and Director: Edinburgh Internat. Fest. Soc., 2012–; Edinburgh Royal Military Tattoo Ltd, 2012–. Comr, Northern Lighthouse Bd. Chm., Transnational Demos Proj., 2001–. Dir and Trustee, Our Dynamic Earth Charitable Trust, 2012–. Gov., Edinburgh Trades Maiden Fund. Hon. Pres. or Patron of numerous charities and bodies in Edinburgh, 2012–. OStJ. *Recreations:* film, opera, science fiction, computers, antiques. *Address:* City Chambers, High Street, Edinburgh EH1 1YJ. *T:* (0131) 529 4000, *Fax:* (0131) 529 4010. *E:* lord.provost@edinburgh.gov.uk.

WILSON, (Douglas) Colin (Edward); Deputy Government Actuary, since 2012 and Technical Director, Government Actuary's Department, since 2011; *b* Kingston-upon-Thames, 12 July 1962; *s* of Dr Eric Wilson and Joan Wilson; *m* 1986, Caroline Heslop; one *s* two *d*. *Educ:* King's College Sch., Wimbledon; Trinity Coll., Cambridge (BA Hons Maths 1983). FIA 1996; Chartered Enterprise Risk Actuary 2013. Technical Consultant, EDS-Scicon, 1983–93; trainee actuary, Prudential Ltd, 1993–96; Sen. Quantitative Analyst, 1996–98, Dir, Quantitative Res., 1998–2005, Prudential M&G Ltd; Sen. Consultant, Barrie & Hibbert Ltd, 2005–09; Chief Actuary (Investment and Risk), Govt Actuary's Dept, 2009–11. Member, Council: Inst. for Quantitative Investment Res., 2004–09; Inst. of Actuaries, 2002–08; Inst. and Faculty of Actuaries, 2013– (Pres., June 2016–). *Recreations:* violin playing, defending my flower beds from marauding puppies. *Address:* Government Actuary's Department, Finlaison House, 15–17 Furnival Street, EC4A 1AB. *T:* (020) 7211 2601. *E:* colin.wilson@gad.gov.uk.

WILSON, Duncan Henry, OBE 2007; FCA; FSA; Chief Executive, Historic England, since 2015; *b* London, 29 March 1957; *s* of Sir Anthony Wilson and of (Margaret) Josephine Wilson (*née* Hudson); *m* 1992, Kate Emms; three *s*. *Educ:* Sherborne Sch. for Boys, Dorset; Pembroke Coll., Oxford (MA PPE); Inst. of Archaeol., Univ. of Oxford (MPhil Eur. Archaeol.). FCA 1996; FSA 2009. Field archaeologist, 1983–84; trainee accountant, Coopers & Lybrand, 1984–87; Financial Controller, English Heritage, 1987–91; Defence, Industry and Resource Accounting Desks, HM Treasury, 1991–95; Hd, Libraries Div., DNH, 1995–97; Dir, Somerset Hse Trust, 1997–2002; Chief Executive: Greenwich Foundn for Old Royal Naval Coll., 2002–11; Alexandra Park and Palace Trust, 2011–15. Trustee: Royal Armouries, 2007–11; Churches Conservation Trust, 2008–. Community Gov., Corelli Coll., Greenwich, 2004–07. FRSA. *Recreations:* classical singing and listening to music, restoring old buildings, gardening, dogs. *Address:* 3 Terrett's Place, N1 1QZ. *T:* (020) 7973 3247. *E:* duncan.wilson@HistoricEngland.org.uk.

WILSON, Prof. Edward Osborne, PhD; Pellegrino University Research Professor, 1997–2002, now Emeritus, and Hon. Curator in Entomology, since 1997, Harvard University (Curator in Entomology, 1972–97); *b* 10 June 1929; *s* of Edward O. Wilson, Sen. and Inez Freeman; *m* 1955, Irene Kelley; one *d*. *Educ:* Univ. of Alabama (BS 1949; MS 1950); Harvard Univ. (PhD 1955). Harvard University: Jun. Fellow, Soc. of Fellows, 1953–56; Asst Prof. of Biology, 1956–58; Assoc. Prof. of Zoology, 1958–64; Prof. of Zoology, 1964–76; Baird Prof. of Sci., 1976–94; Mellon Prof. of the Scis, 1990–93; Pellegrino University Prof., 1994–97. Hon. DSc Oxon, 1993; 32 other hon. doctorates. Nat. Medal of Sci., USA, 1978; Tyler Prize for Envmtl Achievement, 1984; Crafoord Prize, Swedish Royal Acad. of Sci., 1990; Internat. Prize for Biol., Japan, 1994; King Faisal Internat. Prize for Sci., 2000; Franklin Medal, Amer. Philosophical Soc., 2000, etc. *Publications:* (with R. H. MacArthur) The Theory of Island Biogeography, 1967; (jtly) A Primer of Population Biology, 1971; The Insect Societies, 1971; Sociobiology: the new synthesis, 1975; On Human Nature, 1978 (Pulitzer Prize, 1979); (jtly) Caste and Ecology in the Social Insects, 1978; (jtly) Genes, Mind and Culture, 1981; (jtly) Promethean Fire, 1983; Biophilia, 1984; Success and Dominance in Ecosystems, 1990; The Diversity of Life, 1992; Naturalist (autobiog.), 1994; In Search of Nature, 1996; Consilience, 1998; Biological Diversity, 1999; The Future of Life, 2002; Pheidole in the New World: a hyperdiverse ant genus, 2003; Nature Revealed, 2006; The Creation, 2006 (Sci. and Literature Prize, Stevens Technol. Inst., 2007); with Bert Hölldobler: The Ants, 1990 (Pulitzer Prize, 1991); Journey to the Ants, 1994; The Superorganism, 2009 (Best Biology Book, Library Jl, 2009); The Leafcutter Ants, 2010; The Social Conquest of Earth, 2012; The Meaning of Human Existence, 2014; contrib. learned jls. *Address:* Museum of Comparative Zoology, Harvard University, 26 Oxford Street, Cambridge, MA 02138–2902, USA. *T:* (617) 4952315.

WILSON, Elizabeth Alice, (Mrs W. I. Wilson), OBE 1995; Chairman, Dumfries and Galloway Community NHS Trust, 1995–97; *b* 26 May 1937; *née* Edwards; *m* 1996, William Iain Wilson, MBE. *Educ:* Coleraine High Sch.; Univ. of Edinburgh (BSc Soc. Sci.); SRN, SCM. Staff Nurse, Midwife, Ward Sister and nurse management posts, 1958–72; Principal Nursing Officer, Edinburgh Northern Hosps Gp, 1972–74; Dist Nursing Officer, N Lothian, Lothian Health Bd, 1974–80; Chief Area Nursing Officer: Dumfries and Galloway Health Bd, 1980–88; Tayside Health Bd, 1988–94. Member: Nat. Bd for Nursing, Midwifery and Health Visiting, Scotland, 1983–93 (Dep. Chm., 1985–93); UK Central Council for Nursing, Midwifery and Health Visiting, 1983–88. Chm., Stranraer Cancer Drop In Centre Assoc., 1998–2008. Lady Capt., Stranraer Golf Club, 2015. Hon. Sen. Lectr, Univ. of Dundee, 1988–94. SSStJ 2003. *Publications:* papers on nursing.

WILSON, Erik; Executive Director, Corporate and Support Services, and Member, Executive Board, Competition and Markets Authority, since 2013; *b* London, 29 Nov. 1963; *s* of Roy Wilson and Jean Wilson (now Norley). Prime Minister's Efficiency Unit, 1993; Sec. to Interception, Security and Intelligence Services Comrs, 1994–98; Home Office: Terrorism Bill Manager, Terrorism and Protection Unit, 1998–2000; Home Sec.'s Office, 2000–02; Office of Fair Trading: Principal Private Sec. to Sir John Vickers, 2002–04; Dep. Dir, Bd Secretariat, 2004–06; Director: Exec. Office and Human Resources, 2006–07; Exec. Office and Internat., 2007–12. *Recreations:* reading, antiques, family. *Address:* Competition and Markets Authority, 37 Southampton Row, WC1B 4AD. *T:* (020) 3738 6964. *E:* erik.wilson@cma.gsi.gov.uk.

WILSON, Fraser Andrew, MBE 1980; HM Diplomatic Service, retired; Executive Director, Prospect Burma, 2010–13; *b* 6 May 1949; *s* of William McStravick Wilson and Mary McFadyen Wilson (*née* Fraser); *m* 1981, Janet Phillips; two *s*. *Educ:* Bellahouston Acad.; Surrey Univ. (Dip. Russian Studies). Joined Diplomatic Service, 1967; served: FCO, 1967–70; Havana, 1970–71; SE Asia, 1971–73; Seoul, 1973–77; Salisbury, 1977–80; FCO, 1980–84; Moscow, 1984–85; First Sec. (Commercial), Rangoon, 1986–90; FCO, 1990–94; Dep. Consul Gen., São Paulo, 1994–98; Ambassador to Turkmenistan, 1998–2002; High Comr, Seychelles, 2002–04; Dep. Hd, Overseas Territories, FCO, 2004–06; Ambassador to Albania, 2006–09. *Recreations:* travelling, reading.

WILSON, Geoffrey Alan, OBE 2004; Chairman, Equity Land Ltd, 1994–2012; *b* 19 Feb. 1934; *s* of Lewis Wilson and Doris Wilson (*née* Shrier); *m* 1963, Marilyn Helen Freedman; one *s* two *d*. *Educ:* Haberdashers' Aske's School; College of Estate Management. FRICS. 2nd Lieut RA, 1955–56. Private practice, 1957–60; Director: Amalgamated Investment & Property Co., 1961–70; Sterling Land Co., 1971–73 (and co-founder); Greycoat, 1976–94 (Chm., 1985–94, and co-founder); Perspectives on Architecture (formerly Perfect Harmony) Ltd, 1993–98. Member: W Metropolitan Conciliation Cttee, Race Relations Bd, 1969–71; Council, Central British Fund for World Jewish Relief, 1993–97. Trustee: ORT Trust, 1980–85; Public Art Develt Trust, 1990–95; British Architectural Liby Trust, 1996–2000; AA Foundn, 1998–2002; Buildings at Risk Trust, 1998–2001. English Heritage: Comr, 1992–98; Chm., London Adv. Cttee, 1995–98; Chm., Urban Panel, 2000–03; Chm., Heritage Protection Review Steering Cttee, DCMS, 2004–08. Mem., Governing Council, UCS, 1991–95. Governor: Peabody Trust, 1998–2004; City Literary Inst., 1998–2002; Mus. of London, 2000–10. Hon. FRIBA 1995. *Recreations:* reading, architecture, art. *Address:* 5 Elm Walk, West Heath Road, NW3 7UP. *Club:* Reform.

WILSON, Hon. Geoffrey Hazlitt, CVO 1989; FCA, FCMA; Chairman, Southern Electric plc, 1993–96 (Director, 1989–96); *b* 28 Dec. 1929; *yr s* of 1st Baron Moran, MC, MD, FRCP, and Lady Moran, MBE; *m* 1955, Barbara Jane Hebblethwaite; two *s* two *d*. *Educ:* Eton; King's Coll., Cambridge (BA Hons). JDipMA. Articled to Barton Mayhew (now Ernst & Young), 1952; Chartered Accountant 1955; joined English Electric, 1956; Dep. Comptroller, 1965; Financial Controller (Overseas), GEC, 1968; joined Delta Group as Financial Dir, Cables Div., 1969; elected to Main Board as Gp Financial Dir, 1972; Jt Man. Dir, 1977; Dep. Chief Executive, 1980; Chief Exec., 1981–88; Chm., 1982–94. Director: Blue Circle Industries plc, 1980–97; Drayton English & International Trust, 1978–95; W Midlands and Wales Regl Bd, Nat. Westminster Bank PLC, 1985–92 (Chm., 1990–92); Johnson Matthey plc, 1990–97 (Dep. Chm., 1994–97); UK Adv. Bd, National Westminster Bank, 1990–92. Member: Council, Inst. of Cost and Management Accountants, 1972–78; Accounting Standards Cttee, 1978–79; Financial Reporting Council, 1990–93; London Metal Exchange, 1982–94; Chm., 100 Gp of Chartered Accountants, 1979–80 (Hon. Mem., 1985). Mem. Management Bd, Engineering Employers Fedn, 1979–83 (Vice-Pres., 1983–86 and 1990–94; Dep. Pres., 1986–90); Chm., EEF Cttee on Future of Wage Bargaining, 1980; Dep. Pres., 1986–87, Pres., 1987–88, Counsellor, 1989–94, BEAMA; Member: Administrative Council, Royal Jubilee Trusts, 1979–88, Hon. Treas., 1980–89; Council, Winchester Cathedral Trust, 1985–93; Council, St Mary's Hosp. Med. Sch., 1985–88. Vice-Chm., Campaign Appeal, 1994–97, Fellow Commoner, 1996–, King's Coll., Cambridge. CCMI. Mem. Ct of Assistants, Chartered Accountants' Co., 1982–95 (Master, 1988–89). OStJ 1996. *Recreations:* family, reading, walking, vintage cars. *Club:* Boodle's.

WILSON, Prof. Geoffrey Victor Herbert, AM 1998; PhD; Vice Chancellor and President, Deakin University, 1996–2002; *b* 23 Sept. 1938; *s* of Victor Hawthorne Wilson and Dorothy Eleanor Wilson (*née* Spooner); *m* 1961, Beverley Wigley; two *s* two *d*. *Educ:* Univ. of Melbourne (BSc 1958; MSc 1960; DSc 1977); PhD Monash Univ. 1964. FAIP, MACE, FTSE, FAIM. Postgrad. Schol., Univ. of Melbourne, 1958–60; Teaching Fellow, Monash Univ., 1960–63; Nuffield Foundn Travelling Fellow, Oxford Univ., 1963–65; Sen. Lectr in Physics, Monash Univ., 1965–71; University of New South Wales: Prof. of Physics, 1971–85, Dean, Faculty of Mil. Studies, 1978–86, Royal Mil. Coll.; Rector of University Coll., Aust. Defence Acad., 1984–91; Vice Chancellor, Central Queensland Univ., 1991–96. Director: Australian Maritime Coll., 2004–; Forestry Cooperative Res. Centre, 2009–12. Chm. Bd, AMC Search, 2007–. Vis. Prof., Free Univ. of Berlin, 1977–78. *Recreations:* gardening, theatre, physical recreation. *Address:* 33 Highett Road, Highton, Vic 3216, Australia.

WILSON, Gerald Robertson, CB 1991; FRSE; Treasurer, Royal Society of Edinburgh, since 2012; Chairman, Scottish Biomedical Foundation, 1999–2004; Special Adviser, Royal Bank of Scotland, 2000–11; *b* 7 Sept. 1939; *s* of late Charles Robertson Wilson and Margaret Wilson (*née* Early); *m* 1963, Margaret Anne (*d* 2005), *d* of late John S. and Agnes Wight; one *s* one *d*. *Educ:* Holy Cross Academy, Edinburgh; University of Edinburgh. (MA). FRSE 1999. Asst Principal, Scottish Home and Health Dept, 1961–65; Private Sec. to Minister of State for Scotland, 1965–66; Principal, Scottish Home and Health Dept, 1966–72; Private Sec. to Lord Privy Seal, 1972–74, to Minister of State, Civil Service Dept, 1974; Asst Sec., Scottish Economic Planning Dept, 1974–77; Counsellor, Office of the UK Perm. Rep. to the European Communities, Brussels, 1977–82; Asst Sec., Scottish Office, 1982–84; Under Sec., Industry Dept for Scotland, 1984–88; Sec., Scottish Office Educn, later Educn and Industry, Dept, 1988–99. Non-exec. Dir, ICL (Scotland) Ltd, 2000–02; Advr, ScottishJobs.com, 2004–05. Chm., Scottish Biomed. Res. Trust, 1999–2003. Chm., E Scotland, RIPA, 1990–92. Vice Chm., Royal Scottish Nat. Orchestra, 2002–06 (Bd Mem., 1999–2002); Trustee, Royal Scottish Nat. Orchestra Foundn, 2006–; Hon. Sec., Friends of the Royal Scottish Acad., 2009–. Chm., Scottish Eur. Educnl Trust, 2006–12. Mem. Ct, Strathclyde Univ., 1999–2008 (Vice Chm., 2008–12; Hon. Fellow, 2011); Gov., George Watson's Coll., Edinburgh, 2000–08. Mem., Bd of Mgt, St Andrew's Children's Soc., 2002–11. Mem. Council, Fairbridge in Scotland, 2000–06 (Chm., 2006–11). DUniv Stirling, 1999. *Recreation:* music. *Address:* 17/5 Kinnear Road, Edinburgh EH3 5PG.

WILSON, Gillian Brenda, (Mrs Kenneth Wilson); *see* Babington-Browne, G. B.

WILSON, Gordon; *see* Wilson, Robert G.

WILSON, Guy Murray, MA; FSA; museum and historical consultant; *b* 18 Feb. 1950; *s* of late Rowland George Wilson and Mollie (*née* Munson; later Mrs Youngs); *m* 1972, Pamela Ruth McCredie; two *s* two *d*. *Educ:* New Coll., Oxford (MA); Manchester Univ. (Dip. Art, Gallery and Museum Studies). FSA 1984. Joined Royal Armouries, 1972; Keeper of Edged Weapons, 1978; Dep. Master of the Armouries, 1981–88; Master of the Armouries, 1988–2002. Member: British Commn for Military History, 1978–; Adv. Cttee on History Wreck Sites, 1981–99; Arms and Armour Soc. of GB, 1973– (Vice-Pres., 1995–); Arms and Armour Soc. of Denmark, 1978–; Meyrick Soc., 1980–; Internat. Napoleonic Soc., 2001–; Pres., Internat. Assoc. of Museums of Arms and Military Hist., 2002–03; Chairman: Internat. Cttee of Museums and Collections of Arms and Military Hist., 2003–10; Battle of Crécy Trust, 2007–; Leeds Peace Poetry, 2009–. Dir, Genesis Trio Ltd, 2005–09. Writer, Arms in Action (TV series), 1998, 2000. FRSA 1992. *Publications:* Treasures of the Tower: Crossbows, 1975; (with A. V. B. Norman) Treasures from the Tower of London, 1982; (with D. Walker) The Royal Armouries in Leeds: the making of a museum, 1996; The Vauxhall Operatory: a century of inventions before the Scientific Revolution, 2009; contribs to museum and exhibn catalogues and to Jl of Arms and Armour Soc., Internat. Jl of Nautical Archaeol., Connoisseur, Burlington, Country Life, Museums Jl, Guns Rev., etc. *Recreations:* theatre, music, reading, walking. *Address:* Yeoman's Course House, Thornton Hill, Easingwold, York YO61 3PY.

WILSON, (Iain) Richard, OBE 1994; actor and director; *b* 9 July 1936; *s* of John Boyd Wilson and Euphemia (*née* Colquhoun). *Educ:* Greenock High Sch.; Royal Acad. of Dramatic Art. Associate Director: Royal Court, 2000–07; Sheffield Theatres, 2009–. *Theatre* includes: Uncle Vanya, Edinburgh Traverse Th., 1968; Normal Service, Hampstead, 1979; Operation Bad Apple, 1982, An Honourable Trade, 1984, May Days, 1990, Royal Court; The Weekend, Strand, 1994; What the Butler Saw, NT, 1995; Waiting for Godot, Manchester Royal Exchange, 1999; The Play What I Wrote, West End, 2001–02; Whipping It Up, Bush Th., 2006, transf. New Ambassadors and tour, 2007; Twelfth Night, RSC Stratford and West End, 2009–10; A Little Hotel on the Side, Th. Royal, Bath, 2013; Krapp's Last Tape, Crucible Th., Sheffield, 2014; *plays directed:* Heaven and Hell, 1981, Other Worlds, 1983, Royal Court; An Inspector Calls, Manchester Royal Exchange, 1986; A Wholly Healthy Glasgow, Manchester Royal Exchange, Royal Court and Edinburgh Fest., 1987, 1988; Prin, Lyric, Hammersmith, 1989; Imagine Drowning, Hampstead, 1991; Women Laughing, Manchester Royal Exchange, transf. Royal Court, 1992; Simply Disconnected, Chichester, 1996; Tom and Clem, Aldwych, 1997; Four Knights in Knaresborough, Tricycle Th., 1999; Primo, NT, Hampstead, NY and S Africa, 2004; East Coast Chicken Supper, Traverse Th., 2005; Astronaut Wives Club, NYT, 2006; Royal Court: Four, 1998; Toast, 1999; Mr Kolpert, I Just Stopped By to See the Man, 2000; Nightingale and Chase, 2001; Where Do We Live, Day in Dull Armour, Graffiti, 2002; Under the Whaleback, Playing the Victim, 2003; The Woman Before, 2005; Rainbow Kiss, 2006; That Face, The Pride, Sheffield Crucible, 2010; Lungs, Paines Plough co-prodn with Sheffield Crucible, 2011; Straight, Sheffield Crucible, transf. Bush Th., London, 2012; Smack Family Robinson, Rose Th., Kingston, 2013; May 08, GSMD, 2013; Love Your Soldiers, Sheffield Crucible, 2013; Blasted, Sheffield Crucible, 2015; *television series* include: My Good Woman, 1972; Crown Court, 1973–84; A Sharp Intake of Breath, 1979–81; Only When I Laugh, 1979–82; High and Dry, 1987; Tutti Frutti, 1987; One Foot in the Grave, six series, 1989–2000; High Stakes, 2001; Life - As We Know It, 2001; Jeffrey Archer: The Truth, 2002; King of Fridges, 2004; Born and Bred, two series, 2004–05; Doctor Who, 2005; A Harlot's Progress, 2006; The True Voice of Prostitution, 2006; Reichenbach Falls, 2007; Kingdom, two series, 2007–08; Merlin, 2008–12; New Tricks, 2009; Demons, 2009; Britain's Best Drives, 2009; Two Feet in the Grave, 2009; Dispatches, 2011; Playhouse Presents: Space Age, 2014; Richard Wilson on the Road, 2015; TV film, Danny and the Human Zoo, 2015; *television directed* includes: Commitments, 1982; Remainder Man, 1982; Under The Hammer, 1984; A Wholly Healthy Glasgow, 1987; Changing Step, 1991; The Egg, 2002; Primo, 2008; *films* include: A Passage to India, 1984; Whoops Apocalypse, 1986; Prick Up Your Ears, 1987; How to Get Ahead in Advertising, 1989; Fellow Traveller, 1990; Carry on Columbus, 1992; Soft Top Hard Shoulder, 1993; The Man Who Knew Too Little, 1998; Women Talking Dirty, 2001; Love and Other Disasters, 2006. Rector, Glasgow Univ., 1996–99. Hon. DLitt Glasgow Caledonian, 1995. Top TV Comedy Actor, British Comedy Awards, 1991; Light Entertainment Award, BAFTA, 1991 and 1993. *Recreations:* squash, collecting work of living Scottish painters. *Address:* c/o Conway van Gelder Grant Ltd, 8–12 Broadwick Street, W1F 8HW. *T:* (020) 7287 0077. *Clubs:* Royal Automobile, Groucho.

WILSON, Prof. Ian Andrew, DPhil, DSc; FRS 2000; FRSE; Hansen Professor of Structural Biology, Department of Molecular Biology and Skaggs Institute for Chemical Biology, Scripps Research Institute, since 1982; *b* 22 March 1949; *s* of George Alexander Wilson and Margaret Stewart Wilson (*née* McKillop). *Educ:* Perth Acad.; Univ. of Edinburgh (BSc 1st Cl. Hons 1971); Corpus Christi Coll., Oxford (DPhil 1976; DSc 2000). Jun. Res. Fellow, Corpus Christi Coll., Oxford, 1975–77; Res. Fellow in Biochem., 1977–80, Res. Associate, 1980–82, Harvard Univ.; Asst Mem., 1982–84, Associate Mem., 1984–90, Scripps Clinic and Res. Foundn. Adjunct Prof., UCSD, 1998–. FRSE 2008. *Recreations:* scuba diving, tennis, golf, opera. *Address:* Department of Molecular Biology, BCC206, Scripps Research Institute, 10550 North Torrey Pines Road, La Jolla, CA 92037, USA. *T:* (858) 7849706. *Club:* La Jolla Beach and Tennis.

WILSON, Ian Matthew, CB 1985; Under Secretary, Scottish Education Department, 1977–86; *b* 12 Dec. 1926; *s* of Matthew Thomson Wilson and Mary Lily Barnett; *m* 1st, 1953, Anne Chalmers (*d* 1991); three *s*; 2nd, 1996, Joyce Town (*d* 2012). *Educ:* George Watson's Coll.; Edinburgh Univ. (MA). Asst Principal, Scottish Home Dept, 1950; Private Sec. to Perm. Under-Sec. of State, Scottish Office, 1953–55; Principal, Scottish Home Dept, 1955; Asst Secretary: Scottish Educn Dept, 1963; SHHD, 1971; Asst Under-Sec. of State, Scottish Office, 1974–77. Sec. of Commns for Scotland, 1987–92. Dir, Scottish Internat. Piano Competition, 1997–2004. Mem., Bd of Govs, RSAMD, 1992–2000. Pres., Univ. of Edinburgh Graduates' Assoc., 1995–97. *Address:* 47 Braid Hills Road, Edinburgh EH10 6LD. *T:* (0131) 447 1802. *Club:* New (Edinburgh).

WILSON, Iona Elisabeth Lois; *see* Jones, I. E. L.

WILSON, Ivan Patrick; Lay Member, First-tier Tribunal (Information Rights) (formerly Information Tribunal), 2003–12; *b* 24 Aug. 1941; *s* of William Wilson and Jessie (*née* Bateson); *m* 1966, Kathleen Mary Price; three *s*. *Educ:* Royal Sch., Dungannon; Academy, Omagh; Queen's Univ., Belfast. HM Treasury, 1965–95; Private Sec. to Perm. Sec., Overseas Finance, 1971–73; Press Office, 1973–76; Defence Policy and Budget Div., 1981–84; RCDS 1985; Information Systems, 1986–89; Under-Sec., Industry and Employment Gp, 1989–90; Dir, Govt Centre for Information Systems, 1990–93; Under Sec., Public Enterprises Gp, HM Treasury, 1993–95; Exec. Advr, ICL Enterprises, 1995–98; Partnership Sec., Freshfields, 1998–99; Interim Chief Exec., NI Policing Bd, 2001–02. *Recreations:* foreign travel, sport, walking, member of Manchester United Supporters Trust. *Address:* 88 Redhill Wood, New Ash Green, Longfield, Kent DA3 8QP. *T:* (01474) 874740.

WILSON, Dame Jacqueline, DBE 2008 (OBE 2002); author; Children's Laureate, 2005–07; *b* 17 Dec. 1945; *d* of late Harry Aitken and of Margaret Aitken (*née* Clibbons); *m* 1965, William Millar Wilson (marr. diss. 2004); one *d*. *Educ:* Coombe Girls' Sch. Journalist, D. C. Thomsons, 1963–65. Ambassador, Reading is Fundamental, UK, 1998–; Cttee Mem., Children's Writers and Illustrators Gp, Soc. of Authors, 1997–; Adv. Mem., Costa (formerly Whitbread) Book Awards Panel, 1997–; Judge: Rhône-Poulenc Prizes for Jun. Sci. Books, 1999; Orange Prize for Fiction, 2006; Prince Maurice Prize, 2006; Patron, Children's Film and TV Foundn, 2000–06; Pres., Book Trade Benevolent Soc., 2007–. Roehampton University: Vis. Prof. of Children's Literature, 2008–; Pro-Chancellor, 2011–13; Chancellor, 2014–. FRSL 2006. Hon. DEd: Kingston, 2001; Winchester, 2006; Roehampton, 2007; Hon. DLit Bath, 2006; Hon. DLaws Dundee, 2007. *Publications: fiction:* Hide and Seek, 1972; Truth or Dare, 1973; Snap, 1974; Let's Pretend, 1975; Making Hate, 1977; *for children:* Nobody's Perfect, 1982; Waiting for the Sky to Fall, 1985; Other Side, 1990; Take a Good Look, 1990; The Story of Tracy Beaker, 1991 (adapted for television, 2002); The Suitcase Kid, 1992 (Children's Book of the Year Award, 1993); Video Rose, 1992; The Mum-minder, 1993; The Werepuppy, 1993; The Bed and Breakfast Star, 1994; Mark Spark in the Dark, 1994; Twin Trouble, 1995; Glubbslyme, 1995; Jimmy Jelly, 1995; Dinosaur's Packed Lunch, 1995; Cliffhanger, 1995; Double Act, 1995 (Children's Book of the Year Award; Smarties Prize); My Brother Bernadette, 1995; Werepuppy on Holiday, 1995; Bad Girls, 1996; Mr Cool, 1996; Monster Story-teller, 1997; The Lottie Project, 1997; Girls in Love, 1997; Connie and the Water Babies, 1997; Buried Alive!, 1998; Girls Under Pressure, 1998; The Illustrated Mum (Guardian Children's Book of the Year Award), 1999 (adapted for television, 2003); Girls Out Late, 1999; The Dare Game, 2000; Vicky Angel, 2000; The Cat Mummy, 2001; Sleepovers, 2001; Dustbin Baby, 2001; Girls In Tears, 2002; Secrets, 2002; The Worry Website, 2002; Lola Rose, 2003; Midnight, 2003 (adapted for stage, 2005); The Diamond Girls, 2004; Best Friends, 2004 (adapted for television, 2006); Clean Break, 2005; Love Lessons, 2005; Candyfloss, 2006; Starring Tracy Beaker, 2006; Jacky Daydream (autobiog.), 2007; Kiss, 2007; My Sister Jodie, 2008; Cookie, 2008; My Secret Diary, 2009; Hetty Feather, 2009; Little Darlings, 2010; The Longest Whale Song, 2010; Lily Alone, 2011; Sapphire Battersea, 2011; The Worst Thing About My Sister, 2012; Four Children and It, 2012; Emerald Star, 2012; Queenie, 2013; Diamond, 2013; Opal Plumstead, 2014; Paws and Whiskers, 2014; The Butterfly Club, 2015; Katy, 2015; Little Stars, 2015. *Recreations:* talking to my daughter, reading, swimming, going to art galleries and films. *Address:* c/o David Higham Associates, 7th Floor, Waverley House, 7–12 Noel Street, W1F 8GQ. *T:* (020) 7434 5900.

WILSON, James Millar; Member (UU) Antrim South, Northern Ireland Assembly, 1998–2007; *b* 15 Dec. 1941; *s* of James Millar Wilson and Isobel Wilson; *m* 1965, Muriel Smyth; one *s* one *d*. *Educ:* Ballyclare High Sch.; Belfast Coll. of Technol. Engineer: Port Line Ltd, Merchant Navy, 1962–64; British Enkalon Ltd, 1964–73; partner, retail grocery business, 1972–88. Chief Exec., UU Party, 1987–98. Chief UUP Whip, 1998–2002, Dep. Speaker, 2002, NI Assembly. Dir, Bann System Ltd, 2002–. Mem., NI Water Council, 2000–08. Dir, Countryside Alliance, NI, 2003–08. Mem. Bd, Foyle and Carlingford Irish Lights, 2008–. Mem., UU Council, 1982–87 and 1998– (Mem. Exec. Cttee, 1985–87 and 1998–); Vice Pres., S Antrim UU Assoc., 1996–. *Recreations:* gardening, angling. *Address:* 1 Fairlands, Moorfields, Ballymena, Co. Antrim BT42 3HE. *E:* jim.wilson83@btopenworld.com.

WILSON, Sir James (William Douglas), 5th Bt *cr* 1906; farmer; *b* 8 Oct. 1960; *s* of Captain Sir Thomas Douglas Wilson, 4th Bt, MC, and of Pamela Aileen, *d* of Sir Edward Hanmer, 7th Bt; *S* father, 1984; *m* 1985, Julia Margaret Louise, fourth *d* of J. C. F. Mutty, Mulberry Hall, Melbourn, Cambs; two *s* two *d*. *Educ:* London Univ. (BA Hons French). *Heir:* *s* Thomas Edward Douglas Wilson, *b* 15 April 1990.

WILSON, Jennifer Chase E.; *see* Edgar-Wilson.

WILSON, Jeremy James O'Brien; Vice Chairman, Corporate Banking, Barclays Bank plc, since 2009; Chairman, Barclays Bank Egypt, since 2013; *b* Cape Town, SA, 9 Oct. 1949; *s* of Richard O'Brien Wilson and Anne Florence Wilson; *m* 1978, Joanna Jane Parker; two *s* two *d*. *Educ:* Pembroke Hse, Kenya; Nautical Coll., Pangbourne; Durham Univ. (BA Gen. (French, Geog., Anthropol.)). Dir, Barclays Bank plc; Dir, 2005–07, Chm., 2007–13, Bloomsbury Publishing plc. Chm., Govt Coordination Cttee, UK Payments Industry, 2013–. Dir, TheCityUK, 2011– (Chm., Audit & Risk Cttee, 2011–); Chm., Banking Envmt Initiative Wkg Gp, 2011–. Chm., Clearing House Automated Payments System Clearing Co., 2007–13. British Association for Finance and Trade: Chm., Global Councils, 2006–09; Dir, 2009–; Chm., Nominations Cttee, 2013–. Dir, Barclays Bank Pension Fund Trustees Ltd, 2000–08. Mem., Vice Chancellor's 175 Appeal Cttee, Durham Univ., 2005–07. Chm., Majajani Primary Sch. Trust, 2005–. *Recreations:* cartoons, writing, rowing (support of), corporate sustainability, mowing, early waking, early bed. *Address:* The Globe, Farnham, Bishops Stortford, Herts CM23 1HR; Barclays Bank plc, One Churchill Place, Canary Wharf, E14 5HP. *T:* (020) 7116 3779, 07970 123454, 07527 476642. *E:* jjob.wilson@btinternet.com. *Clubs:* Brooks's; Leander (Henley-on-Thames); Muthaiga Country (Nairobi).

WILSON, Jill Christine; *see* Rubery, J. C.

WILSON, Joe; *see* Wilson, Anthony J.

WILSON, John, FRCM; conductor; *b* Gateshead, 25 May 1972; *s* of Brian Wilson and Margaret Wilson (*née* McKie). *Educ:* Royal Coll. of Music (GRSM; ARCM; FRCM 2011). Founder and Conductor, John Wilson Orch., 1994–; a Principal Conductor: Royal Northern Sinfonia (formerly Northern Sinfonia), 2009–; RTE Concert Orch., Dublin, 2014; regular conductor of most UK orchs. BBC Proms debut, Royal Albert Hall, 2007; operatic debut, Gilbert and Sullivan's Ruddigore, Opera North, 2010, UK tour, 2011; John Wilson Orch. BBC Proms debut, Royal Albert Hall, 2009. Orchestrations for film, radio and television incl. Beyond the Sea (film), 2004. Recordings with John Wilson Orch. *Recreations:* walking, cooking, reading, shouting at the television. *Address:* c/o Intermusica, 36 Graham Street, N1 8GJ.

WILSON, John Armstrong; QC 2011; *b* Wigan, 8 Oct. 1958; *s* of Joe Wilson and late Ann Wilson (*née* Armstrong); *m* 1988, Susan Tilley. *Educ:* Ampleforth Coll.; St John Rigby Sixth Form Coll., Wigan; Pembroke Coll., Cambridge (BA Law 1980). Called to the Bar, Inner Temple, 1981; in practice as barrister, specialising in matrimonial, finance and cohabitation law. Mem., Family Procedure Rule Cttee, 2010–14. Mem., Family Law Bar Assoc., 1995–. Patron, Nat. Family Mediation, 2011–. FRSA 2014. Editor in Chief, Family Affairs. *Publications:* Cohabitation Claims: Law, Practice and Procedure, 2009, 2nd edn 2014; (contrib.) Jackson's Matrimonial Finance and Taxation, 9th edn 2012; (contrib.) Cases that Changed our Lives, vol. 2, 2015. *Recreations:* spending time with my wife, the Alpes Maritimes, trying to finish editing a novel. *Address:* 1 Hare Court, Temple, EC4Y 7BE. *T:* (020) 7797 7070, *Fax:* (020) 7797 7435. *E:* wilson@1hc.com.

WILSON, John Gordon; Member for Scotland Central, Scottish Parliament, since 2007 (SNP, 2007–14, Ind, since 2014); *b* 28 Nov. 1956; *s* of Thomas Wilson and Elizabeth Murray; *m* 1982, Frances M. McGlinchey; one *d*. *Educ:* Univ. of Glasgow (MA Social Scis 1987). Coachbuilder, W. Alexanders Co. Ltd, 1972–82; Project Co-ordinator, Castlemilk Housing Involvement Project, 1987–94; Dir, Glasgow Council of Tenant Assocs, 1994–97; Manager, Glasgow Tenants Resource Centre, 1997–98; Fieldwork Manager, Poverty Alliance, 1998–2001; Dir, Scottish Low Pay Unit, 2001–07. *Address:* Scottish Parliament, Edinburgh EH99 1SP. *T:* (0131) 348 6684, *Fax:* (0131) 348 6686. *E:* john.wilson.msp@scottish.parliament.uk.

WILSON, John Richard; Member, Covent Garden Market Authority, 2004–13; *b* 8 March 1946; *s* of Kenneth Charles Wilson and Mary Edith Wilson (*née* Dalladay); *m* 1968, Anne Margaret Saville; two *s*. *Educ:* Lewes Co. Grammar Sch. for Boys. MCIH 2002. Ministry of Defence: Exec. Officer, Navy Dept, 1965–68; Secretariat Divs, 1968–85; Directing Staff, JSDC, 1985–87; Hd, Br. Personnel and Logistics Div., 1987–89; Project Manager, Quality Assce Relocation, 1989–92; Hd, Plans and Budgets, for Dir Gen. Support Systems (RAF), 1992–94; Hd, Plans and Budgets, for AO CIS, HQ RAF Logistics Comd, 1994–95; Dir, Finance and Secretariat, 1995–99, Chief Exec., 1999–2004, Defence Housing Exec. *Recreations:* walking, DIY, classic cars. *Address:* 20 Rowanwood Avenue, Sidcup, Kent DA15 8WN. *T:* (020) 8300 0916.

WILSON, His Honour John Warley; a Circuit Judge, 1982–2001; *b* 13 April 1936; *s* of late John Pearson Wilson and Nancy Wade Wilson (*née* Harston); *m* 1962, Rosalind Mary Pulford. *Educ:* Warwick Sch.; St Catharine's Coll., Cambridge (MA). Served RA, 1954–56. Called to the Bar, Lincoln's Inn, 1960, in practice, 1960–82; a Recorder of the Crown Court, 1979–82. Dep. Chairman, West Midlands Agricultural Land Tribunal, 1978–82. *Recreations:* gardening, National Hunt racing. *Address:* Victoria House, Farm Street, Harbury, Leamington Spa CV33 9LR. *T:* (01926) 612572.

WILSON, John Willoughby; QC (NI) 1988; Master, Queen's Bench and Appeals, Supreme Court of Northern Ireland, 1993–2006; Clerk of the Crown for Northern Ireland, 1993–2006; *b* 4 Sept. 1933; *s* of late Willoughby Wilson and Martha (*née* Wood); *m* 1st, 1963, Rosemary Frances Turner (*d* 1999); one *s* two *d*; 2nd, 2006, Irenée Sarah, *widow* of Gordon Roger Cree; one step *s* one step *d*. *Educ:* Leys Sch.; Magdalene Coll., Cambridge (MA);

Queen's Univ., Belfast (LLB). Called to the Bar, NI, 1960; in practice, 1960–66; Private Sec., 1966–79, Legal Sec., 1979–80, to Lord Chief Justice of NI; Asst Dir, NI Court Service, 1980–85; Master, High Court, Supreme Court of NI, 1985–93. Under Treas., Inn of Court of NI, 1997–2008; Hon. Bencher, 2008. Gov., Victoria Coll., Belfast, 1970–2012 (Chm., 1990–95). Chancellor, Dio. Connor, 1982–2007. *Recreations:* music, reading, cycling.

WILSON, Rev. Dr Kenneth Brian, OBE 1993; Hon. Senior Research Fellow, Jubilee Centre for Character and Values, School of Education, College of Social Sciences, University of Birmingham, 2012–15; *b* 10 April 1937; *s* of Norman Harold Wilson and Violet Frances Sarah Wilson; *m* 1962, Jennifer Rosemary Floyd; one *s* two *d*. *Educ:* Kingswood Sch., Bath; Trinity Hall, Cambridge (BA 1961; MA); Univ. of Bristol (MLitt; PhD); MA Oxon. Ordained Minister in Methodist Church; Asst Minister, Hinde Street Methodist Church, London, 1964–66; Asst Chaplain, 1966–69, Chaplain, 1969–73, Kingswood Sch., Bath; Rowbotham Prof. of Philosophy and Ethics, Wesley Coll., Bristol, 1973–80; Principal, Westminster Coll., Oxford, 1981–96; Dir of Res., 1996–2001, Sen. Res. Consultant, 2001–04, Res. Centre, Queen's Foundn, Birmingham. Fernley-Hartley Lectr, 1973; Hon. Vis. Fellow, UC Chichester, 2004–11; Hon. Res. Fellow, Canterbury Christ Church Univ., 2005–11; Fellow, Southlands Coll., Univ. of Roehampton, 2007–. Dir, Methodist Newspaper Co., 1991–2002. Director: Hinksey Network, 1981–2012; Ammerdown Centre (formerly Ammerdown Christian Study Centre), Radstock, 1986–2014 (Chm., 2008–13). Chairman: Science and Religion Forum, 1979–81 and 2009–12; Nat. Primary Centre, Oxford, 1987–93; Christian Educn Movt, 1995; Member: Council, CNAA, 1982–92; Cttee, Ian Ramsey Centre, Oxford, 1985–99; Council, Inst. of Educn, Univ. of London, 1991–96 (Chm., 1993–95); CATE, 1992–94; Council, Sarum Coll., 2001–07; Accreditation Cttee, British Accreditation Council, 2010–. Trustee, Higher Educn Foundn, 1985–96. Gov., The Leys Sch., Cambridge, 1990–2002. FRSA. Hon. DTh Lycoming, 1994; Hon. DLL High Point Univ., 1995. *Publications:* Making Sense of It, 1973; Living it Out, 1975; (ed) Experience of Ordination, 1979; (with F. Young) Focus on God, 1986; (ed with N. Timms) Governance and Authority in the Roman Catholic Church, 2000; (ed jtly) Readings in Church Authority, 2003; Learning to Hope, 2005; (ed jtly) Christian Community Now, 2008; Dying to Live?, 2008; Methodist Theology, 2011. *Recreations:* books, poetry, art, religion. *Address:* Knapp Cottage, West Bradley, Glastonbury, Som BA6 8LT. *Club:* Oxford and Cambridge.

WILSON, Louise; *see* Wilson, M. L.

WILSON, Lynton Ronald, OC 1997; Chairman, CAE Inc., 1999–2013; Chancellor, McMaster University, 2007–13, now Chancellor Emeritus; *b* Port Colborne, Canada, 3 April 1940; *s* of Ronald Alfred and Blanche Evelyn Wilson; *m* 1968, Brenda Jean Black; one *s* two *d*. *Educ:* Port Colborne High Sch.; McMaster Univ. (BA Hons 1962); Cornell Univ. (MA 1967). Dep. Minister, Min. of Industry and Tourism, Govt of Ontario, 1978–81; Pres. and CEO, 1981–88, Chm., 1988–89, Redpath Industries Ltd, Toronto; Man. Dir, North America, Tate & Lyle plc, 1986–89; Vice-Chm., Bank of Nova Scotia, Toronto, 1989–90; BCE Inc.: Chief Operating Officer, 1990–92; Pres., 1990–96; CEO, 1992–98; Chm., 1993–2000; Chm., Nortel Networks Corp., 2001–05 (now Chm. Emeritus). Dir, Supervisory Bd, Daimler AG (formerly DaimlerChrysler AG), 1998–2013; Chm., Mercedes-Benz (formerly Daimler Chrysler, then Daimler) Canadian Adv. Council, 2005–. Hon. D*hc* Montreal, 1995; Hon. LLD: McMaster, 1995; UC of Cape Breton, 1998; Mount Allison, 2000; Brock, 2003; Hon. DCL Bishop's Univ., 1997. Vanier Medal, Inst. of Public Admin of Canada, 2014. *Recreation:* golf. *Address:* The Wilson Foundation, 1540 Cornwall Road, Suite 207, Oakville, ON L6J 7W5, Canada. *Clubs:* York, Toronto (Toronto); Rideau (Ottawa); Toronto Golf, Mount Royal.

WILSON, (Marie) Louise; Chief Executive Officer, Signature Sponsorship Ltd (formerly Signature Sponsorship), since 1999; *b* Burnley, Lancs; *d* of Henry Anthony Wilson and Doreen Wilson (*née* Cass). *Educ:* Saints John Fisher and Thomas More RC High Sch.; Univ. of Nottingham (BA Hons Politics 1987). Andersen Consulting, 1987–89; Procter & Gamble, 1989–93; Pepsi-Co., 1993–94; Coca Cola Co., 1994–99. Mem., LOCOG, 2006–09. University of Nottingham, 2007–: Mem. Council, 2008–; Chair: Strategy and Planning Cttee, 2012–14 (Mem., 2009–14); Laureate Awards, 2011, 2012; Member: Estates Planning Cttee, 2007–; Nominations Cttee, 2008–; Finance Cttee, 2009–; Campaign Bd, 2011–. Mem. Bd, Mktg Gp of GB, 2012–. Trustee: David Ross Educn Acad. Trust, 2009–; Historic Royal Palaces, 2012– (Member: Remuneration Cttee, 2012–; Campaign Bd, 2013–; Chm. Search Cttee, 2014). FRSA 2002. *Recreations:* entertaining, historic houses, travelling, making music/singing, live concerts, theatre, art galleries, astrology, yoga. *Address:* The Coach House, Black Horse Yard, Windsor, Berks SL4 1LA. *E:* mlwilson@signaturesponsorship.com.

WILSON, Mark Andrew; Group Chief Executive Officer, Aviva plc, since 2013; *b* Rotorua, NZ, Aug. 1966; *s* of Herbert John Watters Wilson and Lynda Adele Wilson; *m* 1996, Antonia Basile; three *d*. *Educ:* Kelliher Econs Foundn (Econs Schol. 1983); Univ. of Waikato (BMS 1988). Mktg Manager, then Man. Dir, National Mutual Asset Mgt, later Man. Dir, NZ Permanent Trustees, National Mutual, NZ, 1988–99; AXA Asia Pacific Holdings: Chief Gen. Manager, 1999–2001; Chief Executive Officer: SE Asia, 2001–03; AXA China Reg. Ltd, 2003–06; Chief Operating Officer and Pres., 2007–09, CEO and Pres., 2009–10, AIA Gp; Chm. and Chief Exec., Pounamu Private Equity, 2010–13. *Recreations:* tennis, piano, art, Rugby. *Address:* Aviva plc, St Helen's, 1 Undershaft, EC3P 3DQ. *T:* (020) 7662 2710. *E:* officeoftheceo@aviva.com.

WILSON, Martin; *see* Wilson, Alan M.

WILSON, Martin Joseph, FCA; Deputy Chairman, Ulster Bank, 2004–06 (Group Chief Executive, 1998–2004); *b* 13 March 1950; *s* of Michael and Elizabeth Wilson; *m* Paulette Palmer; one *s* two *d*. *Educ:* Oatlands Coll., Dublin. ACA 1975, FCA 1985; FIBI 1991. Articled Clerk, Fay McMahon & Co., Chartered Accountants, 1969–75; Sen. Audit Manager, KPMG, 1975–78; Chief Accountant, Bell Lines Ltd, 1978–80; Financial Controller, 1980–89, Head of Treasury, 1984–89, Ulster Investment Bank; Ulster Bank: Gp Treas., 1989–95; Dir, 1991; Dep. Gp Chief Exec., 1997–98; Chief Exec., Ulster Bank Mkts, 1995–97. Pres., ICAI, 2006–07. *Recreations:* golf, reading, music.

WILSON, Sir Mathew John Anthony, 6th Bt *cr* 1874, of Eshton Hall, Co. York; OBE 1979 (MBE 1971); MC 1972; *b* 2 Oct. 1935; *s* of Anthony Thomas Wilson (*d* 1979; 2nd *s* of Sir Mathew Richard Henry Wilson, 4th Bt) and Margaret (*d* 1980), *d* of late Alfred Holden; *S* uncle, 1991; *m* 1962, Janet Mary, *e d* of late E. W. Mowll, JP; one *s* one *d*. *Educ:* Trinity Coll. Sch., Ontario. Brig. KOYLI, retired 1983. Exec. Dir, Wilderness Foundn (UK), 1983–85. Former Vice-Pres., Internat. Wilderness Leadership Foundn. *Publications:* Taking Terrapin Home: a love affair with a small catamaran, 1994; The Bahamas Cruising Guide with the Turks and Caicos Islands, 1998; The Land of War Elephants: travels beyond the pale—Afghanistan, Pakistan, India, 2003. *Heir: s* Mathew Edward Amcotts Wilson [*b* 13 Oct. 1966; *m* 1995, Imogen Nancy, *yr d* of Richard Thomas Wilson; one *s* one *d*].

WILSON, Michael; *see* Wilson, T. M. A.

WILSON, Michael Anthony; Director: JVM Consultants Ltd, since 2007; Healthwatch Haringey, since 2013; *b* 19 Feb. 1948; *s* of Alan Wilson and Christina Wilson (*née* McFarlane); *m* 1st, 1972, Aileen Athey (marr. diss. 1991); one *s* two *d*; 2nd, 2008, Tanya Braznhikova. *Educ:* Aston Univ. (BSc Hons Behavioural Sci. 1972); DipTP 1977. MRTPI 1979; AIH 1984. Planning Asst, London Borough of Barnet, 1972–74; Res. and Inf. Officer, Harlow Develt Corp., 1974–80; Housing Manager, City of Glasgow, 1980–84; Dir of Housing and Envmtl Services, London Borough of Brent, 1984–92; Chief Exec., Waltham Forest Housing Action Trust, 1992–2002; Dir of Regeneration, NE London Strategic HA, 2002–06; Managing Dir, Mike Wilson Associates Ltd, 2002–09. Chairman: Sports Club Orient, 2003–10; Ocean Estate New Deal for Communities, 2004–07; Member Board: Waltham Forest Community-Based Housing Assoc., 2002–09; Leyton Orient Community Sports Prog., 2003–07. FRSA. JP Waltham Forest, 1999–2009. *Recreations:* watching football (Spurs), cinema, theatre, good food and wine, the children and grandchildren. *Address:* Hollyoaks Cottage, The Chilterns, Leighton Buzzard, Beds LU7 4QD.

WILSON, Michael Anthony, FRCGP; general practitioner; *b* 2 June 1936; *s* of late Charles Kenneth Wilson and Bertha Wilson; *m* 1st, 1959, Marlene (*née* Wilson) (marr. diss. 2011); two *s*; 2nd, 2012, Beryl May Hunt. *Educ:* Roundhay Grammar Sch., Leeds; Medical Sch., Univ. of Leeds (MB ChB 1958). DObst RCOG 1961; MRCGP 1965, FRCGP 1980. British Medical Association: Chm., Gen. Med. Services Cttee, 1984–90 (Dep. Chm., 1979–84); Pres., Yorkshire Regional Council, 1975–79; Mem. Council, 1977–90, 1992–2000; Vice-Pres., 2001–; Fellow, 1979. Member: GMC, 1989–2003; Standing Med. Adv. Cttee to DHSS, 1967–69, 1978–90 (Dep. Chm., 1986–90); NHS Clinical Standards Adv. Gp, 1990–93; Code of Practice Authy, Assoc. of British Pharmaceutical Industry, 1990–2013; Jt Consultants Cttee, 1991–97. Chm., BMA Pension Trustees Ltd, 1994–2000; Dir, Professional Affinity Group Services Ltd, 1987–2000. *Recreations:* golf, Rotary. *Address:* Court Ash, Woodacre Crescent, Bardsey, Leeds LS17 9DQ. *T:* (01937) 572381. *Clubs:* East India; Ampleforth Coll. Golf.

WILSON, Michael Gregg, OBE 2008; producer; Chairman, EON Productions, since 1983; *b* NY, 1942; *s* of Lewis Wilson and Dana Broccoli, and step *s* of Albert R., (Cubby), Broccoli; *m* 1965, Coila Jane Wilson; two *s*. *Educ:* Harvey Mudd Coll., Claremont, Calif (BS); Stanford Univ. (DJur). Legal Advr, Dept of Transportation, Washington, 1966–67; Partner, law firm, Surrey and Morse, Washington, 1967–74; joined legal dept, EON Productions, 1974; asst to Cubby Broccoli, The Spy Who Loved Me, 1977; Executive Producer: Moonraker, 1979; (and screenplay) For Your Eyes Only, 1981; (and screenplay) Octopussy, 1983; Producer: (and screenplay) A View to Kill, 1985; (and screenplay) The Living Daylights, 1987; (and writer) Licence to Kill, 1989; GoldenEye, 1995; Tomorrow Never Dies, 1997; The World is Not Enough, 1999; Die Another Day, 2002; Casino Royale, 2006; Quantum of Solace, 2008; Skyfall, 2012. Chairman: Bd, Albert R. and Dana Broccoli Charitable Foundn, 2004–; Kraszna-Krausz Foundn, 2010–; Science Mus. Foundn, 2012–. Trustee, NMSI, 2004–08 (Chm., Develt Cttee); Chm. Trustees, Nat. Media Mus. (formerly Nat. Mus. of Photography, Film and TV), 2004–12. Founder, Wilson Centre for Photography, London, 1998. Trustee: Carnegie Sci. Foundn; Harvey Mudd Coll., Claremont, CA; Cape Farewell, 2001–; The Art Fund, 2010– (Chm., Develt Cttee). *Address:* c/o EON Productions Ltd, 138 Piccadilly, W1J 7NR.

WILSON, Maj.-Gen. Michael Peter Bruce Grant; Director, WISLON Field Sports Services, since 2008; Chief Executive, Security Industry Authority, 2007–08; *b* 19 Aug. 1943; *s* of Ian Henry Wilson and Catherine Collingwood Wilson; *m* 1967, Margaret Ritchie; two *s* one *d*. *Educ:* Duke of York Sch., Nairobi; Dip. Photogrammetry, UCL. FRICS 1995 (ARICS 1988); FRGS 1990. Commnd RE, 1966; served UK, Kenya, Uganda, Nigeria, BAOR, MoD; UK Exchange Officer, US Defense Mapping Agency, 1978; Sen. Instructor in Air Survey and Cartography, Sch. of Mil. Survey, 1981; Asst Dir, Mil. Survey Systems and Techniques Unit, 1983; CO 512 Special Team RE and Comdr, Geographic Staff, Washington, 1986; Comdr, 42 Survey Engr Gp, 1987; Dir, Geographic Ops, MoD, 1990; Dir-Gen., Mil. Survey and Chief Exec., Mil. Survey Defence Agency, 1993; Dir-Gen. Intelligence and Geographic Resources, MoD, 1995–96; Chief Executive: Defence Vetting Agency, 1996–2004; Gangmasters Licensing Authy, 2005–07. Col Comdt RE, 1997–2002. Mole catcher to the Vicar of Old Malton. FCMI. *Recreations:* mountaineering, rock climbing, shooting, stalking, fishing, golf, cricket. *Clubs:* Geographical, Chartered Surveyor/Sapper; North Wolds Gun (Pres., 2010–); Ampleforth Golf (Captain, 2012–).

WILSON, Michael Sumner, CBE 2012; Joint Founder, and Life President, since 2012, St James's Place (formerly St James's Place Capital) (Chief Executive, 1992–2004; Chairman, 2004–11; Director, 1997–2011); Chairman, St James's Place Foundation, since 2012; *b* 5 Dec. 1943; *s* of late Peter and Margaret Wilson; *m* 1975, Mary Drysdale (marr. diss. 1997); one *d*. *Educ:* St Edward's School, Oxford. Equity & Law, 1963–68; Abbey Life, 1968–71; Allied Dunbar (Hambro Life until 1985, when name was changed), 1971–91: Exec. Dir, 1973; Board Dir, 1976; Dep. Man. Dir, 1982; Man. Dir, 1984; Gp Chief Exec., 1988–91. Non-executive Director: BAT Industries, 1989–91; Vendôme Luxury Gp, 1993–98; RIT Capital Partners plc, 2013–. Trustee, MQ: Transforming Mental Health, 2010–. *Recreations:* tennis, racing. *Clubs:* Raffles, Annabel's, George.

WILSON, Prof. Nairn Hutchison Fulton, CBE 2004; PhD; FDS; Professor of Restorative Dentistry and Dean and Head of King's College London Dental Institute (formerly Guy's, King's and St Thomas' Dental Institute, King's College London), 2001–12, Hon. Professor of Dentistry, since 2012; Deputy Vice Principal Health, King's College London, 2009–11; Lead, Dental Clinical Academic Group, King's Health Partners, 2010–11; *b* 26 April 1950; *s* of William Fulton Wilson and Ann Hutchison Wilson (*née* Stratton); *m* 1st, 1971, Madeleine Christina Munro (marr. diss. 1981); two *d*; 2nd, 1982, Margaret Alexandra Jones; one *s* one *d*. *Educ:* Strathallan Sch.; Univ. of Edinburgh (BDS 1973); Univ. of Manchester (MSc 1979; PhD 1985); Royal Coll. of Surgeons of Edinburgh (FDS 1977; DRD 1980). FACD 1990; FADM 1991; FDS RCS (*ad eundem*) 1994, Hon. FDS RCS 2010; FFGDP (UK) (*ad eundem*) 2002; FFDRCSI 2011. Lectr in Restorative Dentistry (Prosthetics), Univ. of Edinburgh, 1974–75; University of Manchester: Lectr in Conservative Dentistry, 1975–81; Sen. Lectr, 1981–86; Prof. of Restorative Dentistry, 1986–2001; Head, Dept of Conservative Dentistry, 1986–88, Dept of Restorative Dentistry, 1988–92; University Dental Hospital: Head, Unit of Operative Dentistry and Endodontology (formerly of Conservative Dentistry), 1982–2001; Dep. Dean, 1991–92; Dean and Clin. Dir, 1992–95; Pro Vice-Chancellor, Univ. of Manchester, 1997–99. Hon. Vis. Prof. of Restorative Dentistry, Univ. of Manchester, 2001–04; Vis. Prof., Osaka Dental Univ., 2011–. Hon. Consultant in Restorative Dentistry: Central Manchester Healthcare NHS Trust (formerly Central Manchester HA), 1982–2001; King's Coll. Hosp. NHS Trust, 2001–12. Non-exec. Dir, N Manchester Healthcare NHS Trust, 1994–97. Chairman: Jt Cttee for Specialist Trng in Dentistry, 1998–99, 2007–10; Oral and Dental Res. Trust, 2003–09; British Dental Editors Forum, 2004–08; Council of Hds and Deans of Dental Schs, 2006–08. Dean, Faculty of Dental Surgery, RCSE, 1995–98. President: British Assoc. of Teachers of Conservative Dentistry, 1992; Sect. of Odontology, Manchester Med. Soc., 1993–94; British Soc. for Restorative Dentistry, 1994–95; Eur. Sect., Acad. of Operative Dentistry, 1998–2000; Educn Res. Gp, IADR, 1998–2000; GDC, 1999–2003; Eur. Fedn of Conservative Dentistry, 2003–05; Sect. of Odontology, Royal Soc. of Med., 2008–09; Metropolitan Br., BDA, 2012–13; KCL Assoc., 2012–14; Royal Odonto-Chirurgical Soc. of Scotland, 2013–14; BDA, 2015–April 2016. Registrar, UK Public Health Register, 2012–15. Ext. Gov., Univ. of Portsmouth, 2012–. Trustee, Nat. Exams Bd for Dental Nurses, 2014–. Patron, Dental Wellness Trust, 2011–. Ed., Jl of Dentistry, 1986–2000; Ed. in Chief, Quintessentials in Dental Practice Series (44 vols), 2003–09; Chairman, Editorial Board: Primary Dental Jl, 2012–; Dental Practice, 2012–15. FKC 2006; FHEA 2007. Hon. Fellow, Coll. of Dental Surgeons of HK, 1999. Hon. DSc Portsmouth, 2010. Cultura Della Materia, Univ. of Brescia, 2011. *Publications:* (jtly) Advances in Operative Dentistry, vol. 1: contemporary clinical practice, 2001; vol. 2: challenges of the future, 2001; Minimally

Invasive Dentistry, 2007; Clinical Dental Medicine 2020, 2009; Merger to Global Leader: King's College London Dental Institute 1998–2011, 2012; Principles and Practice of Esthetic Dentistry: vol. 1, essentials of esthetic dentistry, 2014; contrib. chaps in contemporary texts and numerous papers in jls. *Recreation:* various. *Address:* 1 Oak Park, Alderley Edge, Cheshire SK9 7GS. *T:* 07815 997086.

WILSON, Nicholas Allan Roy; *see* Wilson of Culworth, Rt Hon. Lord.

WILSON, Nigel Guy, FBA 1980; Fellow and Tutor in Classics, Lincoln College, Oxford, 1962–2002; *b* 23 July 1935; *s* of Noel Wilson and Joan Lovibond; *m* 1996, Hanneke Marion. *Educ:* University Coll. Sch.; Corpus Christi Coll., Oxford (1st Cl. Classics (Mods) 1955; 1st Cl. Lit. Hum. 1957; Hertford Scholar 1955; Ireland and Craven Scholar 1955; Derby Scholar 1957; Hon. Fellow, 2013). Lectr, Merton Coll., Oxford, 1957–62. Jt Editor, Classical Rev., 1975–87. Ospite Linceo, Scuola normale superiore, Pisa, 1977; Visiting Professor: Univ. of Padua, 1985; Ecole Normale Supérieure, Paris, 1986. James P. R. Lyell Reader in Bibliog., Oxford Univ., 2002–03. Gaisford Lectr, 1983. Mem., Accademia Ambrosiana, 2015. Hon. DLitt: Uppsala, 2001; Cyprus, 2013. Gordon Duff Prize, 1968; Premio Anassilaos, Reggio Calabria, 1999. *Publications:* (with L. D. Reynolds) Scribes and Scholars, 1968, 4th edn 2013; An Anthology of Byzantine Prose, 1971; Medieval Greek Bookhands, 1973; St Basil on the Value of Greek Literature, 1975; Scholia in Aristophanis Acharnenses, 1975; (with D. A. Russell) Menander Rhetor, 1981; Scholars of Byzantium, 1983; (with Sir Hugh Lloyd-Jones) Sophoclea, 1990; (ed with Sir Hugh Lloyd-Jones) Sophocles: Fabulae, 1990; From Byzantium to Italy, 1992; Photius: the Bibliotheca, 1994; Aelian: Historical Miscellany, 1997; Pietro Bembo: Oratio pro litteris graecis, 2003; Aristophanes: Comoediae, 2007; Aristophanea, 2007; A Descriptive Catalogue of the Greek Manuscripts of Corpus Christi College Oxford, 2011; (jtly) The Archimedes Palimpsest, 2011; articles and reviews in various learned jls. *Recreations:* bridge, real tennis, wine. *Address:* Lincoln College, Oxford OX1 3DR. *T:* (01865) 279800, *Fax:* 279802.

WILSON, Sir Patrick Michael Ernest David McN.; *see* McNair-Wilson.

WILSON, Pete; Governor of California, 1991–98; Principal and Of Counsel, Morgan Lewis Consulting, since 2014 (Of Counsel, Bingham McCutcheon, and Principal, Bingham Consulting Group, 2004–14); *b* 23 Aug. 1933; *m* Betty Robertson (marr. diss.); *m* 1983, Gayle Edlund. *Educ:* Yale Univ. (BA); Univ. of California at Berkeley (JD). Admitted to California Bar, 1962. Mayor of San Diego, 1971–73; US Senator (Republican) from California, 1983–91. Former Man. Dir, Pacific Capital Gp Inc. Dist. Vis. Fellow, Hoover Inst., Stanford Univ., 1999–. *Address:* Morgan Lewis Consulting, 355 South Grand Avenue, Suite 4400, Los Angeles, CA 90071–3106, USA.

WILSON, Peter James, OBE 2001; freelance cultural buildings consultant, since 2011; Cultural Buildings Advisor, West Kowloon Cultural District Authority, Hong Kong, since 2011; *b* 19 Sept. 1947; *s* of James Arthur Wilson and Edith Mary Wilson (*née* Sillick); *m* 1971, Angela Mary Hawkes; one *s* two *d*. *Educ:* Eltham Coll.; Pembroke Coll., Cambridge (BA 1970). Tate Gallery: DES Studentship in Conservation, 1972–76 (Dip. Conservation, 1976); picture restorer, 1976–80; Head: Tech. Services, 1980–88; Gall. Services, 1988–94; Dir, Projects and Estates, 1994–2005 (incl. openings: Tate Gall. St Ives, 1993; Tate Gall. Liverpool Phase II, 1998; Tate Modern, 2000; Tate Britain Centenary Develt, 2001). Transformation Project Dir, RSC, 2005–11; Project Dir, Shakespeare Birthplace Trust, 2013–. Associate Consultant: Lord Cultural Resources, Toronto, 2006–08; Tate Gall., 2014–; Associate Sen. Consultant, Lordculture Paris, 2008–13. Special Advr, Theatres Trust, 2011–; Client Advr, Made in London Team for Olympicopolis, 2015. Member: CABE Enabling Panel, 2001–04; Steering Cttee, Laban, 2001–04. Chm., Mus. Documentation Assoc., 1988–95. Mem. Bd, Lightbox, Woking, 2001–10. Hon. FRIBA 2007. *Recreations:* reading and watching films whilst flying between London and Hong Kong, struggling with Cantonese, gardening, drawing, cycling, cooking, theatre-going, visiting museums and galleries.

WILSON, Peter Michael; Chairman, Gallaher Group Plc, 1997–2004 (Chief Executive, 1997–99); Chairman, Gallaher Ltd, 1994–2004 (Deputy Chairman, 1987–94; Chief Executive, 1994–99); *b* 9 June 1941; *s* of late Michael Wilson and Mary Wilson; *m* 1964, Lissa Trab; one *s* one *d*. *Educ:* Downside Sch.; Oriel Coll., Oxford (MA Hons Law). Marketing appts, Reckitt & Colman and Beecham Gp, 1963–69; joined Gallaher Ltd, 1969: Gen. Manager, Cigarette Marketing, 1974–79; Man. Dir, Gallaher (Dublin), 1979–81; Marketing Dir, Gallaher Tobacco Ltd, 1981–84; Jt Man. Dir, 1984–85, Dep. Chm., 1986, Gallaher Tobacco (UK) Ltd. Non-executive Director: Beam Inc. (formerly American Brands, then Fortune Brands Inc.), 1994–2014; Powergen plc, 2001–03; Somerfield plc, 2002–05; Kesa Electricals plc, 2003–11. *Address:* The Stable, Old Odiham Road, Alton, Hants GU34 4BW. *T:* (01420) 543892.

WILSON, Hon. Peter Michael Alexander, CMG 2013; HM Diplomatic Service; Deputy Permanent Representative, UK Mission to the United Nations, New York (with rank of Ambassador), since 2013; *b* London, 31 March 1968; *s* of Baron Wilson of Tillyorn, *qv*; *m* 2001, Mónica Quintas Ribeiro Roma Pereira; two *s* one *d*. *Educ:* Eton Coll.; Merton Coll., Oxford (BA Modern Hist.); Kennedy Sch. of Govt, Harvard Univ. (MPA); Westminster Univ. and Univ. of Internat. Business and Econs, Beijing (Operational Mandarin). Entered FCO, 1992; Second Sec. (Commercial), Beijing, 1995–98; Mem., Cabinet of Sir Leon Brittan, Vice Pres., EC, 1999; First Sec., UK Perm. Repn to EU, 1999–2002; Hd, Strategic Policy Team, FCO, 2003–04; Political Counsellor: Islamabad, 2005–06; Beijing, 2007–10; Dir, Asia Pacific, FCO, 2010–13. *Recreations:* walking, reading, photography. *Address:* c/o Foreign and Commonwealth Office, King Charles Street, SW1A 2AH. *T:* (020) 7008 1570. *E:* peter.wilson@fco.gov.uk.

WILSON, Philip; MP (Lab) Sedgefield, since July 2007; *b* 31 May 1959; *s* of Bernard Wilson and Ivy Wilson (*née* Woods); *m* (marr. diss. 1999); two *s*. *Educ:* Trimdon Secondary Modern Sch.; Sedgefield Comprehensive Sch. Civil Servant, Dept for Nat. Savings, 1978–87; res. asst to Rt Hon. Tony Blair, MP, 1987–94; Labour Party organiser, 1994–97; Political Asst to Gen. Sec., Labour Party, 1997–99; Consultant, Brunswick Gp, 1999–2002; Dir, Fellows' Associates, 2002–07. *Recreations:* jazz, reading, writing. *Address:* House of Commons, SW1A 0AA. *T:* (020) 7219 4966. *E:* phil.wilson.mp@parliament.uk.

WILSON, Most Rev. Philip Edward; *see* Adelaide, Archbishop of, (RC).

WILSON, Primrose Eileen, CBE 2007 (OBE 1997); engaged in voluntary projects; *b* 21 April 1947; *d* of Anthony and Sheelagh Clarke; *m* 1969, Edward Brice Wilson (CBE 2003); one *s* two *d*. *Educ:* Glengara Park Sch., Dun Laoghaire, Co. Dublin; Royal Victoria Hosp., Belfast (SRN); Open Univ. (BA Hons). SRN, Royal Victoria Hosp., Belfast, 1969–75. Voluntary Co-ordinator, Eur. Heritage Open Days, 1997–2000. Chairman: Ulster Architectural Heritage Soc., 1987–94; Historic Bldgs Council (NI), 1994–2000. Trustee, Nat. Heritage Meml Fund, 2000–06; Chairman: Assoc. Preservation Trusts (NI), 2004–12; Follies Trust, 2006–. Hon. Mem., RSUA, 2000. *Publications:* (jtly) The Buildings of Armagh, 1992. *Recreations:* admiring, enjoying, conserving and restoring Ireland's and Britain's built heritage. *Address:* Marlacoo House, Portadown, Co. Armagh. *T:* (028) 3887 1238.

WILSON, Richard; *see* Wilson, I. R.

WILSON, (Richard) Andrew; author and writer, since 1989; Director and Partner, Wilson McWilliam Studio (formerly Associates) Garden and Landscape Design, since 2008; Director, London College of Garden Design, since 2009; *b* St Helens, Lancs, 10 July 1959; *s* of Kevin and Edna Wilson; *m* 1985, Barbara Anne Martindale; two *d*. *Educ:* St Helens Cowley High Sch. for Boys; Manchester Poly. (BA Hons Landscape Design; Postgrad. DipLA). Landscape architect, BRB, 1984–91; Dir, Garden Design Studies and Vice Principal, Inchbald Sch. of Design, 1989–2003; Partner, Pockett Wilson Garden and Landscape Design, 1999–2006; Garden Designer, Andrew Wilson Associates, 2006–08; Prog. Dir, Garden Design, Guildford Coll., 2004–09. Visiting Lecturer: Garden Design, Univ. of Greenwich, 2003–06; Postgrad. Landscape Architecture, Birmingham City Univ. (formerly UCE), 2003–. Founding Ed., Garden Design Jl, 1993–97. Columnist, Gardens Illustrated, 2006–10. Consultant, Bord Bia, Ireland for the Bloom Garden Show, 2006–. Ext. examr in garden design for Middx Univ., 1995–98, Univ. of Greenwich, 1998–2003, Writtle Coll., 1999–2002, Falmouth Coll., 2003–08; ext. examr, Univ. of Brighton, 2008–11. Assessor and judge for show gdns, 1994–13 (incl. Bloom Garden Show, Dublin, 2006–), Chair of Assessors, Chair of Gdns Panel and Judge, 2009–11, RHS; Mem. Selection Panel, Internat. Garden Fest., Chaumont sur Loire, 2012. Chm., Soc. of Gdn Designers, 1993–96. Patron, Green Base, St Helens, 2010–. FSGD 1996. *Publications:* The Garden Style Source Book, 1989; The Creative Water Gardener, 1995; (contrib.) The Essential Garden Book, 1998; Influential Gardeners, 2002; The Book of Garden Plans, 2004; The Book of Plans for Small Gardens, 2007; (contrib.) The RHS Encyclopedia of Garden Design, 2009; The Gardens of Luciano Giubbilei, 2010; Contemporary Colour in the Garden, 2011; RHS Small Garden Handbook, 2013. *Recreations:* riding my motorbike, classical singing (tenor; Member of Weybridge Male Voice Choir, 2010–), swimming, good food, messing about on the beach/in the surf in Cornwall, drawing and water-colour painting, travel, photography. *Address:* Laurel Cottage, 12 Bridge Road, Chertsey, Surrey KT16 8JL. *T:* (01932) 563293. *E:* r.a.wilson@btconnect.com, andrew@wmstudio.co.uk, andrewwilson@lcgd.org.uk.

WILSON, Prof. Richard Henry, RA 2006; sculptor; Visiting Research Professor, University of East London, since 2004; Professor of Sculpture, Royal Academy of Arts, since 2011; *b* 24 May 1953; *s* of Arthur and Ivy Wilson; partner, Miyako Narita; one *s* one *d* with Silvia Ziranek, writer and performance artist. *Educ:* London Coll. of Printing (Foundn); Hornsey Coll. of Art (DipAD 1st 1974); Univ. of Reading (MFA 1976). Formed Bow Gamelan Ensemble with Anne Bean and Paul Burwell, 1983–91. Mem., Artistic Records Cttee, Imperial War Mus., London, 1999. DAAD Residency, Berlin, 1992; Henry Moore Fellowship in Sculpture, Univ. of East London, 2002–04; Maeda Vis. Artist, AA, London, 2003. *Solo exhibitions and commissions* include: 11 Pieces, 1976, 12 Pieces, 1978, Coracle Press Gall., London; Viaduct, Aspex Gall., Portsmouth, 1983; Sheer Fluke, 1985, 20:50, 1987, She Came in Through the Bathroom Window, 1990, Watertable, 1994, Matt's Gall., London; Hopperhead, Café Gall., London, 1985; Halo, The Aperto, Venice Biennale, 1986; Heatwave, Ikon Gall., Birmingham, 1986; One Piece at a Time, Tyne Bridge, Newcastle upon Tyne, 1987; Up a Blind Alley, Trigon Biennale, Graz, 1987; Leading Lights, Kunsthallen Brandts Klaedefabrik, Odense, 1989; Sea Level, Arnolfini Gall., Bristol, 1990; High-Tec, MOMA, Oxford, 1990; High Rise, São Paulo Biennial, Brazil, Great Britain/USSR, Kiev, Moscow, 1990; All Mod Cons, Edge Biennial, Newcastle, 1990; Take Away, Centre of Contemp. Art, Warsaw, 1990; Lodger, Valeria Belvedere, Milan, 1991; Swift Half and Return to Sender, Gal. de l'Ancienne Poste, Calais, 1992; Installation, Künstlerhaus Bethanien, Berlin, 1993; Deep End, LA/UK, Fest. MOCA, Los Angeles, 1994; Room 6 Channel View Hotel, Towner Art Gall., Eastbourne, 1996; Formative Processes, Gimpel Fils, London, 1996; Jamming Gears, Serpentine Gall., London, 1996; Going In/Off, Château de Sacy, Picardie, 1997; Hung, Drawn and Quartered, Städtisches Mus., Zwickau, 1997, Ha'Mumche Gall., Tel Aviv, 1999; Irons in the Fire, Globe Gall., South Shields, 1997, UK tour, 2002, Wapping Proj., London, 2003; Tate Christmas Tree, Tate Gall., London, 1997; Pipe Dreams, AA, London, 1999; Turbine Hall Swimming Pool, Clare Coll. Mission Ch, London, 2000; Butterfly, Wapping Proj., London, 2003; Queen & Gantry, Storey Gall., Lancaster, 2005; Curve Gall., London, 2006; 5 Piece Kit, Matthew Bown Gall., London, 2006; RIBA Drawing Show, Liverpool, 2007; Chris Westbrook Gall., London, 2007; Turning the Place Over (lead work for Liverpool, Eur. Capital of Culture 2008), Liverpool, 2007; RA Summer Show, 2007; Objects of Art, Matthew Brown Gall., London, 2007; Galleria Fumagalli, Bergamo, Italy, 2007; Meter's Running, Pula, Croatia, 2007; Richard Wilson, Edinburgh Fest., 2008; Force Quit, Worksprojects, Bristol, 2009; 20:50, Sulaymanyah, Kurdistan, N Iraq, 2009, Saatchi Gall., 2010; Square the Block, LSE, 2009; Matthew Bown Gall., Berlin, 2010; Shack Stack, St James's Develt, Chelsea Dock, 2010; Vertu Global Art Commn, Shanghai, 2010; Hang On A Minute Lads, I've Got a Great Idea, De La Warr Pavilion, UK, 2012; Slipstream, Heathrow Terminal 2, 2014; *group exhibitions* include: Art of Our Time, Saatchi Collection, Royal Scottish Acad., Edinburgh, 1987; Saatchi Collection, London, 1991; Close Encounters of the Art Kind, V&A, 2001; Butterfly, Platform China, Beijing, 2006; Objects of Art, Matthew Bown Gall., London, 2007; Folkestone Triennial, 2008; Still-Film, Tate Britain, 2008; Royal Acad. Summer Show, 2008, 2009; *performance work:* Blast, Birmingham, 2007; Performance Fest., Staglinec, Croatia, 2008; Blast, Performance, Blackpool, 2009; *permanent works:* entrance to Utility Tunnel, Tachikawa Public Art Proj., Tokyo, 1994; Over Easy, The Arc, Stockton, 1999; Slice of Reality, North Meadow Sculpture Proj., Millennium Dome, London, 2000; Set North for Japan (74° 33' 2"), Echigo Tsumari Proj., Japan, 2000; Off Kilter, Millennium Sq., Leeds, 2001; Final Corner, World Cup Proj., Fukuroi City, 2002; Rock n' hole, Lincoln City and Archaeol. Mus., 2005; work in public collections inc. Weltkunst Collection at Irish Mus. of Mod. Art, Boise, BM, Govt Art, Arts Council England, British Council, Ulster Mus., Leeds Mus and Galls, Centre of Contemp. Art, Warsaw and Museet for Samstidskunst, Oslo. Hon. DFA Middx, 2008; Hon. Dr E London. *Recreations:* percussion, cinema, world musics, exhibitions. *Address:* 44 Banyard Road, SE16 2YA. *T:* (020) 7231 7312. *E:* richardwilson.sculptor@virgin.net.

WILSON, Robert, OBE 2008; professional footballer, 1964–74; Presenter: BBC Television Sport, 1974–94; ITV Sport, 1994–2003; *b* 30 Oct. 1941; *s* of William Smith Wilson and Catherine Wingate (*née* Primrose); *m* 1964, Margaret Vera Miles; two *s* (one *d* decd). *Educ:* Tapton House Grammar Sch.; Chesterfield Grammar Sch.; Loughborough Coll. (DipPE). PE teacher, 1963–64; represented England Schoolboys, 1957, Derbyshire Schs, 1957–60, and British Univs, 1960–63, at football; Mem., England Amateur Squad, 1960–63; professional footballer (goalkeeper), Arsenal FC, 1964–74 (winner: Euro Fairs Cup, 1970; League and Cup Double, 1971); internat. appearances for Scotland, 1971–72; Goalkeeping Coach, Arsenal FC, 1975–2003. Chm., London Football Coaches Assoc., 1990–2007. Co-founder, Willow Foundn Charity, 1999– (Life Pres., 2012). Gov., Univ. of Hertfordshire, 1997–2006. Hon. DLitt Loughborough, 1989; DUniv: Derby, 2001; Middlesex, 2004. *Publications:* Goalkeeping, 1970; The Art of Goalkeeping, 1973; You've Got to be Crazy, 1989; Behind the Network (autobiog.), 2003; Googlies, Nutmegs and Bogies, 2006; Rucks, Pucks and Sliders, 2007; Life in the Beautiful Game, 2008. *Recreations:* reading, golf, boating, theatre.

WILSON, (Robert) Gordon; solicitor in private practice, 1960–74 and 1987–2005; politician, retired; *b* 16 April 1938; *s* of R. G. Wilson; *m* 1965, Edith M. Hassall; two *d*. *Educ:* Douglas High Sch.; Edinburgh Univ. (BL). Scottish National Party: Nat. Sec., 1963–71; Exec. Vice-Chm., 1972–73; Sen. Vice-Chm., 1973–74; Dep. Parly Leader, 1974–79; Nat. Convener (formerly Chm.), 1979–90; Vice-Pres., 1992–98. Contested (SNP) Dundee E, 1987. MP (SNP) Dundee E, Feb. 1974–1987. Parly Spokesman: on Energy, 1974–79; on Home Affairs, 1975–76; on Devolution (jt responsibility), 1976–79; SNP spokesman: on energy, 1992–93; on Treasury affairs, 1993–94. Rector, Dundee Univ., 1983–86. Chairman: Marriage Counselling (Tayside) (formerly Dundee Marriage Guidance Council), 1989–92; temp. Chm., Couple Counselling, Dundee, 2006; Solas (Centre for Public Christianity), 2010–13; Director: Dundee Age Concern, 2001–05; Dundee CAB, 2011; Options for

Scotland, 2012–. Mem., Church and Nation Cttee, C of S, 2000–03. Gov., Dundee Inst. of Technology, subseq. Univ. of Abertay, 1991–97. Hon. LLD Dundee, 1986. *Publications:* SNP: the turbulent years 1960–90, 2009; Pirates of the Air: the story of Radio Free Scotland, 2011; Scotland: the battle for independence, 2014. *Recreations:* reading, writing. *Address:* 48 Monifieth Road, Broughty Ferry, Dundee DD5 2RX. *T:* (01382) 779009. *E:* gordonwilson10@blueyonder.co.uk.

WILSON, Sir (Robert James) Timothy, Kt 2011; DL; PhD; Vice-Chancellor and Chief Executive, University of Hertfordshire, 2003–10; *b* 2 April 1949; *s* of John and Joan Wilson; *m* 1972, Jackie Hinds; two *d*. *Educ:* Univ. of Reading (BSc Hons); Univ. of Lancaster (MA); Walden Univ., USA (PhD 1997). Lectr, then Sen. Lectr, Operational Res., Leeds Poly., 1974–84; Dir of Studies, Cranfield Inst. of Technol., 1984–87; Asst Dir, Leicester Poly., 1987–91; Hatfield Polytechnic, later University of Hertfordshire: Dep. Dir, 1991–92; Pro Vice Chancellor and Dep. Chief Exec., 1992–2002; Prof., 2002–10, now Emeritus. Chairman: Herts Prosperity Ltd, 2003–09; UH Holdings Ltd, 2008–10; Board Member: E of England Devel Agency, 2003–09; HEFCE, 2004–11. Head, Wilson Review of Univ.-Business Collaboration for UK govt, 2012. Dir, Raffles Univ., Singapore, 2008–10. Non-executive Director: Unite Gp plc, 2010–; University of Law Ltd, 2012–. Chm., Herts LEP, 2011–12. Trustee, Garden House Hospice, 2012–. DL Herts, 2011. FRSA 2008. Hon. DEd: Hertfordshire, 2013; Plymouth, 2014. *Publications:* numerous articles in jls relating to mathematical modelling and higher educn mgt. *Recreations:* golf, Rugby Union. *E:* wilson.pendleton@gmail.com.

WILSON, Robert Julian, (Robin), MA; Headmaster, Trinity School of John Whitgift, Croydon, 1972–94; *b* 6 July 1933; *s* of late Prof. Frank Percy Wilson, FBA, and Joanna Wilson (*née* Perry-Keene); *m* 1957, Caroline Anne (*née* Maher); two *d* (and one *s* one *d* decd). *Educ:* St Edward's Sch., Oxford; Trinity Coll., Cambridge (MA). Lektor, Univ. of Münster, Westphalia, 1955–58; Assistant Master: St Peter's, York, 1958–62; Nottingham High Sch. (Hd of English), 1962–72. Mem. Cttee, HMC, 1987–94 (Chm., 1993); Vice-Chm., Academic Policy Cttee, 1990–92; Member: Council, GDST (formerly GPDST), 1994–2008; Cttee, GBA, 1999–2002. Governor: Brentwood Sch., 1995–2015; St Peter's Sch., York, 1996–2002. *Publications:* (jtly) Bertelsmann Sprachkursus English, 1959; (ed) The Merchant of Venice, 1971; articles on the teaching of English. *Recreations:* drama, travel, golf. *Address:* 22 Beech House Road, Croydon, Surrey CR0 1JP. *T:* (020) 8686 1915. *Clubs:* East India, Devonshire, Sports and Public Schools; Addington Golf.

WILSON, Robert Nelson; Chairman, A. Nelson & Co. Ltd, since 2001; *b* 23 July 1962; *s* of Robert Wiseman Wilson and Anne Wilson; *m* 1994, Nicola Jane Petrie; two *s* two *d*. *Educ:* St Columba's Coll., Dublin; Trinity Coll., Dublin (BA Hons Hist., MA); Harvard Business Sch. A. Nelson & Co.: Mktg Dir, 1990–93; Man. Dir, 1993–2001. Dir, Wigmore Pubns, 1991–. Trustee: Scottish Civic Trust, 2002–12; Prince's Foundn for Integrated Health, 2005–09; Prince's Initiative for Mature Enterprise, 2010–14; Chairman: Prostate Scotland, 2006–; Barcapel Foundn, 2006–; Co-Founder, Jupiter Artland Foundn, 2006–; Trustee, The Art Room, 2013–. Bd Dir, Edinburgh Arts Festival, 2010– (Chm., 2010–). Gov., Kilgraston Sch., 2005–10. FRSA. Mem., Royal Co. of Archers, 2013–. *Recreations:* shooting, art, golf, travel. *Address:* A. Nelson & Co., Nelson House, 83 Parkside, Wimbledon, SW19 5LP. *T:* (020) 8780 4200, *Fax:* (020) 8789 0141. *E:* RobertWilson@Nelsons.net. *Clubs:* Oriental, Sloane; New (Edinburgh); Bruntsfield Links Golfing Society; Golf House (Elie).

WILSON, Robert O.; MP (C) Reading East, since 2005; Parliamentary Secretary, Cabinet Office, since 2014; *b* 4 Jan. 1965; *m* Jane; one *s* three *d*. *Educ:* Wallingford Sch.; Univ. of Reading (BA Hist.). Entrepreneur, health and communications. Mem. (C), Reading BC, 1992–96, 2004–06. Shadow Minister for Higher Educn, 2007–09; an Opposition Whip, 2009–10; PPS to Sec. of State for Culture, Olympics, Media and Sport, 2010–12, for Health, 2012–13, to Chancellor of the Exchequer, 2013–14. Contested (C): Bolton NE, 1997; Carmarthen W and S Pembs, 2001. *Publications:* 5 Days to Power: the journey to coalition Britain, 2010; The Eye of the Storm, 2014. *Address:* (office) 12a South View Park, Marsack Street, Reading RG4 5AF; House of Commons, SW1A 0AA.

WILSON, Sir Robert (Peter), KCMG 2000; Chairman, Riverstone Energy Ltd, since 2013; *b* 2 Sept. 1943; *s* of late Alfred Wilson and Dorothy (*née* Mathews); *m* 1975, Shirley Elisabeth Robson; one *s* one *d*. *Educ:* Epsom Coll.; Sussex Univ. (BA); Harvard Business Sch. (AMP). With Dunlop Ltd, 1966–67; Mobil Oil Co. Ltd, 1967–70; RTZ Corporation plc, later Rio Tinto plc, 1970–2003: Dir, Main Bd, 1987–2003; Dir, Planning and Develt, 1987–89, Mining and Metals, 1989–91; Chief Exec., 1991–97; Chairman: Rio Tinto plc, 1997–2003; Rio Tinto Ltd, 1999–2003. Non-executive Director: The Boots Co. PLC, 1991–98; Diageo plc, 1998–2003; BP plc (formerly British Petroleum, then BP Amoco), 1998–2002; Economist Newspaper Ltd, later The Economist Gp, 2002–09 (Chm., 2003–09); BG Gp plc, 2002–12 (Chm., 2004–12); GlaxoSmithKline plc, 2003–. Sen. Advr, Morgan Stanley, 2013–14. Chm., Internat. Council for Mining & Metals, 2002–03; Patron, Centre for Energy, Petroleum and Mineral Law and Policy, Dundee Univ., 2010–. FEI 2006; CCMI; FRSA. Hon. DSc: Exeter, 1993; Birmingham, 2002; Sussex, 2004; Hon. LLD Dundee, 2001. *Recreations:* theatre, opera, reading, wine.

WILSON, Robert William Gordon, OBE 2011; Principal Clerk of Select Committees, and Deputy Head, Committee Office, House of Commons, 2001–10; *b* 8 July 1946; *s* of late Gordon Chamberlain Wilson, CBE, and Winifred Wilson (*née* Low); civil partnership 2007, David Ira Wurtzel. *Educ:* Lancing Coll.; Christ Church, Oxford (MA). A Clerk, H of C, 1967–: Clerk: of Eur. Legislation Cttee, 1981–86; of Envmt Cttee, 1986–87; of Foreign Affairs Cttee, 1987–91; Principal Clerk: of Financial Cttees and Treasury and Civil Service Cttee, 1991–92; of Domestic Cttees and Sec., H of C Commn, 1992–95; of Overseas Office, 1995–2001. Jt Sec., Assoc. of Secretaries-General of Parlts, 1977–84. Hon. Steward, Westminster Abbey, 1981–98, 2010–. Chm., Decorative Arts Soc., 2011– (Dep. Chm., 2004–11). Trustee, Erskine May Meml Fund, 2001–10. *Publications:* Guide to the Houses of Parliament, edns from 1988 to 2010. *Recreations:* theatre, opera, travel, swimming. *Address:* 35 Albany Mansions, Albert Bridge Road, SW11 4PG. *Club:* Athenæum.

WILSON, Dr Robert Woodrow; Senior Scientist, Harvard-Smithsonian Center for Astrophysics, since 1994; *b* 10 Jan. 1936; *s* of Ralph Woodrow Wilson and Fannie May Willis; *m* 1958, Elizabeth Rhoads Sawin; two *s* one *d*. *Educ:* Rice Univ. (BA Physics, 1957); Calif Inst. of Technol. (PhD 1962). Post-doctoral Fellowship, Calif Inst. of Technol., 1962–63; Mem. Technical Staff, Bell Labs, Holmdel, NJ, 1963–76; Head, Radio Physics Res. Dept, Bell Telephone Labs, Inc., later AT&T Bell Labs, 1976–94. Member: Phi Beta Kappa; Amer. Acad. of Arts and Sciences, 1978; US Nat. Acad. of Science, 1979. Hon. degrees: Monmouth Coll., 1979; Jersey City State Coll., 1979; Thiel Coll., 1980. Henry Draper Award, 1977; Herschel Award, RAS, 1977; (jtly) Nobel Prize for Physics, 1978. *Publications:* contrib. to Astrophys. Jl. *Address:* 9 Valley Point Drive, Holmdel, NJ 07733–1320, USA. *T:* (201) 6717807; Harvard-Smithsonian Center for Astrophysics, 60 Garden Street #42, Cambridge, MA 02138–1516, USA.

WILSON, Robin; *see* Wilson, R. J.

WILSON, Robin Lee, CBE 1992; FREng; consulting engineer; *b* 4 March 1933; *s* of late Henry Eric Wilson, OBE and Catherine Margaret Wilson; *m* 1956, Gillian Margaret, *d* of late L. J. N. Kirkby and Margaret Kirkby; one *s* two *d*. *Educ:* Glenalmond College; Univ. of Glasgow (BSc Eng. 1955). FICE 1966; FCIHT (FIHT 1966). Joined R. Travers Morgan & Partners, 1956, Partner, 1966, Sen. Partner, 1985; Dir and Gp Chm., Travers Morgan Ltd, Consulting Engineers, 1988–91; Chairman: New Builder Publications Ltd, 1989–94; Thomas Telford Ltd, publishers, 1990–94. Dir, Mid Kent Hldgs, 1994–97. Member Council: ICE, 1977–80, 1983–86, 1987–93 (Pres., 1991–92); ACE, 1985–88; Construction Industry Council, 1990–97 (Chm., 1994–96); Engrg Council, 1991–99 (Chm., Bd for Engineers' Regulation, 1994–99); Glenalmond Coll., 1985–2001 (Chm. Cttee, 1995–2001; Pres., Fellowship, 2011–). Pres., Smeatonian Soc. of Civil Engineers, 2016. Minister's nominee, SE Council for Sport and Recreation, 1987–90. Chm., Coultershaw Trust, 2002–. Master, Paviors' Co., 2003–04. DSc *hc* City Univ., 1991. Coopers Hill Meml Prize, ICE, 1989; Instn of Highways and Transportation Award, 1990. *Publications:* papers in learned jls on highway engineering and related subjects. *Recreations:* sailing, golf. *Address:* The Grove House, Little Bognor, Pulborough, Sussex RH20 1JT. *T:* (01798) 865774. *Clubs:* Sloane; Itchenor Sailing.

WILSON, Rodney Herbert William; Executive Producer for BBC Classical Music, Television, 1998; *b* 21 June 1942; *s* of Herbert Herman Wilson and Vera Anne Faulkner. *Educ:* Windsor Grammar Sch. for Boys; Berkshire Coll. of Art (Intermediate Diploma); Camberwell Sch. of Art (NDD); Hornsey Coll. of Art (ATD). Asst Lectr, Loughborough Coll. of Art, 1965–69; Film Officer, 1970, Head of Film Section, 1980, Arts Council of GB; Dir, Dept of Film, Video and Broadcasting, Arts Council of England, 1986–98. Member: Film, Video and Television Adv. Cttee, British Council, 1983–98; Council, Edinburgh Film Festival, 1984–94; Festival Council, Art Film Fest., Slovakia, 1995–; RTS, 1994. Exec. Producer for Arts Council Films, 1970. *Recreations:* walking, doodling, photography.

WILSON, Air Chief Marshal Sir (Ronald) Andrew (Fellowes), (Sir Sandy), KCB 1991 (CB 1990); AFC 1978; Air Member for Personnel and Air Officer Commanding-in-Chief Personnel and Training Command, 1993–95; Air Aide-de-Camp to the Queen, 1993–95; *b* 27 Feb. 1941; *s* of late Ronald Denis Wilson and Gladys Vera Groombridge; *m* 1979, Mary Christine Anderson; one *d*, and one step *s* one step *d*. *Educ:* Tonbridge Sch.; RAF Coll., Cranwell. Flying Instr, 1963–65; No 2 Sqn, 1966–68; ADC to C-in-C, RAF Germany, 1967–68; Flt Comdr No 2 Sqn, 1968–72; RAF Staff Coll., 1973; HQ STC, 1974–75; CO No 2 Sqn, 1975–77; Air Plans, MoD, 1977–79; CO RAF Lossiemouth, 1980–82; Air Cdre Falkland Islands, 1982–83; Central Staff, MoD, 1983–85; Dir Ops Strike, MoD, 1985; Dir Air Offensive, MoD, 1986–87; SASO, HQ, RAF Strike Comd, 1987–89; AOC No 1 Group, 1989–91; Comdr, British Forces during Op. Granby, ME, Aug.–Dec. 1990; C-in-C, RAF Germany and Comdr Second ATAF, 1991–93. Pres., Aircrew Assoc., 1997–2003. Vice-Chm., Air League, 1997–2005. Mem. Council, Lord Kitchener Meml Fund, 1998–. Freeman, City of London, 1966; Liveryman, 1970, Mem. Court, 1984–87, 1994–, Master, 1999–2000, Worshipful Co. of Skinners. CCMI (CIMgt 1993); FRAeS 1994. *Recreations:* painting, antique restoration, genealogy, golf. *Club:* Royal Air Force.

WILSON, Roy Vernon, CEng; Director, Eastern Region, Property Services Agency, Department of the Environment, 1980–82; *b* 23 July 1922; *s* of late Alfred Vincent Wilson and Theresa Elsie Wilson; *m* 1951, Elsie Hannah Barrett; three *s*. *Educ:* Cheadle Hulme Sch.; Manchester Univ. (BScTech Hons Civil Engrg 1942). MICE. Served Royal Engineers, 1942–44. Civil Engineer, local govt, 1945–51; Harlow Develt Corp., 1951–54; Air Ministry Works Directorate: Warrington, 1954–59; Newmarket, 1959–62; Germany, 1962–65; District Works Officer: Wethersfield, 1965–67; Mildenhall, 1967–72; Area Officer, Letchworth (PSA), 1972–76; Regional Director, Cyprus (PSA), 1976–79; Chief Works Officer, Ruislip, 1979. *Recreations:* lacrosse (played for England *v* USA in 1942–43), tennis (earlier years), golf. *Address:* 12 Diomed Drive, Great Barton, Bury St Edmunds, Suffolk IP31 2TD. *Club:* Civil Service.

WILSON, Ruth Joanna; actress; *b* Ashford, Middx, 13 Jan. 1982; *d* of Nigel and Mary Wilson. *Educ:* Notre Dame Sen. Sch., Cobham, Surrey; Esher Coll.; Nottingham Univ. (BA Hons). Actress: *television:* Jane Eyre, 2006; Capturing Mary, 2007; A Real Summer, 2007; The Doctor Who Hears Voices, 2008; The Prisoner, 2009; Small Island, 2009; Luther, 2010–13; The Affair, 2014–15 (Golden Globe Award, 2015); *theatre:* Philistines, RNT, 2007; A Streetcar Named Desire, Donmar, 2009 (Best Supporting Actress, Olivier Awards, 2010); Through a Glass Darkly, Almeida, 2010; Anna Christie, Donmar, 2011 (Best Actress, Olivier Awards, 2012); The El Train (also dir), Hoxton Hall, 2013; Constellations, Samuel J Friedman Th., NY, 2015; *films:* Anna Karenina, 2012; The Lone Ranger, 2013; Saving Mr Banks, 2013; Locke, A Walk Among the Tombstones, 2014; Suite Française, 2015. *Address:* c/o Troika Talent, 10A Christina Street, EC2A 4PA. *T:* (020) 7336 7868. *E:* info@troikatalent.com.

WILSON, Samuel, (Sammy); MP (DemU) East Antrim, since 2005; *b* 4 April 1953; *s* of Alexander and Mary Wilson. *Educ:* Methodist Coll., Belfast; The Queen's Univ., Belfast (BScEcon; PGCE). Teacher of Economics, 1975–83; Researcher in N Ireland Assembly, 1983–86. Councillor, Belfast CC, 1981–; Lord Mayor of Belfast, 1986–87 and 2000–01. Press Officer for Democratic Unionist Party, 1982–96. Contested (DemU) Antrim E, 2001. Mem. (DemU) Belfast E, 1998–2003, E Antrim, 2003–Aug. 2015, NI Assembly; Minister of the Envmt, 2008–09, of Finance and Personnel, 2009–13, NI. *Publications:* The Carson Trail, 1982; The Unionist Case—The Forum Report Answered, 1984; Data Response Questions in Economics, 1995. *Recreations:* reading, motor cycling, windsurfing, gardening. *Address:* East Antrim DUP, 116 Main Street, Larne BT40 1RG. *T:* (028) 2826 7722. *E:* barronj@parliament.uk.

WILSON, Air Chief Marshal Sir Sandy; *see* Wilson, Air Chief Marshal Sir R. A. F.

WILSON, Simon Charles Hartley; HM Diplomatic Service, retired; consultant; Director, RNVR Officers' Association Ltd, since 2013; *b* 9 Aug. 1957; *s* of late Charles William Wilson and of Brenda Christine Wilson (*née* Hartley); *m* 1984, Heather Graine Richardson; two *s*. *Educ:* Newborough Sch., Liverpool; Liverpool Coll. Entered FCO, 1975; Attaché: Johannesburg, 1978–81; Helsinki, 1981–83; FCO, 1984–87; Vice Consul: Tehran, 1987; Riyadh, 1987–92; Second Sec. (Political), Lisbon, 1992–96; SE Asia Dept, FCO, 1997–2001; Dep. Hd of Mission, Bahrain, 2001–05; Dep. High Comr to Eastern India, at Kolkata, 2006–09. Mem. Bd, Dr Graham's Homes, Calcutta, 2007–09. Advr, Prosperitus Capital Partners, 2011–. Writer and presenter, documentary, Memories Bahrain, Bahrain TV, 2009; actor in film, Gumshuda - The Diamond Murders, 2010. Member: Cttee, Fulham and Hammersmith Asthma Soc., 1985–87; Chilbolton PCC, 1999–2001. *Publications:* articles on monarchy, ornithology, Bahrain history, HMS Hood, Roman Winchester. *Recreations:* birding, taxidermy, philately, ambulist, nargileh, Edward VIII memorabilia, tennis, ski-ing, sports cars, Indian art, reading history. *E:* sheeshawilson@hotmail.com. *Clubs:* Naval; Tollygunge, Bengal (Calcutta).

WILSON, Sophie, FRS 2013; FREng; Senior Technical Director, Broadcom Corporation; *b* Leeds, 1957. *Educ:* Univ. of Cambridge (Computer Sci. and Maths). Acorn Computers, 1979–99; co-founder, Element 14 Ltd, 1999, sold to Broadcom Corp., 2000; designed: Acorn Micro-Computer, 1978; BBC Microcomputer, BBC BASIC, 1980; instruction set for Acorn RISC Machine (ARM), 1983; Acorn Replay, video architecture for Acorn machines. Consultant, ARM Ltd, 1990. FREng 2008. *Address:* Broadcom Corporation, Unit 101 Science Park, Milton Road, Cambridge CB4 0FY.

WILSON, Sir Thomas David, 4th Bt *cr* 1920, of Carbeth, Killearn, co. Stirling; *b* 6 Jan. 1959; *s* of Sir David Wilson, 3rd Bt and of Eva Margareta Wilson (*née* Lindell); *S* father 2014; *m* 1st, 1984, Valerie Stogdale (marr. diss. 2002); two *s*; 2nd, 2006, Briony Jane Roberts (*née* Clark). *Educ:* Harrow. *Heir:* *s* Fergus Wilson, *b* 24 April 1987.

WILSON, Prof. Thomas Michael Aubrey, PhD; CBiol, FRSB; FRSE; Honorary Professor, Warwick-HRI, University of Warwick, 2007–10 (Professor of Biological Sciences, 2004–07); *b* 10 Oct. 1951; *s* of Basil Francis Aubrey Wilson and Elisabeth Mathew Wilson (*née* Hogg); *m* 1975, Judith Lindsey Dring; two *s* one *d*. *Educ:* Univ. of Edinburgh (BSc 1st Cl. Hons Biol Sci. 1973); St John's Coll., Cambridge (PhD Biochem. 1976). CBiol 1995; FRSB (FIBiol 1998); FIHort 1999–2010; FRSE 1999. MRC Res. Fellow, Univ. of Nottingham, 1976–78; Lectr in Biochem., Univ. of Liverpool, 1979–83; SSO, 1983–86, PSO, 1986–89, John Innes Inst., Norwich; Prof., Rutgers Univ., NJ, 1989–92; Head of Virology, 1992–95, Dep. Dir, 1995–99, Scottish Crop Res. Inst., Dundee; Sci. Dir, 1999, CEO, 1999–2004, Horticulture Res. Internat. Hon. Lectr, UEA, 1985–92; Hon. Professor: Univ. of Dundee, 1993–99; Zhejiang Acad. Agricl Scis, China, 1993–; Univ. of Birmingham, 1999–2004; Univ. of Warwick, 1999–2004. Ed., Jl of Horticultural Sci. and Biotechnol., 2004–15. FRSA 2003–07. *Publications:* (with J. W. Davies) Genetic Engineering with Plant Viruses, 1992; Engineering Genesis, 1998; contrib. approx. 100 papers in specialist jls; also over 100 abstracts, proceedings and invited seminars.

WILSON, Sir Timothy; *see* Wilson, Sir R. J. T.

WILSON, Prof. Timothy Hugh, FSA; Barrie and Deedee Wigmore Research Keeper, Department of Western Art, Ashmolean Museum, Oxford, since 2013; Professorial Fellow, Balliol College, Oxford, since 1990; Professor of the Arts of the Renaissance, University of Oxford, since 2010; *b* 8 April 1950; *s* of late Col Hugh Walker Wilson and Lilian Rosemary (*née* Kirke); *m* 1984, Jane Lott; two *s* one *d*. *Educ:* Winchester Coll.; Mercersburg Acad., USA; Corpus Christi Coll., Oxford (BA 1973; MA); Warburg Inst., London Univ. (MPhil 1976); Dept of Museum Studies, Leicester Univ. FSA 1989. Res. Asst, Dept of Weapons and Antiquities, Nat. Maritime Mus., Greenwich, 1977–79; Asst Keeper (Renaissance collections), Dept of Medieval and Later Antiquities, BM, 1979–90; Keeper of Western Art, Ashmolean Mus., Oxford, 1990–2013. Trustee: Ruskin Foundn, 1994–2000; Oxford Preservation Trust, 2006–; Cartoon Art Trust, 2010–; Radcliffe Trust, 2011–. Fellow: Harvard Univ. Center for Renaissance Studies, Villa I Tatti, Florence, 1984; Accademia Raffaello, Urbino, 2003; Frick Center for the History of Collecting, NY, 2012. Hon. Fellow: Royal Soc. Painter-Printmakers, 1991; Accademia Pietro Vannucci, Perugia, 2008. *Publications:* (jtly) The Art of the Jeweller, 1984; Flags at Sea, 1986, 2nd edn 1999; Ceramic Art of the Italian Renaissance, 1987; Maiolica, 1989, 2nd edn 2003; (ed) Italian Renaissance Pottery, 1991; (jtly) Systematic Catalogue of the National Gallery of Art: Western Decorative Arts, Part 1, 1993; (ed jtly) C. D. E. Fortnum and the Collecting and Study of Applied Arts and Sculpture in Victorian England, 1999; (jtly) Le maioliche rinascimentali nelle collezioni della Fondazione Cassa di Risparmio di Perugia, 2006–07; (jtly) Italian Renaissance Ceramics: a catalogue of the British Museum collection, 2009; articles in Apollo, Burlington Mag., Faenza, Jl Warburg and Courtauld Insts, Jl of Hist. of Collections, Ceramic Review, etc; contribs exhibition and museum catalogues. *Address:* Balliol College, Oxford OX1 3BJ; 4 Boults Close, Old Marston, Oxford OX3 0PP. *T:* (01865) 428677; Marlborough Cottage, Durlow Common, Herefordshire HR1 4JQ.

WILSON, Dr William Laurence; Member (SNP) Scotland West, Scottish Parliament, 2007–11; *b* 11 Dec. 1963; *s* of Samuel and Mary Wilson; *m* 2002, Julieta A. Pineda. *Educ:* Glasgow Univ. (BSc Hons Zool.; MSc IT); Aberdeen Univ. (MSc Ecol.); Queen's Univ., Belfast (PhD). Biologist: Glasgow Univ., 1987; Berks, Bucks and Oxon Wildlife Trust and Oxford Univ., 1987–89; Res. Asst, QUB, 1989–91; Res. Officer, Ulster Univ., 1993–96; Res. Fellow, 1996–98, Project Manager, 1998–99, Glasgow Univ.; IT Asst, Glasgow Caledonian Univ., 2001; Systems Developer, Prudent/Standard Life, 2001–05; Statistician, Scottish Funding Council, 2005–07. Contested (SNP): Glasgow Anniesland, 1997, Paisley and Renfrewshire N, 2005; Glasgow Maryhill, Scottish Parlt, 1999, 2003. *Publications:* series of training booklets for researchers, 1999; (contrib.) Is There a Scottish Road to Socialism?, 2007; contrib. scientific jls. *Recreations:* reading, hill walking, travel.

WILSON-BARNETT, Prof. Dame Jenifer, (Dame Jenifer Trimble), DBE 2003; Professor of Nursing, 1986–2004, now Emeritus, and Founding Head of Florence Nightingale School of Nursing and Midwifery, 1999–2004, King's College, London (Head of Division of Nursing and Midwifery, 1994–99); *b* 10 Aug. 1944; adopted by Edith M. Barnett and Barbara M. Wilson; *m* 1975, Michael Robert Trimble. *Educ:* Chichester High School for Girls; St George's Hosp., London (student nurse), 1963–66; Univ. of Leicester, 1967–70 (BA Politics); Edinburgh Univ., 1970–72 (MSc); Guy's Hosp. Med. Sch., London (PhD 1977). FRCN 1984; FKC 1995. Staff Nurse, 1966, Nursing Sister, 1972–74, St George's Hosp.; Researcher, Guy's Hosp., 1974–77; Chelsea College: Lectr in Nursing, 1977; Sen. Lectr, 1983; Reader and Hd of Dept, 1984. Ed.-in-Chief, Internat. Jl of Nursing Studies, 2000–05. Chair, Chichester Cttee, Macmillan Cancer Support, 2013–. Patron, Selsey and Dist Carers Support Gp, 2007–. Chair, St Mary, Our Lady, Sidlesham, Develt Gp, 2010–. Hon. DSc: Hull, 2004; Kingston, 2006. Lifetime Achievement Award, British Jl Nursing, 2008. *Publications:* Stress in Hospital: patients' psychological reactions to illness and health care, 1979; (with Morva Fordham) Recovery from Illness, 1982; Patient Teaching, 1983; Nursing Research: ten studies in patient care, 1983; Nursing Issues and Research in Terminal Care, 1988; Patient Problems: a research base for nursing care, 1988; (with Sarah Robinson) Directions in Nursing Research, 1989; (with Jill Macleod Clark) Health Promotion and Nursing Research, 1993; (with Alison Richardson) Nursing Research in Cancer Care, 1996. *Recreations:* music, writing, 'singing'. *Address:* Jubilee Cottage, Mill Lane, Sidlesham, Chichester, W Sussex PO20 7NA. *Clubs:* Royal Automobile, Royal College of Nursing, Royal Society of Medicine.

WILSON-JOHNSON, David Robert, FRAM; baritone; Professor of Singing, Amsterdam Conservatorium, 2004–10; Director, Ferrandou Singing School; *b* 16 Nov. 1950; *s* of Sylvia Constance Wilson and Harry Kenneth Johnson. *Educ:* Wellingborough School; British Institute, Florence; St Catharine's College, Cambridge (BA Hons 1973); Royal Acad. of Music (Dove Prize, 1976). NFMS Award, 1977; Gulbenkian Fellowship, 1978–81. Royal Opera House, Covent Garden: We Come to the River (début), 1976; Billy Budd, 1982; L'Enfant et les Sortilèges, 1983; Le Rossignol, 1983; Les Noces, Boris Godunov, 1984; Die Zauberflöte, 1985; Werther, Turandot, 1987; Madam Butterfly, 1988; title rôle, St François d'Assise (Messiaen), 1988–89 (Evening Standard Award, 1989); Wigmore Hall recital début, 1978; Edinburgh Fest. début, 1980; BBC Proms début, 1981; Paris Opera début (Die Meistersinger), 1989; US début, Cleveland Orch., 1990; other roles include King Fisher (A Midsummer Marriage), King Priam (Tippett), Merlin (Albeniz), Oedipe (Enescu), The Nose (Shostakovitch); appearances at Netherlands Opera, Brussels, Geneva, Houston, New York, Turin, Salzburg, etc; many collaborations with Pierre Boulez, Frans Bruggen, Charles Dutoit, Robert King, Andre Previn, Simon Rattle, Gennadi Rozhdestvensky, David Owen Norris; numerous recordings, including works by Bach, Schönberg and Schubert. FRAM 1988 (ARAM 1982). *Recreations:* swimming, slimming, gardening and growing walnuts at Dordogne house. *Address:* Highfield Cottage, Overgate Road, Swayfield, Grantham, Lincs NG31 4LG. *T:* (01476) 550432; Prinsengracht 455, 1016 HN Amsterdam, Netherlands. *T:* (20) 7728104. *W:* www.davidwilsonjohnson.com.

WILSON JONES, Prof. Edward, FRCP, FRCPath; Professor of Dermatopathology, Institute of Dermatology, University of London, 1974–91, now Emeritus (Dean, 1980–89); *b* 26 July 1926; *s* of Percy George Jones and Margaret Louisa Wilson; *m* 1952, Hilda Mary Rees; one *s* one *d*. *Educ:* Oundle Sch.; Trinity Hall, Cambridge (MB, BChir 1951); St Thomas' Hosp., London. FRCP 1970; FRCPath 1975. National Service, Army, 1953–54. House Surgeon (Ophthalmic), St Thomas' Hosp., 1951; House Physician (Gen. Medicine), St Helier Hosp., Carshalton, 1951–52; House Physician (Neurology and Chest Diseases), St Thomas' Hosp., 1955; Registrar (Gen. Medicine), Watford Peace Meml Hosp., 1955–57; Registrar (Derm.), St Thomas' Hosp., 1957–60; Inst. of Dermatology, St John's Hosp. for Diseases of the Skin: Sen. Registrar (Derm.), 1960–62; Sen. Registrar (Dermatopath.), 1962–63; Sen. Lectr (Dermatopath.), 1963–74; Hon. Consultant, St John's Hosp. for Diseases of Skin, 1974–. Non-exec. Dir, Crockett & Jones Ltd. Founders Award, Amer. Soc. of Dermatopathology, 1997; Gray Medal, British Assoc. of Dermatology. *Publications:* (contrib.) Textbook of Dermatology, ed Rook, Wilkinson and Ebling, 3rd edn 1979; articles on dermatopath. subjects in British Jl of Derm., Arch. of Derm., Acta Dermatovenereologica, Dermatologica, Clin. and Exptl Derm., Histopath., and in Human Path. *Recreations:* art history, watercolour painting. *Address:* Featherstone House, 89 Wise Lane, NW7 2RH.

WILTON, 8th Earl of, *cr* 1801; **Francis Egerton Grosvenor;** Viscount Grey de Wilton 1801; Baron Ebury 1857; *b* 8 Feb. 1934; *s* of 5th Baron Ebury, DSO and Ann Acland-Troyte; *S* to Barony of father, 1957; *S* to Earldom of kinsman, 1999; *m* 1st, 1957, Gillian Elfrida (Elfin) (marr. diss. 1962), *d* of Martin Soames, London; one *s*; 2nd, 1963, Kyra (marr. diss. 1973), *d* of late L. L. Aslin; 3rd, 1974, Suzanne Jean, *d* of Graham Suckling, Christchurch, NZ; (one *d* decd). *Educ:* Eton; Univ. of Melbourne (PhD). *Recreation:* ornithology. *Heir:* *s* Viscount Grey de Wilton, *qv*. *Address:* PO Box 466, Mt Macedon, Vic 3441, Australia. *Clubs:* Oriental; Melbourne, Melbourne Savage (Melbourne); Hong Kong.

WILTON, Andrew; *see* Wilton, J. A. R.

WILTON, Christopher Edward John, CMG 2003; HM Diplomatic Service, retired; Director, DCW Consultants Ltd, since 2005; Adviser, de Mellow and Co., Wealth Management (St James's Place Group), since 2012; *b* 16 Dec. 1951; *s* of Sir (Arthur) John Wilton, KCMG, KCVO, MC and of Maureen Elizabeth Alison Wilton; *m* 1975, Dianne Hodgkinson; one *s* one *d*. *Educ:* Tonbridge Sch.; Manchester Univ. (Hons Near Eastern Studies); Chartered Insurance Inst. (Dip. Personal Finance 2012). Production Supervisor, Esso Petroleum, 1975–77; HM Diplomatic Service, 1977–98: FCO, 1977; Bahrain, 1978–81; FCO, 1981–84; Tokyo, 1984–88; on loan to Cabinet Office, 1988–90; Commercial Counsellor, Riyadh, 1990–94; Consul Gen., Dubai, 1994–97; Counsellor, FCO, and Comr (non-resident), British Indian Ocean Territories, 1998; Regl Man. Dir, GEC, later BAE Systems, 1999–2001 (on special leave); Counsellor, FCO, 2001–02; Ambassador to Kuwait, 2002–05. Middle East Advisor: to RBS, 2005–08; Selex Sensors and Airborne Systems Ltd, 2005–08; Sen. Advr, EMCIIS Ltd, 2008–10; Dir, Blue Sea UK Ltd, 2009–; Vice Chm., DTZ plc, 2009–10. Dir, Arab-British Chamber of Commerce, 2005–10; Chm. Adv. Council, London Middle East Inst., 2007–08. Chm., Raleigh Internat., 2007–12. Trustee, Wallacea Trust, 2012–; Chm. of Trustees, Rosemary Foundn Hospice at Home Care, 2014–. *Recreations:* walking, cooking, piano. *Club:* Athenæum.

WILTON, (James) Andrew (Rutley), FSA; Visiting Research Fellow, Tate Gallery, since 2003 (Keeper and Senior Research Fellow, 1998–2002); *b* 7 Feb. 1942; *s* of Herbert Rutley Wilton and Mary Cecilia Morris (*née* Buckerfield); *m* 1976, Christina Frances Benn (marr. diss.); one *s*. *Educ:* Dulwich Coll.; Trinity Coll., Cambridge (MA). Assistant Keeper: Walker Art Gallery, Liverpool, 1965; Dept of Prints and Drawings, BM, 1967; Curator of Prints and Drawings, Yale Center for British Art, 1976; Asst Keeper, Turner Collection, BM, 1981; Curator, Turner Collection, 1985–89, Keeper of British Art, 1989–98, Tate Gallery. Hon. Curator of Prints and Drawings, Royal Acad., 2003. Trustee, Turner's House Trust (formerly Sandycombe Lodge Trust), 2005–. Hon. Curator and Hon. Liveryman, Painter-Stainers' Co., 2003. FRSA 1973; FSA 2000. Hon. RWS 1985. *Publications:* Turner in Switzerland (with John Russell), 1976; British Watercolours 1750–1850, 1977; The Wood Engravings of William Blake, 1977; The Life and Work of J. M. W. Turner, 1979; The Art of Alexander and John Robert Cozens, 1979; William Pars: journey through the Alps, 1979; Turner and the Sublime, 1980; Turner Abroad, 1982; Turner in his Time, 1987; Painting and Poetry, 1990; The Swagger Portrait, 1992; The Great Age of British Watercolour, 1992; (ed jtly) Grand Tour, 1996; (ed jtly) Pictures in the Garrick Club: a catalogue, 1997; (ed jtly) The Age of Rossetti, Burne-Jones and Watts: symbolism in Britain, 1997; Five Centuries of British Painting, 2001; American Sublime, 2002; Turner as Draughtsman, 2006; contribs to arts magazines. *Recreations:* music, architecture, travel. *Address:* 10 Farrington Place, Ashfield Lane, Chislehurst, Kent BR7 6BE. *Clubs:* Athenæum, Chelsea Arts.

WILTON, Maxwell William M.; *see* Moore-Wilton.

WILTON, Penelope Alice, OBE 2004; actress; *b* 3 June 1946; *m* 1st, Daniel Massey, actor (marr. diss.; he *d* 1998); one *d*; 2nd, 1991, Sir Ian Holm, *qv* (marr. diss. 2002). *Educ:* Drama Centre. *Theatre* includes: National Theatre, later Royal National Theatre: The Philanderer; Betrayal; Much Ado About Nothing; Man and Superman; Major Barbara, 1982; Sisterly Feelings; The Secret Rapture, 1988; Piano, 1990; Landscape, 1994; Sketches, 2002; The House of Bernarda Alba, 2005; Greenwich Theatre: Measure for Measure; All's Well That Ends Well; The Norman Conquests; King Lear, Nottingham Playhouse; The Deep Blue Sea, Almeida, 1992, transf. Apollo, 1993; Vita and Virginia, Chichester, 1992, transf. Ambassadors, 1993; The Cherry Orchard, RSC, 1995; Long Day's Journey into Night, Young Vic, 1996; A Kind of Alaska, Dublin, 1997, Donmar Warehouse, 1998; The Seagull, RSC, 2000; The Little Foxes, Donmar, 2001; Afterplay, Gielgud, 2002; Women Beware Women, RSC, 2006; Eh Joe, Duke of York's, 2006, Royal Lyceum Th., 2013; John Gabriel Borkman, Donmar, 2007; The Chalk Garden, The Family Reunion, Donmar, 2008; Hamlet, Wyndham's Th., 2009; Taken at Midnight, Chichester, 2014, transf. Th. Royal, Haymarket, 2015 (Best Actress, Olivier Awards, 2015); *television* includes: Othello; King Lear; Country; The Norman Conquests, 1977; The Tale of Beatrix Potter, 1983; Ever Decreasing Circles; Screaming; The Borrowers, 1992; The Deep Blue Sea, 1994; Landscapes, 1995; Talking Heads (Nights in the Gardens of Spain), 1998; Wives and Daughters, 1999; Victoria and Albert, 2001; Bob and Rose, 2001; Lucky Jim, 2003; Downton Abbey, 2010, 2011, 2012, 2013, 2014, 2015; South Riding, 2011; The Girl, 2012; *radio* includes: Jane and Prudence, 1994; North by Northamptonshire, 2011–12; *films* include: The French Lieutenant's Woman, 1981; Clockwise, 1986; Cry Freedom, 1987; The Secret Rapture, 1993; Carrington, 1995; Iris, 2002; Calendar Girls, 2003; Shaun of the Dead, 2003; Pride and Prejudice, 2005; Match Point, 2006; The History Boys, 2006; The Best Exotic Marigold Hotel, 2012; Belle, 2014; The Second Best Exotic Marigold Hotel, 2015. *Address:* c/o Independent Talent Group Ltd, 40 Whitfield Street, W1T 2RH.

WILTS, Archdeacon of; *no new appointment at time of going to press.*

WILTSHIRE, Earl of; Christopher John Hilton Paulet; *b* 30 July 1969; *s* and *heir* of Marquess of Winchester, *qv*; *m* 1992, Christine, *d* of Peter Town; one *s* one *d*. *Heir:* *s* Lord St John, *qv*.

WIMBORNE, 4th Viscount *cr* 1918; **Ivor Mervyn Vigors Guest;** Baron Wimborne 1880; Baron Ashby St Ledgers 1910; Bt 1838; *b* 19 Sept. 1968; *o s* of 3rd Viscount Wimborne and of his 1st wife, Victoria Ann, *o d* of Col Mervyn Vigors, DSO, MC; *S* father, 1993; *m* 2011, Ieva Imsa; one *d*. *Educ:* Eton. *Heir:* *uncle* Hon. Julian John Guest [*b* 12 Oct. 1945; *m* 1st, 1970, Emma Jane Arlette (marr. diss. 1978), *e d* of Cdre Archibald Gray, RN; 2nd, 1983, Jillian, *d* of late N. S. G. Bannatine].

WINCH, Prof. Donald Norman, FBA 1986; FRHistS; Emeritus Professor of Intellectual History (formerly Emeritus Research Professor), University of Sussex, since 2000 (Professor of History of Economics, 1969–2000); *b* 15 April 1935; *s* of Sidney and Iris Winch; *m* 1983, Doreen Lidster. *Educ:* Sutton Grammar Sch.; LSE (BSc Econ 1956); Princeton Univ. (PhD

1960). Vis. Lectr, Univ. of California, 1959–60; Lectr in Economics, Univ. of Edinburgh, 1960–63; University of Sussex: Lectr, 1963–66; Reader, 1966–69; Dean, Sch. of Social Scis, 1968–74; Pro-Vice-Chancellor (Arts and Social Studies), 1986–89. Visiting Fellow: Sch. of Social Sci., Inst. for Advanced Study, Princeton, 1974–75; King's Coll., Cambridge, 1983; History of Ideas Unit, ANU, 1983; St Catharine's Coll., Cambridge, 1989; All Souls Coll., Oxford, 1994; British Council Distinguished Vis. Fellow, Kyoto Univ., 1992. Carlyle Lectr, Oxford Univ., 1995. Vice-Pres., British Acad., 1993–94. Publications Sec., Royal Economic Soc., 1971–; Review Editor, Economic Jl, 1976–83. Fellow, Hist. of Econs Soc., 2007. Hon. Mem., European Soc. for Hist. of Econs, 2012. Hon. DLitt Sussex, 2006. *Publications:* Classical Political Economy and Colonies, 1965; James Mill: selected economic writings, 1966; Economics and Policy, 1969; (with S. K. Howson) The Economic Advisory Council 1930–1939, 1976; Adam Smith's Politics, 1978; (with S. Collini and J. W. Burrow) That Noble Science of Politics, 1983; Malthus, 1987; Riches and Poverty, 1996; Wealth and Life, 2009; Malthus: a very short introduction, 2013. *Address:* Arts B, University of Sussex, Brighton BN1 9QN. *T:* (01273) 678634.

WINCHESTER, 18th Marquess of, *cr* 1551; **Nigel George Paulet;** Baron St John of Basing, 1539; Earl of Wiltshire, 1550; Premier Marquess of England; *b* 23 Dec. 1941; *s* of George Cecil Paulet (*gggs* of 13th Marquess) (*d* 1961), and Hazel Margaret (*d* 1976), *o d* of late Major Danvers Wheeler, RA, Salisbury, Rhodesia; *S* kinsman, 1968; *m* 1967, Rosemary Anne, *d* of Major Aubrey John Hilton; two *s* one *d*. *Heir: s* Earl of Wiltshire, *qv*. *Address:* 6A Main Road, Irene, Centurion, 0062 Gauteng, South Africa.

WINCHESTER, Bishop of, since 2011; **Rt Rev. Timothy Dakin;** *b* Kongwa, Tanzania, 6 Feb. 1958; *s* of Rev. Canon Stanley Frederick Dakin and Judith Dakin (*née* Clark); *m* 1984, Sally Atkinson; one *s* one *d*. *Educ:* Schs in Tanzania and Kenya; University Coll. of St Mark and St John, Plymouth; King's Coll. London (BA Theol. and Phil.; MTh). Ordained deacon, 1993, priest, 1994; Principal, Carlile Coll., Kenya, 1993–2000; Curate, Nairobi Cath., 1993–2000; Gen. Sec., Church Mission Soc., 2000–11. *Recreations:* reading, walking, films, non-western Christianity. *Address:* Wolvesey, Winchester, Hants SO23 9ND. *T:* (01962) 854050. *E:* bishop.tim@winchester.anglican.org.

WINCHESTER, Dean of; *see* Atwell, Very Rev. J. E.

WINCHESTER, Archdeacon of; *no new appointment at time of going to press.*

WINCHESTER, Simon Bernard Adrian, OBE 2006; writer and journalist, since 1967; *b* 28 Sept. 1944; *s* of Bernard Austin William Winchester and Andrée Freda Winchester (*née* de Wael); *m* 1st, 1966, Isobel Judith Brown (marr. diss. 1988); three *s*; 2nd, 1989, Catherine Evans (marr. diss. 1998); 3rd, 2007, Setsuko Sato; also one *d*. *Educ:* Hardye's Sch., Dorchester; St Catherine's Coll., Oxford (BA 1966, MA 1974; Hon. Fellow, 2009). Geologist: Falconbridge of Africa Ltd, Kilembe, 1966; Amoco Offshore Exploration, North Sea, 1967; reporter, then Science Corresp., The Journal, Newcastle upon Tyne, 1967–70; correspondent, variously NE England, NI, Washington, New Delhi, The Guardian, 1970–78; America Corresp., Daily Mail, 1978–80; Chief Foreign Feature Writer, then Asia Corresp., Sunday Times, 1980–84; Hong Kong Corresp., The Guardian, 1985–92; freelance journalist and writer, 1992–; Publisher, Art AsiaPacific, 2005–07; Ed., The Sandisfield Times, 2010–. FRGS 1984; FGS 2000. Hon. LLD Dalhousie, 2010. *Publications:* In Holy Terror, 1974; American Heartbeat, 1976; Their Noble Lordships, 1981; Stones of Empire (photography), 1983; Prison Diary, Argentina, 1984; Outposts, 1985; Korea, 1988; The Pacific, 1991; Pacific Nightmare, 1992; Hong Kong: here be dragons, 1994; Small World, 1996; The River at the Centre of the World, 1997; The Surgeon of Crowthorne, 1998 (US edn as The Professor and the Madman); The Fracture Zone, 1999; America's Idea of a Good Time, 2001; The Map that Changed the World, 2001; The Meaning of Everything, 2003; Krakatoa, 2003; A Crack in the Edge of the World, 2005; Bomb, Book and Compass, 2008 (US edn as The Man Who Loved China); (ed) Best American Travel Writing, 2009; Atlantic, 2010; The Alice Behind Wonderland, 2011; Bering to Baja, 2012; Skulls, 2012; The Men who United the States, 2013; When the Earth Shakes, 2015; Pacific, 2015. *Recreations:* bee-keeping, astronomy, stamp collecting, letterpress printing, hill-walking, being in Scotland west of the Caledonian Canal, being at sea anywhere, cider-making, cycle touring, carpentry. *Address:* c/o William Morris Endeavor Entertainment LLC, 1325 Avenue of the Americas, New York, USA. *Clubs:* Travellers; Century, Coffee House (New York); China (Hong Kong).

WINCHILSEA, 17th Earl of, *cr* 1628, **AND NOTTINGHAM,** 12th Earl of, *cr* 1681; **Daniel James Hatfield Finch Hatton;** Bt 1611; Viscount Maidstone 1623; Bt 1660; Baron Finch, 1674; Custodian of the Royal Manor of Wye; *b* 7 Oct. 1967; *s* of 16th Earl of Winchilsea and 11th Earl of Nottingham, and of Shirley (*née* Hatfield); *S* father, 1999; *m* 1994, Shelley Amanda, *d* of Gordon Gillard; two *s* one *d*. *Educ:* Univ. of the West of England, Bristol. *Heir: s* Viscount Maidstone, *qv*.

WINDEATT, Prof. Barry Alexander Corelli, PhD, LittD; Professor of English, University of Cambridge, since 2001; Fellow of Emmanuel College, Cambridge, since 1978; *b* 5 April 1950; *s* of Edwin Peter Windeatt and Queenie Gladys Windeatt (*née* Rusbridge). *Educ:* Sutton County GS, Surrey; St Catharine's Coll., Cambridge (BA 1971; MA 1975; PhD 1975; LittD 1996). Cambridge University: Res. Fellow, Gonville and Caius Coll., 1974–78; Asst Lectr in English, 1983–87; Lectr in English, 1987–95; Reader in Medieval Lit., 1995–2001; Tutor, 1982–95, Dir of Studies in English, 1979–98, Keeper of Rare Books, 1992–, Vice-Master, 2013–, Emmanuel Coll. *Publications:* (ed and trans.) Chaucer's Dream Poetry: sources and analogues, 1982; (ed) Geoffrey Chaucer, Troilus and Criseyde: A New Edition of The Book of Troilus, 1984, 2nd edn 1990; (trans.) The Book of Margery Kempe, 1985, new edn 2000; (ed with Ruth Morse) Chaucer Traditions, 1990; Oxford Guide to Chaucer: Troilus and Criseyde, 1992, 2nd edn 1995; (ed) English Mystics of the Middle Ages, 1994; Troilus and Criseyde: a new translation, 1998; (ed) Troilus and Criseyde, 2003; (ed with Charlotte Brewer) Traditions and Innovations in the Study of Medieval English Literature, 2013; Julian of Norwich: Revelations of Divine Love; a new translation, 2015; (ed) Revelations of Divine Love: parallel text edition, 2015; articles on medieval English, French and Italian lit. *Recreations:* opera, gardens, visual arts. *Address:* Emmanuel College, Cambridge CB2 3AP. *T:* (01223) 334200.

WINDELER, John Robert; Chairman, Quantum Alpha Ltd, since 2010; *b* 21 March 1943; *s* of Alfred Stewart Windeler and Ethela Windeler (*née* Boremuth); *m* 1965, Judith Lynn Taylor; two *s*. *Educ:* Ohio State Univ. (BA, MBA). Exec. Vice Pres., Irving Trust Co., 1969–89; Chief Financial Officer, Nat. Australia Bank, 1989–94; Dir, Alliance & Leicester Building Soc., subseq. Alliance & Leicester plc, 1995–2005, Dep. Chm., 1998–99, Chm., 1999–2005. Chm., Millen Gp, 2006; non-executive Director: BMS Associates Ltd, 1995–2005; RM plc, 2002–11. Gov., De Montfort Univ., 2005–10. *Recreations:* tennis, skiing, antiques. *Club:* Hurlingham.

WINDER, Robert James; writer; Section Editor, Independent on Sunday, 1998–2001; *b* 26 Sept. 1959; *s* of Herbert James Winder and Mary Nina (*née* Dalby); *m* 1989, Hermione Davies; two *s*. *Educ:* Bradfield Coll.; St Catherine's Coll., Oxford (BA English). Euromoney Publications, 1982–86; Dep. Lit. Ed., 1986–89, Lit. Ed., 1989–95, The Independent; Dep. Ed., Granta Publications, 1996–98. *Publications:* No Admission, 1988; The Marriage of Time and Convenience, 1994; Hell for Leather, 1996; Bloody Foreigners, 2004; The Final Act of Mr Shakespeare, 2010; Open Secrets, 2010; The Little Wonder: 150 years of Wisden, 2013; Half-Time: the glorious summer of 1934, 2015. *Recreations:* reading, writing, walking, talking, etc. *Address:* 125 Elgin Crescent, W11 2JH.

WINDHAM, William Ashe Dymoke; Chairman, Skelmersdale Development Corporation, 1979–85; (Deputy Chairman, 1977); *b* 2 April 1926; *s* of late Lt-Col Henry Steuart Windham and Marjory Russell Dymock; *m* 1956, Alison Audrey, *d* of late Maj. P. P. Curtis, MC and Ellinor Kidston; two *s* one *d*. *Educ:* Bedford Sch.; Christ's Coll., Cambridge (schol.; University prize; MA). Gen. Manager, Runcorn Div., Arthur Guinness Son & Co. (GB), 1972–84. Mem., Runcorn Develt Corp., 1975–77. Steward, Henley Royal Regatta, 1953– (Mem. Cttee of Mgt, 1972–94; Sen. Steward, 2002–); rowed for: winning Cambridge crews, 1947 and 1951; England, Empire Games, 1950; GB, European Championships, 1950 and 1951 (Gold Medal); Olympic Games, 1952. High Sheriff, Powys, 1996. *Recreations:* shooting, fishing, carpentry, gardening. *Clubs:* Hawks (Cambridge); Leander (Henley) (Pres., 1993–98).

WINDLE, Prof. Alan Hardwick, FRS 1997; FIMMM, FInstP; Professor of Materials Science, University of Cambridge, 1992–2009, now Emeritus; Fellow, Trinity College, Cambridge, since 1978; Director, Pfizer Institute for Pharmaceutical Materials Science, since 2005; *b* 20 June 1942; *s* of Stuart George Windle and Myrtle Lillian (*née* Povey); *m* 1968, Janet Susan Carr; one *s* three *d*. *Educ:* Whitgift Sch.; Imperial Coll., London (BSc Eng. 1963; ARSM 1963); Trinity Coll., Cambridge (PhD 1966). FIMMM (FIM 1992); FInstP 1997. Imperial College, University of London: ICI Res. Fellow, 1966–67; Lectr in Metallurgy, 1967–75; Cambridge University: Lectr in Metallurgy and Materials Sci., 1975–92; Hd of Dept of Materials Sci. and Metallurgy, 1996–2001; Trinity College, Cambridge: Lectr and Dir of Studies in Natural Scis, 1978–92; Tutor, 1983–91. Exec. Dir, Cambridge-MIT Inst., 2000–03. Vis. Prof., N Carolina State Univ., 1980. Vice-Pres., Inst. of Materials, 2001. Comr, Royal Commn for Exhibition of 1851, 2001–10. Chm. Trustees, Mission Aviation Fellowship Europe, 2001–03. Gov., Whitgift Foundn, 1997–2001. Fellow, APS, 2001. Foreign Fellow, Nat. Acad. of Scis, India, 2007. Bessemer Medal, Imperial Coll., 1963; Silver Medal, RSA, 1963; Rosenhain Medal and Prize, Inst. Metals, 1987; Swinburne Medal and Prize, PRI, 1992; Founders' Prize, Polymer Physics Gp, Inst. of Physics, RSC and IMMM, 2007; Armourers' and Brasiers' Co. Prize, Royal Soc., 2007. *Publications:* A First Course in Crystallography, 1978; (with A. M. Donald) Liquid Crystalline Polymers, 1992, (with A. M. Donald and S. Hanna) 2nd edn 2006; contribs to learned jls mainly on polymer morphology, polymer glasses, polymer diffusion, liquid crystalline polymers, polymer modelling and the science and technology of carbon nanotubes. *Recreation:* flying light aircraft. *Address:* Department of Materials Science and Metallurgy, 27 Charles Babbage Road, Cambridge CB3 0FS. *T:* (01223) 334321.

WINDLE, Terence Leslie William, CBE 1991; Director, Directorate General for Agriculture, European Commission, 1980–91; *b* 15 Jan. 1926; *s* of Joseph William Windle and Dorothy Windle (*née* Haigh); *m* 1957, Joy Winifred Shield; one *s* two *d*. *Educ:* Gonville and Caius College, Cambridge (MA); London University (Colonial Course). Colonial/HMOCS: Nigeria, 1951–59; Zambia, 1959–69 (Under Sec., Min. of Natural Resources and Tourism); Home Civil Service, MAFF, 1969–73; Commn of EC, 1973–91. *Address:* rue du Fond Agny 20, 1380 Lasne, Belgium. *T:* (2) 6334410.

WINDLESHAM, 4th Baron *cr* 1937; **James Rupert Hennessy;** *b* London, 9 Nov. 1968; *o s* of 3rd Baron Windlesham, CVO, OBE and Prudence (*d* 1986), *d* of Lt-Col Rupert T. W. Glynn; *S* father, 2010; *m* 2004, Deborah Jane Wallace; one *s*. *Educ:* Eton Coll.; Bristol Univ. Hambros Bank Ltd, 1991–98; New Boston Partners Ltd, 1998–2007; MVP Asset Management, 2008–. *Recreations:* sport, reading. *Heir: s* Hon. George Rupert James Hennessy, *b* 19 Nov. 2006. *Address:* 65 Fulham Park Gardens, SW6 4LB. *T:* (020) 7736 0804. *E:* lord@windlesham.net. *Club:* White's.

WINDSOR, Viscount; Ivor Edward Other Windsor-Clive; *b* 19 Nov. 1951; *s* and *heir* of 3rd Earl of Plymouth, *qv*; *m* 1979, Caroline, *d* of Frederick Nettlefold and late Hon. Mrs Juliana Roberts; three *s* one *d*. *Educ:* Harrow; Royal Agricl Coll., Cirencester. Co-founder, and Dir, Centre for the Study of Modern Art, 1973. Chairman: Earl of Plymouth Estates Ltd, 1997–; Ludlow Food Centre Ltd, 2006–. Chm., Heart of England Reg., HHA, 1996–2001. FRSA. *Recreation:* cricket. *Heir: s* Hon. Robert Other Ivor Windsor-Clive, *b* 25 March 1981. *Address:* Oakly Park, Ludlow, Shropshire SY8 2JW; Flat 3, 6 Oakley Street, SW3 5NN. *Club:* Brooks's.

WINDSOR, Dean of; *see* Conner, Rt Rev. D. J.

WINDSOR, Barbara Anne, MBE 2000; actress; *b* 6 Aug. 1937; *d* of John Deeks and Rose Deeks (*née* Ellis). *Educ:* Our Lady's Convent, London; Aida Foster Stage Sch. *Theatre includes:* Love from Judy, Palace; Fings Ain't Wot They Used T' Be, Garrick, 1959; Oh What a Lovely War, NY; Come Spy with Me, Whitehall; Sing a Rude Song, Garrick; The Threepenny Opera, Prince of Wales, 1972; The Owl and the Pussycat; Carry on London, Victoria Palace; A Merry Whiff of Windsor (one women show, UK and world tour); Twelfth Night, Chichester; Calamity Jane (UK tour); Entertaining Mr Sloane, Lyric, Hammersmith, 1981; The Mating Game; Guys and Dolls (tour). *Television includes:* The Rag Trade, 1961–63; Carry on Laughing, 1975; Worzel Gummidge, 1979; Peggy Mitchell in EastEnders, 1994–2003, 2005–10. *Films include:* Lost, 1956; Too Hot to Handle, 1959; Flame in the Street, 1961; On the Fiddle, 1961; Sparrers Can't Sing, 1963; Crooks in Cloisters, 1963; Carry on Spying, 1964; A Study in Terror, 1965; Carry on Doctor, 1968; Carry on Camping, Hair of the Dog, Chitty Chitty Bang Bang, 1969; Carry on Girls, 1971; The Boyfriend, 1971; Carry on Dick, 1974; Comrades, 1987; Double Vision; Alice in Wonderland, 2010. *Radio series:* Barbara Windsor's Ladies of Song, 2012. Numerous albums and radio performances. Freeman, City of London, 2010. Variety Club of GB Award, 1998; Best Actress, Manchester Evening News Awards, 1998; Best Actress, Nat. Soap Awards, 1999; RADAR People of the Year Award, 1999; BBC Hall of Fame Award, 2000; Gold Badge of Merit, BASCA, 2000; Outstanding Contrib. to Entertainment Award, Inside Soap, 2001. *Publications:* Laughter and Tears of a Cockney Sparrow; All of Me: my extraordinary life (autobiog.), 2000. *Address:* c/o Burnett Crowther Ltd, 3 Clifford Street, W1S 2LF.

WINDSOR, Dr Colin George, FRS 1995; FInstP, FInstNDT; Consultant: Culham Centre for Fusion Energy (formerly United Kingdom Atomic Energy Authority, Fusion), since 1998; Tokamak Energy Ltd, since 2013; *b* 28 June 1938; *s* of late George Thomas Macdonald Windsor and Mabel (*née* Rayment); *m* 1st, 1963, Margaret Lee (marr. diss. 2005); one *s* two *d*; 2nd, 2005, Mo Watkins. *Educ:* Beckenham Grammar Sch.; Magdalen Coll., Oxford (BA 1st Cl. Hons Physics; DPhil 1963). FInstP 1975; FInstNDT 1993. Magnetic resonance research, Clarendon Lab., Oxford, 1963; Res. Fellow, Yale Univ., 1964; Neutron scattering research, Harwell, 1964–96; Sen. Scientist, Nat. Non-Destructive Testing Centre, AEA Technology, 1988–96; Programme Area Manager, UKAEA, Fusion, 1996–98; Sen. Consultant, Penop, 1998–2001. Fellow: Japanese Soc. for Promotion of Sci., 1980; Neural Network Applications, 1987–. Hon. Prof. of Physics, Birmingham Univ., 1990. *Publications:* Pulsed Neutron Scattering, 1981; Four Computer Models, 1982; (ed jtly) Solid State Science, Past, Present and Predicted, 1987; contrib. to learned jls. *Recreations:* cycling to work, table tennis, sketching, singing, piano, organ, composing. *Address:* D3, Culham Laboratory, Abingdon, Oxon OX14 3DB. *T:* (01235) 466311. *E:* colin.windsor@ccfe.org.uk. *W:* freespace.virgin.net/colin.windsor; (home) 116 New Road, East Hagbourne, Oxon OX11 9LD. *Club:* Oxford Naturist (Oxford).

WINDSOR, Ven. (Julie) Fiona; Archdeacon of Horsham, since 2014; *b* 2 Sept. 1959; *d* of Rev. Howell Jones and Margaret Jones; *m* 1979, Robin Windsor; one *s* one *d*. *Educ:* Ridley Hall, Cambridge. Ordained deacon, 2000, priest, 2001; Curate, Chertsey, 2000–04; Team

Vicar, 2004–08, Team Rector, 2008–14, St Peter, Papworth; Bishop's Advr on Women's Ministry, Dio. of Ely, 2012–14. Hon. Canon, Ely Cathedral, 2012–14. *Address:* c/o Diocesan Church House, 211 New Church Road, Hove BN3 4ED.

WINDSOR-CLIVE, family name of **Earl of Plymouth.**

WINEGARTEN, Jonathan Isaac; Chief Master of the Senior (formerly Supreme) Court, Chancery Division, 1998–2013 (a Master, 1991–2013); *b* 10 Dec. 1944; *s* of late Moshe Winegarten and Hannah Deborah Winegarten (*née* Cohen). *Educ:* Hasmonean Grammar Sch., Hendon (Head Boy); Gateshead Yeshiva; University Coll. London (LLB Hons 1967); Slabodka Yeshiva, Israel. Chm., Yavneh, 1966. Winston Churchill Award and called to the Bar, Middle Temple, 1969, *ad eundem* Lincoln's Inn, 1972 (Bencher, 1990); in practice, Chancery Bar, 1970–91. Accredited Civil and Commercial Mediator, ADR Gp, 2014. Member: Chancery Bar Assoc. Cttee, 1982, 1983; Supreme Court Procedure Cttee, 1992–2000; Judges' Council of England and Wales, 2008–12; Non-Contentious Probate Rules Cttee, 2009–; Adv. Panel, Chancery Modernisation Review, 2013. Member: Bd of Deputies, 1973–79; Council, Jews' Coll., 1989–2000; Elder, Fedn of Synagogues, 2015– (Vice Pres., 1989–2001). Pres., Shomrei Hadath Synagogue, 1982–2003 (Hon. Life Pres., 2004). Freeman, City of London, 1992. Adv. Editor, Atkin's Court Forms, 1993–2015; Editor: Tristram and Coote's Probate Practice, 1995–2013; Civil Procedure (The White Book), 1999–2013. *Publications:* (ed) Collected works of Rabbi Z. H. Ferber (11 vols), 1983–92; (jtly) Modernising the Civil Courts: the judges' requirements, 2001. *Recreations:* violin playing, painting, esp. glass painting and etching, music, reading, publishing. *Address:* Radcliffe Chambers, 11 New Square, Lincoln's Inn, WC2A 3QB. *E:* clerks@radcliffechambers.com.

WINEMAN, Vivian; President, Board of Deputies of British Jews, 2009–15; Chairman, Mildmay Properties Ltd, since 2010; *b* London, 14 Feb. 1950; *s* of Joseph and Devorah Wineman; *m* 1994, Naomi Helen Greenberg; one *s* two *d*. *Educ:* City of London Sch.; Kerem B'Yavneh Rabbinical Acad.; Gonville and Caius Coll., Cambridge (BA 1971; MA 1975). Admitted solicitor, 1975; Articled clerk, 1973–75, Asst Solicitor, 1975–77, Berwin Leighton; Solicitor, 1977–78, Partner, 1978–81, Clintons; Founder Partner, David Wineman, 1981–2008; DWFM Beckman Solicitors: Partner, 2008–10; Consultant, 2010–11. Sen. Vice Pres., Bd of Deputies of British Jews, 2006–09; Vice Pres., Eur. Jewish Congress, 2009–12 (Chair Council, 2012–); Chair, Council of Members, Jewish Leadership Council, 2009–. Vice Chair, 2007–13, Co-Chair, 2013–, Inter Faith Network for UK; Mem., Adv. Bd, Three Faiths Forum, 2007–. Chairman: British Friends Peace Now, 1987–89; New Israel Fund UK, 1993–95. Dir, Conference for Jewish Material Claims against Germany, 2012– (Mem., Goodwill Guidelines Cttee, 2011–13; Mem., Governance Panel, 2014–). Vice Pres., World Jewish Congress, 2013–. Trustee, Holocaust Meml Day Trust, 2011–. Hon. Legal Counsel, High Premium Gp of Lloyds of London, 2004–. *Publications:* Contracts (Rights of Third Parties) Act 1999, 2001. *Recreations:* music, cycling, mountain walking. *Address:* 76 Meadway, NW11 6QH. *Club:* Royal Automobile.

WINFIELD, Rev. Canon Flora Jane Louise; DL; Archbishop of Canterbury's Secretary for Anglican Relations, since 2007; Priest-in-charge, St Mary-at-Hill, City of London, since 2008; Anglican Communion Representative to United Nations, Geneva, since 2014; *m* 1985, Rev. Canon Jonathan Robin Blanning Gough, *qv*. *Educ:* Portsmouth High Sch. for Girls, GPDST; St David's Univ. Coll., Lampeter (BA Hons 1985); Ripon Coll., Cuddesdon, Oxford (Cert. Theol. 1989); Westminster Coll., Oxford (Dip. Applied Theol. 1996). Lay Worker, Christ Church Abbeydale, Glos, 1986–87; ordained deacon, 1989, priest, 1994; Parish Deacon, Stantonbury and Willen Ecumenical Parish, Milton Keynes, 1989–92; County Ecumenical Officer, Glos, 1992–94; Chaplain and Tutor, Mansfield Coll., Oxford, 1994–97; Sec. for Local Unity, and Advr to House of Bishops, C of E Archbishop's Council, 1997–2002; Canon Residentiary, Winchester Cathedral, 2002–05, now Canon Emerita. Asst Sec. Gen., 2005–06, Special Advr, 2006–, World Conference of Religions for Peace; Hon. Chaplain, St Ethelburga's Centre for Reconciliation and Peace, 2008–13 (Special Advr, 2005–08); Sec. for Internat. Affairs, Churches Together in Britain and Ireland, 2006–09. Mem., Faith and Order Adv. Gp, C of E, 1991–2005. Chaplain: to HM Forces (V), 1997–; to Farriers' Co., 2004–; to Princess Royal's Volunteer Corps, 2007–. Trustee: St Andrew's Trust, 2003–; Community of St Mary the Virgin, Wantage, 2013–. Gov., Sch. of St Helen and St Katharine, Abingdon, 1993–2009. FRSA 1998. DL Gtr London, 2011. Hon. DD Virginia Theol Seminary, 2010. Dame, Order of Francis (First Class). *Publications:* (with Elizabeth Welch) Travelling Together: a handbook on local ecumenical partnerships, 1995; Releasing Energy: how Methodists and Anglicans can grow together, 2000; Growing Together: working for unity locally, 2002; Working with Partner Churches in the Diocese: a handbook for new Bishops, 2002; It's the Thought that Counts in Unpacking the Gift: Anglican resources for theological reflection on the gift of authority, 2003; contributed to: European Women's Experience in the Church, 1991; Reconciliation in Religion and Society, 1994; Community, Unity, Communion: essays in honour of Mary Tanner, 1998; The Table of God's Generosity in Voices of this Calling: experiences of the first generation of woman priests, 2002; articles in Midstream, Ecumenical Review. *Recreations:* country pursuits, gardening, food, music. *Address:* St Andrew's House, 16 Tavistock Crescent, W11 1BA. *Club:* Nikæan.

WINFIELD, Susan Margaret, OBE 2003; Lord-Lieutenant, Tyne and Wear, since 2015; *b* Sunderland, 18 May 1947; *d* of Richard Foster Heron and Margaret Marriott Heron; *m* 1974, Anthony Charles Winfield; one *s* one *d*. *Educ:* Central Newcastle High Sch.; Univ. of Newcastle upon Tyne (LLB 1968); Univ. of Nottingham (DipASS 1969). Durham Probation Service: Probation Officer, 1970–75; Sen. Probation Officer, 1975–82; Asst Chief Probation Officer, 1982–86; Northumbria Probation Service: Asst Chief Probation Officer, 1986–88; Dep. Chief Probation Officer and Dir of Service Delivery, 1988–2002; Chair, Sunderland Teaching PCT, 2002–13. Mem., Home Sec.'s Policy Adv. Cttee on Sexual Offences, 1976–86. Trustee and Manager, and Vice Chair, Bd of Managers, Aycliffe Young People's Centre, Darlington, 1988–2005. Trustee: Derwent Initiative, 1993–; Helix Arts, 2000–09; Community Foundn for Tyne and Wear and Northumberland, 2006–15 (Vice Pres., 2015–). High Sheriff Tyne and Wear, 2010–11. *Publications:* (contrib.) The Golden Age of Probation, 2014. *Recreations:* gardening, walking, singing, tennis, golf. *Club:* Northern Counties (Newcastle).

WINFIELD, William Richard, MA; Headmaster, Mill Hill School, 1995–2007; *b* 19 March 1947; *s* of William Arthur and Paula Constance Winfield; *m* 1986, Margaret Ruth Richards; one *s* one *d*. *Educ:* William Ellis Sch.; Royal Acad. of Music (Jun. Exhibnr); Clare Coll., Cambridge (BA Mod. and Med. Langs 1968; PGCE 1970; MA 1972). Lectr, Maison de l'Europe, Bordeaux, 1968–69; Mill Hill School: Asst Master, 1970–75; Head of Modern Langs, 1975–87; Dir of Studies, 1982–92; Dep. Headmaster, 1992–95. Chief Examr, French Studies, JMB, 1980–87. Governor: Keble Sch., 1999–2009; Berkhamsted Sch. (formerly Berkhamsted Collegiate Sch.), 2007–11. *Publications:* (jtly) Vocational French, 1985; contribs to jls on Section Bilingue and intensive language teaching. *Recreations:* playing chamber music, hill walking. *Address:* The Old School House, Church Road, Slapton, Leighton Buzzard LU7 9BX.

WINGATE, Rev. Canon Andrew David Carlile, OBE 2011; PhD; Director of Inter-Faith Relations (formerly Director of Ministry and Training and Bishop's Inter-Faith Adviser), Diocese of Leicester, 2000–10 (Co-ordinator of Lay Training, 2000–04); Director, St Philip's Centre for Study and Engagement in a Multifaith Society, Leicester, 2004–10; Canon Theologian of Leicester Cathedral, since 2000; Chaplain to the Queen, 2007–14; *b* 2 Aug. 1944; *s* of late Rev. Canon David Hugh Wingate and Olga Wingate; *m* 1967, Angela Beever; one *s* two *d*. *Educ:* Worcester Coll., Oxford (BA 1st class, MA, MPhil); Lincoln Theol Coll.; Univ. of Birmingham (PhD 1995). Asst Master, King Edward's Sch., Birmingham, 1968–70; ordained deacon, 1972, priest, 1973; Asst Curate, Halesowen Parish Church, 1972–75; Lectr, Tamil Nadu Theol Seminary, Madurai, S India, 1975–82; Principal: W Midlands Ministerial Training Course, Queen's Coll., Birmingham, 1982–90; United Coll. of the Ascension, Selly Oak, Birmingham, 1990–2000. Hon. Lectr in Theol., Univ. of Birmingham, 1998–2009; Hon. Lectr in Inter-Religious Relations, De Montfort Univ., 2009–. Hon. DArts De Montfort, 2007. *Publications:* Encounter in the Spirit: Muslim Christian dialogue in practice, 1988, 2nd edn 1991; The Church and Conversion, 1997; (ed) Anglicanism: a global communion, 1998; Does Theological Education Make a Difference?, 1999; Free to Be, 2002; Celebrating Difference: staying faithful - how to live in a multifaith world, 2005; (ed) Discipleship and Dialogue: new frontiers in interfaith engagement, 2013; The Meeting of Opposites? Hindus and Christians in the West, 2014; articles in theol jls. *Recreations:* tennis, swimming, golf, painting, mountain walking. *Address:* 23 Roundhill Road, Evington, Leicester LE5 5RJ.

WINGATE, Captain Sir Miles (Buckley), KCVO 1982; FNI; Deputy Master and Chairman of the Board of Trinity House, London, 1976–88, retired; *b* 17 May 1923; *s* of Terrence Wingate and Edith Wingate; *m* 1947, Alicia Forbes Philip; three *d*. *Educ:* Taunton Grammar Sch.; Southampton and Prior Park Coll., Somerset. Master Mariner. Apprenticed to Royal Mail Lines Ltd, 1939; first Comd, 1957; elected to Bd of Trinity House, 1968. Commonwealth War Graves Comr, 1986–91. Vice-President: Seamen's Hosp. Soc., 1980–; Royal Alfred Seafarers Soc., 1980–; British Maritime Charitable Foundn, 1983–; Pres., Internat. Assoc. of Lighthouse Authorities, 1985–88 (Vice-Pres., 1980–85); Dep. Chm., Gen. Council, King George's Fund for Sailors, 1983–93; Mem., Cttee of Management, RNLI, 1976–98; Council, Missions to Seamen, 1982–93. Liveryman: Hon. Co. of Master Mariners, 1970–; Shipwrights' Co., 1977–90; Freeman, Watermen and Lightermen's Co., 1984. Governor, Pangbourne Coll., 1982–91. *Recreation:* golf. *Address:* Trinity House, Tower Hill, EC3N 4DH. *T:* (020) 7481 6900.

WINGFIELD, family name of **Viscount Powerscourt.**

WINGFIELD, Katrina Elizabeth; Consultant, Penningtons Manches (formerly Penningtons Solicitors) LLP, since 2013 (Partner, 2000–13); *b* Malvern, Worcs, 27 Jan. 1948; *d* of Frederick Wingfield and Elizabeth Wingfield; *m* 1983, Gareth Julian. *Educ:* Worcester Grammar Sch. for Girls; Univ. of Exeter (LLB). Admitted solicitor, 1974; Solicitor, 1974–77, Partner, 1977–2000, Walker Martineau Solicitors. Tribunal Judge, Mental Health Tribunal, 1994–. Chair, Appeal Panel: Specialist Trng Authy of Royal Medical Colls, 1998–2005; PMETB, 2005–10; Dir, Appeals, GDC, 2004–; Chm., Registration and Certification Appeals, GMC, 2010–. Chm., Regulatory Bd, Assoc. of Chartered Certified Accountants, 2008–14. *Recreations:* riding, swimming, sailing, walking the dog. *Address:* Penningtons Manches LLP, Abacus House, 33 Gutter Lane, EC2V 8AR. *T:* (020) 7457 3000, *Fax:* (020) 7457 3240. *E:* katrina.wingfield@penningtons.co.uk.

WINGHAM, Prof. Duncan John, PhD; Chief Executive, Natural Environment Research Council, since 2012; *b* 12 Oct. 1957; *s* of Philip and Margaret Wingham; *m* 1987, Ivana Azanjac; one *d*. *Educ:* City of Bath Boys' Sch.; Univ. of Leeds (BSc Hons Phys 1979); Univ. of Bath (PhD 1985). Res. Seismologist, Seismograph Service Ltd, Kent, 1979–81; Res. Officer, Dept of Phys, Univ. of Bath, 1981–84; University College London: Res. Associate, Mullard Space Sci. Lab., 1985–86; Lectr, 1986–89, Sen. Lectr, 1989–93, Dept of Electronic and Electrical Engrg; Sen. Lectr, 1993–96, Prof. of Climate Phys, 1996–2005, Dept of Space and Climate Phys; Prof. and Hd, Dept of Earth Scis, 2005–12, now Hon. Prof.; Dir, NERC Centre for Polar Observation and Modelling, 2001–08. Lead Investigator, CryoSat, then CryoSat-2 Missions, ESA, 1999–2011. Chairman: Sci. and Innovation Bd, NERC, 2007–11; Steering Bd, UK Collaborative on Develt Scis, 2012–. *Publications:* articles in Nature, Science, Geophysical Res. Letters, Jl of Geophys Res., Jl of Glaciology, Earth & Planetary Sci. Letters, etc. *Address:* Natural Environment Research Council, Polaris House, North Star Avenue, Swindon SN2 1EU.

WINKELMAN, Joseph William, PPRE (RE 1982; ARE 1979); free-lance painter-printmaker, since 1971; President, Royal Society of Painter-Printmakers (formerly Royal Society of Painter-Etchers and Engravers), 1989–95; *b* 20 Sept. 1941; *s* of George William Winkelman and Cleo Lucretia (*née* Harness); *m* 1969, Harriet Lowell Belin; two *d*. *Educ:* Univ. of the South, Sewanee, Tenn (BA English 1964); Wharton School of Finance, Univ. of Pennsylvania; Ruskin Sch. of Drawing; Univ. of Oxford (Cert. of Fine Art 1971). Royal Society of Painter-Etchers and Engravers: Hon. Sec., 1982; Vice-Pres., 1986; Fellow, Printmakers' Council of GB, 1978 (Hon. Fellow, 1988). Former tutor for: Sch. of Architecture, Oxford Polytechnic; Ruskin Sch. of Drawing, Oxford Univ.; Dept for External Studies, Oxford Univ. Artist in Residence, St John's Coll., Oxford, 2004. Work in public collections including: Tate Gall.; V&A; Mus. of London; Science Mus.; London Guildhall Liby; Royal Collection; Nat. Mus. of Wales; Ashmolean Mus., Oxford; Fitzwilliam Mus., Cambridge; Russian State Collection; Musée d'Art Contemporain, Chamalières; Lahti Museum, Finland; Iowa City Art Mus., USA; Bodleian Liby, Oxford; BL; L of C. Mem., Bd of Dirs, Bankside Gall., London, 2002–06. Chm., Oxford Art Soc., 1987–93 (Vice Pres., 1994–). Chm., Nat. Assoc. of Blood Donors, 1994–95. Gov., Windmill First Sch., Headington, Oxford, 1994–98. RBA, 1980–82; RWA, 1990–2006 (ARWA 1983). Hon. RWS 1997. *Publications:* (illustrated) Sewanee Poems, by Richard Tillinghast, 2010. *Recreations:* gardening, theatre, hill walking. *Address:* The Hermitage, 69 Old High Street, Headington, Oxford OX3 9HT. *T:* (01865) 762839. *E:* joe@winkelman.co.uk. *W:* www.winkelman.co.uk. *Club:* Oxford University Yacht.

WINKETT, Rev. Canon Lucy Clare; Rector, St James's, Piccadilly, since 2010; *b* 8 Jan. 1968; *d* of Bryan and Cecilia Winkett. *Educ:* Dr Challoner's High Sch.; Selwyn Coll., Cambridge (BA (Hons) Hist. 1990); RCM (ARCM 1992); Queen's Coll., Birmingham (BD 1994). Ordained deacon, 1995, priest, 1996; Asst Curate, St Michael and All Angels, Manor Park, 1995–97; St Paul's Cathedral: Minor Canon, 1997–2003; Residentiary Canon and Precentor, 2003–10. Chm. of Govs, City Acad. *Publications:* Our Sound is Our Wound, 2010. *Recreations:* reading, singing, cycling. *Address:* St James's Church, 197 Piccadilly, W1J 9LL. *T:* (020) 7734 4511.

WINKLEMAN, Claudia; Host: The Arts Show with Claudia Winkleman, BBC Radio 2, since 2008; Film Show, BBC Television, since 2010; *b* London, 15 Jan. 1972; *d* of Barry Winkleman and Eve Pollard, *qv*; *m* 2000, Kris Thykier; two *s* one *d*. *Educ:* City of London Sch. for Girls; New Hall, Cambridge (BA Hons Hist. of Art 1993). Television includes: host or presenter: Fanorama, 2001–02; Comic Relief Does Fame Academy, 2003–07; Strictly Come Dancing: It Takes Two, 2004–10; Hell's Kitchen, 2009; Let's Dance for Sport Relief, 2009–10; Strictly Come Dancing: The Results, 2010–; The Great British Sewing Bee, 2013–; Strictly Come Dancing, 2014–. *Recreations:* sleeping, cuddling and bothering our children.

WINKLEY, Sir David (Ross), Kt 1999; DPhil; Founder and President, National Primary Trust, 1986–2006; *b* 30 Nov. 1941; *s* of late Donald Joseph Winkley and Winifred Mary Winkley; *m* 1967, Dr Linda Mary Holland; one *s* one *d*. *Educ:* King Edward's Sch., Birmingham; Selwyn Coll., Cambridge (MA); Wadham Coll., Oxford (DPhil 1975; Hon. Fellow 2006). Mem., Centre for Contemporary Cultural Studies, Univ. of Birmingham, 1965; Dep. Head, Perry Common Sch., 1968–71; Head, Grove Primary Sch., 1974–97.

Fellow, Nuffield Coll., Oxford, 1981–82. Vis. Prof., Univ. of Huddersfield, 2003–; Hon. Professor: Univ. of Birmingham, 1999–; Univ. of Warwick, 2004–. Member: CATE, 1985–90; Stevenson Cttee on Information and Communication Technol., 1996. Founder and Chairman: Birmingham Children's Community Venture, 1967–; Health Exchange, 2008–; Founder, Children's Univ., 1992. DLitt Birmingham, 1999; DUniv UCE, 2000. *Publications:* Diplomats and Detectives, 1986; Handsworth Revolution, 2002; The Philosophy Group, 2010; Life Cycle, 2012; The Inspector, 2015; numerous academic articles on educational and philosophical issues. *Recreations:* reading, music, piano playing, writing fiction.

WINKWORTH-SMITH, (Michael) John; mediator; Regional Managing Partner, Leeds Office, Dibb Lupton Alsop (formerly Dibb Lupton Broomhead), 1995–99; *b* 4 May 1944; *s* of late Frank Winkworth-Smith and Marjorie Beaumont Winkworth-Smith (*née* Smith); *m* 1974, Sarah Elisabeth Jackson; two *s* (one *d* decd). *Educ:* Ermysted's Grammar Sch., Skipton. Admitted solicitor, 1970; Partner, Broomhead Wightman & Reed, later Dibb Lupton Broomhead, then Dibb Lupton Alsop, 1972–99; Man. Partner, Birmingham Office, 1993–95. Treas., Royal Sheffield Instn for the Blind, 1972–78; Mem., Sheffield CVS, 1978–90; Dir, Broomgrove Trust, 1980–92; Chairman: Taptonholme Ltd, 1984–2000; Champion Hse, Derby Diocesan Youth Centre, 1988–93. Director: CEDR, 1991–99; Japan Adv. Services Ltd, 1991–97; Consensus Mediation Ltd, 2004–11. Trustee, Sheffield Royal Soc. for the Blind, 2003–14. FRSA 1997. *Recreations:* family, farming, researching local history. *Address:* Churchdale Farm, Ashford-in-the-Water, Bakewell, Derbys DE45 1NX. *T:* (01629) 640912.

WINN, family name of **Baron St Oswald**.

WINN, Allan Kendal, FRAeS; Director and Chief Executive Officer, Brooklands Museum, since 2003; *b* 19 March 1950; *s* of Atkinson Winn and Janet Winn; *m* 1994, Jacqueline Christina Worsley; one step *s* one step *d*. *Educ:* Nelson Coll., NZ; Univ. of Canterbury, Christchurch, NZ (BE(Mech), Diploma in Journalism). FRAeS 1996. Technical Editor, Consulting Engineer, 1975–77; Technical Editor, Editor, Man. Editor, Engineering Today, later New Technology, 1977–85; Editor: Commercial Motor, 1985–88; Flight International, 1989–98; Publisher, Flight International and Airline Business, 1998–2003. Chm., Assoc. of Friends of Brooklands Mus., 1995–2003. Liveryman: Hon. Co. of Air Pilots (formerly GAPAN), 1999–; Coachmakers' and Coach Harness Makers' Co., 2008–. Sir Peter Masefield Gold Medal, British Assoc. Aviation Consultants, 2006; Jeffrey Quill Medal, The Air League, 2014. *Recreation:* vintage motor vehicles. *Address:* Brooklands Museum, Brooklands Road, Weybridge, Surrey KT13 0QN. *T:* (01932) 857381; 39 Heathcote, Tadworth, Surrey KT20 5TH. *T:* (01737) 362760. *Clubs:* Aviation of UK (Chm., 1991–97), Vintage Sports Car, Bentley Drivers.

WINNICK, David Julian; MP (Lab) Walsall North, since 1979; *b* Brighton, 26 June 1933; *s* of late Eugene and Rose Winnick; one *s*; *m* 1968, Bengi Rona (marr. diss.), *d* of Tarik and Zeynep Rona. *Educ:* secondary school; London Sch. of Economics (Dip. in Social Admin). Army National Service, 1951–53. Branch Secretary, Clerical and Administrative Workers' Union, 1956–62 (later APEX GMB; Mem. Exec. Council, 1978–88, Vice-Pres., 1983–88); Advertisement Manager, Tribune, 1963–66; employed by UKIAS, 1970–79 (Chm., 1984–90). Member: Willesden Borough Council, 1959–64; London Borough of Brent Council, 1964–66 (Chair, Children Cttee, 1965–66). Contested (Lab) Harwich, 1964; MP (Lab) Croydon South, 1966–70; contested (Lab): Croydon Central, Oct. 1974; Walsall N, Nov. 1976. Member: Select Cttee on the Environment, 1979–83; Home Affairs Cttee, 1983–87, 1997–; Select Cttee on Procedure, 1989–97; Co-Chm., British-Irish Inter-Parly Body, 1997–2005 (Vice-Chm., 1993–97). *Recreations:* walking, cinema, theatre, reading. *Address:* House of Commons, SW1A 0AA.

WINNIFRITH, Charles Boniface, CB 1998; Clerk of Committees, House of Commons, 1995–2001; *b* 12 May 1936; *s* of Sir John Winnifrith, KCB and late Lesbia Margaret Winnifrith; *m* 1st, 1962, Josephine Poile, MBE (*d* 1991); one *s* two *d*; 2nd, 1993, Sandra (*née* Stewart). *Educ:* Tonbridge Sch.; Christ Church, Oxford (MA). 2nd Lieut, RAEC, 1958–60. Joined Dept of the Clerk of the House of Commons, 1960; Second Clerk of Select Cttees, 1983; Clerk of Select Cttees, 1987; Principal Clerk of the Table Office, 1989. Mem., General Synod of C of E, 1970–90. Member: Soc. of Clerks-at-the-Table in Commonwealth Parlts, 1989–; Assoc. of Secs Gen. of Parlts, 1996–. Governor, Ashford Sch., Kent, 1973–93. *Recreations:* cricket, Rugby, American soap opera. *Address:* Gale Lodge Farm, Long Buckby, Northants NN6 7PH. *T:* (01604) 770396. *Club:* MCC.

WINNINGTON, Sir Anthony (Edward), 7th Bt *cr* 1755, of Stanford Court, Worcestershire; *b* 13 May 1948; *s* of Col Thomas Foley Churchill Winnington, MBE and Lady Betty Marjorie Anson, *d* of 4th Earl of Lichfield; *S* uncle, 2003; *m* 1st, 1978, Karyn (marr. diss. 2007), *d* of F. H. Kettles; one *s* two *d*; 2nd, 2009, Alexandra Fawke, *d* of late Alexander B. MacColl. *Educ:* Eton. FCSI. High Sheriff, Worcs, 2015–16. *Heir:* *s* Edward Alan Winnington, *b* 15 Nov. 1987. *E:* winnington@aol.com. *Clubs:* Boodle's, Hurlingham.

WINNINGTON-INGRAM, Edward John; Managing Director, Mail Newspapers Plc (formerly Associated Newspapers Group), 1986–89, retired; *b* 20 April 1926; *s* of Rev. Preb. Edward Francis and Gladys Winnington-Ingram; *m* 1st, 1953, Shirley Lamotte (marr. diss. 1968); two *s*; 2nd, 1973, Elizabeth Linda Few Brown. *Educ:* Shrewsbury; Keble Coll., Oxford (BA). Served RN (Sub-Lieut), 1944–47. Joined Associated Newspapers, 1949; Circulation Manager, Daily Mail, 1960–65; Gen. Manager, Daily Mail Manchester, 1965–70; Dir, Associated Newspapers, 1971; Managing Director: Harmsworth Publishing, 1973; Mail on Sunday, 1982; Dir, Associated Newspapers Holdings, 1983; non-executive Director: NAAFI, 1987–93; Burlington Gp, 1988–92; Dir, Oxford Diocesan Pubns, 2000–08. *Recreations:* shooting, golf, Byzantine history, music, defending the 1662 Prayer Book. *Address:* Old Manor Farm, Cottisford, Brackley, Northants NN13 5SW. *T:* (01280) 848367. *Club:* Buck's.

WINSER, Ellen; *see* Winser, M. E.

WINSER, Kim Lesley, OBE 2006; Founder and Chief Executive Officer, Winser London Ltd, since 2012; *b* Helensburgh, 11 March 1959; *d* of Terence and Dorothy Haresign; one *s*. *Educ:* Purbrook Park Grammar Sch. Marks & Spencer plc: mgt trainee, 1978; Merchandiser, 1982–84; Merchandise Manager, 1984–89; Exec., Brooks Bros USA and Marks & Spencer Canada, 1989–93; Exec., UK Women's Casualwear, 1993–95; Dir, Womenswear, 1995–2000; President and Chief Executive Officer: Pringle of Scotland, 2000–06; Aquascutum, 2006–09; Chm., Agent Provocateur, 2009–11; Special Advr, Net-A-Porter and French Sole, 2009–. Contributor to Forbes, 2013–. Trustee, Natural Hist. Mus., 2013–. Hon. DLitt Heriot-Watt, 2002. *Recreations:* tennis, swimming, cars. *Address:* Winser London Ltd, The Perfume Factory, Studio G17, 140 Wales Farm Road, W3 6UG. *T:* 0845 600 1521. *E:* emma@kimwinser.co.uk.

WINSER, (Margaret) Ellen, MBE 2012; Chair: Truro and Penwith College, since 2004; Truro & Penwith Academy Trust, since 2013; Vice Lord-Lieutenant for Cornwall, since 2014; *b* London, 6 Sept. 1942; *d* of late Donald Blake Fraser, FRCS, FRCOG and Betsy Rose Fraser (*née* Henderson); *m* 1969, Thomas Ralph Winser (*d* 2014); two step *d* (one step *s* decd). *Educ:* Benenden Sch.; Girton Coll., Cambridge (BA 1964; MA 1972). James Capel & Co. (stockbrokers), 1967–90, Partner, 1973–90. Long distance sailing, 1990–95. Chairman: Liontrust Asset Mgt plc, 1996–2004; Sutton Harbour Hldgs plc, 1998–2007; Dir, Pendennis Shipyard Hldgs Ltd, 2004–09. Member: Objective One Cornwall Strategic Develt Gp, 2002–07; Bd, SW RDA, 2007–12. Mem. Council, Benenden Sch., 1972–2002. Gov., Univ. of Plymouth, 2005–10. Chm., Nat. Maritime Mus. Cornwall Trust, 2002–14; Dir/Trustee, Cornwall Care, 1997–2005. *Address:* Cuby House, Tregony, Cornwall TR2 5TN. *T:* (01872) 530117. *E:* ellen@cubyhouse.com.

WINSHIP, Sir Peter (James Joseph), Kt 2004; CBE 1998; QPM 1990; HM Inspector of Constabulary, 1995–2005; *b* 21 July 1943; *s* of late Francis Edward Winship and Iris May (*née* Adams); *m* 1st, 1963, Carol Ann McNaughton; two *s* one *d*; 2nd, 1989, Janet Mary Bird; one *d*. *Educ:* Bicester Grammar Sch.; St John's Coll., Oxford (BA Eng. Lang. and Lit.; MA). Oxfordshire Constabulary, 1962; Sergeant to Supt, Thames Valley Police, 1968–79; Graduate, FBI Acad., 1980; Chief Supt, Metropolitan Police, 1982; Asst Chief Constable, Thames Valley Police, 1984; Metropolitan Police: Dep. Asst Comr, Policy & Planning, 1987, No 1 Area HQ, 1988; Asst Comr, 1989–95; Management Support and Strategy Dept, 1989–91; Inspection and Review Dept, 1992–95. Dir, Police Extended Interviews, 1993–95. Chm., Technical and Res. Cttee, ACPO, 1992–95. Member: Exec. Council, London Fedn of Boys' Clubs, 1988–95; Exec. Cttee, Royal Humane Soc., 1989–95; Governing Bd, Revolving Doors Agency, 1993–95. Trustee, Police Rehabilitation Trust, 2002–. FCMI. *Publications:* articles in police jls and other periodicals on professionally related subjects, travel, and treatment of police in literature; essay on delinquency and social policy (Queen's Police Gold Medal, Essay Competition, 1969). *Recreations:* reading, gardening, music.

WINSHIP, Sionaidh; *see* Douglas-Scott, S.

WINSKEL, Prof. Glynn, ScD, PhD; Professor of Computer Science, University of Cambridge, since 2000; Fellow, Emmanuel College, Cambridge, since 2000; *b* 23 May 1953; *s* of Thomas Francis Winskel and Helen Juanita Winskel (*née* McCall); *m* 1982, Kirsten Krog Jensen; two *d*. *Educ:* Emmanuel Coll., Cambridge (BA, MA Maths, ScD Computer Sci. 1995); St Catherine's Coll., Oxford (MSc Maths); Univ. of Edinburgh (PhD Computer Sci. 1980). Res. Scientist, Carnegie-Mellon Univ., Pittsburgh, 1982–83; University of Cambridge: Lectr in Computer Sci., 1984–87; Reader, 1987–88; Fellow, King's Coll., 1985–88; Prof. of Computer Sci., 1988–2000, Dir, Basic Res. in Computer Sci., 1994–2000, Aarhus Univ., Denmark. Royal Soc. Leverhulme Sen. Res. Fellow, 2010–11. MAE 2011. Ed., Jl of Mathematical Structures in Computer Science. *Publications:* Formal Semantics of Programming Languages: an introduction, 1993; (contrib.) Handbook of Logic in Computer Science, 1994. *Recreations:* music, art, running, swimming. *Address:* University of Cambridge, Computer Laboratory, 15 JJ Thomson Avenue, Cambridge CB3 0FD.

WINSLET, Kate Elizabeth, CBE 2012; actress; *b* 5 Oct. 1975; *d* of Roger and Sally Winslet; *m* 1st, 1998, Jim Threapleton (marr. diss. 2001); one *d*; 2nd, 2003, Samuel Alexander Mendes, *qv* (marr. diss. 2010); one *s*; 3rd, 2012, Ned Rocknroll; one *s*. *Educ:* Theatre Sch., Maidenhead. *Films include:* Heavenly Creatures, 1995; Sense and Sensibility (Best Supporting Actress, BAFTA), Jude, 1996; Hamlet, 1997; Titanic, 1998; Hideous Kinky, 1999; Holy Smoke, 2000; Quills, Enigma, 2001; Iris, 2002; The Life of David Gale, 2003; Eternal Sunshine of the Spotless Mind, Finding Neverland, 2004; Romance & Cigarettes, All the King's Men, Little Children, The Holiday, 2006; The Reader (Best Actress, Academy Awards and BAFTA; Best Supporting Actress, Golden Globe Awards), Revolutionary Road (Best Actress, Golden Globe Awards), 2009; Contagion, 2011; Carnage, 2012; Labor Day, 2013; Divergent, 2014; Insurgent, A Little Chaos, The Dressmaker, 2015; *television includes:* Mildred Pierce, 2011 (Best Actress, Emmy Awards, 2011; Best Actress, Golden Globe Awards, 2012). *Address:* c/o United Agents, 12–26 Lexington Street, W1F 0LE. *T:* (020) 3214 0800, *Fax:* (020) 3214 0801.

WINSLOW, Peter Anthony, CBE 2012; FCA; Executive Chairman, BGL Group, since 2013 (Group Chief Executive, 1995–2013); *b* London, 9 Feb. 1953; *s* of William Winslow and Babette Winslow; *m* 1977, Janet Young; one *s* one *d*. *Educ:* Uppingham Sch. FCA 1978. Chief Exec., HarperCollins UK, 1990–94. Non-exec. Dir, St Andrew's Healthcare, 1998– (Chm., 2014–). *Recreations:* tennis, ski-ing, flying helicopters, restaurants. *Address:* BGL Group, Pegasus House, Bakewell Road, Orton Southgate, Peterborough PE2 6YS. *E:* peter.winslow@bglgroup.co.uk.

WINSOR, Sir Thomas (Philip), Kt 2015; HM Chief Inspector of Constabulary, since 2012; *b* 7 Dec. 1957; twin *s* of late Thomas Valentine Marrs Winsor and Phyllis Margaret Winsor (*née* Bonsor); *m* 1989, Sonya Elizabeth Field (marr. diss. 2012); two *d*. *Educ:* Grove Acad., Broughty Ferry; Univ. of Edinburgh (LLB Scots Law 1979); Univ. of Dundee (Postgrad. Dip. Petroleum Law 1983). Admitted solicitor, 1981, NP 1981, WS 1984, Scotland; admitted solicitor, England and Wales, 1991; in general practice, Dundee, 1981–83; Assistant Solicitor: Dundas & Wilson, CS, 1983–84; Norton Rose, 1984–91; Partner, Denton Hall, 1991–99; Chief Legal Advr and Gen. Counsel, Office of Rail Regulator, 1993–95; Rail Regulator and Internat. Rail Regulator, 1999–2004; Partner, White & Case LLP, 2004–12. Hon. Lectr, Centre for Energy, Petroleum and Mineral Law and Policy, Univ. of Dundee, 1993–. Member: Law Soc. of Scotland, 1981–; Internat. Bar Assoc., 1983–; Univ. of Dundee Petroleum and Mineral Law Soc., 1987– (Pres., 1987–89); Soc. of Scottish Lawyers in London, 1987– (Pres., 1987–89); Law Soc. of England and Wales, 1991–. Ind. Review of Police Officer and Staff Remuneration and Conditions for Home Sec., 2010–12. Consulting Ed., Vol. 37 (Railways), Halsbury's Laws of England, 2007–. *Publications:* (with M. P. G. Taylor) Taylor and Winsor on Joint Operating Agreements, 1989; contrib. Legal Lines, The Right Side of the Tracks, articles in Modern Railways mag., 1996–99, 2005–09; contrib. articles in newspapers, books and learned jls on oil and gas, electricity, railways law and regulation, policing. *Recreations:* family, literature, theatre, opera, music, cycling, politics, Scottish constitutional history, law, works of Robert Burns. *Address:* HM Inspectorate of Constabulary, 6th Floor, Globe House, 89 Eccleston Square, SW1V 1PN. *Club:* Caledonian.

WINSTANLEY, Rt Rev. Alan Leslie; Team Rector, Shirwell, and Honorary Assistant Bishop, Diocese of Exeter, 2012–14; *b* 7 May 1949; *s* of John Leslie Winstanley and Eva Winstanley; *m* 1st, 1972, Vivien Mary Parkinson (*d* 2013); one *s* one *d* (and one *s* decd); 2nd, 2014, Janet Elizabeth Bowyer. *Educ:* St John's College, Nottingham (BTh, ALCD). Deacon 1972, priest 1973, Blackburn; Curate: St Andrew's, Livesey, Blackburn, 1972–75; St Mary's, Great Sankey, dio. Liverpool, with responsibility for St Paul's, Penketh, 1975–77; Vicar of Penketh, 1978–81; SAMS Missionary in Peru: Lima, 1981–85; Arequipa, 1986–87; Bishop of Peru and Bolivia, 1988–93; Vicar of Eastham, and Hon. Asst Bp, Dio. of Chester, 1994–2003; Vicar of Whittle-le-Woods, and Hon. Asst Bp, Dio. of Blackburn, 2003–12. *Recreations:* vintage aircraft, caravanning, steam locomotives. *Address:* 51 Warrington Rd, Penketh, Warrington WA5 2BW.

WINSTANLEY, Charles Jeffery, TD 1990; JP; DL; DBA; Chairman, NHS Lothian, 2007–13; *b* London, 6 March 1952; *s* of late Jeffery and Elisabeth Winstanley; *m* 1987, Columbine Hobart (marr. diss. 2009); one *s* one *d*. *Educ:* Wellington Coll.; RMA Sandhurst; Henley Management Coll. (MBA 1992; DBA 1997). Lieutenant, 16th/5th Lancers, 1970–76; Major, Royal Yeomanry, 1977–92. Chm., Fitness to Practise Panel, GMC, 2000–07; Member: Nat. Consumer Council for Postal Services, 2002–08; Asylum and Immigration Tribunal, 2003–; Audit Cttee, UK Supreme Court, 2011–; Tribunals Disciplinary Panel, 2014–. Non-executive Director: Norfolk and Norwich Univ. Hosp. NHS Trust, 1999–2006; MoD, 2010–14; Scottish Govt, 2010–13; Chairman: Norfolk Probation Bd, 2001–06; Edinburgh Leisure, 2010–15. Mem., Scottish Adv. Cttee on Distinction Awards, 2008–11. Mem. Council, Erskine, 2012–. JP Thames and Central Norfolk, 1993–2006, supplementary list, 2006–; DL Gtr London, 1997. *Recreations:* motorcycling, sailing, fly fishing. *E:* cjwinstanley@aol.com.

WINSTANLEY, Prof. Peter Andrew, MD; FRCP; Dean of Medicine, University of Warwick, since 2010; *b* Liverpool, 26 May 1956; *s* of Reginald Joseph and Jessie Patricia Winstanley; *m* 1984, Maria Therese Roberts; two *s* one *d*. *Educ:* St Mary's Coll., Crosby; Liverpool Med. Sch., Univ. of Liverpool (MB ChB Hons 1979; MD 1989). DTM&H 1988; FRCP 1997. Tutor in Medicine, Univ. of Leeds, 1982–83; Lectr in Clin. Pharmacol., Univ. of Liverpool, 1983–89; MRC Res. Fellow, Nuffield Dept of Medicine, Univ. of Oxford, 1989–92; University of Liverpool: Prof. of Clin. Pharmacol., 1992–2007; Hd, Sch. of Clin. Scis, 2007–10. *Publications:* (with S. Constable) Medical Pharmacology, 1996, 8th edn 2007. *Recreation:* Roman history. *Address:* 105 Druids Cross Road, Liverpool L18 3HN; Warwick Medical School, University of Warwick, Coventry CV4 7AL. *T:* (024) 7657 3080. *E:* p.winstanley@warwick.ac.uk.

WINSTANLEY, Col Richard Dirdoe, OBE 2007; Clerk to Worshipful Company of Drapers, since 2013; *b* London, 28 May 1964; *s* of John Winstanley, MC, TD and Jane Winstanley; *m* 1989, Caroline Jane Grey Edwards; one *s* one *d*. *Educ:* Wellington Coll.; RMA Sandhurst. Commnd Grenadier Guards, 1984; served 2nd Bn in Belize and NI, 1985–87; Anti-tank Platoon Comdr, 1st Bn, 1988–91; Adjt, 2nd Bn, 1991–93; Comdr, 1st Bn, 1993–95; Guards Co. Comdr, Army Trng Regt, Pirbright, 1995; Staff Coll., 1996; GSO, HQ UK Support Comd, Germany, 1997–99; Co. Comdr, 1st Bn, 1999–2001; Acad. Adjt, RMA Sandhurst, 2001–03; Mil. Asst to COS, HQ ISAF, 2003–04; GSO, HQ Theatre Troops, 2004–05; CO, Support Bn, Allied Rapid Reaction Force, 2005–07; i/c Army's Lesson Learned Cell, Warminster, 2007–08; i/c officer career mgt for Infantry, Armoured Corps and AAC, 2008–10; resp. for personnel mgt and regtl issues for infantry, 2010–12. *Recreations:* fishing, cycling, mahjong, gardening, shooting. *Address:* Drapers' Company, Drapers' Hall, Throgmorton Avenue, EC2N 2DQ. *E:* rwinstanley@thedrapers.co.uk. *Club:* Flyfishers'.

WINSTANLEY, Robert James; His Honour Judge Winstanley; a Circuit Judge, since 1996; *b* 4 Nov. 1948; *s* of late Morgan James Winstanley and of Joan Martha Winstanley; *m* 1972, Josephine Langhorne; two *s*. *Educ:* St Catharine's Coll., Cambridge (MA 1970). Admitted Solicitor, 1973; Asst Solicitor, Dawson & Co., 1973–75; Partner, Winstanley-Burgess, Solicitors, 1975–96. Mem. Council, Law Soc., 1985–96. *Recreations:* golf, cricket, bridge. *Address:* c/o The Court Service, 2nd Floor, Rose Court, 2 Southwark Bridge, SE1 9HS. *T:* (020) 7921 2109. *Clubs:* MCC; Sudbury Golf.

WINSTON, family name of **Baron Winston**.

WINSTON, Baron *cr* 1995 (Life Peer), of Hammersmith in the London Borough of Hammersmith and Fulham; **Robert Maurice Lipson Winston;** Professor of Science and Society, Imperial College London, since 2008; Professor of Fertility Studies, University of London at Imperial College School of Medicine (formerly at the Institute of Obstetrics and Gynaecology, Royal Postgraduate Medical School), 1987–2005, now Professor Emeritus; formerly Consultant Obstetrician and Gynaecologist, Hammersmith Hospital; Director of NHS Research and Development, Hammersmith Hospitals NHS Trust, 1998–2005; *b* 15 July 1940; *s* of late Laurence Winston and Ruth Winston-Fox, MBE; *m* 1973, Lira Helen Feigenbaum; two *s* one *d*. *Educ:* St Paul's Sch., London; London Hosp. Med. Coll., London Univ. (MB, BS 1964). MRCS, LRCP 1964; FRCOG 1983 (MRCOG 1971); FRCP 2002. Jun. posts, London Hosp., 1964–66; Registrar and Sen. Registrar, Hammersmith Hosp., 1970–74; Wellcome Res. Sen. Lectr, Inst. of Obs and Gyn., 1974–78; Sen. Lectr, Hammersmith Hosp., 1978–81; Reader in Fertility Studies, RPMS, 1982–86. Vis. Prof., Univ. of Leuven, Belgium, 1976–77; Prof. of Gyn., Univ. of Texas at San Antonio, 1980–81; Clyman Vis. Prof., Mt Sinai Hosp., New York, 1985. Member, Steering Cttee, WHO: on Tubal Occlusion, 1975–77; on Ovum Transport, 1977–78; Mem., EPSRC, 2007–13 (Chm., Societal Issues Panel, 2007–13). Pres., Internat. Fallopius Soc., 1987–88. Mem. Council, Cancer Res. UK (formerly ICRF), 1998–2004. Vice Pres., Progress (all-party parly campaign for res. into human reprodn), 1992 (Chm., 1988–91). Mem. Bd, POST, 1998–; Mem., Select Cttee on Sci. and Technol., H of L, 1997–2001 (Chm., 1998–2001), 2003–06 and 2010–; Mem., Scottish Science Adv. Council, 2010–. Founder Mem., British Fertility Soc., 1975–; Mem. Bd, Internat. Soc. for Stem Cell Res., 2004–; Pres., BAAS, 2004–05. Dir, Atazoa Ltd, 2004–. Hon. Member: Georgian Obs Soc., 1983–; Pacific Fertility Soc., 1983–; Spanish Fertility Soc., 1985–; Israel Fertility Soc., 1990–. Mem. Council, RPMS, 1992–97; Chm. Council, Royal Coll. of Music, 2008–. Chancellor, Sheffield Hallam Univ., 2001–; Mem. Council, Univ. of Surrey, 2008–. Chm., Genesis Res. Trust, 2010–; Trustee: UK Stem Cell Foundn, 2010–; Royal Institution, 2012–. Presenter, BBC TV: Your Life in their Hands, 1979–87; The Human Body, 1998; The Secret Life of Twins, 1999; A Child of Our Time, 2000–; Superhuman, 2000; Threads of Life, BBC TV, 2001; Human Instinct, BBC TV, 2002; Walking with Cavemen, 2003; The Human Mind, 2003; Frankenstein: birth of a monster, 2003; The Story of God, 2005; Child Against All Odds, 2006; Super Doctors, 2008; Frontiers of Medicine, 2008; presenter, Robert Winston's Musical Analysis, Science and Music, BBC Radio 4. Member, Editorial Board: Internat. Jl of Microsurgery, 1981–; Clinical Reproduction and Fertility, 1985–. Founder FMedSci 1998; FCGI 2011. Hon. Fellow: QMW, 1996; Inst. of Educn. Hon. FRCSE 2006; Hon. FIBiol 2006; Hon. FRCPSGlas, 2007; Hon. FREng, 2008; Hon. Fellow: Clinical Genetics Soc., 2013; Endocrine Soc., 2013. Hon. DSc: Cranfield, 2001; UMIST, 2001; Oxford Brookes, 2001; Strathclyde, 2002; St Andrews, 2002; Salford, 2003; Middlesex, 2003; Sunderland, 2003; Exeter, 2004; Southampton Inst., 2004; QUB, 2005; TCD, 2005; East Anglia, 2006; Auckland, 2008; De Montfort, 2008; Lincoln, 2009; Aberdeen, 2010; Loughborough, 2011; Surrey, 2011; Hon. Dr: Lancaster, 2005; Open, 2014; Birmingham City, 2015; Weizmann Inst., 2015. Chief Rabbinate Award for Contribn to Society, 1992–93; Victor Bonney Prize, RCS, 1991–93; Cedric Carter Medal, Clinical Genetics Soc., 1993; Michael Faraday Gold Medal, Royal Soc., 1999; Gold Medal, RSH, 1999; Gold Medal for Medicine in the Media, BMA, 1999; Wellcome Award for Sci. in the Media, 2001; Edwin Stevens Gold Medal, RSocMed, 2003; Viewers' and Listeners' Award for Best Individual Contrib. to Television, 2003; Maitland Medal, Inst. of Engineers, 2004; Gold Medal, N of England Zool Soc., 2004; Al-Hammadi Medal, RCSE, 2007; Peer of the Year, H of L, 2008. *Publications:* Reversibility of Sterilization, 1978; (jtly) Tubal Infertility, 1981; Infertility, a Sympathetic Approach, 1987; Getting Pregnant, 1990; The IVF Revolution, 2000; (jtly) Superhuman: the awesome power within, 2000; Human Instinct, 2002; The Human Mind, 2003; What Makes Me Me, 2004 (Aventis Prize, Royal Soc.); The Story of God, 2005; Child Against All Odds, 2006; It's Elementary, 2008; Evolution Revolution from Darwin to DNA, 2009; Bad Ideas?: an arresting history of our inventions, 2010; What Goes On in My Head, 2010; Science Experiments, 2011 (Young Peoples' Science Book Prize, Royal Soc.); Science Year by Year, 2013; That's Life, 2013; Utterly Amazing Science, 2014; Utterly Amazing Body, 2015; The Essential Fertility Guide, 2015; scientific pubns on human and experimental reproduction. *Recreations:* theatre (directed award-winning Pirandello production, Each in his Own Way, Edinburgh Fest., 1969), festering, music, wine. *Address:* 11 Denman Drive, NW11 6RE. *T:* (020) 8455 7475. *Clubs:* Athenæum, Garrick, MCC.

WINSTON, Prof. Brian Norman, PhD; The Lincoln Professor, College of the Arts, University of Lincoln, since 2007 (Dean, Faculty of Media and Humanities, 2002–05; Pro-Vice-Chancellor, 2005–07); *b* 7 Nov. 1941; *s* of Reuben and Anita Winston; *m* 1978, Adèle Paul; one *s* one *d*. *Educ:* Kilburn Grammar Sch.; Merton Coll., Oxford (BA Laws; MA); Univ. of Lincoln (PhD 2007). Researcher, 1963–66, Prod. and Dir, 1963–66, 1969–71, Granada TV; Prod. and Dir, BBC TV, 1966–69; Lectr, Bradford Coll. of Art, 1972–73; Head of Gen. Studies, Nat. Film Sch., 1973–79; Res. Dir, Dept of Sociology, Glasgow Univ., 1974–76; Vis. Prof., 1976–77, Prof., 1979–86, Sch. of the Arts, NY Univ.; writer, WNET-TV, NY, 1984–85; Dean, Coll. of Communications, Pennsylvania State Univ., 1986–92; Dir, Centre for Journalism Studies, UWCC, then Univ. of Wales, Cardiff, 1992–97; Hd, Dept of Communication, Media and Design, then Sch. of Communication and Creative Industries, Westminster Univ., 1997–2002. Guest Prof., Beijing Normal Univ., 2013–. Gov., BFI, 1995–2001. Emmy Award for documentary script writing, 1985. *Publications:* Dangling Conversations, vol. 1, the image of the media, 1973, vol. 2, hardware/software, 1974; (jtly) Bad News, 1976; (jtly) More Bad News, 1980; Misunderstanding Media, 1986; (jtly) Working with Video, 1986; Claiming the Real, 1995, rev. edn as Claiming the Real II, 2008; Technologies of Seeing, 1996; Media, Technology and Society: a history, 1998; Fires Were Started, 1999; Lies, Damn Lies and Documentaries, 2000; Messages, 2005; A Right to Offend, 2012 (Internat. Book Award on Human Rights, Vienna, 2013); (ed and contrib.) The BFI Documentary Film Book, 2013; The Rushdie Fatwa and After: a lesson to the circumspect, 2014. *Recreations:* cooking, theatre. *Address:* 24a Minster Yard, Lincoln LN2 1PY; University of Lincoln, Brayford Pool, Lincoln LN6 7TS.

WINSTON, Clive Noel; Assistant Director, Federation Against Copyright Theft Ltd, 1985–88; *b* 20 April 1925; *s* of George and Alida Winston; *m* 1952, Beatrice Jeanette; two *d*. *Educ:* Highgate Sch.; Trinity Hall, Cambridge (BA). Admitted solicitor, 1951. Joined Metropolitan Police, 1951; Dep. Solicitor, Metropolitan Police, 1982–85. Chairman, Union of Liberal and Progressive Synagogues, 1981–85 (Vice-Pres., 1985–); Treas., Eur. Bd, World Union of Progressive Judaism, 1990–95. *Recreations:* golf, gardening, bridge.

WINSTONE, Norma Ann, MBE 2007; jazz singer, since 1965; *b* Bow, E London, 23 Sept. 1941; *née* Norma Ann Short; *d* of Walter Short and Doris Short (*née* Ince, later Clark); partner, Hugh Mitchell; two *s*. *Educ:* County High Sch., Dagenham. Recording artist, 1979–. Hon. Fellow, Trinity Laban Conservatoire of Music and Dance, 2010; Hon. Mem., RAM, 2013. *Recreations:* gardening, walking, family, cinema, music. *Address:* Tideway, 8 Wellington Parade, Walmer, Deal, Kent CT14 8AA. *T:* (01304) 367840. *E:* winstone.norma@gmail.com.

WINTER, Rev. Canon David Brian; Team Minister, Hermitage Team Ministry, 1995–2000; Hon. Canon, Christ Church Cathedral, Oxford, 1995–2000, now Canon Emeritus; *b* 19 Nov. 1929; *s* of Walter George Winter and Winifred Ella Winter; *m* 1st, 1961, Christine Ellen Martin (*d* 2001); two *s* one *d*; 2nd, 2004, Rosalind Anne Lee. *Educ:* Machynlleth County Sch.; Trinity County Grammar Sch., Wood Green; King's Coll., Univ. of London (BA, PGCE). Nat. Service, RAF, 1948–50. Teacher: Ware CE Secondary Sch., 1954–58; Tottenham County Grammar Sch., 1958–59; Editor, Crusade, 1959–70; freelance writer and broadcaster, 1970–71; BBC: Producer, Religious Broadcasting, 1971–75, Sen. Producer, 1975–82; Hd of Religious Progs, Radio, and Dep. Hd, Religious Broadcasting, 1982–87; Hd of Religious Broadcasting, 1987–89. Chm., Arts Centre Gp, 1976–82. Oak Hill Ministerial Trng Course, 1985–87. Deacon, 1987, priest, 1988. Hon. Asst Curate, St Paul and St Luke, Finchley, 1987–89; Priest-in-Charge, Ducklington, 1989–95; Bishop's Officer for Evangelism, Dio. of Oxford, 1989–95. Editor, Bible Reading Fellowship, 1997–2001; Consulting Ed., People's Bible Commentary, 1998–2006. *Publications:* Ground of Truth, 1964; New Singer, New Song (biog. of Cliff Richard), 1967; (with S. Linden) Two a Penny, 1968; Closer than a Brother, 1971; Hereafter, 1972; (ed) Matthew Henry's Commentary on the New Testament, 1974; After the Gospels, 1977; But this I can believe, 1980; The Search for the Real Jesus, 1982; Truth in the Son, 1985; Living through Loss, 1985; Walking in the Light (confessions of St Augustine), 1986; Believing the Bible, 1987; Battered Bride, 1988; What happens after Death?, 1992; You Can Pray, 1993; What's in a Word, 1994; Mark for Starters, 1995; Where do we go from here?, 1996; Forty Days with the 'Messiah', 1996; Message for the Millennium, 1998; (ed) The Master Haunter (anthol.), 1998, re-issued as The Poets' Christ, 2000; Winter's Tale (autobiog.), 2001; With Jesus in the Upper Room, 2001; Hope in the Wilderness, 2003; Making Sense of the Bible, 2004; Old Words, New Life, 2005; The Nation's Favourite Prayers (anthol.), 2006; Journey to Jerusalem, 2007; Seasons of the Son: a journey through the Christian year, 2008; Pilgrim's Way: journeying through the year with the Bible, 2008; One-stop Guide to Christianity, 2009; The Road Well Travelled: exploring traditional Christian spirituality, 2009; Facing the Darkness and Finding the Light: reflections for troubled times from the Book of Revelation, 2011; The Highway Code for Retirement, 2012; At the End of the Day: enjoying life in the departure lounge, 2013. *Recreations:* watching cricket, opera, theatre, talking. *Address:* 51 Nideggan Close, Thatcham, Berks RG19 4HS. *W:* www.davidwinter-author.co.uk.

WINTER, Prof. (David) Michael, OBE 2005; PhD; Professor of Rural Policy and Director, Centre for Rural Policy Research (formerly Centre for Rural Research), University of Exeter, since 2002; *b* 10 Nov. 1955; *s* of David Winter and Nanette Winter (*née* Wellsteed); *m* 1979, Hilary Susan Thomas; one *s* one *d*. *Educ:* Peter Symonds Coll., Winchester; Wye Coll., London (BSc Rural Envmt Studies 1977); Open Univ. (PhD 1986). Res. Asst, Univ. of Exeter, 1980–82; Res. Officer, Univ. of Bath, 1983–87; Dir, Centre for Rural Studies, RAC, Cirencester, 1987–93; Reader, then Prof., Countryside and Community Res. Unit, Cheltenham and Gloucester Coll. of Higher Educn, 1993–2001; Hd, Sch. of Geog., Archaeol. and Earth Resources, Univ. of Exeter, 2003–05. Member, Board: Countryside Agency, 2005–06; Commn for Rural Communities, 2006–13; Mem., Sci. Adv. Council, DEFRA, 2009–11; Vis. Prog. Dir, Wilton Park, 2010–. Chm., 2001–04, Vice-Chm., 2004–08, Hatherleigh Area Proj.; Chairman: South West Rural Affairs Forum, 2002–07; N Devon Biosphere Partnership, 2012–; Uplands Alliance, 2015–; Pres., Devon Rural Network, 2006–09 (Chm., 2002–06); Vice Pres., Community Council of Devon, 2008–13; Trustee/Dir, North Wyke Res., 2008–09. Res. Associate, Inst. of Grassland and Envmtl Res., 1998– (Mem., Bd of Govs, 2006–08); Member: Expert Panel for Nat. Ecosystem Assessment, 2009–14; Bd of Govs, Rothamsted Res., 2014–. Lay Canon, Exeter Cathedral, 2008–. *Publications:* (ed jtly) Agriculture: people and policies, 1986; (jtly) Countryside Conflicts, 1986; (ed with M. Bouquet) Who From Their Labours Rest, 1987; (jtly) The Voluntary Principle in Conservation, 1990; (jtly) Church and Religion in Rural England, 1991; Rural Politics, 1996; (with P. Gaskell) The Effects of the 1992 Reform of the Common Agricultural Policy on the Countryside of Great Britain, 1998; (ed with M. Lobley) What is Land For? The Food, Fuel and Climate Change Debate, 2009. *Recreations:* gardening, hedge-laying, walking, choral singing, music, Church, community, reading, Welsh Rugby. *Address:* Centre for Rural Policy Research, University of Exeter, Department of Politics, Amory Building, Rennes Drive, Exeter EX4 4RJ. *T:* (01392) 263837. *E:* d.m.winter@exeter.ac.uk. *Club:* Athenæum.

WINTER, Sir Gregory (Paul), Kt 2004; CBE 1997; PhD; FRS 1990; FMedSci; scientific researcher and consultant; Master of Trinity College, Cambridge, since 2012; *b* 14 April 1951; *m* 1974, Fiona Jane Winter (marr. diss. 2002); one *s* three *d*. *Educ:* Royal Grammar Sch., Newcastle-upon-Tyne; Trinity College, Cambridge (BA Natural Scis 1973; MA; PhD 1976). Early career in protein chemistry, later in recombinant DNA technology, and enzyme and antibody engrg; Fellow, Trinity College, Cambridge, 1976–80 and 1991–2012; MRC Laboratory of Molecular Biology: Staff Scientist, 1981–2014; Jt Hd, Div. of Protein and Nucleic Acid Chemistry, 1994–2008; Dep. Dir, 2006–11; Acting Dir, 2007–08; Dep. Dir, Centre for Protein Engrg, 1990–2010. Co-Founder and non-executive Director: Cambridge Antibody Technology, 1989–96; Domantis, 2001–06; Bicycle Therapeutics, 2009–; non-exec. Dir, Peptech (Australia), 2001–03. Trustee, Newton Trust. FMedSci 2006. Foreign Fellow, Aust. Acad. of Technol Scis, 2002; Foreign Mem., Royal Swedish Acad. of Engrg Scis, 2007. Hon. FRCP 2003; Hon. Mem., Biochem. Soc., 2007; Hon. FRSocMed, 2009. Dr *hc* Nantes, 2001; Hon. Dr rer. nat. ETH Zurich, 2002. Novo Biotechnology Award, Denmark, 1986; Colworth Medal, Biochem. Soc., 1986; Behring Prize, FRG, 1989; Louis

Jeantet Foundn Award for Medicine, Switzerland, 1989; Pfizer Award, 1989; Milano Award, Italy, 1990; Scheele Award, Swedish Acad. of Pharmaceutical Scis, 1994; Biochemical Analysis Prize, German Soc. for Clin. Chem., 1995; King Faisal Internat. Prize in Medicine, 1995; William B. Coley Award, Cancer Res. Inst., USA, 1999; Jacob Heskel Gabbay Award in Biotechnol. and Medicine, Brandeis Univ., 2002; Jean-Pierre Lecocq Award, Acad. of Scis, France, 2002; Nat. Biotechnology Ventures Award, USA, 2004; Baly Medal, RCP, 2005; Biochemical Soc. Award, 2006; Bioindustry Assoc. Award, 2008; Royal Medal, Royal Soc., 2011; Prince of Asturias Award, Spain, 2012; Canada Gairdner Internat. Award, 2013; Millennium Medal, MRC, 2013. *Publications:* articles in learned jls on protein and gene structure, enzymes, viral proteins, antibodies and peptides. *Address:* The Master's Lodge, Trinity College, Cambridge CB2 1TQ.

WINTER, Henry Oliver; Football Correspondent, Daily Telegraph, since 1994; *b* London, 18 Feb. 1963; *s* of John and Valerie Winter; *m* 1992, Catriona Elliott; one *s* one *d*. *Educ:* The Hall, Hampstead; Westminster Sch.; Edinburgh Univ. (MA Hist.); London Coll. of Printing (Cert. Journalism). Sports journalist, The Independent, 1987–94. Columnist, 4-4-2 Mag., 2000–; contrib. Sky Sports, BBC TV and Radio. *Publications:* (with D. Davies) FA Confidential, 2008; ghost writer: Kenny Dalglish: My Autobiography, 1997; John Barnes: The Autobiography, 1999; Steven Gerrard: The Autobiography, 2006; Kenny Dalglish: My Liverpool Home, 2010. *Recreations:* marathon-running, visiting WW II museums, cycling round Rutland Water, singing out of tune. *Address:* Daily Telegraph, 111 Buckingham Palace Road, SW1W 0DT. *T:* (020) 7931 2600.

WINTER, Michael; *see* Winter, D. M.

WINTER, Peter John, MA; Head, Latymer Upper School, 2002–12; *b* 10 July 1950; *s* of Jack Winter and Ursula Winter (*née* Riddington); *m* 1979, Jennifer Adwoa; one *s* one *d*. *Educ:* Trinity Sch., Croydon; Wadham Coll., Oxford (MA French); Univ. of Reading (PGCE). Asst teacher, French and German, Latymer Upper Sch., 1973–79; Head of Modern Langs, Magdalen Coll. Sch., Oxford, 1979–86; Head of Modern Langs, 1986–90, Housemaster, Internat. Centre, 1987–93, Sevenoaks Sch.; Headmaster, King Edward's Sch., Bath, 1993–2002. Strategic Consultant, PORG Schs, Czech Republic, 2014–. *Recreations:* Chelsea FC, Test Match cricket, France, grandparenting. *Address:* 20 Oyster Wharf, 18 Lombard Road, SW11 3RJ; 60 rue de la Cité, 34480 Magalas, France.

WINTER, Dr Robert James David, OBE 2009; FRCP; Consultant Respiratory Physician, Cambridge University Hospitals (formerly Addenbrooke's Hospital and Papworth Hospital), Cambridge, 2000–15; Programme Director, Integrated Care, University College London Partners, since 2015; *b* 11 March 1953; *s* of David Winter and Margery Joan Winter; *m* 1984, Elizabeth Jane Sowton (marr. diss. 2005); two *d*. *Educ:* Clifton Coll., Bristol; Royal Free Hosp. Sch. of Medicine, Univ. of London (BSc 1974; MB BS 1977; MD 1987). MRCP 1979, FRCP 1995. Registrar, UCL, 1981–84; MRC Trng Fellow, 1984–86; Sen. Registrar, Hammersmith Hosp., 1986–91; Consultant Physician, Barnet Hosp., 1991–2000; Medical Director: Addenbrooke's NHS Trust, subseq. Cambridge Univ. Hosps NHS Foundn Trust, 2002–08; NHS East of England, 2008–11; Dir, Cambridge Univ. Health Partners, 2011–13; Man. Dir, Eastern Academic Health Sci. Network, 2013–14. Associate Lectr, Univ. of Cambridge, 2001–15; Fellow, Hughes Hall, Cambridge, 2013–15. Jt Nat. Clinical Dir for Respiratory Disease, DoH, 2009–13. Mem. Exec. Cttee, and Trustee, British Lung Foundn, 1992–2002 (Vice Pres., 2010–); Trustee, Fund for Addenbrooke's, 2002–07. *Publications:* chapters and articles on quality in health care delivery. *Recreations:* music, walking. *Address:* University College London Partners, 3rd floor, 170 Tottenham Court Road, W1T 7HA. *T:* (020) 3108 2321. *E:* Robert.winter@uclpartners.com; 29 High Street, Barrington, Cambridge CB22 7QX.

WINTER, Robert Rickaby, OBE 2012; Lord-Lieutenant and Lord Provost of Glasgow, 2007–12; *b* 31 March 1937; *s* of Thomas Rickaby Winter and Dona Smillie McKendrick Winter; *m* 1983, Sheena Morgan Duncan; one *d*; four *s* by a previous marriage. CSW; DPA. Dir of Social Work, Greenock and Port Glasgow, 1969–75; Dep. Dir of Social Work, 1975–95, Dir of Social Work, 1995–96, Strathclyde Regl Council; Sec., Assoc. of Dirs of Social Work, 1996–99. Mem., 1996–2005, Panel Chm., 2007–12, GMC. Mem., Gtr Glasgow Health Bd PCT, 1996–2005 (Chm. Panel, until 2007). Mem. (Lab), Glasgow City Council, 1999–2012. Hon. FRCPGlas 2009; Hon. FRIAS 2011. DUniv: Caledonian, 2011; Strathclyde, 2012. *Recreations:* walking, swimming, reading, football spectation.

WINTER, Sophie; *see* Raworth, S.

WINTERBOTTOM, Prof. Michael, MA, DPhil; FBA 1978; Corpus Christi Professor of Latin, University of Oxford, 1992–2001; Fellow, Corpus Christi College, Oxford, 1992–2001, now Emeritus; *b* 22 Sept. 1934; *s* of Allan Winterbottom and Kathleen Mary (*née* Wallis); *m* 1st, 1963, Helen Spencer (marr. diss. 1983); two *s*; 2nd, 1986, Nicolette Janet Streatfeild Bergel. *Educ:* Dulwich Coll.; Pembroke Coll., Oxford. 1st Cl. Hon. Mods and Craven Schol., 1954; 1st Cl. Lit. Hum. and Derby Schol., 1956; Domus Sen. Schol., Merton Coll., 1958–59; MA 1959, DPhil 1964 (Oxon). Research Lectr, Christ Church, 1959–62; Lectr in Latin and Greek, University Coll. London, 1962–67; Fellow and Tutor in Classics, Worcester Coll., Oxford, 1967–92; Reader in Classical Langs, Univ. of Oxford, 1990–92. D*hc* Besançon, 1985. *Publications:* (ed) Quintilian, 1970; (with D. A. Russell) Ancient Literary Criticism, 1972; Three Lives of English Saints, 1972; (ed and trans.) The Elder Seneca, 1974; (ed with R. M. Ogilvie) Tacitus, *Opera Minora*, 1975; (ed and trans.) Gildas, 1978; Roman Declamation, 1980; (ed with commentary) The Minor Declamations ascribed to Quintilian, 1984; (with D. C. Innes) Sopatros the Rhetor, 1988; (with M. Brett and C. N. L. Brooke) rev. edn of Charles Johnson (ed), Hugh the Chanter, 1990; (ed) Cicero, *De Officiis*, 1994; (ed with R. A. B. Mynors and R. M. Thomson) William of Malmesbury, *Gesta Regum Anglorum*, 1998; (ed with R. M. Thomson) William of Malmesbury, Saints' Lives, 2002; (ed with T. Reinhardt) Quintilian Book 2, 2006; (ed) William of Malmesbury, *Gesta Pontificum Anglorum*, vol. 1, 2007; (ed with R. M. Thomson) William of Malmesbury, *Liber super explanationem Lamentationum Ieremiae prophetae*, 2011; (ed with M. Lapidge) The Early Lives of St Dunstan, 2012; (trans.) William of Malmesbury on Lamentations, 2013; articles and reviews in jls. *Recreations:* walking, geology. *Address:* 53 Thorncliffe Road, Oxford OX2 7BA. *T:* (01865) 513066.

WINTERFLOOD, Brian Martin, MBE 2012; Founder, 1988, and Life President, since 2009, Winterflood Securities Ltd (Managing Director, 1988–99; Chief Executive Officer, 1999–2002; Chairman, 2002–09); Chief Executive Officer, Winterflood Gilts, 1999–2002 (Managing Director, 1994–99); Chairman, Gilts and Securities, since 2001; *b* 31 Jan. 1937; *s* of late Thomas G. Winterflood and of Doris M. Winterflood; *m* 1966, Doreen Stella McCartney; two *s* one *d*. *Educ:* Fray's Coll., Uxbridge. National Service, 1955–57. Messenger, Greener Dreyfus & Co., 1953–55; Bisgood Bishop & Co. Ltd, 1957–85: Partner, 1967–71; Dir, 1971–81; Man. Dir, 1981–85; Man. Dir, County Bisgood, 1985–86; County NatWest Securities Ltd: Dir, 1986–87; Exec. Dir, 1986–88, resigned, 1988. Director: Union Discount Co. of London, 1991–93; Close Brothers Group, 1995–2002; PROSHARE, 1998–2003; Monument Securities, 2002–06. Chm., Cttee of USM Initiative, Prince's Youth Bus. Trust, 1989–92; Jt Chm., UK Adv. Bd, EASD, 2000–01. Member: City Gp for Smaller Cos, now Quoted Cos Alliance, 1992–2000 (Mem. Exec. Cttee, 1992–96; Pres., 2010); City Disputes Practitioners Panel, 1994–2000; AIM Adv. Cttee, 1995–; AIM Appeals Cttee, 1995–98; Non FTSE 100 Wkg Party Cttee, 1996–98; Secondary Markets Cttee, 1996–98; Market Adv. Cttee, EASD, 2000–. Mem. Cttee, October Club, 1990–2002; Trustee, Stock Exchange Benevolent Fund, 1995; Pres., Securities Industry Mgt Assoc., 2004 (Lifetime Achievement Award, 2008). Pres., Rehabilitation and Med. Res. Trust, 1998–2007 (Vice Pres., 1989, 2007–); Vice-Pres., Save the Children, 2004–09; Vice-Chm., Lord Mayor's Appeal, 2004; Ambassador, E London Bond Appeal, 2010. Gov., Reeds Sch., 2002–07 (Pres., Sch. Appeal, 1997–98; Hon. Vice Pres., 2007). Member: Boost (City Life) Appeal, 2001–02; Guild of Internat. Bankers, 2002–; Order of St George, 2002–; Heart of the City Cttee, 2002–. Winterflood Theatre, City of London Boys' Sch., 2008. Freeman, City of London, 2002. Liveryman, Internat. Bankers' Co., 2007– (Mem. Ct). FCSI (FSI 1997); FRSA 2001. PLC Achievement Award, Price Waterhouse Coopers, 1994; Assoc. of Private Client Investment Managers and Stockbrokers Award, 2000; Lifetime Achievement Award: Variety Club, 2008; Grant Thornton Quoted Companies Awards, 2011. *Recreations:* family, work, travel. *Address:* Winterflood Securities Ltd, The Atrium Building, Cannon Bridge, 25 Dowgate Hill, EC4R 2GA. *T:* (020) 3100 0000. *Club:* City of London.

WINTERS, Prof. (Leonard) Alan, CB 2012; PhD; Professor of Economics, University of Sussex, since 1999; *b* Walthamstow, 8 April 1950; *s* of Geoffrey Walter Horace Winters and Christine Agnes Winters (*née* Ive); *m* 1997, Zhen Kun Wang; one *s* two *d*. *Educ:* Chingford Co. High Sch.; Univ. of Bristol (BSc 1971); Fitzwilliam Coll., Cambridge (MA 1975; PhD 1979). Res. officer, Dept Applied Econs, Univ. of Cambridge, 1971–80; Lectr, Univ. of Bristol, 1980–86; Economist, World Bank, 1983–85; Professor of Economics: UC of N Wales, Bangor, 1986–90; Univ. of Birmingham, 1990–97; Res. Manager, 1994–99, Dir of Res., 2004–07, World Bank; Chief Economist, DFID, 2008–11. Chair, Global Develt Network, 2011–. Mem., ESRC, 2015–. Ed., World Trade Rev., 2008–. Chair, English Folk Dance and Song Soc., 1981–83. *Publications:* International Economics, 1982, 2nd edn 1991; Eastern Europe's International Trade, 1994; Handbook on International Trade and Poverty, 2001; Regionalisation and Development, 2002; contrib. chapters to acad. books and jl articles. *Recreations:* music, cricket, walking. *Address:* Jubilee Building, University of Sussex, Falmer, Brighton BN1 9SL. *T:* (01273) 678332. *E:* L.A.Winters@sussex.ac.uk.

WINTERSGILL, Dr William, FFPH; Examining Medical Officer (part-time), Department of Health, since 1989; Member, Research and Advisory Committee, Cambridge Applied Nutrition, Toxicology and Biosciences Ltd, since 1984; *b* 20 Dec. 1922; *s* of Fred Wintersgill and May Wintersgill; *m* 1952, Iris May Holland; three *d*. *Educ:* Barnsley Holgate Grammar Sch.; Leeds Medical Sch., Univ. of Leeds (MB, ChB). MRCGP; MFCM, FFCM 1983. House Surgeon, 1948, and Registrar, 1948–49, Pontefract Infirmary; Principal, Gen. Practice, Snaith, Yorks, 1950–66; Dept of Health and Social Security (formerly Min. of Health): Reg. MO, 1967–70; SMO, 1970–72; PMO, 1972–76; SPMO, 1976–83. Specialist in Community Medicine, York HA, 1983–89. Pt-time MO, Cttee on Safety of Medicines, 1987–; Mem., Health Adv. Service Vis. Team, 1987–90; Dist Med. Advr, 1987–88. Chm., British Assoc. of Community Physicians, 1985–89. *Recreations:* gardening, antique collecting, playing the piano, choral singing, painting, old buildings. *Address:* 5 River View Court, Bridge Street, Hereford HR4 9BQ.

WINTERSON, Jeanette, OBE 2006; writer; Professor of New Writing, University of Manchester, since 2012; *b* 27 Aug. 1959; *m* 2015, Susie Orbach. *Educ:* St Catherine's Coll., Oxford (BA Hons English). Hon. FRA 2012. Internat. Fiction Award, Fest. Letteratura, Italy, 1999; 25th Anniversary Medal for Prose, Hay Fest., 2012; Internat. Rapallo Carige Prize for Women, 2014; Lifetime Achievement Award, Univ. of St Louis, Mo, 2014. *Publications:* Oranges are not the only fruit, 1985 (Whitbread Prize, 1st Novel; numerous awards for screenplay, televised 1990); The Passion, 1987 (John Llewellyn Rhys Prize); Sexing the Cherry, 1989 (E. M. Forster Award, Amer. Acad. and Inst. of Arts and Letters); Written on the Body, 1992; Art and Lies, 1994; Great Moments in Aviation (screenplay), 1994; Art Objects: essays on ecstasy and effrontery, 1995; Gut Symmetries, 1997; The World and Other Places (short stories), 1998; The Powerbook, 2000 (adapted for stage, 2002); Lighthousekeeping, 2004; Weight, 2005; The Stone Gods, 2007; (ed) Midsummer Nights: new stories/old dreams (short stories), 2009; Why Be Happy When You Could Be Normal? (memoir), 2011 (Ind. Publishers' Award, Stonewall Award, 2012); The Daylight Gate (horror novella), 2012; The Gap of Time, 2015; *for children*: The King of Capri, 2002; Tanglewreck, 2006; The Lion, the Unicorn, and Me, 2009 (opera version perf. Washington Nat. Opera, 2013); The Battle of the Sun, 2009; Ingenious (screenplay), 2009. *Recreations:* opera, ballet, champagne. *Address:* c/o Caroline Michel, PFD, 34 Russell Street, WC2B 5HA. *E:* mail@jeanettewinterson.com.

WINTERTON, 8th Earl *cr* 1766 (Ire.); **(Donald) David Turnour;** Baron Winterton 1761 (Ire.); Viscount Turnour 1766 (Ire.); *b* 13 Oct. 1943; *s* of Cecil Noel Turnour, DFM, CD (*d* 1987), *yr b* of 7th Earl Winterton and Evelyn Isabel, *d* of Dr C. A. Oulton; *S* uncle, 1991; *m* 1st, 1968, Jill Pauline (marr. diss. 1997), *d* of late John Geddes Esplen; two *d*; 2nd, 2004, Vecide Brigitte Aktelligul. *Educ:* Waterloo Lutheran Univ., Ontario (BA). *Heir: b* Robert Charles Turnour [*b* 30 Jan. 1950; *m* 1st, 1974, Sheila (marr. diss. 1976), *d* of G. H. Stocking; 2nd, 1983, Patricia Ann, *d* of William Avery; two *d*].

WINTERTON, (Jane) Ann, (Lady Winterton); *b* 6 March 1941; *d* of late Joseph Robert Hodgson and Ellen Jane Hodgson; *m* 1960, Nicholas Raymond Winterton (*see* Sir N. R. Winterton); two *s* one *d*. *Educ:* Erdington Grammar Sch. for Girls. MP (C) Congleton, 1983–2010. Opposition spokesman on nat. drug strategy, 1998–2001; Shadow Minister for Agriculture and Fisheries, 2001–02. Mem., Chairmen's Panel, 1992–98, 2005–10. Chm., 1992–2002, Vice-Chm., 2002–10, All Party Parly Pro-Life Gp. Fellow, Industry and Parlt Trust, 1987–2010. Pres., Congleton Div., St John Ambulance, 1984–; Vice Pres., Townswomen's Guilds, 1994–2004. *Recreations:* music, theatre, tennis, ski-ing. *Address:* Whitehall Farm, Mow Lane, Newbold Astbury, Congleton, Cheshire CW12 3NH.

WINTERTON, Nicholas Hugh, OBE 2003; Director, UK Shared Business Services Ltd (formerly RCUK Shared Services Ltd), since 2007; Executive Director (formerly Administrative Secretary), Medical Research Council, 1995–2009; *b* 1 May 1947; *s* of Deryck Winterton and Margaret Winterton (*née* Simms). *Educ:* Chislehurst and Sidcup GS for Boys; Sidney Sussex Coll., Cambridge (BA 1968, MA 1971; DipEcon 1969). Medical Research Council: various admin. posts, 1969–81; Head of Personnel, 1981–88; on secondment to Wellcome Foundn, Dartford, 1988–89; Director: Corporate Affairs, 1989–94; Finance, 1994–95. Director: UK Med. Ventures Mgt Ltd, 1998–2006; Hammersmith Imanet (formerly Imaging Research Solutions) Ltd, 2001–09; Charman, Board: MRC Technol., 2000–09; Ploughshare Innovations Ltd, 2009–13. Non-exec. Dir, Royal Free Hampstead NHS Trust, 1998–2008 (Vice-Chm., 2003–08). Chairman, Trustees: Bridge Theatre Trng Co., 1995–2006; Vinjeru (Educn Concern Malawi), 1999–. *Recreations:* gardening, travel, walking, theatre. *E:* nick.winterton@gmail.com.

WINTERTON, Sir Nicholas (Raymond), Kt 2002; DL; *b* 31 March 1938; *o s* of late N. H. Winterton, Lysways House, Longdon Green, near Rugeley, Staffs; *m* 1960, Jane Ann Hodgson (*see* J. A. Winterton); two *s* one *d*. *Educ:* Bilton Grange Prep. Sch.; Rugby Sch. Commnd 14th/20th King's Hussars, 1957–59. Sales Exec. Trainee, Shell-Mex and BP Ltd, 1959–60; Sales and Gen. Manager, Stevens and Hodgson Ltd, Birmingham (Co. engaged in sale and hire of construction equipment), 1960–71. Chairman: CPC Cttee, Meriden Cons. Assoc., 1966–68; Midland Branch, Contractors Mech. Plant Engrs Assoc., 1968–69. Member: W Midlands Cons. Council, 1966–69, 1971–72; Central Council, Nat. Union of Cons. and Unionist Assocs, 1971–72. Contested (C) Newcastle-under-Lyme, Oct. 1969, 1970. MP (C) Macclesfield, Sept. 1971–2010. Chairman: Select Cttee on Health, 1991–92; Select Cttee on Procedure, 1997–2005; Member: Social Services Select Cttee, 1980–90; Select Cttee on Modernisation of H of C, 1997–2010; Liaison Select Cttee, 1997–2005; Chairmen's Panel,

1986–2010. Additional Dep. Speaker, for sittings in Westminster Hall, 1998–2005. Chairman, All Party Parliamentary: Gp for Cotton and Allied Textiles, 1979–97; Gp for Media, 1992–2000; British Danish Gp, 1992–2010; British Falklands Is Gp, 1997–2010; British Bahamas Gp, 1997–2010; British Austria Gp, 1999–2010; Joint Chairman: All Party Party British Taiwan Gp, 1997–2010; W Coast Mainline Gp, 2001–10; Vice Chairman, All Party Parliamentary: British Swedish Gp, 1992–2010; British Indonesian Gp, 1992–2000; Anglo S Pacific Gp, 1997–2010; Road Transport Study Gp, 1997–2001; Clothing and Textiles Gp, 1997–2010; Manchester 2002 XVII Commonwealth Games Gp, 2000–02. Member Executive: 1922 Cttee, 1997–2010 (Vice-Chm., 2001–05; Treas., 2005–10); UK Br., CPA, 1997–2010 (Treas., 2004–07); Mem., Exec. Cttee, IPU, 2001–10 (Treas., 2007–10). Member: Exec. Cttee, Anglo-Austrian Soc., 1987–2000 (Chm., 1998–2000); Nat. Adv. Cttee, Duke of Edinburgh Award Scheme, 1973–99; Imperial Soc. of Knights Bachelor, 2002–. County Councillor, Atherstone Div. Warwickshire CC, 1967–72. President: Macclesfield Fermain Club, 1973–2010; Poynton Youth and Community Centre, 1971–2010; Upton Priory Youth Club, Macclesfield, 1992–2001; Vice-President: Macclesfield and Congleton District Scout Council; Cheshire Scout Assoc.; E Cheshire Hospice; Nat. Assoc. of Local Councils, 1979–2001; Royal Coll. of Midwives; N Cheshire Cruising Club, 1997–2010. Hon. Mem., Macclesfield Lions Club, 1973–2010; Hon. Life Mem., Macclesfield Rugby Union Football Club; Patron: Macclesfield and District Sheep Dog Trials Assoc., 1972–2014; Internat. Centre for Child Care Studies, 1980–94; Civit Hills Open Air Theatre, 1996–2001; Elizabeth Trust, 1983–94; Poynton Male Voice Choir, 1997–2010; E Cheshire Br., Alzheimer's Soc., 1998–2010. President, Macclesfield Branch: Riding for the Disabled, 1987–2010; Multiple Sclerosis Soc., 1987–2010. Founder Pres., Bollington Light Opera Gp, 1978– (Hon. Life Vice. Pres., 2010). Life Member: Poynton Gilbert and Sullivan Soc.; Bollington Fest. Players. Liveryman, Weavers' Co., 1981 (Mem., Ct of Assts, 1992–2012; Upper Bailiff, 1997–98); Freeman of the City of London, 1981. Hon. Freeman, Borough of Macclesfield, 2002. DL Cheshire, 2006. SBStJ 2000. *Recreations:* squash, tennis, swimming, horse riding, reading, walking, Rugby (spectator). *Clubs:* Cavalry and Guards, Lighthouse; Old Boys and Park Green (Macclesfield).

WINTERTON, Rt Hon. Rosalie, (Rt Hon. Rosie); PC 2006; MP (Lab) Doncaster Central, since 1997; *b* 10 Aug. 1958; *d* of Gordon and Valerie Winterton. *Educ:* Doncaster Grammar Sch.; Hull Univ. (BA Hons Hist.). Asst to John Prescott, MP, 1980–86; Parliamentary Officer: London Borough of Southwark, 1986–88; RCN, 1988–90; Man. Dir, Connect Public Affairs, 1990–94; Hd, private office of John Prescott, MP, 1994–97. Parly Sec., LCD, 2001–03; Minister of State: DoH, 2003–07; DfT, 2007–08; DWP, 2008–09; BIS and DCLG, 2009–10; Minister for Yorkshire and the Humber, 2008–10; Shadow Leader, H of C, 2010; Shadow Chief Whip, 2010–. *Recreations:* sailing, reading. *Address:* House of Commons, SW1A 0AA.

WINTLE, Rev. Canon Ruth Elizabeth; Hon. Assistant Priest, St John-in-Bedwardine, 1994–2006 (Parish Deacon, 1984–94); Canon Emeritus, Worcester Cathedral, since 1998 (Hon. Canon, 1987–97); *b* 30 Sept. 1931; *d* of John Wintle and Vera (*née* Lane). *Educ:* Clarendon Sch., Malvern, and Abergele, Wales; Westfield Coll., London (BA Hons French 1953); St Hugh's Coll., Oxford (MA Theol. 1972); St Michael's House, Oxford (IDC 1966). Teacher, St Hilda's Sch., Jamaica, 1953–60; Travelling Sec., Inter-Varsity Fellowship and Technical Colls Christian Fellowship, 1960–63; Accredited Lay Worker, St Andrew's Church, N Oxford, 1967–69; Tutor, St John's Coll., Durham, 1969–74; Deaconess (C of E), 1972; Selection Sec., ACCM, 1974–83; Organiser, Internat. Diakonia Conf., Coventry, 1983; Diocesan Dir of Ordinands, Worcester, 1984–92; ordained deacon, 1987, priest 1994; Bishop's Advr on Women's Ministry, Worcester, 1995–97. Mem., Third Order, SSF, 1990–. Mem., Bishop's Staff Meeting, Worcs, 1993–97. Member: Church Army Bd, 1985–2000; Crown Appointments Commn, 1990–95; Gen. Synod of C of E, 1990–95; Council, Retired Clergy Assoc., 1998–2004. Mem. Council, Malvern Coll., 1991–2000. Chm., Li Tim-Oi Foundn, 1993–2006. *Recreations:* reading, driving, ornithology. *Address:* 6 Coronation Avenue, Rushwick, Worcester WR2 5TF. *T:* (01905) 427109.

WINTON, Rt Rev. Alan Peter; *see* Thetford, Bishop Suffragan of.

WINTON, Alexander, CBE 1993; QFSM 1987; HM Chief Inspector of Fire Services for Scotland, 1990–93; *b* 13 July 1932; *s* of Alexander and Jean Winton; *m* 1957, Jean Dowie; two *s*. MIFireE. Fireman, Perth, 1958–64; Station Officer: Perth, 1964–67; Lancashire, 1967–69; Assistant Divisional Officer: E Riding, 1969–72; Angus, 1972–73; Divisional Officer III: Angus, 1973–75; Tayside, 1975–76; Divl Comdr (DOI), Tayside, 1976–80; Temp. Sen. Divl Officer, 1980–81; Dep. Firemaster, 1981–85; Firemaster, Tayside Fire Bde, 1985–89. *Recreations:* golf, curling, reading. *Address:* 5 Ferndale Drive, Broughty Ferry, Dundee DD5 3DB. *T:* (01382) 778156.

WINTON, Dr Douglas James, FMedSci; Senior Group Leader, Cancer Research UK Cambridge Institute, University of Cambridge, since 2012; *b* Aberdeen, 13 April 1959; *s* of late James Winton and of Margaret Nelson Winton; *m* 2006, Jean Aline Miller. *Educ:* Eastwood High Sch.; Univ. of Glasgow (BSc Hons 1982); Univ. of Bristol (PhD 1986). Post-doctoral Res. Associate, Inst. of Cancer Res., Surrey, 1986–89; University of Cambridge: Sen. Post-doctoral Res. Associate, Dept of Pathol., 1989–96; Ind. Principal Investigator, Dept of Oncol., 1996–2007; Gp Leader, CRUK Cambridge Inst., 2007–12. FMedSci 2014. Mem., Stickmakers Guild. *Publications:* papers on stem cells, cancer and intestinal biol. *Recreations:* walking stick maker, travel, jam making, collecting books on islands, finding good coffee bars. *Address:* Cancer Research UK Cambridge Institute, University of Cambridge, Li Ka Shing Centre, Robinson Way, Cambridge CB2 0RE. *T:* (01223) 769783. *E:* doug.winton@cruk.cam.ac.uk.

WINTOUR, Anna, OBE 2008; Editor, US Vogue, since 1988; Artistic Director, Condé Nast, since 2013; *b* 3 Nov. 1949; *d* of late Charles Vere Wintour, CBE; *m* 1984, Dr David Shaffer (marr. diss.); one *s* one *d*. *Educ:* Queen's College Sch., London; North London Collegiate Sch. Dep. Fashion Editor, Harpers and Queen Magazine, 1970–76; Fashion Editor, Harpers Bazaar, NY, 1976–77; Fashion and Beauty Editor, Viva Mag., 1977–78; Contributing Editor for Fashion and Style, Savvy Mag., 1980–81; Sen. Editor, New York Mag., NY, 1981–83; Creative Dir, US Vogue, 1983–86; Editor-in-Chief, Vogue, 1986–87; Editor, House and Garden, New York, 1987–88.

See also P. Wintour.

WINTOUR, Patrick; Political Editor, The Guardian, since 2006; *b* 1 Nov. 1954; *s* of late Charles Vere Wintour, CBE and Eleanor Trego Wintour (*née* Baker); *m* 2002, Rachel Sylvester; two *s*, and one *s* one *d* by a previous marriage. *Educ:* Hall Sch., London; Westminster Sch.; Corpus Christi Coll., Oxford (BA). Journalist, New Statesman, 1976–82; The Guardian: Chief Labour Correspondent, 1983–88; Chief Political Correspondent, 1988–96 and 2000–06; Political Ed., The Observer, 1996–2000. *Publications:* Eddie Shah and the Newspaper Revolution, 1985; Labour Rebuilt, 1990. *Recreations:* piano, gardening. *Address:* The Guardian, Kings Place, 90 York Way, N1 9AG. *E:* Patrick.Wintour@theguardian.com. *Club:* Soho House.

See also A. Wintour.

WINYARD, Dr Graham Peter Arthur, CBE 1999; FRCP; FFPH; Postgraduate Dean, Wessex Deanery, Department of Health, 1999–2007; *b* 19 Jan. 1947; *s* of Lyonel Arthur Winyard and Dorothy Elizabeth Payne; *m* 1st, 1979, Sandra Catherine Bent (*d* 2002); one *s* two *d*; 2nd, 2006, Jill Saltmarsh. *Educ:* Southend High Sch.; Hertford Coll., Oxford (MA); Middlesex Hosp. (BM, BCh); Sch. of Oriental and African Studies, Univ. of London (MA 2014). Sen. House Officer, United Oxford Hosps, 1973–75; Registrar in Community Medicine, 1975–77; Provincial Health Officer, Madang, PNG, 1977–79; Sen. Registrar in Community Medicine, Oxford RHA, and Lectr, LSHTM, 1979–82; Dist MO, Lewisham and N Southwark HA, 1982–87; SPMO, DHSS, later Dept of Health, 1987–90; Regl Med. Dir and Dir of Public Health, Wessex RHA, 1990–93; Dep. CMO and Dir Health Services, NHS Exec., DoH, 1993–98. Consultant Advr to Defence Medical Services, 2001–07. Hon. Prof. of Public Health Mgt, Univ. of Southampton, 1999–2007. Vice-Pres., FPH, 2004–07; Chm., Cttee of Postgrad. Deans UK, 2004–07. Member: Steering Gp, Healthcare Professionals for Assisted Dying, 2010–; Bd, Dignity in Dying, 2013–. Treas., Chithurst Buddhist monastery. *Recreations:* Buddhist studies, meditation, music.

WISBECH, Archdeacon of; *see* McCurdy, Ven. H. K.

WISE, family name of **Baron Wise**.

WISE, 3rd Baron *cr* 1951, of King's Lynn; **Christopher John Clayton Wise;** Director, Everysite, since 2010; *b* Banbury, Oxfordshire, 19 March 1949; *er s* of 2nd Baron Wise and of Margaret Annie (*née* Snead); *S* father, 2012; *m* 1988, Rosalind Myrtle Reed; two *s*. *Educ:* Norwich Sch.; Southampton Univ. (BSc; PhD); Harper Adams Coll. (PGDip). Publisher, Procs of British Crop Protection Council, 1978–2003; Policy Dir, Nat. Fedn of Builders, 2003–06; Co. Sec., British Assoc. for Supported Employment, 2006–08; Ops Dir, Construction Industry Accredited Performance Scheme Ltd, 2008–10. Non-exec. Dir, BCPC, 1994–2003. Crop Sci. Advr, NFU, 1994–2003. *Publications:* (contrib.) Modern Crop Protection: developments and perspectives, 1993; contrib. Annals of Applied Biol. *Recreations:* caravanning, ski-ing, sailing. *Heir:* *s* Hon. Thomas Christopher Clayton Wise, *b* 6 June 1989. *Address:* Demeter House, Woodmancote, Cirencester, Glos GL7 7EF. *Club:* Farmers.

WISE, Hon. Lady; Morag Barbara Wise; a Senator of the College of Justice in Scotland, since 2013; *b* 22 Jan. 1963; *d* of Leslie James Wise and late Barbara Gillies or Wise; *m* 1994, Alastair John Angus McEwan; one *s* two *d*. *Educ:* Univ. of Aberdeen (LLB 1st Cl. Hons 1985; DipLP 1986); McGill Univ., Montreal (LLM 1995). Solicitor in private practice, 1989–92; admitted Advocate, 1993; QC (Scot.) 2005; Temp. Judge, Ct of Session, 2008–13. Chair: Advocates Family Law Assoc., 2007–13; Family Law Arbitration Gp (Scotland), 2011–13; Dir and Trustee, Family Mediation Lothian, 2008–13. Hon. LLD Aberdeen, 2015. *Publications:* (ed jtly) Gloag and Henderson, The Law of Scotland, 11th edn 2001 to 13th edn 2012; (contrib.) A Practical Guide to Human Rights Law in Scotland, ed Lord Reed, 2001. *Recreations:* singing, ski-ing (badly), socialising. *Address:* Court of Session, Parliament House, Parliament Square, Edinburgh EH1 1RQ. *T:* (0131) 225 2595. *E:* supreme.courts@scotcourts.gov.uk.

WISE, Christopher Mark, RDI 1998; FREng; FICE; Co-founder and Director, Expedition Engineering, since 1999; *b* 2 Nov. 1956; *s* of Jeffery and Jean Wise; one *s* by Elspeth Beard; two *s* one *d* by Catherine Ramsden. *Educ:* Reigate Grammar Sch.; Univ. of Southampton (BSc Hons 1979). MIStructE 1985; FREng 2003; FICE 2008. Joined Ove Arup and Partners, Consulting Engrs, 1979; Dir, Ove Arup Partnership, 1993–99; *projects* include: Torre de Collserola, Barcelona, 1992; Channel 4 HQ, 1995; Commerzbank HQ, Frankfurt, 1996; American Air Mus., Duxford, 1997; Millennium Bridge, London, 2000; Infinity Footbridge, Stockton (IStructE Supreme Award, 2009); Barcelona Bullring; 2012 Olympic Velodrome; Intesa Sanpaolo Bank HQ Tower, Turin; Greek Nat. Opera House; Library, Athens. Prof. of Civil Engrg Design, ICSTM, 1998–99; Davenport Prof., Sch. of Architecture, Yale Univ., 2006; Prof. of Civil Engrg Design, UCL, 2012–15. Mem., Design Council, 2005–11. Co-founder and Chm., Useful Simple Trust, 2008–. Reconstructions of Roman technology, for Secrets of Lost Empires series, BBC2: Colosseum, 1996; Caesar's Bridge, 1999. Columnist, Building Mag., 2009–. Master, Faculty of RDI, 2007–09. FRSA 1995. Hon. FRIBA 2001. Guthrie Brown Award, 1993, Oscar Faber Medal, 1996, Gold Medal, 2012, IStructE; Silver Medal, RAEng, 2007; Milne Medal, IABSE, 2010; Gold Medal, ICE, 2012. *Publications:* papers on engrg educn projects in IStructE jl. *Recreations:* abstract painting, guitar, cricket, soccer. *Address:* Expedition Engineering, Morley House, 1st Floor, 320 Regent Street, W1B 3BB.

WISE, Fiona; independent health care business consultant; Chief Executive, North West London Hospitals NHS Trust, 2007–12; *b* 1 Aug. 1954; *d* of Duncan and Doreen Lamond; *m*; two *s*. *Educ:* Haberdashers' Aske's Girls' Sch., Acton; St Mary's Grammar Sch., Northwood. DipHSM. Dep. Unit Gen. Manager, Royal Free Hosp., 1984–88; Unit Gen. Manager, Enfield Priority and Community Care, 1988–93; Chief Exec., Enfield Community Care NHS Trust, 1993–2001; interim Chief Exec., Stoke Mandeville Hosp. NHS Trust, 2001–03; Actg Dir of Modernisation, Beds and Herts Strategic HA, 2003; Chief Exec., Ealing Hosp. NHS Trust, 2003–07. *Recreations:* family, tennis, cooking. *E:* f.wise@btinternet.com.

WISE, Ian; QC 2010; *b* Stoke-on-Trent, 8 July 1959; *s* of Derek Wise and Beryl Wise (*née* Haynes); *m* 1992, Denise; two *d*. *Educ:* Newcastle High Sch.; Open Univ. (BA). Called to the Bar, Gray's Inn, 1992; Mem., Doughty Street Chambers, 1994–2014, Hd, public law team, 1998–2011; Mem., Monckton Chambers, 2014–. *Publications:* Enforcement of Local Taxation, 2000; (jtly) Children in Need: local authority support for children and families, 2011, 2nd edn, 2014. *Recreations:* various sports, family, walking my dog through woods and countryside. *Address:* Monckton Chambers, 1–2 Raymond Buildings, Gray's Inn, WC1R 5NR. *T:* (020) 7405 7211, *Fax:* (020) 7405 2084.

WISE, Prof. Michael John, CBE 1979; MC 1945; PhD; FRGS; Emeritus Professor of Geography, University of London; *b* Stafford, 17 Aug. 1918; *s* of Harry Cuthbert and Sarah Evelyn Wise; *m* 1942, Barbara Mary (*d* 2007), *d* of C. L. Hodgetts, Wolverhampton; one *d* one *s*. *Educ:* Saltley Secondary School, Birmingham; University of Birmingham (BA (Hons Geography) and Mercator Prize in Geography, 1939; DipEd 1940; PhD 1951). Served War, Royal Artillery, 80th LAA Regt, 1941–44, 5th Bn The Northamptonshire Regt, 1944–46, in Middle East and Italy; commissioned, 1941, Major, 1944. Assistant Lecturer, Univ. of Birmingham, 1946–48, Lecturer in Geography, 1948–51; London School of Economics: Lecturer in Geography, 1951–54; Sir Ernest Cassel Reader in Economic Geography, 1954–58; Prof. of Geography, 1958–83; Pro-Director, 1983–85; Hon. Fellow, 1988. Chm., Departmental Cttee of Inquiry into Statutory Smallholdings, 1963–67; Mem., Dept of Transport Adv. Cttee on Landscape Treatment of Trunk Roads, 1971–90 (Chm., 1981–90). Mem., UGC for Hong Kong, 1966–73. Recorder, Sect. E, Brit. Assoc. for Advancement of Science, 1955–60 (Pres., 1965); Founder Pres., Transport Studies Soc., 1962; President: Inst. of British Geographers, 1974 (Hon. Mem., 1989); IGU, 1976–80 (Vice-Pres., 1968–76); Geographical Assoc., 1976–77 (Hon. Treasurer, 1967–76, Hon. Mem., 1983); Vice-Pres., Nat. Assoc. for Envmtl Educn, 1977–; Mem., SSRC, 1976–82; Chm., Council for Extra-Mural Studies, Univ. of London, 1976–83; Chm., Exec. Cttee, Assoc. of Agriculture, 1972–83 (Vice-Pres., 1983–93); Mem. Adv. Cttees, UN Univ., 1976–82; Hon. Sec., RGS, 1963–73, Vice-Pres., 1975–78, Hon. Vice-Pres., 1978–80, 1983–, Pres., 1980–82. Chm., Birkbeck Coll., 1983–89 (Governor, 1968–89; Fellow, 1989); Mem. Delegacy, Goldsmiths' Coll., 1984–88. Chm., Dudley Stamp Meml Trust, 1988–2005 (Hon. Sec., 1966–88; Hon. Pres., 2006). Erskine Fellow, Univ. of Canterbury, NZ, 1970. Hon. Life Mem., Univ. of London Union, 1977. Hon. Member: Geog. Soc. of Russia, 1975; Assoc. of Japanese Geographers, 1980; Geog. Soc. of Mexico, 1984; Geog. Soc. of Poland, 1986; Membre d'Honneur, Société de Géographie, 1983. FIEnvSc 1980; FRSA 1983. Hon. FLI 1991. DUniv Open, 1978; Hon. DSc Birmingham, 1982. Received Gill Memorial award of RGS, 1958; RGS Founder's Medal, 1977; Alexander Kőrösi Csoma Medal, Hungarian Geographical Soc., 1980; Tokyo Geographical Soc. Medal, 1981; Lauréat d'Honneur, IGU,

1984. *Publications:* Hon. Editor, Birmingham and its Regional Setting, 1951; A Pictorial Geography of the West Midlands, 1958; General Consultant, An Atlas of Earth Resources, 1979; The Great Geographical Atlas, 1982; (consultant and contrib.) The Ordnance Survey Atlas of Great Britain, 1982; numerous articles on economic and urban geography. *Recreations:* music, gardening. *Address:* 45 Oakleigh Avenue, N20 9JE. *T:* (020) 8445 6057. *Club:* Athenæum.

WISE, Morag Barbara; *see* Wise, Hon. Lady.

WISE, Dr Richard, FMedSci; Consultant Medical Microbiologist, City Hospital, Birmingham, 1974–2005; *b* 7 July 1942; s of late James Wise and Joan Wise; *m* 1979, Jane M. Symonds; one *d* (one *s* decd). *Educ:* Univ. of Manchester (MB ChB; MD 1980). Hon. Prof. of Clin. Microbiol., Univ. of Birmingham, 1995–; Civilian Consultant, Army, 1997–. Advr, Sci. and Technol. Cttee, H of L, 1997–99. Chm., Specialist Adv. Cttee on Antimicrobial Resistance, 2001–07; Mem., Nat. Expert Cttee on New and Emerging Diseases, 2003–07. Non-executive Director: Centre for Applied Microbiol Res., Porton Down, 1999–2003; Health Protection Agency, 2003–07. Pres., British Soc. Antimicrobial Chemotherapy, 1997–2000. Advr, European Centre for Disease Control, Stockholm, 2005–. Vice Chm., W Midlands, 2009–12, Herefordshire, 2011–, CPRE. Trustee, Hereford Nature Trust, 2002–10 (Dep. Chm., 2007–10). FMedSci 2003. Hon. FRCP 1997. *Publications:* numerous contribs on antibiotic therapy. *Recreations:* gardening, wine, food, France, walking, flying. *Address:* Springfield House, Breinton, Hereford HR4 7PB. *Clubs:* East India; Herefordshire Aero.

WISE, Thomas Harold; Member (UK Ind) Eastern Region, European Parliament, 2004–09; *b* 13 May 1948; *s* of Harold Stanley and Helen Wise; *m* 1974, Janet Featherstone; one *s* one *d*. *Educ:* Bournemouth Grammar Sch.; Bournemouth Coll. Police cadet, 1965, PC, 1967–70, Dorset Police; salesman, 1970–73, Nat. Accounts Exec., 1973–74, Aspro-Nicholas; Regl Manager, Cavenham Confectionery, 1974–78; salesman, 1978–82, Nat. Account Sales Manager, 1982–84, Melitta Benz; National Account Manager: Nestlé, 1984–85; Spillers, 1985–87; Pasta Foods, 1987–89; Sales and Mktg Manager, Chineham Internat., 1989–91; Man. Dir, Ostmann Spices, Brynmawr, 1991–94; Retail Sales Manager, Rio Pacific Foods, Watford, 1994–97; Sales Dir, Brand Mktg Internat., 1997–98; portfolio mgt, 1998–2000; Special Projects Manager, Itswine.com, 2000–01; Office Manager and Regl Organiser, E of England, UKIP, 2001–04. *Recreations:* travel, numismatics, wine appreciation.

WISEMAN, Debbie, MBE 2004; composer and conductor, film and television scores, since 1984; *b* 10 May 1963; *d* of Paul Wiseman and Barbara Wiseman; *m* 1987, Tony Wharmby. *Educ:* Henrietta Barnett Sch.; Trinity Coll. of Music, London (Saturday Exhibnr); Kingsway-Princeton Morley Coll., London; GSMD (GGSM 1984). *Film scores include:* Tom and Viv, 1994; Haunted, 1995; Wilde, 1997; Lighthouse, 1998; Tom's Midnight Garden, 1999; Before You Go, 2002; Freeze Frame, Arsène Lupin, 2004; The Truth About Love, 2005; Middletown, 2006; Flood, 2007; Lesbian Vampire Killers, The Hide, 2009; *television scores include:* The Good Guys, 1992–93; Warriors, 2000; Judge John Deed, 2001–06; My Uncle Silas, 2001; Othello, 2001; He Knew He Was Right, 2004; The Man-eating Leopard of Rudraprayag, 2005; Beaten, 2005; The Inspector Lynley Mysteries, 2005; Johnny and the Bomb, 2006; Jekyll, 2007; The Passion, 2008; Stephen Fry in America, 2009; Land Girls, 2009–11; Joanna Lumley's Nile, 2010; The Promise, 2011; Fry's Planet Word, 2011; Joanna Lumley's Greek Odyssey, 2011; Lost Christmas, 2012; Father Brown, 2013; WPC 56, 2013; A Poet In New York, 2014; Wolf Hall, 2015; The Coroner, 2015; *theatre:* Feather Boy: the musical, NT, 2006. Vis. Prof., Composition for Screen course, RCM, 1998–. Hon. FTCL 2006; Hon. FGSM 2007; Hon. DMus Sussex, 2015. *Recreations:* swimming, table tennis, snooker. *Address:* c/o Music Matters International Ltd, Crest House, 102–104 Church Road, Teddington, Middlesex TW11 8PY. *T:* (020) 8979 4580, *Fax:* (020) 8979 4590. *E:* dwiseman10@aol.com.

WISEMAN, Sir John William, 11th Bt *cr* 1628; financial adviser, R. W. Pressprich & Co., Boston, since 1996; *b* 16 March 1957; *o s* of Sir William George Eden Wiseman, 10th Bt, CB, and of Joan Mary, *d* of late Arthur Phelps, Harrow; *S* father, 1962; *m* 1980, Nancy, *d* of Casimer Zyla, New Britain, Conn; two *d*. *Educ:* Millfield Sch.; Univ. of Hartford, Conn, USA. *Heir: kinsman* Thomas Alan Wiseman [*b* 8 July 1921; *m* 1946, Hildemarie Domnik (*d* 1991); (one *s* one *d* decd)].

WISEMAN, Prof. Timothy Peter, DPhil; FSA; FBA 1986; Professor of Classics, University of Exeter, 1977–2001, now Emeritus; *b* 3 Feb. 1940; *s* of Stephen Wiseman and Winifred Agnes Wiseman (*née* Rigby); *m* 1962, Doreen Anne Williams. *Educ:* Manchester Grammar Sch.; Balliol Coll., Oxford (MA 1964; DPhil 1967). FSA 1977. Rome Schol. in Classical Studies, British Sch. at Rome, 1962–63; University of Leicester: Asst Lectr in Classics, 1963–65; Lectr, 1965–73; Reader in Roman History, 1973–76. Vice-Pres., British Acad., 1992–94; President: Roman Soc., 1992–95; Jt Assoc. of Classical Teachers, 1998–99; Classical Assoc., 2000–01. Chm. Council, British Sch. at Rome, 2002–07. Vis. Associate Prof., Univ. of Toronto, 1970–71; Lansdowne Lectr, Univ. of Victoria (BC), 1987; Whitney J. Oates Fellow, Princeton, 1988 and 2008; Webster Lectr, Stanford, 1993. Hon. DLitt Durham, 1988. *Publications:* Catullan Questions, 1969; New Men in the Roman Senate, 1971; Cinna the Poet, 1974; Clio's Cosmetics, 1979; (with Anne Wiseman) Julius Caesar: the battle for Gaul, 1980; (ed) Roman Political Life, 1985; Catullus and his World, 1985; Roman Studies Literary and Historical, 1987; trans., Flavius Josephus, Death of an Emperor, 1991, 2nd edn (as The Death of Caligula), 2013; Talking to Virgil, 1992; Historiography and Imagination, 1994; Remus: a Roman myth, 1995; Roman Drama and Roman History, 1998; (ed) Classics in Progress, 2002; The Myths of Rome, 2004; Unwritten Rome, 2008; Remembering the Roman People, 2009; (with Anne Wiseman) Ovid: times and reasons, 2011; The Roman Audience, 2015. *Address:* 22 Hillcrest Park, Exeter EX4 4SH. *T:* (01392) 273226.

WISHART, Peter; MP (SNP) Perth and North Perthshire, since 2005 (North Tayside, 2001–05); *b* 9 March 1962; *s* of Alex and Nan Wishart; *m* 1990, Carrie Lindsay (separated 2003); one *s*. *Educ:* Moray House Coll. of Educn. Community worker, 1984–85; musician with rock band, Runrig, 1985–2001. Chief Whip, SNP Gp, 2001–07, 2013–; Mem., Scottish Affairs Select Cttee, 2008–10 and 2015– (Chm., 2015–). SNP spokesperson: for Culture, Media and Sport, 2001–15; Internat. Develt, 2001–10; for Constitution and Home Affairs, 2007–15; Shadow Leader of the House, 2015–. *Recreations:* music, hillwalking. *Address:* (office) 35 Perth Street, Blairgowrie PH10 6DL; (office) 63 Glasgow Road, Perth PH2 0PE.

WISHART, Ruth; writer and broadcaster; *d* of Jack Wishart and Margaret Wishart; *m* 1971, Roderick McLeod (*d* 2004). *Educ:* Eastwood Sen. Secondary Sch.; Open Univ. (BA Hons Humanities 2008). Assistant Editor: Daily Record, 1975–78; Sunday Mail, 1978–82; Sunday Standard, 1982–83; Sen. Asst Ed., The Scotsman, 1986–88; Presenter, BBC Radio Scotland, 1986–2008; columnist, The Herald, 1998–. Chair: Centre for Contemporary Arts Glasgow, 1995–2003; Glasgow Common Purpose, 1998–2003; Dewar Arts Awards, 2002–. Trustee: Nat. Galls of Scotland, 2002–10; Columba 1400, 2006–12; Creative Scotland, 2010–. Gov., Glasgow Sch. of Art, 1998–2003. FRSA. DUniv Stirling, 1994. *Recreations:* visual arts, theatre, sport, concerts. *Address:* Clutha, Meikle Aiden Brae, Kilcreggan G84 0JD. *E:* ruth@kilcreggan.demon.co.uk.

WISTRICH, Enid Barbara, PhD; Visiting Professor, School of Social Sciences (formerly of History and Politics), Middlesex University, 1997–Sept. 2016; *b* 4 Sept. 1928; *d* of Zadik Heiber and Bertha Brown; *m* 1950, Ernest Wistrich, CBE (*d* 2015); two *c* (and one *c* decd). *Educ:* Froebel Institute Sch.; Brackley High Sch.; St Paul's Girls' Sch.; London School of Economics (BScEcon, PhD). Research Asst, LSE, 1950–52; Instructor, Mt Holyoke Coll., Mass, USA, 1952–53; Research Officer, Royal Inst. of Public Administration, 1954–56; Sen. Res. Officer, LSE, 1969–72; NEDO, 1977–79; Prin. Lectr, 1979–91, Reader in Politics and Public Admin, 1991–94, Middlesex Poly., subseq. Middlesex Univ. Vis. Lectr, Univ. of Waikato, NZ, 1989. Councillor (Lab): Hampstead Metropolitan Bor. Council, 1962–65; London Bor. of Camden, 1964–68 and 1971–74; GLC, ILEA, 1973–77. Mem., Hampstead Community Health Council, 1984–92 (Chm., 1986–88). Governor: British Film Inst., 1974–81 (also Actg Chm., 1977–78); National Film Sch., 1978–82. Chm. of Governors, Heathlands Sch. for Autistic Children, 1976–86. *Publications:* Local Government Reorganisation: the first years of Camden, 1972; I Don't Mind the Sex, It's the Violence: film censorship explored, 1978; The Politics of Transport, 1983; (jtly) The Migrants' Voice in Europe, 1999; (jtly) Regional Identity and Diversity in Europe, 2007; (jtly) Devolution and Localism in England, 2014; chapters and articles in various books and jls. *Recreations:* experiencing the arts, admiring nature. *Address:* 37B Gayton Road, NW3 1UB. *T:* (020) 7419 1742.

WITCHELL, Nicholas Newton Henshall; Diplomatic Correspondent, since 1995, Royal Correspondent, since 1998, BBC News; *b* 23 Sept. 1953; *s* of late William Joseph Henshall Witchell and Barbara Sybil Mary Witchell (*née* Macdonald); two *d*; *m* 2014, Maria Frances Staples. *Educ:* Epsom Coll.; Leeds Univ. (LLB). Joined BBC, 1976: grad. news trainee, 1976–78; reporter: TV and radio, NI, 1978–82; TV Network News, 1982–83; Ireland Corresp., 1983–84; Presenter: Six O'Clock News, 1984–89; BBC Breakfast News, 1989–94; Associate Producer: News '39, 1989; News '44, 1994; News '45, 1995; Corresp., Panorama, 1994–95. Gov., Queen Elizabeth's Foundn (formerly Queen Elizabeth's Foundn for Disabled People), 1992– (Vice-Pres., 2010–). Hon. Patron, Queen Alexandra Hosp. Home, 2006–. FRGS 1990. Sony Radio Acad. Event Award, 2002. OStJ 1995. *Publications:* The Loch Ness Story, 1974. *Address:* BBC News, BBC Broadcasting House, Portland Place, W1A 1AA. *Club:* Reform.

WITCHER, Sally Anne, OBE 2006; PhD; freelance management and social policy consultant, since 2010; Chief Executive Officer, Inclusion Scotland, since 2013; *b* 11 July 1960; *d* of late Michael James Witcher and of Janet Mary Witcher (*née* Ashford). *Educ:* Slade Sch. of Fine Art (BA Hons); University Coll. London; Edinburgh Univ. (MSc Policy Studies, PhD Social Policy 2006). Teacher, English as a Foreign Language, British Inst., Lisbon, 1984–85; freelance sculptor, 1985–87; Homeless Families Liaison Worker, Earls Court Homelessness Project, 1987–89; Campaign Worker, Disability Alliance, 1989–93; Dir, CPAG, 1993–98; freelance mgt and social policy consultant, 1998–2006. Chair, Disability Employment Adv. Cttee, DWP, 2002–06; Dep. Dir, Office for Disability Issues, DWP, 2006–10. Mem. Bd, Care Inspectorate (formerly Social Care and Social Work Improvement Scotland), 2011–15. *Publications:* (jtly) A Way out of Poverty and Disability, 1991; (jtly) Letters, Lobbies, Legislation: a guide to Parliamentary campaigning in Scotland, 1999; (jtly) Direct Payments: the impact on choice and control for disabled people, 2000; (jtly) Bodies Politic: a guide for voluntary organisations lobbying in Holyrood, Westminster and Brussels, 2002; Reviewing the terms of inclusion: transactional processes, currencies and context, 2003; Inclusive Equality: a vision for social justice, 2013.

WITCOMB, Roger Mark, OBE 2015; Panel Chairman, Competition and Markets Authority, since 2014; *b* Devizes, 5 May 1947; *s* of Cyril and Jo Witcomb; *m* 1970, Marian Stone; two *s*. *Educ:* Eton Coll.; Merton Coll., Oxford (BA Maths 1968); Nuffield Coll., Oxford (MPhil Econs 1970). Economist, Bank of England, 1970–71; Fellow, Churchill Coll., Cambridge, 1972–74; Fellow, Gonville and Caius Coll., Cambridge, 1974–79; Res. Officer, Dept of Applied Econs, Univ. of Cambridge, 1976–79; Commercial Manager, BP, 1980–89; schoolmaster, Winchester Coll., 1989–90; Dir of Planning, 1990–96, Finance Dir, 1996–2000, Nat. Power; Headhunter, Saxton Bampfylde, 2001–02; Senior Adviser: CDC, 2002–04; Actis, 2004–07. Director: Anglian Water, 2002–10; Andrews & Partners, 2005–11; Infraco Ltd, 2005–11; Renewable Energy Hldgs, 2009–10. Mem., Competition Commn, 2009–14 (Chm., 2011–14). Trustee, Opportunity Internat. UK, 2002–14 (Chm., 2004–06). Gov., Univ. of Winchester, 2004–11 (Chm., 2006–11). Hon. DBA Winchester, 2012. *Recreations:* music, golf, walking, cricket. *Address:* Competition and Markets Authority, Victoria House, Southampton Row, WC1B 4AD. *T:* (020) 3738 6000. *E:* roger.witcomb@cma.gsi.gov.uk. *Club:* Reform.

WITCOMBE, Very Rev. John Julian; Dean of Coventry, since 2013; *b* Wimbledon, 1 March 1959; *s* of Dr Dennis Witcombe, OBE, and Patricia Witcombe; *m* 1st, 1983, Rev. Maureen Edwards (*d* 1999); one *s* two *d*; 2nd, 2000, Rev. Ricarda Leask (*née* Anderson); two step *d*. *Educ:* Nottingham High Sch.; Emmanuel Coll., Cambridge (BA Hons Law 1980); St John's Coll., Nottingham (BA Hons Theol. 1983); Univ. of Nottingham (MPhil 1991). Ordained deacon, 1984, priest, 1985; Curate, St John's, Birtley, 1984–87; Team Vicar, St Barnabas, Inham Nook, 1987–91; Vicar, St Luke's, Lodge Moor, 1991–95; Team Rector, Uxbridge, 1995–98; Dean, St John's Coll., Nottingham, 1998–2005; Diocese of Gloucester: Dir of Ordinands, 2005–11; Dir of Discipleship and Ministry, 2011–13. Hon. Canon, 2009–10, Res. Canon, 2010–12, Glos Cath. *Publications:* Renewing the Traditional Church, 2002; The Curate's Guide, 2005; Hanging on to God, 2008. *Recreations:* hill-walking, family, theatre, galleries, film, music, travel. *Address:* Coventry Cathedral, 1 Hill Top, Coventry CV1 5AB. *T:* (024) 7652 1200. *E:* dean@coventrycathedral.org.uk.

WITHALL, Maj.-Gen. William Nigel James, CB 1982; Marketing Director, and Member, Board of Directors, Link-Miles Ltd, 1985–93 (Consultant, 1984); *b* 14 Oct. 1928; *s* of late Bernard Withall and Enid (*née* Hill); *m* 1952, Pamela Hickman; one *s* one *d*. *Educ:* St Benedict's. Army Engr Cadet, 1947–50; Mons OCS, 1950; Commnd RE, 1950; served in Hong Kong, Gulf States, Aden, Germany and India; Staff Coll., 1961; Sqdn Comd, 73 Fd Sqdn, 1964–66; Jt Services Staff Coll., Latimer, 1967; Mil. Asst to MGO, 1968–70; CO 26 Engr Regt, BAOR, 1970–72; Bde Comd, 11 Engr Bde, 1974–76; NDC, India, 1977; No 259 Army Pilots Course, 1978; Dir, Army Air Corps, 1979–83. Col Comdt RE, 1984–97. Chm., Army Football Assoc., 1980–81; Pres., Army Cricket Assoc., 1981–83; Hon. Life Vice Pres., Aircrew Assoc., 1986; Chm., RE Assoc., 1993–97. Chm., Chute Parish Council, 1995–2002. Freeman, City of London, 1981; Liveryman, Hon. Co. of Air Pilots (formerly GAPAN), 1981. *Recreations:* cricket (Army Cricket XI, 1957–67), squash, all games, reading, walking. *Address:* Linden House, Upper Chute, near Andover, Hants SP11 9EL. *Clubs:* MCC, I Zingari, Band of Brothers, Free Foresters, Stragglers of Asia.

WITHERIDGE, Rev. John Stephen, MA; FRHistS; Headmaster of Charterhouse, 1996–2013; Associate Member, Wadham College, Oxford, since 2014; *b* 14 Nov. 1953; *s* of late Francis Edward Witheridge and Joan Elizabeth Witheridge (*née* Exell); *m* 1975, Sarah Caroline, *d* of Rev. Peter Phillips; two *s* two *d*. *Educ:* St Albans Sch.; Univ. of Kent at Canterbury (BA 1st cl. Eng. and Theol.); Christ's Coll., Cambridge (BA 2nd cl. Theol Tripos; MA); Ridley Hall, Cambridge. Ordained deacon, 1979, priest, 1980; Curate, Luton Parish Church, 1979–82; Head of Religious Studies and Asst Chaplain, Marlborough Coll., 1982–84; Chaplain to Archbishop of Canterbury, 1984–87; Conduct (Sen. Chaplain), Eton Coll., 1987–96. Chm., Lomans Trust, 2000–07; Vice-Pres., Eyeless Trust, 2001–07. Mem. Ct, Univ. of Surrey, 1997–2013. Governor: Brambletye Sch., 2008–12; Clifton Coll., 2009–. FRHistS 2013. *Publications:* Frank Fletcher: a formidable headmaster, 2005; Excellent Dr Stanley: the life of Dean Stanley of Westminster, 2013; articles and reviews. *Recreations:* biography, gardening, grandchildren. *Address:* Minster Cottage, Church Street, Charlbury, Oxon OX7 3PR.

WITHEROW, David Michael Lindley, CBE 2004; Executive Chairman, Radio Authority, 2003 (Member, 1998–2003; Deputy Chair, 2000–03); *b* 19 July 1937; *s* of Dr James Witherow and Greta (*née* Roberts); *m* 1st, 1960, Ragnhild Kadow (marr. diss. 1994); two *d*; 2nd, 1994, Elizabeth Anne Wright, *qv*. *Educ:* King Edward's Sch., Birmingham (Foundn Schol.); Pembroke Coll., Cambridge (BA Hons 1960). Nat. service, RCS, 1955–57. Press Assoc., 1960–63; BBC, 1963–96: Ext. Services News, 1963–77, Editor, 1973–77; Editor, Weekly Progs, TV News, 1977–79; Chief Assistant, Regions, 1980; Head, then Gen. Manager, Monitoring Service, Caversham, 1980–85; Controller, Resources and Admin, Ext. Services, 1985–89; Dep. Man. Dir, 1989–94, Policy Consultant, 1994–96, World Service; Project Dir, Digital Audio Broadcasting Services, 1994–96. Pres., World (formerly Europ.) DAB Forum, 1995–97. *Recreations:* theatre, music. *E:* davidmlw2@hotmail.com.

WITHEROW, John Moore; Editor, The Times, since 2013; *b* Johannesburg, 20 Jan. 1952; *m* 1985, Sarah Linton; two *s* one *d*. *Educ:* Bedford Sch.; York Univ. (BA Hons Hist.). Reuters trainee, London and Madrid, 1977–80; home and foreign corresp., The Times, 1980–83; Sunday Times: Defence corresp., 1984–85; Diplomatic Corresp., 1985–87; Focus Ed., 1987–89; Foreign Ed., 1989–92; Man. Ed. (News), 1992–94; Actg Ed., 1994; Ed., 1995–2013. *Publications:* (with Patrick Bishop) The Winter War: the Falklands, 1982; The Gulf War, 1993. *Recreations:* tennis, sailing. *Address:* The Times, 1 London Bridge Street, SE1 9GF. *T:* (020) 7782 5640. *E:* john.witherow@thetimes.co.uk. *Clubs:* Soho House, Hurlingham, Ivy; Campden Hill Tennis.

WITHERS, Prof. Charles William John, PhD; FBA 2006; FRSE, FRGS, FRSGS, FRHistS; Professor of Historical Geography, University of Edinburgh, since 1994 (Head, Institute of Geography, 2006–09); *b* 6 Dec. 1954; *s* of John Alastair Withers and Mary Alicia Withers (*née* Green); *m* 1980, Anne Marshall Hamilton; two *s* one *d*. *Educ:* St Andrews Univ. (BSc Hons); Downing Coll., Cambridge (PhD 1982). FRGS 1978; FAcSS (AcSS 2001); FRHistS 2002; CGeog 2003; FRSGS 2011. University of Gloucestershire: Lectr, 1981–84; Principal Lectr, 1984–92; Prof., 1992–94; Hd of Dept, 1991–94; Associate Dean, 1992–94. MAE 2000. FRSE 2006. FRSA 2000. *Publications:* Gaelic in Scotland 1698–1981, 1984; The Highland Communities of Dundee and Perth 1797–1891, 1986; Gaelic Scotland, 1988; Discovering the Cotswolds, 1990; Urban Highlanders, 1998; Geography, Science and National Identity: Scotland since 1520, 2001; Placing the Enlightenment, 2007; Geography and Science in Britain 1831–1939, 2010; joint editor: Urbanising Britain, 1991; Geography and Enlightenment, 1999; Science and Medicine in the Scottish Enlightenment, 2002; Georgian Geographies, 2004; Geography and Revolution, 2005; Geographies of the Book, 2010; Geographies of Nineteenth-Century Science, 2011; (jtly) Scotland: mapping the nation, 2011; numerous articles in learned jls. *Recreations:* hill-walking, theatre, reading, food and wine. *Address:* Institute of Geography, University of Edinburgh, Drummond Street, Edinburgh EH8 9XP. *T:* (0131) 650 2559, *Fax:* (0131) 650 2524. *E:* c.w.j.withers@ed.ac.uk.

WITHERS, Roger Dean; Chairman: Sportech Plc, since 2011 (Senior non-executive Director, 2000–05); Safecharge Ltd, since 2014; *b* Bradfield, Berks, 15 Aug. 1942; *s* of Frederick Charles Withers and Norah Daisy Withers; *m* 1963, Patricia Margaret Fenn; one *s*. Associate, Booz, Allen and Hamilton, 1968–73; Divl Dir, Ladbroke plc, 1973–86; Bass plc: Divl Dir, 1986–98; Man. Dir, Coral, 1997–98; Chm., Bass Leisure, South Africa, 1996–99; Chairman: Littlewoods Leisure, 1999–2000; Arena Leisure plc, 2001–06; Playtech Ltd, 2006–13. Advr, Scientific Games Inc., 2000–13. *Recreations:* game shooting, golf, travel, food and wine, classic cars. *Address:* PO Box 325, Aylesbury HP17 8BD. *T:* 07802 155255, *Fax:* (01296) 747210. *E:* rogerwithers@compuserve.com. *Club:* Oriental.

WITHERS, Prof. Stephen George, PhD; FRS 2012; FRS(Can) 2002; Professor of Chemistry and Biochemistry, University of British Columbia, since 1991 (Director, Center for High-Throughput Biology, 2006–13); *b* Horton, Somerset, 1 May 1953; *s* of William Eric George Withers and May Avril Withers; *m* 1986, Pamela Anne Miller; one *s*. *Educ:* Ilminster Grammar Sch.; Univ. of Bristol (BSc Chem. 1974; PhD Chem. 1977). Postdoctoral Fellow and Res. Associate, Univ. of Alberta, 1977–82; Asst Prof., 1982–87, Associate Prof., 1987–91, Univ. of BC. Scientific Dir, P.E.N.C.E., 2000–05. *Publications:* contribs to chem. and biochem. jls. *Recreations:* kayaking and canoeing, hiking, cabin life, reading, theatre. *Address:* Department of Chemistry, University of British Columbia, 2036 Main Mall, Vancouver, BC V6T 1Z1, Canada. *T:* 6048223402. *E:* withers@chem.ubc.ca.

WITHEY, Anthony George Hurst, CBE 1997; FCMA, CGMA; Chief Executive, Remploy Ltd, 1988–2000; *b* 4 Oct. 1942; *s* of Walter Ronald Withey and Laura Maria Withey (*née* Thomas); *m* 1967, Yvonne Jeanette Price Thomas; one *s* one *d*. *Educ:* Bishop Gore Grammar Sch., Swansea; Wadham Coll., Oxford (BA Hons Modern Hist.); Henley Business Sch. (GMC). FCMA 1986; CGMA 2012. Gen. Manager, BXL Plastics Ltd, various divs, and Dir, various subsids, 1976–83; Gp Exec., Tarmac Bldg Products Ltd, 1983–85; Chief Exec., Polymers Div., Evered Holdings PLC, 1985–88. Director: Pan Graphics Industries Ltd, 1991–94; Linx Printing Technologies PLC, 1994–2005; Océ (UK) Ltd, 2000–10; Chm., Electron Technologies Ltd, 2003–08. Director: Morriston Hosp. NHS Trust, 1997–99; Swansea NHS Trust, 1999–2002. Dir, Internat. Orgn for Provision of Work to Disabled People, 1993–2000. Mem., S Wales Police Selection Panel, 1998–2002. Mem. Council, Industrial Soc., 1989–2000. *Recreations:* squash, gardening, antiques, theatre. *Clubs:* Swansea Lawn Tennis and Squash Racquets; Coolhurst Lawn Tennis and Squash Racquets.

WITNEY, Nicholas Kenneth James; Senior Policy Fellow, European Council on Foreign Relations, since 2008; *b* 14 Dec. 1950; *s* of Kenneth Witney and Joan Witney (*née* Tait); *m* 1st, 1977, Ann Margaret Ruskell (marr. diss. 2011); one *s* one *d*; 2nd, 2012, Lucy Jane Aspinall. *Educ:* Tonbridge Sch.; Corpus Christi Coll., Oxford (MA Lit Hum). Joined Foreign and Commonwealth Office, 1973: E European and Soviet Dept, 1973; Arabic lang. trng, Lebanon and Jordan, 1974–76; Third, later Second, Sec., Baghdad, 1976–78; Second, later First, Sec. and Private Sec. to Ambassador, Washington, 1978–82; EC Dept, FCO, 1982–83; on secondment, later perm. transfer, to MoD, 1983–2007: Principal: defence policy Africa/Asia, 1983–85; Army budget and plans, 1985–87; Director: (Ops), Saudi Armed Forces Project, 1987–90; Nuclear Policy and Security, 1990–93; sabbatical at Rand Corp., Santa Monica, 1993–94; Hd, Housing Project Team, 1994–96; Dir-Gen., Mgt and Orgn, 1996–98; Asst Under-Sec. of State, Systems, 1998–99; Director-General: Equipment, 1999–2002; Internat. Security Policy, 2002–04; Chief Exec., European Defence Agency, 2004–07. *Publications:* The British Nuclear Deterrent after the Cold War, 1994; (jtly) Western European Nuclear Forces, 1995; (contrib.) The Oxford Handbook of War, 2012. *Recreations:* Rugby, sailing, modern fiction. *Address:* European Council on Foreign Relations, 35 Old Queen Street, SW1H 9JA.

WITT, Karsten; Joint Founder, and Managing Director, Karsten Witt Musik Management GmbH, since 2004; *b* Hamburg, 5 March 1952; *s* of Reimer Witt and Hilde Witt (*née* Vöge); *m* 1st, 1982, Anna Zeijl; three *s*; 2nd, 1996, Marie-Annick Le Blanc. *Educ:* Univ. of Hamburg (BA Philosophy of Sci.); Univ. of Constance (MA). Founder: Junge Deutsche Philharmonie (Nat. Student Orch.), 1974 (Manager, 1974–87); Deutsche Kammerphilharmonie, 1980 (Manager, 1980–89); Ensemble Modern, 1980 (Manager, 1980–91); Manager, ISCM (German Br.), 1986–90; Gen. Sec., Vienna Konzerthaus, 1991–96; Pres., Deutsche Grammophon, 1996–99; CEO, S Bank Centre, London, 1999–2002; Artistic Advr, Megaron Athens, 2005–08; projects with Shaksfin Asia, 2002–04. Governor: Deutsche Ensemble Akad., 1999–; GSMD, 2000–03; Wiener Konzerthausges., 2002–13. Curator, Allianz Cultural Foundn, 2001–08. Ehrenkreuz für Wissenschaft und Kunst (Austria), 1996; Silbernes Ehrenzeichen für Verdienste um das Land Wien, 1997; Cross of Merit (Hungary), 1999. *Address:* (office) Leuschnerdamm 13, 10999 Berlin, Germany.

WITTENBERG, Nicola; *see* Solomon, N.

WITTEVEEN, Dr (Hendrikus) Johannes, Commander, Order of Netherlands Lion; Commander, Order of Orange Nassau; Chairman, Internationale Nederlanden Group, 1991–93 (Member Supervisory Board, 1979–90); Board Member: Royal Dutch Petroleum Co., 1971–73 and 1978–89; Robeco, 1971–73 and 1979–91 (Adviser, 1971–73); *b* Zeist, Netherlands, 12 June 1921; *m* 1949, Liesbeth de Vries Feyens (*d* 2006); two *s* one *d*. *Educ:* Univ. Rotterdam (DEcon). Central Planning Bureau, 1947–48; Prof., Univ. Rotterdam, 1948–63; Mem. Netherlands Parlt, First Chamber, 1959–63 and 1971–73, and Second Chamber, 1965–67; Minister of Finance, Netherlands, 1963–65 and 1967–71; First Deputy Prime Minister, 1967–71; Managing Director, IMF, 1973–78. Chm., Group of Thirty, 1979–85, Hon. Chm., 1985–; Member: Internat. Council, Morgan Guaranty Trust Co. of NY, 1978–85; European Adv. Council, General Motors, 1978–91; Bd Mem., Thyssen-Bornemisza NV, 1978–86; Advr for Internat. Affairs, Amro Bank, Amsterdam, 1979–90. Pres., Internat. Sufi Movt, 2007– (Vice-Pres., 1957–2007). Grand Cross, Order of Crown (Belgium); Order of Oak Wreath (Luxemburg); Order of Merit (Fed. Republic Germany). *Publications:* Loonshoogte en Werkgelegenheid, 1947; Growth and Business Cycles, 1954; Universal Sufism, 1994; Soefisme en Economie, 2001 (Sufism in Action, 2003); Tot de Ene, 2006; Heart of Sufism: anthology of Hazrat Inayat Khan, 2000; (with Dr Saskia Rosdorff) De magie van harmonie (autobiog.), 2012; Het kleine boekje van God, 2012; articles in Economische Statistische Berichten, Euromoney. *Recreation:* hiking. *Address:* 2243 HL Wassenaar, Waldeck Pyrmontlaan 15, The Netherlands.

WITTY, Sir Andrew (Philip), Kt 2012; Chief Executive, GlaxoSmithKline plc, since 2008; *b* 1964; *m* Caroline; one *s* one *d*. *Educ:* Univ. of Nottingham (BA Econs 1985). Joined Glaxo, 1985; Dir, Pharmacy and Distribn; internat. product manager; Man. Dir, Glaxo S Africa; Area Dir, S and E Africa; Vice-Pres., Glaxo Wellcome; Sen. Vice Pres., Asia Pacific; Pres., GlaxoSmithKline Europe, 2003. Non-exec. Dir, BIS, 2011–13. Pres., Eur. Fedn of Pharmaceutical Industries and Assocs, 2010–13. Chancellor, Univ. of Nottingham, 2013–. Hon. FMedSci 2012. Public Service Medal, 2003, Public Service Star, 2012 (Singapore). *Address:* GlaxoSmithKline, 980 Great West Road, Brentford, Middx TW8 9GS.

WITTY, (John) David, CBE 1985; Director, Great Portland Estates PLC, 1987–97; *b* 1 Oct. 1924; *s* of late Harold Witty and Olive Witty, Beverley; *m* 1955, Doreen Hanlan (*d* 2007); one *s*. *Educ:* Beverley Grammar Sch.; Balliol Coll., Oxford (MA). Served War, RN, 1943–46. Asst Town Clerk, Beverley, 1951–53; Asst Solicitor: Essex CC, 1953–54; Hornsey, 1954–60; Dep. Town Clerk: Kingston upon Thames, 1960–65; Merton, 1965–67; Asst Chief Exec., Westminster, 1967–77, Chief Exec., 1977–84. Hon. Sec., London Boroughs Assoc., 1978–84. Chm., London Enterprise Property Co., 1984–85. Lawyer Mem., London Rent Assessment Panel, 1984–92. Order of Infante D. Henrique (Portugal), 1978; Order of Right Hand (Nepal), 1980; Order of King Abdul Aziz (Saudi Arabia), 1981; Order of Oman, 1982; Order of Orange-Nassau, 1982. *Recreation:* golf. *Address:* 14 River House, 23–24 The Terrace, Barnes, SW13 0NR.

WITTY, Mark F.; *see* Featherstone-Witty.

WLACHOVSKÝ, Miroslav; Ambassador of the Slovak Republic to the Court of St James's, 2011–15; *b* Bratislava, 3 Feb. 1970; *s* of Karol Wlachovský and Miroslava Wlachovská; *m* 2009, Jaroslava Nováková; one *s*. *Educ:* Comenius Univ., Bratislava (Magister Philosophy and Sociology). Hd, Editl Dept and Editor-in-Chief of qly Internat. Issues, Slovak Inst. for Internat. Studies, 1994–95; Dir, Res. Centre, Slovak Foreign Policy Assoc., 1995–98; Dir, Analysis and Planning Dept, Min. of Foreign Affairs, 1998–2001; Foreign Policy Advr to Prime Minister of Slovak Republic, 2001–03; Hd, Political Section, 2003–05, Dep. Chief of Mission, 2005–07, Washington, DC; Dir, Strategic Planning Unit, Analysis and Planning Dept, Min. of Foreign Affairs, 2007–09; Sen. Human Rights Expert, Perm. Mission of Slovak Republic to Internat. Orgns, Vienna, 2009–11. *Recreations:* cycling, swimming, hiking, travelling, music, film, cooking. *Address:* c/o Embassy of the Slovak Republic, 25 Kensington Palace Gardens, W8 4QY.

WODEHOUSE, family name of **Earl of Kimberley**.

WODEHOUSE, Lord; David Simon John Wodehouse; *b* 10 Oct. 1978; *s* and *heir* of Earl of Kimberley, *qv*.

WOGAN, Sir Michael Terence, (Sir Terry), KBE 2005 (OBE 1997); DL; jobbing broadcaster; *b* 3 Aug. 1938; *s* of late Michael Thomas and Rose Wogan; *m* 1965, Helen Joyce; two *s* one *d*. *Educ:* Crescent Coll., Limerick, Ireland; Belvedere Coll., Dublin. Joined RTE as Announcer, 1963, Sen. Announcer, 1964–66; various programmes for BBC Radio, 1965–67; Late Night Extra, BBC Radio, 1967–69; The Terry Wogan Show, BBC Radio One, 1969–72, BBC Radio Two, 1972–84 and 1993–2009; Weekend Wogan, BBC Radio Two, 2010–; television shows include: Lunchtime with Wogan, ATV, 1972–73; BBC: The Eurovision Song Contest, 1972–2008; Song for Europe; Come Dancing, 1973–79; Blankety-Blank, 1979–83; Children in Need, 1980–; Wogan's Guide to the BBC, 1982–; Wogan; Terry Wogan's Friday Night; Auntie's Bloomers, 1991–; Do the Right Thing, 1994; Auntie's Sporting Bloomers; Wogan's Island, 1994; Points of View, 2000–; The Terry and Gaby Show, 2003; Wogan Now and Then, UKTV, 2006–; Terry Wogan's Ireland, 2011. Columnist, Sunday Telegraph, 2001–. Freedom of: City of Limerick, 2007; City of London, 2010. DL Bucks, 2007. Hon. DLitt Limerick, 2004; Hon. DLaw Leicester, 2009. Awards include: Pye Radio Award, 1980; Radio Industries Award (Radio Personality 3 times; TV Personality, 1982, 1984, 1985, 1987); TV Times TV Personality of the Year (10 times); Daily Express Award (twice); Carl Alan Award (3 times); Variety Club of GB: Special Award, 1982; Showbusiness Personality, 1984; Radio Personality of last 21 yrs, Daily Mail Nat. Radio Awards, 1988; Sony Radio Award, 1993, 1994, 2002, Sony Gold Award, 2006; Radio Prog. of the Year, 1997, Lifetime Achievement Award, 2010, TRIC Awards; Lifetime Achievement Award, British Comedy Awards, 2009; Harvey Lee Award for Outstanding Contrib. to Broadcasting, Broadcasting Press Guild, 2010. *Publications:* Banjaxed, 1979; The Day Job, 1981; To Horse, To Horse, 1982; Wogan on Wogan, 1987; Wogan's Ireland, 1988; Is it Me? (autobiog.), 2000; Mustn't Grumble, 2006; Wogan's Twelve, 2008; Where Was I?!: the world according to Terry Wogan, 2009; Wogan's Ireland, 2011; Something for the Weekend, 2014; The Little Book of Common Sense, 2014. *Recreations:* tennis, golf, swimming, reading, writing. *Address:* JGPM, 4th Floor, 75A Berwick Street, W1F 8TG. *Clubs:* Garrick, Lord's Taverners, Saints and Sinners; London Irish Rugby Football; Lambourne Golf, Doonbeg Golf, Lahinch Golf.
See also Baron Parmoor.

WOGAN, Patrick Francis Michael, CMG 1991; HM Diplomatic Service, retired; Sensitivity Reviewer, Foreign and Commonwealth Office, since 2008; *m* 1st, 1960, Rosmarie Diederich (marr. diss. 1988); two *s* one *d*; 2nd, 1988, Afsaneh Khalatbari. Joined FO, subseq. FCO, 1959; Second Sec., Bahrain, 1970; Second, then First, Sec., FCO, 1972; Brussels, 1976; FCO, 1981; Counsellor, FCO, 1983, Tehran, 1984; RCDS, 1987; Consul-Gen. and Dep. High Comr, Karachi, 1988; Ambassador to Iceland, 1991–93; Ambassador and Consul-Gen., Qatar, 1993–97. Officer of H of L, 1999–2004.

WOGAN, Sir Terry; *see* Wogan, Sir M. T.

WOJNAROWSKA, Prof. Fenella Theta, DM; FRCP; Professor of Dermatology, University of Oxford, 1999–2009, now Emeritus; Consultant Dermatologist, Oxford Radcliffe NHS Trust, 1984–2009; *b* Oxford, 23 Oct. 1947; *d* of Kostek Wojnarowski and Muriel Wojnarowska; one *s*; *m* 2008, John Gardiner. *Educ:* Oxford High Sch. for Girls; Tonbridge Girls' Grammar Sch.; Somerville Coll., Univ. of Oxford (BA Animal Physiol.; MSc 1971; DM 1995); St Mary's Hosp. Med. Sch., London (BM BCh 1973). FRCP 1993. Dermatology trng, St John's Hosp. for Diseases of the Skin and St Mary's Hosp., London, 1977–84; Sen. Clin. Lectr, 1992–2002, Reader in Dermatol., 1996–99, Univ. of Oxford; Hon. Sen. Res. Fellow, Somerville Coll., Oxford, 2005–. Founder Mem., British Soc. for the Study of Vulval Disease, 1998– (Chm. and Pres., 2000–); Mem. Bd, Eur. Women's Dermatologic Soc., 1999– (Pres., 2007–). Chm., Tumour Site Specific Cancer Gp for skin, Thames Valley Cancer Gp, 2002–08. European Academy of Dermatology and Venereology: UK Bd Mem., 2004–09; Chm., Fostering Dermatology and Venereology Cttee, 2004–; Member: Membership Cttee, 2004–06; CME Cttee, 2004–08; Exec. Cttee, 2008–10; Jt Ed., EADV News, 2004–07; Lead for Skin Diseases in Pregnancy Task Force, 2006–10. Mem., Guidelines Cttee, 2005–, Lead on Eur. Guidelines for Safety of Topical Steroids in Pregnancy, 2006–11, Eur. Dermatology Forum. Maria M. Duran Lect., Internat. Soc. of Dermatology, 2006; Parkes Weber Lect., RCP, 2008; Gerald Levene Meml Lect., RSocMed, 2009. Chm., Bude and Dist U3A, 2013–. Chm., Tresmeer Parish Council, 2013. Volunteer, Royal Med. Benevolent Fund, 2010–; Bursary Sec., Oxford Univ. Cornwall Soc., 2014–. Certificate of Appreciation, Internat. League of Dermatol Socs, 2009; Presidential Recognition Award, Internat. Soc. for Study of Vulvovaginal Disease, 2009. *Publications: contributions to:* Textbook of Dermatology, 3rd edn 1979 to 8th edn 2010; Textbook of Paediatric Dermatology, 2000, 2nd edn 2005; Kidney Transplantation, 5th edn 2001, 6th edn 2008; Dermatology, 2003, 2nd edn 2008; Oxford Textbook of Medicine, 4th edn 2005, 5th edn 2010; more than 300 articles in med. and scientific jls on autoimmune bullous disease, transplant dermatology and women's health (vulval disease, pregnancy dermatoses and their treatment). *Recreations:* gardening, walking, travel. *Address:* c/o Nuffield Department of Clinical Medicine, University of Oxford, Headington, Oxford OX3 9DU. *E:* fenella.wojnarowska@ndm.ox.ac.uk.

WOLF, family name of **Baroness Wolf of Dulwich**.

WOLF OF DULWICH, Baroness *cr* 2014 (Life Peer), of Dulwich in the London Borough of Southwark; **Alison Margaret Wolf,** CBE 2012; Sir Roy Griffiths Professor of Public Sector Management, King's College London, since 2006 (Professor, since 2004); *d* of Herbert Kingsley Potter and Winnie Morrison (*née* Gove); *m* 1970, Martin Harry Wolf, *qv*; two *s* one *d*. *Educ:* Oxford High Sch.; Somerville Coll., Oxford (MA, MPhil). Res. Associate, Nat. Inst. of Educn, Washington, 1975–82; Res. Officer, 1983–85, Sen. Res. Officer, 1985–95, Prof., 1995–2004, Inst. of Educn, Univ. of London. Conducted Wolf Rev. of Vocational Educn, 2010–11, Advr, 2011–, DFE. Member, Council: UN Univ., 2003–11; KCL, 2011–; Chair of Govs, KCL Maths Sch., 2013–. Trustee: Abbeyfield Soc., Newbury, 2000–; Social Market Foundn, 2013–. *Publications:* Does Education Matter?, 2002; An Adult Approach to Further Education, 2009; Education and Economic Performance, 2011; The XX Factor: how working women are creating a new society, 2013. *Recreations:* reading, walking, music. *Address:* Department of Management, King's College London, 150 Stamford Street, SE1 9NH. *T:* (020) 7848 3724. *E:* alison.wolf@kcl.ac.uk.

See also R. Wolf.

WOLF, Prof. (Charles) Roland, OBE 2010; PhD; FMedSci; FRSE; Director, University of Dundee Medical Research Institute (formerly Biomedical Research Centre) and Hon. Director, Cancer Research UK (formerly ICRF) Molecular Pharmacology Unit, since 1992; *b* 26 Feb. 1949; *s* of Werner Max Wolf and Elisabeth Wolf; *m* 1975, Helga Loth; one *s* one *d*. *Educ:* Univ. of Surrey (BSc Chem.; PhD Biochem. 1975). Vis. Fellow, Nat. Inst. of Envmtl Health Scis, N Carolina, 1977–80; Vis. Scientist, ICI Central Toxicology Labs, Macclesfield, 1980–81; Hd of Biochemistry, Inst. of Toxicology, Univ. of Mainz, W Germany, 1981–82; Sen. Scientist, ICRF Med. Oncology Unit, Western Gen. Hosp., Edinburgh, 1982–86; Head, ICRF Molecular Pharmacology Gp, Univ. of Edinburgh, 1986–92. FRSE 1995; FRSA 1999; FMedSci 2000. *Publications:* (ed jtly) Molecular Genetics of Drug Resistance, 1997; over 450 scientific papers on drug develt, toxicol., cancer res. *Recreations:* weaving, piano playing, gardening, poetry, hiking. *Address:* University of Dundee Medical Research Institute, Level 9, Jacqui Wood Cancer Centre, Ninewells Hospital and Medical School, Dundee DD1 9SY. *T:* (01382) 383134.

WOLF, Martin Harry, CBE 2000; Associate Editor, since 1990, and Chief Economics Commentator, since 1996, Financial Times; *b* 16 Aug. 1946; *s* of Edmund Wolf and Rebecca Wolf (*née* Wijnschenk); *m* 1970, Alison Margaret Potter (*see* Baroness Wolf of Dulwich); two *s* one *d*. *Educ:* University College Sch.; Corpus Christi Coll., Oxford (MA 1st cl. Hons Mods 1967; 1st cl. Hons PPE 1969; Hon. Fellow, 2007); Nuffield Coll., Oxford (MPhil (BPhil Econs 1971); Hon. Fellow, 2010). World Bank: Young Professional, 1971; Sen. Economist, India Div., 1974–77, Internat. Trade Div., 1979–81; Dir of Studies, Trade Policy Res. Centre, 1981–87; Chief Economics Leader Writer, Financial Times, 1987–96. Hon. Prof., Economics Dept, Univ. of Nottingham, 2011– (Special Prof., 1993–2011); Vis. Fellow, Nuffield Coll., Oxford, 1999–2007. Member: NCC, 1987–93; Council, REconS, 1991–96; UK Govt Ind. Commn on Banking, 2010–11. Advr and Rapporteur, Eminent Persons Gp on World Trade, 1990. Hon. FKC 2012; Hon. Fellow, Corpus Christi Coll., Oxford; Global Fellow, Columbia Univ., NY, 2013. Hon. DLitt: Nottingham, 2006; Kingston, 2010; Macquarie, 2012. Hon. DSc: (Econs) LSE, 2006; Warwick, 2009. (Jtly) Sen. Prize, Wincott Foundn, 1989 and 1997; RTZ David Watt Meml Prize, 1994; Decade of Excellence Award, 2003, Commentator of the Year, 2008, Business Journalist of the Year Awards; Newspaper Feature of the Year Award, 2003, AMEC Lifetime Achievement Award, 2007, Workworld Media Awards; Journalism Prize, Fundació Catalunya Oberta, 2006; Ludwig Erhard Prize, Ludwig Erhard Stiftung, 2009; Commentariat of the Year, Comment Awards, 2009; Jt Winner for columns in 'giant newspapers', Soc. of American Business Editors and Writers, 2009; Best Radio Prog., Wincott Awards, 2009, 2015; Internat. Award, Premio Ischia di Giornalismo, 2012; James Cameron Meml Trust Award for Journalism, 2012; Best Commentary Award, Overseas Press Club of America, 2014; Journalist of the Year, Green Ribbon Political Awards, 2014. Commemoration Medal (NZ), 1990. *Publications:* India's Exports, 1982; Why Globalization Works, 2004; Fixing Global Finance, 2008; The Shifts and the Shocks, 2014; numerous articles, mainly on internat. econ. policy. *Recreations:* opera, theatre. *Address:* 27 Court Lane, SE21 7DH. *T:* (020) 7873 3673/3421. *Club:* Reform.

See also R. Wolf.

WOLF, Rachel; Senior Vice President, Amplify, since 2013; *b* London, 1985; *d* of Martin Harry Wolf, *qv* and Baroness Wolf of Dulwich, *qv*; *m* 2012, James Frayne. *Educ:* Univ. of Cambridge (BA Natural Scis). DipEcon. Researcher, Boris Johnson, 2006–07; Political Advr, 2008, Educn Advr, 2008–09, Conservative Party; Dir, 2009–13, Chm. of Trustees, 2013–, New Schs Network. *Recreations:* books, music. *Club:* Reform.

WOLF, Roland; *see* Wolf, C. R.

WOLFE, Prof. Charles David Alexander, MD; FRCOG, FFPH; Professor of Public Health Medicine, King's College London School of Medicine (formerly Guy's, King's and St Thomas' School of Medicine at King's College London), since 2002; Head, Division of Health and Social Care, King's College London, since 2004; *b* 30 July 1954; *s* of late Kenneth Wolfe and Doreen Hibbert Wolfe (*née* Anderson). *Educ:* Highgate Sch.; Royal Free Hosp. Sch. of Medicine, Univ. of London (MB BS 1978); MD London 1990. MRCOG 1985, FRCOG 1998; MFPHM 1991, FFPH (FFPHM 1996). Regtl MO, RAMC, 1980–85; United Medical and Dental Schools of Guy's and St Thomas' Hospitals: Res. Fellow in Obstetrics, 1985–87; Lectr in Public Health Medicine, 1988–92; Sen. Lectr, 1992–98; Reader, GKT, 1998–2002; Guy's and St Thomas' Hospital: Hon. Consultant in Public Health Medicine, 1992–; Clinical Dir, Women's Health, 1995–2000; Dir, R&D, 2000–. Lead for Public Health, King's Health Partners, 2011–. National Institute for Health Research: Chm., Res. for Patient Benefit Cttee, 2007–; Sen. Investigator, 2008–; Chm., NHS Confederation Health Services Res. Bd, 2010–. Mem. Bd, Stanley Thomas Johnson Foundn, Switzerland, 2003–13. *Publications:* Stroke Service and Research, 1996; Stroke Services: policy and practice across Europe, 2001; articles in med. jls on health service res. in stroke and women's health. *Recreations:* furniture restoration, classical music, opera. *Address:* Holly Lodge, Queen Street, New Buckenham, Norfolk NR16 2AL. *T:* (office) (020) 7848 6608. *E:* charles.wolfe@kcl.ac.uk.

WOLFE, David Frederick Harris, PhD; QC 2012; *b* Roodeport, South Africa, 9 June 1964; *s* of late (Frederick) John Harris and of (Catherine) Ann Harris (later Wolfe), and step *s* of Martin Stuart Wolfe; *m* 2009, Amanda Marguerite Illing; two *d*. *Educ:* Manchester Univ. (BSc MEng 1987); Univ. of Cambridge (PhD Engrg 1990); City Univ. (DipLaw 1991). Called to the Bar, Middle Temple, 1992; in practice as a barrister, Matrix, 1992–; pt-time Judge, Special Educnl Needs and Disability Tribunal, 2004–08. Chm. Bd, Press Recognition Panel, 2014–. Member, Board: Legal Services Commn, 2005–13; Legal Services Bd, 2008–13. Mem., Cambridgeshire CC, 1989–93. Gov., Leiston High Sch., later Alde Valley Sch., Suffolk, 2009–13. *Recreations:* friends and family, real ale, parties, ski-ing. *Address:* Flat 100, Vesage Court, Leather Lane, EC1N 7RF; Moya, The Street, Charsfield, Suffolk IP13 7PY. *T:* 07740 948536. *E:* davidwolfe@matrixlaw.co.uk.

WOLFE, Gillian Anne, CBE 2005 (MBE 1995); Director, Learning and Public Affairs, Dulwich Picture Gallery, 2009–15 (Head of Education, 1984–2008); freelance education consultant, since 1990; *b* 25 March 1946; *d* of late Noel Henry Humphrey and Anne (*née* Nicholls); *m* 1974, Dr Kenneth Maurice Wolfe; one *s* one *d*. *Educ:* Sydenham Girls' Sch.; Central Sch. of Art (Pre Diploma 1968); Stockwell Coll. (BEd Hons London 1972). Teacher: Rushey Gn Primary Sch., 1974; Greenwich Pk Secondary Sch., 1974–84. Advisory Teacher: for ILEA, 1984–89; for Southwark, 1989–2008; British Deleg., EC Council of Europe, Saltzburg, 1989; Advr, Kyoto and Tokyo Mus. Educn Project, 1996; Mem., Exec. Cttee, Nat. Heritage, 1997–2000; Judge, Mus. of Year Award, 1997–2000; Project Advr, American Fedn of Arts, 1998; Consultant, Royal Collection, 1999–2000; Specialist Advisor: Clore Foundn, 2001–; HLF, 2005–12; Comr, CABE, 2000–03, now Emeritus (Trustee, Educn Foundn, 2003–06); Mem., Steering Gp, Attingham Trust Survey on Learning in Historic Envmt, 2001–03; Chm., jt DCMS-DfES Adv. Cttee on developing envmt as an educn resource, 2003–04. Trustee: Historic Royal Palaces, 2002–05; Charleston Trust, 2009–; Brighton Pavilion and Museums Foundn, 2010–; Arts4Dementia, 2011–; RIBA British Architects Trust, 2014– (Chm., Public Educn Cttee, 2015–). Learning Advr, Historic Houses Assoc., 2012–. FRSA 2004. Hon. HLD St Norbert Coll., USA, 2006; Hon. Dr Canterbury Christ Church, 2014. NACF Award for Educn, 1987; Sustainable City Award, 2009; RSPH Award, 2012. *Publications:* (contrib.) Oxford Children's Encyclopaedia, 7 vols, 1991; Children's Art and Activity Books, 1997 (Gulbenkian Prize, 1992); (contrib.) Oxford Children's Pocket Encyclopaedia, 1999; Oxford First Book of Art, 1999 (Parent Choice Silver Hon. Award, USA, 2002); Look!: zoom in on art, 2002 (English Assoc. Award for Best Children's non-fiction book, 2007); Look!: body language in art, 2004; Look!: seeing the light in art, 2006; Look!: drawing the line in art, 2008; Look!: really smart art, 2010. *Recreations:* gardening, dance. *Address:* 31 Calton Avenue, SE21 7DE. *T:* (020) 8693 6995. *E:* gillian.wolfe@btinternet.com.

WOLFE, John Henry Nicholas, FRCS; Consultant Vascular Surgeon, St Mary's Hospital, London, since 1984; Hon. Consultant Vascular Surgeon, Royal Brompton Hospital, Great Ormond Street Hospital for Children and Edward VII Hospital for Officers, London, since 1984; *b* 4 June 1947; *s* of late Herbert Robert Inglewood Wolfe and Lesley Winifred (*née* Fox); *m* 1st, 1973, Jennifer Sutcliffe; three *s* two *d*; 2nd, 1994, Dorothy May Sturgeon. *Educ:* Eastbourne Coll.; St Thomas's Hosp. Med. Sch., London (MB BS 1971); MS 1981. FRCS 1975. Res. Fellow, Harvard Medical Sch., Brigham Hosp., 1981–82; Sen Registrar, St Thomas' Hosp., 1982–84; Consultant Surgeon, RPMS, Hammersmith, 1984. Hunterian Prof., RCS, 1983; Moynihan Fellow, Assoc. of Surgeons, 1985. Member: Speciality Adv. Bd, Assoc. of Surgeons, 1993–96; Specialities Board of Surgery: RCS, 1994–95; RCSE, 1994–96; Chm., Continuing Med. Educn Cttee, Eur. Div. Vascular Surgery, 1998–2001, Pres., Eur. Bd of Vascular Surgery, 2001–04, European Union of Med. Specialists, Brussels; Council Member: Vascular Soc. of GB and Ire., 1992–96 (Chm., Vascular Adv. Cttee, 1992–96; Pres., 2005–06); Assoc. of Surgeons of GB and Ire., 1998–2002; President: European Soc. of Vascular Surgery, 2007–08; World Fedn of Vascular Surgery, 2012–13. Trustee, Circulation (formerly British Vascular) Foundn, 1999–. Honorary Member: Surgical Soc. of S Africa, 1991; Vascular Soc. of India, 2002; Swiss Vascular Soc., 2004; Soc. of Vascular Technologists, 2004; Vascular Soc. of Germany, 2005; Eur. Assoc. Vascular Surgical Trainees, 2006; Assoc. of Surgeons of India, 2007; Australasian Vascular Soc., 2012; Soc. of Vascular Surgery, USA, 2013. FRGS 1996. Freedom, City of London, 2007. *Publications:* (associate ed) Rutherford's Vascular Surgery, 1984; ABC of Vascular Diseases, 1992, Czech edn 1994, Italian edn 1995; articles on arterial, venous and lymphatic disease, and surgical training. *Recreations:* sailing, sculpture, rudimentary pond management, walking with children. *Address:* Emmanuel Kaye House, 37A Devonshire Street, W1G 6AA. *T:* (020) 7467 4364, *Fax:* (020) 7467 4376. *E:* jwolfe@uk-consultants.co.uk. *Clubs:* Chelsea Arts, Royal Ocean Racing.

WOLFE, Thomas Kennerly, Jr; author and journalist; *b* 2 March 1930; *m* Sheila; one *s* one *d*. *Educ:* Washington and Lee Univ.; Yale Univ. (PhD 1957). Reporter, Springfield (Mass) Union, 1956–59; Reporter and Latin America correspondent, Washington Post, 1959–62; Reporter and magazine writer, New York Herald Tribune, 1962–66; magazine writer, New York World Journal Tribune, 1966–67; Contributing Editor: New York, magazine, 1968–76; Esquire, 1977–. Contributing artist, Harper's, 1978–81; one-man exhibns of drawings, Maynard Walker Gall., NY, 1965, Tunnel Gall., NY, 1974, Forbes Gall., NY, 2000, Nat. Mus. of American Illustration, 2010. *Publications:* The Kandy-Kolored Tangerine-Flake Streamline Baby, 1965; The Electric Kool-Aid Acid Test, 1968; The Pump House Gang, 1968; Radical Chic and Mau-mauing the Flak Catchers, 1970; The New Journalism, 1973; The Painted Word, 1975; Mauve Gloves and Madmen, Clutter and Vine, 1976; The Right Stuff, 1979; In Our Time, 1980; From Bauhaus to Our House, 1981; Bonfire of the Vanities, 1987; A Man in Full, 1998; Hooking Up (essays), 2000; I am Charlotte Simmons, 2004; Back to Blood, 2012. *Address:* c/o Janklow & Nesbit Associates, 445 Park Avenue, New York, NY 10022, USA.

WOLFENDALE, Sir Arnold (Whittaker), Kt 1995; PhD, DSc; FRS 1977; FInstP, FRAS; Professor of Physics, University of Durham, 1965–92, now Emeritus; Astronomer Royal, 1991–95; *b* 25 June 1927; *s* of Arnold Wolfendale and Doris Wolfendale; *m* 1951, Audrey Darby (*d* 2007); twin *s*. *Educ:* Univ. of Manchester (BSc Physics 1st Cl. Hons 1948, PhD 1953, DSc 1970). FInstP 1958; FRAS 1973. Asst Lectr, Univ. of Manchester, 1951, Lectr, 1954; University of Durham: Lectr, 1956; Sen. Lectr, 1959; Reader in Physics, 1963; Head of Dept, 1973–77, 1980–83, 1986–89. Vis. Lectr, Univ. of Ceylon, 1952; Vis. Prof., Univ. of Hong Kong, 1977–78; Kan Tong Po Vis. Prof. of Physics, City Univ. of Hong Kong, 1995; Prof. of Experimental Physics, Royal Instn of GB, 1996–2002. Lectures: H. C. Bhuyan Meml, Gauhati Univ., 1978 and 1993; B. B. Roy Meml, Calcutta Univ., 1978; Norman Lockyer,

Exeter Univ., 1978; E. A. Milne, Oxford Univ., 1982; Rochester, Durham Univ., 1990 and 2006; A. W. Mailvaganam Meml, Colombo Univ., 1990; Perren, QMW, 1991; O'Neill, Glasgow, 1991; Durham Observatory Anniversary, 1992; Cormack, RSE, 1992; Robinson, Armagh, 1992; David Martin, Royal Soc./British Acad., 1992; Preston Guild, Univ. of Central Lancs, 1992; J. H. Holmes Meml, Newcastle Univ., 1993; Irvine Meml, Stirling, 1993; Tompion, Clockmakers' Co., 1993; Courtauld, Manchester Lit. and Phil., 1993; Minerva, Scientific Instrument Makers' Co., 1993; Hess, IUPAP Cosmic Ray Commn, 1993; Poynting, Univ. of Birmingham, 1994; Mme Curie, Inst. of Physics, 1995; Dee, Glasgow Univ., 1995; Harland, Univ. of Exeter, 1996; Temple Chevallier, Univ. of Durham, 1996; Carter Meml, Nat. Observatory of NZ, 1997; Charter, Inst. of Biology, 1997; Manley Meml, Univ. of Durham, 1997; Cockroft & Walton, Inst. of Physics, India, 1998; Wdowczyk Meml, Univ. of Lodz, Poland, 1998; Bakerian, Royal Soc., 2002; Appapillai Meml, Univ. of Peradeniya, 2003; Pniewski, Tech. Univ. of Warsaw, Plock, 2003. Home Office, Civil Defence, later Regl Scientific Advr, 1956–84. Chm., Northern Reg. Action Cttee, Manpower Services Commn's Job Creation Prog., 1975–78; Mem., SERC, 1988–94 (Chm., Astronomy and Planetary Sci. Bd, 1988–93; Chm., Particles, Space and Astronomy Bd, 1993–94). Chm., Cosmic Ray Commn, IUPAP, 1982–84. President: RAS, 1981–83; Antiquarian Horological Soc., 1993–2014; Inst. of Physics, 1994–96; European Physical Soc., 1999–2001. Pres., Durham Univ. Soc. of Fellows, 1988–94. Freeman: Clockmakers' Co., 1991 (Liveryman, 2006; Harrison Medal, 2006); Sci. Instrument Makers' Co., 1993. MAE 1998. Foreign Fellow: INSA, 1990; Indian Nat. Acad. Scis; For. Associate, RSSAf, 1995; Foreign Mem., Polish Acad. of Arts and Scis, 2010; Hon. Fellow: Lancashire Poly., 1991; Sri Lankan Acad. of Sci., 2010; Hon. Professor: Univ. of Yunnan, China, 1995; Univ. of Sci. and Technology, Hefei, China, 1995; Tata Inst. of Fundamental Res., 1996. Hon. DSc: Univ. of Potchefstroom for Christian Higher Educn, 1989; Lodz, 1989; Teesside, 1993; Newcastle upon Tyne, 1994; Paisley, 1996; Lancaster, 1996; Bucharest, 2000; DUniv: Open, 1995; Durham, 2001; SW Bulgaria, 2001; Turku, Finland, 2009; Bolton, 2009; Dip. *hc* Romanian Acad., 2000. Univ. of Turku Medal, 1987; Armagh Observatory Medal, 1992; Marian Smoluchowski Medal, Polish Phys. Soc., 1993; Powell Meml Medal, EPS, 1996. Silver Jubilee Medal, 1977; Fiorino d'Oro, Comune di Firenze, 2004; Chancellor's Medal, Univ. of Durham, 2011; Homi Bhabha Medal, IUPAP/Tata Inst. of Fundamental Res., 2011; INSA-Vainu Bappu Meml Award, Indian Nat. Acad. of Sci., 2013. *Publications:* Cosmic Rays, 1963; (ed) Cosmic Rays at Ground Level, 1973; (ed) Origin of Cosmic Rays, 1974; (ed jtly and contrib.) Origin of Cosmic Rays, 1981; (ed) Gamma Ray Astronomy, 1981; (ed) Progress in Cosmology, 1982; (with P. V. Ramana Murthy) Gamma Ray Astronomy, 1986, 2nd edn 1993; (with F. R. Stephenson) Secular Solar and Geomagnetic Variations in the last 1,000 years, 1988; (ed jtly) Observational Tests of Cosmological Inflation, 1991; original papers on studies of cosmic radiation, aspects of astrophysics and analysis of climate change. *Recreations:* walking, gardening, foreign travel. *Address:* Ansford, Potters Bank, Durham DH1 3RR. *T:* (0191) 384 5642.

WOLFENSOHN, James David, Hon. KBE 1995; Hon. AO 1987; Chairman and Chief Executive Officer, Wolfensohn Fund Management LLC (formerly Wolfensohn & Co. LLC), since 2007; President, International Bank for Reconstruction and Development, 1995–2005; *b* Sydney, 1 Dec. 1933; *s* of Hyman Wolfensohn and Dora Weinbaum; *m* 1961, Elaine Botwinick; one *s* two *d*. *Educ:* Univ. of Sydney (BA, LLB); Harvard Business Sch. (MBA). Lawyer, Allen Allen & Hemsley; Officer, RAAF; former Exec. Dep. Chm. and Man. Dir, Schroders Ltd, London; former Man. Dir, Darling & Co., Australia; Pres., J. Henry Schroder Banking Corp., 1970–76; Chm., Salomon Brothers Internat., 1977–81; Pres., James D. Wolfensohn Inc., 1981–95; Chm. Internat. Adv. Bd, Citigroup Inc., 2006–. Special Envoy for Gaza Disengagement, 2005–06. Mem. Bd, Carnegie Hall, NY, 1970 (Chm. Bd, 1980–91, now Chm. Emeritus); Chm., Kennedy Center for the Performing Arts, 1990–95, now Chm. Emeritus. Trustee: Inst. for Advanced Study, Princeton Univ., 1979– (Chm., 1986–2007, now Chm. Emeritus); Rockefeller Univ., 1985–94; Fellow: American Acad. of Arts and Scis; American Philosophical Soc. David Rockefeller Prize, Mus. of Modern Art, NY. *Address:* Wolfensohn Fund Management LLC, 1350 Avenue of the Americas, 29th Floor, New York, NY 10019, USA.

WOLFF, Prof. Eric William, PhD; FRS 2010; FRSC; Royal Society Research Professor of Earth Sciences, University of Cambridge, since 2013; *b* Bushey, Herts, 5 June 1957; *s* of Henry Wolff and Joan Agnes Wolff (*née* Whitehead); *m* 1983, Theresa Mary Ormiston. *Educ:* Quainton Hall Sch., Harrow; Merchant Taylors' Sch., Northwood; Churchill Coll., Cambridge (BA Nat. Sci. 1978); Univ. of Cambridge (PhD 1992). Contract glaciologist, British Antarctic Survey, 1978–84; Scientist, Water Research Centre, 1984–85; British Antarctic Survey: Res. Scientist, 1985–2000; Principal Investigator, 2000–09; Science Leader (Chemistry and Past Climate), 2009–13; Individual Merit Band 3, 2005–11, Band 2, 2011–13. Hon. Visiting Professor: Univ. of Southampton, 2011–13; UEA, 2012–. Chm., Sci. Sub-gp, Eur. Project for Ice Coring in Antarctica, 2003–; Co-Chm., Internat. Partnerships in Ice Core Scis, 2005–; Mem., Steering Cttee, Past Global Changes, 2007–13. Mem., Internat. Glaciol Soc., 1978– (Vice Pres., 2005–08). MRSC 1978, FRSC 2011; Member: Amer. Geophysical Union, 1992; Eur. Geoscis Union, 2004. Hon. Fellow, British Antarctic Survey, 2013–. Medal, Envmtl Chem. Gp, RSC, 2007; Louis Agassiz Medal, Eur. Geoscis Union, 2009; Lyell Medal, Geol Soc., 2012. *Publications:* over 190 papers in scientific jls. *Recreations:* alpine and coastal walking, ski-ing, good food, watching cricket, interglacials. *Address:* Department of Earth Sciences, University of Cambridge, Downing Street, Cambridge CB2 3EQ. *E:* ew428@cam.ac.uk.

WOLFF, Prof. Heinz Siegfried, FRSB; FIET; Director, Brunel Institute for Bioengineering, Brunel University, 1983–95, Emeritus Professor, since 1995; *b* 29 April 1928; *s* of Oswald Wolff and Margot (*née* Saalfeld); *m* 1953, Joan Eleanor Stephenson (*d* 2014); two *s*. *Educ:* City of Oxford Sch.; University Coll. London (BSc (Hons) Physiology; Fellow, 1987). FIET (FIEE 1993); FIPEM (FBES 1994). National Institute for Medical Research: Div. of Human Physiology, 1954–62; Hd, Div. of Biomedical Engrg, 1962–70; Hd, Bioengrg Div., Clinical Res. Centre of MRC, 1970–83. European Space Agency: Chm., Life Science Working Gp, 1976–82; Mem., Sci. Adv. Cttee, 1978–82; Chm., Microgravity Adv. Cttee, 1982–91. Chm., Microgravity Panel, Brit. Nat. Space Centre, 1986–87. Bd Dir, Edinburgh Internat. Science Fest., 1995–. Vice-President: Coll. of Occupational Therapy, 1990–; Rehabilitation Engrg Movt Adv. Panel, 1995–; Disabled Living Foundn, 1997–. FRSA; Hon. Fellow, Ergonomics Soc., 1991. *Television series:* BBC TV Young Scientist of the Year (contributor), 1968–81; BBC2: Royal Instn Christmas Lectures, 1975; Great Egg Race, 1978–; Great Experiments, 1985–86. Hon. FRCP 1999. DUniv: Open, 1993; De Montfort, 1995; Oxford Brookes, 1999; Hon. Dr Middlesex, 1999; Hon. DSc Brunel, 2003. Harding Award, Action Res. for the Crippled Child/RADAR, 1989; Edinburgh Medal, Edinburgh Internat. Sci. Fest., 1992; Donald Julius Groen Prize, IMechE, 1994; Medal, 1996, Keith Medal for Innovation, 2001, Royal Scottish Soc. of Arts. *Publications:* Biomedical Engineering, 1969 (German, French, Japanese and Spanish trans, 1970–72); about 120 papers in sci. jls and contribs to books. *Recreations:* working, lecturing to children, dignified practical joking. *Address:* Heinz Wolff Building, Brunel University, Uxbridge, Middx UB8 3PH.

WOLFF, Prof. Jonathan; Professor of Philosophy, since 2000, and Dean, Faculty of Arts and Humanities, since 2012, University College London; *b* 25 June 1959; *s* of Herbert Wolff and Doris Wolff (*née* Polakoff); *m* 2004, Elaine Collins; one *s*. *Educ:* University Coll. London (BA; MPhil). Lectr, 1986–92, Sen. Lectr, 1992–96, Reader, 1996–2000, in Philosophy, UCL; Founding Dir, Philosophy Programme, Sch. of Advanced Study, Univ. of London, 1995–98; Dir, Centre for Philosophy, Justice and Health, UCL, 2008–13. Member: Nuffield Council on Bioethics, 2008–14; Bd of Sci., BMA, 2014–15. Mem., Gambling Review Body, 2000–01; Trustee: Gambling Industry Charitable Trust, subseq. Responsibility in Gambling Trust, 2003–09; Responsible Gambling Trust, 2012–. Hon. Sec., Aristotelian Soc., 2001–07; Sec., British Philosophical Assoc., 2004–07. Editor, Procs of Aristotelian Soc., 1994–2000; columnist, Guardian, 2005–. *Publications:* Robert Nozick: property, justice and the minimal state, 1991; An Introduction to Political Philosophy, 1996; Why Read Marx Today?, 2002; (with Avner de-Shalit) Disadvantage, 2007; (ed with Mark Hannam) Southern Africa: 2020 vision, 2010; Ethics and Public Policy: a philosophical inquiry, 2011; The Human Right to Health, 2012; (ed) G. A. Cohen Lectures in the History of Philosophy, 2013; An Introduction to Moral Philosophy, 2016. *Recreations:* reading, music, spectator sport, film, television. *Address:* Department of Philosophy, University College London, Gower Street, WC1E 6BT. *T:* (020) 7679 3067. *E:* j.wolff@ucl.ac.uk.

WOLFF, Michael, RDI 2012; PPCSD; President, Michael Wolff and Company (formerly Newhouse Associates), since 1993; Trustee and Director, Youth at Risk, since 2012; *b* 12 Nov. 1933; *s* of Serge Wolff and Mary (*née* Gordon); *m* 1st, 1976, Susan Kent (marr. diss.); one *d*; 2nd, 1989, Martha Newhouse (*d* 2011). *Educ:* Gresham's Sch., Holt, Norfolk; Architectural Association Sch. of Architecture. Designer: Sir William Crawford & Partners, 1957–61; BBC Television, 1961–62; Main Wolff & Partners, 1964–65; with Wolff Olins Ltd as a founder and Creative Director, 1965–83; Chm., Addison Design Consultants, 1987–92. Design Consultant to: W. H. Smith Gp, 1990–98; MFI Gp, 2000; Mothercare, 2000–; Consultant to: Citigroup, 1998–; Insead, 2003–; Pyjom, 2012–. Non-exec. Dir, Newell & Sorrell, 1995–98. Advr to UK Govt on Inclusive Design, 2011–. President: D&AD, 1971; SIAD, then CSD, 1985–87. Mem., Bd of Trustees, Hunger Project, 1979–2000. FRSA. *Recreations:* enjoying a family, seeing. *Address:* 9 Cumberland Gardens, WC1X 9AG. *T:* (020) 7833 0007.

WOLFFE, (Walter) James; QC (Scot.) 2007; *b* Dumfries, 20 Dec. 1962; *s* of Antony C. Wolffe and Alexandra L. Wolffe (*née* Graham); *m* 1987, Sarah Poyntell LaBudde, (Hon. Lady Wolffe); two *s*. *Educ:* Kirkcudbright Acad.; Univ. of Edinburgh (LLB Hons; DipLP); Univ. of Oxford (BCL). Legal Asst to the Lord Pres. of the Court of Session, 1990–91; Advocate, 1992; First Standing Jun. Counsel to the Scottish Ministers, 2002–07; Advocate Depute, 2007–10; Sen. Advocate Depute, 2007–10; Vice-Dean, 2013–14, Dean, 2014–, Faculty of Advocates; called to the Bar, Middle Temple, 2013. Mem., Police Appeal Tribunal, 2013–. Hd of UK Delegn to CCBE, 2013–. Member: Scottish Council of Law Reporting, 2008–14 (Chm., 2011–14); Scottish Civil Justice Council, 2013–14. Trustee, Nat. Liby of Scotland, 2008–13. *Publications: contributions to:* Finnie et al's Edinburgh Essays in Public Law, 1991; Stair Memorial Encyclopaedia of the Laws of Scotland; Gloag and Henderson's The Law of Scotland, 11th edn; Johnston and Zimmermann's Unjustified Enrichment Key Issues in Comparative Perspective, 2002; Macfadyen's Court of Session Practice; articles in Public Law, Scots Law Times and Edinburgh Law Review. *Address:* Advocates Library, Parliament House, Parliament Square, Edinburgh EH1 1RF. *T:* (0131) 226 5071. *E:* james.wolffe@advocates.org.uk. *Club:* Waverley Tennis.

WOLFSON, family name of **Baron Wolfson of Sunningdale**.

WOLFSON OF ASPLEY GUISE, Baron *cr* 2010 (Life Peer), of Aspley Guise in the County of Bedfordshire; **Simon Adam Wolfson;** Chief Executive, Next plc, since 2001; *b* 27 Oct. 1967; *e s* of Lord Wolfson of Sunningdale, *qv*; *m* 2012, Eleanor, *d* of Hon. William Hartley Hume Shawcross, *qv*; one *s*. *Educ:* Radley Coll.; Trinity Coll., Cambridge. Dir, 1997–, Man. Dir, 1999–2001, Next plc. *Address:* Next plc, Desford Road, Enderby, Leicester LE19 4AT. *T:* (0116) 284 2308.

WOLFSON OF SUNNINGDALE, Baron *cr* 1991 (Life Peer), of Trevose in the County of Cornwall; **David Wolfson,** Kt 1984; Chairman: Next plc, 1990–98; Great Universal Stores, 1996–2000; *b* 9 Nov. 1935; *s* of Charles Wolfson and Hylda Wolfson; *m* 1st, 1962, Patricia E. Rawlings (*see* Baroness Rawlings) (marr. diss. 1967); 2nd, 1967, Susan E. Davis; two *s* one *d*; one *s*. *Educ:* Clifton Coll.; Trinity Coll., Cambridge (MA); Stanford Univ., California (MBA). Great Universal Stores, 1960–78, 1993–2000, Director, 1973–78 and 1993–2000; Secretary to Shadow Cabinet, 1978–79; Chief of Staff, Political Office, 10 Downing Street, 1979–85. Chm., Alexon Group PLC (formerly Steinberg Group PLC), 1982–86; non-executive Director: Stewart Wrightson Holdings PLC, 1985–87; Next, 1989–90; Compco Hldgs plc, 1995–2004; Fibernet Gp plc, 2001–06 (Chm., 2002–06). Chm., Charles Wolfson Charitable Trust, 1971–. Hon. Fellow, Hughes Hall, Cambridge, 1989. Hon. FRCR 1978; Hon. FRCOG 1989. *Recreations:* golf, bridge. *Clubs:* Portland; Sunningdale; Woburn Golf; Trevose Golf (N Cornwall).

See also Baron Wolfson of Aspley Guise.

WOLFSON, David; QC 2009; *b* Liverpool, 19 July 1968; *s* of Bernard and Rosalind Wolfson; *m* 1995, Louise, *d* of Jeffrey, (Jeff), and Rina Durkin; one *s* two *d*. *Educ:* King David High Sch., Liverpool; Yeshivat Hakotel, Jerusalem; Selwyn Coll., Cambridge (BA Hons 1991; MA 1994). Called to the Bar, Inner Temple, 1992 (Squire Schol.; Stuart of Rannoch Award; Inns of Court Sch. of Law Schol.; Inner Temple Major Schol.); in practice as barrister, specialising in commercial law, 1993–. Director: Bar Mutual Indemnity Fund, 2005–; Jewish Chronicle Trust Ltd, 2011–. Chm. Govs, Kerem Sch., London, 2012–. Trustee, Cambridge Univ. Jewish Soc., 2014–. *Publications:* (ed and contrib.) Bank Liability and Risk, 1995; (contrib.) Arbitration in England, 2013. *Recreations:* travel, wine, learning *lishma*. *Address:* One Essex Court, Temple, EC4Y 9AR. *T:* (020) 7583 2000, *Fax:* (020) 7583 0118. *E:* david.wolfson@oeclaw.co.uk.

WOLFSON, (Geoffrey) Mark, OBE 2002; *b* 7 April 1934; *s* of late Captain V. Wolfson, OBE, VRD, RNVR, and Dorothy Mary Wolfson; *m* 1965, Edna Webb (*née* Hardman); two *s*. *Educ:* Eton Coll.; Pembroke Coll., Cambridge (MA). Served Royal Navy, 1952–54; Cambridge, 1954–57; Teacher in Canada, 1958–59; Warden, Brathay Hall Centre, Westmorland, 1962–66; Head of Youth Services, Industrial Soc., 1966–69; Hd of Personnel, 1970–85, Dir, 1973–88, Hambros Bank. MP (C) Sevenoaks, 1979–97. PPS to Minister of State for NI, 1983–84, to Minister of State for Defence Procurement, 1984–85, to Minister of State for Armed Forces, 1987–88. Mem., NI Select Cttee, 1994–97. Officer, Cons. Backbench Employment Cttee, 1981–83. Mem., Parly Human Rights Delegns to Nicaragua, 1982, El Salvador and Baltic States, 1990, and St Helena, 1996. Associate Advr, Industrial Soc., 1997–98. Cttee Mem. and Trustee, Brathay Hall Trust, 1968–2002; Dir, McPhail Charitable Settlement, 1996–2010.

WOLL, Prof. Bencie, PhD; FBA 2012; Professor of Sign Language and Deaf Studies, and Director, Deafness, Cognition and Language Research Centre, University College London, since 2005; *b* 22 Feb. 1950; *d* of Lazar Benzion Woll and Fannie Zifkin Woll. *Educ:* Univ. of Pennsylvania (BA 1970); Univ. of Essex (MA 1971); Univ. of Bristol (PhD 1992). Sen. Lectr/Res. Fellow, Univ. of Bristol, 1973–95; Prof. of Sign Language and Deaf Studies, City Univ., London, 1995–2005. Vice Chm., Royal Assoc. for Deaf People, 2002–08. Trustee, UK Council on Deafness, 2011–. *Publications:* (with J. Kyle) Sign Language: the study of deaf people and their language, 1985; (with R. Sutton-Spence) The Linguistics of BSL, 1999; (jtly) The Signs of a Savant, 2010; (with R. Pfau and M. Steinbach) Sign Language: an international handbook, 2012. *Recreations:* cats, Yiddish language and culture. *Address:* Deafness, Cognition and Language Research Centre, 49 Gordon Square, WC1H 0PD. *T:* (020) 7679 8670, *Fax:* (020) 7679 8691. *E:* b.woll@ucl.ac.uk. *Club:* Penn (New York).

WOLLASTON, Sarah; MP (C) Totnes, since 2010; *b* 1962; *m* Adrian; one *s* two *d*. *Educ:* Tal Handaq Service Children's Sch., Malta; Watford Grammar Sch. for Girls; Guy's Hosp. Med. Sch. (BSc Pathol. 1983; MB BS 1986). DRCOG 1991; MRCGP 1992. Forensic med. examr, Devon and Cornwall Police, 1996–2001; GP, Chagford Health Centre, Devon, 1999–2010; Trainer, Peninsula Med. Sch., Plymouth, 2001–10; teacher, Exeter Postgrad. Centre until 2010. Mem., Health Select Cttee, 2010– (Chm., 2014–). *Address:* House of Commons, SW1A 0AA.

WOLLEN, Siân; *see* Davies, Siân.

WOLMAR, Christian Tage Forter; author and broadcaster, since 1997; *b* London, 3 Aug. 1949; *s* of Boris Semenovich Kougoulsky and Dagmar Birgit Wolmar (*née* Lindblom); one *d* by Sally Brooks; one *d* by Scarlett McGwire; partner, Alice Deborah Maby. *Educ:* Lycée Français de Londres; Univ. of Warwick (BA Hons Econs 1971). Asst Editor, Marketing mag., 1972–73; Sports Writer, Hampstead and Highgate Express, 1973–74; Publications Officer, Release, 1976–79; Asst Editor, Roof mag., Shelter, 1979–82; PR Officer, London Bor. of Camden, 1982–84; News Editor, New Statesman, 1984; Local Govt Corresp., London Daily News, 1986–87; The Independent: reporter, 1989–91; Asst News Editor, 1991–92; Transport Corresp., 1992–97. Mem., RSA. *Publications:* Points of View: censorship, 1990; Points of View: drugs, 1990; Drugs and Sport, 1992; Unlocking the Gridlock, 1997; The Great British Railway Disaster, 1997; Stagecoach, 1998; Forgotten Children, 2000; Broken Rails, 2001; Down the Tube, 2002; The Subterranean Railway, 2004; On the Wrong Line, 2005; Fire and Steam, 2007; Blood, Iron and Gold, 2009; Engines of War, 2010; The Great Railway Revolution, 2012; To the Edge of the World, 2013; The Iron Road, 2014; (ed jtly) Urban Access for the 21st Century, 2014. *Recreations:* cycling, cricket, tennis, running, ski-ing. *Address:* 48 Crayford Road, N7 0ND. *T:* 07931 504555. *E:* christian.wolmar@gmail.com. *W:* www.twitter.com/christianwolmar, www.christianwolmar.co.uk, www.wolmarforlondon.co.uk. *Clubs:* Beamers Cricket, Wood Vale Lawn Tennis.

WOLMER, Viscount; William Lewis Palmer; Managing Director, Blackmoor Estate; *b* 1 Sept. 1971; *s* and *heir* of 4th Earl of Selborne, *qv*; *m* 2001, Victoria Baum; two *s* one *d*. *Educ:* Eton Coll.; Christ Church, Oxford (BA 1993); Sch. of Oriental and African Studies, London Univ. (MA 1996); Univ. of Sussex (PhD 2001). Res. Officer, then Fellow, Inst. of Develt Studies, Univ. of Sussex, 1997–2007. *Publications:* From Wilderness Vision to Farm Invasions, 2007. *Heir:* *s* Hon. Alexander David R. Palmer, *b* 2002.

WOLPERT, Prof. Daniel Mark, DPhil; FRS 2012; FMedSci; 1875 Professor of Engineering, University of Cambridge, since 2005; Fellow, Trinity College, Cambridge, since 2005; Royal Society Noreen Murray Research Professor in Neurobiology, since 2013; *b* 8 Sept. 1963; *s* of Prof. Lewis Wolpert, *qv* and Elizabeth Wolpert (*née* Brownstein); *m* 1990, Mary Anne Shorrock; two *d*. *Educ:* Hall Sch.; Westminster Sch.; Trinity Hall, Cambridge (BA Hons Med. Scis 1985); Magdalene Coll., Univ. of Oxford (BM BCh Clinical Medicine 1988); Lincoln Coll., Univ. of Oxford (DPhil Physiol. 1992). Med. House Officer, Oxford, 1988–89; MRC Trng Fellow, Univ. Lab. of Physiol., Univ. of Oxford, 1989–92; Fulbright Scholarship, 1992–95, Postdoctoral Associate, 1992–94, McDonnell-Pew Fellow in Cognitive Neurosci., 1994–95, Dept of Brain and Cognitive Sci., MIT; Institute of Neurology, University College London: Lectr, 1995–99, Reader in Motor Neurosci., 1999–2002; Prof. of Motor Neurosci. and Vice Chm., Sobell Dept of Motor Neurosci., 2002–05; Co-Dir, Inst. of Movt Neurosci., 1999–2005; Hon. Sen. Res. Fellow, UCL, 2005–08. Francis Crick Prize Lect., Royal Soc., 2005; Fred Kavli Dist. Internat. Scientist Lect., Soc. for Neurosci., 2009. Golden Brain Award, Minerva Foundn, USA, 2010. FMedSci 2004. *Publications:* articles on neuroscience in learned jls. *Recreations:* bread-making, gadgets and games. *Address:* Department of Engineering, University of Cambridge, Trumpington Street, Cambridge CB2 1PZ. *T:* (01223) 748530, *Fax:* (01223) 332662. *E:* wolpert@eng.cam.ac.uk. *W:* www.wolpertlab.com.

WOLPERT, Prof. Lewis, CBE 1990; DIC, PhD; FRS 1980; FMedSci; FRSL; Professor of Biology as Applied to Medicine, London University, at University College London Medical School (formerly at Middlesex Hospital Medical School), 1966–2004, now Emeritus; *b* 19 Oct. 1929; *s* of William and Sarah Wolpert; *m* 1961, Elizabeth Brownstein; two *s* two *d*. *Educ:* King Edward's Sch., Johannesburg; Univ. of Witwatersrand (BScEng); Imperial Coll., London (DIC; FIC 1996); King's Coll., London (PhD; FKC 2001). Personal Asst to Director of Building Research Inst., S African Council for Scientific and Industrial Research, 1951–52; Engineer, Israel Water Planning Dept, 1953–54; King's College, London: Asst Lectr in Zoology, 1958–60; Lectr in Zoology, 1960–64; Reader in Zoology, 1964–66; Hd of Dept of Biology as Applied to Medicine, later Dept of Anatomy and Biology as Applied to Medicine, Middlesex Hosp. Med. Sch., 1966–87. MRC: Mem. Council, 1984–88; Mem., 1982–88, Chm., 1984–88, Cell Bd; Chairman: Scientific Inf. Cttee, Royal Soc., 1983–88; COPUS, 1994–98; Biology Concerted Action Cttee, EEC, 1988–91. President: British Soc. for Cell Biology, 1985–91; Inst. of Information Scientists, 1986–87. Lectures: Steinhaus, Univ. of California at Irvine, 1980; van der Horst, Univ. of Witwatersrand, Johannesburg, 1981; Bidder, Soc. for Experimental Biology, Leicester, 1982; Swirling, Dana-Farber, Boston, 1985; Lloyd-Roberts, RCP, 1986; Royal Instn Christmas Lectures, 1986; R. G. Williams, Univ. of Pennsylvania, 1988; Bernal, Birkbeck Coll., 1989; Radcliffe, Warwick Univ., 1990; Redfearn, Leicester, 1991; Wade, Southampton, 1991; Robb, Univ. of Auckland, 1994; Samuel Gee, RCP, 1995; Hunterian Oration, 1996; Gerald Walters Meml, Bath Univ., 1997; Medawar, 1998, Faraday (also Award), 2000, Royal Soc.; Rose, Marine Biol. Lab., Woods Hole, Mass., 2001. Presenter: Antenna, BBC2, 1987–88; A Living Hell, BBC2, 1999; interviews with scientists, Radio 3, 1981–; radio documentaries: The Dark Lady of DNA, 1989; The Virgin Fathers of the Calculus, 1991. FMedSci 1998; FRSL 1999. Mem., Amer. Philos. Soc., 2002. For. Mem., Polish Acad. of Arts and Scis, 1998. Hon. MRCP, 1986. Hon. Fellow, UCL, 1995. Hon. DSc: CNAA, 1992; Leicester, 1996; Westminster, 1996; Bath, 1997; DUniv Open, 1998. Scientific Medal, Zoological Soc., 1968; Hamburger Award, Amer. Soc. of Develtl Biol., 2003; Waddington Medal, British Soc. of Develtl Biol., 2015. *Publications:* A Passion for Science (with A. Richards), 1988; Triumph of the Embryo, 1991; The Unnatural Nature of Science, 1992; (with A. Richards) Passionate Minds, 1997; Principles of Development, 1998; Malignant Sadness: the anatomy of depression, 1999; Six Impossible Things Before Breakfast, 2006; How We Live and Why We Die: the secret lives of cells, 2009; You're Looking Very Well: the surprising nature of getting old, 2011; Why Can't a Woman Be More Like a Man, 2014; articles on cell and developmental biology in scientific jls. *Recreation:* tennis. *Address:* Cell and Developmental Biology, University College London, Gower Street, WC1E 6BT.

See also D. M. Wolpert.

WOLSELEY, Sir Charles Garnet Richard Mark, 11th Bt *cr* 1628; Partner, Smiths Gore, Chartered Surveyors, 1979–87 (Associate Partner, 1974); *b* 16 June 1944; *s* of Capt. Stephen Garnet Hubert Francis Wolseley, Royal Artillery (*d* 1944, of wounds received in action) and Pamela (*d* 2002), *yr d* of late Capt. F. Barry and Mrs Lavinia Power, Wolseley Park, Rugeley, Staffs; *S* grandfather, Sir Edric Charles Joseph Wolseley, 10th Bt, 1954; *m* 1st, 1968, Anita Maria (marr. diss. 1984), *er d* of late H. J. Fried, Epsom, Surrey; one *s* three *d*; 2nd, 1984, Mrs Imogene Brown. *Educ:* St Bede's School, near Stafford; Ampleforth College, York. FRICS. *Recreations:* shooting, fishing, gardening, painting. *Heir:* *s* Stephen Garnet Hugo Charles Wolseley [*b* 2 May 1980; *m* 2008, Mary-Kate, *d* of Anthony and Nicola Quinlan; two *s*]. *Address:* 3 School Place, Teddesley Park, Penkridge, Staffs ST19 5RW. *Club:* Shikar.

WOLSELEY, Sir James Douglas, 13th Bt *cr* 1745 (Ire.), of Mount Wolseley, Co. Carlow; *b* 17 Sept. 1937; *s* of James Douglas Wolseley (*d* 1960), and Olive, *d* of Carroll Walter Wofford; *S* kinsman, Sir Garnet Wolseley, 12th Bt, 1991, but his name does not appear on the Official Roll of the Baronetage; *m* 1st, 1965, Patricia Lynn (marr. diss. 1971), *d* of William R. Hunter; 2nd, 1984, Mary Anne, *d* of Thomas G. Brown. *Heir:* *kinsman* John Walter Wolseley [*b* 21 April 1938; *m* 1964, Patricia Ann Newland (marr. diss. 1978); two *s*].

WOLSTENCROFT, Ven. Alan; Archdeacon of Manchester, Canon Residentiary of Manchester Cathedral, and Fellow of the College, 1998–2004, now Archdeacon and Canon Emeritus; *b* 16 July 1937; *s* of John Wolstencroft and Jean (*née* Miller); *m* 1968, Christine Mary Hall; one *s* one *d*. *Educ:* Wellington Tech. Sch., Altrincham; St John's Coll. of Further Educn, Manchester; Cuddesdon Coll., Oxford. Nat. Service, RAF, Nat. Mountain Rescue Team, 1955–57. Trainee Manager, W. H. Smith & Co., 1957–59; Regl Wine and Spirit Manager, Bass/Charrington Co., 1959–67; ordained deacon, 1969, priest, 1970; Assistant Curate: St Thomas, Halliwell, 1969–71; All Saints, Stand, 1971–73; Vicar, St Martin, Wythenshawe, 1973–80; Asst Chaplain, Wythenshawe Hosp., 1973–91; Rural, then Area, Dean of Withington, 1978–91; Vicar: St John the Divine, Brooklands, 1980–91; St Peter, Bolton, 1991–98. Manchester Retired Clergy Officer, 2004–. Synodal Sec., York Convocation, 2007–. Theatre Chaplain, Actors' Church Union, 1975–2010; Religious Advr, Granada TV, 2000–10. Mem., Probus. *Recreations:* watching football, sport, theatre, reading, wines, beers, walking. *Address:* The Bakehouse, 1 Latham Row, Horwich, Bolton, Lancs BL6 6QZ. *T:* (01204) 469985. *Clubs:* Royal Air Force; Bolton Wanderers FC.

WOLSTENHOLME, Andrew William Lewis, OBE 2009; FREng, FICE, FRICS; Chief Executive, Crossrail Ltd, since 2011; *b* London, 5 March 1959; *s* of Michael Ashmore Wolstenholme and Vivien Wolstenholme; *m* 1987, Caroline Barnes-Yallowley; five *s*. *Educ:* Univ. of Southampton (BSc Eng 1st Cl. Civil Engrg 1981); RMA Sandhurst; INSEAD (Advanced Mgt and Finance Progs 2009). Army: SSLC, RE, 1978; SSC, QRIH, 1981–84. Ove Arup and Partners, London, 1984–96, Dir, Proj. Mgt Gp, Hong Kong, 1993–96; BAA plc, 1996–2009: Dir, Capital Projects, 1998–2002; Prog. Dir, Terminal 5, Heathrow, 2002–08; Gp Construction Dir, 2008–09; Man. Dir, Balfour Beatty Mgt, 2009–10, Dir, Innovation and Strategic Capability, 2010–11, Balfour Beatty Gp plc. Dir, Inst. of Cancer Res., 2005–11. Non-exec. Dir, Defence Equipment and Support, MoD, 2014. Mem. Council, Eastbourne Coll., 2009–. FICE 2010; FREng 2013; FRICS 2013. Hon. DSc Southampton 2014. *Recreations:* watercolour painting, cooking, opera, tennis, walking, ukulele. *Address:* Crossrail Ltd, 25 Canada Square, E14 5LQ. *T:* (020) 7299 9299. *E:* andrewwolstenholme@crossrail.co.uk.

WOLSTENHOLME, His Honour (John) Scott; a Circuit Judge, 1995–2013; *b* 28 Nov. 1947; *s* of Donald Arthur Wolstenholme and Kaye (*née* Humphrys); *m* 1972, Lynne Harrison; three *s* one *d*. *Educ:* Roundhay Sch., Leeds; University Coll., Oxford (MA). Called to the Bar, Middle Temple, 1971; practised North Eastern Circuit, 1971–92; Chm., Industrial Tribunals, Leeds Region, 1992–95; a Recorder, 1992–95. Mem., Parole Bd, 2010–. *Recreations:* playing the drums, walking, nine grandchildren.

WOLSTENHOLME, Karen Suzanne; HM Diplomatic Service, retired; Ambassador to the Democratic People's Republic of Korea, 2011–12; *b* Hammersmith, 16 Oct. 1962; *d* of Peter and Teresa Vivian; *m* 1986, Jonathan David Wolstenholme (*d* 2011); one *s* two *d*. *Educ:* Penrhos Coll., Colwyn Bay; Open Univ. (MPA 2010). Entered FCO, 1980; Vice-Consul, Moscow, 1984–85; Asst Admin Officer, Harare, 1986–89; FCO, 1990–94; Second Sec., UK Repn to EU, Brussels, 1994–98; First Sec., Wellington, NZ and Dep. Gov., Pitcairn Is, 1998–2002; Dep. Hd, Conflict Prevention Unit, FCO, 2003; Team Leader: S Pacific, FCO, 2003–04; Nigeria, Ghana and Central Africa, FCO, 2004–06; Dep. UK Perm. Rep. to OPCW, The Hague, 2007–11. Gov., British Sch. in Netherlands, 2008–10. *Recreations:* travel, cookery, family. *Club:* Civil Service.

WOLSTENHOLME, Scott; *see* Wolstenholme, His Honour J. S.

WOLTON, Harry; QC 1982; company director (planning and development consultancy), since 2012; *b* 1 Jan. 1938; *s* of late Harry William Wolton and Dorothy Beatrice Wolton; *m* 1971, Julie Rosina Josephine Lovell (*née* Mason); three *s*. *Educ:* King Edward's Sch., Birmingham (Foundn Scholar); Univ. of Birmingham. Called to the Bar, Gray's Inn, 1969; in practice as a barrister, 1969–2012; a Recorder, 1985–2003; authorised to sit as a Dep. High Court Judge, 1990–2003. Dir, Bar Mutual Insurance Fund, 1997–2004. Trustee, Hon. Doctors Assoc., 2015–. *Recreations:* dendrology, bibliophilia, philanthropy. *Address:* Spring Bank, Tunley, Cirencester GL7 6LP. *T:* (01285) 760504; Rue Jeu de Paume, Goult, 84220, France. *Club:* Garrick.

WOLVERHAMPTON, Bishop Suffragan of, since 2007; **Rt Rev. Clive Malcolm Gregory;** *b* 25 Nov. 1961; *s* of late John Gregory and of Aurea Gregory; *m* 1997, Jenny Hyde; one *s* one *d*. *Educ:* Lancaster Univ. (BA Hons English 1984); Queens' Coll., Cambridge (BA Theology 1987, MA 1989); Westcott House Theol Coll. Ordained deacon, 1988, priest, 1989; Asst Curate, St John the Baptist, Margate, 1988–92; Sen. Chaplain, Univ. of Warwick, 1992–98; Team Rector, Coventry E, 1998–2007. Hon. MA Warwick, 1999. *Recreations:* walking, playing cricket, contemporary music. *Address:* 61 Richmond Road, Wolverhampton WV3 9JH. *T:* (01902) 824503, *Fax:* (01902) 824504. *E:* bishop.wolverhampton@lichfield.anglican.org.

WOLVERTON, 8th Baron *cr* 1869; **Miles John Glyn;** artist, art director, film-maker and animator; *b* London, 6 June 1966; *s* of Hon. Andrew John Glyn (*d* 2007) and of Celia (*née* Laws); *S* uncle, 2011; *m* 2007, Louise Riley (marr. diss. 2011); one *d*. *Educ:* Leicester Poly. (BA 1st cl. Hons Fine Art 1988); Bournemouth Univ. (MA 3D Computer Animation 2003). *Recreations:* table tennis, electronic music, camping, bicycling. *Heir:* *half-b* Jonathan Carlin Glyn, *b* 29 Jan. 1990. *Club:* London Fields Table Tennis.

WOLZFELD, Jean-Louis; Ambassador of Luxembourg to United States of America, since 2012; *b* 5 July 1951; *s* of late Gustave Wolzfeld and of Marie Thérèse (*née* Normand). *Educ:* Univ. of Paris I (Master Internat. Law). Entered Luxembourg Foreign Service, 1976; Internat. Econ. Relns Dept, Min. of Foreign Affairs, 1977–80; Dep. Perm. Rep., Geneva, 1981–86; Ambassador to Japan, 1986–93; Perm. Rep. to UN, 1993–98; Dir for Pol Affairs, Min. of Foreign Affairs, 1998–2002; Ambassador to the UK and concurrently to Ireland and Iceland, 2002–07; Ambassador to Italy, 2007–12. Grand Officer: Ordre du Mérite (Luxembourg) (Officer, 1995); Ordre de la Couronne de Chêne (Luxembourg) (Comdr, 2001). *Recreations:* travel, painting. *Address:* c/o Luxembourg Embassy, 2200 Massachusetts Avenue, Washington, DC 20008, USA. *Clubs:* Athenæum, Travellers.

WOMACK, Joanna Mary; Acting Bursar, Clare Hall, Cambridge, 2014; *b* 12 Sept. 1947; *d* of Laurence Paul Hodges and Mary Elizabeth Hodges (*née* Lyon); *m* 1971, Michael Thomas Womack; three *s*. *Educ:* James Allen's Girls' Sch., Dulwich; New Hall, Cambridge (MA 1st Cl. Hons Law). Admitted solicitor, 1972; solicitor, Herbert Smith & Co., 1972–75; New Hall, Cambridge: Coll. Lectr in Law, 1975–83; Fellow, 1975–90; Bursar, 1983–90; Emeritus Fellow, 1996; Trinity Hall, Cambridge: Bursar and Steward, 1990–93; Fellow, 1990–2003; Treasurer, Cambridge Univ., 1993–2003; Clare Hall, Cambridge: Bursar and Develt Dir, 2003–10; Emeritus Fellow, 2011. Gen. Comr of Tax, 1987–2008. Dir, Cambridge Building Soc., 1994–2006. Fellow and Acting Bursar, Murray Edwards Coll., Cambridge, 2013. Trustee: Cambridge Colleges Federated Pension Scheme, 2003– (Chm., 2006–); Sir Halley Stewart Trust, 2003–; The Varrier-Jones Foundn, 2005–14; The Papworth Trust, 2006–;

Edward Storey Foundn, 2006–; Cambridge Building Soc. Retirement Plan, 2008– (Chm., 2009–); King's Junior Voices, 2010–. Gov., Long Road VI Form Coll., Cambridge, 1992–2001. *Recreations:* family life, photography, music, hill-walking. *Address:* Clare Hall, Herschel Road, Cambridge CB3 9AL. *T:* (01223) 332362.

WOMBELL, Paul David; independent photographic curator and writer; *b* 8 Oct. 1948; *s* of Clifford and Katherine Wombell; *m* 1995, Tricia Coral Buckley. *Educ:* St Martin's Sch. of Art, London (BA Fine Art). Midland Gp Art Centre, 1983–86; Director: Impressions Gall., York, 1986–94; The Photographers' Gall., London, 1994–2005; Festival Dir, Hereford Photography Festival, 2006–07. Guest Curator, Le Mois de la Photo à Montréal, 2013. Vis. Prof., 2003–07, Res. Prof., 2007–09, Univ. of Sunderland. Chm., Citigroup Photography Prize, 2003–05. *Publications:* Battle, Passchendale 1917, 1981; Photovideo: photography in the age of the computer, 1991; Sportscape, the evolution of sport photography, 2000; Blink, 2002; Local: the end of globalisation, 2007; 70s Photography and Everyday Life, 2009; Calves and Thighs: Juergen Teller, 2010; End Times: Jill Greenberg, 2012; Drone: the automated image, 2013. *Recreation:* life.

WOMBWELL, Sir George (Philip Frederick), 7th Bt *cr* 1778; *b* 21 May 1949; *s* of Sir (Frederick) Philip (Alfred William) Wombwell, 6th Bt, MBE, and late Ida Elizabeth, *er d* of Frederick J. Leitch; *S* father, 1977, but his name does not appear on the Official Roll of the Baronetage; *m* 1974, (Hermione) Jane, *e d* of T. S. Wrightson; one *s* one *d*. *Educ:* Repton. *Heir: s* Stephen Philip Henry Wombwell [*b* 12 May 1977; *m* 2006, Helen-Sarah, *o d* of Terence William Pattinson; one *d*]. *Address:* Newburgh Priory, Coxwold, York YO61 4AS.

WOMERSLEY, Prof. David John, DLitt; FBA 2009; FRHistS; Thomas Warton Professor of English Literature, University of Oxford, since 2002; Fellow, St Catherine's College, Oxford, since 2002; *b* 29 Jan. 1957; *s* of late John Crossley Womersley and Joyce Womersley; *m* 1982, Carolyn Jane Godlee; one *s* two *d*. *Educ:* Strode's Sch., Egham; Trinity Coll., Cambridge (BA 1979; PhD 1983). DLitt 2015. FRHistS 1997; FEA 2003. Drapers' Co. Res. Fellow, Pembroke Coll., Cambridge, 1981–83; Lectr, Sch. of English, Univ. of Leeds, 1983–84; Fellow and Tutor in English Lit., Jesus Coll., Oxford, 1984–2002; Sen. Proctor, Univ. of Oxford, 2001–02. Governor: Dragon Sch., Oxford, 1998–2010; Harrow Sch., 2001–. *Publications:* The Transformation of the Decline and Fall of the Roman Empire, 1988; Gibbon and the 'Watchmen of the Holy City': the historian and his reputation 1776–1814, 2002; Divinity and State, 2010; James II, 2015; *edited*: Edward Gibbon, The Decline and Fall of the Roman Empire, 3 vols, 1994, 7th edn 2004, facsimile edn, 6 vols, 1997, abridged edn 2000, 10th edn 2004; Edward Gibbon, Reflections on the Fall of Rome, 1995; Religious Scepticism: contemporary responses to Gibbon, 1997; Augustan Critical Writing, 1997; Edmund Burke, Pre-Revolutionary Writings, 1998; Restoration Drama: an anthology, 2000; Samuel Johnson, Selected Essays, 2003; James Boswell, Life of Johnson, 2008; Jonathan Swift, Gulliver's Travels, 2012; E. W. Monatgu, Reflections on the Rise and Fall of the Ancient Republicks, 2015; *edited collections of essays:* Gibbon: bicentenary essays, 1997; A Companion to English Literature from Milton to Blake, 2000; Cultures of Whiggism, 2005; Literary Milieux, 2008. *Recreations:* wine, yachting, cooking, dogs. *Address:* St Catherine's College, Manor Road, Oxford OX1 3UJ. *T:* (01865) 271714, *Fax:* (01865) 271768. *E:* david.womersley@ell.ox.ac.uk. *Clubs:* Athenæum, Saintsbury.

WOMERSLEY, John; *see* Womersley, W. J.

WOMERSLEY, Sir Peter (John Walter), 2nd Bt *cr* 1945; JP; human resources consultant, 1997–2001; *b* 10 Nov. 1941; *s* of Capt. John Womersley (*o s* of 1st Bt; killed in action in Italy, 1944), and of Betty, *d* of Cyril Williams, Elstead, Surrey; *S* grandfather, 1961; *m* 1968, Janet Margaret Grant; two *s* two *d*. *Educ:* Aldro; Charterhouse; RMA, Sandhurst. Entered Royal Military Academy (Regular Army), 1960; Lt, King's Own Royal Border Regt, 1964; Captain, 1967; retd 1968; Personnel, then Human Resources, Manager, later Evaluation Project Manager, Human Resources, SmithKline Beecham, 1968–97. JP Steyning, 1991, Worthing and Dist, 1996. *Publications:* (with Neil Grant) Collecting Stamps, 1980. *Heir: s* John Gavin Grant Womersley, *b* 7 Dec. 1971. *Address:* Broomfields, 23 Goring Road, Steyning, W Sussex BN44 3GF.

WOMERSLEY, (William) John, DPhil; Chief Executive, Science and Technology Facilities Council, since 2011; *b* Torquay, Devon, 22 Sept. 1962; *s* of Leslie Womersley and Patricia Womersley; *m* 1999, Elizabeth Gallas. *Educ:* Torquay Boys' Grammar Sch.; Corpus Christi Coll., Cambridge (BA Hons 1st Cl. Nat. Scis 1983; MA Nat. Scis 1987); Corpus Christi Coll., Oxford (DPhil Experimental Particle Phys 1987). Asst Prof. of Physics, Florida State Univ., 1989–92; Scientist: SSC Lab., Texas, 1992–94; Fermi National Accelerator Lab., 1994–2004; Director: Particle Physics, CCLRC Rutherford Appleton Lab., 2005–07; Sci. Strategy and Sci. Progs, STFC, 2007–11. Visiting Professor: Univ. of Durham, 2005–; UCL, 2005–; Univ. of Oxford, 2005–. FInstP 2006; Fellow, APS, 2002. *Recreations:* railways, travel, music. *Address:* Science and Technology Facilities Council, Polaris House, North Star Avenue, Swindon SN2 1SZ. *E:* john.womersley@stfc.ac.uk.

WONDRAUSCH, Mary, OBE 2000; potter, since 1975; painter; *b* 17 Dec. 1923; *d* of Harold Lambert and Margaret (*née* Montgomery); *m* 1st, 1943, Kenneth Fyfe (marr. annulled); 2nd, 1946, Basil Harthan (marr. diss.); 3rd, 1954, Witold Wondrausch (marr. diss.); one *s* two *d*. *Educ:* Convent IBVM, St Mary's, Ascot; Convent FCJ, Ware, Herts; Kingston Sch. of Art. WAAF (invalided out), 1943. Flibertygibbet, waitress, cook; professional painter, exhibited, Women's Internat. Art Club, FBA, etc; art teacher, Barrow Hills Sch., 1960–75; set up pottery, Godalming, 1975, later Farncombe, then stables at Brickfields, 1984. Lectures on Continental slipware to BM, Fitzwilliam Mus., Cambridge, and Nat. Ethnographic Mus., Budapest. Pots in private and public collections incl. V&A Mus.; pottery exhibitions: Heidelberg Gall.; Craftsman Potters' Assoc.; British Craft Centre; Farnham Gall.; Amalgam; Univ. of Aberystwyth; Stoke-on-Trent Mus.; BM; Abbots Hall, Kendall; Primavera, Cambridge; Haslemere Mus.; painting exhibitions: Canon Gall., Petworth; Farnham Mus.; Cricket Gall., Chelsea. Hon. Fellow, Craft Potters' Assoc., 2005. *Publications:* Mary Wondrausch on Slipware, 1986, 2nd edn 2001; Brickfields: my life as a potter, painter, gardener, writer and cook, 2004, 2nd edn 2005; contrib. articles on Continental slipware to Ceramic Rev., Antique Collector; contribs on history of food to Oxford Encyclopaedia of Food, Petits Propos Culinaires, Oxford DNB, Oxford Symposium of Food. *Recreations:* reading, eating and drinking good food and wine, making wacky fountains from found materials, wild mushroom gathering. *Address:* The Pottery, Brickfields, Compton, Guildford, Surrey GU3 1HZ. *T:* (01483) 414097.

WONG Kin Chow, Michael, GBS 2001; JP; Chairman, Equal Opportunities Commission of Hong Kong, 2003; a Justice of Appeal of the High Court of Hong Kong, 1999–2001; *b* 16 Aug. 1936; *s* of late Wong Chong and Au Ting; *m* 1963, Mae (*née* Fong); two *s* two *d*. *Educ:* Univ. of Liverpool (LLB Hons 1961). Called to the Bar, Middle Temple, 1962; private practice, Hong Kong, 1962–65; Hong Kong Government: Crown Counsel, Legal Dept, 1966–69; Senior Crown Counsel, 1969–72; Asst Principal Crown Counsel, 1973; Presiding Officer, Labour Tribunal, 1973–75; Asst Registrar, Supreme Court, 1975–77; District Judge, 1977; a Judge of the High Court, then of the Court of First Instance of the High Court, Hong Kong, 1985–99. Chm., Release Under Supervision Bd, 1988–94. JP Hong Kong, 2002. *Address:* Flat C, 51st Floor, The Masterpiece, 18 Hanoi Road, Tsimshatsui, Kowloon, Hong Kong. *Clubs:* Chinese, Hong Kong, Hong Kong Jockey, Kowloon Cricket (Hong Kong).

WONG Yin Song, Rt Rev. James Richard; *see* Seychelles, Bishop of the.

WONNACOTT, John Henry, CBE 2000; artist; *b* 15 April 1946; *s* of John Alfred Wonnacott and Ethel Gwendoline Wonnacott (*née* Copeland); *m* 1974, Anne Rozalia Wesolowska; one *s* two *d*. *Educ:* Slade Sch. of Fine Art, London. *Solo exhibitions* include: Minories, Colchester, 1977; Rochdale Art Gall. and tour, 1978; Marlborough Fine Art, London, 1980, 1985, 1988; Scottish NPG, Edinburgh, 1986; Agnew's, London, 1992, 1996, 2005, 2011; Wolsey Art Gall., Christchurch Mansion, Ipswich, 1998; Hirschl & Adler, NY and Agnew's, London, 1999–2000; NPG (Royal Family etc), 2000; Clare Hall, Cambridge, 2013; St John's Coll., Oxford, 2013; Chambers Fine Art, NY, 2014; Norwich Castle Mus., 2014; Norwich Univ. of Arts, 2014; *group exhibitions* include: Painting and Perception, MacRoberts Arts Centre Gall., Univ. of Sterling, 1971; British Painting '74, Haywood Gall.; British Painting 1952–77, RA, 1977; Britain Salutes New York, Marlborough Fine Art, 1983; The Hard-Won Image, Tate Gall., 1984; Foundn Veranneman invites Marlborough, Foundn Veranneman, Kruishoutem, 1986–87; Monet to Freud, Sotheby's, London, 1989; Salute to Turner, Agnew's, London, 1989; The Pursuit of the Real, British Figurative Painting from Sickert to Bacon, Manchester City Art Galls, Barbican Art Gall. and Glasgow City Art Gall., 1990; The New Patrons, Twentieth Century Art from Corporate Collections, Christie's, London, 1992; Contemp. Portraits from Suffolk to Essex, Gainsborough's House, Sudbury, 1995; Contemp. British Artists Celebrate One Hundred Years of the Nat. Trust, Christie's, London, 1995; Painting the Century, NPG, 2001; A Sea of Faces, Nat. Maritime Mus., London, 2001; Visions of London, Art Space Gall., 2004; Annual Exhibn, RP (Ondaatje Prize for Portraiture), 2006–14; work in public collections including: Arts Council, British Council, Imperial War Mus., H of C, NPG, Nat. Maritime Mus., Nat. Trust, Tate Gall., DTI, London; Metropolitan Mus., NY; Christchurch Mus., Ipswich; Scottish NPG; Norwich Castle Mus.; Rochdale Art Gall. Hon. RP 2001. *Address:* 5 Cliff Gardens, Leigh on Sea, Essex SS9 1EY.

WONNACOTT, Mark Andrew; QC 2013; *b* London, 1967; *s* of Richard Wonnacott and Sheila Wonnacott. *Educ:* Perth Acad.; University Coll. London (LLB 1988). Called to the Bar, Lincoln's Inn, 1989; in practice as a barrister, 1989–. *Publications:* Drafting Property Pleadings, 1997; Possession of Land, 2006; History of the Law of Landlord and Tenant, 2012. *Recreation:* teasing academics and annoying judges. *Address:* Maitland Chambers, 7 Stone Buildings, Lincoln's Inn, WC2A 3SZ. *T:* (020) 7406 1200.

WOO, Kwok-Hing, GBS 2002; CBE 1996; Commissioner on Interception of Communications and Surveillance, Hong Kong, 2006–12; *b* 13 Jan. 1946; *s* of late Woo Leung and Leung Yuk-Ling; *m* Rowena Tang; two *s* two *d*. *Educ:* Univ. of Birmingham (LLB); University College, London (LLM). Called to the Bar, Gray's Inn, 1969; QC (Hong Kong), 1987; in private practice, Hong Kong, 1970–92; a High Court Judge, then Judge of the Ct of First Instance, High Ct, 1992–2000; a Justice of Appeal, 2000–03; Vice-Pres., Ct of Appeal, 2004–11. Chairman: Boundary and Election Commn, Hong Kong, 1993–97; Electoral Affairs Commn, 1997–2006; Commissioner: of Inquiry into Garley Bldg Fire, 1997; of Inquiry on New Airport, 1998–99. *Address:* c/o 66a Deep Water Bay Road, Hong Kong. *Clubs:* Hong Kong Jockey, Hong Kong, Hong Kong Country.

WOO, Sir Leo (Joseph), Kt 1993; MBE 1984; Chairman and Chief Executive, Dragon Resources Ltd, since 2006; *b* 17 Oct. 1952; *s* of Gabriel Bernard Woo and Molly Woo; *m* 1973, Emilyn Cha; one *s* two *d*. *Educ:* De La Salle Oakhill Coll., Sydney. Former Chm. and Chief Exec., Woo Hldgs Gp. *Address:* PO Box R399, Royal Exchange, NSW 1225, Australia.

WOO, Prof. Patricia Mang Ming, CBE 2005; PhD; FRCP, FRCPCH, FMedSci; Professor of Paediatric Rheumatology, University College London, 1994–2010, now Emeritus; Consultant Physician, Great Ormond Street and University College London Hospitals, 1994–2010, now Hon. Consultant Physician, Great Ormond Street Hospital Foundation NHS Trust and University College Hospital Foundation NHS Trust; *b* 12 Feb. 1948; *d* of Woo Hing Tak and Woo Lam Chiu Wah. *Educ:* Charing Cross Hosp. Med. Sch., Univ. of London (BSc 1969; MB BS 1972); Darwin Coll., Cambridge (PhD 1979). FRCP 1991; FRCPCH 1997. House physician and house surgeon, Charing Cross Hosp., 1973–74; Senior House Officer: Brompton Hosp., 1974; Northwick Park Hosp., 1974–75; MRC Clin. Trng Fellow and Hon. SHO, Cambridge Univ., 1975–78; Registrar, Northwick Park Hosp., 1979–81; Sen. Registrar, Guy's Hosp., 1981–83; Res. Fellow, Harvard Med. Sch., 1983–85; MRC Clin. Scientist and Consultant Physician, Northwick Park Hosp., 1985–94. FMedSci 2001. *Publications:* (jtly) Paediatric Rheumatology Update, 1989; (ed jtly) Oxford Textbook of Rheumatology, 1993, 3rd edn 2004; Paediatric Rheumatology in Clinical Practice, 2007; 187 original contribs to Jl of Rheumatology and scientific jls; 72 reviews, editorials and book chapters. *Recreations:* music, ski-ing, golf, sailing. *Address:* Rayne Building, University College London, 5 University Street, WC1E 6JF. *T:* (020) 7679 6364, *Fax:* (020) 7679 6212.

WOO, Sir Po-Shing, Kt 1999; FCIArb; Founder, Woo Kwan Lee & Lo, Solicitors & Notaries, Hong Kong, 1973; *b* 19 April 1929; *s* of late Seaward Woo, JP, and of Ng Chiu Man; *m* 1956, Helen Woo Fong Shuet Fun; four *s* one *d*. *Educ:* La Salle Coll., Hong Kong; King's Coll., London (LLB 1956; FKC 1995). Admitted Solicitor, England and Hong Kong, 1960; NP 1966; admitted as Barrister and Solicitor, Supreme Court of Victoria, Australia, 1983. Hon. Prof., Nankai Univ. of Tianjin, China, 1995. Dir of numerous companies in Hong Kong. Member: Inst. Admin. Mgt, 1975; Inst. Trade Mark Agents, 1978. Founder, Po-Shing Woo Charitable Foundn, 1994. Patron: Woo Po-Shing Gall. of Chinese Bronze, Shanghai Mus., 1996–; Sir Po-Shing Woo Auckland Observatory Bldg, 1998–. Fellow, Hong Kong Mgt Assoc., 2000. FCIArb 1966; FCMI (FIMgt 1975); FInstD 1975; World Fellow, Duke of Edinburgh's Award, 1994. Hon. LLD City Univ. of Hong Kong, 1995. Chevalier, Ordre des Arts et des lettres (France), 2004. *Recreations:* travelling, antiques (incl. Chinese paintings, bronze and ceramic), race-horse owner (incl. Derby winners, Helene Star, 1993, and Helene Mascot, 2008). *Clubs:* Royal Automobile; Hong Kong Jockey, Hong Kong (Hong Kong).

WOOBEY, Paul, CEng; Director, Information and Communications Technology, Wellcome Trust Sanger Institute, since 2014; *b* Leeds, 9 May 1956; *s* of Eric and Irene Woobey; *m* 1976, Alison Edwardson; one *s*. *Educ:* High Sch., Glasgow; Univ. of Glasgow (BSc Atomic Physics and Maths). CEng 1979. Scientific Officer (Reactor Physics), AEA, 1978–83; Res. Scientist, Rutherford Labs, 1983–86; Vice Pres., Global Infrastructure, GE Healthcare, 1986–2000; Chief Information Officer, EMEA Corporate IT, Pfizer, 2000–08; Chief Inf. Officer, 2008–13, Dir, Strategy and Standards, 2011–13, ONS. MBCS 1979. *Address:* Wellcome Trust Sanger Institute, Wellcome Trust Genome Campus, Hinxton, Cambridge CB10 1SA. *T:* (01223) 499902. *E:* paul.woobey@sanger.ac.uk.

WOOD, family name of **Earl of Halifax** and **Baron Wood of Anfield**.

WOOD OF ANFIELD, Baron *cr* 2011 (Life Peer), of Tonbridge in the County of Kent; **Stewart Martin Wood,** PhD; Adviser to Ed Miliband, Office of the Leader of the Opposition, since 2010; *b* Tunbridge Wells, 25 March 1968; *s* of Brian James Wood and Gisela Wood; *m* 1998, Camilla Bustani; two *s*. *Educ:* Judd Sch., Tonbridge; University Coll., Oxford (BA 1989; MA); Harvard Univ. (PhD 1997). Fulbright Schol., 1989–90; Jun. Res. Fellow, St John's Coll., Oxford, 1995–96; Fellow and Tutor in Politics, Magdalen Coll., Oxford, 1996–2011. Special Advr to Chancellor of the Exchequer on Treasury's Council of Economic Advrs, 2001–07; Special Advr to Prime Minister on Foreign Policy, NI, Culture, Media and Sport, 2007–10; Hd of Communications, Rt Hon. Edward Miliband's Leadership Campaign, 2010; Shadow Minister without Portfolio, Cabinet Office, 2011–15. *Publications:* (ed jtly) Options for Britain: a strategic policy review, 1996; contrib. articles to pol sci. jls and ed vols on pol economy and public policy in Western Europe. *Recreations:* film, theatre, football, cricket, alt-country music. *Address:* c/o House of Lords, SW1A 0PW. *T:* (020) 7219 5854. *E:* stewart.wood@parliament.uk.

WOOD, Adam Kenneth Compton; HM Diplomatic Service, retired; Lieutenant-Governor, Isle of Man, since 2011; *b* 13 March 1955; *s* of Kenneth Wood and Cynthia Wood; *m* 1993, Katie Richardson; one *d*. *Educ:* Oriel Coll., Oxford (BA Hons). Kenya Programme Manager, ODA, Nairobi, 1988–93; Advr to Dir Gen., EC, 1993–96; Hd, DFID SE Asia, Bangkok, 1996–2000; Counsellor (Develt), UKREP, Brussels, 2000–02; High Commissioner: Uganda, 2002–05; Kenya, 2005–08; Dir (Africa), FCO, 2008–10. *Recreations:* birding, golf, tennis. *Address:* Government House, Onchan, Isle of Man IM3 1RR. *E:* government.house@gov.im.

WOOD, Prof. Adrian John Bickersteth, CBE 2005; Professor of International Development, University of Oxford, 2005–11, now Emeritus; *b* 25 Jan. 1946; *s* of John Henry Francis Wood and Mary Eva Bickersteth Wood (*née* Ottley); *m* 1971, Joyce Miriam Teitz; two *d*. *Educ:* King's Coll., Cambridge (BA, PhD 1973); Harvard Univ. (MPA). Fellow, King's College, Cambridge, 1969–77; Asst Lectr, then Lectr, Cambridge Univ., 1973–77; Economist, then Sen. Economist, World Bank, 1977–85; Professorial Fellow, Inst. Develt Studies, Univ. of Sussex, 1985–2000; Chief Economist, DFID, 2000–05. *Publications:* A Theory of Profits, 1975; A Theory of Pay, 1978; (jtly) China: long-term development issues and options, 1985; North-South Trade, Employment and Inequality, 1994; contrib. articles to learned jls. *Recreations:* music, tennis. *Address:* Court House, The Green, Rottingdean, Brighton BN2 7HA.

WOOD, Tan Sri Alan John, CBE 1971; PSM 1972; Chief Executive Officer (formerly Executive Vice President), Malwood Global, Inc., Simpsonville, SC, 1993–2007; *b* 16 Feb. 1925; *s* of late Lt-Col Maurice Taylor Wood, MBE and Ethel Mabel Hill; *m* 1950 (marr. diss.); one *s* (one *d* decd); *m* 1978, Marjorie Anne (*née* Bennett). *Educ:* King Edward VI Royal Grammar Sch., Guildford, Surrey, UK; Indian Mil. Acad., Dehra Dun (grad 1945). Served Army, 1943–47; demobilised rank Captain. Various exec. and managerial positions with Borneo Motors Ltd, Singapore and Malaya, 1947–64 (Dir, 1964); Dir, Inchcape Bhd, 1968–73, Exec. Dep. Chm. 1973–74; Exec. Vice Pres., Sowers, Lewis, Wood Inc., Old Greenwich, Conn, 1975–78; Gen. Manager, India, Singer Sewing Machine Co., 1979–82; Asst Dir, Delaware River Port Authority, World Trade Div., then World Trade and Econ. Develt Div., 1983–93. Pres., Malaysian Internat. Chamber of Commerce, 1968–72; Chairman: Nat. Chambers of Commerce of Malaysia, 1968 and 1972; Internat. Trade Cttee, Chamber of Commerce of Southern NJ, 1990–93. Mem. Bd, Malaysia-US Business Council, 2003–. *Recreation:* listening to books on tape for the legally blind. *Address:* 102 Woodtrace Circle, Greenville, SC 29615, USA. *Clubs:* Lake (Kuala Lumpur); Penang (Penang).

WOOD, Alan John, CBE 2005; FREng; Chairman, Siemens Holdings plc, 2007–12; *b* 20 March 1947; *s* of Joseph Wood and Ivy Wood (*née* Larcombe); *m* 1973, Jennifer Margaret Lynn; two *d*. *Educ:* King Edward VII Sch., Sheffield; Manchester Univ. (BSc 1st Cl. Hons 1968; Hon. LLD 2003); Harvard Univ. (MBA 1975). MIMechE 1973, FIMechE 2002. Unilever plc, 1968–73; Head of Production, Crittall Construction, 1975–78; Man. Dir, Small Electric Motors, 1978–81; joined Siemens, 1981: Siemens AG, 1981–82; Production Dir, 1982–84, Man. Dir, 1984–87, Siemens Measurements Ltd; Managing Director: Electronic Components & Telecom Networks, 1987–91; Energy & Industry, 1991–98; Chief Exec., Siemens plc, 1998–2007. Chairman: North West Reg., CBI, 1996–98; Nat. Mfg Council, CBI, 2000–02; German-British Chamber of Industry and Commerce, 2001–12; Econ. Policy Cttee, EEF, 2003–05; South East Reg., CBI, 2005–07. Pres., EEF, 2005–08. FREng 2005. Hon. DTech Loughborough, 2009. Bundesverdienstkreuz Erste Klasse, 2008. *Recreations:* family, travel, gardening.

WOOD, Alan Thorpe Richard, CBE 2011; Director, Children Services, London Borough of Hackney, since 2006; *b* Romford, 4 April 1954; *s* of Henry Thorpe Peter Wood and Isabel Patricia Smith; *m* 2003, Eleanor Schooling; one *s* one *d*. *Educ:* Stepney Green Comprehensive Sch.; York Univ. (BA Hons Social Scis); Birmingham Univ. (PGCE); Inst. of Educn, Univ. of London (Dip. SEN). Director of Education: Lambeth LBC, 2000; Hackney LBC, 2001–02; Chief Exec., Learning Trust, 2002–06. *Recreations:* cycling, cinema, reading. *Address:* Hackney Service Centre, 1 Hillman Street, E8 1DY. *T:* (020) 8356 4573. *E:* alan.wood@hackney.gov.uk.

WOOD, Aloun; *see* Ndombet-Assamba, A.

WOOD, Dr Andrew Charles, OBE 2013; Chief Executive, Adnams plc, since 2010; *b* London, 1960; *s* of Charles Wood and Doris Wood (*née* Lewin); *m* 1985, Sonya Clabburn; one *d*. *Educ:* Brockley Co. Grammar Sch.; Anglia Poly. Univ. (MBA 1994); Cranfield Univ. (DBA 2007). Norwich Union Insce Gp, 1976–94; Adnams plc: Customer Services, 1994–2000; Sales and Mktg Dir, 2000–06; Man. Dir, 2006–10. Non-exec. Chm., SG Wealth Mgt, 2014–. Chairman: Norcas, 2005–12; New Anglia Local Enterprise Partnership, 2010–. Hon. DBA Anglia Ruskin, 2010; Hon. DSc Cranfield, 2013. *Address:* 59 Drewray Drive, Taverham, Norwich NR8 6XS. *E:* wood.andy1@gmail.com.

WOOD, Sir Andrew (Marley), GCMG 2000 (KCMG 1995; CMG 1986); HM Diplomatic Service, retired; Senior Adviser: ITE, since 2002; Associate Fellow, Chatham House, since 2008; *b* 2 Jan. 1940; *s* of Robert George Wood; *m* 1st, 1972, Melanie LeRoy Masset (*d* 1977); one *s*; 2nd, 1978, Stephanie Lee Masset; one *s* one *d*. *Educ:* Ardingly Coll.; King's Coll., Cambridge (MA 1965). Foreign Office, 1961; Moscow, 1964; Washington, 1967; FCO, 1970; seconded to Cabinet Office, 1971; First Sec., FCO, 1973; First Sec. and Hd of Chancery, Belgrade, 1976; Counsellor, 1978; Hd of Chancery, Moscow, 1979; Hd of W European Dept, 1982, Hd of Personnel Operations Dept, 1983, FCO; Ambassador to Yugoslavia, 1985–89; Minister, Washington, 1989–92; Chief Clerk, FCO, 1992–95; Ambassador to Russian Fedn and to Moldova, 1995–2000. Director: The PBN Co., 2002–11 (Chm., 2007–10); Mechel, 2004–06. Director: Foreign and Colonial Trust, 2000–07; Russo-British Chamber of Commerce, 2000–07 (Chm., 2005–06); Member, Advisory Council: British Expertise (formerly British Consultants Bureau), 2000–08; Renaissance Capital, 2003–08; Adviser: European Round Table, 2004–09; Toyota Europe, 2007–09; Special Representative: BP, 2002–14; Petrofac, 2012–13. Pres., King's Coll. (Cambridge) Assoc., 2006–14. Trustee, Victor Zorza Hospice Trust, 2000–12. *Publications:* (with Lilia Shevstova) Change or Decay: Russia's dilemma and the West's response, 2011; pubns with Chatham Hse, American Interest.

WOOD, Anne, CBE 2000; Founder, Ragdoll Productions Ltd, since 1984; *b* 18 Dec. 1937; *d* of Jack Savage and Eleanor Savage (*née* Thomson); *m* 1959, Barrie Wood; one *s* one *d*. *Educ:* Tudhoe Colliery Primary Sch.; Alderman Wraith Grammar Sch.; Bingley Teachers' Trng Coll. Teacher, Spennymoor Secondary Modern Sch., 1959–65; Founder: Books for Your Children mag., 1965, Ed. and publisher, 1965–95; Fedn of Children's Book Gps, 1969; Consultant, Tyne Tees TV, 1977–79; Children's Producer, Yorkshire TV (The Book Tower, Ragdolly Anna), 1979–82; Hd, Children's Progs, TV-am (originator of Rub a dub tub, Roland Rat), 1982–84. FRTS 1998. Eleanor Farjeon Award, 1969; Ronald Politzer Award, 1974; BAFTA Awards, 1979 and 1982, Prix Jeunesse, 1980, for The Book Tower; BAFTA Awards, 1996 and 1997, for Tots TV; Japan Prize, 1997, BAFTA Award, 1998, Most Edgy Children's Prog. in Last Fifty Years, Prix Jeunesse, 2014, for Teletubbies, and BAFTA Award, 2002, for Teletubbies Everywhere; Veuve Clicquot Business Woman of Year Award, 1998; Olswang Business Award, Women in Film & Television, 2003; Japan Foundn President's Prize, 2004, for Open a Door; BAFTA Awards, 2007 and 2008, and Best Children's TV Prog., Voice of the Listener and Viewer Excellence in Broadcasting Awards, 2010, for In the Night Garden; BAFTA Award for Best Ind. Production Co., 2008; Lifetime Achievement Award, Mother and Baby mag., 2010; BAFTA Award for Dipdap, 2011. Hon. DLitt: Birmingham, 2013; Sheffield, 2015. *Recreations:* reading, gardening. *Address:* Ragdoll Productions Ltd, Timothy's Bridge Road, Stratford upon Avon, Warwickshire CV37 9NQ. *T:* (01789) 404100.

WOOD, Anthony, PhD; Senior Vice President, and Head, Worldwide Medicinal Chemistry, Pfizer, since 2008; *b* Gateshead, 12 Sept. 1965; *s* of Alan Wood and Linda Winifred Wood; *m* 2008, Dr (Jane) Sarah Houlton; one *s* by a previous marriage. *Educ:* Newcastle Univ. (BSc Hons 1987; PhD 1990). Pfizer: Scientist, Dept of Discovery Chemistry, 1992–99; Manager, 1999–2001; Dir, 2001–04; Hd, Chemistry, 2004–07; Hd, Chemistry and Exploratory Medicinal Scis, 2007–08. Mem., EPSRC, 2010–13. Discovered maraviroc (Selzentry), a new HIV medicine. Malcolm Campbell Prize, RSC, 2005; Heroes of Chemistry Award, ACS, 2008; PhRMA Discoverers Award, 2010; UCB-Ehrlich Award, Eur. Fedn of Medicinal Chemistry, 2010. *Publications:* (ed) Annual Reports in Medicinal Chemistry, vol. 41, 2006. *Recreations:* mountain biking, cooking. *Address:* Pfizer, 620 Memorial Drive, Cambridge, MA 02139, USA.

WOOD, Sir Anthony John P.; *see* Page Wood.

WOOD, Anthony Richard; HM Diplomatic Service, retired; *b* 13 Feb. 1932; *s* of late Rev. T. J. Wood and of Phyllis Margaret (*née* Bold); *m* 1st, 1966, Sarah Drew (marr. diss. 1973); one *s* one *d*; 2nd, 2006, Charlotte Olivia Ryder (*née* Strutt). *Educ:* St Edward's Sch.; Worcester Coll., Oxford (BA). HM Forces, 1950–52. British Sch. of Archaeology in Iraq, Nimrud, 1956; joined HM Foreign Service, 1957; served: Beirut, 1957; Bahrain, 1958; Paris, 1959; Benghazi, 1962; Aden, 1963; Basra, 1966; Tehran, 1970; Muscat, 1980; Counsellor, FCO, 1984–87. *Recreations:* walking, singing. *Clubs:* Army and Navy, Rifle Officers'.

WOOD, Ven. Antony Charles M.; *see* MacRow-Wood.

WOOD, Prof. Bernard Anthony, PhD, DSc; Director, Center for the Advanced Study of Human Paleobiology, and University Professor of Human Origins, since 2006, and Professor of Human Evolutionary Anatomy, since 1997, George Washington University (Henry R. Luce Professor of Human Origins, 1997–2006); Hon. Senior Scientist, Smithsonian Institution, since 1997; *b* 17 April 1945; *s* of Anthony Wood and Joan Wood (*née* Slocombe); *m* 1st, 1965, Hazel Francis (marr. diss. 1980); one *s* one *d*; 2nd, 1982, Alison Richards (marr. diss. 2003); one *d*; 3rd, 2008, Sally Furze. *Educ:* King's Sch., Gloucester; Middlesex Hosp. Med. Sch., Univ. of London (BSc 1966; MB BS 1969; PhD 1975; DSc 1996). Lectr, Charing Cross Hosp. Med. Sch., 1973–74; Middlesex Hospital Medical School: Asst Lectr, 1971–73; Lectr, subseq. Sen. Lectr, 1974–78; Reader in Anatomy, 1978–82; S. A. Courtauld Prof. of Anatomy, 1982–85; Derby Prof. of Anatomy, 1985–97, and Dean, Faculty of Medicine, 1996–97, Univ. of Liverpool. Non-executive Director: Royal Liverpool and Broad Green NHS Trust, 1994–96; Liverpool HA, 1996–97. West Meml Lecture, Univ. of Wales, Cardiff, 1996. Chairman: Science-based Archaeol. Cttee, SERC, 1992–95; Science-based Archaeol. Strategy Gp, NERC, 1995–96; President: Primate Soc., 1986–89; Anatomical Soc. of GB and Ireland, 1996–97; Vice-Pres., Royal Anthropological Inst., 1989–92. *Publications:* (ed) Food Acquisition and Processing in Primates, 1984; (ed) Major Topics in Primate and Human Evolution, 1986; Koobi Fora Research Project: hominid cranial remains, 1991; (ed) Wiley-Blackwell Encyclopedia of Human Evolution, 2011; articles on palaeoanthropology, hominid palaeobiology, and human morphology in scientific jls. *Recreations:* English salt glaze stoneware, Verdi, Bach. *Address:* Center for the Advanced Study of Human Paleobiology, George Washington University, Science and Engineering Hall, 800 22nd Street NW, Suite 6000, Washington, DC 20052, USA.

WOOD, Prof. Bernard John, PhD; FRS 1998; Research Professor, University of Oxford, since 2007; *b* 10 May 1946; *s* of Sidney James Wood and Marjorie Ethel Wood; *m* 1st, 1968, Susan Brightmore (marr. diss.); two *d*; 2nd, 1982, Kristin Vala Ragnarsdottir (marr. diss.); one *s* one *d*; 3rd, 2004, Susan Prosser. *Educ:* Northern Poly. (BSc London); Univ. of Leeds (MSc); Univ. of Newcastle upon Tyne (PhD 1971). Lectr in Geol., 1973–78, Reader, 1978–79, Univ. of Manchester; Principal Scientist, Rockwell Hanford Ops, Richland, Washington, 1980–81; Prof., Northwestern Univ., 1982–89; Prof. of Earth Sciences, Univ. of Bristol, 1989–2005; Fedn Fellow, Nat. Key Centre for Geochem. Evolution and Metallogeny of Continents, Macquarie Univ., 2005–07. Vis. Prof., Univ. of Chicago, 1979–80. Award, Mineralogical Soc. of America, 1984; Schlumberger Medal, Mineralogical Soc. of GB, 1991; Holmes Medal, Eur. Union of Geoscis, 1997; Murchison Medal, Geol. Soc., 1997; Goldschmidt Medal, Geochem. Soc., 2003; Hess Medal, American Geophys. Union, 2013; Roebling Medal, Mineralogical Soc. of America, 2014. *Publications:* (with D. G. Fraser) Elementary Thermodynamics for Geologists, 1976; (with J. R. Holloway) Simulating the Earth, 1988. *Address:* Department of Earth Sciences, University of Oxford, South Parks Road, Oxford OX1 3AN.

WOOD, Catherine; QC 2011; a Recorder, since 2007; *b* Walsall, 27 Aug. 1963; *d* of late Bernard Michael Wood and of Margaret R. Wood; *m* 1991, Simon Derek John Wheatley; three *s* one *d*. *Educ:* Queen Mary's High Sch. for Girls, Walsall; Queen Mary Coll., Univ. of London (LLB). Called to the Bar, Middle Temple, 1985; in practice as a barrister, 1985–; 4 Paper Buildings, 1993–. *Recreations:* family, friends, cricket, Mallorca. *Address:* 4 Paper Buildings, Temple, EC4Y 7EX. *T:* (020) 7427 5200, *Fax:* (020) 7353 4979. *E:* cw@4pb.com. *Club:* St George's Hill Lawn Tennis.

WOOD, Charles; Chief Executive, London Borough of Brent, 1986–95; *b* 16 May 1950; *s* of Sir Frank Wood, KBE, CB and Lady (Olive May) Wood (*née* Wilson); *m* Carolyn Hall; three *s* two *d*. *Educ:* King's College London (BSc Hons); Polytechnic of Central London (DipTP). Engineer, GLC, 1971–76; Planner, and Dep. Dir of Housing, London Borough of Hammersmith and Fulham, 1976–82; Dir of Develt, London Borough of Brent, 1982–86. *Recreations:* walking, tennis.
See also W. J. Wood.

WOOD, Charles Gerald, FRSL 1984; writer for films, television and the theatre, since 1962; *b* 6 Aug. 1932; *s* of John Edward Wood, actor and Catherine Mae (*née* Harris), actress; *m* 1954, Valerie Elizabeth Newman, actress; one *s* one *d*. *Educ:* King Charles I Sch., Kidderminster; Birmingham Coll. of Art. Corp., 17/21st Lancers, 1950–55; Factory worker, 1955–57; Stage Manager, advertising artist, cartoonist, scenic artist, 1957–59; Bristol Evening Post, 1959–62. Member: Drama Adv. Panel, South Western Arts, 1972–73; Council, BAFTA, 1991–93. Consultant to Nat. Film Develt Fund, 1980–82. *Wrote plays:* Prisoner and Escort, John Thomas, Spare, (Cockade), Arts Theatre, 1963; Meals on Wheels, Royal Court, 1965; Don't Make Me Laugh, Aldwych, 1966; Fill the Stage with Happy Hours, Nottingham Playhouse, Vaudeville Theatre, 1967; Dingo, Bristol Arts Centre, Royal Court, 1967; H, National Theatre, 1969; Welfare, Liverpool Everyman, 1971; Veterans, Lyceum, Edinburgh, Royal Court, 1972; Jingo, RSC, 1975; Has 'Washington' Legs?, Nat. Theatre, 1978; Red Star, RSC, 1984; Across from the Garden of Allah, Comedy, 1986; adapted Pirandello's Man, Beast and Virtue, Nat. Theatre, 1989 and The Mountain Giants, Nat. Theatre, 1993; Dumas's The Tower, Almeida, 1995. *Screenplays include:* The Knack, 1965 (Grand Prix, Cannes; Writers Guild Award for Best Comedy); Help!, 1965; How I Won the War, 1967; The Charge of the Light Brigade, 1968; The Long Day's Dying, 1969; Cuba, 1980; Wagner, 1983; Red Monarch, 1983; Puccini, 1984; Tumbledown, 1988 (Prix Italia, RAI Prize, 1988; BAFTA,

Broadcasting Press Guild and RTS awards, 1989); Shooting the Hero, 1991; An Awfully Big Adventure, 1995; (with Richard Eyre) Iris, 2001; (with Richard Eyre) The Other Man, 2008; Will, 2009; *adapted:* Bed Sitting Room, 1973. Numerous *television* plays incl. Prisoner and Escort, Drums Along the Avon, Drill Pig, A Bit of a Holiday, A Bit of an Adventure, Do As I Say, Love Lies Bleeding, Dust to Dust; creator of Gordon Maple in series, Don't Forget to Write; Company of Adventurers (series for CBC), 1986; My Family and Other Animals (series for BBC), 1987; The Settling of the Sun, 1987; Sharpe's Company, 1994; A Breed of Heroes, 1994; (with John Osborne) England My England, 1996; Sharpe's Regiment, 1996; Sharpe's Waterloo, 1997; Mute of Malice, 1997; Briefs Trooping Gaily, 1998; Monsignor Renard, 2000. Evening Standard Awards, 1963, 1973. *Publications:* plays: Cockade, 1965; Fill the Stage with Happy Hours, 1967; Dingo, 1967; H, 1970; Veterans, 1972; Has 'Washington' Legs?, 1978; Tumbledown, 1987; Man, Beast and Virtue, 1990; The Mountain Giants, 1993; (trans.) Dumas, The Tower, or Marguerite of Bourgogne, 1995; Plays One, 1997; Plays Two, 1997; Plays Three, 2005. *Recreations:* military and theatrical studies; gardening. *Address:* c/o Sue Rodgers, Independent Talent Group Ltd, 40 Whitfield Street, W1T 2RH. *T:* (020) 7636 6565. *Clubs:* Royal Over-Seas League, British Playwrights' Mafia.

WOOD, Rear Adm. Christopher Lainson, CB 1991; *b* 9 Feb. 1936; *s* of Gordon and Eileen Wood; *m* 1962, Margot Price; two *s* (one *d* decd). *Educ:* Pangbourne College. Seaman Officer, RN, 1954; joined submarine service, 1958; CO's qualifying course, 1966; in comd, HMS Ambush, 1966–68; JSSC, 1970; nuclear submarine training, 1971; in comd, HMS Warspite, 1971–73; Staff of FO Submarines, 1973–75; Staff of Dir, Naval Op. Requirements, 1975–77; Underwater Weapons Acceptance, 1978–81; Dep. Dir, Naval Op. Requirements, 1981–83; Dir Gen., Underwater Weapons, 1983–85; Dir Gen., Fleet Support, 1986–88; ACDS, Operational Requirements (Sea Systems), 1988–91. Dir, ALVA, 1992–96. *Recreations:* reading, fishing, sporting interests, voluntary service.

WOOD, Christopher Terence; HM Diplomatic Service; Director, British Office (formerly British Trade and Cultural Office), Taipei, since 2013; *b* Wolverhampton, 19 Jan. 1959; *s* of Terry and late Joyce Wood. *Educ:* Cotwall End Prim. Sch., Sedgley; High Arcal Grammar Sch., Sedgley; Fitzwilliam Coll., Cambridge (BA Hons Mod. and Medieval Langs 1981). Desk Officer, W Eur. Dept, FCO, 1981–82; lang. trng, London and Hong Kong, 1982–84; Asst Pol Advr, Hong Kong Govt, 1984–87; Hong Kong Dept, FCO, 1987–89; Security Co-ordination Dept, FCO, 1989–91; DoE, subseq. DETR, 1992–98, Private Sec. to Minister of State, 1995–98; Econ. and Domestic Secretariat, Cabinet Office, 1998–2001; ODPM, 2001–02; Consul-Gen., Guangzhou, 2003–06; Dir, Americas, FCO, 2007–08; Dep. Hd of Mission, Beijing, 2008–12. *Recreations:* cinema, theatre, swimming. *Address:* c/o Foreign and Commonwealth Office, King Charles Street, SW1A 2AH.

WOOD, Rt Rev. Clyde Maurice, BA, ThL; Bishop of North Queensland, 1996–2002; *b* 7 Jan. 1936; *s* of Maurice O. Wood and Helen M. Wood; *m* 1957, Margaret Joan Burls; two *s* one *d*. *Educ:* Perry Hall, Melbourne (ThL 1964); Monash Univ. (BA 1974). Deacon 1965, priest 1965; Curate: St John's, Bentleigh, 1965–66; St Paul's, Ringwood, 1966–67; in Dept of Evangelism and Extension, 1967–70; Curate-in-Charge: St Philip's, Mount Waverley, 1967–70; Armadale/Hawksburn, 1970–73; Rector and Canon Res., Christ Church Cathedral, Darwin, 1974, Dean 1978–83; on leave, Rector St Timothy's Episcopal Church, Indianapolis, USA, 1981; Bishop of the Northern Territory, 1983–92; Bishop of the Western Region, and Asst Bishop, dio. of Brisbane, 1992–96. OStJ 1980; ChStJ 1985. *Recreations:* golf, sailing. *Address:* 21 Wilton Court, Gunn, NT 0832, Australia.

WOOD, David, OBE 2004; actor, playwright, writer, composer, theatrical producer and director; *b* 21 Feb. 1944; *s* of Richard Edwin Wood and Audrey Adele Wood (*née* Fincham); *m* 1975, Jacqueline Stanbury; two *d*. *Educ:* Chichester High Sch. for Boys; Worcester Coll., Oxford. BA (Hons). Acted with OUDS and ETC at Oxford; first London appearance in ETC prodn, Hang Down Your Head and Die (also co-writer), Comedy, 1964; later performances include: A Spring Song, Mermaid, 1964; Dr Faustus (OUDS), 1966; Four Degrees Over, Edinburgh Festival and Fortune, 1966 (also contrib. lyrics and sketches); repertory, 1966–69; RSC's After Haggerty, Aldwych 1970, and Criterion 1971; A Voyage Round My Father, Greenwich, 1970, Toronto, 1972; Me Times Me, tour, 1971; Mrs Warren's Profession, 1972, and revue Just the Ticket, 1973, Thorndike, Leatherhead; The Provok'd Wife, Greenwich, 1973; Jeeves, Her Majesty's, 1975; Terra Nova, Chichester, 1980. *Films include:* If…, 1968; Aces High, 1975; Sweet William, 1978; North Sea Hijack, 1979. *TV plays and series include:* Mad Jack, Fathers and Sons, Cheri, The Vamp, Sporting Scenes, Disraeli, The Avengers, Van der Valk, Danger UXB, Huntingtower, Enemy at the Door, Jackanory, Jim'll Fix It, When the Boat Comes In, The Brack Report, Tricky Business, Watch, Longitude. Wrote various theatre revues in collaboration with John Gould; music and lyrics, The Stiffkey Scandals of 1932, Queen's, 1967 (revived as The Prostitutes' Padre, Norwich Playhouse, 1997); with John Gould formed Whirligig Theatre, touring children's theatre company, 1979; for Whirligig directed many of own plays on tour and at Sadler's Wells Theatre, annually 1979–2004; has directed nat. tours and West End productions for Clarion Productions, including The BFG, 1991–92, 1993–94, 2001–03 and 2009, The Witches, 1992–93 and 1996–97, Noddy, 1993–94, and More Adventures of Noddy, 1995–96, Guess How Much I Love You, 2010; has performed David Wood Magic and Music Show in theatres all over UK, incl. Polka Theatre, Arts Theatre and Purcell Room, 1983–; David Wood's Storytime, Rose Th., Kingston and Arts, 2010; wrote The Queen's Handbag, for children's Party at the Palace for the Queen's 80th birthday, 2006 (also televised); wrote (with Richard Taylor) The Go-Between (musical, based on book by L. P. Hartley), W Yorks Playhouse, 2011 (Best Musical Prodn, UK Th. Awards, 2012); Goodnight Mister Tom (adaptation of book by Michelle Magorian), Chichester Fest. Th., then tour, 2013 (Olivier Award for Best Entertainment and Family, 2013). Chm., Action for Children's Arts, 1998–. Formed, jointly: Verronmead Ltd, ind. TV producing co., 1983; Westwood Theatrical Productions Ltd, 1986; W2 Productions Ltd, 1995. *TV series scripts:* Chips' Comic; Chish 'n' Fips; Seeing and Doing; The Gingerbread Man; Watch; *screenplays:* Swallows and Amazons, 1974; Back Home, 1989; Tide Race, 1989; *radio play:* Swallows and Amazons, 1999. Hon. MA Chichester, 2005. *Publications: musical plays for children:* (with Sheila Ruskin) The Owl and the Pussycat went to see…, 1968; (with Sheila Ruskin) Larry the Lamb in Toytown, 1969; The Plotters of Cabbage Patch Corner, 1970; Flibberty and the Penguin, 1971; The Papertown Paperchase, 1972; Hijack over Hygenia, 1973; Old Mother Hubbard, 1975; The Gingerbread Man, 1976; Old Father Time, 1976; (with Tony Hatch and Jackie Trent) Rock Nativity, 1976; Nutcracker Sweet, 1977; Mother Goose's Golden Christmas, 1977; Tickle, 1978; Babes in the Magic Wood, 1978; There Was an Old Woman…, 1979; Cinderella, 1979; Aladdin, 1981; (with Dave and Toni Arthur) Robin Hood, 1981; Dick Whittington and Wondercat, 1981; Meg and Mog Show, 1981; The Ideal Gnome Expedition, 1982; Jack and the Giant, 1982; The Selfish Shellfish, 1983; (with ABBA and Don Black) Abbacadabra, 1984; (with Dave and Toni Arthur) Jack the Lad, 1984; (with Peter Pontzen) Dinosaurs and all that Rubbish, 1985; The Seesaw Tree, 1986; The Old Man of Lochnagar (based on book by HRH the Prince of Wales), 1986; (with Dave and Toni Arthur) The Pied Piper, 1988; Save the Human, 1990; The BFG (based on book by Roald Dahl), 1991; The Witches (based on book by Roald Dahl), 1992; Rupert and the Green Dragon, 1993; Noddy (based on books by Enid Blyton), 1994; More Adventures of Noddy, 1995; Babe, the Sheep-Pig (based on book by Dick King-Smith), 1998; The Forest Child (children's opera based on book by Richard Edwards), 1998; The Twits (based on book by Roald Dahl), 1999; David Wood Plays 1, 1999; David Wood Plays 2, 1999; Spot's Birthday Party (based on books by Eric Hill), 2000; Tom's Midnight Garden (based on book by Philippa Pearce), 2000; Fantastic Mr Fox (based on book by Roald Dahl), 2001; James and the Giant Peach (based on book by Roald Dahl), 2001; Clockwork (opera, based on book by Philip Pullman), 2004; The Lighthouse Keeper's Lunch (based on book by Ronda and David Armitage), 2005; Danny the Champion of the World (based on book by Roald Dahl), 2005; Fimbles Live! (based on TV series), 2006; The Tiger Who Came to Tea (based on book by Judith Kerr), 2008; George's Marvellous Medicine (based on book by Roald Dahl), 2009; Guess How Much I Love You (based on book by Sam McBratney), 2010; Goodnight Mister Tom (based on book by Michelle Magorian), 2011; Shaun's Big Show (Shaun the Sheep) (based on Aardman Animations TV series), 2011; The Forest Child (based on book by Richard Edwards), 2012; The Magic Finger (based on book by Roald Dahl), 2013; *books for children:* The Gingerbread Man, 1985; (with Geoffrey Beitz) The Operats of Rodent Garden, 1984; (with Geoffrey Beitz) The Discorats, 1985; Chish 'n' Fips, 1987; Sidney the Monster, 1988; Save the Human, 1991; The BFG: plays for children, 1993; Meg and Mog: plays for children, 1994; The Christmas Story, 1996; (with Peters Day) The Phantom Cat of the Opera, 2000; The Witches: plays for children, 2001; The Twits: plays for children, 2003; Jack and the Baked Beanstalk, 2007; (with Dana Kubick) A Present for Father Christmas, 2008; Danny the Champion of the World: plays for children, 2009; Lady Lollipop: the play (based on book by Dick King-Smith), 2005; Cinderella, 2012; The Porridge Pincher, 2012; with Richard Fowler: Play-Theatres, 1987; Happy Birthday, Mouse, 1991 (USA 1990); Baby Bear's Buggy Ride, 1993; Pop-up Theatre (Cinderella), 1994; Bedtime Story, 1995; The Magic Show, 1995; Mole's Summer Story, 1997; Silly Spider, 1998; Mole's Winter Story, 1998; Funny Bunny's Magic Show, 2000; The Toy Cupboard, 2000; Under the Bed, 2006; Scary Mary, 2012; *book for adults:* (with Janet Grant) Theatre for Children: guide to writing, adapting, directing and acting, 1997; articles in Drama, London Drama, Stage, ArtsBusiness, Encore. *Recreations:* crosswords, conjuring (Mem. of the Inner Magic Circle with Gold Star), collecting old books. *Address:* c/o Casarotto Ramsay Ltd, Waverley House, 7–12 Noel Street, W1F 8GQ. *T:* (020) 7287 4450, *Fax:* (020) 7287 9128.

WOOD, Rear-Adm. David John, CB 1998; CEng, FRAeS; defence aviation consultant; *b* 12 June 1942; *s* of John Herbert Wood and Nesta (*née* Jones); *m* 1966, Hilary Jolly; two *s* one *d*. *Educ:* St Paul's Sch.; BRNC Dartmouth; RNEC Manadon (BScEng 1965). Joined BRNC 1960; service in 892, 846, 707 Sqdns and HMS Ark Royal, 1967–73; Aircraft Dept (Navy), 1973–76; Air Engineer Officer, Lynx IFTU, 1976–77; Army Staff Course, 1978; Helicopter Procurement, MoD (PE), 1979–81; Naval Sec's Dept, MoD, 1981–84; Staff of FONAC, 1984–86; NATO Defence Coll., 1986–87; Asst Dir, EH101, MoD (PE), 1987–89; Dir, Aircraft Support Policy (Navy), 1989–91; Dir, Maritime Projects, MoD (PE), 1991–95; DG Aircraft (Navy), MoD, 1995–98. Mem. Council, RAeS, 1996. Trustee, Bishop's Palace, Wells, Som, 2010– (Chm., 2013–). *Recreations:* cross-country and long distance running, choral singing.

WOOD, David M.; *see* Muir Wood.

WOOD, His Honour David Russell; a Circuit Judge, 1995–2013; *b* 13 Dec. 1948; *s* of Christopher Russell Wood and Muriel Wynn Wood (*née* Richardson); *m* 1979, Georgina Susan Buckle; two *s* one *d*. *Educ:* Sedbergh Sch.; Univ. of East Anglia (BA). Called to the Bar, Gray's Inn, 1973; Recorder, 1989–95. Pres., Council of Circuit Judges, 2008. *Recreations:* country pursuits, tennis, walking, music. *Club:* Northern Counties (Newcastle upon Tyne).

WOOD, Maj.-Gen. Denys Broomfield, CB 1978; Independent Inquiry Inspector, 1984–93; General Commissioner for Taxes, 1986–98; *b* 2 Nov. 1923; *s* of late Percy Neville Wood and Meryl Broomfield; *m* 1948, Jennifer Nora Page (*d* 1999), *d* of late Air Cdre William Morton Page, CBE; one *s* two *d*. *Educ:* Radley; Pembroke Coll., Cambridge (MA). CEng, FIMechE. Commissioned into REME, 1944; war service in UK and Far East, 1944–47; Staff Captain, WO, 1948–49; Instructor, RMA, Sandhurst, 1949–52; Staff Coll., 1953; DAA&QMG, 11 Infantry Bde, 1955–57; OC, 10 Infantry Workshop, Malaya, 1958–60; jssc 1960; Directing Staff, Staff Coll., 1961–63; Comdr, REME, 3rd Div., 1963–65; Operational Observer, Viet Nam, 1966–67; Col GS, Staff Coll., 1967–69; idc 1970; Dir, Administrative Planning, 1971–73; Dep. Military Sec. (2), 1973–75; Dir of Army Quartering, 1975–78. Exec. Sec., 1978–82, Sec., 1982–84, CEI. Col Comdt, REME, 1978–84. Lay Mem., Law Soc. Adjudication Cttee, 1986–92. Volunteer Speaker for Nat. Trust, 1999–2011. FRSA. *Recreations:* walking, gardening, reading. *Address:* 20 Franklin Court, Brook Road, Wormley, Godalming, Surrey GU8 5US. *T:* (01428) 681829.

WOOD, Derek Alexander, CBE 1995; QC 1978; a Recorder, since 1985; Principal, St Hugh's College, Oxford, 1991–2002, now Hon. Fellow; *b* 14 Oct. 1937; *s* of Alexander Cecil Wood and Rosetta (*née* Lelyveld); *m* 1st 1961, Sally Teresa Clarke (marr. diss. 2001); two *d*; 2nd, 2001, Barbara Kaplan (*née* Spector). *Educ:* Tiffin Boys' Sch., Kingston-upon-Thames; University Coll., Oxford (MA, BCL; Hon. Fellow, 2002). Called to the Bar, Middle Temple, 1964 (Bencher, 1986; Treas., 2006; Dir of Advocacy, 2011–). Department of the Environment: Mem., Adv. Gp on Commercial Property Develt, 1975–78; Mem., Property Adv. Gp, 1978–94; Mem., Working Party on New Forms of Social Ownership and Tenure in Housing, 1976; Chairman: Review of Rating of Plant and Machinery, 1991, 1997–98; Property Industry's Working Gp on Code of Practice for Commercial Leases, 1995; Standing Adv. Cttee on Trunk Road Assessment, Dept of Transport, 1987–94. Drafter of new Code of Statutes, 2002, and Regulations, 2002–04, Univ. of Oxford; Chm., review of bar vocational course, 2008, pupillage, 2009, continuing professional develt, 2010, Bar Standards Bd. Dep. Chm., Soc. of Labour Lawyers, 1978–90. Chm., Chislehurst Constituency Labour Party, 1972–76, 1979–84. Chm., Oxfordshire Community Foundn, 1995–2001; Trustee, Attlee Foundn, 2003–10 (Chm., 2004–10). Mem. Council, London Bor. of Bromley, 1975–78. Gov., Quintin Kynaston Sch., 2003–. Fellow, CAAV, 1988; FCIArb 1993. FRSA 1992. Hon. RICS (Hon. ARICS 1991; Mem., Governing Council, 2003–06). *Publications:* (jtly) Handbook of Arbitration Practice, 2nd edn 1993 to 4th edn 2003; (contrib.) Landlord and Tenant Law: past, present and future, 2006; (contrib.) The Judicial House of Lords, 2009. *Recreation:* music. *Address:* Falcon Chambers, Falcon Court, EC4Y 1AA. *Clubs:* Athenæum, Royal Automobile, Architecture; Kent Valuers' (Hon. Mem.).

WOOD, Donald Edward, CBE 2005; Chairman, Orders of St John Care Trust, since 2013 (Trustee, 2007–12); *b* 10 May 1945; *s* of Thomas Wood and Mary (*née* Burton); *m* 1970, Barbara Schumacher; three *s* three *d*. *Educ:* King's Coll. Sch., Wimbledon; Bristol Univ. (BSc Hons (Civil Engrg) 1966); Manchester Business Sch. (DipBA 1970). W S Atkins & Partners, 1966–69; Rio Tinto Zinc Corp., 1970–73; Circle 33 Housing Trust, 1973–74; GEP Project Management, 1974–76; Dir, New Islington & Hackney Housing Assoc., 1976–87; Chief Exec., later Gp Chief Exec., London & Quadrant Housing Trust, 1987–2008. Mem. Nat. Council, Nat. Housing Fedn, 1985–91; Chairman: London Connection, 1991–99; London Housing Foundn, 2008–13 (Bd Mem., 1999–); Board Member: Focus Housing Gp, 1995–98; English Churches Housing Gp, 1999–2002; Homes and Communities Agency, 2008–12. Member Management Committee: St Luke's House Community Centre, 1980–85; Carr-Gomm Soc., 1988–91. Cttee Mem., Catholic Inst. for Internat. Relns, 1976–81. Chm., Barn Educn Assoc., 1977–82; Gov., Queen's Sch., Kew, 1979–83; Mem. Bd of Govs, St Mary's Coll., Twickenham, 2000–03. KM 2012. *Recreations:* music, family. *Address:* 6 The Avenue, Kew Gardens, Richmond, Surrey TW9 2AJ. *T:* (020) 8940 7043. *E:* wood.don6@gmail.com.

WOOD, Dudley Ernest, CBE 1995; Secretary, Rugby Football Union, 1986–95; *b* 18 May 1930; *s* of Ernest Edward and Ethel Louise Wood; *m* 1955, Mary Christina Blake (*d* 2010); two *s*. *Educ:* Luton Grammar School; St Edmund Hall, Oxford (MA Modern Languages). Sen. Manager, ICI, 1954–86. Rugby Football: Oxford Blue, 1952, 1953; played Rugby for Bedford, Rosslyn Park, Waterloo, and Streatham-Croydon, 1949–65; Pres., Surrey County

RFU, 1983–85. Pres., St Edmund Hall Assoc., 1996–99. Pres., Bedfordshire CCC, 1998–2006; Hon. Life Mem., Squash Rackets Assoc., 1984. Hon. DArts De Montfort, 1999. *Recreations:* walking with dogs, watching cricket, attending reunions and socializing. *Address:* Mead Hall, Little Walden, Saffron Walden, Essex CB10 1UX. *Clubs:* East India, Lord's Taverners.

WOOD, Eric; Finance Director (formerly Finance Officer), University of Bristol, 1979–91; *b* 22 Sept. 1931; *s* of late Herbert Francis and Eva Wood; *m* 1955, Erica Twist; three *d. Educ:* West Hartlepool Grammar Sch.; Blandford Grammar Sch.; St Peter's Coll., Oxford (MA). CPFA. National Service, Army, 1950–51. Finance Depts, Cheshire, Durham and Notts County Councils, 1954–65; Finance Dept, London Transport, 1965–67; Asst Treasurer, GLC, 1967–73; Dir, CIPFA, 1973–79. *Publications:* articles in prof. accountancy press. *Recreations:* ski-ing, squash, hill-walking, bridge. *Address:* 6 Royal York Mews, Royal York Crescent, Clifton, Bristol BS8 4LF. *T:* (0117) 946 6311.

WOOD, Prof. Graham Charles, FRS 1997; FREng; Professor of Corrosion Science and Engineering, University of Manchester Institute of Science and Technology, 1972–97, now Emeritus Professor, University of Manchester; *b* 6 Feb. 1934; *s* of Cyril Wood and Doris Hilda Wood (*née* Strange); *m* 1959, Freda Nancy Waithman; one *s* one *d. Educ:* Bromley Grammar Sch., Kent; Christ's Coll., Cambridge (MA 1960, PhD 1959, ScD 1972). CChem 1969; FRSC 1969; FIMMM (FIM 1969); FICorr (FICorrST 1968); FIMF 1972; FREng (FEng 1990). University of Manchester Institute of Science and Technology: Lectr, 1961, Sen. Lectr, 1966; Reader in Corrosion Sci., 1970–72; Hd, Corrosion and Protection Centre, 1972–82; Vice-Principal for Acad. Develt, 1982–84; Dep. Principal, 1983; Dean, Faculty of Technol., 1987–89; Pro-Vice-Chancellor, 1992–97. Pres., ICorrST, 1978–80. Chm., Internat. Corrosion Council, 1993–96. Hon. DSc UMIST, 2001. Sir George Beilby Medal and Prize, Inst. of Metals, SCI and RIC, 1973; U. R. Evans Award, Instn of Corrosion Sci. and Technol., 1983; Carl Wagner Meml Award, Electrochem. Soc., 1983; Cavallaro Medal, Eur. Fedn of Corrosion, 1987; Hothersall Medal, Inst. of Metal Finishing, 1989; Griffith Medal and Prize, Inst. of Materials, 1997; Eur. Corrosion Medal, Eur. Fedn of Corrosion, 1999. *Publications:* numerous papers in Phil Trans Royal Soc., Proc. Royal Soc., Nature, Phil Mag., Corrosion Sci., Oxidation of Metals, Jl Electrochem. Soc. and Trans Inst. Metal Finishing. *Recreations:* travel, cricket, walking, reading about history of art, science and politics.

WOOD, Graham Nash; QC 2002; **His Honour Judge Graham Wood;** a Circuit Judge, since 2011; a Deputy High Court Judge (Administrative Court), since 2010; a Senior Circuit Judge and Designated Civil Judge, since 2014; *b* 21 May 1957; *s* of late Benjamin Leslie Wood and Mary Valerie Wood; *m* 1984, Janet Helen Winstanley; three *s. Educ:* Liverpool Coll.; Leeds Univ. (LLB Hons). Called to the Bar, Middle Temple, 1979, Bencher, 2010; in practice as barrister, specialising in medical, public law, human rights and criminal fraud, 1980–2011. Asst Recorder, 1997–2000; Recorder, 2000–11. Legal Assessor: GDC, 2006–11; GMC, 2009–11. Tribunal Judge, Mental Health Rev. Tribunal (Restricted Patients Panel), 2007–. Dep. Chancellor: Dio. Liverpool, 2002–; Dio. Chester, 2008–. Chm. Govs, Liverpool Coll., 2009–12. Lay Reader, Church of England. *Publications:* (jtly) Bingham's Negligence Cases, rev. edn 1994, 4th 2002. *Recreations:* sailing, supporting Liverpool FC, writing novels and short stories in the hope that one day something may be published. *Address:* Liverpool Civil and Family Court, 35 Vernon Street, Liverpool L2 2BX. *E:* woodqc@btinternet.com.

WOOD, (Gregory) Mark, FCA; non-executive Chairman, Digitalismedia, since 2010; *b* 26 July 1953; *s* of William and Anne Wood; *m* 2009, Lisa Claire Walden; one *s* two *d* by a previous marriage. *Educ:* Cambridgeshire Coll. of Arts and Technol. (BA Hons Econ). FCA 1979. Work with Price Waterhouse, Commercial Union, Barclays, BZW, British & Commonwealth; Chairman: Wagon Finance Ltd, 1991–94; Safeguard Insce Services, 1991–94; Divl Chief Exec., UK Retail Financial Services, MAI plc, 1991–94; Man. Dir, AA Insce, Financial Services and Retail, 1994–96; Chief Exec., AXA Equity & Law, 1997; Gp Chief Exec., AXA in the UK (formerly Sun Life & Provincial Hldgs), 1997–2001; Chief Exec., Prudential Assurance Co. Ltd, 2001–05; Exec. Dir, Prudential PLC, 2001–05; Founder and Chief Exec., 2006–09, Dep. Chm., 2009–11, Paternoster Assurance; non-exec. Chm., 2010–13, CEO, 2013, JLT Benefit Solutions; CEO, JLT Employee Benefits, 2013–15. Non-exec. Chm., Chaucer Syndicates, 2011–14; non-exec. Dir, RAC Ltd, 2011–. Dep. Chm., ABI, 1999–2001 (Chm., Gen. Insce Cttee, 1999–2001); Chm., Govt's Property Crime Reduction Action Team, 1999–2001. Chm. Trustees, NSPCC, 2010–15 (Trustee, 1999–2007; Dep. Chm., 2003–07). Chm. Govs, Amesbury Sch., 2002–07. MCSI (MSI 1986). Hon. DBA Anglia Ruskin, 2010. *Recreations:* tennis, ski-ing. *Address:* Faraday House, 30 Blandford Street, W1A 4AU. *E:* wood@walbrookadvisors.co.uk. *Club:* Royal Automobile.

WOOD, Hugh Bradshaw; composer; University Lecturer in Music, Cambridge University, and Fellow of Churchill College, Cambridge, 1977–99; *b* 27 June 1932; *s* of James Bonar Wood and Winifred Bradshaw Wood; *m* 1960, Susan McGaw; one *s* one *d* (and one *d* decd). *Educ:* Oundle Sch.; New Coll., Oxford (Major Scholar; 2nd Cl. Hons Modern History, 1954). ARCM (private study with Dr W. S. Lloyd Webber), 1955. Studied: composition with Iain Hamilton, and harmony and counterpoint with Anthony Milner, 1956–58; composition with Mátyás Seiber, 1958–60; taught at: Morley Coll., 1958–67; Royal Acad. of Music, 1962–65; Univ. of Glasgow (Cramb Res. Fellow), 1966–70; Univ. of Liverpool, 1971–75; Univ. of Leeds, 1975–76; teacher, Dartington Summer Sch. of Music, 1959–74. *Main compositions: for orchestra:* Scenes from Comus (with soprano and tenor), 1965; Concerto for Cello, 1969; Chamber Concerto, 1971; Concerto for Violin, No 1, 1972, No 2, 2005; Symphony, 1982; Concerto for Piano, 1991; Variations for Orchestra, 1997; Serenade and Elegy (for string quartet and string orch.), 1999; Epithalamion, 2015; *chamber music:* Variations for Viola and Piano, 1958; String Quartet No 1, 1962, No 2, 1970, No 3, 1976, No 4, 1993, No 5, 2001; Piano Trio, 1984; Horn Trio, 1989; Clarinet Trio, 1997; Overture for Trio, 2005; *for voice(s) and ensembles:* Logue Songs, 1961; Song Cycle to Poems of Pablo Neruda, 1974; Cantata, 1989; Tenebrae, 2003; From the Pisan Cantos, 2012; *songs:* Robert Graves Songs, 4 sets, 1976–93; Robert Graves cycle, 2006. Hon. DMus Liverpool, 2006. *Recreation:* thinking about going to Greece. *Address:* 32 Woodsome Road, NW5 1RZ. *T:* (020) 7267 0318.

WOOD, Humphrey; *see* Wood, J. H. A.

WOOD, Sir Ian (Clark), Kt 1994; CBE 1982; FRSE; Chairman, 1981–2012, and Chief Executive (formerly Managing Director) 1967–2006, John Wood Group plc (formerly John Wood & Son); Chairman, J. W. Holdings Ltd, since 1981; *b* 21 July 1942; *s* of John Wood and Margaret (*née* Clark); *m* 1970, Helen Macrae; three *s. Educ:* Aberdeen Univ. (BSc Psychology, First Cl. Hons 1964). Joined John Wood & Son, 1964. Dir, Royal Bank of Scotland, 1988–97. Chairman: Aberdeen Beyond 2000, 1986–90; Grampian Enterprise, 1990–94. Member: Aberdeen Harbour Bd, 1972–89; Sea Fish Industry Authority, 1981–87; Offshore Industry Adv. Bd, 1989–93; Offshore Industry Export Adv. Gp, 1989–93; British Trade Internat. Oil and Gas Export Bd (formerly Oil & Gas Projects & Supplies Office), 1994–2000 (Chm., 1997–2000); Bd, Scottish Develt Agency, 1984–90; Scottish Econ. Council, 1988–98; Scottish Enterprise Bd, 1995–2000 (Chm., 1997–2000); Bd, Scottish Business Forum, 1998–99; Scottish Sub-Cttee, UGC, subseq. UFC, 1988–91; SHEFC, 1991–97; Nat. Trng Task Force, 1988–91; PILOT, 2000–06; Scottish Sea Fisheries Council, 2007–. Chancellor, Robert Gordon Univ., 2004–. Chm., Commn on Developing Scotland's Young Workforce, 2013–; Chm., UK Continental Shelf Maximising Recovery Rev., 2013–14. Sen. Trustee, The Wood Foundation (formerly Sir Ian Wood Family Charitable Trust, then Wood Family Trust), 2007– (Chm.). CCMI (CBIM 1983); FCIB 1998; FRSE 2000; FSQA; FRSA; Fellow, Scottish Vocational Educn Council. Hon. LLD Aberdeen, 1984; Hon. DBA Robert Gordon, 1998; Hon. DTech Glasgow Caledonian, 2002; Hon. DEng Heriot-Watt, 2012; Hon. DSc Strathclyde, 2013. Scottish Free Enterprise Award, 1985; (jtly) Scottish Business Achievement Award Trust Award, 1992; Corporate Elite Leadership Award, 1992; Corporate Elite World Player Award, 1996; Business Ambassador for Scotland, Scottish Business Insider, 2002; Chief Exec. of the Year, Business Insider/PricewaterhouseCoopers, 2003; Glenfiddich Spirit of Scotland Award for Business, 2003; Entrepreneurial Exchange Philanthropist of the Year Award, 2008; Offshore Energy Centre Hall of Fame, Houston, 2009; Wallace Award, American Scottish Foundn, 2012; Lifetime Achievement Award, Oil and Gas UK, 2012; Chm. of the Year, Broadwalk Asset Mgt LLP, 2012. Silver Jubilee Medal, 1977; Cadman Medal, Energy Inst., 2010; President's Award, SCDI, 2011; Royal Medal, Royal Soc. of Edinburgh, 2013; Lifetime Achievement Award: Northern Star Business Awards, 2014; Oil Council, 2014. *Recreations:* family, art, tennis. *Address:* Marchmont, 42 Rubislaw Den South, Aberdeen AB15 4BB. *T:* (01224) 313625.

WOOD, James Alexander Douglas; QC 1999; a Recorder, since 2000; *b* 25 June 1952; *s* of Alexander Blyth Wood and Cynthia Mary Wood (*née* Boot); two *s* by Ros Carne; *m* 1999, Janet Allbeson. *Educ:* Haileybury Coll.; Warwick Univ. (LLB 1974). Called to the Bar, Middle Temple, 1975; criminal defence barrister specialising in civil liberties and human rights; has appeared in many leading terrorist cases and miscarriages of justice, incl. both appeals of Birmingham 6, and Carl Bridgwater case; Asst Recorder, 1998–2000. *Publications:* The Right to Silence, 1989; Justice in Error, 1993; reports. *Recreations:* travel, painting. *Address:* Doughty Street Chambers, 54 Doughty Street, WC1N 2LS. *T:* (020) 7404 1313. *Club:* Blacks.

WOOD, James Douglas Graham, FRSL; Staff Writer, The New Yorker, since 2007; *b* 1 Nov. 1965; *s* of Dennis William Wood and Sheila Graham Wood (*née* Lillia); *m* 1992, Claire Denise Messud; one *s* one *d. Educ:* Eton Coll.; Jesus Coll., Cambridge (BA 1st cl. Hons (Eng. Lit.) 1988). Chief Literary Critic, The Guardian, 1991–95; Sen. Editor, The New Republic, 1995–2007. Weidenfield Vis. Prof. of Eur. and Comparative Lit., Oxford Univ., 2011. Vis. Lectr, subseq. Prof. of the Practice, Harvard Univ., 2003–. Mem. Editl Bd, London Review of Books, 1995–. Fellow, Amer. Acad. of Arts and Scis, 2007. FRSL 2011. Young Journalist of the Year, British Press Awards, 1990; Award in Literature, AAAL, 2001; Nat. Mag. Award for Criticism, American Soc. of Mag. Eds, 2009. *Publications:* The Broken Estate: essays on literature and belief, 1999; The Book Against God (novel), 2003; The Irresponsible Self: on laughter and the novel (essays), 2004; How Fiction Works, 2008; The Fun Stuff (essays), 2013; The Nearest Thing to Life (essays), 2015. *Recreations:* playing the piano, reading. *Address:* c/o Jonathan Cape Ltd, 20 Vauxhall Bridge Road, SW1V 2SA.

WOOD, Prof. James Lionel Norman, PhD; Alborada Professor of Equine and Farm Animal Science, since 2008, and Head, Department of Veterinary Medicine, since 2013, University of Cambridge; Fellow, Wolfson College, Cambridge, since 2009; *b* Wegberg, Germany, 19 May 1963; *s* of Lt-Col Lionel David Wood and Belinda Mary Wood; *m* 2004, Rosamund Anne Rivett; two *d. Educ:* University Coll. London (BSc Physiol. and Basic Medicine Scis 1985); Royal Veterinary College (BVetMed 1988); London Sch. of Hygiene and Tropical Medicine (MSc Epidemiol. 1991); Open Univ. (PhD 1998); MA Cantab 2009. MRCVS 1988. Veterinary Res. Officer, Central Veterinary Lab., 1990; Animal Health Trust, Newmarket: Equine Epidemiologist, 1990–93; Hd of Epidemiology, 1993–2004; Dir, Cambridge Infectious Diseases Consortium, Univ. of Cambridge, 2005–10. Pres., Soc. for Vet. Epidemiol. and Preventive Medicine, 2003; Hon. Pubns Officer, British Equine Vet. Assoc., 2005–. Trustee: Survival Internat., 1990– (Chm., 2009–); Animal Health Trust, 2005–10; Charity Trustee, Univ. of Cambridge Vet. Sch. Trust, 2014–. Diplomat, Eur. Coll. of Vet. Public Health, 2002. Hon. Res. Fellow, Zoological Soc. of London, 2014–. FRSocMed 1998–2008; FSS 2005; FRSB (FSB 2012). *Publications:* author or co-author of more than 200 papers in scientific and learned jls. *Recreations:* walking, cooking, boating, cycling. *Address:* Department of Veterinary Medicine, University of Cambridge, Madingley Road, Cambridge CB3 0ES. *T:* (01223) 337600, *Fax:* (01223) 764667. *E:* jlnw2@cam.ac.uk.

WOOD, James Peter, FRCO, FRAM; conductor, composer, musicologist and former percussionist; *b* 27 May 1953; *s* of Peter Ley Wood and Elizabeth Gillian Wood; *m* 1977, Penelope Anne Irish (marr. diss. 2010); one *s* one *d. Educ:* Radley Coll.; Sidney Sussex Coll., Cambridge (BA 1975); Royal Acad. of Music. ARCO 1968, FRCO 1971; ARAM 1990, FRAM 2000. Dir, New London Chamber Choir, 1982–2007; Prof. of Percussion, Internat. Ferienkürse für Neue Musik, Darmstadt, 1982–94; Dir, Critical Band, 1990–. Worked with: BBCSO; Netherlands Radio Symphony Orch.; London Sinfonietta; Ensemble InterContemporain (Paris); L'Itinéraire (Paris); Ensemble 2e2m (Paris); Champ d'Action (Antwerp); Ictus (Brussels); MusikFabrik (Cologne); Percussion Gp The Hague; Amadinda (Budapest); Ju Percussion Gp (Taipei); Netherlands Radio Choir; Netherlands Chamber Choir; Berlin Radio Choir; WDR Choir; RIAS Kammerchor; Rundfunk Chor, Berlin; Tokyo Philharmonic Choir. *Compositions* include: Rogosanti, 1986; Stoicheia, 1988; Oreion, 1989; Two Men Meet, each presuming the other to be from a distant planet, 1995; The Parliament of Angels, 1996; Mountain Language, 1998; Jodo, 1999; Autumn Voices, 2001; Hildegard, 2002–04; De telarum mechanicae, 2007; Cloud-Polyphonies, 2011; Sea Dances, 2012; Gulliver, 2014; Stylistic reconstruction of Gesualdo, Sacrae Cantiones, Liber Secundus, 2011. *Recreations:* mountain hiking, wine, instrument building, carpentry, gardening, cooking. *Address:* Dorfstrasse 32, 14913 Schlenzer, Germany. *T:* (33) 74680508. *E:* james.wood@gmx.net. *W:* www.choroi.net.

WOOD, Sir (James) Sebastian (Lamin), KCMG 2014 (CMG 2002); HM Diplomatic Service; Ambassador to Federal Republic of Germany, since 2015; *b* 6 April 1961; *s* of John Lamin Wood and Gillian Margaret Wood (*née* Neason, now Bohan); *m* 1990, Sirinat Pengnuam; one *s* three *d. Educ:* Emanuel Sch.; Magdalen Coll., Oxford (BA Hons Maths and Philos. 1982). FCO, 1983–85; Second Sec., Bangkok, 1985–89; Second, then First Sec., FCO, 1989–92; First Sec., Sino-British Jt Liaison Gp, Hong Kong, 1992–96; Security Policy Dept, FCO, 1996–97; Dep. Hd, UN Dept, FCO, 1998; Principal Private Sec. to Cabinet Sec., Cabinet Office, 1998–2000; Fellow, Weatherhead Centre for Internat. Affairs, Harvard Univ., 2000–01; Counsellor, Washington, 2001–05; Dir, Asia-Pacific, FCO, 2005–08; Advr on Global Corporate Develt, Rolls Royce, 2008–09 (on secondment); Ambassador to the People's Republic of China, 2010–15. *Recreations:* Bach, blues guitar, gadgets, hill walking. *Address:* c/o Foreign and Commonwealth Office, King Charles Street, SW1A 2AH.

WOOD, John, CB 1989; Solicitor, Morgan Lewis & Bockius, 1997–99; *b* 11 Jan. 1931; *s* of Thomas John Wood and Rebecca Grand; *m* 1958, Jean Iris Wood; two *s. Educ:* King's College Sch., Wimbledon. Admitted Solicitor, 1955. Director of Public Prosecutions: Legal Assistant, 1958; Sen. Legal Asst, 1963; Asst Solicitor, 1971; Asst Director, 1977; Principal Asst Dir, 1981; Dep. Dir, 1985–87; Head of Legal Services, Crown Prosecution Service, 1986–87; Dir of Serious Fraud Office, 1987–90; DPP, Hong Kong, 1990–94; Consultant Solicitor, Denton Hall, 1995–97. Pres., Video Appeals Cttee, 1996–2011. *Recreations:* cricket, Rugby football, music, theatre.

WOOD, John David; Chief Executive, since 2012, and Director of Environment, since 2002, Hertfordshire County Council; *b* London, 9 June 1962; *s* of Cliff Wood and Barbara Wood; *m* 1989, Annmarie Leeming; three *s. Educ:* Highams Park Sen. High Sch.; City Univ. (BSc Hons Civil Engrg). MICE 1985. Trainee, then Asst Engr, Lambeth LBC, 1980–88; Sen. Engr, Newham LBC, 1988–91; Hertfordshire County Council: Principal Transport Engr, 1991–96;

Hd of Forward Planning, 1996–2000; Asst Dir, Strategy, 2000–02; Dep. Chief Exec., 2009–12. *Recreations:* socialising with family and friends, playing sport (especially tennis), walking the dog. *Address:* Hertfordshire County Council, County Hall, Pegs Lane, Hertford SG13 8DE. *T:* (01992) 555200. *E:* john.wood@hertfordshire.gov.uk.

WOOD, John Edwin, PhD; FInstP; Director of Underwater Engineering, British Aerospace Dynamics Division, 1988–90; *b* 24 July 1928; *s* of late John Stanley Wood and Alice (*née* Hardy); *m* 1953, Patricia Edith Wilson Sheppard (marr. diss. 1978); two *s* two *d*. *Educ:* Darlington Grammar Sch.; Univ. of Leeds (BSc, PhD). Joined Royal Naval Scientific Service at HM Underwater Countermeasures and Weapons Estabt, 1951; Admiralty Underwater Weapons Estabt, 1959; Head of Acoustic Research Div., 1968; Head of Sonar Dept, 1972; Admiralty Surface Weapons Establishment: Head of Weapons Dept, 1976; Head of Communications, Command and Control Dept, 1979; Chief Scientist (Royal Navy), and Director General Research (A), 1980; joined Sperry Gyroscope (subseq. British Aerospace), Bracknell, 1981; Exec. Dir, BAe, Bristol, 1984–88. Pres., Gp 12, Council for British Archaeology, 1984–93. *Publications:* Sun, Moon and Standing Stones, 1978, 2nd edn 1980; (jtly) The Treasure of Rennes-le-Château, 2003, 2nd edn 2005; papers and book reviews in technical and archaeological jls. *Recreations:* archaeology, making home videos. *Address:* 7 Pennant Hills, Bedhampton, Havant, Hants PO9 3JZ. *T:* (023) 9247 1411.

WOOD, (John) Humphrey (Askey); a Managing Director, Consolidated Gold Fields plc, 1979–89; Chairman, Vitec (formerly Vinten) Group plc, 1991–99; *b* 26 Nov. 1932; *s* of late Lt-Col Edward Askey Wood and Irene Jeanne Askey Wood; *m* 1st, 1965, Jane Holland; one *s*; 2nd, 1981, Katherine Ruth Stewart Reardon (*née* Peverley); one step *s* one step *d*. *Educ:* Abberley Hall; Winchester College; Corpus Christi College, Cambridge. MA (Mech. Scis). De Havilland Aircraft Co. Ltd, 1956; Hawker Siddeley Aviation Ltd, 1964, Dir and Gen. Manager, Manchester, 1969–76; Man. Dir, Industrial and Marine Div., Rolls-Royce Ltd, 1976–79; Chm., Amey Roadstone Corp., 1979–86. Director: Gold Fields of South Africa Ltd, 1986–89; Blue Tee Corp., USA, 1986–89; non-executive Director: Birse Gp plc, 1989–95; Albrighton plc, 1990–96 (Chm., 1993–96); Ennstone plc, 1996–98. Butten Trustee, PA Consulting Gp, 1991–97. Vice-Pres., Nat. Council of Building Material Producers, 1985–89. Mem. Council, CBI, 1983–89. Chm., SW Rivers Assoc., 2002–11 (Vice Pres., 2011–); Trustee, Westcountry Rivers Trust, 2002–14; Mem., SW Reg. Fisheries, Ecology and Recreation Adv. Cttee, Envmt Agency, 2002–08. *Recreations:* salmon conservation, fly fishing, sailing, painting, gardening. *Address:* Albyn House, 239 New King's Road, SW6 4XG. *T:* (020) 7371 0042.

WOOD, Sir John (Kember), Kt 1977; MC 1944; a Judge of the High Court of Justice, Family Division, 1977–93; President, Employment Appeal Tribunal, 1988–93 (Judge, 1985–88); *b* Hong Kong, 8 Aug. 1922; *s* of John Roskruge Wood and Gladys Frances (*née* Kember); *m* 1952, Kathleen Ann Lowe; one *s* one *d*. *Educ:* Shrewsbury Sch.; Magdalene Coll., Cambridge. Served War of 1939–45: Rifle Brigade, 1941–46; ME and Italy; PoW, 1944. Magdalene Coll., 1946–48. Barrister (Lincoln's Inn), 1949, Bencher, 1977; QC 1969; a Recorder of the Crown Court, 1975–77. Vice-Chm., Parole Bd, 1987–89 (Mem., 1986–89). *Recreations:* sport, travel. *Address:* 22 Addison Avenue, Holland Park, W11 4QR. *Clubs:* Garrick, MCC; Hawks (Cambridge).

WOOD, Prof. John Nicholas, PhD, DSc; FMedSci; FRS 2009; Professor of Molecular Neurobiology, University College London, since 2000; *b* Plymouth, 23 Nov. 1950; *s* of late Charles Wood and Dorothy Wood; *m* 2005, Min Liu, PhD; one *d*. *Educ:* Univ. of Leeds (BSc 1971); Univ. of Warwick (MSc 1972; PhD 1976; DSc 1997). Post Doctoral Scientist, Institut Pasteur, Paris, 1976–79; Sen. Scientist, Wellcome Foundn, 1981–84; Hd of Neuroimmunol., Sandoz Inst. for Med. Res., 1984–95; Reader in Neurosci., UCL, 1995–2000. Vis. Prof., Neurobiol., Harvard Univ., 1984. FMedSci 2009. Grand Prix Scientifique de l'Institut de France, 2009. *Publications:* Capsaicin in the Study of Pain, 1996; Molecular Basis of Pain Induction, 2000. *Recreations:* jazz, travel, sailing. *Address:* Wolfson Institute for Biomedical Research, University College London, Gower Street, WC1E 6BT. *T:* (020) 7679 6954, *Fax:* (020) 7679 6609. *E:* j.wood@ucl.ac.uk.

WOOD, Prof. John Vivian, CBE 2007; PhD, DMet; FIMMM, FInstP, FREng; Secretary General, Association of Commonwealth Universities, since 2010; *b* 10 Sept. 1949; *s* of Vivian Wood and Lois Wood (*née* Hall); *m* 1976, Alison Lee; one *s* one *d*. *Educ:* St Lawrence Coll., Ramsgate; Sheffield Univ. (BMet 1971, DMet 1994); Darwin Coll., Cambridge (PhD 1975). CEng 1984; FIMMM (FIM 1989); CPhys, FInstP 1998; FREng 1999. Goldsmiths' Jun. Res. Fellow, Churchill Coll., Cambridge, 1974–78; Lectr, then Sen. Lectr in Materials, Open Univ., 1978–89; University of Nottingham: Cripps Prof. and Hd, Dept of Materials Engrg, 1989–2001; Dean of Engrg, 1998–2001; Chief Exec., CCLRC (on secondment), 2001–07; Principal, Faculty of Engrg, 2007, Internat. Relns Advr, 2008–10, Imperial Coll. London. Chairman: Internat. Network for Availability of Scientific Pubns, 2009–; Oxeta, 2011–; Director: M4 Technologies, 1994–2013; Maney Publg, 2003–12; Bio Nano Consulting, 2008–. Chairman: UK Foresight Panel on Materials, 1997–2001; Eur. Strategy Forum for Res. Infrastructure, 2002–08; Eur. Res. Area Bd, 2008–12; Res. Information Network, 2012–; Co-Chm., Res. Data Alliance, 2012–; Member: Eur. Res. and Innovation Bd, 2012–14; EC Res. Innovation and Sci. Bd, 2014–. Mem. Council, RAEng, 2008–11. Trustee: Industrial Trust, 2000–13; Tomorrow Project, 2006–13; Daphne Jackson Trust, 2008–; CRAC, 2013–. Hon. Prof. of Materials, Imperial Coll. London, 2010–; Hon. Chair of Nanotechnol., UCL, 2014–. Hon. DSc Tech. Univ. of Cluj-Napora, Romania, 1994; Hon. DSc A. H. Rahman Univ., Chennai, 2014. Grunfeld Medal, 1986, Ivor Jenkins Award, 2000, Inst. Materials; William Johnson Internat. Gold Medal, Internat. Conf. of Advanced Materials and Processes, 2001. *Publications:* (contrib.) Ultra Rapid Quenching of Metals, 1978; contrib. numerous res. pubns and patent applications. *Recreations:* woodlands, chamber music and serious contemporary music, affordable wine, reading. *Address:* Association of Commonwealth Universities, Woburn House, 20–24 Tavistock Square, WC1H 9HF. *T:* (020) 7380 6700. *E:* john.wood@acu.ac.uk. *Club:* Foundation Universitaire (Brussels).

WOOD, Prof. Laurie, PhD; Professor, 2000–10, and Executive Director, Enterprise and Development, 2007–10, University of Salford; Chairman, Museum of Science and Industry, Manchester, 2001–11; Director, Laurie Wood Associates, since 2010; *b* Manchester, 25 Dec. 1952; *d* of Walter and Muriel Brown; *m* 1972; one *d*. *Educ:* Fairfield High Sch. for Girls; Manchester Poly. (BA 1st Cl. Hons Business Studies 1982); Victoria Univ. of Manchester (PGCE 1986); Univ. of Salford (PhD 1993). Dip. Mktg CIM 1982; Chartered Marketer 1998. Asst to Gp Mktg Manager, CWS Packaging Technol. Gp, 1971–73; accounting and mktg consultant, 1973–75; Mktg Services Manager, Nat. Westminster Bank, Manchester, 1975–80; Nat. Develt Manager, CWS Milk Gp, Manchester, 1982–84; Sen. Lectr, Mktg and Planning and Industrial Liaison Tutor, Manchester Poly., 1984–87; University of Salford: Sen. Lectr in Strategic Mgt and Mktg Information Systems, 1987–2000; Dir, Centre for Audience Develt Res., 1997–2001; Associate Dean, Enterprise, Faculty of Business and Informatics, 1999–2001; Dir, Acad. Enterprise and Chief Exec., Univ. of Salford Enterprises, 2001–07. Chm., UK Mktg Council, 2000–02; Bd Mem., UK Sci. Enterprise Centres, 2006–09. Non-exec. Dir, Tameside and Glossop Acute Services NHS Trust, 1997–2000. Chm., Arts About Manchester, 1993–97. Mem. Bd, Acad. Mktg Res., 2001–. Chartered Institute of Marketing: Internat. Vice Chm., 1996–99, Internat. Chm., 1999–2001; Dir, Commercial Bd, 1997–2002; Professorial Senate Mem., 2001–06; Internat. Trustee, 2004–; Benevolent Fund Trustee, 2009–; Hon. Fellow, 2001. Trustee and Dep. Chm., Communications, Advertising and Mktg Foundn, 2000–02. MMRS 1987; MInstD 2006. FRSA 1997; FCMI 2003; FHEA 2007. Freeman, City of London, 2001; Liveryman, Marketors' Co., 2001. *Publications:* contribs to learned jls in field of mktg and communications. *Recreations:* reading, film and music, family. *Address:* The Rivals, 39 Springmeadow Lane, Uppermill, Oldham OL3 6HL. *T:* (01457) 878582; 07767 270473. *E:* lauriewood@btinternet.com.

WOOD, Leanne; Member (Plaid Cymru) South Wales Central, National Assembly for Wales, since 2003; Leader, Plaid Cymru, since 2012; *b* 13 Dec. 1971; *d* of Jeff Wood and Avril Wood; one *d* by Ian Brown. *Educ:* Univ. of Glamorgan (BA Hons Public Admin); Univ. of Wales, Cardiff (Dip. in Social Work). Probation Officer, Mid Glamorgan Probation Service, 1997–2000; pt-time Pol Researcher to Jill Evans, MEP, 2000–01; Univ. Lectr, Social Work and Social Policy, Cardiff Univ., 2000–03 (pt-time, 2000–02); pt-time Community Support Worker, Cwm Cynon Women's Aid, 2001–02. Shadow Minister for Social Justice, 2003, for Housing and Regeneration, Nat. Assembly for Wales. Mem. (Plaid Cymru) Rhondda Cynon Taf CBC, 1995–99. *Address:* National Assembly for Wales, Cardiff Bay, Cardiff CF99 1NA. *T:* 0300 200 7202. *E:* leanne.wood@assembly.wales.

WOOD, Maj. Gen. Malcolm David, CBE 2002 (MBE 1988); Director General Joint Supply Chain, Defence Equipment and Support (formerly Director General Logistics (Supply Chain), Defence Logistics Organisation), 2003–08; *b* 14 May 1953; *s* of late Stanley Andrew Wood and of Elsie Blackley Wood (*née* Stamper); *m* 1977, Nora Ann (*née* Smith); three *d*. *Educ:* Hampton Sch.; RMA, Sandhurst; St John's Coll., Cambridge (MA). Staff Officer, Grade 2, UKCICC, 1986–87; Comdr, 32 Ordnance Co., 1988–89; Staff Officer, Grade 2, Personnel Br., 1990; CO, 5 Ordnance Bn, 1991–93 (mentioned in despatches, 1993); Directing Staff, Army Staff Coll., 1993–94; Dep. COS, 3 UK Div., 1995–96; Director: Logistic Support Services, 1997; Materiel Support (Army), 1998–99; Comdr, 101 Logistic Bde, 2000–01; rcds 2002. QCVS 1996. *Recreations:* Army Football (former Chm.), supporter of Burnley FC and Lancs CCC.

WOOD, Mark; *see* Wood, G. M.

WOOD, Mark William; Chief Executive, Ten Alps plc, since 2014; *b* 28 March 1952; *s* of Joseph Hatton Drew Wood and Joyce Wood; *m* 1st, 1986, Helen Lanzer (*d* 2007); one *s* one *d*; 2nd, 2010, Jane Louise Jones (*d* 2012). *Educ:* Univs of Leeds (BA Hons), Warwick (MA) and Oxford. Joined Reuters, 1976; corresp. in Vienna, 1977–78, East Berlin, 1978–81, Moscow, 1981–85; Chief Corresp., West Germany, 1985–87; Editor, Europe, 1987–89; Editor-in-Chief, 1989–2000; Hd, strategic media investments and alliances, 2000–02. Dir, Reuters Hldgs, 1990–96; Chm., Reuters Television, 1992–2002; Independent Television News: Dir, 1993–2009; Chm., 1998–2009; Chief Exec., 2003–09; Chief Exec., Future Publishing UK, 2010–11; Chief Exec., 2011–14, non-exec. Dir, 2014–, Future plc. Non exec. Dir, Citywire, 2002–; Mem., Adv. Bd, PWC, 2015–. Chairman: Library and Inf. Commn, 1999–2000 (Mem., 1995–2000; Vice Chm., 1998–99); MLA (formerly Resource: Council for Museums, Archives and Libraries), 2003–08 (Bd Mem., 2000–08); Member: Commonwealth Press Union, 1996–2000; Rathenau Gesellschaft, Germany, 1999–. *Recreations:* opera, ski-ing, supporting Spurs, tennis, theatre. *Address:* Ten Alps plc, 1 New Oxford Street, WC1A 1NU. *Club:* Garrick.

WOOD, Sir Martin (Francis), Kt 1986; OBE 1982; FRS 1987; DL; Hon. President, Oxford Instruments Group plc, since 2000 (Deputy Chairman, 1983); Fellow, Wolfson College, Oxford, 1967–94, Hon. Fellow, 1994; *b* 19 April 1927; *s* of late Arthur Henry Wood and Katharine Mary (*née* Cumberlege); *m* 1955, (Kathleen) Audrey (OBE 2006), *d* of Rev. John Howard Stanfield; one *s* (one *d* decd) and one step *s* one step *d*. *Educ:* Gresham's; Trinity Coll., Cambridge (BA Engrg, MA); Imperial Coll. (RSM) (BSc); Christ Church, Oxford (MA; Hon. Student, 2003). Nat. Service, Bevin Boy, S Wales and Derbyshire coalfields, 1945–48. Mgt Trainee, NCB, 1954–55; Sen. Res. Officer, Clarendon Lab., Oxford Univ., 1955–69; Founder, Oxford Instruments Ltd, 1959 (co. floated, 1983). Chm., Nat. Cttee for Superconductivity, SERC/DTI, 1987–92; Member: ABRC, 1983–89; ACOST, 1990–93; NRPB, 1991–96; Council, Central Lab. of the Res. Councils, 1995–98. Co-Founder, CONECTUS, 1994. Pres., FARM/Africa Ltd, 2000 (Vice-Chm. Council, 1985); Mem. Council, Royal Soc., 1995–97. Founder Trustee, Northmoor Trust (for nature conservation); Sylva Foundn (to promote sustainable forest mgt); Founder, Oxford Trust (for encouragement of study and application of science and technol.); Director: Oxford Econ. Partnership; Oxford Technol. Venture Trust. Lectr, UK and abroad. DL Oxon, 1985. Hon. FREng (Hon. FEng 1994). Hon. Fellow: UMIST, 1989; Cardiff Univ., 1998. Hon. DSc: Cranfield Inst. of Technol., 1983; Nottingham, 1996; Oxford Brookes, 2000; Hon. DTech Loughborough Univ. of Technol., 1985; Hon. DEng Birmingham, 1997; DUniv Open, 1999; Hon. DCL Oxon, 2004; Hon. Dr York, 2004. Mullard Medal (jtly), Royal Soc., 1982. *Publications:* articles in prof. jls. *Address:* c/o Oxford Instruments Group plc, Tubney Woods, Abingdon, Oxon OX13 5QX.

WOOD, Sir Michael (Charles), KCMG 2004 (CMG 1995); barrister; HM Diplomatic Service, retired; *b* 5 Feb. 1947; *s* of Walter Wood and Hilda Wood (*née* Forrester). *Educ:* Solihull Sch.; Trinity Hall, Cambridge (MA, LLM); Free Univ., Brussels. Called to the Bar, Gray's Inn, 1968, Bencher, 2000. HM Diplomatic Service, 1970–2006: Asst Legal Advr, FCO, 1970–81; Legal Advr, Bonn, 1981–84; Legal Counsellor, FCO, 1986–91 and 1994–96; Counsellor (Legal Advr), UK Mission to UN, NY, 1991–94; Dep. Legal Advr, FCO, 1996–99; Legal Advr, FCO, 1999–2006. Sen. Fellow, Lauterpacht Centre for Internat. Law, Univ. of Cambridge, 2006–. Mem., UN Internat. Law Commn, 2008–. Mem. Editl Cttee, British Yearbook of Internat. Law, 2001–. *Publications:* The Legal Status of Berlin, 1987; (with A. Pronto) The International Law Commission 1999–2009, Vol. IV 2010; articles on internat. law. *Recreations:* walking, music, travel. *Address:* 20 Essex Street, WC2R 3AL.

WOOD, Prof. Michael David; film maker, broadcaster and historian; Director, Maya Vision International Ltd, since 1989; Professor of Public History, University of Manchester, since 2013; *b* Manchester, 23 July 1948; *s* of George Wood and Elsie Bell; *m* 1988, Rebecca Ysabel Dobbs; two *d*. *Educ:* Manchester GS (Foundn Scholar); Oriel Coll., Oxford (Open Scholar; BA Hons; Postgrad. Scholar). Journalist: ITV, 1973–76; BBC, 1976–79; documentary film maker: BBC, 1979–86; Central TV, 1987–91. Has made over 100 documentaries for British and US TV. FRHistS 2001; FSA 2008. Gov., RSC. DUniv Open, 2003; Hon. DLitt: Birmingham, 2005; Lancaster, 2007; Stafford, 2008; Sunderland, 2009; Leicester, 2011. Numerous awards; Medlicott Medal, Histl Assoc., 2011. *Publications:* In Search of the Dark Ages, 1981, 6th edn 2005; In Search of the Trojan War, 1985, 6th edn 2005; Domesday, 1986, 5th edn 2005; Legacy, 1992, 3rd edn 2005; The Smile of Murugan, 1995, 3rd edn 2007; In the Footsteps of Alexander the Great, 1997, 3rd edn 2005; In Search of England, 1999; Conquistadors, 2000; Shakespeare, 2003; (contrib.) Chidambaram, 2004; In Search of Myths and Heroes, 2005; The Story of India, 2007; (contrib.) Lay Intellectuals in the Carolingian World, 2008; The Story of England, 2010; England and the Continent in the Tenth Century, 2011; In Search of Myths and Heroes: exploring four epic legends of the world, 2013; (ed) Essays and Reviews 1959–2002, by Bernard Williams, 2014. *Recreations:* theatre, music, reading history, walking in Greece. *Address:* Maya Vision International Ltd, 6 Kinghorn Street, EC1A 7HW. *T:* (020) 7796 4842.

WOOD, Rear Adm. Michael George, CBE 1995; JP; DL; logistic support consultant, since 2003; *b* 8 June 1948; *s* of George William Wood and late Margaret Jean Wood (*née* Cottier); *m* 1972, Judith Vivienne Tickle; one *s* two *d*. *Educ:* Plymouth Coll.; BRNC Dartmouth; RNEC Manadon. BSc, CNAA; CEng, FIMechE. Joined RN, 1968; served HM Ships Tenby, Torquay, Hermes, HM Yacht Britannia, Minerva, and ashore at RNC Greenwich, Raleigh, RNEC and staff of Flag Officer Sea Training, 1968–85; exchange with US Navy, 1986–88; SMEO to Captain Seventh Frigate Sqn, 1988–90; jsdc 1990; Naval Asst to First Sea

Lord, 1991–92; rcds 1993; staff of FO Portsmouth, 1994; Captain Fleet Maintenance, Devonport, 1994–96; Sec. to Chiefs of Staff Cttee, 1996–98; Dir Naval Logistic Policy, MoD, 1998–99; Dir Gen. Fleet Support (Ops and Plans), MoD, 1999–2000; Dir Gen. Defence Logistics (Ops and Business Develt), subseq. Dir Gen. Ops (Defence Logistics Orgn), MoD, 2000–03; Chief Naval Engr Officer, 2001–03. Senior Military Adviser: Mowlem plc, 2003–06; Carillion plc, 2006–10. Mem., Plymouth Area Business Council, 2005–. Chm., Devonport Naval Base Visitors Centre and Museum Trust, 2005–14. Gov., Drake Foundn, 2009–. Pres., RN Engrs Quart Club, 2004–13; Vice Pres., Combined Services Hockey Assoc., 2004–11. Chm. Trustees, China Fleet Club, 2013–. JP Plymouth, 2009 (Dep. Chm., S and W Devon Magistrates' Bench, 2013–); DL Cornwall, 2014. *Recreations:* family, sailing, travelling, ski-ing, tennis. *Address:* c/o Naval Secretary, Fleet Headquarters, Whale Island, Portsmouth PO2 8BY. *Club:* Royal Naval Sailing Assoc.

WOOD, Michael John Andrew; a District Judge (Magistrates' Courts), Durham, 2004–12; *b* 26 March 1950; *s* of Leslie Harold Thomas Wood and Irene Mary Wood; *m* 1973, Margaret (*née* Bellamy); three *d. Educ:* Headlands Sch., Bridlington; Univ. of Newcastle upon Tyne (LLB Hons 1972; J. H. Renoldson Meml Prize). Admitted solicitor, 1975; Assistant Solicitor: Messrs Linsley & Mortimer, 1975–77; Messrs Hay & Kilner, 1977–79; sole practitioner, Messrs Michael J. Wood & Co., 1979–2004. Dep. Dist Judge (Civil), 1993–99; Actg Stipendiary Magistrate, 1998–2000; Dep. Dist Judge (Magistrates' Courts), 2000–04. *Recreations:* golf, painting (watercolours), classic cars. *Club:* Whickham & District 41.

WOOD, Michael Jon; MP (C) Dudley South, since 2015; *b* 17 March 1976; *s* of Brian Wood and Jacqueline Susan Wood (*née* Priest); *m* 2008, Laura Chadderton; one *s* one *d. Educ:* Old Swinford Hosp. Sch.; Univ. of Wales, Aberystwyth (BScEcon Hons Econs and Law 1997); Cardiff Univ. (Postgrad. DipLaw 1999). Asst to Earl of Stockton, MEP, 1999–2002; Policy Advr, Eur. Parlt, 2002–06; Sen. Researcher, JDS Associates, 2006–08; Constituency Organiser, Cons. Party, 2009–10; Caseworker to Andrew Griffiths, MP, 2010–11; Parly Asst, H of C, 2011–14. Mem. (C) Dudley MBC, 2014–. *Address:* House of Commons, SW1A 0AA.

WOOD, Michael Mure; QC 1999; a Recorder, since 1999; Advocate, Public Defender Service, since 2014; *b* 22 Oct. 1953; *o s* of John Craig Mure Wood and Jean Margaret Wood; *m* 1st, 1978, Marianne Smith (marr. diss. 2012); one *d*; 2nd, 2012, Suzanne Eleanor Jane Dixey; one *s. Educ:* Rugby Sch.; Southampton Univ. (LLB Hons). Called to the Bar, Middle Temple, 1976, Bencher, 2012; an Asst Recorder, 1994–99; admitted: Grand Court, Cayman Is., 2004–06; Dubai Internat. Financial Centre Court, 2007. Member: Criminal Bar Assoc. Cttee, 1992–94; Bar Human Rights Cttee, 1995–2000. *Publications:* articles for Criminal Bar Assoc. and Law Commn. *Recreations:* food, wine, travel, golf. *Address:* Luckington Manor Stables, The Street, Luckington, Wilts SN14 6NP. *T:* 07841 816611. *E:* mwoodqc@hotmail.com. *Club:* Bar Golfing Soc.

WOOD, Michael Roy; *b* 3 March 1946; *s* of late Rowland L. Wood and Laura M. Wood; *m* 1999, Christine O'Leary; two step *d*; one *s* one *d* by a previous marriage. *Educ:* Nantwich and Acton Grammar Sch.; Salisbury and Wells Theol Coll. (CTh 1974); Leeds Univ. (CQSW 1981); Leeds Metropolitan Univ. (BA 1989). Probation officer, Liverpool, Bradford, Leeds, and social worker, Calderdale, Leeds, 1965–97. Mem. (Lab), Kirklees DC, 1980–88. Contested (Lab) Hexham, 1987. MP (Lab) Batley and Spen, 1997–2015.

WOOD, Nicholas Leslie; Executive Chairman, Leach and Burton Ltd, 1988–2012; *b* 25 Sept. 1948; *s* of Harold Edward Wood and Joyce Winifred Wood (*née* Clark); *m* 1974, Elizabeth Ann Ketteridge; two *s. Educ:* Forest Sch.; Sch. of Pharmacy, Univ. of London (BPharm). FRPharmS; FIPharmM. Community pharmacy br. manager, 1974–82, Man. Dir, 1982–2000, N. L. Wade Ltd. Gen. Sec., 1999–2003, Pres., 2007–, Inst. of Pharmacy Mgt. Member Council: Royal Pharmaceutical Soc., 1985–97, 2003–05 (Vice-Pres., 1992–93; Pres., 1993–94, 2004–05); Pet Health Council, 1990–97; Fedn Internat. Pharmaceutique, 1992–94; Commonwealth Pharmaceutical Assoc., 1995–97. Member: Standing Pharmaceutical Adv. Cttee, DoH, 1987–96; Jt Formulary Cttee, British Nat. Formulary, 1987–2007 (Dep. Chm., 1995–2007); Nurse Prescribers Formulary Cttee, 1998–2007; Health Policy Cttee, N Essex HA, 1999–2002; Council for Healthcare Regulatory Excellence, 2004–05. Mem. Council, Sch. of Pharmacy, Univ. of London, 1993–99, 2000–09 (Vice-Chm., 2006–09). Membership Sec., Lib Dem Health Assoc., 1988–92. Fellow, Sch. of Pharmacy, 2010. Freeman, City of London, 1970; Liveryman, Soc. of Apothecaries, 1990– (Mem., Court of Assts, 1995–; Chm., Charity Cttee, 2000–07; Master, 2008–09; Gideon de Laune Lectr, 2009; Curator, 2013–). *Recreations:* motor boating, medical and family history, gardening, playing rock guitar badly. *Address:* Tintern House, Melton Road, Woodbridge, Suffolk IP12 1NH. *Clubs:* East India; City Livery Yacht.

WOOD, Nicholas Marshall; His Honour Judge Nicholas Wood; a Circuit Judge, since 2007; *b* Sydney, 8 Oct. 1955; *s* of Geoffrey Ingham Wood and Hazel Esther Wood; *m* 1989, Sophie McCallum Kneebone; one *s* one *d. Educ:* Leeds Grammar Sch.; Queen's Coll., Oxford (BA Hons 1976); Indiana Univ. Sch. of Law (LLM 1978). Called to the Bar, Middle Temple, 1980; in practice as barrister specialising in criminal law: Francis Taylor Bldg, 1982–95; QEB Hollis Whiteman Chambers, 1995–2007; Asst Recorder, 1997–2000; Recorder, 2000–07. Sec., Criminal Bar Assoc., 1996–98; Vice Chm., Remuneration Cttee, Bar Council, 2003–05. *Recreations:* hill-walking, cricket, football, cinema, theatre. *Address:* Isleworth Crown Court, 36 Ridleway Road, Isleworth TW7 5LP. *T:* (020) 8380 4500.

WOOD, Peter Anthony; Finance Director, Standard Chartered Bank, 1993–2000; *b* 4 Feb. 1943; *s* of Roger Sydney Wood and Winifred May (*née* Hine); *m* 1965, Janet Catherine Brown; one *s* one *d. Educ:* Oldershaw Grammar Sch.; Manchester Univ. (BSc Hons Maths); Birkbeck Coll., London Univ. (MSc Stats). ACIB; FCT; FSS. NCB, 1964–66; Barclays Bank, 1966–93: Treas., 1985–91; Finance Dir, 1991–93. *Recreations:* golf, birdwatching. *Club:* Wildernesse (Sevenoaks).

WOOD, Prof. Peter Anthony, PhD; CGeog; Professor of Geography, University College London, 1996–2005, now Emeritus; *b* 24 Aug. 1940; *s* of Peter Barron Wood and Mary Theresa Wood. *Educ:* Univ. of Birmingham (BSc 1961; PhD 1966). CGeog 2002. University College London: Asst Lectr, 1965–68; Lectr, 1968–82; Sen. Lectr, 1982–92; Reader, 1992–96; Hd, Dept of Geog., 1997–2002. Sec., Council of British Geog., 2010–. Co-Chair, Chartered Geog. Assessors Panel, RGS, 2003–14; Chair, Frederick Soddy Trust, 2015–. Hon. FRGS 2015. *Publications:* (with G. M. Lomas) Employment Location in Regional Economic Planning, 1970; (with K. E. Rosing) Character of a Conurbation: a computer atlas of the West Midlands Conurbation, 1971; (jtly) Housing and Labour Migration in England and Wales, 1974; Industrial Britain: the West Midlands, 1974; (ed with H. D. Clout) London: problems of change, 1986; (ed with P. Damesick) Regional Problems, Problem Regions and Public Policy in the United Kingdom, 1987; (with J. N. Marshall) Services and Space: aspects of urban and regional development, 1995; (ed) Consultancy and Innovation: the business service revolution in Europe, 2002; (jtly) The Competitive Performance of English Cities, 2006; (contrib.) Handbook of Innovation and Services, 2010; (contrib.) Global Migration, Ethnicity and Britishness, 2011; numerous contribs to Trans of IBG, Progress in Human Geog., Geog., Regl Studies, Envmt and Planning A, Internat. Small Business Jl, Entrepreneurship and Regl Develt, Geoforum, Global Networks, L'Espace Géographique, Tijdschrift voor Econ. En Sociaale Geografie, Papers in Regl Sci., Service Industries Jl, Growth and Change. *Recreations:* music, opera, golf, travel. *Address:* Department of Geography, University College London, Gower Street, WC1E 6BT. *T:* (020) 7679 0587.

WOOD, Peter John, CBE 1996; Chairman, Esure, since 2000 (Chief Executive, 2000–12); *m* (marr. diss.); five *d.* Founder, 1985, Chief Exec., 1985–96, Chm., 1996–97, Direct Line Insurance. Non-executive Director: Plymouth Rock Corp., USA, 1995–; The Economist Newspaper Ltd, 1998–2003. *Address:* Esure, The Observatory, Reigate, Surrey RH2 0SG.

WOOD, Peter (Lawrence); theatrical, operatic and television director; *b* 8 Oct. 1925; *s* of Frank Wood and Lucie Eleanor (*née* Meeson). *Educ:* Taunton School; Downing College, Cambridge. Resident Director, Arts Theatre, 1956–57; Associate Dir, NT, 1978–89. Director: The Iceman Cometh, Arts, 1958; The Birthday Party, Lyric, Hammersmith, 1958; Maria Stuart, Old Vic, 1958; As You Like It, Stratford, Canada, 1959; The Private Ear and The Public Eye, Globe, 1962, Morosco, New York, 1963; Carving a Statue, Haymarket, 1964; Poor Richard, Helen Hayes Theatre, New York, 1964; Incident at Vichy, Phœnix, 1966; The Prime of Miss Jean Brodie, Wyndham's, 1966; White Liars, and Black Comedy, 1968; In Search of Gregory (film), 1968–69; Design for Living, Los Angeles, 1971; Jumpers, Burgtheater, Vienna, 1973, Billy Rose Theatre, NY, 1974; Dear Love, Comedy, 1973; Macbeth, LA, 1975; The Mother of Us All (opera), Santa Fé, 1976; Long Day's Journey into Night, LA, 1977; Così Fan Tutte, Santa Fé, 1977; She Stoops to Conquer, Burgtheater, Vienna, 1978; Night and Day, Phoenix, 1978, NY, 1979; Il Seraglio, Glyndebourne, 1980, 1988; Don Giovanni, Covent Garden, 1981; Macbeth, Staatsoper, Vienna, 1982; The Real Thing, Strand, 1982; Orione (opera), Santa Fé, 1983; Orion, King's Theatre, Edinburgh, 1984; Jumpers, Aldwych, 1985; Wildfire, Phoenix, 1986; Otello, Staatsoper, Vienna, 1987; Les Liaisons Dangereuses, LA, 1988; Hapgood, Aldwych, 1988, LA, 1989; Map of the Heart, Globe, 1991; Midsummer Night's Dream, Zurich, 1992; Arcadia, Zurich, 1993; The Bed Before Yesterday, Almeida, 1994; Indian Ink, Aldwych, 1995; *Chichester:* The Silver King, 1990; Preserving Mr Panmure, 1991; She Stoops to Conquer, 1992; Arcadia, 2000; On the Razzle, 2001; *Royal Shakespeare Company:* Winter's Tale, 1960; The Devils, 1961; Hamlet, 1961; The Beggar's Opera, 1963; Co-Dir, History Cycle, 1964; Travesties, 1974 (NY, 1975); Dr Jekyll and Mr Hyde, 1991; *National Theatre:* The Master Builder, 1964; Love for Love, 1965 (also Moscow); Jumpers, 1972; The Guardsman, The Double Dealer, 1978; Undiscovered Country, 1979; The Provok'd Wife, 1980; On the Razzle, 1981; The Rivals, 1983; Rough Crossing, 1984; Love for Love, 1985; Dalliance, 1986; The Threepenny Opera, 1986; The American Clock, 1986; The Beaux Stratagem, 1989; The School for Scandal, 1990; *television:* Hamlet, USA, 1970; Long Day's Journey Into Night, USA, 1973; Shakespeare, episode I, 1976; Double Dealer, 1980; The Dog it was that Died, 1988. *Recreation:* gastronomy. *Address:* The Old Barn, Batcombe, Somerset BA4 6HD.

WOOD, Philip, CB 1997; OBE 1979; Director General, Office of the Deputy Prime Minister (formerly Department of the Environment, Transport and the Regions, then Department for Transport, Local Government and the Regions), 1997–2003; *b* 30 June 1946; *s* of late Frank and Eleanor Wood; *m* 1971, Dilys Traylen Smith; one *s. Educ:* Queen Elizabeth Grammar Sch., Wakefield; Queen's Coll., Oxford. Entered Civil Service, 1967; Min. of Transport, 1967–70; DoE, 1970–75; a Private Sec. to the Prime Minister, 1975–79; Dept of Transport, 1979–97: Sec. to Armitage Inquiry into Lorries and the Envmt, 1980; Under Sec., 1986–95; seconded to BRB, 1986–88; Dep. Sec., 1995–97.

WOOD, Philip Richard, CBE 2015; Special Global Counsel, since 2002, and Head, Global Law Intelligence Unit, since 2009, Allen & Overy LLP; *b* Livingstone, N Rhodesia, 20 Aug. 1942; *s* of Frank Leslie Wood and Mary Florence Wood (*née* Dews); *m* Marie-Elisabeth Marciniak; three *s* one *d. Educ:* St John's Coll., Johannesburg; Univ. of Cape Town (BA 1963); Univ. of Oxford (MA English Lit.). Joined Allen & Overy, 1967: admitted Solicitor, 1970; Partner, 1973–2002; Hd, Banking Dept, 1992–98. Yorke Dist. Fellow, Cambridge Univ., 2001–. Visiting Professor: QMW, subseq. QMUL; of Internat. Financial Law, Univ. of Oxford, 2002–; LSE, 2003–08; Vis. Fellow, Bingham Centre for Rule of Law, 2013–. Founder, World Univs Comparative Law Project, 2010. Hon. QC 2010. Hon. LLD Lund. *Publications:* books on internat. financial law; contrib. articles to jls. *Recreations:* marathon-running, book-writing, travelling, speaking, digging paths, non-fiction, popular piano. *Address:* Allen & Overy LLP, One Bishop's Square, E1 6AD. *E:* philip.wood@allenovery.com; Knowle Grange, Hound House Road, Shere, Surrey GU5 9JH. *T:* (01483) 202108, 07785 500831. *Club:* Reform.

WOOD, (René) Victor; Director: Sun Life Corp. plc, 1986–96; Wemyss Development Co. Ltd, 1982–2006; *b* 4 Oct. 1925; *e s* of late Frederick Wood and Jeanne Wood (*née* Raskin); *m* 1950, Helen Morag (*d* 2013), *o d* of late Dr David S. Stewart. *Educ:* Jesus Coll., Oxford (BA 1948; Queen Elizabeth I Fellow, 2014). FFA. Chief Exec., 1969–79, Chm. 1974–79, Hill Samuel Insurance and Shipping Holdings Ltd; Chm., Lifeguard Assurance, 1976–84. Director: Haslemere Estates, 1976–86; Coalite Gp, 1977–89; Chandros Insce Co., 1979–89; Colbourne Insce Co., 1980–90; Criterion Insce Co., 1984–90; Scottinvest SA, 1985–95; Wemyss Hotels France SA, 1985–95; Les Résidences du Colombier SA, 1985–93; Domaine de Rimauresq SARL, 1985–2006; Worldwide and General Investment Co., 1992–2008. Vice-Pres., British Insurance Brokers' Assoc., 1981–84. *Publications:* (with Michael Pilch): Pension Schemes, 1960; New Trends in Pensions, 1964; Pension Scheme Practice, 1967; Company Pension Schemes, 1971; Managing Pension Schemes, 1974; Pension Schemes, 1979. *Address:* Helen Morag House, c/o Roca Corba 37, Can Diumenge - Escaldes, Andorra AD700. *T:* 869149.

WOOD, Prof. Richard Dean, PhD; FRS 1997; Grady F. Saunders Distinguished Professor in Molecular Biology, M. D. Anderson Cancer Center, University of Texas, since 2008; *b* 3 June 1955; *s* of Robert Dean Wood and Maxine Louise (*née* Hargis); *m* 1975, Enid Alison Vaag. *Educ:* Farmington High Sch., New Mexico; Westminster Coll., Salt Lake City (BS 1977); Univ. of Calif, Berkeley (PhD 1981). Grad. Fellow, NSF, 1977–80; Postdoctoral Fellow, Yale Univ., 1982–85; Imperial Cancer Research Fund: Postdoctoral Fellow, 1985–88; Res. Scientist, 1988–92; Sen. Scientist, 1992–95; Principal Scientist, 1995–2001; Richard Cyert Prof. of Molecular Oncology and Leader, Molecular and Cellular Biology (formerly Oncology) Prog., Univ. of Pittsburgh Cancer Inst., 2001–08. Hon. Prof., UCL, 1998. Mem., EMBO, 1998. Trustee, Marie Curie Cancer Care, 2000–01 (Chm., Scientific Cttee, 2000–01). Fellow, AAAS, 2013. Meyenburg Award for Cancer Res., 1998; Westminster Coll. Alumni Award, 1999. *Publications:* DNA Repair and Mutagenesis, 2nd edn 2006; papers in scientific res. jls. *Recreations:* playing bass, jazz, acoustic music, cycling, hiking. *Address:* Department of Epigenetics and Molecular Carcinogenesis, University of Texas, M. D. Anderson Cancer Center, PO Box 389, 1808 Park Road 1C, Smithville, TX 78957, USA.

WOOD, Prof. Robert Anderson, FRCSE, FRCPE, FRCPGlas, FRCPsych; Postgraduate Dean, and Professor in Clinical Medicine, University of Aberdeen Medical School, 1992–99; *b* 26 May 1939; *s* of late Dr John Fraser Anderson Wood and Janet Meikle Wood (*née* Hall); *m* 1966, Dr Sheila Margaret Pirie; one *s* three *d. Educ:* Edinburgh Academy; Univ. of Edinburgh (BSc Hons, MB ChB). FRCPE 1976; FRCSE 1994; FRCPGlas 1997; FRCPsych 1999. House Officer, Royal Infirmary, Edinburgh, 1963–64, Asst Lectr, Univ. of Edinburgh, 1964–65; Registrar and Sen. Registrar in Medicine, Dundee Teaching Hosps, 1965–69; Lectr in Therapeutics, Univ. of Aberdeen, 1969–72; Sen. Lectr in Therapeutics, 1972–92, Dep. Dir, Postgrad. Med. Educn, 1986–92, Univ. of Dundee; Consultant Physician, Perth Royal Infirmary, 1972–92. Member: Criminal Injuries Compensation Tribunal (formerly Appeals Panel), 2000–11; Advocates Disciplinary Tribunal, 2000–. HM Inspector of Anatomy for Scotland, 2007–14. Trustee, RCPE, 2005– (Mem. Council, 1990–92; Dean, 1992–95; Treas., 1999–2003). Mem. Bd, Med. and Dental Defence Union of Scotland, 2003–09 (Mem. Council, 1992–2003; Mem. Mgt Cttee, 1997–2003). *Publications:* papers on clinical pharmacology and medical education. *Recreations:* golf, sheep-husbandry. *Address:* Ballomill

House, Abernethy, Perthshire PH2 9LD. *T:* (01738) 850201. *E:* robertwood127@btinternet.com. *Clubs:* Royal & Ancient Golf (St Andrews); Craigie Hill Golf (Captain, 1999–2001) (Perth).

WOOD, Air Vice-Marshal Robert Henry, OBE 1977; *b* 24 Jan. 1936; *s* of Jack Cyril Wood and May Doris Wood; *m* 1957, Amy Cameron Wright; one *s* two *d*. *Educ:* Maldon Grammar School; cfs, psc, ndc, rcds. Commnd RAF, 1956; served Nos 617 and 88 Sqns, 1957–63; CFS, 1965–67; No 44 Sqn, 1967–69; attended Indian Staff Coll., 1970; MA to COS Far East Command, Singapore, 1970–71; PSO to Air Sec., 1972; NDC, Latimer, 1973; OC 51 Sqn, 1974; MoD Policy and Plans Dept, 1977; OC RAF Cranwell, 1978; OC RAF Linton-on-Ouse, 1979; Gp Capt. Flying Trng, HQ RAFSC, 1981–83; Dir Personal Services 1 (RAF), 1983–85; RCDS, 1985; Dep. Comdt, RAF Staff Coll., Bracknell, 1986; AOC and Comdt, RAF Coll., Cranwell, 1987–89; retd 1990. Director: Airways Flight Trng, 1992; British Red Cross, Leicestershire, 1993–96. *Recreations:* golf, music. *Clubs:* Royal Air Force; Luffenham Heath Golf (Captain, 2004).

WOOD, Hon. Sir Roderic (Lionel James), Kt 2004; **Hon. Mr Justice Roderic Wood;** a Judge of the High Court of Justice, Family Division, since 2004; *b* 8 March 1951; *s* of Lionel James Wood and Marjorie Wood (*née* Thompson). *Educ:* Nottingham High Sch.; Lincoln Coll., Oxford. Called to the Bar, Middle Temple, 1974; Bencher, 2001. QC 1993; a Recorder, 1997–2002; a Circuit Judge, 2002–03; Family Div. Liaison Judge for Wales, 2007–12. Member: Cttee, Family Law Bar Assoc., 1988–2002; Bar Council, 1993–95; Professional Conduct Cttee of the Bar, 1993–2000 (Vice-Chm., 1997–98; Chm., 1999–2000); Legal Aid and Fees Cttee, Gen. Council of the Bar, 1995–98 (Vice-Chm., Family, 1998); Court of Appeal (Civil Div.) User Cttee, 1995–2000. Jt Chm., Barristers/Clerks Liaison Cttee, 1994–95. Mem., Editl Bd, Longman Practitioner's Child Law Bull., 1993–94. *Recreations:* music, theatre, travel. *Address:* Royal Courts of Justice, Strand, WC2A 2LL.

WOOD, Roger Nicholas Brownlow; Chairman, Reliance HiTech, 2009–11; *b* 21 July 1942; *s* of Reginald Laurence Charles Wood and Jean Olive Wood; *m* 1966, Julia Ellen Mallows (*d* 2013); two *d*. *Educ:* Sherborne Sch.; Grad. Sch. of Management, Northwestern Univ., USA. With ICL, 1962–89 (Dir, ICL (UK) Ltd, 1987–89); Man. Dir, STC Telecoms Ltd, 1989–91; Gp Vice Pres., NT Europe SA, 1991–93; Dir Gen. Adjoint, Matra Marconi Space NV, 1993–96; Man. Dir, British Gas Services Ltd, 1996–2001; Dir, Centrica plc, 1996–2004; Man. Dir, Automobile Assoc., 2001–04. Director: Paypoint plc, 2004–10; Reliance plc, 2006–09. Mem., Parly Space Cttee, 1993–96. FBCS 1991; FCMI (FIMgt 1984); FInstD 1990. *Recreations:* music, Provence, Thai culture. *Address:* 16 Albany Reach, Queens Road, Thames Ditton, Surrey KT7 0QH. *Club:* Molesey Boat.

WOOD, Prof. Ronald Karslake Starr, FRS 1976; Senior Research Fellow, and Emeritus Professor, Imperial College, University of London, since 1986 (Professor of Plant Pathology, 1964–86); *b* 8 April 1919; *s* of Percival Thomas Evans Wood and Florence Dix Starr; *m* 1947, Marjorie Schofield; one *s* one *d*. *Educ:* Ferndale Grammar Sch.; Imperial College. Royal Scholar, 1937; Forbes Medal, 1941; Huxley Medal, 1950. Research Asst to Prof. W. Brown, 1941; Directorate of Aircraft Equipment, Min. of Aircraft Production, 1942; Imperial College, London University: Lectr, 1947; Reader in Plant Pathology, 1955; Head of Dept of Pure and Applied Biol., 1981–84; Gov., Imperial Coll. Commonwealth Fund Fellow, 1950; Research Fellow, Connecticut Agric. Experiment Stn, 1957. Mem. Council, British Mycological Soc., 1948; Sec., Assoc. of Applied Biologists; Mem., 1949, Chm., 1987–91, Biological Council; Mem., Parly and Scientific Cttee; Consultant, Nat. Fedn of Fruit and Potato Trades, 1955; Mem. Council, Inst. of Biology, 1956 (Vice-Pres., 1991–); Chm., Plant Pathology Cttee, British Mycological Soc.; Mem. Governing Body, Nat. Fruit and Cider Inst., Barnes Memorial Lectr, 1962; Sec., First Internat. Congress of Plant Pathology, 1968; Hon. Pres., 7th Internat. Congress of Plant Pathology, 1998. Mem. Governing Body: East Malling Research Stn, 1966 (Vice-Chm.); Inst. for Horticultural Res., 1987; Pres., Internat. Soc. for Plant Pathology, 1968 (Hon. Mem., 1988); Mem., Nat. Cttee for Biology, 1978; Chm., British Nat. Sub-Cttee for Botany, 1978; Dean, RCS, 1975–78; Founder Pres. and Hon. Mem., British Soc. for Plant Pathol., 1987. Scientific Dir, NATO Advanced Study Institute, Pugnochiuso, 1970, Sardinia, 1975, Cape Sounion, 1980; Consultant, FAO/UNDP, India, 1976. Fellow, Amer. Phytopathological Soc., 1972; Corresp. Mem., Deutsche Phytomedizinische Gesellschaft, 1973. Otto-Appel-Denkmünster, 1978. Thurburn Fellow, Univ. of Sydney, 1979; Sir C. V. Raman Prof., Univ. of Madras, 1980; Regents' Lectr, Univ. of California, 1981; Scholar, Rockefeller Foundn Bellagio Center; Visiting Professor: Univ. of Hong Kong; Univ. of Illinois; W Virginia Univ. *Publications:* Physiological Plant Pathology, 1967; (ed) Phytotoxins in Plant Diseases, 1972; (ed) Specificity in Plant Diseases, 1976; (ed) Active Defence Mechanisms in Plants, 1981; (ed) Plant Diseases: infection, damage and loss, 1984; numerous papers in Annals of Applied Biology, Annals of Botany, Phytopathology, Trans British Mycological Soc. *Recreation:* gardening. *Address:* Pyrford Woods, Pyrford, near Woking, Surrey GU22 8QL. *T:* (01932) 343827.

WOOD, Maj.-Gen. Roy; Chairman, Map Action, since 2011 (International Director, 2006–11); *b* 14 May 1940; *s* of Alec and Lucy Maud Wood; *m* 1963, Susan Margaret Croxford; two *s*. *Educ:* Farnham Grammar Sch.; Welbeck College; RMA; Cambridge Univ. (MA); University College London (MSc 1971). FRICS; FRGS. Commissioned RE 1960; Mapping Surveys, Sarawak, Sierra Leone and Sabah, 1964–70; Instructor, Sch. of Military Survey, 1972–75; MoD, 1975–77; OC 14 Topo. Sqn, BAOR, 1977–79; CO Mapping and Charting Estabt, 1979–81; Defense Mapping Agency, USA, 1981–83; MoD, 1984; Comdr, 42 Survey Engr Gp, 1985–87; Dir, Military Survey, 1987–90; Dir Gen., Military Survey, MoD, 1990–94. Col Comdt, RE, 1994–2003; Hon. Col, 135 Ind. Topographic Sqn RE (V), 1994–99. Chm., Geo-UK Ltd, 1994–2005. Pres., Photogrammetric Soc., 1993–95; Chairman: Assoc. for Geographic Information, 1996–97; RE Assoc., 2000–03; BSES, 2003–08; Member: Cttee of Mgt, Mt Everest Foundn, 2002–08; Council, RGS, 2008–11. *Publications:* articles on surveying and mapping in professional and technical jls. *Recreations:* rowing, ski-ing, hill walking, travel. *Club:* Geographical.

WOOD, Sir Samuel Thomas H.; *see* Hill-Wood.

WOOD, Scott F.; *see* Furssedonn-Wood.

WOOD, Sir Sebastian; *see* Wood, Sir J. S. L.

WOOD, Simon Edward; His Honour Judge Simon Wood; a Circuit Judge, since 2008; *b* North Shields, 23 Oct. 1958; *s* of Walter Scott Wood and Shirley Wood (*née* Bittermann); *m* 1984, Catherine Mary, *d* of George Edward Taylor Walton and Margaret Walton; four *s*. *Educ:* Chorister Sch., Durham; Royal Grammar Sch., Newcastle upon Tyne; Univ. of Newcastle upon Tyne (LLB Hons 1980). Called to the Bar, Middle Temple, 1981 (Harmsworth Schol.); in practice on NE Circuit, 1982–2008; Asst Recorder, 1998–2000; Recorder, 2000–08. NE Circuit Rep., Council of HM Circuit Judges, 2015–. Dep. Chancellor, Dio. of Newcastle, 2013–. Gov., Royal GS, Newcastle upon Tyne, 1999–2009. Trustee, Northern Sinfonia Trust, 2008–13 (Chm. Trustees, 2011–13). *Publications:* (ed with Christopher Walton) Charlesworth & Percy on Negligence, 12th edn 2010. *Recreations:* music (mem., Chorus of the Royal Northern Sinfonia (formerly Northern Sinfonia Chorus), 1983–), playing the piano, family history, walking. *Address:* The Law Courts, The Quayside, Newcastle upon Tyne NE1 3LA. *T:* (0191) 201 2000, *Fax:* (0191) 201 2001.
See also C. T. Walton.

WOOD, Sotiroula Maria, (Roula); *see* Konzotis, S. M.

WOOD, Timothy John Rogerson; Chairman, Autotronics plc, 1998–2000; *b* 13 Aug. 1940; *s* of Thomas Geoffrey Wood and Norah Margaret Annie (*née* Rogerson); *m* 1969, Elizabeth Mary Spencer; one *s* one *d*. *Educ:* King James's Grammar Sch., Knaresborough, Yorks; Manchester Univ. (BSc Maths). Joined Ferranti Ltd as Lectr in Computer Programming, 1962; joined ICT Ltd (later ICL), 1963; subseq. involved in develt of ICL systems software; Sen. Proj. Management Consultant advising on introdn of large computer systems, 1977; Sen. Proj. Manager on application systems, 1981; resigned from ICL, 1983. MP (C) Stevenage, 1983–97; contested (C) same seat, 1997. PPS to: Minister for Armed Forces, 1986–87; Minister of State, 1987–89, Sec. of State, 1989–90, Northern Ireland; Asst Govt Whip, 1990–92; Lord Comr of HM Treasury (Govt Whip), 1992–95; Comptroller of HM Household, 1995–97. Chm., Wokingham Cons. Assoc., 1980–83; Pres., Bracknell Cons. Assoc., 1998–2003; Vice Chairman: National Assoc. of Cons. Graduates, 1975–76; Thames Valley Euro Constituency Council, 1979–83; Mem., Bow Gp, 1962– (Mem. Council, 1968–71). Member: Bracknell DC, 1975–83 (Leader, 1976–78; Mem. Bd, Bracknell Develt Corp., 1977–82); (C) E Devon DC, 2007–. Governor: Princess Helena Coll., 2000–09 (Vice Chm., 2005–09); Littleham Sch., 2004– (Chm., 2005). *Publications:* Bow Group pamphlets on educn, computers in Britain, and the Post Office. *Recreations:* gardening, chess, reading. *Club:* Carlton.

WOOD, Victor; *see* Wood, R. V.

WOOD, Victoria, CBE 2008 (OBE 1997); writer and comedian; *b* 19 May 1953; *d* of late Stanley and Helen Wood; *m*; one *s* one *d*. *Educ:* Bury Grammar School for Girls; Univ. of Birmingham (BA Drama, Theatre Arts). Performed regularly on television and radio as singer/songwriter, 1974–78. First stage play, Talent, performed at Crucible Th., Sheffield, 1978; TV production of this, broadcast, 1979 (3 National Drama awards, 1980); wrote Good Fun, stage musical, 1980; wrote and performed, TV comedy series: Wood and Walters, 1981–82; Victoria Wood As Seen On TV, 1st series 1985 (Broadcasting Press Guilds Award; BAFTA Awards, Best Light Entertainment Prog., Best Light Entertainment Perf.), 2nd series 1986 (BAFTA Award, Best Light Entertainment Prog.), Special, 1987 (BAFTA Best Light Entertainment Prog.); An Audience with Victoria Wood, 1988 (BAFTA Best Light Entertainment Prog., BAFTA Best Light Entertainment Perf.); Victoria Wood, 1989; Victoria Wood's All Day Breakfast, 1992 (Writers' Guild Award); Victoria Wood Live in Your Own Home, 1994; dinnerladies, 1998–2000 (Best New TV Comedy, Nat. TV Awards, 1999; Best TV Comedy, British Comedy Awards, 2000; Press Prize, Montreux Fest., 2000); Still Standing (Special), 1998; Christmas Special, 2000; Victoria Wood's Sketch Show Story, 2001; Victoria Wood's Big Fat Documentary, 2004; Moonwalking (documentary), 2004; Housewife, 49 (TV drama), 2006 (Best Actress, Best Single Drama, BAFTA, 2007); Victoria's Empire (documentary), 2007; Ballet Shoes (TV drama), 2007; Victoria Wood's Midlife Christmas, 2009; Eric and Ernie (TV drama), 2011; The Borrowers (TV drama), 2011; Case Histories (TV drama), 2011; Loving Miss Hatto (TV drama), 2012; Victoria Wood's Nice Cup of Tea, 2013 (documentary) (Fortnum and Mason Food and Drink Award for TV Prog. of the Year, 2014); That Musical We Made, 2014 (documentary). *Screenplay:* Pat and Margaret, 1994 (BPG Award, Best Single Drama Critic's Award, Monte Carlo, and Nymphe d'Or) (adapted for stage, 2003). Appeared in stage revues, Funny Turns, Duchess Th., 1982, Lucky Bag, Ambassadors, 1984; own shows include: Victoria Wood, Palladium, 1987; Victoria Wood Up West, 1990; Victoria Wood - At It Again, Royal Albert Hall, 2001; wrote and performed, Acorn Antiques the Musical!, Th. Royal, Haymarket, 2005, (dir) UK tour, 2007; wrote and dir, That Day We Sang, Opera House, Manchester, 2011, (TV play) 2014. Variety Club BBC Personality of the Year, 1987; British Comedy Awards: Top Female Comedy Performer, 1996; Writer of the Year, 2000; Best Female TV Comic, 2011; BAFTA Tribute Award, 2005; Lifetime Achievement Award, Women in Film and TV Awards, 2011. Hon. DLitt: Lancaster, 1989; Sunderland, 1994; Bolton, 1995; Birmingham, 1996. *Publications:* Victoria Wood Song Book, 1984; Up to you, Porky, 1985; Barmy, 1987; Mens Sana in Thingummy Doodah, 1990; Chunky, 1996. *Recreation:* brain training. *Address:* c/o Phil McIntyre, 85 Newman Street, W1T 3EU. *T:* (020) 7291 9000.

WOOD, Rt Rev. Wilfred Denniston, KA 2000; Area Bishop (formerly Bishop Suffragan) of Croydon, 1985–2002; *b* Barbados, WI, 15 June 1936; *s* of Wilfred Coward and Elsie Elmira Wood; *m* 1966, Ina Eileen, *d* of L. E. Smith, CBE, Barbadian MP; three *s* two *d*. *Educ:* Combermere Sch. and Codrington Coll., Barbados. Lambeth Dip. in Theol., 1962. Ordained deacon, St Michael's Cath., Barbados, 1961; ordained priest, St Paul's Cath., London, 1962. Curate of St Stephen with St Thomas, Shepherd's Bush, 1962–66, Hon. Curate, 1966–74; Bishop of London's Officer in Race Relations, 1966–74; Vicar of St Laurence, Catford, 1974–82; RD of East Lewisham, 1977–82; Archdeacon of Southwark, 1982–85; Hon. Canon of Southwark Cathedral, 1977–85. Mem., General Synod, 1987–91. Chairman: Martin Luther King Meml Trust; Cttee on Black Anglican Concerns, 1986–91. Member: Royal Commn on Criminal Procedure, 1978–80; Archbishop of Canterbury's Commn on Urban Priority Areas, 1983–85; Housing Corp. Bd, 1986–95. Non-exec. Dir, Mayday Healthcare NHS Trust, 1993–2002 (Vice-Chm., 2000). JP Inner London, 1971–85. Hon. Freeman, London Bor. of Croydon, 2002. Hon. DD Gen. Theol Seminary, NY, 1986; DUniv Open, 2000; Hon. LLD West Indies, 2002. *Publications:* (contrib.) The Committed Church, 1966; (with John Downing) Vicious Circle, 1968; Keep the Faith, Baby!, 1994; Faith for a Glad Fool, 2010. *Recreations:* listening to audio-books, poetry and music, cricket; armchair follower of most sports. *Address:* 69 Pegwell Gardens, Christ Church, Barbados, West Indies. *T:* 4201822. *E:* wilfredwoodbarbados@gmail.com.

WOOD, William James; QC 1998; *b* 10 July 1955; *s* of Sir Frank Wood, KBE, CB, and Lady (Olive May) Wood (*née* Wilson); *m* 1986, Tonya Mary Pinsent; one *s* one *d*. *Educ:* Dulwich Coll.; Worcester Coll., Oxford (BA, BCL, both 1st cl.); Harvard Law Sch. (LLM). Called to the Bar, Middle Temple, 1980, Bencher, 2006. Member: Panel of Ind. Mediators; Internat. Acad. of Mediators, 2012–; Civil Justice Council, 2014–. Adjunct Prof. of Dispute Resolution, Hong Kong Shue Yan Univ., 2014–. *Recreations:* fishing, ski-ing. *Address:* The Old Rectory, Church Lane, Charlbury, Oxon OX7 3PX; Brick Court Chambers, 7–8 Essex Street, WC2R 3LD.
See also C. Wood.

WOOD, William Murray, TD 2003; Sheriff of Tayside, Central and Fife at Perth, since 2014; *b* Fraserburgh, 1963; *s* of William Murray Diack Wood and Madelina Jack Wood (*née* Anderson); *m* 1990, Monica McLaughlin; two *s* one *d*. *Educ:* High Sch. of Dundee; Univ. of Aberdeen (LLB 1984; DipLP 1985); RMA, Sandhurst. Commnd Regular Army, 1986; served with 1st Bn, Gordon Highlanders, 1986–90. Trainee and solicitor, Inverness, 1990–93; admitted as solicitor, 1991; Solicitor, Alloa, Hamilton and Uddingston, 1993–2012. Fee Paid Immigration Judge, 2001–13; Convener, Mental Health Tribunal for Scotland, 2005–13; Chair, Pensions Appeal Tribunal for Scotland (War Pensions), 2008–13; Fee Paid Dep. Upper Tribunal Judge (Immigration and Asylum Chamber), 2010–13; Fee Paid Social Security Judge, 2012–13; pt-time Sheriff, 2012–13; Floating Sheriff of Tayside, Central and Fife at Stirling, 2013. Served TA, 1990–2013; Lt Col, 2006; i/c Glasgow and Strathclyde Univs OTC, 2006–08. Mem., Guildry of Stirling, 2013–. *Recreations:* obligatory gardening, moderate running and cycling, light squash, reading, films. *Address:* Sheriff's Chambers, Sheriff Court House, Tay Street, Perth PH2 8NL.

WOOD, William Rowley; QC 1997; **His Honour Judge William Wood;** a Circuit Judge, since 2002; *b* 22 March 1948; *s* of Dr B. S. B. Wood and Elizabeth Wood; *m* 1973, Angela Beatson-Hird; one *s* two *d*. *Educ:* Bradfield Coll., Berks; Magdalen Coll., Oxford (MA). Called to the Bar, Gray's Inn, 1970. A Recorder, 1990–2002. Chm., Birmingham DAC, 1999–2006. *Recreations:* sailing, tennis, theatre. *Clubs:* Buckland (Birmingham); Bentley Drivers; Edgbaston Priory Lawn Tennis.

WOODARD, Rear-Adm. Sir Robert (Nathaniel), KCVO 1995; DL; Flag Officer Royal Yachts, 1990–95; an Extra Equerry to the Queen, since 1992; *b* 13 Jan. 1939; *s* of Francis Alwyne Woodard and Catherine Mary Woodard (*née* Hayes); *m* 1963, Rosamund Lucia, *d* of Lt-Col D. L. A. Gibbs, DSO and Lady Hilaria Gibbs (*née* Edgcumbe); two *s* one *d*. *Educ:* Lancing College; Coll. of Air Warfare. Joined Royal Navy as Cadet, 1958; specialised in flying; served HM Ships Undaunted, Ark Royal, Eagle, Victorious, Bulwark in 800, 801, 845, 846 and 848 Sqns (active service Malaya, Borneo); DS, BRNC Dartmouth, 1971–73; Commands: 771 Sqn, 1973–74; 848 Sqn, 1974–75; HMS Amazon, 1978–80; Dir, JMOTS, 1981–83; HMS Glasgow, 1983–84; HMS Osprey, 1984–86; MoD Op. Requirements, 1986–88; Cdre, Clyde, 1989–90. Dir, Crownhill Estates, 1996–2012. Dir, Woodard (Western Div.) plc, 1985–2005; Fellow, Western Div., 1985–2005, Trustee, 2001–11, Vice Pres., 2011–, Woodard Corp.; Patron, Sir Robert Woodard Acad., 2009–. Vice-Pres., Falmouth Br., Royal Naval Assoc. Pres., SSAFA, Cornwall, 1995. Chm., Regl Cttee, Devon and Cornwall, NT, 1997–2002. Chairman of Governors: King's Coll., Taunton, 2000–05; King's Hall, Pyrland, 2000–05; Vice-Chm., Govs, Bolitho Sch., Penzance, 1994–2010. Pres., Helford River Children's Sailing Trust, 1997–2014; Pres., Type 21 Club, 2014–. Younger Brother, Trinity House, 1994–. DL Cornwall, 1999. FCMI (FBIM 1979); MInstD 1995. Comdr, Ordre Nat. du Mérite (France), 1992. *Recreations:* shooting, fishing, painting, sailing, mowing. *Clubs:* Royal Yacht Squadron, Royal Cornwall Yacht.

WOODBRIDGE, Anthony Rivers; Senior Partner, The Woodbridge Partnership, 1997–2009; Consultant Solicitor, Thomas A Deegan, since 2011; *b* 10 Aug. 1942; *s* of late John Nicholas Woodbridge and Patricia Madeleine (*née* Rebbeck); *m* 1976, Lynda Anne Nolan; one *s*. *Educ:* Stowe; Trinity Hall, Cambridge (MA). Admitted solicitor, 1967; Partner, Woodbridge & Sons, Uxbridge, 1969–83; Sen. Partner, Turberville Woodbridge, 1983–97. Company Secretary: Abbeyfield Uxbridge Soc. Ltd, 1974–96 (Vice-Chm., 1996–98); Burr Brown Internat. Ltd, 1992–96. Adminr, Uxbridge Duty Solicitor Scheme, 1983–91. Clerk to Comrs of Income Tax, 1985–2009. Mem., Hillingdon HA, 1990–92; Chairman: Hillingdon Community Health NHS Trust, 1992–94; Harrow and Hillingdon Healthcare NHS Trust, 1994–2001; Stoke Mandeville Hosp. NHS Trust, 2001–02; Hillingdon Hosp. NHS Trust, 2002–05. Trustee, The Hillingdon Partnership Trust, 1994–2003 and 2011– (Chm., 2014–). Hon. Solicitor: Samaritans, Hillingdon, 1973–; Age Concern, Hillingdon, 1989–. Mem., Law Soc., 1967–. Mem. Ct, Brunel Univ., 1995–. FInstD 1999. Gov., Fulmer Sch., Bucks, 1984–2003 (Chm. Govs, 1988–94). DUniv Brunel, 2000. *Recreations:* walking, cycling, touring. *Address:* 16 Fairfield Park Road, Fairfield Park, Bath, Avon BA1 6JN. *T:* (office) (01895) 876586, 07802 414590. *E:* tonywoodbridge@hotmail.co.uk.

WOODBURN, Christopher Hugh, FCA; Chief Executive, General Insurance Standards Council, 1999–2005; *b* 6 Nov. 1947; *s* of Leonard Arthur and Phyllis Lydia Woodburn; *m* 1972, Lesley Avril Mohan; two *d*. *Educ:* St John's Sch., Leatherhead. FCA 1972. Articled Clerk and Audit Senior, Deloitte & Co., 1966–72; London Stock Exchange, 1972–88 (Hd, Financial Regulation, 1987–88); Securities Assoc., 1988–91 (Dep. Chief Exec., 1990–91); SFA, 1991–99 (Chief Exec., 1997–99). Hon. FCII 2006. *Recreations:* sailing, history. *Address:* Oak House, Heathfield Road, Burwash, E Sussex TN19 7HN. *T:* (01435) 883196.

WOODCOCK, Prof. Ashley Arthur, OBE 2006; MD; FRCP; Professor of Respiratory Medicine, since 1998, and Head, Institute of Inflammation and Repair, since 2012, University of Manchester (Head, School of Translational Medicine, 2008–12); Consultant Respiratory Physician, University Hospital of South Manchester, since 1988; *b* Stoke-on-Trent, 13 April 1951; *s* of Arthur and Vera Woodcock; *m* 1974, Fiona; two *s* one *d*. *Educ:* Hanley High Sch., Stoke-on-Trent; Univ. of Manchester (BSc 1972; MB ChB 1975; MD 1982). FRCP 1992. Consultant Physician: Bandar Seri Begawan Brunei, SE Asia; Manchester Royal Infirmary, 1985. Co-chair, Med. Tech. Options Cttee to Montreal Protocol for Protection of Ozone Layer, 1996–2013. FMedSci 2008. *Publications:* contribs on treatment of asthma, allergy and respiratory symptoms. *Recreations:* golf, walking in Wales. *Address:* University Hospital South Manchester, Southmoor Road, Manchester M23 9LT. *E:* ashley.woodcock@manchester.ac.uk. *Clubs:* Hale Golf, Aberdovey Golf.

WOODCOCK, John Charles, OBE 1996; cricket writer; *b* 7 Aug. 1926; *s* of late Rev. Parry John Woodcock and Norah Mabel Woodcock (*née* Hutchinson). *Educ:* Dragon Sch.; St Edward's Sch., Oxford; Trinity Coll., Oxford (MA; DipEd; OUHC *v* Cambridge, 1946, 1947). Manchester Guardian, 1952–54; cricket writer, The Times, 1954–; Cricket Corresp. to Country Life, 1962–91; Editor, Wisden Cricketers' Almanack, 1980–86; has covered over 40 Test tours, 1950–98, to Australia, 18 times, S Africa, W Indies, New Zealand, India, Pakistan and Sri Lanka. Mem., MCC Cttee, 1988–91 and 1992–95 (Trustee, 1996–99; Hon. Life Vice-Pres., 2001). Pres., Cricket Writers' Club, 1986–2005. Patron of the living of Longparish. Hon. Fellow, Winchester Univ., 2012. Sports Journalist of the Year, British Press Awards, 1987. *Publications:* The Ashes, 1956; (with E. W. Swanton) Barclays World of Cricket, 1980 (Associate Editor, 2nd edn 1986, Consultant Editor, 3rd edn 1986); The Times One Hundred Greatest Cricketers, 1998. *Recreations:* the countryside, golf. *Address:* The Old Curacy, Longparish, Andover, Hants SP11 6PB. *T:* (01264) 720259. *Clubs:* MCC; Vincent's (Oxford); St Enodoc Golf.

WOODCOCK, John Zak; MP (Lab Co-op) Barrow and Furness, since 2010; *b* Sheffield, 14 Oct. 1978; *m* 2004, Amanda Telford; two *d*. *Educ:* Edinburgh Univ. (MA 2002). Journalist, Scotsman; Special Adviser: to Rt Hon. John Hutton, MP, 2005; to Cabinet Sec., 2005; to Sec. of State for Work and Pensions, 2005–07; to Sec. of State for Business, Enterprise and Regulatory Reform, 2007–08; to the Prime Minister, 2009. Shadow Transport Minister, 2010–12; Shadow Education Minister, 2015. Mem., Defence Select Cttee, 2010. *Address:* House of Commons, SW1A 0AA.

WOODCOCK, Michael, (Mike); JP; company director, consultant, researcher and writer; *b* 10 April 1943; *s* of Herbert Eric Woodcock and Violet Irene Woodcock; *m* 1969, Carole Ann (*née* Berry); one *s* one *d*. *Educ:* Queen Elizabeth's Grammar Sch., Mansfield, Notts; DLitt IMCB, 1988. Successively: Accountant, Personnel Officer, Management Development Adviser, Head of Small Business Development Unit, Consultant, Vice-Pres. of US Corp., Founder of six UK companies. Underwriting Mem. of Lloyd's, 1984–. Proprietor of Estates in Scotland: Glenrinnes; Rigg; Carron Bridge; Corbiewells. MP (C) Ellesmere Port and Neston, 1983–92. Member: Trade and Industry Select Cttee, 1984–87; Home Affairs Select Cttee, 1987–92; Secretary: Cons. Smaller Business Cttee, 1990–92; All Party Transpennine Gp of MPs, 1990–92. Parly Advr, Chamber of Coal Traders, 1985–93. Nat. Vice Pres., Ramblers' Assoc., 1993–. Vis. Prof., Univ. of Lancaster Mgt Sch., 1992–96; Vis. Fellow, Leeds Business Sch., 1994–97. Pres. and Chm. of Council, Royal Masonic Trust for Girls and Boys, 2008–; Gov., Royal Masonic Sch. for Girls, 2013–; Trustee, Royal Masonic Instn for Girls Endowment Trust, 2013–; Chm. of Trustees, Lifelites, 2010–. Companion, IMCB, 1990. JP Mansfield, Notts, 1971. *Publications:* People at Work, 1975; Unblocking Your Organisation, 1978 (UK, USA and Holland); Team Development Manual, 1979 (UK, USA and Indonesia); Organisation Development Through Teambuilding, 1981 (UK and USA); The Unblocked Manager, 1982 (UK, USA and four foreign edns); 50 Activities for Self Development, 1982 (UK, USA and eight foreign edns); Manual of Management Development, 1985; 50 Activities for Teambuilding, 1989 (UK, USA and 11 foreign edns); (jtly) Clarifying Organisational Values, 1989 (UK and Sweden); 50 Activities for Unblocking Your Organisation, vol. 1, 1990, vol. 2, 1991; The Self Made Leader, 1990; Unblocking Organisational Values, 1990; Change: a collection of activities and exercises, 1992; The Woodcock Francis series of Management Audits, 1994; Teambuilding Strategy, 1994 (UK and India); The Teambuilders Toolkit, 1996; The Problem Solvers Toolkit, 1996; The New Unblocked Manager, 1996; 25 Interventions for Improving Team Performance, 1997; Developing Your People, 1998; Interventions for Developing Managerial Competencies, 1998; Management Skills Assessment, 1999; The Agile Organisation, 1999; Audits for Organisational Effectiveness, 2004; Team Metrics: resources for measuring and improving team performance, 2005. *Recreation:* walking. *Address:* Inkersall Farm, Bilsthorpe, Newark, Notts NG22 8TL; 13 Denny Street, SE11 4UX.

WOODCOCK, Vice Adm. Simon Jonathan, OBE 2008; Second Sea Lord, since 2015; *b* Sandown, IoW, 5 July 1962; *s* of Roger Fairhurst Woodcock and Phyllis Margaret Woodcock; *m* 1985, Joanna Leigh Clarke; one *s* one *d*. *Educ:* Ryde Sch.; Britannia Royal Naval Coll.; RNEC Manadon (BSc Hons Eng). CEng 1996; MIMechE 1996. Joined RN, 1980; Hd, Machinery Trials Unit, 1999–2001; Comdr (Marine Engrg), HMS Ark Royal, 2001–03; COS to Capability Manager (Precision Attack), 2003–05; Captain: RN Sch. of Marine Engrg, 2005–08; HMS Raleigh, 2008–09; rcds 2010; Hd, Pay and Manning, MoD, 2010–12; Cdre, Naval Personnel, 2012; Naval Sec. and ACNS (Personnel), 2012–15. Trustee, RN Benevolent Trust, 2009–. FCIPD 2014. *Recreations:* country sports, ski-ing, gardening, bee keeping. *Address:* Office of the Second Sea Lord, Navy Command Headquarters, Mail Point 2.1, Leach Building, Whale Island, Portsmouth PO2 8BY. *E:* Jonathan.woodcock569@mod.uk.

WOODCOCK, Thomas, CVO 2011 (LVO 1996); DL; FSA; Garter Principal King of Arms, since 2010; Genealogist, Order of the Bath, since 2010; *b* 20 May 1951; *s* of late Thomas Woodcock, Hurst Green, Lancs, and Mary, *d* of William Woodcock, Holcombe, Lancs; *m* 1998, Lucinda Mary Harmsworth, *d* of late Lucas Michael Harmsworth King. *Educ:* Eton; University Coll., Durham (BA); Darwin Coll., Cambridge (LLB). FSA 1990. Called to Bar, Inner Temple, 1975, Bencher, 2010. Research Assistant to Sir Anthony Wagner, Garter King of Arms, 1975–78; Rouge Croix Pursuivant, 1978–82; Somerset Herald, 1982–97; Norroy and Ulster King of Arms, 1997–2010. Advr on Naval Heraldry, 1996–; Inspector of Regtl Colours and of RAF Badges, 2010–. Chm., Harleian Soc., 2004–; Pres., Lancs Parish Register Soc., 2004–. DL Lancs, 2005. *Publications:* (with John Martin Robinson) The Oxford Guide to Heraldry, 1988; (ed with D. H. B. Chesshyre) Dictionary of British Arms: Medieval Ordinary, vol. 1, 1992, vol. 2 (ed with Hon. J. Grant and I. Graham), 1996, vol. 3 (ed with Sarah Flower), 2009, vol. 4 (ed with Sarah Flowers), 2014; (with John Martin Robinson) Heraldry in National Trust Houses, 2000. *Address:* College of Arms, 130 Queen Victoria Street, EC4V 4BT. *T:* (020) 7236 3634, (020) 7248 1188. *Clubs:* Travellers, Beefsteak.

WOODFORD, Air Vice-Marshal Anthony Arthur George, CB 1989; Home Bursar and Fellow, Magdalen College, Oxford, 1992–2001; *b* 6 Jan. 1939; *s* of Arthur and May Woodford; *m* 1965, Christine Barbara Tripp; one *s* two *d*. *Educ:* Haberdashers' Aske's Hampstead School; RAF College, Cranwell. BA Hons Open Univ. 1978. Commissioned pilot, 1959; served Nos 12, 44, 53, 101 Sqns and 4017th CCTS USAF; Asst Air Attaché, British Embassy, Washington, 1978–81; Comdr RAF St Mawgan, 1982–83; Comdr British Forces Ascension Island, 1982; ADC to the Queen, 1982–83; RCDS 1984; HQ Strike Command: Air Cdre Plans, 1985–87; AOA, 1987–89; ACOS Policy, SHAPE, 1989–92, retd. *Address:* Filkins Moor, Filkins, Lechlade, Glos GL7 3JJ. *Club:* Royal Air Force.

WOODFORD, Maj.-Gen. David Milner, CBE 1975; retired; Member, Lord Chancellor's Panel of Independent Inspectors, 1988–2000; *b* 26 May 1930; *s* of late Major R. M. Woodford, MC, and Marion Rosa Woodford (*née* Gregory); *m* 1st, 1959, Mary E. Jones (marr. diss. 1987); 2nd, 1995, Carole M. Westoby. *Educ:* Prince of Wales Sch., Nairobi; Wadham Coll., Oxford. psc, jsdc, rcds. National Service, then Regular, 1st Royal Fusiliers, Korea, 1953, then Regtl service, Egypt, Sudan, UK, 1953–55; ADC/GOC Berlin, 1956–58; Adjt and Co. Comd 1RF, Gulf, Kenya, Malta, Cyprus, Libya, UK, 1958–61; GSO3 Div./Dist, UK, 1962; sc Camberley, 1963; GSO2 MO 1, then MA/VCGS, 1964–66; Co. Comd 1RF, BAOR, UK, Gulf and Oman, 1966–68; GSO1 (DS) Staff Coll., 1968–70; CO 3 RRF, Gibraltar, UK, N Ireland, 1970–72; Col GS NEARELF (Cyprus), 1972–75; Comd 3 Inf. Bde (N Ireland), 1976–77; Dep. Col, RRF, 1976–81; RCDS 1978; D Comd and COS SE Dist, UK, 1979–80; Dir Army Training, 1981–82; Sen. Army Mem., RCDS, 1982–84; Comdt, JSDC, 1984–86. Col RRF, 1982–86. *Recreations:* literary, historical; passionate golfer. *Address:* c/o Regimental Headquarters, The Royal Regiment of Fusiliers, HM Tower of London, EC3N 4AB. *Clubs:* Army and Navy, New Zealand Golf.

WOODFORD, F(rederick) Peter, PhD; FRCPath; FRSC; FIPEM, FSA; Chief Scientific Officer, Department of Health (formerly of Health and Social Security), 1984–93; *b* 8 Nov. 1930; *s* of Wilfrid Charles Woodford and Mabel Rose (*née* Scarff); *m* 1964, Susan Silberman, NY; one *d*. *Educ:* Lewis Sch., Pengam, Glam; Balliol Coll., Oxford (Domus Exhibnr; BA (Hons Chem.) 1952; MA 1955); PhD Leeds 1955. FRCPath 1984; CChem, FRSC 1990; FIPEM (FBES 1993; MBES 1991). Res. Fellow, Leiden Univ., 1958–62; Vis. Scientist/Lectr, Univ. of Tennessee Med. Sch. and NIH, USA, 1962–63; Guest Investigator, Rockefeller Univ., NY, 1963–71; Scientific Historian, Ciba Foundn, and Scientific Associate, Wellcome Trust, 1971–74; Exec. Dir, Inst. for Res. into Mental and Multiple Handicap, 1974–77; PSO (Clin. Chem.), DHSS, 1977–84. Distinguished Visitor, Royal Free Hosp. Sch. of Med., 1994–; Gov., Royal Free London NHS Foundn Trust (formerly Royal Free Hosp. NHS Trust), 2012–14 (Shadow Gov., 2008–11). Mem., Quality of Life Panel, Camden Council, 2009–12. Editorial Consultant: Clin. Res. Inst., Montreal, 1970–90; Inst. of Pharmacology, Milan Univ., 1995–. Chm., Council of Biology Editors (USA), 1969–70; Managing/Executive Editor: Jl of Atherosclerosis Res., 1960–62; Jl of Lipid Res., 1963–69; Procs of Nat. Acad. of Scis, USA, 1970–71; Editl Consultant, King's Fund Centre for Health Service Develt, 1990–93; Pubns Editor, Camden History Soc., 1993– (meetings co-ordinator, 2008–12, 2013–; website manager, 2010–; publisher, Hampstead Manorial 17C Court Records, 2010–). Student Gov., City Lit. Inst., 1999–2001. Chm., Hampstead Music Club, 1996–99; Patron, Cavatina Chamber Music Trust, 2003–; Patron Friend, Hampstead Town Hall. FSA 2010. First non-med. ARCP, 2000; Hon. Fellow, Assoc. of Clin. Biochemistry, 2005. Hon. DSc Salford, 1993. Waverley Gold Medal for scientific writing, 1955; Meritorious Award, Council of Biology Editors, USA, 1984. *Publications:* Scientific Writing for Graduate Students, 1969, 4th edn 1986; Medical Research Systems in Europe, 1973; The Ciba Foundation: an analytic history 1949–1974, 1974; Writing Scientific Papers in English, 1975; In-Service Training series: of Physiological Measurement Technicians, 1988; of Medical Physics Technicians, 1989; of Medical Laboratory Assistants, 1991; of Rehabilitation Engineering Technicians, 1992; (ed) From Primrose Hill to Euston Road, 1995; Atherosclerosis X, 1995; A Constant Vigil: 100 years of the Heath and Old Hampstead Society, 1997; (ed) Streets of Bloomsbury and Fitzrovia (a historical survey), 1997; (ed) East of Bloomsbury, 1998; How to Teach Scientific Communication, 1999; (ed) Streets of Old Holborn, 1999, 2nd edn 2010; (ed) The Streets of Hampstead, 3rd edn, 2000; (ed) The Good Grave Guide to Hampstead Cemetery, Fortune Green, 2000; (ed) Streets of St Giles, 2000; (ed) Victorian Seven Dials, 2001; (ed) 200 Years of Local Justice in Hampstead and Clerkenwell, 2001; (ed) The Railways of Camden, 2002; (ed jtly) Streets of St Pancras, 2002; (ed jtly) 20th-Century Camden Recalled, 2002; (ed jtly) Streets of Camden Town, 2003; (ed jtly) Streets of Kentish Town, 2005; (ed) Wartime St Pancras, 2006; (ed jtly) Streets of Gospel Oak and West Kentish Town, 2006; (ed) The Greville Estate: the history of a Kilburn neighbourhood, 2007; (ed) Buried in Hampstead, 2nd edn, 2007; (ed jtly) Streets of Highgate, 2007; (ed jtly) George Morland: a London artist in eighteenth-century Camden, 2008; (ed) Streets of Belsize, 2009; (ed) A Better Life: oral histories of Italian immigrants to Clerkenwell, London from 1850, 2011; (ed jtly) Streets of St Giles, 2012; The King's Cross Fraudster Leopold Redpath: his life and times, 2013; articles on scientific writing, lipids of the arterial wall, editing of biomed. jls, prevention and treatment of handicapping disorders, screening for spina bifida, quality in pathology labs, costing and ethics in clin. chem., history of Heath and Old Hampstead Soc., 18th-century doctors in Bloomsbury, clinical significance of antioxidants, institutional invasion of Queen Square, London between 1846 and 2011, life in Hampstead in the 17th century, inspiration for Debussy's Golliwogg Cakewalk. *Recreations:* chamber music (pianist), local history. *Address:* 1 Akenside Road, NW3 5BS.

WOODFORD, Neil Russell, CBE 2013; Head of Investment, Woodford Investment Management, since 2014; *b* Cookham, 2 March 1960. *Educ:* Univ. of Exeter (BA Econs and Agricl Econs 1981); London Business Sch. (postgrad. studies in finance). Fund Manager, Eagle Star, 1987–88; Hd, UK Equities, and Fund Manager, Invesco Perpetual, 1988–2014. *Address:* Woodford Investment Management, 9400 Garsington Road, Oxford OX4 2HN. *T:* (01865) 809000. *E:* info@woodfordfunds.com.

WOODFORD, Stephen William John; Chairman, Lexis Agency, since 2013; *b* 11 Feb. 1959; *s* of John and Barbara Woodford; *m* 1988, Amelia Wylton Dickson; two *s* two *d*. *Educ:* Tomlinscote Sch., Frimley; City Univ. (BSc Hons). Grad. trainee, Nestlé Co. Ltd, 1980–82; Account Manager, Lintas Advertising, 1982–85; Account Dir, Waldron Allen Henry & Thompson, 1985–89; Account Dir, subseq. Gp Account Dir, WCRS, 1989–91; Dep. Man. Dir, Leo Burnett, 1991–94; Client Services Dir, 1994–95, Man. Dir, 1995–99, CEO, 1999–2005, WCRS; CEO, Engine, 2005–07; Chm. and CEO, DDB London, 2007–12; Chm., adam&eve/DDB, 2012–13. Co-founder and non-exec. Dir, Ffrees Family Finance, 2011–. Non-exec. Dir, Brighton and Sussex Univ. Hosps NHS Trust, 2013–. Mem. Bd, Creative Skillset, Learning and Skills Council for creative industries, 2011–. Pres., Inst. Practitioners in Advertising, 2003–05; Pres. and Trustee, Nat. Advertising Benevolent Soc., 2009–. Trustee: Changing Faces Charity, 2003– (Chm., 2003–07); History of Advertising Trust. *Recreations:* family, riding, running, the countryside. *Address:* Lexis Agency, 75 Bermondsey Street, SE1 3XF.

WOODFORD-HOLLICK, Susan Mary; *see* Hollick, Lady.

WOODGATE, Terence Allan, RDI 2003; furniture and lighting designer; *b* 5 Feb. 1953; *s* of Charles and Ethel Woodgate; *m* 1979, Paula Casey; two *s*. *Educ:* Westminster Coll.; London Coll. of Furniture. Work exhibited in perm. collections of Museu d'Art Decoratives, Barcelona and V&A Mus. British Design Award, Design Council, 1992; Red Dot Best of the Best Award, Design Zentrum Nordrhein Westfalen, Germany, 1992; Industrie Form Ecology Award, Germany, 1995. *Address:* West Hill, Little Trodgers Lane, Mayfield, E Sussex TN20 6PW. *T:* (01435) 872800. *E:* terence@terencewoodgate.com. *W:* www.terencewoodgate.com.

WOODHALL, David Massey, CBE 1992; Partner, The Woodhall Consultancy, 1992–2010; *b* 25 Aug. 1934; *s* of Douglas J. D. and Esme Dorothy Woodhall; *m* 1954, Margaret A. Howarth; two *s*. *Educ:* Bishop Holgate's Sch., Barnsley; Royds Hall, Huddersfield; Henley Administrative Staff Coll. Dip. Leeds Sch. of Architecture and Town Planning. West Riding CC, 1951–60; Cumberland CC, 1960–63; Northamptonshire CC, 1963–82: County Planning Officer, 1971–80; Asst Chief Executive, 1980–82; Chief Exec., Commn for New Towns, 1982–92. Dir, Adnams Co. plc, 1986–2006. Consultant, Caws and Morris, Chartered Surveyors, 1992–2004. A Countryside Comr, 1996–99; Mem., Countryside Agency, 1999–2001. *Recreations:* National Hunt racing, landscape, food and wine. *Address:* 2 Hardingstone Lane, Hardingstone, Northampton NN4 6DE. *T:* (01604) 764654.

WOODHAM, Prof. Jonathan Michael; Professor of History of Design, 1993–2015, now Research Professor, Director, Centre for Research Development (Arts and Architecture), since 1998, and Director of Research and Development (Arts and Humanities), 2012–15, University of Brighton; *b* 8 June 1950; *s* of Ronald Ernest Woodham and Kathleen Isabel Woodham (*née* Malone); *m* 1981, Amanda Grace Callan Smith; two *s*. *Educ:* Downside Sch.; Edinburgh Coll. of Art, Univ. of Edinburgh (MA 1st cl. Hons (Fine Art) 1973); Courtauld Inst. of Art, London (MA (British Romantic Art) 1974). Lectr, 1974–75, Sen. Lectr, 1975–82, in Hist. of Art and Design, Staffordshire Polytech.; Brighton Polytechnic, later University of Brighton: Course Dir, Hist. of Design, 1982–93; Dir, Design Hist. Res. Centre, 1993–2001. Member: Hist. of Art and Design Bd, 1984–87, Register of Special Advrs, 1987–92, CNAA; Quality Assessment Panel, 1996–98, RAE Panel, 2001, HEFCE; Postgrad. Qualifications Res. Panel, Visual Arts & Media, AHRB, 1998–2004; Bd, Internat. Conference for Design Hist. and Design Studies, 1999–; AHRC Peer Review Coll., 2004–15; ESRC Peer Review Coll., 2010–; Social Scis and Humanities Res. Council Canada, 2008, 2011; Icelandic Res. Fund, 2011, 2012; Panel Mem., AHRC Block Grant Partnerships, 2011; AHRC Strategic Reviewer, 2011–. Mem., Hong Kong Accreditation Council, 1987–; Expert Scientific Advr, Culture and Soc. Panel, Acad. of Finland, 2003–09. Chm., Design Hist. Soc., 1995–97. Member, Editorial Board: Jl of Design History, 1987–2004 (Mem., Editl Adv. Bd, 2004–); Design Issues, 1994–; Art Design and Communication in Higher Educn, 2002–10; Design History (Japan), 2003–; Animation: an Interdisciplinary Jl, 2006–15; Jl of Media and Communications, 2012–. *Publications:* The Industrial Designer and the Public, 1983; Twentieth-Century Ornament, 1991; Twentieth-Century Design, 1997; Design and Popular Politics in the Postwar Period: the Britain Can Make It Exhibition 1946, 1999; A Dictionary of Modern Design, 2004; (ed jtly) Image, Power and Space: studies in consumption and identity, 2007; (ed jtly) Art and Design at Brighton 1859–2009: from arts and manufactures to the creative and cultural industries, 2009; Jiří Pelcl - Czech Design, 2012; contribs to jls, incl. Jl of Design Hist., Design Issues, Design Hist. Japan, Temes de Disseny, L'Arca, Design, Crafts, and Architecture, and to Procs British Acad. 2010. *Recreations:* cookery, gardening, travel, drinking wine. *Address:* 116 Hollingbury Park Avenue, Brighton BN1 7JP. *T:* (01273) 506319. *E:* j.m.woodham@brighton.ac.uk.

WOODHAMS, Stephen Robert; designer (gardens and exteriors); design director, since 1990; Founder, Stephen Woodhams Design Ltd, London and Ibiza, since 2008; *b* 17 July 1964; *s* of late Robert and Joy Woodhams. *Educ:* RHS Certificate. Paul Temple Ltd, 1982; buyer, Moyses Stevens, 1984; Dir, Horticultural Innovations, 1986; Founder, Woodhams Ltd, 1990–2007, Woodhams Landscapes Ltd, 1994–2007. Accredited RHS Judge, 2009. *Publications:* Flower Power, 1999; Portfolio of Contemporary Gardens, 2000. *Recreations:* photography, running. *T:* (020) 7735 3798. *E:* stephen@stephenwoodhams.com. *Club:* Blacks.

WOODHEAD, Vice-Adm. Sir (Anthony) Peter, KCB 1992; DL; Prisons' Ombudsman, 1994–99; *b* 30 July 1939; *s* of Leslie and Nancy Woodhead; *m* 1964, Carol; one *s* one *d*. *Educ:* Leeds Grammar Sch.; Conway; BRNC Dartmouth. Seaman Officer; Pilot, 1962; Aircraft Carriers, Borneo Campaign; CO, HM Ships Jupiter, 1974, Rhyl, 1975; NDC 1976; Naval Plans Div., MoD, 1977; CSO to Flag Officer, Third Flotilla, 1980; COS to FO Comdg Falklands Task Force, 1982; Captain, Fourth Frigate Sqdn, 1983; RCDS 1984; Dir, Naval Ops, 1985; CO HMS Illustrious, 1986; Flag Officer: Flotilla Two, 1988; Flotilla One, 1989. Dep. SACLANT, 1991–93. Lay Reader: Guildford, 1991; Chichester, 1997. Pres., Marriage Resource, 1995–2004. Dep. Chm., BMT, 1996–2011. Chm., Crime Reduction Initiatives, 2001–10; Member: Security Vetting Appeals Panel, 1997–2009; Armed Forces Pay Review Body, 2001–04. Dir, Beaconlight Trust, 2004–13. Gov., Aldro Sch., 1996–2013; Trustee, Kainos prison therapeutic community, 1999–2013. DL E Sussex, 2012. *Recreations:* ball games, antique restoration. *Club:* Royal Navy of 1765 and 1785.

WOODHEAD, David James; education consultant, since 2004; National Director, Independent Schools Council Information Service (formerly Independent Schools Information Service), 1985–2004; Deputy General Secretary, Independent Schools Council, 1998–2004; *b* 9 Nov. 1943; *s* of late Frank and Polly Woodhead; *m* 1974, Carole Underwood; two *s*. *Educ:* Queen Elizabeth Grammar Sch., Wakefield; Univ. of Leicester (BA Hons). Journalist: Cambridge Evening News (educn corresp.), 1965–68; Sunday Telegraph, 1968–75; ILEA Press Office: Press Officer, 1975–78; Chief Press Officer, 1978–85; Hon. Press Officer, London Schs Symphony Orch., 1975–84. Led UK Repn at first internat. conf. on private schs in China, Beijing, 1999. Trustee: Jt Educnl Trust, 1988–2004; Oratory Gp, 1995–98; EAC Educnl Trust, 2005–13; Founder-Trustee, Nat. Youth String Orch. (formerly Nat. ISIS Strings Acad., then Nat. Youth Strings Acad.), 1995–. Mem., Dresden Trust, 1995– (Trustee, 2005–; Jt Vice Chm., 2011–13; Founder, Dresden Scholars' Scheme, 2001). Member: NW Herts Community Health Council, 1976–79; Adv. Develt Bd, Rudolf Kempe Soc. for Young Musicians, 2000– (Trustee, 2004–); Adv. Bd, Global Educn Mgt Systems Ltd, 2005–07 (Special Advr, 2007–09); British-German Assoc. Youthbridge Cttee, 2008–; European Movement Surrey Cttee, 2015–. University of Leicester: Schs and Colls Liaison Consultant, 2005–; Mem. Council, 2000–09; Mem. Court, 2000–09; Life Mem. Court, 2009. Consultant, Cherwell Schs Gp, 2010–12. Governor: Battle Abbey Sch., 1988–91; St John's Sch., Leatherhead, 1994–2011 (Vice-Chm., 2006–11; Chm., Educn Cttee, 2001–10); Feltonfleet Prep. Sch., Cobham, 1998–2001; City of London Sch. for Girls, 2002–06; Purcell Sch., 2004–13; Hon. Gov., Wakefield Grammar Sch. Foundn, 2004–09. FRSA 1990. Medal of Honour, Soc. for Reconstruction of the Frauenkirche, Dresden, 2007. *Publications:* Choosing Your Independent School, annually, 1985–99; (ed) Good Communications Guide, 1986, 2nd edn 1989; The ISC Guide to Accredited Independent Schools, annually, 2000–04; (contrib.) Education in the UK, 2002; (ed jtly and contrib.) A Trust for Our Times: the story of the Dresden Trust, 2015; numerous newspaper and magazine articles. *Recreations:* family, classical music, opera (a Wagner fanatic), books, German and Austrian history, travel. *Address:* 29 Randalls Road, Leatherhead, Surrey KT22 7TQ. *T:* (01372) 373206.

WOODHEAD, Prof. Linda Jane Pauline, MBE 2013; Professor of Sociology of Religion, Lancaster University, since 2006; *b* Taunton, 15 Feb. 1964; *d* of Ronald Woodhead and Penelope Woodhead; *m* 2007, Alexander Mercer. *Educ:* Richard Huish Coll., Taunton; Emmanuel Coll., Cambridge (BA Theol. and Religious Studies 1985). Lectr, Ripon Coll., Cuddesdon, 1988–92; Lancaster University: Lectr, 1992–2000; Sen. Lectr, 2000–06. Dir, AHRC/ESRC Religion and Society Prog., 2007–13; Mem., ESRC, 2013–. Co-Founder and Organiser, Westminster Faith Debates, 2012–. Pres., Modern Church, 2014–. Hon. DD Uppsala 2009; Hon. PhD Zurich 2014. *Publications:* (ed jtly) Diana: the making of a media icon, 1999; (ed jtly) Religion in Modern Times, 2000; (ed) Reinventing Christianity: nineteenth century contexts, 2001; (ed jtly) Religions in the Modern World: traditions and transformations, 2002, 2nd edn 2009; (ed) Peter Berger and the Study of Religion, 2002; (ed jtly) Predicting Religion, 2003; (ed jtly) Congregational Studies in the UK, 2004; Christianity: a very short introduction, 2004; An Introduction to Christianity, 2004; (with Paul Heelas) The Spiritual Revolution, 2005; (with Ole Riis) A Sociology of Religious Emotions, 2010; (ed with Rebecca Catto) Religion and Change in Modern Britain, 2012; (ed jtly) Everyday Lived Islam in Europe, 2013; (ed) The Westminster Faith Debates, 2013; (ed jtly) A Sociology of Prayer, 2015. *Recreations:* friends and social media, American muscle cars, fashion, gardening, sleeping. *Address:* Department of Politics, Philosophy and Religion, Lancaster University LA1 4YD. *T:* (01524) 510819. *E:* l.woodhead@lancaster.ac.uk.

WOODHEAD, Prof. Martin, PhD; Professor of Childhood Studies, Open University, 2003–14, now Emeritus; *b* Birmingham, 4 Dec. 1949; *s* of Maurice Woodhead and Eunice Woodhead; *m* 1974, Judith M. Park; three *s* one *d*. *Educ:* Moseley Grammar Sch., Birmingham; Univ. of Manchester (BA 1st Cl. Hons Psychol. 1971); Univ. of Leicester (MA 1972); Open Univ. (PhD 1984). NFER, 1973–77; Faculty of Educn, Open Univ., 1977–2014. Sen. Associate, Univ. of Oxford/Young Lives Study, 2005–. Advr, All Our Children, BBC TV series, 1984–90; Consultant, UN Cttee on the Rights of the Child, 2005; Chm., Adv. Bd, Early Childhood Prog., Open Soc. Foundn, 2008–15; Trustee, UNICEF UK, 2012– (Vice Chm., 2014–). Co-Editor, Children and Society Jl, 2003–11. *Publications:* Intervening in Disadvantage, 1976; Pre-school Education in Western Europe, 1979; In Search of the Rainbow, 1996; (ed jtly) Cultural Worlds of Early Childhood, 1998; (ed jtly) Changing Childhoods: local and global, 2003. *E:* martinwoodhead@me.com.

WOODHEAD, Vice-Adm. Sir Peter; *see* Woodhead, Vice-Adm. Sir A. P.

WOODHEAD, Robin George; Chairman, Sotheby's International, since 2008 (Chief Executive, 2000–08); *b* 28 April 1951; *s* of Walter Henry Woodhead and Gladys Catherine (*née* Ferguson); *m* 1980, Mary Fitzgerald Allen, *qv* (marr. diss. 1991). *Educ:* Mt Pleasant Sch., Salisbury, Rhodesia; UC of Rhodesia and Nyasaland (LLB Hons London ext.). Admitted Solicitor, 1978; Man. Dir, Premier Man Ltd, 1980–86; Chief Executive: Nat. Investment Gp, 1986–90; London Commodity Exchange, 1991–97; Man. Dir, 1998–99, Chief Exec., 1999–2000, Sotheby's Europe; Chief Exec., Sotheby's Europe and Asia, 2000–06. Chairman: Internat. Petroleum Exchange, 1980–86; Hofesh Shechter Co., 2008–. Chairman: Rambert Dance Co., 1995–2000; Music Research Inst., 1997–2000. Dep. Chm. and Gov., S Bank Centre, 2004–. Trustee and Chm., David Rattray Meml Trust, 2007–; Trustee, African Arts Trust, 2011–. *Recreations:* game reserve development in Zululand, riding, music, visual arts, performing arts. *Address:* Sotheby's, 34–35 New Bond Street, W1A 2AA. *T:* (020) 7293 6066.

WOODHOUSE, family name of **Baron Terrington**.

WOODHOUSE, Rev. Canon Alison Ruth; Vicar, St Luke's, Formby, 1995–2007; Chaplain to the Queen, 2005–13; *b* 14 Aug. 1943; *d* of Harold and May Woodhouse. *Educ:* Bedford Coll. of Educn (Cert Ed 1964); DipTh London Univ. 1971 (ext.). Primary sch. teacher, Huncoat CP Sch., Accrington, 1964–68; licensed as Parish Worker, Lichfield dio., 1971; ordained deaconess, 1978, deacon, 1987, priest, 1994; Parish Deacon, then Curate, Burscough Bridge, 1987–95; Area Dean, Sefton, 2000–05. Hon. Canon, Liverpool Cathedral, 2002–07. *Recreations:* singing in a choir, music, cinema. *Address:* 16 Fountains Way, Liverpool L37 4HF.

WOODHOUSE, Ven. Andrew Henry, DSC 1945; MA; Archdeacon of Hereford and Canon Residentiary, Hereford Cathedral, 1982–91, now Archdeacon Emeritus; *b* 30 Jan. 1923; *s* of H. A. Woodhouse, Dental Surgeon, Hanover Square, W1, and Woking, Surrey, and Mrs P. Woodhouse; unmarried. *Educ:* Lancing Coll.; The Queen's Coll., Oxford. MA 1949. Served War, RNVR, 1942–46 (Lieut). Oxford, 1941–42 and 1946–47; Lincoln Theological Coll., 1948–50. Deacon, 1950; Priest, 1951; Curate of All Saints, Poplar, 1950–56; Vicar of St Martin, West Drayton, 1956–70; Rural Dean of Hillingdon, 1967–70; Archdeacon of Ludlow and Rector of Wistanstow, 1970–82. *Recreations:* photography, walking. *Address:* Orchard Cottage, Bracken Close, Woking, Surrey GU22 7HD. *T:* (01483) 760671. *Club:* Naval.

See also R. M. Woodhouse.

WOODHOUSE, Ven. (Charles) David (Stewart); Archdeacon of Warrington, 1981–2001, now Emeritus; Vicar of St Peter's, Hindley, 1981–92; *b* 23 Dec. 1934; *s* of Rev. Hector and Elsie Woodhouse. *Educ:* Silcoates School, Wakefield; Kelham Theological College; Lancaster Univ. (MA 1995). Curate of St Wilfrid's, Halton, Leeds, 1959–63; Youth Chaplain, Kirkby Team Ministry, Diocese of Liverpool, 1963–66; Curate of St John's, Pembroke, Bermuda, 1966–69; Asst Gen. Secretary, CEMS, 1969–70; Gen. Sec., 1970–76; Rector of Ideford, Ashcombe and Luton and Domestic Chaplain to Bishop of Exeter, 1976–81. Hon. Canon, Liverpool Cathedral, 1983. *Address:* 9 Rob Lane, Newton-le-Willows WA12 0DR.

WOODHOUSE, Charles Frederick, CVO 1998; DL; Partner, Farrer and Co., Solicitors, 1969–99 (Consultant, 1999–2001); Solicitor to the Duke of Edinburgh, 1983–2001; *b* 6 June 1941; *s* of late Wilfrid Meynell Woodhouse and Peggy Woodhouse (*née* Kahl); *m* 1969, Margaret Joan Cooper; one *s* two *d*. *Educ:* Marlborough; McGill Univ.; Peterhouse, Cambridge (BA Hons 1963; MA Hons). Hon. Legal Advr, Commonwealth Games Council for England, 1983–2007; Legal Advr, CCPR, 1971–99 (Mem., Inquiry on Amateur Status, 1986–88). Pres., British Assoc. for Sport and Law, 1997–2000; Founder and Chm., Sports Dispute Resolution Panel, 1997–2007. Dir, Santos USA Corp., 1992–2002. Chm., Rural Regeneration Cumbria, 2003–06; Dir, Cumbria Vision Ltd (formerly Cumbria Vision Renaissance Ltd), 2006–08. Mem., Royal Parks Rev. Gp, 1992–96. Chairman: Cheviot Trust, 1991–97; Rank Pension Plan Trustee Ltd, 1992–2001; Trustee: Mulberry Trust, 1988–; Aim Foundn, 1988–2007; LSA Charitable Trust, 1991–; Brian Johnston Meml Trust, 1996–99; Yehudi Menuhin Meml Trust, 1999–2001; Cumbria Community Foundn, 2002–08; Hospice at Home, Carlisle and N Lakeland, 2002–11; Athletics Foundn, 2004–15; Lowther Castle and Gardens Trust, 2007–11. Governor: Nelson Thomlinson Sch., Wigton, 2003–11; St Bees Sch., 2004–08. DL Cumbria, 2007. *Publications:* articles on sports law, incl. The Law and Sport, 1972; The Role of the Lawyer in Sport, 1993; contrib. to Jl British Assoc. for Sport and Law. *Recreations:* cricket, golf, gardens and trees, Owen's Southsea, Cumbria's historic environment, writing (Mem., Mungrisdale Writers). *Address:* Quarry Hill House, Mealsgate, Cumbria CA7 1AE. *T:* (01697) 371225. *E:* cfwoodhouse@btinternet.com. *Clubs:* Oxford and Cambridge, MCC; Hawks (Cambridge); Worplesdon Golf; Silloth on Solway Golf (Capt., 2010); Free Foresters, Guildford Cricket (Pres., 1991–2002), Surrey County Cricket, Lord's Taverners.

WOODHOUSE, Ven. David; *see* Woodhouse, Ven. C. D. S.

WOODHOUSE, James Stephen; Director, ISIS East, 1994–2000; *b* 21 May 1933; *s* of late Rt Rev. J. W. Woodhouse, sometime Bishop of Thetford, and late Mrs K. M. Woodhouse; *m* 1957, Sarah, *d* of late Col Hubert Blount, Cley, Norfolk; three *s* one *d*. *Educ:* St Edward's Sch.; St Catharine's Coll., Cambridge. BA (English) Cantab, 1957; MA 1961. Nat. Service, 14th Field Regt RA, 1953. Asst Master, Westminster Sch., 1957; Under Master and Master of the Queen's Scholars, 1963; Headmaster, Rugby Sch., 1967–81; Headmaster, Lancing Coll., 1981–93. Chairman: NABC Religious Adv. Cttee, 1971–93; Bloxham Project, 1972–77; Head Masters' Conf., 1979; Joint Standing Cttee of HMC, IAPS and GSA, 1981–86; Vice-Chm., E-SU Schoolboy Scholarship Cttee, 1973–77. Director: The Norfolk Boat, 1993–2012; Holkham Pageant, 1994. Mem. Council (formerly Cttee of Mgt), RNLI, 1994–2006. Trustee and Dir, Assoc. for Educn and Guardianship of Internat. Students, 2001–13. Gov., Norwich Cathedral Inst., 2000–11. *Recreations:* sailing, music, hill walking. *Address:* Welcome Cottage, Wiveton, Holt, Norfolk NR25 7TH.

WOODHOUSE, Prof. John Henry, PhD; FRS 2000; Professor of Geophysics, 1990–2014, now Emeritus, and Head of Department of Earth Sciences, 2000–03, 2011–12, University of Oxford; Fellow of Worcester College, Oxford, 1990–2014; *b* 15 April 1949; *s* of G. B. Woodhouse. *Educ:* Southall Grammar Sch.; Bristol Univ. (BSc 1970); King's Coll., Cambridge (MA, PhD 1975). Fellow, King's Coll., Cambridge, 1974–78; Vis. Asst Res. Geophysicist, Inst. of Geophysics and Planetary Physics, Univ. of Calif., San Diego, 1976–77; Asst Prof., 1978–80, Associate Prof., 1980–83, Prof. of Geophysics, 1983–90, Harvard Univ. Chm., Commn on Seismological Theory, Internat. Assoc. of Seismol. and Physics of Earth's Interior, 1983–87. Fellow, Amer. Geophys. Union (Macelwane Award, 1984; Inge Lehmann Medal, 2001). Beno Gutenberg Medal, Eur. Geoscis Union, 2008; Gold Medal for Geophysics, RAS, 2010. *Publications:* many contribs to learned jls. *Address:* Department of Earth Sciences, Parks Road, Oxford OX1 3AN; Worcester College, Oxford OX1 2HB.

WOODHOUSE, Prof. John Robert, FBA 1995; Fiat Serena Professor of Italian Studies, Oxford, 1989–2001; Fellow, Magdalen College, Oxford, 1990–2001, now Emeritus; *b* 17 June 1937; *s* of Horace Woodhouse and Iris Evelyn Pewton; *m* 1967, Gaynor Mathias. *Educ:* King Edward VI Grammar School, Stourbridge; Hertford College, Oxford (MA, DLitt); Univ. of Pisa; PhD Wales. Nat. Service, RAF, 1955–57. Asst Lectr in Italian, Univ. of Aberdeen, 1961–62; British Council Scholar, Scuola Normale Superiore, Pisa, 1962–63; Asst Lectr and Lectr, UCNW, Bangor, 1963–66; Lectr and Sen. Lectr, Univ. of Hull, 1966–73; Oxford University: Univ. Lectr in Italian and Fellow of St Cross Coll., 1973–84; Lectr at Jesus Coll., 1973, St Edmund Hall, 1975, Brasenose Coll., 1976; Fellow, 1984–89, Supernumerary Fellow, 1991, Pembroke Coll.; Founding Chm., Oxford Italian Assoc., 1990–2010. Harvard Old Dominion Foundn Fellow, Villa I Tatti, 1969; Founding Fellow, Centro Studi Dannunziani, Pescara, 1979; Corresponding Fellow: Accad. lett. ital. dell'Arcadia, 1980; Accad. della Crusca, 1991; Commissione per i Testi di Lingua, Bologna, 1992; Sen. Res. Fellow, Center for Medieval and Renaissance Studies, UCLA, 1985; Fellow: Huntington Liby, Calif., 1986; Newberry Liby, Chicago, 1988. Mem., Exec. Cttee, Soc. for Italian Studies, 1979–85 and 1989–95; Pres., MHRA, 2008 (Mem., Exec. Cttee, 1984–94; Hon. Life Mem., 1994). Editor (Italian), Modern Language Review, 1984–94; Mem., Editl Bd, Italian Studies, 1987–91. Gov., British Inst. of Florence, 1991–2001. Serena Medal, British Academy, 2002. Cavaliere Ufficiale, Order of Merit (Italy), 1991. *Publications:* Italo Calvino: a reappraisal and an appreciation of the trilogy, 1968; (ed) Italo Calvino, Il barone rampante, 1970; (ed) V. Borghini, Scritti inediti o rari sulla lingua, 1971; (ed) V. Borghini, Storia della nobiltà fiorentina, 1974; Baldesar Castiglione, a reassessment of the Cortegiano, 1978; (ed) G. D'Annunzio, Alcyone, 1978; (ed with P. R. Horne) G. Rossetti, Lettere familiari, 1983; (ed jtly) G. Rossetti, Carteggi, I, 1984, II, 1988, III, 1992, IV, 1996, V, 2002, VI, 2006; (ed jtly) The Languages of Literature in Renaissance Italy, 1988; From Castiglione to Chesterfield: the decline in the courtier's manual, 1991; (ed) Dante and Governance, 1997; Gabriele D'Annunzio: defiant archangel, 1998 (trans. Italian, 1999; Premio D'Annunzio, 2000); Gabriele D'Annunzio tra Italia e Inghilterra, 2003; Il Generale e il Comandante: Ceccherini e D'Annunzio a Fiume, 2004; L'Ottavo Giurato: Giuseppe Sovera con D'Annunzio a Fiume, 2008; articles in learned jls. *Recreation:* gardening. *Address:* Magdalen College, Oxford OX1 4AU.

WOODHOUSE, Rev. Jonathan, CB 2014; Chaplain-General, HM Land Forces, 2011–14; Chaplain, Moorlands College, since 2015; *b* Cardiff, 29 March 1955; *s* of Herbert and Joan Woodhouse; *m* 1978, Jackie Evetts; one *s* one *d*. *Educ:* Whitchurch Grammar Sch.; London Bible Coll., Spurgeon's Coll.; BA Hons CNAA; Open Univ. (BSc); MTh Wales. Ordained to Baptist Ministry, 1980; Asst Minister, Eastbourne, 1980–85; Minister, Selsdon, 1985–90; Regtl Chaplain in Germany, Cyprus, UK and Hong Kong, 1990–2000; Chaplain, HQ Land Comd, 2000–01; Staff Chaplain to Chaplain Gen., Upavon, 2001–02; Senior Chaplain: 16 Air Assault Bde, Colchester, 2002–05; RMA Sandhurst, 2005–06; Asst Chaplain-Gen., Germany, 2006–08; Dep. Chaplain-Gen., 2008–11. Convenor, United Navy, Army and Air Force Bd, 2015. QHC 2008–14. *Recreations:* enjoyable interest in Cardiff City FC, Welsh Rugby, England cricket, downhill ski-ing at a Padre's pace. *Address:* Henbury, New Inn Road, Bartley, Hampshire SO40 2LR. *T:* (023) 8081 3776. *E:* jonandjackie@hotmail.com.

WOODHOUSE, Prof. Kenneth Walter, MD; FRCP; Professor of Geriatric Medicine, 1990–2012, now Emeritus, and Professor of Medicine, 2010–12, now Emeritus, School of Medicine, Cardiff University (formerly University of Wales College of Medicine); *b* 18 July 1954; *s* of Walter and Marion Woodhouse; *m* 1994, Judith Paul; three *s*. *Educ:* Southampton University Med. Sch. (BM Hons 1977); Univ. of Newcastle upon Tyne (MD 1985). FRCP 1990. MRC Trng Fellow, 1980–83; MRC Travelling Fellow, Karolinska Inst., 1984–85; Sen. Lectr in Medicine (Geriatrics) and Clinical Pharmacol., and Consultant Physician, Univ. of Newcastle upon Tyne, 1985–90; University of Wales College of Medicine (later School of Medicine, Cardiff University): Vice Dean of Medicine, 1997–2000; Dean of Medicine, 2000–04; Pro Vice-Chancellor, 2004–10. Member: Cttee on Safety of Medicines, 1998–2005; Pharmacovigilance Cttee, MHRA, 2006–12; Chm., Nat. Commng Bd, Health Commn Wales, 2002–08. *Publications:* (ed jtly) Topics in Ageing Research in Europe, vol. 13, The Liver, Metabolism and Ageing, 1989; (with J. Pascual) Hypertension in Elderly People, 1996; (with M. Hasan) Managing Hypertension in Practice, Book 2, The Elderly Hypertensive Patient, 1997; (ed jtly) Drug Therapy in Old Age, 1998; (ed jtly) Brocklehurst's Textbook of Geriatric Medicine and Gerontology, 2010. *Recreations:* hill walking, scout leader, science fiction. *Address:* Department of Geriatric Medicine, Academic Centre, University Hospital Llandough, Penlan Road, Penarth CF64 2XX. *T:* (029) 2071 6986, *Fax:* (029) 2071 1267. *E:* woodhousekw@cf.ac.uk.

WOODHOUSE, Michael; *see* Woodhouse, R. M.

WOODHOUSE, Prof. the Hon. Nicholas Michael John, PhD; FInstP, FIMA; Professor of Mathematics, University of Oxford, 2006–10, now Emeritus (Chairman of Mathematics, 2001–10; Deputy Head, Mathematical, Physical and Life Sciences Division, 2011–12); Fellow of Wadham College, Oxford, since 1977 (Sub-Warden, since 2014); *b* Knebworth, Herts, 27 Feb. 1949; *s* of 5th Baron Terrington, DSO, OBE and Lady Davina Woodhouse (*née* Lytton), *widow* of 5th Earl of Erne; *m* 1973, Mary Jane Stormont Mowat, *qv*; one *s*. *Educ:* Christ Church, Oxford (BA 1970); King's Coll. London (MSc 1971; PhD 1973). FInstP 2002; FIMA 2004. University of Oxford: Lectr, 1977–97; Reader, 1997–2006; Sen. Tutor, Wadham Coll., 1982–86; Mem., North Commn of Inquiry, 1994. Fellow, Eton Coll., 1995–2007. Mem. Council, 1998–2009, Treas., 2002–09, London Mathematical Soc.; Pres., Clay Math. Inst., 2012–. *Publications:* Geometric Quantization, 1979, 2nd edn 1991; Introduction to Analytical Dynamics, 1987; (with L. J. Mason) Integrability, Self-duality, and Twistor Theory, 1995; Special Relativity, 2003; General Relativity, 2007. *Recreations:* walking, gardening. *Address:* Wadham College, Oxford OX1 3PN. *T:* (01865) 277900. *E:* Nick.Woodhouse@maths.ox.ac.uk.
See also Baron Terrington.

WOODHOUSE, (Ronald) Michael, CVO 2000; Chairman, Rexam PLC (formerly Bowater), 1993–96 (Director, 1988–96); Chairman, Prince's Trust Volunteers, 1991–2000; *b* 19 Aug. 1927; *s* of Henry Alfred Woodhouse and Phyllis Woodhouse (*née* Gemmell); *m* 1955, Quenilda Mary (*d* 1997), *d* of Rt Rev. Neville Vincent Gorton; one *s* three *d*. *Educ:* Lancing Coll.; Queen's Coll., Oxford (BA Mod. History). Courtaulds plc, 1951–91: Dir, 1976–91; Dep. Chm., 1986–91; Man. Dir, 1972–79, Chm., 1979–84, Internat. Paint Co.; Chm., British Cellophane Ltd, 1979–86. A Director: RSA Exam. Board, 1991–95; RSA Exams and Assessment Foundn, 1995–97; Mem., Prince's Trust Council, 1995–2000. Dir, London Mozart Players, 1990–97; Mem. Council of Mgt, Friends of Royal Acad., 1996–2003; Trustee, Royal Acad. Pension Fund, 1997–2003. CCMI (CBIM 1978); FRSA 1979. *Recreations:* walking in Lake District, watching Rugby and cricket, opera, music, gardening, art, reading. *Address:* Tankards, Wonersh, Guildford, Surrey GU5 0PF. *T:* (01483) 892078; Dalehead, Hartsop, Patterdale, Cumbria CA11 0NZ. *Clubs:* Carlton; Vincent's (Oxford).
See also Ven. A. H. Woodhouse.

WOODLEY, Anthony; Executive Officer, Unite the Union, since 2011 (Joint General Secretary, 2007–11; General Secretary, Transport and General Workers' Union, 2003–07, on merger with Amicus); *b* 2 Jan. 1948; *s* of George Woodley. Ellesmere Port factory, Vauxhall Motors, 1967–89; Dist Official, 1989–91, Nat. Official, 1991–2002, Dep. Gen. Sec., 2002–03, TGWU. *Address:* Unite the Union, Unite House, 128 Theobalds Road, WC1X 8TN.

WOODLEY, Karin Lee; Chief Executive, Cambridge House, since 2013; *b* London, 11 Aug. 1961; *d* of Wilfred Trevor Woodley and Hon. Juliet Priscilla Mary Duncombe; one *s*; *m* 2008, Michael Kenneth Herbert (marr. diss. 2015). *Educ:* Goldsmiths Coll., Univ. of London (BMus Hons 1982). Chief Exec., Minorities' Arts Adv. Service, 1985–89; Partner, Keya Associates, 1987–90; Dep. Dir, Camden Arts Centre, 1990–2000; Dir, Tabernacle Centre for Arts and Learning, 2000–05; Chief Executive: Stephen Lawrence Charitable Trust, 2005–09; ContinYou, 2010–13. Mem., ESRC, 2015–. Director: Inst. of Race Relns, 1984–87; Cultural Partnerships Ltd, 1985–88; Nat. Campaign for the Arts Ltd, 1985–89; Chair: (and Founder) Haringey Black Arts Forum, 1983–87; Haringey Arts Council, 1984–89; (and Founder) Arts Media Gp, 1985–90; Black Art Gall., 1989–93; Funding Panel, Royal Bor. of Kensington and Chelsea Neighbourhood Renewal Fund, 2003; (and Founder) Race Equality Partnership, Kensington and Chelsea, 2004–08; Vice Chair: W Midlands Ethnic Minority Arts Service, 1984–89; London South Bank Univ. Student Union, 2013–; Advisory Member: Educn Cttee, Royal Opera House, 1988–91; Credit Framework Steering Gp, Learning Skills Council, 2002–05; Member: Exec. Cttee, GLAA, 1988–92; Exec. Cttee, British-Amer. Proj., 1999–2001; Community Advr, Scotland Yard Gold Task Gp for Notting Hill Carnival Policing Strategy, 2001–05. Trustee: Metronomes Steel Orch. Ltd, 2004–09; Harrow Club, 2004–07; Locality, 2013–; Magdalene Coll. Youth Trust, 2013–. Visiting Lecturer: Poly. of Central London, 1988; Wolverhampton Poly., 1989; Kingsway Coll., 1991; Univ. of Amsterdam, 1993; Dillard Univ., 2003; Birkbeck, Univ. of London, 2002–05; Siberian Federal Univ., 2010. Associate Trainer, Nat. Police Improvement Assoc., 2010–11. Governor: Coleridge Prim. Sch., 1996–2001 (Treas., 1996–2001); Alexandra Park Comp. Sch., 2003–05. Judge: London Educn Partnership Awards, 2007–08; Business in Community Opportunity Now Awards, 2008–09; Creating the Future Awards, Home and Communities Acad., 2009; Parly Premiership Rugby Community Awards, 2011. Fellow, British-Amer. Proj., 1996; FRSA 2015. Mem., Inst. of Fundraising, 2013. *Publications:* articles in jls incl. Regeneration Mag., British Amer. Arts Assoc. Jl, Black Arts in London mag., Disability Arts in London mag., City Limits mag. *E:* kwoodley@ch1889.org.

WOODLEY, Keith Spencer, OBE 2014; FCA; chartered accountant; *b* 23 Oct. 1939; *s* of Charles Spencer Woodley and Hilda Mary Woodley (*née* Brown); *m* 1962, Joyce Madeleine Toon; one *s* two *d*. *Educ:* Stationers' Co. Sch. Articled Clerk, Senior Deloitte Plender Griffiths & Co., 1959–69; Partner, Deloitte Haskins & Sells, 1969–90: Nat. Personnel Partner, 1978–82; Mem., Partnership Bd, 1985–90. Complaints Commissioner: SIB, 1990–94; SFA, 1990–2001; FIMBRA, 1990–2001; LSE, 1994–2009; PIA, 1995–2001; Ind. Investigator, Investors' Compensation Scheme, 1991–2002. Director: Royscot Trust, 1990–96; National & Provincial Building Soc., 1991–96; Abbey National Plc, 1996–2010 (Dep. Chm., 1999–2004); Abbey National Treasury Service Plc, 1998–2002; Alliance & Leicester plc, 2008–10; Santander UK plc, 2010–11. Member Council: ICAEW, 1988–98 (Pres., 1995–96); NACAB, 1991–94 and 1997–99 (Hon. Treas., 1991–94); Univ. of Bath, 1996–2013 (Treas.,

2002–07; Pro-Chancellor, 2008–13). Trustee, Methodist Ministers' Pension Scheme, 1998–. Gov., Kingswood Sch., Bath, 2004–10. *Recreations:* theatre, music, hill walking. *Address:* Rectory Cottage, Combe Hay, Bath BA2 7EG.

WOODLEY, Leonard Gaston; QC 1988. *Educ:* Univ. of London (Dip. Internat. Affairs). Called to the Bar, Inner Temple, 1963, now Bencher; a Recorder, 1989–2000. Called to Trinidad and Tobago Bar. Mem., Royal Commn on Care of the Elderly, 1997–99. Chm., Laudat Enquiry under Mental Health Act; Mem., internat. enquiry into illegal hanging in Trinidad. First black person to be appointed QC and Recorder. Patron, Plan Internat. UK. *Recreations:* sports, music.

WOODLEY, Ven. Ronald John; Archdeacon of Cleveland, 1985–91, Emeritus, since 1991; *b* 28 Dec. 1925; *s* of John Owen Woodley and Maggie Woodley; *m* 1959, Patricia Kneeshaw; one *s* two *d*. *Educ:* Montagu Road School, Edmonton; St Augustine's Coll., Canterbury; Bishops' Coll., Cheshunt. Deacon 1953, priest 1954; Curate: St Martin, Middlesbrough, 1953–58; Whitby, 1958–61; Curate in Charge 1961–66, and Vicar 1966–71, The Ascension, Middlesbrough; Rector of Stokesley, 1971–85; RD of Stokesley, 1977–84. Canon of York, 1982–2000, Emeritus, 2001–. *Address:* The Old Joiners Cottage, Cross Lane, Ingleby Arncliffe, Northallerton DL6 3ND. *T:* (01609) 882983.

WOODLEY, Sonia; QC 1996; a Recorder, since 1985; *b* 8 Oct. 1946; *d* of Stanley and Mabel Woodley; *m* 1973, Stuart McDonald (marr. diss. 1986; he *d* 2007); two *s* one *d*. *Educ:* Convent High Sch., Southampton. Called to the Bar, Gray's Inn, 1968, Bencher, 2004. *Recreations:* travel, gardening. *Address:* Furnival Chambers, 32 Furnival Street, EC4A 1JQ.

WOODMAN, Ian Michael; Director Maritime (formerly Maritime and Dangerous Goods), Department for Transport, since 2007; *b* 19 Dec. 1958; *s* of Stanley Albert Woodman and Eva Woodman (*née* Crawford); *m* 1989, Ruth Angela Sparkes. *Educ:* Univ. of Manchester (BA Hons 1980); Trinity Coll., Cambridge (BA Hons 1986). With RN, 1980–84; joined Min. of Defence, 1986; Asst Pvte Sec. to Sec. of State, 1989–90; Principal, 1990–99; Dir, Resource Mgt, Equipment Support Air, 1999–2002; Dir, Perf. Analysis, 2002–05; Dir, Planning and Perf., DfT, 2005–07. *Recreations:* music, walking, DIY. *Address:* Department for Transport, Great Minster House, 33 Horseferry Road, SW1P 4DR.

WOODMAN, Janet; *see* Beer, J.

WOODMAN, Rev. Dr Simon Patrick; Joint Minister, Bloomsbury Central Baptist Church, since 2012; *b* Sevenoaks, 5 Aug. 1972; *s* of Colin and Davida Woodman; *m* 1994, Elizabeth Mary Gleed. *Educ:* Judd Sch.; Sheffield Univ. (BA Biblical Studies 1994); Bristol Baptist Coll.; Univ. of Bristol (MLitt 2001); Cardiff Univ. (PhD 2012). Minister, Counterslip Baptist Church, Bristol, 1999–2004; Tutor in Biblical Studies, S Wales Baptist Coll., Cardiff, 2004–12; Sen. Hon. Tutor in Biblical Studies, Cardiff Univ., 2004–12. Associate Baptist Chaplain, KCL, 2013–. Jt Editor, Baptist Qly, 2012–. FHEA 2008. *Publications:* The Book of Revelation, 2008; (ed jtly) The 'plainly revealed' Word of God: Baptist hermeneutics in theory and practice, 2011; (ed jtly) Prayers of the People, 2011. *Recreations:* reading, photography, drinking coffee, playing the guitar, watching Formula 1, subverting empire. *Address:* Bloomsbury Central Baptist Church, 235 Shaftesbury Avenue, WC2H 8EP. *T:* (020) 7240 0544. *E:* simonw@bloomsbury.org.uk.

WOODROFFE, Jean Frances, (Mrs J. W. R. Woodroffe), CVO 1953; *b* 22 Feb. 1923; *d* of late Capt. A. V. Hambro; *m* 1st, 1942, Capt. Hon. Vicary Paul Gibbs, Grenadier Guards (killed in action, 1944), *er s* of 4th Baron Aldenham; one *d* (and one *d* decd); 2nd, 1946, Rev. Hon. Andrew Charles Victor Elphinstone (*d* 1975), 2nd *s* of 16th Lord Elphinstone, KT; one *d* (one *s* decd); 3rd, 1980, Lt-Col John William Richard Woodroffe (*d* 1990). Lady-in-Waiting to the Queen as Princess Elizabeth, 1945; Extra Woman of the Bedchamber to the Queen, 1952–. *Address:* 1 Church Street, Mere, Warminster, Wilts BA12 6DS. *T:* (01747) 860159.

WOODROFFE, Simon, OBE 2006; Founder: YO! Sushi, 1997; YO! Company, 2002; Yotel, 2007; YO! Home, 2012; *b* 14 Feb. 1952; *s* of John and Pippa Woodroffe; one *d*. *Educ:* Marlborough (two 'O' levels). Roadie, 1970–75; stage designer, 1975–85; TV Exec., SuperChannel, 1985–92; skier, Chamonix, 1992–95. Appeared on Dragons' Den, BBC TV, 2005. *Publications:* The Book of Yo!, 2004. *Recreations:* polo, climbing, sailing. *Address:* Houseboat Victory, Cheyne Walk, SW10 0DG.

WOODROW, William Robert, (Bill), RA 2002; sculptor; *b* 1 Nov. 1948; *s* of late Geoffrey W. Woodrow and Doreen M. (*née* Fasken); *m* 1970, Pauline Rowley; one *s* one *d*. *Educ:* Barton Peveril GS, Eastleigh; Winchester Sch. of Art; St Martin's Sch. of Art (DipAD); Chelsea Sch. of Art. Trustee: Tate Gall., 1996–2001; Imperial War Mus., 2003–11. Chm., Roche Court Educnl Trust, New Art Centre, Salisbury, 2011–. Gov., Univ. of the Arts, London, 2003–08. Solo exhibns in UK, Europe, Australia, USA and Canada, 1972–, including: Fools' Gold, Tate Gall., London, 1996; Regardless of History, for Fourth Plinth, Trafalgar Square, 2000; The Beekeeper, S London Gall. and Mappin Art Gall., Sheffield, 2001, and Glynn Vivian Art Gall., Swansea, 2002; Bill Woodrow: Sculpture, Waddington Galleries, London, 2006; Brood—Sculpture from The Beekeeper series 1996–2007, Great Hall, Winchester, 2007; Skulpturen und Zeichungen, 2008, Revelator, 2012, Lullin & Ferrari, Zürich; Bill Woodrow: Sculptures 1981–1988, Waddington Custot Galls, London, 2011; Bill Woodrow - Sculpture, RA, 2013; work in group exhibitions worldwide, including: British Sculpture in the 20th Century, Whitechapel Art Gall., 1981; An International Survey of Recent Painting and Sculpture, Mus. of Modern Art, NY, 1984; Skulptur Im 20. Jahrhundert, Basle, Switzerland, 1984; Carnegie Internat. Mus. of Art, Pittsburgh, 1985; British Sculpture since 1965, USA tour, 1987; Great Britain-USSR, Kiev and Moscow, 1990; Metropolis, Berlin, 1991; Arte Amazonas, Rio de Janeiro, Brasilia, Berlin, Dresden and Aachen, 1992–94; Ripple across the Water, Tokyo, 1995; Un Siècle de Sculpture Anglaise, Jeu de Paume, Paris, 1996; Forjar el Espacio, Las Palmas, Valencia and Calais, 1998–99; Bronze, Holland Park, 2000–01; Field Day, Taipei Fine Arts Mus., Taiwan, 2001; Turning Points: 20th Century British Sculpture, Tehran Mus. of Contemp. Art, Iran, 2004; Drawing and Works on Paper from the Collection, Irish Mus. of Modern Art, Dublin, 2005; Eldorado, Mus. of Modern Art, Luxembourg, 2006; In Focus: Living History, Tate Modern, London, 2006; Sculpture in the Close, Jesus Coll., Cambridge, 2007; Punk. No One is Innocent, Kunsthalle Wien, Vienna, 2008; Modern British Sculpture, RA, 2011. Represented GB at Biennales of Sydney, 1982, Paris, 1982 and 1985, São Paulo, 1983 and 1991, Havana, 1997. Anne Gerber Award, Seattle Mus. of Art, USA, 1988. *Publications:* The Sculpture of Bill Woodrow, 2013. *E:* bill@billwoodrow.com.

WOODRUFF, Prof. (David) Phillip, PhD, DSc; FRS 2006; Professor of Physics, University of Warwick, since 1987; *b* 12 May 1944; *s* of Cyril and Dora Woodruff; *m* 1969, Angela Grundy; two *s*. *Educ:* Univ. of Bristol (BSc 1st Cl. Hons Physics 1965); Univ. of Warwick (PhD Physics 1968; DSc 1983). Lectr, 1969–83, Sen. Lectr, 1983–87, in Physics, Univ. of Warwick. Consulting Scientist, Bell Labs, NJ, 1979, 1981, 1985; Vis. Scientist, 1982 and 2002–11, Scientific Consultant, 1998–2002, Fritz-Haber-Inst., Berlin; EPSRC Sen. Res. Fellow, 1998–2003. *Publications:* The Solid/Liquid Interface, 1973; (with T. A. Delchar) Modern Techniques in Surface Science, 1986, 2nd edn 1994; over 500 articles in scientific jls. *Recreations:* gardening, walking, cookery, travel. *Address:* Physics Department, University of Warwick, Coventry CV4 7AL. *T:* (024) 7652 3378, *Fax:* (024) 7615 0897. *E:* d.p.woodruff@warwick.ac.uk.

WOODS, Very Rev. Alan Geoffrey, TD 1993; Clergy Retirement Officer, Sherborne Area, Salisbury Diocese, since 2010; Dean of Gibraltar, 2003–08, now Emeritus; Archdeacon of Gibraltar, 2005–08; *b* 18 July 1942; *s* of Samuel and Grace Woods; *m* 1968, Barbara (*née* Macdonald); three *d*. *Educ:* Bristol Cathedral Sch.; Salisbury Theol Coll. ACCA 1965, FCCA 1980. Auditor, Goodyear Tyre & Rubber Co., 1965–67. Ordained deacon, 1970, priest, 1971; Curate, St Francis, Ashton Gate, Bristol, 1970–73; Swindon Archdeaconry Youth Chaplain and Warden, Legge House Residential Youth Centre, 1973–76; Priest i/c, Neston, 1976–79; Team Vicar, Greater Corsham, 1979–81; Priest i/c, Charminster, 1981–83; Vicar: Charminster and Stinsford, 1983–90; Calne and Blackland, 1990–96; Sen. Chaplain, Malta and Gozo, and Chancellor, St Paul's Cathedral, Valletta, 1996–2003; Vicar Gen. to Bishop in Europe, 2003–05; Priest i/c, Malaga, 2006–07. Rural Dean: Dorchester, 1985–90; Calne, 1990–96. CF (TA), 1980–94; Chaplain: Dorchester Hosps, 1986–87; St Mary's Sch., Calne, 1990–96; Canon and Preb., Salisbury Cathedral, 1992–96. *Recreations:* travel, music. *Address:* 6 Maumbury Square, Weymouth Avenue, Dorchester DT1 1TY. *T:* (01305) 264877.

WOODS, Albert John, OBE 2012; Vice Chairman, British Olympic Association, 1999–2013, now Hon. Life Vice President; *b* Nottingham, 6 June 1949; *s* of Thomas Woods and Ourania Woods; *m* 1987, Helen Armitage. *Educ:* Nottingham High Sch.; Peoples Coll. of Further Educn (ONC Mechanical and Electrical Engrg 1968). Man. Dir, Maltby Heating Engineers, 1970–. President: British Canoeing (formerly British Canoe Union), 1992–; Eur. Canoe Assoc., 1993–; Mem. Bd of Dirs, Internat. Canoe Fedn, 1988–. Hon. MSc Nottingham Trent, 2005. *Recreations:* canoeing, shooting, koi carp. *Address:* 35 Killerton Park Drive, West Bridgford, Nottingham NG2 7SB. *T:* (0115) 984 5068. *E:* albert.woods@TeamGB.com. *Clubs:* Midland Canoe; Old Nottinghamians Rifle.

WOODS, Prof. Andrew William, PhD; BP Professor of Petroleum Science, BP Institute, University of Cambridge, since 2000; Fellow, St John's College, Cambridge, since 2000; *b* 2 Dec. 1964; *s* of Prof. William Alfred Woods and Dorothy Elizabeth Woods; *m* 1996, Dr Sharon Jane Casey; three *s* one *d*. *Educ:* St John's Coll., Cambridge (BA 1st Cl. Maths 1985, Part III Maths 1986, MA 1988; PhD Applied Maths 1989). Green Scholar, Scripps Instn of Oceanography, UCSD, 1989–90; University of Cambridge: Res. Fellow, 1988–90, Teaching Fellow, 1991–96, St John's College; Lectr, Inst. of Theoretical Geophysics, 1991–96; Prof. of Applied Maths, Univ. of Bristol, 1996–99. Italgas Prize, Turin, 1997; Marcello Carapezza Prize, Gp. Nat. per la Volcanologia, Rome, 1997; Wager Medal, IAVCEI, 2002. *Publications:* (jtly) Volcanic Plumes, 1997. *Address:* BP Institute, Bullard Laboratories, Madingley Rise, Madingley Road, University of Cambridge, Cambridge CB3 0EZ. *T:* (01223) 765702.

WOODS, Christopher Matthew, CMG 1979; MC 1945; HM Diplomatic Service, retired; Special Operations Executive Adviser, Foreign and Commonwealth Office, 1982–88; *b* 26 May 1923; *s* of Matthew Grosvenor Woods; *m* 1st, 1954, Gillian Sara Rudd (*d* 1985); four *s* one *d*; 2nd, 1992, Mrs Patricia Temple Muir. *Educ:* Bradfield Coll.; Trinity Coll., Cambridge. HM Forces, KRRC and SOE, 1942–47; Foreign Office, 1948; served Cairo, Tehran, Milan, Warsaw, Rome; FO, later FCO, 1967. *Publications:* (contrib.) Mission Accomplished: SOE in Italy 1943–45, 2011; (contrib.) Target Italy: the official history of SOE Operations against Fascist Italy 1940–43, 2014; papers in English and Italian on SOE in Italy. *Recreations:* birds, churches, music, books. *Address:* 31 Friars Street, Sudbury, Suffolk CO10 2AA. *T:* (01787) 882544. *Club:* Special Forces.

WOODS, Dr David Randle, DPhil; FRSSAf; Chairman, SANTRUST, since 2006; *b* Pietermaritzburg, 18 July 1940; *s* of Arthur Phillips Woods and Katherine Isabella Woods (*née* Straffen); *m* 1965, Anne Charlotte Abbott; one *s* one *d*. *Educ:* Michaelhouse Sch.; Rhodes Univ. (BSc Dist. Botany; BSc Hons Dist. Botany); University Coll., Oxford (DPhil 1966). Rhodes Schol., Natal, 1963–66; Asst Lectr in Microbiol., Dept of Botany and Microbiol., QMC, 1966–67; Rhodes University: Sen. Lectr in Microbiol., 1967–71; Prof. and Head of Microbiol., 1972–79; University of Cape Town: Dir, Microbial Genetics and Industrial Microbiol. Res. Unit, 1975–96; Prof. and Head of Dept of Microbiol., 1980–87; Fellow, 1985; Dep. Vice-Chancellor, 1988–96; Dir, Foundn for Res. Develt/Univ. of Cape Town Microbial Genetics Res. Unit, 1980–96; Vice-Chancellor, Rhodes Univ., 1996–2006. Research Fellow: Institut Pasteur, Paris, 1973–74; Dept of Biochem., Trondheim Univ., Norway, 1974–75; R. F. Cherry Prof. for Dist. Teaching, Baylor Univ., USA, 1992–93. Member, Editorial Board: Jl Bacteriol., 1987–89; Anaerobe Microbiol., 1994–98. Chm., Bacteriol. and Applied Microbiol. Div., and Mem., Exec. Bd, Internat. Union of Microbiol Socs, 1995–99. Member: S African Soc. for Microbiol., 1970 (Pres., 1982–84); S African Soc. for Biochem., 1970–96; Amer. Soc. for Microbiol., 1980; Acad. of Sci. of SA, 1995–. FRSSAf 1987; Fellow: Acad. of Sci. of SA, 1994; Amer. Acad. Microbiol., 1995. Hon. DCL Oxford, 2003; Hon. DLaws Rhodes, 2007. *Publications:* (ed) The Clostridia and Biotechnology (series), 1993; jt author numerous res. papers. *Recreations:* squash, reading, music, hiking.
See also T. P. Woods.

WOODS, Eldrick, (Tiger); golfer; *b* 30 Dec. 1975; s of late Lt-Col Earl Woods and of Kultida Woods; *m* 2004, Elin Nordegren (marr. diss. 2010); one *s* one *d*. *Educ:* Western High Sch., Anaheim, Calif; Stanford Univ. Professional golfer, 1996–; wins include: US Masters, 1997 (youngest winner), 2001 (first player ever to hold all four major professional titles concurrently), 2002, 2005; US PGA Championship, 1999, 2000, 2006, 2007; US Open, 2000, 2002, 2008; The Open, St Andrews, 2000, 2005, Hoylake, 2006; numerous other tournaments; Mem., US Ryder Cup Team, 1997, 1999, 2002, 2004, 2006, 2010, 2012. *Publications:* (jtly) How I Play Golf, 2001. *Address:* PGA Tour, 112 PGA Tour Boulevard, Ponte Vedra Beach, FL 32082, USA.

WOODS, Elisabeth Ann; a Commissioner, HM Customs and Excise, 1991–97; *b* 27 Oct. 1940; *d* of late Norman Singleton, CB and Cicely Margaret Singleton (*née* Lucas); *m* 1976, James Maurice Woods. *Educ:* South Hampstead High Sch.; Girton Coll., Cambridge (BA Hons Cl. 1 Modern Languages, 1963). Asst Principal, Min. of Pensions and Nat. Insurance, 1963–69 (Asst Private Sec. to the Minister, and Private Sec. to Permanent Sec.); Principal, DHSS, 1969–76 (Sec. to Cttees on Nursing and on Allocation of Resources to Health Authorities); Asst Sec., DHSS, 1976–88 (responsible for mental handicap policy, later for liaison with health authorities, finally for aspects of supplementary benefit); seconded to HM Treasury, 1980–82; Grade 3, DHSS Central Resource Management, 1988; Hd of Finance, DSS, 1988–91; HM Customs and Excise: Dir, VAT Control, 1991–94; Dir, Ops (Compliance), 1994–97; pt-time consultant on mgt and policy issues for UK and overseas govt depts and other orgns, 1998–2005. Non-executive Director: S Wilts PCT, 2003–06; NHS Wilts (formerly Wilts PCT), 2007–13. Chair, George Herbert in Bemerton Gp, 2013–14; Mem., HFEA, 1999–2002 (Chm., Audit Cttee, 2000–02). Mem., Wilts Children and Young People's Trust Bd, 2007–13; Gov., Salisbury Foundn Trust, 2007–13; Volunteer advr, Salisbury CAB, 1999–; Mem., Salisbury Civic Soc. Gen. Purposes Cttee, 2012–. *Recreations:* walking, travel, reading, cooking, being with friends. *Address:* West Wing, 43 Church Lane, Lower Bemerton, Salisbury SP2 9NR. *E:* lisandjames@gmail.com.

WOODS, Gordon Campbell, MA; Warden, Glenalmond College, Perth, 2003–15; *b* 5 Nov. 1955; *s* of late Ian and Margot Woods; *m* 1984, Emma, *d* of late Michael Godwin and Elizabeth Godwin; one *s* one *d*. *Educ:* Durham Sch.; Mansfield Coll., Oxford (BA Geog., MA 1978; PGCE 1979). Shrewsbury School, 1979–2003: Hd of Geog., 1984–89; Master i/c Rowing, 1988; Housemaster, 1989–99; Second Master (Dep. Hd), 1999–2003. Member: Bd of Mgt, SCIS, 2004–14; Exec. Cttee, Boarding Schs Assoc., 2010–14. Chm., Field Studies Working Gp, Geographical Assoc., 1989. Governor: Cargilfield Prep. Sch., 2003–15; Malsis

Prep. Sch., 2003–14; Belhaven Hill Prep. Sch., 2015–. *Recreations:* sailing, golf, railways (steam), industrial archaeology, watching live sport. *Clubs:* East India; Leander (Henley-on-Thames).

WOODS, Maj.-Gen. Henry Gabriel, CB 1979; MVO 2014; MBE 1965; MC 1945; Vice Lord-Lieutenant, North Yorkshire, 1985–99; Vice-President, St William's Foundation, since 1998 (Secretary, then Director, 1984–98); *b* 7 May 1924; *s* of late G. S. Woods and F. C. F. Woods (*née* McNevin); *m* 1953, Imogen Elizabeth Birchenough Dodd; two *d*. *Educ:* Highgate Sch. (Scholar); Trinity Coll., Oxford (Exhibnr; MA 1st Cl. Hons Mod. History). psc, jssc, rcds. Commnd 5th Royal Inniskilling Dragoon Guards, 1944; served NW Europe, 1944–45; Korea, 1951–52; Adjt, 1952–53; Sqdn Leader, 1954–55 and 1960–62; Army Staff Coll., 1956; Jt Services Staff Coll., 1960; Mil. Asst to Vice CDS, MoD, 1962–64; comd 5th Royal Inniskilling Dragoon Gds, 1965–67; Asst Mil. Sec. to C-in-C BAOR, 1968–69; Comdt, RAC Centre, 1969–71; RCDS, 1972; Mil. Attaché, Brit. Embassy, Washington, 1973–75; GOC NE Dist, 1976–80, retd. Head, Centre for Industrial and Educnl Liaison (W and N Yorks), 1980–87. Chairman: SATRO Panel, 1982–83; W and N Yorks Regl Microelectronics Educn Programme, 1982–86; Yorks and Humberside Industry/Educn Council, 1982–87; Bradford and W Yorks Br., BIM, 1982–84; N Yorks Scouts, 1982–2000; Yorks Region, Royal Soc. of Arts, 1982–92 (Mem. Council, 1984–92); Vice Chm., W Yorks Br. Exec. Cttee, Inst. of Dirs, 1985–91; Mem., Yorks Br. Exec. Cttee, BAAS, 1982–87. Vice Pres., Duke of York's Community Initiative, 2012– (Trustee, 2011–12). Trustee, Second World War Experience Centre, 1998–. Mem. Council, RUSI, 1981–84. Mem. Court, Univ. of Leeds, 1980–2001 (Mem. Council, 1980–91). Chm., 5th Royal Inniskilling Dragoon Guards Regtl Assoc., 1979–92; Pres., Royal Dragoon Guards Regtl Assoc., 1992–. Pres., York and Humberside Br., Royal Soc. of St George, 1986–88; Member: Trinity Soc., 1947–; Oxford Soc., 1987– (Pres., York Br., 1997–2001). FRSA; MInstD; FCMI. Hon. Mem., Yorks Reg., RIBA, 1994. Mayor, Co. of Merchants of Staple of England, 1991–92; Mem., Merchant Adventurers of the City of York. DL N Yorks, 1984–2006. Hon. DLitt Bradford, 1988. Officier, Ordre de Léopold, Belgium, 1965. *Publications:* Change and Challenge: the story of 5th Royal Inniskilling Dragoon Guards, 1978; contrib. Everyone's War: tanks - a brief history. *Recreations:* hunting (foot follower), fencing, sailing, military history. *Address:* Grafton House, Tockwith, York YO26 7PY. *T:* (01423) 358735. *Club:* Ends of the Earth (UK section).

WOODS, Prof. Hubert Frank, CBE 2001; FRCP, FRCPE; Sir George Franklin Professor of Medicine, University of Sheffield, 1990–2003, now Emeritus Professor; *b* 18 Nov. 1937; *s* of Hubert George Woods and Julia Augusta Woods; *m* 1st, 1966, Hilary Sheila Cox (*d* 1999); one *s* two *d*; 2nd, 2004, Rosemary Gaye Statham (*née* Starling). *Educ:* St Bees Sch., Cumbria; Leeds Univ. (BSc 1962); Pembroke Coll., Oxford (BM BCh 1965; DPhil 1970). MRCP 1968, FRCP 1978; FFPM 1989; FRCPE 1991. House appts, Radcliffe Infirmary and Hammersmith Hosp., 1965–67; Lectr in Medicine, Oxford Univ., 1967–72; Mem., MRC Ext. Clinical Scientific Staff and Hon. Sen. Registrar, MRC Clinical Pharmacology Unit, Radcliffe Infirmary, 1972–76; University of Sheffield: Prof. of Clinical Pharmacology and Therapeutics, 1976–90; Dean, Faculty of Medicine, 1989–99; Dir, Div. of Clinical Scis (South), Sheffield Med. Sch., 2000–03; Collins Meml Lectr, 1992; Public Orator, 1993–2007; Hon. Consultant Physician: Royal Infirmary, Sheffield, 1976–88; Middlewood Psychiatric Hosp., 1976–91; Royal Hallamshire Hosp., 1976–2003. Visiting Professor: Maryland Med. Center, 2000; Meml Sloan Kettering Cancer Center, 2000. Non-executive Member: Sheffield HA, 1990–96; Rampton Hosp. Authy, 1996–99. Chairman: Adv. Cttee on Toxicity of Chemicals in Food, Consumer Products and the Environment, DoH, 1992–2002; Department of Health Working Group: on Peanut Allergy, 1997–98; on Organophosphates, 1998–99; on Phyto-oestrogens, 1999–2003; on risk assessment for mixtures of Pesticides, 2000–02; on Lowermoor, 2002–13; Member: Jt Cttee on Higher Med. Trng, 1990–94; Adv. Cttee on Novel Foods and Processes, MAFF, 1992–2002; Food Adv. Cttee, MAFF, 1992–2001; Task Force on Food Incidents, Food Standards Agency, 2005–07. Mem. Council, RCP, 1987–89; Mem., GMC, 1994–2002 (Mem., 1994–2002, Dep. Chm., 1996–99, Chm., 1999–2002, Health Cttee; Mem., Review Bd for Overseas Practitioners, 1997–2002). Special Trustee, Former United Sheffield Hosps, 1989–2000; Trustee: Harry Bottom Charitable Trust, 1989–2003; Cavendish Hip Foundn, 2005–07 (Chm. Trustees, 2006–07). Gov., St Bees Sch., Cumbria, 1985–2009, 2013– (Chm., 2013–). Founder FMedSci 1998. Hon. FFOM 1995. Hon. MD Sheffield, 2007. *Publications:* (with R. D. Cohen) Lactic Acidosis, 1976; papers on metabolism and pharmacogenetics in med. and sci. jls. *Recreations:* gardening, fly fishing, works of Raymond Chandler. *Address:* Minshulls, 21 London Road, Aston Clinton, Bucks HP22 5HG. *T:* (01296) 630986. *Club:* Athenæum.

WOODS, Prof. John David, CBE 1991; PhD; Professor of Oceanography, Department of Earth Science and Engineering (formerly Department of Earth Resources Engineering, then T. H. Huxley School of the Environment, Earth Sciences and Engineering), Imperial College, University of London, 1994–2006, now Emeritus Professor of Oceanography and Complex Systems; Adjunct Fellow, Linacre College, Oxford, since 1991; *b* 26 Oct. 1939; *s* of late Ronald Ernest Goff Woods and Ethel Marjorie Woods; *m* 1971, Irina (marr. diss. 1996), *y d* of Bernd von Arnim and Elizabeth Gräfin Platen-Hallermund; one *s* one *d*. *Educ:* Imperial College, Univ. of London. BSc Physics 1961, PhD 1965. Research Asst, Imperial Coll., 1964–66; Sen., later Principal, Research Fellow, Meteorol Office, 1966–72; Prof. of Physical Oceanography, Southampton Univ., 1972–77; Ordinarius für Ozeanographie, Christian Albrechts Universität und Direktor Regionale Ozeanographie, Kiel Institut für Meereskunde, Schleswig-Holstein, 1977–86; Dir, Marine and Atmospheric Sci., NERC, 1986–94; Imperial College, London: Hd, Dept of Earth Resources Engrg, 1994–97; Dean, Graduate Sch. of the Envmt, 1994–97. Vis. Prof. Atmospheric Scis, Miami Univ., 1969; Hon. Prof. of Oceanography, Southampton Univ., 1994–. Jt Founding Dir, Foto Zerüi, 2005–. Member: NERC, 1979–82; Meteorol Res. Cttee, Meteorol Office, 1976–77, 1987–96; OST Foresight Marine Panel, 1996–2006. Council Member: Underwater Assoc., 1967–72 (Hon. life mem., 1987); RMetS, 1972–75; RGS, 1975–77, 1987–92 (Vice-Pres., 1989–91; Patron's Medal, 1996); Member, international scientific committees for: Global Atmospheric Research Prog., 1976–79; Climate Change and the Ocean, 1979–84; World Climate Research Prog., 1980–86; World Ocean Circulation Experiment, 1983–89 (Chm., 1984–86); Internat. Geosphere Biosphere Prog., 1987–91; Global Ocean Observing System, 1994– (Chm., Eur. Consortium, 1994–); Global Envmt Facility, 1994–98; Lead Author, Intergovtl Panel for Climate Change, 1989. Associate, Italian Nat. Res. Council, 2008. MAE 1988. Lectures: Iselin, Harvard, 1989; Linacre, Oxford, 1991; Adye, Fellowship of Engrg, 1991; European Geophys. Soc., Edinburgh, 1992; Bruun, Unesco, 1993, 1999. Inventor and developer of Virtual Ecology Workbench, 1992–2007. Hon. DSc: Liège, 1980; Plymouth, 1991; Southampton, 2004. L. G. Groves Prize, MoD, 1968; Medal of Helsinki Univ., 1982. *Publications:* (with J. Lythgoe) Underwater Science, 1971; (with E. Drew and J. Lythgoe) Underwater Research, 1976; (with N. Pinardi) Ocean Forecasting, 2002; The Joy of Swimming, 2010; Ix-Xlendi and its Ancient Shipwrecks, 2011; Winter water colours, 2012; Spring water colours, 2013; papers on atmospheric physics and oceanography in learned jls. *Recreations:* history, photography (www.fotozerui.com), filmmaking (vimeopro.com/goff/alps). *Address:* Department of Earth Science and Engineering, Imperial College, SW7 2AZ. *T:* (020) 7594 7414. *Clubs:* Athenæum, Geographical, Royal Over-Seas League.

WOODS, Kenneth Allen; 'cellist; Principal Conductor and Artistic Director, English Symphony Orchestra, since 2013; *b* Madison, Wisconsin, 6 June 1968; *s* of Prof. R. Claude Woods and Charlotte O. Woods; *m* 2004, Suzanne Casey; one *s* one *d*. *Educ:* James Madison Meml High Sch.; Indiana Univ. Sch. of Music (BM Cello Performance 1991); Univ. of Wisconsin-Madison Sch. of Music (MM Cello Performance 1993); Univ. of Cincinnati Coll.-Conservatory of Music (DMA-ABD Conducting and Cello). Conducting Asst, Cincinnati SO, 1998–99; Asst Prof. of Cello and Conducting, and Hd of Strings and Chamber Music, Eastern Oregon Univ., 1999–2002; Music Director: Grande Ronde Symphony, 1999–2002; Oregon E Symphony, 2000–09; Principal Guest Conductor, Orch. of the Swan, 2009–14. Cellist: Taliesin Piano Trio, 1993–98; Quatuor Masala, 1996–99; Ensemble Epomeo, 2008–. Mem., Bd of Dirs, Conductors' Guild, 2001–02. Hon. Patron, Hans Gál Soc., 2014–. *Recreations:* writing (fiction, poetry, political analysis and blogging on music), composition and song-writing, cycling, camping, time with family, film, cooking, wine, beer and good coffee. *Address:* c/o English Symphony Orchestra, 16–20 Deansway, Worcester WR1 2ES. *T:* 07973 906206. *E:* ken@kennethwoods.net. *W:* www.kennethwoods.net.

WOODS, Sir Kent (Linton), Kt 2011; MD; FRCP; Professor of Therapeutics, University of Leicester, 1996–2013, now Emeritus; *b* 5 June 1948; *s* of Stephen and Mary Woods; *m* 1970, Rose Whitmarsh; three *s* (one *d* decd). *Educ:* Lawrence Sheriff Sch., Rugby; Clare Coll., Cambridge (MA, MB BChir 1972; MD 1980 (Horton Smith Prize)); Birmingham Univ.; Harvard Sch. of Public Health (SM Epidemiology 1983). MRCP 1974, FRCP 1988. Clinical trng posts, Birmingham, 1972–75; Sheldon Res. Fellow and MRC Trng Fellow, 1975–78; Lectr in Clinical Pharmacology, Birmingham Univ., 1978–84; MRC Travelling Fellow, Harvard, 1982–83; Sen. Lectr in Clinical Pharmacology, 1984–94, Reader, 1994–96, Univ. of Leicester. Regl Dir of R&D, Trent, NHS Exec., DoH, 1995–99; Dep. Dir, 1998, Dir, 1999–2003, NHS Health Technol. Assessment Programme. Chief Exec., Medicines and Healthcare products Regulatory Agency, 2004–13; Chm., Eur. Medicines Agency, 2011–13. Hon. Consultant Physician, Leicester Royal Infirmary, 1984–2013. FMedSci 2008. Hon. FFPM, 2009. *Publications:* contrib. numerous papers to med. and scientific jls, mainly on cardiovascular topics. *Recreations:* travel, books. *Club:* Athenaeum.

WOODS, Maurice Eric; Regional Chairman, Employment (formerly Industrial) Tribunals (Bristol), 1990–98; *b* 28 June 1933; *s* of late Leslie Eric Woods and of Winifred Rose Woods (*née* Boniface); *m* 1956, Freda Pauline Schlosser; two *s* two *d*. *Educ:* Moulsham Secondary Modern Sch., Chelmsford. LLB London. National Service (Army), 1951–53. Clerk with Essex CC, 1948–51; Police Constable, Essex Police Force, 1954–59; Claims Assistant, Cornhill Insce, 1959–61; Solicitors' Clerk and Articled Clerk, Barlow Lyde and Gilbert, 1961–65; admitted Solicitor, 1965; private practice, 1965–84; Dep. County Court Registrar, 1977–84; Chairman: Suppl. Benefit Appeal Tribunals and Social Security Appeal Tribunals, 1981–84; Industrial Tribunals, Bristol, 1984–90. *Recreations:* music, travel, painting.

WOODS, Prof. Ngaire Tui, DPhil; Director, Global Economic Governance Programme, since 2003, Dean, Blavatnik School of Government, since 2011, and Professor of Global Economic Governance, since 2011, University of Oxford; Fellow, University College, Oxford, since 1993; *b* Wellington, NZ, 13 Feb. 1963; *d* of N. Rowland Woods and Tui Clark; *m* 1995, Eugene L. Rogan; one *s* one *d*. *Educ:* Univ. of Auckland (BA, LLB Hons); Balliol Coll., Oxford (MPhil; DPhil 1992). Jun. Res. Fellow, New Coll., Oxford, 1990–92; University of Oxford: Lectr in Internat. Relns, Dept of Politics and Internat. Relns, 1993–2008; Prof. of Internat. Political Econ., 2008–11; Academic Dir, Blavatnik Sch. of Govt, 2011. Vis. Lectr, Govt Dept, Harvard Univ., 1992. *Publications:* (ed and contrib.) Explaining International Relations since 1945, 1996; (ed jtly and contrib.) Inequality and World Politics, 1999; (ed) The Political Economy of Globalization, 2000; The Globalizers: the IMF, the World Bank and their borrowers, 2006; (ed with J. Welsh) Exporting Good Governance, 2007; (ed with D. Brown) Making Self-Regulation Effective in Developing Countries, 2007; (ed with W. Mattli) The Politics of Global Regulation, 2009; (ed with L. Martinez) Networks of Influence, 2009. *Recreations:* sailing, ski-ing, hiking. *Address:* University College, High Street, Oxford OX1 4BH. *T:* (01865) 276602, *Fax:* (01865) 276659. *E:* geg@univ.ox.ac.uk.

WOODS, Nigel Dermot, FRICS; Chief Executive and Commissioner of Valuation for Northern Ireland, Valuation and Lands Agency, 1998–2007; *b* 21 Feb. 1947; *s* of Victor and Sheila Woods; *m* 1974, Alison Grant; one *s* two *d*. *Educ:* Bangor Grammar Sch. FRICS 1983 (ARICS 1970). Worked in estate agency, Belfast, 1964–67; with Valuation Office, subseq. Valuation and Lands Agency, 1967–2007. Vis. Prof., Sch. of Built Envmt, Univ. of Ulster, 2003–. *Recreations:* golf, bridge. *Club:* Bangor Golf.

WOODS, Robert Barclay, CBE 2003; Chief Executive, Peninsular and Oriental Steam Navigation Co., 2004–06 (Executive Director, 1996–2006); *b* 23 Sept. 1946; *s* of Robert Wilmer Woods and Henrietta Wilson; *m* 1975, Georgiana Garton; three *s* one *d*. *Educ:* Winchester Coll.; Trinity Coll., Cambridge (MA); Harvard Business Sch. (SMP). Joined P&O Gen. Cargo Div., 1971; seconded to J. Swire & Sons, Japan, 1972–73; Overseas, subseq. P&O, Containers: Dubai, 1980–84; Gen. Manager, FE Trade, 1984–86; Trade Dir, Aust. and NZ, 1986–89; Dir, 1987; Managing Director: P&O Containers, 1990–96; P&O Nedlloyd, 1997–2003; Chairman: P&O Ports, 2002–06; P&O Ferries, 2003–. Chm., Southampton Container Terminal, 1989–; non-executive Director: J. Swire & Sons, 2002–; Cathay Pacific Airways, 2006–10; Caledonia Investments plc, 2011–; Advr to Bd, Dubai Ports World, 2006– (Dir, 2014–). Chm., Maritime London, 2007–10. Chm., Far Eastern Freight Conf., 1996–2003; President: Chamber of Shipping, 2002–04; Inst. of Chartered Shipbrokers, 2014–. Chairman: Council of Trustees, Oxford House Community Centre, 1993–2005; Council, Mission to Seafarers, 2007–; Mem., Sea Cadet Council, 2005–. Younger Brother, Trinity House, 2005–. Hon. Capt. RNR, 2002–. Fellow, Winchester Coll., 2007–. Hon. DUniv Anglia Ruskin, 2007. *Recreations:* field sports, music, vintage cars and aircraft, sailing. *Address:* Old Rectory, Frilsham, Newbury, Berks RG18 9XH. *T:* (01635) 201249. *E:* robert.woods@dpworld.com. *Clubs:* White's; Vintage Sports-Car; Keyhaven Yacht.

WOODS, Sir Robert (Kynnersley), Kt 2000; CBE 1986; Judge, District Court of New South Wales, 2000–11; *b* 12 Nov. 1939; *s* of Frederick Kynnersley Smythies Woods, OBE and Ruth Cecilia Woods (*née* Shaw). *Educ:* Univ. of Sydney (LLB). Solicitor, NSW, 1966–69; Legal Officer, PNG Govt, 1969–81; Justice, Nat. and Supreme Courts of PNG, 1982–99. PNG Scout Association: Scout Leader, 1969–74; Scout Comr, 1974–2000 (Leader Trainer, 1992–96); Chief Comr, 1996–99. Chancellor, Anglican Dio. of Bathurst, NSW, 2003–. KStJ 2004. *Address:* 737 Parkes Road, Wellington, NSW 2820, Australia. *T:* (2) 68453707.

WOODS, Robert Stockley; Director, HM Treasury, since 2014; *b* Southport, 20 Oct. 1966; *s* of John and Mary Woods; *m* 1999, Maria del Carmen Frieyro de Lara; two *d*. *Educ:* Rainford High Sch.; Girton Coll., Cambridge (BA Hons Econs 1988); Warwick Univ. (MSc Econs). HM Treasury: Head: Forecast Report and Modelling Br., 1992–95; Monetary Policy Br., 1996–98; EU Econs and EMU Br., 1999–2001; Fiscal and Macroeconomic Policy, 2002–06; Global Econs, 2006–08; Dir, Macroeconomics, and Chief Macroeconomist, 2008–10; Head, Macro Financial Analysis Div., 2010–12; Head, Conjunctural Assessment and Projections Div., 2012–14; Project Leader, Monetary Analysis Directorate, Bank of England, 2014. *Publications:* contribs to learned jls. *Recreations:* swimming, tennis, football, piano, reading, gardening, socialising with friends and family. *Address:* HM Treasury, Horse Guards Road, SW1A 2HQ. *E:* robert.woods@hmtreasury.gsi.gov.uk.

WOODS, Prof. Robert Thomas, FBPsS, FAcSS; Professor of Clinical Psychology of the Elderly, since 1996, and Co-Director, Dementia Services Development Centre, since 1999, Bangor University (formerly University of Wales, Bangor); *b* 9 April 1952; *s* of Walter T. W. Woods and Kathleen Ellen Woods (*née* Brooks); *m* 1972, Joan Doreen Foster; one *s* one *d*. *Educ:* Gravesend Sch. for Boys; Churchill Coll., Cambridge (BA 1973; MA 1977); Univ. of Newcastle-upon-Tyne (MSc 1975). CPsychol 1988; FBPsS 1992. Clinical psychologist,

Newcastle Gen. Hosp., 1975–80; Lectr, then Sen. Lectr, Inst. of Psychiatry, Univ. of London and Hon. Clinical Psychologist, Maudsley and Bethlem Royal Hosps, 1980–92; Head, Psychol. Services for Older People, Camden and Islington Community Health Services NHS Trust, 1992–96; Hon. Sen. Lectr in Psychol., UCL, 1992–96; Hon. Clinical Psychologist, Betsi Cadwaladr University Health Bd (formerly Gwynedd Community Health, then NW Wales, NHS Trust), 1996–. Mem., Med. and Scientific Adv. Panel, Alzheimer's Soc. (formerly Alzheimer's Disease Soc.), 1987–2007, and Alzheimer's Disease Internat., 1997–; Ambassador, Alzheimer's Soc., 2007–. Associate Specialist Advr, Health Adv. Service 2000, 1998–2003. Associate Editor, Aging and Mental Health, 1997–. FAcSS (AcSS 2014). 25th Anniversary Award, Alzheimer's Soc., 2004; M. B. Shapiro Award, BPsS, 2006; Barry Reisberg Award, Hearthstone Alzheimer Care, USA, 2011. *Publications:* (with U. Holden) Reality Orientation, 1982, 3rd edn as Positive Approaches to Dementia Care, 1995; (with C. Lay) Caring for the Person with Dementia: a guide for families and other carers, 1982, 3rd edn 1994; (with P. Britton) Clinical Psychology with the Elderly, 1985; Alzheimer's Disease: coping with a living death, 1989; (ed) Handbook of the Clinical Psychology of Ageing, 1996, (ed with L. Clare) 2nd edn, 2008; (ed) Psychological Problems of Ageing, 1999; (with J. Keady and D. Seddon) Involving Families in Care Homes, 2007. *Recreations:* football, cooking. *Address:* Dementia Services Development Centre, Bangor University, Ardudwy, Holyhead Road, Bangor, Gwynedd LL57 2PZ. *T:* (01248) 383719.

WOODS, Roberta C.; *see* Blackman-Woods.

WOODS, Hon. Ronald Earl; Diplomat in Residence, then Professor of United States Foreign Policy, University of Washington, 1996–2007; *b* 10 Oct. 1938; *s* of Earl L. Woods and Marie C. Woods; *m* 1959, Judith M. Wishner; two *d. Educ:* Georgetown Univ.; School of Foreign Service (BSFS 1961). Joined US Foreign Service, 1961; served: Cairo, 1962; Washington, 1963; Rome, 1966; Paris, 1969; Strasbourg, 1971; Washington, 1974; Madrid, 1979; Oslo, 1982; Brussels, 1985; Minister, London, 1989–93; Exec. Dir, World Affairs Council, 1993–96. *Recreations:* tennis, ski-ing, walking. *Address:* 4527 52 Avenue South, Seattle, WA 98118–1501, USA. *T:* (206) 7227208. *E:* ronaldwoods@mac.com.

WOODS, Tiger; *see* Woods, E.

WOODS, Timothy Phillips, MA, DPhil; Head of History, Trent College, 1985–2004; *b* 24 Dec. 1943; *s* of late Arthur Phillips Woods and of Katherine Isabella Woods; *m* 1969, Erica Lobb. *Educ:* Cordwalles Prep. Sch., Natal; Michaelhouse Sch., Natal; Rhodes Univ. (BA Hons, MA; UED); Oxford Univ. (DPhil). Cape Province Rhodes Scholar, 1968; Felsted School: Asst Master, 1971; Head of History, 1975; Headmaster, Gresham's Sch., 1982–85. *Recreations:* golf, gardening, music, history and architecture of cathedrals. *Address:* 63 Curzon Street, Long Eaton, Nottingham NG10 4FG. *T:* (0115) 972 0927. *Club:* Vincent's (Oxford).
See also D. R. Woods.

WOODS, Victoria Patricia Ann, (Vicki), (Mrs F. A. Woods Walker); Contributing Editor, Vogue (USA), since 1994; *b* 25 Sept. 1947; *d* of Frederick Woods and Barbara Joan (*née* Hinchliffe); *m* 1980, Frank A. Walker; one *s* one *d. Educ:* Lancaster Girls' Grammar Sch.; Univ. of Lancaster (BA). Sub-editor, Harpers & Queen, 1970–73; Chief sub-editor, Radio Times, 1973–75; Exec. Editor, Harpers & Queen, 1975–79; Associate Editor, then Dep. Editor, Tatler, 1982–87; Femail Editor, Daily Mail, 1987–89; Contributing Editor, Vogue (USA) and Associate Editor, Spectator, 1989–91; Editor, Harpers & Queen, 1991–94.

WOODS-WILFORD, Dr (Jacqueline Lee) Penelope; Chief Executive, British Lung Foundation, since 2012; *b* London, 3 May 1963; *d* of Peter Woods and Lucia Woods; *m* 2011, Julian Wilford; one *d. Educ:* Sidney Sussex Coll., Cambridge (BA 1984; MA 1987); Guy's Hosp. Med. Sch. (MB BS 1987); INSEAD Business Sch. (MBA 1992). Jun. doctor, NHS, 1987–89; mgt consultant, Arthur Andersen, Booz Allen and ISO Healthcare, 1989–2000; Sen. Vice Pres., BTG plc, 2000–07; Chief Exec., Picker Inst. Europe, 2009–12. Angel investor and non-exec. dir, private and public sectors, 1998–. Member: RSocMed; BMA; RSA. *Recreations:* deciding what I want to be when I grow up, adrenaline sports, travel, family. *Address:* British Lung Foundation, 73–75 Goswell Road, EC1V 7ER. *T:* (020) 7688 5566. *E:* penny.woods@blf.org.uk.

WOODSTOCK, Viscount; William Jack Henry Bentinck; Count of the Holy Roman Empire; consultant, specialising in startup recruitment and team-building, since 2014; Career Specialist, Makers Academy, since 2014; *b* 19 May 1984; *s* and *heir* of Earl of Portland, *qv. Educ:* Harrow Sch.; Heythrop Coll., Univ. of London (BA Hons Philosophy 1st cl.). Co-founder: Ragged Project (London), 2010–11; Levantine Links, 2010–14; Develt Manager, IDEA UK, 2011–12. Key Account Manager, Enternships Ltd, 2012–14. Dir, ISOWORG, 2014–. Mem. Cttee, BCS Entrepreneurs, 2012–; Catalyst, Global Wkg Gp on Decent Work for Youth, ILO, 2012–13; Head of Marketing, Business Governance Solutions, 2014; Member: Steering Gp, SEE Change, UnLtd, 2013–; Adv. Bd, EdTech UK, 2015–; Steering Gp, Learning Futures Prog., Educn and Trng Foundn, 2015–. Advisor: E-Skills UK, then The Tech Partnership, 2012–; Advocate, Tech London Advocates, 2013– (Chm., Supporting Educn Gp, 2013–); Course Leader, Accelerator Acad., 2013–; Becon, Beconomy, 2013–; Mentor: Wayra UK, 2014–; Wayra UnLtd, 2014–. World of Difference winner, Vodafone Foundn, 2011. Croupier, London Clubs Internat., 2005–08. *Heir: b* Hon. Jasper James Mellowes Bentinck, *b* 1988. *Clubs:* Eccentric, King's Head, Union.

WOODTHORPE BROWNE, Robert, MBE 2014; Managing Director, Robert Browne and Partners, since 1984; *b* Little Gaddesden, Herts, 26 May 1943; *m* 1966, Barbara Zwiauer; one *s. Educ:* Birkbeck Coll., Univ. of London (BA Hons Spanish); Univ. de Barcelona (Estudios Hispánicos); Univ. de Poitiers. Chief Underwriter, Reinsurance Co. of Mauritius, 1969–73; Man. Dir, Africa and Middle East, Sedgwick Gp, 1973–84; Exec. Dir, Citicorp Insce Brokers, subseq. Nelson Hurst, 1988–96; Exec. Dir, Bain Hogg, subseq. Aon Gp, 1996–2002. Contested (Lib Dem): Harlow, 1979; Kensington and Chelsea, 1997, Nov. 1999; Mid Worcs, 2001; Sedgefield, 2005; Staffordshire S, 2015; European Parliament: Central London, 1997; East of England, 1999; Chairman: Lib Dem Parly Candidates Assoc., 1998–2001; Internat. Relns Cttee, Lib Dems, 2006–. Member: Cttee, British German Assoc., 2000–; Cttee, Gresham Soc., 2002–; Council, RIIA, 2011–. Court Asst, World Traders' Co., 2006– (Jun. Warden, 2014–). Treas., Liberal Internat., 2010–. FRGS 1980. *Recreations:* forestry, 17th century English ceramics, theatre, international travel. *Address:* 136 Coleherne Court, Redcliffe Gardens, SW5 0DY. *T:* 07770 605978. *E:* robertbrowne@cix.co.uk. *Club:* National Liberal.

WOODWARD, Barbara Janet, CMG 2011; OBE 1999; HM Diplomatic Service; Ambassador to the People's Republic of China, since 2015; *b* 29 May 1961; *d* of late Arthur Claude Woodward, MC, FRICS, and of Rosemary Monica Gabrielle Woodward (*née* Fenton). *Educ:* Univ. of St Andrews (MA Hons (Hist.) 1983); Yale Univ. (MA (Internat. Relns) 1990). Joined HM Diplomatic Service, 1991; Asst European Corresp., FCO, 1991–93; Second, then First, Sec., Moscow, 1994–98; Hd, EU Enlargement Section, FCO, 1999–2001; Dep. Hd, Human Rights Policy Dept, FCO, 2001–03; Political Counsellor, Beijing, 2003–06; Minister and Dep. Hd of Mission, Beijing, 2006–09; Internat. Dir, UK Border Agency, 2009–11; Dir Gen., Econ. and Consular, FCO, 2011–14. Chm., Adv. Bd, Hua Dan, 2009– (Mem., 2006–). *Recreations:* sport (competitive swimming, mountain biking, tennis), bridge. *Address:* c/o Foreign and Commonwealth Office, King Charles Street, SW1A 2AH. *Club:* Otter Swimming (Hon. Sec., 1998–2002).

WOODWARD, Christopher John Paul; Director, Garden Museum (formerly Museum of Garden History), since 2006; *b* Welwyn Garden City, 13 Sept. 1969; *s* of David Woodward and Janet Woodward (*née* Musther); *m* 2000, Anna Bacigalupi (marr. diss. 2011); one *s. Educ:* Hitchin Boys' Sch.; Peterhouse, Cambridge (BA Hist. of Art 1990). Asst Curator, Sir John Soane's Mus., 1995–2000; Dir, Holburne Mus. of Art, Bath, 2000–05. Trustee: Heritage Lottery Fund, 2006–13; Nat. Heritage Meml Fund, 2006–13. *Publications:* In Ruins, 2001. *Recreations:* open water swimming (crossing of Hellespont and the Strait of Gibraltar), ruins, guerrilla gardening. *Address:* c/o Garden Museum, Lambeth Palace Road, SE1 7LB. *T:* (020) 7401 8865.

WOODWARD, Sir Clive (Ronald), Kt 2004; OBE 2002; Director of Sport, British Olympic Association and Director of Olympic Performance, Team 2012, 2006–12; Founder and Chief Executive Officer, Captured; *b* 6 Jan. 1956; *m* Jayne; two *s* one *d. Educ:* HMS Conway; Loughborough Coll. Rugby Football Union player: début for England U-23, 1976; 21 England caps, 1980–84; British Lions tours, 1980, 1983; Leicester RFC, 1979; Manly, Australia, 1985; Coach: Henley RFC, 1993–95; London Irish RFC, 1995; Bath RFC, 1996–97; Head Coach: England Rugby Football Union team, 1997–2004; winning England team, World Cup, 2003; British Lions tour, NZ, 2005; Technical Dir, Southampton FC, 2005–06; a Dep. Chef de Mission, GB Team, London Olympics, 2012. Dir, Leicester RFC, 2008–. Hon. Pres., British Assoc. of Ski (later Snowsport) Instructors, 2007–12; Mem., Perf. Mgt Gp, Amateur Boxing Assoc. of England, 2008–. *Publications:* Winning!: the story of England's rise to Rugby World Cup glory, 2004.

WOODWARD, David John, CMG 2000; Director, Cross Government Studies, National Audit Office, 2006–09; *b* 12 Dec. 1949; *s* of Lionel John Innes Woodward and Ethel Woodward; *m* 1st, 1973, Agnes Kane (marr. diss. 1985); 2nd, 1985, Yvonne Yee Fun Wong; one *s. Educ:* Reigate Grammar Sch.; Woolwich Poly.; City of London Poly. (Dip. Auditing and Accounting). With BR, 1969–75; Nat. Audit Office, 1975–2009: Associate Dir, 1987–93; Director: Internat., London, 1993–94; Audit Ops, UN HQ, NY, and Chm. Tech. Gp, UN Panel of External Auditors, 1995–2001; Conseiller Maître en Service Extraordinaire, Cour des Comptes, France (on exchange), 2001–02; UK Mem., Internat. Bd of Auditors for NATO, Brussels, 2002–06 (Chm., 2003–05). Gov., Grove Park Primary Sch., 2014– (Chm., Resources Cttee, 2014–). *Recreations:* English history, exploring the River Thames. *E:* woodwardaccount@yahoo.co.uk.

WOODWARD, Edward Gareth; Executive Vice Chairman, Manchester United Football Club, since 2012; *b* Chelmsford, Essex, 9 Nov. 1971; *s* of David Garry Woodward and Susan Carol Woodward (*née* Mayo); *m* 2001, Isabelle Nicole Caprano; one *s* one *d* (twins). *Educ:* Brentwood Sch.; Bristol Univ. (BSc Physics 1993). ACA 1996. Corporate Tax, PricewaterhouseCoopers, 1993–99; Mergers and Acquisitions, Robert Fleming & Co., 1999–2000, J. P. Morgan, 2000–05; with Manchester United FC, 2005–. *Recreation:* food and wine. *Address:* Manchester United Football Club, Old Trafford, Sir Matt Busby Way, Manchester M16 0RA. *T:* (020) 7484 1202. *E:* kay.hayes@manutd.co.uk.

WOODWARD, Prof. (Frank) Ian, PhD; Professor of Plant Ecology, Department of Animal and Plant Sciences, University of Sheffield, since 1991; *b* 15 Dec. 1948; *s* of Frank Clement Woodward and Gwenda Agnes Woodward (*née* Allen); *m* 1972, Pearl May Chambers; one *s* one *d. Educ:* Mansfield Coll., Oxford (BA Hons Botany 1970); Univ. of Lancaster (PhD 1973); MA Cantab 1979. NERC Res. Fellow, Univ. of Lancaster, 1973–75; Higher Scientific Officer, Grassland Res. Inst., 1975–76; Lectr, Dept of Plant Scis, UWCC, 1976–79; Lectr, Dept of Botany, 1979–91, Fellow, Trinity Hall, 1981–91, Univ. of Cambridge. Henry J. Oosting Lectr, Duke Univ., USA, 1996. FLS 1990; FAAAS 2003. W. S. Cooper Award, Ecological Soc. of America, 1991; Marsh Award for Climate Change Res., British Ecol Soc., 2010. *Publications:* Principles and Measurements in Environmental Biology, 1983; Climate and Plant Distribution, 1987 (trans. Japanese 1993); Vegetation and the Terrestrial Carbon Cycle: modelling the first 400 million years, 2001; Global Change and the Terrestrial Biosphere, 2011; numerous articles in jls on influences of climate and carbon dioxide on plants and vegetation. *Recreations:* wood turning, music. *Address:* 16 Ecclesall Road South, Ecclesall, Sheffield S11 9PE. *T:* (0114) 266 0399.

WOODWARD, Guy Andrew; Associate Editor: Harrods Publishing, since 2014; Le Pan Magazine, since 2015; *b* Birmingham, 30 May 1973; *s* of Ray Woodward and Susan Woodward; *m* 2012, Vanessa Miller. *Educ:* King Edward's Sch., Edgbaston; Univ. of Manchester (BMus). Editor, AB Europe, 1997–2001; Sub-Editor, Sport, The Guardian, 2001–03; Dep. Editor, 2003–06, Editor, 2006–12, Decanter; Editor, Food and Travel, 2012–14. Mem. Cttee, BSME, 2012– (Vice Chm., 2013; Chm., 2014). Advr, All-Party Parly Wine and Spirit Gp Enquiry into impact of tax changes on UK wine industry, 2009. Broadcaster on wine, TV progs, BBC News, Market Kitchen, 2010–12, This Morning, 2010–12. *Publications:* freelance writing on sport, travel and wine for The Guardian, Independent, Daily Mail, Observer, FT, Independent on Sunday, Esquire, ShortList, TIME Mag., Christie's, Condé Nast Traveller; columnist, Harpers Wine & Spirit. *Recreations:* sport (football, tennis, golf), music (classical), gambling. *Address:* Harrods Publishing, 68 Hammersmith Road. *T:* W14 8YW.

WOODWARD, Ian; *see* Woodward, F. I.

WOODWARD, Rev. Canon Dr James Welford; Principal, Sarum College, Salisbury, since 2015; *b* Durham, 23 Feb. 1961; *s* of Colin Woodward and Patricia Woodward (*née* Welford). *Educ:* Spennymoor Grammar Sch.; King's Coll. London (BD 1982; AKC 1982); Westcott House, Cambridge; STh Lambeth 1985; Univ. of Birmingham (MPhil 1991); Open Univ. (PhD 1999). Ordained deacon, 1985, priest, 1986; Curate, Consett, 1985–87; Bishop of Oxford's Domestic Chaplain, 1987–90; Hd of Chaplaincy, Queen Elizabeth Hosp., Birmingham, 1990–96; Priest-in-charge, Middleton and Wishaw, 1996–98; Bishop of Birmingham's Advr for Health and Social Care, 1996–2001; Master, Foundn of Lady Katherine Leveson and Vicar, St Mary the Virgin, Temple Balsall, 1998–2009; Dir, Leveson Centre for Study of Aging, Spirituality and Social Policy, Temple Balsall, 2000–09; Canon Steward, St George's Chapel, Windsor, 2009–15; Hon. Canon and Preb., Salisbury Cathedral, 2015–. Associate Lectr, Dept of Health and Social Welfare, Open Univ., 1992–2001; Associate Res. Fellow, Warwick Business Sch., Univ. of Warwick, 2002–05; Hon. Lectr, Dept of Theology, Univ. of Birmingham, 1993–2005; Hon. Res. Fellow, Practical Theology, Univ. of Cardiff, 1999–2003. Non-exec. Dir, Solihull PCT, 2003–06. Trustee, St Martins Trust, Birmingham, 2013–. Lay Mem., Patient Liaison Cttee, RCAnaes, 2000–03. Gov., SCM Press Trust Ltd, 1994–99. *Publications:* Embracing the Chaos: theological reflections on AIDS, 1990; Encountering Illness: voices in pastoral and theological perspective, 1995; Finding God in Illness, 1997; (with S. Pattison) The Blackwell Reader in Pastoral and Practical Theology, 1999; Befriending Death, 2005; Services for Weekdays: readings, reflections and prayers, 2006; Praying the Lectionary: prayers and reflections for every week's readings, 2006; Valuing Age: mission and ministry among older people, 2008; Between Remembering and Forgetting: the spiritual dimensions of dementia, 2010; (with P. Gooder and M. Pryce): Journeying with Mark, 2011; Journeying with Luke, 2012; Journeying with Matthew, 2013; Journeying with John, 2014. *Recreations:* modern political biography, cooking, photography, Wales, walking, art, cinema. *Address:* Sarum College, 19 The Close, Salisbury, Wilts SP1 2EE.

WOODWARD, John Collin; Managing Director, Arts Alliance, since 2010; *b* 18 Feb. 1961; *s* of Anthony and Anne Woodward; *m* 2000, Emma Jeffery; one *s* one *d. Educ:* Shiplake Coll.; Poly. of Central London (BA Hons Media Studies). Co-ordinator, 25% Campaign, 1986–87; Dir, Independent Access Steering Cttee, 1987–88; Dep. Dir, Independent Producers

Programme Assoc., 1988–90; Chief Executive: Producers Assocs, 1990–92; Producers Alliance for Cinema and Television, 1992–98; Dir, BFI, 1998–99; CEO, UK Film Council (formerly Film Council), 1999–2010. Member: Govt Film Policy Rev. Gp, 1997; Film Policy Rev. Action Cttee, 1998; former Mem., Video Consultative Council, BBFC. *Recreations:* fatherhood, cinema, reading. *Address:* Arts Alliance, 5 Young Street, W8 5EH. *Club:* Ivy.

WOODWARD, Nicholas Frederick; His Honour Judge Nicholas Woodward; a Circuit Judge, since 2001; *b* 12 March 1952; *s* of Frederick Cyril Woodward and Joan Woodward; *m* (marr. diss.); one *s*. *Educ:* Trent Poly., Nottingham (BA). Called to the Bar, Lincoln's Inn, 1975; in practice as barrister, Chester, 1977–2001. *Address:* Chester Crown Court, The Castle, Chester CH1 2AN. *Club:* City (Chester).

WOODWARD, Patricia Mary Alice; *see* Bey, P. M. A.

WOODWARD, Paul Scott; Chairman, Buckinghamshire Care Ltd, since 2013; *b* Cardiff, 16 July 1950; *s* of William and Jean Woodward; two *s* three *d*. *Educ:* St John's Coll. Sch., Cambridge; Worksop Coll. CA 1973. Articled clerk, 1967–72, tax accountant, 1972–73, Everetts; Investment Analyst, ICI Pension Fund, 1973–74; Eur. Project Accountant, SGB Gp Ltd, 1974–76; Beecham Pharmaceuticals: Finance Manager, Internat. Div., 1976–79; Area Manager, Saudi Arabia, 1979–81, Francophone Africa, 1981–83; Manager, Gulf States, Yemen and Egypt, 1983–85; Gen. Manager, ME, 1985–90; Business Develt Dir, Europe, SmithKline Beecham, 1990–95; Schering Healthcare Ltd: Mktg Dir, 1995–2000; CEO, 2000–06; CEO, Sue Ryder Care, then Sue Ryder, 2007–14. Mem., Eur. Bd, Schering AG, 2000–06. Vice Chm., FPA, 2007–12 (former Chm., Finance and Audit Sub-Cttee, 2007–12). Chm., St John's Coll. Choir Assoc., Cambridge, 2009–14. Trustee: Voluntary Orgns Disability Gp, 2010–14; St Peter and St James Charitable Trust, 2012–14; St Elizabeth Hospice, Ipswich, 2015–. Hon. Fellow, Coll. of Pharmacy Practice, 2006. *Recreations:* ski-ing, sailing, music, reading. *Address:* Buckinghamshire Care Ltd, Easton Street, High Wycombe HP11 1NH. *T:* (01494) 586557. *E:* paul.woodward@yahoo.co.uk.

WOODWARD, Robert Stanley Lawrence; Chief Executive, STV Group plc (formerly SMG plc), since 2007; *b* 30 Nov. 1959; *s* of Frederick Stanley Woodward and Freda Mary Williams; *m* 2009, Patricia Mary Alice Bey, *qv*. *Educ:* Marr Coll., Troon; Univ. of Durham (BSc 1980); Univ. of Edinburgh (MBA 1981). Deloitte & Touche, 1986–97: Partner, Deloitte & Touche Consulting, 1992–97; Man. Dir, Braxton Associates, 1995–97; Man. Dir, UBS Warburg, 1997–2001; Commercial Dir, Channel 4 Television, 2001–05; Sen. Advr, Longacre Partners, 2005–07. Non-exec. Dir, Regenersis plc, 2013–. Trustee, NESTA, 2009–. Pro Chancellor and Chm. Council, City Univ. London, 2012– (Mem. Council, 2006–; Dep. Pro Chancellor, 2009–12). Member: Council, NYT, 2006–12; BAFTA, 2010–. FRSA 2010. *Recreations:* photography, ski-ing, travel, cheese-making. *Address:* Crawfordston Farm, Maybole, Ayrshire KA19 7JS. *T:* (01655) 750215. *Clubs:* MCC; Scottish Arts (Edinburgh).

WOODWARD, Roger Robert, AC 1992; OBE 1980; concert pianist, conductor, writer and composer; Founding Director, School of Music, and Professor of Keyboard Performance Practice, San Francisco State University, since 2002; *b* Sydney, 20 Dec. 1942; *s* of Francis William Wilson Woodward and Gladys Alma Bracken; *m* 1989, Patricia May Ludgate, *d* of Edward and Hazel Ludgate; two *s* one *d*. *Educ:* Higher State Sch. of Music, Warsaw; Chopin Nat. Acad., Warsaw; Univ. of Sydney (DMus 1999). Débuts: Polish Nat. Philharmonic Orch., Warsaw, 1967; RPO, RFH, London, 1970; since then has appeared with major orchestras and conductors incl. Claudio Abbado, Zubin Mehta, Lorin Maazel, Kurt Masur, Witold Rowicki, Charles Mackerras, Erich Leinsdorf, Charles Dutoit, Walter Susskind, and at principal concert centres and festivals in Europe, USA, Japan, China, Australia, NZ; performed complete works of Beethoven, Chopin and Debussy; premières of works by Xenakis, Donatoni, Dillon, Stockhausen, Takemitsu, Feldman, Radulescu, Boyd, Meale, Sitsky. Founder and Artistic Director: London Music Digest, 1972; Alpha Centauri Chamber Ensemble, 1989; Sydney Spring Internat. Fest. of New Music, 1989; Koetschach Mauthen Musiktage (Austria), 1992; Joie et Lumière (Burgundy), 1997: Co-founder and Artistic Dir, Sydney Internat. Piano Comp., 1963; Co-founder, Music Teachers Assoc., NSW, 1975. Chair of Music, Univ. of New England, 2000. Has made numerous recordings; awarded Goethe Prize, Diapason d'Or and German Critics' Award. Order of Merit (Poland), 1993; Chevalier des Arts et des Lettres (France), 2005; Order of Solidarity (Poland), 2007; Gloria Artis Medal Gold Class (Poland), 2011. *Publications:* Beyond Black and White, 2013; numerous contribs to scholastic pubns. *W:* www.rogerwoodward.com.

WOODWARD, Rt Hon. Shaun (Anthony); PC 2007; *b* 26 Oct. 1958; *s* of Dennis George Woodward and late Joan Lillian (*née* Nunn); *m* 1987, Camilla Davan, *e d* of Rt Hon. Sir Timothy Sainsbury, *qv*; one *s* three *d*. *Educ:* Bristol Grammar Sch.; Jesus Coll., Cambridge (first class double MA). Parly Lobbyist, Nat. Consumer Council, 1981–82; BBC TV: Researcher, That's Life!, 1982–85; Producer: Newsnight, 1985–87; Panorama, 1988–89; Editor, That's Life!, 1989–91; Researcher, Lost Babies, 1983; Producer: Drugwatch, 1985; The Gift of Life!, 1987; Dir of Communications, Cons. Party, 1991–92; Vis. Professorial Fellow, QMW, 1992–96; Fellow, Inst. of Politics at Kennedy Sch., Harvard Univ., 1994–95. MP Witney, 1997–2001 (C, 1997–99, Lab, 1999–2001). MP (Lab) St Helens S, 2001–10, St Helens S and Whiston, 2010–15. Opposition front bench spokesman for London, 1999; Parly Under-Sec. of State (Minister for Security and Health Service), NI Office, 2005–06; Parly Under-Sec. of State (Minister for Creative Industries and Tourism), DCMS, 2006–07; Sec. of State for NI, 2007–10; Shadow Sec. of State for NI, 2010–11. Member, Select Committees: EU, 1997–99; Foreign Affairs, 1999–2001; Human Rights, 2001–05. Director: Jerusalem Productions, 1989–96; ENO, 1994–2002 (Chm., Redevelt Campaign, 1994–2002). Chairman: Understanding Industry, 1995–97; Oxford Student Radio, 1995–97; Dep. Chm., LAMDA, 2013– (Chm., Capital Campaign, 2013–); Hon. Chair, Hamptons Internat. Film Fest., 2013–. Chm., Ben Hardwick Meml Fund, 1984–93; Trustee, 1993–2005, Dep. Chm., 1993–97, Childline; Trustee, Human Dignity Trust, 2012– (Dep. Chm., 2014–). Mem., Foundn Bd, RSC, 1998–2002; Mem., Fundraising Council, Southwark Cathedral, 2011–; Dir, Marine Stewardship Council, 1998–2002. *Publications:* (with Ron Lacey) Tranquillisers, 1983; (with Esther Rantzen) Ben: the story of Ben Hardwick, 1985; (with Sarah Caplin) Drugwatch, 1986. *Recreations:* opera, architecture, gardening, reading, travel.

WOODWARD, Sir Thomas (Jones), (Sir Tom Jones), Kt 2006; OBE 1999; entertainer; *b* 7 June 1940; *s* of Thomas Woodward and late Freda (*née* Jones); *m* 1956, Melinda Trenchard; one *s*. Singing début at age of 3; sang in clubs and dance halls; first hit record, It's Not Unusual, 1964; toured US, 1965; many internat. hit records, incl. Reload, 2000 (most successful album in career); radio and TV appearances, incl. series, This is Tom Jones, 1969–71; The Voice, 2012–15; King of the Teds (TV play), 2012; Under Milk Wood, 2014; has toured worldwide. Score for musical play, Matador, 1987. *Films:* Mars Attacks, 1997; Agnes Brown, 1999. Appeared as character in Disney animated feature, Emperor's New Groove, 2000. Silver Clef Award, Nordoff Robbins Music Therapy, 2001. Hon. FRWCMD (Hon. FWCMD 1994). MTV Video Award, 1988; Brit Award, 2003. *Recreations:* music, history. *Address:* Tom Jones Enterprises, 1801 Avenue of the Stars, Suite 200, Los Angeles, CA 90067, USA. *T:* (310) 5520044. *E:* office@tomjones.com. *Clubs:* Home House; Friars (Los Angeles and New York).

WOODWARD, William Charles; QC 1985; a Recorder, 1989–2010; a Deputy High Court Judge, 1997–2010; President, Mental Health Review Tribunal, 2000–10; a Justice of Appeal, Court of Appeal of St Helena, 2002–13; *b* 27 May 1940; *s* of Wilfred Charles Woodward and Annie Stewart Woodward (*née* Young); *m* 1965, Carolyn Edna Johns; two *s* one *d*. *Educ:* South County Junior Sch.; Nottingham High Sch.; St John's Coll., Oxford (BA Jurisp). Marshall to Sir Donald Finnemore, Michaelmas 1962. Called to the Bar, Inner Temple, 1964; pupillage with Brian J. Appleby, QC; Midland (formerly Midland and Oxford) Circuit, 1964–; Head of Ropewalk Chambers, Nottingham, 1987–94. Member: E Midlands Area Cttee, Law Soc., 1972–; Bar Eur. Gp, 1998–; Founder Member: Notts Medico-Legal Soc., 1985–; E Midlands Business and Property Bar Assoc., 1994–. Special Prof., Univ. of Nottingham Sch. of Law, 1998–2010. *Recreations:* family, friends, holidays, Austin 7. *Address:* (chambers) 24 The Ropewalk, Nottingham NG1 5EF. *T:* (0115) 947 2581, *Fax:* (0115) 947 6532. *Clubs:* Pre War Austin Seven; Nottingham and Notts United Services.

WOODWARK, Susan Margaret; *see* Sharland, S. M.

WOOL, Dr Rosemary Jane, CB 1995; FRCPsych; Independent Consultant in Health Care in a Secure Environment, 1996–2010; Founder and Director, Prison Health Care Practitioners, 2003–12. *Educ:* University of London (Charing Cross Hospital Medical School). MB BS, DPM, DRCOG. Dir of Health Care, Prison Medical Service, later Prison Service, 1989–96; Hd of Educn and Trng Unit, Dept of Psychiatry of Addictive Behaviour, St George's Hosp. Med. Sch., 1996–98; Specialist in Psychiatry, specialising in drug and alcohol misuse, W Herts Health Care Trust, 1998. Sec. Gen., Internat. Council of Prison Med. Services, 1995–2001. Trustee, Druglink, 2005–. *Address:* Wicken House, 105 Weston Road, Aston Clinton, Bucks HP22 5EP.

WOOLARD, Edgar Smith; Chairman, 1989–97, and Chief Executive Officer, 1989–96, Du Pont; *b* 15 April 1934; *s* of Edgar S. Woolard and Mamie (Boone) Woolard; *m* 1956, Peggy Harrell; two *d*. *Educ:* North Carolina State Univ. (BSc Indust. Eng. 1956). Joined Du Pont 1957; industrial engineer, Kinston, NC, 1957–59; group supervisor, industrial engrg, 1959–62; supervisor, manufg sect., 1962–64; planning supervisor, 1964–65; staff asst to Prodn Manager, Wilmington, 1965–66; product supt, Old Hickory, Tenn, 1966–69; engrg supt, 1969–70; Asst Plant Manager, Camden, SC, 1970–71; Plant Manager, 1971–73; Dir of products marketing div., Wilmington, 1973–75; Man. Dir, textile marketing div., 1975–76; Manager, corp. plans dept, 1976–77; Gen. Dir, products and planning div., 1977–78; Gen. Manager, textile fibers, 1978–81; Vice-Pres., textile fibers, 1981–83; Exec. Vice President, 1983–85; Vice Chm., 1985–87; Pres. and Chief Operating Officer, 1987–89. Dir, Citicorp; former Dir, N Carolina Textile Foundn; Advr, Acorn Energy, 2010–; Mem., Bd of Trustees, N Carolina State Univ., 1987–95; former member: Bd of Trustees, Winterthur Mus.; Med. Center of Delaware; Protestant Episcopal Theol Seminary, Virginia; Exec. Cttee, Delaware Roundtable; Bretton Woods Cttee; World Affairs Council; Business Roundtable. *Address:* c/o Du Pont, 1007 Market Street, Wilmington, DE 19898, USA.

WOOLAS, Philip James; Founder and Director, Wellington Street Partners Ltd, since 2011; *b* 11 Dec. 1959; *s* of late Dennis Woolas and of Maureen Woolas (*née* White); *m* 1988, Tracey Jane Allen; two *s*. *Educ:* Univ. of Manchester (BA Hons Philosophy 1981). Treas., 1983–84, Pres., 1984–86, NUS; journalist, Television South, 1987; Asst Prod., BBC Newsnight, 1988–90; Prod., Channel Four News, 1990–91; Head of Communications, GMB, 1991–97. MP (Lab) Oldham East and Saddleworth, 1997–Nov. 2010. PPS to Minister for Transport, 1999–2001; an Asst Govt Whip, 2001–02; a Lord Comr of HM Treasury (Govt Whip), 2002–03; Parly Sec., Privy Council Office, and Dep. Leader, H of C, 2003–05; Minister of State: (Minister for Local Govt and Community Cohesion), ODPM, subseq. DCLG, 2005–07; DEFRA, 2007–08; Minister of State (Minister for Immigration), HM Treasury and Home Office, 2008–10; Minister for the NW, 2009–10; Shadow Minister for Immigration, 2010. Chm., All Party Parly Clothing and Textile Gp, 1998–2001; Mem., PLP Leadership Campaign Team, 1997–99 (Dep. Chm., 1998–99). Chm., Tribune Publications Ltd, 1997–2001. Chm., ACE Centre, 2014–. FRSA 2007. *Recreations:* photography, reading, Roxy Music, French wine, cricket, Manchester United supporter. *Address:* 16 Church Walk, Brentford, Middlesex TW8 8DB. *Clubs:* Groucho; Lancashire County Cricket.

WOOLER, Stephen John, CB 2005; HM Chief Inspector, Crown Prosecution Service, 1999–2010 (became statutory independent inspectorate, 2000); *b* 16 March 1948; *s* of Herbert George Wooler and Mabel Wooler; *m* 1974, Jonquil Elizabeth Wilmshurst-Smith; one *s* one *d*. *Educ:* Bedford Modern Sch.; University Coll. London (LLB Hons 1969). Called to the Bar, Gray's Inn, 1969, Bencher, 2008; in practice at Common Law Bar, 1970–73; joined Office of Director of Public Prosecutions, 1973: Legal Asst, 1973–76; Sen. Legal Asst, 1976–82; Asst DPP, 1982–83; on secondment to Law Officers' Dept, 1983–87; Chief Crown Prosecutor (London North), 1987–89; on secondment to Law Officers' Dept, 1989–99: Dep. Legal Sec. to Law Officers, 1992–99. Asst Boundary Comr for England, 2011–14. Member: Lord Chancellor's Adv. Sub-Cttee for Bucks, 2012–14, for Thames Valley, 2014–; Case Mgt Cttee, Financial Reporting Council, 2013–; Ind. Bd, Legal Services Agency for NI (formerly NI Legal Services Commn), 2014–. Review of Attorney Gen.'s Chambers for I of M Govt, 2012; Ind. Reviewer, RSPCA prosecution functions, 2013–14; Adv. Gp to the Victims' Comr, 2014–. *Recreations:* campanology, Rugby, walking, gardening. *Address:* 29 Vicarage Road, Marsworth, Tring, Herts HP23 4LT.

WOOLEY, Prof. Trevor Dion, PhD; FRS 2007; Professor of Pure Mathematics, University of Bristol, since 2007. *Educ:* Gonville and Caius Coll., Cambridge (BA Hons Maths 1987; Cert. of Adv. Study in Maths 1988); Imperial Coll. of Sci. and Technol., Univ. of London (PhD 1990). Department of Mathematics, University of Michigan: Asst Prof., 1991–95; Associate Prof., 1995–98; Prof., 1998–2007; Chm. of Dept, 2002–05. *Publications:* articles in jls. *Address:* Department of Mathematics, University of Bristol, University Walk, Clifton, Bristol BS8 1TW.

WOOLF, family name of **Baron Woolf**.

WOOLF, Baron *cr* 1992 (Life Peer), of Barnes in the London Borough of Richmond; **Harry Kenneth Woolf,** CH 2015; Kt 1979; PC 1986; Lord Chief Justice of England and Wales, 2000–05; Chartered Arbitrator/Mediator, since 2006; *b* 2 May 1933; *s* of late Alexander Woolf and Leah Woolf (*née* Cussins); *m* 1961, Marguerite Sassoon, *d* of late George Sassoon; three *s*. *Educ:* Fettes Coll.; University Coll., London (LLB; Fellow, 1981). Called to Bar, Inner Temple, 1954; Bencher, 1976. Commnd (Nat. Service), 15/19th Royal Hussars, 1954; seconded Army Legal Services, 1955; Captain 1955. Started practice at Bar, 1956. A Recorder of the Crown Court, 1972–79; Jun. Counsel, Inland Revenue, 1973–74; First Treasury Junior Counsel (Common Law), 1974–79; a Judge of the High Court of Justice, Queen's Bench Div., 1979–86; Presiding Judge, SE Circuit, 1981–84; a Lord Justice of Appeal, 1986–92; a Lord of Appeal in Ordinary, 1992–96; Master of the Rolls, 1996–2000; Judge, Hong Kong Court of Final Appeal, 2003–; Pres., Qatar Financial Services Court, 2006–. Held inquiry into prison disturbances, 1990, Part II with Judge Tumin, report 1991; conducted inquiry, Access to Justice, 1994–96; held inquiry into BAE Systems, 2008 (report: Business Ethics, Global Companies and the Defence Industry, 2008); Chm., LSE Inquiry into LSE's relationship with Libya, 2011. Member: Senate, Inns of Court and Bar, 1981–85; Bd of Management, Inst. of Advanced Legal Studies, 1985–94 (Chm., 1986–94); World Bank Internat. Adv. Council on Law and Justice, 2001–; Chairman: Lord Chancellor's Adv. Cttee on Legal Educn, 1986–91; Middx Adv. Cttee on Justices of the Peace, 1986–90; Lord Chancellor's Adv. Cttee on Public Records, 1996–2000; Council of Civil Justice, 1998–2000; Rules Cttee, 1998–2000; Bank of England's Financial Markets Law Cttee, 2005–; President: Assoc. of Law Teachers, 1985–89; Central Council of Jewish Social Services, 1987–2000; SW London Magistrates Assoc., 1987–93; Assoc. of Mems of Bds of Visitors, 1994–; Public Records Soc., 1996–2000. Vice-Pres., Royal Over-Seas League, 2001–. Pro-Chancellor, London Univ., 1994–2002. Chairman: Trustees, Butler Trust, 1992–96 (Trustee, 1991–96; Pres., 1996–); Special Trustees, St Mary's Hosp., Paddington, 1993–97; Magna Carta Trust, 1996–2000; Prison Reform Trust, 2011–. Patron: Jewish Mus., 1998–; Woolf Institute: Muslim, Jewish and

Christian Inter-faith Relns, 2000–. Visitor: Nuffield Coll., Oxford, 1996–2000; UCL, 1996–2000 (Chm., Council, 2005–). Chancellor, Open Univ. of Israel, 2005–. Gov., Oxford Centre for Postgrad. Hebrew Studies, 1989–93. Hon. Mem., SPTL, 1988. Hon. Bencher, King's Inns, Dublin. Hon. FBA 2000; Hon. FMedSci 2002. Hon. Fellow, Leeds Poly., 1990. Hon. LLD: Buckingham, 1992; Bristol, 1992; London, 1993; Anglia Poly. Univ., 1994; Manchester Metropolitan, 1994; Hull, 2001; Richmond, 2001; Cambridge, 2002; Birmingham, 2002; Exeter, 2002; Wolverhampton, 2002; Hon. DSc Cranfield, 2001; Hon. DLit London. Hon. Freeman and Mem., Drapers' Co., 1999. *Publications:* Protecting the Public: the new challenge (Hamlyn Lecture), 1990; (ed with J. Woolf) Declaratory Judgement, 2nd edn, 1993, 3rd edn 2002; (ed jtly) de Smith, Judicial Review of Administrative Action, 5th edn, 1995, 7th edn (jtly) as de Smith's Judicial Review, 2008; (ed jtly) Principles of Judicial Review, 1999. *Address:* House of Lords, SW1A 0PW. *Clubs:* Athenæum, Garrick, Royal Automobile.

WOOLF, Dame (Catherine) Fiona, DBE 2015 (CBE 2002); Partner, CMS Cameron McKenna, since 1981; President, Law Society, 2006–07 (Vice President, 2005–06); Lord Mayor of London, 2013–14; *b* 11 May 1948; *d* of Richard and Margaret Swain; *m* 1990, Nicholas Woolf; one step *s* one step *d*. *Educ:* Keele Univ. (BA Law 1970); Strasbourg Univ. (Dip. Comparative Law 1969). Solicitor of Supreme Court, 1973. Coward Chance, 1973–78; CMS Cameron McKenna, 1981–, energy and projects practice, work on power sector restructurings, privatisations and power and transmission projects. Mem., Competition Commn, 2005–14. Non-exec. Dir, Affinity Water Ltd (formerly Three Valleys Water plc, then Veolia Water Central plc), 2006–13; Chair, Adv. Bd, Base London. Sen. Fellow, Harvard Univ., 2001–02. Pres., Chelsea Opera Gp (Chm., 2008); Trustee: Raleigh Internat., 2007–; Sci. Mus. Gp, 2015–. Gov., Guildhall Sch. of Music and Drama, 2011–14; Chancellor, Univ. of Law, 2014–. Alderman, Candlewick Ward, City of London, 2007–; Sheriff, City of London, 2010–11; Mem. Council, London Regt, 2011–. Hon. Pres., Aldersgate Gp. Hon. LLD: Coll. of Law, 2007; Keele, 2008. *Publications:* Global Transmission Expansion: recipes for success, 2003; co-author of three World Bank pubns; many articles and papers in energy jls. *Recreations:* singing, music, furniture history, theatre, art, occasional golf, turned wood. *Address:* CMS Cameron McKenna, Mitre House, 160 Aldersgate Street, WC1A 4DD. *T:* (020) 7367 3000. *E:* fiona.woolf@cms-cmck.com. *Clubs:* Royal Automobile, East India.

WOOLF, Prof. Clifford John; Professor of Neurology and Neurobiology, Harvard Medical School, since 2010 (Richard Kitz Professor of Anesthesia Research, 1997–2010); Director, F. M. Kirby Neurobiology Center, Children's Hospital Boston, since 2010; Director, Neurobiology Program, Harvard Stem Cell Institute, since 2013; *b* 30 Jan. 1952; *s* of Jeffry and Lorna Woolf; *m* 1976, Fredia Maltz; two *s*. *Educ:* Univ. of the Witwatersrand, Johannesburg (MB, BCh, PhD). MRCP. Lectr, Middlesex Hosp. Med. Sch., London, 1979–81; Lectr, 1981–88, Reader, 1988–92, Prof. of Neurobiology, 1992–97, UCL. Dir, Neural Plasticity Res. Gp, Massachusetts Gen. Hosp., 1997–2010. Schmidt Lectr, MIT, 2010. Hon. Fellow, Faculty of Pain Medicine, Coll. of Anaesthetists, Ireland, 2015. Distinguished Res. Award, Amer. Soc. for Anesthesia, 2004; Wall Medal, RCAnaes, 2009; Javits Award, NIH, 2011; F. E. Bennett Meml Lectureship Award, American Neurol Assoc., 2012; Magnes Medal (Israel), 2013; Frederick W. L. Kerr Basic Sci. Res. Award, American Pain Soc., 2015. *Publications:* numerous articles in scientific jls on the pathophysiology of pain and the regeneration of the nervous system. *Recreation:* mind surfing. *Address:* F. M. Kirby Neurobiology Center, Children's Hospital Boston, 300 Longwood Avenue, CLS 12258, Boston, MA 02115, USA.

WOOLF, Dame Fiona; *see* Woolf, Dame C. F.

WOOLF, Geoffrey David; photographer; *b* 15 April 1944. *Educ:* Polytechnic of Central London (BSc Econ). Lecturer in History, Southgate Technical College, 1974–89; Gen. Sec., NATFHE, 1989–94; Trade Union Manager, LV Gp, 1996–97; Organiser, Prospect (formerly Inst. of Professionals, Managers and Specialists), 1997–2005. *Recreation:* politics. *Address:* 23 Sawyers Court, Chelmsford Road, Shenfield, Essex CM15 8RH. *E:* geoffwoolf@outlook.com.

WOOLFE, Richard; Director, WoolfeTV, media consultants, since 2012; *b* Brighton, 14 Aug. 1962; *s* of Julian Woolfe and Laurel Woolfe; *m* 1988, Hilary Berg; one *s* one *d*. *Educ:* Brighton Coll.; Manchester Poly. (BEd Hons). Freelance reporter/producer, BBC Radio Sussex, 1985–86; Researcher, then Producer, later Exec. Producer, That's Life!, Hearts of Gold, Nat. Lottery Live, Noel's Christmas Presents, The Family Show, Good Fortune, BBC TV, 1986–96; Man. Dir, Real TV, 1996–97; Ed., Entertainment, Granada TV, 1998–99; Hd of Entertainment, Planet 24 Productions, 1999–2001; Dir of Television, Living TV, 2001–06; Dir of Progs, Sky 1, 2, 3, 2006–08; Channel Controller, Five, 2009–10; Creative Director: Prime Focus Productions, 2011–12; Prizeo.com, 2012–15. Member: RTS 2002; BAFTA 2007. *Recreations:* reading, wine. *Clubs:* Ivy, Soho House.

WOOLFE, Steven Marcus; Member (UK Ind) North West Region, European Parliament, since 2014; *b* Moss Side, Manchester, 9 Oct. 1967; *m*. *Educ:* St Bernard's RC Sch.; St Bede's RC Ind. Coll.; Univ. of Wales, Aberystwyth (LLB 1990); Inns of Court Sch. of Law. Called to the Bar, Inner Temple, 1992; in practice as barrister, specialising in commercial, criminal and common law, 1992–96; Legal and Compliance Analyst, UBS, 1996–97; Counsel: Taylor Wessing, 1997–99; DLA Piper, 1999–2000; Sen. Compliance Consultant and Partner, Aurelius Compliance Consultants, 2000–07; Dep. Hd, Compliance Dept, Standard Bank, 2003–04; Gen. Counsel, Boyer Allen Investment Mgt LLP, 2006–12; Gen. Counsel Consultant, MercuryJove Advrs, 2012–14. UKIP spokesman on financial affairs and City of London, 2010–14, on econs, 2014, on migration and financial affairs, 2014–. Contested (UK Ind) Stockport, 2015. *Address:* European Parliament, 60 Rue Wiertz, 1047 Brussels, Belgium; (office) 62 Northgate Street, Chester CH1 2HT.

WOOLFENDEN, Guy Anthony, OBE 2007; freelance composer and conductor; *b* 12 July 1937; *s* of late Harold Woolfenden and Kathleen Woolfenden (*née* Groom); *m* 1962, Jane Aldrick; three *s*. *Educ:* Westminster Abbey Choir Sch.; Whitgift Sch.; Christ's Coll., Cambridge (BA 1959; MA 1963); Guildhall Sch. of Music and Drama, London (LGSM 1960). Joined Royal Shakespeare Co., 1961, Hd of Music, 1963–98; Artistic Dir, Cambridge Fest., 1986–91. Composed scores for: RSC (over 150 scores); Comédie-Française, Paris; Burgtheater, Vienna; Teatro Stabile, Genoa; Nat. Theatre, Norway; arranged music for four full-length ballets by choreographer André Prokovsky: Anna Karenina (conducted Russian premiere, Kirov Ballet, St Petersburg, 1993); The Three Musketeers; La Traviata - The Ballet; The Queen of Spades. Chm., British Assoc. of Symphonic Bands and Wind Ensembles, 1999–2002; Pres., ISM, 2002–03. Vice-Pres., Denne Gilkes Meml Fund (Chm., 1985–2013; Vice-Pres., 2014–). FBC (FBSM 1990). Hon. LCM 1998. *Address:* Malvern House, Sibford Ferris, Banbury, Oxfordshire OX15 5RG. *T:* (01295) 780679, *Fax:* (01295) 788630. *E:* guy@arielmusic.co.uk.

WOOLFSON, Prof. Michael Mark, FRS 1984; FRAS; FInstP; Professor of Theoretical Physics, University of York, 1965–94, now Emeritus; *b* 9 Jan. 1927; *s* of Morris and Rose Woolfson; *m* 1951, Margaret (*née* Frohlich); two *s* one *d*. *Educ:* Jesus College, Oxford (MA; Hon. Fellow, 1999); UMIST (PhD, DSc). Royal Engineers, 1947–49. Research Assistant: UMIST, 1950–52; Cavendish Lab., Cambridge, 1952–54; ICI Fellow, Univ. of Cambridge, 1954–55; Lectr, 1955–61, Reader, 1961–65, UMIST; Head of Dept of Physics, Univ. of York, 1982–87. Hughes Medal, Royal Soc., 1986; Patterson Award, Amer. Crystallographic Assoc., 1990; Aminoff Medal, Royal Swedish Acad. of Scis, 1992; Dorothy Hodgkin Prize, British Crystallographic Assoc., 1997; Ewald Prize, Internat. Union of Crystallography, 2002. *Publications:* Direct Methods in Crystallography, 1961; An Introduction to X-Ray Crystallography, 1970, 2nd edn 1997; The Origin of the Solar System, 1989; Physical and Non-Physical Methods of Solving Crystal Structures, 1995; An Introduction to Computer Simulation, 1999; The Origin and Evolution of the Solar System, 2000; Planetary Science, 2001, 2nd edn 2013; Mathematics for Physics, 2007; Formation of the Solar System, 2007, 2nd edn 2013; Everyday Probability and Statistics, 2008, 2nd edn 2012; Time, Space, Stars and Man, 2009; Materials, Matter and Particles, 2009; On the Origin of Planets, 2010; The Fundamentals of Imaging, 2011; Resonance, 2014; Time and Age, 2015; papers in learned jls. *Recreation:* writing. *Address:* 24 Sandmoor Green, Leeds LS17 7SB. *T:* (0113) 266 2166.

WOOLGAR, Prof. Stephen William, PhD; Professor of Sociology and Marketing, and Head of Science and Technology Studies, University of Oxford, since 2000; Fellow, Green Templeton College (formerly Green College), Oxford, since 2000; *b* 14 Feb. 1950; *s* of late William Thomas Woolgar, III, and Constance Lillian Stuart Woolgar (*née* Hinkes); *m* 1983, Jacqueline Stokes; three *d*. *Educ:* Brentwood Sch.; Emmanuel Coll., Cambridge (BA 1st Cl. Hons 1972; MA 1976; PhD 1978). Brunel University: Lectr in Sociol., 1975–88; Reader 1988–92; Prof. of Sociol., 1992–2000; Dir, Centre for Res. into Innovation, Culture and Technol., 1991–98; Hd, Dept of Human Scis, 1996–98; Dir, ESRC prog. Virtual Society? the social sci. of electronic technologies, Univ. of Oxford (formerly at Brunel Univ.), 1997–2002. Vis. Prof., McGill Univ., Canada, 1979–81; Exxon Fellow, MIT, 1983–84; Maître de Recherche Associé, Ecole Nationale Supérieure des Mines, Paris, 1988–89; ESRC Sen. Res. Fellow, 1994–95; Fulbright Sen. Schol., Dept of Sociol., UC San Diego, 1995–96. Member: OST Technology Foresight Panel: Leisure and Learning, 1994–96; IT, Electronics and Communications, 1996–99; Sociol. Panel, HEFCE RAE 1996 and 2001; Council, Consumers' Assoc., 2000–. *Publications:* (with B. Latour) Laboratory Life: the construction of scientific facts, 1979, 2nd edn 1986; (ed) Knowledge and Reflexivity, 1988; Science: the very idea, 1988; (ed jtly) The Cognitive Turn: sociological and psychological perspectives on science, 1989; (ed with M. Lynch) Representation in Scientific Practice, 1990; (with K. Grint) The Machine at Work: technology, work and organisation, 1997; Virtual Society?: technology, cyberbole, reality, 2002; numerous articles. *Address:* Saïd Business School, University of Oxford, Park End Street, Oxford OX1 1HP. *T:* (01865) 288934. *E:* steve.woolgar@sbs.ox.ac.uk.

WOOLHOUSE, Prof. Mark Edward John, OBE 2002; FRSE; FMedSci; Professor of Infectious Disease Epidemiology, University of Edinburgh, since 2005; *b* Shrewsbury, 25 April 1959; *s* of late Prof. John George Woolhouse, CBE and of (Ruth) Carolyn Woolhouse; *m* 2004, Dr Francisca Mutapi; one *d*. *Educ:* New Coll., Oxford (BA Zool. 1980); Univ. of York (MSc Biol Computation 1981); Queen's Univ., Kingston, Ont (PhD Biol. 1985). Res. Fellow, Dept of Biol Scis, Univ. of Zimbabwe, 1985–86; MRC Trng Fellow, Dept of Biol., Imperial Coll. London, 1986–89; Department of Zoology, University of Oxford: Beit Meml Fellow for Med. Res., 1989–92; Royal Soc. Univ. Res. Fellow, 1992–97; Prof. of Veterinary Public Health and Quantitative Epidemiol., Centre for Tropical Veterinary Medicine, Univ. of Edinburgh, 1997–2005. FRSE 2004; FMedSci 2010. *Publications:* contrib. book chapters and articles to scientific jls. *Recreations:* walking, fishing, Everton FC. *Address:* Centre for Immunity, Infection and Evolution, Ashworth Laboratories, Kings Buildings, University of Edinburgh, Charlotte Auerbach Road, Edinburgh EH9 3FL. *T:* (0131) 650 5456, *Fax:* (0131) 650 6564. *E:* mark.woolhouse@ed.ac.uk.

WOOLHOUSE, Richard; Chief Economist, British Bankers' Association, since 2013; *b* Cambridge, 6 Aug. 1967; *s* of Geoffrey and June Woolhouse; *m* Susanna; one *s* two *d*. *Educ:* Fitzwilliam Coll., Cambridge (BA 1990; MA). PA, Cambridge Econ. Consultants, 1990–94; Economist/Strategist, Citibank: London, 1994–97; Hong Kong, 1997–98; London, 1998–2000; McKinsey & Co., London, 2000–02; Economist, HMRC/HM Treasury, 2002–04; Strategist, Credit Suisse First Boston, 2004–05; Public and Corporate Econ. Consultants, 2005–08; Economist: Centre for Cities, 2008–09; CBI, 2009–13. *Recreation:* cricket. *Address:* British Bankers' Association, Pinners Hall, 105–108 Old Broad Street, EC2N 1EX. *T:* 07785 257224. *E:* richard.woolhouse@gmail.com.

WOOLLAM, Her Honour Suzanna Elizabeth; a Circuit Judge, 2001–06; *b* 6 Dec. 1946; *d* of late John Martin Woollam and Elizabeth Mary Woollam (*née* Brennan). *Educ:* various convents; Trinity Coll., Dublin (MA Philosophy 1969). Called to the Bar, Gray's Inn, 1975; law reporting for the Weekly Law Reports and Times Law Reports, 1975–77; Army Legal Service, 1977–79; Solicitor to Scotland Yard, 1980–88; Sen. Legal Asst, office of JAG, 1988–90; Asst JAG, 1990–2001. *Recreations:* walking, gardening, reading, films, theatre.

WOOLLARD, John Ian; a District Judge (Magistrates' Courts), Essex, since 2011; *b* 13 July 1954; *s* of Charles and Joy Woollard; *m* 1981, Angela Margaret Lee; one *s* one *d*. *Educ:* Brentwood Sch. Admitted Solicitor, 1977; Asst Solicitor, T. V. Edwards & Co., 1977–78; County Prosecuting Solicitors' Office, Essex, 1978–82; Partner, Mitchell Maudsley & Wright, Basildon, 1982–87; freelance solicitor advocate, 1987–98; a Stipendiary Magistrate, then Dist Judge (Magistrates' Courts), Hants, 1998–2006; a Dist Judge (Magistrates' Courts), NE London, 2006–11. *Recreations:* music, reading, tennis. *Address:* c/o Essex Magistrates' Courts, Osprey House, Hedgerows Business Park, Springfield, Chelmsford CM2 5PF. *T:* (01245) 313500.

WOOLLEY, David Rorie; QC 1980; barrister-at-law; a Recorder of the Crown Court, 1982–94; *b* 9 June 1939; *s* of Albert and Ethel Woolley; *m* 1988, Mandy, *d* of Donald and Barbara Hutchison, Upper Dicker, Sussex. *Educ:* Winchester Coll.; Trinity Hall, Cambridge (BA Hons Law). Called to the Bar, Middle Temple, 1962, Bencher, 1988. Vis. Scholar, Wolfson Coll., Cambridge, 1982–87. Inspector, DoE inquiry into Nat. Gall. extension, 1984. *Publications:* Town Hall and the Property Owner, 1965; (jtly) Environmental Law, 2000, 2nd edn, 2009; (jtly) History of the Middle Temple, 2011; (contrib.) Pantaudi: nawab of cricket, 2013; contribs to various legal jls. *Recreations:* opera, mountaineering, Real tennis. *Address:* White Lodge, Lockeridge, Wilts SN8 4EQ. *Clubs:* MCC; Swiss Alpine.

WOOLLEY, Janice Joanne; *see* Graham, J. J.

WOOLLEY, John Maxwell, MBE 1945; TD 1946; Clerk, Merchant Taylors' Company, and Clerk to The Governors, Merchant Taylors' School, 1962–80; *b* 22 March 1917; *s* of Lt-Col Jasper Maxwell Woolley, IMS (Retd) and Kathleen Mary Woolley (*née* Waller); *m* 1952, Esme Adela Hamilton-Cole; two *s*. *Educ:* Cheltenham College; Trinity College, Oxford. BA (Oxon) 1938, MA (Oxon) 1962. Practising Solicitor, 1950–55; Asst Clerk, Merchant Taylors' Company, 1955–62. Hon. Mem. CGLI, 1991. *Address:* Flat 27, 15 Grand Avenue, Hove, E Sussex BN3 2NG. *T:* (01273) 733200.

WOOLLEY, (John) Moger; DL; Chairman, Bristol Water Holdings, 1998–2012; *b* 1 May 1935; *s* of Cyril Herbert Steele Woolley and Eveline Mary May Woolley; *m* 1960, Gillian Edith Millar; one *s* one *d*. *Educ:* Taunton Sch.; Bristol Univ., 1956–59 (BSc). National Service, 1954–56. Various management positions, DRG plc, 1959–89, Chief Exec., 1985–89; Chairman: Dolphin Packaging, 1990–95; API plc, 1992–2001; Brunel (Hldgs) plc (formerly BM Gp), 1992–2002. Non-executive Director: Staveley Industries, 1990–99; United Bristol Hosp. Trust, 1991–93; Avon Rubber, 1992–96. Chm. Council, 1997–2006, Pro-Chancellor, 2006, Univ. of Bristol. DL 2000, High Sheriff, 2002–03, Glos. Hon. Fellow, Univ. of Bristol, 2014. Hon. LLD Bristol, 2005. *Recreations:* cricket, hockey, golf, gardening. *Address:* Matford House, Northwoods, Winterbourne, Bristol BS36 1RS. *T:* (01454) 772180. *Clubs:* MCC; Merchant Venturers' (Bristol) (Master, 1998–99).

WOOLLEY, Mary Elizabeth; *see* Lewis, M. E.

WOOLLEY, Moger; *see* Woolley, (John) Moger.

WOOLLEY, Simon; Co-Founder and Director, Operation Black Vote, since 1996; *b* Leicester, 24 Dec. 1961; *s* of Daniel and Phyliss Fox; partner, Begona Juarros; one *s*. *Educ:* BA Hons Lit. and Spanish; MA Hons Spanish Lit. Mem., Equality and Human Rights Commn, 2009–12. Chair, At Home in Europe, Open Soc. Foundn, 2012–. Vis. Lectr, Nottingham Univ., 2006–. Hon. Dr Westminster, 2012. *Publications:* How to Achieve Better Black and Minority Ethnic Representation. *Recreations:* football, swimming. *Address:* 18A Victoria Park Square, E2 9PB. *E:* simon@obv.org.uk.

WOOLLEY, Trevor Adrian, CB 2007; non-executive Director, Oil and Pipelines Agency, since 2012; Lay Member, Hounslow Clinical Commissioning Group, since 2013; *b* 9 Aug. 1954; *s* of late Harry George Woolley and Doreen Vera Woolley (*née* O'Hale). *Educ:* Latymer Upper Sch., Hammersmith; Peterhouse, Cambridge (MA Hist.). Ministry of Defence, 1975–2012: Private Sec. to Sec. of Cabinet, 1986–90 (on secondment); Dir, Procurement Policy, 1990–93; Head, Resources and Progs (Army), 1993–97; Asst Under Sec. of State (Systems), 1997–98; Dir Gen., Resources and Plans, 1998–2002; Comd Sec., Land, 2002–03; Finance Dir, 2003–08; Dir Gen., Police Study Team, 2009–10; Chief of Corporate Services, then Dir Gen., Resources, Defence Equipment and Support Orgn, 2010–12. Mem., Adv. Council, Nat. Archives, 2014–. *Publications:* Unnatural Selection: 50 years of England Test teams, 2015. *Recreations:* cricket, golf, travel, trekking. *E:* trvrwool@aol.com. *Clubs:* MCC; Windlesham Golf.

WOOLMAN, Hon. Lord; Stephen Errol Woolman; a Senator of the College of Justice in Scotland, since 2008; *b* 16 May 1953; *s* of late Errol Woolman, architect, and Frances Woolman (*née* Porter); *m* 1977, Dr Helen Mackinnon; two *d*. *Educ:* George Heriot's Sch., Edinburgh; Aberdeen Univ. (LLB). Lectr, 1978–87, Associate Dean, Faculty of Law, 1981–84, Edinburgh Univ.; admitted to Faculty of Advocates, 1987; Standing Junior Counsel in Scotland: Office of Fair Trading, 1991–95; MoD (Procurement Exec.), 1995–96; Inland Revenue, 1996–98; QC (Scot.) 1998; Advocate Depute, 1999–2002. Chm., Scottish Council of Law Reporting, 2007–08; Dep. Chm., Boundary Commn for Scotland, 2009–. Keeper, Advocates' Liby, 2004–08. Trustee, Nat. Liby of Scotland, 2004–08. Chm. Council, St George's Sch., Edinburgh, 2011–15. Hon. LLD Aberdeen, 2012. Liveryman, Woolmen's Co., 2014. *Publications:* An Introduction to the Scots Law of Contract, 1987, 5th edn 2014. *Recreations:* cinema, swimming. *Address:* Court of Session, Parliament House, Edinburgh EH1 1RQ. *Club:* New (Edinburgh).

WOOLMAN, Andrew Paul Lander; His Honour Judge Woolman; a Circuit Judge, since 2006; *b* 10 Feb. 1950; *s* of Sydney and Anita Woolman; *m* 1977, Telsa Phillipson; two *s* one *d*. *Educ:* Leeds Grammar Sch.; Pembroke Coll., Cambridge (BA 1971). Called to the Bar, Inner Temple, 1973; Asst Recorder, 1992–97; a Recorder, 1997–2006. *Recreations:* tennis, classics, football, music, theatre, fell-walking, talking. *Address:* c/o Preston Combined Courts, The Law Courts, Openshaw Place, Ringway, Preston, Lancs PR1 2LL. *T:* (01772) 844700.

WOOLMAN, Stephen Errol; *see* Woolman, Hon. Lord.

WOOLMER, family name of **Baron Woolmer of Leeds**.

WOOLMER OF LEEDS, Baron *cr* 1999 (Life Peer), of Leeds in the county of West Yorkshire; **Kenneth John Woolmer;** Partner: Halton Gill Associates, consultants on central and local government relations, 1999–2009 (Principal, 1979–97); Anderson McGraw, 2001–07; *b* 25 April 1940; *s* of Joseph William and Gertrude May Woolmer; *m* 1961, Janice Chambers; three *s*. *Educ:* Gladstone Street County Primary, Rothwell, Northants; Kettering Grammar Sch.; Leeds Univ. (BA Econs). Research Fellow, Univ. of West Indies, 1961–62; Teacher, Friern Rd Sec. Mod. Sch., London, 1963; Lecturer: Univ. of Leeds (Economics), 1963–66; Univ. of Ahmadu Bello, Nigeria, 1966–68; Univ. of Leeds, 1968–79; Dir, MBA Progs, 1991–97, Dean of Ext. Relns, 1997, Chm., subseq. Dean, 1997–2000, Sch. of Business and Econ. Studies, Leeds Univ., later Leeds Univ. Business Sch. Councillor: Leeds CC, 1970–78; West Yorkshire MCC, 1973–80 (Leader, 1975–77; Leader of Opposition, 1977–79). Chairman, Planning and Transportation Cttee, Assoc. of Metropolitan Authorities, 1974–77. Contested (Lab) Batley and Spen, 1983, 1987. MP (Lab) Batley and Morley, 1979–83; Opposition spokesman on trade, shipping and aviation, 1981–83; Mem., Select Cttee on Treasury and Civil Service, 1980–81; Chm., 1981, Vice-Chm., 1982, PLP Economics and Finance Gp; House of Lords: Mem., 1999–2002, Chm., 2002–06, EU Sub Cttee B (Industry, Energy, Telecoms and Transport); Mem., EU Select Cttee, 2002–06; Mem., EU Sub Cttee A (Economic and Financial Affairs and Internat. Trade), 2007–12; Mem., Secondary Legislation Scrutiny Cttee, 2013–. Dir, UK Japan 21st Century Gp, 2005–10; Mem., Internat. Adv. Bd, White Rose E Asia Centre, 2007–. Dir, Leeds United AFC, 1991–96. Non-executive Director: Thornfield Develts Ltd, 1999–2002; Thornfield Ventures Ltd, 2002–04; Saiinfo plc, 2000–02; Courtcom Ltd, 2001–03. Chm. Govs, Leeds Metropolitan Univ., 2010–13; Mem. Adv. Bd, Warwick Business Sch., 2012–.

WOOLRICH, John; composer; *b* 3 Jan. 1954; *s* of Derek Holland Woolrich and Una Woolrich (*née* MacDougall). *Educ:* Manchester Univ. (BA); Lancaster Univ. (MLitt). Northern Arts Fellow, Durham Univ., 1982–85; Composer in Residence, Nat. Centre for Orchestral Studies, 1985–86; Artistic Dir, Composers' Ensemble, 1989–; Composer in Association, Orch. of St John's, Smith Square, 1994–95; Dir of Concerts, Almeida Opera, 1999–; Artistic Associate, Birmingham Contemporary Music Gp, 2002–; Associate Artistic Dir, Aldeburgh Fest., 2005–10 (Guest Artistic Dir, 2004); Artistic Director: Dartington Internat. Summer Sch., 2010–13; Mirepoix Musique, 2013–. Lectr in Music, RHBNC, 1994–98; Prof. of Music, Brunel Univ., 2010–13. Vis. Fellow, Clare Hall, Cambridge, 1999–2001. Hon. FTCL 1996. *Compositions* include: orchestral: The Barber's Timepiece, 1986; The Ghost in the Machine, 1990; The Theatre Represents a Garden: Night, 1991; Concerto for Viola, 1993; Concerto for Oboe, 1996; Cello Concerto, 1998; Concerto for Orchestra, 1999; Violin Concerto, 2008; Falling Down, 2009; chamber music: Ulysses Awakes, 1989; Lending Wings, 1989; The Death of King Renaud, 1991; It is Midnight, Dr Schweitzer, 1992; A Farewell, 1992; Capriccio, 2009. *Address:* c/o Faber Music, Bloomsbury House, 74–77 Great Russell Street, WC1B 3DA. *T:* (020) 7908 5310.

WOOLTON, 3rd Earl of, *cr* 1956; **Simon Frederick Marquis;** Baron Woolton, 1939; Viscount Woolton, 1953; Viscount Walberton, 1956; *b* 24 May 1958; *s* of 2nd Earl of Woolton and Cecily Josephine (later Countess Lloyd George of Dwyfor), *e d* of Sir Alexander Gordon Cumming, 5th Bt; *S* father, 1969; *m* 1st, 1987, Hon. Sophie Frederika (marr. diss. 1997), *o c* of Baron Birdwood; three *d*; 2nd, 1999, Mrs Carol Chapman (*née* Davidson). *Educ:* Eton College; St Andrews Univ. (MA Hons). Company director. Merchant banker, S. G. Warburg & Co. Ltd, 1982–88; Founder Director: Woolton Elwes Ltd, 1994–2000; New Boathouse Capital Ltd, 2000–08; Quayle Munro Ltd, 2008–; Dir, Quayle Munro Hldgs Ltd, 2012–. Trustee: Woolton Charitable Trust; Titsey Foundn; Balcarres Heritage Trust; Keats-Shelley Meml Assoc. Gov., Tonbridge Sch. Liveryman, Skinners' Co. *Recreation:* golf. *Address:* Broom Villa, 27 Broomhouse Road, SW6 3QU. *Clubs:* White's, Brooks's, MCC; Royal and Ancient; Swinley Forest Golf.

WOOLVERTON, Kenneth Arthur; Head of Latin America, Caribbean and Pacific Department, Overseas Development Administration of the Foreign and Commonwealth Office, 1985–86; *b* 4 Aug. 1926; *s* of Arthur Eliott Woolverton and Lilian Woolverton; *m* 1957, Kathleen West; one *s*. *Educ:* Orange Hill Grammar Sch. Colonial Office, 1950–61; CRO, 1961–66 (2nd Sec., Jamaica); Min. of Overseas Development, 1966–79; Hd of Middle East Develt Div., ODA, 1979–81; Hd of British Develt Div. in the Caribbean, ODA, and UK Dir, Caribbean Develt Bank, 1981–84. ARPS 1992. *Recreations:* photography, archaeology, sailing. *Address:* 47 Durleston Park Drive, Great Bookham, Surrey KT23 4AJ. *T:* (01372) 454055.

WOOLWICH, Area Bishop of, since 2012; **Rt Rev. Michael Geoffrey Ipgrave,** OBE 2011; PhD; *b* 18 April 1958; *s* of Geoffrey William Ipgrave and Ellen Ruth Ipgrave; *m* 1981, Julia Dawn Bailey; three *s*. *Educ:* Magdalen College Sch., Brackley; Oriel Coll., Oxford (BA 1978, MA 1994); Ripon Coll., Cuddesdon; St Chad's Coll., Durham (PhD 1999); SOAS, Univ. of London (MA 2005). Ordained deacon, 1982, priest, 1983; Asst Curate, All Saints, Oakham, 1982–85; Asst Priest, Ch of the Resurrection, Chiba, Japan, 1985–87; Team Vicar, The Ascension, Leicester, 1987–90; Team Vicar, 1990–95, Team Rector, 1995–99, The Holy Spirit, Leicester; Inter Faith Relns Advr, Archbishops' Council, and Sec., Chs' Commn on Inter Faith Relns, 1999–2004; Priest-in-charge, St John with St Andrew, Peckham, 2009–10; Archdeacon of Southwark, 2004–12, and Canon Missioner, Southwark Cathedral, 2010–12. Hon. DLitt De Montfort, 2015. *Publications:* Christ in Ten Thousand Places, 1994; Trinity and Inter Faith Dialogue, 2003; The Road Ahead: Christian-Muslim dialogue, 2003; (ed) Scriptures in Dialogue, 2004; (ed) Bearing the Word, 2005; (ed) Building a Better Bridge, 2008; (ed) Justice and Rights: Christian and Muslim perspectives, 2010; (ed) Humanity: texts and contexts, 2011. *Recreations:* walking, all things Japanese. *Address:* Trinity House, 4 Chapel Court, Borough High Street, SE1 1HW. *T:* (020) 7939 9407, *Fax:* (020) 7939 9465. *E:* bishop.michael@southwark.anglican.org.

WOOLWICH, Sian Mary; *see* Williams, S. M.

WOOSNAM, Ian Harold, OBE 2007 (MBE 1992); professional golfer, since 1976; golf course designer; *b* 2 March 1958; *s* of late Harold Woosnam and of Joan Woosnam; *m* 1983, Glendryth Mervyn Pugh; one *s* two *d*. *Educ:* St Martin's Modern Sch. 47 professional tournament wins, 1982–, including: World Cup (individual), 1987 and 1991; World Match Play, 1987, 1990 and 2001; PGA, 1988 and 1997; PGA Grand Slam of Golf, 1991; US Masters, 1991; British Masters, 1994. Hon. Mem., PGA European tour. Captain, Ryder Cup team, (winners) 2006. Pres., World Snooker, 1999–. *Publications:* Ian Woosnam's Golf Masterpieces, 1988; Power Golf, 1989, new edn 1991; Golf Made Simple: the Woosie Way, 1997; (with Edward Griffiths) Woosie: the autobiography, 2002. *Recreations:* snooker, water ski-ing, shooting. *Address:* c/o IMG, McCormack House, One Burlington Lane, Hogarth Business Park, W4 2TH. *Clubs:* Llanmynech Golf, Oswestry Golf, La Moye Golf.

WOOTTON, Adrian; Chief Executive Officer: Film London, since 2003; British Film Commission, since 2011; *b* 18 May 1962; *s* of Ronald Oliver Wootton and Unity Wootton; *m* 1986, Karen Sarah Goodman; one *d*. *Educ:* Univ. of East Anglia (BA Hons English and Amer. Studies, MA Film Studies). Director: Bradford Playhouse and Film Theatre, 1986–89; Nottingham Media Centre Ltd, 1989–93; Hd, BFI Exhibn (incl. Exec. Hd, NFT and Dir, London Film Fest., 1993–2002); Dep. Dir, BFI, 2002–03. Director: Shots in the Dark, Internat. Crime, Mystery and Thriller Fest., Nottingham, 1991–2001; Crime Scene, fest. of crime and mystery genre, NFT, 2000–; Co-Curator, Soundtracking, Fest. of Popular Music and Cinema, Sheffield, 1999–2000; Chair of Bd, Sensoria Music and Film Fest., Sheffield, 2009–. Board Member: Skillset Craft and Tech. Skills Acad., 2011–; British Screen Adv. Council, 2011–; Mayor of London's Strategy Bd, 2012–. Foreign Consultant, Noir in Fest., Italy, 1999–; Advr to Venice Film Fest., 2004–. Vis. Prof., Film and Media, Norwich University Coll. of the Arts, 2012–. Member: BAFTA, 1996–; Eur. Film Acad., 2006–. Hon. DArts Norwich Univ. Coll. of the Arts, 2012; Hon. DLitt UEA, 2014. *Publications:* (contrib.) 100 Great Detectives, 1992; (ed jtly) Celluloid Jukebox, 1995; (ed) David Goodis, Black Friday and Selected Stories, 2006; contribs to arts magazines and Guardian newspaper. *Recreations:* film, literature, music, theatre. *Address:* Film London, Suite 6.10, The Tea Building, 56 Shoreditch High Street, E1 6JJ. *T:* (020) 7613 7676. *Clubs:* Groucho, Soho House.

WOOTTON, Sir David (Hugh), Kt 2013; Partner, Allen & Overy LLP, 1979–2015; Lord Mayor of London, 2011–12; *b* Bradford, W Yorks, 21 July 1950; *s* of James Wootton and Muriel Wootton (*née* Comfort); *m* 1977, Elizabeth Rosemary Knox; two *s* two *d*. *Educ:* Bradford Grammar Sch.; Jesus Coll., Cambridge (BA 1972; MA; Hon. Fellow, 2014). Admitted Solicitor, 1975; Asst Solicitor, Allen & Overy LLP, 1975–79. Dir, Local Partnerships LLP, 2009–11. Mem. Council, Nat. Trust, 2004–07. Pres., City of London Br., IoD, 2013–. Chairman: Misys Charitable Foundn, 2004–11; Local Partnership LLP, 2012–; Northern Ballet, 2013–; Morden Coll., 2013–; Trustee: Jesus Coll., Cambridge Soc., 2008–; King's Fund, 2008–14; St Paul's Cathedral Chorister Trust, 2009–; Nat. Opera Studio, 2013–; Chm. Trustees, Charles Dickens Mus., 2009–14 (Vice Chm., 2014–). Governor: City of London Acad., Southwark, 2003–; GSMD, 2004–13; King Edward's Sch., Witley, 2006–; Bradford Grammar Sch., 2012–; Almoner, Christ's Hosp., 2008–09. Mem., Court of Common Council, 2002, Alderman, 2005, Sheriff, 2009–10, City of London; Master: Fletchers' Co., 2005–06; City of London Solicitors' Co., 2010–11. Pres., Soc. of Young Freemen, 2008–. Pres., City Livery Club, 2014–. Steward, Henley Royal Regatta, 2012–. KStJ 2011. Hon. DLaws City, 2012; Hon Dr Staffordshire, 2013. Hon. FGS, 2012. *Recreations:* opera, ballet, theatre, cinema, rowing, railway architecture. *Address:* City of London Corporation, Members' Room, Guildhall, EC2P 2EJ. *E:* dhwootton@gmail.com. *Clubs:* Athenæum, Oxford and Cambridge, Pilgrims, East India; Hawks (Cambridge); Leander; London Rowing.

WOOTTON, Prof. (Harold) John, CBE 1997; FREng; FICE; FCILT; Rees Jeffreys Professor of Transport Planning, University of Southampton, 1997–2001, now Visiting Professor; *b* 17 Nov. 1936; *s* of Harold Wootton and Hilda Mary (*née* Somerfield); *m* 1960, Patricia Ann Riley; two *s*. *Educ:* Queen Mary's Grammar Sch., Walsall; QMC, Univ. of London; Univ. of Calif, Berkeley. FCIHT (FIHT 1980); FCILT until 2014 (FCIT 1987; FILT 1999); CEng 1990, FREng 2000; FICE 1996. Lectr, Dept of Civil Engrg, Univ. of Leeds, 1959–62; Technical Dir, Freeman Fox Wilbur Smith, 1963–67; Jt Man. Dir, SIA Ltd, 1967–71; Chm., Wootton Jeffreys Consultants Ltd, 1971–91; Chief Exec., Transport and Road, subseq. Transport, Res. Lab., 1991–97. Visiting Professor in: Computing, KCL, 1987–89; Transport Studies, UCL, 1989–92. Pres., Instn of Highways and Transportation, 1997–98. Chm., Motorway Archive Trust, 2006–15; Mem., Public Policy Cttee, RAC Foundn, 2001–10. Trustee, Rees Jeffreys Road Fund, 2001–10. *Publications:* numerous papers on transport, planning and computer topics. *Recreations:* cricket, golf, Rotary, photography, travel, investment strategies. *Address:* Transportation Research Group, Department of Civil Engineering and the Environment, University of Southampton, Highfield, Southampton SO17 1BJ. *T:* (023) 8059 2192.

WOOTTON, Ian David Phimester, MA, MB, BChir, PhD; FRSC, FRCPath, FRCP; Professor of Chemical Pathology, Royal Postgraduate Medical School, University of London, 1963–82; *b* 5 March 1921; *s* of D. Wootton and Charlotte (*née* Phimester); *m* 1946, Veryan Mary Walshe; two *s* two *d*. *Educ:* Weymouth Grammar School; St John's College, Cambridge; St Mary's Hospital, London. Research Assistant, Postgraduate Med. School, 1945; Lecturer, 1949; Sen. Lecturer, 1959; Reader, 1961. Consultant Pathologist to Hammersmith Hospital, 1952. Member of Medical Research Council Unit, Cairo, 1947–48; Major, RAMC, 1949; Smith-Mundt Fellow, Memorial Hosp., New York, 1951. Chief Scientist (Hosp. Scientific and Technical Services), DHSS, 1972–73. *Publications:* Microanalysis in Medical Biochemistry, 1964, ed 6th edn, 1982; Biochemical Disorders in Human Disease, 1970; papers in medical and scientific journals on biochemistry and pathology. *Recreation:* bookbinding. *Address:* Coombe House, The Coombe, Streatley on Thames, Reading RG8 9QL. *T:* (01491) 873050.

WOOTTON, John; *see* Wootton, H. J.

WOOTTON, Ronald William, CBE 1991; Head of West and North Africa and Mediterranean Department, Overseas Development Administration, 1986–91; *b* 7 April 1931; *s* of late William George and Lilian Wootton; *m* 1954, Elvira Mary Gillian Lakeman; one *s* one *d*. *Educ:* Christ's College, Finchley. Served Royal Signals, 1950–52. Colonial Office, 1952–63; Commonwealth Relations Office, 1963–65; ODM/ODA, 1965–91: Head of Overseas Manpower and Consultancies Dept, 1976–79; Head of UN Dept, 1979–82; Head of British Develt Div. in the Pacific, 1982–85. Mem., Internat. Cttee, Leonard Cheshire Foundn, 1992–98. Chm., Caterham Probus, 2001–02; Pres., Ashburton Men's Probus, 2009–10. *Address:* 4 Birchside Lane, Ashburton 7700, New Zealand.

WOOTTON, Sarah Donaldson; Chief Executive: Dignity in Dying, since 2008; Compassion in Dying, since 2008; *b* Shrewsbury, 30 Sept. 1966; *d* of Anthony James Wootton and Seonaid Moira Beaton Wootton; *m* 2012, Michael Faulkner; one *d*. *Educ:* Queen Anne Grammar Sch., York; Univ. of Sussex (BSc Neurobiol. 1988). Grad. trainee, SmithKline Beecham, 1990–92; Officer, Tequila Sales Promotion Agency, 1992–93; Volunteer Prog. Officer, CSV, 1994–97; Dir of Communications, FPA, 1997–2000; Hd of Communications and Change, EOC, 2001–07. Mem., Internat. Women's Forum, 2015–. Trustee: Women's Resource Centre, 1995–99; Abortion Rights, 2000–05. *Recreation:* over-thinking. *Address:* Dignity in Dying/Compassion in Dying, 181 Oxford Street, W1D 2JT. *T:* (020) 7479 7735. *E:* Sarah.Wootton@dignityindying.org.uk.

WORCESTER, Marquess of; Henry John Fitzroy Somerset; *b* 22 May 1952; *s* and *heir* of 11th Duke of Beaufort, *qv*; *m* 1987, Tracy Louise, *yr d* of Hon. Peter Ward and Hon. Mrs Claire Ward; two *s* one *d*. *Educ:* Eton; Cirencester Agricultural College. *Recreations:* golf, shooting, rock music, selective television watching. *Heir:* *s* Earl of Glamorgan, *qv*. *Club:* Turf.

WORCESTER, Bishop of, since 2007; **Rt Rev. John Geoffrey Inge,** PhD; Lord High Almoner to the Queen, since 2013; *b* 26 Feb. 1955; *s* of Geoffrey Alfred and Elsie Inge; *m* 1989, Denise Louise Longenecker (*d* 2014); two *d*. *Educ:* Kent Coll., Canterbury; Univ. of Durham (BSc 1977; MA 1994; PhD 2002); Keble Coll., Oxford (PGCE 1979); Coll. of the Resurrection, Mirfield. Ordained deacon, 1984, priest, 1985; Asst Chaplain, Lancing Coll., 1984–86; Jun. Chaplain, 1986–89, Sen. Chaplain, 1989–90, Harrow Sch.; Vicar, St Luke, Wallsend, 1990–96; Canon Res., 1996–2003, and Vice-Dean, 1999–2003, Ely Cathedral; Bishop Suffragan of Huntingdon, 2003–07. Mem., Faith and Order Commn, 2010–. Visitor: Community of the Holy Name, 2007–; Mucknell Abbey, 2009–. Trust Protector, Common Purpose, 2011– (Trustee, 2005–11). Pres., Three Counties Show, 2012. Hon. DLitt Worcester, 2011. *Publications:* A Christian Theology of Place, 2003; Living Love, 2007. *Address:* The Old Palace, Deansway, Worcester WR1 2JE. *Clubs:* Athenæum, Farmers; Worcestershire Cricket.

WORCESTER, Dean of; *see* Atkinson, Very Rev. P. G.

WORCESTER, Archdeacon of; *see* Jones, Ven. R. G.

WORCESTER, Sir Robert (Milton), KBE 2005; DL; Founder, Market & Opinion Research International (MORI) Ltd, 1969 (Managing Director, 1969–94; Chairman, 1973–2005); International Director, Ipsos, 2005–08; Senior Advisor, Ipsos MORI, since 2008; *b* 21 Dec. 1933; *s* of late C. M. and Violet Ruth Worcester, of Kansas City, Mo, USA; adopted dual citizenship, 2004; *m* 1st, 1958, Joann (*née* Ransdell) (decd); two *s*; 2nd, 1982, Margaret Noel (*née* Smallbone). *Educ:* Univ. of Kansas (BSc). Consultant, McKinsey & Co., 1962–65; Chief Financial Officer, Opinion Research Corp., 1965–68. Non-exec. Dir, Kent Messenger Gp, 2004–08; Chm., Maidstone Radio Ltd, 2004–06. Member, Advisory Board: Media Standards Trust, 2006–; GovNet, 2008–; Camelot Corp. Responsibility Adv. Bd, 2006–11. Pres., World Assoc. for Public Opinion Research, 1983–84. Vice President: Internat., Social Science Council, UNESCO, 1989–94; UNA, 1999–. Visiting Professor: City Univ., 1990–2002; LSE, 1992– (Gov., 1995–; Hon. Fellow, 2005); Strathclyde Univ., 1996–2001; Hon. Prof., Warwick Univ., 2005–; Chancellor's Lectr, Univ. of Kansas, 2012–14 (Adjunct Prof., 2012; Dist. Graduate, 2006). Chm., Pilgrims' Soc. of GB, 1993–2010 (Vice Pres., 2010–); Co-Chairman: Jamestown 2007 British Cttee, 2004–07; Magna Carta 2015 800th Anniversary Cttee, 2010–15. Governor: Ditchley Foundn; ESU. Comr, US-UK Fulbright Commn, 1995–2005. Vice-Pres., Royal Soc. of Wildlife Trusts, 1995–; Pres., Envmtl Campaigns Ltd, 2002–06. Trustee: Magna Carta Trust, 1993– (Dep. Chm., 2009–); Wildfowl and Wetlands Trust, 2002–08; WWF (UK), 1995–2001. Patron, Battlefields Trust, 2015–. Mem., Adv. Council, Inst. of Business Ethics (Pres., 2010–13). Member: Ct, Middlesex Univ., 2001–; Ct and Council, Univ. of Kent, 2002–13 (Chancellor, 2006–13; Hon. Prof. of Politics, 2002–). Kent Ambassador, Kent CC, 2008–. Freeman, City of London, 2001. DL Kent, 2004. Fellow: Market Res. Soc., 1997; Royal Statistical Soc., 2004. Founding Co-Editor, Internat. Jl of Public Opinion Research. Hon. FKC 2007. Hon. DSc Buckingham, 1998; Hon. DLitt Bradford, 2001; DUniv Middlesex, 2001; Hon. LLD Greenwich, 2002; Hon. DCL: Kent, 2006; Warwick, 2012. Hon. DLaws Richmond, Amer. Internat. Univ. in London, 2009. *Publications:* (ed) Consumer Market Research Handbook, 1971, 3rd edn 1986; (with M Harrop) Political Communications, 1982; (ed) Political Opinion Polling: an international review, 1983; (with Lesley Watkins) Private Opinions, Public Polls, 1986; (with Eric Jacobs) We British, 1990; British Public Opinion: history and methodology of political opinion polling, 1991; (with Eric Jacobs) Typically British, 1991; (with Samuel Barnes) Dynamics of Societal Learning about Global Environmental Change, 1992; (with Roger Mortimore): Explaining Labour's Landslide, 1999; Explaining Labour's Second Landslide, 2001; (with R. Mortimore and P. Baines) Explaining Labour's Landslip, 2005; (jtly) Explaining Cameron's Coalition: how it came about: an analysis of the 2010 General Election, 2011; contrib. Financial Times, Observer; papers in tech. and prof. jls. *Recreations:* castles, choral music, gardening. *Address:* Ipsos MORI, 3 Thomas More Square, E1W 1YW. *T:* (020) 3059 5000. *E:* rmworcester@yahoo.com. *Clubs:* Beefsteak, Reform, Walbrook; Brook (New York).

WORDEN, Prof. (Alastair) Blair, FBA 1997; Fellow, and Tutor in Modern History, St Edmund Hall, Oxford, 1974–95, now Emeritus Fellow; *b* 12 Jan. 1945; *s* of late Prof. Alastair Norman Worden and of Agnes Marshall Scutt; *m* 2014, Victoria Jane Drummond. *Educ:* St Edward's Sch., Oxford; Pembroke Coll., Oxford (BA 1966; MA 1971). Res. Fellow, Pembroke Coll., Cambridge, 1969–72; Fellow, and Dir of Studies in History, Selwyn Coll., Cambridge, 1972–74; Prof. of Early Modern History, Univ. of Sussex, 1996–2003. Vis. Prof. of Modern History, Univ. of Oxford, 2003–11; Res. Prof. of History, Royal Holloway Coll., Univ. of London, 2005–10. Trustee, London Liby, 2002–04. *Publications:* The Rump Parliament, 1974; (ed) Edmund Ludlow, A Voyce from the Watch Tower, 1978; (ed) Stuart England, 1986; (ed) David Wootton, Republicanism, Liberty and Commercial Society, part I, 1994; The Sound of Virtue: Philip Sidney's 'Arcadia' and Elizabethan politics, 1996; Roundhead Reputations: the English Civil Wars and the passions of posterity, 2001; Literature and Politics in Cromwellian England, 2007; The English Civil Wars, 2009; God's Instruments: political conduct in the England of Oliver Cromwell, 2012; (ed) Marchamont Nedham, The Excellencie of a Free-State, 2012; articles on early modern English history and lit. *Address:* Appleton Lodge, Souldern, Bicester OX27 7JR. *T:* (01869) 346842. *E:* blair.worden@history.ox.ac.uk.

WORDSWORTH, Barry; conductor; Music Director: Birmingham Royal Ballet, 1990–2008 (Music Director Laureate, since 2011); Royal Ballet, 1990–94 and since 2007; *b* 20 Feb. 1948; *s* of Ronald and Kathleen Wordsworth; *m* 1970, Ann Barber; one *s*. *Educ:* Royal College of Music. Conductor, Royal Ballet, 1974–84; Music Dir, New Sadler's Wells Opera, 1982–84; Musical Dir and Prin. Conductor, Brighton Philharmonic Orch., 1989–; Prin. Conductor, 1989–2006, Conductor Laureate, 2006–, BBC Concert Orch. Joint winner, Sargent Conductor's Prize, 1970; Tagore Gold Medal, RCM, 1970. *Recreations:* swimming, photography, cooking. *Address:* c/o IMG Artists, The Light Box, 111 Power Road, W4 5PY.

WORDSWORTH, Prof. (Bryan) Paul, FRCP; Clinical Reader in Rheumatology, since 1992, and Titular Professor of Rheumatology, since 1998, University of Oxford; Fellow, since 1992, and Dean, since 2013, Green Templeton College (formerly Green College), Oxford; *b* 4 April 1952; *s* of Victor Pargiter Wordsworth and Dora Mary Wordsworth; *m* 1981, Christine Brow; two *s* one *d*. *Educ:* Whitgift Sch.; Westminster Med. Sch., London Univ. (MB BS 1975); MA Oxon 1992. MRCP 1978, FRCP 1996. Registrar in Rheumatology, Middx Hosp., 1978–80; Sen. Registrar in Rheumatology, Oxford Hosps, 1980–87; University of Oxford: Res. Fellow, Nuffield Depts of Pathology and Medicine, 1983–85 and 1987–92; Sen. Tutor, Green Coll., 1997–2000. Gov., Whitgift Sch., 2014–. Michael Mason Prize, 1992, Heberden Orator, 2012, British Soc. for Rheumatology. *Publications:* (with R. Smith) Clinical and Biochemical Disorders of the Skeleton, 2005; contribs to over 500 books and learned jls on musculoskeletal diseases and arthritis. *Recreation:* cricket. *Address:* Nuffield Orthopaedic Centre, Windmill Road, Headington, Oxford OX3 7LD. *T:* (01865) 737545.

WORDSWORTH, Samuel Sherratt; QC 2013; *b* Warborough, 27 June 1964; *s* of Jonathan Fletcher Wordsworth and Dorothy Ann Sherratt Wordsworth; *m* 2009, Claudia Josephs; one *s* two *d*. *Educ:* Magdalen College Sch., Oxford; University Coll. London (BA Hons 1st Cl.); London Sch. of Econs and Pol Sci. (LLM Internat. Law). Admited as solicitor, 1991; Solicitor, Paris, 1991–97; Avocat à la Cour, barreau de Paris, 1994; called to the Bar, Lincoln's Inn, 1997; in practice as a barrister, 1997–; Mem., Attorney Gen.'s Panel of Counsel, 2002–13. Vis. Prof. KCL, 2009–; Professeur Invité, Univ. de Paris, Paris X, 2011–12. *Publications:* (jtly) International Relations Law, in Halsbury's Laws of England, Vol. 61, 5th edn 2010. *Address:* Essex Court Chambers, 24 Lincoln's Inn Fields, WC2A 3ED. *T:* (020) 7813 8000, *Fax:* (020) 7813 8080. *E:* swordsworth@essexcourt.net.

WORDSWORTH, Stephen John, CMG 2011; LVO 1992; HM Diplomatic Service, retired; Executive Director, Council for At-Risk Academics, since 2012; *b* 17 May 1955; *s* of Christopher Wordsworth and Ruth Wordsworth (*née* Parrington); *m* 1981, Nichole Mingins; one *s*. *Educ:* St John's Sch., Porthcawl; Epsom Coll.; Downing Coll., Cambridge (MA). Joined HM Diplomatic Service, 1977; FCO, 1977–79; Third, later Second Sec., Moscow, 1979–81; FCO, 1981–83; First Sec. (Econ. and Commercial), Lagos, 1983–86; on loan to Cabinet Office, 1986–88; First Secretary: FCO, 1988–90; (Political), Bonn, 1990–94; Counsellor (Dep. Internat. Affairs Advr), SHAPE, Mons, 1994–98; FCO, 1998–2002, Hd, Eastern Adriatic Dept, 1999–2002; Minister and Dep. Hd of Mission, Moscow, 2003–06; Ambassador to Serbia, 2006–10. Hon. Dr Liberal Arts Arbertay, Dundee, 2014. Bundesverdienstkreuz (FRG), 1992. *Recreations:* travel, walking the dog, family history research, good food and drink.

WORKMAN, Prof. Paul, PhD; FMedSci; Chief Executive and President, Institute of Cancer Research, since 2014; Harrap Professor of Pharmacology and Therapeutics, University of London, since 1997; *b* Cumbria, 30 March 1952; *s* of late Lancelot John Workman and Thomasina Workman; *m* 1975, Elizabeth Williams; one *s* one *d*. *Educ:* Workington Co. Grammar Sch.; Univ. of Leicester (BSc Hons 1973); Univ. of Leeds (PhD 1977). FRSB (FIBiol 2001); FRSC 2010. MRC Clinical Oncology Unit, Cambridge: Postdoctoral Scientist, 1976–79; Staff Scientist, 1979–87; MRC Special Appt, 1987–90; CRC Prof. of Experimental Cancer Therapy, Univ. of Glasgow, 1991–93; Hd, Biosci. Section, Zeneca Gp plc, 1993–97; Institute of Cancer Research: Chm., Section of Cancer Therapeutics, 1997–2011; Team Leader, Signal Transduction and Molecular Pharmacol. Team, 1997–; Dir, CRUK Cancer Therapeutics Unit, 1997–; Hd, Div. of Cancer Therapeutics, 2011–; Dep. Chief Exec., 2011–14. Non-exec. Dir, Royal Marsden NHS Foundn Trust, 2014–. Founder: Chroma Therapeutics, 2001 (Consultant, Chm., Mem. Bd, and Mem. Sci. Adv. Bd, 2001–12); Piramed Pharma, 2003 (Consultant and Mem. Adv. Bd, 2003–08). European Organisation for Research and Treatment of Cancer: Mem. Council, 1987–93; Mem. Bd, 1991–93; Chm., Pharmacol. and Molecular Mechanisms Gp, 1987–91. Mem., Progs Cttee, CRUK (formerly Scientific Cttee, CRC), 1999–. UICC Vis. Fellow, Stanford Univ., 1990. Lectures: Bruce Cain Meml, NZ Cancer Soc., 2003; New Drug Develt Office Award, 2006; Tom Connors, British Assoc. for Cancer Res., 2009. Life Fellow, CRC, 1991. FMedSci 2002; FRSocMed 2007; Fellow, Eur. Acad. of Cancer Scis, 2014. Hon. DSc Leicester, 2009. Award for Excellence in Oncol. Res., Eur. Sch. of Oncol., 1985; George and Christine Sosnovsky Award, 2010, World Entrepreneur of the Year Award, 2012, RSC; Raymond Bourgine Award, Internat. Congress on Anticancer Treatment, 2014. Writer of blog, The Drug Discoverer, www.icr.ac.uk/blogs/the-drug-discoverer. *Publications:* papers on cancer res. and drug discovery in scientific jls. *Recreations:* family, music, sport, travel. *Address:* Institute of Cancer Research, 237 Fulham Road, SW3 6JB. *T:* (020) 7153 5209. *E:* paul.workman@icr.ac.uk. *Club:* Sloane.

WORKMAN, Timothy (Henry), CBE 2007; a District Judge (Magistrates' Courts) (formerly Metropolitan Stipendiary Magistrate), 1986; Chief Magistrate and Senior District Judge (Magistrates' Courts), 2003–10 (Deputy Chief Magistrate and Deputy Senior District Judge, 2000–03); a Chairman, Inner London Youth Court (formerly Juvenile Panel), 1989–2010, and Family Proceeding Court, 1992–2010; a Recorder, 1994–2012; *b* 18 Oct. 1943; *s* of late Gordon and Eileen Workman; *m* 1971, Felicity Ann Caroline Western; one *s* one *d*. *Educ:* Ruskin Grammar Sch., Croydon. Probation Officer, Inner London, 1967–69; admitted Solicitor, 1969; Solicitor, subseq. Partner, C. R. Thomas & Son, later Lloyd Howorth & Partners, Maidenhead, 1969–85. Mem., Sentencing Guidelines Council, 2004–10. Hon. Bencher, Gray's Inn, 2007. *Recreations:* woodturning, shepherding, pottery. *Address:* c/o Westminster Magistrates' Court, 181 Marylebone Road, NW1 5BR. *T:* (020) 3126 3100. *E:* timworkman@mail.com.

WORMALD, Christopher; Permanent Secretary, Department for Education, since 2012; *b* London, 30 Oct. 1968; *s* of Peter John Wormald, *qv*; *m* 1997, Claire McCoy; one *s* two *d*. *Educ:* Rutlish Sch.; St John's Coll., Oxford (BA 1990); Imperial Coll. London (MBA 1999). Department for Education, later Department for Education and Employment, then Department for Education and Skills: fast stream trainee, 1991–95; Team Leader, Finance Directorate, 1995–98; Standards and Effectiveness Unit, 1998–2001; Principal Private Sec. to Sec. of State, 2001–04; Policy Advr to Sec. of State, 2004–05; Dir of Academies and Capital, 2005–06; Dir Gen., Local Govt and Regeneration, DCLG, 2006–09; Dir Gen., Domestic Policy Gp and Hd of Econ. and Domestic Affairs Secretariat, 2009–11, Hd, Dep. Prime Minister's Office, 2010–12, Cabinet Office. *Address:* Department for Education, Sanctuary Buildings, Great Smith Street, SW1P 3BT.

WORMALD, Peter John, CB 1990; Director, Office of Population Censuses and Surveys, and Registrar General for England and Wales, 1990–96; *b* 10 March 1936; *s* of late H. R. and G. A. Wormald; *m* 1962, Elizabeth North; three *s*. *Educ:* Doncaster Grammar Sch.; The Queen's Coll., Oxford (MA). Assistant Principal, Min. of Health, 1958, Principal, 1963; HM

Treasury, 1965–67, Asst Sec., 1970; Under Sec., DHSS, 1978; Dep. Sec., Dept of Health (formerly DHSS), 1987. *Recreations:* music, golf, contract bridge. *Club:* Oxford and Cambridge.

See also C. Wormald.

WORMINGTON, Veronique Eira; *see* Buehrlen, V. E.

WORMWELL, Denis; Chief Executive Officer, Shearings Holidays Group, since 2007; *b* Colne, Lancs, 27 Aug. 1961; *s* of Peter and Kathleen Wormwell; *m* 2002, Amanda Whalley; two *s* two *d. Educ:* Colne Park High Sch.; Blackburn Coll. Univ. Centre (HNC Business Studies). Hd of Dept, Buoyant Upholstery, 1980–86; Overseas Area Manager, Club 18–30 Holidays, 1986–91; Sales Director: Elvington Ltd, 1991–95; Flying Colours Leisure Gp, 1995–98; Sales and UK Service Delivery Dir, Thomas Cook, 1998–2001; Chief Executive: Nat. Express Coaches, 2002–06; Nat. Express Bus, 2006–07. *Recreations:* music, football, cinema, art. *Address:* Shearings Group Ltd, Miry Lane, Wigan WN3 4AG. *T:* (01942) 823402, *Fax:* (01942) 824075. *E:* denis.wormwell@shearings.com.

WORNE, John Philip; Director of Strategy, British Council, since 2007; *b* Sheffield, 13 Sept. 1968; *s* of Brian Patrick George Worne and Rita Worne; partner, Eleanor Street; one *s* one *d. Educ:* Jesus Coll., Oxford (BA Hons PPE 1990). Graduate trainee, then Market Planner, Cable & Wireless plc, 1990–93; Hd, Mktg, then Hd, Advertising, Bouygues Telecom, France, 1993–98; Hd, Business Mobile and Data Products, Cable & Wireless UK, 1998–2000; Dir, Brand and Global Campaigns, Cable & Wireless Global, 2000–01; Public Service Reform Policy Advr, Cabinet Office, 2001–02; Dep. Dir, NHS and DoH Communications, 2002–05; Dir, Communications, Cabinet Office, 2005–07. *Recreations:* family, writing, current affairs, science, arts, sports (particularly cricket, cycling and football). *Address:* British Council, 10 Spring Gardens, SW1A 2BN. *E:* john.worne@britishcouncil.org. *W:* www.johnworne.com. *Club:* MCC.

WORRALL, Anna Maureen, (Mrs G. H. G. Williams); QC 1989; a Recorder, 1987–2003; *b* 16 Sept. 1938; *er d* of T. B. Worrall and S. F. Worrall (*née* Cushman); *m* 1964, (George Haigh) Graeme Williams, QC (*d* 2013); two *d. Educ:* Hillcrest Sch., Bramhall; Loreto Coll., Llandudno; Manchester Univ. Called to the Bar, Middle Temple (Harmsworth Scholar), 1959, Bencher, 1996; in practice, 1959–63 and 1971–2012; Lectr in Law, Holborn Coll. of Law, Language and Commerce, 1964–69; Dir, ILEA Educnl Television Service, 1969–71. Pres., Mental Health Review Tribunals, later a Judge, First-tier Tribunal, 1995–2011. Mem., Home Office Cttee on Review of Sexual Offences, 2002–03. *Recreations:* theatre, music, cooking, walking, travel. *Address:* Lamb Building, Ground Floor, Temple, EC4Y 7AS. *T:* (020) 7797 7788, *Fax:* (020) 7353 0535. *Club:* Reform.

WORRALL, Denis John, PhD; Chairman: Omega Investment Research Ltd (Chief Executive, 1990); African Business Advisors (Pty) Ltd; *b* 29 May 1935; *s* of Cecil John Worrall and Hazel Worrall; *m* 1965, Anita Ianco; three *s. Educ:* Univ. of Cape Town (BA Hons, MA); Univ. of South Africa (LLB); Cornell Univ. (PhD). Teaching and research positions, Univs of Natal, S Africa, Ibadan, Witwatersrand, California, Cornell; Rearch Prof. and Dir, Inst. of Social and Economic Research, Rhodes Univ., 1973. Senator, 1974; elected to Parlt, 1977; Chm., Constitutional Cttee, President's Council, 1981; Ambassador: to Australia, 1983–84; to the UK, 1984–87; Co-Leader, Democratic Party, 1988–90; MP (Democratic Party) Berea (Durban), South Africa, 1989–94. Advocate of Supreme Court of S Africa. *Publications:* South Africa: government and politics, 1970. *Recreations:* tennis, reading, music. *Address:* PO Box 23599, Claremont, 7700, South Africa.

WORRALL, Peter Richard, CB 2015; OBE 2000; CEng, FREng, FIMechE; Chief of Materiel (Joint Enablers), Defence Equipment and Support Organisation, Ministry of Defence, since 2011; *b* W Midlands, 1961; *s* of Frederick and Janet Worrall; *m* 1989, Claire Levenberg. *Educ:* King's Coll., London (BSc 1st Cl. Hons Mech. Engrg 1986; AKC 1986). CEng 1992; FIMechE 2000; FREng 2011; RCNC 1992. Ministry of Defence, 1980–: Team Leader, Challenger 2 Main Battle Tank, 1996–99; rcds 2000; Sen. Civil Service, 2000; Team Leader: Future Artillery Weapons Systems, 2000–02; Bowman and Land Digitisation, 2002–04; NATO Gen. Manager, NATO Eurofighter Typhoon and Tornado Mgt Agency, 2005–08; Dir, Defence Equipment and Support Orgn, 2008–11. Non-exec. Dir, HRW Ltd, 2009–. FAPM 2000; FCMI 2003. *Recreations:* horology, contemporary ceramics, Jack of many trades. *Address:* Chief of Materiel (Joint Enablers), Maple 2c #2219, Defence Equipment and Support Organisation, Abbey Wood, Bristol BS34 8JH. *Club:* Army and Navy.

WORRALL THOMPSON, (Henry) Antony (Cardew); TV chef; restaurateur; *b* 1 May 1951; *s* of late Michael Worrall Thompson and Joanna Duncan; *m* 1st, 1974, Jill Thompson (marr. diss.); 2nd, 1983, Militza Millar (marr. diss.); two *s*; 3rd, 1996, Jacinta Shiel; one *s* one *d. Educ:* King's Sch., Canterbury; Westminster Hotel Sch. (HND). Head chef, Brinkley's Restaurant, Fulham Rd, 1978–80; head chef, Dan's Restaurant, Chelsea, 1980–81; opened Ménage à Trois, Knightsbridge, 1981; first chef/patron, restaurant at One Ninety, Queen's Gate, 1989 (Best New Restaurant, Time Out, 1990); restaurants opened: Managing Director: Bistrot 190, 1990; dell 'Ugo, Frith St, 1992; Palio, Notting Hill Gate, 1992; Zoe, St Christopher's Place, 1993; Cafe dell 'Ugo, City of London, 1993; The Atrium, Westminster, 1994; Drones, Belgravia, 1995; De Cecco, Parsons Gn, 1995; The Greyhound Free House & Grill, 2005–; Kew Grill, 2005–; The Lamb Free House and Kitchen, 2006–09; Barnes Grill, 2006–09; Windsor Grill, 2007–14; chef/proprietor: Woz, N Kensington, 1997–99; Wiz, Holland Park, 1998–2002; Bistrorganic, N Kensington, 1999; Notting Grill, Holland Park, 2002–09. Restaurant consultant, Bombay, Melbourne, Stockholm and NY, 1981–88. Man. Dir, Simpson's of Cornhill Gp, 1995–97. Numerous TV appearances, incl. Ready, Steady, Cook, 1994–; Food and Drink prog., 1997–2003; Saturday Kitchen, 2003–06; Saturday Cooks, 2006–07; Daily Cooks Challenge, 2008–. FIH (FHCIMA 1989). Meilleur Ouvrier de GB, 1987. *Publications:* The Small and Beautiful Cookbook, 1984; (with M. Gluck) Supernosh, 1993; Modern Bistrot Cookery, 1994; 30 Minute Menus, 1995; Simply Antony, 1998; The ABC of AWT, 1998; Food and Drink Cookbook, 2002; Raw (autobiog.), 2003; How to Cook and Buy Real Meat, 2003; Healthy Eating for Diabetes, 2003; Antony Worrall Thompson's GI Diet, 2005; Antony's Weekend Cookbook, 2006; Barbecues and Grilling, 2006; The GL Diet Made Simple, 2006; AWT's The Diabetes Weight Loss Diet, 2007; The People's Cookbook, 2007; Saturday Cooks Cookbook, 2008; The Sweet Life, 2008; Fast Family Food, 2008; Antony Makes It Easy, 2010; The Essential Diabetes Cookbook, 2010 (Best Health and Nutrition Book, Cordon Bleu Media Awards, 2010); Slow Cooking, 2011; The Essential Low Fat Cookbook, 2011. *Recreations:* gardening, antiques, interior design, eating, cooking. *Address:* c/o Limelight Management, 10 Filmer Mews, 75 Filmer Road, SW6 7JF. *T:* (020) 7384 9950. *E:* antony@awtrestaurants.com. *W:* www.twitter.com/AntonyWT. *Club:* Groucho.

WORSDALE, Godfrey James; Director, The Henry Moore Foundation, since 2015; *b* Doncaster, S Yorks, 19 Oct. 1967; *s* of John Raymond Worsdale and Alice Avril Worsdale; *m* 2001, Dr Alia Al-Khalidi; one *s* one *d. Educ:* Camberwell Coll. of Art (BA Hons Art Hist. 1989; HND Conservation Studies 1991). Curator, BM, 1991–95; Curator, 1995–99, Dir, 1999–2002, Southampton City Art Gall.; Director: Middlesbrough Inst. of Modern Art, 2002–08; BALTIC Centre for Contemporary Art, 2008–15. Trustee: Northern Canon, 2007–; ARC Stockton Arts Centre, 2015–; Chairman: Visual Art and Galls Assoc., 2010–15; Contemporary Visual Arts Network, 2010–15. Mem. Jury, Turner Prize, 2011. Patron, Crisis Commn, 2011–14. Vis. Fellow, Cleveland Coll. of Art and Design, 2015–. FRSA 2012. Hon. DCL Northumbria, 2012. *Publications:* Douglas Allsop: Lacunae, 1995; Co-Operators, 1996; Chris Ofili, 1998, 2nd edn 1999; Martin Creed Works, 2000; (with E. Chaney) The Stuart Portrait: status and legacy, 2001; Graham Dolphin, 2005; Draw, 2007. *Recreation:* antiques – particularly glass. *Address:* The Henry Moore Foundation, Dane Tree House, Perry Green, Much Hadham, Herts SG10 6EE. *T:* (01279) 843333. *E:* godfrey.worsdale@henry-moore.org.

WORSLEY, Lord; George John Sackville Pelham; *b* 9 Aug. 1990; *s* and *heir* of 8th Earl of Yarborough, *qv*.

WORSLEY, Daniel; His Honour Judge Worsley; a Circuit Judge, since 1999; *b* 27 March 1948; *s* of Francis Arthur Worsley and Mary Worsley; *m* 1971, Virginia Caroline Wilkinson; one *s* one *d. Educ:* Ampleforth Coll.; Emmanuel Coll., Cambridge (BA). Called to the Bar, Gray's Inn, 1971; Barrister, 1971–99. *Publications:* Contrib. Ed., Halsbury's Laws of England, 4th edn, 1998; (jtly) I am Horatio Nelson, 2005; contrib. to legal textbooks. *Recreations:* East Anglia, sailing, trout streams, wine, the Pyrenees.

WORSLEY, Francis Edward, (Jock), OBE, 2002; non-executive Director, Brewin Dolphin Holdings plc, 2003–14; *b* 15 Feb. 1941; *s* of late Francis Arthur Worsley and Mary Worsley; *m* 1962, Caroline Violet (*née* Hatherell); two *s* two *d. Educ:* Stonyhurst College. FCA. Articled, Barton, Mayhew & Co., 1959–64; with Anderson Thomas Frankel, Chartered Accountants, 1964–69; Financial Training Co., 1969–93 (Chm., 1972–92). Dir, 1990–94, Dep. Chm., 1992–94, Lautro; Complaints Comr, SIB, then FSA, 1994–2001. Non-executive Director: Cleveland Trust PLC, 1993–99; Reece Plc, 1994–98; Accident Exchange Gp plc, 2004–05. Chm., Lloyds Members Agency Services Ltd, 1994–2012. Pres., Inst. of Chartered Accountants in England and Wales, 1988–89. Mem., Building Socs Commn, 1991–2002. Trustee, 1994–2002, Chm., 1998–2002, Cancer Res. Campaign; Trustee, Cancer Res. UK, 2002–03. *Recreations:* golf, wine, travel, cooking.

WORSLEY, Lucy, DPhil; Chief Curator, Historic Royal Palaces, since 2003; *b* 18 Dec. 1973; *d* of Peter and Enid Worsley; *m* Mark Hines. *Educ:* New Coll., Oxford (BA Hons (Ancient and Mod. Hist.) 1995); Univ. of Sussex (DPhil (Art Hist.) 2001). FRHistS 2001. Administrator, Wind and Watermill Section, SPAB, 1995–97; Inspector of Ancient Monuments and Historic Bldgs, English Heritage, 1997–2002. Presenter, TV series: Elegance and Decadence: the age of Regency, 2011; If Walls Could Talk: the history of the home, 2011; Fit to Rule: how Royal illness changed history, 2013; A Very British Murder, 2013; The First Georgians: the German Kings who made Britain, 2014; Dancing Cheek to Cheek: an intimate history of dance, 2014; presenter: Tales from the Royal Bedchamber, 2013; Tales from the Royal Wardrobe, 2014; Lucy Worsley's 100 Years of the WI, 2015; Lucy Worsley's Reins of Power, 2015. *Publications:* Hardwick Old Hall, 1998; Bolsover Castle, 2000; Kirby Hall, 2000; The Official Illustrated History of Hampton Court Palace, 2005; Cavalier: a tale of passion, chivalry and great houses, 2007; Courtiers: the secret history of Kensington Palace, 2010; If Walls Could Talk: an intimate history of the home, 2011; A Very British Murder: the story of a national obsession, 2013; various articles in jls. *Recreation:* treasure hunts. *Address:* Apartment 25, Hampton Court Palace, Surrey KT8 9AU. *T:* (020) 3166 6400. *E:* lucy.worsley@hrp.org.uk.

WORSLEY, Michael Dominic Laurence; QC 1985; *b* 9 Feb. 1926; *s* of Paul Worsley and Magdalen Teresa Worsley; *m* 1962, Pamela (*née* Philpot) (*d* 1980); one *s* (and one *s* decd); *m* 1986, Jane, *d* of Percival and Mary Sharpe. *Educ:* Bedford School; Inns of Court School of Law. RN 1944–45. Lived in Africa, 1946–52; called to the Bar, Inner Temple, 1955, Bencher, 1980; Standing Prosecuting Counsel to Inland Revenue, 1968–69; Treasury Counsel at Inner London Sessions, 1969–71; Junior Treasury Counsel, 1971–74, Senior Treasury Counsel, 1974–85, CCC. *Recreations:* music, travelling. *Clubs:* Garrick, Lansdowne.

WORSLEY, Paul Frederick; QC 1990; **His Honour Judge Paul Worsley;** a Circuit Judge, since 2006; Senior Circuit Judge, since 2007; *b* 17 Dec. 1947; *s* of Eric Worsley, MBE, GM and Sheila Mary Worsley (*née* Hoskin); *m* 1974, Jennifer Ann, JP, *d* of late Ernest Avery; one *s* one *d. Educ:* Hymers College, Hull; Mansfield College, Oxford (MA). Called to the Bar, Middle Temple, 1970 (Astbury Scholar), Bencher, 1999; practised NE Circuit, 1970–2006; Asst Recorder, 1983–87; Recorder, 1987–2006. Mem., Parole Bd, 2007–14; Course Dir, Judicial Studies Bd, 2007–14. Governor: Scarborough Coll., 1996–2011; Leeds Girls' High Sch., 2001–05; Leeds Grammar Sch., 2005–08. Trustee, Stephen Joseph Theatre, 2011–. Freeman: City of London, 2009; Coopers' Co., 2007; Co. of Merchants of Staple of England, 2013. *Recreations:* Vanity Fair prints, opera, sailing, croquet, dogs. *Address:* c/o Central Criminal Court, Old Bailey, EC4M 7EH. *Clubs:* Athenæum; Bar Yacht; Brompton Fly Fishing.

WORSLEY, Rt Rev. Ruth Elizabeth; *see* Taunton, Bishop Suffragan of.

WORSLEY, Sir William (Ralph), 6th Bt *cr* 1838, of Hovingham, Yorkshire; DL; *b* York, 12 Sept. 1956; *s* of Sir William Marcus Worsley, 5th Bt and Hon. Bridget Assheton, *d* of 1st Baron Clitheroe, KCVO, PC; *S* father, 2012; *m* 1987, Marie-Noelle Dreesmann; one *s* two *d. Educ:* Harrow; RAC Cirencester. FRICS 1992; ARAgS 2012. Consultant, Humberts, 1986–92; Director: Scarborough Building Soc., 1996–2009 (Chm., 2002–09); Brunner Investment Trust plc, 2000–14; Skipton Building Soc., 2009–11. Member: N York Moors Nat. Park Authy, 1994–98; Adv. Panel, Forestry Commn, 1998–2006; Indep. Panel on Forestry, 2011–12; Chm., Howardian Hills Area of Outstanding Beauty Cttee, 2004–07. Pres., CLA, 2009–11 (Vice Pres., 2005–07; Dep. Pres., 2007–09). DL N Yorks, 2007. Lieut, QOY, 1975–80; Hon. Col, Yorks Sqdn, QOY, 2008–15. *Recreations:* walking, reading, skiing. *Heir: s* Marcus William Worsley, *b* 2 Nov. 1995. *Address:* Hovingham Hall, York YO62 4LU. *T:* (01653) 628771. *E:* office@hovingham.co.uk. *Club:* White's.

WORSTHORNE, Sir Peregrine (Gerard), Kt 1991; writer; Editor, Comment Section, Sunday Telegraph, 1989–91; *b* 22 Dec. 1923; *s* of Col Koch de Gooreynd, OBE (who assumed surname of Worsthorne by deed poll, 1921), and Baroness Norman, CBE; *m* 1st, 1950, Claude Bertrand de Colasse (*d* 1990); one *d*; 2nd, 1991, Lady Lucinda Lambton (*see* L. Lambton), *d* of Viscount Lambton. *Educ:* Stowe; Peterhouse, Cambridge (BA); Magdalen Coll., Oxford. Commnd Oxf. and Bucks LI, 1942; attached Phantom, GHQ Liaison Regt, 1944–45. Sub-editor, Glasgow Herald, 1946; Editorial staff: Times, 1948–53; Daily Telegraph, 1953–61; Deputy Editor, Sunday Telegraph, 1961–76, Associate Editor, 1976–86, Editor, 1986–89. *Publications:* The Socialist Myth, 1972; Peregrinations: selected pieces, 1980; By the Right, 1987; Tricks of Memory (autobiog.), 1993; In Defence of Aristocracy, 2004. *Recreation:* reading. *Address:* The Old Rectory, Hedgerley, Bucks SL2 3UY. *T:* (01753) 646167. *Clubs:* Beefsteak, Garrick, Pratt's, City University.

See also Sir S. P. E. C. W. Towneley.

WORSWICK, Dr Richard David, CChem, FRSC; Chairman, Cobalt Light Systems Ltd, since 2009; *b* 22 July 1946; *s* of (George) David (Norman) Worswick, CBE, FBA and of Sylvia Ellen Worswick; *m* 1970, Jacqueline Brigit Isobel Adcock; two *d* (and one *d* decd). *Educ:* New College, Oxford (BA Hons Nat. Sci. 1969; MA 1972; DPhil 1972). CChem, FRSC 1991. SRC post-doctorate res. asst, Inorganic Chem. Lab., Oxford, 1972–73; Res. Admin, Boots Co., Nottingham, 1973–76; Harwell Lab., UKAEA, 1976–91: marketing and planning, 1976–85; Head, Res. Planning and Inf. Services, 1985–87; Head, Safety Branch, 1988; Head, Envmtl and Med. Scis Div., 1988–90; Dir, Process Technology and Instrumentation, AEA Industrial Technology, 1990–91; Chief Exec., Lab. of Govt Chemist, DTI, 1991–96; Govt Chemist, 1991–2002. Chief Exec., 1996–2005, Dep. Chm., 2005–07, LGC Gp Hldgs plc (formerly LGC (Hldgs) Ltd); Chm., Pipeline Develts Ltd, 1998–2002. Mem., STFC, 2013–. UK Entrepreneur of the Year (business products and services), Ernst & Young, 2003.

Publications: LGC: the making of a company, 2011; research papers in sci. jls. *Recreations:* listening to music, playing the violin, walking. *Address:* Cobalt Light Systems Ltd, 174 Brook Drive, Milton Park, Abingdon, Oxon OX14 4SD.

WORTH, Abbot of; *see* Jamison, Rt Rev. P. C.

WORTH, Anthony James Longmore, CVO 2015; FRAgS; Lord-Lieutenant of Lincolnshire, 2008–15 (Vice Lord-Lieutenant, 2002–08); farmer; Chairman, A. H. Worth and Co. Ltd, 2000–10; *b* 23 Feb. 1940; *s* of late George Arthur Worth, MBE and Janet Maitland Worth, *d* of Air Chief Marshal Sir Arthur Murray Longmore, GCB, DSO; *m* 1964, Jennifer Mary Morgan; three *s* one *d*. *Educ:* Marlborough Coll.; Iowa State Coll.; Sidney Sussex Coll., Cambridge (BA 1962, MA 1966). Farm mgt consultant, Vic, Australia, 1964; Managing Director: Holbeach Marsh Co-op., 1970–2005; A. H. Worth and Co. Ltd, 1972–2000; QV Foods Ltd, 1994–99. Chairman: S Holland Internal Drainage Bd, 1978–87; Welland and Nene Local Flood Defence Cttee, EA, 2000–05 (Mem., 1987–2005); Mem., Anglian Regl Flood Defence Cttee, EA, 2000–05. Chm., LEAF (Linking Envmt and Farming), 2005–09. Mem., Lincs Probation Bd, 1993–2007 (Chm., 1999–2001). Mem. Council, Lincs Agricl Soc., 1994– (Pres., 1994). Gov., Lincoln Univ., 1996–2005. High Sheriff, 1990–91, DL, 1994, Lincs. FIAgrM 1997; FRAgS 2002. MInstD 1985. Hon. DBA Lincoln, 2005. Freeman, City of London, 1993; Liveryman, Co. of Farmers, 1993–. CStJ 2011. Bledisloe Gold Medal for Landowners, RASE, 1995. *Recreations:* walking, gardening, shooting, fishing. *Address:* Old White House, Holbeach Hurn, Spalding, Lincs PE12 8JP. *E:* tony.worth@qvfoods.com.
See also H. B. H. Carlisle.

WORTHINGTON, Baroness *cr* 2011 (Life Peer), of Cambridge in the County of Cambridgeshire; **Bryony Katherine Worthington;** Founder and Director, Sandbag Climate Campaign, since 2008; consultant on climate change and energy policy; an Opposition Whip, since 2012; *b* Wales; *m* 2010, Dr Srivas Chennu; one *s*. *Educ:* Queens' Coll., Cambridge (BA 1993). Fundraiser, Operation Raleigh; Leader, Friends of the Earth Climate Change Campaign, 2000; public awareness campaigns and drafting Climate Change Bill, DEFRA; Policy Advr to Scottish and Southern Energy. Non-exec. Dir, 10:10 Climate Campaign Gp. Mem., Guardian Sustainable Business Adv. Panel. *Address:* House of Lords, SW1A 0PW.

WORTHINGTON, Anthony, (Tony); *b* 11 Oct. 1941; *s* of late Malcolm and Monica Worthington; *m* 1966, Angela Oliver; one *s* one *d*. *Educ:* LSE (BA Hons); Univ. of Glasgow (MEd). Lecturer, Social Policy and Sociology: HM Borstal, Dover, 1962–66; Monkwearmouth Coll. of Further Educn, Sunderland, 1967–71; Jordanhill Coll. of Educn, Glasgow, 1971–87. Councillor, Strathclyde Region, 1974–87 (Chm., Finance Cttee, 1986–87). MP (Lab) Clydebank and Milngavie, 1987–2005. Opposition front bench spokesman: on educn and employment in Scotland, 1989–92; on overseas develt, 1992–93; on foreign affairs, 1993–94; on Northern Ireland, 1995–97; Parly Under-Sec. of State, NI Office, 1997–98. Member: Home Affairs Select Cttee, 1987–89; Internat. Develt Select Cttee, 1999–2005; Treas., All Party Population and Develt Gp, 1989–97; Chm., All Party Gp on Overseas Develt, 2000–05. British Pres., Parliamentarians for Global Action, 2001–05; a Dir, Parliamentarians Network on the World Bank, 2002–05. Chm., Labour Campaign for Criminal Justice, 1987–89. *Recreation:* gardening. *Address:* 24 Cleddans Crescent, Hardgate, Clydebank G81 5NW. *T:* (01389) 873195. *Club:* Radnor Park Bowling.

WORTHINGTON, Ian Alan, OBE 1999; HM Diplomatic Service; Ambassador to the Dominican Republic and (non-resident) to Haiti, 2006–09; *b* 9 Aug. 1958; *s* of Alan Worthington and Bette Worthington (*née* Wright). *Educ:* Parish Church Primary Sch., Spring Gardens, Stockport; Stockport Sch., Mile End. Joined FCO, 1977; Moscow, 1980–82; Lusaka, 1982–85; Second Sec., FCO, 1985–88; Second Sec., Seoul, 1988–91; Dep. Head of Mission, Vilnius, 1991–92; Second Sec., Kingston, 1992–95; Consul Gen., Ekaterinburg, 1995–98; FCO, 1998–2001; First Sec., Berlin, 2001–06. *Recreations:* family history, walking, languages, meeting new and interesting people. *Address:* 44 Forbes Road, Stockport SK1 4HN.

WORTHINGTON, Sir Mark, Kt 2014; OBE 2005; consultant; *b* Leek, Staffs, 23 Jan. 1961; *s* of Percy and Marjorie Worthington. *Educ:* Westwood High Sch., Leek; King's Coll. London (BA Hons Hist. 1982). Parly Advr, 1986–92; Private Sec. to Rt Hon. Baroness Thatcher, 1992–2013. Dir, Margaret Thatcher Foundn, 1992–2011. *Recreations:* reading, history, politics, gardening, opera. *Address:* 96 Telford Avenue, SW2 4XG. *T:* (020) 3674 3969.

WORTHINGTON, Prof. Michael Hugh, PhD; Professor of Geophysics, 2001–11, and Senior Research Scientist, since 2001, Oxford University; Supernumerary Fellow, Wolfson College, Oxford, 2002–11; *b* 16 June 1946; *s* of Air Vice-Marshal Sir Geoffrey Worthington, KBE, CB, and late Margaret Joan (*née* Stevenson); *m* 1975, Mary Archange Mackintosh; one *s* one *d*. *Educ:* Wellington Coll.; Durham Univ. (BSc 1968; MSc 1969); ANU (PhD 1973). Univ. Lectr in Geophysics, and Fellow of Exeter Coll., Oxford, 1973–85; Prof. of Geophysics, 1985–2001, Hd, Dept of Geol., 1993–97, ICSTM. Vis. Prof., Dept of Applied and Engrg Physics, Cornell Univ., 1978. Member: Soc. of Exploration Geophysicists; European Assoc. of Geoscientists and Engineers; FGS. William Smith Medal, Geol Soc., 2007. *Publications:* (jtly) Seismic Data Processing, 1986; contribs to professional jls. *Recreations:* sailing, painting. *Address:* Department of Earth Sciences, Oxford University, South Parks Road, Oxford OX1 3AN. *T:* (01865) 272000.

WORTHINGTON, Prof. Sarah Elizabeth, FBA 2009; Downing Professor of the Laws of England, University of Cambridge, since 2011; Fellow, Trinity College, Cambridge, since 2011; *b* Barnsley, 18 Feb. 1955; *d* of Bernard and Frances Monks; *m* 1978, Peter Worthington; two *s* two *d*. *Educ:* Australian Nat. Univ. (BSc 1974); Univ. of Qld (DipEd 1977; LLB 1986); Univ. of Melbourne (LLM 1990); Wolfson Coll., Cambridge (PhD 1995). Departmental Tutor, Biochem. Dept, Univ. of Qld, 1975–77; Sen. Sci. Teacher, San Sisto Girls' Sch., 1978–79; Lectr in Law, Dept of Business Law, then Faculty of Law, 1988–92, Univ. of Melbourne; Lectr in Law, 1994–96, Sen. Lectr in Law, 1996–97, Dept of Law, Birkbeck Coll., London; Sen. Lectr in Law, 1997–2001, Reader, 2001–03, Prof. of Law, 2003–11, Dept of Law, and Pro-Dir, 2005–10, LSE. Professorial Fellow, Univ. of Melbourne, 2005–; Francqui Chair, Univ. of Leuven, 2009–10; Cheng Yu Tong Dist. Vis. Prof., Univ. of Hong Kong, 2010–. Called to the Bar, Middle Temple, 2005, Bencher, 2010; Academic Mem., 3–4 South Sq., Gray's Inn, 2005–; Pres., Soc. of Legal Scholars, 2007–08. Member, Council: AHRC, 2010–13; British Acad., 2011–14 (Treas., 2015–); Mem., Panel of Recognised Internat. Market Experts in Finance, 2011–. Hon. QC 2010. FRSA 1995. Ed., Palmer's Company Law, 2003–; Syndic, CUP, 2012–. *Publications:* Proprietary Interests in Commercial Transactions, 1996; Personal Property: text and materials, 2000; (ed) Commercial Law and Commercial Practice, 2003; Equity, 2004, 2nd edn 2006; (ed with L. Sealy) Sealy's Cases and Materials in Company Law, 8th edn 2007, 10th edn as Sealy and Worthington's Cases and Materials in Company Law, 2013; Equity and Property: fact, fantasy and morals, 2009; (ed with P. L. Davies) Gower and Davies, Principles of Modern Company Law, 9th edn 2012; (jtly) Law of Personal Property, 2013. *Recreations:* theatre, art, walking, ski-ing, dinners with friends. *Address:* Faculty of Law, University of Cambridge, 10 West Road, Cambridge CB3 9DZ. *E:* sew1003@cam.ac.uk.

WORTHINGTON, Stephen Anthony; QC 2006; a Recorder, since 2001; *b* 14 April 1953; *s* of Dennis and Moya Worthington; *m* 1981, Julie Evans; two *s* one *d*. *Educ:* Trinity Coll., Cambridge (BA 1975). Called to the Bar, Gray's Inn, 1976, Bencher, 2009; barrister. *Recreations:* sport, wine, walking. *Address:* 12 King's Bench Walk, Temple, EC4Y 7EL. *T:* (020) 7583 0811, *Fax:* (020) 7583 7228. *E:* worthington@12kbw.co.uk.

WOSNER, John Leslie; Chairman and Senior Partner, PKF, accountants, 1999–2005; *b* 8 June 1947; *s* of Eugen and Lucy Wosner; *m* 1974, Linda Freedman; two *s* one *d*. *Educ:* Univ. of Sheffield (BA Econ 1969). FCA 1972; ATII 1973. Trained with Arthur Andersen & Co., 1969–74; PKF: joined, 1974; Partner, 1976–2005; Managing Partner, 1994–99. *Publications:* articles in British Tax Review, Taxation, Accountancy. *Recreations:* opera, country walking, history. *Club:* Travellers.

WÖSSNER, Dr Mark Matthias; Chairman, Supervisory Board: Heidelberger Druckmaschinen AG, 2004–11; Citigroup Global Markets Deutschland, 2002–08; *b* 14 Oct. 1938. *Educ:* Karlsruhe Technical University (DrIng). Management Asst, Bertelsmann AG, Gütersloh, 1968; Mohndruck (Bertelsmann largest printing operation): Production Manager, 1970; Technical Dir, 1972; Gen. Manager, 1974; Mem. Exec. Bd, Bertelsmann, 1976; Dep. Chm. of Bd, 1981, Chm. and CEO, 1983–98; Chm., Supervisory Bd, Bertelsmann AG, 1998–2000; Chm. and CEO, Bertelsmann Foundn, 1998–2000. Chm., Supervisory Bd, eCircle AG, 2000–10; Member, Supervisory Board: DaimlerChrysler AG, 1998–2009; Douglas Hldg AG, 2003–13.

WOTHERS, Peter David, MBE 2014; PhD; FRSC; Teaching Fellow, Department of Chemistry, University of Cambridge, since 1996; Fellow, and Director of Studies, St Catharine's College, Cambridge, since 1997; *b* Swindon, 21 Jan. 1969; *s* of Geoffrey Wothers and June Wothers. *Educ:* Bedford Modern Sch.; St Catharine's Coll., Cambridge (BA Hons 1991; PhD 1996). FRSC 2005. Mem., UK Chemistry Olympiad, 1997–; Chm., Cambridge Chemistry Challenge, 2011–; Chm., Steering Cttee, Internat. Chemistry Olympiad, 2011–. Presenter: The Big Experiment, Discovery Channel, 2008; Royal Instn Christmas Lectures, 2012. Pres.'s Prize, 2011, Nyholm Prize for Educn, 2013, RSC. *Publications:* (jtly) Organic Chemistry, 2000; (with J. H. Keeler) Why Chemical Reactions Happen, 2003; (with J. H. Keeler) Chemical Structure and Reactivity, 2008, 2nd edn 2013. *Recreations:* collecting rare chemistry books 1500–1800, devising interesting chemistry questions, rowing, cycling. *Address:* St Catharine's College, Cambridge CB2 1RL. *T:* (01223) 336320. *E:* peter@wothers.com. *Club:* Hawks (Cambridge).

WOTTON, John Prier; Consultant, Allen & Overy LLP, 2007–12 (Partner, 1984–2007); *b* Hounslow, Middx, 7 May 1954; *s* of Arthur John Wotton and Persis Rubena (*née* Spearing); *m* 1976, Linde Diana Lester; one *s* two *d*. *Educ:* Latymer Upper Sch.; Jesus Coll., Cambridge (BA 1975). Admitted solicitor, 1978; Allen & Overy LLP, 1976–2012. Mem. Council, Law Soc. of England and Wales, 2007–13 (Pres., 2011–12; Chair, Educn and Trng Cttee, 2012–15). Mem., Co-operation and Competition Panel for NHS-funded Services, 2009–14; Mem., Reporting Panel, Competition Commn, 2013–14; Inquiry Chair (formerly Panel Dep. Chm.), CMA, 2014–; External Expert, Monitor, 2014–. Gov., Latymer Foundn at Hammersmith, 2000–15. Mem. Council, Fauna & Flora Internat., 2006–. Vice Chair, Kent Historic Buildings Cttee, CPRE, 2015–. *Publications:* articles on EU and competition law, media and utilities regulation. *Recreations:* cricket, gardening, conservation, music. *Address:* Goddards Green, Angley Road, Cranbrook, Kent TN17 3LR. *E:* jpwotton@gmail.com. *Clubs:* Travellers, MCC.

WOUDHUYSEN, Deborah Jane; *see* Loudon, D. J.

WOUDHUYSEN, Prof. Henry Ruxton, DPhil; FBA 2010; FSA; Rector, Lincoln College, Oxford, since 2012; *b* London, 24 Oct. 1954; *s* of Lewis Woudhuysen and Alice Woudhuysen (*née* Roberts); *m* 1987, Deborah Jane Loudon, *qv*; two *s*. *Educ:* St Paul's Sch., London; Pembroke Coll., Oxford (MA 1981; DPhil 1981; Hon. Fellow, 2014). Jun. Res. Fellow, Lincoln Coll., Oxford, 1979–82; Department of English, University College London: Lectr, 1982–95; Sen. Lectr, 1995–97; Prof. of English, 1997–2012; Hd of Dept, 2002–07; Dean, Faculty of Arts and Humanities, 2008–12; Lyell Reader in Bibliography, Univ. of Oxford, 2013–14. Member: Council, Malone Soc., 1984–; Council, Bibliographical Soc., 1985–88, 2001–06, 2008– (Vice-Pres., 2010–14; Pres., 2014–); Curators of Bodleian Libraries, 2007–12. Gov., City Lit, 2010–12. *Publications:* (ed with D. Norbrook) The Penguin Book of Renaissance Verse, 1509–1659, 1992; Sir Philip Sidney and the Circulation of Manuscripts, 1558–1640, 1996; (ed) Love's Labour's Lost, 1998; (ed) AEH AWP: a classical friendship, 2006; (ed with K. Duncan-Jones) Shakespeare's Poems, 2007; (ed with M. F. Suarez, SJ) The Oxford Companion to the Book, 2010; contribs to learned jls and to TLS on sales of books and manuscripts. *Address:* Lincoln College, Oxford OX1 3DR. *T:* (01885) 279804. *E:* rector@lincoln.ox.ac.uk.

WOUK, Herman; author, US; *b* New York, 27 May 1915; *s* of Abraham Isaac Wouk and Esther Wouk (*née* Levine); *m* 1945, Betty Sarah Brown (*d* 2011); two *s* (and one *s* decd). *Educ:* Townsend Harris High Sch.; Columbia Univ. (AB). Radio script writer, 1935–41; Vis. Professor of English, Yeshiva Univ., 1952–57; Presidential consultative expert to the United States Treasury, 1941. Served United States Naval Reserve, 1942–46, Deck Officer (four campaign stars). Member Officers' Reserve Naval Services. Trustee, College of the Virgin Islands, 1961–69. Hon. LHD Yeshiva Univ., New York City, 1954; Hon. DLit: Clark Univ., 1960; American Internat. Coll., 1979; Trinity Coll., Hartford, Conn, 1998; George Washington Univ., Washington, 2001; Hon. PhD: Bar-Ilan, 1990; Hebrew, 1997. Columbia University Medal for excellence, 1952; Alexander Hamilton Medal, Columbia Univ., 1980; Berkeley Medal, Univ. of Calif, 1984; Golden Plate Award, Amer. Acad. of Achievement, 1986; Lone Sailor Award, US Navy Meml Foundn, 1987; Kazetnik Award, Yad Vashem, 1990; Guardian of Zion Award, Bar Ilan Univ., 1998; UCSD Medal, Univ. of Calif, San Diego, 1998. *Publications: novels:* Aurora Dawn, 1947; The City Boy, 1948; The Caine Mutiny (Pulitzer Prize), 1951; Marjorie Morningstar, 1955; Youngblood Hawke, 1962; Don't Stop The Carnival, 1965; The Winds of War, 1971 (televised 1983); War and Remembrance, 1978 (televised 1989); Inside, Outside (Washingtonian Book Award), 1985; The Hope, 1993; The Glory, 1994; A Hole in Texas, 2004; The Lawgiver, 2012; *plays:* The Traitor, 1949; The Caine Mutiny Court-Martial, 1953; Nature's Way, 1957; *non-fiction:* This Is My God, 1959; The Will to Live On, 2000; The Language God Talks, 2010. *Address:* c/o BSW Literary Agency, 303 Crestview Drive, Palm Springs, CA 92264, USA. *Clubs:* Cosmos, Metropolitan (Washington); Bohemian (San Francisco); Century (New York).

WRACK, Matt; General Secretary, Fire Brigades Union, since 2005; *b* 23 May 1962. *Educ:* Open Univ. (BSc); London Sch. of Econs (MSc). Joined London Fire Brigade, 1983. *Address:* Fire Brigades Union, Bradley House, 68 Coombe Road, Kingston-upon-Thames, Surrey KT2 7AE. *T:* (020) 8541 1765. *E:* matt.wrack@fbu.org.uk.

WRAGG, John, RA 1991 (ARA 1983); sculptor; *b* 20 Oct. 1937; *s* of Arthur and Ethel Wragg. *Educ:* York Sch. of Art; Royal Coll. of Art. *Work in public collections:* Israel Mus., Jerusalem; Tate Gall.; Arts Council of GB; Arts Council of NI; Contemp. Art Soc.; Wellington Art Gall., NZ; work in private collections in GB, America, Canada, France and Holland. *One-man exhibitions:* Hanover Gall., 1963, 1966 and 1970; Galerie Alexandre Iolas, Paris, 1968; York Fest., 1969; Bridge Street Gall., Bath, 1982; Katherine House Gall., Marlborough, 1984; Quinton Green Fine Art, London, 1985; Devizes Mus. Gall., 1994; England & Co., London, 1994; L'Art Abstrait, London, 1995; Handel House Gall., Devizes, 2000; Bruton Gall., Leeds, 2000; *exhibitions:* Lord's Gall., 1959; L'Art Vivant, 1965–68; Arts

Council Gall., Belfast, 1966; Pittsburgh Internat., 1967; Britische Kunst heute, Hamburg, Fondn Maeght, and Contemp. Art Fair, Florence, 1968; Bath Fest. Gall., 1977 and 1984; Artists Market, 1978; Biennale di Scultura di Arese, Milan, and King Street Gall., Bristol, 1980; Galerie Bollhagen Worpswede, N Germany, 1981 and 1983; Quinton Green Fine Art, London, 1984, 1985, 1986 and 1987; Best of British, Simpsons, 1993; Connaught Brown, London, 1993; Monumental '96, Belgium, 1996; Courcoux & Courcoux, 1997; Bruton Gall., Leeds, 1999; Bruton St Gall., London, 1999; Discerning Eye, Mall Galls, London, 2000; Cobham Fest., 2001; Bohun Gall., Henley-on-Thames, 2001; RWA Gall., 2001; Hotbath Gall., Bath, 2002. Sainsbury Award, 1960; Winner of Sainsbury Sculpture Comp., King's Road, Chelsea, 1966; Arts Council Major Award, 1977; Chantry Bequest, 1981. *Relevant publications:* chapters and articles about his work in: Neue Dimensionen der Plastik, 1964; Contemporary British Artists, 1979; British Sculpture in the Twentieth Century, 1981; Studio Internat., Art & Artiste, Sculpture Internat., Arts Rev., and The Artist. *Recreation:* walking. *Address:* 6 Castle Lane, Devizes, Wilts SN10 1HJ. *T:* (01380) 727087. *E:* johnwragg.ra@virgin.net.

WRAGG, William Peter; MP (C) Hazel Grove, since 2015; *b* Stockport, 11 Dec. 1987; *s* of Peter Wragg and Julie Wragg. *Educ:* Poynton High Sch. and Sixth Form; Univ. of Manchester (BA Hist.); Liverpool John Moores Univ. (PGCE). Former primary sch. teacher. Mem. (C) Stockport Council, 2011–15. *Address:* House of Commons, SW1A 0AA.

WRAIGHT, Margaret Joan; *see* Hustler, M. J.

WRATTEN, Donald Peter; Director, National Counties Building Society, 1985–96; *b* 8 July 1925; *er s* of late Frederick George and Marjorie Wratten; *m* 1947, Margaret Kathleen (*née* Marsh); one *s* one *d*. *Educ:* Morehall Elem. Sch. and Harvey Grammar Sch., Folkestone; London Sch. of Economics. Storehand, temp. clerk, meteorological asst (Air Min.), 1940–43; service with RAF Meteorological Wing, 1943–47. LSE, 1947–50. Joined Post Office, 1950; Private Sec. to Asst Postmaster Gen., 1955–56; seconded to Unilever Ltd, 1959; Private Sec. to Postmaster Gen., 1965–66; Head of Telecommunications Marketing Div., 1966–67; Director: Eastern Telecommunications Region, 1967–69; Exec. Dir, Giro and Remittance Services, 1969–74 (Sen. Dir, 1970–74); Sen. Dir, Data Processing Service, 1974–75; Sen. Dir, Telecom Personnel, 1975–81. Member: Industrial Adv. Panel, City Univ. Business Sch., 1974–81 (Chm., 1977–81); Court, Cranfield Inst. of Technology, 1976–81; Business Educn Council, 1977–83; Council: Intermediate Technology Develt Gp, 1982–85; Internat. Stereoscopic Union, 1987– (Vice-Pres., 2001–03); Pres., Stereoscopic Soc., 1996–98 (Vice-Chm., 1990–92; Chm., 1993–95). Pres., Radlett Soc. & Green Belt Assoc., 1996–2004 (Chm., 1989–96). *Publications:* The Book of Radlett and Aldenham, 1990. *Recreations:* 3-D photography, social history. *Address:* 11 Brampton Apartments, Brampton Valley Lane, Chapel Brampton, Northampton NN6 8GB. *T:* (01604) 850731.

WRATTEN, Air Chief Marshal Sir William (John), GBE 1998 (KBE 1991; CBE 1982); CB 1991; AFC 1973; Chief Military Adviser, Rolls-Royce Defence (Europe), 1998–2000; *b* 15 Aug. 1939; *s* of William Wellesley Wratten and Gwenneth Joan (*née* Bourne); *m* 1963, Susan Jane Underwood; two *s* two *d*. *Educ:* Chatham House Grammar Sch., Ramsgate; RAF Coll., Cranwell. OC, RAF Coningsby, 1980–82; Sen. RAF Officer, Falkland Is, 1982; RCDS, 1983; Dir, Operational Requirements (RAF), MoD, 1984–86; SASO, HQ 1 Gp, 1986–89; AOC No 11 Gp, 1989–91; Air Comdr British Forces ME, and Dep. to Comdr (on attachment), Nov. 1990–March 1991; Dir Gen., Saudi Armed Forces Project, 1992–94. AOC-in-C Strike Comd, and Comdr Allied Air Forces Northwestern Europe, 1994–97; Air ADC to the Queen, 1995–97. CCMI (CIMgt 1996). QCVSA 1968. Legionnaire, Legion of Merit (USA), 1993. *Recreation:* photography. *Address:* 14 College Road, Cheltenham GL53 7HX. *Club:* Royal Air Force.

WRAW, Rt Rev. John Michael; *see* Bradwell, Area Bishop of.

WRAXALL, 3rd Baron *cr* 1928, of Clyst St George, co. Devon; **Eustace Hubert Beilby Gibbs,** KCVO 1986; CMG 1982; HM Diplomatic Service, retired; Vice Marshal of the Diplomatic Corps, 1982–86; *b* 3 July 1929; *s* of 1st Baron Wraxall, PC; *S* brother, 2001; *m* 1st, 1957, Evelyn Veronica Scott (*d* 2003); three *s* two *d*; 2nd, 2006, Caroline Mary (*née* Burder), *widow* of Lt-Col Philip Fielden, MC. *Educ:* Eton College; Christ Church, Oxford (MA). ARCM 1953. Entered HM Diplomatic Service, 1954; served in Bangkok, Rio de Janeiro, Berlin, Vienna, Caracas, Paris. *Recreations:* music, golf. *Heir: s* Hon. Antony Hubert Gibbs [*b* 19 Aug. 1958; *m* 1st, 1988, Caroline Jane Gould (marr. diss. 1994); two *d*; 2nd, 1995, Virginia, *d* of Colin Gilchrist; two *s*]. *Address:* Oakley House, Upper Street, Oakley, Diss, Suffolk IP21 4AT.

WRAXALL, Sir Charles (Frederick Lascelles), 9th Bt *cr* 1813; Assistant Accountant, Morgan Stanley International, since 1987; *b* 17 Sept. 1961; *s* of Sir Morville William Lascelles Wraxall, 8th Bt, and of Lady (Irmgard Wilhelmina) Wraxall; *S* father, 1978; *m* 1983, Lesley Linda, *d* of late William Albert and Molly Jean Allan; one *s* one *d*. *Educ:* Archbishop Tenison's Grammar School, Croydon. *Recreations:* choral singing (Mem., Choir Cttee), Overseas Link Officer, St Mary the Virgin, Ashford, watching football and cricket. *Heir: s* William Nathaniel Lascelles Wraxall, *b* 3 April 1987.

WRAY, Prof. David; Dean, Hamdan Bin Mohammed College of Dental Medicine (formerly Dubai School of Dental Medicine), since 2012; Professor of Oral Medicine, Glasgow University, 1993–2011, now Emeritus; *b* 3 Jan. 1951; *s* of Arthur Wray and Margaret Wray (*née* Craig); *m* 1st, 1974, Alison Young (marr. diss. 1997); two *s*; 2nd, 1997, Alyson Urquhart (marr. diss. 2009); two *s* one *d*; 3rd, 2012, Jennifer McCallum. *Educ:* Uddingston Grammar Sch.; Glasgow Univ. (BDS 1972; MBChB 1976; MD 1982). FDSRCPSGlas 1979; FDSRCSE 1987. Fogarty Vis. Associate, NIH, Bethesda, 1979–81; Wellcome Res. Fellow, Royal Dental Sch., Univ. of London, 1982; Sen. Lectr, Dept of Oral Medicine and Pathology, Univ. of Edinburgh, 1983–93; Glasgow University: Associate Dean for Res., Dental Sch., 1995–2000; Dean of Dental Sch., 2000–05; Clinical Dir, Glasgow Dental Hosp., 2004–09. Hon. Consultant in Oral Medicine, Greater Glasgow and Clyde NHS (formerly North Glasgow NHS Trust), 1993–2011. Founder FMedSci, 1998. *Publications:* Oral Medicine, 1997; Oral Candidosis, 1997; Textbook of General and Oral Medicine, 1999; Textbook of General and Oral Surgery, 2003. *Recreations:* golf, wine, cooking. *Address:* Hamdan Bin Mohammed College of Dental Medicine, Dubai Healthcare City, PO Box 505097, Dubai, United Arab Emirates.

WRAY, Edward James; Co-Founder, 1999, and Chairman, 2006–12, Betfair Group plc; *b* Coulsdon, 27 March 1968; *s* of Philip and Brenda Wray; *m* 2003, Catherine Pickering; one *s* two *d*. *Educ:* Worcester Coll., Oxford (MA Hons Engr, Econs and Mgt). Joined JP Morgan, 1991; Vice Pres., 1994–99. *Recreations:* golf, sailing, horseracing, wine. *Address:* Matrix Complex, 91 Peterborough Road, SW6 3BU. *T:* (020) 7736 4699. *E:* edward.j.wray@gmail.com.

WRAY, Nigel William; non-executive Director: Prestbury Investment Holdings, since 2003; Chapel Down Group plc (formerly English Wines Group plc), since 2004; *b* 9 April 1948. *Educ:* Mill Hill Sch.; Univ. of Bristol (BSc). Chairman: Fleet Street Letter plc, 1976–90; Burford Hldgs plc, 1988–2001; Nottingham Forest plc, 1997–99; British Seafood Gp, 2006–10; Dir, Saracens Ltd, 1995– (Chm., 1996–); non-executive Director: Carlton Communications plc, 1976–97; Singer and Friedlander Gp plc, 1986–2001; Peoples Phone, 1989–96; Columbus Gp, 1991–2000; Urbium (formerly Trocadero, then Chorion) plc, 1995–2005; SkyePharma plc, 1995–2000; Domino's Pizza UK & IRL plc (formerly Domino's Pizza Group plc), 1997–2013; Carlisle Hldgs, 1998–2001; Hartford Gp, 1998–2000; Safestore plc, 1999–2003; Seymour Pierce Gp (formerly Talisman House) plc, 2000–04; Electric Word plc, 2000–06 (Chm., 2002–04); Invox plc, 2000–06; Extreme Gp, 2002–05; Play Hldgs Ltd, 2004–; WILink.com (formerly Knutsford) plc, 2005–06 (non-exec. Chm., 1999–2005); Greenhouse Fund Ltd, 2006–07; Networkers International plc, 2006–; Premier Team Hldgs, 2006–; Franchise Brands Worldwide, 2008–; non-exec. Chm., Environ Gp (Investments) plc (formerly Southern Bear plc), 2010–12. Hon. LLD Bristol, 2005. *Address:* Cavendish House, 18 Cavendish Square, W1G 0PJ. *T:* (020) 7647 7647.

WREN, Simon William, CBE 2003 (MBE 1997); Director of Communication, Home Office, since 2012; *b* Stevenage, Herts, 10 May 1965; *s* of late Terence Roy Wren and Mary Christine Wren; *m* 2002, Sheila Elizabeth Houghton. *Educ:* King Harold Comprehensive Sch., Waltham Abbey. Ministry of Defence: various posts, 1985–2000; Chief Press Officer, 2000–02; Head of News: Dept for Transport, 2002–05; MoD, 2005–06; Home Office, 2006–11; Dir, Media and Communication, MoD, 2011–12. *Recreation:* attending heavy metal concerts (Member of Motorheadbangers). *Address:* Home Office, 2 Marsham Street, SW1P 4DF. *Club:* Tottenham Hotspur.

WREN-LEWIS, Prof. Simon Jeremy Quentin; Professor of Economic Policy, Blavatnik School of Government, University of Oxford, since 2014 (Professor of Economics, 2007–14); Fellow and Tutor in Economics, Merton College, Oxford, 2007–14, now Emeritus; *b* London, 11 July 1953; *s* of John Wren-Lewis and Shirley Wren-Lewis; *m* 1979, Joanna Lynne Gura; two *s*. *Educ:* Cavendish Sch., Chiswick; Latymer Upper Sch., Hammersmith; Clare Coll., Cambridge (BA 1974); Birkbeck Coll., Univ. of London (MSc 1979). Economic Asst and Advr, HM Treasury, 1974–81; Sen. Res. Officer and Sen. Res. Fellow, NIESR, 1981–90; Lectr, Queen Mary Coll., Univ. of London, 1985; Prof. of Macroecon. Modelling, Univ. of Strathclyde, 1990–95; Prof. of Econs, Univ. of Exeter, 1995–2006. Res. Fellow, Centre for Econ. Policy Res., 1986–97; Member, Academic Panel: HM Treasury, 1986–95; ONS, 1997–2002; Member: Res. Grants Bd, ESRC, 1992–96; Adv. Panel, Office for Budget Responsibility, 2011–. Mem. Council, Royal Econ. Soc., 1998–2003. Consultant, Bank of England, 1999–2004; Vis. Prof., Reserve Bank of NZ, 2003–04. Gov., NIESR, 1995–. *Publications:* papers on nat. and internat. macroecons in professional jls. *Recreations:* gardening, watching swallows, writing a blog. *Address:* Merton College, Oxford OX1 4JD. *T:* (01865) 271080, *Fax:* (01865) 271094. *E:* simon.wren-lewis@economics.ox.ac.uk.

WRENBURY, 4th Baron *cr* 1915, of Old Castle, Sussex; **William Edward Buckley;** *b* 19 June 1966; *s* of 3rd Baron Wrenbury and of Penelope Sara Frances Buckley (*née* Fort); *S* father, 2014; *m* 1996, Emma Clementson; two *s*. *Heir: s* Hon. Jamie Paul Buckley, *b* 20 Nov. 2001.

WRENCH, Peter Nicholas; consultant and writer; *b* 5 April 1957; *s* of late Cyril Wrench and of Edna Mary Wrench; *m* 1978, Pauline Jordan; two *d*. *Educ:* Clitheroe Royal Grammar Sch.; Royal Holloway Coll., London (BA). Home Office, 1980–2010: Private Sec. to Perm. Sec., 1987–88; Immigration and Nationality Dept, 1988–93; Organised and Internat. Crime Directorate, 1993–2000; Dep. Dir Gen., Immigration and Nationality Directorate, 2000–03; Dir of Resettlement, HM Prison Service, 2003–05; Dir of Strategy and Assurance, Nat. Offender Mgt Service, 2005–07; Sen. Dir, Simplification Project, Border and Immigration Agency, later UK Border Agency, 2007–10; Hd, Core Learning Prog., Nat. Sch. of Govt (on loan), 2010. Member: Fitness to Practise Cttee, Gen. Pharmaceutical Council, 2010–; Ind. Review Panel, Equitable Life Payments Scheme, HM Treasury, 2011–; Planning, Resources and Performance Cttee, Bar Standards Bd, 2011–; Audit Cttee, Office of Immigration Services Comr, 2012–; Panel, Judicial Appts Commn, 2012–; Disciplinary Panels, Judicial Conduct Investigations Office, 2012–; Ind. Appeals Body, PhonepayPlus, 2012–; Bd of Trustees, RoadPeace, 2014–; Disciplinary Tribunal, CILEx Regulation, 2015–; Chm., Professional Conduct Cttee, UK Council for Psychotherapy, 2012. *Publications:* (contrib.) Zusammenarbeit der Polizei- und Justizverwaltungen in Europa, 1996; (contrib.) Crime Sans Frontières: international and European legal approaches, 1998; Saint Dominic's Flashback, 2012. *Recreations:* obscure music, family, friends, co-owner, Tom Thumb Theatre, Margate. *Address:* 38 Millers Road, Brighton BN1 5NQ. *W:* www.edenontheline.co.uk.

WREXHAM, Bishop of, (RC), since 2012; **Rt Rev. Peter Malcolm Brignall;** *b* Whetstone, 5 July 1953; *s* of Charles V. Brignall and Marie E. Brignall (*née* Stilz). *Educ:* Finchley Catholic High Sch.; Barnet Coll. of Further Educn; Allen Hall Seminary; Univ. of Wales, Swansea (Dip. Med. Ethics 1993). Ordained deacon, 1977, priest, 1978; Deacon, St David's, Mold, 1977–78; Assistant Priest: Blessed Sacrament, Connah's Quay, 1978–79; Our Lady Star of the Sea, Llandudno, 1979–80; Chaplain, Univ. Coll. of N Wales, Bangor, 1979–84; Asst Priest, St David and St Patrick, Haverfordwest, 1984–85; Parish Priest: Knighton and Presteigne, 1985–89; Our Lady and St James, Bangor, 1989–99; Dean, Cathedral of Our Lady of Sorrows, Wrexham, 1999–2012. Member: Council, Coll. of Health Care Chaplains, 1998–2008; Historic Churches Cttee for Wales and Herefordshire, 2000–12; Liturgy Cttee, Bishops' Conf., 2010–12. Gov. and Trustee, Churches Tourism Network Wales, 2008–. Chaplain: Bangor NHS Hosps, 1980–84, 1998–99; Carmelite Monastery, Presteigne, 1985–89; Wrexham NHS Hosps, 1999–2012. *Recreations:* food and cooking from source to plate, strolling with a purpose (natural history, historic routes, visiting antiquities), listening to classical music, learning to sign British Sign Language. *Address:* Bishop's House, Sontley Road, Wrexham LL13 7EW. *T:* (01978) 262726, *Fax:* (01978) 354257. *E:* curia@wrexhamdiocese.org.

WREY, Benjamin Harold Bourchier; Chairman, Henderson Global Investors Ltd (formerly Henderson Administration Group and Henderson Investors), 1992–2004; Director, Henderson Global Investors (Holdings) plc, 1998–2005; *b* 6 May 1940; *s* of Christopher B. Wrey and Ruth Wrey (*née* Bowden); *m* 1970, (Anne) Christine (Aubrey) Cherry; one *d*. *Educ:* Blundell's Sch.; Clare Coll., Cambridge (Hons in Econs; MA). Legal and General Assurance Soc., 1963–66; Investment Dept, Hambros Bank, 1966–69; joined Henderson Administration, 1969; Director, 1971; Jt Man. Dir/Dep. Chm., 1982; Director: Henderson Electric and General Investment Trust plc (formerly Electric and General Investment Co.), 1977–2000; Henderson American Capital and Income Trust plc, 1996–99; CCLA Investment Management, 1999–2005. Chm., Institutional Fund Managers' Assoc., 1996–98 (Dep. Chm., 1994–96); Member: Institutional Investors Adv. Cttee, London Stock Exchange, 1994–2000; Exec. Cttee, Assoc. of Investment Trust Cos, 1997–2002 (Dep. Chm., 1999–2002); Investment Cttee, 1999–2010 (Chm., 2003–10), Council, 2003–10, BHF; Investment Cttee, Cambridge Univ. Assistants Pension Scheme, 2004–. Dir, 1998–2005, Chm., 2005–09, COIF Charities Funds. Mem., Adv. Council, Nat. Opera Studio, 1996–2005. *Publications:* articles on investment. *Recreations:* shooting (rep. Cambridge Univ., England and GB in full bore target rifle shooting; winner, Bisley Grand Aggregate, 1966, 1969; runner-up, HM the Queen's Prize, 1963, 1977), fishing, mountain-walking, ballet, photography. *Address:* 8 Somerset Square, Addison Road, W14 8EE. *Clubs:* Boodle's, City of London; Hurlingham.

WREY, Sir (George Richard) Bourchier, 15th Bt *cr* 1628, of Trebitch, Cornwall; *b* 2 Oct. 1948; *s* of Sir Bourchier Wrey, 14th Bt and Sybil Mabel Alice Wrey, *d* of Dr George Lubke, S Africa; *S* father, 1991; *m* 1981, Lady Caroline Lindesay-Bethune, *d* of 15th Earl of Lindsay; two *s* one *d*. *Educ:* Eton. *Recreation:* shooting. *Heir: s* Harry David Bourchier Wrey, *b* 3 Oct. 1984. *Address:* Hollamoor Farm, Tawstock, Barnstaple, Devon EX31 3NY. *T:* (01271) 373466.

WRIGGLESWORTH, family name of **Baron Wrigglesworth**.

WRIGGLESWORTH, Baron *cr* 2013 (Life Peer), of Norton on Tees in the County of Durham; **Ian William Wrigglesworth,** Kt 1991; Chairman, Durham Group (formerly Bluehall Properties) (Chief Executive, 2008); Chairman, Port of Tyne, 2005–12 (Director, 2003–05); *b* Dec. 1939; *s* of Edward and Elsie Wrigglesworth; *m* 1967, Patricia Truscott; two *s* one *d*. *Educ:* Stockton Grammar Sch.; Stockton-Billingham Technical Coll.; Coll. of St Mark and St John, Chelsea. Formerly: Personal Assistant to Gen. Sec., NUT; Head of Research and Information Dept of Co-operative Party; Press and Public Affairs Manager of National Giro. Chm., Govt Policy Consultants Ltd, 1998–2000; Dep. Chm., John Livingston & Sons Ltd, 1987–95; Chm., UK Land Estates, 1995–2008; Dir, CIT Hldgs Ltd, 1987–2003; Divl Dir, Smiths Industries PLC, 1976–2000; Dir, Tyne Tees TV, 2002–06. Contested (SDP/Alliance) Stockton South, 1987. MP (Lab and Co-op, 1974–81, SDP, 1981–87) Teesside, Thornaby, Feb. 1974–1983, Stockton South, 1983–87. PPS to Mr Alec Lyon, Minister of State, Home Office, 1974; PPS to Rt Hon. Roy Jenkins, Home Secretary, 1974–76; Opposition spokesman on Civil Service, 1979–80; SDP spokesman on industry, 1981, on industry and economic affairs, 1983–87. Treas., Liberal Democrats, 2012– (Pres., 1988–90). Chairman: Northern Reg., CBI, 1992–94; Newcastle-Gateshead Initiative, 1999–2004; Baltic Centre for Contemporary Art, Gateshead, 2004–09. Gov., Univ. of Teesside, 1993–2002. DL Tyne and Wear, 2005. Hon. DMus Northumbria, 2011; Hon. DBus Teesside, 2012. Freeman, City of London, 1995; Liveryman, Co. of Founders, 1994. *Address:* House of Lords, SW1A 0PW. *E:* wrigglesworthi@parliament.uk. *Clubs:* Reform, Groucho.

WRIGHT, family name of **Baron Wright of Richmond**.

WRIGHT OF RICHMOND, Baron *cr* 1994 (Life Peer), of Richmond-upon-Thames in the London Borough of Richmond-upon-Thames; **Patrick Richard Henry Wright,** GCMG 1989 (KCMG 1984; CMG 1978); HM Diplomatic Service, retired; *b* 28 June 1931; *s* of late Herbert H. S. Wright and Rachel Wright (*née* Green); *m* 1958, Virginia Anne Gaffney; two *s* one *d*. *Educ:* Marlborough; Merton Coll. (Postmaster), Oxford (MA; Hon. Fellow, 1987). Served Royal Artillery, 1950–51; joined Diplomatic Service, 1955; Middle East Centre for Arab Studies, 1956–57; Third Secretary, British Embassy, Beirut, 1958–60; Private Sec. to Ambassador and later First Sec., British Embassy, Washington, 1960–65; Private Sec. to Permanent Under-Sec., FO, 1965–67; First Sec. and Head of Chancery, Cairo, 1967–70; Dep. Political Resident, Bahrain, 1971–72; Head of Middle East Dept, FCO, 1972–74; Private Sec. (Overseas Affairs) to Prime Minister, 1974–77; Ambassador to: Luxembourg, 1977–79; Syria, 1979–81; Dep. Under-Sec. of State, FCO and Chm., Jt Intelligence Cttee, 1982–84; Ambassador to Saudi Arabia, 1984–86; Permanent Under-Sec. of State and Head of Diplomatic Service, 1986–91. Mem., Security Commn, 1993–2002. Member: H of L Sub-Cttee on Home Affairs, 2001–07 (Chm., 2004–07); EU Select Cttee, 2005–07; H of L Sub-Cttee on Law and Instns, 2007–12; Jt Cttee on Conventions, 2006. Director: Barclays Bank plc, 1991–96; BP Amoco (formerly British Petroleum Co.), 1991–2001; De La Rue, 1991–2000; Unilever, 1991–99; BAA, 1992–98. Trustee, Home Start Internat., 1999–2007 (Chm., 2004–07). Chm., RIIA, 1995–99 (Mem. Council, 1992–99); Member: Council, RCM, 1991–2001 (FRCM 1994); Atlantic Coll., 1993–2000; ICRC Consultative Gp of Internat. Experts, 1992–95. Governor: Ditchley Foundn, 1986–2012; Wellington Coll., 1991–2001; Edward VII Hosp., 2005–07. KStJ 1990; Registrar, 1991–95, Dir of Overseas Relations, 1995–97, Order of St John of Jerusalem. House Mag. Award for Best Parly Speech of the Year, 2004. *Publications:* (contrib.) The Arabists of Shemlan; (contrib.) Envoys to the Arab World. *Recreations:* stamp collecting, cooking. *Address:* c/o House of Lords, Westminster, SW1A 0PW. *Club:* Oxford and Cambridge.
See also Sir S. G. McDonald.

WRIGHT, Alan; *see* Wright, R. A.

WRIGHT, Alan John; a Master of the Supreme Court, Supreme Court Taxing Office, 1972–91; *b* 21 April 1925; *s* of late Rev. Henry George Wright, MA and Winifred Annie Wright; *m* 1952, Alma Beatrice Ridding (*d* 2014); one *s* one *d* (and one *s* decd). *Educ:* St Olave's and St Saviour's Grammar Sch., Southwark; Keble Coll., Oxford. BA 1949, MA 1964. Served with RAF, India, Burma and China, 1943–46. Solicitor 1952; in private practice with Shaen Roscoe & Co., 1952–71; Legal Adviser to Trades Union Congress, 1955–71. Lay Reader, 1989. *Recreations:* Germanic studies, walking, travel, foreign languages. *Address:* 49 Grange Road, Billericay, Essex CM11 2RG.

WRIGHT, Alec Michael John, CMG 1967; *b* Hong Kong, 19 Sept. 1912; *s* of Arthur Edgar Wright and Margery Hepworth Chapman; *m* 1948, Ethel Surtees; one *d*. *Educ:* Brentwood Sch. MRICS (ARICS 1934); ARIBA 1937. Articled pupil followed by private practice in London. Joined Colonial Service, 1938; appointed Architect in Hong Kong, 1938. Commissioned Hong Kong Volunteer Defence Corps, 1941; POW in Hong Kong, 1941–45. Chief Architect, Public Works Dept, Hong Kong, 1950; Asst Director of Public Works, 1956; Dep. Director, 1959; Director, 1963–69; Commissioner for Hong Kong in London, 1969–73. *Address:* 13 Montrose Court, Princes Gate, SW7 2QQ. *T:* (020) 7584 4293. *Club:* Hong Kong (Hong Kong).

WRIGHT, Sir Allan Frederick, KBE 1982; farmer, retired; *b* Darfield, 25 March 1929; *s* of Quentin A. Wright; *m* 1953, Dorothy June Netting; three *s* two *d*. *Educ:* Christ's Coll., Christchurch. Nat. Pres., Young Farmers' Clubs, 1957–58; President: N Canterbury Federated Farmers, 1971–74; Federated Farmers of NZ, 1977–81 (formerly Sen. Nat. Vice-Pres.). Mem., NZ Cricket Bd of Control, 1967–90; Manager, NZ Cricket Team to England, 1983; Pres., NZ Cricket, 1993–94 (Life Mem., 1993). Chairman: NZ Rail, 1991–94; Lincoln Hldgs Ltd, 1995–2003; The Crossings (Marlborough) Ltd, 1998–2006; Dir, Richina Pacific Ltd, 1996–2004 (Chm., 1998–2001); former Dir, Orion Ltd. Chancellor, Lincoln Univ., 1990–94 (Chm. Council, Lincoln Coll., 1985–89, Mem., 1974–89). Hon. DCom Lincoln, 1997. *Recreations:* cricket (played for N Canterbury), Rugby, golf. *Address:* Annat, RD Sheffield, Canterbury, New Zealand.

WRIGHT, Rev. Andrew David Gibson; Secretary General, Mission to Seafarers, since 2013; *b* Redditch, 18 May 1958; *s* of David and Anita Wright; *m* 1984, Julia Savage; one *s* three *d*. *Educ:* Dragon Sch., Oxford; St Edward's Sch., Oxford; Univ. of St Andrews (MTh 1981); Ridley Hall, Cambridge. Ordained deacon, 1983, priest, 1984; Assistant Curate: Church of the Good Shepherd, W Derby, 1983–86; Holy Trinity and St Barnabas, Carlisle, 1986–88; Vicar, St James with St Thomas, Wigan, 1988–91; Chaplain, Hd of Religious Studies, and Housemaster, St Edward's Sch., Oxford, 1991–2007; Mission Chaplain and Dir of Ops, Royal Nat. Mission to Deep Sea Fishermen, 2007–13. *Recreations:* walking, sailing, theatre, history of art. *Address:* The Mission to Seafarers, St Michael Paternoster Royal, College Hill, EC4R 2RL. *T:* (020) 7248 5202, *Fax:* (020) 7248 4761. *E:* andrew.wright@missiontoseafarers.org.

WRIGHT, Andrew Paul Kilding, OBE 2001; PPRIAS, RIBA; architect and heritage consultant in private practice, Andrew P. K. Wright, since 2001; Commissioner, Royal Fine Art Commission for Scotland, 1997–2005; *b* 11 Feb. 1947; *s* of Harold Maurice Wright, ARIBA and Eileen May Wright; *m* 1970, Jean Patricia Cross; one *s* two *d*. *Educ:* Queen Mary's Grammar Sch., Walsall; Univ. of Liverpool (BArch Hons). RIBA 1973; ARIAS 1976, FRIAS 1987; FSAScot 1998. Weightman & Bullen, Liverpool, 1970–72; Rowand Anderson Kininmonth & Paul, Edinburgh, 1972–73; Sir Basil Spence, Glover & Ferguson, Edinburgh, 1973–78; Law & Dunbar-Nasmith, 1978–2001: Partner, 1981–2001; Chm., 1999–2001. Dir, Exec. Bd, UK City of Architecture and Design, Glasgow 1999 Festival Co. Ltd, 1995–2004. Archt, dio. of Moray, Ross and Caithness, 1988–98; Cons. Archt, Mar Lodge Estate, NT for Scotland, 1996–99; Hon. Archtl Advr, Scottish Redundant Churches Trust, 1996–; Architectural Adviser: Holyrood Progress Gp, Scottish Parlt, 2000–04; Scottish Churches Trust (formerly Scottish Churches Architectural Heritage Trust), 2011–; Conservation Advr, Highland Bldgs Preservation Trust, 2001–14. Member: Ancient Monuments Bd for Scotland, 1996–2003; Historic Envmt Adv. Council for Scotland, 2003–09 (Vice-Chm., 2003–06); Panel, Fundamental Review of Historic Scotland, 2003; Post Completion Adv. Gp, Scottish Parlt, 2004–06; Nat. Casework Panel, Scottish Civic Trust, 2011–; non-exec. Mem., Adv. Cttee, Historic Scotland, 2012–; Mem., Transition Adv. Bd, Historic Scotland and Royal Commn on Ancient and Histl Monuments of Scotland, 2013–15. Member Council: Inverness Archtl Assoc., 1981–90 (Pres., 1986–88); RIAS, 1986–94, 1995–99 (Vice-Pres., 1986–88; Convener, Memship Cttee, 1992–94; Pres., 1995–97); RIBA, 1988–94, 1995–97. Member: Ecclesiastical Archts and Surveyors Assoc., 1989; Conservation Adv. Panel, Hopetoun Hse Preservation Trust, 1997–2007 (Co-Chair, 2005–07); C of S Adv. Cttee on Artistic Matters, 2000–05; Arts and Crafts in Architecture Award Panel, Saltire Soc., 2001–06; Conservation Cttee, NT for Scotland, 2007–11. Trustee: Clan Mackenzie Charitable Trust, 1998–; Cawdor Maintenance Trust, 2010–; Cawdor Heritage Charity, 2010–; Scottish Lime Centre Trust, 2011–. Founding Fellow, Inst. of Contemp. Scotland, 2001; FRSA; FSA Scot. *Recreations:* cycling, fishing, industrial heritage, music. *Address:* Andrew P. K. Wright, Chartered Architect, 16 Moy House Court, Forres, Moray IV36 2NZ. *T:* (01309) 676655.

WRIGHT, Dr Anne Margaret, CBE 1997; Chair: National Lottery Commission, 2005–13; School Teachers' Review Body, 2008–11; *b* 26 July 1946; *d* of Herbert and Florence Holden; *m* 1970, Martin Wright; one *d*. *Educ:* Holy Trinity Ind. Grammar Sch., Bromley; King's Coll., London (BA Hons English I, 1967; Inglis Teaching Studentship, 1967–68; PhD 1970). Lectr in English, Lancaster Univ., 1969–71; Lectr, then Sen. Lectr, Principal Lectr and Reader in Modern English Studies, Hatfield Poly., 1971–84; British Acad. Res. Award, Univ. of Texas at Austin, 1979; Registrar for Arts and Humanities, CNAA, 1984–86; Dep. Rector (Academic), Liverpool Poly., 1986–90; Rector and Chief Exec., Sunderland Poly., 1990–92, Vice Chancellor and Chief Exec., Univ. of Sunderland, 1992–98; Chief Exec., UFI Ltd, 1998–2001; educational consultant, 2001–08. Member: English Studies Bd, 1978–84, Arts and Humanities Res. Sub-Cttee, 1979–84, CNAA; Cttee I of Cttee for Internat. Co-op. in Higher Educn, British Council, 1990–97; Council for Industry and Higher Educn, 1994–97; Armed Forces Pay Review Body, 2002–08; Bar Standards Bd, 2012–; NMC, 2013–; Director: FEFC, 1992–97; Hong Kong UPGC, 1992–2003; HEQC, 1993–97. Member: EOC, 1997–98; Bd, English Partnerships, 2004–08. Chairman: City of Sunderland (formerly Wearside) Common Purpose, 1990–97; Nat. Glass Centre, 1997–98; Director: Everyman Theatre, Liverpool, 1988–90; The Wearside Opportunity, 1990–93; Northern Sinfonia, 1990–96; Northern Arts, 1991–95; Wearside TEC, 1992–98; Chair of Trustees, Youth Music Theatre, 2009–11. CCMI (CIMgt 1994; Mem. Bd of Companions, 1999–2006); FRSA 1992. DL Tyne and Wear, 1997–2001. *Publications:* (ed jtly) Heartbreak House: a facsimile of the revised typescript, 1981; Literature of Crisis 1910–1922, 1984; Bernard Shaw's Saint Joan, 1984; articles in jls and entries in dictionaries of lit. biog. *Recreations:* singing, theatre, opera, the arts.

WRIGHT, Prof. Anthony, DM; FRCS; Professor of Otorhinolaryngology, University College London, 1991–2006, now Emeritus Professor of Otolaryngology (Director, Ear Institute (formerly Institute of Laryngology and Otology), 1991–2006); Consultant Ear, Nose and Throat Surgeon, Royal National Throat, Nose and Ear Hospital, 1993–2010; *b* 21 Nov. 1949; *s* of Arthur Donald and Hilda Wright; *m* 1989, Linda Steele; two *d*. *Educ:* Mill Hill Sch.; Emmanuel Coll., Cambridge (Sen. Schol.; Captain, Univ. Boxing Team, 1970; Full Blues, 1969, 1970); Lincoln Coll., Oxford (Full Blue, Boxing, 1972). DM Oxon 1986; LLM UWC Cardiff, 1995; FRCSE 1979; FRCS *ad eundem* 1995. Sen. Lectr in ENT Surgery, Inst. of Laryngology and Otology, 1984–89; Consultant ENT Surgeon, Royal Free Hosp., 1989–91. Queen's Award for Technol., 1998. *Publications:* Dizziness: a guide to disorders of balance, 1988; (ed with Harold Ludman) Diseases of the Ear, 6th edn 1997; scientific articles on the structure and function of the inner ear and on medico-legal aspects of ENT surgery. *Recreation:* still attempting to make coffee that tastes as good as it smells. *Address:* 4 Grange Road, Highgate, N6 4AP. *T:* (020) 8340 5593. *Clubs:* Athenæum; Hawks (Cambridge).

WRIGHT, Anthony David; *b* 12 Aug. 1954; *s* of late Arthur Wright and of Jean Wright; *m* 1988, Barbara Fleming; one *s* one *d*, and one step *d*. *Educ:* secondary modern sch. Engineer. Mem. (Lab) Great Yarmouth BC, 1980–82, 1986–98. Dir, Great Yarmouth Tourist Authority, 1994–97; Mem., Great Yarmouth Marketing Initiative, 1992–97 (Chm., 1996–97). MP (Lab) Great Yarmouth, 1997–2010; contested (Lab) same seat, 2010. Member: Public Admin Select Cttee, 2000–02; Trade and Industry Select Cttee, 2005–08; Business Enterprise and Regulatory Reform Cttee, 2008–10.

WRIGHT, Rev. Canon (Anthony) Robert, LVO 2010; Canon, 1998–2010, Sub-Dean, 2005–10 and Archdeacon, 2009–10, of Westminster; Rector of St Margaret's, Westminster, and Chaplain to the Speaker of the House of Commons, 1998–2010; *b* 24 April 1949; *s* of Kenneth William Wright and Christabel Annie Wright (*née* Flett); *m* 1970, Leah Helen Flower; one *s* one *d*. *Educ:* Lanchester Poly. (BA Hons Modern Studies); St Stephen's House, Oxford (CTh Oxon). Ordained deacon, 1973, priest, 1974; Curate: St Michael, Amersham, 1973–76; St Giles-in-Reading, 1976–78; Vicar: Prestwood, 1978–84; Wantage, 1984–92; RD of Wantage, 1984–92; Vicar of Portsea, 1992–98. *Recreations:* abstract painting, walking, reading.

WRIGHT, Dr Anthony Wayland; *b* 11 March 1948; *s* of Frank and Maud Wright; *m* 1973, Moira Elynwy Phillips; three *s* (and one *s* decd). *Educ:* Desborough County Primary Sch.; Kettering Grammar Sch.; LSE (BSc Econ 1st Cl. Hons); Harvard Univ. (Kennedy Schol.); Balliol Coll., Oxford (DPhil). Lectr in Politics, UCNW, Bangor, 1973–75; Lectr 1975, Sen. Lectr 1987, Reader 1989, in Politics, Sch. of Continuing Studies, Univ. of Birmingham. Educnl Fellowship, IBA, 1979–80; Chm., S Birmingham CHC, 1983–85. MP (Lab) Cannock and Burntwood, 1992–97, Cannock Chase, 1997–2010. PPS to the Lord Chancellor, 1997–98. Chm., Public Admin Select Cttee, 1999–2010. Hon. Prof., Univ. of Birmingham, 1999–; Vis. Prof. in Governance and Public Policy, UCL; Professorial Fellow, Birkbeck, Univ. of London. Jt Editor, Political Qly, 1994–. *Publications:* G. D. H. Cole and Socialist Democracy, 1979; Local Radio and Local Democracy, 1982; British Socialism, 1983; Socialisms: theories and practices, 1986; R. H. Tawney, 1987; (ed jtly) Party Ideology in Britain, 1989; (ed jtly) The Alternative, 1990; (ed jtly) Consuming Public Services, 1990; (ed jtly) Political Thought since 1945, 1992; Citizens and Subjects, 1993; (ed with G. Brown) Values, Visions and Voices, 1995; Socialisms: old and new, 1996; Who Do I Complain to?, 1997; Why Vote Labour?, 1997; (jtly) The People's Party, 1997; The British Political Process, 2000; British Politics: a very short introduction, 2003; contribs to learned jls. *Recreations:* tennis, walking, gardening.

WRIGHT, Brian; *see* Wright, G. B.

WRIGHT, Caroline Jane; Her Honour Judge Caroline Wright; a Circuit Judge, since 2009; *b* Oxford, 10 Aug. 1959; *d* of Frederick and Lilian Wright; *m* 1st, 1997, Dan Gardiner (marr. diss. 2002); one *s* one *d*; 2nd, 2007, Matthew John Hale. *Educ:* Oxford High Sch.; Univ. of York (BSc Psychol.); Univ. of Westminster (Dip. Law). Called to the Bar, Gray's Inn, 1983; in practice as barrister, specialising in family and public law, Albion Chambers, Bristol, 1992–2003, 29 Bedford Row, London, 2003–09; Fee-paid Immigration Judge, 1998–2009; a Recorder, 2004–09. Mem., Bar Standards Bd, 2008–09. Tutor in public and private family law, JSB, 2010–. *Recreations:* my diverse and entertaining family, painting, music, cycling, travel, swimming on Hampstead Heath. *Address:* Principal Registry of the Family Division, First Avenue House, 42–49 High Holborn, WC1V 6NP; Inner London Crown Court, Newington Causeway, SE1 6AZ. *E:* HHJudge.Wright@judiciary.gsi.gov.uk.

WRIGHT, Caroline Janet Pamela; Director, British Educational Suppliers Association, since 2012; *b* 29 Dec. 1973; *d* of Peter Richard Wright and Janet Anne Wright; *m* 2007, Jonathan Rubidge; one *s* one *d*. *Educ:* Chingford Sch.; Royal Holloway and Bedford New Coll., London (BSc Hons Geog. 1995). Regl journalist, 1995–98; Communications Manager, Post Office, 1998–2000; Department of Trade and Industry: Dep. Dir of News, 2000–03; Hd, Strategic Communications, 2003; Hd, News and Mktg, Ofsted, 2003–05; Dir of Communications, Partnerships for Schs, 2005–06; Dir of Communications, DES, later DCSF, then DFE, 2006–11. Non-exec. Dir, Barking, Redbridge and Havering NHS Trust, 2011–13. *Recreation:* swimming. *Address:* British Educational Suppliers Association, 20 Beaufort Court, Admirals Way, E14 9XL. *E:* caroline@besa.org.uk.

WRIGHT, Christopher John; Deputy Team Leader, Iraq Study, Ministry of Defence, 2009–10; *b* 22 March 1953; *s* of James Wright and Ruby Wright (*née* Galbraith); *m* 1995, Barbara Ann Spells. *Educ:* Royal Grammar Sch., Newcastle upon Tyne; Univ. of York (BA). Joined MoD, 1974; Private Sec. to Air Mem. for Supply and Orgn, 1981; Office of Manpower Econs, 1982–85; Private Sec. to Perm. Under-Sec. of State, 1987–90; Asst Sec., 1990; Head: Central Services, 1990–93; NATO and European Policy Secretariat, 1993–94; Cost Review Secretariat, 1994–95; Dir of Orgn and Mgt Develt, 1995–98; Comd Sec., RAF Strike Comd, 1998–2001; Fellow, Center for Internat. Affairs, Harvard Univ., 2001–02; Hd, New Security Issues Prog., RIIA, 2002–04; Dir, Security and Intelligence, Cabinet Office, 2004–09. *Recreations:* reading, cinema, modern art, house refurbishment.

WRIGHT, Christopher Norman, CBE 2005; Director, Lasgo Chrysalis Ltd, since 2011; Chairman: Chrysalis plc (formerly Chrysalis, later Chrysalis Group plc), 1969–2011; Digital Rights Group, since 2007; *b* 7 Sept. 1944; *s* of Walter Reginald Wright and Edna May (*née* Corden); *m* 1st, 1972, Carolyn Rochelle Nelson (marr. diss. 1999); two *s* one *d*; 2nd, 2003, Janice Ann Stinnes (*née* Toseland); one *d*. *Educ:* King Edward VI Grammar Sch., Louth; Manchester Univ. (BA Hons 1966); Manchester Business Sch. Co-Founder, Ellis Wright Agency, 1967; name changed to: Chrysalis, 1968; Chrysalis Gp plc, 1985. Chm., Loftus Road plc (incorp. Queen's Park Rangers Football and Athletic Club), 1996–2001; Founder, Shareholder and Dir, London Wasps RFC, 1996–2008 (Chm., 1996–2007); Chm., Portman Film and Television, 2004–07. Chm., British Phonographic Industry, 1980–83; Director: Phonographic Performance Ltd, 1980–94; Internat. Fedn of Phonographic Industry, 1981–95 (Vice-Pres., 1981–91). *Recreations:* playing tennis, breeding race horses, music, collecting art and fine wines, watching sport of all kinds. *Club:* Turf.

WRIGHT, Prof. Crispin James Garth, PhD, DLitt; FBA 1992; FRSE, FAAAS; Professor of Philosophy, New York University, since 2008; *b* 21 Dec. 1942; *s* of Geoffrey Joseph Wright and Jean Valerie Holford; *m* 1985, Catherine Steedman (*née* Pain); two *s*, and one step *s* one step *d*. *Educ:* Birkenhead Sch.; Trinity Coll., Cambridge (BA Hons 1964; MA, PhD 1968); BPhil 1969, DLitt 1988, Oxon. Oxford University: Jun. Res. Fellow, Trinity Coll., 1967–69; Prize Fellow, All Souls Coll., 1969–71; Lectr, Balliol Coll., 1969–70; Lectr, UCL, 1970–71; Res. Fellow, All Souls Coll., Oxford, 1971–78; University of St Andrews: Prof. of Logic and Metaphysics, 1978–2008; Wardlaw Prof. 1997–2008; Dir, Arché Res. Centre, 1998–2009; Prof. of Phil., 1987–92, Nelson Prof. of Phil., 1992–94, Univ. of Michigan, Ann Arbor. Leverhulme Res. Prof., 1998–2003; Dir, Northern Inst. of Philosophy, 2009–15, Regius Prof. of Logic, 2013–15, Univ. of Aberdeen. FRSE 1996; FAAAS 2012. *Publications:* Wittgenstein on the Foundations of Mathematics, 1980; Frege's Conception of Numbers as Objects, 1983; Realism, Meaning and Truth, 1986; Truth and Objectivity, 1993; (with Bob Hale) The Reason's Proper Study, 2001; Rails to Infinity, 2001; Saving the Differences, 2003. *Recreations:* gardening, mountain-walking, running, P. G. Wodehouse, Liverpool FC. *Address:* Department of Philosophy, 5 Washington Place, New York, NY 10003, USA.

WRIGHT, David; *b* 22 Dec. 1966; *s* of Kenneth William Wright and Heather Wright; *m* 1996, Lesley Insole. *Educ:* Wolverhampton Poly. (BA Hons Humanities). MCIH 1994. With Sandwell MBC, 1988–2001 (Housing Strategy Manager, 1995–2001). MP (Lab) Telford, 2001–15; contested (Lab) same seat, 2015. An Asst Govt Whip, 2009–10; Opposition Whip, 2010–12. *Recreations:* watching football (AFC Telford Utd) and cricket (Surrey), visiting old towns and cities. *Clubs:* Wrockwardine Wood and Trench Labour, Dawley Social.

WRIGHT, David Alan, OBE 1983; HM Diplomatic Service; Joint Head (formerly Assistant Director), PROSPER, Human Resources Command, Foreign and Commonwealth Office, since 2002; *b* 27 May 1942; *s* of Herbert Ernest Wright and Ivy Florence (*née* Welch); *m* 1966, Gail Karol Mesling; four *s* one *d*. *Educ:* Surbiton Grammar Sch.; Univ. of Birmingham (BSocSc 1963). VSO, Chad, 1963; Inf. Officer, BoT, 1964; entered Foreign Office, 1965: Asst Private Sec. to Minister of State, FO, 1966–68; MECAS, 1968–70; Baghdad, 1970–73; Doha, 1973–76; on secondment to DHSS, 1976–78; FCO, 1978–80; Durban, 1980–83; Baghdad, 1983–87; FCO, 1987–92 (Head: Communications Dept, 1988–90; Inf. Systems Div. (Resources), 1990–92); Consul Gen., Atlanta, 1992–97; Ambassador and Consul Gen., Qatar, 1997–2002. Member: (C) Guildford BC, 2003– (Chm., Licensing, 2003–07; Lead Mem. for Community Safety, 2007–11; Dep. Leader, 2011–12); Surrey Probation Bd, 2006–09; Vice Chm., 2007–14, Chm., 2014–, Surrey Hills Bd. Chm., SurreySave Credit Union, 2012–. *Recreations:* jogging, sailing, pottery, travel, music. *Address:* Newlands House, Newlands Corner, Guildford GU4 8SE. *Club:* Royal Over-Seas League.

WRIGHT, David Arthur, FRCS; Consultant Otolaryngologist: Mount Alvernia Hospital, Guildford, 1970–2004; Royal Surrey County Hospital, 1970–99, now Consultant Emeritus; President, British Association of Otorhinolaryngologists and Head and Neck Surgeons, 1997–99; *b* 13 April 1935; *s* of Arthur Albert Wright and Ena May (*née* Claxton); *m* 1969, Hillery Drina Seex; one *s* one *d*. *Educ:* Repton; Jesus Coll., Cambridge (MB BChir, MA 1960); Guy's Hosp. LRCP 1959; MRCS 1959, FRCS 1966. Hon. Consultant Otolaryngologist: Cambridge Mil. Hosp., 1981–96; King Edward VII Hosp., Midhurst, 1995–2003. Ear, Nose and Throat Adviser: British Airways, 1987–97; CAA, 1994–; Army, 1999–. Asst Ed., Jl Laryngology and Otology, 1981–88. Pres., TWJ Otological Foundn, 2010– (Chm., 1974–2008). Sec. Gen., Eur. Bd Otolaryngology, 1998–2000. Member: BMA, 1960–98; Council, RCS, 1995–2000; Pres., Section of Otology, RSocMed, 1992. Examr, Intercollegiate Bd Otolaryngology, 1990–94. Mem. Senate, Royal Surgical Colls, 1997–2000 (Chm., Specialist Adv. Cttee, 1988–94). Patron, British Soc. of Hearing Therapists, 1999–; Master, British Academic Conf. in Otolaryngology, 2003–06. George Davey Howells Meml Prize, RSocMed, 1989; Walter Jobson Horne Prize, BMA, 1997; Gold Medal, British Assoc. of Otorhinolaryngologists, 1999. *Publications:* (ed) Scott-Brown's Otolaryngology, vol. 1, Basic Sciences, 5th edn 1988; chapters in text books; contrib. articles in med. jls on noise induced hearing loss, multi-channel hearing aids and functional endoscopic sinus surgery. *Recreations:* off-shore sailing, ski-ing, golf, weather forecasting, fly-fishing. *Address:* Eastbury Farmhouse, Compton, Guildford, Surrey GU3 1EE. *T:* (01483) 810343. *Clubs:* Royal Society of Medicine; Royal Southern Yacht (Hamble); Liphook Golf (Hants).

WRIGHT, Sir David (John), GCMG 2002 (KCMG 1996; CMG 1992); LVO 1990; HM Diplomatic Service, retired; Vice-Chairman, Barclays (formerly Barclays Capital), since 2003; *b* 16 June 1944; *s* of J. F. Wright; *m* 1968, Sally Ann Dodkin; one *s* one *d*. *Educ:* Wolverhampton Grammar Sch.; Peterhouse, Cambridge (MA; Hon. Fellow, 2001). Third Secretary, FO, 1966; Third Sec., later Second Sec., Tokyo, 1966–72; FCO, 1972–75; Ecole Nationale d'Administration, Paris, 1975–76; First Sec., Paris, 1976–80; Private Sec. to Secretary of the Cabinet, 1980–82; Counsellor (Economic), Tokyo, 1982–85; Head of Personnel Services Dept, FCO, 1985–88; Dep. Private Sec. to HRH the Prince of Wales, 1988–90 (on secondment); Ambassador to Republic of Korea, 1990–94; Dep. Under-Sec. of State, FCO, 1994–96; Ambassador to Japan, 1996–99; Gp Chief Exec. (Perm. Sec.), British Trade Internat., 1999–2002. Non-exec. Dir, Balfour Beatty, 2003–05; Member: Internat. Adv. Bd, All Nippon Airways, 2003–07; Internat. Adv. Council, China Develt Bank, 2010–. Chm., Govt Wine Cttee, 2004–. Vice-Pres., China Britain Business Council, 2003–09; Member: Bd, UK-Japan 21st Century Gp, 2003–; Adv. Council, British Consultants and Construction Bureau, 2003–05. Chm. and Trustee, Daiwa Anglo-Japanese Foundn, 2001–04; Chm., UK-Korea Forum, 2008–14. Gov., RSC, 2004–08. Chm., Develt Cttee, Peterhouse, Cambridge, 2004–10; Mem. Bd, 2020 Vision Campaign, Cambridge Biomed. Campus, 2011–13. Chm., Peterhouse Soc., 2010–13. Hon. LLD: Wolverhampton, 1997; Birmingham, 2000. Grand Cordon, Order of the Rising Sun (Japan), 1998. *Recreations:* golf, cooking, military history. *Address:* c/o Barclays, 5 The North Colonnade, Canary Wharf, E14 4BB. *Clubs:* Travellers, Garrick, Saintsbury.

WRIGHT, Elizabeth Anne, CMG 2015; Chair, Advisory Board, China Policy Institute, University of Nottingham, since 2005 (Executive Chair, China Policy Institute, 2003); *b* Coventry, 6 Feb. 1946; *d* of John Wright and Anne Wright; *m* 1994, David Michael Lindley Witherow, *qv*. *Educ:* Nuneaton High Sch. for Girls; School of Oriental and African Studies, Univ. of London (BA Hons Chinese 1968; MA Area Studies 1971). Res. Officer, FCO, 1969–72; Second Sec., British Embassy, Beijing, 1972–75; Dep. Dir, 1976–78, Dir, 1978–84, Great Britain-China Centre; BBC World Service, 1984–2003: Hd, Chinese Service, 1989–93; Hd, Asia and Pacific Reg., 1993–2003. Trustee: Needham Res. Inst., 2009–; Governing Bd, SOAS, 2003–14 (Vice-Chm., 2011–14); Chm., Univs China Cttee, 2013–. *Publications:* The Chinese People Stand Up, 1989. *Recreations:* classical music, opera, theatre, painting, fiction. *E:* ew25@soas.ac.uk.

WRIGHT, Eric; Chairman, Yorkshire and Humberside Development Agency (formerly Association), 1993–99; *b* 17 Nov. 1933; *s* of Alec Wright and Elsie (*née* Worthington); *m* 1st, 1955, Pauline Sutton (marr. diss. 1993); three *s* (and one *s* decd); 2nd, 1993, Hazel Elizabeth Story. *Educ:* Wolstanton Grammar Sch.; Keble Coll., Oxford (BA 1st Cl. Hons Mod. Hist.). 2nd Lieut RASC, 1955–57. Ministry of Fuel and Power, 1957–65; Civil Service Commission, 1965–67; Min. of Technology, 1968–70; Sloan Fellow, London Business Sch., 1970–71; Principal Private Sec. to Secretary of State, DTI, 1971–72; Dept of Trade, 1972–77; Dept of Industry, 1977–83; Under-Sec., 1979–; DTI, 1983–93 (Regl Dir, Yorks and Humberside, 1985–93). *Recreations:* music, tennis, chess. *Address:* 17 Foxhill Crescent, Leeds LS16 5PD. *T:* (0113) 275 4309.

WRIGHT, Prof. Ernest Marshall, PhD, DSc; FRS 2005; Professor of Physiology, since 1974, Sherman M. Mellinkoff Distinguished Professor of Medicine, since 1999, Distinguished Professor of Physiology, since 2004, School of Medicine, University of California, Los Angeles; *b* Belfast, N Ireland, 8 June 1940; *m* 1961, Brenda W. Keys; two *s*. *Educ:* Chelsea Coll. of Sci. and Technol., Univ. of London (BSc Physiol. and Chem. 1961); Univ. of Sheffield (PhD Physiol. 1964); Univ. of London (DSc Physiol. 1978). Res. Fellow, Biophysics, Harvard Univ., 1965–66; University of California, Los Angeles: Asst Prof. of Physiol., 1967–70; Associate Prof. of Physiol., 1970–74; Chair, Dept of Physiol., 1987–2000. Visiting Professor: Center for Advanced Studies, Nat. Poly. Inst., Mexico City, 1973; Max Planck Inst. for Biophysics, Frankfurt, 1974–75; Queen Elizabeth Coll., London, 1977. Senator Jacob K. Javits Neurosci. Investigator, 1985–92. Horace W. Davenport Dist. Lectr, Exptl Biol. 2000, San Diego, 2000. Mem., Adv. Bd, Broad Med. Res. Prog., 2001–. Chm., Physiol. Study Section, NIH, 1983–86; Councilor: Soc. of Gen. Physiologists, 1986–89; Gastrointestinal Sect. Steering Cttee, Amer. Physiol Soc., 1999–2002. Mem. Review Panel, Structural Biol., Nat. Center of Competence in Res., Swiss Nat. Sci. Foundn, 2002–. Fellow, Biophysical Soc., 2005. Member: German Acad. Scis Leopoldina, 2006; Nat. Acad. of Scis, USA, 2013. Award for Sustained Achievement in Digestive Scis, Janssen/Amer. Gastroenterol. Soc., 2004. *Publications:* (with M. Martin) Congenital Intestinal Transport Defects, in Pediatric Gastrointestinal Disease, 4th edn 2004; (contrib.) Sugar Absorption, in Physiology of the Gastrointestinal Tract, 4th edn 2005; numerous articles in learned jls, incl. Nature, Science, Jl Biol Chem., Jl Membrane Biol., Jl Physiol., Biochemistry, Physiol Reviews. *Address:* Department of Physiology, David Geffen School of Medicine at UCLA, 10833 Le Conte Avenue, Los Angeles, CA 90095–1751, USA. *T:* (310) 8256905, *Fax:* (310) 2065661. *E:* ewright@mednet.ucla.edu.

WRIGHT, Freya Patricia; *see* Newbery, F. P.

WRIGHT, (George) Brian; JP; Head of Educational Broadcasting Services, BBC, 1989–93; *b* 9 April 1939; *s* of George Wright and Martha Blair Wright (*née* Dundee); *m* 1963, Joyce Avril Frances Camier; two *s*. *Educ:* Trinity Coll., Dublin (MA, HDipEd). Schoolmaster, 1961–67; Local Govt Administrator, 1967–69; BBC Educn Officer, Belfast, Nottingham, Birmingham, 1969–81; Chief Educn Officer, BBC, 1981–89. Occasional Lectr, Henley Management Coll., 1994–95. Mem., Lord Chancellor's Nottingham Div. Adv. Cttee, 1997–2001. Mem., City and Co. of Notts Adv. Bd, Salvation Army, 1999–2001. Burgess, Ancient Corp. of St Pancras, Chichester, 2015. JP Ealing, 1992–93, Nottingham, 1993. *Publications:* How Britain Earns Its Living, 1980; (with John Cain) in a class of its own, 1994; In the Name of Decent Citizens: the trials of Frank De Groot, 2006. *Recreations:* reading, crosswords, watching Rugby. *Address:* 56 Lyndhurst Road, Chichester, W Sussex PO19 7PE. *T:* (01243) 773432.

WRIGHT, George Henry, MBE 1977; Vice-Chairman, Wales Co-operative Development Centre, since 1985 (Chairman, 1983–85); Regional Secretary, Wales, Transport and General Workers Union, 1972–99; *b* 11 July 1935; *s* of William Henry and Annie Louisa Wright; *m* 1956, Margaret Wright; two *d*. *Educ:* Tinkers Farm Sch., Birmingham. Car worker, 1954–65. T&GWU: District Officer, West Bromwich, 1966–68; District Secretary, Birmingham, 1968–72. Gen. Sec., Wales TUC, 1974–84 (Chm., 1989–90). Member: MSC Wales, 1976–88; Employment Appeal Tribunal, 1985–; Welsh Trng Adv. Gp, 1989–; Bd, Welsh Develt Agency, 1994–; Central Arbitration Cttee, Dept of Employment, 1994–; Econ. and Social Cttee, EC, 1994–; S Wales Police Authority, 1994–. *Recreations:* fishing, gardening. *Address:* 5 Kidwelly Court, Caerphilly CF83 2TY. *T:* (029) 2088 5434.

WRIGHT, Graeme Alexander; Editor, Wisden Cricketers' Almanack, 1986–92 and 2000–02; *b* 23 April 1943; *s* of Alexander John Wright and Eileen Margaret Wright. *Educ:* St Patrick's Coll., Wellington, NZ; St Patrick's High Sch., Timaru, NZ; Univ. of Canterbury, Christchurch, NZ. Copywriter, NZ Broadcasting Corp., 1965–67; Sub-editor, BSI, 1968–69; Editor and writer, Publicare Ltd, 1969–72; Managing Editor, Queen Anne Press, 1973–74; freelance editor and writer, 1974–; cricket writer, Independent on Sunday, 1990–94; Dir, John Wisden & Co. Ltd, 1983–86. *Publications:* (with Phil Read) Phil Read, 1977; The Illustrated Handbook of Sporting Terms, 1978; Olympic Greats, 1980; (with George Best) Where do I go from here?, 1981; (with Patrick Eagar): Test Decade 1972–1982, 1982; Botham, 1985; (with Joe Brown) Brown Sauce, 1986; Merrydown: forty vintage years, 1988; Betrayal: the struggle for cricket's soul, 1993; Chelton: the first 50 years, 1997; (ed) Wisden on Bradman, 90th Birthday Edition, 1998; (ed) A Wisden Collection, 2004; (ed) Wisden at Lord's, 2005; (ed) Bradman in Wisden, 2008; Behind the Boundary: cricket at a crossroads, 2011; Mackie's Law, 2012. *Recreations:* reading, thinking, coffee houses. *Address:* 14 Field End Road, Eastcote, Pinner, Middx HA5 2QL.

WRIGHT, Helen Mary, EdD; Headmistress, Ascham School, Sydney, 2013–14; education adviser; writer and speaker; *b* Perth, 22 Aug. 1970; *d* of Gordon Kendal and Patricia Kendal (*née* Foggo); *m* 1993, Brian Wright; one *s* two *d*. *Educ:* James Gillespie's High Sch., Edinburgh; Lincoln Coll., Oxford (BA 1992; PGCE 1993); Univ. of Leicester (MA 1998); Univ. of Exeter (EdD 2004). French and German teacher, Reed's Sch., Cobham, 1993–95; Hd of Dept, Bishop's Stortford Coll., 1995–97; Hd of Dept and Dep. Housemistress, St Edward's Sch., Oxford, 1997–2000; Dep. Headmistress, 2000, Headmistress, 2001–03, Heathfield Sch., Ascot; Headmistress, St Mary's School, Calne, 2003–12. Teacher-educator and PGCE mentor, 1997–2000; Examr and Sen. Examr (Higher Level), Internat. Baccalaureate, 1999–2009; Inspector, ISI, 2000–12. Consultant, Scholastic Books, 1998–2001; Internat. Educn Advr, Australian Educn City, 2014–15. Dir, Dalton Foundn Ltd (HK), 2014–; non-exec. Dir, Global Trails, 2015–; Director and Trustee: ESU (Scotland), 2014–; Changing the Chemistry, 2015–; Mem. Adv. Bd, Obrussa, 2014–. Chair, World Leading Schs Assoc. Res. Gp, 2012–. Member: Assoc. for Language Learning, 1993–2012; Ind. Schs' Modern Langs Assoc., 1993– (Mem. Cttee, 1997–2000; Ed. of Newsletter, 1997–2000; Patron, 2005–); ASCL (formerly SHA), 2000–12 (Mem. Council, 2009–12); GSA, 2001–12 (Mem. Council, 2009–12; Pres., 2011; Hon. Mem., 2012); Vice Chm., ISC, 2011–12. Mem. Bd, Oxford Univ. Soc., 2008–; Mem. Editl Adv. Bd, Oxford Today, 2011–. MInstD 2009. FRSA 2003. Ed., Francophonie, 1999–2002. *Publications:* trans., Elizabeth Behr-Sigel, A Monk of the Eastern Church, 1999; French Fries My Brain!, 2001; Learning Through Listening, 2004; Decoding Your 21st Century Daughter, 2013; numerous articles and reviews. *Recreations:* reading, studying, travelling, making jam, indoor gardening, writing. *W:* www.drhelenwright.com, www.twitter.com/drhelenwright. *Club:* Caledonian.

WRIGHT, Hugh Raymond, MA; Chief Master, King Edward's School, Birmingham, 1991–98; *b* 24 Aug. 1938; *s* of Rev. Raymond Blayney Wright and Alice Mary Wright (*née* Hawksworth); *m* 1962, Jillian Mary McIldowie Meiklejohn; three *s*. *Educ:* Kingswood Sch., Bath; The Queen's Coll., Oxford (Bible Clerk; MA Lit. Hum.). Asst Master, Brentwood Sch., 1961–64; Cheltenham Coll., 1964–79: Hd of Classics, 1967–72; Housemaster, Boyne House, 1971–79; Headmaster: Stockport Grammar Sch., 1979–85; Gresham's School, Holt, 1985–91. Headmasters' Conference: Chm., 1995; Chm., NW Dist, 1983; Chm., Community Service Sub-Cttee, 1985–90 (Mem., 1980–90); Rep. on ISC (formerly ISJC) Europe Cttee, 1997–2001; Mem., Assisted Places Wkg Pty, 1992–97. Mem., Chaplaincy Team, Shepton Mallet Prison, 2001–13. Member: Bloxham Project Cttee, 1993–98 (Trustee, 1998–2006); Admty Interview Bd Panel, 1982–95; ABM (formerly ACCM), C of E, 1982–; GBA Cttee, 2000–03. Chm., Nat. Steering Cttee, Children's Univ., 1995–2001. Gov., Kingswood Sch., Bath, 1995–2006 (Chm., 1998–2006). Mem., Cttee, Friends of Bath Internat. Fest., 1995–2013 (Chm., 2008–13). Co-writer, Into Your Satisfaction, diaries and music of Benjamin Britten, perf. Gresham's Sch., Holt, 2013. *Publications:* film strips and notes on The Origins of Christianity and the Medieval Church, 1980; Thomas Tropenell: builder of Great Chalfield, 2011; The Story of Great Chalfield: the lives and times of the owners and occupiers of the Manor 1553–1913, 2011; Widows, Wives and Daughters: the women who shaped the story of Great Chalfield, 2013; contribs The Greshamian. *Recreations:* music, theatre, walking, wildfowl, biographical research, butterflies. *Address:* 5 The Paddock, Kingston Road, Bradford on Avon BA15 1FN. *Club:* East India.

WRIGHT, Iain David; MP (Lab) Hartlepool, since Sept. 2004; *b* 9 May 1972; *m* Tiffiny; three *s* one *d*. *Educ:* Manor Comprehensive Sch., Hartlepool; University Coll. London (BA, MA). ACA 2003. Deloitte & Touche, 1997–2003; chartered accountant, One NorthEast, 2003–04. Mem. (Lab), Hartlepool BC, 2002–05. Parly Under-Sec. of State, DCLG, 2007–09, DCSF, 2009–10. Chm., Select Cttee on Business, Innovations and Skills, 2015–. *Address:* (office) 23 South Road, Hartlepool TS26 9HD; House of Commons, SW1A 0AA.

WRIGHT, Prof. Ian Craig, PhD; Director, Science and Technology, National Oceanography Centre, since 2013; *b* Wellington, NZ, 14 Dec. 1958; *s* of Peter Wright and Margaret Wright; *m* 1981, Barbara Stewart; one *s* one *d*. *Educ:* Wellington Coll., Wellington, NZ; Victoria Univ. of Wellington (BSc Hons 1981; PhD 1986). Jun. Lectr, Victoria Univ. of Wellington, 1982–86; Res. Scientist, NZ Oceanographic Inst., 1987–92; sabbatical, UK, 1993; National Institute of Water and Atmospheric Research, NZ: Res. Scientist, 1993–98; Principal Scientist, 1998–2004; Coasts and Oceans Centre Leader, 2004–08; National Oceanography Centre: Gp Leader, 2008–10; Dep. Dir, Sci. and Technol., 2010–12. *Publications:* over 70 articles in learned jls. *Recreations:* golf, tennis, rambling. *Address:* National Oceanography Centre, University of Southampton Waterfront Campus, Southampton SO14 3ZH. *T:* (023) 8059 6017. *E:* ian.wright@noc.ac.uk.

WRIGHT, Prof. Ian Peter, PhD; Professor of Planetary Sciences, Open University, since 2005; *b* Birmingham, 28 Nov. 1956; *s* of Ronald Wright and Vera Wright; *m* 1986, Prof. Monica Mary Grady, *qv*; one *s*. *Educ:* King Edward VI Five Ways Grammar Sch.; Univ. of Birmingham (BSc Geol Scis 1978); Darwin Coll., Cambridge (PhD 1982). Post-doctoral Res., Univ. of Cambridge, 1982–83; Open University: Post-doctoral Res., 1983–88; Res. Fellow, 1988–96; Sen. Res. Fellow, 1996–2005. Fellow, Inst. of Advanced Study, Durham Univ., 2010. FRAS 1989. *Publications:* articles in scientific jls. *Recreations:* denizen of virtual worlds, theatre, music, gardening, cooking, art, outreach, education. *Address:* Department of Physical Sciences, Open University, Walton Hall, Milton Keynes MK7 6AA. *T:* (01908) 653898. *E:* ian.wright@open.ac.uk.

WRIGHT, Prof. Jack Clifford, MA, BA; Professor of Sanskrit, 1964–96, Research Fellow, 1996–99, Research Associate, since 1999, Professor Emeritus, since 2000, and Hon. President, Centre of Jaina Studies, since 2004, School of Oriental and African Studies, University of London; *b* 5 Dec. 1933; *s* of late Jack and Dorothy Wright, Aberdeen; *m* 1958, Hazel Chisholm (*née* Strachan), Crathes, Banchory; one *s*. *Educ:* Robert Gordon's Coll., Aberdeen; Univ. of Aberdeen (MA Hons in French and German, 1955); University of Zürich; Univ. of London (BA Hons in Sanskrit, 1959). Lectr in Sanskrit, 1959–64, Head, Dept of Indology and Mod. Langs and Lits of S Asia, 1970–83, SOAS, Univ. of London. *Address:* Faculty of Languages and Cultures, School of Oriental and African Studies, University of London, Thornhaugh Street, Russell Square, WC1H 0XG.

WRIGHT, James Robertson Graeme, CBE 2001; DL; Vice-Chancellor, University of Newcastle upon Tyne, 1992–2000; *b* 14 June 1939; *s* of John Wright and Elizabeth Calder (*née* Coghill); *m* 1966, Jennifer Susan Greenberg; two *d*. *Educ:* Inverness Royal Acad.; Dundee High Sch.; Univ. of Edinburgh (MA 1st cl. Hons Classics 1961, Guthrie Fellowship in Classical Lit., C. B. Black Scholarship in New Testament Greek); St John's Coll., Cambridge (Major Scholar, BA 1st cl. Classical Tripos Pt II 1963, MA 1968, Henry Arthur Thomas Studentship, Denney Studentship, Ferguson Scholarship in Classics, 1962). University of Edinburgh: Asst Lectr in Humanity (Latin), 1965; Lectr, 1966–78; Sen. Warden, Pollock Halls of Residence, 1973–78; Mem., Univ. Court, 1975–78; St Catharine's College, Cambridge: Fellow, 1978–87; Professorial Fellow, 1987–91; Hon. Fellow, 1992–; Dir, Studies in Classics, 1978–87; Bursar, 1979–87; Cambridge Bursars' Committee: Sec., 1983–86; Chm., 1986–87; Sec.-Gen. of Faculties, Univ. of Cambridge, 1987–91. Non-executive Member: Cambridge Dist HA, 1990–91; Northern and Yorks RHA, 1994–96. Mem. Council, CVCP, 1996–2000. Chm., Higher Educn Management Statistics Gp, 1995–2000; Mem., SHEFC, 1992–99; Associate Comr, Hamlyn Nat. Commn on Educn, 1992–93; Dir, UCAS, 1997–2000; Chm. Exec. Cttee, UKCOSA: Council for Internat. Educn, 1998–2002. British Council: Mem., CICHE, 1993–2000; Mem., CICHE Cttee 2 (Asia and Oceans Reg.), 1992–94. Dir, Newcastle Initiative, 1993–2000; Chm., Connexions Tyne & Wear, 2002–08. Mem., Governing Body, Shrewsbury Sch., 1986–2000. Trustee: Nat. Heritage Meml Fund, 2000–06 (Chm., Audit Cttee, 2003–06); Homerton Coll., Cambridge, 2002–10; Chm., Homerton Sch. of Health Studies, 2003–05. Age Concern England, later Age UK: Trustee, 2001–05, 2007–13; Chm., 2002–05; Dir, Age Concern Hldgs, 2005–14 (Chm., 2007–14); Trustee, Age Concern Scotland, 2002–09; Chm., Age Scotland, 2009–13 (Trustee, 2009–13). DL 1995, High Sheriff, 2003–04, Tyne and Wear. Hon. LLD Abertay Dundee, 1999; Hon. DEd Naresuan, Thailand, 2000; Hon. DCL Newcastle upon Tyne, 2001. *Publications:* articles and reviews in classical jls. *Recreations:* walking, travel in France, food, wine. *Address:* 10 Montagu Avenue, Gosforth, Newcastle upon Tyne NE3 4JH. *Clubs:* Athenæum; Northern Counties (Newcastle upon Tyne).

WRIGHT, James Roland; High Commissioner for Canada in the United Kingdom, 2006–11; *b* Montreal, 19 July 1950; *s* of David Stuart Wright and Jean Gertrude Percy; *m* 1977, Donna Thomson, *d* of James Thomas and Marjorie McKeown; one *s* one *d*. *Educ:* McGill Univ., Montreal (BA 1972; MA 1973). Joined Dept of Foreign Affairs, Ottawa, 1976; Third Sec., Moscow, 1978–80; Soviet Desk Officer, E Eur. Div., Ottawa, 1980–83; First Sec., Washington, 1983–87; Office of the Prime Minister, Ottawa, 1987–88; Dir, Pol/Econ. Personnel Div., Ottawa, 1989–92; Minister, Pol and Public Affairs, London, 1992–96; Dir Gen., Central, E and S Europe Bureau, Ottawa, 1996–2000; Pol Dir and Asst Dep. Minister, Global and Security Br., Ottawa, 2000–04; Pol Dir and Asst Dep. Minister, Internat. Security Br., 2005–06. Sen. Advr, The World Remembers, 2012–; Mem. Bd, Citizen Advocacy, 2013–; Advr, Plan Inst., 2014–. Fellow, Norman Patterson Sch. for Internat. Affairs, Carleton Univ., 2012–. Hon. Dr Ulster, 2008. Queen's Diamond Jubilee Medal, 2013. *Recreations:* golf, tennis, ski-ing, hiking. *Address:* 523 Tillbury Ave, Ottawa, ON K2A 0Z1, Canada. *E:* jameswrightca@gmail.com.

WRIGHT, Rt Hon. Jeremy (Paul); PC 2014; QC 2014; MP (C) Kenilworth and Southam, since 2010 (Rugby and Kenilworth, 2005–10); Attorney General, since 2014; *b* 24 Oct. 1972; *s* of John and Audrey Wright; *m* 1998, Yvonne Salter; one *s* one *d*. *Educ:* Taunton Sch.; Trinity Sch., NYC; Univ. of Exeter (LLB Hons). Called to the Bar, Inner Temple, 1996; in practice on Midlands and Oxford Circuit, specialising in criminal law, 1996–2005. An Opposition Whip, 2007–10; a Lord Comr of HM Treasury (Govt Whip), 2010–12; Parly Under-Sec. of State, MoJ, 2012–14. Mem., Select Cttee on Constitutional Affairs, 2005–07. Trustee, Community Develt Fund, 2007–09. *Recreations:* golf, music, cinema. *Address:* House of Commons, SW1A 0AA. *T:* (020) 7219 8299. *E:* jeremy.wright.mp@parliament.uk.

WRIGHT, Sir (John) Michael, Kt 1990; a Judge of the High Court of Justice, Queen's Bench Division, 1990–2003; Presiding Judge, South Eastern Circuit, 1995–98; *b* 26 Oct. 1932; *s* of Prof. John George Wright, DSc, MVSc, FRCVS, and Elsie Lloyd Razey; *m* 1959, Kathleen, *er d* of F. A. Meanwell; one *s* two *d*. *Educ:* King's Sch., Chester; Oriel Coll., Oxford (BA Jurisprudence 1956; MA 1978; Hon. Fellow, 2000). Served Royal Artillery, 1951–53; TA, 1953–57. Called to Bar, Lincoln's Inn (Tancred Student), 1957, Bencher 1983, Treasurer, 2003–04; QC 1974; a Recorder, 1974–90; Leader, SE Circuit, 1981–83; Chm. of the Bar, 1983–84 (Vice-Chm., 1982–83). Member: Bar Council, 1972–73; Senate of the Four Inns of Court, 1973–74; Senate of the Inns of Court and the Bar, 1975–84. Mem. Supreme Court Rules Cttee, 1973–74. Legal Assessor to the Disciplinary Cttee, RCVS, 1983–90; Vice-Chm., Appeal Cttee, ICA, 1989–90. Hon. Member: American Bar Assoc.; Canadian Bar Assoc. Trustee, Thalidomide Trust, 1997–2011 (Chm., 2008–11). Gov., Reigate Grammar Sch., 2004–08 (Chm. of Govs, 2004–08). *Recreations:* books, music. *Address:* Angel Shades, Angel Street, Petworth, W Sussex GU28 0BG.

WRIGHT, John Robertson; Chairman: XM International Associates Ltd, since 2004; Boomer Industries, since 2007; Qube GB Ltd, since 2012; Lagan Ashphalt Ltd, since 2012; *b* 10 Sept. 1941; *s* of George Alexander Wright and Jean Robertson Wright (*née* Buchanan); *m* 1971, Christine Greenshields; one *s* one *d*. *Educ:* Daniel Stewart's Coll., Edinburgh. ACIBS; FIBI. Posts with Bank of Montreal, Canada and Hong Kong, Bank of North Lagos, Nigeria, Grindlays Bank Ltd, London, Calcutta and Colombo, Clydesdale Bank Ltd, 1958–74; Vice Pres., First Interstate Bank of California, 1974–79; Asst Gen. Manager, Internat. Div., Bank of Scotland, 1979–86; Dir and CEO, Oman International Bank, 1986–93; Chief Executive and Director: Northern Bank Ltd, 1993–96; Northern & National Irish Banks, 1996–97; Chief Exec. and Chief Gen. Manager, Gulf Bank KSC, Kuwait, 1997–98; Chief Exec., Clydesdale Bank plc and Yorkshire Bank, 1998–2001. Chairman: Edinburgh Fund Managers plc, 2001–02; Toughglass Ltd, 2002–06; BIC Systems Ltd, 2002–05; Claridge Ltd, Bermuda, 2006–07; EZD Ltd, 2006–07; Alphaplus Gp, 2008–11; non-executive Director: ECGD, 2001–06; Bank of N. T. Butterfield UK Ltd, 2001–; Bank of N. T. Butterfield, Bermuda, 2002–; Glasgow Univ. Retail Heritage Ltd, 2004–; Scottish Enterprise Borders, 2004–08; Alliance Housing Bank Ltd, Muscat, Oman, 2005–08; Kainos Ltd, 2006–13; Derby House Ltd, 2006–10; Sutherlands Ltd, 2006–09; Mazoon Electric Co., Oman, 2011–14; Majan Electric Co., Oman, 2011–14; Muscat Electric Distribn Co., Oman, 2011–; European Islamic Investment Bank, 2012–; Damac plc, 2013–. Director: Arab-British Chamber of Commerce, 1998–2010; Glasgow Chamber of Commerce, 1999–2005; Mem., Arab Financial Forum, 2005. External Mem., Audit Cttee, Scottish Borders Council, 2003–13. Vis. Prof. and Mem. Adv. Bd, Glasgow Univ. Business Sch., 2005–. Chm., Borders Coll., 2011–. Trustee, Abbotsford House, Melrose, 2008–. *Recreation:* watching Rugby. *Clubs:* New (Edinburgh); Hong Kong; Edinburgh Academicals Sports, Hong Kong Football.

WRIGHT, (John) Stephen; Chairman, International Classical Artists (formerly Van Walsum), since 2008; *b* 12 Feb. 1946; *s* of late Eustace McDonald Wright and Hilde Wright; *m* 1977, Jadwiga Maria Rapf (*d* 2007); two *s* one *d*. *Educ:* Dragon Sch., Oxford; Westminster; Magdalene Coll., Cambridge (Hons Mod. Langs and Law). Co-founder and Dir, Oxford and Cambridge Shakespeare Co., 1969–71; Dir, Shawconcerts Ltd, 1971–75; Dir, later Jt Man. Dir, Harold Holt, 1975–90; Man. Dir and Sen. Internat. Vice-Pres., IMG Artists Europe, later IMG Artists, 1991–2005. *Recreations:* cricket, wine, classic cars. *Address:* 36 Walcot Square, SE11 4TZ. *Clubs:* Garrick, Soho House, Savile.

WRIGHT, Rt Rev. Kelvin; *see* Dunedin, Bishop of.

WRIGHT, Lester Paul; Under Secretary, Department for Culture, Media and Sport (formerly of National Heritage), 1992–99; *b* 2 July 1946; *s* of late Christopher Percy Wright and Mary Wright (*née* Sutton); *m* 1969, Jill Wildman (*d* 2008); one *s* (and one *s* decd). *Educ:* Bedford Sch.; Gonville and Caius Coll., Cambridge (BA 1967; PhD 1971); Harvard Univ.; Open Univ. (BSc 2007). Lectr in History, Univ. of Reading, 1970–71; Home Office, 1971; Asst Private Sec. to Home Sec., 1972; Harkness Fellow, Harvard Univ. and Univ. of California at Berkeley, 1976–77; Private Sec. to Perm. Under Sec., 1980–82; Asst Sec., 1983–92. *Recreations:* music, walking, looking at pictures. *Address:* 9 Broom Hall, High Street, Broom, Biggleswade, Beds SG18 9ND. *T:* (01767) 314633.

WRIGHT, Margaret; Development Executive, The Law Society, 1988–91; *b* 18 Oct. 1931; *d* of Harry Platt and Edith Baxter; *m* 1991, Bill Wright (*d* 1999). *Educ:* Bedford College, Univ. of London (BA Hons 1st Cl., History). Called to the Bar, Gray's Inn, 1956. Estate Duty Officer, Inland Revenue, 1952–63; Inst. of Professional Civil Servants, 1963–87 (Dep. Gen. Sec., 1980–87); Gen. Sec., Clearing Bank Union, 1987–88. Mem., Industrial Disputes Panel, Jersey, 1989–. *Recreations:* renovating old houses, travel, reading. *Address:* Flat 5, St James Court, The Vinefields, Bury St Edmunds, Suffolk IP33 1YD. *T:* (01284) 755399.

WRIGHT, Martin; Senior Research Fellow, Faculty of Health and Life Sciences, De Montfort University, Leicester, since 2007; Visiting Research Fellow, Sussex Law School (formerly Centre for, then School of, Legal Studies), University of Sussex, 1995–2007; *b* 24

April 1930; *s* of late Clifford Kent Wright and Rosalie Wright, Stoke Newington; *m* 1957, Louisa Mary Nicholls; three *s* one *d* (and one *d* decd). *Educ:* Repton; Jesus Coll., Oxford; PhD LSE, 1992. Librarian, Inst. of Criminology, Cambridge, 1964–71; Dir, Howard League for Penal Reform, 1971–81; NAVSS, later Victim Support, 1985–94: Information Officer, 1985–88; Policy Officer, 1988–94. Chm., Lambeth Mediation Service, 1989–92; Mem. Exec. Cttee, Mediation UK (formerly Forum for Initiatives in Reparation and Mediation), 1984–99; Board Member: Inst. for Food, Brain and Behaviour (formerly Natural Justice), 1999–; European Forum for Victim/Offender Mediation and Restorative Justice, 2000–06; Vice-Chm., Restorative Justice Consortium, 2001–07. Hon. Fellow, Inst. of Conflict Resolution, Sofia, Bulgaria, 2005. Eur. Restorative Justice Award, Eur. Forum, 2012. *Publications:* (ed) The Use of Criminological Literature, 1974; Making Good: Prisons, Punishment and Beyond, 1982, repr. 2008; (ed jtly) Mediation and Criminal Justice, 1989; Justice for Victims and Offenders: a restorative response to crime, 1991, 2nd edn 1996; Restoring Respect for Justice, 1999, 2nd edn 2008 (trans. Polish 2005, Russian 2007); Towards a Restorative Society, 2010; (ed jtly) Civilising Criminal Justice: an international restorative agenda for penal reform, 2013. *Recreation:* suggesting improvements. *Address:* 19 Hillside Road, SW2 3HL. *T:* (020) 8671 8037. *W:* www.martinwright.eu.

WRIGHT, Hon. Sir Michael; *see* Wright, Hon. Sir J. M.

WRIGHT, Prof. Michael, CBE 2010; DL; Vice-Chancellor, Canterbury Christ Church University, 2005–10, now Emeritus Professor; *b* 24 May 1949; *s* of Gordon Huddart Wright and Nancy (*née* Murgatroyd); *m* 1971, Pamela Stothart; one *s* one *d* (and one *s* decd). *Educ:* Durham Johnston Grammar Sch.; Bearsden Acad.; Univ. of Birmingham (LLB 1969, LLM 1970). Lectr in Law, Bristol Poly., 1970–79; Hd of Dept, Glasgow Coll. of Technology, 1980–83; Asst Principal, Napier Coll., subseq. Napier Poly., 1983–92; Dep. Vice Chancellor, Napier Univ., 1992–97; Principal, Canterbury Christ Ch Coll., subseq. Canterbury Christ Ch Univ. Coll., 1997–2005. Vice Pres., Inst. of Personnel and Develt, 1991–94. Member: Kent & Medway LSC, 2001–07; Kent (formerly Kent & Medway) Economic Bd, 2005–10; Dir, Kent & Medway Strategic HA, 2003–06. Comr, Duke of York's Royal Mil. Sch., 2000–12. Lay Canon, Canterbury Cathedral, 2004–14 (Mem. of Chapter, 2010–14); Mem. Council, Rochester Cathedral, 2007–10. Chm. Bd, Canterbury Arts Fest., 2011–14 (Vice Chm., 2009–11). Chm. Govs, Northbourne Park Sch., 2010–14; Chm., E Kent Coll. Governing Body (formerly Thanet Coll. Corporation), 2010–14. Chm., Lambeth Conference Co., 2012–. DL Kent, 2006. *Publications:* Labour Law, 1974, 4th edn (with C. J. Carr) 1984; articles in legal jls. *Recreations:* choral singing, golf. *E:* michael.wright@canterbury.ac.uk. *Clubs:* Nobody's Friends; Goswick Golf.

WRIGHT, Monica Mary; *see* Grady, M. M.

WRIGHT, Nathalie Marie Daniella; *see* Lieven, N. M. D.

WRIGHT, Nicholas; playwright; *b* Cape Town, 5 July 1940; *s* of Harry and Winifred Wright. *Educ:* Rondebosch Boys' Sch.; London Acad. of Music and Dramatic Art. Casting Dir, 1967, Asst Dir, 1968, Royal Court Th.; Dir, Royal Court Th. Upstairs, 1969–70 and 1972–74; Jt Artistic Dir, Royal Court Th., 1975–77; Associate Dir, NT, 1984–89 and 1991–98. Member Board: Royal Court Th., 1992–2003; NT, 2003–09; Nat. Council for Drama Trng, 2005–. *Plays:* Treetops, Riverside Studios, 1978 (George Devine Award); The Gorky Brigade, Royal Court Th., 1979; One Fine Day, Riverside Studios, 1980; The Crimes of Vautrin (after Balzac), Joint Stock, 1982; The Custom of the Country, RSC, 1983; The Desert Air, RSC, 1984; Mrs Klein, NT, 1988; Cressida, Almeida Th. at the Albery, 2000; Vincent in Brixton, NT, 2002 (Best New Play, Olivier Award); His Dark Materials (based on trilogy by Philip Pullman), NT, 2003, revived 2004; The Reporter, NT, 2007; He's Talking, NT Connections, 2008; Rattigan's Nijinsky, Chichester Fest., 2011; The Last of the Duchess, Hampstead Th., 2011; Travelling Light, NT, 2012; A Human Being Died That Night, Hampstead Th., 2013; *play adaptations:* Slave Island, RADA, 1985; Six Characters in Search of an Author, NT, 1987; Thérèse Raquin, Chichester Fest., 1990, NT, 2006; John Gabriel Borkman, NT, 1996; Naked, Almeida Th., 1998; Lulu, Almeida Th., 2001; Three Sisters, NT, 2003; Alice's Adventures in Wonderland, Royal Ballet, Covent Garden, 2011; Regeneration, Royal Northampton, 2014; television adaptations: Armistead Maupin's More Tales of the City, 1998; No 1 Ladies' Detective Agency (episodes), 2009; *opera libretti:* The Little Prince (after St Exupéry), premièred by Houston Grand Opera, 2003; Buzz on the Moon, C4, 2006. The Art of the Play column, Independent on Sunday, 1993–94. *Publications:* 99 Plays, 1992; (with Richard Eyre) Changing Stages, 2000; *plays:* Five Plays (Treetops, One Fine Day, The Custom of the Country, The Desert Air, Mrs Klein), 2000; Cressida, 2000; Vincent in Brixton, 2002; His Dark Materials, 2003, rewritten version 2004; The Reporter, 2007; Rattigan's Nijinsky, 2011; The Last of the Duchess, 2011; Travelling Light, 2012. *Address:* c/o Judy Daish Associates, 2 St Charles Place, W10 6EG.

WRIGHT, Sir Nicholas (Alcwyn), Kt 2006; MD, PhD, DSc; FRCS, FRCP, FRCPath; Professor of Histopathology, since 2011, and Centre Lead, Centre for Tumour Biology, Barts Cancer Institute, since 2013, Queen Mary University of London (Warden, Barts and The London (formerly Bart's and The London, Queen Mary's) School of Medicine and Dentistry, 2001–11); *b* 24 Feb. 1943; *s* of late Glyndwr Alcwyn Wright and Hilda Lilian (*née* Jones); *m* 1966, Vera, (Ned), Matthewson; one *s* one *d*. *Educ:* Bristol Grammar Sch.; Durham Univ. (MB BS 1965); Newcastle Univ. (MD 1974; PhD 1975; DSc 1984); MA (Oxon) 1979. FRCPath 1986; MRCP 1998, FRCP 2001; FRCS 1999. University of Newcastle upon Tyne: Demonstrator in Pathology, 1966–71; Res. Fellow, 1971–74; Lectr in Pathology, 1974–76; Sen. Lectr, 1976–77; Clinical Reader in Pathology, Univ. of Oxford, 1977, Nuffield Reader, 1978; Fellow, Green Coll., Oxford, 1979–80; Prof. of Histopathology, RPMS, 1980–96; Dir of Histopathology, Hammersmith Hosp., 1980–96; Dean, RPMS, 1996–97; Clin. Dir of Path., Hammersmith Hosps NHS Trust, 1994–96; Vice Principal for Res., 1996–2001, Dep. Principal, 1997–2001, ICSM, Univ. of London; Imperial Cancer Research Fund, later Cancer Research (UK): Asst Dir, 1988; Associate Dir, 1989; Dep. Dir, 1990; Dir of Clinical Res., 1991–96; Dir, Histopathology Unit, London Res. Inst., 1988–2011. Chm., Research for Health Charities Gp, 1994–96. Editor, Cell and Tissue Kinetics, 1980–87. President: Pathol Soc. of GB and Ireland, 2001–06; British Soc. for Gastroenterology, 2003–04 (Mem. Council, 1986, 1990); Mem. Council, RCPath, 1982, 1986, 1990. Lectures: Avery Jones, Central Middx Hosp., 1989; Kettle, RCPath, 1990; Showering, Southmead Hosp., 1991; Morson, 1991, Sir Arthur Hurst, 1997, British Soc. of Gastroenterology; Burroughs Wellcome, Yale Univ., 1993; Watson Smith, RCP, 1998; Sidney Truelove, Internat. Soc. for Inflammatory Bowel Disease, 1999; Dow, Dundee Univ., 2006. Fellow, Faculty of Medicine, Imperial Coll. London, 2011; Founder FMedSci 1998. Hon. DSc: Hertfordshire, 2007; Durham, 2008; Bristol, 2011; Aston, 2015; Hon. MD St Andrews, 2008; Hon. LLD Dundee, 2012. *Publications:* Introduction to Cell Population Kinetics, 1977; (ed) Psoriasis: cell proliferation, 1982; The Biology of Epithelial Cell Populations, 1984; (ed) Colorectal Cancer, 1989; (ed) Oxford Textbook of Pathology, 1991; (ed) Clinical Aspects of Cell Proliferation, 1991; (ed) Molecular Pathology of Cancer, 1993; (ed) Growth Factors and Cytokines of the Gut, 1996; (ed) The Gut as a Model for Cell Molecular Biology, 1997; papers on cell proliferation and differentiation in the gut. *Recreations:* Rugby football, cricket, military history, cooking. *Address:* Barts Cancer Institute, Barts and The London School of Medicine and Dentistry, Queen Mary University of London, Charterhouse Square, EC1M 6BQ. *T:* (020) 7882 8956. *Club:* Athenæum.

WRIGHT, Capt. Nicholas Peter, CVO 2010 (LVO 1994); RN; Private Secretary to the Princess Royal, since 2002; *b* 11 Nov. 1949; *s* of late Lt Comdr Edward J. Wright and Peggy Wright; *m* 1976, Venetia, *d* of Vice-Adm. Sir Stephen Ferrier Berthon, KCB; one *s* three *d*. *Educ:* Ampleforth Coll. Joined BRNC Dartmouth, 1968; served HMS Whitby and HMS Diomede, 1969–73; Flag Lt to FO Medway, 1973–75; HMS Norfolk, 1976–77; Allied Forces, Northern Europe, Oslo, 1978–80; HMS Lowestoft, 1980–82; Asst Sec. to Second Sea Lord, 1982–84; Staff of BRNC Dartmouth, 1985–87; HMS Illustrious, 1987–89; Sec. to FO Portsmouth, 1989–91; JSDC RNC Greenwich, 1991; HM Yacht Britannia, 1992–94; Sec. to ACNS, 1995–97; CSO Personnel to FONA, 1998–2000; Exec. Asst to Dep. SACLANT, Virginia, 2000–02; retd RN, 2002. Younger Brother, Trinity House, 2013. *Recreations:* squash, ski-ing, tennis, cricket. *Address:* c/o Buckingham Palace, SW1A 1AA. *T:* (020) 7024 4199, *Fax:* (020) 7930 4180. *Club:* Jesters.

WRIGHT, Rt Rev. Prof. (Nicholas) Thomas, DPhil, DD; FRSE; Bishop of Durham, 2003–10; Research Professor of New Testament and Early Christianity, University of St Andrews, since 2010; *b* 1 Dec. 1948; *s* of Nicholas Irwin Wright and Rosemary (*née* Forman); *m* 1971, Margaret Elizabeth Anne Fiske; two *s* two *d*. *Educ:* Sedbergh Sch.; Exeter Coll., Oxford (BA 1st cl. Hons LitHum 1971; MA 1975; DPhil 1981; DD 2000); Wycliffe Hall, Oxford (BA 1st cl. Hons Theology 1973). Ordained deacon, 1975, priest 1976; Jun. Res. Fellow, 1975–78, Jun. Chaplain, 1976–78, Merton Coll., Oxford (Hon. Fellow, 2004); Fellow and Chaplain, Downing Coll., Cambridge, 1978–81 (Hon. Fellow, 2003); Asst Prof. of New Testament Studies, McGill Univ., Montreal, and Hon. Prof., Montreal Dio. Theol Coll., 1981–86; Lectr in Theology, Oxford Univ., and Fellow, Tutor and Chaplain, Worcester Coll., Oxford, 1986–93; Dean of Lichfield, 1994–99; Canon of Westminster, 2000–03. Fellow, Inst. for Christian Studies, Toronto, 1992–; Canon Theologian, Coventry Cathedral, 1992–99. Visiting Professor: Hebrew Univ., Jerusalem, 1989; Harvard Div. Sch., 1999; Gregorian Univ., Rome, 2002; Fuller Theol Seminary, Pasadena, 2009; Vis. Res. Fellow, Merton Coll., Oxford, 1999. Member: Doctrine Commn of C of E, 1979–81, 1989–95; Internat. Anglican Doctrinal and Theological Commn, 1991, 2001–08; Lambeth Commn, 2004. Presenter, various radio and television series, 1996–: Jesus Then and Now, BBC1, 1996; presenter and writer: Resurrection, Channel 4, 2004; Spring Journey, Radio 3, 2004; Evil, Channel 4, 2005; participant, The Brains Trust, Radio 3, 1999–2002. FRSE 2015. Hon. DD: Aberdeen, 2001; Wycliffe Coll., Toronto, 2006; Nashotah House, Wisconsin, 2006; Durham, 2007; St Andrews, 2009; Northumbria, 2010; London, 2010; St Mary's Univ., Baltimore, 2012; Fribourg, 2014; Univ. of the South, Sewanee, 2015; Huron Coll., Ont, 2015; Hon. DLitt Gordon Coll., Mass, 2003. Burkitt Medal for Biblical Studies, British Acad., 2014. *Publications:* Small Faith, Great God, 1978; The Work of John Frith, 1983; The Epistles of Paul to the Colossians and to Philemon, 1987; (ed jtly) The Glory of Christ in the New Testament, 1987; (with S. Neill) The Interpretation of the New Testament 1861–1986, 1988; The Climax of the Covenant, 1991; New Tasks for a Renewed Church, 1992; The Crown and the Fire, 1992; The New Testament and the People of God, 1992; Who Was Jesus?, 1992; Following Jesus, 1994; Jesus and the Victory of God, 1996; The Lord and His Prayer, 1996; What Saint Paul Really Said, 1997; For All God's Worth, 1997; Reflecting the Glory, 1998; (with M. Borg) The Meaning of Jesus, 1999; The Myth of the Millennium, 1999; (ed jtly) Romans and the People of God, 1999; Holy Communion for Amateurs, 1999, reissued as The Meal Jesus Gave Us, 2002; The Challenge of Jesus, 2000; Twelve Months of Sundays, Year C, 2000; (with Paul Spicer) Easter Oratorio, 2000; Twelve Months of Sundays, Year A, 2001; Luke for Everyone, 2001; Mark for Everyone, 2001; Paul for Everyone: Galatians and Thessalonians, 2002; Matthew for Everyone, 2002; Paul for Everyone: the prison letters, 2002; John for Everyone, 2002; Twelve Months of Sundays, Year B, 2002; (contrib.) New Interpreters Bible, vol. X, 2002; The Contemporary Quest for Jesus, 2002; The Resurrection of the Son of God, 2003; Paul for Everyone: 1 Corinthians, 2003; Paul for Everyone: 2 Corinthians, 2003; Quiet Moments, 2003; Hebrews for Everyone, 2003; For All the Saints?, 2003; Paul for Everyone: the pastoral letters, 2003; Paul for Everyone: Romans, 2004; (ed jtly) Dictionary for Theological Interpretation of Scripture, 2005; Scripture and the Authority of God, 2005, 2nd edn 2011; Paul: fresh perspectives, 2005; The Scriptures, the Cross and the Power of God, 2005; Simply Christian, 2006; Evil and the Justice of God, 2006; (jtly) The Resurrection of Jesus: John Dominic Crossan and N. T. Wright in dialogue, 2006; Judas and the Gospel of Jesus, 2006; The Cross and the Colliery, 2007; Surprised by Hope, 2007; Acts for Everyone, 2008; (with C. Evans) Jesus: the final days, 2008; (ed jtly) Theological Interpretation of the New Testament: a book-by-book survey, 2008; (with J. I. Packer) Anglican Evangelical Identity: yesterday and today, 2008; Justification: God's plan and Paul's vision, 2009; Lent for Everyone—Luke, 2009; Virtue Reborn, 2010; Lent for Everyone—Matthew, 2011; The New Testament for Everyone (new translation), 2011; Early Christian Letters for Everyone, 2011; Revelation for Everyone, 2011; Simply Jesus, 2011; Lent for Everyone—Mark, 2012; How God Became King, 2012; New Testament Prayers for Everyone, 2012; New Testament Wisdom for Everyone, 2013; The Case for the Psalms, 2013; Perspectives on Paul (Collected Essays, 1978–2013), 2013; Paul and the Faithfulness of God, 2013; Finding God in the Psalms: sing, pray, live, 2014; Surprised by Scripture, 2014; Simply Good News, 2015; The Paul Debate, 2015; Paul and his Recent Interpreters, 2015. *Recreations:* music, hill walking, poetry, golf. *Address:* St Mary's College, South Street, St Andrews, Fife KY16 9JU. *T:* (01334) 462850. *E:* ntw2@st-andrews.ac.uk.

WRIGHT, Rev. Dr Nigel Goring; Principal, Spurgeon's College, 2000–13, now Principal Emeritus and Senior Research Fellow; *b* Manchester, 13 May 1949; *s* of Charles Somerville Wright, MBE and Muriel Cooper Wright; *m* 1971, Judith Mary Biggin; one *s* one *d*. *Educ:* Manchester Central Grammar Sch.; Univ. of Leeds (BA 1970); Univ. of London (BD 1973); Univ. of Glasgow (MTh 1987); King's Coll., London (PhD 1994); Spurgeon's Coll. Ordained Minister, 1973; Minister, Ansdell Baptist Church, Lytham St Annes, 1973–86; Res. Fellow, Univ. of Glasgow, 1986–87; Lectr, Spurgeon's Coll., 1987–95; Sen. Minister, Altrincham Baptist Church, 1995–2000. Pres., Baptist Union of GB, 2002–03. FHEA; FRHistS 2012. *Publications:* You Are My God, 1982; The Church, 1983; The Radical Kingdom, 1986; The Fair Face of Evil, 1988; Challenge to Change, 1991; Charismatic Renewal, 1993; The Radical Evangelical, 1996; Power and Discipleship, 1996; Disavowing Constantine, 2000; New Baptists, New Agenda, 2002; A Theology of the Dark Side, 2003; Free Church, Free State, 2005; God on the Inside, 2006; Baptist Basics, 2008; The Real Godsend, 2009; Jesus Christ: the alpha and omega, 2010; Truth that Never Dies, 2014; The Convictions of the Christian Community, 2015; *festschrift:* (ed Pieter J. Lalleman) Challenging to Change: dialogues with a radical baptist theologian: essays presented to Dr Nigel G. Wright on his sixtieth birthday, 2009. *Recreations:* walking, reading, travel. *Address:* 4 Chesterfield Close, Winsford, Cheshire CW7 2NS. *T:* (01606) 227828. *E:* nigelgoringwright@gmail.com.

WRIGHT, Norman Alfred; His Honour Judge Wright; a Circuit Judge, since 2006; *b* 20 Jan. 1951; *s* of late Alfred Wright and of Thea Wright (now Mason); *m* 1976, Susan Whittaker; one *s* one *d*. *Educ:* Bradford Grammar Sch.; Univ. of Liverpool (LLB 1973); College of Law. Called to the Bar, Gray's Inn, 1974 (Gerald Moody Entrance Schol. 1972; Albion Richardson Schol. 1974); in practice at the Bar, 1974–2006; Asst Recorder, 1994–99; a Recorder, 1999–2006; Liaison Judge: Burnley, Pendle and Rossendale Magistrates, 2007–12; Liverpool Univ., 2013–. Pt-time Tutor, Univ. of Liverpool, 1974–78. *Recreations:* oenology, golf, travel. *Address:* Queen Elizabeth II Law Courts, Derby Square, Liverpool L2 1XA. *Club:* Heswall Golf.

WRIGHT, Oliver; Whitehall Editor, The Independent, since 2010; *b* Manchester, 30 June 1973; *s* of Ian and Lydia Wright. *Educ:* Univ. of Edinburgh (MA Hons Pols and Mod. Hist.). Reporter, Sheffield Star, 1997–2000; The Times: Midlands Corresp., 2000–02; Health

Corresp., 2002–04; Asst News Ed., 2004–05; Home News Ed., 2005–08; News Ed., Independent, 2008–10. *Recreations:* walking, failing newspaper shorthand examinations. *Address:* The Independent, Press Gallery, House of Commons, SW1A 0AA. *T:* (020) 7334 0079. *E:* O.Wright@independent.co.uk. *Club:* Shoreditch House.

WRIGHT, Ven. Paul; Archdeacon of Bromley and Bexley, since 2003; *b* 12 Feb. 1954; *s* of Cecil Edwin John Wright and Bessie Wright; *m* 1981, Jill Rosemary Yvonne Rayner; two *s* one *d*. *Educ:* King's Coll., London (BD, AKC 1978); Ripon Coll., Cuddesdon; Heythrop Coll., Univ. of London (MTh 1990); Univ. of Wales, Lampeter (DMin 2009). Ordained deacon, 1979, priest, 1980; Curate: St George, Beckenham, 1979–83; St Mary and St Matthias, Richmond, 1983–85; Chaplain, Christ's Sch., Richmond, 1983–85; Vicar, St Augustine, Gillingham, 1985–90; Rector, St Paulinus, Crayford, 1990–99; RD, Erith, 1994–97; Vicar, St John the Evangelist, Sidcup, 1999–2003. Hon. Canon, Rochester Cathedral, 1998–2003. *Recreations:* riding my Harley-Davidson, going to the cinema, France, walking Dolly the dog, swimming. *Address:* The Archdeaconry, The Glebe, Chislehurst, Kent BR7 5PX. *T:* (020) 8467 8743. *E:* archdeacon.bromley@rochester.anglican.org.

WRIGHT, Prof. Paul Stanley, PhD; FDSRCS, FFGDP(UK); Professor of Prosthetic Dentistry, Barts and The London (formerly Barts and The London, Queen Mary's) School of Medicine and Dentistry, Queen Mary, University of London, 2000–11, now Emeritus (Dean for Dentistry, 1999–2007); Consultant Adviser to the Chief Dental Officer, Department of Health, 2007–12; *b* 1 May 1946; *s* of late William and Eileen Wright; *m* 1970, Mary Lawrence; three *s*. *Educ:* London Hosp. Med. Coll. Dental Sch. (BDS; PhD 1980). FDSRCS 1973; FFGDP(UK) 2005. London Hospital Medical College Dental School, later Barts and The London, Queen Mary's School of Medicine and Dentistry, subseq. Barts and The London School of Medicine and Dentistry, Queen Mary, University of London: Lectr in Prosthetic Dentistry, 1972–80; Sen. Lectr in Prosthetic Dentistry, 1981–99; Hon. Consultant in Restorative Dentistry, 1982–2011; Specialist in Prosthodontics, 2000–11. Gen. dental practitioner (pt-time), 1970–2001. Founding Ed., Eur. Jl Prosthodontics and Restorative Dentistry, 1992–2003. Chairman: Council, Heads and Deans of Dental Schs, 2004–06; Central Commn, Academic Dental Staff, BDA, 2009–11. President: Eur. Prosthodontic Assoc., 2005–06; British Soc. of Gerodontology, 2007–08; Barts and The London Alumni Assoc., 2012–. FHEA (ILTM 2002). Gold Medal, British Soc. for Study of Prosthetic Dentistry, 2011. *Publications:* (jtly) The Clinical Handling of Dental Materials, 1986, 2nd edn 1994; numerous contribs to jls. *Recreations:* swimming, ski-ing, gardening, family, touring in classic Jaguar replica. *Address:* The Lodge, Station Road, Eynsford, Dartford, Kent DA4 0ER. *T:* (01322) 863608, 07711 636952.

WRIGHT, Rev. Canon Paul Stephen; Sub-Dean, HM Chapels Royal, Deputy Clerk of the Closet, Sub-Almoner and Domestic Chaplain to the Queen, since 2015; *b* Winstanley, Wigan, Lancs, 26 Dec. 1966; *s* of William and Dorothy Wright; *m* 2006, Georgina Elisabeth Peek; two *s* two *d*. *Educ:* Lancs Poly. (BA 1988); Liverpool Univ. (MA 1996); Westcott House, Cambridge; Cardiff Univ. (MTh 2011). Ordained deacon, 1993, priest, 1994; Curate, Up Holland, Lancs, 1993–96; Chaplain to the Forces, 1996–2015: Dover Castle, 2004–08; Guards Chapel, 2008–10; HQ ARRC, 2010–12; RMA Sandhurst, 2012–14; HM Chapels Royal, 2015; RAuxAF, 2015. Guest Curator, Soldiers of Solace, Talbot House, Belgium, 2015. Mem., Anglo-Belgian Soc. *Recreations:* The Book of Common Prayer, battlefield walks, Tristram Shandy. *Address:* Chapel Royal, St James's Palace, SW1A 1BL. *Clubs:* Royal Air Force; Talbot House (Belgium).

WRIGHT, Penelope Ann, (Mrs D. C. H. Wright); *see* Boys, P. A.

WRIGHT, Peter; Editor Emeritus, Associated Newspapers, since 2012; *b* 13 Aug. 1953; *s* of Nigel and June Wright; *m* 1974, Dorothy Manders; three *s* one *d*. *Educ:* Marlborough Coll.; Clare Coll., Cambridge (MA History). Reporter, Evening Echo, Hemel Hempstead, 1976–79; Daily Mail: Reporter, 1979; Asst News Editor, 1980–85; Associate News Editor (Foreign), 1985; Asst Features Editor, 1986–88; Femail Editor, 1988–91; Asst Editor (Features), 1991; Associate Editor, 1992–95; Dep. Editor, 1995–98; Editor, Mail on Sunday, 1998–2012. Mem., Editor's Code Cttee, 2004–08; Comr, Press Complaints Commn, 2008–14; Mem., Complaints Cttee, IPSO, 2014–. *Address:* Associated Newspapers, Northcliffe House, 2 Derry Street, W8 5TT.

WRIGHT, Peter Duncan; QC 1999; a Recorder, since 2001; *b* 2 Nov. 1957; *s* of Harvey Wright and Margaret Wright; *m* 1982, Stephanie Maria Mandziuk; one *s* two *d*. *Educ:* Hull Univ. (LLB Hons). Called to the Bar, Inner Temple, 1981. Sen. Treasury Counsel, 2006–10. *Recreations:* Rugby, travel. *Address:* 2 Hare Court, Temple, EC4Y 7BH. *T:* (020) 7353 5324.

WRIGHT, Peter Malcolm; His Honour Judge Wright; a Circuit Judge, since 2006; Designated Family Judge, Watford and Hertfordshire, since 2006; *b* 5 June 1948; *s* of late Malcolm Wright, QC, County Court Judge and Peggy Wright (*née* Prince), BEM; *m* 1975, Eleanor Charlotte Madge; one *s* one *d*. *Educ:* Kingswood Sch., Bath; Trinity Hall, Cambridge (BA 1971). Called to the Bar, Middle Temple, 1974 (Bencher, 2005); Tenant, Queen Elizabeth Bldg, Temple, 1975–2006; specialized in family law, clinical negligence and personal injury law; Asst Recorder, Western Circuit, 1998–2000; Recorder, 2000–06. Legal Assessor, NMC, 1994–2006. Vice-Chm., Appeal Cttee, CIMA, 2001–05. Trustee, Lambeth Palace Liby, 2002–. Gov., Kingswood Sch., Bath, 1998–. *Recreations:* walking, sailing, music, gardening, country sports, Retriever training. *Address:* Watford County Court, Cassiobury House, 11–19 Station Road, Watford WD17 1EZ.

WRIGHT, Peter Michael, FRCO(CHM); Organist and Director of Music, Southwark Cathedral, since 1989; *b* 6 March 1954; *s* of Dudley Cyril Brazier Wright and Pamela Deirdre (*née* Peacock). *Educ:* Highgate Sch. (Music Schol.); Royal Coll. of Music (Exhibnr; ARCM); Emmanuel Coll., Cambridge (Organ Schol.; MA). LRAM. Sub-Organist, Guildford Cathedral, and Music Master, Royal Grammar Sch., Guildford, 1977–89. Conductor: Guildford Chamber Choir, 1984–94; Surrey Festival Choir, 1987–2001. Freelance conductor, recitalist (organ), adjudicator and broadcaster. Royal College of Organists: Mem. Council, 1990–2002; Hon. Sec., 1997–2002; Vice-Pres., 2003–05, 2008–; Pres., 2005–08; Mem. Council, Friends of Cathedral Music, 2001–04. Hon. Lay Canon, Southwark Cathedral, 2014–. FRSCM 2011. Hon. FGCM 2000. *Recreations:* travel, theatre, reading, good food. *Address:* 52 Bankside, SE1 9JE. *T:* (020) 7261 1291.

WRIGHT, Sir Peter (Robert), Kt 1993; CBE 1985; Director Laureate, The Birmingham (formerly Sadler's Wells) Royal Ballet, since 1995 (Director, 1977–95); *b* 25 Nov. 1926; *s* of Bernard and Hilda Mary Wright; *m* 1954, Sonya Hana; one *s* one *d*. *Educ:* Bedales School; Leighton Park Sch. Dancer: Ballets Jooss, 1945–47, 1951–52; Metropolitan Ballet, 1947–49; Sadler's Wells Theatre Ballet, 1949–51, 1952–56; Ballet Master, Sadler's Wells Opera, and Teacher, Royal Ballet Sch., 1956–58; freelance choreographer and teacher, 1958–61; Ballet Master and Asst Dir, Stuttgart Ballet, 1961–63; BBC Television Producer, 1963–65; freelance choreographer, 1965–69; Associate Dir, Royal Ballet, 1969–77. Special Prof., Sch. of Performance Studies, Birmingham Univ., 1990–. Governor: Royal Ballet Sch., 1976–2002; Sadler's Wells Theatre, 1987–2001. Pres., Benesh Inst., 1993–; Vice Pres., Royal Acad. of Dancing, 1995–. *Creative Works:* Ballets: A Blue Rose, 1957; The Great Peacock, 1958; Musical Chairs, 1959; The Mirror Walkers, 1962; Quintet, 1962; Namouna, 1963; Designs for Dancers, 1963; Summer's Night, 1964; Danse Macabre, 1964; Variations, 1964; Concerto, 1965; Arpege, 1974; El Amor Brujo, 1975; Summertide, 1976; own productions of classics: Giselle: Stuttgart, 1966; Staatsoper Ballett, Cologne, 1967; Royal Ballet, 1968, 1985, 2014; Canadian National Ballet, 1970; Bavarian State Ballet, Munich, 1976; Dutch National Ballet, 1977; Houston Ballet, Texas, 1979; Staatsoper Ballett, Frankfurt, 1980; Ballet Municipale de Rio de Janeiro, Brazil, 1982; Royal Winnipeg Ballet, 1982; Star Dancers Ballet, Tokyo, 1989; Karlsruhe Ballet, 2004; The Sleeping Beauty: Staatsoper Ballett, Cologne, 1968; Royal Ballet, 1968; Bavarian State Ballet, Munich, 1974; Dutch National Ballet, 1981; Sadler's Wells Royal Ballet, 1984; Vienna State Opera Ballet, 1995; Ballet de Santiago, Chile, 2003; Coppelia: Royal Ballet Touring Co., 1976; Sadler's Wells Royal Ballet, 1979; Scottish Ballet, 1992; Star Dancers Ballet, Tokyo, 1997; Karlsruhe Ballet, 2005; Birmingham Royal Ballet, 2012; Swan Lake: Sadler's Wells Royal Ballet, 1981; Bavarian State Ballet, Munich, 1984; Birmingham Royal Ballet, 1991; Royal Swedish Ballet, 2001; Colon Teatro, Buenos Aires, 2013; Nutcracker: Royal Ballet, 1984 (revised 1999); Birmingham Royal Ballet, 1990; Star Dancers Ballet, Tokyo, 1998; Australian Ballet, Melbourne, 2007. FBSM (Conservatoire Fellow), 1991; Fellow, Birmingham Soc., 1995. Hon. DMus London, 1990; Hon. DLitt Birmingham, 1994. Evening Standard Award for Ballet, 1982; Queen Elizabeth II Coronation Award, Royal Acad. of Dancing, 1990; Digital Premier Award, 1991; Critics Circle Award, 1995; Nat. Dance Award for Outstanding Achievement, 2004; Critics' Circle Centenary Award for Lifetime Achievement in Dance, 2013. *Recreation:* all forms of theatre. *Address:* Flat 5, Wedderburn House, 95 Lower Sloane Street, SW1W 8BZ.

WRIGHT, Richard Irwin V.; *see* Vane-Wright.

WRIGHT, Richard James; QC 2013; a Deputy District Judge (Magistrates' Courts), since 2006; a Recorder, since 2012; *b* Ipswich, 1 July 1976; *s* of Gordon Wright and Andrea Wright (*née* Price, now Ridgeon); *m* 2011, Emma Haley. *Educ:* Orwell High Sch., Felixstowe; Univ. of Leeds (LLB Hons 1997); Inns of Court Sch. of Law. Called to the Bar, Middle Temple, 1998; Jun., NE Circuit, 2004. *Recreations:* countryside, beer, vintage tractors. *Address:* 6 Park Square, Leeds LS1 2LW. *T:* (0113) 245 9763, *Fax:* (0113) 242 4395. *E:* wrightqc@psqb.co.uk.

WRIGHT, Sir Richard (Michael) C.; *see* Cory-Wright.

WRIGHT, Rev. Canon Robert; *see* Wright, Rev. Canon A. R.

WRIGHT, (Robert) Alan, PhD; Public Sector Policy Adviser, Iron Mountain (UK), 2007–11; Director, Office of Manpower Economics, 2003–07; freelance pay and governance consultant, since 2008; *b* 8 Oct. 1949; *s* of late John Haig Wright and Elsie Eileen Wright (*née* Hill); *m* 1975, (Veronica) Anne Dennis. *Educ:* Moseley Grammar Sch., Birmingham; Univ. of Birmingham (BA (Medieval and Mod. Hist.) 1971; PhD 1977; PGCE). Joined Civil Service, 1975; Private Sec. to Chm. of MSC, 1982; Head: Secretariat, HSE, 1987–88; Admin, NII, 1988–91; Dir, Finance Policy, Employment Dept, 1991–94; Department of Trade and Industry: Director: Pay and Working Time, 1995–98; Coal Health Claims Unit, 1998–99; Finance, 2000–03. Member: Perf. and Best Value Cttee, Bar Standards Bd, 2007–11; Planning, Resources and Perf. Cttee, 2012. Volunteer: Elmbridge and Runnymede Talking News, 2009– (Mem., Exec. Cttee, 2015–); Surrey History Centre, 2010–. Associate Gov., Heathside Sch., Weybridge, 2015–. *Recreations:* history, modern literature, watching cricket and Rugby. *T:* 07956 919838.

WRIGHT, Air Marshal Sir Robert (Alfred), KBE 2004; AFC 1982; Controller, Royal Air Force Benevolent Fund, 2007–12; *b* 10 June 1947; *s* of Leslie Dominic Wright and Marjorie Wright; *m* 1970, Maggie Courtliff; one *s* one *d*. *Educ:* Maidstone Grammar Sch. No 8 (Day Fighter Ground Attack) Sqn (Hunters), 1969–71; No 17(F) Sqn (Phantoms), 1971–74; No 1 Tactical Weapons Unit (Hunters), 1974–76; Exchange Duty, USN (Phantoms), 1976–79; No 208 Sqn (Buccaneers), 1979–82; RAF Staff Coll., 1982; Operational Requirements Div., MoD, 1982–84; Directing Staff, RAF Staff Coll., 1984–87; OC, No 9 Sqn (Tornados), Bruggen, 1987–89; PSO to CAS, 1989–91; OC, RAF Bruggen, 1992–94; Asst COS, Policy and Plans, HQ AirNorthWest, 1994–95; Air Cdre Ops, and Dep. Dir Franco British Air Gp, HQ STC, 1995–97; MA to High Rep., Sarajevo, 1997–98; COS to Air Mem. for Personnel, and Dep. C-in-C, HQ PTC, 1998–2000; Asst COS (Policy and Requirements), Supreme HQ Allied Powers in Europe, 2000–02; UK Mil. Rep. to NATO and EU, 2002–06. President: RAF Athletics Assoc., 1998–2005; RAF Winter Sports Assoc., 2003–06; Combined Services Winter Sports Assoc., 2003–06; Naval 8/208 Sqn Assoc., 2003–. Liveryman, Hon. Co. of Air Pilots (formerly GAPAN), 2011. FRAeS 1997; FCMI 2006. *Publications:* contrib. articles to RUSI Jl. *Recreations:* golf, tennis, ski-ing, walking. *Clubs:* Royal Air Force; New (Cheltenham).

WRIGHT, Robert Douglas John; management consultant; *b* 2 March 1951; *s* of Douglas Norman Wright and Nora Hermione Wright (*née* Hatton-Jones); *m* 1983, Jane Clare Augier; one *s* two *d*. *Educ:* Canford Sch.; Southampton Univ. (BSc Psychol. 1973). CSD, 1975–81; attachment to Canadian Govt, Ottawa, 1981–82; Cabinet Office (Mgt and Personnel Office), 1982–85; on secondment to Hong Kong Govt, Hong Kong, 1985–88; Cabinet Office (OPSS), 1988–94; Dir, Internat. Affairs, OST, 1994–98; Department of Trade and Industry: Director: Personnel Ops, 1999–2001; Coal Policy, 2001–02; Energy Strategy, 2002–04; Export Control and Non-Proliferation, 2004–07. Mem., Cabinet Office Security Vetting Appeals Panel, 2009–; Ind. Mem., Civil Nuclear Police Authy, 2010–. Sen. Consultant, Transparency Internat. UK, Defence and Security Prog. (formerly Transparency, Internat. Defence and Security Prog.), 2010–13. Dir, Wrighthand Ltd, 2007–13; Dir, Meadowcott Ltd, 2014–. Associate: Nat. Sch. of Govt, 2007–12; Civil Service Coll. Ltd, 2012–13. Gov., Bohunt Community Sch., Liphook, 2002–08. Mem., Inst. of Dirs, 2007–. *Recreations:* family, walking (Nat. Deaf Children's Soc. Cuba Trek, 2001), theatre. *Address:* Meadowcott Ltd, c/o Unity Chambers, 34 High East Street, Dorchester, Dorset DT1 1HA.

WRIGHT, Roger William, CBE 2015; Chief Executive, Aldeburgh Music, since 2014; *b* 1956; *m*; two *c*. *Educ:* Chetham's Sch., Manchester; Royal Holloway College, London Univ. (BMus 1977; Pres., Students' Union, 1977–78; Hon. Fellow, 2002). Manager, then Dir, British Music Inf. Centre, 1978–87; Sen. Producer, BBC SO, 1987–89; Artistic Administrator, Cleveland Orch., 1989–92; Exec. Producer, then Vice-Pres., Deutsche Grammophon, 1992–97; Head of Classical Music, BBC, 1997–98; Controller, BBC Radio 3, 1998–2014; Dir, BBC Proms, 2007–14. FRCM 2007; Fellow, Radio Acad. *Publications* include: (with M. Finnissy) New Music 1989, 1989. *Address:* Aldeburgh Music, Snape Maltings Concert Hall, Snape, Suffolk IP17 1SP.

WRIGHT, Rosalind, CB 2001; Independent Member, Regulatory Board, Association of Chartered Certified Accountants, since 2012; *b* 2 Nov. 1942; *d* of late Alfred Kerstein and Felicie Kerstein; *m* 1966, Dr David Julian Maurice Wright; three *d*. *Educ:* University College London (LLB Hons). Called to the Bar, Middle Temple, 1964, Bencher, 2001; in practice at the Bar, 1965–69; Department of the Director of Public Prosecutions, then Crown Prosecution Service: Legal Asst, 1969–72; Sen. Legal Asst, 1972–81; Asst Dir, 1981–87 and Head of Fraud Investigation Gp (London), 1984–87; Head of Prosecutions, Securities Assoc., later SFA, 1987–94; Exec. Dir (Legal and Investor Protection Policy) and Gen. Counsel, SFA, 1994–97; Dir, Serious Fraud Office, 1997–2003. Chm., Fraud Adv. Panel, 2003–14; non-exec. Dir, OFT, 2003–07; Member: Supervisory Cttee, European Anti-Fraud Office, 2005–12 (Chm., 2005–07); Exclusion Cttee, European Investment Bank, 2012–. Independent Director: BIS (formerly DTI, then BERR) Legal Services Gp, 2002–08; Insolvency Service Steering Bd, 2006–11. Complaints Comr, London Metal Exchange, 2010–. Lay Member, Disciplinary Panel: Nat. Register of Public Sector Interpreters, 2012–; AAT, 2012–. Mem. of the Bar, NI, 1999–. Mem., Gen. Council of the Bar, 1998–2003. Trustee, 1999–2015, Vice Chm., 2003–15, Jewish Assoc. for Business Ethics. Hon. QC 2006. *Recreations:* music, theatre, Jewish jokes.

WRIGHT, Roy Kilner; Deputy Editor, The London Standard (formerly Evening Standard), 1979–88; *b* 12 March 1926; *s* of Ernest Wright and Louise Wright; *m* 1st (marr. diss.); two *d;* 2nd, 1969, Jane Barnicoat (*née* Selby). *Educ:* elementary sch., St Helens, Lancs. Jun. Reporter, St Helens Reporter, 1941; Army Service; Sub-Editor: Middlesbrough Gazette, 1947; Daily Express, Manchester, 1951; Daily Mirror, London, 1952; Features Editor, Daily Express, London; Dep. Editor, Daily Express, 1976, Editor, 1976–77; Dir, Beaverbrook Newspapers, 1976–77; Senior Asst Editor, Daily Mail, 1977. *Address:* 3 The Square, Cranebridge Road, Salisbury, Wilts SP2 7TW. *T:* (01722) 414464.

WRIGHT, Hon. Ruth Margaret; *see* Richardson, Hon. R. M.

WRIGHT, Simon; *b* 15 Sept. 1979; *m* Rosalind. *Educ:* Dereham Neatherd High Sch.; Imperial Coll. London (BSc Maths); King's Coll. London (PGCE). Teacher of Maths, Alderman Peel High Sch., Wells Next the Sea, Norfolk, 2002–03; Campaigns Officer for Norman Lamb, MP, 2003–07. Mem. (Lib Dem) N Norfolk DC, 2003. MP (Lib Dem) Norwich S, 2010–15; contested (Lib Dem) same seat, 2015. Mem., Envmtl Audit Select Cttee, 2010–15.

WRIGHT, Stephen; *see* Wright, J. S.

WRIGHT, Stephen James; *see* Lowe, Stephen.

WRIGHT, Sir Stephen (John Leadbetter), KCMG 2006 (CMG 1997); HM Diplomatic Service, retired; Senior Adviser: Good Governance Group (G3), since 2008; Mitsui & Co. Europe plc, since 2011; *b* 7 Dec. 1946; *s* of late J. H. Wright, CBE and Joan Wright; *m* 1st, 1970 (marr. diss. 2000); one *s* one *d;* 2nd, 2002, Elizabeth Abbott Rosemont. *Educ:* Shrewsbury Sch.; The Queen's Coll., Oxford (BA Mod. History, 1968). HM Diplomatic Service, 1968; Havana, 1969–71; CS Coll., 1971–72; FCO, 1972–75; British Information Services, NY, 1975–80; UK Permanent Repn to EC, Brussels, 1980–84; FCO, 1984–85; seconded to Cabinet Office, 1985–87; Counsellor and Hd of Chancery, New Delhi, 1988–91; Counsellor (Ext. Relations), UK Perm. Repn to EC, Brussels, 1991–94; Asst Under Sec. of State, later Dir, EU affairs, FCO, 1994–97; Minister, Washington, 1997–99; Dir, Wider Europe, FCO, 1999–2000; Dep. Under-Sec. of State, FCO, 2000–02; Ambassador to Spain, 2003–07; Chief Exec., Internat. Financial Services London, 2008–10; Sen. Advr, TheCityUK, 2010–11. *Recreations:* photography, rowing, books. *E:* stephenjlwright@gmail.com.

WRIGHT, Stephen Neill; Headmaster, Merchant Taylors' School, Northwood, 2004–13; *b* 4 Sept. 1956; *s* of Neill and Kathleen Wright; *m* 1985, Penelope Susan Gill; one *s* two *d. Educ:* King's Sch., Macclesfield; Queens' Coll., Cambridge (BA Hons (Hist.) 1979; PGCE 1980). Teacher, Woolverstone Hall Sch., Suffolk, 1980–83; Housemaster, Framlingham Coll., 1983–94; Dep. Headmaster, Judd Sch., Tonbridge, 1994–98; Headmaster, Borden Grammar Sch., Sittingbourne, 1998–2004. *Recreations:* village cricket, gardening.

WRIGHT, Rt Rev. Thomas; *see* Wright, Rt Rev. N. T.

WRIGHT, Thomas Charles Kendal Knox, CBE 2007; Chief Executive, Age UK (formerly Age Concern England and Help the Aged), since 2009; *b* 22 Feb. 1962; *s* of David Andrew Wright and Penelope Jane Wright; *m* 1986, Charlotte Annabel Mudford; one *d. Educ:* Marlborough Coll.; Ealing Coll. (BA Hons Business Studies 1985). Dip. Market Res.; DipM. Graduate trainee, various marketing roles, United Biscuits, 1981–87; Gp Product Manager, British Tissues, 1987–89; Gp Marketing Manager, Anchor Foods, 1989–95; R&D Dir, Carlsberg-Tetley, 1995–96; Sales and Marketing Dir, Center Parcs (UK), 1996–98; Marketing, Sales and Develt Dir, Center Parcs (NV), 1998–99; Man. Dir, Saga Holidays, 1999–2002; Dir, Saga Gp, 1999–2002; CEO, British Tourist Authy, later VisitBritain, 2002–09. Director: VisitLondon (formerly London Tourist Bd), 2002–09; SW Tourism, 2003–09. Chm., Soc. of Ticket Agents and Retailers, 2002–15; Dir, European Travel Commn, 2004–09. Chm., British Gas Energy Trust, 2009–12. Non-exec. Dir, Southern Health Foundn Trust, 2012–14; Dir, Leeds Castle Enterprises, 2014–. Chm., Fuel Poverty Adv. Gp, 2015–. Trustee: Imperial War Mus., 2004–12; Imperial War Mus. Develt Trust, 2012–; DEC, 2009–15; Royal Green Jackets Mus., 2011–; Go ON, 2012–. *Recreations:* running, walking, history, motor racing, travel.

WRIGHT, Rt Rev. Dr Dom Timothy Martin, OSB; Abbot of Ampleforth, 1997–2005; *b* 13 April 1942; *s* of Monty Wright and Marjorie (*née* Brook). *Educ:* Ampleforth Coll.; St Benet's Hall, Oxford (MA); London Univ. (BD (ext.) 1972); Univ. of Wales (PhD 2012). Ordained priest, 1972; Master of Ceremonies, 1971–80, Jun. Master, 1985–88, Ampleforth Abbey; Appeal Dir, Ampleforth Abbey Trust, 1994–97. Ampleforth College: Head of Religious Studies, 1977–91; Housemaster, 1980–97; Dep. Head, 1988–97. Spiritual Dir, Beda Coll., Rome, 2006–13; Tutor, Benedictine Univ., Illinois, 2013–. Member, Religious Studies Panel: Midland Examining Gp, 1984–96; Univ. of Cambridge Local Exams Syndicate, 1988–94; SEAC, 1988–93. Mem., Abbey Farm Bd, 1985–97. Governor: Bar Convent Direct Grant Sch., York, 1980–85; All Saints RC Comprehensive Sch., York, 1985–96; Westminster Cathedral Choir Sch., 1995–2007. *Publications:* The Eucharist, 1988; Jesus Christ, the Way, the Truth and the Life, 1994; (jtly) Doing Business with Benedict, 2002; No Peace without Prayer: encouraging Muslims and Christians to pray together - a Benedictine perspective, 2013; papers on Islamic-Catholic dialogue and religious freedom. *Recreations:* sport, travel, cycling. *Address:* Ampleforth Abbey, York YO62 4EN. *T:* (01439) 766700.

WRIGHTSON, Sir (Charles) Mark (Garmondsway), 4th Bt *cr* 1900; Chairman, Close Brothers Corporate Finance Ltd, 1999–2006 (Managing Director, 1996–99); *b* 18 Feb. 1951; *s* of Sir John Garmondsway Wrightson, 3rd Bt, TD, and Hon. Rosemary (*d* 1998), *y d* of 1st Viscount Dawson of Penn, GCVO, KCB, KCMG, PC; *S* father, 1983; *m* 1975, Stella Virginia, *d* of late George Dean; three *s. Educ:* Eton; Queens' Coll., Cambridge (BA 1972). Called to the Bar, Middle Temple, 1974. Hill Samuel & Co. Ltd, 1977–96 (Dir, 1984–96). *Heir: s* Barnaby Thomas Garmondsway Wrightson [*b* 5 Aug. 1979; *m* 2008, Clare Nancy Louise, *d* of Hon. David Dugdale; two *s* (twins) one *d*]. *Address:* 39 Westbourne Park Road, W2 5QD.

WRIGHTSON, Prof. Keith Edwin, PhD; FRHistS; FBA 1996; Randolph W. Townsend Professor of History, Yale University, since 2004 (Professor of History, 1999–2004); *b* 22 March 1948; *s* of Robert Wrightson and Evelyn Wrightson (*née* Atkinson); *m* 1972, Eva Mikušová; one *s* one *d. Educ:* Dame Allan's Boys' Sch., Newcastle upon Tyne; Fitzwilliam Coll., Cambridge (BA 1970; MA 1974; PhD 1974). FRHistS 1986. Research Fellow in Hist., Fitzwilliam Coll., Cambridge, 1972–75; Lectr in Modern Hist., Univ. of St Andrews, 1975–84; University of Cambridge: Univ. Lectr in Hist., 1984–93; Reader in English Social Hist., 1993–98; Prof. of Social Hist., 1998–99; Fellow, Jesus Coll., 1984–99 (Hon. Fellow, 2008). Visiting Professor: Univ. of Toronto, 1984, 1992; Univ. of Alberta, 1988; Centre for Northern Studies, Northumbria Univ., 2003–08; Univ. of Newcastle upon Tyne, 2008–14. Pres., N American Conference on British Studies, 2013–15 (Vice Pres., 2011–13). Hon. Prof., Univ. of Durham, 2008. Hon. DLitt: Durham, 2011; Newcastle, 2013. *Publications:* (with D. Levine) Poverty and Piety in an English Village, 1979, 2nd edn 1995; English Society 1580–1680, 1982; (ed jtly) The World We Have Gained, 1986; (with D. Levine) The Making of an Industrial Society, 1992; Earthly Necessities: economic lives in early modern Britain, 2000; Ralph Tailor's Summer: a scrivener, his city and the plague, 2011; numerous essays and articles on English social history. *Recreation:* modern jazz. *Address:* Department of History, Yale University, PO Box 208324, New Haven, CT 06520–8324, USA.

WRIGHTSON, Sir Mark; *see* Wrightson, Sir C. M. G.

WRIGLEY, Andrea; *see* Young, Andrea.

WRIGLEY, Prof. Christopher John, PhD; Professor of Modern British History, 1991–2012, now Emeritus, and Head of the School of History and Art History, 2000–03, Nottingham University; *b* 18 Aug. 1947; *s* of late Arthur Wrigley and Eileen Sylvia Wrigley; *m* 1987, Margaret Walsh. *Educ:* Goldsworth Primary Sch., Woking; Kingston Grammar Sch.; Univ. of E Anglia (BA 1968); Birkbeck Coll., London (PhD 1973). Lecturer in Econ. and Social Hist., QUB, 1971–72; Loughborough University: Lectr in Econ. Hist., 1972–78; Sen. Lectr, 1978–84; Reader, 1984–88; Reader in Econ. Hist., Nottingham Univ., 1988–91. Team Assessor (Hist.), Teaching Quality Assessment, HEFCE, 1993–94; Mem., Hist. Panel, HEFCE RAE, 1997, 2001; Coll. Mem. (Hist.), ESRC, 2002–05. Ed., The Historian, 1993–98. Member of Council: Historical Assoc., 1980–2008 (Pres., 1996–99); Econ. Hist. Soc., 1983–92, 1994–2000 and 2002–08; a Vice-President: RHistS, 1997–2001; Soc. for Study of Labour History, 2012– (Exec. Mem., 1983–2005; Vice Chm., 1993–97; Chm., 1997–2001); Trustee, Arkwright Soc., 2012– (Mem., Consultative Council, 2011–12). Mem. (Lab) Leics CC, 1981–89 (Labour Chief Whip, 1985–86; Leader, Labour Gp, 1986–89); Mem. (Lab) Charnwood BC, 1983–87 (Dep. Leader, Labour Gp). Contested: (Lab) Blaby, 1983; (Lab and Co-op) Loughborough, 1987. CMILT (MILT 2000); AcSS 2001. Hon. LittD E Anglia, 1998. *Publications:* (ed jtly) The Working Class in Victorian Britain, 4 vols, 1973; David Lloyd George and the British Labour Movement, 1976, 2nd edn 1992; A. J. P. Taylor: a complete bibliography, 1980; (ed) A History of British Industrial Relations: Vol. 1: 1875–1914, 1982; Vol. 2: 1914–1939, 1986, 2nd edn 1992; Vol. 3: 1939–1979, 1996; (ed) William Barnes: the Dorset poet, 1984; (ed) Warfare, Diplomacy and Politics, 1986; Arthur Henderson, 1990; Lloyd George and the Challenge of Labour, 1990; (ed jtly) On the Move, 1991; Lloyd George, 1992; (ed) Challenges of Labour, 1993; (ed) A. J. P. Taylor: From Napoleon to the Second International, 1993; (ed) A. J. P. Taylor: From the Boer War to the Cold War, 1995; (jtly) An Atlas of Industrial Protest in Britain 1750–1990, 1996; (ed) British Trade Unionism 1945–95, 1997; (ed) A. J. P. Taylor: British Prime Ministers and other essays, 1999; (ed) A. J. P. Taylor: Struggles for Diplomacy: diplomatic essays, 2000; (ed) The First World War and the International Economy, 2000; Churchill: a biographical dictionary, 2002; British Trade Unions since 1933, 2002; (ed) A Companion to Early Twentieth-Century Britain, 2003; (ed jtly) The Emergence of European Trade Unionism, 2004; A. J. P. Taylor: radical historian of Europe, 2006; Churchill, 2006; (ed jtly) The Second Labour Government 1929–1931, 2011. *Recreations:* swimming, music, visiting art galleries, reading even more history. *Address:* School of History, Nottingham University, Nottingham NG7 2RD. *E:* chris.wrigley@nottingham.ac.uk; (home) 8 Tavistock Road, West Bridgford, Nottingham NG2 6FH.

WRIGLEY, Sir Edward Anthony, (Sir Tony), Kt 1996; PhD; FBA 1980; Master of Corpus Christi College, Cambridge, 1994–2000; President, British Academy, 1997–2001; *b* 17 Aug. 1931; *s* of Edward Ernest Wrigley and Jessie Elizabeth Wrigley; *m* 1960, Maria Laura Spelberg; one *s* three *d. Educ:* King's Sch., Macclesfield; Peterhouse, Cambridge (MA, PhD). William Volker Res. Fellow, Univ. of Chicago, 1953–54; Lectr in Geography, Cambridge, 1958–74; Peterhouse, Cambridge: Fellow, 1958–74, Hon. Fellow, 1997; Tutor, 1962–64; Sen. Bursar, 1964–74; Co-Dir, Cambridge Gp for History of Population and Social Structure, 1974–94; Prof. of Population Studies, LSE, 1979–88; Sen. Res. Fellow, 1988–94, Dist. Fellow, 2002–05, Academic Sec., 1992–94, All Souls Coll., Oxford; Prof. of Econ. History, Univ. of Cambridge, 1994–97. Leverhulme Emeritus Res. Fellow, 2008–09. Pres., Manchester Coll., Oxford, 1987–96. Mem., Inst. for Advanced Study, Princeton, 1970–71; Hinkley Vis. Prof., Johns Hopkins Univ., 1975; Tinbergen Vis. Prof., Erasmus Univ., Rotterdam, 1979. President: British Soc. for Population Studies, 1977–79; Econ. History Soc., 1995–98; Chm., Population Investigation Cttee, 1984–90; Treas., British Acad., 1989–95. Chm., Newton Trust, 2000–07. Editor, Economic History Review, 1986–92. Mem., Amer. Philosophical Soc., 2001; Hon. Foreign Mem., Amer. Acad. of Arts and Scis, 2001. Hon. LittD: Manchester, 1997; Sheffield, 1997; Bristol, 1998; London, 2004; Hon. DLitt: Oxford, 1999; Leicester, 1999; Hon. DSc Edinburgh, 1998. IUSSP Laureate, 1993; Founder's Medal, RGS, 1997; Leverhulme Medal, British Acad., 2005. *Publications:* Industrial Growth and Population Change, 1961; (ed) English Historical Demography, 1966; Population and History, 1969; (ed) Nineteenth Century Society, 1972; (ed) Identifying People in the Past, 1973; (ed with P. Abrams) Towns in Societies, 1978; (with R. S. Schofield) Population History of England, 1981; (ed jtly) The Works of Thomas Robert Malthus, 1986; People, Cities and Wealth, 1987; Continuity, Chance and Change, 1988; (ed with R. A. Church) The Industrial Revolutions, 1994; (jtly) English Population History from Family Reconstitution, 1997; Poverty, Progress and Population, 2004; Energy and the English Industrial Revolution, 2010; The Early English Censuses, 2011. *Recreation:* gardening. *Address:* 13 Sedley Taylor Road, Cambridge CB2 8PW. *T:* (01223) 247614.

WRIGLEY, Prof. Neil, PhD, DSc; FBA 2012; Professor of Geography, University of Southampton, since 1991; *b* Denton, Lancs, 27 March 1948; *s* of Fred and Eva Wrigley; *m* 1st, 1972, Susan Broom (marr. diss. 1995); two *d;* 2nd, 1996, Michelle Lowe; two *s* one *d. Educ:* Audenshaw Grammar Sch., Lancs; University Coll. of Wales, Aberystwyth (BA 1st Cl. Hons 1970); St Catharine's Coll., Cambridge (PhD 1976); Univ. of Bristol (DSc 1990). Lectr in Geog., Univ. of Southampton, 1973–76; Lectr, then Reader in Geog., Univ. of Bristol, 1976–86; Prof. of City and Regl Planning, Univ. of Wales Coll. of Cardiff, 1986–91 (Hd of Dept, 1989–91); Hd of Dept of Geog., Univ. of Southampton, 1992–95, 1999–2001. Ed., Trans IBG, 1988–93; Founding Ed., Jl Econ. Geog., 2001–. Visiting Professor: UCSB, 1981; Boston Univ., 1981; Macquarie Univ., 1984; Karlsruhe Univ., 1985; UCLA, 1986, 1989; Univ. of Toronto, 1987, 2000; George Mason Univ., 1993; Univ. of Canterbury, NZ, 1995. Erskine Fellow, NZ, 1995; Vis. Schol., St Catharine's Coll., Cambridge, 1995–96; Sen. Res. Fellow, St Peter's Coll., Oxford, 1996–97; Leverhulme Trust Res. Fellow/Individual Award, 1997–99. Member: Res. Resources and Methods Cttee, 1983–91, Dir, Retail Ind. Business Engagement Network, 2008–13, ESRC; Future High Streets Forum, DCLG, 2013–. Mem., Acad. Develt Bd, Worldwide Univs Network, 2001–03. Mem. Council, IBG, 1988–89; Chair, Royal Geographical Annual Conf. 2010, 2009–11. FAcSS (AcSS 2003). Ashby Prize, Pion Ltd, 2004; Murchison Award, RGS, 2008; Outstanding Impact in Business Prize, ESRC, 2014. *Publications:* (ed) Statistical Applications in the Spatial Sciences, 1979; (ed with R. J. Bennett) Quantitative Geography: a British view, 1981; Measuring the Unmeasurable: the analysis of quantitative spatial data, 1985; Categorical Data Analysis for Geographers and Environmental Scientists, 1985, 2nd US edn 2002; Store Choice, Store Location and Market Analysis, 1988, repubd 2014; (ed jtly) Urban Dynamics and Spatial Choice Behaviour, 1989; (ed with M. Lowe) Retailing, Consumption and Capital: towards the new retail geography, 1996, repr. 1998; (with M. Lowe) Reading Retail: a geographical perspective on retailing and consumption spaces, 2002; (ed with N. Coe) The Globalization of Retailing, 2 vols, 2009; (ed with E. Brookes) Evolving High Streets: resilience and reinvention, 2014; (with D. Lambiri) British High Streets: from crisis to recovery? a comprehensive review of the evidence, 2015; contrib. papers to internat. jls incl. Envmt & Planning A, Econ. Geog., Trans IBG, Jl Econ. Geog., Progress in Human Geog., Urban Studies, Regl Studies, Global Networks. *Recreations:* travel, wine, Manchester City FC, over-turning established academic pecking orders. *Address:* 18 St Thomas Street, Winchester, Hants SO23 9HJ. *T:* (01962) 865796; School of Geography and Environment, University of Southampton, Southampton, Hants SO17 1BJ. *T:* (023) 8059 3762. *E:* n.wrigley@soton.ac.uk.

WRIGLEY, Sir Tony; *see* Wrigley, Sir E. A.

WRIXON-BECHER, Sir John William Michael; *see* Becher.

WROATH, His Honour John Herbert; a Circuit Judge, 1984–97; *b* 24 July 1932; *s* of Stanley Wroath and Ruth Ellen Wroath; *m* 1959, Mary Bridget Byrne; two *s* one *d*. *Educ:* Ryde Sch., Ryde, IoW. Admitted Solicitor, 1956; private practice, 1958–66; Registrar, Isle of Wight County Court, 1965; County Prosecuting Solicitor, 1966; full-time County Court Registrar, 1972; a Recorder of the Crown Court, 1978–84. Chm., Independent Schs Tribunal, 1998–2003. *Recreations:* sailing, bowling, reading, painting. *Address:* 8 Tides Reach, Birmingham Road, Cowes, Isle of Wight PO31 7NU. *T:* (01983) 293072. *Clubs:* Island Sailing, Corinthian Yacht.

WRONG, Henry Lewellys Barker, CBE 1986; Director, Barbican Centre, 1970–90; *b* Toronto, Canada, 20 April 1930; *s* of Henry Arkel Wrong and Jean Barker Wrong; *m* 1966, Penelope Hamilton Norman; two *s* one *d*. *Educ:* Trinity Coll., Univ. of Toronto (BA). Stage and business administration, Metropolitan Opera Assoc., New York, 1952–64; Director Programming, National Arts Center, Ottawa, 1964–68; Dir, Festival Canada Centennial Programme, 1967; Chm., Spencer House (St James's) Ltd, 1989–92; Dir, European Arts Foundn, 1990–95. Member: Royal Opera House Trust, 1989–95; Adv. Cttee, ADAPT (Access for Disabled People to Arts Premises Today). Trustee: Henry Moore Foundn, 1990–2012; LSO, 1990–; Royal Fine Art Commn, 1995–2003; Governor, Compton Verney House Trust, 1995–2002. Liveryman, Fishmongers' Co., 1987. FRSA 1988. Hon. DLitt City, 1985. Pro Cultura Hungarica, 1989. Centennial Medal, Govt of Canada, 1967; Chevalier, Ordre Nat. du Mérite (France), 1985 (Officier, 1985). *Address:* Yew Tree House, Much Hadham, Herts SG10 6AJ. *T:* (01279) 842106. *Clubs:* White's; Badminton and Rackets (Toronto).

WROTTESLEY, family name of **Baron Wrottesley**.

WROTTESLEY, 6th Baron *cr* 1838; **Clifton Hugh Lancelot de Verdon Wrottesley;** Bt 1642; yacht broking, since 1997, property, since 2003, and fine wine investment management, since 2005; *b* 10 Aug. 1968; *s* of Hon. Richard Francis Gerard Wrottesley (*d* 1970) (2nd *s* of 5th Baron) and of Georgina Anne (who *m* 1982, Lt-Col Jonathan L. Seddon-Brown), *er d* of Lt-Col Peter Thomas Clifton, CVO, DSO; *S* grandfather, 1977; *m* 2001, Sascha, *d* of Urs Schwarzenbach; three *s* one *d*. *Educ:* Eton; Edinburgh Univ. Commnd 1st Bn Grenadier Guards, 1990; Lieut, 1993, Capt. 1994; retd, 1995. *Heir: s* Hon. Victor Ernst Francis de Verdon Wrottesley, *b* 28 Jan. 2004. *Address:* New Quadrant Partners Ltd, 22 Chancery Lane, WC2A 1LS. *Clubs:* White's, Turf; Brook (New York); St Moritz Tobogganing; St Moritz Bobsleigh; Corviglia Ski; Dracula (St Moritz).

WROUGHTON, Sir Philip (Lavallin), KCVO 2008; Lord-Lieutenant of Berkshire, 1995–2008; Chairman and Chief Executive, C. T. Bowring & Co. Ltd, 1988–96; *b* 19 April 1933; *s* of Michael Lavallin Wroughton and Elizabeth Angela Wroughton (*née* Rate); *m* 1957, Catriona Henrietta Ishbel MacLeod; two *d*. *Educ:* Eton Coll. Nat. Service, 1951–53, 2nd Lieut KRRC. Price Forbes & Co. Ltd, 1954–61; C. T. Bowring & Co. Ltd, 1961–96; Dir, Marsh & McLennan Cos, Inc., 1988–96 (Vice Chm., 1994–96); Chm., Venton Underwriting Agencies Ltd, 1996–99. Mem., Council of Lloyds, 1992–95. President: Newbury & Dist Agricl Soc., 1985–86; Berks Community Foundn, 1995–2008; SE RFCA, 2000–04; South of England Agricl Soc., 2008–09. Trustee, 1991–2000, Vice-Pres., 2000–12, Princess Royal Trust for Carers; Trustee, Prince Philip Trust, 1995–2008. Gov., St Mary's Sch., Wantage, 1986–2006. High Sheriff, Berks, 1977; DL Berks, 1994. Hon. LLD Reading, 2004. KStJ (Pres., Council of St John, Berks, 1995–2008). *Recreations:* shooting, racing. *Address:* North Lodge, Woolley Park, Wantage OX12 8NJ. *T:* (01488) 638214. *E:* plw@northlodge.biz. *Club:* White's.

WU, Prof. Duncan, DPhil; Professor of English, Georgetown University, Washington, since 2008; *b* 3 Nov. 1961; *s* of Spencer Yin-Cheung Wu and Mary (*née* Sadler); *m* 1st, 1997, Caroline Beatrice Carey (marr. diss. 2008); 2nd, 2011, Catherine Mary Payling (MBE 2003). *Educ:* St Catherine's Coll., Oxford (MA; DPhil 1990). British Acad. Postdoctoral Res. Fellow, 1991–94; Reader in English Lit., 1995–98, Prof. of English Lit., 1998–2000, Univ. of Glasgow; Lectr in English Lit., 2000–03, Prof. of English Lang. and Lit., 2003–07, Univ. of Oxford; Fellow, St Catherine's Coll., Oxford, 2000–07. Trustee: Charles Lamb Soc., 1991–; Keats-Shelley Meml Assoc., 1998–. FRSA. *Publications:* Wordsworth's Reading 1770–1799, 1993; (ed with S. Gill) Wordsworth: a selection of his finest poems, 1994; Romanticism: an anthology, 1994, 4th edn 2012; Six Contemporary Dramatists: Bennett, Potter, Gray, Brenton, Hare, Ayckbourn, 1995; Romanticism: a critical reader, 1995; Wordsworth's Reading 1800–1815, 1996; William Wordsworth: the Five-Book Prelude, 1997; Women Romantic Poets: an anthology, 1997; A Companion to Romanticism, 1998; William Hazlitt, The Plain Speaker: key essays, 1998; The Selected Writings of William Hazlitt, 1998; Making Plays: interviews with contemporary British dramatists and directors, 2000; Wordsworth: an inner life, 2002; (ed with M. Demata) British Romanticism and the Edinburgh Review, 2002; The Blackwell Essential Literature Series, 7 vols, 2002; William Wordsworth: the earliest poems 1785–1790, 2002; Wordsworth's Poets, 2003; (ed jtly) Metaphysical Hazlitt: bicentenary essays, 2005; New Writings of William Hazlitt, 2007; Hazlitt: the first modern man, 2008; The Happy Fireside: Romantic poems about dogs and cats, 2011; Immortal Bird: the nightingale in Romantic poetry, 2011; Poetry of Witness: the tradition in English, 1500-2000, 2014; All that is worth remembering: selected essays of William Hazlitt, 2014; 30 Great Myths about the Romantics, 2015. *Recreations:* jazz, walking, cinema, visiting art museums and American Civil War battlefields, book collecting. *Address:* Department of English, 306 New North, Georgetown University, Washington, DC 20057–1131, USA. *E:* dw252@georgetown.edu.

WU, Sir Gordon (Ying Sheung), GBS 2004; KCMG 1997; Chairman, Hopewell Holdings Group, since 1972 (Managing Director, 1972–2001); *b* Hong Kong, 3 Dec. 1935; *s* of Chung Wu and Sum Wu (*née* Chang); *m* 1970, Kwok, (Ivy), San-Ping; two *s* two *d*. *Educ:* Princeton Univ. (BS Civil Engrg 1958). Architect; civil engr. Founder: Central Enterprises Co. Ltd, 1962; Gordon Wu and Associates, 1962; Hopewell Construction Co. Ltd, 1963; Hopewell Hldgs Ltd, 1972; Consolidated Electric Power Asia Ltd, 1993. *Projects* include: Hopewell Centre, Hong Kong (66 storey building); China Hotel, Guangdong, China; Shajiao B and C (coal-fired power stations), Guangdong, China; G-S-Z Superhighway (motorway linking Hong Kong and China). Vice Pres., Real Estate Developers Assoc. of Hong Kong, 1970–; Mem., Chinese People's Political Consultative Conf., 1983–2013 (Vice Chm., Cttee for Liaison with HK, Macao, Taiwan and Overseas Chinese, 2003–13). *Address:* Hopewell Holdings Ltd, 64th Floor, Hopewell Centre, 183 Queen's Road East, Hong Kong.

WULF-MATHIES, Dr Monika; Executive Vice President (formerly Managing Director), Corporate Public Policy and Sustainability (formerly Managing Director, Policy and Environment), Deutsche Post World Net, 2001–08 (Policy Adviser, Board of Management, since 2009); *b* 17 March 1942; *d* of Carl-Hermann Baier and Margott Meisser; *m* 1968, Dr Carsten Wulf-Mathies. *Educ:* Univ. of Hamburg (DrPhil 1968). Br. Asst, Federal Ministry of Econs, Germany, 1968–71; Hd, Dept for Social Policy, Federal Chancellery, 1971–76; joined Gewerkschaft Öffentliche Dienste, Transport und Verkehr (Public Services and Transport Workers' Union), 1971; Mem., Man. Exec. Cttee, 1976–95; Chm., 1982–95; Mem., European Commn, 1995–99. Policy Mem., Inst. for Study of Labour, Bonn, 2005–; Dep. Chm., Supervisory Bd, Univ. of Bonn, 2008–13; Mem. Senate, Leibniz Gemeinschaft, 2010–. Pres., Beethoven-Stiftung für Kunst und Kultur, 2005–. *Recreations:* garden, painting in watercolours.

WULFF, Christian; President, Federal Republic of Germany, 2010–12; *b* Osnabrück, 19 June 1959; *s* of Rudolf Wulff and Dagmar Wulff; *m* 1st, 1988, Christiane Vogt (marr. diss.); one *d*; 2nd, 2008, Bettina Körner; one *s*, and one step *s*. *Educ:* Univ. of Osnabrück (Law degree specialising in Econs 1986); Hanover (state exams in law). Legal trng, Oldenburg Higher Regl Court, 1987–90, then joined a law firm. Mem. (CDU), Osnabrück Council, 1986–2001 (Leader, CDU Gp, 1989–94). Landtag of Lower Saxony: Mem. (CDU), 1994–2010; Leader, CDU Parly Gp, 1994; Minister-Pres., 2003–10. Chm., Lower Saxony, CDU, 1994–2010; Dep. Federal Chm., CDU, 1998–2010. Patron, Nat. Orgn, German Multiple Sclerosis Soc., 2001–. Hon. Senator, Eur. Acad. of Scis and Arts, Salzburg. Hon. Dr Tongji Univ., Shanghai.

WULSTAN, Prof. David; Hon. Professor, Department of European Languages, Aberystwyth University (formerly University of Wales, Aberystwyth), since 2010; *b* 18 Jan. 1937; *s* of Rev. Norman and (Sarah) Margaret Jones; *m* 1965, Susan Nelson Graham; one *s*. *Educ:* Royal Masonic Sch., Bushey; Coll. of Technology, Birmingham; Magdalen Coll., Oxford (Academical Clerk, 1960; Burrowes Exhibnr, 1961; Mackinnon Sen. Schol., 1963; Fellow by examination, 1964). MA, BSc, BLitt; ARCM. Lectr in History of Music, Magdalen Coll., Oxford, 1968–78; also at St Hilda's and St Catherine's Colls; Vis. Prof., Depts of Near Eastern Studies and Music, Univ. of California, Berkeley, 1977; Statutory (Sen. Lectr), University Coll., Cork, 1979, Prof. of Music, 1980–83; Gregynog Prof. of Music, UCW, Aberystwyth, 1983–90. Member: Council, Plainsong and Mediaeval Music Soc.; Soc. for Old Testament Studies. Dir, Clerkes of Oxenford (founded 1961); appearances at Cheltenham, Aldeburgh, York, Bath, Flanders, Holland, Krakow, Zagreb, Belgrade Fests, BBC Proms; many broadcasts and TV appearances, gramophone recordings; also broadcast talks, BBC and abroad. Fellow, Royal Soc. of Musicians, 2001. Hon. Fellow, St Peter's Coll., Oxford, 2007. Consulting Ed., Spanish Academic Press. *Publications:* Septem Discrimina Vocum, 1983; Tudor Music, 1985; Musical Language, 1992; The Emperor's Old Clothes, 1994, 2nd edn 2001; The Poetic and Musical Legacy of Heloise and Abelard, 2003; Music from the Paraclete, 2004; editor: Gibbons, Church Music, Early English Church Music, vol. 3, 1964, vol. 27, 1979; Anthology of Carols, 1968; Anthology of English Church Music, 1971; Play of Daniel, 1976, 3rd edn 2008; Victoria, Requiem, 1977; Tallis, Puer Natus Mass, 1977; Coverdale Chant Book, 1978; Sheppard, Complete Works, 1979–; Weelkes, Ninth Service, 1980; St Peters Chantbook, 2011; (contrib.) Canterbury Dictionary of Hymnology, 2013; (contrib.) Liber Amicorum Gerardo Huseby, 2013; (contrib.) Mapping the Medieval Mediterranean, 2014; Listen Once More: a new history of music, 2015; many edns of anthems, services etc; entries in Encyclopédie de Musique Sacrée, 1970; chapter in: A History of Western Music, ed Sternfeld, 1970; The Secular Latin Motet in the Renaissance, 1990; chapters in Cobras e Som, 2001; contrib. periodicals and learned jls incl. Plainsong and Medieval Music, Music and Letters, Early Music, Jl of Theol Studies, Jl of Semitic Studies, Iraq, Jl of the Amer. Oriental Soc., English Histl Review, Notes, al-Masāq (guest ed., 2010), Bull. of Cantigueiros of Santa Maria, Faith and Worship, The Consort, Prayer Bk Soc. Jl, Comparative Drama. *Recreations:* cooking, eating, aikido, self-defence (instructor), being politically incorrect, bemoaning the decline of the English language and of British universities. *Address:* Hillview Croft, Lon Tyllwyd, Llanfarian, Aberystwyth, Cardiganshire SY23 4UH. *T:* (01970) 617832.

WULWIK, Peter David; His Honour Judge Wulwik; a Circuit Judge, since 2004; Principal Judge for estate agents' appeals to the First-Tier Tribunal (General Regulatory Chamber) and a Judge of the Upper Tribunal (Administrative Appeals Chamber), since 2009; a Judge of the Upper Tribunal (Tax and Chancery Chamber), since 2014; *b* 15 Sept. 1950; *s* of Eddie and Mona Wulwik; *m* 1975, Joanna Rosenberg; two *s* one *d*. *Educ:* St Marylebone Grammar Sch.; Univ. of London (LLB Hons ext.). Called to the Bar, Gray's Inn, 1972; Asst Recorder, 1995–2000; a Recorder, 2000–04. Part-time Chairman: London Rent Assessment Panel and Leasehold Valuation Tribunal, 1999–2004; Consumer Credit and Estate Agents Appeals Panel, 2003–. Pres., Consumer Credit Appeals Tribunal, 2008–09. *Publications:* (contrib.) Bennion's Consumer Credit Law Reports, 1990–2000; (contrib.) Goode's Consumer Credit Reports, 2000–04. *Recreations:* reading, opera, theatre, classical music, antique fairs, playing bridge, tennis, watching Tottenham Hotspur. *Club:* Radlett Lawn Tennis and Squash.

WURTH, Hubert; Permanent Representative of Luxembourg to the United Nations in Vienna and to the Organization for Security and Co-operation in Europe, since 2011; *b* Luxembourg, 15 April 1952; *s* of Ernest Wurth and Denise Wurth (*née* Conrath); *m* 1998, Francisca Passchier; two *d*. *Educ:* Univ. of Paris II (law degree 1975); Inst. of Political Studies, Paris (Dip. Internat. Relns 1976). Min. of Foreign Affairs, Luxembourg, 1978–89; Ambassador: to USSR, Poland, Finland and Mongolia, 1988–91; to Netherlands, 1992–98; Ambassador and Perm. Rep. to UN, NY, 1998–2003; Ambassador to France, OECD and UNESCO, 2003–07; Ambassador to the Court of St James's, and concurrently to Ireland and Iceland, 2007–11. Ambassador, Special Mission for Former Yugoslavia, 1996–98. *Recreations:* painter (self-taught), various exhibitions (incl. 'Dark', EU Commn Gall., London, 2008) and publications. *W:* www.wurthhubert.com.

WÜTHRICH, Prof. Kurt, PhD; Professor: of Biophysics, Eidgenössische Technische Hochschule, Zürich, since 1980; of Structural Biology, Scripps Research Institute, California, since 2004; *b* 4 Oct. 1938; *s* of Herrmann Wüthrich and Gertrud Wüthrich-Kuchen; *m* 1963, Marianne Briner; one *s* one *d*. *Educ:* Univ. of Bern (MS Chemistry, Physics and Maths 1962); Univ. of Basel (PhD Chemistry 1964); Eidgenössisches Turn- und Sportlehrerdiplom 1964. Postdoctoral training: Univ. of Basel, 1964–65; Univ. of California, Berkeley, 1965–67; Bell Telephone Labs, Murray Hill, 1967–69; Eidgenössische Technische Hochschule, Zürich, 1969–: Asst Prof., 1972–76; Associate Prof., 1976–80; Chm., Dept of Biology, 1995–2000. Vis. Prof. of Structural Biol., Scripps Res. Inst., La Jolla, 2001–04. Mem. Council, 1975–78, 1987–90, Sec. Gen., 1978–84, Vice Pres., 1984–87, IUPAB; Mem. Gen. Cttee, 1980–86, Standing Cttee on Free Circulation of Scientists, 1982–90, ICSU. Member: EMBO, 1984; Deutsche Akad. der Naturforscher Leopoldina, 1987; Academia Europea, 1989; Schweizerische Akad. der Technischen Wissenschaften, 2001; Schweizerische Akad. der Medizinischen Wissenschaften, 2002. Editor: Qly Rev. Biophysics, 1984–91, 1996–2001; Macromolecular Structures, 1990–2000; Jl Biomolecular NMR, 1991–2011. Hon. Member: Japanese Biochem. Soc., 1993; American Acad. of Arts and Scis, 1993; Nat. Magnetic Resonance Soc., India, 1998; Swiss Chemical Soc., 2003; World Innovation Foundn, 2003; Internat. Soc. Magnetic Resonance in Medicine, 2004; Hungarian Acad. of Sci., 2004; World Acad. of Young Scientists, 2004; Eur. Acad. Arts, Scis and Humanities, 2004; Latvian Acad. Scis, 2004; Groupement Ampère, 2004; NMR Soc. of Japan, 2004; Indian Biophysical Soc., 2005; Korean Magnetic Resonance Soc., 2005. Foreign Associate: US Nat. Acad. of Scis, 1992; Acad. of Scis, Inst. of France, 2000; RSChem, 2003; RSE, 2003. FAAAS 1998; Foreign Mem., Royal Soc., 2010. Foreign Fellow: Indian Nat. Sci. Acad., 1989; Korean Acad. of Sci. and Technol., 2005; Nordrhein-Westfälische Acad. der Wissenschaften, 2005; Hon. Fellow: NAS, India, 1992; Latvian Inst. of Organic Synthesis, Riga, 2008. Hon. Dr Chem.: Siena, 1997; Univ. del Norte, Asunción, Paraguay, 2007; Hon. PhD Zürich, 1997; Doctor *hc*: Ecole Poly. Fédérale Lausanne, 2001; Valencia, 2004; Sheffield, 2004; King George's Med. Univ., Lucknow, 2005; Pécs, 2007; Lomonosov Moscow State Univ., 2007; Verona, 2007; Univ. René Descartes, Paris, 2007; Naples, 2012. Friedrich Miescher Prize, Schweizerische Biochemische Ges., 1974; Shield, Fac. of Medicine, Tokyo Univ., 1983; P. Bruylants Medal, Catholic Univ. of Louvain, 1986; Stein and Moore Award, Protein Soc., USA, 1990; Louisa Gross Horwitz Prize, Columbia Univ., 1991; Gilbert N. Lewis Medal, Univ. of California, Berkeley, 1991; Marcel Benoist Prize, Switzerland, 1992; Dist. Service Award, Miami Winter Symposia, 1993; Prix Louis Jeantet de Médecine, Geneva, 1993; Kaj Linderstrøm-Lang Prize, Carlsberg Foundn, Copenhagen, 1996; Eminent Scientist of RIKEN, Tokyo, 1997; Kyoto

Prize in Advanced Technol., 1998; Günther Laukien Prize, Exptl NMR Conf., 1999; Otto Warburg Medal, Soc. for Biochem. and Molecular Biol., Germany, 1999; World Future Award, M. Gorbatschow Foundn, 2002; (jtly) Nobel Prize for Chemistry, 2002; Swiss Soc. award, Swiss Awards, 2002; Ehrenpreis, Wallisellen, Switzerland, 2002; Johannes M. Bijvoet Medal, Utrecht Univ., 2008; Paul Walden Medal, Riga Tech. Univ., 2008; Jabir ibn Hyyan (Geber) Medal, Saudi Chemical Soc., 2009; Ralph and Helen Oesper Award, Univ. of Cincinnati, 2010; President's Gold Medal (India), 2012; Theodor Bücher Medal, FEBS, 2013. Hon. Citizen, Lyss, Switzerland, 2003. *Publications:* NMR in Biological Research: Peptides and Proteins, 1976; NMR of Proteins and Nucleic Acids, 1986; NMR in Structural Biology: a collection of papers, 1995; contrib. to learned jls. *Address:* Department of Integrative Structural and Computational Biology, The Scripps Research Institute, 10550 N Torrey Pines Road, La Jolla, CA 92037, USA; Institute of Molecular Biology and Biophysics, ETH Zürich, Otto Stern-Weg, 8093 Zürich, Switzerland.

WYAND, Roger Nicholas Lewes; QC 1997; a Recorder, since 2000; a Deputy High Court Judge, since 2004; *b* 31 Oct. 1947; *s* of John Blake Wyand and Diana Wyand (*née* Williams); *m* 1973, Mary Elizabeth Varley; three *s*. *Educ:* Lakefield Coll. Sch., Canada; Rugby Sch.; Downing Coll., Cambridge (MA Nat. Sci.). Called to the Bar, Middle Temple, 1973, Bencher, 2005; Asst Recorder (Patents County Court), 1994–2000. Vice-Chm., Intellectual Property Bar Assoc. *Recreations:* theatre, golf, Arsenal FC. *Address:* Hogarth Chambers, 5 New Square, Lincoln's Inn, WC2A 3RJ. *T:* (020) 7404 0404.

WYATT, Prof. Adrian Frederick George, DPhil; FRS 2000; Professor of Physics, 1976, now Emeritus, and former Director, Centre for Energy and the Environment (formerly Energy Studies Unit), University of Exeter; *b* 1 Oct. 1938. *Educ:* Univ. of Bristol (BSc 1960); DPhil Oxford 1963. Lectr, then Sen. Lectr, in Physics, Univ. of Nottingham, 1964–76. *Publications:* (ed with H. J. Lauter) Excitations in Two-dimensional and Three-dimensional Quantum Fluids, 1991; contrib. to learned jls. *Address:* School of Physics, University of Exeter, Stocker Road, Exeter EX4 4QL.

WYATT, (Alan) Will, CBE 2000; Chairman, ToniandRosi Films Ltd, 2010–14; *b* 7 Jan. 1942; *s* of Basil Wyatt and Hettie Evelyn (*née* Hooper); *m* 1966, Jane Bridgit Bagenal; two *d*. *Educ:* Magdalen College Sch., Oxford; Emmanuel Coll., Cambridge. Trainee reporter, Sheffield Telegraph, 1964; Sub-Editor, BBC Radio News, 1965; moved to BBC television, 1968; Producer: Late Night Line Up, In Vision, The Book Programme, B. Traven—a mystery solved, *et al*, 1970–77; Asst Hd of Presentation (Programmes), 1977; Hd of Documentary Features, 1981; Hd of Features and Documentaries Gp, 1987; Asst Man. Dir, 1988–91, Man. Dir, 1991–96, BBC Network Television; Chief Exec., BBC Broadcast, 1996–99. Chm., BBC Guidelines on Violence, 1983, 1987; Director: BARB, 1989–91; BBC Subscription TV, 1990–93; BBC Enterprises, 1991–94; BBC Worldwide Television, 1994–96; UKTV, 1997–99; Coral Eurobet, 2000–02; Vitec Gp plc, 2002–11; Racing UK, 2004–11; Amalgamated Racing, 2008–11 (Chm., 2010–11); Chairman: Human Capital Ltd, 2001–08; Goodwill Associates (Media) Ltd, 2003–13; Racecourse Media Gp, 2008–11. Vice-Chm., Shadow Racing Trust, 2003–07. Chairman: Adv. Bd, POLIS, 2006–09; Teaching Awards Trust, 2008–13. Governor: Univ. of the Arts London (formerly London Inst.), 1990–2007 (Chm., 1999–2007); Nat. Film and TV Sch., 1991–97; Magdalen Coll. Sch., Oxford, 2000–06. Vice-Pres., EBU, 1998–99. Trustee, Services Sound and Vision Corp., 2007–13; Trustee, Welsh Nat. Opera, 2013–. Prod. and dir, Toni and Rosi, BBC documentary film, 2012. FRTS 1992 (Vice-Pres., 1997; Pres., 2000–04). *Publications:* The Man Who Was B. Traven, 1980; (contrib.) Masters of the Wired World, 1999; The Fun Factory: a life in the BBC, 2003; numerous articles on broadcasting etc. *Recreations:* fell walking, horse racing, opera, theatre. *Address:* Abbey Willows, Rayford Lane, Middle Barton, Oxon OX7 7DD. *E:* will.wyatt@btinternet.com. *Clubs:* Garrick, Century.

WYATT, Caroline Jane; Religious Affairs Correspondent, BBC, since 2014; *b* Darlinghurst, 21 April 1967; *d* of David Joseph Wyatt, *qv* and Annemarie Wyatt (*née* Angst). *Educ:* Convent of the Sacred Heart, Woldingham; Southampton Univ. (BA Hons English and German); Rutgers Univ. (exchange prog.); City Univ. (Dip. Journalism). BBC: news trainee, 1991–92; asst producer, BBC World TV, 1993; Berlin stringer, 1994–97; Bonn Corresp., 1997–99; Berlin Corresp., 1999–2000; Moscow Corresp., 2000–03; Paris Corresp., 2003–07; Defence Corresp., 2007–14. Mem. Council, Chatham Hse, 2010–. Trustee, Nat. Army Mus., 2014–. Hon. DLitt Southampton, 2010. Op. Telic Medal, 2003. *Publications:* (contrib.) From Our Own Correspondent, 2005; (contrib.) More From Our Own Correspondent, 2008; (contrib.) Oxford Handbook of War, 2012; (contrib.) Contemporary Writing on Conflict: reportage, 2014. *Address:* c/o Home Affairs Unit, BBC Broadcasting House, Portland Place, W1A 1AA. *Clubs:* Naval and Military, Royal Air Force.

WYATT, (Christopher) Terrel, FREng, FICE, FIStructE; Chairman, W. S. Atkins plc, 1987–98; *b* 17 July 1927; *s* of Lionel Harry Wyatt and Audrey Vere Wyatt; *m*; four *s*; *m* 1990, Patricia Perkins. *Educ:* Kingston Grammar Sch.; Battersea Polytechnic (BScEng); Imperial Coll. (DIC). FICE 1963; FIStructE 1963; FREng (FEng 1980). Served RE, 1946–48. Charles Brand & Son Ltd, 1948–54; Richard Costain Ltd, 1955–87: Dir, 1970–87; Gp Chief Exec., 1975–80; Dep. Chm., 1979–80; Chm., Costain Group PLC, 1980–87. *Recreation:* sailing. *Address:* Ryderswells Farm, Uckfield Road, Lewes, E Sussex BN8 5RN.

WYATT, David; HM Diplomatic Service, retired; owner, The Lime Leaf restaurant, Basingstoke; *b* 18 April 1946; *s* of Ernest Wyatt and Eva Mabel Wyatt (*née* Hayles); *m* 1st, 1969, Rosemary Elizabeth Clarke (*d* 2000); one *s* one *d*; 2nd, 2002, Sunthian Phujarn. *Educ:* Sandown Grammar Sch. Entered Diplomatic Service, 1965; Lusaka, 1968–71; SOAS, 1971–72; Third Sec. (Commercial), Bangkok, 1972–76; Second Secretary: Yaoundé, 1976–77; FCO, 1977–79; NDC, 1980; First Secretary: (Commercial), Athens, 1981–84; and Hd of Chancery, Bangkok, 1984–88; FCO, 1988–94; Dep. High Comr, Accra, 1994–98; Commercial Counsellor, Bangkok, 1999–2001; Dep. High Comr, Lagos, 2001–07. *Recreations:* running, reading, music.

WYATT, David Joseph, CBE 1977; Chairman, Crown Bio Systems, 2004–05 (consultant, 2003); HM Diplomatic Service, 1949–85; *b* 12 Aug. 1931; *s* of late Frederick Wyatt and Lena (*née* Parr); *m* 1st, 1957, Annemarie Angst (*d* 1978); two *s* one *d*; 2nd, 1990, Dr Wendy Baron, *qv*. *Educ:* Leigh Grammar Sch. National Service, RAF, 1950–52. Entered Foreign Service, 1949; Berne, 1954; FO, 1957–61; Second Sec., Vienna, 1961; First Sec., Canberra, 1965; FCO, 1969–71; First Sec., Ottawa, 1971; Counsellor, 1974; seconded Northern Ireland Office, Belfast, 1974–76; Counsellor and Head of Chancery, Stockholm, 1976–79; Under Sec. on loan to Home Civil Service, 1979–82; UK Mission to UN during 1982 General Assembly (personal rank of Ambassador); Minister and Dep. Comdt, British Mil. Govt, Berlin, 1983–85. Acting Dir Gen., Jan.–July 1990, Dir, Internat. Div., 1985–92, Advr on Internat. Relations, 1992–99, BRCS; Chm., Internat. Red Cross/Red Crescent Adv. Commn, 1996–97. FRSA 1991.

See also C. J. Wyatt.

WYATT, Derek Murray; *b* 4 Dec. 1949; *s* of late Reginald Swythin Wyatt and of Margaret Eira (*née* Holmden); *m* (marr. diss.); one *d* one *s*. *Educ:* St Luke's Coll., Exeter; Open Univ. (BA Hons); St Catherine's Coll., Oxford. History teacher, 1972–81; journalist and writer, 1982–84; editor, George Allen & Unwin Ltd, 1984–85; Dir and Publisher, William Heinemann Ltd, 1986–88; Dir, TSL Ltd, 1988–91; consultant, writer and journalist, 1992–94; Head of Programmes, Wire TV, 1994–95; Founder and Dir, Computer Channel, BSkyB, 1995–97. MP (Lab) Sittingbourne and Sheppey, 1997–2010. Mem., Select Cttee on Culture, Media and Sport, 1997–2005; Public Accounts Cttee, 2007. Chairman: All Party Parly Internet Cttee (founder), 1997–2007; All Party Parly Rugby Union Cttee, 1997–2010; All Party Parly British Council, 2000–10; (also Founder) All Party Zimbabwe Gp, 2003–05; All Party London Olympic and Paralympic Gp 2012, 2004–10; Co-Chairman: All Party Adventure and Recreation in Society Gp, 2004–06; All Party Parly Communications Gp, 2007–10. Parliamentary Private Secretary: DCMS, 2007–09; FCO, 2009. Member: Exec. Bd, CAABU, 2008–12; Egypt British Business Council, 2010–12. Dir, Crowdbnk, 2012–; Chairman: Great Retail Revival Foundn, 2013–; NICE NHS SE Innovation Hub, 2014–. Member: Bd, CITI, Columbia Univ., 2012–; Sounding Bd, Design Council, 2014–; SE RFU Legacy Gp, Rugby World Cup 2015, 2013–. Founder: Women's Sports Foundn (UK), 1985; Oxford Internet Inst., 2000; Digital Day for the Nation, 2007. Chm., Develt Cttee, Book Trust, 2014–; Trustee: Major Stanley's (Trustee Gp for OURFC), 1986– (Chm., 2012–); Citizen's Online, 2005–09; Patron: Time Bank, 2008– (Trustee, 2004–08); RIBA, 2013–14 (Mem., Liby Cttee, 2013–). Chm., Royal Trinity Hospice (formerly Trinity Hospice), 2011–. UK Ambassador for Eur. Year of the Brain 2014–15, 2013–15. Freeman, City of London, 2001; Liveryman, Co. of Information Technologists, 2012– (Mem., 2001–). Commendation for work on sport and apartheid, UNO, 1987. Elected Representative New Media Award, New Statesman, 2006; Internet Hero Award, Internet Services Providers' Assoc., 2006; Winner, MPs Awards, British Computer Society, 2007 and 2008. *Publications:* Wisecracks from the Movies, 1987; The International Rugby Almanack 1994, 1993; The International Rugby Almanack 1995, 1994; Rugby Disunion, 1995; (with Colin Herridge) Rugby Revolution, 2003; (with Colin Herridge) Rugby 2011: the teams, the stats, the history of the World Cup, 2011. *Recreations:* Rugby (played for Oxford University, Barbarians, England), film, jazz, reading, software, travelling, writing. *E:* derekwyatt@aol.com. *W:* www.derekwyatt.co.uk. *Clubs:* Royal Automobile; Vincent's (Oxford).

WYATT, Prof. Derrick Arthur; QC 1993; Professor of Law, 1996–2009, now Emeritus, and Visiting Professor of Law, 2009–14, University of Oxford; Fellow, St Edmund Hall, Oxford, since 1978; *b* 25 Feb. 1948; *s* of Iris Ross (formerly Wyatt, *née* Thompson) and step *s* of Alexander Ross; *m* 1970, (Margaret) Joan Cunnington; one *s* one *d*. *Educ:* Alsop High Sch.; Emmanuel Coll., Cambridge (MA, LLB); Univ. of Chicago Law Sch. (JD). Lectr in law, Univ. of Liverpool, 1971–75; called to the Bar, Lincoln's Inn, 1972; Fellow, Emmanuel Coll., Cambridge, 1975–78; CUF Lectr in Law, Oxford Univ., 1978–96; in practice as barrister (door tenant), Brick Court Chambers, 1986–. Vis. Prof., Florida State Univ., 1987. Mem., Acad. Adv. Bd, Jean Monnet Inter-Univ. Centre of Excellence, Opatija, 2010–. Member: Vale of White Horse DC, 1983–87; Abingdon Town Council, 1983–87. Mem. Editl Cttee, British Yearbook of Internat. Law, 1992–2012; Mem. Editl Bd, Croatian Yearbook of European Law and Policy, 2005–. Mem. Panel, Kuala Lumpur Regl Centre for Arbitration, 2014–. *Publications:* Wyatt and Dashwood's Substantive Law of the EEC, 1980, 6th edn as European Union Law, 2011; (ed with A. Barav) Yearbook of European Law, 1988–97; articles and reviews in learned jls. *Recreations:* walking, reading. *Address:* St Edmund Hall, Oxford OX1 4AR.

WYATT, Hugh Rowland, CVO 2009; Lord-Lieutenant of West Sussex, 1999–2008; *b* 18 Nov. 1933; *s* of late Brig. Richard John Penfold Wyatt, MC, TD and Hon. Margaret Agnes, *d* of 1st Baron Ebbisham, GBE; *m* 1959, Jane Ann Elizabeth Eden; one *s* two *d*. *Educ:* Winchester. 2nd Lieut, The Royal Sussex Regt, 1952–54; Captain, TA, 1954–61. Dir, McCorquodale plc, 1964–85; farmer. Chairman: Chichester Cathedral Trust, 1991–98; Chichester Dio. Bd of Finance, 1997–2001; Chichester Cathedral Council, 2001–09. High Sheriff of West Sussex, 1995–96. Pres., Royal Sussex Regtl Assoc., 1997–2008. KStJ 2001. *Recreations:* travel, opera. *Address:* The White Cottage, Nepcote, Findon, West Sussex BN14 0SD. *T:* (01903) 873328. *Club:* Sussex.

WYATT, Matthew Stephen Spence; Head, Syria Crisis Unit, Department for International Development, since 2013; *b* 2 June 1961; *s* of Ralph William Peter Wyatt and Susan Jennifer Wyatt; *m* 1994, Simonetta Fucecchi; one *s* one *d*. *Educ:* Lady Margaret Hall, Oxford (BA PPE 1983); College of Europe, Bruges (Dip. Higher European Studies 1984). Head: E Europe and Central Asia Dept, DFID, 1999–2001; DFID, Kenya, 2001–04; Permanent Rep. to UN Food and Agric. Agencies, Rome, 2004–06; Asst Pres., Ext. Affairs Dept, IFAD, 2006–09; Hd, Climate and Envmt Dept, 2009–13. *Recreations:* football, theatre, hiking. *Address:* Department for International Development, 22 Whitehall, SW1A 2EG. *Club:* Railway Wanderers (Nairobi).

WYATT, Prof. Terence Richard, (Terry), DPhil; FRS 2013; Professor of Physics, University of Manchester, since 2004; *b* Watford, 29 June 1957; *s* of Ernest Lawrence Wyatt and Pearl Evelyn Wyatt (*née* Sparkes); *m* 2001, Anne Marie Ryan; two *s*. *Educ:* Queen Elizabeth's Grammar Sch., Tamworth; Imperial Coll. London (BSc 1st Cl. Hons 1979; Govs' Prize for Phys 1979; ARCS); St Edmund Hall, Oxford (DPhil 1983). Computer programmer, Cosmic Ray and Space Phys Gp, Imperial Coll. London, 1975–76; research, Deutsches Elektron-Synchrotron, Hamburg, 1980–83; Res. Fellow, CERN, Geneva, 1984–86; Res. Associate, QMC, 1986–89; PPARC Advanced Res. Fellow, CERN/Univ. of Manchester, 1989–96; University of Manchester: Lectr in Phys, 1996–99; Reader in Phys, 1999–2004; PPARC Sen. Res. Fellow, 2003–06. Vis. Scientist, Fermi Nat. Accelerator Lab., 2002–03. Mem., Adv. Panel, Nurse Review, UK Res. Councils, 2015–. Mem., UK Cttee on CERN, BIS (formerly BERR), 2007–; Mem., Scientific Policy Cttee, 2007–, Chm., LHC Experiments Cttee, 2007–10, CERN. Member, Editorial Board: Eur. Phys. Jl C, 2010–; Progress of Theoretical and Experimental Physics, 2012–. Chadwick Medal and Prize, Inst. of Phys, 2011. *Publications:* approx. 800 articles in learned jls. *Recreations:* music (including playing the guitar), hill walking. *Address:* Particle Physics Group, School of Physics and Astronomy, University of Manchester, Oxford Road, Manchester M13 9PL. *T:* (0161) 275 4173, *Fax:* (0161) 275 0480. *E:* Terry.Wyatt@manchester.ac.uk. *W:* www.hep.man.ac.uk/u/wyatt.

WYATT, Terrel; *see* Wyatt, C. T.

WYATT, Wendy, (Mrs D. J. Wyatt); *see* Baron, O. W.

WYATT, Will; *see* Wyatt, A. W.

WYBAR, Linda; Headteacher, Tunbridge Wells Girls' Grammar School, since 1999; *b* 21 June 1959; *d* of late Thomas Smith Clough and of Mary Clough; *m* 1995, Geoffrey Wybar; two *s*. *Educ:* Blyth Grammar Sch.; Univ. of Hull (BA Hons Eng. Lang. and Lit. 1980; PGCE Dist. 1981); Open Univ. (MA Educn Mgt 1996). English Teacher: Rede Sch., Strood, 1981–82; Highworth Grammar Sch., Ashford, 1982–86; Hd of English, Norton Knatchbull Boys' Grammar Sch., Ashford, 1986–92; Dep. Headteacher, Highworth Grammar Sch., Sittingbourne, 1992–99. Chm., Kent and Medway Grammar Schs Assoc., 2004–. *Recreations:* reading modern fiction, theatre-going, wine-tasting, relaxing in Cornwall. *Address:* Tunbridge Wells Girls' Grammar School, Southfield Road, Tunbridge Wells, Kent TN4 9UJ. *T:* (01892) 520902, *Fax:* (01892) 536497. *E:* admin@twggs.kent.sch.uk.

WYETH, Mark Charles; QC 2009; *b* Kingsbury, London, 27 Sept. 1960; *s* of Derek Wyeth and Rosemary Jean Wyeth; *m* 1987, Mary Patricia Austin; one *s* two *d*. *Educ:* Abbotsfield Sch., Middx; Leicester Poly. (BA Hons Law); London Sch. of Econs (LLM Commercial Law). Called to the Bar, Inner Temple, 1983; Founder and Hd of Chambers, 2 Paper Buildings, Temple, 1988–99; 5 Paper Buildings, 1999–. Panel List QC, Serious Fraud Office, 2010–. Mem. Cttee, Bar Standards Bd, 2005–10. Organiser with Amer. Bar Assoc. Accreditation, London Law Consortium, 1991–. Chm., Disciplinary Appeals Cttee, CIPFA, 2010–13. Vis. Prof., Coll. of Law, Univ. of Iowa, 1995–. *Recreations:* founder of Club Ska records and films, bass player with Symarip, sleeve notes for various music CD and DVD releases, articles for music and sport periodicals, Chelsea Football Club. *Address:* 5 Paper Buildings, Temple, EC4Y 7HB. *T:* (020) 7583 6117, *Fax:* (020) 7353 0075. *E:* clerks@5pb.co.uk. *Clubs:* MCC, Bar Yacht.

WYKE, Prof. John Anthony, PhD; Professor, Faculty of Medicine, University of Glasgow, 1991–92, now Professor Emeritus; Director, Scottish Cancer Foundation, since 2002 (Chairman, 2002–10); *b* 5 April 1942; *s* of late Eric John Edward Wyke and Daisy Anne Wyke (*née* Dormer); *m* 1968, Anne Wynne Mitchell; one *s*. *Educ:* Dulwich Coll.; St John's Coll., Cambridge (Schol.; VetMB, MA); Univ. of Glasgow; UCL (PhD). MRCVS. FRSE 1989. Postdoctoral res., Univ. of Washington and Univ. of Southern California, 1970–72; Imperial Cancer Research Fund: scientific staff, London, 1972–83; Head, ICRF Labs at St Bartholomew's Hosp., 1983–87; Asst Dir, 1985–87; Dir, Beatson Inst. for Cancer Res., 1987–2002. Dir, Worldwide Cancer Res. (formerly Assoc. for Internat. Cancer Res.), 2003–. Mem. Council, RVC, 2008–12; Trustee, RSE Scotland Foundn, 2012–. Founder FMedSci 1998. Hon. FRCVS 1999. Hon. Fellow, Univ. of Glasgow, 2004. *Publications:* more than 100 scientific articles. *Recreations:* hill walking, ski-ing, gardening. *Address:* 6 Ledcameroch Road, Bearsden, Glasgow G61 4AA. *E:* johnwyke@hotmail.co.uk.

WYKES, Dr David Lewis; Director, Dr Williams's Trust and Library, since 1998; Co-Director, Dr Williams's Centre for Dissenting Studies, 2004–15; *b* 29 June 1954; *s* of Christopher Lewis Wykes, FCA and Joan Margaret Wykes; *m* 1997, Dr Elizabeth Jane Clapp. *Educ:* Univ. of Durham (BSc); Univ. of Leicester (PhD 1987). Mem. of Ct, Leicester Univ., 1985–. Hon. Reader, QMUL, 2007–15. FRHistS 2002. *Publications:* (ed with Dr S. J. C. Taylor) Parliament and Dissent, 2005; (with Prof. I. Rivers) Joseph Priestley, Scientist, Philosopher, and Theologian, 2008; (with Prof. I. Rivers) Dissenting Praise: religious dissent and the hymn in England and Wales, 2011; numerous articles in academic and learned jls. *Recreations:* chamber music, walking, history. *Address:* Dr Williams's Library, 14 Gordon Square, WC1H 0AR. *T:* (020) 7387 3727.

WYLD, David John Charles; Secretary General, International Law Association, 1993–2014; *b* Inverness, 11 March 1943; *s* of John Wyld and Helen Leslie Wyld; *m* 1st, 1970, Sally Morgan (marr. diss.); two *s*; 2nd, 1987, Caroline Alexander; three *d*. *Educ:* Harrow Sch.; Christ Church, Oxford (BA Eng. Lit. 1961); Coll. of Law; Queen Mary, Univ. of London (LLM Internat. Law 2007). Admitted as solicitor, 1974; Partner: Macfarlanes, 1980–2001; David Wyld & Co., 2001–13. Clerk to Governing Body, St Paul's Sch., 2013–. Chm., City of London Law Soc., 2000–04. *Recreations:* reading, walking, golf, theatre. *Address:* Ground Floor Flat, 20 Cresswell Road, Twickenham, Middx TW1 2DZ. *T:* 07771 531951. *E:* davidwyld1943@gmail.com. *Clubs:* Garrick; Berkshire Golf, Honourable Company of Edinburgh Golfers (Muirfield).

See also M. H. Wyld.

WYLD, Martin Hugh, CBE 1997; painting conservator; Chief Restorer, National Gallery, 1979–2009; *b* 14 Sept. 1944; *s* of John Wyld and Helen Leslie Melville; one *s* one *d*. *Educ:* Harrow School. Assistant Restorer, National Gallery, 1966. *Recreation:* travel. *Address:* Flat 5, 23 Clapham Common West Side, SW4 9AN. *T:* (020) 7978 5036. *Club:* MCC.

See also D. J. C. Wyld.

WYLDE, Dr Richard John, FREng; Owner and Managing Director, Thomas Keating Ltd, scientific instrument manufacturers, since 1983; *b* London, 16 Feb. 1958; *s* of John Wylde and Nancy Wylde (*née* Stewart); *m* 1986, Lucy Wilcock; two *s*. *Educ:* Eton Coll.; Sidney Sussex Coll., Cambridge (BA Nat. Sci. 1979); Queen Mary Coll., Univ. of London (PhD Physics 1985). FIET 1999; FInstP 2013. Sen. Vis. Fellow, Dept of Phys, QMC, subseq. QMW, 1986–2002; Hon. Reader, Dept of Phys and Astronomy, Univ. of St Andrews, 2002–. Associate Scientist, ESA Planck Mission, 2009–. FREng 2013. Mem., Cave Diving Section, Nat. Speleological Soc. Liveryman, Innholders' Co., 1990–. *Publications:* contrib. papers to microwave and antenna jls. *Recreations:* mapping underwater caves, ski touring, horse riding, quantum field theory. *Address:* Churchwood, Fittleworth, W Sussex RH20 1HP. *T:* (01798) 865324, *Fax:* (01403) 785464. *E:* r.wylde@terahertz.co.uk. *Club:* Downhill Only (Wengen).

WYLIE, Alexander Featherstonhaugh; *see* Kinclaven, Hon. Lord.

WYLIE, Andrew; President, The Wylie Agency, since 1980; *b* 4 Nov. 1947; *s* of Craig and Angela Fowler Wylie; *m* 1969, Christina Meyer; one *s*; *m* 1980, Camilla Carlini; one *s* one *d*. *Educ:* St Paul's Sch.; Harvard Coll. (BA *magna cum laude* 1970). Established: Wylie Agency, NY, 1980; London office, 1996; Madrid office, 1999. Mem., Council on Foreign Relns, 2006–. *Recreations:* running, bicycling, tennis. *Address:* The Wylie Agency LLC, 250 West 57th Street, Suite 2114, New York, NY 10107, USA. *T:* (212) 2460069; The Wylie Agency (UK) Ltd, 17 Bedford Square, WC1B 3JA. *T:* (020) 7908 5900. *Clubs:* Knickerbocker, Harvard, River (New York); Southampton, Bathing Corporation, Meadow Club (Southampton, NY).

WYLIE, Prof. Christopher Craig; William Schubert Professor of Developmental Biology, and Director, Developmental Biology Division, Children's Hospital Medical Center, Cincinnati, 2000–13, now Emeritus Professor of Pediatrics; *b* 15 Sept. 1945; *s* of Joseph and Edna Wylie; *m* 1st, 1969, Christine Margaret Hall; 2nd, 1976, Janet Heasman; three *s* one *d*. *Educ:* Mombasa Primary Sch.; Duke of York Sch., Nairobi; Chislehurst and Sidcup County Grammar School for Boys; University College London (BSc, 1st cl. Hons Anatomy 1966; PhD 1971). Lectr in Anatomy, University College London, 1969; St George's Hospital Medical School: Sen. Lectr in Anatomy, 1975; Reader, 1983; Prof., 1985; F. J. Quick Prof. of Biol., Cambridge Univ., 1988–94, now Prof. Emeritus; Fellow, Darwin Coll., Cambridge, 1989–94; University of Minnesota: Martin Lenz Harrison Prof. of Develtl Biol. and Genetics, 1994–2000; Dir, Develtl Biol. Centre, 1994–2000; Dir, Develtl Genetics Prog., Sch. of Med., 1994–2000. Vis. Asst Prof. in Biology, Dartmouth Coll., 1975; Vis. Associate Prof. of Anatomy, Harvard Med. Sch., 1981. Editor in Chief, Development (internat. jl of develt biol.), 1987–2003; Series Ed., Develtl and Cell Biol. Monographs, 1986–. *Publications:* (ed jtly) Development and Evolution, 1983; (ed jtly) Current Problems in Germ Cell Differentiation, 1983; (ed jtly) A History of Embryology, 1984; (ed jtly) Determinative Mechanisms in Early Development, 1986; 176 papers and review articles in sci. jls of biology. *Recreations:* relaxing with the family, racket sports, golf, history of biomedical science. *Address:* 66 Harvey Farm Road, Waterbury Center, VT 05677, USA.

WYLIE, Dr Ian Martin; Chief Executive, Royal College of Obstetricians and Gynaecologists, since 2010; *b* 22 Oct. 1955; *s* of Charles Ronald Wylie and Margaret (*née* Catanach); *m* 1987, Siân Meryl Griffiths, *qv*; one *s*, and two step *d*. *Educ:* Bedford Modern Sch.; St Peter's Coll., Oxford (MA Hons); DPhil Oxon 1985. Manager, Homeless Services, Bloomsbury HA, 1982–84; Primary Care Officer, 1984–86, PR Consultant, 1986–88, City and Hackney HA; Press and Information Manager, Oxford CC, 1988–92; Dir, Public Relns, Oxford RHA, 1992–94; King's Fund: Hd, Communications, 1994–97; Dir, Corporate Affairs, 1997–2000; Chief Exec., BDA, 2001–05; Associate Prof., Faculty of Social Sci., Chinese Univ. of Hong Kong, 2006; Chief Exec., TreeHouse (nat. charity for autism educn), 2006–09; Sen. Officer, Service Planning and Develt, Hong Kong Hosp. Authy, 2009–10. Chairman: Thames Vale Youth Orch., 2003–05; Autism Educn Trust, 2007–08. Trustee: Crouch End Festival Chorus, 2009–10; Faculty of Med. Leadership and Mgt, 2013–. *Publications:* Young Coleridge and the Philosophers of Nature, 1989; (with Sarah Harvey) Patient Power, 1999. *Recreations:* writing, opera, family. *Address:* Royal College of Obstetricians and Gynaecologists, 27 Sussex Place, Regent's Park, NW1 4RG. *Club:* Garrick.

WYLIE, Rose, RA 2015; artist and painter, since 1951; *b* Hythe, Kent, 14 Oct. 1934; *d* of Alexander Forrest Wylie, OBE and Barbara Wylie (*née* Hewat Gillmon); *m* 1957, Roy Oxlade, artist, painter (*d* 2013); one *s* two *d*. *Educ:* Folkestone and Dover Sch. of Art (NDD 1956); Royal Coll. of Art (MA 1981). Foundn Lectr, Art Sch., Denbighshire Tech. Coll., 1965–68; Sen. Lectr, Art Dept, Sittingbourne Coll. of Educn, 1972–79; Sen. Lectr (pt-time), Tunbridge Wells Adult Educn Centre, 1986–2000. Exhibitions include: retrospective, Jerwood Gall., Hastings, 2012; BP Spotlight, Tate Britain, 2013. Dupree Award, 1999, Charles Wollaston Award, 2015, RA; Paul Hamlyn Prize for Visual Arts, 2011; John Moores Painting Prize, 2014. *Recreations:* film, music, literature, art. *Address:* c/o UNION Gallery, 94 Teesdale Street, E2 6PU. *T:* (020) 3176 7303, *Fax:* (020) 7729 9461. *E:* info@union-gallery.com.

WYLIE, Siân Meryl, (Mrs Ian Wylie); *see* Griffiths, S. M.

WYLLIE, Andrew, CBE 2015; FREng; Chief Executive, Costain Group, since 2005; *b* 24 Dec. 1962; *s* of Kenneth David Wyllie and Margaret Emily Wyllie; *m* 1990, Jane Morag Hudson; one *d*. *Educ:* Dunfermline High Sch.; Univ. of Strathclyde (BSc Hons 1984); London Business Sch. (MBA 1993). CEng 1991; FICE; FREng 2009; CCMI 2009. With Taylor Woodrow, 1984–2005, Man. Dir, Taylor Woodrow Construction Ltd, 2001–05. Non-exec. Dir, Scottish Water, 2009–. Vice Pres., ICE, 2015–. Fellow, British American Project, 2003–. FInstD. *Address:* Costain Group plc, Costain House, Vanwall Business Park, Maidenhead, Berks SL6 4UB. *T:* (01628) 842444, *Fax:* (01628) 842554.

WYLLIE, Prof. Andrew David Hamilton, FRS 1995; FRSE; FMedSci; Professor of Pathology and Fellow of St John's College, Cambridge University, 1998–2011. *Educ:* Aberdeen Univ. (BSc 1964; MB ChB 1967; PhD 1975). MRCP 1971; MRCPath 1975, FRCPath 1987; FRCPE 1993. Res. Fellow, Hammersmith Hosp., 1969; Res. Fellow, then Lectr in Pathol., Aberdeen Univ., 1970–72; Edinburgh University: Lectr, 1972–77; Sen. Lectr, 1977–85; Reader, 1985–92; Prof. of Experimental Pathology, 1992–98. FRSE 1991; FMedSci 1998. Hon. DSc Aberdeen, 1998. *Publications:* scientific papers on colorectal cancer and apoptosis. *Address:* St John's College, Cambridge CB2 1TP.

WYLLIE, Very Rev. Hugh Rutherford; Moderator of the General Assembly of the Church of Scotland, 1992–93; Minister at the Old Parish Church of Hamilton, 1981–2000; *b* 11 Oct. 1934; *s* of late Hugh McPhee Wyllie and Elizabeth Buchanan; *m* 1962, Eileen Elizabeth Cameron, MA; two *d*. *Educ:* Shawlands Acad., Glasgow; Hutchesons' Grammar Sch., Glasgow; Univ. of Glasgow (MA; Pitcairn Miller Frame Awards, 1961, 1962). The Union Bank of Scotland, 1951–53 (MCIBS). RAF Nat. Service, 1953–55. Licensed and ordained by Presbytery of Glasgow, 1962; Asst Minister, Glasgow Cathedral, 1962–65; Minister: Dunbeth Church, Coatbridge, 1965–72; Cathcart South Church, Glasgow, 1972–81. General Assembly: Convener: Stewardship and Budget Cttee, 1978–83; Stewardship and Finance Bd, 1983–86; Assembly Council, 1987–91; Member: Bd of Nomination to Church Chairs, 1985–91, 1993–99; Bd of Practice and Procedure, 1991–95; Bd of Communication, 1999–2003. Presbytery of Hamilton: Moderator, 1989–90; Convener, Business Cttee, 1991–95; Chaplain: Royal British Legion (Hamilton Br.), 1981–2001; Lanarks Burma Star Assoc., 1983–2001; Strathclyde Police 'Q' Div., 1983–2001. Master, Hamilton Hosp., 1982–2001; Vice-Chm., Lanarkshire Healthcare NHS Trust, 1996–99 (non-exec. Dir, 1995–99); Trustee, Lanarkshire Primary Care NHS Trust, 1999–2001. Established Centre for Information for the Unemployed, Hamilton, 1983; introduced Dial-a-Fact on drugs and alcohol, 1986; established Hamilton Church History Project, 1984–87; Pres., Glasgow Univ. SCM, 1958; Chm., SCM Scottish Council, 1958. Mem. Council, Scout Assoc., 1993–2004. Pres., Hamilton Burns Club, 1990. Hon. Freeman, District of Hamilton, 1992; Freeman, City of Winnipeg, Canada, 1992. Dr William Barclay Meml Fund Lectr, 1994. Hon. FCIBS 1997. Hon. DD Aberdeen, 1993. George and Thomas Hutcheson Award, Hutchesons' Grammar Sch., Glasgow, 2002. *Recreations:* gardening, bowling, the internet. *Address:* 18 Chantinghall Road, Hamilton ML3 8NP.

WYLLIE, Prof. Peter John, PhD; FRS 1984; Professor of Geology, California Institute of Technology, 1983–99, now Emeritus (Chairman, Division of Geological and Planetary Sciences, 1983–87; Academic Officer, 1994–99); *b* 8 Feb. 1930; *s* of George William and Beatrice Gladys Wyllie (*née* Weaver); *m* 1956, Frances Rosemary Blair; one *s* one *d* (and one *s* one *d* decd). *Educ:* Univ. of St Andrews. BSc 1952 (Geology and Physics); BSc 1955 (1st cl. hons Geology); PhD 1958 (Geology). Nat. Service, 1948–49: Aircraftsman First Cl. (Best Recruit, Basic Trng, Padgate, 1948). Heavyweight boxing champion, RAF, Scotland, 1949. Glaciologist, British W Greenland Expedn, 1950; Geologist, British N Greenland Expedn, 1952–54; Asst Lectr in Geology, Univ. of St Andrews, 1955–56; Research Asst, 1956–58, Asst Prof. of Geochemistry, 1958–59, Pennsylvania State Univ.; Research Fellow in Chemistry, 1959–60, Lectr in Exptl Petrology, 1960–61, Leeds Univ.; Associate Prof. of Petrology, Pennsylvania State Univ., 1961–65 (Acting Head, Dept Geochem. and Mineralogy, 1962–63); University of Chicago: Prof. of Petrology and Geochem., 1965–77; Master Phys. Scis, Collegiate Div., Associate Dean of Coll. and of Phys. Scis Div., 1972–73; Homer J. Livingston Prof., 1978–83; Chm., Dept of Geophysical Scis, 1979–82. Louis Murray Vis. Fellow, Univ. of Cape Town, 1987; Hon. Prof., Chinese Univ. of Geosciences, Beijing, 1996–. Man. Ed., Jl Petrology, 1965–67; Ed., Jl Geol., 1967–83; Ed.-in-Chief, Minerals and Rocks monograph series (25 vols), 1967–88. President: Mineralogical Soc. of America, 1977–78 (Vice Pres., 1976–77); Internat. Mineralogical Assoc., 1986–90 (Vice Pres., 1978–86); Internat. Union of Geodesy and Geophysics, 1995–99 (Vice Pres., 1991–95). Foreign Associate, US Nat. Acad. of Scis, 1981 (Chm. Cttee on Solid-Earth Sciences and Society, report published 1993); Fellow: Amer. Acad. of Arts and Scis, 1982; Amer. Geophys. Union; Geol Soc. Amer.; Mineral Soc. Amer., 1965; Corresp. Fellow, Edin. Geol Soc., 1985–; Hon. Fellow, IUGG, 2015; Foreign Fellow: Indian Geophys. Union, 1987; Indian Nat. Sci. Acad., 1991; Nat. Acad. of Scis, India, 1992; Foreign Member: Russian (formerly USSR) Acad. of Scis, 1988; Chinese Acad. of Scis, 1996; Academia Europaea, 1996. Hon. Member: Mineralogical Soc. of GB and Ireland, 1986–; Mineralogical Soc. of Russia, 1986–; German Geological Soc., 2001–. Hon. DSc St Andrews, 1974. Polar Medal, 1954; Mineralogical Soc. of America Award, 1965; Quantrell Award for excellence in undergrad. teaching, Univ. of Chicago, 1979; Wollaston Medal, Geol Soc. of London, 1982; Abraham-Gottlob-Werner Medal, German Mineral Soc., 1987; Roebling Medal, Mineralogical Soc. of America, 2001; Leopold von Buch Medal, Deutschen Geologischen Ges., 2001. *Publications:* Ultramafic and Related Rocks, 1967; The Dynamic Earth, 1971; The Way the Earth Works, 1976; (ed) Solid-Earth Sciences and Society, 1993; numerous papers in sci. jls. *Address:* Division of Geological and Planetary Sciences, 170–25 California Institute of Technology, Pasadena, CA 91125, USA.

WYMAN, Peter Lewis, CBE 2006; DL; FCA; Senior Advisor, Albright Stonebridge Group LLC, since 2010; Principal, Peter Wyman Private Clients, since 2010; Chairman: Yeovil District Hospital NHS Foundation Trust, since 2011; Sir Richard Sutton Estates Ltd (formerly Sir Richard Sutton's Settled Estates), since 2011 (Director, since 2010); *b* 26 Feb. 1950; *s* of late John Bernard Wyman and Joan Dorethea Wyman (*née* Beighton); *m* 1978, Joy Alison Foster; one *s* one *d*. *Educ:* Epsom Coll. ACA 1973, FCA 1978. Chartered Accountant; articled clerk, Ogden Parsons & Co. and Harmood Banner, 1968–73; Deloitte Haskins & Sells, then Coopers & Lybrand, subseq. PricewaterhouseCoopers LLP: Manager, 1973–78; Partner, 1978–2010; Hd of Tax, 1993–98; Hd of External Relations, 1998–2000; Hd of Regulatory Policy, 2003–04; Hd of Professional Affairs and Regulatory Policy, 2004–09; Global Leader, Public Policy and Regulatory Matters, 2008–10. Mem. Cttee, London Soc. of Chartered Accountants, 1981–90 (Chm., 1987–88); Institute of Chartered Accountants in England and

Wales: Mem. Council, 1991–2009; Chm., Faculty of Taxation, 1991–95; Chm., Educn and Trng Directorate, 1995–99; Chm., Professional Standards Office, 1999–2000; Mem., Exec. Cttee, 1996–2003; Vice Pres., 2000–01; Dep. Pres., 2001–02; Pres., 2002–03; Chm., Outstanding Achievement Award Selection Panel, 2011–14; International Federation of Accountants: Member: Transnat. Auditors' Cttee, 2006–08; Planning and Finance Cttee, 2006–08; Internat. Regulatory Liaison Cttee, 2008–10. Chairman: Common Content for Accountancy Qualifications Steering Gp, 2002–06; Consultative Cttee of Accountancy Bodies, 2002–03; Rev. Gp, Financial Reporting Adv. Bd, 2010–11; Dep. Chm., Financial Reporting Council, 2002–03. Special Advr on Deregulation and Taxation to Parly Under-Sec. of State for Corporate Affairs, 1993–94; Member: Deregulation Task Force, 1994–97; Panel on Takeovers and Mergers, 2002–03. External Overseer, Contributions Agency/IR Jt Working Prog., 1995–97; Member: Regulation of Accounting Profession Implementation Working Party, 1999–2001; Steering Gp, Rev. of Regulatory Régime of Accountancy Profession, 2003–04; Audit, Risk and Governance Cttee, RSA, 2005–11; EU Adv. Gp, City of London, 2004–09; Bd, Companies Hse, 2011– (Chm., Audit Cttee, 2011–); Supervisory Bd, Focal & Co., 2012–14. Chairman: Somerset Community Foundn, 2009–15 (Dir, 2003–04); Adv. Bd, Pasco Risk Mgt Ltd, 2011–13 (Mem., 2010–13). Dir, City of London Sinfonia, 2011–. FRSA. Freeman, City of London, 1988; Freeman, 1988, Master, 2006–07, Almoner, 2011–14, Chartered Accountants' Co. Member: Council, Univ. of Bath, 2003–06 and 2009– (Mem., Finance Cttee, 2003–; Treas., 2011–); Adv. Bd, BPP Business Sch., 2010–11; Develt Adv. Council, Inst. Econ. Affairs, 2011–13. Gov., Aylwin Girls' Sch., Southwark, 2001–06 (Vice-Chm., 2001–03; Chm., 2003–06); Chm., F & GP Cttee, Harris Acad., Bermondsey, 2006–07; Trustee, Five Bridges Sch., Vauxhall, 2002–05. Trustee, Hestercombe Gdns Trust, 2010–11. DL Somerset, 2015. Award for Outstanding Achievement, ICAEW, 2006; Award for Outstanding Industry Contribution, Accountancy Age, 2008. *Publications:* various professional jls on taxation and accountancy matters. *Recreations:* music, history, family history, equestrian sports, gardening. *Address:* Plainsfield Court, Plainsfield, Over Stowey, Somerset TA5 1HH. *T:* 07711 776128; Flat 1, Priory House, 3 Burgon Street, EC4V 5DR. *Club:* 1900.

WYN, Eurig; *b* 10 Oct. 1944; *s* of Albert and Alvira Davies; *m* 1972, Gillian; one *s* one *d. Educ:* Univ. of Wales, Aberystwyth. Journalist/presenter, BBC Wales, 1970–75; Organiser, Plaid Cymru Party, 1975–78; Develt Officer, Community Co-operative Movt, 1978–82; freelance journalist, newspapers and BBC radio, 1982–85. Mem. (Plaid Cymru) Gwynedd CC, 1982–99. MEP (Plaid Cymru) Wales, 1999–2004. Mem. and Vice Pres., Cttee of the Regions, EU, 1994–99. Contested (Plaid Cymru) Ynys Môn, 2005. *Address:* Y Frenni, Waunfawr, Caernarfon, Gwynedd LL55 4YY. *T:* (01286) 650512.

WYN GRIFFITH, Martin Peter; Commercial Director, Department for Business, Innovation and Skills, 2009–10; *b* 2 Feb. 1957; *s* of Hugh and Simone Wyn Griffith; *m* 2006, Jo; one step *s* one step *d. Educ:* Manchester Grammar Sch.; Univ. of Bristol (BA Jt Hons); Henley Mgt Coll. (MBA). EMI Records Ltd, 1978–84; Man. Dir, AWGO Ltd, 1984–92; Mktg Dir, EMI Music, 1994–96; Business Advr, 1996–97, Manager, 1997–99, and Chief Exec., 1999–2001, Business Link Wilts; Chief Exec., Business Link Berks and Wilts, 2001–02; Chief Exec., Small Business Service, DTI, later Enterprise Directorate, BERR, 2002–08; Dir, Service Transformation, BIS, 2008–09. Chm. Trustees, UnLtd, 2013– (Trustee, 2008–). *Publications:* contribs on entrepreneurship in entertainment and the future for multimedia to Jl Strategic Mgt. *Recreations:* motor racing, ski-ing, golf, Manchester United.

WYN-ROGERS, Catherine; mezzo-soprano; *b* 24 July 1954; *d* of Geoffrey Wyn Rogers and Helena Rogers (*née* Webster). *Educ:* St Helena High Sch. for Girls, Chesterfield; Royal Coll. of Music. Studied with Meriel St Clair, Ellis Keeler and Diane Forlano. Performances: with various European orchs and choirs, incl. BBC SO, LPO, CBSO, RSNO, BBC Scottish Orch., RLPO, Accademia di Santa Cecilia, Rome, and Concertgebouw; with various opera cos incl. Royal Opera, Scottish Opera, WNO, Opera North, ENO, Bavarian State Opera and Teatro Real, Madrid; frequent appearances at BBC Proms, Aldeburgh, Salzburg and Edinburgh Fests; Glyndebourne début, 2013. Numerous recordings. *Address:* c/o Askonas Holt, Lincoln House, 300 High Holborn, WC1V 7JH.

WYNDHAM, family name of **Baron Egremont and Leconfield**.

WYNDHAM, Henry Mark; Chairman, Sotheby's Europe, since 1997; *b* London, 19 Aug. 1953; *s* of Hon. Mark Hugh Wyndham, OBE, MC and Anne Wyndham; *m* 1978, Rachel Sarah Pritchard; three *s. Educ:* Eton; Univ. Paris Sorbonne. Dir, Christies, 1982; Proprietor, Henry Wyndham Fine Art, 1987–93; Chm., Sotheby's UK, 1994–2004. Trustee: Glyndebourne, 2004–14; Chatsworth House Trust, 2004–; Towner Art Gall., Eastbourne, 2014–. Mem. Court, Goldsmiths' Co., 2008–12. *Recreations:* many sports, tennis, golf, supporting Brighton and Hove Albion, travelling, music, going to the bottle bank, bonfires, growing vegetables, picking up rubbish off beaches on Colonsay, spending time with my family. *Address:* 18 St Leonards Terrace, SW3 4QG. *T:* (office) (020) 7293 5057. *E:* henry.wyndham@sothebys.com. *Clubs:* MCC (Mem. Cttee, 1988–91; Chm., Arts and Liby Cttee, 1993–98), White's, Pratt's, Saints & Sinners, Aberdino, Grillions, Mark's, George, 5 Hertford Street.

WYNESS, James Alexander Davidson; Senior Independent Director, Spirent (formerly Bowthorpe) plc, 1999–2006 (Director, 1979–2006; Acting Chairman, 2002); *b* 27 Aug. 1937; *s* of late Dr James Alexander Davidson Wyness and Millicent Margaret (*née* Beaton); *m* 1966, Josephine Margaret Worsdell; three *d. Educ:* Stockport Grammar Sch.; Emmanuel Coll., Cambridge (MA, LLB). National Service, 2 Lieut, RA. Articled Clerk, A. F. & R. W. Tweedie, 1964–66 (qualified 1965); Linklaters & Paines, 1966–97: Partner, 1970–97; Managing Partner, 1987–91; Jt Sen. Partner, 1991–93; Sen. Partner, 1994–96. Dir, Saracens Ltd, 1996– (Chm., 1996–2002). Mem., Law Soc. Mem., Co. of City of London Solicitors. Life Member: Saracens FC (RFU) (Captain, 1962–65); Middx RFU; London Div. RFU. *Recreations:* visiting France, growing vegetables, Rugby football, reading. *Address:* c/o Linklaters, One Silk Street, EC2Y 8HQ.

WYNFORD, 9th Baron *cr* 1829, of Wynford Eagle, co. Dorset; **John Philip Robert Best;** chartered surveyor; Executive Partner, Wynford Eagle Partners, running family estate in Dorset, since 1981; *b* 23 Nov. 1950; *o s* of 8th Baron Wynford, MBE and Anne Daphne Mametz (*née* Minshull Ford); *S* father, 2002; *m* 1981, Fenella Christian Mary Danks; one *s* one *d. Educ:* Radley Coll.; Keele Univ. (BA Hons 1974); RAC Cirencester (MRAC 1977). MRICS (Land Agency Div.) 1979. Mem., Wynford Eagle Parish Council, 1996–. *Recreations:* reading, music, fine claret, 17th century oak furniture. *Heir: s* Hon. Harry Robert Francis Best, *b* 9 May 1987. *Address:* The Manor, Wynford Eagle, Dorchester, Dorset DT2 0ER. *T:* (01300) 320763.

WYNFORD-THOMAS, Prof. David, PhD, DSc; FRCPath; Pro-Vice Chancellor, Dean of Medicine and Head of College of Medicine, Biological Sciences and Psychology, University of Leicester, 2008–15; *b* 28 Feb. 1955; *s* of Richard and Eunice Wynford-Thomas; *m* 2004, Theresa; one *s* two *d. Educ:* Welsh Nat. Sch. of Medicine (MB BCh Hons 1978; PhD 1981); DSc Wales 1995. FRCPath 1996. MRC/NIH Postdoctoral Res. Fellow, Univ. of Colorado, 1982–83; University of Wales College of Medicine: Lectr, 1983–86, Sen. Lectr, 1986–92, in Pathology; Prof. and Hd, Dept of Pathology, 1992–2005; Dean and Hd of Sch. of Medicine, Cardiff Univ., 2005–08. Hon. Consultant in Molecular Pathology, 1986–. FMedSci 2003. Subject Editor, British Jl of Cancer, 1995–. *Publications:* (ed with E. D. Williams) Thyroid Tumours, 1989; co-author of over 150 peer-reviewed papers in scientific and med. jls. *Recreations:* chess, walking, reading. *Address:* Maurice Shock Medical Sciences Building, University of Leicester, PO Box 138, University Road, Leicester LE1 9HN.

WYNGAARDEN, James Barnes, MD; FRCP; Principal, Washington Advisory Group, 1996–2002; Foreign Secretary, National Academy of Sciences, Washington, 1990–94; *b* 19 Oct. 1924; *s* of Martin Jacob Wyngaarden and Johanna Kempers Wyngaarden; *m* 1946, Ethel Dean Vredevoogd (marr. diss. 1976); one *s* four *d. Educ:* Calvin College; Western Michigan University; University of Michigan. MD 1948; FRCP 1984. Investigator, NIH, 1953–56; Associate Prof. of Medicine, Duke Univ. Med. Center, 1956–61; Prof. of Medicine, Duke Univ. Med. Sch., 1961–65; Chairman, Dept of Medicine: Univ. of Pennsylvania Med. Sch., 1965–67; Duke Univ. Med. Sch., 1967–82; Dir, NIH, 1982–89; Assoc. Dir, Life Scis, Exec. Office of the President of USA, 1989–90. Hon. DSc: Michigan, 1980; Ohio, 1984; Illinois, 1985; George Washington, 1986; S Carolina, 1989; Western Michigan, 1989; Duke, 2006; Hon. PhD Tel Aviv, 1987. *Publications:* (ed jtly) The Metabolic Basis of Inherited Disease, 1960, 5th edn 1983; (with O. Sperling and A. DeVries) Purine Metabolism in Man, 1974; (with W. N. Kelley) Gout and Hyperuricemia, 1976; (with L. H. Smith) Review of Internal Medicine; a self-assessment guide, 1979, 3rd edn 1985; (ed jtly) Cecil Textbook of Medicine, 15th edn 1979 to 19th edn 1992. *Recreations:* tennis, ski-ing, painting.

WYNN, family name of **Baron Newborough**.

WYNN, Sir (David) Watkin W.; *see* Williams-Wynn.

WYNN, Terence; Member (Lab) North West Region, England, European Parliament, 1999–2006 (Merseyside East, 1989–94, Merseyside East and Wigan, 1994–99); *b* 27 June 1946; *s* of Ernest Wynn and Lily (*née* Hitchen); *m* 1967, Doris Ogden; one *s* one *d. Educ:* Leigh Technical Coll.; Riversdale Technical Coll., Liverpool (OND); Liverpool Polytechnic (Combined Chief Engrs Cert); Salford Univ. (MSc Manpower Studies and Industrial Relns 1984). Seagoing Marine Engr Officer, MN, 1962–74; Engr Surveyor, ICI, Runcorn, 1975–76; Ship Repair Man., Manchester Dry Docks, 1976–78; Trng Advr, Shipbuilding ITB, 1978–82; Sen. Trng Exec., Marine Trng Assoc., 1982–89. Member, Ethics Cttee, EC, 2010–. Trustee, Action for Children (formerly NCH), 2007–13. Adjunct Sen. Fellow, Nat. Centre for Res. on Europe, Univ. of Canterbury, NZ, 2007–. Methodist local preacher, 1978–. Mem. Bd, Trustees for Methodist Church Purposes, 2007–15. Sec., Billy Boston Statue Trust, 2014–. Performed playwright: Gerrumonside, Turnpike Theatre Co., Leigh, 1995; For The Love of the Game, Acad. of Live and Recording Arts, Mill at the Pier, Wigan, 2014. *Publications:* Onward Christian Socialist, 1996; Where are the Prophets, 2007. *Recreation:* Rugby League supporter.

WYNN-EVANS, Charles Andrew; Partner, Dechert LLP, since 1997; a Fee-paid Employment Judge, Midlands West Region, since 2009; *b* Royal Leamington Spa, 12 Dec. 1967; *s* of Anthony Wynn-Evans and Margaret Wynn-Evans; *m* 1997, Karen Wendy Alexandra, (Alex), McColl; one *s* one *d. Educ:* King Henry VIII Sch., Coventry; Univ. of Bristol (LLB 1988); Coll. of Law, Chester; Merton Coll., Oxford (BCL 1990). Titmuss, Sainer & Webb, later Dechert LLP: Trainee Solicitor, 1990–92; admitted solicitor, 1992; Solicitor, 1992–97. Member, Employment Law Committee: Law Soc. of England and Wales, 2007–; City of London Law Soc., 2008–. Ind. Person, London Bor. of Southwark, 2015–. *Publications:* Blackstone's Guide to the New Transfer of Undertakings Legislation, 2006; The Law of TUPE Transfers, 2013; articles in various jls. *Recreations:* tennis, cricket, watching Rugby, tending an allotment. *Address:* Dechert LLP, 160 Queen Victoria Street, EC4V 4QQ. *T:* (020) 7184 7545, *Fax:* (020) 7184 7001. *E:* charles.wynn-evans@dechert.com.

WYNN OWEN, Philip, CB 2008; Member, European Court of Auditors, Luxembourg, since 2014; *b* 10 June 1960; *s* of late Emrys and Ruth Wynn Owen; *m* 1989, Elizabeth Mary Fahey; three *s. Educ:* Maidstone Grammar Sch.; University Coll., Oxford (MA Mod. Hist.); London Business Sch. (MBA Dist.); Harvard Business Sch. (AMP 2008). HM Treasury, 1981–99: Asst Private Sec. to Chancellor of Exchequer, 1984–86; Private Sec. to Perm. Sec., 1991–93; Team Leader: Transport Team, 1993–96; Tax and Budget Team, 1996; Tax Policy Team, 1997–99; Director: Regulatory Impact Unit, Cabinet Office, 1999–2003; Financial Sector, HM Treasury, 2003–04; Director General: Strategy and Pensions, and Chair, Shared Services Business, DWP, 2004–09; Nat. Climate Change and Consumer Support, DECC, 2009–11; Dir Gen., Internat. Climate Change and Energy Efficiency, DECC, 2011–13; Acting Perm. Sec., DECC, 2012–13. Alternate Dir, EIB, 1994–96. Non-exec. Dir, Maidstone and Tunbridge Wells NHS Trust, 2008–13 (Dep. Chm., 2009–13). Mem., RBL, 2010–. *Recreations:* cricket, tennis, running. *Clubs:* MCC; Leigh Cricket (Kent).

WYNNE, Sir Graham (Robert), Kt 2010; CBE 2003; Chief Executive, Royal Society for the Protection of Birds, 1998–2010; *b* 29 May 1950; *s* of late Arthur Robert Wynne and of Joan Brenda Wynne (*née* Chapman); *m* 1994, Janet Anne Stewart. *Educ:* Brentwood Sch., Essex; Pembroke Coll., Cambridge (BA Hons 1971; MA). DipTP 1975; MRTPI (RTPI 1975). Various planning posts, Lewisham, 1972–78; Shoreditch Area Team Leader, 1978–86, Hd, Planning Policy, 1986–87, Hackney; Reserves Dir, 1987–90, Conservation Dir, 1990–98, RSPB. Sen. Advr to Prince of Wales' Internat. Sustainability Unit, 2010–. Member: UK Biodiversity Steering Gp, 1994–2000; UK Round Table on Sustainable Develt, 1998–2000; Sustainable Develt Commn, 2000–03; Policy Commn on Future of Farming and Food, 2001–02; Cttee on Climate Change (Adaptation), 2009–. Mem. Council, Birdlife Internat., 1998–2010. Trustee, Green Alliance, 2011–. *Publications:* Biodiversity Challenge: an agenda for conservation action in the UK, 1995; (contrib.) Conservation Science and Action, 1997; contrib. various RSPB and local authy pubns. *Recreations:* natural history, football, restoring a C16th house, gardening.

WYRKO, David John, QPM 1995; DL; Chief Constable of Leicestershire, 1997–2002; *b* 15 July 1948; *s* of late Wasyl John Wyrko and of Stella Doreen Wyrko (*née* Witts); *m* 1973, Beryl Case; one *s* one *d. Educ:* City of Bath Technical Sch.; Univ. of Surrey (BSc Electrical, Electronic and Control Engineering 1969). Police Constable to Chief Superintendent, Northants, 1972–91; Asst Chief Constable, Northants, 1991–93; Dep. Chief Constable, Leics, 1993–97. Co-Dir, Police Extended Interviews, 1999–2002. FBI Nat. Acad., Quantico, 1984; Cabinet Office Top Mgt Prog., 1995. Hon. Treas., 1994–98, Chm., Inf. Mgt Cttee, 1997–2000, ACPO; Mem., PITO Bd, 1997–2002. Sen. Vis. Fellow, Scarman Centre, Univ. of Leicester, 2003–. Council Mem., Shrievalty Assoc., 2005–07. Mem. Council, Leics and Rutland Wildlife Trust, 2007–11. Pres., Hope Against Cancer, 2012– (Chm. Trustees, 2007–11). High Sheriff, 2008–09, DL 2010, Leics. BUniv Surrey, 2011. *Recreations:* cabinet making, golf, cycling, gardening. *Address:* c/o Leicestershire Constabulary HQ, St John's, Narborough, Leics LE9 5BX. *T:* (0116) 222 2222.

WYVER, Clare; *see* Paterson, C.

XYZ

XI JINPING; General Secretary, Central Committee, Communist Party of China, since 2012; President, People's Republic of China, since 2013 (Vice-President, 2008–13); Chairman, Central Military Commission, since 2013 (Vice-Chairman, 2010–13); *b* Fuping Co., Shaanxi Province, June 1953; *s* of Xi Zhongxun; *m* 1987, Peng Liyuan; one *d*. *Educ:* Tsinghua Univ., Beijing (BSc Chem. Engrg 1979; LLD 2002). Work as an educated youth, Liangjiahe Bde, Shaanxi Province, 1969–75; joined Communist Party, 1974; Sec., Gen. Office of State Council and Gen. Office of Central Mil. Commn (as officer in active service), 1979–82; Communist Party of China: Dep. Sec., 1982–83, Sec., 1983–85, Zhengding Co. Cttee, Hebei Province; Mem., Standing Cttee of Municipal Party Cttee and Vice Mayor, Xiamen, Fujian Province, 1985–88; Secretary: Ningde Prefectural Cttee, Fujian Province, 1988–90; Fuzhou Municipal Cttee, 1990–96; Fujian Provincial Committee: Mem., Standing Cttee, 1993–95; Dep. Sec., 1995–2002; Chm., Standing Cttee, Fuzhou Municipal People's Congress, Fujian Province, 1990–96; Actg Gov., 1999–2000, Gov., 2000–02, Fujian Province; Dep. Sec., 2002, Sec., 2002–07, Zhejiang Provincial Cttee, and Actg Gov., Zhejiang Province, 2002–03; Chm., Standing Cttee, Zhejiang Provincial People's Congress, 2003–07; Sec., Shanghai Municipal Cttee, 2007; Central Committee, Communist Party of China: Member: Standing Cttee of Central Cttee, 2007–10 and 2012–, Central Cttee, 2012–, Political Bureau; Secretariat, 2007–10; Pres., Party Sch., 2007–10; Sec. Gen., Nat. Congress, 2012–. *Publications:* The Governance of China, 2014. *Address:* Office of the President, Zhong Nan Hai, Beijing, People's Republic of China.

YACOUB, Sir Magdi (Habib), OM 2014; Kt 1992; FRCS; FRS 1999; British Heart Foundation Professor of Cardiothoracic Surgery, National Heart and Lung Institute (formerly Cardiothoracic Institute), Imperial College London (formerly British Postgraduate Medical Federation, University of London), since 1986; Director of Research, Magdi Yacoub Institute (formerly Harefield Research Foundation), Heart Science Centre; *b* Cairo, 16 Nov. 1935; *m*; one *s* two *d*. *Educ:* Cairo University. FRCS, FRCSE, FRCSGlas, 1962; LRCP 1966, MRCP 1986, Hon. FRCP 1990. Rotating House Officer, Cairo Univ. Hosp., 1958–59; Surgical Registrar, Postgrad. Surgical Unit, Cairo Univ., 1959–61; Resident Surgical Officer, 1962–63, Surgical Registrar, 1963–64, London Chest Hosp.; Rotating Sen. Surgical Registrar, Nat. Heart and Chest Hosps, 1964–68; Asst Prof. of Cardiothoracic Surgery, Chicago Univ., 1968–69; Consultant Cardiothoracic Surgeon, Harefield Hosp., Middx, 1969–92, Royal Brompton and Harefield NHS Trust, 1986–2001 (now Hon.); Consultant Cardiac Surgeon, Nat. Heart Hosp., 1973–89. Hon. Consultant: Royal Free Hosp. Med. Sch.; King Edward's Coll. of Medicine, Lahore, Pakistan; Hon. Prof. of Surgery, Univ. of Sienna; Hon. Prof. of Cardiac Surgery, Charing Cross and Westminster Hosp. Med. Schs. Has developed innovations in heart and heart-lung transplants. Founder and Pres., Chain of Hope, 1995–. Mem., Soc. Thoracic Surgeons; FRSocMed; Founder FMedSci 1998. Hon. DSc: Brunel, 1985; Amer. Univ. at Cairo, 1989; Loughborough, 1990; Hon. MCh Cardiff, 1986; Hon. PhD Lund, 1988. Editor: Annual of Cardiac Surgery; Current Opinion in Cardiology: coronary artery surgery. *Publications:* papers on pulmonary osteoarthropath, aortic valve homografts, surgical treatment of ischaemic heart disease, valve repairs, and related subjects. *Address:* Imperial College London, Heart Science Centre, Harefield, Middx UB9 6JH.

YALE, David Eryl Corbet, FBA 1980; Reader in English Legal History, Cambridge University, 1969–93, now Emeritus; Fellow, Christ's College, Cambridge, since 1950; *b* 31 March 1928; *s* of Lt-Col J. C. L. Yale and Mrs Beatrice Yale (*née* Breese); *m* 1959, Elizabeth Ann, *d* of C. A. B. Brett, Belfast; two *s*. *Educ:* Malvern Coll., Worcs; Queens' Coll., Cambridge (BA 1949, LLB 1950, MA 1953). Called to the Bar, Inner Temple, 1951, Bencher, 2009; Asst Lectr and Lectr in Law, Cambridge Univ., 1952–69. Pres., Selden Soc., 1994–97. Hon. QC 2000. *Publications:* various, mainly in field of legal history. *Recreation:* fishing. *Address:* Christ's College, Cambridge CB2 3BU. *T:* (01223) 334900; Saethon, Porthmadog, Gwynedd LL49 9UR. *T:* (01766) 512129.

YAM Yee-Kwan, David; a Judge of the Court of First Instance of the High Court (formerly Judge of the High Court), Hong Kong, 1994–2012; *b* 4 Oct. 1948; *s* of Yam Fat-Shing Frank and Ng Yuet-Hing Nora; *m* 1977, Dr Stella T. P. Wong; two *s*. *Educ:* Hong Kong Univ. (BSc 1971; LLB 1975); Inns of Court Sch. of Law. Called to the Bar, Middle Temple, and to Hong Kong Bar, 1976; in practice, 1977–87; District Court Judge, 1987–94. Chm., Insider Dealing Tribunal, 1995–97. *Recreations:* golf, music, travelling. *T:* 92727314. *Clubs:* Hong Kong Jockey, Shek O Country (Hong Kong).

YAMEY, Prof. Basil Selig, CBE 1972; FBA 1977; Professor of Economics, University of London, 1960–84, now Emeritus; Member (part-time), Monopolies and Mergers Commission, 1966–78; *b* 4 May 1919; *s* of Solomon and Leah Yamey; *m* 1st, 1948, Helen Bloch (*d* 1980); one *s* one *d*; 2nd, 1991, Demetra Georgakopoulou. *Educ:* Tulbagh High Sch.; Univ. of Cape Town; LSE. Served as Lieut, SAAF, 1941–45. Lectr in Commerce, Rhodes Univ., 1945; Senior Lectr in Commerce, Univ. of Cape Town, 1946; Lectr in Commerce, LSE, 1948; Associate Prof. of Commerce, McGill Univ., 1949; Reader in Economics, Univ. of London, 1950. Managing Trustee, IEA, 1986–91. Trustee: National Gall., 1974–81; Tate Gall., 1979–81; Member: Museums and Galls Commn, 1983–84; Cinematograph Films Council, 1969–73. Mem. Committee of Management: Courtauld Inst., 1981–84; Warburg Inst., 1981–84; Mem., Governing Body, London Business Sch., 1965–84. *Publications:* Economics of Resale Price Maintenance, 1954; (jt editor) Studies in History of Accounting, 1956; (with P. T. Bauer) Economics of Under-developed Countries, 1957; (jt editor) Capital, Saving and Credit in Peasant Societies, 1963; (with H. C. Edey and H. Thomson) Accounting in England and Scotland, 1543–1800, 1963; (with R. B. Stevens) The Restrictive Practices Court, 1965; (ed) Resale Price Maintenance, 1966; (with P. T. Bauer) Markets, Market Control and Marketing Reform: Selected Papers, 1968; (ed) Economics of Industrial Structure, 1973; (jt editor) Economics of Retailing, 1973; (jt editor) Debits, Credits, Finance and Profits, 1974; (with B. A. Goss) Economics of Futures Trading, 1976; Essays on the History of Accounting, 1978; (jt editor) Stato e Industria in Europa: Il Regno Unito, 1979; Further Essays on the History of Accounting, 1983; Arte e Contabilità, 1986; Análisis Económico de los Mercados, 1987; Art and Accounting, 1989; (ed) Luca Pacioli, Exposition of Double Entry Book-keeping, Venice 1494, 1994; (jt editor) Accounting History: some British contributions, 1994; articles on economics, economic history and law in learned journals. *Address:* 27B Elsworthy Road, NW3 3BT. *T:* (020) 7586 9344.

YANDELL, Claire Louise; *see* Armitstead, C. L.

YANG, Chen Ning, FInstP; physicist, educator; Einstein Professor and Director, Institute for Theoretical Physics, State University of New York at Stony Brook, New York, 1966–99, now Emeritus Professor and Director; Distinguished Professor-at-Large, Chinese University of Hong Kong, since 1986; Professor, Tsinghua University, Beijing, since 1998; *b* Hefei, China, 22 Sept. 1922; *s* of Ke Chuen Yang and Meng Hwa Lo; naturalized US citizen, 1964; *m* 1950, Chih Li Tu (*d* 2003); two *s* one *d*; *m* 2004, Fan Weng. *Educ:* National Southwest Associated Univ., Kunming, China (BSc), 1942; University of Chicago (PhD), 1948. FInstP 1998. Institute for Advanced Study, Princeton, NJ: Member, 1949–55; Prof. of Physics, 1955–66; several DSc's from universities. Member of Board: Rockefeller Univ., 1970–76; AAAS, 1976–80; Salk Inst., 1978–; Ben Gurion Univ.; Member: Amer. Phys. Soc.; Nat. Acad. Sci.; Amer. Philos. Soc., Sigma Xi; Brazilian, Venezuelan, Royal Spanish and Chinese Acads of Sci; Academia Sinica; Foreign Member: Royal Soc., 1992; Russian Acad. of Sciences, 1994. Nobel Prize in Physics, 1957; Rumford Prize, 1980; Nat. Medal of Science, 1986; Benjamin Franklin Medal, Amer. Phil Soc., 1993; Bower Prize, Franklin Inst., 1994; King Faisal Internat. Prize, 2001. *Publications:* contrib. to Physical Review, Reviews of Modern Physics. *Address:* Department of Physics, Chinese University of Hong Kong, Shatin, New Territories, Hong Kong; Tsinghua University, Beijing, China.

YANG, Prof. Fujia; President, University of Nottingham, Ningbo, China, since 2004; Professor of Physics, Fudan University, since 1980; *b* Shanghai, 11 June 1936; *s* of Yang Shanqing and Zhu Qin; *m* Peng Xiuling; one *d*. *Educ:* Fudan Univ. (Physics degree 1958). Postdoctoral Researcher, Niels Bohr Inst., Copenhagen, 1963–65; Fudan University: Lectr; Pres., 1993–99; Niels Bohr Prof., Fudan Univ., 1999–2009. Dir, Shanghai Inst. of Nuclear Res., Chinese Acad. of Scis, 1987–2001; Chancellor, Univ. of Nottingham, UK, 2001–12. Chm., Shanghai Assoc. for Sci. and Technol., 1992–96; Vice Chm., Chinese Assoc. for Sci. and Technol., 2001–12. Academician, Chinese Acad. of Scis, 1991–. Fellow, 48 Group Club. Hon. degrees, Soka, New York State, Hong Kong, Nottingham, Connecticut, Chinese Univ. Hong Kong and Misr Univ. of Sci. and Technol. *Publications:* Atom Physics, 1984, 2008; Atomic and Nuclear Physics, 1993; Applied Nuclear Physics, 1994; Quest for Excellence, 1995; (with J. H. Hamilton) Modern Atomic and Nuclear Physics, 1996; Boxue Duzhi, 2001; Chinese contemporary educator's work: Yang Fujia vol., 2006; Approaching to the top universities: comparison of Chinese and Western education, 2009; From Fudan to Nottingham, 2013; Liberal Arts Education, 2014. *Recreations:* reading, walking, swimming. *Address:* Fudan University, 220 Handan Road, Shanghai 200433, China. *E:* fjyang@fudan.edu.cn.

YANG, Hon. Sir Ti Liang, Kt 1988; Member Executive Council, Hong Kong Special Administrative Region, 1997–2002; Chairman, Exchange Fund Investment Ltd, 1998–2003; Chief Justice of Hong Kong, 1988–96; *b* 30 June 1929; *s* of late Shao-nan Yang and Elsie (*née* Chun); *m* 1954, Eileen Barbara (*née* Tam) (*d* 2006); two *s*. *Educ:* The Comparative Law Sch. of China; Soochow Univ., Shanghai; UCL (LLB Hons 1953; Fellow 1989). FCIArb 1990. Called to the Bar (with honours), Gray's Inn, 1954, Hon. Bencher, 1988. Magistrate, Hong Kong, 1956; Sen. Magistrate, 1963; Rockefeller Fellow, London Univ., 1963–64; District Judge, Dist Court, 1968; Judge of the High Court, Hong Kong, 1975; Justice of Appeal, Hong Kong, 1980; Pres., Court of Appeal of Negara Brunei Darussalam, 1988–92. Candidate for selection of Chief Exec., HKSAR, 1996. Chairman: Kowloon Disturbances Claims Assessment Bd, 1966, Compensation Bd, 1967; Commn of Inquiry into the Rainstorm Disasters, 1972; Commn of Inquiry into the Leung Wing-sang Case, 1976; Commn of Inquiry into the MacLennan Case, 1980; Mem., Law Reform Commn, 1980–96 (Chm., Sub-cttee on law relating to homosexuality, 1980). Mem., Chinese Lang. Cttee (Chm. Legal Sub-cttee), 1970. Chairman: University and Polytechnic Grants Cttee, 1981–84; Hong Kong Univ. Council, 1987–2001; Pro-Chancellor, Hong Kong Univ., 1994–2001. Chm., Hong Kong Red Cross, 1998–2012 (Pres., 2012–). Pres., Bentham Club. Hon. LLD: Chinese Univ. of Hong Kong, 1984; Hong Kong Poly., 1992; Hon. DLitt Hong Kong Univ., 1991. Order of Chivalry, First Class, SPMB, Negara Brunei Darussalam, 1990; Grand Bauhinia Medal (Hong Kong), 1999. *Publications:* (trans.) General Yue Fei, by Qian Cai (Qing Dynasty novel), 1995; (trans.) Peach Blossom Fan, (novel by Gu Shifan, 1948), 1998; (trans.) Officialdom Unmasked, (novel by Li Boyuan, 1903), 2001. *Recreations:* philately, reading, walking, oriental ceramics, travelling, music. *Address:* A10 Carolina Gardens, 20 Coombe Road, The Peak, Hong Kong. *Clubs:* Hong Kong, Hong Kong Country.

YANG, Prof. Ziheng, PhD; FRS 2006; R. A. Fisher Professor of Statistical Genetics, University College London, since 2010; *b* 1 Nov. 1964; *s* of Yi Yang and Weiying Wang; *m* 1991, Fan Yang; two *d*. *Educ:* Gansu Agricl Univ. (BSc 1984); Beijing Agricl Univ. (MSc 1987; PhD 1992). Lectr, Beijing Agricl Univ., 1992–97; postdoctoral res., Pennsylvania State Univ. and Univ. of Calif. at Berkeley; University College London: Lectr, 1997–2000; Reader, 2000–01; Prof. of Statistical Genetics, 2001–10. *Publications:* Computational Molecular Evolution, 2006; Molecular Evolution: a statistical approach, 2014. *Address:* Department of Biology, University College London, Darwin Building, Gower Street, WC1E 6BT.

YANNAKOUDAKIS, Marina; Member (C) London Region, European Parliament, 2009–14; *b* London, 16 April 1956; *d* of Lefteris and Toulla Yallouros; *m* 1983, Zacharias Yannakoudakis; two *s* one *d*. *Educ:* Brunel Univ. (BSc Hons); Open Univ. (MA). Financial Dir, Viamare Travel Ltd, 1984–2008. Mem. (C), Barnet LBC, 2006–10. Contested (C) London Reg., EP, 2014. *Recreation:* family and friends.

YANUKOVYCH, Viktor Fedorovych; President of Ukraine, 2010–14; *b* Yenakiyeve, Donetsk Region, Ukraine, 9 July 1950; *m* Lyudmyla; one *s* (one *s* decd). *Educ:* Donetsk Poly. Inst. (Mech. Engrg 1980); Ukrainian Acad. of Foreign Trade (MA Internat. Law 2001). Regl transport exec. Gov., Donetsk Reg., 1997; Mem., Donetsk Regl Council, 1999; Prime

Minister of Ukraine, 2002–04 and 2006–07; MP (Party of Regions), Ukraine, 2006. Leader, Party of Regions, 2003–10, now Hon. Leader. Fellow, Acad. of Econ. Scis of Ukraine. Order for Merit, 1st, 2nd and 3rd degrees, Honored Transport Worker of Ukraine.

YAPP, John William; HM Diplomatic Service, retired; High Commissioner, Belize, 2007–08; *b* 14 Jan. 1951; *s* of late William Yapp and Pamela Yapp (*née* Clarke); *m* 2010, Elizabeth Anne, *d* of late John March and of Loris March; one *s* four *d* by previous marriages. *Educ:* St Augustine's Coll., Ramsgate. Joined HM Diplomatic Service, 1971: Islamabad, 1973–75; Third Sec. (Consular), Kuala Lumpur, 1976–77; Asst Private Sec. to Ministers of State, FCO, 1978–80; Second Sec. (Commercial), Dubai, 1980–84; Second Sec. (Economic), The Hague, 1984–88; Jt Export Promotion Directorate, FCO/DTI, 1988–91; First Sec. (Political/PR), Wellington, NZ, 1992–95 (concurrently Dep. Governor, Pitcairn Is); Dep. Head, N American Dept, FCO, 1995–97; High Comr, Seychelles, 1998–2002; First Sec. (Political-Military), Washington, 2003; Dep. Hd, S Asia Gp, FCO, 2004–07. *Recreations:* photography, reading, cooking, Rugby Union (now as a spectator). *E:* jwyapp@hotmail.co.uk.

YARBOROUGH, 8th Earl of, *cr* 1837; **Charles John Pelham;** Baron Yarborough, 1794; Baron Worsley, 1837; *b* 5 Nov. 1963; *o s* of 7th Earl of Yarborough and Ann, *d* of late John Herbert Upton; *S* father, 1991; *m* 1990, Anna-Karin Zecevic, *d* of George Zecevic; four *s* one *d*. High Sheriff, Lincs, 2014–15. *Heir: s* Lord Worsley, *qv*. *Address:* Brocklesby Park, Lincs DN41 8FB.

YARD, John Ernest, CBE 2000; freelance consultant specialising in change management and outsourcing, since 2004; *b* 29 July 1944; *s* of Ernest Alfred and Kathleen Lilian Yard; *m* Jean Pamela Murray; one *s* one *d*; two *s* one *d* from a previous marriage. *Educ:* St Marylebone Grammar Sch. FBCS 2003; MCIPS 2004. Inland Revenue: Exec. Officer and PAYE Auditor, 1963–71; Inspector of Taxes, 1971–84; Dep. Dir (Systems and Policy), 1984–91; Dir of Change Mgt, 1992; Dir, Business Services (IT) Office, then Business and Mgt Services Div., subseq. Business Services Div., 1993–2004. *Recreations:* travel, eating, golf. *E:* john@johnyard.com.

YARDE-BULLER, family name of **Baron Churston**.

YARMOUTH, Earl of; William Francis Seymour; *b* 2 Nov. 1993; *s* and *heir* of Marquess of Hertford, *qv*. *Educ:* British Sch., Rio de Janeiro; Winterfold House Sch.; Shrewsbury Sch.; Haileybury Sch.; Royal Agricl Univ., Cirencester.

YARNOLD, Patrick; HM Diplomatic Service, retired; professional genealogical and historical researcher; *b* 21 March 1937; *s* of late Leonard Francis Yarnold and Gladys Blanche Yarnold (*née* Merry); *m* 1961, Caroline, *er d* of late Andrew J. Martin; two *d*. *Educ:* Bancroft's School. HM Forces, 1955–57. Joined HM Foreign (now Diplomatic) Service, 1957; served: FO, 1957–60; Addis Ababa, 1961–64; Belgrade, 1964–66; FO (later FCO), 1966–70; 1st Sec., Head of Chancery, Bucharest, 1970–73; 1st Sec. (Commercial), Bonn, 1973–76; FCO, 1976–79; Counsellor (Economic and Commercial), Brussels, 1980–83; Consul-Gen., Zagreb, 1983–85; Counsellor and Head of Chancery, Belgrade, 1985–87; Hd of Defence Dept, FCO, 1987–90; Consul-Gen., Hamburg, 1990–94; Consul-Gen., Marseilles, 1995–97. *Publications:* Wanborough Manor: school for secret agents, 2009. *Recreations:* travel, photography, walking, local history, Chinese cooking, etc. *Address:* Cherry Cottage, The Street, Puttenham, Guildford, Surrey GU3 1AT.

YARNTON, David Nigel; Managing Director, Equinox Talent (formerly Global Talent Group), since 2012; *b* London, 25 Feb. 1959; *s* of Albert Edward Yarnton and Minnie Florence Evelyn Yarnton; *m* 1985, Sally Elizabeth Withers; one *s* one *d*. *Educ:* Defence Force Acad. (Duntroon Scholar); South Australian Inst. of Technol.; Australian Inst. of Mgt (Cert. Applied Mgt 1982); Univ. of New England (Co. Dirs Dip. 1990). Industrial Sales Rep., Stanley Tools, 1979–82; State Manager, Vic, Sidchrome Pty Ltd, 1982–84; State Sales Manager, Vic, British Paints Pty Ltd, 1984–86; Nat. Sales and Mktg Manager, Action Hi-Tech Pty Ltd, 1986; Gen. Manager and Dir, IAD Pty Ltd, 1987–95; Dir, Sales and Mktg, Nintendo Australia Ltd, 1995–2003; Gen. Manager, Nintendo UK, 2003–12. Non-executive Director: GfK Charttrack, 2007–12; Eyes on Athletes, 2012–. Dir, Aust. Toy Assoc., 2000; Dir and Co-Founder, Interactive Entertainment Assoc. of Australia, 2002; Mem. Bd and Vice Chm., UK Interactive Entertainment Assoc., 2004–11. Mem. Bd, Edinburgh Interactive Fest., 2004– (Chm., 2011–). Founder and Chm., British Inspiration Awards, 2009–. Associate, Aust. Inst. of Mgt, 1984; FAICD 1990; Hon. Mem., Acad. of Interactive Arts and Scis, LA, 1997. Athletics Coach, Level 1, Aust. Athletics Coaches Assoc., 1998. *T:* 07717 600800. *E:* dyarnton@aol.com.

YARROW, Alan Colin Drake; JP; Chairman, Chartered Institute for Securities and Investment, since 2009; Chairman, Kleinwort Benson Group, since 2010; Lord Mayor of London, 2014–15; *b* Jahor Bahru, 1951; *s* of Colin Yarrow and Paula Yarrow; *m* 1975, Gilly; two *s*. *Educ:* Harrow; Manchester Business Sch. Work in graphic design studio, Paris, 1968; Grieveson Grant, later Kleinwort Benson: joined Grieveson Grant, stockbrokers, 1972; Mem., Stock Exchange, 1978; Partner, 1981; Hd, UK Institutional Sales, 1989–92; Hd, Global Distribution, 1992–94; Man. Dir, Kleinwort Benson Securities, 1994; Mem. Bd, Kleinwort Benson Gp, 1995; Global Hd, Equities, 1995; Mem. Mgt Bd, Dresdner Kleinwort Benson, 1995; Vice Chm., 2000; CEO, UK Reg., 2007–09. Member: Takeover Panel, 2002–10; Chancellor of the Exchequer's High Level Stakeholder Gp, 2006–09; Dep. Chm., FSA Practitioner Panel, 2004–10. Chm., LIBA, 2004–09; Vice Pres. and Mem. Council, BBA, 2004–09. Non-executive Director: Complinet, 2002–10 (Chm., 2002–08); Baikal Global Ltd, 2009–10; Turquoise Global Hldgs Ltd, 2010–; Fixnetix, 2010–. Hon. Chartered FCSI 2010. Gov., City of London Freemen's Sch., 2011–13; Almoner, Christ's Hosp., 2007–. Alderman, Ward of Bridge and Bridge Without, City of London, 2007–; Sheriff, City of London, 2011–12; JP 2007. Liveryman: Fishmongers' Co., 2007; International Bankers' Co., 2008; Glaziers' Co., 2012; Hon. Liveryman, Launderers' Co., 2011. KStJ 2014. *Recreations:* tennis, bridge, golf, art. *Address:* Chartered Institute for Securities and Investment, 8 Eastcheap, EC3M 1AE. *T:* (020) 7645 0603. *E:* alan.yarrow@cisi.org. *Clubs:* Hurlingham, Boodle's, City of London; Royal Wimbledon Golf.

YARROW, Dr Alfred, FFPH; Honorary Member, Epidemiology Unit, Ministry of Health, Jerusalem, 1987–96; *b* 25 May 1924; *s* of Leah and step *s* of Philip Yarrow; *m* 1953, Sheila Kaufman; two *d*. *Educ:* Hackney Downs Grammar Sch.; Edinburgh Univ. (MB, ChB); London Sch. of Hygiene and Trop. Medicine (Hons DPH). FFPH (Foundn FFCM 1972). Dep. Area MO, Tottenham and Hornsey, 1955–60; Area MO, SE Essex, 1960–65; MOH, Gateshead, 1965–68; Dir, Scottish Health Educn Unit, 1968–73; SMO, 1973–77, SPMO, 1977–84, DHSS. Temp. Consultant, WHO, 1975–76. Brit. Council Lectr, 1975; Council of Europe Fellow, 1978. *Publications:* So Now You Know About Smoking, 1975; Politics, Society and Preventive Medicine, 1986; scientific papers on demography, epidemiology, preventive medicine and health educn. *Recreations:* lawn bowls, travelling, reading. *Address:* 9/4 Nof Harim, Jerusalem 96190, Israel. *T:* 6438792.

YARROW, Sir Eric Grant, 3rd Bt *cr* 1916; MBE (mil.) 1946; DL; FRSE; Chairman, Clydesdale Bank PLC, 1985–91 (Director 1962–91, Deputy Chairman, 1975–85); Director: Standard Life Assurance Co., 1958–91; National Australia Bank Ltd, 1987–91; *b* 23 April 1920; *o s* of Sir Harold Yarrow, 2nd Bt and 1st wife, Eleanor Etheldreda (*d* 1934); *S* father, 1962; *m* 1st, 1951, Rosemary Ann (*d* 1957), *yr d* of late H. T. Young, Roehampton, SW15; (one *s* decd); 2nd, 1959, Annette Elizabeth Françoise (marr. diss. 1975), *d* of late A. J. E. Steven, Ardgay; three *s* (including twin *s*); 3rd, 1982, Mrs Joan Botting, *d* of late R. F. Masters, Piddinghoe, Sussex. *Educ:* Marlborough Coll.; Glasgow Univ. Served apprenticeship, G. & J. Weir Ltd. Served Burma, 1942–45; Major RE, 1945. Asst Manager Yarrow & Co., 1946; Dir, 1948; Man. Dir, 1958–67; Chm., 1962–85; Pres., Yarrow PLC, 1985–87. Mem. Council, RINA, 1957–65; Vice-Pres., 1965; Hon. Vice-Pres., 1972. Mem., General Cttee, Lloyd's Register of Shipping, 1960–87; Prime Warden, Worshipful Co. of Shipwrights, 1970; Deacon, Incorporation of Hammermen of Glasgow, 1961–62; Retired Mem. Council, Institution of Engineers & Shipbuilders in Scotland; Mem. Council, Inst. of Directors, 1983–90; Mem., Glasgow Action, 1985–91. Pres., Scottish Convalescent Home for Children, 1957–70; Hon. Pres., Princess Louise Scottish Hospital at Erskine, 1986– (Chm., 1980–86). President: British Naval Equipment Assoc., 1982–90; Smeatonian Soc. of Civil Engineers, 1983; Marlburian Club, 1984; Scottish Area, Burma Star Assoc., 1990–2010; Vice President: RHAS, 1990–91; Glasgow Br., RNLI, 1988–96; Chm., Blythe Sappers, 1989. DL Renfrewshire, 1970. FRSE 1974. OStJ. *Recreation:* family life. *Heir: g s* Ross William Grant Yarrow, *b* 14 Jan. 1985. *Address:* Craigrowan, Porterfield Road, Kilmacolm, Renfrewshire PA13 4PD. *T:* (01505) 872067. *Club:* Royal & Ancient Golf (St Andrews).

YARWOOD, Michael Edward, OBE 1976; entertainer, since 1962; *b* 14 June 1941; *s* of Wilfred and Bridget Yarwood; *m* 1969, Sandra Burville (marr. diss. 1987); two *d*. *Educ:* Bredbury Secondary Modern Sch., Cheshire. First television appearance, 1963; *BBC TV:* Three of a Kind, 1967; Look—Mike Yarwood, and Mike Yarwood in Persons (series), 1971–82; *ATV:* Will the Real Mike Yarwood Stand Up? (series), 1968; *Thames:* Mike Yarwood in Persons, 1983–84; Yarwood's Royal Variety Show, the Yarwood Chat Show, and Mike Yarwood in Persons, 1986; *stage:* Royal Variety performances, 1968, 1972, 1976, 1981, 1987, 1993; One for the Pot, UK tour, 1988. Variety Club of Gt Britain award for BBC TV Personality of 1973; Royal Television Society award for outstanding creative achievement in front of camera, 1978. Mem., Grand Order of Water Rats, 1968. *Publications:* And This Is Me, 1974; Impressions of my life (autobiog.), 1986. *Recreations:* golf, tennis. *Club:* Lord's Taverners.

YASAMEE, Heather Jacqueline, (Mrs S. J. Gagen), CMG 2006; Assistant Director (Information Management), Directorate for Strategy and Information, Foreign and Commonwealth Office, 2004–06; *b* 12 Aug. 1951; *d* of Dennis Gordon Fenby and Betty Mitchell Fenby (*née* Linford); *m* 1st, 1979, Feroze Abdullah Khan Yasamee (marr. diss. 1999); 2nd, 2005, Stephen John Gagen, JP. *Educ:* Lawnswood High Sch. for Girls, Leeds; St Anne's Coll., Oxford (MA Mod. Hist.). Foreign and Commonwealth Office: joined, 1973; Historians, 1973–95, Hd of Historians, 1990–95; Editor, Documents on British Policy Overseas, 1988–95; Departmental Record Officer, 1995–2006: Hd, Records and Histl Services, 1995–99; Hd, Records and Histl Dept, 1999–2003. *Publications:* (Asst Ed.) Documents on British Policy Overseas: Potsdam, 1984; Schuman Plan, 1986; London Conferences, 1987; (ed) German Rearmament, 1989; Korea, 1991; various articles. *Recreations:* family life, gardening. *Address:* 32 Station Road, SW19 2LP. *E:* heather@yasamee.com.

YASS, Irving, CB 1993; freelance transport policy consultant, since 2010; Policy Adviser, London First, 2008–09 (Director: Transport, 1995–2001; Policy, 2001–08); *b* 20 Dec. 1935; *s* of late Abraham and Fanny Yass; *m* 1962, Marion Leighton; two *s* one *d*. *Educ:* Harrow County Grammar School for Boys; Balliol Coll., Oxford (Brackenbury Schol.; BA). Assistant Principal, Min. of Transport and Civil Aviation, 1958; Private Sec. to Joint Parliamentary Secretary, 1960; HM Treasury, 1967–70; Asst Secretary, Dept of the Environment, 1971; Secretary, Cttee of Inquiry into Local Govt Finance, 1974–76; Dept of Transport, 1976–94 (Under Sec., 1982); Dir, Planning and Transport, Govt Office for London, 1994–95. *Address:* 5a Templewood Avenue, NW3 7UY. *T:* (020) 7419 2879.

YASSAIE, Sir Hossein, Kt 2013; PhD; Chief Executive Officer, Imagination Technologies Ltd, since 1998; *b* Iran, 1956; adopted British nationality, 1984; *m* Maha; two *d*. *Educ:* Birmingham Univ. (BSc 1st Cl. Hons Electronics and Communications 1979; PhD 1982). Res. Fellow, Birmingham Univ., 1982–84; with Inmos, subseq. STMicroelectronics, 1984–92; Chief Technol. Officer, 1992–98, Dir, 1995–, Imagination Technologies Ltd. Non-exec. Dir, Toumaz Gp (formerly Toumaz Ltd), 2009–. *Address:* Imagination Technologies Ltd, Imagination House, Home Park Estate, Kings Langley, Herts WD4 8LZ.

YASSUKOVICH, Stanislas Michael, CBE 1991; Chairman, S. M Yassukovich & Co. Ltd, 1997–2010; *b* 5 Feb. 1935; adopted British nationality, 1993; *s* of Dimitri and Denise Yassukovich; *m* 1961, Diana (*née* Townsend); two *s* one *d*. *Educ:* Deerfield Academy; Harvard University. US Marine Corps, 1957–61. Joined White, Weld & Co., 1961: posted to London, 1962; Branch Manager, 1967; General Partner, 1969; Managing Director, 1969; European Banking Co. Ltd: Managing Director, 1973; Group Dep. Chm., 1983. Sen. Advr, Merrill Lynch & Co., 1989–90; Dir, Merrill Lynch Europe Ltd, 1985–90 (Chm., 1985–90); Chairman: Flextech, 1989–97 (Dep. Chm., 1997–99; Dir, Telewest plc, 1999–2003); Park Place Capital, 1991–; Henderson Euro Trust PLC, 1992–2008; Hemingway Properties, 1993–98; Gallo & Co., 1995–98; Easdaq, 1997–2000; Manek Investment Management, 1998–; Cayzer Continuation PCC Ltd, 2004–; Prometheus Energy, 2007–08; BMCE Internat. Hldgs plc (formerly Medicapital Hldgs Ltd), 2007–11; Vice-Chm., Bristol & West plc, 1991–99; Dep. Chm., ABC Internat. Bank, 1993–2007; Director: Mosimann's Ltd, 1989–98; Henderson plc, 1991–98; SW Water, 1992–99 (Dep. Chm., 1997–99); Tradepoint Financial Network, 1997–99; Atlas Capital Ltd, 2002–07; Fortis Investments SA, 2007–09. Jt Dep. Chm., Internat. Stock Exchange, 1986–89; Chm., Securities Assoc., 1988–91. Chairman: City Res. Project, 1991–95; City Disputes Panel, 1994–98. *Publications:* articles in financial press. *Recreations:* hunting, shooting, polo. *Address:* 42 Berkeley Square, W1J 5AW. *T:* (020) 7318 0825. *Clubs:* Buck's, White's; Travellers (Paris).

YATES, Prof. (Anthony) David; Warden, Robinson College, Cambridge, since 2001; *b* 5 May 1946; *s* of Cyril Yates and Violet Ethel Yates (*née* Mann); *m* 1st, 1974, Carolyn Paula Hamilton (marr. diss. 1988); 2nd, 1992, Susanna Margaret McGarry. *Educ:* Bromley Grammar Sch. for Boys; St Catherine's Coll., Oxford (Exhibnr; BA 1967, MA 1971; Hon. Fellow, 2003). Admitted solicitor, 1972; Lecturer in Law: Univ. of Hull, 1969–72; Univ. of Bristol, 1972–74; University of Manchester: Lectr in Law, 1974–76; Sen. Lectr, 1976–78; Principal, Dalton Hall, 1975–80; Foundn Prof. of Law, 1979–87, Dean, Sch. of Law, 1979–84, and Pro-Vice-Chancellor, 1985–87, Univ. of Essex; Dir, Professional Develt, 1987–93, Dir of Strategy, 1993–97, Partner, 1993–2001, and Chief Operating Officer, 1997–2001, Baker & McKenzie. Visiting Professor: Univ. of Manchester, 1979; Univ. of NSW, 1985; Univ. of Essex, 1987–91; Parsons Vis. Fellow, 1985, Adjunct Prof. of Law, 2007–15, Univ. of Sydney. Mem., Educn and Trng Cttee, SRA, 2013–15. Mem., Law Soc., 1970– (Mem. Council, 1992–97). Chm. of Govs, Coll. of Law, England and Wales, 2009–12 (Gov., 2002–05; Dep. Chm., 2005–09). Hon. LLD Univ. of Law, 2013. FRSA 2006. *Publications:* Exclusion Clauses in Contracts, 1978, 2nd edn 1982; Leases of Business Premises, 1979; (with A. J. Hawkins) Landlord and Tenant Law, 1981, 2nd edn 1986; (with A. J. Hawkins) Standard Business Contracts, 1986; (Ed. in Chief) The Carriage of Goods by Land, Sea and Air, annually, 1993–2005; (with Malcolm Clarke) The Carriage of Goods by Land and Air, 2005, 2nd edn 2008. *Recreations:* opera, food, wine, Rugby football. *Address:* Warden's Lodge, Robinson College, Cambridge CB3 9AN. *Club:* Oxford and Cambridge.

YATES, Brian Douglas; Consumer Director, TrustMark, 2008–12; *b* 1 May 1944; *s* of Bertram Yates and Barbara (*née* Wenham); *m* 1971, Patricia, *d* of Arthur Hutchinson, DFC; one *s*. *Educ:* Uppingham Sch.; Clare Coll., Cambridge (MA); London Business Sch. (MBA).

CEng; Eur Ing. RHP Bearings, 1973–81; Thorn EMI, 1981–85; Dexion, 1985–88; Morris Material (formerly Morris Mechanical) Handling, 1988–2004. Member: Northampton BC, 1979–83; Hampshire CC, 1985–89. Mem. Council, 1986–2014, Chm., 1994–2007, Consumers' Assoc.; Member: Council, Ombudsman for Estate Agents, 1998–2005; Fitness to Practise (formerly Professional Conduct) Cttee, GMC, 2001–13; Genetics Insce Cttee, DoH, 2002–06; Hardship Panel, Assoc. of Investment Trust Cos, 2003–06; Immigration Appeal Tribunal, 2003–14; Insolvency Licensing Cttee, ICAEW, 2006–13; Fitness to Practise Cttee, NMC, 2009–; Appeals Cttee, Law Soc. of Scotland, 2014–; Chm., Probate Cttee, ICAEW, 2013–. Public Mem., Network Rail, 2008–11. Mem., Lunar Soc., Birmingham. FRSA. *Recreations:* tennis, cross country ski-ing. *Address:* 19 Park Avenue, Harpenden AL5 2DZ. *T:* (01582) 768484. *Clubs:* Athenæum, Royal Over-Seas League; Hatfield House Tennis, Harpenden Lawn Tennis.

YATES, David; *see* Yates, A. D.

YATES, Prof. David William, FRCS; Professor of Emergency Medicine, University of Manchester, 1990–2004, now Emeritus; *b* 19 Nov. 1941; *o s* of Bill and Lena Yates; *m* 1977, Veronica Mary Henderson; two *s*. *Educ:* Bradford Grammar Sch.; Emmanuel Coll., Cambridge (MB BChir 1967; MD 1990); St Thomas' Hosp., London. FRCS 1972. Med. posts in orthopaedic surgery; first Prof. of Emergency Medicine in UK, 1990. First Dean, Faculty of A&E Medicine, RCS, 1993–98. Founding Dir, Trauma Audit and Res. Network, 1990. *Address:* c/o Trauma Audit and Research Network, Salford Royal Hospital, Salford M6 8HD. *T:* (0161) 206 4397.

YATES, Edgar; *see* Yates, W. E.

YATES, Ian Humphrey Nelson, CBE 1991; Director, 1989–90, Chief Executive, 1975–90, The Press Association Ltd; *b* 24 Jan. 1931; *s* of James Nelson Yates and Martha (*née* Nutter); *m* 1956, Daphne J. Hudson, MCSP; three *s*. *Educ:* Lancaster Royal Grammar Sch.; Canford Sch., Wimborne. Royal Scots Greys, Germany and ME (National Service Commn), 1951–53. Management Trainee, Westminster Press Ltd, 1953–58 (Westmorland Gazette, and Telegraph & Argus, Bradford); Asst to Man. Dir, King & Hutchings Ltd, Uxbridge, 1958–60; Bradford and District Newspapers: Asst Gen. Man., 1960; Gen. Manager, 1964; Man. Dir, 1969–75; Dir, Westminster Press Planning Div., 1969–75. Chairman: Universal News Services Ltd, 1988–90; Tellex Monitors Ltd, 1988–90; CRG Communications Gp Ltd, 1990–91. President: Young Newspapermen's Assoc., 1966; Yorks Newspaper Soc., 1968. Member: Council, Newspaper Soc., 1970–75; Council, Commonwealth Press Union, 1977–90; Pres., Alliance of European News Agencies, 1987–88. FRSA 1989. *Recreations:* walking, reading, theatre.

YATES, John Michael, QPM 2006; Head of Security, Scentre Group, since 2014; *b* Liverpool, 17 Feb. 1959; *s* of Dr Godfrey and Dr Muriel Yates; *m* 2012, Felicity Ross; one *d*; one *s* one *d* by previous marriage. *Educ:* Marlborough Coll.; King's Coll., London (BA Hons Medieval and Modern Hist.); Fitzwilliam Coll., Cambridge (Dip. Applied Criminol. 2003). Metropolitan Police Service, 1981–2011: Comdr, Crime, 2003–04; Dep. Asst Comr, and Dir of Intelligence, 2004–06; Asst Comr, Professional Standards, 2006–07; Hd of Serious and Organised Crime, 2008–09; Asst Comr, Specialist Ops, 2009–11; Sen. Consultant, G3 Security, 2013; Hd of Security (Global), Westfield Australia, 2013–14. ACPO lead for Rape and Serious Sexual Offences, 2003–09; Mem., Internat. Gp of Experts on Corruption, 2006–; Chair, Terrorism and Allied Matters, and nat. lead for Counter Terrorism, ACPO, 2009. *Recreations:* long-distance cycling, Liverpool Football Club, cooking.

YATES, Roger Philip; Chief Executive Officer, Pioneer Investments, 2010–12 (non-executive Director, since 2012); *b* 4 April 1957; *s* of Eric Yates and Joyce Yates; *m* 2003, Catriona Louise Maclean; three *s* one *d*. *Educ:* Worcester Coll., Oxford (BA Hons Mod. Hist.); Univ. of Reading (postgrad. res.). GT Management plc, 1981–88, Dir, 1985; Chief Investment Officer: Morgan Grenfell Asset Mgt, 1988–94 (Dir, 1990–94); LGT Asset Mgt, 1994–98; Invesco Asset Mgt, 1998–99; Chief Exec. and Dir, Henderson Global Investors, 1999–2009; Chief Exec., Henderson Gp (formerly HHG), 2003–09 (Dir, 2003–09). Non-exec. Dir, IG Gp plc, 2006–; Director: JPMorgan Elect, 2008–; Electra Private Equity, 2012– (Chm., 2014–). *Recreations:* ski-ing, golf, tennis, climbing.

YATES, Prof. (William) Edgar, MA, PhD; FBA 2002; Professor of German, University of Exeter, 1972–2001, now Emeritus; *b* 30 April 1938; *s* of Douglas Yates and Doris Yates (*née* Goode); *m* 1963, Barbara Anne Fellowes; two *s*. *Educ:* Fettes Coll. (Foundn Schol.); Emmanuel Coll., Cambridge (Minor Open Schol.; MA, PhD). 2nd Lieut, RASC, 1957–58. Lectr in German, Univ. of Durham, 1963–72; University of Exeter: Hd of Dept of German, 1972–86; Dep. Vice-Chancellor, 1986–89. Vice-Pres., Conf. of Univ. Teachers of German, 1991–93. Lewis Fry Meml Lectr, Univ. of Bristol, 1994. Vice-Pres., Wiener Shakespeare-Ges., 1992–2002; Member: Cttee, MHRA, 1980–2015; Council, English Goethe Soc., 1984–2009; Council, Internat. Nestroy-Ges., 1986– (Vice-Pres., 1997–). Germanic Editor, MLR, 1981–88; Editor, 1992–2001, Jt Editor, 2002–09, Nestroyana; Co-ordinating Gen. Editor, historisch-kritische Nestroy-Ausgabe, 1992–2012. Corresp. Fellow, Austrian Acad. of Scis, 1995. Gov., Exeter Sch., 1986–2011 (Chm., 1994–2008). J. G. Robertson Prize, Univ. of London, 1975. Ehrenkreuz für Wissenschaft und Kunst, 1. Klasse (Austria), 2001; Silver Medal, Schwechat, 2005. *Publications:* Grillparzer: a critical introduction, 1972; Nestroy: satire and parody in Viennese popular comedy, 1972; Humanity in Weimar and Vienna: the continuity of an ideal, 1973; Tradition in the German Sonnet, 1981; Schnitzler, Hofmannsthal, and the Austrian Theatre, 1992; Nestroy and the Critics, 1994; Theatre in Vienna 1776–1995: a critical history, 1996; (with B. Pargner) Nestroy in München, 2001; Bin Dichter nur der Posse: Johann Nepomuk Nestroy. Versuch einer Biographie, 2012; *edited:* Hofmannsthal: Der Schwierige, 1966; Grillparzer: Der Traum ein Leben, 1968; Nestroy: Stücke 12–14 (Hist.-krit. Ausgabe), 1981–82, Stücke 34, 1989, Stücke 18/I, 1991, Stücke 22, 1996, Stücke 17/II, 1998, (jtly) Stücke 2, 2000, (jtly) Nachträge (2 vols), 2007; (jtly) Viennese Popular Theatre, 1985; (jtly) Grillparzer und die europäische Tradition, 1987; Vom schaffenden zum edierten Nestroy, 1994; Nestroys Reserve und andere Notizen, 2000, 2nd edn 2003; (jtly) From Perinet to Jelinek, 2001; Der unbekannte Nestroy, 2001; Nestroys Alltag und dessen Dokumentation, 2001; (jtly) Hinter den Kulissen von Biedermeier und Nachmärz, 2001; (jtly) Briefe des Theaterdirektors Carl Carl und seiner Frau Margaretha Carl an Charlotte Birch-Pfeiffer, 2004; (jtly) Theater und Gesellschaft im Wien des 19. Jahrhunderts, 2006; numerous articles on Austrian literary and cultural history, on German literature of the Biedermeier period, and on German lyric poetry; *festschrift:* The Austrian Comic Tradition, 1998. *Recreations:* music, theatre, opera, French wine. *Address:* 7 Clifton Hill, Exeter EX1 2DL. *T:* (01392) 254713.

YATES, William Hugh, MBE 2007; Senior Partner, Knight Frank (formerly Knight Frank & Rutley), 1992–96; *b* 18 Dec. 1935; *s* of late Brig. Morris Yates, DSO, OBE and Kathleen Rosanna Yates (*née* Sherbrooke, later Mrs Hugh Cowan); *m* 1st, 1963, Celia Geraldine Pitman (marr. diss. 1972); one *s*; 2nd, 1979, Elisabeth Susan Mansel-Pleydell (*née* Luard); four step *s*. *Educ:* Lancing Coll.; RMA Sandhurst. FRICS. Commissioned, Royal Dragoons, 1955; ADC to Governor of Aden, 1959. Articled surveyor, Rylands & Co., 1961; Knight Frank & Rutley, 1964–96: Man. Dir, Geneva, 1968–72; Partner, 1972; Man. Partner, 1978–82; Head of Residential Div., 1982–92. Director: INCAS SA, 1970–78; European Property Investment Co. NV, 1973–81; Ecclesiastical Insurance Group, 1985–2006 (Dep. Chm., 1995–2006); Woolwich plc (formerly Woolwich Building Soc.), 1990–2000 (Dep. Chm., 1996–2000); Roxton Sporting Ltd, 2001–03. Save the Children Fund: Chm., Fund Raising Cttee, 1980–86; Hon. Treasurer, 1986–92; Dep. Chm., Suzy Lamplugh Trust, 2002–05. *Recreations:* riding, gardening, golf, music. *Address:* Upper Farm, Milton Lilbourne, Pewsey, Wilts SN9 5LQ. *T:* (01672) 563438. *Club:* Turf.

YAXLEY, John Francis, CBE 1990; HM Overseas Civil Service, 1961–94, retired; *b* 13 Nov. 1936; *s* of late Rev. Canon R. W. and Dorothy Yaxley; *m* 1960, Patricia Anne Scott; one *s*. *Educ:* Hatfield Coll., Durham Univ. National Service, 1958–60. Joined HMOCS, 1961; posts in New Hebrides and Solomon Islands, 1961–75; seconded FCO, 1975–77; Hong Kong, 1977–89: posts included Dir of Industry, Sec. for Econ. Services, and Dep. Financial Sec.; Comr, Hong Kong Govt, London, 1989–93. Mem., Salvation Army Nat. Adv. Bd, 1990–98; Chm., Oxford Diocesan Bd of Finance, 1996–2001. Mem. Council, Durham Univ., 1995–2001; Mem. Governing Body, Hatfield Coll., Durham, 1997–2001. Treasurer: W Mercia NADFAS, 1995–2000; Northleach DFAS, 2001–04. Trustee: Triumph over Phobia UK, 1995–2000; Oxford Historic Churches Trust, 2002–16 (Vice Chm., 2013–16); Trustee and Jt Financial Dir, Prayer Book Soc., 2005–06. *Publications:* The Population of the New Hebrides (with Dr Norma McArthur), 1968; (ed) Public Sector Reform in the Hong Kong Government, 1989. *Recreations:* walking, church crawling, history, gardening. *Address:* Old Housing, Fifield, Oxon OX7 6HF.

YEA, Philip Edward; Chairman, Board of Trustees, British Heart Foundation, 2009–15 (Trustee, 2008–15); non-executive Chairman, bwin.party digital entertainment plc, since 2014; *b* 11 Dec. 1954; *s* of John Yea and Beryl Yea (*née* Putman); *m* 1981, Daryl Walker; two *s* one *d*. *Educ:* Wallington High Sch.; Brasenose Coll., Oxford (MA Mod. Langs). FCMA. Perkins Engines, 1977–82; Klix (Mars), 1983; Guinness PLC, 1984–88; Cope Allman plc, 1988–91; Dir, Financial Control, 1991–93, Finance Dir, 1993–97, Guinness PLC; Finance Dir, Diageo plc, 1997–99; Man. Dir, Investcorp, 1999–2004; Chief Exec., 3i Gp plc, 2004–09. Chm., Rose Partnership LLP, 2011–12. Non-executive Director: Halifax plc, subseq. HBOS plc, 1999–2004; Manchester United plc, 2000–04; Vodafone Gp, 2005– (Sen. non-exec. Dir, 2015–); Aberdeen Asian Smaller Cos Investment Trust, 2014–; Rocket Internet SE, 2014–; Sen. non-exec. Dir, Computacenter, 2015–. Mem., Adv. Gp, PricewaterhouseCoopers Services (UK), 2009–14. Sen. Business Advr to the Duke of York, 2009–14. Ind. Dir and Trustee, Francis Crick Inst., 2011–. *Recreation:* travel. *Address:* Farm Street Advisors Ltd, 29 Farm Street, W1J 5RL.

YEANG, Dr Kenneth King Mun; architect and planner; Principal, T. R. Hamzah & Yeang (Malaysia) Sdn Bhd, since 1976; *b* 6 Oct. 1948; *s* of Yeang Cheng Hin and Louise Yeang; *m* 1986, Priscilla Khoo; two *s* two *d*. *Educ:* Cheltenham Coll.; AA Sch., London (Grad. in Architecture 1971); Wolfson Coll., Cambridge (PhD 1981; Hon. Fellow, 2015). Principal, 2005–10, Chm., 2010–12, Llewelyn Davies Yeang. Major projects include: Menara Mesiniaga, Subang, Malaysia, 1992; Nat. Liby Building, Singapore, 2005; Mewah Oils HQ, Port Kelang, Malaysia, 2005; Gt Ormond St Hosp. Extension, 2010; Solaris, Singapore, 2010; Putrajaya 2C5 Mixed-use Complex, Malaysia, 2010. Graham Willis Vis. Prof., Sheffield Univ., 1994–98, 1999–2005; Distinguished Plym Prof., Univ. of Illinois, 2005–; Adjunct Prof., Tongji Univ., Shanghai, 2005–08. Hon. DLitt Sheffield, 2003. *Address:* T. R. Hamzah & Yeang Sdn Bhd, 8 Jalan Satu, Taman Sri Ukay, off Jalan Ulu Kelang, 6800 Ampang, Selangor, Malaysia. *T:* (603) 42571966, *Fax:* (603) 42561005. *E:* kynnet@pc.jaring.my.

YEATMAN, Prof. Eric Morgan, PhD; FREng, FIET, FIMMM, FIEEE; Professor of Micro-Engineering, since 2005, and Head, Department of Electrical and Electronic Engineering, since 2015, Imperial College London; *b* Oslo, 1 Feb. 1963; *s* of Richard Harry Martin Yeatman and Rannveig Havig Yeatman (*née* Omang); *m* 2002, Antonia Szigeti. *Educ:* Dalhousie Univ., Halifax (BSc 1983; MSc Phys 1986); Technical Univ. of Nova Scotia, Halifax (BEng 1985); Imperial Coll. of Sci., Technol. and Medicine, London (PhD 1989). FIET 2005; FIMMM 2005; FREng 2012; FIEEE 2013. Imperial College London: Lectr, 1989–96; Sen. Lectr, 1996–2001; Reader, 2001–05; Chm., Acad. Trng Cttee, Grad. Sch. of Engrg and Physical Scis, 2002–11; Dep. Hd, Dept of Electrical and Electronic Engrg, 2008–15; Mem., Adv. Bd, Inst. for Security Sci. and Technol., 2010–; Co-Dir, Digital Economy Lab., 2011–. Dir, 2001–, Chm., 2004–11, 2012–13, Microsaic Systems plc (formerly Microsaic Systems Ltd) (Actg Chief Exec., 2011–12). Member: Tech. Adv. Bd, Lambda Crossing, Caesarea, 2001–05; Adv. Bd, West Steag Partners, Essen, 2002–04; Tech. Adv. Bd, Young Associates, London, 2002–05. Advr, Wingate Scholarships, 2005–12; Chm., Internat. Adv. Cttee, Body Sensor Networks conf. series, 2009–; Acad. Dir, Vodafone Tech. Excellence Prog., 2011–; Chief Internat. Acad. Advr, Harbin Inst. of Technol., 2011–. Hon. Sec., Electronic Applications Divl Bd, Inst. of Materials, 1990–2002. Editor-in-Chief, Internat. Jl of Electronics, 1998–2001. Silver Medal, RAEng, 2011. *Publications:* over 200 articles in scientific jls and procs; book chapters; patents. *Recreations:* travel, walking, music, history. *Address:* Department of Electrical and Electronic Engineering, Imperial College London, Exhibition Road, SW7 2AZ. *T:* (020) 7594 6204, *Fax:* (020) 7594 6308. *E:* e.yeatman@imperial.ac.uk.

YELLAND, David Ian; Founder, Kitchen Table Partners Ltd, since 2015; *b* Harrogate, 14 May 1963; *s* of John Michael Yelland and Patricia Ann (*née* McIntosh); *m* 1st, 1996, Tania Farrell (*d* 2006); one *s*; 2nd, 2010, Charlotte, *d* of Prof. Jeremy Elston and Gill Elston; one *d*. *Educ:* Brigg Grammar Sch., Lincs; Coventry Univ. (BA Hons Econs 1984); Harvard Business Sch. (AMP 2003). Grad. trainee, Westminster Press, 1985; trainee reporter, Buckinghamshire Advertiser, 1985–87; industrial reporter, Northern Echo, 1987–88; gen. news and business reporter, North West Times and Sunday Times, 1988–89; city reporter, Thomson Regl Newspapers, 1989–90; joined News Corporation, 1990: city reporter, city editor and NY corresp., The Sun, 1990–93; Dep. Business Ed., Business Ed., Dep. Ed., New York Post, 1993–98; Editor, The Sun, 1998–2003; Sen. Vice Pres., News Corp., NY, 2003; Sen. Vice-Chm., Weber Shandwick UK and Ireland, 2004–06; Partner, Brunswick Gp LLP, 2006–15. Life Patron, NSPCC, 2007; Trustee and Mem. Bd, Action on Addiction, 2012–. FRSA 2003. *Publications:* The Truth About Leo, 2010. *Recreations:* reading, writing, swimming, sleeping, recovering, Manchester City FC. *T:* (020) 7652 4348. *E:* david@kitchentablepartners.com. *Clubs:* Savile, Royal Automobile.

YELTON, Michael Paul; His Honour Judge Yelton; a Circuit Judge, since 1998; *b* 21 April 1950; *s* of Joseph William Yelton and Enid Hazel Yelton; *m* 1973, Judith Sara Chaplin; two *s* one *d*. *Educ:* Colchester Royal Grammar Sch.; Corpus Christi Coll., Cambridge (BA 1971; MA 1973). Called to the Bar, Middle Temple, 1972; in practice at the Bar, 1973–98; Fellow and Dir of Studies in Law, Corpus Christi Coll., Cambridge, 1977–81. *Publications:* Fatal Accidents: a practical guide to compensation, 1998; (jtly) Martin Travers, 1886–1948: an appreciation, 2003; Trams, Trolleybuses, Buses and the Law, 2004; Peter Anson, 2005; Anglican Papalism 1900–1960, 2005; Alfred Hope Patten and the Shrine of Our Lady of Walsingham, 2006; Empty Tabernacles, 2006; (jtly) Anglican Church-Building in London 1915–1945, 2007; Alfred Hope Patten: his life and times in pictures, 2007; (jtly) West Mon, 2008; The Twenty One: an Anglo-Catholic rebellion in London, 2009; Outposts of the Faith: Anglo-Catholicism in some rural parishes, 2009; Blackwells of Earls Colne, 2009; An Anglo-Catholic Scrapbook, 2010; The South India Controversy and the Converts of 1955–6, 2010; Bedwas & Machen UDC, 2010; Gelligaer UDC, 2011; (jtly) Guide to the Family Procedure Rules, 2011; Caerphilly UDC, 2013; (jtly) Anglican Church Building in London 1946–2012, 2013; More Empty Tabernacles, 2014; contribs to transport jls. *Recreations:* ecclesiology, history of road passenger transport, Association football. *Address:* Cambridge County Court, 197 East Road, Cambridge CB1 1BA. *T:* (01223) 224500.

YENTOB, Alan; Creative Director, BBC, since 2004; *b* 11 March 1947; *s* of Isaac Yentob and Flora Yentob (*née* Khazam); one *s* one *d* by Philippa Walker. *Educ:* King's School, Ely; Univ. of Grenoble; Univ. of Leeds (LLB). BBC general trainee, 1968; producer/director, 1970–; arts features, incl. Omnibus, and Arena (Best Arts Series, British Acad. Awards, 1982, 1983, 1984, BPG Awards, 1985); Editor, Arena, 1978–85; Co-Editor, Omnibus, 1985; Hd of Music and Arts, BBC TV, 1985–88; Controller: BBC2, 1988–93, responsible for progs incl. The Late Show, Have I Got News For You, Absolutely Fabulous, Rab C. Nesbitt; BBC1, 1993–96; Dir of Progs, BBC TV, 1996–97; Dir of Television, BBC, 1997–2000; Dir, Drama, Entertainment and Children's Progs, BBC, 2000–04. Member: Bd of Directors, Riverside Studios, 1984–91; BFI Production Board, 1985–93; Council, English Stage Co., 1990; Chm., ICA, 2002–10. Governor: Nat. Film and TV School, 1988; S Bank Bd, 1999; Trustee, Architecture Foundn, 1992; Patron, Timebank (Trustee, 2001). FRTS; Fellow, BFI, 1997. Hon. Fellow: RCA, 1987; RIBA, 1991. Programming Supremo of Year, Broadcast Prodn Awards, 1997. *Recreations:* swimming, books.

YEO, Rt Rev. (Christopher) Richard, JCD; OSB; Abbot President, English Benedictine Congregation, since 2001; *b* 7 July 1948; *s* of Peter and Patricia Yeo. *Educ:* Downside Sch.; Lincoln Coll., Oxford (MA; Hon. Fellow, 2010); St Benet's Hall, Oxford; Pontifical Gregorian Univ., Rome (JCD). Entered monastery, 1970; ordained priest, 1976; Sec. of Abbot Primate of the Benedictines, 1980–86; Parish Priest, Bungay, 1986–93; Official, Congregation for Consecrated Life, 1993–98; Abbot of Downside, 1998–2006; Superior of Buckfast Abbey, 2007–09. *Publications:* The Structure and Content of Monastic Profession, 1982. *Address:* St Elizabeth, Hall Road, Scarisbrick, Ormskirk L40 9QE.

YEO, Diane Helen; consultant; Chairman, Encouragement Through the Arts and Talking, since 2014; *b* 22 July 1945; *d* of Brian Harold Pickard, FRCS and late Joan Daisy Pickard; *m* 1970, Timothy Stephen Kenneth Yeo, *qv*; one *s* one *d*. *Educ:* Blackheath High Sch.; London Univ.; Institut Français de Presse. BBC Radio, 1968–74; Africa Educnl Trust, 1974–79; Girl Guides' Assoc., 1979–82; YWCA, 1982–85; Dir, Inst. of Charity Fundraising Managers, 1985–88; Charity Comr, 1989–95; Chief Exec., Malcolm Sargent Cancer Fund for Children, subseq. Sargent Cancer Care for Children, 1995–2001; Chief Exec., UK for UNHCR, 2001–03; Diane Yeo Associates not for profit consultancy, 2003–; Chief Executive: Muscular Dystrophy Campaign, 2003–05; Chelsea and Westminster Health Charity, 2005–08. Chm., Charity Standards Cttee, 1991–95 (Rowntree Report 1991); Member: Nathan Cttee on Effectiveness and the Voluntary Sector, 1989–90 (Report 1990); Adv. Council, NCVO, 1994–; Council and Audit Cttee, Advertising Standards Authy, 1997–2003; Fundraising Regulation Adv. Gp, Home Office (Charities Act 2003), 2001–. Chm., NCVO/Charity Commn Cttee on Trng of Trustees, 1989–92 (report, On Trust, 1990). Chm. Mgt Bd, 151 Proprietors Ltd, 2009–. Chm., SOS Westminster, 2010–; Ambassador, Save the Children, 1986; Patron, CANCERactive, 2004–. Chm., The Arts Educational Schools, 2004–13. Mem. Ct of Govs, Univ. of Westminster, 2008– (Chm., Nominations Cttee; Member: Develt Cttee; Audit Cttee). Judge, Third Sector Excellence Awards, 2006–. FInstF; FRSA 1989. Paul Harris Fellow, Rotary Internat., 2000. Charity Accounts Award, ICAEW and Charities Aid Foundn, 2002; Local Campaign of the Year Award, Leonard Cheshire Disability, 2011. *Publications:* contribs to professional jls. *Recreations:* tennis, photography, piano, gardening. *E:* diyeo@outlook.com.

See also J. Yeo.

YEO, Jonathan; portrait artist; *b* London, 18 Dec. 1970; *s* of Timothy Stephen Kenneth Yeo, *qv* and Diane Helen Yeo, *qv*; *m* 2006, Shebah Ronay; two *d*. *Educ:* Westminster Sch.; Univ. of Kent. *Solo exhibitions:* Jonathan Yeo's Sketchbook, Eleven, London, 2006; Blue Period, 2008, You're Only Young Twice, 2012, Lazarides, London; Porn in the USA, Lazarides LA, 2010; (I've Got You) Under My Skin, Circle Culture Gall., Berlin, 2013; Jonathan Yeo Portraits, Nat. Gall., London, 2013–14, Lowry Gall., 2014, Laing Art Gall., 2014–15. Painting commissions include portraits of: Archbishop Trevor Huddleston, private collection, 1993; Tony Blair, William Hague and Charles Kennedy (triptych), H of C, 2001; Rupert Murdoch, NPG, 2006; Claire's Room (Grayson Perry), NPG, 2006–13; Prince Philip, Duke of Edinburgh, Muscular Dystrophy Campaign, 2008; Tony Blair, Lincoln's Inn, 2008; Sir Michael Parkinson, NPG, 2010; David Attenborough, Royal Collection, 2011; Girl Reading (Malala Yousafzai), Malala Fund, 2013; Damien Hirst, NPG, 2013; HRH Duchess of Cornwall, Clarence House, 2014. Art consultant for Soho House, 2009–. Judge: Art Fund Prize for Mus, 2010; BP Portrait Award, 2014. *Relevant publication:* The Many Faces of Jonathan Yeo, 2013. *E:* info@jonathanyeo.com. *Clubs:* Groucho, Soho House, Chelsea Arts.

YEO, Rt Rev. Richard; *see* Yeo, Rt Rev. C. R.

YEO, Timothy Stephen Kenneth; *b* 20 March 1945; *s* of late Dr Kenneth John Yeo and Norah Margaret Yeo; *m* 1970, Diane Helen Pickard (*see* D. H. Yeo); one *s* one *d*; one *d*. *Educ:* Charterhouse; Emmanuel Coll., Cambridge (Open Exhibnr 1962; MA 1971). Asst Treas., Bankers Trust Co., 1970–73; Director, Worcester Engineering Co. Ltd, 1975–86. Chief Exec., Spastics Soc., 1980–83, Mem., Exec. Council, 1984–86. MP (C) S Suffolk, 1983–2015. PPS to Sec. of State for Home Dept, 1988–89, to Sec. of State for Foreign Affairs, 1989–90; Parly Under Sec. of State, DoE, 1990–92, DoH, 1992–93; Minister of State, DoE, 1993–94. Opposition spokesman on local govt and envmt, 1997–98; Shadow Minister of Agric., 1998–2001; Shadow Culture, Media and Sport Sec., 2001–02; Shadow Trade and Industry Sec., 2002–03; Shadow Health and Educn Sec., 2003–04; Shadow Transport and Envmt Sec., 2004–05. Member: Social Services Select Cttee, 1985–88; Employment Select Cttee, 1994–96; Treasury Select Cttee, 1996–97; Chairman: Envmtl Audit Select Cttee, 2005–10; Energy and Climate Change Select Cttee, 2010–15; Jt Sec., Cons. Pty Finance Cttee, 1984–87. Captain, Parly Golfing Soc., 1991–95. Director: Genus plc, 2002–04; ITI Energy Ltd, 2006–12; Groupe Eurotunnel SA, 2007–; Chairman: AFC Energy plc, 2007–; Eco City Vehicles plc, 2007–12; TMO Renewables Ltd, 2010–. Hon. Treasurer, International Voluntary Service, 1975–78. Pres., Renewable Energy Assoc., 2012–. Trustee: African Palms, 1970–85; Tanzania Development Trust, 1980–97; Victoria Univ., Kampala, 2010–; Chm., Tadworth Court Trust, 1983–90. Golf Correspondent: Country Life, 1994–; Financial Times, 2004–08. *Publications:* Public Accountability and Regulation of Charities, 1983; Green Gold, 2010. *Recreation:* ski-ing. *Clubs:* Garrick, MCC; Sudbury Conservative (Sudbury); Royal and Ancient Golf (St Andrews); Royal St George's (Sandwich); Sunningdale Golf.

See also J. Yeo.

YEOMAN, Maj.-Gen. Alan, CB 1987; *b* 17 Nov. 1933; *s* of George Smith Patterson Yeoman and Wilhelmina Tromans Elwell; *m* 1960, Barbara Joan Davies; two *s* (one *d* decd). *Educ:* Dame Allan's School, Newcastle upon Tyne. Officer Cadet, RMA Sandhurst, 1952; commnd Royal Signals, 1954; served Korea, Malaysia, Singapore, Cyprus, UK, BAOR and Canada, 1954–70 (Staff Coll., 1963); CO 2 Div. Sig. Regt, BAOR, 1970–73; HQ 1 (BR) Corps, BAOR, 1973–74; MoD, 1974–77; Col AQ, HQLF Cyprus, 1978–79; Comd Trng Gp, Royal Signals and Catterick Garrison, 1979–82; Brig. AQ, HQ 1 (BR) Corps, BAOR, 1982–84; Comd Communications, BAOR, 1984–87; retd 1988. Dir, Army Sport Control Bd, 1988–95 (Army Rugby League Challenge Cup named Yeoman Cup, 1994). Col Comdt, Royal Corps of Signals, 1987–93. Hon. Col, 37th (Wessex and Welsh) Signal Regt, T&AVR, 1987–95. Chm., Royal Signals Assoc., 1995–2000. *Recreation:* bridge. *Address:* c/o Lloyds Bank, 3 South Street, Wareham, Dorset BH20 4LX.

YEOMAN, Rt Rev. David, PhD; Assistant Bishop of Llandaff, 2004–09, now Honorary; *b* 5 March 1944; *s* of Thomas Walter and Doreen Yeoman; *m* 1969, Janice Flower; one *s* one *d*. *Educ:* UC Cardiff (BTh; PhD 2004); St Michael's Coll., Llandaff. Local govt officer, 1963–66. Ordained deacon, 1970, priest, 1971; Curate: St John Baptist, Cardiff, 1970–72; Caerphilly, 1972–76; Vicar: Ystrad Rhondda, 1976–81; Mountain Ash, 1981–96; Rector, Coity with Nolton, 1996–2004; Archdeacon of Morgannwg, 2004–06. Chaplain: Princess of Wales Hosp., 1996–2004; Welsh Guards Assoc., Bridgend, 1996–2001; RBL, Bridgend, 2003–04. Priory Chaplain, St John Priory for Wales, 2010–. *Publications:* (jtly) Christ in AIDS, 1997; (contrib.) Sexuality and Spirituality, 2000. *Recreations:* reading, poetry, music, photography, theatre, sport. *Address:* 4 Llety Gwyn, Bridgend CF31 1RG. *T:* (01656) 649919. *Club:* Rotary International (Bridgend).

YEOMAN, Prof. Michael Magson, PhD; FRSE; Regius Professor of Botany, 1978–93, now Emeritus, and Curator of Patronage, 1988–93, University of Edinburgh; *b* 16 May 1931; *s* of Gordon Yeoman and Mabel Ellen (*née* Magson), Newcastle upon Tyne; *m* 1962, Erica Mary Lines; two *d*. *Educ:* Gosforth Grammar Sch.; King's Coll., Univ. of Durham (BSc 1952, MSc 1954, PhD 1960); FRSE 1980. National Service, Royal Corps of Signals, 1954–56. Demonstrator in Botany, King's Coll., Newcastle upon Tyne, 1957–59; Edinburgh University: Lectr in Botany, 1960; Sen. Lectr, 1968; Reader, 1973; Dean, Fac. of Science, 1981–84; Vice-Principal, 1988–91. Vis. Prof., NENU, Changchun, China, 1986–. Chm., Univs Council for Adult and Continuing Educn (Scotland), 1989–91. Member: Governing Bodies, Nat. Vegetable Res. Stn and Scottish Plant Breeding Stn, 1978–82; SERC Biological Scis Cttee, 1982–85; SERC Biotechnology Management Cttee, 1983–85; British Nat. Cttee for Biology, 1981–89. Chm., Edinburgh Centre for Rural Res., 1989–93; Governor: East of Scotland Coll. of Agriculture, 1984–93; Scottish Crops Res. Inst., 1986–89. Chm. Trustees, Edinburgh Botanic Gdn (Sibbald) Trust, 1996–2003 (Trustee, 1986–2003); Trustee, Royal Botanic Gdn, Edinburgh, 1992–98 (Chm., Scientific Adv. Bd, 1995–98). Convener, N Northumberland Gp, Scottish Rock Garden Club, 1999–2002. Mem. Council, RSE, 1985–91 (Fellowship Sec., 1986–91). Gov. and Chm., Ellingham C of E First Sch., 1993–99; Churchwarden, St Maurice, Ellingham, 1996–2000. Member Editorial Board: Jl of Experimental Botany, 1981–85; Plant Science Letters, 1974–83; New Phytologist, 1977–93 (Trustee); Botanical Jl of Scotland, 1992–99. *Publications:* (ed) Cell Division in Higher Plants, 1976; (jtly) Laboratory Manual of Plant Cell and Tissue Culture, 1982; (ed) Plant Cell Technology, 1986; contrib. scientific jls; chapters, articles and revs in books. *Recreations:* military history, photography, gardening, walking. *Address:* 116 Allerburn Lea, Alnwick, Northumberland NE66 2QP. *T:* (01665) 605822.

YEOMANS, Prof. Julia Mary, DPhil; FRS 2013; Professor of Physics, University of Oxford, since 2002; Pauline Chan Fellow and Tutor in Physics, St Hilda's College, Oxford, since 1983; *b* Derby, 15 Oct. 1954; *d* of Anthony Harold Hickling Yeomans and Edna Maud Yeomans; *m* 1989, Prof. Peter John Hore; four *d*. *Educ:* Manchester High Sch. for Girls; Somerville Coll., Oxford (BA Phys 1976); Wolfson Coll., Oxford (DPhil Theoretical Phys 1979). Postdoctoral Res. Associate, Cornell Univ., 1979–81; Lectr, Univ. of Southampton, 1981–83; University of Oxford: Lectr, 1995–98; Reader in Phys, 1998–2002. Member: Council, Eur. Phys. Soc., 2010–14; Commn C3, IUPAP, 2011–. FInstP 2000. Gov., Francis Holland Schs, 2009–. Eur. Phys. Jl E—Pierre-Gilles de Gennes Lect. Prize, 2013. *Publications:* Statistical Mechanics of Phase Transitions, 1992; articles on soft matter physics in learned jls. *Recreations:* family, hiking, running, tango. *Address:* Rudolf Peierls Centre for Theoretical Physics, University of Oxford, 1 Keble Road, Oxford OX1 3NP. *T:* (01865) 273992, *Fax:* (01865) 273947. *E:* J.Yeomans1@physics.ox.ac.uk.

YEOMANS, Lucy; Editor-in-Chief, Net-A-Porter.com, since 2012; Editor, Porter, since 2014; *b* 1 Nov. 1970; *d* of Harry Hammond Light Yeomans and Margaret (*née* Boyle). *Educ:* Univ. of St Andrews (MA Hons Hist. of Art 1992). Ed., Boulevard mag., Paris, 1993–95; Lit. Ed. and Features Ed., The European, 1995–98; Features Ed., Dep. Ed. and Actg Ed., Tatler, 1998–2000; Ed., Harpers & Queen, later Harper's Bazaar, 2000–12. FRSA. *Recreations:* theatre, horse-riding, music, poetry. *Address:* Net-A-Porter Group Ltd, 1 The Village Offices, Westfield London, Ariel Way, W12 7GF. *Club:* Soho House.

YERBURGH, family name of **Baron Alvingham**.

YEVTUSHENKO, Yevgeny Aleksandrovich; poet, novelist, film director, film actor, photographer; *b* 18 July 1933; *m*; five *s*; *m* 4th, 1986, Maria Novikova. *Educ:* Moscow Literary Inst., 1952–56 (expelled). Elected Mem., Congress of People's Deputies of USSR, 1989. Distinguished Professor: Queen's College, New York; University of Tulsa. Has visited 94 countries; Vice-Pres., Russian PEN, 1990–93; Hon. Mem., Amer. Acad. of Arts and Letters, 1987; Mem., European Acad. of Scis and Arts; hon. degrees from numerous Univs. Film actor: Take Off, 1979 (silver prize, Moscow Internat. film fest.); film director: Kindergarten, 1984; Stalin's Funeral, 1990. *Publications: in Russian:* Scouts of the Future, 1952; The Third Snow, 1955; The Highway of Enthusiasts, 1956; The Promise, 1959; The Apple, 1960; A Sweep of the Arm, 1962; Tenderness, 1962; Mail Boat, 1966; Bratsk Power Station, 1967; Kazan's University, 1971; A Father's Hearing, 1975; Morning People, 1978; Talent is not a Miracle by Chance (essays), 1980; Wild Berries Places (novel), 1981; Mother and Neutron Bomb and other poems, 1983; Almost at the End, 1986; A Wind of Tomorrow (essays), 1987; Selected Poetry, 3 vols, 1987; Don't Die Before You're Dead (novel), 1993; Late Tears (poetry), 1995; The Best from the Best (poetry), 1995; Strophes of the Century (anthology), 1995; God Could be Each of Us, 1996; If All Danes were Jews (play), 1996; Wolf's Passport (memoirs), 1998; words to Shostakovich's 13th Symphony (Babi Yar) and Execution of Stepan Razin Oratorio; *in English:* Zima Junction, 1961; A Precocious Autobiography, 1963; Bratsk Power Station, 1966; Stolen Apples, 1972; From Desire to Desire, 1976; The Face Behind the Face, 1979; Dove in Santiago, 1982; Invisible Threads (photography), 1981; Wild Berries (novel), 1984; Ardabiola (novel), 1985; Almost at the End, 1987; Divided Twins (photography), 1987; Last Attempt, 1988; Politics—everybody's privilege (essays), 1990; Collected Poems 1952–90, 1991; Fatal Half Measures, 1991; (ed) Twentieth-Century Russian Poetry, 1993; Pre-morning (poetry), 1995; Collected Works, vols 1–2, 1997; The Thirteen, 1997; The Evening Rainbow, 1999; Selected Prose, 1999. *Address:* 2256 South Troost Avenue, Tulsa, OK 74114–1348, USA.

YIANNI, Steven John, FREng; Chief Executive, Transport Systems Catapult, since 2013; *b* Barnet, 9 April 1962; *s* of Antony Yianni and Marianne Yianni; *m* 1984, Pamela Lesley Paton; two *s* one *d*. *Educ:* Highgate Sch.; Haberdashers' Aske's Boys' Sch., Elstree; King's Coll., Cambridge (BA Engrg 1983; MA 1985); London Business Sch. (MBA 1990). CEng 1988; FIMechE 2002. Ford Motor Co.: graduate trainee, 1983–85; Develt Engr, 1985–87; Powertrain Product Planner, 1988–89; Sen. Strategy Analyst, 1990–91; J.C. Bamford Excavators Ltd: Gen. Manager, JCB Res., 1991–93; Engrg Manager, JCB Wheeled Loader Div., 1993–95, JCB Loadall Div., 1995–97; Gen. Manager, Hydraulic Ram Div., 1998–99; Dir, 1999–2007; Dir, Engrg, Network Rail, 2008–13. Chm., 2010–13, non-exec. Dir, 2013–, Welding Inst. FREng 2014. *Recreations:* theatre, walking, family, running, swimming. *Address:* Transport Systems Catapult, The Pinnacle, 170 Midsummer Boulevard, Milton Keynes MK9 1BP. *T:* (01908) 359999. *E:* steve.yianni@ts.catapult.org.uk.

YIP, Amanda Louise; QC 2011; a Recorder, since 2009; a Deputy High Court Judge, since 2013; *b* Liverpool, 23 April 1969; *d* of Rt Hon. Sir John William Kay, PC (Rt Hon. Lord Justice Kay) and Jeffa Kay; *m* 1991, David Yip; one *s* two *d*. *Educ:* Merchant Taylors' Sch. for Girls, Crosby, Liverpool; Emmanuel Coll., Cambridge (BA Law 1990). Called to the Bar, Gray's Inn, 1991; in practice as a barrister, Exchange Chambers, 1991–. *Recreations:* spending time with family and friends, swimming, ski-ing. *Address:* Exchange Chambers, 1 Derby Square, Liverpool L2 9XX. *T:* (0151) 236 7747, *Fax:* (0151) 236 3433. *E:* yip@exchangechambers.co.uk.

YIP, Prof. George Stephen; Professor of Strategy (formerly of Management), and Co-Director, Centre on China Innovation, China Europe International Business School, since 2011; *b* 24 Sept. 1947; *s* of Teddy Yip and Susie (*née* Ho); *m* 1970, Moira Winsland; one *s* one *d*. *Educ:* Peak Sch., Hong Kong; East Grinstead County Grammar Sch.; Dover Coll.; Magdalene Coll., Cambridge (BA Hons 1970; MA 1973); Cranfield Univ. (MBA 1976); Harvard Business Sch. (MBA 1976; DBA 1980). Account Executive, 1970–72, Account Supervisor, 1973–74, Lintas London; Product Manager, Birds Eye Foods, 1972–73; Business Manager, Data Resources Inc., 1976–78; Asst Prof., Harvard Business Sch., 1980–83; Sen. Associate, MAC Gp, 1983–86; Sen. Manager, Price Waterhouse, 1986–87; Vis. Associate Prof., Georgetown Univ., 1987–91; Adjunct Prof., UCLA, 1991–99; Beckwith Prof. of Mgt Studies, Judge Inst. and Fellow, Magdalene Coll., Univ. of Cambridge, 1998–2000; Prof. of Strategic and Internat. Mgt, 2001–06, Associate Dean, 2001–03, London Business Sch.; Vice-Pres., and Dir of Res. and Innovation, Capgemini Consulting, 2006–08; Dean, Rotterdam Sch. of Mgt, Erasmus Univ., 2008–11. Visiting Professor: Stanford Business Sch., 1997; Imperial Coll. London Business Sch., 2011–; Vis. Fellow, Templeton Coll., Oxford, 1998; Sen. Fellow, Advanced Inst. Mgt Res., 2003. Fellow: World Economic Forum, 1998; Acad. of Internat. Business, 1999. *Publications:* Barriers to Entry, 1982; Total Global Strategy, 1992; Asian Advantage, 1998; Strategies for Central and Eastern Europe, 2000; Managing Global Customers, 2007; Strategic Transformation, 2013; articles in internat. mgt and mkting jls. *Recreations:* theatre, opera, classical music, tennis, sailing, rural Maine. *Address:* 39 Halsey Street, SW3 2PT. *T:* (020) 7225 3868.

YOCKLUNN, Sir John (Soong Chung), KCVO 1977; Kt 1975; Associate University Librarian, Monash University Library, 1993–98 (Chief Librarian, Gippsland Institute of Advanced Education, then Monash University College, 1983–92); *b* Canton, China, 5 May 1933; *s* of late Charles Soong Yocklunn and Ho Wai-lin, formerly of W Australia; *m* 1981, Patricia Ann Mehegan. *Educ:* Perth Modern Sch.; Northam High Sch., W Australia; Univ. of W Australia (BA); Aust. Nat. Univ. (BA); Univ. of Sheffield (MA). MCLIP; ALAA. Dept of the Treasury, Canberra, 1959–63; Nat. Library of Australia, Canberra, 1964–67; Librarian-in-Charge, Admin. Coll. of Papua New Guinea, Port Moresby, 1967–69; Exec. Officer, Public Service Board of Papua New Guinea, 1969–70; Librarian, Admin. Coll., 1970–72; Principal Private Sec. to Chief Minister, 1972–73; study in UK, under James Cook Bicentenary Schol., 1973–74; on return, given task of organising a national library; Sen. Investigation Officer, Public Services Commn, 1974–77; Asst Sec. (Library Services), Dept of Educn (National Librarian of PNG), 1978–83. Chm., PNG Honours and Awards Cttee, 1975–83; Advr on Honours to PNG Govt, 1984–85; Consultant on estabt of new honours system, 1985–86. Vice-Pres., Pangu Pati, 1968–72; Nat. Campaign Manager for Pangu Pati for 1972 general elections in Papua New Guinea; Treasurer, Pangu Pati, 1973–80. Asst Dir, Visit of Prince of Wales to PNG, 1975; Dir, Visits of the Queen and Prince Philip to PNG, 1977 and 1982. Mem. Nat. Adv. Council, Aust. Broadcasting Corp., 2001–03. Australian Library and Information Association: Chm., Gippsland Regional Gp, 1984–94; Mem., Vict. Br. Council, 1986–94; rep. on Commonwealth Library Assoc., 1988–91; Mem. Exec. Cttee, Vict. Div., Aust. Council for Library and Inf. Servs, 1989–94; Vice Pres., University Liby Soc. of Rockhampton, 1999–2003. Pres., Regl Arts Develt Fund Council, Rockhampton, 2004–06 (Vice-Pres., 1999–2003); Mem. Adv. Council, CARE Aust., 1988–92. Trustee, 1986–98, Chm. of Friends, 1985–88, Vice-Chm., 1992–98, Mus. of Chinese Australian Hist.; Sec., Rockhampton Chinese Assoc., 2003–04 (Vice Pres., 1999–2000; Pres., 2001–03). *Publications:* The Charles Barrett Collection of Books relating to Papua New Guinea, 1967, 2nd edn 1969; articles on librarianship, etc., in various jls. *Recreations:* orders and medals research, heraldry, languages. *Address:* Unit 68, Settlers Village, 14 Pauline Martin Drive, Rockhampton, Qld 4700, Australia. *T:* (7) 49273960.

YONATH, Prof. Ada E., PhD; Martin S. and Helen Kimmel Professor of Structural Biology, Director, Mazer Center for Structural Biology, and Director, Kimmelman Center for Biomolecular Structure and Assembly, Weizmann Institute of Science; *b* Jerusalem, 22 June 1939; *d* of Hillel and Esther Lifshitz; one *d*. *Educ:* Hebrew Univ. of Jerusalem (BSc 1962; MSc 1964); Weizmann Inst. of Sci. (PhD 1968). Postdoctoral studies, Carnegie-Mellon Univ. and MIT, 1968–70; Weizmann Inst. of Sci., 1970–; Gp Leader, Max Planck Inst. for Molecular Genetics, 1979–84; Hd, Res. Unit for Ribosome Structure, Max Planck Unit of Structural Molecular Biol., DESY, Hamburg, 1986–2004. Vis. Prof., Univ. of Chicago, 1977–78. Mem., EMBO. Member: NAS; Amer. Acad. Arts and Scis; Israel Acad. Scis and Humanities; Eur. Acad. Scis and Art. (Jtly) Nobel Prize in Chem., 2009. *Address:* Department of Structural Biology, Weizmann Institute of Science, PO Box 26, Rehovet 76100, Israel.

YONG, Rt Rev. Datuk Ping Chung; Bishop of Sabah, 1990–2006; Archbishop of South East Asia, 2000–06; *b* 20 Feb. 1941; parents decd; *m* 1969, Julia Yong; two *d*. *Educ:* Meml Univ., Newfoundland (BA 1968); Queen's Coll., Newfoundland (LTh 1969). Ordained, Sabah, 1970; Canon, 1974–90, Archdeacon, 1976–90, Sabah. Chairman: ACC, 1984–90; Council of Churches of E Asia, 1996–99; President: Christian Fedn of Malaysia, 1997–2001; Council of Churches of Malaysia, 1997–2001; Sabah Council of Churches, 1997–2003. *Address:* c/o PO Box 10811, 88809 Kota Kinabalu, Sabah, Malaysia.

YORK, Archbishop of, since 2005; **Most Rev. and Rt Hon. John Tucker Mugabi Sentamu;** PC 2005; PhD; *b* 10 June 1949; *s* of John Walakira and Ruth; *m* 1973, Margaret (*née* Wanambwa); one *s* one *d*. *Educ:* Masooli, Kyambogo and Kitante Hill and Old Kampala Sch., Uganda; Makerere Univ. (LLB 1971); Selwyn Coll., Cambridge (Pattison Student; BA 1976; MA, PhD 1984; Hon. Fellow, 2005); Ridley Hall, Cambridge; Dip. in Legal Practice, Uganda, 1972. Advocate, Uganda High Ct, 1972–74. Ordained deacon and priest, 1979; Asst Chaplain, Selwyn Coll., Cambridge, 1979; Asst Curate, St Andrew, Ham, and Chaplain, HM Remand Centre, Latchmere House, 1979–82; Asst Curate, St Paul, Herne Hill, 1982–83; Priest-in-charge, Holy Trinity, and Vicar, St Matthias, Tulse Hill, 1983–84, Vicar of jt parish, 1985–96; Priest-in-charge, St Saviour, Brixton Hill, 1987–89; Area Bp of Stepney, 1996–2002; Bp of Birmingham, 2002–05. Hon. Canon, Southwark Cathedral, 1993–96. Mem., Gen. Synod of C of E, 1985–96 (Mem., Standing Cttee, 1988–96, Policy Cttee, 1990–96); Chm., Cttee for Minority Ethnic Anglican Concerns, 1990–99. Member: Young Offenders Cttee, NACRO, 1986–95; Council, Family Action (formerly Family Welfare Assoc.), 1989–; Stephen Lawrence Judicial Inquiry, 1997–99; Chairman: Islington Partnership, 2002–04; EC1 New Deal for Communities, 2000–02; London Marriage Guidance Council, 2000–03 (also Pres.); Damilola Taylor Investigation and Prosecution Review, 2002; NHS Haemoglobinopathy Screening Prog., 2001–13; Living Wage Commn, 2013–14; Sponsor, York Fairness Commn, 2011–12. President: Youth for Christ, 2004–; YMCA, 2005–. Trustee, John Smith Inst., 2002–. Gov., Univ. of N London, 1997–2002; Chancellor: York St John Univ., 2006–; Univ. of Cumbria, 2007–. FRSA. Freeman: City of London, 2000; City of Montego Bay, 2007. Hon. Bencher, Gray's Inn, 2007. Hon. Fellow: Canterbury Christ Church UC, 2001; QMW, 2001; St Margaret's Coll., Dunedin, 2014. Harold Turner Vis. Fellow, Univ. of Otago, 2014. DUniv Open, 2001; Hon. DPhil Glos, 2002; Hon. DLitt West Indies, 2007; Hon. DCL Northumbria at Newcastle, 2008; Hon. DD: Birmingham, 2003; Hull, 2007; Cambridge, 2008; Nottingham, 2008; Wycliffe Coll., Toronto, 2009; Sewanee, Tennessee, 2010; London, 2010; Aberdeen, 2013; Huron Univ. Coll., London, Ont, 2013; Hon. LLD: Leicester, 2005; Teeside, 2009; Leeds, 2010; Hon. DLitt Sheffield, 2007; Hon. Dr: Birmingham City, 2008; DUniv York, 2010; Hon. DTheol Chester, 2009. Midlander of the Year, 2003; Yorkshire Man of the Year, 2007. *Recreations:* music, cooking, reading, Rugby, football, athletics. *Address:* Bishopthorpe Palace, Bishopthorpe, York YO23 2GE.

YORK, Dean of; *see* Faull, Very Rev. V. F.

YORK, Archdeacon of; *see* Bullock, Ven. S. R.

YORK, David; independent consultant, since 2004; *b* 20 April 1950; *s* of George William York and Ann (*née* Morgan); *m* 1982, Lindsey Anne Murgatroyd (marr. diss. 2006). *Educ:* Manor Park Sch., Newcastle upon Tyne; Salford Univ. (BSc 1973). MICE 1976. Joined Dept of Transport, 1970; Project Engr, 1977–83; Principal Engr, 1983–87; Superintending Engr, 1987–90; Director: NW Network Mgt, 1990; Yorks and Humberside Construction Prog., 1990–93; Motorway Widening Unit, 1993–95; Dep. Road Prog. Dir, 1995–96, Road Prog. Dir, 1996; Highways Agency: Project Services Dir, 1996–2001; Operations Dir, 2001–03; Nat. Traffic Dir, 2003–04. *Recreations:* flying, scuba diving, golf. *E:* davidyork@davidyork.plus.com.

YORK, Col Edward Christopher, OBE 2015; TD 1978; Vice Lord-Lieutenant of North Yorkshire, 1999–2014; Chairman and Managing Director, Hutton Wandesley Farms Co., and others, 1984–2014; *b* 22 Feb. 1939; *o s* of late Christopher York and Pauline Rosemary York (*née* Fletcher); *m* 1965, Sarah Ann, *d* of late Major James Kennedy Maxwell, MC; one *s* one *d*. *Educ:* Eton Coll. 1st Royal Dragoons, 1957–64. Chm., Thirsk Racecourse Co., 1993–2008. Vice Pres., Northern Assoc. of Building Socs, 1987–91; Pres., Yorks Agricl Soc., 1989 (Mem. Council, 1970–99); Hon. Show Dir, 1992–96, Pres., 1997, Chm. of Council, 1998–2002, Vice Patron, 2003–, RASE; Mem., N Yorks Br., 1978–2005, RASE Rep. on Council, 1999–2002, CLA. Chm., Royal Armouries Develt Trust (Leeds), 1995–99. CO, Queen's Own Yeomanry, 1979–81 (Hon. Col, 1998–2003); Dep. Comdr, 15 (NE) Bde, 1981–85; ADC to the Queen, 1982–86; Col Comdt, Yeomanry, 1994–99. Chm., Yorks and Humberside RFCA (formerly TAVRA), 1998–2003; Vice-Chm. (Army), Council of RFCAs, 2001–04; Co. Chm., N Yorks Scouts, 1999–2008; President: Army Benevolent Fund, N Yorks, 1999–; SSAFA, N Yorks, 2003–14. Mem. Bd, Yorks Mus. of Farming, 1979–2001. Chm., Christopher Topham's Apprenticing Charity, 1974–2011; Trustee, Arthur Rank Centre, NAC, 2002–14; Gov., William Akroyd's Charity, 1996–2008; Patron, MIND, York, 2009–. FRAgS 1998. DL 1988, High Sheriff, 1988, N Yorks. *Recreations:* racing, field sports. *Address:* Hutton Wandesley Hall, York YO26 7NA. *T:* (home) (01904) 738240, (office) (01904) 738755, *Fax:* (01904) 738468. *E:* ecy@huttonwandesley.co.uk. *Club:* Boodle's.

YORK, Giles Tristan, QPM 2015; Chief Constable, Sussex Police, since 2014; *b* Tonbridge, Kent, 10 Feb. 1967; *s* of Carl Peter Francis Andrew York and Deidre Gabrielle York (*née* MacDonald); *m* 1995, Sally Gail Hargreaves; one *s* two *d*. *Educ:* Judd Sch., Tonbridge; Univ. of Durham (BSc); Roffey Park, Sussex (MBA). With Kent Police, 1990–2004, Divl Comdr, Medway, 1999–2002, Hd, Special Br., 2002–04; Asst Chief Constable, S Wales Police, 2005–08; Dep. Chief Constable, Sussex Police, 2008–14. FRSA. *Recreations:* photography, Land Rover owner (Series 3). *Address:* Sussex Police Headquarters, Malling House, Church Lane, Lewes, E Sussex BN7 2DZ.

YORK, Michael, (Michael York-Johnson), OBE 1996; actor; *b* 27 March 1942; *s* of Joseph Johnson and Florence Chown; *m* 1968, Patricia Frances McCallum. *Educ:* Hurstpierpoint College; Bromley Grammar School; University College, Oxford (MA). *Stage:* Dundee Repertory Theatre, 1964; National Theatre Co., 1965; Outcry, NY, 1973; Bent, NY, 1980; Cyrano de Bergerac, Santa Fe, 1981; Whisper in the Mind, 1991; The Crucible, NY, 1992; Someone Who'll Watch Over Me, NY, 1993; Camelot, US tour, 2007; Strauss Meets Frankenstein, Long Beach, 2008; Lisztian Loves, 2011; My Fair Lady, 2012; King Lear, 2013; *films:* The Taming of the Shrew, Accident, 1966; Romeo and Juliet, 1967; Cabaret, England Made Me, 1971; The Three Musketeers, 1973; Murder on the Orient Express, 1974; Logan's Run, 1975; The Riddle of the Sands, 1978; Success is the Best Revenge, 1984; Dawn, 1985; Vengeance, 1986; The Secret of the Sahara, Imbalances, 1987; The Joker, Midnight Blue, The Return of the Musketeers, 1988; The Long Shadow, 1992; Rochade, 1992; Eline Vere, 1992; Wide Sargasso Sea, 1993; Discretion Assured, 1993; The Shadow of a Kiss, 1994; Gospa, 1995; Austin Powers, 1997; Wrongfully Accused, 1998; Lovers and Liars, The Omega Code, 1999; Borstal Boy, 2000; Megiddo, 2001; Austin Powers in Goldmember, 2002; Moscow Heat, 2004; Testimony, 2009; The Justice of Wolves, 2010; The Mill and the Cross, 2011; *television* includes: Jesus of Nazareth, 1976; A Man Called Intrepid, 1978; For Those I Loved, 1981; The Weather in the Streets, The Master of Ballantrae, 1983; Space, 1984; The Far Country, 1985; The Four Minute Mile, The Heat of the Day, 1988; Till We Meet Again, 1989; The Night of the Fox, 1990; Fall from Grace, 1994; September, 1995; Not of This Earth, 1996; The Ring, 1996; True Women, Dark Planet, The Ripper, 1997; The Search for Nazi Gold, A Knight in Camelot, 1998; Perfect Little Angels, 1999; The Haunting of Hell House, 2000; The Lot, 2001; Curb Your Enthusiasm, 2002; La Femme Musketeer, 2004; Icon, 2005; Law and Order: Criminal Intent, 2006; The Four Seasons, 2008; Coming Home, 2009; British Legends of Stage and Screen, 2012. Chm., Calif Youth Theatre, 1987–. Hon. DFA S Carolina, 1988. *Publications:* (contrib.) The Courage of Conviction, 1986; (contrib.) Voices of Survival, 1987; Travelling Player (autobiog.), 1991; A Shakespearean Actor Prepares, 2000; Dispatches from Armageddon, 2002; Are My Blinkers Showing?, 2005. *Recreations:* travel, music, collecting theatrical memorabilia. *W:* www.michaelyork.net.

YORK-JOHNSON, Michael; *see* York, M.

YORKE, family name of **Earl of Hardwicke**.

YORKE, David Harry Robert, CBE 1993; FRICS; Senior Partner, Weatherall Green & Smith, Chartered Surveyors, 1984–92 (Consultant, 1992–97); *b* 5 Dec. 1931; *s* of late Harry Yorke and Marie Yorke, Minera, N Wales; *m* 1955, Patricia Gwynneth Fowler-Tutt; one *d*. *Educ:* Dean Close Sch., Cheltenham; College of Estate Management; Open Univ. (BA (Hons) 2005). FRICS 1966 (ARICS 1956); FCIArb 1994. Articled to Tregear & Sons, 1948–54. 2nd Lieut RA, 1955–56. Weatherall Green & Smith, 1960–97, Partner, 1961. Dir, London Auction Mart, 1981–92; Chm., Belgravia Property Co. Ltd, 1993–95. Mem., Bristol Develt Corp., 1988–96; Dir, British Waterways Bd, 1988–2000 (Vice-Chm., 1998–2000). Royal Institution of Chartered Surveyors: Mem., Gen. Council, 1978–92; Pres., Gen. Practice Div., 1981–82; Pres., 1988–89; Chm., RICS Insurance Services, 1991–96. Mem. Council, British Property Fedn, 1990–94. Pres., British Chapter, Internat. Real Estate Fedn, 1974. Freeman, City of London, 1979; Liveryman, Co. of Chartered Surveyors, 1979. *Recreations:* reading, crosswords, occasional cookery. *Address:* Beech House, The Croft, Kintbury, Berks RG17 9TS. *T:* (01488) 608788. *E:* dhryorke@gmail.com. *Clubs:* Buck's, Sloane, East India.

YORKE, John; Managing Director, Company Pictures, 2013–15; *b* 9 July 1962; *s* of Sydney Yorke and Valerie Yorke. *Educ:* Univ. of Newcastle upon Tyne (BA 1st Cl. Hons English Lit. 1984). BBC Radio Five, Drama: Producer, 1990–92; Sen. Producer, 1992–93; Chief Producer, 1993–94; BBC 1: Script Editor, 1994, Series Script Editor, 1994, Story Editor, 1995–98, Eastenders; Producer, City Central, 1998–2000; Exec. Producer, Eastenders, 2000–03; Dep. Hd of Drama Series, BBC, 2003–04; Hd of Drama, Channel 4 Television, 2004–05; Controller, Continuing Drama Series and Head of Independent Drama, BBC, 2005–06; Controller, Drama Production, subseq. Drama Production and New Talent, BBC, 2006–12. Founder, BBC Writers' Acad., 2004. Vis. Prof., Univ. of Newcastle upon Tyne, 2007–. *Publications:* Into The Woods: a five act journey, 2013.

YORKE, Very Rev. Michael Leslie; Dean of Lichfield, 1999–2004, now Dean Emeritus; *b* 25 March 1939; *s* of late Leslie Henry and Brenda Emma Yorke; *m* 1st, 1964, Michal Sara Dadd (*d* 1987); one *s* one *d*; 2nd, 1988, Frances Grace Archer. *Educ:* Midhurst Grammar Sch.;

Brighton Coll.; Magdalene Coll., Cambridge (BA 1962; MA 1966); Cuddesdon Theol Coll., Oxford. Ordained deacon, 1964, priest, 1965; Curate, Croydon Parish Church, 1964–68; Precentor and Chaplain, 1968–73, Dep. Dir of Res. and Trng, 1972–74, Chelmsford Cathedral; Rector, Ashdon with Hadstock, 1974–78; Canon Residentiary, 1978–88, Vice Provost, 1984–88, now Canon Emeritus, Chelmsford Cathedral; Vicar, St Margaret's with St Nicholas, King's Lynn, 1988–94; Hon. Canon, Norwich Cathedral, 1992–94, now Canon Emeritus; Provost of Portsmouth, 1994–99. Nat. Chm., Samaritans Inc., 1976–79; Vice-Chairman: Help the Aged, 1980–85; Mid-Essex Health Authy, 1981–87 (Acting Chm., 1987–88). *Publications:* (with C. Proot) Life to be Lived: challenges and choices for patients and carers in life-threatening illnesses, 2012. *Recreations:* opera, 20th century military history, contemporary art. *Address:* The Old Chapel, West Street, North Creake, Fakenham, Norfolk NR21 9LQ. *Club:* Norfolk.

YORKE, Robert Anthony, FSA; finance director and management consultant, since 1981; *b* 27 June 1944; *s* of late Patrick Langdon Yorke and Pamela Mary (*née* Rudgard; later Mrs Robert Michael Clive); *m* 1975, Morag, *d* of late J. S. M. Dow; one *s* one *d*. *Educ:* Marlborough Coll.; Clare Coll., Cambridge (MA); London Business Sch. (MSc Econ). Financial Controller, Bowater Corp., 1975–77; Chief Exec., Ridham Freight Services, 1977–81; Finance Dir, London and Devonshire Trust Ltd, 1987–2009. Comr, RCHME, 1991–99; Member: Ancient Monuments Adv. Cttee, English Heritage, 1998–2003; English Heritage Adv. Cttee, 2003–04; Sussex Inshore Fisheries Conservation Authy, 2011. Chairman: Nautical Archaeol. Soc., 1987–91; Jt Nautical Archaeol. Policy Cttee, 1995– (Vice-Chm., 1988–95). FSA 2001. Gov., Coll. of Richard Collyer, Horsham, 2012–. *Publications:* contribs to learned jls. *Recreations:* nautical archaeology, tennis. *Address:* Silver Birches, Bashurst Hill, Itchingfield, Horsham, W Sussex RH13 0NY. *T:* (01403) 790311.

YORKE, Thomas Edward; singer and guitarist; *b* Wellingborough, Northants, 7 Oct. 1968; *m* 2003, Rachel Owen; one *s* one *d*. *Educ:* Abingdon Sch., Oxon; Univ. of Exeter. Lead singer, Radiohead, 1991–. *Albums:* with Radiohead: Pablo Honey, 1993; The Bends, 1995; OK Computer, 1997 (Grammy Award, 1997); Kid A, 2000 (Grammy Award, 2000); Amnesia, 2001; Hail to the Thief, 2003; In Rainbows, 2007 (Ivor Novello Award, 2008; Grammy Award, 2008); The King of Limbs, 2011; solo: The Eraser, 2006; Tomorrow's Modern Boxes, 2014; with Atoms for Peace: Amok, 2013. *Address:* c/o XL Recordings, One Codrington Mews, W11 2EH.

YOSHIDA, Miyako, Hon. OBE 2007; Principal Dancer, Royal Ballet, 1995–2010; *b* 28 Oct. 1965; *d* of Eiji Yoshida and Etsuko (*née* Fukuda). *Educ:* Royal Ballet Sch. Joined Sadler's Wells Royal Ballet, later Birmingham Royal Ballet, 1984; soloist, 1987; Principal, 1988; transf. to Royal Ballet, 1995. *Performances* include leading rôles in: Swan Lake, Sleeping Beauty, The Nutcracker, Giselle, Elite Syncopations, La Fille Mal Gardée, Hobson's Choice, The Dream, Don Quixote, Paquita, Allegri Diversi, Theme and Variations, Concerto Barroco, Les Sylphides, Divertimento No 15, Danses Concertantes, Les Patineurs, Romeo and Juliet, The Firebird, Coppélia. Prix de Lausanne, 1983; Global Award, 1989; Nakagawa Einosuke Award, 1995; Akiko Tachibana Award, 1996, 2002; Arts Encouragement Prize for New Artists, Min. of Educn, Sci., Sports and Culture, 1997; Hattori Chieko Award, 1998; Artist for Peace, Unesco, 2004; Japan Soc. Award, 2007; Best Female Dancer, Dance Critics, 2007. *Recreations:* reading, watching films. *Address:* Blooming Agency Co. Ltd, 5–1–10–501 Minami Aoyama, Minato-ku, Tokyo 107–0062, Japan.

YOUARD, Richard Geoffrey Atkin; The Investment Ombudsman (formerly Investment Referee), 1989–96; *b* 27 Jan. 1933; *s* of Geoffrey Bernard Youard, MBE and Hon. Rosaline Joan Youard (*née* Atkin); *m* 1960, Felicity Ann Morton; one *s* two *d*. *Educ:* Bradfield Coll., Berks; Magdalen Coll., Oxford (BA Jurisprudence; MA 1998). Admitted Solicitor, 1959. Commnd (2nd Lieut) RA, 1952 (Nat. Service); Lieut TA, 1954. Slaughter and May, London: Articled Clerk, 1956–59; Asst Solicitor, 1959–68; Partner, 1968–89. Inspector, DTI, 1987. Ind. Investigator, SIB, 1994–97. Hon. Sen. Res. Fellow, KCL, 1988–. Chairman: Nat. Fedn of Consumers Groups, 1968; Cttee of Inquiry, Accountants Jt Disciplinary Scheme, 1989; Mem., Home Office Cttee on London Taxicab and Car Hire Trade, 1967. Clerk to Governors, Bradfield Coll., 1968–89, Governor, 1989–95. Mem., Chancellor's Court of Benefactors, Oxford Univ., 1995–2000. Mem. Council, Pali Text Soc., 1991–2000. Trustee, Elizabeth Garrett Anderson Hosp. Appeal, 1997–2005. *Publications:* (contrib.) Sovereign Borrowers, 1984; (contrib.) Current Issues of International Financial Law, 1985; (jtly) Butterworths Banking Documents, 1986; (contrib.) Butterworths Banking and Financial Law Review, 1987; contribs on legal aspects of internat. finance to Jl of Business Law, Euromoney and Internat. Financial Law Review. *Recreations:* gardening, electronics (holder of Amateur Transmitting Licence), map collecting, reading, jazz, Welsh language/history. *Address:* Hill Fort House, Ruckhall, Eaton Bishop, Herefordshire HR2 9QG. *T:* (01981) 251754; Cwm Mynach Ganol, Bontddu, Dolgellau, Gwynedd LL40 2TU.

YOUNG; *see* Hughes-Young, family name of Baron St Helens.

YOUNG, family name of **Barons Kennet, Young of Cookham, Young of Graffham** and **Young of Norwood Green**.

YOUNG OF COOKHAM, Baron *cr* 2015 (Life Peer), of Cookham in the Royal County of Berkshire; **George Samuel Knatchbull Young,** CH 2012; PC 1993; Bt 1813; *b* 16 July 1941; *s* of Sir George Young, 5th Bt, CMG, and Elisabeth (*née* Knatchbull-Hugessen); *S* father as 6th Bt, 1960; *m* 1964, Aurelia Nemon-Stuart, *er d* of late Oscar Nemon, and of Mrs Nemon-Stuart, Boar's Hill, Oxford; two *s* two *d*. *Educ:* Eton; Christ Church, Oxford (Open Exhibitioner); MA Oxon, MPhil Surrey. Economist, NEDO, 1966–67; Kobler Research Fellow, University of Surrey, 1967–69; Economic Adviser, PO Corp., 1969–74. Councillor, London Borough of Lambeth, 1968–71; Mem., GLC, for London Borough of Ealing, 1970–73. MP (C) Ealing, Acton, Feb. 1974–1997, NW Hampshire, 1997–2015. An Opposition Whip, 1976–79; Parly Under Sec. of State, DHSS, 1979–81, DoE, 1981–86; Comptroller of HM Household, 1990; Minister of State, DoE, 1990–94; Financial Sec. to HM Treasury, 1994–95; Sec. of State for Transport, 1995–97; Shadow Leader, H of C, 1998–2000 and 2009–10; Lord Privy Seal and Leader, H of C, 2010–12; Parly Sec. to HM Treasury (Govt Chief Whip), 2012–14. Chm., Acton Housing Assoc., 1972–79. Dir, Lovell Partnerships Ltd, 1987–90. Trustee, Guinness Trust, 1986–90. *Publications:* Accommodation Services in the UK 1970–1980, 1970; Tourism, Blessing or Blight?, 1973. *Recreation:* bicycling. *Heir:* (to Baronetcy) *s* George Horatio Young [*b* 11 Oct. 1966; *m* 1999, Marianne, *e d* of Dr Peter Toghill]. *Address:* House of Lords, SW1A 0PW.

YOUNG OF GRAFFHAM, Baron *cr* 1984 (Life Peer), of Graffham in the County of W Sussex; **David Ivor Young,** CH 2015; PC 1984; DL; Chairman, Young Associates Ltd, since 1996; *b* 27 Feb. 1932; *s* of late Joseph and of Rebecca Young; *m* 1956, Lita Marianne Shaw; two *d*. *Educ:* Christ's Coll., Finchley; University Coll., London (LLB Hons; Fellow, 1988). Admitted solicitor, 1956. Exec., Great Universal Stores Ltd, 1956–61; Chairman: Eldonwall Ltd, 1961–74; Manufacturers Hanover Property Services Ltd, 1974–84; Cable and Wireless, 1990–95; Neoscorp Ltd (formerly Inter Digital Networks), 1997–2002; CDT Holdings plc, 1997–99; Pixology Ltd, 1997; Autohit, then Accident Exchange Gp, plc, 2000–06; Spectrum Interactive plc, 2004; Euortel Ltd, 2006; Director: Town & City Properties Ltd, 1971–74; Salomon Inc., 1990–94; Business for Sterling. Chm., British ORT, 1975–80 (Pres., 1980–82); Pres., World ORT Union, 1990–93 (Chm., Admin. Cttee, 1980–84). Dir, Centre for Policy Studies, 1979–82 (Mem., Management Bd, 1977); Mem., English Industrial Estates Corp., 1980–82; Chm., Manpower Services Commn, 1982–84; Mem., NEDC, 1982–89. Industrial Adviser, 1979–80, Special Adviser, 1980–82, DoI; Minister without Portfolio, 1984–85; Sec. of State for Employment, 1985–87; Sec. of State for Trade and Industry, 1987–89; Dep. Chm., Cons. Party, 1989–90. Pres., Inst. of Directors, 1993–2002. Chairman: EU-Japan Business Forum (formerly EU-Japan Assoc.), 1991–97; W Sussex Econ. Forum, 1996–; formerly Dir, Prince of Wales Business Leaders Forum. Pres., Jewish Care, 1990–97 (formerly Mem., Community Foundn); Chairman: Internat. Council of Jewish Social and Welfare Services, 1981–84; Central Council for Jewish Community Services, 1993; Bd of Govs, Oxford Centre for Postgrad. Hebrew Studies, 1989–93. Chm., Chichester Festival Theatre Ltd, 1997–2012; Director: Royal Opera House Trust, 1990–95; South Bank Foundn Ltd; formerly Dir, Centre for Performing Arts; Chairman: London Philharmonic Trust, 1995–98; Council, UCL, 1995–2005. Hon. FRPS 1981. DL West Sussex, 1999. *Publications:* The Enterprise Years: a businessman in the Cabinet, 1990; Degrees of Isolation, 2005. *Recreations:* music, book-collecting, photography. *Address:* Young Associates Ltd, 100 Marylebone Road, NW1 5DX. *Club:* Savile.

See also Rt Hon. Sir B. A. Rix.

YOUNG OF HORNSEY, Baroness *cr* 2004 (Life Peer), of Hornsey in the London Borough of Haringey; **Lola Young,** OBE 2001; PhD; freelance arts and heritage consultant, since 2004; *b* 1 June 1951; *d* of Maxwell Fela Young and Yele Santos; *m* 1984, Barrie Birch; one *s*. *Educ:* Middlesex Univ. (BA Hons; PhD 1995). Social worker, 1971–73; actor, 1976–85; Arts Develt Officer, Haringey Arts Council, 1985–89; freelance arts consultant, 1989–90; Lecturer: (pt-time) in Media Studies, 1989–90; Thames Valley Univ., 1990–92; Lectr, 1992–97, Prof. of Cultural Studies, 1997–2001, Emeritus Prof., 2002, Middx Univ.; Hd of Culture, GLA, 2002–04. Vis. Prof., Birkbeck, Univ. of London, 2004–. Chm., Nitro, theatre co., 2004–09. Advr to Arts Council England, 1988–2002. Mem., RCHME, 2000; Member Board: RNT, 2000–03; Resource: Council for Museums, Archives & Libraries, 2000–02; South Bank Centre, 2002–; Chairman: Arts Adv. Cttee, British Council, 2004–08; Commonwealth Gp on Culture and Develt, 2009–; non-exec. Dir, Nat. Archives, 2007–10; Comr, Historic England (formerly English Heritage), 2011–. FRSA 2000. *Publications:* Fear of the Dark: race, gender and sexuality in cinema, 1996; contrib. articles and chapters in edited books; contrib. articles to academic jls, incl. Women: A Cultural Rev., Cultural Studies from Birmingham, Oxford Art Jl, Parallax. *Recreations:* hiking, cinema, theatre, reading. *Address:* House of Lords, SW1A 0PW. *Club:* Hospital.

YOUNG OF NORWOOD GREEN, Baron *cr* 2004 (Life Peer), of Norwood Green, in the London Borough of Ealing; **Anthony Ian Young,** Kt 2002; *b* 16 April 1942; *m* 1st, 1962, Doreen Goodman (marr. diss. 1984); one *s* two *d*; 2nd, 1985, Margaret Newnham; one *s* one *d*. *Educ:* Kenmore Park Primary Sch.; Harrow County GS. Joined GPO as telecommunications apprentice, 1958; Union Br. Officer, 1967, Mem. NEC, 1978–89, PO Engrg Union; Gen. Sec., Nat. Communications Union, 1989–95; Jt Gen. Sec., 1995–98, Sen. Dep. Gen. Sec., 1998–2002, Communication Workers' Union. A Lord in Waiting (Govt Whip) and Parly Under-Sec. of State, DIUS, later BIS, 2008–10. Mem., Gen. Council, TUC, 1989–2002 (Pres., 2001–02); Eur. Co-Pres., Union Network Internat., 1999–2003 (Eur. Pres., Communications Internat., 1997–99). Trade Union Liaison Officer, Ethical Trading Initiative, 2002– (Vice Chm.). Member: Employment Tribunal Steering Bd, 1997–2003; Wilton Park Academic Council, 1997–2006. A Governor, BBC, 1998–2002. Chm., One World Broadcasting Trust, 2002–09. Gov., Three Bridges Primary Sch., 2002–. *Recreations:* reading, music, cycling, tennis, skating, walking, spasmodic gardening and cooking. *Address:* House of Lords, SW1A 0PW.

YOUNG OF OLD SCONE, Baroness *cr* 1997 (Life Peer), of Old Scone, in Perth and Kinross; **Barbara Scott Young;** Chief Executive, Diabetes UK, since 2010; *b* 8 April 1948; *d* of George Young and Mary (*née* Scott). *Educ:* Perth Acad.; Edinburgh Univ. (MA Classics); Strathclyde Univ. (Diploma Sec. Sci.); DipHSM, 1971. Various posts, finally Sector Administrator, Greater Glasgow Health Bd, 1975–78; Dir of Planning and Develt, St Thomas' Health Dist, 1978–79; Dist Gen. Administrator, NW Dist, Kensington and Chelsea and Westminster AHA, 1979–82; Dist Administrator, Haringey HA, 1982–85; District General Manager: Paddington and N Kensington HA, 1985–88; Parkside HA, 1988–91; Chief Exec., RSPB, 1991–98; Chm., English Nature, 1998–2000; Vice-Chm., Bd of Govs, BBC, 1998–2000; Chief Exec., Envmt Agency, 2000–08; Shadow Chair, 2008–09, Chair, 2009–10, Care Quality Commission, DoH. Member: BBC Gen. Adv. Council, 1985–88; Cttee, King's Fund Inst., 1986–90; Delegacy, St Mary's Hosp. Med. Sch., 1991–94; Cttee, Sec. of State for the Envmt's Going for Green initiative, 1994–96, UK Round Table on Sustainability, 1995–2000; Commn on Future of Voluntary Sector, 1995–96; Exec. Cttee, NCVO, 1997 (Mem., Trustee Bd, 1993–97); COPUS, 1996–97; Minister for Agriculture's Adv. Gp, 1997–98; EU Envmtl Adv. Forum, 1999–2001. Pres., Inst. of Health Services Management, 1987–88. Internat. Fellow, King's Fund Coll., 1985–87 and 1990. Non-exec. Dir, AWG plc, 1998–2001. Member: World Council, Birdlife Internat., 1994–98; Green Globe Task Force, 1997–98; Adaptation Sub-Cttee, Cttee on Climate Change, 2009–10. Patron, Inst. of Ecol and Envmt Management, 1993–; Vice President: Flora & Fauna Internat., 1998–; Birdlife Internat., 1999–; RSPB, 2000–; President: Cambs, Beds, Northants and Peterborough Wildlife Trust, 2002–; British Trust for Ornithology, 2005–13 (Vice Pres., 2004–05); S Georgia Heritage Trust, 2010–; Beds SO, 2013–. Trustee, IPPR, 1999–2009. Chancellor, Cranfield Univ., 2010–. Patron, Lantra, 2013–. Hon. RICS 2000; Hon. Fellow: Geologists Assoc., 2000; Sidney Sussex Coll., Cambridge, 2002; Hon. FCIWEM 2001. DUniv: Stirling, 1995; York, St Andrews, Aberdeen, 2000; Open, 2001; Hon. DSc: Hertfordshire, 1997; Cranfield, 1998; Anglia Ruskin, 2009; Gloucestershire, 2009. *Publications:* (contrib.) What Women Want, 1990; (contrib.) Medical Negligence, 1990; articles in Hosp. Doctor. *Recreations:* obsessive cinema going, gardening, dressage. *Address:* House of Lords, SW1A 0PW.

YOUNG, Andrea, PhD; Director, Digital Economy Unit, Department for Culture, Media and Sport and Department for Business, Innovation and Skills, since 2014; *b* Oadby, Leics, 30 July 1964; *d* of Alec Young and Janette Young; *m* 1994, Ave Wrigley; two *d*. *Educ:* Bristol Univ. (BSc Botany and Zoology 1982; PhD 1991). Hd, Sustainable Develt Unit, 2002–03, Hd, Farm Regulation, 2004–06, DEFRA; Hd, Econ. and Envmt, 2006–08, Actg Regl Dir, 2008, Govt Office for the East of England; Department for Environment, Food and Rural Affairs: Dir, Climate Change, Exotic Disease and Agency Relationship Portfolio, Food and Farming Gp, 2008–11; Dir, Strategy, 2011–12; Dir, Triennial Rev. Team, Envmt Agency and Natural England, 2012–13; Dir, Enterprise, 2013–14. *Address:* Department for Culture, Media and Sport, 100 Parliament Street, SW1A 2BQ.

YOUNG, Andrew; Chairman, Andrew J. Young Foundation, since 2003; *b* New Orleans, La, 12 March 1932; *s* of Andrew J. Young and Daisy Fuller; *m* 1954, Jean Childs (*d* 1994); one *s* three *d*; *m* 1996, Carolyn Watson. *Educ:* Howard Univ., USA; Hartford Theological Seminary. Ordained, United Church of Christ, 1955; Pastor, Thomasville, Ga, 1955–57; Associate Dir for Youth Work, Nat. Council of Churches, 1957–61; Admin. Christian Educn Programme, United Church of Christ, 1961–64; Mem. Staff, Southern Christian Leadership Conf., 1961–70, Exec. Dir, 1964–70, Exec. Vice-Pres., 1967–70; elected to US House of Representatives from 5th District of Georgia, 1972 (first Black Congressman from Georgia in 101 years); re-elected 1974 and 1976; US Ambassador to UN, 1977–79; Mayor of Atlanta, 1982–89. Co-Chm., Atlanta Cttee for Olympic Games 1996. Chm., Law Cos Internat. Gp, Inc., 1990–93; Vice-Chm., Law Cos Gp, Inc., 1993–97; Co-Chm. and Co-founding Partner, GoodWorks Internat., 1997–2012. Pres., Nat. Council of the Churches of Christ, 2000–01. Chairman: Atlanta Community Relations Commn, 1970–72; National Democratic voter registration drive, 1976; during 1960s organized voter registration and community develt programmes. Mem. Bd of Dirs, Martin Luther King, Jr Center. Hon. Prof. of Policy Studies, Andrew Young Sch. of Policy Studies, Georgia State Univ. Holds numerous hon. degrees and awards, including: Presidential Medal of Freedom, 1980; Légion d'Honneur (France). *Publications:* A Way Out of No Way, 1994; An Easy Burden, 1996. *Address:* Andrew J. Young Foundation, 260 14th Street NW, Atlanta, GA 30318, USA.

YOUNG, Dr Andrew Buchanan, FRCPE; Deputy Chief Medical Officer, Scottish Office Department of Health (formerly Scottish Office Home and Health Department), 1989–97; *b* 11 Aug. 1937; *s* of Alexander and Elizabeth Young; *m* 1965, Lois Lilian Howarth; one *s* one *d*. *Educ:* Falkirk High School; Edinburgh Univ. (MB ChB). DTM&H. Supt, Presbyterian Church of E Africa Hosps, Kenya, 1965–72; Fellow in Community Medicine, Scottish Health Service, 1972–75; Scottish Home and Health Department: MO 1975; SMO 1978; PMO 1985. Pres., Edinburgh Medical Missionary Soc., 1992–97. QHP, 1993–96. *Recreations:* trying to learn computing, reading. *Address:* 101 Hawthornden Road, Christchurch 8042, New Zealand. *E:* abylly@xtra.co.nz.

YOUNG, Andrew George; Strategy Actuary, Pensions Regulator, since 2009; *b* 15 June 1949; *s* of James Cameron Young and Agnes Young; *m* 1st, 1975, Victoria Leslie (marr. diss. 2009); one *s* three *d*; 2nd, 2010, Sara Victoria, two *d*. *Educ:* Univ. of Glasgow (BSc 1st Cl. Hons Maths, Natural Philosophy). Government Actuary's Dept, 1973–2009; Directing Actuary, 1995–2005; Sen. Consulting Actuary, 2005–09. *Recreations:* music, theatre, travel. *Address:* 95 Stanford Road, Brighton BN1 5PR. *T:* (01273) 563443.

YOUNG, Prof. Andrew William, PhD, DSc; FBA 2001; Professor of Neuropsychology, University of York, since 1997; *b* 14 March 1950; *s* of Alexander Young and Winnifred Doris Young; *m* 1976, Mavis Langham; one *s* two *d*. *Educ:* Bedford Coll., London (BSc 1971); PhD Warwick 1974; DSc London 1990. Lectr in Psychol., Univ. of Aberdeen, 1974–76; Lectr, then Reader in Psychol., Univ. of Lancaster, 1976–89; Prof. of Psychol., Univ. of Durham, 1989–93; Special Appt, MRC Scientific Staff, Applied Psychol. Unit, Cambridge, 1993–97. Dr *hc* Liège, 2000. Cognitive Psychol. Award, 1994, 2007, President's Award, 1995, Book Award, 2001, Hon. Fellow, 2005, Lifetime Achievement Award, 2013, BPsS. *Publications:* (with A. W. Ellis) Human Cognitive Neuropsychology, 1988, 2nd edn 1996; (with V. Bruce) In the Eye of the Beholder: the science of face perception, 1998; (with V. Bruce) Face Perception, 2012. *Recreation:* jukebox collector and partially reformed trainspotter. *Address:* Department of Psychology, University of York, Heslington, York YO10 5DD. *T:* (01904) 323159.

YOUNG, Prof. Archibald, MD; FRCP, FRCPGlas, FRCPE; Professor of Geriatric Medicine, Edinburgh University, 1998–2007; *b* 19 Sept. 1946; *s* of Dr Archibald Young and Mary Downie Young (*née* Fleming); *m* 1st, 1973, Alexandra Mary Clark (marr. diss. 1995); one *s* one *d*; 2nd, 2006, Susann Mary Dinan. *Educ:* Glasgow Univ. (BSc 1st Cl. Hons 1969; MBChB 1971; MD 1983). MRCP 1973, FRCP 1989; FRCPGlas 1985; FRCPE 1999. Hon. Consultant Physician in Rehabilitation Medicine, Nuffield Dept of Orthopaedic Surgery, Oxford Univ., 1981–85; Consultant Physician in Geriatric Medicine, Royal Free Hosp., 1985–87; Royal Free Hospital School of Medicine: Hon. Sen. Lectr, 1985–87, Sen. Lectr, 1987–88, in Geriatric Medicine; Prof. and Head, Univ. Dept of Geriatric Medicine and Hon. Consultant Physician, 1988–98. *Publications:* contribs to learned jls on effects of ageing, use and disuse on muscle and exercise physiology. *Recreation:* physical. *Address:* 45 Polton Road, Lasswade, Midlothian EH18 1LT. *Club:* Junior Mountaineering of Scotland.

YOUNG, Sir Brian (Walter Mark), Kt 1976; MA; Director General, Independent Broadcasting Authority (formerly Independent Television Authority), 1970–82; *b* 23 Aug. 1922; *er s* of late Sir Mark Young, GCMG and Josephine (*née* Price); *m* 1947, Fiona Marjorie (*d* 1997), *o d* of late Allan, 16th Stewart of Appin, and Marjorie (*née* Ballance); one *s* two *d*. *Educ:* Eton (King's Schol.); King's College, Cambridge (Schol.). FSA 1994. Served in RNVR, mainly in destroyers, 1941–45. First class hons in Part I, 1946, and Part II, 1947, of Classical Tripos; Porson Prize, 1946; Winchester Reading Prize, 1947; BA 1947; MA 1952. Assistant Master at Eton, 1947–52; Headmaster of Charterhouse, 1952–64; Dir, Nuffield Foundn, 1964–70. Chm., Christian Aid, 1983–90. Member: Central Advisory Council for Education, 1956–59 (Crowther Report); Central Religious Adv. Cttee of BBC and ITA, 1960–64; Bd of Centre for Educn Develt Overseas, 1969–72; Arts Council of GB, 1983–88; Exec. Cttee, British Council of Churches, 1983–90; Chm., Associated Bd of the Royal Schs of Music, 1984–87. Pres., British and Foreign Sch. Soc., 1991–2003. A Managing Trustee, Nuffield Foundn, 1978–90; Trustee: Lambeth Palace Liby, 1984–97; Imperial War Mus., 1985–92. Hon. RNCM, 1987. Hon. DLitt Heriot-Watt, 1980. *Publications:* Via Vertendi, 1952; Intelligent Reading (with P. D. R. Gardiner), 1964; The Villein's Bible: stories in Romanesque carving, 1990. *Recreations:* music, travel, history, problems. *Address:* Hill End, Woodhill Avenue, Gerrards Cross, Bucks SL9 8DJ. *T:* (01753) 887793.

See also Maj. Gen. A. P. Grant Peterkin, T. M. S. Young.

YOUNG, Charmaine Carolyn, CBE 2003; Chief Executive, Berkeley Foundation, since 2013; *b* 24 July 1952; *d* of Leonard and Dolly Danks; *m* 1992, Robert Michael Young. *Educ:* Birmingham Polytech. (pt-time; ONC, HNC Bldg Construction). Architectural Technician, 1974–81, Project Team Leader, 1981–83, Birmingham CC; Asst Dir of Housing, Sheffield CC, 1983–89; Urban Renewal Manager, Wimpey Homes, 1989–96; Business Develt Dir, Lovell Partnerships, 1996–99; Regeneration Dir, St George Regeneration Ltd, 1999–2012; Dir, St George plc, 2010–12. Ind. Expert, Bd, Homes for London, 2012–. FInstD 2008. *Publications:* (ed) Working Together: delivering growth through localism, 2011. *Recreations:* trying to recapture my youth, getting the construction industry to value women. *Address:* (office) 19 Portsmouth Road, Cobham, Surrey KT11 1JG. *T:* (01932) 868555. *E:* charmaine.young@berkeleygroup.co.uk.

YOUNG, His Honour Christopher Godfrey; a Circuit Judge, 1980–97; a Deputy High Court Judge, 1992–97; *b* 9 Sept. 1932; *s* of late Harold Godfrey Young, MB, ChB, and Gladys Mary Young; *m* 1969, Jeanetta Margaret (*d* 1984), *d* of Halford and Dorothy Vaughan; one *s*. *Educ:* Bedford Sch.; King's Coll., Univ. of London (LLB Hons 1954; MA 1999). Called to the Bar, Gray's Inn, 1957; Midland and Oxford Circuit, 1959; a Recorder of the Crown Court, 1975–79; Resident Judge: Peterborough Crown Court, 1980–87; Leicester Crown Court, 1987–97. Mem., Parole Bd, 1990–93, 1997–2003 (Appraiser, 2003–05); Pt time Chm., Immigration Appeal Tribunal, 1997–98. Hon. Pres., De Montfort Univ. Sch. of Law, 1996–98. Postgraduate research: in Byzantine Studies, RHC, 1999–2005; in Faculty of Oriental Studies, Oxford Univ., 2005– (Mem., Pembroke Coll., Oxford). Mem., Cttee, Soc. for the Promotion of Byzantine Studies, 2004–07. Chm., Maidwell with Draughton Parish Council, 1973–76. *Recreations:* music, travel, Eastern Mediterranean. *Address:* Stockshill House, Duddington, Stamford, Lincs PE9 3QQ. *T:* (01780) 444658. *Club:* Athenæum.

YOUNG, Rt Rev. Clive; Bishop Suffragan of Dunwich, 1999–2013; *b* 31 May 1948; *s* of late William Alfred Young and Dorothy Young; *m* 1971, Susan Elizabeth Tucker. *Educ:* King Edward VI Grammar Sch., Chelmsford; St John's Coll., Durham (BA Hons); Ridley Hall, Cambridge. Ordained: deacon, 1972; priest, 1973; Assistant Curate: Neasden cum Kingsbury St Catherine, London, 1972–75; St Paul, Hammersmith, 1975–79; Priest-in-charge, 1979–82, Vicar, 1982–92, St Paul with St Stephen, Old Ford; Area Dean, Tower Hamlets, 1988–92; Archdeacon of Hackney and Vicar of Guild Church of St Andrew, Holborn, 1992–99. *Recreations:* music, gardening. *Address:* The Sycamores, Ewyas Harold, Herefordshire HR2 0JD. *T:* (01981) 240776.

YOUNG, Colin, CBE 1994 (OBE 1976); Senior Consultant, Ateliers du Cinéma Européen, since 1996 (Director, 1993–96); Director, National Film and Television School of Great Britain (formerly National Film School), 1970–92; *b* 5 April 1927; *s* of Colin Young and Agnes Holmes Kerr Young; *m* 1st, 1960, Kristin Ohman; two *s*; 2nd, 1987, Constance Yvonne Templeman; one *s* one *d*. *Educ:* Bellahouston Academy, Glasgow; Univs of Glasgow, St Andrews and California (Los Angeles). Theatre and film critic, Bon Accord, Aberdeen, 1951; cameraman, editor, writer, director, 1953–; producer, 1967–; UCLA (Motion Pictures): Instructor, 1956–59; Asst Prof., 1959–64; Assoc. Prof., 1964–68; Prof., 1968–70, Head, Motion Picture Div., Theater Arts Dept, UCLA, 1964–65; Chm., Dept of Theater Arts, 1965–70. Res. Associate, Centre Nat. de Recherche Scientifique, Paris, 1984 and 1987; Andrew W. Mellon Vis. Prof. in Humanities, Rice Univ., Houston, Texas, 1985–86. Tutor, Arista Story Editing Workshops, 1996–2006. Vice-Chm., 1972–76, Chm., 1976–91, Edinburgh Film Festival; Chm., Edinburgh Internat. Film and Television Council, 1990–91; Governor, BFI, 1974–80. Member: Arts Council Film Cttee, 1972–76; Public Media Panel, Nat. Endowment for Arts, Washington, 1972–77; Gen. Adv. Council, BBC, 1973–78; Council of Management, BAFTA, 1974–81; Exec. Cttee, Centre International de Liaison des Ecoles de Cinéma et de Télévision, 1974–94 (Pres., 1980–94); Nat. Film Finance Corp., 1979–85; British Screen Adv. Council, 1990–; Bd, Moonstone Film Labs Internat., 1997–2007; Lottery Film Prodn Cttee, Scottish Arts Council, 1998–2000; Lottery Film Prodn Cttee, Scottish Screen, 2000–05. Consultant, Goldcrest Films & Television Ltd, 1985–86. FBKS 1975. Chm., Cttee on Educational Policy, UCLA, 1968–69. London Editor, Film Quarterly, 1970–91 (Los Angeles Editor, 1958–68). Hon. Gov., Nat. Film and Television Sch., 2007– (Mentor, documentary dept, 2006–). Michael Balcon Award, 1983, Fellow, 1993, BAFTA; Lifetime Achievement Award, British Ind. Film Awards, 2000. Chevalier de l'Ordre des Arts et des Lettres (France), 1987. *Publications:* various articles in collections of film essays including Principles of Visual Anthropology, 1975; experimental film essay for Unesco, 1963; ethnographic film essay for Unesco, 1966; contribs to Film Quarterly, Sight and Sound, Jl of Aesthetic Education, Jl of the Producers Guild of America, Kosmorama (Copenhagen), etc. *Address:* Turret House, Ivy Hatch Court, Ivy Hatch, Sevenoaks, Kent TN15 0PQ.

YOUNG, Sir Colville (Norbert), GCMG 1994; MBE 1986; JP; DPhil; Governor-General of Belize, since 1993; *b* 20 Nov. 1932; *s* of Henry Oswald Young and Adney Wilhelmina (*née* Waite); *m* 1956, Norma Eleanor Trapp; three *s* one *d*. *Educ:* Univ. of West Indies (BA 1961); Univ. of York (DPhil 1971). Principal, St Michael's Coll., Belize, 1974–76; Lectr in English and Gen. Studies, Belize Tech. Coll., 1976–86; University College of Belize: Pres., 1986–90; Lectr, 1990–93. JP Belize, 1985, now supplementary list. *Publications:* Creole Proverbs of Belize, 1980, rev. edn 1988; From One Caribbean Corner (poetry), 1983; Caribbean Corner Calling, 1988; Language and Education in Belize, 1989; Pataki Full, 1990; contrib. poetry and drama in various anthologies; articles in Belizean Affairs, Jl Belizean Affairs, Belcast Jl, Caribbean Dialogue, Handbook on World Educn. *Recreations:* creative writing, playing and arranging steelband music. *Address:* Belize House, PO Box 173, Belmopan, Belize, Central America. *T:* (8) 222521, 223081, *Fax:* (8) 222050.

YOUNG, David Edward Michael; QC 1980; a Recorder, 1987–2006; *b* 30 Sept. 1940; *s* of George Henry Edward Young and Audrey Young; *m* 1968, Ann de Bromhead (*d* 2010); two *d*. *Educ:* Monkton Combe Sch.; Hertford Coll., Oxford (MA). Called to the Bar, Lincoln's Inn, 1966, Bencher, 1989; practised at Chancery Bar, specialising in intellectual property work. Dep. Judge, Patent County Court, 1990–2006; a Dep. High Court Judge, 1993–2006. Chm., Plant Varieties and Seeds Tribunal, 1987–2008. *Publications:* (co-ed) Terrell on the Law of Patents, 12th edn 1971 to 14th edn 1994; Passing Off, 1985, 3rd edn 1994. *Recreations:* gentleman farmer, francophile.

YOUNG, David Ernest, CBE 2007; Chairman, Higher Education Funding Council for England, 2001–07; *b* 8 March 1942; *s* of late Harold Young and Jessie Young (*née* Turnbull); *m* 1st, 1964, Norma Robinson (marr. diss. 1996); two *d*; 2nd, 1998, Margaret Pilleau. *Educ:* King Edward VII Sch., Sheffield; Corpus Christi Coll., Oxford (BA Hons). Ministry of Defence, 1963–82: Private Secretary: to 2nd Perm. Sec., 1966–68; to CAS, 1968–70; to Minister of State for Defence, 1973–75; seconded to Central Policy Rev. Staff, Cabinet Office, 1975–77; Head of Defence Secretariat, 1979–82; John Lewis Partnership, 1982–2002: Finance Dir, 1987–2001; Dep. Chm., 1993–2002. Chm., John Lewis Partnership Trust for Pensions, 1989–2004. Director: Ocado plc, 2001–12; Orbit Gp, 2013–. Treas., Open Univ., 1998–2001; Hon. Treas., Soil Assoc., 2004–10. Mem. Adv. Panel, Greenwich Hosp., 2002–07. Trustee: RAF Mus., 1999–2005; Textile Ind. Children's Trust, 2000–08. Mem. Council, 2008–, Treas., 2010–, Sheffield Univ. Hon. DLitt Sheffield, 2005; Hon. DBA Beds, 2008. *Recreations:* theatre, food and wine, bridge, walking. *Address:* Gable Cottage, Fairmile, Henley on Thames RG9 2JX. *Club:* Phyllis Court (Henley on Thames).

YOUNG, David Tyrrell; Chairman, City and Guilds of London Institute, 1999–2006; *b* 6 Jan. 1938; *s* of late Tyrrell F. Young and Patricia M. Young (*née* Spicer); *m* 1965, Madeline Helen Celia Philips; three *d*. *Educ:* Charterhouse. Trained as Chartered Accountant; joined Spicer & Pegler, later Spicer & Oppenheim, 1965 (merged with Touche Ross, 1990): Partner 1968; Managing Partner, 1982; Sen. Partner, 1988–90; Dep. Chm., 1990–93. Chm., N Herts NHS Trust, 1995–2000. Director: Lombard Insce Gp, 1993–2000; Asprey, then Asprey & Garrard, 1993–2000; Wates City of London Properties, 1994–2000; Nomura Bank Internat., 1996–2010; Berkshire Hathaway Internat. Insce Ltd, 1998–2014; Marlborough Underwriting Agency, 2000–11; Capita Syndicate Mgt, 2001–08. Mem. Council, ICAEW, 1979–82. Mem. Court, Fishmongers' Co., 1981–. FRSA 1992. Hon. FCGI 1995. *Recreations:* golf, limited gardening. *Address:* Lovegrove Barn, Fieldside, Long Wittenham, Oxon OX14 4QB. *T:* (01865) 407763. *Clubs:* Honourable Artillery Company, Royal Worlington Golf, Huntercombe Golf.

YOUNG, Rt Rev. Donald Arthur; Bishop of Central Newfoundland, 2000–04; *b* 11 Nov. 1944; *s* of Harold and Frances Young; *m* 1966, Sylvia Joan Spurrell; one *s* three *d*. *Educ:* Univ. of Newfoundland; Atlantic Sch. of Theology; Queen's Coll., St John's, Nfld (LTh). Ordained deacon, 1977, priest, 1977; Deacon in charge, Buchans, 1977; Rector: Buchans, 1977–81; Port Rexton, 1981–89; (pro tem.) Hermitage, 2011–12; (pro tem.) Deer Lake, 2013–14; Diocesan Progs and Exec. Officer, Central Newfoundland, 1989–2000. *Address:* 24A Park Street, Grand Falls-Windsor, NL A2B 1C7, Canada. *T:* and *Fax:* (709) 4891804.

YOUNG, Hon. Douglas; *see* Young, Hon. M. D.

YOUNG, Edward, CVO 2015 (LVO 2010); Deputy Private Secretary to the Queen, since 2007 (Assistant Private Secretary, 2004–07); *b* 24 Oct. 1966; *s* of Dr Edward Young and late Sally Rougier Young (*née* Chapman); *m* 2003, Nichola O'Brien Malone; one *d*. *Educ:* Reading Sch. (Boarder). Trade finance specialist, Internat. Services Br., Barclays, 1985–97; Project Manager, Barclays Corporate Euro Prog., 1997; Dep. Hd, Corporate Bank Public Relns, Barclays Bank plc, 1997–99; Adviser: to Shadow Chancellor, 1999–2000; to Leader of the Opposition, 2001; Hd, Corporate Communications, Granada plc, 2001–04. Mem., Westminster Abbey Inst. Council of Reference, 2013–. *Address:* Buckingham Palace, SW1A 1AA.

YOUNG, Eve J.; *see* Jardine-Young, E.

YOUNG, Rev. Prof. Frances Margaret, OBE 1998; PhD; FBA 2004; Edward Cadbury Professor of Theology, University of Birmingham, 1986–2005; Methodist minister, since 1984; *b* 25 Nov. 1939; *d* of A. Stanley Worrall and Mary F. Worrall (*née* Marshall); *m* 1964, Robert Charles Young; three *s*. *Educ:* Bedford Coll., Univ. of London (BA); Girton Coll.,

Univ. of Cambridge (MA, PhD). Research Fellow, Clare Hall, Cambridge, 1967–68; University of Birmingham: Temp. Lectr, 1971–73; Lectr, 1973–82; Sen. Lectr, 1982–86; Hd, Dept of Theol., 1986–95; Dean, Faculty of Arts, 1995–97; Pro-Vice-Chancellor, 1997–2002. Hon. DD Aberdeen, 1994; Hon. DTh MF Norwegian Sch. of Theol., Oslo, 2008; DUniv Oxford Brookes, 2010; Hon. DD Liverpool Hope Univ., 2013. *Publications:* Sacrifice and the Death of Christ, 1975; (contrib.) The Myth of God Incarnate, 1977; From Nicaea to Chalcedon, 1983, 2nd edn 2010; Face to Face, 1985, 2nd edn 1990; (with David Ford) Meaning and Truth in 2 Corinthians, 1987; The Art of Performance, 1990; The Theology of the Pastoral Epistles, 1994; Biblical Exegesis and the Formation of Christian Culture, 1997; (ed) Encounter with Mystery, 1997; (ed jtly) The Cambridge History of Early Christian Literature, 2004; (ed jtly) The Cambridge History of Christianity: origins to Constantine, 2006; Brokenness and Blessing, 2007; (with Morna Hooker) Holiness and Mission, 2010; God's Presence: a contemporary recapitulation of Early Christianity, 2013; Arthur's Call: a journey of faith in the face of learning disability, 2014; numerous articles, etc. *Recreations:* outdoor pursuits, music. *Address:* 142 Selly Park Road, Birmingham B29 7LH. *T:* (0121) 472 4841.

YOUNG, Gavin Neil B.; *see* Barr Young.

YOUNG, Helen, (Mrs K. Rees), FRMetS; broadcast meteorologist, 1993–2005, Broadcast Manager, 2000–05, BBC Weather Centre; *b* 10 June 1969; *d* of Derek and Lyn Young; *m* 1997, Kerith Rees; one *s* one *d*. *Educ:* Univ. of Bristol (BSc Geog.); Meteorological Office (qualified as forecaster). Dep. Manager, BBC Weather Centre, 1998–2000. *Recreations:* ski-ing, swimming, gardening. *Address:* c/o 1st Choice Speakers UK Ltd, PO Box 562, Chesham, Bucks HP5 1ZJ.

YOUNG, Prof. (Hobart) Peyton, PhD; FBA 2007; James Meade Professor of Economics, University of Oxford, and Fellow of Nuffield College, Oxford, since 2007; Research Principal, Office of Financial Research, US Treasury Department, since 2012; *b* 9 March 1945; *s* of Hobart Paul Young and Louise B. Young; *m* 1982, Fernanda F. Toueg; two *s*. *Educ:* Harvard Univ. (AB cum laude Gen. Studies 1966); Univ. of Michigan (PhD 1970). Prof. of Econs and Public Policy, Univ. of Maryland, 1981–94; Scott and Barbara Black Prof. of Econs, Johns Hopkins Univ., 1994–2007. Sen. Fellow in Econ. Studies, Brookings Instn, 1998–; Ext. Prof., Santa Fe Inst., 2001–05, 2007–10; Fulbright Dist. Chair in Econs, Univ. of Siena, 2003–04. Pres., Game Theory Soc., 2006–. Fellow, Econometric Soc., 1995. *Publications:* (with M. L. Balinski) Fair Representation: meeting the ideal of one man one vote, 1984, 2nd edn 2002; Equity in Theory and Practice, 1994; Individual Strategy and Social Structure: an evolutionary theory of institutions, 1998; Strategic Learning and Its Limits, 2004; articles in learned jls. *Address:* Nuffield College, Oxford OX1 1NF. *T:* (01865) 271086, *Fax:* (01865) 271094. *Clubs:* Oxford and Cambridge; Cosmos (Washington, DC); Chevy Chase.

YOUNG, Ian Robert, OBE 1985; PhD; FRS 1989; FREng; consultant; *b* 11 Jan. 1932; *s* of John Stirling Young and Ruth Muir Young (*née* Whipple); *m* 1956, Sylvia Marianne Whewell Ralph; two *s* one *d*. *Educ:* Sedbergh Sch., Yorkshire; Aberdeen Univ. (BSc, PhD). FIET; FREng (FEng 1988). Hilger & Watts Ltd, 1955–59; Evershed & Vignoles Ltd (and affiliates), 1959–76; EMI Ltd, 1976–81; GEC plc, 1981–97. Visiting Professor: of Radiology, RPMS, 1986; Dept of Electrical and Electronic Engrg, Imperial Coll. London, 2005–. Hon. FRCR 1990; Hon. Mem., Amer. Soc. of Neuroradiology, 1995. Hon. DSc Aberdeen, 1992. *Publications:* over 200 papers in Proc. IEE, Magnetic Resonance in Medicine, Magnetic Resonance Imaging, Jl Magnetic Resonance, Computer Assisted Tomography, etc; 50 separate patents; ed. 5 books. *Recreations:* bird watching, golf, gardening. *Address:* High Kingsbury, Kingsbury Street, Marlborough, Wilts SN8 1HZ. *T:* (01672) 516126.

YOUNG, Prof. Ian Robert, AO 2012; PhD; Vice-Chancellor and President, Australian National University, since 2011; *b* Cunnamulla, Qld, 17 Jan. 1957; *s* of Richard and Mary Stella Young; *m* 1985, Heather Beckwith; one *d*. *Educ:* James Cook Univ. (BE Hons; MEngSc; PhD 1984). FIEAust 1990, Hon. FIEAust 2011; FTSE 2000. Sen. Lectr, 1986–94, Prof. of Civil Engrg, 1994–98, Univ. of NSW; Exec. Dean, Faculty of Engrg, Computer and Mathematical Scis, 1999–2003, Pro Vice-Chancellor (Internat.), 2001–03, Univ. of Adelaide; Vice-Chancellor, Swinburne Univ. of Technol., 2003–11. Chm., Gp of Eight, 2014. Fellow, Acad. of Technol Scis and Engrg, 2000. C. N. Barton Medal, Engineers Australia, 1979; Lorenz G. Staub Medal, Univ. of Minnesota, 1986; Centenary Medal (Australia), 2003. *Publications:* (with G. J. Holland) Atlas of the Oceans: wind and wave climate, 1996; Wind Generated Ocean Waves, 1999; contrib. papers to jls. *Address:* Office of the Vice-Chancellor, Australian National University, Canberra, ACT 0200, Australia. *T:* (2) 61252510, *Fax:* (2) 62573292. *E:* vc@anu.edu.au.

YOUNG, James Edward D.; *see* Drummond Young.

YOUNG, Sir Jimmy; *see* Young, Sir L. R.

YOUNG, John Adrian Emile; Partner, Markby, Stewart & Wadesons, subseq. Cameron Markby Hewitt, 1965–95; *b* 28 July 1934; *s* of John Archibald Campbell Young and Irene Eugenie Young (*née* Bouvier); *m* 1959, Yvonne Lalage Elizabeth Bankes (*d* 2008); three *s* one *d*. *Educ:* Cranbrook Sch., Kent; London Univ. (LLB). Admitted solicitor, 1958; Asst Sec., Law Soc., 1958–64. Adjudicator (formerly Legal Officer), Office of the Banking Ombudsman, 1996–98. Nat Chm., Young Solicitors Gp, 1965–66; Pres., Assoc. Internat. des Jeunes Avocats, 1968–69; Law Society: Mem. Council, 1971–95; Dep. Vice-Pres., 1993–94; Vice-Pres., 1994–95; Mem. Council, Internat. Bar Assoc., 1983–94. FRSA 1989. Master, City of London Solicitors' Co., 1989–90. *Publications:* sundry legal articles. *Recreations:* music (runs local church choir), gardening, family! *Address:* Stonewold House, The Street, Plaxtol, Sevenoaks, Kent TN15 0QH. *T:* (01732) 810289.

YOUNG, Sir John (Kenyon Roe), 6th Bt *cr* 1821; Purchasing Manager; *b* 23 April 1947; *s* of Sir John William Roe Young, 5th Bt, and Joan Minnie Agnes (*d* 1958), *d* of M. M. Aldous; *S* father, 1981; *m* 1977, Frances Elise, *o d* of W. R. Thompson; one *s* one *d*. *Educ:* Hurn Court; Napier College. Joined RN, 1963; transferred to Hydrographic Branch, 1970; qualified Hydrographic Surveyor, 1977; retired from RN, 1979; attended Napier Coll., 1979–80. Member: Hydrographic Soc.; Inst. of Purchasing Mgt. *Recreation:* fishing. *Heir:* *s* Richard Christopher Roe Young, *b* 14 June 1983.

YOUNG, John Robert Chester, CBE 1992; Nominated Member, 1996–2002, and Deputy Chairman, 1997–2002, Council of Lloyd's; Chairman, Lloyd's Regulatory Board, 1997–2002; *b* 6 Sept. 1937; *s* of Robert Nisbet Young and Edith Mary (*née* Roberts); *m* 1963, Pauline Joyce (*d* 1997); one *s* one *d* (and one *s* decd). *Educ:* Bishop Vesey's Grammar Sch.; St Edmund Hall, Oxford Univ. (MA); Gray's Inn, London. Joined Simon & Coates, members of the Stock Exchange, 1961; Partner, 1965; Dep. Sen. Partner, 1976; London Stock Exchange (formerly Stock Exchange, subseq. Internat. Stock Exchange): Mem. Council, 1978–82; Dir of Policy and Planning, 1982–87; Vice-Chm. (non-exec.), Managing Bd, 1987–90. Chief Exec. and Dir, SFA (formerly Securities Assoc.), 1987–93; Dir, 1993–97, Chief Exec., 1993–95, SIB. Non-executive Director: Darby Gp plc, 1996–97; Elderstreet Millennium (formerly Gartmore) Venture Capital Trust, 1996–2006; E Surrey Healthcare (formerly E Surrey Hosp. and Community Healthcare) NHS Trust, 1992–96. Public Interest Dir, Financial Services Compensation Scheme Ltd, 2000–04. Mem. Ethics Cttee, Securities Inst., 1995–2009 (Hon. Fellow, 2003). Lay Mem., Legal Services Consultative Panel, DCA, subseq. MoJ, 2004–09. Advr, Royal Sch. for the Blind, 1997–2001. Formerly internat. athlete, Rugby player (England and British Lions) and England Rugby selector. *Recreations:* cooking, grandsons, Rugby football. *Clubs:* Vincent's (Oxford); Harlequins, Achilles.

See also L. Botting.

YOUNG, Sir John Robertson, (Sir Rob), GCMG 2003 (KCMG 1999; CMG 1991); HM Diplomatic Service, retired; High Commissioner, New Delhi, 1999–2003; *b* 21 Feb. 1945; *s* of late Francis John Young and Marjorie Elizabeth Young; *m* 1967, Catherine Suzanne Françoise Houssait; one *s* two *d*. *Educ:* King Edward VI Sch., Norwich; Leicester Univ. (BA 1st Cl. Hons, French). Entered FCO, 1967; MECAS, Lebanon, 1968; Third Sec., Cairo, 1970; Second Sec., FCO, 1972; Private Sec. to Minister of State, 1975; First Sec., Paris, 1977; Asst Head, Western European Dept, FCO, 1982; Counsellor, Damascus, 1984; Head of Middle East Dept, FCO, 1987; Minister, Paris, 1991; Dep. Under-Sec. of State, 1994–98, and Chief Clerk, 1995–98, FCO. Comr, Commonwealth War Graves Commn, 2003–11. Non-executive Director: Hirco plc, 2006–10; Aguas de Barcelona, 2008–10; GDF SUEZ Energy Internat. (formerly Internat. Power), 2011–. Chairman: Calcutta Tercentenary Trust, 2003–; Adv. Bd, World Appreciation of Music, 2008–. Mem., Conseil d'Admin, Fêtes Musicales en Touraine, 2012–15. Patron, Loomba Trust, 2005–. Hon. DLaws Leicester, 2001. *Recreations:* music, sailing, theatre, carpentry. *Address:* Les Choiseaux, La Planche des Chaqueneaux, 37260 Artannes-sur-Indre, France. *Clubs:* Beefsteak, Royal Over-Seas League.

YOUNG, John Todd; Co-Chair, Hogan Lovells, 2010–12 (Senior Partner, Lovells, 2004–10); *b* 14 Jan. 1957; *s* of Ian Taylor Young and Flora Leggett Young (*née* Todd); *m* 1981, Elizabeth Jane Grattidge. *Educ:* Manchester Grammar Sch.; Sidney Sussex Coll., Cambridge (BA 1978; MA 1982). Admitted solicitor, 1981; Hogan Lovells (formerly Lovell, White & King, then Lovell White Durrant, later Lovells): articled clerk, 1979–81; Solicitor, 1981–87; Partner, 1987–2004; Hd, Corporate Insce Practice, 1997–2011; Hd, Financial Instns Gp, 2004–09. Non-executive Director: JLT Reinsurance Brokers Ltd, 2012–; Mitsui Sumitomo Insurance (London Mgt) Ltd, 2012–; Forester Life Ltd, 2013–. Trustee, Farm Africa, 2013–. Gov., Manchester Grammar Sch., 2014–. Liveryman, Solicitors' Co., 2009; Liveryman, Insurers' Co., 2014. *Publications:* (consultant ed.) A Practitioner's Guide to the FSA Regulation of Insurance, 2002, 4th edn 2011; numerous articles on insce related topics. *Recreations:* Scottish and alpine mountaineering, ski-ing, windsurfing. *E:* john@johntyoung.eu. *Club:* Caledonian.

YOUNG, John William Garne; Group Chief Executive, Wolseley plc, 1996–2000; *b* 6 Jan. 1945; *s* of David Richard Young and Pamela Mary Young (*née* Garne); *m* 1971, Eleanor Louise Walsh; three *s*. *Educ:* Shaftesbury Grammar Sch. Apprentice, Tube Investment Gp, 1962–67; Man. Dir, P. J. Parmiter & Sons Ltd, 1967–85; Wolseley plc: Chief Exec., Agricl Div., 1982–90, Agricl, Photographic & Technical Services Div., 1990–95; Dep. Chief Exec., 1994–96. Pres., Agricl Engrs Assoc., 1987–88. Pres., Comité Européen de Constructeurs de Mechanisme Agricole, 1995–96. *Recreations:* fishing, golf. *Address:* Garne House, 23 Bimport, Shaftesbury, Dorset SP7 8AX.

YOUNG, Jonathan Piers; Editor, The Field, since 1991; *b* 23 Sept. 1959; *s* of Peter and Mavis Young; *m* 1993, Caroline Bankes; one *s* one *d*. *Educ:* Blundell's; Univ. of Leicester (BA). Ed., Shooting Times and Country Magazine, 1986–90. Liveryman, Gunmakers' Co., 1992 (Mem., Ct of Assts, 2012–). *Publications:* A Pattern of Wings, 1989. *Recreations:* shooting, fishing, horsing around. *Address:* The Field, Blue Fin Building, 110 Southwark Street, SE1 0SU. *T:* (020) 3148 4772. *Clubs:* Tyburn Angling Society; Silkie.

YOUNG, Air Vice-Marshal Julian Alexander, CB 2013; OBE 2000; Director Helicopters, Defence Equipment and Support, since 2015; *b* Cambridge, 18 Dec. 1961; *s* of Ronald Emsley Young and Mrs Rosemary Eunice Young (now Perrin); *m* 1986, Helen Hewetson; two *s* one *d*. *Educ:* Royal Latin Sch., Buckingham; City Univ. (BSc Hons Air Transport Engrg); Cranfield Univ. (Master Defence Admin; MSc Leadership Studies); King's Coll. London (MA Internat. Studies). RAF Univ. Cadet, 1980–85; Jun. Engr Officer, No 7 Sqdn, RAF Odiham, 1985–87; Engr Officer, No 78 Sqdn, RAF Mt Pleasant, 1987; OC No 1 Aircraft Repair Flt, Repair and Salvage Sqdn, RAF Abingdon, 1987–90; Sen. Engr Officer, No 18 Sqdn, RAF Gütersloh and RAF Laarbruch, 1990–93; PSO to AO Engrg and Supply, HQ Strike Comd, 1993–96; RAF Staff Coll., 1996; Harrier Support Authy, RAF Wyton, 1996–99; OC Engrg and Supply Wing, RAF Cottesmore, 1999–2000; Gp Captain, Logistics Policy and Strategy, 2000–02; CO, RAF Cosford, 2002–03; Dir, End-to-End Rev. Air Implementation and Defence Logistics Transformation Prog., 2003–06; rcds 2006; ACOS A4 Logistics, HQ Air Comd, 2007–09; Dir, Defence Support Review, 2009–10; Defence Career Partnering (placement in industry), 2010; COS Support, HQ Air Comd, 2010–11; Exec. Officer, HQ Air Comd and Chief Engr (Air Comd), 2011–12; Dir Technical, 2012–15, Chief Inf. Officer, 2013–15, Defence Equipment and Support. *Recreations:* family, Impressionist art, military and British history, Radio 4, supporter of Peterborough United FC. *Address:* c/o RAF Personnel Management, HQ Air Command, RAF High Wycombe, Bucks HP14 4UE. *T:* 07704 186651. *E:* julian.young523@mod.uk. *Club:* Royal Air Force.

YOUNG, Kirsty Jackson, (Mrs N. K. A. Jones); Presenter: Desert Island Discs, BBC Radio Four, since 2006; Crimewatch UK, since 2008; *b* 23 Nov. 1968; *d* of John and Catherine Young; *m* 1999, Nicholas Keith Arthur Jones, *qv*; two *d*. *Educ:* High Sch. of Stirling. Newsreader and news presenter, BBC Radio Scotland, 1990–93; news anchor and presenter, Scottish Television, 1993–95; reporter, Holiday and Film 96, BBC TV, 1995–96; News Anchor: Channel Five News, 1996–2000; ITV, 2000–01; Five News, Channel Five, 2001–07. *Recreations:* family, food, laughter. *Address:* c/o KBJ, 22 Rathbone Street, W1T 1LG. *Club:* Soho House.

YOUNG, Prof. Lawrence Sterling, PhD, DSc; FRCPath, FRCP; FMedSci; FRSB; Pro Vice-Chancellor (Academic Planning and Resources), University of Warwick, since 2013; *b* 28 Oct. 1958; *s* of Bernard Young and late Joan Young (*née* Black); *m* 1979, Alison Hilton; one *s*. *Educ:* Univ. of Birmingham (BSc 1981; PhD 1984; DSc 1998). MRCPath 1993, FRCPath 2000; FRSB (FSB 2009); FRCP 2012. University of Birmingham: Res. Fellow, 1984–89, Lectr and Sen. Lectr, 1989–94, Dept of Cancer Studies; Professor of Cancer Biology, 1994–2013; Head: Div. of Cancer Studies and Dir, Cancer Res. UK Inst. for Cancer Studies, 2001–07; Coll. of Medical and Dental Scis, 2008–12; Pro Vice-Chancellor, 2009–12; Pro Vice-Chancellor for Res. and Capital Develt, Univ. of Warwick, 2013. Adjunct Prof., Monash Univ., 2014; Vis. Prof., Cancer Center, Sun Yat-sen Univ., Guangzhou, 2014. Member: Med. and Scientific Adv. Panel, Leukaemia Res. Fund, 1996–99; Grants Cttee, CRC, 1996–2001; Molecular Cell Medicine Bd, MRC, 2003–07; Cancer Sub-panel, 2001 and 2008 RAEs; Yorks Cancer Res. Scientific Adv. Cttee, 2008–. Non-executive Director: Birmingham Children's Hosp., 2008–10; Alta Innovations, 2009–12; Biosciences Ventures, 2010–12; Alta Bioscience, 2010–12. Pres., Internat. Assoc. for Res. on Epstein-Barr Virus and Associated Diseases, 2008–10. Chm., CORE Res. Awards Cttee, 2010–. FMedSci 2007 (Mem., Sectional Cttee 2, 2012–14). Hon. MRCP 1998. *Publications:* contrib. articles to learned jls on cancer, viruses and novel cancer therapies. *Recreations:* Gilbert and Sullivan operas, travel, poetry, learning to play the ukulele. *Address:* University House, University of Warwick, Coventry CV4 8UW. *T:* (024) 7652 8164. *E:* L.S.Young@warwick.ac.uk.

YOUNG, Sir Leslie (Clarence), Kt 1984; CBE 1980; Chairman: Enterprise plc, 1999–2000 (Director, Lancashire Enterprises, later Enterprise, plc, 1992–99); Eatonfield Group plc, 2006–09; *b* 5 Feb. 1925; *s* of late Clarence James Young and of Ivy Isabel Young; *m* 1st, 1949, Muriel Howard Pearson (*d* 1998); one *s* one *d*; 2nd, 1999, Margaret Gittens. *Educ:* London School of Economics (BScEcon). Courtaulds Ltd: held range of senior executive appts, incl. chairmanship of number of gp companies, 1948–68; J. Bibby & Sons Ltd, 1968–86: Managing

Director, J. Bibby Agriculture Ltd, 1968; Chm. and Man. Dir, J. Bibby Food Products Ltd, 1970; Gp Man. Dir, 1970, Dep. Chm. and Man. Dir, 1977, Chm., 1979–86, J. Bibby & Sons Ltd. Director: Bank of England, 1986–90; National Westminster Bank, 1979–90 (Regl Dir, 1979–90, Chm., 1986–90, Northern Regl Bd); Swiss Pioneer Life (formerly Pioneer Mutual Insce Co.), 1986–92; Sibec Developments PLC, 1988–91; Britannia Cable Systems Wirral plc, 1990–92. Chairman: NW Regional Council, CBI, 1976–78; NW Industrial Development Board, 1978–81; Merseyside Develt Corp., 1980–84; British Waterways Bd, 1984–87. Trustee, Civic Trust for the North West, 1978–83. Non-executive Director: Granada Television Ltd, 1979–84; Blue Max plc, 2000–. Chm. Trustees, Nat. Museums and Galls on Merseyside, 1986–95. Member Council: N of England Zoological Soc., 1979–85; Royal Liverpool Philharmonic Soc., 1980–2000. DL Merseyside, 1983–2007. Hon. Col, Liverpool Univ. OTC, 1989–94. Hon. LLD Liverpool, 1988. *Recreations:* fly-fishing, walking. *Address:* The Meadows, Grovefields, Hampton Lucy, Warwicks CV35 8AT. *T:* (01926) 624320, 07808 137160.

YOUNG, Sir Leslie Ronald, (Sir Jimmy), Kt 2002; CBE 1993 (OBE 1979); Presenter, Jimmy Young Programme, BBC Radio Two, 1973–2002 (Radio One, 1967–73); *b* 21 Sept. 1921; *s* of Frederick George Young and Gertrude Woolford; *m* 1st, 1946, Wendy Wilkinson (marr. diss.); one *d*; 2nd, 1950, Sally Douglas (marr. diss.); 3rd, 1996, Alicia Plastow. *Educ:* East Dean Grammar Sch., Cinderford, Glos. RAF, 1939–46. First BBC radio broadcast, songs at piano, 1949; pianist, singer, bandleader, West End, London, 1950–51; first theatre appearance, Empire Theatre, Croydon, 1952; regular theatre appearances, 1952–; first radio broadcast introd records, Flat Spin, 1953; BBC TV Bristol, Pocket Edition series, 1955; first introd radio Housewives' Choice, 1955; BBC radio series, incl.: The Night is Young, 12 o'clock Spin, Younger Than Springtime, Saturday Special, Keep Young, Through Till Two, 1959–65; presented progs, Radio Luxembourg, 1960–68. BBC TV: series, Jimmy Young Asks, 1972; The World of Jimmy Young, 1973. First live direct BBC broadcasts to Europe from Soviet Union, Jimmy Young Programme, 16 and 17 May 1977; Jimmy Young Programmes broadcast live from Egypt and Israel, 9 and 12 June 1978, from Zimbabwe-Rhodesia, 9 and 10 Aug. 1979; Host for Thames TV of first British Telethon, 2nd and 3rd Oct. 1980; Jimmy Young Programmes live from Tokyo, 26th, 27th and 28th May 1981, from Sydney, 4–8 Oct. 1982, from Washington DC, 3–7 Oct. 1983. ITV series: Whose Baby?, 1973; Jim's World, 1974; The Jimmy Young Television Programme, 1984–87. Hit Records: 1st, Too Young, 1951; Unchained Melody, The Man From Laramie, 1955 (1st Brit. singer to have 2 consec. no 1 hit records); Chain Gang, More, 1956; Miss You, 1963. Weekly Column, Daily Sketch, 1968–71; Sunday Express columnist, 2003–14. Hon. Mem. Council, NSPCC, 1981–. Freeman, City of London, 1969. Hon. DArts Gloucestershire, 2012. Variety Club of GB Award, Radio Personality of the Year, 1968; Sony Award, Radio Personality of the Year, 1985; Sony Radio Awards Roll of Honour, 1988; Radio Broadcaster of the Year, BPG Radio Awards, 1994; Sony Gold Award, for Service to the Community, 1995, for Outstanding Service to Radio, 1997; Jimmy Young Programme: Radio Industries Award, Prog. of the Year, 1979; BBC Current Affairs Prog. of the Year, Daily Mail Nat. Radio Awards, 1988; Radio Prog. of the Year, TV and Radio Inds Club Award, 1989. Silver Jubilee Medal, 1977. *Publications:* Jimmy Young Cookbook: No 1, 1968; No 2, 1969; No 3, 1970; No 4, 1972; (autobiogs) JY, 1973, Jimmy Young, 1982, Forever Young, 2003; contrib. magazines, incl. Punch, Woman's Own. *Address:* PO Box 39715, W4 3YF.

YOUNG, Hon. M. Douglas; PC (Canada) 1993; QC (Canada) 2009; Chairman: Summa Strategies Canada, Inc., 1997; CPCS Transcom Inc., 2006; *b* 20 Sept. 1940; *s* of Douglas Young and Annie Young (*née* Wishart); *m* 1979, Jacqueline David; one *s* two *d*. *Educ:* St Thomas Univ. (BA 1972); Univ. of New Brunswick (LLB 1975); New Brunswick Teachers' Coll. Cert., 1957. Lawyer and businessman. MLA for Tracadie, New Brunswick, 1978–88; Leader, New Brunswick Liberal Party, 1981–83; Provincial Minister of Fisheries and Aquaculture, 1987–88; MP (L) Gloucester, renamed Acadie-Bathurst, 1988–97; Canadian Minister: of Transport, 1993–96; of Human Resources, 1996; of Nat. Defence and of Veteran Affairs, 1996–97. Hon. LLD St Thomas, 2013. *Recreations:* tennis, reading, travelling. *Address:* PO Box 1042, Bathurst, NB E2A 4H8, Canada.

YOUNG, Madeleine Mary, (Lady Young); *see* Arnot, M. M.

YOUNG, Malcolm, (Mal); independent television producer, since 2011; *b* 26 Jan. 1957; *s* of late Charles Young, Liverpool, and of Maria (*née* Williams); *m* 2014, Mari Wilson. *Educ:* Liverpool Sch. of Art (DipAD). Design Manager, Littlewoods Orgn, 1975–81; actor/singer, 1981–84; Mersey Television, 1984–96: Design Asst on Brookside, then Asst Floor Manager and Floor Manager, 1986–91; Producer, Brookside and Dir, Brookside Prodns, 1991–95; Series Producer, Brookside, 1995–96 (also devised and produced And The Beat Goes On, Channel 4); Hd of Drama, Pearson TV, 1996–97; Hd of Drama Series, 1997–2001, Controller of Continuing Drama Series, 2001–04, BBC, responsible for: EastEnders, Casualty, Holby City, Waking the Dead, Doctors, Murder in Mind, In Deep, Judge John Deed, Down to Earth, Dalziel and Pascoe, and Dr Who; Dir of Drama, 19 TV, 2005–10; writer and creator: Born in the USA, for Fox TV (US), 2005; Austin Golden Hour, TV drama pilot for CW/Paramount (US), 2008; writer and executive producer: If I Can Dream, for Hulu, 2010; Desperate Scousewives, for Channel 4, 2011–12; writer and creative consultant, Sony Pictures Internat. TV, 2012–; co-writer and creator: Young Americans, for ABC, 2013–14; Blocked, for NBC TV, 2014–15; storyline writer and consultant producer, River City, BBC Scotland, 2015; Founder and Co-Owner, Dynamo Prodns, 2012–15; Founder and Owner, Pool of Life Prodns, 2014–. Hon. Prof., TV Scriptwriting, Glasgow Caledonian Univ., 2014–. Member: BAFTA, 1997; RTS, 1999; Writers Guild of Great Britain, 2013; Writers Guild of America West, 2013. Huw Wheldon Meml Lecture, RTS, 1999. Special Award for Creative Contribution to TV, British Soap Awards, 2004. *Publications:* Sinbad's Scrapbook, 1996. *Recreations:* music, tennis, snooker.

YOUNG, Prof. Malcolm Philip, PhD; Chief Executive, e-Therapeutics plc, since 2007; *b* 11 Sept. 1960; *s* of James Guthrie Philips Young and Shirley Joyce Young (*née* Smith); *m* 1987, Deborah Anne Howse; one *s* two *d*. *Educ:* Bristol Univ. (BSc 1st cl. Hons (Psychol.) 1987); Univ. of St Andrews (PhD (Neurosci.) 1990). Royal Soc. Japan Sci. and Technol. Sci. Exchange Fellow, Riken Inst., Japan, 1990–91; Oxford University: MRC Res. Associate, 1991–92, Royal Soc. Univ. Res. Fellow, 1992–94, Univ. Lab. of Physiol.; British Telecommunications Jun. Res. Fellow, Brasenose Coll., 1993–94; Newcastle upon Tyne University: Dir, Inst. for Neurosci., 1999–2001; Prof. and Chair in Psychol., 1994–2009; Hd, Dept of Psychol., 1994–2001; Provost, Faculty of Sci., Agriculture and Engrg, 2001–05; Pro-Vice-Chancellor for Strategic Develt, 2005–07; Vis. Prof., Inst. of Neurosci., 2009–. Vis. Prof., Agency of Industrial Sci. and Technol., Tsukuba, Japan, 1995. Chairman and Chief Technology Officer: In Rotis Technologies Ltd, 2001–; e-Therapeutics plc, 2003–07; non-executive Chairman: Novotech Investment Ltd, 2007–; Searchbolt (formerly OGS Search) Ltd, 2007–; Chm., Lisles Research Ltd, 2012–. Mem., Soc. for Neurosci., USA, 1990–. Ernst and Young Innovation Entrepreneur of the Year, N and Midlands, 2010. *Publications:* The Analysis of Cortical Connectivity, 1996; many articles in learned jls inc. Nature, Science, Procs of Royal Soc., Philosophical Transactions of Royal Soc., Jl of Neuroscience, etc. *Recreations:* sailing, ski-ing, hiking, music. *Address:* Executive Office, e-Therapeutics, Fenlock Court, Blenheim Office Park, Oxon OX29 8LN.

YOUNG, Marianne; HM Diplomatic Service; Deputy Head (Climate), Science, Innovation and Climate Department, Foreign and Commonwealth Office, since 2015; *b* UK, 8 Aug. 1971; *d* of James and Andrea Darch; *m* 2002, Barry Young; one *s* two *d*. *Educ:* St Teresa's Sch., Effingham; Wellington Coll.; Univ. of Warwick (BA); City Univ., London (Postgrad. Dip.). Grad. trainee, The Times, 1994–95; staff ed., then Asia Ed., Fairplay Gp Singapore, 1995–2000; Sen. Corresp., Fairplay Gp UK, 2000–01; entered FCO, 2001; deptl report writer, then Press Officer, Press Office, 2001–03; Hd, Great Lakes Section, then Hd, E Africa and Horn Section, Africa Directorate, 2003–05; Head: communications engaging with Islamic World Gp, 2005–06; Ext. Political Section, Pretoria and Dep. High Comr, Kingdoms of Lesotho and Swaziland, 2006–11; High Comr, Namibia, 2011–15. *Recreations:* literature, photography, scuba diving, travel, story writing. *Address:* c/o Foreign and Commonwealth Office, King Charles Street, SW1A 2AH.

YOUNG, Neil; *see* Young, R. N.

YOUNG, Sir Nicholas (Charles), Kt 2000; Chief Executive, British Red Cross, 2001–14; *b* 16 April 1952; *s* of late Leslie Charles Young and Mary Margaret Young (*née* Rudman); *m* 1978, Helen Mary Ferrier Hamilton; three *s*. *Educ:* Wimbledon Coll.; Birmingham Univ. (Hons LLB 2.1). Qualified Solicitor, 1977; Articled Clerk and Solicitor, Freshfields, 1975–78; Solicitor, later Partner, Turner, Martin & Symes, 1979–85; Sec. for Develt, Sue Ryder Foundn, 1985–90; Dir, UK Ops, BRCS, 1990–95; Chief Exec., 1995–2001 and Vice-Pres., 2001–, Macmillan Cancer Support (formerly Cancer Relief Macmillan Fund, later Macmillan Cancer Relief). Vice Chm., Nat. Council for Hospice and Specialist Palliative Care Services, 1996–99; Member: Exec. Cttee, Healthwork UK, 1998–2002; NCVO Charity Law Reform Gp, 1998–2001; NHS Modernisation Bd, 2000–01; Foreign Secretary's Human Rights Adv. Gp, 2010–14; Cabinet Office Nat. Honours Cttee, 2011–; Trustee, 2000–, and Chm., 2005–, Monte San Martino Trust; Mem., Steering Cttee, The Giving Campaign, 2000–03; Mem., Adv. Bd, Nat. Council of Voluntary Orgns, 2010–; Trustee: Disasters Emergency Cttee, 2001–14; Guidestar UK, 2003–06; Wimbledon Foundn, 2015–; Trustee and Dep. Chm., Humanitarian Forum, 2006–; Mem. and Vice Chm., Humanitarian Worker Meml Cttee, 2015–. Chm., Judging Panel, Asian Women of Achievement Awards, 2006–. Mem., Stumblers Assoc., 1978–. Gov., Wimbledon Coll., 1998–2000. Patron, Escape Lines Meml Soc., 2009–. MCMI 2009. Freeman, City of London, 2007. Queen's Badge of Honour, 2013, Hon. Vice Pres., 2014, British Red Cross. *Recreations:* theatre, walking, amateur dramatics, travel, reading, writing. *E:* youngs2city@yahoo.com.

YOUNG, Peter Lance; Group Chief Executive, RMC Group, 1996–2000; *b* 26 June 1938; *s* of Harry Aubrey Young and Ethel Freda Young; *m* 1962, Susan Mary Wilkes; three *s* one *d*. *Educ:* Chippenham Grammar Sch. Joined RMC Group, 1961; Dir, 1977; Dep. Man. Dir, 1992; Man. Dir, 1993. *Recreations:* tennis, gardening.

YOUNG, Peter Michael Heppell, OBE 1995; HM Diplomatic Service, retired; *b* 23 April 1939; *s* of late Denis and Constance Young; *m* 1st, 1969, Maria Laura Aragon; 2nd, Verona Buchan; two step *s*. *Educ:* Haileybury Coll.; Williston Acad., USA (ESU Scholarship); Emmanuel Coll., Cambridge (MA). Chartered FCIPD. Royal Marines and Royal West Africa Frontier Force (2nd Lieut), 1958–60; FCO, 1964; served: Sofia, 1967–70; Geneva, 1970–72; Pretoria/Cape Town, 1972–74; FCO 1974–77; First Sec., Lagos, 1977–79; Dep. High Comr, Ibadan, 1979–80; Consul (Commercial), Lyon, 1981–84; FCO, 1985–89; Counsellor, Lagos, 1989–93; seconded to Dept of National Heritage (Events Director, D-Day and VE-Day 50th Annivs), 1993–95; High Comr, Bahamas, 1996–99. Pres., Bahamas Hon. Consular Corps, 2010–13. Dir, Nassau Inst.; former Mem., Exec. Cttee, Bahamas Nat. Trust. Mem. Bd, Tribune Media Gp, 2013–. *Recreations:* tennis, golf, African history. *Address:* PO Box EE 16944, Nassau, Bahamas. *Clubs:* Oxford and Cambridge, MCC; Lyford Cay, Royal Nassau Sailing (former Hon. Sec.); Nassau Lawn Tennis (Pres., 2012–).

YOUNG, Peyton; *see* Young, H. P.

YOUNG, Raymond Kennedy, CBE 2007 (OBE 1989); Chairman, Architecture and Design Scotland, 2004–10; *b* 23 Jan. 1946; *s* of Sharp and Christina Neil, (Neilina), Young; *m* 1972, Jean; three *s*. *Educ:* Univ. of Strathclyde (BArch Hons). FRIAS. Project Architect, ASSIST/Univ. of Strathclyde, 1971–74; Housing Corp., 1974–89 (Dir, Scotland); Dir North, and Dir Res. and Innovation, Scottish Homes, 1989–97; self-employed, 1997–. Hon. Sen. Res. Fellow, Dept of Urban Studies, Univ. of Glasgow, 1997–2009; Hon. Prof., Dept of Architecture, Univ. of Strathclyde, 2007–11. Mem., UK Sustainable Develt Commn, 2000–04. Non-exec. Dir, Historic Scotland, 2007–. *Publications:* Annie's Loo: the Govan origins of Scotland's community based housing associations, 2013; gen. professional pubns. *Recreations:* theatre, music, no sports. *Address:* Willowbank, Upper Granco Street, Dunning PH2 0RX.

YOUNG, Richard; photographer; Co-Founder and Co-Director, Richard Young Gallery, London, since 2008; *b* Welwyn Garden City, 17 Sept. 1947; *s* of David Young and Hilda Young; *m* 1985, Susan Walker; two *s* one *d*. Social photographer, 1974–. *Solo exhibitions* include: Richard Young: An Early Retrospective, Olympus Gall., London, 1979; By Invitation Only, 1981, PAPARAZZO!, 1989, Hamilton's Gall., London; Richard Young Two Thousand, Blains Fine Art, London, 1999; 15 Minutes: 30 Years Retrospective, The Hospital, London, 2004; Richard Young Gallery: Icons, 2009; GQ Man of the Year Awards 11 Year Retrospective, 2010; Pret-a-Photo II, 2011; Elizabeth Taylor, 2012, also Stephen Webster, LA and Colombaia Mus., Ischia, 2012; David Bowie, 2013; RY40, 2014; *group exhibitions* include: Olympus Gall., London, 1986; Four Stages of Innocence, RCA, 1993; Warholesque?, 2009, Pret-a-Photo, 2010, Richard Young Gall.; George Harrison, GRAMMY Mus., LA, 2011; photograph of Freddie Mercury inducted into NPG, 2013. Hon. Dr Univ. of Arts, London, 2013. Ischia Art Award, Ischia Global Film and Music Fest., 2012; Le Prix Champagne de la Joie de Vivre, 2013; Ordre des Coteaux de Champagne, 2014; Chairman's Award, UK Picture Editors' Guild, 2015. *Publications:* By Invitation Only, 1981; Paparazzo!, 1989; Shooting Stars, 2004; Nightclubbing, 2014. *Recreations:* riding my Harley, walking, good food. *Address:* Richard Young Gallery, 4 Holland Street, W8 4LT. *T:* (020) 7937 8911. *E:* office@richardyoungonline.com. *Clubs:* Chelsea Arts, Groucho.

YOUNG, Sir Rob; *see* Young, Sir J. R.

YOUNG, Robert; Principal, European Economic Research Ltd, 2004–14, now Special Adviser; *b* 27 March 1944; *s* of Walter Horace Young and Evelyn Joan Young; *m* 1965, Patricia Anne Cowin; one *s* one *d* (and one *s* decd). *Educ:* Magdalen College, Oxford (BA Hons 1965; MA 1996). Graduate apprentice, Rolls-Royce, 1965; IBM UK, 1969–71; Rolls-Royce Motors, 1971–81: Man. Dir, Military Engine Div., 1977–79; Dir and Gen. Manager, Diesel Div., 1979–81; Vickers, 1981–85 (Group Commercial Dir, 1981–83); Man. Dir, Crane Ltd, 1985–88; Chief Exec., Plastics Div., McKechnie plc, 1989–90; Dir, Beauford plc, 1990–92; Competition Policy Consultant, Coopers & Lybrand, 1993–98; Dir, PricewaterhouseCoopers, 1998–2000; Principal, 2000–04, Dir, 2001–04, LECG Ltd. Member: Central Policy Review Staff, 1983; No 10 Policy Unit, 1983–84; CBI W Midlands Regional Council, 1980–81 (Chm., CBI Shropshire, 1981); Monopolies and Mergers Commn, 1986–92; Fulbright Commn, 1994–2004. *Recreations:* Mozart, railways, cats, photography. *Address:* 12 Beechcroft Road, SW14 7JJ. *Club:* Oxford and Cambridge.

YOUNG, Prof. Robert Joseph, PhD; FRS 2013; FREng, FIMMM; FInstP; Professor of Polymer Science and Technology, University of Manchester (formerly University of Manchester Institute of Science and Technology), since 1986 (Head, School of Materials, 2004–09); *b* 29 May 1948; *s* of Joseph and Florence Young; *m* 1971, Sheila Winifred Wilson; two *d*. *Educ:* St John's Coll., Cambridge (MA, PhD). Res. Fellow, St John's Coll., Cambridge, 1973–75; Lectr in Materials, QMC, 1975–86. Wolfson Res. Prof. in Materials Science, Royal Soc., 1992–97. Visiting Professor: Hong Kong Poly. Univ., 2008–11; King Fahd Univ. of

Petroleum and Minerals, Saudi Arabia, 2011–12. Zeneca Lect., 1996, BAAS Public Lect., 1997, Royal Soc. Panel Chm., HEFCE RAE, 1996, 2001. FREng 2006. Silver Medal, Plastics and Rubber Inst., 1991; Griffith Medal, Inst. of Materials, 2002; Plueddemann Internat. Award, 2010; Leslie Holliday Prize, 2011, Swinburne Medal and Prize, 2012, IMMM. *Publications:* Introduction to Polymers, 1981, 3rd edn (jtly), 2011; (jtly) Fracture Behaviour of Polymers, 1983; more than 350 papers in learned jls. *Recreations:* tennis, piano, gardening; former athlete (four blues, 1967–70; British Univs' Sports Fedn 110m Hurdles Champion, 1970). *Address:* Materials Science Centre, School of Materials, University of Manchester, Oxford Road, Manchester M13 9PL. *T:* (0161) 306 3550.

YOUNG, Sir Robin (Urquhart), KCB 2002; Permanent Secretary, Department of Trade and Industry, 2001–05; Chairman: Circle Anglia, since 2009; A4e Ltd, since 2012; *b* 7 Sept. 1948; *s* of late Col Ian U. Young and Mary Young; *m* 1998, Madeleine Mary Arnot, *qv*. *Educ:* Fettes Coll., Edinburgh; University Coll., Oxford (BA 1971). Joined DoE, 1973; Private Sec. to Parly Sec., Planning and Local Govt, 1976; Private Sec. to Minister of Housing, 1980–81; Local Govt Finance, 1981–85; Private Sec. to successive Secs of State, 1985–88; Under Secretary: Housing, 1988–89; Envmt Policy, 1989–91; Local Govt Review, 1991–92; Local Govt, DoE, 1992–94; Dep. Sec., 1994–98; Regl Dir, Govt Office for London, 1994–97; Hd of Econ. and Domestic Affairs Secretariat, Cabinet Office, 1997–98; Permanent Sec., DCMS, 1998–2001. Chairman: Dr Foster Intelligence Ltd, 2006–11; Euro RSCG Apex Commns, 2006–11; First Columbus Investments, 2007–09. Non-executive Director: Bovis Construction Ltd, 1989–94; Dr Foster Ltd, 2005–15; A4e Ltd, 2007–12; Cambridge Cleantech Ltd, 2012–. Chairman: E of England Sci. and Industry Council, 2006–09; E of England Internat. Ltd, 2006–10; Board Member: IoD, 2007–14; Film London, 2012–; Adv. Bd, Solar Cloth Co. Ltd, 2014–. *Recreations:* tennis, cinema, house in France. *Address:* 47 Moreton Terrace, SW1V 2NS.

YOUNG, (Roderic) Neil; Investment Consultant, 1989–2006; *b* 29 May 1933; *s* of late Dr F. H. Young and S. M. Young (*née* Robinson); *m* 1962, Gillian Margaret Salmon; two *s* one *d*. *Educ:* Eton; Trinity College, Cambridge (MA). FCA. 2nd Lieut Queen's Own Royal West Kent Regt, 1952–53. Howard Howes & Co., 1956–59; Fenn & Crosthwaite, 1960–63; Brown Fleming & Murray, 1964–68; Director: Murray Johnstone, 1969–70; Kleinwort Benson, 1971–88. Director: Malvern UK Index Trust, 1990–98; London and SE Bd, Bradford and Bingley Bldg Soc., 1990–97. City of London: Mem., Court of Common Council, 1980; Alderman, Ward of Bread Street, 1982–94; Sheriff, 1991–92; Master, Gunmakers' Co., 1994–95. Adv. Cttee, Greenwich Hosp., 1983–2002. *Recreations:* gardening, DIY. *Address:* Down Farm House, Lamberhurst Down, Lamberhurst, Kent TN3 8HA. *T:* (01892) 891792.

YOUNG, Roger; President, FPL Group Inc., 1999, retired; *b* 14 Jan. 1944; *s* of Arnold and Margaret Young; *m* 1970, Sue Neilson; one *s* two *d*. *Educ:* Gordonstoun Sch.; Edinburgh Univ. (BSc Engrg); Cranfield Business Sch. (MBA). Rolls-Royce Ltd, 1961–72; Alidair Ltd, 1972–73; Wavin Plastics Ltd, 1973–76; Aurora Holdings Ltd, 1976–80; Low & Bonar plc, 1980–88; Chief Exec., Scottish Hydro-Electric plc, 1988–98. Non-executive Director: Friends Ivory & Sime (formerly Ivory & Sime) plc, 1993–99; Bank of Scotland, 1994–99. *Recreations:* family, flying, hill walking.

YOUNG, Roger Dudley; Chairman, Clex Developments, since 1976; *b* 7 Jan. 1940; *s* of Henry G. Young and Winifred G. Young; *m* 1st, 1965, Jennifer J. Drayton (marr. diss. 2010); one *s* two *d*; 2nd, 2011, Hilary C. Vaughan (*née* Rushworth). *Educ:* Dulwich Coll. Drayton Group, 1958–69; Imperial Group, 1969–73; Robert Fleming, 1971–73; Director: Henry Ansbacher Group, 1973–82; Touche Remnant Group, 1982–85; Chief Executive: Bank Julius Baer (London), 1985–89; March Group, 1989–91; Dir Gen., Inst. of Mgt, 1992–98. Dir Gen., Inst. of Enterprise, 1998–2001. Chairman: Andrews and Partners Ltd, 2000–05; Andrews Estate Agents Ltd, 2000–05; Bicon Hldgs Ltd, 2000–13; Lunar (formerly Apollo) Diagnostics Ltd, 2005–07; Chic Sheds Ltd, 2014–; non-exec. Dir, PMP Plus, subseq. Apollo Medical Partners, Ltd, 2000–05. Dir, Ipswich Hosp. NHS Trust, 1992–99. Trustee, 1998–2005, Chm., 2000–03, World in Need, subseq. Andrews Charitable Trust Ltd. CCMI; FRSA. *Recreations:* small businesses, sculpture, travel. *Address:* Hardy House, 32 Benton Street, Hadleigh, Ipswich IP7 5AT. *T:* (01473) 828878. *Club:* Honourable Artillery Company.

YOUNG, Sir Roger (William), Kt 1983; MA; STh, LHD, FRSE; Principal of George Watson's College, Edinburgh, 1958–85; *b* 15 Nov. 1923; *yr s* of late Charles Bowden Young and Dr Ruth Young, CBE; *m* 1950, Caroline Mary Christie (*d* 2013); two *s* two *d*. *Educ:* Dragon Sch., Oxford; Westminster Sch. (King's Scholar); Christ Church, Oxford (Scholar). Served War of 1939–45, RNVR, 1942–45. Classical Mods, 1946, Lit. Hum. 1948. Resident Tutor, St Catharine's, Cumberland Lodge, Windsor, 1949–51; Asst Master, The Manchester Grammar Sch., 1951–58. 1st Class in Archbishop's examination in Theology (Lambeth Diploma), 1957. Participant, US State Dept Foreign Leader Program, 1964. Scottish Governor, BBC, 1979–84. Member: Edinburgh Marriage Guidance Council, 1960–75; Scottish Council of Christian Educn Movement, 1960–81 (Chm., 1961–67; Hon. Vice-Pres., 1981–85); Gen. Council of Christian Educn Movement, 1985–94 (Vice-Pres., 1989–2002); Management Assoc., SE Scotland, 1965–85; Educational Research Bd of SSRC, 1966–70; Court, Edinburgh Univ., 1967–76; Public Schools Commn, 1968–70; Consultative Cttee on the Curriculum, 1972–75; Adv. Cttee, Scottish Centre for Studies in Sch. Administration, 1972–75; Royal Soc. of Edinburgh Dining Club, 1972–; Scottish Adv. Cttee, Community Service Volunteers, 1973–78; Edinburgh Festival Council, 1970–76; Independent Schs Panel of Wolfson Foundn, 1978–82; Gen. Adv. Council of BBC, 1978–79; Scottish Council of Independent Schs, 1978–85; Royal Observatory Trust, Edin., 1981–93; Council, RSE, 1982–85; ISJC, 1988–94. Hon. Sec., Headmasters' Assoc. of Scotland, 1968–72, Pres., 1972–74; Chairman: HMC, 1976; BBC Consult. Gp on Social Effects of TV, 1978–79; Bursary Bd, Dawson International Ltd, 1977–85; Bath Film Soc., 1990–93; Catch-up Prog. for World in Need, 1996–2000; Caxton Trust, 1998–2000; Dep. Chm., GBA, 1988–94. Trustee: Campion Sch., Athens, 1984–91; Wells Cathedral Sch., 1987–2005; Chm. Council, Cheltenham Ladies' Coll., 1986–93; Member, Governing Body: Westminster Sch., 1986–97; Royal Sch., Bath, 1987–99; Mem. Council, Bath Univ., 1993–96, 1997–2001. Conducted Enquiry on Stirling Univ., 1973. Hon. LHD, Hamilton Coll., Clinton, NY, 1978. *Publications:* Lines of Thought, 1958; Everybody's Business, 1968; Everybody's World, 1970; Report on the Policies and Running of Stirling University 1966–1973, 1973; Outdoor Adventures: third year projects at George Watson's College, 2003. *Recreations:* gardening, films, photography, music, knitting. *Address:* 11 Belgrave Terrace, Bath BA1 5JR. *T:* (01225) 336940. *Club:* East India.

YOUNG, Sally; *see* MacDonald, S.

YOUNG, Prof. Stephen John, PhD; FREng; Professor of Information Engineering, Cambridge University, since 1995 (Senior Pro-Vice Chancellor, 2009–15); Fellow of Emmanuel College, Cambridge, since 1985; *b* 23 Jan. 1951; *s* of John Leonard Young and Joan Young (*née* Shaw); *m* 1976 (marr. diss. 1996); two *d*; *m* 1999, Sybille Wiesmann. *Educ:* Maghull GS; Jesus Coll., Cambridge (MA, PhD). FIET, CEng; FREng 2002; FIEEE 2009. Res. Engr, GEC Hirst Res. Centre, 1973–74; Univ. Lectr in Computation, UMIST, 1977–84; Lectr in Engrg, 1984–95, Reader, 1995, Cambridge Univ.; Tech. Dir, Entropic Cambridge Res. Lab., 1996–99; Architect, Microsoft Corp., 1999–2001; Cambridge University: Chm., Sch. of Technol., 2002–04; Hd of Inf. Engrg, 2002–09. Chairman: Phonetic Arts Ltd, 2008–10; VocalIQ Ltd, 2011–. Member of Council: Univ. of Cambridge, 2006–09; RAEng, 2006–. Chm., Speech and Lang. Tech. Cttee, IEEE, 2009–10. Fellow, Internat. Speech Communication Assoc., 2008 (Medal for Scientific Achievement, 2010). Tech. Achievement Award, Eur. Assoc. for Signal Processing, 2013; James L. Flanagan Award, IEEE, 2015. FRSA. Editor, Computer Speech and Language, 1993–2005. *Publications:* Real Time Languages, 1982; An Introduction to Ada, 1985; (ed) Corpus-based Methods, 1997; articles in jls. *Recreations:* ballet, film, music. *Address:* Engineering Department, Trumpington Street, Cambridge CB2 1PZ. *T:* (01223) 332654.

YOUNG, Sir Stephen Stewart Templeton, 3rd Bt *cr* 1945; QC (Scot.) 2002; Sheriff Principal of Grampian, Highland and Islands, 2001–12; *b* 24 May 1947; *s* of Sir Alastair Young, 2nd Bt, and Dorothy Constance Marcelle (*d* 1964), *d* of late Lt-Col Charles Ernest Chambers, and *widow* of Lt J. H. Grayburn, VC, Parachute Regt; *S* father, 1963; *m* 1974, Viola Margaret Nowell-Smith, *d* of Prof. P. H. Nowell-Smith and Perilla Thyme (she *m* 2nd, Lord Roberthall, KCMG, CB); two *s*. *Educ:* Rugby; Trinity Coll., Oxford; Edinburgh Univ. Voluntary Service Overseas, Sudan, 1968–69. Sheriff: of Glasgow and Strathkelvin, March–June 1984; of N Strathclyde at Greenock, 1984–2001. *Heir:* *s* Charles Alastair Stephen Young, *b* 21 July 1979. *Address:* Beechfield, Newton of Kinkell, Conon Bridge, Ross-shire IV7 8AS.

YOUNG, Timothy Mark Stewart; Director of Education (in charge of School Leadership and the Rank Fellowship), Rank Foundation, since 2007; *b* 6 Oct. 1951; *s* of Sir Brian Walter Mark Young, *qv*; *m* 1990, Dr Alison Mary Keightley, MRCP, FRCR; two *s*. *Educ:* Eton (King's Schol.); Magdalene Coll., Cambridge (BA 1974; MA 1978); Bristol Univ. (PGCE 1975). Asst Master, Eton, 1975–83 and 1985–87; Asst Master, Wanganui Collegiate Sch., NZ, 1984; Teacher, Harvard Sch., Los Angeles, 1987–88; Housemaster, Eton, 1988–92; Headmaster, Royal Grammar Sch., Guildford, 1992–2006. Hon. Treas., HMC, 1999–2002. Mem. Court, Univ. of Surrey, 1992–2006. Governor: Abbots Hosp., 1992–2006; Westminster Sch., 2005–15. Consultant, Internat. Inst. of Educn, 2010–12. Trustee, Young Carers Develt Trust, 2011–. *Recreations:* music, cinema, travel, Watford FC. *Address:* Cobbetts, Mavins Road, Farnham, Surrey GU9 8JS. *Clubs:* East India, Devonshire, Sports and Public Schools, Lansdowne.

YOUNG, Timothy Nicholas; QC 1996; barrister; *b* 1 Dec. 1953; *s* of William Ritchie Young and Patricia Eileen Young; *m* 1981, Susan Jane Kenny; two *s* one *d*. *Educ:* Malvern Coll.; Magdalen Coll., Oxford (BA, BCL). Called to the Bar, Gray's Inn, 1977, Bencher, 2004; in practice at the Commercial Bar, 1977–. Vis. Lectr, St Edmund Hall, Oxford, 1977–80. *Publications:* Voyage Charters, 1993, 3rd edn 2007. *Recreations:* watercolours, drawing, cricket, guitar, theatre, television. *Clubs:* Thebertons Cricket, Worcs CC; Dulwich and Sydenham Golf.

YOUNG, Toby Daniel Moorsom; journalist and author; *b* 17 Oct. 1963; *s* of Baron Young of Dartington and Sasha Young; *m* 2001, Caroline Bondy; three *s* one *d*. *Educ:* Creighton Comp. Sch.; King Edward VI Comp. Sch.; William Ellis Comp. Sch.; Brasenose Coll., Oxford (BA 1986); Harvard Univ.; Trinity Coll., Cambridge. Teaching Fellow, Graduate Sch. of Arts and Scis, Harvard, 1987–88; Teaching Asst, Soc. and Pol Scis Fac., Univ. of Cambridge, 1988–90; Editor, The Modern Review, 1991–95; Contrib. Editor, Vanity Fair, 1995–98; Drama Critic, 2001–06, Associate Editor, 2007–, The Spectator; Restaurant Critic, ES magazine, 2002–07; blogger, Daily Telegraph, 2010–15. Trustee, 2004–10, Ambassador, 2010–, Orbis UK; CEO and Dir, W London Free Sch. Academy Trust, 2014– (Co-Founder, Chm. Govs and Trustee, 2011–14). Vis. Fellow, Univ. of Buckingham, 2011–. Mem., Fulbright Commn, 2013–. *Plays* (co-author): How to Lose Friends and Alienate People, 2003 (co-prod. of film, 2008); Who's the Daddy?, 2005 (Best New Comedy, Theatregoers' Choice Awards, 2006); A Right Royal Farce, 2006; *TV drama* (co-author and co-prod.), When Boris Met Dave, 2009. *Publications:* How to Lose Friends and Alienate People, 2001; The Sound of No Hands Clapping, 2006; How to Set Up a Free School, 2011; What Every Parent Needs to Know, 2014. *Recreation:* food and drink. *Address:* West London Free School, Cambridge Grove, W6 0LB. *E:* tobyyoung@mac.com. *Club:* Soho House.

YOUNG, Sir William Neil, 10th Bt *cr* 1769; Chairman, Napo Pharmaceuticals Inc., 2007–14; *b* 22 Jan. 1941; *s* of Captain William Elliot Young, RAMC (killed in action 27 May 1942), and Mary (*d* 1997), *d* of late Rev. John Macdonald; *S* grandfather, 1944; *m* 1965, Christine Veronica Morley, *o d* of late R. B. Morley, Buenos Aires; one *s* one *d*. *Educ:* Wellington Coll.; Sandhurst. Captain, 16th/5th The Queen's Royal Lancers, retired 1970. Dir, Kleinwort Benson International Investment Ltd, 1982–87; Head: Investment Management, Saudi Internat. Bank, 1987–91; ME Dept, Coutts & Co., 1991–94; Dir, Barclays Private Bank Ltd, 1994–99. Chm., High Ham Br., RBL, 2004–. Gov., High Ham Sch., 2010–. *Recreation:* tennis. *Heir:* *s* William Lawrence Elliot Young [*b* 26 May 1970; *m* 2001, Astrid Bartsch, Vienna; one *s* one *d*].

YOUNGE, Patrick Anthony; Founder and Director, WeCreate Associates Ltd, since 2014; Co-founder and Managing Director, Sugar Films Ltd, since 2015; *b* Greenwich, 14 Feb. 1964; *s* of Patrick Colonso Younge and Reba Anelda Younge (*née* Stoute); *m* 1994, Jill Carter (marr. diss. 2007); one *s* one *d*; *m* 2010, Amy Girdwood; one *s*. *Educ:* Nobel Comprehensive Sch., Stevenage; University Coll. Cardiff (BSc Hons Mineral Exploitation). BBC News and Current Affairs, 1994–99; Commng Ed., Channel 4 TV, 1999–2001; Hd, Progs and Planning, BBC Sport, 2001–05; Pres. and Gen. Manager, Travel Channel Media, USA, 2005–10; Chief Creative Officer, BBC Production, 2010–13. Gov., Univ. of W London, 2014–. FRTS; FRSA. *Recreations:* cinema, sport, reading. *E:* patrickyounge@gmail.com.

YOUNGER, family name of **Viscount Younger of Leckie**.

YOUNGER OF LECKIE, 5th Viscount *cr* 1923, of Alloa, Clackmannanshire; **James Edward George Younger;** Bt 1911; a Lord in Waiting (Government Whip), since 2015; *b* 11 Nov. 1955; *e s* of 4th Viscount Younger of Leckie, KT, KCVO, TD, PC, DL and of Diana Rhona (*née* Tuck); *S* father, 2003; *m* 1988, Jennie Veronica (*née* Wootton); one *s* two *d*. *Educ:* Cargilfield Sch., Edinburgh; Winchester Coll.; St Andrews Univ. (MA Hons Medieval Hist. 1979); Henley Mgt Coll. (MBA 1993). MCIM 1994. Personnel Mgr, Coats Patons, 1979–84; Recruitment Consultant, Angela Mortimer Ltd, 1984–86; Exec. Search Consultant, Stephens Consultancies, 1986–92; Director: MacInnes Younger, 1992–94; HR, UBS Wealth Mgt, 1994–2004; Culliford Edmunds Associates, 2004–07; Consultant, Eban Internat., 2007–10. Chm., Bucks Cons. Constituency Assoc., 2006–10. Member: Assoc. of Cons. Peers, 2006–; Area Bd, Oxon and Bucks Conservatives, 2008–13; Chm., Milton Keynes Conservatives, 2011–13. Elected Mem., H of L, 2010. Cons. Party Whip, 2011–12; a Lord in Waiting (Govt Whip), 2012–13; Parly Under-Sec. of State, BIS, 2013–14. Vice Pres., War Widows' Assoc., 2012–. Mem., Royal Co. of Archers (Queen's Body Guard for Scotland). Pres., Highland Soc. of London, 2012–; Hon. Pres., Kate Kennedy Club Life Members Assoc., St Andrews Univ. *Recreations:* sailing, tennis, shooting, Highland dancing, ski-ing, country pursuits, cricket. *Heir:* *s* Hon. Alexander William George Younger, *b* 13 Nov. 1993. *Address:* The Old Vicarage, Dorton, Aylesbury, Bucks HP18 9NH. *T:* (01844) 238396. *E:* jeg.younger@virgin.net. *Club:* White Hunters Cricket (Hampshire).

YOUNGER, Alexander William, CMG 2011; Chief, Secret Intelligence Service, since 2014; *b* 4 July 1963; *m* 1993, Sarah Hopkins; two *s* one *d*. Served Army. Second Sec., FCO, 1991; First Secretary: UK Mission to IAEA, Vienna, 1995–98; FCO, 1998–2002; (Pol), Dubai, 2002–05; Counsellor, FCO, 2005–14. *Address:* PO Box 1300, London, SE1 1BD.

YOUNGER, Sir David; *see* Younger, Sir J. D. B.

YOUNGER, (James) Samuel, CBE 2009; Chief Executive, Charity Commission, 2010–14; *b* 5 Oct. 1951; *s* of Rt Hon. Sir Kenneth Gilmour Younger, KBE, PC and Elisabeth Kirsteen (*née* Stewart); *m* 1984, Katherine Anne Spencer; one *s*. *Educ:* Westminster Sch.; New Coll., Oxford (BA Hons). Asst Editor, Middle East International, 1972–78; BBC World Service: Sen. Asst, Central Current Affairs Talks, 1979–84; Sen. Producer and Exec. Producer, Current Affairs, 1984–86; Asst Head, Arabic Service, 1986–87; Head, Current Affairs, 1987–89; Head, Arabic Service, 1989–92; Controller, Overseas Services, 1992–94; Director of Broadcasting, 1994; Man. Dir, 1994–98; Dir-Gen., BRCS, 1999–2001; Chm., Electoral Commn, 2001–08. Chair, QAA, 2004–09; Interim Chief Executive: Shelter, 2009; Electoral Reform Soc., 2010; Bell Educnl Trust, 2010. Vice Chm., and Chm., UK Cttee, VSO, 2014–. Ind. Mem., Standards Cttee, GLA, 2008–12. Mem. Council, ASA, 2014–. Mem. Council, Univ. of Sussex, 1998–2007 (Chm. Council, 2001–07). Dir, English Touring Opera, 1999–2010. Gov., Commonwealth Inst., 1998–2005. Patron, Windsor Leadership Trust, 1998–. *Recreations:* sport, choral singing.

YOUNGER, Captain Sir (John) David (Bingham), KCVO 2013 (LVO 2007); Lord-Lieutenant of Tweeddale, 1994–2014 (Vice Lord-Lieutenant, 1992–94); Co-founder and Managing Director, Broughton Brewery Ltd, 1979–95; *b* 20 May 1939; *s* of Major Oswald Bingham Younger, MC, A and SH, and Dorothea Elizabeth Younger (*née* Hobbs); *m* 1962, Anne Rosaleen Logan (*d* 2012); one *s* two *d*. *Educ:* Eton Coll.; RMA Sandhurst. Regular Army, Argyll and Sutherland Highlanders, 1957–69; Scottish and Newcastle Breweries, 1969–79. Dir, Broughton Ales, 1995–96. Chairman: Belhaven Hill Trust, 1986–94; Scottish Borders Tourist Board, 1989–91; Peeblesshire Charitable Trust, 1994–2014; Bowmen Ltd, 2008–. Director: Queen's Hall (Edinburgh) Ltd, 1992–2001; Eastgate Theatre and Arts Centre (Peebles) Ltd, 2014–. Vice Pres., RHASS, 1994. Mem., Queen's Body Guard for Scotland, Royal Company of Archers, 1969– (Sec., 1993–2007; Brig., 2002; Ensign, 2010). River Tweed Comr, 2002–. President: Lowland RFCA, 2006–14; SSAFA (formerly SSAFA Forces Help) (Borders), 2006–; Peebles CCC, 2006–. Trustee, Chambers Instn, 2012–. DL Tweeddale, 1987. *Recreation:* the countryside. *Address:* Glenkirk, Broughton, Peeblesshire ML12 6JF. *T:* (01899) 830570.

YOUNGER, Sir Julian William Richard, 4th Bt *cr* 1911, of Auchen Castle, co. Dumfries; *b* 10 Feb. 1950; *s* of Maj.-Gen., Sir John Younger, 3rd Bt, CBE and Stella Jane Dodd (*née* Lister); *S* father, 2002; *m* 1st, 1981, Deborah Ann Wood (marr. diss. 2002); one *s*; 2nd, 2006, Anthea Jane Stainton. *Educ:* Eton; Grinnell Univ., USA. *Heir: s* Andrew William Younger Thieriot, *b* 14 Jan. 1986.

YOUNGER, Prof. Paul Lawrence, PhD; FREng, FICE, FIChemE, CEng, CGeol, CSci; Rankine Chair of Engineering and Professor of Energy Engineering, Glasgow University, since 2012; *b* Hebburn, Co. Durham, 1 Nov. 1962; *s* of Norman and Joan Younger; *m* 1988, Emma Louise Bryan; three *s*. *Educ:* Newcastle Univ. (BSc 1st Cl. Hons Geol.; PhD Water Resources Engrg); Oklahoma State Univ. (MS Hydrogeol.). CGeol 1996; CEng 2001; FIChemE 2004; CSci 2005; FREng 2007; FICE 2010. Harkness Fellow, 1984–86; Hydrogeologist, NRA, 1989–91; Volunteer Hydrogeologist, Centro YUNTA, Bolivia, 1991–92; Newcastle University: Lectr, 1992–99; Reader, 1999–2001; Professor, 2001–12; Public Orator, 2007–10; Pro-Vice-Chancellor (Engagement), 2008–10; Dir, Newcastle Inst. for Res. on Sustainability, 2010–12. Director: NuWater Ltd, 1995–; Project Dewatering Ltd, 2000–; Cluff Geothermal Ltd, 2010–; Five-Quarter Energy Ltd, 2010–; Energy Technol. Partnership (Scotland), 2015–. Chairman: River Tyne Sediments Steering Gp, 2010–; Global Scientific Cttee, Planet Earth Inst., 2011–; Scientific Adv. Panel, British Geological Survey, 2013–. DL Tyne and Wear, 2009–12. Hon. Freeman, Gateshead Metropolitan Bor., 2011. FGS 1996. Dr *hc*: Univ. Nacional de San Agustín, Arequipa, Perú, 2010; Oviedo, Spain, 2010. *Publications:* Mine Water: hydrology, pollution, remediation, 2002; Groundwater in the Environment: an introduction, 2007; Water: all that matters, 2012; Energy: all that matters, 2014; more than 350 articles in learned jls. *Recreations:* singer-songwriter and musician (guitar, mandolin, Northumbrian pipes), Gaelic music (Mem., Glasgow Gaelic Musical Assoc.), hill walking, languages (Spanish, Scottish Gaelic). *Address:* School of Engineering, James Watt South Building, University of Glasgow, Glasgow G12 8QQ. *T:* (0141) 330 5042. *E:* paul.younger@glasgow.ac.uk.

YOUNGER, Samuel; *see* Younger, J. S.

YOUNGER-ROSS, Richard; Member (Lib Dem), Devon County Council, since 2013; *b* 29 Jan. 1953; *m* 1982, Susan Younger. *Educ:* Walton-on-Thames Secondary Modern Sch.; Ewell Tech. Coll. (HNC); Oxford Poly. Architectural consultant, 1970–90; design consultant, 1990–2001. Joined Liberal Party, 1970 (Mem. Council, 1972–82). Contested (Lib Dem): Chislehurst, 1987; Teignbridge, 1992, 1997. MP (Lib Dem) Teignbridge, 2001–10; contested (Lib Dem) Newton Abbot, 2010, 2015.

YOUNGHUSBAND, Jan; Commissioning Editor, BBC Music and Events, since 2009; *b* Portsmouth, 8 May 1954; *d* of John Younghusband and Joyce Younghusband (*née* Browning); one *s*. *Educ:* Portsmouth High Sch.; Millfield Sch.; Royal Holloway Coll., London. Asst Prodn Manager, Glyndebourne, 1974–79; Prodn Manager, Nuffield Th., Southampton, 1979–80; Asst Producer to Peter Hall, NT, 1980–88; freelance television producer and writer, 1988–2000; Commissioning Ed., Channel 4, 2000–09, Arts and Performance, 2001–09. Mem., BAFTA, 2002–. *Publications:* Orchestra, 1990; Concerto, 1991; A Genius in the Family, 1997. *Recreations:* playing the piano, reading, ski-ing, golf.

YOUNGSON, Prof. George Gray, CBE 2009; PhD; FRCSEd; Professor of Paediatric Surgery, University of Aberdeen, 1999–2010, now Emeritus; *b* Glasgow, 13 May 1949; *s* of Alexander Keay Youngson, MBE and Jean O'Neil Youngson; *m* 1973, Sandra Jean Lister; one *s* two *d*. *Educ:* Buckhaven High Sch.; Aberdeen Univ. (MB ChB 1973; PhD 1979). FRCSEd 1977. Lectr in Surgery, 1975–83, Resident in Cardiothoracic Surgery, 1977–79, Univ. of Western Ontario; Fellow in Paediatric Surgery, Hosp. for Sick Children, Toronto, 1981–82; Consultant Gen. Surgeon, Aberdeen Royal Infirmary, 1984–88; Consultant Paediatric Surgeon, Royal Aberdeen Children's Hosp., 1984–2010. Mem. Council, RCSE, 2005–10 (Vice Pres., 2009–12). Hon. FRCPE 2011. *Publications:* Emergency Abdominal Surgery, 1996; Enhancing Surgical Performance: a primer in non-technical skills, 2015. *Recreations:* squash, golf, hill walking, bagpipes, guitar. *Address:* Birken Lodge, Bieldside, Aberdeen AB15 9BQ; Royal College of Surgeons of Edinburgh, Nicolson Street, Edinburgh EH8 9DG. *T:* (0131) 527 1642. *E:* ggyrach@abdn.ac.uk. *Clubs:* Deeside Golf (Aberdeen); Kippie Lodge Sports and Country.

YOUSAF, Humza; Member (SNP) Glasgow, Scottish Parliament, since 2011; Minister for Europe and International Development, since 2014; *b* Glasgow, 7 April 1985; *s* of Muzaffar Yousaf and Shaaista Yousaf; *m* 2010, Gail Lythgoe. *Educ:* Glasgow Univ. (BA Hons Politics). Parliamentary researcher: to Bashir Ahmad, MSP, 2007–09; to Anne McLaughlin, MSP, 2009; Parly aide to Rt Hon. Alex Salmond, MSP, 2009–10; Communications and Policy Officer, SNP, 2010–11. Minister for Ext. Affairs and Internat. Develt, 2012–14. *Recreations:* football, running, badminton, riding my motorbike. *Address:* Scottish Parliament, Holyrood, Edinburgh EH99 1SP. *E:* humza.yousaf.msp@scottish.parliament.uk.

YOUSAFZAI, Malala; campaigner for education; *b* Swat Valley, Pakistan, 12 July 1997; *d* of Ziauddin Yousafzai and Toor Pekai Yousafzai. Co-Founder, Malala Fund. Nat. Youth Peace Prize, Pakistan, 2011; Tipperary Internat. Peace Award, Tipperary Peace Convention, 2012; Premi Internacional Catalunya, Spain, 2013; Simone de Beauvoir Prize, Éditions Gallimard and Culturesfrance, 2013; Ambassador of Conscience Award, Amnesty Internat., 2013; Sakharov Prize for Freedom of Thought, EP, 2013; Internat. Children's Peace Prize, KidsRights Foundn, 2013; Anna Politkovskaya Award, Reach All Women in War, 2013; (jtly) Nobel Peace Prize, 2014. *Publications:* (with C. Lamb) I Am Malala: the girl who stood up for education and was shot by the Taliban, 2013 (trans. 40 langs); (with P. McCormick) I Am Malala (young readers' edn), 2014.

YOXALL, Basil Joshua; Master of the Senior (formerly Supreme) Court, Queen's Bench Division, since 2002; *b* 24 April 1952; *s* of Cecil Ezra Yoxall-Harary and Grace Yoxall-Harary; *m* 1981, Sally Anne Eagle; two *s* one *d*. *Educ:* Wallington Grammar Sch.; St Catharine's Coll., Cambridge (MA). Called to the Bar, Inner Temple, 1975; known professionally as Basil Yoxall; in practice as barrister, specialising in common law, 1975–2002. *Publications:* (ed jtly) The White Book Service: Civil Procedure, annually 2004–; (contrib.) Atkin's Court Forms (on Judgments and Orders), 2004, 2014. *Recreations:* cinema, classical music, history. *Address:* Royal Courts of Justice, Strand, WC2A 2LL. *Club:* Travellers.

YOXALL-HARARY, Basil Joshua; *see* Yoxall, B. J.

YU, David; Chief Product Officer, Funding Circle, since 2015; *b* Seattle, 6 Nov. 1967; *s* of Donald and Jean Yu; *m* 1995, Philana Dee Chow. *Educ:* Univ. of Calif, Berkeley (BS Electrical Engrg and Computer Sci.); Stanford Univ. (MS Computer Sci.). Engrg Dir, Zip2 Corp., 1997–99; Vice-Pres., Engrg, Alta Vista Co., 1999–2001; Betfair Group Ltd: Chief Technol. Officer, 2002–05; Chief Operating Officer, 2005–06; CEO, 2006–11. *Recreations:* travel, photography, food and wine.

YU, Prof. Hai-Sui, DPhil, DSc; Professor of Geotechnical Engineering, since 2001, Founding Director, Nottingham Centre for Geomechanics, since 2002, and Pro-Vice-Chancellor, since 2011, University of Nottingham; *b* 12 Aug. 1964; *s* of Dahei Yu and Xinghua Xiao; *m* 1988, Xiu-Li Guan; one *s* one *d*. *Educ:* Shijiazhuang Railway Univ., China (BE Civil Engrg 1985); Imperial Coll. London (MSc Rock Mechanics 1987; DIC 1987); St Anne's Coll., Oxford (DPhil Soil Mechanics 1990); Univ. of Newcastle, NSW (DSc Geomechanics 2000). FREng 2011. University of Newcastle, New South Wales: Lectr in Civil Engrg, 1991–94; Sen. Lectr in Civil Engrg, 1994–98; Associate Prof. of Civil Engrg, 1998–2000; University of Nottingham: Dep. Hd, 2003–07, Hd, 2007–08, Sch. of Civil Engrg; Dean, Faculty of Engrg, 2008–11. *Publications:* Cavity Expansion Methods in Geomechanics, 2000; Plasticity and Geotechnics, 2006; (ed with W. Wu) Modern Trends in Geomechanics, 2006; (ed jtly) Advances in Transportation Geotechnics, 2008; Memories of My Heart: Hai-Sui's Poems (in Chinese), 2012. *Recreations:* poetry (writing and reading), walking, literature. *Address:* Pro-Vice-Chancellor's Office, Trent Building, University of Nottingham, University Park, Nottingham NG7 2RD. *T:* (0115) 823 2487. *E:* Hai-sui.yu@nottingham.ac.uk.

YU, Rt Rev. Patrick Tin-Sik; a Suffragan Bishop of Toronto (Area Bishop of York-Scarborough), since 2006; *b* 8 July 1951; *s* of Cheung Tok Yu and Sin Yuk Law; *m* 1978, Kathy Cheung; one *s* two *d*. *Educ:* McMaster Univ. (BA Hons 1974); Wycliffe Coll., Univ. of Toronto (MDiv 1981); Toronto Sch. of Theology (DMin 1997). Ordained priest, 1982; Asst Curate, Church of Epiphany, 1981–83; Incumbent: Parish of Coldwater-Medonte, 1985–90; St Theodore of Canterbury, 1990–97; St Timothy Agincourt, 1997–2006. Sec., Adv. Cttee for Postulants for Ordination, N and W Ontario, 1983–87; Co-ord. of Internship and Instructor, Supervised Ministry, Wycliffe Coll., Univ. of Toronto, 1995–2006. Convenor, Evangelism and Church Growth Initiative, Anglican Communion, 2010–. Hon. DD Wycliffe Coll., 2006. *Publications:* Being Christian in Multi-Faith Context, 1997, new edn 2013; The Wycliffe Internship Manual, 2000; (contrib.) Canadian Anglicanism at the Dawn of a New Century, 2001; (contrib.) The Homosexuality Debate: faith seeking understanding, 2003; (in Chinese) Preaching the True and Living Word, 2009. *Recreations:* cooking, travel, music. *Address:* Diocese of Toronto, 135 Adelaide Street East, Toronto, ON M5C 1L8, Canada. *T:* (416) 3636021, *Fax:* (416) 3633683.

YUEH, Linda, DPhil; Chief Business Correspondent, BBC, since 2013. *Educ:* Yale Univ. (BA); Harvard Univ. (MPP); New York Univ. (JD Law); Univ. of Oxford (MA; DPhil Econs). Attorney, Paul, Weiss, Rifkind, Wharton & Garrison, 1997–99; Economics Ed., Bloomberg TV, 2010–12. Adjunct Prof. of Econs, London Business Sch., 2006–; Fellow in Econs, St Edmund Hall, Oxford, 2007–; Vis. Prof. of Econs, Peking Univ., 2013. *Publications:* (with Graeme Chamberlin) Macroeconomics, 2006; (jtly) Globalisation and Economic Growth in China, 2006; (ed) The Law and Economics of Globalisation, 2009; (ed) The Future of Asian Trade and Growth, 2009; The Economy of China, 2010; Enterprising China: business, economic and legal development since 1979, 2011; (ed) China and Globalisation, 4 vols, 2012; China's Growth: the making of an economic superpower, 2013.

YUKON, Bishop of, since 2010; **Rt Rev. Larry Robertson;** *b* Toronto, 11 July 1954; *m* 1976, Sheila; three *s*. *Educ:* St John's Coll., Winnipeg (BMin, DD); Church Army, Canada (Evangelist Dip.). Ordained priest, 1986; Lay Evangelist, later Priest, Dio. of the Arctic; Suffragan Bishop of the Arctic, 1999–2010. *Address:* Diocese of Yukon, Box 31136, Whitehorse, Yukon, Y1A 5P7, Canada. *E:* synodoffice@klondiker.com.

YULE, Prof. William, PhD; Professor of Applied Child Psychology, King's College London, 1987–2005, now Emeritus; *b* Aberdeen, 20 June 1940; *s* of Peter Cocker Yule and Mary Ann Yule (*née* Moir); *m* 1st, 1967, Vivien Walters (marr. diss. 1971); 2nd, 1972, Bridget Ann Osborn; one *s* one *d*. *Educ:* Aberdeen Grammar Sch.; Aberdeen Univ. (MA Psychol. 1962); Univ. of London Inst. of Psychiatry (Dip. Abnormal Psychol. 1963); Univ. of London (PhD Psychol. 1979). MRC Social Psychiatry Res. Unit, 1963–64; Res. Officer, 1965–68, Lectr, 1969, Univ. of London Inst. of Educn; Institute of Psychiatry: Lectr, 1969–73; Sen. Lectr, 1973–80; Reader, 1980–87; Hon. Clin. Psychologist, Bethlem Royal and Maudsley Hosp., 1969–2005 (Hd, Clin. Psychol. Services, 1979–94); Hon. Consultant in Clin. Psychol. to British Army, 2000–10; Vis. Lectr in Clin. Psychol., Univ. of Colombo, Sri Lanka, 2008–10. Fellow, Leverhulme Trust, 2005–06, now Emeritus. Hon. FBPsS 2006. Hon. LLD Roehampton, 2011. Lifetime Achievement Award, Internat. Soc. for Traumatic Stress Studies, 2005; Aristotle Prize, Eur. Fedn of Psychol Assocs, 2007. *Publications:* (jtly) A Neuropsychiatric Study in Childhood, 1970; (ed with J. Carr) Behaviour Modification for the Mentally Handicapped, 1980; (ed jtly) The Lead Debate: the environment, toxicology and child health, 1986; (ed with M. Rutter) Language Development and Disorders, 1987; (jtly) Treatment of Autistic Children, 1987; (with O. Udwin) Infantile Hypercalcaemia and Williams Syndrome: guidelines for parents, 1988; (with A. Gold) Wise Before the Event: coping with crises in school, 1993; (ed jtly) International Handbook of Phobic and Anxiety Disorders in Children and Adolescents, 1994; (ed with G. O'Brien) Behavioural Phenotypes, 1995; (ed jtly) Perspectives on the Classification of Specific Developmental Disorders, 1998; (ed) Post Traumatic Stress Disorder, 1999; (ed with J. Green) Research and Innovation on the Road to Modern Child Psychiatry: vol. 1: Festschrift for Professor Sir Michael Rutter, 2001; (jtly) Fostering Changes: how to improve relationships and manage difficult behaviour: training pack, 2005; (jtly) Managing Difficult behaviour: a handbook for foster carers of the under 12s, 2008; (jtly) Post Traumatic Stress Disorder: cognitive therapy with children and young people, 2010. *Recreations:* watercolour painting, theatre, family, reading detective stories, gardening, people watching. *Address:* Institute of Psychiatry, Psychology and Neuroscience, (PO77), De Crespigny Park, SE5 8AF. *E:* william.yule@kcl.ac.uk.

YUNUS, Muhammad, PhD; Founder, 1983, and Managing Director, 2000–11, Grameen Bank, Bangladesh; *b* Chittagong, 28 June 1940; *s* of Haji Muhammad Dula Meah and Sufia Khatun; *m* 1980, Afrozi; one *d*; one *d* by former marriage. *Educ:* Chittagong Collegiate Sch.; Chittagong Coll.; Dhaka Univ. (BA 1960; MA 1961); Vanderbilt Univ. (Fulbright Scholar;

PhD 1969). Res. Asst, Bureau of Econs 1961; Lectr in Econs, Chittagong Coll., 1962–65; Asst Prof. of Econs, Middle Tennessee State Univ., 1969–72; Dep. Chief, Gen. Econs Div., Planning Commn, Govt of Bangladesh, 1972; Associate Prof. of Econs and Hd, Dept of Econs, Chittagong Univ., 1972–75; Prof. of Econs, Chittagong Univ. and Dir, Rural Econs Prog., 1975–89. Project Dir, Grameen Bank, Bangladesh, 1976–83. Chancellor, Glasgow Caledonian Univ., 2012–. Hon. DLitt Glasgow Caledonian, 2008. (Jtly) Nobel Peace Prize, 2006. Presidential Medal of Freedom (USA), 2009. *Publications:* Banker to the Poor, 1999; (jtly) Creating a World Without Poverty, 2008. *Address:* c/o Grameen Bank, Mirpur-2, Dhaka 1216, Bangladesh.

YURKO, Allen Michael; Industry Executive, Avista Capital Partners, since 2010; *b* 25 Sept. 1951; *s* of Mike Yurko and Catherine (*née* Ewanishan); *m* 1991, Gayle Marie Skelley; two *s* one *d*. *Educ:* Lehigh Univ. (BA Bus. and Econs); Baldwin-Wallace Coll., USA (MBA). Divl Controller, Joy Mfg, 1978–81; Gp Controller, Eaton Corp., 1981–83; Chief Financial Officer and Gp Vice-Pres., Mueller Hldgs, 1983–89; Robertshaw Controls: Vice-Pres. of Finance, 1989–90; Pres., 1990–91; Pres. and Chief Operating Officer, Siebe T. & A. Controls, 1991–92; Siebe plc: Chief Operating Officer, 1992–93; CEO, 1994–99; Chief Exec., Invensys plc, 1999–2001; Partner: Compass Partners, 2002–07; DLJ Merchant Banking Partners, 2007–10. Non-exec. Dir, Tate & Lyle plc, 1996–2005. *Recreations:* boating, golf, sports cars, theatre. *Address:* Avista Capital Europe LLP, 42 Brook Street, W1K 5DB. *Clubs:* Annabel's; Sunningdale Golf.

YUVAL-DAVIS, Prof. Nira, PhD; FAcSS; Professor, since 2003, and Director, since 2009, Centre of Research on Migration, Refugees and Belonging, University of East London; *b* Tel-Aviv, 22 Aug. 1943; *d* of Itzhak and Rivka Yuval; *m* Alain Hertzmann; one *s* by a previous marriage. *Educ:* Hebrew Univ., Jerusalem (BA Sociol. and Psychol. 1966; MA 1st Cl. Sociol. 1972); Sussex Univ. (PhD Sociol. 1979). Res. Fellow, Richardson Inst. for Conflict and Peace Res., London, 1973–74; Sociol. Div., Thames Poly., later Univ. of Greenwich, 1974–2003, Prof. of Gender and Ethnic Studies, 1995–2003; Prof. and Dir, Post-Grad. Studies Prog. in Gender, Sexualities and Ethnic Studies, Sch. of Humanities and Social Scis, Univ. of E London, 2003–09. Arts Faculty Vis. Prof., ANU, 1998; Visiting Professor: Dept of Behavioural Scis, Ben-Gurion Univ., Israel, 2000; Dept of Sociol., Tel-Aviv Univ., 2002; Univs of Aalborg and Roskilde, Denmark, 2007; Maria Jahoda Vis. Prof., Dept of Women's Studies, Ruhr Univ., 2003; Benjamin Meacker Vis. Prof., Dept of Sociol., Bristol Univ., 2004; Guest Prof. (pt-time). Res. Centre for Gender Studies, Univ. of Umeå, Sweden, 2009–; Hon. Prof., Faculty of Social Scis, Aalborg Univ., Denmark, 2012–; Vis. Fellow, Dept of Sociol., Hebrew Univ., Jerusalem, 1980–81; Elizabeth Poppleton Vis. Fellow, Peace Res. Centre, ANU, 1989; Morris Ginsburg Fellow, Dept of Sociol., LSE, 1990–91; Visiting Research Fellow: Inst. of Social Studies, The Hague, 1992; Dept. of Sociol., Univ. of Umeå, Sweden, 2000; Schol. in Residence, Havens Centre, Dept of Sociol., Univ. of Wisconsin, Madison, 2003; Rockefeller Fellow, prog. on Gender, Globalization and Human Security, Grad. Sch., CUNY and USA Nat. Council for Res. on Women, 2004. Mem., Sociol. Sub-panel, RAE, 2008, REF, 2014. Pres., Res. Cttee on Racism, Nationalism and Ethnic Relns RC05, Internat. Sociol Assoc., 2002–06. Founder Member: Women Against Fundamentalism, 1989; Internat. Res. Network of Women in Militarized Conflict Zones, 1993. FAcSS (AcSS 2003). Ed., book series, Politics of Intersectionality, 2009–; Mem. internat. editl bds of 8 learned jls, incl. Signs: Jl of Women in Culture and Soc., and Sociol. of Race and Ethnicity. *Publications:* (ed jtly) Israel and the Palestinians, 1975; (ed jtly) Power and the State, 1978; Israeli Women and Men: divisions behind the unity, 1982; Worlds Apart: women under immigration and nationality laws in Britain, 1985; (ed with F. Anthias) Women - Nation - State, 1989; (ed with H. Bresheeth) The Gulf War and the New World Order, 1991; (with F. Anthias) Racialised Boundaries: race, nation, gender, colour and class and the anti-racist struggle, 1992; (ed with G. Sahgal) Refusing Holy Orders: women and fundamentalism in Britain, 1992; (ed jtly) Women and Citizenship in Europe: borders, rights and duties, 1992; (ed with D. Stasiulis) Unsettling Settler Societies: articulations of gender, ethnicity, race and class, 1995; (ed jtly) Crossfires: nationalism, racism and gender in Europe, 1995; Gender and Nation, 1997; (ed with P. Werbner) Women, Citizenship and Difference, 1999; (ed with A. Imam) Warning Signs of Fundamentalisms, 2004; (ed jtly) Situating the Politics of Belonging, 2006; The Politics of Belonging: intersectional contestations, 2011; (ed with P. Marfleet) Racism, Migration and the Politics of Belonging, 2012; (ed with S. Dhaliwal) Women Against Fundamentalism: stories of dissent and solidarity, 2014; (with G. Wymess and K. Cassidy) Bordering, 2016; books and articles trans. more than 10 langs. *Recreations:* reading, dancing, visual and audio art and entertainment, sea, sun and sand. *Address:* Centre of Research on Migration, Refugees and Belonging, School of Social Sciences, University of East London, Docklands Campus, E16 2RD. *T:* (020) 7249 9718. *E:* n.yuval-davis@uel.ac.uk.

YVON, Christopher; HM Diplomatic Service; UK Permanent Representative to Council of Europe, Strasbourg (with personal rank of Ambassador), from summer 2016; *b* 11 Nov. 1969; *m* 2011, Aneta Michalska; one *s* two *d*. *Educ:* Marling Grammar Sch., Stroud. Entered FCO, 1989; Migration and Visa Dept, FCO, 1989–91; Attaché, Prague, 1991–93; Hong Kong Dept, FCO, 1994; Visa Officer, Bangkok, 1995; Vice Consul, Riyadh, 1995–99; Second Sec., Port Louis, 1999–2002; Desk Officer, Human Rights Policy Dept, FCO, 2003–04; Hd, Sanctions Team, 2005–06, Dep. Hd, 2007–10, Internat. Orgns Dept, FCO; Ambassador to Macedonia, 2010–14; Chargé d'Affaires, Ljubljana, 2014–15. *Recreations:* snooker, cinema, cycling. *Address:* c/o Foreign and Commonwealth Office, King Charles Street, SW1A 2AH. *E:* christopher.yvon@fco.gov.uk. *Clubs:* Rileys Snooker (Vic); Lions (Macedonia).

ZACHARIAH, Joyce Margaret; Secretary of the Post Office, 1975–77; *b* 11 Aug. 1932; *d* of Robert Paton Emery and Nellie Nicol (*née* Wilson); *m* 1978, George Zachariah (marr. diss. 2006). *Educ:* Earl Grey Sch., Calgary, Canada; Hillhead High Sch., Glasgow; Glasgow Univ. (MA 1st cl. Hons French and German, 1956). Post Office: Asst Principal, 1956; Private Sec. to Dir Gen., 1960; Principal, 1961; Asst Sec., 1967; Dir, Chairman's Office, 1970. *Address:* Kelvinbrae, Wisborough Lane, Storrington, W Sussex RH20 4ND.

ZACKLIN, Ralph, CMG 2006; Chairman, United Nations Independent Panel on Accountability, since 2008; international law consultant; *b* 13 Oct. 1937; *s* of Joseph and Anna Zacklin; *m* 1961, Lyda Aponte; two *s*. *Educ:* University Coll. London (LLB Hons; Hon. Fellow, 2012); Columbia Univ. (LLM); Institut des Hautes Etudes Internationales, Geneva (PhD). Dir, Internat. Law Prog., Carnegie Endowment for Internat. Peace, NY, 1967–73; United Nations: Office of Legal Affairs, UN Secretariat, NY, 1973–2005; Officer-in-Charge, Office of High Comr for Human Rights, Geneva, 1997; Asst Sec. Gen. for Legal Affairs, 1998–2005. Sen. Advr, Macro Adv. Partners LLP, 2013. Legal Consultant, ICRC, 2010–11, 2013. Member: Kyrgyzstan Inquiry Commn, 2010–11; UN Ind. Special Inquiry Commn for Timor Leste, 2006–07; UN Ind. Inquiry into violent demonstration against UN peacekeepers, Gao, Mali, 2015. Sen. Fellow, Faculty of Law, Univ. of Melbourne, 2006–08 (Sir Ninian Stephen Vis. Scholar, 2013). *Publications:* Amendment of the Constitution Instruments of the United Nations and Specialized Agencies, 1968, 2nd edn 2005; The Challenge of Rhodesia, 1969; The United Nations and Rhodesia, 1974; The Problem of Namibia in International Law, 1981; The United Nations Secretariat and the Use of Force in a Unipolar World: power *v* principle, 2010; articles in various jls. *Recreations:* travel, sports, reading, music. *Address:* 400 Central Park West, New York, NY 10025, USA. *T:* (212) 2220680. *E:* ralph@zacklin.com. *Club:* Yale (New York).

ZAFFAR, Dame Naila, DBE 2010; Executive Principal, Ambassador Schools, 2014–Dec. 2016; *b* Nairobi, 27 April 1955; *d* of Abdul Karim and Mumtaz Begum; *m* 1975, Shaukat Zaffar; two *d*. *Educ:* Fairfax Grammar Sch.; Wentworth Castle Coll., Barnsley (CertEd); Bradford and Ilkley Coll. (BEd 1st Cl. Hons). Teacher: West Bowling Lang. Centre, Bradford, 1983–84; Newby Primary Sch., Bradford, 1984–85; Atlas Primary Sch., Bradford, 1985–88; Teacher Fellowship, Bradford and Ilkley Coll., 1988–89; Dep. Headteacher, Feversham Primary Sch., Bradford, 1989–92; Headteacher, Copthorne Primary Sch., 1992–2012; Exec. Headteacher, Lapage Primary Sch., Bradford, 2009–10; Vice Principal, Sch. of Research Sci., Dubai, 2012–13. Mem., Gen. Teaching Council for England, 2000–05; Primary Strategy Consultancy Leader, 2004–07; Inspector, OFSTED, 2006–. *Recreation:* spending time with grandchildren. *Address:* Block D, Masakin Al Furjan, Dubai. *T:* 07979 811182, (UAE) 528492485. *E:* nzaffar@ymail.com.

ZAFIROPOULOS, Vassilis; Ambassador of Greece to the Court of St James's, 1996–99, retired; *b* Corfu, 24 Jan. 1934; *s* of Sarantis and Helen Zafiropoulos; *m* 1963; one *s*. *Educ:* Univ. of Athens. Joined Greek Civil Service, 1962; Min. of Finance, 1962–67; Head of Press Affairs, UN Information Centre for Greece, Israel, Turkey and Cyprus, 1967–71; joined Greek Diplomatic Service, 1971; Third Sec., Min. of Foreign Affairs, 1971–73; Second Sec., Liège, 1973–76; First Sec., Nicosia, and Dir, Greek Press Office in Cyprus, 1976–78; Counsellor, Nicosia, 1978–80; Counsellor (Political), London, 1980–84; Head of Cyprus Affairs, Min. of Foreign Affairs, 1984–86; Minister and Dep. Permt Rep. to NATO, Brussels, 1986–90; Ambassador to Australia and New Zealand, 1991–93; Permt Rep. to NATO, 1993–96. Special Rep., Greek Presidency of EU, S Caucasus, 2003. DUniv N London, 1998. Higher Comdr, Order of Phoenix (Greece). *Recreation:* tennis. *Address:* 20B Sirinon Street, Athens 175 61, Greece.

ZAHAWI, Nadhim; MP (C) Stratford-on-Avon, since 2010; *b* Baghdad, 2 June 1967; *s* of Harith and Najda Zahawi; *m* 2004, Lana Saib; two *s* one *d*. *Educ:* University Coll. London (BSc Chem. Eng.). Marketing Director: Global Inc. Ltd, 1990–95; Allen (Hinckley) Ltd, 1995–98; Eur. Mktg Dir, Smith & Brooks Ltd, 1998–2000; CEO and Co-founder, YouGov plc, 2000–10. Non-exec. Dir, SThree plc, 2008–; Chief Strategy Officer, Gulf Keystone, 2015–. Mem., Foreign Affairs Select Cttee, 2014–. Mem. (C), Wandsworth BC, 1994–2006. Patron, Peace One Day, 2008–. *Publications:* (with M. Hancock) Masters of Nothing: the crash and how it will happen again unless we understand human nature, 2011. *Recreations:* show jumping, cinema, spending time with family and friends. *Address:* House of Commons, SW1A 0AA. *Clubs:* Annabel's, Soho House.

ZAHEDI, Saeed, OBE 2000; RDI 2013; PhD; CEng, FREng; FIMechE; Chief Technical Officer, and Technical Director, Chas A. Blatchford & Sons Ltd, since 2013 (Technical Director, 2005–13); *b* Tehran, 23 May 1957; *s* of Ahmad Zahedi and Mehri Zahedi (*née* Mahloudji); *m* 1988, Shirin Sadeghian; one *s* two *d*. *Educ:* Poly. of Central London (BSc Hons Mech. Engrg); Univ. of Strathclyde (PhD Biomed. Engrg 1978). CEng 1985, FREng 2010; FIMechE 1998; CDir. Chas A. Blatchford & Sons: Res. Asst, 1979–85; Sen. Med. Physicist, 1985–88; Project Coordinator, 1988–92; Design Gp Leader, 1992–98; Res. Manager, 1998–2000; Hd of Technol., 2000–04; R&D Manager and Dir Designate, 2004–05. Visiting Professor: Univ. of Surrey, 2006–; Bournemouth Univ. Vice-Chm., Internat. Soc. for Prosthetics and Orthotics, 2013–. Chm., Manufg Cttee, American Orthotic and Prosthetic Assoc., 2007–10. Mem., ISO CEN, BSI, 1999–. Fellow, LSE. *Publications:* Advances in Prosthetics, 1996; Conference of European Society of Biomechanics, 1996; Review of Current Advances in Prosthetics, 1997; Atlas of Amputation and Limb Deficiencies, 2004; Principle of Design, 2004; Design Matters, 2008; contrib. articles to jls. *Recreations:* practical philosophy, economics with justice, mountaineering. *Address:* 10 Washington Road, Barnes, SW13 9BH. *T:* (020) 8748 2418, 07715 071086. *E:* Saeed.Zahedi@ic24.net.

ZAKHAROV, Prof. Vasilii, (Basil), PhD, DSc; consultant; Director of Information Processing, International Organization for Standardization, Geneva, 1990–95 (Head of Information Processing, 1989–90); *b* 2 Jan. 1931; *s* of Viktor Nikiforovich Zakharov and Varvara Semyenovna (*née* Krzak); *m* 1959, Jeanne (*née* Hopper) one *s* one *d*. *Educ:* Latymer Upper Sch.; Univ. of London (BSc: Maths 1951, Phys 1952; MSc 1958; PhD 1960; DIC 1960; DSc 1977). Research in Computer systems and applications, Birkbeck Coll., 1953–56; digital systems development, Rank Precision Instruments, 1956–57; Research Fellow, Imperial Coll., 1957–60; Physicist, European Organisation for Nuclear Res. (CERN), Geneva, 1960–65; Reader in Experimental Physics, Queen Mary Coll., London, 1965–66; Head of Computer Systems and Electronics Div., as Sen. Principal Sci. Officer, SRC Daresbury Laboratory, 1966–69, Dep. Chief Sci. Officer, 1970–78; Dir, London Univ. Computing Centre, 1978–80, and Prof. of Computing Systems, 1979–80; Sen. Associate, CERN, Geneva, 1981–83; Invited Prof., Univ. of Geneva, 1984–87. Vis. Scientist: JINR Dubna, USSR, 1965; CERN, 1971–72; Consultant to AERE Harwell, 1965; Hon. Scientist and Consultant, CCLRC, 2006–10; Vis. Prof. of Physics, QMC London, 1968; Vis. Prof., Westfield Coll., 1974–78. Member, SRC Comp. Sci. Cttee, 1974–77. *Publications:* Digital Systems Logic, 1968; No Snow on Their Boots, 2003, and other books; scientific papers in professional jls on photoelectronics, computer systems, elementary particle physics and computer applications. *Recreations:* collecting Russian miscellanea, amateur radio; grape growing, wine making, wine drinking.

ZAMBELLAS, Adm. Sir George (Michael), KCB 2012; DSC 2001; DL; FRAeS; First Sea Lord and Chief of the Naval Staff, since 2013; First and Principal Naval Aide-de-Camp to the Queen, since 2013; *b* 4 April 1958; *s* of late Michael George Zambellas and of Rosemary Frederique Zambellas (*née* Lindsay); *m* 1982, Amanda Jane LeCudennec; three *s*. *Educ:* Shabani Primary Sch., Zimbabwe; New College Sch.; Peterhouse Sch., Zimbabwe; Stowe; Univ. of Southampton (BSc Hons Aeronautical and Astronautical Engrg 1980). FRAeS 2009. Served 814, 829 and 815 Naval Air Sqdns, 1982–89; RN staff course, 1990; Command: HMS Cattistock, 1991; HMS Argyll, 1995; Corporate Planner, MoD, 1997; Comd HMS Chatham, 1999; HCSC, 2001; Dep. Flag Officer Sea Trng, 2002; PSO to CDS, 2002–05; Comdr Amphibious Task Gp, 2005–06; C of S (Fleet Transformation), 2006–07; Comdr, UK Maritime Force, 2007–08; COS (Ops), 2008–10; Dep. C-in-C Fleet, COS Navy Comd HQ and Chief Naval Warfare Officer, 2011; Fleet Comdr and Dep. Chief of Naval Staff, 2012; NATO Maritime Comdr (Northwood), 2012–13. Younger Brother, Trinity House, 2009; Upper Freeman, Hon. Co. of Air Pilots (formerly GAPAN), 2012; Freeman, Shipwrights' Co., 2014. DL Dorset, 2013. Hon. DSc Southampton, 2014. *Address:* Ministry of Defence, Main Building, Whitehall, SW1A 2HB.

ZAMBELLO, Francesca; theatre and opera director; Artistic Director, Washington National Opera, since 2013 (Artistic Advisor, 2011–12); *b* New York, 24 Aug. 1956. *Educ:* American Sch. of Paris; Colgate Univ. (BA). Assistant Director: Lyric Opera of Chicago, 1981–82; San Francisco Opera, 1983–84; Co-Artistic Dir, The Skylight, opera and music th. co., Milwaukee, 1984–91; Artistic Advr, San Francisco Opera; Gen. and Artistic Dir, Glimmerglass Opera, NY, 2010–. Dir of prodns at major theatre and opera cos in Europe and USA incl. Royal Opera House, Bastille Opera, Houston Grand Opera, Bolshoi Opera and NY Metropolitan Opera. Prodns incl. Fidelio, Tosca, War and Peace, Turandot, Arianna, Madama Butterfly, Iphigénie en Tauride, La Traviata, Emmeline, Tristan und Isolde, Boris Godunov, Dialogues of the Carmelites, Luisa Miller, Napoleon, Prince Igor, Peter Grimes, Queen of Spades, Of Mice and Men, The Bartered Bride, Thérèse Raquin, Don Giovanni, Les Troyens, Lady in the Dark, Street Scene, La Bohème, Carmen, Cyrano, Die Walküre, William Tell and The Tsarina's Slippers. Olivier awards for: Khovanshchina, ENO, 1994;

Billy Budd, 1995, Paul Bunyan, 1998, Royal Opera House. Chevalier, Ordre des Arts et des Lettres (France), 2008. *Address:* c/o Opus 3 Artists, 470 Park Avenue South, 9th Floor North, New York, NY 10016, USA.

ZAMBONI, Richard Frederick Charles, FCA; Managing Director, 1979–89 and a Vice-Chairman, 1986–89, Sun Life Assurance Society plc; Chairman, AIM Distribution Trust PLC, 1996–2000; *b* 28 July 1930; *s* of Alfred Charles Zamboni and Frances Hosler; *m* 1st, 1960, Pamela Joan Marshall (*d* 1993); two *s* one *d*; 2nd, 1996, Deirdre Olive Baker (*née* Kingham). *Educ:* Monkton House Sch., Cardiff. Gordon Thomas & Pickard, Chartered Accountants, 1948–54; served Royal Air Force, 1954–56; Peat Marwick Mitchell & Co., 1956–58; British Egg Marketing Board, 1959–70, Chief Accountant, from 1965; Sun Life Assurance Society plc, 1971–89, Director, 1975–89; Chairman: Sun Life Investment Management Services, 1985–89; Sun Life Trust Management, 1985–89. Deputy Chairman: Life Offices' Assoc., 1985 (Mem., Management Cttee, 1981–85); Assoc. of British Insurers, 1986–88 (Dep. Chm., 1985–86, Chm., 1986–88, Life Insurance Council); Member: Council, Chartered Insurance Inst., 1983–85; Lautro's steering gp, 1985–86; Hon. Treasurer, Insurance Institute of London, 1982–85. Dir, 1984–97, and Chm., 1990–97, Avon Enterprise Fund Ltd. Member, Management Cttee, Effingham Housing Assoc. Ltd, 1980–86; Chairman: Council of Management, Grange Centre for People with Disabilities, 1991–96; Governing Body, Little Bookham Manor House Sch. Educnl Trust Ltd, 1999–2003. Pres., Insurance Offices RFU, 1985–87. *Recreations:* ornithology, gardening, golf. *Address:* Riverbank House, 80A Church Street, Leatherhead, Surrey KT22 8ER. *T:* (01372) 812398. *Club:* Royal Automobile.

ZANDER, Prof. Michael, FBA 2005; Professor of Law, London School of Economics, 1977–98, now Emeritus; *b* 16 Nov. 1932; *s* of late Dr Walter Zander and Margarete Magnus; *m* 1965, Betsy Treeger; one *d* one *s*. *Educ:* Royal Grammar Sch., High Wycombe; Jesus Coll., Cambridge (BA Law, double 1st Cl. Hons; LLB 1st Cl. Hons; Whewell Scholar in Internat. Law); Harvard Law Sch. (LLM). Solicitor of the Supreme Court. National Service, RA, 1950–52, 2nd Lieut. Cassel Scholar, Lincoln's Inn, 1957, resigned 1959; New York law firm, 1958–59; articled with City solicitors, 1959–62; Asst Solicitor with City firm, 1962–63; London Sch. of Economics: Asst Lectr, 1963; Lectr, 1965; Sen. Lectr, 1970; Reader, 1970; Convener, Law Dept, 1984–88, 1997–98. Legal Correspondent, The Guardian, 1963–87. Mem., Royal Commn on Criminal Justice, 1991–93. Hon. QC 1997. Hon. LLD KCL, 2010. *Publications:* Lawyers and the Public Interest, 1968; (ed) What's Wrong with the Law?, 1970; (ed) Family Guide to the Law, 1971, 2nd edn 1972; Cases and Materials on the English Legal System, 1973, 10th edn 2007; (with B. Abel-Smith and R. Brooke) Legal Problems and the Citizen, 1973; Social Workers, their Clients and the Law, 1974, 3rd edn 1981; A Bill of Rights?, 1975, 4th edn 1996; Legal Services for the Community, 1978; (ed) Pears Guide to the Law, 1979; The Law-Making Process, 1980, 7th edn 2015; The State of Knowledge about the English Legal Profession, 1980; The Police and Criminal Evidence Act 1984, 1985, 6th edn 2013; A Matter of Justice: the legal system in ferment, 1988, rev. edn 1989; The State of Justice, 2000; articles in jls incl. Criminal Law Rev., Mod. Law Rev., Law Soc.'s Gazette, New Law Jl, Criminal Law & Justice Weekly, Solicitors' Jl, Amer. Bar Assoc. Jl. *Address:* 12 Woodside Avenue, N6 4SS. *T:* (020) 8883 6257. *E:* mandbzander@btinternet.com.

ZANI, John Andrew; a District Judge (Magistrates' Courts), Inner London, since 2001; *b* 14 Feb. 1953; *s* of Primo and Alda Zani; *m* 1978, Cinthia Gallian. *Educ:* Highgate Sch.; Coll. of Law. Admitted solicitor, 1977; Partner, 1979, Sen. Partner, 1986–2000, Whitelock & Storr. Chm., Professional Matters Sub-Cttee, Holborn Law Soc., 1994–96. Mem. Founder Cttee, British Italian Law Assoc., 1982. Trustee, Friends of Highgate Sch., 1996–; Mem. Cttee, Old Cholmeleian Soc., 1994–; Chm., Old Cholmeleian CC, 1990–. *Recreations:* cricket, football, the arts. *Address:* c/o Westminster Magistrates' Court, 181 Marylebone Road, NW1 5BR.

ŽANTOVSKÝ, Michael; Ambassador of the Czech Republic to the Court of St James's, 2009–15; President, Aspen Institute, Prague, since 2012; *b* Prague, 3 Jan. 1949; *s* of Jiri Žantovský and Hana Žantovská; *m* 2001, Jana Nosekova; two *s* two *d*. *Educ:* Charles Univ., Prague (MA 1973); McGill Univ., Montreal. Freelance translator and author, 1980–88 (trans. into Czech works of contemporary English and American fiction, poetry, drama and non-fiction); Prague corresp., Reuters, 1988–90; Press Sec. and spokesman for Pres., Czech and Slovak Fed. Republic, 1990–92; Ambassador, of Czech and Slovak Fed. Republic, 1992, then Czech Republic, 1993–96, to USA; Chm., Cttee on Foreign Affairs, Defence and Security, Senate of Parlt, 1996–2002; Ambassador to Israel, 2003–09. Founding Mem., Civic Forum (umbrella orgn that coordinated overthrow of communist regime), 1989; Pres., Civic Democratic Alliance, 1997 and 2001. Co-founder, Prog. of Atlantic Security Studies, 2003. Founding Mem., Czech chapter, PEN, 1989. *Publications:* Havel: a life, 2014. *Club:* Travellers.

ZAOUI, Michael Alexandre; Co-Founder and Partner, Zaoui & Co., since 2013; *b* Fez, Morocco, 30 Dec. 1956; *s* of Charles Zaoui and Violette Zaoui (*née* Cohen); *m* 1995, Anna Benhamou; one *s* one *d*. *Educ:* Institut d'Etudes Politiques, Paris (Diploma); Univ. de Paris (Masters Law); Univ. Panthéon-Sorbonne, Paris (DESS Dr Law); London Sch. of Econs and Political Sci. (post-grad. res. prog.); Harvard Business Sch. (MBA). Banque Rothschild, Paris, 1978–81; Mgt Consultant, MAC Gp, London, 1983–85; Morgan Stanley: Vice Pres., NY, 1986–90; Exec. Dir, 1991–93; Man. Dir, London, 1993–97; Co-Hd, 1997–99, Chm., 1999–2008, Eur. M&A; Vice Chm., Institutional Securities Gp, London, 2006–08; advr to major corporations and investors, 2009–12. Dir of several privately owned cos. Counsellor, Commerce Extérieur de la France, London, 2011–. Gov., Southbank Centre, London, 2012–. Mem., Bd of Dean's Advrs, Harvard Business Sch., 2007–; Mem., Belfer Internat. Council, 2012–, Mem., Littauer Soc., 2014–, Kennedy Sch. of Govt, Harvard Univ. *Recreations:* symphony music, opera, classical and contemporary art, history, sport, cycling. *Address:* Zaoui & Co., 11 Hill Street, W1J 5LF. *T:* (020) 7290 5580. *Clubs:* Annabel's, Harry's Bar and Mosimann's.

See also Y. Zaoui.

ZAOUI, Yoël; Co-Founder and Partner, Zaoui & Co., since 2013; *b* Casablanca, 11 Jan. 1961; *s* of Charles Zaoui and Violette Zaoui (*née* Cohen); one *s* one *d*. *Educ:* HEC, Paris; Univ. Paris-Dauphine (DEA Dr Finance 1983); Stanford Univ. (MBA 1988). Sen. Auditor, Arthur Andersen, Paris; Goldman Sachs, 1988–2012: Partner, 1998–2012; Co-Hd, then Hd, Eur. M&A; Co-Hd, then Hd, Eur. Investment Banking; Mem., Mgt Cttee, 2008–12; Global Hd, M&A. *Recreations:* sports, reading, travel. *Address:* Zaoui & Co., 11 Hill Street, W1J 5LF. *T:* (020) 7290 5585.

See also M. A. Zaoui.

ZAPATERO, José Luis Rodríguez; *see* Rodríguez Zapatero.

ZARA, Robert Joseph; a District Judge (Magistrates' Courts), Birmingham, since 2004, and Family Court, Coventry, since 2014; *b* 20 July 1947; *s* of Alfred and Naomi Zara; *m* 1st, 1986, Alicia Edkins (*d* 2000); one *s*; 2nd, 2004, Catherine Edwards. *Educ:* Tonbridge Sch.; Bristol Univ. (LLB 1969). Community Lawyer, Coventry Community Develt Project, 1973–75; Solicitor: Coventry Legal and Income Rights Service, 1975–81; in private practice in Coventry, 1981–2002; a District Judge (Magistrates' Cts), Nottingham, 2002–04. *Publications:* (contrib.) Handbook for Widows, 1978; (contrib.) Survival Guide for Widows, 1986; contrib. occasional articles and book reviews to New Law Jl. *Recreations:* bridge, crosswords, digging my allotment. *Address:* Victoria Law Courts, Corporation Street, Birmingham B4 6QA.

ZARNECKI, Prof. Jan Charles, (John), PhD; Professor of Space Science, Open University, 2004–13, now Emeritus; Director, International Space Science Institute, Berne, since 2013; *b* London, 6 Nov. 1949; *s* of Jerzy, (George), Zarnecki and Anne Leslie Zarnecki (*née* Frith); *m* 1st, 1976, Gillian Elizabeth Fairbanks (marr. diss. 1993); one *s* one *d*; 2nd, 2009, Catherine Philomena O'Donoghue. *Educ:* Highgate Sch., London; Queens' Coll., Cambridge (Open Exhibnr; BA 1971); Mullard Space Science Lab., University Coll. London (PhD 1977). FRAS 1972; CPhys 1978; FInstP. Res. Asst, Mullard Space Sci. Lab., UCL, 1974–79; Sen. Systems Engr, Dynamics Gp, British Aerospace, 1979–81; Unit for Space Sciences, University of Kent: Sen. Experimental Officer, 1981–85; Lectr, 1985–87; Sen. Lectr, 1987–96; Reader, 1996–2000; Reader, Planetary and Space Scis Res. Inst., Open Univ., 2000–04. Space projects include: Faint Object Camera for Hubble Space Telescope, 1978–81; Co-investigator for Dust Impact Detection System on Giotto Comet Halley Probe, 1982–92; Principal Investigator, Surface Sci. Package on Huygens Probe Titan, 1992–2006. Royal Astronomical Society: Mem. Council, 1995–98; Vice-Pres., 2009–11; Pres., May 2016–. Member: Solar System Wkg Gp, ESA, 1995–98 (Chm., 2014–); Eur. Space Sci. Cttee, ESF, 1997–2000; PPARC, 2005–07. Mem., Shareholder's Cttee, Eurotunnel plc, 2003–06. Mem. Bd, Milton Keynes Gall., 2002–06. Mem. IAU, 1982–. Gold Medal, RAS, 2014. *Publications:* over 200 scientific and technical articles. *Address:* Planetary and Space Sciences Research Institute, Open University, Walton Hall, Milton Keynes MK7 6AA. *T:* (01908) 659599, *Fax:* (01908) 655667. *E:* j.c.zarnecki@open.ac.uk.

ZEALLEY, Christopher Bennett; trustee and company director; *b* 5 May 1931; *s* of Sir Alec Zealley and Lady Zealley (*née* King); *m* 1966, Ann Elizabeth Sandwith; one *s* one *d*. *Educ:* Bramcote; Sherborne Sch.; King's Coll., Cambridge (Choral Schol.; MA Law). Commnd RNVR, 1953; ICI Ltd, 1955–66; IRC, 1967–70; Chairman: Public Interest Res. Centre, 1972–2012; Social Audit Ltd, 1972–; Charity Appointments, 1988–92; Accreditation Bureau for Fundraising Orgns, 1997–2007; Dir and Trustee, Dartington Hall Trust, 1970–88. Mem. Council, Which? (formerly Consumers' Assoc., later Assoc. for Consumer Res.), 1976–92, 1994–2007 (Chm., 1975–82). Trustee: NACRO, 1974–82; Charities Aid Foundn, 1982–90; Ricability (formerly Res. Inst. for Consumer Affairs), 1989–. Director: British United Trawlers, 1969–81; JT Group Ltd; Grant Instruments Ltd. Chairman: Dartington Coll. of Art, 1973–91; Dartington Summer Sch. of Music, 1980–97; Plymouth Symphony Orch., 2013–. *Publications:* Creating a Charitable Trust, 1994. *Recreations:* rural affairs, music. *Address:* Sneydhurst, Broadhempston, Totnes, Devon TQ9 6AX. *Clubs:* Lansdowne, Naval.

ZEALLEY, Dr Helen Elizabeth, OBE 1998; MD; FRCPEd, FFPH; Director of Public Health and Chief Administrative Medical Officer, 1988–2000, Executive Director, 1991–2000, Lothian Health Board; *b* 10 June 1940; *d* of late Sir John Howie Flint Brotherston and Lady Brotherston; *m* 1965, Dr Andrew King Zealley; one *s* one *d*. *Educ:* St Albans High Sch. for Girls; Edinburgh Univ. (MB, ChB 1964; MD 1968). FRCPEd 1987; FFPH (FFPHM 1980). Virologist, City Hosp., Edinburgh, 1965–70; Consultant in Public Health Medicine, Lothian Health Bd, 1974–88, with a special interest in the health of children. Non-exec. Dir, NHS Health Scotland, 2003–09; Board Member: Scottish Envmtl Protection Agency, 2006–13; Central Scotland Green Network, 2011–14; Hon. Fellow, Scottish Envmt LINK, 2011– (Pres., 2008–11). Vice-President: Med Act, 1980–2014; Early Education, 1998–2006. Chm., Friends of the Earth, Scotland, 2003–08. Mem. Court, Edinburgh Univ., 1992–98. QHP 1996–2000. Kentucky Colonel, 1961. Hon. DCCH 1993. *Recreations:* family, gardening, sailing, ski-ing. *Address:* Viewfield House, 12 Tipperlinn Road, Edinburgh EH10 5ET. *T:* (0131) 447 5545.

ZEBEDEE, Graham; HM Diplomatic Service; Ambassador to the Democratic Republic of Congo, since 2015; *b* Southampton, 27 Nov. 1973; *s* of Roger Zebedee and Brenda Zebedee; *m* 2009, Lucy Katherine Ryan; one *s* one *d*. *Educ:* Wadham Coll., Oxford (BA Phys and Philos.). Joined FCO, 1999; UK Perm. Rep. to EU, 1999–2000; EC (on secondment), 2001–02; Counter-Proliferation Dept, FCO, 2003–05; Kabul, 2005–07; Dep. Hd, Africa Directorate, FCO, 2007–10; Hd, Nat. Security Unit, 2010–13, Hd, Border and Visa Policy, 2013–15, Home Office (on secondment). *Recreations:* mountains, marathons, managing messy mealtimes. *Address:* c/o Foreign and Commonwealth Office, King Charles Street, SW1A 2AH. *E:* graham.zebedee@fco.gov.uk.

ZEDNER, Prof. Lucia Helen, DPhil; FBA 2012; Professor of Criminal Justice, University of Oxford, since 2005; Fellow, Corpus Christi College, Oxford, since 1994; *b* Kingston, Surrey, 20 Feb. 1961; *d* of Thomas and Ruby Zedner; *m* Prof. Joshua Getzler; two *d*. *Educ:* Univ. of York (BA); Nuffield Coll., Oxford (DPhil). Prize Res. Fellow, Nuffield Coll., Oxford, 1984–89; Lectr in Law, LSE, 1989–94; Lectr, 1994–99, Reader, 1999–2005, Law Faculty, Univ. of Oxford. Adjunct Prof., Faculty of Law, Univ. of NSW, 2007–. Member: Res. Coll., ESRC, 2005–08; Adv. Panel, Leverhulme Trust, 2013–; Projects Cttee, British Acad., 2013–. Mem., Editl Bd, Clarendon Series in Criminol., Oxford Univ. Press., 1994– (Gen. Ed., 2010–12). *Publications:* Women, Crime and Custody in Victorian England, 1991; (with J. Morgan) Child Victims, Crime, Impact and Criminal Justice, 1992; (ed with Andrew Ashworth) The Criminological Foundations of Penal Policy, 2003; Criminal Justice, 2004; (ed with Benjamin Goold) Crime and Security, 2006; Security, 2009; (ed with Julian Roberts) Principles and Values in Criminal Law and Criminal Justice, 2012; (ed jtly) Prevention and the Limits of the Criminal Law, 2013; (with Andrew Ashworth) Preventive Justice, 2014; chapters in books. *Address:* Corpus Christi College, Oxford OX1 4JF.

ZEEMAN, Sir (Erik) Christopher, Kt 1991; PhD; FRS 1975; Principal, Hertford College, Oxford, 1988–95, now Honorary Fellow; *b* 4 Feb. 1925; *s* of Christian Zeeman and Christine Zeeman (*née* Bushell); *m* 1st, 1950, Elizabeth Jones; one *d*; 2nd, 1960, Rosemary Gledhill; three *s* two *d*. *Educ:* Christ's Hospital; Christ's Coll., Cambridge (MA, PhD; Hon. Fellow, 1989). Served RAF, 1947–51; Commonwealth Fellow, 1954; Fellow of Gonville and Caius Coll., Cambridge, 1953–64 (Hon. Fellow, 1997); Lectr, Cambridge Univ., 1955–64; Prof., and Dir of Maths Res. Centre, Warwick Univ., 1964–88, Hon. Prof. 1988. Sen. Fellow, SRC, 1976–81. Visiting Prof. at various institutes, incl.: IAS; Princeton; IHES, Paris; IMPA, Rio; Royal Instn; also at various univs, incl.: California, Florida, Pisa. Hon. Dr: Strasbourg, Hull, Claremont, York, Leeds, Durham, Hartford, Warwick, Open. *Publications:* numerous research papers on topology, dynamical systems, catastrophe theory, and applications to biology and the social sciences, in various mathematical and other jls. *Recreation:* family. *Address:* 23 High Street, Woodstock, Oxon OX20 1TE. *T:* (01993) 813402.

ZEFF, Jonathan Charles; Director, BBC Trust, 2014–15; *b* London, 23 May 1966; *s* of Brian and Paula Zeff; *m* 1996, Alison Beat; one *s* one *d*. *Educ:* University Coll. Sch., London; Univ. of Warwick (BA Hons Maths). Admin Trainee, 1991–94, Employment Service Review Leader, 1995, Dept for Employment; Asst Dir, Employment Relns, DTI, 1995–98; Department for Culture, Media and Sport: Head: Film Policy, 1998–99; Nat. Lottery Div., 1999–2001; Policy Innovation and Delivery Unit, 2001–03; Broadcasting Policy, 2003–08; Dir, Media, 2008–11; Dir, Broadband, Spectrum and Communications, 2011–14. *Recreations:* contemporary literature, theatre, music, playing piano and video games, country walks, Queens Park Rangers FC.

ZEFFIRELLI, Gian Franco (Corsi), Hon. KBE 2004; opera, film and theatrical producer and designer since 1949; *b* 12 Feb. 1923. *Educ:* Florence. Designer: (in Italy): A Streetcar Named Desire; Troilus and Cressida; Three Sisters. Has produced and designed numerous operas at La Scala, Milan, 1952–, and in all the great cities of Italy, at world-famous festivals, and in UK and USA; *operas include:* Covent Garden: Lucia di Lammermoor, Cavalleria Rusticana and Pagliacci, 1959; Falstaff, 1961; Don Giovanni, Alcina, 1962; Tosca, Rigoletto, 1964; Pagliacci, 2003; Metropolitan Opera, NY: Otello, 1972; Antony and Cleopatra, 1973; La Bohème, 1981, 2008; Tosca, Rigoletto, 1985; Turandot, 1983, 1987, 2011; Carmen, 1996; La Traviata, 1998; Falstaff, 2003; La Scala: Otello, 1976; Don Carlos, 1992; La Bohème,

2003; Aida, 2006, 2012; Verona: Carmen, 1995; Il Trovatore, 2001; Aida, 2002, 2003; Carmen, 2003; Madame Butterfly, 2004; Pagliacci, 2011, 2012; Don Giovanni, 2012; L'Elisir d'Amore, Glyndebourne, 1961; Don Giovanni, Vienna, 1972; Aida, Tokyo, 1997, 2003; Rome: Tosca, 2000, 2008; Don Giovanni, and Aida, 2006; Busseto: Aida, 2001, also Moscow, 2004; La Traviata, 2002, 2009, also Moscow, 2003; Falstaff, 2010; Tel Aviv: Traviata, and I Pagliacci, 2005; Turandot, Muscat, 2011; *stage:* Romeo and Juliet, Old Vic, 1960; Othello, Stratford-on-Avon, 1961; Amleto, Nat. Theatre, 1964; After the Fall, Rome, 1964; Who's Afraid of Virginia Woolf, Paris, 1964, Milan, 1965; La Lupa, Rome, 1965; Much Ado About Nothing, Nat. Theatre, 1966; Black Comedy, Rome, 1967; A Delicate Balance, Rome, 1967; Saturday, Sunday, Monday, Nat. Theatre, 1973; Filumena, Lyric, 1977; Six Characters in Search of an Author, RNT, 1992; Absolutely! (perhaps), Wyndham's, 2003; *films:* The Taming of the Shrew, 1965–66; Florence, Days of Destruction, 1966; Romeo and Juliet, 1967; Brother Sun, Sister Moon, 1973 (S Calif Motion Picture Council Award, Olivier d'Or, Prix Femina Belge du Cinema, 1973); Jesus of Nazareth, 1977; The Champ, 1979 (Silver Halo Award, S Calif Motion Picture Council, 1979); Endless Love, 1981; La Traviata, 1983; Cavalleria Rusticana, 1983; Otello, 1986; The Young Toscanini, 1988; Hamlet, 1991; The Sparrow, 1993; Jane Eyre, 1996; Tea with Mussolini, 1999; Callas Forever, 2002; (documentary with Tourist Office of Rome) Omaggio a Roma, 2009. Produced Beethoven's Missa Solemnis, San Pietro, Rome, 1971. Senator of the Italian Republic, 1992–98. Member: Acad. of Motion Picture Arts and Scis; Directors Guild of America; United Scenic Artists; Artistic Directorate, Shakespeare's Globe; Hon. Cttee, Amici Opificio di Firenze; Pres., Roma per il Teatro dell'Opera di Roma. Hon. Member: Friends of Florence; Boys' Town, New York. Hon. Citizen of towns and cities incl. New York, Busseto, Gubbio, Catanzaro. Hon. DHL: San Diego, 1978; Loyola Marymount, 1979; Hon. DLitt Kent, 1986; Hon. PhD Tel Aviv, 1993. Blason D'Oro, 1967; XIII San Giuseppe Award, Florence, 1980; Rudolph Valentino Award, 1995; Two Presidents Award, Italy and Russia, 2004. Grande Ufficiale dell'Ordine al Merito della Repubblica Italiana, 1977; Commandeur, Ordre des Arts et des Lettres (France), 1978. *Publications:* Zeffirelli (autobiog.), 1986, 2006. *Address:* Via Lucio Volumnio 45, Rome 00178, Italy.

ZEICHNER, Daniel Stephen; MP (Lab) Cambridge, since 2015; *b* Beckenham, 9 Nov. 1956; *s* of Eric Zeichner and Mary Zeichner (*née* Mead); partner, Barbara, (Budge), Ziolkowska. *Educ:* King's Coll., Cambridge (BA 1979). Milk roundsman, Co-op, 1976; trainee computer programmer, Cambs CC, 1979–81; computer programmer, Perkins Engines, Peterborough, 1981; Database Adminr, Pye Electronics, Cambridge, 1982; computer programmer, Whitbread, Reading and London, 1983; estabd and ran Red and Green Nurseries, Norfolk, retail and wholesale herbaceous plant specialists, 1983–91; computer programmer and systems designer, Norwich Union, 1984–91; Political Assistant: to John Garrett, MP, 1992–97; to Clive Needle, MEP, 1995–99; Labour Link Policy and Campaigns Officer, UNISON, 2002–15. Mem. (Lab), S Norfolk DC, 1995–2003. *Recreations:* enjoying music, especially at Cambridge's Kettles Yard, Cambridge United season ticket holder. *Address:* House of Commons, SW1A 0AA. *T:* (01223) 423252. *E:* daniel.zeichner.mp@parliament.uk.

ZEIDMAN, Martyn Keith; QC 1998; **His Honour Judge Zeidman;** a Circuit Judge, since 2001; *b* Cardiff, 30 May 1952; *s* of Abe and Jennie Zeidman; *m* 1977, Verity, *d* of His Honour Aron Owen; one *s* one *d*. *Educ:* Univ. of London (LLB Hons ext.). Called to the Bar, Middle Temple, 1974; Asst Recorder, 1995–99; a Recorder, 1999–2001. Pres., Mental Health Review Tribunal (Restricted Cases), 1998–2010. Chm., Jewish Marriage Council, 2004–. Judicial Mem., London Courts Bd, 2007–. *Publications:* A Short Guide to The Landlord & Tenant Act 1987, 1987; A Short Guide to The Housing Act 1988, 1988; Steps to Possession, 1989; A Short Guide to The Courts and Legal Services Act 1990, 1990; A Short Guide to The Road Traffic Act 1991, 1991; Making Sense of The Leasehold Reform Housing & Urban Development Act 1993, 1994; Archbold Practical Research Papers on: Law of Mistake, 1997; Law of Self Defence, 1997. *Recreations:* family, studying Jewish religious texts, cycling. *Address:* Snaresbrook Crown Court, The Court House, Hollybush Hill, E11 1QW.

ZEILER, Gerhard; President, Turner Broadcasting System International, since 2012; *b* Vienna, 20 July 1955. *Educ:* Univ. of Vienna (Psychol., Sociol. and Educnl Sci.). Freelance journalist, 1979; Press Spokesman for Minister for Educn and the Arts, subseq. for Chancellor of Austria, 1979–86; Sec.-Gen., ORF (Public Broadcasting Corp. of Austria), 1986–91; Chief Executive Officer: Tele 5, Germany, 1991–92; RTL II, Germany, 1992–94; ORF, 1994–98; RTL Television, Cologne, 1998–2005; RTL Gp, 2003–12; Mem. Exec. Bd, Bertelsmann AG, 2005–12. Personality of Year Award, MIPCOM, 2004; Brandon Tartikoff Legacy Award, Nat. Assoc. TV Prog. Execs, USA, 2011. *Address:* TBS International, One CNN Center, Atlanta, GA 30303, USA.

ZEKI, Prof. Semir, FRS 1990; Professor of Neuroesthetics, University College London, since 2008 (Fellow, 2000); *b* 8 Nov. 1940; *m* 1967, Anne-Marie Claire Blestel; one *d* one *s*. *Educ:* University College London (BSc Anat. 1964; PhD 1967). Asst Lectr, UCL, 1966–67; Res. Associate, St Elizabeth's Hosp., Washington DC, 1967–68; Asst Prof., Univ. of Wisconsin, 1968–69; Lectr in Anatomy, UCL, 1969–75; Henry Head Res. Fellow, Royal Soc., 1975–80; University College London: Reader in Neurobiol., 1980–81; Prof. of Neurobiol., 1981–2008; Co-hd, Wellcome Dept of Cognitive Neurol., 1996–2001. Vis. Professorial Fellow, RPMS, Hammersmith Hosp., 1991–96. Visiting Professor: Duke Univ., 1977; Ludwig Maximilians Univ., Munich, 1982–87; Univ. of California, Berkeley, 1984, 2003 and 2006; St Andrews, 1985; Vis. Upjohn Prof., Erasmus Univ., Brussels, 1997–98; Visiting Scholar: J. Paul Getty Mus., 1996; Center for Advanced Study, Stanford, 2001. Lectures include: David Marr, Cambridge Univ., 1989; Philip Bard, Johns Hopkins Univ., 1992; Ferrier, Royal Soc., 1995; Woodhull, Royal Instn, 1995; Royal Soc. Humphry Davy, Acad. des Scis, Paris, 1996; Carl Gustave Bernhard, Royal Swedish Acad., 1998. Member: Neuroscience Res. Program and Neurosci. Inst., NY, 1985–; Wellcome Trust Vision Panel, 1985–93 (Chm., 1987–93); Bd of Scientific Govs, Scripps Res. Inst., Calif., 1992–2012; Nat. Sci. Council of France, 1998–2002. Trustee: Fight for Sight, 1992–97; Minerva Foundn, Berkeley, 1995–2012; Guarantor, Brain, 1994–2006. Mem., Cttee of Honour, Paris DFAS, 1996–. Ed., Philosophical Trans of Royal Soc., series B, 1997–2003. Exhibn, Bianco su bianco: oltre Malevich, Museo Pecci d'arte contemporanea, Milan, 2011. Founder FMedSci 1998; MRI, 1985; Member: Academia Europaea, 1990; Eur. Acad. of Scis and Arts, 1992; Amer. Phil Soc., 1998; Hon. Mem., Italian Primatological Assoc., 1988. Hon. DSc: Aston, 1994; Aberdeen, 2008; Athens, 2012. Minerva Foundn Prize, USA, 1985; Prix Science pour l'Art, LVMH, Paris, 1991; Rank Prize, 1992; Zotterman Prize, Swedish Physiol Soc., 1993; Electronic Imaging Award, Internat. Soc. for Optical Engrg, 2002; King Faisal Internat. Prize in Sci. (Biology), King Faisal Foundn, 2004; Erasmus Medal, Academia Europea, 2008; Segerfalk Award, Segerfalk Foundn, 2009; Aristotle Medal, World Psychiatric Fedn, 2011; Rome Prize, Atena Onlus Foundn, 2012. *Publications:* A Vision of the Brain, 1993; (with Balthus) La Quête de l'Essential, Paris, 1995; Inner Vision: an exploration of art and the brain, 1999; Splendors and Miseries of the Brain, 2008; (with Ludovica Lumer) La bella e la bestia: arte e neuroscienza, 2011; articles on vision and the brain in professional jls. *Recreations:* reading (esp. about the darker side of man), music, deep sleep. *Address:* Wellcome Department of Imaging Neuroscience, University College London, WC1E 6BT. *T:* (020) 7679 7316. *Clubs:* Athenæum, Garrick.

ZELDIN, Dr Theodore, CBE 2001; FBA 1995; FRSL, FRHistS; President, Oxford Muse, since 2001; Fellow, St Antony's College, Oxford, 1957–2001; *b* 22 Aug. 1933; *s* of Jacob Zeldin, civil engr, and Emma Zeldin, dentist; *m* 1975, Deirdre Wilson, *qv*. *Educ:* Aylesbury Grammar Sch.; Birkbeck Coll., London (BA 1951); Christ Church, Oxford (schol.; BA 1954; MA); St Antony's Coll., Oxford (DPhil 1957). Oxford University: Lectr, Christ Church, and Univ. Lectr in Modern Hist., 1959–76; Dean, Sen. Tutor, and Tutor for Admissions, St Antony's Coll., 1963–76; Dir, Future of Work Project, 1997–2000. Res. Fellow, CNRS, Paris, 1952–53; Visiting Professor: Harvard Univ., 1969–70; Univ. of Southern Calif, 1980–83. Mem., EC Cttee for Eur. Voluntary Service, 1997–99; Vice-Pres., Culture Europe, 2000–. Pres., Planning Commn, Nord-Pas-de-Calais, 1993–95; Advr, French Millennium Commn, 1999; Hon. President: Centre du Paysage, France, 2000; Maison du Temps et de la Mobilité, Belfort, 2001. Pres., Internat. Fest. of Geography, 1999; Chm., Oxford Food Symposium; Member: Council, Vivendi-Universal Inst de Prospective; Adv. Council, Demos; Mgt Cttee, Soc. of Authors; Attali Commission pour la Libération de la Croissance Française, 2007–11. Trustee: Wytham Hall Med. Charity for the Homeless; Amar Internat. Appeal for Refugees. MAE 1993. Wolfson Prize for History. Comdr, Ordre des Arts et des Lettres (France); Comdr, Légion d'Honneur (France), 2012. *Publications:* The Political System of Napoleon III, 1958; (ed) Journal d'Emile Ollivier, 1961; Emile Ollivier and the Liberal Empire of Napoleon III, 1963; Conflicts in French Society, 1971; France 1848–1945: vol. 1, Ambition, Love and Politics, 1973, vol. 2, Intellect, Taste and Anxiety, 1977, both vols re-issued 1993 as History of French Passions; The French, 1983; Happiness (novel), 1987; An Intimate History of Humanity, 1994; Flirtations (filmscript), 1994; Conversation, 1998; The Hidden Pleasures of Life, 2015; contrib. nat. press and learned jls. *Recreations:* painting, gardening, mending things. *Address:* Tumbledown House, Cumnor, Oxford OX2 9QE.

ZELENSKY, Igor Anatolyevich; ballet dancer; Artistic Director: Novosibirsk State Academic Opera and Ballet Theatre, Siberia, since 2006; Moscow Stanislavsky Ballet, since 2011; *b* Georgia, 13 July 1969. *Educ:* Tbilisi Sch. of Choreography; Vaganova Sch. of Choreography, St Petersburg. With Kirov (now Mariinsky) Ballet, 1989–2013 (Principal, 1991–2013); with New York City Ballet, 1992–97; guest dancer: Deutsche Oper, Berlin, 1990–; Royal Ballet, 1996– (Principal, 1997–2001); also with companies in Europe, Asia and America; Asst Dir, Athens Opera House, 2001–06. Rôles include Basil in Don Quixote, Siegfried in Swan Lake, Solor in La Bayadère, Albrecht in Giselle; leading rôles in Romeo and Juliet, Apollo, Le Corsaire, Manon, Sleeping Beauty. *Address:* c/o Mariinsky Theatre, Teatralnaya ploschad 1, St Petersburg, Russia.

ZELLICK, Prof. Graham John, CBE 2009; PhD; FAcSS; President, Valuation Tribunal for England, 2009–15; Member, Investigatory Powers Tribunal, since 2013; *b* 12 Aug. 1948; *s* of R. H. and B. Zellick; *m* 1975, Jennifer Temkin, *qv*; one *s* one *d*. *Educ:* Christ's Coll., Finchley; Gonville and Caius Coll., Cambridge (MA, PhD; Hon. Fellow, 2001); Stanford Univ. Called to the Bar, Middle Temple, 1992, Bencher, 2001 (Reader, 2013); Assoc. Mem., 3 Verulam Bldgs, Gray's Inn, 1993–2010. Ford Foundn Fellow, Stanford Law Sch., 1970–71; Queen Mary College, later Queen Mary and Westfield College, London: Lectr, 1971–78; Reader in Law, 1978–82; Prof. of Public Law, 1982–88; Dean of Faculty of Laws, 1984–88; Head, Dept of Law, 1984–90; Drapers' Prof. of Law, 1988–91; Prof. of Law, 1991–98, now Emeritus; Sen. Vice-Principal and Acting Principal, 1990–91; Principal, 1991–98; Vis. Prof. of Law, 2007–12; University of London: Dean, Faculty of Laws, 1986–88; Dep. Chm., Academic Council, 1987–89; Dep. Vice-Chancellor, 1994–97; Vice-Chancellor and Pres., 1997–2003. Vis. Fellow, Centre of Criminology, 1978–79, and Vis. Prof. of Law, 1975, 1978–79, Toronto Univ.; Vis. Scholar, St John's Coll., Oxford, 1989; Hon. Prof., Sch. of Law, Univ. of Birmingham, 2004–11; Dist. Vis. Fellow, NZ Law Foundn, 2010. Lectures: Noel Buxton, NACRO, 1983; Webber, Jews' Coll., London, 1986; Sir Gwilym Morris, UWIST, Cardiff, 1986; Wythe, Coll. of William and Mary, Va, 1989; Atkin, Reform Club, 2000; White, Indiana Univ., 2002; Van Der Zyl, Leo Baeck Coll., London, 2003; Lund, British Acad. Forensic Scis, 2006. Editor: European Human Rights Reports, 1978–82; Public Law, 1981–86; Member of Editorial Board: British Jl of Criminology, 1980–90; Public Law, 1981–91; Howard Jl of Criminal Justice, 1984–87; Civil Law Library, 1987–91. Member: Council and Exec. Cttee, Howard League for Penal Reform, 1973–82; Jellicoe Cttee on Bds of Visitors of Prisons, 1973–75; Sub Cttee on Crime and Criminal Justice, 1984–88, and Sub Cttee on Police Powers and the Prosecution Process, 1985–88, ESRC; Lord Chancellor's Legal Aid Adv. Cttee, 1985–88; Newham Dist Ethics Cttee, 1985–86; Data Protection Tribunal, 1985–96; Lord Chancellor's Adv. Cttee on Legal Educn, 1988–90; S Thames RHA, 1994–95; E London and the City HA, 1995–97; Criminal Injuries Compensation Appeals Panel, 2000–03; Competition Appeal Tribunal (formerly Competition Commn Appeal Tribunals), 2000–03; Criminal Justice Council, 2003–06; Valuation Tribunal Service Bd, 2009–15; Chm., Criminal Cases Review Commn, 2003–08; Electoral Comr, 2001–04. Chairman: Prisoners' Advice and Law Service, 1984–89; Legal Cttee, All-Party Parly War Crimes Gp, 1988–91; Dep. Chm., Justice Cttee on Prisoners' Rights, 1981–83. Dir, UCAS, 1994–97. Chairman: Cttee of Heads of Univ. Law Schs, 1988–90; E London Strategic Forum for Nat. Educn and Trng Targets, 1993–95; Vice-Chm., Acad. Study Gp for Israel and ME, 1995–2003; Mem. Council, CVCP, 1993–97. Pres., West London Synagogue, 2000–06 (Chm., Senate, 2006–14); Member: Council: UCS, 1983–92; City and East London Confedn for Medicine and Dentistry, 1991–95; St Bartholomew's Hosp. Med. Coll., 1991–95; Council of Govs, London Hosp. Med. Coll., 1991–95; Court of Governors: Polytechnic of Central London, 1973–77; Polytechnic of N London, 1986–89; Univ. of Greenwich, 1994–97; Chairman: Bd of Govs, Leo Baeck Coll., 2005–06; Bd of Trustees, Richmond, Amer. Internat. Univ. in London, 2005–06 (Trustee, 2002–06; Acad. Gov., 1999–2003); Governor: Pimlico Sch., 1973–77; Tel Aviv Univ., 2000–09 (Chm., Lawyers' Gp, 1984–89, and Trustee, 1985–87, Tel Aviv Univ. Trust); Visitor, Bancroft's Sch., 2009–10. Mem. Council, Spitalfields Heritage Centre, 1992–98; Patron, Redress Trust, 1993–; Trustee: William Harvey Res. Inst., 1995–2000; Samuel Courtauld Trust, 1997–2003; Gov., William Goodenough Trust, 1997–2003; Chm., Reform Club Conservation Charitable Trust, 2003–13. JP Inner London (N Westminster), 1981–85. Freeman, City of London, 1992; Mem., Ct of Assts, Drapers' Co., 2000– (Freeman, 1992; Liveryman, 1995; Master, 2009–10; Renter Warden, 2013–14). CCMI (FBIM 1991; CIMgt 1997); FRSA 1991; FRSocMed 1996; Founding FICPD, 1998; FAcSS (AcSS 2000). Fellow, Heythrop Coll., Univ. of London, 2005. Hon. QC 2010. Hon. Fellow: Soc. of Advanced Legal Studies, 1997; Burgon Soc., 2001 (Patron, 2009–); Leo Baeck Coll., 2007; Hon. FRAM 2003. Hon. LHD New York, 2001; Hon. LLD: Richmond, Amer. Internat. Univ. in London, 2003; Birmingham, 2006; Hon. DLit London, 2010. *Publications:* Justice in Prison (with Sir Brian MacKenna), 1983; (ed) The Law Commission and Law Reform, 1988; (contrib.) Halsbury's Laws of England, 4th edn 1982; contribs to collections of essays, pamphlets, the national press, and professional and learned periodicals incl. British Jl of Criminology, Civil Justice Quarterly, Criminal Law Rev., Modern Law Rev., Public Law, Univ. of Toronto Law Jl, William and Mary Law Rev., Medicine, Sci. and the Law, Manitoba Law Jl. *Address:* 63 Hampstead Way, NW11 7DN; Wykeham House, Wothorpe, Stamford PE9 3LA. *E:* graham.zellick@gmail.com.

ZELLICK, Jennifer, (Mrs G. J. Zellick); *see* Temkin, J.

ZEMAN, Miloš; President of the Czech Republic, since 2013; *b* 28 Sept. 1944; *m* 1st, 1971 (marr. diss. 1978); one *s*; 2nd, 1993; one *d*. *Educ:* Sch. of Economics, Kolín; Univ. of Economics, Prague (graduated *summa cum laude* 1969). Worked at engrg plant Tatra Kolín, 1963–67; teacher of econ. forecasting, Univ. of Econs, Prague, 1969; Sportpropag Co., 1971–84; Agrodat, 1984–89; Economic Forecasting Inst., 1990. Mem., Federal Assembly, 1990–92 (Civic Forum, 1990–92, Czech Social-Democratic Party, 1992) (Chm., Budget Cttee). Leader, Czech Social-Democratic Party, 1993–2001; Chm., Chamber of Deputies, Parliament of Czech Republic, 1996; Prime Minister, 1998–2002. Founder, Party of Citizen

Rights, 2009 (Leader, 2010; Hon. Chm., 2010). *Publications:* All My Mistakes in Politics (memoir), 2005. *Address:* Office of the President, Pražskýhrad, 11908 Prague 1, Czech Republic.

ZEPHANIAH, Benjamin Obadiah Iqbal; writer and poet; Professor of Poetry and Creative Writing, Brunel University, since 2011; *b* 15 April 1958; *s* of Oswald Springer and Leneve Faleta Wright. *Educ:* Broadway Comprehensive Sch., Birmingham; Glen-Parva Borstal, Leicester. Poet, 1977–. DUniv: N London, 1998; Staffordshire, 2001; Open, 2004; Hon. DLitt: W England, 1999; South Bank, 2002; E London, 2003; Leicester, 2004; Hon. DArts Oxford Brookes, 2002; Hon. MA Northampton, 2003. *Publications: poetry:* Pen Rhythm, 1980; The Dread Affair, 1985; Inna Liverpool, 1988; City Psalms, 1992; Propa Propaganda, 1996; School's Out, 1997; (ed) Bloomsbury Book of Love Poems, 1999; Too Black Too Strong, 2001; To Do Wid Me, 2013; *prose:* Rasta Time in Palestine, 1990; Kung Fu Trip, 2011; *for children:* Talking Turkeys, 1994; Funky Chickens, 1996; Wicked World, 2000; A Little Book of Vegan Poems, 2000; (with Prodeepta Das) We Are Britain, 2002; When I Grow Up, 2011; *novels:* Face, 1999; Refugee Boy, 2001; Gangsta Rap, 2004; Teacher's Dead, 2007; Liam, 2012. *Recreation:* collecting money. *Address:* PO Box 1153, Spalding, Lincs PE11 9BN.

ZERHOUNI, Elias A., MD; Professor of Radiology and Biomedical Engineering, and Senior Adviser, Johns Hopkins University School of Medicine, since 2009; President, Global Research and Development, Sanofi, since 2011 (Member, Executive Committee and Management Committee, since 2011); *b* 12 April 1951. *Educ:* Univ. of Algiers Sch. of Medicine (MD 1975). Johns Hopkins University School of Medicine: Residency in Diagnostic Radiol., 1975–78 (Chief Resident, 1977–78); Instructor, 1978–79, Asst Prof., 1979–81, Dept of Radiol.; Asst Prof., 1981–83, Associate Prof., 1983–85, Dept of Radiol., Eastern Virginia Med. Sch.; Johns Hopkins University School of Medicine: Associate Prof., 1985–92; Prof. of Radiol., 1992–2002; Prof. of Biomedical Engrg, 1995–2002; Chm., Dept of Radiol., 1996–2002; Exec. Vice Dean, Vice Dean for Clin. Affairs and Pres., Clin. Practice Assoc., 1996–99; Vice Dean for Res., 1999–2002; Exec. Vice Dean, 2000–02. Vice Chm. and Dir, Body Imaging Section, De Paul Hosp., Eastern Virginia Med. Sch., 1982–85; Johns Hopkins Medical Institutions: Co-Dir, MRI and Body CT, and Co-ordinator of Clin. Res., 1985–88; Dir, Divs of Thoracic Imaging and MRI, 1988–96; Radiologist-in-Chief, Johns Hopkins Hosp., 1996–2002; Dir, Nat. Insts of Health, USA, 2002–08. Sen. Fellow for Global Health, Bill & Melinda Gates Foundn, 2009–. Mem., Bd of Trustees, King Abdullah Univ. of Sci. and Technol., 2009–. Dr Emeritus, Univ. of Algiers, 2005. Fellow, Internat. Soc. for Magnetic Resonance in Medicine, 1998–. *Publications:* contrib. chapters to books; numerous contribs to peer-reviewed jls incl. Radiol., Jl Thoracic Imaging, JCAT, Circulation, Jl MRI.

ZERNICKA-GOETZ, Prof. Magdalena, PhD; FMedSci; Wellcome Trust Senior Research Fellow, Gurdon Institute, since 2002, and Professor of Mammalian Development and Stem Cell Biology, since 2010, University of Cambridge; *b* Warsaw, 30 Aug. 1963; *d* of Boguslaw and Danuta Zernicki; *m* 2000, Prof. David Moore Glover, *qv*; one *s* one *d*. *Educ:* Univ. of Warsaw (PhD). Adjunkt, Dept of Embryol., Univ. of Warsaw, 1993–97; University of Cambridge: EMBO Fellow, 1995–97; Lister Sen. Res. Fellow, Gurdon Inst., 1997–2002; Sen. Res. Fellow, Sidney Sussex Coll., 1997–2003; Reader in Develtl Biol., 2007–10. FMedSci 2013. *Publications:* contribs to scientific jls. *Address:* Department of Physiology, Development and Neuroscience, University of Cambridge, Downing Street, Cambridge CB2 3DY. *T:* (01223) 763291. *E:* mz205@cam.ac.uk.

ZETLAND, 4th Marquess of, *cr* 1892; **Lawrence Mark Dundas;** Bt 1762; Baron Dundas, 1794; Earl of Zetland, 1838; Earl of Ronaldshay (UK), 1892; DL; *b* 28 Dec. 1937; *e s* of 3rd Marquess of Zetland, DL and Penelope, *d* of late Col Ebenezer Pike, CBE, MC; *S* father, 1989; *m* 1964, Susan, 2nd *d* of late Guy Chamberlin, Oatlands, Wrington Hill, Wrington, Bristol, and late Mrs Chamberlin; two *s* two *d*. *Educ:* Harrow School; Christ's College, Cambridge. Late 2nd Lieut, Grenadier Guards. Founding Dir, British Horseracing Bd, 1993–97. DL N Yorks, 1994. *Heir: s* Earl of Ronaldshay, *qv*. *Address:* The Orangery, Aske, Richmond, N Yorks DL10 5HE. *T:* (01748) 823222. *Clubs:* All England Lawn Tennis and Croquet, Jockey (Steward, 1992–94).

ZETTER, Paul Isaac, CBE 1981; Chairman, Zetters Group Ltd, 1972–2000; *b* 9 July 1923; *s* of late Simon and Esther Zetter; *m* 1954, Helen Lore Morgenstern; one *s* one *d*. *Educ:* City of London Sch. Army, 1941–46. Family business, 1946–2000; became public co., 1965. Chm., Southern Council for Sport and Recreation, 1985–87; Member: Sports Council, 1985–87; National Centres Bd, Sports Council, 1987–88; Governor, 1975–, and Hon. Vice-Pres., 1985–, Sports Aid Foundation (Chm., 1976–85); Vice-Chm., World Ice Skating Championships, 1994–95. Trustee: Thames Salmon Trust, 1988–92; Foundn for Sports and Arts, 1991–96 (Chm., Sports Working Party, 1991–94). President: John Carpenter Club, 1987–88; Restricted Growth Assoc., 1993–96. Liveryman, Glovers' Co., 1981–2009; Freeman, City of London, 1981. Olympic torch bearer, W Sussex, 2012. *Publications:* It Could Be Verse, 1976; Bow Jest, 1992; Zero Risk, 2000; Global Warming, 2001; London Roundabout, 2007. *Recreations:* National Hunt horse racing (owner), walking, writing. *Address:* Willowbrook, The Ride, Ifold, W Sussex RH14 0TQ.

ZEWAIL, Prof. Ahmed H., PhD; Linus Pauling Professor of Chemistry and Professor of Physics, since 1995, and Director, Physical Biology Center for Ultrafast Science and Technology, since 2005, California Institute of Technology; United States Science Envoy, since 2009; *b* 26 Feb. 1946; *s* of Hassan A. Zewail and Rawhia Dar; *m* Dema; two *s* two *d*. *Educ:* Alexandria Univ., Egypt (BSc 1st Cl. Hons 1967; MS 1969); Univ. of Pennsylvania (PhD 1974). IBM Postdoctoral Fellow, Univ. of Calif, Berkeley, 1974–76; California Institute of Technology: Asst Prof. of Chemical Physics, 1976–78; Associate Prof., 1978–82; Prof. of Chemical Physics, 1982–89; Linus Pauling Prof. of Chemical Physics, 1990–94; Dir, NSF Lab. for Molecular Scis, 1996–2007. Jtly, patent, Solar Energy Concentrator Devices, 1980. Mem., President Obama's Council of Advrs on Sci. and Technol., 2009–. Foreign Mem., Royal Soc., 2001. Awards include: King Faisal Internat. Prize in Sci., 1989; Wolf Prize in Chem., 1993; Robert A. Welch Award in Chem., 1997; Benjamin Franklin Medal, Franklin Inst., USA, 1998; Nobel Prize in Chemistry, 1999; G. N. Lewis Medal, Univ. of Calif, Berkeley, 2010; Priestley Medal, American Chem. Soc., 2011; Davy Medal, Royal Soc., 2011. OM 1st Cl. (Scis and Arts) (Egypt), 1995; Grand Collar of the Nile (Egypt), 1999; Order of Zayed (UEA), 2000; OM (Tunisia), 2000; Order of Cedar (Lebanon), 2000; Order of ISESCO 1st Cl. (Saudi Arabia), 2000; Order of the Two Niles 1st Cl. (Sudan), 2004; Chevalier, Légion d'Honneur (France), 2012. *Publications:* Femtochemistry: ultrafast dynamics of the chemical bond, Vols I and II, 1994; Voyage through Time: walks of life to the Nobel Prize (autobiog.), 2002; numerous contribs to scientific jls incl. Science (USA), Nature and other professional jls. *Recreations:* reading, music, family-time travel. *Address:* California Institute of Technology, Arthur Amos Noyes Laboratory of Chemical Physics, Mail Code 127–72, Pasadena, CA 91125, USA. *T:* (626) 3956536. *Clubs:* Hon. Life Member: Athenaeum Faculty (Pasadena); Gezira, Automobile, Cairo Capital (Cairo); Alexandria Sporting (Egypt).

ZIA, Hon. Khaleda; Prime Minister of Bangladesh, 1991–96 and 2001–06; *b* 15 Aug. 1945; *m* 1960, Gen. Ziaur Rahman (*d* 1981), President of Bangladesh; two *s*. *Educ:* Surendranath Coll., Dinajpur. Vice-Chm., 1982–84, Chm., 1984–, Bangladesh Nat. Party.

ZIEGLER, Philip Sandeman, CVO 1991; author; *b* 24 Dec. 1929; *s* of Major Colin Louis Ziegler, DSO, DL, and Mrs Dora Ziegler (*née* Barnwell); *m* 1st, 1960, Sarah Collins; one *s* one *d*; 2nd, 1971, (Mary) Clare Charrington; one *s*. *Educ:* Eton; New Coll., Oxford (1st Cl. Hons Jurisprudence; Chancellor's Essay Prize). Entered Foreign Service, 1952; served in Vientiane, Paris, Pretoria and Bogotà; resigned 1967; joined William Collins and Sons Ltd, 1967, Editorial Dir 1972, Editor-in-Chief, 1979–80. Chairman: The London Library, 1979–85; Soc. of Authors, 1988–90; Public Lending Right Adv. Cttee, 1994–97. FRSL 1975; FRHS 1979. Hon. DLitt: Westminster Coll., Fulton, 1988; Buckingham, 2000. *Publications:* Duchess of Dino, 1962; Addington, 1965; The Black Death, 1968; William IV, 1971; Omdurman, 1973; Melbourne, 1976 (W. H. Heinemann Award); Crown and People, 1978; Diana Cooper, 1981; Mountbatten, 1985; Elizabeth's Britain 1926 to 1986, 1986; The Sixth Great Power: Barings 1762–1929, 1988; King Edward VIII, 1990; Harold Wilson: the authorised life, 1993; London at War 1939–45, 1995; Osbert Sitwell, 1998; Britain Then and Now, 1999; Soldiers: fighting men's lives, 1901–2001, 2001; Rupert Hart-Davis: man of letters, 2004; Legacy: the Rhodes Trust and the Rhodes Scholarships, 2008; Edward Heath: the authorised biography, 2010 (Elizabeth Longford Prize, Soc. of Authors, 2011); Queen Elizabeth II: a photographic portrait, 2010; Olivier, 2013; George VI: the dutiful king, 2014; *edited:* the Diaries of Lord Louis Mountbatten 1920–1922, 1987; Personal Diary of Admiral the Lord Louis Mountbatten 1943–1946, 1988; From Shore to Shore: the diaries of Earl Mountbatten of Burma 1953–1979, 1989; (with Desmond Seward) Brooks's: a social history, 1991. *Address:* 22 Cottesmore Gardens, W8 5PR. *T:* (020) 7937 1903. *E:* philipziegler@me.com. *Club:* Brooks's.

ZILKHA, Selim Khedoury; Principal: Zilkha Renewable Energy, 2001–05; Zilkha Biomass, since 2005; *b* 7 April 1927; *s* of Khedoury Aboodi Zilkha and Louise (*née* Bashi); *m* (marr. diss.); one *s* one *d*. *Educ:* English Sch., Heliopolis, Egypt; Horace Mann Sch. for Boys, USA; Williams Coll., USA (BA Major Philos.). Dir, Zilkha & Sons Inc., USA, 1947–87; Chm. and Man. Dir, Mothercare Ltd and associated cos, 1961–82; Dir, Habitat Mothercare Gp, 1982; Chairman: Amerfin Co. Ltd, GB, 1955–68; Spirella Co. of Great Britain Ltd, 1957–62; Chm./Jt Man. Dir, Lewis & Burrows Ltd, 1961–64; Chairman and Chief Executive Officer: Towner Petroleum Co., Houston, 1983–85; SKZ Inc., Houston, 1986; Zilkha Energy Co., Houston, 1987–98; non-executive Director: Sonat Inc., 1998–2000; El Paso Energy and Gas, 2000–02. Owner, Laetitia Winery and Vineyard, 2002–. Founder, Zilkha Neurogenetic Inst., 2002. *Recreations:* bridge, backgammon, tennis. *Address:* 750 Lausanne Road, Los Angeles, CA 90077–3316, USA. *Club:* Portland.

ZILLMAN, Dr John William, AO 1996; Director of Meteorology, Australia, 1978–2003; President, World Meteorological Organization, 1995–2003; Vice-Chancellor's Fellow, School of Earth Sciences, University of Melbourne, 2009–12 (Professor of Earth Sciences, 1999–2009); *b* 28 July 1939; *s* of late Charles H. S. Zillman and of Thelma Flora Fraser. *Educ:* Nudgee Coll.; Univ. of Queensland (BSc Hons 1960; BA 1970); Melbourne Univ. (MSc 1971); Univ. of Wisconsin (PhD 1972). Australian Bureau of Meteorology: forecaster and research scientist, 1957–74; Asst Dir (Res.), 1974–78. Perm. Rep. of Australia with WMO, 1978–2004 (Mem., Exec. Council, 1979–2004); Chm., Steering Cttee for Global Climate Observing System, 2006–09. President: Royal Soc. of Victoria, 1993–94; Aust. Acad. of Technol Scis and Engineering, 2003–06 (Vice-Pres., 1995–98); Internat. Council of Acads of Engrg and Technol Scis, 2005; Aust. Nat. Academics Forum, 2005–06. *Publications:* (ed jtly) Climate Change and Variability: a southern perspective, 1978; (ed jtly) Climate of the South Pacific, 1984; numerous contribs to learned jls. *Recreations:* reading, music. *Address:* GPO Box 1289, Melbourne, Vic 3001, Australia. *T:* (3) 96694250. *Club:* Melbourne (Melbourne).

ZIMMER, Hans Florian; film score composer; Co-founder and Partner, Remote Control Productions (formerly Media Ventures Entertainment Group); *b* Frankfurt-am-Main, 12 Sept. 1957; *m* Vicki Carolyn (marr. diss.); one *d*; *m* Suzanne; one *s*. Keyboard player with Buggles (album, The Age of Plastic, 1980), with Ultravox, with Krisma (album, Cathode Mama, 1981); formerly Asst to Stanley Myers, London; Hd of Music Dept, DreamWorks SKG, 1994–. *Film scores include:* with Stanley Myers: Moonlighting, 1982; Eureka, Success is the Best Revenge, 1984; Insignificance, 1985; My Beautiful Laundrette, 1986; score producer, The Last Emperor, 1986; sole composer: A World Apart, 1988; Rain Man, Black Rain, Driving Miss Daisy, 1989; Bird on a Wire, Days of Thunder, Pacific Heights, Green Card, 1990; Regarding Henry, Thelma & Louise, Backdraft, 1991; The Power of One, A League of their Own, Toys, 1992; True Romance, Cool Runnings, 1993; I'll Do Anything, The Lion King (Acad. Award; Golden Globe Award), Drop Zone, Renaissance Man, 1994; Nine Months, Something to Talk About, Beyond Rangoon, Crimson Tide (Grammy Award, 1996), 1995; Broken Arrow, The Rock, The Fan, Muppet Treasure Island, The Preacher's Wife, 1996; The Peacemaker, As Good as it Gets, 1997; Prince of Egypt, 1998; The Thin Red Line, Chill Factor, The Last Days, 1999; The Road to El Dorado, Gladiator (Golden Globe Award), Mission Impossible 2, An Everlasting Piece, 2000; Pearl Harbor, Hannibal, 2001; Black Hawk Down, 2002; Pirates of the Caribbean: The Curse of the Black Pearl, The Last Samurai, Something's Gotta Give, 2003; King Arthur, Thunderbirds, Shark Tale, 2004; The Da Vinci Code, Pirates of the Caribbean: Dead Man's Chest, 2006; The Simpsons Movie, Pirates of the Caribbean: At World's End, 2007; Kung Fu Panda, The Dark Knight, Frost/Nixon, 2008; Sherlock Holmes, 2009; Inception, 2010; The Dark Knight Rises, 2012; Man of Steel, 2013; 12 Years a Slave, 2014; Interstellar, 2014. Composer of the Year and Outstanding Contribution to Music, Classic BRIT Awards, 2013. *Address:* Remote Control Productions, 1547 14th Street, Santa Monica, CA 90404, USA.

ZIMMER, Prof. Robert J., PhD; President, and Professor, Department of Mathematics, University of Chicago, since 2006. *Educ:* Brandeis Univ. (AB 1968); Harvard Univ. (AM 1971; PhD 1975). University of Chicago: L. E. Dickson Instructor of Maths, 1977–79; Associate Prof., 1979–80; Prof., Dept of Maths, 1980–2002; Vice-Pres. for Res. and for Argonne Nat. Lab., 2000–02; Provost, Brown Univ., 2002–06. *Publications:* Ergodic Theory and Semisimple Groups, 1984; Essential Results of Functional Analysis, 1990. *Address:* Office of the President, University of Chicago, 5801 S Ellis Avenue, Suite 501, Chicago, IL 60637, USA. *E:* president@uchicago.edu.

ZIMMERMAN, Robert Allen, (Bob Dylan); singer, musician and composer, since 1960; *b* 24 May 1941; *s* of Abe Zimmerman and Beatrice Rutman; *m* 1965, Sarah Lowndes (marr. diss. 1978); three *s* one *d*, and one step *d*; *m* 1986, Carolyn Y. Dennis (marr. diss. 1992); one *d*. *Educ:* Hibbing High Sch., Minn; Univ. of Minnesota. Albums include: Bob Dylan, 1962; The Free Wheelin' Bob Dylan, 1963; The Times They Are A-Changin', 1964; Another Side of Bob Dylan, 1964; Bringing It All Back Home, 1965; Highway 61 Revisited, 1965; Blonde on Blonde, 1966; John Wesley Harding, 1967; Nashville Skyline, 1969; Self Portrait, 1970; New Morning, 1970; Dylan, 1973; Planet Waves, 1974; Before the Flood, 1974; The Basement Tapes, 1975; Blood on Tracks, 1975; Desire, 1976; Street Legal, 1978; Slow Train Coming, 1979; Saved, 1980; Shot of Love, 1981; Infidels, 1983; Empire Burlesque, 1985; Biograph, 1985; Knocked Out Loaded, 1986; Down in the Groove, 1988; Oh Mercy, 1989; Under the Red Sky, 1990; Bootleg Series, vols 1–3, 1991; Good as I Been to You, 1992; World Gone Wrong, 1993; Time Out of Mind, 1997; Bootleg Series, vol. 4, 1998; Love and Theft, 2001; Bootleg Series, vol. 5, 2002, vol. 6, 2004, vol. 7, 2006; Modern Times, 2006; Together Through Life, 2009; Christmas in the Heart, 2009; Tempest, 2012; The Basement Tapes Complete, 2014; Shadows in the Night, 2015. Actor in films: Pat Garrett and Billy the Kid, 1973; Hearts of Fire, 1987; Masked and Anonymous, 2003. Exhibitions of paintings: Drawn Blank Series, Halcyon Gall., 2008 and 2010; Bob Dylan: Face Value, NPG, 2013; Mood Swings, Halcyon Gall., 2013. Presidential Medal of Freedom (USA), 2012; Officier, Légion d'Honneur (France), 2013. *Publications:* Tarantula, 1966; Writings and Drawings,

1973; Lyrics: 1962–85, 1985; Drawn Blank, 1994; Lyrics: 1962–1997, 1999; Lyrics: 1962–2001, 2004; Chronicles, vol. 1 (autobiog.), 2004. *Address:* c/o Jeff Rosen, PO Box 870, New York, NY 10276, USA.

ZINKERNAGEL, Prof. Rolf Martin, MD, PhD; Professor of Experimental Immunology, and Director, Institute of Experimental Immunology, University of Zürich, 1992–2008, now Emeritus; *b* 6 Jan. 1944; *s* of Robert Zinkernagel and Susanne Zinkernagel-Staehlin; *m* 1968, Kathrin Lüdin; one *s* two *d*. *Educ:* Mathematisch-Naturwissenschaftliches Gymnasium; Univ. of Basel (MD 1970); Univ. of Zürich; ANU (PhD 1975). Extern, Glen Cove Community Hosp., Long Island, NY, 1966; Intern, Surgical Dept, Clara-Spital, Univ. of Basel, 1969; Fellow: Lab. for Electron Microscopy, Inst. of Anatomy, Univ. of Basel, 1969–70; Inst. of Biochemistry, Univ. of Lausanne, 1971–73; Vis. Fellow, Dept of Microbiology, John Curtin Sch. of Med. Res., ANU, 1973–75; Asst Prof., subseq. Associate Prof., 1976–79, Prof., 1979, Dept of Immunopathology, Res. Inst. of Scripps Clinic, Calif; Adjunct Associate Prof., Dept of Pathology, UCSD, 1977–79; Associate Prof., 1979–88, Prof., 1988–92, Dept of Pathology, Univ. Hosp., Univ. of Zürich. Member: Swiss Soc. of Allergy and Immunology, 1971–; Amer. Assoc. of Immunologists, 1977–; Swiss Soc. of Pathology, 1981–; Sci. Adv. Council, Cancer Res. Inst., 1988–; Academia Europea, 1989–; Founding Cttee, Max-Planck-Inst. of Infectiology, 1990–92; US Acad. of Scis, 1996–; Foreign Mem., Royal Soc., 1998. Member: editl bd, numerous jls; numerous scientific adv. bds. Hon. DSc Liège, 1996. Awards include: Cloëtta Stiftung, Zürich, 1981; Paul Ehrlich Preis, Frankfurt, 1983; Lasker Award, 1995; (with Peter Doherty) Nobel Prize in Physiology or Medicine, 1996. *Address:* Institute of Experimental Immunology, University of Zürich, University Hospital, Schmelzbergstrasse 12, 8091 Zürich, Switzerland.

ZISSERMAN, Prof. Andrew Peter, PhD; FRS 2007; Microsoft/Royal Academy of Engineering Professor of Computer Vision Engineering, University of Oxford, since 2006; Fellow of Brasenose College, Oxford. *Educ:* Fitzwilliam Coll., Cambridge (BA 1978; PhD); MA Oxon. Univ. of Edinburgh, 1984–87; Univ. of Oxford, 1987–, Prof. of Engrg Sci., 1999–2006. *Publications:* (with Andrew Blake) Visual Reconstruction, 1987; (with Richard Hartley) Multiple View Geometry in Computer Vision, 2nd edn 2004. *Address:* Department of Engineering Science, University of Oxford, Parks Road, Oxford OX1 3PJ.

ZISSMAN, Sir Bernard (Philip), Kt 1996; Chairman: CDI Group Ltd, since 1999; Cerebrum Partners, since 2011; AbbeyQC Ltd, since 2013; JWZ LLP, since 2013; *b* 11 Dec. 1934; *s* of Hannah and David Zissman; *m* 1958, Cynthia Glass; one *s* two *d*. *Educ:* King Edward's Grammar Sch., Five Ways. Sales Dir, 1960–70, Man. Dir, 1970–85, Zissman Bros (Birmingham); Dir, Hyatt Regency (Birmingham), 1992–95; Chm., Communication Hub Ltd, 1995–97; Dir of Communications, Bucknall Austin, 1996–99; Chief Exec., Confident Communications, 1997–. Chaiman: Private Equity Builders (formerly Business Angels Bureau Ltd), 2005– (Dep. Chm., 2004–05); Early Equity plc, 2008–10; Rewired PR Ltd, 2011–14. Non-executive Director: Severn Trent Water Authy, 1983–89; Birmingham Broadcasting, 1994–2000; Capolito Roma, 1996–99. Chm., Good Hope NHS Hosp. Trust, 1998–2004. Birmingham City Council: Mem. (C), 1965–95; Lord Mayor, 1990–91; Leader, Conservative Gp, 1992–95; Hon. Alderman, 1995–. Pres., Edgbaston Cons. Assoc., 2013– (Chm., 1996–99). Member: Council, Birmingham Chamber of Commerce and Industry, 1991–2009; W Midlands Police Authy, 1994–95. Chairman: Adv. Bd, Japan Centre, Birmingham Univ., 1992–2001; Midlands Cttee, Princess Royal Trust for Carers, 1999–2006; Millennium Point Trust, 2007–12. Mem., Regl Council, Nat. Meml Arboretum, 2008–. Trustee, CBSO, 1992–. Life Mem., Fedn of Clothing Designers and Execs, 1991–. Patron, Marie Curie Hospice, Solihull, 2012–. Freeman, City of London. President: Birmingham Hebrew Congregation, 1999–2004; Repr. Council, Birmingham and Midland Jewry, 2006– (Mem., 1992–2000). FRSA 1997. Hon. LLD Birmingham, 1997; DUniv Central England, 2000. *Publications:* A Knight Out with Chamberlain in Birmingham, 2002; Herzl's Journey, 2008. *Recreations:* family, photography, travel. *Address:* 14 Walled Garden Court, Hampton Road, Stanmore HA7 3GE. *T:* (020) 3759 1795.

ZITCER, Diane; *see* Kenwood, D.

ZITTER, Guy; Group Managing Director, Mail Newspapers, 2008–14; *b* London, 26 Feb. 1954; *s* of late Gerald Zitter and of Ina Zitter; *m* 1987, Julie Polk; one *s* one *d*. *Educ:* Edinburgh Univ. (BSc Commerce; Cert. Advertising and Mktg). Sen. Finance Officer, Seychelles Govt, 1976–77; night club proprietor, 1977–79; sales exec., Sunday Express, 1980–81; restaurant proprietor, 1981–84; Mail on Sunday: Sen. Sales Exec., 1981–83; Sales Manager, 1983–84; Advertising Manager, 1984–89; Daily Mail: Advertisement Dir, 1989–94; Man. Dir, 1994–2008. Chm., People Bank Ltd, 1996–99; Director: Free Publishing Services, 1995–98; Metro, 2003; Evening Standard, 2003–08; Boiling Oil Ltd, 2014–. Gilt Cross, Scout Assoc., 1966. *Recreations:* ski-ing, shooting, fishing, fine wine, Cuban cigars. *Clubs:* Harry's Bar; St Moritz Yacht.

ZOLLINGER-READ, Paul John, CBE 2012; Chief Medical Officer, BUPA, since 2012; *b* Birmingham, 18 Feb. 1962; *s* of Eric Ernest Read and Mary Irene Read; *m* 1988, Heidi Carris Zollinger; one *s* one *d*. *Educ:* Gonville and Caius Coll., Cambridge (BA 1983); Guy's Hosp. (MB BS 1986). Dip. Geriatric Medicine 1989; DRCOG 1990; Dip. Child Medicine 1991; MRCGP. Gp Partner, Braintree, Essex, 1991–2012. Dir, Modernisation Agency, NHS, 2000–02; Chief Executive Officer: Braintree Care Trust, 2002–06; Chelmsford PCT, 2004–06; NE Essex PCT, 2006–10; Gt Yarmouth and Waveney PCT, 2009; Cambs NHS, 2010–11; NHS Peterborough, 2010–11; Director: E of England SHA, 2010–12; Midlands and E SHA, 2012. Med. Advr and Primary Care Lead, King's Fund, 2011–12. Hon. PhD Anglian Ruskin, 2013. *Publications:* contrib. Lancet. *Recreations:* long distance running, playing piano, photography, family. *Address:* Flaglands, 25 Queen Street, Castle Hedingham, Essex CO9 3HA. *T:* 07515 507855. *E:* paul.zollingerread@btinternet.com.

ZOUCHE, 18th Baron *cr* 1308, of Haryngworth; **James Assheton Frankland;** Bt 1660; company director; President, Multiple Sclerosis Society of Victoria, 1981–84; *b* 23 Feb. 1943; *s* of Major Hon. Sir Thomas William Assheton Frankland, 11th Bt, and Mrs Robert Pardoe (*d* 1972), *d* of late Captain Hon. Edward Kay-Shuttleworth; *S* to father's Btcy, 1944; *S* grandmother, 17th Baroness Zouche, 1965; *m* 1978, Sally Olivia, *y d* of R. M. Barton, Bungay, Suffolk; one *s* one *d*. *Educ:* Lycée Jaccard, Lausanne. Served 15/19th the King's Royal Hussars, 1963–68. Mem. (C), Somerset CC, 2009–13. *Heir: s* Hon. William Thomas Assheton Frankland, *b* 23 July 1984. *Address:* The Abbey, Charlton Adam, Somerton, Somerset TA11 7BE.

ZUCKER, His Honour Kenneth Harry; QC 1981; a Circuit Judge, 1989–2005; *b* 4 March 1935; *s* of Nathaniel and Norma Zucker; *m* 1961, Ruth Erica, *y d* of Dr H. Brudno; one *s* one *d*. *Educ:* Westcliff High Sch.; Exeter Coll., Oxford, 1955–58 (MA). Served in Royal Air Force, 1953–55. Bacon Scholar, Gray's Inn, 1958; called to Bar, Gray's Inn, 1959; Atkin Scholar, Gray's Inn, 1959. A Recorder, 1982–89. *Recreations:* reading, walking, photography, bookbinding, table tennis.

ZUCKERMAN, Adrian; *see* Zuckerman, A. A. S.

ZUCKERMAN, Prof. Arie Jeremy, MD, DSc; FRCP, FRCPath, FMedSci; Professor of Medical Microbiology in the University of London, 1975–2014, now Emeritus, and Dean, Royal Free Hospital School of Medicine, then Royal Free and University College Medical School, 1989–99; *m* 1951, Alice Adamson (*d* 2011); one *s* one *d*. *Educ:* Birmingham Univ. (BSc 1953; MSc 1962; DSc 1973); London Univ. (MB BS 1957; MD 1963; DipBact 1965). MRCS, LRCP, 1957; DObst, RCOG, 1958; MRCPath 1965, FRCPath 1977; MRCP 1977, FRCP 1982. Ho. Surg., Royal Free Hosp., 1957–58; Ho. Phys., 1958, Casualty Surg. and Admissions Officer, 1958–59, Whittington Hosp.; Flt Lieut, then Sqn Leader, Medical Branch, RAF, 1959–62: Unit MO and Tutor in Aviation Medicine, Advanced Flying Sch., 1959–60; Epidemiol Res. Lab., PHLS, 1960–62; seconded to Dept of Pathol., Guy's Hosp. Med. Sch., 1962–63; Sen. Registrar, PHLS, 1963–65; London School of Hygiene and Tropical Medicine: Sen. Lectr, Dept of Bacteriol. and Immunol., 1965–68; Reader in Virology, 1968–72; Prof. of Virology, 1972–75; Dir, Dept of Med. Microbiol., 1975–88; Member Council: Univ. of London, 1995–99 (Mem. Court, 1992–95); UCL, 1995–2003. Chm., Conf. of Metropolitan Deans, 1992–95. Hon. Consultant Microbiologist: UCH, 1982–89; Royal Free Hosp., 1989–2003; Hon. Consultant Virologist: Charing Cross Hosp., 1982–95; NE Thames Regl Blood Transfusion Centre, Brentwood, 1970–94; Nat. Blood Authy, 1994–99. World Health Organisation: Consultant on hepatitis, 1970–2005; Member: expert adv. gps, DoH, 1970–2007; Adv. Gps on hepatitis, HIV/AIDS, transfusion-transmitted viruses and liver disease strategy, DoH, 1970–2011; Expert Adv. Panel on Virus Diseases, 1974–2005; Dir, Collaborating Centre for Ref. and Res. on Viral Diseases, 1990–2006; Dir, Collaborating Centre for Ref. and Res. on Viral Hepatitis, London, 1974–89. Non-exec. Dir, Royal Free Hampstead NHS Trust, 1990–99; Dir, Anthony Nolan Bone Marrow Trust, 1990–2003. Mem. Council, Zool Soc. of London, 1989–92. Chm., Hepatitis B Foundn UK, 2006–12. Founder FMedSci 1998. Stewart Prize, BMA, 1981; James Blundell Medal and Award, British Blood Transfusion Soc., 1992. Editor: Jl of Med. Virology, 1976–2015; Jl of Virological Methods, 1979–2015. *Publications:* Virus Diseases of the Liver, 1970; Hepatitis-associated Antigen and Viruses, 1972, 2nd edn as Human Viral Hepatitis, 1975 (trans. Japanese 1980); (with C. R. Howard) Hepatitis Viruses of Man, 1979 (trans. Japanese 1981); A Decade of Viral Hepatitis: abstracts 1969–1979, 1980; (ed) Viral Hepatitis: clinics in tropical medicine and communicable diseases, 1986; (ed jtly) Principles and Practice of Clinical Virology, 1987 (trans. Italian 1992), 6th edn 2009; (ed) Viral Hepatitis and Liver Disease, 1988; (ed) Recent Developments in Prophylactic Immunization, 1989; (ed) Viral Hepatitis, 1990 (trans. Spanish 1991); (ed with H. Thomas) Viral Hepatitis: scientific basis and clinical management, 1993, 4th edn 2013 (trans. Turkish 2006, Chinese 2007); (ed) Prevention of Hepatitis B in the Newborn, Children and Adolescents, 1996; (ed) Hepatitis B in the Asian-Pacific Region, vol. 1, 1997, vol. 2, 1998, vol. 3, 1999; (ed jtly) Diabetes and Viruses, 2012; contribs to many learned jls. *E:* arie.zuckerman@ucl.ac.uk.

ZUCKERMAN, Prof. (Azriel) Adrian (Sorin); Professor of Civil Procedure, University of Oxford, 2006–14, now Emeritus; Fellow and Praelector in Jurisprudence, University College, Oxford, 1973–2011, now Emeritus Fellow; *b* Bucharest, Romania, 18 Jan. 1943; *s* of Bercu-Avram and Anna Zuckerman; *m* 1st, 1969, Orna Rabinowitz (marr. diss. 1972); one *d*; 2nd, 1995, Lady Joanna Edwina Doreen Knatchbull, *d* of 7th Baron Brabourne, CBE and of Countess Mountbatten of Burma, *qv*; one *s*. *Educ:* Natanya Municipal Sch.; Hebrew Univ., Jerusalem (LLB, LLM); Univ. of Oxford (MA). Jun. Res. Fellow, Balliol Coll., Oxford, 1971–73. *Publications:* The Principles of Criminal Evidence, 1989; (ed) Reform of Civil Procedure: essays on access to justice, 1995; (ed) Justice in Crisis (essays), 1999; Civil Procedure, 2003, 3rd edn as Zuckerman on Civil Procedure, 2013; (with P. Roberts) Criminal Evidence, 2004, 2nd edn 2010. *Recreations:* sailing, opera, gardening, perfecting espresso coffee. *Address:* Law Faculty, St Cross Building, Manor Road, Oxford OX1 3UL. *T:* (01865) 271490. *E:* adrian.zuckerman@univ.ox.ac.uk.

See also Baron Brabourne, Hon. P. W. A. Knatchbull.

zu GUTTENBERG, Karl-Theodor Freiherr; Founder and Chairman, Spitzberg Partners LLC, New York, since 2013; *b* 5 Dec. 1971; *m* 2000, Stephanie Gräfin von Bismarck-Schönhausen; two *d*. *Educ:* Univ. of Bayreuth (Law); Univ. of Munich (Pol Sci.). Mil. service, Light Mt Infantry, Mittenwald (non-commnd officer of reserve). Hd, family business, Munich until 2002 (worked in Frankfurt, NY and Berlin); Mem., Bd of Dirs, Rhön-Klinikum AG, 1996–2002. Mem., Bundestag, 2002–11; Speaker, CDU/CSU Parly Gp, 2005–08; Mem., Foreign Affairs Cttee, 2005–08; spokesman of CDU/CSU Parly Gp on disarmament, non-proliferation and arms control, 2005–08; Chm., CSU Foreign Policy Expert Cttee, 2005–08; Federal Minister of Econs and Technol., 2009, of Defence, 2009–11. Chm., CSU Upper Franconian Dist Exec., 2007–11; Sec. Gen., CSU, 2008–09. Distinguished Statesman, Center for Strategic and Internat. Studies, 2011–. *Address:* Spitzberg Partners LLC, 270 Lafayette Street, Suite 1005, New York, NY 10012, USA.

ZUKERMAN, Pinchas; conductor, concert violinist and violist; Music Director, National Arts Centre Orchestra, Canada, since 1999; *b* Tel Aviv, Israel, 16 July 1948; *s* of Yehuda and Miriam Zukerman; *m* 2004, Amanda Forsyth; two *d* from former marriage. *Educ:* Juilliard School of Music. Début, USA, 1963, Europe, 1970. Violin soloist with every major orchestra in USA and Europe; tours of USA, Europe, Israel, Scandinavia, Australia; extensive recordings. Music Director: South Bank Festival, 1978–80; St Paul Chamber Orch., 1980–87; Principal Guest Conductor: Dallas SO, 1993–95 (Principal Conductor, Internat. Summer Music Fest., 1990–95); RPO, 2009–. First prize, Leventritt Internat. Violin Competition, 1967. *Address:* c/o Kirshbaum Demler & Associates, 711 West End Avenue, New York, NY 10025, USA. *T:* (212) 2224843.

ZUMA, Jacob Gedleyihlekisa; President: of South Africa, since 2009; African National Congress, since 2007; *b* Inkandla, KwaZulu-Natal, 12 April 1942; *s* of Gcinamazwi Zuma and Nokubhekisisa Zuma; *m* 1973, Sizakele Khumalo; *m* Kate Mantsho (*d* 2000); *m* Nkosazana Dlamini (marr. diss. 1998); *m* 2008, Nompumelelo Ntuli; *m* 2010, Thobeka Madiba; *m* 2012, Gloria Bongekile Ngema; twenty *c*. Mem., ANC, 1958–; arrested and convicted for conspiring to overthrow govt, 1963 and sentenced to 10 years imprisonment on Robben Island; after release in 1973, mobilised internal resistance and re-estabt of ANC underground structures, 1974–75; based in Swaziland, then Mozambique, 1975–87; returned to SA, 1990; African National Congress: Mem., Nat. Exec. Cttee, 1977–; Dep. Sec. Gen., 1991–94; Nat. Chm., Council, 1995–97; Dep. Pres., 1997–2007. Mem., Exec. Council, Econ. Affairs and Tourism, KwaZulu-Natal Provincial Govt, 1994–99; Leader, Govt Business, Nat. Assembly, 1997–2005; MP (ANC), 1999–2005; Dep. Pres., SA, 1999–2005. *Address:* Office of the President, Union Buildings, Private Bag X1000, Pretoria 0001, South Africa.

ZUMLA, Prof. Alimuddin; Grand Comdr, Order of Dist. Service, First Div. (Zambia), 2012; PhD; FRCP, FRCPE, FRCPath; FRSB; Professor of Infectious Diseases and International Health, UCL Medical School (formerly Royal Free and University College Medical School), University College London, since 1998; Consultant Infectious Diseases Physician, University College London Hospitals NHS Foundation Trust, since 1994; Honorary Consultant, Royal Free Hospital NHS Foundation Trust, since 2000; *b* Fort Jameson, Zambia, 1956; *s* of Ismail Bagas and Aminaben Zumla; *m* 1986, Farzana Gulam Bhuta; two *s* one *d*. *Educ:* Univ. of Zambia (BSc Human Biol. (Dist.) 1976; MB ChB 1979); London Sch. of Hygiene and Tropical Medicine, Univ. of London (MSc Tropical Medicine 1981 (Frederick Murgatroyd Medal and Prize); PhD 1987 (Alan Woodruff Medal)). MRCP 1984, FRCP 1994; FRCPE 1999; FRCPath 2009; FRSB (FSB 2012). Clin. Fellow and SHO in Gen. Medicine, RPMS, Hammersmith Hosp., 1981–83; Registrar in Gen. Medicine, Royal Northern Hosp., London, 1983–84; Beit Meml Res. Fellow and Hon. Registrar, LSHTM, 1984–87; Registrar, Rush Green and Oldchurch Hosps, Romford, 1987–88; Sen. Registrar and Hon. Lectr, Depts of Medicine and Immunol., RPMS, Hammersmith Hosp., 1988–92; Associate Prof., Center for Infectious Diseases, Univ. of Texas Health Sci. Center at Houston, Med. Sch. and Sch. of Public Health, Houston, Texas, 1992–94; University College London: Sen. Lectr, 1994–95, Reader in Infectious Diseases, 1995–98, Dept of Medicine, Royal Free and University Coll.

Med. Sch.; Dir, Centre for Infectious Diseases and Internat. Health, 1994–2011. Visiting Professor: Univ. of Zambia Sch. of Medicine, 1992–; Univ. of Cape Town, 2007–; Univ. of Amsterdam, 2011; Hon. Professor: Liverpool Sch. of Tropical Medicine and Hygiene, 2003–08; Centre for Internat. Child Health, Inst. of Child Health, 2004–. Bayer UK Award, British Soc. for Study of Infection, 1991; Weber-Parkes Trust Medal and Prize, RCP, 1999; Albert Chalmers Medal and Prize, Royal Soc. of Tropical Medicine and Hygiene, 2000; Windrush Award for Professional Achievement, Windrush Anserhouse, 2003; Gold Award, 2004, Platinum Award, 2008, NHS Adv. Cttee on Clin. Excellence Awards; Ibn Sina (Avicenna) Award for Excellence in Medicine and Sci., Muslim News Health Professional Awards, 2005; Zambia Med. Assoc. Medal, 2006; Bharuch Spinoza Award, Univ. of Amsterdam, 2011; India Internat. Foundn Award, 2011; Clinical Sci. Prize, Karolinska Inst., Sweden, 2012; Lifetime Achievement Award, Zambia Min. of Health, 2012; Best Internat. Collaboration Award, Times Higher Educn, 2013; Donald MacKay Medal, RSTM&H, 2014; Clinical Excellence Award for World Class Res., UCL Hosps NHS Foundn Trust, 2015. Ed., Current Opinions in Pulmonary Diseases Infectious Diseases (annually), 1998–. *Publications:* (jtly) A Guide to the MRCP Part 2 Written Examination, 1993, 2nd updated edn, as A Guide to the MRCP Part 2 Written Paper, 2006; (jtly) Multiple Choice Questions for the MRCP Part 1 Exam, 1993; (jtly) 100 Short Cases for the MRCP Clinical Exam, 1994; (ed jtly) AIDS and Respiratory Medicine, 1997; (ed with D. J. James) Granulomatous Disorders, 1999; (ed with O. P. Sharma) Tropical Lung Disease: clinics in chest medicine, 2002; (ed with M. Gandy) The Return of the White Plague: global poverty and the new tuberculosis, 2003; (ed with G. C. Cook) Manson's Tropical Diseases, 21st edn, 2003, 22nd edn 2009; (ed jtly) Tuberculosis: a comprehensive clinical treatise, 2009; (ed jtly) Perspectives in Medicine: tuberculosis, 2015; contribs to WHO reports and internat. guidelines; over 390 peer-reviewed pubns cited on PubMed. *Recreations:* cricket, philately, gardening. *Address:* UCL Medical School, University College London, Royal Free Campus, Division of Infection and Immunity, Centre for Clinical Microbiology, 2nd Floor, Royal Free Hospital, Rowland Hill Street, NW3 2PF. *T:* 07901 638375. *E:* a.zumla@ucl.ac.uk. *Club:* MCC.

ZUNZ, Sir Gerhard Jacob, (Sir Jack), Kt 1989; FREng; consulting engineer; *b* 25 Dec. 1923; *s* of Wilhelm Zunz and Helene (*née* Isenberg); *m* 1948, Babs Maisel; one *s* one *d* (and one *d* decd). *Educ:* Athlone High Sch., Johannesburg; Univ. of the Witwatersrand (BScCivEng); FICE, FIStructE; FREng (FEng 1983). War service, Egypt and Italy, with SA Artillery, 1943–46. Asst Engr, Alpheus, Williams & Dowse, 1948–50; Structural and Civil Engr with Ove Arup & Partners, London, 1950–54; Co-founder and Partner, Ove Arup & Partners (S Africa), 1954–61; Ove Arup & Partners: Associate Partner, 1961–65; Sen. Partner, and Partner in all overseas partnerships, 1965–77; Dir and Chm., 1977–84; Co-Chm., Ove Arup Partnership, and Dir, Ove Arup & Partners, 1984–89, Consultant, 1989–95. Non-exec. Dir, Innisfree PFI Fund, 1996–2006. Chairman: Ove Arup Foundn, 1992–96; AA Foundn, 1993–2005; Pres., CIRIA, 1996–98; former mem., various cttees associated with the construction industry. Industrial Fellow Commoner, Churchill Coll., Cambridge, 1967–68; Hon. Mem., AA, 2011. Hon. Fellow, Trevelyan Coll., Durham Univ., 1996. Hon. FRIBA 1990; FCGI 1990. Hon. DSc W Ontario, 1993; Hon. DEng Glasgow, 1994. Oscar Faber Silver Medal (jtly, with Sir Ove Arup), 1969; IStructE Gold Medal, 1988. *Publications:* (some jtly) number of technical papers to learned socs, incl. papers on Sydney Opera House and Hongkong & Shanghai Bank. *Recreations:* theatre, music, golf, tribal art. *Address:* c/o 13 Fitzroy Street, W1P 6BQ.

zur HAUSEN, Prof. Harald, MD; Scientific Director, German Cancer Research Centre, Heidelberg, 1983–2003, now Professor Emeritus; *b* Gelsenkirchen, Germany, 11 March 1936; *m* 1st, 1964; three *s*; 2nd, Dr Ethel-Michele de Villiers. *Educ:* Univ. of Bonn; Univ. of Hamburg; Univ. of Düsseldorf (MD 1960). Internships in Wimbern, Isny, Gelsenkirchen and Düsseldorf, 1960–62; Research Fellow: Inst. of Microbiol., Univ. of Düsseldorf, 1962–65; Div. of Virology, Children's Hosp. of Philadelphia, 1966–69; Asst Prof., Univ. of Pennsylvania, 1968; Sen. Scientist, Inst. of Virology, Univ. of Würzburg, 1969–72; Chm. and Prof. of Virology, Univ. of Erlangen-Nürnberg, 1972–77; Chm. and Prof. of Virology, Univ. of Freiburg, 1977–83. Ed.-in-Chief, Internat. Jl of Cancer, 2000–09. Mem. Bd of Dirs, UICC, 2006–10. Vice-President: German Nat. Acad. for Natural Scis and Medicine, 2003–10; Eur. Acad. of Cancer, 2010–. (Jtly) Nobel Prize in Physiology or Medicine, 2008. Special Order of Merit with Star (Germany). *Address:* German Cancer Research Centre, im Neuenheimer Feld 280, 69120 Heidelberg, Germany.

ZUYDAM, (David) Mel; Principal, ProSynergy, since 2012; *b* 29 Sept. 1961; *s* of late Willem Zuydam and of Sheila Zuydam (*née* Toff); *m* 2003, Melissa Christina Sophie Jones; one *s* one *d*. *Educ:* Univ. of Edinburgh (BSc Hons 1984). ACA 1991, FCA 2001. Subsidiary Finance Dir, Stylo plc, 1991–97; Balfour Beatty plc, 1997–2002: Financial Controller; Subsidiary Finance Dir; E Commerce Dir; Subsidiary Finance Dir, Serco plc, 2002–03; Consultant, EEF, 2003–04; Finance Dir, Highways Agency, DfT, 2004–08; Chief Financial Officer, Grontmij NV, 2009–12. Non-exec. Mem., Audit Cttee, DFID, 2007–. Volunteer, Disabled Sailing, RYA, 1995–2008. MInstD 2010. *Recreations:* having fun with my wife, daughter and son, singing, sailing, flying (private pilot licence, 1997); Three Peaks Challenge (1997 and 2008). *E:* MelZuydam@upcmail.nl.